Collins

Collins
Spanish
Dictionary

Collins
Spanish
Dictionary

HarperCollins Publishers
Westerhill Road
Bishopbriggs
Glasgow
G64 2QT
Great Britain

First Desktop Edition 2005

Previously published as Collins Concise
Spanish Dictionary

© William Collins Sons & Co. Ltd. 1985
© HarperCollins Publishers 1993, 1998, 2002,
2004

ISBN 0-00-719648-2

Collins® and Bank of English® are
registered trademarks of HarperCollins
Publishers Limited

www.collins.co.uk

A catalogue record for this book is available
from the British Library

Grupo Editorial Random House Mondadori,
S.L.
Travessera de Gràcia, 47-49
08021 Barcelona

www.diccionarioscollins.com

ISBN 84-253-3843-3

HarperCollins Publishers, Inc.
10 East 53rd Street, New York, NY 10022

ISBN 0-06-073380-2

Library of Congress Cataloging-in-
Publication Data has been applied for

www.harpercollins.com

First HarperCollins edition published 1993

HarperCollins books may be purchased for
educational, business, or sales promotional
use. For information, please write to:
Special Markets Department, HarperCollins
Publishers Inc., 10 East 53rd Street, New
York, NY 10022

Computer typeset by HarperCollins
Publishers, Glasgow, Great Britain

Printed in Italy by Amadeus S.r.l.

Acknowledgements
We would like to thank those authors and
publishers who kindly gave permission for
copyright material to be used in the Collins
Word Web. We would also like to thank
Times Newspapers Ltd for providing
valuable data.

CONTENTS		ÍNDICE DE MATERIAS

Series Editor/Directora de publicaciones
Lorna Sinclair Knight

General Editor/Dirección general
Jeremy Butterfield

Project Management/Dirección editorial
Gerard Breslin   Helen Newstead

Senior Editors/Responsables de redacción
Teresa Álvarez García   Cordelia Lilly

Editorial Coordination/Coordinación editorial
Emma Aeppli   Val McNulty

Contributors/Colaboradores
Diarmuid Bradley   Harry Campbell   Fernando León Solís
Julia Muleba   Victoria Ordóñez Diví   José María Ruiz Vaca
Alison Sadler   Carol Styles Carvajal   José Martín Galera

Editorial Assistance/Ayudantes de redacción
Elspeth Anderson   Irene Lakhani   Maggie Seaton   Pat Cook

Data Management/Informática
Jane Creevy   Robert Scovell-Lightfoot   Thomas Callan

Corpus Acknowledgements
We would like to acknowledge the assistance of the many hundreds of individuals and companies who have kindly given permission for copyright material to be used in the Bank of English. The written sources include many national and regional newspapers in Britain and overseas; magazine and periodical publishers; and book publishers in Britain, the United States and Australia. Extensive spoken data has been provided by radio and television broadcasting companies; research workers at many universities and other institutions; and numerous individual contributors. We are grateful to them all.

Structure of English entries

headword / **lema**	**Jersey** ['dʒɜːzɪ] N Isla *f* de Jersey, Jersey *m* ➤ **Jersey cow** vaca *f* de Jersey
	jersey ['dʒɜːzɪ] N (= *garment*) jersey *m*, suéter *m*

words starting with lower case follow those starting with upper case

palabras que comienzan con minúscula siguen aquéllas que comienzan con mayúscula

homograph number / **número de homógrafo**	**incense**[1] ['ɪnsens] N incienso *m* ➤ **incense burner** incensario *m*
IPA phonetics / **transcripción fonética**	**incense**[2] [ɪn'sens] VT indignar, encolerizar
	incensed [ɪn'senst] ADJ [*person*] furioso, furibundo

part of speech

categoría gramatical

calculate ['kælkjʊleɪt] (A) VT calcular; **his words were ~d to cause pain** había planeado expresamente sus palabras para hacer daño; **a move ~d to improve his popularity** una operación diseñada *or* pensada para darle mayor popularidad (B) VI (*Math*) calcular, hacer cálculos ➤ **calculate on** VI + PREP contar con

letters for different parts of speech

letras para las distintas categorías gramaticales

numbers for different senses / **números para las distintas acepciones**	**jack** [dʒæk] (A) N [1] (*Aut, Tech*) gato *m*, gata *f* (*LAm*) **2** (*Elec*) toma *f* de corriente, enchufe *m* hembra **3** (*Cards*) jota *f*; (*in Spanish pack*) sota *f* (B) CPD ➤ **jack plug** enchufe *m* de clavija

inflected form / **forma inflexionada**	**calf**[1] [kɑːf] N (*pl* **calves**) **1** (= *young cow*) becerro/a *m/f*, ternero/a *m/f*; (= *young seal, elephant etc*) cría *f*; (= *young whale*) ballenato *m* **2** (*also* **~skin**) piel *f* de becerro
	calf[2] [kɑːf] N (*pl* **calves**) [*of leg*] pantorrilla *f*, canilla *f* (*esp LAm*)

meaning indicator

indicador de acepción

typical subject of verb / **sujeto típico del verbo**	**jackknife** ['dʒæknaɪf] (A) N (*pl* **jackknives**) navaja *f*, chaveta *f* (*LAm*) (B) VI [*lorry*] colear

non-hyphenated compound nouns / **nombres compuestos sin guión**	**cable** ['keɪbl] (A) N cable *m* (B) VT [+ *news, money*] mandar por cable, cablegrafiar; [+ *person*] mandar un cable a (C) CPD ➤ **cable car** (*suspended*) teleférico *m*; (*on rail*) funicular *m* ➤ **cable railway** (*suspended*) teleférico *m*; (*with rail*) funicular *m* aéreo ➤ **cable television** televisión *f* por cable

typical objects of verb

objetos típicos del verbo

word which typically appears with headword / **palabra que por regla general aparece con el lema**	**jolly** ['dʒɒlɪ] (A) ADJ (*compar* **jollier**; *superl* **jolliest**) (= *cheerful*) alegre; (= *amusing*) divertido; [*laugh*] gracioso (B) ADV (*Brit**) muy, la mar de*, bastante; **we were ~ glad** estábamos la mar de contentos*, nos alegramos muchísimo; **you've ~ well got to** no tienes otro remedio, no te queda otra (*LAm*); **~ good!** ¡estupendo!, ¡macanudo! (*Per, SC*)

~ stands in for headword

~ sustituye al lema

translation / **traducción**	**jet**[1] [dʒet] N (= *stone*) azabache *m* ➤ **jet black** negro *m* azabache
	jet[2] [dʒet] (A) N **1** [*of liquid, steam*] chorro *m* **2** (= *plane*) avión *m* a reacción, reactor *m* (B) CPD [*fighter, plane*] a reacción ➤ **jet engine** [*of plane*] motor *m* a reacción, reactor *m* ➤ **jet lag** jet lag *m* (*desfase debido a un largo viaje en avión*); **to be suffering from ~ lag** tener jet lag ➤ **jet propulsion** propulsión *f* a reacción, propulsión *f* a chorro ➤ **the jet set** la jet set (*Sp*), el jet set (*LAm*) ➤ **jet stream** corriente *f* en chorro

Spanish gender

género en español

Estructura de las entradas españolas

headword / **lema**	**Acuario** SM (= *signo*) Aquarius **acuario** Ⓐ SM (= *pecera*) aquarium Ⓑ SMF INV (*Astron*) (= *persona*) Aquarius; **soy ~** I'm Aquarius	**words starting with lower case follow those starting with upper case** / **palabras que comienzan con minúscula siguen aquéllas que comienzan con mayúscula**
homograph number / **número de homógrafo**	**acre¹** ADJ [*olor*] acrid, pungent; [*crítica*] sharp, biting, mordant **acre²** SM acre	
reference to verb tables / **remisión a la tabla de conjugaciones**	**aburrir** /3a/ Ⓐ VT to bore Ⓑ **aburrirse** VPR to be bored, get bored (**con, de, por** with); ✦ MODISMO **~se como una ostra** to be bored stiff	
	dentadura SF teeth *pl*; **tener mala ~** to have bad teeth ➤ **dentadura postiza** false teeth *pl*, dentures *pl*	**part of speech** / **categoría gramatical**
letters for different parts of speech / **letras para las distintas categorías gramaticales**	**agente** Ⓐ SMF (= *representante*) agent; (= *policía*) policeman/policewoman ➤ **agente comercial** business agent ➤ **agente de bolsa** stockbroker ➤ **agente de seguros** insurance agent ➤ **agente de tránsito** (*Arg, Méx*) traffic policeman/policewoman ➤ **agente literario** literary agent ➤ **agente secreto** secret agent ➤ **agentes sociales** social partners (*employers and unions*) Ⓑ SM (*Quím*) agent	
numbers for different senses / **números para las distintas acepciones**	**dama** SF **1** (= *señora*) lady; **~s y caballeros** ladies and gentlemen; **primera ~** (*LAm Pol*) First Lady ➤ **dama de honor** [*de reina*] lady-in-waiting; [*de novia*] bridesmaid **2** (= *mujer noble*) lady **3** (= *pieza*) (*Ajedrez, Naipes*) queen; (*en damas*) king **4 damas** (*juego*) draughts (*Brit*), checkers (*EEUU*)	
	aficionado/a Ⓐ ADJ **1** (= *entusiasta*) keen, enthusiastic; **es muy aficionada a la pintura** she's really into painting, she's very keen on painting (*Brit*) **2** (= *no profesional*) amateur Ⓑ SM/F **1** (= *entusiasta*) (*de hobby*) enthusiast; (*como espectador*) lover; **los ~s a la ópera** opera lovers **2** (= *no profesional*) amateur; **partido de ~s** amateur game; **somos simples ~s** we're just amateurs **3** [*de equipo, grupo*] fan, supporter	**meaning indicator** / **indicador de acepción**
	agitar /1a/ Ⓐ VT **1** [+ *mano, bandera, arma*] to wave; [+ *alas*] to flap; **el viento agitaba las hojas** the wind stirred the leaves **2** [+ *botella, líquido*] to shake; **agítese antes de usar** shake well before use **3** (= *inquietar*) to worry, upset **4** (= *convulsionar*) [+ *multitud*] to stir up Ⓑ **agitarse** VPR **1** (= *moverse*) [*ramas*] to stir; [*bandera, toldo*] to flap; [*mar*] to get rough; [*barco*] to toss **2** (= *inquietarse*) to get worried *o* upset **3** (= *moverse inquieto*) **el enfermo se agitaba en la cama** the patient was tossing and turning	**typical objects of verb** / **objetos típicos del verbo**
typical subject of verb / **sujeto típico del verbo**		
	densidad SF **1** (= *concentración*) [*de sustancia, tráfico*] density; [*de humo, vegetación*] thickness, denseness; [*de caracteres*] (*Inform*) pitch ➤ **densidad de población** population density **2** [*de discurso, relato*] denseness **3** (*Fís*) density	**compound noun** / **nombre compuesto**
words which typically appear with headword / **palabras que por regla general aparecen con el lema**	**agobiante** ADJ **1** [*calor, ambiente, lugar*] oppressive; **un día de verano ~** a stifling *o* sweltering summer's day **2** (= *insoportable*) [*trabajo, día*] stressful; [*pena, ritmo*] unbearable; [*responsabilidad*] overwhelming; **es ~ verla sufrir y no poder hacer nada** it's unbearable watching her suffer and being unable to do anything; **una ~ sensación de soledad** an overwhelming sense of loneliness	**~ stands in for headword** / **~ sustituye al lema**
translation / **traducción**	**denso** ADJ **1** (= *concentrado*) [*sustancia*] dense; [*tráfico*] heavy; [*humo, vegetación*] thick, dense **2** [*discurso, relato*] dense **3** (*Fís*) dense	

Structure of English entries

---

region used
uso regional

queue-jump ['kju:dʒʌmp] VI (*Brit*) colarse*

* = informal register
* = informal

---

quickie* ['kwıkı] N **to have a ~** (= *drink*) tomarse una copita*; (= *sex*) echar un polvo rápido**

slang or very informal
(*** = offensive)
argot o muy informal
(*** = ofensivo)

---

region where translation is used
región donde se emplea la traducción

jobless ['dʒɒblıs] **Ⓐ** ADJ sin trabajo, desempleado, parado (*Sp*), cesante (*Chi*) **Ⓑ** NPL **the ~** los desempleados, los parados (*Sp*), los cesantes (*Chi*)

---

joke [dʒəʊk] **Ⓐ** N (= *witticism, story*) chiste *m*; (= *practical joke, hoax*) broma *f*; **to treat sth as a ~** tomar algo a broma; **it's (gone) beyond a ~** (*Brit*) esto no tiene nada de gracioso; **for a ~** en broma; **is that your idea of a ~?** ¿es que eso tiene gracia?; **to make a ~** hacer un chiste (**about sth** sobre algo); **it's no ~ having to go out in this weather** no tiene nada de divertido salir con este tiempo

set phrases are alphabetized according to underlined key element for ease of reference
frases fijas en orden alfabético según el elemento clave subrayado para facilitar la referencia

examples and phrases
ejemplos y frases

Ⓑ VI (= *make jokes*) contar chistes, hacer chistes; (= *be frivolous*) bromear; **I was only joking** lo dije en broma, no iba en serio; **I'm not joking** hablo en serio; **you're joking!** ◇ **you must be joking!** ¡no lo dices en serio!

---

saint [seınt] N santo/a *m/f*; **she's no ~** (*iro*) ella no es una santa, que digamos

---

note about usage
nota de uso

> When used before a man's name, the word **Santo** is shortened to **San**, the exceptions being **Santo Tomás** and **Santo Domingo**.

Saint John San Juan; **Saint Theresa** Santa Teresa ➤ **All Saints' Day** día *m* de Todos los Santos (*1 de noviembre*)

QC N ABBR (*Brit*) = **Queen's Counsel**

QC/KC

> **QC** o **KC**, abreviaturas de **Queen's** o **King's Counsel**, es el título que se les da a los abogados de más alto rango en el Reino Unido. Los letrados denominados **barristers** (o **advocates** en Escocia) que hayan practicado la abogacía durante al menos diez años pueden solicitar este título al **Lord Chancellor**, quien a su vez los recomienda a la Corona para su designación. Pasar a ser un **QC** o **KC** se conoce como **taking silk** (recibir la seda), haciendo referencia al material de la túnica que llevan estos letrados.

cultural note to help Spanish native speaker
nota cultural de ayuda al hablante de español

---

inch [ıntʃ] N pulgada *f* (= 2,54 cm); **not an ~ of territory** ni un palmo de territorio; **the car missed me by ~es** faltó poco para que me atropellara el coche; **~ by ~** palmo a palmo; **we searched every ~ of the room** registramos todos los rincones del cuarto; **every ~ of it was used** se aprovechó hasta el último centímetro; **he's every ~ a soldier** es todo un soldado; **to be within an ~ of death/disaster** estar a dos dedos de la muerte/del desastre; **✦ IDIOM give him an ~ and he'll take a mile** dale un dedo y se toma hasta el codo; ◇ *IMPERIAL SYSTEM*

cross-reference to cultural note
remisión a nota cultural

IDIOM
MODISMO

phrasal verb
verbo con preposición o adverbio

➤ **inch forward** VI + ADV avanzar muy lentamente

---

glitter ['glıtə'] **Ⓐ** N [*of gold etc*] brillo *m* **Ⓑ** VI [*gold etc*] relucir, brillar; **✦ PROV all that ~s is not gold** no es oro todo lo que reluce

PROVERB
REFRÁN

---

cross-reference to equivalent
remisión a un equivalente

glamor ['glæmə'] N (*US*) = **glamour**

January ['dʒænjʊərı] N enero *m*; *see July*

---

cross-reference
remisión

gab* [gæb] N *see gift*

---

cross-reference to a similar entry where more examples are shown
remisión a una entrada similar donde se indican más ejemplos

fabric ['fæbrık] **Ⓐ** N **1** (= *cloth*) tela *f*, tejido *m*; (= *textiles*) tejidos *mpl* **2** (*Archit*) estructura *f*; **the ~ of society** el tejido social, la estructura de la sociedad **Ⓑ** CPD ➤ **fabric conditioner, fabric softener** suavizante *m*

---

false friend warning
aviso de un caso de falso amigo

> ⚠ **fabric** ≠ *fábrica*

Estructura de las entradas españolas

region where translation
is used

región donde se emplea
la traducción

agarrador* **Ⓐ** ADJ (*And*) [*bebida*] strong **Ⓑ** SM (*LAm*) (*para la cocina*) oven cloth

region used

uso regional

gallina **Ⓐ** SF 1 (= *ave*) hen; ✦ MODISMOS **acostarse con las ~s** to go to bed early; **matar la ~ de los huevos de oro** to kill the goose that lays the golden eggs ➤ **gallina clueca** broody o (*EEUU*) brooding hen 2 (*Culin*) chicken; **caldo de ~** chicken broth **Ⓑ** SMF (*) (= *cobarde*) chicken*, coward

* = informal register
(** = slang; *** = offensive)

* = informal
(** = argot; *** = ofensivo)

demasiado **Ⓐ** ADJ 1 (= *excesivo*) too much; **hace ~ calor** it's too hot; **¡esto es ~!** that's the limit!; **no tengo ~ tiempo** I don't have much time; **¡qué ~!*** wow!* 2 **demasiados** too many **Ⓑ** ADV (= *en exceso*) (*con adjetivos, adverbios*) too; (*con verbos*) too much; **es ~ pesado** it is too heavy; **comer ~** to eat too much

examples and phrases

ejemplos y frases

> **Demasiado** se traduce por **too** delante de adjetivos y adverbios: "Hace demasiado calor", *It's too hot*; "Hablas demasiado deprisa", *You talk too quickly*. Se traduce por **too much** delante de sustantivos incontables o cuando modifica al verbo: "demasiada sal", *too much salt*; "Habla demasiado", *He talks too much*. En plural la traducción es **too many**: "Tiene demasiadas preocupaciones", *He has too many worries*.

note about usage

nota de uso

gana SF 1 **hacer algo** con **~s** to do sth willingly o enthusiastically; **comer/reírse con ~s** to eat/laugh heartily; **un chico joven y con ~s de trabajar** a young lad willing to work; **jóvenes con ~s de divertirse** young people eager o keen to enjoy themselves; **con ~s de pelea** spoiling for a fight; **dar ~s: esto da ~s de comerlo** it makes you want to eat it; **dan ~s de pegarle una patada** you feel like kicking him; **le** entran **~s de hacer algo** he gets the urge to do sth; **quedarse con las ~s** to be left disappointed, be left wanting; **nos quedamos con las ~s de saberlo** we never got to find out; **quitársele** a algn las **~s de algo: se me han quitado las ~s de ir** I don't feel like going now o any more; **hacer algo** sin **~s** to do sth reluctantly o unwillingly; **tener ~s de hacer algo** to feel like doing sth

set phrases are
alphabetized according
to underlined key element
for ease of reference

frases fijas en orden
alfabético según el
elemento clave subrayado
para facilitar la referencia

> Recuérdase que las preposiciones en inglés rigen gerundio y no infinitivo, de ahí **to feel like doing sth**.

note about usage

nota de uso

IDIOM

MODISMO

agosto SM August; ✦ MODISMO **hacer su ~** to feather one's nest, make one's pile; *ver tb* **septiembre**

cross-reference to a similar
entry where more
expressions are shown

remisión a una entrada
similar donde se indican
más ejemplos

> En inglés los meses se escriben con mayúscula.

denominación SF 1 (= *acto*) naming 2 (= *nombre*) name

DENOMINACIÓN DE ORIGEN

cultural note to help
English native speaker

nota cultural de ayuda
al hablante de inglés

The **Denominación de Origen**, abbreviated to **D.O.**, is a prestigious product classification which is awarded to food products such as wines, cheeses, sausages and hams that are produced in designated Spanish regions according to stringent production criteria. **D.O.** labels serve as a guarantee of quality.

cross-reference to
cultural note

remisión a una nota cultural

décimo **Ⓐ** ADJ, PRON tenth; *ver tb* **sexto** **Ⓑ** SM (*tb ~ de lotería*) ≈ lottery ticket; ⇨ *EL GORDO*

cross-reference to entry
where treated

remisión a entrada donde
se trata el lema

hay *ver* **haber**

actualmente ADV 1 (= *en este momento*) currently, at present, presently (*EEUU*); **~ está rodando una nueva serie** he's currently making a new series, he's making a new series at present 2 (= *hoy día*) nowadays; **~ se usan métodos más eficaces** nowadays more efficient methods are used

> ⚠ **actualmente** ≠ *actually*

false friend warning

aviso de un caso de
falso amigo

Special treatment for key entries

menu box showing parts of speech

recuadro de ayuda para la búsqueda de categoría gramatical

in

A PREPOSITION   **C** ADJECTIVE
B ADVERB   **D** NOUN

When ‣in is the second element in a phrasal verb, eg **ask in**, **fill in**, **look in**, *etc, look up the verb. When it is part of a set combination, eg* **in the country**, **in danger**, **dressed in**, *look up the other word.*

clear cross-references

remisiones ilustrativas

in [ɪn] **A** PREPOSITION
1 (*in expressions of place*) en; (= *inside*) dentro de; **it's in London/Scotland/Galicia** está en Londres/Escocia/Galicia; **in the garden** en el jardín; **in the house** en casa; (= *inside*) dentro de la casa; **our bags were stolen, and our passports were in them** nos robaron los bolsos, y nuestros pasaportes iban dentro

usage notes

notas de uso

When phrases like **in Madrid**, **in Germany** are used to identify a particular group, **de** is the usual translation:

our colleagues in Madrid nuestros colegas de Madrid; **in here/there** aquí/allí dentro
2 (*in expressions of time*)
2.1 (= *during*) en; **in 1986** en 1986; **in May/spring** en mayo/primavera; **in the eighties/the 20th century** en los años ochenta/el siglo 20; **in the morning(s)/evening(s)** por la mañana/la tarde; **at four o'clock in the morning/afternoon** a las cuatro de la mañana/la tarde
2.2 (= *for*) **she hasn't been here in years** hace años que no viene
3 (*indicating manner, medium*) en; **in a loud/soft voice** en voz alta/baja; **in Spanish/English** en español/inglés; **to pay in dollars** pagar en dólares
4 (= *clothed in*) **she opened the door in her dressing gown** abrió la puerta en bata; **they were all in shorts** todos iban en *or* llevaban pantalón corto; **you look nice in that dress** ese vestido te sienta bien

When phrases like **in the blue dress**, **in the glasses** are used to identify a particular person, **de** is the usual translation:

translation exception

ejemplo con una traducción distinta a la general

the man in the hat el hombre del sombrero; **the boy in the checked trousers** el chico de los pantalones de cuadros; *BUT* **the girl in green** la chica vestida de verde
5 (*giving ratio, number*) **one person in ten** una persona de cada diez; **he had only a one in fifty chance of survival** sólo tenía una posibilidad entre cincuenta de sobrevivir; **20 pence in the pound** 20 peniques por (cada) libra; **once in a hundred years** una vez cada cien años; **in twos** de dos en dos
6 (= *among*) entre; **this is common in children/cats** es cosa común entre los niños/los gatos
7 (*talking about people*) **she has it in her to succeed** tiene la capacidad de triunfar; **it's not in him to do that** no es capaz de hacer eso; **it's something I admire in her** es algo que admiro de *or* en ella
8 (*in profession etc*) **to be in teaching** dedicarse a la enseñanza; **to be in publishing** trabajar en el mundo editorial
9 (*after superlative*) de; **the biggest/smallest in Europe** el más grande/pequeño de Europa
10 (*with verb*) **in saying this** al decir esto
11 (*in set expressions*)

set structures and expressions

estructuras y expresiones fijas

✦ **in all** en total
✦ **in itself** de por sí
✦ **in that** (= *since*) puesto que, ya que
✦ **what's in it for me**: **I want to know what's in it for me** quiero saber qué gano yo con eso

Tratamiento especial a entradas claves

decir /3o/

Ⓐ VERBO TRANSITIVO
Ⓑ VERBO INTRANSITIVO
Ⓒ VERBO PRONOMINAL
Ⓓ SUSTANTIVO MASCULINO

Para otras expresiones con el participio, ver **dicho.**

decir Ⓐ VERBO TRANSITIVO
1 (= *afirmar*) to say; **ya sabe ~ varias palabras** she can already say several words, she already knows several words; **viene y dice: —estás despedido*** he goes "you're fired"*; <u>como</u> **dicen los madrileños** as they say in Madrid; **como iba diciendo ...** as I was saying ...; **¿cómo ha dicho usted?** pardon?, what did you say?; **~ para** *o* **entre <u>sí</u>** to say to o.s.
◆ **decir que** to say (that); **mi amigo dice que eres muy guapa** my friend says (that) you're very pretty; **~ que sí/no** to say yes/no

2
◆ **decir algo a algn** to tell sb sth; **¿quién te lo dijo?** who told you?; **tengo algo que ~te** there's something I want to tell you, I've got something to tell you
◆ **decir a algn que** (+ INDIC) to tell sb (that); **me dijo que no vendría** he told me (that) he wouldn't come
◆ **decir a algn que** (+ SUBJUN) (= *ordenar*) to tell sb to do sth; (= *pedir*) to ask sb to do sth; **la profesora me dijo que esperara fuera** the teacher told me to wait outside; **dile que venga a cenar mañana con nosotros** ask him to come and have supper with us tomorrow
3 (= *contar*) [+ *mentiras, verdad, secreto*] to tell; **~ tonterías** to talk nonsense
4 (= *llamar*) to call; **¿cómo le dicen a esto en Perú?** what do they call this in Peru?; **en México se le dice "recámara" al dormitorio** in Mexico they say "recámara" instead of "dormitorio"
5 (= *opinar*) to say; **¿tu familia qué dice de la boda?** what does your family say about the wedding?
6 (*rectificando*) **había ocho, digo nueve** there were eight, I mean nine; **dirá usted aquel otro** you must mean that other one
7 [*texto*] to say; **no puedo leer lo que dice** I can't read what it says; **como dice el <u>refrán</u> ...** as the saying goes ...
8 [+ *misa*] to say
9 (*locuciones en* <u>*indicativo*</u>) <u>**digo**</u> **...** well, er ...; <u>como quien</u> <u>dice</u> so to speak; <u>lo mismo</u> <u>digo</u> likewise; **pues si esto te parece mucha gente, no te digo** <u>nada</u> **en verano** if you think this is a lot of people, you should see it in summer; **no lo digo** <u>por</u> **ti** I'm not referring to you; **¿qué me dices?** you don't say!, well I never!; **si tú lo dices** if you say so; **eso digo yo** that's (just) what I say; **deberías buscar trabajo, vamos, digo yo** you ought to look for a job, that's what I think anyway; **¡y que lo digas!** you can say that again!; ◆ MODISMOS **no dijo ni pío** ◇ **no dijo esta boca es mía** she never once opened her mouth; ◆ REFRÁN **dime con quien andas y te diré quien eres** a man is known by the company he keeps
10 (*locuciones en infinitivo*) **<u>es</u> ~** that is (to say); **es <u>mucho</u> ~** that's saying something; **<u>ni que</u> ~ tiene que ...** it goes without saying that ...; **no hay más que ~** there's nothing more to say; **<u>por así</u> ~lo** so to speak; **<u>querer</u> ~** to mean; **¿qué quiere ~ "spatha"?** what does "spatha" mean?; **¿querrás ~ un millón, no un billón?** do you mean a million rather than a billion?; **<u>ya es</u> ~** that's saying something
11 (*locuciones en subjuntivo, imperativo*) **es, digamos, un comerciante** he's a dealer, for want of a better word, he's a sort of dealer; **¡haberlo dicho!** ◇ **¡me lo hubieras dicho!** you could have told me *o* said!; **y <u>no</u> digamos ...** not to mention ...; **no estuvo muy cortés, que digamos** he wasn't what you'd call polite, he wasn't exactly polite; **¡no me**

Spanish Pronunciation

The pronunciation of Spanish is generally regular and the notes below should be sufficient to enable an English speaker to read most Spanish words. Because of this, the only pronunciations shown on the Spanish-English side of the dictionary are those of foreign words or other words which are pronounced in a way you would not expect. Pronunciations, where shown, are transcribed using the International Phonetic Alphabet, which is explained below.

Stress in Spanish words falls on the second last syllable if the word ends in a vowel, n or s; if a word ends in a consonant the last syllable is stressed. If the stress falls anywhere else in the word, this is shown by an acute accent over the stressed vowel.

Vowels and diphthongs

Spanish vowels are always pronounced clearly and are not relaxed in unstressed syllables as in English.

a	[a]	Between English **a** as in *pat* and **u** as in *hut*	**pata, amara**
e	[e]	Similar to English **e** as in *set*	**me, pelo, sangre**
i	[i]	Between English **i** as in *bit* and **ee** as in *been*	**iris, filo**
o	[o]	Similar to English **o** as in *pot*	**poco, cosa, bomba**
u	[u]	Between English **u** as in *rule* and **oo** as in *foot*. Silent after **q** and in **gue**, **gui**, unless marked by a diaeresis (*argüir, fragüe*)	**luna, aquel, pague**
y	[i]	When used as a vowel it is pronounced like **i**	**y**
ai, ay	[ai]	Like **i** in English *side*	**baile, hay**
au	[au]	Like **ou** in English *sound*	**áureo, causa**
ei, ey	[ei]	Like **ey** in English *they*	**reina, rey**
eu	[eu]	Like the vowel sounds in English **may-you**, without the sound of the **y**	**deuda, feudo**
oi, oy	[oi]	Like **oy** in English *boy*	**oiga, soy**

Semiconsonants

i, y	[i]	Like **y** in English *yes, yacht*	**bien, yunta**
u	[w]	Like **w** in English *well*	**huevo, agua**

Consonants

b, v		These letters have the same value.	
	[b]	At the start of the word and after written **m** and **n** the sound is like English **b**	**bomba, boda, enviar**
	[β]	In all other positions the sound is between English **b** and **v** in which the lips do not touch	**haba, severo**
c	[k]	**c** before **a**, **o**, **u** or a consonant is like English **k** in keep	**calco, acto**
	[θ]	**c** before **e**, **i** is like English **th** in *thin* or in parts of Andalusia and Latin America like **s** in English *same*. In words like *acción, sección* both types of c sound are heard [kθ]	**celda, cinco**
ch	[tʃ]	Like **ch** in English *church*	**mucho, chorro**
d	[d]	At the start of the word and after **l** and **n** the sound is like English **d**	**dama, aldea**
	[ð]	Between vowels and after consonants other than **l** and **n** the sound is similar to English **th** in *this*	**pide, cada, pardo**
		In the final position it is often not pronounced	**verdad, usted**
g	[x]	Before **e**, **i** it is similar to Scottish lo**ch**	**Gijón, general**
	[g]	At the start of the word and after **n** it is pronounced like English **g** in *get*	**gloria, rango**
	[ɣ]	In other positions the sound is softer than in *get*	**haga, agosto**
h		This is always silent	
j	[x]	Similar to Scottish *loch* or German *Achtung*	**jota, jején**
ll	[ʎ]	Similar to English **lli** in *million*, but often like English *yet* or *pleasure*	**calle, ella, lluvia**
ñ	[ɲ]	Similar to English **ni** in *onion*	**uña, ñoño**
q	[k]	Like English **k** in *kick*. Always written in combination with **u**, which is silent	**que, quinqué**
r	[r]	A single like trill the Scots **r**. Pronounced like **rr** at the start of a word and also after **l, n, s**	**coro, rápido**

rr	[rr]	Strongly trilled in a way that does not exist in English	**torre, burro**
s	[s]	Except in the instances mentioned next, like English **s** in *same*	**casa, soso**
	[z]	Before **b, d, g, l, m, n** like English *rose, phase*	**desde, asgo, mismo**
w		Usually pronounced like Spanish **b, v**, or like English **v**, or kept as English **w**	**wáter, week-end, wolframio**
y	[j]	As English *yes, youth*	**mayo, yo**
z	[θ]	Like English **th** in *thin* or in parts of Andalusia and Latin America like English **s** in *same*	**zapato, zorro, luz**

f, k, l, m, n, p, t, x are pronounced as in English

Spanish Spelling

Use of capitals

As in English, capital letters are used to begin words in the following cases:

– for the first letter of the first word in a sentence
– for proper names (but see also below)

María, el Papa, el Rey, la Real Academia Española, Viernes Santo, el Partido Laborista, Dios

Note that where the article is an integral part of the proper name, it also begins with a capital – **El Escorial, La Haya, La Habana** – but where the article is generally or optionally used with the name of a country, it does not begin with a capital – **la India, la Argentina**

– for abbreviations of titles:

Sr., D., Excmª

In the following cases usage differs from English:

– names of days and months:

lunes, mayo

– the pronoun **yo**, unless it begins a sentence
– while capitals are used for names of countries, they are not used for the adjectives derived therefrom:

Francia, but **francés**

Similarly, adjectives derived from proper names do not begin with a capital:

... en los estudios lorquianos, las teorías einsteinianas

– in the titles of books, films, plays etc, only the first word begins with a capital letter:

Lo que el viento se llevó, Cien años de soledad

– points of the compass begin with lower case:

norte, sur etc

(though they are capitalized if part of a name: **Korea del Sur**)

– official and noble titles:

el duque de Alba, el ministro de Interior

Note that capital letters can be accentuated in the same way as lower case letters.

Spelling changes

Spelling changes may occur in inflected forms, to reflect the pronunciation, eg:

c to **z**: *vencer, (yo) venzo*
z to **c**: *la luz, las luces*
g to **gu**: *pagar, (yo) pague*
gu to **g**: *distinguir, (yo) distingo*
g to **j**: *dirigir, (yo) dirijo*

The acute accent may be added or dropped in inflected forms to show a change in the stressed syllable:

un francés, but *dos franceses*
el carácter, but *los caracteres*
situar, but *(yo) sitúo*

Punctuation

Other than the differences listed below, punctuation in English and Spanish is very similar.

Exclamation marks and question marks

An inverted exclamation mark (¡) or question mark (¿) is required at the start of the exclamation or question in addition to the standard exclamation mark or question mark at the end. The position of these marks does not always coincide with the beginning of the sentence:

¡Qué calor hace!
Pues, ¿vamos o no vamos?
Son trece en total, ¿verdad?

Full stops

These are used very much as in English, except that:

– they are generally used after abbreviations:

Sr. Solís

They are used in numbers where English uses a comma:

English	Spanish
10,587	10.587

Commas

A comma is used instead of the decimal point:

English	Spanish
10.1	10,1 *(diez coma uno)*

Colons

These may be used instead of a comma after the name of the recipient of a letter.

Querida Dolores:
Muy Señor mío:

Hyphens

The tendency is for compound nouns and adjectives to be written as a single word:

antifranquista, proeuropeo, antihistamínico

When the two adjectives refer to different things, the hyphen is used:

el eje franco-alemán, el pensamiento anglo-americano

Hyphens are also used as in English to join nouns:

misiles tierra-aire, el eje Roma-Berlín

Dashes

The dash is often used to insert parenthetical material:

la moción de censura fue aprobada por unanimidad – algo cada vez más raro en el parlamento – a últimas horas de la sesión.

The dash is used to represent continuous dialogue where English would use inverted commas. It is used both to show a change of speaker and the resumption of dialogue after a pause:

–¿Vas a venir? –dijo suavemente
–No puedo –contesté

Note that punctuation in direct speech is placed after the dash.

Pronunciación del inglés

Sistema de signos

Se emplean los signos de la IPA (International Phonetic Alphabet).

Acentuación

En las transcripciones el signo ['] se coloca delante de la sílaba acentuada. El signo [ˌ] se pone delante de la sílaba que lleva el acento secundario o más débil en las palabras largas, p.ej. **acceleration** [ækˌseləˈreɪʃən]. Dos signos de acento principal indican que las dos sílabas, o bien dos de las sílabas, se acentúan igualmente, p.ej. **A1** [ˈeɪˈwʌn], **able-bodied** [ˈeɪblˈbɒdɪd].

Signos impresos en cursiva

En la palabra **annexation** [ˌænekˈseɪʃən], la [ə] en cursiva indica que este sonido puede o no pronunciarse; bien porque muchos hablantes la pronuncian pero otros muchos no, o bien porque es un sonido que se oye en el habla lenta y cuidada pero que no se oye en el habla corriente y en el ritmo de la frase entera.

Transcripciones alternativas

En los casos donde se dan dos transcripciones, ello indica que ambas pronunciaciones son igualmente aceptables en el uso culto, p.ej. **medicine** [ˈmedsɪn, ˈmedɪsɪn], o bien que la pronunciación varía bastante según la posición de la palabra en la frase y el contexto fonético, p.ej. **an** [æn, ən, n].

Vocales y diptongos

[æ]	Con los labios en la posición de **e** en *pena* y luego se pronuncia el sonido **a** parecido a la **a** de *carro*	**bat, apple**
[ɑː]	Entre **a** de *caro* y **o** de *noche*	**farm, calm**
[e]	Como en *perro*	**set, less**
[ə]	Vocal neutra parecida a una **e** u **o** casi muda	**above, porter**
[ɜː]	Entre **e** abierta y **o** cerrada, sonido alargado	**fern, work**
[ɪ]	Más breve que en *sí*	**tip, pity**
[iː]	Como en *vino*	**see, been**
[ɒ]	Como en *corra, torre*	**rot, wash**
[ɔː]	Como en *por*	**ball, board**
[ʊ]	Sonido muy breve, más cerrado que *burro*	**soot, full**
[uː]	Sonido largo, en *uno, supe*	**root, fool**
[ʌ]	**a** muy breve	**come, rum, blood**
[aɪ]	Como en *fraile, vais*	**lie, fry**
[aʊ]	Como en *pausa, sauce*	**now, plough**
[eɪ]	**e** cerrada seguida por una **i** débil	**fate, say, waiter**
[əʊ]	[ə] seguido por una breve **u**	**ago, also, note**
[ɛə]	Casi como en *vea*, pero el sonido **a** se mezcla con el indistinto [ə]	**there, rare, fair**
[ɪə]	Como en *manía*, mezclándose el sonido **a** con el indistinto [ə]	**here, interior, fear**
[ɔɪ]	Como en *voy*	**toy, voice**
[ʊə]	**u** bastante larga más el sonido indistinto [ə]	**allure, pure**

Consonantes

[b]	Como en *tumbar, umbrío*	**bet, able**
[d]	Como en *conde, andar*	**dime, mended**
[g]	Como en *grande, rango*	**go, agog**
[h]	Como la jota hispanoamericana	**hit, reheat**
[j]	Como en *cuyo, reyes*	**you, pure**
[ŋ]	Como en *banco, rango*	**bank, singer**
[r]	Se pronuncia con la punta de la lengua hacia atrás y sin hacerla vibrar	**rate, sorrow**
[ʳ]	Indica que la **r** final se pronuncia en inglés británico cuando la palabra siguiente empieza con vocal	**bear, after**
[s]	Como en *casa, sesión*	**sit, scent**
[v]	Como **f**, pero se retiran los dientes superiores vibrándolos contra el labio inferior	**vine, river**
[w]	Como la **u** de *huevo, puede*	**wine, bewail**
[z]	Como en *desde, mismo*	**zero, roses**

[ʒ]	Como en las palabras francesas *jour, jalousie*	**rouge, leisure**
	Este sonido aparece a menudo en el grupo [dʒ], parecido al grupo **dj** de la palabra francesa *adjacent*	**page, jail**
[ʃ]	Como en las palabras francesas **ch**am*bre, fi*che	**shame, ocean**
	Este sonido aparece a menudo en el grupo [tʃ], parecido al grupo **ch** del español *mu*cho, *cho*cho	**much, chuck**
[θ]	Como en **z**um*bar,* **c**iento	**thin, maths**
[ð]	Como en to**d**o, habla**d**o	**this, other**
[x]	Se encuentra en el inglés de Escocia; como en **j**oven, **r**ojo	**loch**

f, k, l, m, n, p, t, x iguales que en español

Sonidos extranjeros

El grado de corrección con que un hablante de inglés pronuncia las palabras extranjeras que acaban de incorporarse al idioma depende – como en español – de su nivel cultural y de los conocimientos que pueda tener del idioma de donde se ha tomado la palabra. Las transcripciones que damos de tales palabras representan una pronunciación más bien culta. En las transcripciones la tilde [~] indica que la vocal tiene timbre nasal (en muchas palabras de origen francés). En las pocas palabras tomadas del alemán aparece a veces la [x], para cuya explicación véase el cuadro de las consonantes.

La ortografía del inglés

Vamos a hablar aquí de una serie de reglas ortográficas del inglés que pueden resultar de utilidad para los hablantes de español, así como de las diferencias ortográficas entre el inglés británico y el norteamericano. Nos referiremos, en primer lugar, al inglés británico.

Consonantes dobles

Ⓐ En las palabras monosílabas que acaban en una sola consonante, esta consonante se dobla cuando se añade un sufijo que empieza por vocal.

knot + -ed = knotted; cut + -er = cutter; hit + -ing = hitting

EXCEPCIONES: Cuando en la palabra hay dos vocales juntas, o cuando la consonante final es doble.

feel → feeling; hand → handed

Ⓑ En las palabras de dos o tres sílabas acabadas en consonante precedida de una sola vocal, esta consonante se dobla al añadírsele un sufijo, siempre que el énfasis de la raíz recaiga en la última sílaba.

regret + -ing = regretting; begin + -er = beginner

NOTA: cuando la última sílaba no va acentuada esto no ocurre.

enter + -ed = entered; answer + -ing = answering

Sin embargo, existen algunas excepciones como:

kidnap → kidnapper, kidnapped etc; **worship → worshipping, worshipped** etc

Ⓒ En algunas palabras acabadas en **-l**, esta **l** se suele hacer doble en los dos casos siguientes:

– en las palabras acabadas por **-l** precedida de una sola vocal.

equal → equalling; instil → instilled; repel → repellent

– en las palabras acabadas en dos vocales que formen un diptongo.

real → really; fuel → fuelled

Cuando desaparece la -e final

Ⓐ En las palabras acabadas en una sola **-e** precedida de consonante, la **-e** desaparece cuando se añade un sufijo que empiece por vocal.

retrieve → retrieving; love → lovable

NOTA: La excepción a esta regla la constituye la palabra **likeable** – aunque también existe la forma "likable" – así como algunas palabras que terminan por **-ce** o **-ge** (ver más abajo).

Ⓑ Cuando se añade a la palabra un sufijo que empiece por consonante, la **-e** final se mantiene.

hate → hateful

EXCEPCIONES: Cuando la palabra acaba en **-able** o **-ible** y se le añade el sufijo adverbial **-ly**.

possible → possibly; arguable → arguably

En determinadas palabras, entre las que cabe destacar:

whole → wholly; argue → argument; true → truly;

Palabras terminadas en -ce y -ge

Ⓐ Tanto en las palabras que terminan por **-ce** como en las que terminan por **-ge**, la **-e** final se mantiene al añadirles un sufijo que empiece por **a** o por **o**, a fin de que se mantenga el sonido suave de la **c** y la **g**.

change → changeable; replace → replaceable

Ⓑ En las palabras que terminan en **-ce**, la **-e** se convierte en **i** antes del sufijo **-ous**.

space → spacious; malice → malicious

Palabras terminadas en -y

Ⓐ Cuando las palabras que terminan por **-y** van precedidas de una consonante, la **y** se convierte en **i** al añadírseles cualquier sufijo que empiece por vocal.

try → tried; funny → funnier; easy → easily

NOTA: Esto ocurre también en los sustantivos en singular acabados en **-y** precedida de consonante, que forman el plural añadiendo el sufijo **-es**. Así: **baby → babies; lorry → lorries.** Y lo mismo en la formación de la tercera persona del presente: **hurry → she hurries; cry → she cries.**

EXCEPCIÓN: La única excepción a esta regla la constituye el sufijo **-ing**.

try + -ing = trying; carry + -ing = carrying.

Ⓑ Cuando la **-y** va precedida de vocal, esta **y** se mantiene.

convey → conveyed; lay → layer; boy → boys; stay → stays

Grupos vocálicos -ie- y -ei-

En la mayoría de los casos, el orden de las letras de estos grupos vocálicos en el interior de una palabra es **-ie-**, a menos que la **i** vaya precedida de **c**, en cuyo caso ocurre lo contrario.

retrieve, believ e pero **receive, deceipt**

Sin embargo, existen unas cuantas excepciones a esta regla, que son, entre otras, las siguientes palabras:

beige	freight	neither	their	weight
eight	height	rein	veil	weird
either	leisure	seize	vein	
foreign	neighbour	sleigh	weigh	

Sustantivos terminados en -o

Estos sustantivos forman el plural añadiendo el sufijo **-es.**

tomato, tomatoes; hero, heroes; potato, potatoes

EXCEPCIONES: Cuando terminan en dos vocales.

studio, studios; radio, radios.

Cuando los sustantivos son, en origen, palabras abreviadas.

kilo, kilos; photo, photos.

Palabras terminadas en -ence y -ense

En inglés británico los verbos derivados de ciertos sustantivos que se escriben con **-c-** se escriben con **-s-**. Esto no ocurre en inglés americano.

a licence pero **to license**
the practice pero **to practise**

Mayúsculas

Las mayúsculas se emplean en inglés en los siguientes casos donde se escribe minúscula en español:

A Los nombres de los días y meses: **Monday, Tuesday, May, June**

B El pronombre personal de sujeto, primera persona: **I** (yo). Pero, a diferencia del español, en que se escribe Ud., Uds., el pronombre de segunda persona (igual que el resto de los pronombres) se escribe siempre con minúscula.

C Los gentilicios: **I like the French, two Frenchwomen, French cheese, a text in old Castilian.** Sin embargo, el adjetivo de nacionalidad puede escribirse con minúscula en algún caso cuando se refiere a una cosa corriente u objeto conocido por todos, p. ej. **a french window, german measles.**

D En los nombres y adjetivos derivados de otras clases de nombres propios: **a Darwinian explanation, the Elizabethans.**

E En los sustantivos y adjetivos principales en los títulos de libros, películas, artículos etc: **A Clockwork Orange, Gone with the Wind.**

Apóstrofes

El apóstrofe se usa fundamentalmente en inglés:

A En la formación del posesivo, para la que se añade una **s** precedida de apóstrofe al singular de cualquier sustantivo o al plural que no acabe en **-s.**

my father's car; women's talk

En los plurales de los sustantivos acabados en **-s** se añade solamente un apóstrofe.

their friends' house; my daughters' social life

B En determinadas contracciones de palabras, para señalar la omisión de una o más letras.

I am → **I'm; you are** → **you're; he is** → **he's; I had/ I would** → **I'd** etc

Diferencias ortográficas entre el inglés británico y el norteamericano

Palabras con el grupo vocálico -ou-

A En las palabras terminadas en **-our** en inglés británico derivadas del latín, la **u** se suprime en inglés americano. Así, por ejemplo: inglés británico **colour** = inglés americano **color**; inglés británico **labour** = inglés americano **labor**. (Esto no afecta a los monosílabos como **dour, flour, sour,** donde no hay diferencia).

B En inglés americano también se suprime la **u** cuando este grupo de letras se encuentra en el interior de la palabra. Así: inglés británico **mould** = inglés americano **mold**; inglés británico **smoulder** = inglés americano **smolder.**

Palabras terminadas en -re *(Brit)*

Cuando esta terminación va precedida de consonante y el énfasis no recae en esta sílaba en inglés británico, normalmente cambia a **-er** en inglés americano: inglés británico **centre** = inglés americano **center**; inglés británico **metre** = inglés americano **meter**. (Pero no existe diferencia en **acre, genre, lucre, massacre, mediocre, ogre**).

Vocales finales

Ciertas vocales finales, que no tienen valor en la pronunciación, se escriben en inglés británico pero se suprimen en inglés americano: inglés americano **catalog** = inglés británico **catalogue**; inglés americano **program** = inglés británico **programme.**

Diptongos de origen griego o latino

En inglés americano se suele simplificar los diptongos de origen griego o latino **ae, oe,** escribiéndose sencillamente **e**: inglés americano **anemia** = inglés británico **anaemia**; inglés americano **anesthesia** = inglés británico **anaesthesia.**

Palabras terminadas en -ence *(Brit)*

En algunos casos las palabras que en inglés británico terminan en **-ence** se escriben **-ense** en inglés americano: inglés británico **defence** = inglés americano **defense**; inglés británico **offence** = inglés americano **offense.**

Consonantes dobles

Algunas consonantes que en inglés británico se escriben dobles, en inglés americano se escriben sencillas: inglés británico **waggon** = inglés americano **wagon** (aunque **wagon** se admite también en el Reino Unido). Pero esto ocurre sobre todo en formas verbales, al añadirse sufijos a verbos que acaban en consonante. Así, por ejemplo: inglés británico **kidnapped** = inglés americano **kidnaped**; inglés británico **worshipped** = inglés americano **worshiped.**

En el caso de la **l** o **ll** intervocálicas, mientras en inglés británico la **l** se hace doble antes de un sufijo en las palabras que terminan en **l** precedida de una sola vocal o de dos vocales que forman un diptongo, en inglés americano estas palabras se escriben con una sola **l**. Así, por ejemplo: inglés británico **councillor** = inglés americano **councilor**; inglés británico **traveller** = inglés americano **traveler**. Sin embargo, en posición de final de sílaba o de palabra, la **l** en inglés británico es a menudo **ll** en inglés americano: inglés americano **enroll** = inglés británico **enrol**; inglés americano **skillful** = inglés británico **skilful.**

Algunas palabras aisladas

Existe una serie de palabras aisladas que se escriben de modo diferente:

(US)	(Brit)	(US)	(Brit)
ax	axe	mustache	moustache
check	cheque	pajamas	pyjamas
cozy	cosy	plow	plough
disk	disc	skeptic	sceptic
gray	grey	tire	tyre
gypsy	gipsy		

Es importante observar, sin embargo, que existen algunas palabras que en inglés británico se escriben con ortografía americano, aunque en general su significado queda restringido a determinados contextos. Así, por ejemplo, encontramos **disk** y **program** con ortografía norteamericana, pero referidos exclusivamente a la Informática, mientras que en todos los demás casos se escribe **disc** y **programme**.

La puntuación

Se usan los mismos signos que en español, con las siguientes excepciones:

Ⓐ Los signos de admiración e interrogación

Los signos de apertura de admiración e interrogación (¡¿) no se emplean en inglés.

What is her name?
Help!

Ⓑ El paréntesis

En inglés el paréntesis se prefiere en muchos casos a la doble raya con función parentética (—...—).

Old people think that the pace of modern life (i.e. from 1940 onwards) is far too fast.

Ⓒ Las comillas

Se utilizan para abrir y cerrar el diálogo y la oración directa, en lugar de la raya.

"Would you like a cup of coffee?" she asked.

Ⓓ La raya

En inglés informal se usa a menudo, en lugar de los dos puntos o del punto y coma, para indicar que lo que sigue es conclusión o resumen de lo anterior.

Everybody was trying to speak at the same time – the noise was deafening.

Y también para separar un comentario o una idea del resto de la frase.

She told me everything she knew – at least that's what I thought at the time.

Ⓔ El guión

Se usa, como en español, para formar palabras compuestas de otras dos o más palabras, así como para dividir palabras al final de renglón.

También se usa en ocasiones en inglés británico para separar determinados prefijos, en los siguientes casos:

– cuando el prefijo acaba en la misma vocal con la que empieza la siguiente palabra.

co-opting, pre-eminent

– cuando va delante de una palabra escrita con mayúscula.

anti-American, pre-Victorian

– siempre que se trate de los prefijos **ex-** y **non-**.

ex-husband, non-proliferation

DICCIONARIO
ESPAÑOL-INGLÉS

SPANISH-ENGLISH
DICTIONARY

Aa

A, **a** SF (= *letra*) A, a

a PREP 1 (*indicando dirección*) 1.1 (*hacia alguna parte*) to; **voy a la playa/al parque** I'm going to the beach/to the park; **ir a trabajar** o **al trabajo** to go to work; **mirar al norte** to look north(wards); **ir a casa** to go home 1.2 (*hacia dentro*) into; **me caí al río/mar** I fell into the river/sea; **subirse a un tren** to get on a train 1.3 **llegar a** [+ *ciudad, país*] to arrive in; [+ *edificio*] to arrive at; **no ha llegado todavía a la oficina** she still hasn't arrived at the office 1.4 (= *encima de*) onto; **se subieron al tejado** they climbed onto the roof

2 (*indicando situación, distancia*) **al final de la calle** at the end of the street; **a la orilla del río** on the riverbank; **siéntate a mi lado** sit next to me, sit beside me; **nos pusimos a la sombra** we moved into the shade; **está a siete km de aquí** it is seven km (away) from here; **estaba sentado a su mesa de trabajo** he was sitting at his desk; **a lo lejos** in the distance; **a la derecha** on the right; **a la izquierda** on the left

3 (*con expresiones de tiempo*) 3.1 (*en un momento concreto*) at; **a las ocho** at eight o'clock; **a los 55 años** at the age of 55; **¿a qué hora llega el tren?** what time o when does the train arrive?; **estamos a tres de julio** it's July the third, it's the third of July (*esp Brit*); **a la mañana siguiente** the following morning; **a medianoche** at midnight; **a la noche** at night; **a la tarde** (*esp RPl*) in the afternoon 3.2 (*con tiempo transcurrido*) **a la semana** a week later; **al año de vivir en Caracas** after living in Caracas for a year; **a los pocos días** after a few days, a few days later; **a los 18 minutos de juego** in the 18th minute, 18 minutes into the game 3.3 (*indicando frecuencia*) **dos veces al día** twice a day; **una vez a la semana** once a week; **día a día vamos mejorando** we're improving with every day, we're improving day by day 3.4 **al** (+ INFIN) **al entrar yo** when I came in; **nos cruzamos al salir** we bumped into each other as we were going out; **al no llegar a tiempo, quedamos fuera de la prueba** since we didn't arrive on time, we were eliminated from the race

4 (*indicando modo*) **a la americana** American-style; **funciona a pilas** it runs on batteries; **una camisa a cuadros** a check o checked shirt; **una camisa a rayas** a striped shirt; **fui a pie/ caballo** I walked/rode; **a oscuras** in the dark; **a lápiz** in pencil; **lo mataron a navajazos** he was stabbed to death; **sabe a queso** it tastes of cheese; **huele a vino** it smells of wine; **a mano** by hand; **hay que lavarlo a mano** it should be washed by hand; **hecho a mano** handmade

5 (*indicando cantidad, precio, velocidad*) **a un precio elevado** at a high price; **a 300 pesetas el kilo** at o for 300 pesetas a kilo; **los huevos están a 250 pesetas la docena** eggs are 250 pesetas a dozen; **al cinco por ciento** at five per cent; **íbamos a más de 120km por hora** we were going at o doing over 120km an hour; **poco a poco** little by little

6 (*indicando finalidad*) 6.1 (*tras verbos*) **voy a verla** I'm going to see her; **ha ido a por agua a la fuente** (*Esp*) she's gone to get some water from the fountain; **empezó a cantar** he began to sing, he started singing; **vengo a que me den un impreso** I've come to get a form 6.2 (*tras sustantivos*) **asuntos a tratar** items to be discussed; **"precio a convenir"** "price negotiable"; **éste será el camino a seguir** this must be the path to take

7 (*con complemento de persona*) 7.1 (*como complemento indirecto*) to; **le enseñé a Pablo el libro que me dejaste** I showed Pablo the book you lent me, I showed the book you lent me to Pablo 7.2 (*como complemento directo*) *no se traduce*; **vi al jefe** I saw the boss 7.3 (*indicando procedencia*) from; **se lo compré a él** I bought it from him

8 (*indicando condición*) **a no ser esto así, me iría** if this were not the case, I'd leave

9 (*indicando desafío*) **a que** I bet; **¿a que no sabes quién ha llamado?** I'll bet you can't guess who called!

10 (*uso imperativo*) **¡a callar!** be quiet!; **¡a trabajar!** let's get down to work!; **¡a comer!** lunch is ready!

11 (= *en cuanto a*) **a supersticioso no hay quien le gane** when it comes to being superstitious, there's nobody quite like him

ábaco SM abacus

abad SM abbot

abadejo SM pollack

abadesa SF abbess

abadía SF abbey

abajeño ADJ lowland, coastal

abajo Ⓐ ADV 1 (*indicando posición*) 1.1 (*gen*) down; **ahí** o **allá** o **allí** ~ down there; **aquí** ~ down here; **de** ~ lower, bottom; **yo duermo en la litera de** ~ I sleep in the lower o bottom bunk; **la sábana de** ~ the bottom sheet; **la parte de** ~ the bottom; **desde** ~ from below; **más** ~ (*en distancia*) further down; (*en altura*) lower down; **vivo tres pisos más** ~ I live three floors below; **de cintura para** ~ from the waist down; **por** ~ (= *en la parte inferior*) at the bottom; (= *por debajo*) underneath; ~ **del todo** right at the bottom, at the very bottom 1.2 (*en edificio, casa*) downstairs; ~ **están la cocina y el salón** the kitchen and lounge are downstairs; **los vecinos de** ~ the downstairs neighbours

2 (*indicando dirección*) 2.1 (*con sustantivos*) **aguas** ~ downriver, downstream; **continuaron aguas** ~ they continued downriver o downstream; **calle** ~ down the street; **cuesta** ~ down the hill; **río** ~ downstream, downriver 2.2 (*con preposición*) **hacia** ~ downward(s), down; **para** ~: **me voy para** ~ I'm going down; **no mires para** ~ don't look down; **la economía va para** ~ the economy is going downhill 2.3 (*con verbo*) **echar** ~ [+ *puerta, barricada*] to break down; [+ *gobierno*] to bring down; [+ *paz*] to break up; **venirse** ~ [*edificio, estructura, economía*] to collapse; [*planes, sueños*] to come to nothing; [*persona*] to go to pieces; **después del divorcio se vino** ~ after the divorce he went to pieces; **este país se ha venido** ~ **por culpa de la guerra** this country has been ruined by war, war has brought this country to its knees

3 (*en un texto*) below; **en la foto de** ~ in the photo below; **el** ~ **firmante** the undersigned

4 (*en una escala*) the bottom; **los de** ~ **siempre salimos perdiendo** those of us at the bottom (of the pile) are always the losers; **para** ~: **los responsables, de ministro para** ~, **deben dimitir** those responsible, from the minister down, should resign; **de 30 años para** ~ 30 years old and under

5 (*esp LAm*) (= *debajo*) underneath

6 ~ **de** (*LAm*) under; ~ **de la camisa** under the shirt Ⓑ EXCL down with!; **¡~ el gobierno!** down with the government!

abalanzarse /1f/ VPR (= *lanzarse*) to rush forward; [*multitud*] to surge forward; ~ **sobre** to spring at, rush at

abalear * /1a/ VT (*And, Ven*) to fire at, shoot up*

abalorio SM glass bead

abanderado/a SM/F 1 (= *portaestandarte*) standard bearer 2 [*de un movimiento*] champion, leader 3 (*Méx*) (= *linier*) linesman, assistant referee

abanderar /1a/ VT [+ *causa*] to champion; [+ *campaña*] to take a leading role in

abanderizarse /1f/ VPR (*Chi Pol*) to take sides, adopt a position

abandonado ADJ 1 (= *sin gente*) [*pueblo, vivienda*] abandoned, deserted; [*fábrica, cantera*] disused; [*edificio en ruinas*] derelict

2 (= *desatendido*) [*jardín, terreno*] neglected; **tienes ~s a los amigos** you've neglected your friends; **tienen el negocio muy** ~ they've allowed their business to decline; **dejar** ~ [+ *cónyuge, hijo*] to abandon, desert; [+ *animal, casa, vehículo*] to abandon; **el autobús nos dejó ~s en la carretera** the bus left us stranded by the roadside, the bus abandoned us by the roadside

3 (= *despreocupado*) slack

4 (= *desaliñado*) scruffy, shabby

5 (= *solitario*) desolate, forlorn (*frm*)

abandonar /1a/ **Ⓐ** VT **1** (= *dejar abandonado*) [+ *cónyuge, hijo*] to abandon, desert; [+ *animal, casa, posesiones*] to abandon; [+ *obligaciones*] to neglect; **no me abandones nunca** never leave me
2 (= *marcharse de*) [+ *lugar, organización*] to leave; **pronto podrán ~ el hospital** they will soon be able to leave the hospital; **miles de refugiados han abandonado la ciudad** thousands of refugees have abandoned the city
3 (= *renunciar a*) [+ *estudios, proyecto*] to give up, abandon; [+ *costumbre, cargo*] to give up; [+ *privilegio, título*] to renounce, relinquish; **he decidido ~ la política** I've decided to give up *o* abandon politics
4 [*buen humor, suerte*] to desert; **el valor la abandonó** her courage deserted her
Ⓑ VI **1** (*Atletismo*) (*antes de la prueba*) to pull out, withdraw; (*durante la prueba*) to pull out, retire
2 (*Boxeo*) to concede defeat, throw in the towel *o* sponge*
3 (*Ajedrez*) to resign, concede
4 (*Inform*) to quit
Ⓒ **abandonarse** VPR **1** (= *no cuidarse*) to let o.s. go
2 (= *entregarse*) to abandon o.s.; **~se a** [+ *alcohol, droga*] to give o.s. over *o* up to, abandon o.s. to; [+ *destino, suerte*] to abandon o.s. to; [+ *sueño*] to surrender to, give in to

abandono SM **1** (= *acción*) **1.1** [*de lugar*] **ordenaron el ~ de la isla** they ordered people to abandon *o* leave the island **1.2** [*de actividad, proyecto*] abandonment **1.3** (*Jur*) [*de cónyuge*] desertion; [*de hijos*] abandonment
➤ **abandono del domicilio conyugal, abandono del hogar** desertion
2 (*Dep*) (*antes de la prueba*) withdrawal; (*durante la prueba*) retirement; (*Ajedrez*) resignation; **ganar por ~** to win by default (*thanks to an opponent's withdrawal*)
3 (= *descuido*) neglect, abandon (*frm*); **es lamentable el ~ que sufre la sanidad pública** it's dreadful how public health has been so neglected

abanicar /1g/ **Ⓐ** VT to fan **Ⓑ** **abanicarse** VPR to fan o.s.
abanico SM **1** (*para darse aire*) fan; **extender las cartas en ~** to fan out one's cards **2** (= *gama*) range ➤ **abanico de posibilidades** range of possibilities ➤ **abanico de salarios** wage scale

abaratamiento SM price reduction
abaratar /1a/ VT to make cheaper, lower the price of
abarcar /1g/ VT **1** (*con los brazos*) to get one's arms round **2** (= *comprender*) to include, take in; (= *contener*) to contain, comprise; **el capítulo abarca tres siglos** the chapter covers three centuries; **sus conocimientos abarcan todo el campo de ...** his knowledge ranges over the whole field of ... **3** [+ *tarea*] to undertake, take on **4** (*con la vista*) to take in; **desde aquí se abarca todo el valle** you can take in the whole valley from here
abarrotar /1a/ VT to pack; **el público abarrotaba la sala** the hall was packed with people; **el estadio estaba abarrotado** the stadium was packed; **abarrotado de** bursting with, stuffed full of
abarrotería SF (*Méx*) grocer's (shop) (*esp Brit*), grocery store (*EEUU*)
abarrotero/a SM/F (*Méx, Chi*) grocer
abarrotes SMPL (*And, Méx, CAm*) groceries; **tienda de ~** grocer's (shop), grocery store
abastecer /2d/ VT to supply, provide (**de** with)
abastecimiento SM (= *acto*) supplying, provision; (= *servicio*) supply, provision
abasto SM **1** (= *provisión*) supply; **no puedo dar ~ (a)** (*fig*) I can't cope *o* keep up (with) **2** (*Ven*) = **abarrotería**
abatible ADJ **asiento ~** tip-up seat; (*Aut*) reclining seat; **mesa de alas ~s** gate-leg(ged) table
abatido ADJ depressed
abatimiento SM depression
abatir /3a/ **Ⓐ** VT **1** (= *derribar*) to demolish, knock down; [+ *árbol*] to cut down, fell; [+ *ave*] to shoot down, bring down **2** [*enfermedad, dolor*] to lay low, prostrate (*frm*)
3 (= *desanimar*) to depress, discourage (= *humillar*) to humble, humiliate **Ⓑ** **abatirse** VPR **1** (= *caerse*) to drop, fall; [*pájaro, avión*] to swoop, dive; **~se sobre** to swoop on

2 (= *desanimarse*) to be depressed, get discouraged
abdicación SF abdication
abdicar /1g/ **Ⓐ** VT to renounce, relinquish; **~ la corona** to give up the crown, abdicate **Ⓑ** VI to abdicate; **~ de algo** to renounce *o* relinquish sth; **~ en algn** to abdicate in favour *o* (*EEUU*) favor of sb
abdomen SM abdomen
abdominal **Ⓐ** ADJ abdominal **Ⓑ** SM **abdominales** (= *ejercicio*) sit-ups
abecedario SM (= *alfabeto*) alphabet; (= *libro*) primer, spelling book
abedul SM birch ➤ **abedul plateado** silver birch
abeja SF bee ➤ **abeja obrera** worker bee ➤ **abeja reina** queen bee
abejorro SM bumblebee
aberración SF aberration; **es una ~ bañarse cinco veces al día** it's crazy to have a bath five times a day
aberrante ADJ aberrant
abertura SF (*gen*) opening, gap; (= *agujero*) hole; (= *corte*) slit
abertzale ADJ **movimiento ~** (Basque) nationalist movement
abeto SM fir, fir tree
abiertamente ADV openly
abierto **Ⓐ** PP *de* **abrir**
Ⓑ ADJ **1** [*puerta, armario, boca, herida*] open; **la puerta estaba un poco abierta** the door was ajar; **me miró con los ojos muy ~s** he looked at me with his eyes wide-open, he looked at me with wide-open eyes; **llevas la bragueta abierta** your fly is undone, your flies are undone (*Brit*); **dejar ~** [+ *ventana, cortina, válvula*] to leave open; [+ *grifo*] to leave running, leave on
2 [*comercio, museo, oficina*] open; **"abierto"** "open"
3 (= *sin obstáculos*) [*competición, billete*] open
4 (= *extrovertido*) [*persona*] open, outgoing; [*carácter, mentalidad*] open; **tiene una mentalidad muy abierta** he's very open-minded, he's got a very open mind
5 estar ~ a [+ *sugerencias, ideas*] to be open to; **tienen una actitud abierta al diálogo** they are open to dialogue
6 (= *directo*) [*contradicción, oposición*] open; [*desafío*] direct; **se encuentran en ~ desacuerdo con él** they openly disagree with him
7 (*TV*) **en ~:** **emitir algo en ~** to broadcast sth unscrambled; **emisión en ~** unscrambled programme
8 (*Ling*) [*vocal, sonido*] open
abigarrado ADJ **1** (= *de diversos colores*) multi-coloured, multi-colored (*EEUU*) **2** (= *variopinto*) motley
abismado ADJ **1** (= *absorto*) lost (*in thought*); **estaba ~ en su lectura** he was engrossed in his reading **2** (*And*) (= *sorprendido*) amazed
abismal ADJ (= *enorme*) vast, enormous; [*diferencia*] irreconcilable
abismante* ADJ (*And*) amazing
abismar /1a/ **Ⓐ** VT (*And*) to amaze **Ⓑ** **abismarse** VPR to be amazed
abismo SM abyss, chasm; **de sus ideas a las mías hay un ~** our views are worlds *o* poles apart
abjurar /1a/ VI **~ de** to abjure, forswear
ablación SF ➤ **ablación del clítoris, ablación femenina** female circumcision
ablandar /1a/ **Ⓐ** VT **1** (= *poner blando*) to soften; (*Culin*) to tenderize **2** (= *conmover*) to touch; (= *calmar*) to soothe **3** (*CS Aut*) to run in (*Brit*), break in (*EEUU*) **Ⓑ** **ablandarse** VPR (= *ponerse blando*) to soften (up), get soft(er); [*persona*] to relent, soften; (*con la edad*) to mellow
ablativo SM ablative
ablución SF ablution
abnegación SF self-denial, abnegation (*frm*)
abnegado ADJ self-denying, self-sacrificing
abobado ADJ bewildered
abocado ADJ **1** (= *encaminado*) **estar ~ al desastre** to be

héading for disaster **2** (*CS, Ven frm*) (= *dedicado*) **estar ~ a algo** to be engaged in sth

abochornado ADJ embarrassed

abochornar /1a/ Ⓐ VT to shame, embarrass Ⓑ **abochornarse** VPR to get embarrassed

abofetear /1a/ VT to slap, hit (in the face)

abogacía SF (= *abogados*) legal profession; (= *oficio*) the law

abogado/a SM/F lawyer, attorney(-at-law) (*EEUU*); **ejercer de ~** to practise *o* (*EEUU*) practice law ➤ **abogado/a defensor(a)** defence counsel, defense counsel (*EEUU*) ➤ **abogado del diablo** devil's advocate ➤ **abogado/a del Estado** public prosecutor, attorney general (*EEUU*) ➤ **abogado/a de oficio** court-appointed counsel, duty solicitor (*Brit*), public defender (*EEUU*) ➤ **abogado/a laboralista** labour lawyer, labor lawyer (*EEUU*)

abogar /1h/ VI **~ por** to advocate, champion

abolengo SM ancestry, lineage; **de rancio ~** of ancient lineage

abolición SF abolition

abolir /3a; *defectivo*/ VT to abolish

abolladura SF (*en metal*) dent

abollar /1a/ Ⓐ VT [+ *metal*] to dent Ⓑ **abollarse** VPR [*metal*] to get dented

abollón SM dent

abombado ADJ **1** (= *convexo*) convex; (= *abovedado*) domed **2** (*LAm*) (= *aturdido*) stunned **3** (*LAm*) [*comida*] rotten; **estar ~** to smell bad, stink

abombarse /1a/ VPR (*LAm*) to go bad, go off (*Brit**)

abominable ADJ abominable

abominación SF abomination

abominar /1a/ VT to abominate, detest

abonado/a SM/F (*a revista, compañía telefónica*) subscriber; (*Teat, Ferro*) season-ticket holder

abonar /1a/ Ⓐ VT **1** (*Agr*) to fertilize; **están abonando el terreno para cambiar la ley** they're preparing the ground for a change in the law **2** (= *pagar*) [+ *cuota, salario*] to pay; [+ *cheque, giro*] to cash; **me ~on los intereses en mi cuenta** the interest was credited to *o* paid into my account Ⓑ **abonarse** VPR **~se a una revista** to subscribe to a magazine, take out a subscription to a magazine; **me he abonado a la ópera** I have bought a season ticket for the opera

abono SM **1** (*Agr*) (= *fertilizante*) manure, fertilizer ➤ **abono químico** chemical fertilizer, artificial manure **2** (*Com*) (= *pago*) payment; (= *plazo*) instalment, installment (*EEUU*) **3** (*a periódico, revista*) subscription; (*Teat, Ferro*) season ticket

aboquillado ADJ tipped, filter-tipped

abordaje SM (*Náut*) (= *invasión*) boarding; **¡al ~!** all aboard!

abordar /1a/ VT **1** (= *acometer*) to tackle; **el libro aborda temas controvertidos** the book tackles some controversial subjects **2** (= *tratar*) to deal with; **se negó a ~ la cuestión en la rueda de prensa** he refused to deal with the subject at the press conference **3** **~ a algn** to approach sb **4** (*Náut*) (= *atacar*) to board; (= *chocar con*) to ram **5** (*Méx*) [+ *automóvil*] to get into; [+ *avión, camión urbano*] to board, get onto

aborigen Ⓐ ADJ aboriginal Ⓑ SMF aborigine, aboriginal

aborrecer /2d/ VT to loathe, detest

abortar /1a/ Ⓐ VI (*accidentalmente*) to have a miscarriage; (*de forma provocada*) to have an abortion Ⓑ VT **1** [+ *plan, aterrizaje*] to abort **2** (= *frustrar*) [+ *complot*] to foil, frustrate; [+ *motín, protesta*] to quell, put down **3** (*Inform*) to abort

abortista Ⓐ ADJ [*clínica*] abortion *antes de s*; [*política*] pro-abortion Ⓑ SMF (= *partidario*) abortion campaigner Ⓒ SF *woman who has had an abortion*

abortivo ADJ **píldora abortiva** abortion pill; **algunas prácticas abortivas** certain methods of abortion

aborto SM **1** (*Med*) (*accidental*) miscarriage; (*provocado*)

abortion ➤ **aborto clandestino** backstreet abortion **2** (= *fracaso*) failure **3** (******) ugly man/woman

abotagado ADJ = **abotargado**

abotagarse /1h/ VPR = **abotargarse**

abotargado ADJ swollen, bloated

abotargarse /1h/ VPR to swell up, become bloated

abotonar /1a/ VT to button up, do up

abovedado ADJ vaulted

abra SF (*Méx, RPl*) (= *claro*) clearing

abrasar /1a/ Ⓐ VT to burn (up); **murieron abrasados** they burned to death Ⓑ **abrasarse** VPR to burn (up); **~se de calor** to be roasting *o* sweltering

abrasión SF abrasion

abrasivo ADJ, SM abrasive

abrazadera SF bracket, clamp

abrazar /1f/ Ⓐ VT **1** [+ *persona*] to hug, hold, embrace **2** [+ *fe*] to adopt, embrace Ⓑ **abrazarse** VPR to hug (each other), embrace (each other); **~se a** (*gen*) to hug, embrace; (*para no caer*) to cling to, clutch

abrazo SM **1** (= *acción*) hug, embrace **2** (*en cartas*) **un ~ afectuoso** *o* **cordial** with best wishes *o* kind regards; **un fuerte ~ (de)** love from

abrebocas SM INV (*Col*) appetizer

abrebotellas SM INV bottle opener

abrecartas SM INV letter opener, paper knife

abrefácil SM **un envase con ~** an easy-open carton; **"abrefácil"** "easy-open"

abrelatas SM INV can opener, tin opener (*Brit*)

abrevadero SM drinking trough

abrevar /1a/ VI to drink

abreviar /1b/ Ⓐ VT [+ *palabra*] to abbreviate; [+ *texto*] to abridge, reduce; [+ *discurso, estancia*] to shorten, cut short Ⓑ VI (= *apresurarse*) to be quick; **bueno, para ~ ...** well, to cut (*Brit*) *o* make (*EEUU*) a long story short ...

abreviatura SF abbreviation, contraction

abridor SM [*de botellas*] bottle opener; [*de latas*] can opener, tin opener (*Brit*)

abrigado ADJ **1** (= *cubierto de ropa*) wrapped up (**con** in); **tengo los pies bien ~s** my feet are nice and warm **2** (*RPl*) (= *que abriga*) [*ropa*] warm **3** (= *protegido*) [*lugar*] sheltered, protected (**de** from)

abrigador ADJ (*And, Méx*) warm

abrigar /1h/ Ⓐ VT **1** (*del frío*) [*persona*] to wrap up; [*ropa, manta*] to keep warm **2** (= *resguardar*) to shelter, protect (**de** from) **3** (= *ayudar*) to support; **tiene un buen equipo que le abriga** he's got a good team supporting him **4** (= *albergar*) [+ *ambición, sospecha, temor*] to harbour, harbor (*EEUU*); [+ *duda*] to entertain, harbour, harbor (*EEUU*); [+ *esperanza, ilusión*] to cherish, harbour, harbor (*EEUU*) Ⓑ VI [*ropa, manta*] to be warm; **esta chaqueta abriga mucho** this jacket is nice and warm Ⓒ **abrigarse** VPR **1** (*con ropa*) to wrap (o.s.) up; **¡abrígate bien!** wrap up well!; **usaban una manta para ~se** they used a blanket to keep themselves warm; **abrígate el cuello con la bufanda** cover your neck up with the scarf **2** (= *resguardarse*) to shelter, take shelter (**de** from)

abrigo SM **1** (= *prenda*) coat; **un ~ de pieles** a fur coat **2** (= *protección*) **2.1** (*contra el frío*) **esta manta te servirá de ~** this blanket will keep you warm; **ropa de ~** warm clothes **2.2** (*contra viento, lluvia*) shelter; ✦ MODISMO **de ~** (*Esp*) [*gastos, presupuesto, pelea*] huge; **tiene una bronquitis de ~** she has really bad bronchitis **3 al ~ de 3.1** (= *protegido por*) [+ *seto, roca*] in the shelter of; [+ *noche, oscuridad*] under cover of; [+ *ley, poder*] under, under the protection of; **la ciudad está situada al ~ de unas colinas** the town is sheltered by hills; **escaparon al ~ de la noche** they escaped under cover of darkness **3.2** (= *protegido de*) [+ *tormenta, viento*] sheltered from; [+ *escándalo, desgracias*] protected from; **nos pusimos al ~ del viento** we took shelter *o* we sheltered from the wind; **al ~ de las miradas indiscretas** away from prying eyes

abril SM April; **una chica de 15 ~es** a girl of 15 summers (*liter*); *ver tb* **septiembre**

En inglés los meses se escriben con mayúscula.

---

abrillantamuebles SM INV furniture polish

abrillantar /1a/ VT to polish

abrir /3a/ (*pp* **abierto**) Ⓐ VT 1 (*algo que estaba cerrado*)
1.1 [+ *puerta, armario, libro, ojos*] to open; [+ *cremallera, bragueta*] to undo; **abrid el libro por la página 50** turn to page 50 in the book, open the book at page 50; ✦ MODISMO **en un ~ y cerrar de ojos** in the twinkling of an eye
1.2 (*desplegando*) [+ *mapa, mantel*] to spread out; [+ *paraguas*] to open, put up; [+ *mano, abanico, paracaídas*] to open
1.3 (*haciendo una abertura*) [+ *pozo*] to sink; [+ *foso, cimientos*] to dig; [+ *agujero, perforación*] to make, bore; **tuvimos que ~ camino cortando ramas** we had to cut a path through the branches; **la explosión abrió una brecha en la pared** the explosion blew a hole in the wall 1.4 (*haciendo un corte*) [+ *sandía*] to cut open; [+ *herida*] to open 1.5 [+ *grifo, luz, agua*] to turn on; [+ *válvula*] to open
2 (= *encabezar*) [+ *manifestación, desfile*] to lead, head; [+ *baile*] to open, lead off; [+ *lista*] to head
3 (= *inaugurar*) 3.1 [+ *acto, ceremonia*] to open; **ya han abierto el plazo de matrícula** registration has already started
3.2 (*Com*) [+ *negocio*] to set up, start; [+ *cuenta*] to open
3.3 (*Tip*) **~ comillas** to open quotes; **~ paréntesis** to open brackets (*Brit*) o parentheses (*EEUU*) 3.4 (*Mil*) **¡abran fuego!** (open) fire!
4 (= *ampliar*) [+ *perspectivas*] to open up
5 [+ *apetito*] **ese olor me esta abriendo el apetito** that smell is making me hungry
Ⓑ VI 1 [*puerta, cajón*] to open
2 [*persona*] to open the door, open up; **¡abre, soy yo!** open the door o open up, it's me!; **llamé pero no abrió nadie** I knocked at the door, but nobody answered; **esta llave no abre bien** this key is a bit stiff
3 [*comercio, museo*] to open; **el banco abre de nueve a uno** the bank is open from nine to one
4 [*flor*] to open
5 (*en operación quirúrgica*) **vamos a tener que ~** we're going to have to open him up
6 (*Meteo*) to clear up
Ⓒ **abrirse** VPR 1 [*paracaídas, paraguas, ventana, libro*] to open
2 (= *extenderse*) **ante nosotros se abría todo un mundo de posibilidades** a whole world of possibilities was opening up before us
3 [*persona*] 3.1 **no te abras tanto en las curvas** stay a bit closer to the side of the road when going around bends; **el delantero se abrió hacia la banda** the forward went wide
3.2 **intentaron ~se paso entre la muchedumbre** they tried to make their way through the crowd; ✦ MODISMO **~se camino en la vida** to make one's way in life 3.3 (******) (= *largarse*) **¡me abro!** I'm off!*, I'm out of here!**
4 **~se a: tenemos que ~nos más al progreso** we have to open up more to progress; **~se a** o **con algn** to confide in sb
5 (= *romperse, rajarse*) [*herida*] to open; **~se la cabeza** to crack one's head open; **se están abriendo las costuras** it's coming apart at the seams; **la madera se está abriendo** the wood is splitting; **~se las venas** to slash one's wrists
6 (*Meteo*) to clear, clear up
7 (*Méx, Ven**) (= *acobardarse*) to back out

abrochar /1a/ Ⓐ VT 1 [+ *botón, cremallera, vestido*] to do up; [+ *broche, hebilla*] to fasten; **¿me abrochas?** can you zip/button *etc* me up?, can you do me up?; **llevas los botones sin ~** your buttons are undone 2 (*LAm*) [+ *papeles*] to staple (together) Ⓑ **abrocharse** VPR [+ *camisa*] to do up; [+ *zapatos*] to tie up; [+ *cinturón de seguridad*] to fasten; **el vestido se abrocha delante con cremallera** the dress does up o fastens at the front with a zip (*Brit*) o zipper (*esp EEUU*)

abrogar /1h/ VT to abrogate, repeal

abrumador ADJ [*responsabilidad*] heavy; [*mayoría*] overwhelming

abrumar /1a/ VT (= *agobiar*) to overwhelm; (= *oprimir*) to oppress, weigh down; (= *cansar*) to wear out, exhaust; **~ a algn de trabajo** to overload o swamp sb with work; **le ~on**

con atenciones they made too much of a fuss of him

abrupto ADJ 1 [*cuesta*] steep; [*terreno*] rough, rugged 2 [*tono*] abrupt

absceso SM abscess

absenta SF absinth(e)

absentismo SM (*Esp*) absenteeism

ábside SM [*de iglesia*] apse

absolución SF (*Rel*) absolution; (*Jur*) acquittal

absolutamente ADV absolutely; **~ nada** nothing at all

absolutista ADJ, SMF absolutist

absoluto ADJ 1 (= *no relativo*) absolute; **mayoría absoluta** absolute majority
2 (= *máximo*) [*prioridad*] top; [*reposo, fe*] complete; [*verdad*] absolute; **tengo la absoluta certeza de que vino** I'm absolutely certain that he came; **guardaron el más ~ silencio** they remained absolutely silent; **viven en la miseria más absoluta** they live in the most abject poverty; **existe compenetración absoluta entre los dos** there is a perfect understanding between them, they understand each other perfectly
3 [*monarquía, poder*] absolute
4 **en ~** not at all; **—¿te importa? —en ~** "do you mind?" — "no, absolutely not o no, not at all"; **esa idea no me atrae en ~** that idea doesn't appeal to me at all o in the slightest; **no dijo nada en ~** he said absolutely nothing (at all)

absolutorio ADJ **fallo ~** verdict of not guilty

absolver /2h/ (*pp* **absuelto**) VT (*Rel*) to absolve; (*Jur*) to acquit, clear (**de** of)

absorbencia SF absorbency

absorbente ADJ 1 [*material*] absorbent 2 (= *interesante*) interesting, absorbing; [*tarea*] demanding; [*amor*] possessive, tyrannical

absorber /2a/ VT 1 [+ *líquido*] to absorb, soak up
2 [+ *información*] to absorb, take in; [+ *recursos*] to use up; [+ *energías*] to take up; [+ *atención*] to command

absorción SF 1 [*de líquidos*] absorption 2 (= *atracción*) absorption 3 (*Com*) takeover

absorto ADJ absorbed, engrossed; **estar ~ (en sus pensamientos)** to be lost in thought

abstemio/a Ⓐ ADJ teetotal Ⓑ SM/F teetotaller

abstención SF abstention

abstencionista SMF abstainer

abstenerse /2k/ VPR (*gen*) to abstain; **~ de hacer algo** to refrain from doing sth

---

Recuérdese que las preposiciones en inglés rigen gerundio y no infinitivo, de ahí **to refrain from doing sth**.

"**abstenerse intermediarios**" "no agencies"

abstinencia SF (*gen*) abstinence; (*Rel*) fasting

abstracción SF abstraction; **hacer ~ de** to leave aside, except

abstracto ADJ abstract; **en ~** in the abstract

abstraer /2o/ Ⓐ VT to abstract Ⓑ **abstraerse** VPR to be lost in thought, be preoccupied; **~se de** to detach o.s. from

abstraído ADJ (= *ensimismado*) withdrawn; (= *inquieto*) preoccupied

absuelto PP *de* **absolver**

absurdo Ⓐ ADJ absurd; **es ~ que** it is absurd that; **lo ~ es que ...** the ridiculous thing is that ... Ⓑ SM absurdity, (piece of) nonsense

abubilla SF hoopoe

abuchear /1a/ VT to boo, jeer at

abucheo SM booing, jeering

abuelo/a SM/F 1 (= *pariente*) grandfather/grandmother; **mis ~s** my grandparents; ✦ MODISMOS **¡cuéntaselo a tu abuela!** who are you trying to kid?*, pull the other one! (*Brit**); **no necesitar** o **tener abuela** (*Esp**) to blow one's own trumpet; (**éramos pocos) y parió la abuela*** and that was

5

the last straw, and that was all we needed **2** (= *anciano*) old man/old woman; **está hecho un ~** he looks like an old man **3** (= *antepasado*) ancestor, forebear

abulense ADJ of/from Ávila

abulia SF total apathy

abúlico ADJ apathetic

abulón SM (*Méx*) abalone

abultado ADJ **1** (= *voluminoso*) bulky, unwieldy; [*labios, libro*] thick **2** (= *exagerado*) exaggerated

abultar /1a/ **Ⓐ** VT **1** (= *aumentar*) to increase; (= *agrandar*) to enlarge **2** (= *exagerar*) to exaggerate **Ⓑ** VI (= *tener bulto*) to be bulky, be big

abundancia SF **1** (= *multitud, copiosidad*) abundance; **había bebida en ~** there was plenty to drink **2** (= *prosperidad*) **la sociedad de la ~** the affluent society; ✦ MODISMO **nadar en la ~** to be rolling in money

abundante ADJ **1** (= *copioso*) abundant, plentiful; **la fauna es ~ en el parque nacional** ◇ **el parque nacional es ~ en fauna** there is abundant wildlife in the national park, there is a wealth of fauna in the national park; **un país ~ en minerales** a country which is rich in minerals, a country which abounds in minerals; **una ~ ración de calamares** a generous portion of squid; **tienes que hervirlos en agua** ~ you have to boil them in plenty of water; **la nubosidad será ~ en Galicia** there will be extensive cloud cover in Galicia **2** (*en plural*) a great many; **un texto con ~s citas** a text with a great many *o* numerous quotations; **los flamencos son muy ~s en toda la zona** there are a great many flamingos throughout the area

abundar /1a/ VI **1** (= *existir en abundancia*) to be plentiful; **el olivo abunda en el sur** olive trees are plentiful in the south **2** (*frm*) (= *tener en abundancia*) ~ **en algo: la zona abunda en gas natural** the area is rich in natural gas, natural gas is plentiful in the area; **los periódicos abundan en anglicismos** the newspapers abound in *o* with anglicisms **3** (= *profundizar*) ~ **en algo** (*frm*) to elaborate on sth; **no quiso ~ más en el asunto** he declined to elaborate **4** (= *estar de acuerdo*) **yo abundo en esa opinión** I absolutely *o* wholeheartedly agree

abur★ EXCL so long!

aburguesado ADJ **un barrio ~** a gentrified area; **un hombre ~** a man who has become bourgeois, a man who has adopted middle-class ways

aburguesarse /1a/ VPR to become bourgeois, adopt middle-class ways

aburrición SF (*Col, Méx*) = **aburrimiento**

aburrido ADJ (= *que aburre*) boring, tedious; (= *que siente aburrimiento*) bored; **un libro ~** a boring book; **una espera aburrida** a tedious wait

---

Aburrido se traduce por **bored** para referirse al hecho de estar aburrido: "*Si estás aburrida podrías ayudarme con esto*", *If you're bored you could help me with this*. Se traduce por **boring** para indicar que alguien o algo es aburrido: "*No me gusta salir con él; es muy aburrido*", *I don't like going out with him; he's very boring*.

---

aburridor ADJ (*LAm*) boring

aburrimiento SM boredom, tedium; **¡qué ~!** what a bore!

aburrir /3a/ **Ⓐ** VT to bore **Ⓑ** **aburrirse** VPR to be bored, get bored (**con, de, por** with); ✦ MODISMO **~se como una ostra** to be bored stiff

abusado (*Méx*) **Ⓐ** EXCL (★) (= *cuidado*) look out!, careful! **Ⓑ** ADJ (= *astuto*) sharp, cunning

abusar /1a/ VI **1** (= *extralimitarse*) **es muy generoso pero no debéis ~** he's very generous but you mustn't take advantage; **~ de** [+ *persona*] to take advantage of; [+ *amistad, hospitalidad, amabilidad, privilegio*] to abuse; **no quiero ~ de su tiempo** I don't want to take up too much of your time; **~ de la confianza de algn** (= *aprovecharse*) to take advantage of sb's good will; (= *traicionar*) to betray sb's trust

2 (= *usar en exceso*) **está bien beber de vez en cuando pero sin ~** drinking every so often is fine as long as you don't overdo it; **no conviene ~ de las grasas** it's not good to eat too much fat **3** (*sexualmente*) **~ de algn** to (sexually) abuse sb

abusivo ADJ (*gen*) unfair; [*precio*] exorbitant, outrageous

abuso SM **1** (= *extralimitación*) [*de privilegios, cargo, fondos*] abuse; **lo que te han cobrado es un ~** it's outrageous what they've charged you ➤ **abuso de autoridad** abuse of authority ➤ **abuso de confianza** (*Pol, Fin*) breach of trust, betrayal of trust ➤ **abuso de poder** abuse of power **2** (= *uso excesivo*) [*de tabaco, drogas*] abuse; [*de disolventes, pesticidas*] overuse; **no es recomendable el ~ de la sal en la comida** it's not advisable to put too much salt in your food; **hicieron uso y ~ del teléfono** they used the phone to excess **3** (*tb* **~ sexual**) sexual abuse ➤ **abuso de menores** child abuse ➤ **abusos deshonestos** indecent assault *sing*

abusón/ona★ (*Esp*) **Ⓐ** ADJ selfish **Ⓑ** SM/F **eres un ~** you're a selfish pig★

abyecto ADJ wretched, abject

acá ADV **1** (*esp LAm*) here, over here; **pasearse de ~ para allá** to walk up and down *o* to and fro; **¡ven *o* vente para ~!** come over here!; **tráelo más ~** move it this way, bring it closer **2** (= *ahora*) at this time, now; **de *o* desde ayer ~** since yesterday; **¿de cuándo ~?** since when?

acabado **Ⓐ** ADJ **1** (= *completo*) finished **2** **estar ~** (*de salud*) to be a wreck; **está ~ como futbolista** he's finished as a footballer, his footballing days are over **Ⓑ** SM (*Téc*) finish

acabar /1a/ **Ⓐ** VT **1** (= *terminar*) [+ *actividad, trabajo*] (*gen*) to finish; (= *dar el toque final a*) to finish off; **me falta poco para ~ la bufanda** I've nearly finished the scarf; **acabó sus días en prisión** he ended his days in prison **2** (= *consumir*) to finish; **ya hemos acabado el aceite** we've used up *o* finished the oil

Ⓑ VI **1** (= *terminar*) to finish, end; **¿te falta mucho para ~?** are you nearly finished?, have you got long to go?; **es cosa de nunca ~** there's no end to it; ✦ MODISMO **acabáramos: acabáramos, ¿así que se trata de tu hijo?** oh, I see, so it's your son, then?

2 ~ **con 2.1** [+ *comida*] to finish off; [+ *injusticia*] to put an end to, stop; [+ *relación*] to end; [+ *reservas*] to exhaust, use up; [+ *esperanzas*] dash, put paid to (*esp Brit*) **2.2** [+ *persona*] (= *atender*) to finish with; (= *matar*) to do away with; **cuando acabe con ella, te lavo la cabeza** when I'm done *o* finished with her, I'll wash your hair; **¡acabemos con él!** let's do away with him!★; **esto acabará conmigo** this will be the end of me

3 ~ **de hacer algo 3.1** (*cuando se ha terminado*) **acabo de leerlo** I have just read it; **acababa de entrar cuando sonó el teléfono** I had just come in when the phone rang **3.2** (*cuando se está haciendo*) **cuando acabemos de pagarlo** when we finish paying for it **3.3** **no acabo de entender por qué lo hizo** I just can't understand why she did it; **ese candidato no me acaba de convencer** I'm not too sure about that candidate

4 (*con complemento de modo*) **la novela acaba bien** the novel has a happy ending; **su relación acabó mal** their relationship came to an unhappy end; **si sigues así vas a ~ mal** if you carry on like that you'll come to a sticky end; **acabé harto de tantas fiestas** I ended up getting sick of *o* fed up with all those parties; **la palabra acaba con *o* por "z"** the word ends in a "z"; ~ **en algo** to end in sth; **espero que no acabe en tragedia** I hope it won't end in tragedy; **todo acabó en nada** it all came to nothing

5 ~ **haciendo algo** ◇ ~ **por hacer algo** to end up doing sth **6** (*en una relación*) to finish, split up; ~ **con algn** to split up with sb, finish with sb

Ⓒ **acabarse** VPR **1** (= *terminarse*) [*acto, reunión*] to finish, come to an end; [*reservas*] to run out; **la impresora te avisa cuando se acaba el papel** the printer tells you when the paper runs out; **¡se acabó!** that's it!; **le das el dinero y se acabó** just give her the money and be done with it **2** (*con complemento indirecto*) **se me ha acabado el tabaco** I'm out of cigarettes **3** (*con valor enfático*) **acábate el café y nos vamos** drink up

your coffee and we'll go
4 [*persona*] (*Méx*) (= *cansarse*) to wear o.s. out

acabóse SM, **acabose** SM **esto es el ~** this is the last straw

acacia SF acacia

academia SF academy; (*Escol*) (private) school; **la Real Academia** the Spanish Academy ➤ **academia de baile** dance school ➤ **academia de idiomas** language school ➤ **academia militar** military academy

ACADEMIA

In Spain **academias** are private schools catering for students of all ages and levels outside normal school and working hours. Some specialize in particular skills such as computing, languages and dressmaking while others offer extra tuition in core school subjects and syllabuses. For people hoping to do well enough in the **oposiciones** to get a post in the public sector, there are **academias** offering special preparatory courses for these notoriously difficult competitive examinations.
◇ OPOSICIONES

académico/a Ⓐ ADJ academic Ⓑ SM/F academician, member (of an academy)

acaecer /2d/ VI to happen, occur

acallar /1a/ VT **1** (= *silenciar*) to silence, quieten, quiet (*EEUU*) **2** (= *calmar*) [+ *furia*] to assuage, pacify; [+ *crítica, duda*] to silence

acalorado ADJ [*discusión*] heated; [*partidario*] passionate

acalorarse /1a/ VPR **1** (= *sofocarse*) to get hot, become overheated **2** (= *enardecerse*) [*persona*] (*al actuar*) to get excited, get worked up (**por** about); (*al hablar*) to get worked up; [*discusión*] to become heated

acalórico ADJ low-calorie *antes de s*, low in calories

acampada SF camping; **ir de** o **hacer una ~** to go camping

acampanado ADJ bell-shaped; [*pantalón*] flared, bell-bottomed

acampar /1a/ VI to camp; (*Mil*) to encamp

acanalado ADJ **1** (*Arquit*) fluted **2** [*hierro*] corrugated

acantilado SM cliff

acantonar /1a/ VT to station

acaparador(a) Ⓐ ADJ (*con cosas*) selfish; (*con personas*) possessive Ⓑ SM/F **1** [*de objetos, mercancías*] hoarder **2** (= *egoísta*) (*con cosas*) selfish person; (*con personas*) possessive person

acaparar /1a/ VT **1** [+ *víveres, bienes*] to hoard **2** (= *tener la totalidad de*) **2.1** [+ *producción, poder, conversación*] to monopolize; **acaparan la distribución de gas en la zona** they have a monopoly on the distribution of gas in the area; **~ el mercado de algo** to corner the market in sth **2.2** (*pey*) to hog*, monopolize; **a ver si no acaparas el teléfono** don't hog* o monopolize the telephone, will you?
3 (= *quedarse con*) to take; **el documental que acaparó todos los premios** the documentary which took all the prizes; **la industria acapara la mayor parte de las ayudas del gobierno** industry gets most of the government aid
4 (= *poseer*) to hold; **la izquierda acapara todos los puestos en el ayuntamiento** the left takes all of the council posts (*esp Brit*) o city government posts (*esp EEUU*)
5 (= *ocupar*) to take up; **el accidente acaparó las primeras páginas de todos los periódicos** the accident took up the front pages in all the newspapers
6 [+ *atención, interés*] to capture; **le gustaba ~ las miradas de todo el mundo** he liked to hog the limelight*

a capella [aka'pela] ADV a cappella

acápite SM (*LAm*) (= *párrafo*) paragraph; (= *título*) subheading; **punto ~** full stop, new paragraph (*Brit*), period, new paragraph (*EEUU*)

acaramelado ADJ [*amantes*] **estaban ~s** they were all lovey-dovey*

acaramelar /1a/ VT to coat with caramel

acariciar /1b/ VT **1** (= *hacer caricias*) to caress, stroke; (= *sobar*) to fondle; [+ *animal*] to pat, stroke
2 [+ *esperanzas*] to cherish, cling to; [+ *proyecto*] to have in mind

ácaro SM mite ➤ **ácaro del polvo** dust mite

acarraladura* SF (*Perú*) run, ladder (*Brit*)

acarrear /1a/ VT **1** (= *transportar*) to transport, carry; (= *arrastrar*) to cart **2** (= *causar*) to cause, bring in its train o wake; **le acarreó muchos disgustos** it caused o brought him lots of problems

acarreo SM (= *flete*) haulage, carriage; **gastos de ~** transport charges

acartonado ADJ [*superficie*] like cardboard; (= *enjuto*) wizened

acartonarse /1a/ VPR (= *ponerse rígido*) to grow stiff; (= *quedarse enjuto*) to become wizened

acaserarse* /1a/ VPR (*And*) to become a regular customer (*of a shop*)

acaso ADV **1** (*en preguntas retóricas*) **¿~ tengo yo la culpa de lo que haga mi hermana?** (how) am I to blame for what my sister does? **2** (*frm*) (= *quizá*) perhaps; **~ no es verdad** perhaps it is not true **3** **si ~: está bueno, si ~ un poco dulce** it's quite good, if perhaps a little too sweet **4** **por si ~** just in case; **llévalo por si ~ hace falta** take it, just in case you need it; **por si ~ viniera** just in case he should come o were to come

acatar /1a/ VT [+ *ley*] to observe, comply with

acatarrado ADJ **estar ~** to have a cold

acatarrar /1a/ Ⓐ VT (*Méx**) to annoy, bother
Ⓑ **acatarrarse** VPR to catch a cold

acaudalado ADJ well-off, affluent

acaudillar /1a/ VT to lead, command

acceder /2a/ VI **1** (= *aceptar*) to agree; **~ a algo** to agree to sth; **~ a hacer algo** to agree to do sth
2 **~ a** (= *entrar*) **2.1** [+ *lugar*] to gain access to; [+ *grupo social, organización*] to be admitted to; **no pueden ~ al mercado laboral** they have no access to the labour o (*EEUU*) labor market; **~ a la universidad** to gain admittance to the university; **si ganan este partido, acceden a la final** if they win this match they go through to the final **2.2** (*Inform*) to access
3 (= *conseguir*) **~ a** [+ *información*] to gain access to, access; **la primera mujer en ~ a este puesto** the first woman to assume this post; **no pueden ~ a una vivienda digna** they have no access to decent housing; **para ~ a estas becas es necesario ser europeo** only European citizens are eligible for these grants; **~ al poder** to assume power; **~ a la propiedad de algo** to become the owner of sth; **~ al trono** to succeed to the throne

accesible ADJ **1** [*lugar, texto, lenguaje, estilo*] accessible **2** [*persona*] approachable **3** [*precio, producto*] affordable

accésit SM (*pl* **~s**) second prize

acceso SM **1** (= *posibilidad de entrar*) (*a edificio, institución, mercado, documentos*) access; (*a competición*) entry; **el ~ público a la educación** public access to education; **"acceso prohibido"** ◇ **"prohibido el acceso"** "no entry", "no admittance"; **(código de) ~ internacional** (*Telec*) international (dialling o (*EEUU*) dialing) code; **eso coincidió con su ~ al poder** this coincided with his assuming power; **dar ~ a** [+ *lugar*] to lead to; [+ *institución*] to give entry to; [+ *competición*] to provide a place in; [+ *información*] to give access to
2 (= *entrada*) entrance; **puerta de ~** entrance gate o door; **carretera** o **vía de ~** (*a ciudad*) approach road; (*a autovía*) slip road
3 (= *camino*) **los ~s a la finca estaban bloqueados por manifestantes** the approaches to the estate were blocked by protesters
4 (*Univ*) (= *ingreso*) entrance; **curso de ~** continuing education course, access course (*Brit*); **prueba de ~** entrance exam
5 (*Inform*) access ➤ **acceso aleatorio** random access ➤ **acceso secuencial** sequential access
6 (= *ataque*) **6.1** (*Med*) [*de asma, fiebre*] attack; [*de tos*] fit

6.2 [*de celos, cólera*] fit; [*de generosidad*] display

accesorio ⒶADJ accessory; [*gastos*] incidental **ⒷSM 1** (*gen*) accessory, attachment, extra; **accesorios** (*Téc*) accessories, spare parts; (*Aut*) spare parts; (*Teat*) props **2** (*de vestir*) accessory

accidentado/a ⒶADJ 1 [*terreno*] rough, uneven **2** (= *turbado*) [*vida*] troubled, eventful; [*viaje*] eventful **3** (*Med*) injured **ⒷSM/F** accident victim, casualty

accidental ADJ (= *contingente*) accidental; [*encuentro*] casual, chance *antes de s*

accidentalmente ADV (= *por casualidad*) by chance; (= *sin querer*) accidentally, unintentionally

accidentarse /1a/ **VPR** to have an accident

accidente SM 1 (= *suceso*) accident; **por ~** by accident, by chance ➤ **accidente aéreo** plane crash ➤ **accidente de coche** car accident ➤ **accidente de trabajo, accidente laboral** industrial accident ➤ **accidente de tráfico** road accident, traffic accident **2** (*Ling*) accidence **3** ~**s** [*de terreno*] unevenness *sing*, roughness *sing*

acción SF 1 (= *actividad*) action; **película de ~** action film (*esp Brit*), action movie (*esp EEUU*); **es hora de pasar a la ~** it's time to take action; **en ~** in action; **puso el plan en** he put the plan in action; **ponerse en ~** to go into action **2** (= *acto*) act; **llevaron a cabo una ~ condenable** they committed a reprehensible act; **deben ser juzgados por sus acciones y no por sus palabras** they should be judged by their deeds, not by their words; **buena ~** good deed ➤ **acción de gracias** thanksgiving **3** (= *efecto*) [*de medicamento, viento*] action; **lo recomiendan por su ~ relajante** it is recommended for its relaxing effect; **de ~ retardada** [*bomba, mecanismo*] delayed-action *antes de s* **4** (*Mil*) (*gen*) action; (= *operación*) operation; **muerto en ~** killed in action ➤ **acción de guerra** military operation **5** (*Teat, Literat, Cine*) (= *trama*) action **6** (= *movimiento*) [*de la cara, cuerpo*] movement **7** (*Jur*) action ➤ **acción judicial, acción legal** (*gen*) legal action; (= *pleito*) lawsuit **8** (*Com, Fin*) share; **capital en acciones** share capital; **emisión de acciones** share issue, stock issue ➤ **acción de oro** golden share

accionamiento SM operation; **una capota de ~ eléctrico** an electrically-operated top

accionar /1a/ **ⒶVT** [+ *mecanismo, motor, alarma*] to activate, operate; [+ *bomba, misil*] to activate, trigger; [+ *interruptor*] to switch; [+ *palanca*] to pull **ⒷVI** to gesticulate

accionariado SM 1 (= *acciones*) shares *pl*, total of shares, shareholding **2** (= *personas*) shareholders *pl*

accionarial ADJ, accionario ADJ (*LAm*) share *antes de s*

accionista SMF shareholder, stockholder

acebo SM holly, holly tree

acechar /1a/ **VT** (= *observar*) to spy on, watch; (= *esperar*) to lie in wait for; [+ *caza*] to stalk; **~ la ocasión** to wait (for) one's chance

acecho SM estar al o en ~ to lie in wait

aceitar /1a/ **VT** to oil

aceite SM oil ➤ **aceite de almendra** almond oil ➤ **aceite de colza** rapeseed oil ➤ **aceite de girasol** sunflower oil ➤ **aceite de hígado de bacalao** cod-liver oil ➤ **aceite de oliva** olive oil ➤ **aceite de oliva virgen** virgin olive oil ➤ **aceite de ricino** castor oil ➤ **aceite de soja** soya oil ➤ **aceite lubricante** lubricating oil

aceitera SF 1 (*Culin*) oil bottle, cruet; **~s** oil and vinegar set, cruet *sing* **2** (*Aut*) oilcan

aceitoso ADJ oily

aceituna SF olive ➤ **aceituna de mesa** table olive ➤ **aceituna rellena** stuffed olive

aceitunado ADJ (= *verdoso*) olive *antes de s*, olive-coloured, olive-colored (*EEUU*); (= *de tez aceitunada*) olive-skinned

aceitunero/a SM/F olive picker

aceituno ADJ [*color*] olive

aceleración SF acceleration

acelerado ADJ 1 (= *rápido*) [*avance, crecimiento, ritmo*] rapid; **con el corazón ~** with her heart racing *o* beating fast; **una década muy acelerada** a decade of hectic activity **2** [*curso*] intensive, crash *antes de s* **3** (*) [*persona*] hyper*

acelerador SM accelerator, gas pedal (*EEUU*); **pisar el ~** to put one's foot down (*esp Brit*), step on the gas (*EEUU*)

acelerar /1a/ **ⒶVT 1** (*Aut*) [+ *coche*] to accelerate; [+ *motor*] to rev, rev up **2** (= *apresurar*) [+ *cambio, proceso, trámite*] to speed up; [+ *acontecimiento*] to hasten; **~ la marcha** to go faster; **~ el paso** to quicken one's pace, speed up; **~ el ritmo de algo** to speed sth up **3** (*Fís*) [+ *partícula, velocidad*] to accelerate **ⒷVI 1** (*Aut*) [*coche, conductor*] to accelerate **2** (*) (= *darse prisa*) to get a move on*, hurry up **Ⓒacelerarse VPR 1** (= *apresurarse*) [*cambio, proceso*] to speed up; **el corazón se le aceleró** her heart beat faster, her heart started racing; **~se a hacer algo** to hurry to do sth, hasten to do sth **2** (*) (= *ponerse nervioso*) to get over-excited **3** (*Fís*) to accelerate

acelga SF Swiss chard

acendrado ADJ pure, unblemished; **de ~ carácter español** typically *o* thoroughly Spanish in nature

acento SM 1 (*Ling*) (*escrito*) accent; (*hablado*) stress, emphasis ➤ **acento agudo** acute accent **2** (= *deje*) accent; **tiene un ~ muy cerrado** he has a very strong *o* broad accent **3** (= *énfasis*) emphasis; **poner el ~ en algo** to put the emphasis on sth, emphasize *o* stress sth **4** (*frm*) (= *tono*) tone (of voice)

acentuación SF accentuation

acentuar /1e/ **ⒶVT 1** (*Ling*) to accent, stress **2** (= *subrayar*) to emphasize, accentuate **Ⓑacentuarse VPR** to become more noticeable, be accentuated

acepción SF (*Ling*) sense, meaning

aceptable ADJ acceptable, passable

aceptación SF (= *acto*) acceptance; (= *aprobación*) approval; (= *popularidad*) popularity; **no tener ~** to be unsuccessful

aceptar /1a/ **VT 1** [+ *oferta, propuesta, dimisión*] to accept; [+ *cheque, tarjeta, trabajo*] to accept, take; [+ *condición*] to accept, agree to; **la impresora sólo acepta este tipo de papel** the printer only takes this type of paper; **se niega a ~ los hechos** he refuses to face the facts; **no han aceptado mi solicitud de trabajo** they have rejected my job application; **"no aceptamos devoluciones"** "no refunds given" **2 ~ hacer algo** to agree to do sth; **no ~ hacer algo** to refuse to do sth; **por fin ~on que se publicara** they finally agreed for it to be published, they finally allowed it to be published **3 ~ a algn** to accept sb; **me ~on muy bien en mi nuevo trabajo** I was made to feel very welcome in my new job; **¿aceptas a María por esposa?** do you take María to be your lawful wedded wife?

acequia SF irrigation ditch, irrigation channel

acera SF pavement (*Brit*), sidewalk (*EEUU*)

acerbo ADJ [*sabor*] bitter, sour; [*crítica*] harsh; **tener un odio ~ a algo** to despise *o* detest sth

acerca de PREP about

acercamiento SM 1 (*a un lugar*) approach **2** (*a un tema*) introduction **3** (= *reconciliación*) (*entre personas*) reconciliation; (*entre países, posiciones*) rapprochement; **la obra trata de conseguir el ~ con el público** the play seeks to forge a closer relationship with the audience

acercar /1g/ **ⒶVT 1** (= *aproximar*) (*gen*) to move closer; (*al hablante*) to bring closer; **acercó la cámara a uno de los actores** he moved the camera up to one of the actors; **acerca un poco la silla** bring your chair a bit *o* a little closer; **un intento de ~ la cultura al pueblo** an attempt to bring culture to the people **2** (= *dar*) (*sin moverse*) to pass; (*desde más lejos*) to bring over; **acércame las tijeras** pass the scissors; **¿puedes ~me**

aquel libro? can you bring me over that book?
3 (= *llevar en coche*) to take; **¿quieres que te acerque al aeropuerto?** do you want me to take you to the airport?
4 (= *unir*) [+ *culturas, países, puntos de vistas*] to bring closer (together)
Ⓑ **acercarse** VPR **1** (= *aproximarse*) **1.1** (*al hablante*) to come closer; (*a algo alejado del hablante*) to get closer; **acércate, que te vea** come closer so that I can see you; **no te acerques más, que te puedes quemar** don't get any closer, you could burn yourself; **unos pasos femeninos se acercaban por el pasillo** a woman's footsteps were coming up the corridor; **~se a: no te acerques tanto a la mesa** don't get so close to the table; **los periodistas no pudieron ~se al avión** the journalists couldn't get near the plane; **me acerqué a la ventana** I went up *o* over to the window; **señores pasajeros, nos estamos acercando a Heathrow** ladies and gentlemen, we're approaching Heathrow **1.2** (= *abordar*) **~se a algn** (*al hablante*) to come up to sb; (*lejos del hablante*) to go up to sb; **se me acercó por la espalda** she came up behind me **1.3 ~se algo al oído** to put sth to one's ear
2 (*en el tiempo*) [*acontecimiento, momento*] to get closer, get nearer; **se acercaba la hora de despedirnos** it was nearly time to say goodbye; **~se a** [+ *fecha*] to approach; [+ *situación*] to get closer to
3 (= *ir*) **acércate a la tienda y trae una botella de agua** go over to the shop (*esp Brit*) *o* store (*EEUU*) and get a bottle of water; **ya me ~é un día a visitaros** one of these days I'll pay you a visit *o* I'll come and see you
4 (= *parecerse*) **~se a algo: los resultados se acercan bastante a lo que esperábamos** the results are fairly close to what we expected

acería SF steelworks, steel mill

acerico SM pincushion

acero SM steel ➤ **acero inoxidable** stainless steel

acérrimo ADJ [*partidario*] staunch; [*enemigo*] bitter

acertado ADJ **1** (= *correcto*) [*diagnóstico, respuesta*] right, correct; [*descripción, resumen*] accurate **2** (= *apropiado*) [*comentario, título, regalo*] appropriate; **la música del funeral no fue muy acertada** the music was not very appropriate for a funeral **3** (= *sensato*) [*juicio, consejo, idea*] wise

acertante Ⓐ ADJ [*quiniela, boleto*] winning Ⓑ SMF [*de quiniela, concurso*] winner

acertar /1j/ Ⓐ VT [+ *respuesta*] to get right; [+ *adivinanza*] to guess; **acertó cinco preguntas** he got five answers right; **a ver si aciertas lo que traigo** see if you can guess what I've brought you
Ⓑ VI **1** (*al disparar*) to hit the target; **la bala le acertó de lleno en el corazón** the bullet hit him right in the heart; **no acertó** he missed
2 (= *adivinar*) to get it right; **¡has acertado!** you got it right!
3 (*al decir, hacer algo*) to be right; **aciertan cuando dicen que la corrupción no tiene solución** they're right when they say that there's no solution to corruption; **~ con algo** (*al escoger*) to get sth right; **habéis acertado con el regalo** you made just the right choice with that present; **~ en algo: habéis acertado en la elección** you have made the right choice; **~on de pleno en sus pronósticos** their forecasts were totally accurate *o* correct
4 **~ a hacer algo** (= *conseguir*) to manage to do sth; (*casualmente*) to happen to do sth; **los médicos no aciertan a dar con lo que tiene** the doctors can't find out what's wrong with him; **no acierto a comprenderlo** I fail to understand it
5 ~ con (= *encontrar*) to manage to find; **tras mucho pensarlo acertamos con la solución** after a lot of thought we managed to find the solution

acertijo SM riddle, puzzle

acervo SM **nuestro ~ común** our collective heritage ➤ **acervo cultural** cultural heritage

acetato SM acetate

acetona SF acetone

achacar /1g/ VT **~ algo a** to attribute sth to, put sth down to; **~ la culpa a algn** to lay the blame on sb

achacoso ADJ sickly, ailing

achantar* /1a/ Ⓐ VT to scare, frighten Ⓑ **achantarse** VPR to back down, eat one's words

achaparrado ADJ [*árbol*] stunted; [*persona*] stocky, thickset

achaque SM ailment, malady ➤ **achaques de la vejez** ailments *o* infirmities of old age

acharolado ADJ polished, varnished

achicar /1g/ Ⓐ VT **1** (= *empequeñecer*) to make smaller; (*Cos*) to shorten, take in **2** (= *desaguar*) to bail out; (*con bomba*) to pump out **3** (= *intimidar*) to intimidate, browbeat Ⓑ **achicarse** VPR (*esp LAm*) to be intimidated, belittle o.s.

achicharrante ADJ **calor ~** sweltering heat

achicharrar /1a/ Ⓐ VT **1** (= *quemar*) to scorch; (*Culin*) to burn **2** (*Chi**) (= *aplastar*) to flatten, crush Ⓑ **achicharrarse** VPR to get burnt; **¡me estoy achicharrando!** I'm getting burnt to a cinder!

achichincle* SM (*Méx*) minion

achicopalado* ADJ (*Méx*) depressed, gloomy

achicoria SF chicory

achinado ADJ [*ojos*] slanting

achiote SM (*LAm*) **1** (= *condimento*) anatto **2** (= *tinte*) anatto dye

achiquillado ADJ (*esp Méx, RPl*) childish

achís EXCL atishoo!

achispado ADJ tipsy

achoclonarse /1a/ VPR (*SAm*) to crowd together

acholado ADJ (*And*) half-caste, part-Indian

acholar /1a/ Ⓐ VT (*Chi*) to embarrass Ⓑ **acholarse** VPR **1** (*And*) (= *acriollarse*) [*indígenas*] to adopt mestizo *o* half-breed ways **2** (*Chi*) to be abashed, become shy

achuchado* ADJ **estar ~** (*CS*) (= *acatarrado*) to have a chill; (= *febril*) to be feverish

achuchar /1a/ Ⓐ VT **~ un perro contra algn** to set a dog on sb Ⓑ **achucharse** VPR **1** [*amantes*] to cuddle, fondle (one another), pet* **2** (*RPl*) (= *asustarse*) to get scared

achuchón SM squeeze

achunchar /1a/ (*Chi*) Ⓐ VT to shame Ⓑ **achuncharse** VPR to be ashamed

achuntar /1a/ VI (*Chi*) **1** (= *dar, pegar*) to hit **2** (= *acertar*) to guess right; (= *dar en el clavo*) to hit the nail on the head

achurar /1a/ VT (*RPl*) [+ *animal*] to gut; [+ *persona*] to kill

achuras SFPL (*RPl*) offal *sing*

aciago ADJ ill-fated, fateful, black*

acicalado ADJ smart, spruce; (*pey*) tarted up (*Brit**), gussied up (*EEUU**), overdressed

acicalar /1a/ Ⓐ VT to dress up, bedeck Ⓑ **acicalarse** VPR to smarten o.s. up, spruce o.s. up

acicate SM incentive

acicatear /1a/ VT [+ *persona*] to spur on; [+ *imaginación*] to fire

acidez SF (*Quím*) acidity; (*Culin*) sourness

ácido Ⓐ ADJ sour, acid Ⓑ SM **1** (*Quím*) acid ➤ **ácido nítrico** nitric acid ➤ **ácido sulfúrico** sulphuric acid **2** (*) (= *droga*) LSD, acid*; (= *pastilla*) acid tab*, LSD tab*

acidulante SM acidulant, acidifier

acierto SM **1** (= *respuesta correcta*) (*en concurso, examen*) correct answer; (*en quiniela, diagnóstico*) correct forecast **2** (= *buena decisión*) good move, good decision; **fue un ~ invitarla a la fiesta** it was a good move *o* decision to invite her to the party **3** (= *cualidad*) **con ~** (= *hábilmente*) skilfully, skillfully (*EEUU*); (= *correctamente*) rightly; **el periódico que con tanto ~ dirige** the paper which he edits so competently; **tener el ~ de hacer algo** to have the good sense to do sth **4** (= *éxito*) success **5** (*Ftbl*) fine shot

acitronar /1a/ VT (*Méx*) to brown

aclamación SF acclamation; **entre las aclamaciones del público** amid applause from the audience

aclamar /1a/ VT (= *proclamar*) to acclaim; (= *aplaudir*) to applaud

aclaración SF (*para hacer entender*) clarification; (*para dar razones*) explanation; **quisiera hacerles una ~** I'd like to clarify something

aclarado SM (*Esp*) rinse

aclarar /1a/ **Ⓐ** VT **1** (= *explicar*) [+ *suceso, motivo*] to clarify; [+ *duda, malentendido*] to clear up; [+ *misterio*] to solve; **con esto ya queda todo aclarado** with this now everything is clear; **~ algo a algn** to explain sth to sb; **me lo explicó dos veces pero no consiguió aclarármelo** she explained it to me twice but couldn't manage to make it clear; **le he escrito para ~ las cosas** I've written to him to make things clear; **~ que** to make it clear that **2** (*Esp*) [+ *ropa, vajilla, pelo*] to rinse; **~ con agua fría** to rinse in cold water **3** (= *diluir*) [+ *pintura, salsa*] to thin, thin down **4** (= *hacer más claro*) [+ *color, pelo*] to make lighter, lighten **5** [+ *bosque*] to clear **Ⓑ** VI **1** (= *amanecer*) to get light **2** (= *despejarse las nubes*) to clear up **3** (*Esp*) (= *enjuagar*) to rinse **Ⓒ aclararse** VPR **1** [*día, cielo*] to clear up **2** (= *hacerse más claro*) [*pelo, color*] to go lighter; [*mancha*] to fade **3 ~se la voz** to clear one's throat **4** (*Esp**) [*persona*] **con tantas instrucciones no me aclaro** I'm confused by all these instructions; **explícamelo otra vez, a ver si me aclaro** explain it to me again and let's see if I understand; **¡a ver si te aclaras!** (= *decídete*) make up your mind!; (= *explícate*) what are you going on about?*

aclaratorio ADJ explanatory

aclimatar /1a/ **Ⓐ** VT to acclimatize, acclime (*EEUU*) **Ⓑ aclimatarse** VPR to acclimatize o.s., get acclimatized; **~se a algo** to get used to sth

acné SF acne

ACNUR SM ABR (= **Alto Comisariado de las Naciones Unidas para los Refugiados**) UNHCR

acobardar /1a/ **Ⓐ** VT to intimidate, cow **Ⓑ acobardarse** VPR (= *asustarse*) to be intimidated, get frightened; (= *echarse atrás*) to flinch, shrink back (**ante** from, at)

acocil SM (*Méx*) freshwater shrimp

acocote SM (*Méx*) *type of gourd used in the production of tequila and pulque*

acodarse /1a/ VPR to lean (**en** on); **acodado en** leaning on

acogedor ADJ [*ambiente*] friendly, cosy, cozy (*EEUU*), warm; [*cuarto*] snug, cosy, cozy (*EEUU*)

acoger /2c/ **Ⓐ** VT **1** (= *albergar*) [+ *huésped, refugiado*] to take in; [+ *visitante*] to receive; [+ *fugitivo*] to harbour, harbor (*EEUU*), shelter; **muchas familias acogen a estudiantes** many families provide accommodation for *o* take in students; **la ciudad acoge todos los años a miles de visitantes** the city receives thousands of visitors every year; **niños acogidos en centros públicos** children housed *o* accommodated in public centres *o* (*EEUU*) centers; **el hotel que acoge a los periodistas extranjeros** the hotel where the foreign journalists are staying **2** (= *recibir*) [+ *noticia, idea, propuesta*] to receive; **nos acogieron con muestras de afecto** they received us with demonstrations of affection **3** (= *ser sede de*) [*ciudad*] to host; [*edificio, auditorio*] to be the venue for; **Atenas acogió por segunda vez los Juegos Olímpicos** Athens hosted the Olympics for the second time **4** (= *contener*) **4.1** [+ *espectadores*] to seat, hold; **el auditorio podrá ~ a 1.500 espectadores** the concert hall will be able to seat *o* hold 1,500 people **4.2** [+ *obras*] **este edificio acoge al Museo de la Ciencia** this building houses the Science Museum; **los pasillos del nuevo centro ~án una exposición fotográfica** the corridors of the new centre *o* (*EEUU*) center will accommodate a photographic exhibition **Ⓑ acogerse** VPR **1** (= *acudir*) **~se a** [+ *ley, derecho*] to invoke; **se acogieron a la protección del santo** they turned to the saint for protection **2** (= *beneficiarse*) **~se a:** **~se a la baja incentivada** to take

voluntary redundancy (*esp Brit*) *o* lay-off (*EEUU*); **~se a la amnistía** to accept the offer of amnesty

acogida SF **1** (= *recibimiento*) [*de noticia, producto, propuesta*] reception; **una fría** ~ a very cold reception; **una calurosa** ~ a warm welcome; **tener buena/mala** ~ to be well/poorly received; **el centro de ~ de visitantes** the visitors' centre *o* (*EEUU*) center **2** (= *albergue*) **2.1** (*Pol*) [*de refugiado, emigrante*] **tras la ~ de miles de refugiados** after accepting thousands of refugees; **un centro de ~** a reception centre *o* (*EEUU*) center; **país de ~** host country **2.2** [*de personas necesitadas*] **un centro de ~ de personas sin hogar** a homeless hostel (*esp Brit*) *o* shelter (*esp EEUU*), a shelter for the homeless; **un centro de ~ de menores** a children's refuge; **dar ~ a algn** to accept sb **➤ acogida familiar** (*Jur*) fostering

acogotar* /1a/ VT (*CS*) (= *estrangular*) to strangle, choke; **el cuello de la camisa le acogotaba** his shirt collar was choking him; **estar acogotado de deudas/de trabajo** to be up to one's eyes in debt/in work

acojonante ** ADJ (*esp Esp*) tremendous, fantastic

acojonar ** /1a/ (*esp Esp*) **Ⓐ** VT **1** (= *atemorizar*) to freak out**, put the wind up (*Brit**) **2** (= *asombrar*) to amaze, overwhelm **Ⓑ acojonarse** VPR **1** (= *acobardarse*) to back down; (= *inquietarse*) to freak out, get the wind up (*Brit**) **2** (= *asombrarse*) to be amazed, be overwhelmed **3** (*de miedo*) to freak out*, shit o.s.***

acojone ** SM, **acojono** ** SM (*esp Esp*) funk*, fear

acolchado **Ⓐ** ADJ [*tela*] quilted, padded; [*sobre*] padded **Ⓑ** SM **1** [*de tela*] quilting; [*de sobre*] padding **2** (*RPI*) eiderdown

acolchar /1a/ VT to quilt, pad

acólito SM **1** (*Rel*) acolyte; (= *monaguillo*) server, altar boy **2** (= *adlátere*) acolyte, minion

acomedido ADJ (*Méx, And*) helpful, obliging; **♦ MODISMO andar *o* ir de ~ con algn** (*Méx* pey*) to suck up to sb*

acomedirse /3k/ VPR (*Méx, And*) to offer to help

acometer /2a/ VT **1** (= *atacar*) to attack, set upon; [*toro*] to charge **2** [+ *tarea*] to undertake, attempt; [+ *asunto*] to tackle, deal with **3** [*sueño*] to overcome; [*miedo*] to seize, take hold of; [*dudas*] to assail

acometida SF (= *ataque*) attack, assault; [*de toro*] charge

acomodadizo ADJ (= *complaciente*) accommodating, obliging; (= *manejable*) pliable

acomodado/a **Ⓐ** ADJ **1** (*económicamente*) well-to-do, well-off **2** (*CS, Méx**) (= *con palanca*) **estar ~** to have contacts **Ⓑ** SM/F **los ~s** people with contacts

acomodador(a) SM/F usher/usherette

acomodar /1a/ **Ⓐ** VT **1** [+ *visitante, huésped*] to put up; **nos ~on en diferentes cuartos** they put us up in different rooms **2** (= *sentar*) **nos ~on en nuestros asientos** they showed us to our seats **3** (= *poner cómodo*) to make comfortable **4** (= *albergar*) [*local*] to seat; [*vehículo*] to take; **una sala con capacidad para ~ a mil personas** a hall with a capacity of one thousand, a hall which can seat one thousand people **5** (*frm*) (= *adaptar*) **~ algo a algo** to adapt sth to (suit) sth; **tendrán que ~ la ley a la directiva europea** they will have to bring the law into line with the European directive **6** (*LAm*) (= *colocar*) to put; **acomoda aquí los libros** put the books here **7** (*CS, Méx*) (= *dar trabajo a*) to get a job for, fix up (with a job)* **Ⓑ acomodarse** VPR **1** (= *ponerse cómodo*) **¡acomódate!** make yourself comfortable; **se acomodó en el sillón** he settled down in the armchair **2** (= *adaptarse*) **~se a algo** to adapt to sth **3** (*LAm*) (= *ajustarse*) [+ *ropa, gafas*] to adjust

acomodaticio ADJ = **acomodadizo**

acomodo SM **1** (= *arreglo*) arrangement; (= *acuerdo*) agreement, understanding **2** (*CS, Méx pey*) (= *palanca*) nepotism, favouritism, favoritism (*EEUU*)

acompañado ADJ **está ~** he's with someone; **los invitados**

no podrán ir ~s a la boda guests can't take someone else along with them to the wedding; **entró acompañada de su padre** she came in with her father, she came in accompanied by her father; **bien/mal ~** in good/bad company

acompañamiento SM **1** (= *cortejo*) (*como escolta*) escort; [*de rey*] retinue **2** (*Mús*) accompaniment **3** (= *acción*) (*tb Culin*) accompaniment

acompañante SMF (= *que acompaña*) companion, escort; (*Mús*) accompanist

acompañar /1a/ **Ⓐ** VT **1** (*a alguna parte*) (*gen*) to go with, accompany (*frm*); **no quiero que me acompañe nadie** I don't want anyone to go with me; **¡te acompaño!** I'll come with you!; **iba acompañada de dos guardaespaldas** he had two bodyguards with him, he was accompanied by two bodyguards; **~ a algn a <u>casa</u>** to see sb home; **~ a algn a la <u>puerta</u>** to see sb to the door, see sb out **2** (= *hacer compañía*) (*por un rato*) to keep company; (*como pareja*) to be companion to; **nos quedamos un rato para ~ a la abuela** we stayed a while to keep grandmother company; **~ a algn en algo** to join sb in sth; **le acompaño en el sentimiento** (*en un entierro*) please accept my condolences **3** (= *ocurrir al mismo tiempo*) to accompany; **el escándalo que acompañó al estreno de la ópera** the scandal that accompanied the opening of the opera **4** [*comida*] **este vino acompaña bien al queso** this wine goes well with cheese; **~ algo <u>con</u>** o **<u>de</u> algo** to serve sth with sth **5** [*documentos*] **la solicitud debe ir acompañada de un certificado** the application should be accompanied by a certificate **6** (*Mús*) to accompany (**a, con** on) **7** (= *ser favorable*) **a ver si la suerte nos acompaña** let's hope we're lucky, let's hope our luck's in; **parece que nos acompaña la mala suerte** we seem to be dogged by o to be having a lot of bad luck **Ⓑ** VI **1** (= *hacer compañía*) to be company; **un perro acompaña mucho** a dog is good company **2** [*comida*] **¿quieres un poco de pan para ~?** would you like some bread to go with it? **3** [*ser favorable*] to be favourable o (*EEUU*) favorable; **es una pena que el tiempo no ~a** it's a shame the weather wasn't more favourable o (*EEUU*) favorable; **si el tiempo acompaña** weather permitting **Ⓒ** acompañarse VPR (*Mús*) to accompany o.s. (**con, de** on)

acompasado ADJ (= *rítmico*) rhythmic, regular; (= *medido*) measured

acomplejado ADJ neurotic, hung-up*; **está ~ por su nariz** he's got a complex about his nose, he's got a thing about his nose

acomplejante ADJ (*LAm*) inhibiting, embarrassing

acomplejar /1a/ **Ⓐ** VT **~ a algn** to give sb a complex **Ⓑ** acomplejarse VPR to get a complex (**con, por** about)

aconcharse /1a/ VPR (*Chi*) [*líquido*] to settle, clarify

acondicionador SM conditioner

acondicionar /1a/ VT **1** (= *arreglar*) to arrange, prepare; [+ *pelo*] to condition **2** (*Com*) to fit out **3** (= *aclimatar*) to air-condition

acongojar /1a/ **Ⓐ** VT to distress, grieve **Ⓑ** acongojarse VPR to become distressed

aconsejable ADJ advisable

aconsejar /1a/ VT to advise

acontecer /2d/ VI to happen, occur

acontecimiento SM event

acopio SM **hacer ~ de** [+ *alimentos*] to stock up with o on; [+ *información*] to gather; [+ *valor*] to summon up

acoplado SM (*CS*) trailer, semitrailer (*EEUU*)

acoplamiento SM (*Mec*) coupling; (*Elec*) connection; [*de astronaves*] docking, link-up

acoplar /1a/ **Ⓐ** VT (= *unir*) (*Téc*) to couple; (*Elec*) to connect, join up; [+ *astronaves*] to dock, link up; (*LAm Ferro*) to couple (up) **Ⓑ** acoplarse VPR **1** (*Aer*) to dock **2** (*Elec*) to cause feedback

acoquinar /1a/ **Ⓐ** VT to scare, intimidate, cow **Ⓑ** acoquinarse VPR to get scared, take fright

acorazado **Ⓐ** ADJ [*cámara*] security **de** s; [*vehículo*] reinforced, armoured, armored (*EEUU*), armour-plated, armor-plated (*EEUU*) **Ⓑ** SM battleship

acordar /1l/ **Ⓐ** VT **1** (= *decidir*) [+ *precio, fecha*] to agree, agree on; **eso no es lo que acordamos** that is not what we agreed; **han acordado la suspensión provisional de las obras** it was agreed that the works should be suspended temporarily; **~ hacer algo** to agree to do sth; **~ que** to agree that **2** (= *recordar*) **~ a algn de hacer algo** ◊ **~ a algn que haga algo** (*And*) to remind sb to do sth **3** (*LAm*) (= *conceder*) to grant, accord (*frm*) **Ⓑ** acordarse VPR to remember; **no me acuerdo** I don't o can't remember; **no quiero ni ~me** I don't even want to think about it; **<u>ahora</u> que me acuerdo** now that I think of it, come to think of it; **~se de algo/algn** to remember sth/sb; **nadie se acordaba del número** nobody could think of o remember the number; **ya no me acordaba de que tenía una reunión** I'd completely forgotten that I had a meeting; **el otro día me acordé de ti cuando ...** I thought of you the other day when ...; **me acuerdo mucho de mi infancia** I often think about o recall my childhood; **desde que te has ido, me acuerdo mucho de ti** since you left, I've missed you a lot

> Nótese la diferencia de significado entre **to remember to do sth** y **to remember doing sth** en los siguientes ejemplos:
>
> **~se de <u>hacer</u> algo** to remember to do sth; **~se de <u>haber hecho</u> algo** to remember doing sth; **me acuerdo de haber leído un artículo sobre eso** I remember reading an article about that

acorde **Ⓐ** ADJ **1 ~ a** o **con** [+ *situación, posición*] appropriate to; [+ *ley, directiva*] in conformity o compliance with; **un motor ~ a** o **con las normas ecológicas** an engine that complies with environmental regulations **2** (*frm*) (= *coincidente*) **estar ~s** to be agreed, be in agreement **Ⓑ** SM (*Mús*) chord

acordeón SM **1** (*Mús*) accordion **2** (*Méx**) (*en examen*) cheat-sheet*

acordeonista SMF accordionist

acordonar /1a/ VT (*con guardias*) to cordon off

acorralar /1a/ VT **1** (*Agr*) [+ *ganado*] to pen, corral **2** (= *arrinconar*) to corner; (= *intimidar*) to intimidate

acortamiento SM shortening, reduction

acortar /1a/ **Ⓐ** VT [+ *vestido, falda, traje*] to take up, shorten; [+ *artículo, texto*] to shorten, cut down; [+ *periodo, duración*] to shorten, reduce; **yendo por aquí acortamos camino** it's shorter if we go this way; **tuve que ~ las vacaciones** I had to cut short my holidays (*esp Brit*) o vacation (*EEUU*); **el Barcelona está acortando distancias con el Real Madrid** Barcelona is catching up with Real Madrid **Ⓑ** acortarse VPR to get shorter

acosar /1a/ VT **1** (= *atosigar*) to hound, harass; **~ a algn a preguntas** to pester sb with questions; **ser acosado sexualmente** to suffer (from) sexual harassment, be sexually harassed **2** (= *perseguir*) to pursue relentlessly

acosijar /1a/ VT (*Méx*) to pester

acoso SM **1** (= *atosigamiento*) harassment; **es víctima del ~ de la prensa** she's a victim of press harassment; **una operación de ~ y derribo contra el presidente** a campaign to hound the president out of office ➤ **acoso sexual** sexual harassment **2** (= *persecución*) relentless pursuit

acostado ADJ **estar ~** to be in bed

acostar /1l/ **Ⓐ** VT **1** (*en cama*) to put to bed **2** (*Náut*) to bring alongside **Ⓑ** acostarse VPR (= *tumbarse*) to lie down; (= *ir a dormir*) to go to bed; **Pilar se acostó con Juan** Pilar went to bed o slept with Juan; **es hora de ~se** it's bedtime

acostumbrado ADJ **1** (= *normal*) usual, customary (*frm*); **el lugar ~** the usual o (*frm*) customary place; **antes de lo ~** earlier than usual **2 ~ a algo** used to sth; **estar ~ a hacer**

algo to be used to doing sth

Recuérdese que **to be used to** rige que el verbo que le siga inmediatamente aparezca en gerundio y no en infinitivo:

---

está ~ a trabajar de noche he's used to working at night **3 mal ~: sus hijos están muy mal ~s** her children are very spoilt

acostumbramiento SM (CS) **producir ~** to be addictive

acostumbrar /1a/ ❶ VT **~ a algn a algo** to get sb used to sth; **~ a algn a hacer algo** to get sb used to doing sth; **aquí no se acostumbra a decir eso** people don't say that o that isn't said here
❷ VI **~ (a) hacer algo** to be used o accustomed to doing sth, be in the habit of doing sth; **los sábados acostumbra (a) ir al cine** he usually goes to the cinema (esp Brit) o movies (EEUU) on Saturdays; **acostumbraba a levantarme temprano** I used to get up early
❸ **acostumbrarse** VPR **~se a (hacer) algo** to get accustomed o used to (doing) sth; **se acostumbró a tomar té** he got into the habit of drinking tea

acotación SF marginal note

acotamiento SM (Méx) hard shoulder (Brit), shoulder (EEUU), berm (EEUU)

acotar /1a/ VT **1** (= poner cotos en) to limit, set bounds to **2** [+ mapa] to mark elevations on; [+ página] to annotate

ácrata ❶ ADJ anarchist(ic), libertarian ❷ SMF anarchist, libertarian

acre¹ ADJ [olor] acrid, pungent; [crítica] sharp, biting, mordant

acre² SM acre

acrecentar /1j/ ❶ VT to increase, augment
❷ **acrecentarse** VPR to increase, grow

acreditación SF (= acto) accreditation; (= autorización) authorization, sanctioning

acreditado ADJ (Pol) accredited; (= estimado) reputable; **nuestro representante ~** our official agent; **una firma acreditada** a reputable firm

acreditar /1a/ ❶ VT **1** (= dar reputación a) to do credit to, give credit to **2** (= avalar) to vouch for, guarantee; (= probar) to prove; (= autorizar) to sanction, authorize **3** (Pol) [+ embajador] to accredit **4** (Com) to credit
❷ **acreditarse** VPR to prove one's worth; **~se como** to get a reputation for

acreditativo ADJ **documentos ~s** supporting documents

acreedor(a) ❶ ADJ **~ a** worthy of, deserving of ❷ SM/F creditor

acribillar /1a/ VT to riddle, pepper; **~ a balazos** to riddle with bullets; **~ a algn a preguntas** to bombard sb with questions

acrílico ADJ acrylic

acriollarse /1a/ VPR (esp CS) to go native

acristalamiento SM (Esp) glazing; **doble ~** double glazing

acristalar /1a/ VT (Esp) to glaze

acrobacia SF acrobatics sing ➤ **acrobacia aérea** aerobatics sing, aerial acrobatics sing

acróbata SMF acrobat

acrobático ADJ acrobatic

acrónimo SM acronym

acta SF **1** [de reunión] minutes pl; **constar en ~: las pruebas documentales constan en ~** the documentary proof is in the minutes; **pidieron que su oposición al plan constara en ~** they asked for their opposition to the plan to be noted; **levantar ~ de** [+ reunión, sesión parlamentaria] to write up the minutes of; [+ acontecimiento, delito] to make a(n official) report on
2 [de congreso] proceedings pl; [de organismo] records pl **3** (Esp Educ) [de notas] student's achievement record, grade card (EEUU)
4 (= certificado) certificate ➤ **acta de bautismo** certificate of baptism ➤ **acta de defunción** death certificate ➤ **acta de**

diputado (Esp Pol) certificate of election ➤ **acta de matrimonio** marriage certificate ➤ **acta de nacimiento** birth certificate ➤ **acta matrimonial** marriage certificate ➤ **acta notarial** affidavit
5 (Pol) ➤ **Acta Única Europea** Single European Act

actitud SF **1** (= comportamiento, disposición) attitude; **no vas a conseguir nada con esa ~** you won't get anywhere with that attitude **2** (= postura física) posture; **tenía el mentón levantado, en ~ desafiante** he had his chin raised in a defiant posture; **adoptó una ~ pensativa** she adopted a thoughtful pose **3** (= estado de ánimo) frame of mind, mood

activar /1a/ VT (= poner en marcha) to activate; [+ trabajo] to expedite, speed up, hurry along; [+ fuego] to brighten up, poke; [+ economía] to stimulate

actividad SF **1** (= acción) activity; **ha sido una jornada de escasa ~ bursátil** trading was slow o sluggish on the stock exchange today; **el volcán aún está en ~** the volcano is still active **2** (= tarea profesional) work; **los pescadores han reanudado su ~** the fishermen have gone back to work ➤ **actividad docente** teaching ➤ **actividad lucrativa** gainful employment **3 actividades** (= actos) activities pl; **~es deportivas** sporting activities

activismo SM activism

activista SMF activist

activo ❶ ADJ **1** (= que actúa) active; (= vivo) lively, energetic; (= ocupado) busy **2** (Ling) active ❷ SM **1** (Com) assets pl ➤ **activo fijo** fixed assets pl ➤ **activo y pasivo** assets and liabilities pl **2** (Mil) **oficial en ~** serving officer; **estar en ~** to be on active service **3** ✦ MODISMO **por activa y por pasiva: se lo he dicho por activa y por pasiva** I don't know how many times I've told him

acto SM **1** (= acción) act, action; **la atraparon en el ~ de falsificar la firma** they caught her in the act of forging the signature; **no es responsable de sus ~s** he's not responsible for his actions; **hacer ~ de presencia** (= asistir) to attend, be present; (= aparecer) to appear; (= dejarse ver brevemente) to put in an appearance; **morir en ~ de servicio** to die on active service; **el ~ sexual** the sexual o sex act ➤ **acto reflejo** reflex action
2 (= ceremonia) **celebrar un ~** to hold a function ➤ **acto oficial** official function ➤ **acto religioso** (religious) service **3** (Teat) act
4 en el ~ (= inmediatamente) there and then; **la ingresaron y la operaron en el ~** she was admitted and operated on there and then o on the spot; **murió en el ~** he died instantly; **"reparaciones en el acto"** "repairs while you wait"
5 ~ seguido immediately after(wards)

actor SM actor ➤ **actor de cine** film actor (esp Brit), movie actor (EEUU) ➤ **actor de doblaje** dubber ➤ **actor de reparto** supporting actor

actriz SF actress ➤ **actriz de cine** film actress (esp Brit), movie actress (EEUU) ➤ **actriz de doblaje** dubber ➤ **actriz de reparto** supporting actress

actuación SF **1** (= intervención) [de cantante, deportista] performance; [de actor] acting; **su ~ es lo peor de la película** the worst thing in the film (esp Brit) o movie (esp EEUU) is his acting
2 (= espectáculo) show; **todas sus actuaciones tuvieron un gran éxito de público** all his shows were a great success with the public; **habrá dos actuaciones de jazz** there will be two jazz sessions
3 (= acción) action; **su línea de ~** their plan of action; **las actuaciones policiales fueron vanas** police action was to no avail; **criticaron la ~ del presidente ante la crisis** they criticized the president's handling of the crisis
4 (= conducta) behaviour, behavior (EEUU), conduct; **la ~ de la policía en la manifestación** the conduct o behaviour o (EEUU) behavior of the police at the demonstration

actual ADJ **1** (= de ahora) [situación, sistema, gobernante] current, present; [sociedad] contemporary, present-day; [moda] current, modern; **el ~ campeón de Europa** the reigning o current o present European champion; **en el momento ~** at the present moment; **la ~ literatura francesa** French literature today, present-day French literature

2 (= *de actualidad*) [*cuestión, tema*] topical; **temas muy ~es** highly topical issues
3 (= *moderno*) up-to-date, fashionable; **ha cambiado su peinado por otro algo más ~** he's changed his hairstyle for a more up-to-date *o* fashionable one; **corbatas de diseño muy ~** very fashionable-looking ties; **las técnicas más ~es** the most up-to-date *o* up-to-the-minute techniques, the latest techniques

⚠ actual ≠ *actual*

actualidad SF **1 en la ~** (= *hoy día*) nowadays; (= *en este momento*) currently, at present, presently (*EEUU*); **es un juego muy de moda en la ~** it's a very popular game nowadays; **hay en la ~ más de dos millones de parados** there are currently over two million unemployed, there are over two million unemployed at present
2 (= *cualidad*) **las obras de Shakespeare no han perdido ~** the works of Shakespeare have not lost their topicality; **de ~** [*noticia, tema*] topical; [*modelo, diseño*] up-to-date, up-to-the-minute; **poner algo de ~** to focus attention on sth
3 (*Periodismo*) **la ~** (= *asuntos*) current affairs *pl*; (= *noticias*) news, current news; **una revista sobre la ~ francesa** a magazine on French current affairs; **y ahora vamos a pasar a la ~ internacional** and now (for) international news
actualización SF updating
actualizar /1f/ VT to bring up to date, update; (*Inform*) to refresh
actualmente ADV **1** (= *en este momento*) currently, at present, presently (*EEUU*); **está rodando una nueva serie** he's currently making a new series, he's making a new series at present **2** (= *hoy día*) nowadays; **~ se usan métodos más eficaces** nowadays more efficient methods are used

⚠ actualmente ≠ *actually*

actuar /1e/ VI **1** [*actor*] to act; [*cantante, banda, compañía, equipo*] to perform
2 (= *obrar*) to act; **actúa como** *o* **de mediador en el conflicto** he's acting as a mediator in the conflict; **actúa de manera rara** he's acting *o* behaving strangely; **la indecisión no le dejaba ~** indecision prevented him from taking any action
3 (*Jur*) (= *proceder*) to institute (legal) proceedings; [*abogado*] to act; **el abogado que actúa en nombre de mi familia** the lawyer acting for my family
4 (= *tener efecto*) to act; **la crema actúa directamente sobre la herida** the cream acts directly on the wound
acuarela SF watercolour, watercolor (*EEUU*)
Acuario SM (= *signo*) Aquarius
acuario ⒶSM (= *pecera*) aquarium Ⓑ SMF INV (*Astron*) (= *persona*) Aquarius; **soy ~** I'm Aquarius
acuárium SM aquarium
acuartelamiento SM (= *alojamiento*) quartering, billeting; (*por posibles disturbios*) confinement to barracks
acuartelar /1a/ Ⓐ VT (= *alojar*) to quarter, billet; (*por posibles disturbios*) to confine to barracks Ⓑ **acuartelarse** VPR to withdraw to barracks
acuático ADJ aquatic, water *antes de s*
acuatizaje SM (*LAm*) touchdown (*on water*), landing (*on water*)
acuatizar /1f/ VI (*LAm*) to come down (*on water*), land (*on water*)
acuchillar /1a/ VT **1** (= *rajar*) to knife, stab; [+ *vestido*] to slash **2** [+ *persona*] to stab (to death), knife **3** (*Téc*) to sand
acuciante ADJ [*problema*] pressing; **necesidad ~** dire necessity, urgent *o* pressing need
acuciar /1b/ VT (= *estimular*) to urge on; (= *acosar*) to harass; **acuciado por el hambre** driven on by hunger
acudir /3a/ VI **1** (*indicando movimiento*) (= *ir*) to go; (= *venir*) to come; **señor Martínez, acuda a información por favor** Mr Martínez, please go to the information desk; **dijo que ~ía a**

declarar voluntariamente he said that he would testify voluntarily; **el perro acude cuando lo llamo** the dog comes when I call; **sólo diez trabajadores acudieron a sus puestos** only ten workers showed up for work; **acudieron en su ayuda** they went to his aid; **no acudió a la cita** he did not keep the appointment, he did not turn up (for the appointment); **~ a una llamada** to answer a call; **~ a la mente** to come to (one's) mind; **~ a las urnas** to go to the polls
2 (= *participar*) to take part; **el pasado año acudieron 130 expositores** last year 130 exhibitors took part
3 (= *recurrir*) **~ a** to turn to; **no tenemos a quién ~** we have nobody to turn to; **acudo a ustedes para quejarme sobre ...** I am writing to complain about ...; **~ a los tribunales** to go to court
acueducto SM aqueduct
acuerdo SM **1** (= *decisión conjunta*) agreement; (*implícito, informal*) understanding; (*de negocios*) deal; **llegar a un ~** to come to *o* reach an agreement; **tenemos una especie de ~ para no hacernos la competencia** we have a sort of understanding that we will not become competitors; **llegaron a un ~ sin necesidad de acudir a juicio** they settled out of court; **de común ~** by mutual agreement, by mutual consent; **de** *o* **por mutuo ~** by mutual agreement, by mutual consent ➤ **acuerdo de paz** peace agreement ➤ **acuerdo de pesca** fishing agreement ➤ **Acuerdo General sobre Aranceles Aduaneros y Comercio** General Agreement on Tariffs and Trade ➤ **acuerdo marco** framework agreement
2 de ~ 2.1 (*independiente*) OK, all right **2.2 estar de ~** to agree, be in agreement (*frm*); **en eso estamos de ~** we agree on that, we're in agreement on that (*frm*); **estoy totalmente de ~ contigo** I totally agree with you; **estoy de ~ con que deberíamos mudarnos de casa** I agree that we should move house **2.3 ponerse de ~** to come to an agreement, reach (an) agreement; **no se ponían de ~ en nada** they couldn't agree on anything **2.4 de ~ con** according to, in accordance with (*frm*); **todo se hizo de ~ con las reglas** everything was done according to *o* (*frm*) in accordance with the regulations; **una casa de ~ con sus necesidades** a house to suit their needs
acuicultura SF aquaculture
acuífero Ⓐ ADJ aquiferous, water-bearing Ⓑ SM aquifer
acumulación SF accumulation; **una ~ de gas** a build-up of gas
acumulador SM storage battery
acumular /1a/ Ⓐ VT [+ *posesiones*] to accumulate; [+ *datos*] to amass, gather Ⓑ **acumularse** VPR to accumulate, gather, pile up; **se me acumula el trabajo** the work is piling up (on me)
acumulativo ADJ cumulative
acunar /1a/ VT to rock, rock to sleep
acuñación SF [*de moneda*] minting; [*de frase*] coining
acuñar /1a/ VT [+ *moneda*] to mint; [+ *medalla*] to strike; [+ *frase*] to coin
acuoso ADJ [*ojos, líquido, solución*] watery; [*fruta*] juicy
acupuntor(a) SM/F acupuncturist
acupuntura SF acupuncture
acurrucarse /1g/ VPR to snuggle up, curl up
acusación SF **1** (= *inculpación*) accusation; (*Jur*) (= *cargo*) charge, indictment; **negar la ~** to deny the charge
2 (= *acusador*) prosecution ➤ **la acusación particular** (the counsel for) the prosecution
acusado/a Ⓐ ADJ **1** (*Jur*) accused **2** (= *marcado*) (*gen*) marked, pronounced; [*acento*] strong; [*contraste*] marked, striking Ⓑ SM/F accused, defendant
acusador(a) Ⓐ ADJ accusing, reproachful Ⓑ SM/F accuser ➤ **acusador/a público/a** public prosecutor, prosecuting *o* district attorney (*EEUU*)
acusar /1a/ VT **1** (= *culpar*) to accuse; **nos acusan de racistas** they are accusing us of being racists; **~ a algn de**

hacer algo to accuse sb of doing sth

> Recuérdese que •las preposiciones en inglés rigen gerundio y no infinitivo, de ahí **to accuse sb of doing sth**.

2 (*Jur*) (= *incriminar*) to charge; **le han acusado de asesinato** he has been charged with murder; **~ a algn de hacer algo** to charge sb with doing sth

> Recuérdese que las preposiciones en inglés rigen gerundio y no infinitivo, de ahí **to charge sb with doing sth**.

3 (= *mostrar*) to show signs of; **sus caras acusaban el cansancio** tiredness showed in their faces
4 (= *registrar*) to pick up, register; **este sismógrafo acusa la más leve vibración** this seismometer picks up *o* registers the least vibration
5 (*Correos*) **~ recibo de algo** to acknowledge receipt of sth **B** acusarse VPR **1** (= *confesarse*) to confess; **~se de (haber hecho) algo** to confess to (having done) sth
2 (= *notarse*) **mañana se ~á un aumento de las temperaturas** temperatures will rise tomorrow, tomorrow there will be a rise in temperature; **esta deficiencia se acusa aquí claramente** this deficiency is clearly noticeable here, this deficiency shows clearly here

acusatorio ADJ accusatory, accusing

acuse SM ➤ **acuse de recibo** acknowledgement of receipt

acusetas* SMF (*Ven*), **acusete*** SMF (*And, CS*) telltale, sneak, tattler (*EEUU**)

acusica* SMF (*Esp*), **acusique*** SMF telltale, sneak, tattler (*EEUU**)

acústica SF acoustics

acústico ADJ acoustic

adagio SM (= *proverbio*) adage, proverb; (*Mús*) adagio

adalid SM leader, champion

Adán SM Adam

adán SM (= *sucio*) scruffy fellow; (= *vago*) lazy fellow; **estar hecho un ~** to be terribly shabby

adaptabilidad SF adaptability, versatility

adaptable ADJ adaptable, versatile

adaptación SF adaptation

adaptador SM adaptor ➤ **adaptador universal** universal adaptor

adaptar /1a/ **A** VT to adapt **B** adaptarse VPR to adapt (**a** to)

a. de C. ABR (= *antes de Cristo*) BC

adecentar /1a/ **A** VT to tidy up **B** adecentarse VPR to tidy o.s. up

adecuación SF adaptation

adecuado ADJ **1** (= *apropiado*) [*actitud, respuesta, tratamiento*] appropriate; [*documento, requisito*] appropriate, relevant; **es el traje más ~ para la primavera** it is the most suitable *o* appropriate outfit for spring; **exigen un uso ~ de los recursos** they are demanding that resources be used appropriately *o* properly; **estar en el momento y el lugar ~s** to be in the right place at the right time; **el hombre ~ para el puesto** the right man for the job; **lo más ~ sería ...** the best thing *o* the most appropriate thing would be to ...
2 (= *acorde*) **un precio ~ a mis posibilidades** a price within my budget *o* reach

adecuar /1d/ **A** VT to adapt **B** adecuarse VPR **~se a** to adapt to

adefesio SM (= *persona fea*) disaster*; (= *objeto feo*) monstrosity; **estaba hecha un ~** she looked a sight

a. de J.C. ABR (= *antes de Jesucristo*) BC

adelantado/a **A** ADJ **1** (= *avanzado*) [*país, método, trabajo*] advanced; **lleva la tesis bastante adelantada** she's quite well ahead with her thesis; **estar** *o* **ir ~ en los estudios** to be well ahead in one's studies; **sus ideas eran**

bastante adelantadas entonces his ideas were quite ahead of their time; **está muy ~ para su edad** he's very advanced for his age, he's well ahead of his age
2 [*reloj*] fast
3 (= *prematuro*) [*cosecha, elecciones*] early
4 (= *de antemano*) [*pago*] advance; **por ~** in advance
5 (*Dep*) **un pase ~** a forward pass
B SM/F **ser un ~ en algo** to be a pioneer in sth

adelantamiento SM (*Aut*) overtaking, passing (*esp EEUU*)

adelantar /1a/ **A** VT **1** (= *pasar por delante*) [+ *vehículo, rival*] to overtake (*esp Brit*), pass (*esp EEUU*)
2 (= *mover de sitio*) [+ *ficha, meta*] to move forward; **~on la meta 30 metros** they moved the finishing line 30 metres *o* (*EEUU*) meters further forward
3 (*en el tiempo*) **3.1** [+ *fecha, acto*] to bring forward; **no adelantemos acontecimientos** let's not get ahead of ourselves, let's not jump the gun* **3.2** [+ *reloj*] to put forward; **hoy se adelantan los relojes una hora** today the clocks go forward (by) one hour
4 (= *conseguir*) **no adelantamos nada con decírselo** we'll get nowhere by telling him
5 (= *anticipar*) **5.1** [+ *sueldo, dinero*] to pay in advance, advance **5.2** [+ *información*] to disclose, reveal; **ha adelantado las líneas generales de su plan** he has disclosed *o* revealed the outline of his plan; **lo único que puedo ~te es que ...** the only thing that I can tell you now is that ...
6 (= *apresurar*) [+ *trabajo*] to speed up; **para ~ trabajo** to speed things up
7 (*Dep*) [+ *balón*] to pass forward
B VI **1** (*Aut*) to overtake (*esp Brit*), pass (*EEUU*); **"prohibido adelantar"** "no overtaking" (*esp Brit*), "no passing" (*EEUU*)
2 (= *avanzar*) to make progress; **llevamos un mes negociando sin ~ nada** we have spent a month negotiating without making any progress *o* headway
3 [*reloj*] to gain time; **ese reloj adelanta dos minutos diarios** that clock gains two minutes a day
C adelantarse VPR **1** (= *avanzar*) to go forward, move forward; **se adelantó para darle dos besos** she stepped *o* went *o* moved forward to kiss him
2 (= *ir por delante*) to go ahead; **me ~é a inspeccionar el camino** I'll go ahead and check the way; **~se en el marcador** (*Dep*) to go ahead
3 (= *anticiparse*) [*cosecha, primavera*] to come early
4 ~se a 4.1 [+ *deseos, preguntas*] to anticipate
4.2 [+ *persona*] (= *hacer antes*) to get in before; **alguien se me adelantó** someone beat me to it *o* got in before me; **se adelanta a su tiempo** he is ahead of his time
5 [*reloj*] to gain time

adelante ADV **1** (*indicando dirección*) forward; **tráelo para ~** bring it forward; **echado para ~** (= *inclinado*) leaning forward; (= *seguro de sí mismo*) self-assured; **hacia ~** forward; **el espejo estaba inclinado hacia ~** the mirror was tilted forward; **un paso (hacia) ~** a step forward; **mirar hacia ~** to look ahead; **llevar ~ un proyecto** to carry out a project; **sacar ~ una empresa/un espectáculo** to get a company/a show off the ground; **sacar ~ a los hijos** to give one's children a good education in life; **salir ~** [*proyecto, propuesta*] to go ahead; **hay que trabajar mucho para salir ~** you have to work hard to get ahead *o* (*esp Brit*) get on (in life); **si trabajamos juntos saldremos ~** if we all work together we'll get through this; **la orquesta no podrá salir ~ sin subvenciones** the orchestra won't be able to survive without subsidies; **seguir ~** to go on; **tuvimos una avería y no pudimos seguir ~** we broke down and couldn't go on any further; **mis hijos me dan fuerzas para seguir ~** my children give me the strength to keep going; **decidieron seguir ~ con sus proyectos** they decided to go ahead *o* carry on with their plans
2 (*indicando posición*) **la fila dos es demasiado ~** row two is too near the front *o* too far forward; **está más ~** [*edificio, calle*] it's further on; **más ~** (*en una sala*) further forward; (*en texto*) below; **la parte de ~** the front
3 (*indicando tiempo*) **en ~** from now on, in future; **de ahora en ~** ◇ **de aquí en ~** from now on; **de hoy en ~** as from today; **más ~** later; **decidimos dejar la reunión para más ~** we decided to leave the meeting till a later date *o* till later
4 (*indicando cantidad*) **en ~** upwards; **para niños de tres años en ~** for children of three and upwards

5 ¡adelante! (*autorizando a entrar*) come in!; (*animando a seguir*) go on!, carry on!; (*Mil*) forward!
6 ~ de (*LAm*) in front of; **se sentó ~ de mí** he sat in front of me

adelanto SM **1** (= *progreso*) **1.1** (= *acción*) advancement; (= *resultado*) step forward; **esa ley supone un gran ~** that law marks a great step forward **1.2 adelantos** (= *descubrimientos*) advances; **los ~s de la ciencia** the advances of science; **una cocina con los últimos ~s** a kitchen with the latest gizmos *o* (*Brit*) mod cons*
2 (*en tiempo*) **piden el ~ de las elecciones** they are asking for the elections to be brought forward; **con una hora de ~** an hour early
3 [*de información*] **el artículo es sólo un ~ de su próximo libro** the article is just a taster of his latest book
4 [*de dinero*] (= *anticipo*) advance; (= *depósito*) deposit

adelfa SF oleander

adelgazamiento SM slimming

adelgazante Ⓐ ADJ slimming, weight-reducing Ⓑ SM slimming product, weight-reducing product

adelgazar /1f/ Ⓐ VT [+ *persona*] to make thin, make slender; [+ *kilos*] to lose, take off Ⓑ VI to lose weight

ademán SM **1** [*de mano*] gesture, movement; (= *postura*) posture, position; **en ~ de hacer algo** as if to do sth, getting ready to do sth; **hacer ~ de hacer** to make as if to do, make a move to do **2 ademanes** (= *modales*) manners

además ADV **1** (= *también*) (*para añadir otro elemento*) also, in addition (*frm*); (*para reforzar un comentario*) what's more, besides, furthermore (*frm*), moreover (*frm*); **hay, ~, pistas de tenis y campos de golf** there are also tennis courts and golf courses, in addition, there are tennis courts and golf courses (*frm*); **estoy cansado y, ~, no me apetece** I'm tired, and what's more, *o* besides, I don't feel like it; **quiero decirle, ~, que ésa no era mi intención** furthermore, *o* moreover I want to tell you that that was not my intention (*frm*)
2 ~ de as well as, besides; **~ del alojamiento, necesitamos la comida** as well as *o* besides somewhere to stay we need food; **el examen fue largo, ~ de difícil** the exam was long as well as difficult; **~ de que** (+ INDIC) as well as + *ger*; **~ de que estaba cansado, no había comido** as well as being tired he hadn't eaten

adentrarse /1a/ VPR **~ en** to go into, get inside; **~ en la selva** to go deep(er) into the forest

adentro Ⓐ ADV **1** (*esp LAm*) = **dentro 1 2 mar ~** out at sea, out to sea; **tierra ~** inland; **¡adentro!** come in! Ⓑ PREP **~ de** (*LAm*) (= *dentro de*) inside; **~ mío*** inside myself Ⓒ **adentros** SMPL **dijo para sus ~s** he said to himself

adepto/a SM/F (= *partidario*) follower, supporter; (*Rel*) adept, initiate

aderezar /1f/ VT [+ *ensalada*] to dress; [+ *guiso*] to season

aderezo SM **1** (*Culin*) dressing **2** (= *joyas*) set of jewels ➤ **aderezo de diamantes** set of diamonds

adeudar /1a/ VT [+ *dinero*] to owe; **~ una suma en una cuenta** to debit an account for a sum

adeudo SM (*en cuenta*) debit, charge; (= *deuda*) debt

adherencia SF **1** (= *calidad*) adherence **2** (*Aut*) road holding

adherente ADJ adhesive

adherir /3i/ Ⓐ VT to adhere, stick (**a** to) Ⓑ **adherirse** VPR (= *pegarse*) to adhere, stick (**a** to); **~se a** (= *seguir*) to follow; (= *afiliarse*) to join, become a member of

adhesión SF (*Téc*) adhesion; (= *apoyo*) adherence, support; (= *afiliación*) membership

adhesivo Ⓐ ADJ adhesive, sticky Ⓑ SM adhesive

adicción SF addiction

adición SF **1** (*Mat*) addition **2** (*RPI*) (= *cuenta*) bill (*Brit*), check (*EEUU*)

adicional ADJ additional, extra

adictivo ADJ addictive

adicto/a Ⓐ ADJ **1 ~ a algo** addicted to sth; **es ~ a la heroína** he's addicted to heroin, he's a heroin addict
2 (= *fiel*) [*admirador, amigo*] devoted **3** (= *partidario*) loyal; **la**

prensa adicta al Gobierno sections of the press loyal to *o* supportive of the government Ⓑ SM/F addict

adiestrado ADJ trained

adiestramiento SM [*de animal*] training; (*Mil, Dep*) drilling, practice

adiestrar /1a/ VT [+ *animal*] to train; (*Mil*) to drill

adinerado ADJ wealthy, well-off

adiós Ⓐ EXCL (*al irse*) goodbye!; (*al saludar*) hello! Ⓑ SM goodbye, farewell; **ir a decir ~ a algn** to go to say goodbye to sb

adiposidad SF adiposity

adiposo ADJ adipose, fat

aditamento SM (= *complemento*) complement, addition; (= *accesorio*) accessory

aditivo SM additive

adivinación SF (= *predicción*) prophecy, divination; (= *conjeturas*) guessing; **por ~** by guesswork

adivinador(a) SM/F fortune teller

adivinanza SF riddle, conundrum

adivinar /1a/ Ⓐ VT **1** (= *acertar*) [+ *acertijo, adivinanza*] to guess; **¡adivina quién ha llamado!** guess who called!; **~ el pensamiento a algn** to read sb's mind *o* thoughts; **~ las intenciones a algn** to second-guess sb
2 (= *predecir*) [+ *futuro*] to foresee; **es fácil ~ lo que ocurrirá** it's easy to foresee *o* see what will happen
3 (= *entrever*) (*frm*) **su primera novela deja ~ su genio** her first novel gives a glimpse of *o* hints at her genius Ⓑ VI to guess
Ⓒ **adivinarse** VPR (*frm*) **su silueta se adivinaba en la ventana** one could make out her silhouette in the window, her silhouette was just visible in the window

adivino/a SM/F fortune-teller

adjetivo Ⓐ ADJ adjectival Ⓑ SM adjective

adjudicación SF [*de premio*] award; (*en subasta*) sale

adjudicar /1g/ Ⓐ VT to award (**a** to); **~ algo al mejor postor** to knock sth down to the highest bidder; **¡adjudicado!** sold! Ⓑ **adjudicarse** VPR **~se el premio** to win (the prize)

adjuntar /1a/ VT (= *incluir*) to append, attach; (*en carta*) to enclose

adjunto/a Ⓐ ADJ **1** [*información*] attached; **el formulario ~** the attached form; **un órgano consultivo ~ a la Presidencia** a consultative body attached to the presidency; **en el documento ~ a esta carta** in the enclosed document
2 (= *ayudante*) assistant; **profesor ~/a** assistant lecturer; **director(a) ~/a** assistant director
Ⓑ ADV (*en carta*) **remitir** *o* **enviar algo ~** to enclose sth
Ⓒ SM/F **1** (= *ayudante*) **el ~ al** *o* **del director** the assistant to the director, the director's assistant
2 (*en carta*) enclosure; **~s: un folleto informativo y un contrato** enc: one information leaflet and one contract

adlátere SM (*pey*) (= *subordinado*) minion, minder

administración SF **1** (= *organización*) administration; (= *dirección*) management, running ➤ **administración de lotería** (*Esp*) lottery outlet **2** (*Pol*) government, administration ➤ **administración central** central government ➤ **administración pública** civil service, public administration (*EEUU*)

administrador(a) SM/F [*de bienes, distrito*] administrator; [*de organización, empresa*] manager; [*de tierras*] (land) agent; **es buena ~a de la casa** she uses the housekeeping money very efficiently ➤ **administrador(a) de fincas** (*Esp*) land agent ➤ **administrador(a) de redes** system administrator

administrar /1a/ Ⓐ VT **1** (= *organizar*) to administer; (*Com*) to manage, run **2** [+ *justicia, sacramento*] to administer Ⓑ **administrarse** VPR to manage one's own affairs

administrativo/a Ⓐ ADJ administrative; (*Com*) managerial Ⓑ SM/F (= *funcionario*) clerk, office worker; (= *encargado*) administrative officer

admirable ADJ admirable

admiración SF 1 (= *aprecio*) admiration; **un gesto digno de ~** an admirable gesture; **causar** *o* **despertar ~** to be (much) admired; **sentir** *o* **tener ~** *o* **por algn** to admire sb 2 (= *asombro*) amazement; **ante la ~ de todos** to everyone's amazement 3 (*Tip*) exclamation mark

admirador(a) SM/F admirer

admirar /1a/ **Ⓐ** VT 1 (= *estimar*) to admire; **sus progresos son de ~** his progress is admirable 2 (= *contemplar*) [+ *cuadro, panorama*] to admire 3 (= *asombrar*) to amaze, astonish; **me admira tu ingenuidad** your ingenuity amazes *o* astonishes me **Ⓑ admirarse** VPR to be amazed, be astonished

admirativo ADJ admiring

admisible ADJ [*conducta, crítica, propuesta*] acceptable, admissible (*frm*); [*excusa, nivel*] acceptable

admisión SF 1 (= *entrada*) (*en club, organización*) admission; (*en universidad*) acceptance; **"reservado el derecho de admisión"** "the management reserves the right to refuse admission"; **se ha ampliado el plazo de ~ de solicitudes** the closing date for applications has been extended; **las condiciones de ~ al concurso** the conditions of entry to the competition 2 [*de admisión*] admission

admitir /3a/ VT 1 (= *dejar entrar*) (*en organización*) to admit, accept; (*en hospital*) to admit; **fue admitido en la universidad** he got a place at university
2 (= *aceptar*) [+ *opinión, regalo*] to accept; **se admiten apuestas** all bets accepted; **"no se admiten propinas"** "no tipping"; **el juez admitió la demanda a trámite** the judge granted leave to file a lawsuit
3 (= *permitir*) to allow, permit (*frm*); **el contenido de plomo admitido en las gasolinas** the permitted lead content of petrol (*Brit*) *o* gas (*EEUU*), the amount of lead allowed *o* (*frm*) permitted in petrol (*Brit*) *o* gas (*EEUU*); **este asunto no admite medias tintas** there's no room for half measures here; **esto no admite demora** this cannot be put off, this will brook no delay (*frm*); **no admite discusión** it is indisputable; **no admite duda(s)** it leaves no room for doubt
4 (= *reconocer*) [+ *culpabilidad, error*] to admit; **~ haber hecho algo** to admit (to) having done sth; **hay que ~ que no hay nada mejor** it has to be said that there's nothing better
5 (= *tener cabida para*) to hold; **la sala admite 500 personas** the hall holds 500 people

admón. ABR (= **administración**) admin

admonición SF warning

admonitorio ADJ warning *antes de s*

ADN SM ABR (= **ácido desoxirribonucleico**) DNA; **prueba del ~** DNA test

adobar /1a/ VT to marinate

adobe SM adobe, sun-dried brick

adobo SM (= *preparación*) marinating; (= *salsa*) marinade

adocenado ADJ run-of-the-mill

adoctrinamiento SM indoctrination

adoctrinar /1a/ VT to indoctrinate (**en** with)

adolecer /2d/ VI **~ de** to suffer from

adolescencia SF adolescence

adolescente **Ⓐ** ADJ adolescent **Ⓑ** SMF (*Med*) adolescent; (= *joven*) teenager, teen (*EEUU**)

adolorido ADJ (*LAm*) = **dolorido**

adonde CONJ (*esp LAm*) where

adónde (*esp LAm*) **Ⓐ** ADV INTERROG where? **Ⓑ** CONJ where

adondequiera ADV wherever

Adonis SM Adonis; **es un ~** he's gorgeous*

adopción SF 1 [*de niño*] adoption 2 [*de medidas, decisiones*] **es necesaria la ~ de medidas contra la crisis** we need to take *o* adopt measures against the crisis 3 [*de nacionalidad*] adoption

adoptado/a **Ⓐ** ADJ adopted **Ⓑ** SM/F adopted child

adoptar /1a/ VT 1 [+ *niño*] to adopt 2 (= *tomar*) [+ *medida, decisión, postura, actitud*] to take; [+ *papel*] to take on; **en la reunión no se adoptó ningún acuerdo concreto** nothing definite was agreed on in the meeting 3 [+ *postura física*]

durante el sueño adopta una mala postura he sleeps in a bad position; **deberías ~ una postura mejor al sentarte** you should sit better *o* with a better posture 4 (= *empezar a usar*) [+ *nombre, nacionalidad*] to take, adopt; [+ *costumbres*] to adopt; [+ *sistema*] to adopt, introduce

adoptivo ADJ [*padres*] adoptive; [*hijo*] adopted; **patria adoptiva** country of adoption; **hijo ~ de la ciudad** honorary citizen

adoquín SM paving stone, flagstone, cobble

adoquinado SM (= *losas*) paving; (= *piedras pequeñas*) cobbles *pl*

adoquinar /1a/ VT (*con losas*) to pave; (*con piedras pequeñas*) to cobble

adorable ADJ adorable

adoración SF adoration, worship; **una mirada llena de ~** an adoring look **➤ Adoración de los Reyes** Epiphany

adorar /1a/ VT to adore, worship

adormecer /2d/ **Ⓐ** VT to make sleepy, send to sleep **Ⓑ adormecerse** VPR (= *amodorrarse*) to become sleepy, become drowsy; (= *dormirse*) to fall asleep, go to sleep

adormidera SF poppy

adormilarse /1a/ VPR to doze

adornar /1a/ VT (= *decorar*) to adorn, decorate (**de** with); (*Cos*) to trim (**de** with)

adorno SM 1 (= *objeto*) ornament; **una casa llena de ~s** a house full of ornaments **➤ adornos de navidad** Christmas decorations 2 (= *decoración*) ornamentation, adornment; **un estilo literario sin ~ superfluo** a literary style with no superfluous ornamentation *o* adornment; **de ~** decorative; **está de ~** it's just for decoration 3 (*Cos*) trim, trimming

adosado (*Esp*) **Ⓐ** ADJ **casa adosada** ◇ **chalet ~** semi-detached house (*Brit*), duplex (*EEUU*) **Ⓑ** SM semi-detached house (*Brit*), duplex (*EEUU*)

adosar /1a/ VT 1 **~ algo a una pared** to lean sth against a wall, place sth with its back against a wall 2 (*Méx*) (= *adjuntar*) to attach, enclose (*with a letter*)

adquirir /3i/ VT 1 (= *comprar*) [+ *vivienda, billete*] to purchase; (*Fin*) [+ *derechos, acciones, empresa*] to acquire, purchase; **pueden ~se en cualquier tienda especializada** they are available in any specialist shop (*esp Brit*) *o* specialty store (*EEUU*)
2 (= *conseguir*) [+ *cultura, conocimientos, dinero*] to acquire; [+ *fama*] to gain, achieve; **viajando adquirió una gran experiencia** she gained great experience travelling; **ha adquirido renombre con una biografía de Stalin** he became renowned for his biography of Stalin
3 (= *adoptar*) [+ *costumbre*] to adopt; [+ *carácter, identidad*] to take on, acquire; [+ *nacionalidad*] to acquire, obtain; [+ *compromiso*] to undertake; [+ *color*] to take on; **el problema adquirió proporciones de crisis** the problem took on *o* acquired crisis proportions; **el cielo adquirió un color rosado** the sky took on a pinkish colour *o* (*EEUU*) color; **hay que impedir que esas ideas adquieran fuerza** we have to prevent these ideas gaining a hold

adquisición SF 1 (= *compra*) acquisition, purchase; **nuevas adquisiciones** new acquisitions *o* purchases; **una casa de reciente ~** a newly-purchased house
2 (= *artículo comprado*) acquisition; **una de las mejores adquisiciones del museo** one of the museum's finest acquisitions; **el televisor ha sido una buena ~** the television has been a good buy
3 (= *persona*) acquisition; **la última ~ del Atlético** Atlético's latest signing *o* acquisition; **la cocinera ha sido una auténtica ~*** the cook is a real find*
4 [*de conocimientos, datos*] acquisition
5 [*de costumbres*] adoption

adquisitivo ADJ purchasing

adrede ADV on purpose, deliberately

adrenalina SF adrenalin

Adriático SM (*mar*) **~** Adriatic (Sea)

adscribir /3a/ (*pp* **adscrito** *o* (*RPl*) **adscripto**) VT **~ a** to appoint to, assign to; **estuvo adscrito al servicio de ...** he was attached to ...

aduana SF (= *institución*) customs; (= *oficina*) customs house; **derecho de ~** customs duty; **pasar por la ~** to go through customs

aduanero ADJ customs *antes de s*

aducir /3n/ VT (= *alegar*) to adduce, offer as proof; [+ *prueba*] to provide, furnish

adueñarse /1a/ VPR **~ de** to take possession of

adulación SF flattery, adulation

adulador(a) Ⓐ ADJ flattering, fawning **Ⓑ** SM/F flatterer

adular /1a/ VT to flatter

adulteración SF adulteration

adulterar /1a/ VT to adulterate

adulterio SM adultery

adúltero/a Ⓐ ADJ adulterous **Ⓑ** SM/F adulterer/adulteress

adulto/a ADJ, SM/F adult, grown-up

adusto/a ADJ harsh, severe

advenedizo/a SM/F upstart

advenimiento SM advent, arrival **➤ advenimiento al trono** accession to the throne

adverbial ADJ adverbial

adverbio SM adverb

adversario/a SM/F adversary, opponent

adversativo ADJ adversative

adversidad SF (= *problemas*) adversity; (= *revés*) setback, mishap

adverso ADJ adverse

advertencia SF **1** (= *aviso*) warning; **un disparo de ~** a warning shot; **hacer una ~** to give a warning **2** (= *consejo*) piece of advice; **una ~** a word of advice

advertir /3i/ **Ⓐ** VT **1** (= *avisar*) to warn; **estás advertido** you have been warned; **~ a algn de algo** to warn sb about sth; **~ a algn que haga algo** to warn sb to do sth; **te advierto que no pienso ir** I have to let you know that I'm not going; **te advierto que tal vez habría sido mejor que no lo hubiera sabido** mind you, perhaps it would have been better if she hadn't found out about it **2** (= *aconsejar*) to advise, tell **3** (= *notar*) [+ *olor, error*] to notice; **el perro advirtió nuestra presencia** the dog noticed us; **en sus últimas obras se advierten una serie de cambios** one can see *o* observe some changes in her latest works **Ⓑ** VI **~ de** *o* **sobre algo** to warn of sth

Adviento SM Advent

adyacente ADJ adjacent

AEE SF ABR (= **Agencia Europea del Espacio**) ESA

aéreo ADJ (*Fot*) aerial; [*tráfico*] air

aerobic SM, **aerobics** SM INV (*Méx*) aerobics

aerobismo SM (*CS*) aerobics

aerobús SM airbus

aeroclub SM flying club

aerodinámico ADJ (*Fís*) aerodynamic; [*forma*] streamlined

aeródromo SM aerodrome (*esp Brit*), airdrome (*EEUU*)

aeroespacial ADJ aerospace *antes de s*

aerofaro SM beacon

aerografía SF spray painting, airbrushing

aerógrafo SM airbrush

aerolínea SF airline

aerolito SM meteorite

aeromodelismo SM aeromodelling, making model aeroplanes

aeromotor SM aero-engine

aeromozo/a SM/F (*LAm*) steward/stewardess, air steward/stewardess, flight attendant

aeronáutica SF **1** (= *ciencia*) aeronautics *sing* **2** (*RPI Mil*) air force

aeronáutico ADJ aeronautical

aeronaval ADJ air-sea *antes de s*

aeronave SF airship **➤ aeronave espacial** spaceship

aeroplano SM aeroplane (*Brit*), airplane (*EEUU*)

aeropuerto SM airport

aerosol SM aerosol

aerostato SM, **aeróstato** SM balloon, aerostat

aerotransportado ADJ airborne

afable ADJ affable, genial

afamado ADJ famous, noted (**por** for)

afán SM **1** (= *deseo*) eagerness; **en su ~ de marcar un gol** in his eagerness to score a goal; **por ~ de: lo hizo por ~ de superarse** she did it out of a desire to better herself; **tener ~ de algo** to be eager for sth **➤ afán de conocimiento** thirst for knowledge **➤ el afán de lucro** the profit motive **➤ afán de protagonismo: un juez con ~ de protagonismo** a judge who loves publicity *o* always wants to be in the limelight
2 (= *ahínco*) **hacer algo con ~** to do sth eagerly; **rebuscó con ~ en los archivos** he searched eagerly through the files **3** (*frm*) (= *intención*) **una obra con ~ didáctico** an educational work; **sin ~ efectista** with no desire for dramatic effect
4 (*Col, Perú*) (= *prisa*) hurry; **tengo muchísimo ~** I'm in a tearing (*esp Brit*) *o* big (*esp EEUU*) hurry

afanador(a) SM/F (= *ladrón*) thief; (*Méx*) [*de limpieza*] cleaner

afanar /1a/ **Ⓐ** VT **1** (*) (= *birlar*) to pinch*, swipe* **2** (*Col**) (*con prisas*) to rush; (*con preocupaciones*) to worry **Ⓑ afanarse** VPR **~se por hacer algo** to strive to do sth

afanoso ADJ **1** [*trabajo*] hard, heavy **2** (= *concienzudo*) [*temperamento*] industrious; [*actividad, búsqueda*] feverish, hectic

afasia SF aphasia

afear /1a/ VT **1** (= *hacer feo*) to make ugly, disfigure **2** (= *censurar*) to condemn, censure

afección SF (*Med*) trouble, disease **➤ afección cardíaca** heart trouble **➤ afección hepática** liver complaint

afectación SF affectation

afectado ADJ **1** (= *forzado*) [*acento, persona*] affected; [*estilo*] stilted, precious **2** (*Med*) (= *aquejado*) **estar ~ del corazón** to have heart trouble

afectar /1a/ VT **1** (= *repercutir sobre*) to affect; **el paro afecta especialmente a los jóvenes** unemployment affects young people in particular; **por lo que afecta al tema de la contaminación** as far as the question of pollution is concerned
2 (= *entristecer*) to sadden; (= *conmover*) to move; **su muerte nos afectó mucho** we were terribly saddened by his death; **me ~on mucho las imágenes del documental** I was very moved by the pictures in the documentary **3** (*frm*) (= *fingir*) to affect, feign; **~ ignorancia** to affect *o* feign ignorance

afectísimo ADJ **suyo ~** yours truly

afectividad SF emotional nature, emotion

afectivo ADJ affective

afecto SM affection, fondness (**a** for); **tomar ~ a algn** to become attached to sb

afectuosamente ADV affectionately; (*en carta*) yours affectionately

afectuoso ADJ affectionate

afeitado SM **1** [*de barba*] shave **2** (*Taur*) blunting of the horns, trimming of the horns

afeitar /1a/ **Ⓐ** VT (= *rasurar*) to shave; (*Taur*) [+ *cuernos*] to blunt, trim; [+ *toro*] to blunt the horns of, trim the horns of **Ⓑ afeitarse** VPR to shave, have a shave

afeite SM make-up, cosmetic, cosmetics *pl*

afelpado ADJ plush, velvety

afeminado Ⓐ ADJ effeminate **Ⓑ** SM effeminate man, poof (*Brit***), fag (*EEUU***)

aferrado ADJ **seguir ~ a** to stick to, stand by

aferrarse /1j/ VPR **1** (= *agarrarse*) to cling, hang on **2 ~ a** *o* **en** (= *obstinarse en*): **~ a un principio** to stick to a principle;

~ **a una esperanza** to cling to a hope; ~ **a su opinión** to remain firm in one's opinion

Afganistán SM Afghanistan

afgano/a ADJ, SM/F Afghan

afianzar /1f/ Ⓐ VT to strengthen, secure Ⓑ **afianzarse** VPR to become strong, become established

afiche SM (*esp LAm*) poster

afición SF **1** (= *apego*) fondness, liking (**a** for); **tomar** ~ **a** to take a liking to; **tener** ~ **a** to like, be fond of **2** (= *pasatiempo*) hobby, pastime; **pinta por** ~ he paints as a hobby **3 la** ~ (*Dep*) the fans; **aquí hay una gran** ~ support is strong here

aficionado/a Ⓐ ADJ **1** (= *entusiasta*) keen, enthusiastic; **es muy aficionada a la pintura** she's really into painting, she's very keen on painting (*Brit*) **2** (= *no profesional*) amateur Ⓑ SM/F **1** (= *entusiasta*) (*de hobby*) enthusiast; (*como espectador*) lover; **los** ~**s a la ópera** opera lovers **2** (= *no profesional*) amateur; **partido de** ~**s** amateur game; **somos simples** ~**s** we're just amateurs **3** [*de equipo, grupo*] fan, supporter

aficionar /1a/ Ⓐ VT ~ **a algn a algo** to interest sb in sth Ⓑ **aficionarse** VPR ~**se a algo** to get fond of sth, take a liking to sth

afijo SM affix

afilado ADJ sharp

afilador SM knife-grinder

afilar /1a/ VT to sharpen

afiliación SF (*Pol*) affiliation; [*de sindicatos*] membership

afiliado/a Ⓐ ADJ affiliated (**a** to), member *antes de s* Ⓑ SM/F member

afiliarse /1b/ VPR ~ **a** to affiliate to, join

afín ADJ similar

afinador(a) SM/F (= *persona*) tuner

afinar /1a/ VT **1** (*Mús*) to tune **2** (*Aut*) to tune up **3** (= *perfeccionar*) to put the finishing touch to, complete; (= *pulir*) to polish; (*Téc*) to purify, refine; [+ *puntería*] to sharpen, make more precise

afincarse /1g/ VPR to settle

afinidad SF (= *atracción*) affinity; (= *semejanza*) similarity

afirmación SF affirmation

afirmar /1a/ Ⓐ VT (= *declarar*) to assert, state; ~ **que** to affirm that Ⓑ **afirmarse** VPR **1** (= *recobrar el equilibrio*) to steady o.s. **2** ~**se en lo dicho** to stand by what one has said

afirmativo ADJ affirmative, positive; **en caso** ~ if that is the case; **voto** ~ vote in favour *o* (*EEUU*) favor, vote for

aflautado ADJ high, fluty

aflicción SF affliction, sorrow

afligido ADJ grieving, heartbroken

afligir /3c/ Ⓐ VT (= *afectar*) to afflict; (= *apenar*) to pain, distress Ⓑ **afligirse** VPR to get upset

aflojar /1a/ Ⓐ VT **1** (= *dejar suelto*) [+ *corbata, cinturón, nudo*] to loosen; [+ *tuerca, rosca*] to slacken, loosen; [+ *disciplina, restricción, política, presión*] to relax **2** (= *relajar*) (+ *cuerda*) to slacken; [+ *músculo*] to relax **3** (= *ralentizar*) **caminamos sin** ~ **el paso** *o* **la marcha** we walked without slackening our pace *o* without slowing down **4** (***) [+ *dinero*] to fork out*, cough up* **5** (*LAm*) [+ *motor*] to run in Ⓑ VI **1** (*Meteo*) [*viento*] to drop; [*lluvia*] to ease off; [*calor*] to let up **2** [*fiebre*] to subside; [*tensión*] to ease, subside **3** [*ventas*] to tail off; **el negocio afloja en agosto** business slows down *o* eases up in August **4** (*al andar, correr, competir*) to ease up, let up Ⓒ **aflojarse** VPR **1** [*algo apretado, cinturón, corbata*] to loosen; [*nudo, tuerca, rosca*] to come *o* work loose **2** [*algo tenso, cuerda*] to slacken **3** (*Méx*) **se me aflojó el estómago** I had diarrhoea *o* (*EEUU*) diarrhea

aflorar /1a/ VI (*Geol*) to crop out, outcrop; (= *surgir*) to come to the surface, emerge

afluencia SF influx; **la** ~ **de capital extranjero** the influx of foreign capital; **hubo gran** ~ **de público** there was a good turnout; **la** ~ **a las urnas fue escasa** there was a low turnout at the polls

afluente SM tributary

afluir /3g/ VI [*agua, líquido*] to flow (**a** into); [*gente*] to flock (**a** into, to)

afmo./a. ABR = **afectísimo/a**

afonía SF loss of voice, aphonia

afónico ADJ **estar** ~ to have lost one's voice

aforado/a (*Esp*) Ⓐ ADJ [*provincia, territorio*] with a regional charter Ⓑ SM/F *person with parliamentary immunity who can only be tried by the Supreme Court*

aforismo SM aphorism

aforo SM (*Teat*) capacity; **la sala tiene un** ~ **de 2.000 personas** the hall can seat 2,000 people

afortunadamente ADV fortunately, luckily

afortunado ADJ fortunate, lucky; **un comentario poco** ~ a rather inappropriate comment

afrancesado/a Ⓐ ADJ (*pey*) [*costumbre*] frenchified; (*Pol, Hist*) pro-French, supporting the French Ⓑ SM/F (*Pol, Hist*) pro-French person

afrecho SM (*esp RPl*) bran

afrenta SF affront, insult

afrentar /1a/ VT to affront, insult

África SF Africa

africado ADJ affricate

africano/a ADJ, SM/F African

afrikaner ADJ, SMF (*pl* ~**s**) Afrikaner

afroamericano ADJ Afro-American

afrodisíaco ADJ, SM, **afrodisiaco** ADJ, SM aphrodisiac

afrontar /1a/ VT to confront, face up to

after ['after] SM INV, **afterhours** [after'auars] SM INV after-hours club

aftosa SF (*tb* **fiebre** ~) foot-and-mouth disease

afuera Ⓐ ADV out, outside; **¡afuera!** out of the way!, get out!; **por** ~ on the outside; **las hojas de** ~ the outer leaves, the outside leaves Ⓑ PREP ~ **de** (*LAm*) outside Ⓒ **afueras** SFPL outskirts

afuerano/a SM/F (*Chi*), **afuerino/a** SM/F (*Chi*) outsider

agachar /1a/ Ⓐ VT [+ *cabeza*] to bend, bow; ~ **las orejas*** to hang one's head Ⓑ **agacharse** VPR **1** (= *inclinarse*) to bend down, bend over; (= *acuclillarse*) to crouch, squat; (*para evitar algo*) to duck **2** (*Méx*) (= *ceder*) to give in, submit

agalla SF **1** [*de pez*] gill **2 agallas*** (= *valor*) pluck *sing*, guts*; **tener (muchas)** ~**s** to be brave, have guts*

agalludo ADJ **1** (*Méx, CS*) (= *valiente*) daring, bold **2** (*Ven*) (= *tacaño*) mean, stingy **3** (*Col, Ven*) (= *codicioso*) greedy

ágape SM banquet, feast

agarrada SF scrap, brawl

agarradera SF (*LAm*) handle, grip

agarrado ADJ **1** [*persona*] mean, stingy **2 baile** ~ slow dance

agarrador* Ⓐ ADJ (*And*) [*bebida*] strong Ⓑ SM (*LAm*) (*para la cocina*) oven cloth

agarrar /1a/ Ⓐ VT **1** (= *asir*) **1.1** (*sujetando*) to hold (on to); **lo tuvo bien agarrado hasta que llegó la policía** he held on to him until the police arrived; **entró agarrada del brazo de su padre** she came in holding (on to) her father's arm; **me agarró del brazo** he took me by the arm **1.2** (*con violencia*) to grab; **la agarró de los pelos y no la soltaba** he grabbed her hair and refused to let her go **1.3** (*con fuerza*) to grip; **la agarró fuertemente del brazo** he gripped her arm tightly **2** (= *capturar*) to catch; **ya han agarrado al ladrón** they've already caught the thief; ~ **a algn desprevenido** to catch sb unawares **3** [+ *resfriado*] to catch **4** (*esp LAm*) (= *tomar*) **agarré otro pedazo de pastel** I took

another piece of cake; ~ **un tren** to catch a train; **es un tema tan complicado que no sé por dónde ~lo** it's such a complicated subject I don't know where to start;
◆ MODISMO ~**la con algn*** to have (got) it in for sb*
5 (*LAm**) (= *captar*) to get*, understand
6 (*LAm* = *empezar a sentir*) ~ **cariño a algn** to grow fond of sb; ~ **la impresión de que ...** to get the impression that ...; ~ **odio a algo/algn** to take a strong dislike to sth/sb
Ⓑ VI **1** (= *asir*) **agarra por este extremo** hold it by this end, take hold of it by this end
2 (*Bot*) [*planta*] to take (root)
3 [*color*] to take
4 (*esp LAm*) (= *tomar*) **agarre por esta calle** take this street; **agarró y se fue*** he upped and went*; ~ **para** (= *salir*) to set out for
Ⓒ **agarrarse** VPR **1** (= *asirse*) to hold on; **¡agárrate bien!** hold (on) tight!; ~**se a** o **de algo** to hold on to sth
2 (*Aut*) [*coche*] to hold the road; [*neumático*] to grip, hold the road; **el coche se agarra bien en las curvas** the car handles corners well
3 (*como excusa*) ~**se a algo: se agarra a su mala salud para conseguir lo que quiere** she uses her poor health as an excuse to get whatever she wants
4 (*) (= *cogerse*) **se agarró una buena borrachera** he got well and truly plastered*; **se agarró un buen berrinche cuando se enteró** she threw a tantrum o fit when she found out
5 (*esp LAm*) (= *pelear*) to have a fight; **se ~on a puñetazos** they started hitting each other
6 (*Culin*) (= *pegarse*) to stick

agarre SM (*Aut*) [*de coche*] road-holding, road-handling; [*de neumático*] grip

agarrón SM = **agarrada**

agarrotamiento SM [*de músculos*] stiffening; (*Aut*) seizing up

agarrotar /1a/ **Ⓐ** VT [+ *músculos*] to stiffen **Ⓑ** **agarrotarse** VPR (*Med*) to stiffen, get numb; (*Aut*) to seize up

agasajar /1a/ VT to entertain, fête

ágata SF agate

agazaparse /1a/ VPR (= *ocultarse*) to hide; (= *agacharse*) to crouch down, squat; **estaba agazapada tras las rocas** she was hidden behind the rocks

agencia SF (= *empresa*) agency; (= *oficina*) office, bureau
➤ **agencia de noticias, agencia de prensa** news agency
➤ **Agencia de Protección de Datos** (*Esp*) *data protection agency* ➤ **agencia de publicidad** advertising agency
➤ **agencia de seguridad** security company ➤ **Agencia Tributaria** Inland Revenue (*Brit*), Internal Revenue (*EEUU*)
➤ **agencia de transportes** haulage company ➤ **agencia de viajes** travel agent's, travel agency

agenciar /1b/ **Ⓐ** VT to wangle* **Ⓑ** **agenciarse** VPR **1 yo me las ~é para llegar allí** I'll manage to get there somehow, I'll work out how to get there **2** ~**se algo** to get hold of sth

agenda SF **1** (= *libro*) [*de citas, anotaciones*] diary (*esp Brit*), datebook (*EEUU*); [*de direcciones*] address book **2** [*de reunión*] agenda **3** [*de actividades*] agenda, schedule; **una ~ apretada** a very busy agenda o schedule ➤ **agenda electrónica** PDA

agente **Ⓐ** SMF (= *representante*) agent; (= *policía*) policeman/policewoman ➤ **agente comercial** business agent ➤ **agente de bolsa** stockbroker ➤ **agente de seguros** insurance agent ➤ **agente de tránsito** (*Arg, Méx*) traffic policeman/policewoman ➤ **agente literario** literary agent ➤ **agente secreto** secret agent ➤ **agentes sociales** social partners (*employers and unions*) **Ⓑ** SM (*Quím*) agent

agigantado ADJ **a pasos ~** by leaps and bounds

agigantar /1a/ **Ⓐ** VT (= *aumentar*) to enlarge, increase greatly; (= *exagerar*) to exaggerate **Ⓑ** **agigantarse** VPR (*gen*) to seem huge; [*crisis*] to get much bigger, get out of proportion

ágil ADJ agile, nimble

agilidad SF agility, nimbleness

agilipollado* ADJ (*Esp*) stupid, daft (*Brit*)

agilizar /1f/ **Ⓐ** VT (= *acelerar*) to speed up; (= *mejorar*) to improve, make more flexible **Ⓑ** **agilizarse** VPR to speed up

ágilmente ADV nimbly, quickly

agiotaje SM speculation

agiotista SMF (= *especulador*) speculator; (*Méx*) (= *usurero*) usurer

agitación SF (*Pol*) agitation; (= *bullicio*) bustle, stir; (= *intranquilidad*) nervousness; (= *emoción*) excitement

agitado ADJ **1** [*mar*] rough, choppy; [*aire*] turbulent; [*vuelo*] bumpy **2** (= *trastornado*) agitated, upset; (= *emocionado*) excited **3** [*vida*] hectic

agitador(a) SM/F (*Pol*) agitator

agitanado ADJ gypsy-like, gipsy-like

agitar /1a/ **Ⓐ** VT **1** [+ *mano, bandera, arma*] to wave; [+ *alas*] to flap; **el viento agitaba las hojas** the wind stirred the leaves
2 [+ *botella, líquido*] to shake; **agítese antes de usar** shake well before use
3 (= *inquietar*) to worry, upset
4 (= *convulsionar*) [+ *multitud*] to stir up
Ⓑ **agitarse** VPR **1** (= *moverse*) [*ramas*] to stir; [*bandera, toldo*] to flap; [*mar*] to get rough; [*barco*] to toss
2 (= *inquietarse*) to get worried o upset
3 (= *moverse inquieto*) **el enfermo se agitaba en la cama** the patient was tossing and turning

aglomeración SF agglomeration; ~ **de gente** mass of people; ~ **de tráfico** traffic jam

aglomerado SM chipboard, Masonite® (*EEUU*)

aglomerar /1a/ **Ⓐ** VT to agglomerate, crowd together **Ⓑ** **aglomerarse** VPR (= *juntarse*) to agglomerate, form a mass; (= *apiñarse*) to crowd together

aglutinante ADJ agglutinative

aglutinar /1a/ **Ⓐ** VT **1** (*Med*) to agglutinate **2** (= *unir*) to draw together, bring together **Ⓑ** **aglutinarse** VPR **1** (*Med*) to agglutinate **2** (= *unirse*) to come together, gel

agnóstico/a ADJ, SM/F agnostic

agobiado ADJ **estamos ~s de trabajo** we're up to our necks o (*Brit*) eyes in work*; **estaba agobiada por tantas visitas** she found all these visitors overwhelming o a bit too much*

agobiante ADJ **1** [*calor, ambiente, lugar*] oppressive; **un día de verano** ~ a stifling o sweltering summer's day
2 (= *insoportable*) [*trabajo, día*] stressful; [*pena, ritmo*] unbearable; [*responsabilidad*] overwhelming; **es ~ verla sufrir y no poder hacer nada** it's unbearable watching her suffer and being unable to do anything; **una ~ sensación de soledad** an overwhelming sense of loneliness

agobiar /1b/ **Ⓐ** VT **1** (= *oprimir*) [*problemas, responsabilidad, pena*] to overwhelm; [*ropa*] to stifle; **estamos agobiados por las incesantes llamadas telefónicas** we're overwhelmed with constant phone calls
2 (= *angustiar*) **le agobian mucho los espacios cerrados** he gets really anxious in enclosed spaces; **me agobian las grandes ciudades** big cities are too much for me*, I find big cities very stressful; **me agobia un montón oír el fútbol por la radio*** hearing football on the radio really gets to me*
3 (= *molestar*) to pester, harass; **estaban agobiándola con tantas preguntas** they were pestering o harassing her with so many questions
4 (*) (= *meter prisa*) **no me agobies** please, give me a break o get off my back*
Ⓑ **agobiarse** (*) VPR **no se agobia con nada** he doesn't let anything get on top of him o get to him*

agobio SM **1** (= *malestar*) **el calor y el ~ provocaron algunos mareos entre el público** it was so hot and crowded that some of the audience fainted **2** (= *angustia*) **soñaban con unas vacaciones lejos del ~ del trabajo doméstico** they dreamed of holidays (*esp Brit*) o vacations (*EEUU*) away from the stress of housework; **¡cuántos deberes! ¡qué ~!*** so much homework! it's a nightmare!*

agolpamiento SM throng, crush

agolparse /1a/ VPR (= *apiñarse*) to throng, crowd together; (= *acumularse*) [*problemas*] to come one on top of another; [*lágrimas*] to come in a flood

agonía SF **1** [*de muerte*] death agony, death throes *pl*; (= *últimos momentos*) dying moments *pl*; **acortar la ~ a un**

animal to put an animal out of its misery **2** (= *angustia*) anguish

agonías* SMF INV (*Esp*) moaner, whiner

agonizante ADJ dying

agonizar /1f/ VI to be dying, be in one's death throes

ágora SF main square

agorafobia SF agoraphobia

agorero ADJ ominous; **ave agorera** bird of ill omen

agosto SM August; ✦ MODISMO **hacer su ~** to feather one's nest, make one's pile; *ver tb* **septiembre**

En inglés los meses se escriben con mayúscula.

agotado ADJ **1** (= *cansado*) **estar ~** to be exhausted, be worn out **2** (= *acabado*) [*mercancía, producto*] sold out; [*existencias, provisión*] finished, exhausted; [*libro*] out of stock **3** [*pila*] flat

agotador ADJ exhausting

agotamiento SM (= *cansancio*) exhaustion
➤ **agotamiento nervioso** nervous strain

agotar /1a/ Ⓐ VT **1** (= *cansar*) wear out, tire out; **las fiestas me agotan** parties wear *o* tire me out, parties are exhausting
2 (= *terminar con*) [+ *recursos naturales, reservas*] to use up, exhaust; [+ *posibilidades*] to exhaust; **el público agotó las entradas en dos horas** all the tickets (were) sold out within two hours; **las jugueterías ~on sus existencias** the toystores sold out; **han agotado todas las vías legales** they have exhausted all legal avenues; **antes de eso prefieren ~ la vía diplomática** they prefer to try all diplomatic options first; **agotamos todos los temas de conversación** we ran out of topics of conversation
3 (= *llegar al final de*) **decidí ~ el plazo** I decided to take as much time as I was allowed; **el gobierno pretende ~ la legislatura** the government aims to last out its term
Ⓑ **agotarse** VPR **1** (= *cansarse*) to get exhausted, tire o.s. out, wear o.s. out
2 [*mercancía, artículo, género*] to sell out; **ese producto se nos ha agotado** we've sold out of that product, that product is *o* has sold out
3 [*recursos, reservas*] to run out; **se me está agotando la paciencia** my patience is running out *o* wearing thin
4 [*prórroga, tiempo*] to run out; **el plazo se agota mañana** the deadline is tomorrow

agraciado ADJ **1** (= *atractivo*) attractive; **poco ~** plain
2 (= *con suerte*) lucky; **salir ~** to be lucky, be the winner

agradable ADJ pleasant, agreeable; **es un sitio ~** it's a nice place; **no era muy ~ a la vista** it was not a pretty sight

agradar /1a/ VI **esto no me agrada** I don't like this; **su presencia siempre agrada** your presence is always welcome

agradecer /2d/ Ⓐ VT (= *dar las gracias a*) to thank; (= *sentirse agradecido*) to be grateful for; **(te) agradezco tu ayuda** thanks for your help; **le ~ía me enviara** I would be grateful if you would send me Ⓑ **agradecerse** VPR **¡se agradece!** much obliged!, thanks very much!; **una copita de jerez siempre se agradece** a glass of sherry is always welcome

agradecido ADJ **1 estar ~ (por algo)** to be grateful (for sth); **le quedaría muy ~ si me enviara un ejemplar** I should be very grateful if you would send me a copy **2 ser ~** [*persona*] to be appreciative **3** [*planta, tierra*] **son terrenos muy ~s** this land is easy to grow things on, this land is very easy to cultivate; **los olivos son árboles muy ~s** olive trees are very easy to grow

agradecimiento SM gratitude

agrado SM **ser del ~ de algn** to be to sb's liking; **tengo el ~ de informarle que ...** I have pleasure in informing you that ..., I am glad to tell you that ...

agrandar /1a/ Ⓐ VT (= *hacer más grande*) to make bigger, enlarge; (= *exagerar*) to exaggerate, magnify Ⓑ **agrandarse** VPR to get bigger

agrario ADJ agrarian; **política agraria** agricultural policy; **reforma agraria** land reform

agrarismo SM (*Méx*) agrarian reform movement

agrarista SMF (*Méx*) supporter of land reform

agravamiento SM worsening

agravante SM *o* SF additional problem; (*Jur*) aggravating circumstance; **con la ~ de que** with the further difficulty that; **robo con ~** robbery with aggravation

agravar /1a/ Ⓐ VT (= *hacer más grave*) [+ *pena*] to increase; [+ *dolor*] to make worse; [+ *situación*] to aggravate Ⓑ **agravarse** VPR to worsen, get worse

agraviar /1b/ VT to offend, insult

agravio SM offence, offense (*EEUU*), insult; (*Jur*) grievance, injustice ➤ **agravio comparativo** inequality, resentment arising from inequality

agredir /3a/ VT (*físicamente*) to assault, set upon; (*verbalmente*) to attack

agregado/a SM/F **1** (*Esp*) (= *profesor*) assistant **2** (*Pol*) ➤ **agregado/a comercial** commercial attaché ➤ **agregado/a cultural** cultural attaché ➤ **agregado/a de prensa** press attaché ➤ **agregado/a militar** military attaché **3** (*Col*) (= *aparcero*) sharecropper

agregar /1h/ Ⓐ VT **1** (= *añadir*) to add; **~ algo a algo** to add sth to sth **2** [+ *trabajador, empleado*] to appoint Ⓑ **agregarse** VPR **~se a algo** to join sth

agresión SF (= *acometida*) aggression; (*contra persona*) attack, assault ➤ **agresión sexual** sexual assault

agresividad SF aggressiveness

agresivo ADJ aggressive

agresor(a) Ⓐ ADJ **país ~** aggressor country Ⓑ SM/F (= *atacante*) aggressor, attacker; (*Jur*) assailant

agreste ADJ [*paisaje*] wild

agriar /1b *o* 1c/ Ⓐ VT **1** (= *avinagrar*) to turn sour **2** (= *amargar*) to sour Ⓑ **agriarse** VPR **1** (= *avinagrarse*) to turn sour **2** (= *amargarse*) to turn sour; **con la edad se le ha agriado el carácter** he's turned into a sour old man

agrícola ADJ agricultural, farming *antes de s*

agricultor(a) SM/F farmer

agricultura SF agriculture, farming ➤ **agricultura biodinámica, agricultura biológica** organic farming ➤ **agricultura de subsistencia** subsistence farming ➤ **agricultura ecológica** organic farming ➤ **agricultura intensiva** intensive farming

agridulce ADJ bittersweet; **cerdo ~** sweet and sour pork

agrietar /1a/ Ⓐ VT (= *resquebrajar*) to crack, crack open; [+ *piel*] to chap Ⓑ **agrietarse** VPR (= *resquebrajarse*) to crack; [*piel*] to become chapped

agrimensor(a) SM/F surveyor

agringado ADJ (*LAm*) like a gringo, like a foreigner

agringarse /1h/ VPR (*LAm*) to act *o* behave like a gringo, act *o* behave like a foreigner

agrio Ⓐ ADJ (*al gusto*) sour, tart; (= *desabrido*) bitter, disagreeable Ⓑ **agrios** SMPL citrus fruits

agriparse /1a/ VPR (*And*) to get flu (*esp Brit*), get the flu (*esp EEUU*); **estar agripado** to have flu (*esp Brit*) *o* the flu (*esp EEUU*)

agro SM agriculture

agrónomo/a Ⓐ ADJ **ingeniero ~** agricultural scientist Ⓑ SM/F agronomist, agricultural expert

agropecuario ADJ farming *antes de s*; **sector ~** agriculture and fishing

agroturismo SM rural tourism

agrupación SF **1** (= *grupo*) group, association **2** (= *acción*) grouping

agrupamiento SM grouping

agrupar /1a/ Ⓐ VT to group, group together Ⓑ **agruparse** VPR (*Pol*) to form a group; (= *juntarse*) to gather together, come together (**en torno a** round)

agua SF **1** (*para beber, lavar*) water; **dame ~** give me a drink of water; **dos ~s con gas y una sin gas, por favor** two sparkling *o* (*esp EEUU*) carbonated mineral waters and one still *o* (*esp EEUU*) non-carbonated one, please; **¡hombre al ~!** man overboard!; **caer ~** to rain; **¡~ va!** look out!, careful!;

✦ MODISMOS **bailar el ~ a algn** (*Esp*) (= *adular*) to dance attendance on sb; **hacérsele la boca ~ a algn** (*Esp*) ◇ **hacérsele ~ la boca a algn** (*LAm*): **se me hace la boca ~ sólo de pensar en la sopa** just thinking about the soup makes my mouth water, my mouth is watering just thinking about the soup; **quedar en ~ de borrajas** [*promesas, proyectos*] to come to nothing; **como ~ para chocolate** (*Méx**) furious; **estar con el ~ al cuello** to be in it up to one's neck*; **echar a algn al ~** (*Chi**) to give sb away; **como ~ de mayo** (*Esp*): **esperan la privatización como ~ de mayo** they are eagerly awaiting privatization; **es ~ pasada** that's all water under the bridge; **de primera ~** (*Chi*) first hand; ✦ REFRANES **~ que no has de beber déjala correr** don't be a dog in the manger; **nunca digas de esta ~ no beberé** never say never; **~ pasada no mueve molino** it's no good crying over spilt milk; **lo que por ~ viene, por ~ se va** (*Col*) easy come, easy go* ➤ **agua bendita** holy water ➤ **agua blanda** soft water ➤ **agua corriente** running water ➤ **agua de colonia** eau de cologne ➤ **agua de lluvia** rainwater ➤ **agua de rosas** rosewater ➤ **agua destilada** distilled water ➤ **agua dulce** fresh water ➤ **agua dura** hard water ➤ **agua mineral** mineral water; ▪ **mineral sin gas** still mineral water ➤ **agua nieve** sleet ➤ **agua oxigenada** hydrogen peroxide ➤ **agua potable** drinking water ➤ **agua salada** salt water

2 (*CAm, And*) (= *gaseosa*) pop, fizzy drink (*Brit*), soda (*EEUU*); (= *infusión*) herbal tea; **~ de manzanilla** camomile tea **3** (*CAm*) (= *zumo*) juice; **~ de pera** pear juice **4 aguas** [*de mar, río*] waters; [*de la marea*] tide *sing*; **~s abajo** downstream, downriver; **~s arriba** upstream, upriver; **hacer ~s** [*barco*] to take in water; [*explicación, teoría*] to be full of holes, not to hold water; [*relación, organización, proyecto*] to founder; **romper ~s**: **rompió ~s camino del hospital** her waters broke on the way to the hospital; ✦ MODISMOS **estar** o **nadar entre dos ~s** to sit on the fence; **volver las ~s a su cauce**: **las ~s están volviendo a su cauce** things are returning to normal ➤ **aguas fecales** sewage *sing* ➤ **aguas internacionales** international waters ➤ **aguas jurisdiccionales** territorial waters ➤ **aguas mayores** (*euf*) faeces *sing* (*frm*), feces *sing* (*EEUU frm*); **hacer ~s mayores** to have a bowel movement ➤ **aguas menores** (*euf*) urine *sing*; **hacer ~s menores** to pass water ➤ **aguas termales** thermal springs ➤ **aguas territoriales** territorial waters **5 aguas** (= *ondulación*) veins; **un papel azul haciendo ~s** a blue paper with a marbled design **5.2** [*de tejado*] pitch, slope; **tejado a dos ~s** gabled roof

aguacate SM (= *fruto*) avocado pear; (= *árbol*) avocado pear tree

aguacero SM shower, heavy shower, downpour

aguachento ADJ (*CS*) (= *aguado*) watery

aguachirle* SF (*Esp*) slops *pl*, dishwater

aguadilla SF (*Esp*) ducking; **hacer una ~ a algn** to duck sb, hold sb's head under water

aguado ADJ **1** [*sopa*] thin, watery; [*leche, vino*] watered down; [*café*] weak **2** (*Méx, CAm*) (= *aburrido*) boring

aguafiestas SMF INV spoilsport, killjoy

aguafuerte SF **1** (*Quím*) nitric acid **2** (*Arte*) etching; **grabar algo al ~** to etch sth

aguaitar* /1a/ Ⓐ VT (= *mirar*) to watch; (= *vigilar*) to keep an eye on; (= *espiar*) to spy on Ⓑ VI **~ por la ventana** to look out of the window

aguamala SF (*Col, Méx, Ven*) jellyfish

aguamanil SM (= *jarro*) water jug; (= *jofaina*) washbasin (*esp Brit*), bathroom sink (*esp EEUU*)

aguamar SM jellyfish

aguamarina SF aquamarine

aguamiel SF (*CAm, Méx*) fermented maguey juice, fermented agave juice

aguanieve SF sleet

aguantador ADJ (*LAm*) **1** [*persona*] long-suffering **2** [*material*] hard-wearing

aguantar /1a/ Ⓐ VT **1** (= *soportar deliberadamente*) [+ *dolor, ofensas*] to put up with, endure; **no ~é tus impertinencias ni un minuto más** I won't stand for o take o put up with

your cheek o (*EEUU*) sass a minute longer; ✦ MODISMO **~ el chaparrón** to weather the storm **2** (= *tener capacidad de resistir*) to stand up to; **esta planta aguanta bien el calor** this plant withstands o can take heat well, this plant stands up well to heat; **no sé si podré ~ ese ritmo** I don't know if I'll be able to stand the pace; **sabe ~ bien las bromas** he can take a joke; **no ~: no aguanto a los cotillas** I can't bear o stand gossips; **no aguantaba la presión** he couldn't cope with o take the pressure; **no hay quien te aguante** you're impossible o insufferable; **este frío no hay quien lo aguante** this cold is just unbearable; **no hay quien aguante una ópera tan larga** who could sit through an opera that long? **3** (= *sostener*) [*persona*] to hold; [*muro, columna*] to support, hold up; **la pierna que aguanta la guitarra** the leg that supports the guitar; **estas vigas pueden ~ cualquier peso** these beams can take any weight; **esta estantería no podrá ~ tantos libros** these shelves won't take so many books **4** (= *contener*) [+ *respiración*] to hold; [+ *risa, llanto*] to hold back; **~ las ganas de hacer algo** to resist the urge to do sth **5** (= *durar*) to last; **este abrigo no ~á otro invierno** this coat won't last another winter

Ⓑ VI **1** [*persona*] **ya no aguanto más** I can't bear it o stand it o take it any longer, I can't bear o stand o take any more; **cuando empezaba a correr no aguantaba más de diez minutos** when she started running she couldn't keep going o last for more than ten minutes; **~é en Madrid hasta que pueda** I'll hang on o hold on in Madrid as long as I can; **yo me emborracho enseguida, pero él aguanta mucho** I get drunk straight o right away but he can really hold his drink; **tienes que ~ hasta el año que viene con esos zapatos** you'll have to make do with those shoes until next year; **yo ya no aguanto mucho, a las diez estoy en la cama** I can't take the pace any more, I'm in bed by ten; **bailaremos hasta que el cuerpo aguante** we'll dance till we drop **2** [*clavo, columna*] to hold; **esa columna va a ~ poco** that pillar won't hold (out) much longer **3** (*LAm**) (= *esperar*) to hang on*, hold on; **¡aguanta!** hang on* o hold on a minute!

Ⓒ **aguantarse** VPR **1** (= *contenerse*) **¿no puedes ~te hasta que lleguemos a casa?** can't you hold on until we get home? **2** (= *conformarse*) **me tuve que ~** I had to grin and bear it; **¡ahora te aguantas!** that's tough! o you can lump it!* **3** (*Méx*) (= *callarse*) to keep quiet, keep one's mouth shut*

aguante SM **1** (= *paciencia*) patience **2** (= *resistencia*) (*ante el dolor*) endurance; (*ante el cansancio*) stamina, staying power

aguar /1i/ VT **1** [+ *vino*] to water, water down **2** (= *estropear*) to spoil, mar; **~ la fiesta a algn** to spoil sb's fun

aguardar /1a/ Ⓐ VT to wait for, await; **no sabemos el futuro que nos aguarda** we don't know what's in store for us Ⓑ VI to wait

aguardentoso ADJ [*voz*] husky, gruff

aguardiente SM brandy, liquor; (*tb ~ de orujo*) *liquor distilled from grape remains*

aguarrás SM turpentine

aguate SM (*Méx*) prickle, spine

aguatero/a SM/F (*And, CS*) water carrier, water seller

aguaviva SF (*RPl*) jellyfish

aguayo SM (*And*) multicoloured woollen o (*EEUU*) multicolored woolen cloth (*for adornment, or carried as shoulder bag*)

agudeza SF **1** [*de los sentidos, de la mente*] acuteness, sharpness **2** (= *ingenio*) wit, wittiness **3** (= *comentario, golpe*) witticism

agudización SF [*de los sentidos, de la mente*] sharpening; [*de crisis*] deterioration, worsening

agudizar /1f/ Ⓐ VT [+ *los sentidos, la mente*] to sharpen, make more acute; [+ *crisis*] to aggravate Ⓑ **agudizarse** VPR [*los sentidos, la mente*] to sharpen; (= *empeorarse*) worsen; **el problema se agudiza** the problem is becoming more acute

agudo ADJ **1** [*filo*] sharp **2** [*ángulo, acento*] acute **3** [*voz,* *sonido*] piercing; [*nota*] high, high-pitched **4** [*dolor, enfermedad*] acute **5** [*mente, sentido*] sharp, keen; [*ingenio*] ready, lively; [*crítica*] penetrating; [*observación*] smart, clever **6** (= *gracioso*) witty

agüero SM omen, sign; **de mal ~** of ill omen, unlucky

aguerrido ADJ hardened, veteran

agüevarse** /1a/ VPR (*Cam, Méx*) to cower, shrink

aguijón SM **1** (= *puya*) goad; [*de insecto*] sting **2** (= *incitación*) **el ~ de la carne** sexual desire

aguijonear /1a/ VT to urge, spur on

águila SF **1** (= *ave*) eagle; ✦ MODISMO **ser un ~** to be a genius, be terribly clever ➤ **águila real** golden eagle **2** [*de moneda*] **¿~ o sol?** (*Méx*) heads or tails?

aguileño ADJ [*nariz*] aquiline

aguilucho SM (= *cría*) eaglet, young eagle; (*LAm*) (= *halcón*) hawk, falcon

aguinaldo SM **1** (= *propina*) Christmas tip, Christmas box (*Brit*); (= *plus*) Christmas bonus **2** (*Ven*) (= *canción*) Christmas carol

agüita SF (*Chi*) herb tea, herbal tea

aguja SF **1** (*Cos, Med*) needle; ✦ MODISMO **buscar una ~ en un pajar** to look for a needle in a haystack ➤ **aguja de ganchillo** crochet hook ➤ **aguja de hacer punto** knitting needle ➤ **aguja de tejer** (*LAm*) knitting needle ➤ **aguja hipodérmica** hypodermic needle **2** (= *indicador*) [*de reloj*] hand; (*Téc*) pointer, hand; (*Mil*) firing pin; [*de tocadiscos*] stylus, needle **3** (= *chapitel*) spire, steeple **4** **agujas** (*Culin*) (= *costillas*) shoulder *sing*, rib *sing* **5** (= *pez*) garfish

agujereado ADJ full of holes

agujerear /1a/ VT (= *hacer agujeros en*) to make holes in; (= *penetrar*) to pierce

agujero SM **1** (= *abertura*) hole; **hacer un ~ en** to make a hole in ➤ **agujero de ozono** ozone hole, hole in the ozone layer ➤ **agujero negro** black hole **2** (*Fin*) (= *deuda*) hole, drain, deficit

agujeta Ⓐ ADJ (*Méx*) (= *listo*) sharp Ⓑ SF **1** (*Méx*) (= *cordón*) shoelace **2 agujetas** (*Esp*) (= *rigidez*) stiffness *sing*; **tengo ~s en las piernas** my legs are stiff

agur* EXCL bye*

agustino ADJ, SM Augustinian

aguzar /1f/ VT to incite, stir up; [+ *ingenio*] to sharpen; [+ *apetito*] to whet; **~ el oído** to prick up one's ears; **~ la vista** to keep one's eyes peeled*

ah EXCL **1** (*para expresar sorpresa*) ah!, ha!, oh! **2** (*LAm*) (*para interrogar*) **¿ah?** what?

ahí ADV **1** (*en un lugar*) there; **ponlo ~** put it there; **~ está Antonio** there's Antonio; **~ llega el pelotón** here comes the pack; **¿Nina, estás ~?** Nina, are you there?; **~ abajo** down there; **~ arriba** up there; **~ dentro** in there, inside; **~ fuera** out there, outside; **~ mero** (*Méx*) ◇ **~ mismo** right there; **~ no más** (*LAm*) right (near) here; **por ~** (*indicando dirección*) that way; (*indicando posición*) over there; **entra por ~** go in that way; **busca por ~** look there; **las tijeras deben de estar por ~** the scissors must be around somewhere; **ir a cenar por ~** to go out for dinner, eat out; **lleva muchos años viviendo por ~ fuera** he has been living abroad for many years; **unos cincuenta o por ~** about fifty or so; **por ~ se le ocurre llamar** (*CS*) he might think to call; **~ tiene** there you are; **~ tiene sus libros** there are your books; **¡~ va!: va el balón, ¡cógelo!** there goes the ball, — catch it!; **¡~ va, qué bonito!** wow, it's lovely!; **¡~ va, no me había dado cuenta de que eras tú!** well, well! I didn't realize it was you; ✦ MODISMO **~ donde lo ves** believe it or not **2** (*en una situación*) **~ está la clave de todo** that's the key to everything; **¡~ está el problema!** that's the problem!; **~ está, por ejemplo, el caso de Luis** there's the case of Luis, for example; **¡hombre, haber empezado por ~!** why didn't you say so before?; **de ~** that's why; **de ~ que me sintiera un poco decepcionado** that's why I felt a little let down; **de ~ se deduce que ...** from that it follows that ...; **hasta ~:** **hasta ~ llego yo** I can work that much out for myself; **hasta ~ de acuerdo** I agree with you up to there o that point; **¡hasta ~ podíamos llegar!** what a nerve!, that's the limit!, can you credit it!; **he ~ el dilema** that's the

dilemma, there you have the dilemma; **~ sí que** (*esp LAm*): **si hubiéramos ido más rápido, ~ sí que nos matamos** if we'd gone any faster, ~ sí que definitely have been killed; **~ sí que me pillaste** you've really got me there **3** (*en el tiempo*) **~ mismo** (*LAm*) ◇ **~ no más** (*Chi*) there and then; **a partir de ~** from then on

ahijado/a SM/F (*por bautizo*) godson/goddaughter; (= *protegido*) protégé/protégée

ahijar /1a/ VT to adopt

ahijuna*** EXCL (*CS*) you bastard!***

ahínco SM (= *empeño*) effort; (= *resolución*) determination, perseverance; **con ~** eagerly, hard, earnestly

ahíto ADJ gorged, satiated

ahogado/a Ⓐ ADJ **1** [*persona*] (*en agua*) drowned; (*por falta de aire*) suffocated; **morir ~** (*en agua*) to drown; (*por falta de aire*) to suffocate **2** (= *apagado*) [*voz, llanto*] stifled; [*grito*] muffled **3** (= *sin dinero*) **nos vimos ~s por las deudas** we were up to our eyes in debt **4** (*Méx**) (= *borracho*) drunk Ⓑ SM/F drowned man/woman

ahogador SM (*Méx*) choke

ahogar /1h/ Ⓐ VT **1** (= *matar*) (*en agua*) to drown; (*quitando el aire*) to suffocate; ✦ MODISMO **~ las penas** to drown one's sorrows **2** (= *asfixiar*) [*humo, espina, emoción*] to choke; [*angustia, pena*] to overcome; **su voz tiembla, ahogada por la emoción** her voice trembles, choked with emotion; **la angustia me ahoga** I am overcome with anguish **3** (*económicamente*) [+ *empresa, país*] to cripple **4** (= *reprimir*) [+ *bostezo, tos*] to stifle; [+ *llanto*] to stifle, choke back **5** (= *detener*) [+ *fuego, llamas*] to smother; [+ *lucha, rebelión*] to crush, put down; [+ *voces, protestas*] to stifle; [+ *desarrollo, posibilidades, plan*] to hinder, block; **los aplausos ahogaban sus palabras** her words were drowned (out) by the applause **6** (= *bloquear*) to block **7** (*Aut*) [+ *motor*] to flood Ⓑ **ahogarse** VPR **1** (*en agua*) (*accidentalmente*) to drown; (*suicidándose*) to drown o.s.; ✦ MODISMO **~se en un vaso de agua** to make a mountain out of a molehill **2** (= *asfixiarse*) **2.1** (*por falta de aire*) to get out of breath **2.2** (*por el calor*) to suffocate **2.3** (*con humo, espina*) to choke (**con** on) **3** (*Aut*) [*motor*] to flood

ahogo SM **1** (= *asfixia*) breathlessness; **el asma le produce ~** asthma makes him breathless **2** (= *angustia*) feeling of distress **3** (= *apuro económico*) financial difficulty

ahondar /1a/ VI **~ en** to study thoroughly, explore

ahora Ⓐ ADV **1** (= *en este momento*) now; **~ o nunca** now or never; **de ~ en adelante** from now on; **de ~** of today; **la juventud de ~** the youth of today, today's youth; **no es una cosa de ~** it's not a recent thing; **desde ~** from now on; **hasta ~** up to now, so far; **~ mismo** right now; **a partir de ~** from now on; **por ~** for the moment, for now; **es todo lo que podemos hacer por ~** it's all we can do for the moment o for now; **por ~ ha dirigido sólo dos películas** up to now he has only directed two films (*esp Brit*) o movies (*esp EEUU*); **~ que** now that; **~ que lo pienso** come to think of it, now that I think of it; **~ sí que me voy** I'm definitely going this time **2** (= *hace poco*) just now; **me lo acaban de decir ~** they've just told me; **~ tiempo** (*Chi*) a while ago; **~ último** (*Chi*) recently **3** (= *enseguida*) in a minute; **~ lo apunto** I'll write it down in a minute; **¡hasta ~!** see you in a minute! Ⓑ CONJ **1** (= *sin embargo*) **~, yo entiendo que eso no fue lo acordado** I understand, though, that that is not what was agreed; **es muy barato; ~, si no te gusta no lo compro** it's very cheap; then again, if you don't like it I won't buy it; **~ bien** however; **~ que** although; **es listo, ~ que bastante vago** he's bright, although quite lazy **2** (*uso distributivo*) **~ la quitan, ~ la ponen** one minute they take it away, the next they put it back

ahorcado/a SM/F hanged person

ahorcamiento SM hanging

ahorcar /1g/ **Ⓐ** VT to hang; ✦ MODISMO **a la fuerza ahorcan** there is no alternative **Ⓑ** **ahorcarse** VPR to hang o.s.

ahorita ADV (esp LAm), **ahoritica** ADV (LAm), **ahoritita** ADV (Méx) (= en este momento) right now, this very minute; (= hace poco) a minute ago, just now; (= dentro de poco) in a minute; **¡~ voy!** I'm just coming!, I'll be with you in a minute!

ahorrador ADJ thrifty

ahorrar /1a/ **Ⓐ** VT 1 [+ dinero, energía, tiempo, trabajo] to save; **tienen bastante dinero ahorrado** they have quite a lot of money saved up o put by
2 (= evitar) [+ disgustos, molestias, problemas] to save; [+ peligro] to avoid; **me gustaría ~te las molestias** I'd like to save you the trouble; **te ~é los detalles** I'll spare you the details; **lo contó sin ~ detalles** she told it in great detail; **no ~ ataques/críticas contra algn** to show no mercy in one's attacks/criticism of sb; **no ~ elogios con algn** to be unstinting in one's praise of sb; **no ~ esfuerzos** to spare no effort, be unstinting in one's efforts
Ⓑ VI to save; **está ahorrando para comprarse un coche** he's saving (up) to buy a car; **no encienden el aire acondicionado para ~** they don't put the air conditioning on to save money o to economize
Ⓒ **ahorrarse** VPR 1 [+ dinero, tiempo] to save
2 (= evitarse) to save o.s.; **un regalo que te ahorras** it saves you having to buy a present, you save yourself having to buy a present; **podías haberte ahorrado los comentarios** I could have done without your comments

ahorrativo ADJ thrifty

ahorro SM 1 (= acto) [de dinero, energía, trabajo] saving; **una política que fomenta el ~** a policy which promotes saving; **un plan de ~ energético** an energy saving scheme 2 ahorros (= dinero) savings 3 (= cualidad) thrift

ahuchar /1a/ VT (Col) = **azuzar**

ahuecar /1g/ **Ⓐ** VT 1 (= excavar) to hollow, hollow out; **~ la mano** to cup one's hand 2 [+ voz] to deepen 3 **~ el ala** to make o.s. scarce 4 (Agr) to loosen, soften 5 (Cos) to fluff out **Ⓑ** VI **¡ahueca!** beat it!*

ahuizote SM 1 (CAm, Méx) (= persona) pain*, pain in the neck*, nuisance 2 (= maleficio) evil spell, curse

ahumado ADJ (Culin) smoked; (= lleno de humo) smoky; [vidrio] tinted

ahumar /1a/ VT 1 (Culin) to smoke, cure 2 [+ superficie] to make smoky; [+ sala] to fill with smoke

ahuyentar /1a/ VT 1 (= espantar) to frighten off, frighten away; (= mantener a distancia) to keep off 2 [+ temores, dudas] to banish, dispel

aimará (pl **aimaraes**) **Ⓐ** ADJ, SMF Aymara (Indian) **Ⓑ** SM (Ling) Aymara

aindiado ADJ (LAm) Indian-like, Indianized

airado ADJ angry

aire SM 1 (= elemento) air; **al ~**: **lanzar algo al ~** to throw sth into the air; **la fruta se deja secar al ~** the fruit is left to dry uncovered; **un vestido con la espalda al ~** a backless dress; **estar en el ~** [balón, paracaidista] to be in the air; (Radio) to be on (the) air; **todo está en el ~ hasta que se conozcan los resultados** it's all up in the air until the results are known; **dejar una pregunta/problema en el ~** to leave a question/ issue up in the air; **al ~ libre** (con verbo) outdoors, in the open air; (con sustantivo) outdoor antes de s, open-air antes de s; **actividades al ~ libre** outdoor activities; **saltar por los ~s** to blow up, explode; **tomar el ~** to get some fresh air; **volar por los ~s** to blow up, explode; ✦ MODISMO **a mi/tu/su ~: le gusta hacer las cosas a su ~** he likes to do things his own way; **ir a su ~** to go one's own way, do one's own thing*; ➤ **aire acondicionado** air conditioning; **un vehículo con ~ acondicionado** an air-conditioned vehicle
2 (Meteo) (= viento) wind; (= corriente) draught, draft (EEUU); **entra mucho ~ por la puerta** there's a strong draught o (EEUU) draft coming in through the door; **hoy hace mucho ~** it's very windy today; **entraba un ~ muy agradable de la calle** there was a lovely breeze coming in from the street; **dar ~ a algn** to fan sb; ✦ MODISMO **cambiar** o **mudar de ~s** to

have a change (of scene)
3 (= aspecto) air; **los techos altos le daban un ~ señorial a la casa** high ceilings gave a stately air to the house; **le respondió con ~ cansado** he replied wearily; ✦ MODISMO **darse ~s** to put on airs; **no te des esos ~s de suficiencia conmigo** don't get on your high horse with me
4 (= parecido) **¿no le notas un ~ con Carlos?** don't you think he looks a bit o a little like Carlos?; **darse un ~ a algn** to look a bit like sb ➤ **aire de familia** family resemblance, family likeness
5 (= aerofagia) wind
6 (= garbo) style, panache; **lleva la ropa con mucho ~** she wears her clothes with great style o panache
7 (Mús) air

airear /1a/ **Ⓐ** VT 1 (= ventilar) to air; **~ la atmósfera** to clear the air 2 (= difundir) [+ idea, cuestión] to air; (en prensa) to discuss at length, give a lot of coverage to **Ⓑ** **airearse** VPR to take the air

airoso ADJ **salir ~ de algo** to come through sth unscathed

aislado ADJ 1 (= remoto) isolated 2 (= incomunicado) cut off; **quedamos ~s por las inundaciones** we were cut off by the floods 3 (= suelto) **un caso ~** an isolated case 4 (Elec) insulated

aislamiento SM 1 (= acción) isolation 2 (Elec) insulation ➤ **aislamiento térmico** insulation

aislante **Ⓐ** ADJ insulating **Ⓑ** SM (Elec) insulator

aislar /1a/ **Ⓐ** VT 1 (= dejar solo) to isolate 2 [+ ciudad, fortaleza] to cut off 3 (Elec) to insulate **Ⓑ** **aislarse** VPR to isolate o.s., cut o.s. off (de from)

ajar /1a/ **Ⓐ** VT (= arrugar) to crumple, crush **Ⓑ** **ajarse** VPR [piel] to get wrinkled; [planta] to wither, fade

ajardinar /1a/ VT to landscape; **zona ajardinada** landscaped area

ajedrecista SMF chess player

ajedrez SM chess; **un ~** a chess set

ajenjo SM absinth, absinthe

ajeno ADJ 1 (= de otro) **con el dinero ~** with other people's money; **juegan en campo ~** they are playing away from home; **a costa ajena** at sb else's expense; **trabajador por cuenta ajena** employed worker; **meterse en lo ~** to interfere in other people's affairs
2 (= no relacionado) **~ a** outside; **fuentes ajenas a la empresa** sources outside the company; **"prohibido el paso a toda persona ajena a la obra"** "authorized staff only past this point"; **hablaron de cosas ajenas al trabajo** they talked about things unconnected with work; **se mantendría ~ a la política** he would remain outside of politics; **por razones ajenas a nuestra voluntad** for reasons beyond our control
3 (= indiferente) **nada de lo humano le es ~** (liter) everything human is his concern; **siguió leyendo, ~ a lo que sucedía** she carried on reading, oblivious to what was happening
4 (= extraño) strange; **todo le era ~** everything was strange

ajete SM young garlic

ajetreado ADJ busy

ajetreo SM hustle and bustle

ají SM (pl **~es, ajises**) 1 (SAm) (= pimiento picante) chili; (= pimiento dulce) pepper; ✦ MODISMO **estar hecho un ~** to be hopping mad 2 (And) (= salsa) chili sauce

ajiaco SM (LAm) potato and chili stew

ajillo SM **al ~** with garlic, cooked in garlic

ajo SM garlic; **un ~** a clove of garlic; ✦ MODISMOS **andar en el ~** ◇ **estar en el ~** (= involucrado) to be mixed up in it; (= enterado) to be in on the secret; **echar ~s y cebollas** ◇ **soltar ~s y cebollas** (LAm) to swear like a trooper ➤ **ajo tierno** young garlic

ajoarriero SM dish of cod with oil, garlic and peppers

ajoblanco SM cold garlic and almond soup

ajonjolí SM sesame

ajuar SM [de novia] trousseau; [de niño] layette

ajumado* ADJ tight*, tipsy

ajuntar* /1a/ **Ⓐ** VT (entre niños) to make friends with, be friends with; **¡ya no te ajunto!** I'm not your friend any more! **B** **ajuntarse** VPR (= *amancebarse*) to live together, live in sin; (*entre niños*) **¡no me ajunto contigo!** I'm not your friend any more!

ajustado ADJ **1** (= *ceñido*) tight, tight-fitting; **la blusa le quedaba muy ajustada** the blouse was very tight on her **2** (= *con poco margen*) [*presupuesto*] tight; [*resultado*] tight, close; **los precios más ~s del mercado** the most competitive prices in the market; **hemos tenido que venderlo todo a un precio muy ~** we had to sell everything at a very low profit **3** (= *acertado*) accurate; **un ~ retrato de la sociedad** an accurate portrait of society

ajustar /1a/ **A** VT **1** (*Téc*) **1.1** [+ *pieza, grifo*] (*colocando*) to fit; (*apretando*) to tighten **1.2** (= *regular*) [+ *volumen, temperatura*] to adjust, regulate; [+ *asiento, retrovisor*] to adjust; [+ *cinturón*] to tighten **1.3** (*Chi, Méx*) [+ *motor*] to fix **2** (= *pactar*) [+ *acuerdo, trato*] to reach; [+ *precio*] to agree on; **~ cuentas con algn** (*lit*) to settle accounts with sb; (*fig*) to settle one's scores with sb **3** (= *adaptar*) to adjust (**a** to) **4** (*Cos*) [+ *cintura, manga*] to take in **5** (*CAm, Méx, Chi, Ven*) **~ un golpe a algn** to deal sb a blow; **~ un garrotazo a algn** to beat sb with a club **B** VI **1** (= *encajar*) to fit **2** (*Ven*) (= *agudizarse*) to get worse; **me ajustó el dolor** the pain got worse; **por el camino ajustó el aguacero** on the way, there was a sudden downpour **C** **ajustarse** VPR **1** (= *ceñirse*) **1.1** [+ *corbata, cinturón*] to adjust **1.2** [*zapato*] to fit; [*pantalón, vestido*] to cling; **el zapato debe ~se al pie lo mejor posible** the shoe should fit the foot as well as possible; **se ajusta al cuerpo como una segunda piel** it clings to the body like a second skin **2** (= *encajarse*) to fit **3** (= *adaptarse*) **~se a** [+ *situación, estilo*] to adapt to; [+ *necesidades*] to meet; [+ *norma, regla*] to comply with; **se ajusta al presupuesto** it is within the budget; **tendrán que ~se al guión** they will have to keep to *o* follow the script; **(no) se ajusta a derecho** it is (not) legally admissible **4** (= *coincidir*) **la narración se ajusta a la verdad** the story agrees with the facts

ajuste SM **1** (*Téc*) adjustment **2** (= *adaptación*) adjustment; **se producirá~s de precios** price adjustments will occur **➤ ajuste de plantilla** (*Esp*) redeployment of labour *o* (*EEUU*) labor **➤ ajuste económico** economic adjustment **➤ ajuste laboral** redeployment of labour *o* (*EEUU*) labor **➤ ajuste presupuestario** budget settlement **3** (= *pacto*) **tras el ~ del precio** after fixing the price **➤ ajuste de cuentas** settling of scores **4** (*Chi, Méx*) [*de motor*] overhaul

ajusticiamiento SM execution

ajusticiar /1b/ VT to execute, put to death

al *ver* **a**

ala A SF **1** [*de insecto, pájaro*] wing; **✦** MODISMOS **cortar las ~s a algn** to clip sb's wings; **dar ~s a algn** to encourage sb; **del ~** (*Esp**): **las 1.000 del ~** a cool 1,000 pesetas* **2** [*de avión*] wing **➤ ala delta** (= *deporte*) hang gliding; (= *aparato*) hang glider **3** (*Pol*) wing; **el ~ izquierda del partido** the left wing of the party **4** (*Mil*) wing, flank **5** [*de edificio*] wing **6** (= *parte sobresaliente*) [*de sombrero*] brim; [*de mesa*] leaf, flap **7** (*Dep*) = *banda*) wing **B** SMF (*Dep*) winger; **medio ~** half-back, wing-half

Alá SM Allah

alabanza SF praise; **en ~ de** in praise of; **digno de ~** praiseworthy, commendable

alabar /1a/ VT to praise; **~ a algn por algo** to praise sb for sth

alabastro SM alabaster

alacena SF cupboard (*esp Brit*), closet (*EEUU*)

alacrán SM scorpion

Aladino SM Aladdin

ALALC SF ABR (= **Asociación Latinoamericana de Libre Comercio**) LAFTA

alambicado ADJ [*proceso, estilo*] intricate; [*teoría, misterio*] complex

alambique SM still

alambrada SF wire fence **➤ alambrada de espino** barbed-wire fence

alambrado SM (*LAm*) wire fence

alambre SM wire

alameda SF poplar grove

álamo SM poplar **➤ álamo temblón** aspen

alano SM mastiff

alarde SM **1** display; **un ~ de patriotismo** a display of patriotism; **la decisión fue todo un ~ de serenidad** the decision was a feat of cool-headedness; **en un ~ de generosidad** in a show *o* display of generosity; **hacer ~ de algo** (= *jactarse*) to boast about sth; (= *demostrar*) to display sth, demonstrate sth **2** (*Mil†*) review

alardear /1a/ VI to boast, brag (**de** about)

alargado ADJ long, extended

alargador SM extension lead

alargamiento SM (*gen*) lengthening; (= *prórroga*) extension

alargar /1h/ **A** VT **1** (= *estirar*) [+ *cuerda, goma*] to stretch; [+ *pista de aterrizaje*] to lengthen; [+ *cuello*] to crane; [+ *mano*] to stretch out; [+ *vestido*] to lengthen, let down **2** (*en tiempo*) [+ *visita*] to prolong, extend; [+ *discurso, espera*] to prolong; [+ *relato*] to spin out; **esto alargó nuestra espera** this prolonged our wait, this forced us to wait longer **3** [+ *cable de escalada*] to pay out **4** (*) (= *dar*) to hand, pass (**a** to) **5** [+ *sueldo*] to increase, raise **B** **alargarse** VPR **1** (*en longitud*) to lengthen, get longer **2** (*en tiempo*) [*días*] to grow longer; [*relato*] to drag out; [*orador*] to go on for a long time

alarido SM shriek, yell; **dar ~s** to shriek, yell

alarma SF alarm; **falsa ~** false alarm; **dar la ~** to raise the alarm; **voz de ~** warning note; **señal de ~** alarm signal **➤ alarma antirrobo** [*de coche*] car alarm, anti-theft alarm; [*de casa*] burglar alarm **➤ alarma de incendios** fire alarm **➤ alarma social** public alarm

alarmante ADJ alarming

alarmar /1a/ **A** VT to alarm **B** **alarmarse** VPR to get alarmed, be alarmed

alauí ADJ, **alauita** ADJ Moroccan

Álava SF Álava

alavés ADJ of/from Álava

alazán/ana SM/F sorrel

alba SF dawn, daybreak; **al ~** at dawn; **al rayar** *o* **romper el ~** at daybreak

albacea SMF executor/executrix

albaceteño ADJ of/from Albacete

albahaca SF basil

albanés/esa A ADJ, SM/F Albanian **B** SM (*Ling*) Albanian

Albania SF Albania

albanokosovar ADJ, SMF Kosovar Albanian

albañal SM (*Col*) drain, sewer

albañil SMF (*gen*) builder, construction worker; (*que sólo pone ladrillos*) bricklayer

albañilería SF **1** (= *oficio*) building, construction work **2 trabajo de ~** building (work)

albar ADJ white

albarán SM delivery note, invoice

albarda SF packsaddle

albaricoque SM (*esp Esp*) apricot

albariño SM (*type of*) Galician wine

albatros SM INV albatross

albedrío SM will; **libre ~** free will

alberca SF (= *depósito*) tank, reservoir; (*Méx*) (= *piscina*) swimming pool

albérchigo SM (= *fruto*) peach, clingstone peach; (= *árbol*) peach tree, clingstone peach tree

albergar /1h/ **A** VT **1** (= *acomodar*) [+ *visitante, refugiado,*

inmigrante] to provide accommodation for; [+ *criminal, fugitivo*] to harbour, harbor (*EEUU*)
2 (= *dar cabida a*) [+ *espectadores, público*] to accommodate, hold; [+ *evento, celebración*] to host; **el estadio puede ~ a 30.000 personas** the stadium can accommodate *o* hold 30,000 people, the stadium has a capacity of 30,000; **el edificio que alberga la sede del partido** the building which houses the party's headquarters
3 [+ *esperanza*] to cherish; [+ *rencor*] to harbour, harbor (*EEUU*)
B albergarse VPR **1** (= *refugiarse*) to shelter
2 (= *alojarse*) to stay

albergue SM (= *refugio*) shelter, refuge; (= *alojamiento*) lodging; [*de montaña*] refuge; **dar ~ a algn** to take sb in ➤ **albergue juvenil** youth hostel

albino/a ADJ, SM/F albino

albis ADV **quedarse in ~** not to understand a thing

albóndiga SF meatball

albor SM **1** (= *color*) whiteness **2** (= *luz*) dawn, dawn light ➤ **albor de la vida** childhood, youth **3** (*liter*) **albores** dawn; **en los ~es de la ciencia** at the dawn of science

alborada SF (= *alba*) daybreak, dawn; (*Mús poét*) aubade, dawn song

albornoz SM **1** (= *de baño*) bathrobe **2** (= *prenda árabe*) burnous, burnouse

alborotado ADJ [*persona*] agitated, excited; [*mar*] rough

alborotador(a) A ADJ (= *ruidoso*) boisterous, noisy; (*Pol*) (= *sedicioso*) seditious **B** SM/F (= *agitador*) agitator, troublemaker; (= *alumno*) troublemaker

alborotar /1a/ **A** VT (= *agitar*) to disturb, agitate; (= *amotinar*) to incite to rebel; (= *excitar*) to excite **B** VI to make a racket **C alborotarse** VPR [*individuo*] to get excited, get worked up; [*multitud*] to riot; [*mar*] to get rough

alboroto SM (= *disturbio*) disturbance; (= *vocerío*) racket; (= *jaleo*) uproar; (= *motín*) riot

alborozado ADJ jubilant, overjoyed

alborozo SM joy, jubilation, rejoicing

albricias EXCL (= *¡felicidades!*) **¡albricias! ¡lo conseguí!** whoopee! I got it!

albufera SF lagoon

álbum SM (*pl* **~s** *o* **~es**) album; (= *disco*) album ➤ **álbum de recortes** scrapbook ➤ **álbum de sellos** stamp album ➤ **álbum recopilatorio** greatest hits album

albumen SM albumen

albúmina SF albumin

albur SM (*Méx*) (= *juego de palabras*) pun; (= *doble sentido*) double entendre

ALCA SF ABR (= **Área de Libre Comercio de las Américas**) FTAA

alcachofa SF **1** (= *planta*) artichoke **2** ➤ **alcachofa de (la) ducha** shower head ➤ **alcachofa de regadera** rose

alcahuete/a SM/F **1** (= *proxeneta*) (*hombre*) procurer, pimp; (*mujer*) procuress, go-between **2** (*CS*) (= *chismoso*) gossip

alcahuetear* /1a/ **A** VT (*Col*) (= *tapar*) to cover up **B** VI (*RPl*) (= *chismear*) to gossip

alcaide SM (*Hist*) [*de castillo*] governor; [*de cárcel*] warder (*Brit*), guard (*EEUU*), jailer

alcalde(sa) SM/F mayor/mayoress

alcaldía SF (= *oficio*) mayoralty, office of mayor; (= *oficina*) mayor's office; (= *edificio*) town hall, city hall (*EEUU*)

alcalino ADJ alkaline

alcaloide SM alkaloid

alcance SM **1** (= *posibilidad de acceso*) [*de brazo, persona*] reach; [*de pensamiento*] scope; **al ~ de algn** available to sb; **todos los medios a su ~** all the means available to her; **estar al ~ de algn** (= *cercano*) to be within sb's reach; **estas joyas no están al ~ de cualquiera** not everyone can afford these jewels; **hizo lo que estaba a su ~ por ayudarme** he did what he could to help me; **estar fuera del ~ de algn** (= *alejado, imposible*) to be out of sb's reach, be beyond sb's

reach; (= *incomprensible*) to be over sb's head; (= *caro*) to be beyond sb's means; **"manténgase fuera del alcance de los niños"** "keep out of reach of children"; **al ~ de la mano** at hand, within arm's reach; **poner algo al ~ de algn** to make sth available to sb; **al ~ de la vista** within sight
2 (= *distancia*) (*Mil*) range; **de corto ~** [*arma, misil*] short-range *antes de s*; [*objetivo, proyecto*] short-term *antes de s*; **de gran** *o* **largo ~** [*faros*] full beam *antes de s* (*Brit*), high beam *antes de s* (*EEUU*); [*arma, misil, micrófono*] long-range *antes de s*; [*efecto, repercusiones*] far-reaching
3 (= *importancia*) [*de problema*] extent; [*de noticia, suceso*] importance, significance; **comprendió el verdadero ~ de lo ocurrido** she understood the true significance of what had happened
4 dar ~ a algn (= *capturar*) to capture sb; (= *llegar a la altura*) to catch up with sb
5 alcances (= *inteligencia*) grasp *sing*; **de cortos** *o* **pocos ~s** not very bright
6 (*Chi*) **hacer un ~** to clear sth up, clarify sth ➤ **alcance de nombres**: **no es su padre, es sólo un ~ de nombres** he's not his father, it just happens that their names coincide

alcancía SF (*LAm*) (*para ahorrar*) money box; (*para colectas*) collection box, poor box

alcanfor SM camphor

alcantarilla SF (*para aguas de desecho*) (= *boca*) drain; (= *cloaca*) sewer

alcantarillado SM sewer system, drains *pl*

alcanzado* ADJ hard up*, broke*

alcanzar /1f/ **A** VT **1** (*andando*) to catch up (with); **la alcancé cuando salía por la puerta** I caught up with her just as she was going out of the door
2 [+ *ladrón, autobús, tren*] to catch
3 (= *llegar a*) [+ *cima, límite, edad*] to reach; **dentro de poco ~á a su padre en altura** he'll soon be as tall as his father; **puede ~ una velocidad de 200km/h** it can reach speeds of up to 200km/h; **el termómetro llegó a ~ los cuarenta grados** temperatures rose as high as forty degrees; **~ la mayoría de edad** to come of age; **alcanzó la orilla a nado** he made it to the shore by swimming, he swam ashore; **no llegó a ~ la pubertad** he never made it as far as puberty
3 (= *conseguir*) [+ *acuerdo*] to reach; [+ *éxito, objetivo*] to achieve; **~ la fama** to find fame, become famous
4 [*bala*] to hit; **uno de los dos disparos alcanzó al presidente** the president was hit by one of the two shots
5 (*esp LAm*) (= *dar*) to pass; **¿me alcanzas las tijeras?** could you pass me the scissors?
6 (*) (= *entender*) to grasp, understand; **no alcanza más allá de lo que le han enseñado** he's only capable of understanding what he's been taught
B VI **1** (= *llegar*) to reach (**a, hasta** as far as); **no alcanzo** I can't reach; **hasta donde alcanza la vista** as far as the eye can see
2 ~ a hacer algo to manage to do sth; **no alcanzo a comprender sus razones** I just can't understand her reasons
3 (= *ser suficiente*) to be enough; **con dos botellas ~á para todos** two bottles will be enough for everyone

alcaparra SF caper

alcaravea SF caraway

alcatraz SM gannet

alcaucil SM (*RPl*) artichoke

alcayata SF meat hook, spike

alcazaba SF citadel, castle

alcázar SM (*Mil*) fortress, citadel; (= *palacio*) royal palace; (*Náut*) quarter-deck

alce SM elk, moose

alcista ADJ **mercado ~** bull market, rising market; **la tendencia ~** the upward trend

alcoba SF bedroom

⚠ **alcoba** ≠ *alcove*

alcohol SM alcohol; **lámpara de ~** spirit lamp ➤ **alcohol de quemar, alcohol metílico** methylated spirit

alcoholemia SF alcohol level of the blood; **control de ~** ◇ **prueba de ~** ◇ **test de ~** breath test, Breathalyser® o Breathalyzer® test

alcohólico/a ⓐ ADJ alcoholic; **no ~** [bebida] non-alcoholic, soft **ⓑ** SM/F alcoholic

alcoholímetro SM Breathalyser®, Breathalyzer®

alcoholismo SM alcoholism

alcoholizado ADJ **está ~** he's an alcoholic

alcornoque SM **1** (= árbol) cork tree **2** (*) (= tonto) idiot

alcurnia SF ancestry, lineage; **de ~** of noble family, of noble birth

alcuza SF (Chi) cruet

aldaba SF knocker, door knocker

aldea SF small village, hamlet

aldeano/a ⓐ ADJ **1** (= de pueblo) village antes de s; (= de campo) rustic; **gente aldeana** country people **2** (pey) provincial **ⓑ** SM/F villager

aleación SF alloy

aleatorio ADJ (Estadística) random, contingent; (= fortuito) accidental, fortuitous

alebrestar /1a/ (LAm) **ⓐ** VT **1** (Méx) (= incitar, despertar) **él a mí no me alebresta el menor sentimiento** I don't feel anything for him at all; **el sólo verla le alebresta la pasión** the mere sight of her fills him with passion **2** (Col) (= poner nervioso) to get agitated **3** (Ven*) (= animar) to get excited **ⓑ alebrestarse** VPR (Col) **1** (= ponerse nervioso) to get agitated **2** (Ven*) (= animarse) to get excited; (= indisciplinarse) to get out of hand

aleccionador ADJ instructive, enlightening

aleccionar /1a/ VT (= instruir) to instruct, enlighten; (= regañar) to lecture

aledaños SMPL outskirts

alegación SF (Jur) declaration

alegador ADJ (And) argumentative

alegar /1h/ **ⓐ** VT (= citar) [+ dificultad] to plead; [+ autoridad] to quote; [+ razones] to put forward, adduce; **~ que** to claim that, assert that **ⓑ** VI (LAm) to argue; (= protestar) to complain loudly, make a fuss

alegata SF (Méx) fight

alegato SM **1** (Jur) (escrito) indictment; (= declaración) statement, assertion **2** (And) (= discusión) argument, dispute

alegoría SF allegory

alegórico ADJ allegoric, allegorical

alegrar /1a/ **ⓐ** VT **1** (= poner contento) to cheer up; **le mandamos flores para ~la un poco** we sent her some flowers to cheer her up a little; **me alegra que me preguntes eso** I'm glad you asked me that; **nos alegra saber que ha aprobado** we're pleased to hear that you passed **2** (= animar) [+ fiesta, reunión] to liven up; [+ casa, cuarto] to brighten up, cheer up; **el rojo te alegra la cara** red gives your face a bit of colour o (EEUU) color; **¡alegra esa cara!** cheer up! **ⓑ alegrarse** VPR **1** (= complacerse) to be happy, be pleased; **siempre se alegra cuando la visitamos** she's always happy o pleased when we go and visit her; **me alegro de verte** I'm pleased to see you, it's good to see you; **me alegro por ella** I'm happy o pleased for her; **—he aprobado —¡me alegro!** "I passed" — "I'm pleased to hear it!"; **me alegro muchísimo** I'm delighted; **—ya puedo devolverte el dinero —me alegro de saberlo** "I can pay you back now" — "I'm glad to hear it"; **me alegro de que hayas venido, necesito tu ayuda** I'm glad you've come, I need your help **2** (*) (= emborracharse) to get tipsy*

alegre ADJ **1** (= feliz) [persona] [cara, carácter] happy, cheerful; **recibimos una ~ noticia** we received some happy news; **estar ~ (por algo)** to be happy (about sth); **ser ~** to be cheerful o happy **2** (= luminoso) [día, habitación, color] bright **3** [música, fiesta] lively **4** (*) (= borracho) **estar ~** to be merry o tipsy* **5** (= irresponsable) thoughtless **6** (= inmoral) [vida] fast

alegremente ADV **1** (= felizmente) happily, cheerfully

2 (= irresponsablemente) gaily; **se lo gastó todo ~** he spent it all without a thought for tomorrow

alegría SF **1** (= felicidad) happiness, joy; **¡qué ~!** how marvellous!, that's splendid!; **saltar de ~** to jump for joy **➤ alegría vital** joie de vivre **2** (pey) (= irresponsabilidad) recklessness, irresponsibility **3** (Bot) **➤ alegría de la casa** balsam **4 alegrías** (Mús) type of lively Andalusian dance or song

alejado ADJ **1** (= distanciado) remote; **en un pueblecito ~** in a remote little village; **vivimos algo ~s** we live quite far away, we live quite a distance away; **~ de** [lugar] distant from; [persona] away from; **una lesión lo mantuvo ~ del baloncesto** an injury kept him out of basketball; **ha pasado varios años alejada de los escenarios** she has spent several years off the stage; **viven completamente ~s de la realidad** they live completely cut off from the real world o from reality

2 (= diferente) removed (de from); **muy ~ de nuestro concepto de libertad** very far removed from our concept of freedom

alejamiento SM (= distanciamiento) (gen) distance; (como actividad) distancing; **se ha producido un pequeño ~ entre los dos planetas** the two planets have shifted slightly apart o away from each other; **la obra supone un ~ de la tradición teatral** the work represents a break with o a distancing from theatrical tradition; **se produjo un ~ entre el gobierno y la gente** there was a rift between the government and the people

alejandrino SM alexandrine

alejar /1a/ **ⓐ** VT **1** (= distanciar) to move away (de from); **aleja un poco más el jarrón** move the vase away a little **2** (= hacer irse) (de lugar) to keep away (de from); (de puesto) to remove (de from); **ese olor aleja a los mosquitos** that smell keeps the mosquitoes away; **una enfermedad lo alejó de la vida pública** illness forced him to withdraw from public life; **~ a algn de algn** (= distanciar) to keep sb away from sb; (= causar ruptura) to cause a rift between sb and sb

3 (= desviar) [+ atención] to distract; [+ sospechas] to remove; [+ amenaza, peligro] to remove **ⓑ alejarse** VPR **1** (= irse lejos) to go away, move away (de from); **un coche rojo se alejaba del lugar** a red car was leaving the scene; **vieron ~se corriendo a dos jóvenes** they saw two youths running away; **no conviene ~se de la orilla** it's better not to go too far from the shore; **~se del buen camino** to go o stray off the straight and narrow **2** (= separarse) **~se de algo**: **la carretera se aleja de la costa** the road veers away from the coast; **en esta obra se aleja de los problemas sociales** in this work she moves away from social problems; **poco a poco se fueron alejando de sus amigos** they gradually drifted apart from their friends **3** (= desaparecer) [peligro] to recede; [ruido] to grow fainter; **se aleja la posibilidad de un nuevo recorte de los tipos de interés** the possibility of a new cut in interest rates is becoming increasingly unlikely

alelado ADJ (= aturdido) stupefied, bewildered; (= bobo) foolish, stupid

aleluya ⓐ EXCL hallelujah!, hurray! **ⓑ** SM o SF (Mús, Rel) hallelujah, alleluia

alemán/ana ⓐ ADJ, SM/F German **ⓑ** SM (Ling) German

Alemania SF Germany

alentado ADJ **1** (Chi, Col, Ven) (= sano) healthy **2** (CAm, Méx) (= mejorado) improved, better

alentador ADJ encouraging

alentar /1j/ **ⓐ** VT (= animar) to encourage, hearten; [+ esperanzas] to raise; **en su pecho alienta la esperanza de ...** he cherishes the hope of ...; **~ a algn a hacer algo** to encourage sb to do sth **ⓑ alentarse** VPR (LAm Med) to get better

alergeno SM, **alérgeno** SM allergen

alergia SF allergy; **tener ~ a** to be allergic to **➤ alergia al polen** hay fever, allergy to pollen

alérgico/a ⓐ ADJ allergic (**a** to) **ⓑ** SM/F allergic person

alero SM **1** (Arquit) eaves pl **2** (Dep) winger

alerón SM aileron

alerta Ⓐ EXCL watch out! Ⓑ ADJ, ADV alert, watchful; **estar ~** to be on the alert; **todos los servicios de auxilio están ~(s)** all the rescue services are on stand-by Ⓒ SF alert; **dar la ~** ◇ **dar la voz de ~** to raise the alarm; **en estado de ~** on the alert; **en ~ de 24 horas** on 24-hour stand-by ➤ **alerta roja** red alert

alertar /1a/ VT to alert; **~ a algn de algo** to alert sb to sth

aleta SF 1 (Zool) [de pez] fin; [de foca] flipper; [de natación] flipper ➤ **aleta dorsal** dorsal fin 2 [de coche] wing (Brit), fender (EEUU)

aletargado ADJ drowsy, lethargic

aletargar /1h/ Ⓐ VT to make drowsy, make lethargic Ⓑ **aletargarse** VPR to grow drowsy, become lethargic

aletear /1a/ VI to flutter, flap its wings

alevín SM 1 (= cría de pez) fry, young fish 2 (= joven principiante) youngster, novice

alevosía SF 1 (= traición) treachery 2 (Jur) malice aforethought

alfa SF (= letra) alpha

alfabético ADJ alphabetic, alphabetical

alfabetización SF teaching people to read and write; **campaña de ~** literacy campaign

alfabetizar /1f/ VT 1 (= clasificar) to arrange alphabetically 2 (= enseñar) to teach to read and write

alfabeto SM alphabet ➤ **alfabeto Morse** Morse code ➤ **alfabeto romano** Roman alphabet

alfajor SM (CS, Ven) sweet biscuit with filling; (Esp) sweet eaten at Christmas

alfalfa SF lucerne, alfalfa

alfandoque SM (Col, Perú) caramel bar; (Ven) spiced white fudge

alfanje SM cutlass

alfarería SF (= arte) pottery; (= tienda) pottery shop (esp Brit), pottery store (EEUU)

alfarero/a SM/F potter

alféizar SM [de ventana] window sill

alfeñique SM weakling

alférez SMF second lieutenant, subaltern

alfil SM bishop

alfiler SM (Cos) pin; (= broche) brooch, clip; ✦ MODISMOS **aquí ya no cabe ni un ~** you can't squeeze anything else in; **prendido con ~es** shaky, hardly hanging together ➤ **alfiler de corbata** tiepin ➤ **alfiler de gancho** (CS), **alfiler nodriza** (Col) safety pin

alfiletero SM (= estuche) needle case; (= acerico) pincushion

alfombra SF (grande) carpet; (pequeña) rug, mat ➤ **alfombra de baño** bath mat ➤ **alfombra de oración** prayer mat ➤ **alfombra mágica** magic carpet

alfombrar /1a/ VT to carpet

alfombrilla SF 1 (= estera) mat 2 (Inform) mouse mat 3 (Med) type of mild measles

alforja SF [de jinete] saddlebag; (en bicicleta) pannier; (= mochila) knapsack

alga SF seaweed, alga

algarabía SF hullabaloo

algarada SF outcry

algarroba SF carob, carob bean

álgebra SF algebra

algebraico ADJ algebraic

álgido ADJ [momento] crucial, decisive

algo Ⓐ PRON 1 (en oraciones afirmativas) something; **~ más barato** something cheaper; **~ así: o ~ así** or something like that; **dura ~ como tres horas** it's about three hours long; **~ de: sé ~ de inglés** I know a little English; **nos dieron ~ de comer** they gave us something to eat; **en ~:** **queríamos ser útiles en ~** we wanted to be of some use; **se ha cambiado en ~ el plan** the plan has been changed

slightly; **las dos hermanas se parecen en ~** there is a certain likeness between the two sisters; **llegar a ser ~** to be something; **tomar ~** (de beber) to have a drink; (de comer) to have a bite (to eat); **llegamos a las tres y ~** we arrived at three something; ✦ MODISMOS **~ es ~** it's better than nothing; **darle ~ a algn*:** casi me da **~** cuando falló el penalti I nearly died when he missed the penalty; **un día le va a dar ~** something will happen to him one day; **cuando le da por ~ ...** when he gets something into his head ...; **por ~ será** there must be a reason for it; **ya es ~: ha logrado un estilo propio, lo que ya es ~** she has achieved her own style, which is quite something

2 (en oraciones interrogativas, condicionales) (gen) anything; (esperando respuesta afirmativa) something; **¿hay ~ para mí?** is there anything o something for me?; **¿le has dado ~ más de dinero?** have you given him any more money?; **¿no le habrá pasado ~?** nothing has happened to him, has it? Ⓑ ADV 1 (con adjetivo) rather, a little; **estos zapatos son ~ incómodos** these shoes are rather o a little uncomfortable; **puede parecer ~ ingenuo** he may seem slightly o rather o a little o somewhat (frm) naive

2 (con verbos) a little; **la inflación ha subido ~ más de dos puntos** inflation has gone up by a little over two points Ⓒ SM 1 **un ~: tiene un ~ que atrae** there's something attractive about him o there's something about him that's attractive

2 (Col) mid-afternoon snack

algodón SM 1 (Cos) (= material) cotton; (= planta) cotton plant; ✦ MODISMO **se crió entre algodones** he was always pampered ➤ **algodón en rama** raw cotton 2 (Med) swab ➤ **algodón hidrófilo** cotton wool (Brit), absorbent cotton (EEUU) 3 [de azúcar] candy floss (Brit), cotton candy (EEUU)

algodonal SM cotton plantation

algodonero/a Ⓐ ADJ cotton antes de s Ⓑ SM/F (= cultivador) cotton grower; (= comerciante) cotton dealer Ⓒ SM (= planta) cotton plant

algoritmo SM algorithm

algoterapia SF seaweed wrap treatment

alguacil SM (Jur) bailiff, constable (EEUU); (Taur) (tb **alguacilillo**) mounted official

alguien PRON (gen) somebody, someone; (en frases interrogativas) anybody, anyone; **si viene ~** if somebody comes, if anybody comes; **¿viste a ~?** did you see anybody?; **se cree ~** he thinks he is somebody

alguno/a Ⓐ ADJ (before masc sing **algún**) 1 (antes de s) (en oraciones afirmativas) some; (en oraciones interrogativas, condicionales) any; **llámame si tienes algún problema** call me if you have any problems; **¿conoces algún hotel barato?** do you know a cheap hotel?; **hubo alguna que otra nube** there were one or two clouds, there was the odd cloud; **en alguna parte** somewhere; **alguna vez** (en oraciones afirmativas) at some point; (en oraciones interrogativas, condicionales) ever; **todos lo hemos hecho alguna vez** we've all done it at one time or another o at some point; **alguna vez le he oído hablar de ella** I have heard him mention her sometimes; **¿has estado alguna vez en Nueva York?** have you ever been to New York?

2 (después de s) **no tiene talento ~** he has no talent at all; **sin motivo ~** for no reason at all; **sin interés ~** without the slightest interest; **sin valor ~** completely worthless

3 **algunos** (= varios) several; **salvaron ~s cientos de vidas** they saved several hundred lives Ⓑ PRON 1 (= objeto) one; **estará en ~ de esos cajones** it must be in one of those drawers; **de entre tantas camisas, seguro que alguna te gustará** out of all these shirts, there's bound to be one that you like; **~ que otro** one or two

2 (= persona) someone, somebody; **siempre hay ~ que protesta** there is always one o someone o somebody who complains; **~ de ellos** one of them

3 **algunos** (= cosas) some, some of them; (= personas) some, some of us, you etc; **vinieron ~s, pero no todos** some of them came, but not all; **~s no se han enterado todavía** some (people) haven't found out yet

alhaja SF 1 (= joya) jewel, gem 2 (= persona) treasure, gem; **¡buena ~!** (iró) she's a fine one!

alhajar /1a/ VT (CS) [+ habitación] to furnish, appoint

alhajero SM (CS, Méx), **alhajera** SF (CS, Méx) jewel box

alharaca SF fuss; **hacer ~s** to make a fuss, make a great song and dance (Brit)

alhelí SM wallflower, stock

alhóndiga SF corn exchange

aliado/a Ⓐ ADJ allied Ⓑ SM/F ally; **los Aliados** the Allies

alianza SF 1 (= pacto) alliance ➤ **la Alianza Atlántica** the Atlantic Alliance, NATO 2 (= anillo) wedding ring

aliar /1c/ Ⓐ VT to ally, bring into an alliance Ⓑ **aliarse** VPR to form an alliance; **~se con** to ally o.s. with, side with

alias ADV, SM INV alias

alicaído ADJ downcast, depressed

alicantino ADJ of/from Alicante

alicatado SM tiling

alicatar /1a/ VT to tile

alicate SM 1 = **alicates** 2 (Arg) (= cortaúñas) nail clippers pl

alicates SMPL pliers, pincers

aliciente SM incentive, inducement

alienación SF (= enajenación) alienation; (Psic) alienation, mental derangement

alienar /1a/ VT = **enajenar**

alienígena SMF alien

aliento SM 1 (= hálito) breath; **mal ~** bad breath 2 (= respiración) **sin ~** breathless o out of breath; **me falta al ~** I'm out of breath; **recobrar el ~** to get one's breath back; **paró, tomó ~ y continuó hablando** he stopped to get his breath back, then went on talking 3 (frm) (= ánimo) courage, spirit

aligerar /1a/ Ⓐ VT to lighten Ⓑ VI to hurry, hurry up Ⓒ **aligerarse** VPR [carga] to get lighter; **~se de ropa** to put on lighter clothing

alijo SM contraband, smuggled goods; **un ~ de armas** an arms cache, an arms haul; **un ~ de drogas** a drugs shipment, a consignment of drugs

alimaña SF pest; **~s** vermin

alimentación SF 1 (= acción) feeding; (= comida) food; **hay que cuidar la ~** you need to be sensible about your diet 2 (Téc) feed 3 (Elec) supply

alimentador SM feeder ➤ **alimentador de red** mains power supply

alimentar /1a/ Ⓐ VT 1 (= dar de comer a) to feed; **tengo una familia que ~** I've got a family to feed 2 [+ imaginación, deseo] to fire, fuel; [+ esperanzas, pasiones] to feed, fuel; [+ rencor] to foster 3 [+ hoguera, horno doméstico, fuego] to feed, add fuel to; [+ horno industrial] to stoke Ⓑ VI to be nutritious, be nourishing; **esta comida no alimenta** this food is not nutritious o nourishing; ✦ MODISMO **huele que alimenta** (Esp*) it smells delicious Ⓒ **alimentarse** VPR 1 [animal] to feed 2 [persona] **se alimenta sólo de productos naturales** she eats only natural foods 3 (Mec) **el motor se alimenta de gas-oil** the engine runs on diesel

alimentario ADJ food antes de s; **la industria alimentaria** the food industry

alimenticio ADJ 1 (= nutritivo) nourishing, nutritive 2 (= relativo a comida) food antes de s; **productos ~s** foodstuffs; **valor ~** food value, nutritional value

alimento SM food; **de mucho ~** nourishing; **de poco ~** of little nutritional value ➤ **alimento de primera necesidad** staple food

alimón: **al ~** ADV together, jointly, in collaboration

alineación SF 1 (Téc) alignment 2 (Dep) line-up

alineado ADJ **países no ~s** non-aligned countries

alineamiento SM alignment

alinear /1a/ Ⓐ VT (Téc) to align; [+ alumnos] to line up, put into line; [+ soldados] to form up; (Dep) [+ equipo] to select, pick (con with) Ⓑ **alinearse** VPR (= ponerse en fila) to line up; (Mil) to fall in

aliñar /1a/ VT [+ ensalada] to dress; [+ guiso] to season

aliño SM [de ensalada] dressing; [de guiso] seasoning

alirón Ⓐ EXCL hurray! Ⓑ SM **cantar el ~** to sing a chant celebrating one's team's victory

alisar /1a/ VT 1 [+ vestido] to smooth, smooth down; [+ pelo] to smooth, sleek 2 (Téc) to polish, finish

alisios SMPL **vientos ~** trade winds

alistamiento SM (Mil) enlistment

alistar /1a/ Ⓐ VT (Mil) to enlist Ⓑ **alistarse** VPR 1 (Mil) to enlist, join up 2 (LAm) (= prepararse) to get ready

aliteración SF alliteration

aliviar /1b/ Ⓐ VT 1 [+ dolor, sufrimiento, problema] to ease, relieve 2 [+ carga, peso] to lighten 3 (= consolar) to soothe; **el vino alivia las penas** wine soothes away your troubles; **me alivia saberlo** I'm pleased to hear it Ⓑ **aliviarse** VPR 1 [dolor] to ease 2 [enfermo] to get better; **¡que te alivies!** get well soon! 3 (Méx*) [embarazada] to give birth

alivio SM 1 (= consuelo) relief; **¡qué ~!** what a relief!; **dio un suspiro de ~** he gave a sigh of relief 2 [de un dolor] relief 3 ➤ **alivio de luto** half-mourning

aljama SF (Hist) 1 (= barrio) [de moros] Moorish quarter; [de judíos] Jewish quarter, ghetto 2 (= mezquita) mosque; (= sinagoga) synagogue 3 (= reunión) [de moros] gathering of Moors; [de judíos] gathering of Jews

aljibe SM 1 (= tanque) cistern, tank; (= pozo) well 2 (Perú) (= calabozo) dungeon, underground prison

aljofaina SF washbasin, washbowl

allá ADV 1 (indicando posición, dirección) **~ arriba** up there; **~ abajo** down there; **~ lejos** way off in the distance, away over there; **no tan ~** not so far; **más ~** further away, further over; **más ~ de** beyond; **más ~ de los límites** beyond the limits; **por ~** thereabouts; **¡~ voy!** I'm coming!; ✦ MODISMOS **el más ~** the beyond, the great beyond; **no muy ~*** (= valer poco) no great shakes, not much cop (Brit*); **no está muy ~** (de salud) he isn't very well 2 (indicando desentendimiento) **~ tú** that's up to you, that's your problem; **~ cada uno** that's for the individual to decide 3 (indicando tiempo) **~ por el año 1960** around about 1960

allanamiento SM 1 (LAm) [de policía] raid; **el juez dispuso el ~ del domicilio** the judge granted the police a search warrant for the house 2 ➤ **allanamiento de morada** (Esp) breaking and entering

allanar /1a/ Ⓐ VT 1 [+ superficie] to level, level out, make even 2 [+ problema] to iron out 3 (Jur) [+ casa] (Esp) (= robar) to break into; (LAm) [policía] to raid Ⓑ **allanarse** VPR to level out, level off

allegado/a Ⓐ ADJ 1 (= afín) near, close; **según fuentes allegadas al ministro** according to sources close to the minister 2 [pariente] close Ⓑ SM/F relation, relative

allende (liter) PREP beyond; **~ los mares** beyond the seas; **~ los Pirineos** on the other side of the Pyrenees

allí ADV there; **~ arriba** up there; **~ dentro** in there; **~ cerca** near there; **de ~** from there; **por ~** over there, around there; **hasta ~** as far as that, up to that point; **~ donde va** wherever he goes

alma SF 1 (= espíritu) soul; **no había ni un ~ en la iglesia** there wasn't a soul in the church; **es mi amigo del ~** he's my soulmate; **tenía ~ de poeta** she had a poetic spirit ➤ **alma bendita** kind soul ➤ **alma en pena** lost soul ➤ **almas gemelas** soul mates, kindred spirits (más frm) 2 ✦ MODISMOS **se le cayó el ~ a los pies** his heart sank; **huir o ir como ~ que lleva el diablo** to flee o go like a bat out of hell; **en el ~**: **te lo agradezco en el ~** I'm eternally o deeply grateful; **se me clavó en el ~ = me llegó al alma**; **me dolió en el ~** it broke my heart; **lo siento en el ~** I am truly sorry; **entregar el ~ (a Dios)** (euf) to depart this life; **estar con o tener el ~ en un hilo** to have one's heart in one's mouth o (EEUU) throat; **me llegó al ~** (= me dolió) I was deeply hurt; (= me conmovió) I found it deeply moving o touching; **de mi ~**: **¡madre mía de mi ~!** ◇ **¡Dios mío de mi ~!** good God!, good grief!; **¡hijo de mi ~!** (con cariño) my darling boy!, my precious child!; (con ironía) my dear child!; **no puedo con mi ~** (Esp*) I'm completely bushed o (Brit) shattered*, I'm

ready to drop*; **romperse el ~** (*LAm*) to break one's neck; **me salió del ~** I just said it without thinking, it just came out; **con toda el ~: lo deseo con toda el ~** I want it desperately; **la quiero con toda mi ~** I love her with all my heart; **lo odio con toda mi ~** I detest him, I hate his guts*
3 (= *parte vital*) [*de grupo, organización*] driving force; [*de asunto*] heart, crux; **el ~ de la fiesta** the life and soul of the party

almacén SM **1** [*de mercancías*] warehouse, store **2** (= *tienda*) shop (*esp Brit*), store (*EEUU*); **grandes almacenes** department store *sing*; **Almacenes Pérez** Pérez Department Store **3** (*CS*) [*de comestibles*] grocer's (shop) (*esp Brit*), grocery (*EEUU*); (*CAm, Col*) [*de ropa*] clothes shop

almacenamiento SM (*en almacén, depósito*) warehousing; (*Inform*) storage

almacenar /1a/ VT to store

almacenero/a SM/F (*CS*) grocer

alma máter SF **1** (= *impulsor*) driving force **2** (*Univ*) alma mater

almanaque SM almanac

almeja SF clam

almenas SFPL battlements

almendra SF **1** (*Bot*) almond ➤ **almendra garrapiñada** sugared almond **2** (= *semilla*) kernel, stone

almendrado ADJ [*forma*] almond-shaped; **de ojos ~s** almond-eyed

almendro SM almond tree

almendruco SM green almond

almeriense ADJ of/from Almería

almiar SM hayrick

almíbar SM syrup; **peras en ~** pears in syrup

almibarado ADJ **1** (= *con almíbar*) syrupy; (= *dulce*) honeyed, oversweet **2** (= *meloso*) sugary

almidón SM starch

almidonado ADJ **1** [*ropa*] starched **2** [*persona*] (= *estirado*) stiff, starchy; (= *pulcro*) dapper, spruce

almidonar /1a/ VT to starch

alminar SM minaret

almirantazgo SM admiralty

almirante SMF admiral

almirez SM mortar

almizcle SM musk

almizclero SM musk deer

almohada SF pillow; ✦ MODISMO **consultar algo con la ~** to sleep on sth

almohade ADJ, SMF Almohad

almohadilla SF **1** (*en asiento*) cushion **2** (*para alfileres*) pincushion; (*para sellos*) inkpad

almohadón SM (= *almohada*) large pillow; (*Rel*) hassock

almoneda SF (= *subasta*) auction; (= *liquidación*) clearance sale

almorávide ADJ, SMF Almoravid

almorranas SFPL piles

almorzar /1f, 1l/ ➊ VT (*a mediodía*) to have for lunch, lunch on (*frm*); (*a media mañana*) to have for breakfast, have for brunch ➋ VI (*a mediodía*) to have lunch, lunch (*frm*); (*a media mañana*) to have breakfast

almuecín SM, **almuédano** SM muezzin

almuerzo SM (*a mediodía*) lunch; (*a media mañana*) breakfast, brunch

aló EXCL (*esp SAm Telec*) hello!

alocado ADJ (= *loco*) crazy, mad; (= *irresponsable*) wild; (= *distraído*) scatterbrained

alocución SF speech, address, allocution (*frm*)

áloe SM, **aloe** SM (*Bot*) aloe; (*Farm*) aloes

alojado/a SM/F (*Chi*) guest, lodger, roomer (*EEUU*)

alojamiento SM accommodation; **dar ~** to put up, accommodate

alojar /1a/ ➊ VT to put up, accommodate ➋ **alojarse** VPR to stay; **la bala se alojó en el pulmón** the bullet lodged in the lung

alón SM wing

alondra SF lark, skylark

alopecia SF alopecia

alpaca SF alpaca

alpargata SF rope-soled sandal, espadrille

Alpes SMPL Alps

alpestre ADJ Alpine

alpinismo SM mountaineering, climbing

alpinista SMF mountaineer, climber

alpino ADJ Alpine

alpiste SM **1** (= *semillas*) birdseed, canary seed **2** (*RPl**) (= *alcohol*) drink, booze*

Al Qaeda SM o SF Al Qaeda

alquería SF farmhouse, farmstead

alquilar /1a/ VT **1** [*propietario*] [+ *inmueble*] to let, rent (out); [+ *coche, autocar*] to rent (out), hire (out) (*esp Brit*); [+ *TV*] to rent (out); **"se alquila"** "to let" (*esp Brit*), "for rent" (*EEUU*) **2** [*usuario*] [+ *inmueble*] to rent; [+ *coche, autocar*] to rent, hire (*esp Brit*); [+ *TV*] to rent

alquiler SM **1** (= *acción*) [*de inmueble*] letting, renting; [*de coche, autocar*] rental, hire (*esp Brit*), hiring (*esp Brit*); **coche de ~** hire car (*Brit*), rental car (*esp EEUU*); **contrato de ~** tenancy agreement; **madre de ~** surrogate mother; **pagar el ~** to pay the rent; **vivir de ~** to live in rented accommodation **2** (= *precio*) [*de inmueble*] rent, rental; [*de coche, autocar*] hire charge (*Brit*), rental fee (*EEUU*)

alquimia SF alchemy

alquimista SM alchemist

alquitara SF still

alquitrán SM tar

alquitranar /1a/ VT (*gen*) to tar; [+ *carretera*] to tarmac

alrededor ➊ ADV around; **todo ~** all around; **~ de** (= *en torno a*) around; (= *aproximadamente*) about, in the region of ➋ SM **1** (= *contorno*) **mirar a su ~** to look around o about one **2 alrededores** (*gen*) surroundings, neighbourhood *sing*, neighborhood *sing* (*EEUU*); [*de ciudad*] outskirts; **en los ~es de Londres** in the area round London, on the outskirts of London

alsaciano/a ADJ, SM/F Alsatian

alta SF **1** (*Med*) (*tb* **~ médica**) certificate of discharge; **dar a algn el ~ (médica)** ◇ **dar de ~ a algn** to discharge sb **2** (*en club, organismo*) membership; **solicité el ~ de la línea telefónica** I applied for a phone line; **darse de ~** to join; **nos dimos de ~ en la Seguridad Social** we registered with Social Security

altamente ADV highly

altanería SF haughtiness, arrogance

altanero ADJ haughty, arrogant

altar SM altar; ✦ MODISMO **subir a los ~es** to be beatified, be canonized ➤ **altar mayor** high altar

altavoz SM loudspeaker

alteración SF **1** (= *cambio*) alteration, change **2** (= *aturdimiento*) upset, disturbance ➤ **alteración del orden público** breach of the peace

alterado ADJ upset

alterar /1a/ ➊ VT **1** (= *cambiar*) to modify, alter **2** (= *estropear*) [+ *alimentos*] to spoil; [+ *leche*] to sour **3** (= *conmocionar*) to shake, upset **4 ~ el orden** to disturb the peace ➋ **alterarse** VPR **1** (= *estropearse*) [*alimentos*] to spoil, go bad; [*leche*] to go sour **2** [*voz*] to falter **3** (= *turbarse*) to be shaken, be upset; **¡tranquila, no te alteres!** keep calm!, don't get upset!; **continuó hablando sin ~se** he continued speaking unperturbed

altercado SM argument, altercation

alternador SM alternator

alternancia SF alternation ➤ **alternancia de cultivos** crop rotation ➤ **alternancia en el poder** power switching, taking turns in office

alternar /1a/ **Ⓐ** VT (gen) to alternate; [+ cultivos] to rotate **Ⓑ** VI **1** (= turnar) to alternate (**con** with); (Téc) to alternate, reciprocate **2** (= relacionarse) to mix, socialize; ~ **con la gente bien** to hobnob with top people **Ⓒ** **alternarse** VPR to take turns, change about; **~se en el poder** to take turns in office; **se ~án las nubes con los claros** there will be patchy cloud o cloudy patches

alternativa SF **1** (= opción) alternative, option, choice; **no tener** ~ to have no alternative o option o choice **2** (Taur) **tomar la** ~ to become a fully qualified bullfighter

alternativo ADJ (Elec) alternating; [cultura, prensa] alternative; **fuentes alternativas de energía** alternative energy sources

alterne SM (Esp) (con gente) mixing, socializing; (euf) (= relaciones sexuales) sexual contact, sexual contacts pl; **club de** ~ singles club

alterno ADJ (Bot, Mat) alternate; (Elec) alternating

Alteza SF Highness; **Su ~ Real** His/Her Royal Highness; **sí, ~** yes, your Highness

altibajos SMPL ups and downs

altillo SM (= desván) attic; (= entreplanta) mezzanine

altiplanicie SF high plateau

altiplano SM (= meseta) high plateau; [de los Andes] high Andean plateau, altiplano

altiro* ADV (Chi) right away

altísimo SM **el Altísimo** the Almighty

altisonante ADJ high-flown, high-sounding

altitud SF height, altitude

altivo ADJ haughty, arrogant

alto¹ **Ⓐ** ADJ **1** (en altura) **1.1** [edificio, persona] tall; [monte] high; **está muy ~ para su edad** he is very tall for his age; **los pisos ~s tienen más luz natural** upper flats (Brit) o apartments (EEUU) have more natural light; **jersey de cuello ~** polo neck jumper (esp Brit), turtleneck (EEUU); **camino de alta montaña** high mountain path **1.2** **lo ~:** **en lo ~ de la cuesta** on top of the hill; **desde lo ~ del árbol** from the top of the tree; ✦ MODISMO **lo celebraron por todo lo ~** they celebrated it in style

2 (en nivel) [grado, precio, riesgo] high; [clase, cámara] upper; **una familia de clase alta** an upper class family; **la cámara alta del Parlamento ruso** the upper house of the Russian parliament; **alta burguesía** upper-middle class; ~ **cargo** (puesto) high-ranking position; (persona) senior official, high-ranking official; **alta cocina** haute cuisine; **Alto Comisionado** High Commission; **alta costura** high fashion, haute couture; **altas esferas** upper echelons; **alta fidelidad** high fidelity, hi-fi; **altas finanzas** high finance; ~ **funcionario** senior official, high-ranking official; **oficiales de alta graduación** senior officers, high-ranking officers; **~s hornos** blast furnace; **~s mandos** senior officers, high-ranking officers; **de altas miras: es un chico de altas miras** he is a boy of great ambition; **alta sociedad** high society; **alta tecnología** high technology; **alta tensión** high tension, high voltage; **en voz alta** [leer] out loud; [hablar] in a loud voice

4 (en el tiempo) **hasta altas horas de la madrugada** until the early hours

5 [estilo] lofty, elevated

6 (= revuelto) **estar** ~ [río] to be high; [mar] to be rough

7 (Geog) upper; **el Alto Rin** the Upper Rhine

8 (Mús) [nota] sharp; [instrumento, voz] alto

9 (Hist, Ling) high; **la alta Edad Media** the high Middle Ages **Ⓑ** ADV **1** (= arriba) high; **sube un poco más** ~ go up a little higher; **ha llegado muy ~ en su carrera profesional** he's reached the top in his professional career

2 (= en voz alta) **hablar** ~ (subiendo la voz) to speak loudly; (con franqueza) to speak out, speak out frankly; **¡más ~, por favor!** louder, please!; **pensar (en)** ~ to think out loud, think aloud

Ⓒ SM **1** (= altura) **tiene 5 metros de** ~ it is 5 metres high; **mide 1,80 de** ~ he is 1.80 metres o (EEUU) meters tall; **en** ~: **coloque los pies en** ~ put your feet up; **con las manos en** ~ (en atraco, rendición) with one's hands up; (en manifestación) with one's hands in the air; ✦ MODISMO **dejar algo en** ~: **el resultado deja muy en** ~ **su reputación como el mejor del mundo** the result has boosted his reputation as the best in the world

2 (Geog) hill; **el pueblo está en un** ~ the town lies on a hill

3 (Mús) alto

4 ► **altos y bajos** ups and downs

5 **pasar por** ~ [+ detalle, problema] to overlook

6 (Chi) [de ropa, cartas] pile

7 (Chi) [de tela] length

8 los ~s (esp CS, Méx) [de casa] upstairs; (Geog) the heights; **los ~s de Jalisco** the Jalisco heights ► **Altos del Golán** Golan Heights

alto² **Ⓐ** SM **1** (= parada) stop; **dar el ~ a algn** to order sb to halt, stop sb; **hacer un** ~ (en viaje) to stop off; (en actividad) to take a break; **poner el ~ a algo** (Méx) to put an end to sth ► **alto el fuego** (Esp) ceasefire **2** (Aut) (= señal) stop sign; (= semáforo) lights pl **Ⓑ** EXCL **¡alto!** halt!, stop!; **¡~ ahí!** stop there!

altomedieval ADJ early medieval, of the High Middle Ages

altoparlante SM (LAm) loudspeaker

altozano SM **1** (= otero) small hill, hillock **2** (And, Carib) (= atrio) cathedral forecourt, church forecourt

altramuz SM lupin

altruismo SM altruism

altruista **Ⓐ** ADJ altruistic **Ⓑ** SMF altruist

altura SF **1** [de edificio, techo, persona] height; **hubo olas de hasta tres metros de** ~ there were waves up to three metres o (EEUU) meters high, there were waves of up to three metres o (EEUU) meters in height; **a la ~ de algo:** **la ventana quedaba a la ~ de mi cabeza** the window was level with my head; **sentí un dolor a la ~ de los riñones** I felt a pain around my kidneys

2 (en el aire) height, altitude; **una ~ de 10.000 pies** a height o an altitude of 10,000 feet; **nos encontramos a 3.000 metros de** ~ **sobre el nivel del mar** we are 3,000 metres o (EEUU) meters above sea level; **volaba a muy poca ~ del suelo** it was flying just above the ground ► **altura de crucero** cruising height

3 (= nivel) **estar a la ~ de** [+ persona] to be in the same league as, be on a par with; [+ tarea] to be up to, be equal to; **su último artículo no estaba a la ~ de los anteriores** his last article did not match up to the previous ones; **la novela no estaba a la ~ del concurso** the novel was not up to the standard set by the competition, the novel did not measure up to the competition standards; **supo estar a la ~ de las circunstancias** he managed to rise to the occasion; ✦ MODISMO **dejar o poner a algn a la ~ del betún** o (RPl) **de un felpudo** o (Chi) **del unto*** (estando presente) to make sb feel small; (estando ausente) to lay into sb; **quedar a la ~ del betún** (Esp) if we don't invite them, it'll look really bad

4 (en dirección) (Geog) **a la ~ de** (= latitud) on the same latitude as; **hay retenciones a la ~ de Burgos** it's bumper to bumper near Burgos, there are tailbacks near Burgos (Brit); **¿a qué ~ de la calle quiere que pare?** how far along the street do you want me to stop?

5 (Náut) **pesca de** ~ deep-sea fishing

6 (Dep) (= salto) high jump; (= distancia del suelo) height

7 (Mús) pitch

8 [de ideas, sentimientos] sublimity, loftiness

9 alturas 9.1 (= lugar elevado) (Geog) heights; (Rel) heaven sing; **¡gloria a Dios en las ~s!** glory to God in Heaven! **9.2** [de organización] upper echelons **9.3** **a estas ~s** [de edad] at my/your/his/etc age; [de tiempo] at this stage; **a estas ~s no me preocupan las arrugas** at my age, wrinkles don't worry me; **a estas ~s del año las playas están casi vacías** at this stage of the year the beaches are almost empty; **a estas ~s nadie te va a preguntar nada** at this stage no one is going to ask you anything; **¿todavía no confías en mí a estas ~s?** you still don't trust me after all this time?

alubia SF bean
➤ **alubia pinta** pinto bean ➤ **alubia roja** kidney bean
alucinación SF hallucination
alucinado** ADJ amazed, gobsmacked (*Brit***)
alucinante ADJ **1** (*Med*) hallucinatory **2** (*Esp***) great, fantastic* **3** (*Esp***) (= *inconcebible*) absurd; **es ~** it's mind-blowing*
alucinar /1a/ VI **1** (= *padecer alucinaciones*) to hallucinate **2** (*Esp***) (= *delirar*) **¡tú alucinas!** you're seeing things!; **¡este tío alucina!** this guy must be kidding!*; **yo alucino con esa canción** I love this song; **yo alucinaba al ver tanta cosa** I was amazed *o* (*Brit***) gobsmacked at everything I saw
alucine** SM (*Esp*) **de ~** fantastic*, great*; **¡qué ~!** this is great!*
alucinógeno Ⓐ ADJ hallucinogenic Ⓑ SM (*Med*) hallucinogen
alud SM **1** [*de nieve*] avalanche **2** (= *afluencia*) wave
aludido ADJ **no darse por ~** to pretend not to hear; **no te des por ~** don't take it personally
aludir /3a/ VI **~ a** to allude to, mention
alumbrado SM lighting ➤ **alumbrado público** street lighting
alumbramiento SM birth
alumbrar /1a/ Ⓐ VT **1** (= *iluminar*) [+ *cuarto, calle, ciudad*] to light; [+ *estadio, edificio, monumento*] to light up **2** (= *enfocar*) (*con linterna, foco*) **alumbra aquí** shine the light here Ⓑ VI **1** (= *dar luz*) to give light, shed light; **esta bombilla alumbra bien** this bulb gives a good light **2** (*frm*) (= *dar a luz*) to give birth
aluminio SM aluminium, aluminum (*EEUU*); **papel de ~** aluminium foil, aluminum foil (*EEUU*), silver foil (*Brit*)
aluminosis SF INV (*Constr*) *degeneration of cement used in construction*
alumnado SM (*Univ*) student body; (*Escol*) roll, pupils
alumno/a SM/F (*Escol*) pupil; (*Univ*) student; **antiguo ~** (*Escol*) former pupil, old boy (*Brit*), alumnus (*EEUU*); (*Univ*) old student, former student, alumnus (*EEUU*)
alunizaje SM landing on the moon, moon landing
alunizar /1f/ VI to land on the moon
alusión SF (= *mención*) allusion, reference; (= *indirecta*) hint; **hacer ~ a** to allude to, refer to
alusivo ADJ allusive
aluvión SM **1** (*Geol*) alluvium; **tierras de ~** alluvial soil *sing*, alluvial soils **2** (= *alud*) flood; **un ~ de improperios** a stream *o* torrent of abuse
alveolar ADJ alveolar
alvéolo SM, **alveolo** SM alveolus
alverjilla SF (*LAm*) sweet pea
alza SF **1** (= *subida*) [*de precio, temperatura*] rise; **la bolsa ha experimentado una fuerte ~** the stock market has risen sharply; **al ~** [*tendencia*] upward; [*inflación, precio*] rising; **revisar los precios al ~** to put prices up; **en ~** [*acciones, precio*] on the rise; **un joven escritor en ~** an up-and-coming writer; **jugar al ~** (*Fin*) to speculate on a rising market **2** (*en zapato*) raised insole
alzacristales SM INV (*Esp*) ➤ **alzacristales eléctrico** electric windows *pl*
alzacuello SM, **alzacuellos** SM INV clerical collar, dog collar
alzado/a Ⓐ ADJ **1** (= *levantado*) raised **2** (*Fin*) [*cantidad, precio*] fixed **3** (*Méx, Ven*) (= *engreído*) big-headed **4** (*And, Ven*) (= *sublevado*) arrogant, cocky* **5** (*LAm*) [*animal*] (= *arisco*) wild; **estar ~** (*CS*) to be in *o* (*Brit*) on heat Ⓑ SM/F rebel ➤ **alzado/a en armas** armed insurgent Ⓒ SM (*Arquit*) elevation
alzamiento SM **1** (= *acción*) raising, lifting; **el juez ordenó el ~ del cadáver** the judge ordered the removal of the corpse **2** (= *sublevación*) revolt, uprising **3** (*Com*) (*de precio*) rise, increase; (*en subasta*) higher bid
alzar /1f/ Ⓐ VT **1** (= *levantar*) **1.1** [+ *objeto, persona*] to lift; [+ *objeto muy pesado*] to hoist **1.2** [+ *brazo, cabeza, copa*] to

raise; **~ la mirada** *o* **los ojos** *o* **la vista** to look up; **~ la voz** to raise one's voice
2 (= *erigir*) [+ *monumento*] to raise; [+ *edificio*] to erect
3 (*Rel*) [+ *cáliz, hostia*] to elevate
4 (= *recoger*) (*Méx*) (*del suelo*) to pick up; (*LAm*) (*a un bebé*) to pick up
5 (*Méx*) (= *ordenar*) [+ *casa, recámara*] to tidy up; **~ la mesa** to clear the table; **~ los trastes** to clear away the dishes
6 (*Méx*) [+ *dinero*] to save
Ⓑ **alzarse** VPR **1** (= *ponerse en pie*) to rise
2 [*edificio, monte, monumento*] (= *tener una altura determinada*) to rise; (= *estar situado*) to stand; **la cordillera se alza 2.500m sobre el nivel del mar** the mountain range rises 2,500m above sea level; **el rascacielos se alza por encima del parque** the skyscraper rises *o* towers over the park
3 (= *aumentar*) [*precio, temperatura*] to rise
4 (= *rebelarse*) to rise up, rise, revolt (**contra** against); **~se en armas** to take up arms, rise up in arms
5 (= *llevarse*) **~se con** [+ *premio, votos*] to win; [+ *dinero*] to run off with; **~se con el poder** to take power; **~se con la victoria** to win
6 (*Méx, Ven*) (= *volverse engreído*) to get big-headed
7 (*And, Ven*) (= *rebelarse*) to get awkward, get bolshie (*Brit**); **le llamé la atención y se me alzó** I told her off and she answered me back
8 **~se de hombros** (*Méx*) to shrug one's shoulders
9 (*CS*) [*animal*] to come on heat
ama SF ➤ **ama de cría** wet nurse ➤ **ama de leche** wet nurse ➤ **ama de llaves** housekeeper; *ver tb* **amo**
amabilidad SF (= *generosidad*) kindness; (= *cortesía*) courtesy; **tuvo la ~ de acompañarme** he was kind enough to come with me, he was good enough to come with me; **tenga la ~ de** (+ INFIN) please be so kind as to + *infin*
amable ADJ kind, nice; **si es tan ~** if you would be so kind; **ser ~ con algn** to be kind to sb, be nice to sb; **¡muy ~!** thanks very much, that's very kind, that's very kind of you
amablemente ADV kindly; **muy ~ me ayudó** he very kindly helped me
amado/a Ⓐ ADJ dear, beloved Ⓑ SM/F lover, sweetheart
amadrinar /1a/ VT [+ *niño*] to be godmother to; [+ *soldado, regimiento*] to be patron to
amaestrar /1a/ VT [+ *persona*] to train, teach; [+ *animal*] to train; [+ *caballo*] to break in
amagar /1h/ Ⓐ VT to show signs of Ⓑ VI to threaten, be impending
amago SM **1** (= *amenaza*) threat; (= *inicio*) beginning; (= *indicio*) hint; **con un ~ de sonrisa** with the suggestion of a smile, with a faint smile **2** (*Esgrima*) feint
amainar /1a/ VI [*viento, tormenta*] to abate, die down; [*ira*] to subside
amalgama SF amalgam
amalgamar /1a/ Ⓐ VT (*Quím*) to amalgamate; (= *combinar*) to combine, blend Ⓑ **amalgamarse** VPR to amalgamate
amamantar /1a/ VT to suckle, nurse
amancebado†† ADJ **estar** *o* **vivir ~s** to live together, cohabit
amanecer /2d/ Ⓐ VI **1** (= *hacerse de día*): **amanece a las siete** it gets light at seven **2** [*persona, ciudad*] to wake up (in the morning); **amanecimos en Vigo** the next morning found us in Vigo, the next morning we woke up in Vigo; **el pueblo amaneció cubierto de nieve** morning saw the village covered in snow, when the next day dawned the village was covered in snow Ⓑ SM dawn, daybreak; **al ~** at dawn, at daybreak
amanerado ADJ mannered, affected
amansadora* SF (*RPl*) (= *espera*) long wait
amansar /1a/ VT [+ *caballo*] to break in; [+ *fiera*] to tame; [+ *persona*] to tame, subdue
amante Ⓐ ADJ loving, fond; **nación ~ de la paz** peace-loving nation Ⓑ SMF **1** (= *enamorado*) (= *hombre, mujer*) lover; (= *mujer*) (*pey*) mistress **2** (= *aficionado*) lover; **los ~s**

del cine cinema lovers

amanuense SMF scribe, amanuensis

amañado ADJ **1** (= *falso*) fake, faked **2** (= *diestro*) skilful, skillful (*EEUU*), clever **3** [*resultado, pelea*] fixed, rigged

amañador ADJ (*And, Carib*) pleasant

amañar /1a/ **Ⓐ** VT [+ *resultado*] to alter, tamper with; [+ *elección*] to rig; [+ *cuentas*] to cook* **Ⓑ amañarse** VPR (*Col, Ven*) to become accustomed to; **ya se amaña en Quito** he's beginning to feel at home in Quito

amapola SF poppy

amar /1a/ VT to love

amaraje SM [*de hidroavión*] landing (*on the sea*); [*de nave espacial*] splashdown, touchdown

amaranto SM amaranth

amarar /1a/ VI [*hidroavión*] to land (*on the sea*); [*nave espacial*] to splash down, touch down

amargado ADJ bitter, embittered; **estar ~** to be bitter

amargamente ADV bitterly

amargar /1h/ **Ⓐ** VT [+ *persona*] to embitter; [+ *ocasión*] to spoil; **~ la vida a algn** to make sb's life a misery; ✦ MODISMO **a nadie le amarga un dulce** something's better than nothing **Ⓑ** VI to be bitter, taste bitter **Ⓒ amargarse** VPR [*persona*] to become bitter *o* embittered

amargo **Ⓐ** ADJ [*sabor*] bitter, tart **Ⓑ** SM [*de sabor*] bitterness, tartness

amargura SF (= *aflicción*) bitterness; (= *pena*) grief, sorrow

amariconado** ADJ effeminate

amarillento ADJ yellowish; [*tez*] pale, sallow

amarillismo SM sensationalist journalism

amarillista ADJ [*prensa*] sensationalist

amarillo **Ⓐ** ADJ [*color*] yellow; [*semáforo*] amber, yellow (*EEUU*) **Ⓑ** SM (= *color*) yellow ➤ **amarillo canario** canary yellow ➤ **amarillo limón** lemon yellow

amariposado* ADJ effeminate

amarra SF **1** (*Náut*) mooring line **2 amarras** (*Náut*) moorings; **cortar** *o* **romper las ~s** to break loose, cut adrift; **echar las ~s** to moor

amarradero SM (= *poste*) post, bollard; (*para barco*) berth, mooring

amarrado* ADJ (*Col, Méx*) mean, stingy

amarrar /1a/ **Ⓐ** VT **1** (*esp LAm*) (= *atar*) to fasten, tie up **2** [+ *barco*] to moor, tie up **Ⓑ amarrarse** VPR **amarrársela** (*And, CAm*) to get tight*

amarrete/a* (*CS*) **Ⓐ** ADJ mean, stingy* **Ⓑ** SM/F miser, skinflint, tightwad (*EEUU**)

amartelado ADJ lovey-dovey*

amartizaje SM landing on Mars, Mars landing

amasar /1a/ VT **1** (*Culin*) [+ *masa*] to knead; [+ *harina, yeso*] to mix, prepare **2** [+ *dinero*] to amass

amasijar** /1a/ VT (*RPl*) to canoodle*, smooch*

amasijo SM hotchpotch (*Brit*), hodgepodge (*EEUU*), medley

amateur ADJ, SMF amateur

amatista SF amethyst

amatorio ADJ love *antes de s*

amazacotado ADJ [*arroz*] stodgy; [*masa*] heavy

amazona SF (*Literat*) amazon; (*Dep*) horsewoman, rider

Amazonas SM Amazon

Amazonia SF Amazonia

amazónico ADJ Amazon *antes de s*, Amazonian

ambages SMPL **hablar sin ~** to come straight *o* (*EEUU*) right to the point

ámbar SM amber

ambarino ADJ amber, yellow (*EEUU*)

ambición SF ambition

ambicionar /1a/ VT (= *desear*) to aspire to, seek; (= *codiciar*) to lust after, covet; **~ ser algo** to have an ambition to be sth

ambicioso/a **Ⓐ** ADJ ambitious **Ⓑ** SM/F ambitious person

ambidextro ADJ, **ambidiestro** ADJ ambidextrous

ambientación SF (= *estilo*) atmosphere ➤ **ambientación musical** incidental music

ambientador SM air freshener

ambiental ADJ **1** (= *del aire*) **humedad ~** humidity; **la luz ~ era insuficiente** the lighting was not strong enough **2** (= *medioambiental*) environmental

ambientar /1a/ **Ⓐ** VT **1** (= *dar ambiente a*) **los fans ambientaban el partido** the fans gave the match some atmosphere; **~on la entrada del hotel con decorados exóticos** they livened up the hotel foyer with exotic decoration **2** [+ *película, obra*] to set **Ⓑ ambientarse** VPR (= *adaptarse*) to settle in, adjust; **pondré un poco de música para que nos vayamos ambientando** I'll put some music on to get some atmosphere going

ambiente **Ⓐ** ADJ INV **medio ~** environment; **ruido ~** environmental noise; **trabajamos con 120 decibelios de ruido ~** we work at a noise level of 120 decibels; **temperatura ~** room temperature **Ⓑ** SM **1** (= *aire, entorno*) atmosphere; **un ~ festivo** a festive atmosphere; **no había un buen ~ en la oficina** there wasn't a good atmosphere in the office; **cambiar de ~** to have a change of scene; **crónica de ~** background report; **micrófono de ~** field microphone **2** (= *animación*) **el espléndido ~ cultural de París** the wonderful cultural life *o* ambience of Paris **3** (= *entorno*) environment; **con su familia se siente en su ~** with her family, she really feels in her element; **~ familiar** home environment **4 ambientes** (= *grupo social*) circles; **en ~s universitarios** in the university world, in university circles **5** (**) (*tb* **~ homosexual**) **el ~** the gay scene, the scene**; **de ~** [*bar, discoteca*] gay *antes de s* **6** (*CS*) (= *habitación*) room

ambigú SM buffet

ambiguamente ADV ambiguously

ambigüedad SF ambiguity

ambiguo ADJ ambiguous

ámbito SM **1** (= *campo*) field; **dentro del ~ de** within the limits of, in the context of; **es muy conocido en el ~ nacional** he's nationally famous, he's famous nationwide **2** (= *esfera*) scope, range ➤ **ámbito de acción** sphere of activity

ambivalente ADJ ambivalent

ambo SM (*CS*) two-piece suit

ambos ADJ, PRON both; **~ tienen los ojos azules** they both have blue eyes

ambrosía SF ambrosia

ambulancia SF ambulance

ambulanciero/a SM/F ambulance man/woman

ambulante ADJ [*circo, vendedor*] travelling, traveling (*EEUU*); [*biblioteca*] mobile; [*músico*] itinerant

ambulatorio (*Esp*) **Ⓐ** SM (= *clínica*) national health clinic; (= *sección*) out-patients department **Ⓑ** ADJ **tratar a algn en régimen ~** to treat sb as an out-patient

ameba SF amoeba, ameba (*EEUU*)

amedrentar /1a/ **Ⓐ** VT (= *asustar*) to scare, frighten; (= *intimidar*) to intimidate **Ⓑ amedrentarse** VPR to be scared, be intimidated

amén SM INV **1** (*Rel*) amen; ✦ MODISMOS **decir ~ a todo** to agree to everything; **en un decir ~** in a trice **2 ~ de** (= *salvo*) except for, aside from (*EEUU*); (= *además de*) in addition to

amenaza SF threat ➤ **amenaza de bomba** bomb scare

amenazador ADJ, **amenazante** ADJ threatening, menacing

amenazar /1f/ **Ⓐ** VT to threaten; **~ a algn de muerte** to threaten to kill sb; **la tarde amenazaba lluvia** it looked like rain in the evening **Ⓑ** VI to threaten, impend; **~ con hacer algo** to threaten to do sth

amenizar /1f/ VT (= *hacer agradable*) to make pleasant; [+ *conversación*] to enliven, liven up; [+ *reunión*] to provide entertainment for, entertain

ameno ADJ (= *agradable*) pleasant, agreeable, nice; [*estilo*] engaging; [*libro*] enjoyable, readable; [*lectura*] light

América SF (= *todo el continente*) the American continent, America; (= *Estados Unidos*) America; (= *Latinoamérica*) Latin America ➤ **América Central** Central America ➤ **América del Norte** North America ➤ **América del Sur** South America ➤ **América Latina** Latin America

americana SF (*Esp*) (sports) jacket; *ver tb* **americano**

americanismo SM (*Ling*) Americanism

americanizar /1f/ Ⓐ VT to americanize Ⓑ **americanizarse** VPR to become americanized

americano/a ADJ, SM/F (= *de todo el continente, de Estados Unidos*) American; (= *de Latinoamérica*) Latin American; *ver tb* **americana**

amerindio/a ADJ, SM/F American Indian, Amerindian

ameritado ADJ (*LAm*) worthy

ameritar /1a/ VT (*LAm*) to deserve

amerizaje SM [*de hidroavión*] landing (*on the sea*); [*de nave espacial*] splashdown, touchdown

amerizar /1f/ VI [*hidroavión*] to land (*on the sea*); [*nave espacial*] to splash down, touch down

ametralladora SF machine gun

ametrallar /1a/ VT to machine-gun

amianto SM asbestos

amigable ADJ friendly, sociable

amígdala SF tonsil

amigdalitis SF INV tonsillitis

amigo/a Ⓐ SM/F **1** friend; **Manuel es un ~ mío** Manuel is a friend of mine; **es una amiga de Sofía** she is a friend of Sofía's *o* of Sofía; **el perro es el mejor ~ del hombre** a dog is a man's best friend; **hacer ~s** to make friends ➤ **amigo/a de confianza** very close friend, intimate friend ➤ **amigo/a del alma** soulmate ➤ **amigo/a de lo ajeno** (*hum*) thief ➤ **amigo/a íntimo/a** very close friend, intimate friend **2** (= *novio*) boyfriend/girlfriend Ⓑ ADJ **1 son muy ~s** they are good *o* close friends; **Gonzalo es muy ~ de Pepe** Gonzalo is a good *o* close friend of Pepe's *o* of Pepe; **hacer ~s** to make (new) friends; **hacerse ~s** to become friends; **me hice muy ~ de Antonio** Antonio and I became good friends; **se perdonaron y quedaron tan ~s** they made (it) up and everything was fine **2 ser ~ de algo** to be fond of sth; **no soy muy ~ de las multitudes** I'm not very fond of *o* (*Brit*) keen on crowds; **soy ~ de hablar con franqueza** I like straight talking **3** [*país, fuego*] friendly

amigote SM mate (*Brit**), buddy (*EEUU**); (*pey*) sidekick*, crony

amiguismo SM old-boy network

amilanar /1a/ Ⓐ VT to scare, intimidate Ⓑ **amilanarse** VPR to get scared, be intimidated (**ante, por** at)

aminoácido SM amino acid

aminorar /1a/ VT to reduce

amistad SF **1** (= *cariño*) friendship; (= *relación amistosa*) friendly relationship, friendly connection; **hacer** *o* **trabar ~ con** to strike up a friendship with, become friends with **2 amistades** (= *amigos*) friends; (= *conocidos*) acquaintances

amistarse /1a/ VPR (*Col*) (= *reconciliarse*) to make it up

amistoso ADJ (= *amigable*) friendly, amicable; (*Dep*) friendly

amnesia SF amnesia

amnésico/a ADJ, SM/F amnesiac, amnesic; **es ~** he suffers from memory loss *o* amnesia

amniocentesis SF INV amniocentesis

amniótico ADJ amniotic; **líquido ~** amniotic fluid

amnistía SF amnesty ➤ **Amnistía Internacional** Amnesty International

amnistiado/a Ⓐ ADJ amnestied Ⓑ SM/F *person granted an amnesty*

amnistiar /1c/ VT to amnesty, grant an amnesty to

amo/a Ⓐ SM/F **1** (= *de casa*) master/mistress ➤ **amo/a de casa** house-husband/housewife **2** (= *propietario*) owner Ⓑ SM (= *jefe*) boss; **ser el ~** to be the boss; **ese corredor es el ~ de la pista** that runner rules the track; *ver tb* **ama**

amoblado (*LAm*) Ⓐ ADJ furnished Ⓑ SM furniture

amoblamiento SM (*LAm*) furnishing

amoblar /1l/ VT (*LAm*) to furnish

amodorramiento SM sleepiness, drowsiness

amodorrarse /1a/ VPR to get sleepy, get drowsy

amolar* /1l/ (*esp Méx*) Ⓐ VT **1** (= *estropear*) to ruin, damage **2** (= *fastidiar*) to pester, annoy Ⓑ **amolarse** VPR **1** (= *estropearse*) to be ruined **2** (= *aguantarse*) **¡que se amuele!** that's tough!*

amoldar /1a/ Ⓐ VT to adapt (**a** to), adjust (**a** to) Ⓑ **amoldarse** VPR to adapt o.s., adjust o.s. (**a** to)

amonestación SF **1** (= *reprimenda*) reprimand; (= *advertencia*) warning; (*Ftbl*) caution, yellow card; (*Jur*) caution **2 amonestaciones** (*Rel*) marriage banns; **correr las amonestaciones** to publish the banns

amonestar /1a/ VT **1** (= *reprender*) to reprimand; (= *advertir*) to warn; (*Dep*) to caution, book; (*Jur*) to caution **2** (*Rel*) to publish the banns of

amoniaco SM ammonia

amontillado SM amontillado, amontillado wine

amontonado ADJ heaped, heaped up, piled up; **viven ~s** they live on top of each other

amontonar /1a/ Ⓐ VT (= *apilar*) to pile (up), heap (up); [+ *dinero*] to hoard Ⓑ **amontonarse** VPR (= *apilarse*) to pile up; [*datos*] to accumulate; [*gente*] to crowd, crowd together

amor SM **1** (= *pasión*) love; **por el ~ de** for the love of; **por (el) ~ de Dios** for God's sake; **hacer algo con ~** to do sth lovingly, do th with love; **hacer el ~** to make love; ✦ MODISMO **por ~ al arte** (*hum*) just for the fun of it ➤ **amor a primera vista** love at first sight ➤ **amor libre** free love ➤ **amor maternal** mother love ➤ **amor platónico** platonic love ➤ **amor propio** self-respect, pride; **es cuestión de ~ propio** it's a matter of pride; **picar a algn en el ~ propio** to wound sb's pride **2** (= *persona*) love, lover; **mi ~ ⬦ ~ mío** my love, my darling; **¡eres un ~!** you're a love!, you are sweet! **3** ✦ MODISMO **estar al ~ de la lumbre** to be close to the fire; **¡de mil ~es!** I'd love to!, gladly!

amoral ADJ amoral

amoratado ADJ (= *morado*) purple, purplish; (*de frío*) blue; (= *golpeado*) black and blue, bruised; **ojo ~** black eye, shiner*

amoratarse /1a/ VPR (= *ponerse morado*) to turn purple, go purple; (*de frío*) to turn blue; (*por golpes*) to turn black and blue

amordazar /1f/ VT [+ *persona*] to gag; [+ *perro*] to muzzle; (*fig*) (= *hacer callar*) to gag, silence

amorfo ADJ amorphous, shapeless

amorío SM (*tb* ~s) love affair, romance

amoroso ADJ **1** (= *cariñoso*) [*persona*] loving, affectionate; [*mirada*] amorous; **en tono ~** in an affectionate tone **2** [*poesía*] love *antes de s* **3** (*LAm*) (= *encantador*) lovely, sweet

amortajar /1a/ VT to shroud

amortiguación SF [*de ruido*] deadening, muffling; [*de choque, golpe*] cushioning, absorption; [*de color*] toning down; [*de luz*] dimming, softening

amortiguador SM shock absorber

amortiguar /1i/ VT **1** [+ *ruido*] to deaden, muffle; [+ *choque*] to cushion, absorb; [+ *color*] to tone down; [+ *luz*] to dim, soften **2** (= *mitigar*) to alleviate

amortizable ADJ redeemable

amortización SF [*de bono*] redemption; [*de préstamo*] repayment

amortizar /1f/ VT **1** (= *pagar*) [+ *bono*] to redeem;

[+ *préstamo*] to pay off, repay **2** (= *recuperar*) [+ *inversión, gasto*] to recoup

amoscarse* /1g/ VPR to get cross, be peeved*

amotinado/a Ⓐ ADJ (= *rebelde*) riotous; (*Mil, Náut*) mutinous Ⓑ SM/F (*civil*) rioter; (*Pol*) rebel; (*Mil, Náut*) rebel, mutineer

amotinarse /1a/ VPR (= *causar disturbios*) to riot; (*Pol*) to rise up; (*Mil, Náut*) to mutiny

amparar /1a/ Ⓐ VT **1** (= *proteger*) to protect (**de** from), shelter; (= *ayudar*) to help **2** (*Jur*) [+ *criminal*] to harbour, harbor (*EEUU*) Ⓑ **ampararse** VPR **1** (= *buscar protección*) to seek protection, seek help; **~se con** o **de** o **en** to seek the protection of **2** (*de la lluvia*) to shelter

amparo SM **1** (= *protección*) **buscó ~ en la familia** he sought refuge in his family; **al ~ de la ley** under the protection of the law **2** (= *refugio*) shelter, refuge **3** (*Jur*) **recurso de ~** *appeal on the grounds of unconstitutionality*

amperímetro SM ammeter

amperio SM ampère, amp

ampliación SF (= *acción*) extension; (*Fot*) enlargement; (= *expansión*) expansion ➤ **ampliación de capital, ampliación de capitales** increase of capital

ampliadora SF enlarger

ampliamente ADV (= *cumplidamente*) amply; (= *extensamente*) extensively; **satisfará ~ la demanda** it will more than meet the demand

ampliar /1c/ VT **1** (*en tamaño, cantidad*) to extend; **queremos ~ el salón** we want to extend the living room, we want to make the living room bigger; **lee mucho para ~ su vocabulario** he reads a lot in order to extend o expand his vocabulary; **se fue a Inglaterra a ~ sus estudios** he went to England to further his education
2 (*en número*) to increase; **van a ~ las plazas de profesor** they are going to increase the number of teaching posts; **no ~án la plantilla** they are not going to increase the payroll
3 [+ *prórroga, período*] to extend; **han ampliado el plazo de matrícula** they have put back the closing date for registration, they have extended the period for registration
4 (*Fot*) to enlarge
5 (*Com*) [+ *empresa, compañía*] to expand, grow; [+ *capital*] to increase; **deseamos ~ el campo de acción de la empresa** we want to extend o expand o broaden the company's area of business
6 [+ *sonido*] to amplify
7 [+ *idea, explicación*] to elaborate on
8 [+ *poderes*] to extend, widen

amplificación SF amplification

amplificador SM amplifier

amplificar /1g/ VT to amplify

amplio ADJ **1** (= *espacioso*) [*habitación, interior*] spacious; [*avenida, calle*] wide; **el terremoto afectó a una amplia zona del sur** the earthquake affected a wide area in the south; **una amplia extensión de terreno** a vast tract o stretch of land
2 [*ropa*] loose(-fitting), roomy*; [*falda*] full
3 [*margen*] wide; **un ~ margen a ambos lados** a wide margin on each side; **ganaron por amplia mayoría** they won with a large majority
4 [*conocimiento, vocabulario, poder, gama*] wide, extensive
5 [*sentido*] broad; **en el sentido ~ de la palabra** in the broad sense of the term
6 [*repercusión*] far-reaching; **la noticia tuvo amplia difusión** o **~ eco en la prensa** the news was widely o extensively reported
7 [*informe*] full, detailed

amplitud SF **1** (= *espaciosidad*) [*de sala, habitación, interior*] spaciousness; [*de avenida, calle*] wideness; [*de terreno*] expanse, extent **2** [*de ropa*] looseness; [*de falda*] fullness **3** [*de conocimientos, vocabulario, poder, variedad*] extent ➤ **amplitud de miras** broadmindedness **4 de gran ~** [*reforma, proyecto*] wide-ranging, far-reaching **5** (*Fís*) amplitude

ampolla SF (*en la piel*) blister; (*de inyección*) ampoule; ✦ MODISMO **levantar ~s: la decisión levantó ~s entre los ministros** the decision ruffled a few feathers o put a few backs up in the Cabinet

ampollarse /1a/ VPR to blister, form blisters

ampolleta SF (*Chi*) bulb; ✦ MODISMO **encendérsele a algn la ~*** to have a brainwave

ampulosidad SF bombast, pomposity

ampuloso ADJ bombastic, pompous

amputación SF amputation

amputar /1a/ VT to amputate, cut off

amueblado/a ADJ furnished (**con, de** with)

amueblar /1a/ VT to furnish (**de** with); **sin ~** unfurnished

amuermado* ADJ bored

amuermante* ADJ boring, dull

amuermar* /1a/ Ⓐ VT to bore Ⓑ **amuermarse** VPR to get bored

amuleto SM amulet, charm

amurallar /1a/ VT to wall, fortify

anabólico ADJ anabolic

anabolizante SM anabolic steroid

anacarado ADJ mother-of-pearl *antes de s*

anacardo SM (= *fruto*) cashew, cashew nut; (= *árbol*) cashew tree

anaconda SF anaconda

anacoreta SMF anchorite

anacrónico ADJ anachronistic

anacronismo SM anachronism

ánade SM duck ➤ **ánade real** mallard

anaeróbico ADJ anaerobic

anáfora SF anaphora

anagrama SM anagram

anal ADJ anal

analfabetismo SM illiteracy ➤ **analfabetismo funcional** functional illiteracy

analfabeto/a Ⓐ ADJ illiterate Ⓑ SM/F illiterate, illiterate person

analgesia SF analgesia

analgésico Ⓐ ADJ analgesic, painkilling Ⓑ SM analgesic, painkiller

análisis SM INV (*gen*) analysis; (= *prueba médica*) test ➤ **análisis de sangre** blood test

analista SMF analyst ➤ **analista financiero** financial analyst, market analyst

analítico ADJ analytic, analytical

analizar /1f/ VT to analyse

analogía SF (= *correspondencia*) analogy; (= *semejanza*) similarity

analógico ADJ analogical

análogo Ⓐ ADJ analogous, similar (**a** to) Ⓑ SM analogue

ananá SM (*RPl*) pineapple

anaquel SM (*estante*) shelf; (*Méx*) (*estantería*) bookcase

anaranjado Ⓐ ADJ orange, orange-coloured, orange-colored (*EEUU*) Ⓑ SM orange, orange colour, orange color (*EEUU*)

anarco/a* SM/F anarchist

anarcosindicalismo SM anarcho-syndicalism

anarquía SF anarchy

anárquico ADJ anarchic, anarchical

anarquismo SM anarchism

anarquista Ⓐ ADJ anarchist, anarchistic Ⓑ SMF anarchist

anatema SM anathema

anatematizar /1f/ VT, **anatemizar** /1f/ VT to anathematize

anatomía SF anatomy

anatómico ADJ anatomical; **asiento ~** anatomically

designed seat

anca SF rump, haunch; ✦ MODISMO **llevar a algn a las ~s** o **en ~(s)** (*LAm*) to let sb ride pillion ➤ **ancas de rana** frog's legs

ancestral ADJ ancestral

ancestro SM ancestor

ancho Ⓐ ADJ **1** (= *amplio*) [*camino, puente, habitación*] wide; [*calle, sonrisa, manos*] broad; **un tarro de boca ancha** a wide-necked bottle; **tenía las espaldas anchas** he had a broad back; **era muy ~ de hombros** he was very broad-shouldered; **colocaron una cuerda a lo ~ de la calle** they put a rope across the street
2 (= *holgado*) [*chaqueta, pantalón*] loose, loose-fitting; [*falda*] full; [*manga*] wide; **quedar** o (*Esp*) **estar** o (*Esp*) **venir ~ a algn** to be too wide for sb; **le viene muy ~ el cargo** the job is too much for him; ✦ MODISMO **a sus anchas: puedes hojear a tus anchas todos los libros** you can leaf through all the books at your leisure; **con ellos podrá discutir a sus anchas** you can discuss things freely with them
3 (= *orgulloso*) proud; **iba todo ~ con su traje nuevo** he was very proud in his new suit; ✦ MODISMO **quedarse tan ~: y se quedó tan ~** he felt very pleased with himself
Ⓑ SM **1** [*de camino, ventana*] width; [*de río*] width, breadth; **tiene doce metros de ~** it is twelve metres o (*EEUU*) meters wide ➤ **ancho de banda** band width
2 (*Ferro*) (*tb* ~ **de vía**) gauge; ~ **europeo** European gauge

anchoa SF anchovy

anchura SF **1** (= *amplitud*) [*de camino, ventana*] width; [*de río*] width, breadth; **tiene dos metros de ~** it is two metres o (*EEUU*) meters wide **2** (*Cos*) [*de falda*] fullness

ancianidad SF old age

anciano/a Ⓐ ADJ old, aged Ⓑ SM/F [*de mucha edad*] old man/woman, elderly man/woman; (*Rel*) elder

ancla SF anchor; **echar ~s** to drop anchor; **levar ~s** to weigh anchor

ancladero SM anchorage

anclaje SM anchoring, anchorage

anclar /1a/ Ⓐ VT to anchor Ⓑ VI to anchor, drop anchor; **estar anclado a/en algo** to be anchored to/in sth

áncora SF anchor

andadas SFPL **volver a las ~** to backslide, go back to one's old ways

andaderas SFPL baby walker *sing*

andador Ⓐ ADJ **es ~** he's a good walker Ⓑ SM **1** (*para niños*) baby walker; (*para enfermos*) Zimmer® frame (*Brit*), walker (*EEUU*) **2 andadores** [*de niño*] reins

andadura SF **1** (= *trayectoria*) (*profesional*) career; **comenzó su ~ profesional en la televisión** he began his career in television **2** (= *camino*) path, course

ándale EXCL *ver* **andar A10**

Andalucía SF Andalusia

andalucismo SM **1** (*Ling*) andalusianism, *word or phrase etc peculiar to Andalusia* **2** (= *sentimiento*) *sense of the differentness of Andalusia*; (*Pol*) *doctrine of or belief in Andalusian autonomy*

andaluz(a) ADJ, SM/F Andalusian

andamiaje SM (*Constr*) scaffolding; (*fig*) (= *estructura*) framework, structure

andamio SM (*Constr*) scaffold; **~s** scaffolding *sing*

andanada SF **1** (*Mil*) broadside; (= *reprensión*) reprimand, rocket (*Brit**), tongue-lashing (*EEUU**) **2** (*Dep*) stand, grandstand; (*Taur*) *section of cheap seats*

andante Ⓐ ADJ **caballero ~** knight errant Ⓑ SM (*Mús*) andante

andanzas SFPL deeds, adventures

andar /1p/ Ⓐ VI **1** (= *ir a pie*) to walk; (= *moverse*) to move; (= *viajar*) to travel around; **iremos andando a la estación** we'll walk to the station; **el tren empezó a ~** the train started moving; **anduvieron por Jamaica y Cuba** they travelled o (*EEUU*) traveled around Jamaica and Cuba; ~ **en bicicleta** to cycle; ~ **a caballo** to ride; ~ **tras algo/algn** to be after sth/sb; ~ **tras una chica** to be o chase after a girl;

✦ MODISMO **andando el tiempo** eventually
2 (= *funcionar*) to go, work; **el reloj no anda** the clock won't go, the clock isn't working
3 (*) (= *estar*) to be; **no sé por dónde anda** I don't know where he is; **hay que ~ con cuidado** you have to be careful; **últimamente ando muy liado** I've been very busy lately; **andamos mal de dinero** we're badly off for money, we're short of money; **¿cómo andan las cosas?** how are things?; **¿qué tal andas?** how are you?; **¿cómo andas de tabaco?** how are you off for cigarettes?; **ando escaso de tiempo** I am pushed for time; ✦ MODISMO **de ~ por casa: ropa de ~ por casa** clothes for wearing around the house; **un montaje muy de ~ por casa** a rough-and-ready production; **justicia de ~ por casa** rough-and-ready justice; ✦ REFRÁN **quien mal anda, mal acaba** you get what you deserve
4 (= *rebuscar*) **¡no andes ahí!** keep away from there!; ~ **en** to rummage around in; **no andes en mis cosas** keep out of my things
5 ~ **a: siempre andan a gritos** they're always shouting; **andan a la greña** o **a la gresca** they're at each other's throats
6 ~ **con algn** to go around with sb; **anda con una chica francesa** he goes around with a French girl; ✦ REFRÁN **dime con quién andas y te diré quién eres** a man is known by the company he keeps
7 ~ **en** (= *estar implicado en*) to be involved in; **sospecho que anda en ello Rosa** I suspect Rosa is involved
8 ~ **haciendo** algo to be doing sth; **¿qué andas buscando?** what are you looking for?; **ando buscando un socio** I'm looking for a partner
9 ~ **por** (= *rondar*): **anda por los 50** he's about 50; **anda por los 150 euros** it's around 150 euros
10 (*exclamaciones*) **¡anda!** (= *¡no me digas!*) well I never!; (= *¡vamos!*) come on!; **¡anda!, no lo sabía** well I never, I didn't know that!; **anda, dímelo** go on, tell me; **¡anda, no me molestes!** just stop annoying me, will you?; **¡ándale!** (*Méx**) ◇ **¡ándele!** (*Méx**) (= *¡apúrese!*) come on!, hurry up!; (= *adiós*) bye!*; (= *gracias*) thanks!; (*encontrando algo*) that's it!; **¡andando!** OK, let's get going!; **¡anda ya!**: —**dile que te gusta** —**¡anda ya, para que me suba el precio!** "tell her you like it" — "oh sure, so she can charge me more!"
11 (*) (*imperativos*) **anda y dile a tu padre que ...** go and tell your father that ...
Ⓑ VT **1** (= *recorrer a pie*) [+ *camino, trecho*] to walk; **anduvimos varios kilómetros** we walked several kilometres o (*EEUU*) kilometers; ✦ MODISMO **todo se andará** all in good time
2 (*CAm*) (= *llevar*) [+ *ropa*] to wear; [+ *objeto*] to carry; **yo no ando reloj** I don't wear a watch
Ⓒ **andarse** VPR **1** ~**se con**: **ándate con cuidado** take care; **no puedes ~te con tonterías** you can't afford to mess around; **no podemos ~nos con contemplaciones a la hora de buscar una solución a la crisis** we can't afford to worry about the niceties when looking for a solution to the crisis; **no se anda con chiquitas** he doesn't mess around; **no ~se con rodeos** not to beat about (*Brit*) o around (*EEUU*) the bush
2 ~**se en** [+ *herida, nariz*] to pick; **no te andes en la nariz** don't pick your nose; **se andaba en la herida** he was picking at his wound
Ⓓ SM walk, gait; **es de ~es rápidos** he walks quickly

andariego ADJ fond of travelling

andarín ADJ **es muy ~** he is a great walker

andarivel SM **1** (*Téc*) cable ferry **2** (*LAm*) (= *cerco*) rope barrier; [*de piscina, carretera*] lane

andas SFPL (*Rel*) portable platform *sing*

ándele EXCL *ver* **andar A10**

andén SM **1** (*Ferro*) platform **2** (*CAm, Col*) (= *acera*) pavement (*Brit*), sidewalk (*EEUU*)

Andes SMPL Andes

andinismo SM (*LAm*) mountaineering, climbing

andinista SMF (*LAm*) mountaineer, climber

andino ADJ Andean, of/from the Andes

Andorra SF Andorra

andorrano/a ADJ, SM/F Andorran

andrajo SM rag, tatter

andrajoso ADJ ragged, in tatters

andrógeno SM androgen

androginia SF androgyny

andrógino/a Ⓐ ADJ androgynous Ⓑ SM/F androgyne

androide SM android

andropausia SF male menopause

andurriales SMPL godforsaken place

anduve, anduviera *etc ver* **andar**

anea SF bulrush

anécdota SF anecdote, story

anecdótico ADJ (= *de anécdota*) anecdotal; (= *trivial*) trivial; **el estudio se queda en lo ~** the study does not rise above the merely superficial

anegar /1h/ Ⓐ VT 1 (= *inundar*) to flood 2 (= *abrumar*) to overwhelm Ⓑ **anegarse** VPR (= *inundarse*) to flood, be flooded; **~se en llanto** to dissolve into tears

anejo Ⓐ ADJ attached, joined on (**a** to) Ⓑ SM (*Arquit*) annexe, outbuilding; [*de libro*] supplement, appendix

anemia SF anaemia, anemia (*EEUU*)

anémico ADJ anaemic, anemic (*EEUU*)

anémona SF anemone

anestesia SF (= *sustancia*) anaesthetic, anesthetic (*EEUU*); (= *proceso*) anaesthesia, anesthesia (*EEUU*); **operar sin ~** to operate without (an) anaesthetic ➤ **anestesia general** general anaesthetic, general anesthetic (*EEUU*) ➤ **anestesia local** local anaesthetic, local anesthetic (*EEUU*)

anestesiar /1b/ VT to anaesthetize, anesthetize (*EEUU*), give an anaesthetic to, give an anesthetic to (*EEUU*)

anestesista SMF anaesthetist, anesthesiologist (*EEUU*)

anexar /1a/ VT 1 (*esp LAm Pol*) to annex 2 [+ *documento*] to attach, append

anexión SF, **anexionamiento** SM annexation

anexionar /1a/ Ⓐ VT to annex Ⓑ **anexionarse** VPR to annex

anexo Ⓐ ADJ attached; (*en carta*) enclosed Ⓑ SM (*Arquit*) annexe; (*Rel*) dependency; [*de carta*] enclosure

anfetamina SF amphetamine

anfetamínico/a SM/F amphetamine addict, speed freak*

anfibio Ⓐ ADJ (*Zool*) amphibious; [*avión, vehículo*] amphibian Ⓑ SM amphibian; **los ~s** the amphibia

anfiteatro SM amphitheatre, amphitheater (*EEUU*); (*Univ*) lecture theatre *o* (*EEUU*) theater; (*Teat*) dress circle

anfitrión/ona SM/F host/hostess

ánfora SF 1 (= *cántaro*) amphora 2 (*And, Méx Pol*) ballot box

angarillas SFPL (*para herido*) stretcher; [*de albañil*] handbarrow *sing*; (*en bicicleta*) panniers; (*Culin*) cruet (stand) *sing*

angas SMPL ✦ MODISMO **por ~ o por mangas** (*And*) like it or not

ángel SM 1 (*Rel*) angel ➤ **ángel custodio, ángel de la guarda** guardian angel ➤ **ángel exterminador** angel of death 2 (= *gracia*) **tener ~** to have charm, be very charming

angélica SF angelica

angelical ADJ angelic, angelical

angelito SM (*LAm*) (= *niño fallecido*) dead child

ángelus SM INV angelus

angina SF (*en la garganta*) tonsil; **tener ~s** to have tonsillitis ➤ **angina de pecho** angina (pectoris)

anglicano/a ADJ, SM/F Anglican

anglicismo SM anglicism

anglófilo/a ADJ, SM/F anglophile

anglófobo/a Ⓐ ADJ anglophobe, anglophobic Ⓑ SM/F anglophobe

anglófono/a Ⓐ ADJ English-speaking Ⓑ SM/F English speaker

angloparlante, anglohablante Ⓐ ADJ English-speaking Ⓑ SMF English speaker

anglosajón/ona ADJ, SM/F Anglo-Saxon

Angola SF Angola

angoleño/a ADJ, SM/F Angolan

angolés = **angoleño**

angora SF angora

angorina SF artificial angora

angostar /1a/ Ⓐ VT (= *estrechar*) to narrow; [+ *ropa*] to take in Ⓑ **angostarse** VPR to narrow, get narrow, get narrower

angosto ADJ narrow

angostura SF 1 (= *estrechez*) narrowness 2 (*Náut*) narrows *pl*, strait 3 (= *bebida*) angostura

ángstrom SM (*pl* ~s) angstrom

anguila SF eel

angula SF elver, baby eel

angular Ⓐ ADJ angular Ⓑ SM **gran ~** wide-angle lens

ángulo SM (*Mat*) angle; **en ~** at an angle; **formar ~ con** to be at an angle to ➤ **ángulo muerto** (*Aut*) blind spot ➤ **ángulo recto** right angle; **de o en ~ recto** right-angled

anguloso ADJ [*cara*] angular, sharp

angurria SF (*LAm*) **comer con ~** to eat greedily

angurriento ADJ greedy

angustia Ⓐ SF 1 (= *miedo*) anguish, distress; **una mirada/ sensación de ~** a look/feeling of anguish *o* distress; **da ~ ver esos niños tan delgados** it's distressing to see children as thin as that 2 (= *ansiedad*) (*por estrés, miedo*) anxiety; (*por inseguridad*) angst Ⓑ SMF INV **ser un ~s*** to be a worrier

angustiado ADJ 1 (= *asustado*) [*persona*] distressed; [*expresión, mirada*] anguished 2 (= *preocupado*) anxious

angustiante ADJ distressing

angustiar /1b/ Ⓐ VT 1 (= *agobiar*) to distress; **la angustiaba verlo sufrir** she was distressed to see him suffer, seeing him suffer distressed her 2 (= *preocupar*) to make anxious Ⓑ **angustiarse** VPR 1 (= *agobiarse*) to be distressed (**por** at, on account of) 2 (= *preocuparse*) to get anxious

angustioso ADJ 1 (= *angustiado*) [*sensación*] distressed, anguished; [*voz, mirada*] anguished; **tres horas de angustiosa espera** three hours of anxious waiting 2 (= *agobiante*) [*habitación, espacio*] oppressive; [*problema, recuerdo, situación*] distressing; **tomar decisiones es siempre ~** taking decisions always makes one anxious; **pasamos unos momentos muy ~s** we went through moments of great anguish

anhelante ADJ eager; **esperar ~ algo** to long for sth

anhelar /1a/ VT to long for, yearn for; **~ hacer algo** to be eager to do sth, long to do sth

anhelo SM longing, desire (**de, por** for); **tener ~s de** to be eager for, long for ➤ **anhelo de superación** urge to do better

anhídrido SM ➤ **anhídrido carbónico** carbon dioxide

anidar /1a/ VI 1 (*Orn*) to nest, make its nest 2 (= *morar*) to live, make one's home; **la maldad anida en su alma** his heart is full of evil

aniego SM (*And*) flood

anilina SF aniline

anilla SF 1 [*de cortina*] curtain ring; [*de puro*] cigar band 2 (*Orn*) ring 3 **anillas** (*Gimnasia*) rings

anillar /1a/ VT (*Orn*) to ring

anillo SM ring; ✦ MODISMOS **no creo que se me caigan los ~s por eso** I don't feel it's in any way beneath my dignity; **venir como ~ al dedo** to be just right, suit to a tee ➤ **anillo de boda** wedding ring ➤ **anillo de compromiso** engagement ring ➤ **anillo de pedida** engagement ring

ánima SF soul; **las ~s** (= *oración*) the Angelus *sing* ➤ **ánima bendita, ánima del purgatorio, ánima en pena** soul in purgatory

animación SF 1 (= *alegría*) life; **hemos logrado darle un poco de ~ al bar** we have managed to liven up the bar, we have managed to put some life into the bar 2 (= *bullicio*) activity; **una intensa ~ en la Bolsa** an intense activity on the Stock Market; **en verano aumenta la ~ cultural** there are more cultural things going on in the summer; **departamento de ~ sociocultural** department of culture **3** (*Cine*) animation

animadamente ADV [*charlar*] animatedly, in a lively way; [*bailar*] in a lively way

animado ADJ **1** (= *con ánimo*) **no está muy ~ últimamente** he hasn't been in very high spirits recently; **estar ~ a hacer algo** to be keen to do sth **2** [*lugar*] (= *alegre*) lively; (= *concurrido*) bustling, busy; **una fiesta muy animada** a very lively party **3** (= *con vida*) animate; **un cortometraje ~** a short animation film **4** (*Ling*) animate

animador(a) SM/F (*TV*) host/hostess, presenter ➤ **animador(a) cultural** (*en ayuntamiento*) events organiser; (*en hotel*) entertainment manager ➤ **animador(a) turístico(a)** tourist coordinator

animadora SF (*Dep*) cheerleader

animadversión SF antagonism, ill will

animal Ⓐ ADJ **1** (*Zool*) animal; **instinto ~** animal instinct **2** (*) (= *estúpido*) stupid; **el muy ~ no sabe la capital de España** he's so stupid he doesn't know what the capital of Spain is
3 (*) (= *bruto*) **no seas ~** don't be such a brute; **¡el muy ~ se comió tres platos!** he had three helpings, the pig!
Ⓑ SM animal; **los ~es salvajes** wild animals; **un ~ político** a political animal; **ser ~ de costumbres** to be a creature of habit; ✦ MODISMOS **comer como un ~*** to eat like a pig; **trabajar como un ~*** to work like a slave ➤ **animal de carga** (= *burro, buey*) beast of burden ➤ **animal de compañía** pet ➤ **animal doméstico** [*de compañía*] pet; [*de granja*] domestic animal
Ⓒ SMF (*) **1** (= *estúpido*) fool, moron*
2 (= *bruto*) brute; **el ~ de Juan seguía pegándole** that brute Juan kept on hitting him; **el ~ de Antonio se comió su plato y el mío** that pig Antonio ate all his own dinner and mine too; **eres un ~, lo has roto** you're so rough you've gone and broken it

animalada SF (= *disparate*) silly thing (*to do o say*); (= *atrocidad*) outrage

animar /1a/ Ⓐ VT **1** (= *alegrar*) [+ *persona triste*] to cheer up; [+ *habitación*] to brighten up; **una sonrisa de ilusión animaba sus ojos** an excited smile brightened the look in her eyes
2 (= *entretener*) [+ *persona aburrida*] to liven up; [+ *charla, fiesta, reunión*] to liven up, enliven
3 (= *alentar*) [+ *persona*] to encourage; [+ *proyecto*] to inspire; [+ *fuego*] to liven up; **te estaré animando desde las gradas** I'll be rooting for you *o* cheering you on from the crowd; **~ a algn a hacer** *o* **a que haga algo** to encourage sb to do sth; **ignoramos las razones que lo ~on a dimitir** we are unaware of the reasons for his resignation *o* the reasons that led him *o* prompted him to resign
4 (*Econ*) [+ *mercado, economía*] to stimulate, inject life into **5** (*Biol*) to animate, give life to
Ⓑ **animarse** VPR **1** (= *alegrarse*) **1.1** [*persona*] to cheer up; [*cara, ojos*] to brighten up; **¡venga, anímate!** come on, cheer up! **1.2** [*charla, fiesta, reunión*] to liven up; **si quieres que la fiesta se anime** if you want the party to get going *o* liven up
2 (= *decidirse*) **si te animas, hemos quedado en el Café Central** if you feel like it, we're meeting at the Café Central; **cuando la economía va bien, la gente se anima y gasta** when the economy is doing well people feel more like spending; **nos vamos a París, ¿te animas?** we're going to Paris, do you feel like *o* (*esp Brit*) fancy coming?; **~se a hacer algo: hasta el abuelo se animó a bailar** even grandpa got up and had a dance; **parece que no se anima a llover** it looks as if it's not going to rain after all

animatrónico ADJ animatronics *antes de s*

anímicamente ADV mentally

anímico ADJ mental; **estado ~** state of mind

animista Ⓐ ADJ animistic Ⓑ SMF animist

ánimo SM **1** (= *moral*) spirits *pl*; **tiene mejor ~** he is in better spirits; **hay que mantener el ~ arriba** you've got to keep your spirits up; **admiro su fortaleza de ~** I admire her strength of spirit; **aplacar los ~s** to calm things down;

estar bajo de ~ to be in low spirits; **calmar los ~s** to calm things down; **dar ~s a algn** to cheer sb up; **encrespar los ~s** to rouse passions, inflame passions; **los ~s estaban muy encrespados** feelings were running high
2 (= *aliento*) encouragement; **un mensaje de ~** a message of encouragement; **¡ánimo!** (*para alegrar*) come on!, cheer up!; (*ante un reto*) come on!, go for it!; **dar** *o* **infundir ~(s) a algn** to give encouragement to sb, encourage sb
3 (= *fuerza, coraje*) courage; **hay que afrontar el futuro con mucho ~** you have to face the future with great strength *o* courage; **no me encuentro con ~ de ir** I don't feel up to going
4 (= *intención*) intention; **no he venido con ~ de pelea** I haven't come here to fight *o* with the intention of fighting; **lo dijo sin ~ de ofenderte** he meant no offence, he didn't mean to offend you; **una empresa sin ~ de lucro** a non-profit-making company
5 (= *pensamiento*) mind; **la idea estaba presente en el ~ de todos** the idea was uppermost in everyone's thoughts *o* minds

animosidad SF animosity, ill will

animoso ADJ spirited, lively

aniñado ADJ [*aspecto*] childlike; [*conducta*] childish, puerile

aniquilación SF, **aniquilamiento** SM annihilation, destruction

aniquilador ADJ destructive

aniquilar /1a/ VT [+ *enemigo*] to annihilate, destroy; [+ *equipo rival*] to crush, annihilate

anís SM **1** (*Bot*) anise, aniseed **2** (= *bebida*) anisette; ✦ MODISMOS **estar hecho un ~** (*Perú**) to be dressed up to the nines; **llegar a los anises** (*Perú**) to turn up late

anisado ADJ aniseed-flavoured, aniseed -flavored (*EEUU*)

anisete SM anisette

aniversario SM anniversary

Ankara SF Ankara

ano SM anus

anoche ADV yesterday evening, last night; **antes de ~** the night before last

anochecer /2d/ Ⓐ VI **1** (= *venir la noche*) to get dark **2 anochecimos en Toledo** we got to Toledo as night was falling Ⓑ SM nightfall, dusk; **al ~** at nightfall, at dusk; **antes del ~** before nightfall, before it gets dark

anodino ADJ (= *inocuo*) anodyne, harmless, inoffensive; [*persona*] dull

ánodo SM anode

anomalía SF anomaly

anómalo ADJ anomalous

anonadado ADJ stunned

anonadar /1a/ VT to stun; **me anonadó su descaro** I was stunned *o* left speechless by her cheek *o* (*EEUU*) sass

anonimato SM anonymity; **mantenerse en el ~** to remain anonymous

anónimo Ⓐ ADJ anonymous; *ver* **sociedad 3** Ⓑ SM (= *carta*) anonymous letter; (= *carta maliciosa*) poison-pen letter; (= *obra literaria*) unsigned literary work

anorak SM anorak

anorexia SF anorexia ➤ **anorexia nerviosa** anorexia nervosa

anoréxico/a Ⓐ ADJ anorexic Ⓑ SM/F anorexic

anormal ADJ **1** (= *no normal*) abnormal **2** (*) (= *imbécil*) silly, cretinous

anormalidad SF abnormality

anotación SF **1** (= *nota*) note, annotation (*frm*) ➤ **anotación al margen** marginal note, note in the margin ➤ **anotación en cuenta** (*Com*) account entry **2** (*Baloncesto*) point

anotador(a) SM/F **1** (*Literat*) annotator **2** (*Dep*) scorer

anotar /1a/ Ⓐ VT **1** (= *apuntar*) **1.1** (*en cuaderno*) to make a note of, note down; (*en lista, tabla*) to enter, record; **anotó la matrícula del coche** he took down the registration number of the car; **se han olvidado de ~ los intereses** they have forgotten to record the interest rates **1.2** (*Estadística*) [+ *velocidad, tiempo*] to log

2 (*esp CS*) (= *inscribir*) enrol, enroll (*EEUU*); **anótame para la excursión** put me down for the outing **3** (*Literat*) [+ *texto, libro*] to annotate **4** (*Dep*) [+ *punto*] to score

B anotarse VPR **1** (*Dep*) [+ *punto, gol*] to score; **~se una victoria** to win a victory, gain a victory; ✦ MODISMO **¡anótate un tanto!*** give yourself a pat on the back!* **2** (*Fin*) [+ *precio*] to fetch; [+ *operación, puntos*] to register **3** (*esp CS*) (= *inscribirse*) to enrol, enroll (*EEUU*); **—estamos organizando un viaje —¡yo me anoto!** "we're organizing a trip" — "count me in! *o* I'll come too!"

anovulatorio SM anovulant

anquilosado ADJ **1** [*músculo, miembro*] stiff; (*Med*) ankylosed (*frm*) **2** [*pensamiento, sociedad*] stagnant

anquilosamiento SM **1** [*de músculo, pierna*] stiffness; (*Med*) ankylosis **2** [*de pensamiento, sociedad*] stagnation

anquilosar /1a/ **A** VT **1** [+ *músculo, pierna*] to get stiff; (*Med*) to ankylose (*frm*) **2** (= *detener*) to paralyze **B anquilosarse** VPR to stagnate

ánsar SM goose

ansarino SM gosling

ansia SF **1** (= *anhelo*) yearning, longing; **~ de libertad/amor** yearning *o* longing for freedom/love; **~ de poder/riqueza/ conocimiento/aventura** thirst for power/wealth/knowledge/ adventure; **el ~ de superación** the will to better oneself; **comer con ~** to eat ravenously; **beber con ~** to drink thirstily **2** (= *ansiedad*) anxiety, worry; (= *angustia*) anguish; ✦ MODISMO **no comas ~s** (*Méx*) don't worry

ansiado ADJ longed-for

ansiar /1b/ VT to long for, yearn for; **~ hacer algo** to long to do sth, yearn to do sth

ansiedad SF **1** (= *preocupación*) anxiety, worry **2** (*Med*) anxiety, nervous tension

ansiolítico A ADJ sedative **B** SM sedative, tranquillizer

ansioso ADJ (= *preocupado*) anxious, worried; (= *deseoso*) eager, solicitous; **esperábamos ~s** we waited anxiously

antagónico ADJ antagonistic; (= *opuesto*) opposing

antagonismo SM antagonism

antagonizar /1f/ VT to antagonize

antaño ADV (*liter*) long ago, in years past, in years gone by

antártico A ADJ Antarctic **B** SM **el Antártico** the Antarctic

Antártida SF Antarctica

ante¹ SM **1** (*Zool*) elk, moose **2** (= *piel*) suede **3** (*Méx*) (= *dulce*) macaroon

ante² PREP **1** (= *en presencia de*) [+ *persona*] before **2** (= *enfrentado a*) [+ *peligro*] in the face of, faced with; [+ *dificultad, duda*] faced with; **~ esta posibilidad** in view of this possibility; **~ tantas posibilidades** faced with so many possibilities **3 ~ todo** above all

anteanoche ADV the night before last

anteayer ADV the day before yesterday

antebrazo SM forearm

antecámara SF anteroom, antechamber

antecedente SM **1** (*Mat, Fil, Gram*) antecedent **2 antecedentes** (= *historial*) record *sing*, history *sing*; **no tener ~s** to have a clean record; **poner a algn en ~s** to put sb in the picture ➤ **antecedentes penales** criminal record

anteceder /2a/ VT to precede, go before

antecesor(a) SM/F (*en cargo*) predecessor; (= *antepasado*) ancestor, forebear (*frm*)

antecocina SF (*para muebles*) utility room; (*para comer*) breakfast room

antecomedor SM (*LAm*) room adjoining the dining room

antedatar /1a/ VT to antedate

antedicho ADJ aforesaid, aforementioned

antediluviano ADJ antediluvian

antelación SF **con ~** in advance, beforehand

antemano: de ~ ADV in advance, beforehand

antena SF **1** (*Zool*) feeler, antenna **2** (*Náut*) lateen yard **3** (*Radio, TV, Telec*) aerial, antenna; **estar en ~** to be on the air; **salir en ~** to go out on the air, be broadcast ➤ **antena colectiva** communal aerial ➤ **antena de televisión** television aerial ➤ **antena parabólica** satellite dish, dish antenna (*EEUU*) **4 antenas*** (= *oídos*) ears

antenatal ADJ antenatal, prenatal

anteojeras SFPL blinkers (*Brit*), blinders (*EEUU*)

anteojos SMPL (*esp LAm*) glasses, spectacles, eyeglasses (*EEUU*); (*Aut, Téc*) goggles

antepasado/a SM/F ancestor, forbear (*frm*); **~s** ancestors

antepenúltimo ADJ last but two, antepenultimate (*frm*)

anteponer /2q/ **A** VT **1** (*lit*) to place in front (**a** of) **2** (*fig*) (= *preferir*) to prefer (**a** to) **B anteponerse** VPR to be in front (**a** of)

anteproyecto SM preliminary plan ➤ **anteproyecto de ley** draft bill

anterior ADJ **1** (*en el espacio*) [*parte*] front; **el motor está en la parte ~ del coche** the engine is in the front (part) of the car; **las patas ~es** the forelegs **2** (*en una sucesión*) [*página, párrafo*] previous, preceding; **el capítulo ~ a éste** the chapter before this one; **se subió en la parada ~** he got on at the stop before *o* at the previous stop; **retiro lo ~** I take back what I just said **3** (*en el tiempo*) previous; **en ~es ocasiones** on previous occasions; **el día ~** the day before; **un texto ~ a 1140** a text dating from before 1140; **las horas ~es a la operación** the hours before the operation **4** (*Ling*) anterior

anterioridad SF **con ~** previously, beforehand; **con ~ a esto** prior to this, before this

anteriormente ADV previously, before

antes A ADJ before; **llame el día ~ para pedir cita** call the day before for an appointment; **ocurrió unos momentos ~** it happened a few moments earlier *o* before; **el tren ha llegado una hora ~** the train has arrived an hour early *o* before

B ADV **1** (*en el tiempo*) **1.1** (*con relación a otro acontecimiento*) **yo llegué ~** I arrived first; **el edificio que habían comenzado dos años ~** the building that had been started two years before *o* previously; **no te vayas sin ~ consultarle** don't go without *o* before consulting her first, don't go without *o* before consulting her beforehand; **~ de algo** before sth; **~ de anoche** the night before last; **~ de ayer** the day before yesterday; **~ de una semana no vamos a saber nada** we won't know anything for a week; **el año 27 ~ de Cristo** 27 BC, 27 before Christ; **~ de hacer algo** before doing sth

Recuérdese que las preposiciones en inglés rigen gerundio y no infinitivo, de ahí **before doing sth**.

mucho ~ de algo long before sth; **~ de o que nada** (*en el tiempo*) first of all; (*indicando preferencia*) above all; **poco ~ de algo** just *o* shortly before sth; **~ de que te vayas** before you go; **~ de que termine la década** before the end of the decade **1.2** (*en el pasado*) **~ fumaba un paquete de tabaco al día** before, I smoked a packet of cigarettes a day, I used to smoke a packet of cigarettes a day; **no pasaban estas cosas** these things didn't use to happen before *o* in the past; **de ~: nuestra casa de ~** our old house, our previous house; **ya no soy el mismo de ~** I'm not the same person I was *o* I used to be; **fue una boda de las de ~** it was an old-style wedding; **ya no se hacen trajes como los de ~** they don't make suits like they used to *o* like they did in the old days **1.3** (= *hasta ahora*) before, before now; **nunca ~ he tenido problemas** I've never had any problems before **1.4** (= *más temprano*) earlier; **un poco ~** a little earlier; **no te he podido llamar ~** I couldn't call you sooner *o* earlier; **cuanto ~** as soon as possible; **lo ~ posible** as soon as possible **1.5** (= *más joven*) cada vez se casan los hijos ~ kids get married at a younger *o* an earlier age these days **2** (*en el espacio*) before; **tres páginas** ~ three pages before; ~ **de** algo before sth; **la calle que hay** ~ **del semáforo** the street before the traffic light(s) **©** CONJ (*indicando preferencia*) sooner, rather; **no cederemos:** ~ **gastamos todo nuestro dinero** we shall never give up: we would rather *o* sooner spend all our money; ~ **bien** ◇ ~ **al contrario** but rather; ~ **no** (*Chi, Méx*) just as well, luckily; **vi lo furiosa que estaba,** ~ **no te pegó** I saw how angry she was, just as well *o* luckily she didn't hit you; ~ **que hacer algo** rather than doing sth

Recuérdese que las preposiciones en inglés rigen gerundio y no infinitivo, de ahí **rather than doing sth.**

antesala SF anteroom, antechamber; **en la** ~ **de** on the verge of, on the threshold of
antiabortista ADJ **campaña** ~ anti-abortion campaign
antiadherencia SF non-stick properties *pl*
antiadherente ADJ non-stick
antiaéreo ADJ anti-aircraft
antibalas ADJ INV bullet-proof
antibiótico ADJ, SM antibiotic
antibloqueo SM **sistema de** ~ **de frenos** ABS braking system, anti-lock braking system
anticaspa ADJ INV dandruff *antes de s*, anti-dandruff
anticelulítico ADJ anti-cellulite, cellulite *antes de s*
antichoque ADJ INV, **antichoques** ADJ INV **panel** ~ shock-resistant panel
anticiclón SM anticyclone
anticiclónico ADJ anticyclonic
anticipación SF (= *adelanto*) **hacer algo con** ~ to do sth in good time; **llegar con** ~ to arrive early, arrive in good time; **reservar con** ~ to book in advance
anticipadamente ADV in advance, beforehand
anticipado ADJ early; **pago** ~ advance payment; **gracias anticipadas** thanks in advance; **por** ~ in advance, beforehand
anticipar /1a/ **©** VT **1** [+ *fecha, acontecimiento*] to bring forward; **~on las vacaciones** they took their holiday (*esp Brit*) *o* vacation (*EEUU*) early; **no anticipemos los acontecimientos** let's not cross our bridges before we come to them, let's not get ahead of ourselves; ~ **las gracias a algn** to thank sb in advance **2** [+ *factura*] to pay in advance; [+ *dinero*] to advance, lend, loan **3** (= *prever*) to anticipate, foresee **©** anticiparse VPR **1** [*acontecimiento*] to take place early **2** ~**se a un acontecimiento** to anticipate an event; ~**se a algn** to beat sb to it; **usted se ha anticipado a mis deseos** you have anticipated my wishes; ~**se a su época** to be ahead of one's time
anticipo SM **1** [*de dinero*] advance **2 ser el** ~ **de algo** to be a foretaste of sth
anticlerical ADJ, SMF anticlerical
anticlericalismo SM anticlericalism
anticlímax SM INV anticlimax
anticonceptivo **©** ADJ birth-control *antes de s*, contraceptive; **métodos** ~**s** methods of birth control; **píldora anticonceptiva** contraceptive pill **©** SM contraceptive
anticongelante ADJ, SM antifreeze
anticonstitucional ADJ unconstitutional
anticristo SM Antichrist
anticuado ADJ [*maquinaria, infraestructura, tecnología*] antiquated; [*moda*] old-fashioned, out-of-date; [*técnica*] obsolete; **quedarse** ~ to go out of date
anticuario/a SM/F (= *comerciante*) antique dealer; (= *coleccionista*) antiquarian, antiquary
anticucho SM (*Perú, Chi*) kebab
anticuerpo SM antibody

antidemocrático ADJ undemocratic
antideportivo ADJ unsporting, unsportsmanlike
antidepresivo ADJ, SM antidepressant
antideslizante ADJ (*Aut*) non-skid; [*piso*] non-slip
antidisturbios **©** ADJ INV **policía** ~ riot police, riot control police **©** SMF member of riot police
antidóping ADJ INV, **antidopaje** ADJ INV **control** ~ drugs test, check for drugs
antídoto SM antidote (**contra** for, to)
antidroga ADJ INV **brigada** ~ drug squad; **campaña** ~ anti-drug campaign
antier ADV (*LAm*) = **anteayer**
antiestático ADJ antistatic
antiestético ADJ unsightly, ugly
antifaz SM mask
antígeno SM antigen
antiglobalización SF anti-globalization
antiglobalizador ADJ anti-globalization *antes de s*
antigripal ADJ INV **vacuna** ~ flu vaccine
antigualla SF old thing, relic; ~**s** old junk *sing*
antiguamente ADV in the past, in the old days
antigüedad SF **1** (= *época*) antiquity; **los artistas de la** ~ the artists of antiquity, the artists of the ancient world **2** (= *edad*) antiquity, age; (*en empleo*) seniority; **la fábrica tiene una** ~ **de 200 años** the factory has been going *o* in existence for 200 years **3** (= *objeto*) antique; **tienda de** ~**es** antique shop (*esp Brit*) *o* store (*EEUU*)
antiguo/a **©** ADJ **1** (= *viejo*) [*ciudad, costumbre*] old; [*coche*] vintage; [*mueble, objeto, libro*] antique; **el Antiguo Testamento** the Old Testament; **a la antigua (usanza)** in the old-fashioned way; **de** *o* **desde** ~ from time immemorial; **nuestra amistad viene de** ~ our friendship dates back a long way **2** (*Hist*) [*civilización, restos*] ancient; **la antigua Grecia** ancient Greece; **Antiguo Régimen** ancien régime; *ver tb* **edad 2 3** (= *anterior*) old, former; **un** ~ **novio** an old boyfriend, an ex-boyfriend; **mi** ~ **jefe** my former boss, my ex-boss; **la antigua Yugoslavia** the former Yugoslavia; **más** ~ [*cliente, socio*] longest-standing; [*empleado, prisionero*] longest-serving; **es más** ~ **que yo en el club** he has been in the club longer than me **4** (= *anticuado*) [*traje, estilo, persona*] old-fashioned; [*mentalidad*] outdated **©** SM/F **1** (= *anticuado*) **tu madre es una antigua** your mother is really old-fashioned, your mother is a real fuddy-duddy* **2** (= *veterano*) **el más** ~ the oldest one **3** (*Hist*) **los** ~**s** the ancients
antihigiénico ADJ unhygienic
antihistamínico ADJ, SM antihistamine
antiincendios ADJ INV **equipo** ~ fire-fighting team; **servicio** ~ fire-fighting services
antiinflamatorio ADJ, SM anti-inflammatory
antillano/a ADJ, SM/F West Indian
Antillas SFPL Antilles, West Indies; **el mar de las** ~ the Caribbean, the Caribbean Sea
antílope SM antelope
antimateria SF antimatter
antimilitarista ADJ, SMF antimilitarist
antimisil ADJ, SM antimissile
antimonopolio ADJ INV, **antimonopolios** ADJ INV **ley** ~ anti-trust law
antinatural ADJ unnatural
antiniebla ADJ INV **faros** ~ fog lamps
antinomia SF antinomy (*frm*), conflict of authority
antinuclear ADJ antinuclear
antipatía SF antipathy (**hacia** towards; **entre** between), dislike (**hacia** for)
antipático ADJ unpleasant, disagreeable

antípodas SFPL antipodes

antiproteccionista ADJ anti-protectionist, free-trade *antes de s*

antirreflectante ADJ anti-glare

antirreglamentario ADJ (= *ilegal*) unlawful, illegal; (*Dep*) foul

antirrobo Ⓐ ADJ INV **sistema ~** anti-theft system Ⓑ SM (*tb* **dispositivo ~**) anti-theft device

antisemitismo SM anti-Semitism

antiséptico ADJ, SM antiseptic

antisudoral ADJ, SM (*LAm*) anti-perspirant

antitabaco ADJ INV anti-smoking

antitanque ADJ anti-tank

antiterrorista ADJ **medidas ~s** measures against terrorism; **Ley Antiterrorista** ≈ Prevention of Terrorism Act

antítesis SF INV antithesis

antitético ADJ antithetic, antithetical

antitranspirante ADJ, SM anti-perspirant

antojadizo ADJ **es muy ~** he's always taking a fancy to something or other

antojarse /1a/ VPR **1** (= *apetecer*) **se le antojó ir a la playa** he took it into his head to go to the beach; **se me antoja una cervecita** I could go for a nice beer **2** (= *parecer*) **se me antoja que no estará** I have the feeling that he won't be in

antojitos* SMPL (*Méx*) (= *tapas*) snacks, nibbles

antojo SM **1** (= *capricho*) whim; **hacer a su ~** to do as one pleases **2** [*de embarazada*] craving; **tener ~s** to have cravings **3** (*Anat*) birthmark

antología SF (= *colección*) anthology; (*Arte*) retrospective; **un gol de ~** a goal for the history books, a goal that will go down in history

antológica SF (*Arte*) retrospective

antológico ADJ **1** (*Arte*) **exposición antológica** retrospective **2** (= *destacado*) memorable; **un gol ~** a goal for the history books, a goal that will go down in history

antónimo SM antonym

antonomasia SF antonomasia; **por ~** par excellence

antorcha SF torch ➤ **la antorcha olímpica** the Olympic torch

antracita SF anthracite

ántrax SM anthrax

antro SM (= *cueva*) cavern; (* *pey*) (= *local*) dive* ➤ **antro de corrupción** den of iniquity

antropofagia SF cannibalism

antropófago/a Ⓐ ADJ man-eating *antes de s*, cannibalistic Ⓑ SM/F cannibal; **~s** anthropophagi (*frm*), cannibals

antropología SF anthropology

antropológico ADJ anthropological

antropólogo/a SM/F anthropologist

anual ADJ [*reunión, periodicidad*] yearly, annual; [*planta*] annual

anualidad SF annual payment

anualmente ADV annually, yearly

anuario SM yearbook, annual

anudar /1a/ VT to knot, tie

anuencia SF consent

anulación SF [*de contrato*] annulment, cancellation; [*de ley*] repeal

anular¹ /1a/ Ⓐ VT **1** [+ *contrato*] to cancel, rescind; [+ *ley*] to repeal; [+ *decisión*] to override; [+ *matrimonio*] to annul **2** [+ *elecciones, resultado*] to declare null and void; [+ *gol, tanto*] to disallow **3** [+ *cita, viaje, evento*] to cancel **4** [+ *cheque*] to cancel **5** [+ *efecto*] to cancel out, destroy **6** [+ *persona*] to overshadow; **su fuerte carácter anula a sus amigos** her strong personality overshadows her friends Ⓑ **anularse** VPR **1** (= *amilanarse*) to fade into the

background; **se anula ante su padre** he fades into the background when his father is there **2** (= *neutralizarse*) **los dos campos magnéticos se anulan** the two magnetic fields cancel each other out

anular² Ⓐ ADJ ring-shaped, annular; **dedo ~** ring finger Ⓑ SM ring finger

Anunciación SF (*Rel*) Annunciation

anunciador(a) SM/F (*Méx*) announcer

anunciante SMF advertiser

anunciar /1b/ Ⓐ VT **1** (*Com*) to advertise **2** (= *hacer público*) to announce; **el ministro anunció su dimisión** the minister announced that he was resigning **3** (= *augurar*) **el pronóstico del tiempo anuncia nevadas** they're forecasting snow, the weather forecast says there will be snow **4** (*frm*) (*a una visita*) to announce; **¿a quién debo ~?** who shall I say it is?, what name should I say? Ⓑ **anunciarse** VPR **1** (*Com*) to advertise **2** (= *augurarse*) **el festival se anuncia animado** it promises to be *o* looks like being a lively festival

anuncio SM **1** (*Com*) (*en un periódico*) advertisement, ad*; (*en TV, radio*) advertisement, commercial ➤ **anuncio publicitario** advertisement, commercial ➤ **anuncios clasificados** classified ads*, classified advertisements, classifieds ➤ **anuncios por palabras** classified ads, small ads (*Brit**) **2** (= *notificación*) announcement; **el ~ de su muerte causó mucha tristeza** the announcement of her death caused great sadness **3** (= *presagio*) omen, sign

anverso SM obverse

anzuelo SM (*para pescar*) fish hook; (= *aliciente*) bait, lure; ✦ MODISMO **picar en el ~** ◇ **tragarse el ~** to swallow the bait

añada SF year, season

añadido SM **1** (*Tip*) addition **2** (= *pelo*) hairpiece

añadidura SF **por ~** in addition, on top of that

añadir /3a/ VT to add (**a** to)

añares SMPL (*LAm*) **hace ~ que ...** it's ages since ...

añejo ADJ **1** [*vino, queso*] mature; [*jamón*] well-cured **2** [*noticia, historia*] old, stale

añicos SMPL **hacer un vaso ~** to smash a glass to pieces *o* to smithereens; **hacer un papel ~** to tear a piece of paper into little *o* tiny bits; **hacerse ~** to shatter; **estar hecho ~** (= *cansado*) to be worn out, be bushed*

añil Ⓐ SM (*Bot*) indigo; (= *color*) indigo; (*para lavado*) blue, bluing Ⓑ ADJ INV indigo

año SM **1** (= *periodo de tiempo*) year; **el ~ pasado** last year; **el ~ próximo** ◇ **el ~ que viene** next year; **el ~ entrante** the coming year; **en el ~ 1980** in 1980; **en los ~s 60** in the sixties; **hace ~s** ◇ **~s ha** years ago; ✦ MODISMOS **estar de buen ~** to look well-fed; **el ~ verde** (*LAm**) never ➤ **año bisiesto** leap year ➤ **año fiscal** tax year ➤ **año luz** light-year; **estar a ~s luz de alguien** to be light-years ahead of sb ➤ **Año Nuevo** New Year ➤ **año sabático** sabbatical (year) **2** [*de edad*] **¿cuántos ~s tienes?** how old are you?; **tengo nueve ~s** I'm nine (years old); **una niña de tres ~s** a three-year-old girl, a girl of three; **a mis ~s** at my age; **entrado en ~s** elderly; **llevar diez ~s a algn** to be ten years older than sb; **de pocos ~s** young; **quitarse ~s** to lie about one's age; **con ese lifting te has quitado diez ~s de encima** you look ten years younger after that face-lift; **sacar ~s a algn** to be older than sb

añojo/a SM/F yearling

añoranza SF nostalgia, yearning, longing (**de** for)

añorar /1a/ VT to yearn for, miss, be homesick for

aorta SF aorta

Ap. ABR (= **apartado postal** *o* **de correos**) PO Box

apa EXCL (*Méx*) goodness me!, good gracious!

apabullante ADJ overwhelming, shattering

apabullar /1a/ VT **1** [+ *rival*] to thrash **2** (= *aturdir*) **no le apabulles con tantas explicaciones** don't overwhelm him with all these explanations; **se le ve apabullado por las circunstancias** he's overwhelmed by the situation, the situation is more than he can handle

apacentar /1j/ VT [+ *ganado*] to graze, feed

apache SMF Apache, Apache Indian

apacheta SF (*And, CS*) cairn, wayside shrine

apachurrar /1a/ VT to crush, squash

apacible ADJ [*animal, persona*] gentle, mild; [*temperamento*] gentle, even; [*tiempo*] calm; [*tarde, noche*] pleasant

apaciguar /1i/ Ⓐ VT to calm down Ⓑ **apaciguarse** VPR to calm down, quieten down

apadrinar /1a/ VT 1 (*Rel*) [+ *niño*] to act as godfather to; [+ *novio*] to be best man for 2 [+ *artista*] to sponsor, be a patron to 3 (= *apoyar*) to back, support

apagado ADJ [*volcán*] extinct; **estar ~** [*fuego*] to be out; [*luz, radio*] to be off 2 [*sonido*] muted, muffled; [*voz*] quiet 3 [*color*] dull 4 [*persona, temperamento*] listless, spiritless; [*mirada*] lifeless, dull

apagar /1h/ Ⓐ VT 1 [+ *fuego, vela, cerilla*] to put out; (*soplando*) to blow out; **apagó el cigarrillo en el cenicero** he put out *o* stubbed out his cigarette in the ashtray; **"por favor, apaguen sus cigarrillos"** "please extinguish all cigarettes"
2 (*Elec*) [+ *luz, televisión*] to turn off, switch off; **apagó el motor y salió del coche** she switched off the engine and got out of the car; **~ el sistema** (*Inform*) to close *o* shut down the system
3 [+ *sed*] to quench
Ⓑ **apagarse** VPR 1 [*fuego, vela*] to go out; (*con el viento*) to blow out; [*volcán*] to become extinct
2 [*luz*] to go out; [*aparato*] (*automáticamente*) to switch off, go off; (*por avería*) to stop working
3 [*ira, rencor, entusiasmo*] to subside, die away
4 [*sonido*] to die away

apagón SM power cut

apaisado ADJ oblong

apalabrar /1a/ VT [*dos personas*] to agree on; **ya tengo apalabrada la obra con el albañil** I've arranged with the builder for the work to be done

Apalaches SMPL (*tb* **Montes ~**) Appalachians

apalancado* ADJ 1 (= *apoltronado*) settled 2 (= *apoyado*) propped (up) 3 (= *estancado*) vegetating

apalancar /1g/ Ⓐ VT 1 (*para levantar*) to lever up 2 (= *para abrir*) to prise *o* (*EEUU*) prize off, lever off 3 (*CS**) **~ a algn** to wangle a job for sb* Ⓑ **apalancarse** (*) VPR 1 (= *apoltronarse*) to settle down 2 (= *apoyarse*) to prop o.s. (up) 3 (= *instalarse*) to settle in 4 (= *estancarse*) to vegetate, go to seed

apaleamiento SM beating, thrashing

apalear /1a/ VT to beat, thrash

apanado SM (*Perú*) beating

apanar /1a/ VT (*LAm*) to coat in breadcrumbs

apando SM (*Méx*) punishment cell

apantallar /1a/ VT 1 (*Méx*) (= *impresionar*) to impress 2 (*RPl*) to fan

apañado ADJ 1 (= *práctico*) [*persona*] clever; [*objeto*] handy 2 (= *ordenado*) neat, tidy 3 (*) **¡estás ~!** you've had it!; **estoy ~ si lo hago** I'll be in trouble if I do it; **~s estaríamos si confiáramos en eso** we'd be fools if we relied on that

apañar /1a/ Ⓐ VT 1 (= *arreglar*) to fix 2 (= *amañar*) [+ *elecciones*] to rig*, fix* 3 (*CS*) (= *encubrir*) [+ *delito, error*] to cover up Ⓑ **apañarse** VPR (*tb* **apañárselas**) (*Esp*) to manage, get by; **yo me (las) apaño con poco dinero** I get by *o* manage without much money; **apáñate(las) como puedas** you'll have to manage as best you can; **ya me (las) ~é para llegar a Sevilla** I'll find a way of getting to Seville somehow

apaño SM 1 (= *arreglo*) **me hizo un ~ en el fregadero** he fixed up the kitchen sink for me 2 (= *trampa*) fix*; **hicieron un ~ para ganar las elecciones** the election was fixed *o* rigged* 3 (= *acuerdo*) deal; **un ~ entre los partidos** a deal between the parties

apapachar* /1a/ VT (*Méx*) 1 (= *abrazar*) to cuddle, hug 2 (= *consentir*) to pamper

apapachos* SMPL (*Méx*) (= *abrazos*) cuddles, hugs; (= *caricias*) caresses

aparador SM 1 (= *mueble*) sideboard 2 (*Méx*) (= *escaparate*) shop window, store window

aparato SM 1 (*Téc*) machine; **uno de esos ~s para hacer café** one of those coffee machines *o* coffee-making things*; **un ~ para medir el nivel de contaminación** a device to measure pollution levels ➤ **aparato de medición** measuring instrument ➤ **aparato de relojería** clockwork mechanism
2 (*Elec*) (= *electrodoméstico*) appliance; (= *televisor, radio*) set ➤ **aparato de radio** radio ➤ **aparato de televisión** television set ➤ **aparato de uso doméstico** domestic appliance ➤ **aparato eléctrico** electrical appliance
3 (*Telec*) phone, telephone; **al ~** speaking; **¡Gerardo, al ~!** Gerardo, telephone!; **ponerse al ~** to come to the phone; **tener a algn al ~** to have sb on the line
4 (*Med*) ➤ **aparato auditivo** hearing aid ➤ **aparato circulatorio** circulatory system ➤ **aparato de ortodoncia** brace, braces pl ➤ **aparato digestivo** digestive system ➤ **aparato para sordos** hearing aid ➤ **aparato respiratorio** respiratory system
5 (*Gimnasia*) (= *máquina*) exercise machine, fitness machine; (= *anillas, barras*) piece of apparatus; **los ~s** the apparatus
6 (*Aer*) aircraft, airplane (*EEUU*)
7 (= *formalismo, artificio*) **todo el ~ con el que viaja un rey** all the pomp and ceremony which accompanies a king when he travels; **nos lo contó con gran ~ de misterio** she told us all about it with a great air of mystery
8 (*Pol*) (= *estructura*) [*de base*] machine; [*de control*] machinery; **el ~ del partido** the party machine, the party apparatus; **un fuerte ~ publicitario** a powerful publicity machine
9 (*Meteo*) **una tormenta con gran ~ eléctrico** a storm with a great deal of thunder and lightning
10 (**) (= *pene*) equipment*

aparatosamente ADV spectacularly; **se marcharon ~ de la reunión** they marched out of the meeting in a dramatic way

aparatoso ADJ 1 (= *exagerado*) [*persona, gestos*] showy, ostentatious; [*objeto, ropa*] flamboyant; **la boda fue muy aparatosa** the wedding was very extravagant *o* over the top* 2 [*accidente, caída*] spectacular, dramatic

aparcamiento SM 1 (= *acción*) parking 2 (= *edificio*) car park (*Brit*), parking lot (*EEUU*) ➤ **aparcamiento subterráneo** underground car park (*Brit*) *o* parking lot (*EEUU*); (= *plaza*) parking space

aparcar /1g/ Ⓐ VT 1 [+ *vehículo*] to park 2 (*) (= *aplazar*) [+ *proyecto de ley*] to shelve; [+ *idea*] to put on the back burner Ⓑ VI to park

aparcería SF (*Agr*) share-cropping

aparcero/a SM/F (*Agr*) sharecropper

apareamiento SM mating

aparear /1a/ Ⓐ VT [+ *animales*] to mate Ⓑ **aparearse** VPR to mate

aparecer /2d/ Ⓐ VI 1 (= *presentarse*) to appear, turn up*; **apareció en casa sin avisar** he appeared *o* turned up* at the house without warning
2 [*algo oculto*] to appear, turn up*; **aparecieron dos nuevos cadáveres en la fosa** two more bodies appeared *o* turned up* in the trench
3 [*algo perdido*] to reappear, turn up*; **ya ha aparecido mi paraguas** my umbrella has finally reappeared *o* turned up*
4 (= *surgir*) to appear; **han aparecido los primeros síntomas** the first symptoms have appeared
5 (= *editarse*) [*libro, disco*] to come out
6 (= *figurar*) [*dato, nombre*] to appear; **mi nombre no aparece en el censo electoral** my name does not appear on the electoral register, my name is not on the electoral register
Ⓑ **aparecerse** VPR [*fantasma, espíritu*] to appear

aparecido/a SM/F ghost

aparejado/a ADJ **ir ~ con** to go hand in hand with; **llevar** *o* **traer algo ~** to entail sth

aparejador(a) SM/F quantity surveyor

aparejar /1a/ VT (= *preparar*) to prepare, get ready; [+ *caballo*] to saddle, harness; (*Náut*) to fit out, rig out; [+ *lienzo*] to size, prime

aparejo SM (= *poleas*) lifting gear, block and tackle; (*Náut*) rigging; (*Arquit*) bond, bonding ➤ **aparejos de pesca** fishing tackle

aparentar /1a/ ⒶVT **1** (= *parecer*) to look; **no aparenta su edad** *o* **sus años** she doesn't look her age; **aparenta ser más joven de lo que es** he looks younger than he is **2** (= *fingir*) [+ *interés, sorpresa, indiferencia*] to feign; **aparenta estar estudiando** he pretends to be studying Ⓑ VI to show off

aparente ADJ **1** (= *no real*) apparent; **su interés es sólo ~** he just pretends to be interested, he just feigns interest **2** (= *patente*) apparent; **sin motivo ~** for no apparent reason **3** (*) (= *atractivo*) [*objeto*] pretty; [*persona*] good-looking

aparentemente ADV seemingly, apparently

aparición SF **1** (= *acto*) appearance; (= *publicación*) publication; **un libro de próxima ~** a forthcoming book ➤ **aparición en público** public appearance **2** (= *fantasma*) apparition, spectre

apariencia SF appearance; **bajo su ~ despistada hay un genio** behind his absent-minded appearance he is a genius; **una chica con ~ de alemana** a German-looking girl; **en ~, el coche estaba en perfecto estado** to all appearances, the car was in perfect condition; **guardar** *o* **salvar las ~s** to keep up appearances; ✦ MODISMO **las ~s engañan** appearances can be deceptive

apartado Ⓐ ADJ **1** (= *lejano*) remote, isolated; **un pueblo muy ~** a very remote *o* isolated village; **su casa está un poco apartada** her house is a little out-of-the-way; **~** [*lugar*] far from; [*persona*] isolated from; **ha conseguido mantenerse ~ de los problemas** she's managed to keep out of the problems **2** (= *solitario*) [*vida, persona*] solitary Ⓑ SM **1** (*Correos*) (*tb* **~ de correos, ~ postal**) Post Office box, P.O. Box, box number **2** (= *sección*) (*Literat*) section; (*Jur*) section, sub-section; **en el ~ de sanidad** in the area of health

apartahotel SM aparthotel (*Brit*), apartment hotel (*EEUU*)

apartamento SM apartment

apartamiento SM **1** (= *separación*) separation **2** (= *aislamiento*) seclusion, isolation

apartar /1a/ ⒶVT **1** (= *separar*) **aparta las piezas blancas de las negras** separate the white pieces from the black ones; **si no los apartamos se matarán** if we don't separate them they'll kill each other; **aparta la sartén del fuego** take the pan off the heat; **aparta al niño de la ventana** move the child away from the window; **no podía ~ mi pensamiento de ella** I couldn't get her out of my head; **su enfermedad la apartó de la política activa** her illness kept her away from playing an active role in politics; **~ la mirada/los ojos de algo** to look away from sth, avert one's gaze/one's eyes from sth (*liter*); **no aparta los ojos de la comida** he can't keep his eyes off the food **2** (= *quitar de en medio*) **tuvo que ~ los papeles de la mesa para colocar allí sus libros** he had to push aside the papers on the table to place his books there; **le apartó los cabellos de la frente** she brushed her hair off her forehead; **avanzaban apartando la maleza** they made their way through the undergrowth, pushing *o* brushing it aside as they went; **los guardaespaldas apartaban a las fans** the bodyguards pushed the fans aside *o* away **3** (= *reservar*) to put aside, set aside; **hemos apartado un poco de comida para él** we've put *o* set aside a little food for him; **picar las verduras y ~las a un lado** chop the vegetables and put them to one side Ⓑ **apartarse** VPR **1** (= *quitarse de en medio*) to move out of the way; **se apartó a tiempo para evitar el puñetazo** he moved aside *o* moved out of the way to avoid the punch; **se ~on para dejarla pasar** they moved aside to let her through; **¡apártense! ¡que está herido!** out of the way *o* stand clear! he's wounded!; **~se de** [+ *persona, lugar, teoría*] to move away from; [+ *camino, ruta*] to stray from, wander off; [+ *actividad, creencia*] to abandon; **apártate del fuego**

get *o* move away from the fire; **nunca se aparta de mi lado** she never leaves my side; **no se aparta del teléfono por si suena** she's always sitting by the phone in case it rings; **consiguió ~se de la bebida** he managed to give up drinking; **¡apártate de mi vista!** get out of my sight!; ✦ MODISMO **~se del buen camino** to go off the straight and narrow **2** (= *distanciarse*) [*dos personas*] to part, separate; [*dos objetos*] to become separated; **con el tiempo se han ido apartando** they have drifted *o* grown apart with time; **las cifras se apartan de las predicciones** the figures are far off the predictions; **el libro se aparta del realismo sentimentalista** the book diverges *o* strays from sentimentalist realism

aparte Ⓐ ADV INV separate; **guárdalo en un cajón ~** keep it in a different *o* separate drawer; **lo tuyo es un caso ~** you're a special case; **capítulo ~ merece la corrupción política** another question altogether is political corruption; **mantenerse ~** to keep away Ⓑ ADV **1** (= *a un lado*) **se la llevó ~ para contarle sus confidencias** he took her aside to confide in her; **bromas ~, ¿qué os parece?** joking aside *o* seriously though, what do you think?; **diferencias ideológicas ~, perseguimos el mismo fin** ideological differences aside, we're after the same thing; **poner algo ~** to put sth aside **2** (= *por separado*) separately; **lavar las toallas ~** wash the towels separately **3** (= *además*) besides; **~, yo ya soy mayorcita para que me manden** besides, I'm too old to be bossed around like that; **—¿y se niega a pagar el alquiler? —sí, eso** —"and he doesn't pay the rent?" — "yes, that as well *o* that too" **4** **~ de** apart from; **~ del mal tiempo, las vacaciones fueron estupendas** apart from the bad weather, the holidays were great (*esp Brit*) *o* the vacation was great (*EEUU*); **~ de que** apart from the fact that Ⓒ SM **1** (*Teat*) aside **2** (*Tip*) **punto y ~** new paragraph

apartheid SM apartheid

aparthotel SM aparthotel (*Brit*), apartment hotel (*EEUU*)

apartidista ADJ apolitical, non-party *antes de s*

apasionado ADJ [*persona*] passionate; [*discurso*] impassioned; **~ por algo** passionate about sth

apasionamiento SM passion, enthusiasm

apasionante ADJ exciting, thrilling

apasionar /1a/ ⒶVT **le apasiona el teatro de Shakespeare** he loves Shakespeare's plays; **le apasionan los ordenadores** he's crazy about computers; **el grupo que apasiona a las quinceañeras** the group the teenagers are crazy about; **a mí el fútbol no me apasiona** I'm not exactly passionate about football Ⓑ **apasionarse** VPR to get excited; **~se con algo** to get excited about sth; **~se por algo: se apasionó por la idea de una Europa única** he became very excited by the idea of a united Europe

apatía SF apathy

apático ADJ apathetic

apátrida Ⓐ ADJ **1** (= *sin nacionalidad*) stateless **2** (*CS*) (= *sin patriotismo*) unpatriotic Ⓑ SMF (*CS*) unpatriotic person

Apdo. ABR, **apdo.** ABR (= **apartado postal** *o* **de correos**) PO Box

apeadero SM (*Ferro*) halt, stopping place

apear /1a/ ⒶVT **1** (= *disuadir*) **~ a algn de su opinión** to persuade sb that his opinion is wrong **2** (= *tratamiento a algn*) to drop sb's title Ⓑ **apearse** VPR (*de caballo, mula*) to dismount; (*de tren, autobús*) to get off, alight (*frm*); ✦ MODISMO **no ~se del burro** to refuse to climb *o* back down

apechugar* /1h/ VI **~ con** (= *aguantar*) to put up with, swallow; [+ *cometido*] (= *cargar con*) to take on; **~ con las consecuencias** to take the consequences

apedrear /1a/ VT (*como castigo*) to stone; (*en pelea*) to throw stones at

apegado ADJ attached, devoted (**a** to)

apego SM attachment (**a** to), devotion (**a** to)

apelación SF (*Jur*) appeal; **presentar una ~** to lodge an appeal

apelar /1a/ **Ⓐ** VI 1 (*Jur*) to appeal; **~ contra algo** to appeal (against) sth 2 **~ a** (= *invocar*) to appeal to; **apeló al sentido común** he appealed to people's common sense **Ⓑ** VT (*Jur*) to appeal (against)

apelativo SM 1 (*Ling*) term of address 2 (= *sobrenombre*) nickname

apellidarse /1a/ VPR to be called; **¿cómo se apellida usted?** what's your surname *o* (*EEUU*) last name?

apellido SM surname, last name (*EEUU*) ➤ **apellido de soltera** maiden name

APELLIDO

In the Spanish-speaking world most people use two **apellidos**, the first being their father's first surname, and the second their mother's first surname: e.g. the surname of the children of Juan **García López**, married to Carmen **Pérez Rodríguez** would be **García Pérez**. Married women normally retain their own surnames but in exceptional cases they add their husband's first surname to their first surname: e.g. Carmen Pérez de García. In such cases she could also be referred to as **la señora de García**.

apelmazado ADJ 1 (= *compacto*) [*masa*] compact, solid; [*salsa, líquido*] thick, lumpy; [*pelo*] matted 2 [*estilo*] clumsy

apelotonarse /1a/ VPR [*gente*] to mass, crowd together

apenado ADJ 1 (= *triste*) sad 2 (*LAm*) (= *avergonzado*) embarrassed

apenar /1a/ **Ⓐ** VT to sadden **Ⓑ** **apenarse** VPR 1 (= *afligirse*) to be sad 2 (*LAm*) (= *avergonzarse*) to be embarrassed

apenas **Ⓐ** ADV 1 (= *casi no*) hardly, scarcely (*más frm*); **(si) nos habló durante toda la cena** he hardly *o* barely *o* scarcely said a word to us throughout the whole dinner; **cocinan sin ~ aceite** they cook with hardly any oil; **no sé ~ nada de ese tema** I know hardly anything about that subject, I know almost nothing *o* next to nothing about that subject
2 (= *indicando frecuencia*) hardly ever; **ahora ~ voy** I hardly ever go now
3 (= *indicando tiempo transcurrido*) only; **hace ~ un año que nos conocimos** it's only a year ago that we met; **~ había cumplido quince años cuando ...** he'd only just turned fifteen when ...; **~ me había acostado cuando oí un ruido** hardly *o* scarcely *o* no sooner had I gone to bed when I heard a strange noise
Ⓑ CONJ (*esp LAm*) (= *en cuanto*) as soon as; **~ llegue, te llamo** I'll phone you as soon as I arrive

Apenas suele traducirse por **hardly** o **scarcely**, que es más formal. Cuando modifican a un verbo, estos adverbios van detrás de los auxiliares y modales y delante del verbo principal: "Apenas podía hablar después del accidente", *He could hardly speak after the accident*; "Apenas nos conocemos", *We hardly know each other*. En cambio se traduce por **hardly ever** cuando se refiere a la frecuencia de una acción: "Apenas veo la tele", *I hardly ever watch TV*.

apencar* /1g/ VI to slave away*

apendejarse /1a/ VPR (*Carib, Col*) to get silly, act the fool

apéndice SM 1 (*Anat, Literat*) appendix 2 (= *satélite*) appendage

apendicitis SF INV appendicitis

apercibir /3a/ **Ⓐ** VT 1 (= *avisar*) to warn, advise 2 (*Jur*) to caution **Ⓑ** **apercibirse** VPR **~se de** to notice

apergaminado ADJ [*papel*] parchment-like; [*piel*] dried up, wrinkled; [*cara*] wizened

aperitivo SM (= *comida*) appetizer; (= *bebida*) aperitif

apero SM 1 (*Agr*) implement 2 (*LAm*) (= *arneses*) harness, trappings *pl*

apertura SF 1 (= *acción*) opening; **la ~ de las puertas es automática** the doors open automatically 2 (= *comienzo*) start, beginning; **hoy se celebra la ~ del curso académico** today is the start *o* beginning of the new academic year; **ceremonia de ~** opening ceremony; **sesión de ~** opening session 3 (*Fot*) aperture 4 (*Pol*) (= *liberalización*) opening-up

aperturismo SM (= *liberalización*) liberalization, relaxation; (*Pol*) (= *política*) policy of liberalization

APERTURISMO

In the final years of the Franco régime and after Franco's death in 1975, politicians who wanted to liberalize and democratize the political system were known as **aperturistas** while diehard right-wingers who wanted the régime or something very similar to continue were known as **inmovilistas**.

aperturista **Ⓐ** ADJ liberalizing, liberal **Ⓑ** SMF liberalizer, liberal

apesadumbrado ADJ sad, distressed

apestado ADJ 1 (= *con la peste*) plague-ridden 2 (*CS**) (= *enfermo*) **no te beso porque estoy apestada** I won't kiss you because I don't want you to catch anything

apestar /1a/ VI to stink, reek (**a** of)

apestoso ADJ stinking, reeking; [*olor*] awful, putrid

apetecer /2d/ VI **me apetece un helado** I feel like *o* (*Brit*) I fancy an ice cream

Recuérdese que **feel like** y **fancy** rigen que el verbo que les siga inmediatamente aparezca en gerundio y no en infinitivo:

¿te apetece dar un paseo? do you feel like *o* (*Brit*) fancy going for a walk?; **¿te apetece?** how about it?, would you like to?; **un vaso de jerez siempre apetece** a glass of sherry is always welcome

apetecible ADJ attractive, tempting

apetencia SF hunger (**de** for)

apetito SM (= *gana de comer*) appetite (**de** for); **abrir el ~** to whet one's appetite; **ese olor me está abriendo el ~** that smell is making me hungry; **comer con ~** to eat heartily *o* with appetite; **siempre tiene muy buen ~** he's always got a good *o* hearty appetite ➤ **apetito sexual** sexual appetite

apetitoso ADJ (= *gustoso*) appetizing; (= *sabroso*) tasty; (= *tentador*) tempting, attractive

apiadarse /1a/ VPR **~ de** to pity, take pity on

ápice SM **ni un ~** not a whit; **no ceder un ~** not to yield an inch

apicultor(a) SM/F beekeeper, apiarist (*frm*)

apicultura SF beekeeping, apiculture (*frm*)

apilar /1a/ **Ⓐ** VT to pile up, heap up **Ⓑ** **apilarse** VPR to pile up, mount

apiñado ADJ crammed, packed

apiñar /1a/ **Ⓐ** VT (= *agrupar*) to crowd together, bunch together; (= *apretar*) to pack in **Ⓑ** **apiñarse** VPR to crowd together, press together

apio SM celery ➤ **apio nabo** celeriac

apiolarse* /1a/ VPR (*RPl*) to wise up*

apisonadora SF steamroller, road roller

apisonar /1a/ VT to roll, roll flat

aplacar /1g/ **Ⓐ** VT [+ *persona*] to appease, placate; [+ *hambre*] to satisfy; [+ *sed*] to quench, satisfy; **intenté ~ los ánimos de todos** I tried to calm everyone down **Ⓑ** **aplacarse** VPR [*tormenta*] to die down; **al final se ~on los ánimos** people finally calmed down

aplanacalles* SM INV (*LAm*) idler, lazybones, layabout (*esp Brit**)

aplanado ADJ 1 [*superficie*] levelled, leveled (*EEUU*) 2 (*) [*persona*] **la noticia lo dejó ~** he was stunned by the news

aplanar /1a/ VT to level, make even

aplastante ADJ overwhelming, crushing

aplastar /1a/ ⓐ VT 1 [con pie] to squash, crush 2 (= vencer) to crush, overwhelm ⓑ **aplastarse** VPR (= quedarse plano) to be squashed; [coche] to crash, smash (**contra** on, against)

aplatanarse* /1a/ VPR to become lethargic, sink into lethargy

aplaudir /3a/ ⓐ VT 1 [+ actuación] to applaud 2 (= aprobar) to welcome, approve ⓑ VI (= dar palmadas) to applaud, clap

aplauso SM **un** ~ a round of applause; **~s** applause sing, clapping sing

aplausómetro SM clapometer

aplazamiento SM [de acto] postponement; [de pago] deferment

aplazar /1f/ VT 1 (= posponer) [+ reunión, juicio] (antes de iniciarse) to postpone, put back; (ya iniciado) to adjourn; [+ pago] to defer; **ha aplazado su decisión hasta su regreso** he has postponed o put off the decision until his return 2 (RPI) [+ estudiante] to fail

aplazo SM (RPI) fail

aplicable ADJ applicable; **un ejemplo ~ en la mayoría de los casos** an example applicable o that can be applied to the majority of cases

aplicación SF 1 (= uso externo) (tb Med) use, application (frm); **una o dos aplicaciones diarias** to be applied once or twice daily; **"sólo para aplicación externa"** "for external use only"; ~ **tópica** external use 2 (= puesta en práctica) [de acuerdo, impuesto, medida] implementation, application; [de método] implementation; [de sanción, castigo] imposition; **en ~ de la ley 9/1968** in accordance with law 9/1968 3 (= dedicación) application; **le falta ~ en el estudio** he doesn't apply himself enough to his studies, le lacks application in his studies (frm) 4 **aplicaciones** (= usos) (Téc) uses, applications; (Com, Inform) applications 5 (Bol, Col, Ven) (= solicitud) application

aplicado ADJ 1 [ciencia] applied 2 (= estudioso) conscientious, diligent; **es muy ~ en matemáticas** he works very hard at mathematics

aplicador SM applicator

aplicar /1g/ ⓐ VT 1 (= poner) 1.1 (Med) [+ crema, pomada] to apply; [+ inyección, tratamiento] to give, administer (frm) (**a** to) 1.2 (frm) [+ pintura, pegamento] to apply (frm) 2 (= poner en práctica) [+ teoría] to put into practice; [+ técnica] to use; [+ principio] to apply; [+ descuento] to give; [+ sanción, castigo] to impose, apply; **le ~on la legislación antiterrorista en el interrogatorio** he was questioned under anti-terrorist laws; **durante el verano aplicamos descuentos especiales** during the summer we offer o give special discounts 3 (= dedicar) ~ **a algo** [+ esfuerzo, tiempo] to devote to sth; [+ recursos] to apply to sth ⓑ VI (Bol, Col, Ven) to apply; ~ **a algo** to apply for sth ⓒ **aplicarse** VPR (= esforzarse) **si no te aplicas más, vas a suspender** if you don't work harder o if you don't apply yourself to your studies, you are going to fail; **~se en algo** to work hard at sth

aplique SM (= lámpara) wall lamp; (en mueble) overlay; (Cos) appliqué

aplomo SM assurance, self-possession

apocado ADJ timid

apocalipsis SM INV apocalypse; **el Apocalipsis** (Biblia) Revelations

apocamiento SM timidity

apocopar /1a/ VT to apocopate (frm), shorten

apócope SF apocope, apocopation; **"san" es ~ de "santo"** "san" is an apocopated form of "santo"

apócrifo ADJ apocryphal

apodar /1a/ VT to nickname, dub

apoderado/a SM/F agent, representative; (Jur) proxy, attorney; (Mús, Dep) manager

apoderar /1a/ ⓐ VT 1 (= autorizar) to authorize, empower 2 (Jur) to grant power of attorney to ⓑ **apoderarse** VPR **~se de** to seize, take possession of

apodo SM nickname

apogeo SM peak, height; **estar en el ~ de su fama** to be at the height of one's fame

apolillar /1a/ ⓐ VI (RPI*) to sleep ⓑ **apolillarse** VPR to get moth-eaten

apolíneo ADJ (Mit) Apollonian; (= hermoso) classically handsome

apolítico ADJ apolitical

apología SF defence, defense (EEUU); **una ~ del terrorismo** a statement in support o in defence o (EEUU) in defense of terrorism

⚠ **apología** ≠ **apology**

apoltronarse /1a/ VPR **se apoltronó en el sofá** she settled down on the sofa; **desde que se jubiló se ha apoltronado y no hace nada** he has taken it very easy since he retired and never does anything much

apoplejía SF apoplexy, stroke

apoquinar* /1a/ VT to fork out*, cough up*

aporrear /1a/ VT 1 (= pegar) to beat, club; (= dar una paliza a) to beat up 2 [+ puerta, piano] to hammer at

aportación SF contribution

aportar /1a/ VT 1 [+ bienes, dinero] to contribute; **su estudio no aporta nada nuevo** his study contributes nothing new; **aporta el 25% del calcio necesario** it provides 25% of the calcium requirement 2 [+ pruebas] to provide

aporte SM 1 (= nutricional) intake; **un mayor ~ de vitaminas** higher vitamin intake 2 (RPI) (monetario) contribution ➤ **aporte jubilatorio** pension contribution

aposentar /1a/ ⓐ VT to lodge, put up ⓑ **aposentarse** VPR to lodge, put up (**en** at)

aposento SM (= cuarto) room; (= hospedaje) lodging

aposición SF apposition; **en ~** in apposition

apósito SM (Med) dressing

aposta ADV on purpose, deliberately

apostar¹ /1a/ ⓐ VT (Mil) to station, position ⓑ **apostarse** VPR **~se en un lugar** to position o.s. in o at a place

apostar² /1l/ ⓐ VT to bet; **aposté diez libras al ganador** I bet ten pounds on the winner; **apuesto lo que sea a que es mentira** I'll bet you anything that it's a lie ⓑ VI to bet; ~ **por algo: no todo el mundo apostaba por su éxito** not everyone believed in his success; **han apostado por una política de neutralidad** they have committed themselves to a policy of neutrality; ~ **a que** to bet that; **apuesto a que no lo encontráis** I bet that you don't find it ⓒ **apostarse** VPR to bet; **¿qué te apuestas a que gano yo?** what do you bet that I'll win?

apóstata SMF apostate

apostatar /1a/ VI (Rel) to apostatize (**de** from)

a posteriori ADV 1 (= después) (gen) at a later stage; [comprender] with (the benefit of) hindsight 2 (Lógica, Jur) a posteriori

apostilla SF footnote

apostillar /1a/ VT 1 (= poner apostillas a) to add notes to, annotate 2 (= agregar) to add

apóstol SM (Rel) apostle

apostolado SM apostolate ➤ **apostolado seglar** lay ministry

apostólico ADJ apostolic

apóstrofo SM apostrophe

apostura SF (= elegancia) elegance; (= belleza) good looks pl

apoteósico ADJ huge, tremendous

apoteosis SF INV apotheosis

apoyabrazos SM INV armrest

apoyacabezas SM INV headrest

apoyalibros SM INV book end

apoyar /1a/ Ⓐ VT 1 (= reclinar) to rest, lean; **apoya la cabeza en mi hombro** rest o lean your head on my shoulder; **apoya la bicicleta contra la pared** lean the bicycle against the wall
2 (= ayudar, secundar) to support; **no me apoyan en nada de lo que hago** they don't support me in anything I do Ⓑ **apoyarse** VPR 1 (= reclinarse) to lean (**en** on); **apóyate aquí** lean on this; **~se contra algo** to lean against sth; **la cúpula se apoya en tres pilares** the dome is supported by three pillars
2 (= confiar) **~se en algn** to rely on sb; **se apoyó en sus amigos para pasar la crisis** she relied on her friends to get through the crisis

apoyo SM support; **siempre cuento con el ~ de mis padres** I can always rely on my parents' support ➤ **apoyo psicológico** counselling, counseling (EEUU)

apozarse /1f/ VPR (And, CS) to form a pool

apreciable ADJ [mejora, descenso] appreciable, substantial; [cantidad] considerable; **~ al oído** audible

apreciación SF 1 (= evaluación) appreciation, appraisal; (Com, Fin) valuation, appraisal (EEUU); **según nuestra ~** according to our estimation 2 (= subida) appreciation

apreciado ADJ worthy, esteemed

apreciar /1b/ Ⓐ VT 1 (= sentir afecto por) to be fond of, like; **aprecio mucho a tu padre** I'm very fond of your father
2 (= dar valor a) to value; **~ algo (en) mucho** to value sth highly
3 [+ comida, música] to appreciate; **no sabe ~ un buen vino** he doesn't know how to appreciate a good wine
4 (= agradecer) to appreciate; **aprecio mucho lo que han hecho por mí** I really appreciate what they've done for me
5 (= percibir) **como se aprecia en la radiografía ...** as you can see in the X-ray ...; **no apreció el sarcasmo en sus palabras** he didn't notice o detect the sarcasm in her words
6 (Fin) [+ moneda] to revalue Ⓑ **apreciarse** VPR [moneda] to appreciate, rise (in value)

apreciativo ADJ appreciative

aprecio SM appreciation; **tener a algn en gran ~** to hold sb in high regard

aprehender /2a/ VT [+ persona] to apprehend, detain; [+ bienes] to seize

apremiante ADJ urgent, pressing

apremiar /1b/ Ⓐ VT to urge, urge on, press; **~ a algn a hacer algo** ◇ **~ a algn para que haga algo** to press sb to do sth Ⓑ VI to be urgent; **el tiempo apremia** time is pressing

apremio SM urgency, pressure

aprender /2a/ Ⓐ VT to learn; **~ algo de memoria** to learn sth (off) by heart, memorize sth; **~ a hacer algo** to learn to do sth Ⓑ VI to learn Ⓒ **aprenderse** VPR = Ⓐ

aprendiz(a) SM/F [de oficio] apprentice; (en oficina) trainee, intern (EEUU)

aprendizaje SM 1 [de oficio] apprenticeship; [en oficina] training period, internship (EEUU) 2 (= el aprender) learning; **dificultades de ~** learning difficulties

aprensión SF 1 (= miedo) apprehension, fear 2 (= reparo) misgiving; (= escrúpulos) squeamishness

aprensivo ADJ (= preocupado) apprehensive, worried; (= escrupuloso) squeamish

apresamiento SM capture

apresar /1a/ VT 1 (= coger) to catch; [+ criminal] to capture, catch; [+ buque] to take 2 [animal] to seize

aprestar /1a/ (frm) Ⓐ VT (= preparar) to prepare, get ready; [+ tejido] to size Ⓑ **aprestarse** VPR to prepare, get ready; **~se a** o **para hacer algo** to prepare o get ready to do sth

apresurado ADJ [decisión, movimiento, conclusión] hasty; [paso] quick

apresuramiento SM hurry, haste

apresurar /1a/ Ⓐ VT (= dar prisa a) to hurry, hurry along;

(= acelerar) to speed up; [+ paso] to quicken Ⓑ **apresurarse** VPR to hurry, make haste; **~se a hacer algo** to hurry to do sth

apretado ADJ 1 [tapa, tornillo, ropa] tight 2 (= difícil) difficult; **épocas muy apretadas** quite difficult o hard times; **andamos muy ~s de dinero** we are very short of money 3 (= ocupado) [agenda, programa] busy
4 (= apretujado) (en asiento, vehículo) squashed, cramped
5 (*) (= tacaño) tight-fisted*, tight* 6 (Ven) (= aprovechado) **usa el teléfono sin pedir permiso ¡qué ~ es!** he uses the phone without asking permission, he's got a lot of nerve o a real cheek!*

apretar /1j/ Ⓐ VT 1 [+ tapa, tornillo, nudo] to tighten
2 (= pulsar) [+ interruptor, tecla] to press; [+ gatillo] to squeeze, pull; **~ el acelerador** to put one's foot down (on the accelerator), depress the accelerator (frm)
3 (= apretujar) 3.1 [+ objeto] to clutch; **hay que ~ el compost con los dedos** you have to press the compost down with your fingers; **~ los dientes** to grit one's teeth, clench one's teeth; **~ la mano a algn** to shake sb's hand; **~ el puño** to clench one's fist
3.2 [+ persona] (contra pared, suelo) to pin, press; (con los brazos) to clasp, clutch
4 (= presionar) **~ a algn** to put pressure on sb; ♦ MODISMO **~ las clavijas** o **las tuercas a algn** to put o tighten the screws on sb
5 **~ el paso** to quicken one's pace
6 **aprieta mucho la letra cuando escribe** he bunches up the words when he writes Ⓑ VI 1 (= oprimir) [zapatos] to be too tight, pinch one's feet; [ropa] to be too tight; **este vestido me aprieta en la cintura** this dress is too tight for me around the waist
2 (= aumentar) [dolor, frío] to get worse; [viento] to intensify; **es media mañana y el hambre aprieta** it's half way through the morning and I'm beginning to feel hungry; **donde más aprieta el calor** where the heat is at its worst
3 (= presionar) to put on the pressure
4 (= esforzarse) **si apretáis un poco al final, aprobaréis** if you make an extra effort at the end, you'll pass
5 (Chi) (= irse con prisa) **apretemos que viene la profesora** let's run for it, the teacher's coming; **fueron los primeros en salir apretando después del golpe** they were the first ones to make a getaway after the coup
6 (**) (al defecar) to push Ⓒ **apretarse** VPR 1 (= arrimarse) (en asiento) to move up, squeeze up (esp Brit); (para abrigarse) to huddle together; **los diez sospechosos se apretaban en dos bancos** the ten suspects were squeezed together on two benches
2 **~se el cinturón** to tighten one's belt

apretón SM 1 (= presión) squeeze 2 (= abrazo) hug
➤ **apretón de manos** handshake 3 (euf) [de vientre] urgent call of nature (euf)

apretujar /1a/ VT (= apretar) to press hard, squeeze hard; (= estrujar) to crush, crumple

apretujón SM 1 (= apretón) hard squeeze; (= abrazo) big hug, bear hug 2 (= agolpamiento) press, crush, jam

aprieto SM predicament; **estar** o **verse en un ~** to be in a predicament, be in an awkward situation; **poner a algn en un ~** to put sb in a predicament, put sb in an awkward situation

a priori ADV 1 (= antes) (gen) beforehand; [juzgar] in advance 2 (Lógica, Jur) a priori

aprisa ADV quickly, hurriedly

aprisco SM sheepfold

aprisionar /1a/ VT to imprison, put in prison

aprobación SF [de ley] passing; [de informe, plan, acuerdo] approval, endorsement; **necesito tu ~ para realizar la venta** I need your approval o endorsement to go ahead with the sale

aprobado SM pass (Brit), passing grade (EEUU)

aprobar /1l/ Ⓐ VT 1 [+ ley, proyecto de ley] to pass; [+ informe, plan, acuerdo] to approve, endorse; **el parlamento aprobó el tratado** the treaty was approved o endorsed by Parliament 2 [+ examen, asignatura] to pass; **no he aprobado las matemáticas** I haven't passed mathematics; **no me han aprobado la literatura** I didn't pass literature **3** [+ *decisión, actitud*] to approve of; **no apruebo tu amistad con esa chica** I don't approve of your friendship with that girl **Ⓑ** VI [*alumno*] to pass

aprobatorio ADJ approving

aprontar /1a/ **Ⓐ** VT (*RPl*) to prepare, get ready **Ⓑ** VPR to get ready

apropiación SF appropriation ➤ **apropiación indebida de fondos** misappropriation of funds, embezzlement

apropiado ADJ appropriate, suitable

apropiarse /1b/ VPR ~ **(de)** algo to appropriate sth

aprovechable ADJ **estas tablas son ~s para hacer cajas** those boards can be used to make boxes; **esa camisa es ~ todavía** you can still wear that shirt, that shirt is still wearable

aprovechado/a **Ⓐ** ADJ **1** (= *usado*) **terrenos muy poco ~s** lands that have not been made the best of; **bien ~** [*dinero, tiempo*] well-spent; [*espacio, recursos*] well-exploited; [*oportunidad*] well-taken, well-used; **el espacio está muy bien ~ en esta casa** good use has been made of the space in this house; **mal ~** [*dinero, tiempo, oportunidad*] wasted; [*espacio, recursos*] badly-exploited **2** (= *oportunista*) selfish, self-seeking; **ese vendedor es muy ~** that salesman is a real opportunist **3** (= *aplicado*) [*trabajador*] industrious, hardworking; [*alumno*] resourceful **Ⓑ** SM/F (= *oportunista*) scrounger*, opportunist

aprovechamiento SM **1** (= *utilización*) use; **un mejor ~ del espacio** a better use of space **2** (= *provecho*) **conseguir** o **sacar el máximo ~ de algo** to get the maximum use o advantage out of sth, make the most of sth

aprovechar /1a/ **Ⓐ** VT **1** (= *utilizar*) use; **un intento de ~ los recursos naturales de la zona** an attempt to take advantage of o use the area's natural resources; **ha sabido ~ la ocasión y hacer un buen negocio** he managed to take advantage o use the opportunity to make a profitable deal; **~ algo para hacer algo: vamos a ~ este espacio para hacer un armario** we are going to use this space for a wardrobe; **aproveché que tenía una tarde libre para ir de compras** I took the opportunity of having an afternoon off to go shopping; **quiero ~ esta oportunidad para agradecerles a todos su apoyo** I want to take this opportunity to thank everyone for their support **2** (= *sacar el máximo provecho de*) [+ *tiempo, espacio, ocasión*] to make the most of; [+ *conocimientos, experiencia*] to make use of, make good use of; **saber ~ el tiempo** to know how to make the most of o get the most out of your time; **para ~ mejor el espacio** to make better use of the space **Ⓑ** VI **1** (= *obtener provecho*) **tú que eres soltera, aprovecha** make the most of the fact that you're single; **~ para hacer algo** to take the opportunity to do sth; **salió a pasear y aprovechó para hacer unas compras** he went out for a walk and took the opportunity to do some shopping; **¡que aproveche!** enjoy your meal!, bon appétit!, enjoy! (*EEUU*) **2** (= *progresar*) to progress **Ⓒ** **aprovecharse** VPR **1** (= *abusar*) to take advantage; **todos se aprovechan de mí** everybody takes advantage of me **2** (*Esp*) (= *sacar provecho*) **aprovechaos ahora que tenéis tiempo** make the most of it now that you have time **3** (*en sentido sexual*) **~se de** [+ *adulto*] to take advantage of; [+ *niño*] to abuse

aprovisionar /1a/ **Ⓐ** VT to supply **Ⓑ** **aprovisionarse** VPR **~se de algo** (*para usar*) to get one's supply of sth; (*para almacenar*) to stock up with sth

aproximación SF **1** (*Mat*) approximation (**a** to) **2** (= *acercamiento*) approach (**a** to); (*Pol*) rapprochement

aproximadamente ADV approximately

aproximado ADJ [*distancia, duración, tamaño*] approximate; [*cálculo*] rough

aproximar /1a/ **Ⓐ** VT to bring near, bring nearer (**a** to); **~ una silla** to bring a chair over, draw up a chair **Ⓑ** **aproximarse** VPR **1** (= *arrimarse*) to come near, come closer; **~se a** to near, approach **2** **~se a** [+ *cierta edad*] to be nearly, be getting on for (*Brit*)

aproximativo ADJ [*cantidad, cifra*] approximate; [*cálculo*] rough

aptitud SF **1** (= *conveniencia*) suitability, fitness (**para** for) **2** (= *capacidad*) aptitude, ability ➤ **aptitud para los negocios** business sense

apto ADJ (= *idóneo*) suitable, fit (**para** for, to); **no ~ (para menores)** (*Cine*) unsuitable for children; **~ para el servicio** (*Mil*) fit for military service

apuesta SF **1** (*en juego*) bet; **hagan sus ~s, señores** place your bets, ladies and gentlemen **2** (= *opción*) **nuestra ~ por la modernización** our commitment to modernization

apuesto ADJ handsome

apunamiento SM (*And, CS*) altitude sickness, mountain sickness

apunarse /1a/ VPR (*And, CS*) to get altitude o mountain sickness

apuntador(a) SM/F (*Teat*) prompter; ✦ MODISMO **no se salvó ni el ~*** no-one was spared

apuntalar /1a/ VT (*Min, Arquit*) to prop up, shore up; (*Mec*) to strut

apuntar /1a/ **Ⓐ** VT **1** (= *dirigir*) [+ *cámara, pistola, misil*] to aim (**a** at), train (**a** on) **2** (= *sugerir*) to point out; **apuntó la necesidad de una huelga** he pointed out the need for a strike **3** (= *anotar*) **3.1** (*en cuaderno*) make a note of, note down; (*en lista, tabla*) to enter, record; **apúntalo en mi cuenta** put it on my account **3.2** (*Estadística*) [+ *velocidad, tiempo*] to log **4** (= *inscribir*) (*en lista*) to put down; (*en colegio, curso*) to enrol, enroll (*EEUU*); (*en concurso, competición*) to enter, put down; **¿me puedes ~ para la cena de Navidad?** could you put me down for the Christmas dinner? **5** (= *decir en voz baja*) (*a actor*) to prompt; **~ la respuesta a algn** to whisper the answer to sb **Ⓑ** VI **1** (= *señalar*) (*con arma*) to aim; (*con dedo, objeto*) to point at; **¡apunten! ¡disparen!** take aim! fire!; **~ con: todos le apuntaban con el dedo** everyone pointed their fingers at her; **~ a algn con un arma** to aim a gun at sb, point a gun at sb **2** (= *dirigirse*) to point; **sus declaraciones apuntaban en la dirección opuesta** his statements pointed in the opposite direction **3** (= *anotar*) to note down; **apunta, dos kilos de patatas y uno de uvas** note this down o make a note, two kilos of potatoes and a kilo of grapes **4** (= *brotar*) [*barba*] to sprout; **ya empezaba a ~ el día** the day was dawning; **una tendencia que ya comenzaba a ~ a finales del siglo** a tendency that had already begun to emerge at the end of the century **5** **~ a algo** to point to sth; **una hipótesis apunta al origen romano del yacimiento** one hypothesis suggests that the site is of Roman origin **Ⓒ** **apuntarse** VPR **1** (= *inscribirse*) (*en lista*) to put one's name down; (*en colegio, curso*) to enrol, enroll (*EEUU*), register; (*en partido, asociación*) to join; (*en concurso, competición*) to enter, put one's name down; **como el viaje es tan barato nos hemos apuntado** as the trip is so cheap we've put our names down to go; **he ido a ~me al paro** I went to sign on at the JobCentre (*Brit*), I went to apply for welfare benefits (*EEUU*); **me he apuntado a un curso de inglés** I've signed up for an English course, I've enrolled on an English course **2** (*) **¿alguien se apunta?** anyone interested?; **si vais al museo el domingo, llamadme, que yo me apunto** if you're going to the museum on Sunday, call me, I'll be up for it; ✦ MODISMO **~se a un bombardeo** (*Esp*) to be game for anything, be up for anything* **3** (= *obtener*) **~se un tanto** (*Dep*) to score a point; (*fig*) to chalk up a point, score a point, stay one up; **~se una victoria** to score a win, chalk up a win **4** (= *vislumbrarse*) **a lo lejos se apuntaba el faro** you could make out the lighthouse in the distance

 ⚠ **apuntar ≠ appoint**

apunte SM **1 apuntes** (= *notas*) notes; **tomar ~s** to take notes ➤ **apuntes de campo** nature notes **2** (*Com*) (= *anotación*) entry; ✦ MODISMO **llevar el ~ a algn** (*CS*) to take notice of sb **3** (*Arte*) sketch

apuñalar /*1a*/ VT to stab, knife; **~ a algn por la espalda** to stab sb in the back

apurada* SF (*LAm*) **¿por qué no te echas** *o* **pegas una ~?** why don't you get a move on* *o* hurry up?; ✦ MODISMO **a las ~s** (*RPl*) in a rush

apuradamente ADV (*LAm*) (= *de prisa*) hurriedly, in a rush

apurado Ⓐ ADJ **1** (= *falto*) (*de dinero*) hard up; (*de tiempo*) in a hurry, in a rush; **siempre voy muy ~ de tiempo** I'm always in a hurry *o* rush
2 (= *difícil*) [*situación*] critical; [*triunfo, victoria*] hard-fought; **en tan ~ trance, decidieron entregarse** being in such a critical state, they decided to give in
3 (= *avergonzado*) embarrassed
4 (*Esp*) (= *preciso*) [*limpieza, frenada*] precise, exact; [*afeitado*] close, smooth
5 ✦ MODISMO **casarse ~** (*LAm*) to have a shotgun wedding
Ⓑ SM (= *afeitado*) close shave; **el máximo nivel de ~** the closest shave

apurar /*1a*/ Ⓐ VT **1** (= *agotar*) [+ *bebida*] to drink up; [+ *comida*] to eat up; [+ *provisión, medios*] to use up, exhaust, finish off; **apuró la copa hasta el final** he drained the glass; **apuró hasta el último momento de sus vacaciones** he stretched out his holiday (*esp Brit*) *o* vacation (*EEUU*) until the last moment
2 (= *agobiar*) to put pressure on, pressurize; **deja que haga lo que pueda sin ~lo** let him do what he can without pressurizing him *o* putting him under pressure; **si se me apura, yo diría que es la mejor playa de España** if pushed, I would say that it is the best beach in Spain
3 (= *avergonzar*) to embarrass
4 (*esp LAm*) (= *meter prisa*) to rush, hurry; **¡no me apures!** don't rush *o* hurry me!
Ⓑ VI (*Chi*) to be urgent; **me apura ver al doctor** I have to see the doctor urgently
Ⓒ **apurarse** VPR **1** (= *agobiarse*) to get upset, worry (**por** about, over); **¡no te apures, que todo se arreglará!** don't worry, everything will be all right!
2 (= *esforzarse*) to make an effort, go hard at it; **~se por hacer algo** to strive to do sth
3 (*esp LAm*) (= *apresurarse*) to hurry, hurry up; **¡apúrate!** get a move on!
4 **~se la barba** (*Esp*) to have a close shave

apuro SM **1** (= *aprieto*) predicament; **pueden servir para un caso de ~** they might be useful in an emergency; **vivimos sin ~s gracias a esa pensión** we have no financial worries thanks to that pension; **en ~s: ayudan a empresas en ~s** they help companies in difficulty; **un anciano en ~s** an old man in distress; **llámame si te ves en ~s** call me if you are in trouble; **pasar ~s** [*de dinero*] to suffer hardship; (*al hacer algo*) to have difficulties; **poner a algn en ~s** to put sb in an awkward situation, make things awkward for sb; **sacar a algn de un ~** to get sb out of a mess
2 (= *vergüenza*) embarrassment; **¡qué ~!** how embarrassing!; **me da ~** it embarrasses me, I'm embarrassed
3 (*LAm*) (= *prisa*) rush; **tener ~** [*persona*] to be in a hurry, be in a rush; [*actividad*] to be urgent; ✦ MODISMO **casarse de ~** to have a shotgun wedding

apurón SM ✦ MODISMO **a los apurones** (*RPl*) in a rush

aquejar /*1a*/ VT to afflict; **le aqueja una grave enfermedad** he suffers from a serious disease

aquel(la) ADJ DEM that; **~los/as** those

aquél(la) PRON DEM that, that one; **aquéllos/as** those, those ones; **estos son negros mientras aquéllos son blancos** these ones are black, whereas those ones are white; **~ que está en el escaparate** the one that's in the window; **todo ~ que ...** anyone who ...; **como ~ que dice** so to speak

aquelarre SM witches' coven

aquello PRON DEM INDEF that; **~ no tuvo importancia** that wasn't important; **~ que te conté de mi hermano** that business about my brother I told you about; **~ de que no iba a venir era mentira** when they said he wasn't coming it was a lie

aquerenciarse /*1b*/ VPR **~ a un lugar** to become attached to a place

aquí ADV **1** (*en el espacio*) here; **~ dentro** in here; **ven ~** come here; **soy de ~** I'm from (around) here; **la gente de ~** (the) people here; **a 2km de ~** 2km from here; **andar de ~ para allá** to walk up and down *o* to and fro; **hasta ~** so far, thus far (*frm*), as far as here; **por ~** around here; **por ~ cerca** around here somewhere; **venga por ~** come this way; **he ~ la razón** (*frm*) herein lies the reason (*frm*); ✦ MODISMO **hubo un lío de ~ te espero*** there was a tremendous fuss
2 (*en el tiempo*) **de ~ en adelante** from now on; **de ~ a un mes** a month from now; **de ~ a nada** in next to no time; **hasta ~** up till now
3 **de ~ que** and so, that's why

aquiescencia SF acquiescence

aquietar /*1a*/ Ⓐ VT [+ *persona*] to quieten down (*esp Brit*), quiet down (*EEUU*), calm down; [+ *temor*] to allay
Ⓑ **aquietarse** VPR to calm, calm down

ara¹ SF (= *altar*) altar; (= *piedra*) altar stone; **en ~s de** in honour *o* (*EEUU*) honor of; **en ~s de la exactitud** in the interests of precision

ara² SM (*LAm*) (= *pájaro*) parrot

árabe Ⓐ ADJ Arab; **palabra ~** Arabic word Ⓑ SMF Arab Ⓒ SM (*Ling*) Arabic

arabesco ADJ, SM arabesque

Arabia SF Arabia ➤ **Arabia Saudí, Arabia Saudita** Saudi Arabia

arábigo ADJ [*número*] Arabic

arabista SMF Arabist

arado SM plough, plow (*EEUU*)

Aragón SM Aragon

aragonés/esa Ⓐ ADJ, SM/F Aragonese Ⓑ SM (*Ling*) Aragonese

arancel SM tariff, duty

arancelario ADJ tariff *antes de s*, customs *antes de s*; **barrera arancelaria** tariff barrier

arándano SM bilberry, blueberry

arandela SF washer

araña SF **1** (*Zool*) spider **2** (= *lámpara*) chandelier

arañar /*1a*/ Ⓐ VT **1** (= *herir*) to scratch **2** [+ *audiencia, votos*] to win Ⓑ VI (*RPl*) **aprobó arañando** he scraped through

arañazo SM scratch

arar /*1a*/ VT to plough, plow (*EEUU*), till

araucano/a ADJ, SM/F Araucanian

ARAUCANO

The **Araucanos** or **Mapuches** from Chile and western Argentina resisted both Inca and Spanish attempts to colonize them. Their indomitable spirit is celebrated in Alonso de Ercilla's epic poem **La Araucana**. Their language is today spoken by over 300,000 people and many words of Araucanian origin are used in Chilean and Argentinian Spanish. The name **Chile** is Araucanian for Land's End.

---

araucaria SF araucaria, monkey-puzzle tree

arbitraje SM **1** (= *juicio*) arbitration **2** (*Dep*) refereeing

arbitrar /*1a*/ Ⓐ VT [+ *disputa*] to arbitrate in; (*Tenis*) to umpire; (*Boxeo, Ftbl*) to referee Ⓑ VI to arbitrate; (*Dep*) to umpire, referee; **~ en una disputa** to arbitrate in a dispute

arbitrariamente ADV arbitrarily

arbitrariedad SF **1** (= *cualidad*) arbitrariness **2** (= *acto*) arbitrary act

arbitrario ADJ arbitrary

arbitrio SM **1** (= *libre albedrío*) free will **2** (*Jur*) decision, judgment; **al ~ de** at the discretion of

árbitro/a SM/F (*Jur*) arbiter, arbitrator; (*Tenis*) umpire; (*Boxeo, Ftbl*) referee

árbol SM **1** (*Bot*) tree ➤ **árbol de Navidad** Christmas tree

➤ **árbol frutal** fruit tree ➤ **árbol genealógico** family tree **2** (*Mec*) shaft ➤ **árbol de levas** camshaft **3** (*Náut*) mast

arbolado Ⓐ ADJ **1** [*tierra*] wooded, tree-covered; [*calle*] tree-lined, lined with trees **2** [*mar*] heavy Ⓑ SM woodland

arboladura SF rigging

arbolar /1a/ VT [+ *bandera*] to hoist, raise; [+ *buque*] to fit with masts

arboleda SF grove, coppice

arbóreo ADJ **1** (*Zool*) arboreal, tree *antes de s* **2** (*forma*) tree-like, tree-shaped

arboricultura SF forestry

arbotante SM flying buttress

arbusto SM shrub, bush

arca SF **1** (= *cofre*) chest ➤ **arcas públicas** public funds **2** (*Rel*) ➤ **Arca de la Alianza** Ark of the Covenant ➤ **Arca de Noé** Noah's Ark

arcabuz SM arquebus, harquebus

arcada SF **1** (= *serie de arcos*) arcade **2** [*de puente*] arch, span **3 arcadas** (*Med*) retching *sing*; **me dieron ~s con el olor** the smell made me retch; **sentía ~s pensando aquello** the very thought of it made him feel sick

arcaico ADJ archaic

arcaísmo SM archaism

arcángel SM archangel

arcano Ⓐ ADJ arcane, recondite Ⓑ SM secret, mystery

arce SM maple, maple tree

arcén SM hard shoulder (*Brit*), shoulder (*EEUU*), berm (*EEUU*)

archiconocido ADJ extremely well-known, famous

archidiácono SM archdeacon

archidiócesis SF INV archdiocese

archiduque(sa) SM/F archduke/archduchess

archimillonario/a SM/F multimillionaire

archipiélago SM archipelago

archisabido ADJ extremely well-known

archivador(a) Ⓐ SM/F (*en oficina*) filing clerk (*esp Brit*), file clerk (*EEUU*) Ⓑ SM (= *mueble*) filing cabinet; (= *carpeta*) file

archivar /1a/ VT **1** (= *guardar*) to file, store away **2** [+ *plan*] to shelve, put on the back burner

archivero/a SM/F archivist

archivo SM **1** (= *sitio*) archive, archives *pl*; **fotos de ~** library photos; **imágenes de ~** library pictures ➤ **Archivo Nacional** Public Record Office **2** (= *documentos*) **~s** files ➤ **archivos policiales** police files, police records **3** (*Inform*) file ➤ **archivo adjunto** attachment ➤ **archivo de seguridad** backup file

arcilla SF clay

arcilloso ADJ clayey

arcipreste SM archpriest

arco SM **1** (*Anat, Arquit, Geom*) arch ➤ **arco de herradura** horseshoe arch, Moorish arch ➤ **arco iris** rainbow ➤ **arco triunfal** triumphal arch **2** (= *arma*) bow **3** (*Mús*) bow ➤ **arco de violín** violin bow **4** (*Pol*) ➤ **arco parlamentario** *range of democratic parties represented in parliament* ➤ **arco político** political spectrum **5** (*Mat, Elec*) arc ➤ **arco voltaico** arc lamp **6** (*LAm Dep*) goal

arcón SM large chest

arder /2a/ VI **1** (= *quemarse*) to burn; ✦ MODISMO **la cosa está que arde** things are coming to a head **2** (*esp LAm**) [*herida*] to sting, make smart

ardid SM ruse; **~es** tricks, wiles

ardiente ADJ [*deseo, interés*] burning; [*amor*] ardent, passionate; [*partidario*] fervent, ardent

ardilla SF squirrel

ardor SM **1** (*Med*) ➤ **ardor de estómago** heartburn **2** (= *fervor*) ardour, ardor (*EEUU*), eagerness

ardoroso ADJ ardent, fervent

arduamente ADV arduously

arduo ADJ arduous, hard

área SF **1** (= *zona, superficie*) area ➤ **área de castigo** (*Dep*) penalty area ➤ **área de descanso** (*Aut*) rest area ➤ **área de penalty** (*Dep*) penalty area ➤ **área de servicio** (*Aut*) service area ➤ **área metropolitana** metropolitan area, urban district **2** (= *tema*) **en el ~ de los impuestos** in the field of taxation **3** (= *medida*) area (*100 square metres*)

arena SF **1** (= *tierra*) sand ➤ **arenas movedizas** quicksands **2** (*Dep*) arena

arenal SM sandy spot

arenga SF harangue*, sermon*

arengar /1h/ VT to harangue

arenisca SF sandstone

arenoso ADJ sandy

arenque SM herring ➤ **arenque ahumado** kipper

arepa SF corn pancake

arequipa SF (*Col, Ven*) caramel spread

arete SM earring

argamasa SF mortar

Argel SM Algiers

Argelia SF Algeria

argelino/a ADJ, SM/F Algerian

argentado ADJ (*Téc*) silver-plated; [*voz*] silvery

Argentina SF Argentina; *see also* **www.presidencia.gov.ar**

argentino/a ADJ, SM/F Argentinian, Argentine

argolla SF ring; (*LAm*) [*de boda*] wedding ring

argot [ar'got] SM (*pl* **~s**) slang

argucia SF sophistry (*frm*), hair-splitting

argüende SM (*LAm*) argument

argüir /3g/ VT **1** (= *razonar*) to argue, contend **2** (= *argumentar, justificarse*) to argue, claim; **arguyó que no era culpa suya** he claimed it wasn't his fault

argumentación SF argument, reasoning

argumental ADJ plot *antes de s*; **línea ~** storyline

argumentar /1a/ VT, VI to argue

argumento SM **1** [*de razonamiento*] (*tb Jur*) argument **2** (*Literat, Teat*) plot; (*TV*) storyline

aria SF aria

aridez SF aridity, dryness

árido Ⓐ ADJ arid, dry Ⓑ SMPL **áridos** (*Com*) dry goods

Aries SM (= *signo*) Aries

aries SMF INV (= *persona*) Aries; **soy ~** I'm Aries

ariete SM battering ram

ario/a ADJ, SM/F Aryan

arisco ADJ [*animal*] unfriendly; [*persona*] unsociable, standoffish, surly

arista SF (*Geom*) edge; (*Alpinismo*) arête; (*Arquit*) arris

aristocracia SF aristocracy

aristócrata SMF aristocrat

aristocrático ADJ aristocratic

aristotélico ADJ Aristotelian

aritmética SF arithmetic; *ver tb* **aritmético**

aritmético/a Ⓐ ADJ arithmetical Ⓑ SM/F arithmetician; *ver tb* **aritmética**

arlequín SM buffoon

arma SF **1** (*Mil*) weapon; **los guerrilleros entregaron las ~s** the guerrillas handed over their weapons; **un fabricante de ~s** an arms manufacturer; **nos apuntaba con un ~** he pointed a gun at us; **alzarse en ~s** to rise up in arms; **¡presenten ~s!** present arms!; ✦ MODISMOS **de ~s tomar: es una mujer de ~s tomar** she's not someone you mess with; **pasar a algn por las ~s** to execute sb ➤ **arma arrojadiza** (*lit*) missile; (*fig*) weapon ➤ **arma atómica** atomic weapon ➤ **arma biológica** biological weapon ➤ **arma blanca** knife ➤ **arma de doble filo** double-edged sword ➤ **arma de fuego** firearm ➤ **arma reglamentaria** service weapon ➤ **armas de destrucción masiva** weapons of mass destruction **2** (= *medio de defensa*) weapon; **la movilización popular es su**

su ~ más fuerte popular mobilization is its most powerful weapon **3** (*Mil*) (= *cuerpo*) arm **4** (*Mil*) **las ~s** (= *profesión*) the military, the armed services **5 armas** [*de escudo*] arms

armada SF navy; **la Armada Británica** the British Navy; **un oficial de la ~** a naval officer

armadillo SM armadillo

armado ADJ **1** [*persona, lucha*] armed (**con, de** with); **ir ~ to go armed, be armed; ✦** MODISMO **~ hasta los dientes** armed to the teeth **2** [*hormigón*] reinforced

armador(a) SM/F shipowner

armadura SF **1** (*Mil, Hist*) armour, armor (*EEUU*); **una ~** a suit of armour *o* (*EEUU*) armor **2** (*Téc*) framework

armaduría SF (*Chi*) car assembly plant

armamentista ADJ arms *antes de s*; **carrera ~** arms race

armamento SM armament; **~s** armaments, arms

armar /1a/ ⒶVT **1** [+ *persona, ejército*] to arm (**con, de** with); **se desconoce quién ha armado a los terroristas** it is not known who provided *o* supplied the terrorists with arms **2** (= *montar*) [+ *mueble, ventana, juguete*] to assemble, put together; [+ *tienda de campaña*] to pitch, put up; (*LAm*) [+ *rompecabezas*] to piece together, put together; [+ *cigarrillo*] to roll **3** (*) (= *organizar*) **~ una bronca** to kick up a fuss *o* (*EEUU*) storm; **~on un lío tremendo** they kicked up a real fuss *o* (*EEUU*) storm; **✦** MODISMOS **sin ~ jaleo** without making a racket; **armarla** to stir up trouble; **buena la armó con esa declaración** he really stirred up trouble with that statement; **pienso ~la hasta que consiga lo que quiero** I'm going to make a real fuss until I get what I want **4** [+ *hormigón*] to reinforce **5** (*Mil*) [+ *bayoneta*] to fix; [+ *rifle, cañón*] to load **6** (*Cos*) [+ *chaqueta, solapa*] to stiffen **7 ~ un pleito** (*LAm**) to kick up a fuss*, get ready Ⓑ **armarse** VPR **1** [*soldado, atracador*] to arm o.s. (**con, de** with); **✦** MODISMO **~se hasta los dientes** to be armed to the teeth **2** (= *proveerse*) **~se de algo** to arm o.s. with sth; **armados de prismáticos y teleobjetivos** armed with binoculars and telephoto lenses; **con este tráfico hay que ~se de paciencia** you need a lot of patience in traffic like this; **~se de valor** to pluck up courage **3** (*) (= *organizarse*) **¡que follón se armó!** there was a big fuss; **¡menudo escándalo se armó con lo de esa boda!** what a commotion there was with that wedding!* **4 ~se un lío***: **me armé un lío tremendo con todas las direcciones que me diste** I got into a real muddle* *o* mess with all the addresses you gave me

armario SM [*de ropa*] wardrobe, closet (*EEUU*); [*de cocina*] cupboard, closet (*EEUU*); **✦** MODISMO **salir del ~** to come out (of the closet) ➤ **armario empotrado** built-in cupboard (*esp Brit*), built-in closet (*EEUU*) ➤ **armario ropero** wardrobe, closet (*EEUU*)

armatoste SM (= *objeto*) monstrosity; (= *máquina*) contraption; (*Aut*) jalopy*, old banger (*Brit**)

armazón SM *o* SF [*de mueble*] frame; (*fig*) (= *esqueleto*) framework; (*Aer, Aut*) body, chassis; (*CS*) [*de anteojos*] frame

Armenia SF Armenia

armenio/a ADJ, SM/F Armenian

armería SF gunsmith's, gunsmith's shop

armero SM gunsmith

armiño SM **1** (= *animal*) stoat **2** (= *piel*) ermine

armisticio SM armistice

armonía SF harmony; **en ~** in harmony (**con** with)

armónica SF harmonica, mouth organ

armónico ADJ harmonic

armonioso ADJ harmonious

armonizar /1f/ ⒶVT **1** (*Mús*) to harmonize **2** [+ *diferencias*] to reconcile ⒷVI **1** (*Mús*) to harmonize (**con** with) **2 ~ con** to harmonize *o* be in keeping with; [*colores*] to tone in with

ARN SM ABR (= **ácido ribonucleico**) RNA

arnés SM **1** (*Mil, Hist*) armour, armor (*EEUU*) **2** (*en montañismo, paracaidismo*) harness **3 arneses** (= *arreos*) harness *sing*, trappings

árnica SF arnica

aro SM **1** [*de tonel*] ring, hoop; [*de rueda*] rim; (= *para servilleta*) napkin ring; (*SAm*) (= *arete*) earring; **✦** MODISMO **pasar por el ~** to toe the line **2 aros** (= *juego*) quoits

aroma SM (= *perfume*) aroma, scent; [*de vino*] bouquet

aromaterapia SF aromatherapy

aromático ADJ aromatic, sweet-scented

aromatizador SM air-freshener

aromatizar /1f/ VT (= *perfumar*) to scent; [+ *aire*] to freshen; (*Culin*) to flavour *o* (*EEUU*) flavor with herbs

arpa SF harp

arpegio SM arpeggio

arpía SF (*Mit*) harpy; (= *mujer perversa*) witch

arpillera SF sacking, sackcloth

arpista SMF (*Mús*) harpist

arpón SM harpoon

arponear /1a/ VT to harpoon

arponero ADJ **navío ~** whaler, whaling vessel

arquear /1a/ ⒶVT (= *doblar*) to arch, bend Ⓑ **arquearse** VPR (= *doblarse*) to arch, bend; [*superficie*] to camber

arqueología SF archaeology, archeology (*EEUU*)

arqueológico ADJ archaeological, archeological (*EEUU*)

arqueólogo/a SM/F archaeologist, archeologist (*EEUU*)

arquería SF arcade, series of arches

arquero/a SM/F **1** (*Mil*) archer, bowman **2** (*LAm Ftbl*) goalkeeper

arqueta SF chest

arquetípico ADJ archetypal, archetypical

arquetipo SM archetype

arquitecto/a SM/F architect ➤ **arquitecto/a técnico/a** quantity surveyor

arquitectónico ADJ architectural

arquitectura SF architecture

arrabal SM **1** (= *barrio*) poor suburb **2 arrabales** (= *afueras*) outskirts

arrabalero ADJ **1** (= *de barrio bajo*) of/from the poorer areas **2** (= *basto*) common, coarse

arracada SF pendant earring

arracimarse /1a/ VPR to cluster together

arraigado ADJ [*costumbre*] deep-rooted; [*creencia*] deep-seated

arraigar /1h/ VI [*planta*] to take root; [*costumbre*] to take root, establish itself, take a hold

arraigo SM **de mucho** *o* **viejo ~** deep-rooted

arramblar /1a/ VI **~ con*** to make off with, pinch*

arrancar /1g/ ⒶVT **1** (*tirando con fuerza*) [+ *planta, pelo*] to pull up; [+ *clavo, diente*] to pull out; [+ *pluma*] to pluck; [+ *ojos*] to gouge out; [+ *botón, esparadrapo, etiqueta*] to pull off, tear off; [+ *página*] to tear out, rip out; [+ *cartel*] to pull down, tear down; **le arrancó la oreja de un mordisco** he bit off his ear; **el golpe le arrancó dos dientes** the blow

knocked two of his teeth out
2 (= *arrebatar*) to snatch (**a, de** from); (*con violencia*) to wrench (**a, de** from); **le arrancó al niño de los brazos** she snatched the baby from his arms
3 (= *provocar*) [+ *aplausos*] to draw; [+ *risas*] to provoke, cause; **hemos conseguido ~le una sonrisa** we managed to get a smile out of him; **~ las lágrimas a algn** to bring tears to sb's eyes
4 (= *separar*) **~ a algn <u>de</u>** [+ *lugar*] to drag sb away from; [+ *éxtasis, trance*] to drag sb out of; **no había forma de ~la del teléfono** there was no way I could drag her away from the phone
5 (= *obtener*) [+ *apoyo*] to gain, win; [+ *victoria*] to snatch; [+ *confesión, promesa*] to extract; [+ *sonido, nota*] to produce; **no hubo forma de ~le una palabra** we couldn't get a word out of him
6 (*Aut*) [+ *vehículo, motor*] to start
7 (*Inform*) to boot, boot up, start up
Ⓑ VI **1** [*vehículo, motor*] to start; **esperé hasta que arrancó el tren** I waited until the train left
2 (= *moverse*) to get going, get moving; **¡venga, arranca!** come on, get going *o* get moving!, come on, get a move on!*
3 (= *comenzar*) to start; **¿desde dónde arranca el camino?** where does the road start?; **~ a hacer algo** to start doing sth, start to do sth; **~ <u>de</u>** to go back to, date back to; **esta celebración arranca del siglo XV** this celebration dates *o* goes back to the 15th century
4 (*Chi**) (= *escapar*) **salieron arrancado** they ran away; **arranquemos de aquí** let's get away from here; **tuvieron que ~ del país** they had to get out of the country; **✦** MODISMO **~ a perderse** to make a dash for it*
Ⓒ arrancarse VPR **1** (*con fuerza*) [+ *pelo*] to pull out; [+ *botón*] to pull off
2 (= *empezar*) **se ~on a cantar** they burst into song; **~se por seguiriyas** to break into a seguidilla
3 (*Chi**) (= *escaparse*) **se me arrancó el perro** my dog got away; **se ~on de la cárcel** they escaped from prison
4 (*Chi**) (= *aumentar*) to shoot up*; **hay que evitar que se arranque la inflación** we have to prevent inflation from shooting up*

arranque SM **1** (*Mec*) starting mechanism; **el motor tiene problemas de ~** the engine has problems getting started; **✦** MODISMO **ni para el ~** (*Méx**): **no tengo ni para el ~** I haven't got anywhere near enough ➤ **arranque automático** starter, starter motor
2 (= *impulso*) **necesita un poco más de ~ para ganar el partido** he needs a little more drive to win the match
3 (= *arrebato*) [*de generosidad, franqueza*] outburst; [*de celos, ira, violencia*] fit; [*de energía*] burst
4 (= *ocurrencia*) witty remark
5 (= *base*) [*de columna, arco*] base; [*de escalera*] foot

arras SFPL **1** pledge *sing*, security *sing* **2** (*Hist*) 13 coins given by bridegroom to bride

arrasar /1a/ **Ⓐ** VT **1** [+ *edificio, población*] to raze to the ground; [*ciclón, terremoto*] to devastate **Ⓑ** VI **1** (= *triunfar*) [*partido, equipo*] to sweep the board; [*película, programa*] to be a runaway success **2** **~ con** = A **Ⓒ** arrasarse VPR **se le ~on los ojos de o en lágrimas** her eyes filled with tears

arrastrado ADJ wretched, miserable

arrastrar /1a/ **Ⓐ** VT **1** [+ *objeto pesado*] to drag; [+ *carro*] to pull; [+ *caravana*] to tow; [+ *vestido, capa*] to trail (along the ground); **~ los pies** to drag one's feet, shuffle along; **~ las palabras** to slur one's words
2 (= *transportar*) [*río, viento*] to sweep away *o* along; **la corriente arrastró las ramas** the current swept the branches away *o* along
3 (= *atraer*) [+ *público*] to draw, attract; **~ a algn a hacer algo** to drag sb into doing sth
4 (= *soportar*) **este país arrastra desde hace décadas el problema del paro** this country's been dogged by unemployment for decades; **arrastra un complejo de inferioridad desde la adolescencia** he's had an inferiority complex ever since he was a youth
5 (*Naipes*) to draw
Ⓑ VI [*vestido, capa*] to trail (along the ground), drag; **te arrastra el vestido** your dress is trailing (along the ground) *o* dragging

Ⓒ arrastrarse VPR **1** (= *reptar*) [*bebé, serpiente*] to crawl; [*herido*] to drag o.s.
2 (= *humillarse*) to grovel

arrastre SM **1** (= *acción*) dragging, pulling; (*Aer*) drag; (*Pesca*) trawling; **flota de ~** trawling fleet, fleet of trawlers; **✦** MODISMO **estar para el ~*** to be bushed* **2** (*LAm*) (= *atractivo*) appeal, pulling power; **tener mucho ~** to be very popular, have (a lot of) pulling power

arrayán SM myrtle

arre EXCL gee up!

arreada SF (*CS, Méx*) round-up

arrear /1a/ **Ⓐ** VT **1** (= *estimular*) [+ *ganado*] to drive **2** (*LAm*) [+ *ganado*] to rustle **3** (*) [+ *golpe*] to give **Ⓑ** VI to hurry along; **¡arrea!** get moving!

arrebañar /1a/ VT [+ *comida*] to eat up, clear up

arrebatar /1a/ **Ⓐ** VT **1** (= *quitar violentamente*) to snatch away, wrench (**a** from); [+ *vida*] to take; [*viento*] to carry off, carry away; **le ~on la victoria** they snatched victory from under his very nose **2** (= *cautivar*) to captivate **Ⓑ** arrebatarse VPR to get carried away, get excited

arrebato SM (= *ira*) rage; (= *éxtasis*) ecstasy, rapture; **en un ~ de cólera** in an outburst of anger

arrebol SM (*liter*) **1** [*de persona*] **el ~ de sus mejillas** her rosy cheeks **2** [*de cielo*] red glow **3** **arreboles** (= *nubes*) red clouds

arrebujar /1a/ **Ⓐ** VT **1** [+ *objetos*] to jumble together, jumble up **2** [+ *niño*] to wrap up, cover **Ⓑ** arrebujarse VPR to wrap o.s. up (**con** in, with)

arrecharse /1a/ VPR **1** (*LAm****) (*sexualmente*) to get horny** **2** (*Col, Ven***) (= *enfadarse*) to get angry, get mad (*EEUU**)

arrechera SF **1** (*LAm****) (*sexual*) **tener ~** to get horny** **2** (*Col, Ven***) (= *enojo*) anger; **le dio tremenda ~** he was furious, he got really mad (*EEUU**) **3** (*Col, Ven***) (= *valor*) guts* *pl*

arrecho ADJ **1** (*LAm****) (*sexualmente*) **estar ~** [*persona*] to be horny**; [*animal*] to be in *o* (*Brit*) on heat **2** (*Col, Ven***) (= *furioso*) angry **3** (*CAm, Méx*) (= *valiente*) brave **4** (*Ven***) **¡qué ~!** what a laugh!*

arrechucho* SM **1** [*de cólera*] fit, outburst **2** (*Med*) turn

arreciar /1b/ VI [*tormenta*] to get worse, intensify; [*viento*] to get stronger

arrecife SM reef ➤ **arrecife de coral** coral reef

arredrar /1a/ **Ⓐ** VT **1** (= *asustar*) to scare, frighten **2** (= *hacer retirarse*) to drive back **Ⓑ** arredrarse VPR (= *intimidarse*) to be scared, be frightened; **~se ante algo** to shrink away from sth; **sin ~se** unmoved, undaunted

arreglado ADJ **1** (= *ordenado*) [*habitación, casa*] neat and tidy; [*conducta*] orderly
2 (= *acicalado*) smart, smartly dressed; **¿dónde irá tan arreglada?** where would she going so smart *o* so smartly dressed?
3 [*asunto, pelea*] (= *resuelto*) sorted out; (= *amañado*) arranged
4 **✦** MODISMO **estar ~**: **está arreglada si espera que yo la llame** if she thinks I'm going to call her, she's got another think coming*; **estamos ~s con tantos invitados** we are in a fine mess with so many guests coming*; **¡pues estamos ~s contigo!** you're nothing but trouble, you are!*

arreglalotodo* SM **el señor ~** Mr Fixit*

arreglar /1a/ **Ⓐ** VT **1** (= *reparar*) [+ *electrodoméstico, reloj*] to repair, fix, mend; [+ *coche*] to repair, fix; [+ *zapatos, vestido*] to mend, repair; [+ *casa*] to do up
2 (= *acicalar*) to get ready; **arregló a los niños para ir de paseo** she got the children ready for their stroll
3 (= *resolver*) [+ *asunto*] to sort out; [+ *conflicto, disputa*] to settle; [+ *problema*] to solve, sort out; **pegándole no vas a ~ nada** you're not going to solve anything by hitting him; **~ cuentas con algn** to settle accounts with sb
4 (= *ordenar*) [+ *casa, habitación*] to tidy, tidy up
5 (= *organizar*) to arrange; **ya lo tenemos todo arreglado para la mudanza** we have got everything ready *o* arranged for the move
6 (= *acordar*) [+ *detalles*] to settle; [+ *cita*] to arrange, fix up

7 (*Culin*) [+ *ensalada*] to dress **8** (*LAm*) (= *amañar*) to arrange **9** (*LAm*) [+ *deuda*] to pay, repay **10** (*Chi*) [+ *registro, documento*] to update ⓑ **arreglarse** VPR **1** (= *acicalarse*) **1.1** (*reflexivo*) to get o.s. ready; **yo tardo poco en ~me** I won't take a moment to get myself ready; **se arregla mucho para ir a trabajar** she gets really dressed up to go to work **1.2** **~se la boca** to get one's teeth seen to; **~se la corbata** to adjust one's tie; **~se el pelo** [*uno mismo*] to fix one's hair; (*en peluquería*) to have one's hair done **2** (= *ponerse de acuerdo*) to come to an agreement; **~se a algo** to conform to sth; **las leyes deben ~se a los principios fundamentales** laws should conform to fundamental principles; **~se con algn: me he arreglado con ella para cambiar los turnos** I've arranged to swap shifts with her **3** [*novios*] (= *reconciliarse*) to make up **4** (= *mejorar*) to improve; **si las cosas no se arreglan** if things don't improve; **los problemas no se arreglan solos** problems don't sort themselves out **5** (= *apañarse*) to manage; **con este dinero me arreglo** I can get by *o* I can manage on this money; **~se con/sin algo** to manage with/without sth; ✦ MODISMO **arreglárselas*** to manage; **sabe arreglárselas muy bien solito** he manages perfectly well on his own; **arreglárselas para hacer algo** to manage to do sth

arreglista SMF arranger

arreglo SM **1** (= *reparación*) repair; **"se hacen arreglos"** [*de ropa*] "alterations"; [*de electrodomésticos*] "repairs done"; **el horno no tiene ~** the oven is beyond repair; **ese problema tiene fácil ~** that problem is easy to sort out *o* solve; **mi marido no tiene ~*** my husband is a hopeless case* **2** (= *aseo*) [*de persona*] appearance **3** (= *acuerdo*) agreement; **tenemos un arreglillo con el jefe** we have made a little arrangement with the boss; **con ~ a** [+ *norma, ley*] in accordance with; [+ *circunstancias, criterio*] according to; **llegar a un ~** to reach a compromise ➤ **arreglo de cuentas** settling of old scores **4** [*de amantes*] affair **5** (*tb* **~ orquestal**) arrangement, arrangement for orchestra **6** ➤ **arreglo floral** flower arrangement

arrejuntarse* /1a/ VPR to set up house together, shack up together*; **vivir arrejuntados** to live together

arrellanarse /1a/ VPR, **arrellenarse** /1a/ VPR to lounge, sprawl; **~ en el asiento** to lie back in one's chair

arremangar /1h/ ⓐ VT [+ *mangas, pantalones*] to roll up; [+ *falda*] to tuck up ⓑ **arremangarse** VPR (= *subirse las mangas*) to roll up one's sleeves; (= *subirse los pantalones*) to roll up one's trousers (*Brit*) *o* pants (*EEUU*); (= *subirse la falda*) to tuck up one's skirt

arremeter /2a/ VI to rush forward, attack; **~ contra algn** to attack sb, launch o.s. at sb

arremolinarse /1a/ VPR [*gente*] to crowd around, mill around; [*corriente*] to swirl, eddy; [*bailarines, polvo*] to swirl, whirl

arrendador(a) SM/F landlord/landlady; (*Jur*) lessor

arrendamiento SM **1** [*de vivienda*] renting; [*de máquina*] renting, hiring (*esp Brit*); **tomar una casa en ~** to rent a house **2** (= *precio*) rent, rental

arrendar /1j/ VT **1** [*propietario*] [+ *inmueble*] to rent (out); [+ *máquina*] to rent (out), hire (out) (*esp Brit*) **2** [*usuario*] [+ *inmueble*] to rent; [+ *máquina*] to hire

arrendatario/a SM/F [*de vivienda*] tenant; (*Jur*) lessee, leaseholder

arreo SM **1** (*LAm*) (= *animales*) drove, drove of cattle; (= *acto*) round-up **2 arreos** [*de caballo*] harness *sing*, trappings

arrepentido/a ⓐ ADJ (= *pesaroso*) sorry; (*Rel*) repentant; **terrorista ~** reformed terrorist; **estar ~ de algo** to regret sth, be sorry about sth ⓑ SM/F reformed terrorist

arrepentimiento SM (= *pesar*) regret; (*Rel*) repentance

arrepentirse /3i/ VPR to repent, be repentant; **~ de algo** to regret sth

> Recuérdese que **regret** rige que el verbo que le siga inmediatamente aparezca en gerundio y no en infinitivo:

~ de haber hecho algo to regret doing sth, regret having done sth; **no ~ de nada** to have no regrets, not be sorry for anything

arrestar /1a/ VT to arrest, detain; **~ en el cuartel** to confine to barracks

arresto SM **1** (*Jur*) (= *acción*) arrest; (*Mil*) detention, confinement; **estar bajo ~** to be under arrest ➤ **arresto domiciliario** house arrest ➤ **arresto preventivo** preventive detention **2 arrestos** (= *arrojo*) daring *sing*; **tener ~s** to be bold, be daring

arriar /1c/ VT [+ *bandera*] to lower, strike; [+ *vela*] to haul down; [+ *cable*] to loosen

arriate SM border

arriba ⓐ ADV **1** (*indicando situación*) above; **los platos y las tazas están ~** the cups and saucers are above; **allí ~** up there; **aquí ~** up here; **de ~: el botón de ~** the top button; **los dientes de ~** the top teeth, the upper row of teeth; **la parte de ~** the top; **los de ~** the people above; (= *los que mandan*) the people at the top; **órdenes (que vienen) de ~** orders from above; **desde ~** from above; **está más ~** it's higher *o* further up; **pon esos libros ~ del todo** put those books right at the top **2** (*indicando dirección*) **de ~ abajo** from top to bottom, from head to foot; **vestida de negro de ~ abajo** dressed completely in black, dressed in black from head to foot; **mirar a algn de ~ abajo** to look sb up and down; **andar para ~ y para abajo** ◇ **ir de ~ para abajo** to run back and forth; **hacia ~** up(wards); **mire hacia ~** look up; **hasta ~: subí hasta ~** I climbed to the top; **llenar la copa hasta ~** to fill the glass to the brim; **el estadio está lleno hasta ~** the stadium is chock-a-block; **está hasta ~ de trabajo*** he's up to his neck in work*; **llegar ~** to get to the top; **de la cintura para ~** from the waist up; **un juego para niños de ocho años para ~** a game for children of eight and over; **de diez dólares ~** from ten dollars upwards **3** (*en casa*) upstairs; **los dormitorios ~ están** the bedrooms are upstairs; **los vecinos de ~** our upstairs neighbours *o* (*EEUU*) neighbors **4** (*en texto*) above; **como hemos dicho más ~** as has been said above **5 ~ de** (*esp LAm*) (= *encima de*) on top of; (= *por encima de*) above, over; **lo dejé ~ del refrigerador** I left it on top of the fridge; **viven en el departamento ~ del mío** they live in the flat (*esp Brit*) *o* apartment (*esp EEUU*) above mine **6** ✦ MODISMO **de ~** (*RPl*) (= *gratis*) free ⓑ EXCL (= *a levantarse*) up you get!; **¡~ ese ánimo!** cheer *o* chin up!; **¡manos ~!** hands up!; **¡~ el socialismo!** long live socialism!

arribada SF (*Náut*) arrival

arribar /1a/ VI (*esp LAm*) (= *llegar*) to arrive; (*Náut*) (= *llegar a puerto*) to put into port

arribismo SM social climbing

arribista SMF upstart, arriviste (*frm*)

arribo SM (*esp LAm*) arrival

arriendo SM = **arrendamiento**

arriero SM muleteer

arriesgado ADJ risky, hazardous

arriesgar /1h/ ⓐ VT **1** (= *poner en riesgo*) to risk, hazard **2** [+ *conjetura*] to hazard, venture ⓑ **arriesgarse** VPR to take a risk, expose o.s. to danger; **~se a hacer algo** to risk doing sth

> Recuérdese que **risk** rige que el verbo que le siga inmediatamente aparezca en gerundio y no en infinitivo.

arrimado ADJ **vivir ~ a algn** (*gen*) to live with sb; (*con* *dependencia económica*) to live off sb; (*sexualmente*) to shack up with sb

arrimar /1a/ **A** VT 1 (= *acercar*) to move nearer, move closer (**a** to); **arrima tu silla a la mía** bring your chair nearer *o* closer to mine; **se saludan sólo arrimando la cara** they just touch cheeks when they greet each other; **arrima el sofá contra la pared** move *o* push the sofa against the wall; **~ el oído a la puerta** to put one's ear to the door 2 **~ un golpe a algn** (*Méx**) to hit sb, strike sb **B** **arrimarse** VPR 1 (*a un lugar*) to come nearer, come closer (**a** to); **arrímate un poco más a la pared** get a little nearer to the wall; **no te arrimes mucho al precipicio** don't get too close to the precipice
2 **~se a algn** (*gen*) to come closer to sb; (*para pedir algo*) to come up to sb; (*buscando calor*) to snuggle up to sb; (*para sacar dinero*) to scrounge off sb*; **bailaban muy arrimados** they were dancing cheek-to-cheek, they were dancing very close; **se me fue arrimando hasta que se sentó a mi lado** he edged closer until he was sitting right next to me; **se arriman a los que están en el poder** they ingratiate themselves with those in power
3 (*Méx**) (= *vivir juntos*) to live together

arrimo SM protection; **al ~ de algn/algo** with the support of sb/with the help of sth

arrinconado ADJ 1 (= *abandonado*) forgotten, neglected 2 (= *acorralado*) cornered

arrinconar /1a/ VT 1 [+ *objeto*] to put in a corner 2 (= *abandonar*) to lay aside, discard; (= *marginar*) to leave out in the cold* 3 (= *acorralar*) to corner

arroba SF 1 (= *medida de peso*) 25 pounds; (= *medida de líquidos*) *a variable liquid measure*; ✦ MODISMO **por ~s*** tons*, loads*; **tiene talento por ~s** he has loads of talent, he oozes talent* 2 (= *símbolo*) at (symbol); **"paco arroba canal punto es"** "paco at canal dot es"

arrobamiento SM (= *éxtasis*) ecstasy, rapture; (*Rel*) trance

arrocero ADJ rice *antes de s*; **industria arrocera** rice industry

arrodillarse /1a/ VPR to kneel, kneel down; **estar arrodillado** to be kneeling, be kneeling down

arrogancia SF arrogance, haughtiness

arrogante ADJ arrogant, haughty

arrogarse /1h/ VPR **~ algo** to assume sth, take sth on o.s.

arrojadizo ADJ ➤ **arma arrojadiza** (*lit*) missile; (*fig*) weapon

arrojado ADJ daring, dashing

arrojar /1a/ **A** VT 1 (= *lanzar*) to throw; (*con fuerza*) to hurl; **"no arrojar basura"** "no tipping"
2 [+ *humo, lava*] to send out
3 [+ *resultados*] to produce; **la transacción arrojó un balance positivo** the transaction yielded a profit; **este estudio arroja (alguna) luz sobre el tema** this study sheds some light on the subject; **el accidente arrojó 80 muertos** (*LAm*) the accident left 80 dead
4 (= *expulsar*) to throw out; **lo arrojó de casa** she threw him out of the house
5 (*LAm*) (= *vomitar*) to bring up, vomit **B** **arrojarse** VPR (= *lanzarse*) to throw o.s.; (*con fuerza*) hurl o.s.

arrojo SM daring, fearlessness; **con ~** boldly, fearlessly

arrollado SM (*CS*) (*gen*) roulade; [*de mermelada, crema*] Swiss Roll; **~ de chocolate** chocolate roulade

arrollador ADJ [*mayoría*] overwhelming; [*personalidad*] overwhelming, overpowering

arrollar /1a/ VT 1 (= *enrollar*) (*gen*) to roll up; [+ *cable, cuerda, hilo*] to coil, wind 2 [*riada*] to sweep away, wash away 3 [+ *peatón*] to run over, knock down 4 [+ *persona*] (*en debate, competición*) to crush

arropar /1a/ **A** VT 1 (= *abrigar*) to wrap up, wrap up with clothes; (*en cama*) to tuck in, tuck in bed 2 (= *proteger*) to protect **B** **arroparse** VPR to wrap o.s. up

arrope SM [*de mosto*] grape syrup; [*de miel*] honey syrup

arrorró SM (*LAm*) lullaby

arrostrar /1a/ VT [+ *consecuencias*] to face, face up to;

[+ *peligro*] to brave, face

arroyo SM 1 (= *riachuelo*) stream, brook; (*Méx*) (= *barranco*) gully, ravine 2 (= *cuneta*) gutter; ✦ MODISMO **sacar a algn del ~** to drag sb from the gutter

arroyuelo SM small stream, brook

arroz SM rice ➤ **arroz a la cubana** *rice with banana, tomato sauce and fried egg* ➤ **arroz blanco** white rice ➤ **arroz con leche** rice pudding

arrozal SM rice field, paddy field

arruga SF (*en piel*) wrinkle, line; (*en ropa*) crease

arrugado ADJ [*cara*] wrinkled, lined; [*papel*] creased; [*vestido*] crumpled, creased up

arrugar /1h/ **A** VT [+ *cara*] to wrinkle, line; [+ *ceño*] to knit; [+ *papel*] to crumple, screw up; [+ *ropa*] to ruck up, crumple; **~ el entrecejo** to knit one's brow, frown **B** **arrugarse** VPR 1 [*cara*] to wrinkle, wrinkle up, get wrinkled; [*ropa*] to crease, get creased; [*planta*] to shrivel up 2 (*Méx**) (= *asustarse*) to get scared, get frightened

arruinar /1a/ **A** VT 1 (= *empobrecer*) to ruin 2 (= *destruir*) to wreck, destroy **B** **arruinarse** VPR to be ruined

arrullar /1a/ **A** VT [+ *niño*] to lull to sleep, sing to sleep; [+ *amante*] to say sweet nothings to **B** VI to coo

arrullo SM (*Orn*) cooing; (= *canción*) lullaby

arrumaco SM 1 (= *caricia*) caress 2 **arrumacos** (= *cariñitos*) show of affection *sing*, endearments

arrumar /1a/ VT (*Col*) to pile up

arrumbar¹ /1a/ VT (= *apartar*) to put aside, discard; (= *olvidar*) to neglect, forget

arrumbar² /1a/ (*Náut*) VI to set course (**hacia** for)

arrume SM (*Col*) pile, heap

arruncharse /1a/ VPR (*Col*) to curl up, roll up

arsenal SM (*Náut*) naval dockyard; (*Mil*) arsenal

arsenalera SF (*Chi*) theatre nurse, operating room nurse (*EEUU*)

arsénico SM arsenic

arte SM o SF (*gen m en sing, f en pl*) 1 (= *pintura, música*) art; **~s y oficios** arts and crafts; **bellas ~s** fine arts; **el séptimo ~** the cinema, film; **por ~ de magia** by magic, as if by magic; ✦ MODISMO **no tener ~ ni parte en algo** to have nothing whatsoever to do with sth ➤ **arte abstracto** abstract art ➤ **artes decorativas** decorative arts ➤ **artes gráficas** graphic arts ➤ **artes marciales** martial arts ➤ **artes plásticas** plastic arts
2 (= *habilidad*) skill; (= *astucia*) craftiness; **malas ~s** trickery *sing*
3 (= *artificio*) workmanship, artistry; **sin ~** (*como adj*) clumsy; (*como adv*) clumsily
4 ➤ **arte de pesca** (= *red*) fishing net; (= *caña*) fishing tackle

artefacto SM 1 (*Téc*) device, appliance ➤ **artefactos del baño** (*RPI*) bathroom fixtures 2 (*Arqueología*) artefact, artifact (*EEUU*)

arteria SF 1 (*Med*) artery 2 (= *calle*) artery; **la ~ principal de una ciudad** the main thoroughfare of a town

arterial ADJ arterial

arterioesclerosis SF INV, **arteriosclerosis** SF INV arteriosclerosis

artero ADJ cunning, crafty

artesa SF trough

artesanal ADJ [*método, oficio*] traditional; [*queso, cerámica*] hand-crafted; **productos ~es** (= *objetos*) crafts

artesanía SF (= *arte*) craftmanship; (= *productos*) crafts *pl*; **obra de ~** piece of craftsmanship

artesano/a **A** ADJ = **artesanal** **B** SM/F craftsman/craftswoman, artisan

artesiano ADJ **pozo ~** artesian well

artesonado SM coffered ceiling

ártico **A** ADJ Arctic **B** SM **el Ártico** the Arctic

articulación SF 1 (*Anat*) articulation (*frm*), joint 2 (*Mec*) joint 3 (*Ling*) articulation

articulado ADJ articulated, jointed

articular /1a/ **Ⓐ** VT **1** (Ling) to articulate **2** (Mec) to articulate, join together **3** (Jur) to article **Ⓑ articularse** VPR **~se en torno a** o **sobre** [trama, programa] to be made up of

articulista SMF columnist, contributor (to a paper)

artículo SM **1** (Com) article, item ➤ **artículos alimenticios** foodstuffs ➤ **artículos de consumo** consumer goods ➤ **artículos de escritorio** stationery ➤ **artículos de primera necesidad** basic commodities, essentials ➤ **artículos de tocador** toiletries **2** (= escrito) article, paper; (en libro de consulta) entry, article ➤ **artículo de fondo** leader, editorial **3** (Ling) article ➤ **artículo definido** definite article ➤ **artículo indefinido** indefinite article **4** [de ley, documento] article, section, item

artífice SMF **1** (= responsable) **el ~ de la victoria** the architect of victory **2** (Arte) artist, craftsman/craftswoman

artificial ADJ [flor, luz, inseminación] artificial; [material] artificial, man-made

artificialmente ADV artificially

artificiero/a SM/F explosives expert, bomb-disposal officer

artificio SM **1** (= truco) artifice; (= astucia) cunning, sly trick **2** (= aparato) device, appliance

artificioso ADJ contrived

artillería SF artillery ➤ **artillería antiaérea** anti-aircraft guns pl ➤ **artillería pesada** heavy artillery

artillero SM (Mil) artilleryman; (Aer, Náut) gunner

artilugio SM gadget, contraption

artimaña SF cunning ruse

artista SMF **1** (Arte) artist **2** (Teat, Cine) artist, artiste ➤ **artista de cine** film actor/film actress (esp Brit), movie actor/movie actress (esp EEUU) ➤ **artista invitado/a** guest artist **3** (*) (= persona hábil) **es un ~ haciendo paella** he's an expert at making paella

artístico ADJ artistic

artrítico ADJ arthritic

artritis SF INV arthritis ➤ **artritis reumatoide** rheumatoid arthritis

artrosis SF INV osteoarthritis

arveja SF **1** (= algarroba) vetch **2** (SAm) (= guisante) pea

arvejilla SF (RPl) sweet pea

arzobispado SM archbishopric

arzobispal ADJ archiepiscopal; **palacio ~** archbishop's palace

arzobispo SM archbishop

as SM **1** (Naipes) ace; ✦ MODISMO **guardarse un as en la manga** to have an ace up one's sleeve **2** (*) (= campeón) ace; **es un as** he's a star* ➤ **as del volante** champion driver

asa SF handle

asadera SF (CS) (gen) baking tin (Brit), baking pan (EEUU); (para asados) roasting tin

asado **Ⓐ** ADJ (Culin) (al horno) roast antes de s, roasted; (a la parrilla) grilled (Brit), broiled (EEUU); (a las brasas) barbecued **Ⓑ** SM **1** (Culin) roast, joint **2** (CS) (= comida) barbecue; (= carne asada) barbecued meat

asador¹ SM **1** (= varilla) spit; (= aparato) spit roaster **2** (= restaurante) carvery

asador²(a) SM/F (CS) person who barbecues the food at a barbecue

asadura SF, **asaduras** SFPL offal sing; (Culin) chitterlings

asaetear /1a/ VT to shoot, hit (with an arrow)

asalariado/a **Ⓐ** ADJ wage-earning **Ⓑ** SM/F wage earner

asalmonado ADJ salmon coloured, salmon colored (EEUU)

asaltante SMF [de persona] attacker, assailant; [de banco, tienda] raider

asaltar /1a/ VT **1** [+ persona] to attack, assault; (Mil) to storm; [+ banco, tienda] to break into, raid **2** [dudas] to assail

asalto SM **1** (= atraco) robbery; **~ a un banco** bank raid,

bank robbery **2** (Mil) attack, assault; **el ~ al parlamento** the attack o assault on parliament, the storming of parliament; **tomar por ~** to take by storm **3** (Boxeo) round; (Esgrima) bout **4** (LAm) (= fiesta sorpresa) surprise party

asamblea SF **1** (= reunión) meeting; [de trabajadores] mass meeting **2** (= congreso) assembly ➤ **Asamblea Nacional** National Assembly

asambleísta SMF member of the assembly

asar /1a/ **Ⓐ** VT **1** (Culin) to roast; **~ a la parrilla** to grill (Brit), broil (EEUU); **~ a las brasas** to barbecue **2** (= acosar) to pester, plague (**con, a** with) **Ⓑ asarse** VPR [persona] to roast; **me aso de calor** I'm boiling

asaz ADV (Literat) very, exceedingly

ascendencia SF **1** (= linaje) ancestry; (= origen) origin **2** (= influencia) = **ascendiente**

ascendente **Ⓐ** ADJ [movimiento] ascending; [tendencia] rising, increasing; **en una curva ~** in an upward curve **Ⓑ** SM (Astrol) ascendant

ascender /2g/ **Ⓐ** VI **1** (= subir) [persona] (en montaña) to climb up; (en el aire) to rise, ascend (frm) **2** [temperatura, presión] to go up, rise **3** [empleado, militar] to be promoted; **~ a primera división** [equipo] to go up o be promoted to the first division; **~ al trono** to ascend the throne **4** **~ a** [cantidad] to amount to, come to; **el número de heridos asciende ya a 20** the number of wounded has now reached 20 **Ⓑ** VT [+ empleado, militar] to promote

ascendiente SM ascendancy (frm), (powerful) influence (**sobre** over)

ascensión SF **1** (= subida) (a montaña) ascent; (al poder) rise; **desde su ~ al trono** (frm) since his accession to the throne (frm) **2** (Rel) **la Ascensión** the Ascension

ascenso SM **1** (= subida) (a montaña) ascent; (al poder) rise **2** [de temperatura, precio, popularidad] rise; **temperaturas en ~** rising temperatures, temperatures on the rise **3** [de empleado, militar, equipo] promotion (**a** to)

ascensor SM lift (Brit), elevator (EEUU)

ascensorista SMF lift attendant (Brit), elevator operator (EEUU)

ascetismo SM asceticism

asco SM **1** (= sensación) disgust, revulsion; **¡qué ~!** how disgusting!, how revolting!; **coger ~ a algo** to get sick of sth; **dar ~ a algn** to sicken sb, disgust sb; **me das ~** you disgust me; **poner cara de ~** to look disgusted, pull a face; ✦ MODISMOS **hacer ~s a algo** to turn up one's nose at sth; **poner a algn del ~** (Méx*) to call sb all sorts of names; **morirse de ~** (Esp*) to be bored to tears o to death **2** (= objeto) **es un ~** it's disgusting; **estar hecho un ~** to be filthy

ascua SF live coal, ember; ✦ MODISMOS **arrimar el ~ a su sardina** to look after number one; **estar en ~s** to be on tenterhooks; **pasar por algo como sobre ~s** to rush through sth

aseado ADJ (= limpio) clean; (= arreglado) neat, tidy

asear /1a/ **Ⓐ** VT (= limpiar) to clean up; (= arreglar) to smarten up **Ⓑ asearse** VPR to tidy o.s. up, smarten o.s. up

asechanza SF trap, snare

asediar /1b/ VT **1** (Mil) to besiege **2** (= acosar) to pester; **lo ~on a preguntas** he was bombarded with questions

asedio SM **1** (Mil) siege **2** (= acoso) pestering

asegurado/a **Ⓐ** ADJ **1** (= con seguro) insured (**de, contra** against; **en** for) **2** (= confirmado) **el éxito de la huelga está ~** the success of the strike is assured; **tenemos el éxito ~** we are bound to be successful **Ⓑ** SM/F **el ~** (= que contrata el seguro) the policyholder; (= beneficiario) the insured (frm)

asegurador(a) SM/F insurer

aseguradora SF insurance company

asegurar /1a/ **Ⓐ** VT **1** (= sujetar) to secure; **hay que ~ mejor el cuadro a la pared** the painting needs to be more firmly fixed o secured to the wall; **~ algo con algo** to secure sth with sth **2** (= proteger) [+ zona, edificio] to make secure (**contra** against) **3** (= garantizar) [+ derecho] to guarantee; **si quieres ~te**

el aprobado if you want to be certain of passing; **es posible, pero no lo aseguro** it's possible, but I can't tell you for sure; **se lo aseguro** take my word for it *o* I assure you; **~ a algn que** to assure sb that **4** (= *declarar*) to maintain; **asegura no saber nada del asunto** he maintains *o* affirms that he knew nothing about the matter **5** (*Com, Fin*) [+ *vehículo, vivienda*] to insure (**de, contra** against; **en** for); **deberías ~ el coche a todo riesgo** you should have your car fully insured, you should take out a comprehensive insurance policy **B asegurarse** VPR **1** (= *cerciorarse*) to make sure; **para ~nos del todo** in order to make quite sure **2** (= *garantizarse*) to make sure of, assure o.s. of; **tuvo que luchar para ~se la victoria** he had a struggle to make sure of victory *o* to assure himself of victory **3** (*Com, Fin*) to insure o.s., take out an insurance policy

asemejar /1a/ **A** VT **1** (= *hacer parecido*) to make look alike, make similar **2** (= *comparar*) to liken, compare (**a** to) **B asemejarse** VPR (*en carácter*) to be alike, be similar; (*en aspecto*) to look alike; **~se a** to be like, resemble

asentaderas* SFPL (*hum*) behind* *sing*, bottom *sing*, seat *sing*

asentado ADJ **1** (= *instalado*) [*persona*] settled; [*tropas*] located, positioned; [*ciudad, campamento*] situated, located; **los israelíes ~s en Cisjordania** Israelis settled on the West Bank; **la mesa no está bien asentada** the table is wobbly **2** (= *establecido*) [*costumbre, tradición*] well-established; [*creencia*] deep-rooted, deeply-rooted, firmly held; **marcas firmemente asentadas en el mercado europeo** brands that are well-established in the European market; **una empresa asentada en España desde hace años** a company that has been established in Spain for many years **3** (*esp LAm*) [*persona*] **ser ~** to be well-balanced

asentamiento SM settlement

asentar /1j/ **A** VT **1** (= *colocar*) [+ *objeto*] to place; [+ *campamento*] to set up; ✦ MODISMO **~ la cabeza** to settle down **2** (= *establecer*) [+ *principio*] to lay down; [+ *opinión*] to state **3** (= *aplanar*) [+ *tierra*] to firm down; [+ *costura*] to flatten **4** (*Constr*) [+ *cimientos*] to lay down **5** (*Téc*) [+ *válvula*] to seat **6** (*Méx frm*) (= *afirmar*) to state **B asentarse** VPR **1** (= *estar situado*) [*ciudad*] to stand, be situated **2** (= *posarse*) [*líquido, polvo*] to settle; [*ave*] to alight **3** (= *consolidarse*) to settle **4** (= *basarse*) **~se en** *o* **sobre algo** to be based on sth **5** (*LAm*) (= *adquirir madurez*) to settle down

asentimiento SM assent, consent

asentir /3i/ VI **1** (= *mostrarse conforme*) to assent, agree; **~ con la cabeza** to nod, nod one's head in agreement **2 ~ a** (= *consentir en*) to agree to, consent to

aseo SM **1** (= *acto*) washing, toilet (*frm*); (= *higiene*) cleanliness **2 aseos** (= *retrete*) toilet *sing* (*Brit*), rest room *sing* (*EEUU*)

Asepeyo SF ABR (= **Asistencia Sanitaria Económica para Empleados y Obreros**) *Spanish job-related health insurance scheme*

aséptico ADJ aseptic

asequible ADJ [*precio, producto*] affordable; [*persona, estudio*] accessible

aserción SF (*frm*) assertion

aserradero SM sawmill

aserrar /1j/ VT to saw, saw through

aserrín SM (*LAm*) sawdust

aserruchar /1a/ VT (*LAm*) = **aserrar**

aserto SM (*frm*) assertion

asesinar /1a/ VT to murder; (*Pol*) to assassinate

> **Asesinar** suele traducirse por **to murder**, pero cuando se trata del asesinato de figuras políticas impotantes, como presidentes del gobierno o primeros ministros, se utiliza **to assassinate**: "Robert Kennedy fue asesinado en 1968", *Robert Kennedy was assassinated in 1968.*

asesinato SM (= *acto*) murder, homicide (*EEUU*); (*Pol*) assassination

asesino/a **A** ADJ murderous **B** SM/F murder/murderess, killer; (*Pol*) assassin ➤ **asesino/a en serie, asesino/a múltiple, asesino/a serial** (*LAm*) serial killer

asesor(a) **A** ADJ advisory **B** SM/F adviser, consultant ➤ **asesor(a) de imagen** public relations adviser ➤ **asesora del hogar** (*Chi frm*) maid ➤ **asesor(a) fiscal** tax consultant, tax adviser ➤ **asesor(a) jurídico/a** legal adviser ➤ **asesor(a) técnico/a** technical adviser *o* consultant

asesoramiento SM advice

asesorar /1a/ **A** VT **1** (*Jur*) to advise, give legal advice to, give professional advice to **2** (*Com*) to act as consultant to **B asesorarse** VPR **~se con** to take advice from, consult

asesoría SF consultancy ➤ **asesoría jurídica** legal advice

asestar /1a/ VT [+ *golpe*] to deal; **~ una puñalada a algn** to stab sb

aseveración SF (*frm*) assertion, contention

aseverar /1a/ VT (*frm*) to assert

asexuado ADJ sexless

asexual ADJ asexual

asfaltar /1a/ VT to asphalt

asfalto SM asphalt, blacktop (*EEUU*)

asfixia SF (= *agobio*) suffocation, asphyxiation; (*Med*) asphyxia

asfixiante ADJ [*calor*] suffocating; (*Med, Jur*) asphyxiating

asfixiar /1b/ **A** VT **1** (= *ahogar*) to suffocate **2** (= *agobiar*) **la vida en el pueblo la asfixiaba** village life was suffocating *o* stifling her; **los impuestos han asfixiado el comercio** taxation has suffocated trade **B asfixiarse** VPR **1** (= *ahogarse*) to suffocate; **murieron asfixiados en el incendio** they suffocated (to death) in the fire **2** (= *agobiarse*) to suffocate, feel stifled **3** [*negocio, economía, empresario*] to be strangled

así **A** ADV **1** (= *de este modo*) **1.1** (*con ser*) **—te engañaron, ¿no es ~? —sí, ~ es** "they deceived you, didn't they?" — "yes, they did", "they deceived you, isn't that so?" — "yes, it is"; **usted es periodista ¿no es ~?** you're a journalist, aren't you?; **yo soy ~** that's the way I am; **perdona, pero creo que eso no es ~** excuse me, but I think that's not true; **~ es como lo detuvieron** that's how *o* this is how they arrested him; **~ sea** (*Rel*) Amen **1.2** (*con otros verbos*) like that, like this; **esto no puede seguir ~** things can't go on this way, this can't go on like this; **se iniciaba ~ una nueva etapa** thus *o* so a new phase began; **¡~ se habla!** that's what I like to hear!; **~ ocurrió el accidente** that's how *o* this is how the accident happened; **~ me agradecen lo que hice por ellos** this is the thanks I get for what I did for them; **~ están las cosas** that's the way things are; **puede leer el contrato si ~ lo desea** you can read the contract if you wish; **¿por qué te pones ~?** why do you get worked up like that?; **dijo que llamaría y ~ lo hizo** he said he would call and he did **2** (*acompañando a un sustantivo*) like that; **¿por una cosa ~ se han enfadado?** they got angry over a thing like that? **3 ~ de 3.1** (+ SUSTANTIVO) **tuvieron ~ de ocasiones de ganar** they had so *o* this many chances to win **3.2** (+ ADJ, ADV) **un baúl ~ de grande** a trunk as big as this, a trunk this big; **no para de comer y luego ~ está de gorda** she never stops eating, that's why she's so fat; **~ de feo era que ...** (*LAm*) he was so ugly that ... **4 ~ como** (= *lo mismo que*) the same way as; (= *mientras que*) whereas, while; (= *además de*) as well as; **~ como tú te portes conmigo, me portaré yo** I'll behave the same way as you do to me; **~ como uno de sus hijos es muy listo, el otro no estudia nada** whereas *o* while one of their children is

very bright, the other doesn't study at all; **se necesita el
original ~ como una copia** you need the original as well as
a copy
5 (*otras locuciones*) **por ~ decirlo** so to speak; **no ~** unlike;
los gastos fueron espectaculares, no ~ los resultados the
expenditure was astonishing, unlike the results; **¡~ no
más!** (*Méx**) (= *sin cuidado*) anyhow; (= *sin motivo*) just like
that; **es un tema muy importante para tratarlo ~ no más** it's
a very important issue, you can't just treat it any old how;
se fue ~ no más, sin decir nada he left just like that,
without saying anything; **o ~** about, or so; **20 dólares o ~**
about 20 dollars, 20 dollars or so; **llegarán el jueves o ~**
they'll arrive around Thursday, they'll arrive on Thursday
or thereabouts; **~ sin más** just like that; **y ~ sucesivamente**
and so on and so forth; **~ y todo** even so; **✦** MODISMOS **así
así** so-so; **~ o asá* ✧ ~ o asao* ✧ ~ que asá*** it makes no
odds, one way or another; **~ como ~** just like that; **no
gastan el dinero ~ como ~** they don't spend money willy-
nilly; **no se hace ~ como ~** it's not as easy as all that; **~ es
la vida** such is life, that's life
Ⓑ CONJ **1** (= *aunque*) even if; **~ tenga que recorrer el
mundo entero** even if I have to travel the whole world
2 (= *consecuentemente*) so; **esperan lograr un acuerdo,
evitando ~ la huelga** they are hoping to reach an
agreement and so avoid a strike, they are hoping to reach
an agreement, thereby *o* thus avoiding a strike (*frm*); **~
pues** so; **~ (es) que** so
3 (= *ojalá*) **¡~ te mueras!** I hope you drop dead!*
4 (= *en cuanto*) **~ que** (+ SUBJUN): **~ que pasen unos años
todo se olvidará** in a few years everything will be
forgotten

Asia SF Asia ➤ **Asia Menor** Asia Minor

asiático/a Ⓐ ADJ Asian, Asiatic **Ⓑ** SM/F Asian

asidero SM **1** (= *asa*) handle **2** (= *pretexto*) pretext;
(= *base*) basis

asiduidad SF **1** (= *persistencia*) assiduousness
2 (= *regularidad*) regularity

asiduo/a Ⓐ ADJ (= *persistente*) assiduous; (= *frecuente*)
frequent, regular; **como ~ lector de su periódico** as a
regular reader of your newspaper **Ⓑ** SM/F regular, regular
customer; **es un ~ del museo** he is a frequent visitor to the
museum

asiento SM **1** (= *mueble*) seat; [*de bicicleta*] saddle; **tomar ~**
(*frm*) to take a seat; **✦** MODISMO **calentar el ~: no ha
calentado el ~** he didn't stay long ➤ **asiento de atrás** [*de
coche*] rear seat; [*de moto*] pillion seat ➤ **asiento delantero**
front seat ➤ **asiento trasero = asiento de atrás 2** (= *fondo*)
[*de jarrón, silla*] bottom **3** (*Mec*) seating **4** (= *poso*) sediment
5 (*Arquit*) settling **6** (*Com*) (*en libro*) entry **7** (= *estabilidad*)
stability; (= *juicio*) good sense, judgment

asignación SF **1** (= *acto*) assignment, allocation **2** (*Fin*)
allowance

asignar /1a/ VT (= *adjudicar*) to assign; [+ *recursos*] to
allocate, apportion; [+ *labor*] to set

asignatario/a SM/F (*LAm*) heir/heiress, legatee

asignatura SF subject, course ➤ **asignatura pendiente**
(*Educ*) failed subject, resit *o* retake subject; (= *asunto
pendiente*) unfinished business

asilado/a SM/F (*en institución*) inmate; (*Pol*) refugee,
political refugee

asilar /1a/ **Ⓐ** VT **1** (= *internar*) to put into a home, put
into an institution **2** (*LAm*) (= *dar asilo político a*) to give
political asylum to **Ⓑ asilarse** VPR **1** (= *refugiarse*) to take
refuge (**en** in); (*Pol*) to seek political asylum **2** [*anciano*] to
enter a home, enter an institution

asilo SM **1** (= *institución*) home, institution ➤ **asilo de
ancianos** old people's home **2** (*Pol*) asylum; (= *abrigo*)
shelter, refuge

asimetría SF (= *falta de simetría*) asymmetry;
(= *desequilibrio*) imbalance

asimétrico ADJ asymmetric, asymmetrical

asimilación SF assimilation

asimilar /1a/ **Ⓐ** VT to assimilate **Ⓑ asimilarse** VPR **~se a**
(= *parecerse*) to resemble

asimismo ADV (= *igualmente*) likewise, in the same way;
(= *también*) also

asintomático ADJ asymptomatic

asir /3a; *tiempo presente como salir*/ **Ⓐ** VT to grasp, take
hold of (**con** with; **de** by) **Ⓑ asirse** VPR to take hold; **~se a**
o **de** (= *agarrarse*) to seize

asirio/a ADJ, SM/F Assyrian

asísmico ADJ (*LAm*) [*construcción*] earthquake-resistant;
[*medidas*] anti-earthquake

asistencia SF **1** (= *presencia*) attendance (**a** at) **2** (= *ayuda*)
help, assistance; (*Med*) care, nursing ➤ **asistencia en
carretera** roadside assistance ➤ **asistencia letrada** legal aid
➤ **asistencia médica** medical care ➤ **asistencia pública** (*CS*)
public health authority ➤ **asistencia sanitaria** health care
➤ **asistencia social** welfare work, social work ➤ **asistencia
técnica** technical support

asistencial ADJ social security *antes de s* (*Brit*), welfare
antes de s (*EEUU*)

asistenta SF charwoman, daily help

asistente SMF **1** (= *ayudante*) assistant; (*Mil*) orderly;
(*Ftbl*) linesman ➤ **asistente social** social worker **2 los ~s**
(= *presentes*) those present

asistir /3a/ **Ⓐ** VI **1** (= *acudir*) to attend, go; **no asistió a mi
clase** he did not come to *o* attend my class
2 (= *presenciar*) **~ a algo** to witness sth; **estamos asistiendo
a una nueva revolución tecnológica** we are witnessing a
new technological revolution
3 (*Naipes*) to follow suit
Ⓑ VT **1** (= *ayudar*) to help, assist (*frm*)
2 (*Med*) [+ *paciente, enfermo*] to care for, look after;
[+ *herido, accidentado*] to look after, help; **~ un parto** to
deliver a baby
3 (*Jur*) **su abogado le asistió en la declaración** his lawyer
was present when he gave his statement
4 (*frm*) (= *respaldar*) **le asiste el derecho a recurrir la
sentencia** you have the right to appeal (against) the
sentence; **le asiste la razón** he has right on his side

askenazi ADJ, SMF Ashkenazi

asma SF asthma

asmático/a ADJ, SM/F asthmatic

asno SM donkey, ass

asociación SF (= *acción*) association; (= *sociedad*) society,
association; **por ~ de ideas** by association of ideas
➤ **asociación de vecinos** residents' association

asociado/a Ⓐ ADJ [*compañía, síntoma, problema*]
associated; [*miembro*] associate **Ⓑ** SM/F associate, member

asocial ADJ asocial

asociar /1b/ **Ⓐ** VT to associate; **no quiero que me asocien
con él** I don't want to be associated with him; **asocian
este gen al cáncer de mama** this gene is linked with *o* to
breast cancer **Ⓑ asociarse** VPR **1 ~se (con)** to join together
(with), join forces (with) **2** (*Com, Fin*) **~se (con)** to go into
partnership (with) **3 ~se a algo** to join in sth, become a
member of sth **4** [*circunstancias, hechos*] to combine

asocio SM (*Col*) **en ~** in association (**de** with)

asolador ADJ devastating

asolar /1a/ VT to raze, raze to the ground, destroy

asolear /1a/ **Ⓐ** VT to put in the sun **Ⓑ asolearse** VPR to
sunbathe

asomar /1a/ **Ⓐ** VT [+ *cabeza, hocico*] (*hacia arriba*) to lift;
(*hacia afuera*) to poke out; **asomó la cabeza por encima de
la valla para mirar** he peeped over the fence; **"prohibido
asomar la cabeza por la ventanilla"** "do not lean out of the
window"
Ⓑ VI **1** (= *verse*) [*sol, luna*] (*al salir*) to come up; (*entre las
nubes*) to come out; **le asomaba la cartera** his wallet was
sticking out; **el vestido le asomaba por debajo del abrigo**
her dress was showing below her coat
2 (= *salir*) [*planta*] to come up; [*arruga, cana*] to appear;
por la tarde le asomaba ya la barba by the afternoon he
already had a five o'clock shadow*, by the afternoon his
stubble was beginning to show; **ya le empiezan a ~
algunas canas** he has already got some grey *o* (*EEUU*) gray

hairs coming through o appearing

© **asomarse** VPR **algunas personas se ~on a mirar** some people came out to look; **"prohibido asomarse"** "do not lean out of the window"; **~se a** o **por** [+ *barandilla*] to lean over; [+ *ventana*] (*para mirar*) to look out of; (*sacando el cuerpo*) to lean out of; **asomaos a la terraza para ver la vista** come out on to the terrace to see the view

asombrar /1a/ **Ⓐ** VT to amaze, astonish; **me asombra verte trabajar tanto** I'm amazed o astonished to see you working so hard; **a mí ya nada me asombra** nothing surprises me any more **Ⓑ** **asombrarse** VPR to be amazed, be astonished; **se asombró (de) que lo supieras** she was amazed o astonished that you knew

asombro SM amazement, astonishment; **ante el ~ de todo el mundo** to everyone's amazement o astonishment; **no salgo de mi ~** I can't get over it

asombroso ADJ amazing, astonishing

asomo SM **1** (= *aparición*) appearance **2** (= *indicio*) sign, indication; **sin ~ de violencia** without a trace of violence; **ni por ~** by no means

asonada SF riot, disturbance

asonancia SF (*Literat*) assonance

asonante ADJ assonant

asorocharse /1a/ VPR (*LAm*) to get mountain sickness

aspa SF **1** [*de molino*] sail, arm; [*de ventilador*] blade; **en ~** X-shaped **2** (*CS*) (= *asta*) horn

aspamento SM (*RPl*) = **aspaviento**

aspar /1a/ VT **¡que te aspen!** get lost!*; **¡que me aspen si lo sé!** I'm blowed (*esp Brit*) o darned (*esp EEUU*) if I know!*

aspaventero ADJ excitable

aspaviento SM exaggerated display of feeling; **hacer ~s** to make a great fuss

aspecto SM **1** (= *apariencia*) look; **un hombre de ~ saludable** a healthy-looking man; **¿qué ~ tenía?** what did he look like?; **Juan tiene muy mal ~** Juan isn't looking good o well at all; **esa herida tiene mal ~** that wound looks nasty ➤ **aspecto exterior** outward appearance **2** (= *punto*) aspect; **estudiar todos los ~s de una cuestión** to study all aspects of an issue; **en algunos ~s me parece una obra genial** in some respects I think it is a work of genius **3** (*Ling*) aspect

aspereza SF [*de terreno*] roughness, ruggedness; [*de carácter*] surliness; **contestar con ~** to answer harshly; **✦** MODISMO **limar ~s** to smooth things over

áspero ADJ **1** (*al tacto*) rough; [*terreno*] rough, rugged **2** (*al gusto*) sour, tart **3** [*clima*] harsh; [*trato*] rough **4** [*voz*] rough, rasping; [*tono*] surly, gruff

aspersión SF (*Agr*) spraying; **riego por ~** watering by spray, watering by sprinklers

aspersor SM sprinkler

áspid SM, **áspide** SM asp

aspidistra SF aspidistra

aspiración SF **1** (*Zool, Med*) breathing in, inhalation; (*Ling*) aspiration; (*Mús*) short pause **2** (= *anhelo*) aspiration; **aspiraciones** aspirations, ambition *sing*

aspirado ADJ aspirate

aspiradora SF vacuum cleaner; **pasar la ~** to vacuum, do the vacuuming

aspirante **Ⓐ** ADJ [*persona*] aspiring **Ⓑ** SMF candidate, applicant (**a** for)

aspirar /1a/ **Ⓐ** VT **1** [+ *aire*] to breathe in, inhale; [+ *líquido*] to suck in, take in **2** (*Ling*) to aspirate **Ⓑ** VI **~ a algo** to aspire to sth; **no aspiro a tanto** I do not aim so high

aspirina SF aspirin

asquear /1a/ **Ⓐ** VT to disgust **Ⓑ** **asquearse** VPR to be nauseated, feel disgusted

asquerosidad SF **1** (= *suciedad*) filth; **estar hecho** o **ser una ~** to be filthy **2** (= *dicho*) obscenity

asqueroso ADJ (= *repugnante*) disgusting, revolting; (= *sucio*) filthy

asquiento* ADJ (*LAm*) = **asqueroso**

asta SF **1** [*de banderas*] flagpole; **a media ~** at half mast **2** (*Zool*) horn, antler

astabandera SF (*Méx*) flagpole

asterisco SM asterisk

asteroide SM asteroid

astigmatismo SM astigmatism

astilla SF splinter, chip

astillar /1a/ **Ⓐ** VT to splinter, chip **Ⓑ** **astillarse** VPR to splinter

astillero SM shipyard, dockyard

astracán SM astrakhan

astral ADJ astral

astringente **Ⓐ** ADJ astringent (*frm*), binding **Ⓑ** SM astringent

astro SM **1** (*Astron*) star, heavenly body **2** (*Cine*) star

astrofísica SF astrophysics *sing*

astrofísico/a SM/F astrophysicist

astrolabio SM astrolab

astrología SF astrology

astrólogo/a SM/F astrologer

astronauta SMF astronaut

astronave SF spaceship

astronomía SF astronomy

astronómico ADJ astronomical

astrónomo/a SM/F astronomer

astucia SF (= *inteligencia*) astuteness, cleverness; (= *maña*) guile, cunning; **actuar con ~** to act cunningly, be crafty

astur ADJ, SMF Asturian

asturiano/a **Ⓐ** ADJ, SM/F Asturian **Ⓑ** SM (*Ling*) Asturian

Asturias SF (*tb* **el Principado de ~**) Asturias

astuto ADJ (= *sagaz*) astute, clever; (= *mañoso*) crafty, sly

asueto SM **día de ~** day off; **tomarse una tarde de ~** to take an afternoon off

asumir /3a/ VT **1** (= *responsabilizarse de*) [+ *reto, tarea*] to take on; [+ *cargo*] to take up; [+ *mando*] to take over, assume (*más frm*); **el gobierno asumió el compromiso de crear empleo** the government committed itself o (*más frm*) undertook the commitment to creating employment; **ha asumido la dirección de la empresa** he has taken control of o has taken over the company **2** (= *aceptar*) [+ *consecuencias*] to take, accept; [+ *crítica*] to accept; [+ *problema, enfermedad, derrota*] to come to terms with, accept; **ya he asumido que no podré volver a esquiar** I've already come to terms with o accepted the fact that I won't be able to ski again **3** (= *adoptar*) to adopt, take; **asumió el papel de víctima** he took on the role of victim **4** (= *adquirir*) to assume; **la cuestión del paro ha asumido una dimensión distinta** the question of unemployment has taken on o assumed a different dimension

asunceño ADJ of/from Asunción

Asunción SF (*Geog*) Asunción

asunción SF assumption; **la Asunción** (*Rel*) the Assumption

asunto SM **1** (= *cuestión*) matter; **un ~ familiar grave** an urgent family matter; **el ~ de los impuestos divide al gobierno** the government is divided on the matter o question o issue of taxes; **~s a tratar** agenda; **no te metas en mis ~s** mind your own business; **¡eso es ~ mío!** that's my business o affair!; **¡~ concluido!** that's an end to the matter!; **mal ~** doesn't look good; **el ~ es que ...** the thing is (that) ... **2** (*Pol*) **el ~ Rumasa** the Rumasa affair ➤ **asuntos exteriores** foreign affairs **3** (= *aventura amorosa*) affair; **es un ~ de faldas** there's a woman involved in this somewhere along the line **4** (*CS*) **¿a ~ de qué hiciste eso?** what did you do that for?

asustadizo ADJ **1** [*persona*] (= *que se asusta mucho*) easily frightened; (= *nervioso*) nervy, jumpy

2 [*animal*] shy, skittish

asustar /1a/ Ⓐ VT to frighten, scare Ⓑ **asustarse** VPR to be frightened, get scared; **~se de algo** to be frightened *o* scared by sth

atacante SMF attacker, assailant

atacar /1g/ Ⓐ VT **1** [+ *enemigo, ciudad, fortaleza*] to attack **2** [*enfermedad, plaga, sustancia*] to attack; **ataca al hígado** it attacks the liver; **me estaba atacando el sueño** I was succumbing to sleep; **este niño me ataca los nervios*** that child gets on my nerves* **3** [+ *teoría, planteamiento, propuesta*] to attack **4** [+ *problema*] to tackle, combat Ⓑ VI to attack

atado SM bundle; **~ de cigarrillos** (*CS*) packet of cigarettes (*esp Brit*), pack of cigarettes (*esp EEUU*)

atadura SF tie

atajar /1a/ Ⓐ VT **1** (= *interceptar*) to stop, intercept; (*LAm*) (= *coger*) to catch, catch in flight; **~ un golpe** to parry a blow **2** [+ *proceso*] to end, stop, call a halt to; [+ *abuso*] to put a stop to; **este mal hay que ~lo** we must put an end to this evil Ⓑ VI to take a short cut

atajo SM short cut

atalaya SF watchtower, observation post

atañer /2f; *defectivo*/ VI **~ a** to concern, have to do with; **en lo que atañe a eso** with regard to that, concerning that

atapuzarse* /1f/ VPR (*Carib*) to stuff o.s.

ataque SM **1** (*Mil*) attack; **volver al ~** to return to the attack; **pasar al ~** to go on the offensive; **¡al ~!** charge! ➤ **ataque aéreo** air raid, air strike ➤ **ataque preventivo** pre-emptive strike

2 (*Med*) **un ~ de tos** a coughing fit *o* a fit of coughing ➤ **ataque cardíaco** heart attack ➤ **ataque cerebral** brain haemorrhage *o* (*EEUU*) hemorrhage ➤ **ataque de nervios** fit of panic ➤ **ataque de pánico** panic attack ➤ **ataque epiléptico** epileptic fit

3 (= *arranque*) [*de celos, ira*] fit; **me entró** *o* **dio un ~ de risa** I got a fit of the giggles; **cuando se entere le da un ~*** she'll have a fit when she finds out*

4 (= *crítica*) attack

5 (*Dep*) attack

atar /1a/ VT **1** (= *amarrar*) to tie, tie up; (= *abrochar*) to fasten; ✦ MODISMOS **está de ~** he's raving mad; **dejar algo atado y bien atado** to leave no loose ends, leave everything properly tied up **2** (= *quitar libertad a*) to tie down; ✦ MODISMOS **~ corto a algn** to keep sb on a tight rein; **~ las manos a algn** to tie sb's hands; **verse atado de pies y manos** to be tied hand and foot

atarantado ADJ **1** (*And, Méx*) (= *aturdido*) dazed **2** (*And*) (= *precipitado*) impetuous

atarantar /1a/ Ⓐ VT (*And, Méx*) (= *aturdir*) to stun, daze Ⓑ **atarantarse** VPR **1** (*And, Méx*) to be stunned, be dumbfounded **2** (*Chi*) (= *precipitarse*) to rush

atardecer /2d/ Ⓐ VI to get dark; **atardecía** night was falling Ⓑ SM dusk, evening; **al ~** at dusk

atareado ADJ busy

atascar /1g/ Ⓐ VT [+ *agujero*] to plug, bung up; [+ *cañería*] to clog up Ⓑ **atascarse** VPR **1** [*persona*] (*al avanzar*) to get stuck; (*en discurso*) to dry up*; **se quedó atascado a mitad de la cuesta** he got stuck halfway up the climb **2** [*cañería*] to get clogged up **3** [*plan*] to get bogged down

atasco SM (*Aut*) traffic jam; (= *obstrucción*) obstruction, blockage

ataúd SM coffin, casket (*EEUU*)

ataviar /1c/ (*liter*) Ⓐ VT to dress up (**con, de** in) Ⓑ **ataviarse** VPR to dress up (**con, de** in)

atávico ADJ atavistic

atavío (*liter*) SM attire (*frm*)

atavismo SM atavism

ate SM (*Méx*) **~ de guayaba** guava jelly

ateísmo SM atheism

atejonarse /1a/ VPR (*Méx*) to hide

atembado* ADJ (*Col*) silly, stupid

atemorizar /1f/ Ⓐ VT to frighten, scare Ⓑ **atemorizarse**

VPR to get frightened, get scared (**de, por** at, by)

atemperar /1a/ VT to temper

atemporal ADJ timeless

Atenas SF Athens

atenazar /1f/ VT to grip; **el miedo me atenazaba** I was gripped by fear

atención SF **1** (= *interés*) attention; **¡~, por favor!** attention, please!; **siguen con ~ las explicaciones** they follow the explanations attentively; **en ~ a algo** (*frm*) in view of sth; **en ~ a los intereses de los clientes** in view of the clients' interests; **llamar la ~:** **un coche que no llama la ~ por su diseño** a car with a rather run-of-the-mill design; **le gusta ponerse faldas cortas para llamar la ~** she wears short skirts to be noticed; **llamar la ~ a algn** (= *atraer*) to attract sb's attention; (= *reprender*) to tell sb off; **me llamó la ~ no verte por allí** I was surprised not to see you there; **a mí el chocolate no me llama mucho la ~** I'm not too fond of *o* keen on chocolate; **prestar ~** to pay attention (**a** to); **los niños necesitan que les presten mucha ~** children need to be given a lot of attention

2 (= *precaución*) care; **necesitas poner más ~ en lo que haces** you need to take greater care over what you do; **¡atención!, frenos potentes** beware!: powerful brakes

3 (= *cortesía*) **le agradezco la ~** that's very thoughtful of you; **ha tenido una bonita ~ regalándome ese libro** it was a really nice thought of hers to buy me that book

4 (= *asistencia*) **"horario de atención al público"** (*en oficina*) "hours of business"; (*en tienda*) "opening hours" ➤ **atención al cliente** customer service ➤ **atención médica** medical attention ➤ **atención personalizada** personalized service ➤ **atención primaria** primary health care ➤ **atención psicológica** counselling, counseling (*EEUU*) ➤ **atención psiquiátrica** psychiatric treatment ➤ **atención sanitaria** medical attention

5 (*Correspondencia*) **a la ~ de** (*en carta*) for the attention of; (*en sobre*) attention

atender /2g/ Ⓐ VT **1** (= *ocuparse de*) [+ *asunto*] to deal with; [+ *paciente*] to look after; **atiende primero lo más urgente** deal with the most urgent things first; **sólo atienden los casos urgentes** they only deal with urgent cases

2 (= *recibir*) [+ *cliente*] (*en tienda*) to serve; (*en oficina, consulta*) to see; **¿lo atienden, señor?** are you being served, sir?; **siéntese, enseguida la ~án** take a seat, they'll see you in a minute

3 [+ *consulta, negocio, oficina*] (*como encargado*) to run; (*como trabajador*) to work in; **atiendo la recepción cuando la secretaria no está** I work in reception *o* I man the reception desk when the secretary is not there; **el servicio de habitaciones está mal atendido** the room service is very sloppy

4 (= *prestar atención a*) [+ *ruego, petición*] to respond to, comply with (*frm*); [+ *necesidades, demanda*] to meet; [+ *compromiso, obligación*] to fulfill; [+ *reclamaciones, protesta, queja*] to deal with; [+ *aviso, consejo*] to heed; **Señor, atiende nuestras súplicas** (*Rel*) Lord, heed our prayers

5 (*Telec*) [+ *teléfono, llamada*] to answer

Ⓑ VI **1** (= *prestar atención*) to pay attention; **~ a algo/algn** to listen to sth/sb; **atendiendo a** [+ *criterio, datos*] according to; [+ *situación, circunstancias*] bearing in mind, considering **2** (= *ocuparse de*) **~ a** [+ *detalles*] to take care of; [+ *necesidades, demanda*] to meet

3 (*Com*) (= *servir*) to serve; **¿quién atiende aquí?** who's serving here?

4 ~ por to answer to the name of; **extraviado caniche blanco; atiende por Linda** lost: white poodle; answers to the name of Linda

ateneo SM cultural association, cultural centre, cultural center (*EEUU*)

atenerse /2k/ VPR **~ a 1** (= *ceñirse a*) **aténgase a lo que se le pregunta** confine yourself to answering the question **2** (= *cumplir*) **~ a la ley** to abide by the law, obey the law; **aténgase a lo que se le ordena** follow the orders; **debes atenerte a lo acordado** you must stick to what has been agreed

3 (= *remitirse a*) **me atengo a mis declaraciones previas**

I stand by my previous statements; **contigo nunca sé a qué atenerme** I never know what to expect with you; **si lo haces, atente a las consecuencias** if you do it, you'll have to take the consequences

ateniense ADJ, SMF Athenian

atentado SM attack; **~ a o contra la vida de algn** attempt on sb's life ➤ **atentado contra el pudor, atentado contra la honra** indecent assault➤ **atentado golpista** attempted coup ➤ **atentado suicida** suicide bombing, suicide attack ➤ **atentado terrorista** terrorist attack

atentamente ADV 1 (= con atención) [escuchar, observar] attentively; [leer] carefully; **debes seguir ~ todos sus consejos** you should follow all his advice carefully 2 (= cortésmente) kindly; **Le saluda ~** (en cartas formales) Yours faithfully o sincerely (Brit), Sincerely yours (EEUU)

atentar /1a/ VI **~ contra la honra de algn** to indecently assault sb; **~ contra la ley** to break the law; **~ contra la vida de algn** to make an attempt on sb's life

atento ADJ 1 (= pendiente) [persona] attentive; [mirada] watchful; **tenéis que estar ~s en clase** you have to be attentive in class, you have to pay attention in class; **estate ~ y avísanos si lo ves** stay alert o keep a look out and let us know if you see him; **estar ~ a** [+ explicación] to pay attention to; [+ peligro] to be on the alert for, be on the lookout for; [+ movimiento, ruido] to listen (out) for 2 (= cortés) attentive; **un dependiente muy ~** a very helpful o attentive sales assistant

atenuante Ⓐ ADJ [circunstancias] extenuating, mitigating Ⓑ SM o SF extenuating circumstance, mitigating circumstance

atenuar /1e/ Ⓐ VT (= aminorar) to attenuate; (Jur) [+ crimen] to extenuate; [+ impresión] to tone down; [+ impacto] to cushion, lessen Ⓑ **atenuarse** VPR to weaken

ateo/a Ⓐ ADJ atheistic Ⓑ SM/F atheist

aterciopelado ADJ velvety

aterido ADJ stiff with cold

aterrador ADJ terrifying

aterrar /1a/ Ⓐ VT to terrify Ⓑ **aterrarse** VPR to be terrified (**de** by)

aterrizaje SM landing ➤ **aterrizaje forzoso** emergency landing, forced landing

aterrizar /1f/ VI to touch down, land

aterrorizar /1f/ VT (= aterrar) to terrify; (Mil, Pol) to terrorize

atesorar /1a/ VT [+ dinero, riquezas] to hoard, accumulate; [+ virtudes] to possess; [+ momento, recuerdo] to treasure

atestado¹ SM (Jur) affidavit, statement

atestado² ADJ packed; **~ de** packed with, crammed with, full of

atestar¹ /1a/ VT (Jur) to attest, testify to

atestar² /1j/ VT (= llenar) to pack, stuff (**de** with)

atestiguar /1i/ VT to testify to, give evidence of

atiborrado ADJ **~ de** full of, stuffed with, crammed with

atiborrar /1a/ Ⓐ VT to fill, stuff (**de** with) Ⓑ **atiborrarse** VPR to stuff o.s. (**de** with)

ático SM (= desván) attic; (= apartamento) penthouse

atigrado ADJ (= con manchas) striped; [gato] tabby

atildado ADJ elegant, stylish

atinado ADJ (= correcto) accurate, correct; (= sensato) wise, sensible; (= pertinente) pertinent; (= agudo) penetrating; **una decisión poco atinada** a rather unwise decision

atinar /1a/ VI 1 (= acertar) to be right; **siempre atina** he always gets it right, he always hits the nail on the head; **~ a con o en** to hit upon, find; **~ en el blanco** to hit the mark 2 (= conseguir) **~ a hacer algo** to manage to do sth

atingencia SF (LAm frm) 1 (= relación) connection, relationship 2 (= observación) remark, comment

atípico ADJ atypical, exceptional

atiplado ADJ high-pitched

atirantar /1a/ VT to tighten, tauten

atisbar /1a/ VT 1 (= espiar) to spy on, watch; (a hurtadillas) to peep at 2 (= lograr ver) to see, make out, discern (frm); **atisbamos un rayo de esperanza** we can just see a glimmer of hope

atisbo SM (= indicio) inkling, indication

atizador SM (para el fuego) poker

atizar /1f/ Ⓐ VT 1 [+ fuego] to poke, stir; [+ horno] to stoke 2 [+ discordia] to stir up; [+ pasión] to fan, rouse 3 (*) [+ golpe] to give Ⓑ VI **¡atiza!*** gosh!

atlántico Ⓐ ADJ Atlantic Ⓑ SM **el (Océano) Atlántico** the Atlantic, the Atlantic Ocean

Atlántida SF Atlantis

atlantista Ⓐ ADJ NATO antes de s Ⓑ SMF NATO supporter

atlas SM INV atlas

atleta SMF athlete

atlético ADJ athletic

atletismo SM athletics sing ➤ **atletismo en pista cubierta** indoor athletics

atmósfera SF atmosphere

atmosférico ADJ atmospheric

atochamiento SM (Chi) traffic jam

atole SM Mexican drink thickened with corn meal and often flavoured with chocolate, fruit etc

atolladero SM jam*, fix*; **salir del ~** to get out of a jam o a fix*; **sacar a algn del ~** to get sb out of a jam o a fix*

atolón SM atoll

atolondrado ADJ 1 (= aturdido) bewildered, stunned 2 (= irreflexivo) thoughtless, reckless; (= casquivano) scatterbrained

atómico ADJ atomic

atomización SF 1 (con atomizador) spraying 2 (= desintegración) atomization

atomizador SM atomizer, spray

átomo SM atom; **ni un ~ de** not a trace of

atonal ADJ atonal

atonía SF lethargy, apathy

atónito ADJ amazed, astounded; **me miró ~** he looked at me in amazement o astonishment

átono ADJ atonic, unstressed

atontado ADJ 1 (= aturdido) bewildered, stunned 2 (= tonto) stupid, thick (Brit*), dumb (esp EEUU*)

atorar /1a/ Ⓐ VT 1 (= obstruir) to stop up, obstruct 2 (esp LAm) to stop, hold up Ⓑ **atorarse** VPR (esp LAm) (= atragantarse) to choke

atormentar /1a/ Ⓐ VT 1 (= torturar) to torture 2 (= causar aflicción) to torment Ⓑ **atormentarse** VPR to torment o.s.

atornillar /1a/ VT to screw down

atorrante (And, CS) Ⓐ ADJ lazy Ⓑ SMF tramp, bum (EEUU*)

atortolado ADJ **están ~s** they're like two turtle-doves

atosigar /1h/ VT (= importunar) to harass, plague, pester*; (= presionar) to put pressure on, pressurize, pressure

atracadero SM pier

atracador(a) SM/F (en tienda, banco) armed robber, raider; (en la calle) mugger

atracar /1g/ Ⓐ VT (= robar) [+ banco] to hold up; [+ persona] to mug Ⓑ VI (Náut) to berth Ⓒ **atracarse** VPR 1 (= atiborrarse) to stuff o.s. (**de** with) 2 (Chi) (= acercarse) to come up (**a** to)

atracción SF 1 (Fís) attraction 2 [de persona, lugar] attraction 3 (tb **~ de feria**) attraction, fairground attraction

atraco SM [de banco, tienda] holdup, robbery; [de persona] mugging ➤ **atraco a mano armada** armed robbery

atracón* SM blow-out*, chow-down (EEUU**); **darse un ~** to stuff o.s. (**de** with), pig out* (**de** on)

atractivo Ⓐ ADJ attractive Ⓑ SM attractiveness, appeal

atraer /2o/ Ⓐ VT 1 (Fís) to attract 2 (= interesar) [+ cliente] to attract; **esa chica me atrae mucho** I find that girl very attractive; **no me atrae mucho lo del viaje a Turquía** that

Turkey trip doesn't appeal to me much **3** (= *ganar*) [+ *apoyo*] to win, draw; [+ *atención*] to attract, engage **B** **atraerse** VPR **se atrajo las simpatías de todos** he won everyone's affection, everyone liked him

atragantarse /1a/ VPR **1** (*al comer*) to choke (**con** on); **me atraganté con una espina** I choked on a fish bone; **se me atragantó una miga de pan** a crumb went down the wrong way **2** (*) (= *caer mal*) **el tío ese se me atraganta** I can't stomach that guy*, that guy gets up my nose (*Brit**)

atrancar /1g/ **A** VT [+ *puerta*] to bar, bolt; [+ *cañería*] to clog, block up **B** **atrancarse** VPR (= *atascarse*) to get bogged down (**en** in); (*haciendo algo*) to get stuck

atrapar /1a/ VT (*en trampa*) to trap; [+ *ladrón, resfriado*] to catch; **quedaron atrapados en la montaña** they were trapped on the mountainside

atrás **A** ADV **1** (*posición*) **1.1** (= *a la espalda*) behind; **la pelota le vino de** ~ the ball came from behind; **la panadería está ahí** ~ the bakery is back there; **quedarse** ~ to fall behind, get left behind **1.2** (= *al final*) at the back; **los alumnos de** ~ **estaban fumando** the pupils at the back were smoking; **más** ~ **se ve mejor la pantalla** you can see the screen better if you sit further back; **la parte de** ~ the back, the rear; **está muy** ~ **en la fila** he is a long way down the queue (*esp Brit*) *o* line (*EEUU*); **las patas de** ~ the back legs; **la rueda de** ~ the back *o* rear wheel **2** (*dirección*) backwards; **dar un paso** ~ to take a step back(wards); **ir hacia** *o* **para** ~ to go back(wards) **3** (*en sentido temporal*) **días** ~ days ago; **dejaron** ~ **sus rencores** they put aside their bitterness; **mirar** ~ ◇ **volver la vista** ~ to look back **4** ~ **de** (*LAm*) behind; ~ **del árbol** behind the tree **B** EXCL **¡atrás!** back!, get back!

atrasado ADJ **1** (= *con retraso*) late, behind, behind time; [*pago*] overdue; [*número de revista*] back *antes de s*; [*reloj*] slow; **mi reloj está ocho minutos** ~ my watch is eight minutes slow; **estar** ~ **en los pagos** to be in arrears; **estar** ~ **de noticias** to lack up-to-date information **2** [*país*] backward; [*alumno*] slow, backward

atrasar /1a/ **A** VT [+ *salida*] to delay; [+ *reloj*] to put back **B** VI [*reloj*] to lose time **C** **atrasarse** VPR [*persona*] to stay back, remain behind; [*tren*] to be late; [*reloj*] to lose time; ~**se en los pagos** to be in arrears

atraso SM **1** (*esp LAm*) (= *retraso*) delay; **el tren lleva** ~ the train is late; **llegar con 20 minutos de** ~ to arrive 20 minutes late **2** [*de país*] backwardness; **salir del** ~ to catch up **3** atrasos (*Com, Fin*) arrears

atravesado ADJ **la farola quedó atravesada en la calle** the lamppost fell across the street; ✦ MODISMO **lo tengo** ~* I can't stand him

atravesar /1j/ **A** VT **1** (= *colocar a través*) to put across **2** (= *cruzar*) [+ *calle, puente, frontera*] to cross; **esta avenida atraviesa la capital** this road passes through *o* crosses the capital; **el túnel atraviesa la montaña** the tunnel goes *o* passes under the mountain **3** (= *sufrir*) [+ *periodo, situación, crisis*] to go through; **mi familia atraviesa momentos difíciles** my family is going through a difficult time **4** (= *perforar*) [+ *cuerpo, órgano*] to go through; **la bala le atravesó el cráneo** the bullet went through his skull **B** **atravesarse** VPR **1** (= *colocarse a través*) **el autobús se nos atravesó en la carretera** the bus came out into the road in front of us; **se me ha atravesado una espina en la garganta** I've got *o* I have a fishbone stuck in my throat **2** (*) (= *hacerse insoportable*) **se me ha atravesado Antonio** I've had all I can take of Antonio*

atrayente ADJ attractive

atreverse /2a/ VPR to dare; ~ **a hacer algo** to dare to do sth; **no me atrevo** ◇ **no me atrevería** I wouldn't dare; **¿te atreves?** are you game?, will you?; **¡atrévete!** (= *amenaza*) just you dare!; ~ **con un rival** to take on a rival; **se atreve con todo** he'll tackle anything

atrevido ADJ **1** (= *audaz*) [*persona, pregunta*] daring, bold **2** (= *insolente*) cheeky (*Brit*), sassy (*EEUU*) **3** [*chiste*] daring, risqué

atrevimiento SM **1** (= *audacia*) daring, boldness **2** (= *insolencia*) insolence, cheek

atrezzo SM = **attrezzo**

atribución SF **1** [*de hecho*] attribution **2** (*Pol*) **atribuciones** powers *pl*, functions *pl*

atribuir /3g/ **A** VT **1** ~ **algo a** [+ *autor*] to attribute sth to; [+ *causa*] to put sth down to **2** (*Pol*) [+ *poderes*] to confer **B** **atribuirse** VPR ~**se algo** to claim sth for o.s.; ~**se la responsabilidad de un atentado** to claim responsibility for an attack

atribulado ADJ afflicted, suffering

atributivo ADJ attributive

atributo SM **1** (= *cualidad*) attribute **2** (*Ling*) predicate

atril SM (*para libro*) lectern; (*para partitura*) music stand

atrincherar /1a/ **A** VT to fortify with trenches **B** **atrincherarse** VPR **1** (*Mil*) to entrench o.s., dig in **2** ~**se en** (= *protegerse*) to take refuge in

atrio SM (*Hist*) atrium, inner courtyard; (*Rel*) vestibule, porch

atrocidad SF **1** (= *acto terrible*) atrocity, outrage **2** (*) (*como exageración*) **¡qué** ~**!** how dreadful!, how awful!; **la comedia es una** ~ the play is awful

atrofia SF atrophy

atrofiar /1b/ **A** VT to atrophy **B** **atrofiarse** VPR to atrophy, be atrophied

atronador ADJ deafening

atropelladamente ADV **correr** ~ to run helter-skelter; **hablar** ~ to gabble

atropellado ADJ hasty

atropellar /1a/ **A** VT **1** (= *arrollar*) to knock down, run over; **la atropelló un taxi** she was knocked down *o* run over by a taxi **2** (= *infringir*) [+ *derecho, constitución, estatuto*] to sweep aside, ride roughshod over **B** **atropellarse** VPR **1** (= *empujarse*) **entraron de uno en uno sin** ~**se** they went in one by one without pushing and shoving **2** (= *precipitarse*) to rush

atropello SM **1** (*Aut*) accident; (= *empujón*) shove, push **2** (= *abuso*) abuse (**de** of), disregard (**de** for)

atroz ADJ (= *terrible*) atrocious; (= *cruel*) cruel, inhuman

ATS SMF ABR (*Esp*) (= **ayudante técnico sanitario**) registered nurse

attrezzo SM (*Esp, Méx Teat*) props *pl*

atuendo SM attire

atufado* ADJ (*CAm, Carib*) (= *vanidoso*) proud, stuck-up*

atufar* /1a/ VT [*olor*] to overcome, overpower

atún SM tuna (fish)

atunero **A** ADJ tuna *antes de s* **B** SM (= *barco*) tuna fishing boat

aturdido ADJ bewildered, dazed

aturdimiento SM **1** bewilderment **2** (= *irreflexión*) thoughtlessness, recklessness

aturdir /3a/ **A** VT **1** (*físicamente*) (*con golpe*) to stun, daze; [*ruido*] to deafen; [*droga, movimiento, vino*] to make giddy, make one's head spin **2** (= *atolondrar*) to stun, dumbfound; (= *dejar perplejo*) to bewilder; **la noticia nos aturdió** the news stunned us, we were stunned by the news **B** **aturdirse** VPR (= *atolondrarse*) to be stunned; (= *quedarse perplejo*) to be bewildered

aturrullar* /1a/ **A** VT to bewilder, perplex **B** **aturrullarse** VPR to get flustered

atusar /1a/ **A** VT [+ *pelo*] (= *alisar*) to smooth, smooth down **B** **atusarse** VPR to dress up to the nines; ~**se el bigote** to stroke one's moustache

audacia SF boldness, audacity

audaz ADJ bold, audacious

audible ADJ audible

audición SF **1** (*Med*) hearing **2** (*Teat*) audition **3** (*Mús*) concert

audiencia SF **1** (= *acto*) audience; **recibir a algn en** ~ to grant sb an audience **2** (*Jur*) (= *tribunal*) court ➤ **audiencia pública** (*Pol*) public hearing **3** (*Radio, TV*) audience; **índice de** ~ ratings *pl*, audience ratings *pl*

audífono SM **1** [*de sordo*] hearing aid **2** (*LAm*) **audífonos** (= *cascos*) headphones

audiolibro SM audio book

audiovisual 🅐 ADJ audiovisual **🅑** SM audiovisual presentation

auditar /1a/ VT to audit

auditivo ADJ auditory (*frm*), hearing *antes de s*

auditor(a) SM/F (*Fin*) auditor ➤ **auditor(a) de cuentas** auditor ➤ **auditor(a) externo/a** external auditor; *ver tb* **auditora**

auditora SF firm of auditors, auditors *pl*; *ver tb* **auditor**

auditoría SF (*Com, Fin*) audit, auditing

auditorio SM auditorium, hall

auge SM **1** (= *apogeo*) peak; **está en el ~ de su popularidad** he is at the peak *o* height of his popularity; **ya ha pasado el ~ del tecno** the heyday of techno is over **2** (= *ascendencia*) **el rápido ~ del fundamentalismo** the rapid rise of fundamentalism; **un momento de ~ de la industria** a time of industrial growth; **una moda en ~** an increasingly popular fashion; **el sector turístico está en pleno ~** tourism is booming *o* experiencing a boom

augurar /1a/ VT [*cosa*] to augur; [*persona*] to predict, foresee

augurio SM **1** (= *presagio*) omen; (= *profecía*) prediction **2** augurios (= *deseos*) best wishes (**para** for)

augusto ADJ august

aula SF (*Escol*) classroom; (*Univ*) lecture room ➤ **aula magna** assembly hall, main hall

aullar /1a/ VI to howl, yell

aullido SM howl, yell; **dar ~s** to howl, yell

aumentar /1a/ **🅐** VT **1** [+ *tamaño*] to increase; (*Ópt*) to magnify **2** [+ *cantidad, intensidad, velocidad*] to increase; [+ *sueldo*] to increase, raise; [+ *producción*] to increase, step up; **estas pastillas pueden ~ las molestias** these tablets can make the problem worse **🅑** VI **1** [*tamaño*] to increase **2** [*cantidad, precio, producción*] to increase, go up; **la inflación aumentó en un 2%** inflation increased *o* went up by 2%

3 ~ de to increase in; **~ de peso** [*objeto*] to increase in weight; [*persona*] to put on *o* gain weight; **~ de tamaño** to increase in size

aumento SM **1** [*de tamaño*] increase; (*Ópt*) magnification **2** [*de cantidad, producción, velocidad, intensidad*] increase; [*de precio*] increase, rise; **ir en ~** to be on the increase ➤ **aumento de peso** (*en objeto*) increase in weight; (*en persona*) weight gain ➤ **aumento de población** population increase ➤ **aumento de precio** rise in price ➤ **aumento de sueldo, aumento salarial** (pay) rise (*Brit*), (pay) raise (*esp EEUU*) **3** (*Elec, Radio*) amplification

aun ADV **1** (= *incluso*) even; **yo pagaría mil y ~ dos mil** I'd pay a thousand, even two thousand; **~ siendo tan joven es muy responsable** even though he's so young he's very responsible **2 ~ así: ~ así, no creo que fuera** even so, I don't think I'd go; **es muy rica y ~ así trabaja** she's very rich but she still works **3 ~ cuando: ~ cuando me lo rogara, no se lo daría** even if he begged me I wouldn't give it to him **4 ni ~** not even; **no lo aceptaría ni ~ regalado** I wouldn't accept it even as a present; **y ni ~ así lo haría** and I wouldn't do it even then

aún ADV **1** (= *todavía*) (*temporal*) (*en oraciones afirmativas*) still; (*en oraciones negativas*) yet; **~ está aquí** he's still here; **~ no lo sabemos** we still don't know, we don't know yet; **¿no ha venido ~?** hasn't he come yet? **2** (= *incluso*) even; **más ~** even more

aunar /1a/ **🅐** VT to join, unite **🅑 aunarse** VPR to unite

aunque CONJ **1** (+ INDICATIVO) although, though, even though; **~ estaba cansado vino con nosotros** although *o* though he was tired he came with us; **llevaba un abrigo de piel, ~ era un día muy caluroso** she wore a fur coat, even though it was a very hot day

2 (+ SUBJUNTIVO) even if; **debes ir, ~ no quieras** you must go, even if you don't want to; **me dijo que no me lo diría, ~ lo supiera** he said he wouldn't tell me even if he knew; **~ no me creas, es verdad** you may not believe me, but it's true

> **Aunque** se puede traducir por **although** o **though**, que es más coloquial: "Estoy pensando en ir, aunque no sé cuando", *I'm thinking of going, though I don't know when.* Cuando se trata de un uso más enfático se utiliza **even though**: "Seguí andando, aunque me dolía mucho la pierna", *I went on walking, even though my leg was hurting badly.* Cuando "aunque" significa "incluso si" se traduce por **even if**: "Debes ir, aunque no quieras", *You must go, even if you don't want to.*

3 (*sin verbo*) **es guapa ~ algo bajita** she's pretty but rather short, she's pretty even if she is on the short side

aúpa 🅐 EXCL (*al levantar a un niño*) up!, upsadaisy!; (*para animar*) up!, come on! **🅑** ADJ (*) **una paliza de ~** a good thrashing*; **una tormenta de ~** a hell of a storm*

au pair SMF au pair

aupar /1a/ VT (= *levantar*) to help up; **sus discos la han aupado al primer puesto** her records have lifted her *o* shot her up to top spot

aura SF **1** (= *halo*) aura **2** (= *ave*) vulture, buzzard (*EEUU*)

áureo ADJ (*liter*) golden

aureola SF (*Rel*) halo, aureole (*frm*); (= *gloria*) fame

auricular 🅐 ADJ aural, of the ear; **el pabellón ~** the outer ear **🅑** SM **1** [*de teléfono*] receiver, handset **2 auriculares** (= *cascos*) headphones, earphones

aurífero ADJ gold-bearing

aurora SF dawn ➤ **aurora boreal, aurora borealis** northern lights *pl*

auscultar /1a/ VT to sound, auscultate (*frm*)

ausencia SF absence

ausentarse /1a/ VPR to absent o.s. (**de** from)

ausente 🅐 ADJ **1** (*físicamente*) absent (**de** from); **estar ~ de** to be absent from, be missing from **2** (*mentalmente*) daydreaming **🅑** SMF absentee

ausentismo SM (*LAm*) absenteeism

auspiciar /1b/ VT to back, sponsor

auspicios SMPL **1** (= *patrocinio*) auspices, sponsorship *sing*; **bajo los ~ de** under the auspices of, sponsored by **2** (= *augurio*) omen; **buenos ~** good omen; **malos ~** bad omen

auspicioso ADJ (*esp LAm*) promising

austeridad SF austerity

austero ADJ austere

austral ADJ southern

Australia SF Australia

australiano/a ADJ, SM/F Australian

Austria SF Austria

austríaco/a ADJ, SM/F, **austriaco/a** ADJ, SM/F Austrian

autarquía SF autarky (*frm*), national self-sufficiency

autenticidad SF authenticity

auténtico ADJ **1** (= *legítimo*) authentic; [*persona*] genuine; **es un ~ campeón** he's a real champion **2** (*) (= *estupendo*) great*

autentificar /1g/ VT to authenticate

autillo SM tawny owl

autismo SM autism

autista 🅐 ADJ autistic **🅑** SMF autistic, autistic person; **es ~** he's autistic

autito SM (*CS*) ➤ **autitos chocadores** bumper cars, dodgems

auto[1] SM (*esp CS*) car, automobile (*EEUU*) ➤ **autos de choque** dodgems (*esp Brit*), bumper cars (*EEUU*)

auto² SM **1** (*Jur*) edict, judicial decree ➤ **auto de comparecencia** summons, subpoena (*EEUU*) ➤ **auto de prisión** warrant for arrest ➤ **auto de procesamiento** charge, indictment **2 autos** (= *documentos*) proceedings, court record *sing* **3** (*Rel, Teat*) mystery play, religious play ➤ **auto sacramental** eucharistic play **4** ➤ **auto de fe** (*Hist*) auto-da-fé

autoabastecerse /2d/ VPR (= *autoproveerse*) to supply o.s. (**de** with); (= *ser autosuficiente*) to be self-sufficient

autoabastecimiento SM self-sufficiency

autoadherente ADJ self-adhesive

autoadhesivo ADJ self-adhesive

autoanálisis SM INV self-analysis

autoanalizarse /1f/ VPR to analyze o.s., do self-analysis

autoayuda SF self-help

autobiografía SF autobiography

autobiográfico ADJ autobiographic, autobiographical

autobomba SF (*RPl*) fire engine

autobombo SM self-praise, self-glorification

autobús SM bus ➤ **autobús de línea** long-distance coach (*Brit*) o bus (*EEUU*)

autobusero/a SM/F bus driver

autocalificarse /1g/ VPR ~ **de** to describe o.s. as

autocar SM (*Esp*) coach (*Brit*), bus (*EEUU*) ➤ **autocar de línea** long-distance coach (*Brit*) o bus (*EEUU*)

autocaravana SF camper, motor home (*EEUU*)

autocartera SF holding of its own shares (*by a company*)

autocensura SF self-censorship

autoclave SM (*Med*) autoclave

autocompasión SF self-pity

autocontrol SM self-control, self-restraint

autoconvencerse /2d/ VPR to convince o.s.

autocracia SF autocracy

autócrata SMF autocrat

autocrático ADJ autocratic

autocrítica SF self-criticism

autóctono ADJ indigenous, native

autodefensa SF self-defence, self-defense (*EEUU*)

autodenominarse /1a/ VPR to call o.s.

autodestruirse /3g/ VPR to self-destruct

autodeterminación SF self-determination

autodidacta Ⓐ ADJ [*persona*] self-taught; [*formación, método*] autodidactic (*frm*) Ⓑ SMF autodidact, self-taught person

autodisciplina SF self-discipline

autodisparador SM self-timer

autodominio SM self-control

autoedición SF desktop publishing

autoempleo SM self-employment

autoengaño SM self-deception, self-delusion

autoerótico ADJ autoerotic

autoescuela SF driving school

autoestima SF self-esteem

autoestop SM = **autostop**

autoestopista SMF = **autostopista**

autógeno ADJ autogenous

autogestión SF self-management

autogiro SM autogiro

autogobierno SM self-government

autogolpe SM *coup organized by the government itself to allow it to take extra powers*

autógrafo SM autograph

autohipnosis SF INV autohypnosis, self-hypnosis

autoinculpación SF **1** (= *autoacusación*) self-incrimination **2** (*Jur*) plea of guilty

autoinmune ADJ autoimmune

autoinmunitario ADJ, **autoinmunológico** ADJ autoimmune

autolavado SM car-wash

autolesionarse /1a/ VPR to inflict injury on o.s., injure o.s.

autómata SM automaton, robot

automático Ⓐ ADJ automatic Ⓑ SM press stud (*Brit*), popper (*Brit**), snap (fastener) (*EEUU*)

automatización SF automation

automatizar /1f/ VT to automate

automedicarse /1g/ VPR to treat o.s.

automercado SM (*Carib*) supermarket

automoción SF **la industria de la** ~ the car industry, the automobile industry (*EEUU*)

automontable ADJ self-assembly

automotor Ⓐ ADJ **1** [*tren, máquina*] self-propelled **2** (*LAm frm*) car *antes de s*, automobile *antes de s* (*EEUU*) Ⓑ SM (*Ferro*) diesel train

automóvil SM car, automobile (*EEUU*) ➤ **automóvil de alquiler** hire car (*Brit*), rental car (*EEUU*)

automovilismo SM motoring ➤ **automovilismo deportivo** motor racing

automovilista SMF motorist, driver

automovilístico ADJ car *antes de s*, auto *antes de s* (*EEUU*); **accidente** ~ car accident

automutilarse /1a/ VPR to mutilate o.s.

autonomía SF **1** (= *independencia*) autonomy; (= *autogobierno*) self-government; **Estatuto de Autonomía** (*Esp*) Statute of Autonomy **2** (= *territorio*) autonomous region, autonomy **3** (*Aer, Náut*) range ➤ **autonomía de vuelo** range **4** [*de pila, batería*] battery range

autonómico ADJ (*Pol*) autonomous, self-governing; **elecciones autonómicas** elections for the autonomous regions; **política autonómica** policy concerning the autonomies; **el proceso** ~ the process leading to autonomy; **región autonómica** autonomous region

autónomo/a Ⓐ ADJ **1** (*Pol*) autonomous, self-governing **2** (*Inform*) stand-alone, off-line **3** [*persona*] self-employed; **trabajo** ~ self-employment Ⓑ SM/F self-employed person

autopista SF motorway (*Brit*), freeway (*EEUU*) ➤ **autopista de la información** information superhighway ➤ **autopista de peaje** toll road, turnpike (*EEUU*)

autoproclamarse /1a/ VPR to proclaim o.s.

autopsia SF post mortem, autopsy

autor(a) SM/F **1** [*de obra*] author, writer; [*de idea*] creator, originator, inventor; **el** ~ **del cuadro** the painter **2** [*de delito*] perpetrator; **los presuntos** ~**es del crimen** the suspected killers; **el** ~ **intelectual** the mastermind; **el** ~ **material** *the person directly responsible (for the crime)*

autoría SF authorship; **la** ~ **del atentado** the responsibility for the attack

autoridad SF (= *potestad*) authority; (= *persona*) authority; **las** ~**es** the authorities

autoritario/a ADJ, SM/F authoritarian

autoritarismo SM authoritarianism

autorización SF authorization, permission

autorizado ADJ **1** (= *oficial*) authorized, official **2** (= *fiable*) authoritative **3** (*Com*) approved; **la persona autorizada** the officially designated person, the approved person

autorizar /1f/ VT (= *dar facultad a*) to authorize, empower; (= *permitir*) to approve, license

autorradio SF car radio

autorregulación SF self-regulation

autorretrato SM self-portrait

autoservicio SM **1** (= *tienda*) self-service store, self-service shop (*esp Brit*) **2** (= *restaurante*) self-service restaurant

autostop SM, **auto-stop** SM hitch-hiking; **hacer** ~ to hitch-hike, thumb lifts

autostopista SMF hitch-hiker

autosuficiencia SF **1** (*Econ*) self-sufficiency **2** (= *petulancia*) smugness

autosuficiente ADJ **1** (*Econ*) self-sufficient **2** (= *petulante*) smug

autosugestión SF autosuggestion

autovía SF main road, state highway (*EEUU*)

auxiliar[1] **Ⓐ** ADJ **1** (*Univ*) assistant *antes de s* **2** (*Ling*) auxiliary **3** [*plantilla*] ancillary **Ⓑ** SMF assistant ➤ **auxiliar administrativo** administrative assistant ➤ **auxiliar de clínica, auxiliar de enfermería** auxiliary nurse, nursing auxiliary, nurse's aide (*EEUU*) ➤ **auxiliar de laboratorio** lab assistant, laboratory assistant ➤ **auxiliar de vuelo** steward/stewardess

auxiliar[2] /1b/ VT (= *ayudar*) to help, assist; [+ *agonizante*] to attend

auxilio SM help, assistance (*más frm*); **primeros ~s** (*Med*) first aid; **acudir en ~ de algn** to come to sb's aid

Av. ABR (= **Avenida**) Av., Ave

aval SM **1** (*Com*) endorsement; [*de firma*] guarantee; **dar su ~ a** [+ *fiador*] to be a guarantor for; (*Fin*) to underwrite ➤ **aval bancario** banker's reference **2** (*Pol*) backing, support

avalancha SF **1** [*de nieve*] avalanche **2** (= *gran cantidad*) **una ~ de gente** a flood *o* torrent of people; **una ~ de cartas** an avalanche of letters

avalar /1a/ VT **1** (*Fin*) to underwrite; [+ *individuo*] to act as guarantor for **2** (*Com*) to endorse, guarantee; (= *responder de*) to answer for

avaluar /1e/ VT (*LAm*) to value (**en** at)

avance SM **1** (= *movimiento*) advance; **el ~ de las tropas** the advance of the troops **2** (= *progreso*) advance; **grandes ~s en el terreno de la genética** major advances in the field of genetics; **Pedro ha hecho grandes ~s en matemáticas** Pedro has made great progress in mathematics **3** (*Fin*) advance (payment) **4** (*Cine*) (= *tráiler*) trailer, preview (*EEUU*); **un ~ de la programación matinal** (*TV*) a look ahead at the morning's programmes *o* (*EEUU*) programs ➤ **avance informativo** news headlines, advance news summary

avante ADV (*esp LAm Náut*) ahead

avanzada SF (*LAm*) **de ~** cutting-edge *antes de s*

avanzadilla SF (= *patrulla*) scout, patrol; (= *soldados*) advance party

avanzado ADJ advanced; **de edad avanzada** ◇ **~ de edad** advanced in years; **a una hora avanzada** at a late hour

avanzar /1f/ **Ⓐ** VT **1** (= *mover*) to move forward, advance **2** [+ *dinero*] to advance **3** [+ *opinión, propuesta*] to put forward **4** [+ *resultado*] to predict; [+ *predicción*] to make **Ⓑ** VI **1** (= *ir hacia adelante*) to advance, move forward **2** (= *progresar*) to make progress; **ha avanzado mucho en química** she has made great progress in chemistry; **la genética avanza a ritmo vertiginoso** genetics is progressing *o* advancing at a dizzy speed **3** [*noche, invierno*] to draw on, approach

avaricia SF avarice, greed, greediness

avaricioso ADJ, **avariento** ADJ avaricious, greedy

avaro/a Ⓐ ADJ miserly, mean **Ⓑ** SM/F miser

avasallador ADJ overwhelming

avasallamiento SM subjugation

avasallar /1a/ VT **1** (= *subyugar*) to subjugate **2** (= *obligar*) **~ a algn** to steamroller sb (*into agreement or compliance*)

avatares SMPL ups and downs

Avda. ABR (= **Avenida**) Av., Ave

AVE SM ABR (= **Alta Velocidad Española**) *name given to high-speed train system*

ave SF (= *pájaro*) bird ➤ **ave del paraíso** bird of paradise ➤ **ave de paso** bird of passage ➤ **ave de presa, ave de rapiña** bird of prey ➤ **ave negra** (*CS*) crooked lawyer ➤ **aves de corral** poultry *sing* ➤ **ave zancuda** wader, wading bird

avecinarse /1a/ VPR to approach, come near

avefría SF lapwing

avejentado ADJ **lo encontré muy ~** I thought he'd aged a lot

avejentar /1a/ VT **el pelo blanco te avejentaba mucho** your grey hair made you look much older *o* put years on you

avellana SF hazelnut

avellano SM hazel nut tree

avemaría SF Ave Maria, Hail Mary

avena SF oats *pl*

avenida SF avenue

avenido ADJ **están muy bien ~s** [*personas*] they get on well; [*pareja*] they're well matched

avenimiento SM agreement, compromise

avenir /3a/ **Ⓐ** VT to reconcile, bring together **Ⓑ** avenirse VPR **1** (*Com*) to come to an agreement **2** [*hermanos, amigos*] to get on well together; **no se avienen** they don't get on; **~se con algn** to reach an agreement with sb **3** **~se a hacer algo** to agree to do sth

aventajado ADJ outstanding

aventajar /1a/ VT (= *superar*) to surpass, excel (**en** in); (*en carrera*) to outstrip

aventar /1j/ **Ⓐ** VT (*And, Méx*) (= *arrojar*) to throw **Ⓑ** aventarse VPR **1** (*And, Méx*) (= *tirarse*) to throw o.s. **2** (*Méx**) (= *atreverse*) to dare (**a** to)

aventón* SM (*esp Méx*) **dar ~ a algn** to give sb a ride, give sb a lift (*esp Brit*); **pedir ~** to hitch a lift (*esp Brit*), hitch a ride (*EEUU*); **viajar de ~** to hitch-hike, hitch

aventura SF **1** (= *suceso*) adventure; **una película de ~s** an adventure film **2** (= *riesgo*) **invertir ahora es una ~** investing at this time is a gamble; **se fue a América a buscar trabajo a la ~** he went to America on the off-chance of finding work; **se lanzaron a la ~ de montar un negocio** they embarked on the venture of setting up a business **3** (*) (= *amorío*) fling*, brief affair

aventurado ADJ risky, hazardous

aventurar /1a/ **Ⓐ** VT (= *arriesgar*) to venture, risk; [+ *opinión*] to hazard **Ⓑ** aventurarse VPR to dare, take a chance; **~se a hacer algo** to venture to do sth, risk doing sth

aventurero/a Ⓐ ADJ adventurous **Ⓑ** SM/F adventurer/adventuress

avergonzado ADJ **estar ~** to be ashamed (**de, por** about, at)

avergonzar /1f, 1l/ **Ⓐ** VT **1** (= *hacer pasar vergüenza*) to shame, put to shame; **no me avergüenza nuestra relación** I'm not ashamed of our relationship **2** (= *poner en un aprieto*) to embarrass; **me avergonzaste delante de todos** you embarrassed me in front of everyone **Ⓑ** avergonzarse VPR **1** (= *sentir vergüenza*) to be ashamed (**de, por** about, at, of); **~se de hacer algo** to be ashamed to do sth; **se avergonzó de haberlo dicho** he was ashamed at having said it **2** (= *sentirse violento*) to be embarrassed

avería SF (*Mec*) breakdown; **el coche tiene una ~** there's something wrong with the car

averiado ADJ broken down, faulty; **los faros están ~s** the lights have failed, there's something wrong with the lights; **"averiado"** "out of order"

averiar /1c/ **Ⓐ** VT (*Mec*) to cause a breakdown in, cause a failure in; (= *estropear*) to damage **Ⓑ** averiarse VPR (*Mec*) to have a breakdown; (= *estropearse*) to get damaged; **se averió el arranque** the starter failed, the starter went wrong

averiguación SF inquiry, investigation

averiguar /1i/ **Ⓐ** VT to find out, establish (*frm*); **ya han averiguado la identidad del padre** they have found out *o* (*frm*) established *o* discovered the identity of the father **Ⓑ** VI (*CAm, Méx**) (= *pelear*) to quarrel **Ⓒ** averiguarse VPR (*tb* **averiguárselas**) (*esp Méx*) to manage, get by; **yo me (las) averiguo muy bien solo** I manage *o* get by very well on my own; **tú olvídate, ya me (las) ~é yo con él** don't worry about it I'll sort it out with him

aversión SF aversion; **cobrar ~ a algn/algo** to take a strong dislike to sb/sth

avestruz SM ostrich

avezado ADJ experienced; **los ya ~s en estos menesteres**

those already experienced in such activities

aviación SF **1** (= *locomoción*) aviation ➤ **aviación comercial** commercial aviation **2** (*Mil*) air force; **la ~ francesa** the French air force

aviado* ADJ **estar ~** (*en un lío*) to be in a mess

aviador(a) SM/F **1** (*Aer*) (= *piloto*) pilot, airman; (= *tripulante*) crew member **2** (*Méx**) phantom employee **3** (*And, Carib*) (= *financiador*) mining speculator, mining financier

aviar /1c/ Ⓐ VT **1** (= *preparar*) to get ready, prepare **2** (*LAm*) (= *prestar dinero a*) to advance money to Ⓑ **aviarse** VPR to get ready

avícola ADJ poultry *antes de s*; **granja ~** poultry farm

avicultor(a) SM/F poultry farmer

avicultura SF poultry farming

avidez SF avidity, eagerness (**de** for); **con ~** avidly, eagerly

ávido ADJ avid, eager (**de** for); **~ de sangre** bloodthirsty

avieso ADJ perverse, wicked

avinagrado ADJ [*sabor*] sour, acid; [*persona*] embittered

avinagrar /1a/ Ⓐ VT to sour Ⓑ **avinagrarse** VPR [*persona*] to become embittered; [*vino*] to turn sour

avío SM **1** (*LAm Agr*) loan **2** **avíos** (= *equipo*) gear *sing*

avión SM (*Aer*) aeroplane (*Brit*), airplane (*EEUU*), plane; **por ~** (*Correos*) by airmail; **ir en ~** to go by plane, go by air ➤ **avión a reacción** jet plane ➤ **avión cisterna** fire-fighting plane ➤ **avión de combate** fighter, pursuit plane ➤ **avión de papel** paper dart (*esp Brit*), paper airplane (*EEUU*) ➤ **avión de pasajeros** passenger aircraft

avioneta SF light aircraft

avisar /1a/ VT **1** (= *informar*) to tell, notify (*frm*); **en cuanto ella llegue me avisas** tell me *o* let me know as soon as she comes; **la policía ya ha avisado a los familiares** the police have now told *o* (*frm*) notified *o* (*frm*) informed the family; **me avisó (de) que no comería en casa** she told me she wouldn't be eating at home; **me ~on con una semana de antelación** they gave me a week's notice **2** (= *advertir*) to warn; **te aviso que te denunciaré si no pagas** I warn you I shall report you if you don't pay; **se presentó en casa sin ~** he turned up at home without telling anyone *o* without warning **3** (= *llamar*) to call; **~ un taxi** to call a taxi; **~ al médico** to call the doctor, send for the doctor; **"avisamos grúa"** (*Esp*) "cars parked here will be towed away"

aviso SM **1** (= *notificación*) notice; **hasta nuevo ~** until further notice; **sin previo ~** without warning *o* notice; **dar ~ a algn de algo** to notify *o* inform sb of sth **2** (= *advertencia*) warning; **poner a algn sobre ~** to warn sb **3** (*Com, Fin*) demand note ➤ **aviso de envío** dispatch note, advice note **4** (*esp LAm Com*) advertisement ➤ **avisos clasificados** (*CS*), **avisos limitados** (*Col*) classified advertisements

avispa SF wasp

avispado ADJ sharp, bright

avispero SM **1** (= *nido*) wasps' nest **2** (*) (= *enredo*) hornet's nest, mess

avistamiento SM sighting

avistar /1a/ VT to sight, catch sight of

avituallamiento SM provisioning, supplying

avituallar /1a/ Ⓐ VT to provision, supply with food Ⓑ **avituallarse** VPR to provision o.s.

avivado/a* SM/F (*CS*) smart alec*, smart aleck (*esp EEUU**), wise guy (*EEUU**)

avivar /1a/ Ⓐ VT [+ *fuego*] to stoke, stoke up; [+ *color*] to brighten; [+ *dolor*] to intensify; [+ *pasión*] to excite, arouse; [+ *disputa*] to add fuel to; [+ *interés*] to stimulate Ⓑ **avivarse** VPR (*CS**) to wise up*

avizor ADJ **estar ojo ~** to be on the alert, be vigilant

avocastro SM (*Chi*) ugly devil

avutarda SF great bustard

axila SF armpit

axioma SM axiom

ay Ⓐ EXCL **1** (*dolor*) ow!, ouch! **2** (*pena*) oh!, oh dear!; **¡ay de mí!** whatever shall I do? Ⓑ SM (= *gemido*) moan, groan; (= *grito*) cry

aya SF governess

ayatolá SM, **ayatollah** SM ayatollah

ayer Ⓐ ADV yesterday; **el capítulo de ~** yesterday's episode; **~ por la mañana** yesterday morning; **antes de ~** the day before yesterday; **~ mismamente** *o* **mismo** (*Esp*) *o* **no más** (*LAm*) only yesterday; ✦ MODISMOS **parece que fue ~** it seems like (only) yesterday; **no nací ~** I wasn't born yesterday Ⓑ SM **el ~** (*liter*) yesteryear (*liter*)

aymará ADJ, SMF Aymara

ayo SM tutor

ayte. ABR (= **ayudante**) asst

Ayto ABR = **Ayuntamiento**

ayuda Ⓐ SF help, assistance (*más frm*) ➤ **ayuda a domicilio** home help (*esp Brit*), home helper (*EEUU*) ➤ **ayuda económica** economic aid ➤ **ayuda humanitaria** humanitarian aid Ⓑ SM ➤ **ayuda de cámara** valet

ayudante SMF (= *que ayuda*) helper, assistant; (*Escol, Univ*) assistant ➤ **ayudante de dirección** (*Teat, Cine*) production assistant ➤ **ayudante de laboratorio** lab(oratory) assistant, lab(oratory) technician ➤ **ayudante de realización** (*TV*) production assistant ➤ **Ayudante Técnico Sanitario** (*Esp*) Registered Nurse

ayudar /1a/ Ⓐ VT (= *asistir*) to help, assist, aid; **~ a algn a hacer algo** to help sb to do sth Ⓑ **ayudarse** VPR (*mutuamente*) to help each other

ayunar /1a/ VI to fast

ayunas SFPL **"no tomar en ayunas "** "not to be taken on an empty stomach"; **salir en ~** to go out without any breakfast; ✦ MODISMO **estar en ~** to be completely in the dark

ayuno SM fast, fasting; **guardar ~** to fast; **día de ~** fast day

ayuntamiento SM **1** (= *corporación*) town council, city council **2** (*edificio*) town hall, city hall

azabache SM (*Min*) jet

azada SF hoe

azadón SM large hoe, mattock, pickax (*EEUU*)

azafata SF (*tb* **~ de vuelo**) air hostess, stewardess, flight attendant; (*TV*) hostess ➤ **azafata de congresos** conference hostess

azafate SM (*LAm*) tray

azafrán SM saffron

azahar SM orange blossom

azalea SF azalea

azar SM chance, fate; **al ~** at random; **por ~** accidentally, by chance; **juego de ~** game of chance; **los ~es de la vida** life's ups and downs

azaroso ADJ (= *arriesgado*) risky, hazardous; [*vida*] eventful

Azerbaiyán SM Azerbaijan

azerbaiyaní ADJ, SMF Azerbaijani

azerbaiyano/a ADJ, SM/F Azerbaijani

azerí Ⓐ ADJ Azeri Ⓑ SMF (= *persona*) Azeri Ⓒ SM (*Ling*) Azeri

ázimo ADJ unleavened

azogue SM mercury, quicksilver

azorado ADJ embarrassed, flustered

azorar /1a/ Ⓐ VT to embarrass, fluster Ⓑ **azorarse** VPR to be embarrassed, get flustered

azotaina SF beating, spanking

azotar /1a/ VT **1** (= *zurrar*) to thrash, spank; (*con látigo*) to whip, flog **2** [*lluvia, olas*] to lash

azote SM **1** (= *golpe*) [*de mano*] spanking; [*de látigo*] stroke, lash **2** (= *látigo*) whip, scourge **3** (= *calamidad*) scourge

azotea SF flat roof, terrace roof; ✦ MODISMO **estar mal de la ~*** to be off one's nut*

azteca ADJ, SMF Aztec

azúcar SM *o (ESP IN LAM)* SF sugar ➤ **azúcar blanco/a** white sugar ➤ **azúcar blanquillo/a** white sugar ➤ **azúcar de caña** cane sugar ➤ **azúcar en polvo** (*Col*) icing sugar (*Brit*), confectioners' sugar (*EEUU*) ➤ **azúcar flor** (*Chi*), **azúcar glass**, **azúcar impalpable** (*RPl*) icing sugar (*Brit*), confectioners' sugar (*EEUU*) ➤ **azúcar moreno/a** brown sugar

azucarado ADJ sugary, sweet

azucarar /1a/ VT **1** (= *agregar azúcar a*) to sugar, add sugar to **2** (*fig*) (= *suavizar*) to soften, mitigate; (= *endulzar*) to sweeten

azucarera SF **1** (= *fábrica*) sugar refinery **2** (*LAm*) (= *recipiente*) sugar bowl

azucarero Ⓐ ADJ [*fábrica, industria*] sugar *antes de s*; [*zona*] sugar-producing, sugar-growing Ⓑ SM sugar bowl

azucena SF white lily, Madonna lily

azufre SM sulphur, sulfur (*EEUU*)

azul Ⓐ ADJ blue Ⓑ SM blue ➤ **azul celeste** sky blue ➤ **azul claro** light blue ➤ **azul marino** navy blue ➤ **azul turquesa** turquoise

azulado ADJ blue, bluish

azulejo SM (*vidriado*) glazed tile; (*en el suelo*) floor tile

azulgrana ADJ INV (*Dep*) of Barcelona F.C.

azulina SF cornflower

azulón ADJ, SM deep blue

azuloso ADJ (*LAm*) bluish

azuzar /1f/ VT to egg on, urge on, incite; ~ **a los perros contra algn** to set the dogs on sb, urge the dogs to attack sb

Bb

B, b SF [be] (= *letra*) B, b

baba SF **1** (= *saliva*) [*de persona*] dribble; [*de perro*] slobber; ✦ MODISMO **caerse la ~ a algn: se le cae la ~ por ella** he's completely besotted with *o* smitten with her **2** [*de caracol*] slime

babear /1a/ **Ⓐ** VI [*persona*] to dribble; [*perro*] to slobber **Ⓑ babearse** VPR (*Méx**) **-se por algo** to yearn for sth, drool at the thought of sth

babel SM *o* SF bedlam

babero SM [*de bebé*] bib; (*para el colegio*) smock

babi* SM (*Esp*) (*para el colegio*) smock

Babia SF ✦ MODISMO **estar en ~** to be daydreaming, be in the clouds

bable SM *Asturian dialect*

babor SM port, port side; **a ~** to port, on the port side; **poner el timón a ~** ◇ **virar a ~** to turn to port; **¡tierra a ~!** land to port!

babosa SF slug; *ver tb* **baboso**

babosada* SF (*CAm, Méx*) piece of stupidity; **¡~s!** nonsense!; **decir ~s** to talk nonsense *o* bull

babosear /1a/ **Ⓐ** VT [*perro*] to slobber over; [*niño*] to dribble on **Ⓑ** VI **1** [*perro*] to slobber; [*niño*] to dribble **2** (*Méx**) (= *holgazanear*) to mess around

baboso/a **Ⓐ** ADJ **1** [*caracol, sustancia*] slimy **2** (*) [*persona*] (= *sentimental*) slushy; (= *adulador*) fawning, snivelling **3** (*LAm*) (= *tonto*) silly **Ⓑ** SM/F (*Méx, CAm**) fool, idiot; (*pey*) drip* **Ⓒ** SM (*Méx, CAm*) slug; *ver tb* **babosa**

babucha SF slipper; ✦ MODISMO **llevar a algn a ~** (*RPI*) to give sb a piggyback

babuino SM baboon

baca SF luggage rack, roof rack

bacal SM (*Méx*) corncob

bacaladero ADJ cod *antes de s*

bacaladilla SF blue whiting

bacalao SM cod, codfish; ✦ MODISMO **cortar el ~*** to be the boss, have the final say, run the show

bacán/ana* **Ⓐ** ADJ **1** (*RPI*) (= *rico*) posh*, classy* **2** (*Col*) (= *bueno*) great **Ⓑ** SM/F (*RPI*) wealthy man/woman; **vive como una bacana** to live like a king

bacanal SF orgy

bacano* ADJ (*Col*) great

bacará SM, **bacarrá** SM baccarat

bacenica SF (*Chi*), **bacenilla** SF (*Col*) = **bacinica**

bachata SF (*Carib*) spree

bache SM **1** (*Aut*) hole, pothole **2** (= *mal momento*) bad patch, rough patch; **salir del ~** to get through the bad *o* rough patch, pull through

bachicha* SM (*CS*) wop***

bachiller **Ⓐ** SMF high school graduate (*EEUU*), *person with a secondary-school education* **Ⓑ** SM (*Esp*) = **bachillerato**

bachillerato SM *higher secondary-education course and qualification*

bacilo SM bacillus, germ

bacinica SF, **bacinilla** SF (*Col*) chamber pot

backstage [bak'steitʃ] SM (= *lugar*) backstage area; (= *gente*) (backstage) crew

bacon SM (*Esp*) bacon

bacteria SF bacterium, germ; **bacterias** bacteria, germs

bacteriológico ADJ bacteriological

báculo SM **1** (= *bastón*) stick, staff **2** (= *apoyo*) prop, support; **ser el ~ de la vejez de algn** to be sb's comfort in old age

badajo SM clapper

badana SF sheepskin; ✦ MODISMO **sobarle** *o* **zurrarle la ~ a**

algn* to give sb a good hiding*

badén SM (= *bache*) dip; (*para agua*) gutter

bádminton SM badminton

bafle SM, **baffle** SM speaker, loudspeaker

bagaje SM experience, background ➤ **bagaje cultural** cultural background

bagatela SF **1** (= *objeto*) trinket, knick-knack **2** (= *nimiedad*) trifle

bagayero/a* SM/F smuggler

bagayo* (*RPI*) **Ⓐ** SM (= *contrabando*) (= *acción*) smuggling; (= *artículos*) smuggled goods *pl* **Ⓑ** SF (= *mujer fea*) old hag*

Bagdad SM Baghdad

bagre (*LAm*) **Ⓐ** SM (= *pez*) catfish **Ⓑ** SMF (**) (= *persona*) ugly mug**

bagual (*CS*) SM wild horse, untamed horse

baguala SF *type of folk music originating from north-east Argentina*

baguío SM hurricane, typhoon

bah EXCL bah!, phooey! (*EEUU**)

bahía SF bay

bailable ADJ **música ~** music that you can dance to

bailaor(a) SM/F flamenco dancer

bailar /1a/ **Ⓐ** VI **1** (= *danzar*) to dance; **sacar a algn a ~** to ask sb to dance, ask sb for a dance; **le bailaban los ojos de alegría** her eyes sparkled with happiness; ✦ MODISMOS **éste es otro que bien baila** here's another one (of the same kind); **¡que me quiten lo bailao!*** at least I've lived/I'll have lived!; **~ con la más fea: siempre me toca ~ con la más fea** I always draw the short straw, I always get the short end of the stick (*EEUU*); **~ al son que tocan: los políticos bailan al son que les tocan los militares** the politicians toe the line given them by the military
2 [*peonza*] to spin (around *o* (*Brit*) round)
3 [*mueble*] to be wobbly, be unsteady
4 (*) [*ropa, calzado*] to be miles too big*
Ⓑ VT **1** (= *danzar*) to dance; **~ flamenco** to dance flamenco; **~ el vals** to waltz, dance the waltz
2 (*Méx**) (= *robar*) to nick*, pinch*; **le ~on la cartera** they nicked *o* pinched his wallet*
Ⓒ bailarse VPR **~se a algn** (*Méx**) (= *engañar*) to rip off*, con*; (= *derrotar*) to thrash sb*; **se lo ~on con un billete falso** he was slipped a fake *o* dud* note

bailarín/ina **Ⓐ** ADJ dancing **Ⓑ** SM/F dancer; (*tb* **~ de ballet**) ballet dancer

baile SM **1** (= *acción*) dancing; **lo mío no es el ~** dancing is not my thing* **2** (= *pieza, arte*) dance; **¿me concede este ~?** (*frm*) may I have this dance? (*frm*) ➤ **baile clásico** ballet ➤ **baile de salón** ballroom dance ➤ **baile flamenco** flamenco dancing ➤ **baile folklórico** (= *pieza*) folk dance; (= *arte*) folk dancing **3** (= *fiesta*) dance; (*formal*) ball ➤ **baile de disfraces** fancy-dress ball, costume ball (*EEUU*) ➤ **baile de máscaras** (*LAm*) masked ball **4** (*Med*) ➤ **el baile de San Vito** St Vitus's dance

bailotear* /1a/ VI to dance around, jump around

bailoteo* SM dancing

baja SF **1** (= *descenso*) fall, drop; **a la ~** [*evolución, tendencia*] downward; **el precio del algodón sigue a la ~** the price of cotton continues to fall; **la patronal está presionando los salarios a la ~** employers are forcing wages down; **abrir a la ~** (*Bolsa*) to open down; **cerrar a la ~** (*Bolsa*) to close down; **cotizarse a la ~** (*Bolsa*) to trade low; **estar en ~** [*reputación, popularidad*] to be in decline
2 (= *cese*) (*en organización, subscripción, trabajo*) **hubo muchas ~s en el club** a lot of people left the club; **dar de ~** [+ *socio*] to expel; [+ *abogado, médico*] to strike off; [+ *militar*] to discharge; [+ *empleado*] to dismiss, fire; [+ *empresa, sociedad*] to dissolve; [+ *coche*] to take out of circulation; [+ *avión, tren*] to decommission; [+ *teléfono,*

luz] to have disconnected; **la dieron de ~ del club por no pagar la suscripción** her membership of the club was cancelled because she had failed to pay her subscription; **darse de ~** [*de club, institución, partido*] to leave; [*de revista, periódico*] to cancel one's subscription; **nos dimos de ~ del teléfono** we had the telephone disconnected

3 (= *ausencia laboral*) **dar de ~: se le dará de ~ a partir del día de la operación** she will be on sick leave from the day of the operation; **estar de ~** to be on sick leave, be off sick ➤ **baja permanente** indefinite sick leave ➤ **baja por enfermedad** sick leave; **el número de ~s por enfermedad** the number of people taking sick leave ➤ **baja por maternidad** maternity leave ➤ **baja voluntaria** voluntary redundancy (*esp Brit*), voluntary layoff (*EEUU*)

4 (*Dep*) (*por descalificación*) suspension; (*por lesión*) injury; **el equipo sufrió dos ~s por sendas tarjetas rojas** the team lost two players for red card offences

5 (*Esp Med*) (= *certificado*) medical certificate, sick note*

6 (*Mil*) (= *víctima*) casualty

bajada SF **1** (= *camino*) **la ~ hasta el río** (= *sendero*) the path down to the river; (= *carretera*) the road down to the river; **una ~ muy difícil para un esquiador sin experiencia** a very difficult slope for an inexperienced skier

2 (= *acción*) descent; **en la ~ alcanzamos los 150km/h** on the way down *o* descent we got up to 150km/h; **salimos antes de la ~ del telón** we left the theatre *o* (*EEUU*) theater before the curtain went down ➤ **bajada de bandera** minimum (taxi) fare

3 (= *disminución*) fall, drop; **sufrió una ~ de azúcar** his sugar level fell *o* dropped ➤ **bajada de tensión** drop in blood pressure

4 (*Esp***) [*de drogas*] **cuando le da la ~** when he's coming down

bajamar SF low tide, low water

bajante SF *o* SM drainpipe, downspout (*EEUU*)

bajar /1a/ ⓐ VT **1** (= *llevar abajo*) to take down; (= *traer abajo*) to bring down; **¿has bajado la basura?** have you taken the rubbish (*esp Brit*) *o* trash (*EEUU*) down?; **¿me bajas el abrigo?, hace frío aquí fuera** could you bring my coat down? it's cold out here; **te he bajado la maleta del armario** I got your suitcase down from the wardrobe; **la bajó del caballo** he helped her down off the horse

2 (= *mover hacia abajo*) [+ *bandera, ventanilla, telón*] to lower; [+ *persiana*] to put down, lower; **dimos un paseo para ~ la comida** we had a walk to help us digest our meal

3 (*con partes del cuerpo*) [+ *brazos*] to drop, lower; **bajó la vista** *o* **los ojos** he looked down; **bajó la cabeza** she bowed *o* lowered her head

4 (= *reducir*) [+ *precio*] to lower, put down; [+ *fiebre, tensión, voz*] to lower

5 [+ *radio, televisión, gas*] to turn down; **¡baja la voz!** keep your voice down!

6 ~ la escalera (*visto desde arriba*) to go down the stairs; (*visto desde abajo*) to come down the stairs

7 (= *perder*) [+ *kilos, peso*] to lose

8 (*Inform*) to download

ⓑ VI **1** (= *descender*) (*visto desde arriba*) to go down; (*visto desde abajo*) to come down; **¡ahora bajo!** I'll be right down!

2 (*de autobús, avión, tren, moto, bici, caballo*) to get off; (*de coche*) to get out; **~ de** [+ *autobús, avión, tren, moto, bici, caballo*] to get off; [+ *coche*] to get out of

3 (= *reducirse*) [*temperatura, fiebre, tensión arterial*] to go down, fall, drop; [*hinchazón, calidad*] to go down; **el dólar bajó frente al euro** the dollar fell against the euro; **los coches han bajado de precio** cars have come down in price

4 ~ de: ~ de peso to lose weight; **una cámara buena no baja de 300 dólares** you can't get a good camera for less than 300 dollars; **los termómetros no han bajado de 30 grados** temperatures haven't dropped below 30 degrees

5 [*menstruación*] to start

ⓒ **bajarse** VPR **1** (*de árbol, escalera, silla*) to get down (*de* from); **¡bájate de ahí!** get down from there!

2 (*de autobús, tren, avión, moto, bici*) to get off; (*de coche*) to get out; **~se de** [+ *autobús, tren, avión, moto, bici*] to get off; [+ *coche*] to get out of

3 (*Inform*) to download; **~se algo de Internet** to download

sth from the Internet

> Para decir en inglés **bajar(se) de** en el contexto de coches o taxis se utiliza el verbo **get out of**, mientras que en el caso de trenes, autobuses, aviones, bicicletas, motos o animales sería **get off**: "Bajó del coche y nos saludó", *She got out of the car and said hello*; "No baje del tren en marcha", *Don't get off the train while it is still moving.*

bajativo SM (*CS*) after-dinner liqueur

bajel SM (*liter*) vessel, ship

bajero ADJ **sábana bajera** bottom sheet

bajeza SF **1** (= *maldad*) vileness, baseness **2** (= *acto malvado*) mean deed, vile deed

bajío SM **1** (*Náut*) shoal, sandbank **2** (*LAm*) (= *terreno*) lowland **3 bajíos** (*Méx*) flat arable land on a high plateau

bajista SMF (*Mús*) bassist

bajo ⓐ ADJ **1** (= *de poca altura*) [*objeto*] low; [*persona*] short

2 (= *a poca altura*) (*gen*) low; [*parte*] lower, bottom; [*tierra*] low-lying; [*agua*] shallow; **en la parte baja de la ciudad** in the lower part of the town

3 (= *inclinado*) **contestó con la cabeza baja** she answered with her head bowed; **con los ojos ~s** with downcast eyes

4 (= *reducido, inferior*) [*precios, temperaturas, frecuencia*] low; **de baja calidad** low-quality, poor-quality; **de ~ contenido en grasas** low-fat; **~ en calorías** low-calorie *antes de s*; **la temporada baja** the low season (*Brit*), the off-season (*EEUU*); **estar ~ de ánimo** *o* **de moral** to be in low spirits; **estar ~ de forma (física)** to be unfit, be out of shape

5 [*sonido*] faint, soft; [*voz, tono*] low; **hablar en voz baja** to speak quietly *o* in a low voice; **decir algo por lo ~** to say sth under one's breath

6 (*Hist*) **en la baja Edad Media** in the late Middle Ages

7 (= *humilde*) [*clase*] lower; [*condición*] lowly; [*barrio*] poor; **los ~s fondos** the underworld *sing*

ⓑ SM **1** (*Cos*) [*de vestido*] hem; [*de pantalones*] turn-up (*Brit*), cuff (*EEUU*)

2 [*de edificio*] (= *piso*) ground floor (*Brit*), first floor (*EEUU*) ➤ **bajo comercial** ground-floor (*Brit*) *o* first-floor (*EEUU*) business premises

3 (*Mús*) (= *instrumento*) (= *guitarra*) bass (guitar); (= *contrabajo*) bass; (= *voz*) bass; (= *guitarrista*) bass (guitar) player

4 bajos [*de edificio*] ground floor *sing* (*Brit*), first floor *sing* (*EEUU*); [*de coche*] underside

ⓒ ADV [*volar*] low; [*tocar, cantar*] quietly, softly; **hablar ~** (= *en voz baja*) to speak quietly, speak softly; (= *tener una voz suave*) to be softly spoken, be soft spoken; **¡más ~, por favor!** quieter, please!

ⓓ PREP **1** (= *debajo de*) under; **Juan llevaba un libro ~ el brazo** Juan was carrying a book under his arm; **~ cero** below zero; **~ la lluvia** in the rain; **~ tierra** underground

2 (= *dependiente de, sometido a*) under; **~ los efectos de la droga** under the influence of drugs; **~ el título de ...** under the title of ...; **está ~ la tutela de su tío** her uncle is her legal guardian

bajón SM [*de presión, temperatura, precios*] sudden fall; [*de salud*] sudden decline; **dar** *o* **pegar un ~** [*persona, salud*] to go downhill; [*precios*] to fall away sharply; [*mercado*] to slump

bajoneado* ADJ (*RPl*) down

bajorrelieve SM bas-relief

bajura SF **pesca de ~** shallow-water fishing, coastal fishing

bakaladero/a* (*Esp*) ⓐ ADJ rave *antes de s* ⓑ SM/F raver

bakalao* (*Esp*) ⓐ ADJ INV rave *antes de s* ⓑ SM rave, rave music; **la ruta del ~** weekend-long tour of a series of rave parties

bala ⓐ SF **1** (= *proyectil*) bullet; **sonaron dos disparos de ~** two gunshots rang out; **disparar una ~** to fire a bullet; **a prueba de ~s** bullet-proof; ✦ MODISMOS **como una ~** like a shot; **entró como una ~** he came shooting in, he came in like a shot; **el tren pasó como una ~** the train shot *o* flew past; **no le entran ~s** (*Chi*) he's as hard as nails*; **ni a ~** (*Méx, Col**) no way* ➤ **bala de fogueo** blank (cartridge) ➤ **bala de goma** plastic bullet, rubber bullet **2** (= *fardo*) bale; **una ~ de heno** a bale of hay **3** (*LAm Dep*) shot; **lanzamiento de ~** shot put Ⓑ SMF (*) (= *juerguista*) ✦ MODISMO **ser un ~ perdida** to be a good-for-nothing

balacear /1a/ VT (*CAm, Méx*) to shoot, shoot at

balacera SF (*esp CAm, Méx*) (= *tiroteo*) shooting; (= *enfrentamiento armado*) shoot-out

balada SF (*Mús*) ballad, ballade; (*Literat*) ballad

baladí ADJ trivial, paltry

baladronada SF boast, brag

balance SM **1** (*Fin*) [*de una cuenta*] balance; (= *documento*) balance (sheet); (*Com*) [*de existencias*] stocktaking (*Brit*), inventory (*EEUU*); **hacer ~** [*de existencias*] to do the stocktaking (*Brit*), take inventory (*EEUU*); [*de vida, situación*] to take stock **2** (= *resultado*) **el ~ de víctimas mortales en el accidente** the death toll in the accident, the number of dead in the accident; **el equipo tiene un ~ de dos victorias y tres derrotas** so far the team have had two wins and three defeats **3** (= *evaluación*) [*de hecho, situación*] assessment, evaluation; **hizo ~ de los cinco años de su gobierno** he assessed *o* evaluated *o* took stock of the five years of his government

balancear /1a/ Ⓐ VT to balance Ⓑ **balancearse** VPR (*en mecedora, columpio*) to rock; [*péndulo*] to swing; [*barco, avión*] to roll

balanceo SM (*al mecerse*) rocking; [*de barco, avión*] roll, rolling

balancín SM **1** [*de equilibrista*] balancing pole **2** (*en parque infantil*) seesaw **3** (= *mecedora*) rocking chair

balandrismo SM yachting

balandrista SMF yachtsman/yachtswoman

balandro SM yacht, sloop

balanza SF **1** (= *instrumento*) scales *pl*; (*Quím*) balance; ✦ MODISMO **estar en la ~** to be in the balance ➤ **balanza de cocina** kitchen scales *pl* ➤ **balanza de precisión** precision scales *pl* ➤ **balanza romana** steelyard **2** (*Com, Pol*) ➤ **balanza comercial, balanza de pagos** balance of payments

balar /1a/ VI to bleat, baa

balata SF (*LAm Aut*) brake lining

balaustrada SF balustrade

balazo SM (= *tiro*) shot; (= *herida*) bullet wound; **matar a algn de un ~** to shoot sb dead

balboa SF *Panamanian currency unit*

balbucear /1a/ VT, VI [*adulto*] to stammer, stutter; [*niño*] to babble

balbuceo SM [*de adulto*] stammering, stuttering; [*de niño*] babbling

balbuciente ADJ [*persona, voz*] stammering, stuttering; [*niño*] babbling

balbucir /3f/ VT, VI = **balbucear**

Balcanes SMPL **los ~** the Balkans

balcánico ADJ Balkan

balcanización SF Balkanization

balcón SM **1** (= *terraza*) balcony **2** (= *mirador*) vantage point

balconada SF row of balconies

balda SF shelf

baldado ADJ **1** (= *lisiado*) crippled **2** (*) (= *agotado*) **estar ~** to be bushed*, be knackered (*Brit**)

baldaquín SM, **baldaquino** SM canopy

baldar /1a/ VT **1** (= *lisiar*) to cripple **2** (*) (= *agotar*) to shatter

balde¹ SM (= *cubo*) bucket, pail

balde² SM **1 de ~** (= *gratis*) (for) free, for nothing; **obtener**

algo de ~ to get sth (for) free, get sth for nothing **2 estar de ~** (= *ser superfluo*) to be unwanted; (= *estorbar*) to be in the way **3 en ~** in vain; **los años no pasan en ~** the years don't go by in vain; **por lo menos el viaje no ha sido en ~** at least the journey wasn't in vain

baldear /1a/ VT **1** (= *limpiar*) to wash (down), swill with water **2** (*Náut*) to bail out

baldío Ⓐ ADJ [*campo*] fallow, uncultivated; [*terreno*] waste Ⓑ SM (*Agr*) (= *campo sin cultivos*) uncultivated land, fallow land; (= *solar*) wasteland

baldón SM (= *afrenta*) affront, insult; (= *deshonra*) blot, stain

baldosa SF tile

baldosín SM tile

baleado/a SM/F (*CAm, Méx*) shooting victim, person who has been shot

balear¹ /1a/ VT (*CAm, Méx*) (= *disparar contra*) to shoot, shoot at; (= *matar*) to shoot down, shoot dead; **morir baleado** to be shot dead

balear² ADJ Balearic

Baleares SFPL (*tb* **Islas ~**) Balearics, Balearic Islands

baleo SM (*CAm, Méx*) shooting

balero SM **1** (*LAm*) (= *juguete*) cup-and-ball toy **2** (*Méx Mec*) ball bearing

balido SM bleat, baa

balín SM pellet; **balines** buckshot *sing*

balinera SF (*And*) ball bearings *pl*

balística SF ballistics *sing*

balístico ADJ ballistic

baliza SF (*Náut*) buoy, marker; (*Aer*) beacon, marker

balizaje SM, **balizamiento** SM (*Aer*) runway lights *pl*

ballena SF **1** (*Zool*) whale ➤ **ballena azul** blue whale **2** (*Cos*) [*de corsé*] bone, stay

ballenato SM whale calf

ballenero Ⓐ ADJ whaling; **industria ballenera** whaling industry Ⓑ SM **1** (= *pescador*) whaler **2** (= *barco*) whaler, whaling ship

ballesta SF **1** (*Hist*) crossbow **2** (*Mec*) spring *sing*

ballet [ba'le] SM (*pl* **~s** [ba'les]) (= *disciplina, espectáculo*) ballet; (= *grupo de bailarines*) ballet company ➤ **ballet acuático** synchronized swimming

balneario Ⓐ ADJ **estación balnearia** spa Ⓑ SM **1** (*Med*) spa, health resort **2** (*LAm*) seaside resort

balompié SM soccer, football (*Brit*)

balón SM **1** (*Dep*) ball ➤ **balón de reglamento** regulation ball **2** (= *recipiente*) (*Quím*) bag (*for gas*); (*RPl*) (= *vaso*) balloon glass ➤ **balón de oxígeno** oxygen cylinder; **la noticia fue un ~ de oxígeno para la economía** the news gave the economy a real boost

balonazo SM **me dio un ~** he thumped me with the ball

baloncestista SMF basketball player

baloncesto SM basketball

balonmano SM handball

balonvolea SM volleyball

balota SF (*Perú*) ballot

balotaje SM (*esp RPl*) second round

balotar /1a/ VI (*Perú*) to ballot, vote

balsa¹ SF **1** (*Náut*) (= *embarcación*) raft ➤ **balsa de salvamento, balsa salvavidas** life raft ➤ **balsa neumática** rubber dinghy **2** (*Bot*) balsa, balsa wood

balsa² SF (= *charca*) pool, pond; ✦ MODISMO **ser una ~ de aceite: la reunión fue una ~ de aceite** the meeting went swimmingly; **el pueblo es una ~ de aceite** the village is as quiet as the grave

balsámico ADJ **1** (= *de bálsamo*) balmy **2** (= *relajante*) soothing

bálsamo SM **1** (= *sustancia*) balsam, balm **2** (= *consuelo*) balm, comfort **3** (*Chi*) (*para el pelo*) hair conditioner

balsero/a SM/F **1** (= *piloto de balsa*) ferryman/ferrywoman

2 balseros boat people (*especially Cuban, seeking refuge in the USA*)

báltico ADJ Baltic; **el mar Báltico** the Baltic, the Baltic Sea

baluarte SM bastion

bamba SF (*Esp*) plimsoll (*Brit*), sneaker (*EEUU*)

bambalina SF (*Teat*) drop, drop scene; **entre ~s** behind the scenes

bambolearse /1a/ VPR (*al andar*) to sway; [*péndulo, lámpara*] to swing, sway; [*silla, mesa*] to wobble; [*tren*] to sway

bamboleo SM [*de péndulo, lámpara*] swinging, swaying; [*de silla, mesa*] wobbling, unsteadiness; [*de tren*] rolling

bambú SM bamboo

banal ADJ [*comentario, tema*] banal

banalidad SF 1 (= *cualidad*) banality 2 **banalidades** small talk *sing*, trivialities

banalizar /1f/ VT to trivialize

banana SF (*esp LAm*) banana

bananal SM (*LAm*) banana plantation

bananero (*LAm*) **Ⓐ** ADJ banana *antes de s*; **compañía bananera** banana company; **plantación bananera** banana plantation; **república bananera** banana republic **Ⓑ** SM banana tree

banano SM 1 (= *árbol*) banana tree 2 (*Carib*) (= *fruta*) banana

banca SF 1 (*Com, Fin*) banking; **la ~** the banking community, the banks *pl* ➤ **banca telefónica** telephone banking 2 (*en juegos*) bank; **hacer saltar la ~** to break the bank 3 (*LAm*) (= *asiento*) bench 4 (*Méx*) (= *pupitre*) desk 5 (*Col, RPl*) (= *escaño*) seat; ✦ MODISMO **tener ~** (*RPl**) to have (lots of) pull *o* influence

bancada SF (*Col, RPl*) bench

bancal SM (*Agr*) (= *terraza*) terrace; (= *terreno cultivado*) patch, plot

bancar* /1g/ (*RPl*) **Ⓐ** VT 1 (= *aguantar*) to put up with 2 (= *pagar*) **le tuve que ~ el pasaje** I had to pay for his ticket *o* buy him his ticket; **~ a algn** to give money to sb **Ⓑ** bancarse VPR **~se algo/a algn** to put up with sth/sb

bancario/a **Ⓐ** ADJ bank *antes de s*, banking; **giro ~** bank draft **Ⓑ** SM/F bank clerk (*Brit*), bank teller (*EEUU*)

bancarrota SF bankruptcy; **declararse en** *o* **hacer ~** to go bankrupt

banco SM 1 (= *asiento*) (*gen*) bench; (*en iglesia*) pew; (*LAm*) (= *taburete*) stool; (*SAm*) (= *pupitre*) desk ➤ **banco azul** (*Pol*) ministerial benches *pl* ➤ **banco de abdominales** sit-up bench ➤ **banco de pruebas** (*lit*) test bed; (*fig*) testing ground 2 (*Com, Fin*) bank ➤ **banco central** central bank ➤ **banco de inversiones** investment bank ➤ **banco emisor** issuing bank 3 (= *reserva*) [*de información, órganos*] bank ➤ **banco de datos** data bank ➤ **banco de esperma** sperm bank ➤ **banco de sangre** blood bank 4 (*Geog*) (*en el mar*) bank, shoal ➤ **banco de arena** sandbank ➤ **banco de niebla** fog bank ➤ **banco de nieve** snowdrift 5 [*de peces*] shoal, school

banda SF 1 (= *grupo*) [*de música*] band; [*de delincuentes, amigos*] gang; [*de guerrilleros*] band, flock; **negociaciones a tres ~s** three-party talks, trilateral negotiations ➤ **banda armada** armed gang ➤ **banda terrorista** terrorist group 2 (= *cinta*) (*en la ropa*) band, strip; [*de gala*] sash ➤ **banda magnética** magnetic strip ➤ **banda sonora** [*de película*] soundtrack; (*en carretera*) rumble strip ➤ **banda transportadora** conveyor belt 3 (= *franja*) ➤ **banda ancha** broadband ➤ **banda de frecuencia** band, waveband ➤ **banda salarial** wage scale 4 (= *lado*) side, edge; [*de barco*] side; ✦ MODISMO **coger a algn por ~** (*Esp*): **¡como te coja por ~!** I'll get even with you! ➤ **la Banda Oriental** *former Spanish territories of Uruguay and southern Brazil* 5 (*Dep*) sideline, touchline; **fuera de ~** out of play, in touch; **sacar de ~** to take a throw-in, throw the ball in

➤ **línea de banda** sideline, touchline

6 (*Billar*) cushion

bandada SF [*de aves*] flock; [*de peces*] shoal

bandazo SM 1 (= *sacudida*) (*al andar*) lurch, jolt; (*Náut*) heavy roll; **el coche iba dando ~s** the car swerved from side to side 2 (= *cambio repentino*) marked shift

bandear /1a/ VT (*CS*) (= *cruzar*) to cross, go right across

bandeja SF (*para servir, en nevera*) tray; ✦ MODISMO **poner** *o* **servir algo en ~ (de plata) a algn** to hand sth to sb on a plate (*Brit*) *o* on a silver platter (*EEUU*) ➤ **bandeja de entrada** in-tray ➤ **bandeja de salida** out-tray

bandera SF 1 [*de país, ciudad*] flag; [*de regimiento*] colours, colors *pl* (*EEUU*); **arriar la ~** to lower *o* strike the colours *o* (*EEUU*) colors; **izar la ~** to raise *o* hoist the flag; **jurar ~** to swear allegiance to the flag; ✦ MODISMO **estar hasta la ~*** to be packed ➤ **bandera blanca** white flag ➤ **bandera de conveniencia** flag of convenience ➤ **bandera negra, bandera pirata** Jolly Roger, skull and crossbones ➤ **bandera roja** red flag 2 (= *idea*) banner; **bajo la ~ de la renovación** under the banner of change and renewal 3 [*de taxi*] **bajar la ~** to pick up a fare 4 ✦ MODISMO **de ~** (*Esp**) fantastic; **es una mujer de ~** she's one hell of a woman*

banderazo SM **el ~ de llegada** the chequered flag, the checkered flag (*EEUU*); **el ~ de salida** the starting signal; **dar el ~ de salida** to signal the start, give the starting signal

banderilla SF 1 (*Taur*) banderilla; ✦ MODISMO **clavar ~s a algn** to goad sb 2 (*Culin*) cocktail snack on a stick

banderillear /1a/ VT (*Taur*) *to stick the banderillas into the neck of the bull*

banderillero SM (*Taur*) banderillero, *bullfighter who uses the banderillas*

banderín SM small flag, pennant

banderita SF [*de caridad*] flag (*sold for charity*); **día de la ~** flag day

banderola SF 1 (= *bandera pequeña*) banderole 2 (*CS*) (*en puerta*) transom; (*en ventana*) mullion

bandido SM 1 (= *delincuente*) bandit, outlaw 2 (*) **¡bandido!** you beast!; (*a niño*) you little terror!

bando SM 1 (= *edicto*) edict, proclamation 2 **bandos** (*Rel*) banns 3 (= *facción*) (*Pol*) faction, party; (*Dep*) side; **pasarse al otro ~** to change sides

bandolera SF **llevar algo en ~** to wear sth across one's chest

bandolero/a SM/F bandit

bandoneón SM tango accordion

bandurria SF bandurria (*lute-type Spanish instrument*)

banjo SM banjo

banner ['baner] SM (*Internet*) banner (ad)

banquero/a SM/F banker

banqueta SF 1 (= *taburete*) stool 2 (*CAm, Méx*) (= *acera*) pavement (*Brit*), sidewalk (*EEUU*)

banquete SM banquet, feast ➤ **banquete de boda(s)** wedding reception ➤ **banquete de gala** state banquet

banquillo SM (= *asiento*) bench; (*Dep*) bench, team bench; (*Jur*) dock ➤ **banquillo de los acusados** dock

banquina SF (*RPl*) hard shoulder (*Brit*), shoulder (*EEUU*), berm (*EEUU*)

banquito SM (*RPl*) stool

bantú ADJ, SMF Bantu

bañadera SF 1 (*Arg*) (*para bañarse*) bath (*esp Brit*), bathtub (*esp EEUU*) 2 (*RPl*) (= *autobús*) open-top bus

bañado SM (*LAm*) swamp, marshland

bañador SM (*Esp*) [*de mujer*] swimsuit, swimming costume (*Brit*), bathing suit; [*de hombre*] (swimming) trunks *pl*

bañar /1a/ **Ⓐ** VT 1 **~ a algn** to bath sb (*Brit*), bathe sb (*EEUU*), give sb a bath 2 (= *cubrir*) **he bañado el pastel de** *o* **con chocolate** I've covered the cake with chocolate; **bañado en sangre/sudor** [*persona*] bathed *o* drenched in blood/sweat; [*ropa*] drenched in blood/sweat 3 [*mar, lago*] to wash (*liter*) **4** [*luz, sol*] to flood, bathe **Ⓑ bañarse** VPR (*en bañera*) to have a bath, take a bath; (*en mar, piscina*) to swim; **"prohibido bañarse"** "no swimming"; **¡anda/andá a ~te!** (*CS*) get lost!*, go to hell!**

bañera SF bath (*esp Brit*), bathtub (*esp EEUU*) ➤ **bañera de hidromasaje** whirlpool bath

bañero/a SM/F (*CS*) lifeguard

bañista SMF bather

baño SM **1** (= *acción*) (*en bañera*) bath; (*en mar, piscina*) swim; **darse** o **tomar un ~** (*en bañera*) to have o take a bath; (*en mar, piscina*) to have a swim, go for a swim; **playas aptas para el ~** beaches suitable for bathing ➤ **baño de asiento** hip bath ➤ **baño de espuma** foam bath, bubble bath ➤ **baño de multitudes: darse un ~ de multitudes** to go on a walkabout (*Brit*), mingle with the crowd ➤ **baño de pies** foot bath ➤ **baño de revelado** developing bath ➤ **baño de sangre** bloodbath ➤ **baño de sol: darse** o **tomar un ~ de sol** to sunbathe ➤ **baño de vapor** steam bath ➤ **baño turco** Turkish bath **2** (= *bañera*) bath (*esp Brit*), bathtub (*esp EEUU*); (= *cuarto*) bathroom; (= *aseo*) toilet (*Brit*), bathroom (*esp EEUU*) **3** (*Culin*) **le he dado un ~ de chocolate al pastel** I've covered the cake with chocolate ➤ **baño María: poner algo al ~ María** to cook sth in a double boiler **4** [*de oro, plata*] plating; **el pendiente tiene un ~ de plata** the earring is silver-plated **5** baños (*Med*) spa *sing* ➤ **baños termales** thermal baths

baobab SM baobab

baptista ADJ, SMF Baptist

baqueano/a (*LAm*) ADJ, SM/F = **baquiano**

baquelita SF bakelite

baqueta SF **1** (*Mil*) ramrod **2** (*Mús*) [*de tambor*] drumstick

baquetazo SM **tratar a algn a ~ limpio*** to treat sb harshly

baqueteado ADJ [*persona*] experienced; [*mueble*] worse for wear, battered

baquetear /1a/ VT to treat harshly; **ha sido baqueteado por la vida** life's been hard on him

baquiano/a (*LAm*) Ⓐ ADJ (= *experto*) expert, skilful, skillful (*EEUU*) Ⓑ SM/F (= *guía*) guide, scout

báquico ADJ (*liter*) Bacchic (*liter*)

báquiro SM (*Col, Ven*) peccary

bar SM bar ➤ **bar de alterne** singles bar ➤ **bar de copas** (fashionable) bar

barahúnda SF uproar

baraja SF pack of cards; **jugar a las ~s** (*LAm*) to play cards; ✦ MODISMO **jugar a** o **con dos ~s** to play a double game, double deal

BARAJA ESPAÑOLA

The Spanish deck of cards differs from its British and American counterpart, known in Spain as the **baraja francesa**. The four Spanish suits, **oros, copas, espadas** and **bastos** (golden coins, goblets, swords and clubs) each contain 9 numbered cards, although for certain games only 7 are used, and 3 picture cards: **sota, caballo** and **rey** (jack, queen, king).

barajar /1a/ Ⓐ VT **1** [+ *cartas*] to shuffle **2** (= *considerar*) [+ *nombres, candidatos*] to consider, weigh up; **las cifras que se barajan ahora** the figures now being put o bandied about **3** (*RPl**) (= *atrapar*) to catch; ✦ MODISMO **~ algo en el aire** to be quick to understand sth Ⓑ **barajarse** VPR **barajársele a algn** (*Col**): **y se les barajó el viaje** and bang went their trip*

baranda SF **1** [*de balcón*] rail, railing; [*de escalera*] banisters *pl*; (*en cuesta, pared*) handrail **2** (*Billar*) cushion

barandal SM (*esp Méx*) = **baranda 1**

barandilla SF [*de balcón*] rail, railing; [*de escalera*] banisters *pl*; (*en cuesta, pared*) handrail

barata SF **1** (*Méx*) (= *venta*) sale, bargain sale **2** (*Chi*) (= *cucaracha*) cockroach, roach (*EEUU*)

baratija SF (= *objeto*) trinket; (= *cosa insignificante*) trifle

baratillo SM (= *mercadillo*) street market; **cosa de ~** trash, junk

barato Ⓐ ADJ **1** (= *económico*) cheap; **el café sale más ~ a granel** coffee is cheaper if you buy it in bulk **2** (= *de mala calidad*) [*música, imitación*] cheap; [*novela*] trashy **3** (= *indigno*) [*demagogia, electoralismo*] cheap Ⓑ ADV cheap, cheaply; **en este restaurante se come muy ~** you can eat very cheaply in this restaurant

baraúnda SF = **barahúnda**

barba SF **1** (= *pelo*) beard; **lleva** o **tiene ~ de tres días** he's got three days' stubble, he's got three days' growth of beard; **recortarse la ~** to trim one's beard; **me estoy dejando ~** I'm growing a beard; ✦ MODISMOS **hacer algo en las ~s de algn*** to do sth right under sb's nose; **hacer la ~ a algn** (*Méx**) to fawn on sb, flatter sb; **subirse a las ~s de algn*** to be cheeky (*Brit*) o sassy (*EEUU**) to sb; **por ~***: **dos naranjas por ~** two oranges apiece o per head **2** (= *mentón*) chin **3** [*de ave*] wattle; [*de mejillón, cabra*] beard

Barba Azul SM Bluebeard

barbacana SF [*de defensa*] barbican; (= *tronera*) loophole, embrasure

barbacoa SF **1** (= *asadero*) barbecue **2** (*CAm, Méx, Ven*) (= *carne*) roast pork or goat cooked in an earth oven

barbaridad SF **1** (= *desatino*) **es una ~ conducir con esta niebla** it's crazy to drive in this fog; **es capaz de hacer cualquier ~** he's capable of anything, he will stop at nothing; **decir ~es** to talk nonsense o bull; **¡qué ~!** that's incredible! **2** (= *acción brutal*) atrocity **3** (= *palabrota*) **dice** o **suelta muchas ~es** he says some terrible things **4 una ~*** (= *mucho*): **comimos una ~** we ate loads o tons o masses*, we stuffed ourselves*; **cuesta una ~** it costs a fortune; **nos gustó una ~** we thought it was great o fantastic*; **se nota una ~** it sticks out a mile*

barbarie SF **1** (= *atraso*) barbarism **2** (= *crueldad*) barbarity, cruelty

bárbaro/a Ⓐ ADJ **1** (*Hist*) barbarian **2** (= *cruel*) barbarous, cruel **3** (= *grosero*) rough, uncouth **4** (*) (= *muy bueno*) tremendous, fantastic*; (= *muy grande*) tremendous, massive* Ⓑ ADV (*) **lo pasamos ~** we had a tremendous o fantastic* time Ⓒ SM/F **1** (*Hist*) barbarian **2** (= *bruto*) uncouth person; **conduce como un ~** he drives like a madman

barbas* SM INV bearded guy*

barbecho SM **1** (*Agr*) (= *tierra arada*) ploughed land ready for sowing; **dejar en ~** to leave fallow **2 estar en ~** (*CS*) (*fig*) to be in preparation

barbería SF barber's (shop) (*Brit*), barber shop (*EEUU*)

barbero SM **1** (= *peluquero*) barber **2** (*Guat, Méx**) (= *adulador*) flatterer

barbijo SM (*And, CS*) **1** (= *correa*) chinstrap **2** (= *cicatriz*) slash, scar **3** [*de cirujano*] mask

barbilampiño ADJ **1** (= *sin barba*) beardless, clean-shaven **2** (= *de cara de niño*) baby-faced

barbilla SF chin

barbitúrico ADJ, SM barbiturate

barbo SM barbel ➤ **barbo de mar** red mullet, goatfish (*EEUU*)

barbudo Ⓐ ADJ bearded Ⓑ SM bearded man

barca SF boat, small boat ➤ **barca de pesca** fishing boat

barcaza SF barge ➤ **barcaza de desembarco** (*Mil*) landing craft

barcelonés ADJ of/from Barcelona

barchilón/ona SM/F (*And*) nurse

barco SM (= *embarcación*) boat; [*de gran tamaño*] ship, vessel (*frm*); **en ~** by boat, by ship ➤ **barco de guerra** warship ➤ **barco de pesca** = **barco pesquero** ➤ **barco de vapor** steamer ➤ **barco de vela** sailing boat (*Brit*), sailboat

(*EEUU*) ➤ **barco pesquero** fishing boat

> **Barco** se traduce por **ship** cuando se refiere a un barco grande, de guerra, pasaje o carga. **Boat** refiere a cualquier embarcación; es coloquial hablando de un barco grande, pero es el término que se utiliza para embarcaciones pequeñas.

barda SF (*Méx*) fence

bardo SM bard

baremo SM **1** (= *escala de valores*) scale **2** (= *criterio*) yardstick, gauge, gage (*EEUU*) **3** (*Mat*) ready reckoner

bario SM barium

barítono SM baritone

barlovento SM windward; **a ~** to windward

barman SM (*pl* **~s**) barman, bartender

barniz SM **1** (= *sustancia*) (*para dar brillo*) varnish; (*para cerámica*) glaze; (*en metal*) gloss, polish **2** (= *cualidad superficial*) veneer

barnizar /1f/ VT **1** (= *cubrir con barniz*) [+ *madera, mueble*] to varnish; [+ *cerámica*] to glaze **2** (= *encubrir*) to put a gloss on

barométrico ADJ barometric

barómetro SM barometer

barón SM (= *título*) baron; (*Pol*) chief, bigwig*

baronesa SF baroness

barquero/a SM/F [*de barcaza, barca*] boatman/ boatwoman; [*de embarcadero*] ferryman/ferrywoman

barquilla SF **1** [*de globo*] basket **2** (*Náut*) log

barquillo SM **1** (*Culin*) (= *rollito*) rolled wafer; (= *helado*) ice-cream cone

barra SF **1** (= *pieza alargada*) bar; [*de metal*] bar, ingot; (*en armario*) rail; (*Mec*) rod; [*de bicicleta*] crossbar; ✦ MODISMO **no pararse en ~s** to stick at nothing ➤ **barra de carmín** lipstick ➤ **barra de chocolate** (*CS*) bar of chocolate, chocolate bar, candy bar (*EEUU*) ➤ **barra de cortina** curtain rod ➤ **barra de desplazamiento vertical** (*Inform*) scrollbar ➤ **barra de equilibrio(s)** beam ➤ **barra de espaciado** space bar ➤ **barra de herramientas** (*Inform*) toolbar ➤ **barra de labios** lipstick ➤ **barra de pan** French loaf, French stick (*esp Brit*) ➤ **barra espaciadora** space bar ➤ **barra fija** horizontal bar, fixed bar ➤ **barras asimétricas** asymmetric bars ➤ **barras paralelas** parallel bars **2** (*en un bar*) bar, counter; (*en autoservicio*) counter ➤ **barra americana** singles bar ➤ **barra libre** free bar **3** (*Tip*) (*tb* **~ oblicua**) oblique stroke, slash ➤ **barra inversa** backslash **4** (*Mús*) bar **5** (*Heráldica*) stripe, bar **6** (*Náut*) bar, sandbank **7 la Barra** (*Méx*) the Bar, the legal profession, the Bar Association **8** (*SAm Dep**) fans *pl*, supporters *pl* ➤ **barra brava** *gang of hard-line supporters* **9** (*CS**) (= *pandilla*) gang **10** (*Carib, CS*) [*de río, lago*] river mouth, estuary

barrabasada SF (= *travesura*) piece of mischief; (= *atrocidad*) outrage

barraca SF **1** (*tb* **~ de feria**) stall, booth ➤ **barraca de tiro al blanco** shooting gallery **2** (*en Valencia*) small farmhouse **3** (*And, RPl*) (= *depósito*) large storage shed **4** (*RPl*) [*de la construcción*] builders' yard

barracón SM (= *cabaña*) big hut; (*Mil*) barrack hut

barranco SM, **barranca** SF (*esp RPl*) gully, ravine

barrena SF (= *taladro*) drill; (*de mano, pequeña*) gimlet

barrenar /1a/ VT (= *taladrar*) to drill, bore; (= *volar*) to blast

barrendero/a SM/F street sweeper, road sweeper

barreño SM washing bowl, washbowl (*EEUU*)

barrer /2a/ Ⓐ VT **1** (*con escoba*) to sweep **2** (*Mil, Náut*) to sweep *o* rake (*with gunfire*) **3** (= *eliminar*) [+ *obstáculo*] to sweep aside, sweep away; [+ *rival*] to sweep aside, overwhelm; [+ *dudas*] to sweep aside, dispel; **los candidatos del partido barrieron a sus adversarios** the

party's candidates swept their rivals aside; **~ con todo** to make a clean sweep Ⓑ VI (*con escoba*) to sweep up; ✦ MODISMO **~ para casa** *o* **hacia dentro** to look after number one

barrera SF **1** (= *obstáculo*) barrier; **ya ha traspasado la ~ de los treinta** he has passed the 30-year-old mark ➤ **barrera comercial** trade barrier ➤ **barrera coralina** coral reef ➤ **barrera de seguridad** safety barrier ➤ **barrera generacional** generation gap ➤ **barrera protectora** safety barrier ➤ **barrera racial** colour *o* (*EEUU*) color bar **2** (*Ferro*) crossing gate **3** (*Taur*) (= *valla*) barrier; (= *primera fila*) first row

barriada SF (= *barrio*) quarter, district; (*LAm*) (*marginal*) slum, shanty town

barrial SM (*LAm*) bog

barrica SF large barrel, cask

barricada SF barricade

barrida SF **1** (*con escoba*) sweep, sweeping **2** [*de policía*] sweep, raid

barrido SM **1** (*con escoba*) sweep, sweeping **2** (*Elec*) scan, sweep

barriga SF **1** (*Anat*) belly; (*en lenguaje infantil*) tummy*; **estás echando ~** you're getting a bit of a belly*; **me duele la ~** I have a pain in my stomach; (*niños*) I have a pain in my tummy*; **llenarse la ~** to stuff o.s. **2** [*de jarra*] belly, rounded part

barrigón, barrigudo ADJ potbellied

barril SM (= *tonel*) (*gen*) barrel; [*de madera*] cask; [*de metal*] keg; **cerveza de ~** draught *o* (*EEUU*) draft beer; ✦ MODISMOS **ser un ~ de pólvora** to be a powder keg; **ser un ~ sin fondo** (*RPl**) to be a bottomless pit* ➤ **barril de petróleo** barrel of oil

barrila* SF (*Esp*) **dar la ~ con algo** to go on about sth*

barrilete SM **1** [*de revólver*] chamber **2** (*Téc*) clamp **3** (*RPl*) (= *cometa*) kite

barrio SM area, district, neighborhood (*EEUU*); **un ~ residencial** a residential area *o* district *o* (*EEUU*) neighborhood; **mi ~** my part of town, my neighborhood (*EEUU*); **en un ~ céntrico** in the centre *o* (*EEUU*) center of town; **el ~ judío de Córdoba** the Jewish quarter of Córdoba; **los ~s de la periferia** the outlying suburbs *o* areas, the outskirts; **tiendas de ~** local *o* corner shops (*esp Brit*), local *o* corner *o* neighborhood stores (*EEUU*); ✦ MODISMOS **el otro ~*** the next world; **irse al otro ~*** to snuff it*; **mandar a algn al otro ~*** to do sb in* ➤ **barrio chino** [*de mayoría china*] Chinatown, Chinese quarter; (*Esp*) [*de prostitución*] red-light district ➤ **barrio comercial** [*de negocios*] business quarter, commercial district; [*de tiendas*] shopping area, shopping district ➤ **barrio de tolerancia** (*And*) red-light district ➤ **barrio latino** Latin quarter ➤ **barrio obrero** working-class area, working-class district, working-class neighborhood (*EEUU*) ➤ **barrios bajos** poorer areas (of town)

barriobajero ADJ **1** [*zona, vida*] slum *antes de s* **2** (= *vulgar*) vulgar, common

barrito SM (*RPl*) pimple, spot

barrizal SM mire

barro SM **1** (= *lodo*) mud; **me llené de ~** I got covered in mud **2** (*Arte*) (= *arcilla*) potter's clay; **~ cocido** baked clay; **una vasija de ~** a clay pot **3** (= *loza*) earthenware; **un cacharro de ~** an earthenware dish **4** ➤ **barros jarpa** (*Chi*), **barros luca** (*Chi*) *toasted ham and cheese sandwich*

barroco Ⓐ ADJ **1** [*estilo, período*] baroque **2** (= *recargado*) elaborate Ⓑ SM (= *estilo*) baroque, baroque style; (= *período*) baroque period

barroquismo SM **1** (= *estilo barroco*) baroque, baroque style **2** (= *adorno excesivo*) excess

barrote SM bar

barruntar /1a/ VT to suspect

barrunto SM suspicion

bartola SF ✦ MODISMOS **echarse** *o* **tenderse a la ~** to be lazy, take it easy*; **hacer algo a la ~** (*RPl**) to do sth any old how*

bártulos* SMPL things, belongings; (*Téc*) tools; **liar los ~** to pack up one's things *o* belongings

barullento ADJ (*CS*) noisy, rowdy

barullo SM 1 (= *alboroto*) racket; (= *confusión*) confusion; **armar ~** to make a racket 2 **a ~** in abundance, in great quantities

basa SF base

basalto SM basalt

basamento SM base

basar /1a/ Ⓐ VT to base; **~ algo en algo** to base sth on sth Ⓑ **basarse** VPR 1 (= *tener como base*) **~se en algo** to be based on sth; **la novela está basada en hechos reales** the novel is based on actual events 2 (= *usar como base*) **para la novela me basé en la vida de mi abuela** the novel was inspired by the life of my grandmother, I based the novel on the life of my grandmother; **¿en qué te basas para decir eso?** what basis *o* grounds have you got for saying that?

basca SF 1 (*Esp***) (= *grupo*) crowd; (= *pandilla*) gang, pals *pl* 2 (*Esp*) (= *impulso*) **le dio la ~** he had a sudden urge 3 **bascas** (*esp LAm Med*) nausea *sing*, sick feeling *sing*

báscula SF (*gen*) scales *pl*; (*para camiones*) weighbridge ➤ **báscula de baño** bathroom scales *pl*

basculante SM tipper truck, dumper truck (*Brit*), dump truck (*EEUU*)

bascular /1a/ VI 1 (= *inclinarse*) to tilt, tip up 2 (= *oscilar*) to swing

base Ⓐ SF 1 [*de columna, jarrón, cráneo*] base 2 (= *fondo*) [*de pintura*] background; [*de maquillaje*] foundation; **primero se coloca una ~ de tomate** start by laying a tomato base 3 (= *fundamento*) basis; **ese artículo no tiene ~ científica alguna** that article has no scientific basis at all; **la ~ del éxito está en el trabajo** the key to success is hard work; **carecer de ~** [*acusación*] to lack foundation, be unfounded; [*argumento*] to lack justification, be unjustified; **de ~** [*error, dato*] basic, fundamental; [*activista, apoyo*] grass-roots *antes de s*; **en ~ a** (*uso periodístico*) based on; **partir de una ~: partiendo de esta ~, nos planteamos la necesidad ...** on this assumption, we think it necessary ...; **partir de la ~ que ...** to take as one's starting point that ...; **sentar las ~s de algo** to lay the foundations of sth; **sobre la ~ de algo** on the basis of sth 4 (= *componente principal*) **la leche es la ~ de su alimentación** his diet is milk-based; **a ~ de algo: una dieta a ~ de arroz** a rice-based diet, a diet based on rice; **a ~ de mucho esfuerzo** by *o* after making great efforts; **a ~ de hacer algo** by doing sth; **a ~ de insistir, la convenció para comprar la casa** by *o* through his insistence, he persuaded her to buy the house; ✦ MODISMO **a ~ de bien** (*Esp**): **hoy hemos trabajado a ~ de bien** we've done tons *o* loads of work today*; **cenamos a ~ de bien** we had a really good meal ➤ **base imponible** (*Econ*) taxable income 5 (= *conocimientos básicos*) grounding; **una buena ~ de química** a good grounding in chemistry 6 (*Mil*) base ➤ **base aérea** air base ➤ **base aeronaval** naval air base ➤ **base de operaciones** operations base ➤ **base espacial** space station ➤ **base militar** military base ➤ **base naval** naval base 7 **bases** 7.1 (= *condiciones*) [*de concurso*] conditions, rules; [*de convocatoria*] requirements 7.2 (*Pol*) **las ~s** the rank and file 8 (*Inform*) ➤ **base de datos** database 9 (*Mat, Quím*) base 10 (*Béisbol*) base Ⓑ SMF (*Baloncesto*) guard Ⓒ ADJ INV 1 [*campamento*] base *antes de s* 2 (= *básico*) [*idea*] basic; [*documento, texto*] provisional, draft; [*color*] base

básico ADJ basic

basílica SF basilica

basilisco SM (*Mit*) basilisk; (*Méx*) iguana; ✦ MODISMOS **estar hecho un ~** to be furious; **ponerse como un ~** to get terribly angry

básket SM, **básquet** SM, **básquetbol** SM (*Méx*) basketball

basquetbolista SMF (*LAm*) basketball player

bastante Ⓐ ADJ 1 (= *suficiente*) enough (**para** for); **hay ~ sitio para todos** there is enough room for everyone; **¿no tienes ya ~s?** don't you have enough?; **no había ~ público** there wasn't a big enough audience 2 (= *mucho*) quite a lot of, a fair amount of; **han dejado ~ comida** they've left quite a lot of *o* a fair amount of food; **se marchó hace ~ rato** he left quite some time ago; **la calidad deja ~ que desear** the quality leaves much to be desired 3 (= *muchos*) quite a lot of, quite a few; **había ~s invitados** there were quite a lot of *o* quite a few guests Ⓑ ADV 1 (= *suficiente*) enough; **ya has comido ~** you've eaten enough; **es lo ~ alto como para alcanzarlo** he's tall enough to reach it 2 (= *de forma considerable*) (*con verbos*) quite a lot; (*con adjetivos, adverbios*) quite; **lo he visto ~ últimamente** I've seen a fair amount of him *o* quite a lot of him recently; **el libro está ~ bien** it's a fairly good book, it's quite a good book; **estoy ~ cansado** I'm rather *o* quite tired; **vivo ~ lejos** I live quite a long way away

bastar /1a/ Ⓐ VI 1 (= *ser suficiente*) to be enough; **eso me basta** that's enough for me; **me basta con tu palabra** your word's good enough for me; **baste decir que ...** suffice it to say that ...; **~ para hacer algo** to be enough to do sth; **me bastó una foto para reconocerlo** one look at a photo was enough *o* was all it took for me to recognize him; **me bastó leer el primer párrafo para saber que era un genio** I only had to read the first paragraph to know that he was a genius; **basta que ... para que ...: basta que queramos llegar pronto a casa, para que haya un atasco** just when we want to get home quickly, there's a traffic jam 2 (*uso impersonal*) **con eso basta** that's enough; **con la intención basta** it's the thought that counts; **basta con dar una vuelta por la ciudad para ...** you only need to take a walk around the city to ...; **no basta con ...** it's not enough to ... 3 (*exclamación*) **¡basta!** ◇ **¡basta ya!** that will do!, that's enough!; **¡basta de charla!** that's enough chatter! 4 ✦ MODISMOS **hasta decir basta: nevó hasta decir basta** it snowed like there was no tomorrow; **bailamos hasta decir basta** we danced till we dropped; **es honrado hasta decir basta** he's as honest as the day is long; **~ y sobra** it's more than enough Ⓑ **bastarse** VPR **yo sola me basto para cuidarlo** I'm well capable of looking after him on my own; **~se a sí mismo** to be self-sufficient

bastardilla SF (*Tip*) (*tb* **letra ~**) italic type, italics *pl*

bastardo/a Ⓐ ADJ 1 (= *ilegítimo*) bastard 2 (= *mezquino*) mean, base Ⓑ SM/F bastard

bastedad SF coarseness, vulgarity

bastidor SM 1 (= *armazón*) (*Téc, Cos*) frame; [*de ventana*] frame; [*de lienzo*] stretcher; [*de vehículo*] chassis 2 (*Teat*) wing; **entre ~es** behind the scenes

bastillar /1a/ VT to hem

bastión SM bastion

basto Ⓐ ADJ 1 [*superficie, piel*] coarse 2 [*persona, comportamiento*] rude, vulgar Ⓑ SM **bastos** (*Naipes*) clubs (*one of the suits in the Spanish card deck*); ✦ MODISMO **pintan ~s** things are getting tough, the going's getting tough; ◇ *BARAJA ESPAÑOLA*

bastón SM 1 (*para andar*) (walking) stick ➤ **bastón de esquí** ski pole, ski stick (*Brit*) 2 [*de militar*] baton ➤ **bastón de mando** baton, sign of authority

bastonazo SM blow (*with a stick*)

bastoncillo SM 1 (*para los oídos*) cotton bud (*Brit*), Q-tip® (*EEUU*) 2 (*Anat*) rod, retinal rod

basura SF 1 (= *desechos*) (*en casa*) rubbish (*esp Brit*), garbage (*EEUU*); (*por el suelo*) litter; **"prohibido arrojar basuras (y escombros)"** "no dumping", "no tipping (*Brit*)" ➤ **basura espacial** space junk ➤ **basura radiactiva** radioactive waste 2 (= *recipiente*) (*en casa*) dustbin (*Brit*), trash can (*EEUU*); (*en la calle*) litter bin (*Brit*), trash can (*EEUU*); **tirar algo a la ~** to throw sth in the bin (*Brit*) *o* trash can (*EEUU*)

3 (= *persona o cosa despreciable*) trash*, rubbish (*Brit**); **esta novela es una ~** this novel is rubbish (*Brit*) *o* trash **B** ADJ **comida/televisión ~** junk food/TV

basural SM (*LAm*) tip (*Brit*), rubbish dump (*Brit*), garbage dump (*EEUU*)

basurear* /1a/ VT (*CS*) **~ a algn** to rubbish sb (*Brit**), trash sb (*esp EEUU**)

basurero/a **A** SM/F (= *persona*) dustman/dustwoman (*Brit*), garbage collector (*EEUU*) **B** SM **1** (= *vertedero*) tip (*Brit*), rubbish dump (*Brit*), garbage dump (*EEUU*); (*Agr*) dung heap **2** (= *cubo*) litter bin (*Brit*), trash can (*EEUU*)

bata SF **1** (*para levantarse de la cama*) dressing gown, bathrobe; (*encima de la ropa*) housecoat; [*de playa*] wrap **2** [*de médico*] white coat; [*de científico*] laboratory coat, lab coat ➤ **bata blanca** white coat **3** (= *guardapolvo*) overall (*Brit*), smock

batacazo SM **1** (= *porrazo*) thump **2** (*LAm*) (= *victoria*) surprise win; (= *éxito*) surprise hit

bataclana SF (*RPl*) (*en cabaret*) showgirl; (*licenciosa*) easy woman

batahola* SF (= *ruido*) din, hullabaloo*; (= *jaleo*) rumpus*

batalla SF **1** (= *lucha*) battle; **librar** *o* **trabar ~** to do battle; **ropa de ~** everyday clothes *pl* ➤ **batalla campal** pitched battle **2** (= *sufrimiento*) fight, struggle

batallar /1a/ VI to battle, fight

batallita SF **contar ~s*** to go over old times

batallón SM battalion ➤ **batallón de castigo, batallón disciplinario** punishment squad

batasuno/a **A** ADJ of Herri Batasuna **B** SM/F member/supporter of Herri Batasuna

batata SF sweet potato, yam

batatazo* SM (*LAm*) = **batacazo 2**

bate SM bat, baseball bat

batea SF **1** (= *bandeja*) tray **2** (*LAm*) (= *artesa para lavar*) washing trough **3** (*Náut*) flat-bottomed boat, punt

bateador(a) SM/F batter

batear /1a/ **A** VT to hit **B** VI to bat

batería **A** SF **1** (*Elec*) battery; **se ha agotado la ~** the battery is flat **2** (= *fila*) (*para gallinas*) battery; [*de soldados*] battery; **aparcar en ~** to park at an angle to the kerb (*Brit*) *o* curb (*EEUU*) **3** (*Mús*) (= *instrumento*) drums *pl* **4** (*Culin*) ➤ **una batería de cocina** a set of kitchen equipment **B** SMF (= *persona*) drummer

baterista SMF (*LAm*) drummer

batiburrillo SM hotchpotch (*Brit*), hodgepodge (*EEUU*)

batida SF **1** (*Caza*) beating **2** [*de policía, ejército*] (*buscando algo*) search; (*haciendo detenciones*) raid; **por las noches salíamos a hacer una ~** we used to comb *o* search the area at night

batido SM **1** (= *bebida*) milk shake, shake (*esp EEUU*); **un ~ de frutas** a fruit shake **2** (*LAm*) (= *rebozo*) batter

batidora SF (food) mixer, blender

batiente SM **1** (= *marco*) jamb; (= *hoja*) leaf, panel **2** (*Náut*) open coastline

batifondo* SM (*CS*) uproar, tumult

batín SM dressing gown, bathrobe

batir /3a/ **A** VT **1** (= *vencer, superar*) [*+ adversario, enemigo*] to beat; [*+ récord*] to break, beat **2** (*Culin*) [*+ huevos*] to beat, whisk; [*+ nata, crema*] to whip; [*+ mantequilla, margarina*] to cream **3** (= *recorrer*) (*Mil*) to comb, search; (*Caza*) to beat **4** (= *agitar*) [*+ alas*] to flap; **~ palmas** to clap one's hands **5** (= *golpear*) **5.1** [*+ tambor, metal*] to beat **5.2** [*lluvia, olas, viento*] to beat on *o* against; **el viento batía con fuerza las ventanas** the wind was pounding against the windows **6** (*Mil*) [*+ muro*] to batter, pound **B** VI **1** [*lluvia, olas, viento*] to beat **2** [*tambor*] to ring out, sound **C** batirse VPR **1** (= *luchar*) to fight; **~se con algn** to fight sb, have a fight with sb; **~se en duelo** to fight a duel **2** **~se en retirada** to beat a retreat

batiscafo SM bathyscaph, bathyscaphe

batracio SM batrachian

batuque* SM (*CS*) uproar

batuta SF (*Mús*) baton; ✦ MODISMO **llevar la ~** to be the boss, be firmly in command

baúl SM **1** (= *arca*) trunk **2** (*SAm Aut*) boot (*Brit*), trunk (*EEUU*)

bautismal ADJ baptismal

bautismo SM baptism, christening ➤ **bautismo de fuego** baptism of fire

bautizar /1f/ VT **1** (*Rel*) to baptize, christen; **la ~on con el nombre de Teresa** she was christened Teresa **2** (= *nombrar*) [*+ objeto, barco*] to christen, name **3** (*con un apodo*) to nickname, dub **4** (= *diluir*) [*+ vino*] to water, dilute

bautizo SM **1** (= *acto religioso*) baptism, christening **2** (= *celebración*) christening party

bauxita SF bauxite

baya SF berry

bayeta SF **1** (= *trapo de cocina*) (cleaning) cloth **2** (*Billar*) baize

bayoneta SF bayonet

baza SF **1** (*Naipes*) trick; **hacer una ~** to make *o* win a trick **2** (*en asunto, negocio*) weapon; **una de las principales ~s del equipo** one of the team's main weapons; ✦ MODISMOS **jugar una ~:** **si juega bien su ~** if he plays his cards right; **están jugando su última ~** they are playing their last hand; **España juega una ~ importante en el Mundial** Spain has a good chance of winning the World Cup; **meter ~*** to butt in; **le encanta meter ~** she loves butting in; **no deja meter ~ a nadie** he doesn't let anybody get a word in edgeways; **sacar ~ de algo** (*Esp*) to turn sth to one's (own) advantage

bazar SM **1** (= *mercado*) bazaar **2** (= *tienda*) large retail store **3** (*LAm*) (*de caridad*) bazaar, charity fair

bazo SM spleen

bazofia SF muck

BCE SM ABR (= **Banco Central Europeo**) ECB

be SF *name of the letter B* ➤ **be chica** (*Méx*) V ➤ **be grande** (*Méx*), **be larga** (*LAm*) B

beatería SF (= *santidad*) affected piety; (= *hipocresía*) cant, sanctimoniousness

beatificación SF beatification

beatificar /1g/ VT to beatify

beatitud SF beatitude

beato/a **A** ADJ **1** (*Rel*) (= *beatificado*) blessed **2** (= *piadoso*) devout, pious; (= *santurrón*) sanctimonious **B** SM/F **1** (= *devoto*) devout man/woman **2** (*pey*) (= *hombre*) holy Joe*; (= *mujer*) sanctimonious woman

bebe/a SM/F (*CS*) baby

bebé SM baby; **~ foca** baby seal ➤ **bebé de diseño** designer baby

bebedero SM **1** (*para ganado*) drinking trough **2** (*LAm*) (= *fuente*) drinking fountain

bebedizo SM potion

bebedor(a) **A** ADJ hard-drinking **B** SM/F drinker ➤ **bebedor(a) empedernido/a** hardened drinker

bebé-probeta SMF (*pl* **bebés-probeta**) test-tube baby

beber /2a/ **A** VT **1** [*+ agua, leche, cerveza*] to drink; **no bebe alcohol** he doesn't drink; **~ algo a sorbos** to sip sth; **~ algo a tragos** to gulp sth, gulp sth down **2** (*frm*) (= *absorber*) to drink in; **bebían las palabras del orador** they were drinking in the speaker's words **B** VI **1** (*gen*) to drink **2** (= *beber alcohol*) to drink; **si bebes, no conduzcas** don't drink and drive; ✦ MODISMO **~ como un cosaco** to drink like a fish **3** (= *brindar*) **~ por algo/algn** to drink to sth/sb **C** beberse VPR to drink; **se lo bebió todo** he drank it all

bebercio* SM booze*

bebida SF **1** (= *líquido*) drink, beverage ➤ **bebida no alcohólica** soft drink, non-alcoholic drink ➤ **bebida**

refrescante soft drink **2** (*tb* ~ **alcohólica**) drink, alcoholic drink; **darse a la** ~ to take to drink

bebido ADJ **estar** ~ to be drunk

beca SF (= *ayuda*) (*gen*) grant; (*por méritos o en concurso*) scholarship

becado/a ADJ [*estudiante*] who holds a grant/scholarship

becar /1g/ VT to award a grant/scholarship to

becario/a SM/F (*gen*) grant holder; (*por méritos o en concurso*) scholarship holder

becerrada SF fight with young bulls

becerro SM **1** (= *animal*) yearling calf, bullock ➤ **becerro de oro** golden calf **2** (= *piel*) calfskin

bechamel SF béchamel sauce

bedel(a) SM/F [*de facultad*] ≈ head porter (*Brit*), head custodian (*EEUU*); [*de colegio*] ≈ janitor

beduino/a ADJ, SM/F Bedouin

befa SF jeer, taunt

begonia SF begonia

behaviorista ADJ, SMF behaviourist, behaviorist (*EEUU*)

BEI SM ABR = **Banco Europeo de Inversiones**) EIB

beicon SM bacon

beige [be3] (*LAm*) ADJ, SM beige

beis Ⓐ ADJ (*Esp*) beige Ⓑ SM **1** (*Esp*) beige **2** (*Méx*) baseball

béisbol SM, **beisbol** SM (*Méx*) baseball

beldad SF (*liter*) beauty

Belén SM Bethlehem

belén SM **1** [*de Navidad*] nativity scene, crib, crèche (*EEUU*) ➤ **belén viviente** *representation of the Nativity by real people* **2** (= *confusión*) bedlam; ✦ MODISMO **meterse en belenes** to get into a mess, get into trouble

belenista SMF maker of nativity scenes

belga ADJ, SMF Belgian

Bélgica SF Belgium

Belgrado SM Belgrade

Belice SM Belize

belicista Ⓐ ADJ warmongering, militaristic Ⓑ SMF warmonger

bélico ADJ **1** [*actitud*] warlike **2** [*material, juguete*] war *antes de s*

belicoso ADJ (= *guerrero*) warlike; (= *agresivo*) bellicose, aggressive

beligerancia SF belligerency

beligerante ADJ belligerent

bellaco/a Ⓐ ADJ wicked Ⓑ SM/F scoundrel, rogue

belladona SF deadly nightshade

belleza SF **1** (= *cualidad*) beauty, loveliness **2** (= *persona bella*) beauty; **es una** ~ **(de mujer)** she's a beautiful woman

bello ADJ beautiful, lovely; **es una bella persona** he's a lovely person; **Bellas Artes** Fine Art

bellota SF acorn

bemba** SF (*LAm*) lip

bembo (*LAm*) ADJ, **bembudo** (*LAm*) ADJ thick-lipped

bemol SM (*Mús*) flat; ✦ MODISMO **tener ~es: esto tiene ~es** this is a tough one; **¡tiene ~es la cosa!** (*iró*) that's just great! (*iró**)

benceno SM benzene

bencina SF **1** (*Quím*) benzine **2** (*Chi*) petrol (*Brit*), gas(oline) (*EEUU*)

bencinera SF (*Chi*) petrol station (*Brit*), gas station (*EEUU*)

bendecir /3o/ VT **1** [+ *persona, agua, casa*] to bless; ~ **la mesa** to say grace **2** (= *loar*) to praise

bendición SF [*de persona, agua*] blessing, benediction; **dar** o **echar la** ~ to give one's blessing (**a** to); ➤ **bendición de la mesa** grace (*before meals*)

bendiga *etc*, **bendije** *ver* **bendecir**

bendito/a Ⓐ ADJ **1** (*Rel*) blessed; [*agua*] holy; **¡~s los ojos que te ven!** you're a sight for sore eyes!; **¡~ sea Dios!** (*alivio*)

thank goodness!; (*asombro*) good grief! **2** (*iró*) (= *maldito*) blessed **3** (= *afortunado*) lucky Ⓑ SM/F simple soul; **es un** ~ he's so sweet; ✦ MODISMO **dormir como un** ~ to sleep like a log

benedictino ADJ Ⓐ ADJ Benedictine Ⓑ SM Benedictine; ✦ MODISMO **es obra de ~s** it's a monumental task

benefactor(a) Ⓐ ADJ beneficent Ⓑ SM/F benefactor

beneficencia SF (= *cualidad*) charity; (*tb* **asociación de** ~) charity, charitable organization

beneficiado/a SM/F **el único** ~ the only one to benefit

beneficiar /1b/ Ⓐ VT **1** (= *favorecer*) to benefit; **la empresa más beneficiada por esta ayuda** the company which benefited most from this aid; **esta huelga no beneficia a nadie** this strike is of no benefit to anyone; **esa actitud no te va a** ~ that attitude will do you no favours o (*EEUU*) favors; **la lluvia beneficia al campo** rain is good for the countryside **2** (*Min*) (= *extraer*) to extract **3** (*LAm*) [+ *animal*] to butcher Ⓑ **beneficiarse** VPR ~**se de algo** to benefit from sth

beneficiario/a SM/F [*de herencia, póliza*] beneficiary; [*de beca, subsidio*] recipient; [*de cheque*] beneficiary, payee

beneficio SM **1** (= *ventaja*) benefit; **concederle a algn el** ~ **de la duda** to give sb the benefit of the doubt; **a** ~ **de algn** in aid of sb; **en** ~ **propio** to his own advantage, for his own benefit **2** (*Com, Fin*) profit; **obtener** o **tener ~s** to make a profit **3** (*Min*) [*de mineral*] extraction **4** (*LAm*) [*de animal*] butchering **5** (*CAm*) [*de café*] coffee processing plant

beneficiosamente ADV **influir** ~ **en algo** to have a beneficial effect on sth, be beneficial to sth

beneficioso ADJ beneficial

benéfico ADJ **1** [*acción, influencia*] beneficial **2** [*concierto, función*] charity *antes de s*; **obra benéfica** charity; **organización** o **sociedad benéfica** charity, charitable organization

Benemérita SF **la** ~ the Civil Guard; ⊃ *GUARDIA CIVIL*

benemérito ADJ distinguished

beneplácito SM blessing, approval; **dar su** ~ to give one's blessing

benevolencia SF benevolence, kindness

benevolente ADJ, **benévolo** ADJ benevolent, kind

bengala SF flare

benigno ADJ **1** [*persona*] kind, benevolent **2** [*clima*] mild **3** (*Med*) [*tumor*] benign, non-malignant

benjamín/ina Ⓐ SM/F **1** (*más joven*) baby of the family, youngest child **2** (*Dep*) young player Ⓑ SM (= *botella*) half bottle

beodo ADJ (*frm*) drunk

berberecho SM cockle

berberisco ADJ Berber

berbiquí SM carpenter's brace

berdel SM mackerel

bereber ADJ, SMF, **beréber** ADJ, SMF Berber

berenjena SF aubergine (*Brit*), eggplant (*EEUU*)

berenjenal SM **1** (= *campo*) aubergine field (*Brit*), eggplant field (*EEUU*) **2** (= *lío*) mess, trouble; **en buen** ~ **nos hemos metido** we've got ourselves into a fine mess

bergante SM scoundrel, rascal

bergantín SM brig

berilio SM beryllium

Berlín SM Berlin

berlina SF (*Aut*) saloon car (*Brit*), sedan (*EEUU*)

berlinés/esa Ⓐ ADJ Berlin *antes de s* Ⓑ SM/F Berliner

berma SF (*Chi Aut*) hard shoulder (*Brit*), shoulder (*EEUU*), berm (*EEUU*)

bermejo ADJ reddish

bermudas SMPL o SFPL Bermuda shorts; **unos** o **unas** ~ a pair of Bermuda shorts

Berna SF Bern

berrear /1a/ VI [*animal*] to bellow; [*niño*] to howl, bawl**

berreta ADJ (CS) cheap, flashy

berretín SM (RPI) (= obsesión) obsession; ✦ MODISMO **tener berretines** to think one is something special

berrido SM [de animal] lowing; **berridos** bawling sing

berrinche SM (= rabieta) tantrum; **le dio** o (Méx) **hizo** o (Esp) **cogió un** ~ he had a tantrum; **llevarse un** ~ (Esp) to fly into a rage

berro SM watercress

berza SF cabbage

berzotas SMF INV (Esp) twit*, chump*

besamel SF (Esp) white sauce, bechamel sauce

besar /1a/ **Ⓐ** VT to kiss; ✦ MODISMO ~ **la mano a algn** to pay one's humble respects (**a** to) **Ⓑ** **besarse** VPR to kiss, kiss one another

beso SM kiss; **dar un** ~ **a algn** to kiss sb, give sb a kiss; **tirar un** ~ **a algn** to blow sb a kiss

bestia Ⓐ ADJ (*) **1** (= bruto) **ese tío** ~ that brute o animal* **2 a lo** ~: **parecido a la lucha libre pero más a lo** ~ similar to wrestling but more rough; **hoy hemos entrenado a lo** ~ we trained really hard today; **comimos a lo** ~ we really stuffed ourselves*, we pigged out*; **conducen a lo** ~ they drive like idiots **3** (= ignorante) thick (Brit*), dumb (esp EEUU*) **4** (con admiración, asombro) **¡qué** ~**!** she's amazing o incredible! **Ⓑ** SMF (*) (= bruto) **¡eres un** ~**!** you're a brute!, you're an animal!*; **el muy** ~ that animal*; **es un** ~ **con el trabajo** he works like a dog* **Ⓒ** SF (Zool) beast; ✦ MODISMO **ser una mala** ~ to be a nasty piece of work (esp Brit*), be an SOB (EEUU**) ➤ **bestia de carga** beast of burden, pack animal ➤ **bestia feroz, bestia salvaje** wild animal, wild beast ➤ **bestia negra, bestia parda** bête noire

bestial ADJ (= enorme) terrific*, tremendous*; **la máquina hacía un ruido** ~ the machine made a terrific o tremendous noise*

bestialidad SF **1** (= acción brutal) act of brutality **2** (*) (= disparate) **comer tanto es una** ~ eating so much is just gross*; **no dice más que** ~**es** he's so coarse **3** (*) (= cantidad excesiva) **los precios han subido una** ~ prices have rocketed*; **he dormido una** ~ I slept for absolutely ages*; **una** ~ **de** a mass of*, tons of*; **había una** ~ **de gente** there were masses of people*, there were tons of people*

bestialismo SM bestiality

bestiario SM bestiary

besucón/ona **Ⓐ** ADJ **es muy** ~ he's always dishing out kisses* **Ⓑ** SM/F **es un** ~ he's always dishing out kisses*

besugo Ⓐ SM (= pez) sea bream; **ojos de** ~ bulging eyes **Ⓑ** SMF (*) (= persona) idiot

besuquear /1a/ **Ⓐ** VT to cover with kisses **Ⓑ** **besuquearse** VPR (= besarse) to neck*, smooch*

beta SF beta

betabel SM (Méx) beetroot (Brit), beet (EEUU)

betún SM **1** (para zapatos) shoe polish; **dar (de)** ~ **a algo** to polish sth **2** (Quím) bitumen ➤ **betún de Judea** asphalt

biaba SF (CS) **dar una** ~ **a algn** (= golpear) to beat sb up; (= derrotar) to defeat sb, crush sb

bianual ADJ, SM (Bot) biannual

biberón SM feeding bottle, baby's bottle; **dar el** ~ **al niño** to give the baby his bottle

Biblia SF Bible; ✦ MODISMO **saber la** ~ **en verso** to know everything

bíblico ADJ biblical

bibliobús SM mobile library, bookmobile (EEUU)

bibliografía SF bibliography

bibliográfico ADJ bibliographic(al)

biblioteca SF **1** (= edificio) library ➤ **biblioteca de consulta** reference library ➤ **biblioteca de préstamo** lending library **2** (= mueble) bookcase, bookshelves pl

bibliotecario/a Ⓐ ADJ library antes de s **Ⓑ** SM/F librarian

bibliotecología SF, **biblioteconomía** SF library

science, librarianship

bicameral ADJ (Pol) two-chamber, bicameral

bicarbonato SM (Quím) bicarbonate; (en cocina, digestivo) bicarbonate of soda ➤ **bicarbonato sódico** sodium bicarbonate

bicentenario ADJ, SM bicentenary

bíceps SM INV biceps

biche ADJ (LAm) unripe, immature

bicho SM **1** (Zool) (gen) small animal; (= insecto) bug, creepy-crawly (esp Brit*); ✦ REFRÁN ~ **malo nunca muere** the devil looks after his own **2** (*) (= persona) **es un malo** ~ he's a nasty piece of work (esp Brit), he's an SOB (EEUU**); **todo** ~ **viviente** every living soul, every man-jack of them ➤ **bicho raro** weirdo*

bici SF bike*

bicicleta SF bicycle, bike; **¿vamos en** ~ **al pueblo?** shall we cycle to the village?; **¿sabes andar** o **montar en** ~**?** can you ride a bike? ➤ **bicicleta de carreras** racing bicycle, racing bike ➤ **bicicleta de ejercicio, bicicleta de gimnasio** exercise bike ➤ **bicicleta de montaña** mountain bike

bicicross SM INV cyclo-cross

bicimoto SM (LAm) moped

bicoca SF (= ganga) bargain; (= trabajo fácil) cushy job*

bicolor ADJ two-colour, two-color (EEUU)

BID SM ABR (= **Banco Interamericano de Desarrollo**) IDB

bidé SM, **bidet** [bi'de] SM (pl ~s o **bidets**), **bidel** SM (Col) bidet

bidimensional ADJ two-dimensional

bidireccional ADJ bidirectional

bidón SM (= barril) (grande) drum; (pequeño) can ➤ **bidón de aceite** oil drum

biela SF (Téc) connecting rod

Bielorrusia SF Belorussia

bielorruso/a ADJ, SM/F Belorussian

bien Ⓐ ADV **1** (= satisfactoriamente) well; **hablas** ~ **el español** you speak good Spanish, you speak Spanish well; **no veo muy** ~ I can't see very well; **lo sé muy** ~ I know that perfectly well; ~ **gracias, ¿y usted?** fine thanks, and you?; **¡muy** ~**!** very good!; **oler** ~ to smell good; **saber** ~ to taste good

2 (= correctamente) **¿has puesto** ~ **la rueda?** have you put the wheel on properly?; **se limpia** ~ **el pescado** clean the fish thoroughly o well; **¡** ~ **hecho!** well done!; **has contestado** ~ you gave the right answer, you answered correctly; **no consigo hacerlo** ~ I can't seem to do it right; **haces** ~ you're (quite) right; **hiciste** ~ **en decírselo** you were right to tell him, you did the right thing in telling him

3 estar ~: **¿estás** ~**?** are you all right?, are you OK?; **aquí se está** ~ it's nice here; **¡está** ~**!, lo haré** OK! o all right! I'll do it; **ese libro está muy** ~ that book's very good, that's a very good book; **estás muy** ~ **con ese sombrero** you look really nice in that hat; **está muy** ~ **que ahorres dinero** it's very good that you're saving; **que esté(s)** ~ (Col*) bye*; **¡eso no está** ~**!** that's not very nice!; **te está** ~ **la falda** the skirt fits you fine; **¡ya está** ~**!** that's enough!; **estar** ~ **de algo**: **estar** ~ **de salud** to be well, be in good health; **estar** ~ **de dinero** to be well off; **no está** ~ **de la cabeza** he isn't right in the head

4 (= de acuerdo) **¡bien!** all right!, OK!; **si a ustedes les parece** ~ if it's all right with o by you

5 (= muy) **un café** ~ **caliente** a nice hot coffee; **un coche** ~ **caro** a pretty expensive car; ~ **temprano** pretty early; **hasta** ~ **entrada la noche** until very late at night, until well into the night

6 ~ **de** (Esp*) (= muchos): ~ **de veces** lots of times; **¡te han dado** ~ **de regalos!** you got a lot of presents!; **bebe** ~ **de café** he drinks a lot of coffee

7 (= fácilmente) easily; ~ **se ve que ...** it is easy to see that ...; **¡** ~ **podía habérmelo dicho!** he could have told me!

8 (locuciones) **estar a** ~ **con algn** to be on good terms with sb; **más** ~ rather; **más** ~ **bajo** on the short side, rather short; **más ~ creo que ...** I actually think ...; **pues ~** well; **tener a ~ hacer algo** (frm) to see fit to do sth; **le ruego tenga a ~ comunicarlo a sus lectores** please be kind enough to inform your readers; **~ es verdad que ...** it is of course true that ...

Ⓑ CONJ **1 si ~** although; **si ~ es cierto que ...** although it's true that ...

2 no ~ ◇ **ni ~** (CS): **no ~ llegó, empezó a llover** no sooner had he arrived than it started to rain

3 (en alternancia) **~ por avión, ~ en tren** either by air or by train

Ⓒ ADJ [persona, barrio, familia] well-to-do; **son gente ~** they're well-to-do

Ⓓ SM **1** (= bondad) good; **el ~ y el mal** good and evil; **hacer el ~** to do good; **hombre de ~** good man

2 (= provecho) good; **el ~ común** the common good; **hacer algo para el ~ de** to do sth for the good of; **es por tu ~** it's for your own good

3 bienes (= géneros) goods; (= propiedad) property sing, possessions ➤ **bienes de consumo** consumer goods ➤ **bienes de equipo** capital goods ➤ **bienes gananciales** shared possessions ➤ **bienes inmuebles** real estate sing ➤ **bienes raíces** real estate sing, realty sing (EEUU)

bienal Ⓐ ADJ biennial Ⓑ SF biennial exhibition

bienamado ADJ beloved

bienaventurado ADJ **1** (Rel) blessed **2** (= feliz) happy, fortunate

Bienaventuranzas SFPL Beatitudes

bienestar SM well-being, welfare ➤ **bienestar social** social welfare

bienhechor(a) SM/F benefactor/benefactress

bienintencionado ADJ well-meaning

bienio SM two-year period

bienpensante ADJ sanctimonious, goody-goody*

bienvenida SF welcome; **dar la ~ a algn** to welcome sb; **fiesta de ~** welcome party

bienvenido ADJ welcome

bies SM **al ~** (Cos) on the cross

bifásico ADJ (Elec) two-phase

bife SM (RPI) **1** [de carne] steak; [de pescado] fillet **2** (= bofetada) slap

bífido ADJ forked

bifocal Ⓐ ADJ bifocal; **gafas ~es** bifocals Ⓑ **bifocales** SMPL O SFPL bifocals

bifurcación SF [de calle] fork; (Ferro) junction

bifurcarse /1g/ VPR [camino] to fork; [vía] to diverge

bígamo/a Ⓐ ADJ bigamous Ⓑ SM/F bigamist

bígaro SM winkle

bigote SM (tb ~s) moustache, mustache (EEUU); (Zool) whiskers pl

bigotudo ADJ with a big moustache o (EEUU) mustache

bigudí SM curler, hair curler

bikini SM (SF en Arg) bikini

bilateral ADJ bilateral

bilbaíno ADJ of/from Bilbao

bilet SM (Méx) lipstick

biliar ADJ bile antes de s, gall antes de s; **cálculo ~** gallstone

bilingüe ADJ bilingual

bilingüismo SM bilingualism

bilioso ADJ bilious

bilis SF INV (Med) bile; ✦ MODISMO **descargar la ~ en** o **contra algn** to vent one's spleen on sb

billar SM **1** (= juego) billiards; (con 22 bolas) snooker; **mesa de ~** billiard table/snooker table ➤ **billar americano** pool **2** (= mesa) billiard table/snooker table/pool table **3 billares** [de billar] billiard hall/snooker hall/pool hall; [de otros juegos] amusement arcade

billete SM **1** (Fin) note (Brit), bill (EEUU); **un ~ de cinco libras** a five-pound note; **un ~ de 100 dólares** a 100-dollar bill ➤ **billete de banco** banknote **2** (Esp) [de transporte] ticket;

medio ~ half fare ➤ **billete azul** ticket for off-peak travel ➤ **billete de avión** plane ticket ➤ **billete de ida** single (Brit) o one-way (EEUU) ticket ➤ **billete de ida y vuelta** return (Brit) o round-trip (EEUU) ticket ➤ **billete sencillo** single (Brit) o one-way (EEUU) ticket **3** [de lotería] ticket

billetera SF, **billetero** SM wallet, billfold (EEUU)

billón SM trillion

La palabra inglesa **billion** equivale a mil millones.

bimensual ADJ **1** (= cada dos meses) bimonthly, two-monthly **2** (= dos veces al mes) fortnightly (Brit), semimonthly (EEUU)

bimestral ADJ bimonthly, two-monthly

bimestre SM (= periodo) two-month period; (= pago) two-monthly payment

bimotor Ⓐ ADJ twin-engined Ⓑ SM twin-engined plane

binario ADJ binary

bingo SM **1** (= juego) bingo **2** (= sala) bingo hall

binoculares SMPL binoculars

binóculo SM pince-nez

binomio SM **1** (Mat) binomial **2** (= pareja) **el conocido ~ de humoristas** the famous comedy duo; **el ~ ejército-gobierno** the partnership between government and army; **la falacia del ~ juventud-droga** the fallacy that young people and drugs inevitably go together

bioactivo ADJ bioactive

bioagricultura SF organic farming

biocarburante SM biofuel

biociencia SF bioscience

biodegradable ADJ biodegradable

biodegradar /1a/ Ⓐ VT to biodegrade Ⓑ **biodegradarse** VPR to biodegrade

biodiversidad SF biodiversity

bioética SF bioethics sing

bioético/a Ⓐ ADJ bioethical Ⓑ SM/F bioethicist

biofísica SF biophysics sing

biografía SF biography

biografiar /1c/ VT to write the biography of

biográfico ADJ biographical

biógrafo/a SM/F biographer

biología SF biology

biológico ADJ [ciclo, guerra, padre] biological; [alimento] organic; **cultivo ~** organically-grown produce

biólogo/a SM/F biologist

biomasa SF biomass

biombo SM folding screen

biopsia SF biopsy

bioquímica SF biochemistry

bioquímico/a Ⓐ ADJ biochemical Ⓑ SM/F biochemist

biorritmo SM biorhythm

biosfera SF biosphere

biotecnología SF biotechnology

bioterrorismo SM bioterrorism

bioterrorista Ⓐ SMF bioterrorist Ⓑ ADJ bioterrorist antes de s

bipartidismo SM two-party system

bípedo SM biped

biplano SM biplane

biplaza Ⓐ ADJ INV two-seater antes de s Ⓑ SM (Aer) two-seater

biquini SM (SF en Arg) bikini

birlar* /1a/ VT to pinch*, nick*; **me han birlado la bici** my bike's been nicked o pinched*

Birmania SF Burma

birmano/a ADJ, SM/F Burmese

birome SF (CS) ballpoint pen, Biro®

birra* SF beer

birreta SF (Rel) biretta, cardinal's hat

birrete SM **1** (Univ) mortarboard **2** (Jur) judge's cap **3** (Rel) = **birreta**

birria SF (esp Esp) **la novela es una ~*** the novel is rubbish (Brit) o trash o garbage*

bis Ⓐ ADV (en una calle) **vive en el 24 ~** he lives at 24B Ⓑ SM (Teat) encore

bisabuelo/a SM/F great-grandfather/great-grandmother; **~s** great-grandparents

bisagra SF hinge

bisbisear /1a/ VT to mutter, mumble

bisbiseo SM muttering, mumbling

biscote SM rusk (esp Brit), melba toast (EEUU)

biscúter SM (Aut) three-wheeler

bisel SM bevel, bevel edge

biselar /1a/ VT to bevel

bisemanal ADJ twice-weekly

bisexual ADJ, SMF bisexual

bisiesto ADJ **año ~** leap year

bisnieto/a SM/F great-grandson/great-granddaughter; **~s** great-grandchildren

bisojo ADJ = **bizco A**

bisonte SM bison

bisoñé SM toupée, toupee

bisoño ADJ (= inexperto) green, inexperienced; (Mil) raw

bistec SM (pl **~s**) steak, beefsteak

bisturí SM scalpel

bisutería SF costume jewellery o (EEUU) jewelry, imitation jewellery o (EEUU) jewelry

bit SM (Inform) bit

bitácora SF (Náut) binnacle

Bizancio SM Byzantium

bizantino/a Ⓐ ADJ **1** (Hist) Byzantine **2 discusión bizantina** pointless argument **3** (= decadente) decadent Ⓑ SM/F Byzantine

bizarro ADJ gallant, brave

bizco/a Ⓐ ADJ cross-eyed, squinting; ✦ MODISMO **dejar a algn ~** to leave sb open-mouthed Ⓑ SM/F cross-eyed person, someone with a squint

bizcochería SF (Col, Méx) pastry shop

bizcocho SM (= pastel) sponge cake; (más pequeño) sponge finger, lady finger (EEUU); (Uru) = bollo) bun

bizcochuelo SM (RPl) sponge cake; (Col) cake made with cornmeal

biznieto/a SM/F = **bisnieto**

bizquear /1a/ VI to squint

bizquera* SF (esp LAm) squint

blanca SF **1** ✦ MODISMOS **estar sin ~*** ◇ **no tener ~*** to be broke*, be strapped* **2** (Mús) minim (Brit), half note (EEUU) **3** (Ajedrez) white piece; **yo llevo las ~s** I'll be white **4** (Dominó) blank; ver tb **blanco**

Blancanieves SF Snow White

blanco/a Ⓐ ADJ **1** (= de color blanco) white; **se te está poniendo el pelo ~** your hair is going white; **un vino ~** a white wine; **es de color ~** it's white; ✦ MODISMO **~ como la nieve** as white as snow

2 [raza] white

3 (= pálido) [cara, cutis] fair; **soy muy ~ de piel** I'm very fair-skinned; **estar ~** [cara] to be pale; [cuerpo] to be white; ✦ MODISMO **~ como la cera** o **como el papel** o **como la pared** as white as a sheet

4 (Literat) [verso] blank

Ⓑ SM/F (= persona) white man/woman

Ⓒ SM **1** (= color) white; **casarse de ~** to get married in white, have a white wedding; **en ~ y negro** black and white; ✦ MODISMOS **no distinguir lo ~ de lo negro** to be unable to tell right from wrong; **poner los ojos en ~** to roll one's eyes; **verlo todo ~ o negro** to see everything in black and white ➤ **blanco de España** whiting ➤ **blanco y negro** (Culin) iced coffee with cream

2 (= parte blanca) ➤ **blanco de la uña** half-moon ➤ **blanco del ojo** white of the eye

3 (= objetivo) target; **un ~ fácil** an easy target; **dar en el ~** (lit) to hit the target; **tus críticas han dado en el ~** your criticisms were right on target o (Brit*) were spot on; **hacer ~** to hit the target; **hacer ~ en algo** to hit sth; **la prensa la hizo ~ de sus críticas** the press singled her out for criticism, she was the target of attacks by the press; **ser (el) ~ de** [+ crítica] to be the target of; [+ burla] to be the butt of

4 (= espacio sin escribir) blank, blank (space)

5 en ~ [página, cheque] blank; **rellene los espacios en ~** fill in the blanks; **dejar algo en ~** to leave sth blank; **dejé varias preguntas en ~** there were several questions I didn't answer; **votar en ~** to return a blank ballot paper; ✦ MODISMOS **pasar la noche en ~** not to sleep a wink*, have a sleepless night; **quedarse en ~: el concursante se quedó en ~** the contestant's mind went blank; **se me quedó la mente en ~** my mind went blank

6 (= pausa) gap, break; ver tb **blanca**

blancura SF whiteness

blancuzco ADJ (= parecido al blanco) whitish; (= blanco sucio) dirty-white, off-white

blandengue* ADJ soft, weak

blandir /3a; defectivo; no utilizado en presente/ VT to brandish, flourish

blando ADJ **1** (= tierno) [madera, droga, agua] soft; [carne] tender; (pey) flabby **2** (= indulgente) [persona] soft, indulgent; [carácter] soft, delicate; [política] soft, wet; **~ de corazón** soft-hearted, sentimental; **ser ~ con el crimen** to be soft on crime

blandura SF (gen) softness; [de carne] tenderness

blanqueada SF **1** (LAm) [de pared, casa] whitewashing **2** (Méx Dep*) whitewash

blanqueador SM (Méx) bleach

blanquear /1a/ Ⓐ VT **1** [+ ropa] to bleach; [+ pared, fachada] to whitewash **2** [+ dinero] to launder Ⓑ VI to turn white, go white

blanquecino ADJ off-white, whitish

blanqueo SM **1** [de pared, casa] whitewashing; [de ropa] bleaching **2** ➤ **blanqueo de dinero** money laundering

blanquillo SM **1** (CAm, Méx) (= huevo) egg **2** (Chi, Perú) (= durazno) white peach

blasfemar /1a/ VI **1** (Rel) to blaspheme (**contra** against) **2** (= decir tacos) to curse, swear

blasfemia SF **1** (Rel) blasphemy **2** (= taco) swearword, curse

blasfemo/a Ⓐ ADJ blasphemous Ⓑ SM/F blasphemer

blasón SM **1** (Heráldica) coat of arms **2** (= honor) honour, honor (EEUU), glory

blasonar /1a/ VT **1** [+ escudo] to emblazon **2** (= encomiar) [+ persona] to praise, extol

bledo SM ver **importar²** A **2.1**

blindado ADJ [vehículo] armour-plated, armor-plated (EEUU); [chaleco] bullet-proof; [puerta] reinforced

blindar /1a/ VT [+ vehículo] to armour-plate, armor-plate (EEUU); [+ puerta] to reinforce

bloc SM (pl **~s**) pad, writing pad ➤ **bloc de notas** notepad

blocar /1g/ VT (Dep) [+ jugador] to tackle; [+ balón] to stop, trap

blof SM (LAm) bluff; **hacer un ~ a algn** to bluff sb

blofear /1a/ (LAm) VI to boast, brag

blonda SF blond lace

bloque SM **1** (= trozo) [de piedra, mármol] block; [de helado] brick ➤ **bloque de cilindros** cylinder block ➤ **bloque de pisos** block of flats (Brit), apartment building (EEUU) ➤ **bloque publicitario** commercial break **2** (Pol) bloc; **el ~ comunista** the communist bloc; **en ~** en bloc

bloquear /1a/ Ⓐ VT **1** (= obstaculizar) [+ entrada, salida] to block (off); [+ camino, proyecto, proceso] to block; **un tractor**

bloqueaba la carretera the road was blocked by a tractor, a tractor was blocking the road; **la oposición bloqueó la ley en el parlamento** the opposition blocked the bill in parliament; **la policía nos bloqueó el paso** the police barred our way

2 (= *atascar*) [+ *mecanismo*] to jam (up), block; [+ *cerradura, línea telefónica*] to jam; [+ *volante*] to lock; **los oyentes ~on la centralita de la emisora** listeners jammed the radio station's switchboard

3 (= *aislar*) to cut off; **quedaron bloqueados por la nieve** they were cut off by the snow

4 (*Mil*) to blockade

5 (*Com, Fin*) to freeze; **fondos bloqueados** frozen assets

6 (*Dep*) [+ *jugador*] to tackle; [+ *balón*] to stop, trap

Ⓑ bloquearse VPR **1** (= *paralizarse*) [*persona*] **me bloqueé en el examen** my mind went blank in the exam; **cuando me habla me bloqueo** when he speaks to me I get completely tongue-tied

2 (= *atascarse*) [*mecanismo*] to jam (up); [*cerradura, línea telefónica, centralita*] to jam; [*frenos, volante*] to lock

bloqueo SM **1** (*Mil*) blockade; **burlar** o **forzar el ~** to run the blockade **2** (*Com, Fin*) ➤ **bloqueo de fondos** freezing of assets ➤ **bloqueo informativo** news blackout **3** ➤ **bloqueo mental** mental block

bluejean SM INV (*LAm*) jeans *pl*, denims *pl*

Bluetooth® SF Bluetooth®; **tecnología ~** Bluetooth technology

blusa SF blouse

blusón SM (= *camisa grande*) long shirt, loose shirt; [*de pintor*] smock

BM SM ABR (= **Banco Mundial**) WB

boa SF boa

boatiné SF **bata de ~** padded dressing-gown o bathrobe

boato SM show, ostentation

bobada SF silly thing, stupid thing; **este programa es una ~** this programme is stupid; **decir ~s** to say silly things, talk nonsense; **hacer ~s** to do stupid things

bobalicón/ona Ⓐ ADJ silly **Ⓑ** SM/F nitwit, clot (*Brit**), dumbbell (*EEUU**)

bobería SF **1** (= *cualidad*) silliness, idiocy **2** = **bobada**

bobina SF (*Cos*) reel; (*Téc, Pesca*) spool; (*Fot*) spool, reel; (*Aut, Elec*) coil ➤ **bobina de encendido** ignition coil

bobinar /1a/ VT to wind

bobo/a Ⓐ ADJ (= *tonto*) silly, stupid; (= *ingenuo*) simple, naïve; ✦ MODISMO **estar ~ con algo/algn** to be crazy about sth/sb **Ⓑ** SM/F (= *tonto*) idiot, fool

boca Ⓐ SF **1** (*Anat*) mouth; **no debes hablar con la ~ llena** you shouldn't talk with your mouth full; **tengo que arreglarme la ~** I must get my teeth seen to; **(respiración) ~ a ~** mouth-to-mouth resuscitation; **~ abajo** (*cartas, libro, hoja*) face down; (*vaso*) upside down; **estar tumbado ~ abajo** to be lying face down; **se cuelgan las flores ~ abajo** hang the flowers upside down; **~ arriba** (*cartas, libro, hoja*) face up; (*vaso*) (the) right way up; **poner a algn ~ arriba** to turn sb onto his back

2 en ~ de: suena extraño en ~ de un socialista it sounds odd coming from a socialist; **está en ~ de todos** it's on everybody's lips; **por ~ de** through; **hablan por ~ del negociador** they speak through the negotiator; **lo sabemos por ~ de los propios autores del delito** we know this from the people responsible for the crime

3 ✦ MODISMOS **no abrió la ~ en toda la tarde** he didn't open his mouth o he didn't say a word all afternoon; **coserse la ~*** to keep quiet, keep mum*; **de ~ en ~: la cosa anda de ~ en ~** the story is doing the rounds; **de ~ para afuera: apoyó la idea de ~ para afuera** he paid lip-service to the idea; **eso lo dice de ~ para afuera** he's just saying that, that's what he says (but he doesn't mean it); **decir algo con la ~ chica** o **pequeña** to say sth without really meaning it; **sin decir esta ~ es mía** without a word to anybody; **para hacer ~** as an appetizer; **se me hace la ~ agua** my mouth is watering; **llenársele la ~ a algn: esa Europa con la que se les llena la ~** this Europe that they're always talking about; **se le llena la ~ hablando del coche** all he can talk about is the car; **meterse en la ~ del lobo** to

put one's head in the lion's mouth; **(oscuro) como ~ de lobo** pitch black; **partir la ~ a algn*** to smash sb's face in*; **a pedir de ~: todo salió a pedir de ~** it all turned out perfectly; **quedarse con la ~ abierta** to be dumbfounded; **me lo has quitado de la ~** you took the words right out of my mouth; **tapar la ~ a algn** to keep sb quiet, shut sb up*; **torcer la ~** (= *hacer un gesto*) to make a wry face; (= *burlarse*) to sneer; ✦ REFRANES **en ~ cerrada no entran moscas** silence is golden; **el que tiene ~ se equivoca** we all make mistakes, to err is human; **por la ~ muere el pez** silence is golden, it's best to keep one's own counsel

4 (= *abertura, entrada*) [*de túnel, cueva, vasija*] mouth; [*de tonel*] bunghole; [*de puerto*] entrance; [*de arma*] muzzle ➤ **boca de incendios** hydrant ➤ **boca del estómago** pit of the stomach ➤ **boca de metro** underground (*Brit*) o subway (*EEUU*) entrance ➤ **boca de mina** pithead, mine entrance ➤ **boca de riego** hydrant ➤ **boca de río** river mouth, estuary

5 [*de vino*] flavour, flavor (*EEUU*)

6 ➤ **boca de dragón** (*Bot*) snapdragon

7 bocas (= *personas*) mouths; **son seis ~s las que tengo que alimentar** I have six mouths to feed

Ⓑ SM ➤ **boca a boca: aplicar** o **hacer** o **practicar el ~ a ~ a algn** to give sb mouth-to-mouth resuscitation, give sb the kiss of life

bocacalle SF side street; **la primera ~ a la derecha** the first turning o turn o road on the right

bocadillo SM **1** (*Esp*) sandwich (*made with French bread*) **2** (*en historietas*) balloon, bubble **3** (*Col*) [*de guayaba*] piece of guava cake **4** (*Méx*) snack

bocadito SM snack

bocado SM **1** (= *de comida*) mouthful; (= *aperitivo*) snack; **~ exquisito** titbit, tidbit (*EEUU*); **no he probado ~ en todo el día** I've not had a bite to eat all day; **tomar un ~** to have a bite to eat; ✦ MODISMO **el ~ del león** the lion's share **2** (= *mordisco*) bite; **le he dado sólo un ~ a tu tortilla** I've only had a bite out of your omelette **3** (*para caballo*) bit

bocajarro ADV **a ~** [*disparar*] at point-blank range; **decir algo a ~** to say sth bluntly o without mincing one's words

bocamanga SF cuff, wristband

bocanada SF [*de humo*] puff; [*de viento, aliento*] gust, blast

bocarte SM anchovy

bocasucia* (*RPl*) **Ⓐ** ADJ foul-mouthed **Ⓑ** SMF **ser un ~** to swear like a trooper

bocata* SM (*Esp*) sandwich (*made with French bread*)

bocatería SF (*Esp*) ≈ sandwich bar

bocatoma SF (*And*) water intake, inlet pipe

bocazas* SMF INV (*Esp*) bigmouth*

boceras* SMF INV (*Esp*) loudmouth*

boceto SM (= *esquema*) sketch, outline; (= *maqueta*) model, mock-up

bocha SF **1** (= *bola*) bowl; **juego de las ~s** bowls **2** (*CS***) (= *cabeza*) nut*, noggin (*EEUU***)

bochar* /1a/ VT **1** (*LAm*) (= *rechazar*) to rebuff, reject **2** (*RPl*) (= *en examen*) to fail, flunk*

boche SM (*And*) row, fuss

bochinche SM **1** (*LAm*) (= *jaleo*) uproar, commotion **2** (*Carib*) (= *lío*) muddle, mess

bochinchero/a (*LAm*) **Ⓐ** ADJ rowdy, brawling **Ⓑ** SM/F brawler

bocho* SM (*CS*) **ser un ~** to be brainy, be clever (*esp Brit*), be smart (*esp EEUU*)

bochorno SM **1** (= *calor*) sultry weather, stuffy weather* **2** (= *vergüenza*) embarrassment, shame; **¡qué ~!** how embarrassing!

bochornoso ADJ **1** [*tiempo, día*] close*, stuffy* **2** (= *vergonzoso*) degrading, shameful

bocina SF **1** (*Mús, Aut*) horn; **tocar la ~** (*Aut*) to sound one's horn, blow one's horn **2** (= *megáfono*) megaphone **3** (*LAm*) (= *trompetilla*) ear trumpet **4** (*Méx*) [*de teléfono*] mouthpiece; [*de equipo de música*] speaker

bocinazo SM (*Aut*) toot, blast (*of the horn*)

bocio SM goitre, goiter (*EEUU*)

bocón/ona Ⓐ ADJ **1** (*Méx, Carib*) (= *fanfarrón*) big-mouthed** **2** (*Méx*) (= *poco discreto*) indiscreet Ⓑ SM/F bigmouth

boda SF **1** (= *ceremonia*) wedding, marriage; (= *fiesta*) reception, wedding reception **2** (= *aniversario*) ➤ **bodas de oro** [*de pareja*] golden wedding *sing*, golden wedding anniversary *sing*; [*de asociación*] golden jubilee *sing* ➤ **bodas de plata** [*de pareja*] silver wedding *sing*, silver wedding anniversary *sing*; [*de asociación*] silver jubilee *sing*

bodega SF **1** (= *depósito*) [*de alimentos*] storeroom; [*de vinos*] wine cellar; [*de una casa*] cellar **2** (*tb* ~ **de carga**) (*Aer, Náut*) hold **3** (= *tienda*) [*de vinos, licores*] wine shop (*esp Brit*), off-licence (*Brit*), liquor store (*EEUU*); (*Carib, CAm*) [*de comestibles*] grocer's shop (*esp Brit*), grocery store (*EEUU*) **4** (*esp LAm*) (= *bar*) bar

bodegón SM (*Arte*) still life

bodeguero/a SM/F **1** (= *productor*) wine producer **2** (*Carib, CAm*) (= *tendero*) grocer

bodoque* SM (*Méx*) (= *tonto*) dimwit*

bodrio* SM rubbish (*esp Brit**), garbage (*EEUU**); **ser un** ~ to be rubbish (*Brit**), be garbage (*EEUU**); **un** ~ **de sitio** an awful place

body SM (*pl* **bodies**) body stocking ➤ **body milk** body lotion

BOE SM ABR (*Esp*) (= **Boletín Oficial del Estado**) ≈ Hansard (*Brit*), ≈ The Congressional Record (*EEUU*)

<table><tr><td>BOE</td></tr></table>

The **Boletín Oficial del Estado** is a daily Spanish-government publication in which new laws, directives and executive decisions are published together with advertisements for public-sector posts and contracts. It is provided free of charge to all government agencies and state organizations including schools, embassies and public libraries.

bóer Ⓐ ADJ Boer Ⓑ SMF (*pl* ~**s**) Boer

bofe SM (*Zool*) lung

bofetada SF slap in the face; **dar de** ~**s a algn** to slap sb

bofetón SM slap

boga SF **estar en** ~ to be in fashion, be in vogue

bogar /1h/ VI to row

bogavante SM (*Zool*) lobster

Bogotá SM Bogotá

bogotano/a Ⓐ ADJ of/from Bogotá Ⓑ SM/F native/inhabitant of Bogotá

bohemio/a ADJ, SM/F bohemian

bohío SM (*CAm, Carib*) hut, shack

boicot SM (*pl* ~**s**) boycott; **hacer el** ~ **a algo** to boycott sth

boicotear /1a/ VT to boycott

boina SF beret

boite SF [bwat], **boîte** [bwat] SF nightclub

boj SM (= *planta*) box; (= *madera*) boxwood

bol SM bowl

bola SF **1** (= *cuerpo esférico*) ball; [*de helado*] scoop; (= *canica*) marble; **del susto se me ha hecho una** ~ **en el estómago** my stomach knotted up with fright; ✦ MODISMO **estar hecho una** ~ (= *gordo*) to be round as a barrel, be chubby*; (= *acurrucado*) to be curled up (in a ball) ➤ **bola de cristal** crystal ball ➤ **bola del mundo** globe ➤ **bola de nieve** snowball
2 (*Dep*) ball; [*de petanca*] boule; (*LAm*) (*caza*) **bolas** bolas; ✦ MODISMOS **andar como** ~ **huacha** (*Chi*) ◇ **andar como** ~ **sin manija** (*RPl*) to be at a loose end; **dar** ~ (*CS**) to take notice; **no me da** ~ he doesn't take any notice *o* (*Brit**) a blind bit of notice; **ir a su** ~ (*Esp***) to do one's own thing*; **parar** ~(**s**) (*Col, Ven*) to pay attention ➤ **bola de billar** billiard ball, snooker ball; **tener la cabeza como una** ~ **de billar** to be as bald as a

coot, be as bald as a cue ball (*EEUU*)
3 (*en lana, algodón*) bobble; **para que no le salgan** ~**s** to stop bobbles; **hacerse** ~**s** (*lit*) to get bobbly; (*Méx**) (*fig*) to get confused
4 (*Esp*) (= *músculo*) [*del brazo*] biceps; [*de la pantorrilla*] calf muscle; **sacar** ~ to flex one's muscles
5 bolas* (= *testículos*) balls***; ✦ MODISMOS **en** ~**s*** (= *desnudo*) stark naked*; **hasta las** ~**s*** pissed off***; **pillar a algn en** ~**s*** (= *desprevenido*) to catch sb napping*
6 (*) (= *mentira*) fib; **¡vaya** ~ **que nos metiste!** what a fib you told us!; **nos quiere meter una** ~ he's trying to put one past us*
7 (*Méx*) (= *jaleo*) row, hubbub; **se armó la** ~ all hell broke loose*

bolazo SM **1** (*CS*) (= *tontería*) silly remark, piece of nonsense **2** (*Méx*) ✦ MODISMO **al** *o* **de** ~ at random

bolchevique ADJ, SMF Bolshevik

boleado ADJ (*RPl*) **andar** ~* to be confused

boleador(a) SM/F (*Méx*) (= *limpiabotas*) shoeshine boy/girl

boleadoras SFPL (*CS*) bolas; ◇ *GAUCHO*

bolear /1a/ Ⓐ VT **1** (= *lanzar*) [+ *pelota*] to throw **2** (*CS*) (= *cazar*) to catch with the bolas **3** (*Méx*) [+ *zapatos*] to polish, shine Ⓑ VI (*Billar*) to play for fun, knock the balls around

bolera SF bowling alley, skittle alley

bolero SM **1** (*Mús*) bolero **2** (*Méx*) (= *limpiabotas*) bootblack, shoeshine boy

boleta SF (*LAm*) **1** (= *billete*) ticket; (= *recibo*) receipt ➤ **boleta de calificaciones** (*Méx*) report **2** [*de voto*] ballot paper, voting paper

boletería SF (*LAm*) **1** (*en estación*) ticket office, booking office (*Brit*); (*Teat*) box office **2** (*Dep*) (= *recaudación*) gate, takings *pl* (*Brit*)

boletín SM (= *publicación*) bulletin; (*Univ*) journal, review ➤ **boletín de noticias** news bulletin ➤ **boletín informativo** news bulletin, news sheet ➤ **boletín meteorológico** weather report *o* forecast ➤ **Boletín Oficial del Estado** (*Esp*) ≈ Hansard (*Brit*), ≈ The Congressional Record (*EEUU*); ◇ *BOE*

boleto SM **1** [*de quiniela*] coupon ➤ **boleto de apuestas** betting slip ➤ **boleto de lotería** lottery ticket **2** (*LAm*) [*de transporte*] ticket ➤ **boleto de ida y vuelta** return (*Brit*) *o* round-trip (*EEUU*) ticket **3** (*Méx*) (= *asunto*) business; **ése es mi** ~ that's my business

boli* SM pen, Biro®, ballpoint pen

boliche¹ SM **1** (= *juego*) bowling **2** (= *bola*) jack **3** (= *bolera*) bowling alley **4** (= *juguete*) cup-and-ball toy

boliche²* SM (*CS*) (= *almacén*) small grocery store; (= *café*) cheap snack bar; (= *local nocturno*) club

bólido SM racing car; ✦ MODISMO **iba como un** ~* he was really shifting*

bolígrafo SM pen, ballpoint pen, Biro®

bolilla SF (*CS Univ*) question; ✦ MODISMO **dar** ~ **a algo/algn** to take notice of sth/sb

bolillo SM **1** (*Cos*) bobbin (*for lacemaking*) **2** (*LAm Mús*) drumstick **3** (*Méx*) (= *panecillo*) bread roll

bolinga* (*Esp*) Ⓐ ADJ **estar** ~ to be canned* Ⓑ SF **ir de** ~ to go on the booze*

bolita SF (*CS*) marble

bolívar SM *Venezuelan currency unit*

Bolivia SF Bolivia

boliviano/a ADJ, SM/F Bolivian

bollera* SF (*Esp*) dyke***

bollería SF pastries *pl*

bollo SM **1** [*de pan*] bread roll; (*dulce*) bun **2** (*en el coche*) dent; (*en la cabeza*) bump, lump

bolo¹ SM **1** (= *cilindro*) tenpin **2 bolos** (= *juego*) (tenpin) bowling *sing* **3** (*Méx*) [*de bautizo*] (= *dinero*) *coins thrown into the air by the godparents at a christening for people to catch*; (= *tarjeta*) *souvenir card handed out by the godparents at a christening*

bolo² (*CAm, Cub, Méx*) Ⓐ ADJ drunk Ⓑ SM drunk

bolo³** SM (*Mús*) gig, concert

bols SM INV bowl

bolsa SF **1** (*para llevar algo*) bag; **una ~ de caramelos** a bag of sweets (*esp Brit*) *o* candy (*EEUU*); **una ~ de patatas** *o* (*LAm*) **papas fritas** a packet *o* bag of crisps (*Brit*) *o* chips (*EEUU*); **una ~ de papel** a paper bag; **una ~ de plástico** a plastic bag; ✦ MODISMO **hacer algo ~** (*CS**) to ruin sth; **le pegaron hasta dejarlo hecho ~** they beat him to a pulp ➤ **bolsa de agua caliente** hot-water bottle ➤ **bolsa de aseo** toilet bag (*Brit*), sponge bag (*Brit*), travel kit (*EEUU*) ➤ **bolsa de basura** (*para cubo grande*) rubbish bag (*Brit*), bin bag (*Brit*), garbage bag (*EEUU*); (*para cubo pequeño*) bin liner (*Brit*), trash bag (*EEUU*) ➤ **bolsa de deportes** sports bag ➤ **bolsa de hielo** ice-pack ➤ **bolsa de la compra** shopping bag

2 (*Méx*) [*de mujer*] handbag

3 (*Méx*) (= *bolsillo*) pocket

4 (*Zool*) [*de canguro*] pouch; [*de calamar*] sac

5 (*Anat*) [*de sangre, pus*] build-up ➤ **bolsa escrotal** scrotum

6 (= *acumulación*) [*de gas, personas*] pocket; **una enorme ~ de desempleo** a huge number of unemployed, very high levels of unemployment ➤ **bolsa de aire** air pocket ➤ **bolsa de gas** pocket of gas ➤ **bolsa de petróleo** pocket of oil ➤ **bolsa de pobreza** pocket of poverty

7 (= *arruga*) (*en ojos*) bag; (*en papel pintado*) bubble; **esa blusa te hace ~s** that blouse is all baggy *o* doesn't hang right on you

8 (*Fin*) (= *mercado*) **la Bolsa** the Stock Exchange, the Stock Market; **jugar a la ~** to play the market; **las empresas que cotizan en ~** quoted *o* listed companies; **sacar a ~** to float ➤ **bolsa de empleo** employment office ➤ **bolsa de la propiedad** property section, property page(s) ➤ **bolsa de trabajo** employment exchange ➤ **bolsa negra** (*Chi*) black market

9 [*de dinero*] **¡la ~ o la vida!** your money or your life! ➤ **bolsa de estudios** (study) grant

bolsear /1a/ Ⓐ VT (*CAm, Méx*) ~ **a algn** to pick sb's pocket Ⓑ VI **1** (*CAm, Méx*) (= *robar*) to pick pockets **2** (*CAm, CS, Méx*) (= *estafar*) to cheat, swindle

bolsillo SM **1** [*de chaqueta, pantalón*] pocket; **lo pagué de mi ~** I paid it out of my own pocket; ✦ MODISMOS **meterse a algn en el ~** to have sb eating out of one's hand; **tener a algn en el ~** to have sb eating out of one's hand, have sb in one's pocket **2 de ~** pocket *antes de s*, pocket-size; **edición de ~** pocket edition

bolso SM [*de mano*] bag, handbag, purse (*EEUU*) ➤ **bolso de viaje** travelling bag, traveling bag (*EEUU*)

bolsón SM **1** (*RPl*) (= *bolso*) bag **2** (*Chi*) [*de escuela*] satchel, schoolbag **3** (*Bol Min*) lump of ore

boludear** /1a/ VI (*CS*) to piss about***

boludez** SF (*CS*) (= *acto*) stupid thing to do; **boludeces** shit*** *sing*, crap*** *sing*

boludo/a** (*CS*) Ⓐ ADJ thick (*Brit**), dumb (*esp EEUU**), stupid Ⓑ SM/F arsehole (*Brit****), asshole (*EEUU****), jerk (*EEUU**)

bomba Ⓐ SF **1** (*Mil*) bomb; **arrojar** *o* **lanzar una ~** (*desde un avión*) to drop a bomb; (*desde el suelo*) to throw a bomb; **poner una ~** to plant a bomb; ✦ MODISMOS **caer** *o* **sentar como una ~** [*noticia*] to come as a bombshell, be a bombshell; **la cena me cayó como una ~** dinner did not agree with me at all; **las especias me sientan como una ~ en el estómago** spices really upset my stomach; **a prueba de ~(s)** bomb-proof; **tiene un estómago a prueba de ~** he's got a cast-iron stomach ➤ **bomba atómica** atomic bomb ➤ **bomba de efecto retardado** time bomb ➤ **bomba de hidrógeno** hydrogen bomb ➤ **bomba de neutrones** neutron bomb ➤ **bomba de relojería** time bomb ➤ **bomba fétida** stink bomb ➤ **bomba lapa** limpet mine

2 (*Téc*) [*de agua, aire*] pump; **la ~ de la bicicleta** the bicycle pump ➤ **bomba de aire** (air) pump

3 (*Periodismo*) **3.1** (*tb* **noticia ~**) bombshell **3.2** (*) (= *éxito*) smash hit*

4 (*And, Carib*) (= *burbuja*) bubble

5 (*Col, Ven*) (*tb* **~ gasolinera**) petrol station (*Brit*), gas station (*EEUU*)

6 (*Chi*) [*de bomberos*] (= *vehículo*) fire engine; (= *estación*) fire station; (= *cuerpo*) fire brigade (*Brit*), fire department (*EEUU*)

7 (*CAm, Perú*) (= *borrachera*) drunkenness; **estar en ~** to be drunk

Ⓑ ADJ INV (*Esp†**) (= *estupendo*) **estar ~** [*persona*] to be gorgeous*; **éxito ~** phenomenal success

Ⓒ ADV (*Esp**) **pasarlo ~** to have a whale of a time*, have a super time*

bombacha SF, **bombachas** SFPL **1** (*CS*) (= *prenda interior*) panties *pl* **2** (*And, CS*) (= *pantalón*) baggy trousers *pl*

bombacho Ⓐ ADJ baggy, loose-fitting Ⓑ **bombachos** SMPL baggy trousers

bombardear /1a/ VT **1** (*Mil*) (*desde el aire*) to bomb; (*desde tierra*) to shell **2** (= *lanzar preguntas*) to bombard (**a, con** with)

bombardeo SM **1** (*Mil*) (*desde el aire*) bombing; (*con artillería*) shelling, bombardment **2** [*de preguntas*] bombardment

bombardero SM (*Aer*) bomber

bombazo SM **1** (*Méx*) (= *explosión*) explosion **2** (*) (= *noticia*) bombshell **3** (*) (= *éxito*) smash hit*

bombear /1a/ VT to pump

bombeo SM pumping

bombero/a SM/F **1** (*de incendios*) firefighter, fireman; **cuerpo de ~s** fire brigade (*Brit*), fire department (*EEUU*); **llamar a los ~s** to call the fire brigade (*Brit*) *o* fire department (*EEUU*) **2** (*LAm Aut*) petrol-pump attendant (*Brit*), gas station attendant (*EEUU*)

bombilla SF **1** (*Elec*) bulb, light bulb **2** (*CS*) *tube for drinking maté*

bombillo SM (*Carib, CAm*) light bulb

bombín SM **1** (= *sombrero*) bowler hat (*Brit*), derby (*EEUU*) **2** (*Chi*) [*de aire*] pump

bombita SF (*RPl*) light bulb

bombo SM **1** (*Mús*) bass drum; **tengo la cabeza como un ~** my head's throbbing *o* buzzing; ✦ MODISMO **anunciar algo a ~ y platillo** (*Esp*) *o* **con ~s y platillos** (*LAm*) to announce sth amid a lot of hype, go in for a lot of publicity about sth **2** (*en sorteos*) drum **3** (*) (= *elogio exagerado*) exaggerated praise; (*Teat, Cine*) hype*; **dar ~ a algo** to sing the praises of sth; **darse ~** to blow one's own trumpet*

bombón SM **1** [*de chocolate*] chocolate **2** (*Méx*) [*de caramelo*] marshmallow

bombona SF ➤ **bombona de butano** gas cylinder

bombonera SF sweet box (*esp Brit*), candy box (*EEUU*)

bombonería SF sweet shop (*Brit*), candy store (*EEUU*), confectioner's

bonachón ADJ good-natured, easy-going; (*pey*) simple, naïve

bonaerense ADJ of/from Buenos Aires

bonanza SF **1** (*Náut*) fair weather, calm conditions **2** (= *prosperidad*) prosperity, boom

bonche* SM (*Carib*) (= *fiesta*) party

bonchón/ona* SM/F (*Ven*) party animal

bondad SF (= *cualidad*) goodness; (= *amabilidad*) kindness; **tenga la ~ de pasar** please go in; **tenga la ~ de no fumar** please refrain from smoking

bondadoso ADJ (= *amable*) kind-hearted; (= *de buenas intenciones*) good-natured

bonete SM (*Rel*) biretta; (*Univ*) mortarboard

bongo¹ SM (*LAm Náut*) large canoe; (*And*) small punt

bongó² SM, **bongo²** SM bongo, bongo drum

boniato SM sweet potato, yam

bonificación SF **1** (= *pago*) bonus **2** (*Com*) (= *descuento*) discount

bonificar /1g/ VT to discount

bonito¹ Ⓐ ADJ **1** (= *bello*) pretty; **María es un ~ nombre** María is a pretty name; **el vendedor me lo pintó todo muy ~** the salesman painted me a very pretty picture of it; **lo ~ sería que no hubiera guerras** it would be nice if there were no wars; **¡qué ~!** **¡contestarle así a tu padre!** (*iró*) that's nice, answering your father back like that!; **¡~ lío se armó!***

(*iró*) there was certainly a bit of a fuss!
2 (= *considerable*) **una bonita cantidad** *o* **suma** a tidy little sum*, a pretty penny*
Ⓑ ADV (*LAm**) nicely; **canta ~** she sings nicely; **se te ve ~** it looks good on you

bonito² SM (= *pez*) tuna, bonito

bono SM **1** (= *vale*) voucher, certificate **2** (*Fin*) bond ➤ **bono del estado** government bond ➤ **bono del Tesoro** Treasury bond ➤ **bono de tesorería** debenture bond

bono-bus SM (*Esp*), **bonobús** SM (*pl* **bonobuses**) (*Esp*) bus pass

bono-loto SF, **bonoloto** SF *state-run weekly lottery*

bonsai SM bonsai

bonzo SM bonze; **quemarse a lo ~** to set o.s. alight

boñiga SF [*de vaca*] cowpat; [*de caballo*] horse dung

boom [bum] SM boom ➤ **boom inmobiliario** property boom

boomerang [bume'ran] SM (*pl* **~s**) boomerang

boqueada SF gasp

boquera SF cold sore

boquerón SM fresh anchovy

boquete SM hole; **abrieron un ~ en el muro** they made a hole in the wall

boquiabierto ADJ speechless, open-mouthed

boquilla SF [*de instrumento*] mouthpiece; [*de pipa*] stem; (*para fumar*) cigarette holder; **cigarros con ~** tipped cigarettes; ✦ MODISMO **de ~: sólo apoyó la idea de ~** he was only paying lip service to the idea; **eso lo dice de ~** he's just saying that, that's what he says (but he doesn't mean it)

boquita SF **~ de piñón** pursed lips *pl*

borbónico ADJ Bourbon *antes de s*

borbotón SM **salir a borbotones** [*agua, sangre*] to gush out; **hablar a borbotones** to talk nineteen to the dozen (*Brit**), talk a blue streak (*EEUU**)

borceguí SM high shoe, laced boot

borda SF gunwale, rail; **motor de fuera ~** outboard motor; ✦ MODISMO **echar** *o* **tirar algo por la ~** to throw sth overboard

bordado SM embroidery, needlework

bordadora SF needlewoman

bordar /1a/ VT **1** (*Cos*) to embroider; **bordado a mano** hand-embroidered **2** (= *hacer perfectamente*) to do supremely well; **ha bordado su papel** she was excellent in her part

borde¹ SM **1** [*de asiento, andén, pañuelo*] edge; [*de plato*] rim, lip; [*de vaso, sombrero*] brim; [*de carretera, camino*] side; [*de río*] edge, bank; **fotos con los ~s en blanco** photos with white borders *o* edges
2 al ~ de [+ *precipicio, lago, cráter*] at *o* on the edge of; [+ *quiebra, histeria, crisis*] on the verge of; **estamos al mismo ~ del desastre** we are on the very brink of disaster; **su carrera política está al ~ del abismo** her political career is teetering on the edge of the abyss; **están al ~ de los cuarenta años** they're close to forty, they're hitting *o* pushing forty*; **al ~ del mar** beside the sea; **al ~ de la muerte** at death's door

borde²** (*Esp*) **Ⓐ** ADJ **ponerse ~ (con algn)** to get stroppy (with sb) (*Brit**), get nasty (with sb) **Ⓑ** SMF **¡eres un ~!** you're a nasty piece of work! (*esp Brit**), you're an SOB! (*EEUU***)

bordear /1a/ VT **1** (= *rodear*) to skirt (around); **tuvimos que ~ la montaña** we had to skirt around the mountain; **navegamos bordeando la costa** we sailed along the edge of the coast
2 [*calle, árboles*] (= *estar alrededor de*) to border, border on; (= *flanquear*) to line; **un paseo que bordea el mar** a promenade running along the sea; **un camino bordeado de cipreses** a road lined with cypress trees
3 (= *acercarse a*) [+ *edad*] to be approaching, be close to; [+ *genialidad, obsesión*] to border on; **bordea los sesenta años** he's approaching sixty, he's close to sixty

bordillo SM kerb (*Brit*), curb (*EEUU*)

bordo SM **a ~** aboard, on board; **"bienvenidos a bordo"** "welcome aboard"; **estar a ~ del barco** to be on board the ship

bordó (*RPl*) ADJ INV, SM maroon

boreal ADJ northern; **el hemisferio ~** the northern hemisphere

borgoña SM (*tb* **vino de ~**) Burgundy

bórico ADJ boric

borla SF [*de cortina*] tassel; [*de gorro*] pompom; (*Univ*) tassel; (*para empolvarse*) powder puff

borlote SM (*Méx*) row, uproar

borne SM (*Elec*) terminal

boro SM (*Quím*) boron

borra SF **1** (= *relleno*) [*para colchones*] flock; [*para cojines*] stuffing **2** (= *pelusa*) [*de polvo*] fluff; (*Bot*) down **3** [*de vino*] sediment, lees *pl*; [*de café*] dregs *pl* ➤ **borra de vino** (*RPl*) (= *color*) maroon

borrachera SF (= *estado*) drunkenness; **coger** *o* **pillar** *o* **agarrar** *o* (*Méx*) **ponerse una ~** to get drunk

borrachín/ina SM/F boozer*

borracho/a **Ⓐ** ADJ **1** [*persona*] drunk **2** (= *poseído*) drunk, blind (**de** with) **3** (*Culin*) [*bizcocho*] tipsy (*soaked in liqueur o spirit*); [*fruta*] marinated **Ⓑ** SM/F drunkard, drunk

borrador SM **1** (= *versión*) [*de texto*] first draft, rough copy; [*de pintura, dibujo*] rough sketch **2** (= *cuaderno*) scribbling pad, scratch pad (*EEUU*) **3** [*para pizarra*] board rubber (*Brit*), eraser (*EEUU*)

borraja SF borage

borrar /1a/ **Ⓐ** VT **1** (= *hacer desaparecer*) **1.1** [+ *palabra, dibujo*] (*con goma*) to rub out, erase; (*con borrador*) to rub off, clean off; ✦ MODISMO **a algn/algo del mapa** to wipe sb/sth off the map **1.2** [+ *señal, mancha*] to remove; [+ *pintada*] to clean off; [+ *huellas*] to wipe off, rub off **1.3** [+ *mensaje, fichero*] to delete, erase; [+ *canción, película*] to tape over, erase **1.4** [+ *impresión, recuerdo*] to wipe away, erase; **no podía ~ de su cara las huellas del cansancio** he was unable to wipe away the signs of fatigue from his face
2 (= *limpiar*) [+ *disquete, cinta*] to erase; [+ *pantalla*] to clear; **~ la pizarra** to clean the blackboard
3 (= *dar de baja a*) **~ a algn de** [+ *clase, actividad*] to take sb out of, remove sb from; [+ *lista, curso*] to take sb off, remove sb from
Ⓑ borrarse VPR **1** (= *darse de baja*) **~se de** [+ *club, asociación*] to cancel one's membership of, resign from; [+ *curso*] to drop out of; **se borró de la biblioteca** she cancelled her library membership
2 (= *desaparecer*) [*señal, marca*] to fade away; [*imagen, recuerdo*] to fade; [*duda, sospecha, temor*] to disappear, be dispelled; [*sonrisa*] to vanish

borrasca SF **1** (*Meteo*) area of low pressure, depression; **viene una ~ por el Atlántico** there's low pressure *o* a low approaching from the Atlantic **2** (= *tormenta*) squall

borrascoso ADJ stormy

borrego/a **Ⓐ** SM/F (*Zool*) (= *oveja joven*) lamb, yearling lamb; (= *oveja adulta*) sheep; **lo siguieron como ~s** they followed him like sheep **Ⓑ** SM (*Cub, Méx**) false rumour *o* (*EEUU*) rumor

borreguil ADJ meek, like a lamb

borreguillo SM fleece; **forro de ~** fleece lining

borrico/a SM/F **1** (*Zool*) donkey/she-donkey **2** (= *persona*) fool

borrón SM blot, stain; ✦ MODISMO **hacer ~ y cuenta nueva** (= *olvidar el pasado*) to let bygones be bygones; (= *empezar de nuevo*) to wipe the slate clean

borronear /1a/ VT to scribble, scrawl

borroso ADJ **1** [*foto, imagen*] blurred, indistinct; **lo veo todo ~** everything is blurred **2** [*idea, recuerdo*] vague, hazy

boscaje SM thicket, grove

boscoso ADJ wooded

Bosnia SF Bosnia

bosnio/a ADJ, SM/F Bosnian

bosque SM (= *terreno con árboles*) wood; (*más grande*) forest

> Hay dos palabras en inglés que significan **bosque**: **wood** y **forest**. La diferencia es que por lo general **forest** hace referencia a un bosque mucho más grande que **wood** y además suele estar muy alejado de cualquier población. Cuando se sobrentiende de qué bosque se está hablando se puede utilizar también **the woods**.

bosquejar /1a/ VT 1 (*Arte*) to sketch 2 [+ *idea*] to sketch, outline; [+ *plan*] to draft

bosquejo SM 1 (*Arte*) sketch 2 [*de idea*] sketch, outline; [*de plan*] draft

bosta SF (*CS*) dung

bostezar /1f/ VI to yawn

bostezo SM yawn

bota SF 1 (= *calzado*) boot; ✦ MODISMOS **morir con las ~s puestas** to die with one's boots on; **ponerse las ~s*** (= *enriquecerse*) to strike it rich; (= *comer mucho*) to have a blow-out* ➤ **botas camperas** cowboy boots ➤ **botas de agua** wellingtons ➤ **botas de esquí** ski boots ➤ **botas de fútbol** football boots ➤ **botas de goma**, **botas de hule** (*Méx*) wellingtons ➤ **botas de montaña** walking books, hiking boots ➤ **botas de montar** riding boots 2 ➤ **bota de vino** wineskin

botadero SM (*And*) tip (*Brit*), rubbish dump (*Brit*), garbage dump (*EEUU*)

botado* ADJ 1 (*Col, Méx*) (= *barato*) dirt cheap* 2 (*Col*) (= *muy fácil*) **estar ~** to be a piece of cake 3 (*Col*) (= *despilfarrador*) extravagant

botadura SF launching

botamanga SF (*RPl*) [*de pantalón*] turn-up, cuff (*EEUU*); [*de manga*] cuff

botana SF (*Méx*) snack; ✦ MODISMO **agarrar a algn de ~** to make fun of sb, laugh at sb

botánica SF botany

botánico/a Ⓐ ADJ botanical Ⓑ SM/F botanist

botar /1a/ Ⓐ VT 1 (*Dep*) [+ *pelota*] to bounce 2 (*Náut*) [+ *barco*] to launch 3 (*LAm*) (= *tirar*) to throw away, throw out, chuck out*; **~ un saque de esquina** to take a corner kick 4 (*LAm*) (= *despedir*) to fire*, sack*; **lo ~on de su trabajo** he was fired o sacked* 5 (*Chi, Col, Ven*) (= *derramar*) to spill 6 (*Chi, Col, Ven*) (= *derribar*) [+ *florero, persona*] to knock over; [+ *árbol*] to knock down Ⓑ VI (*Esp*) [*pelota*] to bounce; [*coche*] to bump, jolt; [*persona*] to jump; ✦ MODISMO **está que bota*** he's hopping mad*

botarata* SMF = **botarate 3**

botarate* SM/F 1 (= *loco*) madcap 2 (= *imbécil*) idiot 3 (*And*) (= *despilfarrador*) spendthrift

bote¹ SM 1 [*de pelota*] bounce; **dar un ~** to bounce 2 (*Esp*) [*de persona, caballo*] jump; **se levantó de un ~** he jumped up, he leapt to his feet; **dar** o **pegar un ~** [*persona*] to jump; [*coche*] to bump, jolt; ✦ MODISMO **a ~ pronto*** (just) off the top of one's head*; **dar el ~ a algn*** to chuck sb out*, give sb the boot*; **darse el ~** (*Esp**) to beat it*

bote² SM 1 (= *recipiente*) [*de vidrio*] jar; [*de plástico*] container; [*de metal*] (*para conservas, pintura*) can, tin; (*para bebidas*) can; **un ~ de colonia** a bottle of cologne; **de ~** canned, tinned; **esta sopa es de ~** this is canned o tinned soup; **es rubia de ~*** she's a fake blonde; ✦ MODISMOS **chupar del ~** (*Esp**) to line one's own pocket*, feather one's own nest*; **estar de ~ en ~*** to be packed, be jam-packed*; **estar en el ~** (*Esp**) [*título, premio*] to be in the bag*, be all sewn up*; **meterse a algn en el ~** (*Esp**) to talk sb round (*Brit*), sweet-talk sb*; **pegarse el ~ con algn*** to get on with sb like a house on fire*; **tener algo en el ~** (*Esp**) to have sth in the bag*, have sth all sewn up*; **tener a algn (metido) en el ~** (*Esp**) to have sb in one's pocket* ➤ **bote de basura** (*Méx*) dustbin (*Brit*), trash can (*EEUU*) ➤ **bote de humo** smoke canister

2 (*como propina*) **hemos sacado un ~ de 10 euros** we got 10 euros in tips; **5 euros para el ~** 5 euros for the tips box; **"bote" "**tips"

3 (= *fondo común*) kitty; **pusimos un ~ de diez libras cada uno** we each put ten pounds into the kitty

4 (*en lotería, quiniela*) jackpot

5 (*CAm, Méx, Ven***) (= *cárcel*) jail, nick (*Brit**), can (*EEUU**)

bote³ SM (= *barca*) [*de pesca*] boat; (*deportivo*) skiff ➤ **bote hinchable** inflatable dinghy ➤ **bote salvavidas** lifeboat

botella SF bottle; **cerveza de ~** bottled beer; **media ~** half bottle; **~ de vino** (= *contenido*) bottle of wine; (= *envase*) wine bottle

botellero SM wine rack

botellín SM small bottle, half bottle

botellón SM, **botellona** SF (*Esp*) *gathering of young people in the open air for the purpose of drinking, partying and having a cheap night out*

botica† SF chemist's (shop) (*Brit*), pharmacy, druggist's (*EEUU*); ✦ MODISMO **de todo como en ~** everything under the sun

boticario/a† SM/F chemist (*Brit*), druggist (*EEUU*)

botija Ⓐ SF (= *vasija*) earthenware jug Ⓑ SMF (*Uru**) (= *chaval*) kid*

botijo SM *earthenware drinking jug with spout and handle*

botillería SF (*Chi*) off-licence (*Brit*), liquor store (*EEUU*)

botín¹ SM [*de guerra*] booty, plunder; [*de ladrón*] loot

botín² SM 1 (= *calzado*) ankle boot 2 (*Chi*) (= *borceguí*) bootee

botiquín SM 1 (= *armario*) medicine cabinet; (= *conjunto de medicinas*) first-aid kit ➤ **botiquín de emergencia**, **botiquín de primeros auxilios** first-aid kit 2 (= *enfermería*) first-aid post, first-aid station (*EEUU*), sick bay

botón SM 1 (*Cos, Téc*) button; **apretar** o **pulsar el ~** to press the button ➤ **botón de muestra** example 2 (*Bot*) bud

botones SM INV bellboy, bellhop (*EEUU*)

botulismo SM botulism

boutique [bu'tik] SF boutique

bóveda SF vault ➤ **bóveda craneal** cranial cavity ➤ **bóveda de cañón** barrel vault

bovino Ⓐ ADJ bovine; **carne bovina** beef; **ganado ~** cattle Ⓑ SM bovine; **carne de ~** beef

box SM 1 (*Aut*) pit; **entrar en ~es** to go into the pits, make a pit stop 2 (*Equitación*) stall 3 (*LAm*) (= *boxeo*) boxing

boxeador(a) SM/F boxer

boxear /1a/ VI to box

boxeo SM boxing

boya SF (*Náut*) buoy; (*Pesca*) float

boyante ADJ [*persona*] buoyant; [*negocio*] prosperous

bozal SM 1 [*de perro*] muzzle 2 (*LAm*) [*de caballo*] halter

bozo SM fuzz

bracear /1a/ VI (= *mover los brazos*) to swing one's arms; (*al nadar*) to swim

bracero SM farmhand, farm labourer o (*EEUU*) laborer

braga SF (*Esp*), **bragas** SFPL (*Esp*) panties, knickers (*Brit*); ✦ MODISMOS **dejar a algn en ~s*** to leave sb empty-handed; **estar hecho una ~*** to be knackered (*Brit**), be bushed*; **pillar a algn en ~s*** to catch sb with his pants down*

braguero SM (*Med*) truss

bragueta SF fly, flies *pl* (*Brit*), zipper (*EEUU*)

braguetazo* SM marriage for money; **dar el ~** to marry for money

brahmán SM Brahman, Brahmin

braille ['braile] SM Braille

bramante SM twine, string

bramar /1a/ VI 1 [*toro, elefante*] to bellow; [*león*] to roar 2 [*viento*] to howl, roar; [*mar*] to thunder

bramido SM [*de toro, elefante*] bellow, bellowing; [*de león*] roar, roaring

brandy SM brandy

branquia SF gill; **~s** gills

brasa SF live coal, hot coal; **carne a la ~** grilled meat, barbecued meat

brasero SM **1** (= *como calefacción*) [*de carbón*] brazier; (*eléctrico*) heater **2** (*Méx*) fireplace

brasier SM (*Méx*) bra

Brasil SM Brazil

brasileño/a ADJ, SM/F, **brasilero/a** ADJ, SM/F Brazilian

Brasilia SF Brasilia

brassier SM (*Méx*) bra

bravata SF **1** (= *amenaza*) threat **2** (= *fanfarronada*) boast, brag

bravío Ⓐ ADJ (= *feroz*) ferocious, savage; (= *indómito*) wild, untamed Ⓑ SM ferocity

bravo Ⓐ ADJ **1** [*animal*] fierce, ferocious **2** (*LAm*) [*persona*] (= *enojado*) angry **3** [*mar*] rough, stormy **4** (*Méx Culin*) hot, spicy **5** (*RPl**) (= *difícil*) tricky Ⓑ EXCL bravo!, well done!

bravucón/ona Ⓐ ADJ swaggering Ⓑ SM/F braggart

bravuconada SF boast

bravura SF **1** (= *ferocidad*) ferocity **2** (= *valor*) bravery

braza SF **1** (*Natación*) breaststroke; **nadar a ~** to swim breaststroke **2** (*Náut*) ≈ fathom

brazada SF **1** (*al nadar*) stroke **2** (= *cantidad*) armful

brazal SM **1** (= *banda de tela*) armband **2** (*Agr*) irrigation channel

brazalete SM **1** (= *joya*) bracelet **2** (= *banda de tela*) armband

brazo SM **1** [*de persona*] arm; [*de animal*] foreleg; **se echó a los ~s de su madre** he threw himself into his mother's arms; **dar el ~ a algn** to give sb one's arm; **coger a algn del ~** to take sb by the arm; **iban (cogidos) del ~** they were walking arm in arm; **llevar a algn en ~s** to carry sb in one's arms; ✦ MODISMOS **con los ~s abiertos** with open arms; **dar el ~ a torcer** to give way, give in; **luchar a ~ partido** to fight tooth and nail; **ser el ~ derecho de algn** to be sb's right-hand man/woman ➤ **brazo de gitano** (*Culin*) swiss roll (*Brit*), jelly roll (*EEUU*) **2** [*de sillón, tocadiscos, grúa, cruz*] arm **3** (= *sección*) ➤ **brazo armado** military wing ➤ **brazo político** political wing ➤ **brazo secular** secular arm **4** (*Geog*) ➤ **brazo de mar** inlet, arm of the sea, sound ➤ **brazo de río** channel, branch of river **5** **brazos** (= *trabajadores*) hands, men

brazuelo SM (*Zool*) shoulder

brea SF tar, pitch

brebaje SM potion; (*hum*) brew, concoction

brecha SF **1** (= *abertura*) breach, opening; ✦ MODISMOS **estar en la ~** to be in the thick of things; **seguir en la ~** to go on with one's work, keep at it **2** (*entre personas*) rift; (*entre opiniones*) gap ➤ **brecha generacional** generation gap **3** (*Med*) gash, wound

brécol SM broccoli

brega SF struggle; **andar a la ~** to slog away

bregar /1h/ VI **1** (= *luchar*) to struggle, fight (**con** against, with) **2** (= *trabajar mucho*) to slog away

breke SM (*CAm*), **breque** SM (*CAm*) (*Aut*) brake

brete SM **estar en un ~** to be in a jam*; **poner a algn en un ~** to put sb on the spot

brete SM (*LAm*) [*de vestido*] strap

bretón/ona Ⓐ ADJ, SM/F Breton Ⓑ SM (*Ling*) Breton

breva SF early fig; ✦ MODISMO **¡no caerá esa ~!** no such luck!

breve Ⓐ ADJ **1** (= *corto*) short, brief; **tras un ~ descanso** after a short break *o* a brief pause; **una nota muy ~** a very short note; **seré muy ~** I shall be very brief; **en ~s palabras** briefly; **en ~** shortly, before long **2** [*vocal*] short Ⓑ SF (*Mús*) breve

brevedad SF [*de mensaje*] shortness; [*de texto*] brevity; **con** *o* **a la mayor ~ (posible)** as soon as possible

brevemente ADV briefly, concisely

brevete SM (*Perú Aut*) driving licence (*Brit*), driver's license (*EEUU*)

breviario SM (*Rel*) breviary

brezal SM moor, heath

brezo SM heather

bribón/ona SM/F rascal, rogue

bricolaje SM do-it-yourself, DIY (*Brit*)

brida SF bridle

bridge [briʒ, britʃ] SM (*Naipes*) bridge

briega SF **1** (= *pelea*) fight, brawl **2** (= *trabajo duro*) slog

brigada Ⓐ SF (*Mil*) brigade ➤ **brigada de delitos monetarios** fraud squad ➤ **brigada de estupefacientes** drug squad ➤ **Brigadas Internacionales** International Brigades Ⓑ SMF (*Mil*) sergeant major

brigadier SM brigadier (*Brit*), brigadier-general (*EEUU*)

brigadista SMF ~ **internacional** member of the International Brigade

brik SM (*pl* ~**s**) carton

brillante Ⓐ ADJ **1** (= *reluciente*) [*luz, sol, color*] bright, brilliant; [*superficie pulida*] shiny; [*pelo*] glossy, shiny; [*joyas, lentejuelas*] sparkling, glittering; **¡qué ~ ha quedado el suelo!** the floor is really shiny now!; **tenía los ojos ~s por la emoción** her eyes sparkled with excitement **2** (= *excelente*) brilliant; **su ~ carrera deportiva** her brilliant sporting career; **su actuación fue absolutamente ~** her performance was absolutely outstanding *o* brilliant Ⓑ SM diamond; **un anillo de ~s** a diamond ring

brillantez SF **1** (= *brillo*) brightness **2** (= *excelencia*) brilliance **3** (= *boato*) splendour, splendor (*EEUU*)

brillantina SF brilliantine, hair cream

brillar /1a/ VI **1** (= *relucir*) [*luz, sol*] to shine; [*estrella, ojos*] to shine, sparkle; [*metal, superficie, pelo*] (*gen*) to shine; (*por estar mojado, grasiento*) to glisten; [*joyas, lentejuelas*] to sparkle, glitter; **le brillaban los ojos de alegría** her eyes shone *o* sparkled with happiness; **¡cómo te brillan los zapatos!** what shiny shoes!; **le brillaba la cara por el sudor** his face glistened with sweat **2** (= *sobresalir*) to shine; **Argentina brilló en la segunda mitad** Argentina shone in the second half; ✦ MODISMOS **~ con luz propia** to stand out on one's own; **~ por su ausencia: el ingenio ha brillado por su ausencia** there has a been a distinct lack of ingenuity

brillo SM **1** (= *resplandor*) [*de luz, sol, estrella*] (*gen*) brightness; (*más fuerte*) brilliance; [*de pantalla*] brightness; [*de tela, pelo, zapatos, superficie*] shine, sheen; [*de papel, foto*] glossiness; [*de joyas, lentejuelas*] sparkle, glitter; **el ~ de la luna sobre el agua** the moonlight shining on the water; **lo noté en el ~ de sus ojos** I noticed it in her sparkling eyes; **el ~ de la navaja lo asustó** he was frightened by the gleam of the knife; **¿le revelamos las fotos con ~?** would you like a gloss finish on your photos?; **dar** *o* **sacar ~ a** [+ *suelo, plata, zapatos*] to polish, shine; [+ *muebles*] to polish ➤ **brillo de labios** lip gloss **2** (= *esplendor*) brilliance, splendour, splendor (*EEUU*); **el ~ de la profesión** the splendour *o* (*EEUU*) splendor of the profession; **la ausencia de varios jugadores importantes ha restado ~ al torneo** the absence of several important players has taken the shine off the tournament

brilloso ADJ (*LAm*) shiny

brincar /1g/ VI [*niño*] to jump (up and down); (*con un solo pie*) to hop; [*cordero*] to skip about, gambol

brinco SM (= *salto*) (*gen*) jump, leap; (*al correr*) skip; **de** *o* **en un ~** at one bound; **dar ~s** to hop (around), jump (around); **pegar un ~** to jump, give a start

brindar /1a/ Ⓐ VT (= *ofrecer*) to offer, afford; **le brinda la ocasión** it gives *o* affords him the opportunity **2** (= *dedicar*) to dedicate (**a** to) Ⓑ VI **~ por algn/algo** to drink to sb/sth, toast sb/sth; **~on por los novios** they drank a toast to the newly-weds Ⓒ **brindarse** VPR **~se a hacer algo** (*frm*) to offer to do sth

brindis SM INV toast; **hacer un ~ por algn/algo** to toast sb/sth, drink a toast to sb/sth

brío SM **1** (= *ánimo*) spirit, verve **2** (= *decisión*) determination; **cortar los ~s a algn** to clip sb's wings

brioso ADJ **1** (= *animoso*) spirited, full of verve

2 (= *decidido*) determined

brisa SF breeze

brisca SF *Spanish card game similar to whist but in which it is not necessary to follow suit*

británico/a Ⓐ ADJ British Ⓑ SM/F British person, Britisher (*EEUU*); **los ~s** the British

brizna SF **1** (= *hebra*) [*de hierba*] blade **2** (= *trozo*) piece, fragment; (*muy pequeño*) scrap **3** (*Carib*) drizzle

briznar /1a/ VI (*Carib*) to drizzle

broca SF (drill) bit

brocado SM brocade

brocha SF (= *para pintar*) paintbrush, large paintbrush; **pintor de ~ gorda** (*lit*) painter and decorator; (*fig*) bad painter ➤ **brocha de afeitar** shaving brush

brochazo SM brushstroke

broche SM **1** (*Cos*) clasp, fastener ➤ **broche de gancho** hook and eye ➤ **broche de presión** press stud (*Brit*), snap fastener (*EEUU*) **2** (= *joya*) brooch; ✦ MODISMOS **el ~ final** ✧ **el ~ de oro** the finishing touch **3** (*para papel*) (*LAm*) paperclip; (*Arg*) staple **4** (*Arg*) (*para ropa*) clothes peg (*Brit*), clothespin (*EEUU*) **5** (*Uru*) (*para el pelo*) hair slide (*Brit*), barrette (*EEUU*)

brocheta SF, **brochette** [bro'ʃet] SF (*RPl*) skewer

brócoli SM broccoli

broma SF **1** (= *cachondeo*) **ni en ~** never, not on any account; **lo decía en ~** I was only joking, I was only kidding*; **estar de ~** to be in a joking mood; **tomar algo a ~** to take sth as a joke

2 (= *chiste*) joke; **no es ninguna ~** it's no joke, this is serious; **la ~ me costó caro** the affair cost me dear; **~s aparte ...** joking aside ...; **¡déjate de ~s!** quit fooling!, the joke's over, joke over! (*esp Brit*); **gastar ~s** to tell jokes; **gastar una ~ a algn** to play a joke on sb; **estar para ~s: ¡para ~s estoy!** (*iró*) a fine time for joking!; **no está para ~s** he's in no mood for jokes; **entre ~s y veras** half-joking(ly) ➤ **broma pesada** tasteless joke

bromear /1a/ VI to joke, crack jokes*; **creía que bromeaba** I thought he was joking

bromista Ⓐ ADJ **es muy ~** he's full of jokes, he's a great one for jokes Ⓑ SMF (= *chistoso*) joker; (= *gracioso*) practical joker, leg-puller*; **esto lo ha hecho algún ~** some joker did this

bromuro SM bromide

bronca* SF **1** (= *pelea*) row (*esp Brit*), ruckus (*EEUU**); **armar una ~** to kick up a fuss *o* (*EEUU*) storm; **se armó una ~ tremenda** there was a tremendous rumpus* *o* (*EEUU**) ruckus; **buscar ~** to be looking for a fight, be spoiling for a fight **2** (= *regañina*) telling off*, ticking off (*Brit**); **nos echó una ~ fenomenal** he came down on us like a ton of bricks* **3** (= *ruido*) racket* **4** (*CS**) (= *rabia*) anger, fury; **me da ~** it makes me mad*

bronce SM **1** (= *aleación*) bronze **2** (*LAm*) (= *latón*) brass

bronceado Ⓐ ADJ tanned, brown Ⓑ SM tan, suntan

bronceador SM suntan lotion

broncear /1a/ Ⓐ VT **1** [+ *piel*] to tan **2** (*Téc*) to bronze Ⓑ **broncearse** VPR to get a tan, get a suntan

bronco ADJ **1** [*voz*] hoarse **2** [*superficie*] rough, coarse **3** [*caballo*] unbroken

bronconeumonía SF bronchopneumonia

bronquial ADJ bronchial

bronquios SMPL bronchial tubes; **estaba malo de los ~** he had a bad chest

bronquítico ADJ bronchitic

bronquitis SF INV bronchitis

brotar /1a/ VI **1** (*Bot*) [*planta, semilla*] to sprout, bud; [*hoja*] to sprout, come out; [*flor*] to come out **2** [*agua*] to spring up; [*río*] to rise; [*lágrimas, sangre*] to well (up) **3** (= *aparecer*) to spring up; **han brotado sectas por todos sitios** sects have sprung up all over the place **4** (*Med*) [*epidemia*] to break out; [*erupción, grano, espinilla*] to appear

brote SM **1** (*Bot*) shoot ➤ **brotes de soja** bean sprouts **2** (= *aparición*) [*de violencia, enfermedad*] outbreak; **un ~ de sarampión** an outbreak of measles **3** (= *erupción cutánea*) rash

broza SF **1** (*Bot*) dead leaves, brushwood **2** (*en discurso*) rubbish (*Brit*), garbage

bruces ADV **de ~** face down; **caer de ~** to fall flat on one's face

bruja Ⓐ ADJ **estar ~** (*Carib, Méx***) to be broke*, be flat (*EEUU**) Ⓑ SF **1** (= *hechicera*) witch **2** (*) (= *arpía*) old hag*

brujería SF witchcraft, sorcery, (black) magic

brujo Ⓐ ADJ enchanting Ⓑ SM **1** (= *hechicero*) wizard, sorcerer **2** (*en una tribu*) shaman, medicine man*

brújula SF compass; ✦ MODISMO **perder la ~** to lose one's bearings

bruma SF (= *niebla*) mist; (*en el mar*) sea mist

bruñir /3h/ VT to polish, burnish

brusco ADJ **1** [*descenso, movimiento, cambio*] sudden **2** [*actitud, respuesta*] curt, brusque

Bruselas SF Brussels

brusquedad SF **1** (= *cambio repentino*) suddenness **2** (*en carácter, contestación*) brusqueness

brutal ADJ brutal

brutalidad SF **1** (= *cualidad*) brutality **2** (= *acción*) **una ~** an act of brutality

bruto/a Ⓐ ADJ **1** (= *salvaje*) brutish; **¡no seas ~!** don't be so rough! **2** (= *estúpido*) stupid, ignorant; **es muy ~** he's pretty thick (*Brit*) *o* dumb (*EEUU**) **3** (= *inculto*) uncouth **4** (= *sin alterar*) [*materia*] raw; [*salario, peso*] gross; **en ~** [*diamante*] uncut; [*hierro*] crude; **a lo ~** roughly, crudely Ⓑ SM (= *animal*) brute, beast Ⓒ SM/F **1** (= *salvaje*) brute, boor; **¡bruto!** you beast! **2** (= *idiota*) idiot

Bs.As. ABR (= **Buenos Aires**) BA

bubónico ADJ **peste bubónica** bubonic plague

bucal ADJ [*higiene*] oral; **por vía ~** orally, by mouth

bucanero SM buccaneer

Bucarest SM Bucharest

búcaro SM vase

buceador(a) SM/F diver

bucear /1a/ VI (= *nadar*) to swim under water; (= *sumergirse*) to dive

buceo SM diving

buchaca SF (*CAm, Carib*) (= *bolso*) saddlebag; (*Col Billar*) pocket

buche SM **1** (= *estómago*) [*de ave*] crop; [*de animal*] maw; [*de persona*] belly; ✦ MODISMO **guardar algo en el ~** to keep sth very quiet **2** (= *trago*) mouthful; **hacer ~s con algo** to rinse one's mouth out with sth

bucle SM **1** [*de pelo*] curl, ringlet **2** (*Aer, Inform*) loop

bucodental ADJ [*salud, higiene*] oral; [*tratamiento, clínica*] dental

bucólico ADJ bucolic, pastoral

Buda SM Buddha

budín SM (*dulce*) pudding; (*no dulce*) pie; **~ de pescado** fish pie

budismo SM Buddhism

budista ADJ, SMF Buddhist

buen ADJ *ver* **bueno**

buenamente ADV **1** (= *fácilmente*) easily, without difficulty **2** (= *de buena gana*) willingly

buenamoza ADJ (*CS*) good-looking, pretty

buenaventura SF **1** (= *suerte*) good luck, good fortune **2** (= *adivinación*) fortune; **decir** *o* **echar la ~ a algn** to tell sb's fortune

buenazo/a Ⓐ ADJ (= *buena persona*) kindly, good-natured; (= *sufrido*) long-suffering Ⓑ SM/F good-natured man/woman; **el ~ de Marcos** good old Marcos; **ser un ~** to be kindhearted, be soft (*pey*)

buenmozo ADJ (*CS*) good-looking, handsome

bueno/a Ⓐ ADJ (*before sm sing* **buen**) **1** (*gen*) good; [*tiempo*] fine, good, fair; **es un buen libro** it's a good book; **está muy ~ este bizcocho** this sponge cake is lovely *o* really good; **les gusta la buena vida** they like the good life; **hace buen tiempo** the weather's fine *o* good *o* fair; **los ~s tiempos** the good old days; **¡~ está!** (*LAm*) that's enough!; **¡qué ~!** (*esp LAm*) excellent!, great!; **lo ~ es que ...** the best thing is that ...; **+** REFRÁN **lo ~, si breve, dos veces ~** brevity is the soul of wit **2** (= *bondadoso*) [*persona*] kind, good; **fue muy ~ conmigo** he was very kind *o* good to me; **es usted muy ~** you are very kind; **sé ~** be good; **es buena persona** he's a nice person, he's a good sort; **+** MODISMO **es más ~ que el pan** he's a good soul **3** (= *apropiado*) good; **un buen momento para comprar** a good time to buy; **no es ~ que esté solo** it's not good for him to be alone; **ser ~ para** to be good for **4** (*de salud*) **estar ~** to be well; **ponerse ~** to get better **5** (***) (= *atractivo*) **está muy ~** he's gorgeous*, he's a bit of all right (*Brit**) **6** (= *considerable*) good, large; **un buen número de ...** a good *o* large number of ...; **un buen trozo de ...** a nice big piece of ...; **le di un buen susto** I gave him a real fright **7** (*iró*) **¡ésa sí que es buena!** that's a good one!; **¡buena la has liado o hecho!** you've really gone and done it now!; **¡en buen lío me he metido!** I've got myself into a fine mess!; **¡estaría ~!*** I should hope not!; **estaría ~ que ...** it would be just great if ...; **luego verás lo que es ~*** then you'll see; **lo pusieron ~*** (= *le pegaron*) they beat the living daylights out of him*; (= *lo criticaron*) they slagged him off (*Brit**), they badmouthed him* **8** (*en saludos*) **¡buenas!** hello!; **~s días** good morning; **buenas tardes** (*a primera hora*) good afternoon; (*más tarde*) good evening **9** **+** MODISMOS **estar de buenas** to be in a good mood; **hacer algo a la buena de Dios** to do sth any-old-how; **por las buenas: resolver algo por las buenas** to settle sth amicably; **si no me obedeces por las buenas, tendrás que hacerlo por las malas** you can either do as I say willingly, or I'll have to force you to do it; **de buenas a primeras** suddenly, without warning Ⓑ ADV **¡bueno!** all right!, OK!; (*Méx Telec*) hello!; **~, pues ...** well ...; **~, ¿y qué?** well, so what?, well?; **¡pero ~, cómo puedes ser tan bruto!** honestly, how can you be so stupid!; **pero ~, no nos vamos a meter en historias** but anyway, let's not go into this Ⓒ SM/F **1 el ~** (*de la película*) the goody (*Brit**), the good guy* **2 el ~ de Manolo** good old Manolo

Buenos Aires SM Buenos Aires

buey SM OX; **+** MODISMOS **como ~es** enormous; **hablar de ~es perdidos** (*CS*) to talk about nothing; **sé con los ~es que aro** (*RPI**) I know who I'm dealing with **➤ buey de mar** *variety of crab or crawfish*

búfalo Ⓐ ADJ (*Carib**) great*, fantastic* Ⓑ SM buffalo

bufanda SF scarf

bufar /1a/ VI [*toro*] to snort; [*gato*] to spit; **está que bufa** he's furious; **~ de ira** to snort with rage

bufé SM (*pl* **~s**) = **bufet**

bufet [buˈfe] SM (*pl* **~s**) **1** (= *cena*) buffet supper, cold supper; (= *almuerzo*) buffet lunch **➤ bufet libre** fixed buffet, set-price buffet **2** (*And*) (= *mueble*) sideboard

bufete SM (*de abogado*) (= *oficina*) lawyer's office; (= *negocio*) legal practice

buffer [ˈbufer] SM (*Inform*) buffer

bufido SM snort

bufo ADJ comic, farcical; **ópera bufa** comic opera

bufón SM **1** (= *payaso*) clown **2** (*Hist*) jester

bufonada SF (= *comentario*) jest; (= *acto*) piece of buffoonery

buga* SM (*Esp*) car, wheels* *pl*

buganvilla SF bougainvillea

buhardilla SF **1** (= *desván*) loft **2** (= *ventana*) dormer window, dormer

búho SM owl, long-eared owl

buhonero SM pedlar, peddler (*esp EEUU*), hawker

buitre Ⓐ SM (*Orn*) vulture **➤ buitre leonado** griffon vulture Ⓑ SMF (***) (= *persona gorrona*) scrounger*

buitrear* /1a/ VT to scrounge*

bujarra** SM (*Esp*), **bujarrón**** SM (*Esp*) queer**, fag (*EEUU***)

bujía SF **1** (*Aut*) spark plug **2** (†) (= *vela*) candle **3** (*CAm*) (= *bombilla*) light bulb

bula SF (*Rel*) bull

bulbo SM bulb

bulboso ADJ bulbous

buldog [bulˈdog] SM (*pl* **~s**) bulldog

bule SM (*Méx Bot*) gourd, squash (*EEUU*); (= *cántaro*) water pitcher

bulerías SFPL *Andalusian song accompanied with clapping and dancing*

bulevar SM boulevard, avenue

Bulgaria SF Bulgaria

búlgaro/a Ⓐ ADJ, SM/F Bulgarian Ⓑ SM (*Ling*) Bulgarian

bulimia SF bulimia, binge-eating syndrome (*EEUU*)

bulín SM (*CS*) (*de soltero*) bachelor pad

bulla SF row, racket; **armar** *o* **meter ~** (= *pelea*) to make a row; (= *ruido*) to make a racket*

bullanguero/a Ⓐ ADJ riotous, rowdy Ⓑ SM/F **1** (= *persona ruidosa*) noisy person **2** (= *alborotador*) troublemaker

bullaranga SF (*Col*) noise, row

bulldozer [bulˈdoθer] SM (*pl* **~s** [bulˈdoθer]) bulldozer

bullicio SM **1** (= *ruido*) din, hubbub **2** (= *actividad*) activity, bustle

bullicioso ADJ **1** (= *ruidoso*) [*lugar*] noisy; [*niño*] boisterous **2** (= *con actividad*) busy, bustling

bullir /3h/ VI **1** [*agua*] (= *hervir*) to boil; (= *agitarse*) to bubble (up) **2** (= *moverse*) to move, stir; **la ciudad bullía de actividad** the town was humming with activity

bulo SM hoax

bulón SM (*RPI*) bolt

bulto SM **1** (= *abultamiento*) bulge **2** (= *silueta*) shape; **vimos un ~ moviéndose entre los árboles** we saw a shape moving in the trees **3** (= *volumen*) space, room; **no ocupa** *o* **hace ~** it doesn't take up any space *o* room; **error de ~** glaring error; **de mucho ~** (*lit*) bulky; (*fig*) important; **de poco ~** (*lit*) small; (*fig*) unimportant; **+** MODISMOS **a ~** at a rough guess; **así, a ~, debe de haber unas mil botellas** at a rough guess there must be about a thousand bottles; **calcular algo a ~** to work sth out roughly, make a rough estimate of sth; **decir algo a ~: di algo a ~** just have a guess; **escurrir el ~*** (= *desaparecer*) to duck out*; (= *cambiar de tema*) to dodge the issue*; **ir de ~** *o* **◇ hacer ~** to swell the number(s), make up the number(s) **4** (= *paquete*) bag; [*de compra*] bag; [*de ropa, papel*] bundle; [*de equipaje*] piece of luggage *o* baggage; **el camión trajo todos los ~s pesados** the truck brought all the heavy loads **➤ bulto de mano** item of hand luggage **5** (*Med*) (= *quiste*) lump; (= *chichón*) bump **6** (*Ven*) (*de escolar*) satchel, bag

bumerán SM boomerang

bumerang [bumeˈran] SM (*pl* **~s** [bumeˈran]) boomerang

bungalow [ˈbongalo, bungaˈlo] SM (*pl* **~s** [ˈbongalo, bungaˈlo]) bungalow

bungee [ˈbanji] SM bungee jumping

búnker [ˈbunker] SM (*pl* **~s** [ˈbunker]) **1** (*Mil*) bunker **2** (*Golf*) bunker, sand trap (*EEUU*)

buñuelo SM fritter

BUP SM ABR (*Esp*) (= **Bachillerato Unificado y Polivalente**) *former secondary-school certificate and course for 14-17 age group*

buque SM ship, boat **➤ buque almirante** flagship **➤ buque cisterna** tanker **➤ buque de guerra** warship;

(*Hist*) man-of-war ➤ **buque insignia** flagship ➤ **buque mercante** merchantman, merchant ship ➤ **buque nodriza** mother ship

buraco* SM (*CS*) hole

burbuja SF bubble; **un refresco sin/con ~s** a still/fizzy (*Brit*) *o* carbonated (*esp EEUU*) drink; **hacer ~s** to fizz

burbujear /1a/ VI [*agua hirviendo*] to bubble; [*champán, gaseosa*] to fizz

burdel SM brothel

burdeos Ⓐ ADJ INV maroon, dark red Ⓑ SM INV (*tb* **vino de ~**) claret, Bordeaux, Bordeaux wine

burdo ADJ 1 [*persona*] coarse, rough 2 [*excusa, mentira*] clumsy

burgalés ADJ of/from Burgos

burgués/esa Ⓐ ADJ 1 (= *de clase media*) middle-class; **pequeño ~** lower middle-class 2 (*Pol pey*) bourgeois Ⓑ SM/F (*de clase media*) middle-class person; (*Pol pey*) bourgeois; **pequeño ~** lower middle-class person; (*Pol pey*) petit bourgeois

burguesía SF middle-class, bourgeoisie; **alta ~** upper middle class; **pequeña ~** lower middle class; (*Pol pey*) petite bourgeoisie

buril SM burin, engraver's chisel

burka SM (*a veces* SF) burqa

burla SF gibe, taunt; **burlas** mockery *sing*, ridicule *sing*; **hacer ~ a algn** to make fun of sb, mock sb; **entre ~s y veras** half-joking(ly)

burladero SM covert (*barrier behind which the bullfighter protects himself from the bull*)

burlar /1a/ Ⓐ VT [+ *persona*] to deceive, trick; [+ *enemigo*] to outwit; [+ *vigilancia*] to defeat; [+ *bloqueo*] to run Ⓑ **burlarse** VPR **~se de algn** to mock sb, make fun of sb

burlesco ADJ 1 (= *cómico*) funny, comic 2 (*Literat*) burlesque

burlete SM draught excluder (*esp Brit*), weather strip (*EEUU*)

burlón ADJ (= *bromista*) [*persona*] mocking, teasing; [*risa, voz*] sardonic

buró SM 1 (= *escritorio*) bureau (*Brit*), (roll-top) desk 2 ➤ **buró político** (*Pol*) executive committee 3 (*Méx*) (= *mesita de noche*) bedside table, night stand *o* table (*EEUU*)

burocracia SF bureaucracy

burócrata SMF 1 (*pey*) bureaucrat 2 (*Méx*) (= *funcionario*) civil servant, administrative official, public official

burocrático ADJ 1 (*pey*) bureaucratic 2 (*Méx*) (= *de los funcionarios*) official, civil service *antes de s*

burqa SM (*a veces* SF) burqa

burrada SF 1 (= *tontería*) stupid thing; **decir ~s** to talk nonsense; **hacer ~s** to do stupid things 2 (*) (= *mucho*) **me gusta una ~** I like it a lot; **sabe una ~** he knows a hell of a lot*; **una ~ de cosas** a whole heap of things, tons of things*

burrero/a SM/F (*CS hum*) horse-lover

burro/a Ⓐ ADJ 1 (*) (= *estúpido*) stupid; **¡qué ~! ¡no sabe la capital de Italia!** what a fool *o* moron*, he doesn't know the capital of Italy!
2 (= *bruto*) **¡deja de empujar, no seas ~!** stop pushing, you great oaf *o* you big brute!*; **¡el muy ~ se comió el pastel entero!** he ate the whole cake, the pig!*
3 (= *obstinado*) pig-headed*; **ponerse ~** to dig one's heels in, be pigheaded* Ⓑ SM/F 1 (*Zool*) donkey/she-donkey; **salto de ~** (*Méx*) leapfrog; ◆ MODISMOS **apearse** *o* **bajar(se) del ~*** to back down; **trabajar como un ~** to work like a slave; **no ver tres en un ~*** to be as blind as a bat*; **ver ~s negros** (*Chi**) to see stars; **si los ~s volaran** pigs might fly ➤ **burro de carga trata a su empleados como ~s de carga** he treats his workers like slaves
2 (*) (= *estúpido*) fool, moron*
3 (*) (= *bruto*) **el ~ de Juan seguía pegándole** that brute Juan kept on hitting him; **el ~ de Antonio se comió su plato y el mío** that pig Antonio ate all his own dinner and mine too*
4 (= *obstinado*) stubborn fool Ⓒ SM 1 (*Naipes*) ≈ old maid

2 (*Téc*) sawhorse, sawbuck (*EEUU*)
3 (*Méx*) (= *escalera*) stepladder; (= *caballete*) trestle ➤ **burro de planchar** ironing board

bursátil ADJ stock-exchange *antes de s*, stock-market *antes de s*

burucuyá SF (*RPl*) passionflower

bus SM 1 (= *autobús*) bus 2 (*Inform*) bus

busca Ⓐ SF search; **en ~ de** in search of; **empezó a llamar por teléfono a todas partes en mi ~** he began phoning around (*esp Brit*) *o* calling around (*esp EEUU*) everywhere to try and find me; **se marcharon en ~ de fortuna** they went off to seek their fortune; **el juez dictó orden de ~ y captura del fugitivo** the judge ordered the fugitive's (immediate) capture Ⓑ SM (*Esp*) (= *mensáfono*) bleeper*, pager (*esp Brit*)

buscabullas SMF (*LAm*) troublemaker

buscador(a) Ⓐ SM/F (= *persona*) ➤ **buscador(a) de agua** water-diviner ➤ **buscador(a) de fortuna** fortune-seeker ➤ **buscador(a) de oro** gold prospector ➤ **buscador(a) de tesoros** treasure hunter Ⓑ SM (*Internet*) search engine

buscapleitos SMF INV (*LAm*) troublemaker

buscar /1g/ Ⓐ VT 1 (= *tratar de encontrar*) 1.1 [+ *persona, objeto perdido, trabajo*] to look for

> No se olvide de incluir la preposición **for** después de los verbos **look** y **search**, cuando **buscar** funciona como verbo transitivo:

estuvieron buscando a los montañeros they were searching for *o* looking for the mountaineers; **el terrorista más buscado del país** the most wanted terrorist in the country; **"se busca piso"** "flat wanted" (*Brit*), "apartment wanted" (*EEUU*); **"chico busca chica"** "boy seeks girl"; **las plantas buscan la luz** plants grow towards the light; ◆ MODISMO **~le tres pies al gato** (= *buscar complicaciones*) to complicate matters, make things difficult; (= *buscar defectos*) to split hairs, nitpick* **1.2** (*en diccionario, enciclopedia*) to look up **1.3** (*con la vista*) to try to spot, look for; **lo busqué entre el público pero no lo vi** I tried to spot him *o* looked for him in the crowd but I didn't see him
2 (= *tratar de conseguir*) [+ *solución*] to try to find; **no sé lo que buscas con esa actitud** I don't know what you're aiming to *o* trying to achieve with that attitude; **con esta novela se busca la creación de un estilo diferente** this novel attempts to *o* aims to create a different style; **yo no busco la fama** I'm not looking for fame; **sólo buscaba su dinero** he was only out for *o* after her money; **~ excusas** to make excuses; **~ hacer algo** to seek to do sth, try to do sth; **ir a ~ algo/a algn** to go and get sth/sb; ◆ MODISMOS **~la** ◇ **~ pelea** to be looking for a fight, be looking for trouble; **~ la ruina a algn** to be the ruin of sb
3 (= *recoger*) to pick up, fetch; **¿vais a ir a ~me a la estación?** are you going to pick me up from the station?
4 (*Inform*) to search
5 (= *preguntar por*) to ask for; **¿quién me busca?** who is asking for me?
Ⓑ VI to look; **¿has buscado bien?** have you looked properly?; **busca en la página 45** look on page 45; **¡busca!** (*al perro*) fetch!
Ⓒ **buscarse** VPR 1 [+ *marido, trabajo*] to find (o.s.); [+ *ayuda, patrocinador*] to get, find; ◆ MODISMO **~se la vida*** (= *ganar dinero*) to try to earn *o* make a living; (= *arreglárselas solo*) to manage on one's own, get by on one's own; **no me vengas con historias, búscate la vida** stop bothering me, sort it out for yourself
2 [+ *problemas*] **no te busques más problemas** don't bring more problems on yourself, don't make more trouble for yourself; **él se lo buscó** he brought it on himself, he asked for it*; ◆ MODISMO **buscársela*** to ask for trouble, ask for it*

buscavidas SMF INV go-getter*

buscón/ona[1][†] SM/F petty thief, rogue

buscona[2] SF (*pey*) whore

buseca SF 1 (*And, Carib*) small bus, minibus 2 (*CS*) thick stew

búsqueda SF search (**de** for); ➤ **búsqueda del tesoro** treasure hunt

busto SM 1 (= *escultura*) bust 2 (*Anat*) chest

butaca SF 1 (= *sillón*) armchair, easy chair 2 (*Teat*) seat ➤ **butaca de patio, butaca de platea** seat in the stalls (*Brit*) *o* orchestra (*EEUU*)

butacón SM large armchair

butano SM (*tb* **gas** ~) butane, butane gas; **bombona de** ~ gas cylinder; **color** ~ orange

butifarra SF 1 (= *embutido*) Catalan sausage 2 (*Perú*) *meat and salad roll*

butrón* SM *hole made to effect a break-in*

buzo[1] SM diver

buzo[2] SM 1 (*CS*) (= *conjunto*) tracksuit (*Brit*), sweatsuit

(*EEUU*); (= *parte de arriba*) sweatshirt 2 (*Col, Uru*) (= *suéter*) sweater; (*Col*) [*de cuello alto*] polo-neck (sweater)

buzo[3]* ADJ (*Méx*) **ponerse** ~ to watch out; **ser** ~ **para algo** to be brilliant at sth*

buzón SM (*en casa*) letterbox (*esp Brit*), mailbox (*EEUU*); (*en calle*) postbox, letterbox (*esp Brit*), mailbox (*EEUU*); **echar una carta al** ~ to post (*esp Brit*) *o* mail (*esp EEUU*) a letter; ✦ MODISMO **vender un** ~ **a algn** (*CS**) to pull the wool over sb's eyes ➤ **buzón de sugerencias** suggestions box ➤ **buzón de voz** voice mail

buzonear /1a/ VT to deliver door-to-door

buzoneo SM direct mail

Cc

C¹, c [θe] (*esp LAm*) [se] SF (= *letra*) C, c

C² ABR (= **centígrado**) C

C/ ABR (= **Calle**) St

cabal ADJ 1 (= *exacto*) **500 pesetas ~es** exactly 500 pesetas 2 (= *completo*) **una ~ formación humanística** a thorough classical education; **esto nos proporciona una idea ~ del asunto** this provides us with a clearer and fuller picture of the matter 3 (= *íntegro*) upright

cábala SF 1 (*Rel*) cab(b)ala 2 (= *intriga*) cabal, intrigue 3 **cábalas** (= *conjeturas*): **hacer ~s** to speculate, conjecture

cabales SMPL **no está en sus ~** she isn't in her right mind

cabalgadura SF [*de montar*] mount, horse; [*de carga*] beast of burden

cabalgar /1h/ Ⓐ VT 1 [*jinete*] to ride 2 [*semental*] to cover, serve Ⓑ VI 1 to ride, go riding; **~ en mula** to ride (on) a mule; **~ sin montura** ◇ **~ a pelo** to ride bareback

cabalgata SF (= *desfile*) mounted procession, cavalcade
➤ **cabalgata de Reyes** Twelfth Night procession

CABALGATA DE REYES

The **cabalgata de Reyes** is a float parade held on 5 January, the eve of Epiphany, in most Spanish towns and cities. It celebrates the coming of the Three Kings with their gifts for the infant Jesus. In the course of the **cabalgatas**, the Three Kings throw sweets into the crowd. ◇ REYES, DÍA DE

cabalístico ADJ (= *de la cábala*) cabalistic; (= *misterioso*) occult, mysterious

caballa SF (Atlantic) mackerel

caballada SF (*LAm*) stupid thing

caballar ADJ horse *antes de s*, equine; **ganado ~** horses *pl*

caballeresco ADJ 1 [*sentimiento*] fine, noble; [*conducta*] chivalrous 2 (*Hist*) knightly, chivalric

caballería SF 1 (*Mil*) cavalry ➤ **caballería ligera** light cavalry, light horse 2 (*Hist*) chivalry; (= *orden*) order of chivalry; **libros de ~** books of chivalry ➤ **caballería andante** knight errantry 3 (*para montar*) (= *montura*) mount, steed (*liter*); (= *caballo*) horse; (= *mula*) mule

caballeriza SF (= *cuadra*) stable; [*de cría*] stud, horse-breeding establishment

caballerizo SM groom, stableman ➤ **caballerizo del rey** equerry

caballero SM 1 (= *hombre educado*) gentleman; **es todo un ~** he is a real gentleman; **señoras y ~s** ladies and gentlemen 2 (*frm*) (= *hombre*) **camisa de ~** man's shirt; **peluquería de ~s** gents' hairdresser's; **ropa de ~** menswear; **"caballeros"** (*en una puerta*) "gents", "gentlemen" 3 (*Hist*) knight; **los ~s de la Tabla Redonda** the Knights of the Round Table; **armar ~ a algn** to knight sb ➤ **caballero andante** knight errant

caballerosidad SF (= *cortesía*) gentlemanliness; (= *nobleza*) chivalry

caballeroso ADJ (= *cortés*) gentlemanly; (= *noble*) chivalrous; **poco ~** ungentlemanly

caballete SM 1 (*Arte*) easel; (*Téc*) trestle 2 [*de tejado, de tierra labrada*] ridge 3 (*Anat*) bridge (of the nose)

caballito SM 1 (= *animal*) little horse, pony; ✦ MODISMO **hacer a algn el ~** to give sb a piggy-back ➤ **caballito del diablo** dragonfly ➤ **caballito de mar** sea horse 2 [*de niño*] (*para mecerse*) rocking horse; (*con palo (y rueda)*) hobby-horse 3 **caballitos** [*de feria*] merry-go-round *sing*, carousel *sing* (*esp EEUU*)

caballo SM 1 (= *animal*) horse; **a ~: una mujer a ~** a woman on horseback *o* riding a horse; **vino a ~** he came on horseback, he rode here; **me gusta andar** *o* **montar a ~** I like (going) riding; **paseo a ~** (horse) ride (*Brit*), horseback ride (*EEUU*); **tropas de a ~** mounted troops; ✦ MODISMOS **a ~ entre** halfway between; **vivo a ~ entre Madrid y Barcelona** I spend my time between Madrid and Barcelona, I spend half my time in Madrid, half in Barcelona; **como ~ desbocado** rashly, hastily; ✦ REFRÁN **a ~ regalado no le mires el diente** don't look a gift horse in the mouth ➤ **caballo de batalla: han convertido el asunto en su ~ de batalla personal** the issue has become their hobbyhorse; **esto se convirtió en el ~ de batalla de la reunión** this became the bone of contention in the meeting ➤ **caballo de carga** packhorse ➤ **caballo de carreras** racehorse ➤ **caballo de tiro** carthorse ➤ **Caballo de Troya** Trojan horse
2 (*Ajedrez*) knight; (*Naipes*) *equivalent of queen in the Spanish pack of cards*; ◇ BARAJA ESPAÑOLA
3 (*Mec*) (*tb* **~ de fuerza, ~ de vapor**) horsepower; **un motor de 100 ~s** a 100 horsepower engine; **¿cuántos ~s tiene este coche?** what horsepower is this car?, what's this car's horsepower?
4 [*de carpintero*] sawhorse, sawbuck (*EEUU*)
5 (**) (= *heroína*) smack**, sugar**

caballón SM (*Agr*) ridge

cabaña SF 1 (= *choza*) hut, cabin; (*en mal estado*) hovel, shack ➤ **cabaña de madera** log cabin 2 (*CS*) (= *estancia*) cattle-breeding ranch

cabaré SM, **cabaret** [kaβa're] SM (*pl* **~s** *o* **cabarets**) (= *espectáculo*) cabaret, floor show; (= *boîte*) cabaret, nightclub

cabaretera SF (= *bailarina*) cabaret entertainer, cabaret dancer, showgirl; (= *chica de alterne*) night-club hostess

cabeceada SF (*LAm*) nod (of the head); **dar ~s** to nod off; **echarse una ~** to have a nap

cabecear /1a/ Ⓐ VT [+ *balón*] to head Ⓑ VI 1 (*al dormir*) to nod off; (= *negar*) to shake one's head; [*caballo*] to toss its head 2 [*barco*] to pitch; [*carruaje*] to lurch, sway; [*carga*] to shift, slip

cabeceo SM 1 (*al dormir*) nod; (= *negativa*) shake of the head; [*de caballo*] toss of the head 2 [*de barco*] pitching; [*de carruaje*] lurching, lurch; [*de carga*] shifting, slipping

cabecera SF 1 [*de página*] top; [*de artículo*] heading; [*de carta*] opening; (*Inform*) title-page; **la noticia apareció en la ~ de todos los periódicos** the news made the headlines in all the newspapers
2 [*de río*] headwaters *pl*
3 [*de cama*] headboard; **tenía una bandera a la ~ de la cama** he had a flag at the head of the bed
4 [*de mesa*] head; **se sentó a la ~ de la mesa** he sat at the head of the table
5 [*de organización, ministerio*] top (level); **desde la ~ del ministerio** from top ministerial level

cabecero SM headboard, bedhead (*Brit*)

cabecilla SMF ringleader

cabellera SF 1 (*liter*) (= *pelo*) hair, head of hair 2 (*Astron*) tail

cabello SM hair; **analizaremos sólo un ~** we shall analyse just a single hair; **llevaba el ~ recogido atrás** she had *o* wore her hair tied back; **te deja los ~s brillantes** it leaves your hair shiny ➤ **cabello de ángel** *confectionery and pastry filling made of pumpkin and syrup*

caber /2l/ VI 1 (= *haber espacio para*) to fit (**en** into); **en este baúl no cabe** it won't fit in *o* go into this trunk, there's no room in this trunk; **¿cabe alguien más?** is there room for anyone else?; **¿cabemos todos?** is there room for us all?; ✦ MODISMOS **¡no me cabe en la cabeza!** I can't understand it!; **no ~ en sí** to be beside o.s.; **no cabe en sí de contento** *o* **gozo** he's beside himself with joy, he's over the moon
2 (= *tener cabida*) **en la bandeja de papel caben 100 hojas** the paper tray holds 100 sheets
3 **~ por** to go through; **eso no cabe por esta puerta** that won't go through this door

4 (*Mat*) **veinte entre cinco cabe a cuatro** *o* **caben cuatro** five into twenty goes four (times)
5 [*ser posible*] **5.1** [+ *explicación*] to be possible; **sólo caben dos explicaciones** there are only two possible explanations **5.2** (+ INFIN) **la persona más generosa que cabe imaginar** the most generous person you could imagine, the most generous person imaginable; **cabe preguntar si ...** one might *o* could ask whether ...
5.3 dentro de lo que cabe under the circumstances; **nos llevamos bastante bien, dentro de lo que cabe** we get on quite well, under the circumstances *o* considering; **no cabe duda de que ...** there is *o* can be no doubt that ...; **no cabe más que: no cabe más que esperar a ver lo que pasa** we can only wait *o* all we can do is wait *o* the only thing for it is to wait and see what happens; **cabe la posibilidad de que ...: ¿no cabe la posibilidad de que usted haya sido utilizada?** is it not possible that you might have been used?; **si cabe: ahora está más amable, si cabe** she's even friendlier now
6 (*frm*) (= *corresponder*) **me cabe el honor/la satisfacción de presentarles (a) ...** I have the honour/it gives me great pleasure to introduce ...

cabestrillo SM sling; **con el brazo en ~** with one's arm in a sling

cabestro SM **1** (= *brida*) halter **2** (= *buey*) leading ox, bell-ox

cabeza ⓐ SF **1** [*de persona*] head; **se rascó la ~** he scratched his head; **me duele la ~** I've got a headache, my head aches; **los aviones pasan por encima de nuestras ~s** the planes are flying overhead; **afirmar** *o* **asentir con la ~** to nod (one's head); **caer de ~** to fall headfirst *o* headlong; **se tiró al agua de ~** he dived headfirst into the water; **marcar de ~** (*Dep*) to score with a header; **lavarse la ~** to wash one's hair; **levantar la ~** (= *mirar*) to look up; **negar con la ~** to shake one's head; **por ~**: **cinco dólares por ~** five dollars a head, five dollars per person; **se me va la ~** I feel giddy; **volver la ~** to look around, turn one's head; **me da vueltas la ~** my head's spinning ➤ **cabeza de ajo** bulb of garlic ➤ **cabeza de partido** administrative centre ➤ **cabeza explosiva** warhead ➤ **cabeza nuclear** nuclear warhead
2 ✦ MODISMOS **andar** *o* **ir de ~*** to be snowed under; **no estar bien de la ~*** = **estar mal de la cabeza**; **esconder la ~** to keep one's head down; **irse a algn de la ~**: **se me fue de la ~** it went right out of my mind; **lanzarse de ~ a** (= *atacar*) to rush headlong at; (= *precipitarse*) rush headlong into; **levantar ~** to get back on one's feet again; **hay sectores como la construcción que empiezan a levantar ~** some sectors, such as construction, are starting to pick up; **estar mal de la ~***: **hace falta estar mal de la ~ para hacer eso** you'd have to be out of your mind to do that; **mantener la ~ fuera del agua** to keep one's head above water; **meter algo en la ~ a algn**: **por fin le metimos en la ~ que ...** we finally got it into his head that ...; **meterse a algn en la ~**: **se le ha metido en la ~ hacerlo solo** he's taken *o* got it into his head to do it alone; **esa melodía la tengo metida en la ~** I can't get that tune out of my head; **pasarse a algn por la ~**: **jamás se me pasó por la ~** it never entered my head; **perder la ~ por** to lose one's head over; **quitar algo de la ~ a algn** to get sth out of sb's head; **romper la ~ a algn** to smash sb's face in; **romperse la ~** to rack one's brains; **sacarse una idea de la ~** to get an idea out of one's head; **sentar ~** to settle down; **subirse a la ~**: **el vino se me subió a la ~** the wine went to my head; **tener ~** to be bright; **tener la ~ dura** to be stubborn; **tener la ~ sobre los hombros** to have one's head screwed on (the right way); **estar tocado de la ~** to be soft in the head; **traer de ~ a algn** to drive sb mad
3 (= *frente*) **a la ~ de: a la ~ de la manifestación** at the head *o* front of the demonstration; **con Pérez a la ~ del gobierno** with Pérez at the head of the government; **ir en ~** to be in the lead; **ir en ~ de la lista** to be at the top of the list, head the list
4 (= *distancia*) head; **le saca una ~ a su hermano** he is a head taller than his brother
ⓑ SMF **1** (= *líder*) head, leader
2 ➤ **cabeza cuadrada*** bigot ➤ **cabeza de chorlito*** scatterbrain ➤ **cabeza de familia** head of the household ➤ **cabeza de serie** (*Dep*) seed ➤ **cabeza de turco** scapegoat

➤ **cabeza dura** stubborn person; **es un ~ dura** he's as stubborn as a mule ➤ **cabeza hueca** idiot ➤ **cabeza rapada** skinhead ➤ **cabeza visible** head, leader

cabezada SF **1** (= *cabeceo*) shake of the head, nod; **dar ~s** to nod (sleepily), doze; **dar** *o* **echar una ~** have a nap **2** (*Náut*) pitch, pitching; **dar ~s** to pitch

cabezadita SF **echar una ~*** to have a snooze*, doze

cabezal SM **1** (= *almohada*) pillow, bolster; [*de sillón*] headrest; (*Med*) pad, compress **2** [*de vídeo, casete*] head

cabezazo SM (*gen*) (*a alguien*) head butt, butt; (*contra una puerta*) bump on the head; (*Dep*) header

cabezón ⓐ ADJ **1** (*) (= *cabezudo*) bigheaded, with a big head; (= *terco*) pigheaded **2** [*vino*] heady ⓑ SM (*) (= *cabeza grande*) big head

cabezonada* SF pig-headed thing to do

cabezonería* SF pig-headedness

cabezota* ⓐ ADJ pig-headed ⓑ SMF pig-headed person

cabezudo ⓐ ADJ (*) = **cabezón A** ⓑ SM *carnival figure with an enormous head*

cabida SF **1** (= *capacidad*) (*en depósito, caja*) capacity; (*en vehículo*) space, room; **necesitamos un depósito de mayor ~** we need a tank with a greater capacity; **en este autobús no hay ~ para 60 personas** this bus can't hold *o* take 60 people, there isn't space *o* room in this bus for 60 people; **el auditorio puede dar ~ a más de mil espectadores** the concert hall can accommodate more than a thousand people, the concert hall has a capacity of more than a thousand; **el teatro tiene ~ para 750 personas** the theatre holds 750 people, the theatre has a capacity of 750
2 (= *aceptación*) **en este periódico no se da ~ a las ideas de vanguardia** there's no place *o* room for avant-garde ideas in this newspaper; **personajes de ese tipo no tienen ~ en nuestro programa** there is no place *o* room in our programme for characters like that
3 (*Náut*) capacity
4 (= *terreno*) area

cabildear /1a/ VI to lobby

cabildo SM **1** (*Rel*) (= *personas*) chapter; (= *junta*) chapter meeting **2** (*Pol*) (= *ayuntamiento*) town council; (*Parl*) lobby ➤ **cabildo insular** (*en Canarias*) inter-island council

cabina SF **1** [*de discjockey, intérprete*] booth; (*tb* ~ **telefónica, ~ de teléfono(s)**) telephone box (*Brit*), telephone booth (*EEUU*) ➤ **cabina de prensa** press box ➤ **cabina de proyección** projection room ➤ **cabina electoral** voting booth **2** [*de tren, camión*] cab **3** (*Aer*) [*de pasajeros*] cabin; [*de piloto*] cockpit ➤ **cabina de mando** (*Aer*) flight deck, cockpit **4** (*Náut*) bridge

cabinero/a SM/F (*Col*) (= *hombre*) steward, flight attendant; (= *mujer*) stewardess, flight attendant, air hostess (*Brit*)

cabizbajo ADJ dejected, downcast, crestfallen

cable SM **1** (*Elec*) (= *hilo*) wire; (*con cubierta aislante*) cable; **tiene varios ~s sueltos** there are several loose wires; **el ~ del micrófono/amplificador** the microphone/amplifier cable *o* lead; ✦ MODISMO **se le cruzaron los ~s*** he totally flipped* ➤ **cable de alta tensión** high-voltage cable
2 (*Mec*) [*de acero*] cable; ✦ MODISMO **echar un ~ a algn*** to give sb a helping hand ➤ **cable de remolque** towline, towrope
3 (*Telec*) cable, wire; **televisión por ~** cable television, cable TV
4 (= *cablegrama*) cable; **enviar un ~ a algn** to cable sb

cableado SM wiring

cablear /1a/ VT (*con instalación eléctrica*) to wire up; (*con fibra óptica*) to cable (up)

cablegrafiar /1c/ VI to cable, wire

cablegrama SM cable, cablegram

cabo SM **1** (= *trozo pequeño*) [*de cuerda, hilo*] thread; [*de vela, lápiz*] stub ➤ **cabo de vela** (*Náut*) rope, cable
2 (*locuciones*) **al ~ de** after; **al ~ de tres meses** after three months, three months later; **llevar a ~** [+ *acción, investigación, tarea*] to carry out; [+ *viaje*] to make; **ya hemos llevado a ~ la recogida de firmas** we have already collected

the signatures; **en esta piscina se llevarán a ~ las pruebas de natación** the swimming events will take place in this pool; ✦ MODISMOS **atar ~s: atando ~s, me di cuenta de que ...** I put two and two together and realized that ...; **de ~ a ~** ◇ **de ~ a rabo** from beginning to end, from start to finish; **me recorrí el pueblo de ~ a rabo y no encontré ningún restaurante** I went all through the village and didn't find a single restaurant; **estar al ~ de la calle de algo** (*Esp*) to be fully aware of sth; **no dejar ningún ~ suelto** (*preparando algo*) to leave nothing to chance; (*investigando algo*) to tie up all the loose ends
3 (= *graduación*) [*de militar*] corporal; [*de policía*] sergeant ➤ **cabo primero** first officer
4 (*Geog*) cape ➤ **Cabo Cañaveral** Cape Canaveral ➤ **Cabo de Buena Esperanza** Cape of Good Hope ➤ **Cabo de Hornos** Cape Horn ➤ **Cabo Verde** Cape Verde

cabotaje SM cabotage, coasting trade, coastal traffic

cabra SF goat; ✦ MODISMO **estar como una ~** to be crazy ➤ **cabra montés** Spanish ibex

cabrales SM INV *strong cheese from Asturias*

cabré *etc ver* **caber**

cabreado** ADJ pissed off***

cabrear** /1a/ ❶ VT to piss off*** ❷ **cabrearse** VPR **1** (= *enfadarse*) to get pissed off*** **2** (*Chi*) (= *cansarse*) to get fed up*

cabreo** SM **¡menudo ~ lleva!** she's really pissed off!***; **coger un ~** to fly off the handle*, fly into a rage

cabrero/a ❶ ADJ (*RPl**) bad-tempered; **ponerse ~** to fly off the handle* ❷ SM/F goatherd

cabrestante SM capstan, winch

cabrío ADJ goatish; **macho ~** billy goat, he-goat

cabriola SF gambol, skip; **hacer ~s** [*persona*] to caper about; [*caballo*] to buck, prance around; [*cordero*] to gambol

cabriolé SM cabriolet

cabritas SFPL (*Chi*) popcorn *sing*

cabritilla SF kid, kidskin

cabrito SM **1** (*Zool*) kid **2** (*) (= *cabrón*) swine*; (= *cornudo*) cuckold; **¡cabrito!** you swine!*

cabro/a* SM/F (*Chi*) kid

cabrón/ona* ❶ SM/F bastard!*** ❷ SM (= *cornudo*) cuckold; (*Col*) (= *chulo*) pimp

cabronada* SF dirty trick; **hacer una ~ a algn** to play a dirty trick on sb

cábula SF (*LAm*) **1** (= *complot*) intrigue, cabal **2** (= *trampa*) trick, stratagem

cabuya SF (*Bot*) pita, agave; (= *fibra*) pita fibre; (*LAm*) (= *cuerda*) rope, cord (*especially one made from pita fibre*)

caca* SF **1** (*lenguaje infantil*) poo (*Brit**), poop (*EEUU**); **¿quieres hacer ~?** do you want to do a poo? (*Brit**) o to poop? (*EEUU**); **se ha hecho** o **hecho** o (*EEUU**) pooped his pants; **¡caca!** (= *no toques*) dirty! **2** (= *birria*) rubbish, crap***; **tenemos un ejército que es una ~** our army is rubbish, our army is crap***

cacahual SM (*LAm*) cacao plantation

cacahuete SM (*Esp*), **cacahuate** SM (*Méx*) peanut

cacao SM **1** (*Bot*) cacao; (= *bebida*) cocoa; **~ en polvo** cocoa powder **2** (*Esp**) (= *confusión*) fuss, to-do; ✦ MODISMOS **armar** o **montar un ~** to cause havoc; **se armó un buen ~** all hell broke loose*; **tener un ~ en la cabeza*** to be all mixed up ➤ **cacao mental*** mental confusion

cacarear /1a/ ❶ VT to boast about, make much of; **ese triunfo tan cacareado** that much-trumpeted victory ❷ VI [*gallina*] to cluck; [*gallo*] to crow

cacarizo ADJ (*Méx*) pitted, pockmarked

cacatúa SF **1** (*Orn*) cockatoo **2** (*) (= *vieja*) old bat*, old bag*, old cow*

cacereño ADJ of/from Cáceres

cacería SF **1** (= *actividad*) hunting, shooting (*esp Brit*); **ir de ~** to go hunting, go shooting (*esp Brit*) **2** (= *partida*) hunt, shooting party (*esp Brit*) ➤ **cacería de zorros** fox hunt

cacerola SF pan, saucepan

cacerolazo SM (*CS*) banging on pots and pans (*as political protest*)

cacha SF **1** [*de arma*] butt **2** (*Anat***) (= *muslo*) thigh; ✦ MODISMO **estar ~s** (*Esp*) (= *ser musculoso*) to have plenty of muscles, be well set-up; (= *ser atractivo*) to be a hunk*

cachaco* SM (*Col*) person from Bogotá

cachada SF **1** (*LAm*) (= *embestida*) butt, thrust; (*Taur*) goring **2** (*RPl**) (= *broma*) joke, leg-pull*

cachador* (*RPl*) ❶ ADJ fond of practical jokes ❷ SM practical joker

cachalote SM sperm whale

cachar¹* /1a/ VT (*RPl*) to kid

cachar² /1a/ VT **1** (*CS*) [+ *bus*] to catch **2** (*CAm*) (= *obtener*) to get **3** (*CS*) (= *entender*) [+ *sentido*] to penetrate; [+ *persona, razón*] to understand; **sí, te cacho** sure, I get it* **4** (*And, CAm, Carib Dep*) [+ *pelota*] to catch

cacharpas* SFPL (*RPl*) stuff *sing*, junk *sing*

cacharpaya SF (*And*) farewell party

cacharrazo* SM bash*, bang; **darse** o **pegarse un ~** (*Aut*) to prang the car*

cacharrería SF (*Col*) (= *ferretería*) hardware shop o store

cacharro SM **1** [*de cocina*] pot, dish; **fregar los ~s** to do o wash the dishes ➤ **cacharros de cocina** pots and pans **2** (*) (= *trasto*) useless object, piece of junk; (*Aut*) old crock, jalop(p)y **3** (*) (= *aparato*) gadget

cachaza SF **1** (*) (= *lentitud*) **tener ~** to be slow **2** (= *licor*) Brazilian cane sugar liqueur

cachazudo ADJ (= *lento*) slow; (= *flemático*) calm, easy-going

cache* ADJ (*Arg*) tacky*, kitsch

caché ❶ SM = **cachet** ❷ ADJ (*Inform*) cached

cachear /1a/ VT **1** (= *registrar*) to search, frisk (for weapons) **2** (*LAm Taur*) to butt, gore

cachemir SM, **cachemira** SF cashmere

cacheo SM searching, frisking (for weapons)

cachet [ka'tʃe] SM (*pl ~s*) **1** (= *sello distintivo*) cachet **2** [*de artista*] fee

cachetada SF (*LAm*), **cachetazo** SM (*LAm*) slap

cachete SM **1** (= *golpe*) slap **2** (= *mejilla*) cheek **3 cachetes** (*CS**) (= *culo*) bottom *sing*

cachetear /1a/ (*LAm*) VT to slap o smack in the face

cachetón ADJ (*LAm**) plump-cheeked, fat-faced

cachi ADJ (*Arg*) = **cache**

cachifo/a* SM/F **1** (*Col*) (= *jovenzuelo*) kid* **2** (*Ven*) (= *criado*) servant

cachimba SF pipe

cachimbo SM **1** (*LAm*) (= *pipa*) pipe **2** (*CAm**) (= *montón*) pile, heap

cachiporra SF truncheon (*Brit*), (billy) club (*EEUU*)

cachivache SM **1** (= *vasija*) pot **2 cachivaches** (= *trastos*) trash *sing*, junk *sing*

cacho SM **1** (*) (= *trozo*) bit, small piece; **es un ~ de pan*** he's really kind, he's got a heart of gold; **a ~s** bit by bit; **caerse a ~s** to fall apart, be falling to pieces **2** (*LAm*) (= *cuerno*) horn; (*CS*) (*para beber*) cup (made of horn) **3** (*And, CS*) (= *cubilete*) dice cup; **jugar al ~** to play dice **4** (*RPl*) [*de bananas*] bunch **5** (*Carib***) (= *marijuana*) joint**, spliff**

cachondearse* /1a/ VPR (*Esp*) to take things as a joke; **~ de algn** to make fun of sb, take the mickey out of sb (*Brit***)

cachondeo* SM (*Esp*) **1** (= *bromas*) joking; (= *guasa*) laugh*, messing about; (= *burla*) teasing, nagging; **estar de ~** to be in the mood for a laugh; **hacer algo en plan de ~** to do sth for a lark o a laugh*; **tomar a ~** to treat as a joke **2** (= *juerga*) **estar de ~** to live it up, have a great time **3** (= *desastre*) farce, mess; **¡esto es un ~!** what a farce this is!, what a mess!

cachondo* ADJ (*Esp*) **1** (= *excitado*) horny**, randy (*Brit**); **estar ~** to feel horny o randy (*Brit**) **2** (= *gracioso*) funny, amusing, jokey; **~ mental** crazy but likable **3** (= *juerguista*) fun-loving, riotous

cachorro/a SM/F (*gen*) cub; [*de perro*] puppy, pup

cachucha SF 1 (*Col, Méx***) cap 2 (*RPI****) cunt***

cachudo ADJ 1 (*LAm*) (= *con cuernos*) horned 2 (*Col*) (= *rico*) wealthy 3 (*Chi**) suspicious, distrustful 4 (*Uru**) = **cache**

cachupín/ina SM/F (*CAm, Méx Hist pey*) Spanish settler

cachureo* SM (*Chi*) bric-a-brac, junk, bits and pieces *pl*

cacillo SM ladle

cacique SM (*Hist*) chief, headman; (*Pol*) local party boss; (*fig*) petty tyrant, despot

caciquil ADJ despotic, tyrannical

caciquismo SM (*Pol*) (system of) dominance by the local party boss; (*fig*) petty tyranny, despotism

cacle SM (*Méx*) sandal

caco* SM (= *ladrón*) thief; (= *carterista*) pickpocket; (= *criminal*) crook*

cacofonía SF cacophony

cactus SM INV, **cacto** SM cactus

cada ADJ INV 1 (*uso distributivo*) (*con elementos individuales*) each; (*con números, tiempo*) every; ~ **uno de los jugadores dispone de cuatro fichas** each player has four counters; **habrá una mesa por ~ ocho invitados** there will one table for every eight guests; **han aumentado los beneficios en todos y ~ uno de los sectores** profits have risen in each and every sector; ~ **cual busca la felicidad como quiere** we all seek *o* each one of us seeks happiness in our own way 2 (*indicando frecuencia*) every; **juega al baloncesto ~ domingo** he plays basketball every Sunday; ~ **cierto tiempo** every so often, every now and then; ~ **dos días** every couple of days, every other day; **los problemas de ~ día** everyday problems; **cinco de ~ diez** five out of every ten; ¿~ **cuánto tiempo?** how often?; ~ **vez que** (*Méx*) whenever, every time (that); ~ **vez que** whenever, every time (that); ✦ MODISMO ~ **dos por tres** every other minute, all the time 3 (*indicando progresión*) ~ **vez más** more and more; **encontrar trabajo es ~ vez más difícil** finding a job is increasingly difficult *o* is (getting) more and more difficult; **me siento ~ vez más viejo** I feel (I'm getting) older and older; ~ **vez mejor** better and better; ~ **vez menos** less and less; ~ **vez peor** worse and worse 4 (*uso enfático*) **¡oye una ~ historia!** the things you hear nowadays!

cadalso SM (*Jur*) (= *patíbulo*) scaffold; (*Téc*) stand, platform

cadáver SM [*de persona*] (dead) body; (*más técnico*) corpse; [*de animal*] body, carcass; **¡sobre mi ~!** ✧ **¡por encima de mi ~!** over my dead body!; **ingresó ~** (*Esp*) he was dead on arrival (at hospital)

cadavérico ADJ (= *de cadáver*) cadaverous; (= *pálido*) deathly pale, ghastly

caddie ['kadi] SMF, **caddy** ['kadi] SMF (*Golf*) caddie

cadena SF 1 [*de eslabones, de joyería*] chain; **se me salió la ~ de la bici** the chain came off my bike, my bike chain came off; **la ~ del reloj** the watch chain; **tirar de la ~ (del wáter)** to flush the toilet, pull the chain; **no echó la ~ de la puerta** he didn't put the door-chain on ➤ **cadena (antirrobo)** chain ➤ **cadena de distribución** distribution chain 2 (*Radio, TV*) (= *canal*) channel ➤ **cadena de televisión** TV channel 3 (*Audio*) ➤ **cadena de sonido** sound system ➤ **cadena musical** music centre, sound system 4 (*Com*) [*de hoteles, tiendas, restaurantes*] chain ➤ **cadena comercial** retail chain 5 ➤ **cadena montañosa** mountain range 6 (= *sucesión*) [*de acontecimientos, átomos*] chain; [*de atentados*] string, series; **en ~: colisión en ~** multiple collision, (multiple) pile-up; **efecto en ~** domino effect, knock-on effect (*Brit*); **reacción en ~** chain reaction; **trabajo en ~** assembly-line work ➤ **cadena alimenticia** food chain ➤ **cadena de ensamblaje** assembly line ➤ **cadena de fabricación** production line ➤ **cadena de montaje** assembly line ➤ **cadena de producción** production line 7 ➤ **cadena perpetua** (*Jur*) life imprisonment, life; **el juez**

lo condenó a ~ perpetua the judge sentenced him to life (imprisonment)
8 cadenas (*Aut*) tyre chains, tire chains (*EEUU*)

cadencia SF 1 (= *ritmo*) cadence, rhythm 2 (*Mús*) (*en frase musical*) cadence; [*de solista*] cadenza

cadencioso ADJ [*voz*] melodious; [*música*] rhythmic(al); [*andares*] swinging

cadeneta SF (*Cos*) chain stitch

cadera SF hip

cadete SM (*Mil*) cadet; (*Dep*) junior

cadmio SM cadmium

caducar /1g/ VI 1 (*Com, Jur*) to expire, lapse; [*permiso, plazo*] to run out; [*costumbre*] to fall into disuse; **el abono ha caducado** the season ticket has expired 2 [*comida*] **¿cuándo caduca el yogur?** what's the expiry date on that yogurt?; **está caducado** it's past its sell-by date

caducidad SF expiry, expiration (*EEUU*); **fecha de ~** (*gen*) expiry date, expiration date (*EEUU*); [*de alimentos*] expiry date, expiration date (*EEUU*), best-before date

caduco ADJ 1 (*Bot*) deciduous; **árbol de hoja caduca** deciduous tree 2 [*persona*] senile, decrepit 3 [*ideas*] outdated, outmoded 4 [*belleza*] faded 5 [*placer*] fleeting 6 (*Com, Jur*) lapsed, expired, invalid; **quedar ~** to lapse, be out of date, have expired

---

caer /2n/

Ⓐ VERBO INTRANSITIVO	Ⓑ VERBO PRONOMINAL

Para las expresiones **caer en la cuenta**, **caer en desuso**, **caer en el olvido**, **caer enfermo**, **caer redondo** *etc ver la entrada correspondiente a la otra palabra.*

caer Ⓐ VERBO INTRANSITIVO
1 [*persona, objeto*]
1.1 (*desde la posición vertical*) to fall; **me hice daño al ~** I fell and hurt myself; **cayó al suelo y se dio un golpe en la cabeza** he fell to the ground and hit his head; **tropezó y cayó de espaldas** she stumbled and fell on her back; **cayó muerto de un tiro** he was shot dead
1.2 (*desde una altura*) to fall; **cayó de un tercer piso** he fell from the third floor; **el niño cayó al río** the child fell into the river; **cayó una bomba en el mercado** a bomb fell on the market; **el avión cayó al mar** the plane came down in the sea; **el coche cayó por un barranco** the car went over a cliff; **dejar ~** [+ *objeto*] to drop; [+ *comentario*] to slip in; **dejó ~ la bandeja** she dropped the tray; **dejó ~ que estaba buscando otro trabajo** he let slip that he was looking for another job; **dejarse ~** (*sobre sofá, cama*) to fall; (= *visitar*) to drop in, drop by; **se dejó ~ sobre la cama** he fell onto the bed; **suele dejarse ~ por aquí** he usually drops in o by; ~ **sobre algo/algn** to fall on sth/sb; ✦ MODISMO **estar al ~** to be imminent; **su liberación está al ~** his release is imminent o is expected any day; **el jefe está al ~** the boss will be here any moment
2 [*lluvia, helada*] **la lluvia caía incesantemente sobre Madrid** the rain was falling continuously on Madrid; **cayó un chaparrón** there was a heavy shower; **cayó un rayo en la torre** the tower was struck by lightning
3 (= *colgar*) to hang, fall; **le caía un mechón sobre la frente** a lock of hair fell across his forehead
4 (= *bajar*) [*precio, temperatura*] to fall, drop; **el dólar cayó más de cinco centavos** the dollar fell o dropped more than five cents
5 (= *ser derrotado*) [*ciudad, plaza*] to fall, be captured; **ha caído el gobierno** the government has fallen
6 (= *morir*) to fall, die; **muchos cayeron en el campo de batalla** many fell o died on the field of battle; ✦ MODISMOS ~ **como chinches** ✧ ~ **como moscas** to drop like flies
7 ~ **en** (= *incurrir*): ~ **en un engaño** to be tricked; **no debemos ~ en el triunfalismo** we mustn't give way to triumphalism; ~ **en el error de hacer algo** to make the

mistake of doing sth

> Recuérdese que las preposiciones en inglés rigen gerundio y no infinitivo, de ahí **to make the mistake of doing sth**.

~ en la tentación to give in o yield to temptation; ✦ MODISMO **~ bajo: ¡qué bajo has caído!** (*moralmente*) how low can you get!, how can you sink so low?; (*socialmente*) you've certainly come down in the world! **8** (*) (= *darse cuenta*) **no caigo** I don't get it*, I don't understand; **ya caigo** I see, now I understand, now I get it* **9** [*fecha*] to fall, be; **su cumpleaños cae en viernes** her birthday falls o is on a Friday **10** (= *tocar*) **el gordo ha caído en Madrid** the first prize (in the lottery) o the jackpot went to Madrid; **~ a algn: le pueden ~ muchos años de condena** he could get a very long sentence; ✦ MODISMO **¡la que nos ha caído encima!** that's just what we needed! **11** (= *estar situado*) to be; **¿por dónde cae eso?** whereabouts is that? **12** – **dentro de** [+ *responsabilidad, apartado*] (= *estar comprendido en*) to fall within **13** (= *causar impresión*) **~ bien a algn: me cae (muy) bien** I (really) like him, I like him (very much); **~ gordo o fatal a algn*: me cae gordo o fatal el tío ése** I can't stand that guy; **~ mal a algn: me cae mal** I don't like him **14** (= *sentar*) **14.1** [*información, comentario*] **la noticia cayó como un mazazo** the news was a blow **14.2** [*ropa*] **~ bien a algn** to suit sb; **~ mal a algn** not to suit sb **15** (= *terminar*) **al ~ la noche** at nightfall; **al ~ la tarde** at dusk
Ⓑ caerse VERBO PRONOMINAL
1 [*persona, objeto*]
1.1 (*desde la posición vertical*) [*persona, objeto*] to fall over; [*edificio*] to collapse, fall (down); **¡cuidado, no te caigas!** mind you don't fall!; **se ha caído el perchero** the coat stand has fallen over; **el edificio se está cayendo** the building is falling down; **~se al suelo** to fall to the ground **1.2** (*desde una altura*) to fall; **se cayó al agua** she fell into the water; **se cayó por la ventana** he fell out of the window; **~se de algo** to fall off sth; **se cayó del caballo** he fell off his horse; **el niño se cayó de la cama** the child fell out of bed
1.3 **~se algo a algn: se me cayeron las monedas** I dropped the coins; **sin el botón se te van a ~ los pantalones** without the button your trousers (*Brit*) o pants (*EEUU*) will fall down **2** (= *desprenderse*) [*hoja*] to fall off; [*diente, pelo*] to fall out; **se me ha caído un botón de la chaqueta** a button has come off my jacket **3** **~se de: se cae de cansancio** he's so tired he could drop; **el edificio se cae de viejo** the building is so old it's falling to bits o it's on the point of collapsing

café SM **1** (= *bebida, planta*) coffee ➤ **café cerrero** (*Col*) strong black coffee ➤ **café completo** (*CS*) continental breakfast ➤ **café con leche** white coffee (*Brit*), coffee with cream (*EEUU*) ➤ **café cortado** coffee with a dash of milk ➤ **café descafeinado** decaffeinated coffee ➤ **café instantáneo** instant coffee ➤ **café irlandés** Irish coffee ➤ **café negro** black coffee ➤ **café solo** black coffee ➤ **café tinto** (*Col*) black coffee **2** (= *cafetería*) café, coffee shop **3** (*CS**) (= *reprimenda*) ticking-off* **4** (*tb* **color ~**) brown

cafeína SF caffein(e)

cafeinómano/a Ⓐ ADJ addicted to coffee o caffeine Ⓑ SM/F coffee o caffeine addict

cafetal SM coffee plantation

cafetalero/a Ⓐ ADJ coffee *antes de s*, coffee-growing; **industria cafetalera** coffee industry Ⓑ SM/F coffee grower

cafetalista SMF (*LAm*) coffee grower

café-teatro SM **1** (= *lugar*) café with live theatre **2** (= *espectáculo*) [*de variedades*] live entertainment; [*de comedia*] stand-up comedy

cafetera SF **1** (= *aparato*) coffee maker, coffee machine; (= *cacharro*) coffee pot; ✦ MODISMO **estar como una ~*** to be

---

crazy, be off one's head (*esp Brit**) ➤ **cafetera de filtro** filter coffee maker ➤ **cafetera exprés** espresso coffee maker **2** (*Aut**) jalop(p)y*, old banger (*Brit**); *ver tb* **cafetero**

cafetería SF (*gen*) café, coffee shop; (*en empresa*) canteen; (*Ferro*) buffet car (*Brit*), refreshment car (*EEUU*)

cafetero/a Ⓐ ADJ **1** [*finca, sector*] coffee *antes de s*; [*país*] coffee producing; **industria cafetera** coffee industry **2** (= *aficionado al café*) **soy muy ~** I really like (my) coffee Ⓑ SM/F (= *cultivador*) coffee grower; (= *comerciante*) coffee merchant; *ver tb* **cafetera**

cafeto SM coffee tree

cafiche* SM (*CS*) pimp

caficultor(a) SM/F (*CAm, Col*) coffee grower

cafre Ⓐ SMF savage; **como ~s** like savages, like beasts Ⓑ ADJ uncouth, boorish

cagada*** SF **1** (= *excremento*) shit***, crap***; **~s de perro** dog shit*** *sing* **2** (= *error*) fuck-up***, cock-up (*Brit***), screw-up (*EEUU***)

cagadera*** SF (*LAm*) = **cagalera**

cagado*** ADJ shit-scared***; **no se atreve a salir, está ~ de miedo** he daren't go out, he's shit-scared***

cagalera*** SF **tener ~** to have the shits*** o trots* o runs*

cagar*** /1h/ Ⓐ VI (= *defecar*) to shit***, have a shit***, take a shit (*EEUU***)
Ⓑ VT **1** ✦ MODISMO **~la** to blow it*, fuck up*** **2** (*RPl*) (= *perjudicar*) to mess about* **3** (*RPl*) (= *embromar*) to rip off*
Ⓒ **cagarse** VPR **1** to shit o.s.***; **se cagó en los pantalones** he crapped in his pants***, he shat himself (*esp Brit***) **2** ✦ MODISMOS **~se de miedo** to shit o.s.***; **~se en algn/algo: ¡me cago en diez o en la mar o en la leche!** shit!***, bloody hell! (*Brit***); **¡me cago en el gobierno!** to hell with o sod the government!*; **~se patas abajo: tenía tanto miedo que se cagó patas abajo** he was so frightened, he shat himself***; **que te cagas** (*como adj*) damn**, bloody (*Brit***); **hace un frío que te cagas** it's bloody freezing (*Brit***), it's frigging freezing***

cagarruta SF [*de animal*] pellet, dropping

cagón/ona*** SM/F **1** (= *cobarde*) wimp* **2** (= *bebé*) **ser un ~** to keep dirtying one's nappies

caguama SF (*Méx*) large turtle (*Brit*), large sea turtle (*EEUU*)

caída SF **1** (= *accidente*) fall; [*de caballo*] fall, tumble; **tuvo una aparatosa ~ de la bicicleta** he had a spectacular fall from his bicycle; **sufrir una ~** to have a fall, take a tumble **2** [*de gobierno, imperio*] fall, collapse; [*de un gobernante*] downfall; **la ~ del Muro de Berlín** the collapse o fall of the Berlin Wall; **la crisis ocasionó la ~ del gobierno** the crisis brought down the government **3** (= *pérdida*) [*de cabello, diente*] loss **4** (*Dep*) ➤ **caída al vacío, caída libre** free fall **5** (= *descenso*) [*de precios, ventas*] fall, drop; [*de divisa*] fall; **el gobierno está decidido a frenar la ~ de la peseta** the government is determined to curb the fall of the peseta; **~ de las temperaturas** drop in temperature; **~ de tensión** (*Med*) drop in blood pressure; (*Elec*) drop in voltage; **~ en picado** o **en picada** (*LAm*) sharp fall; **el banco intervino para evitar la ~ en picado del dólar** the bank intervened to stop the dollar taking a nose-dive o plummeting **6 a la ~ del sol** o **de la tarde** at sunset **7** (= *inclinación*) [*de terreno*] slope; (*brusco*) drop **8** [*de tela, ropa*] hang; **esta chaqueta tiene buena ~** this jacket hangs well ➤ **caída de hombros** slope of the shoulders

caído Ⓐ ADJ (*gen*) fallen; [*cabeza*] hanging; [*hombros*] drooping; [*cuello*] turndown; [*flor*] limp, drooping Ⓑ SM **los ~s** the fallen

caigo *etc ver* **caer**

caimán SM **1** (= *cocodrilo*) caiman, alligator **2** (*Méx Téc*) chain wrench

Caín SM Cain; ✦ MODISMO **pasar las de ~*** to go through hell*

Cairo SM **El ~** Cairo

caitearse* /1a/ VPR **caiteárselas** (*CAm*) to run away, beat it*

caja SF 1 (= *recipiente*) box; [*de cervezas, refrescos*] crate; **una ~ de cartón** a cardboard box; **la ~ tonta*** (= *tele*) the box (*Brit**), the boob tube (*EEUU**) ➤ **caja de cerillas** (*llena*) box of matches; (*vacía*) matchbox ➤ **caja de colores** box of crayons ➤ **caja de herramientas** toolbox ➤ **caja de Pandora** Pandora's box ➤ **caja de sorpresas** (= *juego*) jack-in-the-box; **ser una ~ de sorpresas** to be full of surprises ➤ **caja de zapatos** shoebox ➤ **caja negra** [*de avión*] black box
2 (*Com*) (*en supermercado*) checkout; (*en tienda*) till (*Brit*), cash desk (*Brit*), cashier's desk (*EEUU*); (*en banco*) window; **para pagar, pase por ~** (*en tienda*) please pay at the till (*Brit*) *o* cashier's desk (*EEUU*); (*en supermercado*) please pay at the checkout; **hacer ~** to cash up; **hicieron una ~ de 3.500 euros** they took (in) 3,500 euros; **ingresar en ~: hemos ingresado 1.500 pesos en ~** we have taken (in) 1,500 pesos ➤ **caja de ahorros** savings bank ➤ **caja de caudales** safe, strongbox ➤ **caja de pensiones** pension fund ➤ **caja fuerte** safe, strongbox ➤ **Caja Postal de Ahorros** ≈ Post Office Savings Bank ➤ **caja registradora** cash register, till (*Brit*)
3 [*de reloj*] case, casing; [*de radio, TV*] casing, housing; [*de fusil*] stock ➤ **caja de cambios** (*Mec*) gearbox ➤ **caja de fusibles** fuse box
4 (*Mús*) (= *tambor*) drum; [*de piano*] case; [*de violín*] soundbox ➤ **caja de música** music box ➤ **caja de resonancia** [*de instrumento*] soundbox ➤ **caja de ritmos** drum machine, beatbox*
5 (*Anat*) ➤ **caja torácica** thoracic cavity
6 (*) (= *ataúd*) box*, coffin ➤ **caja de muerto** coffin, casket (*EEUU*)

cajero/a SM/F (*gen*) cashier; (*en banco*) cashier, (bank) teller; (*en supermercado*) checkout operator 🅑 SM ➤ **cajero automático** cash machine (*Brit*), ATM (*EEUU*), automated teller machine (*EEUU*)

cajeta SF 1 (*CAm, Méx*) (*para untar*) caramel spread 2 (*RPl***) cunt***

cajetilla SF pack, packet (*esp Brit*) ➤ **cajetilla de tabaco** pack *o* (*esp Brit*) packet of cigarettes

cajón SM 1 [*de mueble*] drawer ➤ **cajón de sastre: esta sección es un ~ de sastre** this section is a bit of a ragbag *o* mixed bag 2 (= *caja grande*) big box, crate ➤ **cajón de embalaje** crate, packing case (*esp Brit*) *o* box (*esp EEUU*)
3 ✦ MODISMO **de ~*: eso es de ~** that goes without saying 4 (*And, CS*) (= *ataúd*) coffin, casket (*EEUU*) 5 (*LAm Geog*) ravine

cajuela SF (*Méx Aut*) boot (*Brit*), trunk (*EEUU*)

cal SF lime; ✦ MODISMOS **cerrar algo a ~ y canto** to shut sth firmly *o* securely; **dar una de ~ y otra de arena** to apply a policy of carrot and stick ➤ **cal viva** quicklime

cala SF cove

calabacín SM courgette (*Brit*), zucchini (*EEUU*)

calabacita SF 1 (*Méx*) courgette (*Brit*), zucchini (*EEUU*) 2 (*Arg*) butternut squash

calabaza SF 1 (*Bot*) pumpkin; (= *recipiente*) gourd, calabash 2 **dar ~s a** [+ *candidato, estudiante*] to fail; [+ *amante*] to jilt

calabobos* SM INV drizzle

calabozo SM (= *celda*) prison cell; (*Mil*) military prison; (*esp Hist*) dungeon

calada SF [*de tabaco*] puff, drag*

caladero SM fishing ground

calado 🅐 ADJ 1 (= *mojado*) soaked; **estar ~ (hasta los huesos)** to be soaked (to the skin) 2 (*Cos*) openwork *antes de s* 3 [*gorro*] **con la boina calada hasta las orejas** with his beret pulled down over his ears 4 [*bayoneta*] fixed 🅑 SM 1 (*Téc*) fretwork; (*Cos*) openwork 2 (*Náut*) depth of water; [*de barco*] draught, draft (*EEUU*); **un descubrimiento de gran ~** a very important discovery

calamar SM squid ➤ **calamares a la romana** squid rings fried in batter

calambre SM 1 (*muscular*) **me dan ~s** I get cramp 2 (*Elec*) shock; **un cable que da ~** a live wire

calamidad SF 1 (= *desastre*) calamity, disaster; **¡vaya ~!** what terrible luck! 2 (= *persona*) **es una ~** he's a hopeless

case*; **estar hecho una ~** to be in a very bad way

calamina SF 1 (*Med, Min*) calamine 2 (*Chi, Bol, Perú*) (= *chapa*) corrugated iron

calamitoso ADJ calamitous, disastrous

calandria SF (*Orn*) calandra lark

calaña SF sort; **gente de esa ~** people of that ilk *o* sort

calar /1a/ 🅐 VT 1 [*líquido, lluvia, humedad*] to soak (through); **la lluvia me caló la ropa** the rain soaked *o* drenched my clothes; **~ a algn (hasta) los huesos** to cut sb through to the bone
2 (*) (= *percatar*) to see through; **lo calé nada más conocerlo** I saw through him as soon as I'd met him
3 [+ *bayoneta*] to fix
4 [+ *mástil*] to fix, fit; [+ *vela*] to lower; [+ *red*] to cast
5 (*And*) (= *aplastar*) to crush, flatten; (= *humillar*) to humiliate
🅑 VI (= *penetrar*) **una ideología que está calando en la sociedad** an ideology that is catching on in society; **su mensaje caló hondo en nuestra generación** her message had a deep effect *o* made a deep impression on our generation
🅒 **calarse** VPR 1 (= *mojarse*) to get soaked, get drenched; **me calé hasta los huesos** I got soaked to the skin
2 [*material, ropa*] to let water in, get wet; [*zapatos*] to let water in; **esos zapatos se calan** those shoes let water in
3 (*Esp*) [*motor, vehículo*] to stall; **se le caló el coche** his car stalled
4 [+ *sombrero, gorra*] to pull down; [+ *gafas, careta*] to put on

calavera 🅐 SF 1 (*Anat*) skull 2 (*Méx Aut*) tail-light, rear light 🅑 SM (= *juerguista*) reveller; (= *libertino*) rake, roué

calcado 🅐 ADJ (= *idéntico*) **ser ~ a algo** to be just like sth; **ser ~ a algn** to be the spitting image of sb 🅑 SM (*Téc*) tracing

calcar /1g/ VT 1 (*Téc*) to trace, make a tracing of 2 (= *plagiar*) to copy, imitate

calcáreo ADJ calcareous, lime *antes de s*

calce SM wedge, shim

calceta SF **hacer ~** to knit

calcetín SM sock

calcificación SF calcification

calcificar /1g/ 🅐 VT to calcify 🅑 **calcificarse** VPR to calcify

calcinación SF calcination

calcinar /1a/ 🅐 VT (= *quemar*) to burn, reduce to ashes, blacken; **cuerpos calcinados** charred bodies; **murió calcinado** he burned to death 🅑 **calcinarse** VPR to calcine

calcio SM calcium

calco SM 1 (*Téc*) tracing 2 (*Ling*) calque (*de* on), loan translation (*de* from) 3 (= *imitación*) copy, imitation; **ser un ~ de algn** to be the spitting image of sb

calcomanía SF transfer, decal (*EEUU*)

calculador ADJ calculating

calculadora SF calculator

calcular /1a/ VT 1 (*Mat*) (*exactamente*) to calculate, work out; **debes ~ la cantidad exacta** you must calculate *o* work out the exact number; **~ la distancia entre dos puntos** to calculate *o* work out the distance between two points; **calculé mal la distancia y me caí** I misjudged the distance and fell
2 (*como estimación*) **~ que** to reckon (that); **¿cuánto calculas que puede costar?** how much do you reckon it might cost?; **calculo que llegará mañana** I reckon *o* (*esp EEUU*) figure he'll come tomorrow
3 (= *planear*) to work out, figure out; **lo calculó todo hasta el más mínimo detalle** he worked it all out down to the last detail
4 (*) (= *imaginar*) —**¿tienes ganas de ir?** —**¡calcula!** "are you looking forward to going?" — "what do you think? *o* you bet (I am)!"*

cálculo SM 1 (*gen*) calculation, reckoning; (= *conjetura*) estimate, conjecture; (*Mat*) calculus; **según mis ~s** by my reckoning, by my calculations ➤ **cálculo mental** mental arithmetic **2** (*Med*) stone ➤ **cálculo biliar** gallstone

Calcuta SF Calcutta

caldeado ADJ lively; **ambiente ~** (= *tenso*) heated atmosphere; **los ánimos estaban ~s** feelings were running high

caldear /1a/ **Ⓐ** VT (= *calentar*) to warm (up), heat (up); **~ los ánimos de la gente** to work people up **Ⓑ caldearse** VPR [*local*] to get hot; [*ambiente*] to get tense *o* heated

caldera SF **1** (*Téc*) boiler; (= *caldero*) cauldron; (*Uru*) kettle (*Brit*), tea kettle (*EEUU*) **2** (*And*) [*de volcán*] crater

caldereta SF [*de pescado*] fish stew; [*de cordero*] lamb stew

calderilla SF small change

caldero SM cauldron

calderón SM (*Mús*) pause (sign)

caldo SM **1** (= *sopa*) soup, broth; (= *consomé*) (clear) soup; ✦ MODISMO **poner a algn a ~*** (= *regañar*) to tell sb off, give sb a ticking-off (*Brit**) **2** [*para guisar*] stock; [*de guiso*] juice; **cubitos de ~** stock cubes ➤ **caldo de cultivo** (*Biol*) culture medium; (*fig*) breeding ground **3** (= *vino*) wine

caldoso ADJ **un guiso ~** a stew with plenty of liquid; **no debe quedar muy ~** it musn't be too liquid

calé Ⓐ ADJ gipsy *antes de s*, gypsy *antes de s* **Ⓑ** SMF gipsy, gypsy

calefacción SF heating ➤ **calefacción central** central heating

calefaccionar /1a/ VT (*CS*) to heat (up)

calefactor SM heater

calefón SM (*CS*) water heater, boiler

caleidoscopio SM kaleidoscope

calendario SM (*gen*) calendar; [*de reforma*] timetable; [*de trabajo*] schedule

caléndula SF marigold

calentador SM heater ➤ **calentador de agua** water heater ➤ **calentador de gas** gas-fired boiler, gas-fired water heater ➤ **calentador eléctrico** electric heater ➤ **calentadores de piernas** legwarmers

calentamiento SM **1** (= *acción*) (*a temperatura alta*) heating; (*a temperatura media*) warming; **a consecuencia de un ~ excesivo** as a result of overheating ➤ **calentamiento del planeta, calentamiento global** global warming **2** (*Dep*) warm-up

calentar /1j/ **Ⓐ** VT **1** [+ *líquido, metal, mineral, comida*] (*a temperatura alta*) to heat (up); (*a temperatura media*) to warm (up); **¿caliento un poco más la sopa?** shall I heat (up) the soup a bit more?; **estaban calentando piernas antes del partido** they were doing leg warm-up exercises before the match; **~ motores** (*lit*) to warm up the engines; (*fig*) to gather momentum; ✦ MODISMO **~ la cabeza** *o* **los cascos a algn*** to pester sb **2** (*) (*sexualmente*) to turn on* **3** (*esp LAm**) (= *enojar*) to make cross, make mad (*esp EEUU**) **4** (*) (= *zurrar*) **~ bien a algn** to give sb a good hiding **5** (*Chi**) [+ *examen, materia*] to cram for* **Ⓑ** VI **1** (= *dar calor*) [*sol*] to get hot; [*estufa, radiador, fuego*] to give off heat, give out heat; **cuando caliente más el sol** when the sun gets hotter; **el radiador apenas calienta** the radiator hardly gives off *o* gives out any heat **2** (*Dep*) to warm up, limber up **Ⓒ calentarse** VPR **1** (= *caldearse*) [*persona*] to warm o.s. up; [*plancha, sartén*] to heat up, get hot; [*habitación*] to warm up; [*motor, coche*] (*al encenderse*) to warm up; (*en exceso*) to overheat; **nos calentamos a la lumbre** we warmed ourselves up by the fire; ✦ MODISMO **~se la cabeza** *o* **los cascos (por algo)*** to agonize (about sth), fret (over sth) **2** (*) (= *exaltarse*) **los ánimos se ~on y acabaron a puñetazos** feelings began to run high *o* things got heated and it ended in a punch-up **3** (*) (*sexualmente*) to get turned on* **4** (*LAm**) (= *enojarse*) to get cross, get mad (*esp EEUU**) **5** (*RPI**) (= *disgustarse*) to get upset

calentura SF **1** (*Med*) fever, (high) temperature; **estar con** *o* **tener ~** to be feverish, have a temperature **2** (*en labios*)

cold sore (*esp Brit*), fever blister (*EEUU*) **3** (*RPI**) (= *furia*) anger

calenturiento ADJ **1** (*Med*) feverish **2** (= *impúdico*) dirty, prurient; (= *exaltado*) rash, impulsive; **las mentes calenturientas** (*Pol*) the hotheads

calesa SF chaise, calash, buggy

calesita SF (*Perú, CS*) merry-go-round, carousel (*EEUU*)

caleta SF **1** (*Geog*) cove, small bay, inlet **2** (*And*) (= *escondite*) cache

calibrado ADJ calibrated

calibrador SM gauge, gage (*EEUU*)

calibrar /1a/ VT (*Téc*) to calibrate; (*fig*) (= *evaluar*) to gauge, gage (*EEUU*), measure

calibre SM **1** (= *diámetro*) [*de bala, proyectil, casquillo, tubo*] calibre, caliber (*EEUU*); [*de pistola, rifle, cañón*] calibre, bore; **de alto** *o* **gran** *o* **grueso ~** large-bore; **de bajo** *o* **pequeño ~** small-bore; **casquillos del ~ 9 parabellum** 0.9 Parabellum cases **2** (= *importancia*) calibre; **no tenemos un poeta del ~ de Lorca** we do not have a poet of the calibre of Lorca; **tienen problemas de gran ~** they have problems of a serious nature **3** (*CS*) **palabras de grueso ~** foul language *sing*; **un chiste de grueso ~** a crude joke

caliche SM (*LAm*) saltpetre bed, caliche

calidad SF **1** [*de objeto, material, producto*] quality; [*de servicio*] quality, standard; **han mejorado la ~ de la enseñanza** they have improved the quality *o* standard of education, they have raised standards in education; **de (buena) ~** good-quality, quality *antes de s*; **vinos de ~** quality wines; **de mala ~** low-quality, poor-quality ➤ **calidad de vida** quality of life **2** (= *condición*) position, status; **en ~ de: te lo digo en ~ de amigo** I'm telling you as a friend

cálido ADJ (*gen*) hot; [*color, sonrisa*] warm; [*aplausos*] enthusiastic

calidoscopio SM kaleidoscope

calienta *etc ver* **calentar**

calientabiberones SM INV bottle warmer

calientapiernas SMPL legwarmers

calientaplatos SM INV hotplate, plate warmer

calientapollas*** SF INV (*Esp*) prick-teaser***, pricktease***, cock-teaser***

caliente ADJ **1** (= *que quema*) hot; **un café bien ~** a piping hot coffee; **comer ~** to have a hot meal, have some hot food; ✦ MODISMOS **en ~: tuvo que responderle en ~** he had to answer him there and then *o* on the spur of the moment; **agarrar a algn en ~** (*Méx**) to catch sb red-handed **2** (= *no frío*) warm; **esta cerveza está ~** this beer is warm; **si te abrigas con la manta estarás más calentito** if you wrap the blanket around you, you'll feel warmer; **me gusta el pan calentito** I like my bread nice and warm **3** (*en juegos*) warm; **¡caliente, caliente!** warm!, getting warmer! **4** (*) (*en sentido sexual*) **poner ~ a algn** to turn sb on*, make sb horny**

califa SM caliph

califato SM caliphate

calificación SF **1** (*Escol*) grade, mark **2** (= *descripción*) description **3** (= *posición*) rating, standing

calificado ADJ (= *competente*) qualified, competent; [*obrero*] skilled

calificar /1g/ VT **1 ~ algo/a algn como** *o* **de algo** to describe sth/sb as sth, call sb/sth sth; **calificó su política como** *o* **de racismo encubierto** he described their policy as covert racism, he called their policy covert racism **2** (*Escol*) [+ *examen*] to mark, grade (*EEUU*); [+ *alumno*] to give a mark to, give a grade to (*EEUU*)

calificativo Ⓐ ADJ qualifying **Ⓑ** SM **sólo merece el ~ de ...** it can only be described as ...; **lo que han hecho estos gamberros no tiene ~s** what these hooligans have done beggars belief

californiano/a ADJ, SM/F Californian

calígine SF (*poét*) (= *neblina*) mist; (= *oscuridad*) gloom

caligrafía SF (= *arte*) calligraphy; (= *letra*) handwriting

calima SF haze, mist

calimocho SM wine and cola

cáliz SM 1 (*Rel*) chalice, communion cup; (= *copa*) goblet, cup 2 (*Bot*) calyx

caliza SF limestone

calizo ADJ **piedra caliza** limestone; **tierra caliza** limy soil

callado ADJ 1 [*persona*] quiet; **se quedó ~** he didn't say a word, he was silent; **¡qué ~ te lo tenías!** you kept pretty quiet about it! 2 [*carácter*] quiet, reserved

callampa SF (*Chi*) 1 (= *hongo*) mushroom 2 **callampas** (= *suburbios*) shanty town *sing*

callandito* ADV softly, very quietly

callar /1a/ Ⓐ VI 1 (= *dejar de hablar*) to be quiet; **su madre le mandó ~** his mother ordered him to be quiet, his mother told him to shut up; **—Ernesto se casa —¡calla! ¡eso no puede ser!** "Ernesto is getting married" — "you're joking! that can't be true!"
2 (= *no hablar*) to say nothing, keep quiet; **al principio optó por ~** initially he decided to say nothing *o* keep quiet; ✦ REFRÁN **quien calla, otorga** silence is *o* gives *o* implies consent
Ⓑ VT (= *ocultar*) to keep to o.s., keep quiet; **será mejor ~ este asunto** it's best to keep this matter to ourselves *o* keep this matter quiet
Ⓒ **callarse** VPR 1 (= *dejar de hablar*) to stop talking, go quiet; **¡cállense, por favor!** please be quiet!; **¡cállate!** shut up!*
2 (= *no decir nada*) to say nothing, keep quiet; **en esas circunstancias es mejor ~se** in those circumstances, it's best to say nothing *o* keep quiet

calle SF 1 (= *vía pública*) (*gen*) street; (*con más tráfico*) road; **~ abajo** down the street; **~ arriba** up the street;
✦ MODISMOS **se los lleva a todos de ~*** they just can't stay away from her, they find her irresistible; **llevar** *o* **traer a algn por la ~ de la amargura*** to make sb's life a misery* ➤ **calle cerrada** (*Ven, Col, Méx*), **calle ciega** (*Ven, Col*), **calle cortada** (*RPI*) dead end, cul-de-sac (*Brit*) ➤ **calle de doble sentido** two-way street ➤ **calle de sentido único, calle de una mano** (*RPI*), **calle de una sola vía** (*Col*), **calle de un solo sentido** (*Chi*) one-way street ➤ **calle peatonal** pedestrianized street, pedestrian street ➤ **calle principal** main street ➤ **calle sin salida** dead end, cul-de-sac (*Brit*)
2 (= *no casa*) 2.1 **la ~: he estado todo el día en la ~** I've been out all day; **a los dos días de su detención ya estaba otra vez en la ~** two days after his arrest he was back on the streets again; **el grupo tiene ya tres discos en la ~** the group already have three records out; **irse a la ~** to go out, go outside; **salir a la ~** (= *persona*) to go outside; (= *disco, publicación*) to come out; **llevo varios días sin salir a la ~** I haven't been out of the house *o* outside for several days; **el periódico salió ayer a la ~ por última vez** the paper came out yesterday for the last time; ✦ MODISMOS **dejar a algn en la ~** to put sb out of a job; **echar a algn a la ~** to throw sb out on the street; **echarse a la ~** to take to the streets; **hacer la ~** (*euf*) to walk the streets; **poner a algn (de patitas) en la ~*** to kick sb out; **quedarse en la ~** (= *sin trabajo*) to be out of a job; (= *sin vivienda*) to be homeless 2.2 **de ~: ropa de ~** everyday clothes *pl*
3 **la ~** (= *gente*) the public; **vamos a oír ahora la opinión de la ~** we're now going to hear what members of the public think
4 (*Natación, Atletismo*) lane; (*Golf*) fairway

calleja SF = **callejuela**

callejear /1a/ VI to wander (about) the streets, stroll around; (*pey*) to loaf around, hang about

callejero Ⓐ ADJ 1 (*gen*) street *antes de s*; **disturbios ~s** street riots 2 [*persona*] **son muy ~s** they are always out and about Ⓑ SM (*guía*) street directory, street plan

callejón SM (= *calleja*) alley, passage; (*Taur*) space between inner and outer barriers; **gente de ~** (*And*) low-class people ➤ **callejón sin salida** dead end, cul-de-sac (*Brit*); (*fig*) blind alley; **las negociaciones están en un ~ sin salida** the negotiations are at an impasse *o* a stalemate

callejuela SF (= *calle*) side street, small street; (= *pasaje*) alley, passage

callicida SM corn cure

callista SMF chiropodist (*Brit*), podiatrist (*EEUU*)

callo SM 1 (*Med*) [*de pie*] corn; [*de mano*] callus, callosity (*frm*); ✦ MODISMO **dar el ~** (*Esp**) to slog, work hard, slave away* 2 (*) (= *persona fea*) **Juan es un ~** Juan is as ugly as sin 3 **callos** (*Culin*) tripe *sing*

callosidad SF callosity (*frm*), hard patch (*on hand etc*)

calloso ADJ calloused, rough

calma SF 1 (= *tranquilidad*) calm; **¡calma!** (*en una discusión*) calm down!; (*ante un peligro*) keep calm!; **hubo un periodo de ~ entre las elecciones municipales y las legislativas** there was a lull between the local and the general elections; **con ~** calmly; **conservar** *o* **mantener la ~** to keep calm, stay calm; **perder la ~** to lose one's cool*; **tomárselo con ~** to take it easy*
2 (= *relajo excesivo*) **me atendieron con una ~ increíble** they served me in a very relaxed fashion
3 (*Náut, Meteo*) calm; **navegamos con la mar en ~** we sailed in a calm sea ➤ **calma chicha** dead calm

calmado ADJ calm; **estar ~** to be calm; **sería mejor esperar a que las cosas estén más calmadas** it would be better to wait until things have calmed down *o* are calmer

calmante Ⓐ ADJ soothing, sedative Ⓑ SM (= *analgésico*) painkiller; (= *sedante*) sedative, tranquillizer

calmar /1a/ Ⓐ VT 1 (= *relajar*) [+ *persona*] to calm (down); [+ *ánimos*] to calm; [+ *nervios*] to calm, steady; **estas pastillas le ayudarán a ~ la ansiedad** these pills will help reduce *o* relieve your anxiety 2 (= *aliviar*) [+ *dolor, picor*] to relieve; [+ *tos*] to soothe; [+ *sed*] to quench Ⓑ **calmarse** VPR 1 [*persona*] to calm down; **¡cálmese!** calm down! 2 (*Meteo*) [*viento*] to drop; [*olas*] to calm down

calmo ADJ (*esp LAm*) calm

calmoso ADJ 1 (= *tranquilo*) calm 2 (= *lento*) slow, sluggish

caló SM gipsy dialect, gypsy dialect

calor SM (A VECES SF) 1 (= *alta temperatura*) heat; **no puedo dormir con este ~** I can't sleep in this heat; **un material resistente al ~** a heat-resistant material; **¡qué ~!** it's really hot!; **nos sentamos al ~ de la chimenea** we sat by the heat of the fire, we sat by the warm fireside; **dar ~:** **esta camiseta me da demasiado ~** this shirt is too hot *o* warm; **entrar en ~** to get warm; **hacer ~** to be hot; **hace muchísimo ~** it's very hot; **pasar ~** to be hot; **nunca he pasado tanto ~ como hoy** I've never been *o* felt as hot as today; **tener ~** to be hot
2 (= *afecto*) warmth and affection ➤ **calor humano** human warmth
3 **calores** [*de la menopausia*] hot flushes (*Brit*), hot flashes (*EEUU*)

caloría SF calorie

calorífico ADJ calorific

calostro SM colostrum

calumnia SF (= *difamación*) slander, calumny (*frm*); (*Jur*) (*oral*) slander (**de** of); (*escrita*) libel (**de** on)

calumniar /1b/ VT (= *difamar*) to slander; (*en prensa*) to libel

caluroso ADJ [*día, tiempo*] warm, hot; [*recibimiento*] warm, enthusiastic; [*aplausos*] enthusiastic

calva SF (= *cabeza*) bald head; (= *parte sin pelo*) bald patch; (*en alfombra, piel, tela*) bare patch, worn place; [*de bosque*] clearing

calvario SM 1 (= *via crucis*) Stations of the Cross *pl* ➤ **el Calvario** (*Biblia*) Calvary 2 (= *martirio*) torment; **pasar un ~** to suffer agonies

calvicie SF baldness

calvinismo SM Calvinism

calvinista ADJ, SMF Calvinist

calvo/a Ⓐ ADJ [*persona*] bald; **quedarse ~** to go bald Ⓑ SM/F bald man/woman

calza SF 1 (*Mec*) wedge, chock 2 (*Col*) [*de diente*] filling

calzada SF road; **el coche se salió de la ~** the car went off *o* left the road ➤ **calzada romana** Roman road

calzado ⒶADJ iba calzada con unos zapatos rojos she was wearing red shoes **ⒷSM** footwear; **fábrica de ~** shoe factory

calzador SM shoehorn

calzar /1f/ **ⒶVT 1** [+ *zapatos, botas etc*] (= *llevar*) to wear; **¿qué número calza usted?** what size shoes do you wear *o* take?, what size do you take? **2** [+ *persona*] (= *colocar calzado*) to put shoes on; (= *proveer de calzado*) to provide with footwear, supply with shoes **3** [*Téc*] [+ *rueda*] to scotch, chock; (*con cuña*) to put a wedge (under) **4** (*Col*) [+ *diente, muela*] to fill **Ⓑcalzarse VPR** to put one's shoes on

calzo SM 1 (*gen*) wedge; (*Mec*) shoe, brake-shoe; (*Náut*) skid, chock **2** (*Ftbl*) professional foul (*euf*)

calzón SM 1 (*Esp*) (= *pantalón corto*) shorts *pl* **2** (*LAm*) (= *ropa interior*) [*de mujer*] panties *pl*, knickers *pl* (*Brit*); [*de hombre*] underpants, pants (*Brit*), shorts (*EEUU*)

calzonazos* SM INV (= *marido*) henpecked husband; (= *débil*) wimp*

calzoncillos SMPL underpants, pants (*Brit*), shorts (*EEUU*)

calzonudo* ADJ (*And, CAm, CS*) (= *débil*) weak-willed, timid; (= *dominado*) under the thumb*

cama SF 1 (= *mueble*) bed; **una habitación con dos ~s** a room with twin beds, a twin-bedded room (*esp Brit*); **está en la ~ durmiendo** he's asleep in bed, he's in bed sleeping; **caer en ~** to fall ill; **estar en ~** to be in bed; **guardar ~** to stay in bed; **hacer la ~** to make the bed; **irse a la ~** to go to bed; **llevarse a algn a la ~** to get sb into bed; **meterse en la ~** to go to bed ➤ **cama de agua** water bed ➤ **cama de matrimonio** double bed ➤ **cama doble** double bed ➤ **cama elástica** trampoline ➤ **cama individual** single bed ➤ **cama litera** bunk bed ➤ **cama nido** truckle bed, trundle bed (*EEUU*) ➤ **cama plegable** folding bed ➤ **cama redonda** group sex ➤ **cama turca** divan bed **2** (*Geol*) layer

camada SF litter, brood

camafeo SM cameo

camaleón SM chameleon

camaleónico ADJ chameleon-like

camanchaca* SF (*And*) thick fog, pea-souper*

cámara Ⓐ SF 1 [*de fotos, televisión*] camera; **a** *o* **en** (*LAm*) **~ lenta** in slow motion ➤ **cámara de cine** film (*esp Brit*) *o* movie (*esp EEUU*) camera ➤ **cámara de fotos** camera ➤ **cámara de vídeo, cámara de video** (*LAm*) video camera ➤ **cámara digital** digital camera ➤ **cámara fotográfica** camera ➤ **cámara oculta** hidden camera ➤ **cámara oscura** camera obscura
2 (†) (= *habitación*) chamber ➤ **cámara acorazada** [*de archivo*] strongroom, vaults *pl*; [*de banco*] vaults *pl* ➤ **cámara de gas** (*de ejecución*) gas chamber ➤ **cámara de tortura** torture chamber ➤ **cámara frigorífica** cold-storage room, refrigerated container ➤ **cámara mortuoria** funeral chamber
3 (*Pol*) house, chamber ➤ **Cámara de Comercio** Chamber of Commerce ➤ **Cámara de los Comunes** House of Commons ➤ **Cámara de (los) Diputados** Chamber of Deputies ➤ **Cámara de los Lores** House of Lords ➤ **Cámara de Representantes** House of Representatives ➤ **Cámara de Senadores** Senate
4 [*de neumático*] (inner) tube; **cubierta sin ~** tubeless tyre, tubeless tire (*EEUU*)
5 (*Mec*) ➤ **cámara de combustión** combustion chamber ➤ **cámara de compresión** compression chamber ➤ **cámara de oxígeno** oxygen tent
ⒷSMF camera operator, cameraman/camerawoman

camarada SMF 1 (*en partido político*) comrade **2** (*en el trabajo*) colleague; (*en el colegio*) school friend **3** (= *amigo*) pal*, mate (*Brit**), buddy (*EEUU**)

camaradería SF (*entre amigos*) camaraderie, matiness*; (*en deportes*) camaraderie, team spirit; (*en partido político*) comradeship

camarera SF (*en hotel*) maid, chambermaid

camarero/a SM/F 1 (*en restaurante*) waiter/waitress

2 (*Náut*) steward/stewardess; (*Aer*) steward/stewardess, flight attendant

camarilla SF 1 [*de presidente*] entourage; (*pey*) clique, coterie **2** (*en organización*) faction

camarín SM 1 (*CS Teat*) dressing room **2** (*LAm*) [*de tren*] sleeping compartment; [*de barco*] cabin

camarógrafo/a SM/F cameraman/camerawoman

camarón SM shrimp

camarote SM cabin

camastro SM rickety old bed

cambalache SM 1 (= *trueque*) swap, exchange **2** (*LAm*) (= *tienda*) second-hand shop, junk shop

cambiado ADJ 1 (= *diferente*) **estás muy cambiada desde la última vez que te vi** you've really changed since the last time I saw you **2** (= *intercambiado*) reversed; **sus padres tenían los papeles ~s** his parents' roles were reversed

cambiante ADJ [*situación*] changing; [*tiempo, viento*] changeable; [*persona, carácter*] moody

cambiar /1b/ **ⒶVT 1** (= *modificar*) to change; **eso no cambia mucho las cosas** that doesn't change things much **2** (= *intercambiar*) to exchange, swap*; **~ algo por algo** to exchange *o* swap* sth for sth; **¿me cambias el sitio?** can we change places?, can we swap places?*
3 (= *reemplazar*) to change; **ha ido a ~le los pañales al niño** she's gone to change the baby's nappy (*Brit*) *o* diaper (*EEUU*); **¿me puede ~ este por otra talla?** could I change *o* exchange this for another size?
4 (= *trasladar*) to move; **nos van a ~ de aula** they are moving us to another classroom
5 (*Fin, Com*) to change; **tengo que ~ 100 euros en** *o* (*LAm*) **a libras** I have to change 100 euros into pounds; **¿tienes para ~me 10 pesos?** have you got change for a 10-peso note?
Ⓑ VI 1 (= *volverse diferente*) [*persona, situación*] to change; [*voz*] to break; **si es así, la cosa cambia** if it's true, that changes things, well that's a different story then; **con doce años ya le había cambiado la voz** his voice had already broken at the age of twelve
2 ~ de [+ *actitud, canal, dirección*] to change; [+ *casa*] to move; **cuando no le interesa algo, cambia de tema** whenever he isn't interested in something, he changes the subject; **necesitas ~ de aires** you need a change of scene; **~ de dueño** to change hands; **~ de idea** *u* **opinión** to change one's mind
3 (*Transporte*) to change; **tienes que ~ en King's Cross** you have to change at King's Cross
4 (*Radio*) **¡cambio!** over!; **¡cambio y corto!** ◇ **¡cambio y fuera!** over and out!
Ⓒ cambiarse VPR 1 [*persona*] to change, get changed; **me cambio y estoy lista** I'll just change *o* I'll just get changed and then I'll be ready
2 [+ *peinado, ropa, camisa*] to change; **¿te has cambiado el peinado?** have you changed your hairstyle?
3 ~se de algo to change sth; **tuve que ~me de chaqueta** I had to change jackets; **~se de casa** to move house
4 (= *intercambiarse*) to exchange, swap*; **siempre están cambiándose la ropa** they are always borrowing each other's clothes; **no me ~ía por ella** I wouldn't want to swap* *o* change places with her

cambiario ADJ exchange rate *antes de s*; **estabilidad cambiaria** exchange rate stability

cambiazo* SM 1 (*Com*) switch; **dar el ~ a algn** to switch the goods on sb; **dar el ~ en un examen** to cheat in an exam

cambio SM 1 (= *modificación*) change; **ha habido un ~ de planes** there has been a change of plan; **necesito un ~ de aires** I need a change of scene; **un ~ para mejor/peor** a change for the better/worse ➤ **cambio de agujas** (*Ferro*) points *pl* (*Brit*), switch (*EEUU*); **hacer un ~ de agujas** to change the points (*Brit*) *o* switch (*EEUU*) ➤ **cambio de guardia** changing of the guard ➤ **cambio de impresiones** exchange of views ➤ **cambio de marchas** (= *acción*) gear change; (= *mecanismo*) gear stick (*Brit*), gearshift (*EEUU*); **un coche con ~ automático de marchas** a car with an automatic gearbox ➤ **cambio de opinión** change of opinion, turn in opinion ➤ **cambio de rasante: prohibido adelantar en un ~ de rasante** no overtaking on the brow of a hill ➤ **cambio de sentido** change of direction ➤ **cambio de sexo** sex change ➤ **cambio de velocidades** = **cambio de marchas**

2 (= *intercambio*) exchange, swap*; **salimos ganando con el ~** the exchange worked out in our favour

3 (*Fin*) **3.1** (= *dinero suelto*) change; **¿tienes ~ de 20 euros?** do you have change for 20 euros?, can you change 20 euros?; **quédese con el ~** keep the change **3.2** [*de moneda extranjera*] (= *tipo*) exchange rate; **son 40 dólares al ~** that is 40 dollars at the current exchange rate; **"Cambio"** "Bureau de Change", "Change" ➤ **cambio de divisas** foreign exchange

4 a ~ in return, in exchange; **a ~ de** in return for, in exchange for; **reclamaba dinero a ~ de su silencio** he demanded money in return o exchange for keeping quiet (about it)

5 en ~ whereas; **yo nunca llego a tiempo, en ~ ella es muy puntual** I never arrive on time, whereas she is very punctual

cambista SMF money changer

Camboya SF Cambodia

camboyano/a ADJ, SM/F Cambodian

cambur SM (*Ven*) banana

camelar /1a/ VT to cajole, win over; **tener camelado a algn** to have sb wrapped around one's little finger

camelia SF camellia

camello SM **1** (*Zool*) camel **2** (******) (= *traficante*) dealer*, pusher*

camellón SM (*Méx*) central reservation (*Brit*), median strip (*EEUU*)

camelo* SM **1** (= *timo*) swindle; **¡esto es un ~!** it's all a swindle! **2** (= *mentira*) humbug; **a mí me da que es un ~** I don't believe a word of it*

camerino SM (*Teat*) dressing room

Camerún SM Cameroon

camilla SF (*Med*) stretcher; (= *mesa*) table with a heater underneath

camillero/a SM/F stretcher-bearer

caminante SMF traveller, traveler (*EEUU*), wayfarer (*liter*)

caminar /1a/ ❹ VI **1** (= *andar*) to walk; **iban caminando por el parque** they were walking in the park; **hemos venido caminando** we walked (here), we came on foot; **salen a ~ después de comer** they go (out) for a walk after lunch; **~ sin rumbo** to walk o wander about aimlessly

2 (= *progresar*) to move; **caminamos hacia una sociedad sin clases** we are moving towards a classless society

3 (*LAm*) (= *funcionar*) to work; **esto no camina** this doesn't work

❺ VT to walk; **caminamos cuatro kilómetros** we walked four kilometres

caminata SF (= *paseo largo*) long walk; (= *campestre*) hike, ramble

caminero ADJ **peón ~** road labourer, road laborer (*EEUU*)

camino SM **1** (*sin asfaltar*) track; (= *sendero*) path; (= *carretera*) road; **~ de tierra** dirt track; ✦ MODISMO **todos los ~s conducen a Roma** all roads lead to Rome ➤ **camino de rosas**: **la vida no es ningún ~ de rosas** life's no bed of roses ➤ **Camino de Santiago** pilgrims' route to Santiago de Compostela, Way of St James ➤ **camino forestal** (*para vehículos*) forest track; (*para paseos*) forest trail ➤ **Caminos, Canales y Puertos** (*Univ*) Civil Engineering ➤ **camino trillado**: **experimentan con nuevas técnicas, huyen de los ~s trillados** they experiment with new techniques and avoid conventional approaches o the well-trodden paths ➤ **camino vecinal** minor road

2 (= *ruta*) way, route; (= *viaje*) journey; **volvimos por el ~ más corto** we took the shortest way o route back; **iba ~ de Nueva York** I was on my way to New York; **abrirse ~ entre la multitud** to make one's way through the crowd; **de ~:** el banco me queda de ~ the bank is on my way; **está a varios días de ~** it's several days' journey away; **después de tres horas de ~** after travelling for three hours; **en ~: tienen dos niños, y otro en ~** they have two children, and another on the way; **ponerse en ~** to set out o off; **a medio ~** halfway

(there); **a medio ~ paramos para comer** halfway there, we stopped to eat

3 (= *medio*) path, course; **el ~ a la fama** the path to fame; **el ~ al desastre** the road to ruin; **el ~ a seguir: me indicaron el ~ a seguir para resolver el problema** they showed me what needed to be done to solve the problem; ✦ MODISMOS **abrirse ~ en la vida** to get ahead (in life); **allanar el ~: eso sería allanar el ~ a sus adversarios** that would make things easy for their rivals; **ir ~ de: va ~ de convertirse en un gran centro financiero** it is on its way to becoming a major financial centre; **vamos ~ del desastre** we are heading for disaster; **ir por buen ~** to be on the right track; **las cosas van por buen ~** things are going well; **ir por mal ~** to be on the wrong track; **quedarse en el ~: varios corredores se quedaron en el ~** several runners didn't make it to the end; **tirar por el ~ de en medio** to take the middle way

---

CAMINO DE SANTIAGO

The **Camino de Santiago** is a medieval pilgrim route stretching from the Pyrenees to Santiago de Compostela in northwest Spain, where tradition has it that the body of Saint James the Apostle (Spain's patron saint) is buried. Those who had made the long, dangerous journey returned proudly wearing on their hat or cloak the **venera** or **concha** (scallop shell) traditionally associated with this pilgrimage - Saint James' body had reportedly been found covered in scallops.

---

camión SM **1** (= *vehículo*) [*de carga*] lorry (*Brit*), truck (*esp EEUU*); [*de reparto*] van; ✦ MODISMO **estar como un ~** (*Esp**) to be a smasher*, be gorgeous ➤ **camión articulado** articulated lorry (*Brit*), trailer truck (*EEUU*) ➤ **camión cisterna** tanker, tank wagon ➤ **camión de carga** haulage truck (*esp Brit*), freight truck (*EEUU*) ➤ **camión de la basura** dustcart (*Brit*), garbage truck (*EEUU*) ➤ **camión de mudanzas** removal van (*Brit*), moving van (*EEUU*) ➤ **camión de reparto** delivery van ➤ **camión de riego** water cart, water wagon ➤ **camión de volteo** (*Méx*) dump truck ➤ **camión frigorífico** refrigerator lorry, refrigerated truck

2 (= *carga*) lorryload (*Brit*), truckload (*esp EEUU*); **dos camiones de alimentos** two lorryloads (*Brit*) o truckloads (*esp EEUU*) of food

3 (*Méx*) (= *autobús*) bus

camionero/a SM/F **1** lorry driver (*Brit*), truck driver (*EEUU*) **2** (*Méx*) (*en autobús*) bus driver

camioneta SF (= *camión*) van, light truck; (= *coche*) estate car (*Brit*), station wagon (*EEUU*) ➤ **camioneta de reparto** delivery van

camisa SF **1** (= *prenda*) shirt; ✦ MODISMOS **jugarse hasta la ~** to put one's shirt on it*, bet one's last penny; **no llegar a algn la ~ al cuerpo: no le llegaba la ~ al cuerpo** he was simply terrified; **meterse en ~ de once varas** to get into it way over one's head; **perder hasta la ~** to lose everything, lose the shirt off one's back ➤ **camisa de dormir** nightdress (*Brit*), nightgown (*EEUU*) ➤ **camisa de fuerza** straitjacket **2** [*de libro*] dust jacket

camisería SF (= *tienda*) outfitter's (*esp Brit*), haberdasher's (*EEUU*); (= *taller*) shirtmaker's

camisero ADJ **vestido ~** shirtwaister, shirt dress

camiseta SF **1** (*interior*) vest (*Brit*), singlet (*Brit*), undershirt (*EEUU*); (*exterior*) T-shirt; **una ~ sin mangas** a sleeveless T-shirt; **una ~ de tirantes** a vest (*Brit*), an undershirt (*EEUU*); ✦ MODISMO **ponerse la ~** (*CS**) to roll up one's sleeves, put one's back into it **2** (*Dep*) shirt, jersey, strip ➤ **camiseta de deporte** sports shirt, sports jersey

camisón SM nightdress (*Brit*), nightgown (*EEUU*)

camomila SF camomile

camorra* SF fight; **armar ~** to make trouble, pick a fight; **buscar ~** to go looking for trouble o a fight

camorrista ❹ ADJ rowdy, troublemaking ❺ SMF rowdy, hooligan

camote SM **1** (*And, Méx*) (= *batata*) sweet potato; (*Méx*) (= *bulbo*) tuber, bulb **2** (*SAm*) (= *enamoramiento*) crush*

3 (*CAm, Méx**) **poner a algn como** ~ (= *regañar*) to give sb a telling off*; (*en juego*) to beat sb hands down*

campal ADJ **batalla** ~ pitched battle

campamento SM camp, encampment ➤ **campamento de refugiados** refugee camp ➤ **campamento de verano** holiday camp

campana SF **1** [*de iglesia, puerta*] bell; [*de orquesta*] bell, chime; ✦ MODISMOS **echar** *o* **lanzar las ~s a vuelo** to celebrate; **hacer de** ~ (*And, RPI*) to keep watch; **oír** ~**s (y no saber dónde)** not to have a clue ➤ **campana de buzo**, **campana de inmersión** diving bell **2** [*de chimenea*] hood ➤ **campana de humos**, **campana extractora** extractor hood

campanada SF **1** [*de campana*] stroke, peal **2** (= *escándalo*) scandal, sensation; **dar la** ~ to cause (quite) a stir

campanario SM belfry, bell tower, church tower

campanazo SM = **campanada**

campanear* /1a/ VI (*And, RPI*) [*ladrón*] to keep watch

campanero SM (*Téc*) bell founder; (*Mús*) bell ringer

campanilla SF **1** (= *campana*) small bell, handbell; (*eléctrica*) bell; ✦ MODISMO **de (muchas) ~s** high-class, grand **2** (= *burbuja*) bubble **3** (*Anat*) uvula **4** (*Bot*) bellflower, campanula

campante ADJ **siguió tan** ~ he went on as if nothing had happened *o* without batting an eyelid; **allí estaba tan** ~ there he sat as cool as a cucumber

campaña SF **1** (*Pol, Com*) campaign; **una** ~ **antidroga** an anti-drugs campaign, a campaign against drugs; **una** ~ **de recogida de firmas** a petition; **hacer** ~ to campaign ➤ **campaña de descrédito**, **campaña de desprestigio** smear campaign ➤ **campaña electoral** election campaign ➤ **campaña publicitaria** advertising campaign **2** (*Mil*) campaign

campar /1a/ VI ~ **a sus anchas** to roam free; ~ **por sus respetos** to please o.s.

campechano ADJ (= *cordial*) good-natured, cheerful, genial; (= *franco*) frank, open

campeón/ona SM/F champion

campeonato SM **1** (*Dep*) championship **2** (*Esp**) **de** ~: **se agarra unas borracheras de** ~ he gets incredibly *o* unbelievably drunk, he gets blind drunk*

campera SF (*RPI*) windcheater, bomber jacket*

campero Ⓐ ADJ **fiesta campera** open-air party Ⓑ SM (*Col*) (= *vehículo*) four-wheel drive (vehicle)

campesinado SM peasantry, peasants *pl*

campesino/a Ⓐ ADJ [*población*] rural; [*familia, revuelta*] peasant *antes de s* Ⓑ SM/F **1** (= *persona del campo*) countryman/countrywoman **2** (= *agricultor*) farmer; (*pey*) peasant

campestre ADJ country *antes de s*, rural

camping ['kampin] SM (*pl* ~**s** ['kampin]) **1** (= *actividad*) camping; **ir de** ~ to go camping; **hacer** ~ to go camping **2** (= *lugar*) campsite, campground (*EEUU*)

campiña SF countryside

campista SMF camper

campo SM **1** (= *terreno no urbano*) **el** ~ the country; **viven en el** ~ they live in the country *o* countryside; **la gente del** ~ country people *o* folk; **los obreros del** ~ farm workers, agricultural workers; **los productos del** ~ farm produce, country produce; **trabajar en el** ~ to work the land; ~ **a través** cross-country **2** (= *terreno acotado*) **un** ~ **de trigo** a wheat field; ~**s de amapolas** poppy fields ➤ **campo de cultivo** farm land **3** (*Dep*) (= *estadio*) ground; (= *cancha*) field, pitch (*Brit*); **jugaron en el** ~ **del Barcelona** they played at Barcelona's ground; **el portero tuvo que abandonar el** ~ the goalkeeper had to leave the pitch *o* field; **el equipo perdió en su** ~ the team lost at home ➤ **campo de deportes** sports ground ➤ **campo de fútbol** football field *o* (*Brit*) pitch ➤ **campo de golf** golf course ➤ **campo de juego** playing field **4** (= *espacio delimitado*) ➤ **campo de aterrizaje** landing field ➤ **campo de minas** minefield ➤ **campo de tiro** firing range ➤ **campo petrolífero** oilfield ➤ **campo santo** cemetery; (*al lado de iglesia*) churchyard, graveyard

5 (*Mil*) (= *campamento*) camp; **levantar el** ~ (*Mil*) to break camp, strike camp; (= *irse*) (*) to make tracks*; ✦ MODISMO **dejar el** ~ **libre** to leave the field open ➤ **campo de aviación** airfield, airdrome (*EEUU*) ➤ **campo de batalla** battlefield ➤ **campo de concentración** concentration camp ➤ **campo de exterminio** extermination camp ➤ **campo de pruebas** testing ground ➤ **campo de refugiados** refugee camp ➤ **campo de trabajo** [*de castigo*] labour *o* (*EEUU*) labor camp; [*de vacaciones*] work camp **6** (= *ámbito*) field; **el** ~ **de las ciencias** the field of science; **investigación** ~ field investigation ➤ **campo de acción**, **campo de actuación** scope, room for manoeuvre *o* (*EEUU*) maneuver ➤ **campo de investigación** field of investigation ➤ **campo magnético** magnetic field ➤ **campo visual** field of vision, visual field **7** (*LAm*) (= *espacio*) space, room; **no hay** ~ there's no room *o* space

camposanto SM cemetery; (*al lado de iglesia*) churchyard, graveyard

campus SM INV (*Univ*) campus

camuflaje SM camouflage

camuflar /1a/ VT to camouflage

can SM dog, mutt*, pooch*

cana¹ SF (*tb* ~**s**) white *o* grey *o* (*EEUU*) gray hair; ✦ MODISMO **echar una** ~ **al aire*** (= *divertirse*) to let one's hair down; (*con sexo*) to get up to some hanky-panky*

cana²* (*SAm*) Ⓐ SF **1** (= *cárcel*) jail **2** (= *policía*) police Ⓑ SM (= *policía*) policeman

canabis SM cannabis

canaca*** SMF (*And*) Chink***

Canadá SM Canada

canadiense ADJ, SMF Canadian

canal Ⓐ SM **1** (*Náut, Geog*) (*natural*) channel; (*artificial*) canal ➤ **Canal de la Mancha** English Channel ➤ **Canal de Panamá** Panama Canal ➤ **Canal de Suez** Suez Canal **2** (*Agr, Ingeniería*) (= *conducto*) channel ➤ **canal de desagüe** drain ➤ **canal de drenaje** drainage channel ➤ **canal de riego** irrigation channel **3** (*TV*) channel; **no cambies de** ~ don't change *o* switch channels ➤ **canal de televentas** shopping channel ➤ **canal de televisión** television channel **4** (= *medio*) channel; **el problema se resolvió por los ~es habituales** the problem was solved through the usual channels ➤ **canal de distribución** distribution channel Ⓑ SF **1** (*Téc*) pipe, conduit **2** [*de columna*] groove **3** (= *res*) dressed carcass

canaleta SF (*CS*) gutter (*on roof*)

canalización SF **1** [*de río*] canalization **2** [*de inversiones*] channelling, channeling (*EEUU*)

canalizar /1f/ VT **1** [+ *río*] to canalize; [+ *agua*] to harness; (*por tubería*) to pipe; [+ *aguas de riego*] to channel **2** [+ *inversiones*] to channel, direct

canalizo SM navigable channel

canalla* Ⓐ SMF swine*; **¡canalla!** you swine! Ⓑ SF rabble

canallada SF dirty trick

canallesco ADJ mean, despicable

canalón SM (*en el tejado*) gutter, guttering; (= *bajante*) drainpipe

canapé SM **1** (= *sofá*) sofa, couch **2** (*Culin*) canapé

Canarias SFPL (*tb* **las Islas** ~) the Canaries, the Canary Islands; *see also* www.gobcan.es

canario¹/a Ⓐ ADJ from/of the Canary Islands Ⓑ SM/F Canary Islander

canario² SM (*Orn*) canary

canasta SF **1** (= *cesta*) (round) basket; (*para comida*) hamper ➤ **canasta familiar** (*LAm*) weekly shopping basket **2** (*Baloncesto*) basket **3** (*Naipes*) canasta

canastilla SF [*de bebé*] (baby's) layette

canasto SM (= *cesto*) large basket; [*de comida*] hamper

cancán SM **1** (= *baile*) cancan **2** (= *enagua*) stiff, flounced petticoat

cancel SM (*Méx*) (= *tabique*) partition, thin wall; (= *mampara*) folding screen

cancela SF wrought-iron gate

cancelación SF cancellation

cancelar /1a/ VT 1 [+ *pedido, reunión, viaje*] to cancel 2 [+ *deuda*] to pay off

Cáncer SM (= *signo*) Cancer

cáncer Ⓐ SM (*Med*) cancer ➤ **cáncer de mama, cáncer de pecho** breast cancer ➤ **cáncer de pulmón** lung cancer Ⓑ SMF INV (*Astron*) (= *persona*) Cancer; **soy ~** I'm Cancer

cancerbero SM (*Ftbl*) goalkeeper

cancerígeno ADJ carcinogenic

canceroso ADJ cancerous

cancha SF 1 (*Dep*) [*de tenis, baloncesto*] court; [*de fútbol*] ground ➤ **cancha de bolos** (*LAm*) bowling alley ➤ **cancha de golf** (*LAm*) golf course 2 (*CS*) (= *espacio*) room; **abrir ~** to make way, make room; ✦ MODISMOS **estar en su ~** to be in one's element; **dar ~ a algn: hay que dar ~ a los jóvenes escritores** we have to give a chance to young writers; **dar** *o* **dejar ~ libre a algn** (*LAm*) to give sb a free hand 3 (*en aeropuerto*) ➤ **cancha de aterrizaje** (*CS*) landing strip, runway 4 (*LAm*) (= *desenvoltura*) **tener ~** to be wordly-wise

canchero ADJ (*CS*) wordly-wise

canciller SMF 1 (= *presidente*) chancellor 2 (*LAm Pol*) (= *ministro*) ≈ Foreign Secretary (*Brit*), ≈ Secretary of State (*EEUU*), Minister for Foreign Affairs

cancillería SF (*en embajada*) chancery, chancellery; (*LAm*) (= *ministerio*) ministry of foreign affairs, ≈ Foreign Office (*Brit*)

canción SF song ➤ **canción de amor** love song ➤ **canción de cuna** lullaby ➤ **canción infantil** nursery rhyme ➤ **canción protesta** protest song

cancionero SM (*Mús*) song book; (*Literat*) anthology, collection of verse

candado SM padlock; **cerrar algo con ~** to padlock sth

candeal Ⓐ ADJ **pan ~** white bread Ⓑ SM (*CS Culin*) egg flip

candela SF 1 (= *vela*) candle 2 (*esp LAm*) (= *fuego*) fire; (*para cigarro*) light; **pegar** *o* **prender ~ a** to set fire to, set alight; ✦ MODISMOS **dar ~*** to be a nuisance; **dar ~ a algn*** to rough sb up*

candelabro SM candelabra

candelero SM candlestick; ✦ MODISMO **estar en el ~** [*persona*] to be in the spotlight *o* limelight; [*tema*] to be in the news

candente ADJ 1 [*metal*] (= *rojo*) red-hot; (= *blanco*) white-hot 2 [*cuestión*] burning; **un tema de ~ actualidad** a red-hot issue, a subject that everyone is talking about

candidato/a SM/F (= *aspirante*) candidate (**a** for); (*para puesto*) applicant (**a** for)

candidatura SF 1 (*a un cargo*) candidature, candidacy; **presentar su ~** to put o.s. forward for a post, stand for a post 2 (= *lista*) list of candidates

candidez SF naïveté

cándido ADJ naïve

⚠ cándido ≠ *candid*

candil SM oil lamp

candombe SM *dance of African origin*

candonga SF (*Col*) earring

candor SM innocence, lack of guile

candoroso ADJ innocent, guileless

caneca SF (*Col*) (*para basura*) rubbish bin (*Brit*), garbage can (*EEUU*)

canela SF cinnamon; ✦ MODISMO **ser ~ fina** *o* **en rama: Ana es ~ fina** *o* **en rama** Ana is wonderful; **prueba estas gambas, son ~ fina** try these prawns, they're exquisite ➤ **canela en**

polvo ground cinnamon ➤ **canela en rama** stick cinnamon

canelo SM cinnamon tree; ✦ MODISMO **hacer el ~** to act *o* play the fool

canelón SM 1 (= *bajante*) drainpipe 2 **canelones** (*Culin*) cannelloni

canesú SM yoke

cangrejo SM [*de mar*] crab; [*de río*] crayfish; ✦ MODISMOS **está más rojo que un ~** (*por el sol*) he is as pink *o* red as a lobster; **ir para atrás como los ~s** to make little headway

canguelo* SM (*Esp*), **canguis*** SM (*Esp*) **le entró el ~** he got the jitters*

canguro Ⓐ SM 1 (*Zool*) kangaroo 2 (= *impermeable*) cagoule Ⓑ SMF (*Esp**) [*de niños*] baby-sitter; **hacer de ~** to baby-sit

caníbal Ⓐ ADJ cannibal(istic) Ⓑ SMF cannibal

canibalismo SM cannibalism

canica SF 1 (= *bola*) marble 2 **canicas** (= *juego*) marbles

caniche SMF poodle

canícula SF 1 (= *verano*) dog days *pl*; (= *calor*) midsummer heat 2 (= *mediodía*) midday sun

canijo* ADJ 1 (= *pequeño*) short, diminutive 2 (*Méx*) (= *malo*) nasty, horrible 3 (*Méx*) (= *difícil*) tricky*, ticklish*

canilla SF 1 (= *espinilla*) shinbone, shin; (= *pierna*) shank, thin leg 2 (*esp RPl*) (= *grifo*) tap (*Brit*), faucet (*EEUU*); [*de tonel*] spigot, tap (*Brit*) 3 [*de máquina de coser*] cop

canillera SF (*LAm Dep*) shin guard

canillita SM (*And, CS*) newsboy

canino Ⓐ ADJ canine, dog *antes de s*; **exposición canina** dog show; **tener un hambre canina** to be ravenous Ⓑ SM canine (tooth)

canje SM exchange

canjeable ADJ exchangeable

canjear /1a/ VT [+ *prisioneros*] to exchange; [+ *cupón*] to cash in

cannabis SM cannabis

cano ADJ 1 [*pelo, barba*] (= *gris*) grey, gray (*EEUU*); (= *blanco*) white 2 [*persona*] (= *con pelo gris*) grey-haired, gray-haired (*EEUU*); (= *con pelo blanco*) white-haired

canoa SF canoe

canódromo SM dog track

canon SM (*pl* **cánones**) 1 (= *modelo*) canon (*frm*); **el ~ de belleza** the model of beauty 2 (= *impuesto*) tax, levy 3 (*Mús*) canon

canónico ADJ canonical; **derecho ~** canon law

canónigo SM canon

canonización SF canonization

canonizar /1f/ VT (*Rel*) to canonize; (*fig*) to applaud, show approval of

canoso ADJ 1 [*persona*] (= *con pelo gris*) grey-haired, gray-haired (*EEUU*); (= *con pelo blanco*) white-haired 2 [*pelo, barba*] (= *gris*) grey, gray (*EEUU*); (= *blanco*) white

canotaje SM (*Méx*) canoeing

canotier SM, **canotié** SM straw hat, boater

cansado ADJ 1 (= *fatigado*) [*persona*] tired (**de** from); [*aspecto, apariencia*] weary, tired; [*ojos*] tired, strained; **lo noto ~ últimamente** he's been looking tired lately; **es que nació cansada** (*iró*) she was born lazy; **con voz cansada** with a weary voice 2 (= *harto*) **estar ~ de algo** to be tired of sth; **estoy ~ de que me hagan siempre la misma pregunta** I'm tired of always being asked the same question; **¡ya estoy ~ de vuestras tonterías!** I've had enough of this nonsense of yours!; **estar ~ de hacer algo** to be tired of doing sth

> Recuérdese que las preposiciones en inglés rigen gerundio y no infinitivo, de ahí **to be tired of doing sth**.

3 (= *pesado*) tiring; **debe de ser ~ corregir tantos exámenes** it must be tiring marking *o* to mark so many exams,

marking so many exams must be tiring
4 ✦ MODISMO a las cansadas (*RPI*) at long last

cansador ADJ (*SAm*) tiring

cansancio SM **1** (= *fatiga*) tiredness; **ya empezaban a acusar el ~** they were already beginning to feel tired *o* weary; **estar muerto de ~** to be dead tired **2** (= *hastío*) boredom; **✦ MODISMO hasta el ~** endlessly

cansar /1a/ **Ⓐ** VT **1** (= *fatigar*) to tire, tire out; **me cansa mucho trabajar en el jardín** gardening really tires me out, I find gardening really tiring; **~ la vista** to strain one's eyes, make one's eyes tired
2 (= *aburrir*) **me cansa ir siempre a los mismos bares** I get tired of always going to the same old bars
Ⓑ VI **1** (= *fatigar*) to be tiring
2 (= *hartar*) **los niños cansan a veces** children can sometimes be tiresome *o* trying
Ⓒ cansarse VPR **1** (= *fatigarse*) to get tired; **se cansa con nada** the slightest effort makes him tired, he gets tired at the slightest effort
2 (= *hartarse*) to get bored; **~se de algo** to get tired of sth, get bored with sth; **se cansó de él y lo dejó** she got tired of him *o* got bored with him and left him; **~se de hacer algo** to get tired of doing sth; **no me canso de repetirle que deje de fumar** I'm always telling him to stop smoking

cansino ADJ weary

Cantabria SF (*gen*) Cantabria; (*frec*) Santander

cantábrico ADJ Cantabrian

cántabro/a ADJ, SM/F Cantabrian

cantado ADJ **✦ MODISMO estar ~** to be totally predictable

cantaleta SF (*LAm*) (= *repetición*) boring repetition *o* chorus; (= *quejas*) constant nagging

cantalupo SM, **cantalupa** (*CAm*) SF cantaloupe

cantamañanas* SMF INV (*Esp*) **es un ~** he talks a lot of nonsense *o* (*esp Brit*) rubbish*

cantante Ⓐ SMF singer **➤ cantante de ópera** opera singer **Ⓑ** ADJ singing

cantaor(a) SM/F Flamenco singer

cantar /1a/ **Ⓐ** VI **1** (*Mús*) to sing
2 [*pájaro*] to sing; [*gallo*] to crow; [*cigarra, grillo*] to chirp
3 (*liter*) (= *alabar*) to sing of, sing the praises of; **los poetas que le cantan a la mar** the poets who sing of *o* sing the praises of the sea
4 (**) (= *revelar*) to spill the beans*; (*a la policía*) to squeal*; **✦ MODISMO los hechos cantan por sí solos** the facts speak for themselves
5 (*Esp***) (= *oler mal*) to stink*, reek; **te cantan los pies** your feet really stink* *o* reek
Ⓑ VT **1** [+ *canción*] to sing; [+ *mantra, canto gregoriano*] to chant; [+ *misa*] to sing, say; [+ *número de lotería*] to call out; **✦ MODISMOS ~ las cuarenta a algn*** to give sb a piece of one's mind*; **~ victoria: es muy pronto para ~ victoria** it is too early to claim victory
2 (*liter*) [+ *mérito, belleza*] to praise, eulogize
3 (= *revelar*) to confess
Ⓒ SM **1** (= *canción*) song; (*Rel*) chant
2 ✦ MODISMO **eso es otro ~** that's another story **➤ cantar de gesta** chanson de geste, epic poem

cántara SF large pitcher

cantarín ADJ [*voz*] singsong, lilting; [*persona*] fond of singing

cántaro SM (= *vasija*) pitcher, jug; (= *cantidad*) jugful; **✦ MODISMO llover a ~s** to rain cats and dogs, rain buckets

cantata SF (*Mús*) cantata

cantautor(a) SM/F singer-songwriter

cante SM **1** (*Mús*) **➤ cante flamenco, cante jondo** Flamenco singing **2 ✦** MODISMO **dar el ~*** to stand *o* stick* out a mile

cantegril SM (*Uru*) shanty town, slum

cantera SF **1** (*Min*) quarry, pit **2** [*de artistas*] source; (*Dep*) reserve of young players

cantero SM (*CS*) [*de plantas*] bed, plot; [*de flores*] flowerbed

cántico SM (*Rel*) canticle; (*fig*) song

cantidad **Ⓐ** SF **1** (= *medida*) amount, quantity; **en ~: hemos recibido mercancía en ~** we have received huge amounts *o* quantities of stock; **✦ MODISMO en ~es industriales** (*hum*): **bebo café en ~es industriales** I drink coffee by the bucketful *o* by the gallon
2 [*de personas, animales, cosas*] number; **había gran ~ de gente** there was a large number of people
3 (*) (= *gran cantidad*) **3.1 ~ de** loads of*; **vino a verme ~ de gente** loads of people came to see me*; **tengo ~ de cosas que hacer** I've loads to do* **3.2** (*SAm*) **cualquier ~*** loads*; **cualquier ~ de errores** loads of mistakes*
4 [*de dinero*] sum, amount; **hay que abonar una ~ a cuenta** a payment must be made on account
Ⓑ ADV (*esp Esp***) **le va el alcohol ~** he's into drinking in a big way**; **me gustas ~** I like you a lot, I think you're really cool**

cantiga SF, **cántiga** SF song, poem

cantimplora SF water bottle, canteen

cantina SF **1** (*Ferro*) refreshment car, buffet (*Brit*) **2** (*Mil*) canteen, cafeteria (*EEUU*) **3** (= *café-bar*) snack bar; (*LAm*) bar, saloon; (*CS*) (= *restaurante*) Italian restaurant **4** (*And*) [*de leche*] milk churn **5 cantinas** (*Méx*) (= *alforjas*) saddlebags

cantinela SF **la misma ~** the same old story

canto[1] SM **1** (*Mús*) (= *arte*) singing; (= *canción*) song; (*Rel*) chant; **clases de ~** singing lessons **➤ canto de sirena** siren call, siren song **➤ canto gregoriano** Gregorian chant, (Gregorian) plainsong **2** [*de pájaro*] song; [*de gallo*] crow; [*de grillo, chicharra*] chirp **➤ canto del cisne** swan song
3 (*liter*) song, hymn; **un ~ a la libertad** a hymn *o* song to freedom

canto[2] SM **1** (= *borde*) [*de mesa, libro*] edge; **de ~: el libro cayó de ~** the book fell on its side; **✦ MODISMOS al ~** (*Esp**): **cada vez que se veían, pelea al ~** every time they saw each other there was inevitably an argument, every time they saw each other an argument was the order of the day; **faltar el ~ de un duro** (*Esp*): **ha faltado el ~ de un duro para que se caiga** he was *o* came this close to falling
2 (= *piedra*) pebble; **✦ MODISMO darse con un ~ en los dientes*** to think o.s. lucky, count o.s. lucky **➤ canto rodado** pebble

cantón SM canton

cantonés/esa **Ⓐ** ADJ, SM/F Cantonese **Ⓑ** SM (*Ling*) Cantonese

cantor(a) **Ⓐ** ADJ singing, that sings; **ave ~a** songbird
Ⓑ SM/F (= *persona*) singer; (*Orn*) songbird

cantoso* ADJ showy*

canturrear /1a/ VT, VI to sing softly

canuto **Ⓐ** SM **1** (= *tubo*) small tube, small container
2 (*Esp**) (= *porro*) joint* **Ⓑ** ADJ **✦** MODISMO **pasarlas canutas** (*Esp**) to have a rough time of it

caña SF **1** (= *junco*) reed; (= *tallo*) stem, stalk; **un techo de ~** a roof of reed thatch; **✦ MODISMO dar** *o* **meter ~**: la policía le dio ~ a los manifestantes** the police laid into the demonstrators*; **tendrás que meterle ~ si quieres acabarlo pronto** you'll have to get stuck into it if you want to finish it soon; **le mete mucha ~ al coche** he really steps on the gas **➤ caña de azúcar** sugar cane **➤ caña de bambú** cane
2 (*tb* **~ de pescar**) fishing rod
3 (*Esp*) (*tb* **~ de cerveza**) small glass of beer
4 [*de bota*] leg; **botas de media ~** calf-length boots
5 (= *aguardiente*) cane liquor

cañabrava SF (*LAm*) reed

cañada SF **1** (= *barranco*) gully, ravine; (= *valle*) glen
2 (*Agr*) (= *camino*) cattle track, drover's road **3** (*LAm*) (= *arroyo*) stream

cañamazo SM embroidery canvas

cáñamo SM (*Bot*) hemp; (= *tela*) hemp cloth

cañaveral SM **1** (*Bot*) reedbed **2** (*Col Agr*) sugar-cane plantation

cañería SF (= *tubo*) pipe; (= *sistema*) pipes *pl*, piping; (= *desagüe*) drain

cañero **Ⓐ** ADJ **1** (*LAm*) sugar-cane *antes de s* **2** (**) [*música*] funky* **Ⓑ** SM (*LAm*) (= *trabajador*) sugar-cane worker; (= *propietario*) sugar-cane plantation owner

cañí ADJ, SMF = **calé**

cañizal SM reedbed

caño SM (= *tubo*) tube, pipe; [*de fuente*] jet, spout; (*Perú*) (= *grifo*) tap (*Brit*), faucet (*EEUU*)

cañón SM 1 [*de artillería*] cannon ➤ **cañón antiaéreo** anti-aircraft gun ➤ **cañón de agua** water cannon 2 [*de escopeta*] barrel; ✦ MODISMO **ni a ~ o cañones** (*CS, Perú*) not at all, no way 3 (= *valle*) canyon, gorge

cañonazo SM 1 (*Mil*) cannon shot; **cañonazos** (= *fuego*) cannon fire *sing*; **salva de 21 ~s** 21-gun salute 2 (*Ftbl*) shot, volley, fierce shot

cañonero/a SM/F (*LAm Dep*) striker

caoba SF mahogany

caolín SM kaolin

caos SM INV chaos ➤ **caos circulatorio** traffic chaos

caótico ADJ chaotic

cap. ABR, **cap.°** ABR (= **capítulo**) ch., c., chap.

capa SF 1 (= *prenda*) cloak, cape; ✦ MODISMOS **andar o estar de ~ caída** (= *estar triste*) to look o be crestfallen, be down in the mouth; (= *estar en decadencia*) to be in o on the decline; **defender algo a ~ y espada** to fight tooth and nail for sth; **cada uno hace de su ~ un sayo** everyone does as he pleases ➤ **capa torera** bullfighter's cape
2 (= *estrato*) layer; **la ~ atmosférica** the atmosphere; **la ~ de ozono** the ozone layer; **amplias ~s sociales o de la población** broad strata of society; **un corte de pelo a ~s** a layered cut
3 (= *recubrimiento*) [*de pintura*] coat; [*de polvo, chocolate*] layer; **una ~ de hielo** a sheet of ice; **una ~ de nieve** a blanket of snow; **una fina ~ de grasa** a film of grease

capacha* SF (*Chi*) nick (*Brit**), can (*EEUU**); **caer en la ~** to fall into the trap

capacho SM wicker basket

capacidad SF 1 [*de vehículo, teatro, depósito*] capacity; **una sala con ~ para 900 personas** a hall with a capacity of 900 people; **un avión con ~ para 155 pasajeros** a 155-seater aircraft ➤ **capacidad de carga** carrying capacity, freight capacity
2 (= *habilidad*) ability; **necesitamos una persona con ~ para afrontar desafíos** we require a person with the ability to face challenges; **~ de reproducción** capacity for reproduction ➤ **capacidad de aprendizaje** learning ability ➤ **capacidad de convocatoria** [*de orador*] pulling power; [*de huelga, manifestación*] appeal, popular appeal ➤ **capacidad de decisión** decision-making ability ➤ **capacidad de trabajo: tiene una enorme ~ de trabajo** she has an enormous capacity for hard work ➤ **capacidad física** physical capacity ➤ **capacidad intelectual** intellectual ability ➤ **capacidad mental** mental ability
3 (= *autoridad*) authority; **no tenemos ~ para modificar las decisiones del gobierno** we do not have the authority to alter government decisions
4 (*Jur*) capacity

capacitación SF 1 (*Educ*) **conseguir la ~ de piloto** to qualify as a pilot 2 (*Jur*) capacitation

capacitado ADJ **estar ~ para hacer algo** to be qualified to do sth

capacitar /1a/ Ⓐ VT 1 (= *preparar*) to prepare; **~ a los jóvenes para incorporarse al mercado laboral** to prepare young people for the job market 2 (= *habilitar*) to qualify; **este título me capacita para ejercer como abogada** this qualification qualifies o entitles me to work as a lawyer Ⓑ **capacitarse** VPR **~se para algo** to qualify for sth

capar /1a/ VT to castrate, geld

caparazón SM shell; **encerrarse en su ~** to withdraw into one's shell; **salir de su ~** to come out of one's shell

capataz SMF foreman/forewoman, overseer

capaz ADJ 1 (= *competente*) capable, able; **es una persona muy ~** he is a very capable o able person; **~ de hacer algo** capable of doing sth

no han sido capaces de localizar las joyas they were unable to find the jewels; **no es ~ ni de freír un huevo** he can't even fry an egg; **¡es ~ de no venir!** he's quite capable of not coming!
2 (= *que se atreve*) **¿no me crees ~?** do you think I won't?; **ser ~** to dare; **¿a que no eres ~?** you wouldn't dare!, I bet you wouldn't!; **si soy ~ de hacerlo** if I can bring myself to do it
3 (*SAm**) **~ que: ~ que llueve** it might rain; **~ que se perdió** he might have got lost

capazo SM (= *cesto*) large basket; (*para niño*) Moses basket, (wicker) carrycot

capcioso ADJ cunning, deceitful; **pregunta capciosa** trick question

capea SF bullfight with young bulls

capear /1a/ VT 1 (*Taur*) to wave the cape at; (*fig*) to take in, deceive 2 (*Náut*) **~ el temporal** (*lit, fig*) to ride out o weather the storm

capellán SM chaplain

capelo SM (= *sombrero*) cardinal's hat; (= *dignidad*) cardinalate

Caperucita Roja SF (Little) Red Riding Hood

caperuza SF [*de tela*] (pointed) hood; [*de bolígrafo*] cap, top

capicúa Ⓐ ADJ palindromic (*frm*) Ⓑ SM palindrome (*frm*), symmetrical number

capilar Ⓐ ADJ hair *antes de s*, capillary; **loción ~** hair lotion; **tubo ~** capillary Ⓑ SM capillary

capilla SF chapel ➤ **capilla ardiente** funeral chapel

capirotazo SM flip, flick

capirote SM 1 (*Univ, Orn*) hood 2 **tonto de ~** dunce, complete idiot

capital Ⓐ ADJ 1 (= *clave*) [*nombre, personaje*] key; [*rasgo*] main; **una figura ~ de la democracia española** a key figure in Spanish democracy; **esto tuvo una importancia ~ en su vida** this was of paramount o cardinal importance in his life
2 (= *mortal*) **pecado ~** mortal sin; **la pena ~** capital punishment
Ⓑ SM (*Fin*) capital ➤ **capital activo** working capital ➤ **capital fijo** fixed capital ➤ **capital flotante** floating capital ➤ **capital humano** human resources *pl* ➤ **capital riesgo** risk capital, venture capital
Ⓒ SF (*Geog*) [*de país*] capital (city); [*de provincia*] main city, provincial capital; **soy de Málaga ~** I am from the city of Málaga (*as opposed to the province*)

capitalino ADJ (*LAm*) of/from the capital

capitalismo SM capitalism

capitalista ADJ, SMF capitalist

capitalización SF capitalization; [*de interés*] compounding

capitalizar /1f/ VT 1 (*Fin*) (*gen*) to capitalize; [+ *interés*] to compound 2 (*fig*) to capitalize on

capitán SM (*Mil*) captain; (*fig*) leader, chief ➤ **capitán de corbeta** lieutenant commander ➤ **capitán de fragata** commander ➤ **capitán del puerto** harbour o (*EEUU*) harbor master ➤ **capitán de navío** captain ➤ **capitán general** [*de ejército*] ≈ field marshal; [*de armada*] chief of naval operations

capitana SF 1 (*Dep, Mil*) (woman) captain 2 (*Náut*) flagship

capitanear /1a/ VT [+ *equipo*] to captain; [+ *rebeldes*] to lead, command

capitanía SF (= *rango*) captaincy; (= *edificio*) headquarters *pl* ➤ **capitanía general** (= *puesto*) *command of a military district*; (= *edificio*) *headquarters of a military district*

capitel SM (*Arquit*) capital

capitolio SM (= *edificio grande*) large edifice, imposing building; (= *acrópolis*) acropolis; **el Capitolio** the Capitol

capitoste* SM bigwig*, boss

capitulación SF 1 (*Mil*) capitulation, surrender 2 (= *convenio*) agreement, pact; **capitulaciones (de boda o**

matrimoniales) marriage contract *sing*, marriage settlement *sing*

capitular /1a/ vi (*Mil*) (= *rendirse*) to capitulate, surrender

capítulo SM **1** [*de libro*] chapter; [*de ley*] section; **eso es ~ aparte** that's another question altogether **2** (= *tema*) subject, matter; **en el ~ de las pensiones ...** on the subject of pensions ...

capo SM [*de la mafia*] capo; (*esp Col*) drug baron

capó SM **1** (*Aut*) bonnet (*Brit*), hood (*EEUU*) **2** (*Aer*) cowling

capón¹* SM rap on the head

capón² SM (= *pollo*) capon

caporal SM (*Méx*) foreman (*on cattle ranch*)

capota SF **1** (= *prenda*) bonnet **2** [*de carruaje, cochecito*] hood **3** (*Aut*) hood, top (*EEUU*) **4** (*Aer*) cowling

capote SM **1** (= *capa*) cloak; (*Mil*) cape, capote; ✦ MODISMO **echar un ~ a algn** to give *o* lend sb a helping hand **2** (*Taur*) (bullfighter's) cape

capricho SM **1** (= *antojo*) whim, (passing) fancy, caprice (*liter*); **es un ~ nada más** it's just a passing fancy; **por puro ~** just to please o.s.; **entra y sale a su ~** he comes and goes as he pleases **2** (*Mús*) caprice, capriccio **3** (*Arte*) caprice

caprichoso ADJ **1** [*persona*] whimsical; **¡qué niño más ~!** what a spoilt brat! **2** (= *azaroso*) [*idea, decisión*] whimsical, fanciful; [*formas*] fanciful; [*suerte, fortuna*] fickle

Capricornio SM (= *signo*) Capricorn

capricornio SMF INV (= *persona*) Capricorn; **soy ~** I'm Capricorn

cápsula SF **1** (*Med, Aer*) capsule; (*Carib*) cartridge ➤ **cápsula espacial** space capsule **2** (*Méx Rad, TV*) spot, short programme *o* (*EEUU*) program; **una ~ informativa/educativa** a news summary/an educational spot

captación SF ➤ **captación de capital** (*Fin*) capital raising ➤ **captación de clientes: es la encargada de la ~ de clientes** she's in charge of attracting new customers ➤ **captación de datos** data capture ➤ **captación de fondos** fundraising ➤ **captación de votos** vote-winning

captar /1a/ vt **1** (= *atraer*) [+ *votos*] to win; [+ *clientes, audiencia*] to attract; **esto no logró ~ el interés del público** this failed to capture public interest **2** [+ *emisora, señal*] to pick up; **un videoaficionado captó esta escena** this scene was caught on amateur video **3** (= *comprender*) [+ *sentido, esencia*] to get, grasp; **no captó la indirecta** he didn't get *o* take the hint **4** [+ *aguas*] to collect

captura SF [*de prisionero, animal*] capture; [*de droga*] seizure; [*de pesca*] catch

capturar /1a/ vt [+ *prisionero, animal, datos*] to capture; [+ *droga*] to seize

capturista SMF (*Méx*) keyboarder, computer operator

capucha SF [*de prenda*] hood; (*Rel*) hood, cowl

capuchino SM **1** (*Rel*) Capuchin **2** (= *café*) cappuccino (coffee)

capuchón SM **1** [*de pluma, bolígrafo*] top, cap **2** [*de prenda*] hood

capullo¹ SM **1** (= *flor*) bud ➤ **capullo de rosa** rosebud **2** (*Zool*) cocoon **3** (***) (*del pene*) head

capullo²/a (*Esp****) SM/F dickhead***

caqui SM khaki, olive drab (*EEUU*)

cara SF **1** (= *rostro*) face; **varias ~s conocidas** several familiar faces; **~ a ~: se encontraron ~ a ~** they met face to face; **un encuentro ~ a ~** a face-to-face encounter; **de ~ a: nos sentamos de ~ al sol** we sat facing the sun; **reformas de ~ a las próximas elecciones** reforms with an eye on the next elections *o* for the next elections; **no soy nada optimista de ~ al futuro** I'm not at all optimistic about the future; **volver la ~ hacia algn** to turn one's face towards sb; **no vuelvas la ~ atrás** don't look back; ✦ MODISMOS **caerse a algn la ~ de vergüenza: se le tendría que caer la ~ de vergüenza** she ought to be ashamed of herself; **cruzar la ~ a algn** to slap sb in the face; **dar la ~** to face the consequences; **dar la ~ por algn** to come to sb's defence; **decir algo a algn la ~ a ~** to say sth to sb's face; **a ~ descubierta** openly; **lo mejor que te puedes echar a la ~** the very best you could wish for; **echar algo en ~ a algn** to reproach sb for sth; **lavar la ~ a algo** to make sth look presentable; **mirar a algn a la ~** to look sb in the face; **partir la ~ a algn** to smash sb's face in; **plantar ~** [+ *persona, críticas*] to stand up to; [+ *problema*] to face up to, confront; **por la ~*: entrar por la ~ en una fiesta** to gatecrash a party; **no me lo van a dar por mi ~ bonita** they're not going to hand it to me on a plate (*esp Brit*) *o* on a silver platter (*EEUU*); **romper la ~ a algn** to smash sb's face in; **nos veremos las ~s** you haven't seen the last of me **2** (= *expresión*) **poner mala ~** to grimace, make a (wry) face; **no pongas esa ~** don't look like that; **puso ~ de alegría** his face lit up; **tener ~ de: tener ~ de estar aburrido** to look bored; **tener buena ~** [*enfermo*] to be looking well; [*comida*] to look appetizing; **tener mala ~** [*enfermo*] to look ill; [*comida*] to look bad; ✦ MODISMOS **poner ~ de circunstancias** to look serious; **tener ~ de palo** to have a wooden expression; **tener ~ de pocos amigos** to look very unfriendly; **tener ~ de vinagre** to have a sour face **3** (*) (= *descaro*) nerve*, cheek*; (= *valor*) nerve*; **¡qué ~ más dura!*** what a nerve *o* cheek!*; **¡qué ~ tienes!** you've got a nerve!*, what a cheek you've got!*; ✦ MODISMO **tener más ~ que espalda** to have an incredible nerve*, be a cheeky devil (*Brit**) **4** (= *lado*) [*de moneda, montaña, figura geométrica*] face; [*de disco, planeta, papel*] side; [*de tela*] face, right side; **escribir por ambas ~s** to write on both sides; **intentaron ascender por la ~ norte** they tried to climb the north face; **~ A** (*en disco*) A side; **~ o cruz** ◇ **~ o ceca** (*Arg*) ◇ **~ o sello** (*Col*) heads or tails; **echar** *o* **jugar** *o* **sortear algo a ~ o cruz** *etc* to toss for sth

carabela SF caravel

carabina SF **1** (*Mil*) carbine, rifle ➤ **carabina de aire comprimido** airgun **2** (= *persona*) chaperone; **hacer** *o* **ir de ~** to go as chaperone, play gooseberry*

carabinero SM **1** (*Mil*) rifleman, carabineer; [*de frontera*] border guard; (*LAm*) policeman **2** (*Esp Zool*) large prawn (*Brit*), large shrimp (*EEUU*)

Caracas SM Caracas

caracho* EXCL (*And, CS*) sugar!*, shoot!*, I'll be darned! (*EEUU**)

caracol SM **1** (*Zool*) snail; (*esp LAm*) (= *concha*) (sea) shell, snail shell **2** (= *rizo*) curl **3 escalera de ~** spiral staircase, winding staircase **4 ¡~es!** (*euf, *) (*sorpresa*) good heavens!; (*ira*) damn it!

caracola SF (*Zool*) large shell

carácter SM (*pl* **caracteres**) **1** [*de persona*] character; **tiene un ~ muy fuerte** he has a strong personality; **no tiene ~** he lacks character, he's a weak character; **tener un ~ abierto** to be open, have an open nature; **tener buen ~** to be good-natured; **persona de ~** person of *o* with character; **imprimir ~** to be character-building, build up character; **tener mal ~** to be ill-tempered; **tener un ~ reservado** to be of a quiet *o* reserved disposition **2** [*de edificio, estilo*] character; **una casa con mucho ~** a house with a lot of character **3** (= *índole*) nature; **problemas de ~ general** problems of a general nature; **una visita con ~ oficial/privado** an official/private visit; **información de ~ reservado** information of a confidential nature; **un aumento de sueldo con ~ retroactivo** a backdated pay rise (*Brit*) *o* raise (*EEUU*) **4** (*Biol*) trait, characteristic ➤ **carácter dominante** dominant trait, dominant characteristic ➤ **carácter hereditario** hereditary trait ➤ **carácter recesivo** recessive trait **5** (*Tip, Inform*) character; **escrito con caracteres góticos** written in Gothic (script) ➤ **caracteres de imprenta** block letters

característica SF **1** (= *rasgo*) characteristic, feature **2** (*RPl Telec*) area code

característico ADJ characteristic (**de** of)

caracterización SF characterization

caracterizar /1f/ Ⓐ vt **1** (*gen*) to characterize; (= *distinguir*) to distinguish, set apart; (= *tipificar*) to typify **2** (*Teat*) [+ *papel*] to play with great effect Ⓑ **caracterizarse** VPR **1 ~se por algo** to be characterized by sth **2** (*Teat*) to make up, dress for the part

caradura Ⓐ SMF (= *persona fresca*) cheeky person (*Brit*), sassy person (*EEUU*) **Ⓑ** SF (= *frescura*) cheek*, nerve*

carajillo SM (*Esp*) *coffee with a dash of brandy, anis etc*

carajito* SM (*LAm*) kid*, small child

carajo*** Ⓐ SM **1** (*con valor enfático*) —**me debes dinero —¡qué dinero ni qué ~!** "you owe me some money" — "I don't owe you a damn thing!" *o* "like hell I do!"** **2 al ~: ¡al ~ con los libros!** to hell with the books!*; **irse al ~: ¡vete al ~!** go to hell!**; **todo el trabajo se fue al ~** all the work went down the tubes*; **mándalo al ~** tell him to piss off***; **del ~: hace un frío del ~** it's absolutely freezing, it's bloody freezing (*Brit***); **un ~: no entendí un ~** I didn't understand a damn *o* (*Brit*) bloody thing*; **me importa un ~** I couldn't give a damn* *o* toss (*Brit***) **Ⓑ** EXCL **¡carajo!** damn (it)!*

caramanchel SM (*And*) (= *puesto*) street vendor's stall

caramba EXCL (*indicando sorpresa*) good gracious!; (*indicando extrañeza*) how strange!; (*indicando protesta*) for crying out loud!

carámbano SM icicle

carambola SF (*Billar*) (= *juego*) billiards *sing*; (= *golpe*) cannon, carom (*EEUU*); ✦ MODISMO **por ~** by fluke

caramelo SM **1** (= *golosina*) sweet (*Brit*), piece of candy (*EEUU*) **2** (*Culin*) caramel; **a punto de ~** [*azúcar*] caramelized **3** (= *incentivo*) sweetener

carancho SM **1** (*Perú*) (= *búho*) owl **2** (*CS*) (= *buitre*) vulture, turkey buzzard (*EEUU*)

carantoña SF caress; **hacer ~s a algn** (= *acariciar*) to caress sb; (= *halagar*) to sweet-talk sb, butter sb up

caraota SF (*Ven*) bean

caraqueño ADJ of/from Caracas

carátula SF **1** (= *portada*) [*de vídeo*] case; [*de disco*] sleeve **2** (= *careta*) mask **3** (*Méx*) [*de reloj*] face, dial

caravana SF **1** (*Aut*) [*de camiones, coches*] convoy; (= *atasco*) tailback (*Brit*), line of traffic (*EEUU*); **ir en ~** to go in convoy **2** (= *remolque*) caravan (*Brit*), trailer (*EEUU*) **3** (*en el desierto*) caravan **4** (*Méx*) (= *reverencia*) bow

caray EXCL = **caramba**

carbohidrato SM carbohydrate

carbón SM **1** (*Min*) coal ➤ **carbón de leña** charcoal ➤ **carbón de piedra** coal ➤ **carbón vegetal** charcoal **2** (*Tip*) (*tb* **papel ~**) carbon paper; **copia al ~** carbon copy **3** (*Arte*) charcoal; **dibujo al ~** charcoal drawing

carbonatado ADJ carbonated

carbonato SM carbonate

carboncillo SM charcoal; **un retrato al ~** a portrait in charcoal

carbonera SF (*en casa*) coal bunker; *ver tb* **carbonero**

carbonería SF coalyard

carbonero/a Ⓐ ADJ coal *antes de s* **Ⓑ** SM/F coal merchant, coalman; *ver tb* **carbonera**

carbónico ADJ carbonic

carbonilla SF **1** (*Min*) coal dust **2** (*LAm Arte*) charcoal

carbonizar /1f/ **Ⓐ** VT **1** (*Quím*) to carbonize **2** [+ *madera*] to make charcoal of; **quedar carbonizado** (= *quemado*) to be charred, be burnt to a cinder; (= *electrocutado*) to be electrocuted **Ⓑ carbonizarse** VPR (*Quím*) to carbonize

carbono SM carbon

carbunclo SM **1** (*Min*) carbuncle **2** (*Med*) anthrax

carbunco SM (*Med*) anthrax

carburador SM carburettor, carburetor (*EEUU*)

carburante SM fuel

carburar /1a/ VI **1** (*Aut*) to carburet **2** (*) (= *funcionar*) **hoy no carburo** I can't think straight today, I'm not very with it today*

carburo SM carbide

carca* ADJ, SMF INV **1** (= *reaccionario*) reactionary **2** (= *anticuado*) square*

carcacha* SF (*Méx Aut*) old crock

carcaj SM **1** (= *para flechas*) quiver **2** (*Méx*) rifle case

carcajada SF loud laugh, guffaw; **reírse a ~s** to roar with laughter; **soltar una ~** to burst out laughing

carcajearse /1a/ VPR to roar with laughter

carcamal* SM, **carcamán*** SM (*RPl*) old crock*

carcasa SF **1** (= *armazón*) casing **2** (*Aut*) [*de motor*] chassis

cárcel SF prison, jail; **meter a algn en la ~** to jail sb, send sb to jail

carcelario ADJ prison *antes de s*

carcelero Ⓐ ADJ prison *antes de s* **Ⓑ** SM jailer, warder (*Brit*), guard (*EEUU*)

carcinógeno SM carcinogen

carcinoma SM carcinoma

carcoma SF woodworm

carcomer /2a/ VT **1** [+ *madera*] to eat into, eat away **2** [+ *salud*] to undermine

carcomido ADJ **1** [*madera*] infested with woodworm **2** (= *podrido*) rotten, decayed

cardamomo SM cardamom

cardar /1a/ VT **1** (*Textiles*) to card, comb; ✦ MODISMO **~ la lana a algn*** to tell sb off, rap sb's knuckles **2** [+ *pelo*] to backcomb

cardenal SM **1** (*Rel*) cardinal **2** (*Med*) bruise

cardenalicio ADJ **capelo ~** cardinal's hat

cárdeno ADJ [*color*] purple, violet; [*agua*] opalescent

cardiaco ADJ, **cardíaco** ADJ cardiac, heart *antes de s*; **ataque ~** heart attack

cárdigan SM (*esp LAm*) cardigan

cardinal ADJ cardinal

cardiograma SM cardiogram

cardiología SF cardiology

cardiólogo/a SM/F cardiologist

cardiopatía SF heart disease

cardiovascular ADJ cardiovascular

cardo SM thistle; ✦ MODISMO **es un ~** (*Esp**) (= *insociable*) he's a prickly customer*; (= *feo*) he's as ugly as sin*

carear /1a/ VT to bring face to face

carecer /2d/ VI **~ de** to lack; **eso carece de sentido** that doesn't make sense

carencia SF (= *ausencia*) lack; (= *escasez*) lack, shortage, scarcity (*frm*); **una ~ absoluta de recursos económicos** a total lack of economic resources; **para compensar las ~s vitamínicas** to make up for vitamin deficiencies

carenciado ADJ (*CS*) deprived

carencial ADJ **enfermedad ~** deficiency disease

carente ADJ **~ de** lacking in, devoid of (*frm*)

careo SM (*Jur*) confrontation, face-to-face meeting

carero* ADJ pricey*

carestía SF **1** (*Com*) high price, high cost ➤ **carestía de la vida** high cost of living **2** (= *escasez*) scarcity, shortage; **época de ~** period of shortage

careta SF mask; **quitar la ~ a algn** to unmask sb ➤ **careta antigás** gas mask ➤ **careta de oxígeno** oxygen mask

careto** SM (*Esp*) ugly mug**

carey SM **1** (= *material*) tortoiseshell **2** (*Zool*) turtle (*Brit*), sea turtle (*EEUU*)

carga SF **1** (= *cargamento*) **1.1** [*de camión, lavadora*] load; [*de barco*] cargo; [*de tren*] freight **1.2** (= *acto*) loading; **"zona reservada para carga y descarga"** "loading only"; **de ~ frontal** front-loading *antes de s*; **de ~ superior** top-loading *antes de s* **1.3** (= *peso*) load; **no puedo con tanta ~** I can't take *o* manage such a heavy load **2** (= *responsabilidad*) burden; **no quiero ser una ~ para mis hijos** I don't want to be a burden to my children; **yo soy quien lleva la ~ de esta casa** I'm the one who takes responsibility for everything in this house ➤ **carga fiscal, carga impositiva** tax burden ➤ **carga tributaria** tax burden

3 (= *contenido*) **el discurso tenía una fuerte ~ emocional** the speech was charged with great emotion; **se caracteriza por un exceso de ~ ideológica** it is characterized by its excessive ideological content ➤ **carga viral** viral load

4 (*en armas*) charge; **una ~ de tres kilos de explosivo** three kilos of explosives ➤ **carga explosiva** explosive charge

5 (= *recambio*) [*de pluma*] cartridge; [*de bolígrafo*] refill; **se le ha acabado la ~ al mechero** the lighter has run out of fuel

6 (= *ataque*) (*Mil, Dep*) charge; **¡a la ~!** charge!;

✦ MODISMO **volver a la ~: a los pocos minutos el equipo volvió a la ~** a few minutes later the team returned to the attack; **el grupo vuelve a la ~ con un nuevo disco** the group are back with a new record

7 (*Elec*) [*de un cuerpo*] charge; [*de generador, circuito*] load ➤ **carga eléctrica** electrical charge, electric charge

cargada SF 1 (*Méx*) ✦ MODISMO **ir a la ~** to jump on the bandwagon 2 (*CS**) practical joke

cargaderas SFPL (*Col*) braces (*Brit*), suspenders (*EEUU*)

cargado Ⓐ PP *de* **cargar**
Ⓑ ADJ 1 (= *con cargamento*) loaded; **el ascensor iba demasiado ~** the lift (*Brit*) *o* elevator (*EEUU*) was overloaded; **la furgoneta iba cargada hasta los topes** the van was packed full; **déjame que te ayude, que vas muy cargada** let me help you, you've got such a lot to carry; **~ de algo: se presentó ~ de regalos** he arrived weighed down *o* loaded down with presents; **iba cargada de joyas** she was dripping with jewels; **estamos muy ~s de trabajo** we're snowed under (with work), we're overloaded with work; **un país ~ de deudas** a country burdened *o* weighed down with debt; **ser ~ de espaldas** *o* **hombros** to be round-shouldered

2 (= *fuerte*) [*café, bebida alcohólica*] strong

3 [*ambiente*] (= *no respirable*) stuffy; (= *lleno de humo*) smoky; (= *tenso*) fraught, tense; **el ambiente de la reunión estaba cada vez más ~** the atmosphere in the meeting became increasingly fraught *o* tense

4 (*Meteo*) (= *bochornoso*) close, overcast

5 (*Mil*) [*arma*] loaded; [*bomba, mina*] live

6 (*Elec*) [*batería, pila*] charged; [*cable*] live

7 [*dados*] loaded

cargador(a) Ⓐ SM/F [*de camión*] loader; [*de muelles*] docker (*Brit*), longshoreman (*EEUU*); [*de horno*] stoker Ⓑ SM 1 (*Téc*) [*de pistola, metralleta*] magazine; [*de pilas, baterías*] battery charger 2 **cargadores** (*Col*) braces (*Brit*), suspenders (*EEUU*)

cargamento SM 1 [*de barco, avión*] (= *mercancías*) cargo; (= *remesa*) shipment; **el ~ del buque** the ship's cargo; **el último ~ de cigarrillos** the last shipment of cigarettes; **se han incautado de un ~ de armas** they have seized an arms shipment 2 [*de camión, tren*] load

cargante* ADJ [*discurso, personaje*] annoying; [*tarea*] irksome; [*persona*] trying

cargar /1h/ Ⓐ VT 1 [+ *peso*] (= *echar*) to load; (= *llevar*) to carry; **~on los sacos en dos camiones** they loaded the sacks onto two lorries; **iba cargando el bulto sobre los hombros** he was carrying the piece of luggage on his shoulders

2 (= *llenar*) 2.1 [+ *vehículo, pistola, lavadora, cámara*] to load; **~on el coche hasta arriba de maletas** they loaded the car up with suitcases 2.2 [+ *mechero, pluma*] to fill; [+ *batería, pilas*] to charge; [+ *horno*] to stoke 2.3 (*en exceso*) **tratamos de no ~ a los alumnos con demasiadas horas de clase** we try not to overburden the students with too many teaching hours; ✦ MODISMOS **~ la mano** ◇ **~ las tintas** to exaggerate 2.4 (*Inform*) to load 2.5 (*RPl*) **~ nafta** to fill up with petrol (*Brit*) *o* gas (*EEUU*)

3 (= *cobrar*) 3.1 (*en cuenta*) to charge; **lo pueden ~ a mi cuenta** you can charge it to my account 3.2 [+ *contribución*] to charge for; [+ *impuesto*] to levy

4 (= *hacer recaer*) **buscan a alguien a quien ~ la culpa** they are looking for somebody to blame *o* to put the blame on

5 (= *agobiar*) **~ a algn de algo: el ser campeones nos carga de responsabilidad** being champions places a lot of responsibility on our shoulders

6 (*) **~ a algn** (= *fastidiar*) to get on sb's nerves*; (*RPl*) (= *tomar el pelo*) to pull sb's leg*

7 (*Mil*) (= *atacar*) to charge, attack

8 [+ *dados*] to load

9 (*Ven*) (= *llevar*) **¿cargas dinero?** have you got any money

on you?; **~ anteojos** to wear glasses; **~ revólver** to carry a gun

Ⓑ VI 1 (= *echar carga*) (*Aut*) to load up; (*Náut*) to take on cargo

2 **~ con** 2.1 [+ *objeto*] (= *levantar*) to pick up; (= *llevar*) to carry 2.2 [+ *culpa, responsabilidad*] to take; [+ *consecuencias*] to suffer; **la empresa ~á con los gastos del viaje** the company will bear the travel expenses

3 (= *atacar*) **la policía cargó contra los manifestantes** the police charged the demonstrators

Ⓒ **cargarse** VPR 1 (= *llenarse*) **~se de** [+ *fruta, dinero*] to be full of, loaded with; [+ *culpa, responsabilidad*] to take; **el árbol se había cargado de manzanas** the tree was heavy *o* laden with apples; **el ambiente se cargó de humo** the air became filled with smoke; **~se de hijos** to have lots of children

2 (*Esp**) (= *destruir*) [+ *jarrón, juguete*] to smash, break; [+ *esperanzas, vida*] to ruin; **¡te lo has cargado!*** you've gone and wrecked it*

3 [*cielo*] to become overcast

4 (*Elec*) to become charged

5 (*Esp**) **~se a algn** (= *suspender*) to fail sb; (= *matar*) to bump sb off*, do sb in**; (= *eliminar*) to get rid of sb, remove sb

6 **cargársela*** to get into hot water*, get it in the neck*; **te la vas a ~** you're in for it*, you've had it*

cargo SM 1 (= *puesto*) post; **ocupa el ~ de comisario europeo desde hace tres años** he has held the office *o* post of European Commissioner for three years; **alto ~** (= *puesto*) high-ranking position, top post; (= *persona*) top official, senior official; **desempeñar un ~** to hold a position; **jurar el ~** to be sworn in; **poner el ~ a disposición de algn** (*euf*) to offer up one's post to sb ➤ **cargo público** (= *puesto*) public office; (= *persona*) person in public office

2 **a ~ de** 2.1 (= *responsable de*) in charge of, responsible for; **los detectives a ~ de la investigación** the detectives in charge of *o* heading the investigation 2.2 (= *bajo la responsabilidad de*) **"formación a cargo de la empresa"** "training will be provided"; **un concierto a ~ de la orquesta de cámara de la ciudad** a concert performed by the city's chamber orchestra; **las reparaciones correrán a ~ del dueño** the cost of repairs will be met by the owner, repairs will be paid for by the owner; **tener algo a su ~** to be in charge of sth, be responsible for sth; **los niños que tengo a mi ~** the children in my care *o* charge (*frm*)

3 **hacerse ~ de** (= *encargarse*) to take charge of; (= *pagar*) to pay for, take care of; (= *entender*) to realize; **cuando él murió, su hijo se hizo ~ del negocio** when he died, his son took charge of *o* took over the business; **el abuelo se hizo ~ del niño** the boy's grandfather took care of him; **la empresa no quiso hacerse ~ de la reparación** the company refused to meet the costs of repair; **—estamos pasando unos momentos difíciles —sí, ya me hago ~** "we're going through difficult times" — "yes, I understand *o* realize"

4 (*Com*) charge; **podrá recibir información sin ~ alguno** you can receive information free of charge

5 (*Jur*) charge; **el fiscal retiró los ~s contra el acusado** the prosecution dropped all the charges against the defendant ➤ **cargo de conciencia: tengo ~ de conciencia por el tiempo perdido** I feel guilty about all that wasted time

6 (*Chi, Perú*) (= *certificación*) date stamp (*providing proof of when a document was submitted*)

cargosear* /1a/ VT (*CS*) to pester, annoy

cargoso* ADJ (*CS*) annoying

carguero SM (*Náut*) cargo boat; (*Aer*) freight plane

cariado ADJ decayed

cariátide SF caryatid

caribe Ⓐ ADJ Caribbean Ⓑ SMF Carib

caribeño/a ADJ, SM/F Caribbean

caricatura SF caricature

caricaturesco ADJ absurd, ridiculous

caricaturizar /1f/ VT to caricature

caricia SF (*a persona*) caress; (*a animal*) pat, stroke; **hacer ~s a** to caress, stroke

caridad SF charity; **vive de la ~ de la gente del barrio** she lives on *o* off the charity of the local people; **obra de ~** act of charity; **¡una limosna, por ~!** could you spare some change *o* a little money, please?

caries SF INV tooth decay, caries; **tengo una ~ en la muela del juicio** I've got some decay in my wisdom tooth

carillón SM carillon

cariño SM **1** (= *afecto*) love, affection; **falta de ~** lack of affection; **coger ~ a algn/algo** to grow *o* become fond of sb/sth, become attached to sb/sth; **con ~: trata a sus plantas con mucho ~** she takes loving care of her plants; **lo recuerdo con ~** I have fond memories of it, I remember it with great affection; **con ~, Luis** (*en carta*) love (from) Luis; **sentir ~ por algn** to be fond of sb, like sb; **tener ~ a algn/algo** to be fond of sb/sth, like sth; **tomar ~ a algn/algo** to grow *o* become fond of sb/sth, become attached to sb/sth
2 (*apelativo*) darling, honey*
3 cariños (*LAm*) (= *saludos*) love

cariñoso ADJ affectionate, loving

carioca ADJ of/from Rio de Janeiro

carisma SM charisma

carismático ADJ charismatic

caritativo ADJ charitable (**con, para** to)

cariz SM look; **este asunto está tomando mal ~** this is beginning to look bad, I don't like the look of this; **en vista del ~ que toman las cosas** in view of the way things are going

carlinga SF cockpit, cabin

carlista ADJ, SMF Carlist

carmelita ADJ, SMF Carmelite

carmelito ADJ (*Col*) brown

carmesí ADJ, SM crimson

carmín SM **1** (= *color*) carmine **2** (= *pintalabios*) lipstick
3 (*Bot*) dog rose

carminativo ADJ carminative

carnada SF bait

carnal Ⓐ ADJ **1** (*Rel*) carnal, of the flesh **2** [*pariente*] full, blood *antes de s*; **primo ~** first cousin Ⓑ SM (*Méx**) pal*, buddy (*EEUU**)

carnaval SM **1** (= *fiesta*) carnival
2 (*Rel*) Shrovetide; **martes de ~** Shrove Tuesday

CARNAVAL

Carnaval is the traditional period of fun, feasting and partying that precedes the start of Lent (**Cuaresma**). The most important day is probably Shrove Tuesday (**Martes de Carnaval**), but throughout **Carnaval** there are fancy-dress parties, parades and firework displays. In some places in Spain, the changeover from **Carnaval** to Lent on Ash Wednesday is marked by the **Entierro de la Sardina**. This is a grotesque funeral parade in which the symbolic cardboard figure of a sardine is marched through the streets and finally ceremonially burnt or buried.

---

carnavalesco ADJ carnival *antes de s*

carnaza SF **1** (= *cebo*) (*para peces*) groundbait; (*para leones*) scraps *pl* of meat **2** [*de escándalo, suceso*] **dar ~ a la gente** to feed people (with) juicy titbits

carne Ⓐ SF **1** (*Culin*) meat; ✦ MODISMOS **poner toda la ~ en el asador** to pull out all the stops, give it one's all; **no ser ~ ni pescado** to be neither fish nor fowl, be neither one thing nor the other; **ser ~ de cañón** to be cannon-fodder ➤ **carne asada** roast meat ➤ **carne blanca** white meat ➤ **carne bovina, carne de bovino** beef ➤ **carne de cerdo, carne de chancho** (*LAm*) pork ➤ **carne de cordero** lamb ➤ **carne de res** (*LAm*) beef ➤ **carne de ternera** veal ➤ **carne de vaca** beef ➤ **carne molida** (*LAm*), **carne picada** (*Esp, RPl*) mince (*esp Brit*), ground meat (*esp EEUU*) ➤ **carne roja** red meat
2 (*Anat*) flesh; ✦ MODISMOS **de ~ y hueso: las marionetas parecían actores de ~ y hueso** the puppets were just like real-life actors; **ser de ~ y hueso** to be only human; **en ~ y**

hueso in the flesh; **en ~ viva: tenía las rodillas en ~ viva** his knees were raw ➤ **carne de gallina** gooseflesh, goose pimples *pl* (*Brit*), goose bumps *pl* (*EEUU*); **me pone la ~ de gallina** [*de frío, emoción*] it gives me goose pimples (*Brit*) *o* goose bumps (*EEUU*); [*de miedo*] it gives me the creeps, it makes my flesh crawl
3 carnes [*de persona*] **entrado** *o* **metido en ~s** plump, overweight
4 (*Rel*) flesh; **la ~ es débil** the flesh is weak
5 (*Bot*) flesh, pulp ➤ **carne de membrillo** quince jelly
Ⓑ ADJ **color ~** flesh-coloured, flesh-colored (*EEUU*)

carné SM = **carnet**

carnear /1a/ VT **1** (*CS*) [+ *ganado*] to slaughter; [+ *persona*] to murder, butcher **2** (*Chi*) (= *engañar*) to deceive, take in*

carnero SM **1** (*Zool*) sheep, ram ➤ **carnero de la sierra** (*LAm*), **carnero de la tierra** (*LAm*) llama, alpaca, vicuña **2** (*Culin*) mutton **3** (= *piel*) sheepskin

carnet [kar'ne] SM (*pl* ~**s** [kar'nes]) card; **tiene ~ del partido socialista** he has a membership card for the Socialist Party ➤ **carnet de conducir** driving licence (*Brit*), driver's license (*EEUU*) ➤ **carnet de estudiante** student card ➤ **carnet de identidad** identity card; ✧ *DOCUMENTO NACIONAL DE IDENTIDAD* ➤ **carnet de prensa** press pass ➤ **carnet de socio** membership card

carnicería SF **1** (*Com*) butcher's, butcher's shop **2** (= *matanza*) slaughter, carnage

carnicero/a Ⓐ ADJ (= *cruel*) cruel, bloodthirsty Ⓑ SM/F butcher

cárnico ADJ meat *antes de s*

carnitas SFPL (*Méx*) barbecued pork *sing*

carnívoro Ⓐ ADJ carnivorous, meat-eating Ⓑ SM carnivore, meat-eater

carnoso ADJ meaty

caro ADJ **1** (= *costoso*) expensive, dear; **un coche carísimo** a very expensive car; **costar ~** to be expensive, cost a lot; **le costó ~ tal atrevimiento** his daring cost him dear; **pagar ~ algo** to pay dearly for sth; **pagó cara su insolencia** he paid dearly for his insolence; **un piso amueblado sale más ~** a furnished flat (*esp Brit*) *o* apartment (*esp EEUU*) is more expensive **2** (= *querido*) (*liter*) dear, beloved

carón ADJ (*LAm*) broad-faced

carótida SF carotid (artery)

carozo SM (*CS*) stone, pit (*EEUU*)

carpa¹ SF (= *pez*) carp ➤ **carpa dorada** goldfish

carpa² SF **1** [*de circo*] big top
2 (= *toldo*) awning
3 (*LAm*) (*para acampar*) tent
4 (*Méx*) travelling show

CARPA

In Mexico a **carpa** is a travelling show held under a big top. Originating in the nationalistic aftermath of the Mexican revolution, **carpas** toured agricultural communities and mining towns offering a menu of satire, slapstick humour, dramatic sketches and humorous monologues, as well as acrobatics, tightrope walking and other circus entertainments. It was in the **carpa** that the Mexican comic character, Cantinflas, started life. ✧ PELADO

---

carpeta SF **1** (*para archivar*) folder, file ➤ **carpeta de anillas** ring binder **2** (*And, RPl*) (= *tapete*) doily

carpetazo SM ✦ MODISMO **dar ~ a algo** to shelve sth, do nothing about sth

carpintería SF **1** (= *arte, oficio*) carpentry, joinery (*esp Brit*) **2** (= *afición*) woodwork **3** (= *taller*) carpenter's shop

carpintero/a Ⓐ SM/F (*Téc*) carpenter Ⓑ SM (*Orn*) woodpecker

carraca SF **1** (*Mús, Dep*) rattle **2** (= *coche*) jalopy*, banger (*Brit**)

carraspear /1a/ VI to clear one's throat

carraspera SF hoarseness

carrasposo ADJ (*Med*) hoarse; (*LAm*) rough, harsh

carrera SF 1 (= *acción*) (*tb Béisbol*) run; **tuvimos que pegarnos una ~ para no perder el tren** we had to run for it so as not to miss the train; **¿nos echamos una ~ hasta el muro?** race you to the wall!; **nos fuimos de una ~ y llegamos en cinco minutos** we ran for it *o* rushed over and got there in five minutes; ✦ MODISMO **a la ~** at (full) speed, hurriedly; **tuvo que hacer el trabajo a la ~** he had to rush through the job *o* do the job in a rush; **a ~ tendida** at full speed, flat out*
2 (= *competición*) race; **las ~s de Fórmula uno** Formula One races ➤ **carrera armamentista, carrera armamentística** arms race ➤ **carrera campo a través** cross country race ➤ **carrera ciclista** (bi)cycle race ➤ **carrera contrarreloj** (*lit*) time trial; (*fig*) race against time ➤ **carrera de armamentos** arms race ➤ **carrera de caballos** horse race ➤ **carrera de coches** motor race (*Brit*), car race (*EEUU*) ➤ **carrera de fondo** long-distance race ➤ **carrera de galgos** greyhound race ➤ **carrera de obstáculos** (*Atletismo, Equitación*) steeplechase; (*para niños*) obstacle race ➤ **carrera de relevos** relay, relay race
3 (*tb* ~ **universitaria**) (university) course; **está en primero de** ~ she's in her first year (at university); **quiere que sus hijos estudien una** ~ she wants her children to go to university; **hacer una** ~: **estoy haciendo la ~ de Económicas** I'm doing a degree in economics ➤ **carrera de ciencias** science degree ➤ **carrera de letras** arts degree
4 (*tb* ~ **profesional**) career; **tuvo una brillante ~ como actriz** she had an outstanding career as an actress; **diplomático de** ~ career diplomat; **militar de** ~ career officer; **hacer** ~ to advance one's career, pursue a career ➤ **carrera artística** [*de actor*] career as an actor; [*de pintor, escultor*] artistic career ➤ **carrera militar** career as a soldier, military career ➤ **carrera política** political career, career as a politician
5 (*en medias*) run, ladder (*Brit*)
6 [*de taxi*] ride, journey
7 (= *avenida*) avenue
8 (*Col*) (= *calle*) street (*running north-south*)

carrerilla SF **de ~** [*recitar, decir*] parrot-fashion; **tomar ~** to take a run up

carreta SF 1 (= *carro*) (*cubierta*) waggon, wagon; (*sin cubrir*) cart; ✦ MODISMO **tener la ~ llena** (*Carib*) to be weighed down by problems 2 (*Col, Ven*) wheelbarrow

carrete SM 1 (*Fot*) film 2 (*Cos*) reel, bobbin 3 (*Pesca*) reel

carretear /1a/ VT (*LAm Aer*) to taxi

carretel SM (*LAm*) spool

carretela SF (*CAm*) (= *carro*) cart

carretera SF 1 (= *carro*) road, highway (*esp EEUU*); **de ~: bar de ~** roadside bar; **accidente de ~** road accident, traffic accident; **control de ~** roadblock; **por ~: un viaje por ~** a road journey, a journey by road; **hemos venido por ~** we drove here ➤ **carretera comarcal** local road, ≈ B road (*Brit*) ➤ **carretera de acceso** approach road ➤ **carretera de circunvalación** bypass, ring road (*Brit*), beltway (*EEUU*) ➤ **carretera de cuota** (*Méx*) toll road ➤ **carretera general** main road ➤ **carretera nacional** ≈ A road (*Brit*), ≈ state highway (*EEUU*)

carretero SM cartwright, wheelwright; ✦ MODISMO **fumar como un ~** to smoke like a chimney

carretilla SF 1 (*tb* ~ **de mano**) wheelbarrow ➤ **carretilla elevadora** fork-lift truck 2 (*CS*) (= *quijada*) jaw, jawbone
3 ✦ MODISMO **de ~: saber algo de ~** to know sth by heart; **aprender algo de ~** to learn sth parrot fashion *o* by rote

carricoche SM (*pey, ***) jalopy*, banger (*Brit**)

carriel SM (*And, CAm*) leather shoulder bag

carril SM 1 (*en carretera*) lane ➤ **carril bici** cycle lane, bikeway (*EEUU*) ➤ **carril bus** bus lane ➤ **carril de adelantamiento** overtaking lane, fast lane (*Brit*) 2 (*Ferro*) rail

carrillo SM cheek, jowl; ✦ MODISMO **comer a dos ~s** to stuff o.s.*, stuff one's face*

carrito SM (*en supermercado*) trolley (*Brit*), cart (*EEUU*); (*para servir alimentos*) tea trolley (*Brit*) *o* cart (*EEUU*), serving trolley (*Brit*) *o* cart (*EEUU*)

carrizo SM (*Bot*) reed; ✦ MODISMO **no nos ayudan un ~** (*Ven*) they do nothing at all to help us

carro SM 1 (= *carreta*) cart, waggon, wagon;
✦ MODISMOS **apearse** *o* **bajarse del ~*** to leave off, give it a rest*; **¡para el ~!*** hold your horses!; **subirse al ~** to climb *o* jump on the bandwagon ➤ **carro de la compra** shopping trolley (*Brit*), shopping cart (*EEUU*)
2 (*Mil*) tank ➤ **carro blindado** armoured car, armored car (*EEUU*), armour-plated car, armor-plated car (*EEUU*) ➤ **carro de asalto, carro de combate** tank
3 (*And, CAm, Méx, Ven*) (= *coche*) car; (= *vagón*) carriage (*Brit*), car (*esp EEUU*) ➤ **carro comedor** (*Méx*) dining car, restaurant car (*Brit*) ➤ **carro dormitorio** (*Méx*) sleeping car ➤ **carros chocones** (*Méx*), **carros locos** (*Col*) dodgems
4 [*de máquina de escribir*] carriage

carrocería SF (*Aut*) bodywork

carromato SM covered wagon

carroña SF carrion

carroñero ADJ **animal ~** animal which feeds on carrion

carroza Ⓐ SF 1 [*de caballos*] coach, carriage 2 [*de carnaval*] float 3 (*Uru*) [*de entierro*] (funeral) hearse Ⓑ SMF (*Esp*)
1 (= *viejo*) old boy*, old geezer**; (= *vieja*) old girl*
2 (= *carca*) old fogey* Ⓒ ADJ INV (*) (= *carca*) **es muy ~** he's an old fogey*

carruaje SM carriage

carrusel SM [*de verbena*] merry-go-round, roundabout (*Brit*), carousel (*EEUU*)

carta SF 1 (*Correos*) letter; **echar una ~ (al correo)** to post (*Brit*) *o* mail (*EEUU*) a letter; ✦ MODISMOS **a ~ cabal** thoroughly, in every respect; **era honrado a ~ cabal** he was totally honest; **es un caballero a ~ cabal** a true *o* real gentleman; **tomar ~s en el asunto** to step in ➤ **carta abierta** open letter ➤ **carta bomba** letter-bomb ➤ **carta certificada** registered letter ➤ **carta de amor** love letter ➤ **carta de recomendación** (*para un trabajo*) letter of recommendation; (*como presentación*) letter of introduction ➤ **carta tipo** standard letter ➤ **carta urgente** special-delivery letter
2 (*Jur, Com*) (= *documento*) ➤ **carta blanca** carte blanche; **tener ~ blanca** to have a free hand, have carte blanche ➤ **carta de ciudadanía** naturalization papers *pl* ➤ **carta verde** (*Aut*) green card, certificate of insurance (*EEUU*)
3 (= *estatuto*) charter ➤ **Carta Magna** (= *constitución*) constitution; (*Brit Hist*) Magna Carta ➤ **Carta Social (Europea)** (European) Social Charter
4 (*Naipes*) card; **echar las ~s a algn** to tell sb's fortune (*with cards*); **jugar a las ~s** to play cards; ✦ MODISMOS **poner las ~s boca arriba** *o* **sobre la mesa** to put *o* lay one's cards on the table; **no saber a qué ~ quedarse** not to know what to think, be undecided
5 (*Culin*) menu; **a la ~** à la carte; **televisión a la ~** pay-per-view TV; **un programa de estudios a la ~** an individually-tailored syllabus (*esp Brit*) *o* course of study (*EEUU*) ➤ **carta de vinos** wine list
6 (= *mapa*) (*Geog*) map; (*Náut*) chart ➤ **carta astral** star chart ➤ **carta de navegación, carta de viaje, carta de vuelo** flight plan
7 (*TV*) ➤ **carta de ajuste** test card

cartabón SM [*de dibujante*] set square, triangle (*EEUU*); [*de carpintero*] square, set square

cartaginés/esa ADJ, SM/F Carthaginian

Cartago SF Carthage

cartapacio SM 1 (= *cuaderno*) notebook 2 (= *carpeta*) folder

cartearse /1a/ VPR to correspond (**con** with); **se cartearon durante dos años** they wrote to each other for two years

cartel SM 1 (= *póster*) poster; **el ~ del Festival** the poster for the Festival; **"se prohíbe fijar carteles"** "stick no bills", "post no bills"; **en ~: esa película todavía no está en ~** that film (*esp Brit*) *o* movie (*esp EEUU*) is not showing *o* on yet; **"Cats" lleva años en ~** "Cats" has been running for years
2 (= *letrero*) sign; **no vi el ~ de "prohibido fumar"** I didn't see the no smoking sign

cártel SM, **cartel** SM (*Com*) cartel

cartelera SF [*de cine*] billboard, hoarding (*Brit*); (*en periódico*) entertainments *pl*, listings; **se mantuvo en ~ durante tres años** it ran for three years

cárter SM (*Mec*) housing, case ➤ **cárter de cigüeñal** crankcase

cartera SF 1 (= *billetera*) wallet, billfold (*EEUU*); (= *monedero*) purse (*Brit*), billfold (*EEUU*) 2 (*SAm*) [*de mujer*] handbag, purse, (*EEUU*) 3 [*de colegial*] satchel, schoolbag 4 (*para documentos*) briefcase 5 (*Pol*) **dimitió de la ~ de Cultura** he resigned from the post of Minister of Culture; **ministro sin ~** minister without portfolio 6 (*Com, Fin*) ➤ **cartera de acciones** stock portfolio, share portfolio ➤ **cartera de pedidos** order book (*Brit*), orders on hand (*EEUU*) ➤ **cartera de valores** securities portfolio; *ver tb* **cartero**

carterista SMF pickpocket

cartero/a SM/F postman/postwoman (*Brit*), mailman/mailwoman (*EEUU*); *ver tb* **cartera**

cartesiano/a ADJ, SM/F Cartesian

cartílago SM cartilage

cartilla SF 1 (*Escol*) primer, first reader; ✦ MODISMO **cantar** *o* **leer la ~ a algn** to take sb to task, give sb a severe ticking-off (*Brit*) 2 (= *documento*) ➤ **cartilla de ahorros** bank book ➤ **cartilla de racionamiento** ration book

cartografía SF cartography, mapmaking

cartográfico ADJ cartographic, cartographical

cartógrafo/a SM/F cartographer, mapmaker

cartomancia SF fortune-telling (*with cards*)

cartomante SMF fortune-teller (*who uses cards*)

cartón SM 1 (= *material*) cardboard ➤ **cartón piedra** papier mâché 2 (= *caja*) ➤ **cartón de huevos** (*lleno*) box of eggs; (*vacío*) egg box ➤ **cartón de leche** (*lleno*) carton of milk; (*vacío*) milk carton ➤ **cartón de tabaco** pack of cigarettes 3 [*de bingo*] card

cartuchera SF 1 [*de balas*] cartridge belt 2 (*RPI*) [*de lápices*] pencil case

cartucho SM 1 (*Mil*) cartridge 2 [*de monedas*] roll

cartuja SF Carthusian monastery

cartujo SM Carthusian

cartulina SF card; **una ~** a piece of card

casa SF 1 (= *vivienda*) house; **una ~ en el campo** a house in the country; **ir de ~ en ~ vendiendo** to sell things from door to door ➤ **casa adosada** terraced house ➤ **la Casa Blanca** the White House ➤ **casa consistorial** (*gen*) town hall; (*en gran ciudad*) city hall ➤ **casa cuartel** Civil Guard police station including living quarters for families of policemen ➤ **casa de alquiler: vivo en una ~ de alquiler** I live in rented accommodation ➤ **casa de campo** country house (*Brit*), country mansion (*EEUU*) ➤ **casa de citas** brothel ➤ **casa de cultura** municipal arts centre ➤ **casa de huéspedes** boarding house ➤ **casa de juego** gambling house ➤ **casa de labor, casa de labranza** farmhouse ➤ **la Casa de la Moneda** Chilean presidential palace ➤ **casa de locos** (= *manicomio*) madhouse, asylum; (= *lugar caótico*) madhouse ➤ **casa de muñecas** doll's house ➤ **casa de putas*** brothel ➤ **casa de socorro** first-aid post ➤ **casa natal: la ~ natal de Lorca** the house where Lorca was born ➤ **casa pareada** semi-detached house (*Brit*), duplex (*EEUU*) ➤ **casa rodante** caravan (*Brit*), trailer (*EEUU*) ➤ **la Casa Rosada** Argentinian presidential palace ➤ **casa rural** (*de alquiler*) holiday cottage; (= *pensión*) rural B & B ➤ **casa solariega** (*habitada*) family seat, ancestral home; (*usada como museo*) stately home (*esp Brit*), house museum (*EEUU*) 2 (= *hogar*) home; **estábamos en ~** we were at home; **ropa de ~** clothes for wearing around the house; **¿está la señora de la ~?** is the lady of the house in?; **está fuera de ~** she's out, she's not at home; **ir a ~** to go home; **ir hacia ~** to head for home; **ir a ~ de Juan** to go to Juan's (place); **llevar la ~** to run the household; **sentirse como en su ~** to feel at home; **siéntase como en su ~** make yourself at home ➤ **casa y comida** board and lodging 3 ✦ MODISMOS **de andar por ~: zapatos de andar por ~** shoes for wearing around the house; **una explicación de andar por ~** a rough-and-ready explanation; **como una ~*:**

una mentira como una ~ a whopper*; **un penalti como una ~** a clear-cut penalty; **echar** *o* **tirar la ~ por la ventana** to spare no expense; **empezar la ~ por el tejado** to put the cart before the horse 4 (= *asociación*) ➤ **casa de España** club for expatriate Spaniards ➤ **casa de Galicia** club for expatriate Galicians ➤ **Casa del Pueblo** (*Pol*) social club run by Spanish socialist party 5 (*Dep*) home ground (*Brit*), home field (*EEUU*); **equipo de ~** home team; **jugar en ~** to play at home; **jugar fuera de ~** to play away (from home) 6 (*en juegos*) home 7 (*en bar, restaurante*) **una botella de vino de la ~** a bottle of house wine; **invita la ~** it's on the house 8 (= *empresa*) firm, company ➤ **casa de discos** record company ➤ **casa de empeños** pawnshop ➤ **casa de (la) moneda** mint ➤ **casa de modas** fashion house ➤ **casa de préstamos** pawnshop ➤ **casa discográfica** record company ➤ **casa editorial** publishing house ➤ **casa matriz** (= *oficina*) head office; (= *empresa*) parent company 9 (= *linaje*) house; **la Casa de Austria** the Hapsburgs ➤ **casa real** royal household

casaca SF dress coat

casación SF cassation, annulment

casa-cuartel SF (*pl* **casas-cuarteles**) residential barracks (*for Civil Guard*)

casadero ADJ marriageable, old enough to get married

casado/a Ⓐ ADJ married; **¿está** *o* (*LAm*) **es usted casada?** are you married?; **está ~ con mi prima** he's married to my cousin Ⓑ SM/F married man/woman; **su apellido de casada** her married name; **los recién ~s** the newlyweds

casamentero/a SM/F matchmaker

casamiento SM (= *ceremonia*) wedding, wedding ceremony; (= *unión*) marriage

casar /1a/ Ⓐ VT 1 (= *unir en matrimonio*) [*cura*] to marry; [*padres*] to marry off 2 (= *hacer coincidir*) to match up Ⓑ VI (= *armonizar*) **hay una serie de datos que no casan** there are a number of details that don't tally *o* match up Ⓒ **casarse** VPR to marry, get married; **¿cuándo te casas?** when are you getting married?; ✦ MODISMO **no ~se con nadie: respeta a todo el mundo, pero no se casa con nadie** he respects everyone but doesn't side with any of them

casba SF, **casbah** SF kasbah

cascabel Ⓐ SM little bell; ✦ MODISMO **poner el ~ al gato** to bell the cat Ⓑ SF rattlesnake, rattler (*EEUU**)

cascabeleo SM jingling, tinkling

cascada SF waterfall, cascade

cascado ADJ 1 [*persona*] worn out 2 (*Mús*) [*voz*] cracked

cascajo SM (= *trasto*) junk, rubbish (*esp Brit*), garbage (*EEUU*); ✦ MODISMO **estar hecho un ~*** to be a wreck*

cascanueces SM INV nutcracker

cascar /1g/ Ⓐ VT 1 (= *romper*) [+ *nuez*] to crack; [+ *huevo*] to break, crack; [+ *taza, plato*] to chip 2 (*) (= *pegar*) **cuando se entere tu padre, te casca** when your father finds out, he'll give you a bashing *o* (*esp Brit*) he'll thump you* 3 (*Esp**) (= *poner*) **me ~on una multa** I was landed with *o* slapped with a fine* 4 ✦ MODISMO **~la**** to kick the bucket* Ⓑ VI (*) (= *charlar*) to chatter, natter (*Brit**) Ⓒ **cascarse** VPR (= *romperse*) [*nuez*] to crack; [*huevo*] to break, crack; [*taza, plato*] to chip

cáscara SF 1 (= *cubierta*) [*de nuez, huevo*] shell; [*de fruta*] peel, rind, skin ➤ **cáscara de huevo** eggshell ➤ **cáscara de plátano** banana skin (*Brit*), banana peel (*EEUU*) 2 (* *euf*) **¡cáscaras!** well I'm blowed!*

En inglés la **cáscara** de la mayoría de los cítricos, como la naranja, el pomelo, etc., se llama **peel**; la cáscara del limón puede llamarse **peel** o **rind**. Cuando la cáscara es más dura, como en el caso de huevos, gambas y nueces, se utiliza la palabra **shell**.

cascarazo* SM (*SAm*) punch

cascarón SM eggshell, broken eggshell; ✦ MODISMO **está recién salido del ~** he's a bit wet behind the ears

cascarrabias SMF INV grouch*

cascarriento* ADJ (CS) filthy, greasy, mucky*

cascarudo SM (RPl) beetle

casco SM 1 (como protección) [de soldado] helmet; [de obrero] protective helmet, safety helmet, hard hat; [de motorista, ciclista] (crash) helmet; **los ~s azules (de la ONU)** the UN blue berets
2 [de ciudad] ➤ casco antiguo: **el ~ antiguo de la ciudad** the old quarter o part of the city ➤ **casco urbano** built-up area ➤ **casco viejo: el ~ viejo de la ciudad** the old quarter o part of the city
3 (Esp, Méx) (= envase) empty bottle
4 **cascos** (= auriculares) headphones
5 **cascos*** (= cabeza) nut* sing; ♦ MODISMO **alegre** o **ligero de ~s** (= irreflexivo) reckless, foolhardy; (= frívolo) flighty
6 (= pezuña) hoof
7 (Náut) [de barco] hull
8 (RPl Agr) ranch house, ranch and outbuildings
9 [de sombrero] crown
10 (Col) (= gajo) segment

cascorros* SMPL (Méx) shoes

cascorvo* ADJ (CAm) bow-legged

cascote SM piece of rubble; **~s** rubble sing

caserío SM country house (Brit), country mansion (EEUU)

casero/a Ⓐ ADJ 1 (= hecho en casa) [comida, sopa, artefacto] home-made; [remedio] household, home antes de s; **cocina casera** home cooking; **un vídeo ~** a home video; **de fabricación casera** home-made (= hogareño) **soy muy ~** I'm the home-loving sort, I'm the stay-at-home type
Ⓑ SM/F 1 (= propietario) landlord/landlady 2 (en casa de campo) caretaker 3 (Chi) (= cliente) customer, client 4 (Carib) (= repartidor) delivery man/woman

caserón SM large house, ramshackle house

caseta SF 1 [de bañista] changing room ➤ **caseta de perro** kennel (esp Brit), doghouse (EEUU) 2 [de feria] stall

casete [ka'set] Ⓐ SF (= cinta) cassette Ⓑ SM (= aparato) cassette player

casi ADV 1 (= indicando aproximación) almost, nearly; **está ~ terminado** it's almost o nearly finished; **son ya ~ las tres** it's almost o nearly three o'clock; **¡huy!, ~ me caigo** oops! I almost o nearly fell over; **ocurre lo mismo en ~ todos los países** the same thing happens in virtually o practically all countries; **~ nada** almost o virtually nothing, hardly anything; **100 dólares, ¡~ nada!** (iró) 100 dollars, a mere trifle!; **~ nunca** hardly ever, almost never; **~ nunca hay sitio en la biblioteca** there is hardly ever any room in the library; **~ siempre** almost always
2 (indicando indecisión) almost; **no sé, ~ prefiero no ir** I don't know, I think I'd rather not go

casilla SF 1 (= compartimento) (para cartas) pigeonhole, mail box (EEUU); (para guardar algo) compartment; [de formulario] box; [de papel] ruled column, section ➤ **casilla de correos** (And) post office box (number), P.O. Box ➤ **casilla electoral** (Méx) polling-station ➤ **casilla electrónica** (LAm) email address ➤ **casilla postal** (And) post office box (number), P.O. Box 2 (en ajedrez, damas) square; ♦ MODISMO **sacar a algn de sus ~s** to infuriate sb, drive sb up the wall*

casillero SM (en oficina) pigeonholes pl, set of pigeonholes; (en oficina de correos) sorting rack

casino SM 1 [de juego] casino 2 (club social) club

caso SM 1 (= circunstancia) 1.1 (gen) case; **ahí tienes el ~ de Pedro** take Pedro's case 1.2 **en ~ afirmativo** if so; **en (el) ~ contrario** if not, otherwise; **en cualquier ~** in any case; **en ~ de** in the event of; **en ~ de necesidad** if necessary; **en ~ de que llueva, iremos en autobús** if it rains, we'll go by bus; **en ese ~** in that case; **en el mejor de los ~s** at best; **en ~ necesario** if necessary; **en ~ negativo** if not, otherwise; **en el peor de los ~s** at worst; **en tal ~** in such a case; **en todo ~** in any case; **en último ~** as a last resort, in the last resort; **en uno u otro ~** one way or the other 1.3 **darse el ~:** **todavía no se ha dado al ~** such a situation hasn't yet arisen; **el ~ es que ...:** **el ~ es que se me olvidó su nombre** the thing is I forgot her name; **el ~ es que tiene razón** the fact is (that) she's right; **el ~ es que no me gustó** basically I

didn't like it; **hacer al ~** to be relevant; **pongamos por ~ que ...** let us suppose that ...; **según el ~** as the case may be; **no tiene ~** (Méx) there's no point (in it); **venir al ~** to be relevant; **no venir al ~** to be beside the point
2 (Med) case ➤ **caso clínico** clinical case
3 (= asunto) affair; (Jur) case; **el ~ Hess** the Hess affair; **es un ~ perdido** [situación] it's a hopeless case; [persona] he's hopeless*, he's a dead loss (Brit*) ➤ **caso límite** extreme case
4 **hacer ~ a** o **de algo** to take notice of sth, pay attention to sth; **no le hagas ~** don't take any notice of him; **hazle ~, que ella tiene más experiencia** listen to her, she has more experience; **ni ~:** **tú a todo lo que te diga ¡ni ~!*** take no notice of what he says!; **hacer ~ omiso de algo** to ignore sth
5 (Ling) case

casona SF large house

casorio* SM wedding, marriage

caspa SF dandruff

Caspio ADJ **mar ~** Caspian Sea

cáspita† EXCL my goodness!

casposo ADJ 1 [pelo] full of dandruff 2 (*) [película, tema] hackneyed

casquería SF tripe and offal shop

casquete SM skullcap ➤ **casquete polar** polar icecap

casquillo SM cartridge case ➤ **casquillo de bala** bullet shell

casquivano ADJ scatterbrained; (pey) [mujer] loose

casta SF 1 (= clan) caste; **el sistema de ~s de la India** the Indian caste system 2 (= estirpe) stock; **eso me viene de ~** it's in my blood; ♦ REFRÁN **de ~ le viene al galgo** it's in the blood o genes 3 (= grupo social) class; **la ~ militar** the military class 4 (= calidad) class; **un toro de ~** a thoroughbred bull

castaña SF 1 (= fruto) chestnut; ♦ MODISMOS **sacar a algn las ~s del fuego** to get sb off the hook; **ser una ~** (Esp*) to be a drag*; **¡toma ~!** (Esp*) (indicando disfrute) take that!; (indicando sorpresa) just imagine! ➤ **castaña de cajú** (RPl) cashew nut ➤ **castaña de Indias** horse chestnut ➤ **castaña del Brasil** Brazil nut 2 (*) (= golpe) punch; **darse una ~** to give o.s. a knock 3 (*) (= borrachera) **cogerse una ~** to get plastered*

castañazo* SM (= choque) bump

castañero/a SM/F chestnut seller

castañetear /1a/ VI [dientes] to chatter; [huesos] to crack

castaño Ⓐ ADJ [pelo] chestnut, chestnut-coloured, chestnut-colored (EEUU); [ojos] brown; ♦ MODISMO **esto pasa de ~ oscuro** this has gone too far, this is beyond a joke (Brit) Ⓑ SM (Bot) chestnut tree; ♦ MODISMO **pelar el ~** (Carib*) to hoof it* ➤ **castaño de Indias** horse chestnut tree

castañuela SF castanet; ♦ MODISMO **estar como** o **hecho unas ~** be in high spirits

castellano/a Ⓐ ADJ (Pol) Castilian; (Ling) Spanish
Ⓑ SM/F Castilian
Ⓒ SM (Ling) Castilian, Spanish

castellanohablante, castellanoparlante Ⓐ ADJ Castilian-speaking, Spanish-speaking Ⓑ SMF Castilian speaker, Spanish speaker

castellonense ADJ = **castellonés**

castellonés ADJ of/from Castellón

casticismo SM **1** (*Ling*) purity, correctness **2** [*de costumbres*] traditional character, authenticity

castidad SF chastity, purity

castigar /1h/ VT **1** (*por delito, falta*) [+ *delincuente, pecador, culpable*] to punish (**por** for); [+ *niño*] (*sin salir*) to ground, keep in; **la profesora me dejó castigado al terminar las clases** the teacher kept me in *o* made me stay behind after school; **lo ~on sin postre** he was not allowed any dessert as punishment; **la carne** (*Rel*) to mortify the flesh; **el socialismo salió muy castigado de las urnas** socialism suffered heavy losses in the elections
2 (= *perjudicar*) [*guerra, crisis*] to afflict, affect; [*sol*] to beat down on; [*frío*] to bite into; **la ciudad más castigada por los bombardeos** the city worst hit by the bombing
3 (= *maltratar*) to damage, harm

castigo SM **1** (*por delito, falta*) punishment; **celda de ~** punishment cell ➤ **castigo divino** divine retribution
2 (*Dep*) penalty; **área de ~** penalty area, penalty box
3 (= *tormento*) **la artillería sometió durante horas a la ciudad a un duro ~** the artillery pounded the city for hours on end

Castilla SF Castile ➤ **Castilla la Nueva** New Castile ➤ **Castilla la Vieja** Old Castile

castillo SM castle; ✦ MODISMO **~s en el aire** castles in the air ➤ **castillo de arena** sandcastle ➤ **castillo de fuego** firework set piece ➤ **castillo de naipes** house of cards ➤ **castillo de popa** aftercastle ➤ **castillo de proa** forecastle

casting ['kastin] SM (*Cine*) casting

castizo ADJ **1** (= *tradicional*) traditional **2** (= *auténtico*) pure, authentic **3** (*Ling*) pure, correct

casto ADJ chaste, pure

castor SM beaver

castración SF castration, gelding

castrar /1a/ VT (*Zool*) [+ *toro*] to castrate; [+ *caballo*] to geld; [+ *gato*] to doctor

castrense ADJ army *antes de s*, military

castro SM (*Hist*) Iron-Age settlement

casual Ⓐ ADJ [*encuentro*] chance *antes de s*; **su éxito no es ~** his success cannot be put down to chance; **nada es ~** nothing happens by chance Ⓑ SM **por un ~*** by any chance

⚠ **casual** ≠ *casual*

casualidad SF **1** (= *azar*) chance; (= *coincidencia*) coincidence; **sería mucha ~** it would be too much of a coincidence; **nuestra victoria no ha sido fruto de la ~** our victory was no fluke; **da la ~ de que ...** it (just) so happens that ...; **ese día dio la ~ de que decidí salir a dar una vuelta** that day I happened to decide to go out for a walk, as luck would have it I decided to go out for a walk that day; **de** *o* **por ~** by chance; **nos enteramos casi por ~** we found out almost by accident; **¿no tendrás un pañuelo, por ~?** you wouldn't (happen to) have a handkerchief, by any chance?; **no toca un libro ni por ~** he would never think of picking up a book; **¡qué ~!** what a coincidence!
2 (= *suceso casual*) coincidence; **por una de esas ~es de la vida** by one of life's little coincidences

casualmente ADV by chance, fortuitously (*frm*); **~ lo vi ayer** I happened to see him yesterday

casuística SF casuistry

casulla SF chasuble

cata SF tasting

cataclismo SM cataclysm

catacumbas SFPL catacombs

catador(a) SM/F taster

catadura SF **1** (= *acto*) tasting **2** (= *aspecto*) looks *pl*, appearance; **de mala ~** nasty-looking

catafalco SM catafalque

catalán/ana Ⓐ ADJ, SM/F Catalan, Catalonian Ⓑ SM (*Ling*) Catalan; ⊅ *LENGUAS COOFICIALES*

catalanismo SM **1** (*Ling*) Catalanism, *word or phrase etc*

peculiar to Catalonia **2** (= *tendencia*) sense of the differentness of Catalonia; (*Pol*) doctrine of Catalan autonomy, belief in Catalan autonomy

catalejo SM spyglass, telescope

catalepsia SF catalepsy

catálisis SF INV catalysis

catalítico ADJ catalytic

catalizador SM **1** (*Quím*) catalyst **2** (*Aut*) catalytic converter

catalizar /1f/ VT to catalyse

catalogable ADJ classifiable

catalogar /1h/ VT **1** (*en catálogo*) to catalogue, catalog (*EEUU*) **2** (= *clasificar*) to classify (**de** as); **una zona catalogada de interés artístico** an area classified *o* designated as "of artistic interest"

catálogo SM catalogue, catalog (*EEUU*)

Cataluña SF Catalonia

catamarán SM catamaran

cataplasma SF (*Med*) poultice

catapulta SF catapult (*Brit*), slingshot (*EEUU*)

catapultar /1a/ VT to catapult

catapún* ADJ **una cosa del año ~** an ancient old thing*

catar /1a/ VT to taste

catarata SF **1** (*Geog*) waterfall, cataract ➤ **Cataratas del Niágara** Niagara Falls **2** (*Med*) cataract

catarro SM cold

catarsis SF INV catharsis

catastral ADJ relating to the property register; **valores ~es** property values, land values

catastro SM property register, land registry

catástrofe SF catastrophe, disaster; **~ aérea** air disaster ➤ **catástrofe natural** natural disaster

catastrófico ADJ catastrophic, disastrous

catastrofista Ⓐ ADJ doom-laden Ⓑ SMF prophet of doom

catavinos SMF INV wine taster

cate* SM (*Esp*) **1** (= *golpe*) punch, bash* **2** (= *suspenso*) **dar un ~ a algn** to fail sb, flunk sb (*EEUU**)

catear /1a/ VT **1** (*Esp**) [+ *candidato, estudiante, examen*] to fail, flunk (*EEUU**) **2** (*SAm Min*) to prospect **3** (*Méx*) [*policía*] to search

catecismo SM catechism

catecúmeno/a SM/F catechumen

cátedra SF **1** (*en universidad*) chair, professorship; **hablar ex ~** (*Rel*) to speak ex cathedra; (*fig*) to speak with authority; **sentar ~ sobre algo** to pontificate about sth **2** (*en enseñanza secundaria*) post of head of department

catedral SF cathedral; ✦ MODISMO **como una ~*** enormous, gigantic

catedralicio ADJ cathedral *antes de s*

catedrático/a SM/F **1** [*de universidad*] professor **2** (*en enseñanza secundaria*) head of department

categoría SF **1** (*en clasificación*) category; **de primera ~** [*hotel, servicio*] first-class *antes de s* ➤ **categoría gramatical** part of speech ➤ **categoría profesional** professional status **2** (= *calidad*) quality; **fue un espectáculo de ~** it was a top-quality show; **telenovelas de ínfima ~** soap operas of the very worst kind; **no hay hoy ningún maestro de su ~** nowadays there are no maestros of his calibre *o* in his class; **de ~** [*deportista, artista*] top-class *antes de s* **3** (= *apartado*) (*en premio*) category; (*en deporte*) event; **en la ~ de ensayo** in the essay section *o* category; **en la ~ femenina** in the women's event
4 (= *rango profesional*) grade; (*Mil*) rank

categórico ADJ [*respuesta*] categorical; [*orden*] express

categorizar /1f/ VT to categorize

catenaria SF (*Elec, Ferro*) overhead power cable

cateo SM **1** (*Méx*) search **2** (*SAm*) prospecting

catequesis SF INV (*Rel*) catechesis

catequista SMF (*Rel*) catechist

catequizar /1f/ VT (*Rel*) to catechize, instruct in Christian doctrine

catering ['katerin] SM INV catering; **empresa de ~** caterer's, catering firm

caterva SF (*pey*) throng, crowd

catéter SM catheter

cateto/a* SM/F (*Esp*) yokel*, hick (*EEUU**)

catinga SF (*And, CS*) body odour

catire/a (*Carib, Col*) Ⓐ ADJ (= *de pelo rubio*) fair, fair-haired; (= *de piel blanca*) fair-skinned Ⓑ SM/F [*de pelo rubio*] fair-haired person; [*de piel blanca*] fair-skinned person

catita SF (*CS*) parrot

catiusca Ⓐ ADJ (*Esp*) **botas ~s** rubber boots, wellington boots (*Brit*) Ⓑ SF rubber boot, wellington boot

catódico ADJ cathodic, cathode *antes de s*

cátodo SM cathode

catolicismo SM Catholicism, Roman Catholicism

católico/a Ⓐ ADJ (*Rel*) Catholic, Roman Catholic; **no ~** non-Catholic; ✦ MODISMO **no estar muy ~*** to be under the weather Ⓑ SM/F Catholic

catorce ADJ, PRON, SM (*cardinal*) fourteen; (*ordinal, en la fecha*) fourteenth; *ver tb* **seis**

catorceavo ADJ, PRON fourteenth; *ver tb* **sexto**

catre SM camp bed (*Brit*), cot (*EEUU*); **irse al ~**** to hit the sack*

catsup SM ketchup, catsup (*EEUU*)

caucasiano/a ADJ, SM/F Caucasian

caucásico/a ADJ, SM/F Caucasian

Cáucaso SM Caucasus

cauce SM 1 (= *lecho*) [*de río, arroyo*] riverbed; [*de canal*] bed; (= *curso*) course; **desviaron el ~ del río** they changed *o* diverted the course of the river; **las aguas han vuelto a su ~** the river has returned to its normal level 2 (= *medio*) channel, means; **por ~s legales** through legal channels *o* means; **las negociaciones volvieron a su ~** negotiations returned to their normal course

cauchero/a SM/F (*LAm*) worker in a rubber plantation

caucho SM 1 (= *material*) rubber 2 (*Ven Aut*) tyre, tire (*EEUU*) 3 (*Col*) (= *gomita*) rubber band

caudal SM 1 [*de río*] volume (of water); **el ~ del río desciende en verano** the level of the river goes down in the summer 2 (= *fortuna*) fortune, wealth 3 [*de información, datos, ideas*] wealth, volume

caudaloso ADJ [*río*] wide, fast-flowing

caudillismo SM autocratic government

caudillo SM leader; **el Caudillo** (*Esp*) the Caudillo, Franco

causa¹ SF 1 (= *motivo*) cause; **algunos protestaron sin ~ justificada** some protested for no good reason *o* without true cause; **por ~s ajenas a nuestra voluntad** for reasons beyond our control; **el fuego se inició por ~s desconocidas** it is not known how the fire was started; **a o por ~ de** because of; **fue aplazado a ~ de la lluvia** it was postponed because of rain; **dos personas han muerto a ~ de una explosión** two people have died in an explosion; **no quiero que sufras por mi ~** I don't want you to suffer for my sake *o* on my account; **relación ~-efecto** cause and effect relationship 2 (= *ideal*) cause; **es por una buena ~** it's for a good cause ➤ **causa perdida** lost cause 3 (*Jur*) (*tb* **~ judicial**) lawsuit, case

causa² SF (*Perú*) *fish and potato pie, served cold*

causal Ⓐ ADJ 1 [*factor, relación*] causal 2 (*Ling*) **oración ~** clause of reason Ⓑ SF (*RPl frm*) reason

causalidad SF causality

causante Ⓐ ADJ **la explosión ~ del incendio** the explosion that caused the fire Ⓑ SMF cause; **el mal tiempo fue el ~ del retraso** the delay was caused by bad weather

causar /1a/ VT [+ *problema, consecuencia, víctima*] to cause; [+ *impresión*] to make; **le causa muchos problemas** it causes

him a lot of problems; **la explosión causó heridas a dos personas** the explosion injured two people, the explosion left two people injured; **el poema le causó una honda impresión** the poem made a great impression on him; **~ asombro a algn** to amaze sb; **~ emoción a algn** to move sb; **~ extrañeza a algn** to puzzle sb

causativo ADJ causative

cáustico ADJ caustic

cautela SF caution, wariness; **con mucha ~** very cautiously

cautelar ADJ precautionary; **prisión ~** preventive detention

cauteloso ADJ cautious, wary, careful

cauterizar /1f/ VT to cauterize

cautivador ADJ captivating

cautivar /1a/ VT to captivate

cautiverio SM, **cautividad** SF captivity

cautivo/a ADJ, SM/F captive

cauto ADJ cautious, wary, careful

cava¹ SM (= *vino*) cava

cava² SF (= *para el vino*) wine cellar

cavar /1a/ Ⓐ VT (*en el suelo*) [+ *fosa, hoyo*] to dig; [+ *pozo*] to sink; (*Agr*) [+ *tierra*] to dig over Ⓑ VI (*en el suelo*) to dig

caverna SF cave, cavern

cavernícola Ⓐ ADJ 1 (= *de caverna*) cave-dwelling, cave *antes de s* 2 (*Pol**) reactionary Ⓑ SMF 1 (= *habitante de caverna*) cave dweller 2 (*Pol**) reactionary, backwoodsman

cavernoso ADJ [*voz*] resounding, deep

caviar SM caviar, caviare

cavidad SF cavity

cavilación SF deep thought, rumination

cavilar /1a/ VI to think deeply, ponder

cayado SM 1 (*Agr*) crook 2 (*Rel*) crozier

cayena SF cayenne pepper

cayendo *etc ver* **caer**

cayo SM key, islet

caza Ⓐ SF 1 (= *acción*) hunting; (*con fusil*) shooting; **la ~ del zorro** foxhunting; **la ~ de la perdiz** partridge shooting; **a la ~ de algo: van a la ~ de nuevos talentos** they are on the hunt for new talent; **dar ~ a** (= *perseguir*) to give chase to, pursue; (= *alcanzar*) to catch up with; **ir de ~** (*gen*) to go hunting; (*con fusil*) to go (out) shooting ➤ **caza de brujas** witch hunt ➤ **caza furtiva** poaching ➤ **caza mayor** game hunting ➤ **caza menor** small game hunting ➤ **caza y captura: estar a la ~ y captura de la noticia** to be on the hunt for news; **operación de ~ y captura de criminales** operation to track down and catch criminals 2 (= *animal cazado*) game; (*Culin*) game ➤ **caza mayor** big game ➤ **caza menor** small game Ⓑ SM (*Aer*) fighter (plane)

caza-bombardero SM fighter-bomber

cazador(a¹) SM/F hunter ➤ **cazador(a) furtivo/a** poacher

cazadora² SF (= *chaqueta*) jacket

cazadotes SM INV fortune-hunter

cazafortunas SMF INV fortune-hunter, gold digger

cazamariposas SM INV butterfly net

cazar /1f/ Ⓐ VT 1 [+ *animales*] (*gen*) to hunt; (*con fusil*) to shoot 2 [+ *ladrón, fugitivo*] to hunt down 3 [+ *corredor, ciclista*] to catch (up with) 4 (*) (= *atrapar*) to land*; **su aspiración es ~ un hombre para casarse** her ambition is to land herself a husband* **5** (*) (= *sorprender*) to catch; **los cazó robando** he caught them stealing **6** (*) (= *comprender*) to understand ⓑ VI to hunt; **salir a ~** (*gen*) to go (out) hunting; (*con fusil*) to go (out) shooting

cazarrecompensas SMF INV bounty hunter

cazatalentos SMF INV talent scout

cazo SM **1** (= *cacerola*) saucepan **2** (= *cucharón*) ladle

cazón SM dogfish

cazuela SF **1** (= *recipiente*) [*de metal*] pan; [*de barro*] casserole (dish) **2** (= *guiso*) stew, casserole

cazurro ADJ stubborn

C.C. ABR (*Elec*) (= **corriente continua**) DC

c.c. ABR (= **centímetros cúbicos**) cc

c/c ABR (= **cuenta corriente**) C/A, a/c (*EEUU*)

CD SM ABR (= **compact disc**) CD

C.D. ABR = **Club Deportivo**

CD-I [θeðe'i] SM ABR (= **Compact Disc Interactive**) CD-I

CD-ROM [θeðe'rom] SM ABR (= **Compact Disc Read-Only Memory**) CD-ROM

CE ⓐ SF ABR (= **Comunidad Europea**) EC ⓑ SM ABR = **Consejo de Europa**

ce SF the name of the letter *c*, C; ✦ MODISMO **por ce o por be** somehow or other

cebada SF barley

cebador SM (*RPl Aut*) choke

cebar /1a/ ⓐ VT **1** [+ *animal*] to fatten (up) **2** [+ *anzuelo, cepo, trampa*] to bait **3** [+ *fuego, horno*] to feed, stoke (up); [+ *arma*] to prime **4** (*frm*) [+ *pasión, odio*] to feed, nourish; [+ *cólera*] to feed **5** (*RPl*) [+ *maté*] to brew ⓑ **cebarse** VPR **~se con algo/algn** (= *criticar duramente*) to savage sth/sb; **la crisis económica se cebó en el sector agrícola** the recession ravaged the agricultural sector

cebellina SF (*Zool*) sable

cebiche SM *South American dish of fish marinated in lime or lemon juice*

cebo SM **1** (*Pesca*) bait **2** [*de arma*] charge, primer

cebolla SF onion ➤ **cebolla de Cambray** spring onion

cebolleta SF, **cebollino** SM (= *planta*) spring onion (*Brit*), green onion (*EEUU*); (= *tallo*) chive

cebón SM fattened animal

cebra SF zebra

cebú SM zebu

ceca SF (*Arg*) tails *pl*; *ver tb* **cara 4**

Ceca SF **andar** *o* **ir de la ~ a la Meca** to go hither and thither, chase about all over the place

cecear /1a/ VI (*por defecto*) to lisp; (*Ling*) to pronounce "s" as "th"

ceceo SM (*por defecto*) lisp; (*Ling*) pronunciation of "s" as "th"

cecina SF **1** (= *carne seca*) cured meat, smoked meat **2** (*CS*) jerked meat, jerked beef

cedazo SM sieve

ceder /2a/ ⓐ VT [+ *propiedad*] to transfer; [+ *territorio*] to cede (*frm*), hand over; **me cedió el asiento** she let me have her seat, she gave up her seat (for me); **cedió los derechos de autor a su familia** she gave up *o* over the authorial rights to her family; **~ la palabra a algn** to give the floor to sb (*frm*), call upon sb to speak; **"ceda el paso"** "give way" (*Brit*), "yield" (*EEUU*); **~ terreno a algn/algo** to give ground to sb/sth ⓑ VI **1** (= *transigir*) to give in, yield (*frm*); **~ a algo** to give in to sth, yield to sth; **~ ante algn/algo** to give in to sb/sth, yield to sb/sth; **~ en algo**: **no ceden en su empeño de ganar la liga** they're not giving in *o* up in their endeavour to win the league **2** (= *disminuir*) [*viento*] to drop, die down; [*lluvia*] to ease up; [*frío*] to abate, ease up; [*fiebre*] to go down; [*dolor*] to lessen **3** [*suelo, viga*] to give way, give **4** [*zapatos, prenda, elástico*] to stretch, give

cedilla SF cedilla

cedro SM cedar

cédula SF **1** (= *documento*) document ➤ **cédula ciudadanía** (*Col*), **cédula de identidad** (*LAm*) identity card, ID **2** (*Com*) warrant

cefalea SF migraine

céfiro SM zephyr

cegador ADJ blinding

cegar /1h, 1j/ ⓐ VT **1** (= *deslumbrar*) to blind **2** (= *ofuscar*) [+ *persona*] to blind; **le ciega la pasión** he is blinded by passion **3** (= *obstruir*) [+ *tubería, agujero*] to block up, stop up; [+ *pozo*] to block up ⓑ **cegarse** VPR **1** (= *ofuscarse*) to be blinded (**de** by) **2** (= *obstruirse*) to block

cegato* ADJ, **cegatón*** ADJ half blind*

cegué *ver* **cegar**

ceguera SF blindness

ceibo SM coral tree

ceja SF **1** (*Anat*) eyebrow; ✦ MODISMOS **estar endeudado hasta las ~s*** to be up to one's eyes in debt*; **se le ha metido entre ~ y ~ hacerlo*** he's taken it into his head to do it **2** (*Mús*) bridge

cejar /1a/ VI (= *retroceder*) to move back, go back; (*en discusión*) to back down; **no ~** to keep it up, keep going; **no ~ en sus esfuerzos** to keep at it

cejijunto ADJ with eyebrows very close together

cejilla SF (*Mús*) bridge

celador(a) SM/F [*de edificio*] guard; [*de cárcel*] warder (*Brit*), guard (*EEUU*); [*de centro escolar*] janitor, caretaker (*Brit*); [*de museo*] attendant; [*de hospital*] hospital orderly, hospital porter (*esp Brit*)

celaje SM ✦ MODISMO **como un ~** (*And, Carib*) in a flash

celda SF cell ➤ **celda de castigo** solitary confinement cell

celdilla SF [*de colmena*] cell

celebérrimo ADJ SUPERL *de* **célebre**

celebración SF **1** (= *fiesta*) (*tb Rel*) celebration **2** (= *realización*) **tras la ~ de las elecciones** after the elections were held

celebrante SM (*Rel*) celebrant, officiating priest

celebrar /1a/ ⓐ VT **1** (= *festejar*) [+ *aniversario, acontecimiento*] to celebrate; **siempre celebramos la Navidad en familia** we always celebrate Christmas as a family; **estamos celebrando que hemos aprobado los exámenes** we're celebrating passing our exams; **en mayo se celebra el día de los trabajadores** Labour *o* (*EEUU*) Labor Day is in May **2** (= *llevar a cabo*) [+ *congreso, juicio, elecciones*] to hold; **la reunión se ~á el viernes por la tarde** the meeting will take place *o* will be held on Friday afternoon; **el partido no pudo ~se a causa de la lluvia** the game could not be played because of rain **3** (*frm*) (= *alegrarse de*) **lo celebro** I'm delighted; **lo celebro por él** I'm very pleased for him; **celebro que hayas aceptado ese trabajo** I'm delighted *o* very pleased that you've accepted that job **4** (= *alabar*) [+ *valor, belleza*] to celebrate, praise; [+ *ventajas*] to preach, dwell on; [+ *bromas, gracias*] to laugh at **5** (*Rel*) [+ *boda, ceremonia*] to perform; **~ una misa** to celebrate mass, say mass ⓑ VI [*sacerdote*] to celebrate mass, say mass

célebre ADJ famous, celebrated, noted (**por** for)

celebridad SF celebrity

celeridad SF speed, swiftness; **con ~** quickly, promptly

celeste ADJ **1** (= *del cielo*) heavenly **2** [*color*] sky blue

celestial ADJ **1** (*Rel*) celestial **2** (= *delicioso*) heavenly

celestina SF procuress

celibato SM celibacy

célibe ADJ, SMF celibate

cello SM cello

celo¹ SM **1** (= *diligencia*) zeal; **hacer algo con ~** to do sth zealously *o* with zeal ➤ **celo profesional** professional commitment, commitment to one's job **2** (*Zool*) [*de hembra*] oestrus, estrus (*EEUU*); [*de macho*] rut; **estar en ~** to be in *o* (*Brit*) on heat, be in season **3** **celos** jealousy *sing*; **dar**

~s a algn to make sb jealous; **tener ~s de algn** to be jealous of sb

celo² ® SM (*Esp*) (= *cinta*) sticky tape (*Brit*), Sellotape® (*Brit*), Scotchtape® (*EEUU*)

celo³ SM (*Mús*) cello

celofán SM cellophane

celosía SF lattice, lattice window

celoso ADJ **1** [*marido, hermano*] jealous (**de** of) **2** (= *ferviente*) zealous; (*en el trabajo*) conscientious

celta Ⓐ ADJ Celtic Ⓑ SMF Celt Ⓒ SM (*Ling*) Celtic

celtíbero/a ADJ, SM/F Celtiberian

célula SF **1** (*Biol, Elec*) cell ➤ **célula fotoeléctrica** photoelectric cell **2** (*Pol*) cell ➤ **célula terrorista** terrorist cell

celular Ⓐ ADJ cellular, cell *antes de s*; **tejido ~** cell tissue Ⓑ SM (= *teléfono*) (*LAm*) mobile

celulitis SF INV (= *grasa*) cellulite; (= *inflamación*) cellulitis

celulítico ADJ [*célula, proceso*] cellulite *antes de s*; [*persona*] with cellulite

celuloide SM celluloid

celulosa SF cellulose

cementerio SM (*municipal*) cemetery; (*en iglesia*) graveyard ➤ **cementerio de coches** used-car dump, junkyard (*EEUU*)

cemento SM **1** [*de construcción*] cement ➤ **cemento armado** reinforced concrete **2** (*LAm*) (= *pegamento*) glue **3** [*de diente*] cement

cena SF (*por la noche, como comida principal*) dinner; (*a última hora*) supper; **la Última Cena** the Last Supper ➤ **cena de gala** dinner function, formal dinner; (*Pol*) state banquet ➤ **cena de negocios** business dinner ➤ **cena de trabajo** working dinner

cenáculo SM group, coterie

cenador SM arbour, arbor (*EEUU*)

cenagal SM bog, quagmire

cenagoso ADJ muddy

cenar /1a/ Ⓐ VI (*por la noche, como comida principal*) to have dinner; (*a última hora*) to have supper; (*en ocasión formal*) to dine (*frm*); **salir a ~** to go out to dinner, dine out (*frm*) Ⓑ VT (*como comida principal*) to have for dinner; (*a última hora*) to have for supper

cencerrada SF *noise made with cowbells, pots and pans etc, on festive occasions or in mockery*

cencerro SM cowbell; ✦ MODISMO **estar como un ~*** to be nuts*, be round the bend (*Brit**)

cenefa SF **1** (*Cos*) edging, border **2** (*Arquit*) border

cenicero SM ashtray

Cenicienta SF **la Cenicienta** Cinderella

ceniciento ADJ ashen (*liter*), ash-coloured, ash-colored (*EEUU*)

cénit SM, **cenit** SM zenith

ceniza SF **1** (= *polvo*) ash; **reducir algo a ~s** to reduce sth to ashes **2** **cenizas** [*de persona*] ashes, mortal remains

cenizo Ⓐ ADJ [*color*] ashen (*liter*), ash-coloured, ash-colored (*EEUU*) Ⓑ SM (*) (= *mala suerte, persona*) jinx*

cenote SM (*CAm, Méx*) natural well

censar /1a/ VT to take a census of

censo SM census ➤ **censo electoral** electoral roll (*Brit*), list of registered voters (*EEUU*)

censor SM **1** (*Pol*) censor **2** (*Com, Fin*) ➤ **censor(a) de cuentas** auditor ➤ **censor(a) jurado/a de cuentas** chartered accountant (*Brit*), certified public accountant (*EEUU*)

censura SF **1** (= *supresión*) censorship; **sometieron todos sus libros a la ~** they censored all his books **2** (= *institución*) censors *pl*; **el autor tuvo problemas con la ~** the author had problems with the censors **3** (= *condena*) censure (*frm*), criticism

censurable ADJ reprehensible

censurar /1a/ VT **1** (*Pol*) to censor **2** [+ *obra, película*] to censor **3** (= *criticar*) to censure (*frm*), criticize

centauro SM centaur

centavo SM **1** (*partitivo*) hundredth, hundredth part **2** (*Fin*) cent

centella SF **1** (= *chispa*) spark **2** (= *rayo*) flash of lightning; **salió como una ~ del cuarto** he was out of the room as quick as a flash *o* in a flash

centelleante ADJ [*luz, diamante*] sparkling; [*estrella*] twinkling; [*metal*] gleaming, glinting

centellear /1a/ VI [*luz, diamante*] to sparkle; [*estrella*] to twinkle; [*metal*] to gleam, glint

centelleo SM [*de luz, diamante*] sparkle; [*de estrella*] twinkle; [*de metal*] glint

centena SF hundred

centenar SM hundred; **a ~es** by the hundred, in hundreds, in their hundreds

centenario/a Ⓐ ADJ centenary, centennial Ⓑ SM/F centenarian, hundred-year-old person Ⓒ SM centenary (*esp Brit*), centennial (*esp EEUU*)

centeno SM rye

centésima SF hundredth, hundredth part; **una ~ de segundo** a hundredth of a second; *ver tb* **centésimo**

centesimal ADJ centesimal

centésimo ADJ, PRON hundredth; *ver tb* **sexto, centésima**

centígrado ADJ centigrade

centigramo SM centigram

centilitro SM centilitre, centiliter (*EEUU*)

centímetro SM centimetre, centimeter (*EEUU*)

céntimo SM **1** (*partitivo*) hundredth part **2** (*Fin*) cent; ✦ MODISMO **no vale un ~** it's worthless

centinela SMF (*Mil*) sentry, guard; **estar de ~** to be on guard

centolla SF, **centollo** SM spider crab

central Ⓐ ADJ **1** (= *principal*) **1.1** [*personaje, idea*] central, main; **el tema ~ de la reunión** the main subject of the meeting **1.2** [*oficina*] head *antes de s*; [*banco*] central; [*ordenador*] mainframe *antes de s* **2** (= *del medio*) [*región, zona*] central **3** (= *no regional*) [*gobierno, administración*] central Ⓑ SF **1** (*tb* **oficina ~**) [*de empresa*] head office; (*a nivel internacional*) headquarters ➤ **central de abasto** (*Méx*) market ➤ **central de correos** main post office, general post office ➤ **central de teléfonos** telephone exchange (*esp Brit*), telephone central office (*EEUU*) ➤ **central sindical** trade union (*esp Brit*) *o* labor union (*EEUU*) confederation ➤ **central telefónica** telephone exchange (*esp Brit*), telephone central office (*EEUU*) **2** (= *factoría*) plant, station; (*tb* **~ nuclear**) nuclear power station ➤ **central azucarera** (*Cub, Perú*) sugar mill ➤ **central eléctrica** power station ➤ **central hidroeléctrica** hydroelectric power station ➤ **central lechera** dairy ➤ **central térmica** power station

centralismo SM centralism

centralita SF (*Telec*) switchboard

centralización SF centralization

centralizar /1f/ VT to centralize

centrar /1a/ Ⓐ VT **1** (= *colocar*) [+ *imagen, texto*] to centre, center (*EEUU*); **la foto no está bien centrada** the photo is not centred correctly **2** (= *concentrar*) [+ *investigación*] to focus, centre, center (*EEUU*); [+ *esfuerzos*] to concentrate; [+ *atención*] to focus; **he centrado mi nueva obra en sólo dos personajes** my new play focuses on *o* centres on only two characters Ⓑ VI (*Dep*) to centre, center (*EEUU*) Ⓒ **centrarse** VPR **1** **~se en** [*estudio, investigación, debate, programa*] to be focused on, centre on, center on (*EEUU*); [*obra, película, exposición*] to focus on; **la atención internacional se centraba en El Salvador** international attention focused on *o* centred on El Salvador **2** (= *equilibrarse*) to settle down; **tuvo una época muy loca pero después se centró** he went through a very wild

céntrico ADJ central; **está muy ~** it's very central

centrífuga SF centrifuge

centrifugadora SF **1** (*para ropa*) spin-dryer **2** (*Téc*) centrifuge

centrifugar /1h/ VT **1** [+ *ropa*] to spin-dry **2** (*Téc*) to centrifuge

centrífugo ADJ centrifugal

centrípeto ADJ centripetal

centrista Ⓐ ADJ centrist Ⓑ SMF centrist, *member of a centrist party*

centro

> En inglés americano se usa **center** en lugar de **centre**.

Ⓐ SM **1** (= *medio*) centre ➤ **centro de gravedad** centre of gravity ➤ **centro de mesa** centrepiece, centerpiece (*EEUU*) ➤ **centro neurálgico** nerve centre **2** [*de ciudad*] centre; **"centro ciudad"** "city centre", "town centre"; **ir al ~** to go into town, go downtown (*EEUU*) **3** (*Pol*) centre; **ser de ~** [*persona*] to be a moderate; [*partido*] to be in the centre **4** (= *foco*) [*de huracán*] centre; [*de incendio*] seat; **ser el ~ de atención** o **atracción** o **interés** to be the focus of attention, be the centre of attention; **ser el ~ de las miradas: Roma es estos días el ~ de todas las miradas** all eyes are on Rome at the moment **5** (= *establecimiento*) centre; **dos alumnos han sido expulsados del ~** two students have been expelled from the school o centre ➤ **centro cívico** community centre ➤ **centro comercial** shopping centre, shopping mall ➤ **centro cultural** (*en barrio, institución*) (local) arts centre; [*de otro país*] cultural centre ➤ **centro de abasto** (*Méx*) market ➤ **centro de acogida: ~ de acogida para mujeres maltratadas** refuge for battered women; **~ de acogida de refugiados** refugee reception centre ➤ **centro de enseñanza** (*gen*) educational institution; (= *colegio*) school ➤ **centro de planificación familiar** family planning clinic ➤ **centro de salud** health centre ➤ **centro de trabajo** workplace ➤ **centro docente** educational institution ➤ **centro médico** (*gen*) medical establishment; (= *hospital*) hospital ➤ **centro penitenciario** prison, penitentiary (*EEUU*) ➤ **centro sanitario** = **centro médico 6** (= *población*) ➤ **centro turístico** (= *lugar muy visitado*) tourist centre; (*diseñado para turistas*) tourist resort ➤ **centro urbano** urban area, city Ⓑ SMF (*Ftbl*) centre; **delantero ~** centre-forward, center-forward (*EEUU*); **medio ~** centre-half, center-half (*EEUU*)

Centroamérica SF Central America

centroamericano/a ADJ, SM/F Central American

centrocampista SMF (*Dep*) midfielder

centroderecha SM centre-right

centroeuropeo/a ADJ, SM/F Central European

centroizquierda SM centre-left, center-left (*EEUU*)

céntuplo Ⓐ ADJ hundredfold, centuple Ⓑ SM centuple

centuria SF century

centurión SM centurion

cenzontle SM (*CAm, Méx*) mockingbird

ceñido ADJ [*vestido*] figure-hugging; [*traje*] tight-fitting; [*vaqueros*] skintight

ceñir /3h, 3k/ Ⓐ VT **1** (= *ajustar*) **el vestido le ceñía el cuerpo** the dress clung to o hugged her body, the dress was really tight-fitting; **la faja le ceñía el talle** the sash fitted tightly around her waist **2** (*liter*) (= *llevar puesto*) **la corona que ciñó nuestro rey** the crown that our king wore, the crown that rested on the head of our king Ⓑ **ceñirse** VPR **1** (= *atenerse*) **~se a algo: ~se al tema** to keep to the topic; **será difícil ~se al presupuesto** it will be difficult to keep to o stay within the budget **2** (*frm*) (= *ponerse*) to put on; **~se la corona** to be crowned, take the crown (*liter*); **~se la espada**†† to put on one's sword, gird one's sword (*liter*)

ceño SM (= *expresión*) frown, scowl; **arrugar** o **fruncir el ~** to frown, knit one's brows

ceñudo ADJ frowning, scowling

CEOE SF ABR (= **Confederación Española de Organizaciones Empresariales**) ≈ CBI

cepa SF **1** (= *tronco*) [*de árbol*] stump; [*de vid*] stock **2** [*de persona*] stock; **es un inglés de pura ~** he's English through and through, he's every inch an Englishman **3** (*Biol*) strain

CEPAL SF ABR (= **Comisión Económica para América Latina y el Caribe**) ECLAC

cepillado SM **1** [*de ropa, dientes, pelo*] brushing **2** [*de madera*] planing

cepillar /1a/ Ⓐ VT **1** [+ *ropa, dientes, pelo*] to brush **2** [+ *madera*] to plane, plane down Ⓑ **cepillarse** VPR **1** [+ *dientes, pelo*] to brush **2** **~se a algn*** (= *matar*) to bump sb off*; (***) (= *copular con*) to screw sb***; (= *suspender*) to fail sb, flunk sb (*EEUU**)

cepillo SM **1** (*para ropa, dientes, pelo*) brush; **lleva el pelo cortado al ~** he has a crew cut ➤ **cepillo de dientes** toothbrush ➤ **cepillo para el pelo** hairbrush ➤ **cepillo para la ropa** clothes brush ➤ **cepillo para las uñas** nailbrush **2** (*para barrer*) brush **3** (*para madera*) plane **4** (*Rel*) poorbox, alms box

cepo SM **1** (*Caza*) trap, snare **2** (*Aut*) (wheel) clamp (*Brit*), Denver boot (*EEUU*)

ceporro* SM idiot

cera SF wax; **depilarse a la ~** to wax one's legs o arms *etc* ➤ **cera de abejas** beeswax ➤ **cera de los oídos** earwax

cerámica SF **1** (*Arte*) ceramics *sing*, pottery **2** (= *conjunto de objetos*) ceramics *pl*, pottery

ceramista SMF potter

cerbatana SF **1** (*Mil*) blowpipe **2** (= *juguete*) peashooter

cerca[1] SF (= *valla*) [*de madera, alambre*] fence; [*de piedra, ladrillo*] wall

cerca[2] ADV **1** (*indicando proximidad*) (*de aquí* o *allí*) near, nearby; (*entre objetos, personas*) close; **no había un hospital ~** there wasn't a hospital near there o nearby; **está aquí ~** it's very o just near here; **¿está ~ la estación?** is the station near here o nearby?; **quería tener más ~ a los amigos** he wanted to be nearer (to) o closer to his friends; **las Navidades están ya ~** Christmas is nearly here, Christmas is not far off now; **~ de** near (to), close to; **viven ~ de la playa** they live near (to) o close to the beach **2 de ~ 2.1** (= *a poca distancia*) [*ver*] close up; [*seguir, observar, vigilar*] closely; **no veo bien de ~** I can't see things close up, I'm long-sighted (*Brit*) o far-sighted (*EEUU*); **pudo ver de ~ la pobreza** she got to see poverty close at hand o at close quarters **2.2** (= *bien*) **los que lo conocen de ~** those who know him well; **no conoce de ~ los problemas de la población** he does not have first-hand o personal knowledge of the people's problems **3 ~ de** (= *casi*) nearly; **~ de 2.500 personas** nearly 2,500 people; **son ~ de las seis** it's nearly six o'clock; **estar ~ de hacer algo** to come close to doing sth **4** (*esp CS*) **~ nuestro/mío** near us/me

cercado SM **1** (= *recinto*) enclosure **2** (= *valla*) fence, wall **3** (*And Hist*) *state capital and surrounding towns*

cercanía SF **1** (= *proximidad*) nearness, proximity **2 cercanías** (= *alrededores*) neighbourhood *sing*, neighborhood *sing* (*EEUU*), vicinity *sing*; (= *suburbios*) outskirts, suburbs; **tren de ~s** suburban train, commuter train

cercano ADJ **1** [*lugar*] nearby; **entraron en un bar ~** they went to a nearby bar; **acudió a la comisaría más cercana** he went to the nearest police station; **~ a** close to, near, near to; **un hotel ~ al aeropuerto** a hotel close to o near (to) the airport; **una cifra cercana a los tres millones de dólares** a figure close to three million dollars **2** [*amigo, pariente*] close (**a** to); **según fuentes cercanas al ministerio** according to sources close to the ministry **3** (*en el tiempo*) **en el futuro ~** in the near future

Cercano Oriente SM Near East

cercar /1g/ VT **1** [+ *campo, terreno*] to enclose; (*con vallas*) to fence in, wall in **2** [+ *persona*] to surround, ring **3** (*Mil*)

[+ *pueblo, ciudad*] to surround, besiege; [+ *tropas*] to cut off, surround

cercenar /1a/ VT **1** (= *recortar*) to cut o trim the edges of **2** [+ *brazo, pierna*] to sever

cerciorarse /1a/ VPR **~ de algo** make sure o certain of sth

cerco SM **1** (*Agr*) (= *recinto*) enclosure **2** (*LAm*) (= *valla*) fence, hedge **3** (= *borde externo*) [*de estrella*] halo; [*de mancha*] ring **4** (*Mil*) siege; **poner ~ a algo** to lay siege to sth, besiege sth

cerda SF **1** (*Zool*) sow; *ver tb* **cerdo 2** (= *pelo*) [*de cepillo, jabalí, tejón*] bristle

cerdada SF dirty trick

Cerdeña SF Sardinia

cerdo[1] SM **1** (*Zool*) pig, hog (*EEUU*); **son unos ~s** (*pey*) they are bastards o swines*; ✦ MODISMO **comer como un ~** (= *mucho*) to stuff o.s; (= *sin modales*) to eat like a pig; *ver tb* **cerda 2** (*Culin*) pork; **carne de ~** pork

cerdo[2]/a• ⒶADJ **1** (= *sucio*) filthy, dirty **2** (= *canalla*) rotten* ⒷSM/F **1** (= *sucio*) slob* **2** (= *canalla*) swine*/cow*; *ver tb* **cerda**

cereal ⒶADJ cereal, grain *antes de s* ⒷSM **1** (= *grano*) cereal, grain **2** (*tb* **~es**) [*de desayuno*] cereal *sing*, cereals

cerebelo SM cerebellum

cerebral ADJ **1** (= *del cerebro*) cerebral, brain *antes de s* **2** (= *calculador*) scheming, calculating

cerebro SM **1** (*Anat*) brain; ✦ MODISMOS **estrujarse el ~*** to rack one's brains; **ser un ~*** to be brilliant, be really brainy **2** (= *dirigente*) brains *pl*; **es el ~ del equipo** he's the brains of the team

ceremonia SF **1** (= *acto*) ceremony **2** (= *afectación*) formality, ceremoniousness; **¡déjate de ~s!** don't stand on ceremony!; **se despidió sin ~s** he said goodbye without a fuss

ceremonial ADJ, SM ceremonial

ceremonioso ADJ [*reunión, saludo, visita*] formal; [*ambiente*] ceremonious

cereza SF cherry

cerezo SM cherry tree

cerilla SF match

cerillo SM (*CAm, Méx*) match

cerner /2g/ ⒶVT [+ *harina*] to sift, sieve; [+ *tierra*] to sieve Ⓑcernerse VPR **1** [*ave*] to hover; [*avión*] to circle **2** [*amenaza*] **~se sobre algo/algn** to hang over sth/sb

cernícalo SM **1** (*Orn*) kestrel **2** (*) (= *persona*) lout, dolt

cernido SM (*And Meteo*) drizzle

cero SM **1** (*Fís*) zero; (*Mat*) zero, nought (*esp Brit*); **ocho grados bajo ~** eight degrees below zero

---

O (pronunciado igual que la letra **o**) se usa en inglés británico en los números de teléfono y al leer números de referencia y de cuentas bancarias:

~ noventa y uno O nine one ✦ MODISMOS **empezar** o **partir de ~** to start from scratch; **ser un ~ a la izquierda** to be useless

2 (*Ftbl, Rugby*) nil (*Brit*), zero (*EEUU*); **ganaron por tres goles a ~** they won by three goals to nil (*Brit*) o nothing (*EEUU*) o zero (*EEUU*), they won three nil (*Brit*) o nothing (*EEUU*) o three (to) zero (*EEUU*); **empataron a ~** they drew nil-nil (*Brit*), they tied zero-zero (*EEUU*), it was a no-score draw (*Brit*), it was a scoreless game (*esp EEUU*); **estamos 40 a ~** (*Tenis*) it's 40-love

3 (*Educ*) zero, nought (*esp Brit*)

cerote SM (*CAm, Méx*) piece of human excrement, stool

cerquillo SM (*LAm*) fringe (*Brit*), bangs *pl* (*EEUU*)

cerrado ADJ **1** (= *no abierto*) [*puerta, ventana, boca*] closed; [*puño*] clenched; [*curva*] sharp, tight; **"cerrado por vacaciones"** "closed for holidays" (*Brit*), "closed for vacation" (*EEUU*); **la puerta no estaba cerrada con llave** the door was not locked; **un sobre ~** a sealed envelope; **¿está el grifo bien ~?** is the tap (*Brit*) o faucet (*EEUU*) turned off

properly?; **el mitin se celebró en un recinto ~** the rally was held indoors; **huele a ~** it smells stuffy in here; **~ a** closed to; **los jardines están ~s al público** the gardens are closed to the public

2 (= *apretado*) [*barba*] thick, full; [*bosque*] dense, thick; [*ambiente, atmósfera*] stuffy; **el candidato fue recibido con una cerrada ovación** the presidential candidate was given a rapturous welcome

3 [*cielo*] cloudy, overcast; [*noche*] dark, black; **era ya noche cerrada** it was completely dark

4 (*Ling*) [*acento*] broad, strong; [*vocal*] closed

5 [*persona*] **5.1** (= *intransigente*) **es un tío muy cerrado** he keeps himself to himself **5.2** (= *torpe*) (*tb* **~ de mollera**) dense, thick (*Brit**) **5.3** (= *reservado*) reserved

cerradura SF lock

cerrajería SF (*Com*) locksmith's, locksmith's shop

cerrajero/a SM/F locksmith

cerrar /1j/ ⒶVT **1** (*hablando de un objeto abierto*) [+ *puerta, ventana, boca*] to close, shut; [+ *cremallera*] to do up; [+ *camisa*] to button, do up; [+ *cortina*] to draw; [+ *paraguas, válvula*] to close; [+ *carta*] to seal; [+ *costura, herida*] to sew up; **cierra los ojos** close o shut your eyes; **~ algo de golpe** to slam sth shut; **cerré la puerta con llave** I locked the door; ✦ MODISMO **cierra el pico*** shut your trap**

2 (= *desconectar*) [+ *gas, grifo, radiador*] to turn off

3 (= *bloquear*) [+ *agujero, brecha, tubo*] to block (up); [+ *frontera, puerto*] to close; **una roca cerraba la entrada a la cueva** a rock was obstructing the entrance to the cave; **~ el paso a algn** to block sb's way

4 [+ *tienda, negocio*] (*al final de la jornada*) to close, shut; (*para siempre*) to close, close down

5 (= *poner fin a*) [+ *debate, narración, programa*] to close, end; [+ *desfile*] to bring up the rear of; **los manifestantes que cerraban la marcha** the demonstrators bringing up the rear o at the rear; **cierra la cabalgata la carroza de Santa Claus** the last float in the procession is the one with Santa Claus

6 ~ un trato to seal a deal

ⒷVI **1** [*puerta, ventana*] to close, shut; [*paraguas, válvula*] to close; [*herida*] to close up; **la puerta cierra mal** the door won't close o shut properly; **un estuche que cierra con llave** a jewellery box with a lock

2 [*persona*] **cierra, que se va a escapar el gato** close o shut the door or the cat will get out; **te dejo las llaves para que cierres** I am leaving you the keys so you can lock up

3 [*tienda, negocio*] to close, shut; **¿a qué hora cierran las tiendas el sábado?** what time do the shops close o shut on Saturday?

4 (*Fin*) (*en la Bolsa*) to close

5 (*en dominó*) to block; (*en Scrabble*) to use one's tiles up; **¡cierro!** I'm out!

Ⓒcerrarse VPR **1** [*puerta, ventana*] to close, shut; [*paraguas, válvula*] to close; [*herida*] to close up; **la ventana se cerró de golpe** the window slammed shut; **se me cierran los ojos** I can't keep my eyes open

2 [*persona*] **ciérrate bien el abrigo** do your coat up properly; **~se la cremallera** to do one's zip (*Brit*) o zipper (*esp EEUU*) up

3 (*Com*) to close, shut; **el museo se cerró por obras** the museum closed for refurbishment

4 (= *obcecarse*) **~se a algo: no hay que ~se a nada sin probarlo primero** you should never dismiss anything without trying it first; ✦ MODISMO **~se en banda** (= *mostrarse inflexible*) to refuse to budge; (= *unirse*) to close ranks

5 (= *terminar*) to close, end; **se ha cerrado el plazo para las votaciones** the period for voting has closed o is over

6 [*cielo*] to cloud over, become overcast; [*invierno, noche*] to close in

cerrazón SF stubbornness, bloody-mindedness (*Brit*)

cerril ADJ **1** [*animal*] untamed, unbroken **2** [*persona*] (= *brusco*) rough, uncouth; (= *de miras estrechas*) small-minded

cerro SM (*Geog*) hill; ✦ MODISMO **andar** o **echarse** o **ir por los ~s de Úbeda** to wander off the point, go off at a tangent

cerrojazo SM slamming; **dar un ~** (*lit*) to slam the bolt; (*fig*) to end unexpectedly

cerrojo SM bolt, latch; **echar el ~** to bolt the door

certamen SM competition, contest

certero ADJ **1** [*respuesta*] accurate; [*decisión*] correct, right **2** [*tiro*] well-aimed

certeza SF **1** (= *seguridad*) certainty; **tener la ~ de que ...** to know for certain that ..., be sure that ... **2** (= *precisión*) accuracy

certidumbre SF **1** (= *seguridad*) certainty **2** (= *confianza*) conviction

certificación SF certification

certificado 🅐 ADJ (*Correos*) [*carta, paquete*] registered; **envié la carta por correo ~** I sent the letter by registered mail *o* (*esp Brit*) post **🅑** SM certificate **➤ certificado de autenticidad** certificate of authenticity **➤ certificado de defunción** death certificate **➤ certificado de nacimiento** birth certificate **➤ certificado médico** medical certificate

certificar /1g/ VT **1** (*Jur*) to certify **2** (*Correos*) to register

cerúleo ADJ (*liter*) cerulean (*liter*), sky blue

cerumen SM earwax

cervantino ADJ Cervantine; **estudios ~s** Cervantes studies

cervatillo SM fawn

cervato SM fawn

cervecería SF bar, public house (*Brit*), beer hall (*EEUU*)

cervecero ADJ beer *antes de s*

cerveza SF beer **➤ cerveza de barril** draught beer, draft beer (*EEUU*) **➤ cerveza negra** stout **➤ cerveza rubia** lager

cervical ADJ **1** (= *del cuello*) neck *antes de s*, cervical **2** (= *del útero*) cervical

cerviz SF nape (of the neck); **✦ MODISMO bajar** *o* **doblar la ~** to submit, bow down

cesación SF cessation, suspension

cesante 🅐 ADJ [*empleado*] laid-off, redundant (*Brit*); [*funcionario*] suspended; [*embajador*] recalled; **el ministro ~** the outgoing minister **🅑** SMF (*CS*) redundant worker (*Brit*), laid-off worker (*EEUU*)

cesantear /1a/ VT (*CS*) to dismiss

cesantía SF (*LAm*) (= *despido*) redundancy, dismissal; (= *paga*) redundancy money, redundancy payment

cesar /1a/ **🅐** VI **1** (= *parar*) to stop; **un ruido que no cesa** an incessant noise; **no ~ de hacer algo: no cesaba de repetirlo** he kept repeating it; **sin ~** incessantly, nonstop; **repetía sin ~ que siempre estaríamos juntos** she kept saying that we would always be together **2** (= *dimitir*) to leave, quit (*EEUU*); **~ en su cargo** [*empleado*] to resign, leave one's job; [*alto cargo*] to leave office **🅑** VT **1** (= *despedir*) to dismiss **2** (*empezar*) [+ *ataque*] to stop

cesárea SF Caesarean (section)

cese SM **1** (= *parada*) cessation; **el ~ de (las) hostilidades** the cessation of hostilities **2** (= *despido*) dismissal; **dar el ~ a algn** to dismiss sb **3** (= *dimisión*) resignation

cesio SM caesium, cesium (*EEUU*)

cesión SF **1** [*de territorio*] cession (*frm*), giving up **2** (*Jur*) granting, transfer

césped SM **1** (= *planta*) grass **➤ césped artificial** artificial turf, Astroturf® **2** (= *terreno plantado*) lawn **3** (*Dep*) field, pitch (*Brit*)

cesta SF **1** (= *canasta*) basket **➤ cesta de la compra** (*Esp*) shopping basket; (*Econ*) *cost of a week's shopping* **➤ cesta de Navidad** Christmas box, Christmas hamper **2** (*en baloncesto, pelota vasca*) basket

cestería SF **1** (= *arte*) basketmaking **2** (= *conjunto de cestas*) wickerwork, basketwork; **silla de ~** wicker chair, wicker-work chair **3** (= *tienda*) basketwork shop

cestillo SM **1** (= *cesto pequeño*) small basket **2** [*de globo*] basket

cesto SM basket, hamper

cetáceo ADJ, SM cetacean

cetrería SF falconry, hawking

cetrino ADJ [*tez*] sallow

cetro SM sceptre, scepter (*EEUU*); **✦ MODISMO empuñar el ~** to ascend the throne

ceutí ADJ from *o* of Ceuta

C.F. ABR (= **Club de Fútbol**) FC

cf. ABR (= **compárese**) cf

CFC SM ABR (= **clorofluorocarbono**) CFC

cfr. ABR (= **confróntese**) cf

cg ABR (= **centígramo(s)**) cg

CGT SF ABR **1** (*en varios países*) = **Confederación General de Trabajadores 2** (*en Argentina*) = **Confederación General del Trabajo**

Ch, ch [tʃe] SF *combination of consonants formerly considered a separate letter of the Spanish alphabet*

chabacanería SF **1** (= *mal gusto*) vulgarity, bad taste **2** (= *comentario*) **una ~** a coarse *o* vulgar remark

chabacano¹ ADJ [*chiste*] vulgar, coarse, in bad taste; [*objeto*] cheap; [*trabajo*] shoddy

chabacano² SM (*Méx*) apricot, apricot tree

chabola SF shack; **chabolas** (*Esp*) (= *barrio*) shanty town

chabolismo SM (*Esp*) *problem of shanty towns*

chacal SM jackal

chácara SF (*CAm*) large bag (*made of leather*)

chacarera SF *folk dance from the Southern Cone*

chacarero/a SM/F (*LAm*) small farmer, market gardener (*Brit*), truck farmer (*EEUU*)

chacha* SF maid, housemaid

cháchara SF **1** (= *charla*) chatter, chit-chat*; **estar de ~*** to chatter, gab* **2 cháchara** (*Méx*) (= *trastos*) junk *sing*

chacharero/a SM/F (*Méx*) junk dealer, rag-and-bone man (*Brit*)

chachi* ADJ, ADV (*Esp*) great*

chacho* SM boy, lad

chacina SF **1** (= *carne para embutidos*) pork **2** (= *embutidos*) cold meats *pl*, cold cuts *pl* (*EEUU*) **3** (= *cecina*) cured meat

chacolí SM *sharp-tasting Basque wine*

chacota* SF **tomarse algo a ~** not to take sth seriously

chacra SF (*And, CS*) small farm

chador SM chador

chafa* ADJ (*Méx*) useless

chafar /1a/ VT **1** [+ *pelo*] to flatten; [+ *ropa*] to crumple, crease; [+ *patatas*] to mash **2** [+ *persona*] **~** *o* **dejar chafado a algn** to crush sb, take the wind out of sb's sails* **3** (= *estropear*) to ruin, spoil

chaflán SM bevel; **la casa que hace ~** the house on the corner

chaflar* /1a/ VT (*Chi*) to expel, fire*

cháguar SM (*LAm*) agave fibre, hemp

chal SM shawl

chala SF (*And, CS*) maize leaf (*Brit*), maize husk (*Brit*), corn husk (*EEUU*)

chalado* ADJ crazy*

chalán SM (*Col*) **1** (= *entrenador*) horse breaker **2** (= *jinete*) good horseman

chalé SM = **chalet**

chaleco SM [*de traje*] waistcoat (*Brit*), vest (*EEUU*); [*de lana*] sleeveless pullover; **✦ MODISMO a ~** (*CAm, Méx*) by hook or by crook **➤ chaleco antibalas** bulletproof vest **➤ chaleco de fuerza** (*LAm*) straitjacket **➤ chaleco salvavidas** life jacket, life preserver (*EEUU*)

chalecón ADJ (*Méx*) tricky, deceitful

chalet [tʃa'le] SM (*pl* **~s**) (*en urbanización*) (detached) house; [*de campo*] villa, cottage; [*de una sola planta*] bungalow; [*de montaña*] chalet **➤ chalet adosado** (*Esp*) terraced house (*Brit*), row house (*EEUU*) **➤ chalet pareado** (*Esp*) semi-detached house (*Brit*), duplex (*EEUU*)

chalupa¹ SF (= *embarcación*) launch, boat; (*Méx*) small canoe

chalupa² SF (*Méx Culin*) stuffed tortilla

chamaco/a SM/F (*esp Méx*) **1** (= *niño*) kid **2** (= *novio*) boyfriend/girlfriend

chamagoso* ADJ (*Méx*) filthy

chamal SM blanket (*worn by Mapuche Indians*)

chamanto SM poncho (*worn by farmers in Chile*)

chamarilero/a SM/F secondhand dealer

chamarra SF jacket

chamba SF **1** (*Méx**) (= *trabajo*) work, business **2** (*And*) (= *zanja*) ditch

chambear* /1a/ (*Méx*) VI to earn one's living

chambelán SM chamberlain

chambergo SM broad-brimmed soft hat

chambón* ADJ (*LAm*) clumsy

chamizo SM **1** (= *cabaña*) thatched hut **2** (= *chabola*) shack

chamo/a* SM/F (*Ven*) kid*, child

champa SF **1** (*And*) (= *tierra*) sod, turf **2** (*And*) [*de pelo*] (= *greña*) mop of hair **3** (*CAm*) (= *cobertizo*) shed; (= *tienda de campaña*) tent

champán SM o SF champagne

champiñón SM mushroom

championes SMPL (*Uru*) trainers (*Brit*), sneakers (*EEUU*)

champú SM shampoo

champurrado SM (*CAm, Méx*) **1** [*de bebidas*] mixture of alcoholic drinks, cocktail **2** (*) (= *lío*) mess **3** [*de chocolate*] *thick chocolate drink*

chamuchina* SF (*LAm*) **1** (= *turba*) rabble, mob **2** (*And, Carib*) (= *jaleo*) shindy*

chamullar** /1a/ VI (*CS*) (= *hablar*) to speak, talk; (= *mentir*) to cook up a story

chamuscar /1g/ Ⓐ VT to scorch, singe Ⓑ **chamuscarse** VPR to get scorched, singe

chamusquina SF singeing, scorching; ✦ MODISMO **esto huele a ~** there's trouble brewing

chamuyar /1a/ VI (*RPl*) = **chamullar**

chan SM (*CAm*) local guide

chancaca SF **1** (*Perú*) [*de maíz*] maize cake (*Brit*), corn cake (*EEUU*) **2** (*And*) (= *azúcar*) dark brown sugar

chancar /1g/ VT (*And*) **1** (= *moler*) to grind, crush **2** (= *pegar*) to beat, ill-treat

chance SF o SM **1** (*LAm*) (= *oportunidad*) chance **2** (*Col*) (= *suerte*) good luck

chancear /1a/ VI (*Col*), **chancearse** VPR (*Col*) (= *bromear*) to joke, make jokes (**de** about); **~se de algn** to make fun of sb

chanchada* SF (*LAm*) **1** (= *mala*) dirty trick **2** (*repugnante*) **no hagas ~s** don't be messy

chanchería SF (*LAm*) pork-butcher's, pork-butcher's shop

chanchero SM (*LAm*) pork butcher

chanchito* SM (*LAm*) **1** (*para dinero*) piggy bank **2** (= *cerdito*) piglet

chancho (*LAm*) Ⓐ ADJ dirty, filthy Ⓑ SM pig, hog (*EEUU*); (= *carne*) pork; ✦ MODISMO **hacerse el ~ rengo*** to pretend not to notice

chanchullo* SM wangle*, fiddle (*Brit**)

chancla SF flip-flop (*esp Brit*), thong (*EEUU*)

chancleta SF **1** (= *chancla*) flip-flop (*esp Brit*), thong (*EEUU*) **2** (*SAm* hum*) baby girl **3** (*Col, Ven*) (= *acelerador*) accelerator

chanclo SM **1** (= *zueco*) clog **2** [*de goma*] overshoe, galosh

chancón/ona* SM/F (*Perú*) swot (*Brit**), grind (*EEUU**)

chandal SM (*Esp*) (*pl* **~s**), **chándal** SM (*Esp*) (*pl* **chándals**) tracksuit (*Brit*), sweatsuit (*EEUU*)

chanfaina SF (*And, CAm*) mess

chanfle SM (*LAm*) **1** (= *efecto*) **darle ~ a la pelota** to put spin on the ball **2** = **chaflán**

changa SF (*And, CS*) odd job; *ver tb* **chango**

changador SM (*And, CS*) porter

changarro SM (*Méx*) small shop (*Brit*), small store (*EEUU*)

chango/a Ⓐ ADJ **1** (*Méx*) (= *listo*) quick, sharp **2** (*Chi*) (= *tonto*) silly Ⓑ SM/F (*Méx*) small monkey; *ver tb* **changa**

changuito SM **1** (*RPl*) shopping trolley (*Brit*), shopping cart (*EEUU*) **2 changuitos** (*Méx*) **hacer ~s** to keep one's fingers crossed

changurro SM crab

chanquetes SMPL whitebait *pl*

chanta** SMF (*CS*) (= *fanfarrón*) loudmouth*; (= *informal*) fraud

chantaje SM blackmail; **hacer ~ a algn** to blackmail sb

chantajear /1a/ VT to blackmail

chantajista SMF blackmailer

chantar /1a/ VT **1** (*Perú, Chi**) (= *arrojar*) to throw, chuck; **~ a algn en la cárcel** to throw sb in jail, put sb in jail; **~ a algn en la calle** to throw sb out **2** (*CS*) (= *abandonar*) to leave in the lurch **3** (*And, CS*) [+ *golpe*] to give

chanza SF joke; **estar de ~** to be joking

chao* EXCL bye*, so long (*esp EEUU**), see ya (*esp EEUU**)

chapa SF **1** (= *material*) sheet metal **2** (= *lámina*) [*de metal*] sheet; [*de acero*] plate; [*de madera*] panel **3** (= *insignia*) [*de policía*] badge; [*de adorno*] badge (*Brit*), button (*EEUU*) **4** [*de botella*] cap, top **5** (*Aut*) bodywork **6** (*CS*) [*de matrícula*] plate **7 chapas** (= *juego*) *game of throwing bottle tops*; ✦ MODISMO **hacer ~s** (*Esp***) (= *prostituirse*) to turn tricks** **8** (*LAm*) (= *cerradura*) lock

chapado ADJ [*metal*] plated; [*muebles*] veneered, finished; **~ de oro** gold-plated; ✦ MODISMO **~ a la antigua** old-fashioned, of the old school

chapar /1a/ Ⓐ VT **1** (= *cubrir*) [+ *metal*] to plate; [+ *muebles*] to veneer, finish; [+ *pared*] to tile **2** (*Esp***) (= *cerrar*) [+ *local, negocio*] to shut, close **3** (*Perú, RPl*) (= *asir*) to seize **4** (*RPl**) (= *atrapar*) [+ *objeto, persona*] to catch; (= *entender*) to get* Ⓑ VI (**) **1** (*Esp*) (= *estudiar*) to cram*, swot (*Brit**) **2** (*Esp*) (= *dormir*) to sleep **3** (*RPl*) [*pareja*] to canoodle*

chaparral SM thicket (*of kermes oaks*), chaparral

chaparreras SFPL (*Méx*) leather chaps

chaparro/a Ⓐ ADJ **1** (= *rechoncho*) squat **2** (*esp LAm*) (= *bajito*) short Ⓑ SM/F short chubby person

chaparrón SM **1** (*Meteo*) downpour, cloudburst; ✦ MODISMO **aguantar el ~** to face the music* **2** [*de insultos*] barrage

chape SM (*Chi*) tress, pigtail

chapeau [tʃaˈpo] Ⓐ EXCL bravo!, well done! Ⓑ SM ✦ MODISMO **hacer ~** to take off one's hat (**ante** to)

chapero** SM (*Esp*) rent boy (*Brit**), hustler (*EEUU**)

chapista SMF (*Aut*) panel beater

chapitel SM [*de columna*] capital; [*de torre*] spire

chapó = **chapeau**

chapopote SM (*Méx*) (= *alquitrán*) tar; (= *asfalto*) asphalt

chapotear /1a/ VI to splash about

chapoteo SM splashing

chapucero/a Ⓐ ADJ [*trabajo, persona*] shoddy, slapdash Ⓑ SM/F bungler

chapulín SM (*Méx*) large grasshopper

chapurrear* /1a/ VT **chapurrea el italiano** he speaks broken o bad Italian

chapuza SF **1** (= *trabajo mal hecho*) botched job, shoddy piece of work **2** (= *trabajo ocasional*) odd job **3** (*Méx*) trick, swindle

chapuzas* SMF INV botcher*

chapuzón SM dip, swim; **darse un ~** to go for a dip, go for a swim

chaqué SM morning coat

chaquet [tʃaˈke] SM (*pl* **~s**) = **chaqué**

chaqueta SF jacket; ✦ MODISMO **cambiar de ~** to change sides ➤ **chaqueta de punto** cardigan

chaquetero/a* SM/F turncoat

chaquetón SM three-quarter coat

charada SF charade

charal SM (Méx) small fish; ✦ MODISMO **estar como ~*** to be as thin as a rake

charanga SF brass band

charango SM small guitar (made out of the shell of an armadillo)

charca SF pond, pool

charco SM pool, puddle; ✦ MODISMO **cruzar** o **pasar el ~** to cross the water; to cross the Pond (the Atlantic)

charcutería SF 1 (= productos) cooked pork products pl 2 (= tienda) delicatessen (specializing in cold meats)

charla SF 1 (= conversación) chat 2 (= conferencia) talk

charla-coloquio SF (pl **charlas-coloquio**) talk (followed by debate)

charlar /1a/ VI to chat (**de** about)

charlatán/ana Ⓐ ADJ talkative Ⓑ SM/F 1 (= hablador) chatterbox 2 (= estafador) trickster, confidence trickster, con man* 3 (= vendedor aprovechado) smooth-tongued salesman

charlatanería SF 1 (= locuacidad) talkativeness 2 (= engaños) quackery, charlatanism 3 [de vendedor] sales talk, patter

charlotada SF (Taur) mock bullfight

charnego/a SM/F (Esp pey) Southern Spanish immigrant who has settled in Catalonia

charol SM 1 (= cuero) patent leather 2 (= barniz) varnish 3 (LAm) (= bandeja) tray

charola SF (LAm) tray

charquear /1a/ VT (LAm) 1 [+ carne] to dry, jerk 2 [+ persona] to slash, cut to pieces

charqui SM (LAm) jerked beef, jerky (EEUU)

charrasquear* /1a/ VT 1 (Méx) (= apuñalar) to knife, stab 2 (And, CAm, Carib) (= rasguear) to strum

charretera SF epaulette

charro Ⓐ ADJ 1 (= de mal gusto) [ropa] loud, gaudy; [objeto] flashy, showy 2 (= salmantino) Salamancan 3 (Méx) [costumbres] traditional, picturesque; ⟳ MARIACHI, CONJUNTO Ⓑ SM (Méx) typical Mexican

charrúa ADJ, SMF 1 (= indígena) Charrua (extinct pre-Columbian tribe) 2 (CS) (= uruguayo) Uruguayan

chárter Ⓐ ADJ INV **vuelo ~** charter, charter flight Ⓑ SM (pl ~s ['tʃarter]) charter, charter flight

chascar /1g/ VT [+ lengua] to click; [+ dedos] to snap; [+ látigo] to crack

chascarrillo SM funny story

chasco SM disappointment; **dar un ~ a algn** to disappoint sb; **llevarse un ~** to be disappointed, be let down

chasis SM INV, **chasís** SM INV (LAm) 1 (Aut) chassis 2 (Fot) plateholder

chasquear /1a/ VT, VI = **chascar**

chasqui SM (LAm Hist) messenger, courier

chasquido SM [de lengua] click; [de dedos] snap; [de madera] crack

chasquilla SF (Chi) fringe (Brit), bangs pl (EEUU)

chat SM (Internet) (= sala) chat room; (= charla) chat

chata SF (LAm) bedpan

chatarra SF scrap, scrap iron

chatarrero/a SM/F scrap dealer, scrap merchant

chatear /1a/ VI (Internet) to chat

chateo* SM 1 (Internet) chatting 2 (= beber) drinking; **ir de ~** to go out for a few glasses of wine

chatero/a Ⓐ ADJ chat antes de n Ⓑ SM/F chat-room user

chato Ⓐ ADJ 1 [nariz] snub 2 [barco] flat 3 (Arquit) low, squat 4 (Perú) [persona] short 5 (RPl) (= mediocre) poor Ⓑ SM [de vino] tumbler, wine tumbler

chau EXCL = **chao**

chaucha SF 1 (RPl) (= judía verde) green bean 2 (Chi, Perú*) (= dinero) dough*; ✦ MODISMO **le cayó la ~** the penny dropped (Brit), the light went on (EEUU)

chauvinista ADJ, SMF chauvinist

chaval(a)* SM/F lad/lass, boy/girl, kid*

chavalo* SM (CAm) lad, kid*

chaveta Ⓐ SF 1 (Téc) cotter, cotter pin; ✦ MODISMO **perder la ~*** to go off one's rocker* 2 (Perú) (= navaja) broad-bladed knife Ⓑ ADJ INV **estar ~**** to be nuts*

chavo/a* SM/F (Méx, CAm) guy*/girl

che¹ SF the (name of the) letter ch

che² EXCL (RPl) hey!; (en conversación) man, boy, friend

che³* SMF (Chi, Méx) Argentinian

checar /1g/ VT (esp Méx) = **chequear**

chécheres SMPL (And, CAm) (= cosas) things, gear sing; (= cachivaches) junk sing, lumber sing

checo/a Ⓐ ADJ, SM/F Czech Ⓑ SM (Ling) Czech

checoslovaco/a ADJ, SM/F Czechoslovakian

chef SM (pl ~s) chef

chele ADJ (CAm) fair, blond/blonde

cheli* SM (Ling) Madrid slang

chelín SM shilling

chelista SMF cellist

chelo SM cello

chepa SF hump

cheque SM

En inglés americano se usa **check** en lugar de **cheque**.

cheque; **cobrar un ~** to cash a cheque; **extender un ~** to make out o write a cheque; **pagar con ~** to pay by cheque ➤ **cheque al portador** cheque payable to bearer ➤ **cheque bancario** banker's cheque ➤ **cheque cruzado** crossed cheque ➤ **cheque de viaje, cheque de viajero** traveller's cheque ➤ **cheque en blanco** blank cheque ➤ **cheque sin fondos** bounced cheque

chequear /1a/ VT 1 (esp LAm) (= comprobar) [+ cuenta, documento, salud] to check; [+ persona] to check on, check up on 2 (LAm) [+ equipaje] to check in 3 (Méx Aut) to service

chequeo SM 1 (Med) check-up 2 (Aut) service

chequera SF cheque book, checkbook (EEUU)

cheto/a* (RPl) Ⓐ ADJ posh* Ⓑ SM/F posh person*

chévere* ADJ (Col, Ven) great*, fabulous*

chic Ⓐ ADJ INV chic, smart Ⓑ SM elegance

chica SF (= criada) maid, servant; ver tb **chico**

chicanear /1a/ VI (Col, Méx) to use trickery, be cunning

chicanero ADJ (Col, Méx) tricky, crafty

chicano/a ADJ, SM/F Chicano

chicato* ADJ (CS) short-sighted (Brit), near-sighted (EEUU)

chicha¹ SF (LAm) (= bebida) maize liquor (Brit), corn liquor (EEUU); ✦ MODISMO **ni ~ ni limonada** o **limoná*** neither fish nor fowl, neither one thing nor the other

CHICHA

Chicha is a strong alcoholic drink made from fermented maize and produced in Peru, where it is associated with ceremonial and ritual occasions. It is now an element of what is known as **chicha** culture, a dynamic blend of traditional Indian and modern imported styles and fashions created out of the migration of the rural poor to major cities. **Chicha** music has become the most popular music in Peru. It combines the traditional Andean **huayno** with tropical, Afro-Hispanic music and electronic instruments.

chicha²* SF (Esp) meat; ✦ MODISMO **tiene poca(s) ~(s)** she's as thin as a rake*

chicha³ ADJ **calma ~** (Náut) dead calm

chícharo SM (*CAm, Méx*) pea

chicharra SF 1 (*Zool*) harvest bug, cicada 2 (*Elec*) (= *timbre*) bell, buzzer

chicharrón SM pork scratchings, pork cracklings (*EEUU*)

chiche ⒜ ADJ (*CAm*) easy, simple; **está ~** it's a cinch* ⒝ SM 1 (*CAm, Méx**) (= *pecho*) breast, tit** 2 (*CS*) (= *joya*) trinket; (= *juguete*) toy

chichi* SF (*Esp*) pussy***; (*Méx*) tit**

chichón SM bump

chicle SM chewing gum

chiclero SM (*Méx, CAm*) gum collector

chico/a ⒜ ADJ 1 (= *pequeño*) small, little
2 (= *joven*) young; **de ~ no me gustaban las verduras** when I was little I didn't like vegetables
⒝ SM/F 1 (= *joven*) boy/girl; **es un buen ~** he's a good lad; **¿sales con algún ~?** are you going out with anyone?, have you got a boyfriend?
2 (= *niño*) boy/girl; **los ~s de la clase** the boys in the class ➤ **chico de los recados** office boy, messenger boy
3 (= *hijo*) boy/girl, child
4 (= *novio*) boyfriend/girlfriend
5 (*apelativo*) 5.1 (*a un adulto*) **mira, ~, déjalo** OK, just leave it, will you? 5.2 (*a un niño*) **¡oye, ~! ¿quieres ganarte un poco de dinero?** hey! do you want to earn yourself a bit of money?; *ver tb* **chica**
⒞ SM (*LAm Billar*) game; (*Snooker*) frame

chicoria SF chicory

chicotazo SM (*LAm*) lash

chicote SM (*LAm*) whip, lash

chicotear /1a/ VT (*LAm*) to whip, lash

chifa SM (*Chi, Perú*) Chinese restaurant

chiflado/a* ⒜ ADJ crazy*; **estar ~ con** o **por algo/algn** to be crazy about sth/sb ⒝ SM/F nutcase*

chifladura* SF (= *locura*) craziness; **una ~** a crazy idea, a wild scheme

chiflar /1a/ ⒜ VT (*esp LAm*) (*gen*) to whistle; (= *abuchear*) to whistle at ⒝ VI 1 (*esp LAm*) (*gen*) to whistle; (*abucheando*) to hiss 2 (*) **me chiflan los helados** I just love ice cream ⒞ **chiflarse** (*) VPR **~se con** o **por algo/algn** to go crazy about sth/sb

chifle SM (*CAm, Carib Hist*) powder horn, powder flask

chiflido SM (*esp LAm*) 1 (= *silbido*) whistle 2 (= *siseo*) hiss

chiflón SM (*LAm*) (sudden) draught o (*EEUU*) draft (*of air*)

chigüín/ina* SM/F (*CAm*) kid*

chihuahua SM Chihuahua

chiíta ADJ, SMF, **chiita** ADJ, SMF Shiite, Shi'ite

chilaba SF jellaba(h)

chilacayote SM gourd

chilango ADJ (*Méx*) of/from Mexico City

chilaquiles SMPL (*Méx*) *tortilla fried in thick chili or green tomato*

Chile SM Chile

chile SM 1 (*Bot, Culin*) chili, chili pepper ➤ **chile morrón** (*Méx*) pepper 2 (*CAm**) (*tb ~s*) (= *broma*) joke

chilear* /1a/ VI (*CAm*) to tell jokes

chilena SF overhead kick, scissors kick

chileno/a ADJ, SM/F Chilean

chilicote SM (*And, CS*) cricket

chilindrón SM **al ~** cooked with tomatoes and peppers

chilla¹ SF (*Chi*) (= *zorro*) small fox

chilla²* SF (*Méx*) **estar en la ~** to be very poor

chillar /1a/ VI 1 (= *gritar*) [*persona*] to shriek, scream; [*gato, animal salvaje*] to screech, yowl; [*ratón*] to squeak; [*cerdo*] to squeal; [*ave*] to screech, squawk 2 [*colores*] to scream, jar, be loud

chillido SM [*de persona*] shriek, scream; [*de gato, animal salvaje*] screech, yowling; [*de ratón*] squeak; [*de cerdo*] squeal; [*de ave*] screech, squawk

chillón* ADJ 1 [*persona*] loud, shrill, noisy 2 [*sonido, tono*] shrill 3 [*color*] loud, garish, lurid

chilpayate* SM (*Méx*) kid*

chimbo* ADJ 1 (*Col, Ven*) (= *gastado*) worn-out, wasted, old 2 (*Col*) (= *falso*) fake; [*cheque*] dud*

chimenea SF 1 (*en el tejado*) chimney; [*de fábrica*] smokestack, chimney 2 (*dentro de casa*) fireplace, hearth; **encender la ~** to light the fire 3 [*de barco*] funnel 4 (*Min*) shaft

chimentos* SMPL (*RPl*) gossip *sing*

chimichurri SM (*CS*) strong barbecue sauce

chimiscolear /1a/ VI (*Méx*) to go around looking for gossip

chimpancé SMF chimpanzee

chimuelo ADJ (*Méx*) toothless

china SF 1 (*Esp*) (= *porcelana*) china, chinaware 2 (= *piedra*) pebble; ✦ MODISMO **tocarle a algn la ~**: **te ha tocado la ~** you drew the short straw 3 (*Esp**) [*de droga*] lump, piece 4 (*Méx*) girl (*of a "charro"*) 5 (*CS*) girl (*of a "gaucho"*) 6 **chinas** (= *juego*) *game played with pebbles*; *ver tb* **chino**

China SF China

chinampa SF (*Méx*) man-made island (*for cultivation on lakes*)

chinchar* /1a/ ⒜ VT to pester, annoy ⒝ **chincharse** VPR **¡para que te chinches!** so there!; **¡y que se chinchen los demás!** and the others can get stuffed!**

chinche SM o SF 1 (= *insecto*) bedbug; ✦ MODISMO **caer** o **morir como ~s** to die like flies 2 (*LAm*) (= *pieza*) drawing pin (*Brit*), thumbtack (*EEUU*) 3 (*CS**) (= *rabieta*) pique, irritation

chincheta SF drawing pin (*Brit*), thumbtack (*EEUU*)

chinchilla SF chinchilla

chin-chin EXCL chin-chin, cheers

chinchorro SM 1 (*Col, Ven*) (= *hamaca*) hammock 2 (*Méx*) (= *red*) fishing net, fishnet (*EEUU*)

chinchudo* ADJ (*CS*) **estar ~** to be in a grumpy mood

chinchulines SMPL (*CS Culin*) chitterlings, chitlins

chinear /1a/ VT (*CAm*) to carry in one's arms

chinela SF 1 (= *zapatilla*) slipper, mule 2 (*LAm*) (*con tacón*) mule

chinesco ADJ *ver* **sombra 1**

chinga* SF (*CAm*) 1 (= *colilla*) cigarette butt, fag end (*Brit*) 2 (= *posos*) dregs *pl*

chingada* SF (*CAm, Méx*) 1 (= *acto sexual*) fuck***, screw***; **hijo de la ~** bastard***, son of a bitch (*EEUU***) 2 (= *molestia*) damn nuisance**

chingadazo* SM (*CAm, Méx*) bash*

chingado* ADJ (*CAm, Méx*) lousy***, bloody (*Brit***)

chingana SF (*And*) dive*, tavern

chingar* /1h/ ⒜ VT (*esp CAm, Méx*) (= *copular*) to fuck***, screw***; ✦ MODISMO **¡chinga tu madre!** fuck off!*** ⒝ VI (*esp CAm, Méx*) (= *copular*) to fuck***, screw*** 2 (*Méx*) (= *fastidiar*) **no chingues** don't mess me around* ⒞ **chingarse** VPR (*CAm, Méx*) **la fiesta se chingó** the party was a disaster*

chingo ⒜ ADJ (*CAm*) (= *desnudo*) naked, half-naked ⒝ SM (*Méx**) **un ~ de algo** loads of sth*

chingón* SM (*Méx*) big shot*, boss

chingue SM (*Chi*) skunk

chinguear /1a/ VT (*CAm*) = **chingar**

chinita SF (*And*) ladybird (*Brit*), ladybug (*EEUU*)

chino/a ⒜ ADJ Chinese; **barrio ~** red-light district ⒝ SM/F 1 (= *persona*) Chinese man/woman 2 (*LAm*) (= *mestizo*) mestizo, person of mixed race (*of Amerindian and European parentage*) ⒞ SM 1 (*Ling*) Chinese; ✦ MODISMO **me suena a ~** (*idioma*) it sounds like double Dutch to me; (*tema*) it's all Greek to me 2 (*Culin*) conical strainer 3 **chinos** (*Méx*) (= *rizos*) curls; *ver tb* **china**

chip SM 1 (*Inform*) chip; ✦ MODISMO **cambiarse el ~** to get up to date, get with it 2 (*Culin*) crisp (*Brit*), chip (*EEUU*)

chipichipi* SM (*CAm, Méx*) continuous drizzle

chipirón SM baby squid

chipote SM (*Méx*) bump

Chipre SF Cyprus

chipriota ADJ, SMF Cypriot

chiquear /1a/ (*Méx*) **Ⓐ** VT to spoil, indulge **Ⓑ chiquearse** VPR to be pampered

chiquero SM pigsty (*esp Brit*), pigpen (*EEUU*)

chiquilín/ina* **Ⓐ** ADJ (*LAm*) (= *inmaduro*) young, immature **Ⓑ** SM/F (*Uru*) kid

chiquillada SF childish prank; **son ~s** it's kid's stuff*

chiquillería SF kids* *pl*

chiquillo/a SM/F kid*, child

chiquitín/ina* **Ⓐ** ADJ tiny **Ⓑ** SM/F tiny tot

chiquito/a **Ⓐ** ADJ (*esp LAm**) small **Ⓑ** SM/F (*) kid*; ✦ MODISMO **no andarse con chiquitas** not to beat about the bush **Ⓒ** SM **1** (= *vaso*) small glass of wine **2** (*CS**) (= *pedacito*) **un ~** a bit, a little

chircal SM (*Col*) brickworks *pl*, tileworks *pl*

chiribita SF **1** (= *chispa*) spark; ✦ MODISMO **estar que echa ~s*** to be hopping mad **2 chiribitas*** (= *destellos*) spots before the eyes; ✦ MODISMO **los ojos le hacían ~s** her eyes sparkled, her eyes lit up

chirigota* SF joke; **estar de ~** to be joking; **tomarse algo a ~** to take sth as a joke; (*pey*) to treat sth too lightly

chirimbolo* SM thingummyjig*, thingamajig (*EEUU**)

chirimiri SM drizzle

chirimoya SF custard apple, cherimoya (*EEUU*)

chirimoyo SM custard apple tree, cherimoya tree (*EEUU*)

chiringuito SM refreshment stall, refreshment stand

chiripa* SF fluke, stroke of luck; **de** *o* **por ~** by a fluke, by chance

chiripá SM *kind of blanket worn over trousers by "gauchos"*

chirivía SF parsnip

chirla SF mussel, clam

chirle ADJ (*RPl*) [*salsa*] thin

chirona* SF jail, nick (*Brit**), can (*EEUU**)

chiros SMPL (*Col*) rags, tatters

chirriar /1b/ VI **1** [*bisagra, puerta*] to creak, squeak **2** [*frenos*] to screech, squeal

chirrido SM **1** [*de bisagra, puerta*] creak, creaking, squeak, squeaking **2** [*de frenos*] screeching, squealing

chirrión SM (*And, CAm, Méx*) whip

chirucas SFPL *canvas mountain boots*

chirusa* SF (*CS*) (= *niña*) girl, kid*; (= *mujer*) poor woman

chis EXCL sh!

chisme SM **1** (= *cotilleo*) **se sabe todos los ~s** he knows all the gossip **2** (*) (= *cosa*) thing; **¿y este ~ para qué sirve?** and what's this thing for?; **un ~ para cortar metal** a thing *o* whatnot *o* thingummyjig* for cutting metal with

chismorrear /1a/ VI to gossip

chismorreo SM gossip

chismoso/a **Ⓐ** ADJ gossiping, scandalmongering **Ⓑ** SM/F gossip

chispa SF **1** [*de luz, fuego*] spark; ✦ MODISMO **echar ~s***: **está que echa ~s** he's hopping mad* **2** (= *gota de lluvia*) drop **3** (= *pizca*) bit, tiny amount; **una ~ de sal** a pinch of salt; **ni ~** not the least bit; **si tuviera una ~ de inteligencia** if he had an ounce of intelligence **4** (= *ingenio*) wit; **Juan tiene ~** Juan's quite witty

chispazo SM spark

chispear /1a/ VI **1** [*leña, fuego*] to throw out sparks **2** (= *destellar*) to sparkle, scintillate **3** (*Meteo*) to drizzle

chispero SM (*CAm*) **1** (= *encendedor*) lighter **2** (*Aut*) spark plug

chisporrotear /1a/ VI [*aceite*] to spit; [*carne*] to sizzle; [*leña*] to crackle; [*fuego*] to throw out sparks

chisporroteo SM [*de aceite*] spitting, spluttering; [*de carne*] sizzling; [*de leña*] sparking, crackling

chistar* /1a/ VI **nadie chistó** nobody said a word; **sin ~** without a word

chiste SM joke; **suena a ~** it's difficult to believe ➤ **chiste verde** blue joke, dirty joke

chistera SF top hat

chistoso/a **Ⓐ** ADJ funny, amusing **Ⓑ** SM/F wit, funny person

chita¹ SF ✦ MODISMO **a la ~ callando** (*Esp**) (= *con disimulo*) on the quiet, on the sly; (= *sin molestar*) unobtrusively

chita²* EXCL (*Chi*) (= *caramba*) damn!*, Jesus!*; **¡por la ~!** damn it!*

chitón EXCL sh!

chiva SF **1** (*LAm*) (= *barba*) goatee, goatee beard **2** (*And, CAm*) (= *autobús*) bus **3** (*Chi**) fib, tall story

chivarse* /1a/ VPR to squeal*, grass (*Brit**); **~ a la maestra** to tell the teacher

chivatazo* SM tip-off; **dar el ~** to inform, give a tip-off

chivatear /1a/ VI **1** (*Col*) to be a pest* **2** (*And, CS*) to jump about

chivato SM **1** (*) (= *soplón*) informer **2** (*Ven**) big shot* **3** (*And*) (= *pillo*) rascal, villain

chivearse* /1a/ VPR (*CAm, Méx*) to get embarrassed

chivera SF (*And, CAm*) goatee, goatee beard

chivito SM **1** (*Uru*) steak sandwich ➤ **chivito canadiense** *steak, bacon, egg and salad sandwich* **2** (*Arg*) roast goat's meat

chivo SM **1** (*Zool*) billy goat ➤ **chivo expiatorio** scapegoat **2** (*Méx**) (= *soborno*) sweetener*, backhander (*Brit**) **3** (*And***) (= *maricón*) queer**, poof (*Brit***)

chocante ADJ **1** (= *sorprendente*) startling, striking **2** (= *raro*) odd, strange **3** (= *escandaloso*) shocking, scandalous **4** (*esp LAm*) (= *desagradable*) offensive, unpleasant

chocar /1g/ **Ⓐ** VI **1** (= *colisionar*) [*coches, trenes*] to collide, crash; [*barcos*] to collide; **los dos coches ~on de frente** the two cars crashed head on *o* were in a head-on collision; **~ con** *o* **contra** [+ *vehículo*] to collide with, crash into; [+ *objeto*] to bang into; [+ *persona*] to bump into; **para no ~ contra el avión** to avoid crashing into *o* colliding with the plane; **el balón chocó contra el poste** the ball hit the post **2** (= *enfrentarse*) [*opiniones, personalidades*] to clash; **~ con** [+ *ideas, intereses*] to run counter to, be at odds with; [+ *obstáculos, dificultades*] to come up against, run into; [+ *personas*] to clash with; **esa propuesta choca con los intereses de EEUU** that proposal runs counter to *o* is at odds with American interests; **por su carácter chocaba a menudo con sus compañeros de trabajo** he often clashed with his colleagues because of his confrontational nature **Ⓑ** VT **1** (= *sorprender*) to shock; **me chocó muchísimo lo que dijo** I was really shocked by what he said, what he said really shocked me; **no me choca que haya dimitido** I'm not surprised that he's resigned **2** (= *hacer chocar*) [+ *vasos*] to clink; [+ *manos*] to shake; **¡chócala!*** ◊ **¡choca esos cinco!*** put it there!* **3** (*Méx*) (= *asquear*) to disgust; **me choca su actitud** I find his attitude offensive **Ⓒ** **chocarse** VPR (*Méx Aut*) to have a crash

chocarrero ADJ coarse, vulgar

chochada* SF (*CAm*) triviality

chochear /1a/ VI **1** (*por la edad*) to dodder, be senile **2** (*por el cariño*) to be soft

chochera SF **1** (= *cualidad*) senility **2** (= *adoración*) **tener ~ por algn** to dote on sb, be crazy about sb

chochez SF = **chochera 1**

chocho*¹ **Ⓐ** ADJ **1** (= *senil*) doddering, senile **2** (= *embelesado*) soft, doting, sentimental; **estar ~ por algn** to dote on sb, be soft on sb **3** (*CS*) (= *contento*) delighted, chuffed (*Brit**) **Ⓑ** EXCL (*CAm*) no kidding!*, really?

chocho²* SM pussy***

choclo¹ SM (*Méx*) low-heeled shoe; ✦ MODISMO **meter el ~*** to put one's foot in it

choclo² SM (*LAm*) (= *planta*) maize (*Brit*), corn (*EEUU*);

(= *mazorca*) corncob; (= *granos*) sweetcorn

choclón SM (*Chi*) crowd

choco ADJ (*Chi*) **1** (= *manco*) one-armed **2** (= *cojo*) one-legged

chocolate Ⓐ ADJ chocolate-coloured, chocolate-colored (*EEUU*) Ⓑ SM **1** (*para comer*) chocolate; (*para beber*) drinking chocolate, cocoa; ✦ MODISMO **dar a algn agua de su propio ~** (*Méx*) to give sb a taste of his own medicine ➤ **chocolate con leche** milk chocolate ➤ **chocolate negro** dark chocolate, plain chocolate (*Brit*) **2** (*****) (= *hachís*) hash*, pot*

chocolatería SF chocolate shop

chocolatina SF chocolate bar

chófer SMF (*Esp*), **chofer** SMF **1** [*de coche privado*] chauffeur **2** (*LAm*) (= *conductor*) driver

cholga SF (*Chi*) mussel

cholla* SF (*Méx*) nut*, noggin (*EEUU**)

chollo* SM snip*, bargain; **¡qué ~ de trabajo!** what a cushy job!*

cholo/a Ⓐ ADJ **1** (*And*) (= *indígena*) Indian; (= *mestizo*) of mixed race, half-breed (*pey*) **2** (*Chi*) (= *miedoso*) cowardly Ⓑ SM/F **1** (*And*) (= *indígena*) Indian; (= *mestizo*) of mixed race, half-breed (*pey*) **2** (*And*) (*apelativo*) darling, honey (*EEUU*)

chomba SF **1** (*Chi*) sweater **2** (*Arg*) polo shirt

chompa SF **1** (*Perú*) sweater **2** (*Col*) jacket

chompipe SM (*CAm*) turkey

chongo SM **1** (*Méx*) (= *moño*) bun **2** **chongos** (*CAm, Méx*) (= *trenzas*) pigtails

chonta SF (*And*) palm shoots *pl*

chop SM (*CS*) draught beer, draft beer (*EEUU*)

chopera SF poplar grove

chopería SF (*CS*) bar, beer bar

chopito SM baby squid

chopo SM (*Bot*) black poplar

choque SM **1** [*de vehículos*] crash, collision ➤ **choque frontal** head-on collision ➤ **choque múltiple** multiple crash, pile-up **2** (= *desavenencia*) clash; **un ~ de culturas** a clash of cultures **3** (= *lucha*) clash; **hubo varios ~s entre la población civil** there were several clashes between civilians **4** (= *conmoción*) **su muerte fue un ~ para ella** his death was a shock for her **5** (*Med*) shock; **~ postraumático** post-traumatic shock

chorcha SF (*Méx*) (= *fiesta*) noisy party; **una ~ de amigos** a group of friends (*out for a good time*)

chorear* /1a/ VT **1** (*Chi*) **me chorea** (= *enojar*) it really pisses me off**; (= *hartar*) I get really fed up with it* **2** (*CS, Perú*) (= *robar*) to pinch*, nick (*Brit**)

choreo SM (*Chi*) complaint

choricear** /1a/ VT to nick*

choripán SM (*RPI*) sausage sandwich

chorizar** /1f/ VT to nick*

chorizo SM **1** (*Esp Culin*) chorizo, pork sausage (*flavoured with paprika, eaten raw or used in cooking*); (*RPI*) sausage; **bife de ~** (*CS*) rump steak **2** (******) (= *ratero*) small-time crook*

chorlito SM plover

choro SM (*And*) mussel

chorra** Ⓐ SF (= *suerte*) luck; **¡qué ~ tiene!** how lucky *o* (*Brit**) jammy can you get! Ⓑ SMF (= *idiota*) fool, idiot

chorrada* SF **1** (= *objeto insignificante*) knick-knack **2** (= *tontería*) **no digas ~s** stop talking drivel

chorrear /1a/ Ⓐ VI **1** (= *salir a chorros*) to gush (out), spout **2** (= *gotear*) to drip; **la ropa chorrea todavía** the clothes are still dripping water *o* wringing wet; **estar chorreando de sudor** to be dripping with sweat Ⓑ VT **1** (*CS*) (= *robar*) to pinch* **2** (*LAm*) (= *manchar*) to spill; **~on toda la alfombra de vino** they spilled wine all over the carpet

chorreo SM **1** (= *flujo*) gushing, spouting **2** (= *goteo*) dripping **3** [*de dinero*] trickle

chorrera SF **1 chorreras** (*Cos*) frill *sing* **2** (*Méx, RPI*)

(= *montón*) stream, string; **una ~ de algo** a stream *o* string of sth

chorro SM **1** (= *caudal de líquido*) jet, stream; **beber a ~** to drink without touching the bottle; **salir a ~s** to gush forth, come spurting out **2** (*Téc*) jet, blast; **un avión con propulsión a ~** jet-propelled plane **3** (= *pequeña cantidad*) **se añade un chorrito de leche** add a drop of milk **4** (*CS**) (= *ladrón*) thief, pickpocket **5** (*CAm*) (= *grifo*) tap (*Brit*), faucet (*EEUU*) **6** (*Méx**) (= *diarrea*) the runs*

chota SF ✦ MODISMO **estar como una ~*** to be hopping mad*

choteo* SM kidding*, joking; **estar de ~** to be kidding*

chotis SM INV *traditional dance of Madrid*

choto SM **1** (*Zool*) (= *cabrito*) kid; (= *ternero*) calf **2** (*CS***) (= *pene*) prick***

chovinismo SM chauvinism

choza SF hut, shack

chubasco SM heavy shower

chubasquero SM cagoule, foul-weather gear (*EEUU*)

chúcaro ADJ (*LAm*) **1** (= *salvaje*) wild, untamed **2** (= *tímido*) shy

chuchería SF **1** (= *golosina*) sweet (*Brit*), candy (*EEUU*) **2** (= *adorno*) trinket

chucho SM **1** (= *perro*) mongrel; **¡chucho!** down boy! **2** (*LAm*) **~s de frío*** the shivers*; (*por fiebre*) the shakes*

chucrut SM sauerkraut

chueco ADJ **1** (*LAm*) (= *torcido*) crooked; **un negocio ~** a crooked deal* **2** (*And, CS*) (= *patizambo*) bandy-legged; (= *patituerto*) pigeon-toed

chufa SF tiger nut; **horchata de ~** *drink made from tiger nuts*

chufla SF joke, merry quip; **tomar algo a ~** to take sth as a joke

chuico SM (*Chi*) demijohn

chulada* SF (*CAm, Esp, Méx*) **¡qué ~ de moto!** wow! what a fantastic bike!*

chulear* /1a/ VT (*Méx*) (= *elogiar*) to compliment; (= *decir piropos a*) to call out flirtatious remarks at

chulería* SF **1** (= *bravuconada*) **déjate de ~s conmigo** don't get all cocky with me* **2** (*CAm, Esp, Méx**) (= *cosa bonita*) **esa moto es una ~** that bike is really nice; **me he comprado una ~ de camiseta** I've bought a really nice *o* gorgeous T-shirt

chuleta SF **1** [*de carne*] chop, cutlet ➤ **chuleta de cerdo** pork chop ➤ **chuleta de cordero** lamb chop **2** (*****) (= *golpe*) punch, bash* **3** (*Esp**) [*de examen*] crib (*Brit**), trot (*EEUU*)

chuletón SM large steak, T-bone steak

chullo SM (*Perú*) woollen cap, woolen cap (*EEUU*)

chulo Ⓐ ADJ (*) **1** (= *arrogante*) cocky*; **ponerse ~:** **se puso en plan ~** he got all cocky with me* **2** (*CAm, Esp, Méx**) (= *bonito*) **¡qué vestido más ~!** what a pretty *o* (*esp Brit*) lovely dress!; **chica, estás chulísima** (*CAm, Méx*) you look gorgeous Ⓑ ADV (*CAm, Méx**) well; **jugar ~** to play well Ⓒ SM **1** (*) (*tb* **~ (de) putas**) pimp **2** (*Col*) (= *buitre*) vulture, buzzard (*EEUU*)

chumado* ADJ (*Arg*) drunk, tight*

chumbar /1a/ VT (*CS*) [*perro*] to attack, go for; **¡chúmbale!** at him, boy!

chumbera SF prickly pear

chuminada* SF **1** (= *tontería*) silly thing, piece of nonsense **2** (= *detalle*) petty detail

chumino*** SM (*Esp*) cunt***

chumpipe SM (*CAm*) turkey

chunche* SM (*CAm*) whatsit*, thingumabob*

chuncho/a Ⓐ ADJ (*Perú*) bashful, shy Ⓑ SM/F Chuncho Indian

chunga SF fun; **estar de ~** to be in a joking mood; **en plan de ~** for a laugh

chungo** ADJ **1** (= *en mal estado*) [*lavadora, televisor*] bust*; [*fruta*] rotten **2** (= *desagradable*) nasty **3** (= *con mala pinta*) shady*, dodgy (*Brit**) **4** (= *enfermo*) rop(e)y*, dodgy*

chuño SM (*LAm*) potato starch

chupa** SF (*Esp*) leather jacket

chupachupa* SM (*RPl*) lollipop

chupada SF 1 [*de biberón, caramelo*] suck 2 (*en pipa, cigarro*) pull, puff; ✦ MODISMO **se cree la última ~ del mate** (*CS**) he thinks he's the cat's pyjamas *o* the bee's knees*

chupado ADJ 1 (= *flaco*) gaunt, skinny*; **está ~ de cara** his face looks *o* he looks very gaunt, he looks very hollow-cheeked 2 (*LAm*) (= *borracho*) drunk 3 **está ~*** (= *fácil*) it's dead easy*

chupamedias** SM INV (*And, CS*) creep**, bootlicker*, brown-nose (*EEUU***)

chupar /1a/ Ⓐ VT 1 (= *succionar*) [+ *biberón, caramelo, bolígrafo*] to suck; [+ *pipa*] to puff at, puff on; **chupó lo que pudo mientras estuvo en la organización** he milked the organization for all he could while he was there; ✦ MODISMOS **~ cámara*** to get as much (media) exposure as possible; **~ la sangre a algn** to bleed sb dry, take sb for everything they've got
2 (*) (= *aguantar*) to put up with, take; ✦ MODISMO **~ banquillo** (*Ftbl*) to sit on the substitutes' bench
3 [*planta*] [+ *agua*] to absorb, take in, take up
Ⓑ VI 1 (*de cigarro, biberón*) to suck; ✦ MODISMO **~ del bote*** to line one's pocket
2 (*LAm**) (= *beber*) to drink
Ⓒ **chuparse** VPR 1 (= *succionar*) **~se el dedo** (*lit*) to suck one's finger; **¿tú te crees que me chupo el dedo?** do you think I was born yesterday?; ✦ MODISMO **~se los dedos*: la paella estaba para ~se los dedos** the paella was absolutely delicious
2 (*) (= *aguantar*) **nos chupamos toda la conferencia de pie** we had to go through the whole of the lecture standing; ✦ MODISMO **¡chúpate esa!** put that in your pipe and smoke it!*

chupatintas* SMF INV (*pey*) penpusher (*Brit*), pencil pusher (*EEUU*)

chupe SM (*And, CS Culin*) stew

chupete SM 1 [*de niño*] dummy (*Brit*), pacifier (*EEUU*) 2 (*And*) (= *caramelo*) lollipop

chupetear /1a/ VT [+ *polo*] to suck; [+ *helado*] to lick

chupetín SM (*RPl*) lollipop

chupetón* SM lovebite, hickey (*EEUU**)

chupín SM (*RPl*) fish and potato stew

chupinazo SM (*Dep*) hard kick, fierce shot

chupito* SM [*de bebida alcohólica*] shot*

chupo SM (*Col*) dummy (*Brit*), pacifier (*EEUU*)

chupón/ona Ⓐ SM/F (*) (= *parásito*) sponger* Ⓑ SM 1 (*Bot*) sucker 2 (*LAm*) (= *chupete*) dummy (*Brit*), pacifier (*EEUU*); [*de biberón*] teat (*EEUU*), nipple (*EEUU*)

churrasco SM 1 (= *filete a la parrilla*) barbecued meat 2 (*CS*) (= *filete*) steak

churrería SF establishment or stall selling churros

churrete SM dirty mark (*esp on a child's face*)

churria SF 1 (*Méx, Col*) stain 2 **churrias** (*And, CAm, Carib**) (= *diarrea*) runs*, trots*

churriento ADJ (*LAm*) (= *suelto*) loose

churrigueresco ADJ 1 (*Arquit*) churrigueresque
2 (= *recargado*) excessively ornate

churro SM 1 (*Culin*) *flour fritter eaten with coffee or hot chocolate*; ✦ MODISMO **venderse como ~s** to sell like hot cakes 2 (*) (= *chapuza*) botch, mess; **el dibujo ha salido hecho un ~** the sketch came out all wrong 3 (*And, CS**) (= *persona*) dish* 4 (*Méx**) (= *suerte*) luck; **¡qué ~!** how lucky!

churruscarse /1g/ VPR to burn

churrusco ADJ (*And, CAm*) kinky, curly

churumbel* SM kid*

churumbela SF 1 (*Mús*) flageolet 2 (*CAm*) maté cup

chus EXCL ✦ MODISMO **no decir ~ ni mus*** not to say a word

chusco¹ ADJ 1 (= *gracioso*) funny, droll 2 (*And*) [*perro*] mongrel; [*caballo*] ordinary; [*persona*] coarse, ill-mannered

chusco² SM **un ~ de pan** a hunk of bread

chusma SF rabble, riffraff

chuspa SF (*LAm*) bag, pouch

chuta** SF (= *jeringuilla*) needle

chutar /1a/ Ⓐ VI (*Dep*) to shoot (*at goal*) Ⓑ **chutarse** (**) VPR [+ *heroína*] to shoot up*

chute SM 1 (*Dep*) shot (*at goal*) 2 (**) [*de droga*] shot*, fix*

chuzo Ⓐ SM 1 (*CAm*) [*de alacrán*] sting 2 ✦ MODISMO **caer ~s de punta*** to rain cats and dogs, pelt down* Ⓑ ADJ (*CAm**) [*pelo*] lank

Cía. ABR (= **Compañía**) Co.

cianuro SM cyanide

ciática SF sciatica

cibercafé SM cybercafe

ciberespacio SM cyberspace

cibernauta SMF cybernaut

cibernética SF cybernetics *sing*

cibernético ADJ cybernetic

cibersexo SM cybersex

ciberterrorista SMF cyberterrorist

cicatería SF stinginess, meanness

cicatero/a Ⓐ ADJ stingy, mean (*esp Brit*) Ⓑ SM/F miser, skinflint

cicatriz SF scar

cicatrizar /1f/ Ⓐ VT to heal Ⓑ **cicatrizarse** VPR to heal, heal up, form a scar

cicerone SMF guide, cicerone

cíclico ADJ cyclic, cyclical

ciclismo SM cycling

ciclista Ⓐ ADJ cycle *antes de s* Ⓑ SMF cyclist

ciclo SM 1 (*en hechos repetidos*) cycle ➤ **ciclo menstrual** menstrual cycle ➤ **ciclo vital** life cycle 2 [*de conferencias*] series; [*de cine, conciertos*] season 3 (*Escol*) **el segundo ~ de primaria** the second stage of primary (*esp Brit*) *o* elementary (*EEUU*) school

ciclomotor SM moped (*Brit*), motorbike (*EEUU*)

ciclón SM cyclone; ✦ MODISMO **como un ~: entró como un ~ en la cocina** he burst into the kitchen

cíclope SM Cyclops

ciclostil SM cyclostyle

cicloturismo SM cycle touring; **hacer ~** to go on a cycling holiday (*esp Brit*) *o* vacation (*EEUU*)

cicuta SF hemlock

cidracayote SM (*LAm*) gourd, calabash

ciego/a Ⓐ ADJ 1 (= *invidente*) blind; **es ~ de nacimiento** he has been blind from *o* since birth, he was born blind; **dejar ~ a algn** to blind sb; **estar ~** to be blind; **pero ¿estás ~ o qué?** are you blind or what?; **quedarse ~** to go blind
2 (*por ofuscación*) 2.1 [*persona*] blind; **~ a las necesidades del resto del mundo** blind to the needs of the rest of the world; **~ de ira** *o* **rabia** blind with rage 2.2 [*violencia*] senseless, mindless (*esp Brit*); [*fanatismo*] unquestioning, mindless (*esp Brit*)
3 (= *total*) [*confianza, fe*] unquestioning, blind (*pey*)
4 (= *bloqueado*) [*arco, entrada*] blind; [*conducto, tubo*] blocked
5 (**) **ponerse ~ a** *o* **de algo** (= *borracho*) to get pissed on sth (*Brit***), get trashed on sth (*EEUU***); (*con drogas duras*) to get high on sth*; (*con drogas blandas*) to get stoned on sth**; (*comiendo*) to stuff o.s. with sth*
6 **a ciegas** 6.1 (= *sin ver*) **avanzamos a ciegas hasta encontrar el interruptor** we groped our way to the light switch 6.2 (= *sin pensar*) [*actuar, decidir*] in the dark; [*obedecer*] unquestioningly, blindly (*pey*)
Ⓑ SM/F (= *invidente*) blind man/blind woman
Ⓒ SM 1 (*Esp***) **¡qué ~ llevaba!** [*de alcohol*] he was blind drunk* *o* pissed! (*Brit***); [*de drogas duras*] he was high as a kite*; [*de drogas blandas*] he was stoned out of his mind**
2 (*Anat*) caecum, cecum (*EEUU*)

cielo SM 1 (*Astron, Meteo*) sky; **a ~ abierto** [*mina, explotación*] opencast (*Brit*), open pit (*EEUU*); ✦ MODISMOS **cambiar del ~ a la tierra** (*Chi*) to change out of all

recognition; **llegar** o **venir (como) caído** o **llovido del ~**
(*inesperado*) to come (totally) out of the blue; (*muy
oportuno*) to be a godsend; **irse al ~ con todo y zapatos**
(*Méx*) **tú te vas al ~ con todo y zapatos** you'll be blessed in
heaven; **remover ~ y tierra** to move heaven and earth;
tocar el ~ con las manos (*CS, Perú, Col*): **conseguir que me
ayude es tocar el ~ con las manos** getting him to help me
would be virtually impossible; **si me lo ganara sería como
tocar el ~ con las manos** if I won it, it would be like a
dream come true
2 (*Rel*) heaven; **¡cielos!** good heavens!; **ganarse el ~** to win
salvation; **ir al ~** to go to heaven; ✦ MODISMOS **clamar al ~:
¡esto clama al ~!** it's an outrage!, it's outrageous!; **estar en
el séptimo ~** to be in seventh heaven; **ver el ~ abierto:
vimos el ~ abierto cuando dijo que podíamos quedarnos en
su casa** it was a great relief when he said we could stay in
his house
3 (*) (*uso afectivo*) **¡mi ~!** ✧ **¡~ mío!** my love, sweetheart; **el
jefe es un ~** the boss is a real sweetie*
4 (= *parte superior*) [*de boca*] roof; (*CAm*) [*de coche*] roof
5 (*Arquit*) (*tb* ~ **raso**) ceiling

ciempiés SM INV centipede

cien ADJ, PRON, SM (*antes de s, apócope de ~to*) (*cardinal*) a
hundred, one hundred; (*ordinal*) hundredth; **~ mil** a
hundred thousand; **~ por ~** a hundred per cent; **es de lana
~ por ~** it's pure wool, it's a hundred per cent wool;
✦ MODISMO **me pone a ~** (*Esp**) (*al enfadarse*) it drives me up
the wall*; (*sexualmente*) it makes me feel horny o (*Brit**)
randy; *ver tb* **seis**

ciénaga SF marsh, swamp

ciencia SF **1** (= *conocimiento*) science; ✦ MODISMOS **saber
algo a ~ cierta** to know sth for certain o for a fact; **no tener
mucha ~: esto no tiene mucha ~** there's nothing difficult
about it ➤ **ciencia ficción** science fiction
2 (= *doctrina*) science, sciences *pl* ➤ **ciencias naturales**
natural science *sing* ➤ **ciencias ocultas** occultism *sing*
3 ciencias (*Educ*) science *sing*, sciences ➤ **Ciencias de la
Educación** Education *sing* ➤ **Ciencias de la Información**
Media Studies ➤ **Ciencias Empresariales** Business Studies
➤ **Ciencias Exactas** Exact Sciences ➤ **Ciencias Políticas**
Political Science *sing*

ciencia-ficción SF science fiction

cieno SM **1** (= *lodo*) mud **2** (= *depósito fluvial*) silt

científico/a Ⓐ ADJ scientific Ⓑ SM/F scientist

cientista SMF (*LAm*) scientist; **~ social** social scientist

ciento ADJ, PRON **1** (= *numeral*) a hundred, one hundred; **~
veinte** one hundred and twenty, a hundred and twenty;
✦ MODISMO **~ y la madre***: **¡allí estaban el ~ y la madre!** the
world and his wife were there*
2 por ~ per cent; **hay un cinco por ~ de descuento** there is
a five per cent discount; **el ~ por ~** a o one hundred per
cent
3 cientos te lo he dicho ~s de veces I've told you
hundreds of times; **a** o **por ~s: casos como éste se
producen a** o **por ~s** there are cases like this by the
hundred, there are hundreds of cases like this

ciernes SMPL **es un ajedrecista en ~** he's a budding chess
champion

cierra *etc ver* **cerrar**

cierre SM **1** (= *acto*) [*de verja, puerta*] (*gen*) closing,
shutting; [*de edificio, establecimiento, frontera*] closing; **el
horario de ~** closing time
2 (= *fin*) [*de una emisión*] closedown; [*de campaña electoral*]
end, close; [*de la Bolsa*] close; [*de año fiscal*] end; **al ~ de
esta edición de noticias** at the end of this news bulletin; **al
~ de impresión** at the time of going to press
3 [*de negocio, carretera, instalaciones*] closure; **los vecinos
piden el ~ de la factoría** local residents are demanding the
closure of the factory
4 (= *mecanismo*) [*de maleta, puerta*] catch; [*de collar, pulsera,
libro*] clasp; [*de vestido*] fastener, snap fastener ➤ **cierre
centralizado** (*Aut*) central locking ➤ **cierre de dirección**
(*Aut*) steering lock ➤ **cierre hermético** air-tight seal
➤ **cierre relámpago** (*CS, Perú*) zip (fastener) (*Brit*), zipper (*esp
EEUU*)

cierro SM (*Chi*) fence

cierto ADJ **1** (= *verdadero*) true; **¿es ~ eso?** is that really
so?, is that true?; **ha mejorado mucho, ¿no es ~?** it has
improved a lot, don't you think?; **es ~, es mejor que nos
vayamos** yes o you're right, I think we'd better go; **~, es un
problema grave** it's certainly a serious problem; **estar en lo
~** to be right; **lo ~ es que** the fact is that, the truth of the
matter is that; **es ~ que** it's true that
2 (= *seguro*) certain, sure; **les espera una muerte cierta** they
are heading for certain death
3 (*uso indefinido*) **3.1** (*en sing*) a certain; **ocurre con cierta
frecuencia** it happens fairly frequently; **había un ~ aire de
misterio** there was a certain air of mystery about it; **en
cierta ocasión** on one occasion, once; **durante ~ tiempo** for
a while **3.2** (*en pl*) some, certain; **es mejor no hablar de
ciertas cosas** some o certain things are better not
discussed
4 por ~ by the way, incidentally; **un libro que, por ~,
recomiendo totalmente** a book which, by the way, o
incidentally, I would thoroughly recommend

ciervo SM (*Zool*) (*gen*) deer; (*macho*) stag, buck; (*Culin*)
venison

cierzo SM north wind

cifra SF **1** (= *dígito*) figure; **un número de seis ~s** a six-figure
number **2** (= *cantidad*) number; **piensa una ~** think of a
number; **la ~ oficial de muertos** the official death toll **3 en
~** (= *codificado*) coded, in code

cifrado ADJ [*mensaje*] coded, in code

cifrar /1a/ Ⓐ VT **1** (= *codificar*) [+ *mensaje*] to code, write in
code; (*Ling*) to encode **2** [+ *esperanzas, ilusiones*] to pin,
place (**en** on) **3** [+ *ganancias, pérdidas*] to calculate
Ⓑ **cifrarse** VPR **todas las esperanzas se cifran en él** all hopes
are centred on him

cigala SF Dublin Bay prawn

cigarra SF cicada

cigarrera SF (= *caja*) cigar case

cigarrería SF (*And*) tobacconist's (shop) (*Brit*), tobacco o
smoke shop (*EEUU*)

cigarrillo SM cigarette; **cajetilla** o **paquete de ~s** pack(et)
of cigarettes

cigarro SM **1** (= *cigarrillo*) cigarette **2** (*tb* ~ **puro**) cigar
➤ **cigarro habano** Havana cigar

cigoto SM zygote

cigüeña SF **1** (*Orn*) stork **2** (*Mec*) crank, handle; (*Náut*)
winch, capstan

cigüeñal SM crankshaft

cilantro SM (*Bot, Culin*) coriander

cilicio SM (= *vestidura áspera*) hair shirt; (= *con pinchos*)
spiked belt or chain etc worn by penitents

cilindrada SF cylinder capacity

cilíndrico ADJ cylindrical

cilindro SM cylinder

cima SF **1** [*de montaña*] top, summit; **la ~ del Aconcagua**
the top o summit of Aconcagua; **las ~s más altas de los
Alpes** the highest peaks in the Alps **2** (= *cúspide*) **está en la
~ de su carrera** she is at the peak o height of her career
3 [*de árbol*] top

cimarra SF **hacer la ~** (*Chi*) to play truant

cimarrón/ona Ⓐ ADJ **1** (*LAm Bot, Zool*) wild, untamed
2 (*LAm*) **negro ~** (*Hist*) runaway slave, fugitive slave Ⓑ SM/F
(*Hist*) runaway slave, maroon Ⓒ SM (*CS*) unsweetened
mate

címbalo SM cymbal

cimborio SM, **cimborrio** SM dome

cimbrar /1a/ VT (= *agitar*) to shake, swish, swing;
(= *curvar*) to bend

cimbreante ADJ swaying

cimbrear /1a/ Ⓐ VT (= *hacer oscilar*) to swish, swing;
(= *curvar*) to bend; (= *agitar*) to shake Ⓑ VI to swing
around Ⓒ **cimbrearse** VPR **1** (= *balancearse*) to sway;
(= *curvarse*) to bend; (= *agitarse*) to shake **2** (= *andar con
garbo*) to walk gracefully

cimbreo SM (= *balanceo*) swaying; (= *agitación*) shaking;

(= *curvado*) bending

cimbrón SM (*And, CAm, CS*) shudder

cimbronada SF (*LAm*), **cimbronazo** SM (*LAm*) **1** = **cimbrón 2** (= *temblor de tierra*) tremor

cimentación SF **1** (= *cimientos*) foundation **2** (= *acción*) laying of foundations

cimentar /1j/ VT to lay the foundations of *o* for

cimero ADJ [*proyecto, figura*] crowning, finest

cimiento SM (*Arquit*) foundation; [*de amistad, sociedad*] foundation; **echar los ~s de algo** to lay the foundations for sth

cimitarra SF scimitar

cinc SM zinc

cincel SM chisel

cincelar /1a/ VT **1** [+ *piedra, mármol*] to chisel, carve, cut; [+ *metal*] engrave **2** [+ *proyecto*] to fine-tune

cinchar /1a/ **Ⓐ** VT [+ *caballo*] to girth, secure the girth of **Ⓑ** VI (*RPl**) (= *trabajar*) to work hard; **~ por** (= *apoyar*) to root for

cinco **Ⓐ** ADJ, PRON (*cardinal*) five; (*ordinal, en la fecha*) fifth; **las ~** five o'clock; **son las nueve menos ~** ◇ **son ~ para las nueve** (*LAm*) it's five to nine; ✦ MODISMOS **estar sin ~*** ◇ **no tener ni ~*** to be broke*; **¡venga esos ~!*** shake on it!* **Ⓑ** SM **1** (= *número*) five; *ver tb* **seis 2** (*Educ*) five (*the pass mark*); **sacar un ~ pelado** to scrape through*

cincuenta ADJ, PRON, SM (*cardinal*) fifty; (*ordinal*) fiftieth; **los (años) ~** the fifties; *ver tb* **seis**

cincuentavo SM fiftieth part; *ver tb* **sexto 2**

cincuentena SF fifty, about fifty; **una ~ de** fifty-odd, fifty or so

cincuentenario SM 50th anniversary

cincuentón/ona **Ⓐ** ADJ fifty-year old, fiftyish **Ⓑ** SM/F *person in his/her fifties*

cine SM **1** (= *arte*) cinema; **el ~ español** Spanish cinema; **hacer ~** to make films (*esp Brit*) *o* movies (*esp EEUU*); **de ~**: **actor de ~** film actor (*esp Brit*), movie actor (*EEUU*); **me lo pasé de ~** (*Esp**) I had a fantastic time, I had a whale of a time* ➤ **cine de autor** auteur cinema ➤ **cine de terror** horror films *pl* (*esp Brit*), horror movies *pl* (*esp EEUU*) ➤ **cine negro** film noir

2 (= *local*) cinema (*esp Brit*), movie theater (*EEUU*); **¿quieres ir al ~?** do you want to go to the cinema (*esp Brit*) *o* the movies (*esp EEUU*) ? ➤ **cine de verano** open-air cinema (*esp Brit*), open-air movie theater (*EEUU*)

cineasta SMF film maker (*esp Brit*), moviemaker (*EEUU*)

cine-club SM (*pl* **~s** *o* **-es**) film club (*esp Brit*), movie club (*EEUU*)

cinéfilo/a SM/F (= *aficionado*) film fan (*esp Brit*), movie fan (*EEUU*); (= *especialista*) film buff (*esp Brit**), movie buff (*EEUU*)

cinegética SF hunting, the chase

cinegético ADJ hunting *antes de s*, of the chase

cinemateca SF film library, film archive

cinematografía SF cinematography, films (*esp Brit*), movies (*EEUU*), film making (*esp Brit*), movie making (*EEUU*)

cinematográfico ADJ film *antes de s*, cinematographic (*frm*)

cinematógrafo SM **1** (= *cine*) cinema (*esp Brit*), movie theater (*EEUU*) **2** (= *aparato*) (film (*esp Brit*) *o* movie (*EEUU*)) projector

cinéreo ADJ ash-grey, ash-gray (*EEUU*), ashen (*liter*)

cinética SF kinetics *sing*

cinético ADJ kinetic

cínico/a **Ⓐ** ADJ cynical **Ⓑ** SM/F cynic

cinismo SM cynicism; **¡qué ~!** how cynical!, what a nerve!*

cinta SF **1** (= *tira*) ribbon ➤ **cinta adhesiva** adhesive tape ➤ **cinta aislante** insulating tape ➤ **cinta elástica** elastic ➤ **cinta métrica** tape measure **2** [*de vídeo, sonido*] tape ➤ **cinta de casete** cassette tape ➤ **cinta de vídeo** video tape ➤ **cinta limpiadora** head cleaner, head-cleaning tape

➤ **cinta virgen** blank tape **3** (*Cine*) film (*esp Brit*), movie (*EEUU*) **4** (*Téc*) ➤ **cinta transportadora** conveyor belt **5** (*Culin*) ➤ **cinta de cerdo, cinta de lomo** loin of pork **6** (*Bot*) spider plant

cinto SM (= *cinturón*) belt; [*de traje típico, militar*] girdle, sash

cintura SF **1** (*Anat*) waist; **tengo 76cm de ~** my waist (measurement) is 76cm; **de ~ para abajo** from the waist down ➤ **cintura de avispa** wasp waist **2** [*de falda, pantalón*] waist; ✦ MODISMO **meter a algn en ~** (*Esp*) to bring sb into line, make sb toe the line

cinturilla SF waistband

cinturón SM **1** (*gen*) belt; [*de traje típico, militar*] girdle, sash; ✦ MODISMO **apretarse** *o* **ajustarse el ~** to tighten one's belt ➤ **cinturón de castidad** chastity belt ➤ **cinturón de seguridad** safety belt **2** (= *zona*) belt, zone; **el ~ industrial de Madrid** the Madrid industrial belt ➤ **cinturón verde** green belt **3** (*Dep*) belt **4** (= *carretera*) ➤ **cinturón de circunvalación, cinturón de ronda** bypass, ring road (*Brit*), beltway (*EEUU*)

cipote **Ⓐ** ADJ (*Col**) **1** (= *estúpido*) stupid, thick (*Brit**) **2** (*intensificador*) **¡~ chica!** terrific girl!*; **¡~ película¡** great film (*esp Brit*) *o* movie (*esp EEUU*) !* **Ⓑ** SM (*Esp****) prick***

ciprés SM cypress (tree)

circense ADJ circus *antes de s*, of the circus

circo SM **1** (= *espectáculo*) circus ➤ **circo ambulante** travelling circus, traveling circus (*EEUU*) ➤ **circo romano** Roman circus **2** (*Geol*) cirque ➤ **circo glaciar** glacier cirque, glacial cirque

circonio SM zirconium

circuito SM **1** (= *pista*) circuit, track; **un ~ de Fórmula-uno** a Formula-One circuit ➤ **circuito de carreras** racetrack, (motor) racing circuit ➤ **circuito urbano** city circuit, town circuit **2** [*de profesionales*] circuit **3** (*Elec*) circuit; **corto ~** short circuit **4** (*Telec*) ➤ **circuito cerrado (de televisión)** closed-circuit (television) **5** (= *gira*) tour

circulación SF **1** (*Aut*) traffic; **"cerrado a la circulación rodada"** "closed to vehicular traffic *o* vehicles" **2** (*Med*) circulation ➤ **circulación de la sangre** circulation of the blood **3** (*Fin*) circulation; **estar fuera de ~** to be out of circulation, be no longer current; **poner algo en ~** to issue sth, put sth into circulation

circular /1a/ **Ⓐ** VI **1** [*vehículo*] to run; **este tren circula a muy alta velocidad** this train goes *o* travels *o* runs at very high speeds; **circule por la izquierda** drive on the left **2** [*peatón*] to walk; **por favor, circulen por la acera** please walk on the pavement (*Brit*) *o* sidewalk (*EEUU*); **¡circulen!** move along!

3 [*ciudadano, mercancía*] to move around
4 [*moneda*] to be in circulation
5 [*sangre*] to circulate; [*agua*] to flow
6 [*rumor*] to go around, circulate
Ⓑ VT to circulate
Ⓒ ADJ circular; **un salón con** *o* **de forma ~** a circular *o* round hall; **una carta ~** a circular
Ⓓ SF (= *carta*) circular

circularidad SF circularity

circulatorio ADJ **1** (*Anat*) circulatory **2** (*Aut*) traffic *antes de s*; **colapso ~** traffic jam, traffic stoppage

círculo SM **1** (= *circunferencia*) circle ➤ **Círculo Polar Antártico** Antarctic Circle ➤ **círculo vicioso** vicious circle **2** (= *grupo*) circle

circuncidar /1a/ VT to circumcise

circuncisión SF circumcision

circundante ADJ surrounding

circundar /1a/ VT to surround

circunferencia SF circumference

circunflejo SM circumflex

circunlocución SF, **circunloquio** SM circumlocution, roundabout expression

circunnavegar /1a/ VT to sail around, circumnavigate

circunscribir /3a/ (*pp* **circunscrito**) **Ⓐ** VT to circumscribe (**a** to) **Ⓑ** **circunscribirse** VPR (= *limitarse*) to be limited, be confined (**a** to)

circunscripción SF (gen) circumscription; (Mil) district; (Pol) constituency, electoral district

circunspección SF circumspection, prudence

circunspecto ADJ [persona] circumspect; [palabras] carefully chosen, guarded

circunstancia SF circumstance; **dadas las ~s** in o under the circumstances; **estar a la altura de las ~s** to rise to the occasion; **en las ~s actuales** under present circumstances, the way things are at the moment ➤ **circunstancias agravantes** aggravating circumstances ➤ **circunstancias atenuantes** extenuating o mitigating circumstances

circunstancial ADJ 1 (= casual) circumstantial; [caso] incidental 2 [arreglo, acuerdo] makeshift, temporary

circunvalación SF **carretera de ~** bypass, ring road (Brit), beltway (EEUU)

cirílico ADJ, SM Cyrillic

cirio SM 1 (Rel) (wax) candle 2 (*) (= jaleo) squabble; **montar un ~** to kick up a fuss

cirro SM cirrus

cirrosis SF INV cirrhosis

ciruela SF plum ➤ **ciruela pasa, ciruela seca** prune

ciruelo SM 1 (Bot) plum tree 2 (*) (= necio) dolt, idiot

cirugía SF surgery ➤ **cirugía estética** cosmetic surgery ➤ **cirugía plástica** plastic surgery

cirujano/a SM/F surgeon

cisco SM 1 (Min) coaldust, dross; ✦ MODISMOS **estar hecho ~** (Esp*) to be a wreck, be all in; **hacer algo ~** (Esp*) to tear sth to bits, smash sth to smithereens 2 (Esp*) (= riña) shindy*; **armar un ~** ◇ **meter ~** to make a racket

Cisjordania SF the West Bank

cisma SM (Rel) schism; (Pol) split

cisne SM 1 (= ave) swan 2 (RPI) (= borla) powder puff

cisterciense ADJ, SM Cistercian

cisterna SF (para agua) tank; (del wáter) cistern (esp Brit), tank (EEUU); **buque ~** tanker

cistitis SF INV cystitis

cita SF 1 (= encuentro) 1.1 (con médico, profesional) appointment; **tengo ~ con el dentista** I have a dental appointment, I have an appointment at the dentist's; **pedir ~** to make an appointment 1.2 [de novios] date; **tener una ~** to have a date ➤ **cita a ciegas** blind date 2 (= reunión) meeting; **acudir a una ~** to attend a meeting; **darse ~** (= quedar citado) to arrange to meet; (= encontrarse) to gather; **lugar de ~** meeting place 3 (= punto de encuentro) event; **los Juegos Olímpicos son la ~ más importante del deporte mundial** the Olympic Games are the most important sporting event in the world; **ser ~ obligada** [acontecimiento] to be a must; [lugar] to be the place to be 4 (= mención literal) [de escrito, libro] quotation; [de parte de discurso, declaraciones] quote ➤ **cita textual** direct quote

citación SF 1 [de un libro] quotation 2 (Jur) summons, citation ➤ **citación judicial** summons, subpoena

citadino/a (LAm) Ⓐ ADJ urban Ⓑ SM/F city dweller; (Méx) inhabitant of Mexico City

citado ADJ aforementioned

citar /1a/ Ⓐ VT 1 (= mencionar) 1.1 [+ ejemplo, caso] to quote, cite 1.2 [+ frase, autor, fuentes] to quote; **~on textualmente varios párrafos** they quoted several paragraphs word for word o verbatim; **no quería que ningún "imbécil" —cito textualmente— le quitara el puesto** he wasn't having any "idiot" — and I quote — taking the job away from him 2 (= convocar) **¿está usted citado?** do you have an appointment?; **la cité para ultimar unos detalles** I arranged to see her to go over some details 3 (Jur) [juez] to summon; [abogado, defensa, fiscal] to call; **~ a algn a declarar** to summon sb to give evidence Ⓑ **citarse** VPR 1 (varias personas) to arrange to meet; **~se con algn** to arrange to meet sb 2 [novios] to make a date

cítara SF zither

citófono SM (And) buzzer

citología SF 1 (= análisis) smear test (Brit), pap test (EEUU) 2 (Biol) cytology

cítrico Ⓐ ADJ citric Ⓑ **cítricos** SMPL citrus fruits

citrícola ADJ citrus antes de s

ciudad SF 1 (de gran tamaño) city; (más pequeña) town; **la ~ de Granada** (the city of) Granada; **la Ciudad Condal** name for the city of Barcelona ➤ **Ciudad del Cabo** Cape Town ➤ **Ciudad del Vaticano** Vatican City ➤ **Ciudad de México** Mexico City ➤ **ciudad dormitorio** dormitory town (Brit), bedroom community (EEUU) ➤ **ciudad natal** home town, native city, native town ➤ **ciudad perdida** (Méx) shanty town 2 (= instalaciones) ➤ **ciudad deportiva** sports complex ➤ **ciudad sanitaria** hospital complex ➤ **ciudad universitaria** university campus

ciudadanía SF 1 (= habitantes) citizens pl 2 (= status) citizenship

ciudadano/a Ⓐ ADJ civic, city antes de s Ⓑ SM/F citizen; **el ~ de a pie** the man in the street

ciudadela SF 1 (Mil) citadel, fortress 2 (Col) block of flats (Brit), apartment building (EEUU)

ciudad-estado SF (pl **ciudades-estado**) city-state

ciudadrealeño ADJ of/from Ciudad Real

cívico ADJ [deber] civic; [persona] public-spirited, civic-minded

civil Ⓐ ADJ 1 (= no militar) [autoridad, aviación] civil; [vida, víctima, población] civilian; **guerra ~** civil war; **va vestido de ~** he's wearing civilian clothes, he's in civilian clothes 2 (= no religioso) civil; **casarse por lo ~** o (RPI) **por (el) ~** to get married in a civil wedding ceremony, have a registry office wedding (esp Brit) 3 (Jur) [responsabilidad, desobediencia] civil Ⓑ SMF 1 (= persona no militar) civilian 2 (= guardia) civil guard Ⓒ SM (RPI) (= matrimonio) civil ceremony

civilismo SM (CS) pro-civilian-government stance

civilización SF civilization

civilizado ADJ civilized

civilizar /1f/ Ⓐ VT to civilize Ⓑ **civilizarse** VPR to become civilized

civismo SM sense of civic responsibility, public-spiritedness

cizaña SF 1 (Bot) darnel; (Biblia) tares 2 (= discordia) discord; **meter** o **sembrar ~** to sow discord (**entre** among), create a rift (**entre** between)

cizañero/a SM/F troublemaker, mischief-maker

clamar /1a/ Ⓐ VT [+ justicia, venganza] to clamour for, clamor for (EEUU), cry out for Ⓑ VI (= protestar) to protest; ✦ MODISMO **~ al cielo** o **a Dios** to be an absolute outrage; **una injusticia que clama al cielo** an absolutely outrageous injustice

clamor SM 1 (= griterío) clamour, clamor (EEUU), roar 2 (= protesta) outcry

clamoroso ADJ 1 [éxito] resounding, enormous; [acogida, recibimiento] rapturous 2 (= vociferante) clamorous

clan SM (Hist) clan; [de gángsters] family, mob*

clandestinamente ADV clandestinely

clandestinidad SF secrecy, clandestinity, secret nature; **en la ~** in secrecy

clandestino/a Ⓐ ADJ 1 [reunión, cita] secret, clandestine; [boda] secret 2 (Pol) [actividad, movimiento] clandestine, underground; [inmigrante] illegal Ⓑ SM/F illegal immigrant

claque SF claque

claqué SM tap dancing

claqueta SF clapperboard (Brit), clapboard (EEUU)

clara SF 1 [de huevo] egg white; **bata las ~s a punto de nieve** whisk the egg whites until they form peaks 2 (Esp) (= cerveza con gaseosa) shandy (Brit), lager shandy (Brit), beer mixed with lemonade 3 (= calva) bald patch

claraboya SF skylight

clarear /1a/ **A** VI **1** (*Meteo*) (= *despejarse*) to clear up **2** (*al amanecer*) [*día*] to dawn, break; [*cielo*] to grow light; **ya empieza a ~** it's starting to get light now **3** (= *escasear*) **con la altura el monte ya clarea** as you go up the vegetation becomes more sparse; **ya le empieza a ~ el pelo** he's beginning to lose his hair **4** [*tela*] to be transparent **B clarearse** VPR **1** [*tela*] to be transparent **2** (*) (= *delatarse*) to give the game away

clarete SM rosé

claridad SF **1** (= *luminosidad*) light; **este cuarto tiene mucha ~** this room is very light **2** [*de explicación*] clarity; **explicar/expresar algo con ~** to explain sth clearly **3** (= *nitidez*) [*de sonido, voz*] clarity; [*de imagen*] sharpness, clarity; **oír/ver algo con ~** to hear/see sth clearly **4** (= *sinceridad*) frankness; **hablar con ~** to speak frankly

clarificación SF clarification

clarificador ADJ, **clarificante** ADJ [*experiencia, charla*] illuminating, enlightening; [*notas, teoría*] explanatory

clarificar /1g/ VT **1** [+ *asunto, problema*] to clarify **2** [+ *líquidos*] to clarify

clarín SM bugle, trumpet

clarinete A SM (= *instrumento*) clarinet **B** SMF (= *persona*) clarinettist

clarinetista SMF clarinettist

clarisa A ADJ **monja ~ = B B** SF nun of the Order of St Clare

clarividencia SF **1** (= *adivinación*) clairvoyance **2** (= *discernimiento*) discernment

clarividente A ADJ **1** (= *que adivina el futuro*) clairvoyant **2** (= *discerniente*) discerning **B** SMF clairvoyant

claro A ADJ **1** (= *no oscuro*) [*piel*] fair; [*color*] light, pale; **un vestido verde ~** a light *o* pale green dress; **una alemana de ojos ~s** a blue-eyed German girl **2** (= *evidente*) **2.1** (*con sustantivos*) [*ejemplo, prueba, ventaja*] clear; [*inconveniente*] obvious; [*desastre*] total, absolute **2.2** (*con verbos*) **dejar** algo **~** to make sth clear; **estar** *o* **quedar ~** to be clear; **tener** algo **~** to be sure of sth, be clear about sth **2.3 ✦** MODISMOS **a las claras: prefiero decírselo a las claras** I prefer to tell him straight (out); **su triunfo deja bien a las claras el buen momento que atraviesa** his victory is a clear indication *o* sign that he is on excellent form; **ser más ~ que el agua** to be crystal-clear; **las cuentas claras: me gustan las cuentas claras** I like to have *o* keep things clear; **llevarlo** *o* (*Esp*) **tenerlo ~** (*iró*): **lo tienes ~** things won't be easy for you; **ver algo ~: lo vi ~ en cuanto oí la noticia** it became clear to me when I heard the news; **sus padres no veían muy ~ el tema** his parents weren't too sure about the matter **3** (= *poco espeso*) [*té, café*] weak; [*caldo*] thin **4** (= *luminoso*) [*día, mañana*] bright; [*habitación, casa*] light, bright **5** (= *transparente*) [*agua*] clear; [*tejido*] transparent **6** (= *nítido*) [*sonido, voz*] clear; [*imagen*] sharp, clear **7** (= *escaso*) [*pelo*] thin; [*bosque*] light, sparse **8** [*idea*] clear **9** (= *sincero*) frank; **ser ~** to be frank **B** ADV **1** (= *con precisión*) [*oír, ver, hablar*] clearly **2** (= *sinceramente*) frankly; **hablar ~** to speak frankly, be frank **3** (*tras invitaciones, peticiones*) sure **4** (*uso enfático*) **¡claro! por eso estaba ayer tan rara** of course! that's why she was acting so funny yesterday; **—¿por qué no te disfrazas tú? —¡~, para que os riáis de mí todos!** "why don't you dress up?" — "oh sure, so you can all laugh at me!"; **¡~ que no!** of course not!; **¡~ que sí!** yes, of course! **C** SM **1** (*Meteo*) bright spell, sunny interval **➤ claro de luna** moonlight **2** [*momento libre*] lull **3** (= *espacio despejado*) (*entre personas*) space; (*entre árboles*) clearing; [*de pelo*] bald patch **4** (= *pausa*) (*en un texto*) gap, space; (*en discurso*) pause

claroscuro SM chiaroscuro

clase SF **1** (*Escol*) **1.1** (= *lección*) lesson, class; **dar ~(s)** [*profesor*] to teach; (*Esp*) [*alumno*] to have lessons;

✦ MODISMO **fumarse** *o* **saltarse** *o* **soplarse la ~*** to skip class*, skive off (*Brit**) **1.2** (= *instrucción*) school; **hoy no tengo ~** I don't have school today; **los viernes salgo de ~ a las cuatro** on Fridays I finish school at four; **faltar a ~** to miss school, be absent **1.3** (= *aula*) classroom **1.4** (= *grupo de alumnos*) class; **la gente de mi ~** my classmates, my class **➤ clase particular** private lesson; **"se dan clases particulares"** "private tuition offered" **2** (*Univ*) **2.1** (*práctica*) (= *lección, instrucción*) class; (= *aula*) classroom; **hoy no tengo ~** I don't have any classes today; **dar** *o* (*LAm frm*) **dictar ~** [*profesor*] to teach; [*alumno*] (*Esp*) to have classes **2.2** (*teórica*) (= *lección*) lecture; (= *aula*) lecture room; **dar ~** [*profesor*] to teach, lecture; [*alumno*] to have lectures **➤ clase magistral** master class **3** (= *tipo*) kind, sort; **gente de todas ~s** all kinds *o* sorts of people, people of all kinds; **con toda ~ de detalles** in great detail, down to the last detail **4** (= *calidad*) quality **5** (*en viajes*) class; **viajar en primera ~** to travel first class **➤ clase preferente** club class **➤ clase turista** tourist class **6** (= *elegancia*) class; **tener ~** to have class **7** (*Sociol*) class **➤ clase media** middle class; **una familia de ~ media** a middle-class family **➤ clase obrera** working class **➤ clase social** social class **8** (*Biol, Bot*) class

clasicismo SM classicism

clásico A ADJ **1** (*Arte, Mús*) classical **2** (= *característico*) classic **B** SM **1** (= *obra, película*) classic **2** (= *artista, escritor*) outstanding figure, big name* **3** (*SAm Ftbl*) classic game (*between two old rivals*)

> El adjetivo **clásico** se traduce por **classic** o **classical**. **Classical** se aplica a lo que es tradicional y a todo lo relativo a las civilizaciones griega y romana: "la música clásica", *classical music*. Se utiliza **classic** para referirse a algo que representa el ejemplo más típico en su género ("Es el clásico ejemplo de niño mimado", *He's a classic example of a spoilt child*), o en relación a un libro o una película de calidad excelente.

clasificación SF **1** (= *categorización*) classification **2** (= *ordenación*) [*de documentos*] classification; (*Inform, Correos*) sorting **3** (*en torneo*) qualification **4** (= *lista*) table, league

clasificar /1g/ **A** VT **1** (= *categorizar*) to classify **2** (= *ordenar*) [+ *documentos*] to classify; (*Correos, Inform*) to sort **B** VI (*LAm*) **= VPR C clasificarse** VPR (*Dep*) **mi equipo se clasificó en segundo lugar** my team came *o* was placed second; **el equipo no se clasificó para la final** the team did not qualify for the final

clasificatoria SF (= *ronda*) qualifying round; (*Atletismo*) heat

clasificatorio ADJ [*fase, prueba*] qualifying

clasismo SM **1** (= *actitud discriminatoria*) classism **2** (= *estructura social*) class structure

clasista A ADJ **1** [*actitud*] class-conscious, classist; (*pey*) snobbish **2** (= *de clases*) class *antes de s* **B** SMF class-conscious person; (*pey*) snob

claudicar /1g/ VI **1** (= *rendirse*) to give in **2** (= *renunciar*) **~ de algo** to renounce sth

claustro SM **1** (*Rel*) cloister **2** (*Univ*) staff, faculty (*EEUU*); (= *junta*) senate; (= *asamblea*) staff meeting **3** (*Anat*) **➤ claustro materno** womb

claustrofobia SF claustrophobia

claustrofóbico ADJ claustrophobic

cláusula SF clause **➤ cláusula de rescisión** opt-out clause, cancellation clause

clausura SF **1** [*de local, edificio*] closure **2** [*de olimpiada, congreso*] closing ceremony; [*de tribunal*] closing session; **discurso de ~** closing speech **3** (*Rel*) (= *recinto*) cloister; (= *reclusión religiosa*) cloister, religious seclusion; **convento de ~** enclosed convent, enclosed monastery

clausurar /1a/ VT **1** [+ *debate, curso*] to close, bring to a close **2** [+ *negocio, edificio*] to close, close down

clava SF club, cudgel

clavada SF 1 (*Méx*) (= *salto*) dive 2 (**) **pegar una ~ a algn** to rip sb off**, overcharge sb

clavadista SMF (*Dep*) diver

clavado Ⓐ ADJ 1 (*con clavos, puntas*) nailed 2 [*ropa*] just right 3 **dejar a algn** ~ to leave sb speechless; **quedó** ~ he was speechless 4 **a las cinco clavadas** at five sharp *o* on the dot 5 (= *idéntico*) **es Pedro** ~ he's the spitting image of Pedro; **es ~ a su padre** he's the spitting image of his father Ⓑ SM (*LAm*) (= *salto*) dive; **tirarse un** ~ to dive, take a dive

clavar /1a/ Ⓐ VT 1 [+ *clavo*] to hammer in; **le clavó un cuchillo en el cuello** he stuck a knife in his throat; **le clavó las uñas en la cara** she dug her nails into his face 2 (*con clavos*) to nail; **ha clavado unas tablas en la puerta** he has nailed some panels onto the door; **clavó con chinchetas un póster de su equipo** he pinned up a poster of his team; ✦ MODISMO ~ **la mirada** *o* **los ojos en algn/algo** to fix one's gaze *o* one's eyes on sb/sth 3 (*) 3.1 (= *cobrar de más*) to rip off* 3.2 (*CS*) (= *engañar*) to cheat; **me ~on con el cambio** I was short-changed 3.3 (*Méx*) (= *robar*) to swipe*, pinch*, nick (*Brit*) 4 (*CS**) (= *dejar plantado*) to leave in the lurch* 5 (*Ven**) [+ *estudiante*] to fail; **me clavó en el examen de química** I failed (in) my chemistry exam Ⓑ **clavarse** VPR 1 [*espina, astilla*] **se me ha clavado una astilla en la mano** I've got a splinter in my hand; **se me clavó una raspa en la garganta** a fishbone got stuck in my throat 2 (*reflexivo*) **se clavó la espada** he stabbed himself with his sword 3 (*CAm, Méx Dep*) to dive 4 (*CS**) ~**se con algo** to get stuck with sth*

clave Ⓐ SF 1 (= *código*) code; **mensaje en** ~ coded message, message in code ➤ **clave de acceso** password 2 (= *porqué*) key 3 (*Mús*) clef ➤ **clave de fa** bass clef ➤ **clave de sol** treble clef 4 (= *sentido*) **una novela escrita en ~ de humor** a novel written in a humorous style *o* tone 5 (*Arquit*) keystone Ⓑ SM (*Mús*) harpsichord Ⓒ ADJ (= *esencial*) [*tema, punto, factor, personaje*] key *antes de s*; **cuestión** ~ key question; **palabra** ~ keyword

clavecín SM spinet

clavel SM carnation

clavellina SF pink

clavicémbalo SM harpsichord

clavicordio SM clavichord

clavícula SF collar bone, clavicle

clavija SF (*Carpintería*) peg, dowel; (*Mús*) peg; (*Elec*) plug; ✦ MODISMO **apretar las ~s a algn** to put the screws on sb*

clavo SM 1 [*de carpintero*] nail; [*de adorno*] stud; ✦ MODISMOS **agarrarse a un ~ ardiendo: estoy tan desesperado que me agarraría a un ~ ardiendo** I'm so desperate I'd do anything *o* I'm capable of anything; **como un** ~ (*Esp*): **llegó a las dos en punto, como un** ~ she arrived at two o'clock on the dot; **dar en el** ~ to hit the nail on the head; **¡por los ~s de Cristo!** for heaven's sake! 2 [*de botas de fútbol*] stud; [*de zapatillas de correr*] spike 3 [*de montañismo*] piton 4 (*Bot*) (*tb* ~ **de olor**) clove 5 (*CS*) (= *cosa desagradable*) **es un ~ tener que levantarse temprano** it's a real pain *o* bind having to get up so early; **¡qué ~ que te vendieron!** they've sold you a dud!*

claxon SM (*pl* ~**s** *o* **cláxones**) horn; **tocar el** ~ to sound *o* blow one's horn, honk, hoot (*esp Brit*)

clemencia SF (= *misericordia*) mercy; (*Jur*) leniency

clemente ADJ (= *misericordioso*) merciful; (*Jur*) lenient

clementina SF clementine, tangerine

cleptomanía SF kleptomania

cleptómano/a Ⓐ ADJ kleptomaniac Ⓑ SM/F kleptomaniac

clerical ADJ clerical

clericalismo SM clericalism

clérigo SM (*católico*) priest; (*anglicano*) clergyman, priest

clero SM clergy

clic SM click; **hacer ~ en algo** (*Inform*) to click on sth; **hacer doble ~ en algo** to double-click on sth

clicar VI (*Inform*) to click; **clica en el icono** click on the icon; **clicar dos veces** to double-click

cliché SM 1 (*Tip*) stencil 2 (= *tópico*) cliché 3 (*Fot*) negative

cliente SMF [*de tienda, bar, restaurante, banco*] customer; [*de abogado, contable*] customer, client; [*de hotel*] guest

> En inglés para referirse a los clientes de una tienda se habla de **customers**, mientras a los de un abogado o un contable se les llama **clients**. Por otro lado, a los clientes de un hotel se les llama **guests**.

clientela SF (*Com*) clientele, customers *pl*; (*Med*) patients *pl*

clientelismo SM patronage system

clima SM climate; [*de reunión*] atmosphere; climate

climático ADJ climatic

climatizado ADJ air-conditioned

climatizador SM air-conditioner

climatología SF (= *ciencia*) climatology; (= *tiempo*) weather

climatológico ADJ climatological; **estudios ~s** studies in climate *o* climatic change

climatólogo/a SM/F climatologist

clímax ['klimas] SM INV climax

clínica SF 1 (= *hospital*) clinic; [*de formación*] teaching hospital ➤ **clínica de reposo** convalescent home, rest home 2 (*Univ*) clinical training; *ver tb* **clínico**

clínico/a Ⓐ ADJ [*asistencia, análisis*] clinical; **hospital ~** teaching hospital Ⓑ SM/F (= *médico*) specialist, consultant (*Brit*); *ver tb* **clínica**

clip [klip] SM (*pl* ~**s**) 1 [*de sujeción*] (*para papeles*) paper clip; [*de collar, pulsera*] fastener; [*de pantalón*] trouser-clip 2 [*de imágenes*] videoclip

clíper SM clipper

cliqueable ADJ clickable

cliquear /1a/ VI (*Inform*) to click; **cliquea en el icono** click on the icon

clisé SM 1 (*Tip*) cliché, stereotype plate; (*Fot*) negative 2 (= *tópico*) cliché

clítoris SM INV clitoris

cloaca SF sewer, drain

cloch(e) SM (*CAm, Méx*) clutch

clon SM clone

clonación SF, **clonaje** SM cloning

clonar /1a/ VT to clone

clónico Ⓐ ADJ clonal, cloned Ⓑ SM (*Inform*) clone

clorar /1a/ VT to chlorinate

clorhídrico ADJ hydrochloric

cloro SM chlorine

clorofila SF chlorophyl(l)

clorofluorocarbono SM chlorofluorocarbon

cloroformo SM chloroform

cloruro SM chloride ➤ **cloruro sódico** sodium chloride

closet SM, **clóset** SM (*LAm*) (*gen*) (built-in) cupboard, closet (*EEUU*); (*para ropa*) (built-in) wardrobe, closet (*EEUU*)

club SM (*pl* ~**s** *o* ~**es**) 1 (= *sociedad*) club ➤ **club de fans** fan club ➤ **club de fútbol** football club 2 (= *bar*) club ➤ **club nocturno** night club

clueca SF broody hen

cm ABR (= **centímetro(s)**) cm

cm² ABR (= **centímetros cuadrados**) sq. cm

cm³ ABR (= **centímetros cúbicos**) cc

CNT SF ABR 1 (*Esp*) = **Confederación Nacional del Trabajo** 2 (*Uru*) = **Convención Nacional de Trabajadores**

coa SF (*Chi*) underworld slang

coacción SF coercion, compulsion

coaccionar /1a/ VT to coerce, pressure

coadyuvar /1a/ VI **coadjuvar a** to contribute to

coagulante SM coagulant

coagular /1a/ **Ⓐ** VT [+ *sangre*] to coagulate, clot, congeal; [+ *leche*] to curdle **Ⓑ** **coagularse** VPR [*sangre*] to coagulate, clot, congeal; [*leche*] to curdle

coágulo SM clot, coagulum (*frm*) ➤ **coágulo de sangre, coágulo sanguíneo** blood clot

coalición SF coalition; **gobierno de ~** coalition government

coartada SF alibi; **alegar una ~** to produce an alibi

coartar /1a/ VT to limit, restrict

coautor(a) SM/F joint author, co-author

coaxial ADJ coaxial

coba* SF **1** (= *adulación*) soft soap*, cajolery; **dar ~ a algn** to suck up to sb, soft-soap sb* **2** (*Ven*) (= *mentira*) fib

cobalto SM cobalt

cobarde **Ⓐ** ADJ (*en lucha, aventura*) cowardly; (*ante sangre, alturas*) faint-hearted **Ⓑ** SMF coward

cobardía SF cowardice, cowardliness

cobaya SF guinea pig

cobear* /1a/ VI (*Ven*) to lie

cobertizo SM **1** (*para animales, herramientas*) shed **2** (= *refugio*) shelter

cobertor SM bedspread, coverlet

cobertura SF **1** [*de noticia, acontecimiento*] coverage; **la ceremonia recibió amplia ~ informativa** the ceremony was widely covered, the ceremony received wide news coverage
2 (= *ámbito*) range; **este teléfono sólo tiene ~ nacional** this phone only has a range within this country; **una emisora de ~ regional** a regional radio station; **estar fuera de ~** to be out of range; **no tengo ~** I'm out of range
3 [*de un crédito*] cover ➤ **cobertura del seguro** insurance cover ➤ **cobertura sanitaria** health care

cobija SF (*LAm*) blanket; **las ~s** the bedclothes

cobijar /1a/ **Ⓐ** VT (= *proteger*) to protect, shelter; (= *hospedar*) to take in, give shelter to; (*Pol, Jur*) to harbour, harbor (*EEUU*) **Ⓑ** **cobijarse** VPR to (take) shelter

cobijo SM shelter

cobista* (*Esp*) **Ⓐ** ADJ oily*, smarmy (*Brit**) **Ⓑ** SMF bootlicker*, toady*

cobra SF cobra

cobrable ADJ, **cobradero** ADJ [*cheque*] cashable; [*precio*] chargeable; [*suma*] recoverable

cobrador(a) SM/F **1** (*Com*) collector **2** (*en bus*) conductor; (*en tren*) guard (*Brit*), conductor (*EEUU*)

cobrar /1a/ **Ⓐ** VT **1** (= *pedir como pago*) to charge; **cobran 200 dólares por arreglarlo** they charge 200 dollars to repair it
2 (= *recibir*) **cobran un sueldo anual de nueve millones** they get *o* earn *o* receive an annual salary of nine million; **nuestro vecino está cobrando el paro** our neighbour is on unemployment benefit; **cantidades a *o* por ~** amounts payable, amounts due; ♦ MODISMO **~ palos** to get a beating
3 (= *recoger dinero de*) [+ *deuda, alquiler, impuesto*] to collect; [+ *cheque*] to cash; [+ *subsidio, pensión*] to draw
4 (= *adquirir*) **los ordenadores han cobrado una gran importancia** computers have become very important; **~ actualidad** to become topical; **~ vida** [*personaje, juego*] to come alive
5 (= *recuperar*) [+ *pieza de caza*] to retrieve, fetch; [+ *cuerda*] to pull in, take in
Ⓑ VI **1** (= *recibir dinero*) **1.1** (*como sueldo*) to be paid; **cobra los viernes** he gets paid on Fridays; **los atletas cobran por participar en la carrera** the athletes get paid *o* receive a fee for taking part in the race **1.2** (*por servicio*) to charge; **~ por los servicios prestados** to charge for services rendered; **¿me cobra, por favor?** how much do I owe you?, can I have the bill (*Brit*) *o* check (*EEUU*), please?
2 (*) (= *recibir golpes*) **¡vas a ~!** you're (in) for it!

Ⓒ **cobrarse** VPR **1** (= *recibir dinero*) **¡cóbrese, por favor!** can I pay, please?
2 [+ *muertos, víctimas*] to claim

cobre SM **1** (*Min*) copper **2** (*LAm**) (= *céntimo*) cent; **no tengo un ~** I haven't a cent/penny; ♦ MODISMO **enseñar el ~** to show one's true colours

cobrizo ADJ coppery, copper-coloured, copper-colored (*EEUU*)

cobro SM **1** (= *recaudación*) [*de cheque*] cashing, encashment (*frm*); [*de salario, subsidio*] receipt, collection; [*de pensión*] collection, drawing; [*de factura, deuda*] collection; **cargo *o* comisión por ~** collection charge ➤ **cobro revertido: llamada a ~ revertido** reverse charge call (*Brit*), collect call (*EEUU*); **llamar a ~ revertido** to reverse the charges (*Brit*), call collect (*EEUU*), call toll-free (*EEUU*)
2 (= *pago*) **nos comprometemos a garantizar el ~ de las pensiones** we make a guarantee that the pensions will be paid

coca SF **1** (*Bot*) coca **2** (*) (= *droga*) coke* **3** (*Culin*) sponge cake

cocada SF macaroon

cocaína SF cocaine

cocainómano/a SM/F cocaine addict

cocal SM coca plantation

cocción SF **1** (*Culin*) (*gen*) cooking; (= *hervor*) boiling; (= *duración*) cooking time; **el agua de ~** cooking liquid **2** (*Téc*) firing, baking

cóccix SM INV coccyx

cocear /1a/ VT, VI to kick (**contra** against)

cocer /2b, 2h/ **Ⓐ** VT **1** (*Culin*) (= *hervir*) to boil **2** (*Culin*) (= *guisar*) to cook; **~ al vapor** to steam **3** (*Téc*) [+ *ladrillos, cerámica*] to fire **Ⓑ** VI [*vino*] to ferment **Ⓒ** **cocerse** VPR **1** (= *hervir*) to boil **2** (= *guisarse*) to cook; (*al vapor*) to steam **3** (*) (= *tramarse*) **algo raro se está cociendo en el comité** something strange is brewing in the committee; **voy a ver qué se cuece por aquí** I'm going to see what's going on here **4** (*) (= *pasar calor*) to bake*, roast*, boil*

cochambre SF filth, muck

cochambroso ADJ filthy

cochayuyo SM (*And*) edible seaweed

coche SM **1** (= *automóvil*) car, automobile (*EEUU*); (*frm*) **fuimos a Almería en ~** we drove to Almería, we went to Almería by car; ♦ MODISMO **en el ~ de San Fernando** on Shanks's pony, on Shanks's mare (*EEUU*) ➤ **coche bomba** car bomb ➤ **coche celular** police van, patrol wagon (*EEUU*) ➤ **coche de alquiler** hire car (*Brit*), rental car (*EEUU*) ➤ **coche de bomberos** fire engine (*Brit*), fire truck (*EEUU*) ➤ **coche de caballos** coach, carriage ➤ **coche de carreras** racing car ➤ **coche de choque** bumper car, dodgem car (*esp Brit*) ➤ **coche de cortesía** courtesy car ➤ **coche de época** vintage car ➤ **coche de línea** coach (*Brit*), long distance bus (*esp EEUU*) ➤ **coche de muertos** hearse ➤ **coche de ocasión** used car, second-hand car ➤ **coche deportivo** sports car ➤ **coche patrulla** patrol car
2 (*Ferro*) coach, car (*esp EEUU*), carriage
3 [*de bebé*] pram (*Brit*), baby carriage (*EEUU*)
4 (*Méx*) (= *taxi*) taxi, cab

coche-bomba SM (*pl* **coches-bomba**) car bomb

coche-cama SM (*pl* **coches-cama**) sleeping car, sleeper (*Brit*), Pullman (*EEUU*)

cochecito SM **1** (= *juguete*) toy car **2** (*para bebé*) pram (*Brit*), baby carriage (*EEUU*); (*para niño*) (baby) buggy, pushchair (*Brit*), stroller (*EEUU*)

cochera SF (*Esp, Méx*) [*de coches*] private car park (*Brit*), private parking lot (*EEUU*) **2** [*de autobuses*] depot (*esp Brit*), bus garage (*EEUU*); [*de trenes*] engine shed; [*de carruajes*] coach house

coche-restaurante SM (*pl* **coches-restaurante**) dining car, restaurant car (*Brit*)

cochinada SF **1** (= *suciedad*) filth, filthiness **2** (= *comentario*) filthy remark **3** (= *cosa*) filthy object, dirty thing **4** (= *canallada*) dirty trick; **hacer una ~ a algn** to play a dirty trick on sb

cochinería SF = **cochinada**

cochinilla SF 1 (*Zool*) woodlouse 2 (*Culin*) cochineal

cochinillo SM (= *animal*) piglet; (= *carne*) suck(l)ing pig

cochino/a Ⓐ ADJ 1 (= *sucio*) filthy, dirty 2 [*trabajo, sueldo, vacaciones*] rotten*, lousy*; [*mentira*] filthy*, rotten* Ⓑ SM/F 1 (= *animal*) pig, hog (*esp EEUU*) 2 (= *mala persona*) swine* 3 (= *guarro*) filthy pig*

cochura† SF 1 (= *acto*) = **cocción** 2 (= *hornada*) batch (of loaves, cakes, bricks *etc*)

cocido Ⓐ ADJ 1 (*Culin*) boiled, cooked 2 (= *acalorado*) **estar ~*** to be roasting* Ⓑ SM (*Esp*) stew (*of meat, bacon, chickpeas etc*)

cociente SM (*Mat*) quotient; (*Dep*) [*de goles*] goal average ➤ **cociente intelectual** intelligence quotient, IQ

cocina SF 1 (= *habitación*) kitchen; **muebles de ~** kitchen units; ✦ MODISMO **llegar hasta la ~** (*Esp Dep*) to slice *o* burst through the defence 2 (= *aparato*) stove, cooker (*esp Brit*) ➤ **cocina de gas** gas stove, gas cooker (*esp Brit*) ➤ **cocina eléctrica** electric cooker (*esp Brit*), electric stove (*esp EEUU*) 3 (= *actividad*) cooking, cookery; (= *arte*) cuisine, cookery; **libro de ~** cookbook, cookery book (*Brit*); **la ~ valenciana** Valencian cuisine, Valencian cookery ➤ **cocina casera** home cooking

cocinar /1a/ VI, VT to cook

cocinero/a SM/F cook

> Aunque en inglés el nombre de muchas profesiones termina en "-er", p.ej., **teacher**, **bus driver**, **photographer**, etc., no es así en el caso de **cocinero** que se traduce por **cook**.

cocineta SF 1 (*Méx*) kitchenette 2 (*Col*) camping stove, camp stove (*EEUU*)

cocker ['koker] SM (*pl ~ o ~s*) cocker (spaniel)

coco¹ SM 1 (*Bot*) (= *fruto*) coconut; (= *árbol*) coconut palm 2 (**) (= *cabeza*) nut*, noggin (*EEUU**), head; **no anda muy bien del ~** she's not right in the head*; ✦ MODISMOS **comer el ~ a algn** (*Esp*): **la tele les ha comido el ~** the TV has got them brainwashed; **comerse el ~** (*Esp*) to worry (one's head) 3 (= *persona lista*) whizz* 4 **cocos** (*CS****) balls***

coco² SM 1 (= *fantasma*) bogeyman (*Brit*), boogeyman (*EEUU**); **¡que viene el ~!** the bogeyman's (*Brit*) *o* boogeyman's (*EEUU*) coming! 2 (= *persona fea*) **es un ~** he's an ugly devil, he's ugly as sin*

coco³ SM (= *bacteria*) coccus

cocoa SF (*LAm*) cocoa ➤ **cocoa en polvo** cocoa powder, drinking chocolate

cocodrilo SM crocodile

cocol SM (*Méx*) sesame seed bun

cocoliche SM (*RPl Ling*) *hybrid Spanish of Italian immigrants*

cocorota SF nut*, noggin (*EEUU**), head

cocotal SM coconut plantation, coconut grove

cocotero SM coconut palm

cóctel ['koktel] SM (*pl ~s o ~es*) 1 (= *bebida*) cocktail 2 (= *entrante*) cocktail ➤ **cóctel de frutas** fruit cocktail 3 (= *reunión*) cocktail party 4 ➤ **cóctel (Molotov)** Molotov cocktail, petrol bomb (*Brit*)

coctelera SF cocktail shaker

cocuyo SM 1 (*LAm*) (= *insecto*) firefly 2 (*Col, Ven Aut*) sidelight, parking light (*EEUU*)

coda SF 1 (*Mús*) coda 2 (*Téc*) wedge

codaste SM stern post

codazo SM **dar un ~ a algn** (*disimuladamente*) to give sb a nudge, nudge sb; (*con fuerza*) to elbow sb; **abrirse paso a ~s** to elbow one's way through

codearse /1a/ VPR **~ con** to hobnob with, rub shoulders with

codeína SF codeine

codera SF (= *parche*) elbow patch; [*de protección*] elbow guard

códice SM codex

codicia SF (= *avaricia*) greed; (*por lo ajeno*) covetousness

codiciado ADJ [*medalla, trofeo*] coveted; [*posesión, casa*] sought-after

codiciar /1b/ VT [+ *dinero, bienes*] to desire; [+ *lo ajeno*] to covet

codicioso ADJ covetous, greedy

codificación SF 1 (*Jur*) codification 2 [*de mensajes, textos*] encoding

codificador SM encoder

codificar /1g/ VT 1 (*Jur*) to codify 2 [+ *mensaje, información*] to encode, code; (*TV*) to encrypt, scramble

código SM 1 (= *reglamento*) code ➤ **código civil** civil code ➤ **código de la circulación** highway code ➤ **código deontológico** code of practice, ethics (*esp EEUU*) ➤ **código penal** penal code 2 [*de signos, números*] code ➤ **código de barras** bar code ➤ **código genético** genetic code ➤ **código postal** postcode (*Brit*), zip code (*EEUU*)

codillo SM 1 (*Zool*) (= *articulación*) elbow; [*de cerdo*] knuckle 2 (*Téc*) elbow (joint), bend

codirigir /3c/ VT to co-direct

codo¹ SM 1 (*Anat*) elbow; [*de caballo*] knee; ✦ MODISMOS **hablar por los ~s** ◇ **hablar hasta por los ~s** (*LAm*) to talk nineteen to the dozen, talk a blue streak (*EEUU*); **hincar los ~s** to cram, swot (*Brit**); **morderse un ~** (*Méx, CS*) to restrain o.s.; **ser del ~** ◇ **ser duro de ~** (*Arg*) to be stingy, be mean (*Brit*) 2 **codo a codo: hubo un ~ por el segundo puesto** there was a close battle for second place, it was neck and neck for second place 3 [*de camisa, chaqueta*] elbow 4 [*de tubería*] elbow, bend

codo²** ADJ (*Méx*) (= *tacaño*) stingy, mean (*Brit*)

codorniz SF quail

coedición SF [*de libro*] joint publication; (= *acto*) joint publishing

coeficiente SM (*Mat*) coefficient; (*Econ*) rate; (*Med*) degree ➤ **coeficiente de incremento** rate of increase ➤ **coeficiente intelectual** intelligence quotient, IQ

coercer /2b/ VT to constrain (*frm*)

coerción SF coercion (*frm*)

coetáneo/a ADJ, SM/F contemporary (**con** with)

coexistencia SF coexistence ➤ **coexistencia pacífica** peaceful coexistence

coexistente ADJ coexistent

coexistir /3a/ VI to coexist (**con** with)

cofia SF cap

cofinanciar /1b/ VT to finance jointly

cofrade SMF member (of a brotherhood); ◇ *SEMANA SANTA*

cofradía SF (*Rel*) brotherhood, fraternity; (= *gremio*) guild, association; ◇ *SEMANA SANTA*

cofre SM (= *baúl*) chest; (*para joyas*) casket, jewellery *o* (*EEUU*) jewelry box, jewel case; (*Méx Aut*) bonnet, hood (*EEUU*)

---

coger /2c/

Ⓐ VERBO TRANSITIVO	Ⓒ VERBO PRONOMINAL
Ⓑ VERBO INTRANSITIVO	

Para las expresiones **coger desprevenido**, **coger in fraganti** *etc ver la entrada correspondiente a la otra palabra.*

coger Ⓐ VERBO TRANSITIVO

1 (= *con la mano*)

1.1 (= *tomar*) to take; **~ un libro de un estante** to take a book from a shelf; **coge un poco más de queso** have a bit more cheese; **ir cogidos de la mano** to walk along holding hands *o* hand in hand

1.2 (= *levantar*) to pick up

1.3 (*con fuerza*) to grasp

1.4 (= *sostener*) to hold

2 (= *escoger*) to pick; **coge el que más te guste** take *o* pick the one you like best; **has cogido un mal momento** you've picked a bad time
3 [+ *flor, fruta*] to pick
4 (= *quitar*) (*gen*) to take; (= *pedir prestado*) (*Esp*) to borrow; **¿quién ha cogido el periódico?** who's taken the newspaper?; **¿te puedo ~ el bolígrafo?** can I borrow your pen?
5 (= *apuntar*) to take (down); **~ apuntes** to take notes
6 (*esp Esp*) (= *conseguir*) to get; **cógeme un buen sitio** get me a good place; **~ hora para el dentista/en la peluquería** to make an appointment to see *o* with the dentist/at the hairdresser's
7 (= *adquirir*)
7.1 [+ *enfermedad*] to catch; **~ un resfriado** to catch a cold; **~ frío** to get cold; **ha cogido una insolación** she's got sunstroke
7.2 [+ *costumbre, hábito*] to get into; [+ *acento*] to pick up
7.3 [+ *fuerzas*] to gather; [+ *velocidad*] to gather, pick up
8 (= *atrapar*)
8.1 (*esp Esp*) [+ *persona, pez, balón*] to catch
8.2 (*esp Esp*) [*toro*] (= *cornear*) to gore; (= *voltear*) to toss
8.3 (*esp Esp*) [*coche*] (= *atropellar*) to knock down, run over
8.4 (*Mil*) to take prisoner, capture
9 (*esp Esp*) (= *sorprender*) to catch; **la cogieron robando** they caught her stealing; **la guerra nos cogió en Francia** the war found *o* caught us in France; **antes de que no coja la noche** before night overtakes us *o* comes down on us;
♦ MODISMO **~ de nuevas a algn** (*Esp*) to take sb by surprise
10 (= *empezar a sentir*) **~ aversión a algo** to take a strong dislike to sth; **~ cariño a algn** to grow *o* become fond of sb, become attached to sb; **~ celos de algn** to become jealous of sb
11 (= *tomarse*) to take; **no sé si podré ~ vacaciones** I don't know if I'll be able to take any holidays (*esp Brit*) *o* a vacation (*EEUU*)
12 (= *entender*) [+ *sentido, giro, chiste*] to get
13 (*Esp*) (= *aceptar*) [+ *empleados, trabajo*] to take on; [+ *alumnos*] to take in; [+ *pacientes*] (*en hospital*) to take in; (*en consultorio*) to take on
14 (= *alquilar*) to take, rent; **cogimos un apartamento** we took *o* rented an apartment
15 (= *viajar en*) [+ *tren, avión, autobús*] to take
16 (= *ir por*) to take; **coja la primera calle a la derecha** take the first street on the right; **no cojas las curvas tan rápido** don't take the bends so fast
17 (= *recibir*) [+ *emisora, canal*] to pick up, get
18 (= *retener*) [+ *polvo*] to gather, collect
19 (= *aprender*) to pick up
20 (*Arg, Méx, Ven****) (*sexualmente*) to fuck***, screw***
Ⓑ VERBO INTRANSITIVO
1 (= *estar*) to be; **¿coge muy lejos de aquí?** is it very far from here?; **el banco me coge de camino** the bank's on my way
2 (= *ir*) **~ por**: **cogió por esta calle** he went down this street
3 (*Esp**) (= *caber*) to fit
4 (*Arg, Méx, Ven****) (*sexualmente*) to fuck***, screw***
5 ♦ MODISMO **cogió y se fue*** he just upped and left *o* offed*
Ⓒ **cogerse** VERBO PRONOMINAL
1 (= *sujetarse*) **~se a** *o* **de algo** to hold on to sth; **cógete a** *o* **de la cuerda** hold on to the rope; **~se a algn** to hold on to sb
2 (*enfático*)
2.1 (= *pillarse*) [+ *catarro, gripe*] to catch; **~se los dedos en la puerta** to catch one's fingers in the door; **~se una borrachera** to get drunk
2.2 (= *tomarse*) [+ *vacaciones*] to take
2.3 (= *agarrar*) [+ *objeto*] to grab; **cógete una silla** grab a chair

cogida SF (*Taur*) goring; **sufrir una ~** to be gored

cognitivo ADJ, **cognoscitivo** ADJ cognitive

cogollo SM **1** (*Bot*) [*de lechuga, col*] heart; [*de árbol*] top **2** [*de asunto, problema*] heart, crux **3** [*de ciudad*] centre, center (*EEUU*)

cogorza* SF **pescar una ~** to get plastered*

cogote SM back of the neck, nape

cohabitar /1a/ VI (= *vivir juntos*) to live together, cohabit (*frm*); (*Pol*) to coexist

cohechar /1a/ VT to bribe

cohecho SM bribery

coherencia SF **1** [*de ideas, razonamiento, exposición*] coherence **2** [*de acciones, proyecto, política*] consistency **3** (*Fís*) cohesion

coherente ADJ **1** [*texto, idea, exposición, argumentación*] coherent **2** [*proyecto, política*] consistent; **~ con** in line with, in tune with

cohesión SF cohesion

cohesionar /1a/ VT to unite, draw together

cohete SM rocket ➤ **cohete espacial** (space) rocket

cohibido ADJ (= *tímido*) shy, timid, self-conscious; (= *incómodo*) awkward, ill-at-ease; **sentirse ~** to feel awkward *o* ill-at-ease

cohibir /3a/ Ⓐ VT (= *incomodar*) to make awkward *o* ill-at-ease; (= *avergonzar*) to make shy, embarrass Ⓑ **cohibirse** VPR (= *incomodarse*) to feel awkward *o* ill-at-ease; (= *avergonzarse*) to feel embarrassed, become shy

cohorte SF cohort

coima* SF (*And, CS*) (= *soborno*) bribe, sweetener*, backhander (*Brit**); (= *acto*) bribing, bribery

coime SM (*Col*) waiter

coimear /1a/ VT (*And, CS*) (= *sobornar*) to bribe; (= *aceptar sobornos*) to take bribes from

coimero/a (*And, CS*) Ⓐ ADJ easily bribed, corrupt, bent (*Brit***) Ⓑ SM/F bribe-taker; **son unos ~s** they're all crooked *o* (*Brit***) bent *o* (*Brit**) on the take

coincidencia SF **1** (= *casualidad*) coincidence; **es pura ~** it's just a coincidence, it's pure coincidence; **dio la ~ de que yo también estaba allí** it was a coincidence that I was also there **2** (= *acuerdo*) agreement; **en ~ con** in agreement with

coincidente ADJ coincident; **ser ~ con algn/algo** to be coincident with sb/sth

coincidir /3a/ VI **1** (*en el tiempo*) to happen at the same time, occur simultaneously (*frm*), coincide; **~ con algo** to coincide with sth
2 (*en un lugar*) to happen to meet; **coincidimos en el teatro** we happened to meet at the theatre *o* (*EEUU*) theater; **he coincidido con él en varias fiestas pero nunca nos han presentado** we've been at several of the same parties but we've never been introduced; **el punto en que las dos líneas coinciden** the point at which both lines meet
3 (= *estar de acuerdo*) **3.1** **~ con algn** to agree with sb; **~ en algo**: **los observadores internacionales coinciden en afirmar que ...** international observers all agree that ...
3.2 [*informes, versiones, resultados*] to coincide; **~ con algo** to agree with sth, coincide with sth
4 (= *ajustarse*) [*huellas, formas*] to match, match up; **~ con algo** to match (up with) sth

coipo SM, **coipu** SM (*LAm*) coypu

coirón SM (*And*) thatch

coito SM intercourse, coitus (*frm*)

cojan *etc ver* **coger**

cojear /1a/ VI **1** [*persona*] (= *estar cojo*) to limp, hobble (along); (= *ser cojo*) to be lame; **cojea de la pierna izquierda** (*temporalmente*) she's limping on her left leg; (*permanentemente*) she's lame in her left leg, she has a limp in her left leg **2** [*mueble*] to wobble, be wobbly

cojera SF (= *estado*) lameness; (*al andar*) limp

cojín SM cushion

cojinete SM **1** (= *almohadilla*) small cushion **2** (*Mec*) bearing ➤ **cojinete a bolas**, **cojinete de bolas** ball bearing ➤ **cojinete de rodillos** roller bearing **3** (*Ferro*) chair

cojo¹/a Ⓐ ADJ **1** (= *de andar defectuoso*) lame; **está un poco ~ por la caída** he's a bit lame from the fall; **~ de un pie** lame in one foot **2** (= *con una sola pierna, pata*) one-legged; **se quedó ~ en la guerra** he lost a leg in the war **3** [*mueble, objeto*] wobbly **4** (= *incompleto*) [*equipo, organización*] weak, lame Ⓑ SM/F **1** (= *de andar defectuoso*) lame person **2** (= *con una sola pierna*) one-legged person

cojo² *ver* **coger**

cojón*** SM **1** (= *testículo*) ball**; ✦ MODISMOS **es un tío con cojones** he's got balls*** *o* guts*; **echar cojones a algo** to brave sth out; **ya estoy hasta los cojones de que me insulte** I'm totally pissed off with being insulted**; **hago lo que me sale de los cojones** I do what I damn well like *o* (*Brit*) bloody well like**; **no tienes cojones de decírmelo a la cara** you haven't got the balls to tell me to my face***; **este tío me está tocando los cojones** this guy is pissing me off**; **se pasa el día tocándose los cojones** he spends all day doing fuck all*** *o* (*Brit*) sod all**

2 (*como exclamación*): **callaos ya, ¡cojones!** shut up, for fuck's sake!***; **¡y un ~!** ◊ **¡los cojones!: —dame el dinero —¡(y) un ~!** *o* **¡los cojones!** "give me the money" — "go fuck yourself!"***

3 (*como intensificador*) **pero, ¿quién cojones se han creído que son?** who the fuck do they think they are?***; **¡hace un frío de cojones!** it's fucking freezing!***; **no aguanto al periodista ese de los cojones** I can't stand that fucking journalist***; **tienes que hacerlo por cojones** you fucking well have to do it***

4 **un ~** (*como adverbio*): **cuesta un ~** it's worth a fucking fortune***; **me importa un ~ lo que tú digas** I don't give a fuck what you think***

cojonudo ADJ **1** (*Esp***) (= *estupendo*) fantastic*, awesome (*EEUU**); **un tío ~** a great guy* **2** (*RPl**) (= *tonto*) thick (*Brit**), dumb (*EEUU**) **3** (*RPl**) (= *valiente*) **ser ~** to have a lot of guts*

cojudo*** ADJ (*And*) stupid

col SF cabbage ➤ **col de bruselas** (Brussels) sprout ➤ **col lombarda** red cabbage

cola¹ SF **1** (*de animal, avión, cometa*) tail; ✦ MODISMO **traer ~: la decisión del árbitro va a traer ~** this is not the last we will hear of the referee's decision ➤ **cola de caballo** (= *en el pelo*) pony tail; (= *planta*) horsetail
2 (*de frac*) tail; (*de vestido*) train
3 (= *hilera*) queue (*esp Brit*), line (*EEUU*); **¡a la ~!** get in the queue! (*esp Brit*), get in line! (*EEUU*); **hacer ~** to queue (up) (*esp Brit*), line up (*EEUU*); **ponerse a la ~** to join *o* get into the queue (*esp Brit*), join *o* get into the line (*EEUU*)
4 (= *parte final*) (*de manifestación*) tail end, back; (*de carrera*) back; **el ciclista estaba en** *o* **a la ~ del pelotón** the cyclist was at the back of *o* at the tail end of the pack; **el equipo está en el tercer puesto por la ~** the team is sitting third place from (the) bottom
5 (*Esp**) (= *pene*) willy (*Brit**), weenie (*EEUU**)
6 (*Ven Aut*) **pedir ~** to ask for a lift (*esp Brit*) *o* ride (*esp EEUU*); **dar la ~ a algn** to give sb a lift (*esp Brit*) *o* a ride (*EEUU*)
7 (*CS**) (= *trasero*) bottom, bum (*Brit***), ass (*EEUU**); (= *cóccix*) coccyx

cola² SF (= *pegamento*) glue, gum (*esp Brit*); ✦ MODISMO **no pegar ni con ~: esas cortinas no pegan ni con ~** those curtains just don't go with the rest; **el verde y el azul no pegan ni con ~** green and blue just don't go together ➤ **cola de carpintero** wood glue ➤ **cola de contacto** contact adhesive ➤ **cola de impacto** impact adhesive

cola³ SF **1** (= *planta*) cola, kola **2** (= *bebida*) cola, Coke®

cola⁴* SM (*Chi*) queer**, poof (*Brit***)

colaboración SF **1** (= *cooperación*) collaboration ➤ **colaboración ciudadana** help from the public **2** (*en periódico*) (*gen*) contribution; (= *artículo*) article **3** (= *donativo*) contribution

colaboracionista SMF collaborator, collaborationist

colaborador(a) SM/F **1** (*en trabajo, misión*) collaborator, co-worker **2** (*en periódico, revista*) contributor **3** (*con dinero*) contributor

colaborar /1a/ VI to collaborate; **~ con algn** to collaborate with sb; **~ en algo: nuestra empresa ~á en el proyecto** our company is to collaborate on the project; **~ en un periódico** to contribute to a newspaper, write for a newspaper

colación SF **1 sacar** *o* **traer a ~** to mention, bring up **2** (= *refrigerio*) light meal, collation (*frm*)

colada SF (*Esp*) washing; **hacer la ~** to do the washing; **tender la ~** to hang out the washing

coladera SF **1** (*Col, Méx Culin*) strainer **2** (*Méx*) (= *alcantarilla*) sewer

colado ADJ **1** (*metal*) cast **2** ✦ MODISMO **estar ~ por algn*** to be madly in love with sb

colador SM (*para té, infusión*) strainer; (*con agujeros*) colander; (*de malla*) sieve; ✦ MODISMO **dejar como un ~** to riddle with bullets

colágeno SM collagen

colapsar /1a/ VT **1** (= *derribar*) to cause to collapse **2** (*+ tráfico, circulación*) to bring to a halt *o* standstill; (*+ entrada*) to block

colapso SM **1** (*Med*) **el boxeador sufrió un ~** the boxer collapsed **2** (*de régimen, imperio, empresa*) collapse **3** (= *paralización*) **el accidente provocó el ~ del tráfico** the accident caused traffic to come to a standstill *o* to grind to a halt

colar /1l/ **Ⓐ** VT **1** (*+ leche, infusión, verduras, caldo*) to strain **2** (*) (*furtivamente*) **2.1** (*+ objetos*) to sneak; **consiguió ~lo por la aduana** he managed to sneak it through customs; **le coló un gol al portero** he sneaked a goal past the goalkeeper **2.2** **~ algo a algn** (= *dar algo malo*) to palm sth off on sb, palm sb off with sth; (= *hacer creer algo*) to spin sb a yarn about sth*; **¡a mí no me la cuelas!** don't give me any of that!* **2.3** **~ a algn** (*en espectáculo, cine*) to sneak sb in
3 (*+ metal*) to cast
Ⓑ VI **diles que estás enfermo, igual cuela** say you're ill, they might swallow it*; **tienes que copiar muy bien la firma para que cuele el cheque** you'll need to copy the signature very well if you want the cheque to go through
Ⓒ **colarse** VPR **1** (= *filtrarse*) **el agua se cuela por las rendijas** the water seeps (in) through *o* gets in through the cracks; **se le coló el balón** the ball slipped past him
2 (*personas*) (*sin pagar*) to get in without paying; (*en lugar prohibido*) to sneak in; (*en fiesta*) to gatecrash
3 (*error*) **se le ~on varias faltas al revisar el texto** he overlooked several mistakes when revising the text
4 (*en una cola*) to jump the queue (*esp Brit*), cut in line (*EEUU*); **¡oiga, no se cuele!** excuse me, there's a queue!
5 (*Esp**) (= *equivocarse*) to get it wrong*
6 (*Esp*) (= *enamorarse*) **~se por algn** to fall for sb

colateral ADJ collateral

colcha SF bedspread, counterpane

colchón SM mattress; ✦ MODISMO **servir de ~ a** to act as a buffer for ➤ **colchón de aire** airbed; (*Téc*) air cushion ➤ **colchón de muelles** spring mattress, interior sprung mattress

colchoneta SF mat

colear /1a/ VI **1** (*perro*) to wag its tail; (*caballo*) to swish its tail; (*pez*) to wriggle **2** (*fig*) **el asunto todavía colea** the affair is still not settled; ✦ MODISMO **estar vivito y coleando** to be alive and kicking

colección SF collection

coleccionable **Ⓐ** ADJ collectable **Ⓑ** SM (= *objeto*) collectable; (= *fascículo*) pull-out section

coleccionar /1a/ VT, VI to collect

coleccionismo SM collecting

coleccionista SMF collector

colecta SF **1** (= *recaudación*) collection (for charity) **2** (*Rel*) collect

colectivero SM (*Arg*) bus driver; (*And*) driver (*of a collective taxi*)

colectividad SF (*gen*) collectivity; (= *grupo*) group, community; **en ~** collectively

colectivización SF collectivization

colectivizar /1f/ VT to collectivize

colectivo **Ⓐ** ADJ **1** (*responsabilidad, esfuerzo*) collective; (*obra, proyecto*) collective, group *antes de s*; **el transporte ~** public transport (*esp Brit*) *o* transportation (*EEUU*); **acción colectiva** joint action **2** (*Ling*) collective **Ⓑ** SM **1** (= *grupo*) group **2** (*de transporte*) (*Arg*) bus; (*And*) collective taxi

colector SM (*Elec*) collector; (*Mec*) sump (*esp Brit*), oil pan (*EEUU*), trap

colega SMF **1** [*de trabajo*] colleague **2** (= *amigo*) (*) pal*, mate (*Brit**), buddy (*EEUU**); (*en oración directa*) man*

colegiado/a Ⓐ ADJ [*médico, profesor, ingeniero*] member of a professional body Ⓑ SM/F (*Dep*) referee; (*Med*) doctor

colegial(a) Ⓐ ADJ school *antes de s* Ⓑ SM/F schoolboy/schoolgirl

colegiarse /1a/ VPR to become a member of a professional body

colegiata SF collegiate church

colegiatura(s) SF(PL) (*Méx*) [*de escuela*] school fees; [*de universidad*] university fees

colegio SM **1** (*Escol*) school; **ir al ~** to go to school ➤ **colegio de curas** Catholic boys' school (*run by priests*) ➤ **colegio de monjas** convent school ➤ **colegio de pago** fee-paying school ➤ **colegio mayor** (*Univ*) hall of residence (*Brit*), dormitory (*EEUU*); (*Hist*) college ➤ **colegio privado** private school ➤ **colegio público** state school (*Brit*), public school (*EEUU*) ➤ **Colegio Universitario** university college **2** (= *corporación*) ➤ **colegio de abogados** bar (association) ➤ **colegio de arquitectos** architects' association ➤ **colegio de médicos** medical association **3** (*Pol*) ➤ **colegio electoral** (= *lugar*) polling station (*Brit*), polling place (*EEUU*); (= *electores*) electoral college

colegir /3c, 3k/ VT (*frm*) **1** (= *juntar*) to collect, gather **2** (= *inferir*) to infer (**de** from)

coleóptero SM coleopteran, coleopteron

cólera Ⓐ SF anger, rage; **montar en ~** to fly into a rage Ⓑ SM (*Med*) cholera

colérico ADJ (= *furioso*) angry, furious; (= *malhumorado*) irritable, bad-tempered

colesterol SM cholesterol

coleta SF [*de pelo*] ponytail; (*Taur*) pigtail; ✦ MODISMO **cortarse la ~** to quit, retire, hang up one's spurs*

coletazo SM **1** [*de animal*] blow or thrash or swipe with the tail **2** (*Aut*) swaying movement; **dar ~s** to sway about; ✦ MODISMO **está dando los últimos ~s** [*régimen, sistema*] it's in its death throes; [*huracán*] it's petering out

coletilla SF (*en carta, discurso*) postscript, afterthought; (*en frase*) tag

coleto SM **1** (*) ✦ MODISMO **echarse algo al ~** (= *comer*) to put sth away; (= *beber*) to drink sth down **2** (*Carib*) (= *fregasuelos*) mop

colgado Ⓐ PP *de* **colgar** Ⓑ ADJ **1** [*pared, cable*] **este cuadro estuvo ~ muchos años en el museo de la ciudad** this picture hung for many years in the city museum; **está ~ del teléfono todo el día** he's on the phone all day long **2** (= *ahorcado*) hanged, hung **3** (*) [*asignatura*] **tengo la física colgada** I have to resit *o* retake physics; **me han dejado el inglés ~** I've failed English **4 dejar ~ a algn*** (*en una situación difícil*) to leave sb in the lurch*; (*en una cita*) to stand sb up* **5** (**) (= *drogado*) spaced out**; (= *chiflado*) nuts*; (= *sin dinero*) broke*, short of money **6** (**) (= *enviciado*) **~ de algo** hooked on sth* **7** (**) (= *enamorado*) **estoy muy ~ de ella** I'm crazy about her* Ⓒ SMF (**) **1** (= *drogadicto*) druggie* **2** (= *chiflado*) nutcase*

colgante Ⓐ ADJ hanging Ⓑ SM pendant

colgar /1h, 1l/ Ⓐ VT **1** (*de pared, cable*) [+ *cuadro, diploma*] to hang, put up; [+ *colada, banderines*] to hang out; [+ *cartel, letrero, lámpara, cortina*] to put up; [+ *ropa*] (*en armario*) to hang up; (*para secar*) to hang out; **cada día cuelgan el cartel de "no hay billetes"** every day the "sold out" sign goes up; ✦ MODISMO **~ los hábitos** to leave the priesthood **2** (= *ahorcar*) to hang; **¡que lo cuelguen!** hang him!, string him up!* **3** [+ *teléfono*] to put down; **colgó el teléfono** he hung up; **dejar el teléfono mal colgado** to leave the phone off the hook

4 (= *atribuir*) [+ *apodo, mote*] to give; **enseguida te cuelgan la etiqueta de envidioso** they label you as jealous straight away Ⓑ VI **1** [*cuadro, lámpara*] to hang; **~ de** [+ *techo*] to hang from; [+ *pared*] to hang on; **llevar algo colgado a** *o* **del cuello** to wear sth around one's neck **2** (= *caer suelto*) [*rizos, tirabuzones*] to hang down **3** (*al teléfono*) to hang up; **no cuelgue, por favor** please, hold the line Ⓒ **colgarse** VPR **1** (= *estar suspendido*) **~se de** to hang from **2** (= *ahorcarse*) to hang o.s. **3** (= *ponerse*) to put on; **se colgó el bolso del** *o* **al hombro** she put her bag on her shoulder **4** (*Esp***) (= *con drogas*) to flip*, blow one's head** **5** (*Chi, Méx*) to plug illegally into the mains

colibrí SM hummingbird

cólico SM colic

coliflor SF cauliflower

coligarse /1h/ VPR to unite, join together, make common cause (**con** with)

colilla SF cigarette butt, cigarette end, fag end (*Brit***)

colimba* (*Arg*) Ⓐ SM recruit, conscript, draftee (*EEUU*) Ⓑ SF military service; **hacer la ~** to do one's military service

colina SF hill

colindante ADJ adjacent, adjoining, neighbouring, neighboring (*EEUU*)

colindar /1a/ VI to adjoin, be adjacent; **~ con** [*país*] to have a border with; [*casa, finca*] to adjoin

colirio SM eye drops *pl*

colisión SF **1** [*de vehículos*] collision, crash ➤ **colisión en cadena** multiple collision, multiple pile-up ➤ **colisión frontal** head-on collision **2** (*entre personas, intereses, ideas*) clash

colisionar /1a/ VI to collide; **~ con** *o* **contra** [*tren, autobús, coche*] to collide with; [*persona, ideas*] to clash with, conflict with

colita* SF (*Esp*) [*de niño*] willy (*Brit**), weenie (*EEUU**)

colitis SF INV colitis

colla SMF Indian from the altiplano

collado SM **1** (= *colina*) hill; (*más pequeña*) hillock **2** (= *puerto*) mountain pass

collage [ko'la:ʒ] SM collage

collar SM **1** (= *adorno*) necklace; (= *insignia*) chain (of office) ➤ **collar de perlas** pearl necklace **2** [*de perro*] (dog) collar **3** (*Mec*) collar, ring

collarín SM surgical collar

collera SF **1** (*Agr*) horse collar **2 colleras** (*Chi*) (= *gemelos*) cufflinks

collie ['koli] SM collie

colmado Ⓐ ADJ [*vaso*] full to the brim (**de** with), full (**de** of); [*plato, cuchara*] heaped (**de** with); **una cucharada colmada** a heaped tablespoonful; **una carrera colmada de incidentes** an eventful race Ⓑ SM grocer's shop (*esp Brit*), grocery store (*EEUU*)

colmar /1a/ VT **1** (= *llenar*) [+ *vaso, recipiente*] to fill to the brim, fill to overflowing, fill right up (**de** with); [+ *cuchara, plato*] to heap (**de** with) **2** [+ *ambición, esperanzas*] to fulfil, fulfill (*EEUU*), realize **3 ~ a algn de algo**: **~ a algn de honores** to shower sb with honours *o* (*EEUU*) honors; **~ a algn de alabanzas** to heap praise on sb

colmena SF beehive, hive

colmenero/a SM/F beekeeper

colmillo SM (*Anat*) eye tooth, canine (tooth); (*Zool*) fang; [*de elefante, morsa, jabalí*] tusk; **enseñar los ~s** to show one's teeth, bare one's teeth

colmo SM **¡eres el ~! ¡deja ya de quejarte!** you really take the biscuit (*Brit*) *o* cake (*EEUU*)! just stop complaining!; **¡esto es el ~! ¡ya no lo aguanto más!** this is the last straw! I can't stand it any longer!; **tu hermano es el ~, no paro de reírme con él** your brother is hilarious *o* is something else*, he makes me laugh so much; **el ~ de la elegancia** the height of elegance; **para ~** to top it all, cap it all; ✦ MODISMO **ser el ~ de los ~s: que la mismísima policía le robe es ya el ~ de los ~s** to be robbed by the police themselves really is the limit

colocación SF 1 (= *acto*) (*gen*) placing; [*de bomba*] planting; [*de baldosa, moqueta, primera piedra*] laying; [*de cuadro*] hanging 2 (= *empleo*) job; **no encuentro ~** I can't find a job; **agencia de colocaciones** employment agency 3 (= *situación*) positioning; **he cambiado la ~ de los muebles** I've rearranged the furniture 4 (*Com*) [*de acciones*] placing, placement

colocado ADJ 1 (*en trabajo*) **estar ~** to be in work, have a job 2 (*Esp***) (= *drogado*) high*; (= *borracho*) pissed (*Brit***), trashed (*EEUU***)

colocar /1g/ **Ⓐ** VT 1 (= *situar*) (*gen*) to place; [+ *cartel, póster*] to put up; [+ *bomba*] to plant, place; [+ *tropas*] to position, place; [+ *baldosa, moqueta, primera piedra*] to lay; [+ *cuadro*] to hang; (*Náut*) [+ *quilla*] to lay down; **coloca las tazas en su sitio** put the cups away; **~ un producto en el mercado** to place a product on the market
2 (= *ordenar*) [+ *muebles, objetos, libros*] to arrange; **he colocado las revistas por orden alfabético** I've arranged the magazines in alphabetical order; **colocó a los niños en fila** he lined the children up
3 (= *dar trabajo*) **~ a algn** [*agencia*] to get sb a job; [*empresario, jefe*] to give sb a job
4 (*Fin*) [+ *acciones, dinero*] to place
5 (*) (= *endilgar*) **~ algo a algn** to palm sth off on sb, palm sb off with sth
Ⓑ VI (*Esp***) [*drogas, alcohol*] **este vino coloca** this wine is pretty strong stuff
Ⓒ colocarse VPR 1 (*en un lugar*) (*de pie*) to stand; (*sentado*) to sit
2 (*en una clasificación*) **se acaban de ~ en quinto lugar** they have just moved into fifth place; **el programa se ha colocado en el primer lugar de la lista de audiencia** the programme is now top of the ratings *o* has reached the top of the ratings
3 (*en un trabajo*) to get a job
4 (*Esp***) (= *emborracharse*) to get pissed (*Brit***), get trashed (*EEUU***) (**con** on); (= *drogarse*) to get high* (**con** on)

colochos SMPL (*CAm*) curls

colocón* SM (*Esp*) **cogerse un ~** to get high**

colofón SM 1 (*Tip*) colophon 2 (*) (= *culminación*) culmination

Colombia SF Colombia

colombiano/a **Ⓐ** ADJ of/from Colombia **Ⓑ** SM/F native/inhabitant of Colombia

colombino ADJ of Columbus, relating to Columbus

colombófilo/a SM/F pigeon-fancier

colon SM (*Anat*) colon

Colón SM Columbus

colón SM monetary unit of Costa Rica and El Salvador

colonia¹ SF 1 (= *territorio*) colony 2 (= *comunidad*) [*de personas*] community; [*de animales, células*] colony 3 (= *grupo de edificios*) ➤ **colonia penal** penal colony 4 (= *campamento*) summer camp; **irse de ~s** to go (off) to summer camp 5 (*Méx*) residential suburb, residential area

colonia² SF (*tb* **agua de ~**) cologne, eau de Cologne

coloniaje SM (*LAm*) (= *época*) colonial period; (= *sistema*) colonial government

colonial ADJ colonial

colonialismo SM colonialism

colonialista ADJ, SMF colonialist

colonización SF [*de país, territorio*] colonization

colonizador(a) **Ⓐ** ADJ [*proceso, país, lengua*] colonizing **Ⓑ** SM/F [*de país, territorio*] colonist, colonizer

colonizar /1f/ VT to colonize

colono/a SM/F 1 [*de país, territorio*] colonist; (= *nativo de una colonia*) colonial 2 (*Agr*) tenant farmer

coloquial ADJ colloquial

coloquio SM 1 (= *debate*) discussion; **un ~ sobre el aborto** a discussion about abortion; **charla-~** ◇ **conferencia-~** talk followed by a discussion 2 (*frm*) (= *diálogo*) dialogue, dialog (*EEUU*), colloquy (*frm*)

color SM (*A VECES* SF)

> En inglés americano se usa **color** en lugar de **colour**.

1 (= *coloración*) colour; **¿de qué ~ es?** what colour is it?; **el ~ azul** blue; **una falda (de) ~ rojo** a red skirt; **fotocopias a ~** colour photocopying; **a todo ~** full-colour; **dar ~ a algo** to colour sth in; **televisión en ~** *o* (*LAm*) **~es** colour television; **tomar ~**: **esa tela no ha tomado bien el ~** that material has not dyed at all well; **el proyecto empieza a tomar ~** the project is starting to take shape ➤ **color pastel** pastel colour ➤ **color primario** primary colour
2 [*de la cara*] colour; **tener buen ~** to have good colour; **tener mal ~** to look off colour; ✦ MODISMOS **ponerse de mil ~es** to go bright red; **sacar los ~es a algn** to make sb blush
3 (= *raza*) colour; **sin distinción de sexo o ~** regardless of sex *o* colour; **persona de ~** coloured person, person of color (*EEUU*)
4 (= *tipismo*) **la feria ha perdido el ~ de antaño** the festival has lost the flavour *o* (*EEUU*) flavor *o* feel it used to have ➤ **color local** local colour
5 ✦ MODISMOS **de ~ de rosa: verlo todo de ~ de rosa** to see everything through rose-tinted *o* rose-coloured spectacles; **la vida no es de ~ de rosa** life isn't all roses; **no hay ~*** there's no comparison; **subido de ~** [*chiste*] risqué; [*discusión*] heated
6 **colores** (*tb* **lápices de ~es**) coloured pencils, crayons
7 **colores** (*Dep*) colours

coloración SF coloration, colouring, coloring (*EEUU*)

colorado **Ⓐ** ADJ 1 (= *rojo*) red; ✦ MODISMOS **~ como un tomate** as red as a beetroot (*Brit*) *o* beet (*EEUU*); **poner ~ a algn** to make sb blush; **ponerse ~** to blush 2 (*Bol, Méx*) [*chiste*] blue **Ⓑ** SM red

colorante **Ⓐ** ADJ colouring, coloring (*EEUU*) **Ⓑ** SM colouring (matter), coloring (matter) (*EEUU*)

coloreado **Ⓐ** ADJ (= *pintado*) coloured, colored (*EEUU*); (= *teñido*) tinted **Ⓑ** SM (*con pintura*) colouring, coloring (*EEUU*); (*con tinte*) tinting

colorear /1a/ **Ⓐ** VT (= *pintar*) to colour, color (*EEUU*); (= *teñir*) to dye, tint; **~ algo de amarillo** to colour *o* (*EEUU*) color/dye sth yellow **Ⓑ** VI 1 [*frutos*] to ripen 2 (= *tirar a rojo*) to be reddish

colorete SM rouge, blusher

colorido SM colour(ing), color(ing) (*EEUU*)

colorín SM 1 (= *color*) bright colour, bright color (*EEUU*); **con muchos colorines** all bright and colourful *o* colorful (*EEUU*); **y ~, colorado, este cuento se ha acabado** and they all lived happily ever after, and that is the end of the story 2 (*Orn*) goldfinch

colorinche* (*And, CS*) **Ⓐ** ADJ bright; (*pey*) loud **Ⓑ** SM bright colour *o* (*EEUU*) color; (*pey*) loud colour *o* (*EEUU*) color

colorista ADJ colouristic, coloristic (*EEUU*)

colosal ADJ [*edificio, montaña*] colossal; [*comida, fiesta*] amazing*, fantastic*

coloso SM colossus

columbrar /1a/ (*liter*) VT 1 (= *divisar*) to make out, glimpse 2 [+ *solución*] to begin to see

columna SF 1 (*Arquit*) column 2 [*de periódico*] column; **un documento escrito a dos ~s** a document in two-columns, a two-column document 3 [*de soldados, tanques*] column; **~ blindada** armoured *o* (*EEUU*) armored column 4 (*Anat*) (*tb* **~ vertebral**) spine, spinal column, backbone

columnata SF colonnade

columnista SMF columnist

columpiar /1b/ **Ⓐ** VT **~ a algn** (*en columpio*) to push sb; (*en mecedora*) to rock sb **Ⓑ** **columpiarse** VPR to swing

columpio SM swing

colza SF (*Bot*) rape, colza; **aceite de ~** rape-seed oil

coma¹ SM (*Med*) coma; **en ~** in a coma; **entrar en (estado de) ~** to go into a coma ➤ **coma diabético** diabetic coma

➤ **coma profundo** deep coma

coma² SF 1 (*Tip*) comma; ✦ MODISMO **sin faltar** o **sin saltarse una ~: recitó todo el poema sin saltarse una ~** he recited the whole poem word perfect o without leaving out a single word 2 (*Mat*) ≈ point (*Spanish uses a comma in place of a point*); **doce ~ cinco** twelve point five 3 (*Mús*) comma

comadre SF 1 (= *chismosa*) gossip 2 (= *vecina*) neighbour, neighbor (*EEUU*); (= *amiga*) friend 3 (= *madrina*) godmother

comadreja SF weasel

comadreo SM, **comadrería** SF chatting, nattering*

comadrona SF midwife

comal SM (*CAm, Méx*) griddle

comandancia SF 1 (= *función*) command 2 (= *grado*) rank of major 3 (= *central*) headquarters *pl*

comandante SMF 1 (= *jefe*) commander, commandant; (*Aer*) (*tb* ~ **de vuelo**) captain ➤ **comandante en jefe** commander-in-chief 2 (= *grado*) major

comandar /1a/ VT to command

comandita SF limited partnership (*Brit*), silent partnership (*EEUU*); **en ~*** all together, as a team; **fuimos todos en ~ a hablar con el jefe** we all went together to talk to the boss

comanditario ADJ **socio ~** sleeping partner (*Brit*), silent partner (*EEUU*)

comando SM 1 (*Mil*) (= *grupo*) commando unit, commando group ➤ **comando de acción** active service unit ➤ **comando suicida** suicide squad ➤ **comando terrorista** terrorist cell, terrorist squad 2 (*Mil*) (= *soldado*) commando 3 (*Mil*) (= *mando*) command 4 (*Inform*) command

comarca SF *administrative division comprising a number of municipalities*

comarcal ADJ [*carretera*] local; [*emisora*] regional

comatoso ADJ comatose

comba SF 1 (= *curvatura*) bend; (*en viga*) warp, sag 2 (*Esp*) (= *cuerda*) skipping rope (*Brit*), jump rope (*EEUU*); (= *juego*) skipping (*esp Brit*), jumping rope (*EEUU*); **saltar a la ~** to skip (*esp Brit*), jump rope (*EEUU*); ✦ MODISMO **no pierde ~** he doesn't miss a trick

combadura SF 1 = **comba** 1 2 (*Aut*) camber

combar /1a/ Ⓐ VT (= *curvar*) to bend, curve Ⓑ **combarse** VPR (= *hacer curva*) to bend, curve; (= *alabearse*) to bulge, warp; [*techo*] to sag

combate SM (*Mil*) combat; (*Boxeo*) contest, fight; [*de ideas, sentimientos*] conflict; **estar fuera de ~** (*lit, fig*) to be out of action; (*Boxeo*) to be knocked out; **dejar** o **poner a algn fuera de ~** (*lit, fig*) to put sb out of action; (*Boxeo*) to knock sb out; **ganar por fuera de ~** to win by a knockout

combatiente SMF combatant

combatir /3a/ Ⓐ VI [*ejército, soldado*] to fight Ⓑ VT [+ *fraude, desempleo, injusticia, enfermedad*] to combat, fight; [+ *frío*] to fight (off)

combativo ADJ combative, spirited

combi* SF, **combinable** SF combi (van)

combinación SF 1 [*de elementos, factores*] combination 2 [*de números*] combination 3 (*Quím*) compound 4 [*de transportes*] connection; **hay muy buena ~ de autobuses** there is a very good bus connection 5 (= *prenda*) slip

combinado SM 1 [*de bebidas*] cocktail 2 (= *equipo*) selection, team

combinar /1a/ Ⓐ VT 1 [+ *esfuerzos, movimientos*] to combine; [+ *colores*] to match, mix 2 [+ *plan, proyecto*] to devise, work out Ⓑ **combinarse** VPR to get together, join together; **~se para hacer algo** to get o join together to do sth

combinatorio ADJ combinatorial, combinative; **análisis ~** (*Mat*) combinatorial analysis

combo Ⓐ ADJ (= *combado*) bent; (= *arqueado*) bulging; (= *torcido*) warped Ⓑ SM 1 (*And*) (= *martillo*) sledgehammer 2 (*And*) (= *puñetazo*) punch 3 (*Col**) (= *pandilla*) gang; [*de música*] band

combustible Ⓐ ADJ combustible Ⓑ SM (= *carburante*) fuel

combustión SF combustion

comecocos* (*Esp*) Ⓐ SM INV 1 (= *obsesión*) obsession, hang-up*; (= *pasatiempo*) brainteaser, idle pastime; (= *lavacerebros*) brainwashing exercise 2 (= *preocupación*) nagging worry 3 (= *videojuego*) Pacman® Ⓑ SMF INV worry

comedero SM 1 (*Agr*) feeding trough, trough; (*Orn*) feeding box, feeder 2 (*Col*) (= *restaurante*) transport cafe (*Brit*), roadside diner (*EEUU*)

comedia SF 1 (*Teat*) (= *obra cómica*) comedy; (= *obra dramática*) play ➤ **comedia de capa y espada** cloak-and-dagger play ➤ **comedia de enredo** comedy of intrigue ➤ **comedia musical** musical 2 (*LAm TV*) soap opera ➤ **comedia de situación** situation comedy, sitcom* 3 (= *fingimiento*) play-acting; **¡déjate ya de tanta ~!** stop your play-acting!

comediante/a SM/F 1 (*Teat*) actor/actress 2 (*pey*) (= *farsante*) play-actor

comedido ADJ 1 (= *moderado*) moderate, restrained 2 (*esp LAm*) (= *solícito*) obliging

comediógrafo/a SM/F playwright

comedirse /3k/ VPR 1 (*en conducta*) (= *mostrar moderación*) to show restraint; **~ en las palabras** to choose one's words carefully 2 **~ a** (*CS*) (+ INFIN) to offer to + *infin*, volunteer to + *infin*

comedor SM 1 (= *lugar*) (*en casa*) dining room; (*en barco, tren*) restaurant; (*en colegio, facultad*) dining hall, lunch room (*EEUU*); (*en trabajo*) canteen 2 (= *mobiliario*) dining-room suite

comedura SF ~ **de coco** o **de tarro** (*Esp**) = **comecocos** A1

comején SM termite, white ant

comelón/ona ADJ, SM/F (*LAm*) = **comilón**

comendador SM knight commander (*of a military order*)

comensal SMF fellow diner (*frm*); **habrá 13 ~es** there will be 13 for dinner, there will be 13 people dining (*frm*); **mis ~es** my fellow diners (*frm*)

comentar /1a/ Ⓐ VT 1 [+ *poema, texto*] to comment on 2 [+ *noticia, hecho*] to discuss; **antes prefiero ~lo con mi mujer** I'd like to discuss it with my wife first; **es un secreto, no lo comentes** it's a secret, don't tell anyone (about it) o don't mention it to anyone 3 (= *decir*) **le estaba comentando que estás muy cambiada** I was saying to o telling him that you've changed a lot; **me han comentado que se casa** I've heard o I gather he's getting married 4 (*TV, Radio*) [+ *partido*] to commentate on Ⓑ VI 1 (= *opinar*) **no quiso ~ al respecto** she didn't want to comment on it; **~ sobre algo** to comment on sth 2 (*) (= *charlar*) to chat

comentario SM 1 (= *observación*) comment; **"sin comentarios"** "no comment"; **sin más ~, pasemos a ver la película** without further ado, let's watch the film (*esp Brit*) o movie (*esp EEUU*); **hacer un ~: le hizo un ~ al oído** she said something in his ear; **no hizo ~ alguno al respecto** he made no comment on the matter 2 (= *redacción*) essay ➤ **comentario de texto** (*literario*) (literary) commentary; (*lingüístico*) textual analysis 3 **comentarios** (= *cotilleo*) gossip *sing*; **dar lugar a ~s** to lead to gossip

comentarista SMF commentator; ~ **deportivo** sports commentator

comenzar /1f, 1j/ Ⓐ VT to begin, start, commence (*frm*) Ⓑ VI [*proyecto, campaña, historia, proceso*] to begin, start; **comenzó diciendo que estaba de acuerdo conmigo** she began by saying that she agreed with me; **comenzó a los diez años haciendo recados** he began o started at the age of ten as a messenger boy; **al ~ el año** at the start o beginning of the year; **~ a hacer algo** to start o begin doing sth, start o begin to do sth; **para ~** to start with; **por: comenzó por agradecernos nuestra presencia** she started o began by thanking us for coming; **todos sois culpables, comenzando por ti** you're all guilty, starting with you

comer /2a/ **Ⓐ** VT **1** [+ *comida*] to eat; **¿quieres ~ algo?** would you like something to eat?; ✦ MODISMO **sin ~lo ni beberlo: sin ~lo ni beberlo, me vi envuelto en un caso de contrabando de drogas** without really knowing how, I found myself involved in a drug smuggling case **2** (= *almorzar*) to have for lunch, eat for lunch **3** (= *hacer desaparecer*) ~ **terreno** (*Esp*): **la derecha les está comiendo terreno** the right is gaining ground on them; **el equipo se dejó ~ el terreno** the team conceded a lot of ground **4** (= *destruir, consumir*) **eso les come la moral** that's eating away at their morale; **le come la envidia por dentro** she is eaten up *o* consumed with envy **5** (*Ajedrez*) to take **Ⓑ** VI **1** (= *ingerir alimento*) to eat; ~ **fuera** to eat out; ✦ MODISMO **no ~ ni dejar ~** to be a dog in the manger **2** (= *tomar la comida principal*) (*esp Esp, Méx*) (*a mediodía*) to have lunch; (*LAm*) (*por la noche*) to have dinner **3 dar de ~** to feed **Ⓒ comerse** VPR **1** [+ *comida*] to eat; **sólo me he comido un bocadillo** all I've had to eat is a sandwich; **¿quién se ha comido mi queso?** who's eaten my cheese?; **~se las uñas** to bite one's nails; ✦ MODISMOS **~se a algn a besos** to smother sb in kisses; **~se a algn con los ojos** *o* **la vista** to devour sb with one's eyes; **¿cómo se come eso?** what on earth is that?; **está para comérsela*** she's really gorgeous *o* (*Brit***) tasty; **~se el mundo** to conquer the world **2** (= *destruir*) **el sol se ha ido comiendo los colores de la alfombra** the sun has bleached the carpet, the sun has caused the colours of the carpet to fade; **el ácido se ha comido el metal** the acid has eaten the metal away **3** (= *saltarse*) [+ *párrafo*] to miss out; [+ *consonante*] to swallow; **se come las palabras** he swallows his words **Ⓓ** SM **el buen ~** good food; **Fernando es de buen ~** Fernando enjoys his food

comercial Ⓐ ADJ **1** (= *de tiendas*) [*área, recinto*] shopping *antes de s* **2** (= *financiero*) [*carta, operación*] business *antes de s*; [*balanza, déficit, guerra, embargo*] trade *antes de s*; [*intercambio, estrategia*] commercial **3** [*aviación, avión, piloto*] civil **4** [*cine, teatro, literatura*] commercial **Ⓑ** SMF (= *vendedor*) salesperson

comercializar /1f/ VT (= *explotar comercialmente*) to commercialize; (= *lanzar al mercado*) to market

comerciante SMF **1** (*gen*) trader, dealer; (*a gran escala*) merchant; (= *tendero*) shopkeeper (*Brit*), storekeeper (*EEUU*) **2** (= *interesado*) **es un ~** he's very money-minded

comerciar /1b/ VI ~ **con** [+ *empresa*] to do business with, have dealings with; [+ *país*] to trade with; [+ *mercancías*] to deal in, trade in, handle

comercio SM **1** (= *actividad*) trade, commerce ➤ **comercio electrónico** (*Internet*) e-commerce ➤ **comercio exterior** foreign trade ➤ **comercio interior** domestic trade **2** (= *tienda*) shop (*esp Brit*), store (*EEUU*) **3** (= *intercambio*) ➤ **comercio carnal** sexual intercourse

comestible Ⓐ ADJ (= *digerible*) edible **Ⓑ comestibles** SMPL (= *alimentos*) food *sing*; (*Com*) foodstuffs; (*en tienda, supermercado*) groceries; **tienda de ~s** grocer's (shop) (*esp Brit*), grocery (*EEUU*)

cometa¹ SM (*Astron*) comet

cometa² SF (= *juguete*) kite

cometer /2a/ VT [+ *crimen, delito, pecado*] to commit; [+ *atentado*] to carry out; [+ *error, falta de ortografía*] to make

cometido SM task, mission

comezón SF **1** (= *picor*) itch, itching; [*de calor*] tingle, tingling sensation **2** (= *inquietud*) itch (**por** for); **sentir ~ de hacer algo** to feel an itch to do sth

cómic ['komik] SM (*pl* **~s** ['komik]) (*Esp*) comic (*esp Brit*), comic book (*esp EEUU*)

comicidad SF funniness, comicalness

comicios SMPL elections, voting *sing*

cómico/a Ⓐ ADJ **1** (= *gracioso*) comic(al), funny **2** (*Teat*) comedy *antes de s* **Ⓑ** SM/F **1** (*Teat*) (comic) actor/actress

2 (= *humorista*) comedian/comedienne

El adjetivo **cómico** se puede traducir por **comic** y **comical**. **Comic** se utiliza cuando algo se hace o dice con la intención de hacer reír. También para todo lo relacionado con la comedia: "un actor cómico", *a comic actor*. **Comical** describe algo o a alguien que resulta gracioso o absurdo: "Tiene un no sé qué que resulta cómico", *There is something slightly comical about him*.

comida SF **1** (= *alimento*) food; **no sirven ~ después de las tres** they don't serve food *o* meals after three o'clock; **acábate la ~** finish your meal ➤ **comida casera** home cooking ➤ **comida para perros** dog food ➤ **comida precocinada, comida preparada** ready meals *pl*, pre-cooked meals *pl* ➤ **comida rápida** fast food **2** (= *acto de comer*) meal; **hacemos la ~ fuerte al mediodía** we have our main meal at midday **3** (*esp Esp, Méx*) (= *almuerzo*) lunch; **la hora de la ~** lunch time ➤ **comida de negocios** business lunch ➤ **comida de trabajo** working lunch **4** (*LAm*) (= *cena*) dinner, evening meal

comidilla SF **ser la ~ del barrio** to be the talk of the town

comienzo SM **1** (= *principio*) [*de película, historia, partido*] beginning, start; [*de proyecto, plan*] beginning; [*de enfermedad*] onset; **ese fue el ~ de una serie de desastres** that was the first in a series of disasters; **en los ~s de este siglo** at the beginning of this century; **una etapa muy difícil en sus ~s** a very difficult stage, initially; **al ~: al ~ no entendía nada** at first I didn't understand anything; **al ~ de la primavera** in early spring, at the start of spring **2 dar ~** [*acto, curso*] to start, begin, commence (*frm*) **3 dar ~ a** [+ *acto, ceremonia*] to begin, start; [+ *carrera*] to start; [+ *etapa*] to mark the beginning of

comillas SFPL quotation marks, quotes (*EEUU*); **entre ~** in inverted commas (*Brit*), in quotes (*EEUU*)

comilón/ona¹ Ⓐ ADJ greedy **Ⓑ** SM/F (= *buen comedor*) big eater; (= *glotón*) glutton, pig* **Ⓒ** SM (*Méx*) feast, blowout*

comilona²* SF feast, blowout*

comino SM cumin, cumin seed; ✦ MODISMO **(no) me importa un ~** I couldn't give a toss**, I couldn't care less

comiquita SF (*Ven*) (= *tira cómica*) comic strip; (= *dibujos animados*) cartoon

comisaría SF police station, precinct (*EEUU*)

comisariado SM commission

comisario/a SM/F **1** (= *delegado*) commissioner; **alto ~** high commissioner ➤ **comisario/a europeo/a** European commissioner **2** [*de policía*] superintendent (*Brit*), captain (*EEUU*) **3** [*de exposición*] organizer

comisión SF **1** (= *encargo*) assignment, task, commission (*frm*); (= *misión*) mission, assignment **2** (*Pol*) commission; (= *junta*) committee ➤ **Comisión Europea** European Commission ➤ **comisión parlamentaria** parliamentary committee ➤ **comisión permanente** standing committee **3** (*Fin*) board **4** (*Com*) (= *pago*) commission; **a ~** on a commission basis ➤ **comisión de apertura de cuenta** new account charge **5** ➤ **comisión de servicio(s)** (= *destino provisional*) secondment (*Brit*), temporary transfer; (= *permiso de ausencia*) leave of absence

comisionado/a SM/F **1** (= *delegado*) commissioner **2** (= *miembro*) (*Pol*) committee member; (*Com, Fin*) board member

comisura SF corner, angle, commissure (*frm*) ➤ **comisura de los labios** corner of the mouth

comité SM **1** (= *grupo*) committee ➤ **comité de empresa** (*Esp*) works committee, shop stewards' committee ➤ **comité de redacción** (*gen*) drafting committee; (*Prensa*) editorial committee ➤ **comité ejecutivo** executive board **2** (*RPl*) [*sede*] local headquarters *pl*

comitiva SF (= *cortejo*) retinue ➤ **comitiva fúnebre** cortège, funeral procession

como Ⓐ ADV **1** (*indicando semejanza*) like; **se portó ~ un imbécil** he behaved like an idiot; **juega ~ yo** he plays like me *o* like I do; **~ éste hay pocos** there are few like this *o*

him; **sabe ~ a queso** it tastes a bit like cheese; **blanco ~ la nieve** as white as snow
2 (*introduciendo ejemplo*) such as; **tiene ventajas, ~ son la resistencia y durabilidad** it has advantages, such as *o* like strength and durability
3 (*con verbos*) **3.1** (+ INDIC) **lo hice ~ me habían enseñado** I did it as I had been taught; **hazlo ~ te dijo ella** do it like* *o* the way she told you; **fue así ~ comenzó** that was how it began; **lo levanté ~ pude** I lifted it as best I could; **tal ~: tal ~ lo había planeado** just as *o* the way I had planned it
3.2 (+ SUBJUN) **hazlo ~ quieras** do it however you want *o* like; **tratan de mantenerse en el poder ~ sea** they will do whatever it takes to stay in power; **sea ~ sea** in any case
4 (= *en calidad de*) as a spectator; **lo dice ~ juez** he says it speaking as a judge
5 (= *más o menos*) about, around; **vino ~ a las dos** he came at about *o* around two
6 (*con valor causal*) **libre ~ estaba** free as he was
B CONJ **1** (+ INDIC) (= *ya que*) as, since
2 (+ INDIC) (= *según*) as; **~ se ve en el gráfico** as you can see from the diagram; **tal (y) ~ están las cosas** the way things are, as things stand
3 (+ INDIC) (= *cuando*) as soon as; **así ~ nos vio lanzó un grito** as soon as he saw us he shouted
4 (+ INDIC) (= *que*) **ya verás ~ les ganamos** we'll beat them, you'll see; **ya verás ~ no vienen** I bet they won't come; **de tanto ~** (*esp Esp*): **tienen las manos doloridas de tanto ~ aplaudieron** they clapped so much their hands hurt
5 (+ SUBJUN) (= *si*); **~ vengas tarde, no comes** if you're late you'll get nothing to eat; **no salimos, ~ no sea para ir a la ópera** we only go out if it's to go to the opera, we don't go out unless it's to go to the opera
6 ~ que as if; **¡~ que yo soy tonto y me creo esas mentiras!** as if I was stupid enough to believe lies like that!; **hizo ~ que no nos veía** he pretended not to see us
7 ~ si as if, as though
8 ~ para: ¡es ~ para denunciarlos! it's enough to make you want to report them to the police!; **tampoco es ~ para enfadarse tanto** there's no need to get so angry about it

cómo **A** ADV **1** (*interrogativo*) **1.1** (= *de qué modo*) how?; **¿~ se hace?** how do you do it?; **¿~ está usted?** how are you?; **¿~ te llamas?** what's your name?; **no sé ~ hacerlo** I don't know how to do it **1.2** (*en descripciones*) **¿~ es tu casa?** what's your house like?; **¿~ es de alto el armario?** how tall is the cupboard?, what height is the cupboard? **1.3** (= *¿por qué?*) why?; **¿~ es que no viniste?** why didn't you come?; **—no fui a la fiesta —¿~ no?** "I didn't go to the party" — "why not *o* how come?"; **—¿me dejas este libro? —¡~ no!** "can I borrow this book?" — "of course!"
1.4 (*indicando extrañeza*) what?; **¿cómo? ¿que tú no lo sabías?** what? you mean you didn't know?; **¿y ~ es eso?** how come?, how can that be?; **—¿~ que no sabes nada? —no me lo creo** "what do you mean, you don't know anything about it?" — "I don't believe you"
1.5 (= *¿perdón?*) sorry?, what's that?; **¿~ dice?** I beg your pardon? **1.6 ¿a ~?: ¿a ~ están** *o* **son las peras?** how much are the pears?; **¿a ~ estamos hoy?** what's the date today?
2 (*exclamativo*) **¡~ llueve!** look at the rain!; **¡~ corre!** he can certainly run!; **¡~ me gusta ir a la playa!** I love going to the beach!; **—toma, ¡un regalito —¡~ eres!** "here's a small present" — "you shouldn't have!"; **está lloviendo ¡y no veas ~!** just look at the rain!
B EXCL **¡cómo! ¿sólo cuatro libros?** what do you mean, four books!; **¡pero ~! ¡todavía no has acabado?** what are you doing! haven't you finished yet?
C SM **el ~ y el por qué de las cosas** the whys and wherefores

cómoda SF chest of drawers

comodidad SF **1** (= *confort*) comfort; **vivir con ~** to live in comfort **2** (= *conveniencia*) convenience **3 comodidades** comforts, amenities

comodín SM **1** (*Naipes*) joker **2** (= *excusa*) pretext, stock excuse **3** (*Inform*) wildcard

cómodo ADJ **1** (= *confortable*) [*cama, silla, habitación*] comfortable; [*trabajo, tarea*] agreeable **2** (= *conveniente*) [*instrumento, objeto*] handy; [*arreglo, horario*] convenient **3** (= *descansado*) comfortable; **así estarás más ~** you'll be more comfortable this way; **ponerse ~** to make o.s.

comfortable **4** [*persona*] (= *perezoso*) lazy; (= *tranquilo*) laid-back*

comodón/ona **A** ADJ (= *regalón*) comfort-loving; (= *pasivo*) easy-going, liking a quiet life; (= *perezoso*) lazy **B** SM/F (= *perezoso*) lazybones*; **es un ~** he likes his home comforts

comodoro SM commodore

comoquiera CONJ **1 ~ que** (+ INDIC) since, in view of the fact that **2 ~ que** (+ SUBJUN) in whatever way

compa * SMF (*CAm, Méx*) pal*, buddy (*EEUU**)

compact SM (*pl* **-s**) (*tb* **~ disc**) compact disc

compacto ADJ compact; **disco ~** compact disc

compadecer /2d/ **A** VT (= *apiadarse de*) to pity, be sorry for; (= *comprender*) to sympathize with **B** compadecerse VPR **~se de = A**

compadre SM **1** (= *padrino*) godfather **2** (*esp LAm**) (= *amigo*) friend, pal*, buddy (*esp EEUU**)

compadrear /1a/ VI (*RPl*) to brag, show off

compadreo SM (*esp LAm*) companionship, close contact

compaginable ADJ compatible

compaginar /1a/ **A** VT **1** (= *armonizar*) to combine **2** (*Tip*) to make up **B** compaginarse VPR (= *concordar*) to agree, tally; **~se con** (*gen*) to tally with; [+ *colores*] to blend with

compañerismo SM (= *camaradería*) comradeship, friendship; (*Dep*) team spirit

compañero/a SM/F **1** (*gen*) companion; (*en pareja*) (*tb Naipes*) partner; (*Dep*) [*de equipo*] team-mate; **¡compañeros!** (*Pol*) comrades! ➤ **compañero/a de baile** dancing partner ➤ **compañero/a de clase** schoolmate, classmate ➤ **compañero/a de piso** flatmate (*Brit*), roommate (*EEUU*) ➤ **compañero/a de trabajo** (*en fábrica*) fellow worker, workmate (*esp Brit*); (*en oficina*) colleague ➤ **compañero/a sentimental** partner
2 ¿dónde está el ~ de éste? where is the one that goes with this?, where is the other one (of the pair)?; **dos calcetines que no son ~s** two odd socks, two socks which do not match

compañía SF **1** (*gen*) company; **en ~ de** with, accompanied by, in the company of; **hacer ~ a algn** to keep sb company; **andar en malas ~s** to keep bad company **2** (*Com, Teat, Rel*) company ➤ **Compañía de Jesús** Society of Jesus ➤ **compañía de seguros** insurance company **3** (*Mil*) company

comparable ADJ comparable (**a** to; **con** with)

comparación SF **1** (= *cotejo*) comparison; **en ~ con** in comparison with, beside **2** (*Literat*) simile

comparado ADJ **1** [*estudio, proyecto*] comparative **2 ~ con** compared with *o* to

comparar /1a/ **A** VT to compare (**a** to; **con** with, to) **B** compararse VPR **~se a** *o* **con** to compare with *o* to

comparativo ADJ, SM comparative

comparecencia SF (*Jur*) appearance (in court); **su no ~** his non-appearance; **orden de ~** summons, subpoena (*EEUU*)

comparecer /2d/ VI (*Jur*) to appear (in court); **~ ante un juez** to appear before a judge

comparsa **A** SF **1** [*de carnaval*] group **2** (*Teat*) **la ~** the extras *pl* **B** SMF (*Teat*) extra

compartimento SM, **compartimiento** SM compartment ➤ **compartimento de carga** (*Aer*) hold ➤ **compartimento de equipajes** luggage compartment, baggage compartment (*esp EEUU*) ➤ **compartimento estanco** watertight compartment

compartir /3a/ VT **1** [+ *casa, cuarto, comida, ropa*] to share; **~ algo con algn** to share sth with sb **2** [+ *ganancias*] to share (out), divide (up); [+ *gastos*] to share **3** [+ *opinión*] to share; [+ *objetivos*] to agree with; [+ *sentimientos*] to share

compás SM **1** (*Mús*) time; (= *ritmo*) beat, rhythm; (= *división*) bar (*Brit*), measure (*EEUU*); **al ~ de la música** in time to the music; **llevar el ~** to keep time; **perder el ~** to lose the beat; **mantenemos el ~ de espera** we are still waiting ➤ **compás de 2 por 4** 2/4 time **2** (*Mat*) (*tb* **~ de**

puntas) compass, pair of compasses **3** (*Náut*) compass

compasión SF (= *pena*) compassion, sympathy; (= *piedad*) pity; **¡por ~!** for pity's sake!; **tener ~ de** to take pity on, feel sorry for

compasivo ADJ compassionate

compatibilidad SF compatibility

compatibilizar /1f/ VT to harmonize, reconcile, bring into line, make compatible (**con** with)

compatible ADJ compatible (**con** with)

compatriota SMF compatriot, fellow countryman/countrywoman

compendiar /1b/ VT to abridge, condense, summarize

compendio SM (= *tratado breve*) compendium; (*Univ, Téc*) summary; **en ~** briefly, in short

compenetración SF mutual understanding, fellow feeling, natural sympathy

compenetrarse /1a/ VPR to understand one another; **~ con algo/algn** to identify with sth/sb; **estamos muy compenetrados** we understand each other very well

compensación SF **1** (= *pago*) compensation; **como o en ~** as compensation ➤ **compensación por daños y perjuicios** damages *pl* **2** (= *recompensa*) **no espero ninguna ~ por mis desvelos** I don't expect any reward for my efforts; **este trabajo me ofrece muy pocas compensaciones** this job is very unrewarding; **en ~ por lo mal que se portó ayer** to make up for his (bad) behaviour yesterday **3** (= *equilibrio*) **medidas de ~** compensatory measures **4** (*Fin*) clearing

compensar /1a/ Ⓐ VT **1** (= *indemnizar*) to compensate (**por** for); **~ económicamente a algn** to compensate sb financially; **lo ~on con 100 dólares por los cristales rotos** he received 100 dollars' compensation for the broken windows
2 (= *equilibrar*) [+ *pérdida, falta*] to compensate for, make up for; [+ *efecto, bajada*] to compensate for, offset; [+ *gastos*] to repay, reimburse; [+ *error*] to make amends for
3 (*Mec*) [+ *ruedas*] to balance
4 (*Fin*) [+ *cheque*] to clear
Ⓑ VI **no compensa** it's not worth it, it's not worthwhile; **te compensa hacerlo** it's worth you doing it, it's worth your while doing it *o* to do it; **el esfuerzo no compensa** it's not worth the effort

compensatorio ADJ [*indemnización*] compensatory; [*educación*] remedial

competencia SF **1** (= *rivalidad*) competition; **existe una fuerte ~ entre las dos empresas por el control del mercado externo** the two companies are vying for control of the foreign market, there is fierce competition between the two companies for control of the foreign market; **~ desleal** unfair competition; **en ~ con algn/algo** in competition with sb/sth; **hacer la ~ a algn/algo** to compete with sb/sth; **libre ~** free competition
2 (= *rival*) competition; **la ~ tiene mejores ofertas** our competitors have better offers, the competition has better offers
3 (= *capacidad*) competence, ability ➤ **competencia lingüística** linguistic competence, linguistic ability
4 (= *responsabilidad*) **esta decisión es ~ exclusiva del gobierno** this decision is the exclusive jurisdiction of the government, only the government is competent to deal with this decision
5 competencias (*Pol*) powers
6 (*LAm Dep*) competition

competente ADJ **1** (= *responsable*) competent (*frm*); **la autoridad ~** the proper *o* (*frm*) competent authority; **de fuente ~** from a reliable source **2** (= *capaz*) competent

competer /2a/ VI **- a algn** to be the responsibility of sb

competición SF (*Esp*) competition; **deporte de ~** competitive sport

competidor(a) Ⓐ ADJ (*gen*) competing, rival Ⓑ SM/F **1** (*gen*) competitor; (*Com*) rival (**a** for) **2** (*en concurso*) contestant

competir /3k/ VI **1** (= *enfrentarse*) to compete; **~ con** *o* **contra algo/algn** to compete with *o* against sth/sb; **~ en algo** to compete in sth; **~ por algo** to compete for sth

2 (= *compararse*) **~ con algo: no hay nada que pueda ~ con un buen vino** you can't beat a good wine, nothing can compare with a good wine; **en cuanto a resistencia Miguel no puede ~ con Andrés** when it comes to stamina Miguel is no match for Andrés

competitividad SF competitiveness

competitivo ADJ competitive

compilar /1a/ VT to compile

compincharse /1a/ VPR to band together, team up; **estar compinchados*** to be in cahoots* (**con** with)

compinche* SMF **1** (= *amigo*) pal*, mate (*Brit**), buddy (*EEUU**) **2** (= *cómplice*) partner in crime, accomplice

complacencia SF **1** (= *placer*) pleasure, satisfaction **2** (= *agrado*) willingness; **lo hizo con ~** he did it gladly **3** (= *indulgencia*) indulgence

complacer /2w/ Ⓐ VT **1** (*gen*) to please; [+ *cliente*] to help, oblige; [+ *jefe*] to humour; **nos complace anunciarles ...** we are pleased to announce ... **2** [+ *deseo*] to indulge, gratify Ⓑ **complacerse** VPR **el banco se complace en comunicar a su clientela que ...** the bank is pleased to inform its customers that ...

complacido ADJ pleased, satisfied; **me miró ~** he gave me a pleased look; **quedamos ~s de la visita** we were pleased with our visit

complaciente ADJ **1** (= *indulgente*) indulgent; [*marido*] complaisant **2** (= *solícito*) obliging, helpful

complejidad SF complexity

complejo Ⓐ ADJ (*gen*) complex
Ⓑ SM **1** (*Psic*) complex ➤ **complejo de culpa, complejo de culpabilidad** guilt complex ➤ **complejo de Edipo** Oedipus complex ➤ **complejo de Electra** Electra complex ➤ **complejo de inferioridad** inferiority complex ➤ **complejo de superioridad** superiority complex **2** (= *instalaciones*) complex ➤ **complejo deportivo** sports complex, sports centre *o* (*EEUU*) center ➤ **complejo residencial** housing development ➤ **complejo turístico** tourist development **3** (*Quím*) complex ➤ **complejo vitamínico** vitamin complex

complementar /1a/ Ⓐ VT to complement
Ⓑ **complementarse** VPR to complement each other

complementariamente ADV in addition (**a** to), additionally

complementariedad SF complementarity

complementario Ⓐ ADJ (*gen*) complementary Ⓑ SM (*en lotería*) bonus number

complemento Ⓐ SM **1** (*Mat*) complement
2 (*Ling*) complement, object ➤ **complemento circunstancial** adverbial ➤ **complemento directo** direct object ➤ **complemento indirecto** indirect object ➤ **complemento preposicional** prepositional complement **3** (= *parte adicional*) **el vino es el ~ ideal de la buena comida** wine is the ideal complement to good food; **sería el ~ de su felicidad** it would complete her happiness
4 (= *pago*) ➤ **complemento de destino** extra allowance (attached to a post) ➤ **complemento de productividad** performance-related bonus ➤ **complemento salarial** bonus, extra pay
Ⓑ **complementos** SMPL [*de coche, vestido*] accessories

completar /1a/ VT **1** (= *terminar*) to complete, finish; (= *perfeccionar*) to finish off, round off **2** (*LAm*) [+ *formulario, solicitud*] to fill out, fill in (*esp Brit*)

completo Ⓐ ADJ **1** (= *entero*) [*dieta*] balanced; [*colección*] complete; [*texto, informe*] full, complete; [*felicidad*] complete, total; [*panorama*] full; **las poesías completas de San Juan de la Cruz** the complete poems of San Juan de la Cruz; **trabajar a tiempo ~** to work full time; **asistió el ayuntamiento al ~** the entire council was present
2 (= *lleno*) full; **"completo"** (*en pensión, hostal*) "no vacancies"; (*en taquilla*) "sold out"; **el hotel estaba al ~** the hotel was fully booked *o* full
3 (= *total*) [*éxito, fracaso*] complete, total; **por ~** [*desaparecer, desconocer*] completely; **se me olvidó por ~** I completely forgot; **el problema quedará resuelto por ~** the problem will be solved once and for all

4 (= *terminado*) **la novela está ya casi completa** the novel is almost finished
5 (= *bien hecho*) **ha entregado un trabajo muy ~** he's handed in a very thorough piece of work; **este libro es pequeño, pero bastante ~** this book is small, but quite comprehensive
6 (= *polifacético*) [*actor, deportista*] all-round
Ⓑ SM (*Chi*) hot dog (*with choice of various sauces*)

complexión SF build, constitution; **un hombre de ~ fuerte** a well-built man, a man with a strong constitution

complicación SF **1** (= *problema*) complication
2 (= *cualidad*) complexity

complicado ADJ (= *complejo*) (*gen*) complicated, complex; [*fractura*] compound; [*estilo*] elaborate; [*persona*] complex; [*método*] complicated, involved; (*Jur*) involved, implicated

complicar /1g/ **Ⓐ** VT **1** (*gen*) to complicate **2** (*Jur*) to involve, implicate (**en** in) **Ⓑ complicarse** VPR to get complicated; **~se la vida** to make life difficult for o.s.

cómplice SMF accomplice

complicidad SF complicity, involvement (**en** in)

compló SM, **complot** SM (*pl* **complots**) plot, conspiracy, intrigue

componente **Ⓐ** ADJ (*gen*) component, constituent **Ⓑ** SM **1** (= *miembro*) member **2** (= *parte*) (*Quím*) component; (*Mec*) part, component **3** (*Meteo*) **un viento de ~ norte** a northerly wind

componer /2q/ (*pp* **compuesto**) **Ⓐ** VT **1** [+ *comité, jurado, organización*] to make up; **los cuadros que componen esta exposición** the pictures that make up this exhibition, the pictures in this exhibition
2 (= *escribir*) [+ *poesía, sinfonía, canción*] to compose, write; [+ *poema, tratado, redacción*] to write
3 (= *arreglar*) [+ *objeto roto*] to mend, repair, fix
4 (= *curar*) to settle
5 (*Tip*) [+ *texto*] to typeset, set, compose **Ⓑ componerse** VPR **1** **~se de** to consist of
2 (= *arreglarse*) to dress up
3 (*Col, CS, Méx*) [*persona*] to get better
4 componérselas* to manage; **siempre se las compone para salirse con la suya** he always manages to get his own way; ✦ MODISMO **¡allá o que se las componga (como pueda)!*** that's his problem, that's his funeral*

comportamiento SM **1** [*de persona*] behaviour, behavior (*EEUU*) **2** [*de mercado, automóvil*] performance
➤ **comportamiento en carretera** road performance

comportar /1a/ **Ⓐ** VT to involve **Ⓑ comportarse** VPR to behave; **~se mal** to misbehave, behave badly

composición SF **1** (*Mús, Quím, Arte*) composition **2** (*Educ*) essay **3** ➤ **composición de lugar** stocktaking, inventory; **hacerse una ~ de lugar** to take stock (of one's situation) **4** (*Tip*) typesetting

compositor(a) SM/F composer

compostelano ADJ of/from Santiago de Compostela

compostura SF **1** (= *dignidad*) composure; **perder la ~** to lose one's composure **2** (= *arreglo*) mending, repair

compota SF compote, preserve ➤ **compota de manzanas** stewed apples

compra SF **1** (= *proceso*) purchase, purchasing, buying; **hacer la ~** to do the shopping; **ir de ~s** to go shopping ➤ **compra al contado** cash purchase ➤ **compra por catálogo** mail order ➤ **compra y venta** buying and selling **2** (= *artículo*) purchase; **es una buena ~** it's a good buy

comprador(a) SM/F (*Com*) buyer, purchaser; (*en tienda*) shopper, customer

comprar /1a/ **Ⓐ** VT **1** [+ *casa, comida, regalo*] to buy, purchase (*frm*); **~ algo a algn** (*para algn*) to buy sth for sb, buy sb sth; (*de algn*) to buy sth from sb; **~ algo al contado** to pay cash (for sth), pay sth in cash; **~ algo a plazos** to buy sth on hire purchase (*Brit*) *o* on an installment plan (*EEUU*); **~ algo al por mayor** to buy sth wholesale; **~ algo al por menor** to buy sth retail
2 [+ *persona*] to bribe, buy off*; **el árbitro está comprado** they've bribed the referee

Ⓑ VI (= *hacer la compra*) to buy, shop

compraventa SF **1** (*gen*) buying and selling, dealing; **negocio de ~** second-hand shop (*esp Brit*) *o* store (*EEUU*) **2** (*Jur*) contract of sale

comprender /2a/ **Ⓐ** VT **1** (= *entender*) to understand; **no comprendo cómo ha podido pasar esto** I don't see *o* understand how this could have happened; **esto bastó para hacernos ~ su posición** this was all we needed to understand his position; **hacerse ~** to make o.s. understood
2 (= *darse cuenta*) to realize; **al final comprendió que yo no iba a ayudarle** he finally realized I wasn't going to help him
3 (= *incluir*) to comprise (*frm*); **el primer tomo comprende las letras de la A a la G** the first volume covers *o* (*frm*) comprises letters A to G; **está todo comprendido en el precio** the price is all-inclusive; **el período comprendido entre 1936 y 1939** the period from 1936 to 1939 *o* between 1936 and 1939
Ⓑ VI **1** (= *entender*) to understand
2 (= *darse cuenta*) **¡ahora comprendo!** now I see!, I get it (now)!*

comprensible ADJ **1** (= *justificable*) understandable
2 (= *inteligible*) **eso no le resulta ~ a nadie** nobody can understand that

comprensión SF **1** (= *entendimiento*) understanding; **los dibujos nos ayudan a la ~ del texto** the drawings help us to understand the text *o* help our understanding of the text; **un ejercicio de ~ auditiva** a listening comprehension test **2** (= *actitud*) understanding

comprensivo ADJ understanding

compresa SF **1** (*para mujer*) sanitary towel (*Brit*), sanitary napkin (*EEUU*) **2** (*Med*) compress

compresión SF compression

compresor SM compressor

comprimido **Ⓐ** ADJ compressed **Ⓑ** SM **1** (*Med*) pill, tablet **2** (*Col, Perú Escol*) cheat-sheet

comprimir /3a/ **Ⓐ** VT **1** (*Téc*) to compress (**en** into); (= *prensar*) to press (down), squeeze down; (*Inform*) to pack; (= *condensar*) to condense **2** (= *controlar*) to control; [+ *lágrimas*] to hold back **Ⓑ comprimirse** VPR (*gen*) to get compressed; [*personas*] to squeeze *o* squash together

comprobable ADJ verifiable, capable of being checked

comprobación SF **1** (= *proceso*) checking, verification **2** (*Col*) (= *examen*) test

comprobante **Ⓐ** ADJ **documento ~** supporting document **Ⓑ** SM (= *documento*) proof, supporting document; (*Com*) receipt (*esp Brit*), sales slip (*EEUU*)

comprobar /1l/ VT **1** [+ *billete, documento, frenos*] to check; **compruebe el aceite antes de salir de viaje** check your oil before setting out; **necesito algún documento para ~ su identidad** I need some document that proves your identity, I need some proof of identity; **compruebe nuestros productos usted mismo** try our products for yourself
2 (= *confirmar*) [+ *teoría, existencia*] to prove; [+ *eficacia, veracidad*] to verify, confirm; **pudimos ~ que era verdad** we were able to verify *o* confirm *o* establish that it was true

comprometedor ADJ compromising

comprometer /2a/ **Ⓐ** VT **1** (= *poner en evidencia*) to compromise
2 (= *implicar*) **~ a algn en algo** (*futuro*) to involve sb in sth; (*pasado*) to implicate sb in sth
3 (= *obligar*) **~ a algn a algo** to commit sb to sth
4 (= *arriesgar*) [+ *conversaciones, éxito, reputación, paz*] to jeopardize
5 (= *apalabrar*) [+ *habitación, entrada*] to reserve, book; **ya he comprometido la casa** I've already promised the house to someone
6 (= *invertir*) to invest, tie up **Ⓑ comprometerse** VPR **1** (= *contraer un compromiso*) to commit o.s.; **~se a algo** to commit o.s. to sth; **~se a hacer algo** to commit o.s. to doing sth; **me comprometí a ayudarte y lo haré** I promised to help you and I will, I said I'd help you and I will

2 (= *implicarse socialmente*) to commit o.s., make a commitment; **~se políticamente (con algo)** to commit o.s. politically (to sth), make a political commitment (to sth)
3 (= *citarse*) **ya me he comprometido para el sábado** I've arranged to do something else on Saturday; **~se con algn** to arrange to see sb
4 [*novios*] to get engaged; **~se con algn** to get engaged to sb

comprometido ADJ **1** (= *difícil*) awkward, embarrassing
2 (*socialmente*) [*escritor, artista*] politically committed, engagé; [*arte*] politically committed; **está ~ con la causa** he's committed to the cause
3 (*por cita, trabajo*) **ya están ~s para jugar el sábado** they've already arranged to play on Saturday, they've booked to play on Saturday; **ya estaba ~ con otro proyecto** he was already committed to another project; **estar ~ a hacer algo** to be committed to doing sth
4 (*antes del matrimonio*) engaged

compromisario/a SM/F convention delegate

compromiso SM **1** (= *obligación*) **1.1** (*por acuerdo, ideología*) commitment; **esperamos que cumplan con su ~ de bajar los impuestos** we hope they'll honour their commitment to lowering taxes; **pida presupuesto sin ~** ask for an estimate without obligation **1.2** (*por convenciones sociales*) **aunque no tenemos ~ con ellos, los vamos a invitar** we're going to invite them even though we're under no obligation to; **si le regalas ahora algo, la pondrás en el ~ de invitarte a cenar** if you give her a present now, you'll make her feel obliged to take you out to dinner; **por ~ no lo hagas** don't feel obliged to do it
2 (= *aprieto*) **poner a algn en un ~** to put sb in an awkward position
3 (= *acuerdo*) agreement; (*con concesiones mutuas*) compromise; **una fórmula de ~** a compromise, a compromise formula ➤ **compromiso verbal** unwritten agreement
4 (= *cita*) **4.1** (*con otras personas*) engagement; **ahora, si me disculpan, tengo que atender otros ~s** now, if you will excuse me, I have other engagements; **¿tienes algún ~ para esta noche?** do you have anything arranged for tonight? **4.2** (*Dep*) game, match (*esp Brit*)
5 [*de matrimonio*] engagement; **soltero y sin ~** single and unattached ➤ **compromiso matrimonial** engagement, engagement to marry

compuerta SF (*en canal*) sluice, floodgate; (*en puerta*) hatch

compuesto ④ PP *de* **componer**; **estar ~ de** to be composed of, consist of; **un grupo ~ por 15 personas** a group of 15 people **⑤** ADJ **1** (*Mat, Fin, Ling, Quím*) compound; (*Bot*) composite **2** (= *elegante*) dressed up, smart (*esp Brit*); ✦ MODISMO **compuesta y sin novio** all dressed up and nowhere to go **3** (= *tranquilo*) composed **⑥** SM **1** (*Quím*) compound ➤ **compuesto químico** chemical compound **2** (*Ling*) compound, compound word

compulsa SF **1** (= *cotejo*) checking, comparison **2** (*Der, Admin*) certified true copy, attested copy

compulsar /1a/ VT **1** (= *comparar*) to collate, compare **2** (*Der, Admin*) to make an attested copy of

compulsión SF compulsion

compulsivo ADJ **1** [*deseo, hambre*] compulsive **2** (= *obligatorio*) compulsory

compungido ADJ (= *arrepentido*) remorseful, contrite; (= *triste*) sad, sorrowful

compungirse /3c/ VPR (= *arrepentirse*) to feel remorseful (**por** about, because of), feel sorry (**por** for); (= *entristecerse*) to feel sad, be sorrowful

computación SF (*esp LAm*) **1** (= *cálculo*) calculation **2** (*esp LAm Inform*) computing

computacional ADJ computational, computer *antes de s*

computadora SF (*esp LAm*), **computador** SM (*esp LAm*) computer ➤ **computadora personal** personal computer ➤ **computadora portátil** (*gen*) portable computer; (*pequeño*) laptop computer

computadorizar /1f/ VT to computerize

computar /1a/ VT to calculate, compute (**en** at)

computerizar /1f/ VT to computerize

computista SMF (*Col*) (computer) programmer

cómputo SM calculation, computation

comulgar /1h/ **④** VT (*Rel*) to administer communion to **⑤** VI **1** (*Rel*) to take communion, receive communion **2** **~ con** (*gen*) to like, accept, agree with; [+ *ideas*] to share; [+ *personas*] to sympathize with

común ④ ADJ **1** (= *compartido*) [*afición, intereses*] common; [*amigo*] mutual; **tienen una serie de características comunes** they share a series of features, they have a series of common features *o* features in common; **~ a algn/algo** common to sb/sth ·
2 (= *colectivo*) [*causa, frente, espacio*] common; [*gastos*] communal; **no tenemos nada en ~** we have nothing in common; **la pareja tuvo dos hijos en ~** the couple had two children together; **hacer algo en ~** to do sth together; **poner en ~** [+ *iniciativas, problemas*] to share
3 (= *frecuente*) [*enfermedad, opinión*] common, widespread; [*costumbre*] widespread; [*cualidad*] common, ordinary; **el concierto fue más largo de lo ~** the concert was longer than usual; **por lo ~** as a rule
4 (*Esp Educ*) [*asignatura*] core
⑤ SM **1** **el ~ de las gentes** the common man; **bienes del ~** public property
2 (*) (= *retrete*) toilet (*Brit*), bathroom
3 (*Pol*) (*en el Reino Unido*) **la Cámara de los Comunes** the House of Commons

comuna SF **1** (= *comunidad*) commune **2** (*And, CS*) (= *municipio*) municipality, ≈ county (*EEUU*)

comunal ADJ **1** (= *de todos*) communal, community *antes de s* **2** (*And, CS*) (= *del municipio*) municipal, ≈ county *antes de s* (*EEUU*)

comunicación SF **1** (= *conexión*) communication; **entre nosotros falla la ~** we just don't communicate well, we have poor communication ➤ **comunicación no verbal** non-verbal communication
2 (= *contacto*) contact; **establecer ~ con algn** to establish contact with sb; **ponerse en ~ con algn** to get in contact *o* touch with sb, contact sb
3 (*por teléfono*) **cortar la ~** to hang up; **dijo su nombre y se cortó la ~** he said his name and the line went dead *o* we were cut off
4 **comunicaciones** (= *transportes*) communications
5 (= *escrito*) (= *mensaje*) message; (= *informe*) report
6 (*Univ*) (*en congreso*) paper; **presentar una ~ (sobre algo)** to give *o* present a paper (on sth)

comunicado ④ ADJ **1** [*habitaciones*] connected **2** [*pueblo, zona*] **el pueblo está bien ~ por tren** the town has good train connections, the town is easily accessible by train **⑤** SM (= *notificación*) statement, press release, communiqué (*frm*) ➤ **comunicado de prensa** press release ➤ **comunicado oficial** official statement

comunicador(a) SM/F communicator; **un buen ~** a good communicator

comunicante SMF **1** (= *informador*) informant **2** (*en congreso*) speaker

comunicar /1g/ **④** VT **1** (= *decir*) **1.1** [+ *decisión, resultado*] to announce; **según ~on fuentes del gobierno** according to government sources **1.2** **~ algo a algn** to inform sb of sth; **comunicamos a los señores pasajeros que ...** we would like to inform passengers that ...; **nos comunican desde Lisboa que ...** we have heard from Lisbon that ...
2 (*al teléfono*) **¿me comunica con la dirección, por favor?** could I speak to the manager, please?, could you put me through to the manager, please?
⑤ VI **1** (*Esp*) [*teléfono*] to be engaged (*Brit*), be busy (*esp EEUU*); **está comunicando** it's engaged (*Brit*), the line's busy (*esp EEUU*)
2 [*cuarto, habitación*] to connect; **la cocina comunica con el comedor** the kitchen connects with the dining-room **⑥** **comunicarse** VPR **1** (= *establecer comunicación*) **1.1** (*uso recíproco*) to communicate; **se comunican en inglés/por email** they communicate in English/by e-mail, they use English/e-mail (to communicate) **1.2** (*uso transitivo*) **nos comunicamos nuestras impresiones** we exchanged impressions **1.3** **~se con algn** to communicate with sb

2 (= *entenderse*) **~se bien con algn** to connect well with sb
3 (= *unirse*) to be connected (**con** to); **sus habitaciones se comunicaban** they had adjoining rooms, their rooms were connected

comunicativo ADJ [*método, función, persona*] communicative; **es muy poco ~** he's very uncommunicative

comunidad SF **1** (*tb Rel*) community; **de** o **en ~** (*Jur*) jointly ➤ **comunidad autónoma** (*Esp*) autonomous region ➤ **Comunidad Británica de Naciones** British Commonwealth ➤ **comunidad de vecinos** residents' association ➤ **Comunidad (Económica) Europea** European (Economic) Community
2 (= *pago*) [*de piso*] service charge, charge for communal services

COMUNIDAD AUTÓNOMA

In Spain the **comunidades autónomas** are any of the 19 administrative regions consisting of one or more provinces and having political powers devolved from Madrid, as stipulated by the 1978 Constitution. They have their own democratically elected parliaments, form their own cabinets and legislate and execute policies in certain areas such as housing, infrastructure, health and education, though Madrid still retains jurisdiction for all matters affecting the country as a whole, such as defence, foreign affairs and justice. The **Comunidades Autónomas** include: Andalucía, Cataluña, Galicia and País Vasco.

comunión SF communion; **hacer la Primera Comunión** to take one's First Communion

comunismo SM communism

comunista Ⓐ ADJ communist Ⓑ SMF communist

comunitario ADJ **1** [*centro, servicios, cooperación*] community *antes de s*; [*jardín, pasillos*] communal **2** (= *de la Comunidad Europea*) Community *antes de s*

con PREP **1** (*indicando compañía, instrumento, medio*) with; **¿~ quién vas a ir?** who are you going with?; **~ su ayuda** with his help; **ducharse ~ agua fría** to have a cold shower; **lo he escrito ~ bolígrafo** I wrote it in pen; **andar ~ muletas** to walk on o with crutches; **~ este sol no hay quien salga** no one can go out in this sun; **lo compramos ~ mi marido** (*LAm*) my husband and I bought it
2 (*indicando características, estado*) **un hombre ~ principios** a man of principle; **llegó ~ aspecto relajado** she arrived looking relaxed; **murió ~ 60 años** she died at the age of 60
3 (*indicando combinación*) and; **pan ~ mantequilla** bread and butter; **vodka ~ naranja** vodka and orange; **café ~ leche** white coffee
4 (*indicando contenido*) **una cazuela ~ agua caliente** a pan of hot water; **encontraron una maleta ~ 800.000 dólares** they found a suitcase containing 800,000 dollars o with 800,000 dollars in it
5 (*indicando modo*) **ábrelo ~ cuidado** open it carefully; **anda ~ dificultad** she walks with difficulty; **estar ~ dolor de muelas/la pierna escayolada** to have toothache/one's leg in plaster (*Brit*) o in a cast (*esp EEUU*); **~ mucho gusto** certainly, by all means
6 (*como complemento personal de algunos verbos*) to; **¿~ quién hablas?** who are you speaking to?; **se ha casado ~ Jesús** she's married Jesús, she's got married to Jesús; **me escribo ~ ella** she and I write to each other
7 (*tras adjetivos*) to, towards; **amable ~ todos** kind to o towards everybody
8 (*con decimales*) **once ~ siete** (*11,7*) eleven point seven (*11.7*); **un dólar ~ cincuenta centavos** one dollar fifty cents
9 (= *pese a*) in spite of; **~ tantas dificultades, no se descorazonó** in spite of all o for all the difficulties he didn't lose heart; **~ todo (y ~ eso), la gente se lo pasó bien** in spite of everything, people had a good time
10 (*en exclamaciones*) **¡vaya ~ el niño!*** the cheeky monkey! (*Brit**), that fresh o saucy brat (*EEUU*); **¡~ lo bien que se está aquí!** and it's so nice here too!
11 (*indicando una condición*) **11.1** (+ INFIN) **~ estudiar un poco apruebas** with a bit of studying you should pass;

cree que ~ confesarlo se librará del castigo he thinks that by owning up he'll escape punishment; **~ llegar a las seis estará bien** if you come by six it will be fine **11.2** **~ que** (+ SUBJUN): **~ que me invite, me conformo** as long as o provided that she invites me, I don't mind; **basta ~ que nos remita la tarjeta cumplimentada** all you have to do is send us the completed card
12 (*LAm*) (*indicando agente*) **¿~ quién te cortas el pelo?** who cuts your hair?, who do you go to to get your hair cut?

conato SM attempt ➤ **conato de robo** attempted robbery

concatenación SF linking, concatenation (*frm*)

concatenar /1a/ VT to link together

cóncavo Ⓐ ADJ concave Ⓑ SM hollow, cavity

concebir /3k/ Ⓐ VT **1** (= *crear*) [+ *plan, proyecto*] to conceive, devise; [+ *personaje*] to create; [+ *historia*] to think up, invent
2 (= *imaginar*) to conceive of, imagine
3 (= *entender*) **una forma diferente de ~ las cosas** a different way of seeing things; **no concibe que haya gente con ideas mejores que las suyas** he can't comprehend that there are people with better ideas than his
4 (= *engendrar*) [+ *hijo*] to conceive; **el gol nos hizo ~ esperanzas de victoria** the goal brought o gave us hopes of victory
Ⓑ VI to conceive, become pregnant

conceder /2a/ VT **1** (= *dar*) [+ *beca, premio*] to award, grant; [+ *crédito, permiso, deseo, entrevista*] to grant; **su mujer no quería ~le el divorcio** his wife didn't want to grant o give him a divorce; **el juez les concedió el divorcio** the judge granted them a divorce; **el árbitro les concedió el gol** the referee awarded them the goal; **¿me concede el honor de este baile?** may I have the pleasure of this dance? **2** (*frm*) (= *admitir*) to concede, admit

concejal(a) SM/F councillor, councilman/councilwoman (*EEUU*)

concejalía SF post of councillor, post of councilman (*EEUU*)

concejero/a SM/F councillor, councilman/councilwoman (*EEUU*)

concejo SM council ➤ **concejo municipal** town/city council

concentración SF **1** (= *centralización*) concentration, centralization **2** (*mental*) concentration **3** (= *reunión*) (*Pol*) gathering, meeting, rally; **una ~ de motos** a motorcycling rally **4** (*Dep*) [*de equipo*] **antes de su ~ ...** before meeting up o getting together ...

concentrado Ⓐ ADJ concentrated Ⓑ SM extract, concentrate ➤ **concentrado de carne** meat extract

concentrar /1a/ Ⓐ VT to concentrate Ⓑ **concentrarse** VPR **1** (*mentalmente*) to concentrate (**en** on) **2** (= *reunirse*) to gather (together) **3** (= *estar reunidos*) to concentrate, be concentrated

concéntrico ADJ concentric

concepción SF (*Biol*) conception

conceptismo SM conceptism, *witty, allusive and involved style of esp 17th century*

conceptista Ⓐ ADJ [*estilo, novela*] witty, allusive and involved Ⓑ SMF (= *escritor*) writer in the style of conceptism

concepto SM **1** (= *idea*) concept, notion **2** (= *opinión*) view, judgment; **tener buen ~ de algn, tener en buen ~ a algn** to think highly of sb **3** (= *condición*) heading, section; **bajo ningún ~** in no way, under no circumstances; **se le pagó esa cantidad en** o **por ~ de derechos** he was paid that amount as royalties **4** (*Literat*) conceit

conceptual ADJ conceptual

conceptualización SF conceptualization

conceptualizar /1f/ VT to conceptualize

concerniente ADJ **~ a** concerning, relating to; **en lo ~ a** with regard to, concerning

concernir /3i; *defectivo*/ VI **~ a** to concern; **eso a mí no me concierne** that does not concern me, that is of no concern to me, that is not of my concern; **por lo que a mí**

concierne as far as I am concerned; **en lo que concierne a ...** with regard to ..., concerning ...

concertación SF 1 (= *acto*) harmonizing; **política de ~** consensus politics *pl* ➤ **concertación social** social harmony 2 (= *pacto*) agreement, pact

concertado ADJ [*centro, colegio, hospital*] officially approved, state assisted

concertar /1j/ Ⓐ VT 1 (*frm*) [+ *entrevista*] to arrange, set up; **~ una cita** to arrange o make an appointment 2 (= *acordar*) [+ *salario, precio*] to agree (on); [+ *póliza, seguro*] to take out; **~ un acuerdo** to reach an agreement 3 (*Mús*) (= *armonizar*) [+ *voces*] to harmonize; [+ *instrumentos*] to tune (up) Ⓑ VI 1 (*frm*) [*cifras, datos*] to agree, match (up) 2 (*Ling*) to agree 3 (*Mús*) [*voces*] to harmonize; [*instrumentos*] to be in tune

concertina¹ SF (= *instrumento*) concertina

concertino/a² SM/F leader of the orchestra (*Brit*), concertmaster (*EEUU*)

concertista SMF soloist, solo performer; **~ de guitarra** concert guitarist

concesión SF 1 (*en acuerdo, negociación*) concession, granting 2 (*Jur, Pol*) [*de nacionalidad, libertad*] granting 3 [*de un premio*] award 4 (*Com*) [*de fabricación*] licence, license (*EEUU*); [*de venta*] franchise; [*de transporte*] concession, contract

concesionario/a SM/F (*Com*) (*gen*) licence holder, license holder (*EEUU*), licensee; [*de venta*] franchisee, authorized dealer; [*de transportes*] contractor

concesivo ADJ concessive

concha SF 1 (*Zool*) shell; ✦ MODISMO **meterse en su ~** to retire into one's shell ➤ **concha de perla** (*And*) mother-of-pearl 2 (= *carey*) tortoiseshell 3 [*de porcelana*] flake, chip 4 (*Ven*) [*de fruta, verduras*] skin; [*de pan*] crust; [*de nuez*] shell; [*de queso*] rind 5 (*Teat*) prompt box 6 (*And, Carib, Méx*) (= *descaro*) nerve, cheek*; **¡qué ~ la tuya!** you've got a nerve!, you've got a cheek!* 7 (*SAm euf*) **coño**

conchabar /1a/ Ⓐ VT (*CS*) [+ *persona*] to hire for work, engage, employ Ⓑ **conchabarse** VPR 1 (= *confabularse*) to gang up (**contra** on), plot (**contra** against); **los dos estaban conchabados** the two were in cahoots* 2 (*CS*) (= *colocarse*) to get a job 3 (*Méx*) (= *conquistar*) to sweet-talk*

cónchale EXCL (*Carib*) **¡cónchale!** well!, goodness!, jeez (*EEUU*)*

Conchinchina* SF ✦ MODISMO **estar en la ~** to be miles away, be on the other side of the world

concho¹ SM 1 (*CS*) (= *poso*) dregs *pl*, sediment; (= *residuo*) residue; ✦ MODISMO **hasta el ~** to the very end 2 **conchos** (= *sobras*) left-overs

concho²* EXCL (*euf*) sugar!*

conchudo* ADJ (*And, Carib, Méx*) **ser ~** to have a cheek o nerve*

conciencia SF 1 (= *moralidad*) conscience; **en ~** in all conscience; **actuar** u **obrar en ~** to act in good conscience; **votar en ~** to vote according to one's conscience; **tener mala ~** to have a guilty conscience; **remorder a algn la ~**: **me remuerde la ~ por haberle mentido** I've got a guilty o bad conscience about lying to him; **tener la ~ tranquila** to have a clear conscience 2 **a ~** (= *con dedicación*) conscientiously; (= *con mala intención*) on purpose; **me tuve que preparar a ~ para el examen** I had to prepare very thoroughly for the exam; **una casa construida a ~** a solidly o well built house; **lo has hecho a ~ para fastidiarme** you deliberately did it to annoy me, you did it on purpose to annoy me 3 (= *capacidad de juicio*) awareness; **tener ~ de algo**: **no tienen ~ de nación** they have no sense of national identity; **tenían plena ~ de lo que hacían** they were fully aware of what they were doing; **tomar ~ de algo** to become aware of sth ➤ **conciencia de clase** class consciousness 4 (*Med*) consciousness; **perder la ~** to lose consciousness

concienciación SF (*Esp*) **una campaña de ~ ciudadana** a campaign to raise public awareness

concienciado ADJ (*Esp*) socially aware

concienciar /1b/ (*Esp*) Ⓐ VT (= *sensibilizar*) **~ a algn de un problema** to raise sb's awareness of an issue Ⓑ **concienciarse** VPR **~se de algo** to become aware of sth

concientización SF (*LAm*) = **concienciación**

concientizado ADJ (*LAm*) = **concienciado**

concientizar /1f/ VT (*LAm*) = **concienciar**

concienzudo ADJ 1 [*estudiante, trabajador*] conscientious 2 [*estudio, esfuerzo*] painstaking, thorough

concierto SM 1 (*Mús*) (= *función*) concert; (= *obra*) concerto ➤ **concierto de cámara** chamber concert ➤ **concierto sinfónico** symphony concert 2 (*frm*) (= *acuerdo*) agreement

conciliábulo SM secret meeting, secret discussion

conciliación SF conciliation, reconciliation

conciliador(a) Ⓐ ADJ conciliatory Ⓑ SM/F conciliator

conciliar¹ /1b/ VT 1 [+ *enemigos*] to reconcile; [+ *ideas*] to harmonize, bring into line 2 **~ el sueño** to get to sleep 3 [+ *respeto, antipatía*] to win, gain

conciliar² ADJ (*Rel*) of a council, council *antes de s*

conciliatorio ADJ conciliatory

concilio SM council; **el Segundo Concilio Vaticano** the Second Vatican Council

concisión SF conciseness, brevity

conciso ADJ concise, brief

conciudadano/a SM/F fellow citizen

conclave SM, **cónclave** SM conclave

concluir /3g/ Ⓐ VT 1 (= *finalizar*) [+ *estudios, trabajo*] to finish, complete, conclude (*frm*) 2 [+ *acuerdo, pacto*] to reach 3 (= *deducir*) to conclude; **el informe concluye que ...** the report concludes that ...; **~ algo de algo** to deduce sth from sth Ⓑ VI (*frm*) (= *finalizar*) [*acto, proceso, evento*] to conclude, finish, end; [*era, etapa*] to end, come to an end; [*plazo*] to expire; **cuando la investigación concluya** when investigations are complete o have been completed; **y para ~ ...** and finally ...

conclusión SF conclusion; **en ~** in conclusion, finally; **llegar a la ~ de que ...** to come to the conclusion that ...

concluyente ADJ conclusive, decisive

concomerse /2a/ VPR **~ de impaciencia*** to be itching with impatience

concomitante ADJ concomitant

concordancia SF 1 (= *acuerdo*) agreement; (= *armonía*) harmony 2 (*Ling*) concord, agreement 3 (*Mús*) harmony

concordante ADJ concordant

concordar /1l/ Ⓐ VT 1 (= *armonizar*) to reconcile, bring into line 2 (*Ling*) to make agree Ⓑ VI 1 (= *armonizar*) to agree (**con** with), tally (**con** with), correspond (**con** to); **esto no concuerda con los hechos** this does not square with o fit in with the facts; **los dos concuerdan en sus gustos** the two have the same tastes 2 (*Ling*) to agree

concordato SM concordat

concordia SF (= *armonía*) concord, harmony; (= *conformidad*) conformity

concreción SF 1 (= *precisión*) precision; **intenta responder a las preguntas con mayor ~** try to be more precise when you reply to the questions 2 (= *materialización*) realization 3 (*Fís*) concretion

concretamente ADV 1 (= *específicamente*) specifically; **estoy buscando esta marca ~** I'm looking for this brand in particular, I'm specifically looking for this brand; **estuvimos en Inglaterra, ~ en Manchester** we were in England, in Manchester to be exact o precise 2 (= *exactamente*) exactly; **¿qué dijo ~?** what exactly did he say?

concretar /1a/ Ⓐ VT 1 (= *precisar*) to specify; (= *concertar*) to settle; **el portavoz no quiso ~ más datos** the spokesman declined to go into details o to be more specific; **llámame para ~ los detalles** call me to fix o settle the details 2 (= *resumir*) to sum up 3 (*Chi Constr*) to concrete

B VI **concretemos** let's be more specific
C **concretarse** VPR **1** [*ley, prohibición*] to come into force; [*esperanzas*] to be fulfilled; [*sueños*] to come true
2 ~**se en algo**: **un avance de la derecha que se concretó en su triunfo electoral** an advance by the right which resulted in its electoral win; **el proyecto se concretaba en tres objetivos principales** in essence the project had three main objectives

concretizar /1f/ VT = **concretar**

concreto **A** ADJ **1** (= *específico*) [*medida, propuesta*] specific, concrete; [*hecho, resultado*] specific; [*fecha, hora*] definite, particular; **en este caso** ~ in this particular case; **lo importante son los hechos** ~**s** the most important thing is the actual facts
2 (= *no abstracto*) concrete
3 en ~ **3.1** (*con verbos*) **nos referimos, en** ~**, al abuso del alcohol** we are referring specifically to alcohol abuse; **he viajado mucho por Africa, en** ~**, por Kenia y Tanzania** I've travelled a lot in Africa, specifically in Kenya and Tanzania *o* in Kenya and Tanzania to be precise **3.2** (*con sustantivos*) **¿busca algún libro en** ~**?** are you looking for a particular *o* specific book?, are you looking for any book in particular?; **no se ha decidido nada en** ~ nothing definite *o* specific has been decided
B SM (*LAm*) (= *hormigón*) concrete

concubina SF concubine

conculcar /1g/ VT (*gen*) to infringe (on); [+ *ley*] to break, violate

concupiscencia SF **1** (= *lujuria*) lustfulness, concupiscence (*frm*) **2** (= *codicia*) greed, avarice

concupiscente ADJ **1** (= *lujurioso*) lustful, lewd, concupiscent (*frm*) **2** (= *avaro*) greedy, avaricious

concurrencia SF **1** (= *coincidencia*) concurrence; (= *simultaneidad*) simultaneity, coincidence **2** (= *público*) (*Dep*) spectators *pl*; (*Cine, Teat*) audience **3** (= *asistencia*) attendance, turnout; **había una numerosa** ~ there was a big attendance *o* turnout

concurrente **A** ADJ **1** [*suceso*] concurrent **2** (*Com*) competing **B** SMF person present, person attending; **los** ~**s** those present, the audience

concurrido ADJ [*local*] crowded, much frequented; [*calle*] busy, crowded; (*Teat*) popular, well-attended, full (of people)

concurrir /3a/ VI **1** (= *acudir*) ~ **a algo** to attend sth; **diez millones de votantes** ~**án a las urnas** ten million voters will go to the polls
2 (= *participar*) to take part; **todos los partidos que concurren a las elecciones** all parties taking part in the election; **concurre como candidato a la presidencia** he's running as a candidate for the presidency
3 (*frm*) (= *combinarse*) **si concurren las circunstancias siguientes** given *o* in the following circumstances; **en ella concurren las mejores cualidades** she combines the best qualities; **numerosos factores concurren en el éxito de esta empresa** many factors combine to make this company a success; **las circunstancias que concurrieron a la ruina del campo** the circumstances that combined to bring about the demise of the countryside, the circumstances that contributed to the demise of the countryside
4 [*ríos, calles*] to meet, converge

concursante SMF **1** (*para empleo*) candidate **2** (*en juego, concurso*) contestant; (*Dep*) competitor

concursar /1a/ VI **1** (*por empleo*) to compete; **va a** ~ **por la vacante** he is going to apply *o* compete for the vacancy
2 (*en concurso*) to take part

concurso **A** SM **1** (*Com*) tender; **presentar algo a** ~ to open sth up to tender, put sth out to tender
2 (= *competición*) competition, contest; (*TV, Radio*) quiz, game show ➤ **concurso de belleza** beauty contest ➤ **concurso de ideas** (*Arquit*) design competition ➤ **concurso hípico** horse show, show-jumping contest *o* competition
3 (= *examen*) examination, open competition; **ganar un puesto por** ~ to win a post in open competition
➤ **concurso de méritos** *first step in selection process for a post* ➤ **concurso oposición** public competition

4 ➤ **concurso de acreedores** (*Jur*) meeting of creditors
5 (= *coincidencia*) coincidence, concurrence
B ADJ **programa** ~ TV game show

condado SM (= *demarcación territorial*) county; (*Hist*) earldom

conde SM earl, count

condecoración SF (= *acción*) decoration; (= *insignia*) decoration, medal; (= *divisa*) badge

condecorar /1a/ VT to decorate, honour, honor (*EEUU*) (**con** with)

condena SF **1** (= *pronunciamiento*) sentence, conviction; (= *período*) term (of imprisonment); **cumplir una** ~ to serve a sentence **2** (= *desaprobación*) condemnation

condenado/a **A** ADJ **1** (*Jur*) condemned, convicted; (*Rel*) damned
2 (= *destinado*) [*cambio, reforma, ley*] doomed; **la reforma estaba condenada al fracaso** the reform was doomed to failure; ~ **al olvido** destined for oblivion; **instituciones condenadas a desaparecer** institutions doomed to disappear
3 (*) (= *maldito*) damn*, flaming (*Brit**)
B SM/F (*Jur*) prisoner; **el** ~ **a muerte** the condemned man; ✦ MODISMO **trabaja como un** ~ he works like a Trojan
2 (*Rel*) damned soul
3 el ~ **de mi tío*** that wretched *o* damned uncle of mine*

condenar /1a/ VT **1** (= *desaprobar, criticar*) to condemn
2 (*Jur*) to convict, find guilty, sentence; (*a pena capital*) to condemn; ~ **a algn a tres meses de cárcel** to sentence sb to three months in jail, give sb a three-month prison sentence **3** (*Rel*) to damn **4** (*Arquit*) to wall up, block up

condenatorio ADJ condemnatory; **declaración condenatoria** statement of condemnation

condensación SF condensation

condensado ADJ condensed

condensador SM condenser

condensar /1a/ **A** VT to condense **B** **condensarse** VPR to condense, become condensed

condesa SF countess

condescendencia SF **1** (= *deferencia*) obligingness; (= *indulgencia*) affability; **aceptar algo por** ~ to accept sth so as not to hurt feelings **2** (*pey*) **tratar a algn con** ~ to patronize sb

condescender /2g/ VI to acquiesce, comply, agree; ~ **a** to consent to, say yes to; ~ **a los ruegos de algn** to agree to sb's requests; ~ **en hacer algo** to agree to do sth

condescendiente ADJ **1** (= *deferente*) obliging; (= *afable*) affable; (= *conforme*) acquiescent **2** (*pey*) **ser** ~ **con algn** to patronize sb

condición SF **1** (= *requisito*) condition; **lo haré con una** ~ I'll do it on one condition; **las condiciones del contrato** the terms *o* conditions of the contract; **a** ~ **de que ...**
✧ **con la** ~ **de que ...** on condition that ...; ~ **previa** precondition; **entregarse** *o* **rendirse sin condiciones** to surrender unconditionally; ~ **sine qua non** essential condition, sine qua non ➤ **condiciones de pago** terms of payment, payment terms ➤ **condiciones de uso** instructions for use ➤ **condiciones de venta** terms of sale, conditions of sale ➤ **condiciones económicas** [*de contrato*] financial terms; [*de profesional*] fees
2 condiciones **2.1** (= *situación*) conditions; **en condiciones normales** under normal conditions *o* circumstances; **estar en buenas condiciones** [*lugar, máquina*] to be in good condition; [*alimentos*] to be fresh; [*deportista*] to be fit; **estar en condiciones de** *o* **para hacer algo** [*enfermo*] to be well *o* fit enough to do sth; [*deportista*] to be fit (enough) to do sth; **estar en malas condiciones** [*coche, libro, campo de juego*] to be in bad condition; **el queso estaba en malas condiciones** the cheese had gone bad, the cheese was off **2.2 en condiciones** (= *decente*) proper; **no tengo tiempo de echarme una siesta en condiciones** I don't have time for a proper siesta **2.3** (= *cualidades*) **no reúne las condiciones necesarias para este trabajo** he doesn't fulfil the requirements for this job; **el edificio no reúne condiciones para museo** the building is not suitable for use as a

museum ➤ **condiciones de trabajo** working conditions
➤ **condiciones físicas** physical condition *sing*
➤ **condiciones laborales** working conditions
3 (= *naturaleza*) condition; **la ~ humana** the human condition; **tiene muy buena ~** he's very good-natured
4 (= *clase social*) social background
5 (= *posición*) position; **su ~ de artista no lo autoriza a hacer eso** his position as an artist does not allow him to do this; **en su ~ de presidente** in his capacity as president

condicional ADJ (*tb Ling*) conditional

condicionamiento SM conditioning

condicionante Ⓐ ADJ determining Ⓑ SM o SF determining factor, determinant

condicionar /1a/ VT **1** (= *influir*) to condition, determine **2** (= *supeditar*) **~ algo a algo** to make sth conditional on sth

condimentación SF seasoning

condimentar /1a/ VT (*gen*) to flavour, flavor (*EEUU*), season; (*con especias*) to spice

condimento SM (*gen*) seasoning, flavouring, flavoring (*EEUU*); (= *aliño*) dressing

condiscípulo/a SM/F fellow student, fellow pupil

condolencia SF condolence, sympathy

condolerse /2h/ VPR **~ de** o **por** to sympathize with, feel sorry for

condominio SM **1** (*Jur*) joint ownership; (*Pol*) condominium **2** (*LAm*) (= *edificio*) block of flats (*Brit*), condominium (*EEUU*)

condón SM condom

condonación SF **1** [*de pena*] reprieve, remission (*Brit*) **2** [*de deuda*] cancellation

condonar /1a/ VT **1** (*Jur*) **~ una pena** to lift a sentence **2** (*Fin*) [+ *deuda*] to cancel, forgive

cóndor SM condor

conducción SF **1** (*Com*) management; [*de líquidos*] piping; (*por cable*) wiring; (*Fís*) conduction **2** (*Aut*) driving **3** (*Téc*) (= *tubo*) pipe; (= *cable*) cabling ➤ **conducción de agua** water pipe ➤ **conducción principal de gas** gas main

conducente ADJ **~ a** conducive to, leading to

conducir /3n/ Ⓐ VT **1** (*Aut*) to drive
2 (= *llevar*) to take, lead; **este pasillo conduce a los pasajeros al avión** this corridor leads o takes passengers to the plane; **la secretaria nos condujo hasta la salida** the secretary showed us out
3 [+ *electricidad, calor*] to conduct; [+ *agua, gas*] to convey **4** (*frm*) (= *estar a cargo de*) [+ *negocio, empresa*] to manage; [+ *equipo*] to lead; [+ *debate*] to chair, lead
Ⓑ VI **1** (*Aut*) to drive; **si bebes, no conduzcas** don't drink and drive
2 (= *llevar*) **~ a algo** to lead to sth; **esta carretera conduce al aeropuerto** this road leads to the airport, this road takes you to the airport; **¿esa actitud a qué conduce?** where will that attitude get you?

conducta SF conduct, behaviour, behavior (*EEUU*); **mala ~** misconduct, misbehaviour, misbehavior (*EEUU*); **cambiar de ~** to mend one's ways

conductibilidad SF conductivity

conductismo SM behaviourism, behaviorism (*EEUU*)

conductista ADJ, SMF behaviourist, behaviorist (*EEUU*)

conducto SM **1** [*de agua, gas*] pipe, conduit; (*Anat*) duct, canal; (*Elec*) lead, cable ➤ **conducto alimenticio** alimentary canal ➤ **conducto de desagüe** drain
2 (= *medio*) channel; (= *persona*) agent, intermediary; **por ~ de** through, by means of

conductor(a) Ⓐ ADJ (*Fís*) **el agua salada es mejor ~ que el agua dulce** salt water is much more conductive than fresh water; **un material ~ de la electricidad** a material that conducts electricity Ⓑ SM/F **1** [*de coche, camión, autobús*] driver, motorist; [*de moto*] rider; **este impuesto afectará a todos los ~es de vehículos** this tax will affect all motorists **2** (*TV, Radio*) host, presenter (*esp Brit*) Ⓒ SM (*Fís*) conductor; **no ~** non-conductor

conduje *etc ver* **conducir**

conectado ADJ connected; **estar ~** [*aparato*] to be on; [*cable*] to be live; (*Internet*) [*persona*] to be on-line

conectar /1a/ Ⓐ VT **1** [+ *cables, tubos*] to connect (up) **2** (= *enlazar*) **~ algo con algo** to link sth to sth **3** (*LAm*) (= *poner en contacto*) **~ a algn con algn** to put sb in touch with sb
Ⓑ VI **1** (*) (= *congeniar*) **un autor que sabe ~ con el público** an author who knows how to get through to o reach the public; **no hemos logrado ~ con el electorado** we didn't manage to get through to the electorate
2 (= *enlazar*) **este tren conecta con el de Málaga** this train connects (up) with the Malaga train; **la obra conecta con la tradición poética española** the work ties in with Spanish poetic tradition
3 (*TV, Radio*) **conectamos con nuestro corresponsal en Londres** and now it's over to our correspondent in London, and now we're going over to our correspondent in London
Ⓒ **conectarse** VPR (*Inform*) **~se a Internet** to get connected to the Internet

conector SM connector

conejera SF **1** (= *madriguera*) warren, burrow; (= *jaula*) rabbit hutch **2** (**) (= *tasca*) den, dive**

conejillo SM ➤ **conejillo de Indias** guinea pig

conejo SM **1** (*Zool*) rabbit **2** (*Esp***) (= *órgano sexual*) pussy***

conexión SF **1** (= *relación*) connection **2** (*Elec*) connection; **~ a tierra** earth, ground (*EEUU*) **3** (*TV, Radio, Telec*) **tenemos ~ con nuestro corresponsal en Londres** we are going over to our London correspondent; **seguimos en ~ telefónica con el presidente** we still have a telephone link with the president ➤ **conexión en directo** live link-up **4** (*Inform*) interface ➤ **conexión en paralelo** parallel interface **5 conexiones** (= *contactos*) contacts

confabulación SF (= *complot*) plot, conspiracy; (= *intriga*) intrigue

confabularse /1a/ VPR to plot, conspire, scheme

confección SF **1** (= *preparación*) making-up, preparation **2** (*Cos*) dressmaking; **industria de la ~** clothing industry; **traje de ~** ready-to-wear suit

confeccionar /1a/ VT **1** [+ *lista*] to make out, write; [+ *informe*] to prepare, write up **2** (*Cos*) to make (up)

confederación SF confederation

confederado/a ADJ, SM/F confederate

confederarse /1a/ VPR to confederate, form a confederation

conferencia SF **1** (*Pol*) (= *congreso*) conference, meeting ➤ **conferencia de prensa** press conference ➤ **conferencia de ventas** sales conference ➤ **conferencia episcopal** synod **2** (= *charla*) lecture; **dar una ~** to give a lecture **3** (*Esp Telec*) call ➤ **conferencia interurbana** long-distance call **4** (*Inform*) conference, conferencing

conferenciante SMF lecturer

conferenciar /1b/ VI to confer (**con** with), be in conference (**con** with)

conferencista SMF (*LAm*) lecturer

conferir /3i/ (*frm*) VT **1** [+ *premio*] to award (**a** to); [+ *honor*] to confer (**a** on), bestow (**a** on) **2** (= *proporcionar*) to lend, give

confesar /1j/ Ⓐ VT **1** (= *admitir*) [+ *error*] to admit, acknowledge; [+ *crimen*] to confess to, own up to **2** (*Rel*) [+ *pecados*] to confess; [*sacerdote*] to confess, hear the confession of Ⓑ VI (= *admitir*) to confess, own up
Ⓒ **confesarse** VPR (*Rel*) to confess, make one's confession; ✦ MODISMO **¡que Dios nos coja confesados!** God help us!, Lord have mercy!

confesión SF confession

confesional ADJ **1** (= *religioso*) confessional, denominational **2** (= *de la confesión*) confessional

confesionario SM, **confesonario** SM confessional (box)

confeso/a Ⓐ ADJ self-confessed Ⓑ SM/F (*Hist*) converted Jew

confesor SM confessor

confeti SM confetti

confiado ADJ **1** (= *seguro*) confident; **se mostró ~ en que obtendría el puesto** he seemed confident that he would obtain the post; **~ en sí mismo** self-confident **2** (= *ingenuo*) trusting

confianza SF **1** (= *credibilidad*) confidence; **de ~** [*producto*] reliable; **una persona de ~** (= *competente*) a reliable person; (= *honrada*) a trustworthy person; **ganarse la ~ de algn** to win sb's confidence; **dar** o **conceder un margen de ~ a algn** to place one's trust in sb; **poner su ~ en algn** to put o place one's trust in sb; **recuperar la ~ de** o **en algo** to regain one's faith o confidence in sth; **tener ~ en algn** to have faith o confidence in sb
2 (= *seguridad*) confidence; **dar ~ a algn** to give sb confidence, make sb confident; **tener ~ en algo** to be confident of sth; **tienen plena ~ en su victoria** they are fully confident of victory; **tener ~ en que ...** to be confident that ...
3 (= *amistad*) **no te preocupes porque estemos nosotros delante, que hay ~** don't mind us, we're all friends here; **podéis tratarme con toda ~** you can treat me as one of yourselves; **un amigo de ~** a close friend, an intimate friend; **en ~:** (**dicho sea**) **en ~** o **hablando en ~, no me fío nada de él** between you and me, I don't trust him at all; **aquí estamos en ~** we're all friends here; **díselo tú, que tienes más ~ con ella** you tell her, you're closer to her **4 confianzas** (= *libertades*) **se toma demasiadas ~s contigo** he takes too many liberties with you, he's a bit too familiar with you; **¿qué ~s son ésas?** don't be so familiar!

confiar /1c/ Ⓐ VT **~ a algn** [+ *misión, tarea, cuidado, educación*] to entrust sb with; [+ *secreto, preocupaciones*] to confide to sb; [+ *voto*] to give sb; **les ~on la gestión de la publicidad** they were put in charge of publicity; **confíenos sus ahorros** trust your savings to us; **confió a sus hijos al cuidado de sus abuelos** he left his children in the care of their grandparents; **~ algo al azar** to leave sth to fate
Ⓑ VI **~ en algn/algo** to trust sb/sth; **confío plenamente en la justicia** I have complete faith o confidence in justice; **confían en él para que resuelva el problema** they trust him to solve the problem; **~ en que** to hope that; **confiemos en que todo salga bien** let's hope that everything goes well; **confían en que este libro sea un gran éxito** they are confident this book will be a success
Ⓒ **confiarse** VPR **1** (*con excesiva seguridad*) **no te confíes, te queda mucho por estudiar** you shouldn't be so over-confident o sure of yourself, you still have a lot more to study
2 (= *sincerarse*) **~se a algn** to confide in sb

confidencia SF (= *secreto*) confidence, secret; (*a policía*) tip-off; **hacer ~s a algn** to confide in sb, tell sb secrets

confidencial ADJ confidential

confidencialidad SF confidentiality; **en la más estricta ~** in the strictest confidence

confidente/a SM/F **1** (= *amigo*) confidant/confidante, intimate friend **2** (*Jur*) informer

configuración SF **1** (*gen*) shape, configuration; **la ~ del terreno** the lie of the land **2** (*Inform*) configuration

configurar /1a/ VT to shape, form

confín SM **1** (= *límite*) boundary **2** (= *horizonte*) horizon **3 confines** confines, limits

confinamiento SM confinement

confinar /1a/ Ⓐ VT (*Jur*) to confine (**a, en** in); (*Pol*) to banish, exile (**a** to) Ⓑ VI (= *limitar*) **~ con** to border on (*tb fig*) Ⓒ **confinarse** VPR (= *encerrarse*) to shut o.s. away

confirmación SF confirmation (*tb Rel*)

confirmar /1a/ Ⓐ VT **1** [+ *noticia, rumor, temor*] to confirm **2** [+ *vuelo, cita*] to confirm **3** (= *reafirmar*) to confirm; **esta victoria le confirma como el mejor atleta mundial** this win confirms him as the best athlete in the world; **esto me confirma más en mi postura** this makes me more convinced that I'm right **4** (*Rel*) to confirm Ⓑ **confirmarse** VPR **1** (*Rel*) to be confirmed **2** (= *reafirmarse*) **me confirmo en la creencia de que es culpable** I stand by my belief that he is guilty

confiscación SF confiscation

confiscar /1g/ VT to confiscate

confitado ADJ **fruta confitada** crystallized fruit

confitería SF **1** (= *arte*) confectionery **2** (= *tienda*) confectioner's (*frm*), sweet shop (*Brit*), candy store (*EEUU*)

confitero/a SM/F confectioner

confitura SF (= *mermelada*) preserve, jam (*Brit*), jelly (*EEUU*); (= *fruta escarchada*) crystallized fruit

conflagración SF **1** (= *perturbación*) flare-up, outbreak **2** (= *incendio*) conflagration

conflictividad SF **1** (= *tensiones*) tensions and disputes *pl*; **la ~ laboral** industrial disputes, labour o (*EEUU*) labor troubles **2** (= *cualidad*) controversial nature

conflictivo ADJ [*sociedad*] troubled; [*asunto*] controversial; [*sistema*] unstable; [*situación*] tense, troubled; **la edad conflictiva** the age of conflict; **punto ~** point at issue; **zona conflictiva** troubled region, trouble spot

conflicto SM **1** (= *enfrentamiento*) conflict; **las partes en ~** (*Pol*) the warring parties o factions; (*Jur*) the parties in dispute; **entrar en ~ con algo/algn** to come into conflict with sth/sb ➤ **conflicto armado** armed conflict ➤ **conflicto bélico** military conflict ➤ **conflicto de intereses** conflict of interests, clash of interests ➤ **conflicto laboral** labour dispute, labor dispute (*EEUU*) **2** (*Psic*) conflict

confluencia SF confluence

confluir /3g/ VI **1** [*ríos*] to meet, come together **2** [*gente*] to gather

conformar /1a/ Ⓐ VT **1** (= *dar forma a*) [+ *proyecto, educación, escultura*] to shape
2 (= *constituir*) to make up; **un universo conformado por millones de estrellas** a universe composed of o made up of millions of stars
3 (= *adaptar*) **trataba de ~ su vida a ese ideal** he tried to make his life conform to that ideal, he tried to shape his life around that ideal
4 [+ *persona*] to keep happy
5 [+ *cheque, talón*] to authorize, endorse
Ⓑ **conformarse** VPR **1** (= *estar satisfecho*) **~se con algo** to be happy with sth; **no se conforma con nada** he's never happy o satisfied; **tuvo que ~se con la medalla de plata** she had to settle for the silver medal, she had to be satisfied with the silver medal; **no hay que ~se con pensar, hay que actuar** thinking is not enough, we have to act
2 ~se con [+ *reglas, política*] to comply with

conforme Ⓐ ADJ **1** (= *satisfecho*) **¿conforme?** (are we) agreed?; **¡conforme!** agreed!, all right!; **he revisado el contrato, está todo ~** I've gone over the contract, everything is in order; **estar ~ con algo/algn** to be happy o satisfied with sth/sb; **no se quedó ~ con la propina** he wasn't happy o satisfied with the tip; **estar ~ en que** to agree that
2 ~ con (= *correspondiente a*) consistent with
3 ~ a (= *según*) according to; **todo marcha ~ a lo previsto** everything is going according to plan
Ⓑ CONJ **1** (= *como*) as; **todo quedó ~ estaba** everything remained as it was
2 (= *a medida que*) as; **~ entraban, se iban sentando** as they came in, they sat down; **~ subes la calle, a mano derecha** on the right as you go up the street
Ⓒ SM (= *aprobación*) approval, authorization; **dar** o **poner el ~** to authorize

conformidad SF **1** (= *acuerdo*) agreement
2 (= *consentimiento*) consent; **hasta que no dé su ~** until he gives his consent **3** (*frm*) (= *resignación*) resignation, forbearance **4 de** o **en ~ con algo** (*frm*) in accordance with sth (*frm*)

conformismo SM conformism, conventionality

conformista ADJ, SMF conformist

confort [kon'for(t)] SM (*pl* ~s [kon'for(t)s]) comfort; **"todo confort"** "all mod cons" (*Brit**), "every comfort" (*EEUU*)

confortable Ⓐ ADJ comfortable Ⓑ SM (*And*) sofa

confortar /1a/ VT **1** (= *consolar*) to comfort **2** (*Med*) to soothe

confraternizar /1f/ VI to fraternize (**con** with)

confrontación SF confrontation

confrontar /1a/ Ⓐ VT **1** [+ *peligro*] to confront, face, face up to **2** (= *carear*) to bring face to face; **~ a algn con otro** to confront sb with sb else **3** [+ *textos*] to compare, collate Ⓑ **confrontarse** VPR **~se con** to confront, face up to

confundido ADJ **1** (= *equivocado*) **puede que esté ~, pero creo que te he visto antes** I could be mistaken *o* wrong, but I think I've seen you before **2** (= *confuso*) confused

confundir /3a/ Ⓐ VT **1** (= *equivocar*) to confuse; **no confundamos las cosas, por favor** let's not confuse things, please; **siempre os confundo por teléfono** I always get you mixed up on the phone; **~ algo/a algn con algo/algn** to get sth/sb mixed up with sth/sb, mistake sth/sb for sth/sb
2 (= *mezclar*) [+ *papeles*] to mix up
3 (= *desconcertar*) to confuse; **me confunde con tanta palabrería** he confuses me *o* I am confused with all that talk of his, I find all that talk of his confusing
Ⓑ **confundirse** VPR **1** (= *equivocarse*) to make a mistake; **lo siento, se ha confundido de número** I'm sorry, you have the wrong number; **se confundió en un cero al hacer la multiplicación** he got a zero wrong *o* he made a mistake over a zero when doing the multiplication
2 (= *mezclarse*) **~se con algo**: **el mar se confundía con el cielo** the sea blended with the sky; **los policías se confundían con los manifestantes** the police mingled with the demonstrators

confusión SF **1** (= *equivocación*) confusion; **para evitar confusiones** to avoid confusion; **esta carta no es para mí, debe de tratarse de una ~** this letter is not for me, there must be some mistake; **por ~** by mistake **2** (= *desconcierto*) confusion

confuso ADJ **1** (= *poco claro*) [*ideas, noticias*] confused; [*recuerdo*] hazy; [*ruido*] indistinct; [*imagen*] blurred; **llegaban noticias confusas** confused reports were coming in; **una situación muy confusa** a very confused situation **2** (= *desconcertado*) confused

conga SF conga

congelación SF **1** [*de alimentos, líquidos*] freezing **2** (*Med*) frostbite **3** (*Fin*) freeze, freezing ➤ **congelación de salarios** wage freeze **4** ➤ **congelación de imagen** [*de vídeo*] freeze-frame

congelado ADJ frozen, chilled; **¡estoy ~!** I'm frozen *o* freezing!

congelador SM freezer, deep freeze

congelar /1a/ Ⓐ VT **1** [+ *carne, líquido*] to freeze **2** (*Med*) to affect with frostbite, block; [+ *proceso*] to suspend, freeze **4** [+ *imagen de vídeo*] to freeze
Ⓑ **congelarse** VPR **1** [*carne, líquido*] to freeze **2** (*Med*) to get frostbitten

congénere SM fellow, person *etc* of the same sort; **el criminal y sus ~s** the criminal and others like him

congeniar /1b/ VI to get on (**con** with)

congénito ADJ congenital

congestión SF congestion

congestionado ADJ **1** [*circulación*] congested **2** (*Med*) [*pecho, pulmones, nariz*] congested; **tener el pecho ~** to be congested, be chesty (*Brit*)

congestionar /1a/ Ⓐ VT to congest, produce congestion in Ⓑ **congestionarse** VPR to become congested

conglomerado SM **1** (*Geol, Téc*) conglomerate **2** (= *aglomeración*) conglomeration

conglomerar /1a/ VT, **conglomerarse** VPR to conglomerate

Congo SM **el ~** the Congo; ✦ MODISMO **¡vete al ~!**✱✱ get lost!✱✱

congoja SF anguish, distress

congoleño/a ADJ, SM/F Congolese

congraciarse /1b/ VPR to ingratiate o.s. (**con** with)

congratular /1a/ Ⓐ VT to congratulate (**por** on) Ⓑ **congratularse** VPR to congratulate o.s., be pleased; **de eso nos congratulamos** we are glad about that

congregación SF **1** (= *asamblea*) gathering, assembly; (= *sociedad*) brotherhood, guild **2** (*Rel*) congregation

congregar /1h/ Ⓐ VT to bring together Ⓑ **congregarse** VPR to gather, congregate

congresal SMF (*SAm*) = **congresista**

congresista SMF delegate, member, member (*of a conference*)

congreso SM **1** (*científico, profesional, político*) conference ➤ **congreso anual** annual conference **2** (*Pol*) **Congreso** (*en Reino Unido*) ≈ Parliament; (*en EEUU*) ≈ Congress ➤ **Congreso de los Diputados** (*Esp Pol*) ≈ House of Commons (*Brit*), ≈ House of Representatives (*EEUU*); ➪ *CORTES GENERALES*

congrio SM conger, conger eel

congruencia SF **1** (*Mat*) congruence **2** (= *coherencia*) suitability

congruente ADJ, **congruo** ADJ **1** (*Mat*) congruent, congruous (**con** with) **2** (= *coherente*) suitable

cónico ADJ [*forma*] conical; [*sección*] conic

conífera SF conifer

conífero ADJ coniferous

conjetura SF conjecture, surmise; **son meras ~s** it's just guesswork

conjeturar /1a/ VT to guess, guess at, surmise (**de, por** from)

conjugación SF conjugation

conjugar /1h/ Ⓐ VT **1** (*Ling*) to conjugate **2** (= *reunir*) to combine Ⓑ **conjugarse** VPR **1** (*Ling*) to be conjugated **2** (= *unirse*) to fit together, blend

conjunción SF conjunction

conjuntado ADJ **1** (= *coordinado*) coordinated **2** (= *unido*) united, combined

conjuntamente ADV jointly, together; **~ con** together with

conjuntar /1a/ Ⓐ VT **1** (= *coordinar*) to coordinate **2** (= *unir*) to unite, combine Ⓑ VI **~ con** to go with, match

conjuntivitis SF INV conjunctivitis

conjunto Ⓐ ADJ joint, combined Ⓑ SM **1** (= *totalidad*) whole; **en ~** as a whole, altogether; **en su ~** in its entirety ➤ **conjunto monumental** *collection of historic buildings* **2** (= *ropa*) ensemble; **un ~ de falda y blusa** a matching skirt and blouse **3** (*Mús*) [*de cámara*] ensemble; (*pop*) group **4** (*Teat*) chorus **5** (*Dep*) (= *equipo*) team **6** [*de muebles*] suite ➤ **conjunto de baño** bathroom suite **7** (*Mat, Inform*) set

conjura SF, **conjuración** SF plot, conspiracy

conjurar /1a/ Ⓐ VT **1** (*Rel*) to exorcise, cast out **2** [+ *peligro*] to ward off; [+ *pensamiento*] to rid o.s. of Ⓑ **conjurarse** VPR to get together in a plot, plot together, conspire together

conjuro SM (*Rel*) exorcism; (= *hechizo*) spell

conllevar /1a/ VT **1** [+ *sentido*] to convey, carry **2** (= *implicar*) to imply, involve

conmemoración SF commemoration

conmemorar /1a/ VT to commemorate

conmemorativo ADJ commemorative

conmigo PRON with me; **¿por qué no vienes ~?** why don't you come with me?; **se portó muy bien ~** he was very good to me; **atento ~** kind to *o* towards me; **no estoy satisfecho ~ mismo** I'm not proud of myself

conminar /1a/ VT (= *amenazar*) to threaten (**con** with)

conmoción SF **1** (*Geol*) shock, tremor **2** (*Med*) ➤ **conmoción cerebral** concussion

conmocionar /1a/ VT **1** (= *conmover*) to move, affect deeply **2** (= *turbar*) to shake profoundly, cause an upheaval in **3** (*Med*) to put into shock, concuss

conmovedor ADJ moving, touching, poignant

conmover /2h/ **Ⓐ** VT **1** (*Geol*) to shake **2** (= *enternecer*) to move, touch **3** (= *turbar*) to upset **Ⓑ conmoverse** VPR **1** (*Geol*) to shake, be shaken **2** (= *enternecerse*) to be moved *o* be touched

conmutación SF **1** [*de pago, pena*] commutation **2** (*Inform*) switching

conmutador SM **1** (*Elec*) switch **2** (*LAm Telec*) switchboard

conmutar /1a/ VT **1** (= *trocar*) to exchange (**con, por** for); (= *transformar*) to convert (**en** into) **2** (*Jur*) to commute (**en, por** to)

connatural ADJ innate, inherent (**a** in)

connivencia SF connivance; **estar en ~ con** to be in collusion with

connotación SF **1** (= *sentido*) connotation **2** (= *parentesco*) distant relationship

connotado ADJ (*SAm*) (= *destacado*) outstanding; (= *famoso*) famous, renowned

connotar /1a/ VT to connote

cono SM cone

conocedor(a) **Ⓐ** ADJ expert (**de** in), knowledgeable (**de** about) **Ⓑ** SM/F expert (**de** in), connoisseur (**de** of)

conocer /2d/ **Ⓐ** VT **1** [+ *persona*] **1.1** (= *saber quién es*) to know; **¿de qué lo conoces?** where do you know him from?; **¿conoces a Pedro?** have you met Pedro?, do you know Pedro?; **la conozco de oídas** I've heard of her, I know of her; **lo conozco de vista** I know him by sight **1.2** (= *ver por primera vez*) to meet; **la conocí en Sevilla** I met her in Seville **1.3** (= *saber cómo es*) to get to know; **cuando la conozcas mejor** when you get to know her better; **✦** MODISMO **la conozco como la palma de la mano** I know her like the back of my hand **1.4** (= *reconocer*) to recognize, know

2 (= *tener conocimiento de*) [+ *método, resultado*] to know; [+ *noticia*] to hear; **queremos ~ de cerca la situación** we want to get to know the situation at first hand; **investigaciones destinadas a ~ la verdad** investigations aimed at establishing the truth; **✦** REFRÁN **más vale lo malo conocido que lo bueno por ~** better the devil you know than the devil you don't

3 [+ *país, ciudad*] **no conozco Buenos Aires** I've never been to Buenos Aires, I don't know Buenos Aires; **quiero ~ mundo** I want to see the world

4 (= *dominar*) to know; **conoce su oficio** he knows his job; **no conozco mucho el tema** I don't know much about the subject

5 (= *experimentar*) **ha conocido dos guerras mundiales** she has lived through two world wars; **los muchos terremotos que ha conocido Italia** the many earthquakes there have been in Italy

6 (= *distinguir*) to know, tell

7 dar a ~ [+ *información*] to announce; [+ *declaración, informe, cifras*] to release; **se dio a ~ en una película de Almodóvar** he made his name in an Almodóvar film (*esp Brit*) *o* movie (*esp EEUU*); **darse a ~ a algn** to make o.s. known to sb

8 (*Jur*) [+ *causa*] to try

Ⓑ VI **1** (= *saber*) **~ de algo: ¿alguien conoce de algún libro sobre el tema?** does anybody know (of) a book on the subject?

2 (*Jur*) **~ de** *o* **en una causa** to try a case

Ⓒ conocerse VPR **1** (*uso reflexivo*) **~se a sí mismo** to know o.s.

2 (*uso recíproco*) **2.1** (= *tener relación con*) to know each other, know one another **2.2** (*por primera vez*) to meet **2.3** (= *familiarizarse*) to get to know each other, get to know one another

3 (= *reconocerse*) [*uno mismo*] to recognize o.s.; [*dos personas*] to recognize each other

4 (*uso impersonal*) **se conoce que ...** apparently ..., it seems that ...; **se conoce que se lo han contado** apparently he's been told about it, it seems that he's been told about it; **se conoce que no le ha sentado bien**

he's obviously not best pleased

> **Conocer** suele traducirse por *to know*: "No conozco muy bien a su familia", *I don't know his family very well*. Pero cuando se refiere al primer encuentro con alguien, se utiliza *to meet*: "La conocí en una fiesta", *I met her at a party*.

conocido/a **Ⓐ** ADJ **1** (= *público*) [*dato*] known; [*persona*] well-known; **más ~ por Michel** better known as Michel **2** (= *familiar*) familiar; **su cara me es conocida** I recognize his face, his face is familiar **Ⓑ** SM/F acquaintance

conocimiento SM **1** (= *saber*) knowledge; **tengo algunos ~s musicales** I have some knowledge of music **2** (= *información*) knowledge; **el encuentro tuvo lugar sin ~ público** the meeting took place without the public's knowledge; **dimos ~ del robo a la policía** we informed the police about the robbery; **no teníamos ~ del accidente** we weren't aware of the accident; **desea ponerlo en ~ público** he wants it brought to the public's attention, he wishes it to be made public **➤ conocimiento de causa: hacer algo con ~ de causa** to be fully aware of what one is doing; **hablar con ~ de causa** to know what one is talking about **3** (= *consciencia*) consciousness; **perder el ~** to lose consciousness; **recobrar** *o* **recuperar el ~** to regain consciousness

4 (= *sentido común*) common sense

Cono Sur SM (*Pol*) Argentina, Chile and Uruguay, Southern Cone

conozca *etc ver* **conocer**

conque* CONJ so, so then; **¿~ te pillaron?** so they caught you then?

conquense ADJ of/from Cuenca

conquista SF **1** [*de lugar, persona*] conquest **2** (*SAm Dep*) goal

conquistador(a) **Ⓐ** ADJ conquering **Ⓑ** SM/F conqueror **Ⓒ** SM (*Hist*) conquistador

conquistar /1a/ VT **1** (*Mil*) to conquer (**a** from) **2** [+ *puesto, simpatía*] to win; [+ *adversario*] to win round, win over; (= *enamorar*) to win the heart of **3** (*SAm*) [+ *gol*] to score

consabido ADJ **1** (= *conocido*) well-known; [*frase*] old, oft-repeated **2** (= *susodicho*) above-mentioned

consagración SF **1** (*Rel*) consecration, dedication **2** [*de costumbre*] establishment

consagrado ADJ **1** (*Rel*) consecrated (**a** to), dedicated (**a** to) **2** (= *tradicional*) hallowed, traditional; **un actor ~** an established actor

consagrar /1a/ **Ⓐ** VT **1** (*Rel*) to consecrate, dedicate (**a** to); [+ *emperador*] to deify **2** [+ *esfuerzo, tiempo, vida*] to devote, dedicate (**a** to) **3** [+ *fama*] to confirm **Ⓑ consagrarse** VPR **1** (*por fama*) to establish o.s. **2 ~se a** to devote o.s. to

consanguíneo ADJ related by blood, consanguineous (*frm*)

consciencia SF = **conciencia**

consciente **Ⓐ** ADJ **1 ser** *o* (*Méx, Chi*) **estar ~ de algo** to be conscious *o* aware of sth **2** (*Med*) **estar ~** to be conscious **3** (*Jur*) fully responsible **Ⓑ** SM conscious, conscious mind

conscripción SF (*esp LAm*) conscription, draft (*EEUU*)

conscripto SM (*esp LAm*) conscript, draftee (*EEUU*)

consecuencia SF **1** (= *resultado*) consequence; **esto es ~ de una mala gestión** this is the consequence *o* result of bad management; **a ~ de algo** as a result of sth; **atenerse a las ~s** to take *o* accept the consequences; **como ~** as a result, in consequence (*frm*); **ha muerto como ~ del frío** it died from *o* as a result of the cold; **esto tuvo** *o* **trajo como ~ el aumento del paro** this led to *o* resulted in an increase in unemployment; **en ~** (*frm*) consequently; **tener ~s: tuvo graves ~s para la economía** it had serious consequences for the economy; **el accidente no tuvo ~s graves** the accident was not serious; **llevar algo hasta sus últimas ~s** to take sth to its logical conclusion **➤ consecuencia directa** direct consequence, direct result

2 (= *conclusión*) conclusion; **sacar ~s de algo** to draw

conclusions from sth ➤ **consecuencia lógica** logical conclusion
3 (= *coherencia*) **actuar** *u* **obrar en ~** to act accordingly
consecuente ADJ **1** (= *coherente*) consistent (**con** with) **2** (*Fil*) consequent
consecutivo ADJ consecutive
conseguido ADJ successful
conseguir /3d, 3k/ VT [+ *meta, objetivo*] to achieve; [+ *resultado*] to obtain, achieve; [+ *premio, campeonato*] to win; [+ *entradas, empleo, dinero*] to get; [+ *documento, visado, beca, permiso*] to get, obtain; [+ *acuerdo*] to reach; **siempre consigue lo que se propone** he always achieves what he sets out to do; **consiguieron la victoria por tres mil votos** they won by three thousand votes; **~ hacer algo** to manage to do sth; **~ que algn haga algo** to get sb to do sth
consejería SF **1** (*Esp Pol*) ministry in a regional government **2** (= *concejo*) council, commission
consejero/a SM/F **1** (= *asesor*) adviser **2** (*Téc*) consultant; (*Com*) director; (*en comisión*) member of a board *etc* ➤ **consejero/a delegado** managing director (*Brit*), chief executive officer (*EEUU*) **3** (*Esp*) [*de autonomía*] minister in a regional government
consejo SM **1** (= *sugerencia*) advice

Advice es incontable y lleva el verbo en singular:

los ~s que me diste me han servido de mucho the advice you gave me has been very useful; **pedir ~ a algn** to ask sb for advice, ask sb's advice

Para decir **un consejo** puede utilizarse **a piece of advice, a bit of advice**, o **some advice**:

¿quieres que te dé un ~? would you like me to give you a piece of advice *o* a bit of advice *o* some advice?
2 (= *organismo*) (*Pol*) council; (*Com*) board; (*Jur*) tribunal ➤ **consejo de administración** board of directors ➤ **Consejo de Europa** Council of Europe ➤ **consejo de guerra** court-martial ➤ **consejo de ministros** (= *entidad*) cabinet; (= *reunión*) cabinet meeting ➤ **consejo de redacción** editorial board ➤ **Consejo de Seguridad** Security Council
consenso SM consensus
consensuado ADJ [*texto*] agreed; **llegaron a un acuerdo ~** they achieved a consensus; **es una solución consensuada** it's a solution that has been reached by consensus
consensual ADJ agreed; **unión ~** common-law marriage
consensuar /1e/ VT to agree on, reach an agreement on, reach a consensus on
consentido/a ❹ ADJ **1** (= *mimado*) spoiled, spoilt **2** [*marido*] complaisant ❺ SM/F **es una consentida** she's totally spoiled
consentimiento SM consent
consentir /3i/ ❹ VT **1** (= *permitir*) to allow; (= *tolerar*) to tolerate; **¡eso no se puede ~!** we can't have *o* allow that!; **no te consiento que vayas** I can't allow you to go **2** (= *soportar*) to stand, bear **3** (= *mimar*) to spoil ❺ VI to agree, consent, say yes; **~ en hacer algo** to agree to do sth
conserje SMF [*de facultad*] head porter (*Brit*), head custodian (*EEUU*); [*de colegio*] janitor; [*de hotel*] doorman, hall porter (*Brit*); [*de edificio oficial, museo*] janitor, caretaker (*Brit*)
conserjería SF porter's lodge *o* office (*Brit*), custodian's office *o* room (*EEUU*)
conserva SF **1** (= *proceso*) preserving **2** (*Culin*) (= *alimentos*) preserve, preserves *pl*; **atún en ~** tinned (*Brit*) *o* canned (*EEUU*) tuna
conservación SF **1** [*del medio ambiente*] conservation; **instinto de ~** instinct of self-preservation **2** (*Culin*) preservation
conservacionismo SM conservationism
conservacionista ❹ ADJ conservationist, conservation *antes de s* ❺ SMF conservationist

conservado ADJ **estar muy bien ~** [*persona*] to look very well for one's age, be very well-preserved (*hum*); [*mueble*] to be in very good condition (*frm*)
conservador(a) ❹ ADJ (*Pol*) conservative ❺ SM/F **1** (*Pol*) conservative **2** [*de museo*] curator
conservadurismo SM conservatism
conservante SM preservative
conservar /1a/ ❹ VT **1** (= *mantener*) [+ *calor*] to retain, conserve; [+ *tradición, costumbre*] to preserve; **el frío conserva los alimentos** the cold preserves food; **todavía conservo las amistades del colegio** I still keep up the friendships I had at school; **un producto para ~ la piel tersa** a product to keep the skin smooth; **conservaba un aspecto juvenil** she still looked youthful; **ante todo hay que ~ la calma** above all we must keep calm **2** (= *guardar*) [+ *secreto*] to keep; **conservo todas mis fotografías en un baúl** I keep all my photographs in a chest; **el museo conserva los mejores cuadros del pintor** the museum has *o* houses the artist's best paintings; **consérvese en lugar fresco y seco** store in a cool dry place **3** (*Culin*) (= *poner en conserva*) to preserve ❺ **conservarse** VPR **1** [*tradición, costumbre, ruinas*] to survive; **los alimentos se conservan mejor en la nevera** food keeps better in a refrigerator **2** [*persona*] **¡qué bien se conserva!** he looks very well for his age!, he's very well-preserved (*hum*); **se conserva muy joven para su edad** she keeps herself looking young
conservatorio SM conservatoire, conservatory
conservero ADJ [+ *industria*] canning *antes de s*
considerable ADJ considerable
consideración SF **1** (= *deliberación*) consideration; **en ~** under consideration; **someter algo a la ~ de algn** to put sth to sb for consideration; **tener** *o* **tomar algo en ~** to take sth into consideration **2** (= *punto a considerar*) **aquí pueden hacerse algunas consideraciones** a few points can be made here; **sin querer entrar en consideraciones acerca de su propia actuación** without entering into a discussion of his actual performance **3** (= *concepción*) conception **4** (= *importancia*) status; **de ~** [*herida, daños*] serious; **daños de poca ~** minor damage; **sufrió quemaduras de diversa ~** he suffered burns of varying degrees of seriousness **5** (= *atención*) consideration; **¡qué falta de ~!** how inconsiderate!; **en ~ a algo/algn** out of consideration for sth/sb; **sin ~: tratar a algn sin ~** to show no consideration for sb; **no tuvieron ninguna ~ con las víctimas** they showed no consideration for the victims **6** (= *estima*) regard **7** (*en cartas*) **le saludo con mi más distinguida ~** (*frm*) I remain yours faithfully (*Brit frm*), Respectfully (yours) (*EEUU*)
considerado ADJ **1** (= *atento*) considerate **2** (= *estimado*) **el robo está ~ un delito** robbery is regarded as *o* considered a crime; **estar bien ~** to be highly regarded; **estar mal ~** (= *no aceptado*) to be frowned upon; (= *menospreciado*) to be undervalued
considerar /1a/ ❹ VT **1** (= *reflexionar sobre*) to consider **2** (= *tener en cuenta*) **considerando lo que cuesta, la calidad podría ser mejor** considering what it costs, the quality could be better; **considera que ésta puede ser tu última oportunidad** bear in mind that this could be your last chance **3** (= *creer*) **~ algo/a algn (como)** (+ ADJ) to consider sth/sb to be + *adj*; **se le considera como uno de los grandes pintores de este siglo** he is considered (to be) *o* regarded as one of the great painters of this century; **lo considero hijo mío** I look on him *o* regard him as my own son; **~ que** to believe that, consider that **4** (*Jur*) **considerando ...** whereas ... (*word with which each item in a judgement begins*) ❺ **considerarse** VPR to consider o.s.
consigna SF **1** (= *orden*) order; **seguir** *o* **cumplir las ~s del gobierno** to follow government orders **2** [*de equipaje*] left-luggage office (*Brit*), checkroom (*EEUU*) ➤ **consigna automática** locker, left-luggage locker (*Brit*)
consignación SF **1** (*Com*) consignment, shipment **2** (*Fin*)

allocation 3 (Col) (en banco) deposit

consignar /1a/ VT **1** (Com) to send, dispatch (**a** to) **2** (Fin) (= asignar) to assign (**para** to, for) **3** (= registrar) to record, register; **el hecho no quedó consignado en ningún libro** the fact was not recorded o set down in any book **4** (Col) [+ cheque, efectivo] to deposit

consignatario/a SM/F **1** (Com) consignee; (Náut) broker, agent **2** (Jur) trustee **3** [de carta] recipient, addressee

consigo[1] ver **conseguir**

consigo[2] PRON **1** (= con él) with him; (= con ella) with her; (= con uno mismo) with you, with one; (= con usted) with you; (= con ellas, ellos) with them; **siempre lleva ~ un paraguas** he always carries an umbrella with him; **la separación llevó o trajo ~ terribles consecuencias** the separation had terrible consequences; ✦ MODISMO **no tenerlas todas ~: lo preparó todo bien y aun así no las tenía todas ~** he prepared it all well enough but he still wasn't quite sure about it **2 ~ mismo** with himself; **estaba contento ~ mismo** he was pleased with himself; **hablaba ~ misma** she was talking to herself

consiguiente ADJ **por ~** consequently, therefore

consistencia SF consistence, consistency

consistente ADJ **1** [material] (= sólido) solid, firm, tough; (= espeso) thick **2** [argumento] sound, valid **3 ~ en** consisting of

consistir /3a/ VI **1 ~ en** (= componerse de) to consist of **2 ~ en** (= ser): **su atractivo consiste en su timidez** her shyness is what makes her attractive; **el secreto consiste en añadir un poco de vino** the secret lies in adding a little wine; **¿en qué consiste el trabajo?** what does the job involve o entail?

consistorial ADJ **1** (Rel) consistorial **2 casa ~** town hall

consistorio SM **1** (Rel) consistory **2** (Pol) town council; (= edificio) town hall

consola SF **1** (= mesa) console table **2** (Inform, Mús) console ➤ **consola de videojuegos** games console

consolación SF consolation

consolador Ⓐ ADJ consoling, comforting Ⓑ SM dildo

consolar /1l/ Ⓐ VT to console, comfort Ⓑ **consolarse** VPR to console o.s. (**por** about)

consolidación SF consolidation

consolidar /1a/ Ⓐ VT **1** (= afianzar) to consolidate, strengthen **2** (Arquit) to shore up **3** (Fin) to fund Ⓑ **consolidarse** VPR to strengthen

consomé SM consommé, clear soup

consonancia SF **1** (= conformidad) **en ~ con** in accordance o harmony with **2** (Mús) harmony, consonance (frm)

consonante SF consonant

consonántico ADJ consonantal

consorcio SM **1** (Com) consortium, syndicate **2** (= unión) relationship **3** [de circunstancias] conjunction

consorte SMF **1** (= esposo/a) consort, spouse; **príncipe ~** prince consort **2 consortes** (Jur) accomplices

conspicuo ADJ eminent, famous

conspiración SF conspiracy

conspirar /1a/ VI to conspire, plot (**con** with; **contra** against)

constancia SF **1** (= perseverancia) perseverance **2** (= evidencia) **no existe ~ de ello** there is no record of it; **tengo ~ de que todo es cierto** I have proof that it is all true **3** (LAm) (= comprobante) documentary proof, written evidence

constante Ⓐ ADJ **1** (= continuado) constant **2** (= frecuente) constant **3** (= perseverante) [persona] persevering **4** (Fís) [velocidad, temperatura, presión] constant Ⓑ SF **1** (= factor predominante) **el mar es una ~ en su obra** the sea is a constant theme o an ever-present theme in his work **2** (Mat) constant **3** (Med) ➤ **constantes vitales** vital signs

constar /1a/ VI **1** (= ser evidente) **me consta que ...** I have evidence that ...

2 (= aparecer, figurar) **~ (en)** to appear (in), be given (in o

on); **en el carnet no consta su edad** his age is not stated on the licence o (EEUU) license; **y para que así conste ...** and for the record ...; **hacer ~** to put on record **3 que conste: que conste que yo no di mi aprobación** let it be clearly understood that I did not approve; **que conste que lo hice por ti** believe me, I did it for your own good **4** (= componerse) **~ de** to consist of, be composed of

constatación SF confirmation, verification

constatar /1a/ VT **1** (= confirmar) **estos datos constatan la existencia de vida en el planeta** this data proves the existence of life on the planet; **pude ~ que era verdad** I was able to establish that it was true **2** (= afirmar) to state

constelación SF constellation

consternación SF consternation, dismay

consternar /1a/ Ⓐ VT to dismay Ⓑ **consternarse** VPR to be dismayed (**con** by)

constipado Ⓐ ADJ **1** (= con resfriado) **estar ~** to have a cold **2** (LAm) (= estreñido) constipated Ⓑ SM (Med) cold; **coger un ~** to catch a cold

constiparse /1a/ VPR to catch a cold

constitución SF **1** (= creación) setting up **2** (= composición) **a causa de la nueva ~ del gobierno** because of the make-up of the new cabinet; **la ~ del equipo** the line-up **3** (= complexión) constitution **4** (Pol) constitution; **la Constitución** the Constitution

constitucional ADJ constitutional

constitucionalidad SF constitutionality

constituir /3g/ Ⓐ VT (frm) **1** (= crear, fundar) [+ comité, asamblea] to set up, constitute (frm); [+ empresa] to set up **2** (= estar formado por) to make up, constitute **3** (= representar) to constitute (frm); **la pesca constituye la principal riqueza de la región** fishing represents o (frm) constitutes the region's main source of wealth; **para mí constituye un gran honor** this represents a great honour for me; **los Beatles pronto llegaron a ~ una leyenda** the Beatles soon became a legend **4** (= nombrar) **~ a algn en árbitro** to appoint sb as arbitrator Ⓑ **constituirse** VPR **1** (= formarse) [sociedad, empresa] to be set up; [estado] to be constituted **2** (= convertirse) to become; **se han constituido en una amenaza para el proceso de paz** they have become a threat to the peace process; **el país tiene derecho a ~se en estado independiente** the country has the right to constitute itself as o to become an independent state

constitutivo Ⓐ ADJ constituent; **ser ~ de delito** to constitute a crime Ⓑ SM constituent element

constituyente Ⓐ ADJ **1** [asamblea, congreso] constituent **2** [elemento, sintagma] constituent Ⓑ SM **1** (= elemento) constituent **2** (Pol) constituent member

constreñir /3h, 3k/ VT **1** (= limitar) to restrict **2** (= obligar) **~ a algn a hacer algo** to compel o force o (frm) constrain sb to do sth **3** (Med) to constrict

construcción SF **1** (= acción) construction, building; **en (vía de) ~** under construction; **"página en construcción"** (Internet) "(page) under construction" **2** (= sector laboral) construction industry **3** (= estructura) structure **4** (Ling) construction

constructivismo SM constructivism

constructivista ADJ, SMF constructivist

constructivo ADJ constructive

constructor(a) Ⓐ ADJ building, construction antes de s Ⓑ SM/F builder ➤ **constructor(a) naval** shipbuilder

constructora SF (tb **empresa ~**) construction company

construir /3g/ VT **1** [+ barco, carretera, hospital] to build **2** (Ling, Geom) to construct; **este verbo se construye con "en"** this verb takes "en"

consuegro/a SM/F father-in-law/mother-in-law of one's son/daughter

consuelo SM solace, comfort

consuetudinario ADJ **1** (= usual) habitual, customary **2 derecho ~** common law

cónsul SMF consul

consulado SM (= *cargo*) consulship; (= *sede*) consulate

consular ADJ consular

consulta SF **1** (= *pregunta*) enquiry; **hice una ~ telefónica al banco** I telephoned the bank to make an enquiry; **¿le puedo hacer una ~?** can I ask you something? ➤ **consulta de saldo** statement request **2** (*Med*) (= *visita*) consultation; (= *oficina*) surgery (*Brit*), consulting room (*Brit*), office (*EEUU*); **horas de ~** *u* **horario de ~** surgery hours (*Brit*), office hours (*EEUU*) **3** (*Pol*) (= *referéndum*) referendum ➤ **consulta popular** referendum, plebiscite

consultar /1a/ **Ⓐ** VT **1** (= *pedir opinión*) to consult; **es mejor que consultes a un médico** you'd better go to *o* see a doctor; **lo ~é con mi abogado** I'll discuss it with my lawyer; ✦ MODISMO **~ algo con la almohada** to sleep on sth **2** [+ *diccionario, libro, base de datos, archivo*] to consult; **consulta la palabra en el diccionario** look the word up in the dictionary; **consulté el saldo de mi cuenta** I checked my account balance
Ⓑ VI **~ con algn: no lo haré sin ~ antes contigo** I won't do it without discussing it with you first

consultivo ADJ consultative

consultor(a) SM/F consultant

consultora SF, **consultoría** SF consultancy (firm)

consultorio SM **1** (*Med*) surgery (*Brit*), doctor's office (*EEUU*) **2** [*de abogado*] office **3** [*de revista*] (*tb* **~ sentimental**) problem page, advice column, agony column (*Brit*) **4** (*Radio*) phone-in [*for listeners' queries*] (*Brit*), call-in (*EEUU*)

consumación SF **1** (*Jur*) commission, perpetration **2** [*de matrimonio*] consummation

consumado ADJ [*artista*] consummate; [*imbécil*] thorough, out-and-out

consumar /1a/ VT **1** (= *acabar*) to complete; [+ *trato*] to close, complete **2** [+ *crimen*] to commit; [+ *asalto, robo*] to carry out **3** [+ *matrimonio*] to consummate **4** (*Jur*) [+ *sentencia*] to carry out

consumición SF **1** (= *acción*) consumption **2** (= *bebida*) drink; (= *comida*) food ➤ **consumición mínima** cover charge

consumidor(a) SM/F consumer

consumir /3a/ **Ⓐ** VT **1** [+ *comida, bebida, droga*] to consume (*frm*); **consúmase inmediatamente después de ser abierto** consume immediately after opening; **no pueden sentarse aquí si no van a ~ nada** you can't sit here if you're not going to have anything to eat or drink; **consuma productos andaluces** buy Andalusian products; **~ preferentemente antes de ...** best before ...
2 [+ *energía, gasolina*] to use, consume (*frm*); **consume cinco litros a los 100km** it does 100km to (every) five litres **3** [+ *tiempo*] to take up
4 (= *extinguir*) [+ *salud*] to destroy; **el cáncer lo está consumiendo** cancer is destroying him, he's being wasted away by cancer; **estos niños me están consumiendo la paciencia** these children are trying *o* taxing my patience, my patience is wearing thin with these children; **el tejado fue consumido por las llamas** the roof was consumed by the flames
5 (= *desesperar*) **los celos lo consumen** he is consumed *o* eaten up with jealousy
Ⓑ VI **1** (= *comer*) to eat; (= *beber*) to drink
2 (= *gastar*) to consume
Ⓒ **consumirse** VPR **1** [*líquido*] to boil away; [*salsa*] to reduce **2** [*vela, cigarro*] to burn down **3** [*enfermo, anciano*] to waste away **4** [*tiempo*] to run out
5 (= *desesperarse*) **se consume de envidia al ver mis triunfos** he's green with envy at my success; **se consumía de pena tras la muerte de su hija** she was consumed with grief after the death of her daughter

consumismo SM consumerism

consumista **Ⓐ** ADJ consumer *antes de s*, consumerist **Ⓑ** SMF consumer

consumo SM consumption; **el ~ de bebidas alcohólicas** alcohol consumption; **ordenadores de bajo ~** low-energy computers; **precios al ~** retail prices; **sociedad de ~** consumer society

consustancial ADJ consubstantial; **ser ~ con** to be inseparable from, be all of a piece with

contabilidad SF (= *práctica*) accounting, book-keeping; (= *profesión*) accountancy; **llevar la ~** to keep the books

contabilizar /1f/ VT **1** (*Fin*) to enter in the accounts **2** (= *tener en cuenta*) to reckon with, take into account

contable **Ⓐ** ADJ countable **Ⓑ** SMF (*Esp*) (= *tenedor de libros*) book-keeper; (= *licenciado*) accountant

contactar /1a/ VI **~ con** to contact, get in touch with

contacto SM **1** (= *acto de tocar*) contact; **entrar en ~ con algo** to come into contact with sth **2** (= *trato*) touch; **estar en ~ con algn** to be in touch with sb; **ponerse en ~ con algn** to get in touch with sb, contact sb **3** (*Aut*) ignition **4** (*Elec*) contact **5** (*Méx*) (= *enchufe*) socket (*Brit*), outlet (*EEUU*) **6** (= *encuentro*) meeting; **sección de ~s** [*de un periódico*] contact section, contacts **7** (*Fot*) contact print

contado **Ⓐ** ADJ (= *reducido*) **en contadas ocasiones** on rare occasions; **son ~s los que ...** there are few who ...; **tiene los días ~s** his days are numbered **Ⓑ** SM **1** (*Com*) **al ~** for cash, cash down; **lo pagué al ~** I paid cash for it; **precio al ~** cash price **2** (*Col*) (= *plazo*) instalment, installment (*EEUU*)

contador(a) **Ⓐ** ADJ counting **Ⓑ** SM/F (*esp LAm Com*) book-keeper, accountant **Ⓒ** SM meter ➤ **contador de agua** water meter ➤ **contador de electricidad** electricity meter ➤ **contador de gas** gas meter ➤ **contador de taxi** taximeter ➤ **Contador Geiger** Geiger counter

contagiar /1b/ **Ⓐ** VT **1** (*Med*) [+ *enfermedad*] to pass on, transmit (*frm*), give (**a** to); [+ *víctima*] to infect (**con** with) **2** (*fig*) **me ha contagiado su optimismo** his optimism has rubbed off on me **Ⓑ** **contagiarse** VPR **1** (*Med*) [*enfermedad*] (= *transmitirse*) to be transmitted; (= *ser contagiosa*) to be contagious, be infectious **2** [*persona*] to become infected; **~se de algo** to become infected with sth, catch sth **3** (*fig*) to be contagious

contagio SM **1** (*Med*) infection **2** (*fig*) contamination

contagioso ADJ **1** [*enfermedad, enfermo*] infectious **2** (*fig*) catching; [*risa*] infectious

contaminación SF [*de aire, mar*] pollution; [*de alimentos, agua potable*] contamination ➤ **contaminación acústica** noise pollution ➤ **contaminación ambiental** environmental pollution ➤ **contaminación atmosférica** air pollution

contaminante SM pollutant

contaminar /1a/ **Ⓐ** VT [+ *aire, mar*] to pollute; [+ *alimentos, agua potable*] to contaminate **Ⓑ** **contaminarse** VPR [*aire, mar*] to become polluted; [*alimentos, agua potable*] to be contaminated, become contaminated (**con** with; **de** by)

contante ADJ **dinero ~ (y sonante)** cash

contar /1l/ **Ⓐ** VT **1** (= *calcular*) [+ *objetos, números, puntos*] to count; [+ *dinero*] to count, count up
2 (= *relatar*) to tell; **cuéntanos lo que ocurrió** tell us what happened; **el paro está peor y la corrupción, ¿qué le voy a ~?** unemployment has got worse and as for corruption, what can I say?; **¿y a mí qué me cuentas?** so what?; **se cuenta que ...** it is said that ...; ✦ MODISMO **¡una obra que ni te cuento!** one hell of a fine work*
3 (= *tener la edad de*) **María cuenta 32 años** María is 32 years of age
4 (= *incluir*) to count; **seis en total, sin ~me a mí** six altogether, not counting me; **1.500 sin ~ las propinas** 1,500, excluding tips, 1,500, not counting tips
Ⓑ VI **1** (*Mat*) to count; **~ con los dedos** to count on one's fingers; ✦ MODISMO **parar de ~*: hay dos sillas, una mesa y para ya de ~** there are two chairs, a table, and that's it
2 (= *relatar*) to tell; **luego te ~é** I'll tell you later; **es muy largo de ~** it's a long story
3 (= *importar, valer*) to count; **este examen no cuenta para la nota final** this exam doesn't count towards the final mark; **los domingos una hora cuenta por dos** on Sundays one hour counts as two; ✦ MODISMO **la intención es lo que cuenta** it's the thought that counts
4 **~ con** **4.1** (= *confiar en*) to count on; **cuenta conmigo** you can rely *o* count on me; **cuento con que no llueva** I'm

counting on it not raining 4.2 (= *tener presente*) **lo calcularon sin ~ con nosotros** they worked it out without taking us into account; **no contábamos con eso** we hadn't bargained for that; **sin ~ con que ...** leaving aside the fact that ... 4.3 (= *incluir*) to count in; **cuenta conmigo para la cena** count me in for dinner 4.4 (= *tener*) to have; **el polideportivo cuenta con una piscina olímpica** the sports centre has *o* boasts an Olympic-size swimming pool **ⓒ contarse** VPR **1** (*al saludar*) **¿qué te cuentas?** how's things?*
2 ~se entre (= *incluirse*): **me cuento entre sus admiradores** I count myself among his admirers, I consider myself one of his admirers; **su película se cuenta entre las nominadas al óscar** his film (*esp Brit*) *o* movie (*esp EEUU*) is amongst those nominated for an Oscar
3 ~se por (= *calcularse*): **sus seguidores se cuentan por miles** he has thousands of supporters, his supporters number several thousand

contemplación SF **1** (= *observación*) (*gen*) contemplation **2** (= *meditación*) meditation **3 contemplaciones**
3.1 (= *indulgencia*) indulgence *sing*; **tener demasiadas contemplaciones con algn** to be too indulgent towards sb, be too soft on sb **3.2** (= *ceremonias*) **no andarse con contemplaciones** not to stand on ceremony

contemplar /1a/ VT **1** (= *observar*) [+ *paisaje, edificio, cuadro*] to gaze at, contemplate; **desde aquí se contempla una vista espectacular** there is a spectacular view from here; **la exposición podrá ~se aquí en octubre** the exhibition can be seen here in October **2** (= *analizar*) **debemos ~ nuestra obra desde otra perspectiva** we must look at *o* consider his work from another perspective **3** (*frm*) (= *considerar*) [+ *idea, posibilidad*] to consider **4** [*ley, tratado*] to provide for

contemplativo ADJ contemplative

contemporáneo/a ADJ, SM/F contemporary

contemporizador(a) Ⓐ ADJ excessively compliant Ⓑ SM/F temporizer

contemporizar /1f/ VI (= *acomodarse*) to be compliant, show o.s. ready to compromise; (*pey*) to temporize (**con** with); **~ con algn** to hedge with sb; (*Pol*) to appease sb

contención SF **1** (= *moderación*) restraint **▸ contención salarial** pay restraint **2 muro de ~** retaining wall

contencioso Ⓐ ADJ **1** (*Jur*) contentious **2** [*carácter*] captious; [*asunto*] contentious Ⓑ SM (= *disputa*) dispute; (= *punto conflictivo*) point of disagreement

contender /2g/ VI **1** (= *competir*) to compete **2** (*Mil*) to fight

contendiente Ⓐ ADJ contending Ⓑ SMF contestant, contender

contenedor SM **1** (*gen*) container **▸ contenedor de basura(s)** skip (*Brit*), Dumpster® (*EEUU*) **2** (*Náut*) container ship

contener /2k/ Ⓐ VT **1** (= *incluir*) to contain; **"no contiene alcohol"** "alcohol-free", "does not contain alcohol" **2** (= *frenar*) [+ *gente, muchedumbre*] to contain, hold back; [+ *revuelta, epidemia, infección*] to contain; [+ *invasión, lágrimas, emoción*] to contain, hold back; [+ *aliento, respiración*] to hold; [+ *hemorragia*] to stop; [+ *inflación*] to check, curb; [+ *precios, déficit, consumo*] to keep down; **no pude ~ la risa** I couldn't help laughing Ⓑ **contenerse** VPR (= *controlarse*) to control o.s., restrain o.s.

contenido Ⓐ ADJ **1** [*persona*] restrained, controlled **2** [*risa, emoción*] suppressed Ⓑ SM **1** [*de recipiente, paquete*] contents *pl*; **el ~ de la maleta** the contents of the suitcase; **alimentos con un alto ~ en proteínas** foods with a high protein content **2** [*de programa, proyecto*] content

contentar /1a/ Ⓐ VT [+ *persona*] to please; (*frm*) [+ *deseo*] to satisfy; **para ~ al cliente** to keep the customer happy Ⓑ **contentarse** VPR **se contenta con cualquier cosa** he's happy with anything; **no quedaba vino, y me tuve que ~ con agua** there was no wine left so I had to make do with water; **me contento con saber que estás bien** I'm happy just knowing that you are all right

contento Ⓐ ADJ **1** (= *alegre, feliz*) happy; **estoy contenta**

de vivir aquí I'm happy living here; **estar loco de ~** (*frm*) to be overjoyed; **✦** MODISMO **estar más ~ que unas castañuelas** *o* **que unas pascuas** to be as happy as a sandboy **2** (= *satisfecho*) pleased; **estar ~ con algn/algo** to be pleased with sb/sth; **quedar ~ con algo** to be satisfied with sth; **tener ~ a algn** to keep sb happy *o* satisfied **3** (= *bebido*) happy, merry (*Brit*); **no me emborraché, pero estaba ~ o contentillo** I didn't get drunk but I was quite happy *o* (*Brit*) merry Ⓑ SM (*frm*) (= *alegría*) happiness, joy; **el anuncio fue motivo de ~** the announcement gave cause for happiness *o* joy

conteo SM (*LAm*) count **▸ conteo regresivo** countdown

contertulio/a SM/F fellow member (*of a social set*)

contestación SF answer, reply

contestador Ⓐ ADJ (*CS*) cheeky (*Brit*), sassy (*EEUU**) Ⓑ SM (*tb* **~ automático**) answering machine, answerphone (*esp Brit*)

contestar /1a/ Ⓐ VT **1** (= *responder*) to answer, reply; [+ *saludo*] to return; **~ al teléfono** to answer the telephone; **~ una carta** to reply to a letter; **le pregunté que si vendría y contestó que sí** I asked him if he would come and he replied that he would **2** (= *replicar*) to answer back; **no le contestes así a tu madre** don't answer your mother back like that, don't talk back to your mother like that Ⓑ VI **1** (= *responder*) to answer, reply; **no contestan** there's no reply *o* answer **2** (*Pol*) to protest

⚠ **contestar ≠ contest**

contestatario/a Ⓐ ADJ rebellious; **movimiento ~** protest movement Ⓑ SM/F non-conformist

contestón* ADJ given to answering back, argumentative

contexto SM context; **sacar algo (fuera) de ~** to take sth out of context; **~ histórico** historical context

contextualizar /1f/ VT to provide a context for, set in a context

contienda SF contest, struggle

contigo PRON with you; (*Rel*) with thee; **quiero ir ~** I want to go with you; **necesito hablar ~** I need to talk to you; **estamos ~** we're behind you, we're on your side

contiguo ADJ adjacent, contiguous (*frm*) (**a** to); **en un cuarto ~** in an adjoining room

continencia SF continence

continental ADJ continental

continente Ⓐ ADJ continent Ⓑ SM **1** (*Geog*) continent; **el viejo ~** Europe, the Old World **2** (= *recipiente*) container

contingencia SF (*gen*) contingency; (= *posibilidad*) eventuality, possibility

contingente Ⓐ ADJ contingent Ⓑ SM **1** (*Mil*) contingent **2** (*Com*) quota

continuación SF **1** [*de acto, proceso, calle*] continuation; **el mal tiempo impidió la ~ del desfile** the bad weather prevented the parade from continuing; **esta película es la ~ de Rocky** this film is the sequel to Rocky **2 a ~** (*en conversación*) next; (*en texto*) below **3 a ~ de** following, after; **a ~ del sorteo ofrecerán una rueda de prensa** following *o* after the draw, they will give a press conference; **se sentaron uno a ~ del otro** they sat down one after another

continuado Ⓐ ADJ continual Ⓑ SM (*CS*) *a cinema showing films in continuous performance*

continuamente ADV **1** (= *repetidamente*) constantly, continually **2** (= *sin interrupción*) constantly, continuously

continuar /1e/ Ⓐ VT to continue; **continuó su vida como antes** he went on with *o* continued with his life as before Ⓑ VI **1** [*historia, espectáculo, guerra*] to continue, go on; **continúe, por favor** please continue, please go on; **"continuará"** "to be continued" **2** (*en una situación*) **continúa muy grave** she is still in a critical condition, she remains in a critical condition (*frm*); **Pablo continúa con Irene** Pablo is still (together) with

Irene; ~ **haciendo algo: continuó leyendo** she continued to read *o* reading, she went on reading; **continúa lloviendo** it's still raining; **en cualquier caso continúo siendo optimista** in any case, I remain optimistic *o* I am still optimistic
3 [*camino, carretera*] to continue, go on, carry on

continuidad SF **1** (= *permanencia*) continuity **2** (= *continuación*) continuation

continuo Ⓐ ADJ **1** (= *ininterrumpido*) [*línea, fila*] continuous; [*dolor, movimiento, crecimiento*] constant, continuous; [*pesadilla, molestia*] constant **2** (= *frecuente, repetido*) [*llamadas, amenazas, críticas, cambios*] constant, continual **3** (*Fís*) [*movimiento*] perpetual **4** (*Elec*) [*corriente*] direct **5** (*Ling*) continuous **6 de ~ = continuamente** Ⓑ SM (*Fís*) continuum

contonearse /1a/ VPR to swing *o* wiggle one's hips

contorno SM **1** (= *perfil*) outline; (*Geog*) contour **2** (= *medida*) girth; **el ~ de un árbol** the girth of a tree **3 contornos** neighbourhood *sing*, neighborhood *sing* (*EEUU*), surrounding area *sing*; **en estos ~s** in these parts, hereabouts

contorsión SF contortion

contorsionarse /1a/ VPR to contort o.s.

contorsionista SMF contortionist

Contra SF **la ~** (*Nic Hist*) the Contras *pl*

contra Ⓐ PREP **1** (*indicando oposición*) against; **no tengo nada ~ ti** I have nothing against you; **el Sevilla juega ~ el Betis** Seville are playing (against) Betis; **unas pastillas ~ el mareo** some (anti-)travel sickness pills; **en ~: ¿quién está en ~?** who is against?; **tres votos a favor y dos en ~** three votes in favour and two against; **en ~ de lo que habíamos pensado** contrary to what we had thought; **por ~** on the other hand
2 (*indicando posición*) against; **apoyó la bici ~ la pared** she leaned the bike against the wall
3 (*indicando dirección*) against; **fue muy cansado remar ~ la corriente** it was very tiring rowing against the current
Ⓑ SF **1** (*) (= *contraria*) **llevar la ~ a algn** to contradict sb **2** (*Col, Ven Med*) antidote
Ⓒ SM (= *inconveniente*) disadvantage, drawback
Ⓓ EXCL (*) (*indicando enfado*) damn it*

contraanálisis SM INV follow-up test, counter-test

contrabajo Ⓐ SM **1** (= *instrumento*) double bass **2** (= *cantante, voz*) low bass, contrabasso Ⓑ SMF (= *músico*) double bass player, double bassist

contrabandista SMF smuggler

contrabando SM **1** (= *actividad*) smuggling; **introducir** *o* **pasar algo de ~** to smuggle sth in ➤ **contrabando de armas** gun-running ➤ **contrabando de drogas** drug smuggling **2** (= *mercancías*) contraband, smuggled goods *pl*

contracción SF contraction

contracepción SF contraception

contrachapado Ⓐ ADJ **madera contrachapada = B** Ⓑ SM plywood

contracorriente SF cross-current; **ir a ~** (*lit*) to go against the current, go upstream; (*fig*) to go against the tide

contráctil ADJ contractile

contractual ADJ contractual

contractura SF muscular contraction

contracubierta SF back cover (*of book*)

contracultura SF counter-culture

contracultural ADJ alternative, of the counter-culture

contradecir /3o/ Ⓐ VT to contradict Ⓑ **contradecirse** VPR to contradict o.s.

contradicción SF contradiction; **están en ~** they stand in contradiction to each other

contradictorio ADJ contradictory

contraer /2o/ Ⓐ VT **1** [+ *enfermedad*] to contract (*frm*), catch **2** [+ *compromiso*] to make, take on; [+ *obligación*] to take on, contract (*frm*); [+ *deuda, crédito*] to incur, contract (*frm*); **~ matrimonio (con algn)** to marry (sb) **3** [+ *músculo, nervio*] to contract **4** [+ *metal, objeto*] to cause to contract

Ⓑ **contraerse** VPR **1** [*músculo, nervio*] to contract **2** [*objeto, material*] to contract **3** (*Ling*) to contract

contraespionaje SM counter-espionage

contrafuerte SM (*Arquit*) buttress; (*Geog*) spur; (*Mil*) outwork

contragolpe SM **1** (= *reacción*) counter-blow **2** (*Dep*) counter-attack

contrahecho ADJ **1** (*Anat*) hunchbacked **2** (= *falso*) [*moneda*] counterfeit; [*documento, prueba*] fake, faked, forged; [*libro*] spurious

contraincendios ADJ INV **aparato ~** fire-prevention apparatus, fire-alarm system

contraindicación SF counter-indication

contralmirante SM rear admiral

contralor SM (*LAm*) comptroller

contraloría SF (*LAm*) treasury inspector's office

contralto Ⓐ ADJ contralto Ⓑ SMF (= *mujer*) contralto; (= *hombre*) counter tenor

contraluz SM view against the light; **a ~** against the light

contramaestre SMF (*Náut*) boatswain; (*Téc*) foreman/ forewoman

contramano SM **ir a ~** to go the wrong way; **eso queda a ~** that's in the other direction

contraofensiva SF counter-offensive

contraoferta SF counter-offer

contraorden SF countermand

contraparte SF (*And*) other party

contrapartida SF **1** (*Com, Fin*) balancing entry **2** (= *compensación*) compensation; **pero como ~ añade que ...** but in contrast she adds that ...; **como ~ de** as *o* in compensation for, in return for

contrapelo SM **a ~** the wrong way

contrapesar /1a/ VT **1** (= *hacer contrapeso*) to counterbalance **2** (= *compensar*) to offset, compensate for

contrapeso SM counterpoise, counterweight; (*Com*) makeweight

contrapié: a ~ ADV **mi oponente me pilló a ~** my opponent caught me off-balance, my opponent wrongfooted me

contrapoder SM anti-establishment movement

contraponer /2q/ VT **1** (= *cotejar*) to compare, set against each other **2** (= *oponer*) to oppose; **a esta idea ellos contraponen su teoría de que ...** against this idea they set up their theory that ...

contraportada SF back cover

contraposición SF **1** (= *cotejo*) comparison **2** (= *oposición*) contrast, clash; **en ~ a** in contrast to; **pero en ~, ...** but on the other hand, ...

contraprestación SF compensation

contraproducente ADJ counterproductive; **tener un resultado ~** to have a boomerang effect, boomerang

contrapuerta SF storm door

contrapuesto ADJ conflicting, opposing

contrapunto SM counterpoint

contrariado ADJ upset, annoyed, put out

contrariar /1c/ VT **1** (= *contradecir*) to contradict **2** (= *oponer*) to oppose, go against; (= *dificultar*) to impede, thwart; **sólo lo hace por ~nos** he only does it to be contrary *o* awkward *o* difficult **3** (= *fastidiar*) to vex, annoy

contrariedad SF **1** (= *obstáculo*) obstacle; (= *contratiempo*) setback, trouble; (= *pega*) snag, trouble **2** (= *disgusto*) vexation, annoyance

contrario/a Ⓐ ADJ **1** (= *rival*) [*partido, equipo*] opposing; **se pasó al bando ~** he went over to the other *o* opposing side
2 (= *opuesto*) [*extremo, efecto, significado, sexo*] opposite; **mi opinión es contraria a la vuestra** I have the opposite opinion to you; **soy ~ al aborto** I am opposed to *o* against abortion; **intereses ~s** conflicting *o* opposing interests; **sentido ~: un coche que venía en sentido ~** a car coming in

the opposite direction; **el portavoz se expresó en sentido ~** the spokesperson expressed the opposite view; **en sentido ~ a las agujas del reloj** anti-clockwise

3 (*en locuciones*) **al** ~ on the contrary, quite the opposite; **al ~ de: todo salió al ~ de lo previsto** everything turned out the opposite of what we expected; **al ~ de lo que creíamos, hizo muy buen tiempo** contrary to what we thought, the weather turned out very nice; **al ~ que ella, yo no estoy dispuesto a aguantar** unlike her, I'm not willing to put up with it; **lo ~: ¿qué es lo ~ de alto?** what is the opposite of tall?; **nunca he dicho lo ~** I never said anything else *o* different; **de lo ~** otherwise, or else; **salga o, de lo ~, llamaré a la policía** please leave, otherwise *o* or else I'll call the police; **por el ~: los inviernos, por el ~, son muy fríos** the winters, on the other hand *o* on the contrary, are very cold; **todo lo ~** quite the opposite, quite the reverse

B SM/F opponent

C SM (= *opuesto*) opposite

D SF ✦ MODISMO **llevar la contraria: ¿por qué siempre tienes que llevar la contraria?** why do you always have to be so contrary?; **siempre me lleva la contraria en todo** he always contradicts me about everything

contrarreloj A ADV against the clock **B** ADJ **prueba ~ = C C** SF time trial

contrarrestar /1a/ VT to counteract; **~ el efecto de una vacuna** to counteract the effect of a vaccine

contrarrevolución SF counter-revolution

contrarrevolucionario/a ADJ, SM/F counterrevolutionary

contrasentido SM **1** (= *contradicción*) contradiction; **aquí hay un ~** there is a contradiction here **2** (= *inconsecuencia*) inconsistency; **es un ~ que él actúe así** it doesn't make sense for him to act like that

contraseña SF **1** (= *seña*) countersign, secret mark **2** (*Mil, Inform*) password

contrastar /1a/ **A** VT [+ *metal*] to assay; [+ *medidas*] to check; [+ *radio*] to monitor; [+ *hechos*] to check, confirm **B** VI to contrast (**con** with)

contraste SM **1** (= *oposición*) contrast; **en ~ con** in contrast to; **por ~** in contrast **2** (*TV*) contrast **3** [*de pesos y medidas*] (*tb* **marca del ~**) (= *sello*) hallmark; (= *acción*) assay

contrata SF contract

contratacar /1g/ VI, VT to counter-attack

contratación SF [*de albañil, fontanero*] hiring; [*de abogado*] hiring, contracting (*frm*); [*de empleado*] recruitment; **se ha prohibido la ~ de jugadores extranjeros** the signing of foreign players has been banned; **este año ha habido diez mil nuevas contrataciones** this year there have been ten thousand new contracts

contrataque SM counter-attack

contratar /1a/ VT [+ *empleado*] to take on; [+ *albañil, abogado*] to hire; [+ *jugador, artista*] to sign (up); **han contratado nuevo personal** they have taken on *o* recruited new staff; **me han contratado por horas** they have hired me by the hour

contratenor SM counter-tenor

contratiempo SM (= *revés*) setback, reverse; (= *accidente*) mishap, accident

contratista SMF contractor ➤ **contratista de obras** building contractor, builder

contrato SM contract (**de** for); ➤ **contrato de alquiler** [*de casa*] lease, leasing agreement; [*de coche*] rental contract, hire contract ➤ **contrato de compraventa** contract of sale ➤ **contrato de trabajo** contract of employment, contract of service ➤ **contrato indefinido** permanent contract

contravalor SM exchange value

contravenir /3r/ **A** VT to contravene, infringe **B** VI **~ a** to contravene, infringe

contraventana SF shutter

contrayendo *ver* **contraer**

contrayente SMF **los ~s** the bride and groom

contribución SF **1** (= *colaboración*) contribution; **su ~ a la victoria** his contribution to the victory, his part in the

victory **2** (*Fin*) tax; **contribuciones** taxes, taxation *sing*; **pagar las contribuciones** to pay one's taxes ➤ **contribución territorial urbana** local tax

contribuir /3g/ VI **1** (= *colaborar*) to contribute; **cada uno contribuyó con diez euros** each person contributed ten euros; **~ a hacer algo** to help to do sth **2** (*Fin*) to pay, pay in taxes

contribuyente SMF taxpayer

contrición SF contrition

contrincante SMF opponent, rival

contrito ADJ (*frm*) contrite

control SM **1** (= *dominio, vigilancia*) control; **bajo ~** under control; **fuera de ~** out of control; **perder el ~** to lose control; **hacerse con el ~ de algo** to take control *o* charge of sth; **~ de** *o* **sobre sí mismo** self-control ➤ **control de la natalidad** birth control ➤ **control del tráfico** traffic control ➤ **control de precios** price control

2 (= *inspección*) (*Jur*) inspection, check; (*Com, Fin*) audit, auditing

3 (= *puesto*) (*tb* **~ de carretera**) roadblock; (*tb* **~ de frontera**) border *o* (*esp Brit*) frontier checkpoint; **montar un ~** to set up a roadblock ➤ **control de pasaportes** passport control ➤ **control policial en carretera** police roadblock

4 [*de un aparato*] control ➤ **control remoto** remote control

5 (= *examen*) (*Educ*) test

6 (*Med*) test ➤ **control antidoping** drug test, dope test ➤ **control de alcoholemia** Breathalyser® test

controlador(a) SM/F (*tb* **~ aéreo**) air-traffic controller

controlar /1a/ **A** VT **1** (= *dominar*) [+ *situación, emoción, balón, vehículo, inflación*] to control; **medidas para ~ la calidad** quality-control measures; **los bomberos consiguieron ~ el fuego** the firefighters managed to bring the fire under control; **no controlo muy bien ese tema*** I'm not very hot on that subject*

2 (= *vigilar*) **inspectores para ~ el proceso electoral** observers to monitor the electoral process; **deberías ~ tu peso** you should watch your weight; **controla que no hierva el café*** make sure the coffee doesn't boil, see that the coffee doesn't boil

3 (= *regular*) to control

B VI (*) **he bebido tanto que ya no controlo** I've drunk so much I can't see straight*

C controlarse VPR to control o.s.

controversia SF controversy

controvertido ADJ controversial

controvertir /3i/ **A** VT to dispute, question **B** VI to argue

contubernio SM **1** (= *confabulación*) conspiracy **2** (= *cohabitación*) cohabitation

contumacia SF **1** (= *terquedad*) obstinacy, stubborn disobedience **2** (*Jur*) contempt, contempt of court

contumaz ADJ **1** (= *terco*) obstinate, stubbornly disobedient **2** [*bebedor*] inveterate, hardened, incorrigible **3** (*Jur*) guilty of contempt, guilty of contempt of court

contundencia SF **1** [*de instrumento*] bluntness **2** [*de argumentación, razonamiento*] forcefulness, convincing nature; [*de prueba*] conclusiveness

contundente ADJ **1** [*arma*] offensive; [*instrumento*] blunt **2** (= *aplastante*) [*argumento*] forceful, convincing; [*prueba*] conclusive; [*derrota, victoria*] crushing, overwhelming; [*tono*] forceful; [*efecto, método*] severe; [*juego*] tough, hard, aggressive

contusión SF bruise, contusion (*frm*)

contusionar /1a/ VT to bruise

conuco SM (*Ven*) smallholding

convalecencia SF convalescence

convalecer /2d/ VI to convalesce, recover (**de** from)

convaleciente ADJ, SMF convalescent

convalidación SF validation; **tengo que solicitar la ~ de mis títulos** I need to have my qualifications validated

convalidar /1a/ VT to validate

convección SF convection

convecino/a SM/F neighbour, neighbor (*EEUU*)

convector SM convector

convencer /2b/ **Ⓐ** VT **1** ~ **a algn (de algo)** to convince sb (of sth), persuade sb (of sth); **al final la convencí de que era verdad** I eventually convinced o persuaded her it was true; **no me ~éis de lo contrario** you won't convince o persuade me otherwise
2 ~ **a algn (de** o **para hacer algo)** to persuade sb (to do sth) **3** (= *satisfacer*) **ninguno de los dos candidatos me convence** neither of the two candidates seems very convincing o good to me; **el torero convenció a su afición** the bullfighter did not disappoint his fans; **parece buena gente, pero no me acaba de** ~ he seems nice enough but I'm not too sure about him
Ⓑ convencerse VPR **¡convéncete ya, esta enfermedad no tiene cura!** I wish you'd understand, there's no cure for this illness!; **¿te convences ahora de que decía la verdad?** now do you believe that I was telling the truth?; **me convencí de que lo mejor era callarse** I came to the conclusion that it would be better to keep quiet

convencido ADJ [*pacifista, cristiano*] committed, convinced; **estar** ~ **de algo** to be convinced of sth, be certain of sth, be sure of sth

convencimiento SM conviction, certainty; **llegar al** ~ **de algo** to become convinced of sth; **tener el** ~ **de que** to be convinced that

convención SF convention ➤ **Convención de Ginebra** Geneva Convention

convencional ADJ conventional

convencionalismo SM conventionalism

conveniencia SF **1** (= *utilidad*) advisability; **ser de la** ~ **de algn** to be convenient to sb, suit sb **2** (= *provecho propio*) **a su** ~ at your (own) convenience; **por** ~: **lo hace por** ~ he does it because it suits him o because it's in his own interest(s); **se ha casado por** ~ she made a marriage of convenience; **te lo digo por tu** ~ I'm telling you for your own sake o in your own interests

conveniente ADJ **1** (= *aconsejable*) advisable; **ser** ~ **hacer algo** to be advisable to do sth; **es** ~ **que consulte con su abogado** it is advisable to consult your lawyer; **sería** ~ **que nos levantásemos temprano** it might be a good idea for us to get up early o if we got up early **2** (= *indicado*) suitable **3** (= *provechoso*) convenient **4** (= *correcto*) proper

convenio SM agreement ➤ **convenio colectivo** collective bargain, general wages agreement ➤ **convenio comercial** trade agreement

convenir /3r/ **Ⓐ** VI **1** (= *ser adecuado*) ~ **hacer algo**: **conviene recordar que éste es un tema serio** it should be remembered that this is a serious matter; **conviene reservar asiento** reservation is advisable; **convendría hacer algo al respecto** it might be desirable o advisable o appropriate to do something about it
2 (= *ser de interés*) to suit; **esa hora no me conviene** that time is not convenient for me, that time doesn't suit me; **esa amistad no te convenía nada** that friendship was not good o right for you; ~ **a algn hacer algo: no te conviene fumar** in your case, smoking isn't good for you; **te convendría olvidar ese asunto** you would be well advised to forget all about this business
3 ~ **en algo** to agree on sth; ~ **en hacer algo** to agree to do sth; ~ **en que** to agree that
Ⓑ VT [+ *precio, hora*] to agree on, agree; **nos vimos a la hora convenida** we met at the agreed time; **"precio/sueldo a convenir"** "price/salary to be agreed", "price/salary negotiable"; ~ **hacer algo** to agree to do sth

⚠ **convenir ≠ convene**

conventillero/a (*And, RPl*) **Ⓐ** ADJ gossipy **Ⓑ** SM/F scandalmonger, gossip

conventillo SM (*CS*) tenement house

convento SM [*de monjes*] monastery; [*de monjas*] convent, nunnery

conventual ADJ conventual

convergencia SF **1** (*Mat, Fís, Econ*) convergence **2** (= *tendencia común*) common tendency, common direction

convergente ADJ **1** (*Mat, Fís*) convergent, converging **2** (= *concurrente*) having a common tendency, tending in the same direction

converger /2c/ VI, **convergir** /3c/ VI **1** (*Mat, Fís*) to converge (**en** on) **2** (*fig*) to tend in the same direction (**con** as) **3** (*Pol*) to come together

conversa SF (*esp LAm*) talk, chat; *ver tb* **converso**

conversación SF conversation, talk; **cambiar de** ~ to change the subject

conversador(a) **Ⓐ** ADJ talkative, chatty **Ⓑ** SM/F conversationalist

conversar /1a/ VI to talk, chat

conversión SF **1** (= *cambio*) conversion **2** (*Mil*) wheel

converso/a **Ⓐ** ADJ converted **Ⓑ** SM/F convert; (*Hist*) converted Jew/Jewess; *ver tb* **conversa**

conversor SM converter

convertible **Ⓐ** ADJ convertible **Ⓑ** SM (*LAm Aut*) convertible

convertidor SM converter

convertir /3i/ **Ⓐ** VT **1** ~ **algo/a algn en algo** to turn sth/sb into sth; **la victoria lo convirtió en un héroe** the victory turned him into a hero, the victory made him a hero; ~ **dólares en libras** to convert dollars to pounds **2** (*Dep*) [+ *penalti*] to convert, score; [+ *gol, tanto*] to score **Ⓑ convertirse** VPR **1** ~**se en algo** to turn into sth; **la rana se convirtió en un príncipe** the frog turned into a prince; **todos sus deseos se convirtieron en realidad** all her wishes came true
2 (*Rel*) to be converted, convert; **se convirtió al Islam** he converted to Islam

convexo ADJ convex

convicción SF conviction

convicto/a **Ⓐ** ADJ convicted **Ⓑ** SM/F (*LAm*) convict

convidado/a SM/F guest

convidar /1a/ VT **1** (= *invitar*) to invite; ~ **a algn a hacer algo** to invite sb to do sth; ~ **a algn a una cerveza** to buy sb a beer **2** (*LAm*) (= *ofrecer*) to offer; ~ **a algn con algo** to offer sth to sb

convincente ADJ convincing

convite SM **1** (= *invitación*) invitation **2** (= *función*) banquet, feast

convivencia SF **1** [*de personas*] cohabitation, living together **2** (*fig*) (*Pol*) coexistence **3** (*Rel*) **irse de** ~**s** to go on a retreat

convivir /3a/ VI **1** (= *vivir juntos*) to live together; ~ **con algn** to live with sb **2** (= *coexistir*) [*personas*] to live together, live together in harmony; [*ideologías, razas*] to coexist

convocar /1g/ VT **1** [+ *elecciones, referéndum, huelga*] to call; [+ *asamblea, reunión*] to call, convene; [+ *manifestación*] to call for; [+ *concurso, oposiciones*] to announce **2** ~ **a algn:** ~**on a los periodistas a una rueda de prensa** they called journalists to a press conference; **los españoles serán convocados a las urnas en abril** Spaniards will go to the polls in April; **los jugadores convocados por el entrenador** the players selected by the trainer

convocatoria SF **1** (= *anuncio*) [*de concurso, oposiciones*] official announcement; **han anunciado la** ~ **de elecciones generales** they have announced the date for the general election; ~ **de huelga** strike call **2** (= *ronda*) ~ **de septiembre** September's exams; **en primera** ~ in the first round

convoy SM (*Mil, Náut*) convoy; (*Ferro*) train

convulsión SF **1** (*Med*) convulsion **2** (*Geol*) tremor **3** (*Pol*) upheaval

convulsionar /1a/ VT to convulse

convulsivo ADJ convulsive

convulso ADJ convulsed (**de** with)

conyugal ADJ conjugal (*frm*), married; **vida** ~ married life

cónyuge SMF spouse, partner; **cónyuges** married couple *sing*, husband and wife

coña*** (*Esp*) SF piss-taking***; **estar de** ~ to be taking the piss***; **tomar algo a** ~ to take sth as a joke

coñac [koˈɲa] SM (*pl* **-s**) brandy, cognac

coñazo** (*Esp*) SM pain*; **dar el** ~ to be a real pain

coñete ADJ (*Chi, Perú*) stingy, mean (*Brit*)

coño¹*** Ⓐ SM (= *sexo femenino*) cunt***; ◆ MODISMOS **estar hasta el** ~ **de algn/algo** to have had it up to here with sb/sth; **el quinto** ~ (*Esp*) the arse (*Brit*) o ass (*EEUU*) end of nowhere***, the back of beyond*
Ⓑ EXCL **1** (*como expresión de enfado*) hell!*, shit!***; **¡vámonos ya,** ~**!** come on, let's get a fucking*** o (*Brit***) bloody move on!; **¡qué ~/dónde** o **...?** what/where the fucking*** o (*Brit***) bloody hell ...?; **que lo haga él, ¡qué ~!** let him do it for Christ's sake!**
2 (*como expresión de sorpresa*) good God!**
Ⓒ SMF ➤ **coño de madre** (*Ven****) bastard***, motherfucker (*esp EEUU****)

coño²/a SM/F **1** (*Chi** *pey*) (= *español*) Spanish guy*/woman **2** (*Ven****) (= *tipo*) **¡qué ~ con más suerte!** (what a) lucky bastard!***

cooficial ADJ **dos lenguas ~es** two languages equally recognized as official

cool* ADJ INV cool*

cooperación SF cooperation

cooperador(a) Ⓐ ADJ cooperative, collaborating, participating Ⓑ SM/F collaborator, co-worker

cooperante SMF (overseas) voluntary worker

cooperar /1a/ VI to cooperate (**con** with); ~ **en** to collaborate in, work together on

cooperativa SF cooperative, co-op*

cooperativismo SM cooperativism; (*como movimiento*) cooperative movement

cooperativista SMF member of a cooperative

cooperativo ADJ cooperative

coordenada SF coordinate

coordinación SF coordination

coordinado Ⓐ ADJ (= *armonizado*) coordinated; (*Mil*) [*operación*] combined Ⓑ SMPL **coordinados** (= *ropa*) separates

coordinador(a) Ⓐ ADJ coordinating Ⓑ SM/F coordinator

coordinadora SF coordinating committee

coordinar /1a/ Ⓐ VT [+ *movimientos, actividades, equipo, esfuerzo, trabajo*] to coordinate Ⓑ VI (*) **ha bebido tanto que ya no coordina** he's had so much to drink that his coordination has gone; **hasta que no me tomo un café por las mañanas no coordino** I can't think straight in the mornings until I've had a coffee

copa SF **1** (= *recipiente*) (*para bebidas*) glass; (*para postres*) dessert glass ➤ **copa de champán** champagne glass ➤ **copa de coñac** brandy glass
2 (= *contenido*) drink; **os invito a una** ~ let me buy you a drink; **ir(se)** o **salir de ~s** to go out for a drink; **tomarse una** ~ to have a drink; **se tomó una ~ de más** he had one too many
3 [*de árbol*] top, crown; ◆ MODISMO **como la ~ de un pino***: **es un artista como la ~ de un pino** he's a real star; **es una idiotez como la ~ de un pino** that's the stupidest thing I've ever heard
4 (*Dep*) (= *trofeo, competición*) cup ➤ **Copa de Europa** European Cup ➤ **Copa del Mundo** World Cup ➤ **Copa del Rey** (*Esp*) *Spanish FA Cup*
5 **copas** (*Naipes*) one of the suits in Spanish card deck, represented by a goblet; ⇨ *BARAJA ESPAÑOLA*
6 [*de sombrero*] crown
7 [*de sujetador*] cup

copar /1a/ VT **1** (*Mil*) to surround, cut off **2** (*Econ*) to corner; ~ **el mercado** to corner the market **3** (*Naipes*) (*tb* ~ **la banca**) to win, win all the tricks

copartícipe SMF (= *socio*) partner; (= *colaborador*) collaborator (**en** in)

Copenhague SM Copenhagen

copera SF (*Col, RPI*) hostess

copete SM **1** [*de persona*] tuft (of hair), quiff (*esp Brit*); [*de caballo*] forelock; [*de pájaro*] tuft, crest; ◆ MODISMOS **estar hasta el ~*** to be really fed up; **de alto** ~ aristocratic, upper-crust* **2** (= *altanería*) arrogance

copetín SM (*RPI*) drink, aperitif

copetudo ADJ **1** (*Zool*) tufted, crested **2** (= *engreído*) haughty, stuck-up*

copia SF **1** (= *reproducción*) [*de fotografía, documento*] copy; (*Fin*) duplicate ➤ **copia certificada** certified copy ➤ **copia de respaldo, copia de seguridad** (*Inform*) backup, backup copy; **hacer una ~ de seguridad** to make a backup copy ➤ **copia impresa** (*Inform*) hard copy **2** [*de obra de arte, edificio*] copy

copiadora SF photocopier, Xerox® machine

copiar /1b/ Ⓐ VT **1** (= *reproducir*) to copy (**de** from); [+ *estilo*] to imitate **2** [+ *dictado*] to take down; ~ **al pie de la letra** to copy word for word; ~ **por las dos caras** (*Téc*) to make a double-sided copy Ⓑ VI (*en un examen*) to cheat

copihue SM Chilean bell flower (*national symbol of Chile*)

copiloto SMF **1** (*Aut*) co-driver **2** (*Aer*) co-pilot

copión/ona* SM/F **1** (= *alumno*) cheat **2** (= *imitador*) copycat*

copioso ADJ (= *abundante*) copious, abundant; [*lluvia*] heavy

copista SMF copyist

copistería SF copy shop

copla SF **1** (*Literat*) verse (*esp of 4 lines*) **2** (*Mús*) popular song, ballad; ◆ MODISMOS **la misma ~*** the same old song*; **¿os vais quedando con la ~?** do you follow?, do you get my drift? **3** (*LAm Téc*) pipe joint

copo SM ➤ **copo de nieve** snowflake ➤ **copos de avena** oatmeal *sing*, rolled oats ➤ **copos de maíz** cornflakes

copón SM (= *copa*) large cup; (*Rel*) pyx; **un susto del ~*** a tremendous fright, a hell of a fright**

coproducir /3n/ VT to co-produce, produce jointly

copropietario/a SM/F co-owner, joint owner

copto ADJ Coptic

copucha SF (*Chi*) gossip

copuchar /1a/ VI (*Chi*) to gossip

cópula SF **1** (*Biol*) copulation **2** (*Ling*) conjunction

copular /1a/ VI to copulate (**con** with)

copulativo ADJ copulative

coque SM coke

coquear /1a/ VI (*And*) to chew coca

coqueta SF (= *mueble*) dressing table; *ver tb* **coqueto**

coquetear /1a/ VI to flirt (**con** with)

coqueteo SM, **coquetería** SF (= *cualidad*) flirtatiousness, coquetry; (= *acto*) flirtation

coqueto/a Ⓐ ADJ **1** [*vestido*] smart, natty*, attractive **2** (= *juguetón*) flirtatious, flirty **3** (= *presumido*) **es muy ~** he's very fussy about his appearance, he's very clothes-conscious Ⓑ SM/F **1** (= *juguetón*) flirt **2** (= *presumido*) **es una coqueta** she's very fussy about her appearance, she's very clothes-conscious; *ver tb* **coqueta**

coraje SM **1** (= *valor*) courage **2** (*) (= *rabia*) **hemos perdido el autobús, ¡qué ~!** we've missed the bus, what a pain!*; **me da ~ que me mientas** it makes me mad* o it really annoys me when you lie to me

coral¹ (*Mús*) Ⓐ ADJ choral Ⓑ SM chorale Ⓒ SF choir

coral² SM (*Zool*) coral

coralino ADJ coral *antes de s*, coralline

Corán SM Koran

coránico ADJ Koranic

coraza SF **1** (*Mil, Hist*) cuirass; (= *protección*) protection **2** (*Zool*) shell

corazón SM **1** (*Anat*) heart; **estar enfermo** o **mal del** ~ to have heart trouble o problems; **ser operado a** ~ **abierto** to have open heart surgery

2 ✦ MODISMOS **abrir el ~ a algn** to open one's heart to sb, pour one's heart out to sb; **de ~** sincerely; **te lo digo de ~** I mean it sincerely; **se lo agradezco de todo ~** I thank you with all my heart *o* from the bottom of my heart; **encoger a algn el ~: aquellas imágenes me encogieron el ~** those scenes made my heart bleed; **un grito en la noche me encogió el ~** a scream during the night made my heart miss a beat; **con el ~ en la mano** with one's hand on one's heart; **partir** *o* **romper el ~ a algn** to break sb's heart; **tener el ~ en un puño** to have one's heart in one's mouth, be on tenterhooks; **tener un ~ de oro** to have a heart of gold; **tener el ~ de piedra** to have a heart of stone; **una mujer sin ~** a heartless woman; **no tener ~** to have no heart, be heartless

3 (*Prensa*) **la prensa del ~** gossip magazines *pl*; **una revista del ~** a gossip magazine

4 (*apelativo*) **sí, ~** yes, sweetheart; **¡hijo de mi ~!** (my) darling!

5 (= *centro*) [*de ciudad, zona, alcachofa*] heart; [*de manzana*] core

6 corazones (*Naipes*) hearts

corazonada SF **1** (= *presentimiento*) hunch **2** (= *impulso*) impulsive act

corbata SF tie, necktie (*EEUU*) ➤ **corbata de humita** (*Chi*), **corbata de lazo**, **corbata de moño** (*LAm*) bow tie

corbatín SM bow tie

corbeta SF corvette

corcel SM steed, charger

corchea SF quaver (*Brit*), eighth (note) (*EEUU*)

corchete SM **1** (*Cos*) (= *broche*) hook and eye; (= *macho*) hook **2 corchetes** (*Tip*) square brackets **3** (*Chi*) (= *grapa*) staple

corchetear /1a/ VT (*Chi*) to staple, staple together

corchetera SF (*Chi*) stapler

corcho SM **1** [*de botella*] cork **2** (= *corteza*) cork bark; **de ~** cork *antes de s* **3** (*Pesca*) float

corcholata SF (*Méx*) bottle top

córcholis* EXCL good Lord!, dear me!

corcova SF **1** (*Med*) hump, hunch **2** (*Perú*) (= *fiesta*) all-night party

corcovado/a Ⓐ ADJ hunchbacked **Ⓑ** SM/F hunchback

cordel SM cord, line; **a ~** in a straight line

cordero/a Ⓐ SM/F (*Zool*) lamb ➤ **Cordero de Dios** Lamb of God ➤ **cordero lechal** young lamb **Ⓑ** SM (= *piel*) lambskin; (= *carne*) lamb

cordial Ⓐ ADJ warm, cordial **Ⓑ** SM tonic, cordial (*Brit*)

cordialidad SF warmth, cordiality

cordialmente ADV warmly, cordially; (*en carta*) Yours sincerely (*Brit*), Sincerely yours (*EEUU*)

cordillera SF mountain range, mountain chain

cordillerano ADJ (*And*) Andean

córdoba SM (*Nic*) *monetary unit of Nicaragua*

cordón SM **1** (= *cuerda*) cord, string; [*de zapato*] lace, shoelace **2** (*Náut*) strand; (*Mil*) braid **3** (*Anat*) cord ➤ **cordón umbilical** umbilical cord **4** [*de policía*] cordon ➤ **cordón sanitario** cordon sanitaire **5** (*RPl*) (= *bordillo*) kerb (*Brit*), curb (*EEUU*) **6** (*Geog*) ➤ **cordón de cerros** (*CS*) chain of hills

cordoncillo SM braid, piping

cordura SF **1** (*Med*) sanity **2** (= *sensatez*) good sense; **con ~** sensibly, wisely

Corea SF Korea ➤ **Corea del Norte** North Korea ➤ **Corea del Sur** South Korea

coreano/a ADJ, SM/F Korean

corear /1a/ VT to chorus; [+ *eslogan*] shout in unison, chant; (*Mús*) to sing in chorus, sing together

coreografía SF choreography

coreógrafo/a SM/F choreographer

corintio ADJ Corinthian

corinto ADJ INV maroon, purplish

corista Ⓐ SMF (*Rel, Mús*) chorister **Ⓑ** SF (*Teat*) chorus girl

cormorán SM cormorant

cornada SF butt, goring; **dar una ~ a** to gore

cornamenta SF **1** [*de toro*] horns *pl*; [*de ciervo*] antlers *pl*. **2** (*hum*) [*de marido*] cuckold's horns

cornamusa SF (= *gaita*) bagpipe; (= *cuerna*) hunting horn

córnea SF cornea

corneal ADJ corneal

cornear /1a/ VT to butt, gore

corneja SF crow

córner ['korner] SM (*pl* **~s**) corner, corner kick; **¡córner!** (*excl*) corner!; **enviar a ~** to send (out) for a corner; **sacar un ~** to take a corner

corneta Ⓐ SF (= *instrumento*) [*de orquesta*] cornet; (*Mil*) bugle; (*Carib, Méx Aut*) horn **Ⓑ** SMF [*de orquesta*] cornet player; (*Mil*) bugler

cornetín/ina Ⓐ SM (= *instrumento*) cornet **Ⓑ** SM/F (= *instrumentista*) cornet player

cornezuelo SM ergot

cornisa SF cornice; **la Cornisa Cantábrica** the Cantabrian coast

corno SM **1** (*Mús*) horn ➤ **corno inglés** cor anglais, English horn (*EEUU*) **2** (*RPl**) (*como intensificador*) **¿dónde ~/qué ~ ...?** where/what on earth ...?; **✦** MODISMO **no sabe un ~** he doesn't have a clue*

cornucopia SF cornucopia, horn of plenty

cornudo Ⓐ ADJ **1** (*Zool*) horned **2** [*marido*] cuckolded **Ⓑ** SM cuckold

coro SM **1** (= *agrupación*) choir; **niño de ~** choirboy **2** (= *composición*) (*en obra musical, tragedia*) chorus; **una chica del ~** a girl from the chorus, a chorus girl; **decir algo a ~** to say sth in a chorus *o* in unison **3** (*Arquit*) choir **4** [*de ángeles*] choir ➤ **coro celestial** celestial choir, heavenly choir

corola SF corolla

corolario SM corollary

corona SF **1** [*de rey, reina*] crown; [*de santo*] halo; (*tb ~ de flores*) (*para la cabeza*) garland ➤ **corona de espinas** crown of thorns ➤ **corona de laurel** laurel wreath **2** [*de difuntos*] wreath **3 la Corona** (= *monarquía*) the Crown; (*Hist*) (= *reino*) the kingdom **4** [*de muela*] (*natural*) crown; (*artificial*) crown, artificial crown **5** (*Mec*) [*de coche*] crown wheel; [*de bicicleta*] chain wheel; [*de reloj*] winder, crown **6** (*Fin*) crown **7** (*Astron*) corona; **la ~ solar** the sun's corona

coronación SF **1** [*de rey*] coronation **2** (= *fin*) end, culmination **3** (*Arquit*) = **coronamiento 2**

coronamiento SM **1** (= *fin*) end, culmination **2** (*Arquit*) crown

coronar /1a/ VT **1** [+ *persona*] to crown; **~ a algn rey** to crown sb king **2 ~ la cima** to reach the summit **3** (= *completar*) to crown, culminate, end

coronel(a) SM/F colonel

coronilla SF crown, top of the head; **estar hasta la ~** to be utterly fed up (**de** with)

coronta SF (*And, RPl*) deseeded corncob

coroto SM **1** (*Ven*) (= *poder*) power; **tomar el ~** to take power **2 corotos** (*Col, Ven**) (= *trastos*) odds and ends

corpiño SM (= *almilla*) bodice; (*RPl*) (= *sostén*) bra

corporación SF corporation

corporal ADJ corporal, bodily; **castigo ~** corporal punishment; **higiene ~** personal hygiene

corporativismo SM corporate spirit

corporativo ADJ corporate

corpóreo ADJ corporeal, bodily

corpulencia SF burliness, stoutness

corpulento ADJ [*persona*] burly, heavily-built; [*árbol*] stout, solid, massive

corpus SM INV corpus, body ➤ **corpus lingüístico** language corpus

corpúsculo SM corpuscle

corral SM **1** (*Agr*) (= *patio*) farmyard; [*de aves*] poultry yard; (= *redil*) pen, corral (*EEUU*) **2** [*de niño*] playpen

corralón SM **1** (= *patio*) large yard; (= *maderería*) timberyard **2** (*Perú*) (= *terreno*) vacant site *o* (*EEUU*) lot **3** (*Méx*) car pound

correa SF **1** (= *cinturón*) belt; (= *tira*) strap; (*para afilar una navaja*) strop; **la ~ de mi reloj** my watchstrap, my watchband (*EEUU*) **2** [*de perro*] leash, lead (*esp Brit*) **3** (*Mec*) ➤ **correa del ventilador** (*Aut*) fan belt ➤ **correa de seguridad** safety belt ➤ **correa de transmisión** driving belt, drive **4** (= *aguante*) give, elasticity; ✦ MODISMO **tener ~: por cualquier cosa se enfada, tiene muy poca ~** she gets angry at the slightest thing, she has a very short fuse

correaje SM (*Agr*) harness; (*Téc*) belting

corrección SF **1** (= *arreglo*) correction ➤ **corrección de pruebas** (*Tip*) proofreading **2** (= *perfección*) correctness

correccional SM reformatory

correctamente ADV **1** (= *exactamente*) correctly, accurately **2** (= *decentemente*) correctly, politely

correctivo ADJ, SM corrective

correcto ADJ **1** [*respuesta*] correct, right; **¡correcto!** right! **2** (= *educado*) [*persona*] correct; [*conducta, comportamiento*] courteous

corrector(a) Ⓐ SM/F ➤ **corrector(a) de estilo** (*Prensa*) copy editor ➤ **corrector(a) de pruebas** (*Tip*) proofreader Ⓑ SM **1** (= *líquido*) correcting fluid **2** ➤ **corrector ortográfico** (*Inform*) spell checker, spelling checker **3** (*tb ~ dental*) brace, tooth brace

corredera SF (*Téc*) slide; (= *ranura*) track, rail, runner; **puerta de ~** sliding door

corredizo ADJ [*puerta*] sliding; [*nudo*] running, slip *antes de s*

corredor(a) Ⓐ SM/F **1** (*Dep*) (= *atleta*) runner; [*de coches*] driver ➤ **corredor(a) de fondo** long-distance runner **2** (*Com*) agent, broker; (*RPl*) sales rep ➤ **corredor(a) de bolsa** stockbroker ➤ **corredor(a) de casas** house agent Ⓑ SM **1** (*en edificio*) corridor, passage ➤ **corredor de la muerte** death row ➤ **corredor de popa** (*Náut*) stern gallery **2** (*Geog, Mil*) corridor ➤ **corredor aéreo** corridor, air corridor

correduría SF brokerage

corregible ADJ rectifiable

corregidor SM (*Hist*) chief magistrate

corregir /3c, 3k/ Ⓐ VT **1** (= *rectificar*) [+ *error, defecto, rumbo, pruebas de imprenta*] to correct; [+ *vicio*] to get rid of; [+ *comportamiento*] to improve; [+ *tendencia*] to correct, counteract; (*Econ*) [+ *déficit*] to counteract; **¡deja ya de ~me!** stop correcting me!; **corrígeme si me equivoco** correct me if I'm wrong **2** (*Educ*) [+ *examen, dictado, tareas*] to mark, grade (*EEUU*) Ⓑ **corregirse** VPR **1** [*persona*] to reform, mend one's ways **2** [*defecto*] **nadando se te ~á la desviación de columna** swimming will help to correct the curvature of your spine; **la miopía no puede ~se sola** shortsightedness does not cure itself

correlación SF correlation

correlativo ADJ, SM correlative

correligionario/a SM/F **1** (*Rel*) co-religionist **2** (*Pol*) **el presidente y sus ~s** the president and his fellow party members

correntada SF (*CS*) rapids *pl*, strong current

correntoso ADJ (*LAm*) strong-flowing, rapid

correo SM **1** (= *correspondencia*) mail, post (*esp Brit*) ➤ **correo basura** (*Internet*) spam, junk e-mail **2** (= *servicio*) mail, post (*esp Brit*); **echar algo al ~** to post sth (*esp Brit*), mail sth (*esp EEUU*); **por ~** by mail *o* (*esp Brit*) post, through the mail *o* (*esp Brit*) post; **a vuelta de ~** by return (of post) (*esp Brit*), by return mail (*EEUU*) ➤ **correo aéreo** airmail ➤ **correo certificado** registered mail, registered post (*Brit*) ➤ **correo electrónico** e-mail, electronic mail ➤ **correo urgente** special delivery ➤ **correo web** webmail **3** (= *oficina*) **Correos** (*Esp*) post office *sing* **4** (= *mensajero*) courier; (*Mil*) dispatch rider

correoso ADJ **1** (*Culin*) tough, leathery **2** [*asunto, situación*] difficult, tricky*

correr /2a/ Ⓐ VI **1** (= *ir deprisa*) [*persona, animal*] to run; [*vehículo*] to go fast; **subió las escaleras corriendo** he ran up the stairs; **¡cómo corre este coche!** this car's really fast!, this car can really go some!; **no corras tanto, que hay hielo en la carretera** don't go so fast, the road's icy; ✦ MODISMO **~ como un galgo** *o* **gamo** to run like a hare **2** (= *darse prisa*) to hurry, rush; **¡corre!** hurry (up)!; **corre que llegamos tarde** hurry (up) or we'll be late; **me voy corriendo, que sale el tren dentro de diez minutos** I must dash, the train leaves in ten minutes; **hacer algo a todo ~** to do sth as fast as one can **3** (= *fluir*) [*agua*] to run, flow; [*aire*] to flow; [*grifo, fuente*] to run; **corre mucho viento** there's a strong wind blowing, it's very windy; **voy a cerrar la ventana porque corre un poco de aire** I'm going to shut the window because there's a bit of a draught *o* (*EEUU*) draft; **han corrido ríos de tinta sobre el asunto** reams and reams have been written on the subject; **por sus venas corre sangre china** he has Chinese blood; ✦ MODISMO **dejar las cosas ~** to let matters take their course **4** [*tiempo*] **¡cómo corre el tiempo!** time flies!; **corría el año 1965** it was 1965; **al** *o* **con el ~ del tiempo** over the years; **en estos** *o* **los tiempos que corren** nowadays, these days **5** [*rumor*] to go around; **las noticias corren muy deprisa** news travels fast; **la noticia corrió como la pólvora** the news spread like wildfire **6** (= *hacerse cargo*) **eso corre de mi cuenta** I'll take care of that; **~ a cargo de algn**: **eso corre a cargo de la empresa** the company will take care of that; **la entrega del premio corrió a cargo del ministro de Cultura** the prize was presented by the Minister for Culture; **~ con algo**: **~ con los gastos** to meet *o* bear the expenses; **el inversor corre con los riesgos** the investor bears the risk **7** (*Fin*) [*sueldo*] to be payable; [*moneda*] to be valid Ⓑ VT **1** (*Dep*) [+ *distancia*] to run; [+ *prueba*] to compete in; **corre cinco kilómetros diarios** she runs five kilometres a day; **Carl Lewis ha decidido no ~ los 100 metros** Carl Lewis has decided not to run (in) *o* compete in the 100 metres; **ha corrido medio mundo** he's been around half the world **2** (= *desplazar*) [+ *objeto*] to move along; [+ *silla*] to move; [+ *balanza*] to tip; [+ *nudo*] to adjust; [+ *vela*] to unfurl; **corre la cortina** draw the curtain **3** [+ *caballo*] to run, race **4** (= *tener*) [+ *riesgo*] to run; [+ *suerte*] to suffer, undergo; **no corréis peligro** you're not in (any) danger **5** (= *extender*) **el agua corrió la pintura** the water made the paint run; **las lágrimas le corrieron el maquillaje** her tears made her make-up run Ⓒ **correrse** VPR **1** (= *desplazarse*) [*objeto, persona*] to move; [*peso*] to shift; **córrete un poco** move over *o* up a bit; **el dolor se me ha corrido hacia la pierna** the pain has moved to my leg; **~se de asiento** to move up a seat **2** (= *extenderse*) [*colores, maquillaje, tinta*] to run **3** (*Bol, CS*) **se me corrió la media** I've got a run *o* (*Brit*) ladder in my tights **4** (*Esp****) (= *tener un orgasmo*) to come***

correría SF raid, foray

correspondencia SF **1** (= *cartas*) mail, post (*esp Brit*) **2** (= *relación por correo*) correspondence; **mantener ~ con algn** to correspond with sb; **un curso de dibujo por ~** a correspondence course in drawing **3** (*en el metro*) connection; **"correspondencia con las líneas tres y cinco"** "change here for lines three and five" **4** (*Mat*) correspondence

corresponder /2a/ Ⓐ VI **1** (= *tocar*) **1.1** (*en reparto*) **nos correspondieron 20 euros a cada uno** each of us got 20 euros as our share **1.2** (*como derecho*) **le corresponde un tercio de los beneficios** a third share of the profits goes to him; **me corresponde un día de vacaciones cada dos semanas** I am due one day's holiday (*esp Brit*) *o* vacation (*EEUU*) every two weeks **1.3** (*en sorteo, competición*) [*honor, victoria*] to go to; **la victoria final correspondió a Escartín** the final victory was Escartín's, the final victory went to Escartín; **al primer premio le correspondieron 30.000 euros** the winner of the first prize received 30,000 euros **2** (= *incumbir*) **~ a algn** [*responsabilidad*] to fall to sb; **le corresponde a ella decidir** it's up to her to decide; **nos**

corresponde a todos garantizar la calidad it's everyone's job to ensure quality; **"a quien corresponda"** "to whom it may concern"
3 (= *deberse*) **~ a algo: de los 50 millones de ganancias, 40 corresponden a ventas en el extranjero** out of profits of 50 million, 40 million comes from overseas sales *o* overseas sales account for 40 million
4 (*frm*) (= *ser adecuado*) **~ a: se vistió como correspondía a la ocasión** she dressed suitably for the occasion; **fue recibido como corresponde a una persona de su cargo** he was received in a manner befitting a person of his rank, he was received as befitted a person of his rank
5 (= *concordar*) **~ a** *o* **con** to match with, match up with; **los dos cadáveres hallados corresponden a los dos secuestrados** the two bodies found are those of the two kidnap victims; **esa forma de actuar no corresponde con sus principios** such behaviour is not in keeping with his principles
6 (= *retribuir*) **~ a** [+ *cariño, amor*] to return; [+ *favor, generosidad*] to repay, return; **amor no correspondido** unrequited love; **nunca podré ~ a tanta generosidad** I can never adequately repay *o* return such generosity
Ⓑ corresponderse VPR **1** (= *ajustarse*) **~se con algo** to match sth; **esas muestras no se correspondían con las del laboratorio** these samples did not match (up with) the laboratory ones; **eso no se corresponde con su modo de actuar** that is not in keeping with his usual behaviour
2 (= *coordinarse*) [*colores, piezas*] to match, go together

correspondiente ADJ **1** (= *apropiado*) appropriate **2 ~ a: los datos ~s al año anterior** the figures for the previous year; **facturas ~s a gastos de viajes** invoices for travel expenses **3** (= *respectivo*) respective; **cada regalo con su tarjeta ~** each present with its own card

corresponsable ADJ jointly responsible (**de** for)

corresponsal SMF correspondent, newspaper correspondent ➤ **corresponsal de guerra** war correspondent

corretaje SM **1** (*Fin*) brokerage **2** (*RPl Com*) wholesaling

corretear /1a/ **Ⓐ** VT **1** (*LAm*) (= *acosar*) to harass **2** (*CAm, Chi*) (= *ahuyentar*) to scare off **3** (*RPl Com*) to wholesale **Ⓑ** VI to run about

correveidile SMF (*Esp*) (= *acusica*) tell-tale; (= *chismoso*) gossip

corrida SF **1** (= *carrera*) run; **dar una ~** to make a dash; **decir algo de ~** to rattle off sth **2** (*tb* **~ de toros**) (*Taur*) bullfight **3** (*Esp****) (= *orgasmo*) orgasm **4** (*Geol*) outcrop **5** (*Chi*) (= *fila*) row, line

corrido Ⓐ ADJ **1** [*habitación, galería*] continuous
2 [*cortinas*] drawn
3 (*Esp*) (= *avergonzado*) abashed, embarrassed
4 [*estilo*] fluent, confident; **de ~** fluently; **decir algo de ~** to rattle sth off; **se lo sabía todo de ~** he knew it all right through, he could say it all from memory
Ⓑ SM (*Méx*) ballad

corriente Ⓐ ADJ **1** (= *frecuente*) [*error, apellido*] common; **un término de uso ~** a common term, a term in common use; **poco ~** unusual
2 (= *habitual*) usual, customary
3 (= *no especial*) ordinary; **fuera de lo ~** out of the ordinary; **normal y ~** perfectly ordinary; **salirse de lo ~** to be out of the ordinary; **✦** MODISMO **~ y moliente** (*Esp*) very ordinary
4 (*en curso*) [*déficit, mes, año*] current; **el día 2 del ~ mes** (on) the second of this month
5 [*agua*] running
Ⓑ SM **1 al ~ 1.1** (= *al día*) up to date; **estoy al ~ de mis pagos a Hacienda** I'm up to date with *o* on my tax payments **1.2** (= *informado*) **estar al ~ (de algo)** to know (about sth); **mantener a algn al ~ (de algo)** to keep sb up to date (on sth), keep sb informed (about sth); **poner a algn al ~ (de algo)** to bring sb up to date (on sth), inform sb (about sth); **ponerse al ~ (de algo)** to get up to date (with sth), catch up (on sth); **tener a algn al ~ (de algo)** to keep sb up to date (on sth), keep sb informed (about sth)
2 (*en cartas*) **el día 9 del ~** *o* **de los ~s** the 9th of this month
Ⓒ SF **1** [*de fluido*] current; **✦** MODISMOS **ir** *o* **navegar** *o* **nadar contra (la) ~** to swim *o* go against the tide; **seguir la ~ a algn** to humour *o* (*EEUU*) humor sb ➤ **corriente de agua** stream of water ➤ **corriente del Golfo** Gulf Stream ➤ **corriente sanguínea** bloodstream ➤ **corriente submarina** undercurrent, underwater current
2 [*de aire*] draught, draft (*EEUU*); **hay mucha ~** it's very draughty ➤ **corriente de aire** (*gen*) draught, draft (*EEUU*); (*Téc*) air current, air stream
3 (*Elec*) current; **anoche se cortó la ~** there was a power cut (*esp Brit*) *o* power outage (*EEUU*) last night; **me dio (la) ~** I got a shock, I got an electric shock ➤ **corriente alterna** alternating current ➤ **corriente continua** direct current
4 (= *tendencia*) (*ideológica*) tendency; (*artística*) trend ➤ **corriente de opinión** current of opinion

corrientemente ADV usually, normally

corrillo SM (= *grupo*) huddle, small group; (*pey*) clique, coterie

corrimiento SM (*Geol*) slip ➤ **corrimiento de tierras** landslide

corro SM **1** [*de gente*] ring, circle; **la gente hizo ~** the people formed a ring *o* circle **2** (= *baile*) ring-a-ring-a-roses

corroborar /1a/ VT to corroborate

corroer /2a/ **Ⓐ** VT **1** (*Téc*) to corrode **2** (*Geol*) to erode **3** (= *reconcomer*) to corrode, eat away; **le corroen los celos** he is eaten up with jealousy **Ⓑ corroerse** VPR to corrode, become corroded

corromper /2a/ **Ⓐ** VT **1** (= *pudrir*) [+ *madera*] to rot; [+ *alimentos*] to turn bad **2** (= *estropear*) [+ *costumbres, lengua, persona joven*] to corrupt; [+ *placeres*] to spoil **3** (= *sobornar*) to bribe **Ⓑ corromperse** VPR **1** (= *pudrirse*) [*madera*] to rot; [*alimentos*] to go bad **2** [*personas*] to become corrupted

corrompido ADJ **1** [*cosas*] rotten, putrid **2** [*personas*] corrupt

corrosión SF (*Quím*) corrosion; (*Geol*) erosion

corrosivo Ⓐ ADJ [*sustancia*] corrosive; [*lenguaje, estilo*] caustic **Ⓑ** SM corrosive

corrupción SF **1** (= *pudrición*) rot, decay **2** (*moral*) corruption **3** (*Jur*) corruption, graft (*esp EEUU*); (= *soborno*) bribery, graft (*esp EEUU*) ➤ **corrupción de menores** corruption of minors

corruptela SF **1** (= *corrupción*) corruption **2** (= *abuso*) corrupt practice, corrupt practise (*EEUU*), abuse

corrupto ADJ corrupt

corruptor(a) Ⓐ ADJ corrupting **Ⓑ** SM/F corrupter, perverter

corsario SM privateer, corsair

corsé SM corset; (*fig*) straitjacket

cortaalambres SM INV wire cutters

cortacésped SM lawnmower

cortacircuitos SM INV circuit breaker, trip switch

cortada SF **1** (*Col*) (= *corte*) cut **2** (*RPl*) (= *calle*) no through road

cortado Ⓐ ADJ **1** (= *recortado, partido*) cut; **la carne cortada en trozos grandes** meat cut into large chunks
2 [*leche*] off, sour
3 [*piel, labios*] chapped
4 [*calle, carretera*] closed; **"carretera cortada por obras"** "closed for roadworks"; **"carretera cortada al tráfico"** "road closed"

5 [*café*] with a little milk
6 (*Esp**) [*persona*] shy; **es un tío muy ~** he's a really shy guy *o* (*Brit*) bloke*; **está ~ porque no os conoce** he's shy because he doesn't know you; **dejar ~** to cut short; **quedarse ~: no te quedes ~, hombre, di algo** come on, don't be shy, say something; **me quedé ~ cuando entré en la habitación y los vi besándose** I was left speechless when I came into the room and found them kissing
Ⓑ SM *coffee with a little milk*

cortador(a) Ⓐ ADJ cutting **Ⓑ** SM/F cutter **Ⓒ** SM
➤ **cortador de cristal** glass cutter

cortadora SF cutter, cutting-machine ➤ **cortadora de césped** lawnmower

cortafrío SM cold chisel

cortafuego(s) SM (INV) fire-break, fire lane (*EEUU*)

cortante ADJ **1** [*instrumento*] cutting, sharp **2** [*viento*] cutting, biting; **hace un frío ~** it's bitterly cold **3** [*respuesta*] sharp, cutting

cortapisa SF **1** (= *restricción*) restriction, condition; **sin ~s** with no strings attached **2** (= *traba*) snag, obstacle; **poner ~s a algo/algn** to restrict *o* hold back sth/sb; **hablar sin ~s** to talk freely

cortaplumas SM INV penknife

cortapuros SM INV cigar cutter

cortar /1a/ **Ⓐ** VT **1** (*con algo afilado*) (*gen*) to cut; (*en trozos*) to chop; (*en rebanadas*) to slice; **corta la manzana por la mitad** cut the apple in half; **¿quién te ha cortado el pelo?** who cut your hair?
2 (= *partir*) [+ *árbol*] to cut down; [+ *madera*] to saw; **~ la cabeza a algn** to cut sb's head off
3 (= *dividir*) to cut
4 (= *interrumpir*) **4.1** [+ *comunicaciones, agua, corriente*] to cut off; [+ *carretera, puente*] (= *cerrar*) to close; (= *bloquear*) to block; **han cortado el gas** the gas has been cut off; **~ la hemorragia** to stop the bleeding **4.2** [+ *relaciones*] to break off; [+ *discurso, conversación*] to cut short
5 (= *censurar*) to cut
6 [*frío*] to chap, crack; **el frío me corta los labios** the cold is chapping *o* cracking my lips
7 [+ *baraja*] to cut
Ⓑ VI **1** (= *estar afilado*) to cut
2 (*Inform*) **"cortar y pegar"** "cut and paste"
3 (= *acortar*) **podemos ~ por el parque** we can take a shortcut through the park; **es mejor que cortéis por el atajo** it would be better if you took the shortcut
4 **~ con** (= *terminar*): **con el pasado** to make a break with the past; **hay que ~ con este comportamiento** we must put a stop to this behaviour; **ha cortado con su novia** he's broken up with *o* finished with his girlfriend
5 **¡corta!*** give us a break!*
6 (*Naipes*) to cut
7 (*Radio*) **¡corto!** over!; **¡corto y cierro!** over and out!
8 (*CS Telec*) to hang up; **cortó** he hung up
Ⓒ **cortarse** VPR **1** (*con algo afilado*) **1.1** [*persona*] to cut o.s.
1.2 **me corté el dedo con un cristal** I cut my finger on a piece of glass; **~se las uñas** to cut one's nails; **ha ido a ~se el pelo** she's gone to get her hair cut, she's gone to the hairdresser's, she's gone for a haircut; **se cortó las venas** she slashed her wrists
2 [*manos, labios*] to get chapped
3 (*Culin*) [*mayonesa, natillas*] to curdle; [*leche*] to go off
4 (*) (= *cohibirse*) to get embarrassed; **no te cortes** don't be shy; **no se corta a la hora de decir lo que piensa** she doesn't hold back at all when it comes to saying what she thinks
5 (= *interrumpirse*) [*luz*] to go off, go out

cortaúñas SM INV nail clippers

corte¹ SM **1** (= *incisión, herida*) cut; **le hizo un ~ a la madera** he made a cut in the wood; **hacerse un ~** to cut o.s.; **me he hecho un ~ en el dedo** I've cut my finger ➤ **corte longitudinal** lengthwise section, longitudinal section ➤ **corte transversal** cross section
2 (*tb* ~ **de pelo**) cut, haircut ➤ **corte a navaja** razor cut ➤ **corte a tijera** scissor cut
3 (*Cos*) (= *diseño*) cut; **un traje de ~ muy moderno** a suit

with a very modern cut ➤ **corte y confección** dressmaking
4 (= *interrupción*) cut ➤ **corte de carretera** (*para obras, accidente*) road closure; (*como protesta*) roadblock ➤ **corte de digestión** severe attack of indigestion ➤ **corte de luz** power cut (*esp Brit*), power outage (*EEUU*) ➤ **corte publicitario** commercial break
5 (*esp LAm*) (= *reducción*) [*de presupuesto*] cut
6 (= *estilo*) **literatura de ~ tradicional** traditional (type) literature; **un discurso de ~ fascista** a speech with fascist undertones
7 (= *trozo*) [*de carne*] cut; [*de helado*] (*Esp*) wafer, ice cream sandwich (*EEUU*)
8 (*) (= *respuesta contundente*) **dar un ~ a algn: ¡vaya ~ que te dieron!** that was one in the eye for you, wasn't it? ➤ **corte de mangas: hacer un ~ de mangas a algn** to give sb the finger
9 (*Esp**) (= *vergüenza*) **¡qué ~!** how embarrassing!; **me da ~ que me vean contigo** I'm embarrassed to be seen with you
10 (= *borde*) edge
11 [*de disco*] track
12 (*RPl*) (= *importancia*) **darse ~s** to put on airs

corte² SF **1** [*de un rey*] (= *residencia*) court; (= *séquito*) court, entourage, retinue
2 **hacer la ~ a algn** (= *cortejar*) to pay court to sb; (= *halagar*) to win favour with sb, lick sb's boots*, suck up to sb*
3 (*Jur*) law court ➤ **Corte de Justicia** Court of Justice ➤ **Corte Suprema** Supreme Court
4 **las Cortes** (*Esp Pol*) Spanish parliament ➤ **Cortes Constituyentes** constituent assembly ➤ **Cortes Generales** Parliament

---

CORTES GENERALES

The Spanish parliament consists of a lower house, the **Congreso de los Diputados**, and an upper house, the **Senado**. Members of the lower house are called **diputados** and members of the **Senado** are **senadores**.

---

cortejar /1a/ VT to court, woo

cortejo SM **1** (= *séquito*) entourage, retinue **2** (*Rel*) procession ➤ **cortejo fúnebre** funeral cortège, funeral procession **3** (= *acción*) wooing, courting

cortés ADJ **1** (= *atento*) courteous, polite **2** **amor ~** courtly love

cortesana SF courtesan

cortesano Ⓐ ADJ of the court, courtly **Ⓑ** SM courtier

cortesía SF **1** (= *conducta*) courtesy, politeness; **visita de ~** courtesy call; **por ~** as a courtesy **2** (= *etiqueta*) social etiquette **3** (= *regalo*) present, gift

córtex SM cortex

corteza SF [*de árbol*] bark; [*de pan*] crust; [*de fruta*] peel, skin; [*de queso, tocino*] rind ➤ **corteza cerebral** cerebral cortex ➤ **corteza de cerdo** pork rind ➤ **corteza terrestre** earth's crust

corticoide SM corticoid

cortijo SM (*Esp*) farmhouse

cortina SF (*para ventana*) curtain, drape (*EEUU*); (*fig*) screen ➤ **cortina de ducha** shower curtain ➤ **cortina de hierro** (*LAm Pol*) iron curtain ➤ **cortina de humo** smoke screen ➤ **cortina musical** (*CS TV*) musical interlude

cortisona SF cortisone

corto Ⓐ ADJ **1** [*longitud, distancia*] short; **una camisa de manga corta** a short-sleeved shirt; **el vestido se le ha quedado ~** the dress has got too short for her
2 [*periodo, visita, reunión*] short, brief; **los días se van haciendo más ~s** the days are getting shorter; **la película se me hizo muy corta** the film was over *o* went very quickly
3 (= *escaso*) **dos niñas de corta edad** two very young girls; **~ de algo: un café con leche, pero ~ de café** a coffee with plenty of milk, a milky coffee; **ando** *o* **voy ~ de dinero** I'm short of money; **ando** *o* **voy muy ~ de tiempo** I'm short of time, I'm pressed *o* (*Brit*) pushed for time; **~ de vista** shortsighted (*Brit*), nearsighted (*EEUU*); **quedarse ~: costará**

unos tres millones, y seguro que me quedo ~ it will cost three million, and I'm probably underestimating; **le dijo lo que pensaba de él, pero se quedó** ~ she told him what she thought of him, but it still wasn't enough
4 (= *tímido*) shy; ✦ MODISMO **ni ~ ni perezoso** as bold as brass
5 (= *torpe*) dim*, thick (*Brit**)
B SM **1** (*Cine*) short, short film
2 (*Esp*) [*de cerveza, vino*] small glass; [*de café*] black coffee
3 (*Chi*) [*de alcohol*] shot
4 cortos (*Col, Ven*) [*de película*] trailer *sing*
C SF **a la corta o a la larga** sooner or later

cortocircuito SM short-circuit

cortometraje SM short

coruñés ADJ of/from Corunna

corva SF back of the knee

corvina SF sea bass, croaker

corvo ADJ (= *curvo*) curved, bent; [*nariz*] hooked

corzo/a SM/F roe deer

cosa SF **1** (= *objeto*) thing; **cogí mis ~s y me fui** I picked up my things and left; **para el dolor de cabeza no tengo otra ~ que aspirina** all I have for headaches is aspirin; **~s de comer** things to eat; ✦ MODISMO **es ~ fina*** it's excellent stuff*
2 (*uso indefinido*) **¿alguna ~ más?** anything else?; **o ~ así: 20 kilos o ~ así** 20 kilos or thereabouts; **y ~s así** and suchlike; **cualquier** ~ anything; **haría cualquier ~ por ella** I'd do anything for her; **este vino no es cualquier ~** this isn't just any old wine; **poca ~: vive bien con poca ~** she lives well on very little; **no te preocupes por tan poca ~** don't worry about a little thing like that; **la chica es muy poquita ~** there's not much of her; **una ~** something; **hay una ~ que no me gusta** there is one thing I don't like; **¿me puedes decir una ~?** can you tell me something?; **una ~, se me olvidaba preguntarte por el precio** by the way, I forgot to ask you about the price
3 (= *asunto*) **eso es ~ tuya** that's your affair; **¿has visto ~ igual?** did you ever see the like?; **¡qué ~ más extraña!** how strange!; **la ~ es que ...** the thing is (that) ...; **no es ~ de broma** o **risa** it's no laughing matter; **no es ~ de que lo dejes todo** there's no need for you to give it all up; **no sea ~ que** in case; **~ rara: y, ~ rara,** nadie lo vio and, oddly o funnily enough, nobody saw it; ✦ MODISMOS **a otra ~, mariposa** it's time to move on; **como quien no quiere la ~: lo miraba como quien no quiere la ~** she cast a casual glance at the boy; **se levantó y se fue como quien no quiere la ~** she got up and left as inconspicuously as possible; **como si tal ~ se quedó como si tal ~** he barely reacted
4 (= *nada*) **no hay ~ peor** there's nothing worse; **¡no hay tal ~!** nothing of the sort!; ✦ MODISMO **no es ninguna ~ del otro jueves** o **mundo** it's nothing to write home about
5 cosas 5.1 (= *acciones, asuntos*) **son ~s de la edad** it's just old age; **¡~s de niños!** kids will be kids!; **¡qué ~s dices!** you do say some silly things!; **¡tienes unas ~s!** the things you say!; ✦ MODISMO **decir cuatro ~s a algn** to give sb a piece of one's mind **5.2 las ~s** (= *situación*) things; **tal como están las ~s** as things stand; **¡lo que son las ~s!** just imagine!, fancy that!; ✦ MODISMO **las ~s de palacio van despacio** it all takes time, the mills of God grind slowly
6 ~ de (*indicando tiempo*) about; **es ~ de un par de semanas** it takes about a couple of weeks; **en ~ de diez minutos** in about ten minutes
7 (*SAm*) (*como conj*) **~ de** so as to; **apurémonos, ~ de estar listos cuando llegue** let's be quick, so as to be ready when he arrives o so we're ready when he arrives; **~ que: camina lento, ~ que no te canses** walk slowly so (that) you don't get tired; **no le digas nada, ~ que no se ofenda** don't say anything to him, that way he won't get offended

cosaco/a ADJ, SM/F Cossack; ✦ MODISMO **beber como un ~** to drink like a fish

coscarse* /1g/ VPR to catch on, get it*

coscorrón SM **1** (= *golpe*) bump on the head
2 (= *contratiempo*) setback, knock

cosecha SF **1** (= *recogida*) harvest; (= *temporada*) harvest, harvest time; **la ~ de 1972** (= *vino*) the 1972 vintage
2 (= *producto*) crop; **de ~ propia** home-grown, home-

produced; ✦ MODISMO **cosas de su propia ~** things of one's own invention **3** (= *producción*) yield

cosechadora SF combine (harvester)

cosechar /1a/ VT **1** (= *recoger*) [+ *cereales*] to harvest, reap; [+ *frutas*] to harvest, pick **2** (*Esp*) (= *cultivar*) to grow, cultivate **3** (= *ganar*) [+ *admiración, premios*] to win; [+ *respeto*] to win, earn; [+ *fracasos , éxitos*] to achieve; [+ *enemigos*] to earn, make

cosechero/a SM/F producer

coseno SM cosine

coser /2a/ **A** VT **1** [+ *vestido*] to sew, sew up; [+ *botón*] to sew on, stitch on; ✦ MODISMO **es cosa de ~ y cantar** it's easy as pie*, it's as simple as ABC* **2** (*Med*) to stitch, stitch up; **~ con grapas** to staple **3** ✦ MODISMOS **~ a algn a balazos** to riddle sb with bullets; **~ a algn a puñaladas** to stab sb repeatedly, carve sb up* **B** VI to sew

cosher ADJ INV kosher

cosificar /1g/ VT to treat as an object

cosmética SF cosmetics *pl*

cosmético ADJ, SM cosmetic

cósmico ADJ cosmic

cosmogonía SF cosmogony

cosmografía SF cosmography

cosmógrafo/a SM/F cosmographer

cosmología SF cosmology

cosmonauta SMF cosmonaut

cosmopolita ADJ, SMF cosmopolitan

cosmos SM INV cosmos

cosmovisión SF world view

coso¹ SM (= *recinto*) enclosure; (*esp Taur*) bullring

coso² SM (= *insecto*) woodworm

coso³* SM (= *cosa*) thingummy*, thingamajig (*EEUU**), what-d'you-call-it

cospel SM (*Arg*) telephone token

cosquillas SFPL tickling, tickling sensation; **buscar las ~ a algn** to tease sb; **me hace ~** it tickles; **hacer ~ a algn** to tickle sb; **tener ~** to be ticklish

cosquillear /1a/ VT to tickle

cosquilleo SM tickling, tickling sensation

costa¹ SF **1 a ~ de algo/algn: nos estuvimos riendo a ~ suya** we had a laugh at his expense; **lo ha conseguido a ~ de muchos sacrificios** he has achieved it by making many sacrifices; **a toda ~** at all costs **2 costas** (*Jur*) costs

costa² SF **1** (*Geog*) [*del mar*] coast; **la ~ mediterránea** the Mediterranean coast; **la ~ del Atlántico es muy accidentada** the Atlantic coastline is very rugged ➤ **la Costa Azul** the Côte d'Azur **2** (*Náut*) shore **3** (*CS*) [*de un río*] bank, riverbank; [*de un lago*] shore

Costa de Marfil SF Ivory Coast

costado SM **1** [*de objeto*] side **2** (*Anat*) side; **de ~** [*tumbarse*] on one's side; [*moverse*] sideways; ✦ MODISMO **español por los cuatro ~s** Spanish through and through

costal SM sack, bag

costalada SF, **costalazo** SM (= *caída*) bad fall; **darse una ~** to fall on one's back

costanera SF (*CS*) **1** [*de mar*] (= *paseo*) seaside promenade; (= *carretera*) coast road **2** [*de río*] (= *paseo*) riverside promenade; (= *carretera*) riverside road

costar /1l/ **A** VT **1** (*en dinero*) to cost; **¿cuánto te ha costado el libro?** how much did you pay for the book?, how much did the book cost (you)?; **¿cuánto cuesta este libro?** how much is this book?, how much does this book cost?; ✦ MODISMO **~ un ojo de la cara*** to cost an arm and a leg*
2 (*en esfuerzo, tiempo*) **me ha costado lo mío llegar adonde he llegado** it's taken a lot to get where I am; **cada traducción nos cuesta muchas horas de trabajo** each translation takes us many hours of work; **¿te ha costado trabajo encontrar la casa?** did you have trouble finding the house?; ✦ MODISMO **cueste lo que cueste** whatever it takes

3 (*en consecuencias*) to cost; **ese error te ~á el puesto** that mistake will cost you your job *o* will lose you your job; **el accidente por poco le cuesta la vida** the accident nearly cost him his life; **la violación le costó doce años de cárcel** the rape earned him twelve years in prison, he got twelve years in prison for the rape
🅑 VI **1** (*en dinero*) **este abrigo me ha costado muy barato** this coat was very cheap
2 (*en dificultad*) to be hard, be difficult; **cuesta reconocerlo, pero es verdad** it's hard *o* difficult to admit it, but it's true; **~ a algn: lo que más me cuesta es el inglés** the thing I find hardest *o* most difficult is English; **no me cuesta nada llevarte** it's no trouble to give you a ride *o* (*esp Brit*) lift
3 (*en consecuencias*) **~ caro a algn** to cost sb dear

Costa Rica SF Costa Rica

costarricense ADJ, SMF, **costarriqueño/a** ADJ, SM/F Costa Rican

coste SM (*Esp*) cost; **a precio de ~** at cost, at cost price (*Brit*) ➤ **coste de fabricación** manufacturing cost ➤ **coste de la vida** cost of living ➤ **coste de mantenimiento** upkeep, maintenance cost ➤ **costes de producción** production costs

costear¹ /1a/ 🅐 VT (= *financiar*) to pay for, finance (*más frm*); (*Com, Fin*) to finance; **no lo podemos ~** we can't afford it 🅑 **costearse** VPR **~se los estudios** to pay for one's studies; **~se los caprichos** to pay for one's little indulgences

costear² /1a/ VT (*Náut*) to sail along the coast of; [+ *río*] to sail close to the banks of

costeño/a 🅐 ADJ coastal 🅑 SM/F coastal dweller

costero ADJ coastal; [*barco, comercio*] coasting

costilla SF **1** (*Anat*) rib **2** (*Culin*) sparerib ➤ **costilla de cerdo** pork chop, pork cutlet **3** (*) (= *mujer*) wife, better half (*hum**); (*Perú*) (= *novia*) girl, girlfriend

costillar SM **1** (*Anat*) ribcage **2** (*Culin*) ribs *pl*

costo SM **1** (*esp LAm Fin*) cost ➤ **costo de expedición** shipping charges *pl*; *ver tb* **coste 2** (*Esp***) (= *hachís*) dope**

costoso ADJ costly, expensive

costra SF **1** (= *corteza*) crust **2** (*Med*) scab

costumbre SF **1** (*tradicional*) custom; **novela de ~s** novel of (local) customs and manners
2 [*de una persona*] habit; **persona de buenas ~s** respectable person, decent person; **he perdido la ~** I've got out of the habit; **tener la ~ de hacer algo** ◇ **tener por ~ hacer algo** to be in the habit of doing sth

> Recuérdese que las preposiciones en inglés rigen gerundio y no infinitivo, de ahí **to be in the habit of doing sth**.

3 de ~ (*adj*) usual; (*adv*) usually; **como de ~** as usual; **más que de ~** more than usual

costumbrismo SM (*Literat*) *literature of local customs and manners*

costumbrista ADJ (*Literat*) of local customs and manners

costura SF **1** (= *puntadas*) seam; **sin ~** seamless **2** (= *labor*) sewing, needlework; (= *confección*) dressmaking; **alta ~** haute couture, high fashion

costurera SF dressmaker, seamstress

costurero SM (= *caja*) sewing box; (= *cuarto*) sewing room

cota¹ SF **1** (*Hist*) ➤ **cota de malla** coat of mail **2** (*Carib*) (= *blusa*) blouse

cota² SF **1** (*Geog*) height above sea level; (= *altura*) height, level **2** (= *cifra*) number, figure

cotarro* SM **dirigir el ~** to be the boss, rule the roost

cotejar /1a/ VT to compare, collate

cotejo SM **1** (= *comparación*) comparison, collation **2** (*Dep*) game, match (*esp Brit*)

cotelé SM (*Chi*) corduroy

cotidianeidad SF daily nature, routine character

cotidiano ADJ daily, everyday; **la vida cotidiana** daily life, everyday life

cotiledón SM cotyledon

cotilla* SMF (*Esp*) gossip

cotillear* /1a/ VI (*Esp*) to gossip

cotilleo* SM (*Esp*) gossip, gossiping

cotillón SM ≈ New Year's Eve party

cotización SF **1** (*Fin*) price ➤ **cotización de apertura** opening price ➤ **cotización de cierre, cotización de clausura** closing price **2** [*de club*] dues *pl*, subscription; (*a la Seguridad Social*) National Insurance contributions *pl* ➤ **cotización empresarial** employer contribution
3 (= *cambio*) exchange rate **4** (*And*) [*de antigüedad, joya*] valuation; [+ *de proyecto, obra*] estimate

cotizado ADJ (= *solicitado*) in demand, sought-after; (= *estimado*) valued, esteemed

cotizar /1f/ 🅐 VI **1** (= *contribuir*) to make contributions, pay contributions; **~ a la Seguridad Social** to pay National Insurance contributions
2 (*Fin*) **nuestra empresa cotiza ahora en Bolsa** our company is now quoted on the Stock Exchange; **al cierre cotizó a 12,35 euros** it closed at 12.35 euros, at the close it stood at 12.35 euros
🅑 VT **1** [+ *cuota, recibo, impuesto*] to pay
2 (*And*) [+ *antigüedad, joya*] to value; [+ *proyecto, obra*] to estimate for
🅒 **cotizarse** VPR **1** [*acciones*] to stand at, be quoted at; [*divisa*] to stand at; **estas acciones se están cotizando a once dólares** these shares are standing *o* (being) quoted at eleven dollars; **éste es el valor que más se cotiza** this is the most commonly quoted price; **el dólar se cotizó hoy a 102,32 yenes** the dollar stood at 102.32 yen today
2 (= *valorarse*) to be valued; **los conocimientos de inglés se cotizan muy alto** knowledge of English is highly valued

coto¹ SM **1** (= *reserva*) reserve ➤ **coto de caza** game preserve ➤ **coto de pesca** fishing preserve ➤ **coto privado** private reserve **2** **poner ~ a algo** to put a stop to sth

coto² SM (*And, Ven Med*) goitre, goiter (*EEUU*)

cotón SM printed cotton, cotton fabric

cotona SF (*Chi*) *tightly woven cotton shirt*

cotonete SM (*Méx*) cotton bud (*Brit*), Q-tip® (*EEUU*)

cotorra SF **1** (*Orn*) (= *loro*) parrot; (= *urraca*) magpie **2** (*) (= *persona*) chatterbox*, windbag (* *pey*) **3** (*Ven**) (= *conversación*) long chat; (= *mentira*) story*, lie

cotorrear* /1a/ VI to chatter

cotorro* ADJ chatty, talkative

cototo SM (*Chi*) bump, bruise, bruise on the head

cotudo ADJ **1** (*And, Ven Med*) suffering from goitre *o* (*EEUU*) goiter **2** (*Col*) (= *tonto*) stupid

cotufas SFPL (*Ven*) popcorn *sing*

COU SM ABR (*Esp*) (= **Curso de Orientación Universitaria**) *formerly, preparatory one-year course for the university entrance examinations*

covacha* SF hovel

covadera SF (*And*) guano deposit

coxis SM INV coccyx

coyón* ADJ (*Méx*) cowardly

coyote SM **1** (*Zool*) coyote, prairie wolf **2** (*Méx, CAm**) (= *intermediario*) fixer*; (= *guía*) people-smuggler

coyuntura SF **1** (*Anat*) joint **2** (= *momento*) juncture; **en esta ~** at this juncture, at this moment in time; **esperar una ~ favorable** to wait for a suitable moment
3 (= *situación*) situation; **la ~ política** the political situation

coyuntural ADJ **datos ~es** relevant data; **medidas ~es** immediately relevant measures; **solución ~** interim solution

coz SF **1** (= *patada*) kick; **dar (de) coces a** to kick **2** [*de fusil*] (= *retroceso*) recoil, kick; (= *culata*) butt

cps. ABR (= **caracteres por segundo**) cps

crac¹ SM (*Com, Fin*) crash; **el ~ del 29** the 1929 Stock Exchange crash

crac² EXCL crack!, snap!

crack SM **1** (*LAm Dep*) (= *persona*) top player, star player; (= *caballo*) champion horse **2** (*) (= *droga*) crack**

cranear* /1a/ Ⓐ VT (*And*) to dream up* Ⓑ **cranearse** VPR **1** (*And*) to dream up* **2** (*Chi*) (= *estudiar*) to cram* **3** (*Chi*) (= *pensar*) to think hard

cráneo SM skull, cranium (*frm*); ✦ MODISMO **ir de ~***: **voy de ~** it's all going wrong for me

crápula Ⓐ SF (= *embriaguez*) drunkenness; (= *disipación*) dissipation Ⓑ SM wastrel

craso ADJ **1** (= *gordo*) [*persona*] fat; [*líquido*] greasy, thick **2** [*error*] gross, crass

cráter SM crater

crayón SM (*Méx, RPI*) crayon, chalk

creación SF **1** (= *acción*) **1.1** [*de obra, objeto, empleo, ambiente*] creation **1.2** [*de empresa, asociación*] **incentivos para la ~ de empresas** incentives aimed at creating new businesses; **piden la ~ de una comisión de investigación** they are asking for a committee of inquiry to be set up; **desde su ~** since its creation *o* foundation **2** (= *cosa creada*) creation **3 la Creación** (*Rel*) the Creation

creador(a) Ⓐ ADJ creative Ⓑ SM/F **1** [*de movimiento, organización, personaje*] creator **2** (= *artista*) artist; (= *diseñador*) designer Ⓒ SM **el Creador** (*Rel*) the Creator

crear /1a/ VT **1** (= *hacer, producir*) [+ *obra, objeto, empleo*] to create **2** (= *establecer*) [+ *comisión, fondo, negocio, sistema*] to set up; [+ *asociación, cooperativa*] to form, set up; [+ *cargo, puesto*] to create; [+ *movimiento, organización*] to create, establish, found **3** (= *dar lugar a*) [+ *condiciones, clima, ambiente*] to create; [+ *problemas*] to cause, create; [+ *expectativas*] to raise; **el vacío creado por su muerte** the gap left *o* created by her death; **la nicotina crea adicción** nicotine is addictive **4** (*liter*) (= *nombrar*) to make, appoint

creatividad SF creativity

creativo/a Ⓐ ADJ creative Ⓑ SM/F (*tb* ~ **de publicidad**) copywriter

crecepelo SM hair-restorer

crecer /2d/ Ⓐ VI **1** (= *desarrollarse*) [*animal, planta*] to grow; **me he dejado ~ la barba** I've grown a beard; **crecí en Sevilla** I grew up in Seville **2** (= *aumentar*) [*cantidad, producción, sentimiento*] to grow; [*gastos*] to increase, rise; [*inflación*] to rise; [*desempleo*] to increase, grow, rise; **la economía española ~á un 4%** the Spanish economy will grow by 4%; **el viento fue creciendo en intensidad** the wind increased *o* grew in intensity **3** (= *extenderse*) [*ciudad*] to grow; [*río, marea*] to rise; [*luna*] to wax Ⓑ **crecerse** VPR **1** (= *tomar fuerza*) **pocos jugadores saben ~se ante la adversidad** there are few players who can stand up and be counted in the face of adversity **2** (*) (= *engreírse*) to get full of o.s.

creces SFPL **con ~ amply, fully; superó las expectativas con ~** she far exceeded *o* surpassed all expectations; **pagó con ~ lo que debía** he paid back the full amount and more, he gave back everything he owed and more; **devolver un favor/el cariño con ~** to return a favour/sb's affection hundredfold

crecida SF [*de río*] (= *aumento del cauce*) rise in level; (= *inundación*) flooding

crecido ADJ **1** [*persona*] **está muy ~ para su edad** he's very tall *o* big for his age; **está ya crecidita para saber lo que se hace** (*iró*) she's old enough to know what she's doing **2** [*río*] high **3** [*cantidad, número*] large **4** [*pelo, barba*] **tienes el pelo mucho más ~ que cuando te vi la última vez** your hair is much longer than last time I saw you **5** (= *engreído*) vain, conceited

creciente Ⓐ ADJ **1** [*tendencia, demanda, volumen*] growing, increasing **2** [*luna*] waxing Ⓑ SM (*Astron*) [*de la luna*] crescent ➤ **el Creciente Rojo** the Red Crescent

crecimiento SM **1** (*en seres vivos*) growth **2** (= *aumento*) growth; **el ~ del gasto público** the growth *o* increase in public spending; **una población en ~** a growing population

➤ **crecimiento demográfico** population growth
➤ **crecimiento sostenido** sustained growth

credencial SF **1** (= *documento*) document confirming appointment **2 credenciales** credentials

credibilidad SF credibility

crédito SM **1** (= *fe*) credit; **dar ~ a algo** to believe sth, credit sth; **persona (digna) de ~** reliable person **2** (= *fama*) standing, reputation **3** (*Com, Fin*) credit; **a ~** on credit ➤ **crédito a corto plazo** short-term credit ➤ **crédito a la exportación** export credit ➤ **crédito a largo plazo** long-term credit ➤ **crédito bancario** bank credit ➤ **crédito de vivienda** mortgage ➤ **crédito hipotecario** mortgage loan ➤ **crédito personal** personal credit **4** (*Univ*) credit **5** (*Cine, TV*) ~**s** credits

credo SM (*Rel*) creed; **el Credo** the Creed

credulidad SF credulity

crédulo/a Ⓐ ADJ gullible, credulous Ⓑ SM/F **es tan ~** he's so gullible

creencia SF belief (**en** in); **en la ~ de que ...** in the belief that ...

creer /2e/ Ⓐ VI **1** (= *pensar*) **es de Madrid, según creo** I believe she's from Madrid; **no creo** I don't think so; **es difícil, no creas** it's hard enough, I can tell you **2** ~ **en** to believe in; **creen en Dios** they believe in God; **creo en la igualdad** I believe in equality Ⓑ VT **1** (= *considerar cierto*) to believe; **nadie me cree** nobody believes me; —**¿quieres un café?** —**¡ya lo creo!** "do you want some coffee?" — "you bet!"*; **¡ya lo creo que está roto!** you bet it's broken!, it certainly is broken!; **¿que yo voy a ir andando hasta el faro? ¡ya lo creo!** (*iró*) you think I'm going to walk all the way to the lighthouse? you must be joking!* **2** (= *pensar*) to think; **creo que es sincera** I think she's sincere, I believe her to be sincere; **creo que sí** I think so; **no se vaya usted a ~ que ...** don't go thinking that ..., I wouldn't want you to think that ... **3** (= *considerar*) to think; **lo creo mi deber** I think *o* consider it (to be) my duty Ⓒ **creerse** VPR **1** (= *considerar cierto*) to believe; **no me lo creo** I don't believe it; **¡que te crees tú eso!*** you must be joking!*; **¡no te lo crees ni tú!*** come off it!* **2** (= *pensar*) to think; **¿de dónde te crees que sacan el dinero?** where do you think they get their money?; **¿pero tú qué te crees, que soy millonario?** what do you think I am, a millionaire or something? **3** (= *considerarse*) to think; **se cree muy listo** he thinks he's pretty clever; **¿qué se ha creído?** who does he think he is?

creíble ADJ believable, credible

creído/a Ⓐ ADJ **1** (= *engreído*) conceited **2** (= *crédulo*) credulous, trusting Ⓑ SM/F **es un ~** he's very full of himself

crema Ⓐ SF **1** (*en cosmética, de zapatos*) cream ➤ **crema antiarrugas** anti-wrinkle cream ➤ **crema bronceadora** suntan lotion, suntan cream ➤ **crema de afeitar** shaving cream ➤ **crema de manos** hand cream ➤ **crema depilatoria** hair removing cream, depilatory cream ➤ **crema de zapatos** shoe cream ➤ **crema hidratante** moisturizer, moisturizing cream **2** (= *licor*) cream liqueur, crème **3** (*Culin*) (*tb* ~ **de leche**) cream; ~ **líquida** pouring cream, single cream (*Brit*), light cream (*EEUU*); **una ~ de champiñones** cream of mushroom (soup) ➤ **crema agria** sour cream, soured cream ➤ **crema catalana** *dessert similar to crème brûlée* ➤ **crema de cacao, crema de chocolate** chocolate filling ➤ **crema pastelera** confectioner's cream, custard, crème pâtissière **4 la ~** (= *lo mejor*) the cream **5** (*Tip*) (= *diéresis*) diaeresis, dieresis (*EEUU*) Ⓑ ADJ INV [*color*] cream, cream-coloured, cream-colored (*EEUU*)

cremación SF cremation

cremallera SF **1** (*Cos*) zip (*Brit*), zipper (*esp EEUU*); **cerrar la ~** do the zip (*Brit*) *o* zipper (*esp EEUU*) up **2** (*Téc*) rack

cremar /1a/ VT (*Méx*) to cremate

crematístico ADJ financial, economic

crematorio Ⓐ ADJ **horno ~ = B** Ⓑ SM crematorium

cremoso ADJ creamy

crep[1] SM (= *tela*) crêpe, crepe; (= *caucho*) crêpe (rubber), crepe (rubber)

crep[2] SM, **crepa** SF (*Méx Culin*) pancake, crêpe

crepe SM o SF pancake, crêpe

crepé SM 1 (= *tela*) crêpe, crepe; (= *caucho*) crêpe (rubber), crepe (rubber) 2 (*Méx*) (= *peluca*) wig

crepería SF pancake restaurant, crêperie

crepitar /1a/ VI [*leño*] to crackle; [*bacon*] to sizzle

crepuscular ADJ twilight *antes de s*, crepuscular (*liter, frm*); **luz ~** twilight

crepúsculo SM twilight, dusk

crescendo SM crescendo; **ir en ~** to increase, get louder o greater *etc*

crespo Ⓐ ADJ (= *rizado*) [*pelo*] curly; [*hoja*] curled Ⓑ SM (*LAm*) (= *rizo*) curl, ringlet

crespón SM crêpe, crepe, crape

cresta SF 1 (*Orn*) (*gen*) crest; [*de gallo*] comb 2 (*Geog*) crest 3 [*de ola*] crest; ✦ MODISMO **en la ~ de la ola** on the crest of a wave

cretino/a Ⓐ ADJ cretinous Ⓑ SM/F cretin

cretona SF cretonne

creyendo *etc ver* **creer**

creyente SMF believer; **no ~** non-believer, unbeliever

cría SF 1 (*Agr*) (= *actividad*) rearing; (*para la reproducción*) breeding ➤ **cría de ganado** cattle breeding, stockbreeding 2 (*Zool*) (= *camada*) litter; (= *individuo*) baby animal; **una ~ de ballena** a baby whale; **una ~ de león** a lion cub

criadero SM 1 (*Bot*) nursery 2 (*Zool*) breeding place, breeding ground ➤ **criadero de ostras** oyster bed ➤ **criadero de peces** fish hatchery, fish farm

criadilla SF (*Culin*) testicle

criado/a Ⓐ ADJ reared, brought up; **bien ~** well-bred Ⓑ SM/F (= *hombre*) servant; (= *mujer*) servant, maid

crianza SF 1 (*Agr*) (= *actividad*) rearing; (*para la reproducción*) breeding 2 (*Med*) lactation 3 [*de vinos*] vintage ➤ **vinos de crianza** vintage wines 4 (= *educación*) breeding; **mala ~** lack of breeding

criar /1c/ Ⓐ VT 1 (= *educar*) [+ *niño*] to bring up, raise; ✦ REFRÁN **Dios los cría y ellos se juntan** birds of a feather flock together 2 (= *amamantar*) to nurse, suckle, feed; **~ con biberón** to bottle-feed; **~ con el pecho** to breast-feed 3 [+ *ganado*] to raise, rear (*esp Brit*); [+ *aves de corral*] to breed; (*para competición*) to breed 4 [+ *hortalizas*] to grow 5 (= *producir*) **los perros crían pulgas** dogs get fleas; **~ barriga** to get a belly*; **~ polvo** to gather dust Ⓑ VI 1 (= *tener crías*) to breed 2 [*vino*] to age, mature Ⓒ **criarse** VPR to grow up; **se ~on juntos** they grew up together; **se ha criado con sus abuelos** he was brought up o raised by his grandparents

criatura SF 1 (= *ser creado*) creature 2 (= *niño pequeño*) child 3 (*dicho cariñosamente*) **¡pobre ~!** poor little thing!; **pero ~, ¿cómo no te has dado cuenta antes?** you silly thing, how come you didn't realize before?

criba SF 1 (= *instrumento*) sieve 2 (= *acto*) sifting, selection; ✦ MODISMO **hacer una ~** to sort out the sheep from the goats

cribar /1a/ VT to sieve, sift

crimen SM 1 (= *asesinato*) murder; (= *delito grave*) crime ➤ **crimen de guerra** war crime ➤ **crimen organizado** organized crime ➤ **crimen pasional** crime of passion, crime passionnel (*frm*) 2 (*) (= *barbaridad*) **es un ~ dejar aquí al niño** it's criminal to leave the child here

criminal Ⓐ ADJ [*comportamiento, acto*] criminal Ⓑ SMF (= *asesino*) murderer, killer ➤ **criminal de guerra** war criminal

criminalidad SF 1 (= *cualidad*) criminality 2 (= *índice*) crime rate

criminalista SMF 1 (*Univ*) criminologist 2 (*Jur*) criminal lawyer

criminología SF criminology

criminólogo/a SM/F criminologist

crin SF (*Zool*) mane; (*Téc*) horsehair

crío/a SM/F kid*, child; (*pey*) little brat*; **¡no seas ~!** grow up!, don't be such a baby!

criogenizar /1f/ VT to freeze cryogenically

criollo/a Ⓐ ADJ 1 (*Hist*) Creole; (= *de origen español*) of Spanish extraction 2 (*LAm*) (= *no extranjero*) (native) Peruvian/Colombian/Ecuadorean *etc* Ⓑ SM/F 1 (*Hist*) Creole 2 (*LAm*) (native) Peruvian/Colombian/Ecuadorean *etc* Ⓒ SM (*Ling*) Creole; **como dicen en ~** as they say in Latin America/Peru *etc*

criosfera SF cryosphere

cripta SF crypt

críptico ADJ cryptic

criptografía SF cryptography

criptográfico ADJ cryptographic, cryptographical

criptógrafo/a SM/F cryptographer

criptograma SM cryptogram

críquet SM cricket

crisálida SF chrysalis

crisantemo SM chrysanthemum

crisis SF INV 1 (*Econ, Pol, Sociol*) crisis; **nuestro matrimonio está en ~** our marriage is in crisis o going through a crisis ➤ **crisis de fe** crisis of faith ➤ **crisis de gobierno** government crisis ➤ **crisis de identidad** identity crisis ➤ **crisis de los cuarenta** midlife crisis ➤ **crisis energética** energy crisis 2 (*Med*) ➤ **crisis cardíaca** cardiac arrest, heart failure ➤ **crisis epiléptica** epileptic fit, epileptic attack ➤ **crisis nerviosa** nervous breakdown

crisma[1] SF 1 (*Rel*) chrism 2 (**) (= *cabeza*) nut**, noggin (*EEUU***), head; **romperse la ~** to split one's head open

crisma[2] SM (*Esp*), **crismas** SM INV (*Esp*) Christmas card

crisol SM (*Téc*) crucible; (*fig*) melting pot

crispación SF tension, nervousness

crispado ADJ tense, on edge

crispar /1a/ Ⓐ VT 1 [+ *músculo*] to cause to twitch, cause to contract; **con el rostro crispado por la ira** with his face contorted with anger; **eso me crispa (los nervios)** that gets on my nerves* 2 (= *enfadar*) **~ a algn** to annoy sb intensely, really get on sb's nerves* Ⓑ **crisparse** VPR [*músculo*] to twitch, contract; [*cara*] to contort; [*nervios*] to get all on edge

cristal SM 1 (= *vidrio fino*) crystal; **una estatuilla de ~** a crystal statuette 2 (*Esp*) (= *vidrio normal*) glass; **una puerta de ~** a glass door; **un vaso de ~** a glass ➤ **cristal antibalas** bullet-proof glass ➤ **cristal blindado** reinforced glass ➤ **cristal esmerilado** frosted glass ➤ **cristal tallado** cut glass 3 (*Esp*) (= *trozo de cristal*) piece of glass; **hay ~es en el suelo** there's broken glass o there are pieces of broken glass on the floor; **se ha roto el ~ de la mesa** the glass table top has got cracked 4 (*Esp*) [*de ventana*] window pane; [*de coche*] window; [*de gafas*] lens ➤ **cristal de aumento** lens, magnifying glass 5 (*Min*) crystal ➤ **cristal de cuarzo** quartz crystal ➤ **cristal de roca** rock crystal ➤ **cristal líquido** liquid crystal

cristalera SF (*Esp*) (*fija*) window; (*corredera*) French windows *pl*

cristalería SF 1 (= *arte*) glassmaking 2 (= *fábrica*) glassworks; (= *tienda*) glassware shop (*esp Brit*) o store (*EEUU*) 3 (= *vasos*) glassware; (= *juego*) set of glasses

cristalino Ⓐ ADJ (*Fís*) crystalline; [*agua, explicación*] crystal-clear Ⓑ SM crystalline lens

cristalizar /1f/ Ⓐ VT to crystallize Ⓑ VI 1 (*Fís*) to crystallize 2 [*proyecto, idea*] to crystallize, take shape Ⓒ **cristalizarse** VPR 1 (*Fís*) to crystallize 2 [*proyecto, idea*] to crystallize, take shape

cristalografía SF crystallography

cristianamente ADV in a Christian way

cristiandad SF Christendom

cristianismo SM Christianity

cristianizar /1f/ VT to Christianize

cristiano/a Ⓐ ADJ Christian Ⓑ SM/F (*Rel*) Christian ➤ **cristiano viejo** (*Hist*) *Christian with no Jewish or Moorish blood* Ⓒ SM 1 (= *persona*) person; **eso no hay ~ que lo entienda** that is beyond anyone's comprehension 2 **hablar en ~** (= *claramente*) to talk sense; (= *en español*) to speak Spanish

Cristo SM (*Rel*) 1 (= *Jesucristo*) Christ; **en el año 41 antes/ después de** ~ in 41 B.C./A.D. 2 (= *imagen*) figure of Christ; **un ~ barroco** a Baroque figure of Christ

cristo SM 1 (= *crucifijo*) crucifix; **volvió hecho un ~ de la pelea** (*Esp*) he returned from the fight in a terrible mess *o* looking a terrible sight; ✦ MODISMO **ni ~*: eso no lo entiende ni ~** no one on earth can understand that, absolutely no one can understand that; **no había ni (un) ~ en la manifestación** there wasn't a soul at the demonstration 2 (*Esp**) (= *pelea*) **¡vaya ~!** what a to-do!*; **armar** *o* **montar un ~** to raise hell, make an almighty fuss*

criterio SM 1 (= *método*) criterion; **tenemos que unificar ~s** we have to agree on our criteria 2 (= *juicio*) judgement; **tiene buen ~** he has good *o* sound judgement; **lo dejo a su ~** I leave it to your discretion *o* judgement 3 (= *punto de vista*) opinion, view; **en mi ~** in my opinion *o* view; **depende del ~ de cada uno** it depends on each person's *o* individual's viewpoint

crítica SF 1 (= *censura*) criticism; **recibir duras ~s** to be severely criticized, come in for severe criticism 2 (*en periódico, revista*) review; (= *ensayo, libro*) critique 3 **la ~** (= *los críticos*) the critics *pl* 4 (= *actividad*) criticism; (= *chismes*) gossip ➤ **crítica literaria** literary criticism ➤ **crítica teatral** dramatic criticism; *ver tb* **crítico**

criticable ADJ [*conducta, actitud*] reprehensible

criticar /1g/ Ⓐ VT 1 (= *censurar*) to criticize 2 (= *hablar mal*): **siempre está criticando a la gente** he's always criticizing people, he's always finding fault with people 3 (*Arte, Literat, Teat*) [+ *libro, obra*] to review Ⓑ VI to gossip

crítico/a Ⓐ ADJ critical Ⓑ SM/F critic ➤ **crítico/a de arte** art critic ➤ **crítico/a de cine** film critic ➤ **crítico/a literario/a** literary critic ➤ **crítico/a musical** music critic; *ver tb* **crítica**

criticón/ona* Ⓐ ADJ hypercritical, critical, faultfinding Ⓑ SM/F faultfinder

Croacia SF Croatia

croar /1a/ VI to croak

croata ADJ, SMF Croat, Croatian; **los ~s** the Croats, the Croatians

croché SM crochet; **hacer ~** to crochet

croissantería [krwazante'ria] SF croissant shop

crol SM (*Natación*) crawl

cromado Ⓐ ADJ chromium-plated, chrome Ⓑ SM chromium plating, chrome

cromático ADJ chromatic

cromo SM 1 (*Quím*) chromium, chrome 2 (= *estampa*) picture card; ✦ MODISMO **iba hecho un ~** (*Esp**) he was a sight*

cromosoma SM chromosome

cromoterapia SF chromotherapy, colour therapy

crónica SF 1 [*de periódico*] feature, article; (*Radio, TV*) report; **"Crónica de sucesos"** "News in Brief" ➤ **crónica deportiva** sports page ➤ **crónica de sociedad** society column, gossip column 2 (*Hist*) chronicle

crónico ADJ [*enfermedad, déficit, problema*] chronic; [*vicio*] ingrained

cronista SMF 1 [*de periódico*] reporter, columnist ➤ **cronista deportivo** sports writer 2 (*Hist*) chronicler

crono SM (*Esp*) 1 (= *reloj*) stopwatch 2 (*tiempo*) time, recorded time; **ganó con un ~ de 6,59** she won with a time of 6.59

cronología SF chronology

cronológico ADJ chronological; **en orden ~** in chronological order

cronometraje SM timekeeping

cronometrar /1a/ VT to time

cronómetro SM (*Téc*) chronometer; (*Dep*) stopwatch

croqueta SF croquette

croquis SM INV sketch; **hacer un ~** to do *o* draw a sketch

cross [kros] SM INV 1 (*Atletismo*) cross-country running 2 (*Motociclismo*) moto(r)cross

crótalo SM 1 (*Zool*) rattlesnake, rattler (*EEUU**) 2 **crótalos** (*Mús*) castanets

croto* SM (*RPl*) 1 (= *mendigo*) layabout (*esp Brit**) 2 (= *inepto*) useless player*; **un ~ como yo** someone as useless as me*

cruce SM 1 (*Aut*) [*de carreteras, autopistas*] junction (*esp Brit*), intersection (*esp EEUU*); [*de cuatro esquinas*] crossroads; [*para peatones*] crossing (*Brit*), crosswalk (*EEUU*) 2 **luces de ~** dipped headlights 3 (= *acto*) **hubo un ~ de acusaciones entre ellos** there was an exchange of accusations between them; ✦ MODISMO **tener un ~ de cables*** to lose one's head* 4 (*Telec*) crossed line; **hay un ~ en las líneas** the wires are crossed 5 (*Biol*) (= *proceso*) crossbreeding; (= *resultado*) cross

crucero SM 1 (= *barco*) cruise ship, (cruise) liner; (*Mil*) cruiser 2 (= *viaje*) cruise; **hacer un ~** to go on a cruise 3 (*Arquit*) transept 4 (= *misil*) cruise missile 5 (*Méx*) [*de trenes*] level crossing (*Brit*), grade crossing (*EEUU*); [*de calles*] crossroads

cruceta SF 1 (= *viga*) crosspiece; (*Náut, Mec*) crosstree 2 (*Mec*) crosshead

crucial ADJ crucial

crucificar /1g/ VT (*Rel*) to crucify

crucifijo SM crucifix

crucifixión SF crucifixion

crucigrama SM crossword (puzzle)

cruda* SF (*CAm, Méx*) (= *resaca*) hangover

crudeza SF 1 [*de imágenes, descripción*] coarseness, crudeness, crudity 2 [*del invierno*] harshness, bleakness

crudo Ⓐ ADJ 1 (*Culin*) **1.1** (= *sin cocinar*) [*carne*] raw; [*verduras*] raw, uncooked **1.2** (= *poco hecho*) underdone 2 **de color** ~ natural 3 [*clima, invierno*] harsh, severe 4 [*descripción*] crude, coarse; [*imágenes*] harrowing; **la cruda realidad** the harsh reality 5 (*) (= *difícil*) **lo tienen ~ para encontrar un trabajo** they're having a hard *o* tough time finding a job; **lo veo muy ~** it doesn't look (too) good Ⓑ SM crude (oil)

cruel ADJ cruel; **ser ~ con algn** to be cruel to sb

crueldad SF 1 (= *cualidad*) cruelty; **tratar a algn con ~** to treat sb cruelly 2 (= *acción*) cruelty; **¡es una ~!** that's so cruel!, it's such a cruel thing to do *o* say!

cruento ADJ (*liter*) bloody, gory

crujido SM 1 [*de papel, hojas, seda*] rustle, rustling; [*de madera, mueble, rama*] creak, creaking; [*de leña ardiendo*] crackle, crackling 2 [*de articulaciones, huesos*] crack, cracking; [*de dientes*] grinding

crujiente ADJ [*galleta*] crunchy; [*pan*] crunchy, crusty; [*seda*] rustling; [*madera*] creaking

crujir /3a/ VI 1 [*papel, seda, hojas*] to rustle; [*madera, mueble, rama*] to creak; [*leña ardiendo*] to crackle; [*galletas*] to crunch 2 [*articulación, hueso*] to crack; [*dientes*] to grind; **le crujen los dientes** his teeth are grinding

crupier SMF croupier

crustáceo SM crustacean

cruz SF 1 (= *figura*) cross; **con los brazos en ~** with one's arms outstretched; ✦ MODISMO **¡~ y raya!** that's quite enough!, no more! ➤ **cruz de Malta** Maltese Cross ➤ **cruz gamada** swastika ➤ **cruz griega** Greek cross ➤ **cruz latina** Latin cross ➤ **Cruz Roja** Red Cross 2 (= *suplicio*) **¡qué ~ tengo con estos hijos!** these kids of mine are a nightmare!*; **cada uno lleva su ~** each of us has his cross to bear 3 [*de moneda*] tails; **¿cara o ~?** heads or tails?

cruza SF (*LAm*) cross, hybrid

cruzada SF crusade

cruzado Ⓐ ADJ 1 (= *atravesado*) **con los brazos ~s** with one's arms folded *o* crossed; **no podemos quedarnos con los brazos ~s** we can't sit back and do nothing, we can't just sit idly by and do nothing 2 [*chaqueta, americana*] double-breasted 3 [*cheque*] crossed 4 (*Zool*) crossbred Ⓑ SM 1 (*Hist*) crusader 2 (= *moneda*) cruzado (*Brazilian currency unit*)

cruzar /1f/ Ⓐ VT 1 [+ *calle, río, frontera, puente*] to cross; **~ la (línea de) meta** to cross the finishing line; **~on el lago a nado** they swam across the lake
2 [*arrugas, líneas*] **una profunda cicatriz le cruzaba la mano** a deep scar ran across his hand; **el corte le cruzó la espalda de un lado a otro** the cut ran right across his back
3 (= *poner cruzado*) **~ la espada con algn** to cross swords with sb; **~ los dedos** (*lit, fig*) to cross one's fingers; **~ las piernas** to cross one's legs
4 [+ *palabras*] to exchange
5 [+ *apuestas*] to place, make
6 (*Biol*) [+ *plantas, razas*] to cross
Ⓑ VI [*peatón*] to cross; **~ por el puente** to cross over the bridge; **~ por el paso de peatones** to cross at the zebra crossing
Ⓒ **cruzarse** VPR 1 [*dos cosas, líneas*] to intersect, cross; [*caminos*] to cross; **se ~on las miradas de los dos** their eyes met; **se le ~on los cables*** (*por enfado*) he just lost it*, he flipped*; (*por confusión*) he just lost track*
2 [*personas, vehículos*] 2.1 (= *encontrarse*) to pass each other; **se cruzó con ella en la escalera** he passed her on the stairs; **hace tiempo que no me cruzo con él** I haven't seen him for a long time 2.2 (= *pasar por delante*) **se le cruzó otro coche y para evitarlo, se salió de la carretera** another car pulled out in front of him and he swerved off the road to avoid it

CSIC [θe'sik] SM ABR (*Esp*) = **Consejo Superior de Investigaciones Científicas**

cta. ABR, **c.ta** ABR (= *cuenta*) a/c, acc., acct

cu SF Q, *name of the letter Q*

cuaco SM (*Méx*) nag

cuaderno SM (*para notas*) notebook; (*Escol*) jotter, exercise book (*esp Brit*), workbook (*EEUU*); **~ de espiral** spiral notebook, spiral-bound notebook **➤ cuaderno de bitácora** logbook **➤ cuaderno de campo** field diary

cuadra SF 1 (*para caballos*) stable 2 (*LAm*) (*entre calles*) block; **vivo a dos ~s de aquí** I live two blocks from here 3 (= *medida*) (*CS*) ≈ 125.50 metres

cuadrado Ⓐ ADJ 1 (*Mat*) square; **dos metros ~s** two square metres 2 [*objeto, superficie*] square 3 (= *corpulento*) **estar ~** to be well-built, be hefty* 4 (*LAm**) (= *poco flexible*) **ser ~** to be narrow-minded Ⓑ SM square; **cinco (elevado) al ~** five square(d), the square of five

cuadragésimo ADJ, PRON fortieth; *ver tb* **sexto**

cuadrangular ADJ quadrangular

cuadrante SM 1 (*Mat, Náut*) quadrant; **el ~ noroccidental de la Península** the northwestern part *o* corner of the Peninsula 2 [*de radio*] dial; [*de reloj*] face **➤ cuadrante (solar)** sundial

cuadrar /1a/ Ⓐ VI 1 [*cuentas, cifras*] to tally; **los números no cuadran** the numbers don't tally; **~ con algo** to square with sth, tally with sth
2 [*misterio, historia*] to fit together; **todo parecía ~ perfectamente** everything seemed to fit together perfectly; **~ con algo** to fit in with sth
3 **~ a algn** to suit sb; **ven mañana si te cuadra** come tomorrow if it suits you *o* if that's convenient
4 (*Ven**) (= *quedar*) to arrange to meet Ⓑ VT 1 (*Mat*) to square
2 (*Téc*) to square, square off
3 (*Perú*) (= *aparcar*) to park
Ⓒ **cuadrarse** VPR 1 [*soldado*] to stand to attention
2 (*en una actitud*) to dig one's heels in
3 (*Col**) (= *ennoviar*) **~se con algn** to go out with sb
4 (*Chi, Ven**) (= *solidarizarse*) **~se con algn** to side with sb
5 (*Chi**) **~se con algo** to donate sth
6 (*Col, Ven, Perú*) (= *aparcar*) to park

7 (*Perú, Ven**) **~se a algn** to take sb on

cuadratura SF (*Mat*) quadrature; **la ~ del círculo** squaring the circle

cuadrícula SF (*Tip*) grid, ruled squares; [*de mapa*] grid

cuadriculado ADJ **papel ~** squared paper, graph paper; **mapa ~** grid map

cuadricular /1a/ VT to draw squares on, draw a grid on

cuadrilátero Ⓐ ADJ quadrilateral, four-sided Ⓑ SM (*Mat*) quadrilateral; (*Boxeo*) ring

cuadrilla SF 1 [*de amigos*] party, group; [*de obreros*] gang, team 2 (*Taur*) bullfighting team 3 (*Mil*) squad

cuadrito SM (*Culin*) cube; **cortar en ~s** to dice

cuadro SM 1 (= *cuadrado*) square; **una camisa/un vestido a o de ~s** a checked *o* check shirt/dress; **~s escoceses** tartan (pattern); **◆** MODISMOS **quedarse a ~s*** to be flabbergasted*; **ser del otro ~** (*Uru**) to be gay **➤ cuadro de diálogo** dialog box
2 (*Arte*) (= *pintura*) painting; (= *reproducción*) picture; **dos ~s de Velázquez** two paintings by Velázquez, two Velázquez paintings; **pintar un ~** to do a painting, paint a picture; **◆** MODISMO **ir hecho un ~** to be a (real) sight* **➤ cuadro de honor** roll of honour (*Brit*), honor roll (*EEUU*)
3 (= *escena*) (*Teat*) scene; (*fig*) scene, sight; **¡vaya ~!** what a sight!
4 (= *gráfico*) table, chart **➤ cuadro sinóptico** synoptic chart
5 (= *tablero*) panel **➤ cuadro de instrumentos** (*Aer*) instrument panel; (*Aut*) dashboard **➤ cuadro de mandos** control panel
6 (= *armazón*) [*de bicicleta, ventana*] frame
7 **cuadros** (*tb* **~ de mando**) (*en empresa*) managerial staff; (*Admin, Pol*) officials; (*Mil*) commanding officers
8 (*Med*) symptoms pl, set of symptoms **➤ cuadro clínico** symptoms pl, clinical symptoms pl
9 (= *descripción*) picture **➤ cuadro de costumbres** (*Literat*) description of local customs
10 (*Dep*) team; **el ~ argentino** the Argentinian team
11 (*Chi*) (= *bragas*) panties pl, knickers pl (*Brit*)

cuadrúpedo SM quadruped, four-footed animal

cuádruple Ⓐ ADJ quadruple, fourfold Ⓑ SM **yo he pagado el ~** I paid four times that

cuadruplicado ADJ quadruplicate; **por ~** in quadruplicate

cuadruplicar /1g/ Ⓐ VT to quadruple Ⓑ **cuadruplicarse** VPR to quadruple, increase fourfold

cuádruplo Ⓐ ADJ fourfold, quadruple Ⓑ SM = **cuádruple** B

cuajada SF [*de leche*] curd; (*como postre*) junket

cuajado Ⓐ ADJ 1 [*leche*] curdled; [*sangre*] coagulated, congealed 2 (= *lleno*) **~ de** full of, filled with; **un cielo ~ de estrellas** a star-spangled sky, a star-studded sky, a sky studded with stars; **una situación cuajada de peligros** a situation fraught with dangers 3 (= *asombrado*) **estar ~** to be dumbfounded Ⓑ SM **➤ cuajado de limón** lemon curd

cuajar /1a/ Ⓐ VT 1 [+ *leche*] to curdle; [+ *gelatina*] to set; [+ *sangre*] to coagulate, clot; [+ *grasa*] to congeal
2 **~ algo de** (= *cubrir*) to cover sth with, adorn sth with; (= *llenar*) to fill sth with
Ⓑ VI 1 [*nieve*] to lie; [*leche*] to curdle
2 [*moda, producto*] to catch on, take off; [*plan*] to take shape; [*idea, propuesta*] to be well received, be acceptable; [*truco*] to come off, work; **el acuerdo no cuajó** the agreement didn't come off *o* work out
Ⓒ **cuajarse** VPR 1 [*leche*] to curdle; [*sangre*] to congeal, coagulate; [*gelatina*] to set
2 **~se de** to fill (up) with

cuajo SM 1 (*Zool, Culin*) rennet 2 **arrancar algo de ~** to tear sth out by its roots; **arrancar una puerta de ~** to wrench a door out of its frame 3 (= *cachaza*) phlegm, calmness; **tiene mucho ~** he's very phlegmatic 4 **coger un ~*** to cry one's eyes out

cual Ⓐ PRON 1 **el ~/la ~/ los ~es/las ~es** 1.1 (*aplicado a cosas*) which; **un balcón desde el ~ se puede ver toda la bahía** a balcony from which you can see the whole bay;

obtuvo una beca, gracias a la ~ pudo subsistir varios años
he got a grant, which gave him enough to live on for
several years **1.2** *(aplicado a personas) (como sujeto)* who;
(como objeto) who, whom; *(tras preposición)* whom; **tengo
gran amistad con el director, al ~ conozco desde hace
muchos años** the director, who *o* whom I have known for
many years, is a great friend of mine; **había ocho chicos,
tres de los ~es hablaban en inglés** there were eight boys,
three of whom were speaking in English
2 lo ~ which; **se han construido dos escuelas más, con lo ~
contaremos con más de 2.000 plazas escolares** two more
schools have been built, with the result that *o* which
means that we will have more than 2,000 school places;
por lo ~ and therefore, consequently
3 cada ~: **cada ~ puede hacer lo que crea conveniente**
everyone may do what they think fit; **depende del gusto
de cada ~** it depends on individual taste, it depends on
each individual's taste; **allá cada ~** everyone must look out
for themselves
4 sea ~ sea *o* **fuese** *o* **fuere** whatever
Ⓑ ADV, CONJ *(liter)* like; **~ si** as if
Ⓒ ADJ *(Jur)* said, aforementioned

cuál Ⓐ PRON **1** *(interrogativo)* what, which (one); **¿~
quieres?** which (one) do you want?; **ignora ~ será el
resultado** he does not know what the outcome will be **2 a
~ más: son a ~ más gandul** each *o* one is as lazy as the
other; **una serie de coches a ~ más rápido** a series of cars
each faster than the last; **~ más ~ menos** some more, some
less **3** *(exclamativo)* **¡~ no sería mi asombro!** imagine the
surprise I got!, imagine my surprise!
Ⓑ ADJ *(esp LAm)* which?; **¿~es carros?** which cars?

cualidad SF **1** *(= virtud)* quality; *(= talento)* talent; **tiene
buenas ~es** he has good qualities; **hizo una demostración
de sus ~es como actriz** she demonstrated her talent as an
actress **2** *(= atributo)* attribute, characteristic **3** *(Fís, Fil)*
property

cualificado ADJ **1** *[obrero]* skilled, qualified; **obrero no ~**
unskilled worker **2 estar ~ para hacer algo** to be qualified
to do sth

cualitativo ADJ qualitative

cualquier(a¹) *(pl* **cualesquier(a))** ADJ INDEF **1** *(antes de s)*
any; **como en ~ otro país europeo** as in any other
European country; **~ día se presenta aquí** he could turn up
here any day; **~ persona de por aquí te diría lo mismo**
anyone from round here would tell you the same; **en ~
caso** in any case; **~ cosa** anything; **en ~ lugar del mundo**
anywhere in the world; **en ~ momento** at any time, (at)
any moment
2 *(después de s)* any; **—¿cuál prefieres? —me da igual, uno
~a** "which one do you prefer?" — "it doesn't matter, any
one (will do)"; **sucedió un día ~a** it happened on a day like
any other day; **éste no es un coche ~a** this is not just any
old car

cualquiera² *(pl* **cualesquiera) Ⓐ** PRON INDEF **1** *(= cualquier
persona)* anyone, anybody; *(= cualquier cosa)* any one; **tal
como gritaban los niños, ~ diría que los estaba torturando**
the way the children were screaming anyone would think
I was torturing them; **puedes coger ~** you can choose any
one (you like); **es una costumbre como otra ~** it is a
custom like any other
2 ~ de any, any of; **~ de mis alumnos podría realizar este
proyecto** any *o* any one of my pupils could do this project;
~ de los dos either (one) of them, either of the two; **~ de
los dos equipos** either team *o* either (one) of the two teams
3 ~ que (+ SUBJUN) **3.1** *(en general)* whatever; *(ante una
elección)* whichever; **~ que sea tu problema** whatever your
problem is, no matter what your problem is; **respetaremos
el resultado de la votación, ~ que sea** we will respect the
result of the vote, whatever that may be **3.2** *(= persona)*
anyone who, anybody who
4 *(en exclamaciones)* **¡~ sabe!** who knows?; **¡~ le interrumpe
ahora!** I wouldn't interrupt him at the minute!; **¡así ~!** it's
all right for some!*
Ⓑ SM **un ~** a nobody
Ⓒ SF *(pey)* **una ~** a hussy*

cuan ADV *(liter)* **tan estúpidos ~ criminales** as stupid as
they are criminal

cuán ADV how; **¡~ agradable fue todo eso!** how delightful
it all was!

cuando Ⓐ CONJ **1** *(con valor temporal)* *(en un momento
concreto)* when; *(en cualquier momento)* whenever; **te lo diré
~ nos veamos** I'll tell you when I see you; **ven ~ quieras**
come when(ever) you like; **lo dejaremos para ~ estés mejor**
we'll leave it until you're better
2 *(con valor condicional, causal)* if; **~ él lo dice, será verdad** if
he says so, it must be true
3 *(con valor adversativo)* when; **yo lo hago todo, ~ es él
quien debería hacerlo** I'm the one that does it all, when it
should be him
Ⓑ ADV **1 en abril es ~ más casos hay** April is when there
are most cases, it's in April that there are most cases; **de ~
en ~ ◇ de vez en ~** from time to time, now and again,
every so often
2 ~ más at (the) most; **tardaremos, ~ más, una semana** it
will take us a week at (the) most *o* at the outside; **~ menos**
at least; **esperamos llegar, ~ menos, a las semifinales** we are
hoping to reach the semifinals, at least; **~ no** if not
Ⓒ PREP **eso fue ~ la guerra** that was during the war; **~ niño
yo era muy travieso** as a child *o* when I was a child I was
very naughty

cuándo ADV **1** *(en oraciones interrogativas)* when; **no sé ~
será** I don't know when it will be; **¿desde ~?** since when?;
¿hasta ~? how long?; **¿para ...?** when ... by? **2 ¡~ no!**
(LAm) just to make a change!

cuantía SF **1** *(= cantidad)* quantity, amount; **¿cómo se
calcula la ~ de la pensión?** how is the amount *o* level of
pension calculated?; **el fraude supera la ~ de cinco
millones** the fraud amounts to more than five million
2 *(= importancia)* importance; **de mayor ~** more important,
more significant

cuantificable ADJ quantifiable

cuantificar /1g/ VT **1** [+ *daños, pérdidas*] to quantify *(frm)*,
assess **2** *(Fís)* to quantize

cuantioso ADJ *[suma, beneficios, daños]* substantial,
considerable; *[pérdidas]* substantial, heavy

cuantitativo ADJ quantitative

cuanto Ⓐ ADJ **1** *(indicando cantidad)* **daremos ~s créditos
se precisen** we will give as many loans as (are) needed *o*
whatever loans are needed
2 *(en correlación)* **~ más** the more; **~s más invitados vengan
más comida habrá que preparar** the more guests come, the
more food we'll have to prepare; **~ menos** the less
3 unos ~s *(= no muchos)* a few; *(= bastantes)* quite a few
Ⓑ PRON **1** *(indicando cantidad)* all; **tome ~ quiera** take as
much as you want, take all you want
2 *(en correlación)* **~s más** the more; **~s más mejor** the more
the better; **~s menos** the fewer
3 unos ~s *(= no muchos)* a few; *(= bastantes)* quite a few
Ⓒ ADV, CONJ *(expresando correlación)* **~ antes mejor** the
sooner the better; **~ más** the more; **~ menos** the less
2 *(locuciones)* **2.1 ~ antes** as soon as possible **2.2 en ~**
(= tan pronto como) as soon as; *(= en calidad de)* as; **iré en ~
pueda** I'll go as soon as I can; **el cuento infantil, en ~
género literario** children's stories, as a literary genre
2.3 en ~ a as regards, as for; **en ~ a mí** as for me **2.4 en ~
que** insofar as **2.5 ~ más** especially **2.6 ~ menos** to say the
least; **esta interpretación es, ~ menos, discutible** this
interpretation is debatable to say the least **2.7 por ~** in
that, inasmuch as *(frm)*; **es un delito por ~ vulnera los
derechos constitucionales** it is a crime in that *o* inasmuch
as *(frm)* it violates constitutional rights; **llama la atención
por ~ supone de innovación** it attracts attention because of
its novelty value

cuánto Ⓐ ADJ **1** *(en oraciones interrogativas)* **1.1** *(en
singular)* how much; **¿cuánta sal echo?** how much salt
shall I add?; **¿~ tiempo llevas viviendo en Perú?** how long
have you been living in Peru (for)? **1.2** *(en plural)* how
many; **¿~s días libres tienes al año?** how many days off do
you have a year?; **no sabe ~s cuadros hay en su casa** he
doesn't know how many paintings there are in his house
2 *(en exclamaciones)* **¡cuánta gente!** what a lot of people!;
¡~ borracho hay por las calles!* the streets are full of
drunks!
Ⓑ PRON **1** *(en preguntas, uso indirecto)* **1.1** *(tb ~ dinero)*

how much; **¿~ has gastado?** how much have you spent?; **no sé ~ es** I don't know how much it is; **¿a ~ están las peras?** how much are (the) pears? **1.2** (*tb* **~ tiempo**) how long; **¿~ durará esto?** how long will this last?; **¿cada ~?** how often? **1.3** (*en plural*) how many; **¿a ~s estamos?** what's the date today?, what date is it today?

2 (*en exclamaciones*) **¡~ has tardado!** you've been ages!, you took ages!; **¡~s has comprado!** you've bought so many!, you've bought loads!

3 no sé ~s: el señor no sé ~s Mr So-and-So, Mr Something-or-other

☉ ADV **1** (*en preguntas, uso indirecto*) **1.1** (*de cantidad*) how much; **¿~ pesas?** how much do you weigh?; **no sé ~ quieres** I don't know how much you want **1.2** (*de distancia*) how far; **¿~ hay de aquí a Bilbao?** how far is it from here to Bilbao?

2 (*en exclamaciones*) **¡~ has crecido!** how you've grown!; **¡~ me alegro!** I'm so glad!

cuáquero/a ADJ, SM/F Quaker

cuarenta ADJ, PRON, SM (*cardinal*) forty; (*ordinal*) fortieth; **"Los cuarenta principales"** (*Radio, TV*) "the Top Forty" (*Spanish hit parade*); **♦** MODISMOS **cantar las ~** (*Naipes*) *to have the king and queen of trumps;* **cantar las ~ a algn** to tell sb a few home truths, tell sb a thing or two; *ver tb* **seis**

cuarentavo ☉ ADJ **1** (= *ordinal*) fortieth **2** (= *partitivo*) **la cuarentava parte** a fortieth **☉** SM fortieth

cuarentena SF **1** (= *número*) about forty, forty-odd; **ambos rondan la ~** they're both around forty (years old); **una ~ de** some forty, forty or so **2** (= *aislamiento*) quarantine; **poner a algn en ~** (*Med*) to put sb in quarantine, quarantine sb; (*fig*) to give sb the silent treatment, send sb to Coventry (*Brit*)

cuarentón/ona ☉ ADJ forty-something; **es ya ~** he's in his forties, he's forty-something **☉** SM/F person in their forties

cuaresma SF Lent; **⋄** *CARNAVAL*

cuaresmal ADJ Lenten

cuark SM (*pl* **~s**) quark

cuarta SF **1** (*Mat*) quarter **2** (= *palmo*) span **3** (*Aut*) fourth gear, fourth; **meter la ~** to go into fourth (gear), put it *o* the car into fourth (gear) **4 ♦** MODISMO **a la ~** short of money; *ver tb* **cuarto**

cuartear /1a/ **☉** VT to cut up **☉** **cuartearse** VPR **1** (= *agrietarse*) to crack, split **2** (*Taur*) to dodge, step aside **3** (*Méx*) (= *desdecirse*) to go back on one's word

cuartel SM **1** (*Mil*) barracks **➤ cuartel de bomberos** (*RPl*) fire station **➤ cuartel general** headquarters *pl* **2** (= *tregua*) **no dar ~** to give no quarter, show no mercy; **lucha sin ~** fight to the death

cuartelazo SM, **cuartelada** SF military uprising

cuartelero ADJ barracks *antes de s*

cuartelillo SM police station

cuarterón/ona ☉ SM quarter pound, quarter **☉** SM/F (*LAm*) quadroon

cuarteta SF quatrain

cuarteto SM **1** (*Mús*) (= *conjunto, composición*) quartet, quartette **➤ cuarteto de viento** wind quartet **2** (*Literat*) quatrain

cuartilla SF **1** (= *hoja*) (*en general*) sheet (of paper); (= *medio folio*) A-5 sheet of paper; **un sobre tamaño ~** an A-5 envelope **2 cuartillas** (*Tip*) copy; (= *apuntes*) notes, jottings

cuarto ☉ ADJ, PRON fourth; **en ~ lugar** in fourth place; **la cuarta parte** a quarter; *ver tb* **sexto, cuarta** **☉** SM **1** (= *habitación*) room; **el ~ de los niños** children's room **➤ cuarto de aseo** toilet (*Brit*), bathroom (*EEUU*) **➤ cuarto de baño** bathroom **➤ cuarto de estar** living room, sitting room **➤ cuarto oscuro** (*Fot*) darkroom; (= *trastero*) broom cupboard (*Brit*), broom closet (*EEUU*); (*RPl*) voting booth **➤ cuarto trastero** lumber room **2** (= *cuarta parte*) quarter; **un ~ (de) kilo** a quarter (of a) kilo; **♦** MODISMOS **de tres al ~** worthless, third-rate; **tres ~s**

de lo mismo: su amigo es un inútil, y él ... tres ~s de lo mismo his friend is useless, and, as for him, he's not much better; **en otros países ocurre tres ~s de lo mismo** it's the same story *o* it's more of the same in other countries **➤ cuarto creciente** first quarter **➤ cuarto menguante** last quarter **➤ cuartos de final** quarter finals

3 (*en la hora*) quarter; **son las seis menos ~ ◇ es un ~ para las seis** (*LAm*) it's a quarter to six; **a las seis y ~** at (a) quarter past six **➤ cuarto de hora** quarter of an hour

4 (*de animal, de cerdo, vaca*) roast, joint (*Brit*) **➤ cuartos delanteros** forequarters **➤ cuartos traseros** hindquarters **5 cuartos** (*Esp**) (= *dinero*) dough* *sing;* **♦** MODISMOS **aflojar los ~s** (*Esp*) to cough up*; **¡qué coche ni qué ocho ~s!** car, my foot!

6 (*Tip*) quarto

cuarzo SM quartz

cuásar SM quasar

cuate (*CAm, Méx*) **☉** ADJ twin **☉** SMF **1** (= *gemelo*) twin **2** (= *compadre*) pal*, mate (*Brit**), buddy (*EEUU**) **3** (= *tipo*) guy*/girl

cuaternario ☉ ADJ quaternary; (*Geol*) Quaternary **☉** SM **el ~** the Quaternary

cuatrero/a SM/F (*de ganado*) rustler, stock thief; (*de caballos*) horse thief

cuatrienal ADJ four-year *antes de s*, quadrennial (*frm*)

cuatrillizo/a SM/F quadruplet

cuatrimestral ADJ **1** (= *de cada cuatro meses*) four-monthly, every four months **2** (= *de cuatro meses*) four-month(-long)

cuatrimestre SM four-month period

cuatrimotor ☉ ADJ four-engined **☉** SM four-engined plane

cuatriplicado ADJ quadruplicate

cuatro ☉ ADJ, PRON **1** (*cardinal*) four; (*ordinal, en la fecha*) fourth **2** (= *pocos*) **sólo había ~ muebles** there were only a few sticks of furniture; **cayeron ~ gotas** a few drops fell; **sólo había ~ gatos** the place was dead*, there was hardly a soul **☉** SM **1** (= *número*) four; *ver tb* **seis 2** (*Ven Mús*) four-stringed guitar **3** (*Aut*) **➤ cuatro latas*** Renault 4L **➤ cuatro por cuatro** four-wheel drive vehicle **☉** **➤ cuatro ojos*** SMF INV four-eyes*

cuatrocientos ADJ, PRON, SM (*cardinal*) four hundred; (*ordinal*) four hundredth; *ver tb* **seiscientos**

cuba¹ SF (= *tonel*) cask, barrel; (= *tina*) tub, vat; **♦** MODISMO **estar como una ~** to be as drunk as a lord

cuba² SM (*Col*) (= *hijo*) youngest child

Cuba SF Cuba; **♦** MODISMO **más se perdió en ~** it's not the end of the world

cubalibre SM, **cuba-libre** SM (*pl* **cubas-libres** *o* **cuba-libres**) (*de ron*) (white) rum and Coke®; (*de ginebra*) gin and Coke®

cubano/a ADJ, SM/F Cuban

cubata* SM = **cubalibre**

cubertería SF cutlery (*Brit*), flatware (*EEUU*); **una ~ de plata** a set *o* canteen of silver cutlery (*Brit*), a silver flatware service (*EEUU*)

cubeta SF **1** (*Fot, Quím*) tray **2** (*de barómetro, termómetro*) bulb **3** (*para hielo*) ice tray

cubetera SF (*Chi*) ice tray

cubicar /1g/ VT **1** (*Mat*) to cube **2** (*Fís*) to determine the volume of

cúbico ADJ cubic; **metro ~** cubic metre; **raíz cúbica** cube root, cubic root

cubículo SM cubicle

cubierta SF **1** (= *cobertura*) cover(ing); (*de libro*) cover, jacket; (*de edificio*) roof; **~ de lona** tarpaulin **2** (*de rueda*) tyre, tire (*EEUU*) **3** (*Náut*) deck **➤ cubierta de aterrizaje** flight deck **➤ cubierta de botes** boat deck **➤ cubierta de paseo** promenade deck **➤ cubierta de popa** poop deck **➤ cubierta de proa** foredeck

cubierto ☉ PP *de* **cubrir** **☉** ADJ **1** (*gen*) covered (**de** with, in)

2 [*cielo*] overcast
3 [*vacante*] filled
C SM **1** (= *techumbre*) cover; **a** *o* **bajo ~** under cover; **ponerse a ~** to take shelter, take cover; **ponerse a ~ de algo** to shelter from sth
2 (*para comer*) a piece of cutlery (*Brit*), a piece of flatware (*EEUU*); **coge el ~ con la mano derecha** take the spoon/fork/knife with your right hand; **los ~s** the cutlery (*Brit*), the flatware (*EEUU*)
3 (= *servicio de mesa*) place setting
4 (= *comida*) **precio del ~** price per person *o* per head

cubil SM den, lair

cubilete SM **1** [*de dados*] cup **2** (*Col*) (= *chistera*) top hat

cubismo SM cubism

cubista ADJ, SMF cubist

cubitera SF ice-tray

cubito SM **1** (*tb ~ de hielo*) ice cube **2** ➤ **cubito de caldo** stock cube

cubo SM **1** (= *balde*) bucket, pail ➤ **cubo de (la) basura** (*en casa*) dustbin (*Brit*), trash can (*EEUU*); (*en la calle*) litter bin (*Brit*), trash can (*EEUU*) **2** (= *contenido*) bucketful, bucket, pailful, pail **3** (*Mat*) cube; **cinco elevado al ~** five cubed **4** (*Geom*) cube ➤ **cubo de Rubik** Rubik cube **5** (*Mec*) barrel, drum **6** [*de rueda*] hub

cubrecama SM coverlet, bedspread

cubrerradiadores SM INV *cover for radiator*

cubrimiento SM [*de objeto*] covering; [*de noticia*] coverage

cubrir /3a/ (*pp* **cubierto**) **A** VT **1** (= *ocultar*) to cover; **un velo le cubría el rostro** a veil covered her face; **no te metas donde te cubra el agua** don't go out of your depth; **queremos ~ parte del patio** we want to roof (over) part of the patio
2 (= *llenar*) [+ *agujero*] to fill in; [+ *hueco*] to fill; **~ a algn de atenciones** to lavish attention on sb; **~ a algn de besos** to smother sb with kisses
3 (*Dep, Mil*) to cover
4 (= *recorrer*) [+ *ruta, distancia*] to cover; **cubrió 80km en una hora** he covered 80km in an hour; **el autocar cubría el trayecto entre León y Madrid** the coach was travelling between León and Madrid
5 [+ *vacante, plaza*] to fill
6 [+ *gastos, déficit, préstamo*] to cover
7 [+ *necesidades, demanda*] to meet
8 [+ *suceso*] to cover
9 (*Zool*) (= *montar*) to cover
10 (= *disimular*) to cover up, conceal; ✦ MODISMO **~ las apariencias** *o* **las formas** to keep up appearances
B **cubrirse** VPR **1** [*persona*] **1.1** (= *ocultarse*) to cover o.s.; **~se la cabeza** to cover one's head; **~se el rostro** to cover one's face **1.2** (= *ponerse el sombrero*) to put on one's hat
2 (= *llenarse*) **~se de algo** to be covered with *o* in sth; **~se de gloria** (*lit*) to cover o.s. with *o* in glory; (*iró*) to show o.s. up
3 (= *protegerse*) to cover o.s.; **~se contra un riesgo** to cover *o* protect o.s. against a risk; ✦ MODISMO **~se las espaldas** to cover o.s., cover one's back
4 (*Meteo*) [*cielo*] to become overcast

cucaña SF greasy pole

cucaracha SF cockroach

cucha SF (*Arg*) (= *cama*) bed; (= *caseta de perro*) kennel (*esp Brit*), doghouse (*EEUU*); *ver tb* **cucho**

cuchara SF **1** (*para comer*) spoon; ✦ MODISMO **meter algo a algn con ~** to spoon-feed sb sth ➤ **cuchara de postre** dessert spoon ➤ **cuchara de servir** serving spoon, tablespoon ➤ **cuchara de sopa** soup spoon **2** (*Téc*) scoop, bucket **3** (*RPl*) (= *llana*) flat trowel

cucharada SF spoonful; **una ~ rasa** a level spoonful

cucharadita SF teaspoonful

cucharilla SF, **cucharita** SF teaspoon

cucharón SM ladle

cuché SM art paper

cucheta SF (*RPl*) bunk beds *pl*

cuchi (*Perú*) **A** EXCL *call to a pig or hog* **B** SM (*en lenguaje*

infantil) pig, hog (*esp EEUU*)

cuchichear /1a/ VI to whisper (**a** to)

cuchicheo SM whispering

cuchilla SF **1** (*afilada*) blade ➤ **cuchilla de afeitar** razor blade **2** [*de arado*] coulter, colter (*EEUU*) **3** (*Geog*) ridge, crest; (*SAm*) (= *colinas*) sharp ridge

cuchillada SF (= *corte*) stab; (= *herida*) stab wound; **dar una ~ a algn** to stab sb; **matar a algn a ~s** to stab sb to death

cuchillazo SM = **cuchillada**

cuchillo SM **1** (*gen*) knife; ✦ MODISMO **pasar a ~** to put to the sword ➤ **cuchillo de carne** steak knife ➤ **cuchillo de cocina** kitchen knife ➤ **cuchillo del pan** breadknife ➤ **cuchillo de trinchar** carving knife **2** (*Arquit*) upright, support

cuchipanda* SF blow-out*, chow-down (*EEUU***); **ir de ~** to go out on the town

cuchitril SM hole*, hovel

cucho/a **A** ADJ (*Méx*) (= *torcido*) **estar ~** to be on the slant **B** SM/F **1** (*Col**) **1.1** (= *padre*) dad*; (= *madre*) mum (*Brit**), mom (*EEUU**); **fui a visitar a los ~s** I went to see my mum (*Brit*) *o* mom (*EEUU*) and dad* **1.2** (= *profesor*) teacher **1.3** (= *anciano*) old man/old woman; **~s** oldsters*, oldies (*Brit**) **2** (*Chi*) (= *gato*) puss; *ver tb* **cucha**

cuchufleta SF joke, crack*

cuclillas SFPL **en ~** squatting, crouching; **ponerse en ~** to squat; **sentarse en ~** to sit on one's heels

cuclillo SM cuckoo

cuco **A** ADJ **1** (*Esp*) [*persona*] (= *taimado*) sly, crafty; (= *astuto*) shrewd **2** (= *bonito*) pretty, cute **B** SM **1** (*Orn*) cuckoo **2** (*And, RPl*) (= *fantasma*) bogeyman (*Brit*), boogeyman (*EEUU*)

cucú SM (= *canto*) cuckoo

cucufato/a* SM/F **1** (*And*) (= *mojigato*) prude **2** (*Chi*) (= *loco*) nut**

cucurucho SM **1** [*de papel*] (paper) cone, (paper) twist, cornet; (*para helado*) cone, cornet (*Brit*) **2** (= *helado*) (ice-cream) cone **3** (*Rel*) penitent's hood, pointed hat

cuelgue* * SM (*Esp*) high**; **lleva un ~** he's completely high *o* spaced out**, he's really out of it**

cuello SM **1** (*Anat*) neck; **cortar el ~ a algn** to cut sb's throat; ✦ MODISMOS **apostar el ~*: me apuesto el ~ a que no te atreves** I bet you anything you don't dare; **jugarse el ~*** to stick one's neck out, put one's neck on the line ➤ **cuello del útero, cuello uterino** cervix, neck of the womb
2 [*de prenda*] collar; (= *talla*) (collar) size; ✦ MODISMO **de ~ blanco** white-collar *antes de s* ➤ **cuello (a la) caja** crew neck ➤ **cuello alto** polo neck (*esp Brit*), turtle neck (*EEUU*) ➤ **cuello (de) cisne** polo neck (*esp Brit*), turtleneck (*EEUU*) ➤ **cuello de pico** V-neck
3 [*de botella*] neck ➤ **cuello de botella** (*Aut*) bottleneck

cuenca SF **1** (*Geog*) bowl; (*fluvial*) basin ➤ **cuenca minera** coalfield **2** [*del ojo*] socket

cuenco SM **1** (= *recipiente*) earthenware bowl **2** (= *concavidad*) hollow

cuenta SF **1** (*Mat*) (= *operación*) calculation, sum; **hacer una ~** to do a calculation
2 (= *cálculo*) count; **llevar la ~ (de algo)** to keep count (of sth); **perder la ~ (de algo)** to lose count (of sth); **salir a ~:** **sale más a ~** it works out cheaper; **no sale a ~** it isn't worth it; ✦ MODISMO **más de la ~: habla más de la ~** she talks too much; **ha bebido más de la ~** he's had one too many; **me cobraron más de la ~** they charged me over the odds ➤ **cuenta atrás** countdown; **ha empezado la ~ atrás para las próximas Olimpiadas** the countdown to the next Olympics has already begun
3 (= *factura*) bill; [*de restaurante*] bill (*Brit*), check (*EEUU*); **¿nos puede traer la ~?** could we have *o* could you bring us the bill (*Brit*) *o* check (*EEUU*), please?; **pedir la ~** to ask for the bill (*Brit*) *o* check (*EEUU*); **vivir a ~ de algn** to live at sb's expense
4 (*en banco, tienda*) account; **habían cargado los gastos en mi ~** they had charged the expenses to my account; **a ~ on**

account; **un dividendo a ~** an interim dividend; **retenciones a ~ del impuesto sobre la renta** income tax deducted at source; **le dieron una cantidad a ~ de lo que le debían** they paid him part of the money they owed him; **abrir una ~** to open an account ➤ **cuenta a plazo (fijo)** fixed-term deposit (*Brit*) *o* savings (*esp EEUU*) account ➤ **cuenta corriente** current account (*Brit*), checking account (*EEUU*) ➤ **cuenta de ahorro(s)** deposit account (*Brit*), savings account (*esp EEUU*) ➤ **cuenta de correo** (*Internet*) email account ➤ **cuenta personal** personal account ➤ **cuenta vivienda** mortgage account
5 (*en disputa*) **ajustar ~s con algn** to settle one's scores with sb; **voy a ajustarle las ~s** I'm going to have it out with him; **tener ~s pendientes con algn** to have unfinished business with sb; **no querer ~s con algn** to want nothing to do with sb
6 (= *explicación*) **dar ~ de algo** (= *informar*) to recount sth, report sth; (= *acabar*) to finish sth off; **no tiene que dar ~s a nadie** he's not answerable to anyone; **dar buena ~ de una botella** to finish off a bottle; **exigir** *o* **pedir ~s a algn** to call sb to account, bring sb to book; **en resumidas ~s** in short, in a nutshell
7 (= *consideración*) **caer en la ~ (de algo)** to see the point (of sth); **por fin cayó en la ~** he finally caught on, the penny finally dropped (*esp Brit*); **cuando cayó en la ~ de que lo engañaban** when he realized that they were deceiving him; **darse ~** (= *enterarse*) to realize; (= *ver*) to notice; **perdona, no me había dado ~ de que eras vegetariano** sorry, I didn't realize (that) you were a vegetarian; **¿te has dado ~ de que han cortado el árbol?** did you notice (that) they've cut down the tree?; **hay que darse ~ de que ...** one must not forget that ...; **¿te das ~?** (*enfático*) can you believe it!; **habida ~ de eso** bearing that in mind; **tener en ~** to take into account, bear in mind; **también hay que tener en ~ su edad** you must also take her age into account, you must also bear in mind her age; **es otra cosa a tener en ~** that's another thing to remember *o* be borne in mind; **tomar algo en ~ a algn** to hold sth against sb; **traer ~:** **no me trae ~** it's not worth my while going; **lo harán por la ~ que les trae** *o* **tiene** they'll do it if they know what's good for them
8 (= *responsabilidad*) **esta ronda corre de mi ~** this round's on me; **yo he de resolver esto por mi ~** I have to resolve this on my own; **trabajar por ~ ajena** to be an employee; **trabajar por ~ propia** to work for o.s., be self-employed; **por ~ y riesgo de algn** at one's own risk
9 (*Esp*) (*en embarazo*) **está fuera de ~s** ◆ **ha salido de ~s** she's due
10 [*de rosario, collar*] bead; **~s de cristal** glass beads

cuentacuentos SMF INV storyteller

cuentagotas SM INV dropper; ✦ MODISMO **a** *o* **con ~** drop by drop, bit by bit

cuentakilómetros SM INV **1** [*de distancias*] ≈ mil(e)ometer (*Brit*), odometer (*esp EEUU*) **2** (= *velocímetro*) speedometer

cuentarrevoluciones SM INV tachometer (*frm*), rev counter (*Brit*)

cuente *etc ver* **contar**

cuentero/a* SM/F (*RPl*) liar, fibber*

cuentista SMF liar, fibber*

cuento¹ SM **1** (= *historia corta*) short story; (*para niños*) story, tale; **contar un ~** to tell a story; **de ~: un héroe de ~** a storybook *o* fairytale hero; **una casita de ~** a fairytale house; **ir con el ~: en seguida le fue con el ~ a la maestra** he went straight off and told the teacher; ✦ MODISMOS **aplicarse el ~** to take note; **el ~ de la lechera: eso es como el ~ de la lechera** it's a case of wishful thinking; **es el ~ de nunca acabar** it's a never-ending story ➤ **cuento corto** short story ➤ **cuento de hadas** a fairytale ➤ **cuento infantil** children's story
2 (*) (= *mentira*) **todo eso es puro ~ para no ir al colegio** he just made it all up because he doesn't want to go to school; **¡no me cuentes ~s!** ◆ **¡no me vengas con ~s!** ◆ **¡déjate de ~s!** don't give me that!*; **tener ~: tu hermanito tiene mucho ~** your little brother is a big fibber*; ✦ MODISMO **vivir del ~** to live by one's wits ➤ **cuento chino** tall story, cock-and-bull story*; **¡no me**

vengas con ~s chinos! don't give me that (nonsense)!* ➤ **el cuento del tío** (*CS*) confidence trick (*esp Brit*), confidence game (*EEUU*)
3 (*otras locuciones*) **¿a ~ de qué?: ¿a ~ de qué sacas ese tema ahora?** what are you bringing that up for now?; **traer algo a ~** to bring sth up; **venir a ~: eso no viene a ~** that's irrelevant, that doesn't come into it, that has nothing to do with it; **todo esto viene a ~ de lo que acaba de pasar** all this has some bearing on what has just happened; **lo dijo sin venir a ~** she said it for no reason at all
4 (*frm*) (= *cómputo*) **sin ~** countless

cuento² SM [*de bastón*] point, tip

cuerazo SM **1** (*Col, Ven*) (= *latigazo*) lash **2** (*Chi, Méx**) (= *persona*) dish*

cuerda SF **1** (*gruesa*) rope; (*fina*) string, cord; (*para saltar*) skipping rope (*Brit*), jump rope (*EEUU*); **un metro de ~** a metre (length) of rope; **se ha roto la ~ de la persiana** the cord on the blind has broken; ✦ MODISMO **bajo ~: ha conseguido un visado bajo ~** she's got hold of a visa under the counter; **han llegado a un acuerdo bajo ~** they have reached an agreement in secret, they have made a secret agreement ➤ **cuerda de salvamento** lifeline ➤ **cuerda floja** tightrope; ✦ MODISMO **caminar en la ~ floja** to walk a tightrope
2 (*Mec*) [*de reloj*] winder; [*de juguete*] clockwork mechanism; **un reloj de ~** a wind-up watch; **dale ~ al reloj** wind up the clock; ✦ MODISMO **dar ~ a algn*: no para de hablar, parece que le han dado ~** he never stops talking, you'd think he'd been wound up; **quedar ~ a algn*: a ese viejo aún le queda mucha ~** the old boy's still got plenty of life *o* steam left in him*; **tener ~*: después de dos años sin verse, estos tienen ~ para rato*** after two years apart, those two have got enough to keep them going for a while yet
3 (*Mús*) [*de instrumento*] string; **sección de ~** string section, strings *pl*
4 (*Anat*) ➤ **cuerdas vocales** vocal cords
5 cuerdas (*Boxeo*) ropes; (*Hípica*) rails; ✦ MODISMO **contra las ~s** on the ropes

cuerdo ADJ **1** [*persona*] sane **2** [*acto*] sensible, wise

cuerear /1a/ VT (*LAm*) [+ *animal*] to skin; [+ *persona*] to beat, whip, flay

cuerna SF **1** (*Zool*) horns *pl*; [*de ciervo*] antlers *pl* **2** (= *vaso*) drinking horn

cuerno SM **1** (*Zool*) horn; [*de ciervo*] antler; **¡cuerno(s)!** gosh!*, blimey! (*Brit***); ✦ MODISMOS **¡(y) un ~!** my foot!, you must be joking!; **irse al ~** [*negocio*] to fail, go to the wall*; [*proyecto*] to fall through; **¡que se vaya al ~!** he can go to hell!; **mandar a algn al ~** to tell sb to go to hell*; **mandar algo al ~** to consign sth to hell; **poner los ~s a algn** to cheat on sb, cuckold sb†; **romperse los ~s** to break one's back working, work one's butt off (*EEUU**); **saber a ~ quemado: esto me sabe a ~ quemado** it makes my blood boil ➤ **cuerno de la abundancia** horn of plenty
2 (*Culin*) roll, croissant; (*Mús*) horn ➤ **cuerno alpino** alpenhorn

cuero SM **1** (= *piel*) (*curtida*) leather; (*sin curtir*) skin, hide; [*de conejo*] pelt; **una chaqueta de ~** a leather jacket; ✦ MODISMOS **andar en ~s** to go about stark naked; **dejar a algn en ~s** to clean sb out* ➤ **cuero cabelludo** scalp ➤ **cuero de cocodrilo** (*CS*) crocodile skin **2** (= *odre*) wineskin **3** (*Dep*) (= *balón*) ball

cuerpo SM **1** (*Anat*) body; **de ~ entero** [*retrato, espejo*] full-length; **de medio ~** [*retrato, espejo*] half-length; **¡~ a tierra!** hit the ground!; ✦ MODISMOS **a ~: fue una lucha ~ a ~** it was hand-to-hand combat; **un ~ a ~ entre los dos políticos** a head-on *o* head-to-head confrontation between the two politicians; **en ~ y alma** body and soul, wholeheartedly; **a ~ de rey: vive a ~ de rey** he lives like a king; **nos trataron a ~ de rey** they treated us like royalty; **hacer de(l) ~** (*euf*) to defecate, have a bowel movement; **sacar el ~ a algn/algo** (*LAm**) to stay clear of sb/sth
2 (= *cadáver*) body, corpse; **de ~ presente: su marido aún estaba de ~ presente** her husband had not yet been buried; **funeral de ~ presente** funeral (service)
3 (= *grupo*) ➤ **cuerpo de baile** corps de ballet ➤ **cuerpo de bomberos** fire brigade (*esp Brit*), fire department (*EEUU*) ➤ **cuerpo de leyes** body of laws ➤ **cuerpo de policía**

police force ➤ **cuerpo diplomático** diplomatic corps ➤ **cuerpo legislativo** legislative body
4 (= *parte*) [*de mueble*] section, part; [*de un vestido*] bodice; (= *parte principal*) main body; **un armario de dos ~s** a cupboard in two sections *o* parts
5 (= *objeto*) body, object ➤ **cuerpo celeste** heavenly body ➤ **cuerpo del delito** corpus delicti ➤ **cuerpo extraño** foreign body ➤ **cuerpo geométrico** geometric shape
6 (= *consistencia*) [*de vino*] body; **un vino de mucho** ~ a full-bodied wine; **dar** ~ **a algo: el suavizante que da** ~ **a su cabello** the conditioner that gives your hair body; **hay que darle un poco más** ~ **a la salsa** the sauce needs thickening a bit more; **tomar** ~ [*plan, proyecto, personaje, historia*] to take shape
7 (*Tip*) [*de letra*] point, point size

cuervo SM raven

cuesco SM **1** (*Bot*) stone **2** (*) (= *pedo*) fart**

cuesta SF **1** (= *pendiente*) hill, slope; **mi casa está al final de la** ~ my house is at the top of the hill; **una** ~ **empinada** a steep slope; **bajamos la** ~ **corriendo** we ran down the hill; **la** ~ **de enero** *period of financial stringency following Christmas spending*; ~ **abajo** downhill; **ir** ~ **abajo** to go downhill; ~ **arriba** uphill
2 a ~s on one's back; **siempre va con su guitarra a ~s** he always goes around with his guitar on his back *o* slung over his shoulder; **se echa todas las responsabilidades a ~s** she takes all the responsibilities on her own shoulders

cuestación SF charity collection

cueste *etc ver* **costar**

cuestión SF **1** (= *asunto*) matter, question; **eso es otra** ~ that's another matter; **¡sigue gritando, la** ~ **es no dejarme tranquilo!** (*iró*) carry on shouting, don't mind me!; **no sé por qué, pero la** ~ **es que ahora soy más pobre*** I don't know why, but the fact is that I'm poorer now than I was; ~ **de: una** ~ **de honor** a matter of honour; **resolver el problema no es sólo** ~ **de dinero** the answer to the problem is not just a question of money; **que se entregue a la policía es solo** ~ **de tiempo** it's only a matter of time before he gives himself up to the police; **todo es** ~ **de proponérselo** it's all a matter *o* question of telling yourself you can do it; **será** ~ **de irse ya a casa** it's time we were thinking of going home; **en** ~ in question; **la persona en** ~ **resultó ser mi padre** the person in question turned out to be my father; **falleció en** ~ **de segundos** she died in a matter of seconds
2 (= *pregunta*) question; **poner algo en** ~ to call sth into question, raise doubts about sth

cuestionar /1a/ **Ⓐ** VT to question **Ⓑ** VI to argue **Ⓒ** **cuestionarse** VPR to ask o.s., question

cuestionario SM [*de sondeo*] questionnaire; (*Escol, Univ*) question paper

cuete Ⓐ ADJ (*Méx**) drunk **Ⓑ** SM **1** (*Perú*) (= *pistola*) pistol **2** (*LAm*) = **cohete 3** (*Méx, RPI**) (= *embriaguez*) drunkenness **4** (*Méx Culin*) steak

cueva SF cave ➤ **cueva de ladrones** den of thieves

cuezo SM ✦ MODISMO **meter el ~*** to poke *o* stick one's nose in*

cui SM (*pl* ~**s** *o* ~**ses**) (*SAm*) guinea pig

cuico/a SM/F (*Chi pey*) Bolivian

cuidado Ⓐ SM **1** (= *precaución*) **1.1** (*como advertencia directa*) **¡cuidado!** look out!, watch out!; **¡~ con el techo!** mind the ceiling!; **"cuidado con el perro"** "beware of the dog"; ~ **con hacer algo: ¡cuidadito con abrir la boca!** keep your mouth shut, remember!; **¡~ con perderlo!** mind you don't lose it! **1.2 tener** ~ **(con algo)** to be careful (of sth); **¡ten ~!** careful!; **ten** ~ **con el jarrón** careful with the vase (*esp Brit*); **tener** ~ **con algn** to watch out for sb, watch sb*, be careful of sb; **tener** ~ **de no hacer algo** to be careful *o* take care not to do sth **1.3 andarse con** ~ to tread carefully, tread warily; **¡ándate con ~!** watch how you go!, watch your step!
2 (= *atención*) care; **las prendas delicadas deben lavarse con** ~ delicate garments should be washed with care; **analicemos con** ~ **el último de los ejemplos** let's analyse the last of the examples carefully; **poner/tener** ~ **en algo** to

take care over sth
3 [*de niño, enfermo, planta, edificio*] care; **estar al** ~ **de** (= *encargado de*) [+ *niños, familia, plantas*] to look after; [+ *proyecto*] to be in charge of; (= *cuidado por*) [*niños, jardín*] to be in the care of; [*departamento, sección*] to be run by; **dejó a su hija al** ~ **de una amiga** she left her daughter in the care of a friend; **la sección de publicidad está al** ~ **de M. Moyano** M. Moyano is in charge of the advertising department ➤ **cuidado personal** personal care ➤ **cuidados intensivos** intensive care *sing*; **unidad de ~s intensivos** intensive care unit
4 (= *preocupación*) worry, concern; **pierda usted ~, ya me hago yo cargo de todo** don't worry about it, I'll take care of everything; ✦ MODISMOS **tener** *o* **traer sin ~: me tiene sin** ~ **lo que pase a partir de ahora** I don't care at all *o* I couldn't (*Brit*) *o* could (*EEUU*) care less what happens from now on; **¡allá ~s!** let others worry about that!, that's their funeral!*
5 de ~* [*chapuza, bromista*] real; **les echó una bronca de** ~ he gave them a real telling-off*; **traía una intoxicación de** ~ she had bad food poisoning
Ⓑ ADJ [*aspecto*] impeccable; [*trabajo, selección*] meticulous, careful

cuidador(a) SM/F **1** [*de niños*] nanny, baby-sitter, childminder (*Brit*); [*de enfermos*] carer (*Brit*), caretaker (*EEUU*) **2** [*de caballos*] trainer; [*de zoo*] keeper, zookeeper; [*de terreno*] caretaker

cuidadoso ADJ **1** (= *atento*) [*persona, observación, estrategia*] careful **2** (= *prudente*) careful

cuidar /1a/ **Ⓐ** VT **1** (= *atender*) [+ *familia, jardín, edificio*] to look after, take care of; [+ *rebaño*] to tend; **se dedica a niños por las noches** she does baby-sitting in the evenings
2 (= *preocuparse por*) [+ *muebles, propiedades, entorno, salud*] to look after, take care of
3 (= *poner atención en*) [+ *detalles, ortografía*] to pay attention to, take care over
Ⓑ VI ~ **de** to look after, take care of; ~ **de hacer algo** to take care to do sth; ~ **de que no pase nadie** make sure nobody gets in; **cuidó de que todo saliera bien** he made sure that everything went smoothly
Ⓒ **cuidarse** VPR **1** [*persona*] to look after o.s., take care of o.s.; **se cuida mucho** she takes good care of herself; **¡cómo te cuidas!** you do know how to look after yourself well!; **¡cuídate!** (*al despedirse*) take care!
2 ~**se de algo** (= *encargarse*) to take care of sth; (= *preocuparse*) to worry about sth; **no se cuida del qué dirán** she doesn't worry about what people think; ~**se de hacer algo** to be careful to do sth, take care to do sth; ~**se muy mucho de hacer algo** to take good *o* great care to do sth

cuita SF (*liter*) (= *preocupación*) worry, trouble; (= *pena*) grief, affliction; (*civil, doméstica*) strife

culantro SM coriander

culata SF **1** (*Mec*) [*de fusil*] butt; [*de cañón*] breech; [*de cilindro*] head **2** (= *parte trasera*) rear, back

culatazo SM kick, recoil

culear /1a/ VI, VT (*And, Col****) to fuck***, screw***

culebra SF **1** (*Zool*) snake **2** (*Col**) (= *deuda*) debt **3** (*Ven**) (= *culebrón*) soap opera, soap*

culebrear /1a/ VI [*culebra*] to wriggle, wriggle along; [*carretera*] to zigzag, wind; [*río*] to wind, meander

culebrón* SM soap opera, soap**

culeco ADJ (*Col*) broody

culera SF (*Esp*) seat (*of trousers*)

culero/a Ⓐ ADJ lazy **Ⓑ** SM/F (*Méx**) coward

culillo* SM (*And, CAm, Carib*) fear; **tener** ~ to be scared

culín SM (*Esp*) (= *gota*) drop

culinario ADJ culinary, cooking *antes de s*

culmen Ⓐ SM **1** (= *colmo*) **el** ~ **de la ignorancia** the height of ignorance; (= *persona*) the epitome of ignorance **2** (= *punto culminante*) **el** ~ **de su carrera** the crowning moment of his career; **llegar a su** ~ to reach its height **Ⓑ** ADJ = **culminante 2**

culminación SF culmination

culminante ADJ **1** (*Geog*) highest, topmost **2** [*momento*] culminating; **el momento ~ de la revolución** the culminating moment of the revolution, the climax of the revolution; **este fue el momento ~ de su carrera** this was the crowning moment of his career; **en el momento ~ de la fiesta, se apagaron las luces** at the high point of the party, the lights went out

culminar /1a/ Ⓐ VT [+ *objetivo*] to reach, attain; [+ *acuerdo*] to conclude; [+ *tarea, carrera*] to finish Ⓑ VI to culminate (**en** in)

cúlmine ADJ (*And*) = **culminante**

culo SM **1** (*) (*in much of Latin America this is much ruder than in Spain*) (= *nalgas*) backside*, bum (*Brit**), arse (*Brit****), ass (*EEUU***), butt (*EEUU**); (= *ano*) arsehole (*Brit***), asshole (*EEUU***); **le dio un puntapié en el ~** he kicked him in the backside*; **le limpió el culito al niño** he wiped the baby's bottom; **caer de ~** to fall on one's backside*; **dar a algn por el ~*** (= *sexualmente*) to bugger sb; (= *fastidiar*) to piss sb off***; **¡que te den por (el) ~!*** fuck you!***, screw you!***; ♦ MODISMOS **el ~ del mundo**: **está en el ~ del mundo** it's in the back of beyond; **es el ~ del mundo** it's the arsehole (*Brit*) o asshole (*EEUU*) of the world***; **ir de ~** (*Esp**): **con tanta llamada, esta mañana voy de ~** with all these calls this morning I'm way behind*; **si no apruebas esta asignatura vas de ~** if you don't pass this subject you've had it*; **en cuanto al paro, el país va de ~** the country's unemployment record is disastrous; **lamer el ~ a algn**** to lick sb's arse (*Brit***) o ass (*EEUU***), kiss sb's arse (*Brit***) o ass (*EEUU***); **meterse algo por el ~***: **¡métetelo por el ~!** stick it up your arse (*Brit*) o ass (*EEUU*)!***; **partirse el ~**: **me partí el ~ de risa con él** I laughed myself silly with him; **ser un ~ de mal asiento**: **se mudó cinco veces en un año, es un ~ de mal asiento** she moved house five times in one year, she just can't stay in one place; **tomar por ~** (*Esp***): **¡vete a tomar por ~!*** screw you!***, fuck off!***, piss off!***; **el proyecto se fue a tomar por ~** the project went down the toilet**; **los mandó a tomar por ~** he told them to fuck off o piss off***; **su casa está a tomar por ~** her house is in the back of beyond
2 (*) [*de vaso, botella*] bottom; **gafas de ~ de vaso** pebble glasses

culote SM, **culottes** SMPL **1** (*Dep*) cycling shorts *pl* **2** (= *prenda íntima*) French knickers *pl* (*Brit*), panties

culpa SF **1** (= *responsabilidad*) fault, blame; **es ~ suya** it's his fault, he's to blame; **la ~ fue de los frenos** the brakes were to blame; **echar la ~ a algn de algo** to blame sb for sth; **por ~ del mal tiempo** because of the bad weather; **tener la ~ de algo** to be to blame for sth **2** (*Jur*) guilt **3** (= *pecado*) sin

culpabilidad SF **1** (= *culpa*) guilt, culpability (*frm*) **2** (*Jur*) guilt; **veredicto de ~** verdict of guilty

culpabilizar /1f/ VT = **culpar**

culpable Ⓐ ADJ **1** [*persona*] guilty; **confesarse ~** to plead guilty; **declarar ~ a algn** to find sb guilty **2** [*acto*] blameworthy Ⓑ SMF **1** (= *responsable*) person to blame, person at fault **2** (*Jur*) (= *responsable de un delito*) culprit; (= *condenado por un delito*) offender, guilty party

culpar /1a/ VT (= *acusar*) to blame; **~ a algn de algo** to blame sb for sth

culteranismo SM (*Literat*) latinized, precious and highly metaphorical style (*esp 17th century*)

cultismo SM learned word

cultivable ADJ cultivable, arable

cultivado ADJ [*campo, superficie*] cultivated; [*persona*] cultured, cultivated; [*perla*] cultured

cultivador(a) SM/F farmer, grower; **~ de vino** winegrower; **~ de café** coffee grower, coffee planter

cultivar /1a/ VT **1** (*Agr*) [+ *tierra*] to farm, cultivate, till; [+ *cosecha*] to grow, raise **2** (*Biol*) to culture **3** [+ *amistad, arte, estudio*] to cultivate; [+ *talento*] to develop; [+ *memoria*] to develop, improve

cultivo SM **1** (= *acto*) cultivation, growing **2** (= *cosecha*) crop; **el ~ principal de la región** the chief crop of the area;

rotación de ~s crop rotation **3** (*Biol*) culture

culto Ⓐ ADJ **1** [*persona*] cultured, educated; (*pey*) (= *afectado*) affected **2** [*palabra, frase*] learned Ⓑ SM **1** (*Rel*) (= *veneración*) worship; (= *ritual*) cult (**a** of); **rendir ~ a** (*lit*) to worship; (*fig*) to pay homage o tribute to **2** (= *admiración*) cult; **una película de ~** a cult movie

cultura SF **1** (= *civilización*) culture **2** (= *saber*) **un hombre de gran ~** a very knowledgeable o cultured man ➤ **cultura general** general knowledge ➤ **cultura popular** popular culture **3** (= *artes*) culture; **Ministerio de Cultura** Minister of Culture

cultural ADJ cultural; **tiene un bajo nivel ~** he's not very (well-)educated

culturismo SM body building

culturista SMF body builder

culturizar /1f/ Ⓐ VT to educate, enlighten Ⓑ **culturizarse** VPR to educate o.s., improve one's mind

cuma SF (*CAm*) curved machete, curved knife

cumbia SF (= *música*) Colombian dance music; (= *baile*) popular Colombian dance

cumbre Ⓐ SF (*Geog*) summit, top; (*fig*) top, height; **conferencia en la ~** (*Pol*) summit, summit conference; **hacer ~** to make it to the top Ⓑ ADJ INV **conferencia ~** summit conference; **momento ~** culminating point

cumpleaños SM INV birthday; **¡feliz ~!** happy birthday!, many happy returns!

cumplido Ⓐ ADJ **1** (= *perfecto*) complete, full; **un ~ caballero** a perfect gentlemen **2** (= *cortés*) courteous, correct; (= *formal*) formal **3** (*Col*) (= *puntual*) punctual; **ser ~** to be punctual, be on time **4** **tiene sesenta años ~s** he's sixty years old Ⓑ SM **1** (= *alabanza*) compliment **2** (= *cortesía*) **visita de ~** courtesy call

cumplidor ADJ reliable, trustworthy

cumplimentar /1a/ VT **1** [+ *formulario*] to complete, fill out, fill in (*esp Brit*) **2** [+ *órdenes*] to carry out; [+ *deber*] to perform **3** (*frm*) [+ *superior, jefe*] to pay one's respects to (**por** on)

cumplimiento SM **1** (= *satisfacción*) **el ~ de sus obligaciones** keeping o fulfilling his obligations; **le felicitó por el ~ de todos los objetivos propuestos** he congratulated him on achieving all the proposed aims **2** [*de ley*] observance, compliance; **dar ~ a** to fulfil; **falta de ~** non-fulfilment

cumplir /3a/ Ⓐ VT **1** (= *llevar a cabo*) [+ *amenaza*] to carry out; [+ *promesa*] to keep; [+ *objetivo, sueño*] to achieve; [+ *papel*] to play; **les ha acusado de no ~ su palabra** he has accused them of failing to keep o breaking their word **2** (= *obedecer*) [+ *ley, norma, sentencia*] to observe, obey; [+ *orden*] to carry out, obey; **~ la voluntad del difunto** to carry out the wishes of the deceased; **hacer ~ la ley/un acuerdo** to enforce the law/an agreement **3** [+ *condición, requisito*] to comply with, fulfil, fulfill (*EEUU*), meet **4** (= *realizar*) [+ *condena, pena*] to serve; [+ *servicio militar*] to do, complete **5** (*con periodos de tiempo*) **5.1** [+ *años*] **hoy cumple ocho años** she's eight today, it's her eighth birthday today; **cumple 40 años en diciembre** she'll be 40 in December; **cuando cumplas los 21 años** when you're 21, when you reach the age of 21; **¡que cumplas muchos más!** many happy returns! **5.2** [+ *aniversario, días*] **la democracia cumple su vigésimo aniversario** democracy is celebrating its twentieth anniversary; **el paro en el transporte cumple hoy su cuarto día** this is the fourth day of the transport strike Ⓑ VI **1** (= *terminar*) [*plazo*] to end, expire; [*pago*] to fall due **2** (= *hacer lo correcto*) to do one's duty; **yo siempre cumplo en mi trabajo** I always do my job properly; **prepárales una sopita y con eso cumples** just make them a bit of soup, that's as much as can be expected of you **3** **~ con** [+ *compromiso, acuerdo*] to honour, honor (*EEUU*); [+ *ley*] to observe, obey; [+ *condición, requisito, criterio*] to fulfil, fulfill (*EEUU*), comply with, meet; **estaba cumpliendo con su deber** he was doing his duty; **tendrán que ~ con el calendario acordado** they will have to comply with the schedule we agreed on; **para ~ con los criterios de**

Maastricht in order to comply with *o* meet the Maastricht criteria

4 ~ por algn to act on sb's behalf

ⓒ cumplirse VPR **1** (= *realizarse*) [*deseo, sueño, vaticinio*] to come true; [*plan, proyecto*] to be implemented **2** (= *acabarse*) [*plazo*] to expire; **el viernes se cumple el plazo para entregar las solicitudes** Friday is the deadline *o* last day for handing in applications; **hoy se cumple el 40 aniversario de su muerte** today is the 40th anniversary of her death

cúmulo SM **1** (= *montón*) heap, accumulation (*frm*); **un ~ de datos** a heap of facts; **es un ~ de virtudes** he's full of virtues, he's a paragon of virtue **2** (*Meteo*) cumulus

cumulonimbo SM cumulonimbus

cuna SF **1** [*de bebé*] cot (*Brit*), crib (*EEUU*); (*con balancines*) cradle ➤ **cuna portátil** carrycot (*Brit*), portable baby carrier (*EEUU*) **2** (= *lugar de nacimiento*) [*de persona*] birthplace; [*de tendencia, movimiento*] cradle; **Escocia, la ~ del golf** Scotland, the home of golf **3** (= *linaje*) **de noble ~** of noble birth

cundir /3a/ VI **1** (= *rendir*) to produce a good quantity; **hoy no me ha cundido el trabajo** I didn't get very far with my work today, I didn't get much work done today; **no me cunde el tiempo** I'm not getting very far, I'm not getting a lot done, I'm not making very much headway **2** (= *extenderse*) to spread; **¡que no cunda el pánico!** there's no need for panic!, don't panic! **3** (= *multiplicarse*) to increase **4** (= *hincharse*) [*arroz*] to swell

cuneiforme ADJ cuneiform

cuneta SF **1** [*de calle*] gutter; [*de carretera*] ditch **2** (*Chi*) [*de acera*] kerb, curb (*EEUU*)

cuña SF **1** (*Téc*) wedge; [*de rueda*] chock **2 meter ~** to sow discord **3** (*CS**) (= *palanca*) pull, influence **4** (*CAm, Carib Aut*) two-seater car **5** (*Radio, TV*) spot, slot; (*Prensa*) space filler, brief item ➤ **cuña publicitaria** commercial

cuñado/a SM/F brother-/sister-in-law

cuño SM **1** (*Téc*) die-stamp; **de nuevo ~** [*palabra*] newly-coined; [*persona*] new-fledged **2** (= *sello*) stamp, mark

cuota SF **1** (= *parte proporcional*) share ➤ **cuota de mercado** market share ➤ **cuota de pantalla** (*TV*) share of the viewing figures **2** (= *parte asignada*) quota **3** (= *cantidad a pagar*) [*de club*] membership fee, membership fees *pl*; [*de sindicato*] dues *pl* ➤ **cuota de conexión** connection charge, connection fee ➤ **cuota de inscripción** (*a un curso*) enrolment fee, enrollment fee (*EEUU*); (*a una conferencia*) registration fee ➤ **cuota de socio** membership fee **4** (*LAm*) (= *plazo*) **por ~s** by instalments *o* (*EEUU*) installments ➤ **cuota inicial** (*LAm*) down payment **5** (*Méx*) (= *peaje*) toll

cupe *etc ver* **caber**

cupé SM coupé

cupiera *etc ver* **caber**

cuplé SM *type of light, sometimes risqué song originally sung in variety shows*

cupletista SF cabaret singer, singer of "cuplés"

cupo SM **1** (*Fin, Com*) quota ➤ **cupo de importación** import quota **2** (*LAm*) capacity; **no hay ~** there's no room **3** (*CAm, Col, Méx*) (*en vehículo*) seat **4** (*Mil*) draft

cupón SM **1** (= *vale*) coupon ➤ **cupón de racionamiento** ration coupon ➤ **cupón de regalo** gift voucher, gift token (*Brit*), gift certificate (*EEUU*) ➤ **cupón obsequio** gift voucher, gift token (*Brit*), gift certificate (*EEUU*) **2** (*Esp*) [*de lotería*] ticket

cuponazo* SM special lottery prize

cuprero ADJ (*Chi*) copper *antes de s*

cúpula SF **1** (*Arquit*) dome, cupola **2** (= *personas*) (*Pol*) party leadership, leading members; (*Com, Fin*) top management

cura¹ SM (*Rel*) priest ➤ **cura párroco** parish priest

cura² SF (*Med*) (= *curación*) cure; (= *tratamiento*) treatment; **no tiene ~** (*lit*) there is no cure for it; (*fig*) there's no remedy, it's quite hopeless ➤ **cura de reposo** rest therapy ➤ **cura de sueño** sleep therapy ➤ **cura de urgencia** emergency treatment, first aid

curable ADJ curable

curaca SM (*And*) Indian chief, Indian native authority

curación SF (= *proceso*) cure, healing; (= *tratamiento*) treatment

curado ⒶADJ **1** (*Culin*) cured; [*pieles*] tanned, prepared **2** (*And*) (= *borracho*) drunk **3** (= *endurecido*) **estar ~ de espanto(s)** to have seen it all before ⒷSM (*Culin*) curing

curador(a) SM/F **1** (*Jur*) guardian **2** [*de museo*] curator

curandero/a SM/F quack, quack doctor

curar /1a/ ⒶVT **1** (*Med*) (= *tratar*) to treat; (= *sanar*) to cure; **este tratamiento me curó la bronquitis** this treatment cured my bronchitis; **le curó la herida con alcohol** she treated *o* dressed his wound with alcohol; **no le consiguió ~ la herida** he couldn't get his wound to heal **2** [+ *carne, pescado*] to cure; [+ *queso*] to mature; [+ *piel*] to tan; [+ *tela*] to bleach; [+ *madera*] to season ⒷVI [*fármaco, medicamento*] to work; (*frm*) [*paciente*] to get better, recover Ⓒcurarse VPR **1** [*enfermo*] to get better, recover; **ya me he curado de la gripe** I've got over the flu now; ✦ MODISMO **~se en salud** to take precautions; **para ~se en salud** in order to be on the safe side **2** [*herida*] to heal (up)

curare SM curare, curari

curativo ADJ curative

curcuncho/a (*And, Chi*) SM/F hunchback

curda* SF drunkenness; **agarrar una ~** to get sloshed (*Brit**), get pissed (*Brit***), get trashed (*EEUU***); **tener una ~** to be sloshed (*Brit**), be pissed (*Brit***), be trashed (*EEUU***)

curdo/a ⒶADJ Kurdish ⒷSM/F Kurd

curia SF **1** (*Rel*) (*tb ~ romana*) papal Curia **2** (*Jur*) legal profession, the Bar, the Bar Association (*EEUU*)

curiosear /1a/ ⒶVT **1** (= *husmear*) to nose out **2** (= *mirar*) (*en una tienda*) to look over, look around ⒷVI **1** (= *husmear*) to snoop, pry **2** (= *mirar*) (*en una tienda*) to look around, wander around; (= *explorar*) to poke about

curiosidad SF **1** (= *interés*) curiosity; (= *indiscreción*) inquisitiveness; **despertar la ~ de algn** to arouse sb's curiosity; **estar muerto de ~** to be dying of curiosity; **tenemos ~ por saber si …** we are curious to know if … **2** (= *objeto*) curiosity, curio **3** (= *aseo*) neatness, cleanliness

curioso/a ⒶADJ **1** [*persona*] (= *interesado*) curious; (= *indiscreto*) inquisitive **2** (= *raro*) [*acto, objeto*] curious, odd; **¡qué ~!** how odd!, how curious! **3** (= *aseado*) neat, clean, tidy ⒷSM/F **1** (= *presente*) bystander, onlooker **2** (= *cotilla*) busybody

curita SF (*LAm*) plaster (*Brit*), sticking plaster (*Brit*), Band-Aid® (*EEUU*)

currante* SMF (*Esp*) worker

currar* /1a/ VI **1** (*Esp*) to work **2** (*RPl*) (= *estafar*) to rip off**

currelar* /1a/ VI (*Esp*) to work

curricular ADJ curriculum *antes de s*

currículo SM curriculum

curriculum SM, **currículum** SM (*tb ~ vitae*) curriculum vitae (*esp Brit*), résumé (*EEUU*)

currito* SM working man

curro* SM **1** (*Esp*) (= *trabajo*) work **2** (*RPl*) (= *estafa*) rip-off**

currusco* SM hard crust (*at the end of French bread*)

currutaco/a* (*Col, Ven*) ⒶADJ short, squat ⒷSM/F shortie*

curry SM **1** (= *especia*) curry powder; **pollo al ~** curried chicken **2** (= *plato*) curry

cursar /1a/ VT **1** (= *procesar*) [+ *orden, mensaje*] to send, dispatch; [+ *solicitud*] to deal with **2** [+ *asignatura*] to study; [+ *curso*] to take, attend

cursi* ⒶADJ **1** [*persona*] (= *amanerado*) affected; (= *remilgado*) prissy*; (*en sus gustos*) twee (*Brit**), tacky* **2** [*objeto*] twee (*Brit**), kitsch ⒷSMF **es una ~** (= *amanerada*) she's so affected; (= *niña remilgada*) she's so prissy*; (*en sus gustos*) she's so twee (*Brit**) *o* tacky*

cursilada* SF, **cursilería*** SF **no soporto las ~s que dice** I can't stand her affected way of speaking; **hizo la ~ de cortarle el pelo al caniche** he was twee (*Brit*) *o* tacky enough to get the poodle's hair cut *

cursillo SM (= *curso*) short course; (= *conferencias*) short series of lectures

cursiva SF (*Tip*) italics *pl*; (= *escritura*) cursive writing

curso SM **1** (*Escol, Univ*) (= *año escolar*) year; (= *clase*) year, class (*esp EEUU*); **los alumnos del segundo ~** second year pupils, the second years; **es el único chico de mi ~** he's the only boy in my year **2** (= *estudios*) course; **un ~ de informática** a course in computing; **apertura/clausura de ~** beginning/end of term ➤ **Curso de Orientación Universitaria** = **COU** ➤ **curso de reciclaje** refresher course ➤ **curso escolar** school year, academic year ➤ **curso intensivo** crash course, intensive course ➤ **curso lectivo** academic year ➤ **curso por correspondencia** correspondence course **3** [*de río*] course ➤ **curso de agua, curso fluvial** watercourse **4** (= *desarrollo*) course; **deja que las cosas sigan su ~** let matters take their course; **la recuperación del enfermo sigue su ~ normal** the patient is recovering normally; **el año en ~** the present year, the current year **5** (*frm*) **dar ~ a algo: dar ~ a una solicitud** to deal with an application; **dimos libre ~ a la imaginación** we let our imagination run wild **6** (*Com*) **moneda de ~ legal** legal tender

cursor SM **1** (*Téc*) slide **2** (*Inform*) cursor

curtido ⒶADJ **1** [*cuero*] tanned **2** [*piel*] hardened, leathery; [*cara*] (*por sol*) tanned; (*por intemperie*) weather-beaten **3** (= *experimentado*) **estar ~ en** to be expert at, be skilled in Ⓑ SM **1** (= *acto*) tanning **2** (= *cuero*) tanned leather, tanned hides *pl*

curtidor SM tanner

curtir /3a/ Ⓐ VT **1** [+ *cuero*] to tan **2** [+ *piel*] to tan, bronze **3** (= *acostumbrar*) to harden, inure Ⓑ **curtirse** VPR **1** (*por sol*) to become tanned; (*por intemperie*) to get weather-beaten **2** (= *acostumbrarse*) to become inured (**contra** to)

curul SF (*Col Pol*) seat (in parliament)

curva SF **1** [*de carretera, camino*] bend **2** (= *línea*) curve ➤ **curva de la felicidad** (*hum*) paunch, beer-belly **3 curvas*** [*de mujer*] vital statistics; **¡tiene unas ~s!** what a body she's got!

curvar /1a/ Ⓐ VT to bend Ⓑ **curvarse** VPR [*material*] to bow; [*estante*] to sag, bend; [*madera*] to warp

curvatura SF curvature ➤ **curvatura terrestre** Earth's curvature

curvilíneo ADJ curved, curvilinear

curvo ADJ curved

cuscús SM INV couscous

cúspide SF **1** (*Anat*) cusp **2** (*Geog*) summit, peak; (*fig*) pinnacle, apex

custodia SF **1** (= *cuidado*) care, safekeeping, custody; **bajo la ~ de** in the care *o* custody of **2** (= *escolta*) guard, escort **3** (*Rel*) monstrance

custodiar /1b/ VT **1** (= *vigilar*) to guard, watch over **2** [+ *derechos, libertades*] to defend

custodio/a Ⓐ ADJ **ángel ~** guardian angel Ⓑ SM/F (= *guardián*) custodian; (*Méx, Perú*) police officer

cususa SF (*CAm*) home-made liquor, home-made rum

cutacha SF (*LAm*) = **cuma**

cutáneo ADJ cutaneous, skin *antes de s*

cúter SM cutter

cutícula SF cuticle

cutis SM INV skin, complexion

cutre* ADJ **1** [*persona*] (= *tacaño*) mean, stingy; (= *vulgar*) vulgar, coarse **2** (*Esp*) [*lugar*] squalid, shabby; **un sitio ~** a dive*, a hole* **3** (*Esp*) [*objeto*] tacky*

cutter ['kuter] SM (*pl* **-s**) [*de carpintero*] Stanley knife®, razor knife (*EEUU*); [*para papel*] artist's scalpel

cuy(e) (*pl* **cuis** *o* **cuyes**) SM (*LAm*) guinea pig

cuyo ADJ REL **1** [*de persona*] of whom (*frm*), whose; [*de cosa*] of which, whose; **la señora en cuya casa nos hospedábamos** the lady in whose house we were staying; **el asunto ~s detalles conoces** the matter of which you know the details **2 en ~ caso** in which case

CV Ⓐ SM ABR (= **curriculum vitae**) CV Ⓑ SMPL ABR (= **caballos de vapor**) HP, h.p.

C y F ABR (= **costo y flete**) CAF, c.a.f., C and F

Dd

D, d [de] SF (= *letra*) D, d

D. ABR = **Don**; ◇ *DON/DOÑA*

D.ª ABR = **Doña**; ◇ *DON/DOÑA*

dactilar ADJ **huellas ~es** fingerprints

dactilografía SF typing, typewriting

dactilógrafo/a SM/F typist

dadá SM, **dadaísmo** SM dadaism

dádiva SF gift

dadivoso ADJ generous, open-handed

dado[1] SM die; **dados** dice; **echó** o **tiró los ~s** he threw the dice; **jugar a los ~s** to play dice

dado[2] ADJ 1 (= *determinado*) **en un caso** ~ in a given case; **dada su corta edad** in view of his youth; **dadas estas circunstancias** in view of o given these circumstances 2 **ser ~ a algo** to be given to sth; **es muy ~ a discutir** he is much given to arguing 3 ✦ MODISMO **ir ~*: si crees que te voy a pagar los estudios, vas** ~ if you think I'm going to pay for your education, you've another think coming! 4 ~ **que** (+ SUBJUN) provided that, so long as; (+ INDIC) given that

daga SF dagger

daguerrotipo SM daguerreotype

daiquiri SM daiquiri

dalia SF dahlia

dalle SM scythe

dálmata SMF Dalmatian

daltónico ADJ colour-blind, color-blind (*EEUU*)

daltonismo SM colour blindness, color blindness (*EEUU*)

dama SF 1 (= *señora*) lady; **~s y caballeros** ladies and gentlemen; **primera** ~ (*LAm Pol*) First Lady ➤ **dama de honor** [*de reina*] lady-in-waiting; [*de novia*] bridesmaid 2 (= *mujer noble*) lady 3 (= *pieza*) (*Ajedrez, Naipes*) queen; (*en damas*) king 4 **damas** (*juego*) draughts (*Brit*), checkers (*EEUU*)

damajuana SF demijohn

damasco SM 1 (= *tela*) damask 2 (*CS*) (= *árbol*) apricot tree; (= *fruto*) apricot

damasquinado Ⓐ ADJ [*espada, metal*] damascene Ⓑ SM damascene, damascene work

damero SM 1 (= *pasatiempo*) type of crossword 2 (= *tablero*) draughtboard (*Brit*), checkerboard (*EEUU*)

damnificado/a SM/F victim

dandi, dandy ['dandi] SM dandy, fop

danés/esa Ⓐ ADJ Danish Ⓑ SM/F 1 (= *persona*) Dane 2 (= *perro*) (*tb* **gran ~**) Great Dane Ⓒ SM (= *idioma*) Danish

danta SF (*LAm*) tapir

dantesco ADJ nightmarish

dantzari [dan'sari] SMF *Basque folk-dancer*

Danubio SM Danube

danza SF dance; ✦ MODISMOS **siempre está en** ~ he's always on the go*; **no metas los perros en** ~ let sleeping dogs lie ➤ **danza contemporánea** contemporary dance

danzar /1f/ Ⓐ VI to dance; ✦ MODISMO **llevo toda la mañana danzando*** I've been on the go all morning* Ⓑ VT to dance

danzarín/ina Ⓐ ADJ (= *nervioso*) jumpy Ⓑ SM/F dancer

dañar /1a/ Ⓐ VT 1 [+ *objeto, piel, salud*] to damage, harm; **el alcohol le ha dañado el hígado** alcohol has damaged his liver; ✦ MODISMO ~ **la vista: es tan feo que daña la vista** it's an eyesore

2 [+ *cosecha*] to damage, spoil

3 [+ *reputación, carrera, proyecto*] to damage, harm

Ⓑ **dañarse** VPR 1 (= *hacerse daño*) to be hurt, be injured; **se dañó el brazo** she hurt o injured her arm

2 [*objeto*] to be damaged; **los cimientos no llegaron a ~se en el incendio** the foundations were not damaged in the fire

3 [*cosecha*] to be damaged, be spoiled

dañino ADJ 1 (*para la salud*) harmful 2 (*para el desarrollo de algo*) damaging (**para** to)

daño SM 1 (*a algo*) damage, harm; **el granizo ha producido grandes ~s en los cultivos** the hail has caused extensive damage to crops; **estas medidas han ocasionado un gran ~ a la industria** these measures have caused a great deal of harm to the industry; **~s y perjuicios** damages ➤ **daños colaterales** collateral damage

2 (*a alguien*) (*físico, emocional*) pain; (*económico*) harm; **¡ay, qué ~!** ow, that hurts!; **hacer ~ a algn** to hurt sb; **tanta comida picante hace ~ al estómago** all that spicy food is bad for the stomach; **hacerse ~** to hurt o.s.; **se hizo ~ en el pie** he hurt his foot ➤ **daños corporales** physical injury sing

---

dar /1a/

Ⓐ VERBO TRANSITIVO Ⓒ VERBO PRONOMINAL
Ⓑ VERBO INTRANSITIVO

Para las expresiones **dar importancia, dar ejemplo, dar las gracias, dar clases, dar a conocer, dar a entender, darse prisa** *etc, ver la entrada correspondiente a la otra palabra.*

---

dar Ⓐ VERBO TRANSITIVO

1 (= *entregar, conceder*) [+ *objeto, mensaje, permiso*] to give; [+ *naipes*] to deal (out); [+ *noticias*] to give, tell; **le dio un bocadillo a su hijo** he gave his son a sandwich; **se lo di a Blanca** I gave it to Blanca; **deme dos kilos** I'll have two kilos, two kilos, please

2 (= *realizar*) [+ *paliza*] to give; [+ *paso*] to take; ~ **un alarido** to shriek; ~ **una bofetada a algn** to slap sb; **dio un golpe en la mesa** he banged on the table; ~ **un grito** to let out a cry, give a cry; ~ **un paseo** to go for a walk, take a walk

3 (= *celebrar*) [+ *fiesta*] to have, throw; **la embajada ~á una recepción** the embassy will hold a reception

4 (= *presentar*) [+ *obra de teatro*] to perform, put on; [+ *película*] to show, screen; **dan una película de Almodóvar** there's an Almodóvar film on, they're showing o screening an Almodóvar film

5 (*Esp*) (= *encender*) [+ *luz*] to turn on; **¿has dado el gas?** have you turned on the gas?

6 (= *hacer sonar*) [*reloj*] to strike; **el reloj dio las tres** the clock struck three; **ya han dado las ocho** it's past o gone eight o'clock

7 (= *producir*) [+ *fruto*] to bear; [+ *ganancias, intereses*] to yield; ~ **flores** to flower; **este negocio da mucho dinero** there's a lot of money in this business

8 (= *tener como resultado*) **la suma dio 99** the total worked out at 99; **el atleta dio positivo en el control antidoping** the athlete tested positive for drugs

9 (= *hacer sentir*) [+ *placer*] to give; **me dio mucha alegría verla** I was very pleased to see her; **las babosas me dan asco** I find slugs disgusting o revolting; **tu padre me da miedo** I'm scared o frightened of your father; **me da pena tener que tirarlo** it's a pity to have to throw it away; **el vino me da sueño** wine makes me sleepy

10 (*Esp**) (= *fastidiar*) to ruin; **¡me estás dando la fiesta!** you're ruining the party for me!

11

✦ **dar por** (= *considerar*) to consider; **doy el asunto por concluido** I consider the matter settled, I regard the matter as settled; **doy el dinero por bien empleado** I consider it money well spent; **lo podemos ~ por terminado** we can consider it finished; **los dieron por muertos** they were given up for dead

12 ✦ MODISMOS **¡y dale!** (= *¡otra vez!*) not again!; **estar/seguir dale que dale** o **dale que te pego** o (*LAm*) **dale y dale** to go/keep on and on; **la vecina está dale que dale al piano** our neighbour is pounding away at the piano; **a mí no me la das*** you can't fool me; **¡ahí te las den todas!*** you just couldn't care less!; **para ~ y tomar: tenemos botellas para ~**

y tomar we've got loads *o* stacks of bottles; **aquí hay papeles para ~ y tomar** there's tons of papers here; **me da que ...** I have a feeling (that) ...; **me da que no va a venir** I have a feeling (that) he's not going to come
B VERBO INTRANSITIVO
1 (= *entregar*) to give; **dame, yo te lo arreglo** give it here, I'll fix it for you
2 (= *entrar*) **si te da un mareo siéntate** if you feel giddy, sit down; **le dio un infarto** he had a heart attack
3 (= *importar*) **¡qué más da!** ✧ **¡da igual!** it doesn't matter!, never mind!; **¿qué más te da?** what does it matter to you?; **¿qué más da un sitio que otro?** surely one place is as good as another!; **lo mismo da** it makes no difference *o* odds; **me da igual** ✧ **lo mismo me da** ✧ **tanto me da** it's all the same to me, I don't mind
4 (*seguido de preposición*)
◆ **dar a** (= *estar orientado*) [*cuarto, ventana*] to look out onto, overlook; [*fachada*] to face; **mi habitación da a la calle** my room looks out onto *o* overlooks the street
◆ **darle a** (= *hacer funcionar*) [+ *botón*] to press; (= *golpear*) to hit; [+ *balón*] to kick; **dale a la tecla roja** hit *o* press the red key; **no es capaz de ~le al balón de cabeza** he can't head the ball
◆ **dar con** (= *encontrar*) [+ *persona*] to find; [+ *idea, solución*] to hit on, come up with; **dimos con él dos horas más tarde** we found him two hours later; **~ consigo en** to end up in
◆ **dar contra** (= *golpear*) to hit; **el barco dio contra el puente** the ship hit the bridge
◆ **dar de:** **~ de palos a algn** to give sb a beating; **~ de puñetazos a algn** to punch sb; **~ de beber a algn** to give sb something to drink; **~ de comer a algn** to feed sb; **~ de sí** [*comida, bebida*] to go a long way
◆ **dar en** [+ *blanco, suelo*] to hit; [+ *solución*] to hit on, come up with; **el sol me da en la cara** the sun is in my eyes; **~ en hacer algo**† to take to doing sth

---

Recuérdese que las preposiciones en inglés rigen gerundio y no infinitivo, de ahí **to take to doing sth**.

◆ **darle a algn por hacer algo: les dio por venir a vernos** they took it into their heads to come and see us; **últimamente le ha dado por el golf** he's taken up golf lately
◆ **dar para** (= *ser suficiente*) to be enough for; **con eso da para cuatro personas** this is enough for four people
5
◆ **dar que** (+ INFIN) **~ que hablar** to set people talking; **un libro que da en qué pensar** a thought-provoking book, a book which gives you a lot to think about
C **darse** VERBO PRONOMINAL
1 (= *entregarse*) to give in
2 (= *golpearse*) to hit o.s.; **¿dónde te has dado?** where did you hit yourself?; **me he dado contra la esquina del escritorio** I bumped into the edge of the desk
3 (= *ocurrir*) [*suceso*] to happen; **si se da el caso** if that happens; **se han dado muchos casos** there have been a lot of cases
4 (= *crecer*) to grow; **los pepinos se dan bien en esta tierra** cucumbers grow well on this land
5 (*seguido de preposición*)
◆ **darse a** to take to; **~se a la bebida** to take to drink, start drinking
◆ **darse de sí** [*cuero, tela*] to give, stretch
◆ **dárselas de** to make o.s. out to be; **se las da de experto** he makes himself out to be an expert; **¡no te las des de listo!** stop acting clever!
◆ **darse por:** **no se dio por aludido** he didn't take the hint; **me doy por vencido** I give up, I give in
6
◆ **dársele bien a algn: se me dan bien las ciencias** I'm good at science
◆ **dársele mal a algn: se me dan muy mal los idiomas** I'm very bad at languages
7 ✦ MODISMO **dársela (con queso) a algn*** to fool sb, put one over on sb*

dardo SM dart; **jugar a los ~s** to play darts

dársena SF **1** (*Náut*) dock **2** [*de autobuses*] bay

darvinista ADJ, SMF Darwinian

datación SF date, dating; **de difícil ~** hard to date
➤ **datación con carbono** carbon dating

datar /1a/ **A** VT to date **B** VI **~ de** to date from, date back to; **esto data de muy atrás** this goes a long way back

dátil SM (*Bot*) date

datilera SF date palm

dativo SM dative

dato SM **1** (= *información*) piece of information; **un ~ interesante** an interesting fact *o* piece of information; **no tenemos todos los ~s** we don't have all the facts; **otro ~ a tener en cuenta es ...** another thing to bear in mind is ... ➤ **datos personales** personal details, particulars **2** (*Inform*) **datos** data **3** (*Mat*) datum

dcha. ABR (= **derecha**) R

d. de C. ABR (= **después de Cristo**) AD

DDT SM ABR (= **diclorodifeniltricloroetano**) DDT

---

de

---

de PREP
1 (*relación*) of; **las calles de Lima** the streets of Lima; **el alcalde de Valencia** the mayor of Valencia; **en el mes de agosto** in the month of August; **un libro de consulta** a reference book; **un millón de pesos** a million pesos; **la carretera de Bilbao** the Bilbao road, the road to Bilbao; **ya era hora de que vinieses** it's about time you got here; **el hecho de que yo no supiera nada** the fact that I didn't know anything about it
2 (*pertenencia*) **el coche de mi amigo** my friend's car; **un familiar de mi vecina** a relative of my neighbour's; **los coches de mis amigos** my friends' cars; **es de ellos** it's theirs
3 (*característica, material*) **una cadena de oro** a gold chain; **no es de oro** it's not gold; **un billete de primera clase** a first-class ticket; **la niña del pelo largo** the girl with the long hair
4 (*contenido*) **una caja de bombones** a box of chocolates; **una copa de vino** (*llena*) a glass of wine; (*vacía*) a wine glass; **una bolsita de té** a tea bag
5 (*origen, distancia, espacio temporal*) from; **soy de Galicia** I'm from Galicia; **vuelo 507 (procedente) de Londres** flight 507 from London; **vive a 20 km de Quito** she lives 20 km from Quito; **el tren de Santiago** the Santiago train; **salir del museo** to come out of the museum
◆ **de ... a ...: vivió de 1898 a 1937** he lived from 1898 to 1937; **de mi casa a la suya hay 5 km** it is 5 km from my house to his; **de mayo a julio** from May to July
6 (*causa*) **murió de viejo** he died from old age; **me dolían los pies de tanto andar** my feet were sore from all that walking; **no podía moverse del miedo** he was rigid with fear; **estar loco de alegría** to be wild with joy
7 (*manera*) **lo derribó de un solo puñetazo** he felled him with a single blow; **se puso a mi lado de un salto** he jumped to my side; **se lo bebió de un trago** he drank it all down in one gulp *o* (*Brit*) go
◆ **de ... en ...: iban entrando de dos en dos** they came in two by two; **bajó la escalera de tres en tres** he came down the stairs three at a time; **de puerta en puerta** from door to door
8 (= *respecto de*) **estar mejor de salud** to be in better health, be better; **es muy ancho de hombros** he is very broad-shouldered
9 (*tema*) about; **un libro de biología** a biology book, a book on *o* about biology; **hablaba de política** he was talking about politics; **no sé nada de él** I don't know anything about him; **una clase de francés** a French class
10 (*uso*) **máquina de coser** sewing machine; **goma de mascar** chewing gum
11 (*cantidad, medida, valor*) **un chico de quince años** a fifteen-year-old boy; **un viaje de dos días** a two-day journey; **tiene 1 m de alto** it's 1 m high
12 (*con horas y fechas*) **a las siete de la mañana** at seven o'clock in the morning, at seven a.m.; **son las dos de la tarde** it's two o'clock in the afternoon, it's two p.m.; **muy de mañana** very early in the morning; **el 3 de mayo** 3 May (*leído* May the third *o* the third of May)
13 (*tiempo*) **de día** during the day(time); **de noche** at

night; **de niño** as a child; **de mayor voy a ser médico** when I grow up I'm going to be a doctor

14 (*proporción*) **tres de cada cuatro** three out of every four

15 (*uso partitivo*) of; **uno de nosotros** one of us; **comió un poco de pastel** she ate a bit of *o* a little cake; **¡había (una) de gente!*** there were tons of people there!*

16 (*autoría*) by; **un libro de Cela** a book by Cela, a book of Cela's; **las películas de Almodóvar** Almodóvar's films

17 (*como complemento agente*) by; **el rey entró seguido de su séquito** the king entered, followed by his entourage; **tiene dos hijos de su primera mujer** he has two children by his first wife

18 (*en aposición a sustantivos o adjetivos*) **el bueno/pobre de Pedro** good/poor old Pedro; **el imbécil de Fernández** that idiot Fernández; **es un encanto de persona** he's a lovely person

19 (*en comparaciones*) than; **es más difícil de lo que creía** it's more difficult than I thought; **más/menos de siete** more/less than seven

20 (*con superlativos*) in; **el peor alumno de la clase** the worst pupil in the class; **el más caro de la colección/mundo** the most expensive in the collection/world

21 (+ INFIN) **un problema fácil de resolver** an easily solved problem; **un libro agradable de leer** a nice book to read

◆ **ser de** (+ INFIN) **su lealtad es de admirar** his loyalty is admirable; **es de esperar que recibamos una pronta respuesta** it is to be hoped that we receive a prompt reply

22 (*dependiente de formas verbales*) **la acusaban de (ser una) hipócrita** they accused her of being a hypocrite; **disfrutar de la vida** to enjoy life; **¿qué esperabas de él?** what did you expect from him?; **trabaja de camarero** he works as a waiter; **lo uso de despensa** I use it as a pantry; **(vestido) de azul** dressed in blue

23 (*uso condicional*) if; **de ser posible** if possible; **de haberlo sabido no habría venido** if I had known, I wouldn't have come; **de no ser así** if it were not so, were it not so; **de no** (*LAm*) (= *si no*) otherwise

dé *ver* **dar**

deambulador SM walking frame (*Brit*), Zimmer® (*Brit*), walker (*EEUU*)

deambular /1a/ VI to wander (about)

debajo ADV **1** (= *en la parte de abajo*) underneath; **antes de pintar la silla, pon un periódico ~** before you paint the chair, put some newspaper underneath; **ahí ~** down there; **la capa de ~ no se ve** you can't see the layer underneath *o* beneath
2 ~ **de** under; ~ **de este árbol** under *o* beneath this tree; **vive en el piso ~ del nuestro** he lives in the flat (*esp Brit*) *o* apartment (*esp EEUU*) below ours; **pasamos (por) ~ del puente** we went under *o* underneath the bridge; **el Barcelona sigue por ~ del Atlético** Barcelona is still (trailing) behind Atlético; **por ~ de la media** below average

debate SM debate; **un ~ parlamentario** a parliamentary debate; **esos conceptos están a ~** those concepts are being re-evaluated; **poner** *o* **sacar un tema a ~** to raise an issue for discussion

debatir /3a/ Ⓐ VT **1** [+ *ley, presupuesto*] to debate
2 [+ *punto de vista, problema*] to discuss, debate
Ⓑ **debatirse** VPR to struggle; **~se entre la vida y la muerte** to be fighting for one's life

debe SM (*en cuenta*) debit side; **~ y haber** debit and credit

deber /2a/ Ⓐ VT [+ *dinero, explicación, respeto*] to owe; **me debes cinco dólares** you owe me five dollars; **¿qué te debo?** (*en bares, tiendas*) how much (is it)?, how much do I owe you?
Ⓑ VI **1** (+ INFIN) (*obligación*) **debo intentar verla** I must try to see her; **no debes preocuparte** you mustn't worry; **no debes comer tanto** you shouldn't eat so much; **como debe ser** as it ought to *o* should be; **~ía cambiarse cada mes** it ought to *o* should be changed every month; **deberías haberlo traído** you ought to have *o* should have brought it; **no ~ías haberla dejado sola** you shouldn't have left her alone
2 (+ INFIN) (*suposición*) **debe (de) ser brasileño** he must be a Brazilian; **he debido (de) perderlo** I must have lost it; **no debe (de) ser muy caro** it can't be very dear; **no debía (de) tener más de dieciocho años** she couldn't have been more

than eighteen

Ⓒ **deberse** VPR **1** ~**se a algo** (= *tener por causa*) to be due to sth; **el retraso se debió a una huelga** the delay was due to a strike; **el accidente se debió al mal tiempo** the accident was caused by the bad weather; **¿a qué se debe esto?** what is the reason for this?, why is this?
2 ~**se a algn** (= *tener obligación hacia*) to have a duty to sb; **yo me debo a mis lectores** I have a duty to my readers
Ⓓ SM **1** (= *obligación*) duty; **nunca hubiera faltado a su ~** he would never have failed in *o* to do his duty; **últimos ~es** last rites ➤ **deber ciudadano** civic duty
2 (= *deuda*) debt
3 deberes (*Escol*) homework *sing*; **hacer los ~es del colegio** to do one's homework

debidamente ADV [*ajustar, comer*] properly; [*cumplimentar*] duly

debido ADJ **1** (= *adecuado*) due, proper; **a su ~ tiempo** in due course; **como es ~** as is (only) right and proper; **no lo hizo como es ~** he didn't do it properly; **una fiesta como es ~** a real *o* proper party; **más de lo ~** more than necessary
2 ~ **a** owing to, because of; ~ **a la falta de agua** owing to *o* because of the water shortage; ~ **a que** owing to *o* because of the fact that

débil ADJ **1** [*persona*] (*gen*) weak; (*extremadamente*) feeble; (*por mala salud o avanzada edad*) frail; **se encuentra un poco ~ de salud** he is in pretty poor health **2** [*carácter*] weak; [*esfuerzo*] feeble, half-hearted **3** (= *poco intenso*) [*voz, ruido*] faint; [*luz*] dim

debilidad SF **1** (= *falta de fuerzas*) (*gen*) weakness; (*extrema*) feebleness; (*por mala salud o avanzada edad*) frailty **2** [*de carácter*] weakness; [*de esfuerzo*] feebleness, half-heartedness **3** (= *poca intensidad*) [*de voz, ruido*] faintness; [*de luz*] dimness **4** (= *inclinación*) **los niños son mi ~** I love *o* adore children; **tengo ~ por el chocolate** I have a weakness for chocolate; **tener ~ por algn** to have a soft spot for sb

debilitar /1a/ Ⓐ VT **1** [+ *persona, sistema inmunológico*] to weaken, debilitate; [+ *salud*] to weaken **2** [+ *resistencia*] to weaken, impair Ⓑ **debilitarse** VPR **1** [*persona*] to grow weaker, weaken **2** [*voz, luz*] to grow *o* become fainter

débilmente ADV [*sonreír, golpear, moverse*] weakly; [*lucir, brillar*] dimly

debitar /1a/ VT to debit

débito SM (= *debe*) debit; (= *deuda*) debt ➤ **débito directo** (*LAm Com*) direct debit

debut [de'βu] SM (*pl* **~s**) début

debutante Ⓐ ADJ novice *antes de s*; **jugador ~** new player, rookie (*EEUU*) Ⓑ SMF **1** (= *principiante*) beginner; (*en sociedad*) debutante **2** (*Dep*) new player

debutar /1a/ VI to make one's debut

década SF decade

decadencia SF (= *proceso*) decline, decay; (= *estado*) decadence; **estar en ~** to be in decline

decadente ADJ [*moral, sociedad*] decadent; [*imperio, salud*] declining

decaer /2n/ VI **1** [*imperio, país*] to decline; **desde que cerraron la fábrica el pueblo ha decaído** since they closed the factory the town has gone downhill **2** (= *disminuir*) [*entusiasmo, interés*] to wane, fade (away); [*esperanzas*] to fade; **su ánimo decayó tras la muerte de su padre** he lost heart after his father's death; **¡ánimo, que no decaiga!** bear up, don't lose heart! **3** (= *empeorar*) [*salud*] to fail, decline; [*enfermo*] to deteriorate, fail **4** (*Com*) [*demanda*] to fall off; [*calidad*] to decline, fall off

decaído ADJ down, low; **estar ~** to be down *o* low

decaimiento SM **sentir ~** to feel down

decálogo SM decalogue

decano/a SM/F **1** (*Univ*) dean **2** [*de junta, grupo*] (= *de mayor edad*) senior member; (= *de más antigüedad*) doyen/doyenne

decantarse /1a/ VPR ~ **hacia algo** to move towards sth, evolve in the direction of sth; ~ **por algo/algn** to opt for sth/sb, choose sth/sb; ~ **por hacer algo** to opt to do sth, choose to do sth

decapante SM [*de pintura*] paint stripper

decapar /1a/ VT [+ *pintura, barniz*] to strip off

decapitar /1a/ VT to behead, decapitate

decatlón SM decathlon

deceleración SF deceleration

decena SF **una ~ de barcos** (= *diez*) ten ships; (= *aproximadamente diez*) some o about ten ships; **~s de miles de manifestantes** tens of thousands of demonstrators

decenal ADJ decennial; **plan ~** ten-year plan

decencia SF (= *pudor*) decency; (= *honestidad*) respectability

decenio SM decade

decente ADJ **1** (= *pudoroso*) decent; (= *honesto*) respectable **2** (= *aceptable*) [*sueldo, empleo*] decent **3** (= *aseado*) clean, tidy

decepción SF disappointment; **llevarse** o **sufrir una ~** to be disappointed

⚠ **decepción** ≠ **deception**

decepcionado ADJ disappointed

decepcionar /1a/ VT to disappoint

deceso SM (*LAm frm*) decease, passing

dechado SM model; **no es ningún ~ de perfección** it isn't a model of perfection; **es un ~ de virtudes** she's a paragon of virtue

decibelio SM decibel

decididamente ADV **1** (= *con decisión*) decisively; **tenemos que afrontar ~ el futuro** we have to face the future decisively; **entró ~ en la sala** he entered the room purposefully **2** (= *obviamente*) decidedly; **un poema ~ romántico** a decidedly romantic poem **3** (= *sin duda*) definitely; **~, vuelven a estar de moda los tacones** high heels are definitely back in fashion

decidido ADJ **1** (= *firme*) [*apoyo*] wholehearted; [*paso, gesto*] purposeful; [*esfuerzo, intento*] determined; [*defensor, partidario*] staunch, strong; [*actitud, persona*] resolute; **andaba con paso ~** she walked purposefully o with a purposeful stride; **los más ~s saltaron al agua** the most resolute jumped into the water **2 estar ~: voy a dejar el trabajo, ya estoy ~** I'm going to leave my job, I've made up my mind o I've decided; **estar ~ a hacer algo** to be resolved o determined to do sth

decidir /3a/ **Ⓐ** VT **1** (= *tomar una decisión sobre*) to decide; **¿habéis decidido lo que vais a hacer?** have you decided what you are going to do?; **~ hacer algo** to decide to do sth

2 (= *determinar*) [+ *futuro, resultado*] to decide; [+ *asunto, disputa*] to settle, resolve; **el penalti decidió el partido** the penalty decided the match

3 (= *convencer*) **la huelga de trenes me decidió a ir en coche** the rail strike made me decide to take the car

Ⓑ VI to decide; **nadie va a ~ por ellos** no one will make the decision o choice for them

Ⓒ **decidirse** VPR to decide, make up one's mind; **¡decídete ya!** make up your mind!; **~se a hacer algo** to decide to do sth, make up one's mind to do sth; **ojalá se decida a visitarnos** I hope she decides to visit us; **parece que no se decide a llover** it looks as if it's not going to rain just yet; **~se por algo** to decide on sth

décima SF [*de segundo, grado*] tenth; **tiene 37 y tres ~s** his temperature is 37.3 (degrees); **tiene sólo unas ~s (de fiebre)** he's only got a slight temperature

decimal ADJ, SM decimal

decímetro SM decimetre, decimeter (*EEUU*)

décimo **Ⓐ** ADJ, PRON tenth; *ver tb* **sexto** **Ⓑ** SM (*tb ~ de lotería*) ≈ lottery ticket; ⟳ *EL GORDO*

decimoctavo ADJ eighteenth; *ver tb* **sexto 1**

decimocuarto ADJ fourteenth; *ver tb* **sexto 1**

decimonónico ADJ nineteenth-century *antes de s*

decimonoveno ADJ nineteenth; *ver tb* **sexto 1**

decimoprimero ADJ eleventh; *ver tb* **sexto 1**

decimoquinto ADJ fifteenth; *ver tb* **sexto 1**

decimosegundo ADJ twelfth; *ver tb* **sexto 1**

decimoséptimo ADJ seventeenth; *ver tb* **sexto 1**

decimosexto ADJ sixteenth; *ver tb* **sexto 1**

decimotercero ADJ, **decimotercio** ADJ thirteenth; *ver tb* **sexto 1**

decir /3o/

Ⓐ VERBO TRANSITIVO   **Ⓒ** VERBO PRONOMINAL
Ⓑ VERBO INTRANSITIVO   **Ⓓ** SUSTANTIVO MASCULINO

Para otras expresiones con el participio, ver **dicho**.

decir **Ⓐ** VERBO TRANSITIVO

1 (= *afirmar*) to say; **ya sabe ~ varias palabras** she can already say several words, she already knows several words; **viene y dice: —estás despedido*** he goes "you're fired"*; **como dicen los madrileños** as they say in Madrid; **como iba diciendo ...** as I was saying ...; **¿cómo ha dicho usted?** pardon?, what did you say?; **~ para** o **entre sí** to say to o.s.

◆ **decir que** to say (that); **mi amigo dice que eres muy guapa** my friend says (that) you're very pretty; **~ que sí/no** to say yes/no

2

◆ **decir algo a algn** to tell sb sth; **¿quién te lo dijo?** who told you?; **tengo algo que ~te** there's something I want to tell you, I've got something to tell you

◆ **decir a algn que** (+ INDIC) to tell sb (that); **me dijo que no vendría** he told me (that) he wouldn't come

◆ **decir a algn que** (+ SUBJUN) (= *ordenar*) to tell sb to do sth; (= *pedir*) to ask sb to do sth; **la profesora me dijo que esperara fuera** the teacher told me to wait outside; **dile que venga a cenar mañana con nosotros** ask him to come and have supper with us tomorrow

3 (= *contar*) [+ *mentiras, verdad, secreto*] to tell; **~ tonterías** to talk nonsense

4 (= *llamar*) to call; **¿cómo le dicen a esto en Perú?** what do they call this in Peru?; **en México se le dice "recámara" al dormitorio** in Mexico they say "recámara" instead of "dormitorio"

5 (= *opinar*) to say; **¿tu familia qué dice de la boda?** what does your family say about the wedding?

6 (*rectificando*) **había ocho, digo nueve** there were eight, I mean nine; **dirá usted aquel otro** you must mean that other one

7 [*texto*] to say; **no puedo leer lo que dice** I can't read what it says; **como dice el refrán ...** as the saying goes ...

8 [+ *misa*] to say

9 (*locuciones en indicativo*) **digo ...** well, er ...; **como quien dice** so to speak; **lo mismo digo** likewise; **pues si esto te parece mucha gente, no te digo nada en verano** if you think this is a lot of people, you should see it in summer; **no lo digo por ti** I'm not referring to you; **¿qué me dices?** you don't say!, well I never!; **si tú lo dices** if you say so; **eso digo yo** that's (just) what I say; **deberías buscar trabajo, vamos, digo yo** you ought to look for a job, that's what I think anyway; **¡y que lo digas!** you can say that again!; ◆ MODISMOS **no dijo ni pío** she never once opened her mouth; ✧ **no dijo esta boca es mía** she never once opened her mouth; ◆ REFRÁN **dime con quien andas y te diré quien eres** a man is known by the company he keeps

10 (*locuciones en infinitivo*) **es ~** that is (to say); **es mucho ~** that's saying something; **ni que ~ tiene que ...** it goes without saying that ...; **no hay más que ~** there's nothing more to say; **por así ~lo** so to speak; **querer ~** to mean; **¿qué quiere ~ "spatha"?** what does "spatha" mean?; **¿querrás ~ un millón, no un billón?** do you mean a million rather than a billion?; **ya es ~** that's saying something

11 (*locuciones en subjuntivo, imperativo*) **es, digamos, un comerciante** he's a dealer, for want of a better word, he's a sort of dealer; **¡haberlo dicho!** ✧ **¡me lo hubieras dicho!** you could have told me o said!; **y no digamos ...** not to mention ...; **no estuvo muy cortés, que digamos** he wasn't what you'd call polite, he wasn't exactly polite; **¡no me**

digas! you don't say!, well I never!; **¿qué quieres que te diga?** what can I say?
12 (*locuciones en condicional*) **¡quién lo diría!** would you believe it!, who would have thought it!
13
♦ **el qué dirán: se preocupa mucho por el qué dirán** she's always worried about what people will say *o* think
Ⓑ VERBO INTRANSITIVO
1 (*invitando a hablar*) **—¿te puedo pedir algo? —dime** "can I ask you something?" — "go ahead"; **¿diga?** ◇ **¿dígame?** (*al teléfono*) hello?; **usted dirá** (*invitando a hablar*) go ahead; (*sirviendo bebida*) say when; (*en tienda*) can I help you?
2 (= *indicar*) **su nombre no me dice nada** her name doesn't mean anything to me; **su mirada lo dice todo** her expression says it all *o* speaks volumes; **eso dice mucho de su personalidad** that says a lot about her personality
Ⓒ decirse VERBO PRONOMINAL
1 (*uso reflexivo*) **yo sé lo que me digo** I know what I'm talking about *o* saying; **él se lo dice todo** he seems to have all the answers; **al verlo me dije: —han pasado muchos años** when I saw him, I said *o* thought to myself "it's been a long time"
2 (*uso impersonal*) **¿cómo se dice "cursi" en inglés?** what's the English for "cursi"?, how do you say "cursi" in English?; **y no se diga ...** not to mention ...; **se diría que no está** she doesn't seem to be here; **alto, lo que se dice alto, no es** he's not what you'd call tall, he's not exactly tall;
♦ MODISMO **eso se dice muy pronto** that's easier said than done
Ⓓ SUSTANTIVO MASCULINO **es un ~: pongamos, es un ~, que Picasso hubiera nacido en Madrid ...** let's suppose, just for the sake of argument, that Picasso had been born in Madrid ...

decisión SF **1** (= *determinación*) decision; (*Jur*) judgment; **tomar una ~** to make *o* take a decision **2** (= *firmeza*) decisiveness **3** (= *voluntad*) determination

decisivo ADJ [*resultado, factor, papel*] decisive; [*argumento*] winning; [*voto*] deciding; **una etapa decisiva de mi vida** a crucial *o* decisive stage in my life

declamar /1a/ VT **Ⓐ** VT (*gen*) to declaim; [+ *versos, poema*] to recite **Ⓑ** VI to declaim

declaración SF **1** (= *proclamación*) declaration ➤ **declaración de guerra** declaration of war ➤ **declaración de principios** declaration of principles
2 declaraciones (*a la prensa*) statement *sing*; **no quiso hacer declaraciones a los periodistas** he refused to talk to journalists, he refused to make a statement to journalists **3** (*a Hacienda*) tax return; **hacer la ~** to do one's tax return ➤ **declaración conjunta** joint tax return ➤ **declaración de la renta** income tax return
4 (*ante la policía, en juicio*) statement; **las declaraciones de los testigos** the evidence given by the witnesses, the witnesses' statements; **prestar ~** (*ante la policía*) to make a statement; (*en un juicio*) to give evidence, testify; **tomar (la) ~ a algn** to take a statement from sb ➤ **declaración jurada** sworn statement, affidavit

declaradamente ADV openly

declarado ADJ [*actitud, intención*] professed; **un ateo ~** a professed atheist

declarar /1a/ **Ⓐ** VT **1** (= *proclamar*) [+ *guerra, independencia*] to declare; **fue declarado el estado de sitio** a state of siege was declared; **yo os declaro marido y mujer** I pronounce you man and wife; ♦ MODISMOS **tener declarada la guerra a algo** to have declared war on sth; **tener declarada la guerra a algn** to have it in for sb*
2 (= *considerar*) to declare; **el bosque fue declarado zona protegida** the forest was declared a conservation area; **el premio fue declarado desierto** the prize was not awarded; **~ culpable a algn** to find sb guilty; **~ inocente a algn** to find sb innocent
3 (= *manifestar*) (*en público, ante el juez*) to state; (*como anuncio, noticia*) to announce; **el ministro declaró no saber nada del asunto** the minister stated that he knew nothing of the matter; **según declaró un portavoz del gobierno** as a government spokesperson announced
4 (*en la aduana, a Hacienda*) to declare; **¿(tiene) algo que ~?** (do you have) anything to declare?

5 (*Naipes*) to bid
Ⓑ VI **1** (= *testificar*) to give evidence, testify
2 (= *declarar impuestos*) to submit one's tax return **3** (*Naipes*) to bid
Ⓒ declararse VPR **1** (= *reconocerse*) to declare o.s.; **~se a favor de algo** to declare o.s. in favour *o* (*EEUU*) favor of sth; **~se en bancarrota** *o* **quiebra** to declare o.s. bankrupt; **~se culpable** to plead guilty; **~se en huelga** to go on strike; **~se inocente** to plead not guilty
2 **~se a algn** to declare one's love to sb
3 [*epidemia, guerra*] to break out; **se declaró un incendio en el almacén** a fire broke out in the warehouse; **el incendio se declaró en la cocina y se extendió por toda la casa** the fire started in the kitchen and spread throughout the house

declinación SF declension

declinar /1a/ **Ⓐ** VT **1** (= *rechazar*) [+ *honor, invitación*] to decline; **declinamos cualquier responsabilidad** we cannot accept responsibility; **~ hacer algo** to decline to do sth **2** (*Ling*) to decline **Ⓑ** VI **1** (= *decaer*) to decline, decay **2** (*liter*) [*día*] to draw to a close

declive SM **1** [*de terreno, superficie*] incline, gradient; **un terreno en ~** sloping ground **2** (= *decadencia*) decline; **en ~: es una ciudad en ~** it's a city in decline; **el consumo de alcohol está** *o* **va en ~** alcohol consumption is declining *o* is on the decline

decodificar /1g/ VT = **descodificar**

decolaje SM (*SAm*) take-off

decolar /1a/ VI (*And, Chi*) to take off

decolorante SM bleaching agent

decolorar /1a/ **Ⓐ** VT [+ *pelo*] to bleach; [+ *piel, ropa*] to discolour, discolor (*EEUU*) **Ⓑ** decolorarse VPR [*piel, ropa*] to get discoloured, become discolored (*EEUU*), fade; **~se el pelo** to have one's hair bleached

decomisar /1a/ VT to seize, confiscate

decomiso SM seizure, confiscation

decoración SF decoration ➤ **decoración de escaparates** window dressing ➤ **decoración de interiores** interior decorating

decorado SM (*Cine, Teat*) scenery, set

decorador(a) SM/F **1** [*de interiores*] decorator, interior decorator ➤ **decorador(a) de escaparates** window dresser **2** (*Teat*) set designer

decorar /1a/ VT to decorate

decorativo ADJ decorative

decoro SM decorum, decency

decoroso ADJ [*conducta, lenguaje*] decorous; [*empleo, sueldo*] decent

decrecer /2d/ VI **1** (= *disminuir*) [*importancia, interés*] to decrease; [*nivel de agua*] to subside, go down **2** [*días*] to draw in

decreciente ADJ decreasing, diminishing

decrépito ADJ decrepit

decretar /1a/ VT **1** (= *ordenar*) to order; (*por decreto*) to decree **2** [+ *premio*] to award (**a** to)

decreto SM decree, order; (*Parl*) act; **real ~** royal decree

decreto-ley SM (*pl* **decretos-leyes**) government decree, order in council (*Brit*)

decúbito SM (*frm*) ➤ **decúbito supino** supine position

dedal SM thimble

dedicación SF **1** (= *entrega*) dedication (**a** to); **trabajar con ~ plena** to work full-time **2** [*de discurso, libro*] dedication

dedicar /1g/ **Ⓐ** VT **1** [+ *obra, canción*] to dedicate; **me dedicó una copia firmada de su última novela** she presented me with a signed copy of her latest novel; **quisiera ~ unas palabras de agradecimiento a ...** I should like to address a few words of thanks to ...; **el festival dedicó un homenaje al actor** the festival paid tribute to the actor
2 [+ *tiempo, espacio, atención*] to devote, give; [+ *esfuerzo*] to devote; **ha dedicado toda su vida a los derechos humanos** she has dedicated *o* devoted her whole life to human

rights; **un documental dedicado a los deportes de invierno** a documentary about o on winter sports
Ⓑ dedicarse VPR **1** (*como profesión*) **~se a: se dedica a la enseñanza** he is a teacher, he's in teaching; **¿a qué se dedica usted?** what do you do (for a living)?
2 (*como afición*) **~se a: se dedica a ver la tele todo el día** he spends the whole day watching TV
3 (= *entregarse*) **~se a** to devote o.s. to; **se dedicó completamente a cuidar de sus padres** she devoted herself entirely to taking care of her parents
dedicatoria SF dedication, inscription
dedillo SM **saber algo al ~** to know sth like the back of one's hand
dedo SM **1** [*de mano, guante*] finger; [*de pie*] toe; **con la punta** o **la yema de los ~s** with one's fingertips; **apuntar** o **señalar algo/a algn con el ~** to point at sth/sb; **meterse el ~ en la nariz** to pick one's nose; **✦ MODISMOS a ~*: vine a ~** I hitched here*; **he viajado por toda Alemania a ~** I hitched all round Germany*; **ha entrado a ~** he got the job because he knew somebody, he got the job through contacts; **han adjudicado a ~ todas las obras** they handed out all the building contracts to people they knew; **contarse con los ~s: mis amigos se pueden contar con los ~s de una mano** I can count my friends on the fingers of one hand; **escaparse de entre los ~s** to slip through one's fingers; **hacer ~** (*Esp**) to hitch*; **hacer ~s** (*Mús*) to practise one's scales; **no levantar** o **mover un ~** not to lift a finger; **pillarse los ~s** (*Esp*) to get one's fingers burned; **poner el ~ en la llaga** (*de error*) to put one's finger on it; (*de tema delicado*) to touch a raw nerve; **poner el ~ en el renglón** (*Méx*) to put one's finger on it **➤ dedo anular** ring finger **➤ dedo (del) corazón** middle finger **➤ dedo gordo** [*de la mano*] thumb; [*del pie*] big toe **➤ dedo índice** index finger, forefinger **➤ dedo meñique** [*de la mano*] little finger, pinkie (*EEUU, Escocia**); [*del pie*] little toe **➤ dedo pulgar** thumb
2 (= *medida*) [*de altura, grosor*] about an inch; [*de cantidad*] drop; **unos dos ~s** a couple of inches; **ponme un ~ de coñac** give me a drop of brandy; **✦ MODISMO no tener dos ~s de frente*** to be as thick as two short planks (*Brit**), be three bricks shy of a load (*EEUU**); **si tuvieras dos ~s de frente** if you had any sense at all
deducción SF **1** (= *método*) deduction; (= *razonamiento*) inference **2** (*Com*) deduction
deducir /3n/ VT **1** (= *inferir*) [+ *razonamiento, conclusión*] to deduce, infer (**de** from); [+ *fórmula*] to derive (**de** from)
2 (= *descontar*) to deduct; **deducidos los gastos** less charges
deductivo ADJ deductive
defecar /1g/ VI to defecate
defección SF defection
defectivo ADJ (*Ling*) defective
defecto SM **1** [*de persona*] (*físico*) defect; (*moral*) fault, shortcoming **➤ defecto de fonación, defecto del habla, defecto de pronunciación** speech defect, speech impediment **➤ defecto de visión: tiene un ~ de visión** he has defective eyesight
2 [*de máquina, sistema*] fault; [*de tela, objeto*] flaw, defect; **tiene un ~ de fábrica** it has a manufacturing defect o fault, it's faulty o defective
3 (*Jur*) **➤ defecto de forma** technicality
4 en su ~: el director, o en su ~, su delegado the director, or failing that, his delegate; **por ~** (*Inform*) by default
defectuoso ADJ defective, faulty
defender /2g/ **Ⓐ** VT [+ *país, territorio, intereses*] to defend; [+ *causa, ideas*] to defend, champion; **defienden el título de campeón** they are defending the championship title, they are the defending champions; **nos defendió de los atracadores** he defended us against the muggers
Ⓑ defenderse VPR **1** (= *protegerse*) **~se de** o **contra** [+ *calor, lluvia, sol*] to protect o.s. from; [+ *agresor, ataque*] to defend o.s. from o against
2 (= *desenvolverse*) to get by; **me defiendo en inglés** I can get by o along in English; **ya eres mayor, ya puedes ~te solo** you're old enough, you can get by o manage on your own now; **se defendió muy bien en la entrevista** she performed very well in the interview; **✦ MODISMO ~se como un gato panza arriba** to fight tooth and nail (to

defend o.s.)
defendido/a SM/F (*Jur*) **mi ~** my client
defensa **Ⓐ** SF

En inglés americano se usa **defense** en lugar de **defence**.

1 (= *protección*) defence; **salió en ~ de su hermano** he came to his brother's defence; **en ~ propia** in self-defence o (*EEUU*) self-defense; **Ministerio de Defensa** Ministry of Defence, Defense Department (*EEUU*) **➤ defensa personal** self-defence **2** (*Jur*) (= *abogado, argumentación*) defence **3** (*Dep*) **la ~** (= *jugadores*) the defence **4 defensas** (*Med*) defences **Ⓑ** SMF (*Dep*) defender
defensiva SF defensive; **estar a la ~** to be on the defensive
defensivo ADJ defensive
defensor(a) **Ⓐ** SM/F **1** (= *protector*) [*de territorio, intereses*] defender; [*de causa, idea, derechos*] defender, champion **➤ defensor(a) del pueblo** ombudsman **2** (*Jur*) defence lawyer, defense attorney o lawyer (*EEUU*) **Ⓑ** ADJ **1** (= *protector*) **una asociación ~a de los animales** an animal welfare organization **2** (*Jur*) **abogado ~** defence lawyer, defense attorney o lawyer (*EEUU*)
defeño ADJ of/from Mexico City
deferencia SF deference; **nos trató con ~** she treated us with deference o respect; **no tuvo la ~ de informarnos** he didn't have the courtesy to let us know; **en** o **por ~ a** o **hacia algn** out of o in deference to sb
deficiencia SF **1** (= *defecto*) defect (**de** in, of) **2** (= *falta*) deficiency **➤ deficiencia auditiva** hearing impairment **➤ deficiencia mental, deficiencia psíquica** mental deficiency, mental handicap **➤ deficiencia visual** visual impairment
deficiente **Ⓐ** ADJ **1** (= *imperfecto*) [*mercancía, motor*] defective; [*sistema, estructura*] inadequate **2** (= *falto*) deficient (**en** in) **Ⓑ** SMF **➤ deficiente mental, deficiente psíquico** mentally handicapped person **➤ deficiente visual** visually handicapped person
déficit SM (*pl ~s*) **1** (*Com, Fin*) deficit **➤ déficit comercial, déficit exterior** trade deficit **➤ déficit presupuestario** budget deficit **2** (= *falta*) lack, shortage
deficitario ADJ **1** [*empresa, operación*] loss-making **2 ser ~ en algo** to be short of sth, be lacking in sth
definible ADJ definable
definición SF definition
definido ADJ **1** [*línea*] clearly defined; [*preferencia*] definite, clear **2** (*Ling*) definite
definir /3a/ **Ⓐ** VT **1** [+ *concepto, palabra*] to define
2 (= *calificar*) to describe; **definió el partido como aburrido** she described the match as boring
3 (= *aclarar*) [+ *actitud, posición*] to define; [+ *contorno, silueta*] to define, make sharp
4 (= *establecer*) [+ *poder, jurisdicción*] to define, establish **Ⓑ definirse** VPR **1** (= *calificarse*) to define o.s.; **se definió como liberal** he defined himself as a liberal
2 (= *decidirse*) **no se ha definido con respecto al tema** he has not yet defined his position on the subject, he has not yet said where he stands on the subject
definitivamente ADV **1** (= *con seguridad*) definitely
2 (= *para siempre*) permanently; **se ha instalado ~ en la capital** he has settled permanently in the capital, he has settled in the capital for good **3** (= *claramente*) definitely; **~, es la peor película del año** it's definitely the worst movie of the year
definitivo ADJ **1** (= *final*) definitive, final; **la clausura definitiva de la línea ferroviaria** the permanent closure of the railway line **2** (= *inamovible*) [*proyecto, fecha, respuesta*] definite; **ya es ~ que las elecciones son en mayo** the election will now definitely be in May **3** [*prueba*] definitive, conclusive **4 en definitiva: es, en definitiva, una pésima película** in short, it's a terrible movie
deflación SF deflation
deflacionario ADJ, **deflacionista** ADJ deflationary

defoliar /1b/ VT to defoliate

deforestación = **desforestación**

deformación SF (= *alteración*) [*de manos, superficie*] deformation; [*de madera*] warping ➤ **deformación profesional: es ~ profesional** it's a habit you pick up in this job

deformante ADJ **espejo ~** distorting mirror

deformar /1a/ **Ⓐ** VT **1** [+ *cuerpo*] to deform
2 [+ *objeto*] to distort, deform; **no te pongas mis zapatos que me los deformas** don't wear my shoes, you'll put them out of shape; **el calor deformó la madera** the heat warped the wood **3** [+ *imagen, realidad*] to distort
Ⓑ deformarse VPR **1** [*cuerpo, miembro*] to become deformed **2** [*madera, puerta*] to become warped, become twisted; **se le deformó el sombrero con la lluvia** her hat lost its shape in the rain, the rain made her hat lose its shape
3 [*imagen*] to distort, become distorted

deforme ADJ **1** (= *de forma anormal*) [*espécimen, cuerpo*] deformed; [*cabeza, sombra*] misshapen **2** (= *feo*) ugly

deformidad SF deformity, malformation

defraudación SF defrauding ➤ **defraudación de impuestos, defraudación fiscal** tax evasion

defraudar /1a/ VT **1** (= *decepcionar*) [+ *persona*] to disappoint; [+ *esperanzas*] to dash, disappoint; [+ *amigos*] to let down **2** [+ *acreedores*] to cheat, defraud; **~ impuestos** to evade one's taxes

defunción SF death, decease (*frm*)

degeneración SF degeneration

degenerado/a **Ⓐ** ADJ degenerate **Ⓑ** SM/F (*moralmente*) degenerate; (*sexualmente*) pervert

degenerar /1a/ VI **1** (= *empeorar*) [*enfermedad*] to get worse; [*discusión, situación*] to degenerate (**en** into) **2** (= *decaer*) to decline

degenerativo ADJ degenerative

degollar /1m/ VT [+ *persona*] to cut the throat of, slit the throat of; [+ *animal*] to slaughter

degradación SF **1** (= *deterioro*) deterioration **2** (= *bajeza*) degradation

degradante ADJ degrading

degradar /1a/ **Ⓐ** VT **1** (= *deteriorar*) to cause to deteriorate **2** (*Mil*) to demote, downgrade **Ⓑ degradarse** VPR to demean o.s., degrade o.s.

degüello SM shaft; **entrar a ~ en una ciudad** to put the people of a city to the sword

degustación SF tasting, sampling

degustar /1a/ VT to taste, sample

dehesa SF estate

deidad SF deity

deificar /1g/ VT to deify

dejadez SF **1** (*en el trabajo*) (= *falta de esfuerzo*) laziness; (= *falta de cuidado, atención*) carelessness **2** (= *falta de aseo*) slovenliness

dejado ADJ **1** (= *desaliñado*) (*en las costumbres*) slovenly; (*en la apariencia*) scruffy **2** (= *negligente*) careless, sloppy; **no te escribe porque es una dejada** she doesn't write to you because she couldn't care less

---

dejar /1a/

Ⓐ VERBO TRANSITIVO   **Ⓒ** VERBO PRONOMINAL
Ⓑ VERBO INTRANSITIVO

Para las expresiones **dejar caer, dejarse caer, dejar que desear, dejar dicho, dejarse llevar, dejar paso** *etc, ver la entrada correspondiente a la otra palabra.*

---

dejar **Ⓐ** VERBO TRANSITIVO

1 (= *poner, soltar*) to leave; **he dejado las llaves en la mesa** I've left the keys on the table; **se lo dejo en la oficina** I'll leave it for you at the office; **~ atrás** [+ *corredor, vehículo adelantado, competidor*] to leave

behind; **~ algo a un lado** to set sth aside
2 (*al desaparecer, morir*) to leave; **el agua ha dejado una mancha en la pared** the water has left a stain on the wall; **dejó todo su dinero a sus hijos** he left all his money to his children
3 (= *guardar*) **¿me habéis dejado algo de tarta?** have you left any cake for me?
4 (= *abandonar*)
4.1 [+ *actividad, empleo*] to give up; **ha dejado los estudios por el tenis** he has given up his studies to pursue a career in tennis; **lo dejamos porque era muy difícil** we gave up because it was too hard; **~ la bebida** to give up drink *o* alcohol, give up drinking
4.2 [+ *persona, lugar*] to leave; **su novio la ha dejado** her boyfriend has left her
4.3 (*en coche*) to drop off; **¿te dejo en tu casa?** shall I drop you off at your place?
5 (= *no molestar*) **déjame, quiero estar solo** leave me be, I want to be alone; **¡déjalo!** (= *¡no hagas eso!*) stop it!; (= *no te preocupes*) forget it!, don't worry about it!; **dejémoslo así** let's leave it at that; **¡déjame en paz!** ✧ **déjame tranquilo** leave me alone!
6 (= *posponer*) **~ algo para** to leave sth till; **~ algo para mañana** to leave sth till tomorrow; **he dejado el italiano para cuando tenga más tiempo** I've put off learning Italian till I have more time
7 (*Esp*) (= *prestar*) **le dejé mi libro de física** I lent him my physics book; **¿me dejas el coche?** can I borrow the car?, will you lend me the car?
8 (= *permitir*) (+ INFIN) to let; **mis padres no me dejan salir de noche** my parents won't let me go out at night; **~ entrar a algn** to let sb in; **~ pasar a algn** to let sb by *o* through *o* past; **~ salir a algn** to let sb out
✦ **dejar que** (+ SUBJUN) **~ que las cosas vayan de mal en peor** to let things go *o* allow things to go from bad to worse
9 (*indicando resultado*) (+ ADJ) **dejó la ventana abierta** she left the window open; **nos dejó a todos asombrados** he stunned us all; **hay algo que quiero ~ bien claro** there is one thing I want to make perfectly clear; **esa ducha me ha dejado como nueva** I feel like a different person after that shower
10 (= *producir*) [+ *dinero*] **el negocio le deja lo justo para vivir** the business brings in just enough for him to live on
11
✦ **dejar que** (= *esperar*): **deja que acabe de llover** wait for it to stop raining
Ⓑ VERBO INTRANSITIVO (*con una actividad*) **deja, ya lo hago yo** leave it, I'll do it
✦ **dejar de hacer algo** (*por un momento*) to stop doing sth

---

Recuérdese que **stop** *en este sentido rige que el verbo que le siga inmediatamente aparezca en gerundio y no en infinitivo.*

(*por una temporada*) to give up doing sth, stop doing sth

Recuérdese que **stop** *en este sentido y* **give up** *rigen que el verbo que les siga inmediatamente aparezca en gerundio y no en infinitivo.*

---

cuando deje de llover when it stops raining, when the rain stops; **~ de fumar** to give up smoking, stop smoking
✦ **no dejar de** (+ INFIN) **no deja de preguntarme por ti** he's always asking me about you; **eso no deja de tener gracia** it has its funny side; **no dejes de visitarlos** make sure you visit them
Ⓒ dejarse VERBO PRONOMINAL
1 (= *abandonarse*) to let o.s. go; **empezó a ~se después de tener su primer hijo** she started to let herself go after she had her first child
2 (= *olvidar*) to leave; **se dejó el paraguas en un taxi** she left her umbrella in a taxi
3 (= *dejar crecer*) to grow; **~se las uñas largas/el pelo largo** to grow long nails/hair; **~se barba** to grow a beard
4 (= *permitir*) (+ INFIN) **~se convencer** to allow o.s. to be persuaded; **el gato no se dejaba acariciar** the cat wouldn't

let anyone stroke it; —¿**está bien el vídeo? —se deja ver**
"is the video any good?" — "it's watchable"
5 (= *poderse*) (+ INFIN) **ya se deja sentir el frío** it's starting to
get colder
6
◆ **dejarse de** (= *terminar de*): **déjate de bromas** stop
kidding around; **déjate de tanto hablar y estudia** stop
talking all the time and do some studying
deje SM accent
dejo SM **1** (= *sabor*) aftertaste **2** [*toque*] touch **3** (*Ling*)
accent, trace of accent
del = **de + el**; *ver* **de**
delación SF denunciation
delantal SM **1** (*de cocina*) apron **2** (*RPl*) [*de colegial*] overall,
smock
delante ADV **1** (*gen*) in front; **en el coche me gusta
sentarme ~** I like to sit in the front of the car; **no hables de
Antonio ~ de mis amigos** don't talk about Antonio in front
of my friends; **no tengo el documento ~** I don't have the
document in front of me; **de ~: la parte de ~** the front
part; **siempre se sentaba en el banco de ~** she always sat
on the front bench; **el coche de ~** the car in front; **hacia ~:
hizo un movimiento hacia ~** he moved forward(s); **por ~: un
vestido que se abre por ~** a dress that opens at the front;
tenemos todavía cuatro horas por ~ we still have four
hours in front of us; **todavía tiene mucha vida por ~** she
still has her whole life ahead of her; **destruye al que se le
pone por ~** he destroys anyone who gets in his way;
llevarse a algn por ~ (= *atropellar*) to run sb over;
(= *maltratar*) to ride roughshod over sb; **el camión se llevó
una farola por ~** the truck went off the road and took a
lamppost with it
2 ~ **de** in front of; **había un autobús ~ del banco** there was
a bus in front of the bank; **te espero ~ de la bolera** I'll
meet you outside the bowling alley
3 (*esp CS*) ~ **mío/tuyo** in front of me/you
delantera SF **1** [*de casa, vestido*] front **2** (*Dep*) (= *línea de
ataque*) forward line; **llevar la ~** to be in the lead; **llevar la ~
a algn** to be ahead of sb
delantero/a ⓐ ADJ **1** (= *de delante*) [*parte, fila, rueda*]
front *antes de s*; [*patas de animal*] fore *antes de s*, front
2 (*Dep*) [*línea, posición*] forward ⓑ SM/F (*Dep*) forward
➤ **delantero centro** centre-forward, center-forward
(*EEUU*)
delatar /1a/ VT **1** [*persona*] to denounce, inform against
2 [*actitud, mirada*] to betray, give away
delator(a) ⓐ ADJ [*sonrisa, comentario*] revealing;
[*mancha*] incriminating ⓑ SM/F informer; **sabía quienes
habían sido sus ~es** he knew who had informed on *o*
against him
delectación SF delectation
delegación SF **1** (= *acto*) delegation **2** (= *sucursal*) (*Com*)
local office; [*del Estado*] *local office of a government
department* ➤ **delegación del gobierno** *office of the
government delegate to an autonomous community*
3 (= *representantes*) delegation ➤ **delegación comercial**
trade mission **4** (*Méx*) (= *comisaría*) main police station
delegado/a SM/F (= *representante*) delegate; (*Educ*)
representative ➤ **delegado/a del Gobierno** *government
delegate to an autonomous community* ➤ **delegado/a
sindical** shop steward
delegar /1h/ ⓐ VT to delegate; ~ **algo en algn** to delegate
sth to sb ⓑ VI to delegate
deleitar /1a/ ⓐ VT to delight, charm ⓑ **deleitarse** VPR to
delight (**con, en** in)
deleite SM delight, pleasure
deletrear /1a/ VT to spell
deleznable ADJ **1** (= *despreciable*) atrocious **2** [*argumento,
construcción*] weak
delfín SM **1** (*Zool*) dolphin **2** (*Hist*) dauphin
delgadez SF **1** [*de persona*] (= *flaqueza*) thinness;
(= *esbeltez*) slimness **2** [*de tabla, muro*] thinness
delgado ADJ **1** [*persona*] (= *esbelto*) slim; (= *flaco*) thin

2 [*tabla, muro, hebra*] thin
deliberación SF deliberation
deliberado ADJ deliberate
deliberar /1a/ ⓐ VT to debate ⓑ VI to deliberate (**sobre**
on), discuss (**si** whether)
delicadeza SF **1** (= *suavidad*) [*de tejido, piel*] softness; [*de
tela*] fineness; [*de color*] softness
2 (= *cuidado*) gentleness; **con mucha ~** very gently
3 (= *amabilidad*) **no tuvo la ~ de comunicárnoslo** he didn't
have the decency to let us know
4 (= *tacto*) tact, delicacy; **tendrás que presentar la queja
con mucha ~** you will have to make the complaint very
tactfully *o* delicately; **falta de ~** tactlessness, indelicacy
5 (= *dificultad*) delicacy, delicate nature
6 (= *finura*) [*de rasgos*] delicacy; **la ~ con que ejecutó la
pieza** the delicacy with which she performed the piece
7 (= *sensibilidad excesiva*) hypersensitiveness
delicado ADJ **1** (= *suave*) [*tejido, piel*] delicate; [*tela*] fine;
[*color*] soft **2** (= *frágil*) [*máquina*] sensitive; [*salud*]
delicate; **está ~ del estómago** he has a delicate stomach
3 (= *fino*) [*rasgos*] delicate, fine; [*gusto*] delicate, subtle
4 (= *difícil*) [*situación*] delicate, tricky **5** (= *difícil de
contentar*) hard to please, fussy; **es muy ~ con la comida**
he's very choosy about his food* **6** (= *sensible*)
hypersensitive **7** (= *discreto*) tactful **8** (= *atento*)
considerate
delicia SF delight; **un libro que ha hecho las ~s de muchos
niños** a book which has delighted many children
delicioso ADJ **1** [*comida, bebida*] delicious **2** [*momento,
sonido*] delightful
delictivo ADJ criminal *antes de s*
delimitar /1a/ VT to delimit
delincuencia SF crime; **las cifras de la ~** the crime figures
➤ **delincuencia informática** computer crime
➤ **delincuencia juvenil** juvenile delinquency
delincuente SMF criminal ➤ **delincuente común**
common criminal ➤ **delincuente habitual** habitual
offender ➤ **delincuente juvenil** juvenile delinquent
delineación SF delineation ➤ **delineación industrial**
technical drawing
delineador SM eyeliner
delineante SMF draughtsman/draughtswoman,
draftsman/draftswoman (*EEUU*)
delinear /1a/ VT **1** [+ *contornos*] to outline **2** [+ *plan,
propuesta*] to delineate
delinquir /3e/ VI (*frm*) to commit an offence *o* (*EEUU*)
offense
delirante ADJ **1** (*Med*) delirious, raving **2** (= *disparatado*)
[*idea*] crazy; [*chiste*] hilarious
delirar /1a/ VI **1** (*Med*) to be delirious **2** (= *desatinar*) to
rave, talk nonsense; **¡tú deliras!*** you must be crazy!
delirio SM **1** (*Med*) delirium **2** (= *frenesí*) **cuando acabó de
hablar fue el ~** when he finished speaking the place went
wild; **el chocolate me gusta con ~** I absolutely adore
chocolate **3** (= *manía*) ➤ **delirios de grandeza** delusions of
grandeur
delito SM (= *acción criminal*) crime; (= *infracción*) offence,
offense (*EEUU*) ➤ **delito de sangre** violent crime ➤ **delito
fiscal** tax offence *o* (*EEUU*) offense
delta ⓐ SM (*Geog*) delta ⓑ SF (= *letra*) delta
demacrado ADJ drawn
demagogia SF demagogy, demagoguery
demagógico ADJ demagogic
demagogo SM demagogue, demagog (*EEUU*)
demanda SF **1** (= *solicitud*) request (**de** for); (*exigiendo*)
demand (**de** for); **escribir en ~ de ayuda** to write asking for
help ➤ **demanda de extradición** extradition request
2 (*Com*) demand; **hay una gran ~ de profesores** teachers are
in great demand **3** (*Jur*) action, lawsuit; **presentar ~ de
divorcio a algn** to sue sb for divorce
demandado/a SM/F defendant; (*en divorcio*) respondent
demandante SMF **1** (*Jur*) plaintiff **2** ➤ **demandante de**

empleo job seeker

demandar /1a/ VT **1** (= *exigir*) to demand **2** (*Jur*) to sue, file a lawsuit against; **~ a algn por daños y perjuicios** to sue sb for damages

demarcación SF demarcation

demás Ⓐ ADJ **los ~ libros** the other books, the rest of the books
Ⓑ PRON **1 lo ~** the rest (of it); **los ~** the others, the rest (of them); **todo lo ~** all the rest, everything else; **las ~ no tenían dinero** the others didn't have any money, the rest (of them) didn't have any money
2 por lo ~ otherwise, apart from that
3 y ~ and so on, and so forth
4 por ~ (*frm*) **4.1** (= *en vano*) **está por ~ presentar una queja** it is pointless to make a complaint **4.2** (= *demasiado*) excessively; **un informe extenso por ~** an excessively long report

demasía SF excess; **con** o **en ~** too much, excessively

demasiado Ⓐ ADJ **1** (= *excesivo*) too much; **hace ~ calor** it's too hot; **¡esto es ~!** that's the limit!; **no tengo ~ tiempo** I don't have much time; **¡qué ~!*** wow!* **2 demasiados** too many Ⓑ ADV (= *en exceso*) (*con adjetivos, adverbios*) too; (*con verbos*) too much; **es ~ pesado** it is too heavy; **comer ~** to eat too much

> **Demasiado** se traduce por **too** delante de adjetivos y adverbios: "Hace demasiado calor", *It's too hot*; "Hablas demasiado deprisa", *You talk too quickly*. Se traduce por **too much** delante de sustantivos incontables o cuando modifica al verbo: "demasiada sal", *too much salt*; "Habla demasiado", *He talks too much*. En plural la traducción es **too many**: "Tiene demasiadas preocupaciones", *He has too many worries*.

demencia SF madness, insanity ➤ **demencia senil** senile dementia

demencial ADJ mad, demented

demente Ⓐ ADJ mad, demented Ⓑ SMF lunatic; (*Med*) mental patient

demo SF demo

democracia SF democracy

demócrata Ⓐ ADJ **1** [*valores, país*] democratic **2** (*en EEUU*) Democrat Ⓑ SMF **1** (*gen*) democrat **2** (*en EEUU*) Democrat

democratacristiano/a ADJ, SM/F Christian Democrat

democráticamente ADV democratically

democrático ADJ democratic

democratizar /1f/ VT to democratize

democristiano/a ADJ, SM/F Christian Democrat

demografía SF demography

demográfico ADJ demographic; **la explosión demográfica** the population explosion

demoledor ADJ **1** [*ataque, efecto*] shattering **2** [*argumento*] overwhelming; [*crítica*] devastating

demoler /2h/ VT to demolish

demolición SF demolition

demoniaco ADJ, **demoníaco** ADJ demoniacal, demonic

demonio SM **1** (= *diablo*) devil; **ese ~ de niño** that demon o little devil of a child
2 (*) ✦ MODISMOS **esto pesa como un ~** this is hellishly heavy; **¡que se lo lleve el ~!** to hell with it!; **un ruido de todos los** o **de mil ~s** a hell of a noise*; **esto sabe a ~s** this tastes awful; **tiene el ~ en el cuerpo** he can't sit still for five minutes
3 (*) (*frases de sentido exclamativo*) **¡qué ~s!** (*con ira*) hell!, damn it!; (*con sorpresa*) well, I'll be damned!, what the devil?; **¿quién ~s será?** who the devil can that be?

demora SF delay; **sin ~** without delay

demorar /1a/ Ⓐ VT [+ *viaje*] to delay; [+ *llegada, terminación*] to hold up Ⓑ VI (*LAm*) **~ en hacer algo** to take a long time to do sth; **¡no demores!** don't be long!; **¿cuántos días se demora para ir allá?** how many days does it take to get there? Ⓒ **demorarse** VPR to take a long time; **~se en**

hacer algo to take a long time to do sth

demorón ADJ (*LAm*), **demoroso** ADJ (*LAm*) slow; **ser ~ en hacer algo** to take a long time to do sth, be slow in doing sth

demos *ver* **dar**

demoscopia SF public opinion research

demoscópico ADJ **sondeo ~** public opinion poll

demostración SF **1** (= *comprobación*) [*de ejemplo, producto*] demonstration; [*de teorema, teoría*] proof; **hicieron una ~ del funcionamiento** they gave a demonstration of how it worked **2** (= *manifestación externa*) [*de cariño, fuerza*] show; [*de amistad*] gesture; [*de cólera*] display

demostrar /1l/ VT **1** (= *probar*) to prove; **usted no puede ~ nada** you can't prove anything; **ha demostrado ser muy buena amiga** she has shown herself to be a very good friend **2** (= *enseñar*) to show, demonstrate; **nos ~on cómo funcionaba** they showed us o demonstrated to us how it worked **3** (= *mostrar*) [+ *emoción, sentimiento*] to show, display; **no demostró ningún interés** he showed no interest

demostrativo ADJ, SM demonstrative

demudado ADJ [*rostro*] upset, distraught

demudar /1a/ VT [+ *rostro*] to change, alter

denegación SF [*de permiso, petición*] refusal; [*de derechos*] denial

denegar /1h, 1j/ VT **1** (= *rechazar*) [+ *permiso, petición*] to refuse; [+ *derechos*] to deny **2** (*Jur*) [+ *cargo*] to deny

denier SM denier

denigrante ADJ **1** (= *difamante*) degrading **2** (= *injurioso*) insulting

denigrar /1a/ VT (= *difamar*) to denigrate, run down; (= *injuriar*) to insult

denigratorio ADJ denigratory; **campaña denigratoria** campaign of denigration, smear campaign

denodadamente ADV boldly, dauntlessly, intrepidly; **luchar ~** to fight bravely

denodado ADJ bold, brave

denominación SF **1** (= *acto*) naming **2** (= *nombre*) name

DENOMINACIÓN DE ORIGEN

The **Denominación de Origen**, abbreviated to **D.O.**, is a prestigious product classification which is awarded to food products such as wines, cheeses, sausages and hams that are produced in designated Spanish regions according to stringent production criteria. **D.O.** labels serve as a guarantee of quality.

denominado ADJ named, called; **el ~ jet lag** so-called jet lag

denominador SM denominator ➤ **denominador común** (*Mat*) (*fig*) common denominator

denominar /1a/ VT to name, designate

denostar /1l/ VT (*frm*) to insult

denotar /1a/ VT **1** (= *significar*) (*tb Ling*) to denote **2** (= *indicar*) to indicate, show; **eso denota un cambio en su política** that indicates a change in policy

densidad SF **1** (= *concentración*) [*de sustancia, tráfico*] density; [*de humo, vegetación*] thickness, denseness; [*de caracteres*] (*Inform*) pitch ➤ **densidad de población** population density **2** [*de discurso, relato*] denseness **3** (*Fís*) density

denso ADJ **1** (= *concentrado*) [*sustancia*] dense; [*tráfico*] heavy; [*humo, vegetación*] thick, dense **2** [*discurso, relato*] dense **3** (*Fís*) dense

dentado ADJ [*borde*] serrated; (*Bot*) dentate; **rueda dentada** cog

dentadura SF teeth *pl*; **tener mala ~** to have bad teeth ➤ **dentadura postiza** false teeth *pl*, dentures *pl*

dental ADJ dental

dentellada SF bite, nip; **partir algo a ~s** to sever sth with one's teeth

dentera SF **dar ~ a algn** to set sb's teeth on edge

dentición SF teething; **estar con la ~** to be teething

dentífrico Ⓐ ADJ tooth *antes de s*; **pasta dentífrica** toothpaste Ⓑ SM toothpaste

dentina SF dentine, dentin (*EEUU*)

dentista SMF dentist

dentro ADV 1 (*en la parte interior*) inside; **María está ~** María is inside; **allí ~** in there; **de** o **desde ~** from inside, from within (*frm*); **por ~** inside; **el edificio es precioso por ~** the building is beautiful inside; **la sandía es roja por ~** a watermelon is red on the inside 2 **~ de** 2.1 (= *en el interior de*) in, inside; **~ de la casa** in(side) the house; **tenía un pañuelo ~ del bolsillo** she had a handkerchief in *o* inside her pocket 2.2 (= *después de*) in; **~ de tres meses** in three months, in three months' time; **llegará ~ de poco** he'll be here shortly 2.3 (= *en los límites de*) within; **esto no está ~ de mi competencia** this is not within my area of responsibility; **~ de lo posible** as far as possible; **su reacción estaba ~ de lo previsto** her reaction was what one might have expected

denuedo SM (*liter*) valour, valor (*EEUU*)

denuncia SF 1 [*de delito, infracción, accidente*] **hice** o **presenté** o **puse una ~ por el** o **del robo de la cartera** I reported the theft of the wallet 2 (= *crítica*) condemnation, denunciation

denunciar /1b/ VT 1 [+ *delito, accidente, persona*] to report; **denuncié en comisaría el robo de mi bolso** I reported the theft of my handbag to the police 2 (= *criticar*) to condemn, denounce; **denunció la política derechista del gobierno** he condemned *o* denounced the government's right-wing policies

deontología SF (= *ciencia*) deontology; (*profesional*) professional ethics *pl*

D.E.P. ABR (= **descanse en paz**) RIP

deparar /1a/ VT (*frm*) to provide with, afford (*frm*); **nos deparó la ocasión de conocer a su familia** it provided us with *o* (*frm*) afforded us the opportunity to meet his family

departamental ADJ departmental

departamento SM 1 [*de empresa, universidad*] department 2 [*de caja, tren*] compartment 3 (*LAm*) (= *piso*) flat (*Brit*), apartment (*EEUU*) 4 (*LAm*) (= *división administrativa*) *term covering various different sorts of administrative region*

departir /3a/ VI (*frm*) converse (**con** with; **de** about)

depauperar /1a/ Ⓐ VT to impoverish Ⓑ **depauperarse** VPR 1 (= *empobrecerse*) to become impoverished 2 (= *debilitarse*) to become weak

dependencia SF 1 (= *estado*) dependence (**de** on); ➤ **dependencia psicológica** psychological dependence, psychological dependency 2 (= *habitación*) room; **permanecer en ~s policiales** to remain in police custody 3 **dependencias** [*de edificio, castillo*] outbuildings

depender /2a/ VI 1 —**¿vas a ir?** —**depende** "are you going?" — "it depends" 2 **~ de algn/algo** to depend on sb/sth

> Recuérdese que **depend** rige la preposición **on** y nunca **of**:

mi futuro depende de este examen my future depends on this exam; **depende de lo que diga mi madre** it depends (on) what my mother says; **no te eches atrás ahora, que dependo de ti** don't back out now, I'm relying *o* depending on you; **sin coche, dependes de los demás** without a car you depend on *o* you're dependent on other people, without a car you have to rely on other people 3 **~ de** [*empleado, institución*] to be accountable to, be answerable to; **esta oficina depende de la Generalitat** this office is accountable *o* answerable to the Generalitat 4 **~ de algn** (= *corresponder a*): **lo siento, su aceptación no depende de mí** I'm sorry, it's not up to me whether you are accepted or not

5 (*Pol*) **un territorio que depende de Gran Bretaña** a British dependency

dependiente¹ ADJ dependent (**de** on)

dependiente²/a SM/F (*en tienda*) shop assistant (*Brit*), sales assistant (*Brit*), salesclerk (*EEUU*)

depilación SF, **depilado** SM (*con crema, con depiladora*) hair removal, depilation; (*con cera*) waxing; (*con pinzas*) plucking

depilar /1a/ Ⓐ VT (*con crema, con depiladora*) to remove (unwanted) hair from; (*con cera*) to wax; (*con pinzas*) to pluck Ⓑ **depilarse** VPR **~se las piernas** to wax one's legs; **~se las cejas** to pluck one's eyebrows

depilatorio Ⓐ ADJ depilatory Ⓑ SM hair remover, depilatory

deplorable ADJ [*conducta*] deplorable; [*estado*] appalling

deplorar /1a/ VT to deplore

deponer /2q/ Ⓐ VT 1 (= *dejar*) [+ *armas*] to lay down; [+ *actitud*] to change 2 (= *quitar*) [+ *rey*] to depose; [+ *gobernante*] to oust, overthrow; [+ *ministro*] to remove from office Ⓑ VI (*CAm, Méx*) (= *vomitar*) to vomit

deportación SF deportation

deportar /1a/ VT to deport

deporte SM sport; **es muy aficionada al ~** she is really into sports ➤ **deportes de invierno** winter sports

deportista Ⓐ ADJ **es muy ~** she is really into sports Ⓑ SMF sportsman/sportswoman

deportivamente ADV 1 (= *sin agresividad*) sportingly 2 (= *relacionado con el deporte*) **viste ~** she wears sports clothes

deportividad SF sportsmanship

deportivo Ⓐ ADJ 1 [*club, periódico, zapatillas*] sports *antes de s* 2 [*actitud*] sporting, sportsmanlike 3 [*ropa*] casual Ⓑ SM (*Aut*) sports car

deposición SF 1 (= *derrocamiento*) [*de rey*] deposition; [*de gobernante*] overthrow, ousting; [*de ministro*] removal from office, sacking 2 (*Jur*) (= *testimonio*) deposition, evidence 3 (*euf*) (= *acto*) bowel movement; (= *excremento*) stool; **hacer una ~** to have a bowel movement

depositar /1a/ Ⓐ VT 1 (*frm*) (= *colocar*) [+ *flor, ofrenda*] to place; **"depositen las bolsas en información"** "please leave your bags at the information desk"; **~ la confianza en algn** to place one's trust in sb 2 (*Fin*) [+ *dinero, joyas*] to deposit Ⓑ **depositarse** VPR [*líquido, polvo*] to settle

depositario/a SM/F [*de dinero*] depository, trustee; [*de secreto*] repository ➤ **depositario/a judicial** official receiver

depósito SM 1 (= *contenedor*) tank ➤ **depósito de agua** water tank, cistern ➤ **depósito de gasolina** petrol tank (*Brit*), gas tank (*EEUU*) 2 (= *almacén*) [*de mercancías*] warehouse, depot; [*de animales, coches*] pound ➤ **depósito de cadáveres** mortuary, morgue 3 (*Com, Fin*) deposit; **dejar una cantidad en ~** to leave a sum as a deposit 4 (*Quím*) sediment, deposit

depravación SF depravity

depravado/a Ⓐ ADJ depraved, corrupt Ⓑ SM/F degenerate

depre* Ⓐ SF (= *depresión*) **tiene la ~** she's feeling a little low Ⓑ ADJ **estar ~** to be feeling down

depreciación SF depreciation

depreciar /1b/ Ⓐ VT to depreciate, reduce the value of Ⓑ **depreciarse** VPR to depreciate

depredador Ⓐ ADJ [*animal, instinto*] predatory Ⓑ SM (*Zool*) predator

depredar /1a/ VT 1 (= *saquear*) to pillage 2 (*Zool*) to prey on

depresión SF 1 (= *abatimiento*) depression ➤ **depresión nerviosa** nervous breakdown ➤ **depresión posparto** postnatal depression 2 (= *hondonada*) (*en terreno*) depression; (*en horizonte, camino*) dip 3 (*Econ*) depression, recession 4 (*Meteo*) depression

depresivo/a Ⓐ ADJ [*carácter, persona*] depressive; **es una persona depresiva** she's a depressive, she's always feeling depressed Ⓑ SM/F depressive

deprimente ADJ depressing

deprimido ADJ depressed

deprimir /3a/ ♠ VT 1 (= *abatir*) to depress; **este tiempo me deprime** I find this weather depressing, this weather gets me down* 2 [+ *mercado, economía*] to depress; [+ *consumo*] to slow (down) 3 [+ *sistema inmunológico*] to depress ⓑ **deprimirse** VPR to get depressed, become depressed

deprisa ADV *ver* **prisa**

depuración SF [*de agua*] treatment, purification; [*de aguas residuales*] treatment; [*de estilo*] refinement

depurado ADJ [*estilo*] pure, refined

depuradora SF [*de agua*] water-treatment plant; (*en piscina*) filter system ➤ **depuradora de aguas residuales** sewage plant *o* farm

depurar /1a/ VT 1 (= *purificar*) [+ *agua*] to treat, purify; [+ *aguas residuales*] to treat; [+ *sangre*] to cleanse 2 (*Pol*) to purge

derecha SF 1 (= *lado derecho*) **la** ~ the right; **adelantar por la** ~ to overtake on the right; **se sentó a la** ~ **del embajador** he sat on the right *o* to the right of the ambassador; **seguir por la** ~ to keep (to the) right; **torcer a la** *o* **mano** ~ to turn right 2 (*Anat*) (*tb* **mano** ~) right hand; (*tb* **pierna** ~) right leg 3 (*Pol*) **la** ~ the Right; **ser de** ~**s** to be right-wing

derechista ADJ right-wing

derecho ♠ ADJ 1 [*línea, dirección*] straight; **anda derecha** walk upright, stand straight when you walk; **poner algo** ~ (= *no torcido*) to put sth straight, straighten sth; (= *no caído*) to stand sth upright
2 (= *del lado derecho*) [*brazo, pierna, oreja*] right; [*lado, cajón*] right-hand
ⓑ ADV 1 (= *en línea recta*) **siga todo** ~ carry *o* (*Brit*) go straight on
2 (= *directamente*) straight; **fui** ~ **a Londres** I went straight to London
ⓒ SM 1 (= *estudios, legislación*) law; **no actuó conforme a** ~ he acted unlawfully; **lo que me corresponde por** ~ what is legally mine, what is mine by law; **por** ~ **propio** in one's own right ➤ **derecho canónico** canon law ➤ **derecho civil** civil law ➤ **derecho comunitario** Community law ➤ **derecho internacional** international law ➤ **derecho laboral** labour law, labor law (*EEUU*) ➤ **derecho penal** criminal law ➤ **derecho romano** Roman law
2 [*de persona, entidad*] right; **"se reserva el derecho de admisión"** "the management reserve(s) the right to refuse admission"; **¿con qué** ~ **me hablas así?** what right have you to talk to me that way?; **¡no hay** ~**!** it's not fair!; ~ **a la educación** right to education; ~ **a la intimidad** right to *o* of privacy; ~ **al voto** right to vote; (*como derecho civil*) franchise, right to vote; **con** ~ **a algo** entitled to sth; **declaraciones de la renta con** ~ **a devolución** tax returns entitled to a rebate; **entrada con** ~ **a consumición** *entrance ticket including one free drink*; **dar** ~ **a hacer algo** to give the right to do sth; **estar en su** ~ to be within one's rights; **claro, estás en tu** ~ **de decir lo que quieras** of course, you are perfectly entitled to say whatever you like; **tener** ~ **a algo** to be entitled to sth; **tener** ~ **a hacer algo** to have a *o* the right to do sth ➤ **derecho de asilo** right of asylum ➤ **derecho de huelga** right to strike ➤ **derechos civiles** civil rights
3 **derechos** (*Com*) rights; **"reservados todos los derechos"** "all rights reserved" ➤ **derechos de autor** copyright *sing* ➤ **derechos de emisión** (*TV, Radio*) broadcasting rights ➤ **derechos humanos** human rights
4 **derechos** (= *honorarios*) [*de arquitecto, notario*] fee(s); (= *impuestos*) duty *sing* ➤ **derechos de autor** royalties
5 (*tb* **lado** ~) [*de tela, papel*] right side; [*de calcetín, chaqueta*] outside; **¿cuál es el** ~ **de esta tela?** which is the right side of this fabric?; **puedes planchar la falda por el** ~ you can iron the skirt on the outside; **poner algo al** *o* **del** ~ to put sth the right side *o* way up; **ponte la camiseta al** ~ put your T-shirt on the right way around

deriva SF drift; **ir** *o* **estar a la** ~ to drift

derivación SF (*Ling, Mat*) derivation

derivado ♠ ADJ derived ⓑ SM 1 (*Ling*) derivative 2 (*Ind, Quím*) by-product ➤ **derivado del petróleo** oil product

➤ **derivados lácteos** dairy products

derivar /1a/ ♠ VI 1 ~ **de algo** (= *provenir de*) to derive from sth; **esta palabra deriva del griego** this word derives from *o* is derived from the Greek; **esta crisis deriva de una mala política financiera** this crisis stems from *o* springs from bad financial policy
2 ~ **en algo** (= *tener como resultado*) to lead to sth, result in sth; **esto derivó en la pérdida de las colonias** this led to *o* resulted in the loss of the colonies
3 ~ **hacia algo** to turn to sth; **la conversación derivó hacia otros temas** the conversation moved on to *o* turned to different topics
ⓑ VT 1 [+ *carretera, río*] to divert
2 [+ *conversación, charla*] to divert, steer
3 (*Mat*) to derive
ⓒ **derivarse** VPR ~**se de algo** [*palabra, término*] to derive from sth, be derived from sth

dermatólogo/a SM/F dermatologist

derogación SF [*de ley*] repeal; [*de contrato*] revocation

derogar /1h/ VT [+ *ley*] to repeal; [+ *contrato*] to revoke

derramamiento SM [*de líquido*] spilling ➤ **derramamiento de sangre** bloodshed

derramar /1a/ ♠ VT [+ *líquido*] to spill; [+ *sangre, lágrimas, luz*] to shed ⓑ **derramarse** VPR [*líquido*] to spill; [*harina*] to pour out, spill out

derrame SM (*Med*) **tiene un** ~ **en el ojo** he's got a burst blood vessel in his eye ➤ **derrame cerebral** brain haemorrhage *o* (*EEUU*) hemorrhage

derrapar /1a/ ♠ VI (*Aut*) to skid ⓑ **derraparse** VPR (*Méx*): ~**se por algn*** to be crazy about sb*

derrape SM (*Aut*) skid

derredor SM **al** *o* **en** ~ **(de)** around, about

derrengado ADJ **estar** ~ to be worn out; **dejar** ~ **a algn** to wear sb out

derretir /3k/ ♠ VT [+ *mantequilla, helado*] to melt; [+ *metal*] to melt, melt down; [+ *nieve*] to melt, thaw ⓑ **derretirse** VPR [*mantequilla, helado, metal*] to melt; [*nieve*] to thaw, melt

derribar /1a/ VT 1 (= *derrumbar*) [+ *edificio*] to knock down, pull down; [+ *puerta*] to batter down; [+ *barrera*] to tear down; **el huracán derribó varias casas** the hurricane blew down *o* brought down a number of houses
2 [+ *persona*] to knock down; (*Boxeo*) to floor 3 [+ *gobierno*] to bring down, topple

derribo SM 1 [*de edificio*] knocking down, demolition
2 **derribos** (= *escombros*) rubble *sing*, debris *sing*

derrocar /1g/ VT [+ *gobierno*] to overthrow, topple; [+ *ministro*] to oust

derrochar /1a/ VT 1 [+ *dinero, recursos*] to squander, waste
2 [+ *energía, salud*] to be bursting with, be full of

derroche SM 1 (= *despilfarro*) waste, squandering; **es un** ~ **de agua** it's a waste of water; **no se puede tolerar tal** ~ such extravagance *o* wastefulness cannot be tolerated
2 (= *abundancia*) abundance, excess; **con un** ~ **de buen gusto** with a fine display of good taste

derrochón/ona* ADJ, SM/F spendthrift

derrota SF defeat

derrotado ADJ defeated

derrotar /1a/ VT [+ *ejército*] to defeat; [+ *equipo*] to defeat, beat

derrotero SM (*Náut*) course; ✦ MODISMO **tomar otro(s)** ~**(s)** to adopt a different course

derrotista ADJ, SMF defeatist

derruir /3g/ VT to demolish, tear down

derrumbamiento SM [*de edificio*] collapse; [*del techo*] collapse, cave-in

derrumbar /1a/ ♠ VT [+ *edificio*] to knock down, demolish ⓑ **derrumbarse** VPR 1 (= *hundirse*) [*edificio*] to collapse, fall down; [*techo*] to fall in, cave in
2 (= *precipitarse*) [*persona*] to fling o.s., hurl o.s. (**por** down, over)

desabastecer /2d/ VT to leave short

desabastecido ADJ estar ~ **de algo** to be out of sth

desaborido/a Ⓐ ADJ [*comida*] insipid, tasteless; [*persona*] dull Ⓑ SM/F **es un** ~ he's so dull *o* boring

desabotonar /1a/ Ⓐ VT to unbutton, undo Ⓑ **desabotonarse** VPR [*camisa, pantalón*] to come undone; **se desabotonó la camisa** he unbuttoned *o* undid his shirt

desabrido ADJ **1** (= *comida*) tasteless **2** [*persona*] (= *sin gracia*) boring; (= *antipática*) surly **3** [*respuesta*] sharp

desabrigado ADJ **1** [*persona*] **salir** ~ **a la calle** to go out without warm clothes on **2** [*lugar*] exposed

desabrigarse /1h/ VPR (*quitándose ropa*) to take off one's clothes; (*en la cama*) to throw off the bedcovers, kick off the bedcovers; **no te desabrigues** stay well wrapped up

desabrochar /1a/ Ⓐ VT [+ *camisa, zapatos*] to undo; [+ *cremallera, bragueta*] to unfasten Ⓑ **desabrocharse** VPR [*ropa*] to come undone; **¿me ayudas a ~me el vestido?** would you help me undo my dress?

desacato SM **1** (= *desobediencia*) (*a la norma*) failure to comply (**a** with); (*a la autoridad*) disrespect (**a** for) **2** (*Jur*) contempt, act of contempt ➤ **desacato a la justicia, desacato al tribunal** contempt of court

desacelerar /1a/ VI **1** (*Aut*) to decelerate, slow down **2** (*Econ*) to slow down, decline

desacertado ADJ [*diagnóstico, opinión*] mistaken; [*medida*] unwise

desacierto SM mistake

desaconsejar /1a/ VT [+ *persona*] to dissuade, advise against; [+ *proyecto*] to advise against; **los rigores del viaje ~on esa decisión** the difficulties of the journey made that decision inadvisable

desacostumbrado ADJ **1 estamos ~s al frío** we're not used to the cold, we're unsed to the cold **2** (= *insólito*) unusual

desacreditar /1a/ Ⓐ VT [+ *político, gobierno*] to discredit Ⓑ **desacreditarse** VPR to be discredited

desactivar /1a/ VT [+ *bomba*] to defuse, deactivate; [+ *alarma*] to deactivate, neutralize

desacuerdo SM disagreement, discord

desadaptado/a ADJ, SM/F = **inadaptado**

desafiar /1c/ VT **1** [+ *persona*] to challenge, dare **2** [+ *peligro*] to defy

desafilado ADJ blunt

desafinado ADJ out of tune

desafinar /1a/ VI [*instrumento*] to be out of tune; [*cantante*] to sing out of tune; [*músico*] to play out of tune, be out of tune

desafío SM **1** (= *reto*) challenge **2** (*a peligro, muerte*) defiance

desaforadamente ADV **gritar** ~ to shout at the top of one's voice

desaforado ADJ [*comportamiento*] outrageous; [*grito*] earsplitting

desafortunado ADJ unfortunate

desafuero SM outrage, excess

desagraciado ADJ graceless, unattractive

desagradable ADJ unpleasant, disagreeable (*más frm*)

desagradar /1a/ VT **me desagrada ese olor** I don't like that smell; **me desagrada tener que hacerlo** I dislike having to do it

desagradecido/a Ⓐ ADJ **1** [*persona*] ungrateful **2** [*trabajo*] thankless Ⓑ SM/F **eres un** ~ you're so ungrateful

desagrado SM displeasure; **hacer algo con** ~ to do sth unwillingly

desagraviar /1b/ VT [+ *persona*] to make amends to; [+ *agravio, ofensa*] to make amends for

desagravio SM **hacer algo en** ~ **de algo** to make amends for sth by doing sth

desagüe SM **1** (= *acto*) drainage, draining; **tubo de** ~ drainpipe, wastepipe **2** (= *conducto*) [*de bañera, lavadora*] wastepipe, drainpipe; [*de azotea*] drain

desaguisado SM mess

desahogadamente ADV comfortably

desahogado ADJ **1** (= *amplio*) [*habitación, casa*] spacious; [*espacio*] clear, free **2** [*vida, situación*] comfortable; **ahora andamos algo más ~s de tiempo** we're less pressed for time now **3** (= *con dinero*) comfortably off

desahogar /1h/ Ⓐ VT [+ *ira*] to vent (**en** on); **desahogó sus penas** she unburdened herself of her troubles Ⓑ **desahogarse** VPR **1** (= *desfogarse*) (*de estrés*) to let off steam*; (*de enfado*) to get it out of one's system; **me desahogué diciéndole todo lo que pensaba** I got it out of my system by telling him exactly what I thought **2** (= *confesarse*) to get it off one's chest*; **~se con algn** to pour one's heart out to sb

desahogo SM (= *comodidad*) comfort, ease; **vivir con** ~ to be comfortably off

desahuciado ADJ estar ~ to be beyond recovery, be hopelessly ill

desahuciar /1b/ VT **1** [+ *inquilino*] to evict **2** [+ *enfermo*] to declare beyond recovery **3** (*Chi*) [+ *empleado*] to dismiss

desahucio SM **1** [*de inquilino*] eviction **2** (*Chi*) [*de empleado*] dismissal

desairar /1a/ VT to slight, snub

desaire SM slight, snub; **hacer un** ~ **a algn** to slight sb, snub sb

desajustar /1a/ Ⓐ VT **1** (= *desarreglar*) [+ *brillo, color*] to disarrange; [+ *máquina*] to put out of order **2** [+ *planes*] to upset Ⓑ **desajustarse** VPR [*máquina*] to break down; [*clavija, tornillo*] to come loose

desajuste SM [*de hormonas, presupuesto*] imbalance; [*de máquina*] breakdown

desalar /1a/ VT [+ *pescado*] to desalt; [+ *agua salada*] to desalinate

desalentar /1j/ Ⓐ VT to discourage Ⓑ **desalentarse** VPR to get discouraged, lose heart

desaliento SM discouragement

desalinizar /1f/ VT, **desalinar** /1a/ VT to desalinate

desaliñado ADJ slovenly

desaliño SM slovenliness

desalmado ADJ cruel, heartless

desalojar /1a/ VT **1** [+ *inquilino*] to evict, eject **2** (= *desocupar*) [+ *edificio*] to evacuate; [+ *barco*] to abandon; **la policía desalojó el local** the police cleared the premises

desalojo SM **1** [*de inquilino*] eviction, ejection **2** (= *desocupación*) [*de edificio*] evacuation; [*de barco*] abandonment

desamarrar /1a/ VT **1** (*Náut*) to cast off **2** (*Col*) (= *desatar*) to untie

desambiguar /1i/ VT to disambiguate

desamor SM coldness, indifference

desamortización SF (*Esp Hist*) sale of Church lands

desamparado ADJ [*persona*] helpless, defenceless, defenseless (*EEUU*); [*lugar*] exposed

desamparar /1a/ VT **1** [+ *persona*] (= *abandonar*) to desert, abandon; (= *dejar indefenso*) to leave defenceless *o* (*EEUU*) defenseless **2** [+ *lugar*] to leave, abandon

desamueblar /1a/ VT to remove the furniture from, clear the furniture out of

desandar /1p/ VT ~ **lo andado** ◇ ~ **el camino** to retrace one's steps; **no se puede** ~ **lo andado** what's done can't be undone

desangelado ADJ [*lugar*] soulless; [*persona*] charmless, dull, unattractive

desangrar /1a/ Ⓐ VT [+ *persona*] to bleed Ⓑ **desangrarse** VPR (= *perder sangre*) to lose a lot of blood; (= *morir*) to bleed to death

desanimado ADJ downhearted, dejected

desanimar /1a/ Ⓐ VT **1** (= *desalentar*) to discourage **2** (= *deprimir*) to depress, sadden Ⓑ **desanimarse** VPR to get discouraged, lose heart

desánimo SM (= *desaliento*) despondency; (= *abatimiento*) dejection

desanudar /1a/ VT to untie, undo

desapacible ADJ [*tiempo*] unpleasant; [*sabor, carácter*] surly; [*tono*] harsh

desaparecer /2d/ VI 1 [*persona, objeto*] to disappear, go missing; **han desaparecido dos niños en el parque** two children have disappeared *o* gone missing in the park; **el mago hizo ~ una paloma** the magician made a dove disappear; **¡desaparece de mi vista!** get out of my sight! 2 [*mancha, olor, síntoma*] to disappear, go (away)

desaparecido/a Ⓐ ADJ [*persona, objeto*] missing; [*especie*] extinct; **tres continúan ~s** three are still missing; **~ en combate** missing in action, MIA
Ⓑ SM/F missing person; **número de muertos, heridos y ~s** number of dead, wounded and missing

---

LOS DESAPARECIDOS

Los desaparecidos is the name given to those who disappeared during the military dictatorships in the Southern Cone in the 1970s. Thousands of people were taken from their homes, schools and places of work and never seen again. Families of the victims joined forces to form pressure groups like Argentina's **Madres y Abuelas de la Plaza de Mayo**, but although some managed to identify and recover the bodies of their relatives, the perpetrators were rarely brought to justice.

---

desaparición SF 1 [*de persona, objeto*] disappearance 2 [*de especie*] extinction

desapasionado ADJ dispassionate, impartial

desapego SM coolness, indifference (**hacia** towards)

desapercibido ADJ unnoticed; **pasar ~** to go unnoticed

desaprensivo/a Ⓐ ADJ unscrupulous Ⓑ SM/F **es un ~** he's an unscrupulous individual

desaprobación SF disapproval

desaprobar /1l/ VT to disapprove of

desaprovechado ADJ 1 [*oportunidad, tiempo*] wasted 2 [*terreno*] underused, unproductive

desaprovechar /1a/ VT [+ *ocasión, oportunidad*] to waste, miss; [+ *talento*] not to use to the full

desarbolado ADJ treeless

desarmable ADJ **mesa ~** foldaway table

desarmadero SM (*RPl*) scrapyard

desarmador SM (*Méx*) screwdriver

desarmar /1a/ VT 1 (*Mil*) to disarm 2 (= *desmontar*) [+ *juguete*] to take apart, take to pieces; [+ *estantería, mueble*] to dismantle, take apart 3 (= *dejar sin argumentos*) [+ *persona*] to disarm; [+ *ira*] to calm

desarme SM disarmament

desarraigado ADJ [*persona*] rootless, without roots

desarraigar /1h/ VT 1 [+ *árbol*] to uproot 2 [+ *pueblo, persona*] to uproot 3 [+ *costumbre*] to root out, eradicate

desarraigo SM uprooting

desarreglado ADJ (= *desordenado*) untidy; (= *descuidado*) [*aspecto*] slovenly

desarreglar /1a/ Ⓐ VT 1 (= *desordenar*) to mess up 2 (*Mec*) to put out of order Ⓑ **desarreglarse** VPR to get messed up

desarreglo SM 1 (= *desorden*) (*gen*) disorder, confusion; [*de habitación*] mess 2 (*Med*) **~s estomacales** stomach upsets

desarrollar /1a/ Ⓐ VT 1 [+ *capacidad, músculos, industria*] to develop 2 (= *realizar*) [+ *trabajo, proyecto*] to carry out; [+ *técnica, método*] to develop 3 (= *explicar*) [+ *teoría, tema, punto*] to develop 4 (*Mat*) [+ *ecuación, función*] to expand

Ⓑ **desarrollarse** VPR 1 (= *madurar*) [*adolescente*] to develop, reach puberty; [*planta, animal*] to develop, reach maturity; [*país*] to develop
2 (= *ocurrir*) [*suceso, reunión*] to take place; [*trama*] to unfold, develop; **la manifestación se desarrolló sin incidentes** the demonstration went off without incident

desarrollo SM 1 [*de capacidad, persona, industria*] development; **un país en vías de ~ o en ~** a developing country ➤ **desarrollo sostenible** sustainable development 2 (= *realización*) [*de proyecto, plan*] carrying out; [*de técnica, método*] development 3 [*de tema, punto*] development 4 [*de historia, acontecimiento*] development; **el ~ de la trama** the unfolding *o* development of the plot; **seguimos de cerca el ~ de los acontecimientos** we are monitoring developments closely 5 (= *pubertad*) puberty 6 (*Mat*) [*de ecuación, función*] expansion; [*de problema*] working

desarropado ADJ **estar ~** to have lost the covers

desarropar /1a/ Ⓐ VT to take the covers off
Ⓑ **desarroparse** VPR to throw the covers off

desarrugar /1h/ VT [+ *mantel, sábana*] to smooth out; [+ *ropa*] to remove the creases from, remove the wrinkles from (*EEUU*)

desarticular /1a/ VT [+ *máquina, reloj*] to take apart, take to pieces; **~ un grupo terrorista** to force a terrorist group out of action

desaseado ADJ [*persona*] dirty, grubby; [*aspecto, pelo*] untidy, unkempt

desaseo SM [*de persona*] dirtiness, grubbiness; [*de aspecto*] untidiness

desasirse /3a; *presente como salir*/ VPR to extricate *o* free o.s. (**de** from)

desasistir /3a/ VT to neglect

desasosiego SM (= *inquietud*) uneasiness, anxiety; (= *intranquilidad*) restlessness; (*Pol*) unrest

desastrado ADJ [*persona, aspecto*] scruffy, untidy

desastre SM disaster; **¡qué ~!** how awful!; **la función fue un ~** the show was a shambles; **soy un ~ dibujando** I'm terrible *o* hopeless at drawing

desastroso ADJ disastrous, calamitous

desatado ADJ 1 (*cordones*) undone 2 (= *descontrolado*) uncontrolled; **está ~** he's gone absolutely wild*

desatar /1a/ Ⓐ VT 1 [+ *nudo, cuerda, cordones*] to untie, undo; **no consiguió ~ al prisionero** he couldn't manage to untie the prisoner; **la bebida le desató la lengua** the drink loosened his tongue 2 (= *desencadenar*) [+ *guerra, crisis*] to trigger, spark (off); [+ *sentimiento, pasión*] to unleash
Ⓑ **desatarse** VPR 1 (= *soltarse*) [*nudo, cuerda, cordones*] to come undone *o* untied; [*perro*] to break loose; **el prisionero consiguió ~se** the prisoner managed to untie himself 2 (= *desencadenarse*) [*incendio, guerra, motín*] to break out; [*crisis, polémica*] to flare up; [*tormenta, escándalo*] to break; [*desastre*] to strike

desatascador SM plunger, plumber's helper (*EEUU*)

desatascar /1g/ VT [+ *cañería*] to clear, unblock

desatender /2g/ VT 1 (= *descuidar*) [+ *consejo, deseos*] to disregard, ignore; [+ *obligación*] to neglect 2 [+ *persona*] to neglect

desatento ADJ 1 (= *descuidado*) heedless, careless 2 (= *descortés*) discourteous (**con** to) 3 (= *distraído*) **siempre está ~ en clase** he's always daydreaming in class, he never pays attention in class

desatinado ADJ foolish

desatinar /1a/ VI (*al actuar*) to act foolishly; (*al hablar*) to talk nonsense

desatino SM 1 (= *falta de cordura*) foolishness 2 (= *error*) blunder, mistake; (*al actuar*) foolish act 3 **desatinos** (= *disparates*) nonsense *sing*

desatornillador SM (*LAm*) screwdriver

desatornillar /1a/ VT to unscrew

desatracar /1g/ VI (Náut) to cast off

desatrancar /1g/ VT **1** [+ puerta] to force open **2** [+ cañería] to unblock

desautorizar /1f/ VT **1** (= quitar autoridad a) [+ oficial] to deprive of authority; [+ palabras, declaración] to discredit **2** [+ noticia] to deny

desavenencia SF disagreement

desavenido ADJ **están ~s** they have fallen out, they have had a fight

desayunado ADJ **vengo ~** I've had breakfast

desayunar /1a/ Ⓐ VT to have for breakfast Ⓑ VI to have breakfast Ⓒ **desayunarse** VPR (LAm) to have breakfast; **~se algo** to have sth for breakfast

desayuno SM breakfast

desazón SF uneasiness

desbancar /1g/ Ⓐ VT **1** (= quitar el puesto a) to oust; (= suplantar a) to supplant (in sb's affections) **2** (en juegos) [+ banca] to bust*; [+ persona] to take the bank from Ⓑ VI (Naipes) to go bust*

desbandada SF rush (to get away); **cuando empezó a llover hubo una ~ general** when it started to rain everyone rushed for shelter; **retirarse a la ~** to retreat in disorder; **salir en ~** to run off o scatter in all directions

desbandarse /1a/ VPR **1** (= huir) to run off o scatter in all directions **2** (Mil) to disband

desbarajuste SM confusion, chaos; **¡qué ~!** what a mess!

desbaratar /1a/ VT [+ plan] to spoil, thwart; [+ sistema] to disrupt, cause chaos in

desbarrancarse /1g/ VPR (LAm) to fall over a precipice

desbarrar /1a/ VI to talk nonsense

desbastar /1a/ VT (Téc) [+ madera] to plane down; [+ piedra] to smooth down

desbloquear /1a/ VT **1** (= quitar un obstáculo de) [+ tubería] to unblock; [+ tráfico] to free, get moving; [+ negociación] to break the stalemate in **2** (Com, Fin) to unfreeze **3** (Mil) to break the blockade of

desbloqueo SM [de negociación] breaking of the deadlock; [de cuenta] unfreezing, unblocking, freeing

desbocado ADJ [caballo] runaway

desbocarse /1g/ VPR [caballo] to bolt; [multitud] to run riot, get out of control

desbordamiento SM [de lago, río] overflowing

desbordante ADJ **1** (= que rebosa) **una copa ~ de champán** a glass full to the brim with champagne **2** (= abundante) [alegría, entusiasmo, actividad] overwhelming; [humor, imaginación] unbounded, boundless **3 ~ de** [+ salud, entusiasmo, energía] brimming (over) with

desbordar /1a/ Ⓐ VT **1** (= rebosar) **la lluvia ha desbordado el río** the rain has caused the river to burst its banks o to overflow; **han desbordado la centralita con tantas llamadas** the switchboard has been inundated o overwhelmed with calls **2** (= exceder) [+ límite, previsiones] to exceed; [+ persona, tolerancia] to be beyond, be too much for; **su fama ha desbordado las fronteras de este país** her fame has spread far beyond this country; **el trabajo me desborda** the work is just too much for me **3** [+ energía, entusiasmo] to be brimming (over) with; **desborda alegría y buen humor** he's brimming (over) with happiness and high spirits **4** (Dep) (= aventajar) to outplay Ⓑ **desbordarse** VPR **1** (= rebosar) **1.1** [lavabo, río] to overflow; [líquido] to overflow, spill (over); **se ha desbordado el cauce del río** the river has burst its banks o overflowed **1.2** [epidemia, guerra] **~se fuera de** to spread beyond; **la guerra se ha desbordado fuera de nuestras fronteras** the war has spread beyond our borders **2** (= desatarse) [ira] to boil over; **la euforia se desbordó al final del partido** they were unable to contain their euphoria at the end of the match

desborde SM (CS) = **desbordamiento**

desbrozar /1f/ VT [+ camino, campo] to clear

descabalgar /1h/ VI to dismount

descabellado ADJ [plan, idea] crazy, wild, preposterous

descabezado ADJ headless

descacharrante* ADJ hilarious

descacharrar /1a/ VT = **escacharrar**

descafeinado Ⓐ ADJ **1** [café] decaffeinated **2** [lenguaje, ideales] diluted, watered-down Ⓑ SM decaffeinated coffee

descalabrado ADJ **salir ~** to come out the loser (**de** in)

descalabrar /1a/ VT **~ a algn** to split sb's head open

descalabro SM **1** (= contratiempo) disaster **2** (Mil) defeat

descalcificación SF (Med) lack of calcium, calcium deficiency

descalificación SF **1** (Dep) disqualification **2** (= pérdida de crédito) discrediting **3 descalificaciones** (= críticas) smears

descalificar /1g/ VT **1** (Dep) to disqualify **2** (= desacreditar) to discredit

descalzar /1f/ Ⓐ VT [+ rueda] to remove the chocks from; [+ armario, mesa] to remove the wedge(s) from Ⓑ **descalzarse** VPR to take off one's shoes

descalzo ADJ barefoot, barefooted

descambiar* /1b/ VT to change

descaminado ADJ [proyecto] misguided; **andar** o **ir ~** to be on the wrong track; **en eso no andas muy ~** you're not far wrong there

descamisado/a Ⓐ ADJ **1** (= sin camisa) shirtless **2** (= con la camisa abierta) open-shirted **3** (= mal vestido) ragged, shabby **4** (Arg Hist, Pol) Peronist Ⓑ SM/F (Arg Hist, Pol) Peronist

descampado SM open space, area of empty ground

descansado ADJ [persona] rested, refreshed

descansar /1a/ Ⓐ VI **1** (= reposar) to rest, have a rest; **siéntate aquí y descansa** sit down here and have a rest, sit down here and rest; **necesito ~ para despejarme** I need (to have) a rest to clear my head; **no ~á hasta conseguir que dimita el presidente** he will not rest until he gets the president to resign **2** (= dormir) to sleep; **¡hasta mañana! ¡que descanses!** see you in the morning! sleep well! **3 ~ sobre algo** [cúpula, tejado] to be supported by sth, rest on sth **4** (= estar enterrado) **aquí descansan los restos mortales de José Fernández** here lie the mortal remains of José Fernández; **tu tío, que en paz descanse** your uncle, may he rest in peace; **descanse en paz** rest in peace **5** (Mil) **¡descansen!** at ease!, stand at ease! **6** [tierra de labor] to rest, lie fallow Ⓑ VT **1** (= apoyar) to rest; **dejé de leer para ~ la vista** I stopped reading to rest my eyes **2** (Mil) **¡descansen armas!** order arms!

descansillo SM (en escalera) landing

descanso SM **1** (= reposo) rest; **los niños no me dejan ni un minuto de ~** the children don't give me a moment's rest; **tengo tres días de ~** I get three days off **2** (= pausa) break; (Dep) half-time; (Teat) interval (esp Brit), intermission (esp EEUU); **estudió sin ~ hasta aprobar** she studied constantly until she passed **3** (= alivio) relief **4** (en escalera) landing

descapitalización SF **1** (= pérdida) **la empresa sufrió una ~ de 13.000 millones** the net worth of the company fell by 13,000 million **2** (intencionada) asset-stripping

descapitalizar /1f/ VT **1** (no intencionadamente) **~ una empresa** to reduce a company's net worth **2** (intencionadamente) to asset-strip

descapotable ADJ, SM (Aut) convertible

descaradamente ADV (= sin vergüenza) shamelessly, brazenly; (= con frescura) cheekily (Brit), saucily

descarado Ⓐ ADJ **1** [persona] (= desvergonzado) shameless; (= insolente) cheeky (Brit), sassy (EEUU) **2** (= evidente) [mentira] barefaced; [prejuicio] blatant Ⓑ ADV (Esp*) **sí voy, ~** I'm going all right, you bet I'm going

descarga SF **1** [de camión, mercancías] unloading **2** [de adrenalina, emociones] release **3** (*Mil*) firing, discharge (*frm*); **recibió varias ~s en el pecho** he received several shots in his chest **4** (*Elec*) discharge; **recibió una ~ eléctrica** he received an electric shock

descargar /1h/ Ⓐ VT **1** (= *quitar la carga de*) [+ *camión, contenedor, arma*] to unload
2 (= *sacar*) [+ *mercancías*] to unload; **están descargando los sacos del furgón** they are unloading the sacks from the van
3 (= *disparar*) [+ *arma, tiro*] to fire
4 (= *soltar*) [+ *golpe*] to land; [+ *bomba*] to drop, release; **empezó a ~ golpes sobre la mesa** he started banging (on) the table
5 (= *liberar*) [+ *tensión, agresividad*] to release; [+ *enfado, ira*] to vent; [+ *conciencia*] to ease; [+ *responsabilidad, sentimiento*] to offload; **~ a algn de** [+ *obligación, responsabilidad*] to relieve sb of; [+ *deuda*] to discharge sb from; [+ *acusación*] to clear sb of, acquit sb of
6 (*Inform*) to download
Ⓑ VI [*tormenta*] to break; **una fuerte tromba de agua descargó sobre la ciudad** a torrential downpour fell on the city
Ⓒ **descargarse** VPR **1** (= *desahogarse*) to unburden o.s.; **~se de** [+ *carga, problema*] to unburden o.s. of; [+ *responsabilidad*] to unload
2 [*batería*] to go flat; [*pila*] to run down
3 **~se algo de Internet** to download sth from the Internet

descargo SM (*Jur*) **en ~ de algn** in defence *o* (*EEUU*) defense of sb; **quisiera decir algo en mi ~** I would like to say something in my defence *o* (*EEUU*) defense

descarnado ADJ [*estilo, descripción*] straightforward

descaro SM cheek*, nerve*

descarozado ADJ (*CS*) [*fruta*] stoned, pitted

descarriarse /1c/ VPR **1** (= *perder el camino*) [*persona*] to lose one's way; [*animal*] to stray; ✦ MODISMO **ser una oveja descarriada** to be like a lost sheep **2** (= *desviarse de lo correcto*) to go astray

descarrilamiento SM derailment

descarrilar /1a/ Ⓐ VI to be derailed Ⓑ **descarrilarse** VPR to be derailed

descartable ADJ (*RPl*) [*envase, pañal*] disposable

descartar /1a/ Ⓐ VT [+ *candidato, plan, opción*] to rule out, reject; [+ *posibilidad, hipótesis*] to rule out, dismiss Ⓑ **descartarse** VPR (*Naipes*) **se descartó de un as** he threw away *o* discarded an ace

descarte SM (*Naipes*) discard

descascarar /1a/ Ⓐ VT **1** (= *quitar la corteza de*) [+ *naranja, limón*] to peel; [+ *nuez, huevo cocido, gamba*] to shell **2** (*And*) [+ *animal*] to flay, skin **3** (*And*) (= *deshonrar*) to dishonour, dishonor (*EEUU*) Ⓑ **descascararse** VPR to peel, peel off

descascarillar /1a/ Ⓐ VT [+ *plato, vasija*] to chip; [+ *arroz*] to husk Ⓑ **descascarillarse** VPR [*plato, vasija*] to get chipped; [*pintura*] to flake; **las paredes estaban descascarilladas** the paint had flaked off the walls

descatalogado ADJ [*libro*] out-of-print, unlisted; [*disco*] unlisted; [*producto*] discontinued

descendencia SF descendants *pl*; **morir sin dejar ~** to leave no children behind, die without issue (*frm*)

descendente ADJ [*dirección, trayectoria*] downward; [*orden, escala*] descending; [*cantidad*] diminishing; **tren ~** down train

descender /2g/ Ⓐ VT **1** [+ *escalera, colina*] to come down, go down, descend (*frm*); **la canción descendió tres puestos en las listas de éxitos** the song went down three places in the charts
2 (= *llevar abajo*) to lower; **descendieron al bombero al pozo** they lowered the fireman into the well
3 (*en orden, jerarquía*) to downgrade, demote; **lo han descendido de categoría** he has been downgraded *o* demoted
Ⓑ VI **1** (= *disminuir*) [*fiebre*] to go down, abate; [*temperatura, número, nivel*] to go down, fall, drop; [*ventas, demanda, producción*] to fall, drop (off); [*calidad*] to go down, decline

2 (*de un lugar a otro*) [*persona*] to come down, go down, descend (*frm*); [*avión*] to descend
3 (*en orden, jerarquía*) to be downgraded, be demoted; (*Dep*) to be relegated; **el restaurante ha descendido de categoría** the restaurant has been downgraded; **su libro descendió al cuarto puesto** her book went down to fourth place
4 ~ de (= *provenir de*): **el hombre desciende del mono** man is descended from apes

descenso SM **1** [*de temperatura, nivel, demanda*] fall, drop ➤ **descenso térmico** fall *o* drop in temperature **2** (*de un lugar a otro*) descent; **inició el ~ 20 minutos antes de aterrizar** he began his descent 20 minutes before landing; **la prueba de ~** (*Dep*) the downhill event **3** (*en orden, jerarquía*) downgrading, demotion; (*Dep*) relegation; **el CD ha sufrido un ~ de tres puestos** the CD has gone down three places in the charts **4** (= *pendiente*) slope; **el ~ hacia el río** the slope down to the river

descentrado ADJ **1** (*Téc*) [*pieza*] off-centre, off-center (*EEUU*); [*rueda*] out of true **2** [*persona*] disorientated, disoriented (*esp EEUU*)

descentralizar /1f/ VT to decentralize

descerebrado ADJ brainless, mindless

descerrajar /1a/ VT **1** [+ *cerradura, puerta*] to break open, force **2** [+ *tiro*] to let off, fire (**a** at)

descifrar /1a/ VT **1** (= *descodificar*) [+ *escritura*] to decipher, make out; [+ *mensaje*] to decode **2** (= *resolver*) [+ *problema*] to puzzle out; [+ *misterio*] to unravel

desclasificar /1g/ VT (*Dep*) to disqualify

desclavar /1a/ VT to pull out the nails from, unnail

descocado ADJ **1** (= *descarado*) cheeky (*Brit*), sassy (*EEUU*) **2** (= *atrevido*) brazen

descodificador SM decoder

descodificar /1g/ VT [+ *mensaje*] to decode

descojonado*** ADJ (= *cansado*) knackered (*Brit**), pooped (*EEUU***)

descojonarse*** /1a/ VPR (= *reír*) to piss o.s. laughing (*Brit****), shit o.s. laughing (*EEUU****)

descojone*** SM **1** (= *situación graciosa*) **¡qué ~!** what a bloody riot!** **2** (= *caos*) **¡esto es un ~!** what a frigging mess!***, what a bloody shambles! (*Brit***)

descolgar /1h, 1l/ Ⓐ VT **1** [+ *cuadro, cortina*] to take down, get down; **descuelga el abrigo de ahí** take the coat off there *o* down from there **2** [+ *teléfono*] to pick up; **dejó el teléfono descolgado** he left the phone off the hook Ⓑ **descolgarse** VPR **1** (= *bajar por una cuerda*) to let o.s. down, lower o.s.; **~se por** [+ *cuerda*] to slip down, slide down; [+ *pared*] to climb down **2** (*Ciclismo*) **~se del pelotón** to be left behind the group

descollar /1l/ VI to stand out, be outstanding; **descuella entre los demás** he stands out above the others

descolocar /1g/ VT [+ *papeles, libros*] to misplace; [+ *cajón, habitación*] to mess up

descolonizar /1f/ VT to decolonize

descolorido ADJ (*por el lavado*) discoloured, discolored (*EEUU*); (*por el sol*) faded

descomedido ADJ [*tendencia, odio*] excessive, immoderate

descompasado ADJ (= *excesivo*) excessive; (= *sin proporción*) out of all proportion

descomponer /2q/ (*pp* **descompuesto**) Ⓐ VT **1** (= *dividir*) [+ *sustancia, molécula, número*] to break down **2** (= *pudrir*) [+ *alimento*] to rot; [+ *cadáver, cuerpo*] to decompose
Ⓑ **descomponerse** VPR **1** (= *pudrirse*) to decompose, rot **2** (*) (= *alterarse*) **me descompongo con tanto ruido** all this noise gets to me* *o* irritates me; **se le descompuso la cara cuando se lo dije** her face fell when I told her **3** (= *sentirse mal*) **3.1** (*LAm*) to feel unwell **3.2** **se me descompuso el vientre** I had an attack of diarrhoea *o* (*EEUU*) diarrhea **4** (*LAm*) (= *romperse*) to break down

descomposición SF **1** (= *putrefacción*) decomposition

2 (*Med*) ➤ **descomposición de vientre** diarrhoea, diarrhea (*EEUU*)

descompostura SF **1** (*LAm*) (= *diarrea*) diarrhoea, diarrhea (*EEUU*) **2** (*Méx*) [*de aparato*] fault, breakdown **3** (*And*) (= *dislocación*) dislocation

descompresión SF decompression

descompuesto Ⓐ PP *de* **descomponer** Ⓑ ADJ **1** (*LAm*) (= *estropeado*) [*reloj*] broken; [*motor*] broken down **2** (*Med*) **2.1** (*LAm*) (= *indispuesto*) unwell **2.2** (= *con diarrea*) **estar ~** to have diarrhoea *o* (*EEUU*) diarrhea **3** (= *furioso*) angry; **ponerse ~** to get angry, lose one's composure

descomunal ADJ huge, enormous

desconcentrar /1a/ Ⓐ VT [+ *persona*] to distract Ⓑ **desconcentrarse** VPR to lose one's concentration, get distracted

desconcertado ADJ disconcerted

desconcertante ADJ disconcerting

desconcertar /1j/ VT to disconcert; **la pregunta me desconcertó** I was disconcerted by the question

desconchado SM (*en plato, vasija*) chip

desconchar /1a/ Ⓐ VT [+ *pared*] to strip off, peel off; [+ *loza*] to chip off Ⓑ **desconcharse** VPR [*plato, vasija*] to chip; **se ha desconchado la pared** the paint has flaked *o* peeled off the wall

desconcierto SM uncertainty, confusion; **un clima de ~** a climate of uncertainty; **el cambio de táctica provocó ~ en el rival** his opponent was disconcerted by the change of tactics

desconectado ADJ **1 estar ~ de algo** to have no contact with sth **2 estar ~** (*Internet*) to be off-line

desconectar /1a/ Ⓐ VT [+ *gas, teléfono*] to disconnect; [+ *enchufe*] to unplug; [+ *radio, televisor, ordenador*] to switch off, turn off Ⓑ VI (*durante una conversación*) to switch off

desconexión SF **1** (*Elec*) disconnection **2** (*entre personas, capítulos*) lack of connection

desconfiado ADJ distrustful, suspicious (**de** of)

desconfianza SF distrust, mistrust

desconfiar /1c/ VI to be distrustful *o* mistrustful; **~ de algn/algo** to distrust sb/sth, mistrust sb/sth; **"desconfíe de las imitaciones"** "beware of imitations"

desconforme ADJ = **disconforme**

descongelar /1a/ Ⓐ VT **1** [+ *congelador*] to defrost; [+ *alimentos*] to defrost, thaw; [+ *coche*] to de-ice **2** [+ *créditos, salarios*] to unfreeze Ⓑ **descongelarse** VPR [*congelador*] to defrost; [*alimentos*] to defrost, thaw

descongestión SF **1** (= *alivio*) relief, relieving **2** [*de pulmones, nariz*] clearing, decongestion (*frm*)

descongestionar /1a/ VT **1** [+ *calle, ciudad*] to relieve, ease congestion in; [+ *prisión*] to relieve overcrowding in **2** [+ *pulmones, nariz*] to clear, decongest (*frm*); [+ *cabeza*] to clear

desconocer /2d/ VT not to know, be ignorant of; **desconocen los principios fundamentales** they don't know the basic principles, they are ignorant of the basic principles

desconocido/a Ⓐ ADJ **1** (= *no conocido*) unknown; **una explosión de origen ~** an explosion of unknown origin; **su nombre me es totalmente ~** his name is completely unfamiliar to me **2 estar ~: con ese traje estás ~** I'd hardly recognize you *o* you're unrecognizable in your new suit; **después del divorcio está ~** he's a changed person *o* he's like a different person since the divorce Ⓑ SM/F stranger; **un ~ llamó a la puerta** a stranger knocked on the door; **unos ~s le dispararon por la espalda** some unidentified attackers shot him in the back

desconocimiento SM ignorance

desconsideración SF thoughtlessness, inconsiderateness

desconsiderado ADJ thoughtless, inconsiderate

desconsolado ADJ disconsolate

desconsuelo SM distress, grief

descontado ADJ **por ~** of course; **dar algo por ~** to take sth for granted

descontar /1l/ VT **1** (= *deducir*) to deduct, take off; **me lo descuentan del sueldo** it gets deducted from *o* taken off my wages, it comes off my wages **2** (*Com*) (*al pagar*) **te descuentan un 10%** they give you 10% off, there is a 10% discount *o* a discount of 10% **3** (= *excluir*) to exclude; **descontando los gastos de alojamiento** excluding *o* not including accommodation expenses

descontento/a Ⓐ ADJ dissatisfied, discontented (**de** with) Ⓑ SM/F (*Pol*) discontent, unrest

descontrol SM **hay un ~ en la oficina** the office is in chaos

descontrolado ADJ uncontrolled; **estar ~** to be out of control

desconvocar /1g/ VT to call off, cancel

descoordinación SF lack of coordination

descorazonador ADJ discouraging, disheartening

descorazonar /1a/ Ⓐ VT to discourage, dishearten Ⓑ **descorazonarse** VPR to get discouraged, lose heart

descorchar /1a/ VT [+ *botella*] to uncork, open

descorrer /2a/ VT [+ *cerrojo, cortina*] to draw back; [+ *velo*] to remove

descortés ADJ rude, impolite, discourteous (*frm*)

descortesía SF **1** (= *acto*) discourtesy **2** (= *cualidad*) rudeness, impoliteness

descoser /2a/ Ⓐ VT to unstitch, unpick Ⓑ **descoserse** VPR [*costura, manga*] to come unstitched

descosido/a Ⓐ ADJ (*Cos*) unstitched, torn Ⓑ SM/F ✦ MODISMO **como un ~*: habla como un ~** he just rambles on and on* Ⓒ SM (*Cos*) open seam

descoyuntar /1a/ Ⓐ VT **1** (= *dislocar*) to dislocate **2** [+ *hechos*] to twist Ⓑ **descoyuntarse** VPR **1** (= *dislocarse*) **~se el hombro** to dislocate one's shoulder, put one's shoulder out of joint **2** (*) **~se de risa** to split one's sides laughing

descrédito SM discredit, disrepute

descremado ADJ [*leche*] skimmed, low-fat

describir /3a/ (*pp* **descrito**) VT to describe

> Siempre que el verbo **describe** aparece con un objeto indirecto, éste va siempre precedido de **to**:

¿podría ~me lo que ha encontrado? could you describe to me what you found?

descripción SF description

descriptivo ADJ descriptive

descrito PP *de* **describir**

descruzar /1f/ VT [+ *piernas*] to uncross; [+ *brazos*] to unfold

descuajaringar* /1h/ Ⓐ VT to break to pieces Ⓑ **descuajaringarse** VPR (= *partirse*) to come apart; **~se de risa** to split one's sides laughing

descuajeringar /1h/ VT = **descuajaringar**

descuartizar /1f/ VT [+ *animal*] to carve up, cut up; [+ *cuerpo, cadáver*] to quarter

descubierto Ⓐ PP *de* **descubrir** Ⓑ ADJ [*cabeza, pecho*] bare; [*patio, piscina*] open-air; [*autobús, carroza*] open-top; [*cielo*] clear Ⓒ SM **1 al ~** (= *al aire libre*) outdoors, out in the open; **dejar algo al ~** to expose sth (to view); **poner algo al ~** to expose sth; **quedar al ~** to be exposed **2** (*en cuenta corriente*) overdraft; (*en presupuesto*) shortage; **estar en ~** to be overdrawn, be in the red*

descubrimiento SM **1** (= *hallazgo*) [*de país, invento, deportista*] discovery; **este restaurante ha sido todo un ~** this restaurant has been a real find *o* discovery **2** [*de conspiración, estafa*] uncovering **3** [*de secreto*] revelation **4** [*de estatua, placa*] unveiling

descubrir /3a/ (*pp* **descubierto**) Ⓐ VT **1** (= *encontrar*)

[+ *tesoro, tratamiento, persona oculta*] to discover, find; [+ *país, deportista*] to discover; **al revisar las cuentas ha descubierto numerosas irregularidades** when he went over the accounts he discovered *o* found numerous irregularities; **descubra Bruselas, corazón de Europa** discover Brussels, the heart of Europe; **los análisis han descubierto la presencia de un virus** the tests have revealed *o* shown up the presence of a virus; ✦ MODISMO ~ **América** to reinvent the wheel
2 (= *averiguar*) [+ *verdad*] to find out, discover; **descubrió que era alérgica a las gambas** she found out *o* discovered she was allergic to prawns
3 (= *sacar a la luz*) [+ *conspiración, estafa*] to uncover; [+ *secreto, intenciones*] to reveal; **una red de narcotraficantes descubierta en Colombia** a drug-trafficking ring uncovered in Colombia
4 (= *delatar*) to give away; **lo descubrió su voz** his voice gave him away
5 (= *destapar*) [+ *estatua, placa*] to unveil; [+ *cacerola*] to take the lid off; [+ *naipes*] to turn over, lay up; [+ *cara*] to uncover; ✦ MODISMO ~ **el juego a algn** to call sb's bluff
Ⓑ descubrirse VPR **1** (= *quitarse el sombrero*) to take one's hat off; (*para saludar*) to raise one's hat (in greeting); ~**se ante algo/algn** to take one's hat off to sth/sb
2 (= *dejar ver*) [+ *cara, rostro*] to uncover; [+ *cabeza*] to bare; **descúbrase el brazo, por favor** roll up your sleeve, please
3 (= *delatarse*) to give o.s. away

descuento SM (*Com*) discount; **un ~ del 3%** a discount of 3%, a 3% discount; **hacer ~** to give a discount

descuidado ADJ **1** [*persona*] (= *despreocupado*) careless; (= *olvidadizo*) forgetful; (= *desprevenido*) unprepared
2 (= *desaliñado*) [*aspecto*] untidy, slovenly; [*habitación*] untidy, messy **3** (= *abandonado*) neglected

descuidar /1a/ **Ⓐ** VT (= *desatender*) to neglect **Ⓑ** VI (= *no preocuparse*) not to worry; **¡descuida!** don't worry!, it's all right! **Ⓒ descuidarse** VPR **1** (= *desprevenirse*) to drop one's guard; **si te descuidas ◇ como te descuides** if you don't watch out; **en cuanto me descuidé me lo robaron** the moment I dropped my guard *o* stopped watching out they stole it from me **2** (= *abandonarse*) to let o.s. go

descuido SM (= *distracción*) **en un ~ le robaron el dinero** her money was stolen when she wasn't looking *o* in a moment of inattention; **al menor ~ te puedes salir de la carretera** if your attention wanders *o* if you get distracted, even for a moment, the car can go off the road; **la colisión ocurrió por un ~ del maquinista** the crash was caused by a careless mistake on the part of the driver

desde PREP **1** (*indicando origen*) from; **lo llamaré ~ la oficina** I'll call him from the office; **~ Ávila hasta Madrid** from Ávila to Madrid; **~ abajo** from below; **~ arriba** from above; **~ lejos** from a long way off, from afar (*liter*)
2 (*con cantidades, categorías*) from; **camisetas ~ 10 euros** T-shirts from 10 euros
3 (*en el tiempo*) since; **~ el martes** (= *el pasado*) since Tuesday; (= *el próximo*) after Tuesday; **no existe ~ 1960** it ceased to exist in 1960; **~ ahora** from now on; **¿~ cuándo vives aquí?** how long have you been living here?; **~ entonces** since then; **está lloviendo ~ hace tres días** it's been raining for three days; **~ el 4 hasta el 16** from the 4th until *o* to the 16th; **~ siempre** always
4 ~ luego 4.1 (= *por supuesto*) of course; **eso, ~ luego, no es culpa mía** that, of course, is not my fault; **no era muy morena pero rubia ~ luego que no** she wasn't really dark-haired, but she certainly wasn't blonde **4.2** (*como coletilla*) **~ luego, vaya fama estamos cogiendo** we're certainly getting quite a reputation
5 ~ que since; **~ que llegó no ha salido** he hasn't been out since he arrived; **~ que se inventó la televisión** (ever) since television was invented; **escribo ~ que era pequeña** I've been writing since I was little

desdecir /3o/ **Ⓐ** VI **~ de algo** to be unworthy of sth; **esta novela no desdice de las otras** this novel is well up to the standard of the others **Ⓑ desdecirse** VPR to go back on what one has said; **~se de algo** to go back on sth

desdén SM scorn, disdain

desdentado ADJ toothless

desdeñable ADJ contemptible; **nada ~** far from negligible

desdeñar /1a/ VT **1** (= *despreciar*) to scorn, disdain **2** (= *rechazar*) to turn up one's nose at

desdeñoso ADJ scornful, disdainful

desdibujado ADJ [*contorno*] blurred

desdibujarse /1a/ VPR to get blurred, fade

desdicha SF **1** (= *infelicidad*) unhappiness **2** (= *contratiempo*) misfortune; **tuve ~ de tener que trabajar con él** I was unlucky enough to work with him, I had the misfortune to work with him

desdichado ADJ **1** [*persona*] (= *infeliz*) unhappy; (= *desgraciado*) unlucky **2** [*día*] ill-fated

desdoblamiento SM ➤ **desdoblamiento de la personalidad** split personality

desdoblar /1a/ **Ⓐ** VT (= *desplegar*) [+ *pañuelo*] to unfold; [+ *mantel*] to spread out; [+ *alambre*] to untwist **Ⓑ desdoblarse** VPR to divide, split in two

desdramatizar /1f/ VT [+ *situación*] to take the drama out of; [+ *crisis*] to defuse

deseable ADJ desirable

desear /1a/ VT **1** (= *anhelar*) to want; **sólo deseo que me dejen en paz** I just want to be left in peace; **no deseo que le pase nada malo** I don't wish anything bad to happen to him; **un embarazo no deseado** an unwanted pregnancy; **dejar bastante** *o* **mucho que ~** to leave a lot to be desired; **estar deseando algo: estoy deseando que llegue mi cumpleaños** I'm really looking forward to my birthday, I can't wait for *o* till my birthday; **ser de ~: es de ~ que mejoren nuestras relaciones** an improvement in our relations would be desirable; **no hemos avanzado tanto como sería de ~** we haven't made as much progress as we would have liked
2 (*frm*) **2.1** (*en peticiones, fórmulas de cortesía*) [+ *éxito, suerte*] to wish; **el doctor desea hablar un momento con usted** the doctor wishes to speak to you for a moment; **le deseamos una pronta recuperación** we wish you a prompt recovery **2.2** (*en preguntas, sugerencias*) **si lo desea se lo podemos enviar por correo** if you wish we can send it by mail; **¿qué desean beber?** what would you like to drink?; **¿qué desea?** can I help you?
3 (*sexualmente*) to want

desecar /1g/ VT **1** [+ *fruta, planta*] to dry **2** [+ *lago, terreno*] to drain

desechable ADJ disposable

desechar /1a/ VT **1** (= *tirar*) [+ *basura*] to throw out; [+ *objeto inútil*] to scrap, get rid of **2** (= *rechazar*) [+ *consejo, miedo*] to cast aside; [+ *oferta*] to reject; [+ *plan*] to drop

desecho SM **1** (= *residuo*) **productos de ~** waste products ➤ **desecho de hierro** scrap iron **2 desechos** (= *desperdicios*) (*gen*) rubbish *sing* (*Brit*), garbage *sing* (*EEUU*); [*de la industria*] waste *sing*; [*de ropa*] castoffs; [*de animal*] offal *sing*

desembalar /1a/ VT to unpack

desembarazado ADJ free and easy

desembarazar /1f/ **Ⓐ** VT [+ *camino, cuarto*] to clear; **~ un cuarto de trastos** to clear a room of furniture **Ⓑ desembarazarse** VPR **~se de algo** to get rid of sth

desembarazo SM ease, naturalness

desembarcadero SM quay, landing stage

desembarcar /1g/ **Ⓐ** VT [+ *pasajeros*] to disembark; [+ *mercancías*] to unload **Ⓑ** VI (*de barco, avión*) [*pasajeros*] to disembark; [*tropas*] to land, disembark

desembarco SM [*de pasajeros*] disembarkation; [*de tropas*] landing, disembarkation; [*de mercancías*] unloading

desembocadura SF [*de río*] mouth

desembocar /1g/ VI **1 ~ en** [*río*] to flow into, run into; [*calle*] to join, lead into **2 ~ en** (= *terminar en*) to end in, result in; **esto desembocó en una tragedia** this ended in *o* led to tragedy

desembolsar /1a/ VT **1** (= *pagar*) to pay out **2** (= *gastar*) to lay out

desembolso SM outlay, expenditure

desembragar /1h/ VI to declutch, let out the clutch

desembrollar /1a/ VT **1** [+ *madeja*] to unravel **2** [+ *asunto, malentendido*] to sort out

desembuchar /1a/ Ⓐ VT **1** (*) (= *confesar*) to come out with **2** [*ave*] to regurgitate Ⓑ VI (*) (= spill the beans*; **¡desembucha!** out with it!, spit it out!

desempacar /1g/ VT (*esp LAm*) to unpack

desempañar /1a/ VT [+ *cristal*] (*con trapo*) to wipe clean; [*dispositivo antivaho*] to demist, defog (*EEUU*)

desempaquetar /1a/ VT to unpack, unwrap

desempatar /1a/ VI **van a jugar la prórroga para ver si desempatan** extra time will be played to try and break the deadlock *o* to get a result

desempate SM **1** (*Ftbl*) **el ~ llegó con el gol de Roque** the breakthrough came with Roque's goal; **marcó el gol del ~ en el minuto 15** he put his side ahead *o* broke the deadlock in the 15th minute ➤ **desempate a penaltis** penalty shoot-out **2** (*Tenis*) tie break

desempeñar /1a/ Ⓐ VT **1** [+ *propiedades, joyas*] to redeem, get out of pawn, get out of hock (*EEUU*) **2** (= *llevar a cabo*) [+ *deber, función*] to perform, carry out; [+ *papel*] (*tb Teat*) to play **3** (= *ocupar*) [+ *cargo*] to occupy, hold Ⓑ **desempeñarse** VPR (*LAm*) to get along, get on; **~se como** to act as

desempeño SM [*de deber*] performance, carrying out; [*de cargo*] carrying out; **durante el ~ de sus funciones como presidente** in the course of carrying out *o* performing his duties as president

desempleado/a Ⓐ ADJ unemployed, out of work Ⓑ SM/F unemployed man/woman; **los ~s** the unemployed

desempleo SM **1** (= *falta de trabajo*) unemployment **2** (= *subsidio*) unemployment benefit

desempolvar /1a/ VT **1** [+ *libros, muebles*] to dust; [+ *objeto no usado*] to dust off **2** [+ *recuerdos*] to revive

desencadenante Ⓐ ADJ **los factores ~s del accidente** the factors which triggered (off) *o* caused the accident Ⓑ SM cause, trigger

desencadenar /1a/ Ⓐ VT **1** (= *quitar las cadenas de*) [+ *prisionero*] to unchain; [+ *perro*] to unleash **2** (= *desatar*) [+ *ira*] to unleash; [+ *crisis*] to trigger, set off Ⓑ **desencadenarse** VPR **1** (= *soltarse*) to break loose **2** (= *estallar*) [*tormenta*] to burst; [*guerra*] to break out; **se desencadenó una violenta reacción** a violent reaction was unleashed

desencajado ADJ [*cara*] twisted, contorted; [*mandíbula*] dislocated; [*ojos*] wild

desencajar /1a/ Ⓐ VT **1** [+ *hueso*] to throw out of joint; [+ *mandíbula*] to dislocate **2** (*Mec*) to disconnect, disengage Ⓑ **desencajarse** VPR [*cara*] to become distorted *o* contorted; [*ojos*] to look wild; **se le desencajó la mandíbula** he dislocated his jaw

desencaminado ADJ **no vas muy ~** you're not far wrong there

desencanto SM disillusion, disillusionment, disenchantment

desenchufar /1a/ VT to unplug, disconnect

desencolarse /1a/ VPR to come unstuck

desencontrarse /1n/ VPR (*Arg, Col*) to fail to meet up, miss each other; **nos desencontramos** we missed each other

desencuadernar /1a/ Ⓐ VT to unbind Ⓑ **desencuadernarse** VPR to come unbound

desencuentro SM misunderstanding

desenfadado ADJ **1** [*aire, carácter*] free, uninhibited **2** [*persona*] (= *despreocupado*) free-and-easy, carefree; (= *desenvuelto*) self-confident; (*en el vestir*) casual

desenfado SM **1** (= *despreocupación*) free-and-easy manner **2** (= *libertad*) freedom, lack of inhibition **3** (= *desenvoltura*) self-confidence

desenfocado ADJ out of focus

desenfocar /1g/ Ⓐ VT to get out of focus Ⓑ **desenfocarse** VPR to go out of focus

desenfrenado ADJ [*persona*] wild, uncontrolled; [*apetito, pasiones*] unbridled

desenfreno SM abandon

desenfundar /1a/ VT [+ *pistola*] to pull out, draw

desenganchar /1a/ Ⓐ VT (= *soltar*) [+ *cortinas*] to unhook; [+ *vagones*] to uncouple; [+ *caballo*] to unhitch Ⓑ **desengancharse*** VPR to kick the habit*; **~se de algo** to come off sth

desengañado ADJ disillusioned

desengañar /1a/ Ⓐ VT **1** (= *desilusionar*) to disillusion; **es mejor no ~la** it is best not to take away her hopes *o* not to disillusion her **2** (= *decepcionar*) to disappoint **3** (= *abrir los ojos a*) to open the eyes of Ⓑ **desengañarse** VPR **1** (= *desilusionarse*) to become disillusioned (**de** about) **2** (= *decepcionarse*) to be disappointed **3** (= *abrir los ojos*) to see the light, see things as they really are; **¡desengáñate!** wise up!*

desengaño SM **1** (= *desilusión*) disillusion, disillusionment; **los ~s te enseñarán** you'll learn the hard way **2** (= *decepción*) disappointment; **sufrir un ~ amoroso** to be disappointed in love

desengrasado ADJ [*máquina*] rusty, needing oil

desengrasar /1a/ VT to degrease

desenlace SM [*de libro, película*] ending, dénouement (*frm*); [*de aventura*] outcome

desenmarañar /1a/ VT **1** [+ *cuerda, lana, pelo*] to untangle, disentangle **2** [+ *misterio*] to unravel, clear up

desenmascarar /1a/ VT to unmask

desenredar /1a/ Ⓐ VT **1** [+ *pelo, lana*] to untangle, disentangle **2** [+ *dificultad, problema*] to straighten out Ⓑ **desenredarse** VPR (*de un problema*) to extricate o.s. (**de** from)

desenrollar /1a/ Ⓐ VT [+ *alfombra*] to unroll; [+ *cable*] to unwind Ⓑ **desenrollarse** VPR [*alfombra*] to unroll; [*cable*] to unwind

desenroscar /1g/ VT [+ *tornillo*] to unscrew

desensillar /1a/ VT to unsaddle

desentenderse /2g/ VPR **~ de algo** to wash one's hands of sth, want nothing to do with sth

desentendido/a SM/F **hacerse el ~** to pretend not to notice

desenterrar /1j/ VT **1** [+ *cadáver*] to exhume; [+ *tesoro*] to unearth **2** [+ *recuerdo, odio*] to rake up

desentonado ADJ (*Mús*) out of tune

desentonar /1a/ VI **1** (= *no encajar*) [*persona, comentario*] to be out of place; [*colores*] to clash (**con** with); **para no ~** so as to do the right thing, so as to fall into line; **el edificio desentona con el entorno** the building doesn't fit in with the surroundings **2** (*Mús*) to be out of tune

desentrañar /1a/ VT [+ *misterio*] to get to the bottom of, unravel; [+ *significado*] to puzzle out

desentrenado ADJ untrained

desentumecer /2d/ Ⓐ VT [+ *miembro*] to stretch; [+ *músculos*] to loosen up Ⓑ **desentumecerse** VPR to loosen up

desenvainar /1a/ VT [+ *espada*] to draw, unsheathe

desenvoltura SF **1** (= *facilidad*) (*al moverse*) ease; (*al hablar*) fluency **2** (= *falta de timidez*) confidence, self-confidence

desenvolver /2h/ (*pp* **desenvuelto**) Ⓐ VT [+ *paquete*] to unwrap; [+ *rollo*] to unwind, unroll Ⓑ **desenvolverse** VPR **1** [*persona*] to manage; **se desenvolvió muy bien como entrevistador** he did *o* managed very well as an interviewer **2** [*acción, suceso*] (= *suceder*) to go off; (= *desarrollarse*) to develop

desenvuelto Ⓐ PP *de* **desenvolver** Ⓑ ADJ **1** (= *falto de timidez*) confident, self-confident **2** (*al hablar*) fluent

deseo SM **1** (= *anhelo*) wish; **pedir** *o* **formular un ~** to make a wish; **su último ~ fue que la incineraran** her dying wish was to be cremated; **ardo en ~s de conocerla** (*liter*) I have a burning desire to meet her **2** (*tb ~ sexual*) desire

deseoso ADJ **estar ~ de hacer algo** to be anxious *o* eager to do sth

desequilibrado ADJ [persona] unbalanced

desequilibrar /1a/ Ⓐ VT 1 [+ barca, mueble] to unbalance, make unbalanced 2 [+ persona] (físicamente) to throw off balance; (psicológicamente) to unbalance 3 ~ un país/régimen to destabilize a country/regime Ⓑ **desequilibrarse** VPR [balanza] to get out of balance; [persona] to become mentally unbalanced

desequilibrio SM 1 (entre cantidades) imbalance 2 (Med) unbalanced mental condition

deserción SF 1 (Mil) desertion 2 (Pol) defection

desertar /1a/ VI to desert; ~ de to desert

desértico ADJ 1 (= del desierto) desert antes de s 2 (= árido) desert-like, barren 3 (= despoblado) deserted

desertizar /1f/ VT to turn into a desert

desertor(a) SM/F deserter

desescolarizado ADJ niños ~s children deprived of schooling

desesperación SF 1 (= pérdida de esperanza) despair, desperation 2 (= resultado) es una ~ it's maddening

desesperada SF hacer algo a la ~ to do sth as a last resort o in desperation

desesperado/a Ⓐ ADJ 1 (= sin esperanza) [persona] desperate; [caso, situación] hopeless 2 [esfuerzo] furious, frenzied Ⓑ SM/F como un ~ like crazy

desesperante ADJ [situación] infuriating; [persona] infuriating, hopeless

desesperar /1a/ Ⓐ VT mi hermano me desespera my brother drives me crazy, my brother is infuriating o maddening
Ⓑ VI to despair, lose hope; no desesperes don't despair o lose hope; ~ por hacer algo (frm) to despair of doing sth, lose all hope of doing sth
Ⓒ **desesperarse** VPR 1 (= exasperarse) me desespero con tanto trabajo all this work is driving me crazy 2 (= desalentarse) to despair, lose hope

desespero SM (LAm) despair, desperation

desestabilizar /1f/ VT to destabilize

desestimar /1a/ VT [+ demanda, moción] to reject

desexilio SM (CS) return from exile, return home

desfachatez SF 1 (= descaro) brazenness, cheek* 2 una ~ a cheeky (Brit*) o sassy (EEUU*) remark

desfalco SM embezzlement

desfallecer /2d/ VI 1 (= perder las fuerzas) to get weak; ~ de ánimo to lose heart 2 (= desmayarse) to faint

desfallecido ADJ weak; estar ~ de hambre to be weak with hunger

desfasado ADJ behind the times

desfasar /1a/ VT 1 (= dejar anticuado) to phase out 2 (Elec) to change the phase of

desfase SM gap ➤ desfase horario jet lag

desfavorable ADJ unfavourable, unfavorable (EEUU)

desfavorecer /2d/ VT estas medidas ~án a los pequeños agricultores these measures will hurt small farmers o go against the interests of small farmers

desfavorecido ADJ 1 (= discriminado) disadvantaged 2 (= afeado) siempre salgo ~ en las fotos I never look good in photos

desfigurar /1a/ VT [+ cara] to disfigure; [+ cuerpo] to deform; [+ cuadro, monumento] to deface; [+ voz, sonido] to distort, disguise; [+ sentido] to twist

desfiladero SM narrow mountain pass

desfilar /1a/ VI 1 (Mil) to parade; ~on ante el general they marched past the general 2 (= pasar) to come, pass by; por su despacho han desfilado muchos acreedores many creditors have passed through his office 3 [modelo] to model

desfile SM 1 (Mil) parade ➤ desfile aéreo flyby 2 [de carrozas] procession 3 ➤ desfile de modas, desfile de modelos fashion show, fashion parade

desfiscalizar /1f/ VT to exempt from taxation

desflorar /1a/ VT to deflower

desfogar /1h/ Ⓐ VT [+ cólera, frustración] to vent (con, en on) Ⓑ **desfogarse** VPR (de estrés) to let off steam*; (de enfado) to get it out of one's system

desforestación SF deforestation

desgajar /1a/ VT [+ naranja] to split into segments

desgana SF (= falta de apetito) lack of appetite; (= apatía) unwillingness, reluctance; hacer algo a o con ~ to do sth unwillingly o reluctantly

desganado ADJ 1 (= sin apetito) not hungry; estar o sentirse ~ to have no appetite 2 (= sin entusiasmo) half-hearted

desgano SM (Col, RPl) = desgana

desgañitarse* /1a/ VPR to yell one's head off*

desgarbado ADJ [movimiento] clumsy, ungainly; [persona] gawky

desgarrador ADJ [escena, noticia] heartbreaking, heartrending; [grito] piercing; [emoción] heartrending

desgarrar /1a/ VT 1 [+ vestido, papel] to tear, rip 2 [+ corazón] to break

desgarro SM 1 (en tela, papel) tear, rip 2 (Med) sprain

desgastar /1a/ Ⓐ VT 1 [+ tejido, moqueta, neumático] to wear out; [+ tacones, suela] to wear down; [+ superficie] to wear away 2 [+ rival, contrincante] to wear down Ⓑ VI (= debilitar) veinte años de poder desgastan after twenty years in power you get stale o run out of steam Ⓒ **desgastarse** VPR [tejido, neumático] to wear out; [tacones, suela, grada] to wear down; [superficie, roca] to wear away

desgaste SM 1 [de ropa, zapatos, neumático] wear; [de superficie, roca] wearing away, erosion 2 (= agotamiento) su larga enfermedad provocó un ~ en su organismo her long illness exhausted her physically

desglosar /1a/ VT 1 [+ cantidades, cifras] to break down 2 [+ impreso] to detach

desglose SM breakdown

desgobierno SM (Pol) misgovernment, misrule

desgracia SF 1 (= revés) misfortune; la familia ha sufrido una serie de ~s the family has suffered a series of misfortunes; ha ocurrido una ~ something terrible has happened; por ~ unfortunately; ha muerto, ¡qué ~! she has died, what a terrible thing (to happen)! ➤ desgracias personales (= víctimas) casualties 2 caer en ~ to lose favour o (EEUU) favor, fall from favour o (EEUU) favor

desgraciadamente ADV unfortunately, unluckily

desgraciado/a Ⓐ ADJ 1 [persona] (= sin suerte, infeliz) unlucky; fue ~ en su matrimonio he was unhappy in his marriage 2 [vida, existencia] una vida desgraciada a wretched life, a life of misery 3 [accidente, situación] unfortunate; una desgraciada elección an unfortunate choice Ⓑ SM/F 1 (= infeliz) poor wretch 2 (= miserable) swine*

desgraciar /1b/ VT to ruin

desgranar /1a/ VT [+ trigo] to thresh; [+ guisantes] to shell; ~ un racimo de uvas to pick the grapes from a bunch; ~ las cuentas del rosario to tell one's beads

desgravable ADJ tax-deductible

desgravación SF ➤ desgravación de impuestos, desgravación fiscal tax deduction

desgravar /1a/ Ⓐ VT tener un plan de pensiones puede ~ un 10% you can claim a 10% tax deduction if you have a pension plan Ⓑ VI to be tax-deductible

desguace SM 1 (= despiece) [de barco] breaking-up, scrapping; [de coche] scrapping 2 (= lugar) scrapyard

desguarnecer /2d/ VT (Mil) [+ pueblo] to remove the garrison from; [+ plaza fuerte] to dismantle

desguazar /1f/ VT [+ barco] to break up, scrap; [+ coche, avión] to scrap

deshabillé [desabiʎe] SM negligee

deshabitado ADJ [edificio] empty, vacant; [zona, ciudad] uninhabited

deshabituar /1e/ Ⓐ VT ~ a algn de la droga to get sb off drugs **B** **deshabituarse** VPR **1** (*de costumbre*) to get out of the habit **2** **~se de la droga** to kick one's drug habit, conquer one's drug addiction

deshacer /2r/ (*pp* **deshecho**) **A** VT **1** (= *separar*) [+ *nudo, lazo*] to untie, undo; [+ *costura*] to unpick; [+ *fila, corro*] to break up **2** (= *desarreglar*) [+ *maleta*] to unpack; [+ *rompecabezas*] to break up; [+ *paquete*] to undo, unwrap; [+ *cama*] (*al dormir*) to mess up; (*para cambiar las sábanas*) to strip; **deshacía una y otra vez su peinado** she kept redoing her hair; **puede hacer y ~ a su antojo** she is free to do as she wishes; **la cama estaba sin ~** the bed hadn't been slept in **3** (= *derretir*) [+ *nieve, helado*] to melt **4** (= *disolver*) [+ *pastilla, grumos*] to dissolve; (= *desmenuzar*) [+ *bizcocho, pastel, cubito de caldo*] to crumble; **~ algo en agua** to dissolve sth in water **5** (= *estropear*) [+ *vista, proyecto, vida*] to ruin; **la marea deshizo los castillos de arena** the tide washed away *o* broke up our sandcastles **6** [+ *persona*] to shatter **7** [+ *contrato, alianza, acuerdo*] (= *romper*) to break; (= *cancelar*) to annul **8** (= *enmendar*) [+ *agravio*] to right, put right; [+ *equívoco, malentendido*] to resolve; ✦ MODISMO **~ el camino** to retrace one's steps **B** **deshacerse** VPR **1** (= *separarse*) [*nudo*] to come undone, come untied; [*costura*] to come undone, split; [*moño, trenza*] to come undone **2** (= *romperse*) to smash, shatter; **el libro se le deshizo en las manos** the book came apart in his hands; **cuando lo levanté, se me deshizo todo** when I lifted it up it all fell to pieces **3** (= *derretirse*) [*caramelo, hielo*] to melt **4** (= *desmembrarse*) [*organización, manifestación*] to break up **5** **~se de** (*queriendo*) to get rid of; (*sin querer*) to part with; (*Dep*) to dispose of; (*Com*) to dump; **no quiero ~me de eso** I don't want to part with that **6** (= *esforzarse*) **se deshace trabajando** he works incredibly hard; **~se en:** **~se en elogios con algn** to be full of praise for sb, shower sb with praise; **~se en lágrimas** to burst *o* dissolve into tears

desharrapado ADJ ragged

deshecho **A** PP *de* **deshacer** **B** ADJ **1** [*lazo, nudo*] undone; [*cama*] unmade **2** [*objeto*] broken, smashed **3** [*persona*] **estoy ~*** I'm shattered (*Brit**), I'm pooped (*EEUU***); **llegó con los nervios ~s** his nerves were shattered when he arrived

deshelar /1j/ **A** VT [+ *tubería*] to thaw; [+ *congelador*] to defrost; [+ *avión, coche*] to de-ice **B** **deshelarse** VPR [*nieve*] to thaw, melt; [*río, lago*] to thaw

desheredar /1a/ VT to disinherit

deshidratación SF dehydration

deshidratar /1a/ **A** VT to dehydrate **B** **deshidratarse** VPR to become dehydrated

deshielo SM [*de nieve*] thaw; [*de congelador*] defrosting ➤ **deshielo diplomático** diplomatic thaw

deshilachado ADJ frayed

deshilachar /1a/ **A** VT to fray **B** **deshilacharse** VPR to fray

deshilvanado ADJ [*historia, trama*] disjointed, incoherent

deshilvanar /1a/ VT (*Cos*) to untack, take the stitches out of

deshinchar /1a/ **A** VT **1** [+ *neumático*] to let down **2** (*Med*) to reduce the swelling of **B** **deshincharse** VPR **1** [*neumático*] to go down, go flat **2** (*Med*) to go down

deshojar /1a/ VT [+ *árbol*] to strip the leaves off; [+ *flor*] to pull the petals off

deshollinador(a) SM/F chimney sweep

deshonesto ADJ **1** (= *no honrado*) dishonest **2** (= *indecente*) indecent

deshonor SM **1** (= *pérdida del honor*) dishonour, dishonor (*EEUU*), disgrace **2 un ~** an insult, an affront (**a** to)

deshonra SF dishonour, dishonor (*EEUU*), disgrace

deshonrar /1a/ VT **1** [+ *familia, compañeros*] to dishonour,

dishonor (*EEUU*), disgrace **2** (= *afrentar*) to insult **3** (*euf*) [+ *mujer*] to dishonour, dishonor (*EEUU*)

deshonroso ADJ dishonourable, dishonorable (*EEUU*), disgraceful

deshora SF **a ~(s)** at an inconvenient time; **acostarse a ~(s)** to go to bed at some unearthly hour; **comer a ~(s)** to eat at odd times; **llegar a ~(s)** to turn up unexpectedly

deshuesadero SM (*Méx*) scrapyard

deshuesado ADJ [*aceituna*] pitted

deshumanizante ADJ dehumanizing

deshumanizar /1f/ VT to dehumanize

desidia SF idleness

desierto **A** ADJ **1** [*isla, región*] desert *antes de s*; [*paisaje*] bleak, desolate; [*calle, casa*] deserted **2 declarar ~** [+ *oposiciones, premio*] to declare void **B** SM desert

designación SF **1** (*para un cargo*) appointment **2** (= *nombre*) designation

designar /1a/ VT **1** (= *nombrar*) to appoint, designate; **el dictador designó a su sucesor** the dictator appointed *o* designated his successor; **han designado a Sevilla sede del campeonato** Seville has been designated as the host city for the championship **2** (= *fijar*) [+ *fecha*] to fix, set **3** (*frm*) (= *denominar*) **la palabra "rosa" designa a una flor** the word "rose" denotes a flower

designio SM plan, design; **los ~s divinos** divine intentions

desigual ADJ **1** (= *diferente*) different; **las mangas de la chaqueta me han salido ~es** the sleeves of my jacket have come out different sizes; **los ciudadanos reciben un trato ~** people are treated differently, people are not treated equally *o* the same **2** [*lucha, batalla*] unequal **3** (= *irregular*) [*terreno, calidad*] uneven; [*letra*] erratic; **los resultados del alumno son muy ~es** the pupil's results vary widely *o* are not at all consistent

desigualar /1a/ VT **1** [+ *flequillo*] to make uneven; [+ *poderes, capacidades*] to unbalance **2** (*Dep*) to alter the balance of

desigualdad SF (*Econ, Pol*) inequality

desilusión SF **1** (= *decepción*) disappointment; **me llevé una gran ~ cuando lo vi** I was very disappointed when I saw him **2** (= *pérdida de ilusiones*) disillusion, disillusionment

desilusionado ADJ disillusioned

desilusionar /1a/ **A** VT **1** (= *decepcionar*) to disappoint **2** (= *hacer perder las ilusiones a*) to disillusion **B** **desilusionarse** VPR **1** (= *decepcionarse*) to be disappointed **2** (= *desengañarse*) to get disillusioned

desincrustar /1a/ VT to descale (*Brit*), remove the fur from (*EEUU*)

desinencia SF (*Ling*) ending

desinfectante ADJ, SM disinfectant

desinfectar /1a/ VT to disinfect

desinfestar /1a/ VT to decontaminate

desinflado ADJ [*neumático*] flat

desinflar /1a/ **A** VT [+ *neumático*] to let down **B** **desinflarse** VPR [*neumático*] to go down, go flat

desinformación SF **1** (= *información engañosa*) disinformation, misleading information, black propaganda **2** (= *ignorancia*) ignorance, lack of information

desinformar /1a/ VT to misinform

desinhibido ADJ uninhibited

desinhibir /3a/ **A** VT to free from inhibitions **B** **desinhibirse** VPR to lose one's inhibitions

desintegración SF **1** [*de estructura*] disintegration; [*de grupo*] break-up **2** [*de átomo*] splitting

desintegrar /1a/ **A** VT **1** [+ *grupo*] to break up **2** [+ *roca, cohete*] to disintegrate **3** [+ *átomo*] to split **B** **desintegrarse** VPR **1** [*grupo*] to break up **2** [*roca, cohete*] to disintegrate **3** [*átomo*] to split

desinterés SM **1** (= *falta de interés*) lack of interest

2 (= *altruismo*) unselfishness

desinteresado ADJ **1** (= *altruista*) unselfish **2** (= *imparcial*) disinterested

desinteresarse /1a/ VPR to lose interest (**de, por** in)

desintoxicación SF detoxification, disintoxication

desintoxicar /1g/ ⓐ VT **1** (*de toxinas*) to detoxify **2** (*de drogas*) to put sb through detox ⓑ **desintoxicarse** VPR (= *completar un tratamiento*) to undergo detoxification, go through detox; (= *empezar un tratamiento*) to go into detox

desistir /3a/ VI to cease, desist (*frm*); **no desistió en su empeño** she did not cease in *o* (*frm*) desist from her efforts; **~ de algo** to give up sth; **~ de hacer algo** to desist from *o* give up doing sth

---

Recuérdese que las preposiciones en inglés rigen gerundio y no infinitivo, de ahí **to desist from doing sth**. **Give up** también rige gerundio.

---

deslave SM (*Méx*) landslide, rockfall

desleal ADJ **1** (= *infiel*) disloyal (**a, con** to) **2** (*Com*) [*competencia*] unfair

deslealtad SF **1** (= *falta de lealtad*) (*gen*) disloyalty **2** (*Com*) [*de competencia*] unfairness

desleír /3l/ ⓐ VT [+ *sustancia, materia*] to dissolve; [+ *líquido*] to dilute ⓑ **desleírse** VPR **1** (*en un líquido*) to dissolve **2** [*líquido*] to become diluted

deslenguado ADJ foul-mouthed

deslindar /1a/ VT **1** [+ *terreno*] to mark out, mark the limits *o* boundaries of **2** (= *definir*) to define

desliz SM slip; **los deslices de la juventud** the indiscretions of youth

deslizar /1f/ ⓐ VT **deslicé la carta por debajo de la puerta** I slipped *o* slid the letter under the door ⓑ **deslizarse** VPR **1** (= *resbalarse*) to slide; **gotas de sudor se deslizaban por su frente** beads of sweat ran *o* slid down his forehead **2** (= *avanzar*) [*serpiente*] to slither; [*barco*] to glide, slip; **la patinadora se deslizaba elegantemente** the skater was gliding along

deslomar /1a/ ⓐ VT (*lit*) to break the back of; (*fig*) to wear out ⓑ **deslomarse** VPR (*) to work one's tail off

deslucido ADJ **1** (= *sin brillo*) [*metal*] tarnished; [*mármol*] worn, faded **2** (= *aburrido*) dull, lacklustre, lackluster (*EEUU*); **hizo un papel ~** he gave a lacklustre performance

deslucir /3f/ VT **1** [+ *mármol*] to fade; [+ *metal*] to tarnish **2** (= *estropear*) to spoil, ruin

deslumbrante ADJ dazzling

deslumbrar /1a/ VT **1** (*con la luz*) to dazzle **2** (= *impresionar*) to dazzle

deslustrar /1a/ VT **1** [+ *vidrio*] to frost; [+ *loza*] to remove the glaze from **2** [+ *reputación*] to sully, tarnish

desmadejado ADJ worn; **~ en un sofá delante de la televisión** slumped on a sofa in front of the TV

desmadrado* ADJ **está muy ~ últimamente** he's been pretty wild recently*

desmadrarse* /1a/ VPR **1** (= *descontrolarse*) to get out of control, go wild* **2** (= *divertirse*) to let one's hair down* **3** (= *excederse*) **los precios se han desmadrado** prices have gone right through the roof

desmadre* SM **1** (= *exceso*) excess; **esto va de ~ total** this is really getting out of hand **2** (= *confusión*) chaos **3** (= *juerga*) blast*, rave-up (*Brit**)

desmalezar /1f/ VT (*LAm*) to weed

desmán SM **1** (= *exceso*) excess **2** (= *ultraje*) outrage

desmanchar /1a/ VT (*LAm*) to clean, remove the spots *o* stains from

desmandarse /1a/ VPR **1** (= *descontrolarse*) to get out of hand **2** [*caballo*] to bolt, run away

desmano: **a ~** ADV out of the way; **me pilla a ~** it's not on my way

desmantelar /1a/ VT **1** (= *desmontar*) [+ *base, fábrica*] to dismantle; [+ *máquina*] to strip down; [+ *andamio*] to take

down; [+ *casa*] to strip of its contents **2** [+ *organización*] to disband **3** (*Náut*) to unrig

desmañado ADJ **1** (= *torpe*) clumsy **2** (= *lento*) slow

desmaquillador SM make-up remover

desmaquillarse /1a/ VPR to remove one's make-up

desmarcarse /1g/ VPR **1** (*Dep*) to shake off one's attacker, get clear **2** (= *distanciarse*) to distance oneself (**de** from)

desmasificar /1g/ VT [+ *cárceles, hospitales*] to reduce overcrowding in; **~ la universidad** to reduce student numbers

desmayado ADJ (*Med*) unconscious

desmayar /1a/ ⓐ VI [*persona*] to lose heart ⓑ **desmayarse** VPR (*Med*) to faint

desmayo SM **1** (*Med*) faint, fainting fit; **le dio un ~** he fainted **2** (= *languidez*) [*de voz*] faltering; [*del cuerpo*] languidness, limpness; **hablar con ~** to talk in a small voice, speak falteringly

desmedido ADJ **1** [*tamaño, importancia*] (= *excesivo*) excessive; (= *desproporcionado*) out of all proportion **2** [*ambición*] boundless

desmedirse /3k/ VPR to go too far

desmejorado ADJ **está muy desmejorada** she's not looking at all well

desmelenarse* /1a/ VPR to let one's hair down*

desmembración SF, **desmembramiento** SM **1** [*de cadáver, país*] dismemberment **2** [*de partido*] break-up

desmembrar /1j/ ⓐ VT **1** [+ *cadáver, país*] to dismember **2** [+ *partido*] to break up ⓑ **desmembrarse** VPR **1** [*país*] to break up **2** [*partido*] to fall apart

desmemoriado ADJ forgetful

desmentido SM denial

desmentir /3i/ VT [+ *acusación*] to deny, refute; [+ *rumor*] to scotch, squelch (*EEUU*); [+ *carácter, orígenes*] to belie

desmenuzable ADJ crumbly

desmenuzar /1f/ ⓐ VT **1** (*Culin*) [+ *pan*] to crumble; [+ *pescado*] to flake **2** (= *examinar*) to examine minutely ⓑ **desmenuzarse** VPR to crumble

desmerecedor ADJ undeserving

desmerecer /2d/ VI **~ de algo** to compare unfavourably *o* (*EEUU*) unfavorably with sth; **éste no desmerece de sus otros diseños** this is every bit as good as his earlier designs

desmesurado ADJ **1** (= *desproporcionado*) disproportionate **2** (= *enorme*) [*ambición*] boundless; [*dimensiones*] enormous

desmigajar /1a/ ⓐ VT to crumble ⓑ **desmigajarse** VPR to crumble

desmigar /1h/ VT = **desmigajar**

desmilitarizar /1f/ VT to demilitarize

desmineralizar /1f/ VT to demineralize

desmitificar /1g/ VT to demythologize

desmochar /1a/ VT [+ *árbol*] to pollard, cut the top off; [+ *cuernos*] to blunt, file down

desmontable ADJ [*mueble, estantería*] which can be taken apart; [*pieza*] detachable

desmontar /1a/ ⓐ VT [+ *mueble, estantería*] to take apart; [+ *motor*] to strip down; [+ *tienda de campaña*] to take down ⓑ VI to dismount, alight (**de** from)

desmoralizar /1f/ ⓐ VT to demoralize ⓑ **desmoralizarse** VPR to lose heart, get demoralized

desmoronamiento SM crumbling, collapse

desmoronarse /1a/ VPR [*montaña, casa*] to crumble; [*persona*] to go to pieces

desmotivado ADJ unmotivated, lacking motivation

desnacionalizar /1f/ VT to denationalize

desnatado ADJ [*leche*] skimmed, low-fat

desnaturalizado ADJ **1** (*Quím*) denatured; **alcohol ~** methylated spirits *sing* **2** [*persona*] unnatural

desnivel SM **1** [*de terreno*] drop **2** (= *diferencia*) difference (**entre** between) **3** (*Pol, Sociol*) inequality

desnivelado ADJ **1** [*terreno*] uneven **2** (= *desequilibrado*) unbalanced

desnivelar /1a/ VT [+ *composición*] to upset, unbalance; [+ *balanza*] to tip

desnucarse /1g/ VPR to break one's neck

desnuclearizado ADJ **región desnuclearizada** nuclear-free area

desnudar /1a/ Ⓐ VT to undress; **él la desnudaba con la mirada** he was undressing her with his eyes Ⓑ **desnudarse** VPR to undress, get undressed; **~se de cintura para arriba** to strip to the waist

desnudez SF nakedness, nudity

desnudo Ⓐ ADJ **1** (= *sin ropa*) [*persona*] naked; [*cuerpo*] naked, bare; **cavar con las manos desnudas** to dig with one's bare hands **2** (= *sin adorno*) [*árbol, pared*] bare; [*paisaje*] bare, featureless **3** (= *puro*) [*verdad*] plain, naked; [*estilo*] unadorned Ⓑ SM **1** (*Arte*) nude ➤ **desnudo integral** full-frontal nudity **2 poner al ~** to lay bare

desnutrición SF malnutrition, undernourishment

desnutrido ADJ undernourished

desobedecer /2d/ VT, VI to disobey

desobediencia SF disobedience ➤ **desobediencia civil** civil disobedience

desobediente ADJ disobedient

desocupación SF **1** (*esp LAm*) (= *desempleo*) unemployment **2** [*de local*] clearance, clearing

desocupado ADJ **1** (= *libre*) [*asiento*] empty; [*casa*] unoccupied; [*mesa en restaurante*] free **2** (= *sin hacer nada*) free, not busy; (= *sin empleo*) unemployed

desocupar /1a/ Ⓐ VT **1** (= *vaciar*) [+ *casa*] to vacate, move out of **2** (= *desalojar*) [+ *fábrica, sala*] to clear, clear out Ⓑ **desocuparse** VPR to be free; **cuando me desocupe, te llamo** I'll call you when I'm free; **se ha desocupado aquella mesa** that table's free now

desodorante SM deodorant ➤ **desodorante de ambientes** (*RPI*) air freshener

desoír /3p/ VT to ignore, disregard

desolado ADJ **1** [*lugar*] desolate **2** [*persona*] devastated

desolador ADJ [*imagen*] heartbreaking, heartrending; [*noticia*] devastating, distressing; [*paisaje*] bleak, cheerless

desolar /1a/ VT [+ *ciudad, poblado*] to devastate, lay waste (to) (*liter*)

desollar /1l/ VT **1** (= *quitar la piel a*) to skin, flay **2 ~ vivo a algn** (= *hacer pagar*) to fleece sb; (= *criticar*) to tear sb to pieces

desorbitado ADJ **1** (= *excesivo*) [*precio*] exorbitant; [*pretensión*] exaggerated **2 con los ojos ~s** popeyed

desorbitante ADJ excessive, overwhelming

desorbitar /1a/ Ⓐ VT (= *exagerar*) to exaggerate; (= *interpretar mal*) to get out of perspective Ⓑ **desorbitarse** VPR [*asunto*] to get out of hand

desorden SM **1** (= *falta de orden*) [*de objetos, ideas*] chaos; [*de casa, habitación*] mess, untidiness; **no puedo encontrar nada entre tanto ~** I can't find anything amid all this chaos; **en ~** [*gente*] in confusion; [*objetos*] in a mess, in disorder (*más frm*) **2 desórdenes** (= *alborotos*) disturbances; (= *excesos*) excesses; (*Med*) disorders

desordenado ADJ [*habitación, persona*] untidy, messy; [*objetos*] in a mess, jumbled

desordenar /1a/ VT [+ *cajón, armario*] to mess up; [+ *habitación*] to make untidy, mess up; [+ *papeles*] to jumble up

desorganización SF disorganization

desorganizar /1f/ VT to disorganize

desorientado ADJ **1** (= *perdido*) **estoy algo ~** I've lost my bearings **2** [*juventud*] disorientated, disoriented (*esp EEUU*)

desorientar /1a/ Ⓐ VT to disorientate, disorient (*esp EEUU*) Ⓑ **desorientarse** VPR to lose one's way, lose one's bearings

desovar /1l/ VI [*pez, anfibio*] to spawn; [*insecto*] to lay eggs

despabilado ADJ **1** (= *despierto*) wide awake **2** (*) (= *listo*) sharp, quick

despabilar /1a/ Ⓐ VT (= *despertar*) to wake up Ⓑ VI **1** (= *despertar*) to wake up **2** (*) (= *estar alerta*) to wake up; **despabila o te engañarán siempre** wake up, or you'll always end up being taken for a ride* **3** (*) (= *apresurarse*) to hurry up, get a move on*; **despabila si no quieres llegar tarde** better hurry up o get a move on* or you'll be late **4** (*And*) (= *pestañear*) to blink Ⓒ **despabilarse** VPR **1** (= *despertarse*) to wake up **2** (*) (= *estar alerta*) to wake up **3** (*) (= *apresurarse*) to hurry up, get a move on*

despachante SMF (*CS*) (*tb ~ de aduanas*) customs officer

despachar /1a/ Ⓐ VT **1** (= *atender*) [+ *problema, asunto*] to deal with; [+ *correspondencia*] to deal with, see to; **quisiera dejar despachado este asunto hoy** I would like to get this matter settled o out of the way today **2** (= *terminar*) **2.1** [+ *informe, negocio*] to finish **2.2** (*) [+ *libro, tarea*] to knock off*; [+ *comida*] to dispose of*; [+ *bebida*] to knock back* **3** (= *vender*) [+ *fruta, entrada*] to sell **4** (= *servir*) to serve Ⓑ VI **1** [*dependiente*] to serve; [*establecimiento*] to be open (for business); **a partir de las cinco no despachan** they are not open (for business) after five **2** (*Esp*) (*en reunión*) ~ **con** (*gen*) to have a meeting with; [+ *asesor, abogado*] to consult (with); ~ **sobre algo** to discuss sth Ⓒ **despacharse** VPR **1** (*Esp**) (= *criticar*) ~**se bien** o **a gusto con algn** (*delante de algn*) to give sb a piece of one's mind; (*a espaldas de algn*) to really lay into sb*; **se despachó a gusto en su crítica de la película** he didn't pull his punches in his review of the film, he really laid into the film* **2** (*) (= *terminar*) [+ *libro, tarea*] to knock off; [+ *comida*] to dispose of*; [+ *bebida*] to knock back*

despacho SM **1** (= *oficina*) [*de abogado, arquitecto*] office; (*en una casa*) study; **una mesa de ~** an office desk **2** (= *tienda*) shop (*esp Brit*), store (*EEUU*) ➤ **despacho de billetes, despacho de boletos** (*LAm*) booking office ➤ **despacho de lotería** lottery ticket outlet ➤ **despacho de pan** bakery **3** (= *mensaje*) (*Periodismo*) report; (*Mil*) dispatch; (*Pol*) communiqué **4** (= *venta*) sale; **los domingos no hay ~ de billetes** there are no ticket sales on Sundays **5** (= *envío*) dispatch, sending (out)

despachurrar /1a/ VT to crush, squash

despacio ADV **1** (= *lentamente*) slowly; **¿puede hablar más ~?** can you speak more slowly? **2** (= *silenciosamente*) **salí ~ para no molestar a nadie** I left quietly so as not to disturb anybody **3** (= *suavemente*) gently; **llamó ~ a la puerta** he knocked gently at the door

despacioso ADJ (*LAm*) slow

despacito ADV **1** (= *lentamente*) slowly; **¡despacito!** nice and slowly!; ✦ MODISMO ~ **y buena letra** easy does it **2** (= *suavemente*) softly

despampanante ADJ [*chica*] stunning

despancar /1g/ VT (*And*) to husk

despanzurrar /1a/ Ⓐ VT to crush, squash Ⓑ **despanzurrarse** VPR to get squashed, get crushed

desparejo ADJ = **disparejo**

desparpajo SM **1** (= *desenvoltura*) self-confidence **2** (= *descaro*) nerve*, cheek*, sass (*EEUU**)

desparramar /1a/ VT [+ *hojas, lentejas*] to scatter (**por** over); [+ *líquido*] to spill

desparramo SM **1** (*Carib, CS*) (= *esparcimiento*) [*de objetos*] scattering, spreading; [*de líquido*] spilling **2** (*CS*) (= *desorden*) confusion, disorder

despatarrarse /1a/ VPR (= *abrir las piernas*) to open one's legs wide; (*en el suelo, al caer*) to do the splits

despavorido ADJ terrified

despecho SM spite

despechugado ADJ [*hombre*] bare-chested; [*mujer*] bare-breasted

despectivo ADJ **1** (= *despreciativo*) contemptuous, scornful; **hablar de algn en términos ~s** to speak disparagingly of sb **2** (*Ling*) pejorative

despedazar /1f/ VT [+ *objeto*] to tear apart, tear to pieces; [+ *presa*] to tear to pieces

despedida SF **1** (*antes de irse*) goodbye, farewell; **cena/ función de ~** farewell dinner/performance **2** (= *ceremonia*) farewell ceremony ➤ **despedida de soltera** hen party ➤ **despedida de soltero** stag party

despedir /3k/ Ⓐ VT **1** (= *decir adiós a*) (*gen*) to say goodbye to; [+ *visita*] to see out; **fuimos a ~lo a la estación** we went to see him off at the station; **¿cómo vais a ~ el año?** how are you going to bring the new year in? **2** (= *librarse de*) [+ *empleado*] to dismiss, fire*, sack (*Brit**) **3** (= *lanzar*) [+ *objeto*] to hurl, fling; **salir despedido** to fly off* **4** (= *desprender*) [+ *olor, calor*] to give off
Ⓑ **despedirse** VPR **1** (= *decir adiós*) to say goodbye, take one's leave (*frm*); **se despidieron** they said goodbye to each other; **~se de algn** to say goodbye to sb, take one's leave of sb (*frm*); **¡ya puedes ~te de ese dinero!** you can say *o* kiss goodbye to that money!; **se despide atentamente** (*en carta*) yours sincerely (*Brit*), sincerely yours (*EEUU*), yours faithfully (*Brit*), faithfully yours (*EEUU*) **2** (= *dejar un empleo*) to give up one's job

despegado ADJ **1** (= *separado*) detached, loose; **el sobre está ~** the envelope has come unstuck; **el libro está ~** the book is falling apart **2** [*persona*] cold, indifferent

despegar /1h/ Ⓐ VT **1** (= *desprender*) [+ *cosas pegadas*] to unstick; [+ *sobre*] to open; **sin ~ los labios** without uttering a word **2** (= *separar*) to detach Ⓑ VI [*avión*] to take off; [*cohete*] to blast off Ⓒ **despegarse** VPR to come unstuck

despegue SM **1** [*de avión*] takeoff; [*de cohete*] blast-off **2** (= *crecimiento*) boom; **en los años sesenta hubo un ~ económico** in the sixties the economy took off, there was an economic boom in the sixties

despeinado ADJ [*pelo*] ruffled, messed up; **estoy ~** my hair's a mess

despeinar /1a/ Ⓐ VT [+ *pelo*] to ruffle; **¡me has despeinado!** look at the mess you've made of my hair! Ⓑ **despeinarse** VPR to get one's hair in a mess

despejado ADJ **1** (= *sin obstáculos*) [*camino, mente*] clear; [*campo*] open; [*habitación, plaza*] spacious **2** [*cielo, día*] clear **3** (= *despierto*) awake, wide awake

despejar /1a/ Ⓐ VT **1** [+ *lugar*] to clear; **los bomberos ~on el club** the firemen cleared the club of people **2** (*Dep*) [+ *balón*] to clear **3** (= *resolver*) [+ *misterio*] to clear up; (*Mat*) [+ *incógnita*] to find **4** (*Med*) [+ *nariz*] to unblock; [+ *cabeza*] to clear; [+ *persona*] to wake up
Ⓑ VI **1** (*de un lugar*) **¡despejen!** (*al moverse*) move along!; (*haciendo salir*) everybody out! **2** (*Dep*) to clear, clear the ball **3** (*Meteo*) to clear
Ⓒ **despejarse** VPR **1** (*Meteo*) [*cielo*] to clear; [*día*] to clear up **2** [*persona*] (= *despabilarse*) to brighten up; **me lavé la cara con agua fría para ~me** I washed my face with cold water to wake myself up; **voy a salir a ~me un poco** I'm going out to clear my head a little **3** [*misterio*] to be cleared up

despeje SM (*Dep*) clearance

despellejar /1a/ VT **1** [+ *animal*] to skin **2** (= *criticar*) to tear to pieces

despelotado* ADJ **1** (= *desnudo*) half-naked **2** (*LAm*) (= *desorganizado*) disorganized

despelote* SM **1** (= *desnudez*) stripping off **2 ¡vaya ~!** what a laugh! (*Brit**), what a hoot! (*EEUU**) **3** (*LAm*) (= *lío*) mess

despenalización SF legalization, decriminalization

despenalizar /1f/ VT to legalize, decriminalize

despendolado* ADJ uninhibited, wild*

despensa SF **1** (= *armario*) pantry, larder **2** (= *provisión de comestibles*) stock of food **3** (*Náut*) storeroom **4** (*RPl*) (= *almacén*) grocer's (shop)

despeñadero SM cliff, precipice

despeñarse /1a/ VPR [*persona*] to throw o.s. over a cliff; [*coche*] to go over a cliff *o* off the side of the road

desperdiciar /1b/ VT to waste

desperdicio SM **1** (= *derroche*) waste; **el cerdo es un animal que no tiene ~** nothing from a pig is wasted; **el libro no tiene ~** the book is excellent from beginning to end **2 desperdicios** [*de comida*] scraps; (*Biol, Téc*) waste products

desperdigar /1h/ Ⓐ VT to scatter Ⓑ **desperdigarse** VPR to scatter

desperezarse /1f/ VPR to stretch, stretch o.s.

desperfecto SM flaw, imperfection; **sufrió algunos ~s en el accidente** it suffered slight damage in the accident

despersonalizar /1f/ VT to depersonalize

despertador SM alarm clock; **poner el ~** to set the alarm

despertar /1j/ Ⓐ VT **1** (*del sueño*) to wake, wake up, awaken (*liter*) **2** (= *recordar, incitar*) [+ *esperanzas*] to raise; [+ *recuerdo*] to revive; [+ *sentimiento*] to arouse; **me despertó el apetito** it whetted my appetite Ⓑ VI to wake up; **~ a la realidad** to wake up to reality Ⓒ **despertarse** VPR to wake up Ⓓ SM awakening

despiadado ADJ [*persona*] heartless; [*ataque*] merciless

despido SM (*gen*) dismissal; (*con indemnización*) lay-off, redundancy (*Brit*)

despiole* SM (*RPl*) shambles; **¡qué ~!** what a shambles!

despierto ADJ **1** (= *no dormido*) awake **2** (= *listo*) sharp **3** (= *alerta*) alert

despiezar /1f/ VT to quarter, carve up

despilfarrar /1a/ VT [+ *dinero*] to waste, squander; [+ *recursos, esfuerzos*] to waste

despilfarro SM (= *acción*) waste, squandering; (= *cualidad*) extravagance, wastefulness

despintar /1a/ Ⓐ VT (*Chi**) **no ~ algo a algn** not to spare sb from sth Ⓑ **despintarse** VPR **1** [*color*] to fade **2** (*Chi**) **no ~se de algn/algo** never to be without sb/sth

despiojar /1a/ VT to delouse

despistado/a Ⓐ ADJ (= *distraído*) vague, absentminded; **perdona, estaba ~** sorry, I wasn't concentrating Ⓑ SM/F (= *distraído*) scatterbrain, absent-minded person;
✦ MODISMO **hacerse el ~** (*para no entender*) to pretend not to understand; (*para no ver a algn*) to pretend not to be looking

despistar /1a/ Ⓐ VT **1 lograron ~ a sus perseguidores** they managed to give the slip to *o* shake off their pursuers **2** (= *confundir*) to mislead, fox; **esa pregunta está hecha para ~** that question is designed to mislead you
Ⓑ **despistarse** VPR to get distracted; **no puedes ~te ni un momento** you can't let your attention wander for a moment

despiste SM **1** (= *error*) slip; **ha sido un ~** it was just a momentary lapse **2** (= *distracción*) absent-mindedness; **¡qué ~ tienes!** you're so absent-minded!

desplante SM rude remark; **dar** *o* **hacer un ~ a algn** to be short with sb

desplazado ADJ **sentirse un poco ~** to feel a little out of place

desplazamiento SM **1** (= *movimiento*) [*de partículas*] displacement; [*de tropas*] movement **2** (= *viaje*) journey; **utiliza el tren para los ~s cortos** she uses the train for short journeys

desplazar /1f/ Ⓐ VT **1** (= *mover*) [+ *objeto*] to move; [+ *tropas*] to transfer **2** (= *suplantar*) to take the place of; **las cámaras digitales no han conseguido ~ a las convencionales** digital cameras have not taken the place of *o* superseded conventional ones **3** (*Fís, Náut, Téc*) to displace
Ⓑ **desplazarse** VPR **1** [*objeto*] to move, shift **2** [*persona, vehículo*] to go, travel; **tiene que ~se 25 km todos los días** he has to travel 25 km every day **3** [*votos, opinión*] to shift, swing

desplegable ADJ (*Inform*) [*menú*] drop-down

desplegar /1h, 1j/ Ⓐ VT **1** (= *extender*) [+ *mapa, mantel*] to unfold; [+ *periódico*] to open, open up; [+ *alas*] to spread; [+ *bandera, velas*] to unfurl **2** [+ *misiles, tropas*] to deploy **3** (= *utilizar*) [+ *energías*] to use Ⓑ **desplegarse** VPR

1 (= *extenderse*) [*flor*] to open, open out; [*alas*] to spread, spread out **2** [*tropas*] to deploy

despliegue SM **1** [*de misiles, tropas*] deployment **2** [*de fuerzas*] display, show

desplomarse /1a/ VPR **1** [*persona, gobierno*] to collapse **2** [*precios*] to slump, tumble

desplome SM **1** [*de edificio, sistema*] collapse **2** [*de cotización, divisa*] collapse, slump

desplumar /1a/ VT **1** [+ *ave*] to pluck **2** (*) (= *estafar*) to fleece*

despoblación SF depopulation

despoblado 🅐 ADJ (= *con insuficientes habitantes*) underpopulated; (= *con pocos habitantes*) depopulated; (= *sin habitantes*) unpopulated **🅑** SM deserted spot

despoblar /1l/ **🅐** VT ~ **una zona de árboles** to clear an area of trees **🅑 despoblarse** VPR to become depopulated, lose its population

despojar /1a/ **🅐** VT (*de bienes*) to strip; (*de honores, títulos*) to divest; **verse despojado de su autoridad** to be stripped of one's authority **🅑 despojarse** VPR **~se de** [+ *ropa*] to take off; [+ *hojas*] to shed; [+ *poderes*] to relinquish, give up

despojo SM **1** (= *saqueo*) plundering **2** (= *botín*) plunder, loot **3 despojos** [*de comida*] leftovers; [*de animal*] offal *sing*

despolitizar /1f/ VT to depoliticize

desportillar /1a/ **🅐** VT to chip **desportillarse 🅑** VPR /1a/ to get chipped

desposar /1a/ (*frm*) **🅐** VT [*sacerdote, novio*] to marry; **yo te desposo** I take you to be my lawful wedded wife/husband **🅑 desposarse** VPR to marry, get married

desposeído/a SM/F **los ~s** the have-nots, the dispossessed

desposorios SMPL (*frm*) **1** (= *esponsales*) betrothal *sing* **2** (= *ceremonia*) marriage *sing*, marriage ceremony *sing*

déspota SMF despot

despótico ADJ despotic

despotismo SM despotism ➤ **despotismo ilustrado** enlightened despotism

despotricar /1g/ VI to rant and rave (**contra** about)

despreciable ADJ **1** [*persona*] despicable, contemptible **2** (= *sin valor*) [*objeto*] worthless; [*cantidad*] negligible; **una suma nada ~** a not inconsiderable amount

despreciar /1b/ VT **1** [+ *persona*] to despise, scorn; **desprecian a los extranjeros** they look down on foreigners **2** (= *rechazar*) [+ *oferta, regalo*] to spurn, reject

desprecintar /1a/ VT to unseal

desprecio SM **1** (= *desdén*) scorn, contempt; **lo miró con ~** she looked at him contemptuously **2** (= *desaire*) slight, snub; **le hicieron el ~ de no asistir** they snubbed him by not coming

desprender /2a/ **🅐** VT **1** (= *soltar*) [+ *olor*] to give off; [+ *piel, pelo*] to shed **2** (= *separar*) to detach **3** (*RPl*) [+ *botón*] to undo **🅑 desprenderse** VPR **1** (= *soltarse*) [*pieza*] to come off, become detached (*frm*); [*roca*] to come away **2** (*RPl*) [*botón*] to come undone **3 ~se de algo**: **tuvimos que ~nos del coche** we had to part with *o* get rid of the car; **nunca se desprende de su muñequita** she never lets go of her little doll **4** (= *concluirse*) **de esta declaración se desprende que ...** from this statement we can gather that ...

desprendido ADJ **1** (= *suelto*) [*pieza*] loose, detached **2** (= *generoso*) generous

desprendimiento SM **1** [*de pieza*] loosening ➤ **desprendimiento de retina** detachment of the retina; **ha sufrido un ~ de retina** he has a detached retina **2** (= *generosidad*) generosity

despreocupación SF unconcern

despreocupado ADJ unconcerned; **vive ~ de todo** he has a carefree existence

despreocuparse /1a/ VPR **1** (= *descuidarse*) **tú**

despreocúpate del coche, que ya me encargo yo don't you worry about the car, I'll take care of it **2** (= *ser indiferente*) to be unconcerned

desprestigiar /1b/ **🅐** VT to discredit **🅑 desprestigiarse** VPR to lose one's prestige

desprestigio SM discredit, loss of prestige; **campaña de ~** smear campaign

desprevenido ADJ unready, unprepared; **coger** *o* **pillar** *o* (*LAm*) **agarrar a algn ~** to catch sb unawares, catch sb off his guard

desprogramar /1a/ VT to deprogramme, deprogram (*EEUU*)

desprolijo * ADJ (*RPl*) untidy, sloppy*

desproporción SF disproportion, lack of proportion

desproporcionado ADJ disproportionate

despropósito SM **1** (= *salida de tono*) inappropriate remark **2** (= *disparate*) piece of nonsense

desprotección SF vulnerability, defencelessness, defenselessness (*EEUU*)

desprovisto ADJ **~ de algo** devoid of sth, without sth; **estar ~ de algo** to lack sth, be lacking in sth

después ADV **1** (*con sentido temporal*) **1.1** (= *más tarde*) later, later on; (*tras un hecho concreto*) afterwards, after; **nos vemos ~** I'll see you later (on); **no me da tiempo antes de la cena, lo haré ~** I don't have time before the cena, I'll do it after(wards); **poco ~** soon after(wards), not long after(wards); **lo vi en enero, pero ~ no lo he visto más** I saw him in January, but I haven't seen him since (then) **1.2** (= *a continuación*) then, next; **¿qué pasó ~?** what happened then *o* next? **2** (*con sentido espacial*) **primero está el bar y ~ mi casa** first there's the bar and then, next to it, my house; **gire a la derecha dos calles ~** take the second turn on the right after that **3** (*en orden, jerarquía*) then; **primero está el director y ~ el subdirector** first there's the manager, and then the assistant manager **4 ~ de** (*con sentido temporal*) after; **lo saludé ~ del funeral** I said hello to him after the funeral; **~ de aplicarse la mascarilla, relájese** after applying the mask, relax; **nadie llamó ~ de que te fueras** nobody called after you had gone; **no debería llegar ~ de las diez** I shouldn't be any later than ten; **no lo he vuelto a ver ~ de Navidad** I haven't seen him since Christmas; **~ de marcharse no hemos sabido nada de él** we haven't heard anything from him since he left; **en el año 300 ~ de Cristo** in (the year) 300 AD **5 ~ de** (*en orden, jerarquía*) after, next to; **mi nombre está ~ del tuyo** my name comes next to *o* after yours **6 ~ de todo** after all; **~ de todo, no parece tan antipático** he doesn't seem so unpleasant, after all **7 ~ que** * after; **me ducharé ~ que tú** I'll have a shower after you

despuntar /1a/ **🅐** VT [+ *lápiz, cuchillo*] to blunt **🅑** VI **1** [*plantas*] to sprout; [*flores*] to bud **2** [*día*] to dawn; **al ~ el alba** at daybreak, at dawn **3** [*persona*] (= *destacar*) to excel, stand out

desquiciado ADJ deranged, unhinged; **tiene los nervios ~s** his nerves are in tatters *o* shreds

desquiciar /1b/ **🅐** VT **1** [+ *puerta*] to take off its hinges **2** [+ *persona*] to unhinge, drive crazy **3** [+ *orden, situación*] to upset **🅑 desquiciarse** VPR to go crazy

desquicio SM (*CAm, CS*) confusion, disorder

desquitarse /1a/ VPR to get even

desratización SF **campaña de ~** anti-rat campaign

desregular /1a/ VT to free, deregulate, remove controls from

desrielar /1a/ VI (*LAm*) to derail

desrizar /1f/ VT [+ *pelo*] to straighten

destacado ADJ **1** (= *distinguido*) (*gen*) outstanding; [*personaje*] distinguished; [*dato*] noteworthy **2** (*Mil*) stationed

destacamento SM (*Mil*) detachment

destacar /1g/ **Ⓐ** VT **1** (= *hacer resaltar*) to emphasize; **sirve para ~ su belleza** it serves to show off her beauty; **quiero ~ que ...** I wish to emphasize that ... **2** (*Mil*) to detach, detail **Ⓑ** VI to stand out (**por** because of) **Ⓒ destacarse** VPR to stand out; **~se contra** *o* **en** *o* **sobre algo** to stand out *o* be outlined against sth

destajo SM **trabajar a ~** (*lit*) to do piecework; (*fig*) to work one's fingers to the bone; **trabajo a ~** piecework

destapado ADJ **1** (= *sin cubrir*) **dejó la olla destapada** he left the pan uncovered **2** (= *sin sábanas*) **durmió ~** he slept with the covers off

destapador SM (*LAm*) bottle opener

destapar /1a/ **Ⓐ** VT **1** (= *descubrir*) [+ *mueble*] to uncover; [+ *botella*] (*gen*) to open; (*con corcho*) to uncork; [+ *recipiente*] to take the lid off **2** (*en la cama*) to take the covers off; **lo destapó** she took the covers off him **3** (= *hacer público*) [+ *secreto*] to reveal; [+ *escándalo*] to uncover **4** (*LAm*) (= *desatascar*) to unblock **Ⓑ destaparse** VPR **1** (= *descubrirse*) to get uncovered; **el niño se ha destapado** the bedclothes have fallen off the baby **2** (= *revelarse*) to show one's true character

destape SM **1** [*de persona*] (= *estado*) nudity; (= *acto*) undressing **2** [*de costumbres*] permissiveness; (*Pol*) *process of liberalization*

destaponar /1a/ VT to unblock, clear

destartalado ADJ **1** [*casa*] (= *grande, mal dispuesta*) large and rambling; (= *ruinosa*) tumbledown **2** [*coche*] rickety

destejer /2d/ VT to undo

destello SM **1** (= *brillo*) [*de diamante, ojos*] sparkle; [*de metal*] glint; [*de estrella*] twinkling **2** (= *pizca*) glimmer, hint; **tiene a veces ~s de inteligencia** he sometimes shows a glimmer of intelligence

destemplado ADJ **1** (*Mús*) out of tune **2** (*Med*) **estar ~** to have a slight temperature *o* fever

destemplar /1a/ **Ⓐ** VT **1** (*Mús*) to put out of tune **2** (= *alterar*) to upset, disturb **3** (*Col*) [+ *dientes*] to set on edge **Ⓑ destemplarse** VPR **1** (*Mús*) to get out of tune **2** (*Med*) [*persona*] to have a slight temperature *o* (*EEUU*) fever; [*pulso*] to become irregular **3** (*LAm*) (= *irritarse*) to get upset; **con eso me destemplo** that sets my teeth on edge

desteñir /3h, 3k/ **Ⓐ** VI to run; **estos pantalones destiñen** these trousers run **Ⓑ desteñirse** VPR to fade; **se ha desteñido la camisa** this shirt has faded

desternillarse* /1a/ VPR **~ de risa** to split one's sides laughing

desterrar /1j/ VT to exile, banish

destetar /1a/ VT to wean

destiempo SM **a ~** at the wrong time

destierro SM exile, banishment; **vivir en el ~** to live in exile

destilación SF distillation

destilar /1a/ VT **1** [+ *alcohol*] to distil **2** (= *rebosar*) to exude; **la carta destilaba odio** the letter exuded hatred

destilería SF distillery

destinado ADJ **1** (*Correos, Transportes*) **¿a quién va destinada la carta?** who is the letter addressed to? **2** (*en un trabajo*) **está ~ en Córdoba** [*empleado*] he's based in Córdoba; [*militar*] he's stationed in Córdoba **3 ~ a** *o* **para algo** [*dinero, fondos, material*] set aside for sth; **el espacio ~ al olivar** the area given over to olive trees **4 ~ a algo** (= *predestinado*) destined for sth; **la obra estaba destinada al fracaso** the play was destined for failure *o* to fail **5 ~ a algn/algo** (= *pensado para*) intended for sb/sth, aimed at sb/sth; **un libro ~ a los niños** a book intended for *o* aimed at children

destinar /1a/ VT **1** (= *dedicar*) [+ *fondos, espacio*] to allocate; **destinamos el 10% del presupuesto a educación** we allocate 10% of the budget to education **2** (= *enviar*) [+ *empleado, funcionario*] to assign, post; [+ *militar*] to station, post **3** (*frm*) (= *dirigir*) [+ *carta*] to address

destinatario/a SM/F [*de carta*] addressee; [*de giro*] payee

destino SM **1** (= *suerte*) destiny, fate; **el ~ lo quiso así** it

was destined to happen; **rige los ~s del país** he rules the country's fate

2 [*de avión, viajero*] destination; **"a franquear en destino"** "postage will be paid by the addressee"; **van con ~ a Londres** they are going to London; (*Náut*) they are bound for London; **salió con ~ al aeropuerto** she set off for the airport

3 (= *puesto*) [*de empleado*] job, post; [*de militar*] posting; [*de funcionario*] placement

4 (= *uso*) use, purpose; **dar ~ a algo** to find a use for sth

destitución SF dismissal, removal

destituir /3g/ VT [+ *empleado*] to dismiss (**de** from); [+ *ministro, funcionario*] to remove from office; **ha sido destituido de su cargo** he has been removed from his post

destornillador SM screwdriver

destornillar /1a/ **Ⓐ** VT to unscrew **Ⓑ destornillarse** VPR **1** [*tornillo, tuerca*] to come unscrewed **2** (*LAm*) = **desternillarse**

destreza SF skill

destripar /1a/ VT [+ *animal*] to gut; [+ *persona*] to disembowel

destronar /1a/ VT to dethrone

destrozado ADJ **1** [*cristal, cerámica*] smashed, shattered; **quedó ~** [*traje, alfombra, zapato*] it was ruined; [*coche, jardín*] it was wrecked **2** [*persona*] (= *abatido*) shattered, devastated; (*) (= *cansado*) knackered (*Brit**), pooped (*EEUU***); [*corazón*] broken

destrozar /1f/ VT **1** (= *romper*) [+ *cristal, cerámica*] to smash; [+ *edificio*] to destroy; [+ *ropa, zapatos*] to ruin; [+ *nervios*] to shatter; **ha destrozado el coche** he's wrecked the car **2** (= *dejar abatido a*) [+ *persona*] to shatter; [+ *corazón*] to break; [+ *ejército, enemigo*] to crush **3** (= *arruinar*) [+ *persona, vida*] to ruin

destrozo SM **1** (= *acción*) destruction **2 destrozos** (= *daños*) havoc *sing*; **causar** *o* **provocar ~s** to cause *o* wreak havoc (**en** in); **los ~s causados por las inundaciones** the destruction caused by the floods, the havoc wrought by the floods; **los manifestantes provocaron numerosos ~s** the demonstrators caused extensive damage

destrozón ADJ **es muy ~** (*gen*) he's a terrible one for breaking things; (*con la ropa*) he's hard on his clothes

destrucción SF destruction ➤ **destrucción del empleo** job losses *pl*

destructivo ADJ destructive

destructor Ⓐ ADJ destructive **Ⓑ** SM (*Náut*) destroyer

destruir /3g/ VT **1** [+ *objeto, edificio*] to destroy; **el año pasado se destruyeron miles de empleos en la construcción** last year thousands of construction jobs were lost **2** (= *estropear*) [+ *amistad, matrimonio, armonía*] to wreck, destroy; [+ *argumento, teoría*] to demolish; [+ *proyecto, plan*] to wreck, ruin

desubicado ADJ **1** (= *mal situado*) badly positioned **2** (*CS**) (*socialmente*) **¡qué ~ es!** he doesn't have a clue how to behave*

desubicar /1g/ VT (*CS*) to disorientate, disorient (*esp EEUU*)

desunión SF disunity

desunir /3a/ VT **1** (= *separar*) to separate **2** (= *enemistar*) to cause a rift between; **el problema de la herencia ha desunido a la familia** the inheritance problem has split the family

desusado ADJ **1** (= *anticuado*) obsolete, antiquated **2** (= *inusitado*) unusual

desuso SM disuse; **una expresión en ~** an obsolete expression; **caer en ~** to fall into disuse, become obsolete

desvaído ADJ **1** [*color*] pale, washed-out **2** [*contorno*] vague, blurred **3** [*persona*] characterless **4** [*personalidad*] flat, dull

desvalido ADJ helpless, destitute

desvalijar /1a/ VT [+ *persona*] to rob; [+ *cajón, caja fuerte*] to rifle; [+ *casa, tienda*] to ransack

desvalorizar /1f/ VT [+ *moneda*] to devalue, devaluate (*EEUU*); [+ *posesión*] to reduce the value of

desván SM loft, attic

desvanecer /2d/ Ⓐ VT [+ objeto] to make disappear; [+ duda] to dispel; [+ recuerdo, temor] to banish Ⓑ **desvanecerse** VPR 1 [humo, niebla] to clear, disperse; [recuerdo, sonido] to fade, fade away; [duda] to be dispelled 2 (Med) to faint

desvanecido ADJ **caer** ~ to fall in a faint

desvanecimiento SM (Med) fainting fit, fainting spell (EEUU)

desvarar /1a/ VT to refloat

desvariar /1c/ VI 1 (Med) to be delirious 2 (al hablar) to rave

desvarío SM 1 (Med) delirium 2 **desvaríos** (= disparates) ravings

desvelado ADJ sleepless, wakeful; **estar** ~ to be awake, be unable to get to sleep

desvelar /1a/ Ⓐ VT to keep awake; **el café me desvela** coffee keeps me awake o stops me from getting to sleep Ⓑ **desvelarse** VPR 1 (= no poder dormir) to be unable to get to sleep; (Méx) (= estar despierto) to stay up (late) 2 **~se por algo** to take great care over sth; **se desvela porque no nos falte de nada** she works hard so that we should not go short of anything; **~se por hacer algo** to try one's best to do sth

desvelo SM 1 (= falta de sueño) lack of sleep, sleeplessness 2 **desvelos** (= preocupaciones) effort sing

desvencijado ADJ [silla, mueble] rickety; [máquina] broken-down

desvencijarse /1a/ VPR to come apart, fall to pieces

desventaja SF disadvantage; **estar en** ~ to be at a disadvantage

desventajoso ADJ disadvantageous, unfavourable, unfavorable (EEUU)

desventura SF misfortune

desventurado ADJ [persona] unfortunate; [viaje, encuentro] ill-fated

desvergonzado ADJ 1 (= sin vergüenza) shameless 2 (= descarado) insolent

desvergüenza SF 1 (= mala conducta) shamelessness 2 (= descaro) effrontery, impudence; **esto es una** ~ this is disgraceful, this is shameful

desvestir /3k/ Ⓐ VT to undress Ⓑ **desvestirse** VPR to undress, get undressed

desviación SF 1 (= separación) [de trayectoria] deviation (**de** from); [de golpe, disparo] deflection (**de** from); ➤ **desviación de columna** abnormal curvature of the spine ➤ **desviación de fondos** diversion of funds 2 (Aut) diversion

desviar /1c/ Ⓐ VT 1 (= apartar) [+ balón, flecha] to deflect; [+ golpe] to parry; [+ pregunta] to evade; [+ ojos] to avert, turn away; [+ tren] to switch, switch into a siding; [+ avión, circulación] to divert (**por** through); ~ **el cauce de un río** to alter the course of o divert a river 2 [+ persona] ~ **a algn de su vocación** to turn sb from their vocation; ~ **a algn del buen camino** to lead sb astray Ⓑ **desviarse** VPR 1 (de camino) [persona] to turn aside, turn away (**de** from); [carretera] to branch off; **~se de un tema** to stray off a subject 2 (Aut) to make a detour

desvincular /1a/ Ⓐ VT to dissociate Ⓑ **desvincularse** VPR to dissociate o.s.

desvío SM 1 [de trayectoria, orientación] deflection (**de** from), deviation (**de** from) 2 (Aut) (= rodeo) detour; (por obras) diversion

desvirgar /1h/ VT to deflower

desvirtuar /1e/ VT [+ argumento, razonamiento] to detract from; [+ efecto] to counteract; [+ sentido] to distort

desvitalizar /1f/ VT [+ nervio] to numb

desvivirse /3a/ VPR ~ **por los amigos** to do anything for one's friends; **se desvivía por ayudarme** he used to go out of his way to help me

detall: al ~ ADV retail

detalladamente ADV 1 (= con detalles) in detail 2 (= extensamente) at great length

detallado ADJ detailed

detallar /1a/ VT (= contar) to detail; (en una lista, factura) to itemize

detalle SM 1 (= pormenor) detail; **con todo** ~ ◇ **con todos los ~s** in full detail; **me observaba sin perder** ~ he watched my every move 2 (= atención) nice gesture; **¡qué ~!** what a nice gesture!, how thoughtful! 3 (= regalo) small gift 4 (Com) **al** ~ retail antes de s; **vender al** ~ to retail

detallista Ⓐ ADJ 1 (= meticuloso) meticulous 2 (Com) retail antes de s Ⓑ SMF (Com) retailer, retail trader

detectar /1a/ VT to detect

detective SMF detective ➤ **detective privado/a** private detective

detector SM detector ➤ **detector de mentiras** lie detector ➤ **detector de metales** metal detector ➤ **detector de minas** mine detector

detención SF 1 (= parada) holdup, delay 2 (= arresto) arrest; (= prisión) detention ➤ **detención domiciliaria** house arrest ➤ **detención preventiva** police custody

detener /2k/ Ⓐ VT 1 (= parar) to stop; **me detuvo en la calle** he stopped me in the street 2 (= retrasar) to hold up, delay; ~ **el progreso de algo** to hold up the progress of sth 3 (= arrestar) to arrest; (= encarcelar) to detain Ⓑ **detenerse** VPR 1 (= pararse) to stop; **se detuvo a mirarlo** he stopped to look at it 2 (= demorarse) **~se mucho en algo** to take a long time over sth

detenidamente ADV at great length

detenido ADJ 1 (Jur) (por poco tiempo) arrested, under arrest; (por más tiempo) in custody 2 (= sin prisa) [narración, estudio] detailed; [análisis, examen] thorough

detenimiento SM **con** ~ thoroughly

detentar /1a/ VT to hold

detergente ADJ, SM detergent

deteriorar /1a/ Ⓐ VT 1 (= estropear) to damage 2 (Mec) to cause wear and tear to Ⓑ **deteriorarse** VPR 1 (= estropearse) to get damaged 2 (= empeorar) [salud, relaciones] to deteriorate 3 (Mec) to wear, get worn

deterioro SM 1 (= daño) damage 2 (= empeoramiento) deterioration 3 (Mec) wear and tear

determinación SF 1 (= decisión) decision 2 (= valentía) determination, resolution 3 [de fecha, precio] fixing

determinado ADJ 1 (= preciso) certain; **en momentos ~s** at certain times; **no hay ningún tema** ~ there is no particular theme 2 (Ling) [artículo] definite

determinante ADJ, SM determinant

determinar /1a/ Ⓐ VT 1 (= establecer) to determine; **el gen que determina la estatura** the gene which determines height; **"precio por determinar"** "price to be agreed"; ~ **el rumbo** (Aer, Náut) to set a course; **el reglamento determina que ...** the rule lays down o states that ... 2 (= averiguar) [+ peso, volumen, causa] to determine; [+ daños] to assess 3 (= motivar) to bring about, cause 4 (= decidir) to decide; **~on asignarle más fondos al proyecto** they decided to allocate more funds to the project; **esto la determinó a continuar sus estudios** this decided her to continue with her studies 5 (Ling) to determine Ⓑ **determinarse** VPR (= decidirse) to decide, make up one's mind; **~se a hacer algo** to determine to do sth, decide to do sth

determinativo Ⓐ ADJ determinative Ⓑ SM (Ling) determiner

determinista Ⓐ ADJ deterministic Ⓑ SMF determinist

detestable ADJ [persona] hateful; [costumbre] detestable; [sabor, tiempo] foul

detestar /1a/ VT to detest, loathe

detonación SF (= acción) detonation; (= ruido) explosion

detonador SM detonator

detonante Ⓐ ADJ explosive Ⓑ SM 1 (= explosivo)

explosive **2** (= *causa*) trigger (**de** for); **eso fue el ~ de la crisis** that was what sparked off *o* triggered the crisis
detonar /1a/ VI to detonate, explode
detrás ADV **1** (= *en la parte posterior*) **el patio está ~** the patio is at the back; **los más altos que se pongan ~** can the tallest ones please stand at the back?; **en el coche me gusta sentarme ~** when I'm in the car I like to sit in the back; **yo estaba delante y él ~** I was in front and he was behind; **de ~: el asesino salió de ~** the murderer came out from behind; **por ~: la atacaron por ~** she was attacked from behind; **siempre critica a sus amigos por ~*** he's always criticizing his friends behind their backs; **la foto lleva una dedicatoria (por)** ~ the photo has a dedication on the back **2** (= *a continuación*) **primero el nombre y ~ la dirección** first the name and then the address; **paso yo delante y tú vienes ~** I'll go first and you follow; **entraron en el cuarto uno ~ de otro** they went into the room one after the other **3** ~ **de** behind; ~ **del edificio** behind the building; **¿quién está ~ de este complot?** who's behind this plot?, who's behind all this?; **Susana anda ~ de Antonio** Susana's after Antonio; **por ~ de** behind; **dos puestos por ~ del Atlético** two places behind Atlético; **la carretera pasa por ~ del parque** the road goes behind the park **4** ~ **mío/tuyo** (*esp LAm**) behind me/you
detrimento SM detriment; **en ~ de algo** to the detriment of sth
detritus SM INV **1** (*Geol*) detritus **2** (= *desechos*) debris
detuve *etc ver* **detener**
deuda SF **1** (= *obligación*) debt; **estar en ~ con algn** to be indebted to sb **2** (*Com*) debt ➤ **deuda exterior, deuda externa** foreign debt ➤ **deuda pública** national debt **3** (*Rel*) **perdónanos nuestras ~s** forgive us our trespasses *o* sins
deudo/a SM/F (*frm*) relative
deudor(a) SM/F debtor
devaluación SF devaluation
devaluar /1e/ VT to devalue, devaluate (*EEUU*)
devanar /1a/ Ⓐ VT to wind Ⓑ **devanarse** VPR **~se los sesos** to rack one's brains
devanear /1a/ VI to rave
devaneo SM **1** (= *fruslería*) idle pursuit **2** (= *amorío*) flirtation
devastar /1a/ VT to devastate
devengado ADJ [*intereses*] accrued; [*sueldo*] due
devengar /1h/ VT [+ *intereses*] to yield, pay
devenir /3r/ Ⓐ VI **~ en algo** to become sth, turn into sth Ⓑ SM process of development
deveras (*Méx*) Ⓐ ADV *ver* **veras** Ⓑ SF INV **de (a) ~: un amigo de (a) ~** a true *o* real friend; **eso no es querer a alguien de (a) ~** that's not true *o* real love
devoción SF **1** (*Rel*) devotion, devoutness; **la ~ a esta imagen** the veneration of this image **2** (= *admiración*) devotion (**a** to); **sienten ~ por su madre** they are devoted to their mother
devocionario SM prayer book
devolución SF **1** [*de algo prestado, robado*] return **2** (*Com*) [*de compra*] return; [*de dinero*] refund; **"no se admiten devoluciones"** "no refunds will be given", "no goods returnable" **3** [*de poder, territorio*] devolution
devolver /2h/ (*pp* **devuelto**) Ⓐ VT **1** (= *retornar*) [+ *algo prestado, robado*] to give back, return; [+ *carta, llamada, golpe*] to return; [+ *polizón, refugiado*] to return, send back; **¿cuándo tienes que ~ esos libros?** when do you have to take back *o* return those books?; **consiguió que le devolvieran las joyas** he managed to get the jewels back; **leyó la nota y se la devolvió** she read the note and handed *o* gave it back to him; **si nos devuelve el envase le descontamos 30 céntimos** if you bring back *o* return the container you'll get a 30 cent discount; ✦ MODISMO **~ la pelota a algn** to give sb tit for tat **2** (*Com*) **2.1** (= *rechazar*) [+ *producto, mercancía*] (*en mano*) to take back, return; (*por correo*) to send back, return; **si a su hijo no le gusta lo puede** ~ if your son doesn't like it

you can return it *o* bring it back **2.2** (= *reembolsar*) [+ *dinero*] (*de una compra*) to refund, give back; (*de un préstamo*) to pay back; **la máquina me devolvía las monedas** the machine rejected my coins **2.3** [+ *cambio*] to give, give back; **"no devuelve cambio"** "no change given" **2.4** [+ *cheque sin fondos*] to return **3** (= *corresponder*) [+ *cumplido, favor, visita*] to return **4** (= *restituir*) [+ *salud, vista*] to restore, give back **4.2** (*a su estado original*) to restore; **el nuevo tratado ha devuelto la paz a la zona** the new treaty has restored peace to the area; **el sonido del teléfono me devolvió a la realidad** the sound of the telephone brought me back to reality **5** (*liter*) [+ *imagen*] to reflect; **el espejo nos devolvía una imagen distorsionada** the mirror reflected a distorted image of us **6** (= *vomitar*) to bring up Ⓑ VI (= *vomitar*) to throw up* Ⓒ **devolverse** VPR (*LAm*) (= *regresar*) to turn back
devorar /1a/ VT **1** (= *comer ávidamente*) [*animal*] to devour; [*persona*] to devour, wolf down*; **devora las novelas de amor** she laps up love stories; **la devoraba con la mirada** he devoured her with his eyes **2** (= *destruir*) **el fuego lo devoró todo** the fire consumed everything; **lo devoran los celos** he is consumed with jealousy
devoto/a Ⓐ ADJ **1** (*Rel*) [*persona*] devout; [*obra*] devotional; **ser muy ~ de un santo** to have a special devotion to a saint **2** (= *apegado, fiel*) devoted (**de** to); **su ~ servidor** (*frm*) your devoted servant Ⓑ SM/F (*Rel*) devout person; **los ~s** the faithful **2** (= *aficionado*) devotee; **la artista y sus ~s** the artist and her devotees *o* fans
D.F. ABR (*Méx*) = **Distrito Federal**
Dg ABR = **decagramo(s)**
dg ABR = **decigramo(s)**) dg
DGT SF ABR **1** = **Dirección General de Tráfico 2** = **Dirección General de Turismo**
di *etc ver* **dar**, **decir**
día SM **1** (= *período de 24 horas*) day; **todos los ~s** every day; **a los pocos ~s** within *o* after a few days, a few days later; **~ a ~** day in day out, day by day; **el ~ a ~ en la gestión financiera de la empresa** the day-to-day running of the company's financial business; **siete veces al ~** seven times a day; **tres horas al ~** three hours a day; **al otro ~** ✧ **al ~ siguiente** the following day; **menú del ~** today's menu; **pan del ~** fresh bread; **~ (de) por medio** (*LAm*) every other day, on alternate days; **ocho ~s** a week; **quince ~s** two weeks, a fortnight (*esp Brit*); **un ~ sí y otro no** every other day; ✦ MODISMOS **a ~s** at times; **cuatro ~s** a couple of days, a few days; **todo el santo ~** the whole blessed day ➤ **día azul** (*Ferro*) cheap ticket day ➤ **día de diario, día de entresemana** weekday ➤ **día de fiesta** holiday, public holiday (*Brit*), legal holiday (*EEUU*) ➤ **Día de la Hispanidad** Columbus Day (*12 October*) ➤ **día del espectador** *day each week when cinema/movie tickets are discounted* ➤ **Día de los Difuntos** All Souls' Day, Day of the Dead ➤ **día de los enamorados** St Valentine's Day ➤ **día de los inocentes** ≈ April Fools' Day (*1 April*) ➤ **Día de (los) Muertos** (*LAm*) All Souls' Day, Day of the Dead ➤ **Día de Reyes** Epiphany (*6 January*) ➤ **día feriado, día festivo** holiday, public holiday (*Brit*), legal holiday (*EEUU*) ➤ **día hábil, día laborable** working day ➤ **día lectivo** teaching day ➤ **día libre** day off; ✧ *INOCENTES, DÍA DE LOS (SANTOS); REYES, DÍA DE* **2** (= *no noche*) daytime; **durante el ~** during the day(time); **en pleno ~** in broad daylight; **¡buenos ~s!** ✧ **¡buen ~!** (*CS*) good morning!; **dar los buenos ~s a algn** to say good morning to sb; **de ~** by day, during the day; **duerme de ~ y trabaja de noche** he sleeps by day and works by night, he sleeps during the day and works at night; **ya es de ~** it's already light; **mientras sea de ~** while it's still light **3** (= *fecha*) date; **¿qué ~ es hoy?** (*del mes*) what's the date today?; (*de la semana*) what day is it today?; **llegará el ~ dos de mayo** he'll arrive on the second of May (*Brit*), he'll arrive on May second (*esp EEUU*); **~ lunes/martes** *etc* (*LAm*) Monday/Tuesday *etc*; **el ~ de hoy** today; **el ~ de mañana** (*fig*) at some future date **4** (= *momento sin precisar*) **algún ~** some day; **un ~ de éstos** one of these days; **el ~ menos pensado** when you least expect it; **otro ~** some other day, another day; **dejémoslo**

para otro ~ let's leave it for the moment *o* for another day; **¡hasta otro ~!** so long!; ✦ MODISMOS **de un ~ para otro** any day now; **en su** ~ (*referido al futuro*) in due course; (*referido al pasado*) in its/their *etc* day
5 (= *actualidad*) **estar al** ~ (= *actualizado*) to be up to date; (= *de moda*) to be with it; **quien quiera estar al ~ en esta especialidad, que lea ...** anyone who wishes to keep up to date with this area of study, should read ...; **poner al ~** [+ *texto, contabilidad*] to bring up to date; [+ *base de datos*] to update; [+ *diario*] to write up; **ponerse al ~ (en algo)** to get up to date (with sth); **vivir al ~** to live from one day to the next

diabetes SF INV diabetes

diabético/a ADJ, SM/F diabetic

diablillo* SM little devil, little monkey

diablo SM **1** (= *demonio*) devil; **no le hagas caso, es un pobre** ~ don't pay any attention to him, the poor devil; ✦ MODISMOS **como un ~*: esta mesa pesa como un** ~ this table weighs a ton*; **del ~ o de mil ~s*: hace un frío del ~ o de mil ~s** it's hellishly cold*, it's absolutely freezing; **¡~s! ✧ ¡por todos los ~s!*** damn it!**, oh hell!**; **donde el ~ perdió el poncho** (CS*) in some godforsaken spot*, in the back of beyond*; **¡vete al ~!** get lost!*; **mandar al ~*: no podía arreglarlo y lo mandé al** ~ I couldn't fix it so I chucked it out*; **se enfadó y nos mandó al** ~ he got mad and told us to go to hell* ➤ **diablos azules** (LAm) DTs*, pink elephants*
2 (*) (*como intensificador*) **¿cómo ~s se le ocurrió hacer tal cosa?** what on earth *o* what the hell made him do such a thing?*; **¡qué ~s! ¡yo también quiero ser rico!** damn it, I want to be rich too!*

diablura SF prank

diabólico ADJ [*palabras, rito*] diabolic, satanic; (= *malvado*) diabolical; (= *muy difícil*) fiendishly difficult

diábolo SM diabolo

diácono SM deacon

diacrítico ADJ diacritic, diacritical

diacrónico ADJ diachronic

Diada SF *Catalan national day (11th September)*

diadema SF **1** (*para el pelo*) hairband **2** (*de joyas*) tiara

diáfano ADJ **1** (= *translúcido*) [*agua*] crystal-clear, crystalline (*liter*); [*cristal*] translucent; [*tela*] diaphanous **2** [*argumento, explicación*] crystal-clear **3** [*oficina, planta*] open-plan

diafragma SM **1** (*Anat*) diaphragm **2** (= *anticonceptivo*) diaphragm, cap **3** (*Fot*) diaphragm

diagnosis SF INV diagnosis

diagnosticar /1g/ VT to diagnose

diagnóstico SM diagnosis

diagonal ADJ, SF diagonal; **traza una** ~ draw a diagonal line

diagrama SM diagram

dial SM (*Aut, Radio*) dial

dialectal ADJ dialectal, dialect *antes de s*

dialéctica SF **1** (= *enfrentamiento*) dialectic **2** (*Fil*) dialectics *pl*

dialéctico ADJ dialectical

dialecto SM dialect

diálisis SF INV dialysis

dialogante ADJ open to dialogue *o* (EEUU) dialog, willing to discuss

dialogar /1h/ VI (= *conversar*) to have a conversation; ~ **con algn** to engage in a dialogue *o* (EEUU) dialog with sb

diálogo SM **1** (= *conversación*) conversation; (*Pol*) dialogue; ✦ MODISMOS **esto es un ~ de besugos** we are talking at cross purposes; **fue un ~ de sordos** nobody listened to what anyone else had to say, it was a dialogue of the deaf **2** (*Literat*) dialogue, dialog (EEUU)

diamante SM **1** (= *joya*) diamond ➤ **diamante en bruto** (*lit*) uncut diamond; (*fig*) rough diamond **2 diamantes** (*Naipes*) diamonds

diamantina SF (*Méx*) glitter

diametralmente ADV diametrically; ~ **opuesto a algo** diametrically opposed to sth

diámetro SM diameter

diana SF **1** (= *centro de blanco*) bull's-eye; **dar en la** ~ *o* **hacer** ~ (*lit*) to score a bull's-eye; (*fig*) to hit home **2** [*de dardos*] dartboard **3** (*Mil*) reveille; **tocar** ~ to sound reveille

diantre* EXCL dash it all!

diapasón SM (*para afinar*) tuning fork; (*de violín, guitarra*) fingerboard

diapositiva SF slide

diarero SM (*RPl*) paperboy

diariamente ADV daily, every day

diariero SM (*Arg*) paperboy

diario Ⓐ ADJ **1** (= *todos los días*) daily; **tienen peleas diarias** they have arguments every day; **gastos ~s** everyday expenses
2 (= *cada día*) a day; **cien dólares ~s** a hundred dollars a day
3 a ~ every day, daily
4 de ~ everyday; **nuestro mantel de** ~ our everyday tablecloth
Ⓑ ADV (*LAm*) every day, daily
Ⓒ SM **1** (= *periódico*) newspaper, daily ➤ **diario hablado** news, news bulletin
2 (= *libro*) diary ➤ **diario de a bordo, diario de navegación** logbook ➤ **diario de sesiones** ≈ parliamentary report (*Brit*), ≈ congressional report (*EEUU*)

diarrea SF diarrhoea, diarrhea (*EEUU*)

diáspora SF diaspora

diatriba SF diatribe, tirade

dibujante SMF **1** (*Arte*) (*gen*) draughtsman/ draughtswoman, draftsman/draftswoman (*EEUU*); [*de cómics, dibujos animados*] cartoonist; [*de esbozos*] sketcher ➤ **dibujante de publicidad** commercial artist **2** (*Téc*) draughtsman/draughtswoman, draftsman/draftswoman (*EEUU*)

dibujar /1a/ Ⓐ VT **1** (*Arte*) to draw, sketch **2** (*Téc*) to design Ⓑ **dibujarse** VPR **1** (= *perfilarse*) to be outlined (**contra** against) **2** [*emoción*] (*de forma permanente*) to show; (*de forma temporal*) to appear; **el sufrimiento se dibujaba en su cara** suffering showed in his face; **una sonrisa se dibujó en sus labios** a smile appeared on his lips

dibujo SM **1** (= *actividad*) drawing ➤ **dibujo lineal, dibujo técnico** technical drawing **2** (= *representación gráfica*) (*Arte*) drawing; (*Téc*) design; (*en periódico*) cartoon ➤ **dibujos animados** cartoons **3** (*en papel, tela*) pattern; **con ~ a rayas** with a striped pattern

dicción SF diction

diccionario SM dictionary

dicha SF **1** (= *felicidad*) happiness; **es una ~ poder ...** it is a happy thing to be able to ... **2** (= *suerte*) good luck; **por ~** fortunately

dicharachero ADJ **1** (= *gracioso*) witty **2** (= *parlanchín*) talkative

dicho Ⓐ PP *o* ~ **de otro modo ...** or, putting it another way, ..., or, in other words ...; **con esto queda todo** ~ that says it all; **bueno, lo** ~ OK, then; **dejar algo** ~: **antes de morir dejó ~ que la casa era para su hijo** before dying he gave instructions for the house to go to his son; ~ **y hecho** no sooner said than done; ~ **mejor** ~ or rather; ~ **sea de paso** incidentally, by the way
Ⓑ ADJ (= *este*) this; **dicha compañía fue disuelta en 1994** this *o* the said company was dissolved in 1994
Ⓒ SM (= *máxima popular*) saying; ✦ REFRÁN **del ~ al hecho hay mucho trecho** saying is one thing, doing it is another

dichoso ADJ **1** (= *feliz*) happy; **hacer ~ a algn** to make sb happy; **me siento ~ de hacer algo** I feel privileged to do sth **2** (= *afortunado*) lucky, fortunate; **¡~s los ojos!** how nice to see you! **3** (*) (*blessed*) blessed; **¡aquel ~ coche!** that blessed car!

diciembre SM December; *ver tb* **septiembre**

En inglés los meses se escriben con mayúscula.

dicotomía SF dichotomy

dictado SM 1 (= *lectura, texto*) dictation; **escribir al ~** to take dictation 2 **dictados** (= *imperativos*) dictates

dictador(a) SM/F dictator

dictadura SF dictatorship

dictáfono SM Dictaphone®

dictamen SM report ➤ **dictamen facultativo** (*Med*) medical report

dictaminar /1a/ VT to determine, establish

dictar /1a/ Ⓐ VT 1 [+ *carta, texto*] to dictate (**a** to) 2 (*Jur*) [+ *sentencia*] to pass, pronounce; [+ *decreto*] to issue 3 (= *indicar*) to suggest, dictate; **lo que dicta el sentido común** what common sense suggests *o* dictates 4 (*LAm*) [+ *conferencia*] to give, deliver; **~ clase** to teach Ⓑ VI to dictate

dictatorial ADJ dictatorial

didáctica SF didactics *sing*

didáctico ADJ didactic

diecinueve ADJ, PRON, SM (*cardinal*) nineteen; (*ordinal, en la fecha*) nineteenth; *ver tb* **seis**

dieciochesco ADJ eighteenth-century *antes de s*

dieciocho ADJ, PRON, SM (*cardinal*) eighteen; (*ordinal, en la fecha*) eighteenth; *ver tb* **seis**

dieciséis ADJ, PRON, SM (*cardinal*) sixteen; (*ordinal, en la fecha*) sixteenth; *ver tb* **seis**

dieciseisavo Ⓐ ADJ, PRON sixteenth Ⓑ SM **~s de final** *in a tournament, the round before the round before the quarter-finals*

diecisiete ADJ, PRON, SM (*cardinal*) seventeen; (*ordinal, en la fecha*) seventeenth; *ver tb* **seis**

diente SM 1 (*Anat*) tooth; **echar los ~s** to teethe; **lavarse** *o* **cepillarse los ~s** to brush one's teeth; **le están saliendo los ~s** he's teething ➤ **diente canino** canine, canine tooth ➤ **diente de leche** milk tooth ➤ **diente incisivo** incisor 2 ♦ MODISMOS **enseñar los ~s** to show one's claws, turn nasty; **entre ~s: hablar entre ~s** to mumble, mutter; **se le oía maldecir entre ~s** you could hear him cursing under his breath; **hincar el ~ en/a** [+ *comida*] to bite into; [+ *asunto*] to get one's teeth into; **pelar el ~** (*LAm**) to smile affectedly; **poner a algn los ~s largos** to make sb green with envy; **tener buen ~** to be a hearty eater 3 [*de máquina*] cog; [*de peine, sierra*] tooth; [*de hebilla*] tongue 4 (*Bot*) ➤ **diente de ajo** clove of garlic ➤ **diente de león** dandelion

diéresis SF INV diaeresis, dieresis (*EEUU*)

diesel SM 1 (*tb* **motor ~**) diesel engine; **un (coche) ~** a diesel (car) 2 (= *combustible*) diesel

diestra SF right hand; **siéntate a mi ~** sit on my right; ✦ MODISMO **a ~ y siniestra** left, right and centre

diestro Ⓐ ADJ 1 (= *derecho*) right; [*persona*] right-handed; ✦ MODISMO **a ~ y siniestro** left, right and centre 2 (= *hábil*) skilful, skillful (*EEUU*); (*con las manos*) handy Ⓑ SM (*Taur*) matador

dieta SF 1 (*Med*) diet; **estar a ~** to be on a diet 2 **dietas** (*de comida, viajes*) subsistence allowance *sing*, expenses

dietario SM engagement book

dietética SF dietetics *sing*

dietético ADJ dietetic, dietary; **alimento ~** diet food

dietista SMF dietician

diez ADJ, PRON, SM (*cardinal*) ten; (*ordinal, en la fecha*) tenth; **son las nueve menos ~** ◇ **son ~ para las nueve** (*LAm*) it's ten to nine; *ver tb* **seis**

diezmar /1a/ VT to decimate

diezmo SM tithe

difamación SF 1 (*al hablar*) slander (**de** of) 2 (*por escrito*) libel (**de** on)

difamar /1a/ VT (*al hablar*) to slander; (*por escrito*) to libel

difamatorio ADJ [*palabras, afirmación*] slanderous, defamatory; [*artículo, escrito*] libellous, libelous (*EEUU*), defamatory

diferencia SF 1 (= *distinción*) difference; **no debes hacer ~s entre tus hijos** you shouldn't discriminate between your children 2 (= *intervalo*) difference, gap; **hay una ~ de edad de diez años entre ellos** there's an age difference *o* age gap of ten years between them, there's ten years' difference in age between them; **con ~** by far 3 (= *desacuerdo*) **ya han resuelto sus ~s** they've resolved their differences 4 (= *resto*) difference; **pagué la ~ en efectivo** I paid the difference in cash

diferencial Ⓐ ADJ [*ecuación*] differential Ⓑ SM (*Aut*) differential Ⓒ SF (*Mat*) differential

diferenciar /1b/ Ⓐ VT 1 (= *hacer diferencias*) to distinguish, differentiate; **no sabe ~ entre uno y otro** she can't distinguish *o* differentiate between the two 2 (= *hacer diferente*) to make different Ⓑ **diferenciarse** VPR 1 (= *ser diferente*) to differ, be different (**de** from); **no se diferencian en nada** they do not differ at all 2 (= *destacarse*) to stand out; **este producto se diferencia por su calidad** this product stands out because of its quality

diferendo SM (*SAm frm*) dispute

diferente ADJ 1 (= *distinto*) different; **ser ~ de** *o* **a algn/algo** to be different to *o* from sb/sth 2 **~s** (= *varios*) various, several; **por aquí han pasado ~s personalidades** various *o* several celebrities have been here

diferido ADJ **emisión en ~** (*Radio, TV*) recorded programme, recorded program (*EEUU*); **el partido se retransmitirá en ~** a recording of the match will be broadcast

diferir /3i/ (*frm*) Ⓐ VI 1 (= *discrepar*) to differ, disagree; **~ de algo** to disagree with sth; **~ de algn en algo** to differ with sb over sth 2 (= *ser diferente*) to be different, differ Ⓑ VT 1 (= *aplazar*) to defer; **quieren ~ el pago hasta el año 2008** they want to defer payment until the year 2008 2 (= *enviar*) to refer; **han diferido el caso al Tribunal Supremo** the case was referred to the Supreme Court

difícil ADJ 1 (= *complicado*) [*problema*] difficult; [*tiempos, vida*] difficult, hard; [*situación*] difficult, delicate; **es ~ de hacer** it's difficult *o* hard to do; **es ~ que venga** he is unlikely to come; **creo que lo tiene ~** I think he's going to find it difficult 2 [*persona*] difficult; **es un hombre ~** he's a difficult man to get along with

difícilmente ADV 1 (= *con dificultad*) with difficulty 2 (= *apenas*) hardly; **~ se podrá hacer** we'll be hard-pressed to do it, we'll have a hard time doing it *o* trouble doing it

dificultad SF 1 (= *obstáculo, problema*) difficulty; **tuvieron algunas ~es para llegar a casa** they had some trouble getting home; **camina con ~** he has difficulty walking 2 (= *objeción*) objection; **poner ~es** to raise objections; **me pusieron ~es para darme el pasaporte** they made it difficult *o* awkward for me to get a passport

dificultar /1a/ VT 1 (= *obstaculizar*) [+ *camino*] to obstruct; [+ *tráfico*] to hold up 2 (= *hacer difícil*) [+ *trabajo*] to make difficult; [+ *progreso*] to hinder, stand in the way of; [+ *movimientos*] to restrict 3 (*RPl*) (= *dudar*) to doubt; **dificulto que vengan** I doubt (that) they'll win

difteria SF diphtheria

difuminar /1a/ Ⓐ VT to blur Ⓑ **difuminarse** VPR to fade

difundir /3a/ Ⓐ VT 1 [+ *teoría, ideología*] to spread, disseminate; **~ una noticia** to spread a piece of news 2 [+ *programa, imagen*] to broadcast, transmit 3 [+ *calor, luz*] to diffuse Ⓑ **difundirse** VPR 1 [*noticia*] to spread 2 [*calor, luz*] to become diffused

difunto/a Ⓐ ADJ deceased; **el ~ ministro** the late minister Ⓑ SM/F deceased, deceased person

difusión SF 1 [*de programa*] broadcasting; **los medios de ~** the media; **un diario de ~ nacional** a national newspaper

2 [*de noticia, teoría*] dissemination, spreading **3** [*de calor, luz*] diffusion

digerir /3i/ VT **1** [+ *comida*] to digest; **no puedo ~ a ese tío*** I can't stomach that guy* **2** [+ *opinión, noticia*] to absorb, assimilate; **le ha costado ~ su fracaso** he's found it hard to take in his failure

digestión SF digestion; **hacer la ~** to digest (one's food)

digestivo 1 ADJ digestive **2** SM digestive

digital ADJ **1** [*reloj*] digital **2** (= *dactilar*) finger *antes de s*; **huellas ~es** fingerprints

digitalizar /1f/ VT to digitize

dígito SM digit

dignarse /1a/ VPR **~ a hacer algo** to deign to do sth, condescend to do sth; **dígnese venir a esta oficina** (*frm*) please be so kind as to come to this office

dignatario/a SM/F dignitary

dignidad SF **1** (= *cualidad*) dignity **2** (*de sí mismo*) self-respect **3** (= *rango*) rank

dignificar /1g/ VT to dignify

digno ADJ **1** (= *merecedor*) **~ de elogio** praiseworthy; **~ de mención** worth mentioning; **es ~ de nuestra admiración** it deserves our admiration; **es ~ de verse** it is worth seeing **2** [*persona*] (= *honesto*) honourable, honorable (*EEUU*); (= *circunspecto*) dignified **3** (= *decoroso*) decent; **viviendas dignas** decent homes

dije¹ *ver* **decir**

dije²* ADJ (*Chi*) nice, sweet

dije³ SM (= *amuleto*) charm

dilación SF delay

dilapidar /1a/ VT to squander, waste

dilatación SF **1** (*Med*) dilation **2** (*Fís*) expansion

dilatado ADJ **1** [*pupila*] dilated **2** (= *extenso*) [*conocimiento*] extensive; [*período*] long

dilatar /1a/ **Ⓐ** VT **1** (= *extender*) [+ *pupila*] to dilate; [+ *metales*] to expand **2** (= *prolongar*) to protract, prolong **3** (= *retrasar*) to delay **Ⓑ dilatarse** VPR **1** (= *extenderse*) [*pupila*] to dilate; [*cuerpo, metal*] to expand **2** (*CAm, Méx*) (= *tardar*) **~se en hacer algo** to take a long time to do sth, be slow to do sth **3** (*CAm, Méx*) (= *retrasarse*) to be delayed, be late

dilatorio ADJ delaying

dilema SM dilemma

diletante SMF dilettante

diligencia SF **1** (= *cualidad*) (= *esmero*) diligence; (= *rapidez*) speed **2** (= *encargo*) errand **3** (*Jur*) **diligencias** formalities ➤ **diligencias judiciales** judicial proceedings ➤ **diligencias policiales** police inquiries ➤ **diligencias previas** inquest *sing* **4** (= *carruaje*) stagecoach

diligente ADJ **1** (= *esmerado*) diligent; **poco ~** slack **2** (= *rápido*) speedy

dilucidar /1a/ VT [+ *asunto*] to elucidate, clarify; [+ *misterio*] to clear up

diluir /3g/ **Ⓐ** VT **1** [+ *líquido, sustancia*] to dilute **2** (= *aguar*) to water down **Ⓑ diluirse** VPR to dissolve

diluviar /1b/ VI to pour with rain

diluvio SM flood

dimanar /1a/ VT **~ de** (*frm*) to arise from, spring from

dimensión SF **1** (= *magnitud*) dimension; **la cuarta ~** the fourth dimension **2 dimensiones** (= *tamaño*) size *sing*; **de grandes dimensiones** large; **tomar las dimensiones de algo** to take sth's measurements; **las dimensiones de la tragedia** the extent of the tragedy

dimes SMPL **~ y diretes** (= *riñas*) bickering *sing*, squabbling *sing*; (= *chismes*) gossip *sing*

diminutivo ADJ, SM diminutive

diminuto ADJ tiny, diminutive

dimisión SF resignation

dimisionar /1a/ VI, VT = **dimitir**

dimitir /3a/ **Ⓐ** VI to resign (**de** from) **Ⓑ** VT to resign

Dinamarca SF Denmark

dinámica SF **1** (*Fís*) dynamics *sing* **2** (= *funcionamiento*) dynamic; **la ~ de la sociedad** the dynamic of society ➤ **dinámica de grupo** group dynamics *pl*

dinámico ADJ dynamic

dinamismo SM dynamism

dinamita SF dynamite

dinamitar /1a/ VT to dynamite

dinamizar /1f/ VT to invigorate, put new energy into

dinamo SF, **dínamo** SF o (*LAm*) SM dynamo

dinastía SF dynasty

dinástico ADJ dynastic

dineral SM fortune

dinero SM money; **andar mal de ~** to be short of money; **el negocio no da ~** the business does not pay; **es hombre de ~** he is a man of means; **♦** MODISMOS **ganar ~ a espuertas** o **a porrillo** to make money hand over fist; **tirar el ~** to throw money away ➤ **dinero contante y sonante** hard cash ➤ **dinero electrónico** e-money, electronic money ➤ **dinero negro** undeclared money ➤ **dinero para gastos** pocket money ➤ **dinero suelto** loose change

dinosaurio SM dinosaur

dintel SM lintel

diñar* /1a/ VT (*Esp*) **~la** to kick the bucket*

diocesano ADJ diocesan

diócesis SF INV diocese

diodo SM diode

dionisiaco ADJ, **dionisíaco** ADJ Dionysian

dioptría SF dioptre, diopter (*EEUU*); **¿cuántas ~s tienes?** what's your gradation o correction o prescription?

Dios SM **1** (*Rel*) God; **~ Padre** God the Father **2** (*en exclamaciones*) **¡Dios!** (*con sorpresa*) God!; (*con fastidio*) for God's sake!; **¡~ mío!** ◇ **¡~ santo!** my God!, good God!; **¡~ me libre!** God forbid!, Heaven forbid!; **¡por ~!** for heaven's sake!; **—¿puedo fumar? —¡claro, por ~!** "may I smoke?" —"of course! o please do!"; **¡~ quiera que no llueva mañana!** let's hope it doesn't rain tomorrow; **¡vaya por ~!** (*con compasión*) oh dear!; (*con fastidio*) oh, drat!* **3 ♦** MODISMOS **a la buena de ~** (= *sin esmerarse*) any old how; (= *sin planificar*) just like that; **costar ~ y ayuda:** **costó ~ y ayuda convencerlo** it was a real job to persuade him; **dejado de la mano de ~:** **estos pueblos están dejados de la mano de ~** these villages have been abandoned to their fate; **~ dirá** time will tell; **sin encomendarse a ~ ni al diablo** without thought for the consequences; **estar de ~** to be God's will; **como ~ me dio a entender** as best as I could; **a ~ gracias** ◇ **gracias a ~** thank heaven, thank God; **como que hay (un) ~** (*esp CS*) you can bet on it; **como que hay ~ que ...** you can bet (your bottom dollar) that ...; **como ~ manda** (*con verbo*) properly; **como ~ lo echó** o **trajo al mundo*** stark naked, in one's birthday suit†; **si ~ quiere** God willing; **que sea lo que ~ quiera: he decidido hacerlo, y que sea lo que ~ quiera** I've decided to do it, and worry about it later; **sabe ~** God knows; **♦** REFRÁN **~ los cría y ellos se juntan** birds of a feather flock together

dios(a) SM/F god/goddess; **♦** MODISMOS **no hay ~ que*: no hay ~ que entienda eso** no-one on earth could understand that*; **ni ~*** no one; **todo ~*** everyone; **lo sabía todo ~** the world and his dog knew about it*, everyone knew about it

dióxido SM dioxide ➤ **dióxido de carbono** carbon dioxide

dioxina SF dioxin

diploma SM diploma

diplomacia SF diplomacy

diplomado/a **Ⓐ** ADJ qualified **Ⓑ** SM/F **1** (= *con diploma*) holder of a diploma **2** (*Univ*) (= *con diplomatura*) graduate

diplomarse /1a/ VPR (*esp LAm*) to graduate (*from college etc*)

diplomático/a **Ⓐ** ADJ **1** [*carrera, cuerpo*] diplomatic **2** (= *que tiene tacto*) diplomatic, tactful **Ⓑ** SM/F diplomat

diplomatura SF diploma course

diptongo SM diphthong

diputación SF 1 (= *delegación*) deputation 2 (*Pol*)
➤ **diputación provincial** ≈ county council (*Brit*), ≈ county commission (*EEUU*)

diputado/a SM/F ≈ member of parliament (*Brit*), ≈ representative (*EEUU*); ◇ *CORTES GENERALES*

dique SM (*en río*) dyke, dike (*esp EEUU*); (*en puerto*) dock

diré *etc ver* **decir**

dirección SF 1 (= *sentido*) direction; **"dirección prohibida"** "no entry"; **salir con** ~ **a** to leave for; **el tráfico con** ~ **a Barcelona** traffic for Barcelona; **ir en** ~ **contraria** to go the other way; **de dos direcciones** (*Esp*): **calle de dos direcciones** two-way street; **ir en** ~ **a** to go in the direction of, go towards, head for; **el tráfico en** ~ **a Burgos** traffic for Burgos; **calle de** ~ **obligatoria** o **única** one-way street 2 (= *orientación*) way; **desconozco la** ~ **que están siguiendo los acontecimientos** I don't know which way events are going 3 (= *señas*) address; **su nombre y** ~ **completa** your full name and address; **poner la** ~ **a un sobre** to address an envelope ➤ **dirección comercial** business address ➤ **dirección de correo electrónico, dirección electrónica** e-mail address ➤ **dirección de Internet** web address ➤ **dirección IP** IP address 4 (= *control*) [*de empresa, hospital, centro de enseñanza*] running; [*de partido*] leadership; [*de película*] direction; **le han confiado la** ~ **de la obra** he has been put in charge of the work; **se ha hecho cargo de la** ~ **de la orquesta** he's been appointed conductor of the orchestra 5 (= *personal directivo*) **la** ~ [*de empresa, centro escolar*] the management; [*de partido*] the leadership; [*de periódico*] the editorial board 6 (= *cargo*) (*en colegio*) headship (*Brit*), principalship (*EEUU*); (*en periódico, revista*) editorship; (*en partido*) leadership; [*de gerente*] post of manager; [*de alto cargo*] directorship 7 (= *despacho*) (*en colegio*) principal's office, headteacher's office (*Brit*); (*en periódico, revista*) editor's office; [*de gerente*] manager's office; [*de alto cargo*] director's office 8 (*Aut, Náut*) steering ➤ **dirección asistida, dirección hidráulica** (*LAm*) power steering

direccional SF (*Col, Méx Aut*) indicator (*Brit*), turn signal (*EEUU*); **poner la** ~ to signal, indicate (*Brit*)

direccionamiento SM (*Inform*) addressing

directamente ADV directly; **fui** ~ **a casa** I went straight home

directiva SF 1 (= *dirección*) [*de empresa*] board of directors; [*de partido*] executive committee, leadership 2 (= *instrucción*) guideline

directivo/a ❹ ADJ [*junta*] managing; [*función*] managerial, administrative ❺ SM/F (= *gerente*) manager; (= *ejecutivo*) executive

directo ❹ ADJ 1 [*línea*] straight 2 [*pregunta, respuesta, lenguaje*] direct, straightforward; **es muy directa hablando** she's very direct 3 [*tren*] direct, through; [*vuelo*] direct, non-stop 4 **ir** ~ **a** to go straight to 5 (= *sin intermediario*) direct 6 (*Ling*) direct 7 (*Radio, TV*) **en** ~ live; **transmitir en** ~ to broadcast live ❺ SM (*Boxeo*) straight punch

director(a) ❹ ADJ [*consejo, junta*] governing; [*principio*] guiding
❺ SM/F 1 (= *responsable*) [*de centro escolar*] headteacher (*Brit*), headmaster/headmistress (*Brit*), principal; [*de periódico, revista*] editor; (*Cine, TV*) director; [*de orquesta*] conductor; [*de hospital*] manager, administrator; [*de prisión*] governor (*Brit*), warden (*EEUU*) ➤ **director(a) artístico/a** artistic director ➤ **director(a) de cine** film director (*Brit*), movie director (*EEUU*) ➤ **director(a) de departamento** (*Univ*) head of department ➤ **director(a) de escena** stage manager ➤ **director(a) de tesis** thesis supervisor, research supervisor 2 (= *gerente*) manager; (*de mayor responsabilidad*) director ➤ **director(a) adjunto/a** assistant manager ➤ **director(a) ejecutivo/a** executive director, managing director ❻ SM (*Rel*) ➤ **director espiritual** spiritual director

directorio SM 1 (*Inform*) directory 2 ➤ **directorio de teléfonos, directorio telefónico** (*LAm*) telephone directory

directriz SF 1 (= *norma*) guideline 2 (*Mat*) directrix

dirigente ❹ ADJ leading; **la clase** ~ the ruling class ❺ SMF (*Pol*) leader

dirigible ❹ ADJ (*Aer, Náut*) steerable ❺ SM airship

dirigir /3c/ ❹ VT 1 (= *orientar*) [+ *persona*] to direct; [+ *asunto*] **lo dirigió con ayuda de un mapa** she showed him the way o directed him with the help of a map; **estos principios dirigen nuestra política** these are the guiding principles behind our policy; **dirigían sus pasos hacia la iglesia** they made their way o walked towards the church 2 (= *apuntar*) [+ *arma, telescopio*] to aim, point (a, **hacia** at); [+ *manguera*] to turn (a, **hacia** on), point (a, **hacia** at) 3 (= *destinar*) 3.1 [+ *carta, comentario, pregunta*] to address (a to) 3.2 [+ *libro, programa, producto*] to aim (a at); **una publicación dirigida al mercado infantil** a publication aimed at the children's market 3.3 [+ *acusación, críticas*] to make (a, **contra** against), level (a, **contra** at, against); [+ *ataques*] to make (a, **contra** against) 3.4 [+ *esfuerzos*] to direct (a, **hacia** to, towards) 4 (= *controlar*) [+ *empresa, hospital, centro de enseñanza*] to run; [+ *periódico, revista*] to edit, run; [+ *expedición, país, sublevación*] to lead; [+ *maniobra, operación, investigación*] to direct, be in charge of; [+ *debate*] to chair; [+ *proceso judicial*] to preside over; [+ *tesis*] to supervise; [+ *juego, partido*] to referee; **dirigió los destinos del país durante siete décadas** he controlled the fate of the country for seven decades 5 (*Cine, Teat*) to direct 6 [+ *orquesta, concierto*] to conduct; [+ *coro*] to lead ❺ **dirigirse** VPR 1 (= *ir*) ~**se a** o **hacia** to head for; **se dirigía a la oficina cuando lo arrestaron** he was on his way to o heading for the office when he was arrested; **se dirigió en su coche al aeropuerto** he drove to the airport 2 (= *ponerse en contacto*) ~**se a algn** (*oralmente*) to speak to sb, address sb (*frm*); (*por escrito*) to contact sb; **me dirijo a usted para solicitarle su ayuda** I am writing (to you) to request your help 3 (= *estar destinado*) ~**se a algo** to be aimed at sth; **toda sus esfuerzos van dirigidos a conseguir un nuevo récord** she is concentrating all her efforts on setting a new record

dirimir /3a/ VT [+ *disputa*] to settle

discado SM (*And, CS*) dialling, dialing (*EEUU*) ➤ **discado directo** direct dialling o (*EEUU*) dialing

discapacidad SF disability

discapacitado/a ❹ ADJ disabled, incapacitated ❺ SM/F disabled person ➤ **discapacitado/a psíquico/a** mentally disabled person

discar /1g/ VT (*And, CS*) to dial

discernimiento SM discernment

discernir /3k/ ❹ VT to distinguish, discern ❺ VI to discern, distinguish (**entre** between)

disciplina SF 1 (= *normas*) discipline ➤ **disciplina de partido, disciplina de voto** party discipline, party whip 2 (*Dep*) discipline; **ganó en la** ~ **de suelo** she came first in the floor exercises

disciplinar /1a/ VT to discipline

discípulo/a SM/F disciple

discjockey [dis'jokei] SMF disc jockey

Discman® ['disman] SM Discman®

disco SM (*Mús*) record; (*Inform*) disk; (*Dep*) discus; (*Telec*) dial; (*Ferro*) signal; ✦ MODISMO **parece un** ~ **rayado*** he's like a broken record* ➤ **disco compacto** compact disc ➤ **disco de freno** (*Aut*) brake disc ➤ **disco duro** hard disk ➤ **disco rojo** red light ➤ **disco verde** green light ➤ **disco volador** (*CS*) flying saucer

discografía SF records pl; **toda la** ~ **de los Beatles** all the records released by the Beatles

discográfica SF record company, record label

discográfico ADJ record *antes de s*; **casa discográfica** record company, record label; **éxito** ~ chart hit

díscolo ADJ unruly

disconforme ADJ **estar** ~ to be in disagreement, disagree (**con** with)

disconformidad SF disagreement

discontinuo ADJ [*línea*] broken

discordancia SF discord; **eso está en ~ con lo que dijo antes** that contradicts what she said earlier

discordante ADJ 1 (*Mús*) discordant 2 [*opiniones*] clashing

discorde ADJ 1 [*sonido*] discordant 2 [*opiniones*] clashing

discordia SF discord

discoteca SF 1 (= *lugar de baile*) club, nightclub, disco 2 (= *colección de discos*) record collection 3 (*LAm*) (= *tienda*) record shop (*Brit*), record store (*EEUU*)

discotequero ADJ disco *antes de s*; **no soy muy ~*** I'm not into clubbing *o* going to discos

discreción SF 1 (= *prudencia*) discretion; **tenemos que actuar con ~** we must act discreetly; **me callé por ~** I tactfully kept quiet 2 **a ~**: **añadir azúcar a ~** add sugar to taste; **comer a ~** to eat as much as one likes 3 **a ~ de algn** at sb's discretion

discrecional ADJ 1 [*poder*] discretionary 2 (= *facultativo*) optional; **parada ~** request stop (*Brit*), flag stop (*EEUU*); **servicio ~ de autobuses** private bus service

discrepancia SF 1 (= *diferencia*) discrepancy 2 (= *desacuerdo*) disagreement

discrepante ADJ [*visión, opiniones*] divergent; [*voz*] dissenting

discrepar /1a/ VI to disagree (**de** with)

discretamente ADV discreetly

discreto ADJ 1 (= *poco llamativo*) [*color, vestido*] sober; [*advertencia*] discreet 2 [*persona*] (= *prudente*) discreet 3 (= *mediano*) average, middling; **de discreta inteligencia** reasonably intelligent; **unas ganancias discretas** modest profits 4 (*Fís*) discrete

discriminación SF discrimination (**contra** against)

discriminado ADJ **sentirse ~** to feel that one has been unfairly treated *o* has been discriminated against

discriminar /1a/ Ⓐ VT 1 [+ *persona, colectivo*] to discriminate against 2 [+ *colores, sabores*] to differentiate between Ⓑ VI to discriminate (**entre** between)

discriminatorio ADJ discriminatory

disculpa SF 1 (= *pretexto*) excuse 2 (= *perdón*) apology; **pedir ~s a algn por algo** to apologize to sb for sth

disculpar /1a/ Ⓐ VT (= *perdonar*) to excuse, forgive; **disculpa que venga tarde** forgive me for coming late; **¡discúlpeme!** I'm sorry!; **le disculpan sus pocos años** his youth is an excuse, his youth provides an excuse; **te ruego me disculpes con el anfitrión** please make my apologies to the host Ⓑ **disculparse** VPR to apologize (**con** to); **se disculpó por haber llegado tarde** he apologized for arriving late

discurrir /3a/ Ⓐ VT (= *inventar*) to think up Ⓑ VI 1 (= *recorrer*) to roam, wander (**por** about, along) 2 [*río*] to flow 3 [*tiempo*] to pass; **la sesión discurrió sin novedad** the meeting went off quietly 4 (= *meditar*) to meditate (**en** about, on)

discursivo ADJ discursive

discurso SM 1 (= *alocución*) speech; **pronunciar un ~** to make a speech, give a speech 2 (*Ling*) discourse 3 [*del tiempo*] **en el ~ del tiempo** with the passage of time

discusión SF 1 (= *riña*) argument 2 (= *debate*) discussion

discutible ADJ debatable, arguable; **80.000 euros ~s** 80,000 euros (negotiable), 80,000 euros o.n.o. (*Brit*)

discutido ADJ 1 (= *hablado*) much-discussed 2 (= *controvertido*) controversial

discutir /3a/ Ⓐ VT 1 (= *debatir*) [+ *plan, proyecto, idea*] to discuss; [+ *precio*] to argue about 2 (= *contradecir*) to question, challenge; **~ a algn lo que está diciendo** to question *o* challenge what sb is saying; **sus órdenes no se discuten** you don't question his orders; **eso no te lo discuto** I don't dispute that Ⓑ VI 1 (= *dialogar*) to discuss, talk 2 (= *disputar*) to argue (**de, sobre** about, over); **¡no discutas!** don't argue!

disecar /1g/ VT [+ *animal*] to stuff; [+ *planta*] to preserve, mount

disección SF (*Med*) dissection

diseccionar /1a/ VT to dissect, analyse

diseminar /1a/ VT to spread, disseminate (*frm*)

disensión SF disagreement, dissension

disentir /3i/ VI to dissent (**de** from), disagree (**de** with)

diseñador(a) SM/F designer ➤ **diseñador(a) gráfico/a** graphic designer

diseñar /1a/ VT to design

diseño SM 1 (= *actividad*) design; **camisa de ~** designer shirt ➤ **diseño asistido por ordenador, diseño asistido por computador** (*LAm*) computer-aided design ➤ **diseño de interiores** interior design ➤ **diseño gráfico** graphic design ➤ **diseño industrial** industrial design ➤ **diseño textil** textile design 2 (= *dibujo*) (*Arte*) drawing, sketch; (*Cos*) pattern

disertar /1a/ VI to discourse (**acerca de, sobre** upon); **~ largamente sobre algo** to speak at length about sth

disfraz SM (*para una fiesta*) fancy dress, costume; (*para engañar a algn*) disguise

disfrazar /1f/ Ⓐ VT 1 [+ *persona*] (*para ocultarse*) to disguise (**de** as); (*para una fiesta*) to dress up (**de** as) 2 (= *ocultar*) [+ *sentimiento, verdad, intención*] to disguise, conceal; [+ *sabor*] to disguise 3 (*Mil*) to camouflage Ⓑ **disfrazarse** VPR [*persona*] (*para ocultarse de algo*) to disguise o.s. (**de** as); (*para una fiesta*) to dress up (**de** as)

disfrutar /1a/ Ⓐ VT to enjoy Ⓑ VI 1 (= *gozar*) to enjoy o.s.; **¡que disfrutes!** enjoy yourself!; **~ con algo** to enjoy sth; **~ de algo** to enjoy sth 2 **~ de algo** (= *poseer*) to enjoy sth; **disfruta de excelente salud** he enjoys excellent health

disfrute SM enjoyment

disfunción SF malfunction

disgregación SF disintegration, breaking up

disgregar /1h/ Ⓐ VT [+ *grupo*] to break up; [+ *manifestantes*] to disperse Ⓑ **disgregarse** VPR to disintegrate, break up (**en** into)

disgresión SF digression

disgustado ADJ upset

disgustar /1a/ Ⓐ VT to upset; **estaba muy disgustado con el asunto** he was very displeased *o* upset about the matter Ⓑ **disgustarse** VPR to get upset

⚠ **disgustar ≠ disgust**

disgusto SM 1 (= *pena*) **la noticia me causó un gran ~** I was very upset by the news; **nunca nos dio un ~** he never caused us any worry *o* trouble 2 (= *riña*) quarrel 3 **a ~**: **hacer algo a ~** to do sth unwillingly; **estar** *o* **sentirse a ~** to be *o* feel ill at ease

disidencia SF 1 (*Pol*) dissidence 2 (*Rel*) dissent

disidente Ⓐ ADJ (*Pol*) dissident Ⓑ SMF 1 (*Pol*) dissident 2 (*Rel*) dissenter, nonconformist

disimulado ADJ (= *oculto*) covert; **estaba ~ entre unos papeles** it was hidden among some papers; ✦ MODISMO **hacerse el ~** to pretend not to notice

disimular /1a/ Ⓐ VT 1 [+ *emoción, alegría, tristeza*] to hide, conceal 2 [+ *defecto, roto*] to cover up, hide; [+ *sabor, olor*] to hide Ⓑ VI to pretend; **has sido tú, no disimules** it was you, don't pretend it wasn't; **ahí está tu padre, disimula** there's your father, just act normal

disimulo SM **sin el menor ~** quite openly; **se metió el sobre en el bolsillo con ~** he slipped the envelope quietly into his pocket

disipar /1a/ Ⓐ VT [+ *duda, temor*] to dispel, remove Ⓑ **disiparse** VPR 1 [*niebla*] to lift; [*nubes*] to disperse 2 [*dudas*] to be dispelled

diskette [dis'ket] SM diskette

dislate SM 1 (= *absurdo*) absurdity 2 dislates (= *disparates*) nonsense *sing*

dislexia SF dyslexia

disléxico/a ADJ, SM/F dyslexic

dislocar /1g/ **Ⓐ** VT to dislocate **Ⓑ dislocarse** VPR **~se el tobillo** to dislocate one's ankle

disloque* SM **al llegar la medianoche aquello fue ya el ~** when midnight came it was utter chaos

disminución SF **1** (= *reducción*) [*de población, cantidad*] decrease, drop, fall; [*de precios, temperaturas*] drop, fall; [*de velocidad*] decrease, reduction; **la ~ de la capa de ozono** the depletion of the ozone layer **2** [*de dolor*] reduction; [*de fiebre*] drop, fall **3** (*Cos*) [*de puntos*] decreasing

disminuido/a SM/F handicapped person, mentally handicapped person

disminuir /3g/ **Ⓐ** VT [+ *nivel, precio, gastos*] to reduce, bring down; [+ *riesgo, incidencia, dolor*] to reduce, lessen; [+ *temperatura*] to lower, bring down; [+ *prestigio, autoridad*] to diminish, lessen; [+ *fuerzas*] to sap; [+ *entusiasmo*] to dampen; **disminuyó la velocidad para tomar la curva** she slowed down *o* reduced her speed to take the bend

Ⓑ VI **1** (= *decrecer*) [*número, población*] to decrease, drop, fall; [*temperatura, precios*] to drop, fall; [*distancia, diferencia, velocidad*] to decrease; [*fuerzas, autoridad, poder*] to diminish; [*días*] to grow shorter; [*luz*] to fade; [*prestigio, entusiasmo*] to dwindle

2 (= *empeorar*) [*memoria, vista*] to fail

disolución SF **1** (= *acto*) dissolution **2** (*Quím*) solution **3** (*Com*) liquidation **4** (*moral*) dissoluteness, dissipation

disoluto ADJ dissolute

disolvente SM solvent

disolver /2h/ (*pp* **disuelto**) **Ⓐ** VT **1** [+ *azúcar, sal*] to dissolve **2** [+ *contrato, matrimonio, parlamento*] to dissolve **3** [+ *manifestación*] to break up **Ⓑ disolverse** VPR **1** [*azúcar, sal*] to dissolve **2** (*Com*) to go into liquidation **3** (= *deshacerse*) [*manifestación*] to break up; [*parlamento*] to dissolve

disonante ADJ **1** (*Mús*) dissonant **2** (= *discordante*) discordant

dispar ADJ [*opiniones, aficiones*] different, disparate

disparada SF (*LAm*) **ir a la ~** to go at full speed; **irse a la ~** to be off like a shot; **hacer algo a la ~** to rush through sth

disparadero SM trigger, trigger mechanism; ✦ MODISMO **poner a algn en el ~** to drive sb to distraction

disparado ADJ **entrar ~** to shoot in; **ir ~** to go like crazy; **salir ~** to shoot out, be off like a shot

disparador SM [*de arma*] trigger; [*de cámara fotográfica*] release

disparar /1a/ **Ⓐ** VT **1** [+ *arma de fuego, proyectil, tiro*] to fire; [+ *flecha*] to shoot; [+ *gatillo*] to pull **2** (*Dep*) [+ *penalti, falta*] to take **3** [+ *consumo, precio*] **la subida del petróleo ha disparado la inflación** the rise in oil prices has caused inflation to shoot up **4** (= *hacer saltar*) [+ *alarma*] to trigger, set off; [+ *proceso, reacción*] to spark, spark off

Ⓑ VI **1** (*con un arma*) to shoot, fire; **los cazadores ~on al ciervo** the hunters shot *o* fired at the deer; **le ~on a la cabeza** they shot *o* fired at his head; **la policía disparó contra los manifestantes** the police fired on *o* shot at the demonstrators; **apuntó al blanco y disparó** he aimed at the target and fired **2** (*Dep*) to shoot; **el delantero disparó a puerta** the forward shot at *o* for goal **3** (*Fot*) to shoot

Ⓒ dispararse VPR **1** [*arma de fuego*] to go off, fire; [*consumo, precios, inflación*] to shoot up, rocket **2** [*pánico, violencia*] to take hold **3** (*al hablar*) to get carried away*

disparatado ADJ crazy, nonsensical

disparatar /1a/ VI to talk nonsense

disparate SM **1** (= *comentario*) foolish remark; **¡no digas ~s!** don't talk nonsense!; **¡qué ~!** what garbage!, how absurd! **2** (= *acción*) **sacar el coche con esta niebla es un ~** taking the car out in this fog is just crazy *o* is a stupid thing to do; **es capaz de cualquier ~** he's capable of doing

something really stupid **3** (= *error*) blunder; **hiciste un ~ protestando** it was foolish of you to complain

disparejo ADJ (*esp LAm*) **1** (= *desnivelado*) uneven **2** (= *diferente*) different

disparidad SF disparity

disparo SM **1** (= *tiro*) shot; **se oyeron varios ~s** some shooting was heard; **hacer ~s al aire** to fire into the air, shoot into the air **2** (*Dep*) shot

dispendio SM waste

dispensa SF (*Rel*) dispensation

dispensar /1a/ VT **1** (= *conceder*) [+ *ayuda*] to give; [+ *honores*] to grant; [+ *atención*] to pay; [+ *acogida*] to give, accord; [+ *receta*] to dispense **2** (= *perdonar*) to excuse; **¡dispénseme usted!** I beg your pardon!, sorry! **3** (= *eximir*) to exempt (**de** from), excuse (**de** from); **~ a algn de hacer algo** to excuse sb from doing sth

> Recuérdese que las preposiciones en inglés rigen gerundio y no infinitivo, de ahí **to excuse sb from doing sth**.

dispensario SM community clinic

dispersar /1a/ **Ⓐ** VT [+ *multitud, grupo*] to disperse, scatter; [+ *manifestación*] to break up; [+ *enemigo*] to rout **Ⓑ dispersarse** VPR [*multitud, grupo*] to disperse, scatter; [*manifestación*] to break up

disperso ADJ **1** (= *diseminado*) scattered, dispersed **2** [*discurso, mente*] unfocussed, unfocused (*EEUU*)

displicente ADJ offhand, disdainful

disponer /2q/ (*pp* **dispuesto**) **Ⓐ** VT **1** (= *colocar*) (*por orden*) to arrange; (*de otro modo*) to set out; **dispuso los discos por orden alfabético** he arranged the records in alphabetical order; **dispuso los cubiertos sobre la mesa** he set out the silverware on the table **2** (= *preparar*) to prepare, get ready; **dispuso la sala para el concierto** he prepared the hall *o* he got the hall ready for the concert **3** (= *mandar*) [*persona, comisión*] to order; [*juez*] to rule, decree, order; (*en código, testamento*) to lay down, stipulate; **mis padres lo han dispuesto así** my parents have decided that it should be that way

Ⓑ VI **1** **~ de algo** (= *tener*) to have sth (at one's disposal); **disponemos de muy poco tiempo** there is very little time available (to us), we have very little time (at our disposal); **los medios de que disponemos** the means available to us, the means at our disposal; **dispone de quince días para apelar** you have fifteen days to appeal **2** **~ de algo** (= *hacer uso de*) to make use of sth, use sth; **puede ~ de mí para lo que necesites** I am at your disposal for whatever you might need

Ⓒ disponerse VPR **1** **~se a hacer algo** (= *estar a punto de*) to be about to do sth; (= *decidir*) to resolve to do sth **2** (= *colocarse*) **~se para algo** to get into position for sth

disponibilidad SF [*de persona, producto*] availability

disponible ADJ **1** (= *libre*) [*asiento, habitación, dinero*] available; [*tiempo*] spare **2 estar ~** to be available, be free; **la casa ya está ~ para que la ocupéis** the house is now ready for you to move in

disposición SF **1** (= *colocación*) [*de muebles, capítulos*] arrangement; [*de casa, habitación*] layout **2** (= *disponibilidad*) disposal; **a ~ de algn** at sb's disposal; **un número de teléfono a ~ del público** a telephone number for public use *o* at the public's disposal; **puso su cargo a ~ de la asamblea** he offered his resignation to the assembly; **pasar a ~ judicial** to be taken into custody; **tener algo a su ~** to have sth at one's disposal, have sth available **3** (= *voluntad*) willingness; **estar en ~ de hacer algo** to be ready *o* willing to do sth ➤ **disposición de ánimo** frame of mind **4** (= *aptitud*) aptitude, talent (**para** for); **no tenía ~ para la pintura** he had no aptitude *o* talent for painting **5** (*Jur*) (= *cláusula*) provision; (= *norma*) regulation; **última ~** last will and testament **6 disposiciones** (= *medidas*) arrangements

dispositivo SM **1** (= *aparato*) device; (= *mecanismo*) mechanism ➤ **dispositivo de seguridad** (= *mecanismo*) safety catch; (= *medidas*) security measures *pl* ➤ **dispositivo intrauterino** intrauterine device, coil **2 dispositivos** (*Mil*) forces ➤ **dispositivos de seguridad** security forces

dispuesto Ⓐ PP *de* **disponer** Ⓑ ADJ **1** (= *preparado*) arranged, ready; **todo está ~ para las elecciones** everything is set *o* arranged *o* ready for the elections; **¿estáis ~s para salir?** are you ready to leave? **2** (= *decidido*) willing; **es una persona muy dispuesta** she's always ready and willing; **estábamos ~s al diálogo** we were willing *o* prepared to discuss the matter; **estoy ~ a ir a juicio si fuera necesario** I am quite prepared to go to court if necessary; **no estoy ~ a que me insulten** I refuse to be insulted

disputa SF dispute, argument

disputado ADJ [*partido*] close, hard fought

disputar /1a/ Ⓐ VT **1** [+ *partido, encuentro*] to play, contest; [+ *campeonato, liga*] to play; **el Mundial se disputó en Francia** the World Cup was played *o* contested in France **2** **~ algo a algn** (*frm*) to dispute sth with sb Ⓑ VI **~ por algo** to compete for sth Ⓒ **disputarse** VPR **ocho escritores se disputan el premio** eight writers are contending *o* competing for the prize

disquería SF (*LAm*) record shop

disquete SM diskette

disquetera SF disk drive

disquisición SF **1** (= *análisis*) disquisition **2 disquisiciones** (= *comentarios*) asides, digressions

distancia SF **1** (*en el espacio*) distance; **¿a qué ~ está Lugo de Bilbao?** how far (away) is Lugo from Bilbao?, how far is it from Lugo to Bilbao?; **la oficina está a 50 m de ~** the office is 50 m away; **a ~** from a distance; **acortar las ~s** to shorten the distance; **el Real Madrid ha acortado las ~s con el Barcelona** Real Madrid is closing in on Barcelona, Real Madrid is closing the gap with Barcelona; **guardar** *o* **mantener las ~s** ◇ **mantenerse a ~** to keep one's distance; **marcar~s: quieren marcar ~s con la dirección del partido** they want to distance themselves from *o* set themselves apart from the party leadership ➤ **distancia de seguridad** (*Aut*) safe distance **2** (*entre opiniones, creencias*) distance, gap

distanciado ADJ **está distanciada de su familia** she has grown apart from her family; **estamos ~s en nuestras ideas** our ideas are a long way apart *o* poles apart

distanciamiento SM **hay un ~ cada vez mayor entre ellos** they are growing further apart every day

distanciar /1b/ Ⓐ VT **1** [+ *amigos, hermanos*] to cause a rift between **2** [+ *objetos*] to space out, separate Ⓑ **distanciarse** VPR **1** [*dos personas*] to grow apart; **~se de la familia** to grow apart from one's family **2** (*en carrera*) **consiguió ~se del otro corredor** he managed to put some distance between himself and the other runner

distante ADJ **1** [*lugar*] (= *lejano*) distant; (= *remoto*) far-off, remote **2** [*persona, actitud*] distant

distar /1a/ VI **1** (*en el espacio*) **dista 5 km de aquí** it is 5 km from here; **¿dista mucho?** is it far? **2** (= *diferir*) **dista mucho de la verdad** it's very far from the truth

distender /2g/ Ⓐ VT to distend, stretch; **~ las relaciones entre ambos países** to ease *o* steady relations between the two countries Ⓑ **distenderse** VPR [*músculos*] to relax; [*relaciones*] to ease, steady

distendido ADJ [*ambiente, charla*] relaxed

distensión SF **1** (= *relajación*) **ambiente de ~** relaxed atmosphere **2** (*Med*) strain

distinción SF **1** (= *diferencia*) distinction; **hacer una ~ entre ...** to make a distinction between ...; **a ~ de algo** unlike sth, in contrast to sth; **hacer una ~ con algn** to show special consideration to sb; **sin ~: todos serán tratados sin ~** everybody will be treated without distinction; **sin ~ de edad** irrespective *o* regardless of age **2** (= *privilegio*) distinction; **le acaban de otorgar una ~ al valor** he was honoured *o* (*EEUU*) honored for his bravery

➤ **distinción honorífica** honour, honor (*EEUU*)

distingo SM distinction

distinguido ADJ **1** (= *destacado*) [*figura*] distinguished; [*artista, escritor*] celebrated; [*alumno*] outstanding **2** (= *refinado*) [*modales, ropa*] elegant, refined; [*caballero, señora*] distinguished; **~ público, les vamos a presentar ...** ladies and gentlemen, allow me to present ... **3** (*frm*) (*en cartas*) **"Distinguida Sra. Martínez"** "Dear Mrs Martinez"; **"Distinguido Señor"** (*LAm*) "Dear Sir"

distinguir /3d/ Ⓐ VT **1** (= *diferenciar*) **1.1** (= *ver la diferencia entre*) to distinguish; **no distingo bien los sonidos** I can't distinguish the sounds very well; **he puesto una etiqueta a la maleta para ~la** I've put a label on the suitcase to be able to tell it apart from *o* distinguish it from the others; **¿sabes ~ un violín de una viola?** can you tell *o* distinguish a violin from a viola? **1.2** (= *hacer diferente*) to set apart; **lo que nos distingue de los animales** what distinguishes us from the animals, what sets us apart from the animals **1.3** (= *hacer una distinción entre*) to distinguish; **hay que ~ dos períodos** we need to distinguish two periods **2** (= *ver*) [+ *objeto, sonido*] to make out; **no podía ~ la señal** I couldn't make out the sign **3** (= *honrar*) [+ *amigo, alumno*] to honour, honor (*EEUU*); **me distingue con su amistad** I am honoured *o* (*EEUU*) honored to have his friendship Ⓑ VI (= *ver la diferencia*) to tell the difference (**entre** between); (= *hacer una distinción*) to make a distinction (**entre** between); **no era capaz de ~ entre lo bueno y lo malo** he couldn't tell the difference *o* distinguish between good and bad; **en su discurso, distinguió entre el viejo y el nuevo liberalismo** in his speech he made a distinction between the old and the new liberalism Ⓒ **distinguirse** VPR **1** (= *diferenciarse*) [*objeto*] to stand out; [*persona*] to distinguish o.s., make a name for o.s.; **nuestros productos se distinguen por su calidad** our products are distinguished by their quality, our products stand out for their quality; **se distinguió por sus descubrimientos en física cuántica** he made a name for himself through his research into quantum physics **2** (= *reconocerse*) to be identified; **se distinguen por su envoltorio** they can be identified by their packaging

distintivo Ⓐ ADJ [*rasgo, carácter*] distinctive; [*signo*] distinguishing Ⓑ SM (= *insignia*) [*de policía*] badge; [*de equipo*] emblem, badge; [*de empresa*] emblem, logo

distinto ADJ **1** (= *diferente*) different (**a, de** from) **2 distintos** several, various; **hay distintas opiniones sobre eso** there are several *o* various opinions about that

distorsión SF distortion

distorsionar /1a/ VT to distort

distracción SF **1** (= *entretenimiento*) entertainment; **leer es mi ~ favorita** reading is my favourite pastime *o* form of entertainment; **no faltan distracciones para los niños** there is no lack of entertainment for the children **2** [*de preocupaciones, problemas*] distraction; **el trabajo me sirve de ~** my work is a distraction for me; **este libro te servirá de ~** this book will help you take your mind off things **3** (= *despiste*) **en un momento de ~ me robaron la cartera** my attention wandered *o* I got distracted for a moment and I had my wallet stolen; **la causa del accidente podría ser una ~ del conductor** the accident could have been caused by a lapse of concentration on the driver's part

distraer /2o/ Ⓐ VT **1** (= *entretener*) to entertain, amuse; **distrajimos a los niños contándoles cuentos** we kept the children entertained *o* amused by telling them stories; **necesito algo que me distraiga un poco** I need something to take my mind off things; ✦ MODISMO • **el hambre** to keep the wolf from the door **2** (= *despistar*) to distract (**de** from); **"prohibido distraer al conductor"** "do not distract the driver's attention" **3** [+ *dinero, fondos*] to embezzle Ⓑ VI (= *entretener*) [*pesca, ejercicio*] to be relaxing, take your mind off things; [*lectura, espectáculo*] to be entertaining, take your mind off things Ⓒ **distraerse** VPR **1** (= *entretenerse*) to keep o.s. entertained, keep o.s. amused; **deberías salir y ~te** you should get out

and enjoy yourself
2 (= *despistarse*) to get distracted; **se distrae mucho en clase** he gets very easily distracted in class; **me distraje un momento y se me quemó la comida** my attention wandered *o* I got distracted for a moment and the dinner got burnt

distraídamente ADV absent-mindedly

distraído/a Ⓐ ADJ **1** (= *despistado*) **1.1** (*con estar*) **siempre está ~ en clase** he's always daydreaming in class, he never pays attention in class; **iba yo algo ~** I was walking along with my mind on other things; **me miró distraída** she glanced absently at me, she glanced at me absent-mindedly **1.2** (*con ser*) **soy muy ~** I'm very absent-minded **2** (= *entretenido*) entertained, amused **3** (*Esp*) (= *divertido*) entertaining, amusing Ⓑ SM/F **hacerse el ~** to pretend not to notice

distribución SF **1** (= *reparto*) [*de víveres, mercancías, película*] distribution; [*de correo*] delivery; [*de trabajo, tarea*] allocation; [*de folletos*] (*en buzones*) distribution; (*en mano*) handing out **2** (*Estadística*) distribution **3** (*Arquit*) layout, ground plan **4** (*Aut, Téc*) distribution

distribuidor(a) Ⓐ SM/F distributor Ⓑ SM (*LAm Aut*) motorway exit (*Brit*), highway exit (*EEUU*)

distribuir /3g/ VT **1** (= *repartir*) [+ *víveres, mercancía, película*] to distribute; [+ *correo*] to deliver; [+ *trabajo, tarea*] to allocate; [+ *folletos*] (*en buzones*) to distribute; (*en mano*) to hand out **2** [+ *carga*] to stow, arrange; [+ *peso*] to distribute equally **3** (*Arquit*) to plan, lay out

distributivo ADJ distributive

distrito SM district ➤ **distrito electoral** constituency (*Brit*), precinct (*EEUU*) ➤ **distrito postal** postal district

disturbio SM (*de poca importancia*) disturbance; (*más grave*) riot

disuadir /3a/ VT to dissuade, deter; **~ a algn de hacer algo** to dissuade *o* deter sb from doing sth

Recuérdese que las preposiciones en inglés rigen gerundio y no infinitivo, de ahí **to dissuade** *o* **to deter sb from doing sth**.

disuasión SF **1** (= *convencimiento*) dissuasion; **capacidad de ~** powers of persuasion **2** (*Mil*) deterrence

disuasorio ADJ (*Mil*) deterrent

disuelto PP *de* **disolver**

disyuntiva SF **1** (= *opción*) alternative, choice **2** (= *dilema*) dilemma

disyuntivo ADJ disjunctive

DIU SM ABR (= *dispositivo intrauterino*) coil, IUD, IUCD

diurético ADJ, SM diuretic

diurex SM (*Méx*) *ver* **durex**

diurno ADJ (*gen*) day *antes de s*, daytime *antes de s*; [*animal, planta*] diurnal

diva SF prima donna, diva; *ver tb* **divo**

divagación SF digression; **divagaciones** wanderings, ramblings

divagar /1h/ VI **1** (= *salirse del tema*) to digress **2** (= *hablar vagamente*) to ramble

diván SM **1** (= *asiento*) divan **2** [*de psiquiatra*] couch

divergencia SF divergence ➤ **divergencia de opiniones** difference of opinion

divergente ADJ divergent

divergir /3c/ VI **1** [*opiniones*] to differ **2** [*personas*] to differ, disagree **3** [*líneas*] to diverge

diversidad SF diversity

diversificar /1g/ Ⓐ VT to diversify Ⓑ **diversificarse** VPR to diversify

diversión SF **1** (= *entretenimiento*) fun **2** (= *pasatiempo*) hobby, pastime **3** (*Mil*) diversion

diverso ADJ **1** (= *variado*) diverse, varied **2 diversos** several, various; **está en ~s libros** it appears in several *o* various books

divertido ADJ (= *entretenido*) [*libro, película*] entertaining; [*chiste, persona*] funny, amusing; **la fiesta fue muy divertida** the party was great fun *o* very enjoyable

divertir /3i/ Ⓐ VT **1** (= *hacer reír*) **sus imitaciones divierten mucho al público** the audience find his impressions very funny *o* amusing **2** (= *entretener*) to entertain, amuse Ⓑ **divertirse** VPR **1** (= *pasarlo bien*) to have a good time, enjoy o.s.; **¡que te diviertas!** have a good time!, enjoy yourself! **2** (= *distraerse*) to amuse o.s.; **le compré este juego para que se divirtiera** I bought him this game to keep him amused

dividendo SM dividend

dividir /3a/ Ⓐ VT **1** (= *partir*) to divide; **los dividieron en tres grupos** they split them (up) *o* divided them into three groups; **dividía su tiempo entre el cargo y su familia** he divided his time between his job and his family; **la bodega del barco está dividida en cuatro secciones** the hold of the ship is divided into four sections **2** (*Mat*) to divide (**entre, por** by) **3** (= *repartir*) [+ *ganancias, posesiones*] to split up, divide up; [+ *gastos*] to split **4** (= *separar*) to divide; **los Pirineos dividen España y Francia** the Pyrenees divide France from Spain **5** (= *enemistar*) to divide; **la guerra dividió al país** the war divided the country Ⓑ VI (*Mat*) to divide (**entre, por** into) Ⓒ **dividirse** VPR **1** (= *partirse*) [*célula*] to divide; [*grupo, país*] to split; **me encantaría ayudarte, pero no puedo ~me** I'd love to help you, but I can't be in two places at once; **la crítica estuvo muy dividida** the critics were very divided **2** (= *separarse*) [*personas*] to split up; [*camino, carretera*] to fork; **los fundadores se dividieron porque sus ideas eran muy distintas** the founders split up because their ideas were so different **3** (= *repartirse*) [+ *trabajo, ganancias*] to split up, divide up

divieso SM (*Med*) boil

divinamente ADV divinely; **lo pasamos ~** we had a wonderful time

divinidad SF **1** (= *dios*) deity **2** (= *esencia divina*) divinity

divino Ⓐ ADJ **1** (*Rel*) divine **2** (= *precioso*) divine, lovely Ⓑ ADV **pasarlo ~*** to have a wonderful time

divirtiendo *etc ver* **divertir**

divisa SF **1** (= *distintivo*) emblem **2** (*tb* **~s**) (*Fin*) foreign currency; **control de ~s** exchange control

divisar /1a/ VT to make out, distinguish

división SF **1** (= *separación*) [*de célula*] division; [*de átomo*] splitting; [*de gastos, ganancias*] division; **hay ~ de opiniones** opinions are divided ➤ **división del trabajo** division of labour *o* (*EEUU*) labor ➤ **división de poderes** division of powers **2** (*Mat*) division **3** (= *desunión*) [*de partido, familia*] division, split **4** (*Dep, Mil*) division **5** (= *sección*) division ➤ **división administrativa, división territorial** administrative region

divisor Ⓐ ADJ dividing Ⓑ SM (*Mat*) divisor; **máximo común ~** highest common factor, greatest common divisor

divisoria SF dividing line

divisorio ADJ [*línea*] dividing; **línea divisoria de las aguas** watershed

divo/a SM/F star; *ver tb* **diva**

divorciado/a Ⓐ ADJ divorced Ⓑ SM/F divorcé/divorcée

divorciar /1b/ Ⓐ VT to divorce Ⓑ **divorciarse** VPR to get divorced, get a divorce (**de** from)

divorcio SM **1** [*de una pareja*] divorce **2** (= *diferencia*) discrepancy

divulgación SF **1** [*de noticia, ideas*] spreading **2** [*de descubrimiento, secreto*] disclosure; **revistas de ~ científica** popular science magazines

divulgar /1h/ Ⓐ VT **1** [+ *noticia, ideas*] to spread **2** [+ *secreto*] to divulge, disclose Ⓑ **divulgarse** VPR **1** [*secreto*] to leak out **2** [*rumor*] to spread

divulgativo ADJ informative

dizque* ADV (*LAm*) supposedly; **lo hizo ~ por ayudar** he was trying to help, supposedly; **~ vendrán hoy** they're supposed to be coming today

dm ABR (= **decímetro(s)**) dm

DNI SM ABR (*Esp*) (= **documento nacional de identidad**) ID card; ⇨ *DOCUMENTO NACIONAL DE IDENTIDAD*

Dña. = D.ª; ⇨ *DON/DOÑA*

do SM (*Mús*) C

D.O. SF ABR = **denominación de origen;** ⇨ *DENOMINACIÓN DE ORIGEN*

dóberman SM Doberman

dobladillo SM hem

doblaje SM (*Cine*) dubbing

doblar /1a/ **Ⓐ** VT **1** (= *plegar*) [+ *carta, tela, periódico*] to fold; [+ *alambre, pierna*] to bend **2** (= *torcer*) [+ *esquina*] to turn, go around **3** (= *tener el doble de*) **su marido le dobla el sueldo** her husband earns twice as much as her, her husband earns double what she does; **te doblo la edad** I'm twice your age **4** (= *duplicar*) [+ *cantidad, oferta*] to double; **en verano nos doblan el trabajo** in summer our work doubles *o* is doubled **5** (*Cine*) **5.1** (*en la voz*) [+ *película, actor*] to dub **5.2** (*en la acción*) [+ *actor*] to stand in for **Ⓑ** VI **1** (= *girar*) [*persona, vehículo*] to turn; **~ a la derecha** to turn right **2** [*campana*] to toll; **~ a muerto** to sound the death knell **Ⓒ doblarse** VPR **1** (= *plegarse*) [*papel, tela*] to fold (up); [*alambre, barra*] to bend; **se le ~on las rodillas** his knees buckled beneath him **2** [*persona*] (= *encorvarse*) to bend; (= *retorcerse*) to double up; (= *doblegarse*) to give up, give in **3** [*cantidad*] to double; **el número de accidentes se ha doblado** the number of accidents has doubled

doble **Ⓐ** ADJ **1** [*puerta, tela, agente*] double; [*control, nacionalidad*] dual; [*ración, café*] large; [*cuerda*] extra strong; [*ventaja*] twofold; **"no aparcar en doble fila"** "no double-parking"; **una tela de ~ ancho** a double-width piece of fabric; **~ acristalamiento** (*Esp*) double glazing; **~ cristal** double glazing; **~ espacio** double-spacing; **diez páginas impresas a ~ espacio** ten pages printed in double-spacing; **~ juego** double-dealing; **hacer un ~ juego** to play a double game; **~ página** two-page spread, double-page spread; **~ personalidad** split personality; **de ~ sentido** [*calle*] two-way *antes de s*; [*chiste, palabra*] with a double meaning **2** (= *hipócrita*) [*persona*] two-faced **Ⓑ** ADV [*ver*] double; [*beber, comer*] twice as much **Ⓒ** SM **1** (= *cantidad*) **el ~: ahora gana el ~** now he earns twice as much, now he earns double; **necesitamos una casa el ~ de grande** we need a house twice as big as this *o* double the size; **lleva el ~ de harina** it has twice the amount of flour, it has double the amount of flour; **¿cuál es el ~ de diez?** what's two times ten?; **el ~ que** twice as much as **2** (= *copia*) [*de documento*] duplicate copy; [*de llave*] duplicate key **3 dobles** (*Tenis*) doubles; **un partido de ~s** a doubles match **Ⓓ** SMF **1** (*Cine*) double, stand-in **2** (= *persona parecida*) (*gen*) double; [*de algún famoso*] lookalike

doblegar /1h/ **Ⓐ** VT [+ *voluntad*] to break; [+ *enemigo, oponente*] to crush, vanquish (*liter*) **Ⓑ doblegarse** VPR to yield, give in

doblete SM **hacer ~** (*TV, Teat*) to double (**a** for)

doblez **Ⓐ** SM (*Cos*) (= *pliegue*) fold, hem; (= *dobladillo*) turn-up (*Brit*), cuff (*EEUU*) **Ⓑ** SF (= *falsedad*) duplicity

doce ADJ, PRON, SM (*cardinal*) twelve; (*ordinal, en la fecha*) twelfth; *ver tb* **seis**

doceavo ADJ, PRON twelfth

docena SF dozen; **a o por ~s** by the dozen

docencia SF teaching

docente **Ⓐ** ADJ teaching *antes de s*; **centro ~** educational institution; **personal ~** teaching staff; **personal no ~** non-academic staff **Ⓑ** SMF teacher

dócil ADJ [*animal*] docile; [*persona*] submissive, meek

docto ADJ learned, erudite

doctor(a) SM/F (*Med, Univ*) doctor

doctorado SM doctorate, PhD

doctoral ADJ **1** [*tesis, conferencia*] doctoral **2** [*tono*] pedantic, pompous

doctorarse /1a/ VPR to receive *o* get one's PhD *o* doctorate

doctrina SF **1** (= *ideología*) doctrine **2** (= *enseñanza*) teaching

doctrinal ADJ doctrinal

doctrinario/a **Ⓐ** ADJ doctrinaire **Ⓑ** SM/F doctrinarian

documentación SF **1** [*de vehículo*] documentation **2** [*de persona*] papers *pl*, documents *pl*

documentado ADJ **1** (= *informado*) **un libro bien ~** a well documented *o* researched book; **no estaba bien ~** I was not very well informed (about the subject) **2** (= *con documentación*) **no voy ~** I don't have my papers with me

documental ADJ, SM documentary

documentar /1a/ **Ⓐ** VT (= *probar con documentos*) to document **2** (*Méx*) [+ *equipaje*] to check in **Ⓑ** VI (*Méx*) to check in **Ⓒ documentarse** VPR to do one's research

documento SM **1** (= *escrito*) document ➤ **documento adjunto** (*Inform*) attachment ➤ **documento nacional de identidad** identity card ➤ **documentos del coche** car documents **2** (= *testimonio*) document; **un ~ vivo de aquella época** a living document of that period

---

DOCUMENTO NACIONAL DE IDENTIDAD

The Spanish **Documento Nacional de Identidad** is a laminated plastic ID card which is renewable every 5 or 10 years, depending on the age of the holder. All Spanish nationals over the age of 14 are required to carry this card, which have their photo and personal details, at all times. As a legal document it is commonly used as proof of identity and it can be used instead of a passport for travelling around the EU. In Spain it is commonly known as the **DNI**, or else the **carnet (de identidad)**. In Latin America a similar card is called the **cédula (de identidad)**. *See also* www.mir.es/dni

---

dodotis® SM INV nappy (*Brit*), diaper (*EEUU*)

dogma SM dogma

dogmático ADJ dogmatic

dogo SM bull mastiff ➤ **dogo alemán** Great Dane

dólar SM dollar

dolencia SF ailment

doler /2h/ **Ⓐ** VI **1** (*Med*) to hurt; **¿(te) duele?** does it hurt?; **me duele el brazo** my arm hurts; **me duele la cabeza** I have a headache; **me duele el estómago** I have (a) stomach ache; **me duelen las muelas** I have toothache; **me duele la garganta** I have a sore throat **2** (= *afligir*) to hurt; **ese comentario me dolió** I was hurt by that comment, that comment hurt; **no me duele gastarme el dinero en esto** I don't mind spending money on this, spending money on this doesn't bother me; **me duele no poder prestártelo** I'm very sorry I can't lend it to you **Ⓑ dolerse** VPR (*frm*) **~se de algo** to regret sth

dolido ADJ **estar ~ con algn** to be hurt by sb

dolmen SM dolmen

dolor SM **1** (*físico*) pain ➤ **dolor de cabeza** headache ➤ **dolor de espalda** backache ➤ **dolor de estómago** stomach ache ➤ **dolor de muelas** toothache ➤ **dolor de oídos** earache ➤ **dolores de parto** labour pains, labor pains (*EEUU*) **2** (= *pesar*) grief, sorrow; **con gran ~ de mi corazón** much against my will

dolorido ADJ **1** [*cabeza, brazo*] painful, sore; **estaba muy ~** he was in great pain **2** (= *ofendido*) hurt

doloroso ADJ **1** [*parto, muerte*] painful **2** (= *angustioso*) painful, distressing

domador(a) SM/F [*de fieras*] tamer, trainer

domar /1a/ VT **1** [+ *animal salvaje*] (= *amansar*) to tame; (= *adiestrar*) to train **2** [+ *caballo*] to break in **3** [+ *emoción*] to master, control

domesticar /1g/ **Ⓐ** VT to tame, domesticate **Ⓑ domesticarse** VPR to become tame *o* domesticated

doméstico ADJ **1** [*vida*] domestic *antes de s*; **animal** ~ pet; **gastos ~s** household expenses; **las tareas domésticas** housework *sing* **2** [*vuelo*] domestic

domiciliación SF (*tb* ~ **bancaria**) direct debit; ~ **de pagos** payment by direct debit; **con la ~ de su nómina en esta cuenta ...** if your salary is paid into this account ...

domiciliado ADJ ~ **en Valencia** resident in Valencia; **pago** ~ (payment by) direct debit

domiciliar /1b/ **Ⓐ** VT ~ **el pago de algo** to pay sth by direct debit; **tiene que ~ su nómina con nosotros** you'll have to have your salary paid directly into your account here **Ⓑ domiciliarse** VPR to take up residence

domiciliario ADJ **arresto** ~ house arrest

domicilio SM (= *hogar*) home, residence (*frm*); **servicio a** ~ home delivery service; **ventas a** ~ door-to-door sales; **sin ~ fijo** of no fixed abode ➤ **domicilio social** (*Com*) head office, registered office

dominante ADJ **1** [*persona*] domineering **2** (= *predominante*) [*tendencia, opinión, ideología*] dominant, prevailing; [*grupo, cultura, tema*] dominant; [*papel, rol*] dominant, leading; **el consenso ha sido la nota ~ en las negociaciones** consensus has been the keynote *o* tenor of the negotiations

dominar /1a/ **Ⓐ** VT **1** (= *controlar*) [+ *población, territorio*] to dominate; [+ *países*] to rule, rule over; [+ *adversario*] to overpower; [+ *caballo*] to control; **le domina la envidia** he is ruled by envy **2** (= *contener*) [+ *incendio, epidemia*] to check, bring under control; [+ *pasión*] to control, master; [+ *nervios, emoción*] to control **3** [+ *técnica, tema*] to master; **domina bien la materia** she has a good grasp of the subject; **domina cuatro idiomas** he's fluent in four languages **4** (= *divisar*) **desde el castillo se domina toda la vega** from the castle you can look out over the whole plain **Ⓑ** VI [*color, rasgo*] to stand out; [*opinión, tendencia*] to predominate **Ⓒ dominarse** VPR to control o.s.

domingo SM **1** (= *día*) Sunday; **el traje de los ~s** one's Sunday best ➤ **Domingo de Ramos** Palm Sunday ➤ **Domingo de Resurrección** Easter Sunday; ◇ *SEMANA SANTA* **2** (*Méx*) (= *paga*) pocket money (*Brit*), allowance (*esp EEUU*); *ver tb* **sábado**

En inglés los días de la semana se escriben con mayúscula.

dominguero/a SM/F (= *excursionista*) Sunday excursionist; (= *conductor*) Sunday driver

dominical **Ⓐ** ADJ Sunday *antes de s*; **periódico** ~ Sunday newspaper **Ⓑ** SM Sunday supplement

dominicano/a ADJ, SM/F Dominican

dominico SM Dominican

dominio SM **1** (= *control*) control ➤ **dominio de sí mismo** self-control **2** (= *conocimiento*) command; **es impresionante su ~ del inglés** his command of *o* fluency in English is impressive; ◆ MODISMO **es del ~ público** to be common knowledge **3** (= *territorio*) dominion **4** (*Inform*) domain; **nombre de** ~ domain name

dominó SM **1** (= *juego*) dominoes *pl* **2** (= *pieza*) domino

domótica SF home automation, domotics

domótio ADJ home-automation *antes de s*, domotic

don[1] SM **1** (= *talento*) gift; **un ~ especial para la música** a special gift for music ➤ **don de gentes: tener ~ de gentes** to know how to handle people, be good with people ➤ **don de mando** leadership qualities *pl*; (*Mil*) generalship ➤ **don de palabra** gift of the gab*, gift of gab (*EEUU**) **2** (= *deseo*) wish **3** (= *regalo*) gift **3** (= *regalo*) gift

don[2] SM **1** (*tratamiento de cortesía*) **Don** (*en carta, sobre*) Esquire; **Sr. Don Fernando García** (*en correspondencia*) Mr F.

García, Fernando García Esq.; **¿habéis visto a ~ Fernando?** have you seen Mr García? **2** (*Arg, Col**) (*tratamiento popular*) mate (*Brit**), buddy (*esp EEUU**)

dona SF (*Méx*) doughnut, donut (*EEUU*)

donación SF donation

donador(a) SM/F donor

donaire SM grace, elegance

donante SMF donor

donar /1a/ VT to donate

donativo SM donation

doncella[†] SF **1** (= *criada*) maidservant **2** (= *virgen*) maiden

donde **Ⓐ** ADV **1** (+ INDIC) where; **la casa ~ nací** the house where I was born, the house I was born in; **de ~: la caja de ~ lo sacó** the box he took it out of, the box from which he took it; **en ~: fui a la India, en ~ nos conocimos** I went to India, (which is) where we met; **por ~: la puerta por ~ se entra** the door you go in by; **la calle por ~ íbamos andando** the street we were walking along; **va siempre por ~ se le dice** she always goes wherever you tell her to **2** (+ SUBJUN) wherever; ~ **tú quieras** wherever you want; **quiero un trabajo ~ sea** I want a job anywhere *o* wherever; **estén ~ estén** wherever they may be; **vayas por ~ vayas** whichever way you go; ◆ REFRANES (**allí**) ~ **fueres, haz lo que vieres** when in Rome, do as the Romans do; ~ **las dan, las toman** people generally get what they deserve **Ⓑ** PREP **1** (= *al lado de*) **es allí, ~ la catedral** it's over there by the cathedral; **lo guardamos ~ las toallas** we keep it with the towels **2** (= *en/a casa de*) **vamos ~ Ricardo** we're going to Ricardo's

dónde ADV **1** (*en frases interrogativas*) where?; **¿~ están las llaves?** where are the keys?; **¿de ~ eres?** where are you from?; **¿por ~ queda la estación?** whereabouts is the station?; **no recuerdo ~ lo dejé** I can't remember where I left it **2** (*LAm*) (= *¿cómo?*) how?

dondequiera CONJ wherever; ~ **que lo busques** wherever you look for it

donjuan SM, **donjuán** SM casanova, womanizer

donostiarra ADJ of/from San Sebastián

donut SM (*pl* ~**s**) doughnut, donut (*EEUU*)

doña SF **Doña Alicia Pérez** Mrs Alicia Pérez; **¿está ~ Alicia?** is Mrs Pérez in?; ◇ *DON/DOÑA*

dopaje SM [*de caballo*] doping; [*de deportista*] taking performance-enhancing drugs

dopar /1a/ **Ⓐ** VT to dope, drug **Ⓑ doparse** VPR to take performance-enhancing drugs

doquier ADV **por** ~ (*liter*) everywhere, everyplace (*EEUU*)

dorada SF sea bream

dorado ADJ **1** (= *parecido al oro*) gold *antes de s*, golden (*liter*) **2** (*Téc*) gilt, gilded

dorar /1a/ **Ⓐ** VT **1** (*Téc*) to gild **2** (*Culin*) to brown; ◆ MODISMO ~ **la píldora** to sweeten the pill **Ⓑ dorarse** VPR [*cebolla, ajo*] to turn golden, brown

dormido ADJ **1** [*persona*] **estar** ~ (*durmiendo*) to be asleep; (*con sueño*) to be sleepy; **hablar** ~ to talk in one's sleep; **quedarse** ~ to fall asleep **2** [*pierna, brazo*] **tengo la mano dormida** my hand has gone to sleep; **todavía tengo la cara dormida por el frío** my face is still numb from the cold

dormilón/ona Ⓐ ADJ fond of sleeping Ⓑ SM/F sleepyhead

dormilona SF (*Carib*) (= *camisón*) nightdress, nightgown

dormir /3j/ Ⓐ VI **1** (= *descansar*) to sleep; **sólo ha dormido cinco horas** she has only had five hours' sleep, she has only slept (for) five hours; **se fueron a ~ temprano** they went to bed early; **la música no me dejaba ~** the music kept me awake; **~ con algn** (*tb euf*) to sleep with sb; ✦ MODISMOS **~ como un lirón** o **un tronco** ✧ **~ a pierna suelta** to sleep like a log
2 (= *pasar la noche*) to spend the night, stay the night; **dormimos en una pensión** we spent o stayed the night in a guesthouse
3 (= *estar olvidado*) to lie idle; **mi solicitud ha estado durmiendo en el fondo de un cajón** my application has been lying idle at the bottom of a drawer
Ⓑ VT **1** (= *adormecer*) [+ *niño*] to get (off) to sleep; [+ *adulto*] (*por aburrimiento*) to send to sleep; (*con anestesia*) to put to sleep
2 ~ la siesta to have a nap, have a siesta; ✦ MODISMOS **~la*** ✧ **~ la mona*** to sleep it off*
Ⓒ **dormirse** VPR **1** [*persona*] **1.1** (= *quedarse dormido*) to fall asleep, go to sleep; **¡duérmete!** go to sleep!
1.2 (= *despertarse tarde*) to oversleep; **no llegué a la hora porque me dormí** I didn't arrive on time because I overslept
2 [*brazo, pierna*] to go to sleep; (= *descuidarse*) **si te duermes, te quedarás sin trabajo** if you don't stay on your toes, you'll lose your job; ✦ MODISMO **~se en los laureles** to rest on one's laurels

dormitar /1a/ VI to doze, snooze*

dormitorio SM **1** (= *habitación*) bedroom **2** (= *muebles*) bedroom suite **3** (*en internado, cuartel*) dormitory

dorsal Ⓐ ADJ dorsal Ⓑ SM (*Dep*) number (*worn on player's back*)

dorso SM back; **escribir algo al ~** to write sth on the back; **"véase al dorso"** "see overleaf", "please turn over"

dos ADJ, PRON, SM **1** (*numeral*) (*cardinal*) two; (*ordinal, en la fecha*) second; **los ~ libros** both books; **~ piezas** two-piece; ✦ MODISMOS **como ~ y ~ son cuatro** as sure as sure can be; **cada ~ por tres** every five minutes; **en un ~ por tres** in no time at all; *ver tb* **seis 2** (= *dos personas*) **los ~** the two of them/us *etc*, both of them/us *etc*; **vosotros ~** you two; **es para los ~** it's for both of you/us *etc*

doscientos ADJ, PRON, SM (*cardinal*) two hundred; (*ordinal*) two hundredth; *ver tb* **seiscientos**

dosel SM canopy

dosificar /1g/ VT **1** (*Culin, Med, Quím*) to measure out **2** (= *no derrochar*) to be sparing with; **~ las fuerzas** to save one's strength; **el ministro ha dosificado sus apariciones** the minister has chosen his appearances carefully

dosis SF INV **1** (*Med*) dose **2** (= *cantidad*) dose; **en pequeñas ~** in small doses; **una buena ~ de paciencia** a great deal of patience

dossier [dosi'er] SM (*pl* **~s** o **~es** [dosi'er]) dossier ➤ **dossier de prensa** press file

dotación SF **1** (= *dinero*) endowment; **han aumentado la ~ del premio** the value of the prize has been increased, the prize money has been increased **2** (= *plantilla*) staff, personnel; (*Náut*) crew; **una ~ del parque de bomberos** a team of firefighters

dotado ADJ **1** [*persona*] gifted, exceptional (*EEUU*); **los niños excepcionalmente ~s** exceptionally gifted children; **un hombre muy bien ~*** a well-endowed man*; **~ de algo**: **María está dotada de talento musical** María is musically talented o gifted; **~ para algo**: **Adela no está muy dotada para el deporte** Adela does not have a great talent for sports
2 [*máquina, edificio*] **~ de algo**: **un hospital ~ de todos los adelantos técnicos** a hospital equipped with all the latest technology; **un coche ~ de cierre centralizado** a car fitted with central locking
3 [*premio, certamen*] **un premio ~ con 3.000 euros** a prize worth 3,000 euros

dotar /1a/ VT **1** (= *equipar*) **~ (a)** algo de o con algo to provide sth with sth **2 ~ a algn de** o **con algo: dotó a su hija de** o **con un millón de rupias** he provided his daughter with a million rupees as a dowry; **la naturaleza lo dotó de buenas cualidades** he was endowed with good qualities

dote SF **1** [*de novia*] dowry ➤ **dote nupcial** dowry **2 dotes** (= *cualidades*) gifts, talents; **tiene excelentes ~s para la pintura** she has a great gift o talent for painting ➤ **dotes de mando** leadership qualities *pl*

doy *ver* **dar**

Dpto. ABR (= **Departamento**) Dept

Dr. ABR (= **doctor(a)**) Dr

Dra. ABR (= **doctora**) Dr

dracma SM drachma

draconiano ADJ draconian

DRAE SM ABR = **Diccionario de la Real Academia Española**

dragaminas SM INV minesweeper

dragar /1h/ VT **1** [+ *río*] to dredge **2** [+ *minas*] to sweep for

dragón SM **1** (*Mit*) dragon **2** (*Mil*) dragoon **3** (*Bot*) snapdragon

drama SM **1** (= *género*) drama **2** (= *obra*) play

dramático ADJ dramatic; **no seas tan ~** don't make such a drama out of it, don't be such a drama-queen (*hum**)

dramatismo SM drama, dramatic quality

dramatizar /1f/ VT to dramatize

dramaturgo/a SM/F playwright, dramatist

drástico ADJ drastic

drenaje SM drainage

drenar /1a/ VT to drain

driblar /1a/ VT, **driblear** /1a/ VT **~ a algn** to dribble past sb

droga SF **1** (= *estupefaciente, medicamento*) drug ➤ **droga blanda** soft drug ➤ **droga de diseño** designer drug ➤ **droga dura** hard drug **2** (*Méx**) (= *deuda*) debt

drogadicción SF drug addiction

drogadicto/a Ⓐ ADJ addicted to drugs Ⓑ SM/F drug addict

drogar /1h/ Ⓐ VT to drug Ⓑ **drogarse** VPR to take drugs

drogodependencia SF drug addiction

droguería SF **1** (*Esp*) *store that sells household goods, paint etc* **2** (*Col*) (= *farmacia*) chemist's (shop), drugstore (*EEUU*) **3** (*RPl*) (= *empresa*) pharmaceutical wholesaler

dromedario SM dromedary

druida SM druid

dto. ABR (= **departamento**) dept, dpt

dual ADJ, SM dual

dualidad SF duality

dubitativo ADJ [*persona*] hesitant; [*actitud*] uncertain, hesitant

Dublín SM Dublin

dublinés/esa Ⓐ ADJ Dublin *antes de s* Ⓑ SM/F Dubliner

ducado SM **1** (= *territorio*) duchy, dukedom **2** (*Fin*) ducat

ducal ADJ ducal

ducha SF shower; **darse** o **pegarse* una ~** to have o take a shower; ✦ MODISMO **una ~ de agua fría: el rechazo de su propuesta fue una ~ de agua fría para él** the rejection of his proposal was a real shock to the system for him ➤ **ducha de teléfono** detachable-head shower, hand-held shower ➤ **ducha escocesa** alternately hot and cold shower

duchar /1a/ Ⓐ VT to give a shower to Ⓑ **ducharse** VPR to have a shower (*esp Brit*), take a shower (*esp EEUU*)

duchero SM (*RPl*) shower unit

ducho ADJ **~ en algo** experienced in sth

dúctil ADJ **1** [*metal*] ductile **2** [*persona*] easily influenced

duda SF **1** (= *incertidumbre*) doubt; **un hecho que no admite**

~ an unquestionable fact; **no cabe ~ de que ...** there can be no doubt that ...; **no cabe ~ de que vendrá** he'll undoubtedly come; **no te quepa ~ de que se acordarán de ti** you can be sure that they will remember you; **en caso de ~** if in doubt; **estar en ~: su profesionalismo no está en ~** his professionalism is not in doubt; **estoy en la ~ sobre si me iré a esquiar o no** I'm undecided about whether to go skiing or not, I'm in (*Brit*) *o* of (*EEUU*) two minds about whether to go skiing or not; **fuera de toda ~** beyond all doubt; **sin lugar a ~(s)** without doubt, undoubtedly; **poner algo en ~** to question sth, doubt sth; **por (si) las ~s** (*LAm*) just in case; **sacar a algn de ~s** *o* **de la ~** to clear things up for sb; **no me saca de ~s** I'm none the wiser; **salir de ~s: pregúntaselo a él, así saldremos de ~s** ask him, then we'll know; **pues no salimos de ~s** we're none the wiser, then; **sin ~** undoubtedly

2 (= *pregunta*) question, query; **¿alguna ~?** are there any queries?

dudar /1a/ Ⓐ VT **1** (= *no estar seguro de*) to doubt; **espero que venga, aunque lo dudo mucho** I hope she'll come, although I doubt very much (if) she will; **—yo te ayudaré —no lo dudo, pero ...** "I'll help you" — "I'm sure you will, but ..."; **es lo mejor para ti, no lo dudes** it's the best thing for you, believe me; **~ que: dudo que sea verdad** I doubt (whether *o* if) it's true; **~ si: dudaba si había pagado la factura** I wasn't sure if I had paid the bill

2 (= *vacilar sobre*) **lo dudé mucho y al final me decidí por el azul** I thought about it *o* dithered* a lot but in the end I decided on the blue one; **si yo fuera tú, no lo ~ía** if I were you, I wouldn't hesitate

Ⓑ VI **1** (= *desconfiar*) to doubt, have doubts; **~ de algo** to question sth, doubt sth

2 (= *vacilar*) **no sé qué hacer, estoy dudando** I don't know what to do, I'm in (*Brit*) *o* of (*EEUU*) two minds *o* I'm undecided; **dudamos entre ir en autobús o en taxi** we were not sure whether to go by bus or taxi; **dudaba entre los dos** she couldn't decide between the two; **no dudes en llamarme** don't hesitate to call me

dudoso ADJ **1** (= *incierto*) [*diagnóstico, futuro, origen*] doubtful, uncertain; [*resultado*] indecisive **2** (= *vacilante*) [*persona*] hesitant; **estar ~** to be undecided, be in (*Brit*) *o* of (*EEUU*) two minds **3** (= *sospechoso*) [*actuación, dinero, reputación*] dubious; **tácticas dudosas** suspect *o* dubious tactics

duela SF (*Méx*) floorboard

duele *etc ver* **doler**

duelo[1] SM (*Mil*) duel

duelo[2] SM (= *luto*) mourning; **tres días de ~** three days of mourning

duende SM **1** (= *elfo*) goblin, elf **2** (= *encanto*) magic; **tiene ~** it has a certain magic

dueño/a SM/F **1** (= *propietario*) [*de casa, coche, perro*] owner; [*de negocio*] owner, proprietor/proprietress; [*de pensión, taberna*] landlord/landlady; **cambiar de ~** to change hands **2 ser ~ de: ser ~ de la situación** to be the master of the situation, have the situation in hand; **eres ~ de hacer lo que te parezca** you can do as you please; **hacerse ~ de una situación** to take command of a situation

duerma *etc ver* **dormir**

duermevela SM *o* SF **pasé toda la noche en un ~** I tossed and turned all night

Duero SM Douro

dueto SM duet

dulce Ⓐ ADJ **1** [*postre, galleta, vino*] sweet **2** (= *suave*) [*metal, sonido, voz*] soft; [*carácter*] gentle; [*música*] sweet Ⓑ ADV softly Ⓒ SM **1** (= *caramelo*) sweet (*Brit*), candy (*EEUU*) ➤ **dulce de leche** (*Arg*) caramel spread ➤ **dulce de membrillo** quince jelly **2 dulces** (*gen*) sweet things; (= *pasteles*) cakes and pastries **3** (*And, CAm, Carib*) (= *azúcar*) sugar, brown sugar **4** (*RPl*) (= *mermelada*) jam

dulcificar /1g/ Ⓐ VT **1** (*Culin*) to sweeten **2** [+ *consecuencias, carácter, noticia*] to soften Ⓑ **dulcificarse** VPR **1** [*carácter*] to mellow, become milder **2** [*clima*] to become milder

dulzaina SF *type of pipe, similar to a chanter*

dulzón ADJ **1** (= *demasiado dulce*) sickly-sweet; (*esp LAm*) (= *algo dulce*) sweetish **2** (*pey*) (= *empalagoso*) cloying

dulzor SM, **dulzura** SF **1** [*de caramelo, pastel*] sweetness **2** [*de carácter*] sweetness, gentleness; **con ~** sweetly, softly

duna SF dune

dúo SM duo; **cantar a ~** to sing a duet; **me contestaron a ~** they answered me in unison

duodécimo ADJ twelfth; *ver tb* **sexto**

duodenal ADJ duodenal

duodeno SM duodenum

dúplex SM INV duplex apartment (*EEUU*), flat on two floors (*Brit*)

duplicado SM duplicate; **por ~** in duplicate

duplicar /1g/ Ⓐ VT **1** [+ *documento*] to duplicate; [+ *llave*] to copy, duplicate **2** [+ *cantidad*] to double Ⓑ **duplicarse** VPR [*cifra, ganancias*] to double

duplicidad SF duplicity, deceitfulness

duplo Ⓐ ADJ double Ⓑ SM **doce es el ~ de seis** twelve is twice six

duque(sa) SM/F duke/duchess

durable ADJ durable, lasting

duración SF **1** [*de viaje, disco, llamada*] length; **de larga ~** [*parado, paro*] long-term; [*enfermedad*] lengthy; **de poca ~** short **2** [*de batería, pila*] life; **baterías de larga ~** long-life batteries

duradero ADJ [*ropa, tela*] hard-wearing; [*paz, efecto*] lasting; [*relación*] lasting, long-term *antes de s*

duralex® [duraˈleks] SM INV Duralex®

durante PREP (*expresando la duración de algo*) for; (*expresando el período en que ocurre algo*) during; **habló ~ una hora** he spoke for an hour; **¿qué hiciste ~ el verano?** what did you do in *o* during the summer?; **¿ha llovido ~ el fin de semana?** did it rain at *o* over the weekend?; **~ toda la noche** all through the night, all night long

> Si **durante** hace referencia a cuándo ocurre la acción, se traduce por **during**: "Se conocieron durante la guerra", *They met during the war*. Pero si se refiere a la duración de la acción, **durante** se traduce por **for**: "Fue periodista durante 14 años", *He was a journalist for 14 years*.

durar /1a/ VI **1** [*aventura, programa, enfermedad*] to last; **¿cuánto dura la representación?** how long is the play?, how long does the play last?; **¿cuánto dura el trayecto?** how long is the journey?, how long does the journey take?; **la ópera duró cinco horas** the opera was five hours long **2** [*comida, ropa*] to last; **aún me dura el aceite que traje** I still have some of the oil that I brought back

duraznero SM (*LAm*) peach tree

durazno SM (*esp LAm*) (= *fruta*) peach; (= *árbol*) peach tree

durex® SM (*Méx*) Sellotape® (*Brit*), Scotch tape® (*EEUU*)

dureza SF **1** (= *resistencia*) [*de mineral, roca, agua*] hardness; [*de carne*] toughness **2** (= *agresividad*) [*de clima, régimen, crítica*] harshness, severity; [*de deporte, juego*] roughness; [*de ataque*] fierceness; [*de castigo, multa, sentencia*] severity, harshness **3** [*de prueba, examen*] hardness **4** (= *fortaleza*) hardiness, strength **5** (= *callo*) callus

durmiente Ⓐ ADJ sleeping Ⓑ SMF sleeper

duro/a Ⓐ ADJ **1** (= *resistente*) [*material, superficie, cama*] hard; [*cable, alambre, mecanismo*] stiff; [*pan*] hard, stale; [*carne*] tough; [*legumbres*] hard; [*músculo*] firm, hard; ✦ MODISMO **más ~ que una piedra** as tough as nails **2** (= *agresivo*) [*clima, tiempo, crítica*] harsh, severe; [*deporte, juego*] rough; [*ataque*] fierce; [*castigo, sentencia*] severe, harsh; [*carácter, actitud*] tough; **fue un ~ golpe para el partido** it was a severe *o* heavy blow to the party; **el sector ~ del partido** the hardliners in the party; **tener mano dura**

to be firm *o* strict; **rock** ~ hard rock

3 (= *difícil*) [*tarea, prueba, examen*] hard; **este coche ha pasado las pruebas más duras** this car has passed the most stringent tests; **lo tienes ~ para aprobar*** it will be hard *o* difficult for you to pass; ✦ MODISMO **ser ~ de pelar** to be a hard nut to crack

4 (*) (= *torpe*) **~ de mollera** dense*; **~ de oído** (= *medio sordo*) hard of hearing; (*Mús*) tone deaf

B ADV **1** [*trabajar, pegar*] hard

2 (*Col, Ven*) **hablar ~** to speak up

C SM (*Esp†*) (= *cinco pesetas*) five pesetas; (= *moneda*) five-peseta coin; ✦ MODISMOS **estar sin un ~*** to be broke*; **¡lo que faltaba para el ~!*** it's the last straw!

D SM/F **1** (*en película, historia*) tough character; **se hizo el ~** he acted the tough guy

2 (*Pol*) hard-liner

duvet ['duve] SM (= *plumón*) down

DVD SM ABR (= **Disco Versátil Digital**) DVD

Ee

E¹, e [e] SF (= *letra*) E, e

E² ABR (= **este**) E

e CONJ (*before words beginning with i and hi, but not hie*) and; *ver tb* **y**

EAU SMPL ABR (= **Emiratos Árabes Unidos**) UAE

ebanista SMF cabinetmaker, carpenter

ebanistería SF 1 (= *oficio*) cabinetmaking 2 (= *obra*) woodwork, carpentry 3 (= *taller*) cabinetmaker's (workshop)

ébano SM ebony

ebrio ADJ intoxicated (*frm*), drunk; **~ de alegría** beside o.s. with joy

Ebro SM Ebro

ebullición SF 1 [*de líquidos*] boiling; **entrar en ~** to begin to boil, come to the boil; **punto de ~** boiling point 2 (= *alboroto*) turmoil

eccema SM eczema

echada SF (*Méx*) (= *fanfarronada*) boast

echado ADJ **estar ~** to lie, be lying (down); ✦ MODISMO **es muy ~ pa'lante*** he's not backward in coming forward*

echador(a) Ⓐ ADJ (*CAm, Méx*) boastful Ⓑ SM/F 1 ➤ **echador(a) de cartas** fortune teller 2 (*CAm, Méx*) (= *presumido*) boaster

---

echar /1a/

Ⓐ VERBO TRANSITIVO   Ⓒ VERBO PRONOMINAL
Ⓑ VERBO INTRANSITIVO

Para las expresiones **echar abajo, echar en cara, echar la culpa, echar en falta, echar de menos, echar a perder, echar raíces, echar a suertes** *etc ver la otra entrada.*

---

echar Ⓐ VERBO TRANSITIVO

1 (= *tirar*) [+ *pelota, piedra, dados*] to throw; [+ *ancla, red*] to cast; [+ *naipe*] to deal; **échalo a la basura** throw it away; **¿qué te han echado los Reyes?** (*Esp*) ≈ what did you get for Christmas?

2 (= *poner*) to put; **~ carbón a la lumbre** to put coal on the fire; **¿te echo mantequilla en el pan?** shall I put some butter on your bread?; **tengo que ~ gasolina** I need to fill up (with petrol (*Brit*) o gas (*EEUU*))

3 (= *verter*) to pour; **echó un poco de vino en un vaso** he poured some wine into a glass

4 (= *servir*) [+ *bebida*] to pour; [+ *comida*] to give; **échame agua** could you give o pour me some water?; **no me eches tanto** don't give me so much; **tengo que ~ de comer a los animales** I have to feed the animals; ✦ MODISMO **lo que le echen: resiste lo que le echen** she can take whatever they throw at her

5 (= *dejar salir*) **la chimenea echa humo** smoke is coming out of the chimney; **¡qué peste echan tus zapatos!*** your shoes stink to high heaven!*

6 (= *expulsar*) (*de casa, bar, tienda, club*) to throw out; (*del trabajo*) to fire*, sack*; (*de colegio*) to expel; **me echó de su casa** he threw me out of his house; **lo han echado del colegio** he's been expelled from school

7 (= *producir*) [+ *dientes*] to cut; [+ *hojas*] to sprout; **está empezando a ~ barriga** he's starting to get a bit of a belly o paunch

8 (= *cerrar*) **~ la llave/el cerrojo** to lock/bolt the door; **~ el freno** to brake; **echa la persiana** can you draw the blinds?

9 (= *mover*)

9.1 [+ *parte del cuerpo*] **~ la cabeza a un lado** to tilt o cock one's head to one side; **~ el cuerpo hacia atrás** to lean back

9.2 (*empujando*) to push; **~ a algn a un lado** to push sb aside; **~ atrás a la multitud** to push the crowd back

10 (= *enviar*) [+ *carta*] to post (*esp Brit*), mail (*EEUU*); **eché la carta en el buzón** I posted (*esp Brit*) o mailed (*EEUU*) the letter

11 (= *calcular*) to reckon; **¿cuántos años le echas?** how old do you think o reckon he is?; **échale una hora andando** you can reckon on it taking you an hour if you walk

12 (= *dar*) [+ *discurso*] to give, make; **~ una reprimenda a algn** to give sb a telling-off* o reprimand, tell sb off*, reprimand sb; **he ido a que me echen las cartas** I've had my cards read

13 (*con sustantivos que implican acciones*) [+ *trago, partida*] to have; **salió al balcón a ~ un cigarrillo** he went out onto the balcony for a smoke o cigarette

14 (*Esp*) [+ *tiempo*] **hay que ~le muchas horas** it takes a long time; **esta semana he echado cuatro horas extras** I did four hours overtime this week

15 (*Esp**) (*en cine, televisión*) to show; **~on un programa sobre Einstein** there was a programme about Einstein on, they showed a programme about Einstein; **¿qué echan en el cine?** what's on at the cinema? (*Brit*), what's showing at the movies? (*EEUU*)

16 [+ *cimientos*] to lay

Ⓑ VERBO INTRANSITIVO (= *tirar*) **¡echa para adelante!** lead on!; **es un olor que echa para atrás*** it's a smell that really knocks you back*; **echa para allá** move up; **echemos por aquí** let's go this way

✦ **echar a** (+ INFIN) **~ a correr** to break into a run, start running; **~ a reír** to burst out laughing, start laughing

Ⓒ **echarse** VERBO PRONOMINAL

1 (= *lanzarse*) to throw o.s.; **~se en brazos de algn** to throw o.s. into sb's arms; **~se sobre algn** (*gen*) to hurl o.s. at sb; (*atacando*) to fall on sb

2 (= *acostarse*) to lie down; **voy a ~me un rato** I'm going to lie down for a bit

3 (= *moverse*) **échate un poco para la izquierda** move a bit to the left; **me tuve que ~ a la derecha para que adelantara** I had to pull over to the right to let him pass o (*esp Brit*) overtake; **~se atrás** (*lit*) to throw o.s. back(wards), move back(wards); (*fig*) to back out; **échense atrás, por favor** move back please

4 (= *ponerse*) **se echó laca en el pelo** she put some hairspray on; **se echó una manta por las piernas** she put a blanket over her legs

✦ **echarse a** (+ INFIN) **se echó a correr** she broke into a run, she started running

5 (*uso enfático*) **~se una novia** to get o.s. a girlfriend; **~se una siestecita** to have a nap; **~se un trago** to have a drink

6 (*Méx**) (= *romper*) to bust*

7 (*Méx**) ✦ MODISMO **~se a algn al plato** to bump sb off**

8 (*Col**) (= *tardar*) **me echo una hora de aquí a Bogotá** it takes me an hour (to get) from here to Bogotá

echarpe SM (*A VECES* SF) (woman's) stole, scarf

echón/ona* SM/F (*Ven*) braggart, swank*; **¡qué ~!** isn't he full of himself!*

eclecticismo SM eclecticism

ecléctico/a ADJ, SM/F eclectic

eclesial ADJ ecclesiastic(al), church *antes de s*

eclesiástico Ⓐ ADJ (*gen*) ecclesiastic, ecclesiastical; [*autoridades*] church *antes de s* Ⓑ SM clergyman, ecclesiastic

eclipsar /1a/ VT to eclipse

eclipse SM eclipse ➤ **eclipse lunar** eclipse of the moon, lunar eclipse ➤ **eclipse solar** eclipse of the sun, solar eclipse

eclosión SF bloom, blooming; **el modernismo hizo ~ en Latinoamérica muy pronto** modernism burst onto the scene very early in Latin America

eclosionar /1a/ VI (*Entomología*) to hatch, emerge

eco SM 1 (= *sonido*) echo; **hacer ~** to echo 2 (= *reacción*) echo; **hacerse ~ de una opinión** to echo an opinion; **tener ~** to catch on, arouse interest

ecografía SF (= *imagen*) ultrasound scan; (= *técnica*) ultrasound scanning

ecología SF ecology

ecológico ADJ [*desastre, zona, equilibrio*] ecological; [*producto*] environmentally friendly; [*cultivo*] organic, organically grown

ecologista Ⓐ ADJ conservation *antes de s*, environmental Ⓑ SMF ecologist, environmentalist; **los ~s** the Greens

economato SM [*de empresa*] company store; (*Mil*) ≈ NAAFI (*Brit*), ≈ PX (*EEUU*)

econometría SF econometrics *sing*

economía SF 1 [*de país*] economy ➤ **economía de mercado** market economy ➤ **economía de subsistencia** subsistence economy ➤ **economía sumergida** (*Esp*) underground economy, black economy 2 (= *estudio*) economics *sing* 3 (= *ahorro*) economy, saving; **hacer ~s** to make economies, economize 4 (*tb* **Ministerio de Economía**) the Treasury, the Treasury Department (*EEUU*)

económico ADJ 1 [*situación, crisis*] economic; **mis problemas ~s** my financial problems 2 (= *barato*) economical, inexpensive; **edición económica** cheap edition, popular edition 3 (= *ahorrativo*) thrifty

> El adjetivo **económico** se traduce por **economic** cuando se refiere al comercio o a las finanzas: "reformas económicas", *economic reforms*. Se traduce por **economical** cuando hace referencia a la relación calidad-precio: "Mi coche sale muy económico", *My car is very economical to run*.

economista SMF economist

economizar /1f/ Ⓐ VT to economize on; **~ tiempo** to save time Ⓑ VI to economize

ecosistema SM ecosystem

ecotasa SF green tax, eco-tax

ECU SF ABR (= **Unidad de Cuenta Europea**) ECU

ecu SM ecu

ecuación SF equation ➤ **ecuación de segundo grado** quadratic equation

Ecuador SM Ecuador

ecuador SM 1 (*Geog*) equator 2 (= *punto medio*) mid point, half-way point, half-way mark

ecualizador SM equalizer

ecuánime ADJ [*carácter*] level-headed; [*humor, ánimo*] calm; [*juicio*] impartial

ecuatorial ADJ equatorial

ecuatoguineano/a Ⓐ ADJ of/from Equatorial Guinea Ⓑ SM/F native/inhabitant of Equatorial Guinea

ecuatoriano/a ADJ, SM/F Ecuadoran

ecuestre ADJ equestrian

ecuménico ADJ ecumenical

eczema SM eczema

ed. ABR 1 (= **edición**) ed. 2 (= **editor**) ed. 3 = **editorial**

edad SF 1 [*de persona, animal, árbol*] age; **¿qué ~ tiene?** how old is he?, what age is he?; **tenemos la misma ~** we're the same age; **a tu ~ yo ya sabía leer** I could read when I was your age; **jóvenes de ~es comprendidas entre los 18 y los 26 años** young people aged 18 to 26, young people between the ages of 18 and 26; **~ adulta** adulthood; **a la ~ de ocho años** at the age of eight; **murió a los 85 años de ~** she died when she was 85 *o* at the age of 85; **un niño de corta ~** a young child; **una persona de ~** an elderly person; **estar en (la) ~ de hacer algo** ✧ **tener ~ de hacer algo** to be old enough to do sth; **ya no tengo ~ para ir a la discoteca** I'm too old now to go out clubbing; **tercera ~** (= *personas*) senior citizens *pl*, older people *pl*; (= *edad*) old age; ✦ MODISMO **estar en la ~ del pavo** to be at that difficult *o* awkward age ➤ **edad penal** age of legal responsibility, age of criminal responsibility 2 (*Hist*) age ➤ **Edad Antigua** period from the beginning of history to the decline of the Roman Empire ➤ **Edad Contemporánea** Modern Age, Modern Period ➤ **Edad de Bronce** Bronze Age ➤ **Edad de Hierro** Iron Age ➤ **Edad de Piedra** Stone Age ➤ **Edad Media** Middle Ages *pl* ➤ **Edad**

Moderna period from the Middle Ages to the French Revolution

edecán SM 1 (*Mil*) aide-de-camp 2 (*Méx*) (= *acompañante*) assistant

edema SM oedema, edema (*EEUU*)

Edén SM Eden, Paradise

edición SF 1 (= *industria*) publishing; **el mundo de la ~** the publishing world ➤ **edición electrónica** (= *creación*) electronic publishing; (= *texto*) electronic edition 2 [*de libro*] edition ➤ **edición de bolsillo** pocket edition 3 ediciones (= *editorial*) **Ediciones Ramírez** Ramirez Publications 4 (= *celebración*) **es la tercera ~ de este festival** this is the third occasion on which this festival has been held

edicto SM edict, proclamation

edificable ADJ **terreno ~** building land, land available for building

edificante ADJ edifying

edificar /1g/ VT 1 (*Arquit*) to build, construct 2 (*moralmente*) to edify

edificio SM building ➤ **edificio de oficinas** office block

edil SMF (*Esp*) town councillor *o* (*EEUU*) councilor

Edimburgo SM Edinburgh

Edipo SM Oedipus

editar /1a/ VT 1 (= *publicar*) to publish 2 (= *corregir*) (*tb* Inform) to edit

editor(a) Ⓐ ADJ publishing *antes de s* Ⓑ SM/F 1 [*de libros, periódicos*] publisher 2 (= *redactor*) editor Ⓒ SM (*Inform*) editor

editorial Ⓐ ADJ 1 [*industria, mundo, casa*] publishing *antes de s* 2 [*función, política*] editorial Ⓑ SM editorial, leading article (*esp Brit*) Ⓒ SF publishing house

editorialista SMF leader writer (*Brit*), editorialist (*EEUU*)

edredón SM eiderdown (*Brit*), comforter (*EEUU*) ➤ **edredón nórdico** duvet (*Brit*), comforter (*EEUU*)

educación SF 1 (*en centro de enseñanza*) education ➤ **educación a distancia** distance learning ➤ **educación especial** special education ➤ **educación física** physical education ➤ **educación primaria** primary education (*esp Brit*), elementary education (*EEUU*) ➤ **educación secundaria** secondary education ➤ **Educación Secundaria Obligatoria** (*Esp*) *secondary education, for 12- to 16-year-olds* 2 (*en familia*) upbringing; **una ~ muy estricta** a very strict upbringing 3 (= *modales*) manners *pl*; **no tiene ~** she has no manners; **buena ~** good manners *pl*; **con ~:** **se lo pedí con ~** I asked her politely; **falta de ~:** **eso es una falta de ~** that's rude; **mala ~** bad manners *pl* 4 [*de voz, oído, animal*] training

educacional ADJ educational

educado ADJ well-mannered, polite; **mal ~** ill-mannered

educador(a) SM/F educator, teacher

educar /1g/ Ⓐ VT 1 (*en centro de enseñanza*) to educate; **la han educado en un colegio bilingüe** she was educated at a bilingual school 2 (*en familia*) to bring up 3 [+ *voz, oído, animal*] to train Ⓑ **educarse** VPR to be educated

educativo ADJ 1 [*juguete*] educational 2 [*política, sistema*] education *antes de s*; **reforma educativa** educational *o* school reform

edulcorante SM sweetener

EE.UU. ABR (= **Estados Unidos**) US, USA

efectismo SM sensationalism; **la escena final de la película es de un gran ~** the final scene in the film (*esp Brit*) *o* movie (*esp EEUU*) is really dramatic

efectista ADJ, SMF sensationalist

efectivamente ADV 1 (= *verdaderamente*) really; **si ~ es así** if it really is like that 2 (*confirmando algo*) indeed; **~, el robo fue llevado a cabo por dos personas** the theft was indeed carried out by two people; **pensé que iba a llegar tarde, y, ~, así fue** I thought he would be late, and, sure enough, he was

efectivo Ⓐ ADJ 1 [*vacuna, táctica*] effective
2 (= *real*) [*poder*] real; **la orden no será efectiva hasta mañana** the order will not take effect *o* become effective until tomorrow; **hacer ~** [+ *plan*] to put into effect; [+ *multa, pago*] to make payable; [+ *cheque*] to cash; **su dimisión se hizo efectiva el jueves** his resignation took effect *o* became effective on Thursday
Ⓑ SM 1 (= *dinero*) cash; **en ~** in cash; **tres premios en ~** three cash prizes
2 **efectivos** (*Mil*) forces; **~s de la Policía** ◇ **~s policiales** police officers

efecto SM 1 (= *consecuencia*) effect; **los ~s de la anestesia** the effect of the anaesthetic; **conducía bajo los ~s del alcohol** he was driving under the influence of alcohol; **hacer ~** to take effect; **el calmante no le ha hecho ningún ~** the sedative has had no effect on him *o* has not taken effect; **bomba de ~ retardado** delayed-action bomb; **surtir** *o* **tener ~** to have an effect ➤ **efecto 2000** millennium bug, Y2K ➤ **efecto dominó** domino effect ➤ **efecto invernadero** greenhouse effect ➤ **efecto óptico** optical illusion ➤ **efectos colaterales** collateral damage *sing* ➤ **efectos especiales** special effects ➤ **efectos secundarios** side effects ➤ **efectos sonoros** sound effects
2 **en ~** indeed; **en ~, así es** yes, indeed *o* that's right; **y en ~, el libro estaba donde él dijo** sure enough, the book was where he had said it would be
3 (= *vigencia*) [*de ley, reforma*] **una ley con ~ desde 1950** a law that has been in force since 1950; **una subida con ~s retroactivos** a backdated increase; **tener ~** to take effect, come into effect
4 (*frm*) (= *objetivo*) purpose; **a ~s fiscales/prácticos** for tax/ practical purposes; **llevar a ~** [+ *acción, cambio*] to carry out; [+ *acuerdo, pacto*] to put into practice; [+ *reunión, congreso*] to hold; **a tal ~** to this end, for this purpose; **a todos los ~s** to all intents and purposes
5 (= *impresión*) effect; **no sé qué ~ tendrán mis palabras** I don't know what effect my words will have; **es de mal ~ llegar tarde** being late creates a bad impression
6 (*Dep*) (*gen*) spin; (*Ftbl*) swerve
7 **efectos** (*Com*) (= *bienes*) stock *sing*, goods; (= *documentos*) bills

efectuar /1e/ VT [+ *acción, reparación, investigación*] to carry out; [+ *viaje, visita, declaración, pago*] to make; [+ *disparo*] to fire; **el tren ~á parada en todas las estaciones** the train will stop at all stations

efeméride SF event (*remembered on its anniversary*); **"efemérides"** (*en periódico*) "list of the day's anniversaries"

efervescente ADJ 1 [*pastilla, sustancia*] effervescent; [*bebida*] sparkling 2 (= *animado*) high-spirited

eficacia SF [*de ley, remedio, producto, sanción*] effectiveness; [*de persona, método, instrumento*] efficiency

eficaz ADJ [*ley, remedio, producto, sanción*] effective; [*persona, método, instrumento*] efficient

eficiencia SF efficiency

eficiente ADJ efficient

efigie SF 1 (= *busto, escultura*) effigy 2 (= *imagen pintada*) image; **el euro tendrá la ~ del rey** the euro will carry a likeness of the king

efímero ADJ ephemeral

efluvio SM outpour, outflow

efusión SF warmth, effusiveness; **con ~** effusively

efusivamente ADV warmly, effusively

efusivo ADJ [*persona, modales*] effusive; [*gracias*] effusive, warm

EGB SF ABR (*Esp*) (= **Educación General Básica**) *former primary school education*

Egeo SM **el mar ~** the Aegean Sea

égida SF aegis, protection; **bajo la ~ de** under the aegis of

egipcio/a ADJ, SM/F Egyptian

Egipto SM Egypt

égloga SF eclogue

ego SM ego

egocéntrico ADJ egocentric, self-centred, self-centered

(*EEUU*)

egocentrismo SM egocentrism

egoísmo SM egoism, selfishness

egoísta Ⓐ ADJ egoistical, selfish Ⓑ SMF egoist, selfish person

ególatra Ⓐ ADJ egomaniacal Ⓑ SMF egomaniac

egregio ADJ eminent, distinguished

egresado/a SM/F (*LAm*) graduate

egresar /1a/ VI (*LAm*) to graduate

egreso SM (*LAm*) 1 (*Univ*) graduation 2 (*Fin*) expenditure, outgoings *pl* (*Brit*)

eh EXCL 1 (*llamando la atención*) hey!, say! (*EEUU*) 2 (*cuando no se ha entendido algo*) eh?

Eire SM Eire

ej. ABR (= **ejemplo**) ex.

eje SM 1 (*Geog, Mat*) axis; ✦ MODISMO **partir a algn por el ~*** (*en planes*) to ruin sb's plans; (*con preguntas*) to stump sb*, floor sb* ➤ **eje de abscisas** x-axis ➤ **eje de simetría** axis of symmetry 2 [*de rueda*] axle 3 [*de máquina*] shaft, spindle ➤ **eje del cigüeñal** crankshaft 4 (= *centro*) **el ~ de la conversación** the main topic of conversation 5 (*Hist*) **el Eje** the Axis 6 ➤ **eje vial** (*Méx Aut*) arterial road

ejecución SF 1 (= *ajusticiamiento*) execution
2 (= *cumplimiento*) [*de orden*] carrying out, execution; [*de deseos*] fulfilment, fulfillment (*EEUU*); **poner en ~** to carry out 3 (*Mús*) performance

ejecutante SMF (*Mús*) performer

ejecutar /1a/ VT 1 (= *ajusticiar*) to execute 2 (= *hacer cumplir*) [+ *orden, sentencia*] to carry out, execute; [+ *deseos*] to perform, fulfil, fulfill (*EEUU*) 3 (*Mús*) to perform, play 4 (*Inform*) to run

ejecutiva SF (*Pol*) executive body, executive committee

ejecutivo/a Ⓐ ADJ [*función, poder*] executive Ⓑ SM/F (*Com*) executive Ⓒ SM (*Pol*) executive

ejecutor(a) SM/F executor/executrix

ejecutoria SF (*Jur*) final judg(e)ment

ejem EXCL hem! (*cough*)

ejemplar Ⓐ ADJ exemplary, model Ⓑ SM 1 (*Zool*) specimen, example 2 [*de libro*] copy; [*de revista*] number, issue

ejemplificar /1g/ VT to exemplify, illustrate

ejemplo SM example; **dar ~ a algn** to set sb an example; **por ~** for example, for instance; **poner como** *o* **de** *o* **por ~** to give as an example; **servir de** *o* **como ~** to serve as an example

ejercer /2b/ Ⓐ VT 1 [+ *medicina, abogacía*] to practise, practice (*EEUU*) 2 (= *hacer efectivo*) [+ *influencia*] to exert, exercise; [+ *poder*] to exercise, wield 3 [+ *derecho*] to exercise Ⓑ VI [*profesional*] to practise, practice (*EEUU*) (**de** as)

ejercicio SM 1 (*físico*) exercise; **hacer ~** to exercise 2 (*Educ*) exercise ➤ **ejercicio escrito** written exercise 3 (*Mil*) exercise; **los ~s de la OTAN** NATO exercises ➤ **ejercicio acrobático** (*Aer*) stunt ➤ **ejercicios de tiro** target practice *sing* 4 [*de cargo*] **en el ~ de mi cargo** in the exercise of my duties; **abogado en ~** practising *o* (*EEUU*) practicing lawyer 5 (*Com, Fin*) fiscal year, financial year (*Brit*) 6 (*Rel*) ➤ **ejercicios espirituales** retreat *sing*

ejercitar /1a/ Ⓐ VT [+ *músculo, memoria*] to exercise; [+ *tropas*] to drill, train; [+ *alumno*] to train, coach Ⓑ **ejercitarse** VPR [*músculos, memoria*] to exercise; [*tropas*] to drill, train

ejército SM 1 (*Mil*) army; **estar en el ~** to be in the army; **los tres ~s** the forces, the Services ➤ **ejército del aire** Air Force ➤ **ejército de tierra** Army 2 (= *multitud*) army

ejidatario/a SM/F (*esp Méx*) holder of a share in common lands

ejido SM 1 (= *campo*) common land 2 (*Méx*) expropriated land reallocated by the government to a workers' collective

ejote SM (*CAm, Méx*) string bean

el, la, los, las ART DEF 1 (*con nombres de referente único o concreto*) the; **el sol** the sun; **perdí el autobús** I missed the

bus; **¿ha llegado ya el abogado?** has the lawyer arrived yet?
2 (*en algunos casos no se traduce*) **2.1** (*con nombres propios*) **la India** India; **en el México de hoy** in present-day Mexico; **el Real Madrid** Real Madrid; **el Sr. Sendra** Mr Sendra **2.2** (*con nombres en sentido genérico*) **me gusta el baloncesto** I like basketball; **está en la cárcel** he's in jail **2.3** (*con infinitivo*) **el hacerlo fue un error** doing it was a mistake, it was a mistake to do it **2.4** (*con cifras, proporciones*) **la mitad de la población** half of the population; **el 3% más** 3% more
3 (*traducido por el posesivo*)

> El artículo se traduce por el posesivo en inglés cuando se refiere a una parte del cuerpo, una prenda que se lleva puesta o algo que nos pertenece:

se lavó las manos he washed his hands; **me puse el abrigo** I put my coat on
4 (*con expresiones temporales*) **a las ocho** at eight o'clock; **a los quince días** after a fortnight; **el lunes que viene** next Monday
5 (*uso distributivo*) **cuesta 300 pesetas el kilo** it costs 300 pesetas a kilo
6 (*en exclamaciones*) **¡el frío que hacía!** it was freezing!
7 (*posesivo*) **el de:** **mi libro y el de usted** my book and yours; **el de la gorra roja** the one with *o* in the red cap; **prefiero el de Ana** I prefer Ana's; **el idiota de Pedro** that idiot Pedro
8 el que 8.1 (+ INDIC) **el que compramos no vale** the one we bought is no good; **él es el que quiere** it's he who wants to, he's the one who wants to; **los que hacen eso son tontos** anyone who does that is a fool, those who do so are foolish **8.2** (+ SUBJUN) whoever; **el que quiera, que lo haga** whoever wants to can do it

él PRON PERS MASC **1** (*como sujeto*) (= *persona*) he; (= *cosa, animal*) it; **¡es él!** it's him! **2** (*despúes de prep*) (= *persona*) him; (= *cosa, animal*) it; **esto es para él** this is for him **3** (*uso posesivo*) **de él** (= *persona*) his; (= *cosa, animal*) its; **mis libros y los de él** my books and his; **todo eso es de él** all that is his, all that belongs to him

elaboración SF **1** (= *fabricación*) [*de producto*] production; **el proceso de ~ del vino** the wine-making process **2** (= *preparación*) [*de proyecto, presupuesto, lista, candidatura*] drawing up; [*de estrategia*] devising **3** [*de documento, código*] writing, preparation

elaborar /1a/ VT **1** [+ *producto*] to produce, make **2** [+ *proyecto, plan*] to draw up, prepare; [+ *estrategia*] to devise; [+ *presupuesto, lista, candidatura*] to draw up **3** [+ *documento, código*] to write, prepare

elasticidad SF elasticity

elástico 🅐 ADJ [*material*] elastic; [*principio*] flexible; [*superficie*] springy **🅑** SM (= *material*) elastic; (= *trozo*) piece of elastic; (= *goma*) rubber band, elastic band (*esp Brit*)

elección SF **1** (= *selección*) choice; **lo dejo a su ~** I'll leave the choice to you; **no tuve otra ~ que irme** I had no choice *o* alternative but to leave **2** (*Pol*) election (**a** for);
➤ **elecciones autonómicas** regional election *sing*
➤ **elecciones generales** general election *sing* ➤ **elecciones municipales** local elections

eleccionario ADJ (*CS*) electoral, election *antes de s*

electivo ADJ elective

electo ADJ elect; **el presidente ~** the president elect

elector(a) SM/F elector, voter

electorado SM electorate, voters *pl*

electoral ADJ electoral

electoralista ADJ electioneering *antes de s*

eléctrica SF electricity company

electricidad SF electricity

electricista SMF electrician

eléctrico ADJ [*manta, estufa, guitarra*] electric; [*actividad,*

fallo] electrical; **aparatos ~s** electrical appliances

> El adjetivo **eléctrico** se traduce por **electric** cuando se refiere a aparatos que funcionan con la corriente eléctrica: "una guitarra eléctrica", *an electric guitar*. En cambio, **electrical** es menos frecuente y se utiliza sobre todo en el contexto de la física y la mecánica: "un fallo eléctrico", *an electrical fault*; "la ingeniería eléctrica", *electrical engineering*.

electrificar /1g/ VT to electrify

electrizante ADJ electrifying (*tb fig*)

electrizar /1f/ VT to electrify

electrocardiograma SM electrocardiogram

electrochoque SM electroshock

electrocutar /1a/ **🅐** VT to electrocute **🅑** **electrocutarse** VPR to be electrocuted, electrocute o.s.

electrodo SM electrode

electrodoméstico SM electrical household appliance

electroencefalograma SM electroencephalogram

electrólisis SF INV electrolysis

electromagnético ADJ electromagnetic

electrón SM electron

electrónica SF electronics

electrónico ADJ [*juego, sistema, música*] electronic; [*microscopio*] electron *antes de s*

elefante/a SM/F elephant; ✦ MODISMO **como un ~ en una cacharrería** (*Esp*) like a bull in a china shop

elegancia SF (*gen*) elegance; (*en los movimientos*) gracefulness; (*en el vestir*) stylishness, smartness

elegante ADJ (*gen*) elegant; [*traje, fiesta, tienda*] fashionable, smart; [*sociedad*] fashionable, elegant

elegía SF elegy

elegir /3c, 3k/ VT **1** (= *escoger*) to choose, select; **café con bizcochos a ~** coffee with a choice of cakes; **te dan a ~ entre dos modelos** you're given a choice of two models **2** [+ *candidato*] to elect

elemental ADJ **1** (= *básico, rudimentario*) elementary; **un curso de inglés ~** an elementary English course; **nociones ~es de inglés** a basic knowledge of English; **las reglas de cortesía más ~es** the most basic standards of politeness **2** [*derecho, principio*] basic **3** (*Fís*) elemental; **física ~** elemental *o* elementary physics *sing*

elemento SM **1** (= *parte*) element; **el ~ sorpresa** the element of surprise
2 (*Fís, Quím, Elec*) element; [*de pila*] cell
3 (= *ambiente*) **estar en su ~** to be in one's element
4 (= *persona*) **~s subversivos** subversive elements; **¡menudo ~ estás hecho!** (*Esp**) you're a proper little terror!*; **un ~ de cuidado** (*Esp**) a nasty piece of work*
5 (*RPl*) (= *gente*) sort*, crowd*; **a ese lugar va muy mal ~** this place attracts a very bad sort *o* crowd*
6 elementos (= *nociones*) elements, basic principles; (= *fuerzas naturales*) elements ➤ **elementos de juicio** data *sing*, facts

elenco SM [*de actores*] cast; (*LAm*) (= *equipo*) team

elepé SM LP

elevación SF **1** [*de objeto, brazo*] raising **2** (= *aumento*) [*de precios, tipos*] rise, increase; [*de nivel, temperatura*] rise **3** (= *montículo*) hill, elevation (*frm*) **4** (*a dignidad*) elevation **5** (*Jur*) presentation, submission **6** (= *sublimidad*) [*de estilo*] elevation, loftiness; [*de sentimientos*] nobility **7** (*en la misa*) elevation

elevado ADJ **1** (*en nivel*) [*precio, temperatura, cantidad*] high; [*velocidad*] high, great; [*ritmo*] great; **debido al ~ número de accidentes** due to the large number of accidents **2** (*en altura*) [*edificio*] tall; [*montaña, terreno*] high **3** (= *sublime*) [*estilo*] elevated, lofty; [*pensamientos*] noble, lofty **4** [*puesto, rango*] high, important

elevador SM elevator, hoist; (*Méx*) lift (*Brit*), elevator (*EEUU*)

elevalunas SM INV ➤ **elevalunas eléctrico** electric

windows *pl*

elevar /1a/ **Ⓐ** VT **1** (= *levantar*) [+ *objeto, brazos*] to raise; **una sinfonía que eleva el espíritu** a symphony that is spiritually uplifting *o* that uplifts the spirit **2** (= *aumentar*) [+ *precio, tipo, temperatura, calidad*] to raise; **el consumo de huevos eleva el nivel de colesterol** eating eggs increases *o* raises one's cholesterol level; - **el tono de la voz** to raise one's voice **3** [+ *muro*] to raise **4** - **a algn a algo** to elevate sb to sth (*frm*); - **a algn a los altares** to canonize sb **5** [+ *petición, solicitud*] to present, submit **6** (*Mat*) - **al cuadrado** to square; **tres elevado al cuadrado** three squared; - **al cubo** to cube; - **un número a la cuarta potencia** to raise a number to the power of four **7** [+ *voltaje*] to boost **8** (*Chi**) (= *reprender*) to tell off* **Ⓑ elevarse** VPR **1** (= *erguirse*) [*montaña, edificio*] to rise; **la cordillera se eleva 2.500m sobre el nivel del mar** the mountain range rises to 2,500m above sea level **2** (= *ascender*) [*humo*] to rise; [*avión*] to climb **3** (= *aumentar*) [*temperatura, fiebre*] to rise, increase **4** (= *alcanzar*) **~se a** [*cifra, cantidad*] to stand at, amount to; [*temperatura*] to be, reach; **la cifra de heridos se eleva ya a 300** the number of people injured now stands at 300 *o* is now 300

eliminación SF **1** [*de posibilidades*] elimination; **por** - by (a) process of elimination **2** [*de concursante, deportista*] elimination; **3** (= *desaparición*) [*de mancha, obstáculo*] removal; [*de residuos*] disposal **4** [*de incógnita*] elimination **5** (*Fisiol*) elimination

eliminar /1a/ VT **1** (= *quitar*) [+ *mancha, obstáculo*] to remove, get rid of; [+ *residuos*] to dispose of; [+ *pobreza*] to eliminate, eradicate; [+ *posibilidad*] to rule out **2** [+ *concursante, deportista*] to knock out, eliminate **3** (*euf*) (= *matar*) to eliminate, do away with* **4** [+ *incógnita*] to eliminate **5** (*Fisiol*) to eliminate

eliminatoria SF (= *partido*) qualifying round; (= *carrera*) heat; (= *competición*) qualifying competition

eliminatorio ADJ [*carrera, partido, examen*] qualifying; [*fase, ronda*] qualifying, preliminary

elipse SF ellipse

elipsis SF INV ellipsis

elíptico ADJ elliptical, elliptic

élite ['elite] SF, **elite** [e'lite] SF elite

elitismo SM elitism

elitista ADJ, SMF elitist

elixir SM elixir ➤ **elixir bucal** (*Esp*) mouthwash

ella PRON PERS FEM **1** (*como sujeto*) (= *persona*) she; (= *cosa*) it **2** (*después de prep*) (= *persona*) her; (= *cosa*) it; **estuve con ~** I was with her **3** (*uso posesivo*) **de ~** (= *persona*) hers; (= *cosa*) its; **nada de esto es de ~** none of this is hers; **mi sombrero y el de ~** my hat and hers

ellas PRON PERS FPL *ver* **ellos**

ello PRON it; **no tiene fuerzas para ~** he's not strong enough for it; **~ no es obstáculo para que venga** that shouldn't stop him coming

ellos/as PRON PERS MPL/FPL **1** (*como sujeto*) they; **—¿quién lo sabe? —ellos** "who knows?" — "they do" *o* "them"; **ellas no lo saben** they don't know **2** (*después de prep*) them; **dáselo a ~** give it to them; **pregúntales a ellas** ask them; **con ~** with them; **entre ~** between them; **para ~** for them **3** (*en comparaciones*) **no puedo comportarme como ~** I can't behave like them; **tenemos más poder que ~** we're more powerful than them **4** (*uso posesivo*) **de ~** theirs; **el libro es de ~** the book is theirs; **estuvimos en casa de ~** we were at their house

elocución SF elocution

elocuencia SF eloquence

elocuente ADJ eloquent; **un dato ~** a fact which speaks for itself

elogiar /1b/ VT to praise, eulogize (*liter*)

elogio SM praise; **hacer ~ de** to sing the praises of

elogioso ADJ highly favourable, highly favorable (*EEUU*)

elote SM (*CAm, Méx*) (= *mazorca*) corncob, corn on the cob; (= *maíz*) maize (*Brit*), corn (*EEUU*), sweetcorn

El Salvador SM El Salvador

elucidar /1a/ VT to elucidate

elucubrar /1a/ VI to lucubrate

eludir /3a/ VT [+ *problema, responsabilidad*] to evade; [+ *control, vigilancia*] to dodge; [+ *pago, impuesto*] to avoid; **logró ~ a sus perseguidores** she managed to evade her pursuers

elusivo ADJ elusive, evasive

email ['imeil] SM (*gen*) email; (= *dirección*) email address; **mandar un ~ a algn** to email sb, send sb an email

emanación SF emission, emanation (*frm*); **emanaciones de gas** gas emissions; **emanaciones tóxicas** toxic emissions

emanar /1a/ VI **~ de** to emanate from (*frm*), come from

emancipar /1a/ **Ⓐ** VT to emancipate, free **Ⓑ emanciparse** VPR to become emancipated, free o.s. (**de** from)

embadurnar /1a/ VT to daub, smear (**de** with)

embajada SF **1** (= *edificio*) embassy **2** (= *cargo*) ambassadorship

embajador(a) SM/F ambassador (**en** in, to); **el ~ de España en Francia** the Spanish ambassador in *o* to France

embalado* ADJ **1** (= *a toda velocidad*) **el coche pasó ~** the car flew past **2** (*RPl**) (= *entusiasmado*) keen, fired-up*

embalar /1a/ **Ⓐ** VT (*gen*) to pack; (*en cajas resistentes*) to crate **Ⓑ embalarse*** VPR **1** (= *acelerar*) to sprint, make a dash; (= *tomar velocidad*) to gather speed **2** (= *apresurarse*) **se embala hablando** she gets carried away when she's speaking; **no te embales, que hay tiempo** don't rush yourself, there's time **3** (*RPl**) **~se con algo** to get enthusiastic about sth, get all fired-up about sth (*EEUU**)

embaldosar /1a/ VT to tile, pave with tiles

embalsamar /1a/ VT to embalm

embalsar /1a/ VT [+ *río*] to dam, dam up; [+ *agua*] to retain, collect; **este mes se han embalsado 1.000 metros cúbicos** this month reservoir stocks have gone up by 1,000 cubic metres

embalse SM reservoir

embancarse /1g/ VPR (*And*) to silt up, become blocked by silt

embarazada **Ⓐ** ADJ pregnant **Ⓑ** SF pregnant woman

 embarazada ≠ embarrassed

embarazar /1f/ VT **1** (= *estorbar*) to hamper, hinder **2** [+ *mujer*] to make pregnant

embarazo SM **1** [*de mujer*] pregnancy; **interrumpir el ~** to terminate a pregnancy ➤ **embarazo ectópico, embarazo extrauterino** ectopic pregnancy **2** (= *turbación*) embarrassment

embarazoso ADJ (= *molesto*) awkward, inconvenient; (= *violento*) embarrassing

embarcación SF **1** (= *barco*) boat, craft, (small) vessel **2** (= *acto*) embarkation

embarcadero SM pier, jetty

embarcar /1g/ **Ⓐ** VT **1** (*en barco*) [+ *personas*] to embark, put on board; [+ *carga*] to ship, stow **2** (= *implicar*) **~ a algn en algo** to get sb involved in sth **3** (*Ven**) [+ *persona*] (= *dejar esperando*) to keep waiting **Ⓑ embarcarse** VPR **1** (*en barco*) to embark, go on board; **~ para** to sail for **2** (= *enrolarse*) [*marinero*] to sign on **3** (= *implicarse*) **~se en un asunto** to get involved in a matter **4** (*LAm*) (*en vehículo*) to get on

embargar /1h/ VT **1** (*Jur*) to seize, impound **2** [+ *sentidos*] to overpower, overwhelm

embargo SM **1** (*Jur*) seizure, distraint **2** (*Pol*) embargo **3 sin ~** still, however, nonetheless

embarque SM [*de personas*] embarkation, boarding; [*de carga*] shipment, loading; **tarjeta de ~** boarding card

embarrada* SF **1** (*SAm*) (= *metedura de pata*) blunder **2** ~ **de mano** (*Méx**) bribe

embarrado ADJ **1** (= *con barro*) muddy **2** (*Méx**) (= *ceñido*) tight

embarrancar /1g/ **Ⓐ** VI (*Náut*) to run aground; (*Aut*) to run into a ditch **Ⓑ** **embarrancarse** VPR (*Náut*) to run aground; (*Aut*) to run into a ditch

embarrar /1a/ **Ⓐ** VT to cover with mud; **la embarré** (*SAm**) I put my foot in it*, I spoiled things **Ⓑ** **embarrarse** VPR to get covered in mud

embarullar /1a/ VT to bungle, mess up

embate SM [*de mar, viento*] beating, violence; [*de olas*] dashing, breaking, beating ➤ **embates de la fortuna** blows of fate

embaucador(a) SM/F trickster, swindler

embaucar /1g/ VT to trick, fool, lead up (*esp Brit*) *o* down (*esp EEUU*) the garden path*

embeber /2a/ **Ⓐ** VT **1** (= *absorb*) to absorb, soak up **2** (*Cos*) to take in, gather **Ⓑ** **embeberse** VPR **1** (= *abstraerse*) to be absorbed, become engrossed (**en** in) **2** ~**se de** to imbibe, become well versed in

embeleco SM, **embelequería** (*LAm*) SF deceit, fraud

embelesado ADJ spellbound, enraptured

embelesar /1a/ **Ⓐ** VT to enchant, entrance **Ⓑ** **embelesarse** VPR to be enchanted, be enraptured

embeleso SM enchantment, delight

embellecedor SM (*Aut*) hub cap; (= *adorno*) trim

embellecer /2d/ VT to embellish, beautify

embellecimiento SM embellishment

embestida SF (*gen*) attack; [*de olas, viento*] onslaught; [*de toro*] charge

embestir /3k/ **Ⓐ** VT **1** (= *atacar*) to assault, attack **2** (= *abalanzarse sobre*) to rush at, rush upon **3** [*toro*] to charge **Ⓑ** VI **1** (= *atacar*) to attack **2** [*toro*] to rush, charge; ~ **contra algn** to rush at sb

embiste SM (*Carib*) = **embestida**

emblema SM emblem

emblemático ADJ emblematic

embobar /1a/ **Ⓐ** VT to fascinate **Ⓑ** **embobarse** VPR to be amazed (**con, de, en** at), be fascinated (**con, de, en** by); **se quedó embobado mirando los pájaros** he was completely captivated *o* entranced by the birds

embocadura SF **1** [*de río*] mouth **2** [*de flauta, trompeta*] mouthpiece **3** [*de vino*] flavour, flavor (*EEUU*)

embocar /1g/ VT **1** (*Golf*) to hole; (*Billar*) to pocket, pot **2** (*Col, RPl**) (= *acertar*) to get right

embojotar* /1a/ (*Ven*) **Ⓐ** VT to wrap (up) **Ⓑ** VPR to wrap o.s. (up)

embolado* SM jam*, fix*; **meter a algn en un** ~* to put sb in a tight spot*

embolador(a) SM/F (*Col*) bootblack

embolar /1a/ VT **1** (*Taur*) [+ *cuernos*] to tip with wooden balls **2** (*Col*) [+ *zapatos*] to black

embolia SF embolism ➤ **embolia cerebral** brain embolism, blood clot on the brain

émbolo SM piston

embolsar /1a/ VT to pocket

embonar /1a/ VI (*Méx*) to fit (together)

emboquillado ADJ [*cigarrillo*] tipped

emborrachar /1a/ **Ⓐ** VT to make drunk **Ⓑ** **emborracharse** VPR to get drunk (**con, de** on)

emborronar /1a/ **Ⓐ** VT (= *manchar*) to blot, make blots on; (= *garabatear*) to scribble on **Ⓑ** **emborronarse** VPR to get smudged

emboscada SF ambush; **tender una** ~ **a** to lay an ambush for

emboscarse /1g/ VPR to lie in ambush; **estaban emboscados cerca del camino** they were in ambush near the road

embotado ADJ (*lit, fig*) dull, blunt

embotamiento SM dullness, bluntness

embotar /1a/ VT [+ *sentidos*] to dull, blunt

embotellamiento SM traffic jam

embotellar /1a/ VT to bottle

embozar /1f/ **Ⓐ** VT to muffle, muffle up **Ⓑ** **embozarse** VPR to muffle o.s. up (**con, de** in)

embozo SM **1** [*de capa*] top of the cape, fold of the cape **2** [*de sábana*] turnover **3** [*de persona*] **sin** ~ frankly, openly

embragar /1h/ VI to let in the clutch

embrague SM clutch

embravecer /2d/ **Ⓐ** VT to enrage, infuriate **Ⓑ** **embravecerse** VPR **1** [*mar*] to get rough, get choppy **2** [*persona*] to get furious

embravecido ADJ [*mar*] rough, choppy

embrear /1a/ VT to tar, cover with tar

embriagador ADJ [*olor, perfume*] intoxicating; [*vino*] heady

embriagar /1h/ **Ⓐ** VT **1** (= *emborrachar*) to make drunk **2** (= *fascinar*) to delight, enrapture **Ⓑ** **embriagarse** VPR to get drunk

embriaguez SF **1** (= *borrachera*) drunkenness **2** (= *entusiasmo*) rapture, delight

embridar /1a/ VT to bridle, put a bridle on

embriología SF embryology

embrión SM [*de ser vivo*] embryo; [*de proyecto, idea*] germ; **en** ~ (*lit*) in embryo; (*fig*) in its infancy, in its early stages

embrionario ADJ embryonic

embrollar /1a/ **Ⓐ** VT **1** (= *confundir*) to muddle, confuse **2** (= *involucrar*) to involve, embroil (*frm*) **Ⓑ** **embrollarse** VPR to get into a muddle, get into a mess

embrollo SM (= *confusión*) muddle, confusion; (= *aprieto*) fix*, jam*

embromado* ADJ (*LAm*) **1** [*situación*] tricky*, difficult **2 estar** ~ (*gen*) to be in a fix*; (*Med*) to be in a bad way; (*Fin*) to be in financial trouble *o* difficulties

embromar* /1a/ **Ⓐ** VT **1** (*CS*) (= *burlarse de*) to tease, make fun of; (= *engañar*) to hoodwink **2** (*LAm*) (= *molestar*) to annoy **3** (*LAm*) (= *perjudicar*) to harm, set back; (= *echar a perder*) to ruin **Ⓑ** VI (*CS*) **1** (= *molestar*) to bother **2** (= *tomar el pelo*) **¡estás embromando!** you're kidding!* **Ⓒ** **embromarse** VPR (*LAm**) **1** (= *fastidiarse*) **¡que se embrome!** tough!* **2** (= *hacerse daño*) to get hurt; **se embromó la espalda** he hurt his shoulder **3** (= *estropearse*) to damage **4** (= *caer enfermo*) to fall ill, get sick (*EEUU*)

embrujado ADJ [*persona*] bewitched; [*lugar*] haunted

embrujar /1a/ VT [+ *persona*] to bewitch, put a spell on; [+ *lugar*] to haunt

embrujo SM **1** (= *acto*) bewitching **2** (= *maldición*) curse **3** (= *ensalmo*) spell, charm

embrutecer /2d/ **Ⓐ** VT to stupefy, dull the senses of **Ⓑ** **embrutecerse** VPR to be stupefied

embuchar /1a/ VT to stuff with minced (*Brit*) *o* ground (*EEUU*) meat

embudo SM funnel

embuste SM lie

embustero/a **Ⓐ** ADJ lying **Ⓑ** SM/F liar

embutido SM **1** (*Culin*) sausage **2** (*CS, Méx, Ven*) (= *encaje*) lace insert **3** (= *acción*) stuffing

embutir /3a/ **Ⓐ** VT **1** (*Culin*) to stuff (**en** into) **2** (*) (= *atiborrar*) to pack tight, stuff, cram (**de** with; **en** into); **embutida en un vestido apretadísimo** squeezed into a terribly close-fitting dress **Ⓑ** **embutirse*** VPR to stuff o.s. (**de** with)

emergencia SF emergency

emergente ADJ **1** [*nación, ideología, mercado*] emerging, emergent **2** (= *resultante*) resultant, consequent

emerger /2c/ VI (= *aparecer*) to emerge; [*submarino*] to surface

emérito ADJ emeritus

emigración SF [de personas] emigration; [de aves] migration ➤ **emigración golondrina** (Méx) seasonal migration of workers

emigrado/a SM/F emigrant; (Pol etc) émigré(e)

emigrante ADJ, SMF emigrant

emigrar /1a/ VI [personas] to emigrate; [aves] to migrate

emilio* SM (Inform hum) email; **mandar un ~ a algn** to email sb

eminencia SF 1 (= excelencia) eminence 2 (en títulos) **Su Eminencia** His Eminence

eminente ADJ eminent, distinguished

emir SM emir

emirato SM emirate

emisario/a SM/F emissary, envoy

emisión SF 1 (= acción) emission; (Fin etc) issue; (Bolsa) share issue ➤ **emisión de acciones, emisión de valores** flotation 2 (Radio, TV) (= difusión) broadcasting; (= programa) broadcast, programme, program (EEUU)

emisor ⓐ ADJ **banco ~** issuing bank ⓑ SM 1 (Radio, TV) transmitter 2 (Fin) issuing company

emisora SF radio station, broadcasting station ➤ **emisora comercial** commercial radio station

emitir /3a/ VT 1 [+ sonido, olor] to emit, give off, give out 2 [+ dinero, sellos, bonos] to issue 3 [+ opinión] to express; [+ veredicto] to return, issue, give; [+ voto] to cast 4 (Radio, TV) to broadcast; [+ señal] to send out

emoción SF 1 (= sentimiento) emotion; **sentir una honda ~** to feel a deep emotion; **llorar de ~** to be moved to tears 2 (= excitación) excitement; **la ~ de la película no disminuye** the excitement o tension in the film (esp Brit) o movie (esp EEUU) does not flag; **¡qué ~!** (lit) how exciting!; (iró) big deal!; **con la ~ del momento no me di cuenta** in the heat of the moment I just didn't realize; **emociones fuertes** thrills*, excitement sing

emocionado ADJ 1 (= conmovido) deeply moved, stirred 2 (= entusiasmado) excited

emocional ADJ emotional

emocionante ADJ 1 (= conmovedor) moving 2 (= excitante) exciting, thrilling

emocionar /1a/ ⓐ VT 1 (= conmover) to move, touch 2 (= excitar) to excite, thrill ⓑ **emocionarse** VPR 1 (= conmoverse) to be moved, be touched; **me emocioné mucho con la novela** I was very moved by the novel; **se emocionó al volver a ver a su padre** she got emotional when she saw her father again 2 (= entusiasmarse) to get excited; **¡no te emociones!** don't get carried away!

emoticón SM, **emoticono** SM smiley

emotivo ADJ [persona] emotional; [escena] moving, touching; [palabras] emotive, moving

empacadora SF (Agr) baler

empacar /1g/ ⓐ VT (gen) to pack; (Agr) to bale ⓑ VI (LAm) to pack ⓒ **empacarse** VPR (LAm) (= obstinarse) to dig one's heels in

empachado ADJ [estómago] upset; **estoy ~ de comer tanto chocolate** I've got indigestion from eating all that chocolate

empachar /1a/ ⓐ VT 1 (= causar indigestión) to give indigestion to 2 (= aburrir) to bore ⓑ **empacharse** VPR to get indigestion

empacho SM 1 (= indigestión) indigestion 2 (= hartazgo) **darse un ~ de algo** (fig) to get a bellyful of sth* 3 (= reparo) **no tener ~ en hacer algo** to have no objection to doing sth

> Recuérdese que las preposiciones en inglés rigen gerundio y no infinitivo, de ahí **to have no objection to doing sth.**

empachoso ADJ 1 [comida] indigestible 2 [persona] cloying, over-sweet; (= vergonzoso) embarrassing

empadronamiento SM registration

empadronarse /1a/ VPR to register

empalagar /1h/ ⓐ VT [comida] to be too sweet for; **su conversación me empalaga** I find his conversation too sickly-sweet ⓑ VI [chocolate, tarta] to be too sweet ⓒ **empalagarse** VPR to get sick (**de** of)

empalago SM cloying, palling

empalagoso ADJ 1 (= dulce) cloying 2 (= pesado) sickly-sweet

empalar /1a/ VT to impale

empalizada SF palisade, stockade

empalmar /1a/ ⓐ VT 1 [+ tuberías, cables] to connect, join; [+ cuerdas, películas] to splice; **fueron empalmando un tema de conversación tras otro** one subject led to another as they spoke ⓑ VI 1 [carreteras, líneas] to join; [cables, piezas] to connect (**con** with); **esta carretera empalma con la autopista** this road joins the motorway (Brit) o freeway (EEUU) 2 (Ferro) [trenes] to connect; [vías] to join 3 (= sucederse) to follow (on) (**con** from); **su programa empalma con las noticias** her programme follows (on from) the news ⓒ **empalmarse** VPR (Esp***) to get a hard-on***

empalme SM 1 (Téc) joint, connection 2 [de vías, carreteras] junction (esp Brit), intersection (esp EEUU); [de trenes] connection

empanada SF pie ➤ **empanada mental*** confusion

empanadilla SF pasty, pie

empanar /1a/ VT to cover in breadcrumbs

empantanado ADJ [camino] swampy; [proyecto] bogged down

empantanar /1a/ ⓐ VT 1 (= inundar) to swamp 2 [+ negociación, proyecto] to bog down ⓑ **empantanarse** VPR 1 (= inundarse) to be swamped 2 [asunto, negociación] to get bogged down, get held up; **~se en un asunto** to get bogged down in a matter

empañado ADJ [cristal, espejo] misty, steamed-up; **con los ojos ~s en lágrimas** with her eyes moist with tears

empañar /1a/ ⓐ VT [+ cristal, espejo, gafas] to steam up, mist over; [+ superficie, honra] to tarnish ⓑ **empañarse** VPR 1 [cristales, gafas] to get steamed up, mist over; [voz] to falter 2 [reputación] to get tarnished

empañetar /1a/ VT (CAm, Col, Ven) to plaster

empapar /1a/ ⓐ VT 1 (= mojar) to soak, drench; **estar empapado hasta los huesos** to be soaked to the skin 2 (= absorber) to soak up; **empapó toda el agua con una bayeta** she soaked up all the water with a cloth ⓑ **empaparse** VPR 1 (= mojarse) to get soaked; **las patatas se ~on de aceite** the potatoes soaked up the oil 2 (= enterarse) **~se de: se empapó de filosofía griega** he steeped himself in Greek philosophy

empapelar /1a/ VT 1 [+ cuarto, pared] to paper; [+ caja] to line with paper 2 **~ a algn*** to throw the book at sb

empaque SM 1 (= distinción) presence 2 (Col*) (= aspecto) look 3 (Chi, Col, Méx) (= acción, material) (como protección) packing; (para regalo, en plástico) wrapping 4 (Col, Méx, Ven) (= arandela) washer

empaquetar /1a/ VT 1 [+ objeto] to pack, parcel up; (Com) to package 2 (Esp**) [+ soldado] to punish

emparamarse /1a/ VPR (And, Carib) to get soaked

emparar* /1a/ (Perú) VT to catch

emparedado SM sandwich

emparedar /1a/ VT to confine

emparejar /1a/ ⓐ VT 1 [+ cosas, dos personas] to pair, match 2 (= nivelar) to level, make level ⓑ VI (= alcanzar) to catch up (**con** with) ⓒ **emparejarse** VPR to match

emparentado ADJ related by marriage (**con** to)

emparentar /1j/ VI to become related by marriage (**con** to)

emparrado SM trained vine

emparrandarse* /1a/ VPR (Col) to go on a binge*

empastar /1a/ VT 1 [+ diente] to fill, stop 2 (= engomar) to paste **3** (*Tip*) to bind in stiff covers

empaste SM [*de diente*] filling

empatar /1a/ Ⓐ VI **1** (*Dep*) (*resultado final*) to draw (*esp Brit*), tie (*EEUU*); (*durante el partido*) to equalize (*Brit*), tie the score (*EEUU*); **los tres equipos quedan empatados a puntos** the three teams are level on points **2** (*en votación*) to tie Ⓑ VT **1** (*Col, Ven*) (= *conectar*) to connect **2** (*Ven*) (= *juntar*) to join (up)
Ⓒ **empatarse** VPR (*Ven*) **1** [*calles*] to join (up); **se empata con la carretera** it joins (up with) the road **2** (*) (*en relación amorosa*) to get together; **estar empatado con algn** to be (going out) with sb

empate SM **1** (*en partido*) draw; **un ~ a cero** a nil-nil draw; **el gol del ~** the equalizer; **continúa el ~ en el marcador** the scores are still level **2** (*en votación*) tie **3** (*Col, Perú, Ven*) (= *junta*) joint, connection **4** (*Ven**) **4.1** (= *relación amorosa*) relationship; **tienen un año de ~** they've been together for a year **4.2** (= *novio*) boyfriend/girlfriend

empatía SF empathy

empavar* /1a/ VT (*Carib*) to put a jinx on*, bring bad luck to

empecinado ADJ stubborn, pig-headed

empecinarse /1a/ VPR **~ en algo** to be stubborn about sth; **~ en hacer algo** to persist in doing sth

> Recuérdese que las preposiciones en inglés rigen gerundio y no infinitivo, de ahí **to persist in doing sth**.

empedarse* /1a/ VPR (*Méx, RPl*) to get drunk, get sloshed*

empedernido ADJ [*fumador, bebedor*] heavy; [*soltero*] confirmed

empedrado Ⓐ ADJ [*superficie*] paved Ⓑ SM paving

empedrar /1j/ VT to pave

empeine SM instep

empellón SM push, shove; **lo sacaron a empellones** they shoved *o* pushed him out of the door

empelotado* **1** ADJ (*CS*) (= *desnudo*) naked, starkers* **2** (*Méx*) (= *enamorado*) in love

empelotar* /1a/ Ⓐ VT **1** (*Col, CS*) (= *desvestir*) to undress, strip **2** (*Perú**) (= *prestar atención a*) to take notice of, listen to Ⓑ **empelotarse** VPR (*Col, CS*) to strip naked, strip off

empeñado ADJ **1** [*objeto de valor*] pawned **2** (= *endeudado*) in debt; ✦ MODISMO **estar ~ hasta los ojos** to be deeply in debt, be up to one's eyes in debt* **3** (= *empecinado*) determined; **estar ~ en hacer algo** to be determined to do sth

empeñar /1a/ Ⓐ VT **1** [+ *objeto de valor*] to pawn, pledge **2** [+ *palabra*] to give; [+ *persona*] to engage, compel Ⓑ **empeñarse** VPR **1** (= *endeudarse*) to get into debt **2** (= *insistir*) **~se en algo** to insist on sth; **se empeñó en irse a trabajar al extranjero** he insisted on going to work abroad; **me empeñé en que estudiara inglés** I insisted that she should study English

empeño SM **1** (= *resolución*) determination; (= *insistencia*) insistence; **poner ~ en hacer algo** to strive to do sth **2** (= *empresa*) undertaking; **morir en el ~** to die in the attempt

empeñoso ADJ (*LAm*) persevering, diligent

empeoramiento SM deterioration, worsening

empeorar /1a/ Ⓐ VT to make worse, worsen Ⓑ VI to get worse, worsen

emperador SM **1** (= *gobernante*) emperor **2** (= *pez*) swordfish

emperatriz SF empress

emperifollarse* /1a/ VPR to dress up, doll o.s. up*

empero†† CONJ (*liter*) nonetheless

emperrarse* /1a/ VPR to get stubborn, be obstinate; **~ en algo** to persist in sth

empezar /1f, 1j/ Ⓐ VI **1** (*gen*) to start, begin; (*en un puesto de trabajo*) to start; **el curso empieza en octubre** the course

starts *o* begins in October; **el año ha empezado mal** the year got off to a bad start, the year started *o* began badly; **al ~ el año** at the start *o* beginning of the year; **¡no empieces!*** don't you start!*; **para ~** to start with, begin with
2 ~ a hacer algo (*gen*) to start *o* begin to do sth, start *o* begin doing sth; (*en un trabajo*) to start to do *o* doing sth; **ya empiezo a entrar en calor** I'm starting *o* beginning to feel warm now
3 ~ haciendo algo to begin *o* start by doing sth

> Recuérdese que las preposiciones en inglés rigen gerundio y no infinitivo, de ahí **to begin** *o* **start by doing sth**.

4 ~ con algo [*película, curso, año*] to start *o* begin with sth; **¿cuándo empezáis con las clases de inglés?** when do you start your English classes?; **¡no empieces otra vez con lo mismo!** don't start on that again!
5 ~ por algo/algn to start with sth/sb, begin with sth/sb; **"huelga" empieza por hache** "huelga" starts *o* begins with (an) h; **la carcoma empezó por las patas del armario** the woodworm started in the legs of the wardrobe; **~ por hacer algo** to start by doing sth, begin by doing sth

> Recuérdese que las preposiciones en inglés rigen gerundio y no infinitivo, de ahí **to start** *o* **begin by doing sth**.

Ⓑ VT [+ *actividad, temporada*] to start, begin; [+ *botella, jamón*] to start; **hemos empezado mal la semana** the week got off to a bad start for us, the week started badly for us

empinado ADJ [*cuesta*] steep; [*edificio*] high, lofty

empinar /1a/ Ⓐ VT to raise; ✦ MODISMO **~ el codo*** to booze* Ⓑ **empinarse** VPR to stand on tiptoe

empírico/a Ⓐ ADJ empirical, empiric Ⓑ SM/F empiricist

empirismo SM empiricism

emplasto SM (*Med*) poultice

emplazamiento SM **1** (*Jur*) summons **2** (= *sitio*) location; (*Mil*) emplacement **3** [*de producto*] product placement

emplazar /1f/ VT **1** (= *convocar*) to summon, convene; (*Jur*) to summons **2** (= *ubicar*) to site, place **3 ~ a algn a hacer algo** to call on sb to do sth

empleado/a SM/F employee ➤ **empleada del hogar** (*Esp*) servant, maid ➤ **empleado/a de correos** post-office worker ➤ **empleado/a público/a** civil servant

empleador(a) SM/F employer

emplear /1a/ Ⓐ VT **1** (= *usar*) to use; **empleó todo tipo de artimañas para convencerla** he used all sorts of tricks to convince her; **ha empleado mal el término** she has misused the term; ✦ MODISMO **¡le está bien empleado!** (*Esp*) it serves him right!
2 [+ *trabajador*] to employ
3 [+ *tiempo, dinero*] to spend, use; **dinero bien empleado** money well spent; **~ mal el tiempo** to waste time Ⓑ **emplearse** VPR **~se a fondo** to make a great effort; **tendrá que ~se a fondo para ganar** he'll have to give it all he's got if he wants to win

empleo SM **1** (= *uso*) use; **"modo de empleo"** "instructions for use" **2** (= *trabajo*) employment, work; **pleno ~** full employment **3** (= *puesto*) job, post; **buscar un ~** to look for a job, seek employment

emplomadura SF (*RPl*) filling

emplomar /1a/ VT (*RPl*) [+ *diente*] to fill

emplumar /1a/ Ⓐ VT (*Esp*) **le ~on seis meses de cárcel*** they packed him off to prison for six months* Ⓑ VI [*pájaro*] to grow feathers Ⓒ **emplumarse** VPR ✦ MODISMO **emplumárselas** (*Chi**) to leave, split*

empobrecer /2d/ Ⓐ VT to impoverish Ⓑ **empobrecerse** VPR to become poor

empobrecimiento SM impoverishment

empollar /1a/ Ⓐ VT **1** (*Zool*) to incubate, sit on **2** (*Esp**) [+ *asignatura*] to swot up* Ⓑ VI **1** [*gallina*] to sit, brood

2 (*Esp**) [*estudiante*] to swot (*Brit**), grind away (*EEUU**), cram

empollón/ona* SM/F (*Esp*) swot (*Brit**), grind (*EEUU**)

empolvar /1a/ Ⓐ VT [+ *cara*] to powder; [+ *superficie*] to cover with dust Ⓑ **empolvarse** VPR **1** [+ *cara*] to powder one's face **2** [*superficie*] to get dusty

emponchado ADJ (*CS*) wearing *o* covered with a poncho

emponzoñar /1a/ VT to poison

emporio SM **1** (= *gran empresa*) empire; **un ~ económico** a business empire **2** (= *centro*) **un ~ de las artes** an artistic centre *o* (*EEUU*) center **3** (*Hist*) trading centre, trading center (*EEUU*)

empotrado ADJ [*armario*] built-in

empotrar /1a/ Ⓐ VT [+ *armario*] to build in Ⓑ **empotrarse** VPR **el coche se empotró en el muro** the car embedded itself in the wall

empozarse /1f/ VPR (*Col, Perú, Ven*) to form pools

emprendedor ADJ enterprising, go-ahead

emprender /2a/ VT **1** [+ *trabajo*] to undertake; [+ *viaje*] to embark on; **~ la marcha a** to set out for; **~ el regreso** to return; **~ la retirada** to retreat **2 ~la con algn** to take it out on sb; **la emprendieron a botellazos con el árbitro** they threw bottles at the referee

empresa SF **1** (= *compañía*) firm, company; **pequeñas y medianas ~s** small and medium-sized companies ➤ **empresa de trabajo temporal** temp recruitment agency ➤ **empresa pública** public sector company **2** (= *dirección*) management; **la ~ lamenta que ...** the management regrets that ... **3** (= *tarea*) enterprise; **la libre ~** free enterprise

empresarial ADJ [*función, clase*] managerial; **estudios ~es** business studies

empresariales SFPL business studies

empresario/a SM/F **1** (*Com*) businessman/businesswoman **2** [*de ópera, teatro*] impresario **3** (*Boxeo*) promoter

empréstito SM loan

empujada SF (*LAm*) push, shove

empujar /1a/ VT (*gen*) to push; (*con fuerza*) to shove, thrust

empuje SM **1** (= *fuerza*) push, drive; **le falta ~** he lacks drive **2** (*Mec, Fís*) thrust

empujón SM **1** (*con la mano*) push, shove; **abrirse paso a empujones** to push *o* shove one's way through **2** (= *incitación*) push, drive; **dar un ~ a algo** to push sth through, push sth forward

empuñadura SF [*de espada*] hilt; [*de herramienta*] handle

empuñar /1a/ VT **1** (= *coger*) to grasp, clutch; **~ las armas** to take up arms **2** (*Chi*) [+ *puño*] to clench

emú SM emu

emulación SF emulation

emular /1a/ VT to emulate

emulsión SF emulsion

emulsionar /1a/ VT to emulsify

en PREP **1** (*indicando lugar*) **1.1** (= *dentro de*) in; **está en el cajón/en el armario** it's in the drawer/in the wardrobe; **"curvas peligrosas en 2 kilómetros"** "dangerous bends 2 kilometres ahead" **1.2** (= *encima de*) on; **tirado en el suelo** lying on the floor; **la oficina está en el quinto piso** the office is on the fifth floor **1.3** (*con países, ciudades, calles*) **está en Argentina** it's in Argentina; **viven en Granada** they live in Granada; **la biblioteca está en la calle Pelayo** the library is on Pelayo street; **vivía en el número 17** she lived at number 17; **trabaja en un banco** she works in a bank **1.4** (*con edificios*) **en casa** ◊ **en la casa** (*LAm*) at home; **en la oficina** at the office; **te esperé en la estación** I waited for you at the station; **te veo en el restaurante** see you at the restaurant

2 (*indicando movimiento*) into; **entré en el banco** I went into the bank; **me metí en la cama** I got into bed; **entra en el coche** get in(to) the car

3 (*indicando modo*) in; **en inglés** in English; **en pantalón corto** in shorts; **hablar en voz alta** to speak loudly

4 (*indicando proporción*) by; **ha aumentado en un 20 por ciento** it has increased by 20 per cent

5 (*indicando tiempo*) **en 1605** in 1605; **en invierno** in (the) winter; **en enero** in January; **lo hice en dos días** I did it in two days; **no he salido en todo el día** I haven't gone out all day; **en aquella ocasión** on that occasion; **mi cumpleaños cae en viernes** my birthday falls on a Friday; **en aquella época** at that time; **en ese momento** at that moment; **en Navidades** at Christmas; **ayer en la mañana** (*LAm*) yesterday morning

6 (*indicando tema, ocupación*) **un experto en la materia** an expert on the subject; **es bueno en dibujo** he's good at drawing; **trabaja en la construcción** he works in the building industry

7 (*con medios de transporte*) by; **en avión** by plane; **en coche** by car; **en autobús** by bus

8 (*con cantidades*) at, for; **lo vendió en cinco dólares** he sold it at *o* for five dollars; **estimaron las ganancias en unos tres millones de euros** they estimated the profits to be around three million euros

9 (*con infinitivo*) **fue el último en hacerlo** he was the last to do it; **lo reconocí en el andar** I recognized him by his walk

enagua SF, **enaguas** SFPL petticoat

enajenación SF alienation ➤ **enajenación mental** mental derangement

enajenado ADJ deranged

enajenamiento SM = **enajenación**

enajenar /1a/ Ⓐ VT **1** (*Jur*) [+ *propiedad*] to alienate, transfer **2** (*Psic*) to alienate, estrange Ⓑ **enajenarse** VPR **1** (= *enloquecer*) to go insane **2** (= *extasiarse*) to be enraptured, be carried away

enaltecer /2d/ VT to extol

enamoradizo ADJ who easily falls in love

enamorado/a Ⓐ ADJ **1** [*de persona*] in love (**de** with); **estar ~** to be in love **2** (*CS*) = **enamoradizo** Ⓑ SM/F **1** (= *amante*) lover; **el día de los ~s** St. Valentine's Day **2** (= *aficionado*) **es un ~ del baloncesto** he's a real basketball fan, he really loves basketball

enamoramiento SM falling in love

enamorar /1a/ Ⓐ VT to win the love of Ⓑ **enamorarse** VPR to fall in love (**de** with)

enano/a Ⓐ ADJ dwarf *antes de s* Ⓑ SM/F **1** (*en cuento*) dwarf; (= *persona*) dwarf, midget; (*pey*) runt; ✦ MODISMO **disfrutar** *o* **pasárselo como un ~** to have a brilliant time **2** (***) (= *niño*) kid*

enarbolar /1a/ VT [+ *bandera*] to hoist; [+ *espada*] to flourish

enardecer /2d/ Ⓐ VT **1** [+ *pasión*] to inflame **2** [+ *público*] (= *entusiasmar*) to fill with enthusiasm; (= *provocar*) to incite, inflame Ⓑ **enardecerse** VPR to become inflamed

encabalgamiento SM (*Literat*) enjambement

encabestrar /1a/ VT to put a halter on

encabezado Ⓐ ADJ [*vino*] fortified Ⓑ SM (*Chi, Méx*) headline

encabezamiento SM **1** (*en carta*) (= *fórmula*) opening formula; (= *dirección*) heading **2** (*en periódico*) headline

encabezar /1f/ VT **1** [+ *manifestación, delegación*] to lead **2** [+ *lista, liga*] to head, be at the top of **3** [+ *carta, artículo*] to head **4** [+ *vino*] to fortify

encabritarse /1a/ VPR **1** [*caballo*] to rear up **2** (***) (= *enfadarse*) to get riled*, get cross

encabronar** /1a/ Ⓐ VT to make angry Ⓑ **encabronarse** VPR to get riled*, get cross

encachado* ADJ (*Chi*) **1** (= *hermoso*) [*lugar, casa*] beautiful; [*persona*] attractive **2** (= *digno de admiración*) great* **3** (= *entretenido*) amusing

encachar* /1a/ (*Chi*) Ⓐ VT to make nice Ⓑ **encacharse** VPR to spruce o.s. up

encachimbado* ADJ **está ~** (*CAm*) he's livid, he's hopping mad*

encachorrarse /1a/ VPR (*Col*) to get angry

encadenar /1a/ Ⓐ VT **1** (= *atar*) (*lit*) to chain; (*fig*) to tie down **2** [+ *hechos, ideas*] to connect, link Ⓑ VI (*Cine*) to fade in

encajar /1a/ **Ⓐ** VT **1** (= *acoplar*) [+ *pieza, tapón*] to fit; [+ *partes*] to fit together; ~ **algo en algo** to fit sth into sth **2** (= *aceptar*) [+ *broma, crítica*] to take; [+ *desgracia, derrota*] to handle, cope with; **no supo ~ el golpe** he couldn't handle it **3** (*) ~ **algo a algn** (= *endilgar*) to lumber sb with sth*, dump sth on sb*; (= *timar*) to palm sth off on *o* onto sb*; **a mí no me encajas tú esa historia** I won't be taken in by a story like that **4** (= *dar, meter*) [+ *golpe, patada*] to give **Ⓑ** VI **1** (= *ajustar*) [*puerta*] to fit; [*piezas*] to fit (together); ~ **en algo** to fit into sth **2** (= *coincidir*) [*teoría, coartada*] to fit; **aquí hay algo que no encaja** something here doesn't tally *o* fit; ~ **con algo** to tie in with sth, tally with sth **3** (= *integrarse*) ~ **con algn** to fit in with sb; ~ **en** [+ *serie, papel*] to be right for; [+ *ambiente*] to fit in; **no le costó ~ en la oficina** he had no trouble fitting in in the office; **sus ideas encajan dentro de una mentalidad conservadora** her ideas are in keeping with a conservative mentality **Ⓒ** **encajarse** VPR **1** (= *atrancarse*) to get stuck; **el coche se encajó dentro del muro** the car jammed into the wall **2** (= *ponerse*) [+ *abrigo, sombrero*] to put on **3** (*Méx*) (= *aprovecharse*) to take advantage (**con** of)

encaje SM **1** (*Cos*) lace; **una blusa de ~** a lace blouse ➤ **encaje de bolillos** bobbin lace **2** (*Téc*) socket **3** (*Fin*) reserve, stock

encajonar /1a/ **Ⓐ** VT **1** (= *guardar*) to box, box up, put in a box **2** (= *meter en un sitio estrecho*) to squeeze in, squeeze through **Ⓑ** **encajonarse** VPR [*río*] to run between steep banks

encalar /1a/ VT to whitewash

encallar /1a/ VI to run aground, get stranded (**en** on)

encallecerse /2d/ VPR to harden, form corns

encallecido ADJ hardened

encalmarse /1a/ VPR to calm down

encamarse /1a/ VPR to take to one's bed; **estar encamado** to be confined to bed; ~ **con algn** (*And, CS*) to go to bed with sb, sleep with sb

encaminar /1a/ **Ⓐ** VT [+ *plan, esfuerzo*] to direct; [+ *alumno, hijo*] to guide, direct; **el proyecto está encaminado a ayudarles** the plan is designed to help them, the plan is aimed at helping them; **encaminó sus pasos hacia el monasterio** (*liter*) he turned his steps towards the monastery (*liter*) **Ⓑ** **encaminarse** VPR **1** ~**se** *o* **hacia** (= *dirigirse a*) to head for, set out for **2** ~**se a** (= *tener como objetivo*) to be designed to, be aimed at

encamotarse* /1a/ VPR (*LAm*) to fall in love (**de** with)

encanar /1a/ VT (*And, CS*) to throw into jail

encandilado* ADJ **estar ~ con algn** to be all taken with sb

encandilar /1a/ VT (= *fascinar*) to daze, bewilder

encanecer /2d/ VI to go grey, go gray (*EEUU*)

encantado ADJ **1** (= *muy contento*) delighted; **estar ~ con algo/algn** to be delighted with sth/sb; **estar ~ de algo: estoy ~ de tu éxito** I'm delighted at your success; **estoy encantada de poder ayudarte** I'm delighted to be able to help you **2** (*en fórmulas de presentación*) **¡encantado!** "how do you do!", "pleased to meet you!" **3** (= *embrujado*) enchanted

encantador(a) **Ⓐ** ADJ [*persona*] charming, delightful; [*lugar*] lovely **Ⓑ** SM/F magician, enchanter/enchantress ➤ **encantador(a) de serpientes** snake charmer

encantamiento SM enchantment

encantar /1a/ **Ⓐ** VI **me encanta tu casa** I love your house; **me ~ía que vinieras** I'd be delighted if you came, I'd love you to come **Ⓑ** VT to cast a spell *o* over, bewitch

encanto SM **1** (= *atractivo*) charm; **el pueblecito tiene mucho ~** the village has a lot of charm *o* is very charming **2** (= *maravilla*) **el niño es un ~** he's a charming *o* lovely *o* delightful little boy **3** (*uso apelativo*) darling; **¡oye, ~!** hello, gorgeous!* **4** (= *encantamiento*) spell; **desapareció como por ~** it disappeared as if by magic

encañonar /1a/ VT **1** ~ **a algn con un arma** to point a gun at sb; **tener encañonado a algn** to hold sb at gunpoint **2** [+ *agua*] to pipe

encapotado ADJ [*cielo*] cloudy, overcast

encapotarse /1a/ VPR [*cielo*] to cloud over, become overcast

encapricharse /1a/ VPR to take a fancy (**con, por** to)

encapuchado/a **Ⓐ** ADJ hooded **Ⓑ** SM/F hooded man/woman

encarado ADJ **mal ~** evil-looking

encaramarse /1a/ VPR ~ **a algo** to climb on to sth

encarar /1a/ **Ⓐ** VT to face, face up to, confront **Ⓑ** **encararse** VPR ~**se a** *o* **con algn** to confront sb

encarcelamiento SM imprisonment

encarcelar /1a/ VT to imprison, jail

encarecer /2d/ **Ⓐ** VT **1** (*Com*) to put up the price of **2** (= *rogar*) **le encarezco que lo haga** I urge you to do it **Ⓑ** **encarecerse** VPR to get dearer

encarecidamente ADV insistently

encarecimiento SM **1** [*de precio*] increase, rise **2** (= *insistencia*) stressing, emphasizing; **con ~** insistently, strongly

encargado/a **Ⓐ** ADJ **estar ~ de algo** to be in charge of sth, be responsible for sth; **la persona encargada de los impuestos** the person in charge of *o* responsible for taxes **Ⓑ** SM/F [*de tarea, expedición*] person in charge; [*de tienda, restaurante*] manager; [*de parque, cementerio*] groundkeeper, groundskeeper (*EEUU*)

encargar /1h/ **Ⓐ** VT **1** [+ *tarea, misión*] to give; **encargó el cuidado de sus hijos a un familiar** he left his children in the care of a relative; ~ **a algn de algo** to give sb the job of doing sth **2** [+ *obra de arte, informe*] to commission **3** (= *hacer un pedido de*) to order; **encargué los libros por correo** I ordered the books by post; **✦** MODISMOS ~ **familia** to start a family; ~ **un niño: ¿habéis encargado un niño?** do you have a baby on the way?* **4** (= *pedir como favor*) **le encargué dos latas de caviar ruso** I asked him to bring *o* buy me two tins of Russian caviar; **me ha encargado varias cosas del supermercado** she's asked me to get her some things from the supermarket; ~ **a algn que haga algo** to ask sb to do sth **5** (= *aconsejar*) to advise **6** (*Chi Jur*) ~ **reo a algn** to submit sb to trial **Ⓑ** **encargarse** VPR ~**se de** (= *ocuparse de*) to take care of; (= *ser responsable de*) to be in charge of; (= *tomar la responsabilidad de*) to take charge of; **ya me encargo yo de decírselo a todo el mundo** I'll make sure everyone knows, I'll take care of telling everyone; **yo me encargo de los asuntos culturales** I'm in charge of cultural affairs; **cuando ella murió, él se encargó del negocio** when she died, he took over the business *o* he took charge of the business

encargatoria SF (*Chi Jur*) (*tb* **~ de reo**) committal for trial

encargo SM **1** (= *pedido*) order; **o por ~** [*traje, vestido*] tailor made, made to order; [*muebles*] made to order **2** (*profesional*) job, commission; **una exposición realizada por ~ del Ayuntamiento** an exhibition commissioned by the Council **3** (*para comprar algo*) **le hice varios ~s de Nueva York** I asked him to buy a few things in New York, I asked him to bring back a few things from New York **4** **✦** MODISMO **dejar a algn con ~** (*LAm**) to leave sb in the family way*

encariñado ADJ **estar ~ con** to be fond of

encariñarse /1a/ VPR ~ **con** to grow fond of, get attached to

encarnación SF (*Rel*) incarnation; (= *personificación*) embodiment, personification

encarnado ADJ red

encarnar /1a/ **Ⓐ** VT (= *personificar*) to personify; (*Teat*) [+ *papel*] to play, bring to life **Ⓑ** **encarnarse** VPR (*Rel*) to become incarnate, be made flesh

encarnizadamente ADV bloodily, fiercely

encarnizado ADJ bloody, fierce

encarpetar /1a/ VT [+ *papeles*] to file away; [+ *proyecto*] to shelve, bury

encarrilar /1a/ VT **1** [+ *tren*] to put back on the rails **2** (= *dirigir*) to direct, guide; **ir encarrilado** to be on the right lines

encasillado ADJ [*actor*] typecast

encasillar /1a/ VT to pigeonhole, categorize

encasquetar /1a/ VT **1** [+ *sombrero*] to pull down tight **2** (*) ~ **algo a algn** to foist sth on sb

encasquillarse /1a/ VPR [*bala, revólver*] to jam

encatrado SM (*Chi*) frame

encatrinarse* /1a/ VPR (*Méx*) to dress up

encausado/a SM/F accused, defendant

encausar /1a/ VT to prosecute, sue

encauzar /1f/ VT **1** [+ *agua, río*] to channel **2** (= *dirigir*) to channel, direct

encefalitis SF INV encephalitis

encefalograma SM encephalogram

enceguecedor ADJ (*LAm*) blinding, dazzling

enceguecer /2d/ (*LAm*) ⒶVT to blind Ⓑ **enceguecerse** VPR to go blind

encendedor SM lighter

encender /2g/ ⒶVT **1** (= *prender*) [+ *fuego, cigarrillo*] to light; [+ *cerilla*] to strike; [+ *luz, radio*] to turn on, switch on, put on; [+ *gas*] to light, turn on **2** (= *avivar*) [+ *pasiones*] to inflame; [+ *celos, odio*] to awake Ⓑ **encenderse** VPR **1** (= *prenderse*) to light **2** [*cara, ojos*] to light up **3** [*persona*] (= *exaltarse*) to get excited; (= *ruborizarse*) to blush; **~se de ira** to flare up with rage, fly into a temper

encendido Ⓐ ADJ **1** [*colilla, fuego*] lighted, lit; [*luz, radio*] on, switched on **2** (= *rojo vivo*) bright red; [*mejillas*] glowing; [*cara*] (*por el vino*) flushed; (*por la ira*) purple; [*mirada*] fiery, passionate Ⓑ SM (*Aut*) ignition ➤ **encendido eléctrico** electric lighting

encerado Ⓐ ADJ [*suelo*] waxed, polished Ⓑ SM blackboard (*Brit*), chalkboard (*EEUU*)

encerar /1a/ VT [+ *suelo*] to wax, polish

encerrado ADJ **no soporto pasar todo el día encerrada** I can't stand being shut in all day; **el prisionero llevaba siete años ~** the prisoner had been locked up for seven years; **la puerta dio un portazo y me quedé ~** the door slammed shut and I was locked in

encerrar /1j/ ⒶVT **1** (= *meter*) to shut (up); (*con llave*) to lock (up); **encerré el gato en la cocina** I shut the cat (up) in the kitchen; **lo ~on en su celda** they locked him in his cell; **la ~on en un psiquiátrico** they locked her up in a mental hospital **2** (= *contener*) to contain; **el libro encierra profundas verdades** the book contains profound truths **3** (*en ajedrez, damas*) to block Ⓑ **encerrarse** VPR **1** (= *meterse*) to shut o.s. (up); (*con llave*) to lock o.s. (up); **se encerró en su cuarto** she shut herself (up) in her room; **~se en sí mismo** to withdraw into o.s. **2** (*como protesta*) to hold a sit-in, stage a sit-in

encerrona SF trap

encestar /1a/ VI to score (a basket)

encharcado ADJ [*terreno*] swamped

encharcar /1g/ ⒶVT to swamp, flood Ⓑ **encharcarse** VPR **1** [*tierra*] to swamp, get flooded **2** [*agua*] (= *estancarse*) to become stagnant **3** [*pulmones*] to get clogged up

enchastrar /1a/ VT (*RPl*) to dirty, make dirty

enchicharse* /1a/ VPR (*LAm*) to get drunk on chicha

enchilada SF (*CAm, Méx*) filled tortilla

enchilado (*Méx*) Ⓐ ADJ **1** (*Culin*) seasoned with chili **2** (= *rojo*) bright red **3** [*persona*] **estoy ~** my mouth is burning Ⓑ SM stew with chili sauce

enchilar /1a/ (*Méx*) ⒶVT **1** (*Culin*) to season with chili **2** (*) (= *molestar*) to annoy Ⓑ **enchilarse*** VPR **1** (= *enojarse*) to get angry, get mad* **2** (*con algo picante*) **me enchilé con estos jalapeños** those jalapeños were burning my mouth

enchiloso ADJ (*Méx*) [*sabor*] hot

enchinar /1a/ (*Méx*) ⒶVT [+ *pelo*] to curl, perm Ⓑ **enchinarse** VPR **se le enchinó el cuerpo** he got goose bumps *o* goose pimples *o* gooseflesh

enchinchar* /1a/ ⒶVT (*Méx*) to bother Ⓑ **enchincharse** VPR (*RPl*) to get bad-tempered

enchufado/a* Ⓐ SM/F (*en escuela*) teacher's pet; (*en trabajo*) well-connected person, person with pull Ⓑ ADJ **estar ~** to have connections

enchufar /1a/ VT **1** (*Elec*) to plug in **2** (*) (*en un trabajo*) **la han enchufado para el puesto de secretaria** they have set *o* lined her up for the secretary's job (*using contacts*)

enchufe SM **1** (*Elec*) (= *macho*) plug; (= *hembra*) socket ➤ **enchufe múltiple** adaptor **2** (*) (= *influencia*) useful contact; **lo consiguió por ~s** he pulled strings to do it

encía SF gum

encíclica SF encyclical

enciclopedia SF encyclopaedia, encyclopedia

enciclopédico ADJ encyclopaedic, encyclopedic

encierra *etc ver* **encerrar**

encierro SM **1** (*de manifestantes*) sit-in; (*en fábrica*) sit-in, work-in **2** (= *reclusión*) **no hay quien la saque de su ~** no one can persuade her to come out **3** (*Taur*) (= *fiesta*) *running of the bulls*; (= *toril*) bull pen; ⟡ *SANFERMINES*

encima ADV **1** (*en el espacio*) **allí está el cerro y ~ el castillo** you can see the hill there and the castle on top; **déjelo ahí ~** leave it up there; **el gato se me sentó ~** the cat sat on me; **~ de** (*con contacto*) on top of; (*sin contacto*) above; **déjalo ~ de la mesa** leave it on top of the table; **colgó el cuadro ~ del sofá** he hung the painting above the sofa; **llevar** *o* **tener algo ~: no llevaba ~ la documentación** I didn't have the papers on me; **creo que ya tienes bastante ~** I think you've got enough on your plate; **venirse ~ de algn** [*animal, vehículo*] to come (straight) at sb, bear down on sb; [*peso, mueble*] to fall on (top of) sb; **no sabía lo que se le venía ~ cuando llegara a casa** he didn't know what was going to hit him when he got home; ✦ MODISMOS **echarse a algn ~** (*LAm*) to get on the wrong side of sb; **echársele ~ a algn** (= *atrapar*) to catch up with sb; (= *criticar*) to come down (hard) on sb; **estar ~ de algn** (= *estar pendiente*) to stand over sb; (*pey*) to be on someone's back*; **hacerse ~** (*LAm euf*) ⟡ **hacérselo ~** (*Esp euf*) (= *orinarse*) to wet o.s.; (= *defecar*) to mess o.s.; **poner a algn el dedo** *o* **la mano ~** to lay a finger on sb; **quitarse algo/a algn de ~** to get rid of sth/sb

2 (*en el tiempo*) upon; **ya tenemos el invierno ~ otra vez** winter is upon us again; **se nos echó la noche ~** it grew dark, night fell; **se nos viene ~ la fecha de la boda** the wedding is nearly upon us, the wedding is just around the corner

3 por ~ 3.1 (= *por lo alto*) **le eché una manta por ~** I put a blanket over her; **el avión les pasó por ~** the plane passed overhead; **por ~ tiene a su jefe y al director** there's his boss and the director above him; **por ~ de** over; **el avión pasó rozando por ~ de la catedral** the plane skimmed over the top of the cathedral; **por ~ de los 2.500m** above *o* over 2,500m; **estar por ~ de algo** (*en cantidad, nivel*) to be above sth; (*en preferencia*) to come before sth; **por ~ de todo** above all; **la seguridad por ~ de todo** safety first **3.2** (= *superficialmente*) **hemos limpiado muy por ~** we've just done a quick clean; **hicimos una revisión por ~** we had a quick check; **hojear algo por ~** to leaf through sth **4** (= *además*) on top of that; **y ~ no me dio ni las gracias** and on top of that he didn't even thank me; **te lo envían a casa y ~ te regalan un libro** they send it to your house and you get a free book too *o* as well; **le toca la lotería y ~ se queja** she wins the lottery and even then she complains; **~ de** besides, as well as **5** (*esp CS*) **~ mío/tuyo/***etc* above me/you/*etc*; **está siempre ~ mío vigilando lo que hago** he's always on top of me watching everything I do

encimar* /1a/ VT (*Col*) to add as a bonus

encimera SF worktop (*Brit*), countertop (*EEUU*)

encimero ADJ top, upper

encina SF ilex, holm oak

encinar SM holm-oak wood

encinta ADJ pregnant

enclaustrarse /1a/ VPR to shut o.s. away

enclavar /1a/ VT 1 (= *situar*) to place 2 (= *clavar*) to nail; (= *traspasar*) to pierce, transfix 3 (= *empotrar*) to embed, set 4 (*) (= *engañar*) to swindle, con*

enclave SM enclave

enclenque ADJ weak, sickly

encofrado SM form, plank mould

encofrar /1a/ VT to plank, timber

encoger /2c/ Ⓐ VI [*tela*] to shrink Ⓑ **encogerse** VPR 1 [*tela*] to shrink 2 **~se de hombros** to shrug one's shoulders 3 (= *acobardarse*) to cringe

encolar /1a/ VT (= *engomar*) to glue, paste; (= *aprestar*) to size

encolerizar /1f/ Ⓐ VT to anger, provoke Ⓑ **encolerizarse** VPR to get angry

encomendar /1j/ Ⓐ VT to entrust, commend (**a** to, to the charge of) Ⓑ **encomendarse** VPR **~se a** to entrust o.s. to

encomendería SF (*Perú*) grocery store, grocer's

encomendero SM (*Perú*) grocer

encomiable ADJ laudable, praiseworthy

encomiar /1b/ VT to praise, pay tribute to

encomienda SF (*LAm*) package, parcel (*esp Brit*)

encomio SM praise, eulogy

encomioso ADJ (*LAm*) laudatory, eulogistic

enconadamente ADV angrily, bitterly

enconado ADJ [*discusión*] bitter

enconar /1a/ Ⓐ VT [+ *disputa*] to inflame, embitter; [+ *odio, rencor*] to inflame Ⓑ **enconarse** VPR [*agravio*] to fester, rankle; [*disputa*] to become inflamed, become bitter; [*odio, rencor*] to become inflamed

enconcharse* /1a/ VPR 1 (*Col, Méx*) (*psicológicamente*) to go into one's shell 2 (*Ven*) (= *esconderse*) to go into hiding

encono SM 1 (= *rencor*) rancour, rancor (*EEUU*), spite 2 (= *mala voluntad*) bad blood

encontradizo ADJ **hacerse el ~** to contrive an apparently chance meeting, manage to bump into sb

encontrado ADJ [*situación*] conflicting; [*posiciones*] opposing, opposite; **tienen opiniones encontradas sobre el aborto** they have opposing views on abortion

encontrar /1l/ Ⓐ VT 1 (= *hallar buscando*) to find; **no encuentro las llaves** I can't find the keys; **ya no vas a ~ entradas** you won't get any tickets now 2 (*por casualidad*) [+ *objeto, dinero*] to find, come across; [+ *persona*] to meet, run into; [+ *muerte*] to meet; **han encontrado unos restos romanos** they have found some Roman remains; **le ~on un tumor** they found him to have a tumour, he was found to have a tumour; **~ a algn haciendo algo** to find sb doing sth 3 (= *oposición*) to meet with, encounter; [+ *problema*] to find, encounter, come across; **~ dificultades** to encounter difficulties, run into trouble 4 (= *percibir*) to see; **no le encuentro sentido a lo que dices** I can't see the sense in what you're saying; **no sé lo que le encuentran** I don't know what they see in her 5 (= *considerar*) to find; **yo la encuentro bastante atractiva** I find her quite attractive; **te encuentro estupendamente** you look fantastic Ⓑ **encontrarse** VPR 1 (= *descubrir*) to find; **¿qué te has encontrado?** what have you found?; **se ~on la casa llena de gente** they found the house full of people; **me los encontré llorando** I found them crying; **~se con: al llegar nos encontramos con la puerta cerrada** when we arrived we found the door locked; **~se con algo de pura casualidad** to come across sth by pure *o* sheer chance; **~se a sí mismo** to find oneself 2 (= *coincidir*) to meet; **se ~on en Lisboa** they met in Lisbon; **el punto en el que se encuentran las dos calles** the point where the two streets meet; **~se a algn** to bump into sb, meet sb; **~se con** [+ *persona*] to bump into, meet; [+ *obstáculo, dificultad*] to run into

3 (= *chocar*) [*vehículos*] to crash, collide; [*opiniones*] to clash 4 (= *estar*) to be; **no se encontraba en casa** she wasn't at home; **este cuadro se encuentra entre los más famosos de Goya** this is among Goya's most famous paintings 5 (*de salud*) (= *estar*) to be; (= *sentirse*) to feel; **su familia se encuentra perfectamente** his family are all very well; **¿te encuentras mejor?** are you feeling better?; **hoy no me encuentro bien** I don't feel well today

encontronazo SM collision, crash

encoñado** ADJ **estar ~ con algn** to have the hots for sb*; **estar ~ con algo** to be mad keen on sth

encopetado ADJ 1 (= *emperifollado*) dressed to the nines* 2 (= *señorial*) posh*, grand

encorajinar /1a/ VT (*Méx*) to anger, irritate

encorbatado ADJ wearing a tie

encordado SM (*CS*) strings *pl*

encordar /1l/ Ⓐ VT (*Mús*) to fit strings to Ⓑ **encordarse** VPR [*alpinistas*] to rope themselves together

encorsetar /1a/ VT to confine, put into a straitjacket

encorvado ADJ **andar ~** to walk with a stoop

encorvarse /1a/ VPR to stoop

encrespado ADJ [*pelo*] curly; [*mar*] choppy

encrespar /1a/ Ⓐ VT 1 (= *rizar*) [+ *pelo*] to curl; [+ *plumas*] to ruffle; [+ *agua*] to ripple; [+ *mar*] to make rough 2 (= *irritar*) to anger, irritate Ⓑ **encresparse** VPR 1 (= *rizarse*) [*pelo*] to curl; [*agua*] to ripple; [*mar*] to get rough 2 (= *irritarse*) to get cross, get irritated

encrucijada SF crossroads; **poner a algn en una ~** to put sb on the spot

encuadernación SF binding

encuadernar /1a/ VT to bind

encuadrar /1a/ VT 1 (+ *pintura*) to frame 2 (= *clasificar*) to place, classify 3 (= *abarcar*) to contain 4 (*Fot*) to frame

encuadre SM (*Fot*) framing

encubierto Ⓐ PP *de* **encubrir** Ⓑ ADJ (= *oculto*) hidden; (= *secreto*) undercover; [*crítica*] veiled

encubridor(a) SM/F [*de delito*] accessory (after the fact); [*de objeto robado*] receiver, fence*; **lo acusaron de ~ del homicidio** he was accused of helping to cover up the murder

encubrir /3a/ (*pp* **encubierto**) VT 1 (*gen*) (= *ocultar*) to hide 2 [+ *delincuente*] to harbour, harbor (*EEUU*); [+ *delito*] to cover up

encuentro SM 1 (= *reunión*) meeting; **un ~ fortuito** a chance meeting ➤ **encuentro cumbre** summit meeting 2 **ir** *o* **salir al ~ de algn** to go to meet sb 3 (= *partido*) match ➤ **encuentro de ida** first leg ➤ **encuentro de vuelta** return leg 4 (*Aut*) collision, crash 5 [*de opiniones*] clash

encuerado* ADJ (*LAm*) nude, naked, starkers*

encuerar* /1a/ (*LAm*) Ⓐ VT to strip, strip naked Ⓑ **encuerarse** VPR to strip off, get undressed

encuesta SF 1 (= *sondeo*) opinion poll, survey ➤ **encuesta de opinión** opinion poll 2 (= *pesquisa*) inquiry, investigation (**de** into); ➤ **encuesta judicial** post mortem

encuestador(a) SM/F pollster

encuestar /1a/ VT to poll, take a poll of; **el 69% de los encuestados** 69% of those polled

encumbrar /1a/ Ⓐ VT 1 (= *alzar*) to raise, elevate 2 (= *ensalzar*) to extol, exalt Ⓑ **encumbrarse** VPR 1 [*edificio*] to rise, tower 2 (= *engreírse*) to be proud, be haughty

encurtidos SMPL pickles

encurtir /3a/ VT to pickle

ende ADV **por ~** (*frm*) hence (*frm*), therefore

endeble ADJ [*persona*] feeble, weak; [*argumento, excusa*] feeble, flimsy

endecasílabo ADJ, SM hendecasyllabic

endémico ADJ [*enfermedad*] endemic; [*mal*] rife, chronic

endemoniado ADJ 1 (= *poseído*) possessed (of the devil) 2 (= *travieso*) devilish, fiendish

endenantes* ADV (*LAm*) (= *hace algún tiempo*) a short time back; (= *antes*) earlier, before

enderezar /1f/ **Ⓐ** VT **1** [+ *cable, alambre*] to straighten out, straighten up **2** (= *poner vertical*) (*gen*) to set upright, stand vertically; (*Náut*) to right **3** (= *arreglar*) to put in order **4** (*en conducta*) ~ **a algn** to correct sb's faults **Ⓑ enderezarse** VPR (= *ponerse recto*) to straighten up, draw o.s. up; (*Náut*) to right itself

endeudamiento SM indebtedness, (extent of) debt

endeudarse /1a/ VPR to get into debt (**con** with)

endiablado ADJ **1** (= *diabólico*) devilish, diabolical **2** (= *travieso*) impish, mischievous **3** (= *difícil*) [*problema*] tricky; [*carretera*] difficult, dangerous

endibia SF chicory, endive (*EEUU*)

endilgar* /1h/ VT **papá nos endilgó una insoportable disertación política** Dad gave us an unbearable lecture on politics; **siempre me endilgan los peores trabajos** I always get landed *o* saddled with the worst jobs*

endiñar* /1a/ VT (*Esp*) **1** [+ *golpe*] **le endiñó un puñetazo** he thumped him one*; **le endiñó una patada en el culo** she booted him up the backside* **2** = **endilgar**

endiosado ADJ stuck-up*, conceited

endiosamiento SM (= *engreimiento*) vanity, conceit; (= *altanería*) haughtiness

endocrino ADJ endocrine

endogamia SF inbreeding

endomingarse /1h/ VPR to put on one's Sunday best

endorfina SF endorphin

endosar /1a/ VT **1** [+ *cheque*] to endorse **2** (*) ~ **algo a algn** to lumber sb with sth*

endrina SF endorphin

endrino SM blackthorn, sloe

endrogarse /1h/ VPR (*Méx*) to get into debt

endulzante SM sweetener

endulzar /1f/ VT to sweeten

endurecer /2d/ **Ⓐ** VT **1** [+ *material, sustancia*] (= *poner duro*) to harden; (= *hacer más resistente*) to toughen **2** [+ *persona*] (= *curtir*) to toughen up; (= *volver insensible*) to harden **3** [+ *ley, control*] to tighten, tighten up; [+ *pena, castigo*] to make more severe; **han endurecido la política antiterrorista** they're taking a tougher line on terrorism **Ⓑ endurecerse** VPR **1** [*material, sustancia*] (= *ponerse duro*) to harden, get hard; (= *hacerse más resistente*) to toughen **2** [*persona*] (= *curtirse*) to toughen up; (= *volverse insensible*) to harden, become hardened

endurecimiento SM **1** (= *acto*) hardening **2** [*de persona*] (*por curtirse*) toughening up; (*por insensibilidad*) hardening

enebro SM juniper

eneldo SM dill

enema SF enema

enemigo/a **Ⓐ** ADJ enemy, hostile; **ser** ~ **de algo** to be opposed to sth **Ⓑ** SM/F enemy; **pasarse al** ~ to go over to the enemy

enemistad SF enmity

enemistar /1a/ **Ⓐ** VT to make enemies of, cause a rift between **Ⓑ enemistarse** VPR to become enemies; ~**se con algn** to fall out with sb, have a falling out with sb (*EEUU*)

energético ADJ **1** [*política, crisis*] energy *antes de s* **2** [*bebida, comida*] energy *antes de s*; [*componente*] energy-giving

energía SF **1** (= *fuerza*) energy, drive; **obrar con** ~ to act energetically; **reaccionar con** ~ to react vigorously **2** (*Téc*) power, energy ➤ **energía(s) alternativa(s)** alternative energy *sing* ➤ **energía atómica** atomic power ➤ **energía eléctrica** electric power, electricity ➤ **energía eólica** wind power ➤ **energía solar** solar power

enérgico ADJ [*persona*] energetic, vigorous; [*gesto, habla, tono*] emphatic; [*esfuerzo*] determined; [*ejercicio*] strenuous; [*campaña*] vigorous, high-pressure; [*medida, golpe*] bold, drastic; [*ataque*] vigorous, strong; [*protesta*] forceful

energúmeno/a SM/F madman/madwoman; **ponerse**

como un ~* to get mad

enero SM January; *ver tb* **septiembre**

En inglés los meses se escriben con mayúscula.

enervar /1a/ VT **1** (= *poner nervioso a*) to get on sb's nerves **2** (= *debilitar*) to enervate, weaken

enésimo ADJ n^{th}; **elevado a la enésima potencia** (*lit*) raised to the nth power; (*fig*) to the nth degree; **por enésima vez** for the umpteenth time, for the nth time

enfadado ADJ annoyed, angry

enfadar /1a/ **Ⓐ** VT (= *irritar*) to anger, irritate; (= *ofender*) to offend **Ⓑ enfadarse** VPR to get annoyed, get angry (**con** with; **por, de** about, at); **no te enfades con él, lo ha hecho sin intención** don't be angry with him, he didn't mean to do it; **no te enfades, pero creo que lo has hecho mal** don't be offended, but I think you've done it wrong; **se enfadó con su novio** she fell out with her boyfriend

enfado SM annoyance, anger

enfangar /1h/ **Ⓐ** VT to cover with mud **Ⓑ enfangarse** VPR **1** (= *enlodarse*) to get muddy, get covered in mud **2** (= *implicarse*) to dirty one's hands

enfardar /1a/ VT to bale

énfasis SM **1** (*en la entonación*) emphasis; **hablar con** ~ to speak emphatically; **poner el** ~ **en** to stress **2** (= *insistencia*) stress

enfático ADJ emphatic

enfatizar /1f/ VT to emphasize, stress

enfebrecido ADJ feverish

enfermante ADJ (*CS*) irritating, annoying

enfermar /1a/ **Ⓐ** VT **su actitud me enferma** her attitude makes me sick **Ⓑ** VI to fall ill, be taken ill (**de** with); ~ **del corazón** to develop heart trouble **Ⓒ enfermarse** VPR (*esp LAm*) to fall ill, be taken ill (**de** with)

enfermedad SF **1** (= *estado*) illness; **durante su** ~ during his illness **2** (= *agente concreto*) disease

Enfermedad se traduce por **illness** cuando no se especifica la enfermedad de que se trata, o cuando se refiere al tiempo que una persona está enferma: "Adelgazó mucho durante su enfermedad", *He lost a lot of weight during his illness*. Se traduce por **disease** cuando se especifica el tipo de enfermedad: "enfermedades de pulmón", *lung disease*; "enfermedad de Alzheimer", *Alzheimer's disease*.

➤ **enfermedad de la piel** skin disease ➤ **enfermedad del sueño** sleeping sickness ➤ **enfermedad de transmisión sexual** sexually transmitted disease ➤ **enfermedad terminal** terminal illness ➤ **enfermedad venérea** venereal disease

enfermería SF **1** (= *estudios*) nursing **2** (*en centro escolar*) sick bay **3** (*en cárcel, cuartel*) infirmary

enfermero/a SM/F (*male*) nurse/nurse ➤ **enfermero/a jefe/a** head nurse

enfermizo ADJ [*persona*] sickly; [*mente*] morbid; [*pasión*] morbid, unhealthy

enfermo/a **Ⓐ** ADJ ill, sick, unwell; **caer** *o* **ponerse** ~ to fall ill (**de** with) **Ⓑ** SM/F (*gen*) sick person; (*en hospital*) patient ➤ **enfermo/a terminal** terminal patient, terminally ill person

enfervorizar /1f/ VT to arouse (fervour *o* (*EEUU*) fervor in)

enfiestado ADJ (*LAm*) **estar** ~ to be partying*

enfiestarse /1a/ VPR (*LAm*) to party

enfilar /1a/ VT **1** (= *ensartar*) to thread **2** [+ *calle*] to go straight along, go straight down **3** (= *apuntar*) [+ *pistola, cañón*] to aim **4 tener enfilado a algn*** to have it in for sb*

enfisema SM emphysema

enfocar /1g/ **Ⓐ** VT **1** (*Fot*) to focus **2** [+ *cuestión, problema*] to consider, look at; **su modo de** ~ **la cuestión** his approach to the question **B** VI to focus

enfoque SM **1** (*Fot*) (= *acción*) focusing; (= *resultado*) focus **2** [*de tema*] approach

enfrascarse /1g/ VPR ~ **en un libro** to bury o.s. in a book; ~ **en un problema** to get deeply involved in a problem

enfrentamiento SM (= *conflicto*) confrontation; (= *encuentro*) (face-to-face) encounter

enfrentar /1a/ **A** VT **1** (= *enemistar*) to set against; **la herencia enfrentó a los dos hermanos** the inheritance set the two brothers against each other *o* at loggerheads **2** (= *afrontar*) [+ *dificultad*] to face (up to), confront; [+ *realidad*] to face (up to) **3** (= *encarar*) **este partido ~á a los dos mejores tenistas** this match will bring together the two best tennis players **B enfrentarse** VPR [*personas*] to have a confrontation; [*equipos*] to face each other; **~se a** *o* **con** [+ *persona*] to confront; [+ *problema, dificultad*] to face (up to), confront; **la selección de España se enfrentó a la de Italia** the Spanish team came up against *o* faced the Italian team

enfrente ADV **1** (= *en el lado opuesto*) opposite; **Luisa estaba sentada** ~ Luisa was sitting opposite; **la casa de** ~ the house opposite, the house across the road; ~ **de** opposite (to); **mi casa está** ~ **del colegio** my house is opposite the school, my house is across the road from the school; **se sentó** ~ **mío/tuyo** (*esp LAm**) he sat down opposite *o* facing me/you **2** (= *delante*) in front

enfriamiento SM **1** (= *acción*) cooling **2** (= *catarro*) cold, chill

enfriar /1c/ **A** VT **1** [+ *vino, refresco*] to cool, chill; [+ *sopa, motor*] to cool down **2** [+ *economía*] to cool down; [+ *entusiasmo*] to dampen, cool; [+ *pasión, relaciones*] to cool **3** (*Perú**) (= *matar*) to kill, bump off* **B enfriarse** VPR **1** [*alimentos, material*] (*lo suficiente*) to cool down; (*demasiado*) to get cold; **déjalo que se enfríe** leave it to cool (down); **se te va a** ~ **el café** your coffee's going to get cold **2** [*economía*] to cool down; [*pasión, entusiasmo, relaciones*] to cool **3** (= *acatarrarse*) to catch a cold

enfundar /1a/ **A** VT [+ *espada*] to sheathe; [+ *gafas, violín*] to put in its case; [+ *diente*] to cap **B enfundarse** VPR **se enfundó la capa** he wrapped himself (up) in his cape; **una señora enfundada en un visón** a lady wrapped in a mink coat

enfurecer /2d/ **A** VT to enrage, madden **B enfurecerse** VPR to get furious, fly into a rage

enfurruñarse /1a/ VPR to sulk

engalanar /1a/ **A** VT to adorn, deck (**de** with) **B engalanarse** VPR to adorn o.s., dress up

enganchado ADJ hooked* (**a** on)

enganchar /1a/ **A** VT **1** (= *conectar*) (*gen*) to hook; [+ *caballo*] to harness; [+ *carro, remolque*] to hitch up; (*Mec*) to couple, connect; [+ *dos vagones*] to couple up **2** (*) (= *atrapar*) to nab*; **lo enganchó la policía robando en la joyería** the police nabbed him as he was robbing the jeweller's* **3** (*) (= *atraer*) [+ *persona*] to rope in; [+ *marido*] to land; **a mi no me enganchan para cuidar a los niños** they're not going to rope me into looking after the children **B engancharse** VPR **1** (= *quedarse prendido*) to get hooked up, catch (**en** on); (*Mec*) to engage (**en** with); **el vestido se enganchó en un clavo** the dress got caught on a nail; **~se a la droga** to get hooked on drugs*, become addicted to drugs **2** (*Mil*) to enlist, join up

enganche SM **1** (= *acto*) (*gen*) hooking, hooking up; [*de remolque*] hitching; (*Mec*) coupling, connection; (*Ferro*) coupling **2** (= *mecanismo*) hook **3** (*Mil*) recruitment, enlistment **4** (*Méx Com*) (= *depósito*) deposit, initial payment **5** (*Esp Telec*) connection

engañabobos SM INV swindle

engañapichanga * SF (*RPI*) swindle

engañar /1a/ **A** VT **1** [+ *persona*] (= *embaucar*) to deceive, trick; (= *despistar*) to mislead; (*con promesas, esperanzas*) to delude; (= *estafar*) to cheat, swindle; **engaña a su mujer** he's unfaithful to his wife, he's cheating on his wife; **a mí no me engaña nadie** you can't fool me; **no te dejes** ~ don't let yourself be taken in **2 necesito picar algo para** ~ **el hambre** I need to nibble at sth to stop me feeling hungry; ~ **el tiempo** to kill time **B** VI to be deceptive; ✦ REFRÁN **las apariencias engañan** appearances are misleading **C engañarse** VPR **1** (= *equivocarse*) to be wrong, be mistaken; **en eso te engañas** you're wrong there **2** (= *ocultarse la verdad*) to delude o.s., fool o.s.; **no te engañes** don't kid yourself

engañifa * SF swindle

engañito SM (*Chi*) small gift

engaño SM **1** (= *mentira*) deception; **siguió manteniendo el** ~ he continued to keep up the deception; **que nadie se llame a** ~ don't be deceived **2** (= *trampa*) con*; **fue un** ~ it was a con* **3 engaños** (= *astucia*) wiles, tricks

engañoso ADJ [*persona*] deceitful, dishonest; [*apariencia*] deceptive; [*consejo*] misleading

engarce SM setting, mount

engarzar /1f/ **A** VT [+ *joya*] to set, mount; [+ *cuentas*] to thread **B engarzarse** VPR (*Col*) to get tangled, get stuck

engastar /1a/ VT to set, mount

engaste SM setting, mount

engatusar /1a/ VT to coax, wheedle; ~ **a algn para que haga algo** to coax sb into doing sth; **no me vas a** ~ you're not going to get round me

engavetado ADJ (*Ven*) **estar** ~ to be gathering dust

engavetar /1a/ VT (*Ven*) [+ *proyecto, documento*] to allow to gather dust

engendrar /1a/ VT **1** (*Biol*) to beget, breed **2** [+ *problemas, situación*] to cause

engendro SM **1** (*) (= *ser deforme*) freak **2** (= *feto*) foetus, fetus (*EEUU*) **3** (= *invención*) idiotic scheme, impossible plan

engestarse * /1a/ VPR (*Méx*) to scowl

englobar /1a/ VT to include, comprise

engolado ADJ (*fig*) haughty

engomar /1a/ VT to gum, glue

engominar /1a/ VT [+ *pelo*] to put hair cream on; **iba todo engominado** his hair was all smarmed down

engorda SF (*Chi, Méx*) fattening (up)

engordar /1a/ **A** VT **1** [+ *animal, persona*] to fatten (up); [+ *kilos*] to put on, gain **2** [+ *número*] to swell, increase **B** VI **1** (= *ponerse gordo*) to get fat; (= *aumentar de peso*) to put on weight; (*Agr*) to fatten **2** [*comida*] to be fattening

engorde SM fattening (up)

engorro * SM hassle*, bother, nuisance

engorroso ADJ [*asunto*] bothersome, trying; [*situación, problema*] awkward

engranaje SM **1** (= *rueda dentada*) [*de reloj*] cogs *pl*; [*de máquina*] gear teeth *pl*; (= *conjunto de engranajes*) gears *pl*, gear assembly **2** (= *sistema*) mechanism; **el delicado** ~ **de la justicia** the delicate mechanism of the judicial system; **el** ~ **de la dictadura** the machinery of the dictatorship

engranar /1a/ **A** VT to gear **B** VI to interlock; (*Mec*) to engage (**con** with)

engrandecer /2d/ VT **1** (= *aumentar*) to enlarge, magnify **2** (= *ensalzar*) to speak highly of

engrapadora SF (*LAm*) stapler

engrapar /1a/ VT (*LAm*) to staple

engrasador SM grease cup

engrasar /1a/ VT to grease, oil

engrase SM greasing, lubrication

engreído/a **A** ADJ **1** (= *vanidoso*) vain, stuck-up* **2** (*Perú*) (= *mimado*) spoiled, spoilt **B** SM/F **1** (= *vanidoso*) bighead* **2** (*Perú*) (= *mimado*) spoiled brat

engreimiento SM vanity, conceit

engreír /3k/ **A** VT (*Perú*) [+ *niño*] to spoil, pamper

B engreírse VPR to get conceited

engrifarse* /1a/ VPR (Chi, Méx) to get cross, get angry

engriparse /1a/ VPR (CS) to catch the flu

engrosar /1l/ VT to increase; **~ las filas de los desempleados** to swell the ranks of the unemployed

engrudo SM paste

engrupido/a* (Arg) **A** ADJ stuck-up* **B** SM/F show-off*

engrupir* /3a/ VT (CS) (= engañar) to con*

enguantado ADJ [mano] gloved

enguayabado* ADJ **está ~** (And, Carib) he's got a hangover*, he's hung over*

engullir /3a, 3h/ VT to gobble, gulp, gulp down

enharinar /1a/ VT to flour

enhebrar /1a/ VT to thread

enhiesto ADJ erect, upright

enhorabuena SF congratulations pl; **dar la ~ a algn** to congratulate sb; **estar de ~** to be in luck, be on to a good thing

enigma SM enigma

enigmático ADJ enigmatic

enjabonar /1a/ VT 1 (= lavar) [+ manos, ropa] to soap, wash; [+ barba] to lather 2 (*) (= adular) to soft-soap

enjaezar /1f/ VT to harness, saddle up

enjalbegar /1h/ VT to whitewash

enjambre SM swarm

enjaretar* /1a/ VT 1 (= recitar) to reel off, spout 2 (= endilgar) **me enjaretó la tarea de ...** he lumbered me with the task of ...

enjaular /1a/ VT 1 (= guardar) to cage, put in a cage 2 (*) (= encarcelar) to jail, lock up, bang up*

enjoyado ADJ [persona] **todas las señoras iban enjoyadas al teatro** all the ladies wore jewels to the theatre; **iba demasiado enjoyada** she was dripping with jewellery

enjuagar /1h/ VT [+ ropa] to rinse, rinse out; [+ boca] to wash out

enjuague SM 1 (= líquido) (tb ~ **bucal**) mouthwash 2 (= acto) [de ropa] rinsing; [de boca] washing, rinsing 3 (= intriga) scheme 4 (LAm) (para el pelo) conditioner

enjugar /1h/ VT 1 (= secar) [+ sudor] to wipe, wipe off; [+ lágrimas] to wipe away 2 [+ deuda] to wipe out **B enjugarse** VPR **~se la frente** to wipe one's brow, mop one's brow

enjuiciamiento SM judg(e)ment **➤ enjuiciamiento civil** lawsuit **➤ enjuiciamiento criminal** trial

enjuiciar /1b/ VT 1 (= juzgar) to judge, pass judg(e)ment on 2 (Jur) (= acusar) to indict; (= procesar) to prosecute

enjundia SF substance; **una novela con mucha ~** a very weighty novel

enjuto ADJ lean, skinny

enlace SM 1 (= conexión) (Elec) linkage; (Quím) bond; (Ferro) connection; (en autopista) motorway junction (Brit), freeway intersection (EEUU) **➤ enlace telefónico** telephone link-up 2 (tb ~ **matrimonial**) marriage 3 (= mediador) link; (Mil) liaison **➤ enlace sindical** union representative, shop steward (Brit) 4 (Internet) link

enlatado ADJ 1 [alimentos] canned, tinned (Brit) 2 [música] canned

enlatar /1a/ VT 1 [+ alimento] to can, tin (Brit) 2 (TV) to pre-record

enlazar /1f/ **A** VT 1 (= atar) to tie 2 [+ ideas] to link, connect 3 (LAm) [+ caballo] to lasso 4 (Méx frm) (= casar) to marry **B** VI [tren, vuelo] to connect; [carretera] to link (up); [idea, movimiento] to meet, link (up) (**con** with)

enlistado SM (Méx) list

enlistar /1a/ **A** VT (Méx) to make a list of **B enlistarse** VPR (CAm, Carib, Méx Mil) to enlist, join up

enlodar /1a/ VT 1 (= embarrar) to cover in mud 2 (fig) (= manchar) to stain **B enlodarse** VPR to get muddy

enloquecedor ADJ [ruido, trabajo, experiencia] maddening; [dolor] excruciating

enloquecer /2d/ **A** VT to drive crazy **B** VI 1 (= volverse loco) to go mad, go insane 2 (= gustar mucho) **le enloquece la música pop** she's mad o crazy about pop music

enlosar /1a/ VT to pave (with flagstones)

enlozado ADJ (LAm) enamelled, enameled (EEUU), glazed

enlucido SM plaster

enlucir /3f/ VT [+ pared] to plaster; [+ metal] to polish

enlutado ADJ [persona] in mourning, wearing mourning

enlutar /1a/ **A** VT 1 [+ persona] to put into mourning 2 [+ ciudad, país] to plunge into mourning **B enlutarse** VPR to dress in mourning

enmadrado* ADJ (Esp) **está ~** he's tied to his mother's apron strings, he's a mummy's boy (Brit)

enmarañar /1a/ **A** VT 1 [+ madeja, hilo] to tangle, tangle up 2 (= complicar) to complicate; **sólo logró ~ más el asunto** he only managed to make matters worse **B enmarañarse** VPR 1 (= enredarse) to get tangled (up), become entangled 2 (= complicarse) to become involved, become complicated

enmarcar /1g/ **A** VT [+ cuadro] to frame; **la catedral enmarcaba perfectamente la ceremonia** the cathedral was the perfect setting for the ceremony **B enmarcarse** VPR **el acuerdo se enmarca dentro del proceso de paz** the agreement is part of the peace process; **su obra se enmarca en las corrientes vanguardistas** his work forms part of the avant garde movements

enmascarado/a SM/F masked man/woman

enmascarar /1a/ **A** VT 1 [+ cara] to mask 2 [+ intenciones] to disguise **B enmascararse** VPR (lit) to put on a mask

enmendar /1j/ **A** VT 1 [+ texto] to emend, correct; [+ ley, conducta] to amend 2 [+ moral] to reform **B enmendarse** VPR [persona] to mend one's ways

enmicar /1g/ VT (Méx) [+ documento] to cover in plastic, laminate

enmienda SF 1 (= corrección) amendment **➤ enmienda a la totalidad** motion for the rejection of a bill 2 [de comportamiento] reform

enmohecer /2d/ **A** VT 1 [+ metal] to rust 2 (Bot) to make mouldy, make moldy (EEUU) **B enmohecerse** VPR 1 [metal] to rust, get rusty 2 [planta] to get mouldy, get moldy (EEUU)

enmontarse /1a/ VPR (CAm, Col, Méx) to get overgrown

enmoquetar /1a/ VT (Esp) to carpet

enmudecer /2d/ **A** VT to silence **B** VI (= perder el habla) (gen) to go dumb; (por miedo, sorpresa) to be dumbstruck

enmugrar* /1a/ VT (LAm), **enmugrecer*** /2d/ VT, **enmugrentar*** /1a/ VT (Chi) to soil, dirty

ennegrecer /2d/ **A** VT (= poner negro) to blacken; (= oscurecer) to darken **B ennegrecerse** VPR (= ponerse negro) to turn black; (= oscurecerse) to get dark, darken

ennoblecer /2d/ VT 1 (= hacer noble) to ennoble 2 (= adornar) to embellish

enojadizo ADJ (esp LAm) irritable, short-tempered

enojado ADJ angry

enojar /1a/ (esp LAm) **A** VT to annoy **B enojarse** VPR to get angry, get annoyed (**con** with; **por** at, about)

enojo SM anger

enojón ADJ (Chi, Méx) = **enojadizo**

enojoso ADJ irritating, annoying

enólogo/a SM/F oenologist, wine expert

enorgullecer /2d/ **A** VT to fill with pride **B enorgullecerse** VPR to be proud (**de** of), pride o.s. (**de** on)

enorme ADJ enormous, huge

enormidad SF 1 (= inmensidad) enormousness, hugeness 2 [de crimen] enormity 3 (*) **me gustó una ~** I liked it enormously o tremendously

enquistamiento SM 1 (Med) **cuando se produjo el ~ del grano** when the pimple turned into a cyst 2 (= atranque) deadlock; **dado el ~ de la situación** given the current deadlock

enquistarse /1a/ VPR **1** (*Med*) to turn into a cyst **2** [*mal social*] to take hold, fester within

enraizar /1f/ VI to take root

enramada SF **1** (= *follaje*) leafy foliage **2** (*CS*) (= *cobertizo*) arbour, arbor (*EEUU*)

enrarecer /2d/ **A** VT [+ *aire*] to rarefy; [+ *ambiente*] to strain **B** **enrarecerse** VPR **1** [*aire*] to become rarefied, get thin **2** [*relaciones, ambiente*] to become strained, become tense

enrarecido ADJ [*aire*] rarefied; [*relaciones, ambiente*] strained, tense

enratonado* ADJ (*Ven*) hung over*

enrazar /1f/ VT (*Col*) [+ *personas*] to mix (racially); [+ *animales*] to crossbreed

enredadera SF climbing plant, creeper ➤ **enredadera de campo** bindweed

enredador(a) **A** ADJ (= *alborotador*) troublemaking; (= *travieso*) naughty, mischievous **B** SM/F (= *alborotador*) troublemaker; (= *travieso*) naughty child

enredar /1a/ **A** VT **1** [+ *pelo, hilos, cuerda*] to tangle up **2** [+ *situación, asunto*] to make complicated, complicate **3** (*) (= *desordenar*) to get into a mess, mess up **4** (*) (= *involucrar*) to get mixed *o* caught up (**en** in) **5** (*) (= *engañar*) to trick **B** VI (*) (= *juguetear*) to play around, monkey around*; ~ **con algo** to fiddle with sth **C** **enredarse** VPR **1** [*hilos, cuerda*] to get tangled up; **se me ha enredado el pelo** my hair's got all tangled up **2** [*situación, asunto*] to get complicated **3** (*) (= *involucrarse*) to get mixed up, get involved (**con, en** with) **4** (*) (= *liarse*) to get into a tangle*, get into a muddle*; **me enredé haciendo las cuentas** I got into a tangle *o* muddle with the accounts*; **me enredé al pronunciar su nombre** I got tongue-tied when I tried to say his name **5** (*) (*sentimentalmente*) ~**se con algn** to get involved with sb, get embroiled with sb

enredo SM **1** [*de pelos, hilos, cuerda*] tangle **2** [*de datos*] (*gen*) maze, tangle; (= *confusión*) mix-up **3** (= *asunto turbio*) shady business **4** (= *amorío*) love affair **5** **comedia de ~** comedy of intrigue

enrejado SM (= *rejas*) grating; [*de ventana*] lattice; (*en jardín*) trellis

enrejillado SM small-mesh grille

enrevesado ADJ [*asunto*] difficult, complex; [*mente, carácter*] twisted

enrielar /1a/ VT **1** (= *poner rieles a*) to lay rails on **2** (*LAm*) [+ *asunto*] to put on the right track

enriquecer /2d/ **A** VT to make rich, enrich **B** **enriquecerse** VPR to get rich

enriquecido ADJ [*producto*] enriched

enristrar /1a/ VT **1** [+ *cebollas, ajos*] to (put on a) string **2** [+ *lanza*] to take up

enrocar /1g/ VI (*Ajedrez*) to castle

enrojecer /2d/ **A** VT (= *poner rojo*) to redden, turn red; (= *ruborizar*) to make blush **B** VI (= *ruborizarse*) to blush; (*de ira*) to go red (with anger), go red in the face

enrolar /1a/ **A** VT to enlist **B** **enrolarse** VPR to enlist, join up

enrollable ADJ [*colchón, pantalla, persiana*] roll-up *antes de s*

enrollado ADJ **1** (= *liado*) [*alfombra, pergamino*] rolled (up); [*cuerda, cable*] (*en sí mismo*) coiled (up); (*alrededor de algo*) wound (up) **2** (*Esp***) [*persona, música*] cool** **3** (*Esp***) (*en relación amorosa*) **estar ~ con algn** to be going out with sb, be dating sb (*EEUU*) **4** (*Esp***) (*con una actividad*) involved, busy; **estar ~ con algo** to be busy with sth; **estar ~ en algo** to be involved in sth

enrollar /1a/ **A** VT **1** (= *liar*) [+ *papel, persiana, filete*] to roll (up); [+ *cuerda, cable*] (*en sí mismo*) to coil (up); (*alrededor de algo*) to wind (up)

2 (*Esp***) (= *atraer*) **la droga no me enrolla** drugs don't do anything for me, I'm not into drugs* **3** (*Esp***) (= *enredar*) ~ **a algn en algo** to get sb involved in sth **B** **enrollarse** VPR **1** (= *liarse*) [*papel*] to roll up; [*cuerda, cable*] (*en sí mismo*) to coil up; (*alrededor de algo*) to wind up **2** (*Esp***) (= *extenderse demasiado*) (*al hablar*) to go on*; (*sin decir nada*) to waffle on*; **nos enrollamos hablando hasta muy tarde** we were chattering away till very late; **no te enrolles, que tenemos prisa** don't get talking, we've got to hurry; ✦ MODISMO ~**se como una persiana** to go on and on **3** (*Esp***) (= *ser simpático*) **venga, enróllate** come on, be a sport*; ~**se bien** to be cool**; ~**se mal** to be uncool** **4** (*Esp***) (= *tener una relación sexual*) to have it off with algn (*Brit***), make out with sb (*EEUU***); (= *empezar una relación amorosa*) to get off with sb (*Brit**), get it off with sb (*EEUU*) * **5** (*Esp***) (= *involucrarse*) ~**se en algo** to get into sth*, get involved in sth **6** (*Ven***) (= *confundirse*) to get mixed up; (= *preocuparse*) to get worked up*

enronquecer /2d/ VI to grow hoarse

enroque SM (*Ajedrez*) castling

enroscado ADJ [*serpiente, cuerda*] coiled

enroscar /1g/ **A** VT **1** (= *poner*) [+ *tapón*] to screw on; [+ *tornillo*] to screw in **2** [+ *cable, manguera*] to coil **B** **enroscarse** VPR [*serpiente*] to coil up; [*gato*] to curl up; **la manguera se le enroscó en la pierna** the hose coiled round his leg

enrostrar /1a/ VT (*LAm*) to reproach

enrular /1a/ VT (*And, RPl*) to curl

enrumbar /1a/ VI (*And*) to set off

ensaimada SF *spiral-shaped pastry typical of Mallorca*

ensalada SF **1** (*Culin*) salad **2** (= *lío*) mix-up

ensaladera SF salad bowl

ensaladilla SF (*Esp*) (*tb ~ rusa*) Russian salad

ensalmo SM spell, charm

ensalzar /1f/ VT [+ *persona*] to praise; [+ *virtudes*] to extol

ensambladura SF, **ensamblaje** SM (= *acción*) assembly; (= *juntura*) joint

ensamblar /1a/ VT (= *montar*) to assemble; [+ *madera*] to joint

ensanchar /1a/ **A** VT (= *agrandar*) to widen; (= *aumentar*) to expand; (*Cos*) to let out **B** **ensancharse** VPR [*carretera, río*] to get wider, widen; [*vestido, ropa*] to stretch, get stretched out

ensanche SM **1** [*de calle*] widening, expansion **2** [*de ciudad*] (= *acción*) urban growth *o* extension; (= *barrio*) newer part (*of town or city*)

ensangrentado ADJ bloodstained

ensangrentar /1j/ **A** VT to stain with blood, cover in blood **B** **ensangrentarse** VPR to become stained with blood

ensañamiento SM (= *cólera*) rage; (= *crueldad*) cruelty

ensañarse /1a/ VPR ~ **con** to treat brutally

ensartar /1a/ **A** VT **1** (= *pinchar*) [+ *cuentas*] to string; [+ *aguja*] to thread; [+ *carne*] to spit **2** [+ *ideas*] to string together; [+ *disculpas*] to reel off **B** **ensartarse** (*) VPR **1** (*CS*) (= *caer en una trampa*) to be taken for a ride* **2** (*LAm*) (= *en discusión, asunto*) to get involved

ensayar /1a/ **A** VT **1** (= *probar*) to test, try (out) **2** (*Mús, Teat*) to rehearse **B** VI to rehearse

ensayista SMF essayist

ensayo SM **1** (= *prueba*) test, trial; (= *experimento*) experiment; (= *intento*) attempt **2** (*Literat*) essay **3** (*Mús, Teat*) rehearsal; **hicimos un ~ de la obra** we rehearsed the play ➤ **ensayo general** [*de orquesta*] final rehearsal; [*de ópera, teatro*] dress rehearsal

enseguida ADV = **en seguida**; *ver* **seguida**

ensenada SF inlet, cove

enseña SF ensign, standard

enseñado ADJ trained, educated; **bien ~** [*perro*] house-trained

enseñante SMF teacher

enseñanza SF **1** (= *educación*) education; (= *acción, profesión*) teaching; **primera ~** elementary education; **segunda ~** secondary education **2** (= *doctrina*) teaching, doctrine; **la ~ de la Iglesia** the teaching of the Church

enseñar /1a/ **Ⓐ** VT **1** (*Educ*) to teach; **~ a algn a hacer algo** to teach sb (how) to do sth; **enseña francés** he teaches French **2** (= *mostrar*) to show; (= *señalar*) to point out; **estás enseñando el sujetador** your bra's showing; **nos enseñó el museo** he showed us over *o* around the museum **Ⓑ** VI to teach, be a teacher **Ⓒ enseñarse** VPR (*Méx*) (= *acostumbrarse*) to become accustomed (**a** to); **no me enseño aquí** I can't settle down here

enseres SMPL equipment *sing*; **~ domésticos** household goods

ensillar /1a/ VT to saddle (up)

ensimismarse /1a/ VPR to become engrossed, lose o.s.

ensombrecer /2d/ VT to cast a shadow over

ensoñación SF fantasy, fancy, dream

ensopar /1a/ (*Col, RPl, Ven*) **Ⓐ** VT to soak, drench, to dip, dunk **Ⓑ ensoparse** VPR to get soaked

ensordecedor ADJ deafening

ensordecer /2d/ **Ⓐ** VT [+ *persona*] to deafen; [+ *ruido*] to muffle **Ⓑ** VI to go deaf

ensortijado /1a/ ADJ curly

ensuciar /1b/ **Ⓐ** VT **1** (= *manchar*) to get dirty, dirty **2** (*liter*) [+ *reputación, nombre*] to sully, soil (*liter*) **Ⓑ ensuciarse** VPR **1** (= *mancharse*) to get dirty; **me he ensuciado las manos** I've got my hands dirty; **te has ensuciado de barro los zapatos** you've got mud on your shoes **2** [*bebé*] to dirty one's nappy (*Brit*) *o* diaper (*EEUU*)

ensueño SM dream, fantasy; **una cocina de ~** a dream kitchen; **mundo de ~** dream world, world of fantasy

entablar /1a/ VT **1** [+ *conversación*] to strike up; [+ *proceso*] to file; [+ *reclamación*] to put in **2** (*Ajedrez*) to set up

entablillar /1a/ VT (*Med*) to (put in a) splint

entallado ADJ (*Cos*) waisted, with a waist

entallar /1a/ VT (*Cos*) to cut, tailor; (= *ceñir*) to bring in

entarimado SM **1** (*de parquet*) parquet floor; (*de tablas*) floorboarding **2** (= *estrado*) dais, stage, platform

ente SM **1** (= *organización oficial*) body, organization ➤ **ente público** public body, public corporation **2** (*Fil*) entity, being

enteco ADJ weak, sickly, frail

entelequia SF **1** (*Fil*) entelechy **2** (= *plan irrealizable*) pipe dream, pie in the sky

entelerido ADJ (*Méx*) weak

entenado/a SM/F stepson/stepdaughter, stepchild

entendederas* SFPL brains; **ser corto de** *o* **tener pocas ~** to be pretty dim

entendedor(a) SM/F ✦ REFRÁN **a buen ~, pocas palabras bastan** a word to the wise is sufficient

entender¹ /2g/ **Ⓐ** VT **1** (= *comprender*) [+ *pregunta, idioma*] to understand; **lo has entendido todo al revés** you've got it all wrong; **no entiendo tu letra** I can't read your writing; **¿entiendes lo que te quiero decir?** do you know what I mean?, do you know what I'm trying to say?; **dar algo a ~** to imply sth; **nos dieron a ~ que** they gave us to understand *o* led us to believe that; **hacer ~ algo a algn** to make sb understand sth; **hacerse ~** to make o.s. understood; **~ mal** to misunderstand; **no quiero que me entiendas mal** don't get me wrong; **no entendió ni una palabra** he didn't understand a word of it; ✦ MODISMO **no ~ ni jota** *o* (*Esp*) **ni patata*: no entendí ni jota** *o* **ni una patata de lo que decían** I didn't have a clue what they were on about; **no entiendo ni jota de alemán** I don't understand a single word of German **2** (= *opinar*) to think, believe; **entiendo que sería mejor decírselo** I think *o* believe it would be better to tell him **3** (= *interpretar*) to understand; **¿tú qué entiendes por libertad?** what do you understand by freedom? **4** (*) (= *saber manejar*) [+ *aparato*] to know how to use, know how to work **5** (= *oír*) to hear; **no se entiende nada** I can't make out *o* hear a thing **Ⓑ** VI **1** (= *comprender*) to understand; **¡ya entiendo!** now I understand!, now I get it!; **~ de algo** to know about sth **2** (*Jur*) (= *tener competencia*) **entiende en divorcios** he hears divorce cases **3** [*perro, gato*] **entiende por Moncho** he answers to the name of Moncho **Ⓒ entenderse** VPR **1** (*uso reflexivo*) to understand o.s.; **yo me entiendo** I know what I mean; ✦ MODISMOS **entendérselas: que ella se las entienda como pueda** well, that's her problem; **allá tú te las entiendas con tus asuntos** you go and sort out your own affairs; **entendérselas con algn: van a tener que entendérselas conmigo** they're going to have to deal with me **2** (*uso recíproco*) **nosotras nos entendemos** we understand each other; **nos entendimos por señas** we communicated using sign language, we used sign language to communicate; **a ver si nos entendemos** now let's get this straight; **~se con algn** (= *llevarse bien*) to get on *o* along with sb; (= *tener una relación amorosa*) to have an affair with sb **3** (*uso impersonal*) **se entiende que no quiera salir con ellos** it's understandable that she doesn't want to go out with them; **¿cómo se entiende que no nos llamaras antes?** why didn't you call us first?

entender² SM opinion; **a mi ~** in my opinion

entendido/a **Ⓐ** ADJ **1** (= *comprendido*) understood; **¡entendido!** (= *convenido*) agreed!; **tenemos ~ que ...** we understand that ...; **según tenemos ~** as far as we can gather **2** [*persona*] **ser ~ en** to be well up on **Ⓑ** SM/F expert; **el whisky de los ~s** the connoisseur's whisky

entendimiento SM **1** (= *inteligencia*) understanding, mind; **el ~ humano** human understanding, the human mind **2** (= *acuerdo*) understanding

entente SF entente

enteradillo/a* SM/F (*Esp*) little know-all (*Brit*), little know-it-all (*EEUU*), smartypants*

enterado/a **Ⓐ** ADJ (*de una especialidad*) knowledgeable; (*sobre un asunto concreto*) well-informed; **esta muy ~ de política** he's very knowledgeable about politics; **estar ~ de algo** to know sth; **me doy por enterada** I get the message **Ⓑ** SM/F (= *conocedor*) [*de materia*] expert; (*pey*) know-all* (*Brit*), know-it-all* (*EEUU*), bighead*; **para los ~s** for those in the know*

enteramente ADV entirely, completely

enterar /1a/ **Ⓐ** VT **1** (*Chi, Méx*) (= *pagar*) [+ *dinero, deuda*] to pay **2** (*Chi*) (= *completar*) [+ *cantidad*] to make up, complete; **hoy entero dos meses sin fumar** it's two months today since I last smoked **Ⓑ enterarse** VPR **1** (*de noticia, secreto*) **1.1** (*por casualidad*) to hear, find out (**de** about); **no me había enterado** I hadn't heard; **me enteré de tu accidente por Juan** I heard about *o* found out about your accident from Juan; **me enteré del secuestro a través de la prensa** I read about the kidnapping in the paper **1.2** (*haciendo averiguaciones*) to find out (**de** about); **entérate de lo que cuesta** find out what it costs **2** (= *darse cuenta*) to notice; **no se enteró de que le habían quitado la cartera** he didn't notice that his wallet had been stolen; **todavía no se han enterado de qué tipo de persona es** they still don't know what kind of person he is; ✦ MODISMOS **te vas a ~ (de quien soy yo** *o* **de lo que vale un peine)** you'll find out what's what*; **para que te enteres** for your information **3** (*Esp*) (= *comprender, oír*) to understand; **¿te enteras?** do you understand?, do you get it?*; **¡a ver si te enteras!** wise up!*; **no se enteraba de lo que leía** he didn't take in *o* understand what he was reading

entereza SF **1** (= *integridad*) integrity **2** (= *firmeza*) firmness ➤ **entereza de carácter** strength of character

enteritis SF INV enteritis

enterito SM (*RPl*) boiler suit (*Brit*), overalls *pl* (*EEUU*)

enterizo ADJ in one piece, one-piece *antes de s*

enternecedor ADJ touching

enternecer /2d/ **A** VT to affect, move (to pity) **B** **enternecerse** VPR to be affected, be moved (to pity)

entero **A** ADJ 1 (= *completo*) whole, entire; **se comió el paquete** ~ he ate the whole *o* entire packet; **se pasa el día** ~ **quejándose** he spends the whole *o* entire day complaining; **es famoso en el mundo** ~ he's famous the whole world over, he's famous all over the world 2 **por** ~ wholly, fully 3 (*Mat*) whole, integral 4 [*persona*] (= *íntegro*) upright; (= *sereno*) composed **B** SM 1 (*Mat*) integer, whole number 2 (*Com, Fin*) point 3 (*And*) [*de lotería*] whole (lottery) ticket

enterradero SM (*RPl*) safe house

enterrador(a) SM/F gravedigger

enterramiento SM burial, interment (*frm*)

enterrar /1j/ VT to bury (**en** in)

entibiar /1b/ **A** VT 1 [+ *lo caliente*] to cool, cool down 2 [+ *ira*] to cool, cool down **B** **entibiarse** VPR 1 [*lo caliente*] to become lukewarm 2 [*ira, amistad*] to cool off

entidad SF 1 (= *esencia*) entity 2 (*Admin, Pol*) body, organization; (*Com, Fin*) firm, company ➤ **entidad bancaria** bank ➤ **entidad comercial** company, business ➤ **entidad financiera** financial institution 3 **de** ~ of importance

entierro SM 1 (= *acto*) burial, interment 2 (= *funeral*) funeral; ✧ CARNAVAL

entintar /1a/ VT 1 (= *llenar de tinta*) [+ *tampón*] to ink; [+ *blanco*] to ink in 2 (= *manchar*) to stain with ink

entizar /1f/ VT (*LAm Billar*) to chalk

entoldado SM awning

entoldar /1a/ VT to put an awning over

entomología SF entomology

entonación SF intonation

entonado ADJ 1 (*Mús*) in tune 2 (*) [*persona*] **estar más** ~ to have perked up

entonar /1a/ **A** VT 1 (*Mús*) [+ *canción*] to intone, sing; [+ *voz*] to modulate; [+ *nota*] to give, set 2 (*Med*) to tone up **B** VI 1 (*Mús*) (= *cantar*) to intone (*frm*), sing; (= *cantar afinadamente*) to be in tune (**con** with) 2 [*colores*] to match **C** **entonarse** VPR to perk up

entonces ADV 1 (*uso temporal*) then; **desde** ~ since then; **en aquel** ~ at that time; **hasta** ~ up till then; **las costumbres de** ~ the customs of the time; **el** ~ **embajador** the then ambassador; **fue** ~ **que ...** it was then that ..., that was when ... 2 (*uso concesivo*) so, then; ~, **¿qué hacemos?** so, what shall we do?, what shall we do then?

entontecer /2d/ **A** VT to make silly **B** **entontecerse** VPR to get silly

entornado ADJ [*puerta*] ajar; [*ojos*] half-closed

entornar /1a/ VT [+ *puerta*] to leave ajar, half-close; [+ *ojos*] to half-close

entorno SM 1 (= *medioambiente*) environment; (*Literat*) setting, milieu; (= *escenario*) scene; **las personas de su** ~ the people around him; **sacar a algn de su** ~ to take sb away from/out of their normal environment; **el** ~ **cultural** the cultural scene ➤ **entorno social** social setting 2 (*Inform*) environment

⚠ **escenario ≠ scenery**

entorpecer /2d/ VT [+ *tráfico*] to slow down, slow up; [+ *trabajo*] to delay, hinder

entrada SF 1 (= *lugar de acceso*) entrance; **"entrada"** "way in", "entrance"; **le pidieron la identificación a la** ~ they asked for some identification at the door; **las** ~**s a Madrid** roads into Madrid ➤ **entrada de artistas** stage door ➤ **entrada de servicio** tradesman's entrance ➤ **entrada principal** main entrance 2 (= *vestíbulo*) [*de casa*] entrance hall, hall (*Brit*); [*de hotel*] foyer 3 (= *llegada*) 3.1 (*a un lugar*) **no advirtió la** ~ **de su padre**

she didn't notice her father come in; **sus** ~**s y salidas de prisión fueron constantes** he was constantly in and out of jail; **hicieron una** ~ **triunfal en Egipto** they made a triumphal entry into Egypt; **dar** ~ **a un lugar** to give access to a place; **tras la** ~ **en vigor de la ley** after the law came into effect *o* force 3.2 (*Teat*) (*tb* ~ **en escena**) entrance (on stage) 3.3 [*de instrumento, voz*] entry; **el director dio** ~ **a los vientos** the conductor brought in the wind section 3.4 (*Jur*) (*en un domicilio*) entry

4 (= *invasión*) [*de militares*] entry; [*de turistas, divisas*] influx 5 (= *acceso*) (*a espectáculo*) admission, entry; (*a país*) entry; (*a club, institución, carrera*) admission; **"entrada gratuita"** "admission free"; **en su discurso de** ~ **a la Academia** in his introductory *o* opening speech to the Academy; **dar** ~ **a algn** (*en un lugar*) to allow sb in; (*en club, sociedad*) to admit sb; **prohibir la** ~ **a algn** to ban sb from entering 6 (= *billete*) ticket; **"no hay entradas"** "sold out" ➤ **entrada de abono** season ticket 7 (= *público*) (*Teat*) audience; (*Dep*) crowd, turnout 8 (= *recaudación*) (*Teat*) receipts *pl*, takings *pl*; (*Dep*) gate money, receipts *pl* 9 (= *principio*) start; **os deseamos una feliz** ~ **de año** we wish you all the best for the new year; **de** ~ (*desde el principio*) from the start, from the outset; (*al principio*) at first 10 (*Esp*) (= *primer pago*) (*al comprar una vivienda, coche*) down payment, deposit 11 (*Com*) (*en libro mayor*) entry 12 (= *vía de acceso*) (*Mec*) inlet, intake; (*Elec*) input; (*Inform*) input ➤ **entrada de aire** air intake ➤ **entrada de datos** data entry, data input 13 (*Ftbl*) tackle; **hacer una** ~ to tackle sb 14 (*Culin*) starter (*esp Brit*), appetizer (*EEUU*) 15 [*de diccionario*] entry 16 **entradas** 16.1 (*en el pelo*) receding hairline *sing* 16.2 (*Fin*) income *sing* ➤ **entradas y salidas** income and expenditure *sing*

entradilla SF (*Esp Prensa*) lead-in, opening paragraph

entrado ADJ 1 (= *abundante*) **en años** (*euf*) elderly; ~ **en carnes** (*euf*) overweight 2 (= *avanzado*) **hasta bien** ~ **el siglo XIX** until well into the 19th century; **hasta muy entrada la noche** until late at night

entrador ADJ 1 (*LAm*) (= *atrevido*) daring, forward 2 (*RPl*) (= *simpático*) charming, likeable

entramado SM 1 (= *estructura*) framework 2 (= *red*) network

entramparse /1a/ VPR to get into debt

entrante **A** ADJ 1 [*mes, semana*] next 2 [*ministro, presidente*] new, incoming; [*correo*] incoming **B** SM 1 (*Culin*) starter 2 (*Geog*) inlet 3 (*Arquit*) recess

entrañable ADJ [*amigo*] dear, close; [*amistad*] deep; [*paisaje*] beloved, dearly loved; [*recuerdo*] fond

entrañar /1a/ VT to entail

entrañas SFPL 1 (*Anat*) entrails, bowels; **en las** ~ **de la Tierra** in the bowels of the Earth; ✦ MODISMOS **arrancar las** ~ **a algn** to break sb's heart, tear sb's heart out; **echar las** ~* to puke (up)* 2 (= *sentimientos*) heart *sing*, feelings; **no tener** ~ to be heartless

entrar /1a/ **A** VI 1 (*en un lugar*) (*acercándose al hablante*) to come in, enter (*más frm*); (*alejándose del hablante*) to go in, enter (*más frm*); **—¿se puede? —sí, entra** "may I?" — "yes, come in"; **hágalo** ~ show him in; **entré en** *o* (*LAm*) **a la casa** I went into the house; ~**on en mi cuarto anoche** they came into my room last night; **la ayudó a** ~ **en el** *o* (*esp LAm*) **al coche** he helped her (get) into the car; **no me dejaron** ~ **en** *o* (*esp LAm*) **a la discoteca** I wasn't allowed into the club; **entró corriendo en** *o* (*esp LAm*) **a la habitación** she ran into the room; **entra frío por la puerta** there's a draught *o* (*EEUU*) draft coming in through the door 2 (= *encajar*) to fit; **la camisa no entra en el cajón** the shirt won't go *o* fit in the drawer; **las historias de este libro entran de lleno en el surrealismo** the stories in this book are genuinely surrealist, the stories in this book come right into the category of surrealism 3 (= *estar incluido*) **el vino no entra en el precio** the wine is not included (in the price); **eso no entraba en nuestros**

planes that wasn't part of our plans; **en un kilo entran cuatro manzanas** you get four apples to the kilo
4 (= *comenzar*) **4.1** [*persona*] (*en clase, trabajo*) to start; ~ **en una profesión** to take up a profession; ~ **en una asociación** to join a society; **entró a formar parte del comité** he became a member of the committee **4.2** ~ **en calor** to warm up; ~ **en coma** to go into a coma; ~ **en contacto con algn** to contact sb **4.3** [*época, estación*] **el mes que entra** the coming month, next month
5 ~ **a algn** **5.1** (*con sensaciones*) **me entró sueño** I started to feel sleepy; **me ha entrado hambre al verte comer** watching you eat has made me hungry; **me ~on ganas de reír** I felt like laughing **5.2** [*conocimientos, idea*] **no hay forma de que le entre el álgebra** he just can't seem to get the hang of algebra; **no les entra en la cabeza que eso no puede ser así** they can't seem to get it into their heads that this isn't on **5.3** (*) (= *soportar*) **ese tío no me entra** I can't bear *o* stand that fellow
6 (*Inform*) to access
7 [*instrumento, voz*] to come in
8 (*Teat*) to enter
9 (*) (= *abordar a*) to deal with, approach; **sabe ~ a la gente** he knows how to deal with *o* approach people
10 [+ *futbolista*] to tackle
B VT (*) [+ *objeto*] (*acercándose al hablante*) to bring in; (*alejándose del hablante*) to take in

entre PREP **1** (= *en medio de*) **1.1** (*dos elementos*) between; **vendrá ~ las diez y las once** he'll be coming between ten and eleven; ~ **clase y clase** between lessons; **un líquido ~ dulce y amargo** a liquid which is half-sweet, half-sour; **dudo ~ comprar éste o aquél** I'm not sure whether to buy this one or that one **1.2** (*más de dos elementos*) among, amongst; **había un baúl ~ las maletas** there was a trunk in among(st) the cases; **una costumbre muy extendida ~ los romanos** a widespread custom among(st) the Romans; **estamos ~ amigos** we're among(st) friends; **paso el día ~ estas cuatro paredes** I spend the whole day within these four walls; **se abrieron paso ~ la multitud** they forced their way through the crowd
2 (*indicando colaboración, participación*) **lo terminamos ~ los dos** between the two of us we finished it; **esto lo solucionaremos ~ nosotros** we'll sort that out among(st) *o* between ourselves; **la cuento ~ mis mejores amigas** I count her as one of my best friends; **hablaban ~ sí** they were talking among(st) themselves
3 (*uso aditivo*) ~ **niños y niñas habrá unos veinte en total** there are about twenty in total, if you count boys and girls; ~ **que era tarde y hacía frío, decidimos no salir** what with it being late and cold, we decided not to go out; ~ **unas cosas y otras se nos hizo de noche** before we knew it, it was night
4 (*Mat*) **20 ~ 4** 20 divided by 4; **20 ~ 4 es igual a 5** 4 into 20 goes 5 (times)
5 (*esp LAm**) **más estudia más aprende** the more he studies the more he learns
6 ~ **tanto** *ver* **entretanto**

entreabierto ADJ [*puerta*] ajar

entreacto SM interval (*esp Brit*), intermission (*EEUU*)

entrecano ADJ [*pelo*] greyish, grayish (*EEUU*), greying, graying (*EEUU*); [*persona*] going grey *o* (*EEUU*) gray

entrecejo SM space between the eyebrows; **arrugar** *o* **fruncir el ~** to frown, wrinkle one's brow

entrecerrar /1j/ VT (*esp LAm*) to half-close

entrecomillado SM quotation marks *pl*, quotes *pl*, inverted commas *pl* (*Brit*)

entrecomillar /1a/ VT to put in quotation marks *o* (*Brit*) inverted commas

entrecortado ADJ [*respiración*] laboured, labored (*EEUU*), difficult; [*habla*] faltering, hesitant

entrecot SM entrecote, sirloin steak

entrecruzar /1f/ **A** VT to interlace, interweave, intertwine **B** **entrecruzarse** VPR to interweave, intertwine

entredicho SM **1 estar en ~** (= *ser discutible*) to be questionable, be debatable; **su profesionalidad está** *o* **ha quedado en ~** grave doubts have been cast on his professionalism; **poner algo en ~** to raise doubts about sth,

call sth into question **2** (*CS, Perú*) (= *disputa*) (*entre personas*) quarrel; (*territorial*) dispute

entredós SM (*Cos*) insertion, panel

entrega SF **1** (= *acto*) [*de documento, solicitud*] submission; **esta noche es la ~ de premios** tonight is the awards ceremony; **"entrega de llaves inmediata"** "ready for immediate occupancy"; **hacer ~ de** [+ *regalo, premio, cheque*] to present; **le hizo ~ de la medalla al valor** he presented him with an award for bravery
2 [*de cartas, mercancías*] delivery; **"entrega a domicilio"** "we deliver" ➤ **entrega contra reembolso** cash on delivery
3 (*al rendirse*) [*de rehenes*] handover; [*de armas*] surrender, handover
4 (= *sección*) [*de enciclopedia, novela*] instalment, installment (*EEUU*); [*de revista*] issue; [*de serie televisiva*] series
5 (= *dedicación*) dedication, devotion

entregado ADJ **1** (= *dedicado*) **estar ~ a** [+ *causa, creencia, actividad, trabajo*] to be dedicated to, be devoted to; **una vida entregada a ayudar a los más necesitados** a life dedicated *o* devoted to helping those most in need
2 (= *sacrificado*) selfless

entregar /1h/ **A** VT **1** (= *dar*) **1.1** [+ *impreso, documento, trabajo*] to hand in, give in, submit (*frm*); **el proyecto se ~á a la comisión para que lo estudie** the plan will be put before the commission for them to study; **entregó su alma a Dios** he departed this life; ✦ MODISMO **~las** (*Chi***) to kick the bucket** **1.2** (*en mano*) (*gen*) to hand over; [+ *regalo*] to give **1.3** [+ *premio, cheque*] to present
2 (= *distribuir*) (*gen*) to give out; [+ *correo, pedido*] to deliver; **mañana ~emos las notas del examen** we'll give out the exam marks tomorrow; **"para entregar a"** "for the attention of"
3 (= *ceder*) [+ *poderes, botín, rehenes*] to hand over; [+ *armas, país*] to hand over, surrender; **el juez entregó la custodia del niño a su abuela** the judge gave *o* awarded *o* granted custody of the boy to his grandmother
B **entregarse** VPR **1** (= *rendirse*) to give o.s. up, surrender
2 (= *dejarse dominar*) **~se a** [+ *sueño, tentación*] to succumb to; **se entregó a la desesperación** she gave in to despair; **~se a la bebida** to take to drink
3 (= *dedicarse*) **~se a algo** to devote o.s. to sth

entreguerras: de ~ ADJ **el período de ~** the inter-war period, the period between the wars (*i.e.* 1918-39)

entrelazar /1f/ **A** VT to intertwine, interweave **B** **entrelazarse** VPR to intertwine, interweave

entremedias ADV (= *en medio*) in between, halfway; (= *entretanto*) in the meantime

entremés SM **1** (*Teat, Hist*) interlude, short farce
2 (*Culin*) **entremeses** hors d'oeuvres

ENTREMÉS

An **entremés** is a short farce used as an entertaining interval between the first and second act of a **comedia**. It is thought that the **entremés** (derived from the Italian **intermezzo**) was first performed on the Spanish stage in the 16th century and derives from the influential Italian **Commedia dell'Arte**. Often using slapstick, stock characters and situations, **entremeses** had enormous audience appeal and were written by such distinguished writers as Miguel de Cervantes.

---

entremezclar /1a/ **A** VT to intermingle **B** **entremezclarse** VPR to intermingle

entrenador(a) SM/F trainer, coach

entrenamiento SM (= *ejercicios*) training; (= *sesión*) training session; (*por el entrenador*) coaching

entrenar /1a/ **A** VT (*Dep*) to train, coach; [+ *caballo*] to exercise **B** VI to train **C** **entrenarse** VPR to train

entreoír /3p/ VT to half-hear

entrepierna SF **1** (*Anat*) crotch, crutch **2** (= *medida*) inside leg, measurement

entresacar /1g/ VT **1** [+ *información, datos*] to pick out, select 2 [+ *pelo, plantas*] to thin out

entresemana SF **cualquier día de ~** any day midweek, any day in the middle of the week

entresijos SMPL ins and outs

entresuelo SM (*en edificio*) mezzanine, entresol; (*Teat*) dress circle

entretanto ADV meanwhile, meantime

entretecho SM (*Chi*) attic

entretejer /2a/ VT to interweave

entretela SF 1 (*Cos*) interlining 2 **entretelas** [*de organización*] ins and outs

entretelones SMPL (*CS, Perú*) details

entretención SF (*LAm*) entertainment

entretener /2k/ ⓐ VT 1 (= *divertir*) to entertain, amuse; **nos entretuvo con sus chistes** he kept us entertained *o* amused with his jokes 2 (= *retener*) to keep, detain (*frm*); **no le entretengo más** I won't keep *o* (*frm*) detain you any longer 3 (= *distraer*) ~ **a algn** to distract sb's attention; ~ **algo: entretuvieron la espera leyendo** they whiled away the time by reading; **para ~ el hambre** to take the edge off my hunger ⓑ VI **la tele entretiene mucho** TV is very entertaining ⓒ **entretenerse** VPR 1 (= *divertirse*) to amuse o.s. 2 (= *tardar*) to hang about; **¡no te entretengas!** don't hang about!

entretenido ADJ [*libro, obra de teatro*] entertaining, amusing; [*trabajo*] time-consuming

entretenimiento SM entertainment, amusement

entretiempo SM 1 (= *temporada*) **un abrigo de ~** a light coat, a lightweight coat 2 (*Chi Dep*) halftime

entrever /2u/ VT 1 (= *vislumbrar*) to make out; **dejar ~ algo** to suggest sth, hint at sth; **estas manifestaciones dejan ~ fisuras en el partido** these demonstrations seem to suggest divisions within the party 2 (= *adivinar*) to guess 3 (= *presentir*) to glimpse; **podemos ~ una solución** we can glimpse a solution

entreverado ADJ interspersed, intermingled

entrevero SM (*And, CS*) jumble

entrevía SF (*Ferro*) gauge, gage (*EEUU*)

entrevista SF 1 (= *conversación*) interview 2 (= *reunión*) meeting

entrevistado/a SM/F interviewee

entrevistador(a) SM/F interviewer

entrevistar /1a/ ⓐ VT to interview ⓑ **entrevistarse** VPR to meet; **~se con algn** to have a meeting with sb, meet with sb; **los vecinos se ~on con el alcalde** the residents were received by the Mayor yesterday

entripado* SM (*RPl*) problem

entristecer /2d/ ⓐ VT to sadden, make sad ⓑ **entristecerse** VPR to grow sad

entrometerse /2a/ VPR (= *interferir*) to meddle, interfere (**en** in, with); (= *molestar*) to intrude

entrometido/a ⓐ ADJ meddlesome, interfering ⓑ SM/F busybody, meddler

entrón ADJ (*Méx*) flirtatious

entroncar /1g/ VI 1 ~ **con** [*familia*] to be related to, be connected to; (= *estar relacionado*) to be linked to, be related to 2 (*Ferro*) to join, connect (**con** to)

entronizar /1f/ VT to enthrone

entronque SM 1 (= *parentesco*) relationship, link 2 (= *enlace*) connexion, link 3 (*LAm Ferro*) junction (*esp Brit*), intersection (*esp EEUU*)

entuerto SM (= *injusticia*) wrong, injustice

entumecer /2d/ ⓐ VT to numb ⓑ **entumecerse** VPR to go numb, go to sleep

entumecido ADJ numb

entumecimiento SM numbness

entumido ADJ numb

enturbiar /1b/ ⓐ VT 1 [+ *líquido*] to muddy, make cloudy

2 [+ *asunto*] to confuse, fog; [+ *mente, persona*] to confuse ⓑ **enturbiarse** VPR 1 (*líquido*) to get muddy, become cloudy 2 [*asunto*] to become obscured; [*mente, persona*] to get confused 3 [*relaciones*] to be marred

entusiasmar /1a/ ⓐ VT **me entusiasma el trabajo** I love my work; **no le entusiasma mucho la idea** he's not very keen on the idea ⓑ **entusiasmarse** VPR to get enthusiastic, get excited (**con, por** about); **se ha quedado entusiasmada con el vestido** she loves the dress

entusiasmo SM enthusiasm (**por** for); **con ~** (= *con apasionamiento*) enthusiastically; (= *con interés*) keenly

entusiasta ⓐ ADJ (= *apasionado*) enthusiastic (**de** about); (= *interesado*) keen (**de** on) ⓑ SMF (= *aficionado*) enthusiast, fan*; (= *admirador*) admirer

enumeración SF enumeration

enumerar /1a/ VT to enumerate

enunciación SF enunciation

enunciado SM statement

enunciar /1b/ VT [+ *teoría*] to enunciate, state; [+ *idea*] to put forward

envainar /1a/ ⓐ VT [+ *arma*] to sheathe ⓑ **envainarse** VPR (*And, Carib**) to get into trouble

envalentonar /1a/ ⓐ VT to make bold, embolden ⓑ **envalentonarse** VPR (= *cobrar valor*) to pluck up courage; (*pey*) (= *insolentarse*) to become defiant

envanecer /2d/ ⓐ VT to make conceited ⓑ **envanecerse** VPR to become conceited, grow vain

envanecido ADJ conceited, stuck-up*

envanecimiento SM conceit, vanity

envasado SM (*en cajas*) packing; (*en botellas, tarros*) bottling; (*en latas*) canning

envasar /1a/ VT (*en cajas*) to pack; (*en botellas, tarros*) to bottle; (*en latas*) to can, tin (*esp Brit*)

envase SM 1 (= *recipiente*) container; **~ retornable** returnable container; **~ de vidrio** glass container 2 (= *botella*) (*llena*) bottle; (*vacía*) empty 3 (= *lata*) can, tin (*esp Brit*)

envejecer /2d/ ⓐ VT to age, make look old ⓑ VI 1 [*persona*] to age 2 [*vino*] to mature, age

envejecido ADJ 1 [*persona*] old, aged; (*de aspecto*) old-looking; **está muy ~** he's aged a lot 2 [*piel, madera, tela*] distressed

envejecimiento SM ageing

envenenamiento SM poisoning

envenenar /1a/ ⓐ VT 1 (*con veneno*) to poison 2 (= *amargar*) to embitter ⓑ **envenenarse** VPR 1 (*voluntariamente*) to poison o.s., take poison 2 (*por accidente*) to be poisoned

envergadura SF 1 (= *importancia*) importance; **daños de cierta ~** considerable *o* substantial damage; **una operación de cierta ~** an operation of some magnitude *o* size 2 [*de ala*] wingspan

envés SM [*de tela*] back, wrong side; [*de hoja de planta*] underside; [*de espada*] flat

enviado/a SM/F (*Pol*) envoy ➤ **enviado/a especial** [*de periódico, TV*] special correspondent

enviar /1c/ VT to send; **~ a algn a hacer algo** to send sb to do sth; **~ un mensaje a algn** (*por móvil*) to text sb, send sb a text message

enviciar /1b/ ⓐ VT to corrupt ⓑ **enviciarse** VPR **~se con** *o* **en** to become addicted to

envidar /1a/ VT, VI (*Esp Naipes*) to bid

envidia SF envy, jealousy; **dar ~ a algn** to make sb envious *o* jealous; **¡qué ~ me da verte tan contenta!** I'm so envious *o* jealous seeing you so happy!; **tener ~ a algn** to envy sb, be jealous of sb; **✦** MODISMO **estar muerto de ~** to be green with envy

envidiable ADJ enviable

envidiar /1b/ VT 1 [+ *persona*] to envy 2 (= *codiciar*) to desire, covet; **~ algo a algn** to envy sb sth, begrudge sb sth; **su casa no tiene nada que ~ a la tuya** her house is at least as good as yours, her house is quite up to the standard of yours

envidioso ADJ envious, jealous

envilecer /2d/ **Ⓐ** VT to debase, degrade **Ⓑ** envilecerse VPR to degrade o.s., lower o.s.

envilecimiento SM degradation, debasement

envío SM 1 (= acción) (gen) sending; (en barco) shipment; **proponen el ~ de fuerzas de paz** they propose sending peace-keeping forces; **gastos de ~** (cost of) postage and packing (Brit), postage and handling (EEUU) ➤ envío a domicilio home delivery (service) ➤ envío contra reembolso cash on delivery 2 (= mercancías) (gen) consignment, lot; (Náut) shipment

envión SM push, shove

envite SM 1 (= apuesta) stake 2 (= ofrecimiento) offer, bid

enviudar /1d/ VI [mujer] to become a widow, be widowed; [hombre] to become a widower, be widowed; **~ de la primera mujer** to lose one's first wife

envoltorio SM bundle, package

envoltura SF (gen) cover; [de papel] wrapper, wrapping; (Mec) case, casing; (= vaina) sheath

envolver /2h/ (pp **envuelto**) **Ⓐ** VT 1 (= cubrir) (con papel) to wrap (up); (con ropa) to wrap (up), cover (up); **¿quiere que se lo envuelva?** shall I wrap it (up) for you? 2 (= rodear) to surround, shroud; **una niebla espesa envolvía el castillo** the castle was surrounded o shrouded in thick fog; **su muerte está envuelta en misterio** her death is shrouded in mystery 3 (= involucrar) to involve (en in) **Ⓑ** envolverse VPR 1 (con ropa) to wrap o.s. up (en in) 2 (= involucrarse) to become involved (en in)

envuelto PP de **envolver**

enyesado SM plastering

enyesar /1a/ VT 1 [+ pared] to plaster 2 (Med) to put in a (plaster) cast

enzarzarse /1f/ VPR (en una disputa) to get involved; **~ a golpes** to come to blows

enzima SF enzyme

eólico ADJ wind antes de s; **energía eólica** wind power

eón SM aeon, eon (esp EEUU)

epa* EXCL, **épale*** EXCL (LAm) hey!, wow!, say! (EEUU)

epatar* /1a/ VT (= deslumbrar) to startle, dazzle; (= escandalizar) to shock

E.P.D. ABR (= **en paz descanse**) RIP

épica SF epic poetry

epicentro SM epicentre, epicenter (EEUU)

épico ADJ epic

epicúreo/a ADJ, SM/F epicurean

epidemia SF epidemic

epidémico ADJ epidemic

epidérmico ADJ 1 (= de la piel) skin antes de s 2 (= superficial) superficial, skin-deep

epidermis SF INV epidermis

Epifanía SF Epiphany, Twelfth Night

epiglotis SF INV epiglottis

epígrafe SM epigraph

epilepsia SF epilepsy

epiléptico/a ADJ, SM/F epileptic

epílogo SM epilogue

episcopado SM 1 (= cargo) bishopric 2 (= obispos) bishops pl, episcopacy (frm)

episcopal ADJ [autoridad, iglesia] episcopal; [cargo] bishopric; **palacio ~** bishop's palace; **sede ~** (= ciudad) see

episódico ADJ episodic

episodio SM [de aventura, suceso] episode, incident; [de serie, novela] episode, part

epistemología SF epistemology

epístola SF epistle, letter

epistolar ADJ epistolary

epitafio SM epitaph

epíteto SM epithet

epítome SM summary, epitome (frm)

época SF 1 (= momento histórico) age, period, epoch (frm); **la ~ de Carlos III** the age of Charles III; **en aquella ~** at that time, in that period; **muebles de ~** period furniture; **coche de ~** vintage car; **un Picasso de primera ~** an early (period) Picasso; **todos tenemos ~s así** we all go through spells like that; **estoy pasando una mala ~** I'm going through a bad patch; **hacer ~** to be epoch-making, be a landmark 2 (tb ~ **del año**) season, time of year ➤ época de celo (Zool) mating season, rutting season ➤ época de lluvias rainy season

epopeya SF epic

equidad SF fairness, equity (frm)

equidistante ADJ equidistant

equilátero ADJ equilateral

equilibrado ADJ 1 [persona] (= sensato) level-headed, sensible; (= ecuánime) well-balanced 2 [dieta] balanced 3 [partido] close

equilibrar /1a/ **Ⓐ** VT to balance; **~ la balanza de pagos** to restore the balance of payments; **~ el marcador** to level the score **Ⓑ** equilibrarse VPR [persona] to balance o.s. (en on); [fuerzas] to counterbalance each other

equilibrio SM 1 (= estabilidad) balance; **intentó mantener el ~ sobre la cuerda** he tried to keep his balance on the rope; **mantuvo en ~ el palo sobre su dedo** he balanced the stick on his finger; **perder el ~** to lose one's balance; **✦ MODISMO hacer ~s** to do a balancing act ➤ equilibrio ecológico ecological balance ➤ equilibrio presupuestario balanced budget 2 (= armonía) balance, equilibrium ➤ equilibrio de fuerzas, equilibrio de poderes balance of power

equilibrista SMF tightrope walker

equino Ⓐ ADJ equine, horse antes de s **Ⓑ** SM 1 (= caballo) horse 2 [de mar] sea urchin

equinoccio SM equinox ➤ equinoccio de otoño autumnal equinox ➤ equinoccio de primavera vernal equinox

equipaje SM luggage, baggage (esp EEUU); **hacer el ~** to pack, do the packing; **zona de recogida de ~s** luggage o (esp EEUU) baggage collection point ➤ equipaje de mano hand luggage

equipal SM (Méx) wicker chair with seat and back of leather or palm leaves

equipamiento SM equipment ➤ equipamiento de serie standard equipment

equipar /1a/ **Ⓐ** VT 1 [+ casa, coche] to fit, equip (con, de with); **viene equipado con elevalunas eléctrico** it is fitted with electric windows; **un gimnasio muy bien equipado** a very well-equipped gymnasium 2 [+ persona] (con armas, útiles) to equip (con, de with); (con ropa) to kit out (con, de with); **~ a un colegial** to get a child kitted out for school **Ⓑ** equiparse VPR to equip o.s. (con, de with)

equiparable ADJ comparable (con to, with)

equiparación SF comparison

equiparar /1a/ **Ⓐ** VT (= igualar) to put on the same level, consider equal; (= comparar) to compare (con with) **Ⓑ** equipararse VPR **~se con** to be on a level with, rank equally with

equipo SM 1 (Dep) team ➤ equipo de fuera away team ➤ equipo de fútbol football team ➤ equipo local home team ➤ equipo visitante visiting team 2 [de personas] team; **trabajar en ~** to work as a team ➤ equipo de salvamento, equipo de socorro (civil) rescue team; (militar) rescue squad, rescue unit ➤ equipo directivo management team ➤ equipo médico medical team, medical unit 3 (= utensilios, accesorios) (gen) equipment; (para deportes) equipment, kit; **✦ MODISMO caerse con todo el ~*** to make a right mess of things* ➤ equipo de alta fidelidad hi-fi system ➤ equipo de música stereo system ➤ equipo de novia trousseau

equis SF INV (= *letra*) (name of the letter) X; **rayos ~** X-rays; **cada ~ años** every so many years; **durante ~ años** for X number of years; **marcar con una ~ la respuesta correcta** put a cross by the correct answer

equitación SF 1 (= *acto*) riding; **escuela de ~** riding school 2 (= *arte*) horsemanship

equitativo ADJ [*distribución, division, trato*] fair; [*precio*] reasonable; [*reparto*] fair, equitable (*frm*)

equivalencia SF equivalence

equivalente ADJ, SM equivalent

equivaler /2p/ VI ~ **a** to be equivalent to, be equal to; (*en grado, nivel*) to rank as, rank with

equivocación SF mistake, error; **por ~** by mistake, in error

equivocado ADJ 1 [*número, dirección*] wrong; [*persona*] mistaken, wrong; **estás ~** you are wrong, you are mistaken (*más frm*) 2 [*afecto, confianza*] misplaced

equivocar /1g/ ❹ VT 1 (= *confundir*) to get mixed up, mix up; **he equivocado las direcciones** I've got the addresses mixed up, I've mixed up the addresses 2 ~ **a algn** to make sb make a mistake 3 (= *errar*) ~ **el camino** (*lit*) to go the wrong way; (*fig*) to make the wrong choice ❺ **equivocarse** VPR (= *no tener razón*) to be wrong, be mistaken; (= *cometer un error*) to make a mistake; **te equivocas, eso no es así** you're wrong o mistaken, it isn't like that; **me equivoqué muchas veces en el examen** I made a lot of mistakes in the exam; ~**se con algn** to be wrong about sb; ~**se de algo: se ~on de casa** they went to the wrong house; **perdone, me he equivocado de número** sorry, (I've got the) wrong number

equívoco ❹ ADJ equivocal, ambiguous ❺ SM 1 (= *malentendido*) misunderstanding 2 (*al hablar*) (= *juego de palabras*) pun, play on words; (= *doble sentido*) double meaning 3 (*Méx**) (= *error*) mistake

era[1] *ver* **ser**

era[2] SF (*Hist*) era, age ➤ **era cristiana** Christian era ➤ **era espacial** space age

era[3] SF (*Agr*) threshing floor

erais, éramos *ver* **ser**

erario SM (= *Hacienda*) treasury; (= *fondos*) public funds *pl*

erección SF 1 (*Anat*) erection 2 (*Arquit*) [*de edificio*] erection; [*de monumento*] raising

eres *ver* **ser**

ergonomía SF ergonomics *sing*

ergonómico ADJ ergonomic

erguido ADJ erect, straight

erguir /3m/ ❹ VT 1 (= *levantar*) to raise, lift; ~ **la cabeza** (*lit*) to hold one's head up; (*fig*) to hold one's head high 2 (= *enderezar*) to straighten ❺ **erguirse** VPR (*al ponerse en pie*) to straighten up, stand up straight; (*estando sentado*) to sit up straight

erial SM uncultivated land

erigir /3c/ ❹ VT 1 [+ *monumento*] to erect; [+ *edificio*] to build 2 (= *fundar*) to establish, found 3 ~ **a algn en algo** to set sb up as sth ❺ **erigirse** VPR ~ **en algo** to set o.s. up as sth

erizado ADJ [*cepillo, cola*] bristly; [*pelo*] spiky; ~ **de espinas** covered with thorns

erizar /1f/ ❹ VT **el gato erizó el pelo** the cat bristled, the cat's hair stood on end ❺ **erizarse** VPR [*pelo de animal*] to bristle; [*pelo de persona*] to stand on end

erizo SM hedgehog ➤ **erizo de mar, erizo marino** sea urchin

ermita SF chapel, shrine

ermitaño/a SM/F 1 (= *persona*) hermit 2 (*Zool*) hermit crab

erogación SF 1 (*LAm*) (= *gasto*) expenditure, outlay 2 (*Chi*) (= *contribución*) contribution, donation

erogar /1h/ VT 1 (*LAm*) (= *pagar*) to pay; [+ *deuda*] to settle 2 (*Chi*) (= *contribuir*) to contribute

erógeno ADJ erogenous

erosión SF erosion

erosionar /1a/ ❹ VT to erode ❺ **erosionarse** VPR to erode, be eroded

erótico ADJ erotic

erotismo SM eroticism

erotizar /1a/ ❹ VT to eroticize ❺ **erotizarse** VPR to be (sexually) stimulated

erotómano ADJ erotic, pathologically erotic

errabundo ADJ wandering, roving

erradicación SF eradication

erradicar /1g/ VT to eradicate

errado ADJ 1 (= *equivocado*) mistaken 2 [*tiro*] wide of the mark

errante ADJ [*persona*] wandering; [*vida*] nomadic

errar /1k/ ❹ VT [+ *tiro*] to miss with, aim badly; [+ *blanco*] to miss; [+ *vocación*] to miss, mistake; ~ **el camino** to lose one's way ❺ VI 1 (= *vagar*) to wander, rove 2 (= *equivocarse*) to be mistaken; ✦ REFRANES ~ **es humano** ⬦ **de los hombres es ~** to err is human

errata SF misprint, printer's error; **fe de ~s** errata

errático ADJ erratic

erre SF (name of the letter) R; ✦ MODISMO ~ **que ~** stubbornly, pigheadedly

erróneo ADJ (= *equivocado*) mistaken, erroneous; (= *falso*) untrue, false

error SM mistake, error (*más frm*); **salvo ~ u omisión** errors and omissions excepted; **cometer un ~** to make a mistake; **estar en un ~** to be mistaken, be wrong; **inducir a ~** to be misleading; **por ~** by mistake ➤ **error de cálculo** miscalculation ➤ **error de hecho** factual error, error of fact ➤ **error de imprenta** misprint ➤ **error judicial** miscarriage of justice ➤ **error tipográfico** misprint

Los sustantivos **mistake** y **error** tienen el mismo significado, pero **mistake** es una palabra de uso corriente, mientras que **error** suele utilizarse en un contexto formal o en lenguaje técnico. Ambos se utilizan con el verbo **make**, no con **do**.

ertzaina [er'tʃaina] SMF policeman/policewoman, *member of the autonomous Basque police force*

Ertzaintza [er'tʃaintʃa] SF *autonomous Basque police (force)*

eructar /1a/ VI to belch

eructo SM belch

erudición SF learning, scholarship, erudition (*frm*)

erudito/a ❹ ADJ learned, scholarly, erudite (*frm*) ❺ SM/F scholar, learned person; **los ~s en esta materia** those who are expert in this subject, those who really know about this subject

erupción SF eruption; **entrar en ~** to (begin to) erupt ➤ **erupción cutánea** rash, eruption (*frm*)

esa ADJ DEM *ver* **ese**[2]

ésa PRON DEM *ver* **ése**

esbelto ADJ slim, slender

esbirro SM henchman, minion

esbozar /1f/ VT 1 (*Arte*) to sketch, outline 2 [+ *plan*] to outline; ~ **una sonrisa** to smile a faint smile, force a smile

esbozo SM 1 (*Arte*) sketch 2 [*de plan*] outline

escabechar /1a/ VT to pickle, souse

escabeche SM 1 (= *salsa*) pickle, brine 2 (= *pescado*) soused fish

escabechina SF (= *matanza*) slaughter; **hacer una ~** (*Esp**) [*profesor*] to fail a pile of students

escabel SM footstool, footrest

escabroso ADJ 1 [*terreno*] rough, rugged 2 [*problema*] difficult, tough, thorny 3 [*chiste*] risqué, blue, salacious (*frm*)

escabullirse /3a/ VPR to slip away o off

escacharrar* /1a/ ❹ VT to bust* ❺ **escacharrarse** VPR to break

escafandra SF diving suit

escala SF 1 (*en medición, gradación*) scale; **a** ~ [*dibujo, mapa, maqueta*] scale *antes de s*; **un mapa hecho a** ~ a map drawn to scale, a scale map; **una imitación a** ~ **reducida de un objeto real** a scaled-down version of a real object; **a** ~ **real** life-size *antes de s*; **reproducir algo a** ~ to reproduce sth to scale ➤ **escala de valores** set of values, scale of values ➤ **escala Richter** Richter scale ➤ **escala salarial** salary scale 2 [*de importancia, extensión*] **la producción a** ~ **industrial** production on an industrial scale; **un problema a** ~ **mundial** a global problem, a problem on a worldwide scale; **a** o **en gran/pequeña** ~ on a large/small scale 3 (= *parada en ruta*) 3.1 (*Aer*) stopover; **un vuelo sin** ~**s** a non-stop flight; **hacer** ~ to stop over 3.2 (*Náut*) port of call; **el buque hizo** ~ **en Cádiz** the ship put in at Cádiz ➤ **escala técnica** refuelling o (*EEUU*) refueling stop 4 (= *escalera de mano*) ladder ➤ **escala de cuerda** rope ladder 5 (*Mús*) scale

escalada SF 1 [*de montaña*] climb, ascent; **su rápida** ~ **al poder** his rapid rise to power ➤ **escalada en rocas** rock climbing ➤ **escalada libre** free climbing 2 (= *aumento*) escalation; **una** ~ **de la violencia** an escalation of violence; **se ha producido una** ~ **en los precios** prices have escalated

escalador(a) SM/F (*en alpinismo*) climber, mountaineer; (*en ciclismo*) climber, mountain rider; (*en roca*) rock climber

escalafón SM 1 [*de promoción*] promotion ladder; **ascender en el** ~ to go up the ladder, work one's way up 2 (= *ránking*) table, chart

escalar /1a/ **Ⓐ** VT 1 [+ *montaña*] to climb, scale 2 (*en la escala social*) to climb, rise to; ~ **puestos** to move up **Ⓑ** VI 1 [*alpinista*] to climb 2 (*Náut*) to call, put in (**en** at)

escaldado ADJ **salir** ~: **salió** ~ **del negocio** he got his fingers burned in the deal; **salió escaldada de su matrimonio** she came out of the marriage feeling sadder and wiser; **salió** ~ **de la experiencia** he was chastened by the experience

escaldar /1a/ **Ⓐ** VT to blanch, scald **Ⓑ escaldarse** VPR to scald o.s., get scalded

escalera SF 1 [*de edificio*] stairs *pl*, staircase; **se cayó por las** ~**s** she fell downstairs o down the stairs ➤ **escalera de caracol** spiral staircase ➤ **escalera de incendios** fire escape ➤ **escalera de servicio** backstairs *pl* ➤ **escalera mecánica** escalator 2 (*portátil*) ladder ➤ **escalera de mano** ladder ➤ **escalera de tijera** stepladder, steps *pl* ➤ **escalera extensible** extension ladder 3 (*Naipes*) run, sequence; (*en póquer*) straight ➤ **escalera de color** straight flush

escalerilla SF (*en bricolaje, piscina*) ladder; (*en barco*) gangway, companionway; (*Aer*) steps *pl*

escalfar /1a/ VT to poach

escalinata SF steps *pl*

escalofriante ADJ (= *espeluznante*) bloodcurdling, hair-raising; (= *aterrador*) frightening, chilling

escalofrío SM shiver; **aquello me produjo un** ~ **de terror** it made me shiver with fear, it sent a shiver down my spine

escalón SM 1 (= *peldaño*) (*gen*) step, stair; [*de escalera de mano*] rung 2 (*al avanzar*) (= *paso*) step; (*al éxito*) stepping stone

escalonadamente ADV step by step, in a series of steps

escalonar /1a/ VT 1 (= *distribuir*) to spread out at intervals; [+ *horas de trabajo*] to stagger 2 [+ *tierra*] to terrace

escalopa SF (*Chi*) escalope (*Brit*), cutlet (*EEUU*)

escalope SM escalope (*Brit*), cutlet (*EEUU*) ➤ **escalope de ternera** escalope of veal (*Brit*), veal cutlet (*EEUU*)

escalopín SM fillet

escalpelo SM scalpel

escama SF 1 (*Bot, Zool*) scale 2 [*de jabón, pintura*] flake

escamado ADJ wary, cautious

escamar /1a/ **Ⓐ** VT 1 [+ *pez*] to scale 2 (= *producir recelo a*) to make wary; **eso me escama** that makes me suspicious

Ⓑ escamarse VPR to get wary, become suspicious

escamotear /1a/ VT 1 (*) (= *robar*) to lift*, pinch* 2 [+ *hechos, verdad*] to hide, cover up

escampar /1a/ VI 1 [*lluvia*] to stop; [*tiempo*] to clear up 2 (*Carib, Col*) (*de la lluvia*) to shelter

escanciar /1b/ VT to pour, pour out, serve

escandalizar /1f/ **Ⓐ** VT to scandalize, shock **Ⓑ escandalizarse** VPR to be shocked, be scandalized (**de** at, **by**)

escándalo SM 1 (= *tumulto*) scandal, outrage; **¡es un** ~**!** it's outrageous o shocking!; **precios de** ~ (= *caros*) outrageous prices; (= *baratos*) amazing prices 2 (= *ruido*) row, uproar; **armar un** ~ to make a scene, cause an uproar

escandaloso ADJ 1 [*actuación*] scandalous, shocking; [*vida*] scandalous 2 (= *ruidoso*) [*risa*] hearty, uproarious; [*niño*] noisy 3 [*color*] loud

Escandinavia SF Scandinavia

escandinavo/a ADJ, SM/F Scandinavian

escanear /1a/ VT to scan

escaneo SM scanning

escáner SM 1 (= *aparato*) scanner 2 (= *imagen*) scan; **hacerse un** ~ to have a scan

escaño SM (= *banco*) bench; (*Pol*) seat

escapada SF 1 (= *huida*) escape, breakout; ✦ MODISMO **en una** ~ in a spare moment 2 (= *viaje, salida*) **conseguí hacer una** ~ **rápida a Bruselas** I managed to get away to Brussels, I managed a quick getaway to Brussels; **las** ~**s nocturnas del heredero al trono** the heir to the throne's nocturnal jaunts 3 (*Ciclismo*) breakaway

escapado/a **Ⓐ** ADJ (= *rápido*) **salió escapada de aquella casa** she rushed out of the house; **tengo que volverme** ~ **a la tienda** I have to rush back to the shop **Ⓑ** SM/F 1 (= *fugitivo*) fugitive, runaway 2 (*Ciclismo*) **los** ~**s** the breakaway group

escapar /1a/ **Ⓐ** VI 1 (= *huir*) to escape; **sintió una gran necesidad de** ~ he felt a great need to get away o escape; ~ **a algo**: **no pude** ~ **a sus encantos** I could not escape her charms; **hay cosas que escapan a nuestro control** some things are beyond our control; ~ **de** [+ *cárcel, peligro*] to escape from; [+ *jaula*] to get out of; [+ *situación opresiva*] to escape from, get away from; **logramos** ~ **de una muerte cierta** we managed to escape certain death; **dejar** ~ [+ *grito, risa, suspiro*] to let out; [+ *oportunidad*] to let slip; **dejar** ~ **a algn** to let sb get away 2 (*Dep*) (*en carreras*) to break away **Ⓑ escaparse** VPR 1 (= *huir*) [*preso*] to escape; [*niño, adolescente*] to run away; ~**se de** [+ *cárcel, peligro*] to escape from; [+ *jaula*] to get out of; [+ *situación opresiva*] to escape from, get away from 2 (= *filtrarse*) [*gas, líquido*] to leak, leak out (**por** from) 3 (= *dejar pasar*) **me voy, que se me escapa el tren** I'm going, or I'll miss my train; **a nadie se le escapa la importancia de esta visita** everybody is aware of o realizes the importance of this visit; ✦ MODISMO ~**se de las manos**: **la situación se les escapó de las manos** they lost control of the situation 4 (= *dejar salir*) 4.1 [*grito, eructo*] **se me escapó un eructo sin darme cuenta** I accidentally burped o let out a burp; **se me escapó una lágrima** a tear came to my eye 4.2 [*dato, noticia*] **se le escapó la fecha de la reunión** he let slip the date of the meeting 5 (= *soltarse*) [*globo, cometa*] to fly away; [*punto de sutura*] to come undone; **se le escapó un punto en la manga** she dropped a stitch in the sleeve 6 (= *hacerse público*) [*información*] to leak, leak out 7 (= *olvidarse*) to slip one's mind; **ahora mismo se me escapa su nombre** his name escapes me o slips my mind right now

escaparate SM 1 [*de tienda*] window, shop window (*esp Brit*), store window (*EEUU*); **ir de** o **mirar** ~**s** to go window-shopping 2 (*Col*) (= *vitrina*) display cabinet 3 (*Ven*) (= *armario*) wardrobe

escaparatismo SM window dressing

escaparatista SMF window dresser

escapatoria SF way out

escape SM 1 [*de situación opresiva*] escape; **vía de ~** (*lit*) escape route; (*fig*) (form of) escape; ✦ MODISMO **a ~** at full speed; **salir a ~** to rush out 2 (= *fuga*) [*de gas*] leak; [*de líquido, radiación*] leak, leakage; **un ~ de gas** a gas leak 3 (*Mec*) (*tb* **tubo de ~**) exhaust, exhaust fumes; **gases de ~** exhaust, exhaust fumes

escapismo SM escapism

escapulario SM scapular, scapulary

escaquearse** /1a/ VPR (*Esp*) to shirk

escarabajo SM 1 (= *insecto*) beetle ➤ **escarabajo de la patata** Colorado beetle 2 (*Téc*) flaw 3 (*) (= *persona*) dwarf, runt

escaramujo SM 1 (= *planta*) wild rose, briar; (= *fruto*) hip, rosehip 2 (*Zool*) goose barnacle

escaramuza SF 1 (*Mil*) skirmish, brush 2 (= *enfrentamiento*) brush

escarapela SF rosette

escarapelarse /1a/ VPR (*And, Méx*) to go weak at the knees, tremble all over

escarbadientes SM INV toothpick

escarbar /1a/ Ⓐ VT 1 (= *remover*) [+ *tierra*] to scratch; [+ *fuego*] to poke; [+ *dientes*] to pick 2 (= *investigar*) to investigate, delve into; (= *curiosear*) to pry into Ⓑ VI 1 (*buscando*) to scratch 2 **~ en = A2**

escarceo SM, **escarceos** SMPL amateur effort; **en mis ~s con la política** in my occasional dealings with politics ➤ **escarceos amorosos** romantic flings, love affairs

escarcha SF frost

escarchado ADJ [*fruta*] crystallized

escarchar /1a/ Ⓐ VT [+ *tarta*] to ice; [+ *fruta*] to crystallize Ⓑ VI **escarcha** it's frosty, it's freezing

escardar /1a/ VT to weed, weed out

escarlata ADJ INV, SM scarlet

escarlatina SF scarlet fever

escarmentado ADJ wary, cautious; **estoy escarmentada** I've learned my lesson

escarmentar /1j/ Ⓐ VT to teach a lesson to Ⓑ VI to learn one's lesson; **¡para que escarmientes!** that'll teach you!; **no escarmientan** they never learn

escarmiento SM (= *castigo*) punishment; (= *aviso*) lesson, warning; **que esto te sirva de ~** let this be a lesson *o* warning to you

escarnecer /2d/ VT to scoff at, mock

escarnio SM (= *insulto*) jibe, taunt; (= *burla*) ridicule; **para mayor ~** to add insult to injury

escarola SF curly endive, escarole (*EEUU*)

escarpa SF 1 (= *cuesta*) slope; (*Geog, Mil*) scarp, escarpment 2 (*Méx*) (= *acera*) pavement (*Brit*), sidewalk (*EEUU*)

escarpado ADJ steep, sheer

escarpia SF hook

escasamente ADV 1 (= *insuficientemente*) scantily, sparingly 2 (= *apenas*) scarcely, hardly

escasear /1a/ VI to be scarce

escasez SF 1 (= *insuficiencia*) shortage, scarcity (*más frm*); **~ de mano de obra/viviendas** labour/housing shortage 2 (= *pobreza*) poverty; **han pasado muchas escaseces** they suffered great hardships

escaso ADJ 1 (= *limitado*) [*posibilidades*] slim; [*visibilidad*] poor; [*interés*] limited; **el recital tuvo ~ público** the recital was poorly *o* sparsely attended; **un motor de escasa potencia** a not very powerful engine; **iba a escasa distancia del otro coche** he was a short distance behind the other car

2 **~ de algo** short of sth

3 (= *muy justo*) **hay dos toneladas escasas** there are barely *o* scarcely two tons; **duró una hora escasa** it lasted barely *o* scarcely an hour; **ganar por una cabeza escasa** to win by a short head

escatimar /1a/ VT to skimp, be sparing with, stint; **no ~ esfuerzos (para)** to spare no effort (to); **no ~ gastos** to spare no expense

escatológico ADJ 1 (= *de los excrementos*) scatological 2 (*Fil, Rel*) eschatological

escay SM imitation leather

escayola SF (*Esp*) 1 (*Arte*) plaster of Paris 2 (*Constr*) plaster (of Paris) 3 (*Med*) (= *material*) plaster; (= *férula*) plaster cast, cast

escayolar /1a/ VT (*Esp*) to put in a (plaster) cast

escena SF 1 (= *escenario*) stage; **entrar en ~** ◇ **salir a ~** to come on stage, go on stage; **poner en ~** to stage 2 (= *parte de obra, película*) scene ➤ **escena retrospectiva** flashback 3 (= *suceso*) scene; **presenciamos ~s terribles** we witnessed terrible scenes; **hacer o montar una ~** to make a scene 4 (= *ámbito*) scene; **la ~ internacional** the international scene 5 **la ~** (= *el teatro*) the stage

escenario SM 1 (*Teat*) stage 2 (*Cine*) setting 3 (*uso figurado*) scene; **el ~ del crimen** the scene of the crime; **la ceremonia tuvo por ~ el auditorio** the ceremony took place in the auditorium

escénico ADJ stage *antes de s*

escenificar /1g/ VT [+ *comedia*] to stage; [+ *novela*] to dramatize, make a stage version of; [+ *suceso histórico*] to re-enact, reproduce

escenografía SF scenography, stage design

escenógrafo/a SM/F stage designer

escepticismo SM scepticism, skepticism (*EEUU*)

escéptico/a Ⓐ ADJ sceptical, skeptical (*EEUU*) Ⓑ SM/F sceptic, skeptic (*EEUU*)

escindir /3a/ Ⓐ VT to split, divide Ⓑ **escindirse** VPR (= *dividirse*) to split, divide (**en** into); [*facción*] to split off

escisión SF 1 (= *división*) split, division; **la ~ del partido** the split in the party 2 (*Med*) excision (*frm*), surgical removal

esclarecer /2d/ VT [+ *duda*] to explain, clear up, elucidate; [+ *misterio*] to shed light on; [+ *crimen*] to clear up; [+ *situación*] to clarify

esclarecido ADJ illustrious, distinguished

esclarecimiento SM explanation, elucidation, clarification

esclava SF bangle, bracelet; *ver tb* **esclavo**

esclavina SF short cloak, cape

esclavitud SF slavery

esclavizar /1f/ VT to enslave

esclavo/a SM/F slave; **ser ~ del tabaco** to be a slave to tobacco; *ver tb* **esclava**

esclerosis SF INV 1 (*Med*) sclerosis ➤ **esclerosis múltiple** multiple sclerosis 2 (= *fosilización*) fossilization, stagnation

esclerotizado ADJ fossilized, stagnant

esclusa SF (= *cierre*) lock, sluice; (= *compuerta*) floodgate ➤ **esclusa de aire** airlock

escoba SF 1 (*para barrer*) broom, brush; **pasar la ~** to sweep up 2 (*Bot*) broom

escobazo SM blow with a broom; **echar a algn a ~s** to kick sb out

escobilla SF 1 (= *cepillo*) brush; [*de wáter*] toilet brush ➤ **escobilla de dientes** (*And*) toothbrush 2 [*de limpiaparabrisas*] windscreen wiper (*Brit*), windshield wiper (*EEUU*)

escocer /2b, 2h/ VI to sting, smart; **me escuece el labio/la herida** my lip/the cut stings *o* is smarting

escocés/esa Ⓐ ADJ [*persona*] Scottish, Scots; [*whisky*] Scotch; **falda escocesa** kilt; **tela escocesa** tartan, plaid Ⓑ SM/F (= *persona*) Scot, Scotsman/Scotswoman; **los escoceses** the Scots Ⓒ SM 1 (*Ling*) Scots 2 (= *whisky*) Scotch

Escocia SF Scotland

escocido ADJ **el niño está ~** *o* **tiene el culito ~** the baby has nappy (*Brit*) *o* diaper rash (*EEUU*)

escoger /2c/ **A** VT to choose, pick; (*por votación*) to elect; **escogió los mejores vinos para la cena** he picked out *o* chose *o* selected the best wines to go with the meal **B** VI to choose; **no hay mucho donde ~** there isn't much to choose from, there isn't much choice; **hay que ~ entre los dos** you must choose between the two

escogido ADJ [*mercancías*] choice, select; [*obras*] selected

escolar A ADJ [*edad, vacaciones*] school *antes de s*; **año** *o* **curso ~** school year **B** SMF schoolboy/schoolgirl, schoolchild

escolaridad SF schooling, education

escolarizar /1f/ VT to provide with schooling, educate; **niños sin ~** children not in school, children receiving no schooling *o* education

escolástica SF scholasticism

escolástico ADJ scholastic

escoleta SF (*Méx*) **1** (= *banda*) amateur band **2** (= *ensayo*) rehearsal, practice **3** (= *lección de baile*) dancing lesson

escollar /1a/ VI (*CS Náut*) to hit a reef, strike a rock

escollo SM **1** (= *arrecife*) reef, rock **2** (= *obstáculo*) pitfall, stumbling block

escolta A SMF (= *acompañante*) escort; (= *guardaespaldas*) bodyguard; [*de ministro*] minder* **B** SF escort; **dar ~ a** to escort, accompany

escoltar /1a/ VT (*gen*) to escort; (*dando protección*) to guard, protect

escombrar /1a/ VT to clear out, clean out

escombrera SF **1** (= *vertedero*) dump, tip (*Brit*) **2** (*Min*) slag heap

escombros SMPL debris *sing*, rubble *sing*

esconder /2a/ **A** VT to hide, conceal (**de** from) **B esconderse** VPR (= *ocultarse*) to hide, hide o.s., conceal o.s.; (= *estar escondido*) to be hidden, lurk

escondidas SFPL **1 a ~** secretly, by stealth; **hacer algo a ~ de algn** to do sth behind sb's back **2** (*LAm*) hide-and-seek; **jugar a las escondida(s)** to play hide-and-seek

escondite SM **1** (= *escondrijo*) hiding place **2** (= *juego*) hide-and-seek

escondrijo SM (= *escondite*) hiding place, hideout; (= *rincón poco visible*) nook

escoñar** /1a/ (*Esp*) **A** VT to smash up, break, shatter **B escoñarse** VPR **1** [*persona*] to hurt o.s.; **estoy escoñado** I'm knackered* **2** [*máquina*] to break, get broken

escopeta SF shotgun ➤ **escopeta de aire comprimido** air gun, air rifle ➤ **escopeta de cañones recortados** sawn-off shotgun (*Brit*), sawed-off shotgun (*EEUU*) ➤ **escopeta de perdigones** shotgun

escopetado* ADJ **salir ~** to be off like a shot

escoplo SM chisel

escora SF (*Náut*) **1** (= *línea*) level line, load line **2** (= *apoyo*) prop, shore **3** (= *inclinación*) list

escorar /1a/ **A** VT (*Náut*) to shore up **B** VI **1** (*Náut*) to list, heel, heel over **2** (= *inclinarse*) **~ a** *o* **hacia** to lean towards, be inclined towards

escorbuto SM scurvy

escoria SF **1** [*de alto horno*] slag, dross **2** (= *lo más miserable*) scum, dregs *pl*; **la ~ de la humanidad** the scum *o* dregs of humanity

Escorpio SM (= *signo*) Scorpio

escorpio SMF INV (= *persona*) Scorpio; **soy ~** I'm Scorpio

escorpión SM scorpion

escorzo SM foreshortening

escotado ADJ **1** [*vestido*] low-cut **2** (*RPl*) [*zapato*] strapless

escotar /1a/ **A** VT [+ *vestido*] to cut low in front; [+ *cuello*] to cut low **B** VI (= *pagar su parte*) to pay one's share, chip in

escote SM **1** [*de vestido*] neck, neckline; **✦** MODISMO **ir** *o* **pagar a ~** (*entre varios*) to share the expenses; (*entre dos*) to go Dutch, go fifty-fifty ➤ **escote a la caja** round neck ➤ **escote en pico** V-neck **2** [*de mujer*] cleavage

escotilla SF hatchway, hatch

escozor SM stinging, burning

escribanía SF (*RPl*) (= *notaría*) notary's office

escribano/a SM/F (*RPl*) notary (public)

escribiente SMF clerk

escribir /3a/ (*pp* **escrito**) **A** VT, VI **1** [+ *palabra, texto*] to write; **~ a mano** to write in longhand; **~ a máquina** to type **2** (*en ortografía*) to spell; **¿cómo se escribe eso?** how is that spelled?, how do you spell that? **3** [+ *música*] to compose, write **B** VI to write **C escribirse** VPR [*dos personas*] to write to each other, correspond; **~se con algn** to correspond with sb, write to sb

escrito A PP *de* **escribir B** ADJ written, in writing; **examen ~** written exam **C** SM **1** (= *texto*) writing; (= *documento*) document; **por ~** in writing **2 escritos** (*Literat*) writings, works

escritor(a) SM/F writer

escritorio SM (= *mueble*) desk, bureau; (= *despacho*) office; **de ~** desk *antes de s* ➤ **escritorio público** (*Méx*) *stall or kiosk offering help writing letters and filling in forms*

escritura SF **1** (= *sistema de comunicación*) writing; [*de individuo*] writing, handwriting **2 Sagrada Escritura** Scripture, Holy Scripture **3** (*Jur*) deed ➤ **escritura de propiedad** title deed

escriturar /1a/ VT [+ *documentos*] to formalize legally; [+ *propiedad, casa*] to register (legally)

escrofuloso ADJ scrofulous

escroto SM scrotum

escrúpulo SM **1** (= *recelo*) scruple; **sin ~** unscrupulous; **no tuvo ~s en hacerlo** he had no qualms about doing it

> Recuérdese que las preposiciones en inglés rigen gerundio y no infinitivo, de ahí **to have no qualms about doing sth**.

2 (*con la comida*) fussiness, pernicketiness; **me da ~ beber de ahí** I'm wary about drinking from there

escrupulosidad SF scrupulousness

escrupuloso ADJ **1** (= *minucioso*) (*al elegir algo*) particular; (*al hacer algo*) precise **2** (*con la comida*) fussy, pernickety, persnickety (*EEUU*) **3** (= *honesto*) scrupulous

escrutador(a) A ADJ [*mirada*] searching, penetrating **B** SM/F [*de votos*] returning officer, scrutineer

escrutar /1a/ VT **1** (= *examinar*) to scrutinize, examine **2** [+ *votos*] to count

escrutinio SM **1** (= *examen atento*) scrutiny, examination **2** [*de votos*] count, counting

escuadra SF **1** (= *instrumento*) (*para dibujar*) square; (*de carpintero*) carpenter's square; **a ~** square, at right angles **2** [*de hombres*] (*Mil*) squad; (*Náut*) squadron

escuadrilla SF (*Aer*) wing, squadron

escuadrón SM (*Mil, Aer*) squadron ➤ **escuadrón de la muerte** death squad, murder squad

escuálido ADJ skinny, scraggy

escucha A SF (= *acción*) listening; (*Radio*) monitoring; **rogamos que permanezcan a la ~** please stay tuned; **estar a la ~** to listen in ➤ **escuchas telefónicas** phone tapping, wire tapping (*EEUU*) **B** SMF **1** (*Mil*) scout **2** (*Radio*) monitor **3** (*LAm*) (= *oyente*) listener

escuchar /1a/ **A** VT **1** (*con atención*) [+ *música, palabras*] to listen to; [+ *consejo*] to listen to, pay attention to

> Recuérdese que el uso transitivo de **escuchar** se traduce siempre por **listen** más la preposición **to**.

2 (*esp LAm*) (= *oír*) to hear; **se escucha muy mal** (*Telec*) it's a very bad line *o* (*EEUU*) connection **B** VI to listen

escudar /1a/ **A** VT to shield **B escudarse** VPR to shield o.s.

escudería SF motor-racing team (*Brit*), auto-racing team (*EEUU*)

escudero SM squire

escudilla SF bowl, basin

escudo SM 1 [*de protección*] shield 2 (= *moneda*) escudo 3 ➤ **escudo de armas** coat of arms

escudriñar /1a/ VT to scrutinize

escuela SF 1 (= *colegio*) school; **ir a la ~** [*alumno, maestro*] to go to school; **fue a la ~ a hablar con el director** he went to the school to speak to the headmaster ➤ **escuela de primera enseñanza** primary school (*Brit*), elementary school (*EEUU*) ➤ **escuela infantil** nursery school ➤ **escuela primaria** primary school (*Brit*), elementary school (*EEUU*) ➤ **escuela secundaria** secondary school, high school (*EEUU*) 2 (= *centro de enseñanza*) (*gen*) school; (*Chi*) (= *facultad*) faculty, school ➤ **Escuela de Bellas Artes** art school, art college ➤ **escuela de comercio** business school, school of business studies ➤ **escuela de conductores** (*LAm*) driving school ➤ **escuela de enfermería** nursing college ➤ **escuela de manejo** (*Méx*) driving school ➤ **escuela militar** military academy ➤ **escuela naval** naval academy ➤ **escuela nocturna** night school ➤ **escuela normal** teacher training college ➤ **escuela taller** *vocational training centre* ➤ **escuela universitaria** *university college offering diploma rather than degree courses* 3 (*) (= *clases*) school; **mañana no hay** o **no tenemos ~** there's no school tomorrow 4 (= *formación*) experience; **es buen actor pero le falta ~** he's a good actor but he lacks experience; **la ~ de la vida** the university of life, the school of life 5 (= *movimiento*) school; **la ~ veneciana** the Venetian school; **un catedrático de la vieja ~** a professor of the old school; **un escritor que ha creado ~** a writer with a great following; ⇨ COLEGIO

escuerzo SM toad

escueto ADJ [*verdad*] plain, naked; [*estilo*] simple; [*explicación, presentación*] concise, succinct

escuincle/a* SM/F (*Méx*) child, kid*

esculcar /1g/ VT (*Col, Méx*) to search

esculpir /3a/ VT [+ *estatua, piedra*] to sculpt; [+ *madera*] to carve; [+ *inscripción*] to cut

esculque SM (*Méx*) search

escultor(a) SM/F sculptor/sculptress

escultórico ADJ sculptural

escultura SF sculpture, carving ➤ **escultura en madera** wood carving

escultural ADJ statuesque

escupidera SF 1 (*para escupir*) spittoon, cuspidor (*EEUU*) 2 (= *orinal*) chamber pot

escupir /3a/ Ⓐ VI to spit; **~ a algn** to spit at sb; **~ a la cara de algn** to spit in sb's face Ⓑ VT 1 [*persona*] [+ *sangre*] to spit; [+ *comida*] to spit out; [+ *palabra*] to spit, spit out 2 (= *arrojar*) [+ *llamas*] to belch out, spew 3 (*) (= *confesar*) to cough*, sing*

escupitajo* SM gob of spit

escurreplatos SM INV plate rack

escurridizo ADJ 1 [*superficie, objeto*] slippery; [*nudo*] running 2 [*carácter*] slippery; [*idea*] elusive

escurridor SM (= *escurreplatos*) plate rack; (= *colador*) colander

escurrir /3a/ Ⓐ VT [+ *ropa*] to wring, wring out; [+ *platos, líquido, botella*] to drain; [+ *verduras*] to strain Ⓑ VI [*líquido*] to drip Ⓒ **escurrirse** VPR 1 [*líquido*] to drip 2 (= *resbalarse*) [*objeto*] to slip, slide 3 [*comentario*] to slip out

esdrújulo ADJ proparoxytone (*frm*), *stressed on the antepenultimate syllable*

ese¹ SF name of the letter S; ✦ MODISMO **hacer ~s** [*carretera*] to zigzag, twist and turn; [*coche*] to zigzag; [*borracho*] to reel about

ese²/a ADJ DEM that; **esa casa** that house; **esos dibujos** those drawings; **no conozco al tío ese*** I don't know that guy*

ése/a PRON DEM 1 (*gen*) that one; **ése es el mío** that one is mine; **ésos/as** those, those ones; **prefiero ésos** I prefer

those ones; **ésos que te compré yo** the ones I bought you 2 (*en locuciones*) **¡no me vengas con ésas!** don't give me any more of that nonsense!; **y cosas de ésas** and suchlike; **ni por ésas** (= *de ningún modo*) on no account; (= *aun así*) even so

esencia SF 1 (= *base*) [*de teoría*] essence; [*de asunto, problema*] heart; **en ~** essentially, in essence 2 [*de perfume*] essence

esencial ADJ 1 (= *imprescindible*) essential; **es ~ traer ropa de abrigo** it's essential to bring warm clothing 2 (= *principal*) essential, main; **lo ~ es que ...** the main o essential o most important thing is to ... 3 [*aceite*] essential

esfera SF 1 (*Geog, Mat*) sphere ➤ **esfera terrestre** globe 2 (*Téc*) [*de reloj*] face 3 (= *campo*) sphere, field; **las altas ~s** the top authorities, the upper echelons ➤ **esfera de acción** scope, range ➤ **esfera de influencia** sphere of influence

esférico ADJ spherical

esfero* SM (*Col*), **esferográfico** SM (*Col*) ballpoint pen

esfinge SF sphinx

esfínter SM sphincter

esforzar /1f, 1l/ Ⓐ VT [*voz, vista*] to strain; **no esfuerces la vista** don't strain your eyes Ⓑ **esforzarse** VPR to exert o.s., make an effort; **hay que ~se más** you must try harder, you must make more effort; **~se en** o **por conseguir algo** to struggle o strive to achieve sth

esfuerzo SM effort; **sin ~** effortlessly, without strain; **hacer un ~** to make an effort

esfumar /1a/ Ⓐ VT (*Arte*) to tone down, soften Ⓑ **esfumarse** VPR 1 [*apoyo, esperanzas*] to fade away, melt away 2 [*persona*] to vanish, make o.s. scarce; **¡esfúmate!*** get lost!*

esfumino SM (*Arte*) stump

esgrima SF fencing

esgrimidor(a) SM/F (*Dep*) fencer

esgrimir /3a/ Ⓐ VT 1 [+ *espada*] to wield 2 [+ *argumento*] to use; **~ que** to argue that, maintain that Ⓑ VI to fence

esgrimista SMF (*LAm*) fencer

esguince SM sprain

eslabón SM link ➤ **eslabón perdido** missing link

eslabonar /1a/ VT to link, link together

eslálom SM, **eslalon** SM = **slalom**

eslavo/a Ⓐ ADJ Slav, Slavonic Ⓑ SM/F Slav Ⓒ SM (*Ling*) Slavonic

eslip SM (*pl* **~s**) = **slip**

eslogan SM (*pl* **~s**) slogan

eslora SF (*Náut*) length

eslovaco/a Ⓐ ADJ Slovak, Slovakian Ⓑ SM/F Slovak

Eslovaquia SF Slovakia

Eslovenia SF Slovenia

esloveno/a ADJ, SM/F Slovene, Slovenian

esmaltar /1a/ VT [+ *metal*] to enamel; [+ *cerámica, porcelana*] to glaze; [+ *uñas*] to varnish, paint

esmalte SM (*para metal, diente*) enamel; (*para cerámica, porcelana*) glaze ➤ **esmalte de uñas** nail polish, nail varnish (*Brit*)

esmerado ADJ 1 [*trabajo*] careful, neat 2 [*persona*] careful, painstaking

esmeralda SF emerald

esmerarse /1a/ VPR 1 (= *aplicarse*) to take great pains (**en** over); **no se esmera nada en su trabajo** she doesn't take any care over her work; **~ en hacer algo** to take great pains to do sth 2 (= *hacer lo mejor*) to do one's best

esmeril SM emery

esmerilar /1a/ VT to polish with emery

esmero SM 1 (= *cuidado*) care, carefulness; **poner ~ en algo** to take great care o trouble o pains over sth 2 (= *aseo*) neatness

esmirriado ADJ puny

esmoquin SM dinner jacket (*Brit*), tuxedo (*EEUU*)

esnifar* /1a/ VT [+ *cola*] to sniff; [+ *cocaína*] to snort*

esnob Ⓐ ADJ INV [*persona*] snobbish, stuck-up* Ⓑ SMF (*pl* **~s** [ez'noβ]) snob

esnobismo SM snobbery, snobbishness

ESO SF ABR (*Esp*) (= **Enseñanza Secundaria obligatoria**) *compulsory secondary education for 12- to 16-year-olds*

eso PRON DEM that; **¿qué es ~?** what's that?; **¿es verdad ~ que me han contado?** is it true what I've been told?; **¿qué es ~ de que ...?** what's all this about ...?; **¡eso!** that's right!; **~ es** that's it, that's right; **el coche es viejo, ~ sí** the car is certainly old; **~ digo yo** (*indicando acuerdo*) I quite agree; (*respondiendo a pregunta*) that's what I'd like to know; **¡~ no!** ◊ **¡~ sí que no!** no way!; **~ espero** I hope so; **a ~ de las dos** at about two o'clock, round about two; **nada de ~** nothing of the kind, far from it; **¿no es ~?** isn't that so?; **por ~** therefore, and so; **por ~ no vine** that's why I didn't come; **no es por ~** that's not the reason, that's not why, it's not because of that; **¿y ~?** why?, how so?*; **y ~ que llovía** in spite of the fact that it was raining

esófago SM oesophagus (*frm*), esophagus (*EEUU frm*), gullet

esotérico ADJ esoteric

esoterismo SM esotericism

espabilado *ver* **despabilado**

espabilar /1a/ *ver* **despabilar**

espachurrar /1a/ Ⓐ VT to squash, flatten Ⓑ **espachurrarse** VPR to get squashed, get flattened

espaciador SM space bar

espacial ADJ INV 1 (*Aer*) space *antes de s*; **viajes ~es** space travel 2 (*Mat*) spatial

espaciar /1b/ VT 1 [+ *palabras, párrafos*] to space, space out 2 (*en el tiempo*) [+ *noticia*] to spread; [+ *pagos*] to spread out, stagger; **empezó a ~ más sus visitas** his visits became less frequent, there were longer intervals between his visits

espacio SM 1 (*Astron, Fís, Aer*) space; **viajar por el ~** to travel in space ➤ **espacio aéreo** air space ➤ **espacio exterior** outer space ➤ **espacio sideral** outer space 2 (= *sitio*) room, space; **ocupa mucho ~** it takes up a lot of room ➤ **espacio libre** room ➤ **espacio muerto** clearance 3 (= *superficie*) space; **espacios verdes** green spaces 4 (*en un escrito*) space; **un texto mecanografiado a un ~/a doble ~** a single-spaced/double-spaced typescript ➤ **espacio en blanco** blank space 5 [*de tiempo*] space; **en el ~ de una hora** in the space of an hour; **por ~ de** for 6 (*Radio, TV*) (*en la programación*) slot; (= *programa*) programme, program (*EEUU*) ➤ **espacio electoral** party political broadcast (*Brit*), political party advertisement (*EEUU*) ➤ **espacio informativo** news programme ➤ **espacio publicitario** advertising spot, commercial 7 (*Mús*) interval

espacioso ADJ 1 [*cuarto, casa*] spacious, roomy 2 [*movimiento*] slow, deliberate

espada Ⓐ SF 1 (= *arma*) sword; ✦ MODISMO **estar entre la ~ y la pared** to be between the devil and the deep blue sea 2 **espadas** (*Naipes*) one of the suits in the Spanish card deck, *represented by a sword*; ◇ *BARAJA ESPAÑOLA* Ⓑ SMF (*Taur*) matador, bullfighter

⚠ **espada ≠ spade**

espadachín SM skilled swordsman

espadaña SF bulrush

espadín SM 1 (= *espada pequeña*) dress sword, ceremonial sword 2 [*de espadachín*] picklock 3 **espadines** (= *pez*) sprats

espaguetis SMPL spaghetti *sing*

espalda Ⓐ SF 1 (*Anat*) back; **de ~s a algo** with one's back to sth; **atar las manos a la ~** to tie sb's hands behind his back; **caer de ~s** to fall on one's back; **estar de ~s** to have

one's back turned; **volver la ~ a algn** to cold-shoulder sb, turn one's back on sb; **volverse de ~s** to turn one's back; ✦ MODISMOS **cubrirse las ~s** to cover o.s., cover one's own back; **dar la ~ a algo/algn** to turn away from sth/sb, face away from sth/sb; **echarse algo sobre las ~s** to take sth on, take charge of sth; **hacer algo a ~s de algn** to do sth behind sb's back; **tener las ~s cubiertas** to make sure, be on the safe side 2 (*Dep*) backstroke; **la prueba de 200 metros ~s** the 200 metres *o* (*EEUU*) meters backstroke Ⓑ SMF ➤ **espalda mojada** (*Méx**) wetback

espaldar SM 1 (*de silla*) back 2 **espaldares** (*Dep*) wall bars

espaldarazo SM recognition; **ese concierto supuso su ~ definitivo** that concert finally earned him recognition

espaldera SF 1 (*para plantas*) trellis, espalier 2 (*para la espalda*) surgical corset 3 **espalderas** (*Dep*) wall bars

espaldilla SF shoulder blade

espantada SF stampede; **dar la ~** to bolt

espantadizo ADJ timid, easily scared

espantado ADJ frightened, scared; **me quedé espantada cuando lo vi con esos pelos** I was horrified when I saw him with that hair

espantajo SM 1 (= *espantapájaros*) scarecrow 2 (= *persona*) sight*, fright*

espantapájaros SM INV scarecrow

espantar /1a/ Ⓐ VT 1 (= *asustar*) (*gen*) to frighten, scare; (*haciendo huir*) to frighten off *o* away, scare off *o* away; **espantó a los perros con una escoba** she frightened the dogs off *o* away with a broom; **con ese genio espanta a todas las chicas** with that temper of his he frightens *o* scares all the girls (off *o* away) 2 (= *horrorizar*) to horrify, appal; **le espantaba la idea de tener que ir solo** he was horrified *o* appalled at the thought of having to go on his own Ⓑ VI (*And, Ven*) **ahí espantan** that place is haunted Ⓒ **espantarse** VPR 1 (= *asustarse*) to get frightened, get scared 2 (= *horrorizarse*) to be horrified, be appalled

espanto SM 1 (= *susto*) fright 2 (*And, Ven*) (= *fantasma*) ghost 3 (*) (*para exagerar*) **¡qué ~!** how awful!; **hace un frío de ~** it's terribly cold

espantoso ADJ 1 (= *aterrador*) frightening 2 (*para exagerar*) **hizo un frío ~** it was absolutely freezing; **llevaba un traje ~** she was wearing an awful *o* a hideous *o* a frightful *o* ghastly* hat; **había un ruido ~** there was a terrible *o* dreadful noise

España SF Spain; **la ~ de charanga y pandereta** touristy Spain; *see also* www.la-moncloa.es

español(a) Ⓐ ADJ Spanish Ⓑ SM/F Spaniard; **los ~es** the Spaniards, the Spanish Ⓒ SM (*Ling*) Spanish; ◇ *CASTELLANO*

españolada SF (*pey*) film, show etc giving a clichéd, stereotypical image of Spain

españolista Ⓐ ADJ centralist, unionist (*as opposed to regionalist*) Ⓑ SMF pro-centralist

esparadrapo SM (sticking) plaster (*Brit*), Band-Aid® (*EEUU*)

esparcimiento SM 1 (= *dispersión*) spreading 2 (= *descanso*) relaxation 3 (= *diversión*) amusement

esparcir /3b/ Ⓐ VT 1 (= *desparramar*) to spread, scatter 2 (= *divulgar*) to disseminate 3 (= *distraer*) to amuse, divert Ⓑ **esparcirse** VPR 1 (= *desparramarse*) to spread, spread out, scatter 2 (= *descansar*) to relax 3 (= *divertirse*) to amuse o.s.

espárrago SM asparagus; ✦ MODISMOS **estar hecho un ~** to be as thin as a rake *o* (*EEUU*) rail; **mandar a algn a freír ~s** to tell sb to get lost*; **¡vete a freír ~s!** get lost!, go jump in a lake!*, get stuffed!** ➤ **espárrago triguero** wild asparagus

espartano ADJ spartan

esparto SM esparto, esparto grass

espasmo SM spasm

espasmódico ADJ spasmodic

espástico/a ADJ, SM/F spastic

espatarrarse* /1a/ VPR to sprawl

espátula SF **1** (*Constr*) scraper; ✦ MODISMO **estar hecho una ~** to be as thin as a rake *o* (*EEUU*) rail **2** (*Arte*) palette knife **3** (*Culin*) spatula, fish slice (*Brit*) **4** (*Med*) spatula

especia SF spice

especiado ADJ spiced, spicy

especial Ⓐ ADJ **1** (*para un fin concreto*) [*dieta, permiso*] special

2 (= *extraordinario*) special; **un saludo muy ~ para nuestros compañeros** a special hello to all our colleagues

3 en ~ especially, particularly; **¿desea ver a alguien en ~?** is there anybody in particular you want to see?

4 (= *quisquilloso*) fussy; **¡qué ~ eres con la comida!** you're such a fussy eater!

5 (= *extraño*) peculiar; **le encuentro un sabor muy ~ a este café** this coffee has a very peculiar flavour

Ⓑ SM **1** (*TV*) (*tb* **programa ~**) special ➤ **especial informativo** news special

2 (*para comer*) (*RPl*) baguette, submarine sandwich (*EEUU*); (*Chi*) hot dog

especialidad SF **1** (= *ramo*) speciality

> En inglés americano se usa **specialty** en lugar de **speciality**.

ha elegido la ~ de cirugía he has chosen to specialize in surgery, he has chosen surgery as his speciality; **hizo dos años de ~** he did a two year specialization; **la jardinería no es precisamente mi ~** gardening is not exactly my speciality *o* strong point **2** (*Culin*) speciality; **"especialidad de la casa"** "speciality of the house"

especialista Ⓐ ADJ [*técnico, enfermera*] specialist; **un delantero ~ en tiros libres** a forward who specializes in free kicks; **médico ~** specialist Ⓑ SMF **1** (*en estudio, profesión*) specialist, expert; **es el máximo ~ en biología marina** he is the top authority on marine biology **2** (*Med, Dep*) specialist; **~ de la piel** skin specialist **3** (*Cine, TV*) stuntman/stuntwoman

especializado ADJ **1** [*personal, público*] specialized; **un artículo destinado al lector no ~** an article aimed at the general reader; **una cadena especializada en programas culturales** a channel specializing in cultural programmes **2** [*obrero*] skilled, trained **3** [*lenguaje*] technical, specialized

especializarse /1f/ VPR to specialize (**en** in)

especialmente ADV **1** (= *sobre todo*) especially, particularly **2** (= *para un fin concreto*) specially

> En inglés son posibles tanto **especially** como **specially**. En el sentido de "sobre todo" se utiliza más **especially**: "Vuelva a aplicar la crema con filtro solar cada dos horas, especialmente si ha estado en el agua", *Re-apply sunscreen every two hours, especially if you have been swimming*. **Specially** se utiliza hablando de una finalidad concreta: "Un jabón pensado especialmente para pieles sensibles", *A soap specially formulated for sensitive skins*.

especiar /1b/ VT to spice

especie SF **1** (*Biol*) species; **la ~ humana** the human race ➤ **especie protegida** protected species **2** (= *clase*) kind, sort; **una ~ de ...** a kind *o* sort of ... **3 en ~** in kind; **pagar en ~** to pay in kind

especificación SF specification

específicamente ADV specifically

especificar /1g/ VT [+ *cantidad, modelo*] to specify; (*en una lista*) to list, itemize

específico ADJ specific

espécimen SM (*pl* **especímenes**) specimen

espectacular ADJ spectacular

espectacularidad SF spectacular nature; **de gran ~** very spectacular

espectáculo SM **1** (*Teat*) (= *representación*) show; (= *función*) performance; **sección de ~s** entertainment guide, entertainments section; **el deporte como ~** sport presented as show business; ✦ MODISMO **dar un ~** to make

a scene **2** (= *visión asombrosa*) spectacle; **fue un ~ bochornoso** it was an embarrassing spectacle *o* sight

espectador(a) SM/F **1** (*Cine, Dep, Teat*) spectator; **los ~es** (*Dep*) the spectators; (*Teat*) the audience *sing* **2** [*de acontecimiento, accidente*] onlooker

espectral ADJ **1** (*Fís*) spectral **2** (= *fantasmagórico*) ghostly

espectro SM **1** (*Fís*) spectrum; **de amplio ~** wide-ranging, covering a broad spectrum **2** (= *fantasma*) spectre, specter (*EEUU*), ghost; **el ~ del hambre** the spectre *o* (*EEUU*) specter of famine

especulación SF **1** (= *suposición*) speculation **2** (*Com, Fin*) speculation

especulador(a) SM/F speculator

especular /1a/ VI **1** (= *hacer cábalas*) to speculate (**sobre** about, on) **2** (*Com, Fin*) to speculate (**en, con** with)

especulativo ADJ speculative

espéculo SM (*Med*) speculum

espejismo SM **1** (*Ópt*) mirage **2** (= *ilusión*) mirage, illusion

espejo SM mirror ➤ **espejo retrovisor** rear-view mirror

espeleología SF potholing (*Brit*), spelunking (*EEUU*), speleology (*frm*)

espeleólogo/a SM/F potholer (*Brit*), spelunker (*EEUU*), speleologist (*frm*)

espeluznante ADJ hair-raising, horrifying

espera SF wait; **tras una ~ de tres horas** after a three-hour wait; **en ~ de su contestación** awaiting your reply; **en ~ de que llegue** waiting for him to arrive; **estar a la ~ de algo** to be expecting sth

esperanto SM Esperanto

esperanza SF hope; **hay pocas ~s de que venga** there is little hope that he'll come; **con la ~ de que ...** in the hope that ...; **dar ~(s) a algn** to give sb hope; **tener ~(s) de hacer algo** to have hope(s) of doing sth ✦ MODISMO **¡qué ~!** (*LAm*) some hope!, not on your life!*; ✦ REFRÁN **la ~ es lo último que se pierde** there's always hope ➤ **esperanza de vida** life expectancy

esperanzado ADJ hopeful

esperanzador ADJ [*perspectiva*] hopeful; [*noticia, resultado*] encouraging, hopeful, promising

esperanzar /1f/ VT **~ a algn** to give hope to sb; **no quisieron ~lo** they did not want to raise his hopes *o* get his hopes up

esperar /1a/ Ⓐ VT **1** (= *aguardar*) [+ *tren, persona*] to wait for; **esperaban noticias de los rehenes** they were waiting for *o* awaiting news of the hostages; **fuimos a ~la a la estación** we went to meet her at the station; **nos espera un duro invierno** we've got a hard winter ahead of us; **¡la que te espera cuando llegues a casa!** you're (in) for it when you get home!; ✦ MODISMO **de aquí te espero***: **un lío de aquí te espero*** a tremendous row*

2 (= *desear*) to hope; **espero llegar a tiempo** I hope to arrive on time; **eso espero** I hope so; **espero que vengas** I hope you'll come; **espero que no sea nada grave** I hope it isn't anything serious; **espero que no** I hope not; **es de ~ que ...** it is to be hoped that ...

3 (= *contar con*) to expect; **¿esperas visita?** are you expecting someone?; **no me esperes antes de las siete** don't expect me before seven; **¿acaso esperas que pague yo?** you're not expecting me to pay, are you?; **llegaron antes de lo que yo esperaba** they arrived sooner than I expected; **¿qué puedes ~ de él?** what do you expect from him?; **era de ~** it was to be expected; **no esperaba menos de ti** I expected nothing *o* no less of you; **cuando menos te lo esperes** when you least expect it; ✦ MODISMO **~ algo como agua de mayo** to await sth with eager anticipation

4 [+ *bebé*] to expect

Ⓑ VI to wait; **~é aquí** I'll wait here; **¡espera un momento, éste no es mi libro!** hold on *o* wait a minute, this isn't my book!; **~ a** *o* **hasta que algn haga algo** to wait for sb to do sth; **hacer ~ a algn** keep sb waiting; **su respuesta no se hizo ~** his answer wasn't long in coming; ✦ MODISMO **puedes ~ sentado** you've got another think coming; ✦ REFRÁN **el que espera desespera** a watched pot never boils

Ⓒ **esperarse** VPR **1** (*uso impersonal*) to be expected; **no fue**

tan bueno como se esperaba it was not as good as expected
2 (*) (= *uso enfático*) **espérate a que deje de llover** wait until it stops raining; **¡me lo esperaba!** I was expecting this!

esperma SM o SF **1** (*Biol*) sperm; **~ de ballena** spermaceti **2** (*Carib, Col*) (= *vela*) candle

espermatozoide SM, **espermatozoo** SM spermatozoon

espermicida SM spermicide

esperpéntico ADJ grotesque, exaggerated

esperpento SM **1** (= *persona fea*) fright*, sight* **2** (*Teat*) *play which focuses on the grotesque*

ESPERPENTO

Esperpento is a type of theatre developed by Ramón del Valle-Inclán (1869-1936) focusing on characters whose physical and psychological characteristics have been deliberately deformed to the point where they become grotesque caricatures. Valle-Inclán used this **esperpento** as a vehicle for social and political satire.

espesar /1a/ **Ⓐ** VT [+ *líquido, chocolate*] to thicken
Ⓑ espesarse VPR [*líquido*] to thicken, get thicker; [*bosque, niebla, humo*] to get denser, get thicker; [*sangre*] to coagulate, solidify

espeso ADJ (*gen*) thick; [*bosque*] dense

espesor SM (*gen*) thickness; [*de nieve*] depth; **tiene medio metro de ~** it is half a metre thick

espesura SF **en la ~ de la selva** in the thick o heart o depths of the jungle

espetar /1a/ VT **1** [+ *carne*] to skewer, spit **2** [+ *orden*] to rap out; [+ *lección, sermón*] to read; [+ *pregunta*] to fire; **~ algo a algn** to spring sth on sb

espía **Ⓐ** SMF spy **Ⓑ** ADJ INV **satélite ~** spy satellite

espiar /1c/ **Ⓐ** VT to spy on **Ⓑ** VI to spy

espichar /1a/ **Ⓐ** VT **1 ✦** MODISMO **~la(s)** (*Esp***) to kick the bucket**, peg out**
2 (*Col**) (= *apretar*) [+ *botón*] to press; [+ *tubo*] to squeeze; **me ~on en el tren, iba muy lleno** the train was very full, it was a terrible squash o squeeze
3 (*Col**) (= *atropellar*) to run over
4 (*Col, Ven**) [+ *grano, piel*] to squeeze
5 (*Col, Ven**) (= *aplastar*) to squash; **le espichó un huevo en la cabeza** she broke an egg over his head
Ⓑ espicharse VPR **1** (*Méx*) (= *enflaquecer*) to get thin
2 (*Ven*) [*neumático*] to go flat
3 (*Col, Ven*) (= *aplastarse*) to get squashed
4 (*CAm*) (= *asustarse*) to get scared, get frightened

espiga SF [*de trigo*] ear; [*de flores*] spike

espigado ADJ **1** (*Bot*) (= *maduro*) ripe; (= *con grano*) ready to seed **2** [*persona*] tall and slim, willowy

espigador(a) SM/F gleaner

espigar /1h/ **Ⓐ** VI **1** [*cereales*] to come into ear, form ears; [*flor*] to run to seed **2 = B Ⓑ espigarse** VPR [*persona*] to shoot up

espigón SM **1** (*Bot*) ear **2** (= *malecón*) breakwater **3** (*Perú*) (*en aeropuerto*) terminal

espiguilla SF herring-bone pattern

espina SF **1** (*Bot*) [*de rosal*] thorn; [*de chumbera*] prickle; **✦** MODISMOS **mala ~** spite, resentment, ill-will; **me da mala ~** it makes me suspicious; **sacarse la ~** to get even, pay off an old score **2** [*de pez*] bone **3** (*Anat*) (*tb* **~ dorsal**) spine **➤ espina bífida** spina bifida **4** (= *problema*) worry, suspicion

espinaca SF (*Bot*) spinach; **~s** (*Culin*) spinach *pl*

espinal ADJ spinal

espinazo SM spine, backbone; **✦** MODISMO **doblar el ~*** to knuckle under*

espinilla SF **1** (= *tibia*) shin **2** (*en la piel*) (= *punto negro*) blackhead; (= *grano*) spot, pimple, zit (*esp EEUU*)

espinillera SF shin pad, shinguard

espino SM **➤ espino albar, espino blanco** hawthorn **➤ espino negro** blackthorn, sloe

espinoso ADJ **1** [*rosal*] thorny; [*chumbera*] prickly **2** [*problema*] knotty, thorny

espinudo ADJ (*Chi*) = **espinoso**

espionaje SM espionage, spying; **novela de ~** spy story **➤ espionaje industrial** industrial espionage

espiral **Ⓐ** ADJ spiral **Ⓑ** SM [*de reloj*] hairspring **Ⓒ** SF spiral; **la ~ inflacionista** the inflationary spiral; **el humo subía en ~** the smoke went spiralling o (*EEUU*) spiraling up; **dar vueltas en ~** to spiral

espirar /1a/ VT, VI to breathe out, exhale

espiritismo SM spiritualism

espiritista SMF spiritualist

espíritu SM **1** (= *lo inmaterial*) spirit **➤ espíritu de cuerpo** esprit de corps **➤ espíritu de equipo** team spirit **2** (*Rel*) spirit **➤ Espíritu Santo** Holy Ghost, Holy Spirit **3** (= *aparecido*) spirit, ghost **➤ espíritu maligno** evil spirit

espiritual **Ⓐ** ADJ spiritual **Ⓑ** SM spiritual, Negro spiritual

espiritualidad SF spirituality

espiritualismo SM spiritualism

espirituoso ADJ **licores ~s** spirits

espita SF tap (*Brit*), spigot (*EEUU*)

espitoso** ADJ (= *eufórico*) hyper*

espléndido ADJ **1** (= *magnífico*) splendid, magnificent **2** (*generoso*) lavish, generous

esplendor SM splendour, splendor (*EEUU*), magnificence

esplendoroso ADJ magnificent

espliego SM lavender

esplín SM melancholy, depression, the blues

espolear /1a/ VT **1** [+ *caballo*] to spur, spur on **2** (*para estudiar, ganar*) to spur on

espoleta SF **1** (*Mil*) fuse **2** (*Anat*) wishbone

espolón **Ⓐ** SM **1** [*de gallo*] spur **2** (*Geog*) spur **3** (= *malecón*) sea wall; [*de puente*] cutwater **4** (= *paseo*) promenade **Ⓑ** ADJ (*And**) (= *astuto*) sharp, astute

espolvorear /1a/ VT to dust, sprinkle (**de** with)

esponja SF (*para el aseo*) sponge; **✦** MODISMOS **beber como una ~ ✧ ser una ~** to drink like a fish

esponjado ADJ [*material*] spongy; [*toalla, jersey*] fluffy

esponjar /1a/ **Ⓐ** VT to fluff up, make fluffy
Ⓑ esponjarse VPR [*lana*] to fluff up, become fluffy; [*masa*] to rise

esponjoso ADJ (= *blando*) spongy; [*toalla, jersey*] fluffy

esponsales SMPL betrothal *sing*

espónsor SMF sponsor

esponsorizar /1f/ VT to sponsor

espontaneidad SF spontaneity

espontáneo/a **Ⓐ** ADJ **1** (= *sin reflexión*) spontaneous **2** (= *improvisado*) [*discurso, representación*] impromptu; [*persona*] natural **Ⓑ** SM/F (*Taur*) *spectator who rushes into the ring and attempts to take part*

espora SF spore

esporádico ADJ sporadic

esposar /1a/ VT to handcuff

esposas SFPL handcuffs; **poner las ~ a algn** to handcuff sb, put sb in handcuffs

esposo/a SM/F husband/wife; **los ~s** husband and wife, the couple

espray SM = **spray**

esprint [es'prin] SM (*pl* **~s** [es'prin]) sprint

esprínter SMF sprinter

espuela SF spur

espuelear* /1a/ VT (*LAm*) to spur, spur on

espuerta SF basket, pannier; **✦** MODISMO **a ~s** in vast quantities, by the ton

espulgar /1h/ VT to delouse, get the lice *o* fleas out of

espuma SF **1** (= *burbujas*) [*de las olas*] surf, foam; [*de jabón, champú*] foam, lather; [*de cerveza*] head; [*de cava, champán*] froth; [*del caldo*] scum; **echar ~** to foam, froth; **hacer ~** to foam, froth; ✦ MODISMO **crecer como la ~** to mushroom ➤ **espuma de afeitar** shaving foam ➤ **espuma seca** carpet shampoo **2** (= *gomaespuma*) foam, foam rubber; **un colchón de ~** a foam(-rubber) mattress **3** (= *tejido*) (*tb ~ de nylon*) stretch nylon

espumadera SF skimming ladle, skimmer

espumar /1a/ VT to skim off

espumarajo SM froth, foam; **echar ~s (de rabia)** to splutter with rage

espumillón SM tinsel

espumoso ADJ [*cerveza*] frothy; [*baño*] foaming; [*vino*] sparkling

espúreo ADJ, **espurio** ADJ spurious

esputar /1a/ VT to cough up, expectorate (*frm*)

esputo SM sputum

esqueje SM cutting

esquela SF **1** (*Esp*) (*tb ~ de defunción o mortuoria*) announcement of death, death notice **2** (*LAm*) (= *nota*) note **3** (*And*) (= *papel y sobres*) writing set

esquelético ADJ skeletal, skinny*

esqueleto SM **1** (*Anat*) skeleton; ✦ MODISMO **menear** *o* **mover el ~*** to strut one's stuff*, dance **2** [*de edificio, novela*] framework; **en ~** unfinished, incomplete **3** (*Méx*) (= *formulario*) form

esquema SM **1** (= *resumen*) outline; (= *diagrama*) diagram; (= *dibujo*) sketch **2** (= *conjunto de ideas*) thinking, way of thinking; **sus ~s mentales** his thinking *o* way of thinking; ✦ MODISMO **romper ~s** to break the mould

esquemático ADJ schematic; **un resumen ~** an outline

esquí SM (*pl ~s o ~es*) **1** (= *tabla*) ski **2** (= *deporte*) skiing; **hacer ~** to go skiing ➤ **esquí acuático** water skiing ➤ **esquí alpino** alpine skiing ➤ **esquí de fondo, esquí de travesía** cross-country skiing, ski touring (*EEUU*) ➤ **esquí náutico** water skiing

esquiador(a) SM/F skier

esquiar /1c/ VI to ski

esquijama SM winter pyjamas *pl o* (*EEUU*) pajamas *pl*;

esquila SF (= *campanilla*) small bell, handbell; (= *cencerro*) cowbell

esquilador(a) SM/F (= *persona*) (sheep) shearer

esquiladora SF (= *máquina*) shearing machine, clipping machine

esquilar /1a/ VT [+ *ovejas*] to shear; [+ *pelo*] to clip, crop

esquilmar /1a/ VT **1** [+ *tierra*] to impoverish, exhaust **2** (*) [+ *jugador*] to skin*

esquimal Ⓐ ADJ, SMF Eskimo Ⓑ SM (*Ling*) Eskimo

esquina SF **1** (= *vértice*) corner; **a la vuelta de la ~** (*lit*) around the corner; (*fig*) just around the corner; **doblar la ~** to turn the corner; **hacer ~** [*edificio*] to be on the corner; [*calles*] to meet **2** (*Dep*) corner

esquinado ADJ **1** (*Ftbl*) **tiro ~** low shot into the corner of the net **2** [*mueble*] standing in a corner, corner *antes de s*

esquinazo SM **1** (*Chi*) (= *serenata*) serenade **2** ✦ MODISMO **dar ~ a algn** to give sb the slip, shake sb off

esquinero ADJ corner *antes de s*

esquirla SF splinter

esquirol SMF strikebreaker, blackleg, scab*

esquites SMPL (*CAm, Méx*) popcorn *sing*

esquivar /1a/ VT to avoid, shun; (= *evadir*) to dodge, side-step

esquivo ADJ (= *tímido*) shy; (= *huraño*) unsociable; (= *difícil de encontrar*) elusive; (= *evasivo*) evasive

esquizofrenia SF schizophrenia

esquizofrénico/a ADJ, SM/F schizophrenic

esta ADJ DEM *ver* **este**

ésta PRON DEM *ver* **éste**

está *etc ver* **estar**

estabilidad SF stability

estabilizador SM (*gen*) stabilizer; (*Aut*) anti-roll bar

estabilizar /1f/ Ⓐ VT to stabilize Ⓑ **estabilizarse** VPR **1** [*objeto, precios*] to become stable, become stabilized **2** [*persona*] to settle down

estable ADJ **1** [*pareja, mercado, paz*] stable; [*relación*] stable, steady; [*empleo*] steady **2** (*Fís, Quím*) stable

establecer /2d/ Ⓐ VT **1** [+ *relación, comunicación*] to establish; [+ *precio*] to set, fix **2** (= *fundar*) [+ *empresa*] to establish; [+ *colonia*] to settle; **ha establecido su domicilio en Lugo** he's taken up residence in Lugo **3** (= *dictaminar*) to state, lay down; **la ley establece que ...** the law states *o* lays down that ... **4** (= *expresar*) [+ *idea, principio*] to establish; [+ *norma*] to lay down; [+ *criterio*] to set **5** [+ *récord*] to set Ⓑ **establecerse** VPR **1** (= *fijar residencia*) to settle **2** (= *abrir un negocio*) to set up (a business), open up (a business); **~se por cuenta propia** to set up on one's own

establecimiento SM **1** (= *acción*) establishment ➤ **establecimiento de llamada** minimum call charge **2** (= *local*) establishment ➤ **establecimiento comercial** business house, commercial establishment

establishment SM (*pl ~s*) establishment

establo SM stable

estaca SF (= *poste*) stake, post; [*de tienda de campaña*] peg; (= *porra*) cudgel, stick

estacada SF (*Mil*) stockade, palisade; ✦ MODISMO **dejar a algn en la ~** to leave sb in the lurch

estación SF **1** (= *lugar*) station ➤ **estación de autobuses** bus station ➤ **estación de bomberos** (*Col*) fire station ➤ **estación de esquí** ski resort ➤ **estación de ferrocarril** railway station ➤ **estación de policía** (*Col*) police station ➤ **estación depuradora** sewage works, sewage farm ➤ **estación de servicio** service station (*Brit*), petrol station (*Brit*), gas station (*EEUU*) ➤ **estación de trabajo** (*Inform*) workstation ➤ **estación termal** spa **2** (= *parte del año*) season **3** (*LAm*) (*tb ~ de radio*) radio station

estacional ADJ seasonal

estacionamiento SM **1** [*de soldados*] stationing **2** (*Aut*) (= *acción*) parking; (*esp LAm*) (= *sitio*) car park (*Brit*), parking lot (*EEUU*)

estacionar /1a/ Ⓐ VT **1** [+ *soldados*] to station, place **2** (*Aut*) to park Ⓑ **estacionarse** VPR (*gen*) to station o.s.; (*Aut*) to park; (= *no moverse*) to remain stationary; **la inflación/la fiebre se ha estacionado** inflation/the fever has stabilized

estacionario ADJ (*gen*) stationary; (*Med*) stable

estadía SF (*LAm*) stay

estadio SM **1** (= *fase*) stage, phase **2** (*Dep*) stadium **3** (*Mat*) furlong

estadista SMF **1** (*Pol*) statesman/stateswoman **2** (*Mat*) statistician

estadística SF (= *ciencia*) statistics *sing*; **una ~** a figure, a statistic

estadístico/a Ⓐ ADJ [*datos, cifras*] statistical Ⓑ SM/F (= *profesional*) statistician

estado SM **1** (= *situación*) **1.1** [*de objeto, proceso*] state; **estar en buen ~** [*instalación, alimentos*] to be in good condition; **estar en mal ~** [*instalación*] to be in (a) poor condition, be in a bad state; [*alimentos*] to be off; **el ordenador está en perfecto ~** the computer is working perfectly *o* is in perfect working order **1.2** [*de enfermo*] condition

➤ **estado civil** marital status ➤ **estado de alerta** state of alert ➤ **estado de ánimo** (*emocional*) mood; (*mental*) state of mind ➤ **estado de emergencia, estado de excepción** state of emergency ➤ **estado de gracia** [*de creyente*] state of grace; [*de político, gobierno*] honeymoon period; [*de deportista*] run of good form ➤ **estado de la red** (*Inform*)

volume of users ➤ **estado de salud** condition, state of health ➤ **estado de sitio** state of siege
2 (*Fís*) state ➤ **estado gaseoso** gaseous state ➤ **estado líquido** solid state ➤ **estado sólido** solid state
3 en ~ (= *embarazada*): **una mujer en ~** an expectant mother; **estar en ~** to be expecting; **en avanzado ~ de gestación** heavily pregnant, in an advanced state of pregnancy
4 (= *nación*) state; **el Estado español** Spain; **asuntos de ~** affairs of state, state affairs; **hombre de ~** statesman ➤ **estado de derecho** democracy ➤ **estado del bienestar** welfare state ➤ **estado policial** police state
5 (= *región administrativa*) state
6 (*Hist*) (= *clase*) estate
7 (*Mil*) ➤ **el Estado Mayor (General)** the (General) Staff
8 (*Com, Fin*) (= *informe*) report ➤ **estado de cuenta** bank statement, statement of account (*frm*) ➤ **estado de cuentas** [*de una empresa*] statement of account

estado-nación SM (*pl* **estados-nación**) nation state

Estados Unidos SMPL United States (of America)

A menudo se les llama simplemente **The States**.

estadounidense Ⓐ ADJ American, US *antes de s*, of/from the United States Ⓑ SMF American; **los ~s** the Americans

estafa SF swindle, trick

estafador(a) SM/F swindler, trickster

estafar /1a/ VT to swindle, defraud, twist*; **~ algo a algn** to swindle sb out of sth, defraud sb of sth; **¡me han estafado!** I've been done!*

estafeta Ⓐ SF (*tb* **~ de Correos**) sub post office Ⓑ SMF courier; (*Col*) [*de drogas*] drug courier, drug runner

estafilococo SM staphylococcus

estalactita SF stalactite

estalagmita SF stalagmite

estalinista ADJ, SMF Stalinist

estallar /1a/ VI **1** [*pólvora, globo*] to explode; [*bomba*] to explode, go off; [*volcán*] to erupt; [*neumático*] to burst; [*vidrio*] to shatter; **~ en llanto** to burst into tears; **el cristal de la ventana estalló en pedazos** the windowpane shattered; **hacer ~** to set off; (*fig*) to spark off, start **2** [*epidemia, guerra, conflicto, sublevación*] to break out

estallido SM **1** (= *explosión*) explosion **2** [*de guerra, enfrentamientos*] outbreak

estambre SM **1** (*Bot*) stamen **2** (= *tela*) worsted **3** (*Méx*) (= *lana*) wool

Estambul SM Istanbul

estamento SM (*social*) class; (*político*) estate

estampa SF **1** (*Tip*) (= *imagen*) print; (= *grabado*) engraving; (*en libro*) picture; (*típica*) vignette **2** (= *aspecto*) appearance, aspect; **de magnífica ~** fine-looking; **ser la propia ~ de algn** to be the very *o* absolute image of sb, be the spitting image of sb*

estampado Ⓐ ADJ printed; **un vestido ~** a print dress Ⓑ SM **1** (= *impresión*) printing **2** (= *diseño*) pattern **3** (= *tela*) print

estampar /1a/ VT **1** (*Tip*) (= *imprimir*) to print; (= *marcar*) to stamp **2** (*en la mente, memoria*) to stamp, imprint (**en** on) **3** (*) **le estampó un beso en la mejilla** she planted a kiss on his cheek; **lo estampó contra la pared** she flung him against the wall

estampida SF stampede; **se marchó de ~** he went off like a shot

estampido SM [*de pistola, fusil*] bang, report; [*de bomba*] blast, bang

estampilla SF **1** (= *sello de goma*) seal, stamp, rubber stamp **2** (*LAm Correos*) stamp

estampillar /1a/ VT to rubber-stamp

estampita SF *small religious picture*

estancado ADJ **1** [*agua*] stagnant **2** [*negociaciones*] at a standstill; **quedarse ~** to get into a rut

estancamiento SM **1** [*de agua*] stagnation **2** [*de asunto, comercio*] stagnation; [*de negociaciones*] deadlock

estancar /1g/ Ⓐ VT **1** [+ *aguas*] to hold back, stem **2** [+ *progreso*] to hold up, stem; [+ *negociación*] to deadlock; [+ *negocio*] to stop, suspend Ⓑ **estancarse** VPR **1** [*agua*] to stagnate, become stagnant **2** [*economía, industria, persona*] to stagnate

estancia SF **1** (= *permanencia*) stay **2** (*liter*) (= *cuarto*) living room **3** (*CS*) [*de ganado*] farm, cattle ranch

estanciero/a SM/F (*LAm*) farmer, rancher

estanco Ⓐ ADJ (*al agua*) watertight; (*al aire*) airtight Ⓑ SM tobacconist's (shop) (*Brit*), cigar store (*EEUU*)

estándar ADJ, SM standard

estandarizar /1f/ VT to standardize

estandarte SM banner, standard

estanflación SF stagflation

estanque SM pool, pond

estanquero/a SM/F tobacconist (*Brit*), tobacco dealer (*EEUU*)

estanquillo SM (*Méx*) corner shop (*Brit*), convenience store (*EEUU*)

estante SM shelf

estantería SF shelving, shelves *pl*

estaño SM tin; (*para soldar*) solder

estar /1o/

Ⓐ VERBO INTRANSITIVO	Ⓑ VERBO PRONOMINAL

Para las expresiones **estar bien**, **estar mal** *etc ver la otra entrada.*

estar Ⓐ VERBO INTRANSITIVO
1 (*indicando situación*) to be; **la última vez que estuve en Roma** the last time I was in Rome; **el monumento está en la plaza** the monument is in the square; **—hola, ¿está Carmen? —no, no está** "hello, is Carmen in?" — "no, I'm afraid she isn't"; **el día que estuve a verlo** the day I went to see him; **está fuera** (*de casa*) she's out; (*de la ciudad/en el extranjero*) she's away; **ya que estamos** while we are at it
2 (*indicando un estado transitorio*)
2.1 (+ ADJ, ADV) to be; **estoy muy cansada** I'm very tired; **¿estás casado?** (*Esp*) are you married?; **¡qué bueno está este café!** this coffee's really good!; **¿está libre el baño?** is the bathroom free?; **¿qué tal** *o* **cómo estás?** how are you?; **el récord anterior estaba en 33 segundos** the previous record was *o* stood at 33 seconds
2.2 (+ PARTICIPIO) to be; **la radio está rota** the radio is broken; **estaba sentada en la arena** she was sitting on the sand; **él no estaba implicado** he wasn't involved
2.3 (+ GERUNDIO) to be; **me está molestando** he's annoying me; **nos estamos engañando** we're deceiving ourselves
3 (= *existir*) to be; **además están los gastos del viaje** then there are the travel expenses
4 (*indicando el aspecto de algo*) to look; **¡qué elegante estás!** you're looking really smart!; **estás más delgado** you've lost weight, you look slimmer; **el traje te está grande** (*Esp*) that suit is too big for you
5 (= *estar listo*) to be ready; **en seguida está** it'll be ready in a moment; **dos vueltas más y ya está** two more laps and that'll be it; **¡ya está! ¡ya sé lo que podemos hacer!** that's it! I know what we can do!; **¡ya estamos!** (*dicho con enfado*) that's enough!; **¿estamos?** (*al estar listo*) ready?; (*para pedir*

conformidad) are we agreed?, right?, OK?*; **¡ya estuvo!** (*Méx*) that's it!
6 (*indicando fecha, distancia, temperatura*) **estamos en octubre** it's October; **cuando estemos en verano** when it's summer, in the summer
7 (*en estructuras con preposición*)
◆ **estar a: estamos a 8 de junio** it is the 8th of June, today is the 8th of June; **estábamos a 40°C** it was 40°C; **¿a cuántos estamos?** what's the date?; **¿a cuánto estamos de Madrid?** how far are we from Madrid?; **¿a cuánto está el kilo de naranjas?** how much are oranges per kilo?
◆ **estar con: está con la gripe** he's down with flu, he's got the flu; **yo estoy con él** I'm with him
◆ **estar de: está de buen humor** he's in a good mood; **están de charla** they're having a chat; **está de camarero** he's working as a waiter; **están de vacaciones** they are on holiday (*esp Brit*) *o* vacation (*EEUU*)
◆ **estar en: en eso está el problema** that's (exactly) where the problem is; **en ello estamos** we're working on it; **yo estoy en que …** (= *creer*) I believe that …
◆ **estar para: para eso están los amigos** that's what friends are for; **no estoy para bromas** I'm not in the mood for joking; **si alguien llama, no estoy para nadie** if anyone calls, I'm not in
◆ **estar por** (= *en favor de*) [+ *política*] to be in favour *o* (*EEUU*) favor of; [+ *persona*] to support
◆ **estar por** (+ INFIN) **está por ver si es verdad** it remains to be seen whether it's true; **está todavía por hacer** it remains to be done, it is still to be done; **yo estoy por dejarlo** I'm for leaving it, I'm in favour *o* (*EEUU*) favor of leaving it
◆ **estar sin** (+ INFIN) **las camas estaban sin hacer** the beds were unmade, the beds hadn't been made
8 (*en oraciones ponderativas*) **está que rabia*** he's hopping mad*, he's furious; **estoy que me caigo de sueño** I'm terribly sleepy, I can't keep my eyes open
Ⓑ estarse VERBO PRONOMINAL
1 (= *quedarse*)
1.1 (*en un lugar*) to stay; **yo prefiero ~me en casa** I prefer staying at home
1.2 (*en un estado*) **usted estese tranquilo** don't you worry; **¡estate quieto!** keep *o* stay still!
2 (*uso impersonal*) **en la cama se está muy bien** it's nice in bed

estárter SM = **stárter**

estatal ADJ **1** (= *del estado*) state *antes de s* **2** (*Esp*) (= *nacional*) national

estático ADJ static

estatua SF statue

estatuilla SF statuette, figure

estatura SF stature, height; **un hombre de 1,80m de ~** a man 1.80m in height

estatus SM INV status

estatutario ADJ statutory

estatuto SM (*gen*) statute; [*de comité*] (standing) rule
➤ **Estatuto de Autonomía** (*Esp Pol*) statute of autonomy
➤ **estatutos sociales** (*Com*) articles of association

este¹ Ⓐ ADJ INV [*región, orilla*] eastern; [*costa*] east; [*dirección, rumbo*] easterly; [*viento*] east, easterly **Ⓑ** SM **1** (= *punto cardinal*) **el Este** the East, the east; **el sol sale por el Este** the sun rises in the East *o* east **2** (*Pol*) **el Este** the East; **los países de la Europa del Este** East European countries **3** [*de región, país*] east **4** (*Meteo*) (*tb* **viento del ~**) east wind; *ver tb* **sur**

este²/a ADJ DEM **1** (*indicando proximidad*) **1.1** (*sing*) this; **esta silla** this chair; **~ mes** this month **1.2** **estos/estas** these; **estas tijeras** these scissors, this pair of scissors **2** (*) (*con valor enfático*) **¡a ver qué quiere ahora el tío ~!** what does this guy want now!*; **¡~ Pedro es un desastre!** that Pedro is a complete disaster!* **3** (*esp LAm*) (*como muletilla*) **este …** er …, um …

éste/a PRON DEM **1** (*sing*) this one; **ésta me gusta más** I prefer this one; **~ no es el que vi ayer** this is not the one I saw yesterday; **pero ¿dónde está ~?** where on earth is he? **2** **éstos/éstas** these; (*en texto*) the latter **3** **en éstas: en éstas se acerca y dice …** just then he went up and said …

esté *etc ver* **estar**

estela SF (*Náut*) wake, wash; (*Aer*) slipstream, trail; **dejaron tras de sí una ~ de muerte** they left a trail of slaughter behind them

estelar ADJ **1** (*Astron*) stellar **2** (*Teat*) star *antes de s*; **papel ~** star role; **función ~** all-star show

estelarizar /1f/ VT (*Méx*) **~ en** to star in

esténcil SM (*SAm*) stencil

estentóreo ADJ [*voz*] stentorian (*frm*), booming; [*sonido*] strident

estepa SF steppe

estepario ADJ steppe *antes de s*

estera SF **1** (= *alfombra*) mat ➤ **estera de baño** bathmat **2** (= *tejido*) matting

estercolero SM **1** (= *para estiércol*) manure heap, dunghill **2** (= *lugar sucio*) pigsty (*esp Brit*), pigpen (*EEUU*), shit hole***

estéreo ADJ, SM stereo

estereofonía SF stereo, stereophony

estereofónico ADJ stereo, stereophonic, in stereo

estereotipado ADJ stereotyped

estereotipar /1a/ VT to stereotype

estereotipo SM stereotype

estéril ADJ **1** (= *no fértil*) [*persona*] sterile; [*terreno*] sterile, barren **2** [*esfuerzo*] vain, futile

esterilidad SF **1** [*de persona*] sterility; [*de terreno*] sterility, barrenness **2** [*de esfuerzo*] futility, uselessness

esterilización SF sterilization

esterilizar /1f/ VT to sterilize

esterilla SF **1** (= *alfombrilla*) mat **2** (= *tejido*) rush matting **3** (*SAm*) (= *mimbre*) wicker; **silla de ~** wicker chair

esterlina ADJ **libra ~** pound sterling

esternón SM breastbone, sternum (*frm*)

estero SM **1** (*SAm*) (= *pantano*) swamp, marsh **2** (*Chi*) (= *arroyo*) brook

esteroide SM steroid

estertor SM death rattle

esteta SMF aesthete, esthete (*EEUU*)

estética SF **1** (*Arte*) aesthetics *sing*, esthetics *sing* (*EEUU*) **2** (*Med**) cosmetic surgery

esteticién SMF beautician, beauty consultant

esteticismo SM aestheticism, estheticism (*EEUU*)

esteticista SMF beautician, beauty consultant

estético ADJ aesthetic, esthetic (*EEUU*); **cirugía estética** cosmetic surgery

estetoscopio SM stethoscope

estevado ADJ bow-legged, bandy-legged

estiaje SM low water level

estibador(a) SM/F stevedore, docker (*Brit*), longshoreman (*EEUU*)

estiércol SM manure

estigma SM **1** (= *marca, deshonra*) stigma **2** **estigmas** (*Rel*) stigmata

estigmatizar /1f/ VT to stigmatize

estilarse /1a/ VPR **1** (= *estar de moda*) to be in fashion, be in style **2** (= *usarse*) to be used; **estilar hacer algo** to be customary to do sth

estilete SM stiletto

estilismo SM fashion design, fashion designing

estilista SMF **1** (*Literat*) stylist **2** (*Téc*) designer **3** (*Peluquería*) hair stylist

estilístico ADJ stylistic

estilizado ADJ [*persona*] slender

estilizar /1f/ VT (*Arte*) to stylize

estilo SM **1** (= *manera*) style; **un comedor ~ Luis XV** a dining-room suite in Louis XV style; **un ~ inconfundible de andar** an unmistakeable way of walking; ◆ MODISMO **por el ~: algo por el ~** something of the sort *o* kind, something along those lines; **y gentes por el ~** and people like that ➤ **estilo de vida** (= *modo de vida*) way of life; (= *actividades*) lifestyle ➤ **estilo directo** (*Ling*) direct speech (*esp Brit*), direct discourse (*EEUU*) ➤ **estilo indirecto** (*Ling*) reported speech (*Brit*), indirect speech (*esp Brit*), indirect discourse (*EEUU*) **2** (= *elegancia*) style; **tiene mucho ~ vistiendo** he dresses very stylishly **3** (*Natación*) stroke; **~s** medley; **los 400m ~s** the 400m medley **4** (= *punzón*) stylus **5** (*Bot*) style

estilográfica SF fountain pen

estiloso ADJ stylish

estima SF esteem, respect; **tener a algn en gran ~** to hold sb in high esteem, think very highly of sb

estimable ADJ **1** (= *respetable*) estimable (*frm*), esteemed **2** [*cantidad*] considerable, substantial

estimación SF **1** (= *evaluación*) estimate **2** (= *aprecio*) respect

estimado ADJ esteemed, respected; **"Estimado señor Pérez"** "Dear Mr Pérez"

estimar /1a/ VT **1** (*Com*) (= *evaluar*) to estimate; (= *valorar*) to value, appraise (*EEUU*) (**en** at); **los daños se ~on en varios millones** the damage was estimated at several million **2** (= *respetar*) to respect; **una persona muy estimada por los que lo conocían** a person highly respected by those who knew him **3** (= *juzgar*) to consider, deem; **lo que usted estime conveniente** whatever you consider o deem appropriate

estimativo ADJ rough, approximate

estimulante Ⓐ ADJ stimulating Ⓑ SM stimulant

estimular /1a/ VT **1** [+ *persona*] to encourage; **~ a algn a hacer algo** to encourage sb to do sth **2** [+ *apetito, economía, esfuerzos, ahorro*] to stimulate; [+ *debate*] to promote **3** [+ *organismo, célula*] to stimulate

estímulo SM **1** (*Psic*) stimulus **2** (= *incentivo*) incentive

estío SM (*liter*) summer

estipendio SM [*de empleado*] salary; [*de abogado, notario*] fee

estipulación SF stipulation, condition

estipular /1a/ VT to stipulate

estirado Ⓐ ADJ (= *tieso*) stiff, starchy; (= *engreído*) stuck-up* Ⓑ SM [*de pelo*] straightening ➤ **estirado de piel, estirado facial** face lift

estiramiento SM = **estirado B**

estirar /1a/ Ⓐ VT **1** [+ *goma, elástico*] to stretch; [+ *brazos*] to stretch out; [+ *cuello*] to crane; [+ *sábana, mantel*] to smooth out; [+ *piel*] to tighten, make taut; **salir a ~ las piernas*** to go out and stretch one's legs; ✦ MODISMO **~ la pata** to kick the bucket* **2** (*en el tiempo*) [+ *discurso*] to spin out; **~ el dinero hasta fin de mes** to make one's money stretch to the end of the month Ⓑ **estirarse** VPR to stretch

estirón SM **dar** o **pegar un ~*** [*niño*] to shoot up*, take a stretch*

estirpe SF stock, lineage

estitiquez SF (*Chi*) constipation

estival ADJ summer *antes de s*

esto PRON DEM this; **¿y ~ qué es?** whatever is this?; **~ es** that is, that is to say; **~ de la boda es un lío*** this wedding business is a hassle*; **por ~** for this reason; **esto ...** (*vacilando*) er ..., um ...; **en ~ entró su madre** at that point his mother came in; **no tiene ni ~ de tonto** he isn't the least o slightest bit silly

estocada SF **1** (= *acción*) stab, thrust **2** (= *herida*) stab wound **3** (*Taur*) death blow

Estocolmo SM Stockholm

estofa SF **gente de baja ~** riffraff*

estofado Ⓐ ADJ stewed Ⓑ SM stew, hotpot

estofar /1a/ VT to stew

estoico/a Ⓐ ADJ stoic, stoical Ⓑ SM/F stoic

estola SF stole

estolidez SF stupidity

estomacal ADJ stomach *antes de s*

estomagar /1h/ VT **1** (*Med*) to give indigestion to **2** (*Esp**) (= *molestar*) to annoy, bother

estómago SM stomach; **dolor de ~** stomach ache; **"no tomar con el estómago vacío"** "not to be taken on an empty stomach"; **revolver el ~ a algn** to make sb's stomach turn, turn sb's stomach; **tener buen ~** (= *resistir comidas fuertes*) to have a strong stomach; (= *ser insensible*) to be thick-skinned; (= *ser poco escrupuloso*) to have an elastic conscience

estomatólogo/a SM/F stomatologist

Estonia SF Estonia

estonio/a Ⓐ ADJ, SM/F Estonian Ⓑ SM (*Ling*) Estonian

estopa SF **1** [*del cáñamo*] tow **2** (= *tejido*) burlap

estoperol SM (*Chi*) brass tack

estoque SM rapier, sword

estoquear /1a/ VT to stab

estorbar /1a/ Ⓐ VI to be in the way; **siempre estás estorbando** you're always getting in the way Ⓑ VT **1** [+ *paso*] to get in the way of; [+ *trabajo, progreso*] to hinder; [+ *circulación*] to slow down **2** (= *molestar*) to bother

estorbo SM hindrance, nuisance

estornino SM starling

estornudar /1a/ VI to sneeze

estornudo SM sneeze

estoy *ver* **estar**

estrábico ADJ [*persona*] wall-eyed; [*ojo*] squinting, strabismic

estrabismo SM strabismus (*frm*), squint

estrada SF road

estrado SM (= *tarima*) platform; (*Mús*) bandstand; [*de testigo*] stand

estrafalario ADJ **1** [*persona, ideas*] odd, eccentric **2** [*ropa*] outlandish

estragón SM tarragon

estragos SMPL havoc *sing*; **hacer ~** to wreak havoc

estramador SM (*Méx*) comb

estrambote SM (*Literat*) extra lines *pl*, extra verses *pl*, addition

estrambótico ADJ odd, outlandish

estrangis ADV **de ~*** secretly, on the quiet

estrangulación SF strangulation

estrangulador(a) SM/F strangler

estrangulamiento SM strangulation

estrangular /1a/ VT to strangle, throttle

estraperlista SMF black marketeer

estraperlo SM black market

Estrasburgo SM Strasbourg

estratagema SF stratagem

estratega SMF strategist

estrategia SF strategy

estratégico ADJ strategic

estratificar /1g/ VT to stratify

estrato SM **1** (= *capa*) stratum **2** (= *nube*) stratus

estratosfera SF stratosphere

estratosférico ADJ stratospheric

estraza SF rag; **papel de ~** brown paper

estrechamente ADV **1** (= *íntimamente*) closely, intimately **2** (= *austeramente*) austerely

estrechamiento SM **1** [*de valle, calle*] narrowing **2** [*de lazos*] tightening; [*de amistades*] strengthening

estrechar /1a/ Ⓐ VT **1** [+ *calle*] to narrow; [+ *vestido*] to take in **2** [+ *lazos, relaciones*] to tighten; [+ *amistad*] to

strengthen 3 (= *abrazar*) to hug, embrace (*frm*); **me estrechó entre sus brazos** he held me in his arms, he hugged me; ~ **la mano a algn** to shake sb's hand, shake hands with sb **ⓑ estrecharse** VPR **1** [*calle*] to narrow, get narrower **2** (= *abrazarse*) to embrace (*frm*), embrace one another (*frm*), hug; **se ~on la mano** they shook hands **3** [*lazos, relaciones*] to become closer

estrechez SF **1** [*de calle, pasillo*] narrowness; [*de ropa*] tightness **2** (= *dificultad económica*) **vivir en la ~ o con ~** to live in straitened circumstances; **hemos pasado muchas estrecheces** we have been through many difficulties *o* hardships **3 ➤ estrechez de miras** narrow-mindedness

estrecho/a ⓐ ADJ **1** [*calle, pasillo*] narrow; [*zapato, ropa*] tight; **la falda me va muy estrecha** the skirt is very tight on me; **es muy ~ de hombros** he's very narrow-shouldered, he's got very narrow shoulders; **íbamos muy ~s en el asiento trasero** it was a tight squeeze *o* we had to squeeze up tight in the back seat
2 [*amistad, relación*] close; **trabajan en estrecha colaboración** they work in close collaboration; **la sometieron a una estrecha vigilancia** they kept her under close supervision *o* a close watch
3 (*sexualmente*) prudish, prim
4 (*de mentalidad*) narrow-minded; ~ **de miras** *o* **mente** narrow-minded
ⓑ SM (*Geog*) strait, straits *pl* **➤ Estrecho de Gibraltar** Strait(s) of Gibraltar
ⓒ SM/F (*) prude

estrella ⓐ SF **1** (*Astron*) star; **✦** MODISMOS **tener buena ~** to be lucky; **tener mala ~** to be unlucky; **ver las ~s** to see stars **➤ estrella fugaz** shooting star **➤ estrella polar** polar star **2** (= *símbolo*) star; **un hotel de cinco ~s** a five-star hotel **➤ estrella de David** Star of David **➤ estrella de mar** starfish **3** (*Cine, Teat*) star **➤ estrella de cine** film star (*esp Brit*), movie star (*esp EEUU*) **4** (*Mil*) star, pip **ⓑ** ADJ INV star *antes de s*; **el jugador ~** the star player

estrellado ADJ **1** (= *en forma de estrella*) star-shaped **2** [*cielo*] starry, star-spangled

estrellar /1a/ **ⓐ** VT **1** (= *hacer chocar*) to smash, shatter; **lo estrelló contra la pared** he smashed it against the wall; **la corriente amenazaba con ~ el barco contra las rocas** the current threatened to dash the boat on to the rocks **2** (= *decorar con estrellas*) to spangle, cover with stars **ⓑ estrellarse** VPR **1** (= *chocar*) to smash, crash (**contra** into) **2** [*proyecto, plan*] to fail; **~se con** *o* **contra algo** to be thwarted by sth

estrellato SM stardom

estrellón SM (*esp LAm Aut*) crash, collision

estremecedor ADJ alarming, disturbing

estremecer /2d/ **ⓐ** VT to shake **ⓑ estremecerse** VPR **1** [*edificio*] to shake **2** [*persona*] (*de miedo*) to tremble (**ante** at; **de** with); (*de horror*) to shudder (**de** with); (*de frío, escalofrío*) to shudder (**de** with)

estremecimiento SM **1** (= *sacudida*) shake **2** [*de frío*] shiver, shivering

estrenar /1a/ **ⓐ** VT **1** [+ *ropa*] to wear for the first time, put on for the first time; [+ *máquina, coche*] to use for the first time; **voy estrenando zapatos** I'm wearing new shoes; **¿has estrenado ya el coche?** have you tried your new car yet?; **la casa es (nueva) a ~** it's a brand new house **2** (*Cine*) (*Teat*) to premiere; **todavía no han estrenado la película** the film (*esp Brit*) *o* movie (*esp EEUU*) hasn't been released yet, the film (*esp Brit*) *o* movie (*esp EEUU*) is not on release yet; **están a punto de ~ el nuevo montaje de "Yerma"** the new production of "Yerma" is about to open
ⓑ estrenarse VPR **1** [*persona*] to make one's debut; **todavía no se ha estrenado como profesora** she still hasn't started working as a teacher
2 [*película*] to be released
3 (*) (= *pagar*) to cough up*, pay up

estreno SM **1** (= *primer uso*) **hoy voy todo de ~** I'm wearing all new clothes **2** (= *debut*) [*de artista*] debut, first appearance; [*de película*] premiere; [*de obra de teatro*] premiere, first night, first performance

estreñido ADJ constipated

estreñimiento SM constipation

estreñir /3h, 3k/ **ⓐ** VT to constipate **ⓑ** VI to cause constipation **ⓒ estreñirse** VPR to get constipated

estrépito ⓐ SM **1** (= *alboroto*) noise, racket; **reírse con ~** to laugh uproariously **2** (= *bulla*) fuss **ⓑ** ADJ (*Ven*) meddlesome, interfering

estrepitosamente ADV **1** (= *con ruido*) noisily **2** (= *espectacularmente*) spectacularly

estrepitoso ADJ **1** (= *ruidoso*) [*risa, canto*] noisy; [*persona, fiesta*] rowdy; **con aplausos ~s** with loud *o* thunderous applause **2** [*descenso, fracaso*] spectacular

estreptococo SM streptococcus

estreptomicina SF streptomycin

estrés SM stress; ~ **postraumático** post-traumatic stress

estresado ADJ [*persona*] stressed, stressed out*; [*vida, trabajo*] stressful

estresante ADJ stressful

estresar /1a/ VT to cause stress to, put stress on

estría SF **1** (*Anat*) stretch mark **2** (*Arquit*) flute, fluting **3** (*Biol, Geol*) striation

estriado ADJ **1** (*Anat*) stretch-marked **2** (*Arquit*) fluted **3** (*Biol, Geol*) striate, striated

estribación SF (*Geog*) spur; **en las estribaciones del Himalaya** in the foothills of the Himalayas

estribar /1a/ VI ~ **en algo: su felicidad estriba en ver contentos a los demás** her happiness comes from seeing other people being happy; **la dificultad estriba en el texto** the difficulty lies in the text

estribillo SM **1** (*Literat*) refrain **2** (*Mús*) chorus

estribo SM **1** [*de jinete*] stirrup; **✦** MODISMO **perder los ~s** (= *enfadarse*) to lose one's temper, blow one's top* **2** (*Arquit*) [*de edificio*] buttress; [*de puente*] support

estribor SM starboard

estricnina SF strychnine

estricto ADJ strict

estridencia SF stridency, raucousness; **iba vestida sin ~s** she was not loudly dressed

estridente ADJ **1** [*ruido*] strident, raucous **2** [*color*] loud

estrofa SF verse, strophe (*frm*)

estrógeno SM oestrogen, estrogen (*EEUU*)

estroncio SM strontium

estropajo SM scourer, scouring pad

estropajoso ADJ [*lengua*] coated, furry; [*carne*] tough; [*pelo*] straggly; **cuando bebe se le pone la lengua estropajosa** when he drinks he gets tongue-tied

estropeado ADJ **1** (= *averiado*) [*lavadora, televisor*] broken; [*ascensor, vehículo*] broken down
2 (= *dañado*) [*piel*] damaged; [*carne, fruta*] off; **este jersey está ya muy ~** this sweater is falling apart now; **los muebles están muy ~s** the furniture is in very poor condition
3 [*persona*] **3.1** (= *afeado*) **la encontré muy estropeada después del parto** she looked the worse for wear after the birth; **lo he visto muy ~ últimamente** he's been looking a real wreck lately* **3.2** (= *envejecido*) **está muy estropeada para su edad** she looks much older than she is, she looks pretty worn out for her age

estropear /1a/ **ⓐ** VT **1** (= *averiar*) [+ *juguete, lavadora, ascensor*] to break; [+ *vehículo*] to damage
2 (= *dañar*) [+ *tela, ropa, vista*] to ruin; **esa crema le ha estropeado el cutis** that cream has damaged *o* ruined her skin
3 (= *malograr*) [+ *plan, cosecha, actuación*] to ruin, spoil; **el final estropeaba la película** the ending ruined *o* spoiled the film (*esp Brit*) *o* movie (*esp EEUU*)
4 (= *afear*) [+ *objeto, habitación*] to ruin the look of, spoil the look of; [+ *vista, panorama*] to ruin, spoil
5 (= *envejecer*) [+ *persona*] **los años la han estropeado** she has aged really badly
ⓑ estropearse VPR **1** (= *averiarse*) [*lavadora, televisor*] to break; [*ascensor, vehículo*] to break down
2 (= *dañarse*) [*ropa, zapatos, vista*] to get ruined; [*carne,*

fruta] to go off, spoil; **el ante se estropea con la lluvia** suede gets ruined in the rain
3 [*plan, vacaciones*] to be ruined
4 [*persona*] (= *afearse*) to lose one's looks; (= *envejecer*) to age

estropicio* SM **1** (= *rotura*) breakage, smashing **2** (= *jaleo*) rumpus*

estructura SF **1** [*de organización, célula, poema*] structure **2** [*de edificio*] frame, framework

estructural ADJ structural

estructuralismo SM structuralism

estructurar /1a/ VT to structure, arrange

estruendo SM **1** (= *ruido*) din **2** (= *alboroto*) uproar, turmoil

estruendoso ADJ **1** (= *ruidoso*) thunderous **2** [*derrota, fracaso*] outrageous

estrujar /1a/ Ⓐ VT **1** (= *exprimir*) to squeeze **2** (= *apretar*) to press **3** (= *escurrir*) [+ *bayeta, trapo*] to wring **4** (= *aprovecharse de*) to drain, bleed white Ⓑ **estrujarse** VPR ✦ MODISMO **~se la mollera*** to rack one's brains*

estrujón SM squeeze, press

estuario SM estuary

estuche SM [*de gafas, instrumento*] case; [*de lápices*] pencil case; [*de cubiertos*] canteen; [*de joyas*] box, case

estuco SM **1** (*Arte*) stucco, plaster **2** (*CS* hum*) (= *maquillaje*) war paint** (*hum*)

estudiado ADJ [*sonrisa, respuesta*] studied; **una persona de gestos muy ~s** a very mannered *o* affected person

estudiante SMF student

estudiantil ADJ student *antes de s*

estudiantina SF student music group; ⊙ *TUNA*

estudiar /1b/ Ⓐ VT **1** (= *aprender*) [+ *lección, papel*] to learn; **tengo mucho que ~** I've got a lot of work *o* studying to do; **esta tarde tengo que ~ matemáticas** I have to do some maths this evening
2 (= *cursar*) to study; **quería que su hijo estudiase una carrera** she wanted her son to go to university *o* to do a degree
3 (= *examinar*) [*informe*] to examine, look into; [*persona, comportamiento*] to study, look into
4 (= *considerar*, study; **están estudiando la posibilidad de convocar una huelga** they are looking into the possibility of calling a strike, they are considering calling a strike
Ⓑ VI **1** (= *aprender*) to study; **me tengo que ir a ~ ahora** I must go and do some work *o* studying now
2 (= *cursar estudios*) to study; **estudia en un colegio de monjas** she goes to a convent school; **dejé de ~ a los trece años** I left school at thirteen; **~ para algo** to study to be sth

estudio SM **1** (= *investigación*) study; **los últimos ~s en lingüística** the latest work *o* studies in linguistics
➤ **estudio de casos** (*prácticos*) case study ➤ **estudio de mercado** market research ➤ **estudio de viabilidad** feasibility study
2 (= *actividad investigadora*) study; **horas de ~** hours of study
3 (= *análisis*) [*de intención de voto, edificio*] survey; **hacer un ~ del cabello de la víctima** to examine the victim's hair; **estar en ~** to be under consideration
4 **estudios** (= *educación*) education *sing*; **una persona sin ~s** an uneducated person; **dejar los ~s** (*Escol*) to drop out of school; (*Univ*) to drop out of university; **tener ~s** to have an education, be educated ➤ **estudios primarios** primary education *sing* (*esp Brit*), elementary education *sing* (*EEUU*) ➤ **estudios superiores** higher education *sing*; **tener ~s superiores de derecho penal** to have studied criminal law to degree level
5 (*Arte, Mús*) study
6 (= *lugar de trabajo*) (*en una casa*) study; (*profesional*) (*tb Cine, Radio, TV*) studio; (*CS*) [*de abogado*] office ➤ **estudio cinematográfico, estudio de cine** film studio ➤ **estudio de grabación** recording studio ➤ **estudio de televisión** television studio
7 (= *apartamento*) studio flat (*Brit*), studio apartment (*EEUU*)

estudioso/a Ⓐ ADJ studious Ⓑ SM/F expert, scholar

estufa SF **1** (= *para calentarse*) heater ➤ **estufa eléctrica** electric fire **2** (*Col, Méx*) (= *cocina*) stove

estulticia SF (*liter*) stupidity, foolishness

estupefacción SF astonishment, amazement

estupefaciente ADJ, SM narcotic

estupefacto ADJ astonished; **me miró ~** he looked at me in astonishment *o* amazement; **dejar a algn ~** to leave sb speechless

estupendamente ADV marvellously, marvelously (*EEUU*), wonderfully; **estoy ~** I feel great *o* marvellous *o* (*EEUU*) marvelous; **nos lo pasamos ~** we had a fantastic *o* great time*; **le salió ~** he did it very well

estupendo ADJ marvellous, marvelous (*EEUU*), great*; **¡estupendo!** that's great!*, splendid!; **tiene un coche ~** he's got a great *o* fantastic car*

estupidez SF **1** (= *cualidad*) stupidity **2** (= *acto, dicho*) stupid thing; **lo que hizo fue una ~** what he did was stupid, that was a stupid thing to do; **decir estupideces** to talk nonsense

estúpido/a Ⓐ ADJ stupid Ⓑ SM/F idiot

estupor SM **1** (= *sorpresa*) amazement, astonishment **2** (*Med*) stupor

estupro SM sexual intercourse with a minor, statutory rape (*EEUU*)

esturión SM sturgeon

estuve *etc ver* **estar**

esvástica SF swastika

ETA SF ABR (*Esp Pol*) (= **Euskadi Ta Askatasuna**) ETA

etapa SF **1** [*de viaje*] stage; ✦ MODISMO **quemar ~s** to make rapid progress **2** (= *fase*) stage, phase; **la segunda ~ del plan** the second phase of the plan; **lo haremos por ~s** we'll do it gradually *o* in stages **3** (*Dep*) leg, lap

etarra Ⓐ ADJ of ETA Ⓑ SMF member of ETA

etc. ABR (= **etcétera**) etc

etcétera Ⓐ ADV and so on Ⓑ SM **y un largo ~** and a lot more besides, and much much more

éter SM ether

etéreo ADJ ethereal

eternamente ADV eternally, everlastingly

eternidad SF eternity

eternizarse /1f/ VPR **1** [*discurso, reunión*] to drag on (forever), go on forever **2** [*persona*] to take ages*

eterno ADJ **1** (= *duradero*) eternal, everlasting **2** (= *interminable*) never-ending; **el viaje se me hizo ~** I thought the journey would never end, the journey seemed never-ending *o* interminable

ética SF ethics

ético ADJ ethical

etílico ADJ **alcohol ~** ethyl alcohol; **intoxicación etílica** alcohol poisoning; **en estado ~** intoxicated

etilo SM ethyl

etimología SF etymology

etimológico ADJ etymological

etíope ADJ, SMF Ethiopian

Etiopía SF Ethiopia

etiqueta SF **1** (*pegada*) label; (*atada, grapada*) tag; **le han puesto la ~ de cobarde** they've labelled *o* (*EEUU*) labeled him a coward **2** (= *formalismo*) etiquette; **de ~** formal; **baile de ~** gala ball; **traje de ~** formal dress; **ir de ~** to wear formal dress; **"vestir de etiqueta"** (*en invitación*) "dress: formal"

etiquetación SF, **etiquetado** SM, **etiquetaje** SM labelling, labeling (*EEUU*)

etiquetar /1a/ VT to label; **~ a algn de algo** to label sb (as) sth

etnia SF ethnic group

etnicidad SF ethnicity

étnico ADJ ethnic

etnocéntrico ADJ ethnocentric

etnografía SF ethnography

etnográfico ADJ ethnographic

etnología SF ethnology

etnológico ADJ ethnological

etrusco/a Ⓐ ADJ, SM/F Etruscan Ⓑ SM (*Ling*) Etruscan

ETS SF ABR (= **enfermedad de transmisión sexual**) STD

ETT SF ABR (*Esp*) = **Empresa de Trabajo Temporal**

eucalipto SM eucalyptus

eucaristía SF Eucharist

eucarístico ADJ Eucharistic

euclidiano ADJ Euclidean

eufemismo SM euphemism

euforia SF euphoria

eufórico ADJ euphoric

eunuco SM eunuch

eurasiático/a ADJ, SM/F Eurasian

eureka EXCL eureka!

euribor SM (*Fin*) Euribor

euro SM euro

Eurocámara SF Euro Parliament, European Parliament

eurocheque SM Eurocheque

eurocomisario/a SM/F Euro-commissioner

eurócrata SMF Eurocrat

eurodiputado/a SM/F Euro MP, member of the European Parliament

euromisil SM short-range nuclear missile

Europa SF Europe

europarlamentario/a SM/F member of the European Parliament

europeísta ADJ, SMF pro-European

europeo/a ADJ, SM/F European

Eurotúnel® SM Eurotunnel®

Eurovisión SF Eurovision

eurozona SF Eurozone

Euskadi SF the Basque Country

euskaldún/una Ⓐ ADJ 1 (= *vasco*) Basque 2 (*Ling*) Basque-speaking Ⓑ SM/F Basque speaker

euskera SM Basque

EUSKERA

Spoken by over half a million people in the Western Pyrenees, Basque, which is a non-Indo-European language, has been one of Spain's **lenguas cooficiales** (along with **catalán** and **gallego**) since 1982. Under Franco its use was prohibited in the media, but it began to experience a revival in the 1950s through semi-clandestine Basque-language schools called **ikastolas**. Nowadays there is Basque-language radio and television, and under the autonomous government the teaching of the language has become a cornerstone of educational policy. ⇨ LENGUAS COOFICIALES *See also* **www.euskadi.net**

eutanasia SF euthanasia, mercy killing

evacuación SF 1 [*de habitantes, heridos*] evacuation 2 (*Med*) bowel movement

evacuado/a SM/F evacuee

evacuar /1d/ Ⓐ VT to evacuate Ⓑ VI to have a bowel movement

evadir /3a/ Ⓐ VT 1 [+ *problema*] to evade, avoid 2 [+ *impuestos*] to evade Ⓑ **evadirse** VPR to escape; **~se de la realidad** to escape from reality

evaluación SF 1 (= *valoración*) [*de datos*] evaluation; [*de daños, pérdidas*] assessment 2 (*Escol*) (= *acción*) assessment; (= *examen*) test ➤ **evaluación continua** continuous assessment ➤ **evaluación escolar** exam (*forming part of end-*

of-term or end-of-year assessment)

evaluar /1e/ VT 1 (= *valorar*) [+ *datos*] to evaluate; [+ *daños, pérdidas*] to assess 2 (*Escol*) to assess

evangélico ADJ evangelic, evangelical

evangelio SM gospel

evangelista SMF evangelist

evangelizar /1f/ VT to evangelize

evaporación SF evaporation

evaporar /1a/ Ⓐ VT to evaporate Ⓑ **evaporarse** VPR 1 [*líquido*] to evaporate 2 [*persona*] to vanish *o* disappear into thin air

evasión SF [*de lugar*] escape; [*de responsabilidad*] evasion; **literatura de ~** escapist literature ➤ **evasión de capitales** flight of capital ➤ **evasión de impuestos, evasión fiscal** tax evasion

evasiva SF excuse; **contestar con ~s** to avoid the issue

evasivo ADJ [*respuesta*] evasive, noncommittal

evento SM event

eventual Ⓐ ADJ 1 (= *posible*) possible 2 (= *temporal*) [*trabajo, obrero*] temporary, casual; [*solución*] stopgap *antes de s* Ⓑ SMF temporary worker, casual worker

⚠ **eventual** ≠ **eventual**

eventualidad SF eventuality

Everest SM **el (Monte) ~** (Mount) Everest

evidencia SF 1 (= *obviedad*) evidence; **ante la ~ de los hechos** faced with the evidence; **negar la ~** to refuse to face (the) facts; **rendirse ante la ~** to face (the) facts 2 (= *ridículo*) **dejar** *o* **poner algo/a algn en ~** to show sth/sb up; **ponerse en ~** to show o.s. up

evidenciar /1b/ VT to prove, demonstrate

evidente ADJ obvious, clear, evident

evitable ADJ avoidable, preventable

evitar /1a/ Ⓐ VT 1 (= *eludir*) to avoid; **no pude ~lo** I couldn't help it

Recuérdese que **avoid** rige que el verbo que le siga inmediatamente aparezca en gerundio y no en infinitivo:

~ hacer algo to avoid doing sth 2 (= *ahorrar*) [+ *problema, molestia*] to save; **me evita (el) tener que ...** it saves me having to ... Ⓑ **evitarse** VPR 1 (= *ahorrarse*) to save o.s.; **~se trabajo** to save o.s. trouble; **así me evito tener que ir** that saves me having to go, that way I avoid having to go 2 [*dos personas*] to avoid each other

evocación SF 1 [*de recuerdos*] evocation 2 [*de espíritus*] invocation

evocador ADJ 1 (= *sugestivo*) evocative 2 (*del pasado*) reminiscent (**de** of)

evocar /1g/ VT to evoke, conjure up

evolución SF 1 (*Biol*) evolution 2 (= *desarrollo*) evolution, development 3 (*Med*) progress 4 (*Mil*) manoeuvre, maneuver (*EEUU*)

evolucionar /1a/ VI 1 (*Biol*) to evolve 2 (= *desarrollarse*) to evolve, develop 3 (*Med*) to progress 4 (*Mil*) to manoeuvre, maneuver (*EEUU*) 5 (*Aer*) to circle

evolutivo ADJ evolutionary

ex Ⓐ PREF ex-, former; **su ex amante** his former lover, his ex-lover Ⓑ SMF **mi ex*** my ex*, my ex-husband/ex-wife *etc*

exabrupto SM 1 (= *ataque*) broadside 2 (= *observación*) cutting remark

exacerbante ADJ (*esp LAm*) 1 (= *irritante*) irritating, provoking 2 (= *agravante*) aggravating

exacerbar /1a/ VT to aggravate, exacerbate

exactamente ADV exactly

exactitud SF accuracy; **con ~** [*saber, calcular, precisar*] exactly; **siguió las instrucciones con ~** he followed the instructions exactly o to the letter

exacto Ⓐ ADJ 1 (= *preciso*) [*precio, palabras*] exact; **el tren salió a la hora exacta** the train left exactly o bang on time; **tus cálculos no son muy ~s** your calculations are not very accurate; **para ser** ~ to be exact o precise 2 (= *correcto*) correct; **perdone, pero lo que dice no es del todo** ~ excuse me, but what you're saying is not entirely correct 3 (= *fiel*) [*copia, versión*] exact Ⓑ EXCL exactly!, quite right!

exageración SF exaggeration; **—piden diez millones —¡menuda ~!** "they're asking ten million" — "that's way too much! o that's a ridiculous amount!"

exagerado ADJ 1 [*persona*] (*en los gestos*) prone to exaggeration; **¡qué ~ eres!** ◇ **¡no seas ~!** don't exaggerate!, you do exaggerate!; **es un ~ comiendo** he eats an incredible amount 2 [*gesto*] theatrical 3 [*precio*] excessive, steep

exagerar /1a/ Ⓐ VT to exaggerate; **eso sería ~ las cosas** that would be going a bit far o overdoing it a bit Ⓑ VI to exaggerate

exaltación SF 1 (= *sobreexcitación*) overexcitement, elation 2 (= *fanatismo*) hot-headedness 3 (= *ensalzamiento*) exaltation

exaltado/a Ⓐ ADJ 1 (= *acalorado*) [*humor*] overexcited, elated; [*carácter*] excitable; [*discurso*] impassioned; **los ánimos estaban muy ~s** feelings were running high 2 (= *elevado*) exalted Ⓑ SM/F hothead

exaltar /1a/ Ⓐ VT 1 (= *acalorar*) [+ *persona, manifestante*] to work up, excite; [+ *emoción*] to intensify; [+ *imaginación*] to fire 2 (= *elevar*) to exalt 3 (= *enaltecer*) to raise (**a** to) Ⓑ **exaltarse** VPR 1 [*persona*] to get excited, get worked up 2 [*emoción*] to run high

exalumno/a SM/F former student

examen SM 1 (*Escol*) examination, exam; **hacer** o (*CS*) **dar un** ~ to sit o take an examination o exam ➤ **examen de conciencia: hacer ~ de conciencia** to examine one's conscience ➤ **examen de conducir** driving test ➤ **examen de ingreso** entrance examination ➤ **examen oral** oral examination ➤ **examen parcial** (*Univ*) *examination covering part of the course material in a particular subject* 2 (= *estudio*) [*de problema*] consideration; [*de zona*] search; **tras el ~ de la situación** after studying the situation; **someter algo a** ~ to subject sth to examination o scrutiny 3 (*Med*) examination ➤ **examen ocular** eye test

examinador(a) SM/F examiner

examinar /1a/ Ⓐ VT 1 [+ *alumno*] to examine 2 [+ *producto*] to test 3 [+ *problema*] to examine, study 4 [+ *paciente*] to examine Ⓑ **examinarse** VPR (*Esp*) to take an examination o exam

exangüe ADJ weak

exánime ADJ 1 (= *sin vida*) lifeless 2 (= *agotado*) exhausted

exasperación SF exasperation

exasperar /1a/ Ⓐ VT to exasperate, infuriate Ⓑ **exasperarse** VPR to get exasperated, lose patience

Exc.ª ABR = **Excelencia**

excarcelación SF release (*from prison*)

excarcelar /1a/ VT to release (*from prison*)

excavación SF 1 (= *acto*) excavation 2 (= *lugar*) excavation, dig

excavadora SF (= *máquina*) digger

excavar /1a/ VT 1 (*Constr*) to dig, dig out, excavate (*frm*) 2 (*Arqueología*) to excavate

excedencia SF leave of absence

excedentario ADJ surplus *antes de s*; [*país*] surplus-producing

excedente Ⓐ ADJ [*producción*] excess, surplus; [*trabajador*] laid-off, redundant (*Brit*) Ⓑ SM excess, surplus ➤ **excedente laboral** surplus of labour o (*EEUU*) labor, overmanning

exceder /2a/ Ⓐ VT 1 (= *superar*) to exceed, surpass; **los beneficios han excedido el millón de pesetas** profits are in excess of o have exceeded a million pesetas 2 (= *sobrepasar*) to surpass Ⓑ VI ~ **de algo** to exceed sth

Ⓒ **excederse** VPR **no te excedas con la bebida** don't overdo it with the drink; **~se en sus funciones** to exceed one's duty

excelencia SF 1 (= *cualidad*) excellence 2 (= *tratamiento*) **su Excelencia** his Excellency

excelente ADJ excellent

excelso ADJ lofty, exalted, sublime

excentricidad SF eccentricity

excéntrico/a ADJ, SM/F eccentric

excepción SF exception; **asistieron todos los invitados sin** ~ all the guests came without exception; **un libro de** ~ an exceptional book; **hacer una** ~ to make an exception; **a o con** ~ **de** with the exception of, except for

excepcional ADJ 1 (= *anómalo*) [*medidas, circunstancias*] exceptional; **un caso** ~ an exceptional case; **aquí las nevadas son** ~**es** you rarely get any snow here 2 (= *muy bueno*) exceptional

excepcionalmente ADV 1 (= *extraordinariamente*) exceptionally 2 (= *como excepción*) as an exception

excepto PREP except, except for; **todos, ~ Juan** everyone, except (for) o apart from Juan; **se lo perdono todo, ~ que me mienta** I'll forgive him anything, except lying to me

exceptuar /1e/ VT 1 (= *excluir*) to except, exclude; **exceptuando a uno de ellos** except for o with the exception of (*más frm*) one of them 2 (*Jur*) to exempt

excesivo ADJ excessive

exceso SM 1 (= *demasía*) excess; **en o por** ~ excessively, to excess ➤ **exceso de equipaje** excess baggage, excess luggage ➤ **exceso de peso** excess weight ➤ **exceso de velocidad** speeding, exceeding the speed limit 2 **excesos** (= *abusos*) (*al beber, comportarse*) excesses; **los ~s cometidos en su juventud** the overindulgences o excesses of his youth

excipiente SM (*Farm*) excipient

excisión SF (*Med*) excision

excitable ADJ excitable

excitación SF 1 (*Med*) excitation (*frm*); **el café me produce** ~ coffee makes me nervy ➤ **excitación sexual** sexual arousal 2 (= *emoción*) excitement

excitante Ⓐ ADJ 1 (*Med*) stimulating 2 (= *emocionante*) exciting Ⓑ SM stimulant

excitar /1a/ Ⓐ VT 1 (= *intranquilizar*) to get worked up, get excited; **no veas el partido porque te excita mucho** don't watch the game, it'll get you worked up o excited; **el café me excita** coffee makes me nervy 2 (= *entusiasmar*) to make excited 3 (= *provocar*) [+ *curiosidad*] to arouse, excite; [+ *sentimiento*] to arouse, provoke; [+ *apetito*] to stimulate 4 (*sexualmente*) to arouse, excite 5 (*Biol, Elec, Fís*) to excite Ⓑ **excitarse** VPR 1 (= *intranquilizarse*) to get worked up 2 (= *entusiasmarse*) to get excited 3 (*sexualmente*) to get aroused, get excited

exclamación SF 1 (*Ling*) exclamation 2 (= *grito*) cry

exclamar /1a/ VT, VI to exclaim, cry out

exclamativo ADJ exclamatory

excluido/a SM/F (*tb* ~ **social**) socially-excluded person; **los ~s sociales** the socially-excluded; **me siento un** ~ I feel a social outcast

excluir /3g/ VT 1 (*de grupo, herencia*) to exclude (**de** from) 2 (= *eliminar*) [+ *solución*] to reject; [+ *posibilidad*] to rule out

exclusión SF exclusion; **con** ~ **de** excluding

exclusiva SF 1 (*Com*) sole right, sole agency; **tener la** ~ **de un producto** to be sole agent o the sole agents for a product; **venta en** ~ exclusive sale 2 (*Periodismo*) exclusive story, exclusive, scoop; **reportaje en** ~ exclusive story, exclusive

exclusividad SF 1 (= *cualidad*) exclusiveness 2 (*Com*) exclusive rights *pl*, sole rights *pl*

exclusivo ADJ 1 (= *único*) [*distribuidor*] sole; [*derecho*] sole, exclusive 2 (= *selecto*) exclusive

Excmo. ABR = **Excelentísimo**

excombatiente SMF veteran, ex-serviceman/
-servicewoman (Brit)

excomulgar /1h/ VT to excommunicate

excomunión SF excommunication

excoriar /1b/ VT to chafe

excremento SM excrement

excretar /1a/ VT to excrete

exculpar /1a/ VT 1 (de obligación) to exonerate 2 (Jur) to
exonerate (**de** of)

excursión SF 1 (al campo) excursion, trip, outing
➤ **excursión a pie** hike 2 (= viaje) trip, excursion 3 (Mil)
raid

excursionismo SM hiking

excursionista SMF 1 (por campo, montaña) hiker 2 (en un
viaje) tripper

excusa SF excuse

excusado Ⓐ ADJ – **es decir que ...** needless to say ...
Ⓑ SM (†) toilet, lavatory (esp Brit)

excusar /1a/ Ⓐ VT 1 (= disculpar) to excuse; **excúsame con
los otros** apologize to the others for me 2 (= evitar)
excusamos decirle que ... we don't have to tell you that ...
3 (= eximir) to exempt (**de** from) Ⓑ **excusarse** VPR to
apologize (**con** to)

execrable ADJ execrable

execrar /1a/ VT to loathe

exégesis SF INV exegesis

exención SF exemption (**de** from); ➤ **exención
contributiva, exención de impuestos** tax exemption, tax
allowance (Brit), personal allowance (EEUU)

exento ADJ exempt (**de** from), free (**de** from, of); ~ **del
servicio militar** exempt from military service; ~ **de
impuestos** tax free; **un libro** ~ **de interés** a book devoid of
interest

exequias SFPL (frm) funeral rites, exequies (frm)

exfoliación SF exfoliation (frm)

exfoliador SM (Col) tear-off pad, loose-leaf notebook

exfoliante SM exfoliant

exfoliar /1b/ VT to exfoliate

exhalación SF [de suspiro, gemido] exhalation;
✦ MODISMO **pasar como una** ~ to flash past

exhalar /1a/ VT 1 [+ gas] to emit, give off 2 [+ suspiro] to
breathe; ✦ MODISMO ~ **el último suspiro** (euf) to give up
one's last breath, breathe one's last

exhaustivo ADJ exhaustive, thorough

exhausto ADJ exhausted

exhibición SF 1 (= demostración) show, display; **una
impresionante** ~ **de fuerza** an impressive show of strength;
hay varias esculturas en ~ there are various sculptures on
show o on display; **no le gusta hacer** ~ **de sus sentimientos**
he doesn't like to show his feelings ➤ **exhibición aérea**
flying display 2 (Cine) showing 3 (Dep) exhibition, display;
partido de ~ exhibition match

exhibicionismo SM exhibitionism

exhibicionista Ⓐ ADJ, SMF exhibitionist Ⓑ SM (sexual)
flasher*, exhibitionist (frm)

exhibir /3a/ Ⓐ VT 1 (= mostrar) [+ cuadros] to exhibit, put
on show; [+ artículos] to display; [+ película] to screen
2 (= mostrar con orgullo) to show off Ⓑ **exhibirse** VPR
1 (= mostrarse en público) to show o.s. off 2 (indecentemente)
to expose o.s.

exhortación SF exhortation

exhortar /1a/ VT to exhort

exhumación SF exhumation, disinterment

exhumar /1a/ VT to exhume, disinter

exigencia SF demand, requirement, exigency (frm); **tener
muchas** ~**s** to be very demanding

exigente ADJ [persona, trabajo] demanding, exacting;
ser ~ **con algn** to be demanding o exacting of sb, be
hard on sb; **es muy** ~ **con la limpieza** she is very

particular about cleanliness

exigir /3c/ VT 1 [persona] (gen) to demand; [+ dimisión] to
demand, call for; **la maestra nos exige demasiado** our
teacher is too demanding, our teacher asks too much of
us; **exija que le den un recibo** insist on getting a receipt; ~
responsabilidades a algn to call sb to account 2 [situación,
trabajo] to demand, require, call for; **ese puesto exige
mucha paciencia** this job demands o requires o calls for a
lot of patience

exiguo ADJ 1 [cantidad] meagre, meager (EEUU) 2 [objeto]
tiny

exilado/a ADJ, SM/F = **exiliado**

exilar /1a/ VT = **exiliar**

exiliado/a Ⓐ ADJ exiled, in exile Ⓑ SM/F exile

exiliar /1b/ Ⓐ VT to exile Ⓑ **exiliarse** VPR to go into exile

exilio SM exile

eximir /3a/ VT 1 (de impuestos, servicio militar) to exempt
(**de** from) 2 (de obligación) to free (**de** from)

existencia SF 1 [de ser humano, animal] existence; **amargar
la** ~ **a algn** to make sb's life a misery 2 **existencias** (Com)
stock sing; **liquidar** ~**s** to clear stock; **renovar** ~**s** to restock

existencial ADJ existential

existencialismo SM existentialism

existencialista ADJ, SMF existentialist

existente ADJ existing, in existence

existir /3a/ VI 1 (= ser) to exist; **esta empresa existe desde
hace 90 años** the company has been in existence for 90
years; **no existe tal cosa** there's no such thing 2 (= vivir) to
live; **mientras yo exista** as long as I live o I'm alive; **dejar de
** ~ (euf) to pass away

éxito SM 1 (= buen resultado) success; **la operación resultó
con** ~ the operation was successful o was a success; **tiene
mucho** ~ **con los hombres** she's very successful with men,
she has a great deal of success with men; **tener** ~ **en algo**
to be successful in sth, make a success of sth 2 (Mús, Teat)
success, hit; **grandes** ~**s** greatest hits ➤ **éxito de taquilla**
box-office success ➤ **éxito de ventas** best seller ➤ **éxito
editorial** best seller

 éxito ≠ **exit**

exitoso ADJ successful

éxodo SM exodus; **el** ~ **rural** the drift from the land, the
rural exodus

exoneración SF exoneration

exonerar /1a/ VT (de culpa, responsabilidad) to exonerate
(frm); (de un impuesto) to exempt

exorbitante ADJ exorbitant

exorcismo SM exorcism

exorcista SMF exorcist

exorcizar /1f/ VT to exorcise

exótico ADJ exotic

exotismo SM exoticism

expandir /3a/ Ⓐ VT to expand Ⓑ **expandirse** VPR 1 [gas,
metal] to expand 2 [empresa] to expand; [idioma, cultura,
noticia] to spread

expansión SF 1 [de empresa, mercado] expansion; [de
noticia, ideas] spread 2 (= recreo) relaxation

expansionarse /1a/ VPR 1 (= relajarse) to relax
2 (= desahogarse) to unbosom o.s., open one's heart (**con**
to)

expansionista ADJ expansionist

expansivo ADJ 1 [gas] expansive; **onda expansiva** shock
wave 2 (Econ) **una fase/política expansiva** a phase/policy of
expansion

expatriado/a SM/F expatriate

expatriarse /1b/ VPR 1 (= emigrar) to emigrate
2 (= exiliarse) to go into exile

expectación SF (= esperanza) expectation; (= ilusión)
excitement

expectante ADJ (= *esperanzador*) expectant; (= *ilusionado*) excited

expectativa SF 1 (= *esperanza*) expectation; **el resultado superó nuestras ~s** the result surpassed our expectations; **no tiene ~s de que le den el empleo** he isn't expecting to get the job 2 (= *espera*) **estar a la ~ de algo** to be waiting for sth

expectorar /1a/ VT, VI to expectorate

expedición SF 1 [*de personas*] expedition 2 (*Com*) shipment, shipping; **gastos de ~** shipping charges

expedicionario/a Ⓐ ADJ expeditionary Ⓑ SM/F member of an expedition

expedidor SM shipping agent, shipper

expedientar /1a/ VT (*gen*) to make a file on, draw up a dossier on; (*Jur*) to start proceedings against

expediente SM 1 (= *dossier*) dossier; (= *historial*) record; (= *ficha*) file; **alumnos con buen/mal ~** students with a good/poor track record; ✦ MODISMO **cubrir el ~** to do the minimum required; **lo haré por cubrir el ~** I'll do it to keep up appearances ➤ **expediente académico** (*Escol*) student's record, transcript (*EEUU*) ➤ **expediente policial** police dossier

2 (*Jur*) action, proceedings *pl*; **abrir** o **incoar ~** to start proceedings ➤ **expediente de regulación de empleo** labour o (*EEUU*) labor force adjustment plan ➤ **expediente disciplinario** disciplinary proceedings *pl* ➤ **expediente judicial** legal proceedings *pl*

3 (= *medio*) expedient, means; **recurrir al ~ de hacer algo** to resort to doing sth

expedir /3k/ VT [+ *mercancías*] to send, ship off; [+ *documento*] to draw up; [+ *orden, billete*] to issue

expeditar /1a/ VT (*LAm*) to expedite (*frm*)

expeditivo ADJ expeditious (*frm*)

expedito ADJ 1 [*camino*] clear, free; **dejar ~ el camino para** to clear the way for 2 (*LAm*) (= *fácil*) easy

expeler /2a/ VT to expel, eject

expendedor Ⓐ ADJ **máquina ~a** vending machine Ⓑ SM ➤ **expendedor automático** vending machine ➤ **expendedor automático de bebidas** drinks (vending) machine

expendeduría SF [*de tabaco*] tobacconist's (shop) (*Brit*), cigar store (*EEUU*); [*de lotería*] lottery outlet

expender /2a/ VT 1 [+ *dinero*] to expend (*frm*), spend 2 (= *vender*) to sell, retail

expendio SM 1 (*LAm*) (= *tienda*) small shop 2 (*LAm*) (= *venta*) sale ➤ **expendio de boletos** (*Méx*) ticket office

expensas SFPL 1 (*LAm*) (= *costas*) costs; **~ comunes** (*RPl*) service charge *sing* 2 **a ~ de** at the expense of

experiencia SF 1 (= *acontecimientos*) experience; **saber por ~** to know by o from experience; **intercambiar ~s** to swap stories ➤ **experiencia laboral** work experience 2 (= *experimento*) experiment (*en* on); ➤ **experiencia piloto** pilot scheme (*Brit*), pilot program (*EEUU*)

experimentación SF experimentation

experimentado ADJ experienced

experimental ADJ experimental

experimentar /1a/ Ⓐ VT 1 [+ *método, producto*] to test, try out 2 (= *notar*) [+ *cambio*] to experience, go through; [+ *pérdida, deterioro*] to suffer; [+ *aumento*] to show; [+ *sensación*] to feel; **el enfermo ha experimentado una ligera mejoría** the patient has improved slightly Ⓑ VI to experiment (*con* with; *en* on)

experimento SM experiment; **hacer ~s** to experiment

experto/a Ⓐ ADJ expert; **es experta en la materia** she's an expert on the subject; **ser ~ en hacer algo** to be an expert at doing sth

Recuérdese que las preposiciones en inglés rigen gerundio y no infinitivo, de ahí **to be an expert at doing sth**.

Ⓑ SM/F expert

expiación SF expiation (*frm*), atonement

expiar /1c/ VT to expiate (*frm*), atone for

expiración SF expiry, expiration

expirar /1a/ VI to expire

explanada SF area of level ground

explayarse /1a/ VPR (= *esparcirse*) to relax; (*en discurso*) to speak at length; **~ con algn** to confide in sb

explicación SF 1 [*de tema, motivo*] explanation 2 (= *razón*) reason (**de** for); **sin dar explicaciones** without giving any reason

explicar /1g/ Ⓐ VT [+ *motivo, tema, cuestión, problema*] to explain; [+ *teoría*] to expound

Para decir en inglés la expresión explicar algo a algn, hay que usar **to** delante del objeto indirecto: **explain sth to sb**.

¿puedes ~me eso? can you explain that to me?; **os ~é la situación** I'll explain the situation to you
Ⓑ **explicarse** VPR 1 (*al exponer algo*) to explain, explain o.s.; **se explica con claridad** he states things o expresses himself clearly
2 (*al entender algo*) **no me lo explico** I can't understand it, I can't make it out

explicativo ADJ explanatory

explicitar /1a/ VT to state, assert

explícito ADJ explicit

exploración SF 1 [*de terreno*] exploration; (*Mil*) reconnaissance ➤ **exploración submarina** underwater exploration 2 (*Med*) examination, exploration

explorador(a) SM/F (*Geog*) explorer; (*Mil*) scout

explorar /1a/ Ⓐ VT (*Geog*) to explore; (*Mil*) to reconnoitre; (*Med*) to examine, explore Ⓑ VI to explore; (*Mil*) to reconnoitre

exploratorio ADJ exploratory

explosión SF 1 [*de bomba*] explosion; **hacer ~** to explode; **motor de ~** internal combustion engine 2 [*de cólera*] outburst, explosion 3 (= *expansión*) explosion ➤ **explosión demográfica** population explosion

explosionar /1a/ VT, VI to explode, blow up

explosivo ADJ, SM explosive

explotación SF 1 (= *uso*) [*de recursos, riquezas*] exploitation; [*de planta*] running, operation; [*de mina*] working ➤ **explotación agrícola** farm ➤ **explotación forestal** forestry ➤ **explotación minera** mine ➤ **explotación petrolífera** oil exploration 2 (= *uso excesivo*) exploitation

explotador(a) Ⓐ ADJ exploitative Ⓑ SM/F exploiter

explotar /1a/ Ⓐ VT 1 (= *usar*) [+ *recursos, riquezas*] to exploit; [+ *planta*] to run, operate; [+ *mina*] to work 2 (= *usar excesivamente*) to exploit 3 [+ *bomba*] to explode Ⓑ VI [*bomba*] to explode, go off

expoliación SF pillaging, sacking

expoliar /1b/ VT to pillage, sack

expolio SM pillaging, sacking; ✦ MODISMO **armar un ~** to cause a hullaballoo*

exponencial ADJ exponential

exponente Ⓐ SMF (= *persona*) exponent Ⓑ SM 1 (*Mat*) index, exponent 2 (= *ejemplo*) model, prime example

exponer /2q/ (*pp* **expuesto**) Ⓐ VT 1 (*al público*) 1.1 [*museo*] to exhibit, put on show; [*galería, artista*] to show 1.2 (*en tienda*) to display; (*en feria*) to show 2 (*a la luz, al agua*) **no debe ~ la cicatriz al sol** he must not expose the scar to the sun 3 (= *explicar*) [+ *teoría, argumento*] to set out, expound (*frm*); [+ *hechos*] to set out, state; [+ *situación*] to set out 4 (= *arriesgar*) to risk, put at risk 5 (*Fot*) to expose Ⓑ VI [*pintor, escultor*] to exhibit, show Ⓒ **exponerse** VPR 1 (= *someterse*) **~se a algo** to expose o.s. to sth; **se expone a las críticas** she's laying herself open to *o* exposing herself to criticism; **no se exponga al sol durante mucho tiempo** don't go out in the sun for a long time, don't expose yourself to the sun for a long time **2** (= *arriesgarse*) **~se a hacer algo** to risk doing sth, run the risk of doing sth

> Recuérdese que las preposiciones en inglés rigen gerundio y no infinitivo, de ahí **to run the risk of doing sth. To risk** también rige gerundio.

con eso te expones a que te echen del colegio that way you're running the risk of being expelled from school

exportación SF **1** (= *acto*) export, exportation; **comercio de ~** export trade **2** (= *artículos*) exports *pl*

exportador(a) ⓐ ADJ [*país*] exporting **ⓑ** SM/F exporter

exportar /1a/ VT to export

exposición SF **1** (= *muestra*) (*Arte*) exhibition; (*Com*) show, fair ➤ **exposición universal** world fair **2** (= *acto*) (*gen*) exposing, exposure; (*Fot*) exposure; (*Com*) display **3** (= *enunciado*) [*de hechos*] statement; [*de teoría*] exposition

exposímetro SM exposure meter

expositor(a) ⓐ SM/F **1** (*Arte*) exhibitor **2** (*Col*) (= *conferenciante*) speaker **ⓑ** SM (= *vitrina*) showcase, display case; (= *puesto*) sales stand

exprés ADJ **café ~** espresso; **olla ~** (*Esp*) pressure cooker

expresamente ADV (= *concretamente*) expressly; (= *a propósito*) on purpose, deliberately

expresar /1a/ **ⓐ** VT (= *enunciar*) to express; (= *redactar*) to phrase, put; [+ *opiniones, quejas*] to voice; **estaba expresado de otro modo** it was worded differently **ⓑ** expresarse VPR to express o.s.

expresión SF **1** (= *acto*) expression; **expresiones de solidaridad** messages *o* expressions of solidarity ➤ **expresión corporal** self-expression through movement **2** (*Ling*) expression ➤ **expresión familiar** colloquialism, conversational *o* colloquial expression

expresionismo SM expressionism

expresionista ADJ, SMF expressionist

expresividad SF expressiveness

expresivo ADJ (= *que gesticula*) expressive; (= *cariñoso*) tender, affectionate, warm

expreso ⓐ ADJ **1** (= *explícito*) express; (= *exacto*) specific, clear **2** [*tren*] express, fast **3 café ~** espresso **ⓑ** SM (*Ferro*) express train

exprimelimones SM INV lemon squeezer

exprimidor SM (*manual*) lemon squeezer; (*eléctrico*) juice extractor, juicer

exprimir /3a/ **ⓐ** VT **1** [+ *limón, naranja*] to squeeze; [+ *jugo*] to squeeze out **2** (*pey*) [+ *persona*] to exploit **ⓑ** exprimirse VPR ✦ MODISMO **~se el cerebro** *o* **los sesos*** to rack one's brains

ex profeso ADV on purpose, deliberately

expropiación SF (*sin indemnización*) expropriation; (*con indemnización*) compulsory purchase

expropiar /1b/ VT (*sin indemnización*) to expropriate; (*con indemnización*) to place a compulsory purchase order on

expuesto ADJ **1** [*lugar*] (= *al descubierto*) exposed; (= *peligroso*) dangerous **2** [*cuadro, mercancías*] on show, on display, on view **3 estar ~ a un riesgo** to be exposed *o* open to a risk

expulsar /1a/ VT **1** (= *hacer salir*) [+ *alumno, inmigrante*] to expel; [+ *jugador*] to send off, eject (*EEUU*); [+ *intruso, alborotador*] to eject, throw out (**de** from); **la ~on del partido** she was expelled from the party, she was thrown out of the party **2** [+ *gases, humo*] to expel

expulsión SF [*de gases, humo, persona*] expulsion; (*Dep*) sending-off, ejection (*EEUU*)

expurgar /1h/ VT to expurgate

exquisitez SF **1** [*de algo refinado*] exquisiteness **2** [*de comida*] delicacy

exquisito ADJ [*belleza*] exquisite; [*comida*] delicious

extasiar /1c/ **ⓐ** VT to entrance, enrapture, captivate **ⓑ** extasiarse VPR to become entranced, go into ecstasies (**ante** over, about)

éxtasis SM INV **1** (= *estado*) ecstasy, rapture **2** (= *droga*) ecstasy, E*

extático ADJ ecstatic, rapturous

extemporáneo ADJ [*lluvia*] unseasonable; [*comentario, viaje*] untimely

extender /2g/ **ⓐ** VT **1** (= *desplegar*) [+ *manta, mantel*] to spread out; [+ *alas*] to spread, stretch out; [+ *brazo, pierna, tentáculo*] to stretch out; **extendió el mapa encima de la mesa** he opened out *o* spread out the map on the table; **~ la mano a algn** to hold out one's hand to sb, extend one's hand to sb (*frm*) **2** (= *esparcir*) [+ *sellos, arena*] to lay out, spread out **3** (= *untar*) [+ *crema, mantequilla*] to spread **4** (= *difundir*) [+ *noticia, rumor*] to spread; [+ *influencia, poder*] to extend **5** (*frm*) (= *rellenar*) [+ *cheque, receta*] to make out, write out; [+ *certificado*] to issue **ⓑ** extenderse VPR **1** (= *propagarse*) [*tumor, rumor, revolución*] to spread (**a** to) **2** (= *ocupar un espacio*) [*terreno, cultivo*] to stretch, extend; [*especie, raza*] to extend; **la mancha de petróleo se extendía hasta la orilla** the oil slick stretched *o* extended as far as the shore **3** (= *durar*) to last; **el período que se extiende desde ... hasta ...** the period lasting from ... up to ... **4** (= *explayarse*) **~se en** *o* **sobre** [+ *tema, comentarios, respuestas*] to expand on; **nos extendimos demasiado en el debate** we spent too long on the debate

extendido ADJ **1** (= *desplegado*) [*mantel, mapa*] spread out, outspread; [*alas, brazos*] stretched out, outstretched **2** (= *propagado*) widespread; **está muy ~ el uso de esa palabra** that word is very widely used, the use of that word is very widespread; **tenía el tumor muy ~** the tumour had spread all over his body

extensamente ADV **1** (= *mucho*) extensively, widely **2** (= *con detalle*) at length, thoroughly

extensible ADJ **1** [*mesa, escalera*] extending **2** (= *ampliable*) **estas críticas son ~s al resto del equipo** these criticisms can be extended to the rest of the team

extensión SF **1** (= *superficie*) area; **una enorme ~ de agua** an enormous area of water; **una isla con una ~ similar a la de Europa** an island similar in area to Europe **2** (= *duración*) length; **la ~ del relato** the length of the story **3** (= *amplitud*) [*de conocimientos*] extent, range; [*de programa*] scope; [*de significado*] range; **en toda la ~ de la palabra** in every sense of the word; **por ~** by extension **4** (= *ampliación*) [*de incendio*] spread; [*de plazo*] extension; **la ~ del regadío a tierras de secano** the extending of irrigation systems to dry lands **5** [*de cable, cuerda*] extension **6** (*Telec*) extension **7** [*de instrumento, voz*] range, compass **8** (*Internet*) plug-in

extensivo ADJ extensive; **hacer ~ a** to extend to, apply to

extenso ADJ **1** (= *amplio*) [*superficie, objeto*] extensive; [*capítulo, documento*] long, lengthy **2** [*estudio, conocimientos*] extensive; **por ~** in full, at length

extensor SM chest expander

extenuación SF exhaustion

extenuado ADJ exhausted

extenuar /1e/ **ⓐ** VT to exhaust **ⓑ** extenuarse VPR to get exhausted

exterior ⓐ ADJ **1** (= *externo*) [*superficie*] outer; [*pared*] external; [*mundo*] exterior, outside; **una habitación ~** a room facing onto the street **2** (= *extranjero*) [*relaciones, deuda, política*] foreign; [*comercio, ayuda*] foreign, overseas **ⓑ** SM **1 el ~** (= *parte de fuera*) the outside *o* exterior **2 el ~** (= *el extranjero*) abroad; **comercio con el ~** foreign trade, overseas trade **3 exteriores** (*Cine*) location shots; **rodar en ~es** to film on location

exteriorizar /1f/ VT (= *expresar*) to express outwardly; (= *mostrar*) to show, reveal

exteriormente ADV outwardly

exterminar /1a/ VT to exterminate

exterminio SM extermination

externalizar /1f/ VT [+ *servicios*] to outsource

externo/a Ⓐ ADJ [*influencia*] outside, external; [*superficie*] outer; [*pared*] external; **"medicamento de uso externo"** "medicine for external use only" Ⓑ SM/F (= *alumno*) day pupil

extinción SF extinction

extinguido ADJ [*animal, volcán*] extinct; [*fuego*] out, extinguished

extinguidor SM (*LAm*) (*tb* **~ de incendios**) fire extinguisher

extinguir /3d/ Ⓐ VT 1 [+ *fuego*] to extinguish, put out 2 (*Biol*) to exterminate, wipe out Ⓑ **extinguirse** VPR 1 [*fuego*] to go out 2 (*Biol*) to die out, become extinct

extinto ADJ 1 [*especie, volcán*] extinct 2 (*LAm euf*) (= *difunto*) dead, deceased

extintor SM (*Esp*) fire extinguisher

extirpación SF 1 (= *eliminación*) extirpation (*frm*), eradication 2 (*Med*) removal

extirpar /1a/ VT 1 [+ *problema, vicio*] to eradicate, stamp out 2 (*Med*) to remove (surgically)

extorsión SF 1 (*con intimidación*) extortion; (*haciendo chantaje*) blackmail 2 (= *molestia*) inconvenience

extorsionador(a) SM/F (= *intimidador*) extortioner; (= *chantajista*) blackmailer

extorsionar /1a/ VT to extort money from

extra Ⓐ ADJ INV [*tiempo*] extra; **calidad ~** top-quality, best Ⓑ SMF (*Cine*) extra Ⓒ SM 1 (*en cuenta*) extra 2 (= *periódico*) special edition

extracción SF 1 [*de diente*] extraction; [*de bala, astilla*] extraction, removal 2 [*de minerales*] mining, extraction; [*de petróleo*] extraction; [*de pizarra, mármol*] quarrying 3 (*en sorteo*) **vamos a proceder a la primera ~** we shall now draw the first number 4 (= *origen*) origins *pl*; **de ~ humilde** of humble origins, from a humble background 5 (*Mat*) extraction

extracomunitario ADJ **países ~s** countries outside the European Union, non-EU countries

extracto SM 1 (= *resumen*) summary, abstract ➤ **extracto de cuenta** (bank) statement 2 (*Farm, Culin*) extract ➤ **extracto de carne** meat extract

extractor SM extractor ➤ **extractor de humos** extractor fan (*Brit*), ventilator (*EEUU*)

extradición SF extradition

extraditar /1a/ VT to extradite

extraer /2o/ VT 1 [+ *diente, bala, astilla*] to extract 2 [+ *minerales*] to mine, extract; [+ *petróleo*] to extract; [+ *pizarra, mármol*] to quarry 3 [+ *conclusiones*] to draw 4 (*en sorteo*) to draw 5 (*Mat*) to extract

extraescolar ADJ **actividad ~** out-of-school activity

extrafino ADJ superfine

extrajudicial ADJ extrajudicial, out of court

extralargo ADJ [*cigarrillo*] king-size

extralimitación SF abuse (*of authority*)

extralimitarse /1a/ VPR to exceed *o* abuse one's authority, overstep the mark

extramarital ADJ extramarital

extramuros ADV outside the city

extranjería SF **ley de ~** law on aliens

extranjerismo SM foreign word *o* phrase *etc*

extranjero/a Ⓐ ADJ foreign Ⓑ SM/F foreigner; (*Jur*) alien Ⓒ SM **en el ~** abroad

⚠ **extranjero** ≠ *stranger*

extranjis*: de ~ ADV (*Esp*) secretly, on the sly

extrañamiento SM estrangement (**de** from)

extrañar /1a/ Ⓐ VT 1 (= *sorprender*) to surprise; **¡no me ~ía!** I wouldn't be surprised!, it wouldn't surprise me!; **me extrañaba que no hubieras venido** I was surprised you hadn't come; **no es de ~ que ...** it's hardly surprising that ..., it's no wonder that ... 2 (= *echar de menos*) to miss; **esta noche he extrañado mi cama** last night I missed sleeping in my own bed Ⓑ **extrañarse** VPR to be surprised; **~se de algo** to be surprised at sth; **se extrañó de vernos juntos** he was surprised to see us together; **~se de que ...** to be surprised that ...

extrañeza SF surprise, amazement

extraño/a Ⓐ ADJ 1 (= *raro*) strange; **¡qué ~!** how odd *o* strange! 2 (= *ajeno*) **un cuerpo ~** a foreign body; **murió en tierra extraña** he died on foreign soil; **este estilo no es ~ a los lectores de su poesía** this style is not unknown to readers of his poetry Ⓑ SM/F 1 (= *desconocido*) stranger 2 (= *extranjero*) foreigner

extraoficial ADJ unofficial, informal

extraordinario Ⓐ ADJ 1 (= *especial*) extraordinary; **no tiene nada de ~** there's nothing extraordinary *o* special about it 2 (= *destacado*) (*gen*) outstanding; [*edición, numero, descuento*] special; [*cobro*] supplementary, extra Ⓑ SM (*para una ocasión especial*) treat

extraplano ADJ super-slim

extrapolación SF extrapolation

extrapolar /1a/ VT to extrapolate

extrarradio SM suburbs *pl*, outlying area

extrasensorial ADJ extrasensory

extraterrestre Ⓐ ADJ from outer space, extraterrestrial Ⓑ SMF alien, extraterrestrial

extraterritorial ADJ extraterritorial

extravagancia SF 1 (= *cualidad*) outlandishness 2 (= *acción*) **sus ~s** his outlandish behaviour

extravagante ADJ outlandish

extraviado ADJ [*persona, objeto*] lost, missing; [*animal*] lost, stray

extraviar /1c/ Ⓐ VT to lose, mislay, misplace Ⓑ **extraviarse** VPR [*persona*] to get lost, lose one's way; [*animal*] to stray; [*objeto*] to go missing, go astray

extravío SM loss

extremado ADJ extreme

extremar /1a/ Ⓐ VT **~ las medidas de seguridad** to maximize security measures; **las personas alérgicas deben ~ las precauciones** allergic people should take extra precautions Ⓑ **extremarse** VPR to do one's best

extremaunción SF extreme unction

extremeño/a ADJ, SM/F Extremaduran

extremidad SF 1 (= *punta*) tip, extremity; (= *borde*) edge, outermost part 2 **extremidades** (*Anat*) extremities

extremismo SM extremism

extremista ADJ, SMF extremist

extremo¹ ADJ 1 (= *máximo*) extreme; **el nivel de polen era ~** the pollen count was extremely high; **heridas de extrema gravedad** extremely serious wounds; **en caso ~** as a last resort, if all else fails 2 (= *alejado*) furthest 3 (= *radical*) extreme; **extrema derecha** extreme right, far right; **extrema izquierda** extreme left, far left

extremo² Ⓐ SM 1 (= *punta*) end; **vive en el otro ~ de la calle** he lives at the far *o* other end of the street; **el ~ oriental de la península** the easternmost side *o* point of the peninsula; **de ~ a ~** from one end *o* side to the other; **de un ~ a otro** (*lit*) from one end *o* side to the other; (*fig*) from one extreme to another; ✦ MODISMOS **ser el ~ opuesto** to be the complete opposite; **ser los dos ~s** to be complete opposites 2 (= *límite*) extreme; **no me gustan los ~s** I don't like extremes of any kind; **su crueldad alcanzaba ~s insospechados** his cruelty plumbed unheard-of depths; **si la situación se deteriora hasta ese ~ ...** if the situation deteriorates to that extent ...; **en ~** extremely; **hasta el ~** to the full; **es detallista hasta el ~** he pays extremely close attention to detail; **llegar a** o **hasta el ~ de: hemos llegado al ~ de no decirnos ni hola** it's got to the point now that we don't even say hello to each other; **por ahorrar ha llegado al ~ de no comer** he's so desperate to save money he's stopped eating; **en último** ~ as a last resort, if all else fails

3 (= *asunto*) point

Ⓑ SMF (*Dep*) ➤ **extremo derecho** right winger ➤ **extremo izquierdo** left winger

Extremo Oriente SM Far East

extrínseco ADJ extrinsic

extrovertido/a ADJ, SM/F extrovert

exuberancia SF **1** [*de persona, conducta*] exuberance **2** [*de vegetación*] luxuriance, lushness **3** (*en el cuerpo*) fullness, buxomness

exuberante ADJ **1** [*persona, conducta*] exuberant **2** [*vegetación*] luxuriant, lush **3** [*cuerpo, formas*] full, buxom

exudar /1a/ VT to exude

exultante ADJ elated, overjoyed; ~ **de felicidad** flushed with happiness

exvoto SM votive offering

eyaculación SF ejaculation ➤ **eyaculación precoz** premature ejaculation

eyacular /1a/ VT, VI to ejaculate

eyectable ADJ **asiento** ~ ejector seat

eyector SM (*Téc*) ejector

Ff

F, f ['efe] SF (= *letra*) F, f

fa SM (*Mús*) fa, F

fabada SF *rich stew of beans, pork etc*

fábrica SF 1 (= *factoría*) factory; **marca de ~** trademark; **precio de ~** price ex-works, price ex-factory ➤ **fábrica de cerveza** brewery ➤ **fábrica de conservas** canning plant, cannery ➤ **fábrica de papel** paper mill 2 (*Arqu*) **de ~** stone, stonework

⚠️ **fábrica** ≠ **fabric**

fabricación SF manufacture; **de ~ casera** home-made; **de ~ nacional** home-produced; **de ~ propia** our own make

fabricante SMF manufacturer

fabricar /1g/ VT to manufacture, make

fábula SF (*Literat*) fable; (= *historia*) tale, story

fabuloso ADJ 1 (*) (= *maravilloso*) fantastic, fabulous 2 (= *mítico*) mythical, fabulous (*liter*)

facción SF 1 (*Pol*) faction 2 **facciones** (*Anat*) features; **de facciones irregulares** with *o* of irregular features

faccioso/a Ⓐ ADJ [*propaganda, jefe*] rebel; [*bando*] breakaway Ⓑ SM/F (= *rebelde*) rebel; (= *agitador*) agitator

faceta SF facet

facha¹* SF (= *aspecto*) look; **la tarta tiene buena ~** the cake looks really good; **¿adónde vas con esa ~?** where are you going looking like that?; **tener ~ de** to look like; **estar hecho una ~** to look a sight*, look terrible

facha²* ADJ, SMF (*Esp pey*) fascist

fachada SF 1 [*de edificio*] façade, front 2 (= *apariencia*) façade; **no tiene más que ~** it's all just a façade with him, it's all just show with him

fachista ADJ, SMF (*SAm*) fascist

facho/a* ADJ, SM/F (*CS*) fascist

fachoso* ADJ 1 (= *raro*) ridiculous-looking, odd-looking 2 (*Chi*) (= *engreído*) conceited

facial ADJ facial, face *antes de s*; **crema ~** face cream; **mascarilla ~** pack *o* mask

fácil Ⓐ ADJ 1 (= *sencillo*) easy; **el examen fue muy ~** the exam was very easy; **no me lo pones nada ~** you aren't making things very easy for me; **~ de hacer** easy to do; **~ de usar** easy to use, user-friendly 2 (= *afable*) **es de trato ~** he's easy to get on with, he's quite easy-going 3 (*pey*) [*respuesta*] facile, glib; [*chiste*] obvious 4 (= *probable*) **es ~ que venga** he's quite likely to come, he may well come Ⓑ ADV (*) **podría costarte 5.000 ~** it could easily cost you 5,000

facilidad SF 1 (= *sencillez*) easiness; **se me rompen las uñas con ~** my nails break easily 2 (= *habilidad*) **tener ~ para algo** to have a gift for sth; **tener ~ de palabra** to have a way with words 3 **facilidades** (= *condiciones favorables*) **me dieron todas las ~es** they did everything they could for me; **"facilidades de pago"** "credit facilities"

facilitar /1a/ VT 1 (= *hacer fácil*) to make easier, facilitate; **un ordenador facilita mucho el trabajo** a computer makes work much easier; **Internet facilita el acceso a la información** the Internet facilitates access to information 2 (= *proporcionar*) **~ algo a algn** to provide sb with sth, supply sb with sth

fácilmente ADV easily

facineroso/a Ⓐ ADJ 1 (= *de delincuente habitual*) criminal 2 (= *malvado*) evil, wicked Ⓑ SM/F 1 (= *delincuente habitual*) criminal 2 (= *malvado*) evil person, wicked person

facón SM (*CS*) long gaucho knife; ⇨ GAUCHO

facsímil ADJ, SM, **facsímile** ADJ, SM facsimile

factible ADJ feasible

fáctico ADJ real, actual; **los poderes ~s** the powers that be

factor SM 1 (*Mat*) factor 2 (= *elemento*) factor, element; **el**

~ suerte the luck factor, the element of chance ➤ **factor Rh** rhesus factor ➤ **factor sorpresa** element of surprise

factoría SF 1 (= *fábrica*) factory 2 (*And*) (= *fundición*) foundry

factótum SMF factotum

factura SF 1 (*Com*) bill, invoice; ✦ MODISMO **pasar ~: tanto alcohol ha acabado pasándole ~** all that alcohol *o* drink has finally taken its *o* a toll; **nos pasarán (la) ~ por el apoyo que nos dieron en momentos de crisis** they will expect a payback for the support they gave us during the crisis 2 (*frm*) (= *ejecución*) **cuadros de ~ reciente** recently painted pictures 3 (*RPl*) [*de panadería*] cakes and pastries *pl*

facturación SF 1 (*Com*) (= *acto*) invoicing; (= *ventas*) turnover 2 [*de mercancías, equipaje*] (*en aeropuerto*) check-in; (*en puerto, estación*) registration

facturar /1a/ Ⓐ VT 1 [+ *géneros*] to invoice (for), bill (for) 2 (= *tener un volumen de ventas de*) to turn over, have a turnover of 3 [+ *equipaje*] (*en aeropuerto*) to check in; (*en puerto, estación*) to register Ⓑ VI to check in

facultad SF 1 (= *capacidad*) faculty; **está perdiendo sus ~es** she's losing her faculties ➤ **facultades mentales** mental faculties, mental powers 2 (*Univ*) faculty; **está en la ~** he's at the university ➤ **Facultad de Medicina** Faculty of Medicine

facultar /1a/ VT **~ a algn para hacer algo** (= *dar autorización*) to authorize sb to do sth, empower sb to do sth; (= *dar derecho*) to entitle sb to do sth

facultativo/a Ⓐ ADJ 1 (= *opcional*) optional, non-compulsory 2 (*Med*) medical; **dictamen ~** medical report Ⓑ SM/F doctor, physician (*frm*)

faena SF 1 (*gen*) task, job, piece of work; (*en el hogar*) chore; (*Mil*) fatigue; **estar en (plena) ~** to be hard at work ➤ **faena doméstica** housework 2 (*) (*tb* **mala ~**) (= *mala pasada*) dirty trick; **¡menuda ~ la que me hizo!** that was a a terrible thing he did to me! 3 (*Taur*) set of passes (*with the cape*) 4 (*Chi*) (= *obreros*) gang of workers; (= *local*) workplace

faenar /1a/ Ⓐ VI 1 (= *trabajar*) to work, labour, labor (*EEUU*) 2 [*pescador*] to fish Ⓑ VT (*CS*) to slaughter

fagot SM bassoon

faisán SM pheasant

faja SF 1 (= *prenda*) girdle 2 [*de tela*] sash 3 [*de terreno*] strip

fajar* /1a/ VT (*SAm*) to beat up

fajín SM (*Mil*) sash

fajina SF (*CS*) task, job (*to be done quickly*); **tenemos mucha ~** we've a lot to do, we've a tough job on here

fajo SM [*de papeles*] bundle, sheaf; [*de billetes*] roll, wad

falacia SF fallacy

falange SF 1 (*Anat*) phalange 2 (*Mil*) phalanx 3 **la Falange** (*Esp Pol*) the Falange, *the Spanish Falangist movement*

falangista ADJ, SMF Falangist

falaz ADJ false

falda SF 1 (= *prenda*) skirt ➤ **falda de tubo** straight skirt, pencil skirt ➤ **falda escocesa** (*gen*) tartan skirt; (= *traje típico escocés*) kilt ➤ **falda pantalón** culottes *pl*, split skirt ➤ **falda tableada** pleated skirt 2 (= *regazo*) lap; **sentarse en la ~ de algn** to sit on sb's lap 3 **faldas*** (= *mujeres*) women, ladies; **es asunto de ~s** there's a woman behind it somewhere 4 [*de montaña*] (= *ladera*) side; (= *pie*) foot 5 [*de res*] brisket, skirt 6 [*de mesa camilla*] table cover

faldeo SM (*CS*) slope, mountainside

faldero ADJ **hombre ~** ladies' man; **perro ~** lapdog

faldón SM 1 [*de vestido*] tail, skirt; (= *pliegue*) flap 2 [*de bebé*] long dress

falencia SF 1 (*Arg Fin*) bankruptcy 2 (*RPl*) (= *deficiencia*) deficiency

fálico ADJ phallic

falla SF 1 (*Geol*) fault 2 (= *defecto*) [*de tejido*] flaw; [*de mercancías*] fault, defect; (*LAm*) [*de carácter*] failing 3 (*CS, Méx*) (= *mal funcionamiento*) failure; (= *defecto*) fault 4 (*CS, Méx*) (= *error*) mistake 5 (= *figura*) huge ornate cardboard figure burnt in Valencia at the Fallas

fallar /1a/ Ⓐ VI 1 [*freno*] to fail; [*plan*] to fail, go wrong; [*motor*] to misfire; **le falla la memoria** his memory is failing; **me ~on las piernas** my legs gave way; **algo falló en sus planes** something went wrong with his plans; **si le pones la tele se calla, no falla nunca** if you put the TV on for him he'll shut up, it never fails 2 (= *defraudar*) **a algn** to let sb down, fail sb; **mañana hay reunión, no me falles** there's a meeting tomorrow, don't let me down 3 (*Jur*) to pass judg(e)ment; **~ a favor/en contra de algn** to rule in favour *o* (*EEUU*) favor of/against sb, find for/against sb 4 (*Naipes*) to trump Ⓑ VT 1 (= *errar*) **falló las cuatro preguntas** she got all four questions wrong; **fallé el tiro** I missed; **~ el blanco** to miss the target 2 (*Jur*) to deliver judg(e)ment in 3 [+ *premio*] to award

Fallas SFPL *Valencian celebration of the feast of St Joseph*

FALLAS

In the week of March 19 (the feast of San José), Valencia honours its patron saint with a spectacular fiesta called **las Fallas**. **Fallas** is the name given to the huge papier-mâché, cardboard and wooden sculptures depicting politicians and other well-known public figures which, amidst a deafening display of fireworks, are put on bonfires and set alight by members of competing groups, or **falleros**, who will have spent the previous year creating and building them. Only the sculpture which is voted best escapes the flames.
See also www.fallas.com

fallecer /2d/ VI to die, pass away (*euf*)

fallecido/a Ⓐ ADJ deceased, late Ⓑ SM/F deceased

fallecimiento SM death, demise (*frm*), passing (*euf*)

fallero/a Ⓐ ADJ *of/relating to the "Fallas"* Ⓑ SM/F 1 (= *constructor*) maker of "Fallas" 2 (= *participante*) person who takes part in the "Fallas" ➤ **fallera mayor** "Fallas" queen

fallido/a ADJ 1 [*esfuerzo*] unsuccessful 2 (*Carib Com*) bankrupt

fallo SM 1 [*de un tribunal*] judg(e)ment, ruling; [*de concurso, premio*] decision 2 (*Esp*) (= *mal funcionamiento*) failure; (= *defecto*) fault; **debido a un ~ de los frenos** because of brake failure ➤ **fallo cardíaco** heart failure 3 (*Esp*) (= *error*) mistake; **¡qué ~!** what a stupid mistake! ➤ **fallo humano** human error

falluca* SF (*Méx*) smuggling

falluquear* /1a/ VT (*Méx*) to smuggle

falluquero/a* SM/F 1 (*Méx*) (= *contrabandista*) smuggler 2 (*CS*) (= *viajante*) travelling salesman/saleswoman

falluto* ADJ (*CS*) hypocritical, two-faced*

falo SM phallus

falsear /1a/ VT [+ *cifras, datos*] to falsify, doctor; [+ *verdad, hechos*] to distort

falsedad SF 1 [*de acusación, teoría*] falseness, falsity; [*de persona*] falseness, insincerity 2 (= *mentira*) lie, falsehood (*frm*)

falsete SM (*Mús*) falsetto

falsificación SF 1 (= *copia*) forging, forgery; (= *alteracion*) falsification 2 (= *objeto*) forgery

falsificador(a) SM/F forger

falsificar /1g/ VT [+ *billete, firma, cuadro*] to forge; [+ *resultado, elección*] to rig*; [+ *documento*] (= *copiar*) to forge; (= *alterar*) to falsify; [+ *pruebas*] (= *crear*) to fabricate; (= *alterar*) to falsify

falso ADJ 1 [*rumor, alarma, nombre*] false; **lo que dices es ~** what you're saying is false *o* untrue; **~ testimonio** perjury, false testimony 2 [*firma, pasaporte, joya*] false, fake; [*techo*] false; [*cuadro*] fake; [*moneda*] counterfeit 3 (= *insincero*) [*persona*] false, insincere; [*sonrisa*] false 4 [*caballo*] vicious 5 **jurar en ~** to commit perjury

falta SF 1 (= *carencia*) 1.1 [*de recursos, información, control, acuerdo*] lack; **su absoluta ~ de preparación** his total lack of preparation; **~ de respeto** disrespect, lack of respect; **¡qué ~ de respeto!** how rude! 1.2 **a ~ de** in the absence of, for want of; **a ~ de información fiable** in the absence of reliable information, for want of reliable information; **a ~ de champán para celebrarlo, beberemos cerveza** as we don't have any champagne to celebrate with, we'll drink beer; **a ~ de un término/sistema mejor** for want of a better term/system; **a ~ de tres minutos para el final** three minutes from the end; ✦ REFRÁN **a ~ de pan, buenas son tortas** half a loaf is better than none 1.3 **por ~ de** for lack of; **por ~ de pruebas** for lack of evidence; **el rosal se murió por ~ de luz** the rose died due to lack of light 1.4 **echar algo/a algn en ~** to miss sth/sb; **durante el festival se echaron en ~ a las grandes estrellas** the big names were missing from the festival 2 **hacer ~: me hace mucha ~ un coche** I really *o* badly* need a car; **lo que hace ~ aquí es más disciplina** what's needed here is stricter discipline; **aquí no haces ~** you're not needed here; **si hace ~, voy** if necessary, I'll go, if need be, I'll go; **no hace ~ ser un experto** you don't need to be an expert; ✦ MODISMO **ni ~ que hace** (*iró*): **—¿te han invitado al concierto? —no, ni ~ que me hace** "haven't they invited you to the concert?" — "no, and I couldn't care less"* 3 (*Escol*) (*tb* **~ de asistencia**) absence; **poner ~ a algn** to mark sb absent, put sb down as absent; **tiene cinco ~s de asistencia** he has been absent five times 4 (= *infracción*) 4.1 (*Jur*) offence, offense (*EEUU*) 4.2 (*Ftbl, Balonmano*) foul; (*Tenis*) fault; **va a sacar la ~** (*Ftbl*) he's going to take the free kick; (*Balonmano*) he's going to take the free throw ➤ **falta personal** personal foul 5 (= *fallo*) [*de persona*] shortcoming, fault; [*de máquina, producto*] flaw, fault; **sacar ~s a algn** to point out sb's shortcomings, find fault with sb; **siempre le está sacando ~s a todo lo que hago** she's always picking holes in everything I do; **mañana sin ~** tomorrow without fail ➤ **falta de ortografía** spelling mistake 6 (*por estar embarazada*) missed period

faltar /1a/ VI 1 (= *no haber suficiente*) **faltan profesores** there aren't enough teachers; **a la sopa le falta sal** there isn't enough salt in the soup; **faltan dos sillas** we are two chairs short; **~ algo a algn: nos falta tiempo para hacerlo** we don't have enough time to do it; **te faltan dos centímetros para poder ser policía** you're two centimetres too short to be a policeman; ✦ MODISMOS **¡lo que (me) faltaba!** that's all I needed!; **¡no faltaba ~ ía más!** (= *no hay de qué*) don't mention it!; (= *naturalmente*) of course; (= *¡ni hablar!*) certainly not!, no way!*; **¡no faltaba más que eso!** ◇ **¡lo que faltaba!** (= *¡es el colmo!*) that's the last straw!; (= *¡ni hablar!*) certainly not!, no way!* 2 (= *no estar*) to be missing; **faltan 50 euros de la caja** there is 50 euros missing from the till, the till is 50 euros short; **me falta un bolígrafo** one of my pens is missing; **¿quién falta?** who's missing?, who's not here?; **no ~: un libro que**

no debe ~ en su librería a book that should not be missing from your shelves; **no falta ninguno de los ingredientes de la novela policíaca** none of the ingredients of the detective novel are missing

3 (= *no ir*) **no he faltado ni una sola vez a las reuniones** I haven't missed a single meeting; **¡no ~é!** I'll be there!; **~ a una cita** (*de negocios*) to miss an appointment; (*con amigo*) not to show up for a date; **~ a clase** to miss school; **~ al trabajo** to be off work

4 (= *quedar*) **falta todavía bastante por hacer** there is still quite a lot to be done, quite a lot remains to be done; **falta mucho todavía** there's plenty of time to go yet; **¿falta mucho?** is there long to go?; **¿te falta mucho?** will you be long?; **~ para algo: faltan tres semanas para las elecciones** there are three weeks to go to the election, the election is three weeks off; **faltan cinco para las siete** (*LAm*) it's five to seven; **falta poco para las ocho** it's nearly eight o'clock, it's getting on for eight o'clock; **falta poco para que termine el partido** the match is almost over *o* finished

5 (= *estar a punto de*) **faltó poco para que lo pillara un coche** he was very nearly run down by a car

6 (= *insultar*) **¡sin ~!, ¿eh?** keep it polite, right?; **~ a algn al respeto** to be rude to sb, be disrespectful to sb; *ver tb* **promesa 1, respeto 1**

7 (*euf*) (= *estar muerto*) **desde que falta su madre** since his mother passed away; **cuando falte yo** when I'm gone

falto ADJ **~ de** [*recursos, información, ideas, inteligencia*] lacking in; **nos pareció un partido ~ de interés** we thought the match was uninteresting *o* lacking in interest; **estar ~ de personal** to be short of staff

faltriquera SF pocket, pouch

fama SF **1** (= *renombre*) fame; **el libro que le dio ~** the book which made him famous, the book which made his name; **tener ~** to be famous **2** (= *reputación*) reputation; **tiene ~ de duro** he has a reputation for being tough; **este restaurante tiene ~ de barato** this restaurant is (well-) known for its cheap food; **tener mala ~** to have a bad reputation; **una casa de mala ~** a house of ill repute

famélico ADJ starving, famished

familia SF **1** (= *parientes*) family; **es de buena ~** she comes from a good family; **no son ~** they are not related; **ser como de la ~** to be one of the family; **venir de ~** to run in the family ▶ **familia de acogida** foster family ▶ **familia monoparental** one-parent family ▶ **familia política** in-laws *pl* ▶ **familia real** royal family **2** (= *hijos*) **no tienen ~** they haven't got any children; **está por tener ~** (*CS*) she's about to have a baby **3** (*Bot, Ling, Zool*) family

familiar ⒶADJ **1** (= *de la familia*) family *antes de s*; **lazos ~es** family ties; **"pensión Sol, ambiente familiar"** "pensión Sol, friendly atmosphere"; **coche ~** estate car (*Brit*), station wagon (*EEUU*); **envase ~** family-sized *o* family pack; **en la pensión recibes un trato ~** in the guesthouse they treat you like one of the family **2** (= *conocido*) familiar; **tu cara me resulta ~** your face looks familiar **3** [*lenguaje, término*] colloquial ⒷSMF (= *pariente*) relative, relation

familiaridad SF familiarity

familiarizar /1f/ ⒶVT to familiarize, acquaint; **~ a algn con algo** to familiarize *o* acquaint sb with sth
Ⓑfamiliarizarse VPR **~se con** to familiarize o.s. with, get to know, make o.s. familiar with

famoseo SM **una revista de ~** a celebrity magazine, a magazine about celebrities

famoso/a ⒶADJ famous, well-known; **un actor ~** a famous *o* well-known actor; **el pueblo es ~ por su cerámica** the town is famous for its pottery ⒷSM/F celebrity, famous person

fan SMF (*pl* **~s**) fan

fanal SM **1** (*en la costa*) harbour beacon, harbor beacon (*EEUU*) **2** (= *campana*) bell glass **3** (*Méx Aut*) headlight

fanático/a ⒶADJ fanatical ⒷSM/F fanatic

fanatismo SM fanaticism

fancine SM = **fanzine**

fandango SM **1** (*Mús*) fandango **2** (*LAm**) (= *fiesta*) rowdy party, booze-up*

faneca SF *species of flatfish*

fanfarria SF (*Mús*) fanfare

fanfarrón/ona ⒶADJ boastful ⒷSM/F boaster, braggart

fanfarronada SF boasting

fanfarronear /1a/ VI to boast, talk big*

fango SM (= *lodo*) mud, mire; (*fig*) mire, dirt

fantasear /1a/ VI to dream, fantasize

fantasía SF **1** (= *imaginación*) imagination; **es un producto de su ~** it's a figment of his imagination **2** (= *cosa imaginada*) fantasy; **son ~s infantiles** they're just children's fantasies **3** (*Arte, Literat*) fantasy; (*Mús*) fantasia, fantasy **4 de ~** (= *con adornos, colores*) fancy; **botones de ~** fancy buttons; **joyas de ~** costume jewellery

fantasioso ADJ dreamy

fantasma ⒶSM ghost, phantom (*liter*) ⒷSMF (*Esp**) (= *fanfarrón*) boaster, braggart ⒸADJ INV **1** (= *abandonado*) ghost *antes de s*; **buque ~** ghost ship; **ciudad ~** ghost town **2** (= *inexistente*) phantom *antes de s*; **embarazo ~** phantom pregnancy

fantasmagórico ADJ phantasmagoric

fantasmal ADJ ghostly, phantom *antes de s*

fantasmón/ona* ⒶADJ boastful ⒷSM/F boaster

fantástico ⒶADJ **1** (= *imaginario*) fantastic **2** (*) (= *estupendo*) fantastic, great* ⒷEXCL (*) great!, fantastic!

fantoche SM **1** (= *títere*) puppet, marionette **2** (*) (*persona*) (= *mediocre*) mediocrity, nonentity; (= *presumido*) braggart, loudmouth*

fanzine SM fanzine

FAO SF ABR (= **Food and Agriculture Organization**) FAO

faquir SM fakir

farabute SM **1** (*RPl*) (= *fanfarrón*) show-off **2** (*CS*) (= *poco cumplidor*) unreliable person

faramalla* SF (*Méx, Chi*) lie

farándula SF (*Teat, Hist*) troupe of strolling players; **el mundo de la ~** the theatre *o* (*EEUU*) theater world

faraón SM Pharaoh

faraónico ADJ (*Hist*) Pharaonic; [*plan, obra*] overambitious

FARC SFPL ABR (*Col*) = **Fuerzas Armadas Revolucionarias de Colombia**

fardar* /1a/ VI (*Esp*) **1** [*persona*] (= *lucirse*) to show off, put on a display; (= *jactarse*) to boast; **fardaba de sus amigas** he boasted about his girlfriends **2** [*objeto*] to be classy; **es un coche que farda mucho** it's a car with a lot of class

fardo SM bundle

fardón/ona* (*Esp*) ⒶADJ **1** [*objeto*] classy*, swanky, posh (*esp Brit*) **2** (= *elegante*) [*ropa*] natty*; [*persona*] nattily dressed* **3** (= *vanidoso*) stuck-up*, swanky* ⒷSM/F show-off*

farero/a SM/F lighthouse-keeper

farfullar /1a/ ⒶVI (= *balbucear*) to splutter; (= *hablar atropelladamente*) to jabber, gabble ⒷVT **1** (*al hablar*) to jabber, gabble **2** (*al actuar*) to do hastily, botch

faringe SF pharynx

faringitis SF INV pharyngitis

fariseo SM **1** (*Rel*) Pharisee **2** (= *hipócrita*) hypocrite, Pharisee

farlopa** SF (*Esp*) blow**, coke**

farmaceuta SMF (*Col, Ven*) = **farmacéutico** B

farmacéutico/a ⒶADJ [*producto*] pharmaceutical; **la industria farmacéutica** the pharmaceutical *o* drug industry ⒷSM/F (= *persona*) chemist (*Brit*), druggist (*EEUU*), pharmacist (*frm*)

farmacia SF **1** (= *establecimiento*) chemist's (shop) (*Brit*), drugstore (*EEUU*) ▶ **farmacia de guardia** *pharmacy supplying out-of-hours cover* **2** (= *ciencia*) pharmacy

fármaco SM drug, medicine

farmacológico ADJ pharmacological

faro SM **1** (*Náut*) (= *edificio*) lighthouse; (= *señal*) beacon ▶ **faro aéreo** air beacon **2** (*Aut*) headlamp, headlight ▶ **faro antiniebla** fog lamp ▶ **faro halógeno** halogen headlight

farol SM **1** (= *lámpara*) (*en terraza, jardín*) lantern, lamp; (*en la calle*) street light; (*Ferro*) headlamp **2** (*) (= *mentira*) (*gen*) lie, fib; (*Naipes*) bluff; **echarse** o **marcarse** o **tirarse un ~** (*gen*) to shoot a line*, brag; (*Naipes*) to bluff

farola SF (= *lámpara*) street light; (= *poste*) lamppost

farolazo* SM (*CAm, Méx*) swig* (*of liquor*)

farolero/a* **Ⓐ** ADJ boastful **Ⓑ** SM/F boaster

farra SF party; **ir de ~** to go out partying

farragoso ADJ [*discurso*] involved, dense

farrear /1a/ **Ⓐ** VI (*SAm*) to party, be out drinking **Ⓑ** **farrearse** VPR (*RPl**) [+ *dinero*] to squander

farrista ADJ **1** (*CS*) (= *borracho*) hard-drinking, dissipated **2** (= *juerguista*) boisterous, rowdy

farruco* ADJ stroppy (*Brit**), teed off (*EEUU**)

farsa SF **1** (*Teat*) farce **2** (= *engaño*) farce, sham

farsante SMF fraud, phoney*, phony*

fascículo SM part, instalment, installment (*EEUU*)

fascinación SF fascination

fascinante ADJ fascinating

fascinar /1a/ VT to fascinate, captivate

fascismo SM fascism

fascista ADJ, SMF fascist

fase SF **1** (= *etapa*) stage, phase; **el proyecto está en ~ de estudio** the project is still under consideration ➤ **fase clasificatoria** (*Dep*) qualifying stage ➤ **fase terminal** terminal phase **2** (*Astron, Biol, Elec*) phase **3** [*de cohete*] stage

fashion ADJ trendy*

fastidiado* ADJ **1** (= *estropeado*) ruined, bust* **2** **ando ~ del estómago** ◇ **tengo el estómago ~** I've got a bad o (*Brit**) dodgy stomach

fastidiar /1b/ **Ⓐ** VT **1** (= *molestar*) to annoy; **lo que más me fastidia es tener que decírselo** what annoys me most is having to tell him; **su actitud me fastidia mucho** I find his attitude very annoying **2** (*) (= *estropear*) [+ *fiesta, plan*] to spoil, ruin; [+ *aparato*] to break **Ⓑ** VI (= *bromear*) **¡no fastidies!** you're kidding! **Ⓒ** **fastidiarse** VPR **1** (= *aguantarse*) **¿no le gusta la comida? ¡pues que se fastidie!** he doesn't like the food? well, that's tough!* **2** (= *dañarse*) to hurt; **me he vuelto a ~ la rodilla** I've hurt my knee again, I've done my knee in again **3** (*) (= *estropearse*) [*fiesta, plan*] to be spoiled, be ruined; [*aparato*] to break down

fastidio SM annoyance, bother; **¡qué ~!** what a nuisance!, what a pain!*

fasto SM pomp, pageantry

fastuoso ADJ [*palacio, carroza*] magnificent, splendid; [*banquete, fiesta*] lavish, sumptuous

fatal **Ⓐ** ADJ **1** (= *mortal*) [*accidente, desenlace*] fatal **2** (*) (= *horrible*) awful, terrible; **tiene un inglés ~** his English is awful o terrible **Ⓑ** ADV (*) terribly; **cocina ~** he's an awful o a terrible cook; **me encuentro ~** I feel awful o terrible

fatalidad SF **1** (= *destino*) fate **2** (= *desdicha*) misfortune, bad luck

fatalista **Ⓐ** ADJ fatalistic **Ⓑ** SMF fatalist

fatídico ADJ fateful, ominous

fatiga SF **1** (= *cansancio*) fatigue (*frm*), tiredness, weariness ➤ **fatiga cerebral** mental fatigue ➤ **fatiga muscular** muscle fatigue **2** (= *ahogo*) breathlessness; **subir las escaleras me causa ~** I get breathless when I go upstairs **3** (= *reparo*) embarrassment; **me da ~ llamar a estas horas de la noche** I'm embarrassed calling at this time of night **4** **fatigas** (= *penalidades*) hardship *sing*, troubles

fatigar /1h/ **Ⓐ** VT to tire **Ⓑ** **fatigarse** VPR **1** (= *cansarse*) to tire, get tired; **~se al andar** to wear o.s. out walking **2** (= *ahogarse*) to get out of breath, get breathless

fatigoso ADJ **1** (= *cansado*) tiring, exhausting **2** (*Med*) painful, difficult; **respiración fatigosa** laboured o (*EEUU*) labored breathing

fatuo ADJ **1** (= *necio*) fatuous **2** (= *vanidoso*) conceited; *ver*

fuego 1

fauces SFPL (*Anat*) fauces, gullet *sing*; (*fig*) (= *boca*) jaws

faul SM (*pl ~s*) (*LAm Dep*) foul

faulear /1a/ VT (*LAm Dep*) to foul

fauna SF fauna; **toda la ~ del barrio*** all the weirdos in the neighbourhood*

fauno SM faun

fausto **Ⓐ** ADJ fortunate, lucky **Ⓑ** SM splendour, splendor (*EEUU*), magnificence

favor SM

En inglés americano se usa **favor, favorable** etc, en lugar de **favour, favourable** etc.

1 (= *ayuda*) favour; **~ de venir puntualmente** (*Méx*) please be punctual; **hacer un ~ a algn** to do sb a favour; **¿me hace el ~ de bajarme la maleta?** I wonder if you could get my suitcase down for me, please?, could you possibly get my suitcase down for me, please?; **¡haced el ~ de callaros!** will you please be quiet!; **si hace el ~ de pasar** if you'd like o care to go in; **si hace ~** (*LAm*) if you don't mind; **pedir un ~ a algn** to ask sb (for) a favour, ask a favour of sb (*más frm*); **por ~** please **2** (*locuciones*) **2.1 a favor** in favour; **votos a ~** votes in favour; **¿estás a ~ o en contra?** are you for or against it?; **tener el viento a ~** to have the wind behind one o in one's favour **2.2 a ~ de** in favour; **¿está a ~ de poner fin al bloqueo del país?** are you in favour of ending the blockade of the country?; **lo tenía todo a su ~** she had everything going for her; **el partido ya estaba decidido a ~ de la jugadora española** the Spanish player already had the match sewn up **2.3 en ~ de** [*abdicar, manifestarse*] in favour of; [*intervenir*] on behalf of; [*trabajar, luchar*] for; **el director se manifestó en ~ del cine europeo** the director spoke in favour of o expressed his support for the European film industry; **piden a la ONU su intervención en ~ de los detenidos** the UN is being asked to intervene on behalf of those detained; **una recogida de firmas en ~ del indulto de los presos** a petition for the pardon of the prisoners **3** (= *apoyo*) [*del rey, dioses*] favour, protection; [*del público*] support; **ha sabido ganarse el ~ de la audiencia** she has succeeded in winning the audience's affection; **gozar del ~ de algn** to have sb's support o backing, enjoy sb's favour (*frm*)

favorable ADJ

En inglés americano se usa **favorable, favor** etc, en lugar de **favour, favourable** etc.

favourable; **una respuesta ~** a favourable reply; **vientos ~s** favourable winds; **~ a algo** in favour of sth

favorecedor ADJ [*vestido*] becoming; [*retrato*] flattering

favorecer /2d/ **Ⓐ** VT

En inglés americano se usa **favorable, favor** etc, en lugar de **favour, favourable** etc.

1 (= *beneficiar*) to be favourable to, favour; **la devaluación ha favorecido a las compañías exportadoras** devaluation has been favourable to o has favoured exporting companies; **el sorteo favoreció al equipo canadiense** Canada did well out of the draw **2** (= *ayudar a*) [+ *desarrollo, creación, crecimiento*] to contribute to; **las nuevas medidas fiscales ~án la creación de empresas** the new tax measures will contribute to o encourage o favour the creation of new companies **3** (= *tratar con favores*) **~ a algn** to help out sb, do sb favours; **utilizó sus influencias para ~ a sus amigos** she used her influence to help out her friends o to do favours for her friends **4** (= *sentar bien*) [*vestido*] to suit, look good on; [*peinado*] to suit; **las faldas largas no te favorecen** long skirts don't

suit you o look good on you; **el retrato no la favorece** the portrait is not very flattering
Ⓑ VI (= *sentar bien*) to be flattering, look good

favorecido ADJ 1 (= *beneficiado*) (*en el trato*) favoured, favored (*EEUU*); (*por la suerte, el dinero*) fortunate; **trato de nación más favorecida** most-favoured nation treatment; **las clases menos favorecidas** the less fortunate classes; **resultó ~ en la lotería con varios millones de pesetas** he won several million pesetas on the lottery 2 (*físicamente*) **estás muy ~ en esta foto** you look very good in this photo, this is a very good photo of you

favoritismo SM favouritism, favoritism (*EEUU*)

favorito/a ADJ, SM/F favourite, favorite (*EEUU*)

fax SM 1 (= *máquina*) fax (machine); **mandar por ~** to fax, send by fax 2 (= *mensaje*) fax; **mandar un ~** to send a fax

faxear /1a/ VT to fax, send by fax

faz SF face; **en la ~ de la tierra** on the face of the earth

fe SF 1 (*Rel*) faith (**en** in); **la fe católica** the Catholic faith 2 (= *confianza*) faith; **tener fe en algn/algo** to have faith in sb/sth 3 (= *intención*) faith; **mala fe** bad faith; **actuar en** o **de buena fe** to act in good faith 4 (= *testimonio*) **dar fe de algo** to vouch for sth, testify to sth 5 (= *certificado*) ➤ **fe de bautismo** certificate of baptism ➤ **fe de erratas, fe de errores** (*en libro*) errata; (*en periódico*) correction ➤ **fe de vida** *certificate testifying that a person is still alive*

fealdad SF ugliness

febrero SM February; *ver tb* **septiembre**

En inglés los meses se escriben con mayúscula.

febril ADJ 1 (*Med*) fevered, feverish 2 [*actividad*] hectic, feverish

fecal ADJ faecal, fecal (*EEUU*)

fecha SF 1 (= *día preciso*) date; **¿a qué ~ estamos?** what's the date today?; **ya tengo ~ para el dentista** I've got an appointment at the dentist's; **a partir de esa ~ no volvió a llamar** thereafter o from then on he never called again; **una carta con ~ del 15 de agosto** a letter dated August 15th; **hasta la ~** to date, so far; **pasarse de ~** (*Com*) to pass the sell-by date; **poner la ~ a algo** to date sth; **en ~ próxima** soon; **una carta sin ~** an undated letter, a letter with no date ➤ **fecha de caducidad** [*de medicamento, tarjeta*] expiry date; [*de alimento*] best-before date ➤ **fecha de emisión** date of issue ➤ **fecha de entrega** delivery date ➤ **fecha de nacimiento** date of birth ➤ **fecha de vencimiento = fecha de caducidad** ➤ **fecha límite** deadline ➤ **fecha tope** [*de finalización*] deadline; [*de entrega*] closing date
2 **fechas** (= *época*) **siempre viene por estas ~s** he always comes about this time of year; **el año pasado por estas ~s** this time last year

fechar /1a/ VT to date

fechoría SF misdeed, misdemeanour, misdemeanor (*EEUU*)

fécula SF starch

fecundación SF fertilization ➤ **fecundación artificial** artificial insemination ➤ **fecundación in vitro** in vitro fertilization

fecundar /1a/ VT to fertilize

fecundidad SF fertility, fecundity

fecundizar /1f/ VT to fertilize

fecundo ADJ 1 [*persona, tierra*] fertile, fecund (*frm*) 2 [*pintor, escritor*] prolific 3 (= *fructífero*) fruitful, productive; **una década fecunda de los grandes economistas** a fruitful o productive period for great economists

FED SM ABR (= **Fondo Europeo de Desarrollo**) EDF

FEDER SM ABR (= **Fondo Europeo de Desarrollo Regional**) ERDF

federación SF federation

federal ADJ federal

federalismo SM federalism

federar /1a/ **Ⓐ** VT to federate **Ⓑ** **federarse** VPR 1 (*Pol*) to

federate, become federated 2 (= *hacerse socio*) (*en club, asociación*) to become a member; (*en federación*) to affiliate

federativo ADJ federative

fehaciente ADJ reliable

felación SF fellatio

felicidad SF 1 (= *satisfacción*) happiness 2 **¡felicidades!** (= *deseos*) best wishes, congratulations!; (*en cumpleaños*) happy birthday!

felicitación SF 1 (= *enhorabuena*) **mi ~** o **mis felicitaciones al ganador** my congratulations to the winner; **he recibido muchas felicitaciones** lots of people have congratulated me 2 (= *tarjeta*) greetings card, greeting card (*EEUU*) ➤ **felicitación de Navidad** Christmas card

felicitar /1a/ VT to congratulate; **~ a algn por algo** to congratulate sb on sth; **¡le felicito!** congratulations!, well done!; **~ la Navidad a algn** to wish sb a happy Christmas

feligrés/esa SM/F parishioner

felino/a **Ⓐ** ADJ feline, catlike **Ⓑ** SM/F feline, cat

feliz ADJ 1 [*persona, acontecimiento, idea*] happy; **se la ve muy ~** she looks very happy; **¡Feliz Año Nuevo!** Happy New Year!; **hacer ~ a algn** to make sb happy 2 (*frm*) (= *acertado*) [*expresión*] apt

felonía SF felony, crime

felpa SF [*de toalla, camisa, pañal*] (terry) towelling o (*EEUU*) toweling; [*de sillón, moqueta*] plush; **ositos de ~** furry teddies

felpilla SF chenille

felpudo SM doormat

femenil ADJ (*CAm, Méx Dep*) women's *antes de s*; **equipo ~** women's team

femenino **Ⓐ** ADJ 1 (*cualidad de mujer*) feminine; **es muy femenina** she's very feminine 2 [*sexo, representante, población*] female; **el cuerpo ~** the female body 3 (*Dep*) **deporte ~** women's sport; **equipo ~** women's team 4 (*Ling*) feminine **Ⓑ** SM (*Ling*) feminine

Al traducir **femenino**, el adjetivo **female** señala que se está haciendo referencia a algo relativo al sexo femenino por oposición al masculino, p.ej., "el sexo femenino", *the female sex*. El adjetivo **feminine** se utiliza en relación a cualidades que se consideran típicas de la mujer y no del hombre, p.ej., "una chica muy femenina", *a very feminine girl*. Se utiliza además para indicar el género gramatical.

fémina SF (*hum*) woman, female

feminismo SM feminism

feminista ADJ, SMF feminist

femoral **Ⓐ** ADJ [*hueso*] femur *antes de s*; [*arteria, vena*] femoral **Ⓑ** SF femoral artery

fémur SM femur

fenecer /2d/ VI to pass away (*euf*), die

feng shui [ˌfeŋˈʃuːi] SM feng shui

fenicio/a ADJ, SM/F Phoenician

fénix SM phoenix

fenomenal **Ⓐ** ADJ 1 (*) (= *estupendo*) fantastic*, brilliant (*esp Brit**) 2 (= *espectacular*) phenomenal, remarkable **Ⓑ** ADV (*) **lo hemos pasado ~** we've had a fantastic o (*esp Brit*) brilliant time*; **le va ~** he's getting on fantastically well o (*esp Brit*) brilliantly*

fenómeno **Ⓐ** SM 1 (*atmosférico, acústico, psíquico*) phenomenon 2 (= *monstruo*) freak 3 (= *portento*) genius; **Pedro es un ~** Pedro is a genius, Pedro is altogether exceptional **Ⓑ** ADJ (*) (= *fenomenal*) fantastic*, brilliant (*esp Brit**)

feo **Ⓐ** ADJ 1 (= *sin belleza*) [*persona, casa, ropa*] ugly; ✦ MODISMO **más ~ que Picio** o **un grajo** (*Esp*) as ugly as sin 2 (= *desagradable*) [*asunto, tiempo*] nasty, unpleasant; [*jugada*] dirty; **esto se está poniendo ~** things are getting nasty
3 (= *de mala educación*) **es** o (*Esp*) **está muy ~ contestarle así**

a tu madre it's very rude o it's not nice to answer your mother like that; **queda ~ comerse las uñas en público** it's bad manners to bite your nails in public
4 (*LAm*) [*olor, comida*] nasty, unpleasant
Ⓑ SM (= *desaire*) **hacer un ~ a algn** to snub sb; **—no puedo ir a tu boda —¿me vas a hacer ese ~?** "I can't come to your wedding" — "but you can't refuse!" o "how can you refuse?"

feraz ADJ fertile, productive

féretro SM coffin, casket (*EEUU*)

feria SF **1** (= *muestra comercial*) fair ➤ **feria del libro** book fair ➤ **feria de muestras** trade show, trade exhibition
2 (*Agr*) show ➤ **feria agrícola** agricultural show ➤ **feria de ganado** cattle show
3 [*de atracciones*] funfair (*Brit*), carnival (*EEUU*)
4 (= *fiesta*) festival; **durante la ~ habrá corridas de toros todos los días** during the festival there will be bullfights every day; **la Feria de Sevilla** the Seville Fair
5 (*CS*) (= *mercado al aire libre*) street market
6 (*Méx**) (= *cambio*) (small) change; (= *dinero*) dough*; **cuesta unos doscientos pesos y ~** it costs just over two hundred pesos

feriado Ⓐ ADJ **día ~** holiday Ⓑ SM (*LAm*) public holiday, bank holiday

ferial ADJ fair *antes de s*, fairground *antes de s*; **recinto ~** fairground, showground

feriante SMF (*en mercado*) stallholder, trader; (*en feria de muestras*) exhibitor

ferino ADJ **tos ferina** whooping cough

fermentación SF fermentation

fermentar /1a/ Ⓐ VI **1** [*vino, queso, compost*] to ferment **2** [*crisis, violencia*] to ferment Ⓑ VT to ferment

fermento SM **1** [*de queso, cerveza*] ferment **2** [*de crisis, violencia*] ferment

ferocidad SF ferocity, ferociousness

feroz ADJ **1** (= *salvaje*) fierce, ferocious; **tengo un hambre ~** I'm starving, I'm famished **2** (= *cruel*) cruel

férreo ADJ **1** (= *de hierro*) iron *antes de s*; (*Quím*) ferrous; **metal no ~** non-ferrous metal **2** (*Ferro*) rail *antes de s*; **vía férrea** railway track o line, railroad (*EEUU*)
3 (= *tenaz*) [*voluntad*] iron *antes de s*; [*acoso*] fierce, determined; [*cerco, marcaje*] very close, tight
4 (= *estricto*) [*disciplina, control*] strict, tight; [*horario*] strict, rigid

ferretería SF **1** (= *objetos*) hardware, ironmongery (*Brit*) **2** (= *tienda*) hardware store, ironmonger's (shop) (*Brit*)

ferretero/a SM/F hardware dealer, ironmonger (*Brit*)

ferrocarril SM railway (*esp Brit*), railroad (*EEUU*); **por ~** by rail, by train ➤ **ferrocarril de vía estrecha, ferrocarril de trocha angosta** (*CS*) narrow-gauge railway (*esp Brit*) o railroad (*EEUU*)

ferrocarrilero/a (*LAm*) ADJ, SM/F = **ferroviario**

ferroviario/a Ⓐ ADJ [*red, sistema*] rail *antes de s*, railway *antes de s* (*esp Brit*), railroad *antes de s* (*EEUU*) Ⓑ SM/F (= *trabajador*) railway worker (*esp Brit*), railroad worker (*EEUU*)

ferry ['feri] (*pl* **ferries**) SM ferry

fértil ADJ **1** [*tierra, campo*] fertile, rich **2** [*persona, animal*] fertile **3** [*discusión*] fertile, fruitful; [*imaginación*] fertile

fertilidad SF fertility

fertilización SF fertilization ➤ **fertilización in vitro** in vitro fertilization

fertilizante Ⓐ ADJ fertilizing Ⓑ SM fertilizer

fertilizar /1f/ VT to fertilize

ferviente ADJ [*devoto, partidario*] fervent; [*deseo, amor, ambición*] burning

fervor SM fervour, fervor (*EEUU*)

fervoroso ADJ fervent, passionate

festejar /1a/ VT **1** (= *celebrar*) to celebrate **2** [+ *persona*] to wine and dine, entertain

festejo SM celebration; **festejos** (= *fiestas*) festivities

festín SM feast, banquet

festinar /1a/ VT (*LAm*) to hurry along, speed up

festival SM festival

festividad SF **1** (*Rel*) feast, holiday **2** (*tb* **~es**) (= *celebraciones*) festivities, celebrations

festivo ADJ **1** (= *no laborable*) **día ~** holiday **2** (= *alegre*) festive, merry

festón SM festoon, scallop

feta SF (*RPl*) slice

fetal ADJ foetal, fetal (*EEUU*)

fetiche SM fetish

fetichismo SM fetishism

fetichista Ⓐ ADJ fetishistic Ⓑ SMF fetishist

fétido ADJ fetid, foul-smelling, stinking

feto SM foetus, fetus (*EEUU*)

feudal ADJ feudal

feudalismo SM feudalism

feudo SM (*Hist*) fief

FEVE SF ABR = **Ferrocarriles Españoles de Vía Estrecha**

fez SM fez

FF.AA. ABR = **Fuerzas Armadas**

fiabilidad SF reliability, trustworthiness

fiable ADJ reliable, trustworthy

fiaca* (*CS*) Ⓐ ADJ lazy Ⓑ SMF lazy person Ⓒ SF laziness

fiado Ⓐ ADJ on credit Ⓑ SM **al ~** on credit

fiador(a) SM/F (*Jur*) guarantor, bondsman (*EEUU*); **salir ~ por algn** to stand security for sb; (*Jur*) to stand bail for sb

fiambre SM **1** (*Culin*) cold meat, cold cut (*EEUU*); **~s** cold meats, cold cuts (*EEUU*) **2** (*) (= *cadáver*) corpse, stiff*

fiambrera SF lunchbox, dinner pail (*EEUU*)

fiambrería SF (*And, CS*) delicatessen

fianza SF **1** (*Jur*) bail; **bajo ~** on bail **2** (*Com*) (= *anticipo*) deposit; (= *garantía*) surety, security, bond

fiar /1c/ Ⓐ VT to sell on credit
Ⓑ VI **1** (*Com*) to give credit; **"no se fía"** (*en tienda*) "no credit given"; **dejaron de ~le en la tienda** the shop wouldn't let her have anything on credit anymore
2 ser de ~ to be trustworthy, be reliable
Ⓒ **fiarse** VPR (= *confiar*) **~se de algn** to trust sb; **~se de algo** to believe in sth; **no te fíes de lo que digan los periódicos** don't believe what the papers say; **no me fío de su habilidad para resolver el problema** I don't believe in his ability to solve the problem; **no te fíes de las apariencias** don't go o judge by appearances; **¡para que te fíes de los amigos!** with friends like that, who needs enemies!

fiasco SM fiasco

fibra SF fibre, fiber (*EEUU*) ➤ **fibra de vidrio** fibreglass, fiber glass (*EEUU*) ➤ **fibra óptica** optical fibre o (*EEUU*) fiber

fibrosis SF INV fibrosis

fibroso ADJ fibrous

ficción SF **1** (*Literat*) fiction; **obras de no ~** non-fiction books **2** (= *invención*) fiction

ficha SF **1** (*en juegos*) counter; (*en casino*) chip; [*de dominó*] domino; [*de teléfono*] token; ✦ MODISMO **mover ~** to make a move **2** (= *tarjeta*) card; [*de archivo*] index card, record card; (*en hotel*) registration form ➤ **ficha policial** police dossier, police record ➤ **ficha técnica** (*TV*) (list of) credits **3** (*Uru**) (= *persona deshonesta*) crook*

fichaje SM (*Dep*) (= *acción*) signing, signing-up; (= *jugador*) signing

fichar /1a/ Ⓐ VT **1** (= *registrar*) [+ *detenido, trabajador*] to put on file; **está fichado** he's got a record **2** (*Dep*) [+ *jugador*] to sign, sign up **3** (*Pol*) [+ *nuevos miembros*] to sign up, recruit Ⓑ VI **1** (*Dep*) [*jugador*] to sign, sign up

2 [*trabajador*] (*al entrar*) to clock in, clock on; (*al salir*) to clock out, clock off

fichero SM **1** (= *archivo*) card index **2** (= *mueble*) filing cabinet **3** (*Inform*) file

ficticio ADJ [*nombre, carácter*] fictitious; [*historia, prueba*] fabricated

ficus SM INV rubber plant

fidedigno ADJ reliable, trustworthy

fideicomisario/a Ⓐ ADJ trust *antes de s*; **banco ~** trust company Ⓑ SM/F trustee

fideicomiso SM trust

fidelidad SF **1** (= *lealtad*) (*gen*) faithfulness, loyalty; (*sexual*) faithfulness; **~ a una marca** (*Com*) brand loyalty; **jurar ~ a la República** to swear allegiance to the Republic; **renunció al cargo por ~ a sus convicciones** he resigned in order to stay true to his principles **2** (= *exactitud*) [*de dato*] accuracy **3 alta ~** hi-fi

fidelización SF (*Com*) loyalty

fidelizar VT (*Com*) **- a los clientes** to gain o create customer loyalty

fideo SM **1** (*Culin*) noodle **2** (*) (= *delgado*) beanpole*, string bean (*EEUU**)

fiduciario/a Ⓐ ADJ fiduciary Ⓑ SM/F fiduciary, trustee

fiebre SF **1** (= *síntoma*) temperature, fever; **tener ~** to have a temperature **2** (= *enfermedad*) fever ➤ **fiebre aftosa** foot-and-mouth (disease) ➤ **fiebre amarilla** yellow fever ➤ **fiebre del heno** hay fever ➤ **fiebre de Malta** brucellosis ➤ **fiebre palúdica** malaria ➤ **fiebre porcina** swine fever (*Brit*), hog cholera (*EEUU*) ➤ **fiebre tifoidea** typhoid fever

fiel Ⓐ ADJ **1** (*gen*) faithful, loyal; (*sexualmente*) faithful; **un ~ servidor del partido** a loyal o faithful servant of the Party; **seguir siendo ~ a** to remain faithful to, stay true to **2** [*traducción, relación*] faithful, accurate Ⓑ SMF (*Rel*) believer; **los ~es** the faithful Ⓒ SM [*de balanza*] needle, pointer

fielmente ADV **1** [*servir, apoyar*] faithfully, loyally **2** [*reflejar, describir*] faithfully, accurately

fieltro SM felt

fiera Ⓐ SF (*Zool*) wild beast, wild animal; ✦ MODISMO **hecho una ~; ponerse hecho una ~** to be furious, be beside o.s. with rage Ⓑ SMF fiend; **es una ~ para el deporte** he's a sports fiend; **es un ~ para el trabajo** he's a demon for work

fiero ADJ **1** (= *feroz*) fierce, ferocious; (*Zool*) wild; ✦ MODISMO **no es tan ~ el león como lo pintan** (= *persona*) he's not as bad as he's made out to be; (= *situación*) it's not as bad as it's made out to be **2** (*RPI**) (= *feo*) ugly

fierro SM (*LAm*) **1** (= *hierro*) iron; ✦ MODISMO **meterle ~ (a fondo)** (*RPI**) to put one's foot down, step on the gas (*EEUU*) **2** (†) (= *cuchillo*) knife

fiesta SF **1** (= *reunión*) party; ✦ MODISMO **tener la ~ en paz: no os peleéis, ¡tengamos la ~ en paz!** behave yourselves, don't fight! ➤ **fiesta de cumpleaños** birthday party **2** (= *día festivo*) holiday; **mañana es ~** it's a holiday tomorrow ➤ **Fiesta de la Hispanidad** Columbus day ➤ **Fiesta del Trabajo** Labour day, Labor day (*EEUU*) ➤ **fiesta nacional** public holiday, bank holiday ➤ **fiesta patria** (*LAm*) national day **3** (*Rel*) feast day ➤ **fiesta de guardar, fiesta de precepto** day of obligation **4** (= *festejo*) fiesta, festival; **el pueblo está en ~s** o **de ~** the town's having its local fiesta; **la ~ nacional** (*Taur*) bullfighting **5 fiestas** (= *vacaciones*) holiday (*esp Brit*), vacation (*EEUU*); **las ~s de Navidad** the Christmas holiday(s) o (*EEUU*) vacation; **¡Felices Fiestas!** (*en navidad*) Happy Christmas!, Merry Christmas!

FIFA SF ABR (= **Fédération Internationale de Football Association**) FIFA

fifí* Ⓐ ADJ (*RPI*) snobbish Ⓑ SMF (*RPI*) snob Ⓒ SM (*Méx*) playboy

figura Ⓐ SF **1** (= *estatua*) figure; **una ~ de porcelana** a porcelain figure **2** (= *forma*) shape, form; **una chocolatina con ~ de pez** a fish-shaped chocolate, a chocolate in the shape of a fish **3** (= *silueta*) figure; **tener buena ~** to have a good figure **4** (= *personaje*) figure; **una ~ destacada** an outstanding figure **5** (*Geom*) figure ➤ **figura geométrica** geometric figure **6** (*Naipes*) face card **7** (*Ling*) figure ➤ **figura de dicción, figura retórica** figure of speech **8** (*Baile, Patinaje*) figure **9** (*Mús*) note Ⓑ SM **ser un ~** to be a big name, be somebody

figuración SF **1** (*Cine*) extras *pl* **2 figuraciones** (= *imaginación*) **eso son figuraciones tuyas** it's just your imagination, you're imagining things

figurado ADJ figurative

figurante SMF (SF *a veces* **figuranta**) (*Teat*) extra

figurar /1a/ Ⓐ VI **1** (= *aparecer*) to figure, appear (**como** as; **entre** among); **tu nombre no figura en la lista** your name doesn't figure o appear on the list **2** (= *destacar*) **es un don nadie, pero le encanta ~** he's a nobody, but he likes to show off Ⓑ **figurarse** VPR to imagine; **me figuro que Ana ya habrá llegado** I imagine that Ana will have arrived by now; **ya me lo figuraba** I thought as much

figurativo ADJ figurative

figurín SM **1** (= *dibujo*) design **2** (= *persona*) smart dresser

figurinista SMF costume designer

figurita SF (*RPI*) picture card

fija SF (*And, CS Hípica*) favourite, favorite (*EEUU*); **ésa es una ~*** that's for sure

fijación SF **1** (*Psic*) fixation; **tener (una) ~ con** o **por algo/algn** to have a fixation about sth/sb, be fixated on sth/sb **2 fijaciones** (*Esquí*) (safety) bindings

fijador SM **1** (*Fot*) fixative **2** (= *gomina*) setting lotion

fijamente ADV intently, fixedly; **mirar ~ a algn** to stare at sb, look at sb intently o fixedly

fijar /1a/ Ⓐ VT **1** (= *sujetar*) (*gen, Fot*) to fix; (*con clavos*) to secure; (*con pegamento*) to glue; (*con chinchetas*) to pin up; [+ *pelo*] to set; **un gel para ~ el peinado** a gel to hold your hairstyle in place; **"prohibido fijar carteles"** "stick no bills" **2** (= *centrar*) [+ *atención*] to focus (**en** on); [+ *ojos*] to fix (**en** on); **fijando la mirada en sus ojos** looking him straight in the eye **3** (= *determinar*) [+ *fecha, hora, precio, plazo*] to fix, set; [+ *límites, servicios mínimos*] to establish; [+ *condiciones*] to lay down; **el plazo fijado por la ley** the time period established o laid down by law **4** [+ *residencia*] to take up; **fijó su residencia en Suiza** he took up residence in Switzerland Ⓑ **fijarse** VPR **1** (= *prestar atención*) to pay attention; (= *darse cuenta*) to notice; **¿no ves que lo has escrito mal?**

¡es que no te fijas! can't you see you've spelled it wrong? don't you ever pay any attention to what you're doing?; **voy a hacerlo yo primero, fíjate bien** I'll do it first, watch carefully; **¿han pintado la puerta?** no me había fijado has the door been painted? I hadn't noticed; **~se en algo** (= *prestar atención*) to pay attention to sth; (= *darse cuenta*) to notice sth; **no se fija en lo que hace** he doesn't pay attention to what he is doing; **entre tantos candidatos, es muy difícil que se fijen en mí** out of so many candidates, they're hardly likely to notice me
2 (*uso enfático*) **¡fíjate cómo corre!** (just) look at him run!; **¡fíjate lo que me ha dicho!** guess what he just said to me!
3 **~se un objetivo** to set (o.s.) a goal; **~se algo como objetivo** to set one's sights on sth

fijo 🅐 ADJ 1 (= *sujeto*) fixed
2 (= *inmóvil*) [*mirada*] fixed, steady; [*punto*] fixed
3 (= *no variable*) [*fecha, precio*] fixed; **no hay una fecha fija de apertura** there's no definite *o* fixed *o* set date for the opening; **no tengo horario ~ de trabajo** I don't have fixed *o* regular work hours; **una cantidad fija al mes** a fixed monthly sum; **"sin domicilio fijo"** "of no fixed abode"; **imposición a plazo ~** fixed term deposit; **fondos de renta fija** fixed-interest funds
4 (= *regular*) [*sueldo, novio*] steady; [*cliente*] regular; **el padre no tenía trabajo ~** the father didn't have a steady job, the father was not in regular employment (*frm*)
5 (= *permanente*) [*plantilla, contrato, empleado*] permanent; **¿cuándo os van a hacer ~s?** when will you get a permanent contract?; **contrato de ~ discontinuo** permanent seasonal contract
6 [*propósito*] fixed, firm
7 **de ~*** for sure*; **sé de ~ que** I know for sure that*; **de ~ que llueve esta noche** it's definitely going to rain tonight, it's going to rain tonight, that's for sure*
🅑 ADV (*) for sure*; **ya sé que no voy a ganar, eso ~** I know I'm not going to win, that's for sure*

fila SF 1 [*de personas, cosas*] line; **1.1** (*una tras de otra*) line; **una ~ de coches** a line of cars; **ponerse en ~** to line up, get into line; **en ~ india** in single file **1.2** (*una al lado de otra*) row; **había cuatro coches en ~** there were four cars in a row; **en primera/segunda ~** in the front/second row; **estacionar en doble ~** to double-park **1.3** (*Mil*) **¡en ~!** fall in!; **¡rompan ~s!** fall out!, dismiss!
2 **filas 2.1** (*Mil*) **incorporarse a ~s** to join up; **llamar a algn a ~s** to call sb up (*Brit*), draft sb (*EEUU*) **2.2** (*Pol*) ranks;
✦ MODISMO **cerrar ~s** to close ranks

filamento SM filament

filantropía SF philanthropy

filántropo/a SM/F philanthropist

filarmónica SF philharmonic (orchestra)

filarmónico ADJ philharmonic

filatelia SF philately, stamp collecting

filatélico ADJ philatelic

filatelista SMF stamp collector, philatelist

filete SM [*de ternera, cerdo*] steak; [*de pescado*] fillet, filet (*EEUU*)

filetear /1a/ VT to fillet, filet (*EEUU*)

filiación SF 1 (*a partido*) affiliation 2 [*de ideas*] connection, relationship; (= *señas*) particulars *pl*

filial 🅐 ADJ 1 (= *de hijo*) filial 2 (*Com*) subsidiary *antes de s*, affiliated 🅑 SF (*Com*) subsidiary

filibustero SM pirate, freebooter

filigrana SF 1 (*Téc*) filigree (work) 2 **filigranas** (*fig*) delicate work *sing*

Filipinas SFPL **las (Islas) ~** the Philippines

filipino/a 🅐 ADJ Philippine, Filipino 🅑 SM/F Filipino

filisteo/a ADJ, SM/F Philistine

filmación SF filming, shooting

filmadora SF (= *aparato*) [*de cine*] film camera; (*LAm*) [*de video*] camcorder

filmar /1a/ VT to film, shoot

filme SM film (*esp Brit*), movie (*esp EEUU*)

fílmico ADJ film *antes de s* (*esp Brit*), movie *antes de s* (*esp EEUU*)

filmina SF slide, transparency

filmografía SF filmography; **la ~ de Buñuel** Buñuel's films; **la ~ de la estrella** the star's screen career

filmoteca SF film library, film archive

filo SM 1 [*de navaja, espada*] cutting edge, blade; **un arma de doble ~** a double-edged sword 2 (*con horas*) **al ~ de las doce** just before twelve o'clock 3 (*Méx***) (= *hambre*) **tener ~** to be starving

filocomunista ADJ pro-communist, with communist leanings

filología SF philology ➤ **Filología Francesa** (= *carrera*) French Studies

filólogo/a SM/F (= *estudioso*) philologist; (= *licenciado en filología*) language graduate

filón SM (*Min*) vein, lode, seam; (*fig*) gold mine

filoso ADJ 1 (*LAm*) (= *afilado*) sharp 2 (*Méx*) (= *hambriento*) starving

filosofal ADJ **piedra ~** philosopher's stone

filosofar /1a/ VI to philosophize

filosofía SF philosophy; **tomarse las cosas con ~** to take things philosophically

filosófico ADJ philosophic, philosophical

filósofo/a SM/F philosopher

filoxera SF phylloxera

filtración SF 1 (= *proceso*) filtration 2 (= *fuga*) seepage, leakage, loss 3 [*de datos*] leak

filtrar /1a/ 🅐 VT 1 [+ *líquido, luz*] to filter 2 [+ *llamadas, visitantes*] to screen 3 [+ *información, documento, grabación*] to leak 🅑 **filtrarse** VPR 1 [*líquido*] to seep, leak; [*luz, sonido*] to filter 2 (= *desaparecer*) [*dinero, bienes*] to disappear

filtro SM 1 (*Téc*) filter; **cigarrillo con ~** filter-tipped cigarette ➤ **filtro de aire** air filter ➤ **filtro del aceite** oil filter 2 (= *selección*) screening ➤ **filtro de llamadas** call-screening 3 (*Hist*) (= *poción*) love potion, philtre, philter (*EEUU*)

fin SM 1 (= *final*) end; **el ~ del mundo** the end of the world; **en la noche de ~ de año** on New Year's Eve; **~ de curso** end of the school year; **fiesta de ~ de curso** end-of-year party; **dar ~ a** [+ *ceremonia, actuación*] to bring to a close; [+ *obra, libro*] to finish; [+ *guerra, conflicto*] to bring to an end; **estas palabras dieron ~ a tres años de conflicto** these words brought three years of conflict to an end; **llevar algo a buen ~** to bring sth to a successful conclusion; **poner ~ a algo** to end sth, put an end to sth; **deseaban poner ~ a sus vidas** they wished to end their lives; **sin ~** endless; **correa sin ~** endless belt; ✦ MODISMO **llegar a ~ de mes** to make ends meet ➤ **fin de semana** weekend
2 **a fines de** at the end of; **a ~es de abril** at the end of April; **la crisis de ~es del siglo XIX** the crisis at the end of the 19th century, the late 19th century crisis
3 (*otras locuciones*) **3.1 al ~ ◆ por ~** (= *gen*) finally; (*con más énfasis*) at last; (= *gen*) finally; (*con más énfasis*) at last; **¡al ~ solos!** alone at last!; **al ~ y al cabo** after all; **tengo derecho a estar aquí: al ~ y al cabo, soy parte de la familia** I have a right to stay here: after all, I am part of the family; **al ~ y al cabo, lo que importa es que seguimos juntos** at the end of the day, what matters is that we're still together; **a ~ de cuentas** at the end of the day **3.2 en ~** (*quitando importancia*) anyway, oh, well; (*para resumir*) in short; **¡en ~, qué se le va a hacer!** anyway *o* oh, well, there's nothing we can do about it!; **hemos tenido bastantes problemas este año, pero en ~, seguimos adelante** we've had quite a few problems this year, but still *o* anyway, we're still going
4 (= *intención*) aim; **¿con qué ~ se ha organizado esto?** what has been the aim in organizing this?; **a ~ de hacer algo** in order to do sth; **a ~ de que** (+ SUBJUN) so that, in order that (*frm*); **se le ha citado como testigo a ~ de que explique sus relaciones con el acusado** he has been called as a witness in order to explain *o* in order that he explain (*frm*) *o* so that he can explain his relationship with the defendant; **con el ~ de hacer algo** in order to do sth; **a tal ~** with this aim in mind, to this end
5 (= *propósito*) purpose; **con ~es experimentales/militares/políticos** for experimental/military/political purposes

finado/a SM/F deceased

final Ⓐ ADJ (= *último*) [*momento, capítulo, resultado*] final; [*objetivo*] ultimate
Ⓑ SM **1** (= *fin*) [*de ceremonia, vida, aventura, guerra*] end; [*de obra musical*] finale; **no vi el ~ de la película** I didn't see the end of the film; **al ~** in the end; **al ~ de la reunión** at the end of the meeting; **al ~ de la calle** at the end of the street; **al ~ de la lista** at the bottom of the list
2 (= *desenlace*) [*de película, libro*] ending; **la novela tiene un ~ inesperado** the novel has an unexpected ending; **un ~ feliz** a happy ending
3 a finales de at the end of; **a ~es del siglo XIX** at the end of the 19th century
Ⓒ SF (*Dep*) final; **consiguieron pasar a la ~** they managed to get through to the final

finalidad SF **1** (= *propósito*) purpose **2** (*Fil*) finality

finalista Ⓐ ADJ **quedó ~ en dos ocasiones** he was short-listed twice *o* on two occasions Ⓑ SMF finalist

finalización SF ending, conclusion

finalizar /1f/ Ⓐ VT to finish; **muchos universitarios no finalizan la carrera** many university students do not finish their degree; **con el himno se dio por finalizada la ceremonia** the ceremony came to an end *o* ended with the national anthem Ⓑ VI to end; **la jornada finalizó con la prueba de atletismo femenino** the day ended with the women's athletics trials; **hoy finaliza el plazo** today is the deadline

finalmente ADV **1** (= *al final*) finally, in the end; **~ decidimos ir a Mallorca** finally *o* in the end we decided to go to Majorca **2** (= *por último*) lastly; **50% están a favor, 30% en contra y, ~, un 20% se muestra indeciso** 50% are in favour *o* (*EEUU*) favor, 30% are against and lastly, 20% don't know

financiación SF financing, funding

financiar /1b/ VT to finance, fund

financiera SF finance company, finance house

financiero/a Ⓐ ADJ financial; **el mundo ~** the world of finance, the financial world Ⓑ SM/F financier

financista SMF (*LAm*) financier

finanzas SFPL finances

finca SF **1** (= *bien inmueble*) property, land, real estate ➤ **finca urbana** town property **2** (= *casa de recreo*) country house, country estate **3** (= *granja*) farm ➤ **finca cafetera** coffee plantation

finde SM ABBR (= *fin de semana*) weekend

fineza SF **1** (= *cualidad*) fineness, excellence **2** [*de modales*] refinement; (= *cumplido*) compliment

fingido ADJ feigned, false

fingimiento SM pretence, pretense (*EEUU*), feigning

fingir /3c/ Ⓐ VT to feign; **intenté ~ indiferencia** I tried to feign indifference *o* to appear indifferent; **fingió interés** he pretended to be interested; **~ hacer algo** to pretend to do sth Ⓑ VI to pretend Ⓒ **fingirse** VPR **~se dormido** to pretend to be asleep; **~se muerto** to play dead, act dead

finiquitar /1a/ VT [+ *cuenta*] to settle and close, balance up

finiquito SM (*Com, Fin*) settlement

finisecular ADJ fin-de-siècle *antes de s*, turn-of-the-century *antes de s*

finito ADJ finite

finlandés/esa Ⓐ ADJ Finnish Ⓑ SM/F Finn Ⓒ SM (*Ling*) Finnish

Finlandia SF Finland

fino Ⓐ ADJ **1** (= *no grueso*) [*arena, punta, pelo*] fine; [*papel, capa*] thin; [*dedos, cuello*] slender; [*cutis, piel*] smooth; **bolígrafo de punta fina** fine-tipped ballpoint pen
2 (= *de buena calidad*) [*cristal, porcelana, papel*] fine; [*tabaco*] select
3 (= *cortés*) polite, well-bred; (= *refinado*) refined; **no te hagas la fina** you needn't start putting on airs
4 (= *agudo*) [*vista*] sharp; [*oído*] acute; **su fina inteligencia analítica** her fine *o* acute analytical intelligence
5 (= *sutil*) subtle, fine; **me sorprendió su fina ironía** her subtle irony surprised me
6 [*jerez*] fino, dry

Ⓑ SM (= *jerez*) dry sherry, fino sherry

finolis* ADJ INV, **finoli*** ADJ INV (*RPl*) snobbish

finura SF **1** (= *buena calidad*) fineness, excellence **2** (= *cortesía*) politeness, courtesy; (= *refinamiento*) refinement **3** (= *sutileza*) subtlety

fiordo SM fiord

fique SM (*CAm, Col, Méx, Ven*,) sisal

firma SF **1** (= *nombre*) signature; (= *acto*) signing; **me presentó varios documentos a la ~** he handed me several documents to sign; ✦ MODISMO **ponele la ~** (*RPl**) you can be sure of that ➤ **firma digitalizada** digital signature ➤ **firma electrónica** electronic signature **2** (= *empresa*) firm, company

firmamento SM firmament

firmante Ⓐ ADJ signatory (**de** to) Ⓑ SMF signatory; **los abajo ~s** the undersigned

firmar /1a/ Ⓐ VT to sign; **~ un cheque en blanco** to write *o* sign a blank cheque *o* (*EEUU*) check; **~ un contrato** to sign a contract Ⓑ VI to sign; **firme aquí** sign here

firme Ⓐ ADJ **1** [*mesa, andamio*] steady; [*terreno*] firm, solid; **mantén la escalera ~** can you hold the ladder steady?
2 [*paso*] firm, steady; [*voz*] firm; [*mercado, moneda*] steady; [*candidato*] strong; **la libra se ha mantenido ~** the pound has remained steady
3 [*amistad, apoyo*] firm, strong; [*decisión, convicción*] firm; **mantenerse ~** to hold one's ground; **se mostró muy ~ con ella** he was very firm with her; **trabajar de ~** to work hard
4 [*sentencia*] final
5 (*Mil*) **¡~s!** attention!; **ponerse ~s** to come *o* stand to attention
Ⓑ ADV hard; **trabajar ~** to work hard
Ⓒ SM (*Aut*) road surface; **"firme provisional"** "temporary surface"

firmemente ADV (= *con firmeza*) firmly; (= *con fuerza*) securely

firmeza SF **1** [*de una superficie*] firmness **2** [*de carácter, convicciones*] strength, firmness; **se negó con ~** he firmly refused

firuletes* SMPL (*LAm*) **1** (= *objetos*) knick-knacks **2** (*al bailar*) gyrations, contortions

fiscal Ⓐ ADJ (= *relativo a impuestos*) fiscal, tax *antes de s*; (= *económico*) fiscal, financial; **año ~** fiscal year, financial year Ⓑ SMF (*Jur*) public prosecutor, district attorney (*EEUU*) ➤ **fiscal general del Estado** Director of Public Prosecutions (*Brit*), Attorney-General (*EEUU*)

fiscalía SF office of the public prosecutor, District Attorney's office (*EEUU*)

fiscalidad SF taxation

fiscalizar /1f/ VT **1** (= *controlar*) to control; (= *supervisar*) to oversee; (= *registrar*) to inspect (officially) **2** (= *criticar*) to criticize, find fault with

fisco SM treasury, exchequer (*Brit*); **declarar algo al ~** to declare sth to the Internal Revenue Service (*EEUU*) *o* the Inland Revenue (*Brit*)

fisgar* /1h/ Ⓐ VT to snoop on* Ⓑ VI to snoop* (**en** on)

fisgón/ona* Ⓐ ADJ nosey* Ⓑ SM/F snooper*

fisgonear* /1a/ VI to snoop*

física SF physics *sing* ➤ **física cuántica** quantum physics ➤ **física de partículas** particle physics ➤ **física nuclear** nuclear physics; *ver tb* **físico**

físicamente ADV physically

físico/a Ⓐ ADJ physical Ⓑ SM/F physicist Ⓒ SM (*Anat*) physique; (= *aspecto*) appearance, looks *pl*; *ver tb* **física**

fisiología SF physiology

fisiológico ADJ physiological

fisión SF fission ➤ **fisión nuclear** nuclear fission

fisioterapeuta SMF physiotherapist, physical therapist (*EEUU*)

fisioterapia SF physiotherapy, physical therapy (*EEUU*)

fisonomía SF **1** (= *cara*) physiognomy, features *pl* **2** [*de objeto, lugar*] appearance; **la ~ de la ciudad** the appearance of the city

fisonomista SMF **ser buen ~** to have a good memory for faces

fistol SM (*Méx*) tiepin

fístula SF fistula

fisura SF **1** (*en roca*) crack, fissure (*frm*); (*en órgano*) fissure (*frm*); (*en hueso*) crack **2 sin ~s** [*apoyo, fe, convencimiento*] solid

fitosanitario ④ ADJ [*industria, problemas*] phytosanitary **⑧** SM pesticide

flaccidez SF flaccidity (*frm*), flabbiness

fláccido ADJ flaccid (*frm*), flabby

flaco ④ ADJ **1** (= *delgado*) thin, skinny* **2** (= *débil*) weak, feeble; [*memoria*] bad, short; **su punto ~** his weak point, his weakness **⑧** SM (= *defecto*) failing; (= *punto débil*) weakness, weak point

flacura SF thinness, skinniness*

flagelar /1a/ VT to flagellate (*frm*), whip

flagelo SM scourge

flagrante ADJ flagrant; **pillar** o **sorprender a algn en ~ delito** to catch sb in the act, catch sb red-handed, catch sb in flagrante delicto (*frm*)

flama SF (*Méx*) flame

flamable ADJ (*Méx*) flammable

flamante ADJ **1** (= *nuevo*) [*automóvil, traje*] brand-new; [*campeón, director*] new **2** (= *estupendo*) brilliant, fabulous

flambear /1a/ VT to flambé

flamenco¹ SM (= *ave*) flamingo

flamenco²/a ④ ADJ **1** (*Geog*) Flemish **2** (*Mús*) flamenco; **cante ~** flamenco **3 ponerse ~*** (= *engreído*) to get cocky* **⑧** SM/F (= *persona*) Fleming; **los ~s** the Flemings, the Flemish **⑥** SM **1** (*Mús*) flamenco **2** (*Ling*) Flemish

flan SM (*dulce*) creme caramel; (*salado*) mould, mold (*EEUU*); ✦ MODISMO **estar hecho** o **como un ~** to shake like a leaf

⚠️ flan ≠ *flan*

flanco SM **1** [*de animal*] side, flank; [*de persona*] side **2** (*Mil*) flank

flanera SF crème caramel mould o (*EEUU*) mold

flanquear /1a/ VT **1** [+ *persona, construcción*] to flank; [+ *calle, costa, río*] to line **2** (*Mil*) (= *sobrepasar*) to outflank

flaquear /1a/ VI **1** (= *debilitarse*) (*gen*) to weaken, grow weak; [*esfuerzo*] to slacken, flag; [*salud*] to decline (*frm*), get worse; **me flaquean las piernas** my legs are like jelly (*Brit*) o Jell-O® (*EEUU*) **2** (= *desanimarse*) to lose heart, become dispirited

flaqueza SF **1** (= *debilidad*) feebleness, frailty **2 una ~** (= *defecto*) a failing; (= *punto flaco*) a weakness

flash [flas] SM (*pl* **-es** ['flases]) **1** (*Fot*) flash, flashlight ➤ **flash informativo** news flash **2** (*Esp***) (= *sorpresa*) shock; **¡qué ~!** what a shock!

flato SM **tener ~** to have a stitch

flatulencia SF flatulence

flauta SF **1** (= *instrumento*) (*tb* **~ travesera** o **tra(n)versa** (*LAm*) flute; (*tb* **~ dulce**) recorder; ✦ MODISMO **sonó la ~ (por casualidad)** it was a fluke, it was sheer luck **2** (= *barra de pan*) French stick, baguette

flautín SM piccolo

flautista SMF flautist, flute player, flutist (*EEUU*); **el ~ de Hamelin** the Pied Piper of Hamelin

flebitis SF INV phlebitis

flecha SF arrow; **como una ~** like an arrow, like a shot

flechado ④ ADV (*) **el médico vino ~** the doctor came in a flash*; **salir ~** to shoot off* **⑧** ADJ **una calle flechada** (*Uru*) a one-way street

flechar* (= *enamorar*) /1a/ VT **~ a algn** to sweep off sb's feet

flechazo* SM love at first sight

fleco SM **1** (*Méx*) (= *flequillo*) fringe (*Brit*), bangs *pl* (*EEUU*) **2 flecos** (= *adorno*) fringe *sing*; **un mantel con ~s** a fringed tablecloth

flema SF phlegm

flemático ADJ [*persona*] phlegmatic; [*tono, comportamiento*] matter-of-fact, unruffled

flemón SM gumboil

flequillo SM fringe (*Brit*), bangs *pl* (*EEUU*)

fletamiento SM chartering; **contrato de ~** charter

fletán SM **~ negro** Greenland halibut

fletar /1a/ VT **1** [+ *avión, barco*] to charter; (= *cargar*) to load, freight **2** (*LAm*) [*autobús*] to rent, hire (*esp Brit*) **3** (*CS***) (= *despedir*) to get rid of, fire*; (= *expulsar*) to throw out

flete SM **1** (= *alquiler*) **1.1** [*de avión, barco*] charter; **vuelo ~** charter flight **1.2** (*LAm*) [*de autobús, camión*] rent, hire (*esp Brit*); (= *precio*) rental fee, hire charge (*esp Brit*), hiring fee (*esp Brit*) **2** (= *carga*) freight; (*Náut, Aer*) cargo **3** (= *precio del transporte*) freightage, carriage

fletero/a ④ ADJ (*LAm*) [*avión*] charter *antes de s*; [*camión*] for hire (*esp Brit*), for rent (*EEUU*) **⑧** SM/F (*RPl*) (= *transportista*) haulier

flexibilidad SF (*gen*) flexibility; [*del cuerpo*] suppleness; [*de carácter*] flexibility, adaptability ➤ **flexibilidad de plantillas**, **flexibilidad laboral** freedom to "restructure", freedom to hire and fire

flexibilizar /1f/ VT [+ *control, sanción*] to relax; [+ *horario, programa*] to make (more) flexible, adjust, adapt; [+ *plantilla*] to downsize

flexible ADJ **1** [*material, actitud*] flexible; [*cuerpo*] supple; (*Téc*) pliable; [*sombrero*] soft; **horario ~** flexitime **2** [*persona*] flexible, open-minded

flexión SF **1 hacer flexiones (de brazos)** to do press-ups (*Brit*) o push-ups (*EEUU*); **hacer flexiones de cintura** to touch one's toes; **flexiones de piernas** squats **2** (*Ling*) inflection **3** (*Med, Téc*) flexion

flexionar /1a/ VT (*gen*) to bend; [+ *músculo*] to flex

flexo SM adjustable table-lamp

flipado* ADJ (*Esp*) **1** (= *sorprendido*) amazed, gobsmacked (*Brit***); **quedarse ~** to be left speechless (with amazement), be gobsmacked (*Brit***) **2** (= *drogado*) stoned**

flipante* ADJ (*Esp*) **1** (= *estupendo*) great*, cool** **2** (= *pasmoso*) amazing

flipar* /1a/ (*Esp*) **④** VT **1** (= *gustar*) **esto me flipa** I really love this **2** (= *pasmar*) **me flipó lo que pasó** I was amazed at o (*EEUU***) gobsmacked at o (*EEUU***) blown away by what happened **⑧** VI **1** (= *pasmarse*) **yo flipaba al ver a tanta gente famosa en el concierto** I was amazed o (*Brit***) gobsmacked to see so many famous people at the concert; **¡este tío flipa!** this guy must be kidding!* **2** (= *pasarlo bien*) to have a great time; **~ con algo** (= *disfrutar*) to really love sth

flipe* SM (*Esp*) amazing experience, startling revelation

flipper* ['fliper] SM pinball machine; **jugar al ~** to play pinball

flirt [flir, fler] SM (*pl* **-s**) fling*

flirtear /1a/ VI to flirt (**con** with)

flojear /1a/ VI **1** (= *debilitarse*) **me flojean las piernas** my legs are tired **2** (= *flaquear*) **flojeó en el último examen** she did less well in the last exam; **el ritmo flojea hacia el final** the pace slackens towards the end

flojera SF **1** (= *debilidad*) weakness, feebleness **2** (*esp LAm***) (= *pereza*) **me da ~** I can't be bothered; **tener ~** to feel lazy

flojo ADJ **1** [*nudo, tuerca*] loose; [*cable, cuerda*] slack **2** (= *débil*) [*persona*] weak; [*viento*] light **3** (= *mediocre*) [*trabajo, actuación*] poor, feeble; [*estudiante, equipo*] weak, poor; **el guión era muy ~** the script was very weak; **está ~ en matemáticas** he's weak in maths **4** [*té, vino*] weak **5** [*demanda, mercado*] slack **6** (= *holgazán*) lazy, idle

flor SF **1** (*Bot*) flower; **un ramo de ~es** a bunch of flowers; **un vestido de ~es** a floral dress; ✦ MODISMOS **¡ni ~es!***: **de libros sé mucho, pero de cocina ni ~es** I know a lot about books, but I don't know the first thing about cooking*; **ser ~ de un día: su amor fue ~ de un día** their love was short-lived; **su triunfo no fue ~ de un día** his win was no mere flash in the pan; **a ~ de piel: tenía los nervios a ~ de piel** her nerves were all on edge; **tiene la sensibilidad a ~ de piel** she is highly sensitive ➤ **flor de lis** fleur-de-lis, fleur-de-lys

2 en ~ [*planta, campo*] in flower, in bloom; [*árbol*] in blossom, in flower

3 la ~ (= *lo mejor*): **la ~ y nata de la sociedad** the cream of society; **en la ~ de la vida** in the prime of life

4 (*CS**) **~ de: ~ de alegre** really happy, very cheerful; **¡~ de discurso se mandó!** what a brilliant talk he gave!; **~ de reloj me regalaste, ya no funciona** (*iró*) what a great watch you bought me, it doesn't work anymore (*iró*)

flora SF flora

floral ADJ floral

floreado ADJ flowered, floral

florecer /2d/ VI **1** (*Bot*) to flower, bloom **2** (= *prosperar*) to flourish, thrive

floreciente ADJ flourishing, thriving

florecimiento SM **1** (*Bot*) flowering, blooming **2** (= *prosperidad*) blossoming, flowering

florentino/a Ⓐ ADJ Florentine Ⓑ SM/F Florentine

floreo SM (*Esgrima, Mús*) flourish

florería SF florist's (shop)

florero SM vase; ✦ MODISMO **estar de ~** to be just for show o decoration

florete SM (*Esgrima*) foil

floricultor(a) SM/F flower-grower

floricultura SF flower growing

florido ADJ **1** [*campo, jardín*] full of flowers; [*árbol, planta*] in blossom, in flower **2** (= *selecto*) choice, select; **lo más ~ del arte contemporáneo** the pick of contemporary art; **lo más ~ de la sociedad** the cream of society **3** [*estilo*] flowery, florid

florín SM **1** (*holandés*) guilder **2** (*Hist*) florin

florista SMF florist

floristería SF (*esp Esp*) florist's (shop)

floritura SF flourish

flota SF **1** [*de buques*] fleet; **la ~ española** the Spanish fleet ➤ **flota de altura** deep-sea fishing fleet ➤ **flota de bajura** inshore fishing fleet ➤ **flota pesquera** fishing fleet **2** (*Aer, Aut*) fleet **3** (*And*) (= *autobús*) long-distance bus, inter-city bus

flotación SF **1** (*Náut*) flotation ➤ **línea de flotación** waterline **2** (*Fin*) flotation

flotador SM **1** [*de bañista*] (*para la cintura*) rubber ring (*esp Brit*), life preserver (*EEUU*); (*para los brazos*) (inflatable) armband; (*para las manos*) float **2** [*de hidroavión, para medicines*] float; [*de cisterna*] ballcock, floater (*EEUU*)

flotar /1a/ VI **1** (*en líquido*) to float [*bandera*] to flutter; **al viento** [*cabello*] to stream in the wind **3** (*Fin*) to float

flote SM **a ~** afloat; **mantenerse a ~** [*barco, negocio*] to stay afloat; **poner o sacar a ~** [+ *barco*] to refloat; [+ *negocio, economía*] to get back on its feet; **salir a ~** [*negocio, economía, persona*] to get back on one's feet

flotilla SF **1** (*Náut*) flotilla, fleet **2** [*de aviones, taxis*] fleet

fluctuación SF fluctuation

fluctuar /1e/ VI to fluctuate

fluidez SF **1** [*de lenguaje*] fluency; **circular con ~** to flow freely; **habla inglés con ~** he speaks English fluently, he speaks fluent English **2** (*Téc*) fluidity

fluido Ⓐ ADJ **1** [*lenguaje*] fluent; [*estilo*] fluid, free-flowing; **la circulación es bastante fluida** traffic is moving quite freely **2** (*Téc*) fluid Ⓑ SM **1** (*líquido*) fluid ➤ **fluidos corporales** body fluids **2** (*Elec*) current, juice*

fluir /3g/ VI to flow, run

flujo SM **1** (= *corriente*) flow, stream; **~ de lava** lava flow **2** (*Med*) ➤ **flujo menstrual** menstrual flow ➤ **flujo vaginal** vaginal discharge **3** (= *marea*) incoming tide, rising tide

➤ **flujo y reflujo** (*lit, fig*) ebb and flow

fluminense ADJ of/from Rio de Janeiro

flúor SM, **fluor** SM **1** (= *gas*) fluorine **2** (*en agua, pasta de dientes*) fluoride

fluorescente Ⓐ ADJ fluorescent Ⓑ SM (*tb* **tubo ~**) fluorescent tube

fluoruro SM fluoride

fluvial ADJ fluvial, river *antes de s*

flux [flus] SM INV **1** (*Naipes*) flush **2** (*Col, Ven*) (= *traje*) suit of clothes

FM SF ABR (= **Frecuencia Modulada**) FM

FMI SM ABR (= **Fondo Monetario Internacional**) IMF

fobia SF phobia; **yo a esos aparatos les tengo ~** I hate o can't stand these machines

foca SF **1** (*Zool*) seal; (= *piel*) sealskin **2** (*) (= *persona gorda*) fat lump*

focal ADJ focal

foco SM **1** (*Mat, Med, Fís*) focus **2** (= *centro*) focal point, centre, center (*EEUU*); (= *fuente*) source; [*de incendio*] seat; **un ~ de infección** a source of infection **3** (*en monumento, estadio*) floodlight; (*en teatro*) spotlight; (*LAm*) (= *bombilla*) light bulb; (*Aut*) headlamp

fofo ADJ **1** (= *esponjoso*) soft, spongy **2** (*) (= *fláccido*) flabby, podgy, pudgy (*EEUU*)

fogata SF bonfire, blaze

fogón SM **1** (*Culin*) range, stove **2** (*LAm*) (= *hoguera*) bonfire; (= *hogar*) hearth

fogonazo SM explosion

fogosidad SF **1** (= *ímpetu*) ardour, ardor (*EEUU*); (= *temple*) spirit **2** [*de caballo etc*] friskiness

fogoso ADJ (= *apasionado*) ardent; [*caballo etc*] frisky

fogueado ADJ (*LAm*) expert, experienced

fogueo SM **bala** o **cartucho de ~** blank cartridge; **pistola de ~** starting pistol

foja SF (*LAm*) = **hoja 2**

folclore SM, **folclor** SM = **folklore**

folclórico/a ADJ, SM/F = **folklórico**

folículo SM follicle ➤ **folículo piloso** hair follicle

folio SM **1** (*Tip*) folio **2** (= *hoja*) sheet (of paper); [*de libro, documento*] page **3** (*tb* **tamaño ~**) A4 size; **doble ~** A3 size; **un ~** an A4 sheet; **~s** A4 paper

folk ADJ INV, SM folk

folklore SM folklore

folklórico/a Ⓐ ADJ **1** [*música, baile, leyenda*] folk *antes de s*; **es muy ~** it's very picturesque, it's full of local colour o (*EEUU*) color **2** (*pey*) (= *frívolo*) frivolous, unserious Ⓑ SM/F (*Mús*) folk singer

follado* ADJ **ir ~** (*Esp*) to go like fuck***, go like a bat out of hell*

follaje SM **1** (*Bot*) foliage, leaves *pl* **2** (= *palabrería*) verbiage, waffle (*Brit**)

follar* /1l/ VT, VI (*Esp*) to screw***

folletín SM **1** (*en periódico*) newspaper serial; (*Radio*) radio serial **2** (= *sucesos melodramáticos*) drama, saga

folletinesco ADJ melodramatic

folleto SM (*Com*) brochure; (*Pol*) pamphlet; (= *volatín*) leaflet

follón* SM (*Esp*) **1** (= *desorden*) mess; **¡qué ~ de papeles!** what a mess of papers! **2** (= *alboroto*) rumpus*, row (*esp Brit*); **hubo** o **se armó un ~ tremendo** there was a hell of a rumpus*

follonero* ADJ (*Esp*) rowdy

fomentar /1a/ VT [+ *desarrollo, investigación, ahorro, inversión, participación*] to encourage; [+ *turismo, industria*] to promote, boost; [+ *competitividad, producción*] to boost; [+ *odio, violencia*] to foment

fomento SM promotion, encouragement; [*de ventas*] promotion; **Ministerio de Fomento** *ministry responsible for public works, buildings etc*

fonador ADJ [*sistema, aparato, órgano*] speech *antes de s*

fonda SF (= *restaurante*) small restaurant; (= *pensión*) boarding house; (*Hist*) inn, tavern

fondear /1a/ **Ⓐ** VT to anchor **Ⓑ** VI to anchor, drop anchor

fondillo SM (*LAm*), **fondillos** SMPL seat

fondista SMF (*Dep*) long-distance runner

fondo SM **1** (*parte inferior*) [*de caja, botella, lago, mar*] bottom; [*de río*] bed; **los bajos ~s** the underworld; **una maletín con doble ~** a case with a false bottom, a false-bottomed case; **irse al ~** to sink to the bottom; **en el ~ del mar** (*gen*) at the bottom of the sea; (= *en el lecho marino*) on the sea bed; **sin ~** bottomless; ✦ MODISMO **tocar ~** (= *empeorar al máximo*) to reach *o* hit rock bottom; (= *dejar de empeorar*) to bottom out
2 (*parte posterior*) [*de pasillo, calle, nave*] end; [*de habitación, armario*] back; **al ~ del pasillo** at the end of the corridor; **la barra está al ~ de la cafetería** the bar is at the (far) end of the cafe
3 (= *profundidad*) [*de cajón, edificio, bañera*] depth; **¿cuánto tiene de ~ el armario?** how deep is the wardrobe?; **tener mucho ~** to be deep; **tener poco ~** [*bañera*] to be shallow; [*cajón, armario*] not to be deep enough
4 (= *lo fundamental*) **en el ~ de esta polémica late el miedo al cambio** at the heart *o* bottom of this controversy lies a fear of change; **el problema de ~** the basic *o* fundamental *o* underlying problem; **la forma y el ~** form and content; **llegar al ~ de algo** to get to the bottom of sth
5 (= *segundo plano*) background; **verde sobre ~ rojo** green on a red background; **música de ~** background music ➤ **fondo de escritorio, fondo de pantalla** (*Inform*) wallpaper
6 a fondo 6.1 (*como adj*) **una investigación a ~** (*policial*) a thorough investigation; [*de estudio*] an in-depth study; **una limpieza a ~** a thorough clean **6.2** (*como adv*) **no conoce a ~ la situación del país** he does not have a thorough *o* an in-depth knowledge of the country's situation; **la policía investigará a ~ lo ocurrido** the police will conduct a thorough investigation of what happened; **estudiará a ~ nuestra propuesta** he'll look closely at our proposal; **pisar a ~ el acelerador** to put one's foot down (*on the accelerator*)
7 en el fondo (= *en nuestro interior*) deep down; (= *en realidad*) really; (= *en lo fundamental*) fundamentally, essentially; **en el ~ de su corazón** in his heart of hearts, deep down; **lo que se debatirá en la reunión, en el ~, es el futuro de la empresa** what is actually *o* really going to be debated in the meeting is the future of the company; **en el ~ ambos sistemas son muy parecidos** fundamentally *o* essentially, both systems are very similar
8 (*Dep*) **carrera de ~** long-distance race; **esquí de ~** cross-country skiing; **corredor de medio ~** middle-distance runner
9 (= *dinero*) (*Com, Fin*) fund; (*en póker, entre amigos*) pot, kitty; **a ~ perdido** [*crédito, inversión*] non-recoverable, non-refundable; **subvención a ~ perdido** capital grant; **su padre le ha prestado bastante dinero a ~ perdido** his father has given him quite a lot of money on permanent loan ➤ **fondo común** common fund ➤ **Fondo de Ayuda al Desarrollo** Development Aid Fund ➤ **Fondo de Cohesión** Cohesion Fund ➤ **fondo de comercio** goodwill ➤ **Fondo de Compensación Interterritorial** *system of financial redistribution between the autonomous regions of Spain* ➤ **fondo de inversión** investment fund ➤ **fondo de pensiones** pension fund, retirement fund (*EEUU*) ➤ **fondo de previsión** provident fund ➤ **fondo ético** (*Fin*) ethical investment fund ➤ **Fondo Monetario Internacional** International Monetary
10 fondos (= *dinero*) funds; **recaudar ~s** to raise funds; **estar sin ~s** to be out of funds, be broke*; **cheque *o* talón sin ~s** bounced cheque, rubber check (*EEUU*); **el cheque no tenía ~s** the cheque *o* (*EEUU*) check bounced ➤ **fondos bloqueados** frozen assets ➤ **fondos públicos** public funds ➤ **fondos reservados** secret funds
11 (= *reserva*) [*de biblioteca, archivo, museo*] collection; **el ~ de arte del museo** the museum's art collection ➤ **fondo editorial** list of titles
12 (= *carácter*) nature, disposition; **tener buen ~** to be good-natured

13 (= *resistencia*) stamina; **tener mucho ~** to have a lot of stamina; **tener poco ~** to have no staying power

fondón* ADJ big-bottomed*, broad in the beam*

fonema SM phoneme

fonética SF phonetics *sing*

fonético ADJ phonetic

fónico ADJ phonic

fono SM (*Chi*) telephone number

fonobuzón SM voice mail

fonología SF phonology

fonológico ADJ phonological

fonoteca SF record library, sound archive

fontanería SF (*esp Esp*) plumbing

fontanero/a SM/F (*esp Esp*) plumber

footing ['futin] SM jogging; **hacer ~** to jog, go jogging

forajido/a SM/F outlaw, bandit

foral ADJ *relative to the fueros, pertaining to the privileges of a town or region*; **parlamento ~** regional parliament; **policía ~** autonomous police

foráneo ADJ foreign

forastero/a **Ⓐ** ADJ alien, strange **Ⓑ** SM/F stranger, outsider

forcejear /1a/ VI to struggle, wrestle

forcejeo SM struggle

fórceps SM INV forceps

forense **Ⓐ** ADJ forensic **Ⓑ** SMF (*Med*) forensic scientist; (*Jur*) coroner

forestal ADJ (*gen*) forest *antes de s*; [*industria*] timber *antes de s*, lumber *antes de s* (*EEUU*)

forfait [for'fe] SM **1** (*Esquí*) ski pass **2** (= *precio*) flat rate, fixed price; **viajes a ~** package tours **3** (*Dep*) (= *ausencia*) absence, non-appearance

forjar /1a/ VT **1** [+ *hierro*] to forge, shape **2** (= *crear*) (*gen*) to forge, shape; [+ *sueños, ilusiones*] to build up

forma SF **1** (= *figura*) shape; **tiene ~ de pirámide** it is pyramid-shaped; **dar ~ a** [+ *objeto, joya*] to shape; [+ *idea, teoría*] to give shape to; **en ~ de U** U-shaped; **pendientes en ~ de corazón** heart-shaped earrings
2 (= *modo*) way; **yo tengo otra ~ de ver las cosas** I see things in a different way; **no estoy de acuerdo con su ~ de actuar** I don't agree with his way of doing things; **no hubo ~ de convencerle** there was no way we could persuade him; **de ~ directa/inmediata/natural** directly/immediately/naturally; **de esta ~** (*gen*) in this way; (= *por consecuencia*) thus; **de todas ~s** anyway, in any case ➤ **forma de pago** method of payment, form of payment ➤ **forma de ser: es mi ~ de ser** that's how I am, that's the way I am
3 de ~ que (= *por eso*) so that; **el número de socios fue creciendo cada año, de ~ que en 1989 eran ya varios miles** the number of members grew every year, so that *o* such that by 1989 there were several thousand; **de tal ~ que** (= *en un modo que*) in such a way that; (= *tanto que*) so much that; (= *por eso*) so that; **la noticia se filtró de tal ~ que fueron incapaces de evitarlo** news leaked out in such a way that they were unable to stop it; **la empresa ha crecido de tal ~ que es irreconocible** the company has grown so much *o* to such an extent that it is unrecognizable
4 (*tb ~ física*) fitness, form; **estar en (buena) ~** (*para hacer deporte*) to be fit, be in good shape; (*para realizar otra actividad*) to be in (good) form; **estar en baja ~** (*lit*) to be not fully fit; (*fig*) to be in bad shape; **estar bajo de ~** to be in poor shape; **mantenerse en ~** to keep fit
5 (= *aspecto externo*) form; **la ~ y el fondo** form and content
6 formas (*femeninas*) figure *sing*
7 formas (*sociales*) appearances; **guardar *o* mantener las ~s** to keep up appearances
8 (*Rel*) **la Sagrada Forma** the Host
9 (*LAm**) **en ~: una fiesta en ~** a proper party, a blowout*; **va a celebrar su cumpleaños en ~** he's going to have a proper *o* a serious* birthday party; **nos aburrimos en ~** we were seriously bored*

10 (*Méx*) (= *formulario*) form

formación SF **1** (= *creación*) formation; **para prevenir la ~ de hielo** to prevent ice (from) forming, to prevent the formation of ice (*frm*); **la Europa que está en ~** the Europe that is taking shape *o* that is in formation **2** (= *aprendizaje*) (*en un campo concreto*) training; (*en conocimientos teóricos*) education ➤ **formación profesional** vocational training **3** (= *grupo*) (*político*) party; (*musical*) group, band; [*de jugadores*] squad **4** (*Mil*) **en ~ de combate** in battle *o* combat formation **5** (*Geol, Bot*) formation

formal ADJ **1** [*persona*] (= *de fiar*) reliable, dependable; (= *responsable*) responsible; **sé ~ y pórtate bien** be good and behave yourself **2** [*invitación, estilo, lenguaje*] formal **3** (= *oficial*) [*petición, propuesta, compromiso*] official

formalidad SF **1** (= *requisito*) formality; **es pura ~** it's a pure *o* mere formality **2** (= *fiabilidad*) reliability; **esta empresa no tiene ~ ninguna** this company is totally unreliable **3** (= *seriedad*) **¡señores, un poco de ~!** gentlemen, let's be serious!

formalismo SM **1** (*Arte, Literat*) formalism **2** (*pey*) (= *burocracia*) red tape, useless formalities *pl*; (= *convencionalismo*) conventionalism

formalito* ADJ [*adulto*] respectable; [*niño*] well-behaved

formalizar /1f/ Ⓐ VT [+ *contrato*] to formalize; [+ *situación*] to put in order, regularize; **~ sus relaciones** [*novios*] to become formally engaged Ⓑ **formalizarse** VPR [*situación*] to be regularized; [*contrato*] to be formalized; [*nombramiento*] to make official

formar /1a/ Ⓐ VT **1** [+ *figura*] to form, make; **~on un círculo a su alrededor** they formed *o* made a circle around him **2** [+ *organización, partido, gobierno*] to form; **las personas interesadas en ~ un club** people interested in forming a club; **quieren casarse y ~ una familia** they want to get married and start a family **3** (= *constituir*) to make up; **los chiítas forman el 60% de la población** the Shiites make up *o* form 60% of the population; **formamos un buen equipo** we make a good team; **~ equipo con algn** to join forces with sb; **estar formado por** to be made up of; **~ parte de** to be part of **4** (= *enseñar*) [+ *personal, monitor, técnico*] to train; [+ *alumno*] to educate **5** [+ *juicio, opinión*] to form Ⓑ VI **1** (*Mil*) to fall in; **¡a ~!** fall in! **2** (*Dep*) [*equipo*] to line up Ⓒ **formarse** VPR **1** (= *crearse*) to form; **para evitar que se formen grumos** to prevent lumps forming; **se forman colas diarias en el cine** queues (*esp Brit*) *o* lines (*EEUU*) form daily outside the cinema (*esp Brit*) *o* movie theater (*EEUU*) **2** (= *armarse*) **se formó tal follón que ...** there was such an uproar that ... **3** (= *prepararse*) [*profesional, jugador, militar*] to train; [*alumno*] to be educated **4** (*Mil*) to fall in **5** (*Dep*) [*equipo*] to line up **6** [+ *opinión, impresión*] to form; **te formaste una idea equivocada de mí** you got the wrong idea about me

formatear /1a/ VT to format

formativo ADJ formative

formato SM (*Tip, Inform*) format; (= *tamaño*) [*de papel*] size

formica® SF, **fórmica**® (*RPl*) SF Formica®

formidable ADJ **1** [*enemigo, problema*] formidable **2** (= *estupendo*) terrific, tremendous

formol SM formaldehyde

formón SM chisel

fórmula SF **1** (*Quím, Mat*) formula **2** (= *método*) formula; **una ~ para conseguir el éxito** a formula to ensure success ➤ **fórmula mágica** magic formula **3** (= *expresión*) ➤ **fórmula de cortesía** polite set expression **4** (*Aut*) **coches de Fórmula uno** Formula One cars **5** (*Col*) (= *receta*) prescription

formular /1a/ VT **1** [+ *política, teoría*] to formulate; [+ *plan*] to draw up; [+ *pregunta*] to pose; [+ *protesta*] to make, lodge; [+ *demanda*] to file, put in; [+ *deseo*] to express

2 (*Col*) (= *recetar*) to prescribe

formulario SM form; **rellenar un ~** to fill out *o* (*esp Brit*) fill in a form, complete a form

fornicación SF fornication

fornicar /1g/ VI to fornicate

fornido ADJ strapping, hefty

foro SM **1** (*Pol, Hist, Internet*) forum; (= *reunión*) forum, (open) meeting **2** (*Teat*) upstage area; **desaparecer** *o* **marcharse por el ~** (*lit*) to exit stage left; (*fig*) to do a disappearing act

forofo/a* SM/F (*esp Esp*) fan, supporter

forrado ADJ **1** (= *con forro*) lined **2** (***) (= *rico*) **estar ~** to be loaded*, be rolling in it*

forraje SM fodder, forage

forrar /1a/ Ⓐ VT **1** (= *poner forro a*) to line (**de** with) **2** [+ *libro*] to cover (**de** with) Ⓑ **forrarse*** VPR **1** (= *enriquecerse*) make a bundle *o* (*Brit*) packet, to line one's pockets **2** (*Méx, Guat*) (*de comida*) to stuff o.s. (**de** with)

forro SM **1** (*gen*) lining; [*de libro*] cover; ✦ MODISMO **ni por el ~*** not in the least, not a bit ➤ **forro polar** fleece, Polartec® **2** (*Chi*) [*de bicicleta*] tyre, tire (*EEUU*)

fortachón* ADJ strong, tough

fortalecer /2d/ Ⓐ VT to strengthen Ⓑ **fortalecerse** VPR to become stronger

fortalecimiento SM strengthening

fortaleza SF **1** (*Mil*) fortress, stronghold **2** (*moral*) fortitude, strength (of spirit)

fortificación SF fortification

fortificar /1g/ VI **1** (*Mil*) to fortify **2** (= *fortalecer*) to strengthen

fortín SM (small) fort

fortísimo Ⓐ ADJ SUPERL *de* **fuerte** Ⓑ ADV, SM (*Mús*) fortissimo

fortuitamente ADV (= *por casualidad*) fortuitously (*frm*), by chance; (= *por accidente*) accidentally

fortuito ADJ (*gen*) fortuitous (*frm*); [*encuentro*] accidental, chance *antes de s*

fortuna SF **1** (= *riqueza*) fortune; **cuesta una ~** it costs a fortune **2** (= *suerte*) fortune; **por ~** luckily, fortunately; **probar ~** to try one's luck

fórum SM = **foro**

forúnculo SM boil

forzado ADJ **1** (= *obligado*) forced; **verse ~ a hacer algo** to be forced *o* obliged to do sth **2** (= *rebuscado*) [*traducción, estilo, metáfora*] forced

forzar /1f, 1l/ VT **1** (= *obligar*) to force; **~ a algn a hacer algo** to force sb to do sth, make sb do sth **2** [+ *puerta, cerradura*] to force **3** [+ *ojos, voz*] to strain; [+ *sonrisa*] to force; **estás forzando la vista** you're straining your eyes **4** (= *violar*) to rape

forzosamente ADV inevitably; **tiene que crear ~ problemas** it must inevitably create problems; **¿tiene ~ que ser así?** does it have to be like this?

forzoso ADJ (= *necesario*) necessary; (= *inevitable*) inescapable, unavoidable; (= *obligatorio*) compulsory; **aterrizaje ~** forced landing

forzudo/a Ⓐ ADJ (= *fuerte*) tough, brawny Ⓑ SM/F [*de circo*] strongman/strongwoman; (*pey*) (= *matón*) thug

fosa SF (= *hoyo*) pit; (= *sepultura*) grave; (*RPl Aut*) (inspection) pit; (*Teat*) prompt pit ➤ **fosa común** (*para soldados, prisioneros*) mass grave; (*para gente sin familia*) common grave ➤ **fosa marina** oceanic trench ➤ **fosa séptica** septic tank ➤ **fosas nasales** nostrils

fosco ADJ [*pelo*] wild, disordered

fosfato SM phosphate

fosforescente ADJ phosphorescent

fosfórico ADJ phosphoric

fosforito* ADJ INV fluorescent; **amarillo ~** fluorescent yellow, luminous yellow

fósforo SM **1** (*Quím*) phosphorus **2** (*esp LAm*) (= *cerilla*) match

fósil Ⓐ ADJ fossil *antes de s*, fossilized Ⓑ SM fossil

fosilizarse /1f/ VPR to fossilize, become fossilized

foso SM **1** (= *agujero*) (*redondo*) pit, hole; (*alargado*) ditch, trench; (*en castillo*) moat ➤ **foso de agua** (*Dep*) water jump **2** (*Teat*) pit ➤ **foso de la orquesta** orchestra pit

foto SF photo, picture; **sacar una ~** to take a photo *o* picture (**de** of); ✦ MODISMO **salir en la ~** to be in the picture, play one's part ➤ **foto de carnet** passport(-size) photo ➤ **foto fija** still, still photo

fotocomposición SF filmsetting, photosetting (*EEUU*), photocomposition

fotocopia SF photocopy, print

fotocopiadora SF (= *máquina*) photocopier, photocopying machine; (= *local*) photocopier's, photocopying shop (*esp Brit*)

fotocopiar /1b/ VT to photocopy

fotoeléctrico ADJ photoelectric

fotogénico ADJ photogenic

fotograbado SM photogravure, photoengraving

fotografía SF **1** (= *arte*) photography **2** (= *imagen*) photograph

fotografiar /1c/ Ⓐ VT to photograph Ⓑ **fotografiarse** VPR to have one's photograph taken

fotográfico ADJ photographic

fotógrafo/a SM/F photographer ➤ **fotógrafo/a de estudio** portrait photographer ➤ **fotógrafo/a de prensa** press photographer

fotograma SM (*Cine*) still

fotolito SM photolithograph

fotomatón SM photo booth; **una foto de ~** a passport photo

fotómetro SM light meter, photometer

fotomontaje SM photomontage

fotonoticia SF photographic reportage

fotonovela SF *romance or crime story illustrated with photos*

foto-robot SF (*pl ~s*) Photofit® picture

fotosíntesis SF INV photosynthesis

foul [faul] (*pl ~s*) SM (*LAm Dep*) foul

foulard [fu'lar] SM scarf

FP SF ABR (*Esp Educ*) (= **Formación Profesional**) *former vocational courses for 14- to 18-year-olds*

frac SM (*pl ~s o* **fraques**) tailcoat, tails *pl*; **ir (vestido) de ~** to be in morning dress

fracasado/a Ⓐ ADJ failed, unsuccessful Ⓑ SM/F failure

fracasar /1a/ VI to fail

fracaso SM failure ➤ **fracaso escolar** academic failure ➤ **fracaso sentimental** disappointment in love

fracción SF **1** (*Mat*) fraction **2** (= *parte*) part, fragment

fraccionado ADJ **pago ~** payment by instalments *o* (*EEUU*) installments

fraccionamiento SM **1** (*gen*) division, breaking-up (**en** into) **2** (*Méx*) (= *urbanización*) housing estate (*Brit*), real estate development (*EEUU*)

fraccionar /1a/ VT to divide, break up, split up (**en** into); **~ los pagos** to pay by instalments *o* (*EEUU*) installments

fraccionario ADJ fractional; **"se ruega moneda fraccionaria"** "please tender exact fare"

fractura SF fracture

fracturar /1a/ Ⓐ VI to fracture Ⓑ **fracturarse** VPR to fracture

fragancia SF fragrance, perfume

fragante ADJ fragrant, scented

fraganti *ver* **in fraganti**

fragata SF frigate

frágil ADJ **1** [*construcción, material, objeto*] fragile **2** [*anciano*] frail; [*salud*] delicate; [*acuerdo, sistema*] fragile; **una mujer aparentemente ~** a seemingly fragile woman

fragilidad SF (*gen*) fragility; [*de anciano*] frailty

fragmentación SF fragmentation

fragmentar /1a/ Ⓐ VT to fragment Ⓑ **fragmentarse** VPR to fragment

fragmentario ADJ fragmentary

fragmento SM **1** [*de escultura, hueso, roca*] fragment; [*de vasija*] fragment, shard **2** (= *extracto*) [*de novela, discurso, obra musical*] passage; (*ya aislado*) excerpt, extract; **se oían ~s de la conversación** you could hear snippets *o* snatches of their conversation

fragor SM (*gen*) din, clamour, clamor (*EEUU*); [*de trueno*] crash, clash; [*de máquina*] roar

fragua SF forge

fraguar /1i/ Ⓐ VT **1** [+ *metal*] to forge **2** [+ *plan*] to hatch, concoct Ⓑ VI [*hormigón*] to harden, set Ⓒ **fraguarse** VPR [*tormenta*] to blow up; (*fig*) to be brewing

fraile SM friar, monk

frailecillo SM puffin

frambuesa SF raspberry

francamente ADV **1** (= *abiertamente*) frankly **2** (= *realmente*) really

francés/esa Ⓐ ADJ French Ⓑ SM/F Frenchman/ Frenchwoman Ⓒ SM **1** (*Ling*) French **2** (***) (= *felación*) blow job***

franchute/a* (*pey*) Ⓐ ADJ Frog*, French Ⓑ SM/F Frog*, Frenchy*

Francia SF France

franciscano ADJ, SM Franciscan

francmasón SM freemason

franco[1] SM (*Fin*) franc

franco[2] ADJ **1** (= *directo*) frank; **si he de ser ~** frankly, to tell you the truth **2** (= *patente*) clear, evident; **en franca decadencia** in visible decline; **en franca rebeldía** in open rebellion **3** (*Com*) [*puerto*] free; **~ a bordo** free on board; **~ de derechos** duty-free; **~ de porte** carriage-free **4** (*CS*) **estar de ~** to be off duty, be on leave

franco[3] (*Hist*) Ⓐ ADJ Frankish Ⓑ SM Frank

francófilo/a ADJ, SM/F Francophile

francófobo/a Ⓐ ADJ francophobe, francophobic *antes de s* Ⓑ SM/F Francophobe

francófono/a Ⓐ ADJ French-speaking Ⓑ SM/F French speaker

francotirador(a) SM/F sniper

franela SF **1** (= *tela*) flannel **2** (*Col*) (*de ropa interior*) vest (*Brit*), undershirt (*EEUU*)

frangollo SM (*Arg, Uru*) botched job, dog's dinner*

franja SF (= *banda*) strip; [*de uniforme*] stripe; **~ de tierra** strip of land ➤ **franja de edad** age group ➤ **franja horaria** time zone

franquear /1a/ Ⓐ VT **1 ~ el paso a algn** to clear the way for sb; **~ la entrada a** to give free entry to **2** (= *atravesar*) [+ *río*] to cross; [+ *obstáculo*] to negotiate **3** (*Correos*) to frank, stamp; **una carta franqueada** a post-paid letter Ⓑ **franquearse** VPR **~se con algn** to have a heart-to-heart talk with sb

franqueo SM (= *acción*) franking; (= *cantidad*) postage

franqueza SF frankness; **con ~** frankly

franquicia SF **1** (*Com*) franchise **2** (= *exención*) exemption (**de** from); ➤ **franquicia aduanera, franquicia arancelaria** exemption from customs duties ➤ **franquicia postal** Freepost®

franquiciar /1b/ VT to franchise

franquismo SM **el ~** (= *período*) the Franco years, the Franco period; (= *política*) the Franco system; **bajo el ~**

under Franco; **luchó contra el** ~ he fought against Franco

franquista Ⓐ ADJ pro-Franco Ⓑ SMF supporter of Franco

frasco SM bottle

frase SF (= *oración*) sentence; (= *locución*) phrase, expression ➤ **frase hecha** set phrase; [*pey*] cliché, stock phrase

fraseo SM (*Mús*) phrasing

fraternal ADJ brotherly, fraternal

fraternidad SF brotherhood, fraternity

fraternizar /1f/ VI to fraternize

fraterno ADJ brotherly, fraternal

fratricida Ⓐ ADJ fratricidal Ⓑ SMF fratricide

fratricidio SM fratricide

fraude SM fraud ➤ **fraude electoral** electoral fraud ➤ **fraude fiscal** tax evasion

fraudulento ADJ fraudulent, dishonest

fray SM brother, friar

frazada SF (*LAm*) blanket

freático ADJ *ver* **capa**

frecuencia SF frequency; **con** ~ frequently, often ➤ **frecuencia modulada** frequency modulation

frecuentar /1a/ VT to frequent

frecuente ADJ (*gen*) frequent; [*costumbre*] common, prevalent; [*vicio*] rife

frecuentemente ADV frequently, often

freelance [friˈlans] ADJ, SMF INV freelance

freezer [ˈfriser] SM (*LAm*) freezer

fregadera* SF (*LAm*) nuisance, pain*

fregadero SM (kitchen) sink

fregado/a Ⓐ ADJ 1 (*LAm**) (= *molesto*) annoying 2 (*LAm**) (= *difícil*) [*trabajo, tarea*] tricky; [*carácter, persona*] fussy 3 (*LAm**) [*persona*] (= *en mala situación económica*) broke*; (= *deprimido*) down, in a bad way*; (= *dañado, enfermo*) in a bad way* 4 (*LAm**) (= *puñetero*) damn*, lousy* 5 (*Col, Perú*) (= *astuto*) cunning 6 (*Chi, Col, Perú, Ven*) (= *estricto*) strict Ⓑ SM/F (*LAm*) (= *persona difícil*) fussy person Ⓒ SM 1 (*con estropajo, cepillo*) scrubbing 2 (*) (= *lío*) mess

fregar /1h, 1j/ Ⓐ VT 1 (= *limpiar*) (con fregona) to mop, wash; (con estropajo, cepillo) to scrub; (con esponja, trapo) to wash; ~ **los cacharros** o **los platos** to wash o do the dishes, do the washing up (*Brit*), wash up (*Brit*) 2 (*LAm**) (= *fastidiar*) [+ *persona*] to annoy; **lo hicieron para ~ a la competencia** they did it to annoy the competition; **¡no me friegues!** (*expresando molestia*) stop bugging o bothering me!; (*expresando asombro*) you're kidding!*; ✦ MODISMO ~ **la paciencia** o (*Chi**) **la cachimba a algn** to pester sb* 3 (*LAm**) (= *malograr*) [+ *planes*] to ruin, mess up; [+ *fiesta*] to ruin; [+ *aparato*] to wreck; **me ~on con el cambio de horario** the timetable change really messed me up Ⓑ VI 1 (= *fregar los platos*) to wash o do the dishes, do the washing up (*Brit*), wash up (*Brit*) 2 (= *fregar el suelo*) (con fregona) to wash the floor, mop the floor; (con cepillo) to scrub the floor 3 (*LAm**) (= *molestar*) to annoy; **ya viene el vecino a ~ otra vez** here comes the neighbour to annoy us again; **¡no friegues!** (*expresando asombro*) you're kidding!* Ⓒ **fregarse** VPR (*LAm**) 1 (= *aguantarse*) **unos pocos se llenan**

los bolsillos y nosotros nos tenemos que ~ a few line their pockets and we have to grin and bear it; **si nos descubren, nos fregamos** if they find us, we've had it o we're done for* 2 (= *malograrse*) [*planes*] to be ruined, be messed up; [*fiesta*] to be ruined 3 (= *dañarse*) [+ *pierna, rodilla*] to do in*; **me fregué la espalda levantando sacos** I did my back in lifting sacks*

fregón* ADJ (*LAm*) = **fregado** A

fregona SF mop

freidora SF deep-fat frier

freiduría SF (*tb* ~ **de pescado**) fried-fish shop

freír /3l/ (*pp* **frito**) Ⓐ VT 1 (*Culin*) to fry 2 (*) (= *molestar*) to annoy; (= *acosar*) to harass; ~ **a algn a preguntas** to bombard sb with questions 3 (*) (= *matar*) ~ **a algn a tiros** to riddle sb with bullets Ⓑ **freírse** VPR 1 (*Culin*) to fry 2 ~**se de calor*** to be roasting

frenar /1a/ Ⓐ VT 1 (*Aut, Mec*) to brake 2 (= *contener*) [+ *inflación, crecimiento, avance*] to check, slow down; [+ *pasiones, entusiasmo*] to curb; [+ *enemigo, ataque*] to check, hold back Ⓑ VI (*Aut*) to brake Ⓒ **frenarse** VPR (= *contenerse*) to restrain o.s.

frenazo SM (= *acción*) sudden braking; (= *ruido*) squeal of brakes; **dar un** ~ to brake suddenly, brake hard

frenesí SM frenzy

frenético ADJ (= *desenfrenado*) frantic, frenzied; (= *furioso*) furious, wild; **ponerse** ~ to lose one's head

frenillo SM 1 (= *defecto*) **tener** ~ to have a speech defect 2 (*Anat*) fraenum, frenum (*esp EEUU*) 3 (*RPl*) [*de dientes*] brace(s)

freno SM 1 (*Aut, Mec*) brake; **echar el** ~ o **los ~s** to apply the brake(s); **pisé el** ~ I put my foot on the brake, I applied the brake ➤ **freno de disco** disc brake ➤ **freno de mano** handbrake (*Brit*), emergency brake (*EEUU*) ➤ **freno de tambor** drum brake 2 [*de caballo*] bit 3 (= *contención*) brake; **medidas que actúan como** ~ **al crecimiento económico** measures that act as a brake on economic growth, measures that slow down economic growth; **hay que poner** ~ **a la especulación** we must curb speculation

frenopático SM (*Med*) mental home; (*hum**) loony bin**

frentazo SM (*Méx*) disappointment, rebuff; **pegarse un** ~ to feel really let down*

frente Ⓐ SF (*Anat*) forehead, brow (*liter*); ✦ MODISMOS **con la** ~ **(muy) alta** with one's head held high; **lo lleva escrito en la** ~ it's written all over his face; ~ **a** ~ face to face Ⓑ SM 1 (= *parte delantera*) front; **al** ~ in front; **un ejército con su capitán al** ~ an army led by its captain, an army with its captain at the front; **al** ~ **de**: **entró en Madrid al** ~ **de las tropas** he led the troops into Madrid, he entered Madrid at the head of his troops; **el Madrid sigue al** ~ **de la clasificación** Madrid still lead the table o are still top of the league; **espero seguir al** ~ **del festival** I hope to continue as director of the festival; **la casa de en** ~ the house opposite; **hacer** ~ **a** [+ *crisis, problemas*] to tackle; [+ *situación, realidad*] to face up to 2 **de** ~: **atacar de** ~ to make a frontal attack; **chocar de** ~ to crash head-on; **viene un coche de** ~ there's a car heading straight for us 3 (*Mil, Pol*) front; **formar** o **hacer un** ~ **común con algn** to form a united front with sb ➤ **frente de batalla** battle front ➤ **Frente Polisario** Polisario Front ➤ **frente popular** popular front 4 (*Meteo*) front ➤ **frente cálido** warm front ➤ **frente frío** cold front 5 **frente a** 5.1 (= *enfrente de*) opposite; ~ **al hotel** opposite the hotel; **ella está** ~ **a mí** she is facing o opposite me; **el barco encalló** ~ **a la costa irlandesa** the boat ran aground off the Irish coast 5.2 (= *en presencia de*) ~ **a las cámaras** in front of the cameras; **ceder** ~ **a una amenaza** to give way to o in the face of a threat 5.3 (= *en oposición a*) against; **el euro sigue fuerte** ~ **al dólar** the euro remains strong against the dollar; **logró un 39% de los votos,** ~ **al 49% de 1990** she got 39% of the vote, as against 49% in 1990

fresa Ⓐ ADJ INV (*Méx*) (= *tradicionalista*) straitlaced Ⓑ SF 1 (= *fruta*) strawberry; (= *planta*) strawberry plant 2 (*Téc*) milling cutter; [*de dentista*] drill

fresadora SF milling machine

fresca* SF 1 **la ~: saldremos temprano, con la ~** we'll leave early, while it's still cool, we'll leave early, in the cool of the morning; **charlaban en la calle, sentados a la ~** they were sitting in the street chatting in the cool air 2 (*) (= *insolencia*) **decir** o **soltar cuatro ~s a algn** to give sb a lot of lip, give sb a lot of cheek*; *ver tb* **fresco**

frescachón ADJ (= *saludable*) healthy, glowing with health; (= *de buen color*) ruddy

fresco/a Ⓐ ADJ 1 (*Culin*) (= *no congelado, no cocinado*) (*gen*) fresh; (= *no pasado*) [*carne, fruta*] fresh; [*huevo*] fresh, new-laid; (= *no curado*) [*queso*] unripened; [*salmón*] fresh 2 (= *frío*) 2.1 [*brisa, viento*] cool; **salí a respirar un poco de aire ~** I went outside to get a breath of fresh air 2.2 [*bebida*] cool, cold; [*agua*] (*para beber*) cold; (*en piscina, río*) cool 2.3 [*tiempo*] (*desagradable*) chilly; (*agradable*) cool 2.4 [*tela, vestido*] cool 3 (= *reciente*) [*ideas*] fresh; [*pintura*] wet; **la tragedia aún está fresca en mi memoria** the tragic events are still fresh in my memory; **traigo noticias frescas** I have the latest news 4 (= *natural*) [*piel, estilo*] fresh 5 (= *refrescante*) [*colonia, perfume*] refreshing 6 (= *descarado*) cheeky (*Brit**), sassy (*EEUU**); **¡qué ~!** what a cheek!*, what a nerve!*; **me lo dijo y se quedó tan ~** he said it without batting an eyelid Ⓑ SM/F (*) (*sinvergüenza*) **¡usted es un ~!** you've got a nerve!* Ⓒ SM 1 (= *temperatura*) **voy a sentarme fuera, al ~** I'm going to sit outside where it's nice and cool; **dormir al ~** to sleep in the open air, sleep outdoors; **hace ~** (*desagradable*) it's chilly; (*agradable*) it's cool; **tomar el ~** to get some fresh air; ✦ MODISMO **me trae al ~*: que te lo creas o no, me trae al ~** I couldn't care less whether you believe it or not 2 (*Arte*) fresco; **pintar al ~** to paint in fresco 3 (*Col, Perú, Ven*) (= *bebida*) (*sin gas*) fruit drink; (*con gas*) fizzy (*Brit*) o carbonated (*esp EEUU*) fruit drink, soda (*EEUU*); *ver tb* **fresca**

frescor SM [*de temperatura, alimentos*] freshness; [*de lugar, bebida*] coolness; **el ~ nocturno** the cool night air

frescura SF (= *descaro*) nerve*, cheek*

fresno SM ash (tree)

fresón SM (= *fruto*) strawberry; (= *planta*) strawberry plant

fresquera SF meat safe (*esp Brit*), cooler (*EEUU*)

freudiano ADJ Freudian

frialdad SF 1 [*de material, líquido*] coldness 2 (= *indiferencia*) (*en sentimientos, actitudes*) coolness; (*en carácter, mirada*) coldness; **la novela ha sido acogida con ~ por la crítica** the novel has been given a cool reception by the critics; **hemos de actuar con ~ y analizar el problema detenidamente** we have to act dispassionately and analyse the problem at length

fríamente ADV 1 (= *con indiferencia, sin apasionamiento*) coolly; (= *con hostilidad*) coldly; **mirado ~, tiene parte de razón en lo que dice** viewed dispassionately, he is partly right in what he says; **el reo miró ~ a los parientes de sus víctimas** the accused looked with cold detachment at the relatives of his victims 2 (= *a sangre fría*) [*matar*] in cold blood; [*torturar*] coldheartedly

frían *ver* **freír**

fricandó SM, **fricasé** SM fricassee

fricativa SF fricative

fricativo ADJ fricative

fricción SF 1 (= *frotamiento*) rub, rubbing 2 (*Mec*) friction 3 (= *enfrentamiento*) friction, trouble

friccionar /1a/ VT to rub

friega SF 1 (*gen*) rub, rubbing; (*Dep*) rub-down 2 (*LAm**) (= *molestia*) nuisance; (= *problema*) bother

friegaplatos Ⓐ SM INV (= *aparato*) dishwasher Ⓑ SMF INV (= *persona*) dishwasher, washer-up (*Brit*)

frigidez SF frigidity

frígido ADJ frigid

frigorífico Ⓐ ADJ **camión ~** refrigerated lorry (*Brit*), refrigerated truck (*EEUU*); **instalación frigorífica** cold-storage plant Ⓑ SM 1 (= *nevera*) refrigerator, fridge (*esp Brit*) 2 (*CS*) cold-storage plant, meat-packing depot

frigorífico-congelador SM (*pl* **frigoríficos-congeladores**) fridge-freezer

frijol SM, **fríjol** SM 1 (*esp LAm Bot*) (= *judía*) bean ➤ **frijol colorado** kidney bean 2 (*Méx**) (= *comida*) food *sing*; ✦ MODISMO **buscarse los ~es** (*Cuba**) to earn a living

frío Ⓐ ADJ 1 (*en temperatura*) [*aire, invierno, sudor*] cold; **una cervecita bien fría** an ice cold beer; **el café se ha quedado ~** the coffee has got cold; **me quedé ~** I got cold 2 (*en sentimientos, actitudes*) 2.1 [*relaciones, acogida, recibimiento*] cool 2.2 (= *desapasionado*) cool; **mantener la cabeza fría** to keep a cool head, keep one's cool 2.3 (= *insensible, inexpresivo*) cold; **era ~ y calculador** he was cold and calculating; **este público es más ~ que el de otras ciudades** this audience is less responsive than those in other cities 2.4 ✦ MODISMO **dejar ~ a algn** (= *indiferente*) to leave sb cold Ⓑ SM 1 (= *baja temperatura*) cold; **la ola de ~** the cold spell; **hace (mucho) ~** it's (very) cold; **¡qué ~ hace!** it's freezing!, it's so cold! ➤ **frío industrial** industrial refrigeration 2 (= *sensación*) cold; **me entró ~** I got cold; **coger ~** to catch cold; **pasar ~** to be cold; **tener ~** to be cold, feel cold 3 **en ~** 3.1 (= *en calma*) **pactar un acuerdo en ~** to negotiate an agreement with cool heads; **cuando se contemplan las cifras en ~** when one calmly o coolly considers the numbers 3.2 (= *repentinamente*) **me lo dijo en ~ y no supe cómo reaccionar** he sprung it on me out of the blue o he told me just like that and I didn't know quite what to say; ✦ MODISMO **no dar ni ~ ni calor a algn: no me da ni ~ ni calor** I don't mind at all, I'm not at all bothered (*esp Brit*)

friolento ADJ (*LAm*) sensitive to cold

friolera SF trifle, mere nothing; **la ~ de 100 euros** a mere 100 euros

friolero ADJ sensitive to cold

friso SM frieze

fritada SF fry, fry-up (*Brit**)

fritanga SF (= *comida frita*) fry, fry-up (*Brit**); (*pey*) greasy food

fritanguería SF (*And*) (= *tienda*) fried food shop (*esp Brit*) o store (*EEUU*); (= *puesto*) fried food stall

fritar /1a/ VT (*LAm*) to fry

frito Ⓐ PP *de* **freír** Ⓑ ADJ ✦ MODISMOS **dejar ~ a algn*** to do sb in*, waste sb*; **estar ~*** (= *dormido*) to be getting some shuteye*, be out for the count*; (= *muerto*) to have bought it**, have snuffed it (*Brit***); (*Carib, CS*) (= *acabado*) to be finished, be done for*; **quedarse ~*** to go out like a light; **tener ~ a algn*** to get on sb's nerves; **este trabajo me tiene ~** I'm fed up with this job

fritura SF fried food, fry; **~ de pescado** fried fish

frivolidad SF frivolity, frivolousness

frivolizar /1f/ VT (= *trivializar*) to trivialize; (= *quitar importancia a*) to play down

frívolo ADJ frivolous

frondoso ADJ leafy, luxuriant

frontal ADJ 1 [*parte, posición*] front; **choque ~** head-on collision 2 [*enfrentamiento*] direct, frontal; [*rechazo*] outright

frontera SF (= *línea*) border; (= *zona*) border area

fronterizo ADJ border *antes de s*, frontier *antes de s*

frontón SM (*Dep*) (= *cancha*) pelota court; (= *pared*) (main) wall (*of a pelota court*)

frotamiento SM rub, rubbing; (*Mec*) friction

frotar /1a/ Ⓐ VT to rub; **quitar algo frotando** to rub sth off Ⓑ **frotarse** VPR to rub, chafe; **~se las manos** to rub one's hands (together)

frotis SM INV ➤ **frotis cervical** cervical smear (*Brit*), pap smear (*EEUU*)

fructífero ADJ fruitful, productive

fructificar /1g/ VI [*esfuerzos*] to bear fruit; [*plan*] to come to fruition

fructosa SF fructose

fructuoso ADJ fruitful

frufrú SM rustling, rustle

frugal ADJ frugal, thrifty

frugalidad SF frugality

fruición SF delight; **leer con ~** to read with delight; **comer con ~** to eat with relish

frunce SM (*Cos*) gather, shirr

fruncir /3b/ VT 1 (*Cos*) to gather, shirr 2 [+ *labios*] to purse; **~ el ceño** o **entrecejo** to frown, knit one's brow

fruslería SF (= *chuchería*) trinket; (= *nimiedad*) trifle, triviality

frustración SF frustration

frustrado ADJ [*persona*] frustrated; [*intento, plan, atentado*] failed; **delito de homicidio ~** attempted murder

frustrante ADJ frustrating

frustrar /1a/ ④ VT 1 [+ *persona*] to frustrate; [+ *proyecto, aspiración, deseo*] to thwart; **le frustra no poderse comunicar** he finds it frustrating not being able to communicate 2 (= *abortar*) [+ *atentado, operación*] to foil ⑧ **frustrarse** VPR [*persona*] to be frustrated; [*aspiración, deseo*] to be thwarted

fruta SF fruit ➤ **fruta abrillantada** (*RPl*) crystallized fruit ➤ **fruta de la pasión** passion fruit ➤ **fruta del tiempo, fruta de estación** (*RPl*) seasonal fruit ➤ **fruta escarchada** crystallized fruit ➤ **fruta prohibida** forbidden fruit ➤ **fruta(s) seca(s)** (*LAm*) nuts ➤ **frutas del bosque** fruits of the forest, forest fruits

frutal ④ ADJ fruit-bearing, fruit *antes de s*; **árbol ~** fruit tree ⑧ SM fruit tree

frutera SF (*RPl*) fruit dish, fruit bowl

frutería SF fruiterer's (shop), fruit shop (*esp Brit*) o store (*EEUU*), greengrocer's (*esp Brit*)

frutero/a ④ ADJ fruit *antes de s* ⑧ SM/F (= *persona*) fruiterer, greengrocer (*esp Brit*) ⑥ SM (= *recipiente*) fruit dish, fruit bowl

frutilla SF (*And, CS*) strawberry

fruto SM 1 (*Bot*) fruit; **dar ~** to fruit, bear fruit ➤ **frutos secos** nuts 2 (= *resultado*) result, product; (= *beneficio*) profit, benefit; [*de esfuerzo*] fruits *pl*; **dar ~** to bear fruit; **sacar ~ de algo** to profit from sth, derive benefit from sth; **el ~ de esta unión** the offspring of this marriage, the fruit o product of this union (*liter*)

FSE SM ABR (= **Fondo Social Europeo**) ESF

fu SM ✦ MODISMO **ni fu ni fa*** SO-SO

fuchi EXCL (*Méx*) (*asco*) yuk!, ugh!; (*sorpresa*) phew!, wow!

fucsia SF fuchsia

fue *ver* **ser, ir**

fuego SM 1 (= *llamas*) fire; **pegar** o **prender ~ a algo** to set fire to sth, set sth on fire; ✦ MODISMOS **echar ~ por los ojos**: **se marchó echando ~ por los ojos** he went off, his eyes blazing; **jugar con ~** to play with fire ➤ **fuego de artificio** firework; **ha llegado a la cima sin los ~s de artificio típicos de muchas grandes estrellas** she has got to the top without the typical blaze of publicity attached to many big stars ➤ **fuego fatuo** will-o'-the-wisp ➤ **fuegos artificiales** fireworks

2 [*de cocina*] (= *quemador de gas*) burner, ring; (= *quemador eléctrico*) ring; (= *calor*) heat, flame; **se deja cocer a ~ lento 15 minutos** simmer for 15 minutes, cook on o over a low heat for 15 minutes

3 (*para cigarro*) light; **¿tienes** o **me das ~?** have you got a light?

4 (*Mil*) fire; **¡fuego!** fire!; **abrir ~ (contra algo/algn)** to open fire (on sth/sb); **¡alto el ~!** cease fire!; **hacer ~ (contra** o **sobre algo)** to fire (at sth); ✦ MODISMO **estar entre dos ~s** to be caught in the crossfire ➤ **fuego a discreción** fire at will ➤ **fuego amigo** friendly fire

fuel SM fuel oil

fuelle SM 1 (*para el fuego*) bellows *pl*; [*de gaita*] bag; [*de bolso, maleta*] gusset; [*de autobús, tren*] connecting section 2 (= *aguante*) stamina, staying power; ✦ MODISMO **perder ~** to run out of steam

fuel-oil [fuel'oil] SM fuel oil

fuente SF 1 (= *construcción*) fountain; (= *manantial*) spring ➤ **fuente de soda** (*LAm*) *café, selling ice-cream and soft drinks*, soda fountain (*EEUU*) ➤ **fuente termal** hot spring 2 (*Culin*) serving dish, platter ➤ **fuente de horno** ovenproof dish 3 (= *origen*) source, origin; **de ~ desconocida/fidedigna** from an unknown/a reliable source ➤ **fuente de ingresos** source of income 4 (*Tip*) font, typeface

fuer SM **a ~ de** (*liter*) as a

fuera ADV 1 (*de edificio, objeto*) **los niños estaban jugando ~** the children were playing outside; **¡estamos aquí ~!** we're out here!; **el perro tenía la lengua ~** the dog had his tongue hanging out; **¡fuera!** get out!; **ir** o **salir ~** to go out, go outside; **comer ~** (*al aire libre*) to eat outside; (*en restaurante*) to eat out, we're eating out tonight; **de ~** from outside; **trae una silla de ~** bring a chair in from outside; **desde ~** from outside; **por ~** (on the) outside; **por ~ está duro** it's hard on the outside; **esta camisa se lleva por ~** this shirt is worn outside, this shirt is not tucked in 2 (*de ciudad, trabajo*) **estar ~** to be away; **mis padres llevan varios días ~** my parents have been away for several days 3 (*tb ~ del país*) abroad; **toda la maquinaria viene de ~** all the machinery comes from abroad; **ir** o **salir ~** to go abroad

4 (*Dep*) 4.1 (*en un partido*) **estar ~** [*pelota*] (*Ftbl*) to be out of play; (*Rugby*) to be in touch; (*Tenis*) to be out; **~ de juego** offside; **~ de tiempo** *after full time*; **estamos ~ de tiempo** time's up 4.2 (*tb ~ de casa*) away, away from home; **el equipo de ~** the away team; **jugar ~** to play away (from home)

5 **~ de** 5.1 (= *en el exterior de*) outside, out of; **estaba ~ de su jaula** it was outside o out of its cage 5.2 (= *aparte*) apart from, aside from; **pero ~ de eso** but apart o aside from that; **~ de que ...** apart from the fact that ... 5.3 **~ de combate** (*Mil*) wounded; (*Boxeo*) K.O.ed; **dejar a algn ~ de combate** to knock sb out; **~ de lo común** unusual; **estar ~ de lugar** to be inappropriate, be out of place; **~ de peligro** out of danger; **~ de serie** exceptional; **es un ~ de serie** he's quite exceptional

fueraborda SM INV, **fuera-borda** SM INV (= *motor*) outboard engine, outboard motor; (= *bote*) dinghy with an outboard engine

fuereño/a SM/F (*Méx*) outsider

fuero SM 1 (= *carta municipal*) municipal charter; (= *ley local*) local/regional law code; (= *privilegio*) (*tb* **~s**) privilege, exemption; **a ~** according to law; **¿con qué ~?** by what right?; **de ~** de jure, in law 2 (= *autoridad*) jurisdiction; ✦ MODISMOS **en mi ~ interno ...** in my heart of hearts ..., deep down ...; **volver por sus ~s** (= *recuperarse*) to be oneself again; (= *reincidir*) to go back to one's old ways

fuerte ④ ADJ 1 [*persona*] 1.1 (*físicamente*) (*gen*) strong; (= *robusto*) sturdy, powerfully built; (*euf*) (= *obeso*) large 1.2 (*emocionalmente*) strong, tough 1.3 **estar ~ en filosofía/historia** [*estudiante*] to be strong in philosophy/history 2 (= *intenso*) [*sabor, olor, viento*] strong; [*dolor, calor*] intense; [*ejercicio*] strenuous; [*explosión, voz, ruido*] loud; [*golpe*] heavy, hard; [*acento*] strong, thick; [*color*] bright; [*impresión*] strong, powerful; [*deseo*] strong, deep; [*abrazo, beso*] big; **una discusión muy ~** a heated argument; **expresiones muy ~s** strong language; **el taco más ~ que ha pronunciado** the worst swearword he has ever said; **un beso muy ~** (*en cartas*) lots of love; **un ~ abrazo, Carmen** best wishes, Carmen; (*más cariñoso*) love, Carmen 3 (*bebida, medicamento*) strong; [*comida*] heavy; **nunca toma cosas ~s, sólo cerveza y vino** he never drinks spirits o the hard stuff*, just beer and wine 4 (= *resistente*) [*cuerda, tela*] strong; [*economía, moneda, país*] strong 5 (= *importante*) [*aumento, bajada*] sharp; [*crisis*] serious, severe; [*pérdidas*] large, substantial 6 (= *impactante*) [*escena*] shocking, disturbing; **me dijo cosas muy ~s** she said some harsh o nasty* things; **— lo despidió en el acto —¡qué ~!*** "he fired him there and then" — "that's outrageous o appalling!" 7 **hacerse ~** (= *protegerse*) to hole up; (= *volverse fuerte*) to gain strength

⑧ ADV 1 (= *con fuerza*) [*golpear*] hard; [*abrazar*] tight,

tightly; [apostar, jugar] heavily
2 (= en voz alta) [hablar, tocar] loud, loudly; **¡más ~! ¡que no se le oye!** speak up! we can't hear
3 (= gran cantidad) **desayunar ~** to have a big breakfast; **comer ~** to have a big lunch
ⓒ SM **1** (Mil) fort
2 (= especialidad) forte, strong point; **no es mi ~** it's not my forte o strong point

fuertemente ADV **1** (= con fuerza) [golpear] hard; [abrazar, apretar] tightly **2** (= mucho) [apoyar, favorecer, contrastar] strongly; [aumentar, disminuir] sharply, greatly; **la medida ha sido ~ criticada** the measure has been strongly criticized **3** (+ ADJ) **grupos ~ armados** heavily armed groups; **divisas ~ vinculadas al dólar** currencies closely tied to the dollar

fuerza SF **1** [de persona] **1.1** (física) strength; **tienes mucha ~** you're very strong; **con ~** [golpear] hard; [abrazar, agarrar, apretar] tightly, tight; [aplaudir] loudly; **grita con todas tus ~s** shout with all your might; **haced ~** heave! **1.2** [de carácter] strength; **la ~ creadora de Picasso** Picasso's creative energy; **sentirse con ~s para hacer algo** to have the strength to do sth, **tener ~s para hacer algo** to be strong enough to do sth, have the strength to do sth.
✦ MODISMOS **se le va la ~ por la boca*** he's all talk and no action, he's all mouth*; **sacar ~s de flaqueza** to make a supreme effort, gather all one's strength ➤ **fuerza de voluntad** willpower
2 (= intensidad) [de viento] strength, force
3 (= ímpetu) **su nombre ha irrumpido con ~ en el mundo artístico** his name has burst onto the art scene; **la ultraderecha renace con ~** the extreme right is making a strong comeback
4 (= poder) [de fe] strength; [de argumento] strength, force, power; [de la ley] force; **les asistía la ~ de la razón** they were helped by the power of reason; **cobrar ~** [rumores] to grow stronger, gain strength; **la idea ha cobrado ~ últimamente** the idea has gained in popularity o gained momentum recently; **por la ~ de la costumbre** out of habit, from force of habit ➤ **fuerza mayor: por razones de ~ mayor** due to circumstances beyond their control
5 (= violencia) force; **recurrir a la ~** to resort to force; **por la ~:** quisieron impedirlo por la ~ they tried to prevent it forcibly o by force; **por la ~ no se consigue nada** using force doesn't achieve anything, nothing is achieved by force; **imponer algo por la ~** to impose sth forcibly ➤ **fuerza bruta** brute force
6 (locuciones) **6.1 a ~ de** by; **a ~ de repetirlo** by repeating it so much; **a ~ de autodisciplina** by exercising great self control; **a ~ de pasarme horas y horas estudiando** by dint of hours and hours of study; **a ~ de paciencia** by dint of great patience **6.2 a la ~:** hacer algo a la ~ to be forced to do sth; **se lo llevaron de su casa a la ~** he was taken from his home by force, he was taken forcibly from his home; **a la ~ tuvo que oírlos: ¡estaba a su lado!** he must have heard them: he was right next to them!; **alimentar a algn a la ~** to force-feed sb; **entrar en un lugar a la ~** [ladrón] to break into a place, break in; [policía, bombero] to force one's way into a place, enter a place forcibly; ✦ MODISMO **a la ~ ahorcan: dejará el ministerio cuando lo haga su jefe, ¡a la ~ ahorcan!** he'll leave the ministry when his boss does — not that he has any choice, anyway o life's tough!* **6.3 por ~** inevitably; **una región pobre como la nuestra, por ~ ha de ser más barata** in a poor region like ours prices will inevitably be o must be cheaper
7 (Fís, Mec) force ➤ **fuerza centrífuga** centrifugal force ➤ **fuerza centrípeta** centripetal force ➤ **fuerza de (la) gravedad** force of gravity
8 (= conjunto de personas) (Mil, Pol) force ➤ **fuerza(s) aérea(s)** air force sing ➤ **fuerzas armadas** armed forces ➤ **fuerzas del orden (público)** forces of law and order ➤ **fuerzas de seguridad** security forces ➤ **las fuerzas vivas** the powers that be; **las ~s vivas locales** the local power group

fuese ver **ser, ir**

fuetazo SM (LAm) lash

fuete (LAm) SM whip

fuga¹ SF **1** (gen) flight, escape; **darse a la o ponerse en ~** to

flee, take flight; **poner al enemigo en ~** to put the enemy to flight ➤ **fuga de capitales** flight of capital (abroad) ➤ **fuga de cerebros** brain drain **2** [de gas] leak, escape

fuga² SF (Mús) fugue

fugacidad SF fleetingness, transitory nature

fugarse /1h/ VPR [preso] to escape; [niño, adolescente] to run away; [enamorados] to elope; **se fugó de casa** he ran away from home

fugaz ADJ fleeting, brief

fugitivo/a SM/F fugitive

fui, fuimos etc ver **ser, ir**

fulana* SF (pey) slut**, tart (esp Brit**)

fulano* SM **1** (= alguien) so-and-so; **~ de tal** ◇ **Don Fulano** Mr So-and-so, Joe Bloggs (Brit), John Doe (EEUU); **~, zutano y mengano** Tom, Dick and Harry **2** (= tío) guy*

fular SM = **foulard**

fulbito SM (en campo) five-a-side football; (Arg) (de mesa) table football, Foosball® (EEUU)

fulero/a ADJ **1** = **fullero 2** (RPI*) (= feo) nasty, hideous*

fulgor SM brilliance, glow

fulgurante ADJ bright, shining

fulgurar /1a/ VI to shine, glow

full* [ful] **ⓐ** ADJ (Col, Ven) full **ⓑ** SM (CS) **a (todo) ~** flat out

full contact [ful'kontakt] SM full contact sports pl

fullero/a **ⓐ** ADJ **1** (= tramposo) cheating, deceitful **2** (= chapucero) blundering, incompetent; **hacer algo en plan ~** to botch sth* **ⓑ** SM/F **1** (= tramposo) (gen) sneak*, tattler (EEUU); (con cartas) cheat, cardsharp **2** (= chapucero) blunderer

fulminante **ⓐ** ADJ **1** [mirada] withering **2** (= súbito) sudden; **suele ser ~** it tends to be rapidly fatal **3** (*) (= tremendo) terrific, tremendous; **golpe ~** terrific blow; **tiro ~** (Ftbl etc) sizzling shot **ⓑ** SM (LAm) percussion cap

fulminar /1a/ VT to strike down; **murió fulminado por un rayo** he was struck dead o killed by lightning; ✦ MODISMO **~ a algn con la mirada** to look daggers at sb

fumado ADJ **estar ~*** to be stoned*

fumador(a) SM/F smoker; **la sección de no ~es** the no-smoking o non-smoking section ➤ **fumador(a) pasivo/a** passive smoker

fumar /1a/ **ⓐ** VT [+ cigarro, pipa] to smoke **ⓑ** VI to smoke; **fuma en pipa** he smokes a pipe; **"prohibido fumar"** "no smoking"; ✦ MODISMO **~ como un carretero** to smoke like a chimney **ⓒ** **fumarse*** VPR [+ dinero] to squander, blow*; [+ clase] to miss

fumata **ⓐ** SF ➤ **fumata blanca** (Rel) (puff of) white smoke; (fig) indication of success **ⓑ** SMF (**) (= persona) dope-smoker*

fumigación SF **1** [de local, ropa] fumigation **2** (Agr) crop-dusting, crop-spraying

fumigar /1h/ VT **1** [+ local, ropa] to fumigate **2** (Agr) to dust, spray

funambulista SMF, **funámbulo/a** SM/F tightrope walker, funambulist (frm)

función SF **1** (= actividad) (física, de máquina) function; **las funciones cerebrales** the brain functions
2 (= papel) function; **ésa debería ser la ~ de la prensa** that should be the role o function of the press; **es una escultura que también cumple o hace la ~ de puerta** it is a sculpture which also acts as o serves as a door; **desempeñar la ~ de director** to hold o have the position of director; **la ~ de educar corresponde a la escuela** the task of educating falls to the school
3 funciones (= deberes) duties; **en el ejercicio de sus funciones** in the course of her duties; **excederse** o **extralimitarse en sus funciones** to exceed one's duties; **en funciones** [ministro, alcalde, presidente] acting antes de s; **gobierno en funciones** interim government; **entrar en funciones** [funcionario] to take up one's duties o post; [ministro, alcalde, presidente] to take up office, assume office; [organismo] to come into being
4 en ~ de (= según) according to; (= basándose en) on the

basis of; **en ~ de las necesidades de cada país** according to the needs of each country; **el desarrollo cultural está en ~ de la estructura política de un país** cultural development depends on the political structure of a country; **los consumidores realizan sus compras en ~ de la calidad y el precio** consumers make their purchases on the basis of quality and price
5 (= *espectáculo*) [*de teatro, ópera*] performance; [*de títeres, variedades, musical*] show; **ir a ver una ~ de circo** to go to the circus ➤ **función benéfica** charity performance ➤ **función continua** (*LAm*), **función continuada** (*CS*) continuous performance ➤ **función de noche** late performance, evening performance ➤ **función de tarde** matinée
6 la ~ pública the civil service
7 (*Mat*) function
8 (*Ling*) function

funcional ADJ functional

funcionamiento SM **cada 2.000 horas de ~** after every 2,000 hours of operation; **nos explicó el ~ de un carburador** he explained to us how a carburettor works; **poner en ~** to put *o* bring into operation; **para el buen ~ de su motor** in order keep your engine running smoothly

funcionar /1a/ VI **1** [*aparato, mecanismo*] to work; [*motor*] to work, run; [*sistema*] to work, function; **"no funciona"** "out of order" **2** [*plan, método*] to work; [*negocio, película*] to be a success

funcionariado SM civil service, bureaucracy

funcionario/a SM/F **1** (*tb ~ público*) civil servant ➤ **funcionario/a de prisiones** prison officer **2** (*CS, Méx*) (= *empleado*) employee

funda SF **1** (*gen*) case, cover; [*de disco*] sleeve ➤ **funda de almohada** pillowcase, pillowslip ➤ **funda de gafas** spectacles case, glasses case ➤ **funda de pistola** holster **2** [*de diente*] cap

fundación SF foundation

fundadamente ADV with good reason, on good grounds

fundado ADJ well-founded, justified

fundador(a) SM/F founder

fundamental ADJ fundamental, basic

fundamentalismo SM fundamentalism

fundamentalista ADJ, SMF fundamentalist

fundamentar /1a/ VT to base, found (**en** on)

fundamento SM **1** (= *base*) foundation, basis; (= *razón*) grounds, reason; **eso carece de ~** that is completely without foundation; **creencia sin ~** groundless *o* unfounded belief **2 fundamentos** (= *principios*) fundamentals, basic essentials

fundar /1a/ ⓐ VT **1** (= *crear*) [+ *institución, asociación, ciudad, revista*] to found; [+ *partido*] to found, set up, establish **2** (= *basar*) to base (**en** on) ⓑ **fundarse** VPR **~se en** [*teoría*] to be based on, be founded on; [*persona*] to base o.s. on

fundición SF **1** (= *acción*) [*de mineral*] smelting; (*en moldes*) casting; [*de lingotes, joyas*] melting down **2** (= *fábrica*) foundry

fundido/a ⓐ ADJ **1** [*metal, acero, cera*] molten **2** (*) (= *muy cansado*) shattered (*Brit**), whacked (*Brit**), pooped (*EEUU**) **3** (*Perú, CS*) (= *arruinado*) ruined, bankrupt **4** (*Chi**) [*niño*] spoilt ⓑ SM/F (*Chi**) spoilt brat* ⓒ SM (*Cine*) (= *resultado*) fade; (= *acción*) fading ➤ **fundido a negro** fade-to-black

fundillo SM (*LAm*), **fundillos** SMPL (*LAm*) **1** [*del pantalón*] seat **2** (*) (= *trasero*) backside*, bum (*Brit**)

fundir /3a/ ⓐ VT **1** (= *derretir*) (*para hacer líquido*) [+ *metal, cera, nieve*] to melt; [+ *monedas, lingotes, joyas*] to melt down; (*para extraer el metal*) to smelt; (*en molde*) to cast **2** [+ *bombilla, fusible*] to blow
3 (= *fusionar*) [+ *organizaciones, empresas*] to merge, amalgamate; [+ *culturas, movimientos*] to fuse
4 (*Cine*) [+ *imágenes*] to fade
5 (*) [+ *dinero*] to blow*
6 (*Perú, CS*) (= *arruinar*) ruin
7 (*Chi**) [+ *niño*] to spoil
ⓑ **fundirse** VPR **1** (= *derretirse*) [*hielo*] to melt

2 (*Elec*) [*bombilla, fusible*] to blow, go
3 (= *fusionarse*) [*organizaciones, empresas*] to amalgamate, merge; [*partidos políticos*] to merge; **~se en algo** [*organizaciones*] to merge to form sth, amalgamate into sth; [*sonidos*] to merge into sth; [*colores, imágenes*] to merge to form sth, blend together to form sth; **~se con algo**: **el cielo se fundía con el mar** the sea and the sky blended *o* merged into one
4 (*Cine*) [*imagen*] to fade
5 (*Perú, CS*) (= *arruinarse*) to be ruined

fundo SM (*Perú, Chi*) landed property, estate; (= *granja*) farm

fúnebre ADJ **1 coche ~** hearse; **pompas ~s** undertaker's, funeral parlor (*EEUU*) **2** (= *lúgubre*) mournful, funereal (*frm*)

funeral ⓐ ADJ funeral *antes de s* ⓑ SM (*tb ~es*) (= *exequias*) funeral *sing*; (= *oficio religioso*) funeral service *sing*

funerala* SF ✦ MODISMO **ojo a la ~** black eye

funeraria SF undertaker's, funeral parlor (*EEUU*)

funerario ADJ funeral *antes de s*

funesto ADJ (= *maldito*) ill-fated; (= *desastroso*) fatal, disastrous

fungir /3c/ VI (*CAm, Méx*) to act (**de** as)

funicular SM **1** (= *tren*) funicular, funicular railway **2** (= *teleférico*) cable car

furcia* SF whore*, tart (*Brit***), hooker (*EEUU**)

furgón SM (*Aut*) truck, van; (*Ferro*) goods van, boxcar (*EEUU*) ➤ **furgón de cola** guard's-van (*Brit*), caboose (*EEUU*)

furgoneta SF (= *furgón*) (transit) van (*Brit*), panel truck (*EEUU*); (= *coche*) estate (car) (*Brit*), station wagon (*EEUU*) ➤ **furgoneta de reparto** delivery van (*Brit*), delivery truck (*EEUU*)

furia SF fury, rage; ✦ MODISMO **hecho una ~**: **estar hecho una ~** to be furious; **ponerse hecho una ~** to get mad; **salió hecha una ~** she stormed out

furibundo ADJ (= *furioso*) furious; (= *frenético*) frenzied

furioso ADJ furious

furor SM **1** (= *ira*) fury, rage; (= *pasión*) frenzy, passion **2** (= *afición*) rage; **hacer ~** to be all the rage*, be a sensation

furrular* /1a/ VI to work

furtivo ADJ **cazador/pescador ~** poacher; **lágrima furtiva** silent tear

furular /1a/ VI (*Esp**) to work

furúnculo SM boil

fusa SF demisemiquaver (*Brit*), thirty-second note (*EEUU*)

fuselaje SM fuselage

fusible SM fuse

fusil SM rifle, gun

fusilamiento SM execution (*by firing squad*)

fusilar /1a/ VT **1** (= *ejecutar*) to shoot, execute (*by firing squad*) **2** (*) (= *plagiar*) (*Literat, Cine*) to pinch*, rip off**, plagiarize

fusión SF **1** (= *unión*) joining, uniting; (*Com*) merger, amalgamation **2** [*de metal*] melting **3** (*Fís*) fusion ➤ **fusión nuclear** nuclear fusion **4** (*Mús*) crossover

fusionamiento SM (*Com*) merger, amalgamation

fusionar /1a/ ⓐ VT (*gen*) to fuse (together); (*Com*) to merge, amalgamate ⓑ **fusionarse** VPR (*gen*) to fuse; (*Com*) to merge, amalgamate

fusta SF riding whip

fuste SM importance; **de poco ~** unimportant

fustigar /1h/ VT **1** (= *pegar*) to whip, lash **2** (= *criticar*) to upbraid, give a tongue-lashing to*

futbito SM five-a-side football (*Brit*), five-a-side soccer (*EEUU*)

fútbol SM, **futbol** (*Méx, CAm*) SM football (*Brit*), soccer (*esp EEUU*) ➤ **fútbol americano** American football (*Brit*), football (*EEUU*)

Al **fútbol** se le llama **football** en inglés británico y **soccer**, sobre todo, en inglés americano. Lo que en español llamamos **fútbol americano**, el deporte más popular en Norteamérica, se llama **football** en inglés americano y **American football** en inglés británico.

futbolero/a Ⓐ ADJ football *antes de s* (*Brit*), soccer *antes de s* (*esp EEUU*) Ⓑ SM/F football supporter (*Brit*), soccer supporter (*EEUU*)

futbolín SM 1 (= *juego*) table football, Foosball® (*EEUU*) 2 (*tb* **futbolines**) (= *local*) amusement *o* (*EEUU*) video arcade

futbolista SMF footballer (*Brit*), football player (*Brit*), soccer player (*esp EEUU*)

futbolístico ADJ football *antes de s* (*Brit*), soccer *antes de s* (*esp EEUU*)

fútbol-sala SM, **fútbol sala** SM indoor football (*Brit*), indoor soccer (*EEUU*)

fútil ADJ 1 (= *inútil*) futile 2 (= *sin importancia*) trifling, trivial

futón SM futon

futre * SM (*Chi*) toff (*Brit**), dude (*EEUU**)

futurismo SM futurism

futurista Ⓐ ADJ futuristic Ⓑ SMF futurist

futuro Ⓐ ADJ future; **futura madre** mother-to-be Ⓑ SM 1 (= *porvenir*) future; **en el** ~ in (the) future; **en un** ~ **próximo** in the near future 2 (*Ling*) future (tense) 3 **futuros** (*Com*) futures

Gg

G, g[1] [xe] SF (= *letra*) G, g

g[2] ABR (= **gramo(s)**) g, gm(s)

gabacho/a* (*pey*) **Ⓐ** ADJ (= *francés*) Frenchy*, Froggy (*esp Brit***) **Ⓑ** SM/F **1** (= *francés*) Frenchy*, Frog** **2** (*Méx pey*) (= *extranjero*) foreigner, outsider

gabán SM overcoat, topcoat; (*Carib*) jacket

gabardina SF **1** (= *abrigo*) raincoat, mackintosh†; **gambas en ~** (*Esp*) prawns in batter, battered prawns **2** (= *tela*) gabardine

gabarra SF barge, flatboat

gabinete SM **1** [*de abogado, arquitecto*] office; [*de médico, dentista*] surgery (*Brit*), office (*EEUU*) ➤ **gabinete de consulta** surgery (*Brit*), consulting room (*Brit*), doctor's office (*EEUU*) ➤ **gabinete de prensa** press office **2** (*en casa*) study, library; **estratega de ~** armchair strategist **3** (*Pol*) cabinet ➤ **gabinete en la sombra, gabinete fantasma** shadow cabinet

gablete SM gable

gacela SF gazelle

gaceta SF gazette, official journal

gacetilla SF **1** (= *notas sociales*) gossip column; (= *noticias generales*) miscellaneous news section; **"Gacetilla"** "News in Brief"

gacetillero/a SM/F (= *reportero de sociedad*) gossip columnist; (*) (= *periodista*) hack (*pey*)

gacho ADJ **1** (= *encorvado*) bent down, turned downward; [*orejas*] drooping, floppy; **salió con las orejas gachas o con la cabeza gacha** he went out all down in the mouth* **2** (*Méx**) (= *feo, malo*) awful*; (= *desagradable*) [*tarea, persona*] annoying

gachupín/ina SM/F (*Méx pey*) Spaniard

gaditano ADJ of/from Cadiz

gaélico ADJ, SM Gaelic

gafar* /1a/ VT (*Esp*) to jinx*, put a jinx on*

gafas SFPL (*para ver*) glasses, eyeglasses (*EEUU*); (*Dep*) goggles ➤ **gafas de bucear** diving goggles ➤ **gafas de culo de vaso** pebble glasses ➤ **gafas de esquiar** skiing goggles ➤ **gafas de sol** sunglasses ➤ **gafas graduadas** prescription glasses

gafe* (*Esp*) **Ⓐ** ADJ **ser ~** to have a jinx*, be jinxed* **Ⓑ** SMF **ser un ~** to have a jinx*, be jinxed* **Ⓒ** SM (= *mala suerte*) jinx*

gafo ADJ (*Carib*) thick (*Brit**), dumb (*esp EEUU**)

gag SM (*pl* ~**s**) gag

gago/a* SM/F (*Col, Perú*) stammerer, stutterer

gaguear* /1a/ VI (*Col, Perú*) to stammer, stutter

gaita **Ⓐ** SF **1** (*Mús*) bagpipes *pl*; **tocar la ~** to play the bagpipes; **♦ MODISMO templar*** to pour oil on troubled waters ➤ **gaita gallega** Galician bagpipes **2** (*) (= *dificultad*) hassle*; **hoy no estoy para ~s** I don't need any hassle today* **Ⓑ** SMF (*RPl hum*) Galician

gaitero/a SM/F (bag)piper

gajes SMPL ➤ **gajes del oficio** (*hum*) occupational hazards, occupational risks

gajo SM **1** [*de naranja*] slice, segment **2** (*And*) (= *rizo*) curl, ringlet

GAL SMPL ABR (*Esp*) (= **Grupos Antiterroristas de Liberación**) anti-ETA terrorist group

gala SF **1** (= *fiesta*) show ➤ **gala benéfica** charity event **2 de ~**: **cena de ~** gala dinner; **función de ~** gala; **uniforme de ~** full-dress uniform; **traje de ~** (*gen*) formal dress; (*Mil*) full dress; **estar de ~** [*ciudad*] to be in festive mood **3 galas** (= *ropa*) **vestir sus mejores ~s** [*persona*] to put on one's Sunday best; [*edificio, ciudad*] to show one's best face **4 ♦ MODISMOS hacer ~ de algo** (= *jactarse*) to boast of sth; (= *lucirse*) to show sth off; **tener algo a ~** to be proud of sth; **tener a ~ hacer algo** to be proud to do sth; *ver tb* **galo**

galáctico ADJ galactic

galaico ADJ Galician

galán SM **1** (= *novio*) gallant, beau **2** (*Teat*) male lead; (= *protagonista*) hero; **primer ~** leading man ➤ **galán de cine** screen idol **3** ➤ **galán de noche** (= *mueble*) clothes-rack and trouser press

galano ADJ (*Cub*) [*vaca*] mottled (*with red and white patches*)

galante ADJ **1** [*hombre*] (= *caballeroso*) gallant **2** (††) [*mujer*] (*pey*) wanton, licentious

galantería SF **1** (= *caballerosidad*) gallantry **2** (= *cumplido*) compliment

galápago SM **1** (= *tortuga*) freshwater turtle **2** [*de bicicleta*] racing saddle

Galápagos SFPL **las (Islas) ~** the Galapagos (Islands)

galardón SM award, prize

galardonado/a SM/F award-winner, prize-winner

galardonar /1a/ VT [+ *obra, candidato*] to award a prize to, give a prize o award to; **ha sido galardonado con el premio Nobel** he was awarded the Nobel prize

galaxia SF galaxy

galbana SF laziness, sloth

galena SF galena, galenite

galeno SM (*hum*) physician

galeón SM galleon

galeote SM galley slave

galera SF **1** (*Náut*) galley; **condenar a algn a ~s** to condemn sb to the galleys **2** (*CS*) (= *chistera*) top hat **3** (*Tip*) galley

galerada SF (*Tip*) galley proof

galería SF **1** (= *espacio*) (*interior*) gallery; (*exterior*) balcony ➤ **galería comercial** shopping mall ➤ **galería de alimentación** food mall ➤ **galería de arte** art gallery **2** (= *público*) audience; **♦ MODISMO hacer algo para** o **de cara a la ~** to play to the gallery; **ha sido un gesto para la ~** it was just playing to the gallery

galerista SMF (= *propietario*) gallery owner; (= *director*) art gallery director

galerna SF, **galerno** SM *violent north-west wind on North coast of Spain*

galerón SM (*Méx*) (= *sala*) hall

Gales SM Wales

galés/esa **Ⓐ** ADJ Welsh **Ⓑ** SM/F Welshman/ Welshwoman; **los galeses** the Welsh **Ⓒ** SM (*Ling*) Welsh

galga SF gauge, gage (*EEUU*)

galgo/a SM/F greyhound ➤ **galgo afgano** Afghan (hound)

galgódromo SM (*Méx*) dog track

Galia SF Gaul

Galicia SF Galicia; *see also* www.xunta.es

galicismo SM Gallicism

galimatías SM INV (= *asunto*) rigmarole; (= *lenguaje*) gibberish, nonsense

gallada SF **la ~** (*And**) the crowd

gallardía SF **1** (= *belleza*) handsomeness; (= *valentía*) gallantry

gallardo ADJ (= *apuesto*) handsome; (= *valiente*) gallant, brave

gallego/a **Ⓐ** ADJ **1** (= *de Galicia*) Galician **2** (*LAm**) (= *español*) Spanish **Ⓑ** SM/F **1** (= *de Galicia*) Galician **2** (*LAm**) (= *español*) Spaniard **Ⓒ** SM (*Ling*) Galician; ⊃ *LENGUAS COOFICIALES*

galleguista ADJ pro-Galician

gallera SF (*And, Col*) cockpit

gallero/a (*LAm, Canarias*) **Ⓐ** ADJ fond of cockfighting **Ⓑ** SM/F (= *encargado*) owner or trainer of fighting cocks; (= *aficionado*) cockfighting enthusiast

galleta SF **1** (*Culin*) biscuit (*Brit*), cookie (*EEUU*) ➤ **galleta salada**, **galleta de soda** (*And*) cracker **2** (*Esp**) (= *bofetada*) bash*, slap; **se pegó una ~ con la moto** he had a bad smash (*Brit*) *o* wreck (*EEUU*) on the bike* **3 tener mucha ~** (*Méx**) to be very strong **4** (*Arg, Ven**) (= *confusión*) confusion, disorder **5** (*Ven**) [*tráfico*] traffic jam

gallina Ⓐ SF **1** (= *ave*) hen; ✦ MODISMOS **acostarse con las ~s** to go to bed early; **matar la ~ de los huevos de oro** to kill the goose that lays the golden eggs ➤ **gallina clueca** broody *o* (*EEUU*) brooding hen **2** (*Culin*) chicken; **caldo de ~** chicken broth Ⓑ SMF (*) (= *cobarde*) chicken*, coward

gallinaza SF hen droppings *pl*

gallinazo SM **1** (*LAm*) (= *ave*) turkey buzzard **2** (*Col**) (= *hombre*) womanizer

gallinero SM **1** (= *criadero*) henhouse, coop **2** (*Teat*) gods *pl*, top gallery **3** (= *casa de locos*) madhouse

gallito Ⓐ ADJ (*) (= *bravucón*) cocky*, cocksure; **ponerse ~** to get cocky* Ⓑ SM **1** (= *persona*) tough guy*; **es el ~ del grupo** he's top dog* **2** (*Col, Méx Dep*) shuttlecock

gallo[1] SM **1** (= *ave*) cock (*esp Brit*), rooster (*esp EEUU*); (*más pequeño*) cockerel; ✦ MODISMOS **comer ~** (*And, CAm**) to suffer a setback; **haber comido ~** (*Méx**) to be in a fighting mood; **dormírsele a algn el ~** (*CAm, Méx**) to let an opportunity slip; **entre ~s y medianoche** (*Arg*) on the spur of the moment; **matar el ~ a algn** to floor sb, shut sb up*; **en menos que canta un ~** in an instant, in a flash; **otro ~ cantaría** things would be very different; **pelar ~** (*Méx**) (= *salir huyendo*) to make a run for it*; (= *morirse*) to kick the bucket* ➤ **gallo de pelea** gamecock, fighting cock **2** (= *pez*) john dory **3** (*en la voz*) false note; **soltó un ~** (*al cantar*) he sang a false note; (*al hablar*) his voice cracked **4** (*) (= *bravucón*) tough guy* **5** (*Méx*) (= *serenata*) street serenade **6** (*Méx**) (= *ropa usada*) hand-me-down

gallo[2]/a SM/F (*Chi*) guy*/woman; **¡qué galla tan antipática!** she is so unfriendly!

gallón* SM (*Méx*) big shot*

gallumbos** SMPL underpants

galo/a Ⓐ ADJ (*Hist*) Gallic; (*moderno*) French Ⓑ SM/F (*Hist*) Gaul; (*moderno*) Frenchman/Frenchwoman; *ver tb* **gala**

galón[1] SM (*Mil*) stripe, chevron

galón[2] SM (= *medida*) gallon

galopante ADJ (*gen*) galloping; [*inflación*] galloping, runaway; [*déficit*] spiralling, spiraling (*EEUU*); [*paro*] soaring, spiralling, spiraling (*EEUU*); **el número de casos aumentó a un ritmo ~** the number of cases shot up

galopar /1a/ VI to gallop

galope SM gallop; **a ~ al ~** (*lit*) at a gallop; (*fig*) in great haste, in a rush; **a ~ tendido** at full gallop; **alejarse a ~ to** gallop off; **medio ~** canter

galpón SM (*LAm*) shed, storehouse

galvanizar /1f/ VT to galvanize

gama[1] SF **1** (= *serie*) range **2** (*Mús*) scale

gama[2] SF (= *letra*) gamma

gamba SF **1** (= *marisco*) prawn **2** (**) (= *pierna*) leg; ✦ MODISMO **meter la ~** to put one's foot in it*

gamberrada SF (*Esp*) (= *acto vandálico*) piece of hooliganism; (= *grosería*) loutish thing (to do); (= *broma*) lark*, rag*, piece of horseplay; **hacer ~s = gamberrear**

gamberrear /1a/ VI (*Esp*) (*gen*) to go around causing trouble, act like a hooligan; (= *hacer el tonto*) to lark about (*Brit**), goof around (*EEUU**)

gamberrismo SM (*Esp*) hooliganism, loutish behaviour

gamberro/a (*Esp*) Ⓐ ADJ **1** (*pey*) (= *vándalo*) yobbish*; (= *grosero*) loutish, ill-bred **2** (= *bromista*) joking, teasing Ⓑ SM/F **1** (*pey*) (= *vándalo*) hooligan, yob*; (= *grosero*) lout; **hacer el ~** to act like a hooligan **2** (= *bromista*) joker

gambeta SF (*LAm*) dodge

gambito SM gambit

gameto SM gamete

gamín/ina* SM/F (*Col*) street urchin

gamma ADJ INV, SF gamma

gamo SM buck (*of fallow deer*)

gamonal SM (*And, Ven*) = **cacique**

gamonalismo SM (*And, Ven*) = **caciquismo**

gamulán SM (*CS*) sheepskin

gamuza SF **1** (*Zool*) chamois **2** (= *piel*) chamois leather, wash leather **3** (= *paño*) duster, dustcloth (*EEUU*)

gana SF **1 hacer algo con ~** to do sth willingly *o* enthusiastically; **comer/reírse con ~s** to eat/laugh heartily; **un chico joven y con ~s de trabajar** a young lad willing to work; **jóvenes con ~s de divertirse** young people eager *o* keen to enjoy themselves; **con ~s de pelea** spoiling for a fight; **dar ~s: esto da ~s de comerlo** it makes you want to eat it; **dan ~s de pegarle una patada** you feel like kicking him; **le entran ~s de hacer algo** he gets the urge to do sth; **quedarse con las ~s** to be left disappointed, be left wanting; **nos quedamos con las ~s de saberlo** we never got to find out; **quitársele a algn las ~s de algo: se me han quitado las ~s de ir** I don't feel like going now *o* any more; **hacer algo sin ~s** to do sth reluctantly *o* unwillingly; **tener ~s de hacer algo** to feel like doing sth

> Recuérdase que las preposiciones en inglés rigen gerundio y no infinitivo, de ahí **to feel like doing sth**.

tengo ~s de vomitar I feel sick, I'm going to throw up* *o* (*Brit*) be sick; **tengo ~s de ir al servicio** I need (to go to) the toilet *o* bathroom; **tengo ~s de que llegue el sábado** I'm looking forward to Saturday; **tenía ~s de verte** I was hoping I'd see you; **tengo unas ~s locas de verte** I can't wait to see you, I'm dying to see you; **tengo pocas ~s de ir** I don't feel like going much, I don't really want to go; **malditas las ~s que tengo de ir*** there's no way I want to go **2** ✦ MODISMOS **de buena ~** gladly; **con ~s** (= *de verdad*) really; **ser malo con ~s** to be thoroughly nasty; **hacer lo que le da la ~ a uno** to do as one pleases; **hazlo como te dé la ~** do it however you like; **¡no me da la ~!** I don't want to!; **¡las ~s!*** you'll wish you had!; **de mala ~** reluctantly, grudgingly; **ser ~s de: son ~s de molestar** *o* **fastidiar** they're just trying to be awkward; **tenerle ~s a algn*** to have it in for sb*; **venirle en ~ a algn: hacen lo que les viene en ~** they do exactly as they please

ganadería SF **1** (= *crianza*) cattle raising, stockbreeding; (*en estancia*) ranching **2** (= *estancia*) stock farm; (= *rancho*) cattle ranch; **toros de la ~ de Valdemoro** bulls from the Valdemoro ranch **3** (= *ganado*) cattle, livestock

ganadero/a Ⓐ ADJ cattle *antes de s*, stock *antes de s*; (= *de cría*) cattle-raising *antes de s* Ⓑ SM/F **1** (= *criador*) cattle-raiser, stockbreeder; (= *hacendado*) rancher **2** (= *comerciante*) cattle dealer

ganado SM livestock; (*esp LAm*) (*vacuno*) cattle *pl* ➤ **ganado ovino** sheep *pl* ➤ **ganado porcino** pigs *pl* ➤ **ganado vacuno** cattle *pl*

ganador(a) Ⓐ ADJ winning, victorious Ⓑ SM/F winner

ganancia SF profit; **~s y pérdidas** profit and loss

ganancial Ⓐ ADJ profit *antes de s* Ⓑ **gananciales** SMPL joint property *sing*

ganar /1a/ Ⓐ VT **1** [+ *sueldo*] to earn; **¿cuánto ganas al mes?** how much do you earn *o* make a month?; **ha ganado mucho dinero** she has made a lot of money **2** [+ *competición, partido, premio, guerra*] to win; **¿quién ganó la carrera?** who won the race?; **si te toca puedes ~ un millón** if you win you could get a million **3** [+ *contrincante*] to beat; **¡les ganamos!** we beat them!; **no hay quien le gane** there's nobody who can beat him, he's unbeatable; **como orador no hay quien le gane** *o* **no le gana nadie** as a speaker there is no one to touch him, no one outdoes him at speaking **4** (= *conseguir*) [+ *tiempo, peso, terreno*] to gain; **¿qué gano yo con todo esto?** what do I gain *o* get from all this?; **~ popularidad** to win *o* earn popularity **5** (= *alcanzar*) [+ *objetivo*] to achieve, attain; **~ la orilla** to reach the shore **6** (= *convencer*) to win over; **dejarse ~ por algo** to allow o.s.

to be won over by sth

7 (= *aventajar*) **te gana en inteligencia** he's more intelligent than you

8 (*Mil*) [+ *plaza, pueblo*] to take, capture

Ⓑ VI **1** (*trabajando*) to earn; **no gano para comprar un coche** I don't earn enough to buy a car; ✦ MODISMO **no ganamos para sustos** we have nothing but trouble

2 (*en competición, guerra*) to win; **~on por cuatro a dos** they won four-two

3 (= *mejorar*) to benefit, improve; **hemos ganado con el cambio** we've greatly benefited from the change; **su juego ha ganado en confianza** her play has become more confident; **salir ganando** to do well; **salí ganando con la venta del coche** I did well out of the sale of the car

Ⓒ ganarse VPR **1** [+ *afecto, amistad*] to win; **~se la confianza de algn** to win sb's trust

2 [+ *sueldo*] to earn; **~se la vida** to earn a living; **se lo ha ganado** he has earned it *o* deserves it; **se ganó a pulso el título de campeón** he became champion the hard way; **¡te la vas a ~!*** you're in for it!*, you're for it! (*Brit**)

ganchillo SM crochet work; **una colcha de ~** a crocheted quilt; **hacer (labores de) ~** to crochet

gancho SM **1** (= *garfio*) hook; ✦ MODISMO **echar el ~ a algn** (*Esp**) to hook sb, capture sb

2 (*LAm*) (= *horquilla*) hairpin; (= *colgador*) hanger; (*Col, Ven*) (*para tender la ropa*) clothes peg (*Brit*), clothespin (*EEUU*); (*And, CAm*) (= *imperdible*) safety pin

3 (*) (= *atractivo sexual*) sex appeal; (= *atractivo popular*) pulling power; **un actor con mucho ~** an actor with great pulling power; **el nuevo delantero tiene ~** the new forward is a crowd-puller; **esta música tiene ~** this music's really got something; **lo usan de ~ para atraer a la gente** they use it as an attraction to pull the crowds in

4 (*Boxeo*) (= *golpe*) hook; **un ~ hacia arriba** an uppercut

gandalla** SMF (*Méx*) crook*

gandul(a) **Ⓐ** ADJ idle, slack **Ⓑ** SM/F idler, slacker

gandulear /1a/ VI to idle, loaf around

gandulería SF idleness, loafing

ganga SF bargain; **precios de ~** bargain prices, giveaway prices

ganglio SM [*de células nerviosas*] ganglion; (*linfático*) lymph node

gangoso ADJ nasal, twanging

gangrena SF gangrene

gangrenarse /1a/ VPR to become gangrenous

gángster ['ganster] SM (*pl* **~s** ['ganster]) gangster; (= *pistolero*) gunman

gangsterismo SM gangsterism

gansada* SM **decir ~s** to talk nonsense; **hacer ~s** to play the fool, clown around

ganso/a **Ⓐ** ADJ (*) **1** (= *estúpido*) idiotic; (*pey*) (= *bromista*) play-acting; **¡no seas ~!** don't be an idiot! **2** (= *gandul*) lazy **3** *ver* **pasta** **Ⓑ** SM/F (*) (= *torpe*) idiot, dimwit*; (= *rústico*) country bumpkin, hick (*EEUU**) **Ⓒ** SM (= *ave*) (*gen*) goose; (= *macho*) gander; ✦ MODISMO **hacer el ~** to play the fool, clown around ➤ **ganso salvaje** wild goose

ganzúa SF picklock, skeleton key

gañán SM farmhand, labourer, laborer (*EEUU*)

gañir /3h/ VI to yelp, howl; [*perro*] to croak

garabatear /1a/ **Ⓐ** VI **1** (= *escribir*) to scribble, scrawl **2** (*Chi*) (= *decir palabrotas*) to swear **Ⓑ** VT **1** (= *escribir*) to scribble, scrawl **2** (*Chi*) (= *insultar con palabrotas*) to swear at

garabato SM **1** (= *dibujo*) doodle; (= *escritura*) scribble; **hacer ~s** (= *dibujar*) to doodle; (= *escribir*) to scribble **2** (= *gancho*) hook **3** (*Chi*) (= *palabrota*) swearword

garaje SM garage; **una plaza de ~** a parking space

garante **Ⓐ** ADJ responsible, guaranteeing **Ⓑ** SMF (*Fin*) guarantor, surety

garantía SF **1** [*de producto*] guarantee, warranty **2** (= *seguridad*) pledge, security; (= *compromiso*) undertaking, guarantee; **~ de trabajo** job security; **dar ~s a algn** to give sb guarantees ➤ **garantías constitucionales** constitutional guarantees

garantizar /1f/ VT **1** (= *responder de*) [+ *producto, crédito*] to guarantee; **la lavadora está garantizada por dos años** the washing machine is guaranteed for two years, the washing machine has a two-year guarantee **2** (= *avalar*) [+ *persona*] to vouch for **3** (= *asegurar*) to guarantee; **¡te lo garantizo!** I can guarantee it!

garañón SM (*LAm*) stallion

garapiña SF (*Méx*) iced pineapple drink

garbanzo SM chickpea; ✦ MODISMOS **ganarse los ~s** to earn one's living; **ser el ~ negro de la familia** to be the black sheep of the family

garbeo* SM (*Esp*) **darse** *o* **pegarse un ~** to go out and about

garbo SM **1** (= *elegancia*) grace, elegance; (= *porte*) graceful bearing; (= *aire*) jauntiness; **hacer algo con ~** to do sth with grace and ease *o* with style; **andar con ~** to walk gracefully **2** (= *brío*) agility; **empezó a limpiar el cuarto con mucho ~** she went whizzing around the room cleaning up

garcilla SF little egret

garçon [gar'son] SM **con pelo a lo ~**[†] with bobbed hair, with hair in a boyish style

gardenia SF gardenia

garete SM **irse al ~** [*plan, proyecto etc*] to fall through; [*empresa*] to go bust*

garfio SM hook

gargajo SM phlegm, sputum; **echar un ~** to spit up phlegm, hawk

garganta SF **1** (*Anat*) throat; (= *cuello*) neck; **me duele la ~** I have a sore throat **2** [*de botella*] neck **3** (= *barranco*) ravine, gorge; (= *desfiladero*) narrow pass

gargantilla SF choker, necklace

gárgara SF gargle, gargling; **hacer ~s** to gargle; ✦ MODISMO **mandar a algn a hacer ~s*** to tell sb to go to hell; **¡vete a hacer ~s!*** go to blazes!

gargarismo SM **1** (= *acto*) gargling **2** (= *líquido*) gargle, gargling solution

garita SF **1** [*de centinela*] sentry box; [*de conserje*] lodge **2** (= *caseta*) cabin, box

garito SM **1** (*) (= *local*) joint* **2** [*de juego*] gaming house, gambling den

garlar* /1a/ VI (*Col*) to chat

garnacha SF Garnacha grape

garra SF **1** (= *pata*) [*de animal*] claw; [*de águila*] talon; (*) [*de persona*] hand, paw*; ✦ MODISMOS **caer en las ~s de algn** to fall into sb's clutches; **echar la ~ a algn*** to nab sb*, seize sb **2** (= *fuerza*) bite; (*Dep*) sharpness, edge; **esa canción no tiene ~** that song has no edge to it **3** (*Méx*) (= *ropa vieja*) rags *pl*

garrafa SF **1** (= *garrafón*) demijohn; (*para agua*) large glass water container; **de ~*** (*pey*) [*ginebra, vino*] cheap, iffy*, dodgy (*Brit**) **2** (*RPl*) [*de gas*] cylinder

garrafal ADJ (= *enorme*) enormous, terrific; [*error*] monumental, terrible

garrafón SM carboy, demijohn

garrapata SF tick

garrapatear /1a/ VI to scribble, scrawl

garrapiñado ADJ **almendra garrapiñada** sugared almond

garrido ADJ (*liter*) (= *atractivo*) [*hombre*] handsome; [*mujer*] pretty

garrobo SM (*CAm*) iguana

garrocha SF (*Agr*) goad; (*Taur*) spear; (*LAm Dep*) vaulting pole

garrochista SMF (*LAm*) pole vaulter

garrón SM **1** [*de carne*] shank; ✦ MODISMO **vivir de ~** (*RPl*) to sponge*, live off others **2** (*Bot*) snag, spur

garronear* /1a/ VI (*RPl*) to sponge*, live off others

garrotazo SM blow with a stick *o* club

garrote SM **1** (= *palo*) stick, club **2** (= *ejecución*) garrotte **3** (*Méx*) (= *freno*) brake

garrotear /1a/ VT (*LAm*) to club, cudgel

garrotero/a SM/F (Méx Ferro) guard (Brit), brakeman (EEUU)

garrotillo SM (= difteria) croup

garrulo/a Ⓐ ADJ loutish Ⓑ SM/F lout

gárrulo ADJ 1 (= hablador) garrulous 2 (liter) [pájaro] twittering; [agua] babbling, murmuring; [viento] noisy

garúa SF (LAm) drizzle

garuar /1e/ VI (LAm) to drizzle

garufa* SF **ir de ~** (RPl) to go on a spree

garuga SF (CS) = **garúa**

garugar /1h/ VI (CS) = **garuar**

garza SF 1 (tb ~ **real**) heron ➤ **garza imperial** purple heron 2 (Chi) lager glass, beer glass

garzón/ona SM/F (Chi, Uru) waiter/waitress

gas SM 1 (= combustible) gas; **una cocina de ~** a gas stove o (esp Brit) cooker; **esta cerveza tiene mucho ~** this beer is very gassy o (Brit) fizzy; **con ~** [bebida] carbonated, fizzy (Brit); [agua] sparkling; **sin ~** [bebida, agua] still ➤ **gas butano** butane, butane gas ➤ **gas ciudad** town gas ➤ **gas de (efecto) invernadero** greenhouse gas ➤ **gases lacrimógenos** tear gas sing ➤ **gas mostaza** mustard gas ➤ **gas natural** natural gas ➤ **gas propano** propane, propane gas
2 (CAm, Méx) (= gasolina) petrol (Brit), gas (EEUU); **darle ~*** to step on the gas*; ✦ MODISMOS **a medio ~: el equipo jugó a medio ~** the team played with the foot off the pedal; **estar ~** (CAm hum) to be head over heels in love; **a todo ~** (Esp Aut) full out, flat out*; [trabajar] flat out*; **tenían el aire acondicionado a todo ~** they had the air conditioning on full-blast
3 gases (= emanaciones perjudiciales) fumes ➤ **gases de escape** exhaust fumes
4 gases (= flatulencias) wind sing, flatulence sing, gas sing (EEUU); **tener ~es** to have wind, have gas (EEUU)

gasa SF 1 (= tela) gauze 2 (Med) gauze, lint; **una ~** a dressing

gasear /1a/ VT to gas, kill with gas

gaseoducto SM gas pipeline

gaseosa SF 1 (= bebida efervescente) lemonade 2 (= cualquier refresco) fizzy drink (Brit), soda (EEUU)

gaseoso ADJ 1 [estado, densidad, mezcla] gaseous 2 [bebida] sparkling, carbonated, fizzy (Brit)

gásfiter SMF (pl ~s) (Chi) plumber

gasfitería SF (And) plumber's (shop)

gasfitero/a SM/F (Perú) plumber

gasofa* SF juice*, petrol (Brit), gas(oline) (EEUU)

gasoil [ga'soil] SM diesel oil

gasóleo SM diesel oil ➤ **gasóleo de calefacción** central heating oil

gasolina SF petrol (Brit), gas(oline) (EEUU); **echar ~** to put petrol (Brit) o gas(oline) (EEUU) in ➤ **gasolina con plomo** leaded petrol (Brit) o gas(oline) (EEUU) ➤ **gasolina sin plomo** unleaded (petrol (Brit) o gas(oline) (EEUU))

gasolinera SF petrol station (Brit), gas station (EEUU)

gasolinero/a SM/F (= dueño) petrol station owner (Brit), gas station owner (EEUU); (= empleado) petrol pump attendant (Brit), gas station attendant (EEUU)

gasómetro SM gasometer

gastado ADJ 1 (= desgastado) [ropa, neumático, superficie] worn; **las páginas del libro estaban muy gastadas por el uso** the pages of the book were well-thumbed 2 (= trillado) [metáfora] stale, hackneyed; [broma] old, stale; **un político ~** a washed-up politician* 3 [pilas] dead

gastador(a) Ⓐ ADJ extravagant Ⓑ SM/F **es un ~** he's very extravagant, he's a big spender

gastar /1a/ Ⓐ VT 1 [+ dinero] to spend (**en** on); **han gastado un dineral en el arreglo del coche** they've spent a fortune on fixing the car
2 (= consumir) [+ gasolina, electricidad, agua] to use; **un radiocasete como éste gasta más pilas** a radio cassette player like this goes through o uses more batteries; **he gastado todas las velas que tenía** I've used up all the candles I had
3 (= desgastar) [+ ropa, zapato] to wear out; [+ tacones] to wear down
4 (= malgastar) [+ dinero, tiempo, agua] to waste; **~ palabras** to waste one's breath
5 (= llevar) [+ ropa, gafas] to wear; [+ barba] to have; **¿qué número (de zapatos) gasta?** what size (shoes) do you take?; **¿qué talla gasta?** what size are you?
6 [+ broma] to play (**a** on); **~ una broma pesada a algn** to play a practical joke o a hoax on sb
7 gastarlas (Esp*): **no le repliques, que ya sabes como las gasta** don't answer him back, you know what he's like when he gets angry*
Ⓑ VI 1 (= gastar dinero) **a todos nos gusta ~** we all like spending money
2 (= consumir) **este coche gasta poco** this car uses very little petrol (Brit) o gasoline (EEUU); **una bombilla normal apenas gasta** a normal light bulb uses hardly any electricity
Ⓒ gastarse VPR 1 (= consumirse) [pilas] to run out; [vela] to burn down
2 (= desgastarse) [suelas, neumáticos] to wear, wear out; [tacones] to wear down
3 (Esp) (enfático) [+ dinero] to spend; **se lo gasta todo en música** he spends all his money on music
4 (enfático) (= tener) **¡vaya genio que te gastas!** what a filthy temper you've got!; **las bromas que se gasta ése** the jokes he plays on people

Gasteiz SM Vitoria (Basque province)

gasto SM 1 [de dinero] **la inversión nos supondría un ~ de varios millones** the investment would involve an expense o expenditure of several million; **tenemos que reducir el ~** we must cut costs o spending; **no tenías que haberte metido en tanto ~** you needn't have spent so much ➤ **gasto militar** military spending, military expenditure ➤ **gasto público** public spending, public expenditure ➤ **gasto sanitario** health spending, health expenditure ➤ **gasto social** welfare spending, welfare expenditure
2 gastos expenses; **para tus ~s** for your expenses; **he tenido muchos ~s** I have had a lot of expenses; **un viaje con todos los ~s pagados** an all-expenses-paid trip; **cubrir ~s** to cover (one's) costs ➤ **gastos de comunidad** service charges ➤ **gastos de desplazamiento** (por viaje) travelling expenses, traveling expenses (EEUU); (por mudanza) relocation allowance sing ➤ **gastos de envío** postage and packing sing (Brit), postage and handling sing (EEUU) ➤ **gastos de mantenimiento** maintenance costs ➤ **gastos generales** overheads (Brit), overhead sing (EEUU) ➤ **gastos menores (de caja)** petty cash expenses

gástrico ADJ gastric

gastritis SF INV gastritis

gastroenteritis SF INV gastroenteritis

gastronomía SF gastronomy

gastronómico ADJ gastronomic

gata SF 1 (Chi, Perú Aut) jack 2 **a gatas: andar a ~s** to crawl; **subió las escaleras a ~s** he crawled up the stairs; **el niño entró andando a ~s** the baby crawled in; **en este juego tenéis que andar a ~s** in this game you have to crawl on all fours; ver tb **gato**

gatazo* SM ✦ MODISMO **dar el ~** (LAm) to look younger than one is, not show one's age

gatear /1a/ VI (= andar a gatas) to crawl; (= trepar) to climb, clamber (**por** up)

gatera SF cat flap

gatillero SM (Méx) hired gun(man), hitman

gatillo SM trigger; **apretar el ~** to pull o press o squeeze the trigger

gatito/a SM/F (gen) kitten; (como término cariñoso) pussycat

gato/a Ⓐ SM/F 1 (Zool) (gen) cat; (especificando el sexo) tomcat/she-cat; **"El gato con botas"** "Puss in Boots"; ✦ MODISMOS **dar a algn ~ por liebre** to con sb*; **te han dado ~ por liebre** you've been had o conned*, you've been done (Brit*); **cuatro ~s: no había más que cuatro ~s** there was hardly anyone o a soul there; **este programa sólo lo ven**

cuatro ~s hardly anyone watches this programme *o* (*EEUU*) program; **aquí hay ~ encerrado** there's something fishy (going on) here; **jugar al ~ y al ratón con algn** to play cat and mouse with sb, play a cat-and-mouse game with sb; **lavarse como los ~s** to give o.s. a quick wash; **llevarse el ~ al agua** to win the day, pull it off*; **estar para el ~** (*Chi**) to be in a terrible state*; ✦ REFRANES **el ~ escaldado del agua fría huye** once bitten twice shy; **de noche todos los ~s son pardos** everything looks the same in the dark ➤ **gato de Angora** Angora cat ➤ **gato montés** wildcat
2 (*Méx**) (= *criado*) servant
Ⓑ SM **1** (*Téc*) [*de coche*] jack
2 (= *baile*) *popular Argentinian folk dance*
3 (= *juego*) noughts and crosses (*esp Brit*), tic-tac-toe (*EEUU*); *ver tb* **gata**

GATT SM ABR (= **General Agreement on Tariffs and Trade**) GATT

gatuno ADJ catlike, feline

gauchada SF (*Bol, CS*) kind deed, favour, favor (*EEUU*)

gauchaje SM (*RPI*) gauchos *pl*

gauchesco ADJ gaucho *antes de s*

gaucho SM gaucho

GAUCHO

Gaucho is the name given to the men who rode the **Pampa**, the plains of Argentina, Uruguay and parts of southern Brazil, earning their living on cattle farms. Important parts of the **gaucho's** traditional costume include the **faja**, a sash worn round the waist, the **facón**, a sheath knife, and **boleadoras**, strips of leather weighted with stones at either end which were used somewhat like lassos to catch cattle. During the 19th century this vast pampas area was divided up into large ranches and the free-roaming lifestyle of the **gaucho** gradually disappeared.

gavera SF (*Ven*) **1** (*para botellas*) crate **2** (*parar hielo*) ice-tray

gaveta SF drawer

gavia SF **1** (= *vela*) main topsail **2** (= *ave*) seagull

gavilán SM sparrowhawk

gavilla SF sheaf

gaviota SF seagull

gay Ⓐ ADJ INV gay Ⓑ SM (*pl* ~**s**) gay man, gay

gayo ADJ (*liter*) merry, gay; **gaya ciencia** (*Literat, Hist*) art of poetry

gayola* SF (*RPI*) jail

gayumbos** SMPL (*Esp*) underpants

gazapo SM **1** (*Zool*) young rabbit **2** (*) (= *disparate*) blunder* **3** (= *errata*) printing error, misprint

gazmoñería SF (= *mojigatería*) prudery, priggishness; (= *beatería*) sanctimoniousness

gazmoño/a, **gazmoñero/a** Ⓐ ADJ (= *mojigato*) prudish, priggish; (= *beato*) sanctimonious Ⓑ SM/F (= *mojigato*) prude, prig; (= *beato*) sanctimonious person

gaznate SM gullet; ✦ MODISMO **refrescar el ~*** to wet one's whistle*

gazpacho SM *cold vegetable soup*

gazuza* SF ravenous hunger

géiser SM geyser

geisha ['geiʃa] SF geisha girl

gel SM (*pl* ~**s** *o* ~**es**) gel; ~ **de baño** bath gel; ~ **de ducha** shower gel

gelatina SF (= *ingrediente*) gelatin(e); (= *postre*) jelly (*Brit*), Jell-O® (*EEUU*); (*para platos salados*) aspic

gelatinoso ADJ gelatinous

gélido ADJ chill, icy

gema SF gem, jewel

gemelo/a Ⓐ ADJ (= *hermano*) (identical) twin; **torres gemelas** twin towers; **es mi alma gemela** we're two of a

kind Ⓑ SM/F (= *hermano*) (identical) twin Ⓒ SM **1** (= *músculo*) calf muscle **2** [*de camisa*] cufflink **3 gemelos** (= *prismáticos*) binoculars ➤ **gemelos de campo** field glasses ➤ **gemelos de teatro** opera glasses

gemido SM (= *quejido*) groan, moan; (= *lamento*) wail, howl; [*de animal*] whine; [*del viento*] howling, wailing

Géminis SM (= *signo*) Gemini

géminis SMF INV (= *persona*) Gemini; **soy ~** I'm Gemini

gemir /3k/ VI **1** (= *quejarse*) to groan, moan; (= *lamentarse*) to wail, howl; [*animal*] to whine; [*viento*] to howl, wail

gen SM gene

gendarme SMF (*esp LAm*) policeman/policewoman, gendarme

gendarmería SF (*esp LAm*) police, gendarmerie

gene SM gene

genealogía SF genealogy

genealógico ADJ genealogical

generación SF **1** (= *acto*) generation; ~ **de empleo** employment creation; ✦ MODISMO **producirse** *o* **surgir por ~ espontánea** to come out of nowhere, come out of the blue **2** (= *grupo*) generation; **las nuevas generaciones** the rising generation

generacional ADJ generation *antes de s*

generador SM generator

general Ⓐ ADJ **1** (= *común, no detallado*) general; **información de interés ~** information of general interest; **una visión ~ de los problemas del país** an overall *o* general view of the problems of the country; **la corrupción es ~ en todo el país** corruption is widespread in the whole country
2 en ~ 2.1 (*con verbo*) generally, in general; **estoy hablando en ~** I am talking generally *o* in general terms; **en ~, las críticas de la obra han sido favorables** generally (speaking) *o* in general, the play has received favourable criticism **2.2** (*detrás de s*) in general; **literatura, música y arte en ~** literature, music and the arts in general; **el público en ~** the general public
3 por lo ~ generally; **iban a visitarla, por lo ~, dos o tres veces al año** they generally went to see her two or three times a year; **los resultados son, por lo ~, bastante buenos** in general *o* on the whole, the results are pretty good
Ⓑ SMF (*Mil*) general ➤ **general de brigada** brigadier general ➤ **general de división** major general
Ⓒ SF **1** (*tb* **carretera ~**) (*Esp*) main road
2 (*tb* **clasificación ~**) (*Ciclismo*) general classification

generalidad SF (= *vaguedad*) generality

generalista Ⓐ ADJ [*radio, televisión*] general-interest *antes de s*; [*formación*] general; **médico ~ = B** Ⓑ SMF general practitioner, GP, family practitioner (*esp EEUU*)

Generalitat SF **la ~ (de Cataluña)** Catalan autonomous government; **la ~ Valenciana** Valencian autonomous government

generalización SF **1** (= *extensión*) [*de práctica, tendencia*] spread; [*de conflicto*] widening, spread; **la ~ del uso de herbicidas** the increased use of herbicides **2** (= *afirmación general*) generalization

generalizado ADJ [*práctica, tendencia, conflicto*] widespread; **existe la creencia generalizada de que ...** it is commonly *o* widely believed that ..., there is a widely held belief that ...

generalizar /1f/ Ⓐ VT (= *extender*) [+ *práctica, tendencia*] to make (more) widespread; [+ *conflicto*] to widen, spread Ⓑ VI (= *hacer generalizaciones*) to generalize Ⓒ **generalizarse** VPR [*práctica, tendencia, plaga*] to become (more) widespread; [*conflicto*] to widen, spread

generalmente ADV generally

generar /1a/ VT **1** [+ *electricidad, energía*] to generate **2** [+ *empleo, interés, riqueza*] to generate, create; [+ *problemas, tensiones*] to cause; [+ *beneficios*] to generate

generativo ADJ generative

genérico ADJ generic

género SM **1** (= *clase*) kind, type; **este festival es el único**

en su ~ this festival is unique of its kind ➤ **género humano** human race, mankind **2** (*Arte, Literat*) genre, type; **pintor de ~** genre painter ➤ **género literario** literary genre **3** (*Ling*) gender **4** (*Biol*) genus **5 géneros** (*Com*) goods ➤ **géneros de punto** (*Esp*) knitwear *sing* **6** (= *tela*) cloth, material

generosidad SF generosity

generoso ADJ **1** [*persona*] generous; **ser ~ con algn** to be generous to sb; **ser ~ con algo** to be generous with sth **2** [*vino*] rich, full-bodied

génesis SF INV genesis

genética SF genetics *sing*

genético/a Ⓐ ADJ genetic Ⓑ SM/F geneticist

genetista SMF geneticist

genial ADJ **1** (= *de talento*) brilliant, of genius; **fue una idea ~** it was a brilliant idea **2** (= *estupendo*) great, brilliant; **Pablo es ~** Pablo's great *o* terrific

genialidad SF **1** (= *cualidad*) genius **2** (= *acto genial*) stroke of genius, master stroke; **es una ~ suya** (*iró*) it's one of his brilliant ideas

genio SM **1** (= *temperamento*) temper; **¡menudo ~ tiene!** he's got such a temper!; **es una mujer de mucho ~** she's a quick-tempered woman; **tener mal ~** to be bad tempered; ✦ REFRÁN **~ y figura hasta la sepultura** a leopard cannot change his spots **2** (= *estado de ánimo*) **estar de mal ~** to be in a bad temper, be in a bad mood **3** (= *talento*) genius; **¡eres un ~!** you're a genius! **4** (= *ser fantástico*) genie; (= *divinidad*) spirit ➤ **genio del mal** evil spirit

genital Ⓐ ADJ genital Ⓑ **genitales** SMPL genitals, genital organs

genitivo SM (*Ling*) genitive ➤ **genitivo sajón** *possessive genitive with apostrophe*

genocidio SM genocide

genoma SM genome

genotipo SM genotype

genovés/esa ADJ, SM/F Genoese

gente Ⓐ SF **1** (= *personas*) people *pl*; **hay muy poca ~** there are very few people; **son muy buena ~** they are very nice people; **Juan es buena ~*** Juan is a nice guy* ➤ **la gente baja** the lower classes *pl* ➤ **gente bien** well-off people, well-to-do people ➤ **gente de bien** decent people ➤ **gente gorda** (*Esp**) well-to-do people, rich people ➤ **gente guapa**, **gente linda** (*LAm*) beautiful people ➤ **gente menuda** children *pl* **2** (*Méx*) (= *persona*) person; **había dos ~s** there were two people **3** (*) (= *parientes*) family, folks* *pl*; **mi ~** my family, my folks* Ⓑ ADJ **es muy ~** (*Chi**) (= *respetable*) he's very decent*; (*Méx*) (= *amable*) he's very kind

gentil Ⓐ ADJ **1** (= *amable*) kind, helpful **2** (= *no judío*) Gentile Ⓑ SMF (= *no judío*) Gentile

⚠ **gentil** ≠ **gentle**

gentileza SF kindness; **tuvieron la ~ de invitarme** they were kind enough to invite me; **"por gentileza de ..."** "by courtesy of ..."

gentilhombre SM (*pl* **gentileshombres**) (*Hist*) gentleman

gentilicio SM *name of the inhabitants of a country or region etc*

gentío SM crowd, throng

gentuza SF (*pey*) (= *populacho*) rabble, mob; (= *chusma*) riffraff

genuflexión SF genuflexion

genuino ADJ genuine

geoclimático ADJ geoclimatic

geoestadística SF geostatistics *sing*

geofísica SF geophysics *sing*

geografía SF **1** (= *materia*) geography **2** (= *país*) country, territory; **en toda la ~ nacional** all over the country

geográfico ADJ geographical

geógrafo/a SM/F geographer

geología SF geology

geológico ADJ geological

geólogo/a SM/F geologist

geometría SF geometry

geométrico ADJ geometric(al)

geopolítica SF geopolitics *sing*

geopolítico ADJ geopolitical

geosistema SM geosystem

geotermal ADJ geothermal

geranio SM geranium

gerencia SF **1** (= *dirección*) management **2** (= *cargo*) post of manager

gerencial ADJ managerial

gerente SMF manager/manageress

geriatra SMF geriatrician

geriatría SF geriatrics *sing*

geriátrico Ⓐ ADJ geriatric; **centro ~** old people's home Ⓑ SM old people's home

gerifalte SM **1** (= *persona*) bigwig* **2** (= *ave*) gerfalcon

germanía SF criminals' slang, underworld slang

germánico ADJ Germanic

germanista SMF Germanist

germano/a Ⓐ ADJ Germanic, German Ⓑ SM/F German

germanófilo/a ADJ, SM/F Germanophile

germanófobo/a Ⓐ ADJ anti-German Ⓑ SM/F Germanophobe

germen SM **1** (= *microorganismo*) germ **2** (= *brote*) germ ➤ **germen de trigo** wheatgerm **3** (= *origen*) source; **el ~ de una idea** the germ of an idea

germicida Ⓐ ADJ germicidal Ⓑ SM germicide, germ killer

germinación SF germination

germinar /1a/ VI to germinate

gerontocracia SF gerontocracy

gerundense ADJ of/from Gerona

gerundio SM gerund; ✦ MODISMO **arreando, que es ~** (*Esp*) get a move on — now!

gesta SF **1** (= *acción heroica*) heroic deed, epic achievement **2** (*Literat, Hist*) epic poem, epic

gestación SF **1** (*Biol*) pregnancy, gestation; **en avanzado estado de ~** heavily pregnant **2** [*de idea, proyecto*] gestation

gestante Ⓐ ADJ expectant Ⓑ SF expectant mother, pregnant woman

gestar /1a/ Ⓐ VT (*Biol*) to gestate Ⓑ **gestarse** VPR **1** (*Biol*) to gestate **2** (*fig*) to be conceived

gesticulación SF gesticulation

gesticular /1a/ VI (*con ademanes*) to gesticulate; **~ con las manos** to wave one's hands around, gesticulate with one's hands

gestión SF **1** (= *administración*) management **2 gestiones** (= *trámites*) **tenía que realizar unas gestiones in Madrid** he had some business to do in Madrid; **hacer las gestiones necesarias para algo** to take the necessary steps for sth

gestionar /1a/ VT **1** (= *administrar*) to manage **2** (= *tramitar*) [+ *permiso, crédito*] to arrange

gesto SM **1** (= *ademán*) gesture; **con un ~ de cansancio** with a weary gesture; **hacer ~s con la(s) mano(s)** to gesture with one's hand(s); **me hizo un ~ para que me sentara** he gestured for me to sit down **2** (= *expresión*) **hizo o puso un ~ de alivio** he looked relieved; **hizo o puso un ~ de extrañeza** he looked surprised; ✦ MODISMO **poner mal ~ ◇ torcer el ~** to make a wry face **3** (= *acción*) gesture; **un ~ de buena voluntad** a goodwill gesture, a gesture of goodwill

gestor(a) Ⓐ ADJ (= *que gestiona*) managing Ⓑ SM/F manager/manageress; (*tb* **~(a) administrativo/a**) *agent* undertaking business with government departments, insurance companies etc **⊙** SM ➤ **gestor de ficheros** file manager

gestora SF (= comité) management committee

gestoría SF agency (for undertaking business with government departments, insurance companies etc)

GESTORÍA

In Spain **gestorías** are private agencies which specialize in dealing with legal and administrative work. For a fee they carry out the **trámites** involved in getting passports, work permits, car documentation etc and liaise with the Inland Revenue (**Agencia Tributaria**), thereby saving their clients much inconvenience and queueing time.

gestual ADJ gestural; **lenguaje ~** body language

geyser ['yeiser] SM geyser

giba SF [de camello] hump; [de persona] hump, hunchback

gibar** /1a/ VT (Esp) to annoy, bother

Gibraltar SM Gibraltar

gibraltareño ADJ of/from Gibraltar, Gibraltarian

gigante **ⓐ** ADJ giant antes de s, gigantic; **pantalla ~** giant screen; **tamaño ~** giant size **ⓑ** SM 1 (Mit) giant 2 (= persona alta) giant 3 (= genio) giant; **un ~ de la música clásica** one of the giants of classical music 4 (en fiestas populares) giant figure

gigantesco ADJ gigantic, giant antes de s

gigoló [dʒigo'lo] SM gigolo

gijonés ADJ of/from Gijón

gil* SMF (esp CS) fool, nitwit*, twit (esp Brit*)

gili** (Esp) **ⓐ** ADJ stupid, silly **ⓑ** SMF ass*, prat (Brit*), jerk (EEUU*); **hacer el ~** to make an ass o (Brit) prat o (EEUU) jerk of o.s.*

gilipollas*** (Esp) **ⓐ** ADJ INV **no seas ~** don't be such a dickhead o (Brit) wanker*** **ⓑ** SMF INV dickhead***, wanker (Brit***)

gilipollez*** SF (Esp) **es una ~** it's fucking stupid***; **decir gilipolleces** to talk bullshit***

gimnasia SF (Dep) gymnastics sing; (Escol) P.E., gym; (= entrenamiento) exercises pl; **una clase de ~** a P.E. o gym lesson; **hace ~ todas las mañanas** he does exercises every morning ➤ **gimnasia artística** artistic gymnastics ➤ **gimnasia de mantenimiento** keep-fit ➤ **gimnasia mental** mental gymnastics ➤ **gimnasia rítmica** rhythmic gymnastics

gimnasio SM gymnasium, gym*

gimnasta SMF gymnast

gimnástico ADJ [ejercicio, tabla] exercise antes de s; [club, asociación] gymnastic, gymnastics antes de s

gimotear /1a/ VI (= gemir) to whine; (= lamentar) to wail; (= lloriquear) to snivel

gimoteo SM (= gemido) whine, whining; (= lamento) wailing; (= lloriqueo) snivelling, sniveling (EEUU)

gincana SF gymkhana

Ginebra SF Geneva

ginebra SF (= bebida) gin

ginecología SF gynaecology, gynecology (EEUU)

ginecológico ADJ gynaecological, gynecological (EEUU)

ginecólogo/a SM/F gynaecologist, gynecologist (EEUU)

gingival ADJ gum antes de s, gingival; **campaña de salud ~** campaign for healthy gums

gingivitis SF INV gingivitis

ginseng [jin'sen] SM ginseng

gin-tonic [jin'tonik] SM (pl **~s**) gin and tonic

gira SF tour; **estar de ~** to be on tour ➤ **gira artística** artistic tour ➤ **gira de conciertos** concert tour ➤ **gira promocional** promotional tour

girador(a) SM/F drawer

girar /1a/ **ⓐ** VT 1 (= dar vueltas a) [+ llave, manivela, volante] to turn; [+ peonza, hélice, ruleta] to spin; **~ la cabeza** to turn one's head
2 [+ dinero, facturas] to send; [+ letra, cheque] (gen) to draw; (a una persona concreta) to issue **ⓑ** VI 1 (= dar vueltas) (gen) to go (a)round, revolve; [peonza] to spin; [planeta] to rotate; **la tierra gira alrededor del sol** the earth revolves (a)round o goes (a)round the sun
2 (= cambiar de dirección) to turn (a)round; **giró en redondo** he turned right (a)round; **la puerta giró sobre sus bisagras** the door swung on its hinges; **~ sobre sus talones** to turn on one's heel
3 (= torcer) [vehículo] to turn; [camino] to turn, bend; **el conductor giró bruscamente hacia el otro lado** the driver swerved sharply the other way; **~ a la derecha/izquierda** to turn right/left; **el partido ha girado a la izquierda en los últimos años** the party has moved o shifted to the left in recent years
4 **~ alrededor de** o **en torno a** [+ tema, conversación, ideas] to revolve around, centre around (Brit), center around (EEUU); [+ líder, centro de atención] to revolve around; **el número de asistentes giraba alrededor de 500 personas** there were about 500 people in the audience
5 **~ en descubierto** (Com, Fin) to overdraw **ⓒ girarse** VPR to turn around

girasol SM sunflower

giratorio ADJ [movimiento] circular; [eje, tambor] revolving, rotating; [puerta, escenario] revolving; [puente] swing antes de s; [silla] swivel antes de s

giro¹ SM 1 (= vuelta) (gen) turn (sobre around); [de planeta] (sobre sí mismo) rotation; (alrededor de otro planeta) revolution; **el coche dio un ~ brusco** the car swerved suddenly ➤ **giro copernicano** U-turn, complete turnabout ➤ **giro de 180 grados** (lit) U-turn; (fig) U-turn, complete turnabout
2 (= cambio) [de conversación, acontecimientos] turn; **el nuevo ~ que dieron ayer los acontecimientos** the new turn events took yesterday; **el electorado ha dado un ~ a la derecha** the electorate has shifted o moved to the right
3 (= envío de dinero) (por correo) money order; (Com) draft ➤ **giro bancario** bank giro, bank draft ➤ **giro postal** postal order, money order
4 (Ling) turn of phrase, expression

giro² ADJ (LAm) [gallo] with some yellow feathers

gis SM (Méx) chalk

gitano/a ADJ, SM/F gypsy

glaciación SF glaciation

glacial ADJ 1 [era] glacial 2 [viento] icy, bitter 3 [saludo, acogida] icy, frosty

glaciar SM glacier

gladiador SM gladiator

gladiolo SM gladiolus; **un ramo de ~s** a bouquet of gladioli

glamoroso ADJ glamorous

glamour [gla'mur] SM glamour, glamor (EEUU)

glande SM glans

glándula SF gland

glas ADJ INV **azúcar ~** icing sugar (Brit), confectioners' sugar (EEUU)

glasear /1a/ VT 1 [+ papel] to glaze 2 (Culin) to glaze

glauco ADJ (liter) light-green, glaucous

gleba SF (Hist) glebe

glicerina SF glycerin(e)

global ADJ 1 (en conjunto) [cantidad, resultado] overall, total; [investigación, análisis] comprehensive; **estas cifras nos dan una idea ~ del coste** these figures give us an overall picture of the cost 2 (= mundial) global; **la aldea ~** the global village

globalidad SF totality; **abordar la cuestión en su ~** to tackle the issue in its entirety

globalización SF globalization

globalmente ADV globally

globo SM **1** [*de aire*] balloon ➤ **globo aerostático** balloon ➤ **globo sonda** (*Pol*) **lanzar un ~ sonda sobre algo** to test the political waters regarding sth **2** (= *esfera*) globe, sphere ➤ **globo de luz** spherical lamp ➤ **globo ocular** eyeball ➤ **globo terráqueo, globo terrestre** globe **3** (*en un cómic*) balloon **4** [*de chicle*] bubble **5** (*Esp***) (*con drogas*) **tener un ~** to be high* **6** (*Ftbl, Tenis*) lob

globular ADJ globular, spherical

glóbulo SM **1** (= *esfera*) globule **2** (*Anat*) blood cell, corpuscle ➤ **glóbulo blanco** white blood cell, white corpuscle ➤ **glóbulo rojo** red blood cell, red corpuscle

gloria SF **1** (= *cielo*) glory **2** (= *delicia*) delight; (= *éxtasis*) bliss; **esta piscina es una ~** this pool is heavenly; ✦ MODISMOS **a ~: oler a ~** to smell divine; **saber a ~** to taste heavenly; **dar ~: cocina que da ~** she's a wonderful cook; **está que da ~ verla** she looks wonderful; **estar en la ~** to be in heaven **3** (= *fama*) glory **4** (= *personalidad*) great figure, great*; **una de las grandes ~s del cine** one of the greats* *o* great figures of the cinema; **una vieja ~** a has-been*

gloriarse /1b/ VPR **~ de algo** to boast of sth, be proud of sth

glorieta SF **1** (= *pérgola*) bower, arbour, arbor (*EEUU*) **2** (*Aut*) roundabout (*Brit*), traffic circle (*EEUU*)

glorificar /1g/ VT to glorify, praise

glorioso ADJ **1** (= *digno de gloria*) glorious **2** (*Rel*) [*santo*] blessed, in glory; [*memoria*] blessed

glosa SF gloss

glosar /1a/ VT to gloss

glosario SM glossary

glotal ADJ glottal

glotis SF INV glottis

glotón/ona Ⓐ ADJ greedy, gluttonous (*frm*) Ⓑ SM/F glutton

glotonería SF greediness, gluttony

glucosa SF glucose

glutamato SM glutamate

gluten SM gluten

glúteo SM **1** (= *músculo*) gluteus **2** glúteos (= *nalgas*) buttocks, backside *sing*

gnomo ['nomo] SM gnome

gobernabilidad SF governability; **llegar a un pacto de ~** to form a government with the support of minority parties

gobernable ADJ **1** (*Pol*) governable **2** (*Náut*) navigable, steerable

gobernación SF **1** (= *acto*) governing, government **2** (= *residencia*) governor's residence **3** (*esp LAm Pol*) Ministry of the Interior; **Ministro de la Gobernación** Minister of the Interior, ≈ Home Secretary (*Brit*), ≈ Secretary of the Interior (*EEUU*)

gobernador(a) SM/F governor; **el ~ del Banco de España** the governor of the Bank of Spain ➤ **gobernador(a) civil** civil governor ➤ **gobernador(a) general** governor general ➤ **gobernador(a) militar** military governor

gobernanta SF **1** [*de hotel*] staff manageress, housekeeper **2** (*esp LAm*) (= *niñera*) governess

gobernante Ⓐ ADJ ruling, governing Ⓑ SMF ruler

gobernar /1j/ Ⓐ VT **1** (*Pol*) to govern, rule **2** (= *dirigir*) to govern; (= *guiar*) to guide, direct **3** (*Náut*) to steer, sail Ⓑ VI **1** (*Pol*) to govern, rule; **mal** to misgovern **2** (*Náut*) to handle, steer

gobierno SM **1** (*Pol*) government ➤ **gobierno autonómico, gobierno autónomo** autonomous government, regional government ➤ **gobierno central** central government ➤ **gobierno civil** (= *puesto*) civil governorship; (= *edificio*) civil governor's residence **2** (= *dirección*) guidance, direction ➤ **gobierno doméstico, gobierno de la casa** housekeeping, running of the household

goce SM enjoyment

godo/a Ⓐ ADJ (= *gótico*) Gothic Ⓑ SM/F **1** (*Hist*) Goth

2 (*LAm Hist pey*) Spaniard; (*Col, Ven Pol*) (= *conservador*) conservative **3** (*Canarias pey*) (Peninsular) Spaniard

gofio SM (*Canarias, LAm*) *roasted maize or corn meal often stirred into coffee*

gol SM goal; **el ~ del empate** the equalizer; **meter** *o* **marcar un ~** to score a goal

goleada SF hammering*, thrashing*; **les ganaron por ~** they were hammered *o* thrashed*

goleador(a) SM/F (goal) scorer

golear /1a/ Ⓐ VT **el Celta fue goleado por el Betis** Celta were hammered *o* thrashed by Betis*; **el equipo más goleado** the team which has conceded most goals Ⓑ VI to score (a goal)

golero/a SM/F (*CS*) goalkeeper

golf SM golf; **campo de ~** golf course

golfa * SF whore, slut**, tart (*esp Brit***)

golfillo SM urchin, street urchin

golfista Ⓐ ADJ golf *antes de s*, golfing *antes de s* Ⓑ SMF golfer

golfístico ADJ golf *antes de s*, golfing *antes de s*

golfo¹ SM gulf; **la corriente del Golfo** the Gulf Stream ➤ **Golfo de México** Gulf of Mexico ➤ **golfo de Vizcaya** Bay of Biscay ➤ **Golfo Pérsico** Persian Gulf

golfo² SM (= *gamberro*) lout; (= *travieso*) rascal; (= *pilluelo*) street urchin; (= *holgazán*) layabout (*esp Brit**), lazy bum (*EEUU**)

golilla SF **1** (*Cos, Hist*) ruff, gorget **2** (*RPl*) (= *pañuelo*) neckerchief

golondrina SF swallow

golosina SF **1** (= *manjar*) titbit, tidbit (*EEUU*), dainty; (= *dulce*) sweet (*Brit*), piece of candy (*EEUU*) **2** (= *incentivo*) incentive

goloso ADJ **1** (= *aficionado a lo dulce*) sweet-toothed **2** (= *apetecible*) attractive, inviting

golpe SM **1** (= *choque*) knock, hit; (*que duele o hace daño*) bump; **dar un ~: el coche de atrás nos dio un ~** the car behind ran into us; **dar ~s en la puerta** to hammer at the door; **darse un ~: se dio un ~ en la cabeza** he got a bump on his head, he banged his head; **se dio un ~ contra la pared** he hit the wall; ✦ MODISMO **no dar ~*** to be bone idle
2 (*dado por una persona a otra*) blow; **le dio un ~ con un palo** he gave him a blow with his stick, he hit him with his stick; **a ~s: la emprendieron a ~s contra él** they began to beat him; **les molieron a ~s** they beat them up ➤ **golpe de gracia** coup de grâce
3 (*Golf, Tenis*) shot ➤ **golpe bajo** (*Boxeo*) low punch, punch below the belt; **aquello fue un ~ bajo** that was below the belt
4 (= *desgracia*) blow; **ha sufrido un duro ~** he has had a hard knock, he has suffered a severe blow; **la policía ha asestado un duro ~ al narcotráfico** the police have dealt a serious blow to drug traffickers; **acusar el ~** to suffer the consequences
5 (= *sorpresa*) surprise; **dar el ~ con algo** to cause a sensation with sth
6 (*) (= *atraco*) job*, heist
7 (= *salida*) witticism, sally; **¡qué ~!** how very clever!, good one!; **el libro tiene unos ~s buenísimos** the book's got some great lines in it
8 (*Pol*) coup ➤ **golpe de estado** coup d'état ➤ **golpe de mano** rising, sudden attack
9 (*otras expresiones*) **a ~ de: abrir paso a ~ de machete** to hack out a path with a machete; **lo solucionaron a ~ de talonario** they solved the problem by throwing money at it; **de ~: la puerta se abrió de ~** the door flew open; **cerrar una puerta de ~** to slam a door (shut); **de ~ decidió dejar el trabajo** he suddenly decided to give up work; **de un ~** in one go, in one try (*EEUU*); ✦ MODISMO **de ~ y porrazo** suddenly, unexpectedly ➤ **golpe de suerte** stroke of luck ➤ **golpe de tos** fit of coughing ➤ **golpe de vista: al primer ~ de vista** at first glance ➤ **golpe maestro** master stroke, stroke of genius
10 (*Cos*) (= *adorno*) pocket flap; (*Col*) (= *vuelta*) facing

11 (*Méx*) (= *mazo*) sledgehammer
12 (*Carib**) (= *trago*) swig*, slug* (*of liquor*)

golpeador SM (*LAm*) door knocker

golpear /1a/ **Ⓐ** VT **1** (= *dar un golpe a*) to hit; (= *dar golpes a*) [+ *persona, alfombra*] to beat; (*para llamar la atención*) [+ *mesa, puerta, pared*] to bang on; **la ~on en la cabeza con una pistola** (*una vez*) they hit her on the head with a gun; (*varias veces*) they beat her about the head with a gun; **el maestro golpeó el pupitre con la mano** the teacher banged (on) the desk with his hand
2 [*desastre natural*] to hit, strike; **la vida le ha golpeado mucho** life has treated her badly
Ⓑ VI **1** (= *pegar*) to beat; **la lluvia golpeaba contra los cristales** the rain was beating against the windows
2 (*SAm*) (*a la puerta*) to knock
Ⓒ **golpearse** VPR **1** [*persona*] to hit, bang; **me golpeé la cabeza contra el armario** I hit *o* banged my head on the cupboard
2 (*LAm*) [*puerta, ventana*] to bang

golpecito SM (light) blow, tap; **dar ~s en algo** to tap (on) sth, rap (on) sth

golpetear /1a/ VT, VI to drum, tap

golpista **Ⓐ** ADJ **intentona ~** coup attempt; **trama** *o* **conspiración ~** coup plot *o* conspiracy **Ⓑ** SMF (= *participante*) participant in a coup; (= *partidario*) supporter of a coup

golpiza SF (*LAm*) (= *paliza*) beating-up; **dar una ~ a algn** to beat sb up

goma SF **1** (= *sustancia*) (*Bot*) gum; (= *caucho*) rubber; **unos guantes de ~** a pair of rubber gloves ➤ **goma 2** plastic explosive ➤ **goma arábiga** gum arabic ➤ **goma de mascar** chewing gum ➤ **goma espuma** foam rubber **2** (= *banda*) (*para el pelo, papeles, paquetes*) rubber band, elastic band (*esp Brit*); (*en costura*) elastic; (= *tira*) piece of elastic, length of elastic; **jugar** *o* **saltar a la ~** to skip (*with a long elastic*) **3** (*tb* **~ de borrar**) eraser, rubber (*Brit*) **4** (*RPl Aut*) tyre, tire (*EEUU*) **5** (*CAm**) (= *resaca*) hangover

goma-espuma SF, **gomaespuma** SF foam rubber

gomero SM (*CS*) rubber plant

gomina SF (hair) gel

gomita SF **1** (*RPl*) (= *elástico*) rubber band, elastic band **2** (*Ven*) (= *dulce*) marshmallow

gomoso ADJ gummy

gónada SF gonad

góndola SF **1** (= *barca*) gondola **2** (*en supermercado*) gondola

gondolero SM gondolier

gong SM (*pl* **~s**), **gongo** SM gong

gonorrea SF gonorrhoea, gonorrhea (*EEUU*)

gorda SF ✦ MODISMOS **armar la ~*** to kick up a fuss; **armarse la ~*: se armó la ~** all hell broke loose; **se armó la ~ cuando volvieron mis padres** there was a hell of an argument *o* (*esp Brit*) a row when my parents came back*; **ni ~** (*Esp**): **no tener ni ~** to be broke*; **lo hice sin cobrar ni ~** I didn't get a penny for it; **no se oye ni ~** you can hear absolutely nothing; *ver tb* **gordo**

gordinflón/ona* **Ⓐ** ADJ chubby, podgy (*Brit*), pudgy (*EEUU*) **Ⓑ** SM/F fatty*, fatso*

gordo/a **Ⓐ** ADJ **1** [*persona*] fat; ✦ MODISMO **caer ~ a algn*: ese tipo me cae ~** I can't stand that guy*
2 (*) [*cosa, hecho*] big; **ha pasado algo muy ~** something major has happened; **una mentira de las gordas** a big fat lie*; **y lo más ~ fue que ...** and then to cap it all ...*
Ⓑ SM/F fat man/woman
Ⓒ SM **1** (*Culin*) fat, suet
2 (= *premio*) jackpot, big prize; **ganar el ~** to hit the

jackpot, win the big prize; *ver tb* **gorda**

---

gordura SF **1** (= *obesidad*) fat, fatness **2** (*Culin*) grease, fat

gorgojo SM grub, weevil

gorgorito SM trill, warble; **hacer ~s** to trill, warble

gorgotear /1a/ VI to gurgle

gorgoteo SM gurgle

gorila SM **1** (*Zool*) gorilla **2** (*) (= *matón*) tough*, thug*; (= *guardaespaldas*) bodyguard, minder (*esp Brit*); (*Esp*) [*de club*] bouncer* **3** (*CS Pol**) right-winger

gorjear /1a/ VI [*ave*] to chirp, trill

gorjeo SM [*de ave*] chirping, trilling

gorra SF **1** (*para la cabeza*) (*gen*) cap; [*de bebé*] bonnet; (*Mil*) bearskin, busby; ✦ MODISMO **pasar la ~** to pass the hat round ➤ **gorra de baño** (*Méx, RPl*) bathing cap, swimming cap **2** ✦ MODISMO **de ~*: una comida de ~** a free meal; **andar** *o* **ir** *o* **vivir de ~** to sponge*, scrounge*; **comer de ~** to scrounge a meal*; **entrar de ~** to get in free

gorrear /1a/ **Ⓐ** VT **1** (*) (= *gorronear*) to scrounge*, cadge*; **siempre me está gorreando cigarrillos** he's always scrounging *o* cadging cigarettes off me* **2** (*Chi***) (= *poner los cuernos a*) to cuckold **Ⓑ** VI (*) to scrounge*, sponge*

gorrino/a SM/F **1** (= *cerdo*) pig, hog (*EEUU*); **chillaba como un ~** he was squealing like a pig **2** (= *persona*) pig*

gorrión SM sparrow

gorro SM [*de lana*] hat; ✦ MODISMOS **estar hasta el ~*** to be fed up*; **poner el ~ a algn** (*Chi***) to be unfaithful to sb, cuckold sb** ➤ **gorro de baño** swimming cap ➤ **gorro de dormir** nightcap ➤ **gorro de papel** paper hat ➤ **gorro frigio** Phrygian cap, revolutionary cap

gorrón/ona* SM/F (*Esp*) sponger*, cadger*, parasite

gorronear* /1a/ (*Esp*) **Ⓐ** VT to scrounge*, cadge*; **~ algo a algn** to scrounge *o* cadge sth from sb* **Ⓑ** VI to sponge*, scrounge*

gospel SM gospel music

gota **Ⓐ** SF **1** [*de líquido*] drop; [*de sudor*] drop, bead; **unas ~s de coñac** a few drops of brandy; **todo ello mezclado con algunas ~s de humor** all mixed with a few touches of humour *o* (*EEUU*) humor; **~ a ~** drop by drop; **sistema de riego ~ a ~** trickle irrigation; ✦ MODISMOS **la ~ que colma el vaso** the straw that breaks the camel's back, the last straw; **¡ni ~!** not a bit!; **no bebo ni ~ de alcohol** I don't drink a drop of alcohol; **no corre ni ~ de aire** there isn't a breath of air; **no ver ni ~** to see nothing; **parecerse como dos ~s de agua** to be as like as two peas; **sudar la ~ gorda*** to sweat blood ➤ **gota de leche** (*Chi*) (= *institución*) mother-and-child welfare organization ➤ **gota fría** (*Meteo*) severe weather which brings flooding ➤ **gotas amargas** bitters
2 (= *enfermedad*) gout
3 **gotas** (= *medicina*) drops ➤ **gotas nasales** nose drops, nasal drops
Ⓑ SM ➤ **gota a gota** drip, IV (*EEUU*); **le pusieron el ~ a ~** he was put on a drip *o* (*EEUU*) on IV

gotear /1a/ VI **1** [*líquido, grifo, vela*] to drip; [*cañería, recipiente*] to leak **2** (*Meteo*) to rain lightly

goteo SM **1** [*de líquido, grifo*] dripping; [*de cañería, recipiente*] leak; (= *chorrito*) trickle; **el ~ de cartas** the trickle of letters; **un constante ~ de dimisiones** a steady flow *o* stream of resignations; **riego por ~** trickle irrigation **2** (*Med*) drip, IV (*EEUU*)

gotera SF **1** (= *filtración*) leak **2** (= *mancha*) damp stain

gotero SM **1** (*Med*) drip, IV (*EEUU*) **2** (*LAm*) [*de laboratorio*] dropper

gótico ADJ, SM Gothic

gotoso ADJ gouty

gouache [gwaʃ] SM gouache

gourmet [gur'me] SMF (pl ~s [gur'mes]) gourmet, connoisseur (of food)

gozada* SF **es una ~** it's brilliant o fantastic*

gozar /1f/ Ⓐ VT to enjoy Ⓑ VI to enjoy o.s., have a good time (**con** with); **~ de algo** (= disfrutar) to enjoy sth; (= tener) to have sth, possess sth; **~ de buena salud** to enjoy good health

gozne SM hinge

gozo SM (= placer) enjoyment, pleasure; (= júbilo) joy, rejoicing; **no caber (en sí) de ~** to be overjoyed

gozoso/a ADJ joyful

gozque SM (= perro) small yapping dog; (= cachorro) puppy; (Col) (= mestizo) mongrel

gr. ABR (= gramo(s)) gm(s)

grabación SF recording

grabado SM (= impresión) engraving, print; (en un libro) illustration, print ➤ **grabado al agua fuerte** etching ➤ **grabado al agua tinta** aquatint ➤ **grabado en cobre** copperplate ➤ **grabado en madera** woodcut

grabador[1] SM (RPl) tape recorder

grabador[2]**(a)** SM/F (= persona) engraver

grabadora SF tape recorder ➤ **grabadora de sonido** voice recorder ➤ **grabadora de vídeo** video (recorder)

grabadura SF engraving

grabar /1a/ VT 1 (en madera, metal) to engrave; **~ al agua fuerte** to etch 2 [+ sonidos, imágenes] (gen) to record; (en cinta) to tape 3 (= fijar) to etch; **lo tengo grabado en la memoria** it's etched on my memory; **se me quedó grabada la expresión de la niña** I'll never forget the girl's expression

gracejada* SF (CAm, Méx) stupid joke

gracejo SM 1 (= chispa) wit, humour, humor (EEUU); (en conversación) repartee 2 (= encanto) charm, grace

gracia SF 1 [de chiste, persona] **yo no le veo la ~** I don't see what's so funny; **hacer**: **a mí no me hace ~ ese humorista** I don't find that comedian funny; **me hace ~ ver a mi padre en la televisión** it's funny seeing my father on television; **no me hacía ~ su aire de superioridad** I didn't like his air of superiority; **al jefe no le va a hacer ninguna ~ que nos vayamos a casa** our boss is not going to be at all happy about us going home; **¡qué ~!** (gen) how funny!; (iró) it's great, isn't it?; **tener**: [broma, chiste] to be funny; [persona] (= ser ingenioso) to be witty; (= ser divertido) to be funny, be amusing; **tendría ~ que se estropeara el despertador justamente hoy** (iró) wouldn't it be just great if the alarm didn't go off today of all days? (iró)
2 (= encanto) 2.1 (al moverse) gracefulness, grace; **se mueve con ~** she moves gracefully; **tener ~** to be graceful 2.2 (en la personalidad) charm; **tener ~** [persona] to have charm; [objeto] to be nice
3 (= chiste) joke; **hacer una ~ a algn** to play a prank on sb; **hizo una de sus ~s** he showed himself up once again; **reírle las ~s a algn** to laugh along with sb
4 **gracias** 4.1 (para expresar agradecimiento) thanks; **¡~s!** thank you!; **¡muchas ~s!** thank you very much!, thanks a lot!, many thanks! (más frm); **dar las ~ a algn** to thank sb (**por** for); **y ~s que no llegó a más** and we etc were lucky to get off so lightly 4.2 **~s a** thanks to; **han sobrevivido ~s a la ayuda internacional** they have survived with the help of o thanks to international aid; **~s a Dios** thank heaven(s)
5 (Rel) grace; **estar en ~ (de Dios)** to be in a state of grace; **por la ~ de Dios** by the grace of God
6 (Jur) mercy, pardon; **medida de ~** pardon
7 (= favor) favour, favor (EEUU); **te concederé la ~ que me pidas** I will grant you whatever favour o (EEUU) favor you request; ✦ MODISMO **caer en ~ a algn** to warm to sb, take a liking to sb; **nunca me cayó en ~ tu suegra** I never really liked your mother-in-law
8 (Mit) **las tres Gracias** the Three Graces

grácil ADJ graceful

gracilidad SF gracefulness, grace

gracioso/a Ⓐ ADJ 1 (= divertido) funny, amusing; **lo ~ sería que ganaran ellos** it would be funny if they won; **¡qué ~!** how funny! 2 (= mono) cute; **un sombrerito muy ~** a lovely o cute little hat 3 (como título) gracious; **su graciosa Majestad** her gracious Majesty Ⓑ SM/F (iró) joker*; **habrá sido algún ~** it must have been some joker*; **hacerse el ~** to try to be funny

grada SF 1 (= asiento) tier, row of seats; **la(s) ~(s)** (gen) the stands, the grandstand; (Ftbl) the terraces, the terracing 2 (= peldaño) step, stair

gradación SF gradation

gradería SF, **graderío** SM (Esp) the stands pl, the grandstand; (Ftbl) the terraces pl, the terracing; **ambiente crispado en el graderío** o **los graderíos** tense atmosphere on the terraces o the terracing ➤ **gradería cubierta** grandstand

gradiente SF (LAm) gradient

grado SM 1 (= nivel) degree; **un alto ~ de desarrollo** a high degree of development; **quemaduras de primer/segundo ~** first-/second-degree burns; **en mayor ~** to a greater degree o extent; **en menor ~** to a lesser degree o extent; **tercer ~ (penitenciario)** (Esp) lowest category within the prison system which allows day-release privileges
2 (Geog, Mat, Fís) degree; **estamos a cinco ~s bajo cero** it is five degrees below zero; **un ángulo de 45 ~s** a 45-degree angle; **este vino tiene 12 ~s** this wine is 12 per cent alcohol ➤ **grado centígrado** degree centigrade
3 [de escalafón] grade; (Mil) rank
4 (= etapa) stage; **está en el segundo ~ de elaboración** it is now in the second stage of production
5 (esp LAm Educ) (= curso) year (Brit), grade (EEUU); (= título) degree; **tiene el ~ de licenciado** he is a graduate ➤ **grado universitario** university degree
6 (Ling) degree of comparison; **adjetivos en ~ comparativo** comparative adjectives, comparatives
7 (= gusto) **de (buen) ~** willingly; **de mal ~** unwillingly

graduación SF 1 [de volumen, temperatura] adjustment 2 [de bebida] alcoholic strength, proof grading; **bebidas de baja ~** drinks with a low alcohol content ➤ **graduación octánica** octane rating 3 (Esp) [de la vista] testing 4 (Univ) graduation 5 (Mil) rank

graduado/a Ⓐ ADJ 1 [escala] graduated 2 (Educ) graduate antes de s Ⓑ SM/F (= estudiante) graduate Ⓒ SM **graduado escolar** (Esp) formerly, certificate of success in EGB course

gradual ADJ gradual

gradualmente ADV gradually

graduar /1e/ Ⓐ VT 1 (= regular) [+ volumen, temperatura] to adjust; **hay que ~ la salida del agua** the outflow of water has to be regulated 2 (= medir) to gauge, measure; (Téc) to calibrate; [+ termómetro] to graduate; (Esp) [+ vista] to test; **tengo que ~me la vista** I've got to have my eyes tested Ⓑ **graduarse** VPR (Univ) to graduate, take one's degree

GRAE ABR = **Gramática de la Real Academia Española**

grafía SF spelling

gráfica SF 1 (Mat) graph; (= diagrama) chart 2 (= empresa) "Gráficas Giménez" "Giménez Graphics"

gráficamente ADV graphically

gráfico/a Ⓐ ADJ 1 [diseño, artes] graphic; **información gráfica** photographs pl, pictures pl; **reportero ~** press photographer 2 [descripción, relato] graphic Ⓑ SM/F (RPl) printer Ⓒ SM 1 (= diagrama) chart; (Mat) graph ➤ **gráfico de barras** bar chart ➤ **gráfico de sectores**, **gráfico de tarta** pie chart 2 **gráficos** (Inform) graphics

grafismo SM (Arte) graphic art; (Inform) computer graphics pl

grafista SMF graphic artist, graphic designer

grafiti SMPL graffiti

grafito SM graphite, black lead

grafología SF graphology

gragea SF (Med) sugar-coated pill

graifrú SM (CAm, Ven) grapefruit

grajo SM rook

Gral. ABR, **gral.** ABR (= **General**) Gen

grama SF (*Carib*) (= *césped*) lawn

gramática SF (= *estudio*) grammar; (= *texto*) grammar (book) ➤ **gramática generativa** generative grammar ➤ **gramática parda** native wit; **saber** *o* **tener mucha ~ parda** to be worldly-wise, know the ways of the world ➤ **gramática transformacional** transformational grammar; *ver tb* **gramático**

gramatical ADJ grammatical

gramático/a Ⓐ ADJ grammatical Ⓑ SM/F (= *persona*) grammarian; *ver tb* **gramática**

gramínea SF grass

gramo SM gram, gramme (*Brit*)

gran *ver* **grande**

grana SF (*Zool*) cochineal; (= *tinte*) kermes; (= *color*) scarlet; ✦ MODISMO **ponerse como la ~** to go as red as a beetroot

granada SF 1 (= *fruta*) pomegranate 2 (= *bomba*) grenade ➤ **granada de mano** hand grenade ➤ **granada de mortero** mortar shell

granadero SM 1 (*Mil*) grenadier 2 **granaderos** (*Méx*) (= *policía*) riot police

granadilla SF passion fruit

granadino ADJ of/from Granada

granado[1] SM (= *árbol*) pomegranate tree

granado[2] ADJ choice, select; **lo más ~ de la sociedad** the cream of society; **lo más ~ de la prosa en lengua española** the pick of Spanish prose writing

granate Ⓐ SM 1 (= *mineral*) garnet 2 (= *color*) deep red, dark crimson Ⓑ ADJ INV deep red, dark crimson

Gran Bretaña SF Great Britain

Gran Canaria SF Gran Canary

grancanario ADJ of/from Gran Canary

grande Ⓐ ADJ (*antes de sm sing* **gran**) 1 (*de tamaño*) big, large; (*de estatura*) big, tall; [*número, velocidad*] high, great; **¿cómo es de ~?** how big *o* large is it?, what size is it?; **los zapatos le están muy ~s** the shoes are too big for her; **~s cantidades de dinero** large sums of money; **un esfuerzo grandísimo** an enormous effort, a huge effort; **el gran Buenos Aires** greater Buenos Aires; **hacer algo a lo ~** to do sth in style, make a splash doing sth*; **vivir a lo ~** to live in style; ✦ MODISMOS **quedarle algo ~ a algn** to be too much for sb, be more than sb can handle; **pasarlo en ~** to have a tremendous time*

2 (= *importante*) [*artista, hazaña*] great; [*empresa*] big; **un gran pintor** a great painter; **los ~s bancos internacionales** the big international banks; **la gran mayoría** the great majority

3 (= *mucho, muy*) great; **con gran placer** with great pleasure; **fueron ~s amigos** they were great friends; **me llevé una alegría muy ~** I felt very happy; **una actuación de gran éxito** a very successful performance

4 (*en edad*) (= *mayor*) **ya eres ~, Raúl** you are a big boy now, Raúl; **cuando seas ~** when you grow up

5 **¡qué ~!** (*Arg**) how funny!

Ⓑ SMF 1 (= *personaje importante*) **uno de los ~s de la pantalla** one of the screen greats ➤ **Grande de España** grandee

2 (*LAm*) (= *adulto*) grown-up

3 (*LAm*) (= *mayor*) **el más ~ de mis hijos** my eldest son

grandeza SF (= *nobleza*) nobility; **~ de alma** *o* **espíritu** magnanimity

grandilocuencia SF grandiloquence

grandilocuente ADJ grandiloquent

grandioso ADJ (= *magnífico*) grand, magnificent; (*pey*) grandiose

grandullón/ona* SM/F big kid

grandulón/ona SM/F (*And, RPl*) = **grandullón**

granel SM **a ~** (= *en cantidad*) in bulk; (= *sin envasar*) loose; **vender a ~** [+ *líquidos*] to sell by the litre *o* (*EEUU*) liter; [+ *alimentos*] to sell loose; **vino a ~** wine in bulk *o* in the barrel

granero SM granary, barn

granítico ADJ granitic, granite *antes de s*

granito[1] SM (*Geol*) granite

granito[2] SM 1 [*de sal, azúcar etc*] grain; ✦ MODISMO **poner su ~ de arena** to do one's part *o* (*esp Brit**) bit 2 (*Med*) pimple

granizada SF hailstorm

granizado SM ➤ **granizado de café** coffee with crushed ice ➤ **granizado de limón** crushed iced lemon drink

granizar /1f/ VI to hail

granizo SM hail

granja SF farm; **animales de ~** farm animals ➤ **granja avícola** chicken farm, poultry farm ➤ **granja escuela** educational farm

granjear /1a/ Ⓐ VT (= *adquirir*) [+ *respeto, enemigos*] to earn; **su actitud le granjeó una fama de intolerante** his attitude earned him a reputation as a bigot Ⓑ **granjearse** VPR [+ *respeto, enemigos*] to earn

granjero/a SM/F farmer

grano SM 1 (= *semilla*) [*de cereales*] grain; [*de mostaza*] seed; ✦ MODISMO **ir (directo) al ~** to get to the point ➤ **grano de arroz** grain of rice ➤ **grano de café** coffee bean ➤ **grano de trigo** grain of wheat

2 (= *semillas*) grain; **aquí se almacena el ~** the grain is stored here; ✦ MODISMO **apartar el ~ de la paja** to separate the wheat from the chaff

3 (= *partícula*) grain; (= *punto*) speck; **un ~ de arena** a grain of sand; ✦ MODISMO **poner su ~ de arena** to do one's part *o* (*esp Brit**) bit

4 (*en la piel*) pimple, spot, zit (*EEUU*)

5 (*en piedra, madera, fotografía*) grain; **de ~ fino** fine-grained 6 (*Farm*) grain

granuja SMF (= *bribón*) rogue; (*dicho con afecto*) rascal

granujada SF dirty trick; **hacer una ~ a algn** to pull a fast one on sb*

granulado Ⓐ ADJ granulated Ⓑ SM (*Farm*) **un ~ vitamínico** a vitamin powder

granular[1] ADJ granular

granular[2] /1a/ Ⓐ VT to granulate Ⓑ **granularse** VPR to granulate

gránulo SM granule

grapa[1] SF 1 (*para papeles*) staple 2 (*para cables*) cable clip, cable staple (*EEUU*); (*Mec*) dog clamp; (*Arquit*) cramp

grapa[2] SF (*CS*) (= *aguardiente*) grappa

grapadora SF stapler, stapling gun

grapar /1a/ VT to staple

grasa Ⓐ SF 1 [*de alimentos*] fat; **reducir el consumo de ~s** to cut down on fatty foods; **tener mucha ~** [*carne*] to be fatty; [*guiso, plato*] to be (very) greasy ➤ **grasa de ballena** blubber ➤ **grasa de pescado** fish oil ➤ **grasa no saturada** unsaturated fat ➤ **grasa saturada** saturated fat 2 (*Anat*) fat; **eliminar ~s** to get rid of fat 3 (= *suciedad*) grease 4 (*Aut, Mec*) (= *lubrificante*) grease 5 (*Méx**) (*para el calzado*) shoe polish Ⓑ SMF **es un ~** (*RPl**) he's common

grasiento ADJ greasy

graso ADJ 1 [*alimentos, ácidos*] fatty; [*cutis*] greasy, oily; [*pelo*] greasy 2 (= *aceitoso*) [*guiso*] greasy, oily

grasoso ADJ greasy

gratamente ADV pleasantly, pleasingly

gratificación SF 1 (= *recompensa*) reward, recompense; (*como prima*) bonus 2 (= *satisfacción*) gratification

gratificador ADJ (*LAm*) gratifying

gratificante ADJ gratifying

gratificar /1g/ VT 1 (= *recompensar*) to reward, recompense; (*con prima*) to give a bonus to; **"se gratificará"** "a reward is offered" 2 (= *satisfacer*) to gratify

gratinado Ⓐ ADJ au gratin Ⓑ SM dish cooked au gratin; **~ de patatas** potato gratin

gratinar /1a/ VT to cook au gratin

gratis Ⓐ ADV free, for nothing; **te lo arreglarán ~** they'll fix it (for) free *o* for nothing Ⓑ ADJ free; **la entrada es ~** entry is free

gratitud SF gratitude

grato ADJ (= *placentero*) pleasant, pleasing; (= *satisfactorio*) welcome; **recibir una grata impresión** to get a pleasant impression; **una decisión muy grata para todos** a very welcome decision for everybody; **muy ~s recuerdos** very fond memories; **nos es ~ informarle que ...** we are pleased to inform you that ...

gratuidad SF **debemos garantizar la ~ de la enseñanza** we must ensure that education remains free

gratuito ADJ **1** (= *gratis*) free, free of charge **2** [*comentario*] gratuitous, uncalled-for; [*acusación*] unfounded, unjustified

grava SF (= *guijos*) gravel; (= *piedra molida*) crushed stone; (*en carreteras*) road metal

gravable ADJ taxable, subject to tax

gravamen SM **1** (= *impuesto*) tax **2** [*de aduanas*] duty **3** (*Jur*) lien, encumbrance

gravar /1a/ VT **1** (*con impuesto*) to tax; **los impuestos que gravan esta vivienda** the taxes to which this dwelling is subject **2** (*con carga, hipoteca*) to burden, encumber; (*Jur*) [+ *propiedad*] to place a lien upon

grave ADJ **1** [*enfermedad, estado*] serious; **estar ~** to be seriously ill; **hubo 20 heridos ~s** there were 20 people seriously injured **2** (= *serio*) serious; **la situación es ~** the situation is serious **3** [*carácter*] serious, dignified **4** [*nota, tono*] low, deep; [*voz*] deep **5** [*acento*] grave; [*palabra*] stressed on the penultimate syllable

gravedad SF **1** (*Fís*) gravity **2** (*Med*) seriousness; **estar enfermo de ~** to be seriously ill; **parece que la lesión es de poca ~** it seems that the injury is not serious **3** (= *seriedad*) seriousness **4** (= *dignidad*) seriousness, dignity **5** (*Mús*) depth

gravemente ADV **1** [*afectar, perjudicar*] seriously; **estar ~ enfermo** to be seriously ill **2** (*con solemnidad*) gravely; **habló ~** he spoke gravely

gravidez SF (*frm*) pregnancy; **en estado de ~** pregnant

grávido ADJ **1** (= *embarazada*) pregnant **2** (*liter*) (= *lleno*) full (**de** of), heavy (**de** with)

gravilla SF gravel

gravitación SF gravitation

gravitar /1a/ VI **1** (*Fís*) to gravitate (**hacia** towards) **2** **~ sobre algn/algo** (= *apoyarse*) to rest on sb/sth; (= *caer sobre*) to bear down on sb/sth; (*fig*) (= *pesar sobre*) to be a burden to sb/sth; (= *amenazar*) to loom over sb/sth

gravoso ADJ (= *caro*) costly; (= *oneroso*) burdensome

graznar /1a/ VI [*cuervo*] to croak, caw; [*ganso*] to cackle; [*pato*] to quack

graznido SM [*de cuervo*] croak; [*de ganso*] cackle; [*de pato*] quack

greca SF border

Grecia SF Greece

greda SF **1** (*esp Chi*) (= *arcilla*) clay **2** (*Téc*) fuller's earth

gregario ADJ gregarious

gregoriano ADJ Gregorian

greguería SF (*Literat*) brief, humorous and often mildly poetic comment or aphorism about life

greifrú SM (*CAm, Ven*), **grei** SM (*Col*) grapefruit

grelos SMPL turnip tops

gremial ADJ **1** (*Hist*) guild *antes de s* **2** (*LAm*) (= *sindical*) trade-union *antes de s*

gremialista SMF (*LAm*) trade unionist

gremio SM **1** (= *profesión*) trade, profession; **ser del ~** to be in the trade **2** (*Hist*) guild, corporation **3** (*LAm*) (= *sindicato*) (trade) union

greña SF **1** **greñas** (= *cabello*) shock of hair, mat of hair, mop of hair **2** ✦ MODISMO **andar a la ~** to be at daggers drawn, bicker **3 en ~** (*Méx*) [*seda*] raw; [*plata*] unpolished; [*azúcar*] unrefined

gres SM (= *arcilla*) potter's clay; (= *cerámica*) earthenware, stoneware

gresca SF (= *bulla*) rumpus; (= *pelea*) brawl

grey SF flock

Grial SM **Santo ~** Holy Grail

griego/a Ⓐ ADJ Greek Ⓑ SM/F Greek Ⓒ SM (*Ling*) Greek

grieta SF (= *fisura*) crack; (*en la piel*) chap, crack

grifa** SF (= *droga*) dope*; *ver tb* **grifo**

grifería SF taps *pl* (*Brit*), faucets *pl* (*EEUU*)

grifo¹ SM **1** (*Esp*) [*de agua*] tap (*Brit*), faucet (*EEUU*); **agua del ~** tap water; ✦ MODISMO **cerrar el ~** to turn off the tap, cut off the funds **2** (*Perú*) (= *gasolinera*) petrol station (*Brit*), gas station (*EEUU*) **3** (*Chi*) [*de incendios*] fire hydrant

grifo²/a* Ⓐ ADJ **estar ~** (*Méx*) (= *drogado*) to be high*, be doped up* Ⓑ SM/F dope smoker*; *ver tb* **grifa**

grifo ADJ [*pelo*] curly, kinky; *ver tb* **grifa**

grill [gril] SM **1** (= *aparato*) grill **2** (= *local*) grillroom

grillado** ADJ (*Esp*) nutty*, barmy (*Brit**)

grillera SF **1** (= *jaula*) cage for crickets **2** (*) (= *casa de locos*) madhouse, bedlam **3** (**) (= *furgón*) police wagon

grillete SM fetter, shackle

grillo SM **1** (= *insecto*) cricket **2 grillos** (= *cadenas*) fetters, shackles

grima* SF (*Esp*) **dar ~ a algn** (= *dentera*) to set sb's teeth on edge; (= *irritación*) to get on sb's nerves; **me da ~ sentarme ahí** I can't sit there, it's revolting

gringada* SF (*LAm*) **1** (= *extranjeros*) foreigners *pl*; (= *estadounidenses*) Yankees *pl* **2** (= *canallada*) dirty trick

gringo/a (*LAm*) Ⓐ ADJ **1** (= *extranjero*) foreign; (= *estadounidense*) Yankee, North American **2** (*And*) (= *rubio*) blond(e), fair Ⓑ SM/F **1** (= *extranjero*) foreigner; (= *estadounidense*) Yankee, North American **2** (*And*) (= *rubio*) blond(e), fair-haired person

GRINGO

The word **gringo** is a derogatory term used in Latin America to refer to white English-speakers, usually Americans, especially in the context of alleged economic, cultural and political interference in Latin America. One rather fanciful theory traces its origin to the Mexican-American War of 1846-48 and the song "Green Grow the Rushes-oh", supposedly sung by the American troops. According to another theory it is a corruption of **griego** or "Greek", in the sense of anything foreign and unintelligible, as in the English expression "it's all Greek to me".

gringolandia* SF (*LAm pey*) USA, Yankeedom*

gripa SF (*Col, Méx*) flu, influenza

gripal ADJ flu *antes de s*

gripe SF flu, influenza

griposo ADJ **estar ~** to have flu

gris

En inglés americano se usa **gray** en lugar de **grey**.

Ⓐ ADJ [*color*] grey; [*día, tiempo, persona*] grey, dull; **~ marengo** dark grey; **~ perla** pearl-grey, pearl-gray (*EEUU*) Ⓑ SM (= *color*) grey

grisáceo ADJ greyish, grayish (*EEUU*)

grisín SM (*Perú, RPI*) breadstick

grisú SM firedamp

gritadera SF (*And*) loud shouting, clamour, clamor (*EEUU*)

gritar /1a/ Ⓐ VI **1** (= *dar voces*) to shout; **no me grites, que no estoy sorda** don't shout, I'm not deaf **2** (= *chillar*) to scream; **gritaba de dolor** he was screaming with pain **3** (= *abuchear*) to jeer Ⓑ VT [+ *instrucciones, órdenes*] to shout; **le ~on que callara** they shouted at him to be quiet

gritería SF **1** (= *gritos*) shouting, uproar **2** (*CAm Rel*) festival of the Virgin

griterío SM shouting, uproar

grito SM 1 (= *voz alta*) shout; (= *chillido*) scream; [*de animal*] cry, sound; **a ~s** at the top of one's voice; **¡no des esos ~s!** stop shouting like that!; **pegar** *o* **lanzar un ~** to cry out; **✦** MODISMOS **poner el ~ en el cielo** to scream blue murder*; **pedir algo a ~s: estoy pidiendo un corte de pelo a ~s** I badly need a haircut; **a ~ pelado** at the top of one's voice; **es el último ~** it's the very latest, it's the latest thing; **es el último ~ del lujo** it's the last word in luxury; **a voz en ~** at the top of one's voice
2 (= *abucheo*) jeer
3 (*LAm*) (= *proclamación*) proclamation; **el ~ de Dolores** *the proclamation of Mexican independence (1810)* ➤ **grito de independencia** proclamation of independence

groenlandés/esa ⓐ ADJ Greenland *antes de s* ⓑ SM/F Greenlander

Groenlandia SF Greenland

groggy** ADJ, **grogui**** ADJ (= *atontado*) groggy; (= *impresionado*) shattered, shocked, in a state of shock

grosella SF redcurrant

grosería SF 1 (= *mala educación*) rudeness; (= *ordinariez*) coarseness, vulgarity 2 (= *comentario*) rude remark, vulgar remark; (= *palabrota*) swearword

grosero ADJ (= *maleducado*) rude; (= *ordinario*) coarse, vulgar

grosor SM thickness

grosso modo ADV roughly speaking

grotesco ADJ grotesque

grúa SF 1 (*Téc*) crane; (*Náut*) derrick 2 (*Aut*) tow truck, towing vehicle; **avisar** *o* **llamar a la ~** to call for a tow truck; **el coche fue retirado por la ~** the car was towed away

grueso ⓐ ADJ 1 [*persona*] stout, thickset 2 [*jersey, pared, libro, tronco*] thick; [*intestino*] large; [*mar*] heavy 3 (= *basto*) [*tela, humor*] coarse ⓑ SM 1 (= *grosor*) thickness 2 (= *parte principal*) main part, major portion; [*de gente, tropa*] main body, mass; **el ~ del pelotón** (*en carrera*) the pack, the main body of the runners

grulla SF (*tb ~ común*) crane

grullo (*CAm, Méx*) ⓐ ADJ [*caballo*] grey, gray (*EEUU*) ⓑ SM grey horse, gray horse (*EEUU*)

grumete SM cabin boy, ship's boy

grumo SM lump; **una salsa con ~s** a lumpy sauce

grumoso ADJ lumpy

gruñido SM 1 [*de animal*] grunt, growl 2 (= *queja*) grouse*, grumble

gruñir /3h/ VI 1 [*animal*] to grunt, growl 2 [*persona*] to grouse*, grumble

gruñón/ona ⓐ ADJ grumpy, grumbling ⓑ SM/F grumbler

grupa SF crupper, hindquarters *pl*

grupo SM 1 (*gen*) group; **discusión en ~** group discussion ➤ **grupo de investigación** research team, team of researchers ➤ **grupo de noticias** newsgroup ➤ **grupo de presión** pressure group, special interest group ➤ **grupo de riesgo** high-risk group ➤ **grupo de trabajo** working party ➤ **grupo sanguíneo** blood group 2 (*Elec, Téc*) unit, plant; (= *montaje*) assembly ➤ **grupo compresor** compressor unit ➤ **grupo electrógeno** generating set, power plant

grupúsculo SM small group, splinter group

gruta SF cavern, grotto

guaca SF (*And*) (Indian) tomb

guacal SM (*Col, Méx, Ven*) (= *cajón*) wooden crate; (*CAm*) (= *calabaza*) gourd, vessel

guacamaya SF (*Méx*) macaw

guacamayo SM macaw

guacamole SM guacamole

guacarear* /1a/ VI (*Méx*) to throw up*

guachafita SF (*Col, Ven*) 1 (= *batahola*) hubbub, din; (= *desorden*) disorder 2 (= *mofa*) mockery, jeering

guache¹* SM (*Carib, Col*) (= *zafio*) uncouth person

guache² SM (*Arte*) gouache

guachimán SM (*LAm*) watchman

guachinango SM (*Carib, Méx*) red snapper

guacho*/a (*And, CS*) ⓐ ADJ 1 (= *huérfano*) [*niño*] orphaned; [*animal*] motherless, abandoned 2 (*And*) [*zapato etc*] odd ⓑ SM/F (= *expósito*) homeless child, abandoned child; (= *huérfano*) orphan, foundling; (= *animal*) motherless animal; (= *bastardo*) illegitimate child, bastard

guaco SM (*And*) piece of pre-Columbian tomb pottery

guadalajareño ADJ of/from Guadalajara

guadaña SF scythe

guagua¹ SF (*Cub, Canarias*) bus

guagua² SF (*And*) (= *bebé*) baby

guai* ADJ, ADV = **guay**

guaipe SM (*Chi, Perú*) cloth, rag

guaira SF 1 (*CAm*) (= *flauta*) Indian flute 2 (*And, CS Min*) earthenware smelting furnace (*for silver ore*) 3 (*Náut*) triangular sail

guajalote ADJ, SM (*Carib, Méx*) = **guajolote**

guaje/a ⓐ ADJ (*Méx**) (= *estúpido*) silly, stupid; **✦** MODISMO **hacer ~ a algn** to fool sb, take sb in* ⓑ SM/F (*CAm, Méx**) (= *estúpido*) idiot, fool ⓒ SM (*Méx*) (= *calabaza*) gourd, calabash

guajiro/a SM/F 1 (*Cub*) (white) peasant 2 (*Col, Ven*) native/inhabitant of the Guajira region

guajolote SM (*Méx*) turkey

gualdo ADJ yellow, golden

gualdrapa SF horse blanket

gualicho SM 1 (*And, CS*) (= *maleficio*) evil spell 2 (*Arg*) (= *talismán*) good-luck charm, talisman

guama* SF 1 (*And, CAm*) (= *mentira*) lie 2 (*And*) (= *desastre*) calamity, disaster

guampa SF (*CS*) horn

guampudo ADJ (*CS*) horned

guanábana SF (*LAm*) (= *fruta*) soursop, prickly custard apple

guanaco SM 1 (*Zool*) guanaco 2 (*Chi*) (= *camión antidisturbios*) water cannon

guanche ADJ, SMF Guanche (*original inhabitant of the Canary Islands*)

guanera SF guano deposit

guanero ADJ (*LAm*) guano *antes de s*

guango* ADJ (*Méx*) loose

guano SM guano

guantada SF, **guantazo** SM slap

guante SM glove; **✦** MODISMOS **arrojar el ~** to throw down the gauntlet; **ladrón de ~ blanco** gentleman thief; **tratar con ~ blanco** to treat *o* handle with kid gloves; **echar el ~ a algn** to catch hold of sb, seize sb; [*policía*] to catch sb; **echar el ~ a algo** to lay hold of sth ➤ **guantes de boxeo** boxing gloves ➤ **guantes de goma** rubber gloves ➤ **guantes de terciopelo** (*fig*) kid gloves

guantera SF glove compartment

guaperas* SM INV (*Esp*) heart-throb*, dream-boy*

guapetón ADJ good-looking

guapo ⓐ ADJ 1 (= *atractivo*) [*mujer*] attractive, good-looking; [*hombre*] handsome, good-looking; [*bebé*] beautiful
2 (= *elegante*) smart, elegant; **qué ~ estás con ese traje** you look really nice in that suit
3 (*) (= *bonito*) great*; **¡qué camiseta más guapa!** what a great T-shirt!*
4 (*) (*como apelativo*) **¡ven, ~!** (*a un niño*) come here, love!; **¡oye, guapa!** hey!; **¡cállate, ~!** just shut up!
5 (= *valiente*) bold, dashing; (*CS, Méx*) (= *duro*) bold, tough ⓑ SM 1 (*) (= *valiente*) **¿quién es el ~ que entra primero?** who's got the guts to go in first?*, who's brave enough to go in first?
2 (*esp LAm*) (= *bravucón*) bully, tough guy; (= *fanfarrón*) braggart

guapura* SF good looks *pl*

guaquear /1a/ VI (*And*) to rob tombs *o* graves (*in search of archaeological valuables*)

guaquero/a SM/F (*And*) grave robber, tomb robber

guaraca SF (*And*) (= *honda*) sling, catapult (*Brit*), slingshot (*EEUU*); (*para trompo*) whip

guarache SM (*Méx*) **1** (= *sandalia*) sandal, light shoe **2** (*Aut*) patch

guarangada SF (*LAm*) rude remark

guarango ADJ (*And, CS*) (= *grosero*) [*acto*] rude; [*persona*] uncouth

guaraní Ⓐ ADJ, SMF Guarani
Ⓑ SM (*Ling*) Guarani

GUARANÍ

Guaraní is an American Indian language of the **tupí-guaraní** family and is widely spoken in Paraguay, Brazil, Argentina and Bolivia. In Paraguay it is the majority language and has equal official status with Spanish, which is spoken mainly by non-Indians. In parts of southern Brazil, **tupí-guaraní** is the basis for a pidgin known as **Língua Geral**, now losing ground to Portuguese. From **guaraní** and its sister dialect **tupí** come words like "jaguar", "tapir", "toucan" and "tapioca".

guarapear /1a/ VI (*Carib, Perú*) to get drunk

guarapo SM (*LAm*) (= *bebida*) sugar-cane liquor; (*Ven*) [*de piña*] fermented pineapple juice; ✦ MODISMO **se le enfrió el ~** (*Carib**) he lost his nerve

guarda Ⓐ SMF [*de parque, cementerio*] keeper; [*de edificio*] security guard ➤ **guarda de seguridad** security guard ➤ **guarda forestal** (forest) ranger ➤ **guarda jurado** (armed) security guard **Ⓑ** SF [*de libro*] flyleaf, endpaper; [*de cerradura*] ward; [*de espada*] guard

guardaagujas SMF INV pointsman/pointswoman (*Brit*), switchman/switchwoman (*EEUU*)

guardabarrera SMF crossing keeper

guardabarros SM INV mudguard, fender (*EEUU*)

guardabosque SMF, **guardabosques** SMF INV (*en bosque, parque*) ranger, forester; (*en finca*) gamekeeper

guardacalor SM cosy, cover

guardacoches SMF INV parking attendant

guardacostas Ⓐ SMF INV (= *persona*) coastguard **Ⓑ** SM INV (= *barco*) coastguard vessel, revenue cutter

guardaespaldas SMF INV bodyguard, minder*

guardameta SMF goalkeeper

guardamuebles SM INV furniture repository; **llevar algo a un ~** to put sth in storage

guardapolvo SM (= *bata*) overall (*Brit*), duster (*EEUU*); (= *mono*) overalls *pl* (*Brit*), coveralls *pl* (*EEUU*)

guardar /1a/ **Ⓐ** VT **1** [+ *objetos*] **1.1** (= *meter*) (*en un lugar*) to put; (*en su sitio*) to put away; **lo guardó en el bolsillo** he put it in his pocket; **si no vas a jugar más, guarda los juguetes** if you're not going to play any more, put the toys away **1.2** (= *conservar*) to keep; **no tira nunca nada, todo lo guarda** he never throws anything away, he hangs on to *o* keeps everything; **guarda tú las entradas** you hold on to *o* keep the tickets **1.3** (= *reservar*) to save; **te ~é un poco de tarta** I'll save *o* keep you some cake; **¿puedes ~me el sitio en la cola?** can you keep my place in the queue (*esp Brit*) *o* line (*EEUU*)?; **puedo ~le la habitación sólo hasta mañana** I can only keep *o* hold the room for you till tomorrow **1.4** (*Inform*) [+ *archivo*] to save
2 (= *mantener*) [+ *promesa, secreto*] to keep; [+ *recuerdo*] to have; **~ el anonimato** to remain anonymous; **~ las apariencias** to keep up appearances; **~ la calma** (*en crisis, desastre*) to keep calm; (*ante una provocación*) to remain composed; **~ las distancias** to keep one's distance; **~ las formas** to keep up appearances; **~ la línea** (= *mantenerla*) to

keep one's figure; (= *cuidarla*) to watch one's figure; **~ en secreto** [+ *objeto, documento*] to keep in secret, keep secretly; [+ *actividad, información*] to keep secret
3 (= *tener*) [+ *relación*] to bear; [+ *semejanza*] to have; **su teoría guarda cierto paralelismo con la de Freud** his theory has a certain parallel with that of Freud
4 (= *sentir*) [+ *rencor*] to bear, have; [+ *respeto*] to have, show; **no le guardo rencor** I have no ill feeling towards him, I bear him no resentment
5 (= *cumplir*) [+ *ley*] to observe; **~ los Diez Mandamientos** to follow the Ten Commandments
6 (= *cuidar*) to guard; **un mastín guardaba la entrada** a mastiff guarded the entrance; **¡Dios os guarde!**†† may God be with you!
Ⓑ VI **¡guarda!** (*CS**) look out!, watch out!
Ⓒ guardarse VPR **1** (= *meter*) **me guardé en el bolsillo la foto** I put the photo (away) in my pocket
2 (= *conservar*) to keep; **se guardó el dinero del grupo** he kept the group's money for himself, he kept the money that belonged to the group
3 ~se de hacer algo to be careful not to do sth
4 ✦ MODISMO **guardársela a algn** to have it in for sb*; **¡ésta te la guardo!** I won't forget this!, you haven't heard the end *o* last of this!

guardarropa Ⓐ SM **1** (*en teatro, discoteca*) cloakroom (*Brit*), checkroom (*EEUU*) **2** (= *armario, ropa*) wardrobe **Ⓑ** SMF (= *persona*) cloakroom attendant (*Brit*), checkroom attendant (*EEUU*)

guardarropía SF (*Teat*) wardrobe

guardavalla SMF, **guardavallas** SMF INV (*LAm*) goalkeeper

guardavía SMF linesman/lineswoman

guardería SF (*tb ~ infantil*) nursery, day nursery, daycare center (*EEUU*); (*en empresa, tienda*) crèche ➤ **guardería canina** kennels *inv*

guardia Ⓐ SMF (= *policía*) policeman/policewoman; (*Mil*) guardsman ➤ **guardia civil** civil guard, *member of police corps with responsibilities outside towns or cities* ➤ **guardia de tráfico** traffic policeman/policewoman ➤ **guardia forestal** (forest) ranger, warden (*Brit*) ➤ **guardia jurado** (armed) security guard ➤ **guardia marina** midshipman ➤ **guardia municipal, guardia urbano/a** police officer (*of the city or town police*) ➤ **guardias de asalto** riot police; (*Mil*) shock troops
Ⓑ SF **1** (= *vigilancia*) **estar de ~** [*empleado, enfermero, médico*] to be on duty; [*soldado*] to be on sentry duty, be on watch; (*Náut*) to be on watch; **médico de ~** doctor on duty, duty doctor; **oficial de ~** officer on duty, duty officer; **puesto de ~** (*Mil*) guard post, sentry box; **hacer ~** [*médico, empleado*] to be on duty; [*soldado*] to do guard duty, do sentry duty; **montar ~** to stand guard; **montar la ~** (= *empezarla*) to mount guard; ✦ MODISMOS **bajar la ~** to lower one's guard; **estar en ~** to be on (one's) guard; **poner a algn en ~ (contra algo)** to put sb on one's guard (against sth); **se enciende una luz amarilla para poner en ~ al conductor** a yellow light comes on to alert the driver; **ponerse en ~** to be on one's guard
2 (*tb turno de ~*) [*de médico, enfermera*] shift; [*de soldado*] duty session
3 (*Esgrima*) guard, garde
4 (= *cuerpo*) (*Mil*) guard; ✦ MODISMO **la vieja ~** the old guard ➤ **Guardia Civil** Civil Guard ➤ **guardia costera** coastguard service ➤ **guardia de asalto** riot police ➤ **guardia de honor** guard of honour *o* (*EEUU*) honor ➤ **guardia montada** horse guards *pl* ➤ **guardia municipal** city police, town police ➤ **Guardia Nacional** (*Nic, Pan*) National Guard, Army ➤ **guardia pretoriana** (*Hist*) Praetorian Guard; (*pey*) corps of bodyguards ➤ **Guardia Suiza** Swiss Guard ➤ **guardia urbana** city police,

town police

guardián/ana SM/F **1** (= *vigilante*) (*en cárcel*) guard, warden (*esp Brit*); (*en museo*) security guard **2** [*de secreto*] guardian

guarecer /2d/ Ⓐ VT to protect, give shelter to Ⓑ **guarecerse** VPR to shelter, take refuge (**de** from)

guargüero* SM (*LAm*) throat, throttle

guarida SF [*de animales*] den, hideout; [*de persona*] haunt, hideout

guarismo SM figure, numeral

guarnecer /2d/ VT **1** (= *adornar*) to adorn, garnish **2** (*Culin*) to garnish **3** (*Mil*) to man, garrison

guarnición SF **1** (= *adorno*) (*gen*) adornment; (*Cos*) trimming; (*Culin*) garnish; [*de joya*] setting, mount; [*de espada*] guard **2 guarniciones** [*de caballo*] harness *sing*; **guarniciones del alumbrado** light fittings **3** (*Mil*) garrison

guaro SM (*CAm*) liquor, spirits *pl*

guarra SF **1** (*Zool*) sow **2** (*Esp** pey*) (= *mujer*) slut***; *ver tb* **guarro**

guarrada* SF (*Esp*) **1** (= *porquería*) dirty mess, disgusting mess; **hacer una ~** to make a dirty *o* disgusting mess **2** (= *indecencia*) (= *dicho*) filthy thing (to say), disgusting thing (to say); **ese libro es una ~** that book is a piece of filth*; **decir ~s** to talk filth*; **hacer ~s** to do dirty *o* filthy things **3** (= *mala pasada*) dirty trick

guarrazo* SM (= *golpe*) **darse** *o* **pegarse un ~** (*gen*) to take a thump*; (*en coche*) to have a smash (*Brit**), get into a car wreck (*EEUU*)

guarrería* SF = **guarrada**

guarrindongo/a* ADJ, SM/F = **guarro**

guarro/a (*Esp*) Ⓐ ADJ (*) **1** (= *sucio*) dirty, filthy **2** (= *indecente*) dirty, filthy; **un chiste ~** a dirty *o* filthy joke Ⓑ SM/F (*) (= *persona*) (= *sucio*) dirty person; (= *indecente*) filthy person, disgusting person Ⓒ SM (= *animal*) pig, hog (*EEUU*); *ver tb* **guarra**

guarura* SM (*Méx*) bodyguard, minder (*Brit**)

guasa SF **1** (= *chanza*) joking, teasing, kidding*; **con** *o* **de ~** jokingly, in fun; **estar de ~** to be joking *o* kidding; **tomarse algo a ~** to take sth as a joke; **no tengo ganas de ~** I'm not in the mood for jokes **2** (*Col*) (= *arandela*) washer; *ver tb* **guaso**

guasca SF (*And*) leather strap, rawhide thong

guascazo SM (*And*) (= *latigazo*) lash; (= *golpe*) blow, punch

guasch [gwaʃ] SM gouache

guasearse /1a/ VPR to joke, tease, kid*; **~ de algo/algn** to poke fun at sth/sb

guaso/a SM/F **1** (*Chi*) (= *campesino*) peasant, countryman/woman; (*pey*) country bumpkin, hick (*EEUU*) **2** (*And, CS*) (= *grosero*) uncouth person; *ver tb* **guasa**

guasón/ona Ⓐ ADJ **1** (= *bromista*) joking, teasing **2** (= *burlón*) mocking Ⓑ SM/F (= *bromista*) joker, tease; (= *ocurrente*) wag, wit

guata¹ SF (= *algodón*) raw cotton; (= *relleno*) padding

guata²* SF (*And*) paunch, belly; **echar ~** to get fat

guateado ADJ quilted

Guatemala SF (= *país*) Guatemala; (= *capital*) Guatemala City; ✦ MODISMO **salir de ~ y entrar en Guatepeor** to jump out of the frying pan into the fire; *see also* www.congreso.gob.gt

guatemalteco/a Ⓐ ADJ Guatemalan, of/from Guatemala Ⓑ SM/F Guatemalan; **los ~s** the people of Guatemala

guateque† SM (*Esp, Méx*) party

guatero SM (*Chi*) hot water bottle

guatitas SFPL (*Chi*) tripe *sing*

guatón* ADJ (*And*) fat, pot-bellied

guau EXCL woof!, bow-wow!

guay* (*Esp*) Ⓐ ADJ super*, smashing* Ⓑ ADV **pasarlo ~** to have a super *o* smashing time*

guaya SF (*Col, Ven*) steel cable

guayaba SF guava

guayabal SM grove of guava trees

guayabera SF (*LAm*) (= *camisa*) loose shirt with large pockets; (= *chaqueta*) lightweight jacket

guayabo SM **1** (*Bot*) guava tree **2** (*Col, Ven*) (= *murria*) nostalgia **3** (*Col**) (= *resaca*) hangover

Guayana SF Guyana, Guiana ➤ **Guayana Británica** British Guiana ➤ **Guayana Francesa** French Guiana ➤ **Guayana Holandesa** Dutch Guiana

guayuco SM (*Col, Ven*) loincloth

gubernamental ADJ governmental, government *antes de s*

gubernativo ADJ government *antes de s*, governmental; **la decisión gubernativa** the government's decision; **por orden gubernativa** by order of the government

gubia SF gouge

guedeja SF lock

guepardo SM cheetah

güero* ADJ (*CAm, Méx*) (= *rubio*) blond(e), fair; (*de tez*) fair, light-skinned

guerra SF **1** (*Mil, Pol*) war; (= *arte*) warfare; **Primera Guerra Mundial** First World War; **Segunda Guerra Mundial** Second World War; **declarar la ~** to declare war (**a** on); **estar en ~** to be at war (**con** with); **hacer la ~** to wage war (**a** on); ➤ **guerra bacteriológica** germ warfare ➤ **guerra biológica** biological warfare ➤ **guerra civil** civil war ➤ **guerra comercial** trade war ➤ **guerra de guerrillas** guerrilla warfare ➤ **guerra de las galaxias** Star Wars ➤ **guerra de precios** price war ➤ **guerra psicológica** psychological warfare ➤ **guerra santa** holy war, crusade ➤ **guerra sin cuartel** all-out war ➤ **guerra sucia** dirty war **2** (= *problemas*) **dar ~** (*gen*) to be a nuisance (**a** to), make trouble (**a** for); [*niño*] to carry on; **pedir** *o* **querer ~** (*gen*) to look for trouble; (*) (*sexualmente*) to feel randy *o* horny*

guerrear /1a/ VI to wage war, fight

guerrera SF combat jacket; (*Mil*) military jacket

guerrero/a Ⓐ ADJ **1** (= *belicoso*) war *antes de s*; **espíritu ~**

fighting spirit; **hazañas guerreras** fighting exploits **2** (*de carácter*) warlike; **un pueblo** ~ a warlike people **3** (= *en guerra*) warring; **tribus guerreras** warring tribes Ⓑ SM/F warrior, soldier

guerrilla SF **1** (= *grupo*) guerrillas *pl* **2** (= *guerra*) guerrilla warfare

guerrillero/a Ⓐ ADJ guerrilla *antes de s*; **líder** ~ guerrilla leader Ⓑ SM/F guerrilla (fighter)

gueto SM ghetto

güevón/ona* ADJ, SM/F (*And, Ven*) = **huevón**

guía Ⓐ SF **1** (= *libro*) guidebook (**de** to); (= *manual*) handbook; [*de teléfono*] directory ➤ **guía del ocio** "what's on" guide ➤ **guía de teléfonos** telephone directory ➤ **guía gastronómica** food guide ➤ **guía oficial de ferrocarriles** official timetable ➤ **guía telefónica** telephone directory ➤ **guía turística** tourist guide **2** (= *orientación*) guidance; **para que le sirva de** ~ for your guidance ➤ **guía vocacional** vocational guidance **3** (*Inform*) prompt **4** (*Mec*) guide; [*de bicicleta*] handlebars *pl*; [*de planta*] cane Ⓑ SMF (= *persona*) guide ➤ **guía de turismo** tourist guide

guiar /1c/ Ⓐ VT **1** (*gen*) to guide; (= *dirigir*) to lead, direct; **no te dejes** ~ **por la propaganda** don't be influenced or led by propaganda **2** (*Aut*) to drive; (*Náut*) to steer; (*Aer*) to pilot **3** (*Bot*) to train Ⓑ **guiarse** VPR ~**se por algo** to be guided by sth, be ruled by sth, go by sth; ~**se por el sentido común** to follow common sense

guija SF pebble

guijarral SM stony place

guijarro SM (= *piedra*) pebble; (*en camino*) cobblestone, cobble

guillotina SF guillotine; (*para papel*) paper cutter

guillotinar /1a/ VT to guillotine

güincha SM (*And*) = **huincha**

guinda SF **1** (= *fruta*) morello cherry, sour cherry (*EEUU*); (*tb* ~ **confitada**) glacé cherry; ✦ MODISMO **ponerse como una** ~ to turn scarlet **2** (= *remate*) **la** ~ (**del pastel**) the icing on the cake; **como** ~ to cap *o* top it all; **poner la** ~ (= *rematar bien*) to put the icing on the cake; (= *terminar*) to add the finishing touches

guindar /1a/ Ⓐ VT **1** (*Esp***) (= *robar*) to pinch*, swipe* **2** (*Col, Méx, Ven*) (= *colgar*) to hang up Ⓑ VI (*Col, Méx, Ven*) ~ **de algo** to hang from sth **guindarse** VPR (*Col, Méx, Ven*) **1** (= *descolgarse*) to hang (down) **2** (= *colgarse*) ~**se de algo** to hang from sth **3** (*) (= *ahorcarse*) to hang o.s.

guindilla SF chili, hot pepper

guindo SM mazzard cherry tree, morello cherry tree; ✦ MODISMO **caer del** ~ (*Esp***) to cotton on*

Guinea SF Guinea ➤ **Guinea Ecuatorial** Equatorial Guinea

guiñapo SM rag, tatter; ✦ MODISMO **poner a algn como un** ~ to shower sb with insults

guiñar /1a/ Ⓐ VT to wink; ~ **el ojo a algn** to wink at sb Ⓑ VI to wink

guiño SM **1** (= *gesto*) wink; **hacer** ~**s a algn** to wink at sb; ~ **cómplice** (*lit*) knowing wink; (= *apoyo*) tacit support **2** (*Aer, Náut*) yaw

guiñol SM (*Teat*) puppet theatre *o* (*EEUU*) theater, Punch and Judy show

guion SM **1** (*Radio, TV*) script; (*Cine*) (*como transcripción*) script; (*como obra*) screenplay; **salirse del** ~ to depart from the script, improvise **2** (*Tip*) hyphen

guionista SMF scriptwriter

guipar* /1a/ VT to see

güipil SM (*CAm, Méx*) *Indian regional dress or blouse*

guipuzcoano ADJ of/from Guipúzcoa

guiri* SMF (*Esp*) foreigner

guirigay SM (*Esp*) (= *griterío*) hubbub, uproar; (= *confusión*) chaos, confusion; **¡esto es un** ~**!** it's chaos here!

guirlache SM *type of nougat*

guirnalda SF garland

guisa SF **1 a** ~ **de**: **se puso una cinta a** ~ **de pulsera** she wore a strap like a bracelet; **usando el bastón a** ~ **de batuta** using his walking stick like *o* as a baton **2 de tal** ~ in such a way (**que** that)

guisado Ⓐ ADJ **carne guisada** beef stew, beef casserole Ⓑ SM stew; ~ **de alubias** bean casserole

guisante SM (*Esp*) pea

guisar /1a/ Ⓐ VT **1** (= *cocinar*) to cook; (= *en salsa*) to stew; ✦ REFRÁN **él se lo guisa, él se lo come** he's made his bed, so he can lie in it **2** (*) (= *tramar*) to cook up*; **¿qué estarán guisando?** what can they be cooking up?* Ⓑ VI (*Esp*) to cook Ⓒ **guisarse** VPR (*Esp***) (= *tramarse*) **¿qué se estará guisando en la asamblea?** what are they cooking up in the meeting, I wonder?*

guiso SM stew

guita SF **1** (= *cuerda*) twine **2** (***) (= *dinero*) dough*, cash

guitarra Ⓐ SF (= *instrumento*) guitar; ✦ MODISMO **ser como** ~ **en un entierro** to be quite out of place, strike the wrong note ➤ **guitarra eléctrica** electrical guitar Ⓑ SMF guitarist

guitarreo SM strum(ming)

guitarrista SMF guitarist

guitarrón SM (*Méx*) *large six-string acoustic bass guitar*

gula SF gluttony, greed

gurú SMF (*pl* ~**s**) guru

gusa* SF hunger; **tener** ~ to be hungry

gusanillo SM **1** (*) (= *hambre*) **cómete una manzana para matar el** ~ have an apple to keep you going **2** (*) (= *interés*) bug*; **le entró el** ~ **de la gimnasia** he caught the keep-fit bug*, he got hooked on keep-fit* **3 el** ~ **de la conciencia*** the prickings of conscience

gusano SM **1** (*gen*) worm; [*de tierra*] earthworm; [*de mosca*] maggot; [*de mariposa, polilla*] caterpillar; ✦ MODISMO **criar** ~**s** to be dead and buried, be pushing up the daisies* ➤ **gusano de seda** silkworm **2** (*pey*) (= *persona*) worm **3** (*Cuba*** *pey*) *nickname for Cuban refugees post-1959*

gusarapo SM **1** (= *renacuajo*) tadpole **2** (*) (= *bicho*) bug, creature

gustar /1a/ Ⓐ VI **1** (*con complemento personal*) **1.1** (*con sustantivo*) **me gusta el té** I like tea; **¿te gustó México?** did you like Mexico?; **le gustan mucho los niños** she loves children, she's very fond of children, she likes children a lot; **¿te ha gustado la película?** did you enjoy the film?; **el rojo es el que más me gusta** I like the red one best; **eso es, así me gusta** that's right, that's the way I like it; **me gusta como canta** I like the way she sings **1.2** (+ INFIN) **no me gusta nada levantarme temprano** I hate getting up early, I don't like getting up early at all; **le gusta llegar con tiempo de sobra a una cita** she likes to get to her appointments with time to spare **1.3** ~ **que** (+ SUBJUN): **le gusta que la cena esté en la mesa cuando llega a casa** he likes his supper to be on the table when he gets home; **no me gustó que no invitaran a mi hija** I didn't like the fact that *o* I was annoyed that my daughter wasn't invited; **¿te ~ía que te llevara a la ópera?** would you like me to take you to the opera? **1.4** (= *sentir atracción por*) **a mi amiga le gusta Carlos** my friend likes Carlos, my friend fancies Carlos* **2** (*sin complemento explícito*) **es una película que siempre gusta** it's a film that never fails to please; **la obra no gustó** the play was not a success **3** (*en frases de cortesía*) **¿gusta usted?** would you like some?, may I offer you some?; **si usted gusta** if you please, if you don't mind; **como usted guste** as you wish, as you please†; **cuando gusten** (*invitando a pasar*) when you're ready; **puede venir por aquí cuando guste** you can come here whenever you like *o* wish **4** ~ **de algo** to like sth; ~ **de hacer algo** to like to do sth Ⓑ VT **1** (= *probar*) to taste, sample **2** (*LAm*) **¿~ía un poco de vino?** would you like some wine?; **si gustan pasar a la sala de espera** would you like to go through to the waiting room?

gustazo* SM great pleasure; **darse el** ~ **de algo** to treat o.s. to sth

gustillo SM **coger el** ~ **a algo** to get *o* grow to like sth

gusto SM **1** (= *sentido*) taste; **agregue azúcar a** ~ add sugar to taste

2 [*de comida*] taste; **tiene un ~ amargo** it has a bitter taste, it tastes bitter; **helado de tres ~s** Neapolitan ice cream
3 (= *sentido estético*) taste; **tenemos los mismos ~s** we have the same tastes; **es demasiado grande para mi ~** it's too big for my taste; **he decorado la habitación a mi ~** I've decorated the room to my taste; **una habitación decorada con ~** a tastefully decorated room; **buen** ~ good taste; **no es de buen ~ decir eso** it's not in good taste to say that; **tiene buen ~ para la ropa** she has good taste in clothes; **un decorado de buen ~** tasteful décor; **mal** ~ bad taste; **una broma de muy mal** ~ a joke in very poor taste; **un comentario de mal ~** a tasteless remark; ✦ REFRANES **sobre ~s no hay disputa** ◇ **de ~s no hay nada escrito** there's no accounting for tastes
4 (= *placer*) pleasure; **a ~: aquí me encuentro** *o* **siento a ~** I feel at home *o* ease here; **con mucho ~** with pleasure; **lo haré con mucho ~** I'll be glad to do it, I'll be only too happy to do it; **comer con ~** to eat heartily; **dar ~ a algn** to please sb, give pleasure to sb; **da ~ trabajar contigo** it's a pleasure to work with you; **da ~ verlos tan contentos** it's lovely to see them so happy; **tienen un entusiasmo que da**

~ they show a wonderful enthusiasm; **leo por ~** I read for pleasure; **no lo hago por ~** I don't do it out of choice; **tener el ~ de hacer algo** to have the pleasure of doing sth

> Recuérdase que las preposiciones en inglés rigen gerundio y no infinitivo, de ahí **to have the pleasure of doing sth**.

5 (= *agrado*) liking; **ser del ~ de algn** to be to sb's liking; **coger el ~ a algo** ◇ **tomar ~ a algo** to take a liking to sth
6 (*en presentaciones*) **¡mucho ~!** ◇ **¡tanto ~!** how do you do?, pleased to meet you; **el ~ es mío** how do you do?, the pleasure is (all) mine; **tengo mucho ~ en presentar al Sr Peláez** allow me to introduce Mr Peláez

gustosamente ADV gladly, willingly

gutapercha SF gutta-percha

gutural ADJ guttural

Guyana SF Guyana

Hh

H, h[1] ['atʃe] SF (= *letra*) H, h

h[2] ABR (= **hora**) h., hr

h. ABR (= **habitantes**) pop.

Ha. ABR (= **hectárea(s)**)

ha *ver* **haber**

haba SF broad bean; ✦ MODISMOS **en todas partes cuecen ~s** it's the same the whole world over; **son ~s contadas** (*para expresar escasez*) they are few and far between; (= *es seguro*) it's a sure thing

Habana SF **La ~** Havana

habanera SF (*Mús*) habanera

habanero ADJ of/from Havana

habano SM Havana cigar

hábeas corpus SM habeas corpus

haber /2j/ **ⓐ** VERBO AUX **1** (*en tiempos compuestos*) to have; **he comido** I have *o* I've eaten; **había ido al restaurante** he had gone *o* he'd gone to the restaurant; **lo hubiéramos hecho** we would have done it; **¡~lo dicho!** you should have said!; **pero, ¿habráse visto (cosa igual)?** well, have you ever seen anything like it?; **de ~lo sabido** if I had known, if I'd known

2 ~ de 2.1 (*indicando obligación*) **hemos de tener paciencia** we must be patient; **has de saber que ...** you should know that ... **2.2** (*indicando suposición*) **han de ser las nueve** it must be about nine o'clock; **ha de llegar hoy** (*esp LAm*) he should get here today; **has de estar equivocado** (*esp LAm*) you must be mistaken

ⓑ VERBO IMPERS **1 hay** (*con sustantivo en singular*) there is; (*con sustantivo en plural*) there are; **hay mucho que hacer** there is a lot to be done; **¿habrá tiempo?** will there be time?; **no hay plátanos** there are no bananas; **ha habido problemas** there have been problems; **habían muchas personas** (*LAm**) there were many people there; **¿cuánto hay de aquí a Cuzco?** how far is it from here to Cuzco?; **los hay excelentes** some are excellent; **las hay en negro y blanco** they are available in black and white; **oportunistas los hay en todas partes** you'll find opportunists everywhere, there are always opportunists, wherever you go; **no hay: no hay nada mejor que ...** there's nothing better than ...; **no hay como esta playa para disfrutar del surf** there's nothing like this beach for surfing; **no hay más que hablar** there's no more to be said, there's nothing more to say; **¡no hay de qué!** don't mention it!, not at all!; **¿qué hay?** (= *¿qué pasa?*) what's up?; (= *¿qué tal?*) how's it going?, how are things?; **¡qué hubo!** (*Chi, Col, Méx, Ven**) how's it going?, how are things?; ✦ MODISMOS **como hay pocos** ◇ **donde los haya: un amigo como hay pocos** *o* **donde los haya** a friend in a million; **¡eres de lo que no hay!** you're unbelievable! **2 hay que: hay que hacerlo** it has to be done; **no hay que hacer nada** you don't have to do anything; **hay que ser fuertes** we must be strong; **no hay que olvidar que ...** we mustn't forget that ...; **¡había que decírselo!** we'll have to tell him!; **¡había que verlo!** you should have seen it!; **no hay más que: no hay más que leer las normas** all you have to do is read the rules; **no hay más que haber volado un poco para saberlo** anyone who has done a little flying would know; ✦ MODISMO **¡hay que ver!** (*sorpresa*) well I never!

3 (*indicando tiempo*) **tres años ha** (*frm*) three years ago **ⓒ** VT **1** (= *ocurrir*) **en el encuentro habido ayer** in yesterday's game; ✦ MODISMO **habidos y por ~: todos los temas habidos y por ~** every subject under the sun **2** (= *tener*) **los dos hijos habidos en su primer matrimonio** the two children from her first marriage **ⓓ** haberse VPR **habérselas con algn** (= *tener delante*) to be up against sb; (= *enfrentarse*) to have it out with sb **ⓔ** SM **1** (*en balance*) credit side; **¿cuánto tengo en el ~?** how much do I have in my account?; **la autora tiene seis libros en su ~** the author has six books to her credit **2 haberes** (= *ingresos*) salary *sing*; (= *bienes*) assets

habichuela SF kidney bean

hábil ADJ **1** (= *diestro*) skilful, skillful (*EEUU*); **es muy ~ con la aguja** he's very handy *o* good with a needle; **¡muy ~!** (*hum*) very clever!; **ser ~ para algo** to be good at sth **2** (*Jur*) competent

habilidad SF **1** skill; **su ~ con el balón era de leyenda** his ball skills were legendary; **tiene una gran ~ para evitar enfrentamientos** he's very clever *o* skilful *o* (*EEUU*) skillful at avoiding confrontation; **defendió su argumento con ~** he defended his argument cleverly *o* skilfully *o* (*EEUU*) skillfully **2** (*Jur*) competence

habilidoso ADJ handy, good with one's hands

habilitado/a SM/F paymaster

habilitar /1a/ VT **1** (= *dar derecho a*) to qualify, entitle; (= *permitir*) to enable; (= *autorizar*) to empower, authorize **2** (= *preparar*) to equip, fit out; **las aulas están habilitadas con televisores** the rooms are equipped with TVs **3** (*Fin*) to finance

habiloso* ADJ (*Chi*) clever

habitable ADJ inhabitable

habitación SF **1** (= *cuarto*) room ➤ **habitación doble** double room ➤ **habitación individual** single room **2** (*Biol*) habitat, habitation

habitacional ADJ (*CS*) housing *antes de s*

habitáculo SM (*para vivir*) living space; (*en vehículo*) inside, interior

habitado ADJ [*isla, pueblo*] inhabited; [*casa, habitación*] lived-in; [*satélite, cohete*] manned

habitante **ⓐ** SMF **1** (*gen*) inhabitant; **una ciudad de 10.000 ~s** a town of 10,000 inhabitants *o* people, a town with a population of 10,000 **2** (= *vecino*) resident **ⓑ** SM (*hum*) (= *piojo*) louse

habitar /1a/ **ⓐ** VT [+ *zona, territorio*] to inhabit, live in; [+ *casa*] to live in, occupy, be the occupant of **ⓑ** VI (= *vivir*) to live

hábitat SM (*pl* **~s** ['aβitas]) habitat

hábito SM **1** (= *costumbre*) habit; **una droga que crea ~** a habit-forming drug; **tener el ~ de hacer algo** to be in the habit of doing sth

> Recuérdese que las preposiciones en inglés rigen gerundio y no infinitivo, de ahí **to be in the habit of doing sth**.

➤ **hábitos de consumo** buying habits **2** (*Rel*) habit; ✦ MODISMOS **colgar los ~s** to leave the priesthood; **tomar el ~** [*hombre*] to take holy orders, become a monk; [*mujer*] to take the veil, become a nun

habitual **ⓐ** ADJ (= *acostumbrado*) habitual, customary, usual; [*cliente, lector*] regular; [*criminal*] hardened; **mi restaurante ~** my usual restaurant **ⓑ** SMF [*de bar, tienda*] regular

habituar /1e/ **ⓐ** VT to accustom (**a** to) **ⓑ** habituarse VPR **~se a** to become accustomed to, get used to

habla SF **1** (= *facultad*) speech; **dejar a algn sin ~** to leave sb speechless; **perder el ~** to lose the power of speech **2** (= *idioma*) language; (= *dialecto*) dialect, speech; **de ~ francesa** French-speaking **3** (= *acción*) **¡Benjamín al ~!** (*Telec*) Benjamín speaking!; **ponerse al ~ con algn** to get in touch with sb

hablador(a) **ⓐ** ADJ **1** (= *parlanchín*) talkative, chatty* **2** (= *chismoso*) gossip **3** (*Carib, Méx**) (= *mentiroso*) lying **ⓑ** SM/F **1** (= *parlanchín*) chatterbox* **2** (= *chismoso*) gossip **3** (*Carib, Méx**) (= *mentiroso*) liar

habladuría SF rumour, rumor (*EEUU*); **habladurías** gossip *sing*, scandal *sing*, tittle-tattle* *sing*

hablante SMF speaker

hablar /1a/ **ⓐ** VI to speak, talk (**a, con** to; **de** about, of); **necesito ~ contigo** I need to talk *o* speak to you; **acabamos**

de ~ del premio we were just talking *o* speaking about the prize; **¡mira quién fue a ~!** look who's talking!; **los datos hablan por sí solos** the facts speak for themselves; **¡hable!** ◇ **¡puede ~!** (*Telec*) you're through! (*Brit*), go ahead! (*EEUU*); **~ alto** to speak *o* talk loudly; **~ bajo** to speak *o* talk quietly, speak *o* talk in a low voice; **dar que ~ a la gente** to make people talk, cause tongues to wag; **hablaba en broma** she was joking; **vamos a ~ en confianza** this is between you and me; **¿hablas en serio?** are you serious?; **hacer ~ a algn** to make sb talk; **~ por ~** to talk for talking's sake, talk for the sake of it; **~ por teléfono** to speak on the phone; **acabo de ~ por teléfono con ella** I was just on the phone to her; **~ solo** to talk *o* speak to o.s.; ◆ MODISMOS **¡ni ~!** —**¿vas a ayudarlo en la mudanza?** —**¡ni ~!** "are you going to help him with the move?" — "no way!" *o* "you must be kidding!"; **de eso ni ~** that's out of the question; **hablando del rey de Roma ...** talk of the devil ...

B VT **1** [+ *idioma*] to speak; **habla bien el portugués** he speaks good Portuguese, he speaks Portuguese well; **"se habla inglés"** "English spoken"

2 (= *tratar de*) **hay que ~lo todo** we need to discuss everything; **eso habrá que ~lo con tu padre** you'll have to discuss that with your father; **no hay más que ~** there's nothing more to be said about it; **y no hay más que ~** and that's that

3 (*Méx Telec*) to phone; **te habló Luis** Luis phoned

C hablarse VPR **1** (*uso impersonal*) **se habla de que van a comprarlo** there is talk of their buying it; **y no se hable más** and that'll be an end to it

2 (*uso recíproco*) **no se hablan** they are not on speaking terms, they are not speaking (to each other); **no me hablo con él** I'm not speaking to him, I'm not on speaking terms with him

hablilla SF rumour, rumor (*EEUU*), story

habré *etc ver* **haber**

Hacedor SM **el (Supremo)** ~ the Creator, the Maker

hacendado/a **A** ADJ landed, property-owning **B** SM/F landowner

hacendista SMF economist, financial expert

hacendoso ADJ industrious, hard-working

---

hacer /2r/

A VERBO TRANSITIVO	**C** VERBO IMPERSONAL
B VERBO INTRANSITIVO	**D** VERBO PRONOMINAL

Para las expresiones **hacer añicos, hacer gracia, hacerse ilusiones, hacer pedazos, hacerse de rogar, hacer el tonto, hacer las veces de** *etc ver la entrada correspondiente a la otra palabra.*

---

hacer **A** VERBO TRANSITIVO

1 (*indicando actividad en general*) to do; **¿qué haces?** what are you doing?; **¿qué haces ahí?** what are you doing there?; **no sé qué ~** I don't know what to do; **no hizo nada por ayudarnos** she didn't do anything to help us; **haz todo lo posible por llegar a tiempo** do everything possible to arrive on time; **~ el amor** to make love; ◆ MODISMOS **¡qué le vamos a ~!** what can you do?, there's nothing you can do; **no tiene sentido ~ las cosas por ~las** there's no point doing things just for the sake of it; **¡la hemos hecho buena!** (*iró*) we've really gone and done it now!*; **ya ha hecho otra de las suyas** he's been up to his old tricks again

2 (*en lugar de otro verbo*) to do; **él protestó y yo hice lo mismo** he protested and I did the same; **no viene tanto como lo solía ~** he doesn't come as much as he used to

3 (= *crear*) [+ *coche, escultura, ropa*] to make; [+ *casa*] to build; [+ *dibujo*] to do; [+ *novela, sinfonía*] to write

4 (= *realizar*) [+ *apuesta, discurso, oración*] to make; [+ *deporte, deberes*] to do; [+ *caca, pipí*] to do; [+ *nudo*] to tie; [+ *pregunta*] to ask; [+ *visita*] to pay; [+ *milagros*] to do, work; **el gato hizo miau** the cat went miaow, the cat miaowed; **¿me puedes ~ el nudo de la corbata?** could you knot my tie for me?; **~ un favor a algn** to do sb a favour *o* (*EEUU*) favor; **~ un gesto** (*con la cara*) to make *o* pull a face; (*con la mano*) to make a sign; **~ un recado** to do *o* run an

errand; **~ ruido** to make a noise; **~ sitio** to make room; **~ tiempo** to kill time

5 (= *preparar*) [+ *cama, comida*] to make; **~ el pelo/las uñas a algn** to do sb's hair/nails; **~ las maletas** to pack one's bags

6 (= *adquirir*) [+ *amigos, dinero*] to make

7 (= *dedicarse a*) **¿qué hace tu padre?** what does your father do?; **está haciendo turismo en África** he's gone touring in Africa; **~ cine** to make films (*esp Brit*), make movies (*esp EEUU*); **~ teatro** to act

8 (= *actuar*) **~ un papel** to play a role *o* part

9 (= *sumar*) to make; **6 y 3 hacen 9** 6 and 3 make 9; **y cincuenta pesetas, hacen quinientas** five hundred pesetas and fifty change; **éste hace el corredor número 100 en atravesar la meta** he's the 100th runner to cross the line

10 (= *cumplir*) **voy a ~ 30 años la próxima semana** I'm going to be 30 next week, it's my 30th birthday next week

11 (+ ADJ) to make; **~ feliz a algn** to make sb happy; **te hace más delgado** it makes you look thinner

12 (+ INFIN) to make; **les hice venir** I made them come; **hágale entrar** show him in, have him come in; **siempre consigue ~me reír** she always manages to make me laugh; **hicieron pintar la fachada del colegio** they had the front of the school painted

13 **~ que** (+ SUBJUN): **yo haré que vengan** I'll make sure they come

14 (= *pensar*) to think; **yo le hacía más viejo** I thought he was older, I had him down as being older; **te hacíamos en el Perú** we thought you were in Peru

15 (= *acostumbrar*) **~ el cuerpo al frío** to get one's body used to the cold

16 (= *ejercitar*) **~ dedos** to do finger exercises; **~ piernas** to stretch one's legs

B VERBO INTRANSITIVO

1 (= *comportarse*) **haces bien en esperar** you're right to wait; **haces mal no contestando a sus llamadas** it's wrong of you not to answer his calls; **~ como que** *o* **como si** to make as if; **hizo como que no se daba cuenta** *o* **como si no se diera cuenta** he made as if he hadn't noticed, he pretended not to have noticed

2 (*otras expresiones*) **no le hace** (*RPl*) it doesn't matter; **¿qué le hace que sea caro?** what does it matter if it's expensive?; **¿hace?** will it do?, is it all right?; **¿te hace un cigarrillo?** how about a cigarette?, would you like a cigarette?; **dar que ~** to cause trouble; **dieron que ~ a la policía** they caused *o* gave the police quite a bit of trouble; ◆ MODISMO **¡no le hagas!** (*Méx**) you're kidding!*

3 (*seguido de preposición*)

◆ **hacer de** (*Teat*) to play the part of; **~ de malo** to play the villain

◆ **hacer por** (= *intentar*) **haz por verlo si puedes** try to get around to seeing him if you can

C VERBO IMPERSONAL

1 (*tiempo atmosférico*) to be; **hace calor/frío** it's hot/cold; **¿qué tiempo hace?** what's the weather like?; **ojalá haga buen tiempo** I hope the weather's nice

2 (*con expresiones temporales*) **hace tres años que se fue** he left three years ago, it's three years since he left; **hace tres años que no lo veo** I haven't seen him for three years, it's three years since I (last) saw him; **ha estado aquí hasta hace poco** he was here only a short while ago; **no hace mucho** not long ago; **hace un mes que voy** I've been going for a month; **¿hace mucho que esperas?** have you been waiting long?; **desde hace cuatro años** for four years

3 (*esp LAm* hum) (= *tener*) **hace sed** I'm thirsty; **hace sueño** I'm sleepy

D hacerse VERBO PRONOMINAL

1 (= *realizar, crear*) **~se algo** [*uno mismo*] to make o.s. sth; [*otra persona*] to have sth made; **se hizo una bufanda** he made himself a scarf; **¿os hicisteis muchas fotos?** did you take a lot of photos?; **todos los días me hago 3km andando** I walk 3km every day; **~se un retrato** to have one's portrait painted; **se hizo la cirugía estética** she had plastic surgery; **~se caca** to soil one's pants; **~se pipí** to wet o.s.; ◆ MODISMO **hacérsele algo a algn: ¡cuándo se me hará hablar bien inglés!** when will I ever learn to speak good English?

2 (= *cocinarse*) **todavía se está haciendo la comida** the meal's still cooking; **deja que se haga bien la carne** make sure the meat is well done

3 (+ INFIN)
3.1 (= *conseguir*) **deberías ~te oír** you should make your voice heard; **la respuesta no se hizo esperar** the answer was not long in coming
3.2 (= *mandar*) **se hizo traer caviar de Rusia** she had caviar sent over from Russia
4 (*reflexivo*) **se hizo a sí mismo** he's a self-made man
5 (*recíproco*) **se hacían caricias** they were caressing each other
6 (= *llegar a ser*)
6.1 (+ SUSTANTIVO) to become; **se hicieron amigos** they became friends; **~se enfermera** to become a nurse
6.2 (+ ADJ) **quiere ~se famoso** he wants to be famous; **se está haciendo viejo** he's getting old; **se hace tarde** it's getting late
7 (= *parecer*) **se me hizo largo/pesado el viaje** the journey felt long/boring; **se me hace que ...** (*esp LAm*) it seems to me that ..., I get the impression that ...
8 (* = *fingirse*) **~se el interesante** to try to attract attention; **~se de nuevas** to act all innocent; **~se el sordo** to pretend not to hear
9 (= *moverse*) **~se atrás** to move back; **~se a un lado** (*de pie*) to move to one side; (*sentado*) to move over; **hazte para allá, que me siente** move up that way a little so I can sit down
10 (*seguido de preposición*)
◆ **hacerse a** (= *acostumbrarse*) to get used to; **~se a una idea** to get used to an idea; **~se a hacer algo** to get used to doing sth; **¿te has hecho ya a levantarte temprano?** have you got used to getting up early yet?
◆ **hacerse con** [+ *información*] to get hold of; [+ *ciudad, fortaleza*] to take; **logró ~se con una copia** he managed to get hold of a copy; **~se con el control de algo** to gain control of sth

hacha¹ SF (= *herramienta*) axe, ax (*EEUU*); (*pequeña*) hatchet; ◆ MODISMOS **desenterrar el ~ de guerra** to renew hostilities; **enterrar el ~ de guerra** to bury the hatchet; **estar como ~ para algo** (*Chi, Méx**) to be all set for sth*; **ser un ~**: María es un ~ María is a real star; **es un ~ para el tenis** he's fantastic at tennis, he's a fantastic tennis player

hacha² SF (= *vela*) large candle

hachazo SM blow with an axe, blow with an ax (*EEUU*)

hache SF (name of the letter) H; ◆ MODISMOS **por ~ o por be** for one reason or another; **llámalo ~** call it what you will

hachemita ADJ Hashemite, Jordanian

hachís SM hashish, hash

hachón SM large torch, firebrand

hacia PREP **1** (*indicando dirección*) towards, in the direction of; **eso está más ~ el este** that's further (over) to the east; **vamos ~ allá** let's go in that direction, let's go over that way; **~ abajo** down, downwards; **~ adelante** forwards; **~ arriba** up, upwards; **~ atrás** backwards; (*con expresiones temporales*) about, around; **~ las cinco** about five, around five **3** (= *ante*) towards; **su hostilidad ~ la empresa** his hostility towards the firm

hacienda SF **1** (= *finca*) country estate; (*LAm*) ranch **2** (= *bienes*) property **3** (*RPl*) (= *ganado*) cattle, livestock **4** (*Fin*) (*tb* **Ministerio de Hacienda**) ≈ Treasury, ≈ Exchequer (*Brit*), ≈ Treasury Department (*EEUU*); **Hacienda me debe mucho dinero** the Inland Revenue (*Brit*) o the Treasury (*EEUU*) owes me a lot of money ▶ **hacienda pública**: **un desembolso enorme para la ~ pública** a massive outlay of public funds o money

hacinado ADJ [*cosas*] heaped(-up), piled(-up); [*gente, animales*] crowded together, packed together

hacinamiento SM [*de cosas*] heaping (up), piling (up); [*de gente, animales*] crowding, overcrowding

hacinar /1a/ ◆ VT [+ *cosas*] to heap (up), pile (up); [+ *gente, animales*] to cram ⑬ **hacinarse** VPR **~se en** to pack into, cram into

hada SF fairy; **cuento de ~s** fairy tale ▶ **hada buena** good fairy ▶ **hada madrina** fairy godmother

hado SM (*liter*) fate, destiny

haga *ver* **hacer**

hago *ver* **hacer**

haiku ['haiku] SM haiku

Haití SM Haiti

hala EXCL (*Esp*) (*mostrando sorpresa*) wow!; (= *qué exageración*) come off it!*; (= *vamos*) come on!, let's go!; **no quiero, ¡hala!** I don't want to, so there!

halagador(a) ⓐ ADJ [*retrato, opinión*] flattering; [*propuesta*] pleasing, gratifying ⑬ SM/F flatterer

halagar /1h/ VT **1** (= *adular*) to flatter **2** (= *agradar*) to please, gratify; **es una perspectiva que me halaga** it's a pleasant prospect

halago SM flattery

halagüeño ADJ [*perspectiva*] promising, rosy; [*opinión, observación*] flattering

halar [ha'lar] /1a/ VT, VI (*LAm*) = **jalar**

halcón SM **1** (*Zool*) falcon ▶ **halcón peregrino** peregrine falcon **2** (*Pol*) hawk

hale EXCL = **hala**

halibut [ali'βu] SM (*pl* **~s** [ali'βu]) halibut

hálito SM (*liter*) breath

halitosis SF INV halitosis (*frm*), bad breath

hall [xol] SM (*pl* **~s** [xol]) [*de casa*] hall; [*de teatro, cine*] foyer; [*de hotel*] lounge, foyer

hallaca SF (*Ven*) tamale, *Christmas speciality consisting of cornmeal, meat and vegetables wrapped in banana leaves*

hallar /1a/ ⓐ VT **1** (= *encontrar*) **1.1** [+ *objeto, persona, respuesta, solución*] to find; **el cadáver fue hallado ayer** the body was found yesterday **1.2** (*frm*) [+ *apoyo, oposición*] to meet with; **no halló la aprobación que esperaba para su proyecto** his plan did not meet with the approval he had hoped for; **halló la muerte en la montaña** he met his death on the mountain **2** (= *descubrir*) [+ *método*] to find, discover **3** (= *averiguar*) [+ *motivo, razón*] to find out **4** (*Jur*) **ser hallado culpable de algo** to be found guilty of sth
⑬ **hallarse** VPR **1** (= *estar*) to be; **nos hallamos en Sevilla** we are in Seville; **se hallan entre las personas más ricas del mundo** they are among the richest people in the world **1.2** (*indicando estado*) to be; **se hallaban presentes todos los directivos** all the directors were present
2 (= *encontrarse*) to find o.s.; **de repente me hallé en medio de un grupo de desconocidos** I suddenly found myself in the middle of a group of strangers; **nos hallamos ante un ensayo excepcional** we're talking about o this is an exceptional essay
3 (= *sentirse*) to feel; **~se a gusto** to feel comfortable; **no me hallo en una casa tan grande** I don't feel comfortable o right in such a big house

hallazgo SM **1** (= *acto*) discovery; **tras el ~ de unos documentos que le incriminaban** following the discovery of incriminating documents **2** (= *descubrimiento*) [*de la ciencia*] discovery; (*por investigador, institución*) finding; **los últimos ~s científicos** the latest scientific discoveries; **la revista en la que ha difundido sus ~s** the journal in which he published his findings **3** (= *persona, cosa hallada*) find; **el nuevo guitarra ha sido un ~** the new guitarist was a real find

halo SM **1** [*de santo*] halo **2** [*de misterio, genialidad*] aura **3** [*de luna, sol*] halo

halógeno ⓐ ADJ halogenous, halogen *antes de s* ⑬ SM halogen

halterofilia SF weight-lifting

hamaca SF **1** (= *cama*) hammock **2** (*RPl*) (= *mecedora*) rocking chair; (= *columpio*) swing **3** (*plegable*) deckchair

hamacar /1g/ ⓐ VT **1** (*LAm*) (= *mecer*) to rock **2** (*RPl*) (= *columpiar*) to swing ⑬ **hamacarse** VPR **1** (*LAm*) (= *mecerse*) to rock **2** (*RPl*) (= *columpiarse*) to swing

hambre SF **1** (= *necesidad de comer*) hunger; **una huelga de ~** a hunger strike; **dar ~ a algn** to make sb hungry; **entrar ~**: **me está entrando ~** I'm starting to feel hungry, I'm getting hungry; **matar de ~ a algn** to starve sb to death; **en el**

colegio nos mataban de ~ they starved us at school; **morir de** ~ to die of hunger, starve to death; **quedarse con** ~: **se han quedado con** ~ they are still hungry; **tener** ~ to be hungry; **tengo un** ~ **que no veo*** I'm absolutely starving*; ✦ MODISMOS **engañar el** ~ to stave off hunger; **tener un** ~ **canina** o **de lobo** to be ravenous, be ravenously hungry; **juntarse el** ~ **y las ganas de comer: se ha juntado el** ~ **y las ganas de comer** they're two of a kind; **matar el** ~ to keep one going, take the edge off one's appetite; ✦ REFRÁN **a buen** ~ **no hay pan duro** beggars can't be choosers **2** (= *escasez general*) famine **3** (= *deseo*) hunger; **tener** ~ **de justicia** to be hungry for justice

hambreado ADJ (*And, RPl*) starving

hambrear /1a/ VT (*CS*) to starve

hambriento/a Ⓐ ADJ **1** (= *con hambre*) hungry; (= *famélico*) starving; **venimos ~s** we're starving*, we're very hungry; **imágenes de niños ~s** pictures of hungry o starving children **2** ~ **de** hungry for; ~ **de poder** hungry for power **Ⓑ** SM/F (*con hambre*) hungry person; (*en situación desesperada*) starving person; **dar de comer al** ~ to feed the hungry

hambruna SF famine

hambrusia SF (*Col, Méx*) ravenous hunger

hamburguesa SF hamburger, burger

hamburguesería SF burger joint*, burger bar

hampa SF (*gen*) criminal underworld; **gente del** ~ criminals

hámster SM (*pl* ~**s**) hamster

han *ver* **haber**

handicap SM, **hándicap** SM (*pl* ~**s** o **hándicaps**) handicap

handling ['xanlin] SM baggage handling

hangar SM hangar

haragán/ana Ⓐ ADJ idle, lazy **Ⓑ** SM/F idler, layabout (*esp Brit**), lazy bum (*EEUU**)

haraganear /1a/ VI to idle, loaf about, laze around

haraganería SF idleness, laziness

harakiri SM hara-kiri; **hacerse el** ~ to commit hara-kiri

harapiento ADJ tattered, in rags

harapo SM rag

haraquiri SM = **harakiri**

haras SM INV (*CS, Perú, Ven*) stud farm

haré *ver* **hacer**

harén SM harem

harina SF flour; ✦ MODISMO **eso es** ~ **de otro costal** that's a different kettle of fish ➤ **harina animal, harina cárnica** meat and bone meal ➤ **harina de maíz** cornflour (*Brit*), corn starch (*EEUU*) ➤ **harina de trigo** wheat flour

harinoso ADJ floury

harnear /1a/ VT (*LAm*) to sieve, sift

harnero SM sieve

harpillera SF sacking, sackcloth

hartar /1a/ **Ⓐ** VT **1** (= *cansar*) **ya me está hartando que siempre me hable de lo mismo** I'm getting tired of o fed up with* o sick of* him always talking about the same thing **2** (= *atiborrar*) ~ **a algn** a o **de** [+ *comida, alcohol*] to fill sb full of; **lo ~on a palos** they gave him a real beating **Ⓑ hartarse** VPR **1** (= *cansarse*) to get fed up*; **un día se ~á y se marchará** one of these days she'll get tired of o get fed up with* it all and leave; ~**se de algo/algn** to get tired of sth/sb, get fed up with sth/sb*, get sick of sth/sb*; **ya me he hartado de esperar** I've had enough of waiting, I'm tired o fed up with* o sick of* waiting **2** (= *atiborrarse*) ~**se de** [+ *comida*] to gorge o.s. on, stuff o.s. with*; **le gustaría poder** ~**se de marisco** he'd like to be able to pig out on seafood; **me harté de agua** I drank gallons o tons of water* **3** (= *saciarse*) ~**se a** o **de algo: fui al museo para** ~**me de buena pintura** I went to the museum to see plenty of good paintings; **me harté a** o **de tomar el sol** I lay out in the sun all day; **nos hartamos de reír** we laughed till we were fit to

burst; **comieron hasta** ~**se** they gorged o stuffed* themselves; **bebieron champán hasta** ~**se** they drank their fill of champagne; **dormimos hasta** ~**nos** we slept as long as we wanted

hartazgo SM [*de comida*] surfeit, glut; **darse un** ~ [*de comida*] to eat too much, overeat; [*de noticias, televisión*] to have too much

harto Ⓐ ADJ **1** (= *cansado*) fed up*; **¡ya estamos ~s!** we've had enough!, we're fed up!*; **¡me tienes ~!** I'm fed up with you!*; **estar** ~ **de algo/algn** to be tired of sth/sb, be fed up with sth/sb*, be sick of sth/sb*; **está** ~ **de no tener dinero** he's tired o fed up* o sick of* not having any money; **estamos ~s de que lleguen siempre tarde** we're tired of o fed up with* o sick of* them arriving late **2** (= *lleno*) ~ **de algo** stuffed with sth* **3** (= *mucho*) **3.1** (*frm*) **con harta frecuencia** very often o very frequently; **tienen hartas razones** they have plenty of reasons **3.2** (*LAm*) plenty of, a lot of; **usaste harta harina** you used plenty of o a lot of flour; **ha habido ~s accidentes** there have been a lot of o plenty of accidents **Ⓑ** ADV **1** (*con adjetivo*) **1.1** (*frm*) very, extremely; **una tarea** ~ **difícil** a very difficult task, an extremely difficult task **1.2** (*LAm*) very; **llegaron** ~ **cansados** they were very tired when they arrived **2** (*LAm*) (*con adverbio*) very; **lo sé** ~ **bien** I know that very well o all too well **3** (*LAm*) (*con verbo*) a lot; **te quiero** ~ I love you a lot; **dormí** ~ **anoche** I slept a lot last night **Ⓒ** PRON (*LAm*) **hace** ~ **que no lo veo** it's been a long time since I saw him; **falta** ~ **para llegar** there's still a long way to go

hartón* SM **darse un** ~ **de** [+ *pasteles, chocolate*] to stuff oneself with*; **se dio un** ~ **de leer novelas policíacas** he had a binge of reading crime novels

hartura SF **1** (= *cansancio*) **¡qué** ~! I'm fed up with it! o I'm sick of it!* **2** (= *hartazgo*) **da sensación de** ~ it leaves you feeling full

has *ver* **haber**

hasta Ⓐ PREP **1** (*en el espacio*) (*gen*) to, as far as; (= *hacia arriba*) up to; (= *hacia abajo*) down to; **fuimos juntos** ~ **el primer pueblo** we went to o as far as the first village together; **el agua subió** ~ **aquí** the water came up to here; **el vestido me llega** ~ **las rodillas** the dress comes down to my knees; **¿** ~ **dónde vais?** how far are you going? **2** (*en el tiempo*) until, till; **se va a quedar** ~ **el martes** she's staying until o till Tuesday; **¿siempre escuchas música** ~ **tan tarde?** do you always listen to music so late (at night)?; **el** ~ **ayer presidente** the hitherto president (*frm*); ~ **ahora** so far, up to now; ~ **ahora nadie se ha quejado** so far no one has complained, no one has complained up to now; ~ **ahora no se había quejado nadie** no one had complained before o until now o till now; **luego las cosas se tranquilizaron y** ~ **ahora** then things calmed down and since then it's been OK; **¿** ~ **cuándo ...** ? how long ... for?; **¿** ~ **cuándo os quedáis?** how long are you staying (for)?; ~ **entonces** until then, (up) till then; ~ **la fecha** to date; ~ **el momento** so far, up to now, thus far (*frm*); ~ **nueva orden** until further notice **3** (*con cantidades*) (*gen*) up to; (*con valor enfático*) as much as/as many as; **duerme** ~ **diez horas diarias** he sleeps up to ten hours a day; **llegó a haber** ~ **500 invitados*** there were as many as 500 guests **4** (*en expresiones de despedida*) ~ **ahora** see you in a minute; ~ **la vista** see you, so long; ~ **luego** see you, bye*; ~ **más ver** see you again; ~ **nunca** I hope I never see you again; ~ **otra** see you again; ~ **pronto** see you soon; ~ **siempre*** goodbye, farewell (*frm*) **5** (*CAm, Col, Méx*) not ... until, not ... till; **lo hizo** ~ **el martes** he didn't do it until o till Tuesday; ~ **hoy lo conocí** I only met him today, I hadn't met him until o till today **Ⓑ** CONJ ~ **que** until, till; **no me iré** ~ **que (no) me lo des** I won't go until o till you give it to me **Ⓒ** ADV (= *incluso*) even; **se oía** ~ **desde la calle** you could even hear it from the street

hastiar /1c/ **Ⓐ** VT (= *cansar*) to weary; (= *aburrir*) to bore; (= *asquear*) to sicken, disgust **Ⓑ hastiarse** VPR ~**se de** to tire of, get fed up with*

hastío SM (= *cansancio*) weariness; (= *aburrimiento*) boredom; (= *asco*) disgust

hatajo SM lot, collection; **un ~ de sinvergüenzas** a bunch of crooks

hatillo SM = **hato 1, 2**

hato SM 1 [*de ropa*] bundle 2 [*de ganado*] herd; [*de ovejas*] flock 3 (*Carib*) (= *rancho*) cattle ranch

Hawai SM (*tb* **Islas ~**) Hawaii

hawaiano ADJ of/from Hawaii

hay *ver* **haber**

Haya SF **La ~** The Hague

haya¹ *ver* **haber**

haya² SF beech, beech tree

hayal SM, **hayedo** SM beechwood

hayo SM coca

haz¹ SM bundle, bunch; [*de trigo*] sheaf ➤ **haz de luz** beam of light

haz² *ver* **hacer**

hazaña SF feat, exploit, deed

hazmerreír SMF INV laughing stock

he¹ *ver* **haber**

he² ADV (*frm*) **¡heme aquí!** here I am!; **¡helos allí!** there they are!; **he aquí la razón de que ...** ◇ **he aquí por qué ...** that is why ...; **he aquí los resultados** these are the results, here you have the results

heavy ['xeβi] (*pl* **heavies** *o* **~s**) ADJ, SM heavy metal; **los heavies** *o* **~s** heavy metal fans

hebilla SF buckle, clasp

hebra SF 1 [*de hilo*] thread; (= *fibra*) fibre, fiber (*EEUU*); [*de madera*] grain; [*de gusano de seda*] thread; **tabaco de ~** loose tobacco 2 [*de metal*] vein, streak; ✦ MODISMO **pegar la ~*** (= *entablar conversación*) to start *o* strike up a conversation; (= *hablar mucho*) to chatter

hebraico ADJ Hebraic

hebreo/a Ⓐ ADJ Hebrew Ⓑ SM/F Hebrew; **los ~s** the Hebrews Ⓒ SM (*Ling*) Hebrew

hecatombe SF disaster

heces SFPL *ver* **hez**

hechicería SF 1 (= *brujería*) sorcery, witchcraft 2 (= *maleficio*) spell

hechicero/a Ⓐ ADJ 1 [*rito, poder*] magic, magical 2 [*labios, ojos*] enchanting, bewitching Ⓑ SM/F (= *brujo*) sorcerer/sorceress, wizard/witch; [*de tribu*] witch doctor

hechizar /1f/ VT (= *embrujar*) to bewitch, cast a spell on; (= *cautivar*) to fascinate, charm, enchant

hechizo Ⓐ ADJ (*Chi, Méx*) home-made Ⓑ SM 1 (= *maleficio*) spell 2 (= *encanto*) charm

hecho Ⓐ PP *de* **hacer**
Ⓑ ADJ 1 (= *realizado*) done; **si le dijiste que no fuera, mal ~** if you told him not to go, then you were wrong *o* you shouldn't have; **¡hecho!** (= *de acuerdo*) agreed!, it's a deal!; ✦ MODISMO **lo ~, ~ está** what's done is done; ✦ REFRÁN **a lo ~ pecho** it's no use crying over spilt milk
2 (= *manufacturado*) made; **¿de qué está ~?** what's it made of?; **~ a mano** handmade; **se compra la ropa hecha** he buys his clothes off-the-peg (*Brit*) *o* ready-made (*EEUU*)
3 (= *acabado*) done, finished; (= *listo*) ready; **el trabajo ya está ~** the work is done *o* finished; **¿está hecha la comida?** is dinner ready?
4 (*Culin*) 4.1 (= *maduro*) [*queso, vino*] mature; [*fruta*] ripe 4.2 (= *cocinado*) **muy ~** (= *bien*) well-cooked; (= *demasiado*) overdone; **no muy ~** ◇ **poco ~** underdone, undercooked; **un filete poco** *o* **no muy ~** a rare steak
5 (= *convertido en*) **el baño está ~ un asco** the bathroom is disgusting; **usted está ~ un chaval** you look so young
6 [*persona*] **bien ~** well-proportioned; **mal ~** ill-proportioned; ✦ MODISMO **~ y derecho: un hombre ~ y derecho** a (fully) grown man; **soldados ~s y derechos** real soldiers
7 (= *acostumbrado*) **estar ~ a** to be used to

8 (*Col**) (*económicamente*) **está ~** he's (got it) made, he's a made man
Ⓒ SM 1 (= *acto*) **quieren ~s** they want action ➤ **hecho consumado** fait accompli ➤ **Hechos de los Apóstoles** Acts of the Apostles
2 (= *realidad*) fact; (= *suceso*) event; **es un ~** it's a fact; **el ~ es que ...** the fact is that ...; **hay que clarificar los ~s** the facts must be clarified; **un ~ histórico** (= *acontecimiento*) a historic event; (= *dato*) a historical fact; **los ~s acaecidos ayer** yesterday's events; **el lugar de los ~s** the scene of the incident ➤ **hecho imponible** (*Fin*) taxable source of income
3 **de ~** in fact, as a matter of fact

hechura SF 1 (*Cos*) (= *confección*) making-up; (= *corte*) cut 2 (= *forma*) form, shape 3 [*de cuadro, escultura*] craftsmanship, workmanship; **de exquisita ~** of exquisite workmanship

hectárea SF hectare (= *2.471 acres*)

hectogramo SM hectogram, hectogramme (*Brit*)

hectolitro SM hectolitre, hectoliter (*EEUU*)

heder /2g/ VI to stink (**a** of), reek (**a** of)

hediondez SF 1 (= *olor*) stink, stench 2 (*esp CS*) (= *cosa*) stinking thing

hediondo ADJ (= *maloliente*) stinking, foul-smelling; (= *asqueroso*) repulsive

hedonismo SM hedonism

hedor SM stink (**a** of), stench (**a** of)

hegemonía SF hegemony

hégira SF Hegira

helada SF frost, early-morning frost

heladera SF (*RPl*) refrigerator, fridge*; *ver tb* **heladero**

heladería SF ice-cream parlour, ice-cream parlor (*EEUU*)

helado/a Ⓐ ADJ ice-cream *antes de s* Ⓑ SM/F ice-cream seller; *ver tb* **heladera**

helado Ⓐ ADJ 1 (= *congelado*) [*lago, río*] frozen; [*carretera*] icy 2 (= *muy frío*) [*bebida, comida*] ice-cold; [*mirada*] frosty, icy; **¡estoy ~!** I'm frozen!, I'm freezing!; **¡tengo las manos heladas!** my hands are frozen! *o* freezing! *o* like ice!; **sírvase bien ~** (*SAm*) serve chilled 3 (= *pasmado*) **dejar ~ a algn** to dumbfound sb; **¡me quedé ~!** I couldn't believe it! Ⓑ SM ice cream ➤ **helado de agua** (*CS*) sorbet; (*con palo*) ice lolly (*Brit*), Popsicle® (*EEUU*)

helador ADJ [*viento*] icy, freezing; **hace un frío ~** it's icy cold, it's freezing cold

helar /1j/ Ⓐ VT 1 (*Meteo*) to freeze, ice up 2 [+ *líquido*] to freeze; [+ *bebidas*] to ice, chill Ⓑ VI (*Meteo*) to freeze Ⓒ **helarse** VPR 1 (*Aer, Ferro*) to ice up, freeze up 2 [*líquido*] to freeze; [*plantas*] to be killed by frost; [*mirada*] frosty; [*lago, río*] to freeze over 3 [*persona*] **¡me estoy helando!** I'm freezing!; ✦ MODISMO **se me heló la sangre (en las venas)** my blood ran cold

helecho SM bracken, fern

helénico ADJ Hellenic, Ancient Greek

hélice SF 1 (*Anat, Elec, Mat*) helix 2 (*Aer*) propeller; (*Náut*) propeller, screw

helicóptero SM helicopter

helio SM helium

helipuerto SM heliport

helmántico ADJ of/from Salamanca

Helsinki SM Helsinki

helvético ADJ (*Esp*) of/from Switzerland

hematíe SM red (blood) corpuscle

hematología SF haematology, hematology (*EEUU*)

hematoma SM bruise

hembra SF 1 (*Bot, Zool*) female; **el armiño ~** the female stoat, the she-stoat 2 (= *mujer*) female; **cinco hijos: dos varones y tres ~s** five children: two boys and three girls 3 (*Mec*) nut

hemeroteca SF newspaper library

hemiciclo SM 1 (= *anfiteatro*) semicircular theatre,

semicircular theater (*EEUU*) **2** (*Pol*) (= *sala*) chamber; (= *zona central*) floor

hemiplejía SF hemiplegia (*frm*), stroke

hemipléjico ADJ hemiplegic

hemisferio SM hemisphere

hemodiálisis SF INV haemodialysis, hemodialysis (*EEUU*)

hemofilia SF haemophilia, hemophilia (*EEUU*)

hemofílico/a ADJ, SM/F haemophiliac, hemophiliac (*EEUU*)

hemoglobina SF haemoglobin, hemoglobin (*EEUU*)

hemorragia SF haemorrhage, hemorrhage (*EEUU*)
➤ **hemorragia cerebral** cerebral haemorrhage *o* (*EEUU*) hemorrhage ➤ **hemorragia nasal** nosebleed

hemorroides SFPL haemorrhoids, hemorrhoids (*EEUU*), piles

hemos *ver* **haber**

henchir /3h/ Ⓐ VT to fill (up) (**de** with) Ⓑ **henchirse** VPR to swell; **henchido de orgullo** swollen with pride

hendedura SF = **hendidura**

hender /2g/ VT to cleave, split

hendidura SF (= *grieta*) crack; (= *corte*) cleft, split

hendija SF (*LAm*) crack, crevice

hendir /3i/ VT = **hender**

henequén SM (*LAm*) agave, henequen

heno SM hay

hepático ADJ hepatic (*frm*), liver *antes de s*

hepatitis SF INV hepatitis

heptágono SM heptagon

heptatlón SM heptathlon

heráldica SF heraldry

heráldico ADJ heraldic

heraldo SM herald

herbáceo ADJ herbaceous

herbicida SM weed-killer

herbívoro/a Ⓐ ADJ herbivorous Ⓑ SM/F herbivore

herbolario SM (= *tienda*) herbalist's (shop), health food shop

herboristería SF herbalist's, herbalist's shop

hercio SM hertz

hercúleo ADJ Herculean

heredad SF country estate

heredar /1a/ **1** VT [+ *dinero, tradición, problema*] to inherit; **el rey heredó el trono en 1865** the king succeeded to the throne in 1865 **2** [+ *rasgo, ropa, libros*] to inherit; **ha heredado el pelo rubio de su madre** he's inherited his mother's blond hair, he gets his blond hair from his mother; **siempre hereda la ropa de su hermana mayor** her clothes are always handed down from her elder sister

heredero/a SM/F heir/heiress (**de** to), inheritor (**de** of); **príncipe** ~ crown prince

hereditario ADJ hereditary

hereje Ⓐ SMF heretic Ⓑ ADJ (*Ven**) **pasamos un frío** ~ we were terribly cold

herejía SF heresy

herencia SF **1** [*de propiedad, valores*] inheritance, legacy; **me dejó las joyas en** ~ she left *o* bequeathed me her jewels; **es parte de la ~ cultural** it's part of the cultural heritage **2** (*Biol*) heredity ➤ **herencia genética** genetic inheritance

herético ADJ heretical

herida SF (*física*) (*por arma*) wound; (*por accidente*) injury; **me he hecho una ~ en la frente** I've got a cut on my forehead ➤ **herida abierta** open wound ➤ **herida de bala** bullet wound

herido/a Ⓐ ADJ **1** (*físicamente*) (*gen*) injured; (*en tiroteo, atentado, guerra*) wounded; **estaba ~ de muerte** he was fatally injured
2 (*emocionalmente*) hurt; **me sentí herida en mi amor propio** it was a blow to my self-esteem
Ⓑ SM/F (= *lesionado*) (*gen*) injured person; (*en tiroteo, atentado, guerra*) wounded person; **hubo cinco ~s leves** five

people were slightly injured *o* hurt; **el número de los ~s en el accidente** the number of casualties *o* people injured in the accident; **los ~s de guerra** the war wounded

herir /3i/ VT **1** (= *lesionar*) (*gen*) to injure, hurt; (*con arma*) to wound **2** (= *ofender*) to hurt; **me hirió en lo más hondo** it really hurt me deep down **3** (= *irritar*) [*sol, luz*] to beat down on; **un sonido que hiere el oído** a sound which offends the ear

hermafrodita ADJ, SMF hermaphrodite

hermanar /1a/ VT (= *unir*) (*gen*) to unite; [+ *ciudades*] to twin (*Brit*), make sister cities (*EEUU*)

hermanastro/a SM/F (*con padre o madre común*) half brother/sister; (*sin vínculo sanguíneo*) stepbrother/stepsister

hermandad SF [*de hombres*] brotherhood, fraternity; [*de mujeres*] sisterhood

hermano/a Ⓐ ADJ [*barco*] sister *antes de s*; **ciudades hermanas** twin towns (*Brit*), sister cities (*EEUU*)
Ⓑ SM/F **1** brother/sister; **indique el número de ~s** please state number of siblings; **somos ~s de madre** we have the same mother; **medio** ~ half-brother/sister; **primo** ~ first cousin; **mis ~s** (= *sólo chicos*) my brothers; (= *chicos y chicas*) my brothers and sisters; **Gonzalo y Luis son como ~s** Gonzalo and Luis are like brothers; **Rosa y Fernando son como ~s** Rosa and Fernando are like brother and sister ➤ **hermano/a gemelo/a** twin brother/sister ➤ **hermano/a mayor** elder brother/sister, big brother/sister* ➤ **hermano/a político/a** brother-in-law/sister-in-law
2 (*Rel*) brother/sister; **hermanos** brethren
3 [*de un par*] pair; **el ~ de este calcetín** the pair for this sock
4 (*Col, Perú*) (*como apelativo*) pal, buddy

hermenéutica SF hermeneutics *sing*

hermético ADJ **1** (= *cerrado*) (*gen*) hermetic; (*al aire*) airtight; (*al agua*) watertight **2** (= *inescrutable*) [*teoría*] watertight; [*misterio*] impenetrable; [*persona*] reserved, secretive

hermetismo SM [*de teoría, misterio*] tight secrecy, close secrecy; [*de persona*] silence, reserve

hermosear /1a/ VT (*frm*) to beautify, embellish

hermoso ADJ **1** (= *bello*) beautiful, lovely; **un día** ~ a beautiful *o* lovely day **2** (= *robusto, saludable*) **¡qué niño tan ~!** what a fine-looking boy!; **seis ~s toros** six magnificent bulls **3** (= *grande*) nice and big; **la casa tiene una cocina muy hermosa** the house has a nice big kitchen **4** (= *noble*) **un ~ gesto** a noble gesture

hermosura SF **1** (= *cualidad*) beauty **2** (= *persona, cosa hermosa*) **este modelo es una** ~ this model is a beauty, this model is beautiful; **¡qué ~ de niño!** what a lovely *o* beautiful child!

hernia SF rupture, hernia ➤ **hernia discal** slipped disc

herniarse /1b/ VPR to rupture o.s.; **te vas a herniar** (*iró*) you're going to give yourself a hernia (*iró*)

héroe SM hero

heroico ADJ heroic

heroína[1] SF (= *mujer*) heroine

heroína[2] SF (= *droga*) heroin

heroinómano/a SM/F heroin addict

heroísmo SM heroism

herpes SM INV herpes

herrador SM farrier, blacksmith

herradura SF horseshoe; **camino de** ~ bridle path; **curva en** ~ hairpin bend

herraje SM ironwork, iron fittings *pl*

herramienta SF tool

herrar /1j/ VT [+ *caballo*] to shoe; [+ *ganado*] to brand

herrería SF smithy, blacksmith's, blacksmith's workshop (*EEUU*)

herrerillo SM (*Orn*) tit

herrero/a SM/F blacksmith, smith; ✦ REFRÁN **en casa del ~ (cuchillo de palo)** the shoemaker's children always go barefoot

herrete SM metal tip, ferrule

herrumbre SF rust

herrumbroso ADJ rusty

hertzio SM hertz

hervidero SM **un ~ de gente** a swarm of people

hervidor SM kettle

hervir /3i/ Ⓐ VT to boil Ⓑ VI 1 [*agua, leche*] to boil; **~ a fuego lento** to simmer; **empezar** o **romper a ~** to come to the boil, begin to boil; ✦ MODISMO **¡me hierve la sangre!** it makes my blood boil!; **hiervo en deseos de ...** I'm just itching to ... 2 **~ de** o **en** (= *estar lleno de*) to swarm with; **la cama hervía de pulgas** the bed was swarming o alive with fleas

hervor SM boiling; **dar un ~ a algo** to boil sth once

hetero* ADJ, SMF straight

heterodoxia SF heterodoxy

heterodoxo ADJ heterodox, unorthodox

heterogéneo ADJ heterogeneous

heterónimo SM heteronym

heterónomo ADJ heteronomous

heterosexual ADJ, SMF heterosexual

hexagonal ADJ hexagonal

hexágono SM hexagon

hexámetro SM hexameter

hez SF 1 **heces** (= *excrementos*) faeces, feces (*EEUU*) 2 [*de vino*] lees 3 (= *escoria*) dregs, scum

hg ABR (= **hectogramo(s)**) hg

hiato SM (*Ling*) hiatus

hibernación SF hibernation

hibernar /1a/ VI to hibernate

hibisco SM hibiscus

híbrido ADJ, SM hybrid

hice *etc ver* **hacer**

hidalgo/a SM/F nobleman/noblewoman

hidalguía SF nobility

hidrante SM (*CAm, Col*) hydrant ➤ **hidrante de incendios** (fire) hydrant

hidratación SF [*de la piel*] moisturizing

hidratante ADJ moisturizing

hidratar /1a/ VT 1 [+ *piel*] to moisturize 2 (*Quím*) to hydrate

hidrato SM hydrate ➤ **hidrato de carbono** carbohydrate

hidráulico ADJ hydraulic (*frm*), water *antes de s*

hidroavión SM seaplane, flying boat

hidrocarburo SM hydrocarbon

hidroeléctrica SF hydroelectric power station

hidroeléctrico ADJ hydroelectric; **central hidroeléctrica** hydro(electricity) station

hidrófilo ADJ absorbent; **algodón ~** cotton wool (*Brit*), absorbent cotton (*EEUU*)

hidrofobia SF hydrophobia (*frm*), rabies

hidrofóbico ADJ, **hidrófobo** ADJ hydrophobic

hidrofoil SM hydrofoil

hidrógeno SM hydrogen

hidrológico ADJ water *antes de s*; **recursos ~s** water resources

hidromasaje SM hydromassage

hidrosoluble ADJ soluble in water, water-soluble

hidroterapia SF hydrotherapy

hiedra SF ivy

hiel SF 1 (*Anat*) gall, bile; ✦ MODISMO **echar la ~*** to sweat blood*, work one's tail off* 2 (= *amargura*) bitterness 3 **hieles** (= *adversidades*) troubles, upsets

hiela *ver* **helar**

hielo SM ice; ✦ MODISMOS **hacer el ~ a algn** (*Chi, Perú*) to give sb the cold shoulder; **romper el ~** to break the ice

➤ **hielo frappé** (*Méx*), **hielo picado** crushed ice

hiena SF hyena

hierático ADJ (*frm*) [*figura, postura*] hieratic, hieratical; [*aspecto*] stern, severe

hierba SF 1 (= *pasto*) grass; **mala ~** weed; ✦ MODISMO **y otras ~s** and so forth, and suchlike; ✦ REFRÁN **mala ~ nunca muere** it's a case of the proverbial bad penny ➤ **hierba artificial** artificial playing surface, Astroturf® 2 (*Med, Culin*) herb, medicinal plant; **infusión de ~s** herbal tea; **a las finas ~s** cooked with herbs 3 (*) (= *droga*) grass*, pot*

hierbabuena SF mint

hierbajo SM weed

hierbatero/a SM/F (*Chi*), **hierbero/a** SM/F (*Méx*) herbalist

hierro SM 1 (= *metal*) iron; **de ~** iron *antes de s*; ✦ MODISMO **quitar ~ a algo** to play sth down ➤ **hierro colado** cast iron ➤ **hierro forjado** wrought iron ➤ **hierro fundido** cast iron 2 (= *objeto*) iron object; [*de flecha, lanza*] head; ✦ REFRÁN **quien a ~ mata, a ~ muere** those that live by the sword die by the sword 3 (*Golf*) iron; **hierros** irons

hígado SM (*Anat*) liver; ✦ MODISMOS **castigar el ~*** to knock it back*; **echar los ~s*** to sweat one's guts out*; **ser un ~** (*CAm, Méx**) to be a pain in the neck*; **tener (mucho) ~** (*Col, Méx, Ven**) to have (a lot of) guts*

higiene SF hygiene

higiénico ADJ hygienic

higienizar /1f/ VT to clean, cleanse

higo SM fig; ✦ MODISMOS **de ~s a brevas** once in a blue moon; **estar hecho un ~*** to be all crumpled up; **(no) me importa un ~*** I couldn't care less ➤ **higo chumbo** prickly pear ➤ **higo seco** dried fig

higuera SF fig tree; ✦ MODISMOS **caer de una ~** to come down to earth with a bump; **estar en la ~** to be daydreaming, be up in the clouds

hijadeputa*** SF, **hijaputa***** SF bitch**

hijastro/a SM/F stepson/stepdaughter

hijo/a SM/F 1 son/daughter; **una pareja sin ~s** a childless couple; **¿cuántos ~s tiene Amelia?** how many children does Amelia have?; **Pedro Gutiérrez, ~** Pedro Gutiérrez Junior; **ser ~ único** to be an only child; **el Hijo de Dios** the Son of God; ✦ MODISMOS **cada o todo ~ de vecino** any Tom, Dick or Harry*; **como todo ~ de vecino** like everyone else, like the next man; **~ de tigre sale pintado** (*LAm*) like father, like son ➤ **hijo/a adoptivo/a** adopted child ➤ **hijo/a de la chingada** (*Méx****) (= *hombre*) bastard***, son of a bitch***; (= *mujer*) bitch**, cow** ➤ **hijo/a de papá** rich kid* ➤ **hijo/a de puta***** (= *hombre*) bastard***, son of a bitch***; (= *mujer*) bitch**, cow** ➤ **hijo/a natural** illegitimate child ➤ **hijo/a político/a** son-in-law/daughter-in-law ➤ **hijo pródigo** prodigal son

2 (*uso vocativo*) **¡~ de mi alma!** my precious child!; **¡ay ~, qué pesado eres!** you're such a pain!; **¡hijo(s)!** ◇ **¡híjole!** (*Méx**) Christ!**, good God!*

hijodeputa*** SM, **hijoputa***** SM bastard***, son of a bitch***

hijuela SF (*And, CS*) plot of land

hijuelo SM shoot

hilacha SF loose thread; ✦ MODISMOS **mostrar la ~** (*CS*) to show o.s. in one's true colours o (*EEUU*) colors; **dar vuelo a la ~** (*Méx**) to let one's hair down*

hilachento ADJ (*LAm*) 1 (= *persona*) ragged 2 [*ropa*] (= *deshilachado*) frayed; (= *raído*) shabby

hilacho SM (*Méx*) rag

hilachudo ADJ (*Méx, Chi*) = **hilachento**

hilado SM 1 (= *acto*) spinning 2 (= *hilo*) thread, yarn

hilar /1a/ VT to spin; ✦ MODISMO **~ fino** to split hairs

hilarante ADJ hilarious

hilaridad SF hilarity

hilazón SF connection

hilera SF 1 (= *fila*) (*gen*) row, line; (*Mil*) rank, file; (*Arquit*) course; (*Agr*) row, drill 2 (*Cos*) fine thread

hilo SM 1 (*Cos*) thread, yarn; ✦ MODISMO **al ~** (*LAm**) in a row, running; **mover los ~s** to pull strings; **pender de un ~** to hang by a thread ➤ **hilo de bramante** twine ➤ **hilo dental** dental floss ➤ **hilo de zurcir** darning wool **2** (= *cable*) ➤ **hilo directo** direct line, hot line ➤ **hilo musical** piped music **3** (= *chorro*) [*de líquido*] thin stream, trickle; **decir algo con un ~ de voz** to say sth in a thin *o* barely audible voice **4** (*Bot*) fibre, fiber (*EEUU*), filament **5** (= *lino*) linen; **traje de ~** linen suit **6** (= *curso*) [*de conversación*] thread; [*de pensamientos*] train; **el ~ conductor** the theme *o* leitmotiv; **coger el ~** to pick up the thread; **perder el ~** to lose the thread; **seguir el ~** [*de razonamiento*] to follow, understand ➤ **hilo argumental** story line, plot

hilván SM tacking (*Brit*), basting (*EEUU*)

hilvanar /1a/ VT **1** (*Cos*) to tack (*Brit*), baste (*EEUU*) **2** (= *preparar*) [+ *trabajo, discurso*] to cobble together; **bien hilvanado** well put together, well constructed

Himalaya SM **el ~** the Himalayas

himalayo ADJ Himalayan

himen SM hymen, maidenhead (*liter*)

himno SM hymn ➤ **himno nacional** national anthem

hincada SF **1** (*Col, Perú*) (= *dolor*) sharp pain, stabbing pain **2** (*Ven*) (= *herida*) stab wound

hincapié SM **hacer ~ en** to emphasize, stress

hincar /1g/ **Ⓐ** VT (= *meter*) [+ *objeto punzante*] to thrust, drive (**en** into); ✦ MODISMO **~la** (*Esp**) to work one's tail off* **Ⓑ hincarse** VPR **~se de rodillas** (*esp LAm*) to kneel, kneel down

hincha¹ SF **tener ~ a algn** to have a grudge against sb

hincha² SMF (*Dep*) fan, supporter

hinchable ADJ inflatable

hinchada SF supporters *pl*, fans *pl*

hinchado ADJ **1** (= *inflamado*) swollen **2** [*estilo*] pompous, high-flown

hinchador* ADJ (*CS*) (= *molesto*) annoying, tiresome

hinchar /1a/ **Ⓐ** VT **1** [+ *vientre*] to distend, enlarge; (*Esp*) [+ *globo*] to blow up, inflate, pump up **2** (*Esp*) (= *exagerar*) to exaggerate **3** (*CS**) (= *molestar*) to annoy, upset **Ⓑ** VI (*CS*) **1** (*) (= *molestar*) to be annoying **2** **~ por algn** (= *animar*) to cheer on, root for **Ⓒ hincharse** VPR **1** (= *inflamarse*) [*herida, tobillo*] to swell, swell up; [*vientre*] to get distended (*frm*), get bloated **2** (*Esp*) (= *hartarse*) **~se de** [+ *comida*] to stuff o.s. with*; **me hinché de agua** I drank gallons *o* tons of water*; **~se a correr** to run like mad; **~se a reír** to have a good laugh **3** (= *engreírse*) to get conceited, become vain, get swollen-headed

hinchazón SF swelling

hindú ADJ, SMF **1** (*Rel*) Hindu **2** (= *de la India*) Indian

hinduismo SM Hinduism

hinojo¹ SM (*Bot, Culin*) fennel

hinojo² †† SM **de ~s** on bended knee

hip EXCL hic

hipar /1a/ VI to hiccup, hiccough

hiper* SM INV hypermarket

hiperactivo ADJ hyperactive

hipérbaton SM (*pl* **hipérbatos**) hyperbaton

hipérbole SF hyperbole

hiperbólico ADJ hyperbolic (*frm*), hyperbolical (*frm*), exaggerated

hiperenlace SM (*Internet*) hyperlink

hipermercado SM hypermarket

hipermetropía SF long-sightedness (*Brit*), far-sightedness (*EEUU*); **tener ~** to be long-sighted (*Brit*) *o* far-sighted (*EEUU*)

hiperrealismo SM hyper-realism

hipersensible ADJ hypersensitive, over-sensitive, touchy

hipertensión SF hypertension, high blood pressure

hipertenso ADJ **ser ~** to have high blood pressure

hipertexto SM hypertext

hipertrofia SF hypertrophy

hipervínculo SM hyperlink

hípico ADJ horse *antes de s*, equine (*frm*); **club ~** riding club

hipnosis SF INV hypnosis

hipnótico ADJ, SM hypnotic

hipnotizador(a) **Ⓐ** ADJ hypnotizing **Ⓑ** SM/F hypnotist

hipnotizar /1f/ VT **1** (*Psic*) to hypnotize **2** (= *hechizar*) to mesmerize

hipo SM hiccups *pl*, hiccoughs *pl*; **quitar el ~ a algn** to cure sb's hiccups; **tener ~** to have hiccups; ✦ MODISMO **que quita el ~** breathtaking

hipoalergénico ADJ hypoallergenic

hipocondriaco/a, hipocondríaco/a **Ⓐ** ADJ hypochondriac, hypochondriacal **Ⓑ** SM/F hypochondriac

hipocrático ADJ **juramento ~** Hippocratic oath

hipocresía SF hypocrisy

hipócrita **Ⓐ** ADJ hypocritical **Ⓑ** SMF hypocrite

hipodérmico ADJ hypodermic

hipódromo SM racecourse, racetrack

hipoglucemia SF hypoglycaemia, hypoglycemia (*EEUU*)

hipopótamo SM hippopotamus, hippo

hipoteca SF mortgage

hipotecar /1g/ VT [+ *propiedades*] to mortgage; [+ *futuro*] to jeopardize

hipotecario ADJ mortgage *antes de s*

hipotensión SF low blood pressure

hipotenso ADJ **ser ~** to have low blood pressure

hipotenusa SF hypotenuse

hipotermia SF hypothermia

hipótesis SF INV hypothesis

hipotético ADJ hypothetic, hypothetical

hipotetizar /1f/ VI to hypothesize

hippie ['xipi] ADJ, SMF, **hippy** ['xipi] ADJ, SMF (*pl* **~s**) hippy

hiriente ADJ **1** [*observación, tono*] wounding, cutting **2** [*contraste*] striking

hirsuto ADJ [*persona*] hairy, hirsute (*frm*); [*barba*] bristly

hirviendo *ver* **hervir**

hisopo SM **1** (*Bot*) hyssop **2** (*RPl*) [*de algodón*] cotton bud (*Brit*), Q-tip® (*EEUU*)

hispalense ADJ (*Esp liter*) of/from Sevilla

hispánico ADJ Hispanic (*frm*), Spanish

hispanidad SF Spanish world, Hispanic world (*frm*); **Día de la Hispanidad** Columbus Day (*October 12*)

DÍA DE LA HISPANIDAD

El Día de la Hispanidad, on October 12, is a national holiday in Spain in honour of Columbus's arrival in the Americas. It is also a holiday in other Spanish-speaking countries where it is called the **Día de la Raza**.

---

hispanismo SM **1** (= *palabra, expresión*) word etc borrowed from Spanish, hispanicism (*frm*) **2** (*Univ*) Hispanism, Hispanic studies *pl*; **el ~ holandés** Hispanic studies in Holland

hispanista SMF hispanist, hispanicist

hispanística SF Hispanic studies *pl*

hispano/a **Ⓐ** ADJ **1** (= *español*) Spanish, Hispanic (*frm*) **2** (= *latinoamericano*) Hispanic **Ⓑ** SM/F **1** (= *español*) Spaniard **2** (= *latinoamericano*) Hispanic, Spanish-speaking American (*EEUU*)

Hispanoamérica SF Spanish America, Latin America

hispanoamericano/a ADJ, SM/F Spanish American, Latin American

hispanoárabe ADJ Hispano-Arabic

hispanohablante **Ⓐ** ADJ Spanish-speaking **Ⓑ** SMF

Spanish speaker

histamínico ADJ histamine *antes de s*

histerectomía SF hysterectomy

histeria SF hysteria ➤ **histeria colectiva** mass hysteria

histérico/a Ⓐ ADJ **1** (*Med*) hysterical **2** (= *nervioso*) **no seas tan ~** don't get so worked up; **¡me pone ~!*** it drives me crazy *o* mad!, it drives me up the wall* Ⓑ SM/F **1** (*Med*) hysteric **2** (= *nervioso*) **no hagas caso, son unos ~s** pay no attention, they're always having hysterics

historismo SM hysteria

histología SF histology

historia SF **1** [*de país, institución*] history; **es licenciado en ~** he has a degree in history, he has a history degree; **nuestros problemas ya son ~** the problems we had are history now; ✦ MODISMOS **hacer ~** to make history; **pasar a la ~:** **pasará a la ~ como la primera mujer en el espacio** she will go down in history as the first woman in space; **ya ha pasado a la ~** it is a thing of the past; **tener ~** [*objeto*] to have an interesting history; [*suceso*] to be interesting ➤ **historia clínica** medical history ➤ **historia del arte** history of art, art history ➤ **historia natural** natural history ➤ **Historia Sagrada** Biblical history **2** (= *relato*) story; **cuéntame con detalles toda la ~** tell me the whole story in detail; **ésta es la ~ de una princesita** this is the story of a little princess; **la ~ de siempre** *o* **la misma ~** the same old story; **una ~ de amor** a love story **3** (= *excusa*) (*sobre algo pasado*) excuse, story; (*sobre algo presente o futuro*) excuse; **seguro que te viene con alguna ~** she's sure to give you some excuse *o* tell you some story; **¡no me vengas con ~s** *o* **déjate de ~s!** don't give me any of your stories!; **dijo que llegaba tarde por no sé qué ~** he said he was going to be late for some reason or other **4** (= *chisme*) story; **¿quién te ha contado esa ~?** who told you that story *o* that piece of gossip?; **tu amiga siempre viene con ~s** your friend is always gossiping **5** (*) (= *lío*) business*; **andan metidos en una ~ un poco rara** they're mixed up in a pretty strange business* **6** (*) (= *romance*) fling*

> **Historia** se traduce por **history** cuando hace referencia a los sucesos históricos y a su estudio: "libros de historia", *history books*. Se traduce por **story** cuando se trata de ficción, de un relato: "El libro cuenta la historia de dos niños", *The book tells the story of two children*.

historiado ADJ over-elaborate, fussy

historiador(a) SM/F historian

historial Ⓐ ADJ historical Ⓑ SM **1** (= *currículo*) curriculum vitae, CV (*esp Brit*), résumé (*EEUU*) **2** (*Med*) case history

histórico ADJ **1** [*hecho, novela, perspectiva*] historical; **el centro** *o* **casco ~ de la ciudad** the historic city centre *o* (*EEUU*) center; **el patrimonio ~ del país** the country's heritage **2** (= *importante*) [*momento, acontecimiento*] historic; [*récord*] all-time; **el dólar marcó un nuevo mínimo ~ frente al yen** the dollar hit an all-time low against the yen **3** [*miembro, socio*] (*de hace tiempo*) long-serving; (*desde el principio*) founder *antes de s*

> **Histórico** se traduce por **historical** cuando se refiere a algo perteneciente a la historia, o al hablar de una novela o película en la que se narran hechos históricos: "un personaje histórico", *a historical figure*. Se traduce por **historic** al referirse a hechos o lugares que se consideran decisivos desde el punto de vista histórico: "una ciudad histórica", *a historic city*.

historieta SF strip cartoon, comic strip

historiografía SF historiography (*frm*), writing of history

histriónico ADJ histrionic

hitita ADJ, SMF (*Hist*) Hittite

hito SM **1** (= *acontecimiento*) landmark, milestone **2** (= *señal*) milestone; ✦ MODISMO **mirar a algn de ~ en ~** to stare at sb

hizo *ver* **hacer**

hl ABR (= **hectolitro(s)**) hl

hm ABR (= **hectómetro(s)**) hm

Hna(s). ABR (= **Hermana(s)**) Sr(s).

Hno(s). ABR (= **Hermano(s)**) Bro(s).

hobby ['xobi] SM (*pl* ~**s**) hobby

hocico SM **1** [*de animal*] snout, nose **2** (*) [*de persona*] (= *cara*) mug*; (= *nariz*) snout*; ✦ MODISMOS **estar de ~s** (*Esp*) to be in a bad mood; **irse de ~** (*Chi, Méx*) to fall flat on one's face*; **meter el ~** to meddle, stick one's nose in; **poner ~** to scowl; **torcer el ~** to make a (wry) face

hocicón/ona* (*CS, Méx*) ADJ Ⓐ ADJ gossipy* Ⓑ SM/F gossip

hockey ['oki, 'xoki] SM hockey (*Brit*), field hockey (*EEUU*) ➤ **hockey sobre hielo** ice hockey (*esp Brit*), hockey (*EEUU*) ➤ **hockey sobre hierba** hockey (*Brit*), field hockey (*EEUU*) ➤ **hockey sobre patines** roller hockey

hogar SM **1** (= *casa*) home; **artículos de ~ o para el ~** household goods; **se han quedado sin ~** they have become homeless ➤ **hogar conyugal** conjugal home ➤ **hogar de acogida** (*para huérfanos, refugiados*) home ➤ **hogar de ancianos** old folk's home, old people's home ➤ **hogar del pensionista** senior citizens' social club **2** (= *chimenea*) hearth (*liter*); **se sentaron al calor del ~** they sat around the fire

hogareño ADJ [*ambiente*] homely (*esp Brit*), homey (*EEUU*); [*persona*] home-loving

hogaza SF large loaf

hoguera SF **1** (= *fogata*) bonfire; ⊃ *SAN JUAN* **2** (*Hist*) stake; **murió en la ~** he was burned at the stake

hoja SF **1** [*de árbol, planta*] leaf; [*de hierba*] blade ➤ **hoja de parra** fig leaf **2** [*de papel*] leaf, sheet; (= *página*) page; (= *formulario*) form, document ➤ **hoja de cálculo** spreadsheet ➤ **hoja de servicio(s)** record (of service) ➤ **hoja de vida** (*Col, Ven*) curriculum vitae, CV (*esp Brit*), résumé (*EEUU*) ➤ **hoja electrónica** spreadsheet ➤ **hoja informativa** leaflet, handout ➤ **hoja parroquial** parish magazine **3** [*de metal*] sheet; [*de espada, patín*] blade ➤ **hoja de afeitar** razor blade **4** [*de puerta*] leaf; [*de cristal*] sheet, pane

hojalata SF tin, tinplate

hojalatería SF (*Méx*) panel beating (*Brit*), body work (*EEUU*)

hojalatero/a SM/F **1** (*que trabaja con hojalata*) tinsmith **2** (*Méx*) (*que trabaja con carrocerías*) panel beater (*Brit*), body shop worker (*EEUU*)

hojaldre SM puff pastry

hojarasca SF **1** (= *hojas*) dead leaves *pl*, fallen leaves *pl* **2** (*al hablar*) empty verbiage, waffle (*Brit**), yack (*EEUU**)

hojear /1a/ VT to leaf through

hojilla SF (*Ven*) (*tb* **~ de afeitar**) razor blade

hojuela SF (*Col, Méx, Perú, Ven*) flake ➤ **hojuelas de maíz** cornflakes

hola EXCL hello!, hi!*; (*RPl*) (*al contestar el teléfono*) hello?

holá EXCL (*RPl*) hello?

holán SM (*Méx*) (= *volante*) flounce, frill

Holanda SF Holland

holandés/esa Ⓐ ADJ Dutch, of/from Holland Ⓑ SM/F native/inhabitant of Holland Ⓒ SM (*Ling*) Dutch

holding ['xoldin] SM (*pl* ~**s** ['xoldin]) holding company

holgadamente ADV comfortably

holgado ADJ **1** [*ropa*] loose, baggy **2** (*económicamente*) comfortably off, well-to-do; **vida holgada** comfortable life, life of ease **3** **consiguieron una victoria holgada** they won easily *o* comfortably

holgar /1h, 1l/ VI **huelga decir que ...** it goes without saying that ...; **huelga toda protesta** no protest is necessary, it is not necessary to protest

holgazán/ana Ⓐ ADJ idle, lazy Ⓑ SM/F idler, loafer

holgazanear /1a/ VI to laze around, loaf around

holgazanería SF laziness, loafing

holgura SF **1** (= *anchura*) looseness, fullness **2** (= *bienestar*) comfortable living; **vivir con ~** to live comfortably

hollar /1l/ VT (*frm*) to tread, tread on

hollejo SM skin, peel

hollín SM soot

holocausto SM 1 (*Hist*) **el Holocausto** the Holocaust 2 (= *desastre*) holocaust 3 (= *sacrificio*) burnt offering, sacrifice

holograma SM hologram

hombre Ⓐ SM (= *varón adulto*) man; (= *especie humana*) mankind, humankind; **¡ven aquí si eres ~!** come over here if you're a real man!; **es ~ de pocas palabras** he is a man of few words; **creerse muy ~: se cree muy ~** he thinks he's a real tough guy; **el ~ fuerte del partido** the strong man of the party; ✦ MODISMOS **como un solo ~** [*contestar*] with one voice; **hablar de ~ a ~** to talk man to man; **ser un ~ de pelo en pecho** to be a real man, be a he-man; **ser un ~ hecho y derecho** to be a grown man; **si lo compras, me haces un ~*** if you buy it, you'll be doing me a real good turn ➤ **hombre de confianza** right-hand man ➤ **hombre de estado** statesman ➤ **hombre de la calle** man in the street ➤ **hombre del saco** bogeyman ➤ **hombre del tiempo** weatherman ➤ **hombre de mundo** man of the world ➤ **hombre de negocios** businessman ➤ **hombre de paja** stooge* ➤ **hombre lobo** werewolf ➤ **hombre orquesta** one-man band
Ⓑ EXCL **—¿me haces un favor? —sí, ~** "would you do something for me?" — "(yes) of course"; **—¿vendrás? —¡~ claro!** "are you coming?" — "you bet!"; **¡venga, ~, haz un esfuerzo!** come on, make an effort!; **¡~, no me vengas con eso!** oh please *o* oh come on, don't give me that!; **~, yo creo que ...** well, I think that ...; **¡~, Pedro! ¿qué tal?** hey, Pedro! how's it going?; **¡vaya, ~, qué mala suerte has tenido!** dear oh dear, what terrible luck!

hombre-anuncio SM (*pl* **hombres-anuncio**) sandwich-board man

hombre-mono SM (*pl* **hombres-mono**) apeman

hombrera SF (= *almohadilla*) shoulder pad; (*Mil*) epaulette

hombre-rana SM (*pl* **hombres-rana**) frogman

hombrerío SM (*Ven*) men *pl*

hombría SF manliness

hombrillo SM (*Carib Aut*) hard shoulder (*Brit*), shoulder (*esp EEUU*), berm (*EEUU*)

hombro SM shoulder; **a ~s** on one's shoulders; **cargar algo sobre los ~s** to shoulder sth; **en ~s: sacar a algn en ~s** to carry sb out on one's shoulders; **el vencedor salió en ~s** the victor was carried out shoulder-high; ✦ MODISMOS **arrimar el ~** to put one's shoulder to the wheel, lend a hand; **~ con ~** shoulder to shoulder; **mirar a algn por encima del ~** to look down on sb, look down one's nose at sb

hombruno ADJ mannish, butch*

homenaje Ⓐ SM (= *tributo*) tribute; **en ~ a algn** in honour *o* (*EEUU*) honor of sb Ⓑ ADJ **una cena-~ para don Manuel** a dinner in honour *o* (*EEUU*) honor of don Manuel; **partido-~** benefit match, testimonial game

homenajear /1a/ VT to honour, honor (*EEUU*), pay tribute to

homeópata SMF homeopath

homeopatía SF homeopathy

homeopático ADJ homeopathic

homicida Ⓐ ADJ homicidal; **el arma ~** the murder weapon Ⓑ SMF murderer/murderess

homicidio SM (= *intencionado*) murder, homicide (*frm*); (= *involuntario*) manslaughter ➤ **homicidio frustrado** attempted murder

homilía SF homily

homofobia SF homophobia

homogeneizar /1f/ VT to homogenize, level down, equalize

homogéneo ADJ homogeneous

homógrafo SM homograph

homologación SF 1 (= *aprobación*) official approval 2 (= *equiparación*) **le han denegado la ~ del título** they refused to recognize her qualification as equivalent

3 (*Dep*) ratification, recognition

homologar /1h/ VT 1 (= *aprobar*) to approve officially, sanction 2 (= *equiparar*) to bring into line, standardize 3 (*Dep*) [+ *récord*] to ratify, recognize

homólogo/a Ⓐ ADJ equivalent (**de** to) Ⓑ SM/F counterpart, opposite number

homónimo Ⓐ ADJ homonymous Ⓑ SM 1 (*Ling*) homonym 2 (= *tocayo*) namesake

homosexual ADJ, SMF homosexual

homosexualidad SF homosexuality

honda SF [*de cuero*] sling; (*elástica*) catapult (*Brit*), slingshot (*EEUU*)

hondear¹ /1a/ VT (*Náut*) (= *sondear*) to sound; (= *descargar*) to unload

hondear² /1a/ VT (*LAm*) to hit with a catapult (*Brit*) *o* slingshot (*EEUU*)

hondo Ⓐ ADJ 1 (= *profundo*) deep; **en lo más ~ de la piscina** at the deep end (of the pool); **la hirió en lo más ~ de su ser** he wounded her to the depths of her being, she was cut to the quick 2 (= *intenso*) [*pesar*] deep, profound Ⓑ ADV [*respirar*] deeply

hondonada SF hollow, dip

hondura SF depth, profundity (*frm*); ✦ MODISMO **meterse en ~s** to get out of one's depth, get into deep water

Honduras SF Honduras

hondureño/a Ⓐ ADJ of/from Honduras Ⓑ SM/F native/inhabitant of Honduras

honestamente ADV 1 (= *sinceramente*) honestly 2 (= *honradamente*) honourably, honorably (*EEUU*)

honestidad SF 1 (= *sinceridad*) honesty 2 (= *honradez*) honour, honor (*EEUU*)

honesto ADJ 1 (= *sincero*) honest; **sé ~ y dime lo que piensas** be honest and tell me what you think 2 (= *honrado*) honourable, honorable (*EEUU*); **hay pocos políticos ~s** there are very few honourable *o* (*EEUU*) honorable politicians

hongo SM 1 (*Bot*) fungus 2 (= *seta*) (*comestible*) mushroom; (*venenoso*) toadstool; **un enorme ~ de humo** an enormous mushroom cloud of smoke; ✦ MODISMO **crecen** *o* **proliferan como ~s** they sprout up like mushrooms 3 (*Med*) fungal growth; **tengo ~s en los pies** I have athlete's foot, I have a fungal growth on my feet

honor SM

En inglés americano se usa **honor** en lugar de **honour**.

1 (= *cualidad*) honour; **en ~ a la verdad** to be fair; **en ~ de algn** in sb's honour; **hacer ~ a su fama** to live up to it's *etc* reputation ➤ **honor profesional** professional etiquette 2 **honores** honours; **hacer los ~es de la casa** to do the honours of the house; **hacer los debidos ~es a una comida** to do full justice to a meal 3 [*de mujer*] honour, virtue

honorable ADJ honourable, honorable (*EEUU*), worthy

honorario Ⓐ ADJ honorary, honorific Ⓑ **honorarios** SMPL fees, professional fees, charges

honorífico ADJ [*cargo*] honorary; [*mención*] honourable, honorable (*EEUU*)

honra SF

En inglés americano se usa **honor** en lugar de **honour**.

1 (= *orgullo*) honour, pride; **tener a mucha ~ hacer algo** to be proud to do sth, consider it an honour to do sth; **¡y a mucha ~!** and proud of it! ➤ **honra personal** personal honour 2 (†) (= *virginidad*) honour, virtue 3 ➤ **honras fúnebres** funeral rites, last honours

honradez SF 1 (= *honestidad*) honesty 2 (= *integridad*) uprightness, integrity, honourableness (*frm*)

honrado ADJ 1 (= *honesto*) honest 2 (= *honorable*) honourable, honorable (*EEUU*), upright

honrar /1a/ **Ⓐ** VT

En inglés americano se usa **honor** en lugar de **honour**.

1 (= *enorgullecer*) to honour; **un gesto que le honra** a gesture to be proud of **2** (= *respetar*) to honour **Ⓑ honrarse** VPR **~se con algo** to be honoured by sth

honroso ADJ **1** (= *honorable*) honourable, honorable (*EEUU*) **2** (= *respetable*) respectable; **es una profesión honrosa** it is a respectable profession

hora SF **1** (= *periodo de tiempo*) hour; **10 euros la ~** 10 euros an hour; **echar ~s** to put the hours in; **media ~** half an hour; **trabajar por ~s** to work on an hourly basis *o* by the hour ➤ **horas de comercio** business hours ➤ **horas de consulta** opening hours ➤ **horas de mayor audiencia** (*TV*) prime time *sing* ➤ **horas de oficina** business hours, office hours ➤ **horas de visita** visiting hours ➤ **horas de vuelo** (*Aer*) flying time *sing*; (= *experiencia*) experience *sing*; (= *antigüedad*) seniority *sing* ➤ **horas extra, horas extraordinarias** overtime *sing*; **hacer ~s (extra)** to work overtime ➤ **horas libres** free time *sing*, spare time *sing* ➤ **horas muertas** dead period *sing*; **se pasa las ~s muertas viendo la tele** he spends hour after hour watching TV **2** (= *momento*) **2.1** (*concreto*) time; **¿qué ~ es?** what time is it?, what's the time?; **¿tienes ~?** have you got the time?; **¿a qué ~ llega?** what time is he arriving?; **¡la ~!** ◊ **¡es la ~!** time's up!; **llegar a la ~** to arrive on time; **a la ~ en punto** on the dot; **a la ~ justa** in the nick of time; **a la ~ de pagar ...** when it comes to paying ...; **a altas ~s (de la madrugada)** in the small hours, at a late hour; **dar la ~** [*reloj*] to strike (the hour); **poner el reloj en ~** to set one's watch; **no comer entre ~s** not to eat between meals; **a estas ~s:** **a estas ~s ya deben de estar en París** they must be in Paris by now; **ayer a estas ~s** at this time yesterday **2.2** (*oportuno*) **buena ~: es buena ~ para empezar** it's a good time to start; **llegas a buena ~** you've arrived just in time; **es ~ de hacer algo** it is time to do sth; **es ~ de irnos** it's time we went, it's time for us to go; **éstas no son ~s de llegar a casa** what sort of a time is this to get home?; **le ha llegado la ~** her time has come; **mala ~: es mala ~** it's a bad time; **en mala ~ se lo dije** I shouldn't have told her; **en la ~ de su muerte** at the moment of his death; **a primera ~** first thing in the morning; **a última ~** at the last moment, at the last minute; **dejar las cosas hasta última ~** to leave things until the last moment *o* minute; **cambios de última ~** last-minute changes; **"última hora"** (*noticias*) "late news", "stop press (*Brit*)"; **la ~ de la verdad** the moment of truth; **¡ya era ~!** and about time too!; **ya es *o* va siendo ~ de que te vayas** it's high time (that) you went, it's about time (that) you went; ◆ MODISMOS **¡a buena(s) ~(s) (mangas verdes)!** it's too late now!; **¡a buenas ~s llegas!** this is a fine time for you to arrive!; **no ver la ~ de algo** to be hardly able to wait for sth, look forward impatiently to sth ➤ **hora cero** zero hour ➤ **hora de cenar** dinnertime ➤ **hora de comer** (*gen*) mealtime; (*a mediodía*) lunchtime ➤ **hora de entrada: la ~ de entrada a la oficina** the time when we start work at the office ➤ **hora de los brujas** witching hour ➤ **hora de recreo** playtime, recess (*EEUU*) ➤ **hora de salida** [*de tren, avión, autobús*] time of departure; [*de carrera*] starting time; [*de trabajo*] finishing time (*Brit*), quitting time (*EEUU*); [*de escuela*] finishing time (*Brit*), last hour (*EEUU*) ➤ **hora insular canaria** *local time in the Canary Islands* ➤ **hora local** local time ➤ **hora peninsular** *local time in mainland Spain* ➤ **hora pico** (*LAm*) rush hour ➤ **hora punta** (*RPl*) hour off ➤ **hora punta** (*Esp*) [*del tráfico*] rush hour ➤ **horas punta** (*Esp*) [*de electricidad, teléfono*] peak hours ➤ **horas valle** (*Esp*) off-peak times **3** (*Educ*) period; **después de inglés tenemos una ~ libre** after English we have a free period ➤ **horas de clase** (*lectivas*) teaching hours; [*de colegio*] school hours ➤ **horas lectivas** teaching hours **4** (= *cita*) appointment; **pedir ~** to ask for an appointment; **tengo ~ para el dentista** I have an appointment at the dentist's

horadar /1a/ VT (= *perforar*) drill, perforate (*frm*); [+ *túnel*] to make

horario Ⓐ SM **1** [*de trabajo, trenes*] timetable; **"horario de invierno: abierto solo mañanas"** "winter hours: open mornings only" ➤ **horario corrido** (*LAm*) continuous working day ➤ **horario de atención al público** public opening hours *pl* ➤ **horario de máxima audiencia** (*TV*) peak viewing time, prime time ➤ **horario de oficina** office hours *pl* ➤ **horario de visitas** [*de hospital*] visiting hours *pl*; [*de médico*] surgery hours *pl* (*Brit*), (doctor's) office hours *pl* (*EEUU*) ➤ **horario estelar** (*Ven TV*) peak viewing time, prime time ➤ **horario intensivo** continuous working day ➤ **horario partido** split shift(s), *working day with long afternoon break* **2** [*de reloj*] hour hand **Ⓑ** ADJ hourly

horca SF **1** [*de ejecución*] gallows **2** (*Agr*) pitchfork

horcajadas SFPL **a ~** astride

horchata SF [*tb* **~ de chufas**] tiger nut milk

horcón SM (*LAm*) (*para frutales*) forked prop; (*para techo*) prop, support

horda SF horde

horizontal Ⓐ ADJ horizontal **Ⓑ** SF horizontal; ◆ MODISMO **coger *o* tomar la ~*** to crash out* **Ⓒ** SM (*And Dep*) lintel

horizonte SM **1** (= *línea*) horizon; **la línea del ~** the horizon; **en el ~ del año 2000** around the year 2000 **2 horizontes** (= *perspectivas*) **este descubrimiento abrirá nuevos ~s** this discovery will open up new horizons

horma SF (*para hacer zapatos*) last; (*para mantener la forma*) shoetree; ◆ MODISMO **encontrar(se) con la ~ de su zapato** to meet one's match

hormiga SF ant; ◆ MODISMO **ponerse color de ~** (*LAm*) to start to look grim ➤ **hormiga obrera** worker ant ➤ **hormiga roja** red ant

hormigón SM concrete ➤ **hormigón armado** reinforced concrete

hormigonera SF concrete mixer

hormigueo SM (*al quedarse insensible*) tingling; (= *cosquilleo*) pins and needles

hormiguero Ⓐ ADJ *ver* **oso Ⓑ** SM **1** [*de hormigas*] ants' nest, ant hill **2** [*de gente*] **aquello era un ~** it was swarming with people

hormiguillo SM (*Esp*) = **hormigueo**

hormiguita* SF **ser una ~** (= *muy trabajador*) to be hard-working, be always beavering away; (= *ahorrativo*) to be thrifty

hormona SF hormone

hormonal ADJ hormonal

hornacina SF niche, vaulted niche

hornada SF **1** [*de pan*] batch **2** [*de estudiantes, políticos*] collection, crop

hornalla SF (*RPl*) ring

hornazo SM Easter pie (*decorated with eggs*)

horneado SM cooking (time), baking (time)

hornear /1a/ VT to bake

hornero/a SM/F baker

hornillo SM (*portátil*) portable stove; (*para cocina*) ring

horno SM **1** (*Culin*) oven, stove; **¡esta casa es un ~!** it's like an oven in here!; **al ~** [*pescado*] baked; **resistente al ~** ovenproof; ◆ MODISMO **no está el ~ para bollos** this is the wrong moment ➤ **horno de leña** wood-fired oven ➤ **horno microondas** microwave oven **2** (*Téc*) furnace; (*para cerámica*) kiln; **alto(s) ~(s)** blast furnace *sing* ➤ **horno crematorio** crematorium ➤ **horno de fundición** smelting furnace

horóscopo SM horoscope

horqueta SF (*Chi Agr*) pitchfork; (*LAm*) [*de camino*] fork

horquetilla SF (*Ven*) = **horquilla 4**

horquilla SF **1** (*para pelo*) hairpin **2** (*para heno*) pitchfork, garden fork **3** (*en bicicleta*) (front) forks *pl* **4** (*Ven*) **tener ~s** (*en las puntas del pelo*) to have split ends **5** (*Com*) [*de salarios*] wage levels *pl*; [*de inflación*] bracket

horrendo ADJ **1** [*crimen*] horrific **2** [*ropa, zapatos*] hideous, ghastly*; [*película, libro*] dreadful; **hace un frío** ~ it's terribly cold

hórreo SM raised granary

horrible ADJ **1** [*accidente, crimen, matanza*] horrific; **una pesadilla** ~ a horrible nightmare **2** (= *feo*) [*persona, objeto, ropa, cuadro*] hideous **3** (= *malo*) [*tiempo, letra, dolor*] terrible; **hizo un calor** ~ it was terribly hot **4** (= *perverso*) [*persona*] horrible

horripilante ADJ [*escena*] hair-raising, horrifying; [*persona*] creepy*, terrifying

horripilar /1a/ VT ~ **a algn** to make sb's hair stand on end, horrify sb

horror SM **1** (= *miedo*) horror (**a** of), dread (**a** of); **¡qué** ~! how awful *o* dreadful!, how ghastly!*; **la fiesta fue un** ~* the party was ghastly*, the party was dreadful; **se dicen ~es de la cocina inglesa*** awful things are said about English cooking; **tener algo en** ~ (*frm*) to detest sth, loathe sth **2** (= *acto*) atrocity, terrible thing; **los ~es de la guerra** the horrors of war **3** (*) (= *mucho*) **me gusta ~es** *o* **un** ~ I love it!; **me duele ~es** it's really painful, it hurts like hell*

horrorizar /1f/ ⓐ VT to horrify, terrify ⓑ **horrorizarse** VPR to be horrified, be terrified

horroroso ADJ **1** (= *aterrador*) dreadful, ghastly* **2** [*ropa, peinado*] hideous, horrific; [*dolor*] terrible; [*película, libro*] dreadful; **tengo un sueño** ~ I feel really sleepy

hortaliza SF vegetable; **hortalizas** vegetables, garden produce

hortelano/a SM/F market gardener (*Brit*), truck farmer (*EEUU*)

hortensia SF hydrangea

hortera* (*Esp*) ⓐ ADJ INV [*decoración*] tacky*, tasteless, vulgar; [*persona*] lacking in taste; [*gustos*] terrible, crude ⓑ SMF **es un** ~ his taste stinks*, he has lousy taste*

horterada* SF (*Esp*) vulgarity; **ese vestido es una** ~ that dress is a sight*

horticultor(a) SM/F horticulturist, gardener

horticultura SF horticulture, gardening

hortofrutícola ADJ fruit and vegetable *antes de s*

hosco ADJ **1** [*persona*] surly **2** [*tiempo, lugar, ambiente*] gloomy

hospedaje SM (cost of) board and lodging

hospedar /1a/ ⓐ VT to lodge, give a room to ⓑ **hospedarse** VPR to stay, lodge (**en** at)

hospicio SM **1** (*para niños*) orphanage **2** (*Hist*) (*para peregrinos, pobres*) hospice

hospital SM hospital, infirmary ➤ **hospital de campaña** field hospital ➤ **hospital de sangre** field dressing station

hospitalario ADJ **1** (= *acogedor*) hospitable **2** (*Med*) hospital *antes de s*; **estancia hospitalaria** stay in hospital; **atención hospitalaria** hospital treatment

hospitalidad SF hospitality

hospitalización SF hospitalization

hospitalizar /1f/ ⓐ VT to send to hospital *o* (*EEUU*) to the hospital, take to hospital *o* (*EEUU*) to the hospital, hospitalize (*frm*); **estuvo hospitalizado tres meses** he spent three months in hospital *o* (*EEUU*) in the hospital ⓑ **hospitalizarse** VPR (*LAm*) to go into hospital *o* (*EEUU*) into the hospital

hostal SM cheap hotel, boarding house

hostelería SF **1** (= *industria*) hotel trade, hotel business; **empresa de** ~ catering company **2** (= *gerencia*) hotel management

hostería SF **1** (= *posada*) inn, hostelry **2** (*Chi*) (= *hotel*) hotel

hostia SF **1** (*Rel*) host, consecrated wafer **2** (*Esp****) (= *golpe*) punch, bash*; (= *choque*) bang, bash*, smash; **dar de ~s a algn** to kick the shit out of sb***; **le pegué dos** ~**s** I walloped him a couple of times* **3** (*Esp****) (*como exclamación*) **¡hostia!** (*indicando sorpresa*) Christ almighty!**, bloody hell!**; (*indicando fastidio*) damn it all! **4** (*Esp****) (*como intensificador*) **de la** ~: **había un tráfico de**

la ~ the traffic was fucking awful***; **ni** ~: **no entiendo ni** ~ I don't understand a fucking word of it***; **¡qué ~(s)!** (*para negar*) fuck off!***; **¿qué ~s quieres?** what the fuck do you want?***; **¡qué libros ni qué ~s!** books, my foot!* *o* my ass!***

5 (*Esp****) **mala** ~: **estar de mala** ~ to be in a shitty mood***; **tener mala** ~ to have a nasty streak **6** (*Esp****) ✦ MODISMOS **déjate de ~s** stop fucking around***; **ir a toda** ~ to go like nobody's business*; **salió cagando** *o* **echando ~s** he shot out like a bat out of hell; **ser la** ~: **¡ese tío es la ~!** (*con admiración*) he's a hell of a guy!*; (*con enfado*) what a shit he is!***; **y toda la** ~ and all the rest

hostiar* /1b/ VT (*Esp*) to wallop*, sock*, bash*

hostigamiento SM harassment

hostigar /1h/ VT **1** (= *molestar*) to harass, plague, pester **2** (*And*) [*comida*] to be too sweet for

hostigoso ADJ (*And*) [*comida*] sickly, cloying; [*persona*] annoying, tedious

hostil ADJ hostile

hostilidad SF **1** (= *cualidad*) hostility **2 hostilidades** (*Mil*) hostilities; **iniciar las ~es** to start hostilities

hotel SM hotel

hotelería SF = **hostelería**

hotelero/a ⓐ ADJ hotel *antes de s*; **la industria hotelera** the hotel trade ⓑ SM/F hotel manager/manageress, hotelier

hoy ADV **1** (= *en este día*) today; **¿a qué día estamos** ~? what day is it today?; ~ **hace un mes de su boda** their wedding was a month ago today; **de** ~: **en las noticias de** ~ in today's news; **el día de** ~ this very day; **de** ~ **en adelante** from now on; **de** ~ **no pasa que le escriba** I'll write to him this very day; **de** ~ **en ocho días** a week today; **desde** ~ from now on; **hasta** ~: **eso me prometió, ¡y hasta** ~! that's what he promised me, and I've heard no more about it!; **por** ~: **por** ~ **hemos terminado** that's all for today; ✦ MODISMO ~ **por ti, mañana por mí** you can do the same for me some time

2 (= *en la actualidad*) today, nowadays; **la juventud de** ~ the youth of today; ~ **(en) día** nowadays; ~ **por** ~ at the present time, right now

hoya SF (*LAm*) [*de río*] riverbed, river basin

hoyanco SM (*Méx Aut*) pothole

hoyito SM (*en la cara*) dimple

hoyo SM **1** (= *agujero*) (*tb Golf*) hole ➤ **hoyo negro** (*CAm, Méx*) black hole **2** (= *tumba*) grave

hoyuelo SM dimple

hoz SF **1** (*Agr*) sickle; **la ~ y el martillo** the hammer and sickle **2** (*Geog*) gorge, narrow pass, defile (*frm*)

huaca SF = **guaca**

huacalón ADJ (*Méx*) (= *gordo*) fat

huachafo/a (*Perú*) ⓐ ADJ = **cursi** ⓑ SM/F middle-class snob, social climber

huachinango SM (*Carib, Méx*) red snapper

huacho ADJ (*And, RPl*) = **guacho** A

huaco SM (*And Hist*) ancient Peruvian pottery artefact

huaipe SM (*Chi, Perú*) cotton waste

huarache SM (*Méx*) (= *sandalia*) sandal

huaso/a SM/F (*Chi*) = **guaso 2**

huayno SM (*And, Chi*) folk song and dance; ⟳ CHICHA

hube *etc ver* **haber**

hucha SF (*Esp*) (*para ahorrar*) money box; (*para caridad*) collecting tin (*Brit*) *o* can (*EEUU*)

hueco ⓐ ADJ **1** [*árbol, tubo*] hollow; **una nuez hueca** an empty walnut shell; ✦ MODISMO **tener la cabeza hueca*** to be empty-headed **2** [*lana, tierra*] soft **3** [*sonido*] hollow; [*voz*] booming, resonant **4** [*palabras, promesas*] empty ⓑ SM **1** (= *agujero*) (*en valla, muro*) hole; **el ~ del ascensor** the lift (*Brit*) *o* elevator (*EEUU*) shaft; **el ~ de la escalera** the

stairwell; **el ~ de la puerta** the doorway
2 (= *espacio libre*) space; (*entre árboles*) gap, opening; **no hay ni un ~ para aparcar** there isn't a single parking space; **sólo hay ~s en la primera fila** the only places o spaces are in the front row; **hacer (un) ~ a algn** to make room for sb
3 (*en texto*) gap, blank
4 (*en mercado, organización*) gap; **hacerse un ~** to carve o create a niche for oneself; **llenar** u **ocupar un ~** to fill a gap
5 (= *cavidad*) hollow; **el ~ de la mano** the hollow of the o one's hand; **suena a ~** it sounds hollow
6 [*de tiempo*] **en cuanto tenga un ~** as soon as he has a gap in his schedule o as soon as he can fit you in; **hizo un ~ en su agenda para recibirlos** he made space in his schedule to see them, he managed to fit them into his schedule

huecograbado SM photogravure

huela *etc ver* **oler**

huelga SF strike; **estar en ~** to be on strike; **declarar la ~** ◇ **declararse en ~** ➤ **hacer** ~ ◇ **ir a la ~** to go on strike, come out on strike ➤ **huelga de brazos caídos** sit-down strike ➤ **huelga de celo** (*Esp*) work-to-rule (*Brit*), go-slow (*Brit*), slowdown (strike) (*EEUU*) ➤ **huelga de hambre** hunger strike ➤ **huelga general** general strike ➤ **huelga salvaje** wildcat strike

huelguista SMF striker

huelguístico ADJ strike *antes de s*

huella SF **1** (*en el suelo*) (= *pisada*) footprint, footstep; [*de coche, animal*] track; **seguir la ~s de algn** to follow in sb's footsteps ➤ **huella dactilar, huella digital** fingerprint ➤ **huella genética** genetic fingerprint
2 (= *rastro*) trace; **sin dejar ~** without leaving a trace, leaving no sign; **se le notaban las ~s del sufrimiento** you could see the signs of her suffering
3 (= *impronta*) **el presidente dejó una ~ inconfundible en el partido** the president left his unmistakable mark o stamp on the party; **aquello dejó una ~ imborrable** it left an indelible memory

huemul SM (*CS*) southern Andean deer

huérfano/a ⒶADJ **1** [*niño*] orphaned; **una niña huérfana de madre**, a child that has lost her mother **2** (= *desprovisto*) ~ **de** [+ *seguridad, protección*] devoid of; [+ *cariño, amor*] bereft of (*frm*), starved of ⒷSM/F orphan

huero ADJ **1** [*palabras, acciones*] empty, sterile **2** [*huevo*] rotten

huerta SF **1** (= *huerto*) vegetable garden (*Brit*), kitchen garden (*EEUU*) **2** (*Esp*) **la ~ murciana/valenciana** the fertile, irrigated region of Murcia/Valencia

huertero/a SM/F (*Chi*) market gardener, truck farmer (*EEUU*)

huerto SM [*de verduras*] kitchen garden; [*de árboles frutales*] orchard; (*en casa pequeña*) back garden; **el Huerto de los Olivos** (*Rel*) the Mount of Olives; ✦ MODISMO **llevarse a algn al ~*** (= *engañar*) to put one over on sb*; (*a la cama*) to go to bed with sb, sleep with sb, go for a roll in the hay with sb*

hueso SM **1** (*Anat*) bone; **sin ~** boneless; **una blusa de color ~** an off-white blouse; ✦ MODISMOS **dar con los ~s en: dio con sus ~s en la cárcel** he landed o ended up in jail; **estar calado** o **empapado hasta los ~s** to be soaked to the skin; **estar en los ~s** to be nothing but skin and bone; **no dejar ~ sano a algn** to pull sb to pieces ➤ **hueso de santo** filled roll of marzipan
2 (*Bot*) stone (*Brit*), pit (*esp EEUU*); **aceitunas sin ~** pitted olives; ✦ MODISMO **ser un ~*: su profesor es un ~** her teacher is terribly strict; **ser un ~ duro de roer** (*Esp**) to be a hard nut to crack
3 (*CAm, Méx**) (= *sinecura*) government job, sinecure; (= *puesto cómodo*) soft job

huésped SMF (*en casa, hotel*) guest; (*en pensión*) lodger, roomer (*EEUU*), boarder

huestes SFPL (*liter*) **1** (= *ejercito*) host *sing* (*liter*), army *sing*
2 (= *partidarios*) followers

huesudo ADJ bony, big-boned

hueva SF **1** (*tb* **~s**) (*Culin*) roe; (*Zool*) eggs, spawn *sing*
2 huevas (*And****) (= *testículos*) balls***

huevada*** SF (*And*) (= *comentario*) stupid remark; (= *acto*) stupid thing (to do); (= *idea*) crazy idea; **huevadas** (= *tonterías*) crap***

huevear*** /1a/ VI (*Chi, Perú*) to mess around*

huevera SF egg box

huevería SF *shop that specializes in selling eggs*

huevo SM **1** (*Biol, Culin*) egg; ✦ MODISMOS **a ~** (*Méx***) (= *a la fuerza*): **se lo tuvo que comer a ~** she damn well o (*Brit*) bloody well had to eat it**; **poner algo a ~*: nos lo han puesto a ~** they've made it easy for us; **ser como el ~ de Colón** to be simple, be easy ➤ **huevo a la copa** (*Chi*) boiled egg ➤ **huevo cocido** hard-boiled egg ➤ **huevo de corral** free-range egg ➤ **huevo de Pascua** Easter egg ➤ **huevo duro** hard-boiled egg ➤ **huevo escalfado** poached egg ➤ **huevo estrellado, huevo frito** fried egg ➤ **huevo pasado por agua** soft-boiled egg ➤ **huevos al plato** *fried eggs in tomato sauce served with ham and peas* ➤ **huevos pericos, huevos revueltos** scrambled eggs ➤ **huevo tibio** (*Col, Méx*) boiled egg
2 (***) (= *testículo*) ball***; **¡un ~!** like hell!*; **huevos** (= *valor*) balls***; ✦ MODISMOS **estar hasta los ~s de algo/ algn: estoy hasta los ~s de este niño** I've had a fucking bellyful of this kid***; **estar hasta los ~s de hacer algo: estoy hasta los ~s de estudiar** I'm fucking sick of studying***; **tuve que hacerlo por ~s** I had to do it, I had no fucking choice***
3 un ~*** (= *mucho*) a hell of a lot**; **le queremos un ~** we like him a hell of a lot**; **sufrí un ~** I suffered like hell**; **nos costó un ~ terminarlo** it was one hell of a job to finish it**; **el ordenador me costó un ~** the computer cost me an arm and a leg*

huevón/ona** Ⓐ ADJ **1** (*Méx*) (= *holgazán*) lazy, idle **2** (*And, Ven*) (= *estúpido*) stupid, thick* Ⓑ SM/F **1** (*Méx*) (= *holgazán*) lazy bastard*** **2** (*And, Ven*) (= *imbécil*) stupid idiot*, bloody fool**

huida SF **1** (= *fuga*) escape, flight (*liter*); **abandonaron muchas de sus posesiones en la ~** they abandoned many of their possessions when they fled; **el plan es una ~ hacia adelante** the plan is a bit of a leap in the dark; **emprender la ~** to take flight **2** [*de capital, inversores*] flight **3** [*de un caballo*] bolt; *ver tb* **huido**

huidizo ADJ **1** [*persona*] elusive; [*mirada*] evasive
2 [*impresión, luz*] fleeting

huido/a Ⓐ ADJ **1** [*escapado*] [*criminal*] fugitive; [*esclavo*] runaway; **los tres terroristas ~s** the three terrorists on the run, the three fugitive terrorists; **lleva más de un año ~ de la justicia** he has been a fugitive from justice o he has been on the run for over a year; **los rusos ~s del Palacio de Invierno** the Russians that had fled from the Winter Palace **2** (= *receloso*) elusive Ⓑ SM/F fugitive; *ver tb* **huida**

huila* SF **1** (*Méx*) (= *prostituta*) hooker* **2 huilas** (*Chi*) (= *andrajos*) rags

huincha SF (*And*) **1** (= *ribete*) narrow strip of cloth; (= *cinta*) ribbon; (= *para pelo*) headband **2** (= *cinta métrica*) measuring tape, tape measure **3 ¡las ~s!** forget it!

huipil SM (*CAm, Méx*) *Indian regional dress o blouse*

huir /3g/ Ⓐ VI **1** (= *escapar*) to run away, flee (*liter*); **huyó despavorido** he ran away o (*liter*) fled in terror; **huyeron en un vehículo robado** they made their getaway o (*liter*) fled in a stolen vehicle; **huyeron a Chipre** they escaped o (*liter*) fled to Cyprus; **~ de** [+ *enemigo, catástrofe, pobreza*] to flee from; [+ *cárcel, peligro*] to escape from; [+ *familia*] to run away from
2 (= *evitar*) **~ de** [+ *protagonismo, publicidad, tópicos*] to avoid; [+ *calor, frío, realidad*] to escape, escape from; **huye de los periodistas como de la peste** she avoids journalists like the plague
Ⓑ VT (= *esquivar*) to avoid
Ⓒ **huirse** VPR (*Méx*) to escape; **~se con algn** to escape with sb

huira SF (*And*) rope

huiro SM (*And*) seaweed

huitlacoche SM (*CAm, Méx*) *black fungus found on corn cobs, eaten as a delicacy in Mexico and Central America*

hule SM **1** (= *goma*) rubber **2** (= *tela*) oilskin, oilcloth;

(= *mantel*) wipeable table cloth **3** (*CAm, Méx*) (= *árbol*) rubber tree

hulera SF (*CAm*) catapult (*Brit*), slingshot (*EEUU*)

hulla SF soft coal

hullero ADJ coal *antes de s*

humanamente ADV **1** [*posible, comprensible*] humanly **2** (= *con humanidad*) humanely

humanidad SF **1** (= *género humano*) humanity, humankind, mankind **2** (= *benevolencia*) humanity, humaneness (*frm*) **3** (*) (= *gordura*) corpulence **4 humanidades** (*Educ*) humanities

humanismo SM humanism

humanista SMF humanist

humanístico ADJ humanistic

humanitario ADJ humanitarian

humanizar /1f/ **Ⓐ** VT to humanize, make more human **Ⓑ humanizarse** VPR to become more human

humano **Ⓐ** ADJ **1** [*vida, existencia, derechos*] human; ✦ REFRÁN **equivocarse es ~** to err is human **2** (= *benévolo*) humane **Ⓑ** SM human, human being

humanoide ADJ, SMF humanoid

humeante ADJ **1** [*pipa, madera*] smoking; [*mecha, restos*] smouldering, smoldering (*EEUU*); [*cañón, escopeta*] smoking **2** [*caldo, sopa*] steaming

humear /1a/ VI **1** (= *soltar humo*) [*fuego, chimenea*] to smoke, give out smoke **2** (= *soltar vapor*) to steam

humectador SM humidifier

humedad SF **1** (*en atmósfera*) humidity; **en Barcelona siempre hay mucha ~** in Barcelona it's always very humid **2** (*en pared, techo*) damp, dampness; **hay manchas de ~ en el techo** there are stains of damp on the ceiling

humedecer /2d/ **Ⓐ** VT **1** (= *mojar*) [+ *camisa, ropa*] to moisten, dampen; [+ *suelo, sello*] to wet; [+ *piel, labios*] to moisten, wet **2** [+ *ambiente*] to humidify **Ⓑ humedecerse** VPR to get damp, get wet; **se le humedecieron los ojos** his eyes filled with tears, tears came into his eyes

húmedo ADJ [*clima*] damp; [*calor*] humid; [*ropa, pared*] damp; [*pelo*] damp, wet; [*labios, tierra, bizcocho*] moist

húmero SM humerus

humidificador SM humidifier

humidificar /1g/ VT to humidify

humildad SF **1** [*de carácter*] humbleness, humility **2** (= *docilidad*) meekness **3** [*de origen*] humbleness, lowliness

humilde ADJ **1** (= *no orgulloso*) [*carácter, opinión, comida*] humble **2** (= *pobre*) [*clase, vivienda*] low, modest; [*origen*] lowly, humble; **son gente ~** they are humble *o* poor people

humildemente ADV humbly

humillación SF humiliation

humillante ADJ humiliating

humillar /1a/ **Ⓐ** VT to humiliate, humble **Ⓑ humillarse** VPR to humble o.s.

humita SF (*And, RPl*) **1** (*Culin*) tamale **2** (*Chi*) (= *pajarita*) bow tie

humo SM **1** [*de fuego, cigarro*] smoke; (= *gases*) fumes *pl*; (= *vapor*) vapour, vapor (*EEUU*), steam; **echar ~** (*lit*) to smoke; (*fig*) to be fuming; ✦ MODISMO **hacerse ~** (*SAm**) to disappear, split* **2 humos** (= *vanidad*) conceit *sing*, airs; **tener muchos ~s** to think a lot of o.s., have a big head; ✦ MODISMOS **bajar los ~s a algn** to take sb down a peg (or two); **darse ~s** to brag, boast **3 humos**† (= *hogares*) homes, hearths

humor SM **1** (= *estado de ánimo*) mood; **estar de buen/mal ~** to be in a good/bad mood; **me pone de mal ~** it puts me in a bad mood; **no tengo ~ para fiestas** I'm not in a party mood; ✦ MODISMO **un ~ de perros** a foul mood **2** (= *gracia*) humour, humor (*EEUU*), humorousness (*frm*) ➤ **humor negro** black humour *o* (*EEUU*) humor

humorada SF **1** (= *broma*) witticism, joke **2** (= *capricho*) caprice, whim

humorismo SM **1** [*de carácter, momento*] humour, humor (*EEUU*), humorousness (*frm*) **2** (*Teat*) stand-up comedy

humorista SMF **1** (= *cómico*) stand-up comedian/comedienne; (= *dibujante*) cartoonist; (= *escritor*) humorist **2** (= *persona graciosa*) joker

humorístico ADJ humorous, funny

humus SM humus

hundido ADJ **1** [*barco, huellas*] sunken **2** [*ojos*] deep-set, hollow **3** (= *desmoralizado*) downcast, demoralized

hundimiento SM **1** [*de barco*] sinking **2** (= *colapso*) [*de edificio, familia, empresa*] collapse, ruin, fall; [*de terreno*] cave-in, subsidence

hundir /3a/ **Ⓐ** VT **1** (*en agua*) to sink **2** (= *destruir*) [+ *edificio*] to ruin, destroy; [+ *plan*] to sink, ruin **3** (= *desmoralizar*) to demoralize; **me hundes en la miseria** you're driving me to despair **Ⓑ hundirse** VPR **1** (*en agua*) [*barco*] to sink; [*nadador*] to plunge, go down **2** (= *derrumbarse*) [*edificio*] to collapse, fall down, tumble down; [*terreno*] to cave in, subside **3** (= *económicamente*) [*precios*] to slump; [*economía*] to collapse; **el negocio se hundió** the business failed *o* went under **4** (= *moralmente*) to collapse, break down; **~se en la miseria** to get really low *o* depressed

húngaro/a **Ⓐ** ADJ of/from Hungary **Ⓑ** SM/F native/inhabitant of Hungary **Ⓒ** SM (*Ling*) Hungarian

Hungría SF Hungary

huno SM Hun

huracán SM hurricane

huracanado ADJ **viento ~** hurricane-force wind, gale-force wind

huraño ADJ **1** (= *poco sociable*) unsociable **2** (= *esquivo*) shy, elusive

hurgar /1h/ **Ⓐ** VI (= *curiosear*) **~ en** to rummage in; **~ en el bolsillo** to feel in one's pocket, rummage in one's pocket; ✦ MODISMO **~ en la herida** to rub salt in the wound **Ⓑ hurgarse** VPR **~se la nariz** to pick one's nose

hurguetear /1a/ VT (*CS*) **1** (= *rebuscar*) to rummage through **2** (= *fisgonear*) to stick one's nose into*, pry into

hurón SM **1** (*Zool*) ferret **2** (= *huraño*) unsociable person **3** (= *fisgón*) busybody, nosy parker*, snooper*

huronear /1a/ VI to pry, snoop around*

hurra EXCL hurray!, hurrah!

hurtadillas SFPL **a ~** stealthily, on the sly*

hurtar /1a/ VT to steal

hurto SM robbery

húsar SM hussar

husmear /1a/ VT **1** (= *olisquear*) to scent, get wind of **2** (= *fisgonear*) to pry into, sniff out*

huso SM spindle ➤ **huso horario** time zone

hutu ADJ, SMF Hutu

huy EXCL (*de dolor*) ow!, ouch!; (*de asombro*) wow!; (*de sorpresa*) well!, oh!, jeez! (*EEUU*); (*de alivio*) phew!; **¡huy, perdona!** oops, sorry!

Hz ABR (= **hertzio, hercio**) Hz

Ii

I, i [i] SF (= *letra*) I, i ► **I griega** Y, y

I+D ABR (= **Investigación y Desarrollo**) R

iba *etc ver* **ir**

ibérico ADJ Iberian

ibero/a ADJ, SM/F, **íbero/a** ADJ, SM/F Iberian

Iberoamérica SF Latin America

iberoamericano/a ADJ, SM/F Latin American

íbice SM ibex

iceberg SM ['iθeβer] (*pl* ~**s** ['iθeβer]) iceberg; **la punta** *o* **cabeza del** ~ the tip of the iceberg

icono SM icon

iconoclasta Ⓐ ADJ iconoclastic **Ⓑ** SMF iconoclast

iconografía SF iconography

ictericia SF jaundice

id¹ SM id

id² *ver* **ir**

ida SF departure; **viaje de** ~ outward journey; **billete de** ~ **y vuelta** return (ticket) (*esp Brit*), round trip ticket (*EEUU*); ~**s y venidas** comings and goings

idea SF **1** (= *concepto*) idea; **tenía una ~ falsa de mí** he had a false impression of me, he had the wrong idea about me; **formarse una ~ de algo** to form an impression of sth; **hacerse una ~ de algo** to get an idea of sth; **hazte a la ~ de que no va a volver nunca** you'd better get used to the idea that she's never coming back
2 (= *sugerencia*) idea; **tengo una gran** ~ I've had a great idea; ~ **brillante** ◇ ~ **genial** brilliant idea
3 (= *intención*) idea, intention; **mi ~ era salir temprano** I had intended to leave early, my idea *o* intention was to leave early; **cambiar de** ~ to change one's mind; ~ **fija** fixed idea; **ir con la ~ de hacer algo** to mean to do sth; **tiene muy mala** ~ his intentions are not good, he's a nasty piece of work*; **tuvo muy mala ~ al hacer las preguntas** his questions were really malicious *o* nasty; **lo hizo sin mala** ~ he didn't mean any harm; **metérsele una ~ en la cabeza a algn: cuando se le mete una ~ en la cabeza** once he gets an idea into his head; **tener ~ de hacer algo** (*en el pasado*) to mean to do sth; (*en el futuro*) to be thinking of doing sth

> Recuérdese que las preposiciones en inglés rigen gerundio y no infinitivo, de ahí **to be thinking of doing sth.**

✦ MODISMO **tener ~ a algn** (*CS*) to have it in for sb
4 (= *conocimiento*) idea; **no tengo mucha ~ de cocina** I haven't got much (of an) idea about cooking; **no tengo ni ~** I've (got) no idea; **¡ni ~!** no idea!; **tener ~ de algo** to have an idea of sth; **¡no tienes ~ de las ganas que tenía de verte!** you have no idea how much I wanted to see you!; **no tener la menor ~** not to have the faintest *o* the foggiest idea
5 ideas (= *opiniones*) ideas; **sus ~s políticas** his political beliefs *o* ideas; **tengo las ~s muy claras con respecto al aborto** my position on abortion is very clear; **una persona de ~s conservadoras/liberales** a conservative/liberal-minded person

ideal ⒶADJ ideal; **es el marido** ~ he is the ideal husband; **nuestra casa** ~ our dream house *o* home; **lo ~ sería que el aparcamiento fuera gratis** ideally the parking would be free, the ideal thing would be for the parking to be free **Ⓑ** SM **1** (= *modelo, deseo*) ideal; **el ~ de belleza masculina** the ideal of masculine beauty; **mi ~ es vivir junto al mar** my ideal is to live by the sea **2 ideales** (= *valores*) ideals; **jóvenes sin ~es** young people with no ideals

idealismo SM idealism

idealista ⒶADJ idealistic **Ⓑ** SMF idealist

idealizar /1f/ VT to idealize

idear /1a/ VT **1** [+ *proyecto, teoría*] to devise, think up;

[+ *excusa*] to think up **2** (= *diseñar*) [+ *edificio*] to design; [+ *invento, máquina*] to design, devise

ideario SM ideology; **el ~ de la organización** the thinking of the organization

ideático ADJ **1** (*LAm*) (= *maniático*) obsessive; (= *caprichoso*) wilful **2** (*CAm*) (= *inventivo*) ingenious

ídem ADV (*en lengua escrita*) idem; (*en lengua hablada*) ditto

idéntico ADJ identical; **este cuadro es ~ a este otro** this picture is identical to *o* exactly the same as this other one; **llevaba una falda idéntica a la mía** she was wearing an identical skirt to mine; **ser ~ a algn** to be the spitting image of sb*

identidad SF identity ► **identidad corporativa** corporate identity

identificación SF identification

identificador ⒶADJ identifying **Ⓑ** SM ► **identificador de llamadas** caller ID

identificar /1g/ **ⒶVT 1** (= *reconocer*) to identify; **una víctima sin** ~ an unidentified victim
2 (= *equiparar*) **siempre la identificaban con causas humanitarias** she was always identified *o* associated with humanitarian causes
Ⓑ identificarse VPR **1** (= *demostrar la identidad*) to identify o.s.; **la policía les pidió que se ~an** the police asked them to show their identity cards
2 ~se con to identify with; **muchos jóvenes se identifican con este personaje** many young people identify with this character

ideograma SM ideogram

ideología SF ideology

ideológico ADJ ideological

ideólogo/a SM/F ideologist

idílico ADJ idyllic

idilio SM romance, love affair

idioma SM language; **los ~s de trabajo de la UE** the working languages of the EU

> ⚠ **idioma ≠ idiom**

idiomático ADJ idiomatic

idiosincrasia SF idiosyncrasy

idiota ⒶADJ idiotic, stupid **Ⓑ** SMF idiot

idiotez SF idiocy; **¡eso es una ~!** that's nonsense!; **decir idioteces** to talk nonsense; **hacer idioteces** to do silly things

idiotizado ADJ stupefied

ido* ADJ **1** (= *despistado*) absent-minded; **estar** ~ to be miles away **2** (= *chiflado*) crazy, nuts*

idólatra ⒶADJ idolatrous **Ⓑ** SMF idolator/idolatress

idolatrar /1a/ VT **1** [+ *dios*] to worship **2** [+ *amado, cantante*] to idolize

ídolo SM idol

idoneidad SF **1** (= *conveniencia*) suitability, fitness **2** (= *capacidad*) aptitude

idóneo ADJ suitable, fit

IES SM ABR (*Esp*) (= **Instituto de Enseñanza Secundaria**) ≈ state secondary school (*Brit*), ≈ high school (*EEUU*)

iglesia SF church; **casarse por la** ~ o (*Bol, Perú, RPl*) **por** ~ to get married in church, have a church wedding ► **Iglesia Anglicana** Church of England, Anglican Church ► **Iglesia Católica** Catholic Church ► **iglesia parroquial** parish church

iglú SM igloo

ignición SF ignition

ignominia SF **1** (= *deshonor*) disgrace, ignominy **2** (= *acto*) disgraceful act

ignominioso ADJ ignominious, disgraceful

ignorado ADJ (= *desconocido*) unknown; (= *poco conocido*) obscure, little-known

ignorancia SF ignorance

ignorante Ⓐ ADJ ignorant Ⓑ SMF ignoramus

ignorar /1a/ VT 1 (= *desconocer*) to not know, be ignorant of; **ignoramos su paradero** we don't know his whereabouts; **no ignoro que ...** I am fully aware that ..., I am not unaware that ... 2 (= *no tener en cuenta a*) to ignore

ignoto ADJ (*liter*) (= *desconocido*) unknown; (= *no descubierto*) undiscovered

igual Ⓐ ADJ 1 (= *idéntico*) **son todos ~es** they're all the same; **llevaban la corbata ~** they were wearing the same tie; **~ a: éste es ~ al otro** this one is like the other one, this one is the same as the other one; **no he visto nunca cosa ~** I never saw the like *o* anything like it; **partes ~es** equal shares; **~ que: tengo una falda ~ que la tuya** I've got a skirt just like yours, I've got a skirt the same as yours; **es ~ que su madre** (*físicamente*) she looks just like her mother; (*en la personalidad*) she's just like her mother

2 **~ de: es ~ de útil pero más barato** it's just as useful but cheaper; **estoy ~ de sorprendido que tú** I am just as surprised as you are

3 (*en rango, jerarquía*) equal; **todos somos ~es ante la ley** we are all equal in the eyes of the law

4 (*Mat*) equal; **X es ~ a Y** X is equal to Y

5 (= *constante*) [*ritmo*] steady; [*presión, temperatura*] steady, constant; [*terreno*] even

6 (*Dep*) **ir ~es** to be level; **quince ~es** fifteen all; **cuarenta ~es** deuce

Ⓑ ADV 1 (= *de la misma forma*) **se visten ~** they dress the same

2 (*locuciones*) **da ~ ◇ es ~** it makes no difference, it's all the same; **da *o* es ~ hoy que mañana** today or tomorrow, it doesn't matter *o* it makes no difference; **me da ~ ◇ me es ~** it's all the same to me, I don't mind; **por ~** equally; **esta norma se aplica a todos por ~** this rule applies equally to everyone; **~ que** (= *como*) like; **~ que cualquier otro** just like anybody else; **le gusta Brahms, ~ que a mí** like me, he is fond of Brahms; **los chilenos, al ~ que los argentinos, estiman que ...** the Chileans, (just) like the Argentinians, think that ...

3 (*) (= *quizás*) maybe; **~ no lo saben** maybe they don't know, they may not know; **~ voy a la playa** I may go to the beach

4 (*esp CS**) (= *a pesar de todo*) just the same, still; **era inocente pero me expulsaron ~** I was innocent but they threw me out just the same, I was innocent but they still threw me out

Ⓒ SMF (*en la misma escala social*) equal; (*en la misma clase, trabajo*) peer; **tratar a algn de ~ a ~** to treat sb as an equal

Ⓓ SM 1 (*Mat*) equal sign, equals sign (*Brit*)

2 (= *comparación*) **no tener ~** to be unrivalled, have no equal; **sin ~** unrivalled

3 **iguales** (*Esp*) (*en lotería*) lottery tickets

igualada SF (*Esp Dep*) 1 (= *empate*) tie, draw (*esp Brit*) 2 (= *igualdad de puntos*) level score; **rompió la ~** he broke the deadlock

igualado ADJ 1 (= *a la misma altura*) neck and neck; **los dos partidos van ~s en las encuestas** the two parties are running neck and neck in the opinion polls; **el partido quedó ~ a dos** the match finished two all

2 (*indicando posición*) [*competidores, equipos*] evenly-matched; [*competición, partido*] even, evenly-matched; **los dos equipos están ~s a puntos** both teams are level on points

3 [*suelo, césped*] levelled off, leveled off (*EEUU*)

4 (*CAm, Méx**) (= *irrespetuoso*) disrespectful (*to people of a higher class*)

igualar /1a/ Ⓐ VT 1 (= *hacer igual*) 1.1 [+ *cantidades, sueldos*] to make equal, make the same; [+ *resultado*] to equal; **~ algo a *o* con algo** to make sth the same as sth; **han igualado mi sueldo al vuestro** they've put us on the same salary, they've made my salary the same as yours; **si igualamos la x a dos** if x is equal to two 1.2 (*Dep*) [+ *marca, récord*] to equal; **el equipo visitante igualó el marcador** the away team scored the equalizer *o* equalized (*Brit*), the away

team tied the score (*esp EEUU*); **~ el partido** to equalize (*Brit*), tie the score (*esp EEUU*); **~ a puntos a *o* con algn** to be level on points with sb

2 [+ *suelo, superficie*] to level, level off; [+ *flequillo*] to even up; **~ algo con algo** to make sth level with sth

3 (= *poner al mismo nivel*) [+ *precios*] to match, equal; [+ *derechos, fuerzas*] to place on an equal footing; **la constitución iguala los derechos de todos los ciudadanos** the constitution grants equal rights to all citizens; **~ a algn en belleza** to match sb's beauty; **a final de curso consiguió ~ a su hermano en las notas** at the end of the year she managed to get the same marks as her brother

Ⓑ VI 1 (= *ser igual*) **~ con algo** to match sth

2 (*Dep*) (= *empatar*) to score the equalizer (*Brit*), equalize (*Brit*), score the tying goal *etc* (*EEUU*)

Ⓒ **igualarse** VPR **~se a *o* con algn** to be on the same level as sb; **su familia no puede ~se con la nuestra** his family doesn't compare with *o* to ours

igualatorio SM (*Med*) insurance group

igualdad SF equality; **~ de derechos** equal rights; **~ de oportunidades** equal opportunities; **en ~ de condiciones** on an equal basis, on an equal footing

igualitario ADJ egalitarian

igualmente ADV 1 (= *del mismo modo*) equally; **todos mis estudiantes son ~ vagos** all my students are equally lazy, my students are all as lazy as each other 2 (= *también*) likewise 3 (*en saludo*) the same to you, likewise; **—¡Feliz Navidad! —gracias, ~** "Happy Christmas!" — "thanks, the same to you *o* likewise"; **—muchos recuerdos a tus padres —gracias, ~** "give my regards to your parents" — "I will, and to yours too"

iguana SF iguana

ijada SF flank

ikastola SF *school in which Basque is the language of instruction*; ⊳ *EUSKERA*

ikurriña SF *Basque national flag*

ilación SF (= *inferencia*) inference; (= *nexo*) connection, relationship

ilegal ADJ illegal, unlawful

ilegalidad SF illegality, unlawfulness; **trabajar en la ~** to work illegally

ilegalizar /1f/ VT to outlaw, make illegal, ban

ilegible ADJ illegible, unreadable

ilegítimo ADJ 1 (= *no legítimo*) illegitimate 2 (= *ilegal*) unlawful 3 (= *falso*) false, spurious

ileso ADJ unhurt, unharmed; **salió ~** he escaped unscathed

iletrado ADJ (= *analfabeto*) illiterate; (= *inculto*) uneducated

ilícito ADJ illicit, unlawful

ilimitado ADJ unlimited, limitless

Ilma. ABR = **Ilustrísima**

Ilmo. ABR = **Ilustrísimo**

ilocalizable ADJ **ayer seguía ~** he could still not be found yesterday, he was still nowhere to be found yesterday

ilógico ADJ illogical

iluminación SF (*en casa, calle*) lighting; (*en estadio*) floodlighting

iluminado ADJ illuminated, lit

iluminar /1a/ Ⓐ VT 1 [+ *cuarto, calle, ciudad*] to light; [+ *estadio, edificio, monumento*] to light up; **la felicidad iluminó su rostro** his face lit up with happiness

2 [+ *grabado, ilustración*] to illuminate 3 [+ *teoría, tesis*] to illustrate 4 (*Rel*) to enlighten Ⓑ **iluminarse** VPR (= *alegrarse*) [*cara, expresión*] to light up; **el cielo se iluminó con los fuegos artificiales** the sky was lit up with fireworks, fireworks lit up the sky

ilusión SF 1 (= *esperanza*) **su ~ era comprarlo** her dream was to buy it; **hacerse ilusiones** to get one's hopes up; **no me hago muchas ilusiones de que ...** I am not very hopeful that ... 2 (*Esp*) (= *entusiasmo*) **¡qué ~!** how exciting!; **el viaje me hace mucha ~** I am so looking forward to the trip; **tu**

carta me hizo mucha ~ I was thrilled to get your letter **3** (= *imagen no real*) illusion ➤ **ilusión óptica** optical illusion

ilusionado ADJ (= *esperanzado*) hopeful; (= *entusiasmado*) excited; **estaba ~ con el viaje a Francia** he was looking forward to going to France

ilusionar /1a/ **Ⓐ** VT **1** (= *entusiasmar*) to excite, thrill; **me ilusiona mucho el viaje** I'm really excited about the journey **2** (= *alentar falsamente*) **~ a algn** to get sb's hopes up **Ⓑ ilusionarse** VPR **1** (= *entusiasmarse*) to get excited **2** (*falsamente*) to get one's hopes up

ilusionismo SM conjuring

ilusionista SMF conjurer, illusionist

iluso/a Ⓐ ADJ gullible; **¡pobre ~!** poor deluded creature! **Ⓑ** SM/F (= *soñador*) dreamer

ilusorio ADJ (= *irreal*) illusory; (= *sin valor*) empty

ilustración SF **1** (= *ejemplo*) illustration **2** [*de libro*] picture, illustration **3** (= *instrucción*) learning, erudition (*frm*); **la Ilustración** the Enlightenment

ilustrado ADJ **1** [*libro*] illustrated **2** [*persona*] (= *culto*) learned, erudite (*frm*); (= *progresista*) enlightened

ilustrar /1a/ VT **1** [+ *libro*] to illustrate **2** [+ *tema*] to explain, illustrate **3** (= *instruir*) to instruct, enlighten

ilustrativo ADJ illustrative

ilustre ADJ illustrious, famous

ilustrísimo ADJ most illustrious; **Su Ilustrísima** (*al referirse a un obispo*) His Grace

imagen SF **1** (*Fot*, *Ópt*) image; (= *en foto, dibujo, TV*) picture; **las imágenes del accidente** the pictures *o* images of the accident; ✦ REFRÁN **una ~ vale más que mil palabras** a picture is worth a thousand words ➤ **imágenes de archivo** library pictures
2 (= *reflejo*) reflection; **vio su ~ reflejada en el lago** she saw her reflection in the lake; ✦ MODISMOS **a (la) ~ y semejanza de uno** in one's own image; **ser la misma** *o* **la viva ~ de algn** to be the living *o* spitting* image of sb; **ser la viva ~ de algo** to be the picture of sth
3 (= *mental*) image, picture; **guardo una ~ borrosa del accidente** I only have a vague picture of the accident in my mind
4 (= *aspecto*) image; **Luis cuida mucho su ~** Luis takes great care over his appearance *o* image; **un cambio de ~** a change of image
5 (*Rel*) [*de madera, pintura*] image; [*de piedra*] statue
6 (*Literat*) image

imaginable ADJ imaginable, conceivable

imaginación SF **1** (= *capacidad*) imagination; **eso es todo obra de tu ~** it's all a figment of your imagination; **no se me pasó por la ~ que ...** it never even occurred to me that ...; **ni por ~** on no account **2 imaginaciones** (= *lo imaginado*): **eso son imaginaciones tuyas** you're imagining things

imaginar /1a/ **Ⓐ** VT **1** (= *suponer, visualizar*) to imagine; **imagina que tuvieras mucho dinero** suppose *o* imagine that you had a lot of money
2 (= *inventar*) [+ *plan, método*] to think up **Ⓑ imaginarse** VPR **1** (= *suponer*) to imagine; **no te puedes ~ lo mal que iba todo** you can't imagine how bad things were; **sí, ya me imagino** yes, I can imagine; **—¿lo habéis pasado bien? —imagínate** "did you have a good time?" —"what do you think? *o* we sure did"; **me imagino que tendrás ganas de descansar** I imagine *o* suppose *o* guess* you'll need a rest; **imagínate que os pasa algo** suppose something happens to you
2 (= *visualizar*) to imagine, picture; **me la imaginaba más joven** I had imagined *o* pictured her as being younger

imaginario ADJ imaginary

imaginativo ADJ imaginative

imaginería SF (*Rel*) images *pl*, statues *pl*

imam SM, **imán**[1] SM (*Rel*) imam

imán[2] SM magnet

imantar /1a/ VT to magnetize

imbatible ADJ unbeatable

imbécil Ⓐ ADJ **1** (= *idiota*) silly, stupid **2** (*Med*) imbecile **Ⓑ** SMF **1** (= *idiota*) idiot **2** (*Med*) imbecile

imbecilidad SF stupidity, idiocy; **decir ~es** to say silly things

imberbe ADJ **1** (= *sin barba*) beardless **2** (= *sin experiencia*) inexperienced

imbombera* SF (*Ven*) jaundice

imbombo* ADJ (*Ven*) **1** (= *con ictericia*) jaundiced **2** (= *tonto*) silly, stupid

imborrable ADJ indelible

imbricado ADJ **1** [*placa*] overlapping **2** [*asunto*] interwoven

imbuir /3g/ VT to imbue, infuse (**de, en** with)

imitación SF **1** (= *copia*) imitation; **a ~ de** in imitation of; **desconfíe de las imitaciones** beware of imitations; **joyas de ~** imitation jewellery *o* (*EEUU*) jewelry; **una pistola de ~** a fake gun **2** (*Teat*) impression, impersonation

imitador(a) SM/F **1** (= *plagiario*) imitator **2** (= *seguidor*) follower **3** (*Teat*) impressionist, impersonator

imitar /1a/ VT **1** (= *emular*) [+ *maestro, hermano*] to imitate; (*pey*) to ape; **Susana imita a sus padres en todo** Susana copies everything her parents do; **se limita a ~ a los mejores autores** he confines himself to aping the best authors
2 [+ *firma, acento*] to imitate
3 (*por diversión*) to imitate; [+ *personaje*] to do an impression of; **¡deja ya de ~me!** stop imitating me!; **el humorista imitó al rey** the comedian did an impression of the king
4 (= *parecerse a*) **imita el tacto de la seda** it simulates the feel of silk

impaciencia SF impatience

impacientar /1a/ **Ⓐ** VT **1** [*lentitud, retraso*] to make impatient **2** (= *exasperar*) to exasperate **Ⓑ impacientarse** VPR **1** (*por lentitud, retraso*) to get impatient (**ante, por** about, at; **con** with) **2** (= *exasperarse*) to lose patience, get worked up

impaciente ADJ **1** (= *sin paciencia*) impatient (**por** to); **¡estoy ~!** I can't wait! **2** (= *irritable*) impatient

impactar /1a/ **Ⓐ** VT to impress, have an impact on **Ⓑ** VI **1** (= *chocar*) to crash (**contra** against; **en** into) **2** (= *afectar*) **~ en** to affect

impacto SM **1** (= *golpe*) [*de vehículo, disparo*] impact ➤ **impacto de bala** bullet hole **2** (= *efecto*) [*de noticia, cambios, leyes*] impact; **~ ambiental** environmental impact

impagable ADJ unpayable

impago Ⓐ ADJ (*CS*) unpaid **Ⓑ** SM non-payment, failure to pay

impar Ⓐ ADJ odd **Ⓑ** SM odd number

imparable ADJ unstoppable

imparcial ADJ impartial, fair

imparcialidad SF impartiality

impartir /3a/ VT to impart (*frm*), give

impasibilidad SF impassiveness, impassivity; **la golpeó ante la ~ de todos** he hit her and no-one took any notice

impasible ADJ impassive

impasse [im'pas] SM impasse

impávido ADJ dauntless, undaunted

impecable ADJ impeccable, faultless

impedido/a Ⓐ ADJ disabled **Ⓑ** SM/F disabled person

impedimento SM **1** (= *dificultad*) impediment, hindrance; **nos ponen ~s para evitar que lo hagamos** they are putting obstacles in our way to prevent us doing it **2** (*Med*) disability, handicap

impedir /3k/ VT **1** (= *parar*) to prevent, stop; **trataron de ~ la huida de los presos** they tried to prevent the prisoners escaping *o* the prisoners' escape; **~ a algn el acceso al edificio** to prevent sb from entering the building; **un autobús nos impedía el paso** a bus was blocking our way; **a mí nadie me lo va a ~** nobody's going to stop me; **~ a algn hacer algo** ◇ **~ que algn haga algo** to prevent sb (from)

doing sth, stop sb doing sth
2 (= *dificultar*) (*con obstáculos*) to impede, obstruct; (*con problemas*) to hinder, hamper

impeler /2a/ VT **1** (= *empujar*) to drive, propel **2** (= *incitar*) to drive, urge, impel; **impelido por la necesidad** driven by need

impenetrable ADJ **1** [*bosque*] impenetrable **2** [*mirada, rostro*] impassive **3** [*misterio*] impenetrable

impensable ADJ unthinkable

impepinable* ADJ certain

imperante ADJ ruling, prevailing

imperar /1a/ VI **1** (= *prevalecer*) to prevail **2** (= *mandar*) to rule, reign

imperativo Ⓐ ADJ (*gen*) imperative; [*tono*] commanding, imperative Ⓑ SM **1** (= *necesidad*) imperative ➤ **imperativo categórico** moral imperative **2** (*Ling*) imperative, imperative mood

imperceptible ADJ imperceptible

imperdible SM safety pin

imperdonable ADJ unforgivable, unpardonable, inexcusable

imperecedero ADJ [*recuerdo*] immortal, undying; [*legado*] eternal; [*fama*] eternal, everlasting

imperfección SF **1** (= *cualidad*) imperfection **2** (= *fallo*) flaw, fault

imperfecto Ⓐ ADJ **1** [*producto, método*] imperfect, flawed **2** (*Ling*) imperfect Ⓑ SM (*Ling*) imperfect, imperfect tense

imperial ADJ imperial

imperialismo SM imperialism

impericia SF **1** (= *torpeza*) lack of skill **2** (= *inexperiencia*) inexperience; **a prueba de ~** foolproof

imperio SM **1** (*Pol*) empire **2** (= *autoridad*) rule; **el ~ de la ley** the rule of law

imperioso ADJ **1** (= *autoritario*) imperious **2** (= *urgente*) pressing, urgent; **necesidad imperiosa** pressing need, absolute necessity

impermeabilizar /1f/ VT **1** (*Téc*) to waterproof, make watertight **2** (*Aut*) to underseal **3** [+ *frontera*] to seal off

impermeable Ⓐ ADJ **1** (*al agua*) waterproof **2** (= *impenetrable*) impermeable, impervious (**a** to) Ⓑ SM waterproof

impersonador(a) SM/F (*Méx*) impersonator

impersonal ADJ impersonal

impersonar /1a/ VT (*Méx*) to impersonate

impertérrito ADJ unshaken, unmoved

impertinencia SF **1** (= *insolencia*) impertinence **2** (= *comentario*) impertinent remark

impertinente ADJ impertinent

imperturbable ADJ **1** [*ser*] (= *no cambiable*) imperturbable **2** [*estar*] (= *sereno*) unruffled; (= *impasible*) impassive

ímpetu SM **1** (= *impulso*) impetus; (*Mec*) momentum **2** (= *acometida*) rush, onrush **3** (= *impulsividad*) impetuousness, impetuosity

impetuosidad SF impetuosity, impetuousness

impetuoso ADJ **1** [*persona*] impetuous, impulsive **2** [*acto*] hasty, impetuous

impío ADJ impious, ungodly

implacable ADJ implacable, relentless

implantación SF **1** [*de reforma, sistema, modelo*] implementation; **la ~ de la dictadura** the installing of the dictatorship
2 [*de costumbre, ideas*] **una costumbre de reciente ~ a** custom that has only recently become established *o* taken root; **esta moda no tuvo ~ aquí** this fashion never caught on here
3 (= *popularidad*) **un partido con escasa ~ en las ciudades** a party with little support in the cities; **un idioma de fuerte ~ en Nueva York** a language which is firmly established in New York
4 (*Med*) implantation

implantar /1a/ Ⓐ VT **1** [+ *reforma, sistema, modelo*] to implement; [+ *castigo, medidas*] to bring in; [+ *toque de queda*] to impose; **cuando ~on la dictadura** when the dictatorship was installed; **han vuelto a ~ la pena de muerte** they have brought back the death penalty **2** [+ *costumbre, ideas*] to introduce **3** (*Med*) to implant Ⓑ **implantarse** VPR to become established

implante SM implant

implementar /1a/ VT **1** (= *poner en práctica*) to implement **2** (*Ven*) (= *instalar*) to install, instal (*EEUU*)

implemento SM (*LAm*) implement, tool

implicación SF **1** (= *complicidad*) involvement **2** (= *significado*) implication

implicancia SF (*LAm*) (= *consecuencia*) implication

implicar /1g/ VT **1** (= *involucrar*) to involve; **las partes implicadas** the interested parties, the parties concerned **2** (= *significar*) to imply; **esto no implica que ...** this does not mean that ...

implícito ADJ implicit

implorar /1a/ VT to implore, beg, beseech (*liter*)

imponderable Ⓐ ADJ imponderable Ⓑ **imponderables** SMPL imponderables

imponencia SF (*LAm*) impressiveness

imponente ADJ **1** (= *que asusta*) [*persona, castillo, montaña*] imposing **2** (= *magnífico*) [*aspecto*] stunning; [*edificio, fachada*] impressive; [*paisaje, representación*] stunning, impressive

imponer /2q/ (*pp* **impuesto**) Ⓐ VT **1** (= *poner*) [+ *castigo, sanción, obligación*] to impose; [+ *tarea*] to set; **no quiero ~te nada** I don't want to force you to do anything, I don't want to impose anything on you; **el juez le impuso una pena de tres años de prisión** the judge gave him a three-year prison sentence
2 (*frm*) (= *conceder*) [+ *medalla*] to award
3 (= *hacer prevalecer*) [+ *voluntad, costumbre*] to impose; [+ *norma*] to enforce; [+ *miedo*] to instil; [+ *enseñanza, uso*] to lay down, impose; [+ *enseñanza, uso*] to make compulsory; **su trabajo le impone un ritmo de vida muy acelerado** her work forces her to lead a very fast lifestyle; **han impuesto a la fuerza la enseñanza religiosa** they have enforced religious education; **~ la moda** to set the trend; **~ respeto** to command respect; **tu padre me impone mucho (respeto)** I find your father very intimidating; **~ el ritmo** to set the pace
4 [+ *impuesto*] to put, levy (**a, sobre** on); (*Esp*) [+ *dinero*] to deposit
5 (= *instruir*) **~ a algn en algo** to instruct sb in sth
6 (*Rel*) **~ las manos sobre algn** to lay hands on sb
7 (*Chi*) (*a la Seguridad Social*) to pay (in contributions) Ⓑ VI **1** (= *intimidar*) [*persona*] to command respect; [*edificio*] to be imposing; [*arma*] to be intimidating
2 (*Chi*) (*a la Seguridad Social*) to pay contributions Ⓒ **imponerse** VPR **1** (= *obligarse*) [+ *horario, tarea*] to set o.s.
2 (= *hacerse respetar*) to assert one's authority, assert o.s.; **~se a** *o* **sobre algn** to assert one's authority over sb; **siempre acaba imponiéndose sobre sus hermanas** he always ends up getting his own way with his sisters
3 (= *prevalecer*) [*criterio*] to prevail; [*moda*] to become fashionable
4 (*frm*) (= *ser necesario*) [*cambio*] to be needed; [*conclusión*] to be inescapable; **se impone la necesidad de una gran reforma** there is an urgent need for extensive reform
5 (*Dep*) to win; **~se a algn** to defeat sb, beat sb
6 (= *instruirse*) **~se en algo** to acquaint o.s. with sth
7 (*Méx**) (= *acostumbrarse*) **~se a algo** to become accustomed to sth

imponible ADJ **1** [*riqueza, hecho*] taxable, subject to tax; [*importación*] dutiable, subject to duty; **no ~** tax-free (*Brit*), tax-exempt (*EEUU*) **2** (*) [*ropa*] unwearable

impopular ADJ unpopular

importación SF **1** (= *acto*) import, importation; **de ~** [*producto, artículo*] imported; [*comercio, permiso*] import *antes de s* **2 importaciones** (= *mercancías*) imports

importador(a) Ⓐ ADJ importing Ⓑ SM/F importer

importancia SF importance; **no tiene ~** it's not important; **de cierta ~** [*empresa, asunto*] of some importance, important; [*herida*] serious; **conceder** o **dar mucha ~ a algo** to attach great importance to sth; **no quiero darle más ~ de la que tiene** I don't want to make an issue of this; **darse ~** to give o.s. airs; **quitar** o **restar ~ a algo** to make light of sth, play down the importance of sth; **sin ~** [*herida, detalle, comentario*] minor

importante ADJ **1** (= *trascendental*) [*información, persona*] important; [*acontecimiento*] significant, important; [*papel, factor, parte*] important, major; [*cambio*] significant, major; **dárselas de ~** to give o.s. airs; **lo ~ es ...** the main thing is ...; **poco ~** unimportant **2** (*como intensificador*) [*cantidad, pérdida*] considerable; [*herida*] serious; [*retraso*] considerable, serious

importar[1] /1a/ VT (*Com*) to import (**de** from)

importar[2] /1a/ Ⓐ VI **1** (= *ser importante*) to matter; **no importa** never mind, it doesn't matter; **lo que importa es la calidad** the important thing is the quality, what matters is the quality; **¿y eso qué importa?** what does that matter?; **el color importa mucho en su pintura** colour is important in her painting, colour plays an important part in her painting; **no importa el tiempo que haga, allí estaremos** we'll be there whatever the weather
2 (*con complemento de persona*) **2.1** (= *interesar*) **sí que me importa tu opinión** your opinion does matter to me, I do care about your opinion; **¿a quién le importa lo que yo diga?** who cares (about) what I say?; **tú me importas más que nada** I care about you more than anything, you mean more to me than anything; **¿y a ti qué te importa?** what business is it of yours?; **meterse en lo que a uno no le importa** to poke one's nose into other people's business; ✦ MODISMOS **(no) me importa un bledo** o **un comino** o **un pito** o **un rábano*** I couldn't care less*, I don't give a damn**; **(no) me importa un carajo** o **un huevo***** I don't give a shit*** o (*Brit*) a toss** **2.2** (= *molestar*)

En esta acepción **importar** se traduce frecuentemente por **mind**. Recuérdese que **mind** rige que el verbo que le siga inmediatamente aparezca en gerundio y no en infinitivo:

¿te ~ía prestarme este libro? would you mind lending me this book?, could you lend me this book?; **si no le importa, me gustaría que me enviaran la factura** if it's not too much trouble, I'd like you to send me the bill; **no me importa esperar** I don't mind waiting; **no me importa que llegues un poco tarde** I don't mind if you're a bit late, I don't mind you being a bit late
Ⓑ VT (*frm*) [*artículo, producto*] to cost; [*gastos, beneficios*] to amount to

importe SM **1** (= *valor*) [*de compra, cheque*] amount; **¿a cuánto asciende el ~ de los gastos?** how much do the expenses amount to o come to?; **el ~ de la recaudación** (*Cine, Teat*) box office takings *pl*; (*Dep*) gate receipts *pl*; **por ~ de** to the value of ➤ **importe global** grand total **2** (= *coste*) cost; **el ~ de la mano de obra** the cost of labour

importunar /1a/ VT to bother, pester

imposibilitado ADJ **1** (*Med*) disabled **2** (= *impedido*) **estar** o **verse ~ para hacer algo** to be unable to do sth, be prevented from doing sth

imposibilitar /1a/ Ⓐ VT to make impossible, prevent Ⓑ VPR (*Chi, Méx*) to injure o.s.

imposible Ⓐ ADJ **1** (= *no posible*) impossible; **es ~ de predecir** it's impossible to predict; **hacer lo ~ por hacer algo** to do one's utmost to do sth; **¡parece ~!** you'd never believe it! **2** (= *inaguantable*) impossible Ⓑ SM **un ~** (= *tarea*) an impossible task; (= *objetivo*) an impossible goal

imposición SF **1** (= *introducción*) [*de obligación, multa*] imposition; [*de ley, moda*] introduction **2** [*de medalla*] **la ceremonia de ~ de medallas** the medal ceremony **3** (= *impuesto*) taxation **4** (= *ingreso*) deposit; **efectuar una ~** to make a deposit **5** (*Rel*) ➤ **imposición de manos** laying on of hands **6** (*Chi*) (*a la Seguridad Social*) contribution

impositiva SF (*RPl*) **la ~** the Inland Revenue (*Brit*), the IRS (*EEUU*)

impositivo ADJ **1** (*Fin*) tax *antes de s*; **sistema ~** tax system **2** (*And*) (= *autoritario*) domineering

impositor(a) SM/F (*Fin*) depositor

impostor(a) SM/F impostor

impostura SF imposture

impotencia SF **1** (*para hacer algo*) impotence, helplessness **2** (*Med*) impotence

impotente ADJ **1** (*para hacer algo*) impotent, helpless **2** (*Med*) impotent

impracticable ADJ **1** (= *irrealizable*) impracticable, unworkable **2** [*carretera*] impassable

imprecación SF imprecation, curse

imprecar /1g/ VT to curse

imprecisión SF lack of precision, vagueness

impreciso ADJ imprecise, vague

impredecible ADJ unpredictable

impregnar /1a/ VT **1** (= *humedecer*) to impregnate; (= *saturar*) to soak **2** [*olor, sentimiento*] to pervade

imprenta SF **1** (= *acto*) printing; **dar** o **entregar a la ~** to send for printing **2** (= *máquina*) press **3** (= *taller*) printer's

imprescindible ADJ essential, indispensable

impresentable ADJ (*gen*) not presentable; [*acto*] disgraceful; **estás ~** you look a mess; **Juan es (un) ~** you can't take Juan anywhere

impresión SF **1** (= *sensación*) impression; **¿qué ~ te produjo?** what was your impression of it?; **cambiar impresiones** to exchange views; **causar (una) buena ~ a algn** [*persona*] to make a good impression on sb; [*actividad, ciudad*] to impress sb; **dar la ~ de: da la ~ de ser un autor maduro** he appears to be a mature author; **daba la ~ de no caber en la caja** it looked as if it wouldn't fit in the box; **me da la ~ de que ...** I get the impression that ...; **intercambiar impresiones** to exchange views; **primera ~** first impression; **tener la ~ de que ...** to have the impression that ... **2** (= *susto*) shock; **el agua fría da ~ al principio** the cold water is a bit of a shock at first; **su muerte me causó (una) gran ~** her death was a great shock to me **3** (= *huella*) imprint ➤ **impresión digital** fingerprint **4** (*Tip*) (= *acción*) printing; (= *resultado*) print; (= *tirada*) print-run; **un error de ~** a printing error ➤ **impresión en color** colour o (*EEUU*) color printing **5** (*Inform*) (= *acción*) printing; (= *resultado*) printout

impresionable ADJ impressionable

impresionado ADJ **1** (= *sorprendido, asustado*) affected **2** (*Fot*) exposed

impresionante ADJ **1** (= *maravilloso*) [*edificio, acto*] impressive; [*espectáculo*] striking **2** (= *conmovedor*) moving, affecting **3** (= *espantoso*) shocking

impresionar /1a/ Ⓐ VT **1** (= *causar impresión a*) to impress, strike; (= *conmover*) to move, affect; (= *horrorizar*) to shock; **la noticia de su muerte me impresionó mucho** the news of his death had a profound effect on me **2** [+ *foto*] to expose Ⓑ VI (= *causar impresión*) to make an impression; **lo hace sólo para ~** he does it just to impress Ⓒ **impresionarse** VPR (= *sorprenderse, asustarse*) to be affected; (= *conmoverse*) to be moved, be affected

impresionismo SM impressionism

impresionista Ⓐ ADJ **1** (*Arte*) impressionist **2** [*descripción*] impressionistic Ⓑ SMF impressionist

impreso Ⓐ PP *de* **imprimir** Ⓑ ADJ [*papel, libro, material*] printed Ⓒ SM **1** (= *formulario*) form; **un ~ de beca** a grant application form; **cumplimentar** (*frm*) o **rellenar un ~** to fill out a form, fill in a form (*esp Brit*) ➤ **impreso de solicitud** application form **2 impresos** (*en sobre*) printed matter *sing*

impresor(a) SM/F printer

impresora SF (*Inform*) printer

imprevisibilidad SF [*de suceso, problema*] unforeseeable nature; [*de persona*] unpredictability

imprevisión SF lack of foresight

imprevisor ADJ lacking foresight, improvident (*frm*)

imprevisto A ADJ unforeseen, unexpected **B** SM (= *suceso*) contingency; **~s** (= *gastos*) incidentals, unforeseen expenses; (= *emergencias*) contingencies

imprimir /3a/ (pp (en tiempos compuestos) **imprimido**; pp (como adj) **impreso**) VT **1** (*Tip*) [+ *libro, folleto, billetes*] to print **2** (*Inform*) [+ *documento, página*] to print out **3** (= *marcar*) to print; **dejó sus huellas impresas en el jarrón** he left his fingerprints on the vase **4** (= *transmitir*) [+ *estilo*] to stamp; [+ *ritmo*] to set; [+ *velocidad*] to introduce; **el director imprimió su sello a la orquesta** the conductor put his own stamp on the orchestra; **imprime a sus escritos un particular encanto** she brings a special charm to her writing; **~ carácter** to be character-building

improbable ADJ improbable, unlikely

improbidad SF dishonesty

ímprobo ADJ **1** [*tarea, esfuerzo*] enormous **2** [*persona*] dishonest, corrupt

improcedencia SF (*Jur*) inadmissibility

improcedente ADJ (*Jur*) inadmissible; **despido ~** unfair dismissal

improductivo ADJ unproductive

impronta SF stamp, mark

improperio SM insult

impropiedad SF **1** (= *inadecuación*) inappropriateness, unsuitability **2** (= *incorrección*) [*de estilo, palabras*] impropriety, infelicity (*frm*)

impropio ADJ **1** (= *inadecuado*) inappropriate, unsuitable **2** (= *incorrecto*) [*estilo, palabras*] improper, incorrect

improrrogable ADJ [*fecha, plazo*] that cannot be extended

improvisación SF improvisation

improvisado ADJ improvised

improvisar /1a/ **A** VT to improvise **B** VI to improvise

improviso ADJ **de ~** unexpectedly, suddenly

imprudencia SF **1** (= *cualidad*) (*al hacer algo*) imprudence, rashness; (*al averiguar algo*) indiscretion **2** (= *acción*) **fue una ~ del conductor** it was the driver's carelessness ➤ **imprudencia temeraria** criminal negligence

imprudente ADJ **1** (= *irreflexivo*) imprudent, rash **2** (= *indiscreto*) indiscreet **3** [*conductor*] careless

impúber ADJ prepubescent, immature

impúdico ADJ (= *desvergonzado*) immodest, shameless; (= *obsceno*) lewd

impuesto A PP *de* **imponer B** ADJ **1** (= *versado*) **estar ~ en/de algo** to be well versed in/about sth **2** (*Méx*) (= *acostumbrado*) **estar ~ a (hacer) algo** to be used to (doing) sth **C** SM [*del estado*] tax (**sobre** on); (*en operaciones de compraventa*) duty (**sobre** on), levy (**sobre** on); **antes de ~s** pre-tax; **libre de ~s** [*inversión, mercancías*] tax-free; [*bebida, perfume, tabaco*] duty-free ➤ **impuesto al valor agregado** (*LAm*) value added tax ➤ **impuesto de actividades económicas** business tax ➤ **impuesto de circulación** road tax ➤ **impuesto de lujo** luxury tax ➤ **impuesto de plusvalía** capital gains tax ➤ **impuesto de sociedades** corporation tax ➤ **impuesto ecológico** eco-tax, green tax ➤ **impuesto revolucionario** *protection money paid to terrorists* ➤ **impuesto sobre bienes inmuebles** property tax ➤ **impuesto sobre el capital** capital levy ➤ **impuesto sobre el valor añadido, impuesto sobre el valor agregado** (*LAm*) value added tax ➤ **impuesto sobre la renta (de las personas físicas)** income tax

impugnación SF challenge, contestation

impugnar /1a/ VT to contest, challenge

impulsar /1a/ VT **1** (*Mec*) to drive, propel **2** [+ *persona*] to drive, impel; **impulsado por el miedo** driven (on) by fear **3** [+ *deporte, inversión*] to promote

impulsivo ADJ impulsive

impulso SM **1** (= *empuje*) **llevaba tanto ~ que no pudo parar a tiempo** she was going so fast she couldn't stop in time; **coger** o **tomar ~** to gather momentum **2** (= *estímulo*) boost; **un ~ a la economía** a boost to the economy **3** (= *deseo instintivo*) impulse; **un ~ repentino** a sudden impulse; **mi primer ~ fue salir corriendo** my first instinct was to run away; **no pude resistir el ~ de abrazarla** I couldn't resist the impulse o urge to embrace her ➤ **impulso sexual** sexual urge, sex drive **4** (*Fís, Fisiol*) impulse

impulsor(a) A ADJ drive *antes de s*, driving **B** SM/F (= *persona*) promoter, instigator **C** SM (*Mec*) drive; (*Aer*) booster

impune ADJ unpunished

impunemente ADV with impunity

impunidad SF impunity

impuntual ADJ unpunctual

impuntualidad SF unpunctuality

impureza SF impurity

impuro ADJ impure

imputación SF accusation, imputation

imputar /1a/ VT **~ a** to attribute to; **los hechos que se les imputan** the acts with which they are charged

inabarcable ADJ vast, extensive

inabordable ADJ unapproachable

inacabable ADJ endless, interminable

inacabado ADJ [*trabajo, libro*] unfinished; [*problema*] unresolved

inaccesible ADJ [*torre, montaña*] inaccessible; [*precio*] prohibitive; [*persona*] aloof

inaceptable ADJ unacceptable

inactivo ADJ **1** [*persona, máquina*] idle **2** [*volcán*] dormant, inactive **3** [*mercado*] sluggish; [*población*] non-working

inadaptable ADJ unadaptable

inadaptación SF inability to adapt; **~ social** maladjustment

inadaptado/a A ADJ maladjusted **B** SM/F misfit

inadecuado ADJ [*recurso, medida*] inadequate; [*película, momento*] unsuitable, inappropriate

inadmisible ADJ unacceptable

inadvertido ADJ **1** (= *no notado*) unnoticed, unobserved; **pasar ~** to go unnoticed, escape notice **2** (= *despistado*) inattentive

inagotable ADJ [*recursos*] inexhaustible; [*persona, paciencia*] tireless

inaguantable ADJ intolerable, unbearable

inajenable ADJ (*Jur*) inalienable

inalámbrico ADJ [*telefonía, comunicaciones*] wireless; [*teléfono, micrófono*] cordless

in albis ADV **quedarse ~** to be left in the dark

inalcanzable ADJ unattainable

inalienable ADJ inalienable

inalterable ADJ [*materia*] inalterable, unchanging; [*persona, cualidad*] immutable; [*cara*] impassive; [*color*] permanent, fast

inamovible ADJ fixed, immovable

inanición SF starvation

inapelable ADJ (*Jur*) unappealable; **las decisiones de los jueces serán ~s** the judges' decisions will be final

inapetencia SF lack of appetite, loss of appetite

inapetente ADJ **estar ~** to have no appetite

inaplazable ADJ which cannot be put off o postponed, pressing

inapreciable ADJ imperceptible

inaptitud SF unsuitability

inatención SF inattention

inaudito ADJ (*gen*) unheard-of; (= *sin precedente*) unprecedented; (= *increíble*) outrageous

inauguración SF [*de teatro, exposición*] opening,

inauguration (*frm*); [*de monumento*] unveiling; [*de curso*] start; **ceremonia de ~** inauguration ceremony, opening ceremony ➤ **inauguración privada** (*Arte*) private viewing

inaugural ADJ [*ceremonia, competición, discurso*] opening, inaugural; [*concierto*] opening; [*viaje*] maiden *antes de s*

inaugurar /1a/ VT [+ *edificio*] to inaugurate; [+ *exposición*] to open (formally); [+ *estatua*] to unveil

inca SMF Inca

incaico ADJ Inca *antes de s*

incalculable ADJ incalculable

incanato SM (*And*) (= *época*) Inca period; (= *reinado*) reign (*of an Inca*)

incandescente ADJ incandescent (*frm*), white hot

incansable ADJ tireless, untiring

incapacidad SF **1** (= *falta de capacidad*) (*para una actividad*) inability; (*para una profesión*) incompetence **2** (*física*) physical handicap, disability; (*mental*) mental handicap ➤ **incapacidad laboral permanente** invalidity ➤ **incapacidad laboral transitoria** temporary disability **3** (*Jur*) (*tb* ~ **legal**) legal incapacity

incapacitado ADJ **1** (= *inadecuado*) unfit (**para** for) **2** (= *minusválido*) handicapped, disabled

incapacitar /1a/ VT **1** (= *invalidar*) to incapacitate, handicap **2** (*Jur*) to disqualify (**para** for)

incapaz Ⓐ ADJ **1 ser ~: sería ~ de hacer una cosa así** he would never do such a thing; **la policía se mostró ~ de prevenir la tragedia** the police proved unable to prevent the tragedy; **¿es que eres ~ de hablar en serio?** can't you ever talk seriously?; **ser ~ para algo** to be useless at sth **2** (*Jur*) unfit Ⓑ SMF incompetent, incompetent fool

incautación SF seizure, confiscation

incautar /1a/ Ⓐ VT to seize, confiscate Ⓑ **incautarse** VPR **~se de** to seize, confiscate

incauto ADJ **1** (= *crédulo*) gullible **2** (= *imprevisor*) unwary, incautious

incendiar /1b/ Ⓐ VT to set fire to, set alight Ⓑ **incendiarse** VPR (= *empezar a arder*) to catch fire; (= *quemarse*) to burn down

incendiario/a Ⓐ ADJ **1** [*bomba, mecanismo*] incendiary **2** [*discurso, escrito*] inflammatory Ⓑ SM/F fire-raiser, arsonist

incendio SM fire ➤ **incendio forestal** forest fire ➤ **incendio provocado** arson attack

incensario SM censer

incentivar /1a/ VT to encourage; **baja incentivada** voluntary redundancy

incentivo SM incentive ➤ **incentivo fiscal** tax incentive

incertidumbre SF uncertainty

incesante ADJ incessant, unceasing

incesto SM incest

incestuoso ADJ incestuous

incidencia SF **1** (*Mat*) incidence **2** (= *suceso*) incident **3** (= *impacto*) impact, effect; **la huelga tuvo escasa ~** the strike had little impact

incidental ADJ incidental

incidente SM incident

incidir /3a/ VI **~ en** (= *afectar*) to influence, affect; (= *recaer sobre*) to have a bearing on

incienso SM incense

incierto ADJ uncertain

incineración SF [*de basuras*] incineration; [*de cadáveres*] cremation

incinerador SM, **incineradora** SF incinerator

incinerar /1a/ VT [+ *basuras*] to incinerate, burn; [+ *cadáver*] to cremate

incipiente ADJ incipient

incisión SF incision

incisivo Ⓐ ADJ **1** (= *cortante*) sharp, cutting **2** (= *mordaz*) incisive Ⓑ SM incisor

inciso SM **1** (= *observación*) digression, aside; **hacer un ~** to make an aside **2** (*Ling*) (= *oración*) interpolated clause; (= *coma*) comma **3** (*Jur*) subsection

incitación SF incitement (**a** to)

incitante ADJ provocative

incitar /1a/ VT **~ a algn a hacer algo** (*a delito*) to incite sb to do sth; **~ a la violencia** to stir up violence

incivilizado ADJ uncivilized

inclemencia SF (*Meteo*) harshness, inclemency; **las ~s del tiempo** the inclemency of the weather

inclemente ADJ (*Meteo*) harsh, inclement

inclinación SF **1** [*de terreno*] slope, gradient (*Brit*), grade (*EEUU*); [*de objeto*] lean, list; **la ~ del terreno** the slope of the ground, the gradient (*Brit*), the grade (*EEUU*); **la ~ de la Torre de Pisa** the lean of the Tower of Pisa ➤ **inclinación magnética** magnetic dip, magnetic inclination **2** (= *reverencia*) bow; **dio su aprobación con una ~ de cabeza** he nodded (his) approval **3** (= *tendencia*) inclination; **tiene inclinaciones artísticas** she has artistic inclinations, she's artistically inclined; **tener ~ hacia la poesía** to have a penchant for poetry, have poetic leanings ➤ **inclinación sexual** sexual preferences *pl*

inclinado ADJ **1** (*en ángulo*) [*terreno, línea*] sloping; [*plano*] inclined; **la torre inclinada de Pisa** the leaning tower of Pisa **2 sentirse ~ a hacer algo** to feel inclined to do sth

inclinar /1a/ Ⓐ VT **1** (= *ladear*) [+ *objeto vertical*] to tilt, lean; **el peso de los abrigos inclinó el perchero** the hatstand was tilting *o* leaning under the weight of the coats; **inclinó el respaldo del asiento** he reclined his seat **2** [+ *cabeza*] (= *torcer*) to lean; (*para afirmar, saludar*) to nod; (*con reverencia*) to bow; **inclinó la cabeza para olerle el cabello** she leaned her head forward to smell his hair; **~ la balanza** to tip the balance **3** (= *predisponer*) to incline; **la crisis inclina a los consumidores hacia el ahorro** the recession inclines consumers to save their money **4** (= *decidir*) **eso la inclinó a pensar que yo era el culpable** that led her to think that I was guilty Ⓑ **inclinarse** VPR **1** [*objeto vertical*] to lean, tilt **2** (= *encorvarse*) to bend; (*en reverencia*) to bow; **~se hacia adelante** to lean forward **3** (= *tender*) **me inclino a pensar que ...** I am inclined to *o* I tend to think that ...; **me inclino por el segundo** I'm inclined to go for the second *o* I tend to prefer the second

incluir /3g/ VT **1** (= *comprender*) to include, contain; **todo incluido** (*Com*) inclusive, all-in **2** (= *agregar*) to include; (*en carta*) to enclose

inclusión SF inclusion; **con ~ de** including

inclusive ADV inclusive; **del 1 al 10, ambos ~** from the 1st to the 10th inclusive; **hasta el próximo domingo ~** up to and including next Sunday

incluso ADV **1** (= *aun*) even; **~ la pegó** he even hit her **2** (= *incluyendo*) including; **nos gustó a todos, ~ a los más testarudos** we all liked it, even *o* including the most stubborn of us

incoar /1a/ VT to start, initiate

incobrable ADJ irrecoverable

incógnita SF **1** (*Mat*) unknown quantity **2** (= *misterio*) mystery; **queda en pie la ~ sobre su influencia** there is still a question mark over his influence

incógnito Ⓐ ADJ unknown Ⓑ SM incognito; **viajar de ~** to travel incognito

incoherencia SF **1** (*en pensamiento, ideas*) incoherence; (*en comportamiento, respuestas*) inconsistency **2** (= *falta de conexión*) disconnectedness **3 incoherencias** nonsense *sing*

incoherente ADJ **1** [*pensamiento, ideas*] incoherent; [*comportamiento, respuestas*] inconsistent **2** (= *inconexo*) disconnected

incoloro ADJ [*líquido, luz*] colourless, colorless (*EEUU*); [*barniz*] clear

incombustible ADJ [*mueble, ropa*] fire-resistant; [*tela*] fireproof

incomodar /1a/ **A** VT **1** (= *causar molestia a*) to inconvenience, trouble **2** (= *causar vergüenza a*) to make feel uncomfortable, embarrass **3** (= *enfadar*) to annoy **B** **incomodarse** VPR **1** (= *tomarse molestia*) to put o.s. out; **¡no se incomode!** don't bother!, don't trouble yourself! **2** (= *avergonzarse*) to feel uncomfortable, feel embarrassed

incomodidad SF **1** (= *falta de comodidad*) discomfort **2** (= *molestia*) inconvenience

incómodo ADJ **1** [*sofá, situación*] uncomfortable; **un paquete ~ de llevar** an awkward *o* cumbersome package to carry **2** **sentirse ~** to feel ill at ease, feel uncomfortable

incomparable ADJ incomparable

incomparecencia SF failure to appear (*in court etc*), non-appearance

incompatibilidad SF incompatibility; **~ de caracteres** mutual incompatibility; **~ de intereses** conflict of interests

incompatible ADJ incompatible

incompetencia SF incompetence

incompetente ADJ incompetent

incompleto ADJ incomplete

incomprendido/a **A** ADJ [*persona*] misunderstood; [*genio*] not appreciated **B** SM/F misunderstood person

incomprensible ADJ incomprehensible

incomprensión SF incomprehension, lack of understanding

incomunicación SF **1** (= *falta de comunicación*) lack of communication **2** (*para presos*) solitary confinement

incomunicar /1g/ VT **1** (= *aislar*) to cut off, isolate **2** [+ *preso*] to put in solitary confinement

inconcebible ADJ inconceivable

inconcluso ADJ unfinished, incomplete

incondicional **A** ADJ [*retirada, amor, garantía*] unconditional; [*fe*] complete, unquestioning; [*apoyo*] wholehearted, unconditional; [*partidario*] staunch, stalwart **B** SMF stalwart, staunch supporter

inconexo ADJ [*datos*] unrelated, unconnected; [*ideas*] disconnected, disjointed; [*texto*] disjointed; [*lenguaje, palabras*] incoherent

inconfesable ADJ shameful, disgraceful

inconformista ADJ, SMF non-conformist

inconfundible ADJ unmistakable

incongruencia SF **1** (= *falta de coherencia*) inconsistency, contradiction **2** (= *cosa incoherente*) **el paciente decía ~s** the patient was talking incoherently

incongruente ADJ [*relato*] inconsistent; **~ con algo** inconsistent with sth, at odds with sth

inconmensurable ADJ immeasurable, vast

inconmovible ADJ [*persona*] unmoved; [*creencia, fe*] unshakeable

inconsciencia SF **1** (*Med*) unconsciousness **2** (= *ignorancia*) unawareness **3** (= *irreflexión*) thoughtlessness

inconsciente **A** ADJ **1** (*Med*) unconscious **2** (= *ignorante*) unaware (**de** of), oblivious (**de** to) **3** (= *involuntario*) unwitting **4** (= *irresponsable*) thoughtless **B** SM unconscious; **el ~ colectivo** the collective unconscious

inconsecuencia SF inconsistency

inconsecuente ADJ inconsistent

inconsiderado ADJ inconsiderate, thoughtless

inconsistencia SF [*de argumento*] weakness; [*de tela*] flimsiness

inconsistente ADJ [*argumento*] weak; [*tela*] flimsy

inconsolable ADJ inconsolable

inconstancia SF **1** (= *falta de disciplina*) indiscipline **2** (= *veleidad*) fickleness

inconstante ADJ **1** (= *sin disciplina*) undisciplined **2** (= *veleidoso*) fickle

inconstitucional ADJ unconstitutional

inconsumible ADJ unfit for consumption

incontable ADJ countless, innumerable

incontenible ADJ uncontrollable, unstoppable

incontestable ADJ [*argumento*] undeniable, indisputable; [*evidencia, prueba*] irrefutable

incontinencia SF incontinence

incontinente ADJ incontinent

incontrolable ADJ uncontrollable

inconveniencia SF **1** (= *inoportunidad*) inappropriateness **2** (= *comentario*) tactless remark **3** (= *acto*) improper thing to do, wrong thing to do

inconveniente **A** ADJ inappropriate **B** SM **1** (= *problema*) problem; **el ~ es que es muy caro** the problem *o* trouble is that it's very expensive **2** (= *desventaja*) disadvantage; **ventajas e ~s** advantages and disadvantages **3** (= *objeción*) objection; **no hay ~ en pagar a plazos** there is no objection to you paying in instalments; **no tengo ningún ~** I don't mind; **no veo ~ en que llames desde aquí** there's no reason why you shouldn't phone from here

incordiar* /1b/ (*Esp*) **A** VT to annoy, pester, bug* **B** VI to be a nuisance

incordio* SM (*Esp*) pain*, nuisance

incorporación SF (*gen*) incorporation; **~ a filas** enlistment; **"sueldo a convenir, incorporación inmediata"** "salary negotiable, start immediately"

incorporado ADJ (*Téc*) built-in

incorporar /1a/ **A** VT **1** (= *añadir*) (*gen*) to incorporate (**a, en** into, in); (*Culin*) to mix in, add; **~ a filas** (*Mil*) to call up, enlist **2** (= *levantar*) **~ a algn** to sit sb up (*in bed*) **B** **incorporarse** VPR **1** [*persona acostada*] to sit up **2** **~se a** [+ *regimiento, asociación*] to join; **~se a filas** to join up, enlist; **~se al trabajo** to start work, report for work

incorpóreo ADJ incorporeal

incorrección SF **1** [*de datos*] incorrectness, inaccuracy **2** (= *descortesía*) discourtesy; **cometer una ~** to commit a faux pas **3** (*Ling*) mistake

incorrecto ADJ **1** [*dato*] incorrect, wrong **2** [*conducta*] discourteous, bad-mannered

incorregible ADJ incorrigible

incorrupto ADJ incorrupt

incredulidad SF (= *desconfianza*) incredulity; (= *escepticismo*) scepticism, skepticism (*EEUU*)

incrédulo/a **A** ADJ (= *desconfiado*) incredulous; (= *escéptico*) sceptical, skeptical (*EEUU*) **B** SM/F sceptic, skeptic (*EEUU*)

increíble ADJ incredible, unbelievable

incrementar /1a/ **A** VT to increase **B** **incrementarse** VPR to increase

incremento SM **1** (= *subida*) increase **2** (= *diferencia*) increment

increpación SF reprimand, rebuke

increpar /1a/ VT to reprimand, rebuke

in crescendo ADV **ir ~** to increase, spiral upwards

incriminación SF incrimination

incriminar /1a/ VT (= *sugerir culpa de*) [*prueba*] to incriminate; (= *acusar*) to accuse

incruento ADJ bloodless

incrustación SF (*Arte*) inlay, inlaid work

incrustar /1a/ **A** VT [+ *joyas*] to inlay; **una espada incrustada de pedrería** a sword encrusted with precious stones **B** **incrustarse** VPR **~se en** [*bala*] to lodge in, embed itself in

incubadora SF incubator

incubar /1a/ **A** VT to incubate **B** **incubarse** VPR to incubate

incuestionable ADJ unquestionable

inculcar /1g/ VT to instil, instill (*EEUU*), inculcate (**en** in, into)

inculpación SF (*gen*) accusation; (*Jur*) charge

inculpar /1a/ VT (*gen*) to accuse (**de** of); (*Jur*) to charge (**de** with)

inculto ADJ **1** [*persona*] uneducated **2** (*Agr*) uncultivated

incultura SF lack of education

incumbencia SF concern; **no es de mi ~** it is no concern of mine

incumbir /3a/ VI **esto sólo incumbe a los implicados** this only concerns those involved; **no me incumbe (a mí)** it is no concern of mine

incumplido ADJ (*Col, Méx, Perú*), **incumplidor** ADJ (*CS*) unreliable

incumplimiento SM **~ de las promesas electorales** failure to keep electoral promises; **~ de una orden** failure to obey an order; **~ de contrato** breach of contract; **lo expulsaron por ~ del deber** he was expelled for dereliction of duty

incumplir /3a/ **Ⓐ** VT [+ *promesa*] to break, fail to keep; [+ *orden*] to fail to obey; [+ *contrato*] to breach; [+ *regla*] to break, fail to observe **Ⓑ** VI (*Col, Méx, Perú*) **1** (= *fallar*) **~ a algn** to let sb down **2** (= *no acudir*) **~ a una cita** to fail to attend an appointment

incunable SM incunable, incunabulum; **~s** incunabula

incurable ADJ incurable

incurrir /3a/ VI **~ en** [+ *error*] to make; [+ *delito*] to commit; [+ *gasto*] to incur

incursión SF raid, incursion

incursionar /1a/ VI **1** (*Mil*) **~ en** to make a raid into, penetrate into **2** (*LAm*) (= *dedicarse*) **~ en** to try one's hand at

indagación SF investigation, inquiry

indagar /1h/ VT to investigate, inquire into

indebido ADJ (= *injustificado*) undue; (= *incorrecto*) improper; (= *injusto*) illegal, wrongful

indecencia SF **1** (= *cualidad*) (= *falta de decencia*) indecency; (= *obscenidad*) obscenity **2** (= *acto*) indecent act; (= *palabra*) indecent thing **3** (= *porquería*) filth

indecente ADJ **1** [*persona*] (= *falto de decencia*) indecent; (= *obsceno*) obscene **2** [*persona, lugar*] (= *sucio*) filthy

indecible ADJ unspeakable, indescribable; **sufrir lo ~** to suffer terribly

indecisión SF indecision

indeciso ADJ [*ser*] indecisive; **estoy ~** I'm undecided

indecoroso ADJ unseemly, indecorous

indefectiblemente ADV unfailingly

indefendible ADJ indefensible

indefensión SF defencelessness, defenselessness (*EEUU*)

indefenso ADJ defenceless, defenseless (*EEUU*)

indefinible ADJ indefinable

indefinición SF **1** (= *falta de definición*) lack of definition **2** (= *vaguedad*) absence of clarity, vagueness

indefinido ADJ **1** (= *ilimitado*) indefinite; **por tiempo ~** indefinitely **2** (= *vago*) undefined, vague **3** (*Ling*) indefinite

indeformable ADJ that keeps its shape

indeleble ADJ indelible

indemallable ADJ (*CS*) ladderproof (*Brit*), run-resist (*EEUU*)

indemne ADJ [*persona*] unharmed, unhurt

indemnización SF compensation, indemnity; **pagó mil dólares de ~** he paid one thousand dollars in damages *o* in compensation ➤ **indemnización por daños y perjuicios** damages *pl* ➤ **indemnización por despido** redundancy pay

indemnizar /1f/ VT to compensate, indemnify (**de** against, for)

independencia SF independence; **con ~ de (que)** irrespective of (whether)

independentista Ⓐ ADJ pro-independence *antes de s* **Ⓑ** SMF pro-independence campaigner

independiente ADJ, SMF independent

independientemente ADV independently; **~ de que** irrespective *o* regardless of whether

independizar /1f/ **Ⓐ** VT to make independent **Ⓑ independizarse** VPR to become independent (**de** of), gain independence (**de** from); **~se económicamente** to become economically independent; **~se de los padres** to become independent from one's parents

indescifrable ADJ [*código*] indecipherable, undecipherable; [*misterio*] impenetrable

indescriptible ADJ indescribable

indeseable ADJ, SMF undesirable

indesmallable ADJ [*medias*] ladderproof (*Brit*), run-resist (*EEUU*)

indesmayable ADJ unfaltering

indestructible ADJ indestructible

indeterminación SF (*al hablar*) indeterminacy, vagueness; (*sobre el futuro*) indeterminacy, uncertainty

indeterminado ADJ **1** (= *impreciso*) indeterminate; [*resultado*] inconclusive **2** (= *indefinido*) indefinite; **por (un) tiempo ~** indefinitely **3** (*Ling*) indefinite

indexar /1a/ VT (*Fin*) to index-link

India SF **la ~** India

indiada SF **1** (*And, RPl*) (= *grupo*) group of Indians; (*CS pey*) mob **2** (*Col*) (= *acto*) dirty trick

indiano/a SM/F *Spaniard who has made good in America*

indicación SF **1** (= *señal*) sign; **me hizo una ~ con la mano** he gestured *o* signalled *o* (*EEUU*) signaled to me with his hand, he made a sign to me with his hand **2** (= *consejo*) hint, suggestion; **por ~ de algn** at the suggestion of sb; **por ~ del médico** on medical advice, on the doctor's advice **3** [*de termómetro*] reading **4 indicaciones** (= *instrucciones*) instructions, directions; **"indicaciones de uso"** "instructions for use"

indicado ADJ **1** (= *adecuado*) suitable; **no es el momento más ~ para hablar de eso** it isn't the best *o* right moment to talk about this; **tú eres la menos indicada para protestar** you're the last person who should complain; **ser lo más/menos ~** to be the best/worst thing (**para** for) **2** (= *señalado*) [*fecha, hora*] specified

indicador Ⓐ ADJ **sigue las señales ~as** follow the road signs **Ⓑ** SM **1** (= *señal*) sign; **es ~ de su mala salud** it is a sign of his ill health **2** (*Téc*) (= *aparato*) gauge, gage (*EEUU*); (= *aguja*) pointer ➤ **indicador de dirección** (*Aut*) indicator ➤ **indicador de velocidad** (*Aut*) speedometer **3** (*Econ*) indicator ➤ **indicador económico** economic indicator **4** (*Inform*) flag

indicar /1g/ VT **1** (= *señalar*) to show; **me indicó el camino** he showed me the way; **indica con un rotulador rojo dónde están los errores** use a red felt-tip pen to indicate *o* show where the mistakes are; **me indicó un punto en el mapa** he showed me *o* pointed out a point on the map **2** (= *decir*) [*señal, policía*] to indicate; [*portavoz, fuentes*] to state, indicate; **según ~on fuentes policiales** as police sources have stated *o* indicated; **según me indicaba en su carta** as you indicated in your letter; **hice lo que usted me indicó** I did as you instructed; **me indicó con el dedo que me callase** he gestured to me to be quiet; **tome este medicamento como le indicó su médico** take this medicine as directed by your doctor **3** (= *mostrar*) [+ *cantidad, precio, temperatura*] to show; **su actitud indicaba una enorme falta de interés** her attitude showed a complete lack of interest; **todo parece ~ que van a ganar** there is every indication *o* sign that they will win, everything points to them winning; **como su (propio) nombre indica** as its name suggests

indicativo Ⓐ ADJ **1** (= *sintomático*) **ser ~ de algo** to be indicative of sth; **es un síntoma ~ de que la situación está mejorando** this is indicative of the fact that the situation is improving **2** (= *recomendado*) [*horario, precio*] recommended **Ⓑ** SM **1** (*Ling*) indicative; **presente de ~** present indicative **2** (*Radio*) call sign, call letters *pl* (*EEUU*) **3** (*Aut*) ➤ **indicativo de nacionalidad** national identification plate

índice SM **1** [*de libro, publicación*] index ➤ **índice alfabético** alphabetical index ➤ **índice de materias, índice temático** table of contents **2** (= *catálogo*) (library)

catalogue, (library) catalog (*EEUU*) **3** (*Estadística*) rate
➤ **índice de audiencia** (*TV*) audience ratings *pl* ➤ **índice de natalidad** birth rate ➤ **índice de ocupación** occupancy rate **4** (*Econ*) index ➤ **índice de precios al consumo** retail price index (*Brit*), cost of living index (*EEUU*) **5** (= *indicio*) sign, indication **6** (*Anat*) (*tb* **dedo ~**) index finger, forefinger

indiciario ADJ **prueba indiciaria** circumstantial proof

indicio SM **1** (= *señal*) (*gen*) indication, sign; (= *vestigio*) **es ~ de** it is an indication of, it is a sign of **2 indicios** (*Jur*) circumstantial evidence *sing* (**de** to)

indiferencia SF lack of interest (**hacia** in, towards), indifference (*frm*) (**hacia** towards); **ella aparentaba ~** she pretended to be indifferent, she feigned indifference; **ante la ~ de los políticos** faced by the indifference of politicians

indiferente ADJ **1** (= *impasible*) [*actitud, mirada*] indifferent; **un grupo de transeúntes ~s** a group of unconcerned passers-by; **esas imágenes no pueden dejarnos ~s** those images cannot fail to move us; **se mostró ~ a sus encantos** he remained indifferent to her charms **2** (= *que da igual*) **a mí la política me es ~** politics doesn't interest me; **me es ~** it makes no difference to me, I don't mind (*Brit*)

indígena Ⓐ ADJ indigenous (**de** to), native (**de** to) Ⓑ SMF native

indigencia SF poverty, destitution

indigenista ADJ pro-Indian

indigente Ⓐ ADJ destitute Ⓑ SMF destitute person

indigestar /1a/ Ⓐ VT to give indigestion Ⓑ **indigestarse** VPR **1** [*persona*] to get indigestion **2** [*comida*] to cause indigestion; **esa carne se me indigestó** that meat gave me indigestion

indigestión SF indigestion

indigesto ADJ [*alimento*] indigestible, hard to digest; [*artículo, libro*] indigestible, difficult to get through

indignación SF indignation, anger

indignado ADJ indignant, angry (**con, contra** with; **por** at, about)

indignante ADJ outrageous, infuriating

indignar /1a/ Ⓐ VT to anger, make indignant Ⓑ **indignarse** VPR to get angry; **¡es para ~se!** it's infuriating!

indigno ADJ **1** (= *impropio*) unworthy; **tales comentarios son ~s de un ministro** such comments are unworthy of a minister **2** (= *desmerecedor*) unworthy; **ser ~ de algo** to be unworthy of sth **3** (= *despreciable*) despicable

índigo SM indigo

indio/a Ⓐ ADJ Indian Ⓑ SM/F Indian; ✦ MODISMOS **hacer el ~*** to play the fool; **subírsele el ~ a algn** (*Méx**): **se le subió el ~** he got over-excited

indirecta SF hint

indirectamente ADV indirectly

indirecto ADJ **1** [*apoyo, causa, respuesta*] indirect; [*referencia*] oblique; [*amenaza, crítica*] veiled **2** [*impuesto, coste*] indirect **3** [*iluminación, luz*] indirect **4** (*Gram*) [*complemento, estilo*] indirect

indisciplina SF (*gen*) indiscipline, lack of discipline; (*Mil*) insubordination

indisciplinado ADJ **1** [*niño, alumno*] undisciplined **2** [*soldado*] insubordinate

indiscreción SF **1** (= *falta de discreción*) indiscretion **2** (= *acto, dicho*) gaffe, faux pas; **si no es ~** if I may say so; **cometió la ~ de decírmelo** he was tactless enough to tell me

indiscreto ADJ (= *falto de discreción*) indiscreet; (= *falto de tacto*) tactless

indiscriminado ADJ indiscriminate

indiscutiblemente ADV indisputably, unquestionably

indisoluble ADJ **1** [*matrimonio*] indissoluble **2** [*sustancia*] insoluble

indispensable ADJ indispensable, essential

indisponer /2q/ Ⓐ VT **1** (*Med*) to upset, make ill **2** (= *enemistar*) **~ a algn con otro** to set sb against another person Ⓑ **indisponerse** VPR **1** (*Med*) to become ill, fall ill; (*CS euf*) (= *menstruar*) to begin one's period **2** (= *enemistarse*) **~se con algn** to fall out with sb

indisposición SF **1** (*Med*) indisposition **2** (= *desgana*) disinclination, unwillingness

indispuesto ADJ (*Med*) indisposed, unwell; **estar indispuesta** (*CS euf*) (= *menstruar*) to have one's period

indistintamente ADV without distinction; **pueden firmar ~** either may sign

individual Ⓐ ADJ **1** [*trabajo, necesidades, características*] individual **2** [*cama, cuarto*] single Ⓑ SM (*Dep*) singles *pl*, singles match (*esp Brit*)

individualismo SM individualism

individualista Ⓐ ADJ individualistic Ⓑ SMF individualist

individualizar /1f/ Ⓐ VT to individualize; **~ el tratamiento** to individualize the treatment, tailor the treatment to the individual; **~ la enseñanza** to tailor *o* target teaching to each individual's needs Ⓑ VI **prefiero no ~** I prefer not to pick out any individuals *o* single anyone out

individuo SM (*gen*) individual; (*pey*) individual, character; **el ~ en cuestión** the person in question

indivisible ADJ indivisible

indócil ADJ (= *difícil*) unmanageable; (= *testarudo*) headstrong; (= *rebelde*) disobedient

indoctrinar /1a/ VT to indoctrinate

indocumentado ADJ not carrying identity papers

indoeuropeo/a Ⓐ ADJ, SM/F Indo-European Ⓑ SM (*Ling*) Indo-European

índole SF **1** (= *naturaleza*) nature **2** (= *tipo*) kind, sort; **cosas de esta ~** things of this kind

indolencia SF indolence, laziness

indolente ADJ indolent, lazy

indomable ADJ [*espíritu*] indomitable; [*animal*] untameable; [*pelo*] unmanageable; [*energía*] boundless

indomiciliado ADJ homeless

indómito ADJ = **indomable**

Indonesia SF Indonesia

indonesio/a ADJ, SM/F Indonesian

inducción SF **1** (*Fil, Elec*) induction **2** (= *persuasión*) inducement

inducir /3n/ VT **1** (*Elec*) to induce **2** (= *empujar, llevar*) to induce; **~ a algn a error** to lead sb into error

inductivo ADJ inductive

indudable ADJ undoubted, unquestionable; **es ~ que ...** there is no doubt that ...

indulgencia SF **1** (= *tolerancia*) (*tb Rel*) indulgence ➤ **indulgencia plenaria** plenary indulgence **2** (*para perdonar*) leniency

indulgente ADJ (= *tolerante*) indulgent; (*para perdonar*) lenient (**con** towards)

indultar /1a/ VT to pardon, reprieve

indulto SM pardon, reprieve

indumentaria SF clothing, dress

industria SF industry ➤ **industria artesanal** cottage industry ➤ **industria automovilística, industria del automóvil** car industry, auto industry (*EEUU*) ➤ **industria del ocio** leisure industry

industrial Ⓐ ADJ **1** (= *de la industria*) industrial **2** (= *no casero*) factory-made, industrially produced **3** (*) (= *enorme*) huge, massive; **en cantidades ~es** in huge amounts Ⓑ SMF industrialist

industrialización SF industrialization

industrializar /1f/ Ⓐ VT to industrialize Ⓑ **industrializarse** VPR to become industrialized

industriarse /1b/ VPR **industriárselas para hacer algo** to manage to do sth

industrioso ADJ industrious

inédito ADJ **1** [*texto*] unpublished **2** (= *nuevo*) new; (= *nunca visto*) hitherto unheard-of

inefable ADJ indescribable, ineffable

ineficacia SF **1** [*de medida*] ineffectiveness **2** [*de proceso*] inefficiency; [*de gobierno, persona*] inefficiency, incompetence

ineficaz ADJ **1** [*medida*] ineffective **2** [*proceso*] inefficient; [*gobierno, persona*] inefficient, incompetent

ineficiencia SF inefficiency

ineficiente ADJ inefficient

inelástico ADJ inelastic, rigid

ineluctable ADJ (*liter*) ineluctable (*liter*)

ineludible ADJ unavoidable, inescapable

INEM SM ABR (*Esp*) (= **Instituto Nacional de Empleo**) *national employment organization*

inenarrable ADJ inexpressible

inepcia SF (*liter*) ineptitude, incompetence

ineptitud SF ineptitude, incompetence

inepto ADJ inept, incompetent

inequívoco ADJ (= *sin ambigüedad*) unequivocal, unambiguous; (= *inconfundible*) unmistakable

inercia SF **1** (*Fís*) inertia **2** (= *indolencia*) inertia; **por ~** through force of habit, out of habit

inerme ADJ (= *sin armas*) unarmed; (= *indefenso*) defenceless, defenseless (*EEUU*)

inerte ADJ **1** (*Fís*) inert **2** (= *sin vida*) lifeless; (= *inmóvil*) inert, motionless

inescrutable ADJ inscrutable

inesperado ADJ unexpected

inestabilidad SF instability, unsteadiness ➤ **inestabilidad laboral** lack of job security

inestable ADJ unstable, unsteady

inestimable ADJ inestimable, invaluable

inevitable ADJ inevitable

inexactitud SF inaccuracy

inexacto ADJ (= *no preciso*) inaccurate; (= *no cierto*) incorrect, untrue

inexcusable ADJ **1** [*conducta*] inexcusable, unforgivable **2** [*conclusión*] inevitable, unavoidable

inexistente ADJ non-existent

inexorable ADJ inexorable

inexperiencia SF inexperience, lack of experience

inexperto ADJ (= *novato*) inexperienced; (= *torpe*) unskilled, inexpert

inexplicable ADJ inexplicable

inexpresividad SF inexpressiveness, expressionlessness

inexpresivo ADJ expressionless, inexpressive

inexpugnable ADJ impregnable

inextinguible ADJ eternal, inextinguishable

in extremis ADV **1** (= *en el último momento*) at the very last moment **2** (= *como último recurso*) as a last resort

inextricable ADJ [*relación, lío*] inextricable; [*bosque*] impenetrable

infalibilidad SF infallibility

infalible ADJ **1** [*persona*] infallible **2** [*aparato, plan*] foolproof **3** [*puntería*] unerring

infaltable ADJ (*CS*) inevitable

infamante ADJ shameful, degrading

infamar /1a/ VT to defame, slander

infame ADJ [*persona*] odious; [*tarea*] thankless; **esto es ~** this is monstrous

infamia SF **1** (= *calumnia*) calumny, slur **2** (= *deshonra*) disgrace, ignominy **3** (= *canallada*) despicable act; (*hum*) crime

infancia SF **1** [*de persona*] childhood; [*de proyecto, teoría*] infancy; **es un amigo de la ~** he's a childhood friend; **en mi ~** as a child **2** (= *niños*) children

infante/a SM/F **Ⓐ** SM/F (*Hist*) infante/infanta, prince/ princess **Ⓑ** SM **1 ➤ infante de marina** marine **2** (*liter*) (= *niño*) infant; **tierno ~** young child

infantería SF infantry ➤ **infantería de marina** marines *pl*

infanticida SMF infanticide, child killer

infanticidio SM infanticide

infantil ADJ **1** [*educación, población, psicología*] child *antes de s*; [*sonrisa, mirada*] childish, childlike; [*enfermedad*] children's, childhood *antes de s*; [*hospital, libro, programa*] children's; [*mortalidad*] infant, child *antes de s* **2** (*pey*) [*persona, comportamiento*] childish, infantile **3** (*Dep*) ≈ youth

infantilismo SM infantilism

infarto SM **1** (*tb ~ de miocardio*) heart attack **2** **de ~*** heart-stopping

infatigable ADJ tireless, untiring

infausto ADJ (*liter*) (= *infortunado*) unlucky; (= *funesto*) ill-starred, ill-fated

infección SF infection

infeccioso ADJ infectious

infectar /1a/ **Ⓐ** VT to infect **Ⓑ infectarse** VPR to become infected (**de** with)

infectocontagioso ADJ infectious, transmittable

infecundidad SF **1** [*de mujer*] infertility, sterility **2** [*de tierra*] infertility, barrenness

infecundo ADJ **1** [*mujer*] infertile, sterile **2** [*tierra*] infertile, barren

infelicidad SF unhappiness

infeliz **Ⓐ** ADJ [*persona*] unhappy; [*vida*] unhappy, wretched **Ⓑ** SMF poor unfortunate, poor wretch

inferencia SF inference

inferior **Ⓐ** ADJ **1** (*en el espacio*) [*parte, extremidad*] lower; **la parte ~** the lower part; **labio ~** bottom *o* lower lip; **el piso ~ del edificio** the ground (*Brit*) *o* first (*EEUU*) floor of the building
2 (*en categoría, jerarquía*) inferior; **están en un puesto ~ al nuestro en la liga** they're just below us in the league; **le es ~ en talento** he is inferior to him in talent
3 (*con cantidades, números*) lower; **temperaturas ~es a los 20°** temperatures lower than 20°, temperatures below 20°; **renta per cápita ~ a la media** per capita income lower than *o* below the average; **cualquier número ~ a nueve** any number under *o* below *o* less than nine
Ⓑ SMF subordinate

inferioridad SF inferiority; **estar** *o* **encontrarse en ~ de condiciones** to be at a disadvantage

inferir /3i/ VT **1** (= *deducir*) to infer, deduce **2** (= *causar*) [+ *herida*] to inflict (**a, en** on); [+ *daño*] to cause (**a** to)

infernáculo SM (*Esp*) hopscotch

infernal ADJ infernal, hellish; **un ruido ~** a dreadful racket*

infernillo SM = **infiernillo**

infértil ADJ infertile

infestado ADJ **~ de** [+ *parásitos, gérmenes*] infested with; **~ de cucarachas** cockroach-infested; **~ de turistas/ mendigos** crawling with tourists/beggars

infestar /1a/ VT to infest

infición SF (*Méx*) pollution

infidelidad SF infidelity, unfaithfulness ➤ **infidelidad conyugal** marital infidelity

infiel **Ⓐ** ADJ **1** (= *desleal*) unfaithful (**a, con** to); **fue ~ a su mujer** he was unfaithful to his wife **2** (*Rel*) unbelieving, infidel **3** (= *erróneo*) unfaithful, inaccurate; **la memoria le fue ~** (*liter*) his memory failed him **Ⓑ** SMF (*Rel*) unbeliever, infidel

infiernillo SM (*tb ~ de alcohol*) (*para iluminar*) spirit lamp; (*para guisar*) spirit stove

infierno SM hell; **vivieron un ~** they went through hell; **¡vete al ~!*** go to hell!*; **✦ MODISMO mandar a algn al (quinto) ~*** to tell sb to go to hell*

infiltrar /1a/ **Ⓐ** VT **1** [+ *espía, policía*] to infiltrate **2** (*Med*) to infiltrate **Ⓑ infiltrarse** VPR **1** [*espía, policía*] to infiltrate; **se infiltró en la red informática de la NASA** he hacked into NASA's computer network **2** [*ideas, costumbres*] to permeate **3** [*humedad, líquido*] to seep; [*luz*] to filter

ínfimo ADJ [*calidad, grado*] very poor; [*cantidad, porcentaje, nivel*] very small, tiny; **la ayuda que le dieron fue ínfima** the help they afforded him was next to nothing; **viven en ínfimas condiciones** they live in dreadful *o* appalling conditions; **precios ~s** knockdown prices

infinidad SF **1** (*Mat*) infinity **2** (= *gran cantidad*) **~ de veces** countless times, innumerable times; **hay ~ de personas que creen ...** any number of people believe ..., there's no end of people who believe ...

infinitesimal ADJ infinitesimal

infinitivo SM infinitive

infinito Ⓐ ADJ [*universo, variedad, paciencia*] infinite; [*entusiasmo, posibilidades*] boundless; **sonrió con infinita tristeza** she smiled with immense sadness; **tuve que copiarlo infinitas veces** I had to copy it out countless times *o* over and over again **Ⓑ** SM (*Mat*) infinity; **el ~** (*Fil*) the infinite

inflable ADJ inflatable

inflación SF inflation

inflacionario ADJ inflationary

inflacionista ADJ inflationary

inflador SM (*LAm*) bicycle pump

inflamable ADJ inflammable

inflamación SF **1** (*Med*) inflammation **2** (*Fís*) ignition, combustion

inflamar /1a/ **Ⓐ** VT **1** (*Med*) to inflame **2** (= *enardecer*) to inflame, arouse **3** (= *prender fuego a*) to set on fire, ignite **Ⓑ inflamarse** VPR **1** (*Med*) to become inflamed **2** (= *encenderse*) to ignite

inflamatorio ADJ inflammatory

inflar /1a/ **Ⓐ** VT **1** [+ *neumático, globo*] to inflate, blow up **2** (= *exagerar*) (*gen*) to exaggerate; [+ *precios*] to inflate **3** (*Chi*) (= *hacer caso a*) to heed, pay attention to **Ⓑ** VI **1** (*Méx**) (= *beber*) to booze*, drink **2** (*RPl*) (= *molestar*) to be annoying, be irritating **Ⓒ inflarse** VPR **1** (= *hincharse*) to swell **2** (= *engreírse*) to get conceited; **~se de orgullo** to swell with pride **3** (*Méx**) (= *beberse*) to drink

inflexible ADJ (= *rígido*) inflexible; **regla ~** strict rule, hard-and-fast rule

inflexión SF inflection

infligir /3c/ VT to inflict (**a** on)

influencia SF **1** (= *influjo*) influence; **actuó bajo la ~ de las drogas** he acted under the influence of drugs **2 influencias** (= *contactos*) contacts

influenciable ADJ impressionable, easily influenced

influenciar /1b/ VT to influence

influenza SF (*esp LAm*) influenza, flu

influir /3g/ **Ⓐ** VT to influence **Ⓑ** VI to have influence, carry weight; **~ en** *o* **sobre** to influence

influjo SM influence (**sobre** on)

influyente ADJ influential

infografía SF computer graphics

infopista SF information superhighway

información SF **1** (= *datos*) information; (= *oficina*) information desk; (*Telec*) Directory Enquiries (*Brit*), Directory Assistance (*EEUU*); **si desean más** *o* **mayor ~** if you require further information; **pregunte en ~** ask at information *o* at the information desk; **~ internacional ¿dígame?** international enquiries, can I help you?; **"Información"** "Information", "Enquiries" **➤ información genética** genetic information

2 (= *noticias*) news; **según las últimas informaciones** according to the latest reports *o* news **➤ información**

deportiva (*en prensa, radio*) sports section; (*en TV*) sports news **➤ información financiera** (*en prensa, radio*) financial section; (*en TV*) financial news
3 (*Inform*) data *pl*

informado ADJ **estar ~** to be informed (**de, sobre** about); **tenemos derecho a estar ~s** we have a right to know, we have a right to information; **bien ~** well-informed; **mal ~** misinformed, badly informed; **mantener ~ a algn** to keep sb informed

informador(a) Ⓐ ADJ **la comisión ~a** the inquiry commission, the commission of inquiry; **una charla ~a** an informative talk; **el equipo ~ de esta cadena** this channel's team of reporters **Ⓑ** SM/F **1** [*de una noticia*] informant; [*de la policía*] informer **2** (= *periodista*) journalist **➤ informador(a) gráfico/a** press photographer

informal ADJ **1** [*persona*] unreliable **2** [*charla, lenguaje, cena*] informal; [*ropa*] casual, informal **3** (*LAm*) (= *no oficial*) **el sector ~ de la economía** the unofficial sector of the economy, the black economy (*Brit*)

informalidad SF **1** [*de persona*] unreliability **2** [*de lenguaje, reunión*] informality; (*en el vestir*) casualness

informante SMF [*de una noticia*] informant; [*de la policía*] informer

informar /1a/ **Ⓐ** VT **1** (= *dar información a*) **¿dónde te han informado?** where did you get your information?; **le han informado mal** you've been misinformed, you've been badly informed; **~ a algn de algo** to inform sb of sth, tell sb about sth; **el portavoz informó a la prensa de los cambios en el gobierno** the spokesman briefed the press on *o* informed the press about the changes in the government; **~ a algn sobre algo** to inform sb about sth, give sb information on sth
2 (= *comunicar*) **~ que** to report that; **la policía informó que las causas del accidente no estaban claras** the police reported that the cause of the accident was not clear; **~ a algn que** to tell sb that, inform sb that; **nos complace ~le que ha resultado ganadora** we are pleased to inform you that you are the winner
Ⓑ VI [*portavoz, fuentes*] to state, point out, indicate; **según ~on fuentes oficiales** according to official sources; **nuestros representantes ~án de los motivos de la huelga** our representatives will announce the reasons for the strike; **~ de que** to report that; **~ sobre algo** to report on sth **Ⓒ informarse** VPR (= *obtener información*) to find out, get information; **¿te has informado bien?** are you sure your information is correct?; **~se de** *o* **sobre algo** to find out about sth; **he estado informándome sobre los cursos de verano** I've been enquiring about *o* finding out about summer courses

informática SF computing

informático/a Ⓐ ADJ computer *antes de s* **Ⓑ** SM/F (= *técnico*) computer expert; (= *programador*) computer programmer

informativo Ⓐ ADJ **1** (= *que informa*) informative; **un libro muy ~** a very informative book; **un folleto ~** an information leaflet; **boletín ~** news bulletin **2** [*comité*] consultative, advisory **Ⓑ** SM (*Radio, TV*) news programme, news program (*EEUU*)

informatizar /1f/ VT to computerize

informe¹ ADJ [*bulto, figura*] shapeless

informe² SM **1** (= *escrito*) report (**sobre** on); **~ médico/policial/técnico** medical/police/technical report **2 informes** (= *datos*) information *sing*; [*de trabajador*] references; **según mis ~s** according to my information; **pedir ~s** *o* **sobre algo** to ask for information about sth; **pedir ~s de** *o* **sobre algn** (*para trabajo*) to follow up sb's references

infortunio SM (*liter*) (= *mala suerte*) misfortune, ill luck; (= *accidente*) mishap

infracción SF offence, offense (*EEUU*) (**de** against), violation (*EEUU*) (**de** of); **➤ infracción de tráfico** traffic offence, traffic violation (*EEUU*)

infraccionar /1a/ (*Chi, Méx frm*) **Ⓐ** VT to fine **Ⓑ** VI to commit a traffic offence *o* (*EEUU*) violation

infradotado ADJ **1** (= *falto de recursos*) undersupplied, short of resources; (= *falto de personal*) understaffed **2** (*RPl*)

(= *falto de inteligencia*) (*pey*) moronic

infraestructura SF infrastructure

in fraganti ADV **coger** *o* **pillar** *o* **sorprender** ~ **a algn** to catch sb red-handed

infranqueable ADJ [*obstáculo físico*] impassable; [*abismo, distancia*] unbridgeable; [*dificultad*] insurmountable, insuperable

infrarrojo ADJ infrared

infrautilizado ADJ underused

infravalorar /1a/ VT to undervalue

infravivienda SF sub-standard housing

infrecuencia SF infrequency

infrecuente ADJ infrequent

infringir /3c/ VT to infringe, contravene

infructuoso ADJ [*búsqueda, esfuerzo, negociación*] fruitless; [*intento*] unsuccessful; [*empresa, operación*] unprofitable

ínfulas SFPL **darse** ~ to get all high and mighty; **tener (muchas)** ~ **de algo** to fancy o.s. as sth; **un joven con** ~ **de escritor** a young man who fancies himself as a writer

infumable* ADJ (*Esp*) [*espectáculo, película*] unwatchable; [*libro*] unreadable

infundado ADJ unfounded, groundless

infundio SM malicious story

infundir /3a/ VT (*gen*) to instil, instill (*EEUU*) (**a, en** into); [+ *confianza, respeto*] to inspire; ~ **sospechas** to arouse suspicion

infusión SF infusion, herbal tea ➤ **infusión de manzanilla** camomile tea

infuso ADJ *ver* **ciencia 1**

ingeniar /1a/ Ⓐ VT to devise, think up Ⓑ **ingeniarse** VPR **ingeniárselas para hacer algo** to manage to do sth

ingeniería SF engineering ➤ **ingeniería financiera** financial engineering ➤ **ingeniería genética** genetic engineering

Ingeniero SM (*esp Méx*) graduate; (*título*) sir; ~ **Quintanilla** ≈ Dr. Quintanilla

ingeniero/a SM/F engineer ➤ **ingeniero/a aeronáutico/a** aeronautical engineer ➤ **ingeniero/a agrónomo/a** agronomist, agricultural expert ➤ **ingeniero/a de caminos, canales y puertos** civil engineer ➤ **ingeniero/a de minas** mining engineer ➤ **ingeniero/a de telecomunicaciones** telecommunications engineer ➤ **ingeniero/a industrial** industrial engineer ➤ **ingeniero/a naval** naval architect

ingenio SM 1 (= *inventiva*) ingenuity, inventiveness; (= *agudeza*) wit; **aguzar el** ~ to sharpen one's wits 2 (= *aparato*) device 3 (*LAm*) (= *refinería*) ➤ **ingenio azucarero** sugar mill, sugar refinery

ingenioso ADJ 1 [*persona*] (= *mañoso*) clever, resourceful; (= *agudo*) witty 2 [*invento, sistema*] ingenious

ingente ADJ huge, enormous

ingenuidad SF naïveté, ingenuousness

ingenuo ADJ naïve, ingenuous

ingerir /3i/ VT to consume, ingest (*frm*)

ingesta SF, **ingestión** SF consumption, ingestion (*frm*), intake; **la** ~ **de alcohol** alcohol consumption; **la** ~ **diaria de hierro** the daily intake of iron

Inglaterra SF England

ingle SF groin

inglés/esa Ⓐ ADJ English Ⓑ SM/F Englishman/ Englishwoman; **los ingleses** the English, English people; ✦ MODISMO **pagar a la inglesa*** to go dutch Ⓒ SM (*Ling*) English

ingobernable ADJ [*país, ciudad*] ungovernable; [*embarcación*] unsteerable, impossible to steer

ingratitud SF ingratitude

ingrato/a Ⓐ ADJ [*persona*] ungrateful; [*tarea*] thankless, unrewarding Ⓑ SM/F ungrateful person; **¡eres un ~!** you're so ungrateful!

ingravidez SF weightlessness

ingrávido ADJ (= *sin peso*) weightless; (*liter*) (= *ligero*) very light

ingrediente SM 1 [*de comida, compuesto*] ingredient 2 **ingredientes** (*Arg*) (= *tapas*) appetizers

ingresar /1a/ Ⓐ VT 1 (= *internar*) 1.1 (*en institución*) **la ~on en la cárcel** she was put in prison *o* sent to prison; **la cárcel donde están ingresados** the prison where they are being held; ~ **a algn en un colegio** to enrol sb in a school, send sb to a school 1.2 (*en hospital*) to admit (**en** to); **María continúa ingresada** María is still in hospital 2 (*Esp*) [+ *dinero, cheque*] to pay in, deposit; [+ *ganancias*] to take; **he ingresado 5.000 pesos en mi cuenta** I've paid 5,000 pesos into my account; **se han ingresado 200 dólares en su cuenta** 200 dollars have been credited to your account
Ⓑ VI 1 (= *entrar*) 1.1 (*en institución*) [*miembro*] to join; **fue la primera mujer que ingresó en** *o* (*LAm*) **a la Academia** she was the first woman to be elected to the Academy *o* to become a member of the Academy; ~ **en** *o* (*LAm*) **a la cárcel** to go to prison, be sent to prison; ~ **en** *o* (*LAm*) **a un colegio** to enter a school; ~ **en el** *o* (*LAm*) **al ejército** to join the army, join up; ~ **en** *o* (*LAm*) **a la universidad** to start university 1.2 (*Med*) (= *entrar*) (*Esp*) to be dead on arrival; ~ **en el hospital** to be admitted to hospital (*Brit*) *o* to the hospital (*EEUU*) 1.3 (*LAm frm*) (= *introducirse*) ~ **a** to enter 2 [*dinero*] to come in; **hoy no ha ingresado mucho en caja** we haven't taken much today

ingreso SM 1 (*en institución, hospital*) admission; **tras su ~ en la Academia** after he joined the Academy, after his admission to the Academy; **después de su ~ en la marina** after he joined the navy; **examen de** ~ (*Univ*) entrance examination; ~ **en prisión** imprisonment 2 (*Fin*) 2.1 (*Esp*) (= *depósito*) deposit; **hacer un** ~ to pay in some money, make a deposit 2.2 **ingresos** [*de persona, empresa*] income *sing*; [*de país, multinacional*] revenue *sing*; **mi única fuente de ~s** my only source of income; **los ~s por publicidad** advertising revenue, revenue from advertising ➤ **ingresos de taquilla** (*Cine, Teat*) box-office takings; (*Dep*) ticket sales 3 (= *lugar de acceso*) entrance

íngrimo* ADJ **~ y solo** all alone, completely alone

inguinal ADJ inguinal (*frm*), groin *antes de s*

inhábil ADJ 1 [*persona*] (= *torpe*) clumsy; (= *no apto*) unfit 2 **día** = non-working day; **ese día ha sido declarado** ~ **that** day has been declared a holiday

inhabilitación SF disqualification

inhabilitar /1a/ VT 1 (*Pol, Jur*) to disqualify; **el alcalde fue inhabilitado por seis años** the mayor was disqualified *o* barred from holding office for six years 2 (*Med*) to disable, render unfit

inhabitable ADJ uninhabitable

inhalación SF 1 [*de gases*] inhalation 2 **inhalaciones** (*Med*) inhalations

inhalador SM inhaler

inhalar /1a/ VT to inhale

inherente ADJ inherent (**a** in); **la función** ~ **a un oficio** the duties attached to an office

inhibición SF inhibition

inhibidor Ⓐ ADJ inhibiting Ⓑ SM inhibitor ➤ **inhibidor del apetito** appetite depressant

inhibir /3a/ Ⓐ VT to inhibit Ⓑ **inhibirse** VPR 1 (= *no actuar*) to keep out (**de** of), stay away (**de** from) 2 (= *abstenerse*) to refrain (**de** from) 3 (*Biol, Quím*) to be inhibited

inhóspito ADJ inhospitable

inhumación SF burial, interment (*frm*)

inhumano ADJ 1 (= *no humano*) inhuman 2 (= *falto de compasión*) inhumane

inhumar /1a/ VT to bury, inter (*frm*)

iniciación SF 1 (= *comienzo*) beginning 2 (= *introducción*) introduction; **curso de** ~ introductory course 3 (*Rel*) initiation; **ceremonia de** ~ initiation ceremony; **rito de** ~ initiation rite

iniciado/a Ⓐ ADJ initiated Ⓑ SM/F initiate (*frm*); **para los ~s/no ~s** for the initiated/the uninitiated

inicial Ⓐ ADJ [*posición, velocidad, respuesta*] initial; [*sueldo, precio, alineación*] starting; **capital ~** initial capital, starting capital Ⓑ SF (= *letra*) initial

inicialar /1a/ VT to initial

inicializar /1f/ VT to initialize

iniciar /1b/ Ⓐ VT 1 (= *comenzar*) to begin, start, initiate (*frm*) 2 (*en conocimientos, secta*) to initiate (**en** into); **~ a algn en un secreto** to let sb into a secret Ⓑ **iniciarse** VPR 1 (= *comenzar*) to begin, start 2 **~se como actor/escritor** to start out as an actor/writer, take one's first steps as an actor/writer; **~se en política** to start out in politics

iniciático ADJ **ritos ~s** initiation rites

iniciativa SF initiative; **por ~ propia** on one's own initiative; **carecer de ~** to lack initiative; **tomar la ~** to take the initiative ➤ **iniciativa privada** private enterprise

inicio SM start, beginning; **"inicio"** (*Internet*) "home"

inicuo (*frm*) ADJ wicked, iniquitous (*frm*)

inigualable ADJ [*calidad*] unsurpassable; [*belleza, reputación*] matchless; [*oferta, precio*] unbeatable

inimitable ADJ inimitable

ininteligible ADJ unintelligible

ininterrumpido ADJ (*gen*) uninterrupted; [*proceso*] continuous; [*progreso*] steady, sustained; **20 horas de música ininterrumpida** 20 hours of non-stop *o* uninterrupted music; **llovió de forma ininterrumpida** it rained continuously *o* non-stop

injerencia SF interference (**en** in), meddling (**en** in)

injerirse /3i/ VPR to interfere (**en** in), meddle (**en** in)

injertar /1a/ VT to graft (**en** on, on to)

injerto SM 1 (= *acción*) grafting 2 (*Agr, Med*) graft; **~ de piel** skin graft

injuria SF (*gen*) insult; (*Jur*) slander; **~s** abuse *sing*, insults; **demandar a algn por ~s** to sue sb for slander

⚠ **injuria ≠ injury**

injuriar /1b/ VT (*gen*) to insult, abuse; (*Jur*) to slander

injurioso ADJ (*gen*) insulting, offensive; (*Jur*) slanderous

injusticia SF (= *falta de justicia*) injustice; (= *falta de equidad*) unfairness; **es una ~** (= *es inmerecido*) it's unjust, it's an injustice; (= *no es equitativo*) it's unfair

injustificado ADJ unjustified

injusto ADJ [*castigo, crítica*] unjust, unfair; [*detención*] wrongful; [*despido, norma, persona*] unfair; **ser ~ con algn** to be unfair to sb

Inmaculada SF **la ~ (Concepción)** the Immaculate Conception

inmaculado ADJ [*baño, cocina*] immaculate, spotless; [*persona, ropa*] immaculate; [*honradez, reputación*] impeccable

inmadurez SF immaturity

inmaduro ADJ [*persona*] immature; [*fruta*] unripe

inmancable ADJ (*Ven*) infallible

inmanente ADJ immanent

inmaterial ADJ immaterial

inmediaciones SFPL surrounding area *sing*, vicinity *sing*; **en las ~ del bosque** in the area around the forest, in the vicinity of the forest

inmediatamente ADV immediately

inmediatez SF immediacy

inmediato ADJ 1 (= *sin mediar intervalo*) immediate 2 (= *rápido*) prompt; **de ~** immediately; **en el futuro ~** in the immediate future 3 [*lugar*] adjoining; **~ a** close to, next to

inmejorable ADJ (*gen*) excellent, superb; [*precio, récord*] unbeatable

inmemorial ADJ immemorial; **desde tiempo ~** from

time immemorial

inmensamente ADV immensely, vastly; **~ rico** immensely rich, enormously wealthy

inmensidad SF immensity, vastness

inmenso ADJ [*llanura, océano, fortuna*] vast, immense; [*objeto, ciudad, número*] enormous; [*alegría, tristeza, esfuerzo*] tremendous, immense; [*talento*] enormous, immense; **la inmensa mayoría** the vast majority

inmerecido ADJ undeserved

inmersión SF 1 (= *sumergimiento*) immersion 2 (*en tema, idioma*) immersion; **periodos de ~ en el extranjero** periods of intensive exposure abroad ➤ **inmersión lingüística** language immersion

inmerso ADJ 1 (= *sumergido*) immersed 2 (*en actividades, ideas*) immersed (**en** in); **~ en sus meditaciones** deep in thought

inmigración SF immigration

inmigrante ADJ, SMF immigrant

inmigrar /1a/ VI to immigrate

inminente ADJ imminent

inmiscuirse /3g/ VPR to interfere, meddle (**en** in)

inmobiliaria SF 1 (= *agencia de venta*) estate agency (*Brit*), real estate agency (*EEUU*) 2 (= *constructora*) property developer

inmobiliario ADJ real-estate *antes de s*, property *antes de s*; **agente ~** estate agent (*Brit*), real estate agent (*EEUU*); **venta inmobiliaria** sale of property

inmoderado ADJ immoderate

inmodestia SF immodesty

inmolación SF sacrifice, immolation (*frm*)

inmolar /1a/ VT to sacrifice, immolate (*frm*)

inmoral ADJ immoral

inmoralidad SF 1 (= *cualidad*) immorality 2 (= *acto*) immoral act; **es una ~** it's immoral

inmortal ADJ, SMF immortal

inmortalidad SF immortality

inmortalizar /1f/ VT to immortalize

inmóvil ADJ still, motionless; **quedar ~** (*gen*) to stand still *o* motionless; (*Aut*) to remain stationary

inmovilidad SF immobility

inmovilismo SM (= *oposición al cambio*) resistance to change; (*Pol*) ultraconservatism

inmovilista ADJ (= *opuesto al cambio*) resistant to change; (*Pol*) ultraconservative; ⊃ *APERTURISMO*

inmovilizar /1f/ VT 1 [+ *persona, vehículo*] to immobilize 2 (= *paralizar*) to paralyse, bring to a standstill 3 (*Fin*) [+ *capital*] to tie up

inmueble Ⓐ ADJ **bienes ~s** real estate *sing*, real property *sing* Ⓑ SM property, building

inmundicia SF filth, dirt; **esto es una ~** this is absolutely disgusting

inmundo ADJ filthy, dirty

inmune ADJ 1 (*Med*) immune (**a** against, to) 2 (= *no afectado*) immune (**a** to); **~ a las críticas** immune to criticism

inmunidad SF (*Pol, Med*) immunity ➤ **inmunidad diplomática** diplomatic immunity ➤ **inmunidad parlamentaria** parliamentary immunity

inmunitario ADJ immune

inmunización SF immunization

inmunizar /1f/ VT to immunize

inmunodeficiencia SF immunodeficiency

inmunodepresor ADJ immunosuppressive

inmunología SF immunology

inmunológico ADJ [*sistema*] immune; [*tolerancia*] immunological

inmunoterapia SF immunotherapy

inmutable ADJ [*principio, sociedad*] unchanging; [*persona*] impassive; **aguantó ~ los insultos** she took the insults impassively

inmutarse /1a/ VPR **ni se inmutó** he didn't bat an eyelid (*Brit*) *o* eye (*EEUU*), he didn't turn a hair; **siguió sin ~** he carried on unperturbed

innato ADJ innate, inborn

innecesario ADJ unnecessary

innegable ADJ undeniable

innoble ADJ ignoble

innombrable ADJ unmentionable

innovación SF innovation

innovador(a) Ⓐ ADJ innovative Ⓑ SM/F innovator

innovar /1a/ VI to innovate

innumerable ADJ countless, innumerable

inobservancia SF non-observance

inocencia SF [*de acusado*] innocence; (= *ingenuidad*) innocence, naïveté

inocentada SF practical joke, April Fool joke; **pagar la ~** to pay dearly for one's inexperience; ⇨ *INOCENTES, DÍA DE LOS (SANTOS)*

inocente Ⓐ ADJ 1 (= *sin culpa*) innocent (**de** of); (*Jur*) not guilty, innocent; **siempre se ha declarado ~** he has always pleaded his innocence
2 (= *ingenuo*) naïve
3 (= *inofensivo*) [*broma*] harmless
Ⓑ SMF innocent person; **el día de los (Santos) Inocentes** ≈ April Fools' Day

DÍA DE LOS (SANTOS) INOCENTES

28 December, **el día de los (Santos) Inocentes**, is when the Catholic Church in Spain commemorates the New Testament story of King Herod's slaughter of the innocent children of Judaea. Like our April Fools' Day, Spaniards play practical jokes or **inocentadas** on each other. A typical example is sticking a **monigote**, a cut-out paper figure, on someone's back. Whenever someone falls for a trick, the practical joker cries out **Inocente!**

inocentón/ona Ⓐ ADJ gullible, naïve Ⓑ SM/F simpleton

inocuidad SF harmlessness, innocuousness (*frm*)

inoculación SF inoculation

inocular /1a/ VT (*Med*) to inoculate (**contra** against; **de** with)

inocuo ADJ innocuous, harmless

inodoro Ⓐ ADJ odourless, odorless (*EEUU*) Ⓑ SM toilet

inofensivo ADJ inoffensive, harmless

inolvidable ADJ unforgettable

inoperancia SF 1 [*de plan*] inoperative character 2 [*de autoridades, policía*] ineffectiveness

inoperante ADJ [*plan*] inoperative; [*decisión*] ineffective

inopia SF ✦ MODISMO **estar en la ~*** (= *no saber*) to be in the dark, have no idea; (= *estar despistado*) to be dreaming, be miles away

inopinado ADJ unexpected

inoportuno ADJ inopportune, untimely

inorgánico ADJ inorganic

inoxidable ADJ (*gen*) rustproof; [*acero*] stainless

inquebrantable ADJ [*fe*] unshakeable, unyielding; [*fidelidad, lealtad*] unswerving; [*unidad, voluntad*] unbreakable; [*salud*] robust, stout

inquietante ADJ worrying (*esp Brit*), worrisome (*EEUU*), disturbing

inquietar /1a/ Ⓐ VT to worry Ⓑ **inquietarse** VPR to worry

inquieto ADJ 1 (= *preocupado*) anxious, worried (**por** about) 2 (= *agitado*) restless, unsettled

inquietud SF 1 (= *preocupación*) concern; **los rumores han provocado ~ entre los inversores** the rumours have

aroused concern among investors 2 (= *interés*) interest; **es persona de ~es culturales** she has an interest in culture, she has cultural interests

inquilinaje SM 1 (*Chi Agr*) tenancy 2 (*Méx*) (= *arrendatarios*) tenants *pl*

inquilinato SM 1 (= *arrendamiento*) tenancy 2 (*SAm*) (= *edificio*) tenement house 3 (*Chi Agr*) (= *agricultores*) tenant farmers *pl*

inquilino/ɫ SM/F (= *arrendatario*) tenant; (*Chi Agr*) tenant farmer

inquina SF ill will; **tener ~ a algn** to have a grudge against sb, have it in for sb*

inquirir /3i/ VI to inquire; **~ sobre algo** to make inquiries about sth, inquire into sth

Inquisición SF **la ~** the (Spanish) Inquisition

inquisidor SM inquisitor

inquisitivo ADJ inquisitive, curious

inquisitorial ADJ inquisitorial

inri SM **para más ~** (*Esp**) to make matters worse

insaciable ADJ insatiable

insalubre ADJ unhealthy, insalubrious (*frm*)

Insalud SM ABR (*Esp*) = **Instituto Nacional de la Salud**

insano ADJ 1 (= *loco*) insane, mad 2 (= *malsano*) unhealthy

insatisfacción SF dissatisfaction

insatisfactorio ADJ unsatisfactory

insatisfecho ADJ [*condición, deseo*] unsatisfied; [*persona*] dissatisfied

insaturado ADJ unsaturated

inscribir /3a/ (*pp* **inscrito**) Ⓐ VT 1 (= *grabar*) [+ *nombre, iniciales*] to inscribe (**en** on)
2 (= *apuntar*) (*en lista*) to put down; (*en colegio, curso*) to enrol, enroll (*EEUU*)
3 [+ *contrato, nacimiento*] to register; **~ en el registro** to enter in the register, register
4 [+ *figura geométrica*] to inscribe
Ⓑ **inscribirse** VPR 1 (= *apuntarse*) (*en colegio, curso*) to enrol, enroll (*EEUU*), register; (*en partido político*) to join; (*en concurso, competición*) to enter; (*en lista*) to put one's name down, register; **los equipos inscritos** the teams on the list; **~se en el censo electoral** to register o.s. on the electoral roll (*Brit*) *o* list of registered voters (*EEUU*); **~se en el registro** [*pareja*] to sign the marriage register
2 (= *incluirse*) **~se dentro de** *o* **en** [+ *movimiento, tradición*] to fall within; [+ *clasificación*] to be classed among; **la política del gobierno se inscribe dentro de un marco europeo** the government's policy follows the European framework

inscripción SF 1 (= *texto grabado*) inscription 2 (= *acto*) (*en concurso*) entry; (*en curso*) enrolment, enrollment (*EEUU*); (*en congreso, censo*) registration; **el plazo de ~ en el curso finaliza el día 3 de mayo** course applications will be accepted until the 3rd of May, the closing date *o* deadline for enrolment on the course is May 3rd

inscripto (*Arg*) PP *de* **inscribir**

inscrito PP *de* **inscribir**

insecticida SM insecticide

insecto SM insect

inseguridad SF 1 (= *peligro*) lack of safety ➤ **inseguridad ciudadana** lack of safety in the streets, decline in law and order 2 (= *falta de confianza*) insecurity 3 (= *falta de estabilidad*) unsteadiness 4 (= *incertidumbre*) uncertainty ➤ **inseguridad laboral** lack of job security

inseguro ADJ 1 (= *peligroso*) [*zona, negocio, conducción*] unsafe 2 (= *sin confianza*) [*persona*] insecure 3 (= *sin estabilidad*) [*paso, estructura*] unsteady 4 (= *incierto*) [*clima*] unpredictable; [*futuro*] insecure

inseminación SF insemination ➤ **inseminación artificial** artificial insemination

inseminar /1a/ VT to inseminate

insensatez SF foolishness, stupidity; **es una ~** it's foolish *o* stupid; **decir insensateces** to say foolish *o* stupid things

insensato ADJ foolish, stupid

insensibilizar /1f/ VT **1** [+ *persona*] (*ante emociones, problemas*) to render insensitive; (*ante sufrimiento*) to render unfeeling **2** (= *anestesiar*) to anaesthetize, anesthetize (*EEUU*); (*a alérgenos*) to desensitize

insensible ADJ **1** [*persona*] (= *indiferente*) insensitive (**a** to); (= *no afectado*) unaffected (**a** by) **2** [*cambio*] imperceptible **3** (= *inconsciente*) insensible, unconscious; (= *entumecido*) numb

inseparable ADJ inseparable

insepulto ADJ unburied; **funeral** o **misa (de) corpore ~** funeral mass

inserción SF insertion

INSERSO SM ABR (*Esp*), **Inserso** SM ABR (*Esp*) = **Instituto Nacional de Servicios Sociales**

insertar /1a/ VT to insert

inservible ADJ (= *inútil*) useless; (= *averiado*) out of order

insidia SF maliciousness

insidioso ADJ insidious, deceptive

insigne ADJ (= *distinguido*) distinguished; (= *famoso*) famous

insignia SF **1** (= *distintivo*) badge **2** (= *estandarte*) flag, banner; (*Náut*) pennant **3 insignias** [*de dignidad, poder*] insignia

insignificancia SF **1** (= *cualidad*) insignificance **2** (= *cosa insignificante*) trifle

insignificante ADJ [*asunto, cantidad, detalle*] insignificant, trivial; [*persona*] insignificant

insincero ADJ insincere

insinuación SF insinuation; **hacer insinuaciones sobre algo** to make insinuations about sth, drop hints about sth

insinuante ADJ [*tono, movimiento*] insinuating; [*mirada, ropa*] suggestive

insinuar /1e/ Ⓐ VT **1** (= *sugerir*) to insinuate, hint at; **~ que ...** to insinuate o imply that ... **2 ~ una sonrisa** to give the hint of a smile Ⓑ **insinuarse** VPR **1** (= *entreverse*) to begin to appear **2 ~se a algn** to make advances to sb

insípido ADJ [*comida*] insipid, tasteless; [*espectáculo, persona*] dull, tedious

insistencia SF [*de persona*] insistence (**en** on); [*de quejas*] persistence; **a ~ de** at the insistence of

insistente ADJ [*persona*] insistent; [*quejas*] persistent

insistir /3a/ VI **1** (= *perseverar*) **insistió en que se trataba de un error** she insisted that it was a mistake, she was adamant that it was a mistake; **insistió en que nos quedásemos a cenar** she insisted that we should stay to supper; **no insistas, que no pienso ir** don't keep on about it because I'm not going **2** (= *enfatizar*) **~ en** o **sobre algo** to stress o emphasize sth

in situ ADV on the spot, in situ (*frm*)

insociable ADJ unsociable

insolación SF **1** (*Med*) sunstroke; **coger una ~** to get sunstroke **2** (*Meteo*) sunshine; **horas de ~** hours of sunshine

insolentarse /1a/ VPR to become insolent, become rude; **~ con algn** to be insolent to sb, be rude to sb

insolente ADJ insolent, rude

insolidario ADJ unsupportive; **hacerse ~ de algo** to dissociate o.s. from sth

insólito ADJ unusual, unwonted (*frm*)

insoluble ADJ insoluble

insolvente ADJ insolvent, bankrupt

insomne Ⓐ ADJ sleepless, insomniac Ⓑ SMF insomniac

insomnio SM sleeplessness, insomnia

insondable ADJ [*abismo, mar*] bottomless; [*misterio*] unfathomable (*liter*), impenetrable

insonorizar /1f/ VT to soundproof

insoportable ADJ unbearable, intolerable

insoslayable ADJ unavoidable

insospechado ADJ unsuspected

insostenible ADJ untenable

inspección SF (= *revisión*) inspection, examination; (= *control*) check; **una ~ de Hacienda** a tax inspection, an Inland Revenue inspection (*Brit*) ➤ **Inspección de Trabajo** ≈ Industrial Relations Commission ➤ **inspección médica** medical examination ➤ **inspección ocular** visual inspection o examination ➤ **inspección técnica de vehículos** roadworthiness test, ≈ MOT test (*Brit*)

inspeccionar /1a/ VT to inspect

inspector(a) SM/F inspector ➤ **inspector(a) de Hacienda** tax inspector ➤ **inspector(a) de policía** police inspector

inspiración SF **1** [*de artista*] inspiration; **ballets de ~ española** Spanish-inspired ballets **2** (*Med*) inhalation

inspirado ADJ inspired

inspirar /1a/ Ⓐ VT **1** [+ *artista*] to inspire; **eso no inspira confianza al consumidor** that does not inspire confidence in the consumer **2** [+ *aire*] to inhale, breathe in Ⓑ **inspirarse** VPR **~se en algo** to be inspired by sth, find inspiration in sth

instalación SF **1** (= *conexión*) [*de equipo, luz*] installation **2** (= *montaje*) [*de oficina, fábrica*] setting up; [*de tienda de campaña*] pitching **3** (= *equipo*) [*de luz, gas*] system ➤ **instalación eléctrica** electricity system, wiring ➤ **instalación sanitaria** sanitation facilities *pl* **4 instalaciones** (= *recinto*) installations; (= *servicios*) facilities; **durante su recorrido por las instalaciones del museo** during her visit round the museum ➤ **instalaciones deportivas** (= *recinto*) sports grounds; (= *servicios*) sports facilities **5** (*Arte*) installation

instalar /1a/ Ⓐ VT **1** (= *conectar*) [+ *calefacción, teléfono*] to install, instal (*EEUU*); [+ *luz, gas*] to connect, connect up, put in; [+ *antena*] to put up, erect (*frm*); [+ *lavadora, lavaplatos*] to install, instal (*EEUU*), plumb in; [+ *ordenador, vídeo*] to set up; [+ *sistema de control*] to install, instal (*EEUU*), put into operation; **¿te han instalado ya el teléfono?** have you had the phone put in yet?, are you on the phone yet? (*Brit*) **2** (= *montar*) [+ *consulta, oficina*] to set up, open; [+ *campamento, fábrica, espectáculo, exposición*] to set up; [+ *tienda de campaña*] to pitch; **la escultura fue instalada en el centro del escenario** the sculpture was erected in the middle of the stage **3** [+ *invitado*] to put, install Ⓑ **instalarse** VPR **~se en** [+ *casa, oficina*] to settle into; [+ *ciudad*] to set up home in, settle in; [+ *país*] to settle in; **cuando estemos ya instalados** when we're settled in; **¿cuándo os ~éis en las nuevas oficinas?** when are you moving to the new offices?; **me instalé en el sofá y de allí no me moví** I sat o settled myself down on the sofa and didn't move from there; **~se en el poder** to take power, get into power

instancia SF **1** (= *solicitud*) application, request; (*Jur*) petition; **a ~(s) de algn** at the request of sb, at sb's request **2** (= *formulario*) application form **3 en última ~** (= *como último recurso*) as a last resort **4** (= *autoridad*) authority; **altas ~s** high authorities

instantánea SF snap, snapshot

instantáneo ADJ [*respuesta, comunicación*] instantaneous; [*acceso, café, éxito*] instant *antes de s*; **la bala le produjo la muerte instantánea** the bullet killed him instantly

instante SM moment, instant; **se detuvo un ~** he stopped for a moment; **al ~** right now, at once; **(a) cada ~** all the time, every single moment; **en un ~** in a flash; **en ese** o **aquel mismo ~** at that precise moment

instar /1a/ VT to urge, press; **~ a algn a hacer algo** to urge sb to do sth

instauración SF establishment, setting-up

instaurar /1a/ VT to establish, set up

instigación SF instigation

instigador(a) SM/F instigator

instigar /1h/ VT to incite; **~ a algn a hacer algo** to incite *o* induce sb to do sth

instilar /1a/ VT to instil, instill (*EEUU*) (**en** into)

instintivamente ADV instinctively

instintivo ADJ instinctive

instinto SM instinct; **por ~** instinctively ➤ **instinto asesino** killer instinct ➤ **instinto maternal** maternal instinct ➤ **instinto sexual** sexual urge

institución SF **1** (= *organismo*) institution; **un inspector de instituciones penitenciarias** an inspector of prisons; **ese bar es toda una ~ en la ciudad** that bar is something of an institution in the city ➤ **institución benéfica, institución de beneficencia** charitable foundation, charitable organization **2** (= *acción*) establishment **3 instituciones** (*en nación, sociedad*) institutions

institucional ADJ institutional

institucionalizar /1f/ VT to institutionalize

instituto SM **1** (= *organismo*) institute, institution ➤ **instituto de belleza** (*Esp*) beauty parlour, beauty parlor (*EEUU*) **2** (*Esp Educ*) ≈ secondary school, ≈ high school (*EEUU*) ➤ **Instituto de Enseñanza Secundaria** ≈ state secondary school (*Brit*), ≈ high school (*EEUU*) ➤ **Instituto Nacional de Bachillerato** *formerly the name given to state secondary schools/high schools in Spain*

institutriz SF governess

instrucción SF **1** (*Educ*) education; **tener poca ~ en algo** to have a limited knowledge of sth **2** (*Mil*) (= *período*) training; (= *ejercicio*) drill; **los soldados estaban haciendo la ~ en el patio** the soldiers were being drilled in the courtyard; **un vuelo de ~** a training flight **3** (*Dep*) coaching, training **4** (*Jur*) (*tb* **~ del sumario**) preliminary investigation **5 instrucciones** (= *indicaciones*) instructions; **recibir instrucciones** to receive instructions *o* orders; (*Mil*) to be briefed ➤ **instrucciones de uso** directions for use

instructivo ADJ **1** (= *educativo*) educational **2** (= *revelador*) [*conclusión, reunión*] enlightening; [*ejemplo*] instructive

instructor(a) ❹ ADJ [*cabo, sargento*] training; [*fiscal, juez*] examining ❺ SM/F (*Dep*) coach, trainer; (*Mil*) instructor ➤ **instructor(a) de vuelo** flight instructor

instruido ADJ educated

instruir /3g/ ❹ VT **1** (= *formar*) [+ *estudiante*] to instruct; [+ *profesional*] to train; **me instruyeron en el manejo del fusil** I was taught how to use a gun **2** (*Jur*) (= *tramitar*) [+ *caso, causa*] to try, hear; **~ las diligencias** *o* **el sumario** to institute proceedings ❺ VI (= *enseñar*) **la experiencia instruye mucho** experience is a great teacher ❻ **instruirse** VPR to learn, teach o.s. (**de** about)

instrumental ❹ ADJ **1** (*Mús*) instrumental **2** (*Der*) **prueba ~** documentary evidence ❺ SM instruments *pl*

instrumentalizar /1f/ VT **~ a algn** (= *utilizar*) to use sb as a tool, make cynical use of sb; (= *explotar*) to exploit sb, manipulate sb

instrumentar /1a/ VT **1** (*Mús*) to score, orchestrate **2** [+ *medidas, plan*] to implement, bring in

instrumentista SMF (*Mús*) instrumentalist

instrumento SM **1** (*Mús*) instrument ➤ **instrumento de cuerda** string instrument ➤ **instrumento de viento** wind instrument ➤ **instrumento musical** musical instrument **2** (*Téc*) (= *aparato*) instrument; (= *herramienta*) tool, implement ➤ **instrumento de precisión** precision instrument **3** (= *medio*) instrument, tool

insubordinación SF (= *desobediencia*) insubordination; (= *falta de disciplina*) unruliness, rebelliousness

insubordinado ADJ (= *desobediente*) insubordinate; (= *indisciplinado*) unruly, rebellious

insubordinarse /1a/ VPR to rebel

insuceso SM (*Col frm*) unfortunate event

insuficiencia SF **1** (= *escasez*) insufficiency **2** (= *carencia*) lack, shortage; **debido a la ~ de personal** due to shortage of staff **3** (= *incompetencia*) incompetence **4** (*Med*) ➤ **insuficiencia cardíaca** heart failure ➤ **insuficiencia renal** kidney failure ➤ **insuficiencia respiratoria** shortage of

breath **5 insuficiencias** (= *fallos*) inadequacies; (= *carencias*) deficiencies

insuficiente ❹ ADJ [*explicación*] inadequate; [*dinero*] insufficient ❺ SM fail

insuflar /1a/ VT **~ algo a** to breathe sth into; **insufló aires de esperanza a la vida política** he breathed new hope into politics

insufrible ADJ unbearable, insufferable

insular ADJ island *antes de s*

insulina SF insulin

insulso ADJ **1** [*comida*] tasteless, insipid **2** [*charla, persona*] dull

insultar /1a/ VT to insult

insulto SM insult

insumisión SF **1** (= *rebeldía*) rebelliousness **2** (*Esp Mil*) *refusal to do military service or community service*

insumiso ❹ ADJ rebellious ❺ SM (*Esp Mil*) *man who refuses to do military service or community service*

insumos SMPL (*LAm Econ*) supplies, input, materials

insuperable ADJ [*problema*] insurmountable; [*precio*] unbeatable; [*calidad*] unsurpassable

insurgente ADJ, SMF insurgent

insurrección SF revolt, insurrection

insurrecto/a ADJ, SM/F rebel, insurgent

insustancial ADJ insubstantial

insustituible ADJ irreplaceable

intachable ADJ [*conducta*] irreproachable

intacto ADJ **1** (= *sin tocar*) untouched; **dejó el desayuno casi ~** she left her breakfast almost untouched **2** (= *no dañado*) [*vehículo*] intact, undamaged; **conserva ~ su sentido del humor** his sense of humor is intact *o* unaffected

intangible ❹ ADJ intangible ❺ SM intangible, intangible asset

integración SF integration; **~ racial** racial integration

integrado ADJ integrated

integrador ADJ **política ~a** policy of integration, integrationist policy; **proceso ~** process of integration

integral ❹ ADJ **1** (= *entero*) [*cereal*] whole-grain; [*arroz*] brown; [*pan, harina*] wholemeal (*Brit*), wholewheat (*EEUU*) **2** (= *total*) [*plan, reforma, servicio*] comprehensive, all-round; **un desnudo ~** a full frontal **3** (= *integrante*) integral, built-in; **una parte ~ de** an integral part of **4** (= *redomado*) total, complete; **un idiota ~** a total *o* complete fool ❺ SF (*Mat*) integral

íntegramente ADV **1** (= *completamente*) entirely; **el periódico reprodujo ~ la carta** the newspaper published the letter in full **2** (= *con integridad*) uprightly, with integrity

integrante ❹ ADJ [*parte, elemento*] integral; [*país*] member *antes de s* ❺ SMF member

integrar /1a/ ❹ VT **1** (= *componer*) to make up; **la exposición la integran 150 fotografías** the exhibition is made up of 150 photographs; **una enciclopedia integrada por 12 volúmenes** an encyclopaedia consisting of 12 volumes **2** (= *incorporar*) [+ *funciones, servicios*] to incorporate, include; **~ a algn en algo** to integrate sb into sth; **quieren ~ a su club en la federación deportiva** they want their club to become a member of *o* join the sports federation **3** (*Mat*) to integrate **4** (*CS*) (= *pagar*) to pay up ❺ **integrarse** VPR **1** (= *adaptarse*) **~se a** *o* **en** [+ *grupo*] to fit into, integrate into; [+ *conjunto, entorno*] to blend with **2** (= *unirse*) **~se a** *o* **en** [+ *asociación, conjunto*] to join; **el año en que España se integró plenamente en la Alianza Atlántica** the year Spain became a full member of the Atlantic Alliance

integridad SF **1** (= *totalidad*) **publicaron el texto en su ~** they published the text in full *o* in its entirety; **~ física** personal safety, physical well being **2** (= *honradez*) integrity

integrista ADJ, SMF fundamentalist

íntegro ADJ **1** (= completo) [cantidad, pago] whole; [condena] full; [grabación, texto] unabridged; **cumplió la pena íntegra** he served his sentence in full, he served his full sentence; **el libro jamás se publicó ~** the book was never published in full; **en versión íntegra** [película] uncut; [novela] unabridged **2** (= honrado) upright

intelecto SM intellect

intelectual ADJ, SMF intellectual

inteligencia SF **1** (= capacidad) intelligence ➤ **inteligencia artificial** artificial intelligence ➤ **inteligencia verbal** verbal skills pl, verbal ability **2** (= persona inteligente) mind, intellect **3** (Mil) intelligence; **servicio de ~** intelligence service

inteligente ADJ **1** [persona, vida, pregunta] intelligent **2** [misil, edificio, tarjeta] smart

inteligible ADJ intelligible

intemperie SF **la ~** the elements pl; **estar a la ~** to be out in the open, be at the mercy of the elements; **dejar a algn a la ~** to leave sb unprotected

intempestivo ADJ untimely; **a horas intempestivas** at an ungodly hour

intemporal ADJ timeless

intención SF **1** (= propósito) intention; **no ha sido mi ~ despertarte** I didn't mean to wake you; **con la mejor ~ del mundo** with the best (of) intentions; **su ~ era muy otra** he had something very different in mind; **la ~ es lo que cuenta** it's the thought that counts; **con ~** (= a propósito) deliberately, intentionally; **mencionó lo del divorcio con mala ~** he spitefully mentioned the divorce; **la ~ de hacer algo: ha dejado clara su ~ de venir** he has made it clear that he intends to come; **no lo dijo con la ~ de ofenderla** he didn't say it with the intention of offending her, he didn't say it to offend her; **sonrió con la ~ de animarme** he smiled to try to cheer me up; **tenemos la ~ de salir temprano** we intend o plan to start out early **2 intenciones** (= planes) intentions, plans; **no sabes sus intenciones** you don't know what he has in mind; **tener buenas intenciones** to mean well, have good intentions; **tener malas intenciones** to be up to no good **3 doble** o **segunda ~** double meaning; **lo dijo con segunda** o **doble ~** there was a double meaning to what he said

intencionado ADJ (= deliberado) deliberate, intentional; **bien ~** [persona] well-meaning, well-intentioned; [acto] well-meant, well-intentioned

intencional ADJ intentional

intendencia SF **1** (Mil) ≈ service corps, ≈ quartermaster corps (EEUU) **2** (RPl) (= alcaldía) town/city council; (= edificio) town/city hall **3** (Chi, Col) (= división territorial) province

intendente SMF **1** (Mil) quartermaster general **2** (RPl) (= alcalde) mayor **3** (Chi, Col) (= gobernador) provincial governor **4** (Méx, Ecu) (= policía) police inspector

intensamente ADV **1** (= con intensidad) intensely **2** (= con fuerza, vehemencia) powerfully, strongly **3** (= vivamente) vividly, profoundly

intensidad SF **1** [de terremoto, sonido] intensity **2** [de color, olor, dolor] intensity; [de emoción, sentimiento] strength; **Manuel vivió con ~** Manuel lived life to the full

intensificar /1g/ **Ⓐ** VT to intensify **Ⓑ intensificarse** VPR to intensify

intensivo ADJ [búsqueda, tratamiento] intensive; [curso] intensive, crash antes de s

intenso ADJ [frío, dolor, actividad] intense; [emoción] powerful, strong; [color] deep, intense

intentar /1a/ VT to try, attempt (frm); **hemos intentado un acuerdo** we've tried o attempted (frm) to reach an agreement; **¡venga, inténtalo!** come on, have a go o have a try!; **~ hacer algo** to try to do sth, attempt to do sth (frm); **~ que** (+ SUBJUN): **intenta que te lo dejen más barato** try and get them to reduce the price

intento SM **1** (= tentativa) attempt; **~ fallido** o **fracasado** failed attempt ➤ **intento de asesinato** (= acción) murder attempt; (= cargo) attempted murder ➤ **intento de**

suicidio suicide attempt ➤ **intento de violación** attempted rape **2** (Méx) (= propósito) intention; **de ~** (Méx, Col†) by design

intentona SF (Pol) putsch, rising ➤ **intentona golpista** failed coup (d'état), attempted coup (d'état)

interacción SF interaction

interaccionar /1a/ VI to interact (**con** with)

interactivo ADJ interactive

interanual ADJ **promedio ~** year-on-year average; **variación ~** variation from year to year

intercalar /1a/ VT [+ pausa, ejemplo] to put in, include; [+ comentarios, cultivos] to intersperse, alternate; [+ actividad] to fit in, combine; **en el texto se han intercalado bastantes fotografías** a number of photographs have been inserted into the text; **~ algo entre** [+ imágenes, objetos] to insert sth between; [+ cultivos] to intersperse sth between, alternate sth with; **daban unos aperitivos intercalados entre los platos** they served aperitifs between courses

intercambiar /1b/ VT [+ impresiones, presos, ideas] to exchange; [+ sellos, fotos] to swap, exchange

intercambio SM [de impresiones, presos, ideas] exchange; [de sellos, fotos] swap, exchange; **hacemos ~ de conversación** we exchange conversation

interceder /2a/ VI to intercede; **~ con el juez por el acusado** to intercede with the judge on the defendant's behalf, plead with the judge for the defendant

intercentros ADJ INV **comité ~** joint committee (with representatives from all the different workplaces)

interceptar /1a/ VT **1** [+ correspondencia, misil, balón] to intercept **2** [+ tráfico] to stop, hold up; [+ carretera] to block, cut off

intercesión SF **1** (= mediación) mediation **2** (Rel) intercession

interconexión SF interconnection

intercontinental ADJ intercontinental

intercultural ADJ intercultural

interdependencia SF interdependence

interdependiente ADJ interdependent

interés SM **1** (= valor) interest; **ese asunto no tiene ~ para nosotros** this matter is of no interest to us **2** (= curiosidad) interest; **ha seguido con gran ~ la campaña electoral** he has followed the electoral campaign with great interest; **poner ~ en algo** to take an interest in sth; **sentir** o **tener ~ por hacer algo** to be interested in doing sth

> Recuérdese que las preposiciones en inglés rigen gerundio y no infinitivo, de ahí **to be interested in doing sth**.

3 (= beneficio) **3.1** [de persona, país] interest; **te lo digo por tu propio ~** I'm telling you for your own benefit o in your own interest; **en ~ del país** in the interest(s) of the country **3.2** (Fin) interest; **un préstamo a** o **con un ~ del 9%** a loan at 9%; **dar ~** [capital, inversión] to yield interest; [banco, cuenta] to pay interest **4 intereses 4.1** (Com) interests; **hay intereses económicos por medio** there are financial interests involved; **tengo que defender mis intereses** I have to look after my own interests; **tener intereses en algo** to have interests o a stake in sth **4.2** (= aficiones) interests; **¿qué intereses tienes?** what are your interests? ➤ **intereses creados** vested interests

interesadamente ADV **actuaron ~** they had ulterior motives in acting as they did, they acted to protect their own interests

interesado/a **Ⓐ** ADJ **1** (= con interés) interested; **las partes interesadas** the interested parties; **las personas interesadas pueden llamar al 900 100 100** anyone interested can phone 900 100 100 **2** (= egoísta) self-interested, selfish; **su ayuda era muy interesada** she had her own interests at heart in helping us; **actuar de forma interesada** to act selfishly

B SM/F **1** (= *persona interesada*) **los ~s pueden escribir a ...** anyone interested *o* those interested should write to ...; **el consentimiento de los ~s** the consent of those concerned; **todos los ~s en el jazz** all those interested in jazz *o* all jazz fans; **soy el primer ~ en ganar** I have the greatest interest in winning
2 (= *persona egoísta*) **eres un ~** you always act out of self-interest, you're always on the lookout for yourself

interesante ADJ [*persona, película*] interesting; [*precio, sueldo*] attractive; *ver tb* **hacerse**

interesar /1a/ **A** VI **1** (= *despertar interés*) **1.1** [*propuesta, tema*] to be of interest, interest; **un tema que interesa a los jóvenes** a subject of interest to young people, a subject which interests young people **1.2** [*actividad, persona*] **no me interesan los toros** I'm not interested in bullfighting; **sólo le interesa el dinero** his only interest is money, all he's interested in is money
2 (= *concernir*) **~ a algn** to concern sb; **el asunto interesa a todos** the matter concerns everybody
3 (= *convenir*) **ese tipo de negocios no interesa** that sort of business is not worth our while; **no dice nada porque no le interesa desde el punto de vista judicial** he doesn't say anything because, from a legal point of view, it's not in his interest; **este coche podría ~te** this car could be of interest (to you), this car might interest you; **me interesa más este hotel** this hotel suits me better
B VT **1** **~ a algn en algo** to interest sb in sth; **no logré ~lo en mi trabajo** I failed to get him interested in my work
2 (*Med*) [+ *órgano, nervio*] to affect; **la herida interesa la región lumbar** the injury affects the lumbar region
C **interesarse** VPR **~se por algo** to take an interest in sth; **~se por algn** (= *preocuparse*) to show concern for sb; (= *preguntar*) to inquire about sb, ask after sb

interestatal ADJ inter-state

interestelar ADJ interstellar

interétnico ADJ interracial

interface SM *o* SF interface

interferencia SF **1** (*Radio, Telec*) interference; (*intencionada*) jamming **2** (*Ling*) interference

interferir /3i/ **A** VI **1** (= *obstaculizar*) to interfere with, get in the way of **2** (*Radio, Telec*) to interfere with; (*con intención*) to jam **B** VI to interfere (**en** in, with)

interfono SM intercom, entry phone

ínterin SM, **interín** SM **en el ~** in the meantime, in the interim (*frm*)

interinato SM (*LAm*) (= *periodo*) period in a temporary post *o* position; (= *cargo*) temporary post *o* position

interinidad SF (= *estado*) temporary nature; (= *estatus*) provisional status; (*en puesto*) temporary status

interino ADJ [*empleo, empleado*] temporary; [*alcalde, director*] acting *antes de s*; [*medida*] stopgap, interim; **gobierno ~** interim government; **profesor ~** supply teacher (*Brit*), substitute teacher (*EEUU*)

interior **A** ADJ **1** [*espacio*] interior; [*patio*] inner, interior; [*escalera*] internal, interior; [*bolsillo*] inside; [*paz, fuerza*] inner; **en la parte ~** inside, on the inside; **habitación ~** room without a view onto the street; **pista ~** (*Dep*) inside lane; **un joven con mucha vida ~** a reflective young man
2 (= *nacional*) [*comercio, política, mercado*] domestic
B SM **1** (= *parte interna*) **el ~** the inside, the interior; **en el ~ de un vehículo** inside a vehicle; **plantas de ~** house plants; **diseño de ~es** interior design
2 (= *alma*) soul; **un ~ atormentado** a soul in torment; **en mi ~ seguía amándola** in my heart I loved her still; **dije para mi ~** I said to myself
3 (*Geog*) interior; **una tribu del ~ del Brasil** a tribe from the Brazilian interior; **soy del ~** I'm from inland; **en las zonas del ~** in inland areas
4 ➤ **(Ministerio del) Interior** (*Pol*) ≈ Home Office (*Brit*), ≈ Justice Department (*EEUU*)
5 **interiores** (*Cine*) interiors; (*Col, Ven*) (= *calzoncillos*) underpants, pants (*Brit*), shorts (*EEUU*)
C SMF (*Dep*) inside-forward ➤ **interior derecho** inside-right ➤ **interior izquierdo** inside-left

interioridad SF **1** [*de persona*] inner being

2 **interioridades** (= *intimidades*) private *o* personal matters; (= *detalles*) ins and outs

interiorismo SM interior decoration, interior design

interiorista SMF interior decorator, interior designer

interiorizar /1f/ **A** VT **1** (*Psic*) to internalize **2** (*CS*) (= *informar*) to inform (**de, sobre** about) **B** **interiorizarse** VPR (*CS*) **~se de** *o* **sobre algo** to familiarize o.s. with sth

interjección SF interjection

interlocutor(a) SM/F (*gen*) speaker, interlocutor (*frm*); **mi ~** the person I was speaking to, the person who spoke to me ➤ **interlocutor(a) válido/a** (*Pol*) official negotiator, official spokesman

interludio SM interlude

intermediaria SF (*Ven Cine*) evening showing; (*Teat*) evening performance

intermediario/a **A** ADJ intermediary **B** SM/F **1** (= *mediador*) (*gen*) intermediary, go-between; (*Com*) middle-man **2** (*en disputa*) mediator

intermedio **A** ADJ **1** [*etapa, grupo, nivel*] intermediate; [*periodo*] intervening; **un punto ~ entre colonialismo e independencia** a halfway house between colonialism and independence **2** [*tamaño, talla*] medium; **de tamaño ~** medium-sized **B** SM (*Teat*) intermission, interval (*esp Brit*); (*TV*) break; (*Cine*) intermission

interminable ADJ endless, interminable

interministerial ADJ interdepartmental, interministerial

intermitencia SF intermittence

intermitente **A** ADJ (*gen*) intermittent; [*huelga, negociaciones*] on-off; [*luz*] flashing; [*lluvia, nieve*] sporadic, intermittent; **se escuchan disparos de forma ~** shots can be heard now and again *o* intermittently **B** SM (*Aut*) indicator (*esp Brit*), turn signal (*EEUU*)

internacional **A** ADJ international **B** SMF international; **la Internacional** (= *himno*) the Internationale

internacionalista ADJ, SMF internationalist

internacionalizar /1f/ **A** VT to internationalize **B** **internacionalizarse** VPR to become international

internado/a **A** ADJ **estar ~ en** to be (a patient) in **B** SM/F (*Mil*) internee; (*Escol*) boarder; (*Med*) patient **C** SM (= *colegio*) boarding school; (= *alumnos*) boarders *pl*

internalizar /1f/ VT to internalise

internamiento SM (*Pol*) internment; (*Med*) admission (*to hospital*)

internar /1a/ **A** VT (= *ingresar*) (*Mil*) to intern; (*Med*) to admit (**en** to); **~ a algn en un manicomio** to commit sb to a psychiatric hospital **B** **internarse** VPR (= *avanzar*) to advance deep, penetrate; **~se en algo** to go into *o* right inside sth

internauta SMF Net user, Internet user

Internet SM *o* SF, **internet** SM *o* SF Internet

interno/a **A** ADJ internal; [*política*] internal, domestic; **por vía interna** (*Med*) internally **B** SM/F **1** (*Escol*) boarder **2** (*Med*) houseman (*Brit*), intern (*EEUU*) **3** (= *preso*) inmate, prisoner **C** SM (*RPl Telec*) extension, telephone extension

interpelación SF (*frm*) question

interpelar /1a/ VT (*frm*) to question

interpersonal ADJ interpersonal

interplanetario ADJ interplanetary

interpolar /1a/ VT to interpolate

interponer /2q/ **A** VT **1** (= *insertar*) to interpose (*frm*), insert **2** (*Jur*) [+ *apelación*] to lodge **B** **interponerse** VPR [*persona*] to intervene; [*obstáculo*] to stand in the way; **se interpuso entre los dos** he came between the two of them; **grandes obstáculos se interponen en la solución del conflicto** there are great obstacles standing in the way of a solution to the conflict

interpretación SF **1** [*de texto, mensaje*] interpretation; **mala ~** misinterpretation; **admite diversas interpretaciones** it can be interpreted in several different ways
2 (= *traducción hablada*) interpreting **3** (*Mús, Teat*) performance

interpretar /1a/ VT **1** [+ *texto, mensaje*] to interpret; **~ mal** to misinterpret **2** (*Ling*) to interpret **3** (*Mús*) [+ *pieza*] to play, perform; [+ *canción*] to sing; (*Teat*) [+ *papel*] to play

intérprete SMF **1** (*Ling*) interpreter **2** (= *músico*) performer; (= *cantante*) singer

interprofesional ADJ **acuerdo ~** inter-trade agreement; **salario mínimo ~** minimum wage

interregno SM (*Hist, Pol*) interregnum

interrelación SF interrelation

interrelacionar /1a/ VT to interrelate

interrogación SF **1** (= *interrogatorio*) questioning, interrogation **2** (*Tip*) question mark

interrogante SM *o* SF (= *signo*) question mark; (= *incógnita*) question mark, query

interrogar /1h/ VT to interrogate, question; (*Jur*) to question, examine

interrogativo ADJ, SM interrogative

interrogatorio SM **1** (= *preguntas*) interrogation, questioning **2** (*Jur*) questioning, examination

interrumpir /3a/ **Ⓐ** VT **1** (= *cesar*) (*gen*) to interrupt; [+ *vacaciones*] to cut short; [+ *tráfico*] to block, hold up; [+ *embarazo*] to terminate **2** (*Elec*) [+ *luz*] to switch off; [+ *suministro*] to cut off **Ⓑ** VI to interrupt

interrupción SF (*gen*) interruption; [*de emisión*] break ➤ **interrupción (voluntaria) del embarazo** termination ➤ **interrupción del fluido eléctrico** power failure, power cut (*esp Brit*)

interruptor SM (*Elec*) switch

intersección SF intersection; (*Aut*) junction (*Brit*), intersection (*esp EEUU*)

intersticio SM crack, interstice (*frm*)

intertanto SM (*LAm*) **en el ~** in the meantime

intertextualidad SF intertextuality

interurbano ADJ [*autobús, transporte, llamada*] long-distance

intervalo SM **1** [*de tiempo*] (*tb Mús*) interval; (= *descanso*) break; **a ~s** (*gen*) at intervals; (= *de vez en cuando*) every now and then **2** (= *espacio libre*) gap; **situados a ~s de dos metros** placed at two metre intervals; **~s de nubes** cloudy spells *o* intervals; **mantener el ~ de seguridad** (*Aut*) to keep one's distance

intervención SF **1** (= *actuación*) intervention (**en** in) **2** (= *discurso*) speech **3** (= *toma de control*) [*de empresa*] intervention (*by the official receiver*); (*LAm*) [*de periódico, radio*] government takeover; **tras la ~ del banco** after the bank was taken into administration **4** (= *auditoría*) audit, auditing **5** (*Med*) (*tb ~ quirúrgica*) operation **6** [*de droga, contrabando*] seizure, confiscation **7** (*Telec*) tapping

intervencionista ADJ, SMF interventionist

intervenir /3r/ **Ⓐ** VI **1** (= *tomar parte*) to take part; **la reyerta en la que intervino el acusado** the brawl in which the defendant took part *o* was involved **2** (= *injerirse*) [*ejército, estado, policía*] to intervene **3** (= *mediar*) to mediate, intercede; **intervino para que los sacaran de la cárcel** he used his influence to get them out of prison; **las circunstancias que intervinieron en mi dimisión** the circumstances that influenced my resignation **Ⓑ** VT **1** (= *tomar control de*) [+ *banco, empresa*] to take into administration; (*LAm*) [+ *periódico, radio*] to take over, take control of **2** [+ *cuenta*] to audit **3** (*Med*) to operate on **4** [+ *droga, armas, bienes*] to confiscate, seize **5** [+ *teléfono*] to tap

interventor(a) SM/F (*en tren*) ticket inspector; (*en elecciones*) scrutineer (*Brit*), canvasser (*EEUU*) ➤ **interventor(a) de cuentas** auditor ➤ **interventor(a) judicial** receiver, official receiver; (*LAm*) government-appointed manager

interviú SM *o* SF interview

intestinal ADJ intestinal

intestino **Ⓐ** ADJ (*frm*) (= *interno*) internal; [*lucha*]

internecine **Ⓑ** SM intestine, gut ➤ **intestino ciego** caecum ➤ **intestino delgado** small intestine ➤ **intestino grueso** large intestine

inti SM (*Perú*) *former Peruvian monetary unit*

intimación SF announcement, notification

intimar /1a/ **Ⓐ** VI **~ con algn** to be friends with sb **Ⓑ** VT (*frm*) **1** (= *notificar*) to announce, notify **2** (= *mandar*) to order, require

intimidación SF intimidation

intimidad SF **1** (= *amistad*) intimacy, familiarity; **disfrutar de la ~ de algn** to be on close terms with sb **2** (= *ámbito privado*) privacy; **en la ~ familiar** in the privacy of the family **3 intimidades** (= *cosas personales*) personal matters, private matters; (*euf*) (= *genitales*) private parts, privates (*hum*)

intimidar /1a/ **Ⓐ** VT to intimidate **Ⓑ** **intimidarse** VPR to be intimidated

íntimo/a **Ⓐ** ADJ [*secreto, confesión*] intimate; [*amigo, relación*] close, intimate; [*pensamientos, sentimientos*] innermost; [*vida*] personal, private; **una boda íntima** a quiet wedding, a private wedding; **una cena íntima** a romantic meal; **en lo más ~ de mi corazón** in my heart of hearts **Ⓑ** SM/F close friend

intocable ADJ (= *sagrado*) sacred, sacrosanct; [*tema*] taboo **Ⓑ** SMF (*en la India*) untouchable

intolerable ADJ intolerable, unbearable

intolerancia SF intolerance

intolerante **Ⓐ** ADJ intolerant (**con** of) **Ⓑ** SMF intolerant person

intoxicación SF **1** (*Med*) poisoning ➤ **intoxicación alimentaria** food poisoning ➤ **intoxicación etílica** alcohol poisoning; (*euf*) drunkenness **2** (*Pol*) indoctrination

intoxicar /1g/ **Ⓐ** VT to poison **Ⓑ** **intoxicarse** VPR (*con sustancia tóxica*) to be poisoned; (*con alimentos*) to get food poisoning

intraducible ADJ untranslatable

intragable ADJ unpalatable

intramuros ADV within the city, within the walls

intranet [intra'net] SF intranet

intranquilizar /1f/ **Ⓐ** VT to worry, make uneasy **Ⓑ** **intranquilizarse** VPR to get worried, feel uneasy

intranquilo ADJ (= *preocupado*) worried, anxious; (= *desasosegado*) restless

intrascendente ADJ = **intrascendente**

intransferible ADJ not transferable

intransigencia SF intransigence

intransigente **Ⓐ** ADJ intransigent **Ⓑ** SMF diehard

intransitivo ADJ, SM intransitive

intrascendencia SF unimportance, insignificance

intrascendente ADJ unimportant, insignificant

intratable ADJ **1** [*persona*] difficult **2** (*Med*) untreatable

intrauterino ADJ intrauterine

intravenoso ADJ intravenous

intrépido ADJ intrepid

intriga SF (= *maquinación*) intrigue; **novela de ~** thriller; **película de ~** thriller

intrigante **Ⓐ** ADJ **1** (= *enredador*) scheming **2** (= *interesante*) intriguing **Ⓑ** SMF schemer

intrigar /1h/ **Ⓐ** VT to intrigue; **lo que más me intriga del caso es ...** the most intriguing aspect of the case is ...; **me tienes intrigada** you've got me intrigued **Ⓑ** VI to scheme, plot

intrincado ADJ **1** (= *complejo*) complicated; (= *enmarañado*) intricate **2** [*bosque*] dense

intríngulis* SM INV **tiene su ~** it's quite tricky*, it's not as easy as it looks

intrínseco ADJ intrinsic, inherent

introducción SF **1** [*de texto*] introduction; **un curso de ~ al psicoanálisis** an introductory course in psychoanalysis

2 (= *inserción*) [*de objeto*] insertion **3** (= *llegada*) [*de mercancías, cambios*] introduction; **~ de contrabando** smuggling **4** (*Inform*) [*de datos*] input

introducir /3n/ **Ⓐ** VT **1** (= *meter*) [+ *mano, pie*] to put, place (**en** in(to)); [+ *moneda, llave*] to put, insert (**en** in(to)); [+ *enfermedad, mercancías*] to bring (**en** into), introduce (**en** into); [+ *contrabando, droga*] to bring (**en** in(to)); **~ algo de contrabando** to smuggle sth (**en** into); **~ a algn en** [+ *habitación*] to show sb into; [+ *situación real*] to introduce sb to; [+ *situación irreal*] to transport sb to **2** (= *empezar*) [+ *cultivo, ley, método*] to introduce; **para ~ el tema** to introduce the subject **3** (= *realizar*) [+ *medidas, reformas*] to bring in, introduce; **quieren ~ cambios en la legislación** they want to make changes to *o* introduce changes into the current legislation; **las reformas se ~án gradualmente** the reforms will be phased in gradually, the reforms will be brought in *o* introduced gradually **4** (*Inform*) [+ *datos*] to input, enter **Ⓑ introducirse** VPR [*astilla, cristal*] to lodge; **~se en algo** to get into sth, enter sth; **hemos logrado ~nos en el mercado europeo** we've managed to break *o* get into the European market; **muchas palabras se introducen en nuestro idioma procedentes del inglés** many words pass into our language from English

intromisión SF interference

introspección SF introspection

introvertido/a Ⓐ ADJ introverted **Ⓑ** SM/F introvert

intrusión SF intrusion

intruso/a Ⓐ ADJ intrusive **Ⓑ** SM/F intruder

intuición SF intuition; **por ~** intuitively

intuir /3g/ VT (= *saber*) to know intuitively; (= *sentir*) to sense, feel; **intuyo que alguien me sigue** I have a feeling I'm being followed

intuitivo ADJ intuitive

inuit ADJ, SMF Inuit

inundación SF (*acción*) flooding; (*efecto*) flood

inundar /1a/ VT **1** (con agua) to flood **2** (con productos) to flood (**de, en** with), swamp (**de, en** with); **quedamos inundados de ofertas** offers rained in on us, we were flooded *o* swamped with offers **3** [*gente*] to flood, swamp **4** [*pena, sensación*] to overwhelm, sweep over

inusitado ADJ unusual, rare

inusual ADJ unusual

inútil Ⓐ ADJ **1** (= *vano*) [*intento, esfuerzo*] unsuccessful, fruitless; **lo intenté todo, pero fue ~** I tried everything, but it was no use *o* useless; **es ~ que proteste** it's no good *o* use you protesting; **es ~ seguir intentándolo** there's no point in keeping on trying **2** (= *inepto*) useless*, hopeless* **3** (= *inválido*) disabled **4** (= *inservible*) useless **5** (*Mil*) unfit **Ⓑ** SMF **¡es una ~!** she's useless *o* hopeless!*

inutilidad SF uselessness

inutilizable ADJ unusable, unfit for use

inutilizar /1f/ VT (= *hacer inútil*) (*gen*) to make useless, render useless; [+ *mecanismo*] to disable, put out of action; **las carreteras han quedado inutilizadas** the roads have become unusable

inútilmente ADV (= *sin utilidad*) uselessly; (= *en vano*) vainly, fruitlessly

invadir /3a/ VT **1** (*atacar*) [+ *célula, país*] to invade; [+ *espacio aéreo, aguas jurisdiccionales*] to violate, enter; **las malas hierbas invadieron el trigal** the wheatfield was overrun with weeds; **los pájaros invadieron la plantación** birds swooped down onto the field; **~ la intimidad de algn** to invade sb's privacy **2** (= *ocupar*) **2.1** [*multitud*] (*gen*) to pour into/onto; (*protestando*) to storm into/onto; **los fans invadieron el estadio/el escenario** the fans poured into the stadium/ onto the stage **2.2** [*vehículo*] to stray onto; **el autobús invadió el carril contrario** the bus strayed onto the wrong side of the road **3 ~ a algn** [*sentimiento*] to overcome sb; **la invadió una gran tristeza** she was filled with great sadness, a great sadness overcame her

4 (= *usurpar*) [+ *funciones*] to encroach upon

invalidar /1a/ VT [+ *certificado, resultado*] to invalidate, nullify; [+ *decisión*] to reverse; [+ *leyes*] to repeal

invalidez SF **1** (*Med*) disability, disablement; **solicitar la ~ (laboral)** to apply for disability benefit **➤ invalidez permanente** permanent disability **2** (*Jur*) invalidity

inválido/a Ⓐ ADJ **1** (*Med*) disabled **2** (*Jur*) invalid, null and void **Ⓑ** SM/F (*Med*) disabled person; **~ de guerra** disabled ex-serviceman (*Brit*) *o* veteran (*EEUU*)

invalorable ADJ (*LAm*), **invaluable** ADJ (*LAm*) invaluable

invariable ADJ invariable

invasión SF **1** [*de país, cultivos*] invasion **2** [*de pista, calzada*] presence; **la ~ de la pista por un avión de carga causó el accidente** the accident was caused by the presence of a cargo plane on the runway **3** [*de derechos*] encroachment **4** (*Col*) (= *chabolas*) shantytown

invasor(a) Ⓐ ADJ [*ejército, pueblo*] invading; [*tumor*] invasive **Ⓑ** SM/F invader

invectiva SF (*frm*) tirade

invencible ADJ [*enemigo, rival*] invincible, unbeatable; [*obstáculo*] insurmountable

invención SF **1** (= *invento*) invention **2** (= *mentira*) invention, fabrication

inventar /1a/ **Ⓐ** VT (*gen*) to invent; [+ *plan*] to devise; [+ *historia, excusa*] to invent, concoct **Ⓑ inventarse** VPR [+ *historia, excusa*] to invent, concoct

inventariar /1b/ VT to inventory, make an inventory of

inventario SM inventory; **hacer ~** (*Com*) to do the stocktaking (*Brit*), take inventory (*EEUU*); **"cerrado por inventario"** "closed for stocktaking" (*Brit*), "closed for inventory" (*EEUU*)

inventiva SF inventiveness

inventivo ADJ inventive

invento SM invention

inventor(a) SM/F inventor

invernada SF **1** (*And, CS*) (= *pasto*) winter pasture; (= *estación*) winter season **2** (*Carib*) (= *tempestad*) heavy rainstorm

invernadero Ⓐ SM greenhouse; (*con temperatura elevada*) hothouse **Ⓑ** ADJ INV **efecto ~** greenhouse effect

invernal ADJ winter *antes de s*; [*clima, frío*] wintry

invernar /1j/ VI (= *pasar el invierno*) to winter, spend the winter; (*Zool*) to hibernate

inverosímil ADJ (= *improbable*) unlikely, improbable; (= *increíble*) implausible

inversamente ADV inversely

inversión SF **1** (*Com, Fin*) investment (**en** in); **➤ inversión de capital(es)** capital investment **➤ inversiones extranjeras** foreign investment *sing* **2** [*de esfuerzo, tiempo*] investment **3** [*de orden, dirección*] reversal **➤ inversión sexual** homosexuality

inversionista SMF investor

inverso ADJ **1** (= *contrario*) opposite; **en sentido ~** in the opposite direction; **en orden ~** in reverse order; **a la inversa** the other way around; (= *al contrario*) on the contrary **2** [*cara*] reverse **3** (*Mat*) inverse

inversor(a) Ⓐ ADJ investment *antes de s* **Ⓑ** SM/F investor

invertebrado ADJ, SM invertebrate

invertido ADJ [*imagen, objeto*] inverted, upside-down; [*orden*] reversed

invertir /3i/ **Ⓐ** VT **1** (*Com, Fin*) to invest (**en** in) **2** [+ *esfuerzo, tiempo*] to invest (**en** in), put in (**en** on); **invirtieron una hora en recorrer diez kilómetros** they spent an hour covering ten kilometres **3** [+ *figura, objeto*] to invert, reverse **4** (= *cambiar*) [+ *orden*] to reverse **5** (*Mat*) to invert **Ⓑ** VI **~ en algo** to invest in sth **Ⓒ** VPR [*papeles, tendencia*] to be reversed

investidura SF investiture; **discurso de ~** investiture speech; **votación de ~** (*Pol*) vote of confidence (*in the new prime minister*)

investigación SF **1** [*de accidente, delito*] (*por la policía*) investigation; (*por un comité*) inquiry; **ha ordenado la ~ de las cuentas bancarias** he has ordered their bank accounts to be investigated **2** (*científica, académica*) research ➤ **investigación y desarrollo** research and development

investigador(a) Ⓐ ADJ (*gen*) investigative; (*en ciencia*) research *antes de s*; **labor ~a** [*de periodista, policía*] investigative work; (*en ciencia*) research Ⓑ SM/F **1** (= *periodista, policía*) investigator **2** (= *científico*) research worker, researcher

investigar /1h/ Ⓐ VT **1** [+ *accidente, crimen, queja*] to investigate; [+ *cuentas, patrimonio*] to audit **2** (*Univ*) to research, do research into **3** (= *tantear*) to check out; **quédate aquí y yo ~é el terreno** stay here and I'll check out the lie of the land* Ⓑ VI **1** [*policía, comité*] to investigate **2** (*Univ*) to do research

investir /3k/ VT **fue investido doctor honoris causa** he was granted an honorary doctorate; **fue investido como Príncipe de Gales** the title of Prince of Wales was conferred on him; **~ a algn con** *o* **de algo** to confer sth on sb

inveterado ADJ [*fumador, pecador*] inveterate; [*criminal*] hardened; [*hábito*] deep-seated, well-established

inviable ADJ unfeasible, unviable, non-viable

invidente Ⓐ ADJ blind Ⓑ SMF blind person

invierno SM **1** (= *estación*) winter; **deportes de ~** winter sports (*And, CAm, Carib*) (= *meses de lluvia*) rainy season

inviolable ADJ inviolable

invisibilidad SF invisibility

invisible Ⓐ ADJ invisible Ⓑ SM (*Arg*) hairpin

invitación SF invitation (**a** to)

invitado/a Ⓐ ADJ invited; **estrella invitada** guest star Ⓑ SM/F guest ➤ **invitado/a de honor** guest of honour ➤ **invitado/a estelar** star guest

invitar /1a/ VT **1** (= *convidar*) to invite; **me invitó a la fiesta** she invited me to the party **2** (= *pagar*) **invito yo** it's on me; **os invito a una cerveza** I'll buy *o* stand you all a beer; **nos invitó a cenar (fuera)** she took us out for a meal **3** (= *incitar*) to invite; **~ a algn a hacer algo** to invite sb to do sth; (*exhortando*) to call on sb to do sth **4** (= *atraer*) to entice; **una frase que invita a comprar** a slogan which entices you to buy

in vitro ADJ, ADV in vitro

invocar /1g/ VT **1** (= *citar*) to cite, invoke **2** [+ *derecho, principio*] to cite, invoke **3** (= *rogar*) (*gen*) to invoke, appeal for; [+ *divinidad, santo*] to invoke, call on

involución SF regression

involucionista Ⓐ ADJ regressive, reactionary Ⓑ SMF reactionary

involucrar /1a/ Ⓐ VT **1** (= *hacer intervenir*) to involve; **~ a algn en algo** to involve sb in sth; **las personas involucradas en el caso** the people involved in the affair **2** (*LAm*) (= *conllevar*) to involve Ⓑ **involucrarse** VPR to get involved (**en** in)

involuntario ADJ [*gesto, movimiento*] involuntary; [*ofensa*] unintentional; [*agente, causante*] unwitting; **homicidio ~** involuntary manslaughter

invulnerable ADJ invulnerable

inyección SF **1** (= *acción, sustancia*) injection; **ha venido a ponerme una ~** he's come to give me an injection ➤ **inyección intramuscular** intramuscular injection ➤ **inyección intravenosa** intravenous injection **2** [*de optimismo, dinero*] injection **3** (*Mec*) injection; **motor de ~** fuel injection engine

inyectado ADJ **ojos ~s en sangre** bloodshot eyes

inyectar /1a/ Ⓐ VT **1** (*Med*) to inject (**en** into); **~ algo en algn** to inject sb with sth **2** [+ *optimismo, dinero*] to inject **3** (*Mec*) to inject Ⓑ **inyectarse** VPR to give o.s. an injection, inject o.s.

ion SM ion

iónico ADJ ionic

ionizador SM ionizer, negative ionizer

ionizar /1f/ VT to ionize

ionosfera SF ionosphere

IPC SM ABR (= **índice de precios al consumo**) RPI (*Brit*), CPI (*EEUU*)

ir /3s/	
Ⓐ VERBO INTRANSITIVO	Ⓒ VERBO PRONOMINAL
Ⓑ VERBO AUXILIAR	

Para las expresiones **ir de vacaciones**, **ir de veras**, **ir dado**, **irse de la lengua** *etc, ver ver la entrada correspondiente a la otra palabra.*

ir Ⓐ VERBO INTRANSITIVO
1 (= *marchar*)
1.1 (*indicando movimiento, acción*) to go; **anoche fuimos a un restaurante** we went to a restaurant last night; **¿has ido alguna vez a Quito?** have you ever been to Quito?; **¡ya voy!** *✧* **¡ahora voy!** coming!, I'll be right there!; **vamos a casa** let's go home; **¿quién va?** who goes there?
1.2 (*indicando la forma de transporte*) **ir andando** to walk; **ir en avión** to fly; **ir en bicicleta** to ride; **ir a caballo** to ride; **ir en coche** to go by car, drive; **ir a pie** to go on foot; **ir en tren** to go by train *o* rail
1.3 (*con complemento*) **iba muy bien vestido** he was very well dressed; **iban muertos de risa por la calle** they were killing themselves laughing as they went down the street
1.4 ir por *✧* **ir a por** (*Esp*) to go and get; **voy por** *o* (*Esp*) **a por el paraguas** I'll go and get the umbrella; **voy por** *o* (*Esp*) **a por el médico** I'll go and fetch *o* get the doctor; **voy a por él** (*Esp*) (*a buscarle*) I'll go and get him; (*a atacarle*) I'm going to get him; **sólo van a por las pelas** (*Esp**) they're only in it for the money
2 (*indicando proceso*)
2.1 [*persona*] **¿cómo va el paciente?** how's the patient doing?; **el enfermo va peor** the patient has got worse
2.2 [*acción, obra*] to go; **¿cómo va el ensayo?** how's the essay going?, how are you getting on with the essay?; **¿cómo va el partido?** what's the score?; **todo va bien** everything's fine, everything's going well
2.3 ir por: **¿te has leído ya el libro? ¿por dónde vas?** have you read the book yet? whereabouts are you? *o* how far have you got?; **ir por la mitad de algo** to be halfway through sth
3 (*indicando manera, posición*) **ese cuadro debería ir encima del sofá** that picture should go over the sofa; **lo que te dijo iba en serio** he meant what he said (to you)
4 (= *extenderse*) to go, stretch; **la pradera va desde la montaña hasta el mar** the grasslands go *o* stretch from the mountains to the sea; **en lo que va de año** so far this year
5 (*indicando distancia, diferencia*) **va mucho de uno a otro** there's a lot of difference between them; **de 7 a 9 van 2** the difference between 7 and 9 is 2; (*en resta*) 7 from 9 leaves 2
6 (*indicando acumulación*) **con éste van 30** that makes 30 (with this one); **van ya tres llamadas y no contesta** we've called him three times and he doesn't answer
7 (*en apuestas*) **van cinco pesos a que no lo haces** I bet you five pesos you won't do it; **¿cuánto va?** how much do you bet?
8 (= *vestir*) **ir con pantalones** to be wearing trousers (*Brit*) *o* pants (*EEUU*); **¿con qué ropa** *o* **cómo fuiste a la boda?** what did you wear to the wedding?; **iba de rojo** she was dressed in red, she was wearing red
9 irle a algn
9.1 (*indicando importancia*) **nos va mucho en esto** we have a lot riding on this; **le va la vida en ello** his life depends on it; **✦** MODISMO **ni me va ni me viene** it's nothing to do with me
9.2 (*indicando situación*) **¿cómo te va?** how are things?, how are you doing?; **¿cómo te va en los estudios?** how are you getting on with your studies?; **¡que te vaya bien!** take care!
9.3 (= *sentar*) to suit; **¿me va bien esto?** does this suit me?
9.4 (*) (= *gustar*) **no me va nada ese rollo** (*Esp*) I'm not into that sort of thing*; **ese tipo de gente no me va** (*Esp*) I don't get on with that type of people; **le va al Cruz Azul** (*Méx Dep*) he supports Cruz Azul

10 (*seguido de preposición*)
◆ **ir con** (= *acompañar, combinar*) to go with; **iba con su madre** he was with his mother; **esta fotocopia debe ir con la carta** this photocopy has to go (in) with the letter; **el marrón no va bien con el azul** brown and blue don't go together; **eso de ser famosa no va con ella** being famous doesn't agree with her
◆ **ir de** (*Esp*): **¿de qué va el libro?** what's the book about?; **va de intelectual por la vida** he acts the intellectual all the time; **¿de qué vas?*** what are you on about?*
◆ **ir para: va para viejo** he's getting old; **va para cinco años que entré en la Universidad** it's getting on for five years since I started University
◆ **ir por** (*indicando intención*) **eso no va por usted** I wasn't referring to you, that wasn't meant for you; **¡va por los novios!** (here's) to the bride and groom!
◆ **ir tras** to go after; **se dio cuenta de que iban tras él** he realized they were after him
11 (*otras locuciones*) <u>a lo que</u> iba as I was saying; **ir a algn con algo: siempre le iba con sus problemas** he always went to her with his problems; **pues, a** <u>eso</u> **voy** that's what I mean, that's what I'm getting at; **es el** <u>no</u> **va más*** it's the ultimate; **ir de mal en** <u>peor</u> to go from bad to worse; **ir a lo** <u>suyo</u> to do one's own thing; (*pey*) to look after Number One; **ir y** <u>venir</u>: **era un constante ir y venir de ambulancias** ambulances were constantly coming and going; **llevo todo el día yendo y viniendo de un lado al otro de la ciudad** I've spent all day going from one end of town to the other; **ir y: ahora va y me dice que no viene** now he goes and tells me he's not coming; **fue y se marchó** (*Méx**) he just upped and left*
12 (*exclamaciones*)
◆ **¡vaya!** (*indicando sorpresa*) well!; (*indicando enfado*) damn!; **¡vaya! ¿qué haces tú por aquí?** well, what a surprise! what are you doing here?; **¡vaya susto que me pegué!** I got such a fright!, what a fright I got!; **¡vaya con el niño!** that damn kid!*
◆ **¡vamos!** (*dando ánimos*) come on!; (*para ponerse en marcha*) let's go!; **¡vamos! ¡di algo!** come on! say something!; **vamos, no es difícil** come on, it's not difficult; **una chica, vamos, una mujer** a girl, well, a woman
❸ VERBO AUXILIAR
◆ **ir a** (+ INFIN) to go; **vamos a hacerlo** (*afirmando*) we are going to do it; (*exhortando*) let's do it; **¿cómo lo iba a tener?** how could he have had it?; **¡no lo va a saber!** of course he knows!; **¿no irás a decirme que no lo sabías?** you're not going to tell me you didn't know?; **no vaya a** <u>ser</u> **que ...: no salgas no vaya a ser que venga** don't go out in case she comes
◆ **ir** (+ GERUND) **¿quién va ganando?** who's winning?; **fueron hablando todo el camino** they talked the whole way there; **como iba diciendo** as I was saying; **¡voy corriendo!** I'll be right there!; **id pensando en el tema que queréis tratar** be *o* start thinking about the subject you want to deal with
◆ **ir** (+ PARTICIPIO) **van escritas tres cartas** that's three letters I've written
❸ irse VERBO PRONOMINAL
1 (*uso impersonal*) **¿por dónde se va al aeropuerto?** which is the way *o* which way is it to the airport?
2 (= *marcharse*) to go, leave; **se fueron** they went, they left; **se fue de la reunión** she left the meeting; **me voy, ¡hasta luego!** I'm off, see you!; **vete a hacer los deberes** go and do your homework; **¡vete!** go away!, get out!; **¡no te vayas!** don't go away!; **¡vámonos!** let's go!; **¡nos fuimos!** (*LAm**) let's go!, off we go!*
3 (= *actuar*) **vete con cuidado cuando habléis de este tema** you should tread carefully when you mention that subject
4 (= *salirse*) (*por agujero*) to leak out; (*por el borde*) to overflow; **se me fue la leche** the milk boiled over; **a la cerveza se le ha ido el gas** the beer has gone flat
5 (= *desaparecer*) [*luz*] to go out
6 (= *terminarse*) **írsele a algn: se me va el sueldo en autobuses** all my wages go on bus fares; **no se me va este dolor de espalda** I can't seem to get rid of this backache
7 (= *perder el equilibrio*) **parecía que me iba para atrás cuando andaba** I felt as if I were falling over backwards when I walked

8 (*euf = morirse*) (*en presente*) to be dying; (*en pasado*) to pass away; **se nos va el amo** the master is dying; **se nos fue hace tres años** he passed away three years ago

ira SF [*de persona*] anger, rage; [*de elementos*] fury, violence; **ha provocado la ~ de los críticos** he has incurred the wrath of the critics; **las uvas de la ~** the grapes of wrath

iracundo ADJ (= *propenso a la ira*) irascible (*frm*); (= *colérico*) irate

Irak SM Iraq

Irán SM Iran

iraní ❹ ADJ, SMF Iranian **❺** SM (*Ling*) Iranian

Iraq SM Iraq

iraquí ADJ, SMF Iraqi

irascible ADJ irascible (*frm*)

irguiendo *etc ver* **erguir**

iribú SM (*Arg Orn*) turkey buzzard

iridiscente ADJ iridescent

iris SM INV iris

Irlanda SF Ireland ➤ **Irlanda del Norte** Northern Ireland

irlandés/esa ❹ ADJ Irish **❺** SM/F Irishman/Irishwoman; **los irlandeses** the Irish **❻** SM (*Ling*) Irish

ironía SF **1** (= *figura, situación*) irony **2** (= *burla*) sarcasm; (= *comentario*) sarcastic remark

irónico ADJ (*gen*) ironic; (= *mordaz*) sarcastic

ironizar /1f/ VI **~ sobre algo** to be sarcastic about sth

IRPF SM ABR (*Esp*) (= **impuesto sobre la renta (de las personas físicas)**) ≈ personal income tax

irracional ADJ irrational

irradiación SF irradiation

irradiar /1b/ VT **1** (= *emanar*) to irradiate, radiate **2** (*Med*) to irradiate

irreal ADJ unreal

irrealidad SF unreality

irrealizable ADJ [*meta*] unattainable; [*plan*] unworkable

irreconciliable ADJ irreconcilable

irreconocible ADJ unrecognizable

irrecuperable ADJ irrecoverable, irretrievable

irredentista ADJ, SMF irredentist

irreductible ADJ **1** [*enemigo, oposición, voluntad*] implacable, unyielding; [*obstáculo*] insurmountable; **el sector ~ de los terroristas** the hard-line faction of the terrorists **2** [*espíritu, optimismo*] irrepressible

irreemplazable ADJ irreplaceable

irreflexión SF (= *inconsciencia*) thoughtlessness; (= *ímpetu*) rashness, impetuosity

irreflexivo ADJ **1** [*persona*] (= *inconsciente*) thoughtless, unthinking; (= *impetuoso*) rash, impetuous **2** [*acto*] rash, ill-considered

irrefrenable ADJ [*violencia*] uncontrollable; [*deseo*] unstoppable

irrefutable ADJ irrefutable, unanswerable

irregular ADJ **1** (= *desigual*) uneven; [*superficie, terreno*] uneven; [*contorno, línea*] crooked; [*rasgos*] irregular; [*filo*] jagged **1.2** [*latido, ritmo*] irregular; [*rendimiento*] irregular, erratic; [*jugador, equipo*] inconsistent; [*año, vida*] chaotic; **tiene el sueño ~** he has an irregular sleep pattern; **el comportamiento ~ de la Bolsa** the erratic behaviour of the stock market
2 (= *no legal*) **la situación de la pareja es algo ~** the couple's situation is somewhat irregular; **extranjeros en situación ~** foreigners registered illegally
3 [*verbo*] irregular
4 [*figura geométrica*] irregular

irregularidad SF **1** (= *desigualdad*) **1.1** [*de superficie, terreno*] irregularity, unevenness; **las ~es del terreno** the unevenness of the terrain **1.2** [*de latido, ritmo, lluvias*] irregularity; [*de jugador, equipo*] inconsistency, erratic performance **2** (= *ilegalidad*) irregularity; **~es**

administrativas administrative irregularities **3** (*Ling*) irregularity

irrelevante ADJ irrelevant

irrellenable ADJ **botella con tapón** ~ tamper-proof bottle

irremediable ADJ [*daño, decadencia*] irremediable; [*pérdida*] irreparable, irretrievable; [*vicio*] incurable

irremediablemente ADV inevitably

irremisible ADJ irremissible

irrenunciable ADJ [*derecho*] inalienable; **una aspiración** ~ an aspiration which can never be given up

irreparable ADJ irreparable

irrepetible ADJ unrepeatable

irreprochable ADJ irreproachable

irresistible ADJ irresistible

irrespetar /1a/ VT (*Col, Ven*) to show disrespect to *o* for

irrespetuoso ADJ disrespectful

irrespirable ADJ unbreathable

irresponsable ADJ irresponsible

irrestricto ADJ (*LAm*) **apoyo** ~ unconditional support

irreverencia SF irreverence

irreverente ADJ irreverent

irreversible ADJ irreversible

irrevocable ADJ irrevocable

irrigación SF irrigation

irrigar /1h/ VT **1** (= *regar*) to irrigate **2** [+ *cerebro, músculo*] to feed, supply with blood

irrisión SF **1** (= *mofa*) derision, ridicule **2** (= *hazmerreír*) laughing stock

irrisorio ADJ (= *ridículo*) derisory, ridiculous; [*precio*] absurdly low

irritable ADJ irritable

irritación SF irritation

irritar /1a/ Ⓐ VT **1** (= *enfadar*) to irritate **2** (*Med*) to irritate; **tengo la garganta irritada** I've got a sore throat Ⓑ **irritarse** VPR to get irritated; **~se por algo** to get irritated about *o* at sth, get annoyed about *o* at sth

irrompible ADJ unbreakable

irrumpir /3a/ VI ~ **en** to burst into; **los agentes irrumpieron en el bar** the policemen burst into the bar

IRTP SM ABR (*Esp*) = **impuesto sobre el rendimiento del trabajo personal**

isla SF **1** (*Geog*) island ➤ **islas Baleares** Balearic Islands ➤ **islas Británicas** British Isles ➤ **islas Canarias** Canary Islands ➤ **islas Malvinas** Falkland Islands **2** (*Arquit*) block **3** (*en autopista*) (*Ven*) central reservation (*Brit*), median strip (*EEUU*) ➤ **isla peatonal** (traffic) island, safety island (*EEUU*)

Islam SM Islam

islámico ADJ Islamic

islamista ADJ, SMF (*Rel*) Islamist; (= *integrista*) Islamic fundamentalist

islamizar /1f/ VT to Islamize, convert to Islam

islandés/esa Ⓐ ADJ Icelandic Ⓑ SM/F Icelander Ⓒ SM (*Ling*) Icelandic

Islandia SF Iceland

isleño/a Ⓐ ADJ island *antes de s* Ⓑ SM/F islander

isleta SF islet

islote SM small island

ismo SM ism

isobara SF, **isóbara** SF isobar

isométrica SF isometrics *sing*, isometric exercises *pl*

isométrico ADJ isometric

isósceles ADJ **triángulo** ~ isosceles triangle

isoterma SF isotherm

isotérmico ADJ **1** (= *con aislamiento*) [*ropa*] thermal; [*recipiente*] insulated; [*vehículo*] refrigerated **2** (*Geog*) isothermal

isotónico ADJ isotonic

isótopo SM isotope

Israel SM Israel

israelí ADJ, SMF Israeli

israelita ADJ, SMF Israelite

istmo SM isthmus

itacate SM (*Méx*) provisions *pl* (*for journey*), food

Italia SF Italy

italiano/a Ⓐ ADJ, SM/F Italian Ⓑ SM (*Ling*) Italian

ítem SM item

itemizar /1f/ VT (*LAm*) to itemize, list

itinerante ADJ [*biblioteca, exposición*] travelling, traveling (*EEUU*); [*compañía de teatro*] touring; **comando** ~ mobile terrorist unit; **embajador** ~ roving ambassador, ambassador at large

itinerario SM itinerary, route

ITV SF ABR (*Esp*) = **Inspección Técnica de Vehículos**) roadworthiness test, ≈ MOT (*Brit*)

IVA SM ABR (= **impuesto sobre el valor añadido** *o* (*LAm*) **agregado**) VAT

izar /1f/ VT [+ *bandera*] to hoist, raise; [+ *velas*] to hoist, run up; **la bandera está izada** the flag is flying

izq. ABR, **izq.o** ABR, **izqdo.** ABR (= **izquierdo**) L, l

izq.a ABR, **izqda.** ABR (= **izquierda**) L, l

izquierda SF **1** (= *mano*) left hand; (= *lado*) left, left-hand side; **mi casa está a la** ~ my house is on the left *o* on the left-hand side; **está a la** ~ **de tu hermano** he's to the left of your brother; **el árbol de la** ~ the tree on the left *o* on the left-hand side; **tuerza (por) la tercera a la** ~ take the third turn on the left *o* on the left-hand side; **conducen por la** ~ they drive on the left *o* on the left-hand side **2** (*Pol*) **la** ~ the left (wing); **la extrema** ~ the extreme left (wing); **ser de** ~ *o* (*Esp*) **~s** to be on the left

izquierdista Ⓐ ADJ left-wing Ⓑ SMF left-winger

izquierdo ADJ left; **el lateral** ~ **del Barcelona** the Barcelona left-winger; **las dos ruedas del lado** ~ the two wheels on the left-hand side

izquierdoso/a * (*pey*) Ⓐ ADJ leftish Ⓑ SM/F lefty (*Brit**), pinko (*EEUU**)

Jj

J, j ['xota] SF (= *letra*) J, j

jaba SF (*CAm, Méx*) (= *caja*) crate

jabalí SM wild boar

jabalina SF (*Dep*) javelin

jabato SM young wild boar

jábega SF 1 (= *red*) sweep net, dragnet 2 (= *barca*) fishing smack

jabón SM 1 (*para lavar*) soap; **una pastilla de ~** a bar of soap ➤ **jabón de tocador** toilet soap ➤ **jabón en escamas** soap flakes ➤ **jabón en polvo** (*CS*) soap powder 2 (*) (= *adulación*) flattery; **dar ~ a algn** to soft-soap sb 3 (*RPI*) (= *susto*) fright; **pegarse un ~** to get a fright

jabonada SF 1 (= *acción*) soaping 2 (*Chi*) (= *bronca*) telling-off

jabonar /1a/ VT to soap

jabonera SF soap dish

jabonoso ADJ soapy

jaca SF pony

jacal SM (*CAm, Carib, Méx*) shack, hut

jacalear* /1a/ VI (*Méx*) to go around gossiping

jacarandá SM o SF (*pl* **jacarandaes** *o* **~s**) jacaranda, jacaranda tree

jacinto SM hyacinth

jaco SM 1 (= *caballo*) small horse, young horse; (*pey*) nag, hack 2 (**) (= *heroína*) smack**, heroin

jacobeo ADJ (*Rel*) of St James; **la ruta jacobea** the pilgrims' road to Santiago de Compostela

jacobino/a ADJ, SM/F Jacobin

jactancia SF (= *autoalabanzas*) boasting; (= *orgullo*) boastfulness

jactancioso ADJ boastful

jactarse /1a/ VPR to boast, brag (**de** about)

jacuzzi® [ja'kuzi] SM (*pl* **~s**) Jacuzzi®

jade SM jade

jadeante ADJ panting, gasping

jadear /1a/ VI to pant, gasp for breath

jadeo SM panting, gasping

jaez SM 1 (*para el caballo*) harness; **jaeces** trappings 2 (= *ralea*) kind, sort; **y gente de ese ~** and people of that sort

jaguar SM jaguar

jagüel SM (*LAm*), **jagüey** SM (*LAm*) pool

jai* SF (*SAm*) high society

jai alai SM pelota

jaiba SF (*LAm*) crab

jaibol SM (*LAm*) highball

jaibón* ADJ (*Chi*) stuck-up*, pretentious, snobbish

jailoso* ADJ (*Col*) posh*

jalada SF (*Méx*) 1 (= *tirón*) pull, tug, heave 2 **jaladas*** (= *tonterías*) nonsense *sing*

jalapeño SM (*Méx*) jalapeño pepper

jalar /1a/ Ⓐ VT 1 (*LAm*) (= *tirar de*) to pull; **no le jales el pelo** don't pull his hair
2 (*Méx*) (= *tomar*) to take; **jaló un folleto de la mesa** he took a leaflet from the table
3 (*Méx**) (= *llevar*) to pick up, give a lift to
4 (*Méx**) (= *influir*) **lo jalan mucho sus amigos** he's very influenced by his friends
5 (*Esp**) (= *comer*) to eat
Ⓑ VI 1 (*LAm*) (= *tirar*) to pull; **~ de** to pull at, tug at
2 (*LAm*) (= *ir*) to go; **~ para su casa** to head home
3 (*Méx*) (= *funcionar*) to work; **el coche es viejo pero todavía jala** it's an old car but it still works *o* goes
4 (*Méx**) **eso le jala** she's big on that*, she's a fan of that

5 (*And***) [*estudiante*] to flunk*, fail

6 (*CAm, Méx*) [*novios*] to be courting

7 (*And***) (= *fumar*) to smoke dope*

Ⓒ **jalarse** VPR 1 (*LAm*) (= *irse*) to go off
2 (*LAm*) (= *emborracharse*) to get drunk

jalbegue SM whitewash

jalea SF jelly (*Brit*), Jell-O® (*EEUU*) ➤ **jalea real** royal jelly

jalear /1a/ VT to cheer on

jaleo SM 1 (*) (= *ruido*) row, racket; **armar un ~** to kick up a fuss 2 (*) (= *confusión*) mess, muddle; (= *problema*) hassle*; **es un ~ acordarse de tantos nombres** it's such a hassle having to remember all those names*; **con tanto botón me armo unos ~s** I get into such a mess *o* muddle with all these buttons

jalón SM 1 (= *hito*) milestone, watershed 2 (*LAm*) (= *tirón*) pull, tug; **hacer algo de un ~** (*Col, Méx*) to do sth in one go (*Brit*) *o* try (*EEUU*) 3 (*LAm*) (= *distancia*) stretch; **hay un buen ~** it's a good *o* fair way 4 (*CAm, Méx*) (= *trago*) swig*, drink

jalonar /1a/ VT to stake out, mark out

jalonazo SM (*CAm, Méx*) pull, tug

jalonear /1a/ Ⓐ VT (*Méx*) to pull, tug Ⓑ VI 1 (*CAm, Méx*) (= *tirar*) to pull, tug 2 (*Méx*) (= *regatear*) to haggle

Jamaica SF Jamaica

jamaica SF (*Carib, Méx Bot*) hibiscus

jamaicano/a ADJ, SM/F Jamaican

jamás ADV never; (*con negación, en interrogación*) ever; **¡jamás!** never!; **el mejor amigo que ~ ha existido** the best friend ever

jamba SF jamb

jamelgo* SM nag, old hack

jamón SM [*de cerdo*] ham; ✦ MODISMO **¡y un ~!*** get away!*, my foot!* ➤ **jamón cocido** (*LAm*) = **jamón (de) York** ➤ **jamón crudo** (*RPI*) cured ham ➤ **jamón de pata negra** *type of top-quality cured ham made from a special breed of pig that has black legs* ➤ **jamón serrano** cured ham ➤ **jamón (de) York** boiled ham

jamona* SF buxom woman

Japón SM Japan

japonés/esa Ⓐ ADJ, SM/F Japanese Ⓑ SM (*Ling*) Japanese

japuta SF pomfret

jaque SM (*Ajedrez*) check; ✦ MODISMO **tener en ~ a algn** to hold a sword over sb's head ➤ **jaque mate** checkmate; **dar ~ mate a algn** to checkmate sb, mate sb

jaqueca SF (= *dolor*) (severe) headache, migraine

jaquet SM (*CS, Méx*) morning coat

jara SF (*Bot*) rockrose, cistus

jarabe SM 1 (= *líquido*) syrup; **~ contra** *o* **para la tos** cough syrup *o* mixture ➤ **jarabe de palo*** beating 2 ➤ **jarabe tapatío** Mexican hat dance

jarana SF 1 (*) (= *juerga*) binge*; **andar/ir de ~** to be/go out on the town 2 (*Méx Mús*) small guitar 3 (*Perú*) (= *baile*) dance

jaranear* /1a/ VI to be out on the town

jaranero* ADJ merry

jarcha SF kharja

jarcia SF 1 (*Náut*) (*tb* **~s**) rigging 2 (*Cub, Méx*) (= *cuerda*) rope (*made from agave fibre*)

jardín SM garden, flower garden ➤ **jardín botánico** botanical garden ➤ **jardín de infancia, jardín de infantes** (*RPI*) kindergarten, nursery school

jardinear /1a/ VI (*Chi*) to garden

jardinera SF 1 (*para plantas*) (*en ventana, balcón*) window box; (*en la calle*) flower bed 2 (*CS*) (= *pantalón*) dungarees *pl* (*Brit*), overalls *pl* (*EEUU*)

jardinería SF gardening

jardinero/a Ⓐ SM/F gardener Ⓑ SM (CS) dungarees pl (Brit), overalls pl (EEUU)

jareta SF (CAm) (= bragueta) fly, flies pl

jaripeo* SM (Méx) horse show

jarra SF [de leche] jug, pitcher (EEUU); [de cerveza] mug, tankard; **de o en ~s** with arms akimbo

jarrada SF (LAm) jugful, pitcherful (EEUU)

jarro SM jug, pitcher (EEUU); (LAm) (= tazón) mug; ✦ MODISMOS **caer como un ~ de agua fría** to come as a complete shock; **echar un ~ de agua fría a algn** to wipe the smile off sb's face

jarrón SM vase

jaspe SM jasper

jaspeado ADJ speckled, mottled

Jauja SF, **jauja** SF **¡esto es ~!** this is the life!

jaula SF 1 (para animales) (tb Min) cage 2 [de embalaje] crate 3 (Carib*) (= coche celular) Black Maria (Brit*), paddy wagon (EEUU*) 4 (Méx Ferro*) open truck

jauría SF pack of hounds

Java SF Java

jazmín SM jasmine ➤ **jazmín del cabo** (Méx, RPl) gardenia

jazz [jas] SM jazz

jazzístico ADJ jazz antes de s

jeans [jins, dʒins] SMPL jeans

jebe SM (And) (= planta) rubber plant; (= goma) rubber; (= elástico) elastic band

jeep [jip, dʒip] SM jeep

jefatura SF 1 (= liderato) leadership 2 (= sede) headquarters pl ➤ **jefatura de policía** police headquarters pl

jefazo* SM big shot*

jefe/a SM/F 1 (= superior) boss; (= director) head; (Pol) leader; (Com) manager; (Mil) officer in command; [de tribu] chief; **comandante en ~** commander-in-chief; **¿quién es el ~ aquí?** who's in charge around here? ➤ **jefe/a de cocina** head chef ➤ **jefe/a de estación** station master, station manager ➤ **jefe/a de estado** head of state ➤ **jefe/a de estado mayor** chief of staff ➤ **jefe/a de estudios** (Escol) director of studies ➤ **jefe/a de obras** site manager ➤ **jefe/a de redacción** editor-in-chief ➤ **jefe/a supremo/a** commander-in-chief 2 (como apelativo) **¡oiga ~!** hey, man!*

Jehová SM Jehovah

jején SM (LAm Zool) gnat

jengibre SM ginger

jeque SM sheik(h)

jerarca SM leader, chief, hierarch (frm)

jerarquía SF hierarchy

jerárquico ADJ hierarchic, hierarchical

jerarquizado ADJ hierarchical

jeremiquear /1a/ VI (LAm) to snivel, whimper

jerez SM sherry

jerga¹ SF 1 (= lenguaje) jargon 2 (= galimatías) gibberish

jerga² SF (Méx) floor cloth

jergal ADJ jargon antes de s

jergón SM palliasse, straw mattress

jerigonza SF gibberish

jeringa SF 1 (Med) syringe ➤ **jeringa de engrase** grease gun 2 (*) (= molestia) nuisance

jeringar* /1h/ Ⓐ VT to annoy, plague Ⓑ **jeringarse** VPR to put up with it; **¡que se jeringue!** he can lump it!*

jeringuear* /1a/ VT (LAm) = **jeringar** Ⓐ

jeringuilla SF syringe

jeroglífico SM 1 (= escritura) hieroglyph, hieroglyphic 2 (= situación, juego) puzzle

jersey SM (pl ~s) 1 (Esp) (= prenda) sweater, pullover, jersey, jumper (Brit) ➤ **jersey amarillo** (Ciclismo) yellow jersey 2 (LAm) (= tela) jersey

Jerusalén SF Jerusalem

Jesucristo SM Jesus Christ

jesuita ADJ, SM (Rel) Jesuit

jesuítico ADJ Jesuitic, Jesuitical

Jesús SM Jesus; **¡Jesús!** (indicando sorpresa) good heavens!; (al estornudar) bless you!

jet [jet] (pl ~s) Ⓐ SM (Aer) jet, jet plane Ⓑ SF **la ~** the jet-set

jeta Ⓐ SF 1 (*) (= cara) face, mug* 2 (LAm*) (= boca) trap**, gob (Brit**) 3 [de cerdo] snout 4 (*) (= descaro) nerve*; **¡qué ~ tienes!** you've got a nerve!* 5 (Méx*) (= siesta) nap Ⓑ SMF **ser un(a) ~*** to have a nerve*

jet ski ['jeteski] SM jet ski

ji EXCL **¡ji, ji, ji!** (imitando la risa) hee, hee, hee!

jíbaro/a Ⓐ ADJ 1 [pueblo] Jivaro 2 (Carib, Méx) (= rústico) country antes de s, rustic Ⓑ SM/F 1 (= indígena) Jivaro 2 (Col, Ven**) (= traficante) dealer, drug dealer

jibia SF (Zool) cuttlefish

jícama SF (CAm, Méx) edible tuber

jícara SF (CAm, Méx) (= vasija) gourd

jícaro SM (CAm, Méx) 1 (Bot) calabash tree 2 (= plato) bowl

jicote SM (CAm, Méx) wasp

jicotera SF (CAm, Méx) (= nido) wasps' nest; (= zumbido) buzzing of wasps; ✦ MODISMO **armar una ~** to kick up a fuss

jienense ADJ, **jiennense** ADJ of/from Jaén

jijona SM soft nougat (made in Jijona); ◇ TURRÓN

jilguero SM goldfinch

jilote SM (CAm, Méx) green ear of maize o (EEUU) corn

jineta SF (Zool) genet

jinete SM horseman, rider

jinetear /1a/ Ⓐ VT 1 (LAm) (= montar) to ride; (= domar) to break in 2 (Méx*) [+ fondos] to misappropriate Ⓑ VI to ride around

jinetera* SF (Cub) prostitute

jiote SM (Méx) rash

jipijapa (LAm) SF fine woven straw

jirafa SF 1 (Zool) giraffe 2 (TV, Cine) boom

jirón SM 1 (= andrajo) rag, shred; **hacer algo jirones** to tear sth to shreds; **hecho jirones** in shreds 2 (Perú) (= calle) street

jitomate SM (Méx) tomato

jo* EXCL (Esp) (para expresar disgusto) oh!, aw!; (para expresar sorpresa) wow!, blimey! (Brit*), jeez! (EEUU*)

jobar* EXCL (Esp) (para expresar disgusto) oh!, aw!; (para expresar sorpresa) wow!, blimey! (Brit*), jeez! (EEUU*)

jockey ['joki] SM (pl ~s) jockey

jocoque SM (Méx), **jocoqui** SM (Méx) sour cream

jocoso ADJ humorous, jocular

joda*** SF (esp LAm) 1 (= molestia) real hassle* 2 (= broma) joke; **lo dijo en ~** he said it as a joke

joder*** /2a/ Ⓐ VT 1 (= copular) to fuck***, screw*** 2 (= fastidiar) to piss off***; **me jodió mucho que perdiera Colombia** I was really pissed off when Colombia lost***; **esta vez te han jodido** this time you've had it* o you're fucked*** 3 (= estropear) [+ aparato] to bust*, fuck up***; [+ planes] to screw up**, fuck up*** Ⓑ VI 1 (= copular) to fuck***, screw*** 2 (= fastidiar) **jode tener que levantarse tan temprano** it's a drag* o a pain in the arse (Brit***) o ass (EEUU***) having to get up so early; ✦ MODISMO **¡no jodas!** (indicando sorpresa) bloody hell! (Brit**), get out of here! (EEUU*); (indicando rechazo) you must be kidding! Ⓒ **joderse** VPR 1 (= fastidiarse) **ellos a hacerse ricos y los demás a ~se** they get rich and the rest of us can go to hell** o can go screw ourselves***; **¡que se joda!** screw him!***; **¡te jodes!** tough shit!*** 2 (= estropearse) **se me ha jodido el coche** the car's had it*, the car's fucked***; **cuando llegó él se jodió todo** when he arrived it messed* o screwed*** everything up

3 ~se la espalda/una pierna to do one's back/leg in*
Ⓓ EXCL (*Esp*) shit!**, bloody hell! (*Brit***); **cállate ya ¡joder!**
for Christ's sake, shut up!*, shut the fuck up!***, shut up
for fuck's sake!***; **pero ¿cómo no iba a asustarme, ~?** well,
of course I was frightened, for Christ's sake, who wouldn't
be?*

jodido* ADJ **1** (*con ser*) [*situación*] fucking awkward***;
va a ser ~ it'll be fucking*** *o* damn** awkward; **la cárcel es
muy jodida** it's fucking*** *o* damn** hard being in jail; **es
un libro ~** it's a fucking difficult book***, it's a helluva
difficult book*
2 (*con estar*) **2.1** [*persona*] (= *en mal estado*) in a bad way,
fucked***; (= *desanimado*) **estar ~** to feel like shit***
2.2 (= *estropeado*) (= *aparato, vehículo*) bust*, busted (*EEUU*)*
3 (= *maldito*) damn**, bloody (*Brit***)
4 (*LAm**) (= *molesto*) damned annoying**, bloody annoying
(*Brit***)

jodón* ADJ (*LAm*) damned annoying**, bloody annoying
(*Brit***)

jofaina SF washbasin (*Brit*), bathroom sink (*EEUU*)

jogging ['joɣin] SM **1** (*Dep*) jogging; **hacer ~** to jog **2** (*Arg*)
(= *ropa*) jogging suit

jojoba SF jojoba

jojoto SM (*Ven*) (ear of) corn *o* maize

jol SM (*LAm*) hall, lobby

jolgorio SM fun, revelry

jolín* EXCL (*Esp*), **jolines*** EXCL (*Esp*) yikes!*

jónico ADJ Ionic

jonrón SM (*esp LAm*) (*en béisbol*) home run

jopé* EXCL (*Esp*) (*para expresar disgusto*) oh!, aw!; (*para
expresar sorpresa*) wow!, blimey! (*Brit**); jeez! (*EEUU**)

jopo SM **1** (= *rabo*) brush, tail **2** (*CS*) (*en el pelo*) quiff

Jordania SF Jordan

jordano/a ADJ, SM/F Jordanian

jornada SF **1** (= *tiempo de trabajo*) **media ~** half day
➤ **jornada completa** full (working) day ➤ **jornada
continua** = **jornada intensiva** ➤ **jornada de ocho horas**
eight-hour day ➤ **jornada intensiva** *full day's work with no
lunch break* ➤ **jornada laboral** working day ➤ **jornada
partida** split shift
2 (= *día*) day ➤ **jornada de movilización** day of action, day
of protest ➤ **jornada de reflexión** (*Pol*) day before the
election (*on which campaigning is banned*)
3 [*de viaje*] day's journey; (= *etapa*) stage (of a journey)
4 **jornadas** (*Univ*) congress, conference; **"Jornadas
Cervantinas"** "Conference on Cervantes"

jornal SM (= *sueldo*) (day's) wage; (= *trabajo*) day's work;
trabajar a ~ to be paid by the day

jornalero/a SM/F (day) labourer, (day) laborer (*EEUU*)

joroba SF hump

jorobado/a Ⓐ ADJ **1** (= *con chepa*) hunchbacked **2** (*)
(= *fastidiado*) **ando algo ~ con la espalda** my back's giving
me a bit of trouble **3** (*) [*tema, asunto, decisión*] tricky
Ⓑ SM/F hunchback

jorobar* /1a/ Ⓐ VT **1** (= *fastidiar*) to annoy; **lo que más me
joroba es que no reconozcan mi trabajo** what annoys me
most is that they don't acknowledge the work I do
2 (= *estropear*) [+ *aparato*] to mess up, wreck; [+ *planes,
fiesta*] to bust*, ruin, screw up**
Ⓑ VI **sólo lo hace por ~** he only does it to be annoying
Ⓒ **jorobarse** VPR **1** (= *aguantarse*) **tendré que ~me** I'll just
have to grin and bear it; **pues ¡que se jorobe!** well, he can
lump it!*
2 (= *estropearse*) [*aparato*] to be wrecked, be bust*; [*planes,
fiesta*] to be ruined
3 ~se una pierna/una rodilla to mess up one's leg/a knee

jorongo SM (*Méx*) poncho, sleeveless poncho

joropo SM (*Mús*) (*national*) Venezuelan/Colombian dance

jota SF **1** (name of the letter) J; ✦ MODISMO **ni ~: no
entendió ni ~** he didn't understand a word of it; **no saber
ni ~** to have no idea **2** (*Mús*) Spanish dance and tune, *esp
Aragonese* **3** (*Naipes*) knave, jack

jote SM (*CS*) buzzard

joto* SM **1** (*Méx*) (= *homosexual*) queer**, fag (*EEUU***)
2 (*Méx**) (= *cobarde*) coward **3** (*And*) (= *atado*) bundle

joven Ⓐ ADJ [*persona, animal*] young; [*aspecto*] youthful
Ⓑ SMF young man/young woman; (*como apelativo*) young
man/young lady; **los jóvenes** young people, youth, the
young

jovencito/a SM/F youngster

jovial ADJ jolly, cheerful

joya SF **1** (= *adorno*) jewel, gem; **~s** jewels, jewellery,
jewelry (*EEUU*) ➤ **joyas de fantasía** costume jewellery,
imitation jewellery **2** (= *persona, cosa*) gem, treasure

joyería SF **1** (= *tienda*) jeweller's *o* (*EEUU*) jeweler's
2 (= *joyas*) jewellery, jewelry (*EEUU*), jewels *pl*

joyero/a Ⓐ SM/F jeweller, jeweler (*EEUU*) Ⓑ SM (= *estuche*)
jewel case

juana* SF (*Méx*) marijuana

juanete SM bunion

jubilación SF **1** (= *acción*) retirement ➤ **jubilación
anticipada** early retirement **2** (= *pensión*) retirement
pension

jubilado/a Ⓐ ADJ retired Ⓑ SM/F pensioner, retired
person, OAP (*Brit*)

jubilar /1a/ Ⓐ VT **1** [+ *trabajador*] to pension off, retire
2 (* *hum*) (= *desechar*) [+ *objeto*] to discard; [+ *persona*] to
put out to grass Ⓑ **jubilarse** VPR **1** [*trabajador*] to retire
2 (*CAm*) (= *hacer novillos*) to play truant

jubileo SM (*Rel*) jubilee

júbilo SM joy, rejoicing, jubilation

jubiloso ADJ jubilant

jubón SM doublet, jerkin

judaísmo SM Judaism

judas SM INV traitor, betrayer

judeoespañol ADJ, SM Judeo-Spanish

judería SF Jewish quarter

judía SF bean ➤ **judía blanca** haricot bean ➤ **judía pinta**
pinto bean ➤ **judía verde** green bean; *ver tb* **judío**

judicatura SF **1** (= *jueces*) judiciary **2** (= *cargo*) office of
judge

judicial ADJ judicial; **recurrir a la vía ~** to go to law, have
recourse to law

judío/a Ⓐ ADJ **1** [*pueblo, religión*] Jewish **2** (*pey*) (= *tacaño*)
mean, miserly Ⓑ SM/F Jew/Jewess, Jewish man/woman;
ver tb **judía**

judo ['judo] SM judo

judoca SMF, **judoka** [ju'doka] SMF judoist, judoka

juego¹ *ver* **jugar**

juego² SM **1** (= *acto*) play; **el balón está en ~** the ball is in
play; **estar fuera de ~** [*jugador*] to be offside; [*balón*] to be
out of play; **por ~** for fun ➤ **juego limpio** fair play
2 (*como entretenimiento*) game; **el ~ del ajedrez** the game of
chess; ✦ MODISMO **ser un ~ de niños** to be child's play
➤ **juego de azar** game of chance ➤ **juego de cartas** card
game ➤ **juego de computadora** (*LAm*) computer game ➤ **el
juego de la oca** snakes and ladders ➤ **juego de manos**
conjuring trick ➤ **juego de mesa** board game ➤ **juego de
ordenador** (*Esp*) computer game ➤ **juego de palabras** pun,
play on words ➤ **juego de rol** role-playing game
3 juegos (= *competición*) ➤ **Juegos Olímpicos** Olympic
Games ➤ **Juegos Olímpicos de Invierno** Winter Olympics
4 (= *jugada*) (*en tenis*) game; (*de cartas*) hand
5 (*con apuestas*) gambling; **lo perdió todo en el ~** he
gambled everything away, he lost everything through
gambling; **¡hagan ~!** place your bets!; ✦ MODISMOS **estar en
~** to be at stake; **los factores que entran en ~** the factors
that come into play; **poner algo en ~** to place sth at risk
6 (= *estrategia*) game; **le conozco** *o* **veo el ~** I know his
little game, I know what he's up to; ✦ MODISMO **seguir el ~
a algn** to play along with sb
7 (= *conjunto*) [*de vajilla*] set, service; [*de muebles*] suite; [*de
herramientas*] kit; **con falda a ~** with skirt to match, with
matching skirt; **las cortinas hacen ~ con el sofá** the

curtains match the sofa, the curtains go with the sofa ➤ **juego de café** coffee set, coffee service ➤ **juego de cama** set of matching bed linen (*Brit*) *o* bedding (*EEUU*) ➤ **juego de luces** [*de árbol de Navidad*] Christmas lights *pl*, fairy lights *pl* (*Brit*); (*en fiesta, espectáculo*) decorative lights *pl* ➤ **juego de mesa** dinner service **8** [*de mecanismo*] play, movement; **el ~ de la rodilla** the movement of the knee

juerga* SF ~ binge*; **ir de ~** to go out for a good time

juerguista SMF reveller

jueves SM INV Thursday; ✦ MODISMO **no es nada del otro ~** it's nothing to write home about ➤ **Jueves Santo** Maundy Thursday; *ver tb* **sábado**

En inglés los días de la semana se escriben con mayúscula.

juez SMF (SF *a veces* ~**a**) **1** (*Jur*) judge; ✦ MODISMO **ser ~ y parte** to be an interested party ➤ **juez de instrucción** examining magistrate ➤ **juez de paz** justice of the peace, magistrate ➤ **juez de primera instancia** examining magistrate **2** (*Dep*) judge ➤ **juez de banda, juez de línea, juez de raya** (*RPl Ftbl*) linesman

jugada SF **1** (*Dep*) piece of play; (*Ftbl, Ajedrez*) move; **una bonita ~** a lovely piece of play, a lovely move; **hacer una ~** to make a move **2** (*mala*) ~ dirty trick; **hacer** *o* **gastar una mala ~ a algn** to play a dirty trick on sb

jugado ADJ (*And*) expert, skilled

jugador(a) SM/F **1** [*de deporte, juegos de mesa*] player **2** [*de apuestas*] gambler

jugar /1h, 1n/ **Ⓐ** VI **1** [*niño, deportista*] to play; **¡si seguís así yo no juego!** if you carry on like that I'm not playing!; **~ a algo** to play sth; **~ con algo** to play with sth; **~ contra algn** to play (against) sb; ✦ MODISMOS **~ con fuego** to play with fire; **~ con ventaja** to be at an advantage, have the advantage; **~ limpio** to play fair; **~ sucio** to play dirty **2** (= *hacer una jugada*) (*en ajedrez, parchís*) to move; (*con cartas*) to play **3** (= *pretender ser*) **~ a algo** to play at being sth **4** **~ con** **4.1** (= *manosear*) (*gen*) to play around with, mess around with; (*distraídamente*) to toy with, fiddle with **4.2** (= *no tomar en serio*) [+ *sentimientos*] to play with; **solamente está jugando contigo** he's just leading you on; **con la salud no se juega** you can't put your health at risk **4.3** (= *utilizar*) to play with; **esta obra juega con el tema del teatro dentro del teatro** this work plays with the idea of a play within a play **5** (= *influir*) **~ en contra de algo/algn** to work against sth/sb; **la posición del sol jugaba en contra de nuestro equipo** the position of the sun put our team at a disadvantage; **~ a favor de algo/algn** [*situación*] to work in sth's/sb's favour *o* (*EEUU*) favor; [*tiempo, destino*] to be on sb's side **6** (= *apostar*) to gamble **7** (*Bolsa*) to speculate; **~ a la bolsa** to play the stock market **Ⓑ** VT **1** [+ *partida, partido*] to play; ✦ MODISMOS **~ la baza de algo: la oposición ~á la baza de la moción de censura** the opposition will play its trump card and move a motion of censure; **jugársela a algn*** to play a dirty trick on sb, do the dirty on sb (*Brit**); **¡me la han jugado!** I've been had!*; **su mujer se la jugaba con otro** (*LAm*) his wife was two-timing him* **2** [+ *papel*] to play **3** (= *apostar*) to bet; **~ cinco dólares a una carta** to bet *o* put five dollars on a card **4** (*LAm*) [+ *fútbol, tenis, ajedrez, póker*] to play **Ⓒ** **jugarse** VPR **1** [+ *dinero*] (= *apostar*) to bet, stake; (= *perder*) to gamble away; **se jugó la fortuna a la ruleta** he gambled away his fortune at roulette; **jugárselo todo a una carta** (*lit*) to bet everything on one card; (*fig*) to put all one's eggs in one basket **2** (*como reto*) to bet; **me juego lo que quieras a que no te atreves** I bet you anything you won't dare **3** (= *exponerse a perder*) **3.1** (*en una apuesta consciente*) to stake; **jugárselo todo en algo** to stake everything on sth; ✦ MODISMO **jugársela: conducir más deprisa hubiera sido jugársela** to drive any faster would have been too risky;

España se la juega ante Italia esta noche Spain is staking everything on their match with Italy tonight; **~se el todo por el todo** to take the plunge **3.2** (*sin darse cuenta*) **nos estamos jugando el futuro de la democracia** the future of democracy is at stake here; **esto es ~se la vida** this means risking one's life

jugarreta SF dirty trick; **hacer una ~ a algn** to play a dirty trick on sb

juglar SM minstrel, jongleur

juglaría SF minstrelsy, art of the minstrel(s)

jugo SM **1** (= *líquido*) (*gen*) juice; **~ de naranja** (*LAm*) orange juice ➤ **jugos digestivos** digestive juices ➤ **jugos gástricos** gastric juices **2** (= *sustancia*) essence, substance; **sacar el ~ a algo** to get the most out of sth

jugoso ADJ **1** [*alimento*] juicy, succulent **2** (= *rentable*) [*aumento, reducción*] substantial, considerable; [*negocio*] profitable; **un discurso ~** a speech that gives/gave plenty of food for thought

jugué, juguemos *etc ver* **jugar**

juguera SF (*CS*) (*para frutas*) juicer; (*para otros alimentos*) blender

juguete SM **1** (= *objeto*) toy; **un cañón de ~** a toy gun ➤ **juguete educativo** educational toy **2** (*uso figurado*) toy, plaything

juguetear /1a/ VI to play, sport (**con** with)

jugueteo SM playing, romping

juguetería SF **1** (= *tienda*) toyshop (*Brit*), toystore (*EEUU*) **2** (= *industria*) toy business

juguetón ADJ playful

juicio SM **1** (= *inteligencia*) judgment, reason **2** (= *sensatez*) good sense; **estar en su sano ~** to be in one's right mind; **perder el ~** to go mad; **no tener ~** *o* ◇ **tener poco ~** to lack common sense **3** (= *opinión*) opinion; **a mi ~** in my opinion ➤ **juicio de valor** value judgment **4** (*Jur*) (= *proceso*) trial; **llevar a algn a ~** to take sb to court ➤ **juicio civil** criminal trial ➤ **juicio de Dios** trial by ordeal ➤ **Juicio Final** Last Judgment

juicioso ADJ sensible, judicious

julepe SM **1** (*Naipes*) card game **2** (*SAm**) (= *susto*) scare, fright

julepear* /1a/ **Ⓐ** VT (*CS*) to scare, frighten **Ⓑ** **julepearse** VPR (*CS*) to get scared

julia* SF (*Méx*) Black Maria (*Brit**), paddy wagon (*EEUU**)

juliana SF (*Culin*) julienne; **cortar en ~** to cut into thin shreds, cut into julienne strips

Julio SM Julius; **~ César** Julius Caesar

julio SM July; *ver tb* **septiembre**

En inglés los meses se escriben con mayúscula.

jumado* ADJ drunk, plastered*

jumar* /1a/ **Ⓐ** VI to pong**, stink **Ⓑ** **jumarse** VPR to get drunk

jumbo ['jumbo] SM jumbo, jumbo jet

jumento SM donkey

jumo* ADJ (*LAm*) drunk, plastered*

jumper ['dʒumper] SM *o* SF (*pl* ~**s**) (*CS, Méx*) pinafore dress (*Brit*), jumper (*EEUU*)

juncal SM reed bed

junco[1] SM (= *planta*) rush, reed

junco[2] SM (= *barco*) junk

jungla SF jungle ➤ **jungla de asfalto** concrete jungle

junio SM June; *ver tb* **septiembre**

En inglés los meses se escriben con mayúscula.

junior, júnior ['dʒunjor] **Ⓐ** ADJ INV junior **Ⓑ** SMF (*pl* ~**s** *o* **júniors**) junior **Ⓒ** SM (*CS*) office boy

junquera SF rush, bulrush

junta SF 1 (= *reunión*) meeting ➤ **junta general de accionistas** general meeting of shareholders 2 (= *comité*) (*gen*) council, committee; (*Com, Fin*) board ➤ **junta de gobierno** governing body ➤ **junta directiva** board of directors ➤ **junta electoral** electoral board ➤ **junta rectora** governing body 3 (*Mil*) junta 4 (*Esp Pol*) *name given to the governments of some autonomous areas in Spain* 5 (= *acoplamiento*) joint; (= *arandela*) washer, gasket 6 (*LAm*) (= *amistad*) **las malas ~s** the wrong kind of people; **le prohibieron las ~s con esa gente** they forbade him to go out with those people

juntamente ADV **~ con** together with

juntar /1a/ Ⓐ VT 1 (= *colocar juntos*) to put together; **~ on varias mesas** they put several tables together; **junta la librería a la pared** put the bookcase against the wall; **~ dinero** to save, save up 2 (= *reunir*) [+ *amigos, conocidos*] to get together; [+ *participantes, concursantes*] to bring together 3 (= *coleccionar*) [+ *sellos, objetos*] to collect 4 (= *entornar*) [+ *puerta, ventana*] to push to Ⓑ **juntarse** VPR 1 (= *reunirse*) 1.1 (*para una cita*) to get together, meet; **~se con algn** to get together with sb, meet up with sb 1.2 (*en asamblea, trabajo*) to meet 1.3 (*sin citarse*) to come together; **se ~on más de cinco mil personas para oírlo** more than five thousand people assembled *o* came together to listen to him 2 (= *unirse*) **se fue juntando mucha más gente por el camino** many more people joined them along the way; **se juntan un espermatozoide y un óvulo** a sperm and an egg join together; **~se a** *o* **con algn** to join up with sb 3 (= *arrimarse*) [*varias personas*] to move closer together; **si te juntas un poco más cabremos todos en el banco** if you move up a little we can all get on the bench 4 (= *relacionarse*) [*pareja*] to get together; **~se con algn** (*gen*) to mix with sb; (*en pareja*) to get together with sb 5 (= *ocurrir a la vez*) to happen together; **en su poesía se juntan elementos tradicionales y renovadores** traditional and new elements come together in his poetry; **la semana pasada se me juntó todo** it was just one thing after another last week; **se te va a ~ el desayuno con la comida** you'll be having breakfast at the same time as your lunch 6 [*empresas, asociaciones*] to merge 7 [*líneas, caminos*] to meet, join

juntillas *ver* **pie 2**

junto Ⓐ ADJ 1 (= *unido, acompañado*) together; **mételo todo ~ en la maleta** put it all together in the suitcase; **se escribe ~** it is written as one word; **fuimos ~s** we went together; **todos ~s** all together 2 (= *cercano*) close together; **tenía los ojos muy ~s** his eyes were very close together; **poneos más ~s** move a little closer together 3 (= *al mismo tiempo*) together; **las vi entrar juntas** I saw them go in together Ⓑ ADV 1 **~ a** 1.1 (= *cerca de*) close to, near; **tienen un chalet ~ al mar** they have a house close to *o* near the sea 1.2 (= *al lado de*) next to, beside; **fue enterrado ~ a su padre** he was buried next to *o* beside his father; **José permaneció ~ a la puerta** José remained by the door 1.3 (= *en compañía de*) with, together with; **celebró su aniversario ~ a su familia** he celebrated his anniversary (together) with his family; **desea volver ~ a su marido** she wishes to go back to her husband 1.4 (= *conjuntamente*) together with, along with; **nuestro equipo es, ~ al italiano, el mejor de la liga** together with the Italian team, ours is the best in the league 2 **~ con** 2.1 (= *en compañía de*) with, together with; **fue detenido ~ con otros cuatro terroristas** he was arrested (together) with four other terrorists 2.2 (= *conjuntamente*) together with; **el paro es, ~ con el terrorismo, nuestro mayor problema** together with terrorism, unemployment is our biggest problem

juntura SF (*Anat, Téc*) joint

Júpiter SM Jupiter

jura SF (= *juramento*) oath, pledge ➤ **jura de (la) bandera** (taking the) oath of loyalty *o* allegiance

jurado Ⓐ SM (= *tribunal*) (*Jur*) jury; (*en concurso, TV*) panel (*of judges*) Ⓑ SMF (= *miembro*) (*Jur*) juror; (*en concurso, TV*) judge Ⓒ ADJ [*declaración*] sworn

juramentar /1a/ Ⓐ VT to swear in, administer the oath to Ⓑ **juramentarse** VPR to be sworn in, take the oath

juramento SM 1 (= *promesa*) oath; **bajo ~** on oath; **prestar ~** to take the oath (**sobre** on); **tomar ~ a algn** to swear sb in ➤ **juramento hipocrático** Hippocratic oath 2 (= *blasfemia*) oath, curse; **decir ~s** to swear

jurar /1a/ Ⓐ VT 1 (*solemnemente*) to swear; **~ decir la verdad** to swear to tell the truth; **~ (la) bandera** to pledge allegiance (to the flag); **~ el cargo** to be sworn in; **~ la Constitución** to pledge allegiance to the Constitution; **lo juro por mi honor** I swear on my honour *o* (*EEUU*) honor; ✦ MODISMO **tenérsela jurada a algn** (*como venganza personal*) to have it in for sb; (*a nivel político, profesional*) to be after sb's blood 2 (*uso enfático*) to swear; **no he oído nada, se lo juro** I didn't hear a thing, I swear Ⓑ VI (= *blasfemar*) to swear; **~ en falso** to commit perjury

jurel SM horse mackerel

jurídico ADJ legal, juridical

jurisdicción SF 1 (= *autoridad*) jurisdiction 2 (= *distrito*) district, administrative area

jurisdiccional ADJ **aguas ~es** territorial waters

jurisprudencia SF jurisprudence

jurista SMF jurist

justa SF (*Hist*) joust, tournament

justamente ADV 1 (= *exactamente*) 1.1 (*coincidiendo con algo*) just; **~ ahora que ...** just when ...; **ocurrió hace ~ un año** it happened exactly a year ago; **~ lo contrario** exactly the opposite 1.2 (*referido a cosa, lugar*) exactly, precisely; **es aquí ~ donde está la originalidad del autor** it is precisely in this where the author's originality lies; **ésas son ~ las que no están en venta** those are precisely the ones which are not for sale 2 (= *con justicia*) justly; **los monumentos por los que la ciudad es ~ famosa** the monuments for which the city is justly famous 3 (= *escasamente*) frugally; **viven muy ~** they live very frugally

justicia SF justice; **de ~** justly, deservedly; **es de ~ añadir que ...** it is only fair to add that ...; **en ~** (= *por derecho*) by rights; (= *para ser justo*) in all fairness; **hacer ~ a** to do justice to; **tomarse la ~ por su mano** to take the law into one's own hands ➤ **justicia poética** poetic justice

justicialismo SM (*Arg Hist, Pol*) *political movement founded by Perón*; ➭ PERONISMO

justiciero ADJ (*strictly*) just, righteous

justificable ADJ justifiable

justificación SF justification

justificado ADJ justified; **no ~** unjustified

justificante SM [*de dinero*] receipt; [*de enfermedad*] sick note

justificar /1g/ Ⓐ VT 1 (= *explicar*) to account for, explain; **tendrá que ~ su ausencia** she will have to account for *o* explain her absence 2 (= *excusar*) [+ *decisión, comportamiento*] to justify, excuse; **nada justifica tal violencia** nothing can justify *o* excuse such violence 3 (*Inform, Tip*) to justify Ⓑ **justificarse** VPR to justify o.s., make excuses for o.s.

justificativo ADJ **documento ~** voucher, certificate

justo Ⓐ ADJ 1 (= *con justicia*) [*castigo, decisión, sociedad*] fair, just; [*juicio, premio, juez*] fair; [*causa*] just; **me pareció muy ~** it seemed very fair to me; **no es ~** it's not fair; **un reparto más ~ de la riqueza** a more equitable *o* just distribution of wealth 2 (= *exacto*) [*precio, medidas*] exact; **10 euros ~s** exactly 10 euros; **nació a los tres años ~s** he was born exactly three years later; **tengo el tiempo ~ para tomarme un café** I've got just enough time to have a coffee; **estamos los ~s para jugar al bridge** there's just the right number of us to play bridge

3 (= *preciso*) **encontró la palabra justa** she found exactly *o* just the right word; **vino en el momento** ~ he came just at the right moment

4 (= *escaso*) **vivimos muy ~s** we have only just enough to live on; **vamos un poco ~s de tiempo** we're a little pushed for time; **llegaste muy ~ de tiempo** you only just made it; **ando ~ de dinero** money's a little tight at the moment; **vive con lo** ~ he just manages to make ends meet

5 (= *apretado*) [*ropa*] tight; **el traje me queda** *o* **me viene** *o* **me está muy** ~ the suit is very tight for *o* on me

B ADV **1** (= *exactamente*) (*gen*) just; (*con cantidades*) exactly; **llegó ~ cuando yo salía** she arrived just *o* exactly as I was leaving; **su casa está ~ enfrente del banco** his house is just *o* right opposite the bank; **me costó ~ el doble que a ti** it cost me exactly double what it cost you; ~ **lo contrario** exactly the opposite

2 (= *escasamente*) **vivir muy ~** to just manage to make ends meet, have only just enough to live on

C SMPL **los ~s** (*Rel*) the just

juvenil **A** ADJ **1** [*persona*] youthful; **de aspecto** ~ youthful in appearance **2** [*equipo, torneo*] junior **B** SMF (*Dep*) junior, junior player

juventud SF **1** (= *época*) youth; **en mi** ~ in my youth, when I was young; **pecados de** ~ youthful indiscretions **2** (= *los jóvenes*) young people; **la ~ de hoy** young people today, the youth of today **3** (= *cualidad*) youth

juzgado SM court ➤ **juzgado de guardia** police court ➤ **juzgado de instrucción** examining magistrate's court ➤ **juzgado de primera instancia** court of first instance

juzgar /1h/ VT **1** (= *emitir un juicio sobre*) to judge; (*Jur*) to try; ~ **mal** to misjudge; **a ~ por** to judge by, judging by **2** (= *considerar*) to think, consider; **lo juzgo mi deber** I consider *o* (*frm*) deem it my duty

Kk

K[1], k [ka] SF (= *letra*) K, k
K[2] SM ABR (= **kilobyte**) K
Kadsastán SM Kazakhstan
kafkiano ADJ Kafkaesque
káiser SM Kaiser
kaki SM = **caqui**
kale borroka ['kale bo'rroka] SF street violence (*attributed to ETA*)
kamikaze SM kamikaze
kaput* [ka'pu] ADJ kaput*
karaoke SM karaoke
kárate SM, **karate** SM karate
karateka SMF, **karateca** SMF karate expert
karma SM karma
karting ['kartin] SM, **kárting** ['kartin] SM go-kart *o* (*EEUU*) -cart racing
katiuska Ⓐ ADJ (*Esp*) **botas ~s** wellington boots (*esp Brit*), rubber boots Ⓑ SF wellington boot (*esp Brit*), rubber boot
kayac SM, **kayak** SM kayak
kazajo/a Ⓐ ADJ, SM/F Kazak, Kazakh Ⓑ SM (*Ling*) Kazak, Kazakh
k/c ABR (= **kilociclo(s)**) kc
kéfir SM kefir
Kenia SF Kenya
keniano/a ADJ, SM/F Kenyan
keniata ADJ, SMF Kenyan
kepis SM INV, **kepí** SM military style round cap or hat
kg ABR (= **kilogramo(s)**) kg
KHz ABR (= **kilohertzio(s)**, **kilohercio(s)**) KHz
kibutz [ki'βuts] SM (*pl* ~**im** *o* ~) kibbutz
kiki* SM (*Esp*) joint**, reefer**
kiko SM (*Esp*) snack of salted, toasted maize
kilate SM = **quilate**
kilo SM **1** (= *unidad de peso*) kilo **2** (*) (= *un millón de pesetas*) one million pesetas
kilocaloría SF kilocalorie, calorie
kilociclo SM kilocycle
kilogramo SM kilogramme, kilogram (*EEUU*)
kilohercio SM, **kilohertzio** SM kilohertz
kilometraje SM ≈ mileage
kilométrico ADJ **1** (= *de kilómetro*) kilometric; (**billete**) ~ (*Ferro*) ≈ mileage ticket **2** (*) (= *muy largo*) very long;

palabra kilométrica very long word
kilómetro SM kilometre, kilometer (*EEUU*); ~ **cero** starting point
kilovatio SM kilowatt
kilovatio-hora SM kilowatt-hour; **kilovatios-hora** kilowatt-hours
kimono SM kimono
kínder SM (*LAm*), **kindergarten** SM (*LAm*) kindergarten, nursery school
kinesiología SF kinesiology
kiosco SM = **quiosco**
kiosquero/a SM/F = **quiosquero**
Kirguidstán SM, **Kirgidstán** SM, **Kirguisia** SF Kyrgyzstan
kit SM (*pl* ~**s**) kit ➤ **kit de montaje** self-assembly kit
kitsch [kitʃ] ADJ INV, SM kitsch
kiwi SM **1** (= *ave*) kiwi **2** (= *fruta*) kiwi fruit
klaxon SM horn; **tocar el** ~ to blow the horn, toot (the horn)
klínex SM INV tissue, Kleenex®
km ABR (= **kilómetro(s)**) km
km/h ABR (= **kilómetros por hora**) km/h, kmh, kph
knock-out ['nokau] SM, **K.O.** [kaw] SM (= *acto*) knockout; (= *golpe*) knockout blow; **dejar a algn** ~ to knock sb out
kohl SM (*para ojos*) kohl
koljós SM (*pl* **koljoses**), **koljoz** [kol'xos] SM (*pl* **koljozi**) kolkhoz
kosovar Ⓐ ADJ Kosovan, Kosovo *antes de s* Ⓑ SMF Kosovar
Kosovo SM Kosovo
k.p.h. ABR (= **kilómetros por hora**) km/h, kmh, kph
k.p.l. ABR (= **kilómetros por litro**)
kuchen ['kuxen] SM (*Chi*) tart
Kurdistán SM Kurdistan
kurdo/a Ⓐ ADJ Kurdish Ⓑ SM/F Kurd Ⓒ SM (*Ling*) Kurdish
Kuwait SM Kuwait
kuwaití ADJ, SMF Kuwaiti
kv ABR (= **kilovoltio(s)**) kV, kv
kv/h ABR (= **kilovoltios-hora**) kV/h, kv/h
kw ABR (= **kilovatio(s)**) kW, kw
kw/h ABR (= **kilovatios-hora**) kW/h, kw/h

Ll

L, l ['ele] SF (= *letra*) L, l

l ABR (= **litro(s)**) l

la[1] ART DEF **1** (*con sustantivos*) the **2** **la de**: **mi casa y la de usted** my house and yours; **esta chica y la del vestido verde** this girl and the one in the green dress; **la de Pedro es mejor** Peter's is better; **¡la de goles que marcó!** what a lot of goals he scored!; **¡la de veces que se equivoca!** how often he's wrong!; *ver tb* **el**

la[2] PRON PERS (*refiriéndose a ella*) her; (*refiriéndose a usted*) you; (*refiriéndose a una cosa, un animal*) it; *ver tb* **lo**, **laísmo**

la[3] SM (*Mús*) la, A; **la menor** A minor

laberinto SM [*de calles, situaciones*] labyrinth, maze; (*en parque*) maze

labia* SF **tener mucha ~** to have the gift of the gab*

labial ADJ, SF labial

labio SM lip; **labios** lips, mouth *sing*; ✦ MODISMO **sin despegar los ~s** without uttering a word ➤ **labio leporino** harelip, cleft lip ➤ **labios mayores** labia majora

labiodental ADJ, SF labiodental

labor SF **1** (= *trabajo*) labour, labor (*EEUU*), work; **"profesión: sus labores"** "occupation: housewife"; **una ~** job, task, piece of work ➤ **labor de chinos** tedious job ➤ **labor de equipo** teamwork ➤ **labores domésticas** household chores ➤ **labor social** work for a good cause, work in a good cause **2** (= *costura*) needlework; (= *punto*) knitting **3** (*Agr*) ploughing, plowing (*EEUU*)

laborable ADJ [*día*] working

laboral ADJ (*gen*) labour *antes de s*, labor *antes de s* (*EEUU*), work *antes de s*; [*jornada, horario*] working

laboralista ADJ labour *antes de s*, labor *antes de s* (*EEUU*)

laborar /1a/ ▲ VT (*Agr*) to work, till (*liter*) ⓑ VI (*frm*) to work

laboratorio SM laboratory

laborero SM (*And Min*) foreman

laboriosidad SF **1** (= *dedicación*) industry **2** (= *dificultad*) laboriousness

laborioso ADJ **1** (= *dedicado, constante*) hard-working, industrious **2** (= *dificultoso*) [*trabajo, negociaciones*] laborious

laborismo SM labour movement, labor movement (*EEUU*)

laborista

> En inglés americano se usa **Labor** en lugar de **Labour**.

▲ ADJ Labour *antes de s* ⓑ SMF Labour Party member, Labour supporter

labrador(a) SM/F (= *propietario*) (peasant) farmer; (= *labriego*) farmhand, farmworker

labrantío ADJ arable

labranza SF cultivation, farming, tilling (*liter*); **tierras de ~** farmland

labrar /1a/ ▲ VT [+ *metal*] to work; [+ *madera*] to carve; [+ *tierra*] to work, farm, till (*liter*) ⓑ **labrarse** VPR **~se un porvenir** to carve out a future for o.s.

labriego/a SM/F farmhand, labourer, peasant

laburar* /1a/ VI (*CS*) to work

laburo* SM (*CS*) work

laca SF (= *gomorresina*) shellac; (= *barniz*) lacquer; [*de pelo*] hairspray ➤ **laca de uñas** nail polish, nail varnish (*Brit*)

lacar /1g/ VT to lacquer

lacayo SM **1** (= *criado*) footman **2** (*pey*) (= *adulador*) lackey

lacear /1a/ VT (*CS*) [+ *ganado*] to lasso

lacerante ADJ **1** [*dolor*] excruciating **2** [*palabras, comentarios*] wounding, cutting

lacerar /1a/ VT to lacerate

lacho/a* SM/F (*Chi, Perú pey*) live-in lover

lacio ADJ [*pelo*] lank, straight

lacón SM shoulder of pork

lacónico ADJ laconic, terse

lacra SF (*social, moral*) blot, blemish

lacrar /1a/ VT to seal (*with sealing wax*)

lacre ▲ ADJ (*LAm*) bright red ⓑ SM sealing wax

lacrimógeno ADJ **1** [*humo, vapor*] tear-producing; **gas ~** tear gas **2** [*canción, historia*] highly sentimental, weepy*; **novela lacrimógena** tear-jerker

lactancia SF (= *secreción*) lactation; [*de niño*] breast-feeding

lactante ▲ ADJ **mujer ~** nursing mother ⓑ SMF breast-fed baby

lácteo ADJ dairy *antes de s*

lactosa SF lactose

ladeado ADJ tilted, leaning, inclined

ladear /1a/ ▲ VT to tilt, tip ⓑ **ladearse** VPR to lean (**a** towards); (= *torcerse*) to bend; (*Dep*) to swerve

ladera SF hillside

ladilla SF **1** (*Zool*) crab louse **2** (*And, Méx, Ven**) (= *pesado*) pain in the neck*

ladino/a ▲ ADJ **1** (= *astuto*) smart, shrewd; (= *taimado*) cunning, wily **2** (*CAm, Méx*) [*indio*] Spanish-speaking **3** (*CAm, Méx*) (= *mestizo*) half-breed, mestizo **4** (*Méx**) [*voz*] high-pitched, fluty ⓑ SM/F **1** (*CAm, Méx*) (= *indio*) Spanish-speaking Indian **2** (*CAm, Méx*) (= *mestizo*) half-breed, mestizo ⓒ SM (*Ling*) Ladino, Sephardic, Judeo-Spanish

lado SM **1** (= *lateral*) side; **~ derecho** right side, right-hand side; **~ izquierdo** left side, left-hand side; **al otro ~ de la calle** on the other side of the street, across the street; **de ~** sideways; **poner algo de ~** to put sth sideways; **duermo de ~** I sleep on my side; **echarse** o **hacerse a un ~** [*persona*] to move to one side, step aside; [*vehículo*] to swerve out of the way; **por su ~: se fue cada uno por su ~** they went their separate ways; **salieron corriendo cada uno por su ~** they all ran off in different directions; ✦ MODISMOS **dar de ~ a algn** (*Esp*): **a mí eso me da de ~** I couldn't care less about that; **dejar a un ~** to leave aside, forget; **mirar a algn de (medio) ~** to look down on sb; **poner a un ~** to put aside; **estar al otro ~** (*CS**) to be home and dry (*Brit**), be home free (*EEUU**)

2 (= *aspecto*) side; **todo tiene su ~ bueno** everything has its good side; **por un ~ ..., por otro ~ ...** on the one hand ..., on the other hand ...

3 (= *lugar*) **ponlo en cualquier ~** put it anywhere; **en otro ~** somewhere else; **estuvo de un ~ para otro toda la mañana** she was up and down all morning, she was running around all morning; **por todos ~s** everywhere; **rodeado de agua por todos ~s** surrounded by water on all sides, completely surrounded by water; **ir a todos ~s** to go all over

4 (*indicando proximidad*) **no se movió del ~ de su madre** she never left her mother's side; **estar al ~** to be near; **la mesa de al ~** the next table; **la casa de al ~** the house next door; **al ~ de** beside; **viven al ~ de nosotros** they live next door to us; **al ~ de aquello, esto no es nada** compared to that, this is nothing; **a mi/tu ~: se sentó a mi ~** he sat beside me; **estuvo a tu ~ todo el tiempo** she was at your side the whole time

5 (= *bando*) side; **yo estoy de su ~** I'm on his side, I'm with him; **ponerse al ~ de algn** to side with sb

6 (*Mat*) side

7 (*Dep*) end; **cambiar de ~** to change ends

ladrar /1a/ VI [*perro*] to bark; [*persona*] to yell

ladrido SM bark, barking

ladrillazo SM **dar un ~ a algn** to throw a brick at sb

ladrillo SM brick; ✦ MODISMO **ser un ~***: **este libro es un ~** this book is really hard going*

ladrón/ona Ⓐ SM/F thief Ⓑ SM (*Elec*) adaptor

lagaña SF = **legaña**

lagar SM [*de vino*] winepress; (= *edificio*) winery; [*de aceite*] oil press

lagarta** SF (*Esp*) bitch**

lagartear* /1a/ (*Col*) Ⓐ VT to wangle* Ⓑ VI to suck up*

lagartija SF (wall) lizard

lagarto SM 1 (*Zool*) lizard; (*LAm*) (= *caimán*) alligator 2 (= *taimado*) devious person, sly person, fox 3 (*Col**) (= *adulador*) bootlicker*

lago SM lake

lágrima SF tear; **llorar a ~ viva** to cry one's heart out; **se me saltaron las ~s** tears came to my eyes ➤ **lágrimas de cocodrilo** crocodile tears

lagrimal SM corner of the eye

lagrimear /1a/ VI 1 [*persona*] to shed tears easily 2 [*ojos*] to water, fill with tears

laguna SF 1 (*Geog*) (*en el interior*) pool; (*en la costa*) lagoon 2 (*en conocimientos, memoria*) gap

laico/a Ⓐ ADJ 1 (= *seglar*) [*misionero, predicador*] lay 2 [*estado, educación, colegio*] secular Ⓑ SM/F layman/ laywoman

laísmo SM *use of "la" and "las" as indirect objects*; ⋄ LEÍSMO, LOÍSMO, LAÍSMO

laja SF (*LAm*) sandstone

lama[1] SF (*LAm*) 1 (= *cieno*) mud, slime, ooze 2 (= *moho*) mould, mold (*EEUU*), verdigris 3 (= *musgo*) moss

lama[2] SM (*Rel*) lama

lambada SF lambada

lambeta** SMF (*CS*) bootlicker*

lambetear /1a/ VT (*Col, Méx*) to lick

lambiscón/ona* (*Méx*) Ⓐ ADJ fawning Ⓑ SM/F bootlicker*

lambisconear* = **lambonear**

lambisquear* /1a/ Ⓐ VT 1 (*Méx*) (= *adular*) to suck up to* 2 (*Col*) (= *lamer*) to lick Ⓑ VI (*Méx*) to look for sweets (*Brit*) o candies (*EEUU*)

lambón/ona* ADJ, SM/F (*Col, Méx*) = **lambiscón**

lambonear* /1a/ (*Col, Méx*) Ⓐ VT to suck up to* Ⓑ VI to creep*, crawl*

lamé SM lamé

lameculos** SMF INV crawler**, arselicker (*Brit****), brown-nose (*EEUU***)

lamentable ADJ [*conducta*] deplorable; [*error*] regrettable; [*escena, aspecto, estado*] sorry, pitiful; [*pérdida*] sad; **es ~ que ...** it is regrettable that ...

lamentación SF sorrow, lamentation (*frm*); **ahora no sirven lamentaciones** it's no good crying over spilled milk

lamentar /1a/ Ⓐ VT (= *sentir*) to be sorry about, regret; [+ *pérdida*] to lament, bewail, bemoan (*frm*); **lamentamos la muerte de su marido** we're sorry to hear of your husband's death; **no hay que ~ víctimas** fortunately there were no casualties; **lamento lo que pasó** I'm sorry about what happened; **~ que** to be sorry that, regret that Ⓑ **lamentarse** VPR 1 (= *quejarse*) to complain; **de nada sirve ~se** there's no point complaining; **~se de algo: se lamenta del tiempo malgastado** he regrets the time he wasted 2 (*frm*) (= *llorar*) to lament

lamento SM moan

lamer /2a/ VT to lick

lametazo SM lick

lamido ADJ very thin, emaciated (*frm*)

lámina SF (*gen*) sheet; (*Fot, Tip*) plate; (= *grabado*) engraving; (*en libro*) plate, illustration ➤ **láminas de acero** sheet steel *sing*

laminado Ⓐ ADJ (*gen*) laminate(d); **cobre ~** sheet copper, rolled copper Ⓑ SM laminate

laminador SM, **laminadora** SF rolling mill

laminar /1a/ VT (*gen*) to laminate; (*Téc*) to roll

lampa SF (*Chi, Perú*) (= *azada*) hoe; (= *pala*) spade

lampalagua SF (*Chi*) mythical snake

lámpara SF 1 (*Elec*) lamp, light ➤ **lámpara de Aladino** Aladdin's lamp 2 (= *mancha*) stain, dirty mark

lamparín SM (*Chi, Perú*) paraffin lamp (*Brit*), kerosene lamp (*EEUU*)

lamparita SF (*RPl*) lightbulb

lamparón SM stain, dirty mark

lampazo SM (*LAm*) floor mop

lampiño ADJ (= *sin pelo*) hairless; (= *sin barba*) beardless

lamprea SF lamprey

lana SF 1 (*gen*) wool; (= *vellón*) fleece; (= *tela*) woollen cloth, woolen cloth (*EEUU*); (*para labores*) knitting wool; **es de ~** it's woollen, it's woolen (*EEUU*); ✦ REFRÁN **ir por ~ y volver trasquilado** to get more than one bargained for ➤ **lana de acero** steel wool ➤ **lana virgen** pure new wool 2 **lanas*** (*hum*) (= *greñas*) long hair *sing*, locks 3 (*And, Méx**) (= *dinero*) money, dough*

lanar ADJ wool-bearing, wool *antes de s*; **ganado ~** sheep

lance SM 1 (= *episodio*) incident, event ➤ **lance de fortuna** stroke of luck 2 (= *momento difícil*) critical moment, difficult moment 3 (= *riña*) quarrel; ✦ **lance de honor** affair of honour, affair of honor (*EEUU*), duel 4 **tirarse un ~** (*CS*) to take a chance 5 (*Com*) **de ~** secondhand

lancero SM lancer

lanceta SF 1 (*Med*) lancet 2 (*CAm, And*) [*de insecto*] sting

lancha SF (= *barca*) (small) boat; [*de motor*] launch ➤ **lancha de desembarco** landing craft ➤ **lancha de salvamento** lifeboat ➤ **lancha fuera borda** outboard dinghy ➤ **lancha motora** motorboat, speedboat ➤ **lancha neumática** rubber dinghy ➤ **lancha salvavidas** lifeboat

lanchón SM lighter, barge

lanero ADJ wool *antes de s*

langosta SF 1 [*de mar*] lobster; [*de río*] crayfish 2 (= *insecto*) locust

langostino SM prawn (*Brit*), shrimp (*EEUU*); (*grande*) king prawn (*Brit*), king-size shrimp (*EEUU*)

langüetear /1a/ VT (*Chi*) to lick

languidecer /2d/ VI to languish

lánguido ADJ (*gen*) languid (*liter*); (= *débil*) weak, listless

lanilla SF thin flannel cloth

lanolina SF lanolin(e)

lanza Ⓐ SF (*Mil*) lance, spear; ✦ MODISMOS **estar ~ en ristre** to be ready for action; **romper una ~ por algn** to back sb to the hilt; **ser una ~** (*LAm*) to be pretty sharp Ⓑ SMF (*Chi**) (= *ratero*) pickpocket, thief

lanzacohetes SM INV rocket launcher

lanzadera SF shuttle ➤ **lanzadera espacial** space shuttle

lanzado ADJ 1 **ser ~*** (*al hacer algo*) to be full of confidence, be really single-minded; (*en las relaciones*) to be forward 2 (*) (*al moverse*) **salió ~ de la casa** he rushed out of the house; **ir ~** [*coche, moto*] to tear along

lanzador(a) SM/F [*de jabalina, martillo*] thrower; (*Béisbol*) pitcher ➤ **lanzador(a) de peso, lanzador(a) de bala** (*LAm*) shot-putter

lanzagranadas SM INV grenade launcher, mortar

lanzallamas SM INV flamethrower

lanzamiento SM 1 [*de objeto*] (*gen*) throwing; (*con violencia*) hurling; (*desde el aire*) dropping; **~ en paracaídas** parachuting, parachute jumping 2 (*Dep*) (*con la pierna*) kick; (*hacia portería, canasta*) shot ➤ **lanzamiento de bala** (*LAm*) the shot put ➤ **lanzamiento de disco** the discus ➤ **lanzamiento de jabalina** the javelin ➤ **lanzamiento de peso** the shot put 3 [*de nave espacial, misil*] launch 4 [*de acciones, producto*] launch; [*de disco*] release; **oferta de ~** promotional offer

lanzar /1f/ Ⓐ VT 1 [+ *objeto, piedra*] (*gen*) to throw; (*con violencia*) to hurl, fling 2 (= *disparar*) [+ *flecha, proyectil*] to fire; [+ *cohete, misil*] (*hacia el aire*) to launch; (*hacia tierra*) to drop 3 [+ *disco, jabalina, balón*] to throw; [+ *peso*] to put; [+ *pelota*] (*Béisbol*) to pitch; (*Cricket*) to bowl; **~ una falta**

(*Ftbl*) to take a free kick; ~ **un penalti** to take a penalty
4 (= *emitir*) [+ *mensaje*] to deliver; [+ *insulto, ataque*] to hurl; [+ *indirecta*] to drop; [+ *desafío*] to issue, throw down; [+ *grito, suspiro*] to let out; **~on al aire la idea de reducir los impuestos** they floated the idea of reducing taxes; ~ **una mirada** to shoot a glance *o* look
5 [+ *producto, moda*] to launch, bring out; [+ *disco*] to release, bring out
6 (*Mil*) [+ *campaña, ataque*] to launch
B lanzarse VPR **1** (= *arrojarse*) (*al suelo, al vacío*) to throw o.s.; (*al agua*) to throw o.s., jump; **~se en paracaídas** to parachute; **~se en picado** to dive, swoop down; **~se sobre algn** to pounce on sb, leap on sb
2 (= *ir rápidamente*) to hurtle; **se ~on hacia la salida** they hurtled towards the exit; **se ~on a comprar acciones** they rushed to buy shares
3 (*) (= *decidirse*) to take the plunge*
4 ~se a (= *dedicarse*): **~se a la construcción de nuevas viviendas** to embark upon *o* undertake new housing projects; **decidió ~se a la carrera presidencial** he decided to enter the presidential race

lanzatorpedos SM INV torpedo tube

lapa SF (*Zool*) limpet; ✦ MODISMO **pegarse a algn como una ~** to stick to sb like a limpet

laparoscopia SF laparoscopy

La Paz SF La Paz

lapicera SF (*CS*) fountain pen

lapicero SM **1** (= *portaminas*) propelling pencil (*Brit*), mechanical pencil (*EEUU*) **2** (*Esp*) (= *lápiz*) pencil **3** (*CAm, Perú*) (= *bolígrafo*) ballpoint pen **4** (*Arg*) (= *portaplumas*) pen holder

lápida SF gravestone, tombstone ➤ **lápida conmemorativa** commemorative stone plaque

lapidar /1a/ VT to stone

lapidario ADJ lapidary; **frase lapidaria** immortal phrase

lapislázuli SM lapis lazuli

lápiz SM (*gen*) pencil; [*de color*] crayon; **escribir algo a** *o* **con ~** to write sth in pencil ➤ **lápiz a pasta** (*Chi*) ball-point pen ➤ **lápiz de labios** lipstick ➤ **lápiz de ojos** eyebrow pencil ➤ **lápiz óptico** light pen

lapo* SM **1** (*Esp*) (= *escupitajo*) spit **2** (*And, Méx*) (= *golpe*) punch, bash*, swipe

lapón/ona A ADJ of/from Lapland **B** SM/F Lapp **C** SM (*Ling*) Lapp

Laponia SF Lapland

lapso SM **1** (= *tiempo*) lapse; **en un ~ de cinco días** in (the space of) five days ➤ **lapso de tiempo** interval of time, space of time **2** (= *error*) mistake, error

lapsus SM INV (= *error*) mistake; (*tb* ~ **linguae**) slip of the tongue ➤ **lapsus freudiano** Freudian slip

laquear /1a/ VT to lacquer

larga SF **1** ✦ MODISMOS **a la ~** in the long run; **dar ~s a algo/algn** to put sth/sb off; **si te pregunta por el dinero, tú dale ~s** if he asks you about the money, just fob him off* **2** (*Aut*) (*tb* **luz** ~) full beam; **pon las ~s** put the headlights on full beam

largamente ADV at length

largar /1h/ **A** VT **1** (**) (= *dar*) [+ *discurso, regañina, golpe*] to give; [+ *exclamación, suspiro*] to let out; **nos largó un rollo interminable sobre los viejos tiempos** he gave us a never-ending spiel about the old days*, he rabbited on forever about the old days*; **me largó un puñetazo en la boca** he punched me in the mouth, he gave me a punch in the mouth
2 (**) (= *expulsar*) [+ *empleado*] to kick out**, give the boot**; [+ *alumno, huésped*] to kick out**, chuck out**
3 (**) (= *endilgar*) **~ a algn** [+ *tarea, trabajo*] to dump on sb**, foist (off) on sb; [+ *animal, niño*] to dump on sb*
4 (**) (= *deshacerse de*) [+ *novio, marido*] to ditch*, dump*
5 (*Náut*) [+ *cuerda*] (= *soltar*) to let out, pay out; (= *aflojar*) to loosen, slacken; ~ **amarras** to cast off; ~ **lastre** to drop ballast
6 (*CS, Méx**) (= *lanzar*) to throw, hurl
7 (*CS, Méx Dep*) to start

B VI (**) **1** (*Esp*) (= *hablar*) to go on*, rabbit on*; ~ **contra algn** to bad-mouth sb**
2 (= *revelar un secreto*) to spill the beans*
C largarse VPR **1** (*) (= *irse*) to be off*, leave; **¡lárgate!** get lost!*, clear off!*; **~se de casa** to leave home; **~se del trabajo** to quit one's job
2 (*CS*) (= *empezar*) to start, begin; **~se a hacer algo** to start *o* begin doing *o* to do sth
3 (*CS*) (= *tirarse*) **se largó de cabeza al agua** he dived into the water

largavistas SM INV (*CS Téc*) (= *gemelos*) binoculars *pl*

largo A ADJ **1** (*indicando longitud*) [*pasillo, pelo, uñas*] long; **esa chaqueta te queda larga** that jacket is too long for you; **me gusta llevar el pelo ~** I like to wear my hair long; **una camiseta de manga larga** a long-sleeved vest (*Brit*) *o* undershirt (*EEUU*); **ser ~ de piernas** to have long legs; **ponerse de ~** (= *vestirse*) to wear a long dress/skirt; (= *debutar*) to make one's debut
2 (*indicando distancia*) [*camino, recorrido*] long; **pasar de ~** [*persona, autobús*] to go past; [*momento, oportunidad*] to go by; **pasamos de ~ por Valencia** we went straight past Valencia; **no podemos dejar pasar de ~ esta oportunidad** we can't let this opportunity go by
3 (*indicando duración*) [*espera, viaje, película*] long; **es muy ~ de contar** it's a long story; **el resultado de ~s años de investigación** the result of many years of research; **hacerse ~**: **no se me hizo nada larga la clase** the class didn't seem at all long to me; **para ~**: **la reunión va para ~** the meeting looks like being a long one, the meeting looks like going on for some time yet; **cada vez que coge el teléfono tiene para ~** every time he picks up the phone he stays on it for ages; **a ~ plazo** in the long term; **venir de ~**: **este problema viene de ~** this problem goes back a long way, this problem started way back*; ✦ MODISMOS **hablar ~ y tendido sobre algo** to talk at great length about sth; **tú y yo tenemos que hablar ~ y tendido** you and I have to have a long talk; **ser más ~ que un día sin pan** to take forever
4 (*indicando exceso*) good; **media hora larga** a good half-hour; **un kilo ~ de uvas** just over a kilo of grapes
5 (*) [*persona*] tall; **se cayó al suelo cuan ~ era**[†] *o* **todo lo ~ que era** he fell flat on his face, he measured his length on the floor[†]
6 (*locuciones*) **a lo ~** lengthways; **échate a lo ~** stretch yourself full out; **a lo ~ de** [+ *río, pared*] along; [+ *día, mes, año*] all through, throughout; **viajó a lo ~ y a lo ancho de Europa** he travelled the length and breadth of Europe; **a lo ~ de los últimos años** over the last few years; **trabajó mucho a lo ~ de su vida** she worked hard all through *o* throughout her life; **el tiempo mejorará a lo ~ de la semana** the weather will improve in the course of the week
7 (*Esp*) (= *generoso*) generous
B SM **1** (= *longitud*) length; **¿cuánto tiene de ~?** how long is it?, what's its length?; **tiene nueve metros de ~** it is nine metres long
2 (= *unidad de medida*) [*de falda, piscina*] length; [*de cortina*] drop; ~ **de pernera** leg length
3 (*Cine*) (*tb* **~metraje**) (feature) film (*esp Brit*), (feature) movie (*esp EEUU*)
4 (*Mús*) largo
C ADV (*) **¡~ (de aquí)!** clear off!, get lost!

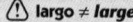

⚠ **largo ≠ large**

largometraje SM (feature) film (*esp Brit*), (feature) movie (*esp EEUU*)

larguero SM (*Arquit*) crossbeam; [*de puerta*] jamb; (*Dep*) crossbar; (*en cama*) bolster

largueza SF generosity, largesse (*frm*)

larguirucho ADJ lanky, gangling

largura SF length

laringe SF larynx

laringitis SF INV laryngitis

larva SF larva, grub, maggot

larvado ADJ hidden, latent

las¹ ART DEF FPL *ver* **los¹**

las² PRON PERS *ver* **los²**

lasaña SF lasagne

lasca SF [*de piedra*] chip; [*de comida*] slice

lascar /1g/ VT (*Méx*) [+ *piel*] to graze, bruise; [+ *piedra*] to chip, chip off

lascivia SF lust, lewdness, lasciviousness

lascivo ADJ [*gesto, mirada, comentario*] lewd, lascivious; [*persona*] lecherous, lascivious

láser SM laser

lasitud SF (*liter*) SF lassitude (*liter*), weariness

lástima SF pity, shame; **es una ~** it's a pity *o* shame; **dar ~**: **toda esta pobreza me da mucha ~** such poverty makes me really sad; **es tan desgraciado que da ~** he's so unhappy I feel really sorry for him *o* I really pity him; **"¡qué ~!"** "what a shame!" *o* "what a pity!"; **¡qué ~ de hombre!** isn't he pitiful?; **sentir** *o* **tener ~ de algn** to feel sorry for sb

lastimadura SF (*LAm*) graze

lastimar /1a/ Ⓐ VT to hurt Ⓑ **lastimarse** VPR to hurt o.s.; **se lastimó el brazo** he hurt his arm

lastimero ADJ pitiful, pathetic

lastimoso ADJ pitiful, pathetic

lastrar /1a/ VT 1 [+ *embarcación, globo*] to ballast 2 (= *obstaculizar*) to burden, weigh down

lastre SM 1 (*Náut, Téc*) ballast 2 (= *inconveniente*) burden

lata SF 1 (= *envase*) [*de comida*] can, tin (*Brit*); [*de bebida*] can; **sardinas en ~** tinned sardines (*Brit*), canned sardines (*esp EEUU*) 2 (= *metal*) tinplate; **suena a ~** it sounds tinny 3 (*) (= *molestia*) pain*, drag*; **es una ~ tener que ...** it's a pain* *o* drag* having to ...; **dar la ~** to be a pain*, drag*; **dar la ~ a algn** to pester sb, go on at sb*; **dar ~ a algn** (*Chi*): **me da ~ tener que estudiar** it's a (real) pain *o* drag having to study*

latente ADJ latent

lateral Ⓐ ADJ 1 [*calle, puerta, salida*] side *antes de s* 2 [*línea, parentesco*] indirect 3 (*Ling*) lateral Ⓑ SM 1 [*de avenida*] side street 2 **laterales** (*Teat*) wings Ⓒ SMF (*Dep*) winger

latero SM (*LAm*) 1 (= *oficio*) tinsmith 2 (*) (= *latoso*) bore, drag*

látex SM latex

latido SM [*de corazón*] beat, beating; [*de herida, dolor*] throb, throbbing

latifundio SM large estate

latifundista SMF *owner of a large estate*

latigazo SM 1 (= *golpe*) lash; (= *chasquido*) crack (*of the whip*) 2 [*de electricidad*] shock

látigo SM whip

latiguillo SM cliché, overworked phrase

latín SM Latin

latinajo SM (= *mal latín*) dog Latin; **soltar ~s** to come out with learned quotations and references

latino/a Ⓐ ADJ 1 (= *latinoamericano*) Latin American 2 (*Hist*) Latin Ⓑ SM/F (= *latinoamericano*) Latin American; **los ~s** Latin Americans

Latinoamérica SF Latin America

latinoamericano/a ADJ, SM/F Latin American

latir /3a/ VI 1 [*corazón*] to beat; [*herida*] to throb 2 (*Chi, Méx, Ven**) (= *parecer*) **me late que todo saldrá bien** something tells me that everything will turn out all right 3 (*Méx**) (= *parecer bien*) to appeal to; **esto no me late nada** that doesn't appeal (to me) at all

latitud SF 1 (*Geog*) latitude; **a 45 grados de ~ sur** 45 degrees south 2 (= *área*) **por estas ~es** in these parts

lato ADJ (*frm*) broad, wide

latón SM 1 (= *metal*) brass 2 (*RPl*) (= *recipiente*) metal bowl

latonería SF (*Col*) panel beating (*Brit*), body work (*EEUU*)

latonero/a SM/F (*Col*) panel beater (*Brit*), body shop worker (*EEUU*)

latoso/a* Ⓐ ADJ (= *molesto*) annoying; (= *pesado*) boring Ⓑ SM/F pain*, drag*

latrocinio SM larceny

latvio/a Ⓐ ADJ, SM/F Latvian Ⓑ SM (*Ling*) Latvian, Lettish

laucha SF (*CS*) *small mouse*; ✦ MODISMO **aguaitar** *o* **catear la ~** (*Chi**) to bide one's time

laúd SM (*Mús*) lute

láudano SM laudanum

laudatorio ADJ (*frm*) laudatory (*frm*)

laudo SM 1 (*Jur*) decision, finding 2 (*RPl*) (*para el personal*) service charge

laureado (*frm*) ADJ [*persona*] honoured, honored (*EEUU*), distinguished; [*obra*] prize-winning

laurear /1a/ VT (*frm*) to honour, honor (*EEUU*)

laurel SM 1 (*Bot*) laurel: **hojas de ~** (*Culin*) bay leaves 2 **laureles** (= *gloria*) laurels; ✦ MODISMO **descansar** *o* **dormirse en los ~es** to rest on one's laurels

lava SF lava

lavable ADJ washable

lavabo SM 1 (= *pila*) sink, washbasin (*esp Brit*) 2 (= *cuarto de baño*) toilet (*Brit*), bathroom (*EEUU*); (*en lugar público*) toilet (*Brit*), rest room (*EEUU*); **¿dónde está el ~ de señoras, por favor?** where is the ladies, please?

lavacoches SM INV car wash

lavada SF 1 [*de ropa*] wash 2 (*Col**) **pegarse una ~** to get soaked

lavadero SM 1 (*público*) laundry, wash house; (*en río*) washing place 2 (*en casa*) (= *habitación*) utility room; (= *pila*) sink 3 (*RPl*) (= *tintorería*) dry cleaner's

lavado Ⓐ SM 1 [*de ropa, vehículo*] wash; **prelavado y ~** pre-wash and wash ➤ **lavado a mano** hand wash ➤ **lavado de automóviles** carwash ➤ **lavado en seco** dry cleaning 2 (*Med*) ➤ **lavado de estómago, lavado gástrico**: **le hicieron un ~ de estómago** he had his stomach pumped 3 (*fig*) **campaña de ~ de imagen** image campaign ➤ **lavado de cara** face lift ➤ **lavado de cerebro** brainwashing; **le han hecho un ~ de cerebro** he's been brainwashed ➤ **lavado de dinero** (*Esp, LAm*) money laundering Ⓑ ADJ (*RPl, Ven*) [*color*] light

lavadora SF washing machine ➤ **lavadora secadora** washer-drier

lavanda SF lavender

lavandera SF 1 (= *mujer*) laundress, washerwoman 2 (*Orn*) wagtail

lavandería SF laundry ➤ **lavandería automática** Launderette® (*esp Brit*), Laundromat® (*EEUU*)

lavandina SF (*Arg*) bleach

lavándula SF lavender

lavaparabrisas SM INV windscreen washer (*Brit*), windshield washer (*EEUU*)

lavapiés SM INV footbath (*at the beach*)

lavaplatos Ⓐ SM INV 1 (= *aparato*) dishwasher 2 (*Chi, Col, Méx*) (= *fregadero*) sink Ⓑ SMF INV (= *empleado*) washer-up, dishwasher

lavar /1a/ Ⓐ VT 1 (= *limpiar*) to wash; **~ los platos** to wash the dishes, do the washing up; **~ en seco** to dry-clean; **~ y marcar** to shampoo and set 2 [+ *dinero*] to launder 3 [+ *honor, ofensa, pecado*] to wash away Ⓑ **lavarse** VPR 1 (= *asearse*) to wash, have a wash; **~se los dientes** to clean one's teeth; **~se las manos** (*lit, fig*) to wash one's hands 2 (*Col*) (= *empaparse*) to to get soaked

lavarropas SF INV (*RPl*) washing machine

lavaseco SM (*Chi*) drycleaner's

lavativa SF 1 (*Med*) enema 2 (*Ven**) (= *molestia*) nuisance, bother, bore

lavatorio SM (*LAm*) (= *mueble*) washstand; (*CS*) (= *lavabo*) sink, washbasin (*esp Brit*)

lavavajillas SM INV (= *aparato*) dishwasher; (= *detergente*) washing-up liquid (*Brit*), (liquid) dish soap (*EEUU*)

laxante ADJ, SM laxative

laxitud SF (*frm*) laxity, laxness, slackness

lazada SF bow

lazar /1f/ VT (*Méx*) to lasso, rope

lazarillo SM blind person's guide

lazo SM 1 (= *nudo*) (*para asegurar*) knot; (*decorativo*) bow 2 [*de vaquero*] lasso, lariat 3 (*Caza*) snare, trap 4 (*Aut*) hairpin bend 5 lazos (= *vínculos*) ties; **~s de parentesco** ties of blood

le PRON PERS 1 (*indirecto*) (= *a él*) (to) him; (= *a ella*) (to) her; (= *a usted*) (to) you; (*a algo*) (to) it; **le hablé** I spoke to him/her; **quiero darle esto** I want to give you this; **le he comprado esto** I bought this for you

> Con partes del cuerpo o con prendas que se llevan puestas se usa el adjetivo posesivo:

le huelen los pies his feet smell; **le arrastra la falda** her skirt is trailing on the floor 2 (*esp Esp*) (*directo*) (= *a él*) him; (= *a usted*) you; **no le veo** I don't see him; **¿le ayudo?** shall I help you?

leal ADJ [*persona*] loyal, faithful; [*competencia*] fair

lealtad SF loyalty, fidelity

leasing ['lizin] SM (= *operación*) leasing

lebrel SM greyhound

lección SF (= *tema*) lesson; (= *clase*) lesson, class; ✦ MODISMOS **aprenderse la ~** to learn one's lesson; **servir de ~**: **¡que te sirva de ~!** let that be a lesson to you!

lechal ADJ sucking, suckling; **cordero ~** baby lamb, young lamb

lechazo SM 1 (= *cordero*) young lamb 2 (*Col, Ven**) (= *golpe de suerte*) stroke of luck

leche SF 1 [*de mamífero, planta*] milk; **café con ~** white coffee, coffee with milk; **chocolate con ~** milk chocolate; ➤ **leche condensada** condensed milk ➤ **leche descremada, leche desnatada** skimmed milk (*Brit*), skim milk (*EEUU*) ➤ **leche en polvo** powdered milk ➤ **leche entera** full-cream milk, whole milk ➤ **leche frita** *dessert made of milk thickened with flour, coated with egg and fried* ➤ **leche limpiadora** cleanser, cleansing milk ➤ **leche materna** mother's milk ➤ **leche maternizada** formula (milk) ➤ **leche semidescremada, leche semidesnatada** semi-skimmed milk (*Brit*), one percent milk (*EEUU*) ➤ **leche UHT** long-life milk, UHT milk (*Brit*)
2 (*Esp***) (= *golpe*) **darse una ~** to come a cropper*; **¡te voy a dar una ~!** I'll thump you!*
3 (*And, Ven**) (= *suerte*) good luck; **¡qué ~ tienes!** you lucky *o* jammy* devil!
4 (***) (= *semen*) cum***, spunk***
5 (*Esp*) ✦ MODISMOS **de la ~**** bloody**; **hace un calor de la ~** (*Esp*) it's bloody hot; **ser la ~**** to be unbelievable; **ir a toda ~**** to go like the clappers*; **mala ~** mala ~ to be in a shitty mood**; **poner a algn de mala ~** to piss sb off***; **tener mala ~** to be a nasty piece of work*

lechera SF 1 (= *recipiente*) milk can, milk churn 2 (*) [*de policía*] police car; *ver tb* **lechero**

lechería SF dairy, creamery

lechero/a Ⓐ ADJ 1 [*producción, cuota*] milk *antes de s*; [*productos, vaca*] dairy *antes de s* 2 (*Col, Perú**) (= *con suerte*) lucky Ⓑ SM/F milkman/milkwoman; *ver tb* **lechera**

lecho SM 1 (*liter*) (= *cama*) bed ➤ **lecho de muerte** deathbed 2 (= *fondo*) [*de río*] bed; (*Geol*) layer

lechón/ona SM/F (= *cochinillo*) piglet; (*Culin*) suckling pig

lechosa SF (*Carib, Col*) papaya

lechoso ADJ milky

lechuga SF lettuce

lechuza SF owl ➤ **lechuza común** barn owl

lectivo ADJ school *antes de s*; **año ~** school year

lector(a) Ⓐ ADJ reading Ⓑ SM/F 1 (= *persona*) reader 2 (*Escol, Univ*) (conversation) assistant Ⓒ SM (= *aparato*) ➤ **lector de código de barras** bar code scanner ➤ **lector de discos compactos** CD player, compact disc player ➤ **lector óptico de caracteres** optical character reader, optical character scanner

lectorado SM (*Univ*) assistantship

lectura SF 1 (= *acción*) reading; **dar ~ a** to read (publicly); **sala de ~** reading room 2 (= *obra*) reading matter; **lista de ~s recomendadas** reading list 3 (= *interpretación*) reading; **hay varias ~s posibles de los resultados** the results can be read in various ways, there are various possible readings of the results

leer /2e/ Ⓐ VT to read; **~ el pensamiento a algn** to read sb's mind *o* thoughts; **~ la mano a algn** to read sb's palm; **~ los labios** to lip-read; ✦ MODISMOS **~ la cartilla a algn** to tell sb off Ⓑ VI to read; **~ entre líneas** to read between the lines; **~ en voz alta** to read aloud; **~ en voz baja** to read quietly

legación SF legation

legado SM 1 (= *enviado*) legate 2 (*Jur*) legacy, bequest

legajo SM file, bundle (of papers)

legal ADJ 1 (= *de ley*) legal 2 (*Esp**) [*persona*] (= *de confianza*) reliable; **es un tío ~** he's a good bloke* 3 (*And*) (= *excelente*) great*

legalidad SF legality, lawfulness

legalización SF [*de partido, droga, situación*] legalization; [*de documentos*] authentication

legalizar /1f/ VT [+ *partido, droga, situación*] to legalize; [+ *documentos*] to authenticate

legalmente ADV legally, lawfully

legaña SF **tener ~s** to have sleep in one's eyes

legar /1h/ VT to bequeath, leave (**a** to)

legendario ADJ legendary

legión SF legion; **son ~** they are legion ➤ **Legión Extranjera** Foreign Legion

legionario SM legionnaire

legionella SF legionnaire's disease

legislación SF legislation, laws *pl*

legislador(a) SM/F legislator

legislar /1a/ VI to legislate

legislativas SFPL parliamentary elections

legislativo ADJ legislative

legislatura SF (*Pol*) 1 (= *mandato*) term of office; (= *año parlamentario*) session 2 (*LAm*) (= *cuerpo*) legislature, legislative body

legitimar /1a/ VT [+ *documento, firma*] to authenticate; [+ *divorcio, elecciones, situación ilegal*] to legalize; [+ *comportamiento*] (= *hacer aceptable*) to legitimize

legítimo ADJ 1 [*dueño*] legitimate, rightful; [*derecho*] legitimate; [*esposo*] lawful; **en legítima defensa** in self-defence 2 (= *auténtico*) [*firma, cuadro*] authentic, genuine

lego/a Ⓐ ADJ 1 (*Rel*) [*hermano, predicador*] lay 2 (= *ignorante*) ignorant; **soy ~ en la materia** I'm ignorant on this subject Ⓑ SM/F 1 (*Rel*) lay brother/lay sister; **los ~s** the laity 2 (= *desconocedor*) layman/laywoman, layperson

legrado SM D & C, scrape*

legua SF league; ✦ MODISMO **eso se ve** *o* **se nota a la ~** you can tell it a mile away

leguleyo/a SM/F (*pey*) pettifogging lawyer, shyster (*EEUU*)

legumbre SF (= *seca*) pulse; (= *fresca*) vegetable

leguminosa SF (= *planta*) leguminous plant; (= *grano*) pulse

leguminoso ADJ leguminous

lehendakari SMF *head of the Basque autonomous government*

leída SF **dar una ~ a** to read

leído ADJ **ser muy ~** to be well-read

leísmo SM *use of "le" instead of "lo" and "la" as direct objects*

leísta Ⓐ ADJ *that uses "le" instead of "lo" and "la" as direct objects* Ⓑ SMF *user of "le" instead of "lo" and "la"*

lejanía SF remoteness; **en la ~** in the distance

lejano ADJ 1 (*en el espacio, en el tiempo*) distant; **en aquellas épocas lejanas** in those distant *o* far-off times; **un país ~** a far-off country; **Lejano Oeste** Far West 2 [*pariente*] distant

lejía SF bleach

lejos ADV 1 (*en el espacio*) far, far away; **está muy ~** it's a long way (away), it's really far (away); **a lo ~** in the distance; **de** *o* **desde ~** at *o* from a distance, from afar (*liter*); **más ~** further away; ✦ MODISMOS **llevar algo demasiado ~** to take sth too far; **llegar ~** to go far; **sin ir más ~** as it happens

2 **~ de algo** a long way from sth, far from sth; **está ~ de la oficina** it is a long way *o* far from the office; **vivo lejísimos de aquí** I live miles away from here; **~ de asustarse, los niños estaban encantados con la tormenta** far from being scared, the children really loved the storm; **nada más ~ de mi intención que hacerte daño** harming you was the last thing on my mind; **nada más ~ de la realidad** nothing could be further from the truth

3 (*en el tiempo*) far off; **junio ya no está tan ~** June is not so far off now; **está ~ ese día** that day is still a long way off; **venir de ~** to go back a long way

4 (*CS*) (= *con mucho*) easily; **es ~ la más inteligente** she's the most intelligent by far, she's easily the most intelligent

lelo/a* Ⓐ ADJ slow Ⓑ SM/F halfwit

lema SM 1 (*Pol*) slogan 2 (= *máxima*) motto 3 (*en diccionario*) headword

lempira SM (*Hond*) *monetary unit of Honduras*

lencería SF 1 (= *ropa interior*) lingerie 2 (= *ropa blanca*) linen

lengua SF 1 (*Anat*) tongue; **según las malas ~s ...** according to gossip ...; **sacar la ~ a algn** to stick one's tongue out at sb; ✦ MODISMOS **¿te ha comido la ~ el gato?** has the cat got your tongue?; **darle a la ~** to chatter, talk too much; **irse de la ~** to let the cat out of the bag; **llegar con la ~ fuera** to arrive out of breath; **no tener pelos en la ~** not to mince one's words, not to pull one's punches; **tener algo en la punta de la ~** to have sth on the tip of one's tongue; **tirar de la ~ a algn** to draw sb out, make sb talk ➤ **lengua de trapo** baby talk

2 (*Geog*) ➤ **lengua de tierra** spit of land, tongue of land 3 (*Ling*) language, tongue; (*Esp Escol*) Spanish language (*as a school subject*) ➤ **lengua franca** lingua franca ➤ **lengua materna** mother tongue ➤ **lengua muerta** dead language ➤ **lengua oficial** official language

lenguado SM sole

lenguaje SM language ➤ **lenguaje corporal** body language ➤ **lenguaje gestual** sign language ➤ **lenguaje periodístico** journalese

lenguaraz ADJ (= *charlatán*) garrulous, talkative; (= *mal hablado*) foul-mouthed

lengüeta SF (*gen*) tab; [*de zapatos*] tongue; (*Mús*) reed

lengüetazo SM lick

lengüetear /1a/ (*LAm*) VT to lick

leninista ADJ, SMF Leninist

lenitivo ADJ lenitive

lenocinio SM pimping, procuring; **casa de ~** brothel

lentamente ADV slowly

lente SF (*a veces* SM) 1 (*gen*) lens ➤ **lente de aumento** magnifying glass ➤ **lentes de contacto** contact lenses ➤ **lentes progresivas** varifocal lenses 2 **lentes** (*esp LAm*) (= *gafas*) glasses, spectacles

lenteja SF lentil

lentejuela SF sequin, spangle

lentilla SF (*Esp*) contact lens

lentitud SF slowness; **con ~** slowly

lento Ⓐ ADJ [*ritmo, movimiento, caída*] slow; [*tráfico, película*] slow, slow-moving; **una muerte lenta** a lingering *o* slow death; **¡qué ~s pasan los días!** the days go so slowly!; **la economía está creciendo a un ritmo ~** the economy is growing sluggishly *o* slowly; **pero seguro** slowly but surely Ⓑ ADV slowly

leña SF 1 (*para el fuego*) firewood; **hacer ~** to gather firewood; ✦ MODISMO **echar ~ al fuego** to add fuel to the fire *o* flames 2 (*) (= *golpes*) thrashing, hiding; **dar ~ a algn** to thrash sb, give sb a good hiding; **repartir ~** to lash out

leñador(a) SM/F woodcutter, logger

leñazo* SM 1 (= *golpe*) knock 2 (= *choque*) bash*

leñe* EXCL (*Esp*) heck*

leño SM log

leñoso ADJ woody

Leo SM (= *signo*) Leo

leo SMF INV (= *persona*) Leo; **soy ~** I'm Leo

león/ona SM/F (*Zool*) lion/lioness; (*LAm*) (= *puma*) puma (*esp Brit*), mountain lion (*EEUU*) ➤ **león marino** sea lion

leonado ADJ tawny, fawn-colored

leonera SF lion's den; **parece una ~** (*Esp*) the place is a pigsty*

leonés ADJ of/from León

leonino ADJ [*contrato*] unfair, one-sided

leopardo SM leopard

leotardo SM, **leotardos** SMPL woollen tights (*Brit*), woolen pantyhose (*EEUU*)

lépero* ADJ (*CAm, Méx*) rude, uncouth

leporino ADJ **labio ~** harelip, cleft lip

lepra SF leprosy

leproso/a Ⓐ ADJ leprous Ⓑ SM/F leper

lerdo ADJ 1 (= *de pocas luces*) slow-witted 2 (= *patoso*) clumsy

leridano ADJ of/from Lérida

les PRON PERS 1 (*indirecto*) (= *a ellos, ellas*) (to) them; (= *a ustedes*) (to) you

Con partes del cuerpo o con prendas que se llevan puestas se usa el adjetivo posesivo:

~ huelen los pies their feet smell; **~ arrastraban los abrigos** their coats were trailing on the floor 2 (*esp Esp*) (*directo*) (= *a ellos, ellas*) them; (= *a ustedes*) you; *ver tb* **le**

lesbiana SF lesbian

lésbico ADJ lesbian

lesera* SF (*Chi*) **eso es una ~** that's stupid; **decir ~s** to talk nonsense

lesión SF injury, lesion (frm) ➤ **lesión cerebral** brain damage

lesionado ADJ injured

lesionar /1a/ **A** VT to injure **B** **lesionarse** VPR to injure oneself; ~**se la pierna** to injure one's leg

lesivo ADJ (frm) **1** (= dañino) harmful, damaging **2** (= perjudicial) detrimental

leso/a A ADJ **1** (frm) **crimen de lesa majestad** lese-majesty, treason **2** (Chi*) (= necio) simple, stupid; **hacer ~ a algn*** to cheat sb, rip sb off** **B** SM/F ✦ MODISMO **hacerse el ~*** to act dumb

letal ADJ deadly, lethal

letanía SF **1** (Rel) litany **2** (= retahíla) long list, litany

letargo SM lethargy

Letonia SF Latvia

letra SF **1** (Tip) letter; ✦ MODISMO **poner cuatro ~s a algn** to drop sb a line; ✦ REFRÁN **la ~ con sangre entra** spare the rod and spoil the child ➤ **letra de imprenta, letra de molde** print; **escriba su nombre en ~s de imprenta o de molde** please print your name in block letters ➤ **letra gótica** Gothic script ➤ **letra mayúscula** capital letter ➤ **letra minúscula** small letter ➤ **letra pequeña** small print **2** (= escritura) handwriting, writing; **no le entiendo la ~** I can't read his handwriting o writing; ✦ MODISMO **despacito y buena ~** easy does it **3** (= sentido literal) letter, literal meaning **4** (Com) (= pago) instalment, installment (EEUU) ➤ **letra de cambio** bill (of exchange), draft **5** (de canción) words pl, lyrics pl **6** **letras** (= cultura) letters, learning sing; **un hombre de ~s** a man of letters; **primeras ~s** elementary education, the three Rs **7** **letras** (Escol, Univ) arts

letrado/a A ADJ **1** (= culto) learned **2** (Jur) legal; **derecho a la asistencia letrada** right to have a lawyer present **B** SM/F lawyer, counsel, attorney (EEUU)

letrero SM sign, notice; (en carretera) sign ➤ **letrero luminoso** neon sign

letrina SF latrine, privy

leucemia SF leukaemia, leukemia (EEUU)

leucocito SM leucocyte, leukocyte (EEUU)

leva SF **1** (Mil) levy **2** (Mec) cam

levadizo ADJ **puente ~** drawbridge

levadura SF yeast ➤ **levadura de cerveza** brewer's yeast ➤ **levadura en polvo** (Esp) baking powder

levantado ADJ up; **no me esperes ~** don't wait up for me

levantador(a) SM/F ➤ **levantador(a) de pesas** weightlifter

levantamiento SM **1** [de objeto] raising, lifting; (con una grúa) hoisting ➤ **levantamiento de pesas** weightlifting **2** [de prohibición, embargo] lifting **3** (Jur) **~ del cadáver** removal of the body **4** (Pol) uprising, revolt **5** (Geog) survey

levantar /1a/ **A** VT **1** (= alzar) **1.1** [+ peso, objeto] to lift; (con una grúa) to hoist; **era imposible ~lo del suelo** it was impossible to lift it off the floor **1.2** [+ pierna, cabeza, cejas] to raise; **~ la mano** to put one's hand up, raise one's hand; **a mí no me levanta la mano nadie** nobody raises their hand to me; **~ los ojos o la vista** to look up; ✦ MODISMO **si tu padre ~a la cabeza ...** your father must be turning in his grave **1.3** [+ cortina, falda] to lift, lift up; [+ persiana, telón] to raise; **~ polvo** to raise dust **2** (= poner de pie) **2.1** **~ a algn** (del suelo) to lift sb, lift sb up; (de la cama) to get sb up; **cuando se sienta en ese sofá no hay quien lo levante** once he sits on that sofa no one can get him off it; **su actuación levantó al público de sus asientos** her performance brought the audience to their feet **2.2** [+ objeto caído] to pick up **3** (= erigir) [+ edificio, pared] to put up; [+ monumento] to erect, put up **4** (= fundar) [+ empresa, imperio] to found, establish **5** (= dar un empuje a) to build up; **todos ayudaron a ~ la empresa** they all helped to build up the company;

tenemos que **~ de nuevo la economía** we've got to get the economy back on its feet **6** [+ ánimo, moral] to lift, raise **7** [+ voz] to raise; **¡no levantes la voz!** keep your voice down! **8** (= desmontar) [+ tienda de campaña] to take down; **~ el campamento** to strike camp; **~ la casa** to move out; **~ la mesa** (LAm) to clear the table **9** (= producir) [+ sospechas] to arouse; [+ dolor] to give; [+ rumor] to spark off; **~ falso testimonio** (Jur) to give false testimony; (Rel) to bear false witness **10** (= terminar) [+ prohibición, embargo] to lift; [+ veda] to end; **~ el castigo a algn** to let sb off **11** (Jur) **11.1** [+ censo, atestado] to make; [+ sesión] to adjourn **11.2** [+ cadáver] to remove **12** (Arquit) [+ plano] to make, draw up **13** (*) (= robar) to pinch*, swipe* **14** (Ven**) (= arrestar) to nick**, arrest **15** (SAm*) [+ mujer] to pick up* **B** VI **1** (hum) [persona] **no levanta del suelo más de metro y medio** she's no more than five foot from head to toe **2** (Naipes) to cut the pack **C** **levantarse** VPR **1** (= alzarse) **1.1** (de la cama, del suelo) to get up; ✦ MODISMO **~se con o (And) en el pie izquierdo** to get out of bed on the wrong side **1.2** (de un asiento) to get up, stand up; **levántense** please stand **2** (= erguirse) [edificio, monumento] to stand **3** (= despegarse) **3.1** [pintura] to come off, peel off; [baldosa, suelo] to come up **3.2** [piel] to peel **4** (Meteo) **4.1** (= disiparse) [niebla, nubes] to lift **4.2** (= producirse) [viento] to get up **5** (= sublevarse) to rise, rise up **6** (Rel) (= resucitar) to rise **7** (SAm*) [+ mujer] (= ligarse a) to pick up*; (= acostarse con) to get off with*

levante¹ SM **1** (= este) east **2** (tb **viento de ~**) east wind

levante² SM (Col, RPl, Ven*) (= conquista) pick-up*

Levante SM **1** (= este de España) east coast **2** (= oriente) Levant

levantisco ADJ [persona] rebellious; [país] turbulent, troubled

levar /1a/ VT (Náut) **~ anclas** to weigh anchor

leve ADJ **1** [falta, heridas] minor **2** (= suave) [brisa] light; [sonrisa, movimiento] slight **3** (= ligero) [carga, peso] light **4** (frm) (= muy fino) light, fine

levedad SF lightness

levemente ADV (= superficialmente) slightly; (= ligeramente) lightly

levita SF frock coat

levitar /1a/ VI to levitate

lexema SM lexeme

léxico A ADJ lexical **B** SM vocabulary

lexicografía SF lexicography

lexicógrafo/a SM/F lexicographer

ley SF **1** (= precepto) law; **por encima de la ~** above the law; **está fuera de la ~** he's outside the law; ✦ MODISMOS **con todas las de la ~: quieren crear una fundación con todas las de la ~** they want to set up a fully-fledged charitable trust; **quiere celebrar su aniversario con todas las de la ~** she wants to celebrate her anniversary in style; **hacerle la ~ del hielo a algn** (Chi, Méx*) to give sb the cold shoulder; **hecha la ~ hecha la trampa** every law has a loophole ➤ **ley de extranjería** (Esp) immigration laws ➤ **ley de (la) fuga** (Chi, Col, Méx): **se le aplicó la ~ de (la) fuga** he was shot while trying to escape ➤ **ley marcial** martial law ➤ **ley seca** prohibition law **2** (= regla no escrita) law ➤ **la ley de la selva** the law of the jungle ➤ **la ley del más fuerte** (the principle of) might is right ➤ **la ley del Talión** (fig) (the principle of) an eye for an eye **3** (= principio científico) law ➤ **ley de la gravedad** law of gravity ➤ **ley de la oferta y la demanda** law of supply and demand ➤ **ley natural** (Fís) law of nature; (Ética) natural law **4** (Rel) **la ~ de Dios** the rule of God, God's law ➤ **ley de**

Moisés the law of Moses
5 (*Metal*) **oro de ~** pure gold, standard gold; **bajo de ~** base

leyenda SF **1** (= *historia*) legend ➤ **leyenda negra** (*Hist*) view of the Conquest of Latin America which emphasised the negative side of Spanish involvement **2** (= *inscripción*) [*de moneda, medalla, lápida*] legend, inscription **3** [*de grabado, mapa*] (= *pie*) caption

leyendo etc ver **leer**

liado* ADJ busy; **está muy ~** he's busy, he has his hands full

liana SF liana

liante/a* SM/F (*Esp*) **esos dos son unos ~s** those two will only get you into trouble

liar /1c/ **Ⓐ** VT **1** [+ *fardos, paquetes*] (= *atar*) to tie up; (= *envolver*) to wrap (up)
2 [+ *cigarrillo*] to roll
3 (= *confundir*) to confuse; **¡no me líes!** don't confuse me!
4 **~la** (*Esp**) (= *provocar una discusión*) to stir up trouble; (= *hacer algo mal*) to make a mess of things; **¡la liamos!** we've done it now!*
Ⓑ **liarse** VPR **1** (= *confundirse*) to get muddled up
2 (*) (*sentimentalmente*) **~se con algn** to have an affair with sb, get involved with sb
3 **~se a** (*Esp**) (+ INFIN): **nos liamos a hablar** we got talking
4 **~se a golpes** o **a palos** (*Esp**) to lay into one another*

libación SF libation

libanés/esa **Ⓐ** ADJ Lebanese **Ⓑ** SM/F Lebanese, Lebanese man/woman

Líbano SM **el** ~ the Lebanon

libar /1a/ VT to suck

libelo SM **1** (= *sátira*) lampoon (**contra** of), satire (**contra** on) **2** (*Jur*) libel

libélula SF dragonfly

liberación SF (*gen*) liberation; [*de preso*] release; [*de precios*] deregulation

liberado/a **Ⓐ** ADJ **1** (*gen*) liberated **2** (*Esp Pol*) full-time **3** (*Com, Fin*) paid-up, paid-in (*EEUU*) **Ⓑ** SM/F (*Esp Pol*) full-time official

liberal **Ⓐ** ADJ liberal **Ⓑ** SMF liberal

liberalismo SM liberalism

liberalizar /1f/ VT to liberalize; [+ *mercado*] to deregulate

liberar /1a/ **Ⓐ** VT **1** [+ *rehén*] to free, release; [+ *país, pueblo*] to liberate **2** **~ a algn de** [+ *carga, obligación*] to free sb of o from; [+ *peligro*] to save sb from; **~ a algn de un pago** to exempt sb from a payment **3** (*Fin*) (= *precios*) to deregulate; [+ *acción*] to pay in full; [+ *deuda*] to release; [+ *tipo de cambio*] to float **4** [+ *energía, oxígeno*] to release **Ⓑ** **liberarse** VPR **~se de algo** to free o.s. from sth **2** (*socialmente*) to liberate o.s.

líbero SMF (*Dep*) sweeper

libertad SF **1** (*gen*) freedom; **estar en ~** to be free; **poner a algn en ~** to set sb free ➤ **libertad bajo fianza** release on bail ➤ **libertad condicional** probation ➤ **libertad de cultos** freedom of worship ➤ **libertad de expresión** freedom of speech ➤ **libertad de prensa** freedom of the press
2 (= *confianza*) **hablar con entera** o **total ~** to speak freely; **tomarse la ~ de hacer algo** to take the liberty of doing sth

Recuérdese que las preposiciones en inglés rigen gerundio y no infinitivo, de ahí **to take the liberty of doing sth.**

tomarse demasiadas ~es con algn to take too many liberties with sb

libertador(a) SM/F liberator; **El Libertador** (*LAm Hist*) the Liberator (*especially Simón Bolívar*)

libertar /1a/ VT to set free, release

libertario/a ADJ, SM/F **1** (= *anarquista*) libertarian **2** (*LAm*) (= *libertador*) liberator

libertinaje SM licentiousness (*frm*), profligacy (*frm*)

libertino/a **Ⓐ** ADJ licentious, profligate (*frm*) **Ⓑ** SM/F libertine

Libia SF Libya

libidinoso ADJ lustful, libidinous (*frm*)

libido SF libido

libio/a ADJ, SM/F Libyan

Libra SM (= *signo*) Libra

libra **Ⓐ** SMF INV (*Astron*) (= *persona*) Libra; **soy ~** I'm Libra **Ⓑ** SF **1** (= *moneda*) pound ➤ **libra esterlina** pound sterling **2** (= *unidad de peso*) pound

librado ADJ **salir bien/mal ~ de algo** to come out of sth well/badly

librador(a) SM/F (*Com*) drawer

libramiento SM (*Com*) order of payment

libranza SF (*Com*) order of payment

librar /1a/ **Ⓐ** VT **1** **~ a algn de** [+ *preocupación, responsabilidad*] to free sb from o of; [+ *peligro*] to save sb from; **¡Dios me libre!** Heaven forbid! **2** [+ *batalla*] to fight **3** (*Com*) to draw; [+ *cheque*] to make out **4** [+ *sentencia*] to pass **Ⓑ** VI (*Esp*) (*en el trabajo*) **libro los sábados** I have Saturdays off **Ⓒ** **librarse** VPR **~se de algo/algn** (= *eximirse*) to escape from sth/sb; (= *deshacerse*) to get rid of sth/sb

libre ADJ **1** [*persona*] free; **cada cual es ~ de hacer lo que quiera** everyone is free to do as they wish; **el martes estoy ~** I'm free on Tuesday
2 (= *exento*) duty-free; **~ de impuestos** free of tax
3 (= *sin ocupar*) [*plaza*] vacant, unoccupied; **¿está ~ este asiento?** is this seat free?; **"libre"** [*parking*] "spaces"
4 [*tiempo*] spare, free
5 **al aire ~** in the open air
6 **por ~** (*Esp*) (= *por cuenta propia*): **examinarse por ~** to take one's exams as an independent candidate; **trabajar por ~** to freelance; **ir por ~** to go it alone
7 (*en natación*) **los 200 metros ~s** the 200 metres freestyle; **estilo ~** freestyle
8 [*traducción, adaptación, verso*] free

librea SF livery

librecambio SM free trade

librecambista **Ⓐ** ADJ free-trade *antes de s* **Ⓑ** SMF free trader

librepensador(a) SM/F freethinker

librería SF **1** (= *tienda*) bookshop (*esp Brit*), bookstore (*esp EEUU*) ➤ **librería de ocasión, librería de viejo** secondhand bookshop (*esp Brit*) o bookstore (*esp EEUU*) **2** (= *estante*) bookcase

⚠ **librería** ≠ **library**

librero¹/a SM/F bookseller

librero² SM (*LAm*) (= *estante*) bookcase

libreta SF (= *cuaderno*) notebook ➤ **libreta de ahorros** savings book ➤ **libreta de manejar** (*Uru*) driving licence (*Brit*), drivers' license (*EEUU*)

libreto SM **1** [*de ópera*] libretto **2** (*LAm*) (= *guión*) script

libro SM **1** (= *obra impresa*) book; ✦ MODISMOS **ser como un ~ abierto** to be an open book; **colgar los ~s** to give up studying ➤ **libro de bolsillo** paperback ➤ **libro de cocina** cookbook, cookery book (*Brit*) ➤ **libro de consulta** reference book ➤ **libro de cuentos** storybook ➤ **libro de estilo** style book ➤ **libro de texto** textbook ➤ **libro electrónico** e-book ➤ **libro sonoro** audio book
2 (= *registro*); **llevar los ~** (*Com*) to keep the books o accounts ➤ **libro de actas** minute book ➤ **libro de caja** cash book, petty cash book ➤ **libro de cuentas** account book ➤ **libro de familia** *booklet containing family details (marriage, births) used for official purposes* ➤ **libro de pedidos** order book ➤ **libro de reclamaciones** complaints book ➤ **libro de visitas** visitors' book
3 (*Pol*) ➤ **libro blanco** white paper

licencia SF

> En inglés americano se usa **license** en lugar de **licence**.

1 (= *documento*) licence ➤ **licencia de armas** gun licence (*Brit*), gun permit (*EEUU*) ➤ **licencia de caza** game licence, hunting permit ➤ **licencia de exportación** (*Com*) export licence ➤ **licencia de manejar** (*CAm, Méx, Ven*) driving licence (*Brit*), driver's license (*EEUU*) ➤ **licencia de obras** building permit, planning permission ➤ **licencia de vuelo** pilot's licence ➤ **licencia fiscal** *registration with the Spanish Inland Revenue formerly required for any commercial activity* **2** (*Mil*) leave, furlough (*EEUU*) **3** [*de trabajo*] leave; **ir de ~** to go on leave **4** (*frm*) (= *permiso*) permission; **dar su ~** to give one's permission, grant permission **5** (*frm*) (= *libertinaje*) licence **6** (*Literat*) ➤ **licencia poética** poetic licence

licenciado/a SM/F **1** (*Univ*) graduate **2** (*CAm, Méx*) (= *abogado*) lawyer, attorney(-at-law) (*EEUU*) **3** (*esp Méx*) (= *título*) ≈ Dr., ≈ Dr. (*EEUU*)

licenciar /1b/ **Ⓐ** VT to discharge **Ⓑ licenciarse** VPR (*Univ*) to graduate, take one's degree

licenciatura SF degree

licencioso ADJ licentious

liceo SM **1** (= *centro cultural*) lyceum **2** (*CS, Ven*) (= *instituto*) secondary school, junior high school (*EEUU*)

lichi SM lychee

licitación SF tender

licitar /1a/ VT [*gobierno*] to put out to tender; [*empresa*] to tender for

lícito ADJ **1** (*Jur*) [*permiso*] legal; [*comercio*] legitimate, legal; [*conducta*] legal, lawful, licit (*frm*) **2** (*frm*) (= *permisible*) permissible; **si es ~ preguntarlo** if one may ask

licor SM **1** (= *bebida dulce*) liqueur ➤ **licor de frutas** fruit liqueur **2 licores** (= *alcohol*) spirits *pl*, liquor *sing* (*EEUU*)

licorera SF **1** (= *botella*) decanter **2** (= *empresa*) distillery

licorería SF **1** (= *fábrica*) distillery; (= *tienda*) off-licence (*Brit*), liquor store (*EEUU*)

licra® SF Lycra®

licuado SM (*tb* **~ de frutas**) (*LAm*) milk shake

licuadora SF blender, liquidizer (*esp Brit*)

licuar /1d/ VT **1** (*Culin*) to blend, liquidize **2** (*Fís, Quím*) to liquefy

lid SF (*frm*) (= *combate*) fight, combat; **en buena ~** fair and square

líder Ⓐ ADJ INV top, leading **Ⓑ** SMF (SF *en Méx* **lideresa**) leader

liderar /1a/ VT to lead, head

liderato SM, **liderazgo** SM leadership

lidia SF **1** (*Taur*) (= *espectáculo, arte*) bullfighting; (= *corrida*) bullfight; **toro de ~** fighting bull **2** (*frm*) (= *lucha*) struggle, fight **3** (*Col, Ven*) (= *molestia*) trouble, nuisance; **dar ~** to be trying, be a nuisance

lidiar /1b/ **Ⓐ** VT (*Taur*) to fight **Ⓑ** VI to fight (**con, contra** against; **por** for)

liebre SF **1** (*Zool*) hare; ✦ MODISMO **levantar la ~** to blow the gaff*, let the cat out of the bag **2** (*Chi*) (= *microbús*) minibus

Liechtenstein SM Liechtenstein

liendre SF nit

lienzo SM **1** (= *tela*) linen **2** (*Arte*) canvas

lifting ['liftin] SM face-lift

liga SF **1** (*Pol, Dep*) league **2** (= *faja*) suspender (*Brit*), garter (*EEUU*) **3** (*LAm*) (*para sujetar*) rubber band, elastic band (*esp Brit*)

ligadura SF **1** (*Med*) ligature ➤ **ligadura de trompas** tubal ligation **2 ligaduras** [*de cuerda, correa*] bonds, ties; (*entre personas*) ties **3** (*Mús*) ligature, tie

ligamento SM ligament

ligar /1h/ **Ⓐ** VT **1** (= *atar*) (*gen*) to tie, bind **2** (= *mezclar*) [+ *metales*] to alloy, mix; [+ *salsa*] to thicken **3** (= *unir*) to join, bind together; **estar ligado por contrato a** to be bound by contract to **4** (*) (= *conquistar*) to pick up*, get off with*, pull* **Ⓑ** VI (*) to pull* **Ⓒ ligarse** VPR **~se a algn*** to get off with sb*

ligazón SF connection, bond, link

ligeramente ADV **1** (= *levemente*) slightly **2** (= *sin sensatez*) flippantly; **hay decisiones que no se pueden tomar ~** there are some decisions which can't be taken lightly

ligereza SF **1** [*de objeto*] lightness **2** (= *rapidez*) speed, swiftness **3** (= *agilidad*) agility, nimbleness; **~ mental** mental agility **4** (= *falta de sensatez*) flippancy; **actuar con ~** to act flippantly; **hablar con ~** to speak without thinking; **juzgar algo con ~** to jump to conclusions about sth, judge sth hastily **5** (= *dicho*) flippant remark; (= *hecho*) indiscretion; **cometí la ~ de contárselo todo** I was foolish enough to tell him everything

ligero Ⓐ ADJ **1** (= *poco pesado*) [*objeto, gas, comida*] light; [*material*] lightweight; **una blusa ligerita** a light *o* lightweight *o* thin blouse; **viajar ~ de equipaje** to travel light; **~ de ropa** lightly dressed; **fotos de chicas ligeras de ropa** photos of scantily clad girls; **tener el sueño ~** to be a light sleeper

2 (= *leve*) [*viento, caricia*] light; [*ruido*] slight; [*perfume, fragancia*] delicate

3 (= *poco importante*) [*enfermedad*] minor; [*castigo*] light

4 (= *rápido*) swift

5 (= *ágil*) agile

6 (= *superficial*) [*conocimiento*] slight; [*sospecha*] sneaking

7 (= *frívolo*) [*carácter, persona*] flippant, frivolous; [*comentario, tema*] flippant; [*mujer*] (*pey*†) loose†

8 (= *sin complicaciones*) [*novela, película*] lightweight; [*conversación, contexto*] light-hearted

9 a la ligera (= *irreflexivamente*) rashly; (= *rápidamente*) quickly; **no podemos juzgar su conducta a la ligera** we shouldn't jump to conclusions about his behaviour, we shouldn't judge his behaviour so hastily; **tomarse algo a la ligera** not to take sth seriously

Ⓑ ADV (= *rápido*) [*andar, correr*] quickly

light [lait] ADJ INV [*tabaco*] low-tar *antes de s*; [*comida*] low-calorie; [*política*] watered-down, toned-down

ligón* (*Esp*) **1** [*persona*] flirtatious; **es muy ~** he's a great one for the girls **2** [*prenda*] (= *bonita*) attractive; (= *sexy*) provocative, sexy

ligue* (*Esp*) **Ⓐ** SM **ir de ~** to look for sb to get off with*, go eyeing up the talent* **Ⓑ** SMF (= *persona*) pick-up*, date ➤ **ligue de una noche** one-night stand

liguero¹ SM suspender belt (*Brit*), garter belt (*EEUU*)

liguero² ADJ (*Dep*) league *antes de s*

liguilla SF (*Dep*) mini-league

lija SF **1** (*Zool*) dogfish **2** (= *papel de lija*) sandpaper

lijar /1a/ VT to sandpaper, sand down

lila¹ SF (*Bot*) lilac

lila² SM (= *color*) lilac

Lima SF Lima

lima¹ SF (*Bot*) lime, sweet-lime tree

lima² SF (= *herramienta*) file; ✦ MODISMO **comer como una ~** to eat like a horse ➤ **lima de uñas** nail file

limar /1a/ VT **1** (*con lima*) to file **2** [+ *artículo, obra*] to polish up; [+ *diferencias*] to iron out

limbo SM **1** (*Rel*) limbo; ✦ MODISMO **estar en el ~** to be miles away **2** (*Bot, Mat*) limb

limeño ADJ of/from Lima

limitación SF **1** (= *restricción*) limitation; **sin ~ de tiempo** with no time limit **2 limitaciones** (= *deficiencias*) limitations

limitado ADJ limited

limitante SF (*CS*) limitation

limitar /1a/ **Ⓐ** VT (= *restringir*) to limit, restrict; **nos han limitado el número de visitas** they have limited *o*

restricted the number of visits we can have
Ⓑ VI **~ con** to border on
Ⓒ limitarse VPR **~se a hacer algo** to limit *o* confine o.s. to doing sth

> Recuérdese que las preposiciones en inglés rigen gerundio y no infinitivo, de ahí **to limit** *o* **confine o.s. to doing sth.**

me he limitado a corregir unos cuantos errores all I've done is correct a few mistakes, I've just corrected a few mistakes, that's all; **tú limítate a escuchar** just be quiet and listen

límite Ⓐ SM **1** (*gen*) limit; **podrá presentarse cualquiera, sin ~ de edad** anyone can apply, regardless *o* irrespective of age, anyone can apply, there's no age limit; **como** *o* **de ~: tenemos como** *o* **de ~ el sábado para presentar el trabajo** the deadline for submitting our work is Saturday; **no tener ~s** to know no bounds; **poner ~ a algo** to limit sth, restrict sth; **sin ~s** limitless ➤ **límite de crédito** credit limit ➤ **límite de velocidad** speed limit **2** (*Geog, Pol*) boundary, border **Ⓑ** ADJ INV [*caso, situación*] extreme

limítrofe ADJ bordering, neighbouring, neighboring (*EEUU*)

limón SM **1** (= *fruta*) lemon; (*LAm*) (= *árbol*) lemon tree **2** (*Carib, Méx*) (*verde*) lime

limonada SF (*natural*) lemonade; (*artificial*) lemon squash

limonar SM lemon grove

limonero SM lemon tree

limosna SF alms† *pl*; **pedir ~** to beg; **vivir de ~** to live by begging, live on charity

limosnear /1a/ VI (*LAm*) to beg

limosnero/a SM/F (*LAm*) beggar

limpiabotas SMF INV bootblack

limpiacabezales SM INV head-cleaner

limpiacristales (*Esp*) **Ⓐ** SM INV (= *líquido*) window cleaner **Ⓑ** SMF INV (= *persona*) window cleaner

limpiada SF (= *acto de limpiar*) clean, clean-up

limpiador(a) Ⓐ ADJ [*líquido, crema*] cleansing **Ⓑ** SM/F (= *persona*) cleaner **Ⓒ** SM (*Méx*) = **limpiaparabrisas**

limpiamente ADV **1** (= *con pulcritud*) cleanly **2** (= *honestamente*) honestly; **nos ganaron ~** they beat us fair and square

limpiametales SM INV metal polish

limpiaparabrisas SM INV windscreen wiper (*Brit*), windshield wiper (*EEUU*)

limpiar /1b/ **Ⓐ** VT **1** [+ *casa*] to tidy, tidy up, clean; [+ *cara, piel*] to cleanse; [+ *marca*] to wipe off, clean off; [+ *maquillaje*] to remove; [+ *zapatos*] to polish, shine; [+ *pescado*] to gut; **~ en seco** to dry-clean; **~ las narices a un niño** to wipe a child's nose **2** (*) (= *robar*) to swipe*, nick* **Ⓑ limpiarse** VPR to clean o.s., wipe o.s.; **~se las narices** to blow one's nose

limpiavidrios Ⓐ SM INV (*LAm*) (= *líquido*) window cleaner **Ⓑ** SM/F INV (*LAm*) (= *persona*) window cleaner **Ⓒ** SM (*Méx*) (= *limpiaparabrisas*) windscreen wiper (*Brit*), windshield wiper (*EEUU*)

límpido ADJ (*frm*) limpid

limpieza SF **1** (= *acción*) cleaning; **la mujer** *o* **señora de la ~** the cleaning lady; **hacer la ~** to do the cleaning ➤ **limpieza en seco** dry cleaning ➤ **limpieza general** spring cleaning **2** (*Pol*) purge; (*Mil*) mopping-up; (*de la policía*) clean-up ➤ **limpieza étnica** ethnic cleansing **3** (= *estado*) cleanness **4 con ~** (= *con integridad*) fair and square

limpio Ⓐ ADJ **1** [*casa, cuarto*] clean; **◆** MODISMO **más ~ que los chorros del oro** as clean as can be **2** (= *despejado*) clear; **~ de algo** free from sth, clear of sth; **el cielo estaba ~ de nubes** there was a cloudless sky, there was not a cloud in the sky **3** (*Dep*) [*jugada*] fair **4** (*Fin*) clear, net; **50 dólares de ganancia limpia** 50 dollars

of clear profit **5** (*) (= *sin dinero*) **estar ~** to be broke; **quedar(se) ~*** to be cleaned out* **6** (*) (*enfático*) **se defendieron a pedrada limpia** they defended themselves with nothing but stones; **◆** MODISMO **a puñetazo ~** with bare fists **Ⓑ** SM **copia en ~** fair copy; **pasar** *o* **poner algo a** *o* **en ~** to make a fair *o* neat *o* clean copy of sth; **◆** MODISMO **sacar algo en ~** to make sense of sth **Ⓒ** ADV **jugar ~** to play fair

limpión SM (*Col*) tea towel

limusina SF limousine

linaje SM lineage, descent

linaza SF linseed

lince SM (*Zool*) lynx; **◆** MODISMO **ser un ~** (= *observador*) to be very sharp-eyed; (= *astuto*) to be very shrewd *o* sharp

linchamiento SM lynching

linchar /1a/ VT to lynch

lindante ADJ bordering (**con** on), adjacent (**con** to)

lindar /1a/ VI **~ con: mis tierras lindan con las suyas** my land borders on theirs; **el banco linda con la biblioteca** the bank is adjacent to the library; **eso linda con el racismo** that is bordering on racism

linde SM *o* SF boundary

lindero Ⓐ ADJ adjoining, bordering **Ⓑ** SM boundary

lindezas SFPL insults, improprieties

lindo Ⓐ ADJ **1** (= *bonito*) nice, lovely, pretty **2** (*esp LAm*) (= *excelente*) fine, excellent, first-rate; **un ~ partido** a first-rate game; **un ~ concierto** a good concert; **◆** MODISMO **de lo ~** a lot, a great deal **Ⓑ** ADV (*LAm*) nicely, well; **baila ~** she dances beautifully

lindura SF (*LAm*) (= *objeto*) lovely thing; **es una ~** it's lovely

línea Ⓐ SF **1** (= *raya*) line; **dibujó una ~ recta** he drew a straight line; **primera ~ de playa** sea-front; **en ~ recta** in a straight line ➤ **línea de flotación** (*Náut*) water line ➤ **línea discontinua** (*Aut*) broken line **2** (*en un escrito*) line; **◆** MODISMOS **leer entre ~s** to read between the lines; **poner unas ~s a algn** to drop a line to sb **3** (= *género, gama*) line; **de primera ~** first-rate, top-ranking ➤ **línea blanca** white goods *pl* ➤ **línea marrón** brown goods *pl* **4** (*Telec*) line; **me he quedado sin ~** I've been cut off ➤ **línea directa** direct line ➤ **línea telefónica** telephone line **5** (*Mil*) line; **primera ~** front line ➤ **línea de fuego** firing line **6** (*Aer, Ferro*) **autobús de ~** service bus, regular bus ➤ **línea aérea** airline ➤ **línea férrea** railway (*esp Brit*), railroad (*EEUU*) ➤ **línea regular** scheduled service **7** (*Dep*) line ➤ **línea de banda** sideline, touchline ➤ **línea de meta** (*en fútbol*) goal line; (*en carrera*) finishing line **8** (*Inform*) **en ~** on-line; **fuera de ~** off-line **9** (= *talle*) figure; **guardar** *o* **conservar la ~** to keep one's figure (trim) **10** (= *moda*) **la ~ del 2002** the 2002 look **11** [*de pensamiento, acción*] line; **explicar algo a grandes ~s** *o* **en sus ~s generales** to set out in broad outline, give the broad outline of sth ➤ **línea de conducta** course of action ➤ **línea dura** (*Pol*) hard line **12** (*genealógica*) line ➤ **línea sucesoria** line of succession, order of succession **Ⓑ** SMF (*Dep*) linesman, assistant referee

lineal ADJ linear; **aumento ~ de sueldos** across-the-board pay increase; **dibujo ~** line drawing

linfa SF lymph

linfático ADJ lymphatic

linfocito SM lymphocyte

lingotazo* SM swig*, shot*

lingote SM ingot

lingüista SMF linguist

lingüística SF linguistics *sing* ➤ **lingüística aplicada** applied linguistics ➤ **lingüística computacional** computational linguistics

lingüístico ADJ linguistic

linier SMF (pl ~s) (Dep) linesman, assistant referee

linimento SM liniment

lino SM 1 (Bot) flax 2 (LAm) (= linaza) linseed 3 (= tela) linen

linóleo SM lino, linoleum

linotipia SF Linotype®

linterna SF (eléctrica) torch (Brit), flashlight (esp EEUU); (= farolillo) lantern

linyera SM (CS) tramp, bum (EEUU*)

lío SM 1 (= fardo) bundle 2 (*) (= jaleo) fuss; (= confusión) muddle, mix-up; **en mi mesa hay un ~ enorme de papeles** my desk is in a real muddle with all these bits of paper; **armar un ~** to make a fuss, kick up a fuss; **se armó un ~ tremendo** there was a terrific fuss; **hacerse un ~** to get into a muddle, get mixed up 3 (= aprieto) **meterse en un ~** to get into trouble 4 (*) (= amorío) affair ➤ **lío de faldas** affair

liofilizado ADJ freeze-dried

lipocito SM fat particle

liposucción SF liposuction

lipotimia SF faint, blackout

liquen SM lichen

liquidación SF 1 [de empresa, negocio] liquidation, winding-up; [de cuenta, deuda] settlement 2 (= rebajas) sale ➤ **liquidación por cierre del negocio** closing-down sale 3 (por despido) redundancy pay 4 (= eliminación) liquidation

liquidar /1a/ Ⓐ VT 1 [+ cuenta] to settle; [+ empresa, negocio] to wind up, liquidate; [+ deuda] to settle, pay off, clear; [+ existencias] to sell off, sell up 2 [+ asunto, problema] to deal with; **y asunto liquidado** and that'll be the end of it 3 (*) (= gastar) to go through*, blow* 4 (*) (= matar) to bump off* 5 (= eliminar) to liquidate 6 (LAm) (= destrozar) to destroy, ruin Ⓑ **liquidarse** (*) VPR [+ ahorros] to blow*

liquidez SF liquidity

líquido Ⓐ ADJ 1 [sustancia] liquid, fluid; **el ~ elemento** water 2 (Fin) net Ⓑ SM 1 (gen) liquid, fluid ➤ **líquido anticongelante** antifreeze ➤ **líquido de frenos** brake fluid 2 (Fin) (= efectivo) ready cash, ready money ➤ **líquido imponible** net taxable income

liquiliqui SM (Carib, Col) Venezuelan national dress

lira SF 1 (Mús) lyre 2 (= moneda) lira

lírica SF lyrical poetry

lírico ADJ 1 (Literat) lyric(al) 2 (Perú, RPl*) [persona] full of idealistic plans

lirio SM iris ➤ **lirio de los valles** lily of the valley

lirismo SM lyricism

lirón SM dormouse; ✦ MODISMO **dormir como un ~** to sleep like a log

lirondo ADJ ver **mondo**

lis SF lily

lisa SF 1 (Carib*) (= cerveza) beer 2 (= pez) mullet

Lisboa SF Lisbon

lisboeta ADJ of/from Lisbon

lisérgico ADJ lysergic

lisiado/a Ⓐ ADJ crippled, lame Ⓑ SM/F cripple; **un ~ de guerra** a wounded veteran

lisiar /1b/ VT (gen) to injure (permanently), hurt (seriously); (= tullir) to cripple, maim

liso ADJ 1 [terreno, superficie] smooth, even; [neumático] bald; [pelo] straight; **los 400 metros ~s** (Esp) the 400-metre flat race; ✦ MODISMO **como la palma de la mano** as smooth as glass 2 (= sin adornos) plain; ✦ MODISMO **lisa y llanamente** (= en términos sencillos) plainly, in plain language; (= evidentemente) quite simply 3 (Perú*) (= descarado) fresh*, cheeky (Brit), sassy (EEUU) 4 (*) (= de poco pecho) flat-chested

lisonja SF flattery

lisonjero/a Ⓐ ADJ flattering Ⓑ SM/F flatterer

lista SF 1 [de nombres, elementos] list; (en escuela) register, school list (EEUU); **pasar ~** (Escol) to call the register o roll ➤ **lista cerrada** (Pol) closed list ➤ **lista de boda** wedding list ➤ **lista de correos** poste restante (esp Brit), general delivery (EEUU) ➤ **lista de espera** waiting list ➤ **lista de éxitos** (Mús) charts pl ➤ **lista de precios** price list ➤ **lista negra** blacklist 2 (= raya) stripe; **tela a ~s** striped material

listado SM (= lista) list, listing; (Inform) printout

listar /1a/ VT to list

listeria SF listeria

listillo/a* SM/F (Esp) know-all (Brit), know-it-all (EEUU), smart alec o (esp EEUU) aleck*

listín SM (Esp) ➤ **listín telefónico, listín de teléfonos** telephone directory

listo Ⓐ ADJ 1 (= dispuesto) ready; **¿estás ~?** are you ready?; **¡preparados, ~s, ya!** ready, steady, go!; **~ para algo** ready for sth 2 (= terminado) finished; **una última lectura y ~** one last read through and that's it o it's finished; **la traducción tendrá que estar lista para mañana** the translation will have to be finished for tomorrow; ✦ MODISMO **estar** o **ir ~***: **¡pues está lista!** she'll be lucky!*; **¡pues estamos ~s!** well, we've really had it now!* 3 (= inteligente) clever, bright, smart*; **¿te crees muy lista, verdad?** you think you're really smart, don't you?; **se las da de ~** he thinks he's so clever; **pasarse de ~** to be too clever by half; ✦ MODISMO **ser más ~ que el hambre** to be as sharp as a needle 4 (Chi, Col, Perú) (indicando conformidad) OK; **¡listo!** OK! Ⓑ SM/F (= inteligente) clever one, smart one*; (pey) cleverclogs*, smart-arse (Brit**), smart-ass (EEUU**)

listón SM 1 [de madera] strip, lath; (Dep) bar; [de goma, metal] strip 2 (= nivel) level; **bajar el ~** to make things too easy 3 (Méx Cos) ribbon

lisura SF 1 [de superficie] evenness, smoothness 2 (And) (= grosería) rude remark

litera SF (en alcoba) bunk, bunk bed; (Náut) bunk, berth; (Ferro) couchette

literal ADJ literal

literalmente ADV literally

literario ADJ literary

literatura SF literature

litigar /1h/ VI to go to law

litigio SM 1 (= pleito) lawsuit 2 (frm) (= disputa) dispute; **en ~** in dispute

litio SM lithium

litografía SF 1 (= proceso) lithography 2 (= cuadro) lithograph

litoral SM seaboard, coast, littoral (frm)

litro SM litre, liter (EEUU)

litrona* SF litre o (EEUU) liter bottle

Lituania SF Lithuania

lituano/a Ⓐ ADJ, SM/F Lithuanian Ⓑ SM (Ling) Lithuanian

liturgia SF liturgy

litúrgico ADJ liturgical

liviano ADJ 1 (esp LAm) (= ligero) (gen) light; [novela, película] lightweight; **tener el sueño ~** to be a light sleeper 2 (= frívolo) frivolous, trivial

lívido ADJ 1 (= pálido) pallid, pale, livid 2 (= amoratado) black and blue, livid

living ['liβin] SM (pl ~s ['liβins]) (esp LAm) living room, lounge

liza SF (Hist) lists pl; (fig) contest

Ll, ll ['eʎe] SF former letter in the Spanish alphabet

llaga SF ulcer, sore

llagar /1h/ VT to cause a sore on, wound

llama¹ SF (Zool) llama

llama² SF 1 [de fuego] flame; **en ~s** burning, ablaze, in flames 2 [de amor, pasión] flame, fire

llamada SF 1 (Telec) call; **gracias por su ~** thank you for your call; **ahora le paso la ~** I'll put you through now; **devolver una ~** to phone back; **hacer una ~** to make a call ➤ **llamada internacional** international call ➤ **llamada**

interurbana *call made between different towns within the same province* ➤ **llamada urbana** local call
2 (*a la puerta*) (*con el puño*) knock; (*con el timbre*) ring **3** (= *aviso*) call; **última ~** last call; **la ~ del deber** the call of duty; **la ~ de la selva** the call of the wild; **acudir a la ~ de algn** to answer sb's call ➤ **llamada al orden** call to order ➤ **llamada de socorro** call for help
4 (*Tip*) mark; **haz una ~ al margen** make a mark in the margin
5 (*Mil*) (*tb* ~ **a las armas**) call to arms

llamado ⒶＡＤＪ **1** (= *con el nombre de*) [*persona*] named, called; [*lugar*] called; **un chico ~ Manuel** a boy named *o* called Manuel; **la llamada generación beat** the so-called beat generation **2** (= *destinado*) **me sentía ~ a hacerlo** I felt destined to do it; **esta ley está llamada a desaparecer** this law is bound *o* destined to disappear ⒷＳＭ **1** (*Arg Telec*) call, phone call **2** (*LAm*) (= *llamamiento*) appeal

llamador ＳＭ doorknocker

llamamiento ＳＭ call; **hacer** *o* **lanzar un ~ (a algo)** to make *o* issue an appeal *o* call (for sth); **han hecho un ~ a la población pidiendo donaciones de sangre** they have appealed for blood donations, they have appealed to people to give blood ➤ **llamamiento a filas** (*Mil*) call-up, draft (*EEUU*)

llamar /1a/ Ⓐ ＶＴ **1** (= *nombrar*) to call; **¿cómo van a ~ al niño?** what are they going to name *o* call the baby?; **me llamó imbécil** he called me an idiot; **la llamó de todo** he called her every name under the sun
2 (= *considerar*) to call; **lo que se dio en ~ la nueva generación** what became known as *o* what came to be called the new generation; **el mal llamado problema** what people wrongly consider a problem
3 (= *avisar*) [+ *médico, fontanero*] to call; [+ *taxi*] (*por teléfono*) to call; (*con la mano*) to hail; **te estuve llamando a voces** I was shouting for you; **me llamó con la mano para que me acercara** he beckoned me over; **no te metas donde no te llaman*** don't poke your nose in where it's not wanted*; **~ a algn al orden** to call sb to order
4 (*Telec*) (*tb* ~ **por teléfono**) to call, phone, ring (*esp Brit*)
5 (= *atraer*) **el chocolate no me llama demasiado** I'm not all that keen on chocolate
6 (= *convocar*) to call, summon (*frm*); **lo ~on a palacio** he was called *o* summoned (*frm*) to the palace; **Dios lo ha llamado a su lado** (*euf*) he has been called to God; **~ a algn a filas** to call sb up
Ⓑ ＶＩ **1** (*Telec*) [*persona*] to call, phone, ring (*esp Brit*); [*teléfono*] to ring
2 (*a la puerta*) (*con el puño*) to knock; (*al timbre*) to ring; **están llamando** there's someone at the door
Ⓒ **llamarse** ＶＰＲ to be called; **mi primo se llama Benjamín** my cousin's name is Benjamín, mi cousin is called Benjamín; **¿cómo te llamas?** what's your name?

llamarada ＳＦ **1** [*de fuego*] flare-up, sudden blaze **2** [*de indignación, ira*] blaze, outburst

llamarón ＳＭ (*Chi, Col*) = **llamarada**

llamativo ＡＤＪ [*color*] loud, bright; **se viste de modo ~** she wears very striking clothes

llamear /1a/ ＶＩ to blaze, flame

llanamente ＡＤＶ *ver* **liso**

llanero/a ＳＭ/Ｆ **1** (*esp Ven*) (*del llano*) plainsman/plainswoman **2** (*Carib*) (= *vaquero*) cowboy/cowgirl ➤ **llanero solitario** lone ranger

llano Ⓐ ＡＤＪ **1** [*superficie, terreno*] (= *sin desniveles*) flat; (= *no inclinado*) level **2** (= *sencillo*) [*persona, trato*] straightforward; [*estilo, lenguaje*] simple **3 palabra llana** *word with the stress on the penultimate syllable* Ⓑ ＳＭ plain

llanta ＳＦ **1** [*de rueda*] rim **2** (*LAm*) (= *neumático*) tyre, tire (*EEUU*) ➤ **llanta de refacción** (*Méx*), **llanta de repuesto** (*LAm*) spare tyre, spare tire (*EEUU*)

llantera* ＳＦ (= *lloros*) sobbing; (= *berridos*) bawling

llantina* ＳＦ sobbing

llanto ＳＭ crying, tears *pl*; **se oía el ~ de un niño** you could hear a child crying; **romper en ~** to burst into tears

llanura ＳＦ (*Geog*) plain; (= *pradera*) prairie

llapa ＳＦ (*LAm*) *ver* **yapa**

llave ＳＦ **1** [*de puerta*] key; **bajo ~** under lock and key; **cerrar con ~** to lock; **echar (la) ~ (a)** to lock up ➤ **llave de contacto** (*Aut*) ignition key ➤ **llave maestra** skeleton key, master key
2 [*de gas, agua*] tap (*Brit*), faucet (*EEUU*); (*Elec*) switch ➤ **llave de paso** [*del agua*] stopcock; [*del gas*] mains tap (*Brit*), shutoff valve (*EEUU*); **cerrar la ~ de paso del agua/gas** to turn the water/gas off at the mains (*Brit*), turn off the shutoff valve (*EEUU*)
3 (*Mec*) spanner (*Brit*), wrench (*EEUU*) ➤ **llave inglesa** monkey wrench, wrench (*Brit*)
4 (*Tip*) curly bracket, brace bracket
5 (*Dep*) [*de lucha libre*] lock; [*de judo*] hold
6 (*Col, Ven**) (= *amigo*) mate (*Brit**), buddy (*esp EEUU**)

llavero ＳＭ key ring

llavín ＳＭ latch key

llegada ＳＦ **1** [*de un viaje*] arrival **2** (*Dep*) (= *meta*) finishing line

---

llegar /1h/

Ⓐ VERBO INTRANSITIVO   Ⓒ VERBO PRONOMINAL
Ⓑ VERBO TRANSITIVO

Para las expresiones **llegar al alma**, **llegar lejos**, **llegar a las manos** *etc, ver la entrada correspondiente a la otra palabra.*

llegar Ⓐ VERBO INTRANSITIVO
1 (*movimiento, destino, procedencia*) to arrive; **~on cubiertos de barro** they arrived covered in mud; **está recién llegado de Roma** he recently arrived from Rome; **el vuelo ~á a las 14:15** the flight gets in at 14:15; **no llegues tarde** don't be late; **~ a** [+ *país, ciudad*] to arrive in; [+ *edificio*] to arrive at

---

arrive *puede ir seguido de* **in** *o* **at** *dependiendo del lugar de llegada, pero nunca aparece seguido de* **to**.

---

cuando llegamos a Bilbao when we got to *o* arrived in Bilbao; **¿a qué hora llegaste a casa?** what time did you get home?; **los vehículos están llegando a la línea de salida** the cars are approaching the starting line; **~le a alguien: ¿te ha llegado ya la carta?** have you got the letter yet?; **estar al ~: Carlos debe de estar al ~** Carlos should be arriving any minute now; **hacer ~ algo a algn** to send sth to sb
2 (= *alcanzar*)
2.1 (*con las manos*) to reach; **no llego al estante de arriba** I can't reach the top shelf
2.2 (*indicando distancia, nivel*) **esta cuerda no llega** this rope isn't long enough, this rope won't reach; **~ a** *o* **hasta** (*en altura*) to come up to; (*en distancia*) to go as far as; **el vestido le llega hasta los pies** the dress comes *o* goes down to her feet; **los pies no le llegaban al suelo** her feet weren't touching the floor; **la cola llegaba hasta la puerta** the queue (*Brit*) *o* line (*EEUU*) went *o* reached back as far as the door; **me llegó muy hondo lo que me dijo** what she said made a very deep impression on me; ✦ MODISMOS **¡hasta allí podíamos ~!** that's the limit!, what a nerve!; **a tanto no llego: soy bastante inteligente pero a tanto no llego** I'm reasonably clever, but not enough to do that
2.3 (*indicando duración*) to last; **este abrigo no te llega al próximo invierno** this coat won't last till next winter; **le falta un año para ~ a la jubilación** he has a year to go till *o* before he retires
3
✦ **llegar a** + SUSTANTIVO **3.1** (= *conseguir*) [+ *acuerdo, conclusión*] to reach, come to; **¿cómo has conseguido ~ a la fama?** how did you manage to achieve fame *o* become famous?; **le costó pero llegó a arquitecto** it wasn't easy, but he eventually managed to become an architect; **por fin ha llegado a catedrático** he's finally made it to professor
3.2 (*con cantidades*) to come to; **los gastos totales ~on a**

10.000 euros the total expenditure came to 10,000 euros; **el público no llegaba a 200 espectadores** there were fewer than 200 spectators there

4

◆ **llegar a** + INFIN **4.1** (= *conseguir*): **llegó a conocer a varios actores** she met *o* got to know several actors; **no llego a comprenderlo** I just can't understand it; **el producto puede ~ a tener éxito** the product could be a success; **si lo llego a saber** if I had known; **~ a ser famoso/el jefe** to become famous/the boss; **~ a ver: no llegó a ver la catedral terminada** he never saw the cathedral finished

4.2 (*como algo extremo*) **llegamos a sospechar de él** we came to suspect him; **puede ~ a alcanzar los 300km/h** it can reach speeds of up to 300km/h; **¿llegó a creer que sería campeón del mundo?** did you ever believe you'd be world champion?

5 (= *bastar*) to be enough; **con ese dinero no le va a ~** you won't have enough money; **no me llega para ropa nueva** I can't afford to buy new clothes

6 [*momento, acontecimiento*] to come; **~á un día en que sea rico** the day will come when I'm rich

Ⓑ VERBO TRANSITIVO (= *acercar*) to bring up, bring over

Ⓒ **llegarse** VERBO PRONOMINAL **llégate a su casa y dile que ...** go over to his house and tell him ...

lleísmo SM *pronunciation of Spanish "y" as "ll"*

llenador ADJ (CS) [*comida*] filling, satisfying

llenar /1a/ **Ⓐ** VT **1** (= *rellenar*) [+ *cubo, vaso, cajón*] to fill; [+ *bañera*] to run; **llenó tanto la maleta que no podía cerrarla** he packed *o* filled the suitcase so full that he couldn't shut it; **no me llenes mucho el plato** don't give me too much food; **siempre llena los auditorios** he always gets full houses; **~ con** *o* **de algo** [+ *contenedor*] to fill with sth; [+ *superficie*] to cover with sth; **llenó la hoja de nombres** he covered the sheet of paper with names;

◆ MODISMO **~le a algn la cabeza de pájaros** to fill sb's head with nonsense

2 (= *ocupar*) [+ *hueco*] to fill

3 (= *satisfacer*) [+ *deseo*] to fulfil, fulfill (EEUU), satisfy; **este trabajo no me llena** I don't find this job satisfying *o* fulfilling; **no me termina de ~ este libro** this book doesn't really convince me

4 (= *colmar*) **~ a algn de** [+ *inquietud, dudas, orgullo*] to fill sb with; **su tono de voz la llenó de inquietud** his tone of voice made her feel uneasy; **verte nos llenó de alegría** we were delighted to see you; **lo ~on de atenciones** they showered him with attention, they made a great fuss of him

5 (= *cumplimentar*) [+ *documento, impreso*] fill out, to fill in (*esp Brit*)

Ⓑ VI [*comida*] to be filling

Ⓒ **llenarse** VPR **1** (= *ocuparse completamente*) to fill, fill up; **los viernes siempre se llena el restaurante** the restaurant always gets full *o* fills up on Fridays; **~se de** [+ *humo, lágrimas*] to fill (up) with; ◆ MODISMO **~se hasta la bandera** *o* **hasta los topes** to be full to bursting, be packed, be packed out (*Brit*)

2 (= *colmarse*): **con esa tarta me he llenado** I'm full after that cake; **se llenó los bolsillos de monedas** she filled her pockets with coins; **~se de** [+ *orgullo, alegría*] to be filled with; [+ *comida*] to stuff o.s. with*

3 (= *cubrirse*) to get covered; **me he llenado los dedos de tinta** I've got ink all over my fingers, my fingers are covered in ink

lleno **Ⓐ** ADJ **1** (= *completo*) [*plato, teatro, tren*] full; **el depósito está ~** the tank is full; **¡~, por favor!** (*en una gasolinera*) fill her up, please!; **no hables con la boca llena** don't talk with your mouth full; ◆ MODISMO **~ a reventar** *o* **hasta la bandera** *o* **hasta los topes** full to bursting, packed, packed out (*Brit*)

2 ~ de 2.1 [*espacio*] full of; [*superficie*] covered in; **tiene la casa llena de gente** she has the house full of people; **llevaba el traje ~ de manchas** his suit was covered in stains **2.2** [*complejos, problemas, aventuras*] full of; [*odio, esperanza*] filled with; **estaba ~ de dudas** I was filled with doubt; **una mirada llena de odio** a hateful look, a look full of hate; **llegué ~ de alegría** I arrived in high spirits

3 de ~ directly; **los cambios nos afectarán de ~** the changes will affect us directly; **la bala le alcanzó de ~ en el** corazón the bullet hit him straight in the heart; **está dedicado de ~ a su familia** he is entirely dedicated to his family; **acertaste de ~ con ese comentario** you hit the nail on the head (with that comment)

4 (= *saciado*) full, full up*

5 (= *regordete*) plump, chubby

6 [*luna*] full

Ⓑ SM (*gen*) sellout; (*Cine, Teat*) full house ➤ **lleno absoluto, lleno hasta la bandera, lleno total** (*Cine, Teat*) packed house; (*Dep*) capacity crowd

llevadero ADJ bearable, tolerable

---

llevar /1a/

Ⓐ VERBO TRANSITIVO	**Ⓒ** VERBO PRONOMINAL
Ⓑ VERBO INTRANSITIVO	

Para las expresiones **llevar adelante, llevar la contraria, llevar las de perder, llevar a la práctica, llevar a término, llevar ventaja** *etc, ver la entrada correspondiente a la otra palabra.*

---

llevar **Ⓐ** VERBO TRANSITIVO

1 (= *transportar*) (*con los brazos*) to carry; (*indicando el punto de destino*) to take; **yo llevaba la maleta** I was carrying the case; **no te olvides de ~ un paraguas** make sure you take an umbrella with you; **lleva los vasos a la cocina** can you take the glasses to the kitchen?; **"comida para ~"** "food to take away", "take-away food"; **¿es para ~?** is it to take away?

2 (*tb* **~ puesto**) to wear; **¿hay que ~ corbata?** do we have to wear a tie?

3 (*tb* **~ encima**) **no llevo dinero (encima)** I haven't got any money on me

4 (= *tener*) [+ *barba, adorno, ingrediente*] to have; **lleva el pelo corto** he has short hair; **este pastel no lleva harina** this cake doesn't have any flour in it; **¿qué lleva el pollo que está tan bueno?** what's in this chicken that makes it taste so good?; **~á el nombre de la madre** she will be named after her mother

5 (= *acompañar*) (*gen*) to take; (*en coche*) to drive; **¿cuándo me llevas a cenar?** when are you going to take me out for a meal?; **Sofía nos llevó a casa** Sofía gave us a lift home, Sofía drove us home; **¿quieres que te lleve?** do you want a lift?

6 (= *conducir*)

6.1 [+ *persona, entidad*] **¿adónde me llevan?** where are you taking me?; **este camino nos lleva a Bogotá** this road takes us to Bogotá; **ha llevado al país a una guerra** he has led the country into a war; **dejarse ~** to get carried away

6.2 [+ *vehículo*] to drive; **yo llevé el coche hasta Santander** I drove the car to Santander

7 (= *dirigir*) [+ *negocio, tienda, finca*] to run; **lleva todos sus negocios en secreto** he conducts all his business in secret; **~ la casa** to run the household; **lleva muy bien la casa** she's a very good housewife; **¿quién lleva la cuenta?** who is keeping count?; **~ las cuentas** *o* **los libros** (*Com*) to keep the books

8 (= *adelantar en*) **me lleva ocho años** he is eight years older than me

9 (= *inducir*) **~ a algn a creer que ...** to lead sb to think that ..., make sb think that ...; **esto me lleva a pensar que ...** this leads me to think that ...

10 (= *tolerar*) **¿cómo lleva lo de su hijo?** how's she coping with what happened to her son?; **lleva muy bien sus sesenta años** he's doing very well for sixty; **hay que saber ~lo** you have to know how to deal with him

11 (*indicando tiempo*)

11.1 (= *haber estado*) to be; **¿cuánto tiempo llevas aquí?** how long have you been here?; **llevo horas esperando aquí** I've been waiting for hours; **el tren lleva una hora de retraso** the train is an hour late

11.2 (= *tardar*) to take; **el trabajo me ~á tres días** the work will take me three days

12 (*Esp*) (= *cobrar*) to charge; **me llevó 100 euros por arreglar el televisor** he charged me 100 euros for fixing the television

13 (= *ir por*) **¿qué dirección llevaba?** what direction was he going in?, which way was he going?; **lleva camino de**

ser como su padre it looks like he's going to turn out just like his father
14 [+ *vida*] to lead; **~ una vida tranquila** to live o lead a quiet life
15 (*CS*) (= *comprar*) to take; **llevo sólo la blusa, por favor** I'll just take the blouse please
16 (*Ven*) (= *recibir*) [+ *susto*] to get; **~ un disgusto** to be upset; **~ malos tratos** to be badly treated
17 (+ PARTICIPIO) **llevo estudiados tres capítulos** I have covered three chapters; **llevaba hecha la mitad** he had done half of it
Ⓑ VERBO INTRANSITIVO [*carretera*] to go, lead
Ⓒ llevarse VERBO PRONOMINAL
1 (= *tomar consigo*) to take; **se llevó todo mi dinero** he took all my money; **¿puedo ~me este libro?** can I borrow this book?; **llévatelo** take it (with you); **me lo llevo** (*al comprar*) I'll take it; **llévate a los niños** take the children with you; **se lo ~on al teatro** they took him off to the theatre; **~se a algn por delante** (= *atropellar*) to run sb over; (= *maltratar*) to ride roughshod over sb; **el camión se llevó una farola por delante** the truck went off the road and took a lamppost with it
2 (= *conseguir*) [+ *premio*] to win; **siempre me llevo la peor parte** I always come off worst; ✦ MODISMO **llevársela**: **¡no lo toques o te la llevas!** don't touch it or you'll live to regret it!
3 (= *sufrir*) **me llevé una alegría** I was so happy; **se llevó un buen susto** he got a real fright
4 (= *arrastrar*) **el mar se lleva la arena** the sea washes the sand away; **el viento se llevó una rama** the wind tore off a branch; ✦ MODISMO **las palabras se las lleva el viento** words are not binding
5 (*en el trato*) **~se bien** to get on well (together); **no se lleva bien con el jefe** he doesn't get on o along with the boss; **nos llevamos muy mal** we get on very badly
6 (= *estar de moda*) to be in fashion, be all the rage; **se vuelven a ~ las gafas negras** dark glasses are coming back into fashion
7 (*con cantidades*) **mi hermano y yo nos llevamos tres años** there are three years between my brother and me; **de doce me llevo una** (*Mat*) I carry one

llorado ADJ (*frm*) [*difunto*] late lamented (*frm*); [*muerte*] lamented (*frm*)

llorar /1a/ **Ⓐ** VI **1** (= *derramar lágrimas*) to cry, weep (*liter*); **¡no llores!** don't cry!; **me dieron o me entraron ganas de ~** I felt like crying; **se puso a ~ desconsoladamente** she began to cry o weep (*liter*) inconsolably; **~ de** [+ *alegría, risa*] to cry with; **echarse a ~** to start to cry; **hacer ~ a algn** to make sb cry; **~ por algo/algn** to cry over sth/sb; ✦ MODISMO **~ a mares** o **a moco tendido** to cry one's eyes out
2 [*ojos*] to water; **me lloran los ojos** my eyes are watering
3 (= *rogar*) **~ a algn** to moan to sb
4 (*Chi**) (= *favorecer*): **a ti te llora el rojo** you look good in red, red looks good on you
Ⓑ VT **1** [+ *lágrimas*] to weep, cry; ✦ MODISMO **~ lágrimas de cocodrilo** to weep crocodile tears
2 (*liter*) (= *lamentar*) [+ *difunto*] to mourn; [+ *muerte*] to mourn, lament; [+ *desgracia*] to bemoan

llorera* SF fit of crying; **una buena ~** a good cry

llorica* (*Esp*) **Ⓐ** ADJ **no seas ~** don't be such a crybaby*
Ⓑ SMF crybaby*

lloriquear /1a/ VI to snivel, whimper

lloro SM crying, weeping, tears *pl*

llorón/ona **Ⓐ** ADJ **1** (= *que llora*): **era muy ~ de pequeño** he was a real crybaby when he was little*; **es una mujer muy llorona** she cries very easily **2** (= *quejica*): **no seas tan ~** don't be such a moaner o whinger* **Ⓑ** SM/F **1** (= *persona que llora*) crybaby* **2** (= *quejica*) moaner*, whinger*

llorona SF (*Méx*) spectre of a wailing woman who wanders the streets

lloroso ADJ [*tono, voz*] tearful; [*ojos*] watery

llovedera SF (*Col, Ven*) (period of) continuous rain

llover /2h/ VI **1** (*Meteo*) to rain; **está lloviendo** it is raining; ✦ MODISMOS **~ a cántaros** to rain cats and dogs, pour (down); **llueve sobre mojado** it's just one thing after another; **ya ha llovido desde entonces** ◇ **ha llovido mucho**

desde entonces a lot of water has flowed under the bridge since then; **nunca llueve a gusto de todos** you can't please everybody; **llueva o truene** rain or shine, come what may
2 **~le algo a algn**: **le llovieron regalos encima** he was showered with gifts

llovida SF (*LAm*) rain, shower

llovizna /1a/ VI to drizzle

lluvia SF **1** (*Meteo*) rain; (= *cantidad*) rainfall; **día de ~** rainy day; **la ~ caída en enero** the rainfall in January, the January rainfall ➤ **lluvia ácida** acid rain ➤ **lluvia radiactiva** (radioactive) fallout **2** (= *abundancia*) [*de balas, misiles*] hail; [*de insultos*] stream, barrage; [*de regalos*] shower; [*de infortunios*] string

lluvioso ADJ rainy, wet

lo¹ ART DEF **1** (*con adjetivos*) **1.1** **el gusto por lo bello** a taste for beautiful things; **no me gusta lo picante** I don't like spicy things; **subimos a lo más alto del edificio** we went right to the top of the building; **lo difícil fue convencerla** the difficult part was convincing her; **yo defiendo lo mío** I defend what is mine; **la física no es lo mío** physics isn't my thing; **en vista de lo ocurrido** in view of what has happened; **sufre lo indecible** she suffers terribly; **es de lo mejor que hay en el mercado** it's among the best you can get; **lo mejor/peor de la obra** the best/worst thing about the play **1.2** (*referido a un estilo*) **construido a lo campesino** built in the peasant style; **un peinado a lo afro** an afro hairstyle **1.3** (*con valor enfático*) **no saben lo aburrido que es** they don't know how boring it is; **sabes lo mucho que me gusta** you know (just) how much I like it
2 **lo de**: **olvida lo de ayer** forget what happened yesterday, forget about yesterday; **lo de siempre** the usual; **lo de la boda** the business about the wedding; **fui (a) lo de Pablo** (*RPl*) (= *a casa de*) I went to Pablo's place
3 **lo que** **3.1** (*relativo*) what; **lo que más me gusta** what I like most; **lo que digo es ...** what I say is ...; **repito lo que he dicho antes** I repeat what I said earlier; **toma lo que quieras** take what o whatever you want; **lo que es eso ...** as for that ...; **en lo que a mi concierne** as far as I'm concerned; **cuesta más de lo que crees** it costs more than you think; **lo que pasa es que ...** the thing is ...; **lo que sea** whatever **3.2** (*con valor intensificador*) **¡lo que has tardado!** how long you've taken!, you've taken so long!; **es lo que se dice feo** he's undeniably ugly **3.3** **a lo que** (*LAm*) (= *en cuanto*) as soon as

lo² PRON PERS **1** (*refiriéndose a él*) him; **no lo conozco** I don't know him; **lo han despedido** he's been sacked
2 (*refiriéndose a usted*) you; **yo a usted lo conozco** I know you
3 (*refiriéndose a una cosa, un animal*) it; **no lo veo** I can't see it; **voy a pensarlo** I'll think about it; **¿el té lo tomas con leche?** do you take milk in your tea?; **lo sé** I know
4 (*referido a un estado, cualidad*) **no parece lista pero lo es** she doesn't seem clever but she is; **guapa sí que lo es** she's certainly pretty; **—¿estás cansado? —sí, lo estoy** "are you tired?" — "yes, I am"

En frases como "No lo sabía", "Se lo diré", este **lo**, que funciona como objeto directo o atributo y sustituye a un concepto o un hecho, no suele traducirse en inglés: *I didn't know, I'll tell him.*

loa SF praise

loable ADV praiseworthy, laudable, commendable

loar /1a/ VT to praise

lobezno/a SM/F wolf cub

lobo/a **Ⓐ** SM/F (= *animal*) wolf ➤ **lobo de mar** old salt, sea dog; (*Chi*) seal ➤ **lobo marino** seal **Ⓑ** ADJ (*) **1** (*Chi*) (= *huraño*) shy **2** (*Col*) (= *de mal gusto*) tacky*

lobotomía SF lobotomy

lóbrego ADJ dark, gloomy

lóbulo SM lobe

loca** SF (= *homosexual*) queen**; *ver tb* **loco**

local **Ⓐ** ADJ [*cultura, producción*] local; [*equipo*] home *antes de s* **Ⓑ** SM [*de negocio*] premises *pl* ➤ **local comercial** (*para oficina*) business premises *pl*; (*para tienda*) shop unit

localidad SF **1** (= *pueblo*) town, place, locality (*frm*) **2** (*Teat*) (= *asiento*) seat; (= *entrada*) ticket; **"no hay localidades"** "house full", "sold out"

localizable ADJ **no estaba ~** we couldn't get hold of him

localización SF **1** (= *acción*) **la ~ de la llamada fue cuestión de segundos** it took a matter of seconds to trace the call **2** (*frm*) (= *ubicación*) location

localizado ADJ localized

localizar /1f/ Ⓐ VT **1** (= *encontrar*) to find, locate **2** [+ *llamada telefónica*] to trace **3** (*Med*) to localize Ⓑ VPR [*dolor*] to be localized

locamente ADV madly, wildly

locatario/a SM/F (*LAm*) tenant, lessee

loción SF lotion ➤ **loción capilar** hair restorer ➤ **loción para después del afeitado** aftershave lotion

loco/a Ⓐ ADJ **1** (= *no cuerdo*) mad, crazy; **¿estás ~?** are you mad *o* crazy?; **no seas ~, eso es muy arriesgado** don't be stupid, that's very risky; **una brújula loca** *a compass whose needle no longer points north*; **estaba ~ de alegría** he was mad *o* wild with joy; **estar ~ con algo** (= *preocupado*) to be worried to death about sth; (= *contento*) to be crazy about sth; **estar ~ por algn** to be mad *o* crazy about sb; **anda** *o* **está loca por irse a Inglaterra** she's mad keen to go to England; **tener ~ a algn** to drive sb crazy; **volver ~ a algn** to drive sb mad, drive sb round the bend; **el marisco me vuelve ~** I'm crazy about seafood; **volverse ~** to go insane, go mad; **este caos es para volverse ~** this is absolute chaos; ✦ MODISMOS **estar ~ de atar** *o* **de remate** to be stark raving mad; **estar más ~ que una cabra** to be as mad as a hatter; **no lo hago ni ~*** no way will I do that*; **hacer algo a lo ~** to do sth any old how
2 (= *frenético*) hectic; **un día ~** a really hectic day **3** (*) (= *enorme*) **he tenido una suerte loca** I've been fantastically lucky*
Ⓑ SM/F lunatic, madman/madwoman; **correr como un ~** to run like mad; **gritar como un ~** to shout like a madman, shout one's head off; **hacerse el ~** to act the fool; **ponerse como un ~** to start acting like a madman/madwoman; ✦ MODISMO **cada ~ con su tema** everyone has their own axe to grind
Ⓒ SM (*Chi*) abalone, false abalone; *ver tb* **loca**

locomoción SF **1** (= *desplazamiento*) locomotion **2** (*Chi*) ➤ **locomoción colectiva** public transport (*esp Brit*), public transportation (*esp EEUU*)

locomotor ADJ **1** [*vehículo, aparato*] locomotive **2** (*Anat*) [*sistema, aparato, conducta*] locomotor

locomotora SF **1** (*Ferro*) engine, locomotive ➤ **locomotora de vapor** steam locomotive **2** [*de la economía, del desarrollo*] driving force

locomotriz ADJ *ver* **locomotor**

locro SM (*LAm*) *meat and vegetable stew*

locuacidad SF (*frm*) loquacity (*frm*), talkativeness

locuaz ADJ (*frm*) loquacious (*frm*), talkative

locución SF expression, phrase

locura SF **1** (= *demencia*) madness, insanity; **un ataque de ~** a fit of madness **2** (= *exceso*) **¡qué ~!** it's madness!; **me gusta con ~*** I'm crazy about it*; **precios de ~*** fantastic prices* **3** (= *acto*) **no hagas ~s** don't do anything silly; **es una ~ ir sola** it's madness to go on your own

locutor(a) SM/F (*Radio, TV*) (*entre programas, en anuncios*) announcer; (*TV*) [*de noticias*] newscaster, newsreader (*Brit*); (= *comentarista*) commentator

locutorio SM **1** (*Telec*) telephone box (*Brit*), phone booth (*EEUU*) **2** (*para visitas*) [*de cárcel*] visiting room; (*Rel*) parlour, parlor (*EEUU*)

lodazal SM quagmire, mudhole

lodo SM mud, mire (*liter*)

logaritmo SM logarithm

logia SF **1** [*de masones*] lodge **2** (*Arquit*) loggia

lógica SF logic; ✦ MODISMO **ser de una ~ aplastante** to be blindingly obvious; *ver tb* **lógico**

lógico/a Ⓐ ADJ **1** [*conclusión, razonamiento, planteamiento*]

logical **2** (= *normal*) natural; **como es ~** naturally; **es ~** it's only natural; **es ~ que ...** it stands to reason that ..., it's understandable that ... Ⓑ SM/F logician; *ver tb* **lógica**

login SM login

logística SF logistics *pl*

logístico ADJ logistic

logo SM logo

logopeda SMF speech therapist

logopedia SF speech therapy

logoterapia SF speech therapy

logotipo SM logo

logrado ADJ successful

lograr /1a/ VT [+ *trabajo*] to get, obtain (*frm*); [+ *éxito, victoria*] to achieve; [+ *perfección*] to attain; **~ hacer algo** to manage to do sth, succeed in doing sth; **~ que algn haga algo** to (manage to) get sb to do sth

logro SM achievement, attainment (*frm*)

logroñés ADJ of/from Logroño

loísmo SM *use of "lo" instead of "le" as indirect object*; ⟲ *LEÍSMO, LOÍSMO, LAÍSMO*

loísta Ⓐ ADJ *that uses "lo" instead of "le" as indirect object* Ⓑ SMF *user of "lo" instead of "le"*

lolo/a* SM/F (*Chi*) teenager, teen (*EEUU**)

loma SF hillock, low ridge

lomada SF (*RPl*) = **loma**

lomaje SM (*Chi*) low ridge

lombarda SF red cabbage

lombriz SF [*de tierra*] worm, earthworm; [*del intestino*] worm

lomo SM **1** [*de cerdo*] loin ➤ **lomo embuchado** (*Esp*) cured loin of pork **2** (*Anat*) back; **iba a ~s de una mula** he was riding a mule ➤ **lomo de burro** (*RPl**), **lomo de toro** (*Chi*) speed hump, speed ramp **3** [*de libro*] spine; [*de cuchillo*] back, blunt edge

lona SF (= *tejido*) canvas; **la ~** (*Dep*) the canvas, the ring

loncha SF (*gen*) slice; [*de bacón*] slice, rasher (*Brit*)

lonche SM (*Perú*) (= *merienda*) tea, afternoon snack

lonchera SF (*LAm*) lunch box

lonchería SF (*LAm*) snack bar, diner (*EEUU*)

londinense Ⓐ ADJ London *antes de s* Ⓑ SMF Londoner

Londres SM London

loneta SF sailcloth

longaniza SF long pork sausage

longevo ADJ long-lived

longitud SF **1** (= *largo*) length; **salto de ~** (*Dep*) long jump ➤ **longitud de onda** wavelength **2** (*Geog*) longitude

longitudinal ADJ longitudinal

lonja¹ SF **1** (= *loncha*) slice; [*de tocino*] slice, rasher (*Brit*) **2** (*RPl*) (= *cuero*) strip of leather

lonja² SF (*Esp*) market, exchange ➤ **lonja de pescado** fish market

lontananza SF **en ~** far away, in the distance

loor SM (*liter*) praise

loquear /1a/ VI (*LAm*) to lark about*, have a high old time*

loquera* SF (*Col, Ven*) **le dio la ~** he went crazy

loquero¹/a* SM/F psychiatric nurse

loquero²* SM madhouse

lord [lor] SM (*pl* **lores**) lord

loro SM **1** (= *ave*) parrot **2** (**) (= *radio*) radio; (= *radiocasete*) radio-cassette; ✦ MODISMO **estar al ~** (*Esp***) (= *alerta*) to be on the alert; (= *informado*) to know the score*; **está al ~ de lo que pasa** he's in touch with what's going on; **¡al ~!** watch out! **3** (= *charlatán*) chatterbox* **4** (*) (= *mujer fea*) old bag*, old bat*

los¹/las¹ ART DEF MPL/FPL the; **las sillas que compramos** the chairs we bought; **mis libros y ~ de usted** my books and yours; **las de Juan son verdes** Juan's are green; *ver tb* **el**

los²/las² PRON PERS (*refiriéndose a ellos, ellas*) them; (*refiriéndose a ustedes*) you; **no te ~ lleves** don't take them away; **señoras, yo las guiaré hasta la salida** ladies, I'll show you the way out; **~ hay y muy buenos** there are some and very good they are too

losa SF (*en el suelo*) (stone) slab, flagstone; (*en un sepulcro*) gravestone, tombstone ➤ **losa radiante** (*Arg*) underfloor heating

loseta SF floor tile

lote SM **1** (*de reparto*) portion, share **2** (*en subasta*) lot **3** (*Inform*) batch **4** (*LAm*) (= *solar*) lot, piece of land, building site **5** ✦ MODISMO **darse** o **pegarse el ~ con algn** (*Esp**) to make it with sb**

lotear /1a/ VT (*esp CS*) to divide into lots

loteo SM (*esp CS*) division into lots

lotería SF lottery; **jugar a la ~** to play the lottery; **le tocó la ~** (= *ganar*) he won the big prize in the lottery; (*fig*) he struck lucky ➤ **lotería primitiva** (*Esp*) *weekly state-run lottery*; ⋄ **EL GORDO**

lotero/a SM/F seller of lottery tickets

lotificación SF (*CAm, Méx, Perú*) division into lots

lotificar /1g/ VT (*CAm, Méx, Perú*) to divide into lots

loto¹ SM lotus

loto²* SF (*Esp*) lottery

loza SF **1** (= *vajilla*) crockery **2** (*fina*) china, chinaware

lozanía SF **1** (*Bot*) freshness **2** [*de persona*] healthiness **3** [*de rostro, mejillas*] freshness

lozano ADJ (*Bot*) fresh; [*persona, animal*] healthy-looking

LSD SM ABR (= **lysergic acid diethylamide**) LSD

lubina SF sea bass

lubricación SF lubrication

lubricante Ⓐ ADJ lubricant, lubricating Ⓑ SM lubricant

lubricar /1g/ VT to lubricate

lubrificar /1f/ VT = **lubricar**

lucas* ADJ INV (*Méx*) crazy, cracked*

lucense ADJ of/from Lugo

lucernario SM skylight

lucero SM (*Astron*) bright star ➤ **lucero del alba, lucero de la mañana** morning star

lucha SF **1** (= *combate*) fight; (= *esfuerzo*) struggle (**por** for); **la ~ contra la droga** the fight against drugs; **la ~ por la supervivencia** the fight o struggle for survival; **esta vida es una ~** life is a struggle; **abandonar la ~** to give up the struggle ➤ **lucha armada** armed struggle ➤ **lucha de clases** class struggle **2** (*Dep*) ➤ **lucha grecorromana, lucha libre** wrestling

luchador(a) Ⓐ ADJ combative Ⓑ SM/F (= *combatiente*) fighter; (*Dep*) wrestler

luchar /1a/ VI **1** (= *combatir*) to fight; (= *esforzarse*) to struggle (**por algo** for sth); **luchó en el bando republicano** he fought on the Republican side; **tuvo que ~ mucho en la vida** life was a constant struggle for her; **~ con** o **contra algo/algn** to fight (against) sth/sb **2** (*Dep*) to wrestle (**con** with)

luche SM (*Chi*) **1** (= *juego*) hopscotch **2** (*Bot*) *edible seaweed*

lucidez SF **1** (= *perspicacia*) lucidity, clarity **2** (*tb* **~ mental**) lucidity

lucido ADJ splendid, magnificent; **una actuación muy lucida** a splendid o magnificent o stunning performance

lúcido ADJ lucid

luciérnaga SF glow-worm

lucimiento SM brilliance, sparkle; **hacer algo con ~** to do sth outstandingly well o very successfully

lucio SM pike

lucir /3f/ Ⓐ VI **1** (= *brillar*) [*estrella*] to shine **2** (= *destacar*) [*persona*] to excel; **no lucía en los estudios** he did not excel as a student **3** (= *aprovechar*) **trabaja mucho, pero no le luce el esfuerzo** he works hard but it doesn't get him very far **4** (*LAm*) (= *parecer*) to look, seem; **(te) luce lindo** it looks

nice (on you) Ⓑ VT (= *ostentar*) to show off; [+ *ropa*] to sport; **lucía un traje nuevo** he was sporting a new suit Ⓒ **lucirse** VPR **1** (= *destacar*) to excel; **Carlos se lució en el examen** Carlos excelled in the exam **2** (= *hacer el ridículo*) (*iró*) to excel o.s.; **¡te has lucido!** you've excelled yourself!

lucrarse /1a/ VPR to do well out of a deal; (*pey*) feather one's (own) nest

lucrativo ADJ lucrative, profitable; **organización no lucrativa** non-profitmaking organization

lucro SM profit

lúcuma* SF (*Chi, Perú, Bol*) *variety of eggfruit*

lúdico ADJ ludic (*liter*), playful

ludópata Ⓐ ADJ addicted to gambling Ⓑ SMF compulsive gambler, gambling addict

ludopatía SF compulsive gambling, addiction to gambling

ludoteca SF children's play-centre

luego Ⓐ ADV **1** (*en el tiempo*) **1.1** (*referido al pasado*) then; **¿y ~ qué pasó?** and then what happened?; **vimos una película y ~ fuimos a cenar** we saw a movie and later (on) o then went out for dinner; **~ de** after **1.2** (*referido al futuro*) later (on), afterwards; **te lo dejo pero ~ me lo devuelves** you can borrow it but you have to give me it back later (on) o afterwards; **~ vuelvo** I'll be back later (on); **te veo ~** I'll see you later (on) o then; **¡hasta ~!** bye!, see you!, see you later! **1.3** (*LAm*) (= *pronto*) soon; **lo vamos a saber muy ~** we'll find out really soon; **espéralo que lueguito viene** wait for him, he's coming in a minute; **lueguito se aburre** he gets bored quickly; **luego luego** (*esp Méx**) straight away **2** (*en el espacio*) then; **primero está la cocina y ~ el comedor** the kitchen is first, then the dining room **3** (= *además*) then; **~ tenemos estos otros colores** then we have these other colours **4** (*Méx*) (= *muy cerca*) nearby; **aquí ~** right here **5 desde ~** of course Ⓑ CONJ therefore; **pienso, ~ existo** I think, therefore I am

lugar SM **1** (= *sitio*) place; **es un ~ muy bonito** it is a lovely spot o place; **el ~ del crimen** the scene of the crime; **algún ~** somewhere; ✦ MODISMO **poner las cosas en su ~** to put things straight ➤ **lugar común** cliché, commonplace ➤ **lugar de encuentro** meeting-place **2** (= *posición*) **2.1** (*en lista, carrera, trabajo*) **ocupar el ~ de algn** to take sb's place; **llegó en último ~** he came last; **en primer ~** [*clasificarse*] in first place; **en primer ~, me gustaría agradecer la invitación** first of all o firstly, I would like to thank you for inviting me **2.2** (= *situación*) **yo, en tu ~, no iría** I wouldn't go if I were you; **usted póngase en mi ~** put yourself in my place o shoes; **dejar a algn en buen/mal ~** [*comportamiento*] to reflect well/badly on sb; [*persona*] to make sb look good/bad; **fuera de ~** out of place **2.3 en ~ de** instead of; **¿puedo asistir yo en su ~?** can I go instead? **3** (= *ocasión*) **dar ~ a algo** to give rise to sth, lead to sth; **sin ~ a dudas** without doubt, undoubtedly; **los datos no dejan ~ a dudas** the figures leave no room for doubt; **no ha ~:** **una reacción tan fuerte, francamente no ha ~** there is no need for such a violent response; **—¡protesto! —no ha ~** (*Jur*) "objection!" — "overruled"; **tener ~** to take place, happen, occur; ✦ MODISMO **a como dé o diera ~** (*LAm*) (= *de cualquier manera*) somehow or other, one way or another; (= *a toda costa*) at any cost **4** (= *localidad*) place; **en un ~ de la Mancha ...** somewhere in La Mancha ...; **del ~** local; **un vino del ~** a local wine; **las gentes del ~** the local people, the locals ➤ **lugar de nacimiento** (*gen*) birthplace; (*en impreso*) place of birth ➤ **lugar de trabajo** workplace

lugareño/a ADJ, SM/F local

lugarteniente SM deputy

lúgubre ADJ (= *triste*) mournful, lugubrious (*frm*), dismal; [*voz, tono*] sombre, somber (*EEUU*), mournful

lujo SM **1** (= *fasto*) luxury; **es un ~** it's a luxury; **un coche de ~** a luxury car; **permitirse el ~ de hacer algo** (*gen*) to allow o.s. the luxury of doing sth; (*económicamente*) to afford to do sth ➤ **lujo asiático***: **¿te vas al Caribe? ¡vaya ~ asiático!** so you're off to the Caribbean? what a life of luxury! **2** (= *abundancia*) profusion, wealth, abundance; **con todo ~ de detalles** with a wealth of detail

lujoso ADJ luxurious

lujuria SF lust, lechery, lewdness

lujurioso ADJ lustful, lecherous, lewd

lumbago SM lumbago

lumbar ADJ lumbar

lumbre SF **1** (= *fuego*) fire; **a la ~** near the fire, by the fireside **2** (†) (*para cigarro*) light

lumbrera SF genius

luminaria SF (*Rel*) altar lamp; **luminarias** illuminations, lights

luminosidad SF brightness, luminosity (*frm*)

luminoso Ⓐ ADJ **1** (*gen*) bright, shining; [*letrero*] illuminated; [*esfera, reloj*] luminous **2** [*idea*] bright, brilliant Ⓑ SM (*Com*) neon sign

luminotecnia SF lighting

luminotécnico ADJ lighting *antes de s*

lumpen Ⓐ ADJ INV lumpen; **el Madrid ~** the Madrid underclass Ⓑ SM INV underclass, lumpen

lumpo SM lumpfish

luna SF **1** (= *astro*) moon; **claro de ~** moonlight; **media ~** half moon; ◆ MODISMOS **estar en la ~** to have one's head in the clouds; **estar en la ~ de Valencia** to be in a dream world; **quedarse en la ~ de Paita** (*And**) to be struck dumb ➤ **luna de miel** [*de novios*] honeymoon; (*fig, Pol*) honeymoon (period) ➤ **luna llena** full moon ➤ **luna nueva** new moon **2** (= *vidrio*) (= *escaparate*) plate glass; (= *espejo*) mirror; [*de gafas*] lens; (*Aut*) window; [*de ventana*] pane; [*de puerta*] panel

lunar Ⓐ ADJ lunar Ⓑ SM **1** (*Anat*) mole ➤ **lunar postizo** beauty spot **2** (*en tejido*) polka-dot, spot; **un vestido de ~es** a polka-dot dress

lunático/a ADJ, SM/F lunatic

lunes SM INV

En inglés los días de la semana se escriben con mayúscula.

Monday; ◆ MODISMO **hacer San Lunes** (*LAm**) to stay away from work on Monday; *ver tb* **sábado**

luneta SF **1** [*de gafas*] lens **2** (*Aut*) window **3** (*Arg*) (*para bucear*) goggles *pl*

lunfardo SM (*Arg*) *local slang of Buenos Aires*

lupa SF magnifying glass; ◆ MODISMO **examinar** o **mirar algo con ~** to go over sth with a fine tooth comb

lúpulo SM (*Bot*) hop, hops *pl*

lurio* (*Méx*) ADJ (= *enamorado*) in love; (= *loco*) crazy, cracked*

lusitano ADJ Portuguese; (*Hist*) Lusitanian

luso/a ADJ, SM/F = **lusitano**

lustrabotas SMF INV (*SAm*) bootblack, shoeshine boy/girl

lustrada* SM (*SAm*) (= *acto*) shine, shoeshine

lustrador(a) SM/F (*SAm*) bootblack, shoeshine boy/girl

lustrar /1a/ VT (*esp LAm*) to shine, polish

lustre SM **1** (= *brillo*) shine, lustre, luster (*EEUU*), gloss; **dar ~**

a to polish, put a shine on **2** (= *sustancia*) polish **3** (= *prestigio*) lustre, luster (*EEUU*), glory

lustrín SM (*Chi*) shoeshine box, shoeshine stand

lustro SM period of five years, five year period, lustrum (*frm*)

lustroso ADJ **1** (= *brillante*) [*zapatos*] shiny; [*pelo*] glossy, shiny **2** (= *saludable*) healthy-looking

luterano/a ADJ, SM/F Lutheran

Lutero SM Luther

luto SM mourning; **medio ~** half-mourning; **estar de ~** ◇ **llevar ~** to be in mourning (**por** for) ➤ **luto riguroso** deep mourning

luxación SF (*Med*) dislocation

Luxemburgo SM Luxembourg

luxemburgués/esa Ⓐ ADJ of/from Luxembourg Ⓑ SM/F native/inhabitant of Luxembourg

luz SF **1** (= *claridad*) light; **una casa con mucha ~** a very bright house, a house that gets a lot of light; **a media ~** in half-darkness; **quitar** o **tapar la ~ a algn** to be in sb's light; ◆ MODISMOS **entre dos luces** (= *al atardecer*) at twilight; (= *al amanecer*) at dawn, at daybreak; **tan claro como la ~ del día** as clear as daylight ➤ **luz de (la) luna** moonlight ➤ **luz del sol** sunlight ➤ **luz eléctrica** electric light ➤ **luz natural** natural light ➤ **luz solar** sunlight ➤ **luz y sonido:** **un espectáculo de ~ y sonido** a son et lumière show **2** (= *lámpara, foco*) light; **apagar la ~** to switch o turn o put the light off; **encender** o (*LAm*) **prender** o **poner la ~** to switch o turn o put the light on; ◆ MODISMO **hacer algo con ~ y taquígrafos** (*Esp*) to do sth openly ➤ **luces altas** (*Chi*) full-beam headlights (*Brit*), high beams (*EEUU*) ➤ **luces bajas** (*Chi*), **luces cortas** dipped headlights (*Brit*), low beams (*EEUU*); **poner las luces cortas** to dip one's headlights (*Brit*), dim one's headlights (*EEUU*) ➤ **luces de carretera** full-beam headlights (*Brit*), high beams (*EEUU*); **poner las luces de carretera** to put one's headlights on full (*Brit*) o high (*EEUU*) beam ➤ **luces de cruce** dipped headlights (*Brit*), low beams (*EEUU*); **poner las luces de cruce** to dip one's headlights (*Brit*), dim one's headlights (*EEUU*) ➤ **luces de estacionamiento** parking lights ➤ **luces de freno** brake lights ➤ **luces de posición** sidelights (*Brit*), parking lights (*EEUU*) ➤ **luces largas = luces de carretera** ➤ **luz de giro** (*Arg*) indicator (*esp Brit*), turn signal (*EEUU*) ➤ **luz de lectura** reading light ➤ **luz roja** red light ➤ **luz verde** green light; **dar ~ verde a un proyecto** to give a project the go-ahead o the green light **3** (= *suministro de electricidad*) electricity; **les cortaron la ~** their electricity (supply) was cut off; **se ha ido la ~** the lights have gone out **4** (*tb* **~ pública**) ◆ MODISMOS **sacar a la ~** [+ *secreto*] to bring to light; [+ *libro, disco*] to bring out; **salir a la ~** [*secreto*] to come to light; [*libro, disco*] to come out; **ver la ~** [*libro, disco*] to appear, come out **5** (*Med*) **dar a ~** [+ *niño*] to give birth **6** (= *aclaración*) light; **a la ~ de un nuevo descubrimiento** in the light of a new discovery; **arrojar ~ sobre algo** to cast o shed o throw light on sth; ◆ MODISMO **a todas luces** by any reckoning **7** (*Arquit*) [*de puerta, hueco*] span; [*de edificio*] window, opening **8** (= *inteligencia*) intelligence *sing*; **corto de luces** ◇ **de pocas luces** dim, stupid **9** (*Hist, Literat*) **el Siglo de las Luces** the Age of Enlightenment

lycra® ['likra] SF Lycra®

Mm

M, m ['eme] SF (= *letra*) M, m

maca SF 1 (= *defecto*) flaw, defect 2 (= *mancha*) (*gen*) spot; (*en fruta*) bruise, blemish

macabro ADJ macabre

macaco SM macaque

macadán SM macadam

macana SF 1 (*LAm*) (= *porra*) (*gen*) club, cudgel; [*de policía*] truncheon (*Brit*), billy (club) (*EEUU*) 2 (*And, CS**) (= *mentira*) lie; **¡macana!** it's all lies!; **macanas** (= *tonterías*) nonsense *sing*, rubbish *sing* (*esp Brit**) 3 (*CS**) (= *contrariedad*) pain*, nuisance; **¡qué ~! el ascensor no funciona** what a pain* *o* nuisance! the lift (*Brit*) *o* elevator (*EEUU*) isn't working

macanear* /1a/ **Ⓐ** VI (*esp And, CS*) (= *mentir*) to lie; (= *decir tonterías*) to talk nonsense, talk rubbish (*esp Brit**) **Ⓑ** VT (*Carib*) to beat, hit

macanudo* ADJ (*LAm*) great*, fantastic*

macarra* SM (*Esp*) 1 (= *bruto*) lout, thug; (= *mal vestido*) vulgar flashy type 2 (= *chulo*) pimp

macarrones SMPL macaroni *sing*

macarrónico* ADJ **habla un inglés ~** his English is awful

macedonia SF ➤ **macedonia de frutas** fruit salad

maceración SF [*de fruta*] soaking, maceration; [*de carne*] marinading; **dejar en ~** [+ *fruta*] to leave to soak; [+ *carne*] to marinate

macerar /1a/ **Ⓐ** VT [+ *fruta*] to soak, macerate; [+ *carne*] to marinate **Ⓑ macerarse** VPR [*fruta*] to soak, macerate; [*carne*] to marinate

maceta SF 1 (= *tiesto*) flowerpot, plant pot (*esp Brit*), planter 2 (= *martillo*) mallet, small hammer 3 (*Méx**) (= *cabeza*) nut*, noggin (*EEUU**)

macetero SM 1 (= *soporte*) flowerpot stand, flowerpot holder 2 (*LAm*) (= *maceta*) flowerpot

machacante ADJ [*publicidad*] constant; [*estribillo*] monotonous, insistent

machacar /1g/ **Ⓐ** VT 1 (= *triturar*) to crush 2 (*) (= *aniquilar*) [+ *contrincante*] to thrash; (*en discusión*) to crush, flatten 3 [+ *precio*] to slash 4 (*) [+ *lección, asignatura*] to swot (up)* 5 (*) (= *insistir sobre*) to go on about; **deja ya de ~ siempre lo mismo** stop going on and on about the same thing **Ⓑ** VI 1 (= *insistir*) to go on; **~ con** *o* **sobre algo** to go on about sth 2 (= *estudiar*) to swot* **Ⓒ machacarse** VPR 1 (*) [+ *dinero, herencia, sueldo*] to blow* 2 **machacársela** (*Esp***) to wank***

machacón/ona **Ⓐ** ADJ (= *insistente*) insistent; (= *monótono*) monotonous, repetitive; (= *pesado*) tiresome, wearisome; **con insistencia machacona** with tiresome *o* wearisome insistence **Ⓑ** SM/F pest, bore

machamartillo SM ✦ MODISMO **a ~: eran cristianos a ~** they were staunch Christians; **creer a ~** (= *firmemente*) to believe firmly; (= *ciegamente*) to believe blindly; **cumplir algo a ~** to carry out sth to the letter

machetazo SM (*esp LAm*) blow with a machete

machete **Ⓐ** SM 1 (= *cuchillo*) machete 2 (*Arg, Col*) (*para exámenes*) crib (*Brit**), trot (*EEUU**) **Ⓑ** ADJ (*RPl**) (= *tacaño*) stingy, mean (*esp Brit*)

machetear /1a/ VT (*LAm*) 1 [+ *caña*] to cut (with a machete) 2 [+ *persona*] to slash (with a machete) 3 (*Uru**) (= *escatimar*) to skimp on, be stingy with

machetero SM 1 (*esp LAm Agr*) cane cutter 2 (*Méx*) (= *cargador*) porter, stevedore 3 (*Méx**) (= *estudiante*) plodder*

machi SM (*CS*) medicine man

machihembrado SM dovetail, dovetail joint

machismo SM male chauvinism, machismo

machista **Ⓐ** ADJ male chauvinist(ic), macho *antes de s* **Ⓑ** SMF male chauvinist

macho **Ⓐ** ADJ 1 (*Biol*) male; **la flor ~** the male flower; **una rata ~** a male rat 2 (*) (= *viril*) manly, brave; **se cree muy ~** he thinks he's very macho* 3 (*Mec*) male **Ⓑ** SM 1 (*Biol*) male ➤ **macho cabrío** he-goat, billy-goat 2 (*) (= *hombretón*) macho man*, he-man* 3 (**) (*uso apelativo*) mate (*Brit**), buddy (*esp EEUU**) 4 (*Mec*) male screw; ✦ MODISMO **atarse** *o* **apretarse los ~s** to pluck up one's courage 5 (*Elec*) male plug 6 (*Cos*) hook

machona* SF (*SAm*) (= *niña*) tomboy; (= *mujer*) mannish woman, butch woman (*pey**)

machote/ta* SM/F (= *hombre*) tough guy*, he-man*; (= *mujer*) butch woman (*pey**)

machucar /1g/ VT (= *aplastar*) to crush; (= *golpear*) to beat; (= *dañar*) to knock about, damage; (= *abollar*) to dent

machucón SM (*LAm*) bruise

macilento ADJ (= *pálido*) wan, pale; (= *demacrado*) haggard, gaunt

macillo SM (*Mús*) hammer

macizo **Ⓐ** ADJ 1 (= *no hueco*) solid; **una mesa de roble ~** a solid oak table 2 (= *fuerte*) [*objeto*] solidly made; [*persona*] stout, well-built 3 (*Esp**) (= *atractivo*) gorgeous*; **está maciza** she's gorgeous* **Ⓑ** SM 1 (*Geog*) massif 2 [*de plantas*] clump 3 (*Arquit*) stretch, section (*of a wall*)

macramé SM macramé

macro SF (*Inform*) macro

macrobiótico ADJ macrobiotic

macroconcierto SM mega-gig*

macrocosmos SM INV macrocosm

macroeconomía SF macroeconomics *sing*

macroeconómico ADJ macroeconomic

macroestructura SF macrostructure

macroproyecto SM large-scale project

macuco* ADJ (*And*) crafty, cunning

mácula SF 1 (*liter*) (= *mancha*) blemish, stain; **sin ~** [*objeto*] immaculate; [*interpretación, actuación*] faultless; [*historial, pasado*] unblemished 2 (*Anat*) blind spot 3 (*Astron*) (*tb ~ solar*) sunspot

macuto SM [*de soldado*] backpack; [*de colegial*] satchel

madama SF **madame** SF madam, brothel keeper

madeja SF [*de lana*] skein, hank; [*de pelo*] tangle, mop; **una ~ de nervios** a bundle of nerves; ✦ MODISMOS **desenredar la ~ de algo** to get to the bottom of sth; **se está enredando la ~** the plot thickens, things are getting complicated; **tirar de la ~** to put two and two together

madera SF 1 (= *material*) (*gen*) wood; (*para la construcción, carpintería*) timber; **dame esa ~** give me that piece of wood; **una silla de ~** a wooden chair; **una escultura en ~** a wooden sculpture; ✦ MODISMO **¡toca ~!** touch wood! (*Brit*), knock on wood! (*EEUU*) ➤ **madera contrachapada** plywood ➤ **madera dura** hardwood ➤ **madera maciza** solid wood ➤ **madera (multi)laminada** plywood 2 **tener ~ de algo** to have the makings of sth; **tiene ~ de torero** he's got the makings of a bullfighter 3 (*Mús*) woodwind section (*of the orchestra*)

maderero/a **Ⓐ** SM/F timber merchant **Ⓑ** ADJ wood *antes de s*, timber *antes de s*; **industria maderera** timber industry

madero SM 1 [*de construcción*] (= *tabla*) (piece of) timber; (= *viga*) beam; (= *tronco*) log 2 (*Náut*) ship, vessel 3 (*Esp***) (= *policía*) cop*, pig**

madrastra SF stepmother

madraza SF doting mother, devoted mother

madrazo* SM (*Méx*) hard blow

madre **Ⓐ** SF 1 (= *pariente*) mother; **ser ~** to be a mother; **futura ~** mother-to-be; **sin ~** motherless; **¡~ mía!** good heavens! ➤ **madre adoptiva** adoptive mother ➤ **madre biológica** biological mother ➤ **madre de alquiler** surrogate mother ➤ **la Madre Patria** the Mother Country, the Old

Country ➤ **madre política** mother-in-law ➤ **madre soltera** single mother, unmarried mother
2 (*Rel*) (*en convento*) mother; (*en asilo*) matron ➤ **madre superiora** Mother Superior
3 ✦ MODISMOS **como su ~ lo trajo al mundo** o **lo parió*** in his birthday suit*, starkers*; **ciento y la ~*** hundreds of people; **ahí está la ~ del cordero*** that's just the trouble, that's the crux of the matter; **mentarle la ~ a algn** to insult sb (*violently*); **¡(me cago en) la ~ que te parió!***** you fucking bastard!***; **¡tu ~!***** up yours!***, get stuffed!***
4 (= *origen*) origin, cradle
5 [*de río*] bed; **salirse de ~** [*río*] to burst its banks; [*persona*] to lose all self-control; [*proceso*] to go beyond its normal limits; ✦ MODISMO **sacar de ~ a algn** to upset sb
6 [*de vino*] dregs *pl*, sediment
Ⓑ ADJ **acequia ~** main channel; **lengua ~** (*Ling*) parent language

madreperla SF (= *nácar*) mother-of-pearl; (= *ostra*) pearl oyster

madreselva SF honeysuckle

Madrid SM Madrid; *see also* www.madrid.org

madridista ADJ *of or relating to Real Madrid football club*

madrigal SM madrigal

madriguera SF **1** [*de animales*] den, burrow; [*de conejos*] warren; [*de tejones*] set **2** [*de ladrones*] den

madrileño ADJ of/from Madrid

madrina SF [*de bautizo*] godmother; [*de boda*] ≈ matron of honour; [*de asociación, inauguración*] patron, patroness

madriza** SF (*Méx*) bashing*, beating-up*

madroño SM **1** (*Bot*) strawberry tree, arbutus **2** (= *borla*) tassel

madrugada SF (= *noche*) early morning, small hours *pl*; (= *alba*) dawn, daybreak; **de ~** in the small hours; **levantarse de ~** to get up early o at the crack of dawn; **a las cuatro de la ~** at four o'clock in the morning, at four a.m.

madrugador(a) **Ⓐ** ADJ **ser ~** to be an early riser **Ⓑ** SM/F early riser

madrugar /1h/ VI (*una vez*) to get up early, get up at the crack of dawn; (*por costumbre*) to be an early riser; ✦ REFRANES **a quien madruga, Dios le ayuda** the early bird catches the worm; **no por mucho ~ amanece más temprano** time will take its course

madrugón* SM **darse** o **pegarse un ~** to get up really early o at the crack of dawn

maduración SF [*de fruta*] ripening; [*de persona, idea*] maturing

madurar /1a/ **Ⓐ** VI **1** [*fruta*] to ripen **2** [*persona*] to mature **Ⓑ** VT **1** [+ *fruta*] to ripen **2** [+ *persona*] (= *hacer mayor*) to mature; (= *hacer fuerte*) to toughen, toughen up **3** [+ *idea, plan*] to think out **Ⓒ madurarse** VPR to ripen

madurez SF **1** [*de fruta*] ripeness **2** [*de carácter, edad*] maturity

maduro **Ⓐ** ADJ **1** [*fruta*] ripe; **poco ~** underripe **2** [*persona, carácter*] mature; **de edad madura** middle-aged **Ⓑ** SM (*Col*) plantain

maestranza SF **1** (*Mil*) arsenal, armoury, armory (*EEUU*) **2** (*Náut*) naval dockyard **3** (= *personal*) staff of an arsenal/a dockyard

maestrazgo SM (*Hist*) office of grand master

maestre SM (*Hist*) grand master (*of a military order*)

maestría SF **1** [*de persona*] (= *dominio*) mastery; (= *habilidad*) skill, expertise **2** (*LAm Univ*) master's degree **3** (*Esp Educ*) vocational qualification

maestro/a **Ⓐ** SM/F **1** (= *profesor*) teacher ➤ **maestro/a de escuela** schoolteacher
2 (*en un arte, un oficio*) master ➤ **maestro/a albañil** master mason ➤ **maestro/a de ceremonias** master of ceremonies ➤ **maestro/a de obras** foreman
Ⓑ SM **1** (= *autoridad*) authority; **beber en los grandes ~s** to absorb wisdom from the great teachers
2 (*Mús*) maestro; **el ~ Falla** the great musician o composer Falla; **¡música, ~!** music, maestro!
3 (*Ajedrez*) master

Ⓒ ADJ (= *principal*) main; **llave maestra** master key, pass key; **viga maestra** main beam

mafia SF mafia; **la Mafia** the Mafia

mafioso/a **Ⓐ** ADJ Mafia *antes de s* **Ⓑ** SM/F (= *de la Mafia*) mafioso, member of the Mafia; (= *criminal*) gangster, mobster (*EEUU*)

magazine [maga'sin] SM (*TV*) magazine

Magdalena SF **La ~** Mary Magdalene; ✦ MODISMO **llorar como una ~** to cry one's eyes out

magdalena SF (*Culin*) fairy cake

magenta SF magenta

magia SF magic; **por arte de ~** (as if) by magic ➤ **magia negra** black magic

mágico ADJ **1** [*alfombra, fórmula, palabras*] magic; [*poderes, propiedades*] magical **2** (= *especial*) magical

---

El adjetivo **mágico** se traduce por **magic** al hablar de algo relacionado con la magia: "Dijo las tres palabras mágicas", *He said the three magic words.* En cambio, al describir cualidades o acontecimientos sobrenaturales, **mágico** se traduce por **magical**: "Creían que el hierro tenía propiedades mágicas", *Iron was believed to have magical powers.* También se usa **magical** para indicar que algo o alguien tiene un encanto especial: "Fue una noche mágica", *It was a magical evening.*

---

magisterio SM **1** (= *enseñanza*) teaching; (= *profesión*) teaching, teaching profession; (= *formación*) teacher training (*Brit*), teacher education (*EEUU*); (= *maestros*) teachers *pl*; **dedicarse al ~** to go in for teaching; **ejerció el ~ durante 40 años** she taught o was a teacher for 40 years **2** (= *maestría*) mastery

magistrado/a SM/F magistrate, judge

magistral ADJ **1** (= *genial*) [*actuación, obra*] masterly **2** [*actitud, tono*] (*gen*) magisterial; (*pey*) pompous, pedantic

magistratura SF (= *cargo*) magistracy, judgeship; (= *jueces*) judges *pl*, magistracy; **alta ~** highest authority ➤ **Magistratura de trabajo** employment tribunal

magma SM magma

magnánimo ADJ magnanimous

magnate SMF tycoon, magnate; **un ~ de la prensa** a press baron

magnavoz SM (*Méx*) megaphone

magnesia SF magnesia

magnesio SM magnesium

magnético ADJ (*lit, fig*) magnetic

magnetismo SM (*lit, fig*) magnetism

magnetofón SM, **magnetófono** SM tape recorder

magnetofónico ADJ **cinta magnetofónica** recording tape

magnicidio SM assassination (*of an important person*)

magnificar /1g/ VT **1** (= *exagerar*) to exaggerate, blow up out of all proportion **2** (= *alabar*) to praise, extol

magnificencia SF magnificence, splendour, splendor (*EEUU*)

magnífico ADJ magnificent, wonderful; **es un jugador ~** he's a magnificent o wonderful player; **¡magnífico!** excellent!, splendid!; **rector ~** (*Esp Univ*) honourable Chancellor, honorable Chancellor (*EEUU*)

magnitud SF magnitude; **de primera ~** (*Astron*) first-magnitude; (*fig*) first-rate *antes de s*, of the first order; **un problema de gran ~** a major problem

magno ADJ (*liter*) great

magnolia SF magnolia

mago/a SM/F **1** (= *prestidigitador*) magician **2** (*en cuentos*) magician, wizard/sorceress; **los Reyes Magos** the Three Wise Men, the Magi (*frm*)

magrear** /1a/ VT (*Esp*) to touch up*, grope*

magrebí ADJ, SMF Maghrebi

magreo** SM (*Esp*) touching up*, groping*

magro Ⓐ ADJ **1** (= *sin grasa*) [*carne*] lean **2** (= *escaso*) meagre, meager (*EEUU*) **3** (*frm*) (= *flaco*) [*persona*] skinny **4** (*liter*) [*tierra*] poor Ⓑ SM loin

magulladura SF bruise

magullar /1a/ Ⓐ VT (= *amoratar*) to bruise; (= *dañar*) to hurt, damage; (= *golpear*) to batter, bash* Ⓑ **magullarse** VPR (= *hacerse un moratón*) to get bruised; (= *hacerse daño*) to get hurt

magullón (*LAm*) SM bruise

maharajá SM maharajah

Mahoma SM Mohammed, Mahomet

mahometano/a ADJ, SM/F Muslim

mahometismo SM Islam

mahonesa SF mayonnaise

maicena SF cornflour (*Brit*), cornstarch (*EEUU*)

mail* SM email

mailing ['mailin] SM (*pl* ~s ['mailin]) mailshot; **hacer un ~** to do a mailshot ➤ **mailing electoral** postal canvassing

maillot [mai'jot] SM (*Dep*) jersey; **el ~ amarillo** the yellow jersey

maitines SMPL matins

maître ['metre] SM head waiter

maíz SM (= *cereal*) maize (*Brit*), corn (*EEUU*); (= *alimento*) sweetcorn ➤ **maíz palomero** (*Méx*) popcorn

maizal SM maize field (*Brit*), cornfield (*EEUU*)

maizena® SF cornflour (*Brit*), cornstarch (*EEUU*)

majada SF **1** (= *corral*) sheep pen **2** (= *estiércol*) dung **3** (*CS*) [*de ovejas*] flock; [*de cabras*] herd

majadería* SF absurdity; **decir ~s** to talk nonsense; **hacer ~s** to be silly

majadero/a* Ⓐ ADJ silly, stupid Ⓑ SM/F idiot, fool

majador SM pestle

majar /1a/ VT to pound, crush; (*Med*) to bruise

majara* (*Esp*), **majareta*** (*Esp*) Ⓐ ADJ nuts*, crackers* Ⓑ SM/F nutter*

maje* ADJ (*Méx*) gullible

majestad SF majesty; **(Vuestra) Majestad** Your Majesty

majestuosidad SF majesty

majestuoso ADJ majestic

majete* (*Esp*) Ⓐ ADJ nice Ⓑ SM guy*, bloke*; **tranquilo, ~** relax, man*

majo/a Ⓐ ADJ (*Esp**) **1** [*persona*] (= *agradable*) nice; (= *guapo*) attractive, good-looking **2** [*cosa*] nice **3** (*uso apelativo*) ¡**hola maja! ¿qué tal te va?** hello, love! how's things?; ¡**oye, majo!, ¡haz el favor de callarte!** do me a favour will you, just shut up? Ⓑ SM/F (*Hist*) *inhabitant of the working-class neighbourhoods of Madrid in the 18th and 19th centuries*

majuelo SM **1** (= *vid*) young vine **2** (= *espino*) hawthorn

mal Ⓐ ADV **1** (= *imperfectamente*) badly; **está muy ~ escrito** it's very badly written; **me entendió ~** he misunderstood me; **oigo/veo ~** I can't hear/see well; **si ~ no recuerdo** if my memory serves me right, if I remember correctly **2** (= *de forma reprobable*) **se portó muy ~ con su mejor amiga** she behaved very badly towards her best friend **3** (= *insuficientemente*) **la habitación estaba ~ iluminada** the room was poorly lit; **sus hijos estaban ~ alimentados** her children were underfed; **un trabajo ~ pagado** a badly paid job **4** (= *sin salud*) ill; **su padre está bastante ~** her father's pretty ill *o* sick; **encontrarse** *o* **sentirse ~** to feel ill **5** (= *desagradablemente*) **lo pasé muy ~ en la fiesta** I had a very bad time at the party; ¡**no está ~ este vino!** this wine isn't bad!; **no estaría ~ ir mañana de excursión** I wouldn't mind going on a trip tomorrow; **caer ~: algn: me cae ~ su amigo** I don't like his friend; **decir** *o* **hablar ~ de algn** to speak ill of sb; **llevarse ~: me llevo ~ con él** I don't get on with him; **los dos hermanos se llevan muy ~** the two brothers don't get on at all; **oler ~: esta habitación huele ~** this room smells (bad); **pensar ~ de algn** to think badly of sb; **saber ~** it doesn't taste nice

6 (*otras locuciones*) **estar a ~ con algn** to be on bad terms with sb; ¡**menos ~!** thank goodness!; **menos ~ que ...** it's just as well (that) ..., it's a good job (that) ...; **ir de ~ en peor** to go from bad to worse; **~ que bien** more or less, just about; **~ que bien lo hemos solucionado** we've more or less *o* just about managed to solve it; **~ que bien vamos tirando** we're just about managing to get by; **tomarse algo (a) ~** to take sth the wrong way
Ⓑ CONJ **~ que le pese** whether he likes it or not
Ⓒ ADJ *ver* **malo A**
Ⓓ SM **1** (= *maldad*) **el bien y el ~** good and evil; **combatir el ~** (*frm*) to fight against evil **2** (= *perjuicio*) harm; **no le deseo ningún ~** I don't wish him any harm *o* ill; **hacer ~ a algn** to do sb harm; **el ~ ya está hecho** the harm *o* damage is done now; **un ~ menor** the lesser of two evils; ✦ REFRANES **no hay ~ que por bien no venga** it's an ill wind that blows nobody any good; **~ de muchos consuelo de tontos** that's no consolation **3** (= *problema*) ill; **los ~es de la economía** the ills afflicting the economy **4** (*Med*) disease, illness ➤ **mal de altura** altitude sickness ➤ **mal de amores** lovesickness; **sufre ~ de amores** she's lovesick **5** ➤ **mal de ojo** evil eye; **le echaron (el) ~ de ojo** they gave him the evil eye

malabar ADJ **juegos ~es** juggling *sing*

malbaratar /1a/ VT (= *malvender*) to sell off cheap, sell at a loss; (= *malgastar*) to squander

malabarismo SM juggling; **hacer ~s** (*lit*) to juggle; (*fig*) to do a balancing act

malabarista SMF juggler

malacate SM **1** (= *torno*) winch, capstan **2** (*CAm*) (= *huso*) spindle

malaconsejado ADJ ill-advised

malacostumbrado ADJ **1** (= *de malos hábitos*) given to bad habits **2** (= *consentido*) spoiled, pampered

malacostumbrar /1a/ VT **~ a algn** (*gen*) to get sb into bad habits; (= *consentir*) to spoil sb

malacrianza SF (*LAm*) rudeness

malagradecido ADJ ungrateful

malagueño ADJ of/from Málaga

Malaisia SF Malaysia

malaisio/a ADJ, SM/F Malaysian

malaleche* * ADJ nasty, horrible

malamente* ADV **1** (= *mal*) badly **2** (= *difícilmente*) hardly

malandrín/ina SM/F (*hum o liter*) scoundrel, rogue

malaria SF malaria

Malasia SF Malaysia

malasio/a ADJ, SM/F Malaysian

malaúva* ADJ mean, miserable

malavenido ADJ **estar ~s** to be in disagreement *o* in conflict; **una pareja malavenida** an unsuited *o* incompatible couple

Malawi SM Malawi

malayo/a Ⓐ ADJ Malay, Malayan Ⓑ SM/F Malay Ⓒ SM (*Ling*) Malay

malcomer /2a/ VI to eat badly

malcriado ADJ (= *grosero*) bad-mannered, rude; (= *consentido*) spoiled, pampered

malcriar /1c/ VT to spoil, pamper

maldad SF **1** (= *cualidad*) evil, wickedness **2 una ~** a wicked thing

maldecir /3o/ Ⓐ VT to curse; **maldecía mi mala suerte** I cursed my bad luck Ⓑ VI to curse; **~ de algn/algo** (= *hablar mal*) to speak ill of sb/sth; (= *quejarse*) to complain bitterly about sb/sth

maldiciendo *etc ver* **maldecir**

maldición SF curse; **la ~ de la bruja** the witch's curse; ¡**maldición!** damn!, curse it!

maldiga *etc ver* **maldecir**

maldito Ⓐ ADJ **1** (= *condenado*) damned; **poeta ~** accursed poet **2** (*Rel*) accursed **3** (*) (*uso enfático*) damn*; **¡maldita sea!** damn it!*; **ese ~ libro** that damn book*; **ese ~ niño** that wretched child; **¡~ el día en que lo conocí!** curse the day I met him!; **¡malditas las ganas que tengo de verlo!** I really don't feel like seeing him! **4** (= *maligno*) wicked Ⓑ SM **el ~** (*Rel*) the Evil One, the Devil

maleable ADJ malleable

maleante SMF crook, villain

malear /1a/ Ⓐ VT to corrupt, pervert Ⓑ **malearse** VPR to be corrupted

malecón SM **1** (= *muelle*) pier, jetty **2** (*Carib*, *SAm*) (= *paseo*) seafront

maledicencia SF slander, scandal

maledicente ADJ slanderous, scandalous

maleducado ADJ bad-mannered, rude

maleducar /1g/ VT to spoil

maleficio SM **1** (= *hechizo*) curse, spell **2** (= *brujería*) witchcraft

maléfico ADJ evil

malentendido SM misunderstanding

malestar SM **1** (= *incomodidad*) discomfort; **un ~ generalizado** a general feeling of discomfort; **el medicamento le produjo ~ en el estómago** the medicine upset his stomach **2** (= *inquietud*) unease; **su conducta le causó un profundo ~** his behaviour disturbed her deeply **3** (= *descontento*) discontent

maleta Ⓐ SF **1** (*para equipaje*) case, suitcase; **hacer la(s) ~(s)** (*lit*) to pack; (*fig*) to pack one's bags; **ya puede ir preparando las ~s** he's on his way out, he can start packing his bags **2** (*Aut*) boot (*Brit*), trunk (*EEUU*) Ⓑ SMF (*) (*gen*) dead loss*; (*Taur*) clumsy beginner; (*Dep*) useless player

maletera SF (*Perú*) boot (*Brit*), trunk (*EEUU*)

maletero SM **1** (*Aut*) boot (*Brit*), trunk (*EEUU*) **2** (= *mozo*) porter

maletilla SMF (*Taur*) *aspiring bullfighter*

maletín SM (= *maleta*) small case; (= *portafolios*) briefcase, attaché case; [*de colegial*] satchel; [*de médico*] bag

malevolencia SF malevolence, spite

malévolo ADJ, **malevolente** ADJ malevolent, malicious

maleza SF **1** (= *malas hierbas*) weeds *pl* **2** (= *espesura*) [*de matas*] undergrowth (*Brit*), underbrush (*EEUU*); [*de zarza*] thicket; [*de broza*] brushwood; **fueron abriéndose camino entre la ~** they gradually beat a path through the undergrowth

malformación SF malformation

malformado ADJ malformed

malgastar /1a/ VT [+ *tiempo, esfuerzo*] to waste; [+ *recursos, dinero*] to squander, waste

malhablado/a Ⓐ ADJ foul-mouthed Ⓑ SM/F **es un ~** he has a foul mouth (on him), he's so foul-mouthed

malhechor(a) SM/F delinquent, criminal; **banda de ~es** bunch of delinquents

malherido ADJ badly injured, seriously injured

malhumorado ADJ bad-tempered

malicia SF **1** (= *mala intención*) malice, spite; **lo dije sin ~** I said it without malice **2** (= *picardía*) [*de persona*] mischief; [*de mirada*] mischievousness; **sonrió con ~** she smiled mischievously **3** (= *astucia*) slyness, guile

maliciar /1b/ VT to suspect, have one's suspicions

malicioso ADJ **1** (= *malintencionado*) malicious, spiteful **2** (= *pícaro*) mischievous **3** (= *astuto*) sly, crafty **4** (= *malo*) wicked, evil

malignidad SF malignancy

maligno Ⓐ ADJ **1** (*Med*) malignant **2** (= *perverso*) [*persona*] evil; [*influencia*] pernicious, harmful; [*actitud, observación*] malicious Ⓑ SM **el ~** the Devil, the Evil One

malinchismo SM (*Méx*) *prejudice in favour of things foreign*

malinformar /1a/ VT to misinform

malintencionado ADJ [*persona, comentario*] malicious

malinterpretación SF misinterpretation

malinterpretar /1a/ VT to misinterpret

malla SF **1** [*de red*] mesh; (= *red*) network; **hacer ~s** to knit; **medias de ~** fishnet stockings ➤ **malla de alambre** wire mesh, wire netting **2** (*para ballet, gimnasia*) leotard; **mallas** (*sin pie*) leggings **3** (*CS*) (*tb* ~ **de baño**) swimming costume, swimsuit **4** (*Dep*) **las ~s** the net *sing*

mallo SM mallet

Mallorca SF Majorca

mallorquín/ina Ⓐ ADJ, SM/F Majorcan Ⓑ SM (*Ling*) Majorcan

malmandado ADJ disobedient

malmirado ADJ **1** (= *mal considerado*) **estar ~** to be disliked **2** (= *desconsiderado*) **ser ~** to be thoughtless, be inconsiderate

malnacido/a** SM/F swine*

malnutrición SF malnutrition

malnutrido ADJ malnourished

malo/a Ⓐ ADJ (*antes de sm sing* **mal**) **1** (= *perjudicial*) bad; **es ~ para la salud** it's bad for your health; ✦ REFRÁN **más vale lo ~ conocido (que lo bueno por conocer)** better the devil you know (than the devil you don't) **2** (= *imperfecto*) bad; **un chiste malísimo** a really bad joke, a terrible joke; **mala calidad** poor quality; **es una tela muy mala** it's a very poor-quality material; **no hay ni un mal bar para tomar algo** there isn't a single little bar where we can get a drink **3** (= *adverso*) bad; **he tenido mala suerte** I've had bad luck, I've been unlucky; **—es tarde y no ha llamado —¡malo!** "it's late and she hasn't called" — "oh dear!"; **lo ~ es que ...** the trouble is (that) ... **4** (= *desagradable*) bad; **un mal día** a bad day **5** (= *podrido*) **esta carne está mala** this meat's off **6** (= *reprobable*) wrong; **¿qué tiene de ~?** what's wrong with that?; **van por mal camino** they're heading off the rails; **es una mala persona** he's a bad person; **una bruja mala** a wicked witch **7** (= *travieso*) naughty; **¡no seas ~!** don't be naughty! **8** (= *enfermo*) ill; **tienes muy mala cara** you look awful *o* really ill; **tengo mala la garganta** I've got a sore throat; **estar ~** (*Esp*) to be ill, be sick; **se puso ~ y se fue a casa** (*Esp*) (*gen*) he felt ill and went home; (*con náuseas*) he felt sick and went home; **creo que me estoy poniendo ~** (*Esp*) I think I'm coming down with something **9** (= *inepto*) bad; **ser ~ para algo** to be bad at sth **10** (= *difícil*) hard, difficult **11** ✦ MODISMOS **a la mala** (*LAm*) (= *a la fuerza*) by force, forcibly; (= *de forma traicionera*) treacherously; **andar a malas con algn** to be on bad terms with sb; **ponerse a malas con algn** to fall out with sb; **estar de malas** (= *de mal humor*) to be in a bad mood; (= *sin suerte*) to be out of luck; **por las malas** by force, willy-nilly Ⓑ SM/F (= *personaje*) (*Teat*) villain; (*Cine*) baddie*

malogrado ADJ **1** (= *difunto*) **el ~ ministro** the late-lamented minister **2** (= *fracasado*) [*proyecto*] abortive, ill-fated; [*esfuerzo*] wasted

malograr /1a/ Ⓐ VT (= *arruinar*) to spoil, ruin; (= *desperdiciar*) to waste Ⓑ **malograrse** VPR **1** (= *fracasar*) to fail; (= *decepcionar*) to fail to come up to expectations, not fulfil its promise **2** (*esp Perú*) [*máquina*] to go wrong, break down **3** [*persona*] to die before one's time

maloliente ADJ stinking

malón SM (*LAm Hist*) Indian raid

malparado ADJ **salir ~** to come off badly; **salir ~ de algo** to get the worst of sth

malpensado ADJ **¡no seas ~!** why do you always have to think the worst of people?

malquerencia SF dislike

malquerer /2t/ VT to dislike

malsano ADJ **1** [*clima*] unhealthy **2** [*curiosidad, fascinación*] morbid; [*mente*] sick, morbid

malsonante ADJ rude, nasty; **usar palabras ~s** to use rude words *o* bad language

malta SF **1** (= *cereal*) malt; **whisky de ~** malt whisky **2** (*Chi*) (= *cerveza*) dark beer **3** (*sin alcohol*) malt drink

malteada SF (*LAm*) malted milk shake

maltraer /2o/ VI to ill-treat; ✦ MODISMO **llevar** *o* **traer a ~ a algn** [*persona*] to give sb nothing but trouble; [*problema*] to be the bane of sb's life

maltratado ADJ [*bebé, mujer*] battered

maltratador(a) SM/F abuser

maltratar /1a/ VT **1** [+ *persona*] (= *tratar mal*) to ill-treat, maltreat; (= *pegar*) to batter **2** [+ *cosas*] to handle roughly **3** (*tb ~ de palabra*) to abuse, insult

maltrato SM **1** (= *conducta*) (*al tratar mal*) mistreatment, ill-treatment; (*al pegar*) battering **2** [*de cosas*] rough handling **3** (= *insultos*) abuse, insults *pl*

maltrecho ADJ **1** [*objeto*] battered, knocked-about; **las maltrechas arcas de la organización** the organization's depleted coffers **2** [*persona*] (= *herido*) injured; (= *agotado*) worn out; **dejar ~ a algn** to leave sb in a bad way

malva ❹ ADJ INV [*color*] mauve ❺ SF (*Bot*) mallow; **(de) color de ~** mauve; ✦ MODISMOS **estar criando ~s** (*Esp**) to be pushing up the daisies*; **estar como una ~** to be very meek and mild

malvado/a ❹ ADJ evil, wicked ❺ SM/F villain

malvarrosa SF hollyhock

malvasía SF malmsey

malvavisco SM marshmallow

malvender /2a/ VT to sell off cheap, sell at a loss

malversación SF embezzlement, misappropriation ➤ **malversación de fondos** embezzlement, misappropriation of funds

malversar /1a/ VT to embezzle, misappropriate

Malvinas SFPL (*tb* **Islas ~**) Falkland Islands, Falklands

malvivir /3a/ VI to live badly, live poorly

malvón SM (*LAm*) geranium

mama SF **1** (= *glándula*) mammary gland; (= *pecho*) breast **2** = **mamá**

mamá* SF mum(my) (*Brit**), mom(my) (*EEUU**); **futura ~** mother-to-be

mamada SF **1** (*esp LAm*) [*de bebé*] feed **2** (***) (= *felación*) blow job*** **3** (**) (= *borrachera*) **coger** *o* **agarrar una ~** to get smashed** **4** (*LAm**) (= *cosa fácil*) cinch*; (= *ganga*) snip*, bargain; (= *trabajo*) cushy number

mamadera SF (*CS*) feeding bottle (*esp Brit*), nursing bottle (*EEUU*)

mamado ADJ **1** (**) (= *borracho*) smashed*, sloshed (*Brit**) **2** (**) (= *fácil*) dead easy* **3** (*Carib**) (= *tonto*) silly, stupid

mamagrande SF (*LAm*) grandmother

mamaíta* SF = **mamá**

mamamama* SF (*And*) grandma*

mamar /1a/ ❹ VI **1** [*bebé*] to suck **2** (= *asimilar*) **lo mamó desde pequeño** he grew up with it from childhood; **nació mamando el oficio** he was born to the trade **3** (***) (= *hacer una felación a*) to suck off***, give a blow job*** ❺ VI **1** [*bebé*] to suck; **dar de ~ a un bebé** to feed a baby; **dar de ~ a una cría** to suckle a baby **2** (**) (= *beber*) to booze*, drink ❻ **mamarse** (**) VPR to get smashed**, get sloshed (*Brit**)

mamario ADJ mammary

mamarrachada* SF (= *acción*) stupid thing; (= *objeto*) monstrosity*, sight*

mamarracho/a* ❹ SM/F (= *persona*) sight*; **estaba hecho un ~** he looked a sight *o* a complete mess* ❺ SM (= *objeto*) monstrosity*, sight*; (= *obra, trabajo*) mess, botch; (= *cuadro*) daub

mambo SM (*Mús*) mambo

mameluco SM **1** (*Hist*) Mameluke **2** (*LAm*) (= *mono*) overalls *pl*; (*tb* **~s de niño**) rompers *pl*, romper suit

mamey SM mammee apple, mamey

mamífero ❹ ADJ mammalian, mammal *antes de s* ❺ SM mammal

mamila SF **1** (*Méx*) (= *biberón*) feeding bottle (*esp Brit*), nursing bottle (*EEUU*); **dar la ~ al niño** to give the baby his bottle **2** (*Col*) (= *chupete*) dummy (*Brit*), pacifier (*EEUU*)

mamografía SF (= *técnica*) mammography; (= *radiografía*) mammogram

mamón ❹ SM (***) prick***, wanker*** ❺ ADJ (*Méx**) cocky*

mamotreto* SM **1** (= *libro*) hefty volume; (= *objeto*) monstrosity*, useless great object

mampara SF screen, partition

mamporro* SM **1** (= *golpe*) (*con la mano*) clout*, bash*; (*al caer*) bump; **liarse a ~s con algn** to come to blows with sb

mampostería SF masonry

mampuesto SM **1** (= *piedra*) rough stone **2** (= *muro*) wall

mamut SM (*pl* **~s**) mammoth

maná SM manna

manada SF **1** [*de ganado, elefantes*] herd; [*de lobos*] pack; [*de leones*] pride **2** (*) [*de gente*] crowd, mob; **los periodistas llegaron en ~** a swarm *o* pack of journalists arrived

manager, mánager ['manaʒer] SMF (*pl* **~s** *o* **mánagers**) manager

Managua SF Managua

managüense ADJ of/from Managua

manantial SM **1** (= *fuente*) spring; **agua de ~** spring water ➤ **manantial termal** hot spring **2** [*de riqueza, conflicto*] (= *origen*) source, origin; (= *causa*) cause

manar /1a/ ❹ VT to run with, flow with; **la herida manaba sangre** blood gushed from the wound ❺ VI **1** [*líquido*] (*gen*) to run, flow; (*a chorros*) to pour out, stream; (= *surgir*) to well up **2** (*fig*) (= *abundar*) to abound, be plentiful; **~ en algo** to abound in sth

manatí SM manatee, sea cow

manazas* ❹ SMF INV **ser (un) ~** to be clumsy ❺ SFPL (= *manos*) big mitts*

mancebo†† SM **1** (= *joven*) youth, young man **2** (= *soltero*) bachelor

mancha SF **1** (= *marca*) [*de aceite, comida, sangre*] stain; [*de óxido, bolígrafo*] mark; [*de pintura de labios*] smudge; **había ~s de sangre por el suelo** there were bloodstains on the floor; **las ~s de grasa salen mejor con agua caliente** oil stains come out better with hot water; **han salido ~s de humedad en la pared** damp patches have appeared on the wall; **quitar una ~** to get a mark *o* stain out, get a mark *o* stain off; ✦ MODISMO **extenderse como una ~ de aceite** [*enfermedad, noticia*] to spread like wildfire; [*movimiento, tendencia*] to spread far and wide

2 (= *área*) [*de hielo, vegetación*] patch; (*en el Sol, en un planeta*) spot ➤ **mancha de petróleo** oil slick ➤ **mancha solar** sunspot

3 (*Zool*) (*grande*) patch; (*redonda*) spot; **un cachorro blanco con ~s marrones** a white puppy with brown patches; **los leopardos tienen la piel a ~s** leopards have spots *o* spotted coats

4 (= *deshonra*) stain; **la ~ del pecado** the taint of sin; **sin ~** [*conducta*] impeccable; [*expediente*] unblemished; [*alma*] pure

5 [*de sarampión, rubeola*] spot; (*en el pulmón*) shadow; **le han salido unas ~s rojizas en la cara** his face has come out in reddish spots ➤ **mancha de nacimiento** birthmark

6 (*RPI*) (= *juego*) **la ~** tag

7 (*Perú*) [*de amigos*] gang

manchado ADJ **1** (= *sucio*) stained, dirty; **~ de algo: el suelo estaba manchado de sangre** the floor was stained with blood; **tenía la chaqueta manchada de café** his jacket had coffee stains on it *o* was stained with coffee; **el folio estaba ~ de tinta** the sheet of paper was smudged with ink **2** [*caballo, perro*] (*con manchas pequeñas*) spotted; (*con manchas más grandes*) dappled; [*ave*] speckled **3** (= *sin honra*) [*reputación*] tarnished

manchar /1a/ ❹ VT **1** (= *ensuciar*) to get dirty, stain; **te has manchado el vestido** you've got your dress dirty,

you've stained your dress, there's dirt on your dress; ~ **algo de algo** (gen) to stain sth with sth; (más sucio) to get sth covered in sth
2 (= desprestigiar) [+ honor, imagen] to tarnish
🅑 VI to stain
🅒 **mancharse** VPR **1** (= ensuciarse) to get dirty; **me he manchado el traje de barro/de tinta** I got my suit covered in mud/ink, I got mud/ink all over my suit
2 (= deshonrarse) to tarnish one's reputation

manchego ADJ of/from La Mancha

mancheta SF [de libro] blurb; [de periódico] masthead

mancilla SF (liter) stain, blemish; **sin ~** unblemished; (Rel) immaculate, pure

mancillar /1a/ VT (liter) to stain, sully (liter)

manco/a **🅐** ADJ **1** (de una mano) one-handed; (de un brazo) one-armed; (= sin brazos) armless **2** (= incompleto) half-finished **3** ✦ MODISMO **no ser ~** (= astuto) to be nobody's fool; (= útil) to be useful o handy; (= sin escrúpulos) to be pretty sharp **🅑** SM/F (de una mano) one-handed person; (de un brazo) one-armed person; (= sin brazos) armless person, person with no arms

mancomunado ADJ joint, jointly held

mancomunar /1a/ **🅐** VT **1** (= unir) [+ personas] to unite, associate; [+ intereses] to combine; [+ recursos] to pool **2** (Jur) to make jointly responsible **🅑** **mancomunarse** VPR to unite

mancomunidad SF **1** (= unión) union, association **2** (= comunidad) (gen) community; [de recursos] pool **3** (Jur) joint responsibility

mancornas SFPL (Col) cufflinks

mancuernas SFPL **1** (= pesas) weights; (pequeñas) dumbbells **2** (CAm, Méx) cufflinks

mancuernillas SFPL (CAm, Méx) cufflinks

manda SF (LAm) religious vow

mandado/a **🅐** SM/F **1** (pey) (= subordinado) dogsbody*; **yo aquí no soy más que un ~** here I just obey instructions, I'm just a dogsbody* o a minion here **2** (Méx*) (= aprovechado) opportunist; **no seas ~** don't take advantage of the situation **🅑** SM **1** (= recado) errand; **hacer un ~** to do o run an errand; **ir a (hacer) los ~s** to do the shopping **2** (Méx) **el ~** the shopping; **ir al ~** to do the shopping

mandamás SMF INV boss*, bigwig*

mandamiento SM **1** (Rel) commandment **2** (Jur) (tb ~ **judicial**) writ, warrant; **notificar a algn un ~ judicial** to serve a writ on sb **3** (Esp Fin) ➤ **mandamiento de pago** banker's order **4** (= orden) order, command

mandanga* SF (*) (= cuento) tale, story; (= excusa) excuse; (= paparrucha) nonsense, rubbish (esp Brit*); **¡no me vengas con ~s!*** don't give me that nonsense o (esp Brit*) rubbish!, who are you trying to kid?*; **hay que dejarse de ~s y decirlo bien claro** you have to stop beating about the bush and say it straight out

mandar /1a/ **🅐** VT **1** (= ordenar, encargar) to tell; **no me gusta que me manden** I don't like being told what to do; **¿hoy no te han mandado deberes?** haven't they given you any homework today?; **~ (a algn) (a) hacer algo**: **lo mandé a comprar pan** I sent him (out) for bread o to buy some bread; **¿quién diablos me ~ía a mí meterme en esto?*** why on earth did I get mixed up in this?*; **~ callar a algn** (gen) to tell sb to be quiet; (con autoridad) to order sb to be quiet; **~ llamar a algn** to send for sb; **~ salir a algn** to order sb out; **~ a algn (a) por algo** to send sb (out) for sth o to do sth; **~ a algn que haga algo** (gen) to tell sb to do sth; (con autoridad) to order sb to do sth
2 (= enviar) to send; **he mandado a los niños a la cama** I've sent the children to bed; **~ algo por correo** to post sth (esp Brit), mail sth (EEUU); **~ recuerdos a algn** to send one's love to sb, send one's regards to sb (frm)
3 (= estar al mando de) [+ batallón] to lead, command; [+ trabajadores, policías] to be in charge of
4 (Dep) to send, hit
5 (Med) to prescribe
6 (LAm) (= lanzar) to throw, hurl
7 (LAm*) **~ un golpe a algn** to hit sb; **~ una patada a algn** to

give sb a a kick, kick sb; **le mandó una bofetada** she slapped him
🅑 VI **1** (= estar al mando) (gen) to be in charge; (Mil) to be in command; **~ en algo** to be in charge of sth; (Mil) to be in command of sth
2 (= ordenar) **¡mande usted!** at your service!, what can I do for you?; **¿mande?** (esp Méx) (= ¿cómo dice?) pardon?, what did you say?; (invitando a hablar) yes?; **le gusta ~** (pey) he likes bossing people around; **según manda la ley** (Jur) in accordance with the law
🅒 **mandarse** VPR **1** (LAm*) **mándese entrar** o **pasar** please come in; **¡mándate cambiar!** (And) ✧ **¡mándense mudar!** (RPI) beat it!*, clear off!*; ✦ MODISMO **~se (guarda) abajo** (Chi*) to come down, come crashing down
2 (LAm*) [+ comida] to scoff*, polish off*; [+ bebida, trago] to knock back*
3 (SAm*) [+ gol] to score; [+ mentira] to come out with; **se manda cada discurso** he's such an amazing speaker
4 (Méx*) (= aprovecharse) to take advantage (of the situation)

mandarín SM **1** (Hist, Ling) Mandarin **2** (pey) (= persona influyente) mandarin

mandarina SF mandarin, tangerine

mandatario/a SM/F **1** (Jur) agent, attorney **2** (= dirigente) leader; (esp LAm Pol) (tb **primer ~**) Head of State

mandato SM **1** (= orden) mandate **2** (= período de mando) term of office, mandate (frm); **bajo** o **durante el ~ de algn** during sb's term of office o mandate (frm) **3** (Jur) (= estatutos) terms of reference pl; (= poder) power of attorney

mandíbula SF (Anat, Téc) jaw; (Zool) mandible; ✦ MODISMO **reír(se) a ~ batiente** to laugh one's head off

mandil SM apron

mandinga* SM (LAm) devil

mandioca SF cassava, manioc

mando SM **1** (= poder) command; **al ~ de** [+ pelotón, flota] in command of; [+ asociación, expedición, país] in charge of; [+ capitán, jefe] under the command o orders of, led by; **estuvo al ~ del país durante muchos años** he was in power for many years, he led the country for many years; **alto ~** high command; **tomar el ~** (Mil) to take command; (Dep) to take the lead ➤ **mando supremo** commander-in-chief
2 [de máquina, vehículo] control; **a los ~s de algo** at the controls of sth; **cuadro de ~s** control panel ➤ **mando a distancia** remote control
3 (= período de mando) term of office
4 mandos (= autoridades) (Mil) high-ranking officers, senior officers; (Pol) high-ranking members, senior members ➤ **mandos militares** high-ranking officers, senior officers

mandoble SM **1** (= golpe) two-handed blow **2** (= espada) broadsword, large sword

mandolina SF mandolin

mandón/ona* **🅐** ADJ bossy **🅑** SM/F bossy-boots*

mandonear* /1a/ VT **~ a algn** to boss sb around

mandrágora SF mandrake

mandril¹ SM (Zool) mandrill

mandril² SM (Téc) mandrel

manduca* SF (Esp) grub*, nosh (Brit*), chow (EEUU*)

manducar* /1g/ VT to scoff*, stuff o.s. with

manear /1a/ **🅐** VT to hobble **🅑** **manearse** VPR (And, Méx) to trip over one's own feet

manecilla SF (gen) pointer; [de reloj] hand

manejable ADJ [asunto, pelo] manageable; [aparato, libro] user-friendly, easy to use; [vehículo] manoeuvrable, maneuverable (EEUU)

manejar /1a/ **🅐** VT **1** (= usar) [+ herramienta, arma] to handle, use; [+ máquina] to operate; [+ idioma] to use
2 (= dirigir) [+ negocio, empresa] to run; [+ asuntos] to look after **3** [+ dinero] to handle **4** **~ a algn**: **mi tía maneja a su marido** my aunt keeps her husband under her thumb
5 (LAm Aut) to drive **🅑** VI (LAm Aut) to drive
🅒 **manejarse** VPR **1** (= desenvolverse) to manage

2 (= *comportarse*) to act, behave

manejo SM **1** (= *uso*) [*de herramienta, arma*] use; [*de máquina*] operation; [*de idioma*] use; **una herramienta de fácil ~** a tool that is easy-to-use **2** [*de negocio, empresa*] running; [*de dinero, fondos*] handling **3 tener buen ~ de** [+ *idioma, tema*] to have a good command of **4 manejos** (= *intrigas*) dealings **5** (*LAm Aut*) driving

manera SF **1** (= *modo*) way; **eso no es ~ de tratar a un animal** that's not the way to treat an animal, that's no way to treat an animal; **¡nunca he visto nevar de esta ~!** I've never seen it snow like this!; **no hubo ~ de convencerla** there was no convincing her, there was no way we could convince her; **a mi/tu/***etc* my/your/*etc* way; **de esta ~** (in) this way, (in) this fashion; **de la misma ~** (in) the same way, (in) the same fashion; **es su ~ de ser** that's the way she is; **cada uno tiene una ~ de ser** everyone has their own character

2 (*locuciones*) **de alguna ~** (= *en cierto modo*) to some extent; (= *de cualquier modo*) somehow; (*al principio de frase*) in a way, in some ways; **en cierta ~** in a way, to a certain extent; **de cualquier ~** (= *sin cuidado*) any old how; (= *de todos modos*) anyway; **en gran ~** to a large extent; **de mala ~:** they really ripped him off*; **me contestó de muy mala ~** he answered me very rudely; **de ninguna ~: eso no lo vamos a aceptar de ninguna ~** there's no way we are going to accept that; **de ninguna ~ deben paralizarse las obras** on no account must the work stop; **¡de ninguna ~!** certainly not!, no way!; **de otra ~** (= *de otro modo*) in a different way; (= *por otra parte*) otherwise; **sobre ~** exceedingly; **de tal ~ que ...** in such a way that ...; **de todas ~s** anyway, in any case

3 de ~ que (*antes de verbo*) so; (*después de verbo*) so that; **¿de ~ que esto no te gusta?** so you don't like this?; **lo hizo de ~ que nadie se dio cuenta** he did it so that nobody noticed

4 maneras (= *modales*) manners; **buenas ~s** good manners; **malas ~s** bad manners, rudeness; **con muy malas ~s** very rudely

manga SF **1** (*en ropa*) sleeve; **estar en ~s de camisa** to be in shirtsleeves; **de ~ corta/larga** short-/long-sleeved; **sin ~s** sleeveless; ✦ MODISMOS **andar ~ por hombro** to be a mess; **ser de** o **tener ~ ancha** (= *tolerante*) to be easy-going; (= *poco severo*) to be too lenient; (*pey*) (= *sin escrúpulos*) to be unscrupulous; **sacarse algo de la ~** to come up with sth; **traer algo en la ~** to have sth up one's sleeve

2 (= *manguera*) (*tb* **~ de riego**) hose, hosepipe ➤ **manga de incendios** fire hose

3 (*Culin*) (= *colador*) strainer; [*de pastelería*] piping bag ➤ **manga pastelera** piping bag

4 (*Aer*) windsock

5 (*Geog*) [*de agua*] stretch; [*de nubes*] cloudburst ➤ **manga de viento** whirlwind

6 (*Náut*) beam, breadth

7 (*Dep*) [*de competición*] round, stage; (*Tenis*) set; (*Bridge*) game

8 (*Méx*) (= *capa*) waterproof cape

9 (*CS**) [*de delincuentes, ignorantes*] bunch

manganeso SM manganese

mangante* SMF (*Esp*) **1** (= *ladrón*) (*gen*) thief; (*en tienda*) shoplifter **2** (= *gorrón*) scrounger*, freeloader* **3** (= *caradura*) rotter*, villain

mangar* /1h/ 🅐 VT to pinch*, nick* 🅑 VI **1** (= *robar*) (*gen*) to pilfer*; (*en tienda*) to shoplift **2** (*CS*) (= *gorronear*) to scrounge*

mangle SM (*Bot*) mangrove

mango¹ SM **1** (*Bot*) mango **2** (*Méx**) (= *hombre*) hunk*; (= *mujer*) stunner* **3** (*RPl**) (= *dinero*) peso

mango² SM (= *asa*) handle ➤ **mango de escoba** broomstick

mangonear* /1a/ 🅐 VT **1** [+ *persona*] to boss about* **2** (= *birlar*) to pinch*, nick* 🅑 VI **1** (= *entrometerse*) to meddle, interfere (**en** in) **2** (= *ser mandón*) (*con personas*) to boss people about; (*con asuntos*) to run everything

mangoneo* SM **1** (= *entrometimiento*) meddling, interference **2** (*con personas*) (= *control*) bossing people about; (= *descaro*) brazenness

mangosta SF mongoose

manguear* /1a/ VI (*CS*) to scrounge*

manguera SF hose, hosepipe ➤ **manguera de incendios** fire hose

mangui** SMF (*Esp*) (= *ladrón*) thief; (= *ratero*) small-time crook*; (= *canalla*) villain, rotter*

manguito SM **1** (*para manos*) muff **2** (*Téc*) sleeve, coupling

maní SM (*pl* **~es** o **manises**) (*esp LAm*) (= *cacahuete*) peanut; (= *planta*) groundnut plant

manía SF **1** (*Med*) mania ➤ **manía persecutoria** persecution mania

2 [*de persona*] (= *costumbre*) odd habit; (= *rareza*) peculiarity, oddity; (= *capricho*) fad, whim; **tiene sus ~s** he has his little ways; **tiene la ~ de comerse las uñas** he has the annoying habit of biting his nails

3 [*de grupo*] (= *afición*) mania; (= *moda*) rage, craze; **la ~ del fútbol** football fever, the football craze

4 (= *antipatía*) dislike; **coger ~ a algn** to take a dislike to sb; **tener ~ a algn** to dislike sb; **el maestro me tiene ~** the teacher's got it in for me

maníaco/a, maniaco/a 🅐 ADJ maniac, maniacal 🅑 SM/F maniac ➤ **maníaco/a sexual** sex maniac

maniaco-depresivo/a ADJ, SM/F manic depressive

maniatar /1a/ VT **1 ~ a algn** (*con cuerdas*) to tie sb's hands; (*con esposas*) to handcuff sb **2** [+ *animal*] to hobble

maniático ADJ (= *obsesionado*) obsessive; (= *excéntrico*) eccentric, cranky*; (= *delicado*) fussy

manicero/a SM/F (*LAm*) peanut seller

manicomio SM lunatic asylum, insane asylum (*EEUU*)

manicura SF, **manicure** SM o SF (*Col, Méx*) manicure

manido ADJ **1** [*tema*] trite, stale; [*frase*] hackneyed **2** [*frutos secos*] stale

manierismo SM mannerism

manierista ADJ, SMF mannerist

manifestación SF **1** (*Pol*) demonstration **2** (= *muestra*) [*de emoción*] display, show; (= *señal*) sign; **han recibido muchas manifestaciones de apoyo** they have received a lot of support **3** (= *declaración*) statement, declaration

manifestante SMF demonstrator

manifestar /1j/ 🅐 VT **1** (= *declarar*) to declare **2** (= *mostrar*) [+ *emociones*] to show; **manifiesta un sincero arrepentimiento** he shows genuine regret 🅑 **manifestarse** VPR **1** (= *declararse*) **el presidente se ha manifestado a favor del pacto** the president came out in favour of the agreement **2** (*Pol*) to demonstrate **3** (= *mostrarse*) to be apparent, be evident

manifiesto 🅐 ADJ (= *claro*) (*gen*) clear, manifest; [*error*] glaring, obvious; [*verdad*] manifest; **poner algo de ~** (= *aclarar*) to make sth clear; (= *revelar*) to reveal sth; **quedar (de) ~** to be plain, be clear 🅑 SM **1** (*Pol, Arte*) manifesto **2** (*Náut*) manifest

manigua (*LAm*) SF (= *ciénaga*) swamp; (= *maleza*) scrubland; (= *selva*) jungle

manija SF **1** (= *mango*) handle **2** (*CS Aut*) starting handle; **dar ~ a algn** to egg sb on

Manila SF Manila

manilargo ADJ **1** (= *generoso*) open-handed, generous **2** (*esp LAm**) (= *ladrón*) light-fingered

manilla SF **1** [*de puerta*] handle, door handle **2** (= *mango*) handle **3** [*de reloj*] hand

manillar SM handlebars *pl*

maniobra SF

En inglés americano se usa **maneuver** en lugar de **manoeuvre**.

1 (= *giro*) (*Aut*) manoeuvre; (*Ferro*) shunting, switching (*EEUU*); **hacer ~s** (*Aut*) to manoeuvre; (*Ferro*) to shunt, switch (*EEUU*) **2** (*Náut*) (= *operación*) manoeuvre; (= *aparejo*) gear, rigging **3 maniobras** (*Mil*) manoeuvres

4 (= *estratagema*) manoeuvre, move; **una ~ política** a political manoeuvre

maniobrar /1a/ **Ⓐ** VT **1** [+ *aparato, vehículo*] (= *manejar*) to handle, operate; (= *mover*) to manoeuvre, maneuver (*EEUU*) **2** (*Ferro*) to shunt, switch (*EEUU*) **Ⓑ** VI to manoeuvre, maneuver (*EEUU*)

manipulación SF **1** (= *manejo*) [*de alimentos*] handling; [*de pieza, máquina*] manipulation **2** [*de información, resultados*] manipulation ➤ **manipulación genética** genetic manipulation

manipulador(a) **Ⓐ** ADJ manipulative **Ⓑ** SM/F **1** [*de mercancías*] handler **2** (= *mangoneador*) manipulator

manipular /1a/ VT **1** (= *manejar*) [+ *alimentos, géneros*] to handle; [+ *aparato*] to operate, use **2** [+ *persona*] to manipulate

maniqueísmo SM **1** (*Hist*) Manicheism, Manichaeism **2** (= *tendencia a simplificar*) tendency to see things in black and white

maniqueo/a **Ⓐ** ADJ **1** (*Hist*) Manichean, Manichaean **2** (= *simplista*) black and white **Ⓑ** SM/F **1** (*Hist*) Manichean, Manichaean **2** (= *simplista*) person who tends to see things in black and white

maniquí **Ⓐ** SM [*de sastre, escaparate*] dummy, mannequin **Ⓑ** SMF (= *modelo*) model

manirroto/a **Ⓐ** ADJ extravagant, lavish **Ⓑ** SM/F spendthrift

manisero (*LAm*) = **manicero**

manitas¹ SFPL ✦ MODISMO **hacer ~** to canoodle*, make out (*EEUU*) (**con** with)

manitas²* SMF INV handyman/handywoman; **ser (un(a)) ~** to be handy, be good with one's hands

manito¹ SM (*Méx*) pal*, mate (*Brit**), buddy (*esp EEUU*)

manito²* SF (*SAm*) = **mano**

manivela SF crank, handle

manjar SM delicacy ➤ **manjar blanco** (*And*) caramel spread

mano¹

*Para las expresiones **manos arriba, al alcance de la mano, frotarse las manos** etc, ver la entrada correspondiente a la otra palabra.*

mano¹ SUSTANTIVO FEMENINO
1 (*Anat*) hand; **lo hice con mis propias ~s** I made it with my own hands, I made it myself; **votar a ~ alzada** to vote by a show of hands; **dar la ~ a algn** (*para saludar*) to shake hands with sb; (*para andar, apoyarse*) to take sb by the hand; **darse la ~** o **las ~s** to shake hands; **los dos iban de la ~** the two were walking hand-in-hand, the two were walking along holding hands; **llevar a algn de la ~** to lead sb by the hand; **¡~s a la obra!** (*como orden*) to work!; (*para darse ánimo*) let's get on with it!, (let's) get down to work ✦ **a mano** (= *sin máquina*) by hand; (= *cerca*) handy, at hand; (= *asequible*) handy, to hand; **hecho a ~** handmade; **¿tienes un bolígrafo a ~?** have you got a pen handy o to hand?; **el supermercado me queda** o (*Esp*) **me pilla* muy a ~** the supermarket is very handy for me, the supermarket is very close o is nearby
✦ **en mano: a entregar en ~** to be delivered by hand; **se presentó allí pistola en ~** he turned up there with a gun in his hand
2 ✦ MODISMOS **~ a ~: se bebieron la botella ~ a ~** they drank the bottle between (the two of) them; **un ~ a ~: hubo un ~ a ~ entre los dos políticos en el parlamento** the two politicians slogged it out between them in parliament; **la corrida será un ~ a ~ entre los dos toreros** the bullfight will be a two-way contest between the two bullfighters; **estar con una ~ adelante y otra atrás** to be broke*; **coger a algn con las ~s en la masa** to catch sb red-handed; **le das la ~ y se toma el codo** an inch and he'll take a mile; **dar una ~ a algn** (*LAm*) to lend o give sb a hand; **echar ~ de** to make use of, resort to; **echar una ~ a algn** to lend o give sb a hand; **tener las ~s largas** (= *ser propenso a robar*) to be light-fingered; (= *ser propenso a*

pegar) to be apt to hit out; **tener las ~s libres** to have full o free rein, be free (to do sth); **llegar a las ~s** to come to blows; **a ~s llenas** lavishly, generously; **meter ~ a algn*** to touch sb up*; **meter ~ a algo: hay que meterle ~ a la corrupción** we have to deal with o tackle corruption; **tengo que meterle ~ a la física** I need to get stuck into my physics*; **ponerle a algn la ~ encima: ¡como me pongas la ~ encima ...!** if you lay one finger on me ...!; **poner la ~ en el fuego: yo no pondría la ~ en el fuego por Juan** I wouldn't risk my neck for Juan, I wouldn't put myself on the line for Juan; **yo pondría la ~ en el fuego por su inocencia** I'd stake my life on his being innocent; **traerse algo entre ~s: ¿qué os traéis entre ~s?** what are you up to?; **se trae entre ~s varios asuntos a la vez** he's dealing with several matters at once; **con las ~s vacías** empty-handed ➤ **mano derecha** right-hand man/woman ➤ **mano de santo** sure remedy; **fue ~ de santo** it was just right, it was just what the doctor ordered ➤ **mano dura** harsh treatment; (*Pol*) firm hand
3 (= *posesión*) hand; **cambiar de ~s** to change hands; **de primera ~** (at) first-hand; **de segunda ~** second-hand; **ropa de segunda ~** second-hand o used clothes
4 (= *control*) **está en tus ~s** it's up to you; **ha hecho cuanto ha estado en su ~** he has done all o everything in his power; **en buenas ~s** in good hands; ✦ MODISMOS **írsele a algn la ~** con algo: **se te ha ido la ~ con la sal** you overdid it with the salt; **írsele algo de las ~s a algn: el asunto se le fue de las ~s** he lost all control of the affair; **dejado de la ~ de Dios** godforsaken
✦ **a manos de** at the hands of; **murió a ~s de los mafiosos** he died at the hands of the mafia; **la carta nunca llegó a ~s del jefe** the letter never reached the boss, the letter never came into the hands of the boss
✦ **en manos de** in the hands of; **me pongo en tus ~s** I place myself entirely in your hands
5 (= *habilidad*) **¡qué ~s tiene!** he's so clever with his hands!; **tener buena ~: tener buena ~ para la cocina** to be a good cook; **tener (buena) ~ para las plantas** to have green fingers (*Brit*) o a green thumb (*EEUU*) ➤ **mano izquierda: tiene ~ izquierda con los animales** he's got a way with animals
6 (= *lado*) side; **a ~ derecha** on the right-hand side; **a ~ izquierda** on the left-hand side
7 (= *trabajadores*) manos hands, workers ➤ **mano de obra** labour, labor (*EEUU*), manpower ➤ **mano de obra especializada** skilled labour o (*EEUU*) labor
8 (*Dep*) handling, handball; **¡mano!** handball!
9 (*Zool*) [*de mono*] hand; [*de perro, gato, oso, león*] front paw; [*de caballo*] forefoot, front hoof; [*de ave*] foot; (= *trompa*) trunk ➤ **manos de cerdo** (*Culin*) pig's trotters
10 (= *instrumento*) [*de reloj*] hand
11 (= *capa*) [*de pintura*] coat; [*de jabón*] wash, soaping
12 (*en juegos, naipes*) (= *partida*) round, game; (= *conjunto de cartas*) hand; **ser** o **tener la ~** to lead
13 (*LAm*) [*de plátanos*] bunch, hand

mano² SM (*Méx*) (*en conversación*) mate*, pal*

manojo SM handful, bunch; ✦ MODISMO **estar hecho un ~ de nervios** to be a bundle o bag of nerves

manómetro SM pressure gauge, manometer (*frm*)

manopla SF **1** (= *guante*) (*gen*) mitten; [*de baño*] bath mitt; (*en béisbol*) glove, mitt **2** (*Hist, Téc*) gauntlet **3** (*LAm*) (= *puño de hierro*) knuckle-duster (*esp Brit*), brass knuckles *pl* (*EEUU*)

manosear /1a/ VT **1** [+ *objeto*] (= *tocar*) to handle, paw*; (= *jugar con*) to fiddle with, mess about with **2** [+ *persona*] to touch up*, grope*

manoseo SM **1** [*de objetos*] handling, pawing* **2** [*de persona*] touching up*, groping*

manotada SF (*LAm*) handful, fistful

manotazo SM slap, smack; **dar un ~ a algn** to give sb a slap, slap sb

manotear /1a/ **Ⓐ** VT to slap, smack **Ⓑ** VI to gesticulate

mansalva SF **a ~** (= *mucho*) in abundance; (= *a gran escala*) on a large scale; (= *sin riesgo*) without risk; **gastan dinero a ~** they spend money as if there were no tomorrow; **le dispararon a ~** they shot him before he could defend himself

mansarda SF attic

mansedumbre SF 1 [*de persona*] gentleness, meekness 2 [*de animal*] tameness

mansión SF mansion

manso ADJ 1 [*persona*] meek, gentle 2 [*animal*] tame

manta[1] SF 1 (*para taparse*) blanket; ✦ MODISMOS **a ~** (*Esp**): **repartieron vino y comida a ~** they handed out food and wine in abundance; **llovía a ~** it was raining buckets; **liarse la ~ a la cabeza** to take the plunge; **tirar de la ~** to let the cat out of the bag, give the game away ➤ **manta de viaje** travelling rug, traveling rug (*EEUU*) ➤ **manta eléctrica** electric blanket
2 (*LAm*) (= *poncho*) poncho
3 (*Esp**) (= *paliza*) hiding; **les dieron una buena ~ de palos** they gave them a real hiding o beating
4 (*Zool*) manta ray
5 (*Méx*) (= *tela*) calico

manta[2]* (*Esp*) Ⓐ ADJ bone-idle Ⓑ SMF idler, slacker Ⓒ SF idleness

mantear /1a/ VT to toss in a blanket

manteca SF 1 (= *grasa*) fat, animal fat ➤ **manteca de cerdo** lard 2 (*esp RPl*) (= *mantequilla*) butter ➤ **manteca de cacahuete** peanut butter ➤ **manteca de cacao** cocoa butter ➤ **manteca de maní** (*RPl*) peanut butter 3 (**) (= *dinero*) dough**, dosh**; (= *géneros*) goods *pl* 4 (*Col*) (= *criada*) servant girl

mantecado SM *Christmas sweet made from flour, almonds and lard*

mantecoso ADJ (= *grasiento*) greasy; (= *cremoso*) creamy, buttery; **queso ~** soft cheese

mantel SM (*para comer*) tablecloth; (*Rel*) altar cloth ➤ **mantel individual** place mat

mantelería SF table linen

mantención SF (*LAm*) = **manutención**

mantener /2k/ Ⓐ VT 1 (= *sostener*) [+ *objeto*] to hold; [+ *puente, techo*] to support
2 (= *preservar*) 2.1 (*en un lugar*) to store, keep; **"una vez abierto manténgase refrigerado"** "once opened keep in a refrigerator"; **"manténgase en un lugar fresco y seco"** "store in a cool dry place" 2.2 (*en un estado o situación*) to keep; **hay que ~ actualizada la base de datos** we have to keep the database up to date; **"mantenga limpia su ciudad"** keep your city clean
3 (= *conservar*) [+ *opinión*] to maintain, hold; [+ *costumbre, ideales*] to keep up, maintain; [+ *disciplina*] to maintain, keep; [+ *promesa*] to keep; **una civilización que lucha por ~ sus tradiciones** a civilization struggling to uphold o maintain its traditions; **~ el orden público** to keep the peace; **al conducir hay que ~ la distancia de seguridad** you have to keep (at) a safe distance when driving; **~ el equilibrio** to keep one's balance; **~ la línea** to keep one's figure, keep in shape; **~ la paz** to keep the peace, maintain peace; ✦ MODISMO **mantenella y no emendalla** (*Esp*) to stand one's ground
4 (*económicamente*) to support, maintain
5 [+ *conversación, contacto*] to maintain, hold; **¿han mantenido ustedes relaciones sexuales?** have you had sexual relations?
6 (= *afirmar*) to maintain; **siempre he mantenido lo contrario** I've always maintained the opposite
Ⓑ **mantenerse** VPR 1 (= *sostenerse*) to be supported; **~se en pie** [*persona*] to stand up, stay on one's feet; [*edificio*] to be still standing
2 (*en un estado o situación*) to stay, remain; **~se en contacto** to keep in touch (**con** with); **~se al día en algo** to keep up to date with sth; **~se en forma** to keep fit, keep in shape; **~se en su puesto** to keep o retain one's post; ✦ MODISMO **~se en sus trece*** to stand one's ground, stick to one's guns
3 (*económicamente*) to support o.s.
4 (= *alimentarse*) **~se a base de algo** to live on sth

mantenimiento SM 1 (= *continuación*) maintenance; **el ~ de la paz** the maintenance of peace
2 (= *conservación*) maintenance; **el ~ de las carreteras** upkeep of the roads, road maintenance; **el coste del ~ de una familia** the upkeep of a family, the cost of running a family; **costes** o **gastos de ~** maintenance costs, upkeep; **servicio de ~** maintenance service
3 (*Dep*) keep-fit; **clase de ~** keep-fit class; **ejercicios** o **gimnasia de ~** keep-fit exercises

mantequera SF 1 (*para batir*) churn 2 (*para servir*) butter dish

mantequería SF (*LAm*) (= *lechería*) dairy, creamery; (= *ultramarinos*) grocer's (shop) (*esp Brit*), grocery (*EEUU*)

mantequilla SF butter; **tostadas con ~** buttered toast; **manos de ~** butter fingers*

mantequillera SF butter dish

mantilla SF 1 [*de mujer*] mantilla ➤ **mantilla de encajes** lace mantilla 2 **mantillas** [*de bebé*] terry nappy (*Brit*), cloth diaper (*EEUU*); ✦ MODISMOS **estar en ~s** [*persona*] to be very naive; [*proyecto, técnica*] to be in its infancy

mantillo SM humus, mould, mold (*EEUU*)

mantis SF INV ➤ **mantis religiosa** praying mantis

manto SM 1 (= *capa*) (*para abrigarse*) cloak; (*Rel, Jur*) robe, gown 2 (*Zool*) mantle 3 (*liter*) (= *velo*) **un ~ de nieve** a blanket of snow

mantón SM shawl ➤ **mantón de manila** embroidered shawl

mantra SM mantra

manual Ⓐ ADJ manual Ⓑ SM manual, guide ➤ **manual de instrucciones** instruction manual

manualidades SFPL handicrafts, craftwork *sing*; **hacer ~** to do craftwork; **talleres de ~** craft workshops

manubrio SM 1 (*Mec*) (= *manivela*) handle, crank; (= *torno*) winch 2 (*LAm*) [*de bicicleta*] handlebar, handlebars *pl* 3 (*Par Aut*) steering wheel

manufactura SF 1 (= *fabricación*) manufacture 2 (= *producto*) product

manufacturar /1a/ VT to manufacture

manumitir /3a/ VT (*frm*) to manumit

manuscrito Ⓐ ADJ handwritten Ⓑ SM manuscript

manutención SF maintenance, upkeep; **le pasa la ~ para sus hijos** he pays for his children's maintenance o upkeep; **gastos de ~** maintenance costs, upkeep

manyar** /1a/ VT, VI (*Carib, CS*) to eat

manzana SF 1 (= *fruta*) apple; **tarta de ~** apple tart; ✦ MODISMO **~ de la discordia** bone of contention 2 ➤ **manzana de Adán** (*esp LAm Anat*) Adam's apple 3 [*de casas*] block (of houses)

manzanar SM apple orchard

manzanilla SF 1 (*Bot*) (= *flor*) camomile; (= *infusión*) camomile tea 2 (= *jerez*) manzanilla sherry

manzano SM apple tree

maña SF 1 (= *habilidad*) skill; **tiene mucha ~ para hacer arreglos caseros** he's a dab hand at mending things around the house 2 (= *ardid*) trick; **con ~** craftily, slyly; **malas ~s** (*gen*) bad habits; [*de niño*] naughty ways

mañana Ⓐ ADV tomorrow; **~ por la ~** tomorrow morning; **¡hasta ~!** see you tomorrow!; **pasado ~** the day after tomorrow Ⓑ SM future; **el día de ~** in the future Ⓒ SF morning; **a las siete de la ~** at seven o'clock in the morning, at seven a.m.; **de** o **por la ~** in the morning; **en la ~ de ayer** yesterday morning; **de la noche a la ~** overnight

mañanero ADJ 1 (= *madrugador*) **ser ~** to be an early riser 2 (= *matutino*) morning *antes de s*

mañanita SF 1 (= *chal*) bed jacket 2 **mañanitas** (*Méx*) (= *canción*) serenade *sing*

maño/a ADJ, SM/F Aragonese

mañosear /1a/ VI (*And, CS*) [*niño*] to be difficult (*esp about food*)

mañoso ADJ 1 [*persona*] (= *hábil*) clever, ingenious; (= *astuto*) crafty, cunning 2 (*LAm*) (= *caprichoso*) difficult 3 (*LAm*) [*animal*] obstinate

maoísmo SM Maoism

mapa SM map; **el ~ político** (= *escena*) the political scene;

(= *abanico*) the political spectrum; ✦ MODISMO **desaparecer del ~** to vanish off the face of the earth ➤ **mapa de carreteras** road map ➤ **mapa del tiempo** weather map

mapache SM racoon, raccoon

mapamundi SM world map

mapear /1a/ VT to map

mapuche (*a veces en fem* **mapucha**) (*esp Chi*) Ⓐ ADJ Mapuche, Araucanian Ⓑ SMF Mapuche (Indian), Araucanian (Indian) Ⓒ SM (*Ling*) Mapuche, Araucanian; ◇ *ARAUCANO*

mapurite SM (*CAm, Carib*), **mapurito** SM (*CAm, Carib*) skunk

maquearse** /1a/ VPR (*Esp*) to get ready (to go out), get dressed up; **ir (bien) maqueado** to be all dressed up

maqueta SF 1 (= *modelo*) model, scale model, mock-up 2 (= *libro*) dummy 3 (*Mús*) demo, demo tape

maquetación SF layout, design

maquetar /1a/ VT to lay out, design

maquetista SMF (*Arquit*) model maker; (*Tip*) typesetter

maquiavélico ADJ Machiavellian

maquiladora SF (*Méx Com*) bonded assembly plant

maquillador(a) SM/F make-up artist

maquillaje SM 1 (= *pintura*) make-up; (= *acto*) making up ➤ **maquillaje base, maquillaje de fondo** foundation 2 (*) [*de cuentas*] massaging*

maquillar /1a/ Ⓐ VT 1 (= *persona*) to make up 2 (*) [+ *cifras, cuentas*] to massage* Ⓑ **maquillarse** VPR to put some make-up on

máquina SF 1 (= *aparato*) (*gen*) machine; **a toda ~** at full speed; **coser algo a ~** to machine-sew sth; **escribir a ~** to type; **hecho a ~** machine-made; **pasar algo a ~** to type sth (up); ✦ MODISMO **forzar la ~** (= *ir deprisa*) to go full steam ahead; (= *abusar de las posibilidades*) to pull out all the stops ➤ **máquina de afeitar** razor, safety razor ➤ **máquina de afeitar eléctrica** electric razor, shaver ➤ **máquina de coser** sewing machine ➤ **máquina de discos** jukebox ➤ **máquina de escribir** typewriter ➤ **máquina de tabaco*** cigarette machine ➤ **máquina expendedora** vending machine ➤ **máquina fotográfica** camera ➤ **máquina tragaperras** slot machine, fruit machine (*Brit*) 2 [*de tren*] engine, locomotive; (*) (= *moto*) motorbike; (*CAm, Cub*) (= *coche*) car 3 (*Pol*) machine ➤ **máquina electoral** electoral machine

maquinación SF machination, plot

maquinar /1a/ VT, VI to plot

maquinaria SF 1 (= *conjunto de máquinas*) machinery ➤ **maquinaria agrícola** agricultural machinery, farm implements *pl* ➤ **maquinaria pesada** heavy plant 2 (= *mecanismo*) mechanism; **la ~ de un reloj** the mechanism of a watch 3 (*Pol*) machine

maquinilla SF (= *máquina*) small machine; (= *torno*) winch; [*de peluquero*] clippers *pl* ➤ **maquinilla de afeitar** razor, safety razor ➤ **maquinilla eléctrica** electric razor, shaver

maquinista SMF 1 (*Ferro*) engine driver (*Brit*), engineer (*EEUU*); (*Náut*) engineer 2 (*Téc*) operator, machinist 3 (*Teat*) scene-shifter; (*Cine*) cameraman's assistant

maquis SM INV (= *movimiento*) resistance movement, maquis; (= *persona*) member of the resistance, maquis

mar SM (A VECES SF) 1 (*Geog*) sea; **una casa al lado del ~** a house by the sea *o* on the coast; **~ adentro** [*ir, llevar*] out to sea; [*estar*] out at sea; **un buque de alta ~** an ocean-going vessel; **pesca de alta ~** deep-sea fishing; **~ de fondo** (*lit*) groundswell; (*fig*) underlying tension; **~ gruesa** heavy sea; **hacerse a la ~** (*liter*) [*barco*] to set sail, to put to sea (*frm*); [*marinero*] to set sail; **por ~** by sea, by boat; ✦ MODISMO **eso es hablar de la ~** that's just wishful thinking, that's just pie in the sky*; **me cago en la ~ (salada)** (*Esp***) shit!**; **mecachis en la ~** (*Esp euf*) sugar! ➤ **mar Caribe, mar de las Antillas** Caribbean Sea ➤ **mar del Norte** North Sea 2 (= *marea*) tide 3 (= *abundancia*) 3.1 **estar hecho un ~ de dudas** to be full of doubt, be beset with doubts (*frm*); **estar hecho un ~ de lágrimas** to be in floods of tears 3.2 **la ~es**: estaba sudando

a ~es he was sweating buckets*; **estuvo lloviendo a ~es** it was raining cats and dogs *o* it was pouring (down) 3.3 ✦ MODISMO **la ~ de***: **tengo la ~ de cosas que hacer** I've got no end of things to do; **hace la ~ de tiempo que no la veo** I haven't seen her for ages; **es la ~ de guapa** she's ever so pretty; **lo hemos pasado la ~ de bien** we had a whale of a time* *o* a great time

marabunta SF 1 [*de hormigas*] plague 2 (= *multitud*) crowd

maraca SF maraca

maracuyá SM passion fruit

marajá SM = **maharajá**

maraña SF 1 (= *maleza*) thicket, tangle of plants 2 [*de hilos*] tangle 3 (= *enredo*) mess, tangle; **una ~ de pasillos** a maze *o* labyrinth of passages

marasmo SM paralysis, stagnation

maratón SM (A VECES SF) marathon ➤ **maratón radiofónico** radiothon

maratoniano ADJ marathon *antes de s*

maravilla SF 1 (= *prodigio*) wonder; **las ~s de la tecnología** the wonders of technology; **¡qué ~ de tiempo tenemos!** what wonderful weather we're having!; **el concierto fue una ~** the concert was wonderful, it was a wonderful concert; **contar** *o* **hablar ~s de algn/algo** to rave about sb/sth; **hacer ~s** to work wonders; **las siete ~s del mundo** the seven wonders of the world; ✦ MODISMO **a las mil ~s** ◇ **de ~** wonderfully, wonderfully well, marvellously 2 (= *caléndula*) marigold; (= *enredadera*) morning glory

maravillar /1a/ Ⓐ VT to astonish, amaze Ⓑ **maravillarse** VPR **~se con** *o* **de algo** to be astonished *o* amazed at *o* by sth

maravilloso ADJ 1 (= *magnífico*) wonderful, marvellous, marvelous (*EEUU*) 2 (= *mágico*) magic

marca SF 1 (= *señal*) mark; **dejó una ~ al principio del libro** he left a mark at the beginning of the book; **haz una ~ en la casilla correcta** tick the appropriate box ➤ **marca de nacimiento** birthmark 2 (= *huella*) [*de pie*] footprint, footmark; [*de dedos*] fingerprint 3 (*Com*) [*de comida, jabón, tabaco*] brand; [*de electrodoméstico, coche*] make; [*de ropa*] label; **ropa de ~** designer-label clothes, designer-label clothing; ✦ MODISMO **de ~ mayor*** [*susto, borrachera*] incredible; **es un imbécil de ~ mayor** he's a total idiot* ➤ **marca registrada** registered trademark 4 (*Dep*) [*de especialidad*] record; [*de deportista*] best time; **su mejor ~ personal** his personal best (time); **batir** *o* **mejorar** *o* **superar una ~** to break a record 5 (*Náut*) (*en tierra*) seamark; (*en el mar*) marker, buoy 6 (*en el ganado*) (= *señal*) brand 7 (*Hist*) march, frontier area

marcado Ⓐ ADJ marked; **con ~ acento argentino** with a marked Argentinian accent; **ese vestido le hacía las caderas muy marcadas** that dress accentuated her hips *o* made her hips stand out; **su visita tiene un ~ significado político** his visit has a strong political significance Ⓑ SM 1 [*de pelo*] set 2 [*de ganado*] branding

marcador SM 1 (*Dep*) scoreboard; **el ~ va dos a uno** the score is 2-1 ➤ **marcador electrónico** electronic scoreboard 2 (= *indicador*) (*gen*) marker; [*de libro*] bookmark (*tb Internet*) 3 (*LAm*) (= *rotulador*) marker

marcaje SM (= *seguimiento*) marking; (= *entrada*) tackle, tackling, one-to-one marking

marcapasos SM INV pacemaker

marcar /1g/ Ⓐ VT 1 (= *señalar*) 1.1 [+ *objeto, ropa*] to mark; [+ *ganado*] to brand; **ha marcado las toallas con mis iniciales** she has put my initials on the towels, she has marked the towels with my initials 1.2 [+ *límites*] to mark 1.3 (*Inform*) [+ *bloque, texto*] to highlight 1.4 [+ *partitura*] to mark up 2 [*experiencia, suceso*] to mark 3 [*termómetro*] to read; **mi reloj marca las dos** it's two o'clock by my watch, my watch says two o'clock; **este reloj marca la hora exacta** this watch keeps good time 4 (= *designar*) [+ *tarea*] to assign; [+ *política, estrategia*] to

lay down; [+ *directrices, pautas*] to lay down, give; [+ *comienzo, período*] to mark; **la empresa nos ha marcado algunas pautas a seguir** the company has given us *o* has issued some guidelines to follow; **la paz marcó el comienzo de una nueva era** peace marked the beginning of a new era; **como marca la ley** as specified by law
5 (= *hacer resaltar*) to accentuate
6 (*Dep*) **6.1** [+ *gol*] to score **6.2** [+ *tiempo*] to record, clock **6.3** [+ *jugador, contrario*] to mark, shadow
7 (*Mús*) ~ **el compás** to keep time, beat time
8 (*Telec*) to dial
9 (*en peluquería*) to set
Ⓑ VI **1** (*Dep*) to score
2 (*Telec*) to dial
3 (*en peluquería*) to set; **"lavar y marcar"** "shampoo and set"
Ⓒ marcarse VPR **1** [*figura, formas*] to stand out
2 (*Esp**) **¿nos marcamos un baile?** do you fancy a dance?; **se marcó un detalle bien majo conmigo** that was a really nice touch of hers
3 (*en peluquería*) **~se el pelo** to have one's hair set, have one's hair styled

marcha SF **1** [*de soldados, manifestantes*] march; **¡en ~!** let's go!, let's get going; (*Mil*) forward march!; **encabezar la ~** to head the march; **a ~s forzadas** against the clock; **ponerse en ~** [*persona*] (*lit*) to set off; (*fig*) to set about; [*máquina, motor*] to start ➤ **marcha a pie** [*de caminantes*] (= *excursión*) hike; (= *actividad*) hiking; [*de manifestantes*] march ➤ **marcha triunfal** [*de ejército*] triumphal march; (*hacia la meta*) winning run
2 (= *partida*) departure; **tras tu ~** after you left
3 (= *velocidad*) speed; **moderar la ~** to slow down; **a toda ~** at top speed
4 (*Mús*) march ➤ **marcha fúnebre** funeral march ➤ **marcha militar** military march ➤ **marcha nupcial** wedding march ➤ **la Marcha Real** *Spanish national anthem*
5 (*Aut*) gear; **cambiar de ~** to change gear (*Brit*), shift gear (*EEUU*); **primera ~** first gear ➤ **marcha atrás** (*en vehículo*) reverse, reverse gear; (*en negociaciones*) withdrawal; (*) (*en el acto sexual*) withdrawal
6 **en ~** (= *en funcionamiento*) [*máquina, sistema*] in operation; [*motor*] running; [*electrodoméstico, ordenador*] on; [*proyecto*] under way, in progress, on the go; **un país en ~** a country on the move *o* that is going places; **poner en ~** [+ *máquina, motor*] to start; [+ *electrodoméstico, ordenador*] to turn on; [+ *proyecto, actividad*] to set in motion; [+ *ley, resolución*] to implement
7 (= *carrera*) walk, hike; (= *excursión*) walk ➤ **marcha atlética** walk
8 (= *desarrollo*) [*de enfermedad*] course; [*de huracán*] progress; **la ~ de los acontecimientos** the course of events; **la larga ~ de las conversaciones** the long drawn-out process *o* course of the talks; ✦ MODISMO **sobre la ~** (= *en el momento*) there and then; (= *durante una actividad*) as I/you/*etc* go along
9 (*Esp***) (= *animación*) **no tengo ganas de ~** I don't feel like going out; **¿dónde está la ~ de Vigo?** where's the nightlife in Vigo?, where are the good bars in Vigo?; **estar/ir o salir de ~** (*a bares*) to be out/go out (on the town)*; (*a discotecas*) to be out/go (out) clubbing*; **tener ~*** [*persona, música*] to be lively; [*ciudad*] to be full of action, be buzzing*

marchamo SM (= *etiqueta*) label, tag; [*de aduana*] customs mark; (*fig*) stamp

marchante/a SM/F **1** (= *comerciante*) dealer, merchant
2 (*esp Méx**) (= *cliente*) client, customer; (= *vendedor*) (*ambulante*) pedlar, peddler (*EEUU*); (*en mercado*) stall holder

marchar /1a/ **Ⓐ** VI **1** (= *ir*) to go; (= *andar*) to walk; **~on hacia el pueblo** they walked towards the village
2 (*Mil*) to march
3 **¡marchando, que llegamos tarde!** get a move on, we'll be late!; **—¡un café!** **—¡marchando!** "a coffee, please" — "right away, sir!"
4 [*mecanismo*] to work; **el motor no marcha** the engine isn't working, the engine won't work
5 (= *desarrollarse*) to go; **todo marcha bien** everything is going well; **¿cómo marcha eso?** ✧ **¿cómo marchan las cosas?** how's it going?, how are things?
Ⓑ marcharse VPR to go (away), leave; **¿os marcháis?** are

you leaving?; **con permiso, me marcho** if you don't mind I must go; **¿cuándo te marchas de vacaciones?** when are you going on holiday (*esp Brit*) *o* vacation (*EEUU*)?

marchitar /1a/ **Ⓐ** VT to wither, dry up **Ⓑ marchitarse** VPR **1** [*flores*] to wither, fade **2** [*belleza, juventud, esperanzas*] to fade; [*ideales*] to fade away **3** [*persona*] to languish, fade away

marchito/a ADJ [*flores*] withered; [*belleza, juventud, esperanzas*] faded

marchoso/a* **Ⓐ** ADJ (= *animado*) lively **Ⓑ** SM/F **un sitio para los más ~s** a place for those who can really take the pace*

marcial ADJ [*ley*] martial; [*porte, disciplina*] military

marciano/a ADJ, SM/F Martian

marco **Ⓐ** SM **1** (*Arquit, Arte*) frame; **poner ~ a un cuadro** to frame a picture; **el ~ de la puerta** the doorframe **2** (*RPI*) [*de anteojos*] frames *pl* **3** (*Dep*) goal posts *pl*, goal **4** (= *escenario*) setting; **un ~ incomparable** a perfect setting **5** (= *contexto*) framework ➤ **marco legal** legal framework **6** (*Fin*) mark
Ⓑ ADJ INV **acuerdo ~** framework agreement; **plan ~** draft *o* framework plan

marea SF **1** (*Geog*) tide ➤ **marea alta** high tide, high water ➤ **marea baja** low tide, low water ➤ **marea negra** oil slick ➤ **marea viva** spring tide **2** (= *flujo*) tide; **una auténtica ~ humana** a real flood of people

mareado ADJ **1 estar ~** (= *con náuseas*) to be *o* feel sick; (*en barco*) to be *o* feel seasick; (= *aturdido*) to feel dizzy
2 (= *achispado*) tipsy

marear /1a/ **Ⓐ** VT **1** (*Med*) **~ a algn** to make sb feel sick
2 (= *aturdir*) **a algn** to make sb (feel) dizzy; **las alturas me marean** heights make me (feel) dizzy
3 (= *emborrachar*) **~ a algn** to make sb feel drunk *o* light-headed
4 (= *confundir*) to confuse; **no marees al pobre chico con tantas preguntas** stop confusing the poor boy with so many questions
5 (= *fastidiar*) **¡decídete y no me marees más!** make up your mind and stop annoying me!
Ⓑ VI (††) (*Náut*) to sail, navigate
Ⓒ marearse VPR **1** (*Med*) to feel sick; (*en coche*) to get carsick, get travel-sick; (*en barco*) to get seasick
2 (= *aturdirse*) to feel dizzy
3 (= *emborracharse*) to get drunk *o* light-headed

marejada SF swell, heavy sea

marejadilla SF slight swell

maremagno SM, **maremágnum** SM **1** (= *cantidad*) ocean, sea **2** (= *confusión*) confusion

maremoto SM seaquake

marengo ADJ INV **gris ~** dark grey

mareo SM **1** (*Med*) sickness; (*en coche*) carsickness, travel sickness; (*en barco*) seasickness; (*en avión*) airsickness
2 (= *aturdimiento*) dizziness, giddiness; **le dio un ~ a causa del calor** the heat made her feel dizzy **3** (= *confusión*) **¡qué ~ de cifras!** all these numbers are making me dizzy
4 (= *pesadez*) pain*, nuisance; **es un ~ tener que ...** it is a pain *o* nuisance having to ...

mareomotriz ADJ [*energía*] wave *antes de s*, tidal *antes de s*

marfil SM ivory

margarina SF margarine

margarita SF **1** (*Bot*) daisy; ✦ MODISMOS **deshojar la ~** (= *juego*) to play "she loves me, she loves me not"; (= *dudar*) to waver; **criar ~s*** to be pushing up the daisies* **2** (= *perla*) pearl; **echar ~s a los cerdos** to cast pearls before swine **3** (*Tip*) daisywheel **4** (= *cóctel*) margarita

margen **Ⓐ** SM **1** [*de página*] margin
2 (= *espacio*) **ganaron por un escaso ~** they won by a narrow margin; **en un escaso ~ de tiempo** in a short space of time ➤ **margen de actuación** scope for action, room for manoeuvre *o* (*EEUU*) maneuver ➤ **margen de confianza** credibility gap ➤ **margen de error** margin of error ➤ **margen de seguridad** safety margin
3 al ~ de [+ *opinión, resultado*] regardless of, despite; **al ~ de lo que tú digas** regardless of *o* despite what you say; **al ~ de que las acusaciones sean o no fundadas** whether the

accusations are true or not; **dejar algo al** ~ to leave sth aside, set sth aside; **mantenerse** o **quedarse al** ~ **de** [+ *negociaciones, situación, escándalo*] to keep out of, stay out of; [+ *sociedad, vida pública*] to remain on the sidelines of, remain on the fringes of
4 (*Econ*) (= *beneficio*) margin ➤ **margen de beneficio** profit margin
Ⓑ SF [*de río*] bank

marginación SF **1** (= *aislamiento*) [*de persona*] alienation; [*de grupo*] alienation, marginalization ➤ **marginación social** (= *discriminación*) social alienation; (= *pobreza*) social deprivation **2** (= *discriminación*) discrimination

marginado/a Ⓐ ADJ **1** (= *aislado*) marginalized; **estar** o **quedar** ~ **de algo** (= *aislado*) to be alienated from sth; (= *excluido*) to be excluded from sth; **sentirse** ~ to feel discriminated against **2** (= *pobre*) deprived Ⓑ SM/F (*por elección*) outsider, drop-out*; (*por discriminación*) underprivileged person, deprived person

marginal ADJ **1** (= *al margen*) [*corrección, nota*] marginal, in the margin **2** (= *pobre*) deprived; **un barrio** ~ a deprived neighbourhood **3** (= *alternativo*) [*teatro*] fringe *antes de s*; [*publicación*] underground *antes de s*; [*artista*] alternative **4** (= *poco importante*) [*asunto*] marginal; [*papel, personaje*] minor **5** (*Econ*) [*coste, tipo*] marginal

marginar /1a/ Ⓐ VT **1** (= *aislar*) [+ *persona*] to alienate; [+ *grupo*] to marginalize; **la marginaban en la escuela** she was alienated at school; **la televisión margina los programas culturales** cultural programmes are marginalized on television
2 (= *discriminar*) **no se ~á a nadie por su ideología** nobody will be discriminated against because of their ideology **3** (= *excluir*) to push out (**de** of), exclude (**de** from); **acabaron marginándola del grupo** they ended up pushing her out of the group o excluding her from the group **4** (*Tip*) [+ *texto*] to write notes in the margin of; [+ *página*] to leave margins on
Ⓑ **marginarse** VPR to alienate oneself (**de** from)

maría¹* SF (*Esp*) (= *marihuana*) grass*, pot*

maría²* SF (*hum o pey*) (= *ama de casa*) traditional housewife

maría³* SF (*Escol*) unimportant subject

maría⁴* SF (*Méx*) *female Indian immigrant from the country to Mexico City*

mariachi SM (= *persona*) mariachi musician; (= *grupo*) mariachi band

marica SM **1** (*) (= *cobarde*) sissy **2** (***) = **maricón**

maricón*** SM **1** (*pey*) (= *homosexual*) queer**, poof (*Brit***), fag (*EEUU***) **2** (= *sinvergüenza*) bastard***; **¡~ de mierda!** you bastard!***

mariconada** SF **¡déjate ya de ~s!** stop pissing about!**, stop behaving like a prat (*Brit***) o jerk! (*EEUU**)

mariconera* SF (man's) handbag

marido SM husband

marihuana, marijuana SF marijuana

marimacho* (*pey*) Ⓐ ADJ butch**, mannish Ⓑ SM mannish woman, butch woman**

marimandón/ona* Ⓐ ADJ overbearing, bossy Ⓑ SM/F bossyboots*

marimba SF **1** (= *xilófono*) marimba; (= *tambor*) *kind of drum* **2** (*CS**) (= *paliza*) beating

marimorena* SF fuss, row; **armar la** ~ to kick up a fuss o a row

marina SF **1** (= *organización*) navy; (= *barcos*) fleet; **la ~ española** the Spanish navy, the Spanish fleet ➤ **marina de guerra** navy ➤ **marina mercante** merchant navy (*Brit*), merchant marine (*EEUU*) **2** (= *marinería*) seamanship; **término de** ~ nautical term **3** (*Arte*) seascape

marinar /1a/ VT to marinate, marinade

marinera SF **1** (= *blusa*) matelot top **2** (*Perú*) (= *baile*) *Peruvian folk dance*; *ver tb* **marinero**

marinero Ⓐ ADJ **1** = **marino A 2** [*gente*] seafaring **3** [*barco*] seaworthy **4** **a la marinera** sailor-fashion; **mejillones a la marinera** (*Culin*) moules marinières Ⓑ SM (*gen*) sailor, mariner (*liter*); (= *hombre de mar*) seafarer, seaman ➤ **marinero de agua dulce** fair-weather sailor, landlubber ➤ **marinero de primera** able seaman; *ver tb* **marinera**

marino Ⓐ ADJ sea *antes de s*, marine Ⓑ SM (= *marinero*) sailor, seaman; (= *oficial*) naval officer ➤ **marino mercante** merchant seaman

marioneta SF puppet, marionette

mariposa SF **1** (*Zool*) butterfly ➤ **mariposa nocturna** moth **2** (*en natación*) butterfly; **100 metros** ~ 100 metres butterfly **3** (= *tuerca*) wing nut, butterfly nut **4** ➤ **mariposa cervical** orthopaedic pillow, butterfly pillow

mariposear /1a/ VI **1** (= *revolotear*) to flutter about, flit to and fro **2** (= *ser inconstante*) to be fickle; (= *coquetear*) to flit from one girl/man to the next

mariposón* SM **1** (= *flirteador*) flirt, Romeo* **2** (*pey*) (= *homosexual*) poof (*Brit***), fag (*EEUU***), fairy**

mariquita Ⓐ SF ladybird (*Brit*), ladybug (*EEUU*) Ⓑ SM (* *pey*) (= *homosexual*) poof (*Brit***), fag (*EEUU***), fairy**

marisabidilla* SF know-all (*Brit*), know-it-all (*EEUU*)

mariscada SF seafood platter

mariscal SM marshal ➤ **mariscal de campo** field marshal

mariscar /1g/ VI to gather shellfish

marisco SM shellfish, seafood; **no me gusta el** ~ o ◇ **no me gustan los ~s** I don't like shellfish o seafood

marisma SF (= *pantano*) salt marsh; (= *tierras de arena*) mud flats *pl*

marisquería SF (= *restaurante*) shellfish bar, seafood restaurant; (= *tienda*) seafood shop (*Brit*), seafood store (*EEUU*)

marital ADJ marital; **convivencia** ~ living together as husband and wife; **hacer vida** ~ to live together as husband and wife

marítimo ADJ (= *de barcos, costeño*) maritime; (= *de navegación*) shipping *antes de s*; (= *del mar*) marine, sea *antes de s*

márketing ['marketin] SM marketing

marmita SF pot

mármol SM marble

marmolista SMF monumental mason

marmóreo ADJ (*liter*) marble *antes de s*, marmoreal (*liter*)

marmota SF **1** (*Zool*) marmot; ♦ MODISMO **dormir como una** ~ to sleep like a log **2** (= *dormilón*) sleepyhead*

maroma SF **1** (= *cuerda*) rope **2** (*LAm*) (= *cuerda floja*) tightrope **3** (*And*) ♦ MODISMO **hacer ~s** to do a balancing act

maromear /1a/ VI (*LAm*) **1** (*en cuerda floja*) to walk the tightrope **2** (*Pol*) (= *ser diplomático*) to do a balancing act; (= *ser chaquetero*) to change one's political allegiance

maromo* SM (*esp Esp*) bloke*, guy*

marqués/esa SM/F marquis/marchioness

marquesina SF (= *cubierta*) glass canopy, porch; [*de parada*] bus shelter

marquetería SF marquetry

marranada* SF, **marranería*** SF **1** (= *inmundicia*) filthiness **2** (= *acto*) filthy act; **decir ~s** to talk filth **3** (= *mala pasada*) dirty trick

marrano/a Ⓐ ADJ (*) filthy, dirty Ⓑ SM (*Zool*) pig, hog (*EEUU*) Ⓒ SM/F **1** (*) (= *persona*) (*despreciable*) swine*; (*sucio*) dirty pig* **2** (*Hist*) converted Jew

marras ADV **1 de ~: es el problema de ~** it's the same old problem; **el individuo de ~** you-know-who **2** (*Col**) **hace ~ que no lo veo** it's ages since I saw him

marrón Ⓐ ADJ brown Ⓑ SM **1** (= *color*) brown **2** (*Culin*) ➤ **marrón glacé** marron glacé **3** (*Esp***) (= *acusación*) charge; (= *condena*) sentence; (= *situación comprometida*) mess; **le pillaron de** o **en un ~** they caught him red-handed; ✦ MODISMO **comerse un ~** to own up

marroquí Ⓐ ADJ, SMF Moroccan Ⓑ SM (= *piel*) morocco, morocco leather

marroquinería SF **1** (= *artículos*) (fine) leather goods *pl*; (= *tienda*) leather goods shop (*esp Brit*), leather goods store (*EEUU*) **2** (= *arte*) (fine) leatherwork

Marruecos SM Morocco

marrullero/a Ⓐ ADJ (= *lenguaraz*) smooth, glib; (= *engatusador*) cajoling, wheedling; [*equipo, jugador*] dirty Ⓑ SM/F smooth type, smoothie*

marsopa SF porpoise

marsupial ADJ, SM marsupial

marta SF (= *animal*) (pine) marten; (= *piel*) sable ➤ **marta cebellina, marta cibelina** sable

martajar /1a/ VT (*CAm, Méx*) to pound, grind

Marte SM Mars

martes SM INV Tuesday; **~ y trece** ≈ Friday 13th; ✦ REFRÁN **en ~, ni te cases ni te embarques** neither marry nor set sail on a Tuesday

En inglés los días de la semana se escriben con mayúscula.

➤ **martes de carnaval** Shrove Tuesday; *ver tb* **sábado**

MARTES Y TRECE

According to Spanish superstition Tuesday is an unlucky day, even more so if it falls on the 13th of the month. As the proverb goes, **En martes, ni te cases ni te embarques**. In many Latin American countries it is Friday 13th that is considered unlucky.

martillar /1a/ VT, VI = **martillear**

martillazo SM (heavy) blow with a hammer; **destrozar algo a ~s** to smash sth to pieces with a hammer

martilleante ADJ insistent, repetitious

martillear /1a/ Ⓐ VT **1** (= *golpear*) [+ *puerta*] to hammer on, pound on; [+ *piano*] to pound away at **2** (= *atormentar*) to worry, torment Ⓑ VI [*motor*] to knock

martilleo SM hammering

martillero/a SM/F (*SAm*) auctioneer

martillo SM (*tb Dep*) hammer; [*de presidente de asamblea*] gavel ➤ **martillo de madera** mallet

martín SM ➤ **martín pescador** kingfisher

martinete SM **1** (*Mús*) hammer **2** (*Zool*) heron

martingala SF **1** (*) (= *engaño*) trick, fiddle* **2** (*RPl*) (= *prenda*) half belt

Martinica SF Martinique

mártir SMF martyr

martirio SM **1** (*Rel*) martyrdom **2** (= *tormento*) torment, torture; (= *persona*) pain* ➤ **martirio chino** Chinese torture

martirizar /1f/ VT **1** (*Rel*) to martyr **2** (= *atormentar*) to torture, torment

marujeo* SM (*hum o pey*) chitchat, gossip

marxismo SM Marxism

marxista ADJ, SMF Marxist

marzo SM March; *ver tb* **septiembre**

En inglés los meses se escriben con mayúscula.

mas CONJ (*liter*) but

---

más

Ⓐ ADVERBIO   Ⓒ SUSTANTIVO MASCULINO
Ⓑ ADJETIVO

Para expresiones como **más aún, más de la cuenta, a más tardar**, *ver la entrada correspondiente a la otra palabra.*

más Ⓐ ADV
1 (*comparativo*)
1.1 (*con adjetivo, adverbio*) more; **~ cómodo** more comfortable; **~ inteligente** more intelligent

La mayoría de los adjetivos y adverbios de una sílaba (o de dos sílabas teminados en **-y**) forman el comparativo añadiendo la terminación **-er**. A veces se produce un cambio ortográfico:

~ barato cheaper; **~ grande** bigger; **~ fácil** easier; **~ lejos** further
1.2 (*con verbo*) **ahora salgo ~** I go out more these days; **correr ~** to run faster; **durar ~** to last longer; **me gusta ~ sin chocolate** I like it better o I prefer it without chocolate; **trabajar ~** to work harder
1.3 (*con numerales, sustantivos*) **quisiera dos libros ~** I'd like another two books, I'd like two more books; **un kilómetro ~ y llegaremos** one more kilometre and we'll be there; **una vez ~** once more, one more time; **¡no aguanto aquí ni un minuto ~!** I can't stand it here a minute longer!
1.4 **~ de** more than; **no tiene ~ de dieciséis años** he isn't more than sixteen; **son ~ de las diez** it's past o gone o after ten o'clock; **~ de lo que yo creía** more than I thought
1.5 **~ que** more than; **el alemán es ~ difícil que el inglés** German is more difficult o harder than English; **tiene ~ dinero que yo** he has more money than I do o than me; **se trata de voluntad ~ que de fuerza** it's a question of willpower rather than of strength, it's more a question of willpower than of strength
2 (*superlativo*)
2.1 (*con adjetivos, sustantivos*) most; **su novela ~ innovadora** his most innovative novel; **él es el ~ inteligente** he is the most intelligent (one)

La mayoría de los adjetivos y adverbios de una sílaba (o de dos sílabas teminados en **-y**) forman el superlativo añadiendo la terminación **-est**. A veces se produce un cambio ortográfico:

el niño ~ joven the youngest child; **el coche ~ grande** the biggest car; **el punto ~ lejano** the furthest point
2.2 (*con verbos*) **salió cuando ~ llovía** he left when it was raining the heaviest o the hardest, he left when the rain was at its heaviest; **el/la que ~: él es el que sabe ~** he's the one who knows (the) most; **el que ~ me gusta es el de flores** the one I like (the) best o most is the flowery one; **trabaja tanto como el que ~** he works as hard as anyone
2.3 **~ ... de: el ~ alto de la clase** the tallest in the class
2.4 **a lo ~** at (the) most; **lo ~ posible** as much as possible; **lo ~ temprano** the earliest; **un libro de lo ~ divertido** a most o highly amusing book; **es un hombre de lo ~ honrado** he's entirely honest; **todo lo ~** at (the) most
3 **algo ~: quisiera decirle algo ~** there's something else I wanted to say to you; **¿desea algo ~?** would you like anything else?; **no dijo nada ~** he didn't say anything else, he said nothing else; **no lo sabe nadie ~** no one else knows, nobody else knows; **¿qué ~?** what else?
4 (*al sumar*) and, plus; **dos ~ tres (son) cinco** two and o plus three is five; **éstos, ~ los que ya teníamos, hacen 200** these together with o plus the ones we had before, make 200
5 (*en frases negativas*)
5.1 (*con sentido restrictivo*) **no veo ~ solución que ...** I see no other solution than o but to ...; **al final no fue ~ que un**

susto it gave us a fright, but that's all; **no hace ~ de tres semanas** only *o* just three weeks ago, no more than three weeks ago

5.2 (= *otra vez*) **no vengas ~ por aquí** don't come round here any more; **nunca ~ le ofreceré mi ayuda** I'll never offer to help her again

6 (*con valor intensivo*) **qué ... ~: ¡qué perro ~ feo!** what an ugly dog!; **¡es ~ bueno!** he's (ever) so kind!

7 (*otras locuciones*) **es ~** what's more, furthermore, moreover; **dos ~, dos menos** give or take two; **ni ~ ni menos: él es uno ~ de entre nosotros, ni ~ ni menos** he's just one of the group, that's all; **desciende ni ~ ni menos que de Carlomagno** he is descended from none other than Charlemagne, he is descended from Charlemagne no less; **~ o menos: me dijo ~ o menos lo mismo de ayer** he said more or less the same thing to me yesterday; **me levanté a las siete ~ o menos** I got up at around *o* about seven o'clock; **por ~ que: por ~ que se esfuerce** however much *o* hard he tries, no matter how (hard) he tries; **por ~ veces que se lo he dicho** no matter how many times I've told him; **sin ~ (ni ~)** without further ado; ✦ MODISMOS **a ~ no poder: está lloviendo a ~ no poder** it really is pouring down; **corrimos a ~ no poder** we ran as fast as we could; **a ~ y mejor: está nevando a ~ y mejor** it really is snowing, it's snowing and then some; **ir a ~: discutieron, pero la cosa no fue a ~** they argued, but things didn't get out of hand; **el problema de la droga va a ~** the drugs problem is getting out of hand *o* out of control

✦ **de más: tenemos uno de ~** we have one too many; **trae una manta de ~** bring an extra blanket; **estar de ~** to be unnecessary, be superfluous; **aquí yo estoy de ~** I'm not needed here, I'm in the way here; **unas copas no estarían de ~** a few drinks wouldn't do any harm; **no estará (por) de ~ preguntar** there's no harm in asking

✦ **no más** (*LAm*) just, only; **así no ~** just like that; **ayer no ~** just *o* only yesterday; **¡espera no ~!** just you wait!; **no ~ llegué me echaron** no sooner had I arrived than they threw me out; **siéntese no ~** please *o* do sit down

B ADJ (*) **esta es ~ casa que la mía** this is a better house than the last one; **es ~ hombre** he's more of a man

C SUSTANTIVO MASCULINO Mat plus, plus sign;

✦ MODISMO **tiene sus ~ y sus menos** it has its good and its bad points, there are things to be said on both sides

masa¹ SF [*de pan*] dough; (*para empanadas etc*) pastry

masa² SF **1** (= *conjunto*) mass; **una ~ de aire** a mass of air; **una ~ de nubes** a bank of clouds

2 (= *volumen*) mass ➤ **masa encefálica** brain matter ➤ **masa molecular** molecular mass

3 (*Sociol*) **las ~s** the masses; **los medios de comunicación de ~s** the mass media

4 en ~ (= *en multitud*) en masse; **fueron en ~ a recibir al equipo** they went en masse to greet the team; **despidos en ~** mass layoffs, mass redundancies (*Brit*)

5 (*Econ*) ➤ **masa salarial** total wage bill

6 (*Elec*) earth (*Brit*), ground (*EEUU*); **conectar un aparato con ~** to earth (*Brit*) *o* ground (*EEUU*) an appliance

7 (*RPl*) (= *pastelillo*) pastry

masacrar /1a/ VT to massacre

masacre SF massacre

masaje SM massage; **dar (un) ~ a algn** to give sb a massage; **salón de ~** massage parlour ➤ **masaje cardíaco** cardiac massage

masajear /1a/ VT to massage

masajista SMF masseur/masseuse; (*Dep*) physio* ➤ **masajista terapéutico/a** physiotherapist

masato SM (*And, CAm*) *drink made from fermented maize, bananas, yucca etc*

mascada SF (*Méx*) scarf

mascar /1g/ **A** VT **1** (= *masticar*) to chew **2** (*) [+ *palabras*] to mumble, mutter; ✦ MODISMOS **~ un asunto** ✧ **dar mascado un asunto** to explain sth in very simple terms **B** VI to chew

máscara SF **1** (= *careta*) mask; **baile de ~s** masked ball ➤ **máscara antigás** gas mask ➤ **máscara de oxígeno** oxygen mask ➤ **máscara facial** face mask *o* pack **2 máscaras** (= *mascarada*) masque *sing*, masquerade *sing*

3 (= *apariencia*) mask; (= *disfraz*) disguise; **bajo su ~ de cinismo** beneath his mask of cynicism; **quitar la ~ a algn** to unmask sb; **quitarse la ~** to reveal o.s.

mascarada SF **1** (= *fiesta*) masque, masquerade **2** (= *farsa*) charade, masquerade

mascarilla SF (= *máscara*) (*tb Med*) mask; (*en cosmética*) face mask *o* pack ➤ **mascarilla capilar** (= *sustancia*) hair oil; (= *tratamiento*) hair-conditioning treatment ➤ **mascarilla facial** face mask, face pack (*Brit*)

mascarón SM ➤ **mascarón de proa** figurehead

mascota SF **1** [*de club, acontecimiento*] mascot **2** (= *animal doméstico*) pet

masculinidad SF masculinity, manliness

masculino **A** ADJ **1** (*Biol*) male; [*apariencia*] masculine **2** (*Ling*) masculine **B** SM (*Ling*) masculine

> Como traducción de **masculino** el adjetivo **male** señala que se está haciendo referencia a algo relativo al sexo masculino y no al femenino, p.ej. "los protagonistas masculinos", *the male characters*. El adjetivo **masculine** se utiliza en relación a cualidades que se consideran típicas del hombre y no de la mujer, p.ej. "rasgos masculinos", *masculine characteristics*. Se utiliza además para indicar el género gramatical.

mascullar /1a/ VT to mumble, mutter

masectomía SF mastectomy

masía SF *traditional Aragonese or Catalan farmstead*

masificación SF (= *abarrotamiento*) overcrowding; (= *propagación*) growth, spread; **la ~ de la universidad** overcrowding in universities; **la ~ de la producción de alimentos** mass production of food

masilla SF (*para ventanas*) putty; (*para agujeros*) filler

masita SF (*CS*) small cake, pastry

masitero SM (*And, Carib, CS*) pastry cook, confectioner

masivamente ADV en masse; **votaron ~ al partido socialista** they voted en masse for the socialist party; **la huelga fue apoyada ~** there was overwhelming support for the strike

masivo ADJ [*ataque, dosis*] massive; [*evacuación, ejecución*] mass *antes de s*; **se espera una asistencia masiva** a huge turnout is expected

masoca* **A** ADJ masochistic **B** SMF masochist

masón SM (free)mason

masonería SF (free)masonry

masónico ADJ masonic

masoquismo SM masochism

masoquista **A** ADJ masochistic **B** SMF masochist

masoterapia SF massage (therapy)

mastectomía SF mastectomy

master, máster **A** ADJ [*copia*] master **B** SM (*pl* **~s**) **1** (*Univ*) master's degree (**en** in) **2** (*Cine, Mús*) master copy **3** (*Dep*) masters' (competition); **el Master de Augusta** the Augusta Masters

masticar /1g/ VT to chew, masticate (*frm*)

mástil SM **1** (= *palo*) pole; (= *sostén*) support; (*para bandera*) flagpole; (*Náut*) mast; (*Arquit*) upright ➤ **mástil de tienda** tent pole **2** [*de guitarra*] neck

mastín SM mastiff

mastodonte SM **1** (= *animal*) mastodon **2** (*) (= *persona*) (great) hulk*; (= *organización*) behemoth

mastodóntico ADJ colossal, huge

mastuerzo SM **1** (*Bot*) cress; (*tb ~ de agua*) watercress **2** (*) (= *persona*) clodhopper*

masturbación SF masturbation

masturbar /1a/ **A** VT to masturbate **B** masturbarse VPR to masturbate

mata SF **1** (= *arbusto*) bush, shrub; (*esp LAm*) (= *planta*) plant; (*en tiesto*) potted plant **2** (= *ramita*) sprig; (= *manojo*) tuft; (= *raíz*) clump **3 matas** (= *matorral*) thicket *sing*, scrub *sing*, bushes **4** ➤ **mata de pelo** mop of hair

matadero SM slaughterhouse, abattoir (*Brit*)

matador(a) Ⓐ ADJ **1** (= *que mata*) killing **2** (*) (= *horrible*) horrible; (= *ridículo*) ridiculous; **el vestido te está ~** that dress looks terrible on you Ⓑ SM/F (*tb* ~ **de toros**) matador, bullfighter

matambre SM (*CS*) stuffed rolled beef

matamoscas SM INV (= *paleta*) fly swat; (= *papel*) flypaper; (= *aerosol*) fly spray

matanza SF (*en batalla*) slaughter, killing; (*Agr*) slaughtering; (= *temporada*) slaughtering season; (*fig*) slaughter, massacre

mataperrada* SF (*And*) dirty trick

mataperrear* /1a/ VI (*And*) to wander the streets

matar /1a/ Ⓐ VT **1** [+ *persona*] to kill; [+ *reses, ganado*] to kill, slaughter; **el jefe me va a ~** the boss will kill me; **~ a algn a golpes** to beat sb to death; **~ a algn a disgustos** to make sb's life a misery; ✦ MODISMO **~las callando** to go about things slyly
2 [+ *tiempo, pelota*] to kill; [+ *sed*] to quench; [+ *sello*] to postmark, cancel; [+ *pieza*] (*en ajedrez*) to take; [+ *cal*] to slake; [+ *ángulo, borde*] to file down; [+ *color*] to dull; **cómete una manzana para ~ el hambre** have an apple to keep you going
3 (*) (= *molestar*) **los zapatos me están matando** these shoes are killing me*
Ⓑ VI to kill; ✦ MODISMO **estar** *o* **llevarse a ~ con algn** to be at daggers drawn with sb
Ⓒ **matarse** VPR **1** (= *suicidarse*) to kill o.s.
2 (= *morir*) to be killed, get killed
3 (= *esforzarse*) to kill o.s.; **~se trabajando** *o* (*Esp*) **a trabajar** to kill o.s. with work; **se mata por sacar buenas notas** he goes all out to get good marks

matarife SM **1** [*de animales*] slaughterman, butcher **2** (= *matón*) thug

matarratas SM INV **1** (= *veneno*) rat poison **2** (*) (= *alcohol*) rotgut, bad liquor

matasanos* SM INV (*hum*) quack (doctor)

matasellar /1a/ VT to postmark, frank

matasellos SM INV (= *marca*) postmark; (= *instrumento*) franking machine; **la carta tenía ~ de Madrid** the letter was postmarked Madrid

matazón SF (*And, CAm, Carib*) = **matanza**

mate[1] ADJ (= *sin brillo*) matt

mate[2] SM (*Ajedrez*) mate; **dar ~ a** (*lit*) to mate, checkmate; (*Méx**) (*fig*) to polish off

mate[3] SM (*LAm*) **1** (= *bebida*) maté **2** (= *vasija*) gourd, maté pot **3** (*CS***) (= *cabeza*) head, nut*, noggin (*EEUU**)

matear /1a/ VI (*LAm*) to drink maté

matemáticas SFPL mathematics *sing* ➤ **matemáticas puras** pure mathematics

matemático/a Ⓐ ADJ **1** (*Mat*) mathematical; [*cálculo*] precise **2** (= *exacto*) exact **3** (*Dep*) **con esa victoria aseguró el ascenso ~** with that win they made sure of promotion **4 es ~** (= *no falla*): **¡es ~!, ¡cada vez que me siento, suena el teléfono!** it's like clockwork!, every time I sit down the phone rings! Ⓑ SM/F mathematician, math specialist (*EEUU*)

materia SF **1** (*Fís*) matter; (= *material*) material, substance ➤ **materia grasa** fat ➤ **materia gris** grey *o* (*EEUU*) gray matter ➤ **materia prima** raw material **2** (= *tema*) subject matter; (*Escol*) subject; **índice de ~s** table of contents; **en ~ de** as regards; **entrar en ~** to get down to business, get to the point; **son expertos en la ~** they are experts on the subject ➤ **materia optativa** (*Escol*) option, optional subject

material Ⓐ ADJ **1** [*ayuda, valor*] material **2** (= *físico*) physical; **la presencia ~ de algn** sb's physical *o* bodily presence; **daños ~es** physical damage, damage to property **3** (= *real*) **la imposibilidad ~ de ...** the physical impossibility of ...; **el autor ~ del hecho** the actual perpetrator of the deed; **no tengo tiempo ~ para ir** I literally don't have time to go

Ⓑ SM **1** (= *materia*) material; **tengo ya ~ para una novela** I've got enough material now for a novel ➤ **materiales de derribo** rubble *sing* ➤ **material impreso** printed matter **2** (= *equipo*) equipment ➤ **material bélico** war material, military equipment ➤ **material de oficina** office supplies *pl*, stationery ➤ **material escolar** school equipment ➤ **material fotográfico** photographic equipment ➤ **material informático** hardware ➤ **material móvil, material rodante** rolling stock **3** (*) (= *cuero*) leather

materialismo SM materialism

materialista Ⓐ ADJ materialist(ic) Ⓑ SMF materialist Ⓒ SM **1** (*Méx*) (= *camionero*) lorry driver (*Brit*), truckdriver (*EEUU*) **2** (*Méx*) (= *contratista*) building contractor

materializar /1f/ Ⓐ VT to materialize Ⓑ **materializarse** VPR to materialize

materialmente ADV **1** (= *de manera material*) materially **2** (= *absolutamente*) absolutely; **nos es ~ imposible** it is quite *o* absolutely impossible for us

maternal Ⓐ ADJ [*instinto*] maternal; [*amor*] motherly, maternal Ⓑ SM (*Carib*) (= *guardería*) nursery

maternidad SF **1** (= *estado*) motherhood, maternity **2** (= *hospital*) maternity hospital

materno ADJ [*lengua*] mother *antes de s*; [*amor, tono*] motherly, maternal; [*casa*] mother's; **el útero ~** the mother's womb; **abuelo ~** maternal grandfather, grandfather on one's mother's side; **leche materna** mother's milk; **hospital ~-infantil** maternity hospital

matete* SM (*CS*) **1** (= *revoltijo*) mess, hash* **2** (= *confusión*) confusion

matinal Ⓐ ADJ morning *antes de s* Ⓑ SF matinée

matinée SF **1** (*Teat*) matinée **2** (*And*) (= *fiesta infantil*) children's party

matiz SM **1** [*de color*] shade **2** [*de sentido*] shade, nuance; (= *ironía*) touch

matización SF **1** (*Arte*) blending **2** (= *aclaración*) qualification; **quiero hacer una ~** I'd like to qualify *o* clarify that

matizar /1f/ VT **1** (*Arte*) to blend; [+ *tono*] to vary, introduce some variety into; [+ *contraste, intensidad de colores*] to tone down **2** (= *aclarar*) to qualify; **creo que deberías ~ lo que acabas de decir** I think what you just said needs qualifying; **~ que ...** to explain that ..., point out that ...

matón SM (= *bravucón*) thug; (*en el colegio*) bully, thug

matorral SM (= *matas*) thicket, bushes *pl*; (= *terreno*) scrubland

matraca SF **1** (= *carraca*) rattle **2** (*) nuisance, pain*; **dar la ~ a algn** to pester sb

matraz SM flask

matrero (*LAm*) Ⓐ ADJ cunning, sly Ⓑ SM fugitive from justice

matriarcado SM matriarchy

matriarcal ADJ matriarchal

matricidio SM matricide

matrícula SF **1** (= *inscripción*) registration, enrolment, enrollment (*EEUU*); **el plazo de ~ finaliza el día 15** the last day for registration *o* enrolment *o* (*EEUU*) enrollment is the 15th; **fui a la universidad a hacer la ~** I went to University to matriculate; **tasas de ~** registration fees **2** (= *nota*) ➤ **matrícula de honor** *top marks in a subject or subjects which gives the student the right to free registration in a corresponding number of subjects the following year* **3** (*Aut*) (= *número*) registration number (*Brit*), license number (*EEUU*); (= *placa*) number plate (*Brit*), license plate (*EEUU*)

matriculación SF **1** (= *inscripción*) registration, enrolment, enrollment (*EEUU*) **2** [*de barco, vehículo*] registration

matricular /1a/ Ⓐ VT **1** (= *inscribir*) to register, enrol, enroll (*EEUU*) **2** [+ *barco, vehículo*] to register Ⓑ **matricularse** VPR to register, enrol, enroll (*EEUU*)

matrimonial ADJ matrimonial; **agencia** ~ marriage bureau; **vida** ~ married life, conjugal life (*frm*)

matrimonio SM **1** (= *institución*) marriage, matrimony (*frm*); **contraer** ~ **(con algn)** to marry (sb); **tras 26 años de** ~ after 26 years of marriage; **hacer vida de** ~ to live together as man and wife ➤ **matrimonio civil** civil marriage ➤ **matrimonio de conveniencia, matrimonio de interés** marriage of convenience ➤ **matrimonio religioso** church wedding **2** (= *pareja*) (married) couple; **el** ~ **García** the Garcías, Mr and Mrs García; **cama de** ~ double bed **3** (*And*) (= *ceremonia*) wedding ceremony

matriz SF **1** (*Anat*) womb, uterus **2** (*Téc*) mould, mold (*EEUU*), die; (*Tip*) matrix **3** [*de talonario*] stub, counterfoil **4** (*Jur*) original, master copy **5** (*Mat*) matrix; (*Inform*) array

matrona SF **1** (= *mujer*) matron **2** (= *comadrona*) midwife

matutino Ⓐ ADJ morning *antes de s* Ⓑ SM morning newspaper

maullar /1a/ VI to mew, miaow

maullido SM mew, miaow

Mauritania SF Mauritania

mausoleo SM mausoleum

maxilar Ⓐ ADJ maxillary Ⓑ SM jaw, jawbone

máxima¹ SF (= *frase*) maxim

máxima² SF (*Meteo*) maximum (temperature), high; **~s de 40 grados** top temperatures *o* highs of 40 degrees

máxime ADV (= *sobre todo*) especially; (= *principalmente*) principally; **y** ~ **cuando ...** and all the more so when ...

maximizar /1f/ VT to maximize

máximo Ⓐ ADJ [*altura, temperatura, velocidad*] maximum; **el** ~ **dirigente** the leader; ~ **jefe** *o* **líder** (*esp LAm*) President, leader; **llegar al punto** ~ to reach the highest point Ⓑ SM maximum; **un** ~ **de 10.000 pesos** a maximum of 10,000 pesos; **el** ~ **de tiempo que se te permite** the maximum time you're allowed; **al** ~ to the maximum; **como** ~ (= *como mucho*) at the most, at the outside; (= *como muy tarde*) at the latest ➤ **máximo histórico** all-time high

maxisingle [maksi'singel] SM twelve-inch (record)

maya (*Hist*) Ⓐ ADJ Mayan Ⓑ SMF Maya, Mayan; **los** ~ the Maya(s)

mayestático ADJ majestic, royal; **el plural** ~ the royal "we"

mayo SM May; **el primero de** ~ May Day; **el Mayo Francés** May 68; *ver tb* **septiembre**

En inglés los meses se escriben con mayúscula.

mayonesa SF mayonnaise

mayor Ⓐ ADJ **1** (*comparativo*) **1.1** (= *más grande*) **un** ~ **número de visitantes** a larger *o* greater number of visitors, more visitors; **son temas de** ~ **importancia** they are more important issues, they are issues of greater importance; **la** ~ <u>parte</u> **de los ciudadanos** most citizens; **ser** ~ **que algo**: **el índice de paro es** ~ **que hace un año** unemployment is higher than (it was) a year ago; ✦ MODISMO **llegar a** ~**es** [*situación*] to get out of hand, get out of control **1.2** (= *de más edad*) older; **es mi hermana** ~ she's my older *o* elder sister; **Emilio es el** ~ **de los dos** Emilio is the older of the two; ~ **que algn** older than sb **2** (*superlativo*) **2.1** (= *más grande*) **su** ~ **problema** his biggest *o* greatest problem **2.2** (= *de más edad*) oldest; **mi hijo (el)** ~ my oldest *o* eldest son **3** (*en frases negativas*) **no tiene** ~ **importancia** it isn't very important; **sin** ~**es complicaciones** with no major problems **4** (= *principal*) [*plaza, mástil*] main; [*altar, misa*] high; **calle** ~ high street (*esp Brit*), main street (*EEUU*) **5** (= *adulto*) grown-up, adult; **nuestros hijos ya son** ~**es** our children are grown-up now; **las personas** ~**es** grown-ups, adults; **ya eres muy** ~ **para hacer esas tonterías** you're too old now to do silly things like that; **ser** ~ **de** <u>edad</u> to be of age; <u>hacerse</u> ~ to grow up **6** (= *de edad avanzada*) old, elderly

7 (= *jefe*) head *antes de s*; **el cocinero** ~ the head chef **8** (*Mús*) major Ⓑ SMF **1** (= *adulto*) grown-up, adult ➤ **mayor de edad** adult, *person who is legally of age* **2** (= *anciano*) **los** ~**es** elderly people Ⓒ SM **al por** ~ wholesale

mayoral SM **1** (= *capataz*) foreman, overseer **2** [*de finca*] farm manager, steward; [*de ovejas*] head shepherd

mayorazgo SM **1** (= *institución*) primogeniture **2** (= *tierras*) entailed estate

mayordomo SM [*de casa*] butler; [*de hacienda*] steward; (*CS*) (= *capataz*) foreman; (*And*) (= *criado*) servant

mayoreo SM (*LAm*) wholesale (trade)

mayoría SF **1** (= *mayor parte*) majority; **la** ~ **de los españoles** the majority of Spaniards, most Spaniards; **en la** ~ **de los casos** in most cases; **en su** ~ mostly; **una** ~ **del 20 por ciento** a 20 per cent majority; **la inmensa** ~ the vast majority ➤ **mayoría absoluta** absolute majority ➤ **mayoría relativa** simple majority, relative majority ➤ **mayoría simple** simple majority **2** ➤ **mayoría de edad** adulthood, majority ➤ **mayoría de edad penal** age of majority; **cumplir** *o* **llegar a la** ~ **de edad** to come of age

mayorista Ⓐ ADJ wholesale Ⓑ SMF wholesaler

mayoritario ADJ majority *antes de s*

mayormente ADV (= *principalmente*) chiefly, mainly; (= *especialmente*) especially; (= *tanto más*) all the more so

mayúscula SF capital (letter); (*Tip*) upper case letter; **se escribe con** ~ it's written with a capital (letter)

mayúsculo ADJ **1** [*letra*] capital **2** (= *enorme*) tremendous

maza SF (= *arma*) mace; (*en polo*) stick, mallet; (*Mús*) drumstick; [*de taco de billar*] handle; (*Téc*) flail ➤ **maza de fraga** drop hammer ➤ **maza de gimnasia** Indian club

mazacote SM **el arroz se ha hecho un** ~ the rice is just one sticky mass

mazamorra (*LAm*) SF **1** [*de maíz*] cornmeal porridge **2** (= *ampolla*) blister

mazapán SM marzipan

mazazo SM heavy blow

mazmorra SF dungeon

mazo SM **1** (= *martillo*) mallet; [*de mortero*] pestle; (= *porra*) club; [*de croquet*] mallet; [*de campana*] clapper; (*Agr*) flail **2** (= *manojo*) bunch, handful; [*de papeles*] sheaf, bundle; [*de naipes*] pack

mazorca SF **1** [*de maíz*] cob, ear ➤ **mazorca de maíz** corncob **2** (*Téc*) spindle

me PRON PERS **1** (*como complemento directo*) me; **me llamó por teléfono** he telephoned *o* rang me; **ya no me quiere** he doesn't love me any more **2** (*como complemento indirecto*) (to) me; **¡dámelo!** give it to me!; **me lo compró** (*de mí*) he bought it from me; (*para mí*) he bought it for me; **me lo dijeron ayer** they told me yesterday **3** (*con partes del cuerpo, ropa*)

Con partes del cuerpo o con prendas que se llevan puestas se usa el adjetivo posesivo:

me rompí el brazo I broke my arm; **me quité el abrigo** I took my coat off **4** (*uso enfático*) **me lo comí todo** I ate it all up; **me leí la novela en dos días** I read the book in (just) two days **5** (*uso reflexivo o pronominal*) **me lavé** I washed (myself); **me miré al espejo** I looked at myself in the mirror; **me marcho** I am going

meada** SF piss***

meadero** SM bog (*Brit***), loo (*Brit**), john (*EEUU***)

meados** SMPL piss*** *sing*

meandro SM meander

mear** /1a/ Ⓐ VI to piss***, have *o* (*EEUU*) take a piss***; ✦ MODISMO ~ **fuera del tiesto** to miss the point completely Ⓑ **mearse** VPR to wet o.s.; ~**se de risa** to piss o.s. laughing***

meca[1] SF **la ~ del cine** the Mecca of the film world

meca[2]*** EXCL (*Chi*) shit!***

meca[3]* SF (*And*) prostitute

Meca SF **La ~** Mecca

mecachis* EXCL (*Esp euf*) sugar!*, shoot!*; **¡~ en la mar!** sugar!*, shoot!*

mecánica SF **1** (= *técnica*) mechanics *sing* ➤ **mecánica cuántica** quantum mechanics *sing* **2** (= *mecanismo*) mechanism, works **3** (= *funcionamiento*) mechanics *pl*; **la ~ del concurso es sencilla** the mechanics of the competition are simple; **la ~ electoral** electoral procedure

mecanicista ADJ mechanistic

mecánico/a Ⓐ ADJ **1** (*gen*) mechanical; (*con motor*) power *antes de s*; (= *de máquinas*) machine *antes de s* **2** (*gesto, trabajo*) mechanical Ⓑ SM/F (*de coches*) mechanic, grease monkey (*EEUU**); (= *operario*) machinist; (*Aer*) rigger, fitter ➤ **mecánico/a de vuelo** flight engineer

mecanismo SM **1** (*de reloj, cerradura, fusil*) mechanism **2** (= *procedimiento*) mechanism ➤ **mecanismo de defensa** defence mechanism

mecanización SF mechanization

mecanografía SF typing

mecanografiar /1c/ VT to type

mecanógrafo/a SM/F typist

mecapal SM (*CAm, Méx*) leather strap (*for carrying*)

mecapalero SM (*CAm, Méx*) porter

mecatazo SM (*CAm, Méx*) **1** (= *golpe*) lash **2** (*) (= *trago*) swig*

mecate SM (*CAm, Méx*) (= *cuerda*) rope, twine; (= *fibra*) strip of pita fibre; ✦ MODISMO **jalar el ~ a algn*** to suck up to sb*

mecateada SF (*CAm, Méx*) lashing, beating

mecatear[1] /1a/ VT (*CAm, Méx*) to lash, whip

mecatear[2] /1a/ VI (*Col*) to snack

mecedora SF rocking chair

mecenas SMF INV patron; **~ de las artes** patron of the arts

mecenazgo SM patronage

mecer /2b/ Ⓐ VT (+ *cuna, niño*) to rock; (*en columpio*) to swing; (+ *rama*) to cause to sway, move to and fro; (*olas*) (+ *barco*) to rock Ⓑ **mecerse** VPR (*en mecedora*) to rock (to and fro); (*en columpio*) to swing; (*rama*) to sway, move to and fro

mecha SF **1** (*de vela, lámpara*) wick; (*de explosivo*) fuse; ✦ MODISMOS **aguantar ~*** to grin and bear it; **a toda ~*** at full speed **2** (*de pelo*) = **mechón**[1] **3 mechas** (*en el pelo*) highlights **4** (*RPl*) (*de taladro*) (drill) bit

mechar /1a/ VT (*Culin*) (*con tocino*) to lard; (= *rellenar*) to stuff

mechero SM (= *encendedor*) cigarette lighter; (= *quemador*) burner; (*And, CS*) (= *candil*) oil lamp

mechón[1] SM (*de pelo*) lock

mechón[2]**/ona*** SM/F (*Chi*) fresher, freshman

mechudo ADJ (*LAm*) tousled, unkempt

medalla SF (*Dep, Mil*) medal; (= *joya*) medallion; **una ~ de la Virgen** a medallion with the Virgin Mary on it; **ser ~ de bronce/plata/oro** to be a bronze/silver/gold medallist *o* (*EEUU*) medalist, get a bronze/silver/gold (medal) ➤ **medalla al valor** medal for bravery

medallero SM medal table

medallista SMF medallist, medalist (*EEUU*)

medallón SM **1** (= *medalla*) medallion **2** (*Culin*) medallion, médaillon

médano SM (*en tierra*) sand dune; (*en el mar*) sandbank

media SF **1 medias** (= *hasta la cintura*) tights (*Brit*), pantyhose (*EEUU*); (*hasta el muslo*) stockings ➤ **medias de compresión** support tights (*Brit*), support hose *sing* (*esp EEUU*) **2** (*LAm*) (= *calcetín*) sock **3** (*Dep*) midfield **4** (= *promedio*) average; **100 de ~ al día** an average of 100 a day ➤ **media aritmética** arithmetic mean

mediación SF mediation, intercession; **por ~ de** through

mediado ADJ (*botella*) half-full; (*trabajo*) halfway through; **mediada la tarde** halfway through the afternoon

mediador(a) SM/F mediator

mediados SMPL **a ~ de marzo** in the middle of March, halfway through March; **a ~ del siglo pasado** around the middle of the last century

mediagua SF (*And*) hut, shack

medialuna SF (*LAm*) croissant

mediana SF **1** (*Aut*) central reservation (*Brit*), median (*EEUU*) **2** (*Mat*) median

medianamente ADV **1** (= *bastante*) fairly; **cualquier persona ~ sensata** any half-sensible person **2** (= *regular*) moderately

medianería SF (*Carib, Méx Com*) partnership; (*Agr*) sharecropping

medianero ADJ (*pared*) party *antes de s*

medianía SF (= *promedio*) average; (= *punto medio*) halfway point; (*en sociedad*) undistinguished social position

mediano ADJ **1** (= *regular*) average; (*en tamaño*) medium-sized; (*empresa*) medium-sized; **una bomba de mediana potencia** a medium-sized bomb; **camisetas de talla mediana** medium T-shirts; **de mediana edad** middle-aged **2** (= *del medio*) middle; **es el hermano ~** he is the middle brother

medianoche SF midnight; **a ~** at midnight

mediante PREP **1** (= *por medio de*) by means of **2 Dios ~** God willing

mediar /1b/ VI **1** (= *llegar a la mitad*) (*tiempo*) **mediaba el mes de julio** it was halfway through July **2** (= *haber en medio*) **media un abismo entre los dos gobiernos** the two governments are poles apart; **sin ~ palabra** without a word **3** (= *interceder*) to mediate (**en** in; **entre** between), intervene; **~ en favor de algn** ◇ **~ por algn** to intercede *o* intervene on sb's behalf; **~ con algn** to intercede with sb

mediático ADJ media *antes de s*

mediatizar /1f/ VT (= *estorbar*) to interfere with, obstruct; (= *influir*) to influence

medicación SF (= *medicinas*) medication; (= *tratamiento*) medication, treatment

medicamento SM medicine

medicar /1g/ Ⓐ VT to give medicine to; **estar medicado** to be on medication Ⓑ **medicarse** VPR to take medicine

medicina SF **1** (= *ciencia*) medicine; **un estudiante de ~** a medical student ➤ **medicina forense** forensic medicine ➤ **medicina general** general medicine, general practice ➤ **medicina interna** internal medicine ➤ **medicina legal** forensic medicine, legal medicine **2** (= *medicamento*) medicine

medicinal ADJ medicinal

medicinar /1a/ Ⓐ VT to give medicine to Ⓑ **medicinarse** VPR to take medicine; **~se con algo** to dose o.s. with sth

medición SF **1** (*de presión, distancia*) (= *acción*) measuring; (= *resultado*) measurement; **un nuevo método de ~** a new measuring system; **¿cómo se realiza la ~ de la temperatura?** how is the temperature measured?; **un método de ~ de audiencias** an audience tracking system; **aparatos de ~** measuring instruments **2** (*de versos*) measuring, scansion

médico/a Ⓐ ADJ medical; **asistencia médica** medical attention; **receta médica** prescription Ⓑ SM/F doctor ➤ **médico/a de cabecera** family doctor, GP ➤ **médico/a (de medicina) general** general practitioner ➤ **médico/a forense** forensic surgeon, expert in forensic medicine; (*Jur*) coroner ➤ **médico/a naturista** naturopath ➤ **médico/a residente** houseman (*Brit*), intern (*EEUU*)

medida SF **1** (= *unidad de medida*) measure; **una ~ de harina y dos de azúcar** one measure of flour and two of sugar ➤ **medida para áridos** dry measure ➤ **medida para líquidos** liquid measure **2** (= *medición*) measuring, measurement **3 medidas** (= *dimensiones*) measurements; **¿qué ~s tiene la mesa?** what are the measurements of the table?; **tomar las ~s a algn/algo** (*lit*) to measure sb/sth, take sb's/sth's

measurements; (*fig*) to size sb/sth up*
4 (= *proporción*) **en cierta ~** to a certain extent; **en gran ~** to a great extent; **en menor ~** to a lesser extent; **en la ~ de lo posible** as far as possible, insofar as it is possible; **a ~ que** as; **a ~ que van pasando los días** as the days go by; **en la ~ en que** (+ INDIC) in that; (+ SUBJUN) if
5 (*Cos*) **a (la) ~** [*ropa, zapatos*] made to measure; [*trabajo, vacaciones*] tailor-made; **un papel hecho a su ~** a tailor-made role; **un hotel a la ~ de tus necesidades** a hotel that suits all your needs
6 (= *disposición*) measure; **~s destinadas a reducir el desempleo** measures aimed at reducing unemployment ➤ **medida de presión** form of pressure ➤ **medidas de seguridad** (*contra ataques, robos*) security measures; (*contra incendios*) safety measures
7 (= *moderación*) **con ~** in moderation; **sin ~** to excess
8 [*de versos*] (= *medición*) measuring, scansion; (= *longitud*) measure

medidor SM (*LAm*) meter

mediero/a SM/F (*Chi*) share-cropper

medieval ADJ medieval

medievalista SMF medievalist

medievo SM Middle Ages *pl*

medio Ⓐ ADJ **1** (= *la mitad de*) half; **~ limón** half a lemon; **acudió media ciudad** half the town turned up; **media pensión** (*en hotel*) half-board; **a media tarde** halfway through the afternoon; **a ~ camino entre ...** halfway between ...; **media hora** half an hour; **una hora y media** an hour and a half; **son las ocho y media** it's half past eight
2 (= *promedio*) average; **la temperatura media** the average temperature
3 (= *normal*) average; **el francés ~** the average Frenchman
4 a medias: está escrito a medias it's half-written; **una verdad a medias** a half truth; **ir a medias** to go fifty-fifty Ⓑ ADV **1** (*con adjetivo*) half; **~ dormido** half asleep; **es ~ tonto** he's not very bright, he's a bit on the slow side
2 (*con verbo, adverbio*) **está a ~ escribir/terminar** it is half-written/finished; **lo dijo ~ en broma** he was only half-joking; **eso no está ni ~ bien** that isn't even close to being right Ⓒ SM **1** (= *centro*) middle, centre, center (*EEUU*); **justo en el ~ de la plaza hay una fuente** there's a fountain right in the middle *o* centre of the square; **de en ~: la casa de en ~** the middle house; **quitar algo de en ~** to get sth out of the way; **quitarse de en ~** to get out of the way; **de por ~: hay droga de por ~** drugs are involved; **hay dificultades de por ~** there are difficulties in the way; **día (de) por ~** (*LAm*) every other day; **en ~: iba a besarla, pero él se puso en ~** I was going to kiss her, but he got between us; **no dejes las cosas por en ~** don't leave your things in the middle of the floor; **en ~ de la plaza** in the middle of the square; **en ~ de tanta confusión** in the midst of such confusion; **por ~ de: pasar por ~ de** to go through (the middle of); ✦ MODISMO **de ~ a ~: equivocarse de ~ a ~** to be completely wrong
2 (*Dep*) midfielder
3 (= *método*) means *pl*, way; **lo intentaré por todos los ~s (posibles)** I'll try everything possible; **poner todos los ~s para hacer algo** to spare no effort to do sth; **por ~ de: lo consiguió por ~ de chantajes** he obtained it by *o* through blackmail ➤ **medio de transporte** means of transport (*esp Brit*) *o* transportation (*esp EEUU*)
4 los medios (*tb* **los ~s de comunicación** *o* **difusión**) the media; **los ~s de comunicación de masas** the mass media
5 medios (= *recursos*) means, resources; **no tienen ~s económicos suficientes** they do not have sufficient financial resources
6 (*Biol*) (*tb* **~ ambiente**) environment
7 (= *círculo*) circle; **en los ~s financieros** in financial circles

medioambiental ADJ environmental

medioambiente SM environment

mediocampista SMF midfield player

mediocre ADJ mediocre

mediocridad SF mediocrity

mediodía SM **1** (= *las doce*) midday, noon; (= *hora de comer*) ≈ lunchtime; **a ~** (= *a las doce*) at midday *o* noon;

(= *a la hora de comer*) ≈ at lunchtime **2** (*Geog*) south; **el ~ de Francia** the French Midi

medioevo SM Middle Ages *pl*

Medio Oriente SM Middle East

medir /3k/ Ⓐ VT **1** (= *tomar la medida de*) [*+ habitación, ángulo*] to measure; [*+ distancia, temperatura*] to measure, gauge, gage (*EEUU*); [*+ tierra*] to survey, plot; **~ algo por millas** to measure sth in miles
2 [*+ ventajas, inconvenientes*] to weigh up
3 (= *enfrentar*) **los dos púgiles ~án sus fuerzas** the two boxers will be pitted against each other *o* will take each other on
4 (= *moderar*) [*+ comentarios*] to choose carefully; **mide tus palabras** (*aconsejando*) choose your words carefully; (*regañando*) watch *o* (*Brit*) mind your language
5 (*Literat*) to scan Ⓑ VI to measure, be; **mido 1,80m** I am 1.80m Ⓒ **medirse** VPR **1** (= *tomarse la medida*) (*uno mismo*) to measure o.s.; [*+ cintura, pecho*] to measure
2 (= *enfrentarse*) **~se con algn** to take on sb
3 (= *moderarse*) to restrain o.s.
4 (*Col, Méx*) [*+ sombrero, zapatos*] to try on

meditabundo ADJ pensive, thoughtful

meditación SF meditation (**sobre** on); ➤ **meditación trascendental** transcendental meditation

meditar /1a/ Ⓐ VT (= *pensar*) to ponder, meditate (on); [*+ plan*] to think out Ⓑ VI to meditate, ponder

Mediterráneo SM **el ~** the Mediterranean

mediterráneo ADJ Mediterranean

médium SMF (*pl* **~s**) (= *persona*) medium

medrar /1a/ VI (= *aumentar*) to increase, grow; (= *mejorar*) to improve, do well; (= *prosperar*) to prosper, thrive; [*animal, planta*] to grow, thrive

médula SF marrow, medulla (*frm*); ✦ MODISMO **hasta la ~** to the core ➤ **médula espinal** spinal cord ➤ **médula ósea** bone marrow

medular ADJ **1** (*Anat*) bone-marrow *antes de s*; **trasplante ~** bone-marrow transplant **2** (= *fundamental*) central, fundamental, essential

medusa SF jellyfish

megabyte ['megabait] SM megabyte

megaciclo SM megacycle

megafonía SF (= *sistema*) public address system; (*en la calle*) loudspeakers *pl*

megáfono SM megaphone

megahercio SM, **megaherzio** SM megahertz

megalítico ADJ megalithic

megalito SM megalith

megalomanía SF megalomania

meiga SF (*Galicia*) wise woman, witch

mejicano/a ADJ, SM/F Mexican

mejilla SF cheek

mejillonero ADJ mussel *antes de s*

mejillón SM mussel

mejor Ⓐ ADJ **1** (*comparativo*) **1.1** (= *más bueno*) [*resultado, producto*] better; [*calidad, oferta*] better, higher; **a falta de otra cosa ~ que hacer** for lack of anything better to do; **nunca he visto nada ~** I've never seen anything better; **~ que algo** better than sth **1.2** (= *preferible*) **ser ~** to be better; **será ~ que te vayas** you'd better go
2 (*superlativo*) **2.1** (*de dos*) better; **de estos dos refrescos, ¿cuál es el ~?** which is the better (out) of these two drinks? **2.2** (*de varios*) [*persona, producto*] best; [*calidad*] top, highest; [*oferta*] highest, best; **está entre las diez ~es** she is among the ten best; **ser el ~ de la clase** to be the best in the class, be top of the class; **vive el ~ momento de su carrera deportiva** he is at the peak of his sporting career; ✦ MODISMO **llevarse la ~ parte** to take the lion's share **2.3 lo ~** the best; **os deseo (todo) lo ~** I wish you all the best, my best wishes (to you); **lo ~ de España es el clima** the best thing about Spain is the climate; **os deseo lo ~ del mundo** I wish you all the best; **lo hice lo ~ que pude** I

did it the best I could, I did it as well as I could; **lo ~ que podemos hacer es callarnos** the best thing we can do is keep quiet

B ADV **1** (*comparativo de bien*) better; **yo canto ~ que tú** I can sing better than you; **lo hace cada vez ~** he's getting better and better; **¿te sientes algo ~?** do you feel any better?; **¡pues si no quieres venir con nosotros, ~!** well, if you don't want to come with us, so much the better!; ~ **dicho** or rather, or I should say; **mucho ~** much better, a lot better*; **~ que ~** so much the better, all the better **2** (*superlativo de bien*) best; **éste es el texto ~ redactado de todos** this text is the best written of all **3** (= *preferiblemente*) ~ **vámonos** we'd better go; **tú, ~ te callas*** you'd better keep quiet* **4** **a lo ~** maybe; **a lo ~ viene mañana** he might come tomorrow, maybe he'll come tomorrow; **a lo ~ hasta nos toca la lotería** we might even win the lottery

mejora SF **1** (= *progreso*) improvement **2** (= *aumento*) increase **3** **mejoras** (= *obras*) improvements, alterations

mejoramiento SM improvement

mejorana SF marjoram

mejorar /1a/ **A** VT **1** [+ *servicio, resultados*] to improve; (= *realzar*) to enhance; [+ *oferta*] to raise, improve; [+ *récord*] to break; (*Inform*) to upgrade; ✦ MODISMO **mejorando lo presente** present company excepted **2** ~ **a algn** (= *ser mejor que*) to be better than sb **B** VI [*situación*] to improve, get better; (*Meteo*) to improve, clear up; (*Fin*) to improve, pick up; [*enfermo*] to get better; **han mejorado de actitud/imagen** their attitude/image has improved **C** **mejorarse** VPR to get better, improve; **¡que se mejore!** get well soon!

mejoría SF improvement

mejunje SM (*pey*) (*gen*) concoction; (= *bebida*) brew

melado SM (*LAm*) cane syrup

melancolía SF melancholy, sadness; (*Med*) melancholia

melancólico ADJ (= *triste*) melancholy, sad; (= *soñador*) wistful

melanina SF melanin

melanoma SM melanoma

melaza SF treacle (*Brit*), molasses *pl* (*EEUU*)

melena SF **1** [*de persona*] long hair; **lleva (una) ~ rubia** she has long blond hair; ✦ MODISMO **soltarse la ~** to let one's hair down **2** [*de león*] mane **3** **melenas** (*pey*) (= *greñas*) mop of hair *sing*

melenudo* **A** ADJ long-haired **B** SM long-haired guy

melifluo ADJ sickly sweet

Melilla SF Melilla; *see also* www.camelilla.es

melillense ADJ of/from Melilla

melindres SMPL (= *afectación*) affected ways; (= *aprensión*) squeamishness *sing*; (= *mojigatería*) prudery *sing*, prudishness *sing*; **déjate de ~ y cómelo** don't be so finicky, just eat it

melindroso ADJ (= *afectado*) affected; (= *aprensivo*) squeamish; (= *mojigato*) prudish; (= *quisquilloso*) finicky, fussy

mella SF (= *rotura*) nick, notch; (*en dientes*) gap; ✦ MODISMO **hacer ~ en algo/algn** to make an impression on sth/sb; **la crisis ha hecho ~ en los bolsillos de los europeos** Europeans are feeling the pinch because of the crisis

mellado ADJ [*filo*] jagged, nicked

mellar /1a/ VT **1** [+ *cuchillo, filo*] to nick, notch; [+ *diente*] to chip; [+ *madera*] to take a chip out of **2** (= *dañar*) to damage, harm

mellizo/a ADJ, SM/F twin

melocotón SM (= *fruto*) peach; (= *árbol*) peach tree

melocotonero SM peach tree

melodía SF **1** (= *música*) melody, tune **2** (= *cualidad*) melodiousness

melódico ADJ melodic

melodioso ADJ melodious, tuneful

melodrama SM melodrama

melodramático ADJ melodramatic

melómano/a SM/F music lover

melón SM **1** (*Bot*) melon **2** (*) (= *cabeza*) head, nut*, noggin (*EEUU**) **3** (*) (= *tonto*) twit*, lemon* **4 melones**** (= *pechos*) melons**, tits***

melonar SM bed of melons, melon plot

melopea* SF **coger** o **agarrar** o **pillar una ~** to get sloshed o plastered*

meloso ADJ **1** (= *dulce*) sweet **2** (= *empalagoso*) [*persona, voz*] sickly-sweet; [*canción, música*] schmaltzy, sickly-sweet

membrana SF membrane

membranoso ADJ membranous

membresía SF (*esp Méx*) membership

membrete SM letterhead, heading; **papel con ~** headed notepaper

membrillo SM **1** (= *fruta*) quince; **(carne de) ~** quince jelly **2** (*) (= *tonto*) fool, idiot

memez* SF stupid thing; **eso es una ~** that's stupid; **decir memeces** to talk nonsense o (*esp Brit*) rubbish

memo¹/a* **A** ADJ silly, stupid **B** SM/F idiot

memo²* SM memo*, memorandum

memorable ADJ memorable

memorando SM, **memorándum** SM (*pl* **memorándums**) **1** (= *nota*) memorandum **2** (= *libreta*) notebook

memoria SF **1** (= *facultad*) memory; **de ~** [*aprender, saber*] by heart; [*hablar, recitar, tocar*] from memory; **hacer ~** to try to remember; **hacer ~ de algo** to recall sth; **perder la ~** to lose one's memory; **refrescar la ~ a algn** to refresh sb's memory, jog sb's memory; **tener buena/mala/poca ~** to have a good/bad/poor memory; **traer algo a la ~** to bring sth back; **venir a la ~: ¡en este sitio me vienen tantos recuerdos a la ~!** this place brings back so many memories!; **no me viene su número a la ~** her number's slipped my mind, I can't remember her number; ✦ MODISMO **tener (una) ~ de elefante** to have the memory of an elephant ➤ **memoria fotográfica** photographic memory **2** (= *recuerdo*) memory; **a la** o **en ~ de algn** [*acto, monumento*] in memory of sb **3** (= *informe*) (*gen*) report; (*Educ*) paper ➤ **memoria anual** annual report ➤ **memoria de licenciatura** dissertation **4** (= *relación*) record **5** (*Inform*) memory ➤ **memoria auxiliar** backing storage ➤ **memoria de acceso aleatorio** random access memory, RAM ➤ **memoria de sólo lectura** read-only memory, ROM ➤ **memoria RAM** RAM ➤ **memoria ROM** ROM **6 memorias** (= *autobiografía*) memoirs

memorial SM (= *escrito*) memorial; (*Jur*) brief

memorístico ADJ [*concurso*] memory *antes de s*; [*aprendizaje, educación*] rote *antes de s*

memorización SF memorizing

memorizar /1f/ VT to memorize

mena SF ore

menaje SM **1** (= *muebles*) furniture, furnishings *pl* **2** (= *utensilios*) (*tb* **artículos de ~**) household items *pl*; **sección de ~** (*en tienda*) hardware and kitchen department

mención SF mention ➤ **mención honorífica** honourable o (*EEUU*) honorable mention; **hacer ~ de algo** to mention sth

mencionado ADJ aforementioned

mencionar /1a/ VT to mention

menda** (*Esp*) **A** PRON (*tb* **~s**) (= *yo*) yours truly; **lo tuvo que hacer este ~ (lerenda)** yours truly had to do it*, muggins here had to do it*; **el ~ no está de acuerdo** I, for one, don't agree **B** SMF (= *persona*) **un ~** a bloke*, a guy*

mendacidad SF untruthfulness, mendacity (*frm*)

mendaz ADJ (*frm*) untruthful, mendacious (*frm*)

mendicante ADJ **1** (*Rel*) mendicant; **las órdenes ~s** the mendicant orders **2** [*actitud*] begging

mendicidad SF begging, mendicity (*frm*)

mendigar /1h/ **A** VT to beg for **B** VI to beg

mendigo/a SM/F beggar

mendrugo SM 1 (= *trozo*) (*tb* ~ **de pan**) crust of bread 2 (*) (= *tonto*) dimwit*

meneallo: más vale no ~* let sleeping dogs lie, the less said the better

menear /1a/ Ⓐ VT 1 [+ *cola*] to wag; [+ *cabeza*] to shake; [+ *líquido*] to stir; [+ *pelo*] to toss; [+ *caderas*] to swing 2 [+ *asunto*] to get on with, get moving on; [+ *negocio*] to handle, conduct
Ⓑ **menearse** VPR 1 (*gen*) to shake; [*cola*] to wag; (= *contonearse*) to swing, sway; **yo de aquí no me meneo** I'm staying right here, I'm staying put; ✦ MODISMOS **de no te menees***: **un vapuleo de no te menees** a good hiding; **meneársela***** to wank*** 2 (= *apresurarse*) to get a move on; **¡~se!** get going!, jump to it!

meneo SM 1 [*de cola*] wag; [*de cabeza*] shake, toss; [*de líquido*] stir, stirring; [*de caderas*] swing(ing), sway(ing); (= *sacudida*) jerk, jolt 2 (*) (= *paliza*) hiding*; (= *bronca*) dressing-down* 3 (= *actividad*) = **movida 1**

menester SM 1 **ser** ~ (*frm*) (= *ser necesario*): **es ~ hacer algo** we must do something, it is necessary to do something; **cuando sea ~** when necessary 2 (= *trabajo*) job; (= *recado*) errand 3 **menesteres** (= *deberes*) duties, business *sing*; (= *ocupación*) occupation *sing*

menesteroso/a Ⓐ ADJ needy Ⓑ SM/F **los ~s** the needy

menestra SF (*tb* ~ **de verduras**) vegetable stew

mengano/a SM/F Mr/Mrs/Miss so-and-so

mengua SF 1 (= *disminución*) decrease, reduction; (= *decadencia*) decay, decline; **ir en ~ de algo** to be to the detriment of sth; **sin ~** (= *íntegro*) complete, whole; (= *intacto*) intact, untouched 2 (= *descrédito*) discredit; **ir en ~ de algn** to be to sb's discredit

menguado Ⓐ ADJ [*ejército, tropas*] depleted; [*esfuerzos*] diminished; [*fuerzas, presupuesto*] reduced Ⓑ SM (*en labor de punto*) decrease

menguante Ⓐ ADJ (= *que disminuye*) decreasing, diminishing; (= *decadente*) decaying; [*luna*] waning; [*marea*] ebb *antes de s* Ⓑ SF 1 (*Náut*) ebb tide 2 [*de luna*] waning

menguar /1i/ Ⓐ VT to lessen, reduce; [+ *labor de punto*] to decrease Ⓑ VI 1 (= *disminuir*) to decrease, dwindle; [*número, nivel del agua*] to go down; [*marea*] to go out, ebb; [*luna*] to wane 2 (= *decaer*) to wane, decay, decline

mengue* SM devil

menhir SM menhir

meningitis SF INV meningitis

menisco SM meniscus

menopausia SF menopause

menopáusico ADJ menopausal

menor Ⓐ ADJ 1 (*comparativo*) 1.1 (*de tamaño*) smaller; **los libros están ordenados de ~ a mayor** the books are arranged by size, from small to large 1.2 (*de cantidad*) fewer, less; **echa sal en ~ cantidad** add less salt; ~ **que algo** less than sth 1.3 (*de importancia, tiempo*) **existe un ~ control en las aduanas** customs controls are not as strict *o* tight as they were; **viene con ~ frecuencia que antes** he doesn't come as often now; **en ~ grado** to a lesser extent 1.4 (*de edad*) younger; **mis dos hermanos ~es** my two younger brothers; ~ **que algn** younger than sb; **ser ~ de edad** to be under age; (*Jur*) to be a minor 1.5 (*Mús*) minor 2 (*superlativo*) 2.1 (*de tamaño*) smallest 2.2 [*de cantidad*] lowest, smallest; **realizó la vuelta en el ~ número de golpes** he finished the round in the lowest number of shots; **hagan el ~ ruido posible** make as little noise as possible 2.3 (*de importancia, tiempo*) least; **no tiene la ~ importancia** it is not in the least important; **en el ~ tiempo posible** in the shortest possible time 2.4 (*de edad*) youngest; **mi hijo ~** my youngest son
Ⓑ SMF (= *niño*) child, minor (*frm en*); **los ~es deben ir acompañados** children who are under age *o* minors (*frm*) must be accompanied; **un ~ de 15 años** a boy of 15; **un campeonato para ~es de 16 años** a championship for under-16s; **"apto para menores acompañados"** (*Cine*) ≈ "certificate PG (*Brit*)", ≈ PG 13 (*EEUU*) ➤ **menor de**

edad (*Jur*) minor
Ⓒ SM (*Com*) **(al) por** ~ retail *antes de s*; **venta (al) por** ~ retail sales

Menorca SF Minorca

menos Ⓐ ADV 1 (*comparativo*) less; **ahora salgo** ~ I go out less these days; **me gusta cada vez** ~ I like it less and less; **una película** ~ **conocida** a less well-known film (*esp Brit*) *o* movie (*esp EEUU*); ~ **aún** even less; ~ **de** (*con sustantivos incontables, medidas, dinero, tiempo*) less than; (*con sustantivos contables*) fewer than; ~ **de lo que piensas** less than you think; **tiene ~ de dieciocho años** he's under eighteen; ~ **de 50 cajas** fewer than 50 boxes; **por ~ de nada** for no reason at all; ~ **que** less than; **me gusta ~ que el otro** I like it less than the other one; **trabaja ~ que yo** he doesn't work as hard as I do 2 (*superlativo*) least; **su novela ~ innovadora** his least innovative novel; **es el que habla ~** he's the one who talks (the) least 3 **al** ~ at least; **hay al ~ cien personas** there are at least a hundred people; **si al ~ lloviera** if only it would rain; **de** ~: **hay siete de** ~ we're seven short, there are seven missing; **me han pagado dos libras de** ~ they have underpaid me by two pounds; **echar de** ~ **a algn** to miss sb; **ir a** ~ to come down in the world; **lo** ~ **diez** at least ten; **es lo** ~ **que se puede esperar** it's the least one can expect; **eso es lo de** ~ that's the least of it; **¡mal!** thank goodness!; ~ **mal que decidimos no esperarla** just as well *o* it's a good job* we decided not to wait for her; **era nada** ~ **que un rey** he was a king, no less; **no es para** ~ quite right too; **por lo** ~ at least; **¡qué** ~!: —**le di dos euros de propina** —**¡qué** ~! "I tipped her two euros" — "that was the least you could do!"; **¿qué** ~ **que darle las gracias?** the least we can do is say thanks!; **venir a** ~ to come down in the world; **y** ~: **no quiero verle y** ~ **visitarle** I don't want to see him, let alone visit him; **¡ya será ~!** come off it!
Ⓑ ADJ 1 (*comparativo*) (*con sustantivos incontables, medidas, dinero, tiempo*) less; (*con sustantivos contables*) fewer; ~ **harina** less flour; ~ **gatos** fewer cats; **no soy ~ hombre que él*** I'm as much of a man as he is; **para no ser ~ que los vecinos** to keep up with the neighbours 2 (*superlativo*) (*con sustantivos incontables, medidas, dinero, tiempo*) least; (*con sustantivos contables*) fewest; **es el que ~ culpa tiene** he is the least to blame; **el examen con ~ errores** the exam paper with the fewest mistakes
Ⓒ PREP 1 (= *excepto*) except
2 (*Mat*) (*para restar*) minus, less; **cinco ~ dos** five minus *o* less two; **son las siete ~ veinte** it's twenty to seven
Ⓓ CONJ **a ~ que** unless
Ⓔ SM minus sign

menoscabar /1a/ VT (= *disminuir*) to lessen, reduce; (= *dañar*) to damage

menoscabo SM (= *disminución*) lessening, reduction; (= *daño*) damage; **con** *o* **en ~ de** to the detriment of

menospreciar /1b/ VT 1 (= *despreciar*) to scorn, despise 2 (= *ofender*) to slight 3 (= *subestimar*) to underrate, underestimate

menosprecio SM 1 (= *desdén*) scorn, contempt 2 (= *subestimación*) underrating, underestimation 3 (= *falta de respeto*) disrespect

mensáfono SM bleeper, beeper, pager (*esp Brit*)

mensaje SM message ➤ **mensaje de la corona** Queen's/King's speech; ➤ **mensaje de texto** text message; **enviar ~s de texto/un ~ de texto a algn** to text-message sb

mensajería SF 1 [*de paquetes*] (= *servicio*) courier service; (= *empresa*) courier firm 2 [*de avisos*] (= *servicio*) messaging service; (= *empresa*) courier firm

mensajero/a SM/F 1 (*para empresa de mensajería*) courier 2 (= *recadero*) messenger

menso* ADJ (*LAm*) silly, stupid

menstruación SF menstruation

menstrual ADJ menstrual; **dolores ~es** period pains

menstruar /1e/ VI to menstruate

mensual ADJ monthly; **50 dólares ~es** 50 dollars a month

mensualidad SF (= *salario*) monthly salary; (= *plazo*) monthly instalment *o* (*EEUU*) installment, monthly payment

mensualmente ADV monthly

menta SF mint

mentada SF (*Méx*) serious insult; **hacer a algn una ~** to seriously insult sb

mental ADJ [*esfuerzo, salud*] mental; [*capacidad, trabajo*] intellectual

mentalidad SF mentality; **tienes la ~ de un niño de tres años** you've got the mentality of a three-year old; **tiene una ~ muy abierta** he is very open-minded, he's got a very open outlook

mentalización SF 1 (= *preparación*) mental preparation 2 (= *concienciación*) **campañas de ~ contra la bebida** campaigns to raise awareness of the risks of drinking

mentalizado ADJ **están ~s para sobreponerse a cualquier dificultad** they are mentally prepared to overcome any problem; **el equipo salió ~ para el triunfo** the team went out with their minds set on victory

mentalizar /1f/ Ⓐ VT 1 (= *preparar*) to prepare mentally 2 (= *concienciar*) to make aware Ⓑ **mentalizarse** VPR 1 (= *prepararse*) to prepare o.s. mentally 2 (= *concienciarse*) to become aware (**de** of)

mentalmente ADV mentally

mentar /1j/ VT to mention; **la tan mentada crisis** the much talked-about crisis; ✦ MODISMO **~ la madre a algn** (*esp Méx*) to insult sb seriously

mente SF 1 (= *pensamiento*) mind; **no me lo puedo quitar de la ~** I can't get it out of my mind; **tener en ~ hacer algo** to be thinking of doing sth

> Recuérdese que las preposiciones en inglés rigen gerundio y no infinitivo, de ahí **to be thinking of doing sth.**

traer a la ~ to call to mind; **venir a la ~** to come to mind 2 (= *mentalidad*) **tiene una ~ muy abierta** she's very open-minded, she's got a very open outlook 3 (= *intelectual*) mind

mentecato/a Ⓐ ADJ silly, stupid Ⓑ SM/F idiot, fool

mentidero SM gossip shop*

mentir /3i/ VI to lie; **nos mintió** he lied to us; **no he mentido en mi vida** I've never told a lie in all my life; **¡miento!** sorry!, I'm wrong!, my mistake!

mentira SF 1 (= *embuste*) lie; **¡mentira!** it's a lie!; **no digas ~s** don't tell lies; **de ~: una pistola de ~** a toy pistol; **parecer ~: aunque parezca ~** strange though it may seem; **¡parece ~!** it's unbelievable!, I can't o don't believe it!; **parece ~ que no te acuerdes** I can't believe that you don't remember; ✦ MODISMO **una ~ como una casa** o **una catedral** o **un templo** a whopping great lie* ➤ **mentira piadosa** white lie 2 (*en uñas*) white mark (*on fingernail*)

mentirijillas* SFPL **es** o **va de ~** it's only a joke; (*a niño*) it's only pretend, it's only make-believe; **lloraba de ~** she was pretending to cry; **jugar de ~** to play for fun (*ie not for money*)

mentiroso/a Ⓐ ADJ lying; **¡mentiroso!** you liar! Ⓑ SM/F liar

mentís SM INV denial; **dar el ~ a algo** to refute sth, deny sth

mentol SM menthol

mentolado ADJ mentholated

mentón SM chin

mentor SM mentor

menú SM 1 [*de comida*] menu 2 (*Inform*) menu ➤ **menú desplegable** drop-down menu

menudear /1a/ Ⓐ VI to be frequent, happen frequently Ⓑ VT (*LAm*) to sell retail

menudencia SF 1 (= *bagatela*) trifle, small thing; **~s** odds and ends 2 (= *minuciosidad*) minuteness; (= *exactitud*) exactness; (= *meticulosidad*) meticulousness 3 **menudencias** (*Culin*) [*de cerdo*] offal *sing*; (= *menudillos*) [*de ave*] giblets

menudeo SM (*Com*) retail trade; **vender al ~** to sell retail

menudez SF smallness, minuteness

menudillos SMPL giblets

menudo Ⓐ ADJ 1 (= *pequeño*) small, minute; [*persona*] diminutive, slight; (*fig*) slight, insignificant; **la gente menuda** the little ones, kids* 2 (*uso admirativo*) **¡~ lío!** what a mess!; **¡~ viento hizo anoche!** it wasn't half windy last night!* Ⓑ ADV **a ~** often

meñique SM (*tb* **dedo ~**) little finger

meollo SM 1 (*Anat*) marrow 2 [*de asunto*] heart, crux 3 [*de persona*] brains *pl*

meón/ona* Ⓐ ADJ **es muy ~** [*niño*] he's always wetting himself; [*adulto*] he's got a weak bladder Ⓑ SM/F 1 **este niño es un ~** this boy's always wetting himself 2 (= *bebé*) baby, baby boy/baby girl

mequetrefe SMF good-for-nothing

mercadear /1a/ Ⓐ VT (= *vender*) to market; (= *regatear*) to haggle over Ⓑ VI to deal, trade

mercadeo SM marketing

mercader SM (*esp Hist*) merchant

mercadería SF merchandise

mercadillo SM street market; (*benéfico*) (charity) bazaar

mercado SM market; **salir al ~** to come on to the market ➤ **mercado bursátil** stock market ➤ **mercado de divisas** currency market, foreign exchange market ➤ **mercado de trabajo** labour o (*EEUU*) labor market ➤ **mercado de valores** stock market ➤ **mercado inmobiliario** property market ➤ **mercado libre** free market ➤ **mercado negro** black market ➤ **mercado único** single market

mercadotecnia SF marketing

mercancía Ⓐ SF merchandise; **~s** goods, merchandise *sing* ➤ **mercancías perecederas** perishable goods Ⓑ SM INV **mercancías** freight train *sing*, goods train *sing* (*Brit*)

mercante Ⓐ ADJ merchant *antes de s* Ⓑ SM merchantman, merchant ship

mercantil ADJ (*gen*) mercantile, commercial; [*derecho*] commercial

mercantilismo SM mercantilism

merced SF 1 **merced a** thanks to 2 **estar a la ~ de algo/algn** to be at the mercy of sth/sb 3 (†) (= *favor*) favour, favor (*EEUU*); **tenga la ~ de hacerlo** please be so good as to do it 4 (††) **vuestra ~** your worship, sir

mercenario Ⓐ ADJ mercenary Ⓑ SM mercenary

mercería SF 1 (= *artículos*) haberdashery (*Brit*), notions *pl* (*esp EEUU*) 2 (= *tienda*) haberdasher's (shop) (*Brit*), notions store (*EEUU*) 3 (*Chi*) (= *ferretería*) hardware store, ironmonger's (*Brit*)

Mercosur SM ABR (= **Mercado Común del Cono Sur**) *common market consisting of Argentina, Brazil, Paraguay and Uruguay*

mercromina® SF Mercurochrome®

Mercurio SM Mercury

mercurio SM mercury

mercurocromo SM Mercurochrome®

merecedor ADJ deserving, worthy (**de** of); **~ de confianza** trustworthy; **ser ~ de algo** to deserve sth, be deserving of sth

merecer /2d/ Ⓐ VT [+ *recompensa, castigo*] to deserve; **merece (que se le dé) el premio** he deserves (to receive) the prize; **no merece sino elogios** she deserves nothing but praise; **merece la pena** it's worth it; **no merece la pena discutir** it's not worth arguing Ⓑ **merecerse** VPR **~se algo** to deserve sth; **tienes unos hijos que no te los mereces** you don't deserve your children; **se lo merece por tonto** (it) serves him right for being so stupid

merecidamente ADV deservedly

merecido Ⓐ ADJ [*premio, descanso*] well-deserved; **bien ~ lo tiene** it serves him right Ⓑ SM just deserts *pl*; **llevarse su ~** to get one's just deserts

merecimiento SM 1 (= *lo merecido*) just deserts *pl* 2 (= *mérito*) merit, worthiness

merendar /1j/ Ⓐ VI to have an afternoon snack, have tea

⑧ VT to have as an afternoon snack, have for tea
⑥ merendarse (*) VPR **1** [+ *adversario*] to thrash*, walk all over* **2** (= *acabar con*) [+ *libro*] to devour; [+ *país, territorio*] to take over

merendero SM (= *café*) open-air café, snack bar; (*en el campo*) picnic area

merengue ⓐ ADJ (*) of/relating to Real Madrid F.C.
⑧ SM **1** (*Culin*) meringue **2** (= *blandengue*) wimp*, weed*; (*LAm*) (= *enfermizo*) sickly person **3** (= *baile*) merengue **4** (*CS*) (= *alboroto*) row, fuss; (= *desorden*) mess

meretriz SF (*liter*) prostitute

meridianamente ADV clearly, with complete clarity

meridiano ⓐ ADJ **1** [*color*] midday *antes de s* **2** [*luz*] very bright **3** [*hecho*] clear as day, crystal-clear; **lo explicó con una claridad meridiana** he explained it perfectly clearly **⑧** SM (*Astron, Geog*) meridian

meridional ⓐ ADJ southern **⑧** SMF southerner

merienda SF tea, afternoon snack; [*de viaje*] packed meal; (*en el campo*) picnic ➤ **merienda-cena** high tea, early evening meal ➤ **merienda de negros** (= *confusión*) bedlam, free-for-all; (*Esp*) (= *chanchullo*) crooked deal

merino ADJ merino

mérito SM merit, worth; **una obra de gran ~ artístico** a work of great artistic merit; **restar ~ a algo** to detract from sth; **eso tiene mucho ~** that's very commendable; **alega los siguientes ~s** he quotes the following facts in support; ✦ MODISMO **hacer ~s** to (try to) earn brownie points* ➤ **méritos de guerra** mention in dispatches *sing*

meritocracia SF meritocracy

meritorio/a ⓐ ADJ meritorious (*frm*), worthy; (= *merecedor*) deserving; **~ de alabanza** praiseworthy; **consiguió una meritoria sexta posición** he achieved a commendable sixth place **⑧** SM/F unpaid trainee

merluza SF **1** (= *pez*) hake **2** (*) (= *borrachera*) **coger una ~** to get sozzled*

merluzo/a* (*Esp*) ⓐ ADJ silly, stupid **⑧** SM/F idiot

merma SF (= *disminución*) [*de interés, ganancia*] decrease; (= *pérdida*) loss

mermar /1a/ ⓐ VT (= *disminuir*) [+ *crecimiento, capacidad*] to reduce; [+ *autoridad, prestigio*] to undermine; [+ *reservas*] to deplete; [+ *pago, raciones*] to cut **⑧** VI, **mermarse** VPR (= *disminuir*) (*gen*) to decrease, dwindle; [*reservas*] to become depleted; [*líquido*] to go down

mermelada SF [*de fresa, ciruela, albaricoque*] jam (*Brit*), jelly (*EEUU*); [*de naranja*] marmalade

mero¹ ⓐ ADJ **1** (= *simple*) mere, simple; **el ~ hecho de ...** the mere *o* simple fact of ...; **soy un ~ espectador** I'm only *o* just a spectator; **fue una mera casualidad** it was pure coincidence
2 (*Méx*) (= *exacto*) precise, exact; **a la mera hora** (*lit*) right on time; (*) (*fig*) when it comes down to it*
3 (*Méx*) (= *mismo*) **el ~ centro** the very centre; **la mera verdad** the plain truth; **en la mera calle** right there on the street; **tu ~ papá** your own father
⑧ ADV (*CAm, Méx*) **1** (= *justo*) right, just; **aquí ~** (= *exacto*) right here, just here; (= *cerca*) near here; **¡eso ~!** right!, you've got it!
2 ahora ~ (= *ahora mismo*) right now; (= *pronto*) in a minute; **¡ya ~!*** just coming!; **ya ~ llega** he'll be here any minute now

mero² SM (= *pez*) grouper

merodeador(a) ⓐ ADJ prowling **⑧** SM/F prowler

merodear /1a/ VI to prowl (about)

merolico* SM (*Méx*) (= *curandero*) quack*; (= *vendedor*) street salesman

mersa* (*RPl*) ⓐ ADJ INV (= *de mal gusto*) common, naff*; (= *ostentoso*) flashy **⑧** SMF INV common person

mes SM **1** [*del año*] month; **50 dólares al ~** 50 dollars a month; **el ~ que viene** ◊ **el ~ próximo** next month
2 (= *sueldo*) month's pay; (= *renta*) month's rent; (= *pago*) monthly payment **3** (*) (= *menstruación*) **estar con** *o* **tener el ~** to have one's period

mesa SF **1** (= *mueble*) table; [*de despacho*] desk; **¡a la ~!**

dinner's ready!; **vino de ~** table wine; **levantar la ~** (*esp LAm*) to clear the table; **poner la ~** to set *o* (*esp Brit*) lay the table; **recoger** *o* (*Esp*) **quitar la ~** to clear the table; **sentarse a la ~** to sit down to table; **servir la ~** to wait at table;
✦ MODISMO **estar sobre la ~** [*asunto*] to be on the table, be under consideration *o* discussion ➤ **mesa auxiliar** side table, occasional table ➤ **mesa de billar** billiard table
➤ **mesa de centro** coffee table ➤ **mesa de comedor** dining table ➤ **mesa de despacho** office desk ➤ **mesa de juntas** conference table ➤ **mesa de luz** (*RPl*) bedside table, night stand *o* table (*EEUU*) ➤ **mesa de mezclas** mixer, mixing desk ➤ **mesa de negociación** negotiating table ➤ **mesa de noche** bedside table, night stand *o* table (*EEUU*) ➤ **mesa de operaciones** operating table ➤ **mesa de trabajo** desk ➤ **mesa ratona** (*RPl*) coffee table ➤ **mesa redonda** (*Pol*) (= *discusión*) round table; (= *conferencia*) round-table conference; (*Hist*) Round Table
2 (= *personas*) (= *comité*) committee; [*de empresa*] board; (*en mitin*) platform
3 (= *pensión*) board; **cama y ~** bed and board; **tener a algn a ~ y mantel** to give sb free board
4 (= *meseta*) tableland, plateau

mesada SF **1** (= *mensualidad*) monthly payment **2** (*RPl*) (= *encimera*) worktop (*Brit*), countertop (*EEUU*)

mesarse /1a/ VPR **~ el pelo** *o* **los cabellos** to tear one's hair (out); **~ la barba** to pull one's beard

mescalina SF mescaline

mesero/a SM/F (*CAm, Col, Méx*) waiter/waitress

meseta SF **1** (*Geog*) tableland, plateau **2** (*Arquit*) landing

mesiánico ADJ messianic

Mesías SM INV Messiah

mesilla SF (*tb* **~ de noche**) bedside table, night stand *o* (*EEUU*) table

mesolítico ⓐ ADJ Mesolithic **⑧** SM **el ~** the Mesolithic

mesón SM **1** (*Hist*) inn; (*moderno*) *restaurant and bar with period décor*, olde worlde inn **2** (*Chi, Ven*) (= *mostrador*) counter

mesonero/a SM/F **1** (*Hist*) innkeeper **2** (*en bar*) landlord/landlady **3** (*Carib*) (= *camarero*) waiter/waitress

mestizaje SM crossbreeding

mestizo/a ⓐ ADJ [*persona*] mixed-race; [*sociedad*] racially mixed; [*raza*] mixed; [*animal*] (*gen*) crossbred; (= *perro*) mongrel *antes de s* (*pey*); [*planta*] hybrid *antes de s*
⑧ SM/F (= *persona*) mestizo, half-caste (*pey*); (= *animal*) (*gen*) crossbreed; (= *perro*) mongrel (*pey*); (= *planta*) hybrid

mesura SF moderation, restraint

mesurado ADJ **1** (= *moderado*) moderate, restrained **2** (= *tranquilo*) calm

meta SF **1** (= *objetivo*) goal, aim; **fijarse una ~** to set o.s. a goal **2** (*Ftbl*) goal; (*en hípica*) winning post; (*en atletismo*) finishing line ➤ **meta volante** (*en ciclismo*) bonus sprint

metabólico ADJ metabolic

metabolismo SM metabolism

metacrilato SM methacrylate

metadona SF methadone

metafísica SF metaphysics *sing*

metafísico/a ⓐ ADJ metaphysical **⑧** SM/F metaphysician

metáfora SF metaphor

metafórico ADJ metaphoric(al)

metal SM **1** (= *material*) metal; (*Mús*) brass; **el vil ~** filthy lucre ➤ **metal noble** precious metal ➤ **metal pesado** heavy metal **2** [*de voz*] timbre

metalenguaje SM metalanguage

metálico ⓐ ADJ [*objeto*] metal *antes de s*; [*color, sonido, brillo*] metallic **⑧** SM (= *dinero*) cash; **pagar en ~** to pay (in) cash; **premio en ~** cash prize

metalizado ADJ metallic

metalurgia SF metallurgy

metalúrgico/a ⓐ ADJ metallurgic(al); **industria metalúrgica** engineering industry **⑧** SM/F (= *trabajador*) metalworker; (= *científico*) metallurgist

metamorfosear /1a/ **Ⓐ** VT to metamorphose (frm), transform (**en** into) **Ⓑ metamorfosearse** VPR to be metamorphosed (frm), be transformed

metamorfosis SF INV metamorphosis (frm), transformation

metano SM methane

metástasis SF INV metastasis

metate SM (CAm, Méx) flat stone for grinding

metedura SF ➤ **metedura de pata*** blunder, clanger*

metelón/ona* (Méx) **Ⓐ** ADJ meddling **Ⓑ** SM/F busybody

meteórico ADJ meteoric

meteorito SM meteorite

meteoro SM meteor

meteorología SF meteorology

meteorológico ADJ meteorological, weather antes de s; **boletín** o **parte ~** weather report

meteorólogo/a SM/F meteorologist

metepatas* SMF INV **eres un ~** you're always putting your foot in it

meter /2a/ **Ⓐ** VT 1 (= poner, introducir) to put; **metió el palo por el aro** she stuck o put the stick through the ring; **~ algo en algo** to put sth in(to) sth; **consiguió ~ toda la ropa en la maleta** she managed to get o fit all the clothes in(to) the suitcase; **~ dinero en el banco** to put money in the bank; **¿quién le metió esas ideas en la cabeza?** who gave him those ideas?; ✦ MODISMO **a todo ~*** as fast as possible

2 (Dep) to score; **~ un gol** to score a goal
3 (Cos) (para estrechar) to take in; (para acortar) to take up
4 (Aut) [+ marcha] to go into; **mete primera** go into first gear
5 (= internar) **~ a algn en la cárcel** to put sb in prison
6 (en una profesión) **lo metieron a trabajar en el banco** they got him a job in a bank
7 (= implicar) **~ a algn en algo** to get sb involved in sth; **él me metió en el negocio** he got me involved in the business; **tú me metiste en este lío** you got me into this mess; **no metas a mi madre en esto** leave my mother out of this
8 (*) (= ocasionar) **~ miedo a algn** to scare o frighten sb; **~ prisa a algn** to hurry sb; (pey) rush sb; **¡no me metas prisa!** don't rush me!; **~ ruido** to make a noise; **~ un susto a algn** to give sb a fright
9 (*) (= dar) **le metieron un golpe en la cabeza** they hit him on the head
10 (*) (= endosar) **me metieron una multa** I was fined; **nos metió un rollo inacabable** he went on and on for ages; **le metieron cinco años de cárcel** they gave him five years in prison
11 (*) (= aplicar) **me metió la maquinilla y me peló al cero** he took the clippers to me and shaved all my hair off; **le quedaba largo el traje y le metió las tijeras** her dress was too long, so she took the scissors to it
12 **~las** (And**) to beat it*

Ⓑ meterse VPR 1 (= introducirse) **métete por la primera calle a la derecha** take the first street on the right; **¿dónde se habrá metido el lápiz?** where can the pencil have got to?; **~se en algo: se metió en la tienda** she went into the shop; **se metió en la cama** she got into bed
2 (= introducir) **métete la camisa** tuck your shirt in; **~se un pico**** to give o.s. a fix**; ✦ MODISMO **¡métetelo donde te quepa!***** you can stuff it!**
3 (= involucrarse) **~se en algo: se metió en un negocio turbio** he got involved in a shady affair; **~se en política** to go into politics; **~se en líos** to get into trouble
4 (= entrometerse) **~se en algo** to interfere in sth, meddle in sth; **¿por qué te metes (en esto)?** why are you interfering (in this matter)?; **¡no te metas en lo que no te importa!** mind your own business!
5 (como profesión) **~se a monja** to become a nun; **~se de aprendiz en un oficio** to go into trade as an apprentice
6 **~se a hacer algo** (= emprender) to start doing sth, start to do sth; **se metió a pintar todas las paredes de la casa** he started painting o to paint the whole house

7 **~se con algn** (= provocar) to pick on sb*; (= burlarse de) to tease sb

meterete/a* (RPl) ADJ, SM/F, **metete/a*** (And) ADJ, SM/F = **metiche**

metiche* (And, CAm, Méx) **Ⓐ** ADJ interfering **Ⓑ** SMF busybody

meticuloso ADJ meticulous

metida* SF = **metedura**

metido* ADJ 1 **estar muy ~ en algo** to be deeply involved in sth; **anda ~ en un lío** he's in a bit of trouble 2 **~ en años** elderly, advanced in years; **está algo metidita en años** she's getting on a bit now; **~ en carnes** plump 3 **~ en sí mismo** introspective 4 (RPl*) (= enamorado) **estar muy ~ con algn** to be in love with sb 5 (LAm) (= entrometido) interfering, meddling

metilo SM methyl

metódico ADJ methodical

metodismo SM Methodism

metodista ADJ, SMF Methodist

método SM 1 (= procedimiento) method ➤ **método anticonceptivo** method of contraception
2 (= organización) **trabajar con ~** to work methodically
3 (= manual) manual

metodología SF methodology

metodológico ADJ methodological

metomentodo* **Ⓐ** ADJ INV interfering, meddling **Ⓑ** SMF busybody, meddler

metonimia SF metonymy

metralla SF shrapnel

metralleta SF submachine gun, tommy gun

métrica SF metrics sing

métrico ADJ metric(al); **cinta métrica** tape measure

metro¹ SM

En inglés americano se usa **meter** en lugar de **metre**.

---

1 (= medida) metre; **mide tres ~s de largo** it's three metres long; **vender algo por ~s** to sell sth by the metre ➤ **metro cuadrado** square metre ➤ **metro cúbico** cubic metre
2 (= regla) rule, ruler; (= cinta métrica) tape measure
3 (Literat) metre

metro² SM underground (Brit), tube (Brit), subway (EEUU)

metrónomo SM metronome

metrópoli SF (= ciudad) metropolis; [de imperio] mother country

metropolitano **Ⓐ** ADJ metropolitan; **área metropolitana de Madrid** Greater Madrid **Ⓑ** SM 1 (Rel) metropolitan
2 (= tren) = **metro²**

mexicano/a ADJ, SM/F Mexican

México SM Mexico; see also www.presidencia.gob.mx

mezcal SM mescal

mezcla SF 1 (= acción) [de ingredientes, colores] mixing; [de razas, culturas] mixing; [de sonidos] mixing; [de cafés, tabacos, whiskies] blending; **la ~ de lo dulce y lo amargo** mixing sweet and sour flavours 2 (= resultado) [de ingredientes, colores] mixture; [de razas, culturas] mix; [de cafés, tabacos, whiskies] blend; **sin ~** [sustancia] pure; [gasolina] unadulterated ➤ **mezcla explosiva** (lit) explosive mixture; (fig) lethal combination 3 (Mús) mix 4 (Constr) mortar

mezclador(a) **Ⓐ** ADJ [vaso, mesa] mixing **Ⓑ** SM/F (Radio, TV) (= persona) mixer ➤ **mezclador(a) de sonido** sound mixer, dubbing mixer **Ⓒ** SM (Radio, TV) (= aparato) (tb **~ de sonido**) mixer, mixing desk 2 (Culin) (tb **vaso ~**) mixing bowl

mezcladora SF mixer; (tb **~ de sonido**) mixer, mixing desk ➤ **mezcladora de hormigón** concrete mixer

mezclar /1a/ **Ⓐ** VT 1 (= combinar) [+ ingredientes, colores] to mix, mix together; [+ estilos] to mix, combine; [+ personas] to mix; **un artista que mezcla estilos diferentes en su obra** an artist who mixes o combines different styles

in his work; **~ algo con algo** to mix sth with sth; **no se debe ~ la religión con la política** one shouldn't mix religion with politics; **la harina y el azúcar se mezclan por partes iguales** equal quantities of flour and sugar are mixed (together)
2 (= *confundir, desordenar*) [+ *fotos, papeles*] to mix up, mess up; [+ *idiomas*] to mix up, muddle up; [+ *naipes*] to shuffle
3 [+ *café, tabaco, whisky*] to blend
4 (*Mús*) [+ *sonido*] to mix
5 (= *implicar*) **~ a algn en algo** to involve sb in sth, get sb involved in sth
Ⓑ VI (*) (*con bebidas alcohólicas*) to mix (one's) drinks
Ⓒ mezclarse VPR **1** (= *combinarse*) [*ingredientes, colores*] to mix; [*culturas, elementos*] to mix, combine
2 (= *confundirse*) [*papeles, intereses*] to get mixed up
3 (= *involucrarse*) **~se en algo** to get involved in sth
4 (= *relacionarse*) **~se con algn** to mix with sb, get involved with sb

mezcolanza SF hotchpotch, hodgepodge (*EEUU*), jumble

mezquinar /1a/ VT (*LAm*) **~ algo** to be stingy with sth, skimp on sth

mezquindad SF **1** (= *tacañería*) stinginess, meanness (*esp Brit*) **2** (= *insignificancia*) paltriness, wretchedness **3** (= *acto vil*) mean thing (to do)

mezquino/a Ⓐ ADJ **1** (= *tacaño*) stingy, mean (*esp Brit*) **2** (= *insignificante*) [*pago*] miserable, paltry **Ⓑ** SM/F (= *tacaño*) miser, stingy *o* (*esp Brit*) mean person **Ⓒ** SM (*And, CAm, Méx*) (= *verruga*) wart

mezquita SF mosque

mezquite SM mesquite (tree *o* shrub)

mezzosoprano ['metso-so'prano] SF mezzo-soprano

mg ABR (= **miligramo(s)**) mg

mi¹ ADJ POSES my

mi² SM (*Mús*) E ➤ **mi mayor** E major

mí PRON (*después de prep*) me; **unos para ti y otros para mí** some for you and some for me; **tengo confianza en mí mismo** I have confidence in myself; **¿y a mí qué?** so what?, what has that got to do with me?; **para mí no hay duda** as far as I'm concerned there's no doubt; **por mí puede ir** as far as I'm concerned she can go; **por mí mismo** by myself

miaja* SF **1** (= *migaja*) crumb **2** (= *poquito*) tiny bit; **ni (una) ~** not the least little bit **3** (*como adv*) a bit; **me quiere una ~** she likes me a bit

miasma SM miasma

miau SM mew, miaow

mica¹ SF (*Min*) mica

mica² SF (*Col*) (= *orinal*) chamber pot; (*para niños*) potty*

miccionar /1a/ VI (*frm*) to urinate

michelín* SM roll of fat, spare tyre (*Brit**)

mico SM **1** (*Zool*) long-tailed monkey; (*como término genérico*) monkey; **¡cállate, ~!*** (*a niño*) shut up, you little monkey! **2** (***) **ser un ~** (= *feo*) to be an ugly devil

micra SF micron

micrero/a SM/F (*CS*) bus driver

micro¹ Ⓐ SM (*And, CS*) (*pequeño*) minibus; (*CS*) (*grande*) bus **Ⓑ** SF (*Chi*) bus

micro² SM (*Inform*) micro, microcomputer

microbiano ADJ microbial

microbio SM microbe (*frm*), germ

microbiología SF microbiology

microbús SM minibus

microchip [mikro'tʃip] SM (*pl* **~s**) microchip

microcirugía SF microsurgery

microclima SM microclimate

microcosmos SM INV microcosm

microficha SF microfiche

microfilm SM (*pl* **~s** *o* **~es**) microfilm

micrófono SM **1** (*Radio, TV*) microphone; **hablar por el ~** to speak over the microphone **2** [*de ordenador*] mouthpiece

microlentillas SFPL contact lenses

microondas SM INV (*tb* **horno ~**) microwave (oven); **apto para ~** microwavable, suitable for microwaving

microorganismo SM microorganism

microprocesador SM microprocessor

microscópico ADJ microscopic

microscopio SM microscope

microsurco SM microgroove

microtransmisor SM micro-transmitter

miéchica EXCL (*And euf*) sugar!*, shoot!*

miedica* SMF chicken*, coward

miedo SM **1** (= *temor*) fear; **~ a las represalias** fear of reprisals; **¡qué ~!** how scary!; **una película de ~** a horror film (*esp Brit*) *o* movie (*esp EEUU*); **pasé mucho ~ viendo la obra** I was very scared watching the play; **me da ~ subir al tejado** I'm scared to go up on the roof; **me da ~ dejar solo al niño** I'm frightened to leave the child alone; **por ~ a** *o* **de algo** for fear of sth; **tener ~** to be scared *o* frightened; **tener ~ a** *o* **de algn/algo** to be afraid of sb/sth; **✦** MODISMO **meterle el ~ en el cuerpo a algn** to scare the wits *o* the hell out of sb
2 ✦ MODISMO **de ~*: lo pasamos de ~** we had a fantastic time; **hace un frío de ~** it's freezing

miedoso/a Ⓐ ADJ (= *cobarde*) scared **Ⓑ** SM/F coward

miel SF [*de abejas*] honey; (= *melaza*) (*tb* **~ de caña, ~ negra**) molasses; **las ~es del triunfo** the sweet taste of success; **✦** MODISMOS **~ sobre hojuelas** so much the better; **dejar a algn con la ~ en los labios** to leave sb feeling cheated

miembro Ⓐ SM **1** (*Anat*) limb, member ➤ **miembro viril** male member, penis **2** (*Ling, Mat*) member **Ⓑ** SMF [*de club*] member; [*de institución, academia*] fellow, associate; **hacerse ~ de** to become a member of, join **Ⓒ** ADJ member *antes de s*

mientes SFPL **¡ni por ~!** never!, not on your life!; **parar ~ en algo** to reflect on sth; **traer a las ~** to recall; **se le vino a las ~** it occurred to him

mientras Ⓐ CONJ **1** (= *durante*) while; **sonreía ~ hablaba** he smiled as he spoke; **~ él estaba fuera** while he was out **2** (*expresando condición*) as long as; **seguiré ~ pueda caminar** I'll carry on (for) as long as I can still walk; **no podemos comenzar ~ no venga** we can't start until he comes
3 (= *en tanto que*) while, whereas; **tú trabajas ~ que yo estoy en el paro** you're working while *o* whereas I'm unemployed
4 (*esp LAm*) (= *cuanto*) **~ más tienen más quieren** the more they have the more they want
Ⓑ ADV (*tb* **~ tanto**) (= *entre tanto*) meanwhile, in the meantime

miércoles SM INV Wednesday ➤ **miércoles de ceniza** Ash Wednesday; *ver* **sábado**

En inglés los días de la semana se escriben con mayúscula.

mierda*** Ⓐ SF **1** (= *excremento*) shit***, crap***; **una ~ de perro** some dog shit***; **estar hecho una ~** (= *sucio*) to be filthy; (= *cansado*) to be knackered*; **mandar a algn a la ~** to tell sb to piss off***
2 (= *suciedad*) crap***; **tienes la casa llena de ~** the house is a pigsty *o* is filthy
3 (= *cosa sin valor*) crap***; **el libro es una ~** the book is crap***; **—¿cuánto te han pagado? —una ~** "how much did they pay you?" — "a pittance"; **de ~** crappy***; **una novela de ~** a crappy novel***
4 (*en exclamaciones*) **¡vete a la ~!** go to hell!*, piss off!***; **—¡ven aquí! —¡una ~!** "come here!" — "piss off!"***
5 (= *borrachera*) **coger** *o* **pillar una ~** to get pissed**, get sloshed**
Ⓑ EXCL shit!***

mierdoso** ADJ filthy

mies SF **1** (= *cereal*) (ripe) corn (*Brit*), (ripe) grain (*EEUU*)
2 mieses cornfields (*Brit*), grain fields (*EEUU*)

miga SF 1 [*de pan*] **la ~** the inside part of the bread, the crumb 2 **migas** (*Culin*) fried breadcrumbs;
✦ MODISMO **hacer buenas ~s con algn** to get on well with sb 3 (= *sustancia*) substance; **esto tiene su ~** there's more to this than meets the eye 4 (= *pedazo*) bit; **hacer algo ~s** to break o smash sth to pieces; **hacer ~s a algn** to shatter sb

migajas SFPL 1 [*de pan*] crumbs 2 (= *trocitos*) bits; (= *sobras*) scraps

migar /1h/ VT to crumble

migra* SF (*Méx*) immigration police

migración SF migration

migraña SF migraine

migrar /1a/ VI to migrate

migratorio ADJ migratory

mijo¹ SM millet

mijo²/a* SM/F (*LAm*) (*a un hombre*) mate*; (*a una mujer*) love*

mil ADJ, PRON, SM a o one thousand; **tres ~ coches** three thousand cars; **doscientos dólares** one thousand two hundred dollars; ✦ MODISMO **a las ~*** at some ungodly hour*; *ver tb* **seis**

milagro SM (*Rel*) miracle; (*fig*) miracle, wonder; **se salvaron de ~** they had a miraculous escape, it was a miracle they escaped; **un buen maquillaje puede hacer ~s** decent make-up can work wonders

milagroso ADJ miraculous

milanesa SF (*Culin*) schnitzel, escalope (*Brit*)

milano SM (*Orn*) kite ➤ **milano real** red kite

milenario ADJ (= *de mil años*) thousand-year-old *antes de s*; (= *antiquísimo*) ancient, age-old

milenio SM millennium

milésima SF thousandth; **una ~ de segundo** a thousandth of a second

milésimo ADJ, PRON thousandth; *ver tb* **sexto**

milhojas SM INV o SF INV millefeuille, *cream cake made with puff pastry*

mili* SF military service; **hacer la ~** to do one's military service

miliar ADJ **piedra ~** milestone

milibar SM millibar

milicia SF 1 (= *arte*) art of war; (= *profesión*) military profession 2 (= *tropa*) militia; **~s armadas** armed militias 3 (= *servicio militar*) military service

miliciano/a SM/F militiaman/militiawoman

milico* SM (*LAm pey*) soldier; **los ~s** the military

miligramo SM milligramme, milligram (*EEUU*)

mililitro SM millilitre, milliliter (*EEUU*)

milimetrado ADJ (*fig*) minutely calculated; **papel ~** graph paper

milimétrico ADJ (= *preciso*) precise, minute; **con precisión milimétrica** with pinpoint accuracy

milímetro SM millimetre, millimeter (*EEUU*); **no ceder ni un ~** not to give an inch; **lo calculó al o hasta el ~** he calculated it very precisely

militancia SF 1 (*en partido*) membership ➤ **militancia de base** rank-and-file members *pl* 2 (*en política*) activism 3 (= *afiliación*) affiliation; **¿cuál es su ~ política?** what is his political affiliation?

militante ❷ ADJ politically active ❸ SMF [*de partido*] member ➤ **militante de base** rank and file member

militar ❷ ADJ military; **ciencia ~** art of war ❸ SM (= *soldado*) soldier, military man; (*en la mili*) serviceman; **los ~es** the military ❹ /1a/ VI 1 (*Mil*) to serve (*in the army*) 2 (*en partido*) to be a member (**en** of) 3 (*en política*) to be politically active

militarista ❷ ADJ militaristic ❸ SMF militarist

militarizar /1f/ VT to militarize

milla SF mile ➤ **milla marina** nautical mile

millar SM thousand; **a ~es** by the thousand

millardo SM thousand million, billion

millón SM million; **un ~ a** o one million; **un ~ y medio de visitantes** a million and a half visitors, one-and-a-half million visitors; **tres millones de niños** three million children; **¡un ~ de gracias!** thanks a million!, thanks ever so much!

millonada* SF **costó una ~** it cost a fortune; **lo vendió por una ~** he sold it for a fortune

millonario/a SM/F millionaire/millionairess

millonésimo/a ADJ, SM/F millionth

milonga SF 1 (= *baile*) *type of dance and music from the River Plate Region* 2 (*RPl**) (= *fiesta*) party

milonguero/a SM/F (*RPl*) party lover

milpa SF (*CAm, Méx*) (= *plantación*) maize field (*Brit*), cornfield (*EEUU*); (= *planta*) maize (*Brit*), corn (*EEUU*)

milpear /1a/ VI (*CAm, Méx*) to sow a field with maize (*Brit*), sow a field with corn (*EEUU*)

milpiés SM INV millipede

milrayas ADJ INV **pantalón ~** fine pin-stripe trousers (*Brit*) o pants (*EEUU*)

mimado ADJ spoiled, pampered

mimar /1a/ VT to spoil, pamper

mimbre SM o SF 1 (*Bot*) osier, willow 2 (= *material*) wicker; **de ~** wicker *antes de s*, wickerwork *antes de s*

mimético ADJ mimetic, imitation *antes de s*

mimetismo SM mimicry

mimetizar /1f/ ❷ VT to imitate ❸ **mimetizarse** VPR to change colour, change color (*EEUU*)

mímica SF 1 (= *arte*) mime; (= *lenguaje*) sign language; (= *gestos*) gesticulation 2 (= *imitación*) imitation, mimicry

mímico ADJ mimic; **lenguaje ~** sign language

mimo/a ❷ SM/F (*Teat*) mime ❸ SM 1 (*Teat*) mime 2 (= *cuidado*) **una casa diseñada con ~** a house designed with loving care; **escribe con ~** she's very careful in the way she writes 3 **mimos** (= *carantoñas*): **hacer ~s a algn** to make a (great) fuss of sb 4 (= *consentimiento excesivo*) pampering; **tratan a Juanito con demasiado ~** they pamper Juanito too much, they spoil Juanito (rotten)

mimosa SF mimosa

mimoso ADJ 1 (= *cariñoso*) affectionate; **¡no te pongas tan ~!** don't be so clingy! 2 (= *mimado*) spoilt, pampered

mina SF 1 (*Min*) mine ➤ **mina a cielo abierto** opencast mine (*Brit*), strip mine (*EEUU*) 2 (= *galería*) gallery; (= *pozo*) shaft 3 (*Mil, Náut*) mine ➤ **mina antipersonal** antipersonnel mine ➤ **mina terrestre** land mine 4 [*de lápiz*] lead 5 (= *ganga*) (*tb ~ de oro*) gold mine; **este negocio es una ~ (de oro)** this business is a gold mine 6 (*CS***) (= *chica*) girl; (= *mujer*) woman

minar /1a/ VT 1 (*Min, Mil, Náut*) to mine 2 (= *debilitar*) to undermine

minarete SM minaret

mineral ❷ ADJ mineral ❸ SM 1 (*Geol*) mineral 2 (*Min*) ore ➤ **mineral de hierro** iron ore 3 (*Chi*) (= *mina*) mine

mineralogía SF mineralogy

minería SF mining

minero/a ❷ ADJ mining ❸ SM/F miner

minga¹ SF (*And*) voluntary communal labour, voluntary communal labor (*EEUU*), cooperative work

minga²*** SF (*Esp*) prick***

mingaco SM (*And*) = **minga¹**

mingitorio SM (*hum*) urinal

mini ❷ SM (*Inform*) minicomputer ❸ SF (= *falda*) mini, miniskirt

miniatura ❷ ADJ miniature ❸ SF miniature; **en ~** in miniature; **relojes en ~** miniature clocks; **un barco en ~** a model ship

miniaturizar /1f/ VT to miniaturize

minibar SM minibar

minicadena SF mini hi-fi, mini stereo system

minicines SMPL *cinema with several small screens*

MiniDisc®, minidisc SM MiniDisc®

minifalda SF miniskirt

minifundio SM smallholding, small farm

minifundismo SM *small-scale farming*

minifundista SMF smallholder

minigolf SM crazy golf

mínima SF (*Meteo*) low, lowest temperature; *ver tb* **mínimo**

minimalismo SM minimalism

minimalista ADJ, SMF minimalist

minimizar /1f/ VT **1** (= *reducir al mínimo*) [+ *gastos, efectos*] to minimize **2** (= *quitar importancia a*) [+ *problema, suceso*] to make light of, minimize, play down

mínimo Ⓐ ADJ **1** (= *inferior*) [*nivel, cantidad*] minimum; **con el ~ esfuerzo** with a o the minimum of effort; **"tarifa mínima: tres euros"** "minimum fare: three euros"; **lo ~: es lo ~ que podemos hacer** it's the least we can do; **el dinero no me interesa lo más ~** I'm not the least o the slightest bit interested in money; **los sueldos no se verán afectados en lo más ~** salaries will not be affected in the least o in the slightest; **en un tiempo ~** in no time at all ➤ **mínimo común denominador** lowest common denominator **2** (= *muy pequeño*) [*habitación, letra*] tiny, minute; [*detalle*] minute; [*gasto, beneficio*] minimal; **este teléfono ocupa un espacio ~** this telephone takes up hardly any space; **me contó hasta el más ~ detalle** he told me everything in minute detail; **un vehículo de consumo ~** a vehicle with minimal fuel consumption **3** [*plazo*] **no existe un plazo ~ para entregar el trabajo** there's no set date for the work to be handed in
Ⓑ SM **1** (= *cantidad mínima*) minimum; **¿cuál es el ~?** what is the minimum?; **bajo ~s** (*Esp*) [*credibilidad, moral*] at rock bottom; [*consumo, presupuesto*] very low; **como ~** at least; **un ~ de algo** a minimum of sth; **necesitamos un ~ de dos millones** we need a minimum of two million; **si tuviera un ~ de vergüenza no vendría más por aquí** if he had any shame at all he wouldn't come back here; **reducir algo al ~** to keep o reduce sth to a minimum **2** (*Fin*) record low, lowest point ➤ **mínimo histórico** all-time low **3** (*Mat*) [*de una función*] minimum **4** (*Meteo*) ➤ **mínimo de presión** low-pressure area, trough

minino/a* SM/F (= *gato*) puss, pussycat

Minipimer® SM electric mixer

miniserie SF miniseries

ministerial ADJ (*de ministro, ministerio*) ministerial; **reunión ~** cabinet meeting

ministerio SM **1** (*Pol*) ministry, department (*esp EEUU*) ➤ **Ministerio de Hacienda** Treasury, Treasury Department (*EEUU*) **2** (*Jur*) **el ~ público** the Prosecution, the State Prosecutor (*EEUU*)

ministro/a SM/F (*en gobierno*) minister, secretary (*esp EEUU*); **primer ~** prime minister; **consejo de ~s** (= *grupo*) cabinet; (= *reunión*) cabinet meeting ➤ **ministro/a de Hacienda** Chancellor of the Exchequer (*Brit*), Secretary of the Treasury (*EEUU*) ➤ **ministro/a del Interior** Home Secretary (*Brit*), Secretary of the Interior (*EEUU*) ➤ **ministro/a portavoz** government spokesperson ➤ **ministro/a sin cartera** minister without portfolio

minivacaciones SFPL minibreak

minoría SF minority; **estar en ~** to be in a o the minority; **gobernar en ~** to govern without an overall majority ➤ **minoría de edad** minority ➤ **minoría étnica** ethnic minority

minorista Ⓐ ADJ retail *antes de s* Ⓑ SMF retailer

minoritario ADJ minority *antes de s*

minucia SF **1** (= *detalle insignificante*) trifle, insignificant detail; **minucias** petty details, minutiae **2** (= *bagatela*) mere nothing

minuciosidad SF **lo limpió con ~** she cleaned it thoroughly o meticulously; **describió la situación con ~** she described the situation in minute detail

minucioso ADJ **1** (= *meticuloso*) thorough, meticulous

2 (= *detallado*) very detailed

minué SM, **minuet** SM minuet

minúscula SF small letter; (*Tip*) lower case letter; **se escribe con ~** it's written with small letters

minúsculo ADJ **1** (= *muy pequeño*) tiny, minuscule **2** (*Tip*) lower-case

minusvalía SF **1** (*Med*) disability, handicap; **personas con ~ disabled** people ➤ **minusvalía física** physical disability o handicap ➤ **minusvalía psíquica** mental disability o handicap **2** (*Com*) depreciation, capital loss

minusválido/a Ⓐ ADJ (*físico*) physically handicapped, physically disabled; (*psíquico*) mentally handicapped, mentally disabled Ⓑ SM/F disabled person, handicapped person; **los ~s** the disabled ➤ **minusválido/a físico/a** physically handicapped person, physically disabled person ➤ **minusválido/a psíquico/a** mentally disabled person, mentally disabled person

minusvalorar /1a/ Ⓐ VT to undervalue, underestimate Ⓑ **minusvalorarse** VPR to hold o.s. in low esteem, have a low opinion of o.s.

minuta SF **1** [*de abogado*] lawyer's bill **2** (= *menú*) menu **3** (= *borrador*) rough draft, first draft **4** (= *lista*) list, roll **5** (*RPl*) (= *comida rápida*) hot snack

minutero SM (= *manecilla*) minute hand; (= *reloj*) timer

minuto SM minute; **volverá dentro de un ~** she'll be back in a minute; **guardar un ~ de silencio** to observe a minute's silence

mío Ⓐ ADJ POSES mine; **es ~** it's mine; **es amigo ~** he's a friend of mine; **¡Dios ~!** my God!, good heavens!; **¡hijo ~!** my dear boy!
Ⓑ PRON POSES **1 el ~/la mía** mine; **éste es el ~** this one's mine; **he puesto lo ~ en esta caja** I've put my stuff o things in this box; **lo ~ con Ana acabó hace tiempo** Ana and I finished a while ago; **el tenis no es lo ~** tennis is not for me, tennis is not my cup of tea o my thing **2 los ~s** (= *mis familiares*) my folks, my family **3 la mía** (= *mi oportunidad*): **¡ésta es la mía!** now's my chance!

> **Mío** se traduce por **mine** y nunca va precedido de artículo cuando hace referencia a lo que pertenece a alguien: "Es (el) mío", *It's mine*. Por otro lado, se traduce por **of mine** cuando significa "uno de mis": "un primo mío", *a cousin of mine*.

miocardio SM myocardium (*frm*); *ver tb* **infarto**

miope Ⓐ ADJ short-sighted (*esp Brit*), near-sighted (*EEUU*), myopic (*frm*) Ⓑ SMF short-sighted person (*esp Brit*), near-sighted person (*EEUU*), myopic person (*frm*)

miopía SF short-sightedness (*esp Brit*), near-sightedness (*EEUU*), myopia (*frm*)

miosis SF INV miosis, myosis

MIR SM ABR (*Esp*) = **Médico interno residente**

mira SF **1** (*Mil, Téc*) sight; ✦ MODISMO **estar con** o **tener la ~ puesta en algo** to have one's sights set on sth **2** (= *intención*) aim, intention; **con ~s a** with a view to **3 miras** (= *actitud*): **corto de ~s** narrow-minded

mirada SF **1** (= *forma de mirar*) look; **con una ~ triste** with a sad look in his eyes; **con la ~ fija en el infinito** staring into space **2** (= *acto*) (*rápida*) glance; (*detenida*) gaze; **le dirigió una ~ de sospecha** he gave her a suspicious look o glance, he looked o glanced at her suspiciously; **le echó una ~ por encima del hombro** she gave him a condescending look, she looked at him condescendingly; **nos dirigimos una ~ de complicidad** we glanced at each other knowingly; **echar una ~ de reojo** o **de soslayo a algo/algn** to look out of the corner of one's eye at sth/sb, cast a sidelong glance at sth/sb ➤ **mirada perdida**: **tenía la ~ perdida en el horizonte** she was gazing into the distance; **tenían la ~ perdida de quienes están próximos a la locura** they had the empty look of people on the verge of madness **3** (= *vista*) **apartar la ~ (de algn/algo)** to look away (from sb/sth); **bajar la ~** to look down; **clavar la ~ en algo/algn** to fix one's eyes on sth/sb; **desviar la ~ (de algn/algo)** (*lit*) to look away (from sb/sth), avert one's eyes (from sb/sth); (fig) to turn one's back (on sb/sth); **dirigir la ~ a** o **hacia algn/algo** (lit) to look at sb/sth; (fig) to turn one's attention to sb/sth; **echar una ~ a algn/algo** (varias veces) to keep an eye on sb/sth, check on sb/sth; (una sola vez) to have a look at sb/sth; **levantar la ~** to look up, raise one's eyes; **tener la ~ puesta en algo** (lit) to have one's gaze fixed on sth; (fig) to be looking towards sth, have one's sights set on sth; **seguir algo/a algn con la ~** to follow sth/sb with one's eyes; **volver la ~** to look back

4 miradas (= atención): **todas las ~s estarán puestas en el jugador brasileño** all eyes will be on the Brazilian player; **me fui, huyendo de las ~s de todo el pueblo** I left, fleeing from the prying eyes of the whole village

mirado ADJ **1** (= estimado) **bien ~** well o highly thought of, highly regarded **2** (= sensato) sensible; (= cauto) cautious, careful; (= considerado) considerate, thoughtful; (= educado) well-behaved **3 bien ~ ...** all things considered ..., when you think about it ...

mirador SM **1** (= lugar de observación) viewpoint, vantage point **2** (= ventana) bay window; (= balcón) (enclosed) balcony

miramiento SM **1** (= consideración) considerateness; (= cortesía) courtesy; **sin ~** without consideration **2 miramientos** (= respeto) respect sing; (= cortesías) courtesies, attentions; **andar con ~s** to tread carefully; **sin ~s** unceremoniously

mirar /1a/ **Ⓐ** VT **1** (= ver) to look at

Recuérdese añadir la preposición **at** después de **look** al traducir el uso transitivo de **mirar**:

me miró con tristeza she looked at me sadly; **~ a algn de arriba abajo** to look sb up and down; **~ algo/a algn de reojo** to look at sth/sb out of the corner of one's eye; **fijamente algo/a algn** to gaze o stare at sth/sb; **~ algo por encima** to glance over sth; ✦ MODISMOS **~ bien** o **con buenos ojos a algn** to approve of sb; **~ mal** o **con malos ojos a algn** to disapprove of sb; **de mírame y no me toques** delicate, fragile

2 [+ televisión] to watch **3** (= observar) to watch; **se quedó mirando cómo jugaban los niños** she stood watching the children play **4** (= comprobar) **le ~on la maleta en la aduana** they searched his suitcase at customs; **mira a ver lo que hace el niño** go and see o check what the boy's up to; **míralo en el diccionario** look it up in the dictionary **5** (= pensar en) **lo hago mirando el porvenir** I'm doing it with the future in mind; **mirándolo bien, la situación no es tan grave** all in all, the situation isn't that bad, if you really think about it, the situation isn't all that bad **6** (= ser cuidadoso con) **deberías ~ lo que gastas** you should watch what you spend; **mira mucho todos los detalles** she pays great attention to detail **7** (uso exclamativo) **7.1** (en imperativo) **¡mira qué cuadro tan bonito!** look, what a pretty painting!; **¡mira lo que has hecho!** (just) look what you've done!; **¡mira quién fue a hablar!** look who's talking!; **¡mira bien lo que haces!** watch what you do! **7.2** (indicando sorpresa, disgusto) **mira que: ¡mira que es tonto!** he's so stupid!; **¡mira que te avisé!** didn't I warn you?; **¡mira que ponerse a llover ahora!** it would have to start raining right now! **7.3** (indicando esperanza, temor) **mira que si: ¡mira que si ganas!** imagine if you win!; **¡mira que si no viene!** just suppose he doesn't come!

Ⓑ VI **1** (con la vista) to look; **estaba mirando por la ventana** he was looking out of the window; **miré por el agujero** I looked through the hole; **~ de reojo** to look out of the corner of one's eye **2** (= comprobar) to look; **¿has mirado en el cajón?** have you looked in the drawer? **3** (= estar orientado hacia) to face **4** (= cuidar) **~ por algn** to look after sb, take care of sb **5** (uso exclamativo) **¡mira! ¡un ratón!** look, a mouse!; ✦ MODISMOS **¡(pues) mira por dónde ...!** you'll never believe it ...! **6 ~ a** (= proponerse) to aim at

7 por lo que mira a (frm) as for, as regards
Ⓒ mirarse VPR **1** (reflexivo) to look at o.s.; **~se al** o **en el espejo** to look at o.s. in the mirror **2** (recíproco) to look at each other o one another

mirilla SF (en puerta) peephole, spyhole; (Fot) viewfinder

miriñaque SM crinoline, hoop skirt

mirlo SM blackbird

mirón/ona* **Ⓐ** ADJ nosey*, curious **Ⓑ** SM/F (= espectador) onlooker; (= mirón) nosey-parker*; (= voyer) voyeur, peeping Tom; **estar de ~** to stand around watching, stand around doing nothing; **ir de ~** to go along just to watch

mirra SF myrrh

mirto SM myrtle

misa SF mass; **decir ~** (lit) to say mass; **¡por mí, que digan ~!** let them say what they like!; **ir a ~** (lit) to go to mass; **lo que yo diga va a ~** what I say goes; **oír ~** to go to mass; ✦ MODISMOS **como en ~: los niños estaban como en ~** the children were really quiet; **estar en ~ y repicando** to have one's cake and eat it; **no saber de la ~ la media** o **la mitad** not to know anything about it, not to have a clue ➤ **misa de campaña** open-air mass ➤ **misa de corpore insepulto, misa de cuerpo presente** funeral mass ➤ **misa de difuntos** requiem mass ➤ **misa del gallo** midnight mass (on Christmas Eve); ○ NOCHEBUENA ➤ **misa negra** black mass

misal SM missal

misantropía SF misanthropy

misántropo/a SM/F misanthrope, misanthropist

miscelánea SF **1** (frm) (= mezcla) miscellany **2** (Méx) (= tienda) corner shop (Brit), corner store (EEUU)

misceláneo ADJ miscellaneous

miserable **Ⓐ** ADJ **1** (= tacaño) stingy, mean (esp Brit); (= avaro) miserly **2** [sueldo] miserable, paltry **3** (= vil) vile, despicable **4** [lugar, habitación] squalid, wretched **Ⓑ** SMF **1** (= desgraciado) wretch **2** (= canalla) swine, wretch; **¡miserable!** you miserable wretch!

miseria SF **1** (= pobreza) poverty, destitution; **vivir en la ~** to live in poverty **2** (= insignificancia) **una ~** a pittance

misericordia SF compassion, mercy

misericordioso ADJ merciful

mísero ADJ **1** (= tacaño) mean, stingy; (= avaro) miserly **2** [sueldo] miserable, paltry **3** (= vil) vile, despicable **4** [lugar, habitación] squalid, wretched

misérrimo ADJ SUPERL ver **mísero**

misil SM missile ➤ **misil (de) crucero** cruise missile ➤ **misil tierra-aire** ground-to-air missile

misión SF **1** (= cometido) mission; (= tarea) task; (Pol) assignment ➤ **misión humanitaria** humanitarian mission **2** (= delegación) mission ➤ **misión diplomática** diplomatic mission **3 misiones** (Rel) overseas missions, missionary work sing

misionero/a SM/F missionary; **postura** o **posición del ~** missionary position

misiva SF (liter) missive (liter)

mismamente* ADV (= sólo) only, just; (= textualmente) literally; (= incluso) even; (= en realidad) really, actually; **~ anoche estuve allí** I was there only o just last night; **~ cerca de mi casa hay uno** there's actually one right near my house

mismísimo ADJ SUPERL very (same); **con mis ~s ojos** with my own eyes; **estuvo el ~ obispo** the bishop himself was there

mismo **Ⓐ** ADJ **1** (= igual) same; **el ~ coche** the same car; **el ~ ... que** the same ... as; **lleva la misma falda que ayer** she's wearing the same skirt as yesterday; **tengo el ~ dinero que tú** I've got the same amount of money as you **2** (reflexivo) **lo hizo por sí ~** he did it by himself; **perjudicarse a sí ~** to harm oneself **3** (enfático) **3.1** (relativo a personas) **yo ~ lo vi** I saw it myself, I saw it with my own eyes; **ni ella misma lo sabe** she doesn't even know herself; **¿quién responde? a ver, tú misma, Ana** who knows the answer? how about you, Ana? **3.2** (relativo a cosas) **—¿cuál quieres? —ese ~** "which one do you want?" — "that one there"; **—¡es un canalla! —eso ~ pienso yo** "he's a swine!" — "my thoughts exactly"; **viven en el ~ centro** they live right in the centre; **en ese ~ momento** at that very moment; **por eso ~: por eso ~ te lo dije** that's exactly why I told you

4 (*como pronombre*) **es el ~ que nos alquilaron el año pasado** it's the same one they rented us last year; **no es la misma desde su divorcio** she hasn't been the same since her divorce; **—¿es usted la señorita Sánchez? —¡la misma!** "are you Miss Sánchez?" — "I am indeed!"; ✦ MODISMO **estamos en las mismas** we're no better off than before, we're no further forward

5 lo mismo 5.1 (= *la misma cosa*) the same (thing); **—¡enhorabuena! —lo ~ digo** "congratulations!" — "likewise" o "the same to you"; **nos contó lo ~ de siempre** she told us the usual story; **—¿qué desea de beber? —lo ~ (de antes), por favor** "what would you like to drink?" — "(the) same again, please"; **cuando le interese a él, o lo que es lo ~, nunca** when it suits him, in other words never; **lo ~ que: le dijo lo ~ que yo** she told him the same thing o the same as she told me **5.2 dar lo ~: da lo ~** it's all the same, it makes no difference; **me da lo ~** I don't mind, it's all the same to me; **da lo ~ que vengas hoy o mañana** it doesn't matter whether you come today or tomorrow **5.3** (*) (= *a lo mejor*) **lo ~ no vienen** maybe they won't come; **no lo sé todavía, pero lo ~ voy** I don't know yet, but I may well come **5.4 lo ~ que** (= *al igual que*): **en Europa, lo ~ que en América** in Europe, (just) as in America; **nos divertimos lo ~ que si hubiéramos ido al baile** we had just as good a time as if we had gone to the dance **5.5 lo ~ ... que** (= *tanto ... como*): **lo ~ te puede criticar que alabar** she's just as likely to criticize you as to praise you; **lo ~ puede durar una hora que dos** it could last anywhere between one and two hours

B ADV (*enfático*) **delante ~ de la casa** right in front of the house; **ahora ~** (= *inmediatamente*) right away o now; (= *hace un momento*) just now; **—¿dónde lo pongo? —aquí ~** "where shall I put it?" — "right here"; **—¿cómo quieres el filete? —así ~ está bien** "how would you like your steak?" — "it's fine just like that"; **he llegado hoy ~** I just arrived today; **mañana ~ te lo traigo** tomorrow, I'll bring it to you tomorrow

misoginia SF misogyny

misógino SM misogynist

miss [mis] SF beauty queen; **concurso de ~es** beauty contest

míster SM trainer, coach

misterio SM **1** (= *incógnita*) mystery; **una novela de ~** a mystery (story) **2** (= *secreto*) secrecy; **¿a qué viene tanto ~?** why all this secrecy?, why are you being so mysterious?; **obrar con ~** to act in secret **3** (*Teat*) mystery play

misterioso ADJ mysterious

mística SF, **misticismo** SM mysticism

místico/a Ⓐ ADJ mystic(al) Ⓑ SM/F mystic

mitad SF **1** (= *parte*) half; **me queda la ~** I have half left; **a ~ de precio** half-price; **~ (y) ~** half-and-half; **es ~ blanco y ~ rojo** it's half white and half red **2** (*Dep*) half; **la primera ~** the first half **3** (= *centro*) middle; **a ~ de la comida** in the middle of the meal, halfway through the meal; **está a ~ de camino entre Madrid y Barcelona** it's halfway between Madrid and Barcelona; **en ~ de la calle** in the middle of the street; **el depósito está a la ~** the tank is half empty; **hacia la ~ del documental** about halfway through the documentary; **cortar por la ~** to cut in half; ✦ MODISMO **me parte por la ~** it upsets my plans

mítico ADJ mythical

mitificar /1g/ VT to mythologize, convert into a myth

mitigar /1h/ VT (*gen*) to mitigate (*frm*); [+ *dolor*] to relieve, ease; [+ *sed*] to quench; [+ *ira*] to calm, appease; [+ *temores*] to allay; [+ *calor*] to reduce; [+ *soledad*] to alleviate, relieve

mitin SM **1** (*Pol*) rally **2** (= *discurso*) political speech

mito SM myth

mitología SF mythology

mitológico ADJ mythological

mitómano/a SM/F mythomaniac

mitón SM mitten

mitote SM (*Méx*) **1** (*Hist*) *Aztec ritual dance* **2** (*) (= *jaleo*) uproar

mitra SF mitre, miter (*EEUU*)

mixto Ⓐ ADJ (= *mezclado*) mixed; [*comité, empresa*] joint; **colegio ~** coeducational school Ⓑ SM (*toasted*) *cheese and ham sandwich*

ml ABR (= *mililitro(s)*) ml

mm ABR (= *milímetro(s)*) mm

mnemotécnica SF, **mnemónica** SF mnemonics *sing*

mnemotécnico ADJ mnemonic

moai SM (*pl* **~s**) Easter Island statue

moaré SM moiré

mobiliario SM (= *muebles*) furniture ➤ **mobiliario de cocina** kitchen units *pl* ➤ **mobiliario de cuarto de baño** bathroom fittings *pl* ➤ **mobiliario de oficina** office furniture ➤ **mobiliario urbano** street furniture

mocasín SM moccasin

mocedad† SF youth

mocetón/ona† SM/F strapping youth/girl

mochar /1a/ Ⓐ VT (*LAm*) to chop off (clumsily), hack off Ⓑ **mocharse** VPR **~se con algn** to split the takings with sb

mochila SF backpack, rucksack (*Brit*); (*Mil*) pack ➤ **mochila portabebés** baby-carrier, baby-sling

mochilero/a SM/F backpacker

mocho/a Ⓐ ADJ **1** (= *desafilado*) blunt, short **2** [*árbol*] lopped, pollarded; [*vaca*] hornless, polled; [*muñón*] stubby **3** (*Carib*) (= *manco*) one-armed Ⓑ SM/F (*Méx*) reactionary Ⓒ SM **1** (*) (= *fregona*) mop **2** [*de utensilio*] blunt end, thick end

mochuelo SM **1** (*Orn*) (*tb* **~ común**) little owl; ✦ MODISMO **cada ~ a su olivo** let's all go back to our own homes **2** ✦ MODISMOS **cargar con el ~** to get landed with it; **colgar** o **echar el ~ a algn** to lumber sb with the job*; (= *culpa*) to make sb carry the can*; (= *crimen*) to frame sb

moción SF motion ➤ **moción de censura** motion of censure, censure motion ➤ **moción de confianza** vote of confidence

mocionar /1a/ VT (*LAm*) to move, propose

mocito/a† Ⓐ ADJ very young Ⓑ SM/F youngster; **mocitas casaderas** girls of marriageable age; **está hecha una mocita** she's a very grown-up young lady

moco SM **1** (*en la nariz*) snot*; **limpiarse los ~s** to wipe one's nose; **sorberse los ~s** to sniff; **tener ~s** to have a runny nose; ✦ MODISMO **llorar a ~ tendido** to cry one's eyes out **2** (*Orn*) crest; ✦ MODISMO **no es ~ de pavo** it's quite something*

mocoso/a* SM/F brat; **ese ~ no tiene derecho a opinar** that little brat has no right to give his opinion; **un ~ de 19 años** a snotty-nosed youth of 19*

moda SF fashion; **la ~ de primavera** spring fashion; **en los noventa llegó la ~ del acid-jazz** in the nineties acid-jazz became fashionable o trendy*; **es sólo una ~ pasajera** it's just a passing fad; **a la ~** fashionable; **tienes que ponerte** o **vestirte un poco más a la ~** you should try and dress a bit more fashionably; **estar de ~** to be in fashion, be fashionable; **pasado de ~** out of fashion, old-fashioned, outdated, out*; **ponerse de ~** to become fashionable, get trendy*

modal ADJ modal

modales SMPL manners; **no tiene ~** he has no manners; **si lo pides con buenos ~** if you ask nicely o politely

modalidad SF **1** (= *tipo*) form, type ➤ **modalidad de pago** (*Com*) method of payment **2** (*Dep*) category **3** (*Ling, Fil*) modality **4** (*Inform*) mode ➤ **modalidad de texto** text mode

modelado SM modelling

modelador(a) SM/F modeller

modelar /1a/ VT (= *dar forma a*) to shape, form; [*escultor*] to sculpt; [*alfarero*] to model

modélico ADJ model, exemplary

modelismo SM modelling, model-making

modelo Ⓐ SM 1 (= *tipo*) model; **un coche último ~** the latest-model car
2 (= *ejemplo*) **presentar algo como ~** to hold sth up as a model; **servir de ~** to serve as a model ➤ **modelo a escala** scale model
3 (= *patrón*) pattern; (*para hacer punto*) pattern
4 (= *prenda*) model, design
Ⓑ SMF (*Arte, Fot, Moda*) model; **desfile de ~s** fashion show; **servir de ~ a un pintor** to sit *o* pose for a painter ➤ **modelo de alta costura** fashion model, haute couture model
Ⓒ ADJ INV (= *ejemplar*) model, exemplary; **cárcel ~** model prison; **niño ~** model child

módem SM (*pl* **~s**) modem

moderación SF 1 (= *mesura*) moderation; **con ~** [*actuar*] with restraint; [*beber, comer*] in moderation 2 (*Econ*) **ha sido necesaria una ~ del gasto** we have had to cut *o* reduce expenses ➤ **moderación salarial** wage restraint 3 [*de debate, coloquio*] **la ~ del debate correrá a cargo de ...** the debate will be chaired by ...

moderado ADJ moderate

moderador(a) Ⓐ ADJ [*papel, poder*] moderating Ⓑ SM/F 1 (*en un debate, coloquio*) moderator, chairperson; (*TV*) host, presenter (*esp Brit*) 2 (*Pol*) moderator

moderar /1a/ Ⓐ VT 1 (= *controlar*) 1.1 [+ *impulsos, emociones*] to restrain, control; [+ *violencia, deseo*] to curb, control; [+ *ambición, opiniones, actitud*] to moderate 1.2 [+ *palabras, lenguaje, tono*] to tone down, watch; **por favor, caballero, modere sus palabras** please watch *o* (*Brit*) mind your language, sir
2 (= *reducir*) [+ *gastos, consumo*] to cut, reduce; [+ *velocidad*] to reduce; [+ *tensión*] to ease; **modere su velocidad** reduce your speed, slow down
3 [+ *debate, coloquio*] to chair, moderate
Ⓑ **moderarse** VPR 1 [*persona*] to restrain o.s., control o.s.; **tuvo que ~se en sus palabras** he had to tone down his language; **hemos tenido que ~nos un poco en los gastos** we've had to cut down our spending a little
2 [*inflación, precio*] **la inflación se moderó relativamente** inflation slowed slightly

modernidad SF modernity

modernismo SM modernism

modernista Ⓐ ADJ modernist(ic) Ⓑ SMF modernist

modernización SF modernization

modernizar /1f/ Ⓐ VT to modernize Ⓑ **modernizarse** VPR to modernize, move with the times

moderno/a Ⓐ ADJ 1 (= *actual*) modern; **siempre va vestida muy moderna** she always wears very trendy clothes*, she always dresses very trendily*; **tiene un equipo de música muy ~** he's got a very up-to-date hi-fi; **tienes unos abuelos muy ~s** your grandparents are very with it* 2 (*Hist*) modern; **la edad moderna** the modern period Ⓑ SM/F trendy*

modestia SF 1 (= *humildad*) modesty; **~ aparte, no soy mal cocinero** though I say so myself *o* (*frm*) modesty aside, I'm not a bad cook; **con ~** modestly; **falsa ~** false modesty 2 (= *escasez*) **con ~ de medios** with quite limited resources

modesto ADJ 1 (= *humilde*) modest; **no seas tan ~** don't be so modest; **en mi modesta opinión** in my humble opinion 2 (= *de poca importancia*) modest; **un ~ paso hacia la paz** a modest step towards peace 3 (= *sin lujo*) modest; **visten de forma muy modesta** they dress very modestly 4 (†) (= *recatado*) [*mujer*] modest

módico ADJ [*precio*] reasonable, modest; [*suma*] modest

modificación SF (*en producto, vehículo, conducta*) modification; (*en texto*) change, alteration; (*en precio*) change

modificar /1g/ VT [+ *producto, vehículo, conducta*] to modify; [+ *texto*] to change, alter; [+ *precio*] to change

modismo SM idiom

modisto/a SM/F (= *sastre*) dressmaker; [*de alta costura*] fashion designer, couturier

modo SM 1 (= *manera*) way, manner (*frm*); **los han distribuido del siguiente ~** they have been distributed in the following way *o* (*frm*) manner; **de un ~ u otro** one way or another; **a mi ~ de pensar** *o* **ver** in my view, the way I see it ➤ **modo de empleo** instructions for use ➤ **modo de producción** mode of production ➤ **modo de vida** way of life
2 (*locuciones*) **a mi/tu ~** (in) my/your (own) way; **a ~ de ejemplo/respuesta** by way of example/reply; **en cierto ~** in a way, to a certain extent; **de cualquier ~** (*antes de verbo*) anyway, in any case; (*después de verbo*) anyhow; **de ~** (+ ADJ): **tenemos que actuar de ~ coherente** we must act consistently; **eso nos afectará de ~ directo** this will have a direct effect on us, this will affect us directly; **de ese ~** (*antes de verbo*) (in) this way; (*después de verbo*) like that; **grosso ~** broadly speaking; **del mismo ~** in the same way; **del mismo ~ que** in the same way as *o* that, just as; **de ningún ~: no quiero implicarla en esto de ningún ~** I don't want to involve her in this in any way; **¡de ningún ~!** certainly not!, no way!*; **de todos ~s** anyway, all the same, in any case
3 **de ~ que** (*antes de verbo*) so; (*después de verbo*) so that
4 (*LAm*) **¡ni ~!** (= *de ninguna manera*) no way*, not a chance*; (= *no hay otra alternativa*) what else can I/you *etc* do?; **ni ~ que lo va a hacer** no way she's going to do it; **si no me quieres, ni ~** if you don't love me, what else can I do?
5 **modos** (= *modales*) manners; **con buenos ~s** politely; **con muy malos ~s** very rudely
6 (*Ling*) [*del verbo*] mood; **adverbio de ~** manner adverb ➤ **modo indicativo** indicative mood ➤ **modo subjuntivo** subjunctive mood
7 (*Inform*) mode
8 (*Mús*) mode

modorra* SF drowsiness; **me entró la ~** I began to feel drowsy

modoso ADJ (= *educado*) well-mannered; (= *recatado*) demure

modulación SF modulation

modulado ADJ modulated

modular /1a/ Ⓐ ADJ modular Ⓑ VT to modulate

módulo SM 1 (*Educ*) module 2 [*de mobiliario*] unit; **estantería por ~s** modular *o* combination shelving units *pl* 3 (*Espacio*) ➤ **módulo de mando** command module ➤ **módulo lunar** lunar module

mofa SF (= *burla*) mockery, ridicule; **hacer ~ de algo/algn** to scoff at sth/sb, make fun of sth/sb

mofarse /1a/ VPR **~ de algo/algn** to mock sth/sb, scoff at sth/sb, sneer at sth/sb

mofeta SF skunk

mofle SM (*CAm, Col, Méx*) silencer (*Brit*), muffler (*EEUU*)

moflete SM chubby cheek

mofletudo ADJ chubby-cheeked

mogollón* Ⓐ SM 1 (= *gran cantidad*) loads *pl*, masses *pl*; **(un) ~ de gente** ◇ **gente a ~** loads *o* masses of people 2 (= *confusión*) commotion, upheaval; (= *lío*) fuss, row; **hay mucho ~ aquí** it's a bit wild here Ⓑ ADV (= *mucho*) **me gusta ~** I think it's great *o* fantastic*

mogollónico* ADJ huge, massive

mohair [mo'xair, mo'air] SM mohair

mohín SM **hacer un ~** to make a face

mohíno ADJ 1 (= *enfadado*) annoyed 2 (= *malhumorado*) sulky, sullen 3 (= *triste*) sad, depressed

moho SM 1 (*en metal*) rust 2 (*en alimentos*) mould, mold (*EEUU*), mildew; **cubierto de ~** mouldy, moldy (*EEUU*); **olor a ~** musty smell

mohoso ADJ 1 [*metal*] rusty 2 [*alimento*] mouldy, moldy (*EEUU*); [*olor, sabor*] musty 3 [*chiste*] stale

moisés SM INV (= *cuna*) Moses basket, cradle; (*portátil*) carrycot

mojado Ⓐ ADJ (= *húmedo*) damp, wet; (= *empapado*) soaked, drenched Ⓑ SM (*Méx*) wetback (*EEUU*), illegal immigrant

mojama SF salted tuna

mojar /1a/ **A** VT **1** (*involuntariamente*) to get wet; (*voluntariamente*) to wet; (= *humedecer*) to damp(en), moisten; (= *empapar*) to drench, soak; **el niño ha mojado la cama** the baby's wet the bed; **moja un poco el trapo** dampen the cloth
2 (= *meter*) to dip; **~ el pan en el café** to dip *o* dunk one's bread in one's coffee
3 (*) [+ *triunfo*] to celebrate with a drink
B **mojarse** VPR **1** (= *humedecerse*) **1.1** (*reflexivo*) to get wet; **~se hasta los huesos** to get soaked to the skin **1.2 ~se el pelo** (*involuntariamente*) to get one's hair wet; (*voluntariamente*) to wet one's hair
2 (*) (= *comprometerse*) to get one's feet wet; **no se mojó** he kept out of it, he didn't get involved

mojarra SF *type of bream*

mojicón SM (= *bizcocho*) sponge cake; (= *bollo*) bun

mojigato/a **A** ADJ (= *santurrón*) sanctimonious; (= *puritano*) prudish, strait-laced **B** SM/F (= *santurrón*) sanctimonious person; (= *puritano*) prude

mojo SM *cold sauce made with oil, vinegar, garlic etc*

mojón SM **1** (= *piedra*) boundary stone; (*tb* **~ kilométrico**) milestone **2** (*Chi**) [*de animal*] turd

molar¹ SM molar

molar²** /1a/ VI (*Esp*) **1** (= *gustar*) **lo que más me mola es ...** what I'm really into is ...*; **¡cómo mola esa moto!** that bike is really cool!**; **no me mola** I don't go for that*, I don't fancy that **2** (= *estar de moda*) to be in*; (= *dar tono*) to be classy*, be real posh* **3** (= *valer*) to be OK*

molcajete SM (*esp Méx*) mortar

molde SM (*Culin*, *Téc*) mould, mold (*EEUU*); (= *vaciado*) cast; (*Tip*) form; ✦ MODISMO **romper ~s** to break the mould *o* (*EEUU*) mold

moldeable ADJ [*material*] malleable; [*carácter, persona*] easily influenced, impressionable

moldeado SM **1** (= *modelado*) moulding, molding (*EEUU*); (*en yeso*) casting **2** [*del pelo*] light perm

moldear /1a/ VT **1** (= *modelar*) to mould, mold (*EEUU*); (*en yeso*) to cast **2** [+ *pelo*] to give a light perm **3** [+ *persona*] to mould, mold (*EEUU*), shape

moldura SF **1** (= *marco*) frame **2** (*Arquit*) moulding, molding (*EEUU*)

mole¹ SF (= *masa*) mass, bulk; (= *edificio*) pile

mole² SM (= *salsa*) thick chile sauce (*typical of Mexican cuisine*); (= *plato*) meat in chile sauce; ✦ MODISMO **ser el ~ de algn** (*Méx**) to be sb's favourite thing ➤ **mole de olla** meat stew

molécula SF molecule

molecular ADJ molecular

moler /2h/ **A** VT [+ *café*] to grind; [+ *trigo*] to mill; (= *machacar*) to crush; (= *pulverizar*) to pound; ✦ MODISMO **~ a algn a palos** to give sb a beating **B** VI (= *molestar*) **~ con algo** to go on and on about sth

molestar /1a/ **A** VT **1** (= *importunar*) to bother, annoy **2** (= *interrumpir*) to disturb; **que no me moleste nadie** I don't want to be disturbed by anyone; **siento ~te, pero necesito que me ayudes** I'm sorry to disturb *o* trouble *o* bother you, but I need your help
3 (= *ofender*) to upset
B VI **1** (= *importunar*) to be a nuisance; **"no molestar"** "(please) do not disturb"
2 (= *incomodar*) to feel uncomfortable, bother; **¿te molesta el humo?** does the smoke bother you?; **me molesta al tragar** it hurts when I swallow; **la radio no me molesta para estudiar** the radio doesn't bother me when I'm studying
3 (= *ofender*) to upset
4 (= *importar*) (*en preguntas*) **¿le molesta que abra la ventana?** do you mind if I open the window?
C **molestarse** VPR **1** (= *tomarse la molestia*) to bother o.s.; **no se moleste, prefiero estar de pie** don't trouble *o* bother yourself, I prefer to stand; **~se en hacer algo** to take the trouble to do sth; **no te molestes en venir a por mí** don't bother to come and pick me up, you needn't take the trouble to come and pick me up; **ni siquiera te has molestado en responder a mis cartas** you didn't even bother to answer my letters
2 (= *disgustarse*) (*con enfado*) to get annoyed, get upset; (*con ofensa*) to take offence, take offense (*EEUU*); **~se con algn** to get annoyed *o* cross with sb; **~se por algo** to get annoyed at sth, get upset about sth

⚠ **molestar** ≠ **molest**

molestia SF **1** (= *trastorno*) bother, trouble; **¿me podrías llevar a casa, si no es mucha ~?** could you take me home, if it's not too much bother *o* trouble?; **perdone la ~, pero ...** sorry to bother you, but ...; **no es ninguna ~** it's no trouble at all; **no tenías que haberte tomado la ~** you shouldn't have bothered *o* taken the trouble, you shouldn't have put yourself out; **"perdonen las molestias"** "we apologize for any inconvenience"
2 (*Med*) discomfort; **si persisten las ~s, consulte a un especialista** if the discomfort *o* trouble persists, consult a specialist; **tengo una pequeña ~ en la garganta** I have a bit of a sore throat

molesto ADJ **1** (= *que causa molestia*) [*tos, ruido, persona*] irritating, annoying; [*olor, síntoma*] unpleasant; **si no es ~ para usted** if it's no trouble to you *o* no bother for you **2** (= *que incomoda*) [*asiento, ropa*] uncomfortable; [*tarea*] annoying; [*situación*] awkward, embarrassing
3 (= *incómodo*) [*persona*] uncomfortable; **me sentía ~ en la fiesta** I felt uneasy *o* uncomfortable at the party; **estaba ~ por la inyección** he was in some discomfort *o* pain after the injection
4 (= *enfadado*) annoyed; (= *disgustado*) upset

molestoso ADJ (*LAm*) annoying

molicie SF **la ~ de la vida moderna** the comforts *o* ease of modern life

molido ADJ **1** [*café, especias*] ground **2 estar ~*** (= *cansado*) to be shattered*

molienda SF [*de café*] grinding; [*de trigo*] milling

molinero/a SM/F miller

molinillo SM hand mill ➤ **molinillo de café** coffee mill *o* grinder

molino SM mill ➤ **molino de agua** water mill ➤ **molino de viento** windmill

molla SF **1** [*de carne*] lean part; [*de fruta*] flesh; [*de pan*] doughy part **2** (*) [*de persona*] flab

molleja SF **1** [*de ave*] gizzard **2 mollejas** [*de res, cordero*] sweetbreads

mollera SF (*) (= *seso*) brains *pl*, sense; **tener buena ~** to have brains, be brainy; ✦ MODISMO **cerrado** *o* **duro de ~** (= *estúpido*) dense*, dim*; (= *terco*) pig-headed

molo SM (*Chi*) breakwater, mole

molón** ADJ **1** (*Esp*) (= *bueno*) fantastic*, brilliant*; (= *elegante*) posh*, classy* **2** (*Méx**) (= *molesto, pesado*) **no seas tan molona** don't be such a pest*

molotov ADJ INV **cóctel ~** Molotov cocktail, petrol bomb (*Brit*)

molusco SM mollusc, mollusk (*EEUU*)

momentáneo ADJ momentary

momento SM **1** (= *instante*) moment; **espera un ~** hold on a minute *o* moment; **éste es un ~ histórico** this is a historic moment; **llegará en breves ~s** she'll be here shortly; **en este ~** at the moment, right now; **en un primer ~** at first; **estuvo a mi lado en todo ~** he was at my side the whole time; **lo hizo en un ~** she did it in next to no time
2 (= *rato*) **los mejores ~s del partido** the highlights of the match; **pasamos ~s inolvidables en Madrid** we had an unforgettable time in Madrid
3 (= *época*) time; **en el ~ actual** at the present time; **el grupo favorito del ~** the most popular group at the moment
4 (= *coyuntura*) **atravesamos un ~ difícil** we are going through a difficult time *o* patch; **llegué en buen ~** I arrived at a good time; **ya te avisarán en su ~** they'll let you know in due course; **ha llegado el ~ de hacer algo** the time has

come to do sth; **ser buen/mal ~ para hacer algo** to be a good/bad time to do sth
5 (*otras locuciones*) **al** ~ at once; **se despertaba a cada** ~ she kept waking up, she was constantly waking up; **en cualquier** ~ any time now; **en un** ~ **dado: en un** ~ **dado, conseguí sujetarlo del brazo** at one stage I managed to grab hold of his arm; **en un** ~ **dado, yo mismo puedo echarte una mano** I could give you a hand some time, if necessary; **de** ~ for the moment; **de** ~ **déjalo** leave it for the moment; **en el** ~ straight away; **de un** ~ **a otro** any minute now; **en el** ~ **menos pensado** when least expected; **por ~s** by the minute; **por el** ~ for the time being, for now
6 (*Mec*) momentum, moment

momia SF mummy

momificar /1g/ Ⓐ VT to mummify Ⓑ **momificarse** VPR to mummify, become mummified

momio/a* (*Chi*) Ⓐ ADJ reactionary, right-wing *antes de s* Ⓑ SM/F reactionary, right winger

mona SF **1** (*Zool*) (= *hembra*) female monkey; (= *especie*) Barbary ape; ✦ MODISMO **mandar a algn a freír ~s*** to tell sb where to go*, tell sb to get lost*; ✦ REFRÁN **aunque la ~ se vista de seda** (**~ se queda**) you can't make a silk purse out of a sow's ear
2 (*) (= *borrachera*) **coger** *o* **pillar una** ~ to get sloshed *o* plastered*; **dormir la** ~ to sleep it off
3 ➤ **mona de Pascua** Easter cake
4 ✦ MODISMO **como la** ~ (*CS**): **ese vestido le queda como la** ~ that dress looks awful on her*; **hiciste los deberes como la** ~ you made a real mess *o* pig's ear** of your homework

monacal ADJ monastic

monacato SM monasticism, monastic life

Mónaco SM Monaco

monada SF **1** (= *cosa*) **la casa es una** ~ the house is gorgeous *o* lovely; **¡qué ~!** isn't it gorgeous *o* lovely?
2 (= *chica*) pretty girl; **¡hola, ~!** hello gorgeous *o* beautiful!*
3 (= *tontería*) **deja de hacer ~s** stop clowning around

mónada SF monad

monaguillo SM altar boy, acolyte

monarca SMF monarch

monarquía SF monarchy

monárquico/a Ⓐ ADJ monarchic(al); (*Pol*) royalist, monarchist Ⓑ SM/F royalist, monarchist

monasterio SM [*de monjes*] monastery; [*de monjas*] convent

monástico ADJ monastic

monda¹ SF **1** (= *peladura*) [*de naranja*] peel; [*de patata*] peelings *pl*; [*de plátano*] skin **2** (= *poda*) pruning; (= *temporada*) pruning season **3** (*Méx**) (= *paliza*) beating

monda²* SF (*Esp*) **¡es la ~!** (= *fantástico*) it's great!*, it's fantastic!*; (= *el colmo*) (*refiriéndose a algo*) it's the limit!; (*refiriéndose a algn*) he's the limit *o* end!*; [*cosa divertida*] it's a scream*; [*persona divertida*] he's a scream*

mondadientes SM INV toothpick

mondadura SF = **monda¹ 1**

mondar /1a/ Ⓐ VT **1** [+ *fruta, patata*] to peel; [+ *nueces, guisantes*] to shell; [+ *palo*] to pare, remove the bark from **2** (*) [+ *persona*] (= *cortar el pelo a*) to scalp*; (= *desplumar*) to fleece*, clean out* **3** (= *podar*) to prune **4** (= *limpiar*) to clean, cleanse Ⓑ **mondarse** VPR **1** (*tb* **~se de risa**) (*) to die laughing* **2** **~se los dientes** to pick one's teeth

mondo ADJ **1** [*cabeza*] completely shorn **2** (= *sin añadidura*) plain; ✦ MODISMO **~ y lirondo*** pure and simple **3** (*) (= *sin dinero*) **me he quedado** ~ I'm cleaned out*, I haven't a cent

mondongo SM (= *entrañas*) guts *pl*, insides *pl*; (= *callos*) tripe

moneda SF **1** (= *pieza*) coin; **una ~ falsa** a counterfeit coin; **una ~ de cinco dólares** a five-dollar piece; **tirar una ~ al aire** to toss a coin
2 [*de un país*] currency; **en ~ española** in Spanish currency *o* money; ✦ MODISMO **pagar a algn con** *o* **en la misma ~** to pay sb back in his own coin *o* in kind ➤ **moneda blanda** soft currency; ➤ **moneda corriente** currency;

✦ MODISMO **es ~ corriente** it's a common occurrence ➤ **moneda de curso legal** legal tender ➤ **moneda fraccionaria** money in small denominations ➤ **moneda única** single currency

monedero SM purse (*Brit*), coin purse (*EEUU*) ➤ **monedero electrónico** electronic purse *o* wallet

monegasco ADJ of/from Monaco, Monegasque

monería SF **1** (= *mueca*) funny face, monkey face **2** (= *payasada*) antic, prank; **hacer ~s** to monkey around, clown around

monetario ADJ monetary

monetarista ADJ, SMF monetarist

mongol(a) Ⓐ ADJ, SM/F Mongol, Mongolian Ⓑ SM (*Ling*) Mongolian

Mongolia SF Mongolia

mongólico/a† Ⓐ ADJ mongoloid†; **niños ~s** children with Down's syndrome Ⓑ SM/F (†) person with Down's syndrome

monigote SM **1** (= *muñeco*) rag doll; [*de papel*] paper doll **2** (*) (= *niño*) little monkey **3** (*) (= *persona sin personalidad*) weak character **4** (= *garabato*) doodle

monitor(a) Ⓐ SM/F (= *persona*) (*Dep*) instructor, coach; [*de gira*] group leader ➤ **monitor(a) de esquí** ski instructor ➤ **monitor(a) de natación** swimming instructor ➤ **monitor(a) deportivo/a** (*gen*) sports coach; (*en escuela*) games coach Ⓑ SM (*tb Inform, Téc*) monitor

monitorizar /1f/ VT to monitor

monitos SMPL (*And, Méx*) cartoon *sing*

monja SF nun ➤ **monja de clausura** cloistered nun, nun in a closed order

monje SM monk

monjil ADJ (*lit*) nun's; (*fig*) (*pey*) excessively demure

mono¹ SM **1** (*Zool*) monkey
2 (= *traje de faena*) overalls *pl* (*Brit*), boiler suit (*Brit*), coveralls *pl* (*EEUU*); [*de calle*] jumpsuit; (*con peto*) dungarees *pl*, overalls (*EEUU*) ➤ **mono de esquí** ski suit
3 (*) [*de drogadicto*] withdrawal symptoms *pl*, cold turkey*; **estar con el** ~ to be suffering withdrawal symptoms, have gone cold turkey*; ✦ MODISMO **tener ~ de algo** to really miss sth
4 (= *figura*) cartoon *or* caricature figure; ✦ MODISMOS **tener ~s en la cara: me miran como si tuviera ~s en la cara** people look at me as if I had two heads*; **ser el último** ~ to be the lowest of the low ➤ **monos animados** (*Chi*) cartoons
5 (*) (= *hombre feo*) ugly devil

mono² ADJ **1** (= *bonito*) pretty, lovely; (= *simpático*) nice, cute; **una chica muy mona** a lovely *o* very pretty girl; **¡qué sombrero más ~!** what a nice *o* cute little hat! **2** (*Mús*) mono

mono³/a Ⓐ ADJ (*Col*) (= *rubio*) blond Ⓑ SM/F (*Col*) (= *rubio*) blond(e) (person)

monocolor ADJ one-colour, of a single colour; **gobierno** ~ one-party government

monocorde ADJ **1** (*Mús*) single-stringed **2** (= *monótono*) monotonous, unvaried

monocromo Ⓐ ADJ monochrome; (*TV*) black-and-white Ⓑ SM monochrome

monóculo SM monocle

monocultivo SM single crop farming, monoculture

monogamia SF monogamy

monógamo ADJ monogamous

monografía SF monograph

monográfico Ⓐ ADJ monographic; **estudio ~** monograph; **número ~** [*de revista*] issue devoted to a single subject; **programa ~** programme devoted to a single subject Ⓑ SM monograph, special edition

monograma SM monogram

monolingüe Ⓐ ADJ monolingual Ⓑ SMF monoglot

monolito SM monolith

monólogo SM monologue, monolog (*EEUU*) ➤ **monólogo interior** stream of consciousness

monomando SM mixer tap (*Brit*), mixing faucet (*EEUU*)

monono* ADJ (*CS*) (= *atractivo*) lovely, pretty; (= *acicalado*) dressed up

monoparental ADJ **familia** ~ single-parent family, one-parent family

monopatín SM **1** (*Esp*) (*sin manillar*) skateboard **2** (*LAm*) (*con manillar*) scooter

monoplano SM monoplane

monoplaza SM single-seater

monopolio SM monopoly

monopolístico ADJ monopolistic

monopolizador ADJ monopolistic; **una empresa ~a del mercado** a company with a monopoly in the market

monopolizar /1f/ VT to monopolize

monosilábico ADJ monosyllabic

monosílabo Ⓐ ADJ monosyllabic Ⓑ SM monosyllable

monoteísmo SM monotheism

monoteísta Ⓐ ADJ monotheistic Ⓑ SMF monotheist

monotemático ADJ **ser** ~ [*discurso, jornada*] to have a single theme; [*persona*] to have only one subject of conversation

monotonía SF monotony; [*de voz, sonido*] monotone; **la ~ (de la existencia) cotidiana** the daily grind

monótono ADJ **1** [*voz, sonido*] monotonous **2** [*trabajo, discurso*] tedious, monotonous; [*vida*] dreary, humdrum

monovolumen Ⓐ ADJ **vehículo** ~ people carrier, minivan (*EEUU*) Ⓑ SM people carrier, minivan (*EEUU*)

monóxido SM monoxide ➤ **monóxido de carbono** carbon monoxide

monseñor SM monsignor

monserga SF (= *pesadez*) boring spiel*; (= *tontería*) drivel*; **¡no me vengas con ~s!** (= *no molestes*) give it a rest!; (= *no te enrolles*) don't talk drivel!*

monstruo Ⓐ SM **1** (*Mit*) monster; ~ **de circo** circus freak **2** (= *persona malvada*) monster **3** (= *prodigio*) giant; **es un ~ del ajedrez** he's a fantastic chess player Ⓑ ADJ INV (*) fantastic, brilliant

monstruoso ADJ **1** (= *terrible*) monstrous **2** (= *horrible*) monstrous, hideous; (= *deforme*) freak *antes de s* **3** (= *enorme*) monstrous, huge

monta SF **1** (= *suma*) total, sum **2** (*en equitación*) (= *caballo*) mount; (= *acción*) mounting **3** (= *apareamiento*) mating; (= *temporada*) mating season **4** ✦ MODISMO **de poca ~** third-rate *antes de s*; **un cantante/hotel de poca ~** a third-rate singer/hotel; **un ladrón de poca ~** a small-time thief

montacargas SM INV service lift (*Brit*), freight elevator (*EEUU*)

montadito SM (*Esp*) small sandwich

montado Ⓐ ADJ **1** [*persona*] **iba ~ a caballo** he was riding a horse, he was on horseback; **estaba montada en la bicicleta** she was riding her bicycle **2** [*caballo*] saddled **3** (*Esp Culin*) [*nata*] whipped; [*clara*] whisked **4** ✦ MODISMO **estar ~ (en el dólar)** (*Esp**) to be rolling in it*, be loaded* Ⓑ SM (*Esp*) small sandwich ➤ **montado de lomo** hot sandwich made with pork loin

montador(a) Ⓐ SM/F **1** [*de máquinas, aparatos*] fitter; [*de joyas*] setter **2** (*Cine, TV*) film editor ➤ **montador(a) de escena** set designer Ⓑ SM (= *poyo*) (*para montar*) mounting block

montaje SM **1** [*de estantería, aparato*] assembly; [*de ordenador*] set up; [*de joyas*] setting **2** [*de exposición*] mounting, setting up; [*de obra de teatro*] staging **3** (*) (= *engaño*) set-up*; **el accidente fue sólo un ~** the accident was just a set-up* ➤ **montaje publicitario** advertising stunt, publicity stunt **4** (*Cine, Fot*) montage ➤ **montaje fotográfico** photomontage **5** (*Radio*) hookup

montante SM **1** (= *suma*) total **2** (*Arquit*) [*de puerta*] transom; [*de ventana*] mullion

montaña SF **1** (= *monte*) mountain; ✦ MODISMO **hacer una ~ de un granito de arena** to make a mountain out of a molehill ➤ **montaña rusa** roller coaster, big dipper

2 (= *sierra*) mountains *pl*; **pasamos un mes en la ~** we spent a month in the mountains

montañero/a Ⓐ SM/F mountaineer, climber Ⓑ ADJ mountain *antes de s*

montañés/esa Ⓐ ADJ (= *de montaña*) mountain *antes de s*; (= *de tierras altas*) highland *antes de s* Ⓑ SM/F highlander

montañismo SM mountaineering, mountain climbing

montañoso ADJ mountainous

montar /1a/ Ⓐ VT **1** (= *cabalgar*) to ride **2** (= *subir*) ~ **a algn en** o **sobre algo** to lift sb onto sth, sit sb on sth **3** [+ *estantería, ventana*] to assemble, put together; [+ *coche*] to assemble; [+ *tienda de campaña*] to put up, pitch **4** (= *instalar*) [+ *consulta, oficina*] to set up, open; [+ *galería de arte, tienda*] to open; [+ *campamento, espectáculo*] to set up; [+ *exposición*] to set up, mount; ~ **un negocio** to set up o start up a business **5** (= *engarzar*) [+ *joya*] to set; [+ *pistola*] to cock **6** [+ *foto, diapositiva*] to mount **7** (= *organizar*) [+ *operación*] to mount; [+ *sistema de control*] to put into operation; **la policía montó un fuerte dispositivo de seguridad** the police put strict security measures into operation; ~ **guardia** to stand guard **8** (*Esp**) (= *crear*) ~ **una bronca** o **un escándalo** to kick up a fuss/scandal*; ~ **un número** o **un show** to make a scene **9** (= *solapar*) **han montado unos colores sobre otros** they have overlapped some colours with others **10** [+ *película*] to edit **11** [+ *decorado*] to put up; [+ *obra*] to stage, put on **12** (*Esp*) [+ *nata*] to whip; [+ *clara*] to whisk, beat **13** (= *aparear*) (*Zool*) to mount **14** (*Cos*) [+ *puntos*] to cast on Ⓑ VI **1** (= *ir a caballo*) to ride **2** (= *subirse*) **2.1** (*a un caballo*) to get on, mount **2.2** (*en un vehículo*) ~ **en avión** to fly, travel by air o by plane; ~ **en barco** to travel by boat; ~ **en bicicleta** to ride a bicycle, cycle **3** (= *sumar*) [*factura, gastos*] to amount to, come to; ✦ REFRÁN **tanto monta (monta tanto, Isabel como Fernando)** (*Esp*) it makes no difference, it's all the same **4** (= *solapar*) ~ **sobre algo** to overlap sth, cover part of sth Ⓒ **montarse** VPR **1** (= *subirse*) **~se en** [+ *coche*] to get in(to); [+ *autobús, tren*] to get on(to); [+ *caballo, bicicleta*] to get on(to), mount; [+ *atracción de feria*] to go on; **~se en barco** to get on a boat, travel by boat **2** ✦ MODISMOS **montárselo** (*Esp**): **montátelo como puedas** you'll have to manage the best you can; **¡tú sí que te lo has montado bien!** you're on to a good thing there!*, you've got it made!*; **se lo ha montado muy mal contigo** he's behaved very badly towards you; **~se en el dólar** to make big money*

montaraz ADJ (= *salvaje*) wild, untamed; (= *tosco*) rough, coarse; (= *huraño*) unsociable

monte SM **1** (= *montaña*) mountain; (= *cerro*) hill; ✦ MODISMO **echarse al** ~ to take to the hills **2** (= *campo*) countryside, country; (= *bosque*) woodland; **un conejo de** ~ a wild rabbit; **batir el** ~ to beat for game, go hunting; ✦ MODISMO **no todo el ~ es orégano** it's not all plain sailing ➤ **monte alto** forest ➤ **monte bajo** scrub **3** ➤ **monte de piedad** pawnshop **4** (*Naipes*) (= *baraja*) pile; (= *banca*) bank **5** ➤ **monte de Venus** mons veneris **6** (*CAm, Carib, Col**) (= *hachís*) hash*, pot*

montepío SM (= *sociedad*) friendly society; (= *fondo*) charitable fund for dependents

montera SF (= *sombrero*) cloth cap; [*de torero*] bullfighter's hat; ✦ MODISMO **ponerse algo por** ~ to laugh at sth

montería SF **1** (= *arte*) hunting; (= *caza*) hunt, chase **2** (= *animales*) game

montés ADJ wild

Montevideo SM Montevideo

montgomery [mon'gomeri] SM (*CS*) duffle coat

montículo SM mound, hump

monto SM amount

montón SM **1** (*gen*) heap, pile; [*de nieve*] pile; ✦ MODISMO **del** ~ ordinary, average **2** (*) (= *mucho*) **sabe un**

~ he knows loads*; **un ~ de gente** loads of people*, masses of people*; **ejemplos hay a montones** there is no shortage of examples

montonera SF (*LAm*) **1** (= *montón*) pile, heap **2** (*CS Hist*) troop of mounted rebels

montonero/a Ⓐ ADJ (*CS*) urban guerrilla *antes de s* Ⓑ SM/F urban guerrilla; **los Montoneros** *armed wing of the Peronist movement in Argentina*

montura SF **1** [*de gafas*] frame; [*de joya*] mount, setting **2** (= *animal*) mount **3** (= *silla*) saddle; (= *arreos*) harness, trappings *pl*; **cabalgar sin ~** to ride bareback

monumental ADJ **1** (= *de monumentos*) **conjunto ~** collection of historical monuments; **la riqueza ~ del país** the country's wealth of monuments **2** (= *enorme*) [*esfuerzo, error, éxito*] monumental; [*atasco*] enormous; [*bronca, paliza*] tremendous **3** (*) (= *excelente*) tremendous*, terrific*

monumento SM **1** (= *construcción*) monument ➤ **monumento a los caídos** war memorial ➤ **monumento al soldado desconocido** tomb of the unknown soldier ➤ **monumento histórico-artístico** (= *edificio*) listed building; (= *zona*) ≈ conservation area **2** (*) (= *mujer*) beauty

monzón SM monsoon

monzónico ADJ monsoon *antes de s*

moña SF **1** (= *cinta*) ribbon; (= *lazo*) bow **2** (*) (= *borrachera*) **cogerse una ~** to get sloshed*

moñita SF (*Uru*) bow tie

moño SM **1** [*de pelo*] bun, chignon; (*en lo alto de la cabeza*) topknot; ✦ MODISMO **estar hasta el ~*** to be fed up to the back teeth* **2** (*Orn*) crest **3** (*LAm*) [*lazo*] bow

moquear /1a/ VI to have a runny nose

moquera SF, **moqueo** SM **tener ~** to have a runny nose

moquero* SM hankie*

moqueta SF fitted carpet

moquette [mo'ket] SF (*RPl*) fitted carpet

moquillo SM [*de perro, gato*] distemper; [*de ave*] pip

mor: **por ~ de** PREP (*liter*) because of, on account of; **por ~ de la amistad** for friendship's sake

mora[1] SF (= *zarzamora*) blackberry; [*del moral*] mulberry

mora[2] SF (*Fin, Jur*) delay

morada SF (*liter*) dwelling (*liter*), abode (*liter*), dwelling place; **última ~** final resting place

morado Ⓐ ADJ purple; **ojo ~** black eye; ✦ MODISMOS **pasarlas moradas** (*Esp**) to have a tough time of it; **ponerse ~ (de algo)** (*Esp**) to stuff one's face (with sth)* Ⓑ SM **1** (= *color*) purple **2** (= *cardenal*) bruise

morador(a) SM/F inhabitant

moral[1] SM (*Bot*) mulberry tree

moral[2] Ⓐ ADJ **1** (= *ético*) moral; **tenemos la obligación ~ de ayudarle** we are morally obliged to help him, we have a moral obligation to help him **2** (= *espiritual*) moral Ⓑ SF **1** (= *ética, moralidad*) morality, morals *pl*; **doble ~** double standards *pl* **2** (= *estado de ánimo*) morale; **la victoria nos dio mucha ~** the victory boosted our morale; **tener baja la ~** ⬦ **estar bajo de ~** to feel a bit low; **levantar la ~ a algn** to raise sb's spirits *o* morale; ✦ MODISMO **tener más ~ que el alcoyano** (*Esp**) to keep going against all the odds, have real fighting spirit **3** (= *valor*) moral courage

moraleja SF moral

moralidad SF morality, morals *pl*; **su falta de ~** his immorality; **faltar a la ~** to behave immorally

moralina SF phoney morality

moralista Ⓐ ADJ moralistic Ⓑ SMF moralist

moralizar /1f/ VI to moralize

morar /1a/ VI (*liter*) (= *vivir*) dwell (*liter*), to live; (= *alojarse*) to stay

moratón SM bruise

moratoria SF moratorium

mórbido ADJ (*liter*) **1** (= *enfermo*) morbid **2** (= *suave*) soft, delicate

morbo SM **1** (*) (= *curiosidad*) morbid curiosity **2** (*) (= *atractivo sexual*) **no es guapa pero tiene ~** she's not pretty but she's sexy **3** (= *enfermedad*) disease, illness

morboso ADJ **1** (= *malsano*) [*persona, mente*] morbid; [*espectáculo*] gruesome; **curiosidad morbosa** morbid curiosity **2** (= *atractivo*) sexually attractive **3** (= *enfermo*) morbid, sickly; [*clima, zona*] unhealthy

morcilla SF blood sausage, black pudding; ✦ MODISMO **¡que te den ~!** (*Esp***) get stuffed!**

mordacidad SF sharpness, bite; **con ~** sharply

mordaz ADJ [*crítica, persona*] sharp, scathing; [*estilo*] incisive; [*humor*] caustic

mordaza SF **1** (*en la boca*) gag **2** (*Téc*) clamp

mordedura SF bite; **una ~ de serpiente** a snake bite

morder /2h/ Ⓐ VT **1** (*con los dientes*) to bite **2** (*CAm, Méx*) **~ a algn** (= *pedir soborno a*) to ask sb for a bribe Ⓑ VI to bite; ✦ MODISMO **está que muerde*** he's hopping mad Ⓒ **morderse** VPR to bite; **~se las uñas** to bite one's nails; ✦ MODISMO **~se la lengua** to bite one's tongue

mordida SF **1** (= *mordisco*) bite **2** (*CAm, Col, Méx**) (= *soborno*) bribe

mordisco SM **1** (= *bocado*) bite; **el perro me dio un ~** the dog bit me **2** (= *trozo*) bite

mordisquear /1a/ Ⓐ VT (*gen*) to nibble (at); [*caballo*] to champ Ⓑ VI (*gen*) to nibble; [*caballo*] to champ

moreno/a Ⓐ ADJ **1** [*persona*] (= *de pelo moreno*) dark-haired; (= *de tez morena*) dark(-skinned), swarthy; (= *bronceado*) brown, tanned; **ponerse ~** to tan, go brown **2** [*pelo*] (dark) brown; [*azúcar, pan*] brown Ⓑ SM/F [*de pelo*] dark-haired man/woman; [*de tez*] dark(-skinned) man/woman; **una morena** a brunette Ⓒ SM (*Esp*) tan

morera SF white mulberry

morería SF (*Hist*) (= *territorio*) Moorish lands *pl*, Moorish territory; (= *barrio*) Moorish quarter

moretón SM bruise

morfar** /1a/ VI (*CS*) to eat, nosh*, chow down (*EEUU**)

morfema SM morpheme

morfina SF morphine

morfinómano/a Ⓐ ADJ addicted to morphine Ⓑ SM/F morphine addict

morfología SF morphology

morfológico ADJ morphological

morfosintaxis SF INV morphosyntax

morganático ADJ morganatic

morgue SF (*esp LAm*) morgue

moribundo/a Ⓐ ADJ **1** [*persona*] dying **2** [*proceso, negocio*] moribund Ⓑ SM/F dying person; **los ~s** the dying

morillo SM firedog

morir /3j/ (*pp* **muerto**) Ⓐ VI **1** [*persona, animal, planta*] to die; **¡muera el tirano!** down with the tyrant!, death to the tyrant!; **~ ahogado** to drown; **~ ahorcado** (*por un verdugo*) to be hanged; (*suicidándose*) to be found hanged; **~ asesinado** [*persona*] to be murdered; [*personaje público*] to be assassinated; **~ de algo** to die of sth; **~ de hambre** to die of hunger, starve to death; **~ de muerte natural** to die a natural death, die of natural causes; ✦ MODISMO **~ al pie del cañón** to die with one's boots on **2** (= *extinguirse*) [*civilización*] to die, die out, come to an end; [*amor*] to die; [*fuego*] to die down; [*luz*] to fade; **las olas iban a ~ a la playa** (*liter*) the waves ran out on the beach; ✦ MODISMO **y allí muere** (*LAm*) and that's all there is to it Ⓑ **morirse** VPR **1** [*persona, animal, planta*] to die; **¡ojalá o así se muera!** I hope he drops dead!; **~se de algo** to die of sth **2** (*) (*para exagerar*) to die; **si me descubren me muero** I'll die if they find me out*; **~se de algo**: **en esta casa me muero de frío** I'm freezing in this house!; **¡me muero de hambre!** I'm starving!; **¡me muero de sed!** I'm dying of thirst!*; **se moría de envidia** he was green with envy; **por**

poco me muero de vergüenza I nearly died of embarrassment*; **me moría de miedo** I was scared stiff*; **se van a ~ de risa** they'll kill themselves laughing*; **me moría de ganas de verte** I was dying to see you*; **~se por algo** (*de deseo*) to be dying for sth*; (*de afición*) to be crazy o mad about sth*; **~se por algn** to be crazy o mad about sb*

morisco/a Ⓐ ADJ Moorish Ⓑ SM/F (*Hist*) Moslem convert to Christianity, subject Moslem (*of 15th and 16th centuries*)

morisqueta SF (*esp RPl*) **hacer ~s** to make faces

mormón/ona SM/F Mormon

moro/a Ⓐ ADJ 1 (*Hist*) Moorish 2 (*Esp* pey*) (= *del norte de África*) North African Ⓑ SM/F 1 (*Hist*) Moor; ✦ MODISMO **¡hay ~s en la costa!** watch out!; **no hay ~s en las costa** the coast is clear 2 (*Esp* pey*) (= *del norte de África*) North African Ⓒ SM (*Esp**) (= *Marruecos*) Morocco; **bajar al ~** to go to Morocco

morocho (*SAm*) Ⓐ ADJ 1 [*pelo*] dark; [*persona*] (= *de pelo oscuro*) dark, dark-haired; (= *de piel oscura*) dark-skinned 2 (*Ven*) (= *gemelo*) twin Ⓑ SM **morochos** (*Ven*) (= *gemelos*) twins

moronga SF (*CAm, Méx*) black pudding (*esp Brit*), blood sausage (*EEUU*)

morosidad SF (*Fin*) slowness in paying; (= *atrasos*) arrears *pl*

moroso/a Ⓐ ADJ slow to pay; **deudor ~** slow payer, defaulter Ⓑ SM/F (*Fin*) bad debtor, defaulter; **cartera de ~s** bad debts *pl*

morral SM (= *mochila*) haversack, knapsack; [*de caza*] pouch, game bag; [*de caballo*] nosebag

morralla SF 1 (= *peces*) small fry, little fish 2 (*) (= *cosas*) junk*; (= *basura*) rubbish (*esp Brit*), garbage (*EEUU*) 3 (*) (= *personas*) rabble, riff-raff 4 (*Méx*) (= *calderilla*) small change

morrazo* SM thump

morrear* /1a/ VT, VI (*Esp*) to snog*, neck

morriña SF (*Esp*) homesickness; **tener ~** to be homesick

morro SM 1 (*Zool*) snout, nose 2 (*Esp**) (= *labio*) (thick) lip; **beber a ~** to drink from the bottle; **partir los ~s a algn** to bash sb's face in*; ✦ MODISMO **estar de ~(s)** to be in a bad mood; **estar de ~(s) con algn** to be cross with sb; **poner morritos** to look sullen 3 (*Esp**) (= *descaro*) cheek*, nerve*; **tener ~** to have a cheek*, have a nerve*; **echarle mucho ~** to have a real nerve*; ✦ MODISMO **tiene un ~ que se lo pisa** he's got a real brass neck*; **por el ~: me lo quedé por el ~** I just held on to it and to hell with them!* 4 [*de coche, avión*] nose 5 (= *promontorio*) headland, promontory; (= *cerro*) small rounded hill

morrocotudo* ADJ 1 (= *fantástico*) smashing*, terrific* 2 (= *grande*) [*riña, golpe*] tremendous; [*susto*] terrible

morrón Ⓐ ADJ **pimiento ~** sweet red pepper Ⓑ SM 1 (= *pimiento*) sweet red pepper 2 (*Esp**) (= *golpe*) blow

morsa SF walrus

morse SM Morse code

mortadela SF mortadella

mortaja SF 1 [*de muerto*] shroud 2 (*Téc*) mortise

mortal Ⓐ ADJ 1 [*ser*] mortal 2 [*herida, golpe*] fatal, deadly; [*disparo, accidente*] fatal; [*veneno, virus, dosis*] deadly, lethal; [*peligro*] mortal; **salto ~** somersault 3 [*pecado*] mortal; [*odio*] deadly Ⓑ SMF (= *ser*) mortal; **como cualquier ~** just like anybody else Ⓒ SM **doble ~** double somersault

mortalidad SF 1 (= *condición de mortal*) mortality 2 (*en demografía*) mortality; (*en accidente*) death toll ➤ **mortalidad infantil** infant mortality

mortandad SF [*de humanos*] loss of life; [*de animales*] death

mortecino ADJ 1 [*luz*] dim, faint; [*color*] dull; [*fuego, llamas*] dying 2 (= *débil*) weak, failing

mortero SM mortar

mortífero ADJ deadly, lethal

mortificación SF 1 (= *sufrimiento*) torture 2 (= *humillación*) humiliation 3 (*Rel*) mortification

mortificar /1g/ Ⓐ VT 1 (= *atormentar*) to torment, plague 2 (= *humillar*) to humiliate 3 (*Rel*) **~ la carne** to mortify the flesh Ⓑ **mortificarse** VPR 1 (= *atormentarse*) to torment o.s., distress o.s. 2 (*Rel*) to mortify the flesh 3 (*CAm, Méx*) (= *avergonzarse*) to feel ashamed, be mortified

mortuorio ADJ mortuary; **coche ~** hearse; **esquela mortuoria** death notice

moruno ADJ Moorish

mosaico SM 1 (*Arte*) mosaic; **un ~ romano** a Roman mosaic; **un suelo de ~** a mosaic floor 2 (*Méx, RPl*) (= *baldosa*) tile; **un piso de ~** tiled floor 3 (= *conjunto*) **un ~ de grupos étnicos** a whole spectrum of ethnic groups

mosca Ⓐ SF 1 (= *insecto*) fly; **pescar a la ~** to fish with a fly, fly-fish; ✦ MODISMOS **caer como ~s** to drop like flies; **cazar ~s** to daydream; **por si las ~s*** just in case; **¿qué ~ te/ le ha picado?*** what's got into you/him?; **tener la ~ en o detrás de la oreja*** to smell a rat* ➤ **mosca artificial** (*en pesca*) fly ➤ **mosca de la carne** meat fly ➤ **mosca tsetsé** tsetse fly 2 (*) (= *pesado*) pest Ⓑ ADJ INV (*Esp**) ✦ MODISMOS **estar ~** (= *suspicaz*) to be suspicious, smell a rat*; (= *preocupado*) to be worried; **estar ~ con algn** to be cross o annoyed with sb

moscada ADJ **nuez ~** nutmeg

moscarda SF bluebottle, blowfly

moscardón SM 1 (= *moscarda*) bluebottle, blowfly; (= *abejón*) hornet 2 (*) (= *pesado*) pest, nuisance

moscatel SM, SM muscatel

moscón SM 1 (= *insecto*) bluebottle, blowfly 2 (*Bot*) maple 3 (*) (= *pesado*) pest, nuisance

moscoso* SM (*Esp*) day off (*for personal matters, not deducted from annual leave*)

moscovita ADJ, SMF Muscovite

Moscú SM Moscow

mosqueado ADJ 1 (*) (= *enfadado*) cross, angry 2 (*) (= *desconfiado*) suspicious

mosqueante* ADJ 1 (= *molesto*) annoying, irritating 2 (= *sospechoso*) suspicious, fishy*

mosquearse* /1a/ VPR 1 (= *enfadarse*) to get cross, get annoyed; (= *ofenderse*) to get offended 2 (= *desconfiar*) to smell a rat* 3 (= *preocuparse*) to worry

mosqueo* SM **coger o pillar o llevarse un ~** (= *enfadarse*) to get cross, get annoyed; (= *ofenderse*) to get offended; (= *desconfiar*) to smell a rat*; (= *preocuparse*) to worry

mosquete SM musket

mosquetero SM (*Hist, Mil*) musketeer

mosquita SF **~ muerta** hypocrite; **hacerse la ~ muerta** to look as if butter wouldn't melt in one's mouth

mosquitero SM mosquito net

mosquito SM (*gen*) mosquito; (*pequeño*) gnat

mostaza SF mustard

mosto SM [*de uva*] grape juice; (*en la elaboración de vino*) must

mostrador SM [*de tienda*] counter; [*de café, bar*] bar; [*de oficina, biblioteca*] desk ➤ **mostrador de facturación** check-in desk

mostrar /1l/ Ⓐ VT to show; **nos mostró el camino** he showed us the way; **~ en pantalla** (*Inform*) to display Ⓑ **mostrarse** VPR (+ ADJ) **se mostró interesado en la oferta** he was interested o showed interest in the offer

mostrenco/a* Ⓐ ADJ 1 [*persona*] (= *bruto*) oafish; (= *poco inteligente*) dense, slow 2 [*objeto*] crude, roughly made Ⓑ SM/F oaf

mota SF 1 (= *partícula*) speck, tiny bit; **~ de polvo** speck of dust; ✦ REFRÁN **ver la ~ en el ojo ajeno** to see the mote in sb else's eye 2 (= *dibujo*) dot; **a ~s** [*dibujo*] dotted 3 (*en tela*) (= *nudillo*) burl; (= *jaspeado*) fleck 4 (*CS*) **motas** (= *pelo*) frizzy hair *sing* 5 (*CAm, Méx*) (= *planta*) marijuana plant; (= *droga*) grass*, pot**

mote[1] SM (= *apodo*) nickname

mote² SM (*And*) (= *trigo*) boiled wheat; (= *maíz*) boiled maize (*Brit*), boiled corn (*EEUU*)

moteado ADJ **1** [*piel*] (= *con manchas pequeñas*) speckled; (= *con manchas grandes*) dappled, mottled; **un caballo gris ~** a dapple-grey horse **2** [*tela*] (= *jaspeado*) flecked; (= *con lunares*) dotted

motejar /1a/ VT to nickname; **~ a algn de algo** to brand sb sth, accuse sb of being sth

motel SM motel

motero/a* SM/F biker*

motete SM motet

motín SM [*de presos*] riot; (*en barco, de tropas*) mutiny

motivación SF **1** (= *estimulación*) motivation **2** (= *motivo*) motive

motivar /1a/ VT **1** (= *estimular*) to motivate **2** (= *causar*) to cause

motivo SM **1** (= *causa*) reason; **por ~s personales** for personal reasons; **con este** o **tal** ~ for this reason; **con ~ de** (= *debido a*) because of, owing to; (= *en ocasión de*) on the occasion of; **sin ~** for no reason, without good reason; **ser ~ sobrado** o **suficiente: es ~ suficiente** o **sobrado para seguir votándolo** that's reason enough to continue voting for him; **hay suficientes** o **sobrados ~s para odiarlo** there are more than enough reasons for hating him ➤ **motivos ocultos** ulterior motives **2** (*Arte, Mús*) motif

moto SF (motor)bike; ✦ MODISMOS **ir como una ~**** to be in a rush; **ponerse como una ~** (*Esp***) (*sexualmente*) to get really turned on**, get horny**; (*con droga*) to get high* ➤ **moto acuática, moto de agua** jet ski

motocarro SM *light delivery van with three wheels*

motocicleta SF motorcycle, motorbike

motociclismo SM motorcycling

motociclista SMF motorcyclist

moto-cross SM INV motocross

motonáutica SF motorboat racing, speedboat racing

motonave SF motor ship, motor vessel

motoneta SF (*LAm*) (motor) scooter

motonieve SF snowmobile

motor ❶ ADJ **1** (*Téc*) motive, motor (*EEUU*) **2** (*Anat*) motor ❸ SM [*de vehículo*] engine; [*de electrodoméstico, barca*] motor; **un ~ de seis cilindros** a six-cylinder engine; **con seis ~es** six-engined; **con ~** power-driven ➤ **motor a chorro, motor a reacción** jet engine ➤ **motor de arranque** starter, starter motor ➤ **motor de búsqueda** (*Internet*) search engine ➤ **motor de inyección** fuel-injected engine ➤ **motor diesel** diesel engine ➤ **motor fuera (de) borda** outboard motor

motora SF motorboat, speedboat

motorismo SM motorcycling

motorista SMF **1** (= *motociclista*) motorcyclist **2** (*esp LAm*) (= *automovilista*) motorist, driver

motorístico ADJ motor-racing *antes de s*

motorizado ADJ motorized; [*tropas*] mechanized, motorized; **trineo ~** motor sleigh; **un largo convoy ~** a long convoy of vehicles; **patrulla motorizada** motorized patrol, mobile unit; **estar ~*** to have wheels*, have a car

motorizar /1f/ ❶ VT (*Mil, Téc*) to motorize ❸ **motorizarse** VPR (*hum**) to get o.s. some wheels*

motosegadora SF motor mower, motorized lawn mower

motosierra SF power saw

motoso ADJ (*SAm*) [*pelo*] frizzy

motricidad SF **1** (= *capacidad*) mobility **2** (*Fisiol*) motor functions *pl*

motriz ADJ **1** (*Téc*) motive, motor (*EEUU*); **potencia ~** motive power; **fuerza ~** driving force **2** (*Anat*) motor; **la actividad ~** motor functions

motu: **de ~ propio** ADV of one's own accord

mousse [muːs] SF (*a veces* SM) **1** (*Culin*) mousse **2** [*de pelo*] (styling) mousse; [*de afeitar*] shaving foam

movedizo ADJ [*terreno, suelo*] moving, shifting; [*objeto*] movable; [*persona, animal*] restless

mover /2h/ ❶ VT **1** (= *cambiar de posición*) **1.1** [+ *objeto, mano, pierna*] to move; **~ a algn de algún sitio** to move sb from somewhere; **"no nos ~án"** "we shall not be moved" **1.2** (*en juegos*) [+ *ficha, pieza*] to move **2** (= *agitar*) to stir; **el perro se acercó moviendo la cola** the dog came up to us wagging its tail; **~ la cabeza** (*para negar*) to shake one's head; (*para asentir*) to nod, nod one's head **3** (= *accionar*) [+ *máquina*] to work, power **4** (= *incitar*) **lo hice movida por la curiosidad** it was curiosity that prompted o moved me to do it; **~ a algn a algo** to move sb to sth; **¿qué fue lo que te movió a actuar de ese modo?** what prompted o moved you to act in that way? **5** (= *agilizar*) [+ *asunto, tema*] to push; [+ *trámite*] to handle **6** [+ *dinero*] to move, handle ❸ VI **1** (*en juegos*) to move; **¿a quién le toca ~?** whose move is it? **2** (= *incitar*) **~ a algo: esta situación mueve a la risa** this situation makes you (want to) laugh ❸ **moverse** VPR **1** (= *cambiar de posición o lugar*) to move; **no te muevas** keep still, don't move **2** (= *agitarse*) [*mar*] to be rough; [*barco*] to roll; [*cortina, hojas*] to move; **¿se ha movido mucho el barco?** was the sea rough? **3** (= *ponerse en marcha*) to move o.s., get a move on* **4** (= *ser activo*) [*persona*] to be on the move*, be on the go*; [*ciudad*] to be lively **5** (= *relacionarse*) (*en un ambiente*) to move; (*entre cierta gente*) to mix

movida SF **1** (*) (= *animación*) scene*; **la ~ madrileña** the Madrid scene* **2** (**) (= *asunto*) thing, stuff**; **a mí no me va esa ~** I'm not into that scene* o stuff**; **¡qué ~! ¡ahora tengo que ponerme a trabajar!** what a pain! I've got to get down to work now!*; **ese tío anda en ~s raras** that guy is into really weird stuff** **3** (*Esp**) (= *pelea*) trouble **4** (*Ajedrez*) move

movido ADJ **1** (*Fot*) blurred **2** [*persona*] (= *activo*) on the move*, on the go*; (= *inquieto*) restless **3** (= *agitado*) **3.1** [*mar*] rough, choppy; [*viaje*] (*en barco*) rough; (*en avión*) bumpy **3.2** [*día, semana*] hectic, busy; [*reunión, sesión*] stormy

móvil ❶ SM **1** (*frm*) (= *motivo*) motive; **un crimen sin ~ aparente** a crime with no apparent motive; **el verdadero ~ de su política** the real reason behind his policies **2** (= *teléfono*) mobile (phone) **3** (*Arte*) mobile ❸ ADJ [*teléfono, unidad*] mobile

movilidad SF mobility

movilización SF **1** (*Mil*) mobilization **2** (*Pol*) **habrá varias jornadas de ~** there will be several days of industrial action; **una llamada a la ~ de los trabajadores** a call for the mobilization of the workforce

movilizar /1f/ VT **1** (= *organizar*) to mobilize **2** (*CS*) (= *desbloquear*) to unblock, free

movimiento SM **1** (*Mec, Fís*) movement ➤ **movimiento de rotación** rotatory movement ➤ **movimiento de traslación** orbital movement o motion ➤ **movimiento sísmico** seismic tremor **2** (= *desplazamiento*) [*de persona, animal*] movement; **esta máquina puede detectar el menor ~** this machine can detect the slightest movement; **no hagas ningún ~** don't move a muscle, don't make a move ➤ **movimiento en falso** false move; **hizo un ~ en falso y tropezó** he missed his step and tripped over ➤ **movimiento migratorio** migratory movement **3 en ~** [*figura, persona*] moving; [*vehículo*] in motion; **una célula en ~** a moving cell o a cell in motion; **mantener algo en ~** to keep sth moving o in motion; **poner en ~** [+ *máquina, motor*] to set in motion; [+ *vehículo*] to get going; [+ *actividad, negocio*] to start, start up **4** [*de cuenta*] transaction; [*de dinero*] movement; **"últimos movimientos"** "most recent transactions" ➤ **movimiento de caja** cash flow **5** (= *actividad*) (*en oficina, tribunal*) activity; (*en aeropuerto, carretera*) traffic **6** (= *tendencia*) movement ➤ **movimiento pacifista** pacifist movement

7 [*de compás*] tempo; [*de sinfonía*] movement **8** (*Inform*) ➤ **movimiento de bloques** block move **9** (= *jugada*) move

moviola® SF **1** (*Cine*) Moviola® **2** (= *repetición*) action replay (*Brit*), instant replay (*EEUU*)

mozalbete SM lad

Mozambique SM Mozambique

mozárabe Ⓐ ADJ Mozarabic **Ⓑ** SMF Mozarab; ▷ *RECONQUISTA*

mozarrón SM big lad, strapping young fellow

mozo/a Ⓐ ADJ **1** (= *joven*) young; **en sus años ~s** in his youth, in his young days **2** (= *soltero*) single, unmarried **Ⓑ** SM/F **1** (= *joven*) lad/girl; **buena moza** good-looking girl **2** (= *criado*) servant **Ⓒ** SM (= *camarero*) waiter; (*Ferro*) porter ➤ **mozo de almacén** warehouse assistant ➤ **mozo de cuadra** stable boy ➤ **mozo de cuerda, mozo de equipajes**, **mozo de estación** porter

MP3 SM MP3; **reproductor (de) ~** MP3 player

mu* SM ✦ MODISMO **no decir ni mu** not to say a word

muchacho/a SM/F **1** (= *joven*) boy /girl **2** (*tb* ~ **de servicio**) (= *hombre*) servant; (= *mujer*) maid, servant

muchedumbre SF crowd, throng; (*pey*) mob, herd

muchísimo Ⓐ ADJ a lot of, lots of; **había muchísima gente** there were a lot of people, there were lots of people; **había muchísima comida** there was a lot of food, there was lots of food; **hace ~ tiempo** a very long time ago, ages ago **Ⓑ** ADV very much, a lot; **me quiere ~** he loves me very much *o* a lot, he really loves me; **llovía ~** it was raining really *o* very hard, it was pouring down

mucho Ⓐ ADJ **1** (*en singular*) (*en oraciones afirmativas*) a lot of, lots of; (*en oraciones interrogativas y negativas*) a lot of, much; **había mucha gente** there were a lot of *o* lots of people there; **¿tienes ~ trabajo?** do you have a lot of *o* much work?; **tengo ~ frío** I'm very cold; **no hace ~ tiempo** not long ago; **llevo aquí ~ tiempo** I've been here a long time

2 (*en plural*) (*en oraciones afirmativas*) a lot of, lots of; (*en oraciones interrogativas y negativas*) a lot of, many; **se lo he dicho muchas veces** I've told him many *o* lots of times; **¿había ~s niños en el parque?** were there a lot of *o* many children in the park?

3 (*) (*con singular colectivo*) **hay ~ tonto suelto** there are a lot of *o* lots of idiots around; **~ beso, pero luego me critica por la espalda** she's all kisses, but then she criticizes me behind my back

4 (= *demasiado*) **es ~ dinero para un niño** it's too much money for a child; **ésta es mucha casa para nosotros*** this house is too big for us **Ⓑ** PRON **1** (*en singular*) **1.1** (*en frases afirmativas*) a lot, lots; (*en frases interrogativas y negativas*) a lot, much; **tengo ~ que hacer** I have a lot *o* lots to do; **su discurso tiene ~ de fascista** his rhetoric contains a lot of fascist elements **1.2** (*referido a tiempo*) long; **no tardes ~** don't be long; **¿falta ~ para llegar?** will it be long till we arrive?; **hace ~ que no salgo a bailar** it's a long time *o* ages since I went out dancing

2 (*en plural*) (*en frases afirmativas*) a lot, lots; (*en frases interrogativas y negativas*) a lot, many; **somos ~s** there are a lot of *o* lots of us; **~s de los ausentes** many of *o* a lot of those absent; **—¿hay manzanas? —sí, pero no muchas** "are there any apples?" — "yes, but not many *o* not a lot"; **¿vinieron ~s?** did many *o* a lot of people come? **Ⓒ** ADV **1** (= *en gran cantidad*) a lot; **come ~** she eats a lot; **viene ~** he comes often *o* a lot; **me gusta ~ el jazz** I really like jazz, I like jazz a lot; **lo siento ~** I'm very *o* really sorry; **trabajar ~** to work hard; **~ antes** long before; **~ más** much *o* a lot more; **~ menos** much *o* a lot less; **muy ~**: **se guardará muy ~ de hacerlo*** he'll jolly well be careful not to do it*; **si no es ~ pedir** if that's not asking too much; **~ peor** much *o* a lot worse

2 (*en respuestas*) **—¿estás cansado? —¡mucho!** "are you tired?" — "I certainly am!"; **—¿te gusta? —no mucho** "do you like it?" — "not much"

3 (*otras locuciones*) **como ~** at (the) most; **con ~** by far, far and away; **tener a algn en ~** to think highly of sb; **ni ~ menos**: **Juan no es ni ~ menos el que era** Juan is nothing

like the man he was; **mi intención no era insultarte, ni ~ menos** I didn't intend to insult you, far from it; **por ~ que**: **por ~ que estudies** however hard you study; **por ~ que quieras no debes mimarlo** no matter how much you love him, you shouldn't spoil him

---

Como traducción de **mucho**, tanto **many** como **a lot of** preceden a sustantivos en plural, p.ej., "Hay mucha gente que no está de acuerdo", *A lot of people o Many people disagree*. En el caso de sustantivos incontables se utilizan **much** o **a lot of**, p.ej. "No tenía mucho dinero", *He didn't have much money o a lot of money.*

---

mucosa SF (= *membrana*) mucous membrane; (= *secreción*) mucus

mucosidad SF mucus

mucoso ADJ mucous

muda SF **1** [*de ropa*] change of underwear **2** (*Zool*) [*de piel*] slough; [*de pelo, plumaje*] moult, molt (*EEUU*) **3** [*de la voz*] breaking

mudanza SF move; **estar de ~** to be moving; **mudanzas** removals; **camión de ~s** removal (*Brit*) *o* moving van (*EEUU*)

mudar /1a/ **Ⓐ** VT **1** (= *cambiar*) to change; (= *transformar*) to change, turn (**en** into); **le mudan las sábanas todos los días** they change his sheets every day; **la han mudado a otra oficina** they've moved her to another office **2** (*Zool*) [+ *piel*] to shed; [+ *pelo, plumaje*] to moult, molt (*EEUU*) **Ⓑ** VI **1** (= *cambiar*) **~ de** to change; **~ de color** to change colour *o* (*EEUU*) color **2** (*Zool*) [+ *piel*] to shed; [+ *pelo, plumaje*] to moult, molt (*EEUU*) **3** [*voz*] to break **Ⓒ** **mudarse** VPR **1** (*tb* **~se de ropa**) to change one's clothes **2** (*tb* **~se de casa**) to move, move house

mudéjar Ⓐ ADJ Mudéjar **Ⓑ** SMF (*Hist*) Mudéjar (*Moslem permitted to live under Christian rule*); ▷ *RECONQUISTA*

mudo ADJ **1** (*Med*) dumb, mute (*frm*); **es ~ de nacimiento** he was born dumb *o* (*frm*) mute **2** (= *callado*) silent, mute; **ser testigo ~ de algo** to stand in mute witness *o* testimony to sth; **quedarse ~ (de)** to be struck dumb (with); **quedarse ~ de asombro** to be left speechless, be dumbfounded **3** (*Ling*) [*letra*] mute, silent; [*consonante*] voiceless **4** [*película*] silent

mueble Ⓐ ADJ movable; **bienes ~s** movable *o* personal property *sing* **Ⓑ** SM piece of furniture; **este ~ es muy valioso** this is a very valuable piece of furniture; **~s** furniture *sing*

El sustantivo **furniture** es incontable, por lo que lleva el verbo en singular:

---

los ~s del salón son muy viejos the dining-room furniture is very old; **con ~s** furnished; **sin ~s** unfurnished ➤ **mueble librería** bookcase ➤ **muebles de cocina** kitchen units ➤ **muebles de época** period furniture *sing* ➤ **muebles de oficina** office furniture *sing*

mueble-bar SM cocktail cabinet, drinks cabinet

mueblería SF (*esp LAm*) (= *tienda*) furniture store; (= *fábrica*) furniture factory

mueca SF (wry) face, grimace; **hacer ~s** to make faces, pull faces (**a** at)

muela SF **1** (*Anat*) (*gen*) tooth; (*para especificar*) back tooth, molar; **dolor de ~s** toothache ➤ **muela del juicio** wisdom tooth **2** [*de molino*] millstone; [*de afilar*] grindstone **3** (= *cerro*) mound, hillock

muelle¹ Ⓐ SM (= *resorte*) spring; **colchón de ~s** interior sprung mattress **Ⓑ** ADJ **1** (= *blando*) soft; (= *delicado*) delicate; (= *elástico*) springy, bouncy **2** [*vida*] soft, easy

muelle² SM **1** (= *puerto*) wharf, quay; (= *malecón*) pier ➤ **muelle de atraque** (*Náut*) mooring quay; (*Aer*) docking bay **2** (*Ferro*) (*tb* ~ **de carga**) loading bay

muera *etc ver* **morir**

muérdago SM mistletoe

muerdo* SM bite

muérgano/a SM/F (*And*) ill-bred person, lout

muermo/a* (*Esp*) **Ⓐ** ADJ (= *pesado*) boring; (= *aburrido*) wet* **Ⓑ** SM/F (= *pesado*) crashing bore*; (= *aburrido*) drip*, wet fish* **Ⓒ** SM **1** (= *aburrimiento*) boredom; (= *depresión*) .the blues* *pl* **2** (= *asunto*) bore

muerte SF **1** (= *por enfermedad, accidente*) death; **murió de ~ natural** he died a natural death *o* of natural causes; **una lucha a ~** a fight to the death; **mantuvo una guerra a ~ con la enfermedad** he fought his illness to the bitter end; **odiar algo/a algn a ~** to detest sth/sb, loathe sth/sb; **pena de ~** death sentence; **un susto de ~** a terrible fright; **✦** MODISMOS **estar de ~** (*Esp**) (= *muy bien*) to be out-of-this-world*; (*Chi**) (= *muy disgustado*) to be extremely upset; **de mala ~*** [*trabajo, película*] crappy***, crap*** *antes de s*; [*casa, pueblo*] grotty**; **cada ~ de obispo** (*LAm**) once in a blue moon **➤ muerte cerebral** brain death **➤ muerte clínica**: **en situación de ~ clínica** clinically dead **➤ muerte prematura** premature death **➤ muerte repentina** sudden death **➤ muerte súbita** (*Med*) sudden death; (*Tenis*) tie-breaker, tie-break (*esp Brit*); (*Golf*) sudden death play-off **➤ muerte violenta** violent death
2 (= *asesinato*) murder; **dar ~ a algn** to kill sb

muerto/a **Ⓐ** PP *de* **morir**
Ⓑ ADJ **1** [*persona, animal*] dead; **el golpe lo dejó medio ~** the blow left him half-dead; **resultó ~ en el acto** he died instantly; **~ en acción** *o* **campaña** killed in action; **dar por ~ a algn** to give sb up for dead; **ser ~ a tiros** to be shot, be shot dead; **vivo o ~** dead or alive; **✦** MODISMOS **estar más ~ que vivo** to be more dead than alive; **estar más que ~*** ◇ **estar ~ y enterrado*** to be as dead as a doornail*, be as dead as a dodo*, be stone dead*; **no tener donde caerse ~** not to have a penny to one's name
2 (*) (*para exagerar*) **2.1** (= *cansado*) dead tired*, ready to drop*; **después del viaje estábamos ~s** we were dead tired *o* ready to drop after the journey*; **caí muerta en la cama** I dropped flat out on the bed **2.2** (= *sin animación*) dead **2.3 estar ~ de algo**: **estaba ~ de la envidia** I was green with envy; **estoy muerta de sueño** I'm dead tired*; **estaba ~ de miedo** I was scared to death; **estaba ~ del aburrimiento** he was dead bored; **estar ~ de risa** [*persona*] to laugh one's head off, kill o.s. laughing; **el piano sigue ahí ~ de risa** the piano is just gathering dust
3 (= *relajado*) [*brazo, mano*] limp; **deja el brazo ~** let your arm go limp
4 (= *apagado*) [*color*] dull
Ⓒ SM/F **1** (= *persona muerta*) (*en accidente, guerra*) **¿ha habido ~s en el accidente?** was anyone killed in the accident?; **el conflicto ha causado 45.000 ~s** the conflict has caused 45,000 deaths *o* the deaths of 45,000 people; **los ~s** the dead; **✦** MODISMOS **¡me cago en los ~s!** (*Esp****) fucking hell!***; **un ~ de hambre** a nobody; **resucitar a un ~**: **esta sopa resucita a un ~** (*hum*) this soup really hits the spot*
2 (*) (= *cadáver*) body; **hacer el ~** (*en el agua*) to float; **hacerse el ~** to pretend to be dead; **✦** REFRÁN **el ~ al hoyo y el vivo al bollo** dead men have no friends
Ⓓ SM **1** (*) (= *tarea pesada*) drag*; **¡vaya ~ que nos ha caído encima!** (*Esp*) what a drag!*; **✦** MODISMO **cargar** *o* **echar el ~ a algn** to pin the blame on sb
2 (*Naipes*) dummy

muesca SF **1** (= *hendidura*) notch, nick; (*para encajar*) groove, slot **2** (= *marca*) mark

muesli SM muesli

muestra SF **1** (= *señal*) sign, indication; **dar ~s de algo** to show signs of sth; **✦** MODISMO **para ~ (basta) un botón** by way of example **2** (= *prueba*) proof **3** (*Com*) sample **➤ muestra gratuita** free sample **4** (*Med*) sample, specimen **5** (= *exposición*) trade fair **6** (= *en estadística*) sample **➤ muestra aleatoria** random sample **7** (*Cos*) pattern

muestrario SM **1** (= *muestras*) collection of samples; (= *libro*) pattern book **2** [*de personajes, objetos*] collection

muestreo SM (= *acto*) sampling; (= *muestra*) sample; **hacer un ~ de la población** to select a sample of the population

mueva *etc ver* **mover**

mufa* SF (*CS*) bad mood

mugido SM [*de vaca*] moo; [*de toro*] bellow

mugir /3c/ VI [*vaca*] to moo; [*toro*] to bellow

mugre SF (= *suciedad*) dirt; (= *inmundicia*) filth; (= *grasa*) grime, grease; **✦** MODISMO **sacarse la ~** (*Chi**) to come a cropper*; **sacarse la ~ trabajando** to work like a dog*

mugriento ADJ (= *sucio*) dirty, filthy; (= *grasiento*) grimy, greasy

mugroso ADJ (*LAm*) dirty, mucky*

muina SF (*Méx*) fury; **tener ~** to be furious

mujer SF **1** (= *persona hembra*) woman; **ropa de ~** women's clothes *o* clothing; **hacerse ~** to become a woman **➤ mujer bandera†** striking woman **➤ mujer de la limpieza** cleaning lady, cleaning woman, cleaner **➤ mujer de la vida** (*euf*), **mujer de mala vida** prostitute **➤ mujer de vida alegre** loose woman **➤ mujer empresaria** businesswoman **➤ mujer fatal** femme fatale **➤ mujer policía** policewoman
2 (= *esposa*) wife; **mi ~** my wife
3 (*uso apelativo*) (*en oración directa no se traduce*) **¡déjalo, mujer, no te preocupes!** forget about it, don't worry!; **¡mujer, no digas esas cosas!** please! don't say such things!

mujeriego **Ⓐ** ADJ **es muy ~** he's a real womanizer **Ⓑ** SM womanizer

mujer-objeto SF (*pl* **mujeres-objeto**) (female) sex object

mujerona SF big woman

mujer-rana SF diver

mujerzuela** SF slut**, tart (*esp Brit***)

mújol SM grey mullet

mula SF **1** (= *animal*) mule **2** (*Méx*) (= *ficha de dominó*) **la ~ de cincos** the double five **3** (*CS**) (= *mentira*) lie; (= *engaño*) trick; **✦** MODISMOS **meter la ~** to tell lies; **meter la ~ a algn** to trick sb

mulato/a ADJ, SM/F mulatto

mulero/a SM/F **1** (= *mozo*) muleteer **2** (*RPl**) (= *mentiroso*) liar

muleta SF **1** (*para andar*) crutch **2** (*Taur*) matador's stick with red cloth attached **3** (= *apoyo*) prop, support

muletazo SM movement of the "muleta" in bullfighting

muletilla SF **1** (= *frase*) pet word, tag **2** (= *bastón*) cross-handled cane; (*Téc*) (= *botón*) wooden toggle, wooden button **3** (*Taur*) = **muleta 2**

mulita SF (*RPl*) armadillo

mullido **Ⓐ** ADJ **1** [*cama, sofá, alfombra*] soft, springy; [*almohada, terreno*] soft; [*pelo, tela*] fluffy **2 dejar a algn ~*** to wear sb out **Ⓑ** SM (= *relleno*) stuffing, filling

mulo SM mule

multa SF fine; **poner una ~ a algn** to fine sb **➤ multa de tráfico** traffic fine

multar /1a/ VT to fine; **~ a algn con 100 dólares** to fine sb 100 dollars

multicine SM multiscreen cinema (*esp Brit*), multiscreen movie theater (*EEUU*), multiplex

multicolor ADJ [*camisa, bandera, pájaro*] multicoloured, multicolored (*EEUU*); [*espectáculo*] colourful, colorful (*EEUU*); [*planta, diseño*] variegated

multiconferencia SF conference call

multicopista SF duplicator; **a ~** duplicated, mimeographed

multicultural ADJ multicultural

multidimensional ADJ multidimensional

multidireccional ADJ multidirectional

multidisciplinar ADJ, **multidisciplinario** ADJ multidisciplinary

multifamiliar SM (*Méx*) block of flats (*Brit*), apartment building (*EEUU*)

multilateral ADJ multilateral

multilingüe ADJ multilingual

multimedia ADJ INV [*equipo, ordenador*] multimedia *antes de s*

multimillonario/a Ⓐ SM/F multimillionaire/multimillionairess Ⓑ ADJ 1 (= *persona*) ser ~ to be a multimillionaire/multimillionairess 2 un contrato ~ a multi-million euro/dollar *etc* contract

multinacional ADJ, SF multinational

multipartidismo SM multi-party system

multiprocesadora SF (*RPl*) food processor

múltiple ADJ 1 [*colisión, embarazo, fractura*] multiple; **enchufe ~** multiple socket (*Brit*), multiple outlet (*EEUU*) 2 **múltiples** [*aplicaciones, problemas, ocasiones*] many, numerous 3 (*Inform*) **de tarea ~** multi-task; **de usuario ~** multi-user

multiplicación SF 1 (*Mat, Biol*) multiplication 2 (= *aumento*) increase

multiplicador Ⓐ ADJ **efecto ~** multiplier effect Ⓑ SM multiplier

multiplicar /1g/ Ⓐ VT (*Mat*) to multiply (**por** by); (= *aumentar*) to increase, multiply Ⓑ **multiplicarse** VPR 1 (*Mat, Biol*) to multiply; (= *aumentar*) to increase, multiply 2 [*persona*] to be everywhere at once

múltiplo Ⓐ ADJ multiple Ⓑ SM multiple

multiprocesador SM multiprocessor

multipropiedad SF time-share; **el sistema de ~** time-sharing

multirracial ADJ multiracial

multitarea Ⓐ ADJ INV multitasking Ⓑ SF multitask

multitud SF 1 (= *gentío*) crowd 2 **~ de: tengo ~ de cosas que hacer** I've got a mountain of things to do; **hay ~ de posibilidades** there are any number of possibilities

multitudinario ADJ [*manifestación*] mass *antes de s*; [*reunión*] large; [*recepción*] tumultuous

multiuso ADJ INV multipurpose

multiusuario ADJ INV multiuser

mundanal ADJ worldly; **lejos del ~ ruido** (*liter o hum*) far from the madding crowd (*liter*); **alejarse del ~ ruido** (*liter o hum*) to get away from it all

mundano/a Ⓐ ADJ 1 (= *del mundo*) worldly 2 (= *de alta sociedad*) society *antes de s*; (= *de moda*) fashionable Ⓑ SM/F society person, socialite

mundial Ⓐ ADJ [*acontecimiento, esfuerzo, organismo*] worldwide; [*economía, figura, población*] world *antes de s*; **una crisis a escala ~** a crisis on a worldwide scale, a global crisis; **la segunda guerra ~** the Second World War, World War II Ⓑ SM world championship; **el Mundial** *o* **los Mundiales (de Fútbol)** the World Cup; **el Mundial** *o* **los Mundiales de Atletismo** the Athletics World Cup *o* Championship

mundialización SF globalization

mundialmente ADV worldwide, universally; **~ famoso** world-famous

mundillo SM world, circle; **en el ~ teatral** in the theatre world, in theatrical circles

mundo SM 1 (= *universo*) world; **es conocido en todo el ~** he is known throughout the world *o* the world over; **el Nuevo Mundo** the New World; **el otro ~** the next world, the hereafter; **irse al otro ~** to pass away; **el Tercer Mundo** the Third World

2 (= *humanidad*) **medio ~** almost everybody; **todo el ~** everyone, everybody

3 (= *ámbito*) world; **el ~ de la moda** the fashion world; **el ~ del espectáculo** show business; **no piensa volver al ~ de la política** she doesn't intend to return to politics

4 (= *vida mundana*) world; **decidió volver la espalda al ~** he decided to abandon worldly things; **los placeres del ~** worldly pleasures

5 ✦ MODISMOS **correr ~** to see the world; **desde que el ~ es ~** since time began; **se le cayó el ~ encima** his world fell apart; **por esos ~s (de Dios)** all over, here there and everywhere; **no es el fin del ~** it's not the end of the world; **por nada del** *o* **en el ~** not for all the world; **no es nada del otro ~** it's nothing special *o* to write home about; **el ~ es un pañuelo** it's a small world; **tener mucho ~** to be very experienced, know one's way around; **traer a algn al ~** to bring sb into the world; **como Dios lo trajo al ~** stark naked, as naked as

the day he was born; **venir al ~** to come into the world, be born; **ver ~** to see the world; **ha visto mucho ~** he's been around a bit

6 **un ~** (= *mucho*): **todo un ~ de posibilidades** a whole world of possibilities; **no debemos hacer un ~ de sus comentarios** there's no need to blow her comments out of proportion, we shouldn't read too much into her comments

munición SF (*tb* **municiones**) (= *balas*) ammunition, munitions *pl*; (= *pertrechos*) stores *pl*, supplies *pl*; **fábrica de municiones** munitions factory

municipal Ⓐ ADJ [*elección*] municipal; [*concejo*] town *antes de s*, local; [*empleado, oficina*] council *antes de s*; [*impuesto*] local, council *antes de s*; [*piscina*] public Ⓑ SMF (= *guardia*) local policeman/policewoman

municipio SM 1 (= *distrito*) municipality; (= *población*) town 2 (= *ayuntamiento*) town council, local council

munido ADJ (*RPl frm*) **~ de** [+ *aparato, objeto*] armed with, bearing

munificencia SF (*liter*) munificence (*liter*)

muñeca SF 1 (*Anat*) wrist 2 (= *juguete*) doll ➤ **muñeca de trapo** rag doll ➤ **muñeca rusa** Russian doll 3 (**) (= *chica*) doll**, chick (*EEUU***) 4 (*CS**) (= *influencia*) pull, influence

muñeco SM 1 (= *juguete*) (*con forma humana*) doll; (*con forma animal*) toy ➤ **muñeco de peluche** soft toy (*Brit*), stuffed toy (*EEUU*) 2 [*de ventrílocuo*] dummy; (= *efigie*) [*de político, famoso*] effigy; (= *dibujo*) figure ➤ **muñeco de nieve** snowman 3 (= *pelele*) puppet, pawn 4 (*) (= *niño*) sweetie*, little angel 5 ✦ MODISMO **entrarle los ~s a algn** (*Perú*): **me entraron los ~s** I had butterflies in my stomach

muñeira SF *popular Galician dance*

muñequera SF wristband

muñón SM stump

mural Ⓐ ADJ mural, wall *antes de s* Ⓑ SM mural

muralla SF 1 [*de ciudad*] (= *muro*) (city) wall, walls *pl*; (= *terraplén*) rampart 2 (*Chi*) (= *pared*) wall

Murcia SF Murcia; *see also* www.carm.es

murciano ADJ of/from Murcia, Murcian

murciélago SM bat

murga SF 1 (*) (= *lata*) nuisance, bind*; **dar la ~** to be a pain*, be a pest 2 (= *banda*) band of street musicians

murmullo SM 1 (= *susurro*) murmur(ing), whisper(ing) 2 [*de hojas, viento*] rustle, rustling; [*de agua*] murmur

murmuración SF gossip

murmurador(a) Ⓐ ADJ (= *chismoso*) gossiping; (= *criticón*) backbiting Ⓑ SM/F (= *chismoso*) gossip; (= *criticón*) backbiter

murmurar /1a/ Ⓐ VT (= *susurrar*) to murmur, whisper Ⓑ VI 1 (= *cotillear*) to gossip (**de** about); (= *quejarse*) to grumble, mutter (**de** about) 2 [*hojas*] to rustle; [*viento*] to whisper; [*agua*] to murmur

muro SM wall ➤ **muro de Berlín** Berlin Wall ➤ **muro de contención** retaining wall ➤ **Muro de las Lamentaciones** Wailing Wall

murria SF depression, the blues *pl*

mus SM *card game*

musa SF Muse

musaraña SF 1 (*Zool*) shrew 2 (= *mota*) speck floating in the eye; ✦ MODISMOS **mirar a las ~s** to stare vacantly *o* into space; **pensar en las ~s** to daydream

musculación SF muscle-building

muscular ADJ muscular

musculatura SF muscles *pl*, musculature (*frm*); **la ~ abdominal** the abdominal muscles

músculo SM muscle

musculoso ADJ (= *de muchos músculos*) muscular; (= *fortachón*) muscly*

muselina SF muslin

museo SM (*gen*) museum; [*de pintura, escultura*] museum, gallery ➤ **museo de arte moderno** modern art gallery ➤ **museo de cera** wax museum, waxworks ➤ **museo de historia natural** natural history museum ➤ **museo de**

pintura art gallery

musgo SM moss

música SF **1** (*gen*) music; **poner ~ a algo** to set sth to music; ✦ MODISMOS **irse con la ~ a otra parte** to clear off*; **ser ~** (*Méx**) (= *egoísta*) to be selfish ➤ **música ambiental** background music ➤ **música antigua** early music ➤ **música celestial** heavenly music; **sus ideas me suenan a ~ celestial** (*iró*) his ideas sound like hot air to me ➤ **música clásica** classical music ➤ **música de cámara** chamber music ➤ **música de fondo** background music ➤ **música étnica** world music ➤ **música ligera** light music ➤ **música pop** pop music ➤ **música sacra** sacred music

2 músicas* (= *tonterías*) drivel *sing*; **no estoy para ~s** I'm not in the mood to listen to such drivel; *ver tb* **músico**

musical ADJ, SM musical

musicalidad SF musicality, musical quality

músico/a Ⓐ ADJ musical Ⓑ SM/F **1** (= *instrumentista*) musician **2** (= *compositor*) musician; *ver tb* **música**

musicología SF musicology

musiquilla SF (= *melodía*) tune

musitar /1a/ VT, VI to mumble, mutter

muslera SF Tubigrip®, thigh strap

muslo SM thigh

mustio ADJ **1** [*planta*] withered; [*lechuga*] limp **2** [*tela, bandera*] faded **3** [*persona*] depressed, gloomy

musulmán/ana ADJ, SM/F Moslem

mutación SF **1** (= *cambio*) change **2** (*Biol*) mutation

mutante ADJ, SMF mutant

mutar /1a/ Ⓐ VI, VT to mutate Ⓑ **mutarse** VPR to mutate (**en** into)

mutilación SF mutilation

mutilado/a Ⓐ ADJ **1** [*persona*] crippled, disabled; [*cadáver*] mutilated **2** [*escultura, monumento*] vandalized, defaced Ⓑ SM/F cripple, disabled person ➤ **mutilado/a de guerra** disabled veteran

mutilar /1a/ VT **1** (*gen*) to mutilate; (= *lisiar*) to cripple, disable **2** [+ *escultura, monumento*] to vandalize, deface; [+ *texto*] to butcher, hack about

mutis SM INV (*Teat*) exit; **¡mutis!** sh!; **hacer ~** (*Teat*) (= *retirarse*) to exit; (*fig*) to say nothing, keep quiet; ✦ MODISMO **hacer ~ por el foro** to make o.s. scarce*

mutismo SM silence; **guardar un ~ absoluto** to remain tight-lipped

mutua SF friendly society (*Brit*), benefit society (*EEUU*)

mutual SF (*And, CS*) friendly society (*Brit*), benefit society (*EEUU*)

mutualidad SF friendly society (*Brit*), benefit society (*EEUU*)

mutuo ADJ (= *recíproco*) mutual; (= *conjunto*) joint

muy ADJ **1** (= *mucho*) very; **~ bueno** very good; **eso es ~ español** that's very Spanish; **fue una reacción ~ suya** it was a very typical reaction of his; **~ bien/tarde** very well/late; **~ bien, que venga** all right, he can come (along); **Muy Señor mío** Dear Sir; **~ pero que ~ guapo** really, really handsome; **~ de: ~ de noche** very late at night; **~ de mañana** very early in the morning; **su apoyo es ~ de agradecer** his support is very much appreciated; **el/la ~:** **el ~ tonto de Pedro** that great idiot Pedro; **¡el ~ bandido!** the rascal!; **por ~:** **por ~ cansado que estés** however tired you are, no matter how tired you are

2 (= *demasiado*) too; **ya es ~ tarde para cenar** it's too late to have dinner now; **es ~ joven para salir contigo** she's too young to be going out with you

3 (*con participio*) greatly, highly; **fue un tema ~ comentado** the topic was very much discussed

Nn

N¹, n ['ene] SF (= *letra*) N, n

N² Ⓐ SF ABR (*Aut*) = **nacional** Ⓑ ABR (= **Norte**) N

nabo SM turnip

nácar SM mother-of-pearl, nacre (*frm*)

nacarado ADJ mother-of-pearl *antes de s*, pearly

nacer /2d/ VI 1 [*persona, mamífero*] to be born; [*ave, insecto, reptil*] to hatch; **nací en Cuba** I was born in Cuba; **cuando nazca el niño** when the baby is born; **al ~** at birth; **~ muerto** to be stillborn; **~ antes de tiempo** to be born prematurely; ✦ MODISMOS **~ de pie** to be born lucky; **nadie nace enseñado** we all have to learn; **~ parado** (*And**) to be born with a silver spoon in one's mouth; **volver a ~** to have a lucky escape
2 [*planta*] to sprout, bud; [*pelo, plumas*] to grow, sprout 3 [*estrella, sol*] to rise; [*día*] to dawn
4 [*revolución, miedo*] to spring (**de** from); **entre ellos ha nacido una fuerte simpatía** a strong friendship has sprung up between them

nacido Ⓐ ADJ born; **recién ~** newborn Ⓑ SM **los ~s a finales de siglo** those born *o* people born at the end of the century

naciente ADJ [*sol*] rising; **el ~ interés por ...** the new-found *o* growing interest in ...

nacimiento SM 1 [*de persona, mamífero*] birth; [*de ave, insecto, reptil*] hatching; **ciego de ~** blind from birth, born blind 2 (= *estirpe*) birth, family 3 (= *manantial*) spring, source 4 [*del pelo*] roots *pl* 5 (= *origen*) [*de nación*] birth; [*de amistad*] beginning, start 6 (*Arte, Rel*) nativity (scene)

nación SF (= *país*) nation; (= *pueblo*) people ➤ **Naciones Unidas** United Nations

nacional Ⓐ ADJ [*deuda, periódico*] national; [*economía, vuelo*] domestic; **sólo consumen productos ~es** they buy only home-produced goods *o* Spanish *etc* goods Ⓑ SMF 1 (*LAm*) (= *ciudadano*) national 2 **los ~es** (*en la guerra civil española*) the Franco forces; ⟳ *GUERRA CIVIL ESPAÑOLA*

nacionalidad SF 1 (*gen*) nationality; **tener doble ~** to have dual nationality 2 (*Esp*) (= *región*) autonomous region

nacionalismo SM nationalism

nacionalista Ⓐ ADJ nationalist, nationalistic Ⓑ SMF nationalist

nacionalización SF [*de industria*] nationalization; [*de persona*] naturalization

nacionalizar /1f/ Ⓐ VT [+ *industria*] to nationalize; [+ *persona*] to naturalize Ⓑ **nacionalizarse** VPR [*industria*] to be nationalized; [*persona*] to become naturalized; **~se español** to become a Spanish citizen, become a naturalized Spaniard

naco/a* (*Méx*) Ⓐ ADJ vulgar, tacky* Ⓑ SM/F (*pey*) Indian

nada Ⓐ PRON 1 (*con el verbo inglés en afirmativo*) nothing; (*con el verbo inglés en negativo*) anything; **no dijo ~** she said nothing, she didn't say anything; **no hay ~ como un café después de comer** there's nothing like a coffee after your meal; **no entiende ~** he doesn't understand a thing *o* anything; **no sabe ~ de español** he knows no Spanish at all, he doesn't know any Spanish at all; **¡~ de eso!** not a bit of it!; **~ de ~** absolutely nothing, nothing at all 2 (*en locuciones*) 2.1 (*con verbo*) **no me falta de ~** I've got everything I need; **a la cocina no le falta de ~** the kitchen has everything; **hace ~** just a moment ago; **no se parecen en ~** they're not at all alike; **quedar(se) en ~** to come to nothing; **no ha sido ~** it's nothing, it doesn't matter 2.2 (*con preposición, adverbio*) **antes de *o* que ~: antes de *o* que ~ tengo que telefonear** before I do anything else I must make a phone call; **a cada ~** (*LAm**) constantly; **como si ~: se lo advertí, pero como si ~** I warned him but it was as if I hadn't spoken; **de ~: —¡gracias! —de ~** "thanks!" — "not at all" *o* "you're welcome"; **¡tanto revuelo por un premio de ~!** all that fuss over such a silly little prize!; **dentro de ~** very soon; **~ más: —¿desea algo más? —~ más, gracias** "can I get you anything else?" — "no, that's all

thank you"; **no dijo ~ más** he didn't say anything else, he said nothing else; **quiero uno ~ más** I only want one; **encendió la tele ~ más llegar** he turned on the TV as soon as he got in; **ocurrió ~ más iniciado el partido** it happened just after the beginning of the game; **~ más que estoy muy cansado** (*And, Méx*) it's just that I'm very tired; **(~ más y) ~ menos que ...** (no more and) no less than ...; **entró ~ menos que el rey** who should come in but the king!; **ni ~** or anything; **es raro que no haya llamado ni ~** it's strange that she hasn't called or anything; **no quiere comer ni ~** he won't even eat; **pues no es feo ni ~** (*iró*) he's really ugly; **para ~** at all; **no los mencionó para ~** he never mentioned them at all; **—¿te gusta? —para ~** "do you like it?" — "not at all"; **por ~: por ~ se echa a llorar** she's always crying over nothing *o* for no reason at all; **no me subiría a un avión por ~ del mundo** I wouldn't get on a plane for anything in the world; **por menos de ~** for no reason at all
3 (*como muletilla*) **pues ~, me voy** well, I'm off then; **—¿qué pasó? —pues ~, que estuve esperando y no llegó** "what happened?" — "well, I was there waiting and he didn't arrive"; **y ~, al final nos fuimos** anyway, in the end we left Ⓑ ADV not at all, by no means; **no es ~ fácil** it's not at all easy, it's by no means easy; **esto no me gusta ~** I don't like this at all; **pues no eres tú ~ ambicioso** you're pretty ambitious, aren't you? Ⓒ SF **la ~** the void; **el avión pareció salir de la ~** the aircraft seemed to come from nowhere

nadador(a) SM/F swimmer

nadar /1a/ VI to swim; **¿no sabes ~?** can't you swim?; **~ a braza** (*Esp*) ✧ **~ de pecho** (*Méx*) ✧ **~ (estilo) pecho** (*CS*) to do (the) breaststroke, swim breaststroke; **~ a** (*Esp*) *o* **de** (*Méx, CS*) **espalda** to do backstroke, swim backstroke; ✦ MODISMOS **~ en la abundancia** to be rolling in it*, be rolling in money*; **querer ~ y guardar la ropa** to want to have it both ways, want to have one's cake and eat it

nadería SF **discutir por ~s** to argue over nothing *o* over stupid things; **me regaló una ~** she just gave me some trifling *o* tiny thing

nadie PRON (*con el verbo inglés en afirmativo*) nobody, no one; (*con el verbo inglés en negativo*) anybody, anyone; **~ lo tiene *o* no lo tiene** nobody has it; **no he visto a ~** I haven't seen anybody; **no vi a ~ más que a Juan** I didn't see anybody apart from *o* except Juan; **no lo sabe ~ más que tú** nobody else knows apart from you, nobody but you knows; ✦ MODISMO **es un don ~** he's a nobody, he's a nonentity

nado SM 1 (*LAm*) swimming ➤ **nado sincronizado** synchronized swimming 2 **cruzar** *o* **pasar a ~** to swim across

nafta SF (= *hidrocarburo*) naphtha; (*RPl*) (= *gasolina*) petrol (*Brit*), gasoline (*EEUU*)

naftalina SF 1 (*Quím*) naphthalene, naphthaline 2 (*para la ropa*) mothballs *pl*

nagual SM (*Méx*), **nahual** SM (*Méx*) 1 (= *animal*) guardian spirit in animal form 2 (= *brujo*) sorcerer, wizard

náhuatl Ⓐ ADJ INV Nahuatl Ⓑ SMF INV Nahuatl Indian Ⓒ SM (*Ling*) Nahuatl language

---

NÁHUATL

Náhuatl is the indigenous Mexican language that was once spoken by the Aztecs and which has given us such words as tomato, avocado, chocolate and chilli. The first book to be printed on the American continent was a catechism in **náhuatl**, edited by a Franciscan monk in 1539. Today **náhuatl** is spoken in the central plateau of Mexico by a million bilingual and monolingual speakers.
See also www.sil.org/mexico/nahuatl/familia-nahuatl.htm

---

naif Ⓐ ADJ (*pl* **~s** *o* **~**) (*Arte*) naive, primitivist

B SM naive art

naipe SM playing card; **naipes** cards

nalga SF buttock; **darse de ~s** to fall on one's bottom

nana SF **1** (*Mús*) lullaby, cradlesong **2** (*CAm, Méx*) (= *niñera*) nanny **3** (*CS**) **hacerse ~** to hurt oneself, get hurt; **tener ~** to have a pain **4** (= *abuela*) grandma*, granny*

nanai* EXCL, **nanay*** EXCL (*tb ~* **de la China**) no way!*

nao SF (*Hist*) ship

napa SF leather

napalm SM napalm

napia* SF, **napias*** SFPL hooter (*esp Brit***), schnozzle (*esp EEUU**)

napoleónico ADJ Napoleonic

napolitano ADJ of/from Naples, Neapolitan

naranja A SF orange; **✦** MODISMOS **¡~s de la China!*** no way!*, nothing doing!*; **encontrar su media ~** to meet one's match **B** ADJ INV orange **C** SM (= *color*) orange

naranjada SF orange drink, orange squash (*Brit*)

naranjero/a A ADJ [*país, comarca, región*] orange-growing **B** SM/F (= *agricultor*) orange grower; (= *vendedor*) orange seller

naranjo SM orange tree

narcisista A ADJ narcissistic **B** SMF narcissist

narciso SM **1** (= *planta*) daffodil; (= *género*) narcissus **2** (= *persona*) narcissist

narco* A SMF = **narcotraficante B** SM = **narcotráfico**

narcodólar SM drug dollar; **~es** drug money *sing*

narcosis SF INV narcosis

narcótico ADJ, SM narcotic

narcotraficante SMF drug(s) trafficker, drug dealer

narcotráfico SM drug trafficking *o* dealing

nardo SM nard, spikenard

narguile SM hookah

narigón ADJ, **narigudo** ADJ big-nosed

nariz SF **1** (*Anat*) nose; **tengo la ~ tapada** I have a stuffy *o* (*Brit*) blocked nose, my nose is stuffed up *o* blocked; **no te metas el dedo en la ~** don't pick your nose ➤ **nariz aguileña** aquiline nose ➤ **nariz respingona** turned-up nose **2 ✦** MODISMOS **darle en la ~ a algn*: me da en la ~ que no está diciendo la verdad** I get the feeling *o* something tells me that she is not telling the truth; **darse de narices con algo/algn*** to bump into sth/sb*; **darse de narices contra el suelo** to fall flat on one's face; **de las narices** (*Esp**) damn*, bloody (*Brit***); **el ruidito ese de las narices** that damn* *o* (*Brit***) bloody noise; **de narices** (*Esp*): **me echó una bronca de narices** he gave me a hell of a telling off*, he chewed me out (*EEUU**); **hace un frío de narices** it's absolutely freezing*; **delante de** *o* **en las narices de algn*** right under sb's nose*; **estar hasta las narices (de algo/algn)*** to have had it up to here (with sth/sb)*; **hinchar las narices a algn** (*Esp**) to get on sb's nerves, get up sb's nose (*Brit**); **meter las narices en algo*** to poke one's nose into sth; **por narices** (*Esp**): **con una alineación así tienen que ganar por narices** with a line-up like this they just have to win; **esto tiene que estar listo para el lunes por narices** this has to be ready by Monday no matter what; **romper las narices a algn*** to smash sb's face in*; **tener narices** (*Esp**): **¡tiene narices la cosa!** it's outrageous!; **tocar las narices a algn** (*Esp**) to get on sb's nerves, get up sb's nose (*Brit**); **tocarse las narices*** to sit around twiddling one's thumbs; **no ven más allá de sus narices*** they can't see beyond the end of their noses **3** (*Esp**) (*exclamación*) **¿dónde narices están?** where on earth are they?*

4 (= *olfato*) nose, sense of smell

5 [*del vino*] nose

narración SF (= *relato, versión*) account; (= *cuento*) story

narrador(a) SM/F narrator

narrar /1a/ VT [+ *historia*] to tell; [+ *suceso, aventuras, experiencia*] to recount

narrativa SF (= *género*) fiction

narrativo ADJ narrative

nasal ADJ nasal

N.ª S.ʳᵃ ABR = **Nuestra Señora**

nata SF **1** (*Esp*) (*en repostería*) cream ➤ **nata líquida** cream ➤ **nata montada** whipped cream **2** (*en leche cocida*) skin

natación SF swimming ➤ **natación sincronizada** synchronized swimming

natal ADJ [*país*] native; [*pueblo*] home *antes de s*

natalicio SM (*frm*) **el ~ de Artigas** the anniversary of Artigas' birth

natalidad SF birth rate

natillas SFPL custard *sing*

natividad SF nativity

nativo/a A ADJ [*persona, país*] native; **lengua nativa** mother tongue **B** SM/F native

nato ADJ born; **un actor ~** a born actor

natura SF **contra ~: un pecado contra ~** a sin against nature

natural A ADJ **1** (= *no artificial*) [*calor, luz*] natural; [*seda*] pure; [*flor*] real; **es rubia ~** she's a natural blonde; **con ingredientes ~es** with natural ingredients

2 (= *a temperatura ambiente*) **este vino se sirve ~** this wine should be served at room temperature

3 (= *innato*) natural; **tiene un talento ~ para la música** she has a natural talent for music

4 (= *normal*) natural; **es ~ que estés cansado** it's natural that you should be tired

5 (= *no afectado*) natural; **has salido muy ~ en la foto** you look very natural in the photo

6 [*hijo*] illegitimate

7 (= *nativo*) **es ~ de Córdoba** he is a native of Cordoba

8 de tamaño ~ life-size(d)

B SMF native

C SM **1** (= *carácter*) nature; **es de ~ reservado** he's reserved by nature

2 al ~ (= *sin aditamentos*) : **fruta al ~** fruit in its own juice; **está muy guapa al ~** she is very pretty just as she is (without make-up)

3 (*Arte*) **del ~**: **pintar del ~** to paint from life

naturaleza SF **1** (= *universo, campo*) nature; **las ciencias de la ~** the natural science(s); **viven en plena ~** they live surrounded by nature **2** (= *carácter*) nature; **es despistado por ~** he's naturally absent-minded **3** (= *constitución*) constitution; **es de ~ fuerte** he has a strong constitution **4** (= *tipo*) nature; **situaciones de ~ poco común** situations of an unusual nature **5** (*Arte*) **naturaleza muerta** still life

naturalidad SF naturalness; **lo dijo con la mayor ~ (del mundo)** he said it as if it were the most natural thing in the world; **siguió caminando con la mayor ~ del mundo** she carried on walking as if nothing had happened

naturalista A ADJ naturalistic **B** SMF naturalist

naturalizar /1f/ **A** VT to naturalize **B** **naturalizarse** VPR to become naturalized

naturalmente ADV **1** (= *de modo natural*) in a natural way **2** (= *por supuesto*) **¡naturalmente!** naturally!, of course!

naturismo SM naturism

naturista ADJ [*remedio*] alternative, natural; [*medicina*] alternative; [*playa*] nudist; **ser ~** to be a naturist

naufragar /1h/ VI **1** [*barco*] to be wrecked, sink; [*gente*] to be shipwrecked **2** [*película, obra, asunto*] to fail; [*negocio*] to go under, fail

naufragio SM **1** (*Náut*) shipwreck **2** (= *fracaso*) failure, ruin

náufrago/a A ADJ shipwrecked **B** SM/F castaway

náusea SF nausea, sick feeling; **dar ~s a algn** (*lit*) to make sb feel sick; (*fig*) to make sb sick; **tener ~s** to feel sick

nauseabundo ADJ nauseating, sickening

náutica SF navigation, seamanship

náutico ADJ nautical; **club ~** yacht club

navaja SF **1** (= *cuchillo*) clasp knife, penknife; (*tb ~* **de afeitar**) razor ➤ **navaja automática, navaja de resorte** flick knife ➤ **navaja (suiza) multiuso(s)** Swiss army knife **2** (= *molusco*) razor shell

navajazo SM knife wound, slash, gash

naval ADJ [*base, bloqueo*] naval; [*compañía, industria*] shipping *antes de s*; [*constructor*] ship *antes de s*

Navarra SF Navarra; *see also* www.navarra.es

navarrica ADJ = **navarro**

navarro ADJ of/from Navarra

nave SF 1 (*Náut*) ship, vessel; ✦ MODISMO **quemar las ~s** to burn one's bridges *o* (*Brit*) boats 2 (*Aer*) ➤ **nave espacial** spaceship, spacecraft 3 [*de iglesia*] nave ➤ **nave central** nave ➤ **nave lateral** aisle 4 (= *almacén*) warehouse ➤ **nave industrial** industrial premises *pl*

navegable ADJ [*río, canal*] navigable; [*barco*] seaworthy

navegación SF (= *arte*) navigation; (= *barcos*) ships *pl*, shipping; **cerrado a la ~** closed to shipping ➤ **navegación aérea** (= *acción*) aerial navigation; (= *tráfico*) air traffic ➤ **navegación fluvial** (= *acción*) river navigation; (= *tráfico*) river traffic

navegador SM (*Internet*) browser

navegante SMF 1 (= *marinero*) seafarer; **un pueblo de ~s** a seafaring nation 2 (= *que lleva el rumbo*) navigator

navegar /1h/ VI 1 (*Náut*) to sail; **a vela** to sail, go sailing 2 (*Inform*) **por internet** to surf the Net

Navidad SF Christmas; (**día de**) ~ Christmas Day; **¡feliz ~!** merry *o* happy Christmas!; **Navidades** Christmas (time)

navideño ADJ Christmas *antes de s*

naviero/a Ⓐ ADJ shipping *antes de s* Ⓑ SM/F shipowner

navío SM ship

nazareno/a Ⓐ ADJ (*Hist*) Nazarene Ⓑ SM/F 1 (*Hist*) Nazarene 2 (*Rel*) penitent in a Holy Week procession; ⇨ *SEMANA SANTA*

nazi ADJ, SMF Nazi

nazismo SM Nazism

N. de la R. ABR = **nota de la redacción**

N. de la T. ABR = **Nota de la Traductora**

N. del T. ABR = **Nota del Traductor**

neblina SF mist, mistiness

nebulizador SM nebulizer

nebulosa SF nebula

nebuloso ADJ 1 (*Astron*) nebular, nebulous 2 (= *impreciso*) nebulous, vague

necedad SF 1 (= *cualidad*) crassness, foolishness, silliness 2 (= *cosa tonta*) **una ~** a silly thing; **~es** nonsense *sing*

necesariamente ADV necessarily

necesario ADJ 1 (*tras sustantivo*) necessary; **no quiero estar aquí más tiempo del ~** I don't want to be here any longer than necessary; **no disponen del dinero ~ para acabar las obras** they do not have the money they need *o* the money necessary to finish the work 2 (*tras verbo*) necessary; **hacer ~: estos incidentes hicieron necesaria la intervención de la policía** these incidents made it necessary for the police to intervene, these incidents made police intervention necessary; **hacerse ~: se hace necesaria una completa renovación** a complete overhaul is now necessary *o* required; **ser ~** to be needed, be necessary; **no será necesaria la intervención del ejército** no military intervention will be needed *o* necessary; **para hacerse monja son ~s dos años en el noviciado** you need to do two years as a novice before you can become a nun; **es muy ~ tener una infraestructura sólida** it is essential *o* vital to have a solid infrastructure; **no es ~ tener pasaporte** you don't need a passport, it is not necessary to have a passport; **es ~ que** (+ SUBJUN): **no es ~ que le pidas disculpas** there is no need for you to apologize to him; **si es ~** if necessary, if need be

neceser SM [*de aseo*] toilet bag, travel kit (*EEUU*); [*de belleza*] vanity case ➤ **neceser de fin de semana** (= *bolsa*) overnight bag; (= *maleta*) overnight case

necesidad SF 1 (= *situación*) 1.1 **la ~ de algo** the need for sth; **la ~ de hacer algo** the need to do sth; **no hay ~ de hacerlo** there is no need to do it; **tener ~ de algo** to need sth; **tienen ~ urgente de ayuda alimenticia** they urgently

need food aid, they are in urgent need of food aid; **y ¿qué ~ tienes de irte a un hotel?** why do you need to go to a hotel?; ✦ MODISMO **hacer de la ~ virtud** to make a virtue of necessity; ✦ REFRÁN **la ~ aguza el ingenio** necessity is the mother of invention 1.2 **de ~: en caso de ~** in an emergency; **una situación de ~** an emergency; **una herida mortal de ~** a fatal wound; **artículos o productos de primera ~** basic essentials, staple items; **por ~: tuve que aprenderlo por ~** I had to learn it out of necessity; **el que se llame John no significa que tenga que ser inglés por ~** the fact that he is called John does not necessarily mean that he is English; **sin ~: no corra riesgos sin ~** don't take unnecessary risks; **sin ~ de algo** without the need for sth; **sin ~ de moverse de casa** without needing to leave the house

2 (*física, emocional*) need; (*cosa indispensable*) necessity; **satisfacer las ~es de algn** to satisfy sb's needs; **un coche no es un lujo, es una ~** a car is not a luxury, it's a necessity 3 (= *pobreza*) need; **están en la mayor ~** they are in great need

4 **necesidades** 4.1 (= *privaciones*) hardships; **pasar ~es** to suffer hardship *sing o* hardships 4.2 ✦ MODISMO **hacer sus ~es** (*euf*) to relieve o.s.

necesitado Ⓐ ADJ 1 (= *falto*) **estar** *o* **verse ~ de algo** to need sth 2 (= *pobre*) in need Ⓑ SMPL **los ~s** the needy

necesitar /1a/ Ⓐ VT to need; **necesitamos dos más** we need two more; **no necesitas hacerlo** you don't need to do it, you needn't do it; **necesito que me lo mandes urgentemente** I need you to send it to me urgently Ⓑ VI ~ **de algo** to need sth

necio/a Ⓐ ADJ foolish, stupid Ⓑ SM/F fool

nécora SF small crab

necrofilia SF necrophilia

necrófilo/a ADJ, SM/F necrophiliac

necrología SF, **necrológica** SF obituary; **necrológicas** obituary column *sing*

necrológico ADJ obituary *antes de s*

necrópolis SF INV necropolis

necrosis SF INV necrosis

néctar SM nectar

nectarina SF nectarine

neerlandés/esa Ⓐ ADJ Dutch Ⓑ SM/F Dutchman/ Dutchwoman Ⓒ SM (*Ling*) Dutch

nefando ADJ (*liter*) unspeakable, abominable

nefasto ADJ 1 (= *funesto*) [*viaje*] ill-fated; [*año*] unlucky; [*resultado*] unfortunate; [*influencia*] harmful, pernicious; [*corrupción*] harmful, damaging 2 (= *atroz*) dreadful, terrible

nefrítico ADJ nephritic

negación SF 1 (*gen*) negation; [*de acusación, culpa*] denial 2 (*Ling*) negative

negado/a Ⓐ ADJ hopeless, useless; **ser ~ para algo** to be hopeless *o* useless at sth Ⓑ SM/F **es un ~** he's a waste of space*, he's a dead loss (*Brit**)

negar /1h, 1j/ Ⓐ VT 1 (= *desmentir*) to deny

Recuérdese que **deny** rige que el verbo que le siga inmediatamente aparezca en gerundio y no en infinitivo:

~ **haber hecho algo** to deny doing sth *o* having done sth; **negó que lo hubieran chantajeado** he denied that they had blackmailed him, he denied having been blackmailed 2 (= *rehusar*) to refuse, deny (**a** to); **nos ~on la entrada al edificio** we were refused *o* denied entry to the building; ~ **el saludo a algn** to blank sb*, snub sb* Ⓑ VI ~ **con la cabeza** to shake one's head Ⓒ **negarse** VPR ~**se a hacer algo** to refuse to do sth

negativa SF refusal

negativamente ADV **contestar** ~ to answer in the negative; **influir** ~ **en algo** to have a negative *o* harmful influence on sth

negativo Ⓐ ADJ (*tb Mat*) negative; **voto** ~ vote against, no vote Ⓑ SM (*Fot*) negative

negligencia SF negligence

negligente Ⓐ ADJ negligent Ⓑ SMF careless person

negociable ADJ negotiable

negociación SF negotiation

negociado SM 1 (= *sección*) department, section 2 (*And, CS*) (= *negocio turbio*) shady deal

negociador(a) Ⓐ ADJ negotiating Ⓑ SM/F negotiator

negociante SMF businessman/businesswoman

negociar /1b/ Ⓐ VT to negotiate Ⓑ VI 1 (*Pol*) to negotiate 2 (*Com*) ~ **en** o **con** to deal in, trade in

negocio SM 1 (*Com, Fin*) (= *empresa*) business; (= *tienda*) shop (*esp Brit*), store (*EEUU*); **montar un** ~ to set up o start a business 2 (= *transacción*) deal, transaction; **hacer un buen** ~ to pull off a good deal, a real bargain ➤ **negocio sucio**, **negocio turbio** shady deal 3 **negocios** (*Com, Fin*) business *sing*, trade *sing*; **estar en viaje de** ~**s** to be (away) on business; **hombre/mujer de** ~**s** businessman/businesswoman

negra SF (*Mús*) crotchet (*Brit*), quarter note (*EEUU*); (*Ajedrez*) black piece; ✦ MODISMOS **tener la** ~ to be out of luck, be having a run of bad luck; *ver tb* **negro**

negrero SM (*Hist*) slave trader; (= *explotador*) exploiter, slave driver (*hum**)

negrita SF (*Tip*) boldface; **en** ~ in bold (type), in boldface

negro/a Ⓐ ADJ 1 [*color, pelo, raza*] black; [*ojos, tabaco*] dark; ✦ MODISMOS **más** ~ **que el azabache** jet-black; ~ **como boca de lobo** pitch-black, pitch-dark 2 (*por el sol*) tanned, brown; **ponerse** ~ to go brown, tan 3 (= *sucio*) filthy, black 4 [*estado de ánimo, humor*] black, gloomy; [*suerte*] terrible, atrocious; **la cosa se pone negra** it's not going well, it looks bad; **lo ve todo** ~ he always sees the negative side of things, he's terribly pessimistic about everything; **ve muy** ~ **el porvenir** he's very gloomy about the future; ✦ MODISMOS **pasarlas negras** to have a tough time of it; **vérselas negras** o **verse** ~ **para hacer algo** to have a tough time doing sth 5 (*) (= *enfadado*) cross, cranky (*EEUU**), peeved*; **estoy** ~ **con esto** I'm getting desperate about it; **poner** ~ **a algn** to make sb cross o (*EEUU**) cranky, upset sb; **ponerse** ~ to get cross o (*EEUU**) cranky 6 (= *ilegal*) [*mercado*] black; **dinero** ~ hot money, black money Ⓑ SM (= *color*) black Ⓒ SM/F 1 (= *persona*) black; ✦ MODISMO **trabajar como un** ~ to work like a dog, slave away* 2 (*) [*de escritor*] ghostwriter; *ver tb* **negra**

negruzco ADJ blackish

nene/a SM/F 1 (= *niño*) baby, small child 2 (*uso apelativo*) dear, darling

nenúfar SM water lily

neocapitalista ADJ, SMF neo-capitalist

neocelandés/esa Ⓐ ADJ of/from New Zealand Ⓑ SM/F New Zealander

neoclásico ADJ neoclassical

neolítico ADJ neolithic

neologismo SM neologism

neón SM neon

neonato/a SM/F newborn baby

neonazi ADJ, SMF neonazi

neoplatónico ADJ neoplatonic

neoyorquino ADJ of/from New York

Nepal SM Nepal

nepalés/esa ADJ, SM/F, **nepalí** ADJ, SMF Nepalese

nepotismo SM nepotism

Neptuno SM Neptune

nervadura SF (*Arquit*) ribs *pl*

nervio SM 1 (*Anat*) nerve; (*en carne*) sinew ➤ **nervio**

ciático sciatic nerve ➤ **nervio óptico** optic nerve 2 **nervios** (= *ansiedad*) nerves; ✦ MODISMOS **crispar los** ~**s a algn** to get o grate on sb's nerves; **de los** ~**s***: **estoy de los** ~**s** my nerves are on edge; **poner de los** ~**s a algn** to get on sb's nerves, put sb's nerves on edge; **ponerse de los** ~**s** to get worked up*; **tener** ~**s de acero** to have nerves of steel; **tener los** ~**s destrozados** ◇ **estar destrozado de los** ~**s** to be a nervous wreck; **tener los** ~**s a flor de piel** to be ready to explode; **poner los** ~**s de punta a algn** to get o grate on sb's nerves

nerviosismo SF nervousness, nerves *pl*; (= *agitación*) agitation, restlessness

nervioso ADJ 1 (*Anat*) [*crisis, sistema*] nervous; **centro** ~ nerve centre 2 (= *excitable*) **ser** ~ to be highly strung, be nervous; **los foxterriers son muy** ~**s** fox terriers are very highly strung 3 (= *intranquilo*) **estar** ~ to be nervous; **está nerviosa porque tiene un examen** she's nervous because she has an exam; **está muy** ~ **porque aún no han llegado** he's very anxious because they haven't arrived yet; **los caballos estaban** ~**s antes de la tormenta** the horses were restless before the storm; **poner** ~ **a algn** to make sb nervous; **ponerse** ~ to get nervous; **¡no te pongas** ~**!** keep cool!*

nervudo ADJ [*mano, brazo*] sinewy

netamente ADV (= *claramente*) clearly; (= *puramente*) purely

neto ADJ 1 (*Com, Fin*) net; **peso** ~ net weight; **sueldo** ~ net salary, salary after deductions 2 (= *claro*) clear; **un perfil** ~ a clear outline

neumático Ⓐ ADJ [*martillo, bomba*] pneumatic; [*freno*] air *antes de s*, pneumatic Ⓑ SM [*de rueda*] tyre, tire (*EEUU*) ➤ **neumático de recambio** spare tyre, spare tire (*EEUU*)

neumonía SF pneumonia ➤ **neumonía asiática** SARS

neura* SF 1 (= *manía*) obsession 2 (= *depresión*) **estar con la** ~ to be down, be in a state

neuralgia SF neuralgia

neurálgico ADJ 1 (*Med*) neuralgic, nerve *antes de s* 2 [*centro*] nerve *antes de s*; [*punto*] crucial, key *antes de s*

neuras* SMF INV **es un** ~ he's neurotic

neurasténico ADJ 1 (*Med*) neurasthenic 2 (*fig*) neurotic, nervy, excitable

neurocirugía SF neurosurgery

neurología SF neurology

neurólogo/a SM/F neurologist

neurona SF brain cell

neurosis SF INV neurosis ➤ **neurosis de guerra** shell shock

neurótico/a ADJ, SM/F neurotic

neurotransmisor SM neurotransmitter

neutral ADJ, SMF neutral

neutralidad SF neutrality

neutralizar /1f/ Ⓐ VT (*gen*) to neutralize; [+ *tendencia, influencia*] to counteract Ⓑ **neutralizarse** VPR (*gen*) to neutralize each other; [*influencias*] to cancel (each other) out

neutro ADJ 1 (*gen*) neutral 2 (*Biol*) neuter, sexless 3 (*Ling*) neuter

neutrón SM neutron

nevada SF snowfall

nevado Ⓐ ADJ (= *cubierto de nieve*) snow-covered; [*montaña*] snow-capped Ⓑ SM (*LAm*) snow-capped mountain

nevar /1j/ VI to snow

nevera SF refrigerator, fridge (*esp Brit**)

nevera-congelador SF fridge-freezer

nevería SF (*Méx*) ice-cream parlour, ice-cream parlor (*EEUU*)

nevisca SF light snowfall, flurry of snow

nexo SM link, connection, nexus (*frm*)

ni CONJ 1 (*con verbo negativo en inglés*) or; (*con verbo afirmativo en inglés*) nor; **no bebe ni fuma** he doesn't smoke or drink; **—a mí no me gusta —ni a mí** "I don't like it" —

"nor do I" *o* "neither do I"; **ni ... ni ...: no tenía ni amigos ni familiares** he had no friends and no family (either), he had no friends or family, he had neither friends nor family; **no vinieron ni Juan ni Pedro** Juan didn't come and neither did Pedro, neither Juan nor Pedro came; **ni lo sé ni me importa** I don't know and I don't care

2 (*para dar más énfasis*) even; **ni a ti te lo dirá** he won't tell even *you*; **no lo compraría ni aunque tuviera dinero** I wouldn't buy it even if I had the money; **no tengo ni idea** I have no idea; **ni siquiera** not even; **ni siquiera me llamó** he didn't even call me; **ni uno**: —**¿cuántos tienes? —ni uno** "how many have you got?" — "not a single one" *o* "none"; **no hemos comprado ni un regalo** we haven't bought a single present; **no me ha dicho ni una palabra** she hasn't said a single word to me

3 (*exclamaciones*) **¡ni hablar!** no way!, not on your life!; **¡ni por ésas!: he intentado convencerla con un regalo, pero ni por ésas** I tried to persuade her with a present but even that didn't work; **ni que: ¡ni que fueras su madre!** anyone would think you were his mother!; **¡ni que fuese un dios!** he must think he's God!

4 ni bien (*RPl*) as soon as; **ni bien me fui, sonó el teléfono** as soon as I left, the phone rang

Niágara SM Niagara

nica* ADJ, SMF (*LAm*) Nicaraguan

Nicaragua SF Nicaragua

nicaragüense ADJ, SMF Nicaraguan

nicho SM niche

nick SM (*Internet*) nickname, user name, nick

nicotina SF nicotine

nido SM **1** (*gen*) nest; ✦ MODISMO **caer del ~** to come down to earth with a bump ➤ **nido de amor** love nest ➤ **nido de víboras** nest of vipers **2** (= *escondrijo*) **un ~ de ladrones** a den of thieves

niebla SF fog; **un día de ~** a foggy day; **hay ~** it is foggy

niego, niegue *etc ver* **negar**

nieto/a SM/F grandson/granddaughter; **~s** grandchildren

nieva *etc ver* **nevar**

nieve SF **1** (*Meteo*) snow; **las primeras ~s** the first snows, the first snowfall **2** (*Culin*) **batir a punto de ~** to beat until stiff **3** (*Méx, CAm*) (= *sorbete*) sorbet, water-ice

NIF SM ABR (= **número de identificación fiscal**) *ID number used for tax purposes*

Nigeria SF Nigeria

nigeriano/a ADJ, SM/F Nigerian

nigromante SM necromancer

nihilista Ⓐ ADJ nihilistic Ⓑ SMF nihilist

niki SM (*Esp†*) T-shirt

Nilo SM **el ~** the Nile

nilón SM nylon

nimbo SM **1** (*Arte, Astron, Rel*) halo **2** (*Meteo*) nimbus

nimiedad SF **1** (= *cualidad*) insignificance, triviality **2 una ~** a trifle, a tiny detail; **discutieron por una ~** they quarrelled over nothing

nimio ADJ insignificant, trivial

ninfa SF (*Mit*) nymph

ninfómana SF nymphomaniac

ningún ADJ *ver* **ninguno**

ningunear* /1a/ VT (*esp CAm, Méx*) **~ a algn** (= *hacer el vacío*) to ignore sb; (= *tratar mal*) to treat sb like dirt*

ninguno Ⓐ ADJ (*con verbo negativo en inglés*) any; (*con verbo afirmativo en inglés*) no; **no han encontrado ninguna pista** they haven't found any clues, they have found no clues; **no voy a ninguna parte** I'm not going anywhere; **no es ningún tonto** he's no fool; **no es molestia ninguna** it's no trouble at all

Ⓑ PRON **1** (*entre más de dos*) (*con verbo negativo en inglés*) any; (*con verbo afirmativo en inglés*) none; **hizo cuatro exámenes pero no aprobó ~** he took four exams but didn't pass any (of them); —**¿cuál te gusta? —ninguno** "which one do you like?" — "none of them"; **~ de: no me creo**

ninguna de sus historias I don't believe any of his stories; **no lo sabe ~ de sus amigos** none of his friends know

2 (*entre dos*) (*con verbo negativo en inglés*) either; (*con verbo afirmativo en inglés*) neither; **no os quiero ver a ~ de los dos** I don't want to see either of you; **no nos ha escrito ~ de los dos** neither of them has written to us; **~ de los dos equipos pasará a la final** neither of the teams *o* neither team will get through to the final

niña SF pupil; ✦ MODISMO **ser la ~ de los ojos de algn** to be the apple of sb's eye; *ver tb* **niño**

niñato* Ⓐ ADJ **no seas tan ~** don't be so childish, don't be such a baby Ⓑ SM brat*

niñera SF nanny (*esp Brit*), nursemaid (*esp EEUU*)

niñería SF (= *acto*) childish thing; (= *trivialidad*) silly thing, triviality

niñez SF childhood

niño/a Ⓐ ADJ **es muy ~ todavía** he's still very young; **¡no seas ~!** don't be so childish!

Ⓑ SM/F **1** (= *crío*) child, (little) boy/(little) girl; **los ~s** the children, the kids*; **de ~** as a child; ✦ MODISMOS **ser el ~ mimado de algn** to be sb's pet; **¡qué coche ni qué ~ muerto!*** all this nonsense about a car!, car my foot!*; **como ~ con zapatos nuevos** (*por regalo, compra*) like a child with a new toy, as pleased as punch; (*por noticia, sorpresa*) as pleased as punch ➤ **niño/a bien, niño/a bonito/a** Hooray Henry* ➤ **niño/a pera** (*Esp*), **niño/a pijo/a** (*Esp**) pampered child, daddy's boy/girl ➤ **niño/a prodigio/a** child prodigy

2 (= *bebé*) baby; **va a tener un ~** she's going to have a baby ➤ **el Niño Jesús** the Christ child; (*con menos formalidad*) the Baby Jesus ➤ **niño/a probeta** test-tube baby

3 (*uso apelativo*) (*a niño*) son/dear; (*a adulto*) darling; **¡~, que te vas a caer!** watch out, you're going to fall!

4 (*LAm esp Hist*) (= *título*) master/mistress, sir/miss; **el ~ Francisco** (young) master Francisco; *ver tb* **niña**

nipón/ona ADJ, SM/F Japanese

níquel SM nickel

niquelar /1a/ VT to nickel-plate

niqui SM (*Esp*) T-shirt

nirvana SM Nirvana

níspero SM medlar ➤ **níspero del japón** loquat

nitidez SF **1** [*de imagen, fotografía*] sharpness, clarity **2** [*de explicación*] clarity

nítido ADJ **1** [*imagen*] sharp, clear **2** [*explicación*] clear

nitrato SM nitrate

nítrico ADJ nitric

nitrógeno SM nitrogen

nitroglicerina SF nitroglycerin(e)

nivel SM **1** (= *altura*) level, height; **a 900m sobre el ~ del mar** at 900m above sea level ➤ **nivel de(l) aceite** (*Aut etc*) oil level

2 (*escolar, cultural*) level, standard; **el ~ cultural del país** the general standard of education in the country; **alto ~ de empleo** high level of employment; **a ~ internacional** at an international level; **estar al ~ de** to be equal to, be on a level with; **no está al ~ de los demás** he is not up to the standard of the others; ✦ MODISMO **dar el ~** to come up to scratch ➤ **nivel de vida** standard of living ➤ **niveles de audiencia** ratings, audience rating *sing*; (*TV*) viewing figures

3 a ~ de (= *en cuanto a*) as for, as regards; (= *como*) as; **a ~ de ministro es un desastre** as a minister he's a disaster

nivelar /1a/ VT **1** [+ *superficie*] to level (out); (*Ferro*) to grade **2** [+ *diferencias, deficiencias*] to even (out), even (up) **3** [+ *presupuesto*] to balance

níveo ADJ (*liter*) snowy, snow-white

nixtamal SM (*CAm, Méx*) (= *maíz cocido*) boiled maize (*Brit*), boiled corn (*EEUU*)

N.o ABR, **n.o** ABR (= **número**) No., no.

NO ABR (= **noroeste**) NW

no Ⓐ ADV **1** (*para negar*) **1.1** (*en respuestas independientes*) no; (*negando una acción*) not; **no, gracias** no, thanks; —**¿te gusta? —no mucho** "do you like it?" — "not really";

todavía no not yet; **¡yo no!** not me!, not I!† **1.2** (*para formar la negación de los verbos*) **no sé** I don't know; **no puedo ir esta noche** I can't come tonight; **no debes preocuparte** you mustn't worry; ✦ MODISMO **el no va más** the ultimate **1.3** **que no: decir que no** to say no; **creo que no** I don't think so; **me rogó que no lo hiciera** he asked me not to do it **1.4** (*con doble negación*) **no conozco a nadie** I don't know anyone

2 (*pidiendo confirmación*) **esto es tuyo, ¿no?** this is yours, isn't it?; **fueron al cine, ¿no?** they went to the cinema, didn't they?; **puedo salir esta noche, ¿no?** I can go out tonight, can't I?

3 (*modificando a adjetivos y sustantivos*) non-; **pacto de no agresión** non-aggression pact; **los países no alineados** the non-aligned nations; **los no fumadores** non-smokers **Ⓑ** SM **un no contundente** a resounding no

Nobel Ⓐ SM (*tb* **Premio ~**) Nobel Prize **Ⓑ** SMF (= *persona*) Nobel prizewinner

nobiliario ADJ **título ~** title

noble Ⓐ ADJ **1** (= *aristocrático*) noble **2** (= *honrado*) noble **3** [*madera*] fine **Ⓑ** SMF nobleman/noblewoman; **los ~s** the nobility *sing*, the nobles

nobleza SF nobility

nobuk SM nubuck

nocaut SM (*LAm*) knockout

noche SF **1** (= *parte del día*) night; **a las once de la ~** at eleven o'clock at night; **a la ~** (*RPl*) at night; **ayer ~** last night; **¡buenas ~s!** (*al atardecer*) good evening!; (*al despedirse o al acostarse*) good night!; **de ~** (*como adv*) at night; (*como adj*) night *antes de s*; **tiene miedo a salir de ~ a la calle** she is afraid to go out after dark *o* at night; **viajaban de ~** they travelled by night; **crema de ~** night cream; **en la ~** (*LAm*) at night; **en la ~ de ayer** last night; **en la ~ de hoy** tonight; **en la ~ del martes** on Tuesday night; **hasta muy entrada la ~** till late into the night, into the small hours; **esta ~** (= *hoy por la noche*) tonight; (= *anoche*) last night; **hacer ~ en un sitio** to spend the night somewhere; **media ~** midnight; **por la ~** at night; **mañana por la ~** tomorrow night; ✦ MODISMOS **de la ~ a la mañana** overnight; **pasar la ~ en blanco** *o* **en vela** to have a sleepless night ➤ **noche de amor** night of passion ➤ **noche de bodas** wedding night ➤ **noche de estreno** (*Teat*) first night, opening night ➤ **noche toledana** sleepless night **2** (= *oscuridad*) **ya es ~ cerrada** it's completely dark now; **es de ~** it's dark; **cuando sea de ~, volveremos al refugio** when night falls *o* when it's dark, we'll go back to the shelter; **hacerse de ~** to get dark

3 **la ~** (= *vida nocturna*) nightlife; **aquí se vive intensamente la ~** the nightlife is very lively here; **es el local de moda de la ~ neoyorquina** it is the trendiest nightspot on the New York scene

Nochebuena SF Christmas Eve

Nochevieja SF, **nochevieja** SF New Year's Eve

noción SF **1** (= *idea*) notion, idea; **no tener la menor ~ de algo** not to have the faintest idea about sth **2 nociones** (= *conocimientos*) [*de electrónica, música*] basics, rudiments; [*de lenguas*] smattering *sing*

nocional ADJ notional

nocivo ADJ harmful, injurious (*frm*) (**para** to)

noctámbulo/a Ⓐ ADJ active at night **Ⓑ** SM/F night owl

nocturno Ⓐ ADJ **1** [*servicio, tarifa, ceguera*] night *antes de s*; **un vuelo ~** a night flight; **locales ~s** nightspots; **vigilante ~** night watchman; **ambiente ~** nightlife; **clases nocturnas** evening classes, night school; **su primera salida nocturna** her first night out **2** (*Zool, Bot*) nocturnal **Ⓑ** SM **1** (*Mús*) nocturne **2** (*Escol*) evening classes *pl*, night school

nodo SM node

nodriza SF wet nurse

nódulo SM nodule

nogal SM (= *madera*) walnut; (= *árbol*) walnut tree

nómada Ⓐ ADJ nomadic **Ⓑ** SMF nomad

nomadismo SM nomadism

nomás ADV (*LAm*) (*gen*) just; (= *tan sólo*) only; *ver tb* **más A7**

nombramiento SM appointment

nombrar /1a/ VT **1** (= *citar*) to name **2** (*para puesto, cargo*) to appoint

nombre SM **1** [*de persona, cosa*] name; **~ y apellidos** full name; **a ~ de: la mesa está reservada a ~ de ...** the table has been booked in the name of ...; **un sobre a ~ de ...** an envelope addressed to ...; **en ~ de** in the name of, on behalf of; **poner ~ a** to call, name; **¿qué ~ le van a poner?** what are they going to call him?; ✦ MODISMOS **llamar a las cosas por su ~** to call a spade a spade; **no tener ~: su conducta no tiene ~** his conduct is utterly despicable ➤ **nombre artístico** stage name ➤ **nombre comercial** trade name ➤ **nombre de pila** first name, Christian name **2** (*Ling*) noun ➤ **nombre común** common noun ➤ **nombre propio** proper name

3 (= *reputación*) name, reputation; **se ha hecho un ~ en el mundo editorial** she's made a name for herself in the world of publishing

nomenclatura SF nomenclature

nomeolvides SF INV forget-me-not

nómina SF **1** (= *lista de empleados*) payroll; **entrar en ~** to be put on the payroll; **estar en ~** to be on the staff **2** (= *sueldo*) salary; (= *hoja de pago*) pay slip (*Brit*), wage statement (*EEUU*)

nominación SF nomination

nominal ADJ **1** [*cargo*] nominal **2** [*valor*] face *antes de s*, nominal **3** (*Ling*) noun *antes de s*

nominar /1a/ VT to nominate

nominativo Ⓐ ADJ **1** (*Ling*) nominative **2** (*Com, Fin*) **un cheque ~ a favor de García** a cheque *o* (*EEUU*) check made out *o* made payable to García **Ⓑ** SM (*Ling*) nominative

non SM odd number; **pares y ~es** odds and evens

nonagenario/a Ⓐ ADJ nonagenarian, ninety-year-old **Ⓑ** SM/F nonagenarian

nonagésimo ADJ, PRON ninetieth; *ver* **sexto**

nonato ADJ born by Caesarean section

nono[1] ADJ ninth

nono[2] SM (*LAm*) **hacer** ~ to sleep; **está haciendo** ~ he's gone to beddy-byes*; **tener** ~ to be sleepy

nopal SM (*Méx*) prickly pear

noqueada SF (*esp LAm*) (= *acto*) knockout; (= *golpe*) knockout blow

noquear /1a/ VT (*esp LAm*) to knock out, K.O*

noray SM bollard

norcoreano/a ADJ, SM/F North Korean

nordeste Ⓐ ADJ [*región*] northeast, northeastern; [*dirección, rumbo*] northeasterly; [*viento*] northeast, northeasterly Ⓑ SM 1 [*de región, país*] northeast 2 (*Meteo*) (*tb* **viento del** ~) northeast wind; *ver tb* **sur**

nórdico/a ADJ, SM/F Northern European

noreste ADJ, SM = **nordeste**

noria SF 1 (*Agr*) waterwheel 2 (*Esp*) [*de feria*] Ferris wheel, big wheel (*Brit*)

norirlandés ADJ Northern Irish

norma SF 1 (= *regla*) (*gen, tb Educ*) rule; (*oficial*) regulation; **una nueva ~ europea sobre emisiones acústicas** a new European regulation on sound emissions; **como** o **por ~ general** as a general rule, as a rule of thumb; **tener por ~ hacer algo** to make it a rule to do sth ➤ **normas de conducta** (*sociales*) rules of behaviour; [*de periódico, empresa*] policy *sing* ➤ **normas de seguridad** safety regulations
2 (= *situación, costumbre*) norm; **un país donde la pobreza es la** ~ a country where poverty is the norm; **como es** ~ **en estos casos** as is standard practice o as is the norm in these cases
3 **la** ~ (*Ling*) the standard form; **la ~ andaluza** standard Andalusian Spanish

normal ADJ 1 (= *usual*) normal; **una persona** ~ a normal person; **es perfectamente** ~ it's perfectly normal; **es ~ que quiera divertirse** it's only natural that he should want to enjoy himself; **no es ~ que no quiera venir** it's unusual for him not to want to come; **lleva una vida muy** ~ he leads a very ordinary life; ~ **y corriente** ordinary; —**¿es guapo? — no, ~ y corriente** "is he handsome?" — "no, just ordinary"; **como alumno es ~ y corriente** he's an average pupil
2 [*gasolina*] three-star petrol (*Brit*), regular gas (*EEUU*)
3 (*Téc*) standard; (*Mat, Quím*) normal

normalidad SF normality, normalcy (*EEUU*); **la situación ha vuelto a la** ~ the situation has returned to normality o normal o (*EEUU*) normalcy; **se comportaba con total** ~ he was behaving perfectly normally; **el acto discurrió con toda** ~ the ceremony passed off without incident

normalista SMF (*Col*) schoolteacher

normalización SF 1 [*de relaciones, servicio, situación*] normalization ➤ **normalización lingüística** *policy of making the local language official within an autonomous region* 2 (*Com, Téc*) standardization

normalizar /1f/ Ⓐ VT 1 [+ *relaciones, servicio, situación*] to restore to normal, normalize 2 (*Com, Téc*) to standardize Ⓑ **normalizarse** VPR to return to normal, normalize

normalmente ADV normally, usually

normando/a ADJ, SM/F Norman

normativa SF rules *pl*, regulations *pl*, guidelines *pl*

normativo ADJ 1 (= *preceptivo*) [*aspecto, carácter*] normative; (*gramática*) prescriptive; **es ~ en todos los coches nuevos** it is mandatory in all new cars 2 (= *legal*) **el marco ~ vigente** the existing regulatory framework; **el actual vacío** ~ the present lack of regulation

noroeste Ⓐ ADJ [*región*] northwest, northwestern; [*dirección, rumbo*] northwesterly; [*viento*] northwest, northwesterly Ⓑ SM 1 [*de región, país*] northwest 2 (*Meteo*) (*tb* **viento del** ~) northwest wind; *ver tb* **sur**

nororiental ADJ north-eastern

norte Ⓐ ADJ [*región, orilla*] northern; [*costa*] north; [*dirección, rumbo*] northerly; [*viento*] north, northerly Ⓑ SM 1 (= *punto cardinal*) **el Norte** the North, the north ➤ **norte magnético** magnetic north 2 [*de región, país*] north

3 (*Meteo*) (*tb* **viento del** ~) north wind 4 (= *meta*) aim, objective; ✦ MODISMO **perder el** ~ to lose one's way, go astray; *ver tb* **sur**

norteafricano/a ADJ, SM/F North African

Norteamérica SF North America

norteamericano/a ADJ, SM/F North American; (*de Estados Unidos*) American

norteño/a Ⓐ ADJ northern Ⓑ SM/F northerner

Noruega SF Norway

noruego/a Ⓐ ADJ, SM/F Norwegian Ⓑ SM (*Ling*) Norwegian

norvietnamita ADJ, SMF North Vietnamese

nos PRON PERS PL 1 (*directo, indirecto*) us; ~ **vinieron a ver** they came to see us; ~ **dio un consejo** he gave us some advice; ~ **lo dará** he'll give it to us; ~ **lo compró** (*de nosotros*) he bought it from us; (*para nosotros*) he bought it for us; ~ **tienen que arreglar el televisor** they have to fix the television for us
2 (*reflexivo*) ourselves; **tenemos que defendernos** we must defend ourselves; ~ **lavamos** we washed

> Con partes del cuerpo o con prendas que se llevan puestas se utiliza el adjetivo posesivo:

~ **dolían los pies** our feet were hurting; ~ **pusimos los abrigos** we put our coats on
3 (*mutuo*) each other; ~ **dimos un beso** we gave each other a kiss; **no** ~ **hablamos** we don't speak to each other; ~ **enamoramos** we fell in love

nosocomio SM (*LAm frm*) hospital

nosotros/as PRON PERS PL 1 (*sujeto*) we; ~ **no somos italianos** we are not Italian; **se lo podemos llevar ~ mismos** we can deliver it to you ourselves 2 (*tras prep*) us; **tu hermano vino con** ~ your brother came with us; **no pedimos nada para** ~ we ask nothing for ourselves

nostalgia SF [*del pasado*] nostalgia; [*de casa, patria, amigos*] homesickness

nostálgico ADJ [*del pasado*] nostalgic; (*de casa, patria, amigos*) homesick

nota SF 1 (= *mensaje*) note
2 (= *apunte*) note; **tomar ~s** to take notes; **tomar (buena) ~ (de algo)** (= *fijarse*) to take (good) note (of sth)
3 (= *comentario*) note ➤ **nota a pie de página** footnote
4 (*Escol*) mark, grade (*EEUU*); **sacar buenas ~s** to get good marks o grades; **¿ya te han dado las ~s?** have you had your report (*Brit*) o report card (*EEUU*) yet?
5 (*Mús*) note; ✦ MODISMO **dar la** ~ to get oneself noticed, act up ➤ **nota discordante** discordant note; **poner la ~ discordante** to strike a discordant note ➤ **nota dominante** dominant feature, dominant element
6 (= *adorno, detalle*) **una ~ de color** a colourful o (*EEUU*) colorful note
7 (*Prensa*) note ➤ **nota de la redacción** editor's note ➤ **nota de prensa** press release
8 (*Com*) (= *recibo*) receipt; (= *vale*) IOU; (= *cuenta*) bill
9 (= *reputación*) **de mala** ~ notorious

notable Ⓐ ADJ 1 (= *destacado*) notable; **una actuación verdaderamente** ~ an outstanding performance, a truly notable performance; **un poema ~ por su belleza lírica** a poem notable for its lyrical beauty 2 (= *considerable*) [*aumento, mejoría, diferencia*] significant, considerable; **la obra fue un fracaso** ~ the play was a signal failure Ⓑ SM (*Esp*) (= *calificación*) mark o grade between seven and eight out of ten; **he sacado un** ~ ≈ I got a B

notablemente ADV significantly, considerably

notación SF notation

notar /1a/ Ⓐ VT 1 (= *darse cuenta de*) to notice; **no lo había notado** I hadn't noticed; **noté que la gente la miraba** I noticed people looking at her, I noticed that people were looking at her; **un niño nota cuando hay tensión en casa** a child can tell when there is tension at home; **dejarse** ~ to be noticeable; **hacer ~ algo** to point sth out; **hacerse ~: las consecuencias se hicieron ~ sin tardanza** the consequences soon became apparent; **sólo se comportan así para hacerse**

~ they only behave like that to get noticed *o* get attention **2** (= *sentir*) [+ *dolor, pinchazo, frío*] to feel; **empiezo a ~ el cansancio** I'm beginning to feel tired **3** (+ ADJ) **te noto muy cambiado** you seem very different; **te noto raro** you're acting strangely

B **notarse** VPR **1** (*uso impersonal*) **1.1** (= *ser obvio*) to be noticeable; **~se algo a algn: no se le nota que es extranjero** you can't tell he's a foreigner, you wouldn't know he's a foreigner; **se le notaba muy agitado** he was obviously very agitated; **~se que: ¡se nota que acabas de cobrar!** you can tell you've just been paid!, you've obviously just been paid! **1.2** (= *sentirse*) to be felt; **la inflación se ha notado en el bolsillo de la gente** people have felt the effect of inflation on their pocket **1.3** (= *verse*) [*mancha, defecto, edad*] to show; **no se nota nada la mancha** the stain doesn't show at all; **~se algo a algn: —tienes una carrera en la media —¿se me nota mucho?** "you've got a run *o* (*Brit*) ladder in your stocking" — "does it show much?" **2** (*uso reflexivo*) to feel; **me noto más relajado** I feel more relaxed

notaría SF **1** (= *profesión*) **gastos de ~** legal fees, lawyer's fees **2** (= *despacho*) notary's office

notarial ADJ (*gen*) notarial; [*estilo*] legal, lawyer's

notario/a SM/F notary, notary public, attorney-at-law (*EEUU*)

noticia SF **1** (= *información*) news

Aunque el sustantivo **news** tiene una terminación plural, es incontable, por lo que para decir una noticia hay que usar **some news, a piece of news** o **a bit of news**:

tengo una buena ~ que darte I've got some good news for you; **fue una ~ excelente para la economía** it was an excellent piece *o* bit of news for the economy; **la última ~ fue sobre las inundaciones** the last news item was about the flooding; **vi las ~s de las nueve** I watched the nine o'clock news ➤ **noticia bomba*** bombshell* **2** (= *conocimiento*) **tener ~s de algn** to have news of sb, hear from sb; **no tener ~ de algo** to know nothing about a matter

⚠ **noticia ≠ notice**

noticiable ADJ newsworthy

noticiero SM (*LAm TV*) news *sing*, news bulletin

noticioso **A** ADJ (*esp RPI*) [*reportaje*] news *antes de s*; [*fuente*] well-informed; [*suceso*] newsworthy **B** SM (*RPI TV, Radio*) news *sing*, news bulletin

notificación SF notification

notificar /1g/ VT to notify, inform

notoriedad SF **1** (= *fama*) fame, renown; (= *mala fama*) notoriety **2** (= *dominio público*) **hechos de amplia ~** widely-known facts

notorio ADJ **1** (= *conocido*) well-known, publicly known; **es ~ que ...** it is well-known that ... **2** (= *obvio*) obvious; [*error*] glaring, blatant, flagrant

⚠ **notorio ≠ notorious**

novatada SF **1** (= *burla*) rag (*Brit*), ragging (*Brit*), hazing (*EEUU*) **2** (= *error*) beginner's mistake, elementary blunder; ✦ MODISMO **pagar la ~** to learn the hard way

novato/a **A** ADJ raw, green **B** SM/F beginner, tyro

novecientos ADJ, PRON, SM (*cardinal*) nine hundred; (*ordinal*) nine hundredth; **línea** *o* **número ~** Freefone® number; *ver tb* **seiscientos**

novedad SF **1** (= *cualidad*) novelty, newness **2** (= *cosa nueva*) novelty; **las ~es discográficas** new releases; **las últimas ~es en moda infantil** the latest in children's fashions; **¿llegó tarde? ¡vaya ~!** so he was late? surprise, surprise! **3** (= *cambio*) **llegar sin ~** to arrive safely; **la jornada ha transcurrido sin ~** it has been a quiet day, it has been a normal day; **el enfermo sigue sin ~** the

patient's condition is unchanged

novedoso ADJ [*idea, método*] novel, new, original

novel ADJ new

novela SF novel ➤ **novela de amor** love story, romance ➤ **novela histórica** historical novel ➤ **novela negra** thriller ➤ **novela policíaca** detective story, whodunit* ➤ **novela rosa** romantic novel

novelar /1a/ VT to make a novel out of, fictionalize

novelero ADJ (= *aficionado*) (*a novedades*) fond of novelty; (*a novelas*) fond of novels; (*a habladurías*) gossipy, fond of gossiping

novelesco ADJ **1** (*Literat*) fictional **2** (= *romántico*) romantic, fantastic

novelista SMF novelist

novena SF (*Rel*) novena

noveno ADJ, PRON ninth; *ver tb* **sexto**

noventa ADJ, PRON, SM (*cardinal*) ninety; (*ordinal*) ninetieth; **los (años) ~** the nineties; *ver tb* **seis**

noviar* /1b/ VI **~ con** (*CS*) to go out with, date, court (*frm*)

noviazgo SM relationship

noviciado SM (*Rel*) novitiate

novicio/a SM/F (*Rel*) novice

noviembre SM November; *ver tb* **septiembre**

En inglés los meses se escriben con mayúscula.

novilla SF heifer

novillada SF (*Taur*) training fight (*bullfight with young bulls and novice bullfighters*)

novillero/a SM/F (*Taur*) apprentice bullfighter

novillo SM **1** (*Zool*) young bull, bullock, steer **2** novillos (*Taur*) = **novillada 3** ✦ MODISMO **hacer ~s** (*Escol*) to play truant, play hookey (*esp EEUU**), skive off (*Brit***)

novio/a SM/F (= *amigo*) boyfriend/girlfriend; (= *prometido*) fiancé/fiancée; (*en boda*) (bride)groom/bride; (= *recién casado*) newly-married man/woman; **los ~s** (= *prometidos*) the engaged couple; (*en boda*) the bride and groom; (= *recién casados*) the newly-weds; **ser ~s formales** to be formally engaged

novísimo ADJ newest, latest, most recent

ntro. ABR = **nuestro**

nubarrón SM storm cloud

nube SF **1** (*gen*) cloud ➤ **nube de verano** (*lit*) summer shower; **fue solo una ~ de verano** (*fig*) it was just a passing phase **2** [*de humo, insectos, polvo*] cloud; [*de gente*] crowd, multitude; **una ~ de periodistas** a crowd *o* pack of journalists **3** (*Med*) (*en el ojo*) cloud, film **4** ✦ MODISMOS **estar en las ~s** to have one's head in the clouds; **los precios están por las ~s** prices are sky high; **poner a algn en** *o* **por** *o* **sobre las ~s** to praise sb to the skies; **ponerse por las ~s** [*precio*] to rocket, soar

nublado **A** ADJ [*cielo*] cloudy, overcast **B** SM storm cloud, black cloud

nublar /1a/ VT [+ *vista*] to blur; [+ *mente*] to cloud; [+ *razón*] to affect, cloud; [+ *felicidad*] to cloud, mar **B** **nublarse** VPR to become cloudy, cloud over; **a veces se me nubla la vista** sometimes my vision goes blurred

nubosidad SF cloudiness, clouds *pl*

nuboso ADJ cloudy

nubuck SM nubuck

nuca SF nape of the neck, back of the neck

nuclear **A** ADJ nuclear **B** SF nuclear power station

núcleo SM (*Biol, Fís, Quím*) nucleus; (*Elec*) core; (*Bot*) kernel, stone; (= *esencia*) core, essence ➤ **núcleo de población** population centre, population center (*EEUU*) ➤ **núcleo duro** hard core ➤ **núcleo rural** (new) village, village settlement ➤ **núcleo tormentoso** thunderstorm ➤ **núcleo urbano** city centre, city center (*EEUU*)

nudillo SM knuckle

nudismo SM nudism

nudista SMF nudist

nudo SM **1** (*en hilo, cuerda*) knot; **el ~ de la corbata** the tie knot; **hacerse el ~ de la corbata** to do up one's tie; **✦** MODISMO **un ~ en la garganta** a lump in one's throat ➤ **nudo corredizo** slipknot ➤ **nudo gordiano** Gordian knot ➤ **nudo marinero** reef knot **2** [*de carreteras, ferrocarriles*] junction **3** (*en tallo*) node; (*en madera*) knot

nudoso ADJ [*madera*] knotty; [*tronco*] gnarled; [*bastón*] knobbly, knobby (*EEUU*)

nueces SFPL *de* **nuez**

nuera SF daughter-in-law

nuestro/a Ⓐ ADJ POSES our; (*tras sustantivo*) of ours; **~ perro** our dog; **un amigo ~** a friend of ours Ⓑ PRON POSES ours; **es ~** it's ours; **esta casa es la nuestra** this house is ours; **es el ~** it is ours; **el tenis no nos gusta, lo ~ es el fútbol** we don't like tennis, we're more into football; **no servimos para pintar, lo ~ es la fotografía** we're no good at painting, we're better at photography; **los ~s** (= *nuestra familia*) our people, our family; (*Dep*) (= *nuestro equipo*) our men, our side; **es de los ~s** he's one of ours, he's one of us

> Nuestro se traduce por **ours** y nunca va precedido de artículo cuando se refiere a las posesiones de alguien: "Es (el) nuestro", *It's ours*. En cambio, se traduce por **of ours** cuando significa "uno de los nuestros": "un compañero nuestro", *a colleague of ours*.

nueva SF (= *noticia*) piece of news; **~s** news; **✦** MODISMOS **coger a algn de ~s** to take sb by surprise; **hacerse de ~s** to pretend to be surprised

Nueva Delhi SF New Delhi

Nueva Guinea SF New Guinea

nuevamente ADV again

Nueva Orleans SF New Orleans

Nueva York SF New York

Nueva Zelanda SF, **Nueva Zelandia** (*LAm*) SF New Zealand

nueve ADJ, PRON, SM (*cardinal*) nine; (*ordinal, en la fecha*) ninth; *ver tb* **seis**

nuevo ADJ **1** (= *no usado*) new; **la casa es nueva** the house is new; **la casa está nueva** the house is as good as new; **como ~: con una mano de pintura quedará como ~** it'll look like new after a coat of paint; **después de una buena siesta quedarás como ~** you'll feel like new after a good nap **2** (= *recién llegado*) new; **soy ~ en el colegio** I'm new at the school **3 de ~** (= *otra vez*) again

Nuevo México SM New Mexico

nuez SF **1** [*del nogal*] walnut; (*Méx*) pecan nut ➤ **nuez de Castilla** (*Méx*) walnut ➤ **nuez de la India** (*Méx*) cashew nut ➤ **nuez moscada** nutmeg **2** (*Anat*) (*tb* **~ de Adán**) Adam's apple

nulidad SF **1** (*Jur*) nullity **2** (= *incapacidad*) incompetence, incapacity **3** (= *persona*) **es una ~** he's a waste of space*, he's a dead loss (*Brit**)

nulo ADJ **1** (*Jur*) void, null, null and void; **el matrimonio fue declarado ~** the marriage was annulled **2** [*persona*] hopeless*; **es ~ para la música** he's hopeless at music* **3** (*en boxeo*) **combate ~** draw

núm. ABR (= **número**) No., no.

numantino ADJ [*resistencia*] heroic, last-ditch; (*pey*) diehard, stubborn

numeración SF **1** (= *acto*) numeration, numbering **2** (= *números*) numbers *pl*, numerals *pl* ➤ **numeración arábiga** Arabic numerals *pl* ➤ **numeración romana** Roman numerals *pl*

numerador SM numerator

numeral Ⓐ ADJ numeral, number *antes de s* Ⓑ SM numeral

numerar /1a/ VT to number

numerario ADJ [*socio, miembro*] full; [*catedrático*] tenured; **profesor ~** permanent member of teaching staff

numérico ADJ numerical

número SM **1** (*Mat*) number; **hacer ~s** to do one's sums, number-crunch; **estar en ~s rojos** to be in the red; **miembro de ~** full member; **problemas sin ~** countless problems ➤ **número arábigo** Arabic numeral ➤ **número cardinal** cardinal number ➤ **número de identificación fiscal** ID number used for tax purposes ➤ **número de teléfono** telephone number, phone number ➤ **número dos** number two; **el ~ dos del partido** the second in command of the party, the number two in the party ➤ **número entero** whole number ➤ **número fraccionario** fraction ➤ **número impar** odd number ➤ **número ordinal** ordinal number ➤ **número par** even number ➤ **número primo** prime number ➤ **número romano** Roman numeral ➤ **número uno** number one; **el jugador ~ uno de su país** the number one player in his country, the top player in his country **2** [*de zapatos*] size **3** [*de periódico, revista*] number, issue ➤ **número atrasado** back number ➤ **número cero** dummy number, dummy run ➤ **número extraordinario** special edition, special issue ➤ **número suelto** single issue **4** (= *billete de lotería*) ticket **5** (*Teat*) act, number; **✦** MODISMO **montar el o un ~*** to make a scene, kick up a fuss **6** (*Gram*) number **7** (*Mil*) man; **un sargento y cuatro ~s** a sergeant and four men

numeroso ADJ numerous; **familia numerosa** large family

numerus clausus SM *system of restricted entry (to university etc)*, quota system

numismática SF numismatics *sing*

numismático/a Ⓐ ADJ numismatic Ⓑ SM/F numismatist

núms. ABR (= **números**) Nos., nos.

nunca ADV (*en frases afirmativas*) never; (*en frases negativas, interrogativas y en comparaciones*) ever; **no viene ~** he never comes; **ninguno de nosotros había esquiado ~** none of us had ever skied before; **casi ~ me escribe** he hardly ever writes to me; **~ más: no lo hizo ~ más** he never did it again; **no lo veré ~ más** I'll never see him again; **✦** REFRÁN **~ es tarde si la dicha es buena** better late than never

nunciatura SF nunciature

nuncio SM (*Rel*) nuncio ➤ **nuncio apostólico, nuncio pontificio** papal nuncio

nupcial ADJ wedding *antes de s*, nuptial (*frm*)

nupcias SFPL **casarse en segundas ~** to get married for the second time, remarry

nutria SF **1** (*carnívoro*) otter **2** (*CS*) (*roedor*) coypu

nutrición SF nutrition

nutricional ADJ nutritional

nutricionista SMF nutritionist

nutrido ADJ **1** (= *alimentado*) **bien ~** well-nourished; **mal ~** undernourished, malnourished **2** (= *grande*) large, considerable; **una nutrida concurrencia** a large crowd, a large attendance; **~s aplausos** enthusiastic applause

nutriente SM nutrient

nutrir /3a/ Ⓐ VT **1** (= *alimentar*) to feed, nourish **2** [+ *confianza, relaciones*] strengthen Ⓑ VPR **nutrirse 1** (= *alimentarse*) to receive nourishment **2** (= *fortalecerse*) to feed (**de** on) **3** (= *abastecerse*) **el lago del que se nutría el río** the lake which fed the river

nutritivo ADJ nutritious, nourishing; **valor ~** nutritional value, food value

nylon ['nailon] SM nylon

Ññ

Ñ, ñ ['eɲe] SF (= *letra*) Ñ, ñ

ña* SF (*LAm*) = **doña**

ñaca-ñaca** SM hanky-panky*

ñam* EXCL ¡**ñam ñam!** yum yum!*

ñame SM yam

ñandú SM South American ostrich, rhea

ñandutí SM Paraguayan lace

ñango* ADJ (*Méx*) awkward, clumsy

ñapa SF (*LAm*) (= *prima*) extra, bonus; (= *propina*) tip; **de ~** as an extra

ñata* SF (*LAm*), **ñatas*** SFPL (*LAm*) nose, conk (*Brit**), beak (*EEUU**)

ñato ADJ (*SAm*) flat-nosed, snub-nosed

ñeque* SM (*And, Ven*) strength

ño* SM (*LAm*) = **don²**

ñoco ADJ (*Col, Ven*) (= *sin un dedo*) lacking a finger; (= *manco*) one-handed

ñoña*** SF (*Chi, Ecu, Ven*) shit***; *ver tb* **ñoño**

ñoñería SF, **ñoñez** SF 1 (= *sosería*) insipidness 2 (= *falta de carácter*) spinelessness; (= *melindres*) fussiness

ñoño/a Ⓐ ADJ 1 (= *soso*) characterless, insipid 2 [*persona*] (= *débil*) spineless; (= *melindroso*) fussy, finicky Ⓑ SM/F spineless person, drip*; *ver tb* **ñoña**

ñoqui SM 1 **ñoquis** (*Culin*) gnocchi 2 (*RPl**) (= *golpe*) thump

ñorbo SM (*And*) passionflower

ñu SM gnu

O¹, o [o] SF (= *letra*) O, o

O² ABR (= **oeste**) W

o CONJ or; **o ... o** either ... or

ó CONJ or; **5 ó 6** 5 or 6

oasis SM INV oasis

obcecación SF (= *ofuscación*) blindness; (= *terquedad*) blind obstinacy; **en un momento de ~** in a moment of blind rage

obcecado ADJ (= *ofuscado*) blind, mentally blinded; (= *terco*) obstinate, stubborn, obdurate (*frm*)

obcecarse /1g/ VPR to become obsessed; **~ con una idea** to become obsessed with an idea

obedecer /2d/ Ⓐ VT [+ *persona, norma*] to obey Ⓑ VI 1 [*persona*] to obey 2 [*mecanismo*] to respond; **el volante no me obedecía** the steering wheel did not respond 3 (= *deberse*) **~ a algo** to be due to sth; **su viaje obedece a dos motivos** there are two reasons for his journey, his journey is due to two reasons

obediencia SF obedience

obediente ADJ obedient

obelisco SM obelisk

obertura SF overture

obesidad SF obesity

obeso ADJ obese

óbice SM (*frm*) obstacle

obispado SM bishopric

obispo SM bishop

obituario SM obituary

objeción SF objection; **poner objeciones** to object, make objections ➤ **objeción de conciencia** conscientious objection

objetar /1a/ Ⓐ VT (*gen*) to object; **¿algo que ~?** any objections?; **le objeté que no había dinero suficiente** I pointed out to him that there was not enough money Ⓑ VI (*Mil*) to be a conscientious objector

objetivamente ADV objectively

objetividad SF objectivity

objetivo Ⓐ ADJ objective Ⓑ SM 1 (= *propósito*) objective, aim 2 (*Mil*) objective, target 3 (*Fot*) lens

objeto SM 1 (= *cosa*) object; **~s perdidos** lost property, lost and found (*EEUU*) ➤ **objetos de valor** valuables ➤ **objeto sexual** sex object ➤ **objeto volante no identificado** unidentified flying object 2 (= *propósito*) object, aim; **al** o **con ~ de hacer algo** with the object o aim of doing sth

> Recuérdese que las preposiciones en inglés rigen gerundio y no infinitivo, de ahí **with the object** o **aim of doing sth.**

estas medidas tienen por ~ reducir la inflación the aim of these measures is to reduce inflation 3 (= *blanco*) object; **fue ~ de sus burlas** she was the butt of their jokes 4 (*Ling*) object ➤ **objeto directo** direct object ➤ **objeto indirecto** indirect object

objetor(a) SM/F objector ➤ **objetor(a) de conciencia** conscientious objector

oblea SF (= *galleta*) wafer-thin slice; (*Rel*) wafer

oblicuo ADJ [*línea*] oblique; [*ojos*] slanting; [*mirada*] sidelong

obligación SF 1 (= *responsabilidad*) obligation, duty; **cumplir con una ~** to fulfil o (*EEUU*) fulfill an obligation; **tener ~ de hacer algo** to have a duty to do sth, be under an obligation to do sth 2 (*Com, Fin*) bond, security

obligado ADJ 1 (= *forzado*) **no estás ~ a dar dinero** you don't have to give any money, you're not obliged to give any money; **sentirse ~ a hacer algo** to feel obliged to do sth; **verse ~ a hacer algo** to be forced to do sth 2 (= *obligatorio*) **normas de ~ cumplimiento** regulations that must be complied with 3 (= *inexcusable*) **este museo es visita obligada para el amante del arte** this museum is a must for the art lover

obligar /1h/ Ⓐ VT 1 (= *forzar*) to force; **~ a algn a hacer algo** to force sb to do sth; **la obligan a estudiar francés** they make her study French 2 [*ley, norma*] **la disposición obliga a todos los contribuyentes** all taxpayers are bound by this requirement 3 (= *empujar*) to force; **sólo se puede cerrar el cajón obligándolo** you can't get the drawer shut except by forcing it Ⓑ **obligarse** VPR **tengo que ~me a ir al gimnasio cada día** I have to force myself to go to the gym every day

obligatorio ADJ obligatory, compulsory; **es ~ hacerlo** it is obligatory to do it; **escolaridad obligatoria** compulsory schooling

obnubilar /1a/ VT = **ofuscar A2**

oboe SM oboe

obra SF 1 (= *acción*) deed; **pecar de ~** to sin by deed; **buenas ~s** good works, good deeds; **ser ~ de algn** to be sb's doing; **esto no puede ser ~ de mi hijo** this can't be my son's doing; **la policía cree que podría ser ~ de la Mafia** the police think this could be the work of the Mafia; **por ~ (y gracia) de** thanks to; **un país destrozado por ~ del turismo** a country totally spoilt by tourism; ✦ MODISMO **ser ~ de romanos** to be a huge task, be a herculean task ➤ **obra benéfica** (= *acción*) charitable deed; (= *organización*) charitable organization, charity; **el dinero se destinará a ~s benéficas** the money will go to charity ➤ **obra de caridad** charitable deed, act of charity ➤ **obra de misericordia** (*Rel*) work of mercy ➤ **obra social** (= *organización*) benevolent fund for arts, sports etc; (= *labor*) charitable work 2 [*de creación artística*] 2.1 (= *producción total*) (*Arte, Literat, Teat, Mús*) work; **el tema de la muerte en la ~ de Lorca** the subject of death in Lorca o in Lorca's work 2.2 (= *pieza*) (*Arte, Mús*) work; (*Teat*) play; (*Literat*) book, work; **~s completas** complete works, collected works ➤ **obra de arte** work of art ➤ **obra de consulta** reference book ➤ **obra de divulgación** *non-fiction book aimed at a popular audience* ➤ **obra de teatro**, **obra dramática** play ➤ **obra maestra** masterpiece ➤ **obra teatral** play 3 (*Constr*) 3.1 = *edificio en construcción*) building site, construction site; **hemos estado visitando la ~** we've been visiting the building o construction site; **¿cuándo acaban la ~?** when do they finish the building work?; ✦ MODISMO **ser** o **parecer la ~ del Escorial** to be a never-ending job 3.2 **de ~** [*chimenea*] brick *antes de s*; [*estantería, armario*] built-in 3.3 **obras** (*en edificio*) building work *sing*, construction work *sing*; (*en carretera*) roadworks; **las ~s de remodelación del estadio** redevelopment work at the stadium; **los vecinos están de ~s** they're having building work done next door, they have the builders in next door*; **"obras"** (*en edificio*) "building under construction"; (*en carretera*) "roadworks"; **"cerrado por obras"** "closed for refurbishment"; **"página en obras"** (*Internet*) "site under construction"; **la autopista está en ~s** there are roadworks on the motorway ➤ **obras públicas** public works 4 (= *ejecución*) workmanship; **la ~ es buena pero los materiales son de mala calidad** the workmanship is good but the materials are of a poor quality; ✦ MODISMO **poner manos a la ~** to get down to work 5 (*Chi*) brickwork 6 **la Obra** (*Esp Rel*) Opus Dei; ⇨ *OPUS DEI*

obrador SM [*de pastelería*] bakery

obraje SM (*CS*) sawmill, timberyard

obrar /1a/ Ⓐ VI 1 (= *actuar*) to act; **~on correctamente** they acted correctly 2 (= *tener efecto*) [*medicinas*] to work, have an effect 3 (*frm*) (= *estar*) **~ en manos** o **en poder de algn** to be in sb's possession Ⓑ VT (*frm*) [+ *mejoría*] to make; [+ *milagro*] to work

obrero/a Ⓐ ADJ [clase] working; [barrio, familia] working-class; [movimiento] labour antes de s, labor antes de s (EEUU) Ⓑ SM/F (= empleado) worker; (= peón) labourer, laborer (EEUU) ➤ **obrero/a calificado/a** (LAm) skilled worker ➤ **obrero/a especializado/a** skilled worker ➤ **obrero/a portuario/a** dock worker

obscenidad SF obscenity

obsceno ADJ obscene

obscu... ver **oscu...**

obsequiar /1b/ VT (frm) **le ~on con un reloj** (Esp) ⬧ **le ~on un reloj** (LAm) they presented him with a watch, they gave him a watch

obsequio SM (= regalo) gift, present; (Com) free gift; **ejemplar de ~** complimentary copy

obsequioso ADJ deferential, obliging

observación SF 1 (= acto) observation; **estar en ~** to be under observation 2 (= comentario) remark, comment, observation; **hacer una ~** to make a remark o comment o observation, comment

observador(a) Ⓐ ADJ observant Ⓑ SM/F observer ➤ **observador(a) extranjero/a** foreign observer

observancia SF observance

observar /1a/ VT 1 (= mirar) to observe, watch 2 (= notar) to see, notice; **se observa una mejoría** you can see o detect an improvement 3 [+ leyes] to observe; [+ reglas] to abide by, adhere to; ~ **buena conducta** to behave o.s.

observatorio SM observatory ➤ **observatorio meteorológico** weather station

obsesión SF obsession

obsesionar /1a/ Ⓐ VT [recuerdo] to haunt; [manía, afición] to obsess; **estar obsesionado con** o **por algo** to be obsessed by sth Ⓑ **obsesionarse** VPR to get obsessed

obsesivo ADJ obsessive

obseso ADJ obsessed

obsoleto ADJ obsolete

obstaculizar /1f/ VT [+ negociaciones, progreso] to hinder, hamper; [+ tráfico] to hold up

obstáculo SM 1 (físico) obstacle 2 (= dificultad) obstacle, hindrance; **no es ~ para que yo lo haga** that does not prevent me (from) o stop me doing it; **poner ~s a algo/algn** to hinder sth/sb

obstante: **no ~** ADV nevertheless, however

obstetra SMF obstetrician

obstetricia SF obstetrics sing

obstinación SF obstinacy, stubbornness

obstinado ADJ obstinate, stubborn

obstinarse /1a/ VPR to dig one's heels in*; ~ **en hacer algo** to persist in doing sth, insist on doing sth

> Recuérdese que las preposiciones en inglés rigen gerundio y no infinitivo, de ahí **to persist in doing sth** y **to insist on doing sth**.

obstrucción SF obstruction

obstruir /3g/ VT 1 (= bloquear) [+ carretera, vena] to obstruct; [+ desagüe, tubería] to block, clog 2 [+ desarrollo, proceso] to hinder, hamper, hold up

obtención SF **el único requisito que se exige para la ~ del permiso** the only requirement for obtaining the permit; **las ventas de acciones orientadas a la ~ rápida de beneficios** the sale of shares with a view to receiving a quick return

obtener /2k/ VT [+ resultado, información, permiso] to get, obtain; [+ mayoría, votos] to win, obtain; [+ premio, medalla, victoria] to win; [+ apoyo] to gain, get, obtain; [+ beneficios] to make; **esperamos ~ mejores resultados este año** we are hoping to get o obtain o achieve better results this year; **ambos obtuvieron el premio Nobel** they both won the Nobel prize; **el equipo español confía en ~ la victoria** the Spanish team is confident of victory; **la empresa está obteniendo grandes beneficios** the company is

making large profits

obturación SF **velocidad de ~** (Fot) shutter speed

obturador SM (Fot) shutter

obtuso ADJ 1 (Mat) obtuse 2 (de mente, entendimiento) obtuse

obús SM (= cañón) howitzer; (= proyectil) shell

obviamente ADV obviously

obviar /1c/ VT 1 (= evitar) to obviate, get around, avoid; ~ **un problema** to get around a problem 2 (= no mencionar) to leave out; **obvió los detalles** he left out the details

obviedad SF **una ~** an obvious remark; **la respuesta parece ser una ~** the answer seems to be obvious

obvio ADJ obvious

oca SF 1 (= ganso) goose 2 **la Oca** (= juego) board game similar to snakes and ladders 3 (= planta andina) oca (root vegetable)

ocarina SF ocarina

ocasión SF 1 (= vez) occasion; **en aquella ~** on that occasion; **en algunas ocasiones** sometimes; **con ~ de** on the occasion of 2 (= oportunidad) chance, opportunity; **una magnífica ~ de gol** a great goal scoring opportunity, a great chance of scoring; **aprovechar la ~** to take one's chance, seize one's opportunity; **dar a algn la ~ de hacer algo** to give sb the chance o opportunity of doing sth 3 **de ~** (Com) secondhand, used; **librería de ~** secondhand bookshop (esp Brit) o bookstore (esp EEUU)

ocasional ADJ 1 (= accidental) chance, accidental 2 (= eventual) [trabajo] casual, temporary; [lluvia, visita, fumador] occasional

ocasionar /1a/ VT to cause; **lamento ~le tantas molestias** I'm sorry to cause you o to be so much trouble

ocaso SM 1 [del sol] sunset, sundown (EEUU); [de astro] setting 2 [de civilización] decline; **en el ~ de su vida** in his declining years, in the twilight of his life (liter)

occidental Ⓐ ADJ western Ⓑ SMF westerner

Occidente SM (Pol) the West, the Western world

occidente SM (= oeste) west

OCDE SF ABR (= **Organización para la Cooperación y el Desarrollo Económico**) OECD

Oceanía SF Oceania

oceánico ADJ oceanic

océano SM ocean ➤ **océano Atlántico** Atlantic Ocean ➤ **océano Glacial Ártico** Arctic Ocean ➤ **océano Índico** Indian Ocean ➤ **océano Pacífico** Pacific Ocean

oceanografía SF oceanography

oceanógrafo/a SM/F oceanographer

ocelote SM ocelot

ochenta ADJ, PRON, SM (cardinal) eighty; (ordinal) eightieth; ver tb **seis**

ocho Ⓐ ADJ, PRON (cardinal) eight; (ordinal, en la fecha) eighth; **dentro de ~ días** within a week Ⓑ SM 1 (= número) eight; ver tb **seis** 2 ochos (Cos) cable stitch sing

ochocientos ADJ, PRON, SM (cardinal) eight hundred; (ordinal) eight hundredth; ver tb **seiscientos**

ocio SM 1 (= tiempo libre) leisure; **ratos de ~** leisure time, spare time, free time; **guía del ~** what's on 2 (= inactividad) idleness

ocioso ADJ 1 [persona] idle 2 (= inútil) [acto] useless, pointless; [promesa] idle, empty; **es ~ especular** there is no point in speculating

oclusivo ADJ (Ling) occlusive, plosive

ocote SM ocote pine

ocre SM ochre

octaedro SM octahedron

octagonal ADJ octagonal

octágono SM octagon

octanaje SM octane number; **de alto ~** high-octane antes de s

octano SM octane

octava SF octave

octavilla SF pamphlet, leaflet

octavo Ⓐ ADJ, PRON (= *numeral*) eighth; *ver tb* **sexto**
Ⓑ **octavos** (*tb* **~s de final**) SMPL (*Dep*) round before the quarterfinals

octeto SM octet

octogenario/a ADJ, SM/F octogenarian, eighty-year-old

octogésimo ADJ, PRON eightieth; *ver tb* **sexto**

octubre SM October; *ver tb* **septiembre**

> En inglés los meses se escriben con mayúscula.

ocular Ⓐ ADJ ocular (*frm*), eye *antes de s*; **mediante examen ~** by visual inspection, with the eye Ⓑ SM eyepiece

oculista SMF ophthalmologist

ocultar /1a/ Ⓐ VT to hide (**a, de** from), conceal (**a, de** from) Ⓑ **ocultarse** VPR to hide (o.s.); **~se tras algo** to hide behind sth; **~se a la vista** to keep out of sight

ocultismo SM occultism

oculto ADJ 1 (= *escondido*) hidden, concealed
2 (= *misterioso*) (*gen*) mysterious; [*pensamiento*] inner, secret; [*motivo*] ulterior 3 [*poderes*] occult

ocupa** SMF (*Esp*) squatter

ocupación SF 1 (= *empleo*) (*en general*) employment; (*en concreto*) occupation; **ha bajado el nivel de ~ entre los jóvenes** the level of employment among young people has dropped; **desea volver a su ~ habitual, la enseñanza** he wishes to return to his usual occupation, teaching
2 (= *actividad*) activity; **cuando sus ocupaciones políticas se lo permiten** when his political activities allow it; **abandonaron sus ocupaciones para unirse a la manifestación** they stopped what they were doing to join the march
3 [*de viviendas*] (= *acción*) occupation; (= *nivel de ocupación*) occupancy; **para fomentar la ~ de viviendas rurales** to encourage the occupation of rural dwellings; **la ~ hotelera ha aumentado este año** hotel occupancy has increased this year
4 (*Mil, Pol*) occupation; **las fuerzas de ~** the occupying forces

ocupacional ADJ [*actividad, taller, terapia*] occupational; **formación ~** job training

ocupado ADJ 1 [*sitio, asiento, plaza*] taken; [*habitación*] taken, occupied; [*retrete*] engaged; **¿está ocupada esta silla?** is this seat taken?; **¿está ~ el baño?** is the toilet occupied *o* engaged?; **"ocupado"** "engaged"
2 (*Telec*) busy, engaged (*Brit*); **la línea está ocupada** the line is busy *o* (*Brit*) engaged; **da señal de ~** the line is busy *o* (*Brit*) engaged, I'm getting the busy (*esp EEUU*) *o* engaged (*Brit*) signal
3 (*Pol, Mil*) [*territorio, país*] occupied
4 [*persona*] 4.1 (= *atareado*) busy (**con** with); **estoy muy ~** I'm very busy; **tenía las dos manos ocupadas** my hands were full, I had my hands full 4.2 (= *empleado*) in work, working; **la población ocupada** the working population

ocupante SMF 1 [*de vehículo*] occupant; [*de vivienda*] occupant, occupier; **~s ilegales de viviendas** squatters
2 (*Pol, Mil*) [*de país*] occupier

ocupar /1a/ Ⓐ VT 1 [+ *espacio*] to take up; **la noticia ocupaba dos páginas del periódico** the story took up two pages in the newspaper; **el espacio que ocupaba el antiguo museo** the site of the old museum
2 [+ *posición*] **ocupan el puesto número diez en la clasificación** they are tenth *o* they are in tenth place in the league table; **vuelvan a ~ sus asientos** go back to your seats
3 [+ *puesto, cargo*] to hold; [+ *vacante*] to fill, the person who held the post before her; **ocupa un escaño en el parlamento desde 1998** he has held a seat in parliament since 1998; **~á su escaño el próximo mes** he will take his seat next month; **él ocupó el puesto que quedó vacante** he filled the position left vacant

4 (*Mil, Pol*) [+ *ciudad, país*] to occupy; **los obreros ~on la fábrica** the workers occupied the factory
5 (= *habitar*) [+ *vivienda*] to live in, occupy; [+ *local*] to occupy; **la vivienda que ocupan desde hace dos años** the house they have been living in *o* have occupied for the last two years; **los jóvenes que ~on la vivienda abandonada** the youths that squatted *o* occupied the empty building
6 [+ *tiempo*] [*labor, acción*] take up; [*persona*] to spend; **las labores de la casa me ocupan mucho tiempo** the housework takes up a lot of my time; **no sabe en qué ~ su tiempo libre** he doesn't know how to fill *o* spend his spare time
7 (= *dar trabajo a*) to employ; **la agricultura ocupa a un 10% de la población** 10% of the population is employed in agriculture, agriculture employs 10% of the working population
8 (= *concernir*) **pero, volviendo al tema que nos ocupa ...** however, returning to the subject under discussion ..., however, returning to the subject we are concerned with *o* that concerns us ...
Ⓑ **ocuparse** VPR 1 **~se de** (*como profesión, obligación*) to deal with; **no se ocupan de cuestiones económicas** they do not deal with economic matters; **ella es quien se ocupó de los detalles de la boda** it was she who took care of *o* saw to the details of the wedding
2 **~se de** (*por interés*) to take an interest in; **me ocupo muy poco de las tareas domésticas** I don't bother much with *o* about the housework, I take very little interest in the housework; **¡tú ocúpate de lo tuyo!** mind your own business!
3 **~se de** [+ *enfermo, niños*] to take care of, look after; [+ *enemigo*] to take care of
4 **~se de** (= *tratar de*): **el libro se ocupa de los aspectos económicos de la crisis** the book deals with the economic aspects of the crisis; **nos ocupamos ahora de la información deportiva** (*Radio, TV*) and now a look at today's sports

ocurrencia SF 1 (= *idea*) idea; **tuvo una ~ genial** he had a brilliant idea; **¡vaya ~!** (*iró*) what a bright idea! 2 (= *dicho gracioso*) funny remark; **tiene unas ~s divertidísimas** he comes out with the funniest remarks

ocurrente ADJ 1 (= *chistoso*) witty 2 (= *gracioso*) entertaining, amusing

ocurrir /3a/ Ⓐ VI to happen; **lo que ocurrió podría haberse evitado** what happened could have been avoided; **¿qué ocurre?** what's going on?; **¿qué te ocurre?** what's the matter?; **lo que ocurre es que ...** the thing is ...
Ⓑ **ocurrirse** VPR **se nos ocurrió una idea buenísima** we had a brilliant idea; **¿se te ocurre algo?** can you think of anything?; **¡ni se te ocurra (hacerlo)!** don't even think about (doing) it!; **si se le ocurre huir** if he takes it into his head to escape; **¿cómo no se te ocurrió pensar que ...?** didn't it cross your mind that ...?; **¿a quién se le ocurre presentarse a medianoche?** who in their right mind would turn up in the middle of the night?

oda SF ode

ODECA SF ABR (= **Organización de los Estados Centroamericanos**) OCAS

odiar /1b/ VT 1 (= *sentir odio por*) to hate 2 (*Chi*) (= *molestar*) to pester, annoy

odio SM 1 (*gen*) hatred; **tener ~ a algn** to hate sb 2 (*Chi*) (= *molestia*) nuisance, bother

odioso ADJ 1 (= *detestable*) odious, hateful 2 (= *repelente*) nasty, unpleasant; **hacerse ~ a algn** to become a nuisance to sb

odisea SF odyssey

odontología SF dentistry, odontology

odontólogo/a SM/F dentist, dental surgeon, odontologist

odre SM wineskin

OEA SF ABR (= **Organización de Estados Americanos**) OAS

OECE SF ABR (= **Organización Europea de Cooperación Económica**) OEEC

oeste Ⓐ ADJ [*región, orilla*] western; [*costa*] west; [*dirección*] westerly; [*viento*] west, westerly Ⓑ SM 1 (= *punto cardinal*)

el Oeste the West, the west **2** [*de región, país*] west; **una película del Oeste** a western **3** (*Meteo*) (*tb* **viento del ~**) west wind; *ver tb* **sur**

ofender /2a/ **Ⓐ** VT **1** (= *agraviar*) to offend; **perdona si te he ofendido** I'm sorry if I've offended you; **(dicho) sin ánimo de ~** no offence meant; **no ofendas la memoria de tu madre** don't insult your mother's memory **2** [+ *sentido*] to offend, be offensive to; **~ a la vista** to offend the eye **Ⓑ** ofenderse VPR to take offence *o* (*EEUU*) offense; **no te ofendas por lo que te voy a decir** don't be offended by what I'm going to tell you

ofendido ADJ offended; **darse por ~** to take offence *o* (*EEUU*) offense

ofensa SF offence, offense (*EEUU*)

ofensiva SF offensive; **pasar a la ~** to go on the offensive ➤ **ofensiva de paz** peace offensive

ofensivo ADJ **1** (= *de ataque*) (*tb Mil*) offensive **2** [*conducta, palabra*] offensive, rude, insulting

oferta SF **1** (= *ofrecimiento*) offer **2** (*Com*) (*gen*) offer; (*para contrato, concurso*) tender; (= *ganga*) special offer; **estar de** *o* **en ~** to be on offer ➤ **oferta pública de adquisición (de acciones)** takeover bid ➤ **oferta pública de venta (de acciones)** share offer ➤ **ofertas de trabajo** (*en periódico*) situations vacant (*Brit*), job openings (*EEUU*) **3** (*Econ*) supply; **la ley de la ~ y la demanda** the law of supply and demand

ofertar /1a/ VT **1** (*esp LAm*) (= *ofrecer*) [+ *suma de dinero, producto*] to offer **2** (*Com*) (*en concurso*) to tender **3** (= *ofrecer barato*) to sell on special offer

ofertorio SM offertory

off [of] SM **en ~** (*Cine*) off-screen

oficial Ⓐ ADJ **1** [*viaje, documento, comunicado*] official **Ⓑ** SMF (*a veces* SF **~a**) **1** (*Mil*) officer **2** (= *obrero*) (*en fábrica*) skilled worker; (*en taller artesano*) craftsman/craftswoman; (*por cuenta ajena*) journeyman; (*en oficina*) clerk ➤ **oficial mayor** head clerk, chief clerk (*esp Brit*)

oficialista ADJ (*LAm*) [*prensa*] pro-government; **el candidato ~** the ruling *o* governing party candidate

oficializar /1f/ VT to make official, give official status to

oficialmente ADV officially

oficiante SM (*Rel*) celebrant, officiant

oficiar /1b/ **Ⓐ** VT [+ *misa*] to celebrate; [+ *funeral, boda*] to conduct, officiate at **Ⓑ** VI (*Rel*) to officiate

oficina SF **1** (= *despacho*) office; **horas de ~** office hours ➤ **oficina de empleo** job centre, employment office (*EEUU*) ➤ **oficina de información** information bureau ➤ **oficina de objetos perdidos** lost property office, lost-and-found department (*EEUU*) ➤ **oficina de prensa** press office **2** (*Chi Min*) nitrate works *sing*

oficinista SMF office worker, clerk

oficio SM **1** (= *profesión*) trade; **aprender un ~** to learn a trade; **sabe su ~** he knows his job; **los deberes del ~** the duties of the post; **mi ~ es enseñar** my job is to teach; **tiene mucho ~** he is very experienced; **✦** MODISMO **sin ~ ni beneficio: un pobre temporero sin ~ ni beneficio** just a poor seasonal worker without a penny to his name; **se encontró sin ~ ni beneficio** he found himself with no means of earning a living **2** (*Rel*) service, mass ➤ **oficio de difuntos** funeral service, mass for the dead, office for the dead **3 Santo Oficio** (*Hist*) Holy Office, Inquisition **4 buenos ~s** good offices; **ofrecer sus buenos ~s** to offer one's good offices

oficiosamente ADV unofficially

oficioso ADJ unofficial, informal; **de fuente oficiosa** from an unofficial source

ofimática SF office automation, office computerization

ofimático ADJ **sistema ~** office computer system; **gestión ofimática integrada** integrated computer system for office management

ofrecer /2d/ **Ⓐ** VT **1** (= *presentar voluntariamente*) **1.1** [+ *servicios, ayuda, dinero*] to offer; **me ofrecieron la posibilidad de trabajar para ellos** they offered me the chance to work for them; **¿cuánto te ofrecieron por el coche?** how much did they offer you for the car? **1.2** [+ *espectáculo, programa*] (*en TV*) to show; **varias cadenas ofrecen el partido en directo** several channels are showing the match live; **los principales espectáculos que ofrece el festival** the main events featured in the festival **1.3** (*frm*) [+ *respetos*] to pay (*frm*) **2** (= *tener*) [+ *ventaja*] to offer; [+ *oportunidad, garantías*] to offer, give; [+ *solución*] to offer, provide; [+ *dificultad*] to present; **no ofrece las suficientes garantías** it's not sufficiently reliable; **la gravedad del caso no ofrece duda** there is no doubt about the seriousness of the case; **el ladrón no ofreció resistencia** the burglar did not put up a struggle, the burglar offered no resistance (*frm*); **el palacio abandonado ofrecía un aspecto desolador** the deserted palace looked depressingly bleak **3** (= *celebrar*) [+ *acto, fiesta, cena*] to hold, give; **un portavoz ofreció una rueda de prensa** a spokesman gave *o* held a press conference **4** [+ *sacrificio, víctima*] to offer up **Ⓑ** ofrecerse VPR **1** [*persona*] **un joven se ofreció como guía** a young man offered to act as a guide; **la vecina se ha ofrecido para cualquier cosa que necesitemos** the woman next door offered to help us in any way she could; **"profesor de inglés se ofrece para dar clases particulares"** "English teacher offers private tuition"; **~se (como) voluntario** to volunteer (**a** for) **2 ofrecérsele a algn** [*oportunidad*] to offer itself (to sb), present itself (to sb); [*obstáculo, dificultad*] to present itself (to sb); **se le ofreció una maravillosa oportunidad** a wonderful opportunity offered *o* presented itself (to him); **se le ofrece ahora la oportunidad de demostrar su valía** he has now been given *o* he now has the opportunity to prove himself **3** (*frm*) (= *desear*) **¿qué se le ofrece?** what can I do for you? *o* what would you like?; **¿se le ofrece algo?** is there anything I can do for you?

ofrecimiento SM offer

ofrenda SF (= *tributo*) tribute; (*Rel*) offering ➤ **ofrenda floral** floral tribute

oftalmología SF ophthalmology

oftalmólogo/a SM/F ophthalmologist

ofuscación SF (*al pensar*) bewilderment, confusion; (*al actuar*) blindness

ofuscar /1g/ **Ⓐ** VT **1** [*luz*] to dazzle **2** [+ *persona*] (= *confundir*) to bewilder, confuse; (= *cegar*) to blind; **estar ofuscado por la cólera** to be blinded by rage **Ⓑ** ofuscarse VPR **~se por algo** to be blinded by sth

Ogino SM **método ~** rhythm method (*of birth-control*)

ogro SM ogre

oída SF **de** *o* **por ~s** by *o* from hearsay

oído SM **1** (*Anat*) ear; **decirle algo a algn al ~** to whisper sth to sb, whisper sth in sb's ear; **✦** MODISMOS **dar ~s a algo** (= *escuchar*) to listen; (= *creer*) to believe sth; **entra por un ~ y sale por otro** it goes in one ear and out (of) the other; **llegar a ~s de algn** to come to sb's attention; **prestar ~s a algo** to pay attention to sth, take heed of sth; **ser todo ~s** to be all ears; **hacer ~s sordos a algo** to turn a deaf ear to sth ➤ **oído externo** external ear ➤ **oído interno** inner ear ➤ **oído medio** middle ear **2** (= *sentido*) (sense of) hearing; **duro de ~** hard of hearing; **tiene un ~ muy fino** he has a very keen sense of hearing **3** (*Mús*) ear; **tocar de ~** to play by ear; **tener (buen) ~** to have a good ear

oigo etc ver **oír**

oír /3p/ **Ⓐ** VT **1** [+ *sonidos*] to hear; **¿me oyes bien desde tu habitación?** can you hear me all right from your room?; **lo oí abrir la puerta** I heard him open the door, I heard him opening the door; **¡no me digas!** really!; **~ hablar de algn** to hear about *o* of sb; **he oído decir que ...** I've heard it said that ..., rumour *o* (*EEUU*) rumor has it that ...; **✦** MODISMOS **lo oyó como quien oye llover** she paid no attention, she turned a deaf ear to it; **¡me van a ~!** they'll be having a few words from me! **2** (= *escuchar*) to listen to; **no han querido ~ nuestras quejas** they didn't want to listen to our complaints **3** [+ *misa*] to attend, hear

4 [+ *confesión*] to hear

5 [+ *ruego*] to heed, answer; **¡Dios te oiga!** I just hope you're right!

B VI **1** (= *percibir sonidos*) ~ **mal** (= *ser medio sordo*) to be hard of hearing; (*al teléfono*) to be unable to hear (properly) **2** ~ **de algn** (*LAm*) to hear from sb

3 (*en exclamaciones*) **¡oye, que te dejas el cambio!** hey, you've forgotten your change!; **oiga, ¿es usted el encargado?** excuse me, are you in charge?; **¡oye, que yo no he dicho eso!** hold on a minute *o* just a minute, that's not what I said!; **¿oiga?** (*Telec*) hello?

OIT SF ABR (= **Oficina** *u* **Organización Internacional del Trabajo**) ILO

ojal SM buttonhole

ojalá **A** EXCL —**mañana puede que haga sol** —**¡ojalá!** "it might be sunny tomorrow" — "I hope so!" *o* "I hope it will be!"; —**¿te darán el trabajo?** —**¡ojalá!** "will you get the job?" — "let's hope so!" **B** CONJ **¡~ venga pronto!** I hope he comes soon!; **¡~ que gane la carrera!** let's hope she wins the race!; **¡~ pudiera!** I wish I could!; **¡~ pudiera andar de nuevo!** if only he could walk again!

ojeada SF glance; **echar una ~ a algo** to glance at sth, take a quick look at sth

ojeras SFPL (= *sombras*) (dark) rings around the eyes; (= *bolsas*) bags under the eyes

ojeriza SF **tener ~ a algn** to have a grudge against sb, have it in for sb*

ojeroso ADJ haggard; **estar ~** to have bags under the eyes

ojete[1] SM **1** (*Cos*) eyelet **2** (***) (= *ano*) arsehole (*Brit***), asshole (*esp EEUU***) **3** (*RPl***) **tener ~** to be fucking lucky***

ojete[2]**/a*** (*Méx*) **A** ADJ (= *cobarde*) yellow-bellied** **B** SM/F (= *cobarde*) fucking coward***; (= *malo*) bastard***

ojival ADJ ogival, pointed

ojo SM **1** (*Anat*) eye; **✦** MODISMOS **a ~: calcular algo a ~ (de buen cubero)** to calculate sth roughly, make a rough guess at sth; **échala a ~** just add roughly the right amount; **abrirle los ~s a algn** to open sb's eyes; **en un abrir y cerrar de ~s** in the twinkling of an eye; **mirar** *o* **ver algo con buenos ~s** to look kindly on sth, approve of sth; **con los ~s cerrados** ◇ **a ~s cerrados** without a second thought; **lo aceptaría con los ~s cerrados** I'd accept it without a second thought; **cerrar los ~s a** *o* **ante algo** to shut one's eyes to sth; **tener ~ clínico** to have good intuition; **costar un ~ de la cara*** to cost an arm and a leg*; **ser el ~ derecho de algn** to be the apple of sb's eye; **echar un ~ a algo/algn** to keep an eye on sth/sb; **tener el ~ echado a algn/algo** to have one's eye on sb/sth; **engordar el ~** (*Chi**) to eye up the talent**; **mirar** *o* **ver algo con malos ~s** to disapprove of sth; **no pegar ~: no pegué ~ en toda la noche** I didn't get a wink of sleep all night; **ponersele a algn los ~s como platos** to be wide-eyed with amazement; **no quitar ~ a algo/algn** not to take one's eyes off sth/sb; **salir de ~** to be obvious; **tener (buen) ~ para algo** to have a good eye for sth, be a good judge of sth; **a ~s vistas** visibly; **✦** REFRANES **~ por ~, (diente por diente)** an eye for an eye, (a tooth for a tooth); **~s que no ven, corazón que no siente** out of sight, out of mind ➤ **ojo a la funerala** (*Esp**) ➤ **ojo a la virulé** (*Esp**) shiner* ➤ **ojo amoratado** black eye ➤ **ojo en compota** (*CS**) shiner*

2 ojos (= *vista*) **paseó los ~s por la sala** he looked around the hall; **torcer los ~s** to squint; **✦** MODISMOS **a los ~s de algn** in sb's eyes; **clavar los ~s en algo/algn** to fix one's gaze on sth/sb, stare at sth/sb; **comerse** *o* **devorar a algn con los ~s** (*con deseo*) to devour sb with one's eyes; (*con ira*) to look daggers at sb; **entrar por los ~s** [*comida*] to look mouth-watering; [*imagen, objeto*] to look wonderful; **irse los ~s tras algo/algn: se le fueron los ~s tras la chica** he couldn't keep his eyes off the girl

3 (= *cuidado*) **¡ojo!** careful, look out!; **~ con el escalón** mind the step; **ir con ~** to keep one's eyes open for trouble

4 (= *orificio*) [*de aguja*] eye; [*de queso*] hole; [*de puente*] span; **el ~ de la cerradura** the keyhole; **un puente de cuatro ~s** a bridge with four arches *o* spans ➤ **ojo de buey** (*Náut*) porthole ➤ **ojo del culo*** hole**, arsehole (*Brit***), asshole (*esp EEUU***) ➤ **ojo del huracán** eye of the hurricane; **el presidente vuelve a estar en el ~ del huracán** the president

is once again at the centre *o* (*EEUU*) center of a controversy

5 (*LAm*) ➤ **ojo de agua** pool, natural pool

ojota SF (*LAm*) flip-flop (*esp Brit*), thong (*EEUU*)

okey EXCL (*esp LAm*) okay!*, OK!*

okupa** SMF (*Esp*) squatter

ola SF [*de mar*] wave; **la ~** (*en un estadio*) the Mexican wave; **✦** MODISMO **la nueva ~** the new wave ➤ **ola de calor** heat wave ➤ **ola de frío** cold spell, cold snap

olán SM (*Méx*) frill

olé EXCL bravo!

oleada SF **1** (*Náut*) big wave **2** (= *gran cantidad*) [*de atentados, huelgas*] spate; **una gran ~ de gente** a great surge of people

oleaginosa SF oil product

oleaginoso ADJ oily, oleaginous (*frm*)

oleaje SM swell, surge

óleo SM **1** (*gen*) oil; **santo(s) ~(s)** (*Rel*) holy oil(s) **2** (*Arte*) oil painting; **pintar al ~** to paint in oils

oleoducto SM pipeline, oil pipeline

oler /2i/ **A** VT **1** (= *percibir por la nariz*) to smell; **me gusta ~ las flores** I like smelling the flowers

2 (*) (= *sospechar*) to suspect; **ha olido lo que estás tramando** he suspects what you're up to, he's smelt a rat*

3 (*) (= *curiosear*) to poke one's nose into*; **siempre anda oliendo lo que hacen los demás** he's always poking his nose into other people's business*

B VI **1** (= *despedir olor*) to smell (**a** of, like); **huele muy bien** [*comida*] it smells very good; [*flor, perfume*] it smells very nice; **huele que apesta** it stinks; **¡qué mal huelen estos zapatos!** these shoes smell awful!; **huele a humedad** it smells of damp; **huele a tabaco** it smells of cigarette smoke; **¡algo huele a quemado** there's a smell of burning in here; **le huele el aliento** his breath smells; **te huelen los pies** your feet smell; **✦** MODISMO **huele que alimenta** (*Esp**) (= *muy bien*) it smells heavenly; (= *muy mal*) it smells foul, it stinks to high heaven*

2 (*indicando desconfianza*) **sus excusas me huelen a camelo*** his excuses sound a bit fishy to me*; **✦** MODISMO **~ a chamusquina: todo esto me huele a chamusquina** the whole thing sounds fishy to me

C olerse (*) VPR (= *sospechar*) to suspect; **nadie se había olido nada** nobody had suspected anything; **se olía que no iban a venir** he had the feeling *o* suspicion that they weren't going to come

olfatear /1a/ VT [+ *comida*] to smell, sniff; [+ *presa*] to scent, smell out

olfativo ADJ olfactory

olfato SM **1** (= *sentido*) smell, sense of smell **2** (= *instinto*) instinct, intuition

oligarca SMF oligarch

oligarquía SF oligarchy

oligárquico ADJ oligarchic, oligarchical

oligoelemento SM trace element

oligofrénico/a **A** ADJ mentally handicapped **B** SM/F mentally handicapped person

oligopolio SM oligopoly

olimpiada SF Olympiad; **las Olimpiadas** the Olympics; **Olimpiada de Invierno** Winter Olympics

olímpicamente ADV **pasó de nosotros ~*** he completely snubbed us

olímpico ADJ **1** [*deporte, título*] Olympic; (*Hist*) Olympian **2** (*) (= *enorme*) **nos despreció de forma olímpica** he was utterly contemptuous of us

Olimpo SM Olympus

olisquear /1a/ VT to smell, sniff (gently)

oliva **A** SF (= *aceituna*) olive **B** ADJ INV olive

olivar SM olive grove

olivarero/a **A** ADJ olive *antes de s* **B** SM/F olive-producer, olive-oil producer

olivo SM olive tree

olla SF **1** (= *cacharro*) pot, pan; ✦ MODISMOS **parar la ~** (*CS**) to bring home the bacon*; **se me va la ~**** (*en conversación*) I'm losing the thread, I'm getting lost; (*por volverse loco*) I'm losing my head ➤ **olla a presión, olla exprés** pressure cooker **2** (*Culin*) stew ➤ **olla podrida** hotpot

olmedo SM elm grove

olmo SM elm, elm tree

ológrafo ADJ, SM holograph

olor SM **1** (*físico*) smell (**a** of); ➤ **olor a quemado** smell of burning ➤ **olor a sudor, olor corporal** body odour *o* (*EEUU*) odor, B.O* **2** (= *atracción*) smell; **acudir al ~ del dinero** to be attracted by the smell of money **3** ➤ **olor de santidad** odour *o* (*EEUU*) odor of sanctity

oloroso Ⓐ ADJ sweet-smelling, fragrant, scented Ⓑ SM (= *jerez*) oloroso, oloroso sherry

olote SM (*CAm, Méx*) corncob

OLP SF ABR (= **Organización para la Liberación de Palestina**) PLO

olvidadizo ADJ forgetful

olvidado ADJ forgotten; **~ de Dios** godforsaken

olvidar /1a/ Ⓐ VT **1** (= *no acordarse de*) to forget; **he olvidado su nombre** I've forgotten his name; **~ hacer algo** to forget to do sth; **¡olvídame!** (*Esp**) get lost!* **2** (= *dejar olvidado*) to forget, leave behind, leave; **no olvides los guantes** don't forget your gloves, don't leave your gloves behind

> Se usa **leave** en vez de **forget** cuando se menciona el lugar donde se ha dejado algo olvidado:

olvidé el paraguas en el tren I left my umbrella on the train Ⓑ **olvidarse** VPR **1** (= *no acordarse*) to forget; **~se de hacer algo** to forget to do sth; **olvidársele algo a algn: se me olvidó por completo** I forgot all about it **2** (= *dejarse olvidado*) **me he olvidado el maletín en casa** I have left my briefcase at home; **olvidársele algo a algn: se me olvidó el paraguas** I forgot my umbrella, I left my umbrella behind

olvido SM **1** (*absoluto*) oblivion; **caer en el ~** to fall into oblivion **2** (= *descuido*) slip, oversight; **fue por ~** it was an oversight

ombligo SM navel, belly button*; ✦ MODISMOS **creerse el ~ del mundo** to think the world revolves around one, think one is the centre of the universe; **mirarse el ~** to contemplate one's navel

ombú SM ombú, ombú tree

ombudsman ['ombudsman] SM ombudsman

OMC SF ABR (= **Organización Mundial del Comercio**) WTO

omega SF omega

OMG SM ABR (= **Organismo Modificado Genéticamente**) GMO

omisión SF omission

omiso ADJ **hacer caso ~ de algo** to ignore sth

omitir /3a/ VT to leave out, miss out, omit

ómnibus SM **1** (*Aut, Hist*) omnibus **2** (*Perú, RPl*) (= *autobús*) bus

omnímodo ADJ (*gen*) all-embracing; [*poder*] absolute

omnipotencia SF omnipotence

omnipotente ADJ omnipotent, all-powerful

omnívoro ADJ omnivorous

omoplato SM, **omóplato** SM shoulder blade

OMS SF ABR (= **Organización Mundial de la Salud**) WHO

onanismo SM onanism

ONCE SF ABR (*Esp*) = **Organización Nacional de Ciegos Españoles**

once Ⓐ ADJ, PRON (*cardinal*) eleven; (*ordinal, en la fecha*) eleventh Ⓑ SM **1** (= *número*) eleven; *ver tb* **seis 2 tomar ~s** (*And*) to have tea (*afternoon snack*)

onceavo ADJ, PRON eleventh; *ver tb* **sexto**

11-S SM 9-11

oncogén SM oncogene

oncología SF oncology

oncólogo/a SM/F oncologist

onda SF **1** (*gen*) wave; ✦ MODISMO **agarrarle la ~ a algo** (*Méx*) to get the hang of sth ➤ **onda corta** short wave; **de ~ corta** shortwave *antes de s* ➤ **onda de choque** shock wave ➤ **onda de radio** radio wave ➤ **onda expansiva** shock wave ➤ **onda explosiva** blast, shock wave ➤ **onda larga** long wave ➤ **onda media** medium wave ➤ **onda sísmica** shock wave ➤ **onda sonora** sound wave **2** (*) (= *ambiente*) **estamos en la misma ~** we're on the same wavelength; ✦ MODISMOS **estar en la ~** (= *de moda*) to be in*; (= *al tanto*) to be on the ball*, be up to date; [*persona*] (= *a la moda*) to be hip*; **¡qué buena ~!** (*Méx*) is that cool or what?**; **¡qué mala ~!** (*Méx*) what a downer!**

ondear /1a/ Ⓐ VT [+ *bandera*] to wave Ⓑ VI [*agua*] to ripple

ondulado ADJ [*carretera*] uneven, rough; [*paisaje, terreno*] undulating, rolling; [*superficie*] undulating, uneven; [*cartón, hierro*] corrugated; [*pelo*] wavy

ondular /1a/ Ⓐ VT [+ *pelo*] to wave; **hacerse ~ el pelo** to have one's hair waved Ⓑ **ondularse** VPR to undulate

oneroso ADJ **1** (= *pesado*) onerous, burdensome **2** (*Jur*) onerous

ONG SF ABR (= **Organización No Gubernamental**) NGO

ónice SM onyx

onírico ADJ oneiric, dream *antes de s*

ónix SM onyx

ONL SF ABR (= **Organización No Lucrativa**) non-profit-making (*esp Brit*) *o* non-profit (*EEUU*) organization

on line ADV, ADJ on-line

onomástica SF saint's day; ⊃ *SANTO*

onomástico ADJ onomastic, name *antes de s*, of names; **fiesta onomástica** saint's day; **índice ~** index of names

onomatopeya SF onomatopoeia

ONU SF ABR (= **Organización de las Naciones Unidas**) UNO; **la ~** the UN

onubense ADJ of/from Huelva

onza SF **1** (= *peso*) ounce **2** (= *animal*) ounce

onzavo/a ADJ, SM/F eleventh; *ver tb* **sexto 1**

op. ABR (= *opus*) op

OPA SF ABR (= **oferta pública de adquisición**) takeover bid ➤ **OPA hostil** hostile takeover bid

opa¹* (*RPl*) Ⓐ ADJ stupid Ⓑ SMF idiot

opa²* EXCL (*RPl*) (*para expresar entusiasmo*) yay!*; (*para saludar*) hi!*, yo!**

opacar /1g/ (*LAm*) Ⓐ VT **1** (= *hacer opaco*) to make opaque; (= *oscurecer*) to darken **2** [+ *persona*] to outshine, overshadow Ⓑ **opacarse** VPR (= *hacerse opaco*) to become opaque; (= *oscurecerse*) to darken, get dark

opaco ADJ opaque; **una pantalla opaca a los rayos X** a screen which does not let X-rays through

ópalo SM opal

opar /1a/ VT to put in a takeover bid (for)

opción SF 1 (= *elección*) option; **no hay ~** there is no other option, there is no alternative *o* choice 2 (= *derecho*) right, option; **tiene ~ a viajar gratis** he has the right *o* option to travel free 3 (*Com*) option (**a** on); ➤ **opción a compra, opción de adquisición, opción de compra** (*gen*) option to buy, option to purchase; (*en Bolsa*) call option ➤ **opción de venta** (*en Bolsa*) put option ➤ **opciones sobre acciones** stock options

opcional ADJ optional

op. cit. ABR (= *opere citato*) op. cit.

OPEP SF ABR (= **Organización de Países Exportadores del Petróleo**) OPEC

ópera SF (= *género*) opera; (= *edificio*) opera, opera house ➤ **ópera bufa** comic opera ➤ **ópera prima** debut, first work

operación SF 1 (*Med*) operation; **una ~ de estómago** a stomach operation, an operation on the stomach ➤ **operación quirúrgica** surgical operation 2 (= *acción*) operation ➤ **operaciones de rescate, operación retorno** (*Esp*) effort to control traffic returning to a big city after a major holiday 3 (*Mil*) operation ➤ **operaciones conjuntas** joint operations 4 (*Com*) transaction, deal 5 (*Mat*) operation

operacional ADJ operational

operador(a) SM/F (*gen*) operator; (*Cine*) [*de rodaje*] cameraman/camerawoman; [*de proyección*] projectionist ➤ **operador(a) de cabina** projectionist, operator ➤ **operador(a) turístico/a** tour operator; *ver tb* **operadora**

operadora SF telecommunications company, telco*; *ver tb* **operador**

operante ADJ operating

operar /1a/ **Ⓐ** VT 1 (= *producir*) [+ *cambio*] to produce, bring about
2 [+ *paciente*] to operate on; **la tienen que ~** she's got to have an operation; **me van a ~ del corazón** I'm going to have a heart operation
3 [+ *máquina*] to operate, use **Ⓑ** VI 1 (= *actuar*) to operate
2 (*Com*) to deal, do business; **hoy no se ha operado en la bolsa** there has been no dealing *o* trading on the stock exchange today **Ⓒ operarse** VPR 1 (*Med*) to have an operation; **me tengo que ~ de la rodilla** I have to have a knee operation
2 (= *producirse*) to occur, come about; **se han operado grandes cambios** great changes have come about, there have been great changes

operario/a SM/F (*gen*) operative; (= *obrero*) worker ➤ **operario/a de máquina** machinist

operativo **Ⓐ** ADJ operative **Ⓑ** SM (*LAm*) (*esp militar, policial*) operation

opereta SF operetta, light opera

operístico ADJ operatic, opera *antes de s*

opiáceo SM opiate

opiante* ADJ (*RPl*) boring; **sus clases son ~s** his lessons are a real drag*, his lessons are really boring

opiarse* /1b/ VPR (*RPl*) to get bored

opinar /1a/ **Ⓐ** VT (= *pensar*) to think; **~ que ...** to think that ..., to be of the opinion that ... **Ⓑ** VI (= *dar su opinión*) to give one's opinion; **fueron opinando uno tras otro** they gave their opinions in turn

opinión SF opinion, view; **en mi ~** in my opinion *o* view; **ser de la ~ (de) que ...** to be of the opinion that ..., take the view that ...; **cambiar de ~** to change one's mind ➤ **opinión pública** public opinion

opio SM 1 (= *sustancia*) opium 2 (*RPl**) (= *tostón*) drag*; **la película es un ~** the film is a drag*

opíparo ADJ [*banquete*] sumptuous

oponente **Ⓐ** ADJ opposing, contrary **Ⓑ** SMF opponent

oponer /2q/ (*pp* **opuesto**) **Ⓐ** VT [+ *resistencia*] to put up **Ⓑ oponerse** VPR 1 [*persona*] **yo no me opongo** I don't object, I'm not against it; **~se a algo** to be against sth, be opposed to sth 2 (*mutuamente*) to oppose each other

oporto SM port

oportunamente ADV 1 (*en el tiempo*) opportunely 2 (= *pertinentemente*) appropriately

oportunidad SF 1 (= *ocasión*) chance, opportunity; **darle una/otra ~ a algn** to give sb a/another chance; **tener la ~ de hacer algo** to have a chance to do sth, have the chance of doing sth; (*Jur*) **igualdad de ~es** equality of opportunity 2 **"oportunidades"** (= *rebajas*) "bargains"

oportunista **Ⓐ** ADJ opportunist, opportunistic **Ⓑ** SMF opportunist

oportuno ADJ 1 [*ocasión*] opportune; **en el momento ~** at an opportune moment, at the right moment; **su llamada no pudo ser más oportuna** his call could not have come at a better moment, his call could not have been better timed 2 (= *pertinente*) appropriate; **no me pareció ~ decírselo** I didn't think it appropriate to tell him; **una respuesta oportuna** an apt reply 3 [*persona*] **¡ella siempre tan oportuna!** (*iró*) you can always rely on her!

oposición SF 1 (*gen*) opposition
2 (*Esp*) (*tb* **oposiciones**) Civil Service examination; **sacar unas oposiciones** to be successful in a public competition; **hacer oposiciones para una cátedra** to compete for a chair

opositar /1a/ VI (*Esp*) to go in for a public competition (*for a post*), sit for a public entrance/promotion examination

opositor(a) SM/F 1 (= *oponente*) opponent 2 (*Esp*) (*a examen*) competitor, candidate (**a** for); ⊳ *OPOSICIONES*

opresión SF 1 (= *sensación*) oppression 2 (*Med*) difficulty in breathing, tightness of the chest

opresivo ADJ oppressive

opresor(a) **Ⓐ** ADJ oppressive **Ⓑ** SM/F oppressor

oprimir /3a/ VT 1 (= *apretar*) [+ *objeto*] to squeeze, press, exert pressure on; **la blusa me estaba oprimiendo el cuello** the blouse was too tight on my neck 2 [+ *botón, tecla*] to press 3 [+ *pueblo, nación*] to oppress

oprobio SM (*frm*) opprobrium (*frm*), ignominy

optar /1a/ VI 1 (*gen*) to choose, decide; **~ por hacer algo** to choose to do sth, opt to do sth 2 **~ a** to compete for; **~ a un premio** to compete for a prize; **ellos no pueden ~ a las becas** they are not entitled to apply for the scholarships

optativa SF (*Educ*) option (*esp Brit*), elective (*EEUU*)

optativo ADJ optional

óptica SF 1 (= *ciencia*) optics *sing* 2 (= *tienda*) optician's 3 (= *punto de vista*) viewpoint, point of view; **desde esta ~** from this point of view

óptico/a **Ⓐ** ADJ [*instrumentos, fibra*] optical; [*nervio*] optic; **una ilusión óptica** an optical illusion **Ⓑ** SM/F optician

óptimamente ADV ideally

optimismo SM optimism

optimista **Ⓐ** ADJ optimistic, hopeful **Ⓑ** SMF optimist

óptimo ADJ ideal, optimum *antes de s*; **condiciones óptimas para la navegación a vela** ideal *o* optimum conditions for sailing; **hemos obtenido ~s resultados con este producto** we've had top *o* the best results with this product

opuesto **Ⓐ** PP *de* **oponer** **Ⓑ** ADJ 1 [*ángulo, lado*] opposite; **el extremo ~ de la ciudad** the opposite side of town; **un coche que venía en dirección opuesta** a car coming in the opposite direction 2 [*intereses, versiones*] conflicting;

tenemos gustos ~s we have very different tastes **3 ser ~ a algo** to be opposed to sth

opulencia SF (= *lujo*) luxury; (= *riqueza*) opulence, affluence; **vivir en la ~** to live in luxury; **sociedad de la ~** affluent society

opulento ADJ (= *lujoso*) luxurious; (= *rico*) opulent, affluent

opus SM (*Mús*) opus

OPUS DEI

The **Opus Dei**, also referred to as **la Obra**, is an influential Catholic association formed in 1928 with the aim of spreading Christian principles in society. It has a direct link to the Vatican which in practice means that it enjoys complete independence from local diocesan authorities. During the Franco era members of the **Opus** formed the intellectual backbone of the régime. Members of the **Opus** are particularly well-represented in educational circles: the universities of Pamplona in Spain and Piura in Peru are run by it.

---

opusino ADJ (*pey*) sanctimonious

OPV SF ABR (= **Oferta Pública de Venta (de acciones)**) *share offer*

ORA SF ABR = **Operación de Regulación de Aparcamientos**

ora ADV (*frm*) **~ A, ~ B** (*uso temporal*) now A, now B; (= *a veces*) sometimes A, sometimes B

oración SF **1** (*Rel*) prayer **2** (*Ling*) sentence; **partes de la ~** parts of speech ➤ **oración compuesta** complex sentence ➤ **oración directa** direct speech ➤ **oración indirecta** indirect speech, reported speech ➤ **oración subordinada** subordinate clause

oráculo SM oracle

orador(a) SM/F speaker, orator (*frm*)

oral ADJ oral; **por vía ~** (*Med*) orally

órale* EXCL (*Méx*) (= *¡vamos!*) come on!; (= *¡oiga!*) hey!

orangután SM orangutan

orar /1a/ VI (*Rel*) to pray (**a** to; **por** for)

oratoria SF oratory

oratorio SM (*Mús*) oratorio; (*Rel*) oratory, chapel

orbe SM **1** (= *globo*) orb, sphere **2** (= *mundo*) world; **en todo el ~** all over the world *o* globe

órbita SF **1** (*gen*) orbit; **poner en ~** to put in orbit; **está fuera de su ~ de acción** it's outside his field **2** (*Anat*) (*ocular*) socket, eye-socket

orca SF killer whale

órdago: **de ~*** ADJ tremendous*; **se cogieron una borrachera de ~** they got well and truly drunk

orden Ⓐ SM **1** (*en colocación, sucesión*) **1.1** (*con objetos, personas*) order; **fueron archivados por ~ alfabético** they were filed alphabetically *o* in alphabetical order; **por ~ de importancia** in order of importance; **poner ~ en algo** to sort sth out **1.2 en ~** in order; **todo en ~, mi capitán** everything is in order, captain; **poner en ~** [+ *papeles, documentos*] to sort out; **poner en ~ las ideas** to sort out one's ideas; ✦ MODISMO **sin ~ ni concierto** without rhyme or reason ➤ **orden del día** agenda ➤ **orden natural** natural order ➤ **orden sucesorio** order of succession **2** (*tb* **~ social**) order; **el ~ establecido** the established order; **las fuerzas del ~** the forces of law and order; **restablecer el ~** to restore *o* reestablish order ➤ **orden público** public order, law and order; **fueron detenidos por alterar el ~ público** they were arrested for breach of the peace *o* for disturbing the peace **3** (= *tipo*) nature; **motivos de ~ moral** moral reasons; **en otro ~ de cosas ...** at the same time ..., meanwhile ...; **de primer ~** [*figura*] leading; [*pensador*] first-rate; [*factor*] prime, of prime importance; [*problema*] major; **en todos los órdenes** on all fronts **4 del ~ de** in the order of, in the region of; **el coste sería del ~ de diez millones de dólares** the cost would be in the order *o* region of ten million dollars; **necesitamos del ~ de**

150.000 euros para comprarlo we need approximately 150,000 euros to buy it **5** (*Arquit*) order ➤ **orden corintio** Corinthian order ➤ **orden dórico** Doric order ➤ **orden jónico** Ionic order **6** (*Biol*) order **7** (*Rel*) (*tb* **~ sacerdotal**) ordination
Ⓑ SF **1** (= *mandato*) order; **tenemos órdenes de no dejar pasar a nadie** we are under orders not to let anybody through; **dar (la) ~ de hacer algo** to give the order to do sth; **hasta nueva ~** until further notice; **por ~ de** by order of; ✦ MODISMO **estar a la ~ del día: los robos están a la ~ del día en esta zona** robberies have become the norm in this area ➤ **orden de arresto, orden de búsqueda y captura** arrest warrant ➤ **orden de registro** search warrant ➤ **orden judicial** court order ➤ **orden ministerial** ministerial order, ministerial decree **2 ¡a la ~!** (*Mil*) yes, sir!; **a sus órdenes** (*Mil*) yes sir; (*esp LAm*) at your service; **estar a las órdenes de algn** (*Mil*) to be at sb's command; (*en la policía*) to be under sb's instructions *o* orders; (*en otros trabajos*) to be under sb **3** (*Mil, Hist, Rel*) (= *institución*) order; **la Orden de Calatrava** the Order of Calatrava ➤ **orden de caballería** order of knighthood ➤ **orden militar** military order ➤ **orden monástica** monastic order ➤ **orden religiosa** religious order **4 órdenes** (*Rel*) orders ➤ **órdenes sagradas** holy orders **5** (*Com, Fin*) order; **cheques a la ~ de Suárez** cheques *o* (*EEUU*) checks (to be made) payable to Suárez ➤ **orden bancaria** banker's order ➤ **orden de pago** money order **6** (*Inform*) command

ordenación SF **1** (= *colocación*) (*estado*) order, arrangement; (*acción*) ordering, arranging ➤ **ordenación del territorio** town and country planning ➤ **ordenación urbana** town planning **2** (*Rel*) ordination

ordenado ADJ **1** (= *en orden*) [*habitación, escritorio*] tidy; [*oficina*] well-organized, ordered; **tiene toda la casa muy limpia y ordenada** she keeps the house very clean and tidy; **los niños entraron de forma ordenada en el museo** the children entered the museum in an orderly fashion **2** [*persona*] (*al colocar algo*) tidy; (*en el trabajo*) organized **3** (*Rel*) ordained, in holy orders

ordenador SM computer ➤ **ordenador de bolsillo** palmtop (computer) ➤ **ordenador de (sobre)mesa** desktop computer ➤ **ordenador personal** personal computer ➤ **ordenador portátil** (*gen*) portable computer; (*pequeño*) laptop computer

ordenamiento SM (= *leyes*) legislation ➤ **ordenamiento jurídico** legal system

ordenanza Ⓐ SF (= *decreto*) ordinance, decree ➤ **ordenanzas municipales** bylaws Ⓑ SMF **1** (= *bedel*) porter **2** (*Mil*)

ordenar /1a/ Ⓐ VT **1** (= *poner en orden*) (*siguiendo un sistema*) to arrange; (*colocando en su sitio*) to tidy; **voy a ~ mis libros** I'm going to sort out *o* organize my books; **ordenó los relatos cronológicamente** he arranged the stories chronologically *o* in chronological order; **nunca ordena sus papeles** he never tidies his paperwork **2** (= *mandar*) to order; **la juez ordenó su detención** the judge ordered his arrest; **les habían ordenado que siguieran al vehículo** they had been ordered to follow the vehicle; **un tono de ordeno y mando** a dictatorial tone **3** (*Rel*) to ordain
Ⓑ **ordenarse** VPR (*Rel*) to be ordained

ordeñadora SF milking machine

ordeñar /1a/ VT to milk

ordinal ADJ, SM ordinal

ordinariez SF **1** (= *cualidad*) coarseness, vulgarity, commonness **2 una ~** (= *comentario*) a coarse remark; (= *broma*) a coarse joke

ordinario ADJ **1** (= *normal*) ordinary; **de ~** usually **2** (= *vulgar*) [*persona*] common; [*comportamiento, modales*] coarse; **son gente muy ordinaria** they're very common people; **sólo cuenta chistes ~s** he only tells crude jokes

orear /1a/ Ⓐ VT [+ *casa, habitación*] to air Ⓑ **orearse** VPR **1** [*ropa*] to air **2** [*persona*] to get some fresh air, take a breather

orégano SM oregano

oreja SF 1 (*Anat*) ear; ✦ MODISMOS **calentar las ~s a algn** (= *pegar*) to box sb's ears; (= *irritar*) to get on sb's nerves; **con las ~s gachas** with one's tail between one's legs, crestfallen; **parar la ~** (*LAm**) to prick up one's ears; **pegar la ~ (en algo)** to eavesdrop (on sth), listen in (on *o* to sth); **sonreír de ~ a ~** (*con alegría*) to beam; (*con autosatisfacción*) to grin from ear to ear; **verle las ~s al lobo** to get a sudden fright; **se le ve la ~** you can see his little game* 2 [*de sillón*] wing

orejeras SFPL 1 [*de gorro*] earflaps 2 (*CS*) (*para el caballo*) blinkers

orejero SM wing chair

orejón SM (= *melocotón*) dried peach; (= *albaricoque*) dried apricot; ✦ MODISMO **ser el último ~ del tarro** (*RPl*) to be the lowest of the low

orensano ADJ of/from Orense

orfanato SM, **orfanatorio** SM (*LAm*) orphanage

orfandad SF orphanage (*frm*)

orfebre SMF silversmith, goldsmith

orfebrería SF 1 (= *oficio*) silversmithing, goldsmithing, craftsmanship in precious metals 2 (= *objetos*) [*de oro*] gold articles *pl*; [*de plata*] silverware

orfelinato SM orphanage

orfeón SM choral society

organdí SM organdie

orgánico ADJ organic

organigrama SM [*de entidad, empresa*] organization chart

organillo SM barrel organ, hurdy-gurdy

organismo SM 1 (*Biol*) organism 2 (*Pol*) (*gen*) organization; (= *institución*) body, institution

organista SMF organist

organito SM (*CS*) barrel organ, hurdy-gurdy

organización SF organization ➤ **Organización de Estados Americanos** Organization of American States ➤ **Organización de las Naciones Unidas** United Nations Organization ➤ **organización no gubernamental** non-governmental organization

organizador(a) Ⓐ ADJ organizing; **el comité ~** the organizing committee Ⓑ SM/F organizer

organizar /1f/ Ⓐ VT 1 [+ *fiesta, espectáculo*] to organize 2 (*) [+ *jaleo, pelea*] **los marineros ~on un auténtico alboroto** the sailors created *o* made a real commotion; **¡menuda has organizado!** you've really stirred things up, haven't you! Ⓑ **organizarse** VPR 1 [*persona*] to organize o.s., get o.s. organized 2 (*) [*jaleo, pelea*] **se organizó una pelea tremenda** there was a major fist fight*

órgano SM 1 (*Anat, Mec*) organ ➤ **órgano sexual** sexual organ, sex organ 2 (*Mús*) organ 3 (= *medio*) means, medium ➤ **órgano de enlace** means of communication

organofosfato SM organophosphate

orgasmo SM orgasm

orgía SF orgy

orgullo SM 1 (= *satisfacción*) pride; **eres el ~ de la familia** you're the pride of the family; **me llena de ~** it makes me really proud 2 (= *altanería*) pride; **su ~ le impedía disculparse** he was too proud to say sorry

orgulloso ADJ 1 (= *satisfecho*) proud; **estar ~ de algo/algn** to be proud of sth/sb 2 (= *altanero*) proud; **es muy orgullosa** she's very proud

orientación SF 1 [*de casa*] aspect; [*de habitación*] position, orientation; **una casa con ~ sur** a house facing south; **la ~ actual del partido** the party's present course *o* position ➤ **orientación sexual** sexual orientation 2 (= *guía*) guidance, orientation ➤ **orientación profesional** careers guidance

oriental Ⓐ ADJ 1 [*persona*] oriental; [*región, zona*] eastern 2 (*CS*) (= *uruguayo*) Uruguayan Ⓑ SMF 1 (= *persona de Oriente*) oriental 2 (*CS*) (= *uruguayo*) Uruguayan

orientalista ADJ, SMF orientalist

orientar /1a/ Ⓐ VT 1 (= *situar*) **~ algo hacia** *o* **a algo** to

position sth to face sth; **la casa está orientada hacia el suroeste** the house faces south-west, the house looks south-west

2 (= *enfocar*) to direct; **tenemos que ~ nuestros esfuerzos hacia un aumento de la productividad** we must direct our efforts towards improving the productivity; **cómics orientados a un público adulto** comics oriented *o* targeted at adult readers

3 (= *guiar*) to guide; **me ha orientado en la materia** he has guided me through the subject, he has given me guidance about the subject

Ⓑ **orientarse** VPR to get one's bearings; **es difícil ~se en esta ciudad** it's hard to get one's bearings in this city, it's hard to find one's way around in this city

orientativo ADJ guiding, illustrative; **los pesos reseñados son puramente ~s** the weights shown are for guidance only

oriente SM 1 (= *este*) east 2 (*Geog*) **el Oriente** the Orient, the East; **el Cercano** *o* **Próximo Oriente** the Near East; **el Extremo** *o* **Lejano Oriente** the Far East; **el Oriente Medio** the Middle East

orificio SM (= *agujero*) orifice (*frm*), hole ➤ **orificio de bala** bullet hole

origen SM 1 (= *causa, principio*) origin; **los orígenes del flamenco** the origins of flamenco; **la policía está investigando el ~ de las llamadas telefónicas** the police are investigating the source of the phone calls; **proteínas de ~ animal/vegetal** animal/vegetable proteins; **dar ~ a** [+ *rumores, movimiento, explosión*] to give rise to; **la gran explosión que dio ~ al Universo** the great explosion that created the Universe; **desde sus orígenes** [*de movimiento, corriente*] from its origins; [*de ciudad, país*] from the very beginning, right from the start; **tener su ~ en** [+ *lugar*] to originate in; [+ *inicio*] to originate from; [+ *fecha*] to date back to; **tiene su ~ en el siglo XV** it dates back to the 15th century

2 [*de persona*] background, origins *pl*; **son gente de ~ humilde** they are from a humble background, they are of humble origins; **de ~ argentino/árabe** of Argentinian/Arab origin *o* (*más frm*) extraction; **país de ~** country of origin, native country

3 **en ~** (*Com, Fin*) at source; **el reciclado de residuos en ~** the recycling of waste at source

original Ⓐ ADJ 1 (= *inicial*) [*idea, documento, idioma*] original; [*edición*] first; **van a intentar devolver la zona a su estado ~** they are going to try to return the area to its original state

2 (= *novedoso*) original; **el guión tiene poco de ~** the script is not very original

3 (= *raro*) unusual, original; (= *extravagante*) eccentric; **él siempre tiene que ser tan ~** (*iró*) he always has to be so different

4 (= *procedente*) **ser ~ de** [*planta, animal*] to be native to Ⓑ SM 1 (= *modelo*) original; **no se parece al ~** it doesn't look like the original

2 (*Tip*) (*tb ~ de imprenta*) manuscript, original, copy

originalidad SF 1 (= *novedad*) originality 2 (= *excentricidad*) eccentricity

originar /1a/ Ⓐ VT to cause; **el terremoto originó la estampida de los elefantes** the earthquake caused the elephants to stampede; **la lucha de clases originó el conflicto** the class struggle led to *o* gave rise to the conflict Ⓑ **originarse** VPR [*enfermedad, conflicto, incendio*] to start, originate; [*universo*] to begin

originario ADJ 1 (= *inicial*) original; **el sentido ~ del término** the original sense of the term 2 **~ de** [*animal, planta*] native to; [*persona*] from; **el lichi es ~ de China** lychees originated in China, the lychee is native to China; **un joven ~ de Cabo Verde** a young man from Cape Verde; **los escoceses son ~s de Irlanda** the Scots originally came from Ireland

orilla SF 1 (= *borde*) [*de río*] bank; [*de lago*] shore, edge; [*de mesa*] edge; [*de taza*] rim, lip; **la ~ del mar** the seashore; **a ~s de** [*de río*] on the banks of; [*de lago*] on the shores of 2 (*Cos*) (= *dobladillo*) hem

orillar /1a/ Ⓐ VT 1 [+ *lago, bosque*] to skirt, go round

2 (= *esquivar*) [+ *dificultad*] to avoid, get around; [+ *tema*] to touch briefly on **3** ~ **a algn a hacer algo** (*Méx*) to lead sb to do sth **ⓑ** **orillarse** VPR (*Méx Aut*) to pull over

orín[1] SM rust

orín[2] SM, **orina** SF urine

orinal SM (= *bacín*) chamber pot; [*de niños*] potty

orinar /1a/ **Ⓐ** VI (*gen*) to urinate **ⓑ** VT ~ **sangre** to pass blood (*in the urine*) **ⓒ** **orinarse** VPR to wet o.s.; ~**se en la cama** to wet one's bed; ~**se encima** to wet o.s.

orines SMPL urine *sing*

oriundo/a **Ⓐ** ADJ ~ **de** [*planta, animal*] indigenous to, native to **ⓑ** SM/F (= *nativo*) native, inhabitant

orla SF **1** (= *borde*) [*de vestido, cuadro*] border **2** (*Esp Educ*) (= *fotografía*) class graduation photograph

ornamental ADJ ornamental

ornamento SM **1** (= *adorno*) ornament, adornment **2 ornamentos** (*Rel*) vestments

ornar /1a/ VT to adorn (**de** with)

ornato SM adornment, decoration

ornitólogo/a SM/F ornithologist

ornitorrinco SM platypus

oro SM **1** (= *metal*) gold; **regla de** ~ golden rule; **tiene una voz de** ~ she has a wonderful voice; ✦ MODISMOS **guardar algo como** ~ **en paño** to treasure sth; **hacerse de** ~ to make a fortune; **prometer el** ~ **y el moro** to promise the earth *o* moon; ✦ REFRÁN **no es** ~ **todo lo que reluce** all that glitters is not gold ➤ **oro negro** black gold, oil **2 oros** (*Esp Naipes*) *one of the suits in the Spanish card deck, represented by gold coins*; ⇨ *BARAJA ESPAÑOLA*

orografía SF orography

orondo ADJ **1** (= *grueso*) potbellied, big-bellied **2** (= *satisfecho*) smug, self-satisfied

oropel SM tinsel; **de** ~ flashy, gaudy

orozuz SM (*esp LAm*) liquorice

orquesta SF orchestra ➤ **orquesta de baile** dance band ➤ **orquesta de cámara** chamber orchestra ➤ **orquesta de cuerda(s)** string orchestra ➤ **orquesta de jazz** jazz band ➤ **orquesta sinfónica** symphony orchestra ➤ **orquesta típica** (*RPl*) *band playing traditional music such as tangos and milongas*

orquestación SF orchestration

orquestal ADJ orchestral

orquestar /1a/ VT to orchestrate

orquestina SF band

orquídea SF orchid

ortiga SF nettle, stinging nettle

orto*** SM (*CS*) arse (*Brit****), ass (*EEUU****)

ortodoncia SF orthodontics *sing*

ortodoxia SF orthodoxy

ortodoxo ADJ orthodox

ortografía SF spelling, orthography (*frm*)

ortográfico ADJ spelling *antes de s*, orthographic(al) (*frm*); **reforma ortográfica** spelling reform

ortopedia SF orthopaedics *sing*, orthopedics *sing* (*EEUU*)

ortopédico ADJ orthopaedic, orthopedic (*EEUU*)

oruga SF **1** (= *insecto*) caterpillar **2** (= *vehículo*) caterpillar, caterpillar track

orujo SM *liquor distilled from grape remains*

orzuelo SM stye, sty

os PRON PERS PL (*Esp*) **1** (*directo*) you; **os quiero mucho** I love you very much; **no os oigo** I can't hear you **2** (*indirecto*) you; **os lo di** I gave it to you; **os lo compré** (= *de vosotros*) I bought it from you; (= *para vosotros*) I bought it for you; **¿os han arreglado ya el ordenador?** have they fixed the computer for you yet? **3** (*reflexivo*) yourselves; **¿os habéis hecho daño?** did you

hurt yourselves?; **cuando os marchéis** when you leave

> Con partes del cuerpo o con prendas que se llevan puestas se usa el adjetivo posesivo:

lavaos las manos wash your hands; **no hace falta que os quitéis el abrigo** you don't need to take your coats off **4** (*mutuo*) each other; **quiero que os pidáis perdón** I want you to say sorry to each other; **¿os conocéis?** have you met?, do you know each other?

osa SF **1** (= *animal*) she-bear **2** (*Astron*) ➤ **Osa Mayor** Ursa Major, Great Bear ➤ **Osa Menor** Ursa Minor, Little Bear

osadía SF **1** (= *audacia*) daring, boldness **2** (= *descaro*) impudence, audacity, temerity

osado ADJ **1** (= *audaz*) daring, bold **2** (= *descarado*) impudent, audacious

osamenta SF **1** (= *esqueleto*) skeleton **2** (= *huesos*) bones *pl*

osar /1a/ VI to dare; ~ **hacer algo** to dare to do sth

osario SM ossuary, charnel house

OSCE SF ABR (= **Organización para la Seguridad y Cooperación en Europa**) OSCE

oscense ADJ of/from Huesca

oscilación SF **1** [*de péndulo*] swinging, swaying, oscillation **2** [*de luz*] winking, blinking; [*de llama*] flickering **3** [*de precios, peso, temperatura*] fluctuation

oscilar /1a/ VI **1** [*péndulo*] to swing, oscillate **2** [*luz*] to wink, blink; [*llama*] to flicker **3** [*precio, peso, temperatura*] ~ **entre** (= *estar comprendido*) to range between; (= *cambiar*) to fluctuate between

oscurantismo SM obscurantism

oscuras: a ~ ADV in the dark; *ver tb* **oscuro**

oscurecer /2d/ **Ⓐ** VT **1** [+ *color, espacio*] to darken **2** (= *quitar importancia a*) [+ *cuestión*] to confuse, cloud; [+ *rival*] to overshadow, put in the shade **3** (*Arte*) to shade **ⓑ** VI, VPR to grow dark, get dark

oscurecimiento SM darkening

oscuridad SF **1** (= *ausencia de luz*) **tiene pánico a la** ~ he's terrified of the dark; **pasaba horas sentado en la** ~ he would sit for hours in the dark *o* in darkness **2** (= *anonimato*) obscurity; **salir de la** ~ to emerge from obscurity

oscuro ADJ **1** (= *sin luz*) dark; **¡qué casa tan oscura!** what a dark house! **2** [*color, cielo, día*] dark; **tiene el pelo castaño** ~ she has dark brown hair **3** [*texto, explicación*] obscure **4** (= *sospechoso*) **oscuras intenciones** dubious intentions, sinister intentions; **un asunto** ~ a shady business **5** (= *poco conocido*) obscure; **un** ~ **escritor** an obscure writer; *ver tb* **oscuras**

óseo ADJ bony, osseous, bone *antes de s*

osito SM teddy, teddy bear ➤ **osito de felpa**, **osito de peluche** teddy, teddy bear

Oslo SM Oslo

osmosis SF INV, **ósmosis** SF INV osmosis

oso SM bear; ✦ MODISMO **hacer el** ~ (*Esp*) to play the fool ➤ **oso de peluche** teddy bear ➤ **oso hormiguero** anteater ➤ **oso panda** panda

ostensible ADJ obvious, evident; **hacer algo** ~ to make sth quite clear

ostentación SF **1** (= *exhibición*) ostentation **2** (= *acto*) show, display; **hacer** ~ **de** to flaunt, parade, show off

ostentar /1a/ VT **1** (= *exhibir*) to show; (= *hacer gala de*) to flaunt, parade, show off **2** (= *tener*) [+ *poderes legales*] to have, possess; [+ *cargo, título*] to have, hold; ~ **el título mundial en patinaje sobre hielo** to hold the world title in ice-skating

ostentoso ADJ ostentatious

osteoartritis SF INV osteoarthritis

osteópata SMF osteopath

osteopatía SF osteopathy

osteoporosis SF INV osteoporosis

ostión SM (*esp LAm*) large oyster

ostra Ⓐ SF (*Zool*) oyster Ⓑ **ostras*** EXCL (*euf*) (*denota sorpresa*) crikey!*; (*denota enfado o desagrado*) sugar!*, shoot! (*EEUU**)

ostracismo SM ostracism

OTAN SF ABR (= **Organización del Tratado del Atlántico Norte**) NATO

otario/a* (*CS*) Ⓐ ADJ gullible Ⓑ SM/F sucker*

otate SM (*Méx*) (= *caña*) cane, stick; (= *junco*) reed, rush

otear /1a/ VT **1** [+ *horizonte*] to scan **2** [+ *objeto lejano*] to make out, glimpse

Otelo SM Othello

otitis SF INV inflammation of the ear, otitis (*frm*)

otomano/a ADJ, SM/F (*Hist*) Ottoman

otoñal ADJ autumnal, autumn *antes de s* (*esp Brit*), fall *antes de s* (*EEUU*)

otoño SM autumn (*esp Brit*), fall (*EEUU*)

otorgar /1h/ VT [+ *privilegio, ayuda, permiso*] to grant (**a** to); [+ *premio*] to award (**a** to); [+ *poderes, título*] to confer (**a** on)

otorrino SMF ear, nose and throat specialist, ENT specialist

otorrinolaringología SF otolaryngology (*frm*), otorhinolaryngology (*frm*)

otorrinolaringólogo SMF ear, nose and throat specialist, otolaryngologist (*frm*)

otro Ⓐ ADJ **1** (= *diferente*) (*en singular*) another; (*en plural*) other; **dame otra revista** give me another magazine; **necesito ~ destornillador más grande** I need a bigger screwdriver; **¿tiene algún ~ modelo?** do you have any other models?; **son ~s tiempos** times have changed; **está en otra parte** it's somewhere else
2 (= *uno más*) (*en singular, con cifras*) another; (*en plural*) other; **¿quieres otra taza de café?** would you like another cup of coffee?; **después volvió con ~s ocho libros** then he came back with another eight books *o* with eight more books
3 (*en una secuencia temporal*) **3.1** (*en el futuro*) next; **se fue y a la otra semana me escribió*** he left and wrote to me the next week **3.2** (*en el pasado*) other; **me encontré con él el ~ día** I met him the other day
Ⓑ PRON **1** (= *diferente*) (*en singular*) another, another one; (*en plural*) others; **tengo ~** I've got another (one); **tengo ~s en el almacén** I've got some others in the warehouse; **todos los países europeos y alguno que ~ de África** all the countries in Europe and some from Africa; **el ~** the other one; **lo ~ no importa** the rest doesn't matter
2 (= *uno más*) (*en singular*) another, another one; (*en plural*) others; **¿quieres ~?** do you want another (one)?; **se me perdieron y me dieron ~s** I lost them, but they gave me some more; **¡otra!** (*en concierto*) encore!; (*en bar*) (the) same again, please
3 (*en una secuencia temporal*) **un día sí y ~ no** every other day; **el jueves que viene no, el ~** a week on Thursday; **¡hasta otra!** see you (later)!
4 (*referido a personas*) (*en singular*) somebody else; (*en plural*) others; **que lo haga ~** let somebody else do it; **parece otra desde que se casó** she's a different person since she got married; **no fue ~ que el obispo** it was none other than the bishop; **unos creen que ganará, ~s que**

perderá some think he'll win, others that he'll lose; ✦ MODISMO **¡~ que tal (baila)!** here we go again!

otrora ADV (*liter*) one-time, former; **el ~ señor del país** the one-time ruler of the country

OUA SF ABR (= **Organización de la Unidad Africana**) OAU

ouija ['wixa] SF, **oui-ja®** ['wixa] SF Ouija® board

ovación SF ovation

ovacionar /1a/ VT to cheer, applaud, give an ovation to

oval ADJ, **ovalado** ADJ oval

óvalo SM oval

ovárico ADJ [*tejido, hormonas, quiste*] ovarian

ovario SM ovary

oveja SF (*sin distinción de sexo*) sheep; (= *hembra*) ewe; ✦ MODISMO **ser la ~ negra de la familia** to be the black sheep of the family; ✦ REFRÁN **cada ~ con su pareja** birds of a feather flock together

ovejero SM ➤ **ovejero alemán** (*esp Arg*) German shepherd, Alsatian

overol SM (*LAm*) (*de una pieza*) overalls *pl* (*Brit*), boiler suit (*Brit*), coveralls *pl* (*EEUU*); (*con peto*) dungarees *pl*, overalls *pl* (*EEUU*)

ovetense ADJ of/from Oviedo

Ovidio SM Ovid

ovillar /1a/ Ⓐ VT to wind, wind into a ball Ⓑ **ovillarse** VPR to curl up into a ball

ovillo SM [*de lana, cuerda*] ball; **hacerse un ~** to curl up into a ball

ovino Ⓐ ADJ ovine (*frm*), sheep *antes de s*; **ganado ~** sheep Ⓑ SM sheep *pl*; **carne de ~** [*de oveja añeja*] mutton; [*de cordero*] lamb

OVNI SM ABR (= **objeto volante** *o* **volador no identificado**) UFO

ovulación SF ovulation

ovular /1a/ VI to ovulate

óvulo SM ovule, ovum

oxidación SF **1** [*de metal*] rusting **2** (*Quím*) oxidation

oxidar /1a/ Ⓐ VT **1** [+ *metal*] to rust **2** (*Quím*) to oxidize Ⓑ **oxidarse** VPR **1** [*metal*] to rust, go rusty **2** (*Quím*) to oxidize

óxido SM **1** (*en metal*) rust **2** (*Quím*) oxide

oxigenación SF oxygenation

oxigenado ADJ **1** (*Quím*) oxygenated **2** [*pelo*] bleached; **una rubia oxigenada** a peroxide blonde

oxigenar /1a/ Ⓐ VT to oxygenate Ⓑ **oxigenarse** VPR **1** (*gen*) to become oxygenated **2** [*persona*] to get some fresh air

oxígeno SM oxygen

oye, oyendo *etc ver* **oír**

oyente SMF **1** (*Radio*) listener; **queridos ~s** dear listeners **2** (*Univ*) unregistered student, occasional student, auditor (*EEUU*); **voy de ~ a las clases de Derecho Romano** I attend the classes on Roman Law as an unregistered student, I audit the classes on Roman Law (*EEUU*)

ozono SM ozone

ozonosfera SF ozonosphere

Pp

P, p [pe] SF (= *letra*) P, p

pa* PREP = **para**

pabellón SM 1 (*Arquit*) [*de muestras, exposiciones*] pavilion; [*de jardín*] summerhouse; [*de hospital*] (= *ala*) wing; (= *anexo*) block, section ➤ **pabellón de caza** hunting lodge ➤ **pabellón de música** bandstand 2 (*Med*) ➤ **pabellón de la oreja** outer ear 3 (*Mús*) [*de trompeta*] bell 4 (= *bandera*) flag ➤ **pabellón de conveniencia** flag of convenience

pabilo SM, **pábilo** SM wick

pábulo SM **dar ~ a** to feed, encourage; **dar ~ a los rumores** to fuel rumours

paca SF (*LAm Zool*) paca, spotted cavy

pacato ADJ (*pey*) 1 (= *tímido*) timid 2 (= *modesto*) excessively modest, prudish

pacense ADJ of/from Badajoz

paceño ADJ of/from La Paz

pacer /2d/ VT, VI to graze

pacha SF (*CAm*) baby's bottle

pachá SM pasha; ✦ MODISMO **vivir como un ~** to live like a king

pachamama SF (*And*) Mother Earth, the earth mother

pachamanca SF (*Perú*) barbecue

pachanga* SF 1 (= *fiesta*) lively party; (= *juerga*) binge*, booze-up** 2 (*Mús*) Cuban dance

pachanguero* ADJ 1 (= *bullicioso*) noisy, rowdy 2 [*música*] catchy

pacharán SM sloe brandy

pachocha* SF (*Perú*) = **pachorra**

pachón* ADJ 1 [*persona*] lackadaisical 2 (*CAm, Méx*) (= *peludo*) shaggy, hairy; (= *lanudo*) woolly, wooly (*EEUU*)

pachorra* SF slowness, sluggishness

pachucho* ADJ (*Esp*) [*persona*] off-colour, off-color (*EEUU*); [*fruta*] overripe

pachuco/a* (*Méx*) Ⓐ ADJ (= *llamativo*) flashy, flashily dressed Ⓑ SM/F 1 (*pey*) (= *chicano*) Chicano, Mexican-American 2 (= *bien vestido*) sharp dresser, snappy dresser

pachulí SM patchouli

paciencia SF patience; **¡paciencia!** (*gen*) be patient!; (*CS*) that's just too bad!; **se me acaba** *o* **agota la ~** my patience is running out *o* wearing thin; **armarse de ~** to resolve to be patient; **perder la ~** to lose patience; **tener ~** to be patient

paciencioso ADJ (*And*) long-suffering

paciente ADJ, SMF patient

pacificación SF pacification

pacificador(a) Ⓐ ADJ pacifying, peace-making Ⓑ SM/F peacemaker

pacíficamente ADV pacifically, peaceably

pacificar /1g/ Ⓐ VT 1 (*Mil*) to pacify 2 (= *calmar*) to calm; (= *apaciguar*) to appease Ⓑ **pacificarse** VPR to calm down

Pacífico SM (*tb* **Océano ~**) Pacific (Ocean)

pacífico ADJ [*lugar, proceso, arreglo*] peaceful; [*carácter*] peaceable; [*ciudadano*] peace-loving

pacifismo SM pacifism

pacifista ADJ, SMF pacifist

paco** SM (*And*) cop**, policeman

pacota* SF (*Méx*) = **pacotilla 1**

pacotilla SF 1 (= *género*) trash, junk, inferior stuff; **de ~** trashy, shoddy 2 (*And, CAm*) (= *muchedumbre*) rabble, crowd, mob

pacotillero SM (*And, Carib, CS*) pedlar, peddler (*EEUU*), hawker

pactar /1a/ Ⓐ VT to agree to; **~ una tregua** to agree to a truce Ⓑ VI to come to an agreement, make a pact

pacto SM agreement, pact; **hacer/romper un ~** to make/break an agreement; ✦ MODISMO **hacer un ~ con el diablo** to make a pact with the devil ➤ **Pacto Andino** Andean Pact ➤ **pacto de no agresión** non-aggression pact ➤ **Pacto de Varsovia** Warsaw Pact ➤ **pacto entre caballeros** gentlemen's agreement ➤ **pacto social** (*gen*) social contract; [*de salarios*] wages settlement

padecer /2d/ Ⓐ VI to suffer; **~ de** to suffer from; **padece del corazón** he has heart trouble Ⓑ VT 1 (= *sufrir*) to suffer 2 (= *aguantar*) [+ *malos tratos, adversidades*] to endure, put up with

padecimiento SM (*gen*) suffering; (*Med*) ailment

padrastro SM 1 (= *pariente*) stepfather 2 (*en dedo*) hangnail

padrazo SM indulgent father

padre Ⓐ SM 1 (= *progenitor*) father; **Gutiérrez ~** Gutiérrez senior, the elder Gutiérrez; ✦ MODISMO **de ~ y muy señor mío**: **una paliza de ~ y muy señor mío** an almighty thrashing, the father and mother of a thrashing ➤ **padre de familia** family man; (*Jur*) head of a household ➤ **padre soltero** single father

2 **padres** (= *padre y madre*) parents
3 (*Rel*) father ➤ **padre espiritual** confessor ➤ **padres de la Iglesia** Church Fathers
4 [*de disciplina*] father; **el ~ de la lingüística moderna** the father of modern linguistics
5 (*) **¡tu ~!** up yours!**
Ⓑ ADJ (*) 1 (= *enorme*) **se armó un lío ~** there was an almighty row
2 (*Méx*) (= *bueno*) great*, fantastic*

padrenuestro SM Lord's Prayer

padrillo SM (*And, CS*) stallion

padrino SM 1 (*en bautizo*) godfather; **padrinos** godparents 2 (*en boda*) ≈ best man 3 (*en duelo*) second 4 [*de mafia*] godfather

padrón SM 1 (= *censo*) census; (*Pol*) electoral register, electoral roll; [*de miembros*] register 2 (*LAm Agr*) stud; (= *caballo*) stallion 3 (*Chi Aut*) car registration documents *pl*

padrote SM 1 (*LAm*) (= *caballo*) stallion; (= *toro*) breeding bull 2 (*CAm, Méx**) (= *chulo*) pimp

paella SF 1 (= *plato*) paella 2 (= *recipiente*) paella dish

paellera SF paella dish

paf EXCL wham!, zap!

pág. ABR (= **página**) p.

paga SF 1 (= *sueldo*) (*semanal*) wages *pl*; (*mensual*) salary; [*de jubilado, viuda*] pension; [*de niño*] pocket money (*esp Brit*), allowance (*esp EEUU*); **14 ~s al año** 14 yearly payments; **día de ~** payday ➤ **paga de Navidad** Christmas bonus (*equivalent to a month's salary*) ➤ **paga extra**, **paga extraordinaria** salary bonus (*usually paid in June and December*)
2 (= *pago*) payment

pagadero ADJ payable; **~ a plazos** payable in instalments

pagado ADJ 1 (= *ya abonado*) paid; **con todos los gastos ~s** with all expenses paid 2 [*asesino, mercenario*] hired 3 (= *satisfecho*) **~ de uno mismo** self-satisfied, smug

pagador(a) Ⓐ ADJ **la entidad ~a** the payer Ⓑ SM/F 1 (= *persona*) payer; **ser buen/mal ~** to be a good/bad payer 2 (*Mil*) paymaster

pagano/a ADJ, SM/F pagan, heathen

pagar /1h/ **Ⓐ** VT **1** (= *abonar*) [+ *factura, rescate, sueldo*] to pay; [+ *compra*] to pay for; [+ *intereses, hipoteca*] to pay off, repay; **paga 200 dólares de alquiler** he pays 200 dollars in rent; **los menores de tres años no pagan entrada** children under three get in free; **¿cuánto pagasteis por el coche?** how much did you pay for the car?; ~ **algo al contado** o **en efectivo** o **en metálico** to pay cash for sth, pay for sth in cash

> Cuando el objeto directo de **pagar** es el producto adquirido, la traducción es **pay** seguido siempre de **for**:

~ **algo a plazos** to pay for sth in instalments o (*EEUU*) installments; ~ **algo con tarjeta de crédito** to pay for sth by credit card; ✦ MODISMO ~ **a algn con la misma moneda** to give sb a taste of their own medicine

2 (= *costar*) to cost; **sus cuadros se pagan a peso de oro** his paintings fetch a very high price

3 (= *corresponder*) [+ *ayuda, favor*] to repay; [+ *visita*] to return; **lo pagó con su vida** he paid for it with his life; ✦ MODISMOS **¡lo ~ás caro!** you'll pay dearly for this!; **¡las vas a ~!** you've got it coming to you!*, you'll pay for this!; **¡que Dios se lo pague!** God bless you!

Ⓑ VI **1** (= *satisfacer un pago*) to pay; **hoy pago yo** I'm paying today, it's my turn to pay today

2 (*Col, Méx*) (= *compensar*) to pay; **el negocio no paga** the business doesn't pay

Ⓒ pagarse VPR **1** [+ *estudios, gastos*] to pay for

2 (= *vanagloriarse*) ~**se de algo** to be pleased with sth; ~**se de uno mismo** to be conceited, be full of o.s.*

pagaré SM promissory note, IOU ➤ **pagaré del Tesoro** Treasury bill, Treasury bond

página SF page; **anuncio a toda** ~ full-page advertisement; **primera** ~ front page ➤ **páginas amarillas** Yellow Pages® ➤ **página de inicio** home page ➤ **páginas doradas** (*Arg*) Yellow Pages® ➤ **página web** Web page

paginación SF pagination

paginar /1a/ VT to paginate

pago¹ SM **1** (*Fin*) payment; **tras el** ~ **de la primera letra** after paying the first instalment; **atrasarse en los** ~**s** to be in arrears ➤ **pago a la entrega** cash on delivery ➤ **pago al contado** cash payment ➤ **pago contra reembolso** cash on delivery ➤ **pago domiciliado** direct debit ➤ **pago en especie** payment in kind ➤ **pago fraccionado** payment in instalments o (*EEUU*) installments, part-payment ➤ **pago inicial** down payment, deposit ➤ **pago por visión** pay per view

2 (= *recompensa*) return, reward; **en** ~ **de** o **por algo** in return for sth, as a reward for sth

pago² SM **por estos** ~**s** round here, in this neck of the woods*

pagoda SF pagoda

págs. ABR (= **páginas**) pp.

pai SM (*LAm*) pie

paiche SM (*And*) dried salted fish

paila SF **1** (*esp SAm*) (= *sartén*) frying pan; (= *cacerola*) large pan **2** (*Chi*) (= *comida*) meal of fried food

país SM **1** (= *nación*) country ➤ **país en vías de desarrollo** developing nation ➤ **país natal** native country ➤ **país satélite** satellite country o state **2** (= *tierra*) land, region; **vino del** ~ local wine

paisaje SM **1** (= *terreno*) landscape; (= *vista*) scenery; **el** ~ **montañoso del Tirol** the mountainous landscape of Tyrol; **contemplar el** ~ to look at the scenery **2** (*Arte*) landscape

paisajista SMF (= *pintor*) landscape painter; (= *jardinero*) landscape gardener

paisajístico ADJ landscape *antes de s*, scenic

paisanada* SF (*CS*) peasants *pl*

paisano/a **Ⓐ** ADJ (= *del mismo país*) from the same country; (= *de la misma región*) from the same region; (= *del mismo pueblo*) from the same town

Ⓑ SM/F **1** (= *civil*) civilian; **traje de** ~ plain clothes *pl*; **vestir de** ~ [*soldado*] to be wearing civilian clothes, be in civvies*; [*policía*] to be in plain clothes

2 (= *del mismo origen*) **es un** ~ **mío** (= *del mismo país*) he's a fellow countryman (of mine); (= *del mismo pueblo*) person from the same town; (= *de la misma región*) person from the same region

3 (*esp RPl*) (= *campesino*) peasant

4 (*Chi*) (= *árabe*) Arab

Países Bajos SMPL **los** ~ (= *Holanda*) the Netherlands; (*Hist*) the Low countries

País Vasco SM **el** ~ the Basque Country; *see also* www.euskadi.net

paja SF **1** (*Agr*) straw; (*de beber*) straw; **sombrero de** ~ straw hat; **techo de** ~ thatched roof; ✦ REFRÁN **ver la** ~ **en el ojo ajeno y no la viga en el propio** to see the mote in sb else's eye and not the beam in one's own **2** (*en libro, ensayo*) padding, waffle*; **hinchar un libro con mucha** ~ to pad a book out **3** (***) **hacerse una** ~ (*Col, RPl*) **la** ~ ◇ **volarse la** ~ (*CAm*) to wank***, jerk off*** **4** (*CAm*) (*tb* ~ **de agua**) (= *grifo*) tap (*Brit*), faucet (*EEUU*) **5** (*And, CAm***) (= *mentira*) lie, fib*

pajar SM straw loft

pájara SF **1** (*) (= *mujer*) sneaky bitch* **2** (*Dep*) collapse

pajarería SF pet shop (*esp Brit*), pet store (*EEUU*)

pajarero/a SM/F (= *vendedor*) bird dealer; (= *cazador*) bird catcher; (= *criador*) bird breeder, bird fancier

pajarita SF **1** (*de papel*) paper bird **2** (*Esp*) (= *corbata*) bow tie

pajarito SM (*Orn*) (= *cría*) baby bird, fledgling; (*hum*) birdie; ✦ MODISMOS **me lo dijo un** ~ a little bird told me; **quedarse como un** ~ to die peacefully

pájaro SM **1** (*Orn*) bird; ✦ MODISMOS **matar dos** ~**s de un tiro** to kill two birds with one stone; **tener la cabeza llena de** ~**s** to be featherbrained; ✦ REFRÁN **más vale** ~ **en mano que ciento volando** a bird in the hand is worth two in the bush ➤ **pájaro bobo** penguin ➤ **pájaro cantor** songbird ➤ **pájaro carpintero** woodpecker ➤ **pájaro de mal agüero** bird of ill omen ➤ **pájaro mosca** (*Esp*) hummingbird

2 (*) (= *astuto*) clever fellow, sharp sort

pajarón* (*CS*) ADJ stupid

pajarraco SM **1** (*Orn*) big ugly bird **2** (*) (= *pillo*) slyboots*

paje SM page

pajita SF (drinking) straw

pajizo ADJ (= *de paja*) straw, made of straw; [*color*] straw-coloured, straw-colored (*EEUU*)

pajolero** ADJ (*Esp*) **no tener ni pajolera idea** not to have a clue*

pajonal SM (*LAm*) scrubland

Pakistán SM Pakistan

pakistaní ADJ, SMF Pakistani

pala SF **1** (*para cavar*) spade; (*para nieve, carbón, tierra*) shovel ➤ **pala mecánica** power shovel **2** (*Culin*) (*para pastel*) cake slice; (*para el pescado*) fish slice (*Brit*), slotted spatula (*EEUU*) **3** (*Dep, Béisbol*) bat; (*en ping-pong*) bat, paddle (*EEUU*); **jugar a las** ~**s** to play beach-tennis **4** [*de hélice, remo*] blade **5** [*de zapato*] vamp

palabra SF **1** (= *vocablo*) word; **no tengo** ~**s** o **me faltan** ~**s para expresar lo que siento** I haven't got the words o there aren't words to express how I feel, words fail to express how I feel; **no dijo ni media** ~ he didn't give us the slightest hint; **en una** ~ in a word; **¡ni una** ~ **más!** not another word!; ✦ MODISMOS **no cruzar (una)** ~ **con algn** not to say a word to sb; **dejar a algn con la** ~ **en la boca** to cut sb off in mid-sentence; **quitar la** ~ **de la boca a algn** to take the words right out of sb's mouth; **tomar la** ~ **a algn** (= *creer*) to take sb at his word; (= *obligar*) to keep sb to his word; **tener la última** ~ to have the final say; ✦ REFRÁN **a** ~**s necias, oídos sordos** it's best not to listen to the silly things people say ➤ **palabras cruzadas** (*CS*) crossword *sing*

2 (= *facultad de hablar*) **la** ~ speech; **he pecado sólo de** ~ I've sinned in word only; **hace tiempo que no me dirige la** ~ he hasn't spoken to me for a long time

3 (*frm*) (= *turno para hablar*) floor; **pedir la** ~ to ask for the floor, ask to be allowed to speak; **tener la** ~ to have the floor; **hacer uso de la** ~ to take the floor, speak

4 (= *promesa*) word; **es hombre de** ~ he is a man of his word; **cumplió su** ~ he kept his word, he was true to his word; ~ **que yo no tengo nada que ver*** I've got nothing to do with it, (I) promise!; **bajo** ~ (*Mil*) on parole; **dar su** ~ to give one's word ➤ **palabra de honor** word of honour, word of honor (*EEUU*)

palabrear /1a/ VT (*And*) (= *acordar*) to agree verbally to; ~ **a algn** to promise to marry sb

palabreja SF strange word

palabrería SF verbiage, hot air

palabrota SF swearword

palacete SM small palace

palaciego ADJ palace *antes de s*, court *antes de s*

palacio SM palace ➤ **palacio de congresos** conference centre, conference hall ➤ **palacio de deportes** sports centre ➤ **palacio de justicia** courthouse ➤ **palacio episcopal** bishop's palace ➤ **Palacio Nacional** (*p.ej. en Guatemala*) Parliament Building ➤ **palacio real** royal palace

paladar SM 1 (*Anat*) (hard) palate, roof of the mouth 2 (= *gusto*) palate

paladear /1a/ VT to savour, savor (*EEUU*)

paladín SM 1 (*Hist*) paladin 2 [*de libertad, justicia*] champion

palafrén SM palfrey

palanca SF 1 (= *barra*) lever ➤ **palanca de cambio** gear lever (*Brit*), gearshift (*EEUU*) ➤ **palanca de freno** brake lever ➤ **palanca de mando** joystick 2 (*) (= *influencia*) pull, influence

palangana Ⓐ SF 1 (= *jofaina*) washbasin, washbowl (*EEUU*) 2 (*And, CAm*) (= *fuente*) platter, serving dish Ⓑ SMF (*CS**) 1 (= *bobo*) idiot 2 (= *jactancioso*) braggart

palanganear* /1a/ VI (*CS*) to brag, show off*

palanquear /1a/ Ⓐ VT 1 (*LAm*) (= *apalancar*) to lever (along), move with a lever 2 (*SAm**) (= *ayudar*) **¿quién te palanqueó?** who got you fixed up? Ⓑ VI (*SAm**) to pull strings

palanqueta SF jemmy, crowbar

p'alante** ADV = **para adelante**; *ver* **adelante**

palapa SF (*Méx*) palm hut

palatal ADJ, SF palatal

palco SM (*Teat*) box; (*Ftbl*) director's box ➤ **palco de autoridades, palco de honor** royal box, box for distinguished persons

palé SM *board game similar to Monopoly*

palear /1a/ Ⓐ VT (*LAm*) [+ *tierra*] to shovel; [+ *zanja*] to dig Ⓑ VI [*piragüista*] to paddle

palenque SM 1 (= *estacada*) stockade, palisade 2 (= *recinto*) arena, ring; [*de gallos*] pit 3 (*RPl*) [*de caballos*] tethering post

palentino ADJ of/from Palencia

paleografía SF palaeography, paleography (*esp EEUU*)

paleolítico ADJ palaeolithic, paleolithic (*esp EEUU*)

paleontología SF palaeontology, paleontology (*esp EEUU*)

Palestina SF Palestine

palestino/a Ⓐ ADJ Palestinian Ⓑ SM/F Palestinian; **los ~s** the Palestinians

palestra SF **salir** *o* **saltar a la ~** (= *participar*) to take the floor; (= *darse a conocer*) to come to the fore

paleta SF 1 (= *herramienta*) (*para cavar*) small shovel, small spade; [*de albañil*] trowel; (*Culin*) (*con ranuras*) fish slice (*Brit*), slotted spatula (*EEUU*); (*plana*) spatula 2 (*Arte*) palette 3 (*Téc*) [*de turbina*] blade; [*de noria*] paddle, bucket 4 (*Anat*) (*de persona*) shoulder blade; (*de animal*) shoulder 5 (*para jugar*) bat, paddle (*EEUU*); **jugar a las ~s** to play beach-tennis 6 (*) (= *diente*) front tooth 7 (*LAm*) (= *polo*) ice lolly (*Brit*), Popsicle® (*EEUU*); *ver tb* **paleto**

paletilla SF shoulder blade

paleto/a* (*Esp*) Ⓐ ADJ boorish, stupid Ⓑ SM/F yokel, country bumpkin, hick (*EEUU*); *ver tb* **paleta**

paliacate SM (*Méx*) bandanna

paliar /1b/ VT [+ *dolor*] to relieve, alleviate, palliate (*frm*); [+ *efectos*] to lessen, mitigate, palliate (*frm*)

paliativo Ⓐ ADJ palliative, mitigating Ⓑ SM palliative; **condenar sin ~s** to condemn unreservedly

palidecer /2d/ VI to turn pale

palidez SF paleness, pallor

pálido ADJ (*gen*) pale, pallid; (= *enfermizo*) sickly

palier SM (*RPl*) landing

palillo SM 1 (= *mondadientes*) (*tb* ~ **de dientes**) toothpick; **unas piernas como ~s de dientes** legs like matchsticks 2 (*Mús*) [*de tambor, batería*] drumstick; **palillos** (= *instrumento*) castanets 3 (*para comida oriental*) chopstick 4 (* *hum*) very thin person; ✦ MODISMO **estar hecho un ~** to be as thin as a rake 5 (*Chi*) (= *aguja de tejer*) knitting needle

palillero SM toothpick holder

palio SM 1 (= *dosel*) canopy 2 (*Rel*) pallium; ✦ MODISMO **recibir bajo ~ a algn** to roll out the red carpet for sb

palique* SM (*Esp*) chat, chitchat; **estar de ~** to chat, natter

palito SM (*RPl*) ice lolly (*Brit*), Popsicle® (*EEUU*)

paliza Ⓐ SF 1 (*en pelea, como castigo*) beating; **dar** *o* **propinar una ~ a algn** to give sb a beating, beat sb up* 2 (*) (= *pesadez*) pain*; **dar la ~** to be a pain*; ✦ MODISMO **darse la ~** to slog away 3 (*Dep**) drubbing, thrashing Ⓑ SMF (*) (= *pesado*) bore, pain*

palizas* (*Esp*) SMF INV bore, pain*

palla SF (*Hist*) Inca princess

pallar SM (*And, CS*) Lima bean

palma SF 1 (*Anat*) palm; **leer la ~ de la mano a algn** to read sb's palm; ✦ MODISMO **conocer algo como la ~ de la mano** to know sth like the back of one's hand 2 **palmas** (= *aplausos*) clapping *sing*, applause *sing*; **batir** *o* **dar** *o* **hacer ~s** to clap (one's hands), applaud; **tocar las ~s** to clap in time 3 (*Bot*) (= *palmera*) palm (tree); (= *hoja*) palm leaf; ✦ MODISMO **llevarse la ~: las tres son muy antipáticas, pero Ana se lleva la ~** the three of them are very unfriendly, but Ana wins hands down

palmada SF 1 [*de amistad*] slap, pat 2 **palmadas** (= *aplausos*) clapping *sing*, applause *sing*; **dar ~s** to clap (one's hands), applaud 3 (*LAm*) (= *azote*) spanking

palmar¹ SM (*Bot*) palm grove, cluster of palms

palmar²** /1a/ Ⓐ VI to kick the bucket*, peg out** Ⓑ VT **~la** to kick the bucket*, peg out**

palmario ADJ obvious, self-evident

palmarés SM 1 (*Dep*) [*de ganadores*] list of winners 2 (= *historial*) record

palmatoria SF candlestick

palmear /1a/ VT (*LAm*) to pat

palmera SF, **palmero¹** SM (*And, Méx*) palm (tree)

palmero² ADJ of/from La Palma

palmeta SF 1 (= *palo*) cane 2 (*RPl*) (*para las moscas*) fly swat

palmípedo ADJ web-footed

palmista SMF (*LAm*) palmist

palmitas SFPL ✦ MODISMO **tener** *o* **llevar** *o* **traer a algn en ~** (= *mimar*) to spoil sb; (= *tratar con cuidado*) to handle sb with kid gloves

palmito SM heart of palm

palmo SM (= *medida*) span; (*fig*) few inches *pl*, small amount; ✦ MODISMOS **~ a ~** inch by inch; **avanzar ~ a ~** to inch forward; **conocer el terreno ~ a ~** *o* **a ~s** to know every inch of the ground; **dejar a algn con un ~ de narices** to disappoint sb, let sb down; **no levantaba un ~ del suelo cuando ...** he was knee-high to a grasshopper when ...

palmotear /1a/ VI to clap, applaud

palmoteo SM clapping, applause

palo SM 1 (= *vara*) (*de poco grosor*) stick; (*fijo en el suelo*) post; [*de telégrafos, tienda de campaña*] pole; [*de herramienta*] handle, shaft; **el ~ de la fregona** the mop handle; ✦ REFRÁN **de tal ~ tal astilla** like father like son ➤ **palo de amasar** (*RPl*) rolling pin ➤ **palo de escoba** broomstick

2 (= *madera*) **cuchara de** ~ wooden spoon; **pata de** ~ wooden leg, peg leg
3 (= *golpe*) blow; **dar** o **pegar un** ~ **a algn** (= *golpear*) to hit sb with a stick; (*) (= *timar*) to rip sb off*; **los críticos le dieron un** ~ **a la obra** the critics slated the play*;
✦ MODISMOS **dar** ~**s de ciego** (*peleando*) to lash out wildly; (*buscando una solución*) to take a stab in the dark; **no dar (ni)** ~ **al agua*** to not lift a finger
4 (*) (= *disgusto*) bummer**, nightmare*; **¡qué** ~ **si suspendo!** it'll be a real bummer** o nightmare* if I fail!; **me daría** ~ **que se enterase** I would hate it if he found out
5 (*Náut*) mast; ✦ MODISMO **a** ~ **seco: nos tomamos el vino a** ~ **seco** we had the wine on its own; **no pasa un día a** ~ **seco** there goes not a single day without a drink; **vermut a** ~ **seco** straight vermouth; **palo de mesana** mizzenmast ➤ **palo de trinquete** foremast ➤ **palo mayor** mainmast
6 (*Dep*) **6.1** [*de portería*] post **6.2** (*para golpear*) (*en hockey*) stick; (*en golf*) club ➤ **palo de golf** golf club
7 (*Tip*) (*de b, d*) upstroke; (*de p, q*) downstroke
8 (*Naipes*) suit; **cambiar de** ~ to change suit ➤ **palo del triunfo** trump suit, trumps *pl*
9 (*Mús*) (*en flamenco*) style
10 (*esp LAm Bot*) tree
11 (*Ven**) [*de licor*] swig*, slug*
12 (*Col, Ven*) **un** ~ **de: un** ~ **de casa** a marvellous house; **es un** ~ **de hombre** he's a great guy; **cayó un** ~ **de agua** the rain came pouring down, there was a huge downpour*
13 (*RPl**) [*de pesos*] million pesos

paloma SF (*gen*) pigeon; (*blanca, como símbolo*) dove ➤ **paloma de la paz** dove of peace ➤ **paloma mensajera** carrier pigeon, homing pigeon ➤ **paloma torcaz** wood pigeon, ringdove

palomar SM dovecot(e)

palomear /1a/ VT (*Perú*) to shoot to kill, shoot dead

palomilla Ⓐ SMF (*And**) (= *niño*) naughty child Ⓑ SF
1 (= *mariposa*) moth; (*esp*) grain moth; (= *crisálida*) nymph, chrysalis **2** (*Téc*) (= *tuerca*) wing nut **3** (*CAm, Méx**) [*de niños*] crowd, band

palomino SM **1** (*Orn*) young pigeon **2** (*LAm*) (= *caballo*) palomino (horse) **3** (*) (*en ropa interior*) skidmark*

palomita SF **1** (*Méx*) (= *aprobación*) tick (*esp Brit*), check (*EEUU**) **2** (*Dep*) full-length dive **3 palomitas** (*tb* ~**s de maíz**) popcorn *sing*

palomo SM (cock) pigeon

palote SM **1** (*en escritura*) (*gen*) downstroke; (*en forma de* "*S*") pothook **2** (*Carib, CS Culin*) [*de amasar*] rolling pin

palpable ADJ **1** (*con las manos*) palpable, tangible **2** (= *claro, evidente*) palpable, obvious, palpable

palpar /1a/ VT **1** (= *tocar*) to touch, feel; (= *tantear*) to feel one's way along; [*+ sospechoso*] to frisk **2** [*+ miedo, ansiedad*] to feel

palpitación SF (*gen*) palpitation; (*nerviosa*) quiver, quivering

palpitante ADJ **1** [*corazón*] throbbing **2** [*interés, cuestión*] burning

palpitar /1a/ VI **1** (*gen*) to palpitate; [*corazón*] to throb, beat; (*nerviosamente*) to quiver; (*con fuerza*) to flutter **2** (*CS*) **me palpita que ...** I have a feeling/hunch that ...

pálpito SM (*CS*) hunch

palta SF (*And, CS*) avocado (pear)

palto SM (*And, CS*) avocado (pear) tree

palúdico ADJ malarial

paludismo SM malaria

palurdo/a* Ⓐ ADJ coarse, uncouth Ⓑ SM/F yokel, hick (*EEUU**)

pamela SF sun hat, picture hat

pampa SF (*Geog*) pampa(s), prairie; **la Pampa** the Pampas; ✦ MODISMO **estar en** ~ **y la vía** (*RPl**) to be flat broke*; ⊙ *GAUCHO*

pampeano ADJ of/from the pampas

pampero SM (*Meteo*) strong westerly wind (*blowing over the pampas from the Andes*)

pampino (*Chi*) ADJ of/from the Chilean pampas

pamplinas SFPL **1** (*) (= *tonterías*) rubbish *sing*, nonsense *sing* **2** (*) (= *zalamerías*) soft soap* *sing*

pamplonés/esa ADJ, **pamplonica** ADJ of/from Pamplona

pan SM **1** (*Culin*) (*gen*) bread; (= *hogaza*) loaf ➤ **pan blanco, pan candeal** white bread ➤ **pan de molde** tin (*Brit*) o pan (*EEUU*) loaf ➤ **pan dulce** (*Méx*) pastry ➤ **pan integral** wholemeal (*Brit*) o wholewheat (*esp EEUU*) bread ➤ **pan molido** (*Méx*), **pan rallado** breadcrumbs *pl* ➤ **pan tostado** toast
2 (= *bloque*) ➤ **pan de azúcar** sugar loaf ➤ **pan de higos** block of dried figs
3 ✦ MODISMOS **con su** ~ **se lo coma** that's his look-out; **ganarse el** ~ to earn one's living; **llamar al** ~ ~ **y al vino vino** to call a spade a spade; **más bueno que el** ~*: **estar más bueno que el** ~ [*persona*] to be gorgeous, be dishy*; **ser más bueno que el** ~ to be as good as gold; **ser el** ~ **nuestro de cada día: aquí los atracos son el** ~ **nuestro de cada día** muggings happen all the time around here

pana[1] SF cord, corduroy

pana[2] SF (*Chi Aut*) breakdown; **quedar en** ~ to break down

pana[3] SF (*Chi*) (= *hígado*) liver

pana[4] SMF (*Carib*) (= *compañero*) pal*, buddy (*EEUU**)

panacea SF panacea

panadería SF baker's (shop), bakery

panadero/a SM/F baker

panal SM honeycomb

Panamá SM (= *país*) Panama; (= *capital*) Panama City

panamá SM panama hat

panameño/a Ⓐ ADJ Panamanian Ⓑ SM/F Panamanian; **los** ~**s** the Panamanians

panamericano Ⓐ ADJ Pan-American Ⓑ SF **la Panamericana** the Pan-American highway

pancarta SF placard, banner

panceta SF streaky bacon

pancha* SF = **panza**

pancho[1] ADJ (= *tranquilo*) calm, unruffled; **estar tan** ~ (*CS, Esp*) to remain perfectly calm, not turn a hair

pancho[2] SM (*RPl Culin*) hot dog

pancita SF (*Méx Culin*) tripe

pancito SM (*LAm*) (bread) roll

páncreas SM INV pancreas

panda[1] SMF (*Zool*) panda

panda[2] SF = **pandilla**

pandear /1a/ VI, **pandearse** VPR [*madera*] to bend, warp; [*pared*] to sag, bulge

pandemonio SM, **pandemónium** SM pandemonium; **fue el** ~* all hell broke loose, there was pandemonium

pandereta SF tambourine

pandero SM **1** (*Mús*) tambourine **2** (*) (= *culo*) backside*, butt (*EEUU***)

pandilla SF **1** [*de amigos*] gang; **la** ~ **de mi hermano** my brother's friends **2** [*de criminales*] gang; [*de gamberros*] bunch, load

pandillero/a SM/F (*esp LAm*) member of a gang

pando ADJ **1** [*pared*] bulging; [*madera*] warped; [*viga*] sagging **2** [*río, persona*] slow **3** [*plato*] shallow; [*terreno*] flat

Pandora SF ✦ MODISMO **la caja de** ~ Pandora's box

pane SM (*And Aut*) breakdown

panecillo SM (bread) roll

panegírico SM panegyric

panel SM **1** [*de pared, puerta*] panel ➤ **panel de información de vuelos** flight information board ➤ **panel de instrumentos** (*Aut*) dashboard ➤ **panel de mandos** (*Aer*) control panel, controls *pl* ➤ **panel solar** solar panel **2** (= *jurado*) panel ➤ **panel de audiencia** TV viewers' panel

panela SF (*LAm Culin*) brown sugar loaf

panelista SMF panelist

panera SF (*para servir*) bread basket; (*para guardar*) bread bin (*Brit*), breadbox (*EEUU*)

pánfilo ADJ (= *crédulo*) simple, gullible; (= *tonto*) stupid

panfletario ADJ cheap, demagogic

panfletista SMF pamphleteer

panfleto SM pamphlet

panga SF (*CAm, Méx*) barge, lighter

pánico SM panic; **le tengo un ~ tremendo** I'm scared stiff of him

panificadora SF bread factory

panizo SM 1 (*Bot*) (= *mijo*) millet 2 (*Chi*) [*de mineral*] mineral deposit

panocha SF 1 (*Bot*) [*de maíz*] corncob; [*de trigo*] ear of wheat 2 (*Méx*) (= *azúcar*) unrefined brown sugar; (= *dulce*) brown sugar candy

panoplia SF 1 (= *armadura*) panoply 2 (= *colección de armas*) collection of arms

panorama SM 1 (*gen*) panorama; (= *perspectiva*) outlook; **el ~ político actual** the present political scene 2 (*Arte, Fot*) view

panorámica SF general view, survey

panorámico ADJ panoramic

panqué SM 1 (*CAm, Carib, Col*) pancake 2 (*Méx*) cake

panqueque SM (*LAm*) pancake

pantaletas SFPL (*CAm, Carib, Méx*) panties

pantalla SF 1 [*de lámpara*] shade, lampshade 2 (*Cine, TV*) screen; **la pequeña ~** ◇ **la ~ chica** (*LAm*) the small screen, the TV; **llevar una historia a la ~** to film a story ➤ **pantalla de plasma** plasma screen ➤ **pantalla grande** big screen ➤ **pantalla panorámica** wide screen 3 (*Inform*) screen, display ➤ **pantalla de cristal líquido** liquid crystal display ➤ **pantalla de rayos** (*en aeropuerto*) X-ray security apparatus ➤ **pantalla táctil** touch screen 4 (*LAm*) (= *abanico*) fan 5 (= *cobertura*) front; **servir de ~ a algo** to be a front for sth 6 [*de chimenea*] fireguard 7 (= *biombo*) screen

pantalón SM, **pantalones** SMPL trousers (*Brit*), pants (*EEUU*); **un ~** ◇ **unos pantalones** a pair of trousers (*Brit*) *o* pants (*EEUU*); **bajarse los pantalones** (*lit*) to take *o* pull one's trousers (*Brit*) *o* pants (*EEUU*) down; (*Esp**) (*fig*) to swallow one's pride; ✦ MODISMO **es ella la que lleva los pantalones*** she's the one who wears the trousers (*Brit*) *o* pants (*EEUU*) ➤ **pantalones cortos** shorts ➤ **pantalón de montar** riding breeches *pl* ➤ **pantalones tejanos, pantalones vaqueros** jeans

pantanal SM marshland

pantano SM 1 (= *ciénaga*) bog, marsh 2 (*Esp*) (= *embalse*) reservoir

pantanoso ADJ 1 [*terreno, región*] boggy, marshy 2 [*situación*] difficult, tricky*

panteísta Ⓐ ADJ pantheistic Ⓑ SMF pantheist

panteón SM 1 (= *monumento*) pantheon; **el ~ de los reyes** the burial place of the royal family ➤ **panteón familiar** family vault 2 (*And, CAm, Méx*) (= *cementerio*) cemetery

pantera SF panther

pantimedias SFPL (*Méx*) tights (*Brit*), pantyhose (*EEUU*)

pantis SMPL tights (*Brit*), pantyhose (*EEUU*)

pantomima SF mime

pantorrilla SF calf

pants SMPL (*CAm, Méx*) tracksuit *sing* (*Brit*), sweatsuit *sing* (*EEUU*)

pantufla SF, **pantuflo** SM (carpet) slipper

panty SM, **pantys** SMPL tights (*Brit*), pantyhose (*EEUU*)

panza* SF belly, paunch

panzada* SF 1 (= *hartazgo*) **nos dimos una ~ de cordero** we stuffed ourselves with lamb; **me he dado una buena ~ de dormir** I had a really good sleep 2 (= *golpe*) (*en el agua*) belly flop; **aterrizaje de ~** belly landing

pañal SM [*de bebé*] nappy (*Brit*), diaper (*EEUU*); ✦ MODISMO **estar todavía en ~es** [*persona*] to be still wet behind the ears; [*ciencia, técnica*] to be still in its infancy

pañito SM [*de mesa*] table-runner; [*de bandeja*] traycloth

paño SM 1 (= *tela*) cloth; ✦ MODISMOS **conocerse el ~** to know the score*; **le conozco el ~** I know his sort 2 (= *pieza*) cloth; (= *trapo*) duster ➤ **paño de cocina** (*para secar los platos*) tea towel (*Brit*), dish towel (*EEUU*); (*para limpiar*) dish cloth ➤ **paño de lágrimas: soy su ~ de lágrimas** I'm a shoulder for him to cry on ➤ **paños calientes** half measures; **no andarse con ~s calientes** (*para solucionar algo*) not to go in for half-measures; (*al criticar algo*) to pull no punches; **poner ~s calientes** to make a half-hearted attempt ➤ **paños menores** underwear *sing*

pañoleta SF 1 [*de mujer*] (*sobre los hombros*) shawl; (*sobre la cabeza*) headscarf 2 [*de torero*] tie

pañuelo SM (*para limpiarse*) handkerchief; (*para la cabeza*) scarf, headscarf; (*para el cuello*) scarf; [*de hombre*] cravat ➤ **pañuelo de papel** paper handkerchief

papa¹ SM (*Rel*) pope

papa² SF 1 (*esp LAm*) (= *patata*) potato; ✦ MODISMO **ni ~***: **no entiendo ni ~** I don't understand a word; **no sabe ni ~** he hasn't got a clue ➤ **papa dulce** sweet potato ➤ **papas fritas** (*de sartén*) French fries, chips (*Brit*); (*de paquete*) crisps (*Brit*), potato chips (*EEUU*) 2 (*Méx**) (= *mentira*) fib*

papá* SM dad*, daddy*, pop (*EEUU**); **mis ~s** my mum (*Brit*) *o* mom (*EEUU*) and dad*, my mom and pop (*EEUU**) ➤ **Papá Noel** Santa Claus, Father Christmas (*Brit*)

papada SF [*de persona*] double chin; [*de animal*] dewlap

papado SM papacy

papagayo SM 1 (= *ave*) parrot; ✦ MODISMO **como un ~** parrot-fashion 2 (*Carib, Méx*) (= *cometa*) large kite 3 (*And, RPl*) (= *bacinilla*) bedpan

papal ADJ (*Rel*) papal

papalote SM (*CAm, Méx*) kite

papamoscas SM INV flycatcher

papamóvil SM popemobile

papanatas* SM INV sucker*, simpleton

papanicolau SM (*LAm*) smear test (*Brit*), pap test (*EEUU*)

paparazzi [papaˈratsi] SMPL **los ~** the paparazzi

paparrucha* SF, **paparruchada*** SF silly thing; **~s** nonsense *sing*, rubbish *sing* (*esp Brit*)

papaya SF papaya, pawpaw (*Brit*)

papayo SM papaya tree, pawpaw tree (*Brit*)

papear** /1a/ VT, VI to eat

papel SM 1 (= *material*) paper; **una bolsa de ~** a paper bag; **un ~** (*pequeño*) a piece of paper; (= *hoja, folio*) a sheet of paper; ✦ MODISMO **sobre el ~** on paper ➤ **papel biblia** India paper ➤ **papel charol** shiny wrapping paper ➤ **papel confort** (*Chi*) toilet paper ➤ **papel de aluminio** tinfoil, aluminium *o* (*EEUU*) aluminum foil ➤ **papel de arroz** rice paper ➤ **papel de envolver** wrapping paper ➤ **papel de estraza** (grey) wrapping paper ➤ **papel de fumar** cigarette paper ➤ **papel del Estado** government bonds *pl* ➤ **papel de lija** sandpaper ➤ **papel de regalo** gift wrap, wrapping paper ➤ **papel (de) seda** tissue paper ➤ **papel higiénico** toilet paper ➤ **papel mojado** scrap of paper, worthless bit of paper; **el documento no es más que ~ mojado** the document isn't worth the paper it's written on ➤ **papel moneda** (*frm*) paper money, banknotes *pl* ➤ **papel pintado** wallpaper ➤ **papel secante** blotting paper ➤ **papel timbrado** stamp, stamp paper ➤ **papel vegetal** tracing paper 2 **papeles** (= *documentos*) papers, documents; (*de identidad*) identification papers; **tiene los ~es en regla** his papers are in order; ✦ MODISMO **perder los ~es** to lose it 3 (= *actuación*) (*Cine, Teat*) part, role; **jugó un ~ muy importante en las negociaciones** he played a very important part in the negotiations; **hacer buen/mal ~** to make a good/bad impression ➤ **papel estelar** star part

papeleo SM (= *trámites*) paperwork; (*pey*) red tape

papelera SF 1 (*en oficina, casa*) wastepaper bin, wastepaper basket; (*en la calle*) litter bin (*Brit*), trash can (*EEUU*); (*Internet*) (*tb ~ de reciclaje*) wastebasket 2 (= *fábrica*) paper mill

papelería SF 1 (= *tienda*) stationer's (shop) 2 (= *artículos de escritorio*) stationery

papelero SM (*RPl*) = **papelera**

papeleta SF 1 [*de rifa*] ticket; (*Univ*) (*tb* ~ **de examen**) *exam results slip*; ✦ MODISMO **¡vaya ~!** (*Esp**) this is a tough one! 2 (*Pol*) ballot paper, voting paper

papelillo SM cigarette paper

papelina* SF paper, sheet (*containing drug*)

papelón SM 1 (*Teat, Cine*) leading role, big part; ✦ MODISMO **hacer un ~** to show o.s. up, make o.s. a laughing stock 2 (*And, Carib*) (= *pan de azúcar*) sugar loaf

papeo** SM grub**, chow (*EEUU***), food

paperas SFPL mumps *sing*

papi* SM dad*, daddy*, pop (*EEUU**)

papila SF papilla ➤ **papila gustativa** taste bud

papilla SF baby food; ✦ MODISMO **estar hecho ~*** (= *cansado*) to be shattered*; (= *roto*) to be smashed to pieces

papiloma SM papilloma

papiro SM papyrus

papiroflexia SF origami

papirotazo SM flick

papista Ⓐ ADJ (*pey*) papist; ✦ MODISMO **es más ~ que el papa** he's a real zealot Ⓑ SMF papist

papo SM [*de persona*] double chin; [*de ave*] crop; [*de animal*] dewlap

paquebote SM packet boat

paquete Ⓐ SM 1 [*de correos*] (*grande*) package, parcel (*esp Brit*); (*pequeño*) package; ✦ MODISMOS **darse ~** (*Méx**) to give o.s. airs, put on airs; **ir** o **viajar de ~*** (*en moto*) to ride pillion ➤ **paquete bomba** parcel bomb ➤ **paquetes postales** (*como servicio*) parcel post *sing* (*Brit*), surface mail *sing* (*EEUU*) 2 [*de cigarrillos, galletas*] packet (*esp Brit*), pack (*esp EEUU*); [*de harina, azúcar*] bag 3 (*Fin, Inform*) package ➤ **paquete accionarial, paquete de acciones** parcel of shares ➤ **paquete de aplicaciones** software package ➤ **paquete de medidas** package of measures 4 (*) (= *castigo*) **meter un ~ a algn** to throw the book at sb 5 (**) (= *genitales*) bulge, lunchbox**; ✦ MODISMO **marcar ~** to wear very tight trousers 6 (*Méx*) (= *asunto*) tough job, hard one Ⓑ ADJ INV (*RPl**) elegant, chic

paquete-bomba SM (*pl* **paquetes-bomba**) parcel bomb (*Brit*), package bomb (*EEUU*)

paquetería SF parcels *pl*; **servicio de ~** parcel service

paquidermo SM pachyderm

paquistaní = **pakistaní**

par Ⓐ ADJ 1 [*número*] even 2 (= *igual*) equal Ⓑ SM 1 (= *pareja*) pair; (= *número indeterminado*) couple; **un ~ de guantes** a pair of gloves; **un ~ de veces** a couple of times ➤ **par de fuerzas** (*Mec*) couple ➤ **par de torsión** (*Mec*) torque 2 (= *igual*) equal; **sin ~** unparalleled, peerless (*frm*) 3 (*Mat*) even number; **~es o nones** odds or evens 4 (*Golf*) par; **dos bajo/sobre ~** two under/over par 5 ✦ MODISMO **de ~ en ~** wide open 6 (*Pol*) peer Ⓒ SF 1 (*esp Com, Fin*) par; **a la ~** on a par 2 **a la ~ que**: **es útil a la ~ que divertido** it is both useful and amusing, it is useful as well as being amusing

---

Par (de) seguido de un sustantivo se traduce por **pair (of)** cuando se refiere a objetos que normalmente se usan por pares: "tres pares de guantes", *three pairs of gloves*. Se traduce por **couple (of)** en los demás casos, cuando se emplea en el sentido de "dos o más de dos": "Me he comprado un par de camisas", *I've bought a couple of shirts*.

---

para PREP 1 (*indicando finalidad, uso*) 1.1 (*con sustantivos, pronombres*) for; **un regalo ~ ti** a present for you; **léelo ~ ti** read it to yourself; **yo no valgo ~ esto** I'm no good at this; **laca ~ el pelo** hairspray; **~ esto, podíamos habernos quedado en casa** if this is it, we might as well have stayed at home 1.2 (*en preguntas*) **¿~ qué lo quieres?** why do you want it?, what do you want it for?; **¿~ qué sirve?** what's it for?; **—¿por qué no se lo dices? —¿~ qué?** "why don't you tell her?" — "what's the point o use?"

2 **~ que** (+ SUBJUN): **lo traje ~ que lo vieras** I brought it so (that) you could see it; **es ~ que lo leas** it's for you to read 3 (+ INFIN) 3.1 (*indicando finalidad*) to; **lo hizo ~ salvarse** he did it (in order) to save himself; **entré despacito ~ no despertarla** I went in slowly so as not to wake her; **no es ~ comer** it's not for eating, it's not to be eaten 3.2 (*indicando secuencia temporal*) **el rey visitará Argentina ~ volar después a Chile** the king will visit Argentina and then fly on to Chile

4 (*con expresiones de tiempo*) **con esto tengo ~ rato** this will take me a while; **lo recordaré ~ siempre** I'll remember it forever; **ahora ~ agosto hará un año** it'll be a year ago this o come August; **va ~ un año desde la última vez** it's getting on for a year since the last time; **lo tendré listo ~ fin de mes** I'll have it ready by o for the end of the month; **~ las dos estaba lloviendo** by two o'clock it was raining; **un cuarto ~ las diez** (*LAm*) a quarter to ten

5 (*indicando dirección*) **~ atrás** back, backwards; **~ la derecha** to the right; **el autobús ~ Marbella** the bus for Marbella, the Marbella bus; **iba ~ la estación** I was going towards the station; **ir ~ casa** to go home, head for home

6 (*indicando opiniones*) **~ mí que miente** in my opinion o if you ask me he's lying

7 (*en comparaciones*) **es mucho ~ lo que suele dar** this is a lot in comparison with what he usually gives; **~ ser un niño lo hace muy bien** he does it very well for a child; **~ ruidosos, los españoles** there's nobody like the Spaniards for being noisy

8 (*indicando trato*) **~ con** to, towards; **tan amable ~ con todos** so kind to o towards everybody

parabién SM congratulations *pl*; **dar el ~ a algn** to congratulate sb (**por** on)

parábola SF 1 (*Mat*) parabola 2 (*Literat*) parable

parabólica SF satellite dish

parabólico ADJ parabolic

parabrisas SM INV windscreen (*Brit*), windshield (*EEUU*)

paraca* SM paratrooper, para*

paracaídas SM INV parachute; **lanzarse** o **saltar** o **tirarse en ~** (*gen*) to parachute; (*en emergencia*) to parachute, bale out; (*una sola vez*) to do a parachute jump

paracaidismo SM parachuting

paracaidista SMF 1 (*gen*) parachutist; (*Mil*) paratrooper 2 (*Méx**) (= *no invitado*) gatecrasher; (= *ocupante de tierras*) squatter

parachoques SM INV (*Aut*) bumper (*Brit*), fender (*EEUU*); (*Ferro*) buffer

parada SF 1 (= *acción*) stop; **hicimos varias ~s en el camino** we made several stops on the way; **un tren sin ~s** a direct train; **el autobús hace ~ en Valencia** the bus stops at Valencia ➤ **parada biológica** temporary fishing ban (*to allow stocks to recover*) ➤ **parada cardíaca** cardiac arrest ➤ **parada en seco** sudden stop 2 (= *lugar*) stop ➤ **parada de autobús** bus stop ➤ **parada de taxis** taxi rank (*Brit*), taxi stand (*EEUU*) ➤ **parada discrecional** request stop 3 (= *desfile*) (*Mil*) parade; ✦ MODISMO **ir a todas las ~s** (*Chi*) to be up for anything* 4 (*Dep*) save, stop 5 (*RPl*) (= *vanidad*) snobbery, pretension 6 (*Perú*) (= *mercado*) open market, farmer's market

paradero SM 1 [*de persona*] whereabouts *pl*; **se halla en ~ desconocido** his whereabouts are unknown 2 (*And*) [*de autobús*] bus stop

paradigma SM paradigm

paradigmático ADJ paradigmatic

paradisiaco ADJ, **paradisíaco** ADJ heavenly

parado/a Ⓐ ADJ **1** (= *detenido*) **me quedé ~ para que no me oyese** I stood still so that he couldn't hear me; **estuve un momento ~ delante de su puerta** I stopped for a moment in front of his door; **¿por qué no nos echas una mano en vez de estar ahí ~?** can't you give us a hand instead of just standing there *o* around?; **no le gusta estar ~, siempre encuentra algo que hacer** he doesn't like to be idle *o* doing nothing, he always finds himself something to do; **¿qué hace ese coche ahí ~?** what's that car doing standing there?; **la producción estuvo parada durante unos meses** production was at a standstill *o* stopped for a few months
2 (*Esp*) (= *sin trabajo*) unemployed
3 (*LAm*) (= *de pie*) standing (up); **estuve ~ durante dos horas** I was standing for two hours
4 (*Esp**) **ser ~** (= *ser tímido*) to be tongue-tied; (= *tener poca iniciativa*) to be a wimp*
5 (*CS*) (= *engreído*) vain
6 salir bien/mal ~: salió mejor ~ de lo que cabía esperar he came out of it better than could be expected; **la imagen del partido ha salido muy mal parada de todo este escándalo** the party's image has suffered because of this scandal
7 (*LAm*) (= *hacia arriba*) [*pelo*] stiff; [*poste*] upright; [*orejas*] pricked-up; **con la cola parada** with its tail held high
Ⓑ SM/F (*Esp*) unemployed person; **los ~s de larga duración** the long-term unemployed

paradoja SF paradox

paradójico ADJ paradoxical

parador SM (*Esp*) (*tb* **~ nacional de turismo**) (state-run) tourist hotel; (*Hist*) inn

PARADOR NACIONAL

In the early days of the Spanish tourist industry in the 1950s, the government set up a network of high-class tourist hotels known as **paradores**. They are sited in rural beauty spots or places of historical interest, often in converted castles and monasteries.
See also www.parador.es

parafarmacia SF chemist's shop (*not selling prescription medicines*)

parafernalia SF paraphernalia

parafina SF (*sólida*) paraffin wax, paraffin (*EEUU*); (*Chi*) (= *combustible*) kerosene, paraffin (*Brit*) ➤ **parafina líquida** liquid paraffin (*Brit*), mineral oil (*EEUU*)

parafrasear /1a/ VT to paraphrase

paráfrasis SF INV paraphrase

paragolpes SM INV (*CS Aut*) bumper (*Brit*), fender (*EEUU*)

paraguas SM INV umbrella

Paraguay SM Paraguay

paraguayo/a Ⓐ ADJ of/from Paraguay Ⓑ SM/F native/inhabitant of Paraguay

paragüero SM umbrella stand

paraíso SM **1** (*Rel*) paradise, heaven ➤ **paraíso fiscal** tax haven ➤ **paraíso terrenal** Garden of Eden **2** (*Teat*) upper gallery, gods *pl* (*Brit*), upper balcony (*EEUU*)

paraje SM place, spot

paralela SF **1** (= *línea*) parallel (line) **2 paralelas** (*Dep*) parallel bars ➤ **paralelas asimétricas** asymmetric bars

paralelamente ADV **la carretera avanza ~ a la vía del tren** the road runs parallel to the rail track

paralelismo SM parallelism, parallel

paralelo Ⓐ ADJ **1** [*líneas*] parallel (**a** to); [*vidas, caracteres*] parallel **2** (= *no oficial*) [*en festival, congreso*] unofficial, fringe *antes de s* Ⓑ SM parallel; **en ~** (*Elec*) in parallel

paralelogramo SM parallelogram

paralímpico/a ADJ, SM/F = **paraolímpico**

parálisis SF INV paralysis ➤ **parálisis cerebral** cerebral palsy

paralítico/a ADJ, SM/F paralytic

paralización SF (*gen*) stoppage; (*Med*) paralysation, paralyzation; (*Com*) stagnation

paralizar /1f/ Ⓐ VT (*gen*) to stop; (*Med*) to paralyse, paralyze; [+ *tráfico*] to bring to a standstill; **estar paralizado de miedo** to be paralysed with fright Ⓑ **paralizarse** VPR **1** [*pierna, brazo*] to become paralysed **2** [*demanda, inversiones, obra*] to grind to a halt

paramédico ADJ paramedic, paramedical

paramento SM **1** [*de pared, piedra*] face **2** (= *colgadura*) hangings *pl* ➤ **paramentos sacerdotales** liturgical vestments

parámetro SM parameter

paramilitar ADJ, SMF paramilitary

páramo SM bleak plateau, high moor

paramuno ADJ (*Col*) upland, highland

parangón SM comparison; **sin ~** incomparable, matchless

paraninfo SM (*Univ*) (= *salón de actos*) assembly hall; (= *auditorio*) auditorium

paranoia SF paranoia

paranoico/a ADJ, SM/F paranoid

paranormal ADJ paranormal

paraolimpiada SF, **paraolimpiadas** SFPL Paralympics, Paralympic Games

paraolímpico/a Ⓐ ADJ Paralympic Ⓑ SM/F Paralympic athlete

parapente SM (= *deporte*) paragliding; (= *aparato*) paraglider

parapetarse /1a/ VPR **1** (= *protegerse*) to protect o.s., shelter (**tras** behind) **2 ~ tras** [+ *excusas*] to take refuge in

parapeto SM (*gen*) defence, defense (*EEUU*), barricade; (*Mil*) parapet

paraplejia SF, **paraplejía** SF paraplegia

parapléjico/a ADJ, SM/F paraplegic

parapsicología SF parapsychology

parar /1a/ Ⓐ VT **1** [+ *persona, coche, respiración*] to stop; **nos paró la policía** we were stopped by the police; **no hay quien pare el avance tecnológico** there is no stopping technological progress
2 [+ *tiro, penalti, gol*] to save, stop; [+ *golpe*] to ward off; (*Esgrima*) to parry
3 (*LAm*) (= *levantar*) to raise; (= *poner de pie*) to stand upright
Ⓑ VI **1** (= *detenerse, terminar*) to stop; **¡pare!** stop!; **paramos a echar gasolina** we stopped to get some petrol (*Brit*) *o* gas (*EEUU*); **¡no para! siempre está haciendo algo** he never stops! he's always doing something; **no ~á hasta conseguirlo** he won't stop *o* give up until he gets it; **~ en seco** to stop dead; **sin ~: los teléfonos sonaban sin ~** the phones never stopped ringing; **lloraba sin ~** he didn't stop crying; **hablar sin ~** to talk non-stop; ✦ MODISMO **¡dónde va a ~!*** there's no comparison!
2 ~ de hacer algo to stop doing sth

Recuérdese que en este sentido **stop** rige que el verbo que le siga inmediatamente aparezca en gerundio y no en infinitivo:

ha parado de llover it has stopped raining; **no para de quejarse** he never stops complaining, he complains all the time
3 ir a ~ to end up; **la empresa podría ir a ~ a manos extranjeras** the firm could end up in foreign hands; **fueron a ~ a la comisaría** they ended up at the police station; **¿dónde habrá ido a ~ todo aquel dinero?** what can have become of *o* happened to all that money?; **¿dónde vamos a ir a ~?** where's it all going to end?, what is the world coming to?
4 (= *hospedarse*) to stay
5 (= *hacer huelga*) to go on strike
Ⓒ **pararse** VPR **1** (= *detenerse*) [*persona*] to stop; [*coche*] to stop, pull up; [*proceso*] to stop, come to a halt; [*trabajo*] to stop, come to a standstill; **~se a hacer algo** to stop to do sth, pause to do sth
2 (*LAm*) (= *ponerse de pie*) to stand (up); (*de la cama*) to get up;

up; [*pelo*] to stand on end
3 ~se en algo (= *prestar atención*) to pay attention to sth
pararrayos SM INV lightning conductor (*Brit*), lightning rod (*EEUU*)

parasitar /1a/ **Ⓐ** VT to parasitize **Ⓑ** VI ~ **en** to parasitize

parasitario ADJ parasitic(al)

parásito Ⓐ ADJ parasitic (**de** on) **Ⓑ** SM 1 (*Biol*) parasite (*tb fig*) 2 **parásitos** (*Radio*) atmospherics *pl*, statics *sing*

parasol SM parasol, sunshade

parcela SF 1 (= *solar*) plot, piece of ground; (*Agr*) smallholding 2 (= *parte*) part, portion ➤ **parcela de poder** (*político*) power base; (*de influencia*) sphere of influence

parcelar /1a/ VT (*gen*) to divide into plots; [+ *finca*] to break up

parchar /1a/ VT (*esp LAm*) to patch, put a patch on

parche SM 1 (= *pieza*) patch; (*para un ojo*) eye patch ➤ **parche de nicotina** nicotine patch 2 (= *solución*) temporary remedy, stopgap solution; **poner ~s** to paper over the cracks 3 (*Chi*) (= *tirita*) sticking plaster (*Brit*), Band-Aid® (*EEUU*) 4 (*Mús*) (= *piel de tambor*) drumhead

parchear /1a/ VT to patch (up)

parchís SM *board game similar to ludo*, Parcheesi® (*EEUU*)

parcial Ⓐ ADJ 1 (= *incompleto*) partial; **examen ~** mid-term exam; **a tiempo ~** part-time 2 (= *no ecuánime*) biased, partial; (*Pol*) partisan **Ⓑ** SM (= *examen*) mid-term exam

parcialidad SF partiality, bias

parco ADJ (*gen*) frugal, sparing; (= *moderado*) moderate, temperate; (*en el gasto*) parsimonious; **~ en elogios** sparing in one's praises

pardal SM (= *gorrión*) sparrow; (= *pardillo*) (*Zool*) linnet

pardiez†† EXCL good heavens!, by gad!††

pardillo/a Ⓐ SM/F (*) (= *ingenuo*) simpleton **Ⓑ** SM (*tb ~ común*) (*Zool*) linnet

pardo/a Ⓐ ADJ grey-brown, brownish-grey **Ⓑ** SM/F (*Carib*, *CS pey*) mulatto, half-breed

pardusco ADJ = **pardo A**

pareado Ⓐ ADJ 1 [*verso*] rhyming 2 [*chalet*] semi-detached **Ⓑ** SM couplet

parear /1a/ VT 1 (= *emparejar*) to pair up 2 (*Biol*) to mate, pair

parecer Ⓐ SM 1 (= *opinión*) opinion, view; **cambiar** o **mudar de ~** to change one's mind
2 (†) (= *aspecto*) **de buen ~** good-looking, handsome **Ⓑ** /2d/ VI 1 (*uso copulativo*) **1.1** (*por el aspecto*) (+ ADJ) to look; (+ SUSTANTIVO) to look like; **esos zapatos no parecen muy cómodos** those shoes don't look very comfortable; **parece una modelo** she looks like a model **1.2** (= *por carácter, comportamiento*) to seem; **parecía una persona muy amable** she seemed very nice
2 (*uso impersonal*) (= *dar la impresión de*) to seem; **aunque no lo parezca** surprising though it may seem; **así parece** so it seems; **al ~ ◆ a lo que parece** apparently, seemingly; **parece como si** (+ SUBJUN): **parece como si quisiera ocultar algo** it's as if he were trying to hide something; **parece que** (+ INDIC): **parece que va a llover** it looks as though o as if it's going to rain, it looks like rain; **parece que fue ayer** it seems only yesterday; **parece que huele a gas** I think I can smell gas; **según parece** apparently, seemingly; **parece ser que** (+ INDIC): **parece ser que ha habido algún problema** it seems o (*más frm*) appears (that) there has been a problem
3 (*indicando opinión*) **~ a algn: ¿qué te pareció la novela?** what did you think of the novel?; **si les parece bien** if that's all right with o by you; **si a usted no le parece mal** if you don't mind; **podríamos ir a la ópera si te parece** we could go to the opera if you like; **como te parezca** as you wish; **~ que: me parece que sí** I think so; **me parece que no** I don't think so; **¿te parece que está bien no acudir a una cita?** do you think it's acceptable not to turn up for an appointment?
Ⓒ parecerse VPR 1 **~se a algn** (*en el aspecto*) to look like sb, be like sb; (*en el carácter*) to be like sb; **su traje se parece al mío** his suit looks o is like mine
2 (*uso recíproco*) (*en el aspecto*) to look alike, be alike; (*en el*

carácter) to be alike; **son hermanas pero no se parecen mucho** they're sisters but they don't look o they aren't very much alike; **¿en qué se parecen estos dos objetos?** what's the similarity between these two objects?, in what way are these two objects alike?

parecido Ⓐ ADJ 1 (= *similar*) similar; **tienen apellidos ~s** they have similar surnames; **nunca he visto cosa parecida** I've never seen anything like it; **ser ~ a algo** to be similar to sth, be like sth; **ser ~ a algn** (*de aspecto*) to look like sb; (*de carácter*) to be like sb 2 **bien ~**† good-looking, nice-looking, handsome **Ⓑ** SM resemblance, likeness; **tiene un cierto ~ con Marlon Brando** he bears a slight resemblance to Marlon Brando

pared SF 1 [*de edificio, habitación*] wall; **estar ~ con ~ con algo** to be right next door to sth; ✦ MODISMOS **se pasa la vida entre cuatro ~es** he spends his life cooped up at home; **es como hablarle a la ~** it's like talking to a brick wall; **las ~es oyen** the walls have ears; **ponerse (blanco) como la ~** to go as white as a sheet; **subirse por las ~es*** to go up the wall* ➤ **pared de carga** load-bearing wall ➤ **pared divisoria** dividing wall ➤ **pared maestra** main wall ➤ **pared medianera** party wall
2 (*Anat*) wall
3 (*Alpinismo*) face wall
4 (*Ftbl*) **hacer la ~** to make o do a one-two*

paredón SM 1 (= *muro*) thick wall 2 [*de roca*] wall of rock, rock face 3 (*Mil*) **llevar a algn al ~** to put sb up against the wall, shoot sb

pareja SF 1 (= *par*) pair; **en este juego hay que formar ~s** for this game you have to get into pairs
2 [*de esposos, compañeros sentimentales*] couple; **vivir en ~** to live as a couple ➤ **pareja de hecho** unmarried couple
3 (= *compañero*) partner; (= *cónyuge*) spouse; **vino con su ~** he came with his partner ➤ **pareja de baile** dancing partner ➤ **pareja estable** regular partner
4 [*de calcetín, guante, zapato*] **no encuentro la ~ de este zapato** I can't find the shoe that goes with this one o my other shoe
5 [*de hijos*] **ya tenemos la parejita** now we've got one of each

---

Pareja referido a dos personas se traduce por **couple** cuando mantienen una relación sentimental: "Algunas parejas prefieren no tener hijos", *Some couples prefer not to have children*. También cuando se refiera a una pareja de baile. En cambio, en el contexto profesional, deportivo, etc., se traduce por **pair**: "Ahora vamos a trabajar por parejas", *Now we're going to work in pairs*.

---

parejo Ⓐ ADJ 1 (= *igual*) similar, alike; **ir ~s** to be neck and neck; **ir ~ con** to be on a par with 2 (*LAm*) (= *nivelado*) (*Téc*) even, flush; [*terreno*] flat, level **Ⓑ** ADV (*LAm*) (= *al mismo tiempo*) at the same time, together **Ⓒ** SM (*CAm, Carib*) [*de baile*] dancing partner

parentela* SF relations *pl*, family

parentesco SF relationship, kinship

paréntesis SM INV 1 (*Tip*) parenthesis, bracket; **entre ~** in parenthesis, in brackets (*Brit*) 2 (*Ling*) (= *pausa*) parenthesis; (= *digresión*) digression; **hacer un ~** (*en discurso, escrito*) to digress; **entre ~** incidentally 3 (= *intervalo*) break, interval; **el ~ vacacional** the break for the holidays

pareo SM beach wrap

paria SMF pariah

parida* SF silly thing, stupid remark; **~s** nonsense *sing* ➤ **parida mental** dumb idea*

paridad SF parity, equality

parienta SF **la ~*** the wife*, the missus*

pariente/a SM/F relative, relation

⚠ **pariente ≠ *parent***

---

parietal Ⓐ ADJ parietal **Ⓑ** SM parietal bone

parihuela SF, **parihuelas** SFPL stretcher

paripé* SM **hacer el ~** to put on a show

parir /3a/ ❹ VI [*mujer*] to give birth, have a baby; [*yegua*] to foal; [*vaca*] to calve; [*cerda*] to farrow; [*perra*] to pup; ✦ MODISMOS **éramos pocos y parió la abuela*** that's the limit*; **poner a ~ a algn*** to slag sb off* ❸ VT [*mujer*] to give birth to, have, bear (*frm*); [*animal*] to have; **¡la madre que te parió!***** you bastard!***

París SM Paris

parisiense ADJ, SMF, **parisino/a** ADJ, SM/F Parisian

paritario ADJ peer *antes de s*

paritorio SM delivery room

parking ['parkin] SM (*pl* ~**s**), **párking** ['parkin] SM (*pl* **párkings**) car park (*Brit*), parking lot (*EEUU*)

párkinson SM, **Parkinson** SM Parkinson's (disease)

parlamentar /1a/ VI to negotiate

parlamentario/a ❹ ADJ parliamentary ❸ SM/F (= *diputado*) member of parliament; (*más veterano*) parliamentarian

parlamento SM **1** (*Pol*) parliament ➤ **Parlamento Europeo** European Parliament **2** (= *discurso*) speech

parlanchín/ina* ❹ ADJ talkative ❸ SM/F chatterbox*

parlante ❹ ADJ talking ❸ SM (*LAm*) (*en lugar público*) loudspeaker; (*de equipo de música*) speaker

parlar* /1a/ VI to chatter

parlotear* /1a/ VI to chatter, prattle

parmesano ADJ, SM Parmesan

paro SM **1** (= *interrupción*) stoppage ➤ **paro biológico** (*Pesca*) temporary fishing ban (*to allow stocks to recover*) ➤ **paro cardíaco** cardiac arrest ➤ **paro del sistema** (*Inform*) system shutdown ➤ **paro técnico** technical breakdown **2** (*Esp*) (= *desempleo*) unemployment; **estar en ~** to be unemployed **3** (*Esp*) (= *subsidio*) unemployment benefit (*Brit*), unemployment insurance (*EEUU*); **cobrar el ~** to be on the dole (*Brit**) *o* on welfare (*EEUU*), receive unemployment benefit (*frm*) **4** (= *huelga*) strike **5** **en ~** (*Col, Ven*) (= *de una vez*) all at once, in one go *o* (*EEUU*) shot

parodia SF parody, takeoff*

parodiar /1b/ VT to parody, take off*

parón SM **la obras sufrieron un ~** building work came to a halt; **parones en una de las líneas del metro** stoppages on one of the underground lines

paroxismo SM paroxysm

parpadear /1a/ VI [*persona*] to blink; [*luz*] to flicker; [*estrella*] to twinkle

parpadeo SM [*de persona*] blinking; [*de luz*] flickering; [*de estrella*] twinkling

párpado SM eyelid

parque SM **1** (= *terreno, recinto*) park ➤ **parque acuático** water park ➤ **parque de atracciones** amusement park ➤ **parque de bomberos** fire station ➤ **parque de diversiones** (*RPl*) amusement park ➤ **parque infantil** children's playground ➤ **parque nacional** national park ➤ **parque natural** nature reserve ➤ **parque tecnológico** technology park ➤ **parque temático** theme park ➤ **parque zoológico** zoo **2** (= *conjunto*) ➤ **parque automotor** (*LAm*), **parque automovilístico** car fleet ➤ **parque móvil** fleet of official cars **3** (*para niños*) playpen **4** (*Méx*) (= *munición*) ammunition, ammo*

parqué SM, **parquet** [par'ke] SM (*pl* **parquets**) **1** (= *entarimado*) parquet **2** (*Fin*) **el ~** the Floor

parqueadero SM (*And*) car park (*Brit*), parking lot (*EEUU*)

parquear /1a/ VT, VI (*LAm*) to park

parquedad SF (= *frugalidad*) frugality, sparingness; (= *moderación*) moderation

parqueo SM (*And*) parking

parquímetro SM parking meter

parra SF (*Bot*) grapevine; (= *trepadora*) climbing vine;

✦ MODISMO **subirse a la ~*** to get all high and mighty

parrafada* SF **1** (= *charla*) chat, talk; **echar la ~** to have a chat **2** (= *discurso*) spiel*, talk

párrafo SM paragraph; **hacer ~ aparte** (*lit*) to start a new paragraph; (*fig*) to change the subject; ✦ MODISMO **echar un ~ (con algn)*** to have a chat (with sb)

parral SM vine arbour, vine arbor (*EEUU*)

parranda* SF spree; **andar** *o* **ir de ~** to go out on the town*

parricida SMF parricide

parricidio SM parricide

parrilla SF **1** (*Culin*) grill (*Brit*), broiler (*EEUU*); **carne a la ~** (*al grill*) grilled (*Brit*) *o* broiled (*EEUU*) meat; (*a la brasa*) barbecued meat **2** (*Dep*) (*tb* **~ de salida**) [*de coches*] starting grid; [*de caballos*] starting stalls **3** (*Aut*) [*de radiador*] radiator grille; (*LAm*) (= *baca*) roof rack (*Brit*), luggage rack (*EEUU*) **4** (= *restaurante*) grillroom, steak restaurant

parrillada SF **1** (= *plato*) (mixed) grill; (*a la brasa*) barbecue **2** (*CS*) (= *restaurante*) grillroom, steak restaurant

párroco SM parish priest

parroquia SF **1** (*Rel*) (= *zona*) parish; (= *iglesia*) parish church; (= *feligreses*) parishioners *pl* **2** (*Com*) customers *pl*, clientele

parroquial ADJ parochial, parish *antes de s*

parroquiano/a SM/F **1** (*Rel*) parishioner **2** (*Com*) patron, customer

parsimonia SF (= *calma*) calmness; (= *flema*) phlegmatic nature; **con ~** calmly, unhurriedly

parsimonioso ADJ (= *tranquilo*) calm, unhurried; (= *flemático*) phlegmatic

parte[1] SM **1** (= *informe*) report; **dar ~ a algn** to report to sb ➤ **parte de alta** certificate of starting employment ➤ **parte de baja (laboral)** (*por enfermedad*) doctor's note; (*por cese*) certificate of leaving employment, ≈ P45 (*Brit*) ➤ **parte de defunción** death certificate ➤ **parte médico** medical report, medical bulletin ➤ **parte meteorológico** weather forecast, weather report **2** (*Mil*) dispatch, communiqué ➤ **parte de guerra** military communiqué, war report **3** (*Radio*[†]) news bulletin **4** (*And Aut*) speeding ticket

parte[2] SF **1** (= *sección*) part; **el examen consta de dos ~s** the exam consists of two parts; **de lo que pasa es culpa mía** I'm partly to blame for the situation; **la ~ de abajo** the bottom; **la ~ de arriba** the top; **la ~ de atrás** the back; **la cuarta ~** a quarter; **la ~ delantera** the front; **la mayor ~ de algo**: **pasé la mayor ~ del tiempo leyendo** I spent most of the time reading; **la mayor ~ de los españoles** most Spanish people ➤ **parte de la oración** part of speech **2** (*en locuciones*) **de ~ de**: **llamo de ~ de Juan** I'm calling on behalf of Juan; **salúdalo de mi ~** give him my regards; **dale esto de mi ~** give her this from me; **¿de ~ de quién?** (*al teléfono*) who's calling?; **en ~** partly, in part; **formar ~ de algo**: **¿cuándo entró a formar ~ de la organización?** when did she join the organization?; **no formaba ~ del equipo** he was not in the team; **forma ~ de sus obligaciones** it is part of his duties; **en gran ~** to a large extent; **por otra ~** on the other hand; **por una ~ ... por otra (parte)** on the one hand, ... on the other; **por ~ de** on the part of; **¡vayamos por ~s!** let's take it one step at a time! **3** (= *participación*) share; **mi ~ de la herencia** my share of the inheritance; **a ~s iguales** in equal shares; **tomar ~ (en algo)** to take part (in sth); **yo no tomé ~ en ese asunto** I had no part in it; ✦ MODISMOS **llevarse la mejor ~** to come off best, get the best of it; **poner de su ~** to do one's bit *o* share; **quedarse con la ~ del león** to take the lion's share **4** (= *lugar*) part; **¿en qué ~ de la ciudad vives?** where *o* whereabouts in the city do you live?; **en alguna ~** somewhere; **en cualquier ~** anywhere; **en ninguna ~** nowhere; **debe de estar en otra ~** it must be somewhere else; **en** *o* **por todas ~s** everywhere; ✦ MODISMO **de algún** *o* **un tiempo a esta ~** for some time now **5** (= *bando*) side; **estar de ~ de algn** to be on sb's side; **estoy de tu ~** I'm on your side; **todo está de su ~** everything is in his favour; **ponerse de ~ de algn** to side with sb, take sb's side **6** (*indicando parentesco*) side; **es primo por ~ de madre** he's a cousin on my mother's side

7 (*Dep*) (*en partido*) half; **primera ~** first half; **segunda ~** second half
8 (*Teat*) part
9 (*Jur*) (*en contrato*) party; **las ~s contratantes** the parties to the contract; ✦ MODISMO **ser juez y ~** to be judge and jury (*in one's own case*) ➤ **parte actora** plaintiff ➤ **parte acusadora** prosecution
10 partes (*euf*) (= *genitales*) private parts (*euf*), privates (*euf*) ➤ **partes íntimas, partes pudendas** private parts
11 (*Méx*) spare part
12 (*CS**) ✦ MODISMO **mandarse la(s) ~(s)** (= *fingir*) to play-act; (= *hacer alarde*) to show off

parteluz SM mullion

partenaire [parte'ner] SMF partner

partero/a SM/F midwife/male midwife

parterre SM flower bed

partición SF (= *reparto*) division, sharing-out; (*Pol*) partition; (*Mat*) division

participación SF **1** (= *acto*) **fomentar la ~ de los ciudadanos en la política** to encourage public participation *o* involvement in politics; **habló de ello durante su ~ en el programa** he spoke about it when he was on the programme ➤ **participación electoral** turnout **2** (*Fin*) (= *parte*) share; (= *inversión*) holding, interest ➤ **participación accionarial** holding, shareholding ➤ **participación en los beneficios** profit-sharing ➤ **participación minoritaria** minority interest
3 (= *número de participantes*) entry; **hubo una nutrida ~** there was a big entry, there were a lot of entries **4** [*de lotería*] (share in a) lottery ticket; ⊳ *EL GORDO* **5** (= *aviso*) notice, notification; **dar ~ de algo** to give notice of sth

participante Ⓐ ADJ participating Ⓑ SMF (*gen*) participant; (*Dep*) entrant

participar /1a/ Ⓐ VI **1** (= *tomar parte*) to take part, participate (*frm*) (**en** in) **2** (*Fin*) **~ en una empresa** to own shares in a company; **~ de los beneficios** to share in the profits **3** (= *compartir*) **~ de una cualidad/opinión** to share a quality/an opinion Ⓑ VT (*frm*) (= *informar*) to inform; **~ algo a algn** to inform sb of sth

participativo ADJ [*sociedad, público*] participative; [*deporte, juego*] participative, participatory; [*democracia*] participatory

partícipe SMF participant; **hacer ~ a algn de algo** (*frm*) (= *informar*) to inform sb of sth; (= *compartir*) to share sth with sb

participio SM participle

partícula SF particle

particular Ⓐ ADJ **1** (= *especial*) special; **nada de ~** nothing special **2** (= *específico*) **en este caso ~** in this particular case; **tiene un sabor ~** it has a flavour of its own; **en ~** in particular **3** (= *privado*) [*secretario, coche, clase*] private Ⓑ SM (*frm*) (= *asunto*) matter; **sin otro ~, se despide atentamente ...** (*en correspondencia*) Yours faithfully (*Brit*), Sincerely yours (*EEUU*) Ⓒ SMF (= *persona*) (private) individual

particularidad SF (= *propiedad*) particularity, peculiarity; (= *rasgo distintivo*) special feature, characteristic

particularizar /1f/ Ⓐ VT **1** (= *distinguir*) to distinguish, characterize **2** (= *especificar*) to specify **3** (= *pormenorizar*) to particularize, give details about Ⓑ **particularizarse** VPR to distinguish itself, stand out

particularmente ADV **1** (= *especialmente*) particularly, specially **2** (= *personalmente*) privately, personally

partida SF **1** (= *documento*) certificate ➤ **partida de bautismo** baptismal certificate ➤ **partida de defunción** death certificate ➤ **partida de matrimonio** marriage certificate ➤ **partida de nacimiento** birth certificate **2** (*Fin*) [*de cuenta*] entry, item; [*de presupuesto*] item, heading ➤ **partida doble** double entry; **por ~ doble** on two accounts **3** (*Com*) (= *envío*) consignment **4** (*Naipes, Ajedrez*) game; **echar una ~** to have a game **5** (= *salida*) departure **6** (= *grupo*) party; (*Mil*) band, group ➤ **partida de caza** hunting party

partidario/a Ⓐ ADJ **ser ~ de algo** to be in favour *o* (*EEUU*) favor of sth Ⓑ SM/F [*de persona*] supporter, follower; [*de idea, movimiento*] supporter

partidismo SM partisanship

partidista ADJ partisan, party *antes de s*

partido SM **1** (*Pol*) party; **sistema de ~ único** one-party system ➤ **partido político** political party **2** (*Dep*) game, match ➤ **partido amistoso** friendly (game *o* match) (*Brit*), exhibition game (*EEUU*) ➤ **partido de desempate** replay ➤ **partido de fútbol** soccer game, football game *o* match (*esp Brit*) ➤ **partido de ida** away game *o* match, first leg ➤ **partido de vuelta** return game *o* match, second leg
3 (= *provecho*) **sacar ~ de algo** to make the most of sth **4** **tomar ~** to take sides; **tomar ~ por algo/algn** to side with sth/sb
5 **ser un buen ~** [*persona*] to be a good match **6** (= *distrito*) district, administrative area ➤ **partido judicial** *district under the jurisdiction of a local court* **7** (*CS*) (= *partida*) game; **un ~ de ajedrez** a game of chess; ✦ MODISMO **¡y se acabó el ~!** (*RPl**) and that's that! **8** (*Arg*) (= *región*) *administrative subdivision of a province*

partir /3a/ Ⓐ VT **1** (= *dividir*) [+ *tarta, sandía, baraja*] to cut; [+ *tableta de chocolate*] to break; [+ *tronco*] to split; **parte la barra de pan por la mitad** (*con cuchillo*) cut the baguette in half; (*con las manos*) break the baguette in half; **¿te parto un trozo de queso?** shall I cut you (off) a piece of cheese?
2 (= *romper*) [+ *hueso, diente*] to break; [+ *rama*] to break off; [+ *nuez, almendra*] to crack; **¡te voy a ~ la cara!** I'm going to smash your face in!*; **~ la cabeza a algn** to split sb's head open; ✦ MODISMO **~ el corazón a algn** to break sb's heart **3** (*) (= *estropear*) to mess up*; **me parte la tarde** it messes up my afternoon*
Ⓑ VI **1** [*persona, expedición*] to set off; [*tren, avión*] to depart (**de** from; **para** for; **hacia** in the direction of)
2 **~ de algo** to start from sth; **partiendo de la base de que ...** working on the principle that ..., assuming that ...
3 **a ~ de** from; **a ~ del lunes** from Monday, starting on Monday; **a ~ de ahora** from now on; **a ~ del puente la carretera se estrecha** the road gets narrower after the bridge; **¿qué podemos deducir a ~ de estos datos?** what can we deduce from these data?
Ⓒ **partirse** VPR to break; **me he partido un brazo** I've broken my arm; **se le partió el labio del golpe** the blow split his lip; ✦ MODISMO **~se (de risa)** to be in stitches*

partisano/a ADJ, SM/F partisan

partitivo ADJ partitive

partitura SF (*Mús*) score

parto SM (*gen*) birth, delivery; (= *contracciones*) labour, labor (*EEUU*); (*Zool*) parturition; **asistir en un ~** to deliver a baby; **estar de ~** to be in labour *o* (*EEUU*) labor; **murió de ~** she died in childbirth ➤ **parto natural** natural childbirth ➤ **parto prematuro** premature birth ➤ **parto sin dolor** painless childbirth

parturienta SF (*antes del parto*) woman in labour *o* (*EEUU*) labor; (*después del parto*) woman who has just given birth

parvada SF (*LAm*) flock

parvulario SM nursery school, kindergarten

párvulo/a SM/F infant; **colegio de ~s** nursery school

pasa SF raisin; ✦ MODISMO **está hecho una ~*** he's as shrivelled *o* (*EEUU*) shriveled as a prune ➤ **pasa de Corinto** currant ➤ **pasa de Esmirna** sultana

pasable ADJ **1** (= *tolerable*) passable, tolerable **2** (*LAm*) [*arroyo*] fordable

pasabocas SMPL (*Col*) snacks

pasacalle SM **1** (= *música*) *type of tune played by street musicians* **2** (= *pancarta*) banner (*stretched across a street*)

pasada SF **1** (*con trapo*) wipe
2 [*de pintura, barniz*] coat
3 (*Cos*) (= *puntada*) **dale una ~ al pantalón** give it a quick sew
4 **de ~** in passing; **sólo estoy aquí de ~** I'm only just passing by *o* through
5 (*) (= *barbaridad*) **¡este coche es una ~!** this car is

amazing!; **¡qué ~! me han cobrado 2,000 euros** what a rip off! they charged me 2,000 euros*; **había una ~ de gente** there were lots *o* tons* of people
6 mala ~ dirty trick; **hacerle** *o* **jugarle una mala ~ a algn** to play a dirty trick on sb

pasadizo SM (*interior*) passage; (*entre calles*) passageway, alley

pasado Ⓐ ADJ **1** (*tiempo*) **el mes ~** last month; **~ mañana** the day after tomorrow; **~s dos días** after two days; **ya eran pasadas las seis** it was already after six; ✦ MODISMO **lo ~, ~ (está)** let bygones be bygones
2 (*Culin*) (*= en mal estado*) [*pan*] stale; [*fruta*] overripe
3 (*Culin*) (*= muy hecho*) [*arroz, pasta*] overcooked; **le gusta la carne muy pasada** he likes his meat very well done
4 (*= no actual*) [*ropa, zapatos*] old-fashioned; [*noticia*] stale; [*idea, costumbre*] antiquated, out-of-date
5 [*tejido, camisa*] worn
Ⓑ SM **1 el ~** (*= tiempo anterior*) the past
2 [*de persona*] past
3 (*Ling*) past (tense)

pasador SM **1** (*Culin*) (*= colador*) colander; [*de té*] strainer; (*= filtro*) filter **2** (*= pestillo*) bolt, fastener; [*de bisagra*] pin **3** [*de corbata*] tie pin **4** [*de pelo*] hair slide (*Brit*), barrette (*EEUU*) **5** (*Perú*) (*= cordón*) shoelace

pasaje SM **1** (*= acción*) passage, passing; (*Náut*) voyage, crossing **2** (*esp LAm*) (*= boleto*) ticket **3** (*= viajeros*) passengers *pl* **4** (*= callejón*) passageway, alleyway; (*con tiendas*) arcade **5** (*Literat, Mús*) passage

pasajero ADJ [*momento*] fleeting, passing; **ave pasajera** bird of passage, migratory bird

pasamanos SM INV, **pasamano** SM (*gen*) handrail, rail; [*de escalera*] banister

pasamontañas SM INV Balaclava (helmet), ski mask

pasante SMF **1** (*gen*) assistant; (*Jur*) articled clerk **2** (*Méx Escol*) assistant teacher

pasapalos SMPL (*Ven*) snacks

pasaporte SM passport

pasapurés SM INV, **pasapuré** SM manual food mill

---

pasar /1a/

Ⓐ VERBO INTRANSITIVO	Ⓒ VERBO PRONOMINAL
Ⓑ VERBO TRANSITIVO	

Para las expresiones **pasar lista**, **pasar desapercibido**, **pasarse de rosca** *etc, ver la entrada correspondiente a la otra palabra.*

pasar Ⓐ VERBO INTRANSITIVO
1 (*= ocurrir*)
1.1 [*suceso*] to happen; **¿qué pasó?** what happened?; **aquí pasa algo misterioso** there's something odd going on here; **siempre pasa igual** *o* **lo mismo** it's always the same; **¿qué pasa?** (*interesándose por lo ocurrido*) what's happening?, what's going on?, what's up?; (*como saludo*) how's things?*; **¿qué pasa que no entra?** why doesn't she come in?; **lo que pasa es que ...** well, you see ..., the thing is that ...; **pase lo que pase** whatever happens, come what may
1.2 ~ a algn: siempre me pasa lo mismo, lo pierdo todo it's always the same, I keep losing things; **tuvo un accidente, pero por suerte no le pasó nada** he had an accident, but fortunately he wasn't hurt; **esto te pasa por no hacerme caso** this is what comes of not listening to me, this wouldn't have happened (to you) if you'd listened to me; **¿qué te pasa?** what's the matter (with you)?
2 (*= cambiar de lugar*)
2.1 [*objeto*] **cuando muera, la empresa ~á al hijo** when he dies, the company will go to his son; **la foto fue pasando de mano en mano** the photo was passed around
2.2 (*= trasladarse*) to go; **~ a un cuarto contiguo** to go into an adjoining room
3 (*= entrar*) **¡pase!** (*desde dentro*) come in!; (*cediendo el paso*) after you!; **no se puede ~** you can't go through, you can't go in; **hacer ~ a algn** to show sb in

4 (*= transitar*) **pasó una bicicleta** a bicycle went past; **ya ha pasado el tren de las cinco** (*= sin hacer parada*) the five o'clock train has already gone by; (*= haciendo parada*) the five o'clock train has already been and gone; **~ de largo** to go *o* pass by; **~ por: el autobús pasa por delante de nuestra casa** the bus goes past our house; **ese autobús no pasa por aquí** that bus doesn't come this way
5 (*= acercarse a*) **~é por el supermercado mañana** I'll go *o* pop into the supermarket tomorrow; **tendrá que ~ por mi despacho** he'll have to come to my office; **pase por caja** please pay at the cash (*Brit*) *o* cashier's (*EEUU*) desk
✦ **pasar a** + INFIN: **te ~é a buscar a las ocho** I'll pick you up at eight; **pasá a verme cuando quieras** come round whenever you like
6 (*= cambiar de situación*) to go; **el equipo ha pasado a primera división** the team has gone up to the first division; **~ de teniente a general** to go from lieutenant to general; **~ a ser** to become
7 (*= transcurrir*) [*tiempo*] to pass, go by; **¡cómo pasa el tiempo!** how time flies!; **ya ha pasado una hora** it's been an hour already
8 (*= acabar*) [*problema, situación*] to be over; [*efectos*] to wear off
9 (*= aceptarse*) **puede ~** it's passable, it's OK; **por esta vez pase** I'll let it go this time
10 (*otras formas preposicionales*)
✦ **pasar a** + INFIN (*= empezar*): **paso ahora a explicar mi postura** I will now go on to explain my position; **ya va siendo hora de ~ a la acción** it is time for action
✦ **pasar de** (*= exceder*): **pasa ya de los 70** he's over 70; **no pasa de ser un jugador mediocre** he's no more than an average player; **de hoy no pasa que le escriba** I'll write to him this very day
✦ **pasar por** (*= atravesar, caber*) [+ *túnel, puerta*] to go through; (*= depender de*) to depend on; (*= ser considerado*) to pass as; **el río pasa por la ciudad** the river flows *o* goes through the city; **está pasando por un mal momento** he's going through a bad patch; **podrían perfectamente ~ por gemelos** they could easily pass as twins; **se hace ~ por médico** he passes himself off as a doctor
✦ **pasar sin: tendrá que ~ sin coche** he'll have to get by *o* manage without a car; **no puede ~ sin ella** he can't manage without her
11 (*Naipes*) to pass; **yo paso** pass
12 (*esp Esp**) (*= mostrarse indiferente*) **yo paso** count me out; **~ de algo/algn: yo paso de política** I'm not into politics; **paso de todo** I couldn't care less
Ⓑ VERBO TRANSITIVO
1 (*= dar, entregar*) (*gen*) to pass; (*en una serie*) to pass on; **¿me pasas la sal, por favor?** could you pass (me) the salt, please?; **cuando termines pásasela a Isabel** when you've finished pass it on to Isabel
2 (*= atravesar*) [+ *río, frontera*] to cross; [+ *límite*] to go beyond
3 (*= llevar*) **nos ~on a otra habitación** they moved us into another room; **he pasado mi despacho al dormitorio** I've moved my office into the bedroom
4 (*= hacer atravesar*) **pasa el alambre por este agujero** put the wire through this hole; **pasó el hilo por el ojo de la aguja** she threaded the thread through the eye of the needle; **~ el café por el colador** to strain the coffee
5 (*= introducir*) [+ *moneda falsa*] to pass (off); [+ *contrabando*] to smuggle
6 (*= deslizar*) to slip; **le pasó el brazo por los hombros/la cintura** she slipped *o* put her arm around his shoulders/waist; **voy a ~le un trapo** I'm going to wipe it down; **~ la mano por algo** to run one's hand over sth; **~ la aspiradora** to do the vacuuming
7 (*= contagiar*) to give; **me has pasado tu catarro** you've given me your cold
8 (*= volver*) [+ *página*] to turn; ✦ MODISMO **~ página** to make a fresh start
9 (*= escribir*) **~ algo a** *o* **en** (*LAm*) **limpio** to make a neat *o* fair *o* clean copy of sth; **~ algo a máquina** to type sth up
10 (*= tragar*) (*lit*) to swallow; (*fig*) to bear, stand; **no puedo ~ esta pastilla** I can't swallow this pill, I can't get this pill down
11 (*= tolerar*) **se lo pasan todo** they let him get away with anything; **no te voy a ~ más** I'm not going to

indulge you any more
12 (= *aprobar*) [+ *examen*] to pass
13 (= *proyectar*) [+ *película, programa*] to show, screen
14 (= *poner en contacto*) **te paso con Pedro** (*al mismo teléfono*) I'll put you on to Pedro; (*a distinto teléfono*) I'll put you through to Pedro
15 (= *superar*) **los pasa a todos en inteligencia** she's more intelligent than any of them; **me pasa ya 3cm** he's already 3cm taller than I am
16 (*Aut*) to pass, overtake (*esp Brit*)
17 (= *sufrir*) **ha pasado una mala racha** she's been through a bad patch; **ya hemos pasado lo peor** we're over the worst now, the worst is behind us now; ~ **frío** to be cold; ~ **hambre** to be hungry
18 [+ *tiempo*] to spend; **voy a ~ el fin de semana con ella** I'm going to spend the weekend with her; **fuimos a ~ el día en la playa** we went to the seaside for the day
♦ **pasarlo** + ADV: **~lo bien** to have a good time; **~lo mal** to have a bad time
🅒 pasarse VERBO PRONOMINAL
1 (= *cesar*) **¿se te ha pasado el mareo?** have you stopped feeling dizzy?; **ya se te ~á** [*enfado, disgusto*] you'll get over it; [*dolor*] it'll stop
2 (= *perder*) to miss; **se me pasó el turno** I missed my turn
3 (= *cambiarse*) to go over; **~se al enemigo** to go over to the enemy
4 (= *estropearse*) [*flor*] to fade; [*carne, pescado*] to go bad *o* off; [*fruta*] to go bad *o* soft
5 (= *recocerse*) **se ha pasado el arroz** the rice is overcooked
6 [*tornillo, tuerca*] to get overscrewed
7 (* = *excederse*) **está bien hacer ejercicio pero no hay que ~se** it's good to exercise but there's no point in overdoing it; **¡no te pases, que te voy a dar una torta!** just watch it or I'll smack you in the face!; **~se de: se pasa de bueno/ generoso** he's too good/generous; **~se de listo** to be too clever by half; **~se de la raya** to go too far, overstep the mark
8 [+ *tiempo*] to spend; **se ha pasado todo el día leyendo** he has spent the whole day reading
9 (= *olvidarse*) **se le pasó la fecha del examen** he forgot the date of the exam; **no se le pasa nada** nothing escapes him, he doesn't miss a thing
10 (*seguido de preposición*)
♦ **pasarse por** [+ *lugar*] **ya que tienes que ~te por el banco** seeing as you have to go to the bank anyway; **se me pasó por la cabeza** *o* **imaginación** it crossed my mind
♦ **pasarse sin algo** to do without sth

pasarela SF (= *puente*) footbridge; [*de modelos*] catwalk; (*Náut*) gangway, gangplank

pasatiempo SM **1** (= *entretenimiento*) pastime; (= *afición*) hobby **2 pasatiempos** (*en periódicos, revistas*) puzzles

Pascua SF (*en Semana Santa*) Easter; **Pascuas** (= *Navidad*) Christmas time, Christmas period; **¡felices ~s!** merry Christmas!; ♦ MODISMOS **de ~s a Ramos** once in a blue moon; **estar como unas ~s** to be as happy as a lark; **hacer la ~ a algn*** (= *molestar*) to annoy sb, bug sb*; (= *perjudicar*) to do the dirty on sb ➤ **Pascua de los judíos** Passover ➤ **Pascua de Resurrección, Pascua florida** Easter

pascual ADJ Paschal; **cordero ~** (older) lamb

pase SM **1** (= *documento*) pass ➤ **pase de favor** complimentary ticket ➤ **pase de prensa** press pass ➤ **pase pernocta** (*Mil*) overnight pass **2** (= *sesión*) (*Cine*) showing ➤ **pase de modas, pase de modelos** fashion show **3** (*Dep*) pass ➤ **pase de pecho** (*Taur*) chest-level pass **4** (*Col*) (= *permiso de conducir*) driving licence (*Brit*), driver's license (*EEUU*)

paseandero ADJ (*CS*) **ser ~** to like to be out and about

paseante SMF (*gen*) walker, stroller; (= *transeúnte*) passer-by

pasear /1a/ **🅐** VI (*gen*) to go for a walk, go for a stroll; (*de un lado a otro*) to walk around; ~ **a caballo** to (horse-)ride, go (horse-)riding **🅑** VT **1** [+ *perro, niño*] to take for a walk, walk **2** (= *exhibir*) [+ *ropa, coche*] to parade, show off

paseíllo SM (*Taur*) ceremonial entry of bullfighters

paseo SM **1** (*gen*) walk, stroll; **dar un ~** (*andando*) to go for

a walk *o* stroll, take a walk *o* stroll; (*en coche*) to go for a ride; **llevar** *o* **sacar a un niño de ~** to take a child out for a walk; **entre las dos casas no hay más que un ~** it's only a short walk between the two houses; ♦ MODISMOS **enviar** *o* **mandar a ~** (*Esp**) [+ *estudios, trabajo*] to jack in*; **enviar** *o* **mandar a algn a** (*Esp*) **~*** to tell sb to go to blazes*, send sb packing, chuck sb out; **¡vete a ~!*** get lost!** ➤ **paseo a caballo** ride (on horseback) ➤ **paseo en barco** boat trip ➤ **paseo en bicicleta** (bike) ride ➤ **paseo en coche** drive, ride
2 (= *avenida*) parade, avenue ➤ **paseo marítimo** promenade, esplanade

pasillo SM (*en casa, oficina*) corridor; (*en avión, teatro*) aisle; **hacer ~s** (*Pol*) to engage in lobby discussions, lobby ➤ **pasillo aéreo** air corridor, air lane ➤ **pasillo móvil, pasillo rodante** travelator

pasión SF **1** (= *amor intenso*) passion; **la quería con ~** he loved her passionately; **tener ~ por algn** to love sb passionately; **tener ~ por algo** to have a passion for sth **2** (*Rel*) **la Pasión** the Passion

pasional ADJ passionate; **crimen ~** crime of passion

pasito ADV (*Col*) gently, softly

pasiva SF (*Ling*) passive (voice)

pasividad SF **1** (= *actitud*) passivity **2** (*RPl*) (= *pensión*) pension

pasivo 🅐 ADJ (*tb Ling*) passive **🅑** SM (*Com, Fin*) liabilities *pl*; [*de cuenta*] debit side

pasma* * (*Esp*) SF **la ~** the fuzz**, the cops* *pl*

pasmado ADJ **1** (= *asombrado*) astonished, amazed; (= *atontado*) stunned, dumbfounded **2** (= *frío*) frozen stiff; (*Bot*) frostbitten **3** (*LAm*) [*fruta*] overripe

pasmar /1a/ **🅐** VT (= *asombrar*) to amaze, astonish; (= *atontar*) to stun, dumbfound **🅑 pasmarse** VPR **1** (= *asombrarse*) to be amazed, be astonished; (= *maravillarse*) to marvel, wonder **2** (*Carib, Méx*) [*fruta*] to wither

pasmarote* SM idiot, halfwit; **¡no te quedes ahí como un ~!** don't just stand there like an idiot!

pasmo SM **1** (= *asombro*) amazement, astonishment; (= *admiración*) wonder **2** (= *enfriamiento*) chill

pasmoso ADJ (= *asombroso*) amazing, astonishing; (= *admirable*) wonderful

paso¹ ADJ dried; **higo ~** dried fig; **ciruela pasa** prune; **uva pasa** raisin

paso² SM **1** (= *acción de pasar*) **para evitar el ~ del aire** to prevent the air getting through; **los detuvieron en el ~ del Estrecho** they were arrested while crossing the Straits; **a su ~ por nuestra ciudad, el presidente ...** during his visit to our city, the president ...; **con el ~ del tiempo** with (the passing of) time; **"prohibido el paso"** "no entry"; **"ceda el ~"** "give way" (*Brit*), "yield" (*EEUU*); **dar ~ a algo: el invierno dio ~ a la primavera** winter gave way to spring; **ahora vamos a dar ~ a nuestro corresponsal en Lisboa** we now go over to our correspondent in Lisbon; **de ~: mencionaron el tema sólo de ~** they only mentioned the matter in passing; **de ~ que vas al banco** on your way to the bank; **de ~ recuérdale que tiene un libro nuestro** remind him that he's got a book of ours while you're at it; **dicho sea de ~** incidentally; **estar de ~** to be passing through ➤ **paso del Ecuador** *party or trip organized by Spanish university students to celebrate the halfway stage in their degree course* ➤ **paso franco, paso libre** free passage
2 (= *camino*) way; (*Geog*) pass; **estás en mitad del ~** you're blocking the way; **¡paso!** make way!; **abrirse ~** to make one's way; **cerrar el ~** to block the way; **dejar el ~ libre** to leave the way open; **dejar ~ a algn** to let sb past; **impedir el ~** to block the way; ♦ MODISMOS **salir al ~ a algn** to collar sb; **han salido al ~ de la acusación** they've been quick to deny the accusation; **salir del ~** to get out of trouble ➤ **paso a desnivel** (*Méx*) underpass ➤ **paso a nivel** level crossing (*Brit*), grade crossing (*EEUU*) ➤ **paso (de) cebra** (*Esp*) zebra crossing (*Brit*), crosswalk (*EEUU*) ➤ **paso de peatones** pedestrian crossing (*Brit*), crosswalk (*EEUU*) ➤ **paso elevado** (*Aut*) flyover (*Brit*), overpass (*EEUU*) ➤ **paso fronterizo** border crossing ➤ **paso subterráneo** underpass, subway (*Brit*)

3 (*al andar*) (= *acción*) step; (= *ruido*) footstep; **he oído ~s** I heard footsteps; **dar un ~** to take a step; **no da ni un ~ sin ella** he never goes anywhere without her; **dirigir sus ~s hacia** to head towards; **dar un ~ en falso** (= *tropezar*) to trip; (= *no pisar bien*) to miss one's footing; (= *equivocarse*) to make a false move; **hacer ~s** (*Baloncesto*) to travel (with the ball); **volvió sobre sus ~s** she retraced her steps;
♦ MODISMOS **a cada ~** at every step, at every turn; **a ~s agigantados** by leaps and bounds; **~ a ~** step by step; **seguir los ~s a algn** to tail sb; **seguir los ~s de algn** to follow in sb's footsteps ➤ **paso adelante** (*lit, fig*) step forward ➤ **paso atrás** step backwards
4 (= *modo de andar*) [*de persona*] walk, gait; [*de caballo*] gait; **caminaba con ~ decidido** he was walking purposefully; **apretar** o **avivar el ~** to start going faster, speed up; **a buen ~** at a good pace; **a ~ ligero** (*gen*) at a swift pace; (*Mil*) at the double; **llevar el ~** to keep in step, keep time; **marcar el ~** (*gen*) to keep time; (*Mil*) to mark time; ♦ MODISMO **a ~ de tortuga** at a snail's pace
5 (= *ritmo*) rate, pace; **a este ~** at this rate
6 (= *distancia*) **vive a un ~ de aquí** he lives round the corner from here; **de eso al terrorismo no hay más que un ~** it's a small step from there to terrorism
7 (= *avance*) step; **el matrimonio es un ~ muy importante en la vida** marriage is an important step in life; ♦ MODISMO **dar el primer ~** ◇ **dar los primeros ~s** to make the first move
8 [*de contador, teléfono*] unit
9 (*Rel*) (*en procesión*) float in Holy Week procession, with statues representing part of Easter story; ⤷ SEMANA SANTA

pasodoble SM paso doble

pasota* Ⓐ ADJ INV (*Esp*) [*persona*] laid-back, apathetic (*pey*); **filosofía ~** couldn't-care-less attitude Ⓑ SMF **¡eres un ~!** you just don't care, do you?; **Jesús va de ~ por la vida** Jesús doesn't care much about anything

pasote* SM (*Esp*) = **pasada 5**

pasotismo SM (*Esp*) couldn't-care-less attitude

paspadura SF (*And, CS*) chapped skin, cracked skin

pasparse /1a/ VPR (*And, CS*) [*piel*] to chap, crack; [*bebé*] to get nappy (*Brit*) o diaper (*EEUU*) rash

paspartú SM passe-partout

pasquín SM **1** (*Pol*) (= *cartel*) satirical poster **2** (*LAm pey*) (= *periódico*) rag (*pey**)

pasta SF **1** (= *masa*) paste ➤ **pasta de dientes** toothpaste ➤ **pasta de madera** wood pulp ➤ **pasta dentífrica** toothpaste ➤ **pasta de papel** paper pulp
2 (*en repostería*) pastry; (*Esp*) (*tb* **~ de té**) biscuit (*Brit*), cookie (*EEUU*) ➤ **pasta quebrada** shortcrust pastry
3 (= *macarrones, fideos*) pasta
4 (*para untar*) paste
5 (*Esp**) (= *dinero*) money, cash, dough*; **me ha costado una ~ gansa** it cost me an arm and a leg*
6 (*Tip*) boards *pl*; **libro en ~** hardback
7 (= *talante*) **tiene ~ de campeón** he has the makings of a champion; **ser de buena ~** to be a good sort

pastar /1a/ VT, VI to graze

pastel Ⓐ SM **1** (*Culin*) (= *dulce*) cake; [*de carne, verduras, etc*] pie; ♦ MODISMO **se descubrió el ~** the scam came to light*; **repartirse el ~** to divide up the cake o (*EEUU*) pie **2** (*Arte*) pastel; **pintura al ~** pastel drawing **3** (*Col**) (*en examen*) cheat-sheet* Ⓑ ADJ pastel

pastelería SF **1** (= *arte*) pastry-making, (art of) confectionery **2** (= *tienda*) baker's, cake shop

pastelero/a Ⓐ ADJ **masa pastelera** pastry; **rodillo ~** rolling-pin Ⓑ SM/F **1** (*Culin*) pastry cook **2** (*Com*) baker **3** (*And***) (= *traficante*) drug trafficker

pasteurizar /1f/ VT to pasteurize

pastiche SM pastiche

pastilla SF **1** (*Med*) tablet, pill ➤ **pastilla para la tos** cough drop **2** [*de jabón*] bar; [*de chocolate*] piece, square;
♦ MODISMO **ir a toda ~** (*Esp**) to go full-belt* ➤ **pastilla de caldo** stock cube ➤ **pastilla de freno(s)** (*Aut*) brake pad o shoe ➤ **pastilla de fuego** firelighter

pastillero¹/a* SM/F (= *persona*) pill popper**

pastillero² SM (= *cajita*) pillbox

pastizal SM pasture

pasto SM (= *sitio*) pasture; (*LAm*) (= *hierba*) grass; (= *césped*) lawn; **fue ~ de las llamas** the flames devoured it

pastón** SM (*Esp*) **un ~** a whole heap of money*

pastor(a) Ⓐ SM/F **1** (*Agr*) shepherd/shepherdess **2** (*Rel*) minister, clergyman/clergywoman Ⓑ SM (*Zool*) sheepdog ➤ **pastor alemán** German shepherd, Alsatian (*Brit*)

pastoral Ⓐ ADJ pastoral Ⓑ SF (*Rel*) pastoral letter

pastoreo SM grazing

pastoril ADJ (*Literat*) pastoral

pastoso ADJ **1** [*masa*] doughy; [*pasta*] pasty **2** [*lengua*] furry; [*voz, vino*] rich, mellow

pata Ⓐ SF **1** (*Zool*) **1.1** (= *pierna*) leg; **~ delantera** front leg; **~ trasera** back o hind leg; **de ~ negra** (*Esp*) [*cerdo, jamón*] prime; **un fútbol de ~ negra** top-notch football*
1.2 (= *pie*) [*de mamífero*] (*tb* Peletería) paw; [*de ave*] foot ➤ **pata de gallo** (*en tela*) hound's-tooth check, dog's-tooth check ➤ **patas de gallo** (*en el ojo*) crow's feet
2 (*) [*de persona*] leg; **a la ~ coja** hopping; **a cuatro ~s** on all fours ➤ **pata de palo** wooden leg, peg leg
3 [*de mueble*] leg; **~s arriba** (= *invertido*) upside down; (= *revuelto*) in a complete mess, topsy-turvy*
4 patas (*Chi**) (= *caradura*) cheek* *sing*; **tener ~s** to be brash, be cheeky*
5 ♦ MODISMOS **estirar la ~*** to kick the bucket*; **hacer la ~ a algn** (*Chi**) to soft-soap sb*, suck up to sb*; **hacer algo con las ~s** (*Col, Méx**) to make a pig's ear of sth*; **mala ~** bad luck; **¡qué mala ~ tuviste!** you were really unlucky!; **meter la ~** to put one's foot in it; **a ~ pelada** (*Chi, Perú**) in bare feet*; **saltar en una ~** (*CS*) to jump with joy; **ser ~** (*Arg*) to be game*, be up for it*; **ser ~ de perro** (*Chi, Méx**) to have itchy feet*; *ver tb* **pato**
Ⓑ SM (*And**) **1** (= *amigo*) pal*, mate (*Brit**), buddy (*EEUU**) **2** (= *tipo*) guy*, bloke (*Brit**)

patada SF **1** (= *puntapié*) kick; **abrieron la puerta de una ~** they kicked the door open; **a ~s: echar a algn a ~s** to kick o boot sb out; **tratar a algn a ~s** to treat sb very badly o like dirt*; **dar ~s** to kick; **dar** o **meter** o **pegar una ~ a algn/algo** to kick sb/sth, give sb/sth a kick; **dar ~s en el suelo** to stamp (the floor)
2 ♦ MODISMOS **ejemplos de eso los hay a ~s*** there are loads of examples of that*; **a las ~s** (*LAm**) really badly; **dar la ~ a*** [+ *empleado*] to kick out*, give the boot to*; [+ *novio, marido*] to ditch*, dump*; **darse ~s por algo: la gente se daba ~s por conseguir una entrada** people would do anything to get a ticket; **me da cien ~s no poder hablar con libertad*** it bugs me that I can't speak freely*; **de la ~** (*CAm, Méx**): **me fue de la ~** it was a disaster, it all went pear-shaped on me*; **me cae de la ~** I can't stand the sight of him*; **en dos ~s*** (= *sin esfuerzo*) with no trouble at all; (= *en seguida*) in a jiffy*; **sentar como una ~ en el estómago*** [*bebida, comida*] to upset one's stomach; [*acción*] to be like a kick in the teeth

patagón ADJ Patagonian

Patagonia SF **la ~** Patagonia

patalear /1a/ VI **1** (*en el suelo*) to stamp (angrily) **2** [*bebé, niño*] to kick out **3** (= *protestar*) to make a fuss

pataleo SM **1** (*en el suelo*) stamping **2** (*en el aire*) kicking **3** (= *protesta*) **derecho al ~** right to protest

pataleta* SF tantrum

patán SM rustic, yokel, hick (*EEUU**); (*pey*) lout

patata SF (*Esp*) **1** (= *tubérculo*) potato; **puré de ~s** mashed potatoes *pl* ➤ **patata caliente** (*fig*) hot potato ➤ **patata de siembra** seed potato ➤ **patatas bravas** *fried potatoes with spicy tomato sauce* ➤ **patatas fritas** (*en tiras*) French fries, chips (*Brit*); (*de bolsa*) crisps (*Brit*), potato chips (*EEUU*)
2 ♦ MODISMO **ni ~*** nothing at all

patatero* ADJ *ver* **rollo 4**

patatín* ♦ MODISMOS **que (si) ~, que (si) patatán** this, that and the other; **y ~ patatán** and so on

patatús* SM fit*; **le dio un ~** he had a fit*

paté SM pâté

pateadura* SF (*RPl*) (= *ataque*) beating; (= *castigo*) spanking

patear /1a/ **Ⓐ** VT 1 (en el suelo) to stamp on; (= dar patadas a) to kick, boot
2 (*Esp**) (= andar por) to tramp round; **tuve que ~ toda la ciudad** I had to tramp round the whole town
3 (*Teat*) (= abuchear) to boo, jeer
4 (*RPl*) (= hacer mal a) to upset; **las cosas fritas me patean el estómago** fried food upsets my stomach o gives me stomach trouble
Ⓑ VI 1 (= patalear) to stamp one's foot
2 (*LAm*) [arma, animal] to kick
3 (*RPl*) (= hacer mal a) **me pateó ese guiso que me comí** that stew I had upset my stomach, that stew I had gave me an upset stomach
Ⓒ **patearse** (*) VPR **nos pateamos todo Madrid** we walked all round o over Madrid

patena SF paten

patentar /1a/ VT to patent

patente Ⓐ ADJ [mentira, muestra] clear; **su enojo era ~** his annoyance was plain to see, he was plainly o patently o clearly annoyed; **hacer algo ~** to reveal sth, show sth clearly; **quedar ~** to become patently clear o obvious
Ⓑ SF 1 [de invento, producto] patent; **derechos de ~** patent rights ➤ **patente de corso: se cree que tiene ~ de corso** he thinks he's got a licence to do whatever he pleases
2 (*CS Aut*) (= matrícula) licence plate, license plate (*EEUU*); (= impuesto) road tax
3 (*Col*) (= carnet) driving licence (*Brit*), driver's license (*EEUU*)

patera SF (*Esp*) boat, (small) boat

paterfamilias SM INV paterfamilias

paternal ADJ fatherly, paternal

paternalista ADJ paternalistic; (*pey*) patronizing

paternidad SF 1 (= estado, situación) fatherhood, parenthood 2 (*Jur*) paternity

paterno ADJ paternal; **abuelo ~** paternal grandfather

patero* ADJ (*Chi*) fawning

patético ADJ pathetic, moving

patetismo SM pathos, poignancy

patíbulo SM scaffold, gallows

patidifuso* ADJ (= estupefacto) astounded, taken aback; (= perplejo) nonplussed

patilla SF 1 [de gafas] sidepiece, temple (*EEUU*) 2 (del pelo) hair that grows down the side of the face in front of the ear; (más larga) sideburn, sideboard 3 (*Carib, Col*) (= sandía) watermelon

patilludo* ADJ (*RPl*) fed up*, sick*

patín SM 1 (*gen*) skate ➤ **patín de ruedas** roller skate ➤ **patines en línea** Rollerblades® 2 (= patinete) scooter
3 (*Náut*) ➤ **patín de pedal** pedalo, pedal-boat

pátina SF patina

patinador(a) SM/F skater

patinaje SM skating ➤ **patinaje artístico** figure skating ➤ **patinaje sobre hielo** ice-skating

patinar /1a/ VI 1 (con patines) (sobre ruedas) to roller-skate; (sobre hielo) to skate, ice-skate 2 (= resbalar) [coche] to skid; [persona] to slide 3 (*) (= equivocarse) to make a blunder, boob*

patinazo SM 1 (*Aut*) skid 2 (*) (= error) boob*, blunder

patineta SF 1 (esp *LAm*) (sin manillar) skateboard 2 (con manillar) scooter

patinete SM scooter

patio SM 1 [de casa] courtyard; [de escuela] playground; ✦ MODISMO **¡cómo está el ~!*: ¡cómo está el ~! hoy todos están de mal humor** what an atmosphere! everybody is in a bad mood today! ➤ **patio de armas** parade ground ➤ **patio de luces** well (of a building) ➤ **patio de recreo** playground 2 (*Teat*) pit ➤ **patio de butacas** stalls pl (*Brit*), orchestra (*EEUU*) 3 (*Méx Ferro*) shunting yard, switching yard (*EEUU*)

patito SM duckling; ✦ MODISMO **los dos ~s*** all the twos*, twenty-two ➤ **patito feo** ugly duckling

patizambo ADJ knock-kneed

pato Ⓐ SM (*Orn*) duck; ✦ MODISMO **pagar el ~*** to carry the can* ➤ **pato silvestre** mallard, wild duck **Ⓑ** ADJ (*CS**) **estar** o **andar ~** to be broke*; *ver tb* **pata**

patochada SF blunder, bloomer*

patógeno SM pathogen

patología SF pathology

patológico ADJ pathological

patoso/a* Ⓐ ADJ clumsy **Ⓑ** SM/F clumsy oaf

patota* SF (*CS*) gang, mob

patotero* SM (*CS*) hooligan

patraña SF tall story

patria SF native land, fatherland; **madre ~** mother country; **luchar por la ~** to fight for one's country; ✦ MODISMO **hacer ~** to fly the flag* ➤ **patria adoptiva** adopted country ➤ **patria chica** home town, home area

patriarca SM patriarch

patriarcado SM patriarchy

patriarcal ADJ patriarchal

patrimonial ADJ hereditary

patrimonio SM 1 (= bienes) (adquiridos) assets pl, wealth; (heredados) inheritance, patrimony (frm); (dejados en herencia) estate 2 (artístico, cultural) heritage ➤ **patrimonio de la humanidad** world heritage ➤ **patrimonio nacional** national heritage

patrio ADJ native, home antes de s; **el suelo ~** one's native land, one's native soil

patriota Ⓐ ADJ patriotic **Ⓑ** SMF patriot

patriotería SF, **patrioterismo** SM chauvinism

patriótico ADJ patriotic

patriotismo SM patriotism

patrocinador(a) Ⓐ ADJ sponsoring **Ⓑ** SM/F sponsor

patrocinar /1a/ VT to sponsor

patrocinio SM sponsorship

patrón/ona Ⓐ SM/F 1 (= jefe) boss*; (= dueño) employer, owner 2 [de pensión] landlord/landlady 3 (*Náut*) (*gen*) skipper; [de barco mercante] master/mistress 4 (*Rel*) (tb **santo ~**) (= santo) patron saint; (= virgen) patron **Ⓑ** SM (*Cos*) pattern; (*Téc*) standard, norm; ✦ MODISMO **parecen cortados por el mismo ~** they seem cast in the same mould o mold (*EEUU*) ➤ **patrón oro** gold standard

patronaje SM pattern designing

patronal Ⓐ ADJ 1 (*Com*) employers' antes de s; **cierre ~** (management) lockout; **organización ~** employers' organization 2 (*Rel*) **fiesta ~** local holiday (on the feast day of the local patron saint) **Ⓑ** SF employers' organization; (= dirección) management

patronato SM (= junta) board of management, board of trustees; (= fundación) trust, foundation; **el ~ de turismo** the tourist board

patronímico ADJ, SM patronymic

patrono/a SM/F 1 (*Com, Fin*) owner, employer 2 (*Rel*) patron saint

patrulla SF patrol; **coche ~** patrol car ➤ **patrulla ciudadana** vigilante group

patrullar /1a/ VT, VI to patrol

patrullera SF patrol boat

patrullero Ⓐ ADJ patrol antes de s **Ⓑ** SM 1 (*Aut*) patrol car 2 (*Náut*) patrol boat

patucos SMPL (*Esp*) bootees

paulatino ADJ gradual, slow

pauperización SF (frm) impoverishment

paupérrimo ADJ very poor, poverty-stricken

pausa SF 1 (= descanso) (en programa, reunión) break; (al hablar, leer) pause; (*Mús*) rest; **con ~** slowly, deliberately ➤ **pausa publicitaria** commercial break 2 (*Téc*) (en casete) pause (button); (en vídeo) hold

pausado ADJ slow, deliberate

pauta SF 1 (= modelo) model; (= guía) guideline; (= regla) rule, guide; **marcar la ~** to set the standard; **servir de ~ a** to act as a model for **2** (*en papel*) lines *pl*

pautado ADJ **papel** ~ ruled paper

pava SF **1** (*Orn*) turkey (hen); ✦ MODISMO **pelar la** ~ (*Esp**) to whisper sweet nothings ➤ **pava real** peahen **2** (*CS*) (*para hervir*) kettle **3** (*Col**) (= *colilla*) cigarette end, fag end** **4** (**) (= *chica*) bird**

pavada SF **1** (*esp RPl**) (= *tontería*) silly thing; **no digas ~s** don't talk nonsense **2** (*CS*) (= *bagatela*) trivial thing; **discutieron por una** ~ they fell out over nothing *o* some little thing

pavear* /1a/ VI (*CS, Perú*) to act the fool, mess about

pavesa SF piece of ash

pavimentar /1a/ VT [+ *exteriores*] to pave; [+ *interiores*] to floor

pavimento SM **1** (*de asfalto*) roadway, road surface **2** (*de losas*) (*gen*) paving; (*en interior*) flooring

⚠ **pavimento** ≠ *pavement*

pavo Ⓐ SM **1** (*Orn*) turkey; ✦ MODISMOS **estar en la edad del** ~ to be at an awkward age; **ir de** ~ (*And**) to travel free, get a free ride ➤ **pavo real** peacock **2** (*) (= *tonto*) silly thing, idiot **3** (*Esp***) (= *moneda*) five peseta coin **4** (**) (= *hombre*) bloke** **5** (*Chi*) (= *cometa*) large kite Ⓑ ADJ (*) silly; **¡no seas ~!** don't be silly!

pavonearse /1a/ VPR (= *presumir*) (*gen*) to show off (**de** about); (*al hablar*) to brag (**de** about); (*al andar*) to swagger, strut

pavoneo SM (*gen*) showing-off; (*al hablar*) bragging; (*al andar*) swagger, strutting

pavor SM dread, terror

pavoroso ADJ terrifying

pavoso ADJ (*Ven*) (= *desafortunado*) unlucky; (= *que trae mala suerte*) that brings bad luck

pay SM (*LAm*) pie

paya SF, **payada** SF (*CS*) *improvised gaucho folksong*

payador SM (*CS*) gaucho minstrel

payar /1a/ VI (*CS*) **1** (= *cantar*) to improvise songs to a guitar accompaniment **2** (*) (= *contar cuentos*) to talk big*, shoot a line*

payasada SF clownish trick, stunt; **payasadas** clowning *sing*

payasear /1a/ VI to clown around

payaso/a SM/F clown (*tb fig*)

payés/esa SM/F (*Cataluña, Baleares*) peasant farmer

payo/a SM/F (*para gitanos*) non-gypsy, non-gipsy

paz SF **1** (= *tranquilidad, no guerra*) peace; **¡déjame en ~!** leave me alone!; **descansar en** ~ to rest in peace; **su madre, que en** ~ **descanse** her mother, God rest her soul; **estar en** ~ (*gen*) to be at peace; (*fig*) to be even, be quits (**con** with); **mantener la** ~ to keep the peace; ✦ MODISMO **¡y en ~!** and that's that!, and Bob's your uncle!* **2** (= *tratado*) peace, peace treaty; **firmar la** ~ to sign a peace treaty; **hacer las paces** (*gen*) to make peace; (*fig*) to make (it) up

pazguato* ADJ simple, stupid

pazo SM (*Galicia*) country house

PC SM ABR (= **personal computer**) PC

PD ABR, **P.D.** ABR (= **posdata**) PS

pe SF (*name of the*) *letter P*; ✦ MODISMO **de pe a pa*** from A to Z, from beginning to end

peaje SM toll; **autopista de** ~ toll motorway (*Brit*), turnpike (*EEUU*)

peana SF base, pedestal

peatón/ona SM/F pedestrian

peatonal ADJ pedestrian *antes de s*

pebete/a (*RPl*) Ⓐ SM/F (*) (= *niño*) kid* Ⓑ SM (*CS*) (= *panecillo*) roll

pebre SM *mild sauce made from vinegar, garlic, parsley and pepper*

peca SF freckle

pecado SM **1** (*Rel*) sin; **un** ~ **de juventud** a youthful indiscretion, a sin of youth; **estar en** ~ to be in a state of sin ➤ **pecado capital** deadly sin ➤ **pecado original** original sin ➤ **pecado venial** venial sin **2** (= *cosa lamentable*) crime, sin

pecador(a) Ⓐ ADJ sinful Ⓑ SM/F sinner

pecaminoso ADJ sinful

pecar /1g/ VI **1** (*Rel*) to sin; (*fig*) to err **2** ~ **de** (+ ADJ) to be too + *adj*; **peca de generoso** he is too generous, he is generous to a fault

pécari SM, **pecarí** SM peccary

pecé SM PC

pecera SF (*redonda*) fishbowl; (*rectangular*) fish tank

pechar* /1a/ Ⓐ VT (*CS*) to tap*, touch for Ⓑ VI ~ **con** (*gen*) to put up with; [+ *cometido*] to shoulder, take on

pechera SF **1** (*Cos*) [*de camisa*] shirt front; [*de vestido*] front **2** (*Anat* hum*) big bosom

pechina SF scallop

pecho SM **1** (= *tórax*) chest; **tenía una herida en el** ~ he had a chest injury; **sacar** ~ (*lit*) to stick one's chest out; **tienes que sacar** ~ don't let it get you down*; (*RPl*) (= *vanagloriarse*) to show off; ✦ MODISMOS **no caberle a algn la alegría en el ~**: **no me/le cabía la alegría en el** ~ I/he was bursting with happiness; **a** ~ **descubierto** (= *sin armas*) unarmed, defenceless, defenseless (*EEUU*); (= *francamente*) openly, frankly; **echarse entre** ~ **y espalda** [+ *comida*] to put away*; [+ *bebida*] to knock back*; **tomarse algo a** ~ to take sth to heart **2** [*de mujer*] **2.1** (= *busto*) bust; **tener mucho** ~ to have a big bust; **tener poco** ~ to be flat-chested **2.2** (= *mama*) breast; **dar el** ~ to breast-feed; **un niño de** ~ a baby at the breast

pechuga SF (*Culin*) breast; (*) [*de mujer*] tits** *pl*, bosom ➤ **pechuga de pollo** chicken breast

pechugón/ona* Ⓐ ADJ **1** (= *de mucho pecho*) busty*, big-bosomed **2** (*Perú*) sponging Ⓑ SM/F (*Perú*) (= *gorrón*) sponger*

pecíolo SM, **peciolo** SM (leaf) stalk, petiole (*Téc*)

pécora SF (*tb* **mala ~**) bitch*

pecoso ADJ freckled

pectina SF pectin

pectoral Ⓐ ADJ (*Anat*) pectoral Ⓑ **pectorales** SMPL (*Anat*) pectorals

pecuario ADJ livestock *antes de s*

peculiar ADJ **1** (= *particular, característico*) particular; **un rasgo** ~ **de su carácter** a particular *o* characteristic trait of his; **tiene un carácter muy** ~ he's got a very individual personality **2** (= *raro*) peculiar, unusual

peculiaridad SF peculiarity, special characteristic

pecuniario ADJ pecuniary, money *antes de s*

pedagogía SF pedagogy

pedagógico ADJ pedagogic(al)

pedagogo/a SM/F (= *profesor*) teacher; (= *teórico*) educationalist (*Brit*), educator (*EEUU*)

pedal SM **1** [*de bicicleta, automóvil*] pedal ➤ **pedal de(l) embrague** clutch (pedal) ➤ **pedal de(l) freno** brake (pedal) **2** (*Esp***) (= *borrachera*) **coger un** ~ to get canned**

pedalear /1a/ VI to pedal

pedanía SF district

pedante Ⓐ ADJ pedantic Ⓑ SMF pedant

pedantería SF pedantry

pedazo SM **1** (= *trozo*) piece; **caerse a ~s** to fall to bits; **hacer ~s** [+ *papel*] to rip, tear (up); [+ *vidrio, cristal*] to shatter, smash; [+ *persona*] to tear to shreds; **estoy hecho ~s** I'm worn out; **hacerse ~s** [*objeto*] to fall to pieces; [*vidrio, cristal*] to shatter, smash; ✦ MODISMO **ser un ~ de pan** to be a really nice person, be an angel **2** (*con insultos*) **es un ~ de alcornoque** *o* **animal** *o* **bruto*** he's a blockhead*, he's an idiot

pederasta SMF paedophile, pedophile (*EEUU*)

pederastia SF paedophilia, pedophilia (*EEUU*)

pedernal SM flint

pederse* /2a/ VPR to fart**

pedestal SM pedestal, stand

pedestre ADJ 1 (= *a pie*) pedestrian; **carrera ~** walking race 2 [*metáfora, arte, razón*] pedestrian

pediatra SMF paediatrician, pediatrician (*EEUU*)

pediatría SF paediatrics *sing*, pediatrics *sing* (*EEUU*)

pediátrico ADJ paediatric, pediatric (*EEUU*)

pedicura SF chiropody (*Brit*), podiatry (*EEUU*)

pedicuro/a SM/F, **pedicurista** SMF (*Méx, And*) chiropodist (*Brit*), podiatrist (*EEUU*)

pedida SF (*Esp*) (*tb* **~ de mano**) engagement

pedido SM 1 (*Com*) order; **cursar** *o* **hacer un ~** to place an order 2 (*LAm*) (= *petición*) request; **a ~ de algn** at the request of sb; **hacer algo bajo** *o* **sobre ~** to make sth to order

pedigrí SM, **pedigree** [pedi'gri] SM pedigree

pedigüeño ADJ cadging (*Brit*), mooching (*EEUU**)

pedir /3k/ Ⓐ VT 1 (= *rogar, solicitar*) to ask for; **¿habéis pedido ya la cuenta?** have you asked for the bill (*Brit*) *o* check (*EEUU*) yet?; **necesito ~te consejo** I need to ask your advice; **una manifestación pidiendo la libertad de los secuestrados** a demonstration calling for the release of the hostages; **llamé para ~ que me pusieran una canción** I phoned to request a song; **~ cuentas a algn** to demand an explanation from sb; **~ algo a Dios** to pray to God for sth; **~ algo por favor: me pidió por favor que fuera discreto** he asked me to please keep it to myself; **te lo pido por favor, quédate conmigo** please stay with me; **~ hora** to make an appointment; **~ limosna** to beg; **~ la palabra** to ask for permission to speak; **~ perdón** (= *disculparse*) to apologize; (*suplicando*) to beg (for) forgiveness; **~ permiso** to ask (for) permission; ✦ MODISMOS **¿qué más se puede ~?** what more can you ask (for)?; **te lo pido por Dios** I'm begging you 2 (*LAm* = *encargar*) to order

3 (*en un restaurante*) to order; (*en un bar*) to ask for, order 4 (*para casarse*) **~ la mano de algn** to ask for sb's hand; **~ a algn en matrimonio** to ask for sb's hand in marriage

5 (= *requerir*) to need; **esta planta pide mucho sol** this plant needs lots of sunlight; **la casa está pidiendo a voces que la pinten** the house is crying out to be painted

6 (*tb* = *prestado*) to borrow; **me pidió prestado el coche** he asked if he could borrow the car, he asked to borrow the car

Ⓑ VI 1 (= *pedir dinero*) [*mendigo*] to beg; [*para causa benéfica*] to collect money

2 (*en un bar, restaurante*) to order

Ⓒ **pedirse** (*) VPR (= *elegir*) to bag*; **yo me pido el de fresa** I bags the strawberry one*, bags I get the strawberry one*

pedo Ⓐ ADJ (**) (= *borracho*) pissed***, sloshed**; (= *drogado*) high** Ⓑ SM 1 (*) fart**; **tirarse un ~** to fart**; ✦ MODISMO **al ~** (*CS**): **lavé el auto al ~** it was a waste of time me washing the car 2 (**) [*de alcohol, drogas*] **agarrar** *o* **coger un ~** (= *emborracharse*) to get pissed***, get sloshed**; (= *drogarse*) to get high**; **estar en ~** (*CS*) to be pissed***, be sloshed**; **¡estás en ~!** (*al hablar*) you must be kidding!

pedofilia SF paedophilia, pedophilia (*EEUU*)

pedorrera** SF string of farts**

pedorreta* SF raspberry*

pedrada SF (= *acción*) throw of a stone; (= *golpe*) hit *o* blow from a stone; **matar a algn a ~s** to stone sb to death

pedrea SF [*de lotería*] minor prizes *pl*

pedregal SM rocky ground, stony place

pedregoso ADJ stony, rocky

pedregullo SM (*CS*) gravel

pedrera SF quarry

pedrería SF precious stones *pl*, jewels *pl*

pedrisco SM (= *granizo*) hail; (= *granizada*) hailstorm

pedrusco SM (= *piedra*) rough stone; (= *trozo de piedra*) piece of stone, lump of stone

pedúnculo SM stem, stalk

pega SF 1 (= *dificultad*) snag, problem; **todo son ~s** there's nothing but problems; **poner ~s** to raise objections 2 **de ~*** (= *falso*) false, dud*; (= *de imitación*) fake, sham, bogus 3 (*And, Carib, Méx*) (= *trabajo*) work

pegada SF 1 (*Boxeo*) punch 2 ➤ **pegada de carteles** (*Pol*): **dio comienzo la campaña con la tradicional ~ de carteles** the campaign began with the traditional sticking up of posters

pegadizo ADJ (*Esp*) 1 [*canción, melodía*] catchy 2 [*risa*] contagious

pegado ADJ 1 (= *adherido*) (*gen*) stuck; (*con pegamento*) glued; **me desperté con los ojos ~s** I woke up with my eyes stuck together

2 (= *junto*) **~ a algo: el estadio está ~ al río** the stadium is right beside the river; **íbamos muy ~s al coche de delante** we were right behind the car in front; **pon el piano ~ a la pared** put the piano right up *o* flush against the wall; **está todo el día ~ a su madre** he's a real mother's boy

3 (= *quemado*) [*arroz, leche*] burned, burnt; **oler a ~** to smell burned *o* burnt; ✦ MODISMO **quedarse ~*** to get an electric shock, get fried (*EEUU**)

pegajoso ADJ 1 [*superficie, suelo, manos*] sticky; [*miel*] sticky, gooey*; **hoy hace un calor ~** it's really sticky today 2 [*persona*] clingy* 3 (*LAm*) [*canción, melodía*] catchy

pegamento SM glue, adhesive

pegar /1h/ Ⓐ VT 1 (= *adherir*) (*gen*) to stick; (*con pegamento*) to glue, stick; [+ *cartel*] to stick up; [+ *dos piezas*] to fix together; (*Inform*) to paste

2 (= *golpear*) (*gen*) to hit; (= *dar una torta a*) to smack 3 (*) (= *dar*) **me pegó un golpe** he hit me; **~ un grito** to shout, cry out; **~ un salto** to jump (*with fright etc*); **~ un susto a algn** to scare sb, give sb a fright; **le ~on un tiro** they shot him

4 (= *arrimar*) **~ una silla a una pared** to move *o* put a chair up against a wall; ✦ MODISMO **~ el oído** *o* **la oreja** to prick up one's ears

5 (*) (= *contagiar*) [+ *gripe*] to give; **él me pegó la costumbre** I picked up the habit off him; ✦ MODISMO **~la** (*And, Arg**) (= *tener suerte*) to be lucky; (= *lograrlo*) to manage it; (= *caer en gracia*) to have a hit (**con** with)

Ⓑ VI (= *adherir*) (*Inform*) to paste

2 (= *poner en contacto*) **~ contra algo** to hit sth; **~ en algo** (= *dar*) to hit sth; (= *rozar*) to touch sth; **el sol pega en esta ventana** the sun beats down through this window

3 (= *armonizar*) to go well, fit; [*dos colores*] to match, go together; **este sillón no pega aquí** this armchair doesn't look right here; **no le pega nada actuar así** it's not like him to act like that; **~ con algo** to match sth, go with sth

4 (*) (= *ser fuerte*) [*vino*] to be strong; **a estas horas el sol pega fuerte** the sun is really hot at this time of day

5 (*) (= *tener éxito*) **ese autor está pegando** that author's a big hit

6 (*) (= *creer*) **me pega que: me pega que no vendrá** I have a hunch that he won't come

7 **~la algo*** to be a great one for sth*; **~le a la bebida** to be a heavy drinker

Ⓒ **pegarse** VPR 1 (= *adherirse*) to stick

2 (= *pelearse*) to hit each other, fight

3 **~se a algn** (= *arrimarse*) to stay close to sb; (*Dep*) to stick close to sb; **si vamos a algún sitio siempre se nos pega** if we go anywhere he always latches on to us; ✦ MODISMO **~se a algn como una lapa** (*Esp*) to stick to sb like glue *o* a limpet

4 (*) (= *contagiarse*) (*lit*) to be catching; (*fig*) to be infectious, be catchy; **se te ha pegado el acento andaluz** you've picked up an Andalusian accent

5 (*) (= *darse*) **~se un tiro** to shoot o.s.; **~se un golpe** to hit o.s.; **se pega la vida padre** he lives the life of Riley; ✦ MODISMOS **pegársela*** (= *fracasar*) to fail, come a cropper*; **pegársela a algn** (= *traicionar*) to double-cross sb; (= *ser infiel*) to cheat on sb

pegatina (*CS*) SF 1 (= *adhesivo*) sticker 2 = **pegada 2**

pego* SM (*Esp*) ✦ MODISMO **dar el ~** [*imitación*] to look like the real thing

pegoste SM (*CAm***) scrounger*

pegote* SM 1 (= *cosa pegajosa*) sticky mess; ✦ MODISMOS **echarse un ~** ✧ **tirarse ~s** to brag*, exaggerate, show off **2** (= *chapuza*) botch

peinado Ⓐ ADJ **bien ~** [*pelo*] well-combed; [*persona*] neat, well-groomed Ⓑ SM **1** [*de pelo*] hairdo, hairstyle **2** (*) (= *redada*) house-to-house search

peinador(a) Ⓐ SM/F (*LAm*) (= *persona*) hairdresser Ⓑ SM **1** (= *bata*) dressing gown, peignoir **2** (*LAm*) (= *tocador*) dressing table

peinar /1a/ Ⓐ VT **1** [+ *pelo*] (*con peine*) to comb; (*con cepillo*) to brush; **~ a algn** (*con peine*) to comb sb's hair; **me peinan en Silvia's** I get my hair done at Silvia's **2** [+ *caballo*] to comb, curry **3** [+ *zona*] to comb Ⓑ **peinarse** VPR (*con peine*) to comb one's hair; (= *hacerse un peinado*) to do one's hair

peine SM comb; ✦ MODISMO **¡te vas a enterar de lo que vale un ~!** (*Esp**) now you'll find out what's what! ➤ **peine de púas** fine-toothed comb, nit comb

peineta SF back comb, ornamental comb

peinilla SF **1** (*And, Carib*) (= *machete*) large machete **2** (*esp Chi*) (= *peine*) comb

p.ej. ABR (= *por ejemplo*) e.g.

pejiguera* SF bother, nuisance

Pekín SM Beijing, Peking

pela* SF **1** (*Esp*) (= *peseta*) peseta; (*tb* **~s**) (= *dinero*) money *sing*; **mucha ~** lots of dough** **2** (*LAm*) (= *zurra*) beating

pelada SF **1** (*LAm*) (= *corte de pelo*) haircut **2** (*CS*) (= *calva*) bald head **3 la Pelada** (*And, Carib, CS*) (= *muerte*) death

peladez* SF (*Méx*) rude word, obscenity

peladilla SF (*Esp*) sugared almond

pelado Ⓐ ADJ **1** (= *sin pelo*) **lleva la cabeza pelada** he has his head shaved
2 (*CS*) (= *calvo*) bald
3 (*por el sol*) **tengo la espalda pelada** my back is peeling
4 [*fruta, verdura*] peeled; [*crustáceo*] shelled; **sólo han dejado los huesos ~s** they left nothing but the bones
5 [*terreno*] treeless, bare; [*paisaje*] bare; [*tronco*] bare, smooth
6 (= *escueto*) bare; **cobra el sueldo ~** he gets just his bare salary; **he sacado un cinco ~** I just scraped a five;
✦ MODISMO **a pie ~** (*Chi*) barefoot
7 (*) (= *sin dinero*) broke*, penniless
8 (*Méx*) (= *grosero*) coarse, rude
Ⓑ SM (*) (= *corte de pelo*) haircut

PELADO

A stock figure in Mexican theatre and film, the **pelado** is a kind of rural anti-hero cum lovable rogue who survives by his quick wits in the foreign environment of the city. The Mexican actor and comedian Mario Moreno (1911-94) based the character **Cantinflas** on the **pelado**, for which he is famous all over the Spanish-speaking world. The **pelado** is closely related to the literary figure of the **pícaro** and forms part of a long line of anti-heroic characters in Hispanic literature.
⇨ PÍCARO, CARPA

---

pelador SM (*Culin*) peeler

peladuras SFPL peel *sing*, peelings

pelagatos* SM INV nobody

pelaje SM **1** (*Zool*) fur, coat **2** (= *apariencia*) **tenía muy mal ~** he looked very suspicious *o* dodgy; **y otros de ese ~** and others of that ilk

pelambre SM **1** (*Zool*) (= *piel*) skin; (= *pelaje*) hair, coat **2** (*Chi*) (= *murmullos*) gossip, slander

pelambrera* SF mop of hair*

pelandusca* SF (*Esp*) floozy**

pelapatatas SM INV, **pelapapas** SM INV (*LAm*) potato peeler

pelar /1a/ Ⓐ VT **1** (= *rapar*) **lo han pelado al cero** *o* **al rape** he's had his head shaved, he's had his hair cropped short
2 [+ *fruta, verdura*] to peel; [+ *habas, crustáceo*] to shell

3 (= *despellejar*) to skin; (= *desplumar*) to pluck
4 (†) (= *quitar el dinero a*) to clean out*, fleece*
Ⓑ VI **1** (*) **que pela: hace un frío que pela** it's bitterly cold **2** (*Chi**) (= *cotillear*) to gossip
Ⓒ **pelarse** VPR **1** (= *cortarse el pelo*) to get one's hair cut **2** [*nariz, hombros*] to peel; **se me está pelando la espalda** my back is peeling
3 ✦ MODISMO **corre que se las pela** he runs like nobody's business*

peldaño SM (*Arquit*) step, stair; [*de escalera portátil*] rung

pelea SF (*a golpes, patadas*) (*tb* Boxeo) fight; (= *discusión, riña*) quarrel, row

peleado ADJ **estoy peleada con dos amigas** I've fallen out with two friends; **María está peleada con su novio** María has broken up *o* split up with her boyfriend

peleador ADJ quarrelsome

pelear /1a/ Ⓐ VI (*físicamente*) to fight; **~ por algo** to fight over sth; **siempre me toca ~ con los niños a la hora del baño** I'm always the one who has to battle with the children at bathtime
Ⓑ **pelearse** VPR **1** (*físicamente*) to fight; **estaban peleándose a puñetazos** they were punching each other *o* laying into each other with their fists; **~se con algn** to fight sb; **~se por algo** to fight over sth
2 (= *discutir*) to argue, quarrel
3 (= *romper una relación*) [*dos amigos*] to fall out; [*novios*] to split up, break up; **se ha peleado con todas sus amigos** he's fallen out with all his friends

pelechar /1a/ VI to moult, molt (*EEUU*)

pelela* SF (*RPl*) potty*

pelele SM **1** (= *figura*) guy, straw doll; (*fig*) tool, puppet **2** [*de bebé*] Babygro®, rompers *pl*, creepers *pl* (*EEUU*)

peleón ADJ **1** (= *belicoso*) aggressive **2** (= *discutidor*) argumentative **3** [*vino*] cheap, rough

peleonero ADJ (*LAm*) = **peleón**

peletería SF (= *tienda*) furrier's, fur shop; (= *oficio*) furriery

peli* SF = **película 1**

peliagudo ADJ [*tema*] tricky

pelícano SM, **pelicano** SM pelican

película SF **1** (*Cine*) film (*esp Brit*), movie (*esp EEUU*);
✦ MODISMO **fue de ~** it was incredible ➤ **película de acción** action film (*esp Brit*) *o* movie (*esp EEUU*) ➤ **película de aventuras** adventure film (*esp Brit*) *o* movie (*esp EEUU*) ➤ **película de dibujos (animados)** cartoon ➤ **película del Oeste** western ➤ **película de miedo** horror film (*esp Brit*) *o* movie (*esp EEUU*) **2** (*Fot, Téc*) film **3** (*) (= *narración*) story, catalogue of events; (= *cuento*) tall story, tale

peliculero* ADJ showy

peligrar /1a/ VI to be in danger

peligro SM (*gen*) danger, peril (*liter*); (= *riesgo*) risk; **en ~ de extinción** in danger of extinction; **estos gases constituyen un ~ para la salud** these gases pose a risk to health, these gases pose a health hazard; **"peligro de incendio"** "fire risk", "fire hazard"; **"peligro de muerte"** "danger"; **correr el ~ de que lo descubran** he runs the risk of being found out; **bajo esta roca no corremos ~** we're in no danger under this rock, we're free from danger under this rock; **estar en ~** to be in danger; **está fuera de ~** he's out of danger; **poner en ~** to endanger, put at risk, jeopardize

peligrosidad SF danger

peligroso ADJ (*gen*) dangerous; (= *arriesgado*) risky; [*herida*] ugly, nasty

pelillo* SM ✦ MODISMO **¡~s a la mar!** (*Esp*) let bygones be bygones!

pelín* SM **un ~** a bit, just a bit; **es un ~ tacaño** he's just a little stingy *o* (*esp Brit*) a bit mean; **te pasaste un ~** you went a little too far

pelirrojo/a Ⓐ ADJ red-haired, red-headed Ⓑ SM/F redhead

pella SF **1** (*gen*) ball, round mass; (*sin forma*) dollop **2** ✦ MODISMO **hacer ~s** to play truant*, play hookey (*esp EEUU**)

pelleja SF skin, hide

pellejerías SFPL (*And*) difficulties

pellejo SM 1 [*de animal*] skin, hide; (*) [*de persona*] skin; [*de uva*] skin; ✦ MODISMOS **no quisiera estar en su ~** I wouldn't like to be in his shoes; **ponte en su ~** put yourself in her shoes 2 (*) (= *vida*) neck*; **arriesgar el ~** to risk one's neck*; **salvar el ~** to save one's skin *o* neck* 3 (= *odre*) wineskin

pelliza SF fur-lined jacket

pellizcar /1g/ VT 1 [+ *persona, mejilla*] to pinch 2 [+ *comida*] to nibble, pick at

pellizco SM 1 (*en mejilla, brazo*) pinch 2 (= *cantidad pequeña*) small bit; **un ~ de sal** a pinch of salt; **un buen ~*** a tidy sum*

pelma* ADJ, SMF = **pelmazo**

pelmazo/a* Ⓐ ADJ boring Ⓑ SM/F bore

pelo SM 1 (*individual*) [*de persona, animal*] hair; [*de barba*] whisker; (*Téc*) fibre, fiber (*EEUU*), strand; **un ~ rubio** a blond hair
2 (*en conjunto*) [*de persona*] hair; [*de animal*] fur, coat; [*de fruta*] down; [*de tejido*] nap, pile; **tienes mucho ~** you have thick hair; **se me está cayendo el ~** I am losing my hair; **cortarse el ~** to have one's hair cut ➤ **pelo de camello** camel-hair, camel's hair (*EEUU*)
3 (= *sierra*) hacksaw blade
4 ✦ MODISMOS **a pelo***: **cabalgar** *o* **montar a ~** to ride bareback; **cantar a ~** to sing unaccompanied; **al ~***: **te queda al ~** it looks great on you, it fits like a glove; **este regalo me viene al ~** this present is just what I needed *o* wanted; **viene al ~ el comentario** that comment is spot on; **caérsele el ~ a algn** (*esp Esp**): **¡se te va a caer el ~!** you're (in) for it now!; **¡Juan viene a cenar y yo con estos ~s!*** Juan is coming to dinner and look at the state I'm in!; **lucirle el ~ a algn***: **así nos luce el ~** and that's the awful state we're in, that's why we're so badly off; **de medio ~** (= *de baja calidad*) second-rate; (= *de baja categoría social*) of no social standing; **de ~ en pecho** manly; **un hombre de ~ en pecho** a real man; **por los ~s** by the skin of one's teeth; **pasó el examen por los ~s** he passed the exam by the skin of his teeth, he scraped through the exam; **parece traído por los ~s** it seems far-fetched; **con ~s y señales** in minute detail; **soltarse el ~*** to let one's hair down*; **no tener ~s en la lengua** not to mince one's words; **no tocar un ~ de la ropa a algn** not to lay a finger on sb; **tomar el ~ a algn** to pull sb's leg; **no ver el ~ a algn*** not to see hide nor hair of sb
5 ✦ MODISMO **un ~*** (= *un poco*): **no me fío un ~ de ellos** I don't trust them an inch; **me temo que te pasas un ~** I am afraid you are going a bit too far; **no tiene un ~ de tonto** he's no fool; **nos escapamos por un ~** we had a close shave

pelón Ⓐ ADJ 1 (= *calvo*) bald, hairless 2 (*And*) (= *con mucho pelo*) hairy, long-haired Ⓑ SM (*CS*) nectarine

pelona SF **la Pelona** (*And, Méx**) (= *muerte*) death

pelota Ⓐ SF 1 (*Dep*) ball; **jugar a la ~** to play ball; ✦ MODISMOS **devolver la ~ a algn** to turn the tables on sb; **hacer la ~ a algn*** to suck up to sb; **pasarse la ~** to pass the buck* ➤ **pelota de goma** (*Mil*) rubber bullet ➤ **pelota vasca** pelota 2 **pelotas*** (= *testículos*) balls***; **en ~s** stark naked, starkers**; ✦ MODISMO **tener ~s** to have balls; ✦ MODISMO **tocar las ~s a algn** to get on sb's tits**, bug sb* Ⓑ SMF (*) creep*

pelotari (*Esp*) SMF pelota player

pelotazo SM 1 (= *golpe*) **me dieron un ~** I got hit by a ball 2 (*) **la cultura del ~** the quick-buck culture

pelotear /1a/ Ⓐ VT (*And**) **~ un asunto** to turn sth over in one's mind Ⓑ VI (*Dep*) to knock a ball about, kick a ball about; (*Tenis*) to knock up

peloteo SM 1 (*Tenis*) (*como entrenamiento*) knock-up; (= *tirada larga*) rally 2 (*Ftbl*) kick-about*; [*de entrada*] warm-up

pelotera* SF row, set-to*

pelotero/a SM/F 1 (*LAm*) (= *jugador*) ball player; [*de fútbol*] football player, soccer player (*EEUU*), footballer (*Brit*); [*de béisbol*] baseball player 2 (*) (= *lameculos*) creep**

pelotilla* SF 1 (= *adulación*) **hacer la ~ a algn** to suck up to sb* 2 [*de moco*] bogey**

pelotillero/a* Ⓐ ADJ crawling*, bootlicking*, brown-nosing (*EEUU***) Ⓑ SM/F crawler*, bootlicker*, brown-nose (*EEUU***)

pelotón SM 1 [*de atletas, ciclistas*] pack 2 (*Mil*) detachment, squad ➤ **pelotón de ejecución, pelotón de fusilamiento** firing squad

pelotudo/a* (*SAm*) Ⓐ ADJ bloody stupid** Ⓑ SM/F bloody fool (*Brit***), jerk (*EEUU**)

peltre SM pewter

peluca SF wig

peluche SM felt, plush

pelucón ADJ (*And*) long-haired

peludo ADJ (= *con mucho pelo*) hairy, shaggy; (= *con pelo largo*) long-haired; [*animal*] furry, shaggy; [*barba*] bushy

peluquear /1a/ (*And*) Ⓐ VT **~ a algn** to cut sb's hair Ⓑ **peluquearse** VPR to have one's hair cut

peluquería SF 1 (= *establecimiento*) hairdresser's 2 (= *oficio*) hairdressing

peluquero/a SM/F hairdresser

peluquín SM hairpiece

pelusa SF 1 (*Bot*) down; (*Cos*) fluff; (*en cara*) down, fuzz; (*bajo muebles*) fluff, dust 2 (*) (*entre niños*) envy, jealousy

pelvis SF INV pelvis

pena SF 1 (= *tristeza*) sorrow; **tengo una ~ muy grande** I'm very sad; **alma en ~** lost soul; **dar ~**: **da ~ verlos sufrir así** it's sad to see them suffer like that; **Pepe me da mucha ~** I feel very sorry for Pepe; ✦ MODISMO **sin ~ ni gloria**: **ese año pasó sin ~ ni gloria** it was an uneventful sort of year; **la exposición pasó sin ~ ni gloria** the exhibition went almost unnoticed
2 (= *lástima*) shame, pity; **¡qué ~!** what a shame *o* a pity!; **mi habitación está que da ~ verla** my room is in a terrible state*; **de ~**: **la economía va de ~** the economy is in a terrible state; **el vestido le quedaba de ~** the dress looked terrible on her
3 penas (= *problemas*) **cuéntame tus ~s** tell me all your troubles; ✦ MODISMOS **ahogar las ~s** to drown one's sorrows; **a duras ~s** with great difficulty
4 (= *esfuerzo*) **merecer** *o* **valer la ~** to be worth; **no merece la ~** it's not worth it; **una obra que vale la ~ ver** a play that's worth seeing
5 (*Jur*) sentence; **el juez le impuso una ~ de tres años de prisión** the judge sentenced him to three years in prison ➤ **pena capital** capital punishment ➤ **pena de muerte** death penalty
6 (*Méx, And*) (= *vergüenza*) embarrassment; **me da mucha ~** I'm very embarrassed; **¡qué ~!** how embarrassing!; **sentir** *o* **tener ~** to be *o* feel embarrassed, be *o* feel ill at ease
7 (*And*) (= *fantasma*) ghost

penacho SM 1 (*Orn*) tuft, crest 2 [*de casco, sombrero*] plume

penal Ⓐ ADJ penal Ⓑ SM 1 (= *prisión*) prison, (state) penitentiary (*EEUU*) 2 (*LAm Dep*) (= *penalty*) penalty (kick)

penalidades SFPL hardship *sing*

penalista SMF expert in criminal law, penologist

penalización SF penalty, penalization

penalizar /1f/ VT to penalize

penalti (*pl* ~s) SM, **penalty** (*pl* **penaltys, ~es**) SM (*Dep*) penalty (kick); ✦ MODISMO **casarse de ~** (*Esp**) to have a shotgun wedding

penar /1a/ Ⓐ VT 1 (*Jur*) to punish; **la ley pena el asesinato** the law punishes murder 2 (*And*) [*difunto*] to haunt Ⓑ VI 1 (= *sufrir*) [*persona*] to suffer; [*alma*] to be in torment 2 (*And*) [*difunto*] **en ese lugar penan** that place is haunted

penca SF (= *hoja*) leaf; (= *nervio*) main rib

pencar /1g/ VI to slog away*, slave away*

pendejada* SF (*LAm*) 1 (= *tontería*) foolish thing 2 (= *acto cobarde*) cowardly act

pendejear* /1a/ VI (*And, Méx*) to act the fool

pendejo/a* Ⓐ ADJ 1 (*LAm*) (= *imbécil*) idiotic; (= *cobarde*) cowardly, yellow* 2 (*Perú*) (= *listo*) smart; (= *taimado*) cunning **3** (*Carib, Méx*) (= *torpe*) ham-fisted **Ⓑ** SM/F **1** (*LAm*) (= *imbécil*) fool, idiot; (= *cobarde*) coward **2** (*CS*) (= *muchacho*) kid* **3** (*Perú*) (= *sabelotodo*) know-all (*Brit*), know-it-all (*EEUU*) **Ⓒ** SM (*LAm****) (= *pelo*) pube**

pendenciero/a Ⓐ ADJ quarrelsome **Ⓑ** SM/F troublemaker

pender /2a/ VI to hang (**de, en** from; **sobre** over); **la amenaza que pende sobre nosotros** the threat hanging over us

pendiente Ⓐ ADJ **1** (= *a la expectativa*) **estar ~ de algo: estaban ~s de su llegada** they were waiting for him to arrive; **estamos ~s de lo que él decida** we are waiting to see what he decides
2 (= *atento*) **estar ~ de algo/algn: está muy ~ de la salud de su madre** he always keeps an eye on his mother's health; **estaban muy ~s de lo que decía** they were listening to her intently
3 [*juicio, caso, asunto*] pending; **tengo la física ~** I have to resit physics
4 [*cuenta*] outstanding, unpaid
5 (= *colgado*) hanging
Ⓑ SM (= *joya*) earring
Ⓒ SF [*de un terreno*] slope; [*de un tejado*] pitch; **en ~** sloping

pendón SM **1** (= *bandera*) banner, standard; [*de forma triangular*] pennant **2** (*Esp**) (= *mujer*) slut**, tart (*esp Brit***)

pendona* SF = **pendón 2**

pendonear* /1a/ VI to loaf around*, hang out*

pendoneo* SM **irse de ~** to go out round the streets*

péndulo SM pendulum

pene SM penis

penetración SF **1** (= *acción*) penetration **2** (= *agudeza*) sharpness, acuteness; (= *visión*) insight

penetrante ADJ **1** [*arma*] sharp; [*frío, viento*] biting; [*sonido*] piercing; [*vista*] acute; [*aroma*] strong; [*mirada*] sharp, penetrating **2** [*genio, mente*] keen, sharp; [*ironía*] biting

penetrar /1a/ **Ⓐ** VI **1** (= *entrar*) **el humo penetraba a través de las rendijas** the smoke was filtering through the cracks; **el agua había penetrado a través de** o **por las paredes** the water had seeped into the walls; **~ en: penetramos en un túnel** we went into o entered a tunnel; **penetramos poco en el mar** we did not go far out to sea
2 (*frm*) (= *descifrar*) to penetrate; **~ en el sentido de algo** to penetrate the meaning of sth
Ⓑ VT **1** (= *atravesar*) to go right through; **un frío glacial le penetró los huesos** an icy cold went right through to her bones
2 (*sexualmente*) to penetrate
3 (*frm*) (= *descubrir*) [+ *misterio*] to fathom; [+ *secreto*] to unlock; [+ *sentido*] to grasp; [+ *intención*] to see through, grasp

penicilina SF penicillin

península SF peninsula ➤ **la Península Ibérica** the Iberian Peninsula

peninsular Ⓐ ADJ peninsular **Ⓑ** SMF **los ~es** peninsular Spaniards

penique SM penny; **~s** pence

penitencia SF penance; **en ~** as a penance; **hacer ~** to do penance

penitenciaría SF prison, (state) penitentiary (*EEUU*)

penitenciario ADJ penitentiary, prison *antes de s*

penitente ADJ, SMF penitent; ⇨ *SEMANA SANTA*

penoso ADJ **1** (= *doloroso*) painful; **me veo en la penosa obligación de comunicarles que ...** I regret to have to inform you that ... **2** (= *difícil*) [*tarea*] arduous, laborious; [*viaje*] gruelling, grueling (*EEUU*) **3** (= *lamentable*) pitiful; **fue un espectáculo ~** it was a sorry o pitiful sight **4** (*And, Méx*) (= *tímido*) shy, timid; (= *embarazoso*) embarrassing

pensado ADJ **un proyecto poco ~** a badly-thought-out o an ill-thought-out scheme; **lo tengo bien ~** I have thought it over o out carefully; **tengo ~ hacerlo mañana** I mean o intend to do it tomorrow; **bien ~, creo que ...** on reflection, I think that ...; **en el momento menos ~** when

you least expect it

pensador(a) SM/F thinker

pensamiento SM **1** (= *facultad, cosa pensada*) thought; **adivinar el ~ a algn** to read sb's thoughts, guess what sb is thinking **2** (= *mente*) mind; **acudir** o **venir al ~ de algn** to come to sb's mind **3** (*Bot*) pansy

pensar /1j/ **Ⓐ** VT **1** (= *opinar*) to think; **~ de: ¿qué piensas de ella?** what do you think of her?; **~ que** to think that **2** (= *considerar*) to think about, think over; **lo ~é** I'll think about it, I'll think it over; **lo pensó mejor** she thought better of it; **pensándolo bien ...** on second thoughts ..., on reflection ...; **¡ni ~lo!** no way!*
3 (= *decidir*) **~ que** to decide that, come to the conclusion that ...
4 (= *tener la intención de*) **~ hacer algo** to intend to do sth; **pienso seguir insistiendo** I intend to keep on trying; **no pienso volver** I have no intention of going back
5 (= *concebir*) to think up
6 (= *esperar*) **cuando menos lo pienses** when you least expect it; **sin ~lo** unexpectedly
Ⓑ VI **1** (= *tener ideas*) to think; **~ en algo/algn** to think about sth/sb; **dar que ~: el hecho de que no llamara a la policía da que ~** the fact that she didn't call the police makes you think; **dar que ~ a la gente** to set people thinking, arouse suspicions; **sin ~** without thinking **2** **~ bien de algo/algn** to think well of sth/sb; **~ mal de algo/algn** to think ill of sth/sb; **¡no pienses mal!** don't be nasty!
Ⓒ **pensarse** VPR **tienes nueve días para pensártelo** you have nine days to think it over o to think about it; **sin pensárselo dos veces** without a second thought; **después de pensárselo mucho** after thinking about it long and hard, after much thought

pensativo ADJ pensive, thoughtful

pensión SF **1** (*por vejez*) pension; (*por invalidez, de divorciada*) allowance ➤ **pensión alimenticia** alimony, maintenance ➤ **pensión asistencial** state pension ➤ **pensión contributiva** contributory pension ➤ **pensión de invalidez** disability allowance ➤ **pensión de jubilación** retirement pension ➤ **pensión de viudedad** widow's/widower's pension ➤ **pensión vitalicia** annuity **2** (= *casa de huéspedes*) boarding house, guest house; (*Univ*) lodgings *pl* **3** (= *precio*) board and lodging; **media ~** half board; **~ completa** full board

pensionado/a Ⓐ SM/F (*Arg*) (= *pensionista*) pensioner **Ⓑ** SM (= *internado*) boarding school

pensionar /1a/ VT (*Perú*) (= *molestar*) to bother; (= *preocupar*) to worry

pensionista SMF **1** (= *jubilado*) (old-age) pensioner **2** (= *huésped*) lodger, paying guest **3** (*Escol*) boarding-school pupil, boarder (*Brit*)

pentágono SM pentagon; **el Pentágono** (*en EEUU*) the Pentagon

pentagrama SM stave (*esp Brit*), staff (*esp EEUU*)

pentámetro SM pentameter

pentatlón SM pentathlon

Pentecostés SM **1** (*cristiano*) Whitsun, Whitsuntide; **domingo de ~** Whit Sunday **2** (*judío*) Pentecost

penúltimo/a ADJ, SM/F penultimate, last but one; ✦ MODISMO **la penúltima*** (*copa*) one for the road*

penumbra SF half-light, semi-darkness; **en la ~** in the shadows

penuria SF (= *pobreza*) poverty; (= *escasez*) shortage, dearth

peña SF **1** (*Geog*) crag **2** (= *grupo*) group, circle; (= *club*) folk club ➤ **peña deportiva** supporters' club ➤ **peña taurina** club of bullfighting enthusiasts **3** (*) (= *gente*) crowd; **hay mucha ~** there's loads of people*

peñasco SM **1** (= *piedra*) large rock, boulder **2** (= *risco*) rock, crag

peñascoso ADJ rocky, craggy

peñazo* (*Esp*) **Ⓐ** ADJ **¡no seas tan ~!** don't be such a pain!* **Ⓑ** SM pain (in the neck)*; **dar el ~** to be a pain*, be a bore*

peñón SM **1** (= *roca*) wall of rock, crag **2 el Peñón** the Rock (*of Gibraltar*)

peo** SM *ver* **pedo**

peón SM **1** (*Téc*) labourer, laborer (*EEUU*); (*esp LAm Agr*) farm labourer *o* (*EEUU*) laborer, farmhand ➤ **peón caminero** navvy, road-mender ➤ **peón de albañil** bricklayer's mate **2** (*Ajedrez*) pawn

peonada SF **1** (= *trabajadores*) gang of labourers *o* (*EEUU*) laborers **2** (= *trabajo*) day's stint, day's shift

peonía SF peony

peonza SF (spinning) top

peor Ⓐ ADJ **1** (*compar de malo*) [*producto, resultado, situación*] worse; [*oferta*] lower; [*calidad*] poorer; **su situación es ~ que la nuestra** their situation is worse than ours; **un vino de ~ calidad** an inferior wine; **ir a ~** to get worse; **y lo que es ~** and what's worse **2** (*superl de malo*) worst; **es el ~ de la clase** he is the worst in the class; **en el ~ de los casos** if the worst comes to the worst; **lo ~ de todo es que ...** the worst thing is that ...
Ⓑ ADV **1** (*compar de mal*) worse; **escribo cada vez ~** my handwriting is getting worse and worse; **~ que nunca** worse than ever; **si no le gusta, ~ para él** if he doesn't like it, that's his loss *o* that's just too bad **2** (*superl de mal*) worst; **la carta ~ redactada que he leído nunca** the most badly *o* the worst written letter I've ever read

pepa SF (*LAm*) [*de uva, tomate*] pip; [*de durazno, dátil*] stone

pepenador(a) SM/F (*CAm, Méx*) scavenger (*on rubbish tip*)

pepenar /1a/ VT **1** (*CAm, Méx*) (= *recoger*) to pick up; (*en la basura*) to search through **2** (*Méx*) (= *agarrar*) to grab hold of

pepinazo* SM **1** (= *explosión*) bang **2** (= *accidente*) smash

pepinillo SM gherkin

pepino SM cucumber; ✦ MODISMO **me importa un ~*** I don't care two hoots*, I don't give a damn*

pepita SF **1** (*Bot*) pip **2** (*Min*) nugget

pepito SM steak sandwich

pepitoria SF (*Culin*) **pollo en ~** chicken fricassee

pepón** ADJ (*Perú*) good-looking, dishy*

pepona SF large cardboard doll

péptico ADJ peptic

pequeñajo/a* (*Esp*) Ⓐ ADJ little, tiny Ⓑ SM/F little rascal, little devil

pequeñez SF **1** [*de tamaño*] smallness, small size; [*de altura*] shortness **2** [*de miras*] pettiness, small-mindedness **3** (= *cosa insignificante*) trifle, trivial thing

pequeñín/ina Ⓐ ADJ tiny, little Ⓑ SM/F little one

pequeño/a Ⓐ ADJ (*gen*) small, little; [*cifra*] small, low; (= *bajo*) short; **el hermano ~** the youngest brother; **un niño ~** a small child; **cuando era ~** ◇ **de ~** when I was a child, when I was little; **un castillo en ~** a miniature castle Ⓑ SM/F child; **los ~s** the children, the little ones; **soy el ~** I'm the youngest

pequeñoburgués/esa Ⓐ ADJ lower middle class; (*Pol pey*) petit bourgeois Ⓑ SM/F lower middle class person; (*Pol pey*) petit bourgeois/petite bourgeoise

pequinés SM (= *perro*) Pekinese, Pekingese

pera¹ SF **1** (*Bot*) pear; ✦ MODISMOS **eso es pedir ~s al olmo** that's asking the impossible; **ser la ~*** to be the limit **2** (*CS**) (= *barbilla*) chin; (= *perilla*) goatee **3** [*de atomizador, bocina*] bulb **4** (= *interruptor*) switch **5 peras*** (= *pechos*) tits*** **6** (*LAm Dep*) punchball

pera²* (*Esp*) ADJ INV posh*

peral SM pear tree

peraltar /1a/ VT to bank, camber

peralte SM [*de curva, carretera*] banking, camber; (*Arquit*) cant, slope

perca SF perch

percal SM, **percala** SF (*And, Méx*) percale; ✦ MODISMO **conocer el ~*** to know what the score is*

percán SM (*Chi*) mould, mold (*EEUU*), mildew

percance SM (= *desgracia*) misfortune, mishap; (*en plan*) setback, hitch

per cápita ADV per capita

percatarse /1a/ VPR **~ de** (= *observar*) to notice; (= *comprender*) to realize

percebe SM **1** (*Zool*) barnacle **2** (*) (= *tonto*) idiot, twit*

percepción SF **1** (*facultad*) perception ➤ **percepción extrasensorial** extrasensory perception **2** (*Com, Fin*) receipt

perceptible ADJ **1** (= *visible*) perceptible, noticeable **2** (*Com, Fin*) payable, receivable

perceptor(a) SM/F (*frm*) recipient ➤ **perceptor(a) de subsidio de desempleo** person who draws unemployment benefit

percha SF **1** (*para ropa*) (clothes) hanger; (= *gancho*) coat hook **2** (*para pájaros*) perch **3** (*) (= *tipo*) build, physique; [*de mujer*] figure

perchero SM [*de pared*] clothes rack; [*de pie*] coat stand

percibir /3a/ VT **1** (= *notar*) to perceive, notice; (= *ver*) to see, observe; [+ *peligro*] to sense, scent **2** (*frm*) [+ *sueldo, subsidio*] to draw, receive

percusión SF percussion

percusionista SMF percussionist

percusor SM (*Téc*) hammer; [*de arma*] firing pin

percutir /3a/ VT to strike, tap

percutor SM = **percusor**

perdedor(a) Ⓐ ADJ [*baza, equipo*] losing Ⓑ SM/F loser; **buen ~** good loser

perder /2g/ Ⓐ VT **1** [+ *objeto, dinero, familiar*] to lose; **he perdido cinco kilos** I've lost five kilos; **~ el conocimiento** to lose consciousness; **~ la costumbre** to get out of the habit; **~ algo de vista** to lose sight of sth; **conviene no ~ de vista que ...** we mustn't forget that ..., we mustn't lose sight of the fact that ... **2** [+ *tiempo*] to waste; **sin ~ un momento** without wasting a moment **3** [+ *aire, aceite*] to leak **4** [+ *tren, avión*] to miss; [+ *oportunidad*] to miss, lose; **no pierde detalle** he doesn't miss a thing **5** (= *destruir*) to ruin; **ese vicio lo ~á** that vice will ruin him, that vice will be his ruin; **lo que le pierde es ...** where he comes unstuck is ... **6** (*Jur*) to lose, forfeit
Ⓑ VI **1** (*en competición, disputa*) to lose; **tienen** *o* **llevan todas las de ~** they look certain to lose; **saber ~** to be a good loser **2** [*tela*] to run (in the wash) **3 echar a ~** [+ *comida, sorpresa*] to ruin, spoil; [+ *oportunidad*] to waste; **echarse a ~** [*comida*] to go off; [*sorpresa*] to be ruined, be spoiled
Ⓒ **perderse** VPR **1** [*persona*] to get lost; **tenía miedo de ~me** I was afraid of getting lost *o* losing my way; **¡piérdete!*** get lost! **2** [*objeto*] **se me han perdido las llaves** I've lost my keys; **¿qué se les ha perdido en Alemania?** what business have you in Germany? **3** [+ *programa, fiesta*] to miss; **¡no te lo pierdas!** don't miss it! **4** (= *desaparecer*) to disappear; **el tren se perdió en la niebla** the train disappeared into the fog **5** (= *arruinarse*) [*persona*] to lose one's way; [*cosecha*] to be ruined, get spoiled; **se perdió por el juego** gambling was his ruin *o* undoing **6 ~se por algo/algn** to be mad about sth/sb; **~se por hacer algo** to be dying to do sth, long to do sth **7** (*LAm*) (= *prostituirse*) to go on the streets

perdición SF (*Rel*) perdition; (*fig*) undoing, ruin; **fue su ~** it was his undoing; **será mi ~** it will be the ruin of me

perdida SF loose woman*; *ver tb* **perdido**

pérdida SF (*gen*) loss; (*Téc*) leakage, wastage; **es una ~ de tiempo** it's a waste of time; **¡no tiene ~!** you can't miss it! ➤ **pérdida de conocimiento** loss of consciousness

perdidamente ADV **~ enamorado** hopelessly in love

perdido/a Ⓐ ADJ 1 (= *extraviado*) lost; [*bala*] stray; **oficina de objetos ~s** lost property office (*Brit*), lost and found department (*EEUU*); **dar algo por ~** to give sth up for lost 2 (= *aislado*) remote, isolated 3 (= *sin remedio*) **estaba borracho ~** he was totally *o* dead* drunk; **es tonto ~** he's a complete idiot; **¡estamos ~s!** we're done for!; ✦ MODISMO **de ~s, al río** in for a penny, in for a pound 4 (= *enamorado*) **estar ~ por algn** to be mad *o* crazy about sb 5 (*Esp**) (= *sucio*) **ponerlo todo ~ de barro** to get everything covered in mud, get mud everywhere; **te has puesto ~ el pantalón** you've ruined your trousers (*Brit*) *o* pants (*EEUU*) Ⓑ SM/F libertine; *ver tb* **perdida**

perdigón SM (= *bala*) pellet; **perdigones** shot *sing*, pellets

perdigonada SF 1 (= *disparo*) shot 2 (= *herida*) shotgun wound

perdigonazo SM 1 (= *impacto*) blast of shot 2 = **perdigonada 2**

perdiguero Ⓐ ADJ **perro ~** gundog Ⓑ SM gundog

perdiz SF partridge; **"y fueron felices y comieron perdices"** "and they lived happily ever after"; ✦ MODISMOS **levantar la ~** (*RPI**) to let the cat out of the bag*; **marear la ~** to mess about*

perdón SM 1 (= *acción*) (*Rel*) forgiveness; (*Jur*) pardon; (*Econ*) write-off; **el ~ de los pecados** the forgiveness of sins; **el ~ de la deuda externa** the write-off of the foreign debt; **con ~** if you don't mind me saying so; **con ~ de la expresión** pardon my language, if you'll pardon the expression; **pedir ~ (a algn)** (*por algo leve*) to apologize (to sb); (*por algo grave*) to ask (sb's) forgiveness; ✦ MODISMO **no tener ~: no tenéis ~ por lo que hicisteis** what you did was unforgivable, there's no excuse for what you did 2 (*independiente*) **¡perdón!** (*disculpándose*) sorry!; (*tras eructar, toser*) excuse me!, pardon me!; (*llamando la atención*) excuse me!, pardon me!; **¿perdón?** (*cuando no se ha entendido algo*) sorry?, pardon?, pardon me? (*EEUU*)

perdonar /1a/ Ⓐ VT 1 [+ *falta, pecado*] to forgive; **~ a algn** to forgive sb; **¿me perdonas?** do you forgive me?; **que Dios me perdone** may God forgive me 2 (= *curiosidad, ignorancia*) to pardon, excuse; **perdone mi ignorancia, pero ...** pardon *o* excuse my ignorance, but ...; **perdona que te interrumpa** (I'm) sorry to interrupt; **perdona que te diga** if you don't mind me saying (so); **"perdonen las molestias"** "we apologize for any inconvenience" 3 [+ *deuda*] (*Econ*) to write off; **~ una deuda a algn** to let sb off a debt; **~ la vida a algn** to spare sb's life; (*Dep*) to let sb off the hook 4 [+ *detalle, ocasión*] to miss; **no perdona ni una sola ocasión de lucirse** he won't miss a single chance of showing off; ✦ MODISMO **no perdona ni una*** he doesn't miss a trick* Ⓑ VI **¿perdona?** ◇ **¿perdone?** (*cuando no se ha entendido algo*) sorry?, pardon?, pardon me? (*EEUU*) ◇ **¡perdone!** (*disculpándose*) (I'm) sorry!; (*llamando la atención*) excuse me!, pardon me!; **perdona, pero yo iba primero** excuse me, but I was first; **~ por algo: perdonen por el retraso** I'm sorry I'm late; ✦ MODISMO **los años no perdonan** time shows no mercy

perdonavidas SMF INV bully, thug

perdurar /1a/ VI (= *durar*) to last, endure; (= *subsistir*) to remain, still exist

perecedero ADJ perishable

perecer /2d/ VI (*liter*) to die, perish (*frm*)

peregrinación SF (*Rel*) pilgrimage

peregrinar /1a/ VI (*Rel*) to go on a pilgrimage, make a pilgrimage

peregrino/a Ⓐ ADJ 1 (*Orn*) migratory 2 (= *extraño*) strange, odd; (= *singular*) rare, extraordinary; **ideas peregrinas** harebrained ideas Ⓑ SM/F pilgrim

perejil SM parsley

perenne ADJ perennial; **de hoja ~** evergreen

perentorio ADJ (*frm*) (= *urgente*) urgent; (= *imperioso*)

peremptory; **plazo ~** final deadline

pereza SF laziness; **me da ~ ducharme** I can't be bothered to have a shower; **tener ~** to feel lazy

perezosa SF (*And, CS*) deckchair

perezoso/a Ⓐ ADJ lazy Ⓑ SM/F (= *vago*) idler, lazybones* Ⓒ SM (*Zool*) sloth

perfección SF perfection; **a la ~** to perfection

perfeccionamiento SM (= *proceso*) perfection; (= *mejora*) improvement

perfeccionar /1a/ VT (*gen*) to perfect; (= *mejorar*) to improve

perfeccionista SMF perfectionist

perfectamente ADV perfectly; **te entiendo ~** I perfectly understand what you mean, I know exactly what you mean; —**¿cómo está tu hermano?** —**¡perfectamente!** "how's your brother?" — "he's doing just fine"

perfecto Ⓐ ADJ 1 (= *ideal*) perfect; **¡perfecto!** fine!; **me parece ~ que lo hagan** I think it quite right that they should do it 2 (= *completo*) complete; **un ~ imbécil** a complete idiot; **era un ~ desconocido** he was a complete *o* total stranger Ⓑ SM (*Ling*) perfect, perfect tense

perfidia SF perfidy, treachery

pérfido ADJ perfidious, treacherous

perfil SM 1 (*gen*) profile (*tb fig*); (= *contorno*) silhouette, outline; (*Geol, Arquit*) section, cross section; (*Fot*) side view; **de ~** in profile, from the side; **ponerse de ~** to stand side on 2 (*profesional*) profile ➤ **perfil del cliente** (*Com*) customer profile ➤ **perfil psicológico** psychological profile

perfilador SM ➤ **perfilador de labios** lip-liner, lip pencil ➤ **perfilador de ojos** eye-liner

perfilar /1a/ Ⓐ VT 1 (*gen*) to outline; (*fig*) to shape 2 (*Aer*) to streamline Ⓑ **perfilarse** VPR 1 [*modelo*] to show one's profile, stand sideways on; [*edificio*] to be silhouetted 2 (*fig*) to take shape; **el proyecto se va perfilando** the project is taking shape

perforación SF 1 (= *orificio*) perforation; (*Cine, Fot*) sprocket; (*Téc*) punch-hole; (*Min*) bore hole 2 (= *proceso*) (*gen*) piercing, perforation; (*Min*) drilling, boring; (*Tip*) punching, perforating

perforadora SF 1 [*de papel*] punch 2 (*Téc*) drill

perforar /1a/ Ⓐ VT (*gen*) to perforate, pierce; (*Min*) to drill, bore; [+ *tarjeta*] to punch, punch a hole in; [+ *ficha*] to punch; [+ *pozo*] to sink; (= *pinchar*) to puncture (*tb Med*) Ⓑ VI (*Min*) to drill, bore Ⓒ **perforarse** VPR [*úlcera*] to get perforated

performance [per'formans, perfor'manse] SF (*LAm*) performance

perfumador SM perfume spray

perfumar /1a/ VT to perfume, scent

perfume SM perfume, scent (*esp Brit*)

perfumería SF perfumery, perfume shop

pergamino SM parchment; **los ~s del mar Muerto** the Dead Sea scrolls

pergenio* SM (*CS hum*) bright boy, clever kid*

pérgola SF pergola

pericia SF (= *habilidad*) skill; (= *experiencia*) expertise

pericial ADJ expert

periclitar /1a/ VI (*frm*) (= *declinar*) to decay, decline; (= *quedar anticuado*) to become outmoded

perico SM 1 (= *ave*) parakeet; ✦ MODISMO **echar ~** (*Méx**) to chat 2 (**) (= *droga*) snow**, cocaine 3 (*Col*) (= *café*) coffee with a little milk

pericote SM (*And*) large rat

periferia SF 1 (*Mat*) periphery 2 [*de población*] outskirts *pl* 3 (*Inform*) peripherals *pl*

periférico Ⓐ ADJ peripheral; **barrio ~** outlying district, peripheral (unit); **carretera periférica** ring road (*Brit*), beltway (*EEUU*) Ⓑ SM 1 **periféricos** (*Inform*) peripherals 2 (*Méx Aut*) ring road (*Brit*), beltway (*EEUU*)

perifollo SM 1 (*Bot*) chervil 2 **perifollos** (= *adornos*) buttons and bows, trimmings

perífrasis SF INV periphrasis

perifrástico ADJ periphrastic

perilla SF 1 (= *barba*) goatee; ✦ MODISMO **venir de ~(s)** to be more than welcome 2 (*Elec*) switch ➤ **perilla del timbre** bellpush 3 (= *tirador*) doorknob

perillán[†*] SM rogue, rascal

perímetro SM perimeter

perimido ADJ (*RPI frm*) [*ideas, teorías*] outdated

perinatal ADJ perinatal

periodicidad SF 1 [*de acción, evento*] regularity; [*de publicación*] frequency 2 (*Téc*) periodicity

periódico Ⓐ ADJ (*gen*) periodic(al); (*Mat*) recurrent Ⓑ SM (= *diario*) newspaper, paper; (= *publicación periódica*) periodical

periodismo SM journalism ➤ **periodismo de investigación** investigative journalism ➤ **periodismo gráfico** photojournalism

periodista SMF journalist ➤ **periodista de radio** radio reporter ➤ **periodista de televisión** television reporter, TV reporter

periodístico ADJ journalistic; **estilo ~** journalistic style, journalese (*pey*); **el mundo ~** the newspaper world; **de interés ~** newsworthy

periodo SM, **período** SM 1 [*de tiempo*] period 2 (= *menstruación*) period

periodoncia SF periodontics *sing*, periodontology

peripecia SF 1 (= *incidente*) adventure, incident 2 (= *vicisitud*) vicissitude, sudden change

periplo SM (*gen*) (long) journey, tour; (*Náut*) (long) voyage

peripuesto* ADJ dressed-up, smart

periquete SM ✦ MODISMO **en un ~*** in a trice, in a tick (*Brit*)

periquito SM parakeet

periscopio SM periscope

peristilo SM peristyle

perita SF ✦ MODISMO **ser una ~ en dulce** to be gorgeous

peritaje SM 1 (= *informe*) specialist's report, expert's report 2 (= *estudios*) professional training

perito/a Ⓐ ADJ (= *experto*) expert; **ser ~ en** [+ *actividad*] to be expert at; [+ *materia*] to be an expert on Ⓑ SM/F (*gen*) expert; (= *técnico*) technician; (= *ingeniero técnico*) technical engineer ➤ **perito/a agrónomo/a** agronomist

peritonitis SF INV peritonitis

perjudicar /1g/ Ⓐ VT to harm; **esta medida ~á a miles de ahorradores** this measure will be harmful for thousands of savers Ⓑ **perjudicarse** VPR to lose out

perjudicial ADJ damaging, harmful, detrimental (*frm*)

perjuicio SM damage, harm; **sufrir grandes ~s** to suffer great damage; **en ~ de algo** to the detriment of sth, at the expense of sth; **redundar en ~ de algo** to be detrimental to sth, harm sth; **sin ~ de** (*Jur*) without prejudice to

perjurar /1a/ VI to perjure o.s., commit perjury

perjurio SM perjury

perjuro/a Ⓐ ADJ perjured Ⓑ SM/F perjurer

perla SF pearl; ✦ MODISMOS **de ~s**: **me parece de ~s** it's absolutely splendid; **me viene de ~s** it suits me perfectly *o* just fine ➤ **perla cultivada** cultured pearl, cultivated pearl

perlado ADJ pearly

permanecer /2d/ VI 1 (*en un lugar*) to stay, remain; **permaneció en cama durante toda la semana** he stayed in bed all week 2 (*en un estado*) to remain; **~ en silencio** to remain silent; **permanezcan sentados** (please) remain seated

permanencia SF 1 (= *continuidad*) **su ~ en el equipo** his presence in the team 2 (= *estancia*) stay

permanente Ⓐ ADJ (*gen*) permanent; [*color*] fast; [*comisión*] standing Ⓑ SM (*Méx*) (*en pelo*) perm (*esp Brit**), permanent (*EEUU*) Ⓒ SF (*en pelo*) perm (*esp Brit**), permanent (*EEUU*); **hacerse una** *o* **la ~** to have a perm (*esp Brit**) *o* permanent (*EEUU*)

permeable ADJ permeable (**a** to)

permisible ADJ permissible

permisionario/a SM/F (*LAm*) official agent, concessionaire

permisividad SF permissiveness

permisivo ADJ permissive

permiso SM 1 (= *autorización*) permission; **¡permiso!** (*para pasar*) excuse me!; **con ~** (*pidiendo ver algo*) if I may; (*queriendo entrar, pasar*) (*esp LAm*) excuse me; **dar ~** to give permission 2 (= *documento*) permit, licence

> En inglés americano se usa **license** en lugar de **licence**.

➤ **permiso de armas** gun licence, firearms certificate ➤ **permiso de conducir** (*Esp*) driving licence (*Brit*), driver's license (*EEUU*) ➤ **permiso de exportación** export licence ➤ **permiso de importación** import licence ➤ **permiso de obras** building permit, planning permission (*Brit*) ➤ **permiso de residencia** residence permit ➤ **permiso de trabajo** work permit, green card (*EEUU*)
3 (*para no trabajar*) leave; **ha pedido unos días de ~** he has asked for a few days' leave; **estar de ~** to be on leave ➤ **permiso por maternidad** maternity leave ➤ **permiso por paternidad** paternity leave

permitir /3a/ Ⓐ VT 1 (= *autorizar*) [+ *entrada, movimiento*] to allow, permit (*más frm*); **no permiten la entrada a menores de 18 años** under-18s are not allowed in; **"no está permitido el uso de teléfonos móviles"** "the use of mobile phones is not permitted"; **si se me permite la expresión** *o* **la palabra** if you'll pardon the expression; **¿me permite?** (*al entrar*) may I (come in)?; (*al pasar al lado de algn*) excuse me, please; (*al ayudar a algn*) may I (help you)?; **~ que**: **permítame que la ayude, señora** please allow me to help you, madam
2 (= *hacer posible*) to allow, permit (*más frm*); **si el tiempo lo permite** weather permitting; **~ (a algn) hacer algo** to allow (sb) to do sth; **~ que** (+ SUBJUN) to allow + *infin* Ⓑ **permitirse** VPR 1 (= *atreverse a*) **se permite demasiadas libertades con su secretaria** he takes too many liberties with his secretary; **me permito recordarle que está prohibido fumar** (*frm*) may I remind you that smoking is forbidden (*frm*)
2 (= *concederse*) to allow o.s.; **poder ~se (hacer) algo** to be able to afford (to do) sth

permuta SF [*de bienes, mercancías*] exchange; [*de puesto de trabajo*] interchange

permutación SF permutation

permutar /1a/ VT 1 (*Mat*) to permute 2 [+ *puesto de trabajo*] to exchange, swap; [+ *acciones, edificios*] to switch, exchange; **~ destinos con algn** to exchange *o* swap postings with sb

pernada SF **derecho de ~** (*Hist*) droit de seigneur

pernera SF trouser leg

pernicioso ADJ pernicious (*tb Med*); [*influencia, sustancia*] harmful

pernil SM 1 (*Zool*) upper leg, haunch; (*Culin*) leg 2 (*Cos*) trouser leg

perno SM bolt

pernocta SF **pase (de) ~** overnight pass

pernoctar /1a/ VI (*frm*) to spend the night, stay the night

pero Ⓐ CONJ 1 (*uso adversativo*) but; **me gusta, ~ es muy caro** I like it, but it's very expensive
2 (*al principio de frase*) **~, ¿dónde está Pedro?** where on earth is Pedro?; **~ bueno, ¿vienes o no?** now look, are you coming or not?; **¡~ qué guapa estás!** you look great!
3 (*uso enfático*) **~ que muy: una chica guapa, ~ que muy guapa** what you call a really pretty girl, a pretty girl and no mistake

B SM **1** (= *falta, defecto*) snag
2 (= *pega*) objection; **encontrar** *o* **poner ~s a algo** to raise objections to sth, find fault with sth; **¡no hay ~ que valga!** there are no buts about it!

perogrullada SF platitude, truism

Perogrullo SM ✦ MODISMOS **verdad de ~** platitude, truism; **ser de ~** to be patently obvious

perol SM (= *cazuela*) (*grande*) pot; (*más pequeño*) saucepan

perola SF saucepan

peroné SM fibula

peronismo SM Peronism

PERONISMO

General Juan Domingo Perón (1895-1974) came to power in Argentina in 1946, on a social justice platform known as **justicialismo. Peronismo** stood for nationalization of industry, trade unions, paid holidays, the welfare state, and the provision of affordable housing. Women were given the vote in 1947, a move championed by Perón's charismatic wife Evita (María Eva Duarte). Following her death in 1952, Perón's support began to crumble and he was driven into exile in 1955. His party was banned and did not regain power until 1973, when he was recalled from exile to become President. He died the following year. **Peronismo** as a movement has survived, and the Peronist party returned to power in 1989 under Carlos Menem.

---

peronista ADJ, SMF Peronist

perorata SF long-winded speech; **echar** *o* **soltar una ~** to rattle on*

perorar /1a/ VI to make a speech

perpendicular **A** ADJ perpendicular (**a** to); **el camino es ~ al río** the road is at right angles to the river
B SF perpendicular

perpetrar /1a/ VT to perpetrate

perpetuar /1e/ VT to perpetuate

perpetuidad SF perpetuity; **a ~** in perpetuity, for ever; **condena a ~** life sentence

perpetuo ADJ (*gen*) perpetual; [*condena, exilio*] life *antes de s*; (*Bot*) perennial

perplejidad SF perplexity, puzzlement

perplejo ADJ perplexed, puzzled

perra SF **1** (*Zool*) bitch **2** (*Esp**) (= *moneda*) copper, penny; **no tener una ~*** to be broke*, be skint* **3** (*) (= *rabieta*) tantrum **4** (*) (= *obsesión*) obsession, crazy idea; **está con la ~ de comprárselo** he's taken it into his head to buy it

perramus SM INV (*RPl*) raincoat

perrera SF **1** (*para perros callejeros*) dog pound; (*para perros con dueño*) kennels *sing y pl*, kennel **2** (= *furgoneta*) dogcatcher's van; *ver tb* **perrero**

perrería SF **1** (*) (= *trampa*) dirty trick **2** (= *palabra*) harsh word, angry word

perrero/a SM/F dog catcher; *ver tb* **perrera**

perrilla SF (*Méx*) stye

perrito/a **A** SM/F puppy ➤ **perrito/a faldero/a** lapdog
B SM **1** ➤ **perrito caliente** hot dog **2** (*Chi*) (*para la ropa*) clothes peg (*Brit*), clothes pin (*EEUU*)

perro **A** SM **1** (*Zool*) dog ➤ **perro callejero** stray (dog) ➤ **perro de caza** hunting dog ➤ **perro de ciego** guide dog (*esp Brit*), seeing-eye dog (*EEUU*) ➤ **perro de presa** bulldog ➤ **perro de raza** pedigree dog ➤ **perro dogo** bulldog ➤ **perro esquimal** husky ➤ **perro faldero** lapdog ➤ **perro guardián** guard dog ➤ **perro guía, perro lazarillo** guide dog (*esp Brit*), seeing-eye dog (*esp EEUU*) ➤ **perro lobo** German shepherd, Alsatian (*Brit*) ➤ **perro pastor** sheepdog ➤ **perro policía** police dog ➤ **perro salchicha*** sausage dog*, dachshund

2 ✦ MODISMOS **atar ~s con longaniza: se cree que allí atan los ~s con longaniza** he thinks it's the land of milk and

honey; **de ~s** foul; **estaba de un humor de ~s** he was in a foul *o* stinking mood; **tiempo de ~s** foul *o* dirty weather; **echarle los ~s a algn*** to come down on sb like a ton of bricks*; **hacer ~ muerto** (*Chi, Perú**) to avoid paying; **llevarse como (el) ~ y (el) gato** to fight like cat and dog; **ser como el ~ del hortelano** to be a dog in the manger; **ser ~ viejo** to be an old hand; **tratar a algn como a un ~** to treat sb like dirt; **vida de ~** dog's life; ✦ REFRANES **a ~ flaco todo son pulgas** it never rains but it pours; **~ ladrador, poco mordedor** his bark is worse than his bite
3 (*Culin*) ➤ **perro caliente** hot dog
4 (* *pey*) (= *persona despreciable*) swine**
B ADJ (*) rotten*; **¡qué perra suerte la mía!** what rotten luck I have!*; **esta perra vida** this wretched life

perruno ADJ (= *de perro*) canine, dog *antes de s*; [*afecto, devoción*] doglike

persa **A** ADJ, SMF Persian **B** SM (*Ling*) Persian

persecución SF **1** (= *acoso*) pursuit **2** (*Pol, Rel*) persecution

persecutorio ADJ **manía persecutoria** persecution complex

perseguidor(a) SM/F **1** (*gen*) pursuer **2** (*Rel, Pol*) persecutor

perseguir /3d, 3k/ VT **1** [+ *presa, fugitivo*] (*gen*) to pursue, chase; (*por motivos ideológicos*) to persecute **2** [+ *persona, empleo*] to chase after, go after; [+ *propósito, fin*] to pursue; **lo persigue la mala suerte** he is dogged by ill luck

perseverancia SF perseverance, persistence

perseverar /1a/ VI to persevere, persist; **~ en** to persevere in, persist with

persiana SF [*de lamas*] (Venetian) blind; (*enrollable*) roller blind; ✦ MODISMO **enrollarse como una ~** (*Esp**) to go on and on

persignarse /1a/ VPR to cross o.s.

persistencia SF persistence

persistente ADJ persistent

persistir /3a/ VI to persist (**en** in)

persona SF **1** (= *individuo*) person; **es una ~ encantadora** he's a charming person

---

Mientras que **persona** en singular se traduce por **person**, el plural tiene dos traducciones: **people** y **persons**. **People** es la forma más utilizada, ya que **persons** se emplea solamente en el lenguaje formal o técnico. Las dos formas llevan el verbo en plural:

20 ~s 20 people; **acaban de llegar tres ~s preguntando por un tal Sr. Oliva** three people have just arrived asking for a Mr Oliva; **aquellas ~s que lo deseen** those who wish; **es buena ~** he's a good sort; **en la ~ de** in the person of; **en ~** in person, in the flesh; **por ~** per person; **sin inmiscuir a terceras ~** without involving third parties ➤ **persona de edad** elderly person, senior citizen ➤ **persona mayor** adult ➤ **persona no grata, persona non grata** persona non grata **2** (*Jur*) ➤ **persona física** natural person ➤ **persona jurídica** legal entity
3 (*Ling*) person; **la tercera ~ del singular** the third person singular
4 (*Rel*) **las tres ~s de la Santísima Trinidad** the three persons of the Holy Trinity

personaje SM **1** (= *sujeto notable*) personage, important person; (= *famoso*) celebrity, personality; **ser un ~** to be somebody, be important **2** (*Literat, Teat*) character

personal **A** ADJ personal **B** SM **1** (= *plantilla*) staff, personnel; (*esp Mil*) force; (*Náut*) crew, complement; **estar falto de ~** to be shorthanded *o* short-staffed ➤ **personal de cabina** cabin staff *o* crew ➤ **personal de tierra** (*Aer*) ground crew, ground staff **2** (*) (= *gente*) people **C** SF (*Baloncesto*) personal foul

personalidad SF **1** (= *modo de ser*) personality; **doble ~** dual personality **2** (= *personaje público*) public figure; **~es** personalities, dignitaries

personalismo SM **1** (= *parcialidad*) partiality; **obrar sin ~s**

to act impartially *o* without favouritism **2** (= *alusión personal*) personal reference; **tenemos que proceder sin ~s** we must carry on without getting personal

personalizar /1f/ Ⓐ VT to personalize Ⓑ VI (= *nombrar en particular*) to name names; (= *hacer alusiones personales*) to get personal Ⓒ **personalizarse** VPR to become personal

personalmente ADV personally

personarse /1a/ VPR ~ **en** to present o.s. at, report to

personería SF (*LAm Jur*) ~ **jurídica** legal status

personero/a SM/F (*LAm Pol*) (= *representante*) (government) official; (= *portavoz*) spokesperson

personificación SF **1** (= *representación*) personification, embodiment; **es la ~ de los celos** he is the embodiment of jealousy, he is jealousy personified **2** (*Literat*) personification

personificar /1g/ VT (= *encarnar*) to personify, embody; **es la codicia personificada** he is greed personified

perspectiva SF **1** (*Arte*) perspective; **en ~** in perspective **2** (= *vista*) view, scene **3** (*de futuro*) prospect; **buenas ~s de mejora** good prospects for *o* of improvement; **tener algo en ~** to have sth in prospect; **las ~s de la cosecha son favorables** the harvest outlook is good

perspicacia SF **1** (= *agudeza mental*) perceptiveness, shrewdness **2** (= *agudeza visual*) keen-sightedness

perspicaz ADJ **1** (= *agudo, sagaz*) perceptive, shrewd **2** [*vista*] keen; [*persona*] keen-sighted

persuadir /3a/ VT to persuade; **~ a algn de algo/para hacer algo** to persuade sb of sth/to do sth; **dejarse ~** to allow o.s. to be persuaded

persuasión SF **1** (= *acción de persuadir*) persuasion **2** (= *convicción*) conviction

persuasivo ADJ [*vendedor, carácter*] persuasive; [*argumento, razones*] persuasive, convincing

pertenecer /2d/ VI ~ **a** to belong to

perteneciente ADJ ~ **a** belonging to; **las personas ~s al organismo** members of the organization

pertenencia SF **1** (= *posesión*) ownership **2 pertenencias** (= *objetos personales*) personal belongings; [*de finca*] appurtenances, accessories **3** (*a club, asociación*) membership (**a** of)

pértiga SF pole; **salto con ~** (*Dep*) pole vault

pertinaz ADJ **1** [*tos*] persistent; [*sequía*] long-lasting, prolonged **2** [*persona*] obstinate

pertinencia SF (= *relevancia*) relevance, pertinence; (= *idoneidad*) appropriateness

pertinente ADJ **1** (= *relevante*) relevant, pertinent; (= *adecuado*) appropriate; **no es ~ hacerlo ahora** this is not the appropriate time to do it **2** ~ **a** concerning; **en lo ~ a libros** as regards books, as far as books are concerned

pertrechar /1a/ Ⓐ VT (*gen*) to supply (**con, de** with); (= *equipar*) to equip (**con, de** with); (*Mil*) to supply with ammunition and stores, equip Ⓑ **pertrecharse** VPR **~se de algo** to provide o.s. with sth

pertrechos SMPL **1** (= *útiles*) gear *sing* **2** (*Mil*) supplies and stores

perturbación SF **1** (*Meteo, Pol*) disturbance ➤ **perturbación del orden público** breach of the peace **2** (*Med*) mental disorder

perturbado/a Ⓐ ADJ mentally unbalanced Ⓑ SM/F mentally unbalanced person

perturbar /1a/ VT **1** (= *alterar*) [+ *orden*] to disturb; [+ *calma*] to disturb, ruffle **2** (*Med*) to disturb, mentally disturb

Perú SM Peru

peruano/a ADJ, SM/F Peruvian

perversidad SF **1** (= *cualidad*) [*de depravado*] depravity; [*de malvado*] wickedness **2** (= *acto*) evil deed

perversión SF perversion ➤ **perversión sexual** sexual perversion

perverso ADJ wicked

pervertido/a Ⓐ ADJ perverted, deviant

Ⓑ SM/F pervert, deviant

pervertidor(a) SM/F corruptor ➤ **pervertidor(a) de menores** child corruptor, corruptor of minors (*frm*)

pervertir /3i/ Ⓐ VT [+ *persona*] to pervert; [+ *texto*] to distort, corrupt; [+ *gusto*] to corrupt Ⓑ **pervertirse** VPR to become perverted

pervivencia SF survival

pervivir /3a/ VI to survive

pesa SF **1** (*Dep*) weight; **hacer ~s** to do weight training, do weights*; **levantamiento de ~s** weightlifting **2** [*de balanza, reloj*] weight

pesadez SF **1** (= *peso*) heaviness ➤ **pesadez de estómago** bloated feeling in the stomach **2** (= *aburrimiento*) tediousness, boring nature; **¡qué ~!** what a bore!

pesadilla SF **1** (= *mal sueño*) nightmare, bad dream **2** (= *tormento*) nightmare

pesado/a Ⓐ ADJ **1** [*paquete, comida*] heavy; **industria pesada** heavy industry **2** [*sueño*] deep, heavy **3** (= *aburrido*) tedious, boring; (= *molesto*) annoying; **el libro me resultaba ~** the book was heavy going; **¡no seas ~!** stop being such a pain!* Ⓑ SM/F pain*

pesadumbre SF grief, sorrow

pesaje SM **1** (= *acción*) weighing **2** (*Dep*) weigh-in

pésame SM condolences *pl*; **dar el ~** to express one's condolences, send one's sympathy (**por** for, on); **mi más sentido ~** my deepest sympathy, my heartfelt condolences

pesar /1a/ Ⓐ VI **1** [*objeto, persona*] **1.1** (= *tener peso*) to weigh; (*Boxeo, Hípica*) to weigh in at; **¿cuánto pesas?** how much *o* what do you weigh? **1.2** (= *tener mucho peso*) to be heavy; **¡cómo pesa esta bolsa!** this bag's really heavy! **2** (= *resultar pesado*) ~ **a algn**: **le pesaba la mochila** his backpack was weighing him down; **los pies me pesan, estoy muy cansado** I'm so tired, I can hardly lift my feet up any more **3** (= *afligir*) **me pesa mucho** I am very sorry about it *o* to hear it; **¡ya le ~á!** he'll be sorry!, he'll regret this! **4** (= *ser una carga*) **le pesa tanta responsabilidad** all that responsibility weighs heavily on him; **me pesan los años** I feel my age; ~ **sobre** [*responsabilidad, preocupación*] to weigh heavily on; [*amenaza, acusación*] to hang over; **pesa sobre mi conciencia** it is weighing heavily on my conscience; **las sospechas que pesan sobre Aguirre** the suspicions surrounding Aguirre; **la maldición que pesa sobre nuestra familia** the curse afflicting our family **5** (= *influir*) to carry weight **6 pese a (que)** in spite of (the fact that), despite (the fact that); **pese a las dificultades** in spite of *o* despite the difficulties; **lo haré pese a quien pese** I'll do it whether people like it or not, I'll do it, no matter who I offend Ⓑ VT **1** [+ *carta, fruta, objeto*] to weigh **2** (= *sopesar*) to weigh up; ~ **las posibilidades** to weigh up one's chances; ~ **los pros y los contras** to weigh up the pros and cons Ⓒ **pesarse** VPR to weigh o.s.; (*Boxeo, Hípica*) to weigh in Ⓓ SM **1** (= *aflicción*) sorrow; **muy a mi ~** much to my regret **2 a pesar de** in spite of, despite; **a ~ del mal tiempo** in spite of *o* despite the bad weather; **a ~ de que** even though; **a ~ de que la quiero** even though I love her

pesaroso ADJ (= *arrepentido*) regretful; (= *afligido*) sorrowful, sad

pesca SF **1** (= *actividad*) fishing; **ir de ~** to go fishing ➤ **pesca de altura** deep sea fishing ➤ **pesca de bajura** coastal fishing, shallow water fishing ➤ **pesca submarina** underwater fishing **2** (= *lo pescado*) catch; **la ~ ha sido mala** it's been a poor catch; ✦ MODISMO **... y toda la ~*** ... and all the rest of it, ... and whatnot*

pescada SF hake

pescadería SF (= *tienda*) fish shop, fishmonger's (shop) (*Brit*); (= *mercado*) fish market

pescadero/a SM/F fishmonger (*Brit*), fish merchant (*EEUU*)

pescadilla SF whiting, small hake

pescado SM fish ➤ **pescado azul** blue fish

pescador(a) Ⓐ ADJ fishing Ⓑ SM/F fisherman/

fisherwoman ➤ **pescador(a) de caña** angler

pescante SM **1** [*de carruaje*] driver's seat, coachman's seat **2** (*Teat*) wire **3** (*Téc*) jib **4** (*Náut*) davit

pescar /1g/ Ⓐ VT **1** [+ *peces, mariscos*] to catch; **pescamos varias truchas** we caught several trout; **fuimos a ~ salmón** we went salmon-fishing **2** (*) (= *agarrar*) to catch; **lo ha pescado la policía** he's been caught *o* nabbed* by the police; **¡vas a ~ una pulmonía!** you'll catch pneumonia!; **me ~on fumando** I got caught smoking **3** (*) (= *entender*) [+ *chiste*] to get
Ⓑ VI [*pescador*] to fish; **ir a ~** to go fishing; **~ al arrastre** to trawl; ✦ MODISMO **~ en río revuelto** to fish in troubled waters

pescozón SM slap on the neck

pescuezo SM (*Zool*) neck; (*Anat*) scruff of the neck; **¡calla, o te retuerzo el ~!** shut up, or I'll wring your neck!

pese PREP *ver* **pesar A6**

pesebre SM **1** (*Agr*) manger **2** (*Rel*) nativity scene, crib

pesero SM (*Méx*) minibus

peseta SF peseta

pesetero* ADJ (*Esp*) money-grabbing*, mercenary

pésimamente ADV awfully, dreadfully

pesimismo SM pessimism

pesimista Ⓐ ADJ pessimistic Ⓑ SMF pessimist

pésimo ADJ awful, dreadful

peso SM **1** (*Fís, Téc*) weight; **no puedo levantar mucho ~** I can't lift much weight; **un vehículo de mucho/poco ~** a heavy/light vehicle; **las telas se venden al ~** the fabrics are sold by weight; **no dar el ~** [*boxeador*] not to make the weight; [*recién nacido*] to be below normal weight, be underweight; **falto de ~** underweight; **ganar ~** to put on weight; **~s y medidas** weights and measures; **perder ~** to lose weight; ✦ MODISMOS **caer por su propio ~** (= *ser obvio*) to go without saying, be obvious; (= *no tener lógica*) not to stand up (to scrutiny); **valer su ~ en oro** to be worth one's weight in gold ➤ **peso atómico** atomic weight ➤ **peso bruto** gross weight ➤ **peso escurrido** net weight ➤ **peso específico** (*lit*) specific gravity; (*fig*) influence ➤ **peso molecular** (*Quím*) molecular weight ➤ **peso muerto** (*Náut*) (*fig*) dead weight ➤ **peso neto** net weight
2 [*de culpa, responsabilidad*] weight; **el ~ de los años** the burden of old age; **me quitarías un buen ~ de encima** it would be a weight off my mind, you would take a weight off my mind
3 (= *importancia*) weight; **su opinión era la de mayor ~ en la reunión** his opinion carried the most weight at the meeting; **de ~** [*persona*] influential; [*argumento*] weighty, forceful; **un argumento de poco ~** a lightweight argument; **razones de ~** good *o* sound reasons
4 (= *balanza*) scales *pl* ➤ **peso de baño** bathroom scales *pl* ➤ **peso de cocina** kitchen scales *pl*
5 (*Dep*) **5.1** (*Esp*) (*Atletismo*) shot; **lanzamiento de ~** shot putting; **lanzar el ~** to put the shot **5.2** (*Halterofilia*) **levantamiento de ~s** weightlifting **5.3** (*Boxeo*) weight ➤ **peso gallo** bantamweight ➤ **peso ligero** lightweight ➤ **peso medio** middleweight ➤ **peso mosca** flyweight ➤ **peso pesado** heavyweight ➤ **peso pluma** featherweight ➤ **peso welter** welterweight
6 (*Fin*) peso

pespunte SM backstitch(ing)

pespuntear /1a/ VT, VI to backstitch

pesquería SF fishing ground, fishery

pesquero Ⓐ ADJ fishing *antes de s* Ⓑ SM fishing boat

pesquisa SF (= *investigación*) investigation, inquiry; (= *búsqueda*) search

pestaña SF **1** [*de ojo*] eyelash; ✦ MODISMO **quemarse las ~s** (= *excederse*) (*gen*) to burn one's fingers; (*estudiando*) to burn the midnight oil **2** (= *saliente*) [*de caja*] flap; [*de neumático*] rim

pestañear /1a/ VI to blink; **sin ~** without batting an eyelid

pestañeo SM blink(ing)

pestazo* SM stink, stench

peste SF **1** (*Med*) plague; ✦ MODISMOS **huir de algo/algn como de la ~** to avoid sth/sb like the plague; **ser la ~*** to be a nuisance, be a pain* ➤ **peste bubónica** bubonic plague ➤ **peste negra** Black Death ➤ **peste porcina** swine fever **2** (= *mal olor*) stink, foul smell **3** ✦ MODISMO **decir** *o* **echar ~s de algn** to slag sb off* **4** (*SAm**) (= *enfermedad*) infection

pesticida SM pesticide

pestilencia SF **1** (= *plaga*) pestilence, plague **2** (= *mal olor*) stink, stench

pestilente ADJ smelly, foul

pestillo SM [*de puerta, ventana*] bolt; [*de cerradura*] latch

pestiño SM (*Esp*) honey-coated fritter

peta* SF (*Esp*) joint**, reefer*

petaca SF **1** (= *caja*) [*de cigarrillos*] cigarette case; [*de puros*] cigar case; [*de pipa*] tobacco pouch; [*de alcohol*] flask; ✦ MODISMO **hacer la ~ a algn** to make an apple-pie bed for sb (*Brit*), short-sheet sb (*EEUU*) **2** (*Méx*) (= *maleta*) suitcase **3 petacas** (*Carib, Méx**) (= *nalgas*) buttocks; (= *pechos*) big breasts

petacón* ADJ **1** (*Méx, And, CS*) (= *rechoncho*) plump, chubby **2** (*Méx*) (= *nalgudo*) fat-bottomed, broad in the beam*

pétalo SM petal

petanca SF pétanque

petar* /1a/ VI (*Esp*) **no le peta trabajar en una oficina** he's not into working in an office; **ahora mismo no me peta** I don't feel like it now

petardazo SM crack, bang

petardo SM **1** (= *cohete*) firecracker, banger (*Brit*); (= *explosivo*) small explosive device; (*Mil*) petard **2** (*) (= *lo que aburre*) bore, drag; **ser un ~** to be dead boring* **3** (**) (= *droga*) joint**

petate SM **1** (= *equipaje*) bundle of bedding and belongings; (*Mil*) kit bag; ✦ MODISMO **liar el ~** to pack up and go, clear out* **2** (*esp LAm*) [*de palma*] mat of palm leaves; (*para dormir*) sleeping mat

petatearse* /1a/ VPR (*Méx*) to peg out**, kick the bucket*

peteneras SFPL (*Esp*) ✦ MODISMO **salir por ~** to say/do something quite inappropriate

petición SF **1** (= *solicitud*) request; (= *documento*) petition; **las peticiones de los oyentes** the listeners' requests; **a ~ de la familia** at the request of the family; **"consulta previa petición de cita"** "consultation by appointment" ➤ **petición de divorcio** petition for divorce ➤ **petición de extradición** request for extradition ➤ **petición de indulto** appeal for a reprieve ➤ **petición de mano** proposal (of marriage) **2** (*Jur*) (= *alegato*) plea; (= *reclamación*) claim

peticionar /1a/ VT (*LAm*) to petition

peticionario/a SM/F petitioner (*frm*), applicant

petimetre Ⓐ ADJ foppish Ⓑ SM fop, dandy

petirrojo SM robin

petiso/a (*LAm*), **petizo/a** (*SAm*) Ⓐ ADJ (= *bajo*) small, short; (= *rechoncho*) chubby Ⓑ SM (= *caballo bajo*) small horse Ⓒ SM/F (= *persona baja*) small person

petisú SM cream puff

peto SM [*de falda*] bodice; [*de pantalón*] bib; (*Mil*) breastplate; (*Taur*) horse's padding; **pantalones de ~** dungarees *pl*, overalls *pl* (*EEUU*)

pétreo ADJ stony, rocky

petrificar /1g/ Ⓐ VT to petrify Ⓑ **petrificarse** VPR (*lit*) to become petrified; (*fig*) to be petrified

petrodólar SM petrodollar

petróleo SM (*Min*) oil, petroleum; (*LAm*) kerosene, paraffin (*Brit*) ➤ **petróleo crudo** crude oil

petrolero Ⓐ ADJ oil *antes de s* Ⓑ SM oil tanker

petrolífero ADJ **1** (*Min*) oil-bearing **2** (*Com*) oil *antes de s*; **compañía petrolífera** oil company

petroquímica SF (= *ciencia*) petrochemistry; (= *fábrica*) petrochemical factory

petroquímico ADJ petrochemical

petulancia SF self-importance

petulante ADJ self-important

petunia SF petunia

peyorativo ADJ pejorative

peyote SM peyote cactus

pez[1] **Ⓐ** SM fish; **tres peces** three fish; ✦ MODISMO **estar como ∼ en el agua** to feel completely at home, be in one's element ➤ **pez de colores** goldfish ➤ **pez espada** swordfish ➤ **pez gordo*** big shot* ➤ **pez martillo** hammerhead **Ⓑ** ADJ (*Esp**) ✦ MODISMO **estar ∼ en algo** to know nothing at all about sth

pez[2] SF (= *brea*) pitch, tar

pezón SM [*de persona*] nipple; [*de animal*] teat

pezuña SF 1 (*Zool*) hoof; (*) [*de persona*] hoof*, foot 2 (*Méx, Perú**) (= *olor*) smell of sweaty feet

piadoso ADJ 1 (*Rel*) pious, devout 2 (= *bondadoso*) kind, merciful (**para, con** to)

piafar /1a/ VI to paw the ground, stamp

pial SM lasso

pianista SMF pianist

piano SM piano; **tocar el ∼** to play the piano; ✦ MODISMOS **aguantar un ∼** (*Méx**) to be a hunk*; **como un ∼** (*Esp**) huge, massive ➤ **piano de cola** grand piano ➤ **piano de media cola** baby grand ➤ **piano vertical** upright piano

piar /1c/ VI to cheep

piara SF herd

piastra SF piastre, piaster (*EEUU*)

PIB SM ABR (= **producto interior bruto**) GDP

pibe/a* SM/F (*esp RPI*) (= *niño*) kid*; (= *muchacho*) boy/girl; (= *novio*) boyfriend/girlfriend

pica SF (*Mil*) pike; (*Taur*) goad; ✦ MODISMO **poner una ∼ en Flandes** to bring off a real coup, achieve a signal success

picacho SM peak, summit

picada SF 1 **caer en ∼** (*LAm*) (*lit*) to nose-dive; (*fig*) to plummet, take a nose-dive 2 (*CS Culin*) nibbles *pl* 3 (*LAm*) (= *senda*) forest trail, narrow path

picadero SM 1 (= *escuela*) riding school 2 (**) (= *apartamento*) bachelor pad*, *apartment used for sexual encounters*

picadillo SM [*de carne*] mince (*esp Brit*), ground meat (*EEUU*); **∼ de cebolla** finely chopped onions *pl*; ✦ MODISMO **los hizo ∼** he made mincemeat out of them

picado Ⓐ ADJ 1 (= *podrido*) [*diente*] rotten, decayed; [*fruta*] rotten; [*metal*] rusty, rusted; **tres muelas picadas** three cavities 2 (*Culin*) [*ajo, cebolla, patata*] chopped; (*Esp, RPI*) [*carne*] minced (*esp Brit*), ground (*EEUU*) 3 (= *triturado*) [*tabaco*] cut; [*hielo*] crushed 4 [*vino*] pricked, sour 5 [*mar*] choppy 6 **∼ de viruelas** pockmarked 7 (*) (= *enfadado*) **estar ∼** to be in a huff* 8 (*) (= *interesado*) **estar ∼ con** o **por algo** to go for sth in a big way* **Ⓑ** SM **caer en ∼** (*Esp Aer*) to plummet, nose-dive; [*precios, popularidad, producción*] to plummet, fall sharply

picador SM 1 [*de caballos*] (*gen*) horse-trainer, horse-breaker; (*Taur*) picador 2 (*Min*) faceworker

picadora SF (*tb* **∼ de carne**) mincer (*Brit*), meat grinder (*EEUU*)

picadura SF 1 [*de abeja, avispa*] sting; [*de serpiente, mosquito*] bite 2 (= *tabaco picado*) cut tobacco

picaflor SM (*LAm*) 1 (*Orn*) hummingbird 2 (*) (= *tenorio*) ladykiller*, Don Juan

picana SF (*LAm*) cattle prod

picante Ⓐ ADJ 1 [*comida, sabor*] hot, spicy 2 (= *malicioso*) [*chiste*] dirty; [*comedia, película*] naughty, spicy **Ⓑ** SM 1 (= *especia*) **esta salsa tiene mucho ∼** this sauce is very hot o spicy 2 (*And, CS*) (= *guisado*) meat stew with chilli sauce

picantería SF (*Perú*) restaurant (*specializing in spicy food*); (*Col pey*) cheap restaurant

picapedrero SM stonecutter

picapica SF **polvos de ∼** itching powder

picapleitos SMF INV (*pey*) lawyer

picaporte SM (= *manija*) door handle; (= *pestillo*) latch

picar /1g/ **Ⓐ** VT 1 [*abeja, avispa*] to sting; [*mosquito, serpiente, pez*] to bite; **∼ el anzuelo** (*lit*) to take o swallow the bait; (*fig*) to rise to the bait, fall for it*; ✦ MODISMO **¿qué mosca le habrá picado?** what's got into her?, what's eating her?* 2 (= *comer*) [*persona*] to nibble at; [*ave*] to peck (at) 3 (= *agujerear*) [+ *hoja, página*] to punch a hole/some holes in; [+ *billete, entrada*] to punch 4 (= *trocear*) 4.1 [+ *ajo, cebolla, patata*] to chop; (*Esp, RPI*) [+ *carne*] to mince (*esp Brit*), grind (*EEUU*) 4.2 [+ *tabaco*] to cut; [+ *hielo*] to crush 4.3 [+ *tierra*] to dig over, break up; [+ *piedra*] (*en trozos pequeños*) to chip at; (*en trozos grandes*) to break up 5 (= *provocar*) [+ *persona*] to needle, goad; [+ *caballo*] to spur on; **eso me picó la curiosidad** that aroused my curiosity; **lo que dijiste lo picó en su amor propio** what you said wounded o hurt his pride 6 (= *corroer*) [+ *diente, muela, madera*] to rot; [+ *hierro, metal*] to rust 7 (*Inform*) [+ *texto*] to key in 8 (*Taur*) [+ *toro*] to stick, prick (*with the goad*) **Ⓑ** VI 1 [*abeja, avispa*] to sting; [*mosquito, serpiente*] to bite; [*ave*] to peck 2 (= *comer*) [*persona*] to nibble, snack; **llevo todo el día picando** I've been nibbling o snacking all day 3 (= *morder el cebo*) [*pez*] to bite; (*) [*persona*] to fall for it* 4 (= *ser picante*) [*comida*] to be hot, be spicy 5 (= *causar picor*) [*herida, espalda*] to itch; **me pica la espalda** my back itches; **me pica la barba** I've got an itchy beard; **¿le pica la garganta?** do you have a tickle in your throat?, do you have a tickly throat?; **me pican los ojos** my eyes are stinging o smarting 6 [*sol*] to burn 7 (= *probar*) **∼ en algo** to dabble in sth 8 (*CS***) (= *largarse*) to split** 9 (*LAm*) [*pelota*] to bounce **Ⓒ** **picarse** VPR 1 (= *corroerse*) [*diente, muela*] to rot, decay; [*hierro, metal*] to rust; [*goma, neumático*] to perish; [*ropa*] to get moth-eaten 2 (*Culin*) [*fruta*] to go rotten; [*vino*] to go sour, turn sour 3 (*) 3.1 (= *enfadarse*) to get into a huff*; ✦ REFRÁN **el que se pica ajos come** if the cap fits, wear it 3.2 (= *sentirse provocado*) **se picó y pisó el acelerador** he rose to the challenge and stepped on the accelerator 3.3 (= *aficionarse*) **∼se con algo** to get hooked on sth* 4 [*mar*] to get choppy 5 (*Carib*) **∼se de pecho** to become consumptive 6 (**) (= *inyectarse droga*) to shoot up*; **∼se heroína** to shoot heroin*

picardía SF 1 (= *cualidad*) (*del taimado*) slyness, craftiness; (*del travieso*) naughtiness 2 (= *acción*) prank, naughty thing (to do)

picardías SM INV baby-doll pyjamas *pl*

picaresca SF 1 (*Literat*) (genre of the) picaresque novel 2 (= *astucia*) guile, chicanery (*liter*), subterfuge

picaresco ADJ picaresque

pícaro/a Ⓐ ADJ 1 (= *taimado*) sly, crafty; (= *travieso*) [*niño*] naughty, mischievous 2 (= *pillo*) roguish 3 (= *precoz*) [*niño*] precocious, knowing (*esp sexually aware before the proper age*)

ⓑ SM/F rogue

PÍCARO

In Spanish literature, especially of the Golden Age, the **pícaro** is a roguish character whose travels and adventures are used as a vehicle for social satire. The anonymous **Lazarillo de Tormes** (1554), which relates the life and adventures of one such character, is thought to be the first of the genre known as the picaresque novel, or **novela picaresca**. Other well-known picaresque novels were written by Cervantes (**Rinconete y Cortadillo**) and Francisco de Quevedo (**El Buscón**).

---

picarón Ⓐ ADJ (*) naughty, roguish **ⓑ** SM (*And Culin*) fritter

picas SFPL (*Naipes*) spades

picatoste SM fried bread

picazón SF 1 (*Med*) (= *picor*) itch; (= *ardor*) sting, stinging feeling 2 (= *desazón*) uneasiness

picha*** SF prick***

pichanga SF (*Chi Dep*) friendly soccer match

pichi SM (*Esp*) pinafore dress

pichí* SM (*CS*) = **pipí**

pichicata* SF (*SAm*) 1 (= *droga*) drugs *pl* 2 (= *cocaína*) coke**

pichicatero/a* SM/F (*SAm*) (= *adicto*) druggie*; (= *comerciante*) drug peddler

pichicato* ADJ (*And, Méx*) stingy

pichincha* SF (*CS*) bargain

pichirre* ADJ (*Ven*) mean, stingy

pichón SM 1 (= *paloma*) young pigeon; (*Culin*) pigeon 2 (*LAm*) (= *cría de ave*) chick 3 (= *apelativo*) darling, dearest; **sí, pichoncito** yes, darling *o* dearest

pichulear* /1a/ VI 1 (*RPl*) (= *regatear*) to haggle; (= *negociar*) to be a small-time businessman 2 (*CAm, Méx, RPl*) (= *gastar poco*) to be careful with one's money

pichulín* SM (*RPl*) winkle*

picia* SF prank

pick-up [piˈkap, piˈku] SM (*LAm*) pickup (truck)

picnic SM picnic

pico SM 1 [*de ave*] beak, bill; [*de insecto*] beak 2 (= *punta*) corner, sharp point; **cuello de ~** V-neck; ✦ MODISMO **irse de ~s pardos*** to go out on the town*, have a night on the town* 3 [*de jarra*] lip, spout 4 [*de montaña*] peak, summit 5 (= *herramienta*) pick, pickaxe, pickax (*EEUU*) 6 [*de una cantidad*] **son las tres y ~** it's just after three; **tiene cuarenta y ~ años** she's forty-odd; **tres mil pesetas y ~** just over three thousand pesetas; ✦ MODISMO **costar un ~*** to cost a fortune* 7 (***) (= *boca*) trap*; **¡cierra el ~!** shut your trap!*, shut up!*; ✦ MODISMOS **darle al ~ ◇ irse del ~** to gab a lot*; **ser un ~ de oro ◇ tener buen o mucho ~** to have the gift of the gab 8 (***) [*de droga*] fix*, shot* 9 (*Chi****) (= *pene*) prick***

picoleto** SM (*Esp*) Civil Guard

picor SM itch

picoso ADJ (*CAm, Méx*) very hot, spicy

picota SF 1 (*Bot*) bigarreau cherry 2 (*Hist*) pillory; ✦ MODISMO **poner a algn en la ~** to pillory sb

picotazo SM peck

picotear /1a/ **Ⓐ** VT to peck (at) **ⓑ** VI (*al comer*) to nibble

pictórico ADJ pictorial

picudo ADJ 1 (= *puntiagudo*) pointed 2 (*Méx**) (= *astuto*) crafty, clever

pida, pido *etc ver* **pedir**

pie SM 1 (*Anat*) foot; **con los ~s descalzos** barefoot ➤ **pie de atleta** athlete's foot ➤ **pie de cabra** crowbar ➤ **pies de barro** feet of clay ➤ **pies planos** flat feet 2 (*locuciones*) **a pie** on foot; **ir a ~** to go on foot, walk; **estar de ~** to be standing (up); **en ~:** **llevo en ~ desde las cuatro** I've been up since four; **mantenerse en ~** [*persona*] to stay standing *o* on one's feet; [*objeto*] to remain upright; **la oferta sigue en ~** the offer still stands; **ponerse de o en ~** to stand up; ✦ MODISMOS **de a ~** common, ordinary; **soldado de a ~** (*Hist*) foot-soldier; **andar con ~s de plomo** to tread carefully *o* warily; **de ~s a cabeza** from head to foot; **es un caballero de ~s a cabeza** he's a gentleman through and through; **caer de ~** to fall on one's feet; **cojear del mismo ~** to suffer from the same problem; **con los ~s por delante** feet first; **no dar ~ con bola*** to get everything wrong; **entrar con buen ~** to get off to a good start; **hacer ~** (*en el agua*) to touch the bottom; **no hacer ~** to be out of one's depth; **a ~s juntillas** blindly; **levantarse con el ~ izquierdo** to get out of the wrong side of the bed; **nacer de ~** to be born lucky; **parar los ~s a algn** take sb down a peg or two; **poner el ~ o los ~s en** to set foot in; **poner los ~s en el suelo** to put your feet firmly on the ground; **poner (los) ~s en polvorosa** to take to one's heels; **salir por ~s*** to take to one's heels, leg it*; **sin ~s ni cabeza** [*argumento*] absurd; **el plan no tiene ni ~s ni cabeza** the plan is totally unworkable 3 (= *base*) [*de columna, estatua, lámpara*] base; [*de cama*] foot; [*de colina, escalera*] foot, bottom; [*de copa*] stem; [*de calcetín*] foot; **a los ~s de la cama** at the foot of the bed; ✦ MODISMO **al ~ del cañón: este fin de semana estará al ~ del cañón** he'll be hard at work this weekend; **ha cumplido 30 años al ~ del cañón** he spent 30 years on the job; **morir al ~ del cañón** to die in harness 4 [*de página*] foot, bottom; [*de foto*] caption; **notas a ~ de página** footnotes; ✦ MODISMO **al ~ de la letra** [*citar*] literally, verbatim; [*copiar*] word for word; [*cumplir*] to the letter, down to the last detail ➤ **pie de imprenta** imprint 5 (*Bot*) [*de árbol*] trunk; [*de planta*] stem; [*de rosa*] stock 6 (= *unidad de medida*) foot 7 (*Teat*) cue 8 (*CS*) (= *entrada*) deposit 9 (= *causa*) **dar ~ a** to give cause for; **dar ~ para que algn haga algo** to give sb cause to do sth 10 (= *posición*) **estar en ~ de igualdad** to be on an equal footing (**con** with); **estar en ~ de guerra** (*lit*) to be on a war footing, be ready to go to war; (*fig*) to be on the warpath

piedad SF 1 (= *compasión, pena*) pity; **ten un poco de ~ con el pobrecillo** show some pity *o* sympathy for the poor boy; **¡por ~!** for pity's sake! 2 (= *clemencia*) mercy; **¡Dios, ten ~ de mí!** God, have mercy on me! 3 (*Rel*) piety

piedra SF 1 (= *material*) stone; (= *trozo*) stone, rock (*EEUU*); **un puente de ~** a stone bridge; **colocar la primera ~** to lay the foundation stone (*Brit*) *o* cornerstone (*EEUU*); ✦ MODISMOS **no dejar ~ sobre ~** to raze to the ground; **menos da una ~** it's better than nothing; **no ser de ~:** **no soy de ~** I'm not made of stone, I do have feelings; **tener el corazón de ~** to be hard-hearted; **tirar ~s a contra su propio tejado** to shoot o.s. in the foot ➤ **piedra angular** cornerstone ➤ **piedra arenisca** sandstone ➤ **piedra caliza** limestone ➤ **piedra de afilar** grindstone ➤ **piedra de molino** millstone ➤ **piedra de toque** touchstone ➤ **piedra filosofal** philosopher's stone ➤ **piedra poma** (*Méx*), **piedra pómez** pumice (stone) ➤ **piedra preciosa** precious stone 2 [*de mechero*] flint 3 (*Med*) stone 4 (*Meteo*) hailstone

piel Ⓐ SF 1 [*de persona*] skin; **tiene la ~ grasa/seca** she has oily/dry skin; **estirarse la ~*** to have a facelift; ✦ MODISMOS **dejarse la ~** to give one's all; **ponerse en la ~ de algn** to put o.s. in sb else's shoes; **se me/le puso la ~ de gallina** I/he came out in goose pimples *o* goose flesh ➤ **piel de naranja** (*por celulitis*) orange-peel skin 2 [*de animal*] (*gen*) skin; [*de vaca, búfalo, elefante*] hide; [*de foca, zorro, visón*] fur; (= *cuero*) leather; **abrigo de ~** fur coat; **una maleta de ~** a leather suitcase; ✦ MODISMO **la ~ de toro** Iberia ➤ **piel de ternera** calfskin 3 [*de frutas*] (*gen*) skin; [*de naranja, limón*] peel; [*de manzana*] skin, peel **ⓑ** SMF ➤ **piel roja** redskin

piélago SM (*liter*) sea

pienso SM feed, fodder; **~s** feeding stuffs

piercing ['pirsiŋ] SM piercing; **lleva tres ~s en la oreja** he's got three piercings in his ear; **me voy a hacer un ~ en el ombligo** I'm going to have my navel pierced

pierna ⒶSF **1** (*Anat*) leg; **estirar las ~s** to stretch one's legs; ✦ MODISMOS **dormir a ~ suelta** o **tendida** to sleep like a log*; **salir por ~s*** to take one's heels, leg it* **2** (= *muslo de animal*) leg; **~ de cordero** leg of lamb ⒷADJ (*RPl**) **es ~ para todo** he's willing to help in any way

pieza SF **1** (= *componente*) **1.1** [*de rompecabezas, colección*] piece; **una vajilla de 60 ~s** a 60-piece dinner service **1.2** [*de una exposición*] exhibit; **la colección expuesta consta de 30 ~s** the collection on display includes 30 exhibits; **una exposición de ~s de cerámica/orfebrería** an exhibition of ceramics/silverware **1.3** [*de mecanismo, motor*] part, component **1.4 de una ~: la silla estaba construida de una ~** the chair was made in one piece; **me quedé de una ~** I was totally dumbstruck o (*Brit***) gobsmacked; ✦ MODISMO **ser de una (sola) ~** (*LAm*) to be as straight as a die
➤ **pieza arqueológica** artefact ➤ **pieza clave** (*lit*) essential part; (*fig*) key element ➤ **pieza de museo** museum piece ➤ **pieza de recambio, pieza de repuesto** spare (part), extra (*EEUU*)
2 (= *ejemplar*) **2.1** [*de carne, fruta*] piece; **dos ~s de fruta** two pieces of fruit; **vender algo por ~s** to sell sth by the piece **2.2** (*Arte*) example; **una ~ única del Románico** a unique example of the Romanesque **2.3** (*tb* **~ de caza**) specimen
3 (*Ajedrez*) piece
4 (*Cos*) (= *remiendo*) patch; (= *rollo de tela*) roll
5 (*esp LAm*) (= *habitación*) room
6 (= *obra*) (*Mús*) piece, composition; (*Literat*) work; (*Teat*) play ➤ **pieza corta** (*Mús*) short piece; (*Teat*) playlet
7 (*Odontología*) tooth
8 (*) (= *persona*) **¡buena ~ estás tú hecho!** you're a fine one!; ✦ MODISMOS **ser una ~ para algo** (*Méx**) to be very good at sth; **ser mucha ~ para algn** (*Méx**) to be in a different league from sb

pífano SM fife

pifia SF **1** (*Billar*) miscue **2** (*) (= *error*) blunder, bloomer* **3** (*And, CS*) (= *burla*) mockery; (= *chiste*) joke; **hacer ~ de** (= *burlarse*) to mock, poke fun at; (= *bromear*) to make a joke of, joke about **4** (*And, CS*) (= *rechifla*) hiss

pifiar /1b/ VT **1** (*And, CS*) (= *arruinar*) to mess up, botch **2** (*And, CS*) (= *chiflar*) to boo, hiss at **3** (*) **~la** to blunder, make a bloomer*

pigmentación SF pigmentation

pigmento SM pigment

pigmeo/a ADJ, SM/F pigmy

pignorar /1a/ VT to pawn

pija[1]*** SF (*RPl*) (= *pene*) prick***; *ver tb* **pijo**

pijada* SF (*Esp*) **1** (= *cosa absurda*) **eso es una ~** that's utter nonsense **2** (= *cosa sin importancia*) trifle

pijama SM pyjamas *pl*, pajama (*EEUU*)

pijo/a[2] (*Esp*) ⒶADJ (*) **1** (*persona, ropa, discoteca*) posh **2** (= *tonto*) stupid Ⓑ SM/F (*) **1** (= *niño bien*) spoilt brat, spoilt rich kid **2** (= *tonto*) berk (*Brit**), twit (*Brit**), jerk (*EEUU**) Ⓒ SM (***) (= *pene*) prick***; ✦ MODISMO **no te oyen un ~** they can't hear you at all; *ver tb* **pija**

pijotero/a* ⒶADJ **1** (*Esp*) (= *molesto*) annoying; (= *condenado*) bloody**, bleeding** **2** (*Arg*) (= *tacaño*) stingy*, mean (*esp Brit*) Ⓑ SM/F (= *persona molesta*) pain*

pijudo* ADJ (*CAm*) great*, terrific*

pila[1] SF **1** [*de libros, juguetes*] pile, stack **2** (*) [*de deberes, trabajo*] heap; **tengo una ~ de cosas que hacer** I have heaps o piles of things to do

pila[2] SF **1** (= *fregadero*) sink; [*de fuente*] basin ➤ **pila de cocina** kitchen sink **2** (*Rel*) (*tb* **~ bautismal**) font ➤ **pila de agua bendita** holy water stoup **3** (*Elec*) battery; ✦ MODISMO **ponerse las ~s*** to get one's act together, put one's skates on ➤ **pila alcalina** alkaline battery, alkaline cell ➤ **pila (de) botón** watch battery, calculator battery

pilar SM **1** (= *poste*) post, pillar; [*de puente*] pier **2** (*fig*) pillar, mainstay; **un ~ de la monarquía** a mainstay of the monarchy

pilastra SF pilaster

Pilatos SM Pilate

pilchas* SFPL (*CS*) clothes

píldora SF pill; ✦ MODISMOS **dorar la ~** to sugar o sweeten the pill; **tragarse la ~** to be taken in ➤ **píldora abortiva** morning-after pill ➤ **píldora anticonceptiva** contraceptive pill ➤ **píldora del día después** morning-after pill

pileta SF (*CS*) [*de cocina*] sink; [*de baño*] wash basin; [*de natación*] swimming pool

pilila* SF willy (*Brit**), peter (*EEUU****)

pillaje SM pillage, plunder

pillar /1a/ ⒶVT **1** (= *atrapar*) to catch; **lo pilló la policía** the police caught o nabbed* him; **me pilló el dedo con la puerta** he got my finger caught in the door; **¡como te pille ... !** if I get hold of you ... !
2 (*) (= *tomar, coger*) to catch, get; **~ el autobús** to catch o get the bus
3 (= *sorprender*) to catch; **lo pillé fumando** I caught him smoking; **¡te he pillado!** caught o got you!
4 (= *alcanzar*) to catch up with
5 (= *atropellar*) to hit, run over; **la pilló una moto** she was hit by a motorbike
6 [+ *resfriado, pulmonía*] to catch, get; **~ una borrachera** to get drunk
7 (*) [+ *puesto*] to get, land
8 [+ *broma, significado*] to get, catch on to
ⒷVI (*Esp**) **me pilla lejos** it's too far for me; **me pilla muy cerca** it's handy o near for me; **me pilla de camino** it's on my way
Ⓒ **pillarse** VPR **1** (= *atraparse*) to catch; **se pilló el dedo con la puerta** he caught his finger in the door **2** (*RPl**) (= *engreírse*) to get conceited, get full of o.s.

pillastre* SMF scoundrel

pillería SF **1** (= *acción*) (*de persona*) dirty trick; (*de niño*) **no hagas ~s** don't be naughty **2** (= *cualidad*) [*de adultos*] craftiness; [*de niños*] naughtiness

pillín/ina SM/F rascal, scamp

pillo/a ⒶADJ [*adulto*] sly, crafty; [*niño*] naughty Ⓑ SM/F (= *adulto*) rogue, scoundrel; (= *niño*) rascal, scamp

pilluelo SM rascal, scamp

pilmama SF (*Méx*) (= *nodriza*) wet-nurse; (= *niñera*) nursemaid

pilón SM **1** (= *poste*) pillar, post; (*Elec*) pylon **2** (= *abrevadero*) drinking trough; [*de fuente*] basin **3** [*de azúcar*] sugar loaf **4** (*Méx**) extra, bonus; (= *propina*) tip; ✦ MODISMO **de ~** to cap it all*; **... y de ~ empezó a llover ...** and then as if that weren't enough o to cap it all, it began to rain*

piloncillo SM (*Méx*) powdered brown sugar

pilotaje SM (*Náut, Aer*) piloting; **fallo de ~** navigational error

pilotar /1a/ VT [+ *avión*] to pilot; [+ *coche*] to drive; [+ *barco*] to steer, navigate

pilote SM pile

pilotear /1a/ VT (*LAm*) = **pilotar**

piloto ⒶSMF [*de avión*] pilot; [*de coche*] driver, racing driver; [*de moto*] rider ➤ **piloto de caza** fighter pilot ➤ **piloto de pruebas** (*Aer*) test pilot; (*Aut*) test driver Ⓑ SM **1** (= *luz*) pilot, pilot light; (*Aut*) tail light, rear light ➤ **piloto automático** automatic pilot **2** (*CS*) (= *prenda*) raincoat Ⓒ ADJ INV [*programa, planta*] pilot *antes de s*; **piso ~** show flat (*esp Brit*), model condominium (*EEUU*)

piltra** SF kip*

piltrafa SF (*tb* **~s**) [*de carne*] scraps **2** (= *cosa*) worthless object; (= *persona*) wretch

pilucho (*Chi*) ⒶADJ (*) naked Ⓑ SM [*de bebé*] bodysuit, body, vest (*Brit*)

pimentero SM pepper pot (*esp Brit*), pepper shaker (*EEUU*)

pimentón SM **1** (= *especia*) (*tb* **~ dulce**) paprika

➤ **pimentón picante** hot paprika, cayenne pepper **2** (*LAm*) (= *fruto*) sweet pepper, capsicum

pimienta SF pepper ➤ **pimienta de cayena** cayenne pepper ➤ **pimienta negra** black pepper

pimiento SM **1** (= *fruto*) pepper; ✦ MODISMO **(no) me importa un ~** I don't care two hoots* ➤ **pimiento morrón, pimiento rojo** red pepper ➤ **pimiento verde** green pepper **2** (= *planta*) pepper plant

pimpante* ADJ **tan ~** smug, self-satisfied

pimplar* (*Esp*) /1a/ Ⓐ VI to booze* Ⓑ **pimplarse** VPR **~se una botella** to down a bottle*, quaff a bottle*

pimpollo SM **1** (*Bot*) (= *brote*) sucker, shoot; (= *capullo*) bud **2 hecho un ~*** (= *elegante*) very smart; (= *joven*) very young for one's age

PIN SM (*CS*) PIN

pin SM (*pl* **~s**) **1** (= *insignia*) badge (*Brit*), button (*EEUU*) **2** (*Elec*) pin

pinacoteca SF art gallery

pináculo SM pinnacle

pinar SM pine grove

pincel SM (*para pintar*) paintbrush; [*de cocina*] brush; ✦ MODISMO **estar hecho un ~** to be very smartly dressed

pincelada SF brushstroke; **última ~** (*fig*) finishing touch

pinchadiscos* SMF INV (*Esp*), **pincha*** SMF INV (*Esp*) disc jockey, D.J.

pinchar /1a/ Ⓐ VT **1** (= *reventar*) [+ *globo, pelota*] to burst; [+ *neumático, rueda*] to puncture; **me han pinchado las ruedas** my tyres have been slashed **2** (= *picar*) **2.1** (*con algo punzante*) to prick; **le pinchó en el brazo con un alfiler** she pricked his arm with a pin **2.2** (*Culin*) to test; **pincha la carne con el tenedor** test the meat with your fork, stick the fork in the meat; ✦ MODISMO **ni ~ ni cortar*** to count for nothing **3** (= *comer*) to nibble (at); **hemos pinchado unos taquitos de queso** we nibbled (at) a few cubes of cheese **4** (*) (= *poner una inyección a*) to give a jab to*, give a shot to*; (= *apuñalar*) to knife **5** (*) (= *presionar*) (*gen*) to prod; (*pey*) to pester; (= *provocar*) to wind sb up*; **siempre me está pinchando** he's always winding me up* **6** (*) [+ *línea, teléfono*] to tap, bug **7** (*Esp Mús**) **~ discos** to deejay*, be a disc jockey Ⓑ VI **1** [*espina*] to prick; [*clavo*] to stick; **te pincha la barba** your beard is bristly *o* prickly **2** (= *tener un pinchazo*) to get a puncture **3** (*Esp**) (= *fracasar*) to come a cropper*; **hemos pinchado con este proyecto** we have come a cropper with this project* **4** (= *hacer clic*) to click (**en** on) **5** (*Chi**) (= *ligar*) **cuando era joven pinchaba harto** when he was young he had a lot of girlfriends; **~ con algn** to get off with sb* Ⓒ **pincharse** VPR **1** (*en dedo, brazo*) to prick o.s.; **me he pinchado con una aguja** I've pricked myself with a needle; **¿te has pinchado en el pie?** did you get something stuck in your foot? **2** (= *reventarse*) [*globo, pelota*] to burst; [*neumático, rueda*] to puncture **3** (*Med*) [+ *antibiótico, insulina*] to inject o.s. with **4** (**) (= *drogarse*) to shoot up*; **se pincha heroína** he shoots heroin*

pinchazo SM **1** (*con objeto punzante*) prick; **me he metido un ~ cosiendo** I've pricked my finger *o* myself sewing **2** (*en neumático*) puncture **3** (*) (= *inyección*) [*de antibiótico, insulina*] jab*, shot; [*de cocaína, heroína*] shot, fix** **4** [*de dolor*] shooting pain, sharp pain **5** (*Telec**) tap*, bug* **6** (*Esp*) (= *fracaso*) fiasco

pinche Ⓐ ADJ **1** (*Méx***) (= *maldito*) bloody**, lousy**; **todo por unos ~s centavos** all for a few measly cents **2** (*CAm, Méx*) (= *miserable*) wretched **3** (*CAm**) (= *tacaño*) stingy, tight-fisted Ⓑ SMF [*de cocina*] kitchen hand, kitchen-boy Ⓒ SM (*Chi*) (= *horquilla*) hairpin, bobby pin (*EEUU*)

pincho SM **1** (= *punta*) point; (= *varilla*) pointed stick,

spike **2** [*de zarza, flor*] thorn, prickle; [*de cactus, animal*] spike, prickle **3** (**) (= *navaja*) knife **4** (*Esp Culin*) tapa; **un ~ de tortilla** a small portion of omelette ➤ **pincho moruno** (*Esp*) kebab

pindonguear* /1a/ VI (*Esp*) to gad about

pinga* SF (*LAm*) (= *pene*) prick***

pingajo SM rag, shred; **ir hecho un ~** to look a right mess*

pingo Ⓐ ADJ INV (*Esp* *pey*) loose*, promiscuous Ⓑ SM **1** (*Esp*) (= *harapo*) rag; **pingos*** (= *ropa*) cheap clothes; ✦ MODISMO **poner a algn como un ~** to slag sb off* **2** (*CS**) (= *caballo*) horse **3** (*Méx*) **el ~** the devil **4** (*CS*) (= *niño*) lively child

pingonear* /1a/ VI to gad about

ping-pong ['pimpon] SM ping-pong

pingüe ADJ [*ganancias*] rich, fat; [*negocio*] lucrative; [*cosecha*] bumper

pingüino SM penguin

pinitos SMPL, **pininos** SMPL (*esp LAm*) **hacer sus ~** [*niño*] to toddle, take his/her first steps; [*novato*] to take his/her first steps; **hago mis ~ como pintor** I play *o* dabble at painting

pino SM **1** (*Bot*) pine, pine tree; ✦ MODISMO **vivir en el quinto ~*** to live at the back of beyond; **eso está en el quinto ~*** that's miles away ➤ **pino albar** Scots pine **2** (*en gimnasia*) **hacer el ~** to do a handstand

pinocha SF pine needles *pl*

pinrel* SM hoof*, foot

pinsapo SM Spanish fir

pinta¹ SF **1** (= *lunar*) (*gen*) spot, dot; (*Zool*) spot **2** [*de líquidos*] drop, spot; [*de lluvia, bebida*] drop; **una ~ de grasa** a grease spot **3** (*) (= *aspecto*) appearance; **por la ~** by the look of it; **tener buena ~** to look good; **tiene ~ de español** he looks like a Spaniard; **con esa(s) ~(s) no puedes ir** you can't go looking like that; ✦ MODISMOS **echar** (*RPl*) *o* **hacer** (*Col*) *o* **tirar** (*Chi*) **~** to impress; **ponerse la ~** (*Col*) to get dressed up **4** ✦ MODISMO **irse de ~** (*CAm, Méx*) to play truant

pinta² SF (= *medida inglesa*) pint

pintada SF piece of graffiti; **~s** graffiti

pintado ADJ **1** (*Zool*) (= *moteado*) spotted; (= *pinto*) mottled, dappled **2** (*) (= *igual*) **el niño salió ~ al padre** the boy turned out exactly like his father *o* identical to his father **3** ✦ MODISMOS **el más ~*** anybody; **sentar/venir que ni ~ a algn*** to suit sb down to the ground*

pintalabios SM INV lipstick

pintar /1a/ Ⓐ VT **1** (*Arte*) (*con óleo, acuarela*) to paint; (*con lápices, rotuladores*) (= *dibujar*) to draw; (= *colorear*) to colour, color (*EEUU*); **~ algo al óleo/temple** to paint sth in oils/tempera **2** [+ *pared, habitación*] to paint; **"recién pintado"** "wet paint"; **~ algo de *o* en blanco/azul** to paint sth white/blue **3** (= *describir*) to paint; **lo pinta todo muy negro** he paints it all very black **4** (*) (= *tener importancia*) **¿pero qué pintamos aquí?** what on earth are we doing here?; **no pinta nada en la empresa** he's nobody important in the company Ⓑ VI **1** (*Arte*) to paint **2** (*para decorar*) to decorate; **cuando terminen la obra ~emos** when they finish the building work we'll decorate *o* do the decorating **3** (= *manchar*) (*de pintura, tinta*) **ten cuidado con ese banco, que pinta** be careful, that bench has wet paint on it; **"¡ojo, pinta!"** "wet paint" **4** (*) (= *escribir*) [*bolígrafo*] to write **5** (*Naipes*) to be trumps **6** (*LAm**) (= *mostrarse*) to look; **no me gusta cómo pinta esto** I don't like the look of this Ⓒ **pintarse** VPR **1** (= *maquillarse*) (*una vez*) to put one's make-up on, make o.s. up; (*con frecuencia*) to use make-up; **~se los labios** to put lipstick on; **~se los ojos: ¿te has pintado los ojos?** have you got any eye make-up on?, did you put on your eye make-up?; **¿con qué te pintas los ojos?** what eye make-up do you use?; **~se las uñas** to paint one's nails; ✦ MODISMO **pintárselas solo: se las pinta solo para conseguir lo que quiere** he's an expert *o* a dab hand at

getting what he wants
2 (= *notarse*) to show; **el cansancio se pintaba en su rostro** you could see the tiredness in her face, the tiredness showed on her face

pintarrajear* /1a/ VT, VI to daub

pintarrajo* SM daub

pintarroja SF dogfish

pintas* SMF INV (*Esp*) scruff*, scruffily dressed person

pintear /1a/ VI to drizzle, spot with rain

pintiparado ADJ (*Esp*) **1** (= *idéntico*) identical (**a** to) **2 ✦** MODISMO **me viene (que ni) ~*** it suits me a treat

pinto ADJ spotted, dappled

pintor(a) SM/F painter ➤ **pintor(a) de brocha gorda** (*de paredes*) painter and decorator; (*de cuadros*) (*pey*) bad painter, dauber

pintoresco ADJ picturesque

pintura SF **1** (= *forma artística, cuadro*) painting; **✦** MODISMO **no lo podía ver ni en ~** she couldn't stand the sight of him ➤ **pintura a la acuarela** watercolour, watercolor (*EEUU*) ➤ **pintura al óleo** oil painting ➤ **pintura al pastel** pastel drawing ➤ **pintura rupestre** cave painting **2** (= *material*) paint ➤ **pintura a la cola, pintura al temple** (*para paredes*) distemper; (*para cuadros*) tempera ➤ **pintura emulsionada** emulsion, emulsion paint **3** (= *lápiz de color*) crayon ➤ **pintura de cera** wax crayon

pinza SF **1** [*de ropa*] clothes peg (*Brit*), clothespin (*EEUU*); (*para el pelo*) hair grip (*Brit*), bobby pin (*EEUU*) **2 pinzas** (*de depilar*) tweezers; (*para hielo, azúcar*) tongs; (*Med*) forceps; **✦** MODISMOS **había que cogerlo con ~s** I had to take it very carefully; **tratar a algn con ~s** (*CS, Méx**) to handle sb with kid gloves **3** (*Cos*) pleat; **pantalones de ~s** trousers (*Brit*) o pants (*EEUU*) with waist pleats **4** [*de cangrejo, langosta*] pincer, claw

pinzón SM finch

piña SF **1** [*de pino*] pine cone **2** (= *fruta*) pineapple **3** (*Esp*) [*de personas*] (= *grupo*) group; (= *conjunto*) cluster, knot; (= *corrillo*) clique, closed circle; **✦** MODISMO **como una ~: estaban unidos como una ~** they were a very close-knit group **4** (*) (= *golpe*) punch, bash*; **darse una ~** to have a crash; **darse ~s** to fight, exchange blows

piñata SF (*en fiestas*) container hung up at parties to be beaten with sticks until sweets or presents fall out

piño** SM (*Esp*) (= *diente*) ivory*, tooth

piñón[1] SM (*Bot*) pine kernel; **✦** MODISMO **estar** o **llevarse a partir un ~** to be the best of buddies, be bosom pals* (**con** with)

piñón[2] SM (*Orn, Téc*) pinion; **✦** MODISMO **seguir a ~ fijo** (= *sin moverse*) to be rooted to the spot; (= *sin cambiar de idea*) to go on in the same old way, be stuck in one's old ways

piñonear /1a/ VI to click

piñoso* ADJ (*Perú*) unlucky

pío[1]/a ADJ **1** (*Rel*) pious, devout; (*pey*) sanctimonious **2** (= *compasivo*) merciful

pío[2] SM (*Orn*) cheep, chirp; **✦** MODISMO **no decir ni ~** not to breathe a word; **¡de esto no digas ni ~!** don't you breathe a word!

piocha SF **1** (*LAm*) (= *piqueta*) pickaxe, pickax (*EEUU*) **2** (*Chi*) (= *distintivo*) badge **3** (*Méx*) (= *barba*) goatee

piojo SM louse

piojoso ADJ **1** (= *con piojos*) lousy **2** (= *sucio*) filthy

piola Ⓐ SF (*And, Carib*) cord, string Ⓑ ADJ INV (*RPl**) (= *astuto*) smart, clever; (= *taimado*) sly; (= *bueno*) great*, terrific*; (= *elegante*) classy*

piolet [pio'le] SM (*pl* **~s**) ice axe, ice ax (*EEUU*)

pionero/a Ⓐ ADJ pioneering Ⓑ SM/F pioneer

piorrea SF pyorrhoea

pipa[1] SF **1** (*de fumar*) pipe; **fumar en ~** o **✧ fumar una ~** to smoke a pipe **2** [*de vino*] (= *barril*) cask, barrel **3** (*Esp Bot*) (= *semilla*) pip, seed; (*tb* **~ de girasol**) sunflower seed; **✦** MODISMO **no tener ni para ~s** to be broke, be skint*

4 (*Mús*) reed **5** (*Col, Perú**) (= *barriga*) belly*; **tener ~** to be potbellied **6** (**) (= *pistola*) rod**, pistol **7 ✦** MODISMO **pasarlo ~** (*Esp**) to have a great time*

pipeta SF pipette

pipí* SM **1** (= *orín*) pee*; (*entre niños*) wee-wee*; **hacer ~** to do a wee-wee*, have a pee*; **me estoy haciendo ~** I need a wee-wee, I need a pee*; **se ha hecho ~** he's wet himself **2** (*Bol, Col, Méx*) (= *pene*) winkle*

pipián SM (*CAm, Méx*) (= *salsa*) thick chili sauce; (= *guiso*) meat cooked in thick chili sauce

pipiar /1c/ VI to cheep, chirp

pipiolo/a* SM/F (= *chico*) little boy/little girl; (= *novato*) novice, greenhorn

pipón* ADJ (*RPl*) full (up)*

pique SM **1** (= *resentimiento*) resentment, pique; (= *inquina*) grudge; (= *rivalidad*) rivalry, competition; **tener un ~ con algn** to have a grudge against sb **2 irse a ~** (*barco*) to sink; [*esperanza, familia*] to be ruined **3 estar a ~ de hacer algo** (= *a punto de*) to be on the point of doing sth **4** (*Chi Min*) (= *galería*) mine shaft **5** (*LAm*) (= *rebote*) bounce, rebound

piquera SF hole, vent

piqueta SF **1** (= *herramienta*) pick, pickaxe, pickax (*EEUU*); [*de tienda de campaña*] peg

piquete SM **1** [*de personas*] (*Mil*) squad, party; (*en huelga*) picket ➤ **piquete móvil** flying picket **2** (*Méx*) (= *pinchazo*) (*con aguja*) prick, jab; [*de insecto*] bite **3** (*Méx*) [*de licor*] dash **4** (= *agujero*) small hole (*in clothing*)

pira SF pyre

pirado/a** Ⓐ ADJ round the bend*, crazy Ⓑ SM/F nutcase*

piragua SF canoe

piragüismo SM canoeing

piragüista SMF canoeist

piramidal ADJ pyramidal

pirámide SF pyramid

piraña SF piranha

pirarse* /1a/ VPR (*Esp*) (*tb* **pirárselas**) (= *largarse*): **me (las) piro** I'm off*, I'm out of here (*EEUU**); **~ las clases** to cut class*

pirata Ⓐ SMF pirate ➤ **pirata aéreo/a** hijacker ➤ **pirata informático/a** hacker Ⓑ ADJ **barco ~** pirate ship; **disco ~** bootleg record; **edición ~** pirated edition; **emisora ~** pirate radio station

piratear /1a/ Ⓐ VT **1** (*Aer*) to hijack **2** [+ *disco, concierto, grabación*] to pirate, bootleg; [+ *libro*] to plagiarize **3** (*Inform*) to hack into Ⓑ VI to buccaneer, practise piracy, practice piracy (*EEUU*)

piratería SF **1** [*de buque*] piracy ➤ **piratería aérea** highjacking **2** [*de disco, concierto, grabación*] pirating, bootlegging ➤ **piratería informática** hacking

pirenaico ADJ Pyrenean

Pirineo SM, **Pirineos** SMPL Pyrenees

pirinola* SF **1** (*And, Méx*) (= *peonza*) (spinning) top **2** (*Chi*) (= *objeto redondo*) knob **3** (*CAm**) (= *pene*) willy (*Brit**), weenie (*EEUU**)

piripi* ADJ (*Esp*) **estar ~** to be sozzled*

pirita SF pyrite

piromanía SF pyromania

pirómano/a SM/F pyromaniac

piropear /1a/ VT to compliment, make a flirtatious remark to

piropo SM (*para ligar*) flirtatious remark; (= *lisonja*) flattery

pirotecnia SF (*gen*) pyrotechnics *pl*, fireworks *pl*; (= *fuegos artificiales*) firework display

pirotécnico ADJ pyrotechnic, firework *antes de s*

pirrar* /1a/ (*Esp*) Ⓐ VI **le pirraba el vino** he was really into wine* Ⓑ **pirrarse** VPR **~se por** to be crazy about*

pirriar* /1b/ VI = **pirrar**

pirueta SF (= *movimiento ágil*) pirouette; (= *cabriola*) caper; ✦ MODISMO **hacer ~s** to perform a balancing act

piruja* SF (Col, Méx) hooker*

pirula** SF **1** ✦ MODISMO **hacer la ~ a** (Esp*) (= *molestar*) to upset, annoy; (= *jugarla*) to play a dirty trick on; (= *embaucar*) to cheat **2** (Anat) willy (Brit*), peter (EEUU***)

piruleta SF (Esp) lollipop

pirulí SM lollipop

pis* SM pee*; **hacer ~** to have a pee*, do a wee*; **hacerse ~ en la cama** to wet the *o* one's bed

pisacorbatas SF INV (Col) tiepin

pisada SF (= *paso*) footstep; (= *huella*) footprint

pisapapeles SM INV paperweight

pisar /1a/ ⒶVT **1** (= *andar sobre*) to walk on; **¿se puede ~ el suelo de la cocina?** can I walk on the kitchen floor?; **"prohibido pisar el césped"** "keep off the grass"
2 (= *poner el pie encima de*) to tread on, step on; **vio una cucaracha y la pisó** she saw a cockroach and trod *o* stood on it; **~ el acelerador a fondo** to step on the accelerator, put one's foot down*; ✦ MODISMO **ir pisando huevos** to tread carefully
3 (= *ir a*) to set foot in; **no volvimos a ~ ese sitio** we never set foot in that place again
4 (= *aplastar*) [+ *uvas*] to tread; [+ *tierra*] to tread down; (RPl) (con tenedor) to mash (up)
5 (= *avasallar*) to trample on, walk all over; **no se deja ~ por nadie** he doesn't let anybody trample on *o* walk all over him
6 (Mús) [+ *tecla*] to strike, press; [+ *cuerda*] to hold down
7 [+ *ave hembra*] to cover; (CAm***) to fuck***, screw***
8 (Esp*) (= *adelantarse a*): **otro le pisó el puesto** somebody got in first and collared the job; **el periódico le pisó la noticia** the newspaper got in first with the news
9 (RPl, Ven) (= *atropellar*) to run over
Ⓑ VI (= *andar*) to tread; ✦ MODISMO **~ fuerte*** to make great strides; **entrar pisando fuerte** to burst onto the scene*
Ⓒ **pisarse** VPR (Col*) to, push off**

pisca SF (Méx) maize harvest (Brit), corn harvest (EEUU)

piscicultor(a) SM/F fish farmer

piscicultura SF fish farming

piscifactoría SF fish farm

piscina SF swimming pool ➤ **piscina climatizada** heated swimming pool ➤ **piscina cubierta** indoor swimming pool ➤ **piscina olímpica** Olympic pool

Piscis SM (= *signo*) Pisces

piscis SMF INV (= *persona*) Pisces; **soy ~** I'm Pisces

pisco SM strong grape liquor ➤ **pisco sauer** (And) pisco cocktail

piscola SF (Chi) pisco and coca cola (drink)

piscolabis* SM INV (Esp) snack

piso SM **1** [de edificio] floor, storey, story (EEUU); [de autobús, barco] deck; [de cohete] stage; [de pastel] layer, tier; **viven en el quinto ~** they live on the fifth floor; **un edificio de ocho ~s** an eight-storey *o* (EEUU) eight-story building; **un autobús de dos ~s** a double-decker bus
2 (esp LAm) (= *suelo*) floor; (= *materiales para suelo*) flooring
3 (esp Esp) (= *apartamento*) [de alquiler] flat (esp Brit), apartment (EEUU); (en propiedad) flat (esp Brit), condominium (EEUU) ➤ **piso franco** (Esp) safe house ➤ **piso piloto** (Esp) show flat (esp Brit), model condominium (EEUU)
4 [de neumático] tread; [de zapato] sole
5 (Perú) (= *estera*) mat; (Chi) (= *alfombra*) rug ➤ **piso de baño** bathmat
6 (Chi) (= *taburete*) stool

pisotear /1a/ VT **1** [+ *papel, suelo*] to trample on
2 (= *humillar*) to trample on **3** [+ *ley*] to flout

pisotón SM stamp; **me ha dado un ~** he trod on my foot

pista SF **1** (= *rastro*) track, trail; **estar sobre la ~ de algn** to be on sb's trail *o* track, be after sb; **seguir la ~ de algn** (gen) to be on sb's trail *o* track; (de cerca) to shadow sb
2 (= *indicio*) clue; **dame una ~** give me a clue; **la policía tiene una ~ ya** the police already have a lead ➤ **pista falsa** (gen) false trail; (= *ardid*) red herring

3 [de atletismo] track; [de circo] ring; (Esp) [de tenis] court ➤ **pista de aterrizaje** (en aeropuerto) runway; (para aviones militares, privados) landing strip ➤ **pista de baile** dance floor ➤ **pista de carreras** racetrack ➤ **pista de esquí** piste, ski run ➤ **pista de hielo** ice rink ➤ **pista de patinaje** skating rink ➤ **pista forestal** forest trail
4 (Aut) trail, track; (Chi) (= *carril*) lane
5 [de cinta] track

pistacho SM pistachio

pistilo SM pistil

pisto SM (Esp) fried vegetable hash, ratatouille; ✦ MODISMO **darse ~*** to show off, swank*

pistola SF **1** (= *arma*) pistol, gun; (Téc) (para pintar) spray gun ➤ **pistola de agua** water pistol ➤ **pistola de engrase** grease gun ➤ **pistola de juguete** toy pistol **2** (Esp) [de pan] French stick, baguette

pistolera SF holster

pistolero SM gunman

pistoletazo SM (= *disparo*) pistol shot; (Dep) (tb ~ **de salida**) starting signal

pistón SM **1** (Mec) piston **2** (Mús) key; (Col) (= *corneta*) bugle, cornet

pita SF (= *planta*) agave, pita; (= *fibra*) pita fibre, pita thread

pitada SF **1** (= *silbido*) whistle; (= *rechifla*) hiss **2** (LAm*) [de cigarrillo] puff, drag*

pitagorín* SM brainbox*

pitanza SF (= *ración*) daily ration; (**) grub**, chow (EEUU**)

pitar /1a/ ⒶVI **1** (= *sonar*) (con silbato) to blow one's whistle; (con claxon) to honk, hoot (esp Brit), blow one's horn; **el conductor me pitó** the driver honked *o* (esp Brit) hooted at us, the driver blew his horn at us **2** (= *abuchear*) to whistle **3** ✦ MODISMO **ir o salir pitando** (Esp*): **salió pitando** he was off like a shot*; **vámonos pitando** let's get a move on* **4** (CS*) (= *fumar*) to smoke Ⓑ VT **el árbitro pitó falta** the referee whistled *o* blew for a foul

pitazo SM (LAm) whistle; ✦ MODISMO **dar el ~ a algn** (Carib, Méx*) to tip sb the wink*

pitear /1a/ VI (LAm) = **pitar A1**

pitido SM (= *silbido*) whistle; (= *sonido agudo*) beep; (= *sonido corto*) pip

pitillera SF cigarette case

pitillo SM **1** (*) (= *cigarrillo*) cigarette; **echarse un ~** to have a smoke **2** (And, Carib) (para beber) drinking straw

pitiminí ✦ MODISMO **de ~** (Esp) trifling, trivial

pito SM **1** [de coche, camión] horn, hooter (Brit); [de tren] whistle, hooter (Brit); **el conductor tocó el ~** the driver honked *o* (esp Brit) hooted (his horn)
2 (= *silbato*) whistle; **tener voz de ~** to have a squeaky voice; ✦ MODISMOS **entre ~s y flautas*** what with one thing and another; **(no) importar un ~***: **no me importa un ~** I don't care two hoots*; **tocar ~** (LAm*): **¿y qué ~ toco yo aquí?** what on earth am I doing here?
3 (*) (= *cigarrillo*) fag*, ciggy*; (Chi) [de marihuana] joint*
4 (*) (= *pene*) willy (Brit*), peter (EEUU**), weenie (EEUU**); ✦ MODISMO **tocarse el ~**** to do damn-all**, be bone-idle

pitón[1] SM (Zool) python

pitón[2] SM (= *cuerno*) horn; [de jarra] spout

pitonisa SF fortune teller

pitorrearse* /1a/ VPR (Esp) **~ de** to scoff at, make fun of

pitorreo* SM (Esp) teasing, joking; **estar de ~** to be in a joking mood

pitorro SM spout

pitote* SM (Esp) fuss, row

pituco*/a (And, CS) Ⓐ ADJ posh* Ⓑ SM/F toff*, posh person*

pituitario ADJ pituitary; **glándula pituitaria** pituitary (gland)

pituto* SM (Chi) useful contact, connection

pivot SMF (Dep) pivot

pivotar /1a/ VI **1** (*Dep*) to pivot **2** (= *oscilar*) ~ **alrededor de** to revolve around

pivote Ⓐ SMF (*Dep*) pivot Ⓑ SM (= *eje*) pivot

píxel SM pixel

piyama SM o SF (*LAm*) pyjamas *pl*, pajama (*EEUU*)

pizarra SF **1** (= *piedra*) slate **2** (*Escol*) blackboard (*Brit*), chalkboard (*EEUU*) **3** (*LAm*) (= *marcador*) scoreboard

pizarrón SM (*LAm Escol*) blackboard (*Brit*), chalkboard (*EEUU*)

pizca SF **1** (= *partícula*) tiny bit; **una ~ de sal** a pinch of salt; ✦ MODISMO **ni ~** not a bit; **no tiene ni ~ de gracia** it's not funny at all; **no tiene ni ~ de verdad** there's not a shred of truth in it **2** (*Méx Agr*) harvest

pizcar /1g/ Ⓐ VT [+ *maíz, algodón*] to pick, harvest Ⓑ VI (= *cosechar*) to harvest

pizpireto* ADJ flirty

pizza ['pitsa] SF pizza

pizzería [pitse'ria] SF pizzeria

placa SF **1** (= *lámina*) sheet; [*de cocina*] plate; (= *radiador*) radiator ➤ **placa conmemorativa** commemorative plaque ➤ **placa de hielo** icy patch ➤ **placa del nombre** nameplate ➤ **placa de matrícula** number plate (*Brit*), license plate (*EEUU*) ➤ **placa dental** (dental) plaque ➤ **placa de silicio** silicon chip ➤ **placa solar** (*en techo*) solar panel; (*en pared*) radiator **2** (*Fot*) (*tb ~ fotográfica*) plate **3** (= *distintivo*) badge, insignia

placaje SM (*Rugby*) tackle

placar /1g/ VT to tackle

placard SM (*RPI*) built-in cupboard (*esp Brit*), (clothes) closet (*EEUU*)

placebo SM placebo; **efecto ~** placebo effect

pláceme SM message of congratulations; **dar el ~ a algn** to congratulate sb

placenta SF placenta, afterbirth

placentero ADJ pleasant, agreeable

placer[1] Ⓐ SM pleasure; **es un ~ hacerlo** it is a pleasure to do it; **tengo el ~ de presentarles a ...** it's my pleasure to introduce ...; **viaje de ~** pleasure trip; **a ~** as much as one wants ➤ **placer de dioses** heavenly delight Ⓑ /2w/ VI **me place poder hacerlo** I am glad to be able to do it

placer[2] SM **1** (*Geol, Min*) placer **2** (*Náut*) sandbank

placero/a SM/F (*Perú*) stallholder, market trader

plácet SM blessing; **dar el ~ a algn** to give one's blessing to sb

placidez SF placidity

plácido ADJ placid

pladur® SM (*Esp*) plasterboard

plaf EXCL bang!, crash!

plafón SM **1** (*en el techo*) (= *rosetón*) ceiling rosette; (= *lámpara*) flush-fitting ceiling light **2** (*Arquit*) (= *panel*) soffit

plaga SF **1** (*Agr, Zool*) pest; [*de langostas*] plague; (*Bot*) blight **2** (= *azote*) scourge; **una ~ de turistas** a plague of tourists

plagar /1h/ Ⓐ VT (= *infestar*) to infest, plague; **han plagado la ciudad de carteles** they have covered o plastered the town with posters; **un texto plagado de errores** a text riddled with errors Ⓑ **plagarse** VPR **~se de** to become infested with

plagiar /1b/ VT **1** (= *copiar*) to plagiarize **2** (*LAm*) (= *secuestrar*) to kidnap

plagio SM **1** (= *copia*) plagiarism **2** (*LAm*) (= *secuestro*) kidnap(ping)

plan SM **1** (= *proyecto*) plan ➤ **plan de estudios** syllabus ➤ **plan de pensiones** pension plan ➤ **plan quinquenal** five-year plan
2 (= *intención*) idea, intention; **mi ~ era comprar otro nuevo** my idea o intention was to buy a new one
3 (*) (= *manera, actitud*) **este niño está en un ~ imposible** this child is really playing up; **como sigas en ese ~** if you go on like that; **viajar en ~ económico** to travel cheap; **en ~ de**: **lo dije en ~ de broma** I said it as a joke o for a laugh; **vamos en ~ de turismo** we're going as tourists; ✦ MODISMOS **eso no es ~** ✧ **tampoco es ~** (*Esp*) that's not on*
4 (*Esp*†*) (= *cita amorosa*) date; (*pey*) fling*

plana SF [*de hoja*] page; **en primera ~** on the front page; ✦ MODISMO **corregir** o **enmendar la ~ a algn** to put sb right; (*pey*) to find fault with sb, improve upon sb's efforts ➤ **plana mayor** (*Mil*) staff; (*fig*) top brass (*Brit**), brass (*EEUU**)

plancha SF **1** (= *lámina*) sheet; (*Tip*) plate; **hacer la ~** [*bañista*] to float **2** (= *utensilio*); (= *acción*) ironing; (= *ropa para planchar*) ironing **3** (*Culin*) griddle; **pescado a la ~** grilled fish **4** (*) (= *error*) bloomer*; **hacer** o **tirarse una ~** to drop a clanger**, put one's foot in it **5** (*Dep*) **entrada en ~** sliding tackle; **lanzarse en ~** to dive (for the ball)

planchado Ⓐ ADJ (*) **1** (*Chi*) (= *sin dinero*) broke* **2** (*RPI*) (= *agotado*) dead beat*, exhausted Ⓑ SM ironing

planchar /1a/ Ⓐ VT [+ *ropa*] to iron; [+ *traje*] to press Ⓑ VI **1** (*con la plancha*) to iron, do the ironing **2** (*RPI*) (= *caerse*) to fall over **3** (*And, RPI**) (*en baile*) to be a wallflower **4** (*Chi**) (= *quedar en ridículo*) to look ridiculous

planchazo* SM = **plancha 4**

plancton SM plankton

planeación SF (*Méx*) planning

planeador SM glider

planear /1a/ Ⓐ VT (= *proyectar*) to plan; ~ **hacer algo** to plan to do sth Ⓑ VI (*Aer*) to glide; (*fig*) to hang, hover (**sobre** over)

planeta SM planet

planetario Ⓐ ADJ planetary Ⓑ SM planetarium

planicie SF plain

planificación SF planning ➤ **planificación familiar** family planning

planificar /1g/ VT to plan

planilla SF **1** (*LAm*) (= *lista*) list; (= *tabla*) table **2** (*LAm*) [*de trabajadores*] (= *nómina*) payroll; (= *personal*) staff; **estar en ~** to be on the payroll **3** (*Méx*) [*de candidatos*] list of candidates **4** (*And, Col, CS*) (*electoral*) electoral roll o register

planning ['planin] SM (*pl* **~s** ['planin]) schedule, agenda

plano Ⓐ ADJ (= *llano*) flat, level; **tiene los pies ~s** he has flat feet; **los 100 metros ~s** (*LAm*) the 100 metres Ⓑ SM **1** (*Mat, Mec*) plane ➤ **plano inclinado** inclined plane **2** (= *posición, nivel*) level; **están en un ~ distinto** they're on a different level
3 (*Cine, Fot*) shot; **un primer ~** a close-up; **en primer ~** (*Cine, Fot*) in close-up; (*Arte*) in the foreground; **estar en (un) segundo ~** (*fig*) to be in the background ➤ **plano general** general view ➤ **plano largo** long shot
4 (*Arquit, Mec*) plan; (*Geog*) map; [*de ciudad*] map, street plan
5 de ~: **caer de ~** to fall flat; **confesar de ~** to make a full confession; **le daba el sol de ~** the sun shone directly on it; **rechazar algo de ~** to turn sth down flat
6 [*de espada*] flat

planta[1] SF (*Bot*) plant ➤ **planta de interior** indoor plant, houseplant

planta[2] SF **1** (= *piso*) floor; **vivo en la tercera ~** I live on the third floor; **un edificio de tres ~s** a three-storey o (*EEUU*) -story building ➤ **planta baja** ground (*Brit*) o first (*EEUU*) floor **2** (*Arquit*) (= *plano*) ground plan; **construir un edificio de (nueva) ~** to build a completely new building **3** (*tb ~ del pie*) the sole of the foot **4** (= *aspecto*) **de buena ~** fine-looking **5** (= *fábrica*) plant ➤ **planta depuradora** water purification plant **6** (*Baile, Esgrima*) position (of the feet)

plantación SF **1** (= *acción*) planting **2** (= *terreno cultivado*) plantation

plantado ADJ **1** (*Bot*) planted (**de** with) **2 dejar ~ a algn*** (*en una cita*) to stand sb up*; (*en relación sentimental*) to dump sb*, ditch sb*; (*en situación difícil*) to leave sb in the lurch*, leave sb high and dry; (*mientras se habla*) to leave sb in mid-sentence **3** (*) (= *de pie*) standing; **sigue ahí ~** he's still standing there **4 bien ~*** (= *persona*) fine-looking

plantar /1a/ Ⓐ VT **1** (*Bot*) [+ *árbol, bulbo, jardín*] to plant;

[+ *semilla*] to plant, sow
2 (= *colocar*) [+ *estaca, poste*] to put, stick; ✦ MODISMO **~ el pie en** to set foot in
3 (*) (= *dar*) [+ *beso*] to plant; [+ *insulto*] to hurl; **~ una bofetada a algn** to slap sb*; ✦ MODISMO **~ cara a** [+ *persona, críticas*] to stand up to; [+ *problema*] to face up to, confront
4 (*) (= *abandonar*) (*en una cita*) to stand up*; [+ *novio*] to dump*, ditch*; [+ *actividad, estudios*] to pack in*, chuck in*
B plantarse VPR **1** (= *colocarse*) to plant o.s., plonk o.s. (*Brit**), plunk o.s. (*EEUU**)
2 (= *llegar*) **~se en** to get to, make it to; **en tres horas se plantó en Sevilla** he got to *o* made it to Seville in three hours
3 (= *mantenerse firme*) **~se en** to stick to; **se plantó en su decisión** she stuck to her decision
4 (= *detenerse*) [*caballo*] to stop dead, pull up short
5 (*Naipes*) to stick

plante SM stoppage, protest strike

planteamiento SM **1** (= *exposición*) [*de novela, película*] first part, exposition (*frm*); **el ~ del problema** (*Mat*) the way the problem is set out **2** (= *punto de vista*) approach; **un ~ nuevo de la cuestión** a new way of looking at *o* approaching the issue; **sus ~s estéticos** his aesthetics

plantear /1a/ **A** VT **1** (= *exponer*) **1.1** [+ *situación, problema*] to bring up, raise; **no me atrevo a ~les el tema a mis padres** I don't dare bring up *o* raise the issue with my parents; **planteado el problema en estos términos ...** with the problem expressed *o* put in these terms ... **1.2** (*Mat*) [+ *ecuación, problema*] to set out
2 (= *proponer*) [+ *cambio, posibilidad*] to suggest
3 (= *causar*) [+ *problema*] to pose, create
B plantearse VPR **1** (= *cuestionarse*) to think about, consider; **yo me planteo la vida como una lucha por sobrevivir** I see life as a struggle for survival; **~se hacer algo** to think of doing sth, consider doing sth

Recuérdese que las preposiciones en inglés rigen gerundio y no infinitivo, de ahí **to think of doing sth.** **Consider** también rige gerundio.

2 (= *presentarse*) [*cuestión, problema*] to arise, come up; **esa cuestión volverá a ~se en el futuro** this question will arise *o* come up again in the future; **en el futuro se nos ~á el mismo dilema** we will be faced with the same dilemma in the future

plantel SM **1** (= *grupo*) **un ~ de jóvenes pintoras** a group of young painters; **un excelente ~ de actores** an excellent pool of actors **2** (*Bot*) nursery **3** (*LAm*) (= *escuela*) school

plantificar* /1g/ **A** VT (= *colocar*) to plonk down (*Brit**), plunk down (*EEUU**), dump down* **B plantificarse** VPR (*en un lugar*) to plant* o.s.

plantilla SF **1** [*de zapato*] inner sole, insole; [*de media*] sole **2** (*Téc*) pattern, template **3** (*Esp*) (= *personas*) staff; **estar en ~** to be on the payroll

plantío SM bed, patch

plantón SM **1** (*) (= *espera*) long wait; **dar (un) ~ a algn** to stand sb up*; **tener a algn de ~** to keep sb waiting **2** (*Méx*) (*de protesta*) sit-in

plañidera SF (paid) mourner

plañidero ADJ mournful, plaintive

plañir /3h/ VT to mourn, grieve over

plaqueta SF platelet

plasma SM plasma

plasmación SF shape, form

plasmar /1a/ **A** VT (*en cuadro, poema*) to capture; (*en estudio, informe*) to embody; **sus ideas quedaron plasmadas en un manifiesto** his ideas were embodied in a manifesto; **la novela plasma perfectamente la angustia del autor** the novel captures *o* reflects the author's anguish perfectly **B plasmarse** VPR **~se en algo** to manifest itself in sth

plasta **A** SF (= *masa*) soft mass, lump **B** SMF (*) (= *pelmazo*) bore **C** ADJ INV boring

plástica SF plastic art, (art of) sculpture and modelling *o* (*EEUU*) modeling

plasticidad SF **1** [*de material*] plasticity **2** (= *expresividad*) expressiveness

plasticina® SF (*CS*) Plasticine®

plástico **A** ADJ **1** (*gen*) plastic; **artes plásticas** plastic arts **2** [*imagen*] expressive; [*descripción*] rich, evocative **B** SM (= *material*) plastic

plastificar /1g/ VT to laminate

plastilina® SF Plasticine®

plata SF **1** (= *metal*) silver; (= *vajilla*) silverware; ✦ MODISMO **hablar en ~** to speak bluntly, speak frankly **2** (*SAm*) (= *dinero*) money; **podrido en ~*** stinking rich*, rolling in it*

platada SF (*Chi*) dish, plateful

plataforma SF **1** (*gen*) platform; **zapatos de ~** platforms, platform shoes ➤ **plataforma continental** continental shelf ➤ **plataforma de lanzamiento** launch pad, launching pad ➤ **plataforma digital** (*TV*) digital platform ➤ **plataforma petrolífera** oil rig **2** (*Pol*) (*tb* **~ electoral**) (= *partido*) platform; (= *programa*) programme **3** (*fig*) (*para lograr algo*) springboard

platal* SM (*LAm*) fortune

platanal SM, **platanar** SM banana plantation

platanero/a **A** ADJ banana *antes de s* **B** SM/F banana grower

plátano SM **1** (= *fruta dulce*) banana; (= *árbol*) banana tree; (*para cocinar*) plantain **2** (= *árbol ornamental*) plane (tree)

platea SF stalls *pl* (*Brit*), orchestra (section) (*EEUU*)

plateado ADJ [*color, objeto*] silver; [*cabello*] silver, silvery; [*brillo*] silvery; (*Téc*) silver-plated

platear /1a/ **A** VT (*Téc*) to silver-plate, silver **B** VI to turn silver

plateresco ADJ plateresque

platería SF **1** (= *arte*) silversmith's craft **2** (= *tienda*) silversmith's **3** (= *objetos*) silverware, silver

platero/a SM/F silversmith

plática SF (*esp Méx*) talk, chat; **estar de ~** to be chatting, be having a talk

platicar /1g/ **A** VI (= *charlar*) to talk, chat **B** VT (*Méx*) (= *decir*) to tell

platija SF plaice, flounder

platillo SM **1** (= *plato*) (*gen*) small plate; (*para taza*) saucer; [*de limosnas*] collecting bowl; [*de balanza*] pan; **pasar el ~** to pass the hat round ➤ **platillo volador** (*LAm*), **platillo volante** (*Esp*) flying saucer **2** (*platillos*) (*Mús*) cymbals **3** (*CAm, Méx*) (*en menú*) course; (= *guiso*) dish; **el tercer ~** the third course

platina SF **1** [*de microscopio*] slide **2** (*Mús*) [*de tocadiscos*] deck; [*de casete*] tape (deck); **doble ~** twin deck **3** (*Tip*) platen

platino **A** SM **1** (= *metal*) platinum **2** (*platinos*) (*Aut*) contact points **B** ADJ **rubia ~** *o* (*LAm*) **platinada** platinum blonde

plato SM **1** (= *recipiente*) (*para comer*) plate; (*de balanza*) pan; **fregar los ~s** to wash *o* do the dishes, wash up; ✦ MODISMOS **pagar los ~s rotos** to carry the can*; **estar en el ~ y en la tajada** to have one's cake and eat it ➤ **plato hondo** soup dish, soup plate ➤ **plato llano**, **plato playo** (*Arg*) dinner plate
2 (= *contenido del plato*) plate, plateful; **un ~ de paella** a plate *o* plateful of paella
3 (*Culin*) (*en menú*) course; (= *guiso*) dish; **un menú de tres ~s** a three-course meal; **es mi ~ favorito** it's my favourite dish ➤ **plato central** (*Ven*) main course ➤ **plato fuerte** (= *comida*) main course; (= *tema*) main topic, central theme ➤ **plato precocinado** pre-cooked meal ➤ **plato preparado** ready-to-serve meal ➤ **plato principal** main course
4 [*de tocadiscos*] turntable
5 ➤ **plato de (la) ducha** shower tray
6 (*Dep*) **tiro al ~** clay pigeon shooting
7 (*SAm**) (= *persona divertida*) (good) laugh*

plató SM set

platónico ADJ platonic

platudo* ADJ (*SAm*) rich, well-heeled*

plausible ADJ 1 [*argumento, motivo*] acceptable, admissible 2 [*intento, esfuerzo*] commendable, praiseworthy

playa SF 1 (= *orilla del mar*) beach 2 (= *costa*) seaside 3 ➤ **playa de estacionamiento** (*CS, Perú*) car park (*Brit*), parking lot (*EEUU*)

playera SF 1 (*CAm, Méx*) (= *camiseta*) T-shirt 2 (= *zapatilla*) canvas shoe; [*de tenis*] tennis shoe

playero ADJ 1 [*ropa*] beach *antes de s* 2 [*persona*] **es muy ~** he loves going down the beach

plaza SF 1 (*entre calles*) square ➤ **plaza de armas** parade ground ➤ **plaza de toros** bullring ➤ **plaza mayor** main square 2 (= *mercado*) market, market place 3 (= *espacio*) [*de vehículo*] seat; **un vehículo de dos ~s** a two-seater vehicle ➤ **plaza de garaje** parking space (*in garage*) ➤ **plaza hotelera** hotel bed 4 (= *puesto de trabajo*) (*gen*) post; (*vacante*) vacancy 5 (†) (= *ciudad*) town, city 6 (*tb* ~ **fuerte**) (*Mil*) fortress, fortified town; (*Pol*) stronghold

plazo SM 1 (= *período*) period; **dentro del ~ previsto** within the specified period; **nos dan un ~ de ocho días** they've given us eight days; **¿cuándo vence el ~?** when is the deadline?; **a ~ fijo** (*Com*) fixed-term; **a corto ~** (*adj*) short-term; (*adv*) in the short term; **a largo ~** (*adj*) long-term; (*adv*) in the long term 2 (= *pago*) instalment, installment (*EEUU*), payment; **pagar algo a ~s** pay for sth in instalments *o* (*EEUU*) installments

plazoleta SF, **plazuela** SF small square

pleamar SF high tide

plebe SF **la ~** (*gen*) the masses *pl*; (*pey*) the mob, the rabble, the plebs* *pl* (*pey*)

plebeyo/a ADJ, SM/F plebeian

plebiscito SM plebiscite

plectro SM plectrum

plegable ADJ [*mesa, cama*] folding, collapsible

plegamiento SM 1 (*Geol*) fold 2 [*de camión*] jack-knifing

plegar /1h, 1j/ **Ⓐ** VT 1 (= *doblar*) to fold 2 (*Cos*) to pleat **Ⓑ plegarse** VPR 1 (= *someterse*) to yield, submit (**a** to) 2 [*mesa, cama*] to fold away 3 (*SAm*) (= *unirse*) **~se a algo** to join in (with) sth

plegaria SF prayer

pleitear /1a/ VI 1 (*Jur*) to go to court; **~ con** *o* **contra algn** to take sb to court 2 (*esp LAm**) (= *reñir*) to argue

pleitesía SF **rendir ~ a algn** to show respect for sb, show sb courtesy

pleito SM 1 (*Jur*) lawsuit, case; **pleitos** litigation *sing*; **poner ~ a algn** to bring an action against sb, take sb to court 2 (= *litigio*) dispute 3 (*esp LAm*) (= *discusión*) quarrel, argument; (= *pelea*) fight, brawl; **estar** *o* **andar de ~** (*Méx*) to be arguing 4 (*LAm Boxeo*) fight, bout

plenamente ADJ [*consciente, recuperado*] fully; [*satisfecho*] completely; **me satisface ~** it gives me complete satisfaction; **acertó ~** he was absolutely right; **vivir la vida ~** to live life to the full

plenario ADJ plenary, full

plenilunio SM full moon

plenipotenciario/a ADJ, SM/F plenipotentiary

plenitud SF **estaba en la ~ de la vida** he was in the prime of life

pleno **Ⓐ** ADJ full; **~ empleo** full employment; **en ~ día** ◊ **a plena luz del día** in broad daylight; **en ~ verano** in the middle of the summer; **vive en ~ centro** he lives right in the center; **en plena vista** in full view **Ⓑ** SM 1 (= *reunión*) plenary, plenary session 2 (*Esp*) (*en quinielas*) maximum *number of points* 3 **en ~:** asistió el gobierno **en ~ al funeral** the entire Cabinet attended the funeral

pleonástico ADJ pleonastic

pletina SF = **platina**

plétora SF (*frm*) plethora (*frm*), abundance

pletórico ADJ **~ de** [+ *energía, entusiasmo*] full of, bursting with; [+ *ilusiones*] full of; [+ *felicidad, salud*] bursting with

pleuresía SF pleurisy

plexiglás® SM Perspex® (*Brit*), Plexiglas® (*EEUU*)

plexo SM (*Anat*) ➤ **plexo solar** solar plexus

pliego SM (= *hoja de papel*) sheet; (*Tip*) section, signature ➤ **pliego de cargos** list of accusations ➤ **pliego de condiciones** specifications *pl* (of a tender) ➤ **pliego de descargo** evidence (for the defendant)

pliegue SM 1 (= *doblez*) fold, crease 2 (*Cos*) pleat 3 (*Geol*) fold

plinto SM plinth

plisado **Ⓐ** ADJ pleated **Ⓑ** SM pleating

plisar /1a/ VT to pleat

plomada SF 1 (*Arquit*) plumb 2 (*Náut*) lead 3 (*Pesca*) weights *pl*, sinkers *pl*

plomazo* SM 1 (= *pelmazo*) bore 2 (*CAm, Méx*) (= *tiro*) shot

plomería SF (*LAm*) plumbing

plomero/a SM/F (*LAm*) plumber

plomífero* ADJ deadly boring

plomizo ADJ [*cielo*] leaden (*liter*), grey, gray (*EEUU*)

plomo SM 1 (= *metal*) lead; **gasolina sin ~** unleaded petrol (*Brit*) *o* gasoline (*EEUU*); **soldadito de ~** tin soldier 2 (= *plomada*) [*de albañil*] plumb line; [*de pesca*] weight, sinker; **a ~** true, vertical(ly); **caer a ~** to fall heavily *o* flat 3 (*Esp Elec*) fuse; ✦ MODISMO **se le fundieron los ~s** he blew his top* 4 (*) (= *pesadez*) bore

plugo, pluguiere *etc ver* **placer**[1]

pluma SF 1 [*de ave*] feather; (*como adorno*) plume, feather; **colchón de ~s** feather bed; ✦ MODISMOS **tener ~** (*Esp**) to be camp 2 (*para escribir*) [*de metal, plástico*] pen; [*de ave*] quill; **escribir algo a vuela ~** to scribble sth down ➤ **pluma atómica** (*Méx*) ballpoint pen ➤ **pluma estilográfica, pluma fuente** (*LAm*) fountain pen 3 (*Bol**) (= *prostituta*) prostitute 4 (*Col, Méx*) (= *grifo*) tap (*Brit*), faucet (*EEUU*)

plumaje SM 1 (*Orn*) plumage, feathers *pl* 2 (= *adorno*) plume, crest

plumazo SM stroke of the pen; ✦ MODISMO **de un ~** at a stroke

plúmbeo ADJ 1 (= *de plomo*) leaden (*liter*) 2 (= *que pesa mucho*) weighty, heavy 3 (= *aburrido*) boring, dull

plumero SM 1 (*para limpiar*) feather duster; ✦ MODISMO **se le ve el ~*** you can see what his game is* 2 (= *portaplumas*) penholder; (= *estuche*) pencil case

plumier SM pencil case

plumífero SM quilted anorak

plumilla SF 1 (*de pluma*) nib 2 (*Dep*) shuttle cock

plumín SM nib

plumón SM 1 (*Orn*) down 2 (= *edredón*) continental quilt, duvet (*Brit*), comforter (*EEUU*); (= *saco de dormir*) quilted sleeping bag 3 (*Esp*) (= *abrigo*) quilted jacket 4 (*Chi*) (= *rotulador*) felt-tip pen

plural **Ⓐ** ADJ 1 (*Ling*) plural 2 (= *diversos*) many **Ⓑ** SM plural; **en ~** in the plural

pluralidad SF plurality

pluralismo SM pluralism

pluralista ADJ pluralist, pluralistic

pluralizar /1f/ VT 1 (*Ling*) to pluralize 2 (= *generalizar*) to generalize

pluriempleado/a **Ⓐ** ADJ having more than one job **Ⓑ** SM/F person with more than one job, moonlighter*

pluriempleo SM having more than one job, moonlighting*

plus SM bonus ➤ **plus de antigüedad** seniority bonus ➤ **plus de nocturnidad** extra pay for unsocial hours ➤ **plus de peligrosidad** danger money ➤ **plus de productividad** productivity bonus

pluscuamperfecto SM pluperfect, past perfect

plusmarca SF record; **batir la ~** to break the record

plusmarquista SMF (= *poseedor*) record holder;

(= *que mejora*) record-breaker

plusvalía SF (*gen*) appreciation, added value; [*de capital*] capital gain

plutocracia SF plutocracy

plutócrata SMF plutocrat

Plutón SM Pluto

plutonio SM plutonium

pluvial ADJ rain *antes de s*

pluviómetro SM rain gauge, pluviometer

pluviosidad SF rainfall

p.m. ABR (= *post meridiem*) pm

PNB SM ABR (= **producto nacional bruto**) GNP

PNV SM ABR (*Esp Pol*) = **Partido Nacionalista Vasco**

P.° ABR (= **Paseo**) Ave, Av.

p.o. ABR = **por orden**

poblacho SM dump, one-horse town

población SF 1 (= *gente*) population ➤ **población activa** working population ➤ **población marginada** marginalized sectors of society *pl* 2 (= *lugar habitado, ciudad*) town; (= *pueblo*) village ➤ **población callampa** (*Chi*) shanty town

poblado Ⓐ ADJ 1 (= *habitado*) inhabited; **poco/densamente** ~ sparsely/densely populated 2 ~ **de** (= *lleno*) full of; (= *cubierto*) covered with 3 [*barba, cejas*] bushy, thick Ⓑ SM (= *pueblo*) village; (= *población*) town; (= *lugar habitado*) settlement; (*Aut*) built-up area

poblador(a) SM/F 1 (= *colonizador*) settler 2 (*Chi*) slum dweller

poblar /1l/ Ⓐ VT 1 [*colonos, conquistadores*] to settle, populate; [*animales, plantas*] to inhabit 2 ~ **una colmena** (*Agr*) to stock a beehive; ~**on el monte de abetos** they planted the trees with fir trees Ⓑ **poblarse** VPR 1 (= *llenarse*) to fill (**de** with) 2 (*Bot*) (= *cubrirse de hojas*) to come into leaf

pobre Ⓐ ADJ 1 [*persona, familia, barrio*] poor 2 (= *escaso*) poor; **una dieta** ~ **en vitaminas** a diet poor in vitamins 3 (*indicando compasión*) poor; **¡~ hombre!** poor man!, poor fellow!; **¡~ Francisco!** poor old Francisco!; **¡~ de él!** poor man!, poor fellow!; **¡~ de ti si te pillo!** you'll be sorry if I catch you!; ~ **diablo** poor wretch, poor devil Ⓑ SMF 1 (= *necesitado*) poor person; (= *mendigo*) beggar; **un** ~ a poor man; **los** ~**s** the poor, poor people 2 (*indicando compasión*) poor thing

pobrecillo/a SM/F poor thing

pobreza SF 1 (= *falta de dinero*) poverty 2 (= *escasez*) ~ **de vocabulario** poverty of vocabulary 3 (*Rel*) **voto de** ~ vow of poverty

pocha SF (*Esp Culin*) haricot bean

pochar /1a/ VT, **pochear** /1a/ VT (*Culin*) to poach

pocho/a Ⓐ ADJ 1 (= *estropeado*) [*fruta*] soft, overripe; [*persona*] peaky (*Brit**), off-colour*, off-color (*EEUU**) 2 (= *deprimido*) depressed, gloomy Ⓑ SM/F (*Méx*) United States national of Mexican origin, Mexican-American

pochoclo SM (*Arg*) popcorn

pocholada* SF nice thing, pretty thing; **es una** ~ it's lovely; **una** ~ **de niño** a sweet *o* cute little baby

pocholo/a* Ⓐ ADJ nice, cute Ⓑ SM/F pretty boy/pretty girl; (*en oración directa*) my little angel, my poppet

pocilga SF 1 (= *porqueriza*) pigsty (*esp Brit*), pigpen (*EEUU*) 2 (= *lugar asqueroso*) pigsty (*esp Brit*), pigpen (*EEUU*)

pocillo SM 1 (= *tazón*) mug 2 (= *cuenco*) (small) bowl, (small) dish

pócima SF, **poción** SF 1 (*Farm*) potion, draught, draft (*EEUU*) 2 (= *brebaje*) concoction

poco Ⓐ ADJ 1 (*en singular*) little, not much; **tenemos** ~ **tiempo** we have little time, we don't have much time; **de** ~ **interés** of little interest

2 (*en plural*) few, not many; ~**s niños saben que ...** few *o* not many children know that ...; ~**s días después** a few days later; **compré unos** ~**s libros** I bought a few books; **todas las medidas son pocas** no measure will be enough Ⓑ PRON 1 (*en singular*) 1.1 (= *poca cosa*) **la reforma servirá**

para ~ the reform won't do much good *o* won't be much use; **una hora da para** ~ you can't get much done in an hour; **ya sabes lo** ~ **que me interesa** you know how little it interests me; **y por si fuera** ~ and as if that weren't enough, and to cap it all **1.2 un** ~ a bit, a little; **he bebido un** ~, **pero no estoy borracho** I've had a bit to drink, but I'm not drunk; **voy a dormir un** ~ I am going to have a little sleep; **espera un** ~ wait a minute *o* moment; **estoy un** ~ **triste** I am rather *o* a little sad; **es un** ~ **lo que yo comentaba** that's more or less what I was saying; **un** ~ **de**: **un** ~ **de dinero** a little money; **dame un** ~ **de vino** can I have some wine?; **¡un** ~ **de silencio!** let's have some quiet here! **1.3** (*referido a tiempo*) not long; **tardaron** ~ **en hacerlo** it didn't take them long to do it, they didn't take long to do it; **lleva** ~ **trabajando aquí** he hasn't been working here long; **a** ~ **de** shortly after; **a** ~ **de haberlo firmado** shortly after signing it; **dentro de** ~ shortly, soon; ~ **después** shortly after; **hace** ~ not long ago; **tu hermana ha llamado hace** ~ your sister called a short while ago; **hasta hace** ~ until recently

2 (*en plural*) few; ~**s son los que ...** there are few who ...

Ⓒ ADV 1 (*con verbos*) not much, little; **cuesta** ~ it doesn't cost much, it costs very little; **habla** ~ he doesn't say much

2 (*con adjetivos: se traduce a menudo por medio de un prefijo*) ~ **dispuesto a ayudar** disinclined to help; ~ **probable** unlikely; ~ **inteligente** unintelligent, not very intelligent; **sus libros son** ~ **conocidos aquí** his books are not very well known here

3 (*otras locuciones*) **a** ~ (*Méx**): **¿a** ~**?** never!, you don't say!; **¡a** ~ **no!** not much!*; **¿a** ~ **no?** (well) isn't it?; **¿a** ~ **crees que ...?** do you really imagine that ...?; **de a** ~ (*LAm*) gradually; ~ **más o menos** more or less; **por** ~ almost, nearly; **por** ~ **me ahogo** I almost *o* nearly drowned; **a** ~ **que**: **a** ~ **que pueda** if at all possible; **a** ~ **que corras, lo alcanzas** if you run now you'll catch it

poda SF 1 (= *acto*) pruning 2 (= *temporada*) pruning season

podadera SF (= *cuchillo*) pruning knife, billhook; (= *tijera*) pruning shears *pl*, secateurs *pl* (*Brit*)

podar /1a/ VT [+ *árbol*] to lop, prune; [+ *rama*] to lop, trim, trim off; [+ *rosal*] to prune

podenco SM hound

---

poder /2s/

Ⓐ VERBO AUXILIAR	Ⓒ VERBO IMPERSONAL
Ⓑ VERBO INTRANSITIVO	Ⓓ SUSTANTIVO MASCULINO

---

poder Ⓐ VERBO AUXILIAR

1 (= *tener la posibilidad o capacidad de*) **puedo hacerlo solo** I can do it on my own *o* by myself; **no puede venir** he can't *o* cannot come; **llevo varios días sin** ~ **salir** I haven't been able to go out for several days; **creo que mañana no voy a** ~ **ir** I don't think I'll be able to come tomorrow; **este agua no se puede beber** this water isn't fit to drink

2 (= *tener permiso para*) **puedes irte** you can *o* may go; **¿puedo abrir la ventana?** can *o* may I open the window?; **aquí no se puede fumar** you aren't allowed to smoke here, you can't smoke here

3 (*en peticiones*) **¿puedes/puede darme un vaso de agua?** can I/may I have a glass of water please?; **¿me puede usted decir cuándo sale el autobús?** can *o* could you tell me when the bus leaves?

4 (*indicando eventualidad*) **puede** *o* **podría estar en cualquier sitio** it could *o* might be anywhere; **¡cuidado, te puedes hacer daño!** careful, you could *o* might hurt yourself!; **por lo que pueda pasar** just in case

5 (*indicando obligación moral*) **¡no pueden tratarnos así!** they can't treat us like this!; **bien podrían cuidarla un poco mejor** they really ought to take better care of her; **no podíamos dejarlo solo** we couldn't leave him alone

6 (*en cálculos, aproximaciones*) **¿qué edad puede tener?** I wonder what age he is?, how old do you reckon he is?; **puede costar unos 50 euros** it could cost as much as 50 euros

7 (*en sugerencias*) **podríamos ir a la playa** we could go to the beach; **siempre puedes volverlo a intentar después** you can always try again later

8 (*en reproches*) **¡podías habérmelo dicho!** you could *o* might have told me!; **¡al menos podrías disculparte!** you could at least say sorry!
B VERBO INTRANSITIVO
1 (= *tener la posibilidad o capacidad*) **no puedo** I can't; **lo haré si puedo** I'll do it if I can; **¡no puedo más!** (= *estoy agotado*) I can't go on!; (= *estoy desesperado*) I can't cope any more!; (= *he comido mucho*) I can't eat another thing!
2 (= *tener permiso*) **¿se puede?** may I come in?; **¿puedo?** may I?
3 (= *tener dominio, influencia*) **los que pueden** those who can, those who are able; **yo le puedo** I'm a match for him; (*entre niños*) I could have him*
♦ **poder con: ¿puedes con la maleta?** can you manage the suitcase?; **no puedo con él** (= *no puedo controlarlo*) I can't handle him; (= *pesa mucho*) he's too heavy for me; **no puedo con la hipocresía** I can't stand hypocrisy
4 (*en locuciones*) **a más no ~: es tonto a más no ~** he's as stupid as they come; **comió a más no ~** he ate until he couldn't eat any more; **no ~ por menos que: no pude por menos que decirle lo que pensaba de él** I just had to tell him what I thought of him
5 (*CAm, Méx**) to upset; **me pudo esa broma** that joke upset me
C VERBO IMPERSONAL
♦ **puede (ser)** (= *es posible*) maybe, it may be so, perhaps; **¡no puede ser!** that can't be!, that's impossible!
♦ **puede (ser) que** + SUBJUN: **puede (ser) que esté en la biblioteca** he could *o* may be in the library, perhaps he's in the library; **puede (ser) que no venga** he may *o* might not come; **puede (ser) que tenga razón** she may *o* could be right; **puede (ser) que sí** maybe (so)
D SUSTANTIVO MASCULINO
1 (= *capacidad, facultad*) power; **tiene un enorme ~ de concentración** she has tremendous powers of concentration ➤ **poder adquisitivo** purchasing power ➤ **poder de convocatoria: tienen un gran ~ de convocatoria** they really pull in the crowds, they're real crowd-pullers*
2 (= *autoridad, influencia*) power; **¡el pueblo al ~!** power to the people!; **subir al ~** to come to power; **el ~ central** central government; **el cuarto ~** the fourth estate; **el ~ establecido** the establishment; **los ~es fácticos** the powers that be; **los ~es públicos** the authorities ➤ **poder absoluto** absolute power ➤ **poder ejecutivo** executive power ➤ **poder judicial** judiciary ➤ **poder legislativo** legislative power
3 (= *potestad*) **poderes** powers; **les dieron amplios ~es para dirigir la empresa** they were given wide-ranging powers to run the company; **tiene plenos ~es para intervenir en el asunto** he has full authority to intervene in the matter
4 (*Jur*) **por ~es** *o* (*LAm*) **poder** by proxy; **casarse por ~es** to get married by proxy
5 (= *posesión*) possession; **tengo en mi ~ información confidencial** I am in possession of confidential information; **estar** *u* **obrar en ~ de algn** to be in sb's hands *o* possession
6 (*Fís, Mec*) power

poderío SM (= *poder*) power; (= *fuerza*) might; (= *señorío*) authority, jurisdiction

poderoso A ADJ powerful **B** SMPL **los ~s** (= *dirigentes*) the people in power; (= *ricos*) the rich and powerful

podio SM podium; **subir al ~** to mount the winners' podium

pódium SM (*pl* **~s**) = **podio**

podología SF chiropody (*Brit*), podiatry (*EEUU*)

podólogo/a SM/F chiropodist (*Brit*), podiatrist (*EEUU*)

podredumbre SF **1** (= *cualidad*) rottenness, putrefaction; (= *parte podrida*) rot **2** (= *corrupción*) rottenness, corruption

podrida SF **armar la ~** (*RPl**) to start a fight

podrido ADJ **1** (= *putrefacto*) rotten **2** (= *corrupto*) rotten, corrupt; **están ~s de dinero*** they're filthy rich* **3** (*RPl**) (= *harto*) fed-up*

podrir /3a/ = **pudrir**

poema SM poem; ♦ MODISMO **ser todo un ~** to be quite a sight

poesía SF **1** (= *arte*) poetry **2** (= *poema*) poem

poeta SMF poet

poética SF poetics *sing*, art of poetry

poético ADJ poetic, poetical

poetisa SF poetess, woman poet

póker SM poker

polaco¹/a A ADJ Polish **B** SM/F Pole **C** SM Polish

polaco²/a* (*pey*) ADJ, SM/F Catalan

polaina SF leggings *pl*

polar ADJ polar

polaridad SF polarity

polarización SF polarization

polarizar /1f/ **A** VT to polarize **B** **polarizarse** VPR to polarize, become polarized (**en torno a** around)

polca SF polka

pólder SM (*pl* **~s**) polder

polea SF (*Téc*) pulley; (*Náut*) tackle, tackle block

polémica SF controversy

polémico ADJ controversial, polemical (*frm*)

polemizar /1f/ VI to argue; **no quiero ~** I have no wish to get involved in an argument

polen SM pollen

poleo SM pennyroyal

polera SF **1** (*Chi*) (= *camiseta*) T-shirt **2** (*RPl*) (= *jersey*) polo neck (*esp Brit*), turtleneck (*EEUU*)

poli* **A** SMF cop* **B** SF **la ~** the cops* *pl*

poliamida SM polyamide

policía A SMF policeman/policewoman, police officer ➤ **policía acostado** (*Ven*) speed ramp ➤ **policía de paisano** plain-clothes policeman ➤ **policía informático/a** *policeman specializing in computer crime* ➤ **policía local, policía municipal** local policeman/policewoman **B** SF (= *organización*) police ➤ **policía antidisturbios** riot police ➤ **policía de barrio** community police ➤ **policía de tráfico, policía de tránsito** (*LAm*) traffic police ➤ **policía municipal** local police (*in charge of traffic and local matters*) ➤ **policía nacional** national police ➤ **policía secreta** secret police

policiaco ADJ, **policíaco** ADJ **novela policíaca** detective story

policial ADJ police *antes de s*

policlínica SF, **policlínico** SM general hospital

policromado ADJ polychrome

policromo ADJ, **polícromo** ADJ polychromatic, polychrome

polideportivo SM sports centre, sports center (*EEUU*)

poliedro SM polyhedron

poliéster SM polyester

polietileno SM polythene (*esp Brit*), polyethylene (*EEUU*)

polifacético ADJ multi-faceted, versatile

polifonía SF polyphony

polifónico ADJ polyphonic

poligamia SF polygamy

polígamo A ADJ polygamous **B** SM polygamist

políglota ADJ, SMF, **polígloto(a)** ADJ, SM/F polyglot

poligonal ADJ polygonal

polígono SM **1** (*Mat*) polygon **2** (*Esp*) (= *terreno*) building lot ➤ **polígono industrial** industrial estate (*Brit*) *o* park (*EEUU*)

poliinsaturado ADJ polyunsaturated

polilla SF [*de ropa*] moth; [*de la madera*] woodworm

Polinesia SF Polynesia

polinesio/a ADJ, SM/F Polynesian

polinización SF pollination

polio SF polio

poliomielitis SF INV poliomyelitis

polipiel® SF imitation leather

pólipo SM polyp, polypus

polipropileno SM polypropylene

Polisario SM ABR (*tb* **El Frente ~**) = Frente Popular de Liberación del Sáhara y Río de Oro

polisemia SF polysemy

polisémico ADJ polysemic

politeísmo SM polytheism

politeísta ADJ polytheistic

política SF 1 (= *ciencia*) politics *sing*; **meterse en ~** to get involved in politics 2 (= *programa*) policy ➤ **política agraria** agricultural policy ➤ **política económica** economic policy ➤ **política exterior** foreign policy ➤ **política interior** domestic policy

políticamente ADV politically; **~ correcto** politically correct

político/a Ⓐ ADJ 1 (*Pol*) political 2 (= *diplomático*) tactful 3 (*pariente*) **padre ~** father-in-law; **familia política** in-laws *pl* Ⓑ SM/F politician

politización SF politicization

poliuretano SM polyurethane

polivalente ADJ (*Quím, Med*) polyvalent 2 (= *versátil*) multi-purpose

polivinilo SM polyvinyl

póliza SF 1 (*tb* **~ de seguro(s)**) insurance policy 2 (= *impuesto*) tax stamp, fiscal stamp

polizón SM stowaway; **viajar de ~** to stow away (**en** on)

polizonte** SM cop*

polla SF 1 (*Esp****) (= *pene*) prick***; ✦ MODISMOS **¡una ~!** like hell!**; **¿qué ~s quieres?** what the hell do you want?** 2 (*CS, Col*) (= *apuesta*) bet 3 (*Chi*) (= *lotería*) lottery; (*Perú*) (= *quiniela*) pools (*Brit*), sports lottery (*EEUU*)

pollada SF (*Orn*) brood

pollera SF (*CS*) (= *falda*) skirt, overskirt

pollería SF poulterer's (shop)

pollero/a SM/F 1 (= *criador*) chicken farmer; (= *vendedor*) poulterer 2 (*Méx**) (= *guía*) guide for illegal immigrants to USA

pollino/a SM/F donkey

pollita* SF (= *chica*) chick**, bird (*Brit***)

pollito/a SM/F chick

pollo SM 1 (*Orn*) (= *adulto*) chicken; (= *cría*) chick; (*Culin*) chicken; **~ asado** o (*LAm*) **rostizado** roast chicken; ✦ MODISMO **montar un ~** (*Esp*) to make a fuss, make a scene ➤ **pollo de corral** free-range chicken ➤ **pollo de granja** broiler chicken 2 (*) (= *joven*) young lad; **¿quién es ese ~?** who's that young lad?*

polluelo SM chick

polo¹ SM 1 (*Geog*) pole ➤ **polo magnético** magnetic pole ➤ **Polo Norte** North Pole ➤ **Polo Sur** South Pole 2 (*Elec*) [*de imán*] pole; [*de enchufe*] pin ➤ **polo negativo** negative pole ➤ **polo positivo** positive pole 3 (= *centro*) centre, center (*EEUU*), focus ➤ **polo de atracción** centre o (*EEUU*) center of attraction 4 (= *extremo*) **son ~s opuestos** they are poles apart; **esto es el ~ opuesto de lo que dijo antes** this is the exact opposite of what he said before 5 (*Esp*) (= *helado*) ice lolly (*Brit*), Popsicle® (*EEUU*)

polo² SM (*Dep*) polo

polo³ SM polo shirt

pololear* /1a/ (*Chi*) VI to be in a relationship; **llevamos dos años pololeando** we've been going out for two years; **~ con algn** to be going out with sb, be dating sb*

pololo/a* SM/F (*Chi*) boyfriend/girlfriend

polonesa SF polonaise

Polonia SF Poland

poltrona SF easy chair

polución SF (= *contaminación*) pollution ➤ **polución nocturna** nocturnal emission (*frm*), wet dream

polvareda SF cloud of dust; ✦ MODISMO **levantar una ~** to create a storm, cause a rumpus*

polvera SF powder compact

polvero SM (*LAm*) cloud of dust

polvo SM 1 (*en el aire*) dust; **lleno de ~** dusty; **limpiar** o **quitar el ~** to dust; ✦ MODISMOS **hacer algo ~** to ruin sth; **hacer ~ a algn*** (= *agotar*) to wear sb out; (= *deprimir*) to depress sb; **hecho ~***: **estoy hecho ~** (= *cansado*) I'm shattered*, I'm knackered**; (= *deprimido*) I feel really down; **el coche está hecho ~** the car is a wreck; **el libro está hecho ~** the book is falling to pieces; **hacer morder el ~ a algn** to humiliate sb 2 (*Quím, Culin, Med*) powder; [*de tocador*] face powder; **ponerse ~s** to powder one's face; **en ~** [*leche, canela*] powdered ➤ **polvos de arroz** rice powder *sing* ➤ **polvos de picapica** itching powder *sing* ➤ **polvos de talco** talcum powder *sing* 3 (***) screw***, shag***; **echar un ~** to have a screw o shag***

pólvora SF 1 (= *explosivo*) gunpowder; ✦ MODISMOS **no ha descubierto** o **inventado la ~** it's not as if he's done anything amazingly original; **propagarse como la ~** to spread like wildfire 2 (= *fuegos artificiales*) fireworks *pl*

polvoriento ADJ dusty

polvorín SM 1 (*Mil*) (= *almacén*) arsenal 2 (= *situación peligrosa*) powder keg

polvorón SM *type of light, crumbly shortbread especially eaten at Christmas*

polvorosa SF ✦ MODISMO **poner pies en ~*** to beat it*, scarper*

pomada SF cream, ointment; ✦ MODISMO **hacer algo ~** (*Méx, RPl**) to break sth to bits, ruin sth

pomelo SM grapefruit, pomelo (*EEUU*)

pómez SF **piedra ~** pumice (stone)

pomo SM 1 [*de puerta*] knob, handle; [*de espada*] pommel 2 (= *frasco*) perfume bottle, scent bottle (*esp Brit*)

pompa SF 1 (= *burbuja*) bubble ➤ **pompa de jabón** soap bubble 2 (= *fasto*) pomp, splendour, splendor (*EEUU*) ➤ **pompas fúnebres** (= *cortejo*) funeral procession *sing*; (= *funeraria*) undertaker's *sing*, funeral parlour *sing* (*Brit*), funeral parlor *sing* (*EEUU*) 3 **pompas** (*Méx**) (= *trasero*) bottom, behind*, butt (*esp EEUU***)

Pompeya SF Pompeii

pompis* SM INV (*Esp*) bottom, behind*, butt (*esp EEUU***)

pomposo ADJ (= *espléndido*) splendid, magnificent; (= *ostentoso*) pompous

pómulo SM (= *hueso*) cheekbone; (= *mejilla*) cheek

ponchada SF (*RPl*) large quantity, large amount; **costó una ~** it cost a bomb*

ponchadura SF (*Méx*) puncture, flat (*EEUU*)

ponchar /1a/ Ⓐ VT (*Méx*) 1 [+ *llanta*] to puncture 2 [+ *boleto*] to punch Ⓑ **poncharse** VPR (*Méx*) [*llanta, balón*] to puncture

ponche SM punch

poncho SM poncho

ponderación SF 1 (*al decir algo*) (= *contrapeso*) weighing, consideration; (= *cuidado*) deliberation 2 (= *alabanza*) high praise 3 [*de índice*] weighting

ponderado ADJ 1 (= *alabado*) praised 2 (= *equilibrado*) balanced 3 (*Estadística*) weighted

ponderar /1a/ VT 1 (= *alabar*) to praise highly, speak highly of 2 (= *considerar*) to weigh up, consider 3 (*Estadística*) to weight

pondré *etc ver* **poner**

ponedora ADJ **gallina ~** laying hen; **ser buena ~** to be a good layer

ponencia SF 1 (= *comunicación*) (learned) paper, communication 2 (= *comisión*) committee, board

ponente SMF speaker (*at a conference*)

poner /2q/

Ⓐ VERBO TRANSITIVO Ⓒ VERBO PRONOMINAL
Ⓑ VERBO INTRANSITIVO

Para las expresiones **poner cuidado, poner en duda, poner por las nubes, poner a parir, poner como un trapo, poner verde, poner de vuelta y media, poner por testigo, ponerse por delante** *etc, ver la entrada correspondiente a la otra palabra.*

poner Ⓐ VERBO TRANSITIVO
1 (= *colocar, situar*) to put; **pon los libros en la estantería** put the books on the shelf; **han puesto un anuncio en el periódico** they've put an advertisement in the paper; **voy a ~ las patatas** I'm going to put the potatoes on; **ponle un poco de mantequilla y verás qué bueno** put some butter in it and you'll see how good it is; **ponlo al sol** leave *o* put it out in the sun; ~ **algo a secar** to put sth out to dry; **ponlo en su sitio** put it back
2 [+ *ropa, calzado*] to put on; **le pusieron un vestido nuevo** they dressed her in a new dress; **ponle los zapatos** can you put his shoes on?
3 (= *añadir*) to add; **ponle más sal** add some salt, put some more salt in it
4 (= *aplicar, administrar*) to put; **le pusieron una tirita en la herida** they put a plaster on her wound; **le han puesto muchas inyecciones** she's been given a lot of injections
5 (= *disponer, preparar*) **pon cubiertos para 12 personas** set the table for 12 people; ~ **la mesa** to set *o* (*esp Brit*) lay the table
6 (= *instalar*)
6.1 [+ *teléfono, calefacción*] to put in; **queremos ~ moqueta** we want to have a carpet fitted
6.2 [+ *tienda*] to open; [+ *casa*] to furnish
7 (= *hacer funcionar*) [+ *radio, televisión, calefacción*] to put on, turn on; [+ *disco*] to put on, play; **¿pongo música?** shall I put some music on?
8 (= *ajustar*) [+ *despertador*] to set; **pon el horno al máximo** put the oven on maximum; ~ **el reloj en hora** to put one's watch right; **ponlo más alto** turn it up
9 (= *adoptar*) **¿por qué pones esa voz?** why are you talking like that?; **puso acento francés** she put on a French accent; **¡no pongas esa cara!** don't look at me like that!; **puso muy mala cara cuando se lo dije** he looked very annoyed when I told him
10 (= *volver*) (+ ADJ, ADV) to make; **me pone furiosa** he makes me mad; **para no ~le de mal humor** so as not to make him cross, so as not to put him in a bad mood; **la has puesto colorada** you've made her blush; **¡cómo te han puesto!** (= *te han manchado*) look what a mess you are!; (= *te han pegado*) they've given you a right thumping!
11 (*Esp*) (= *servir*) **¿qué te pongo?** what can I get you?, what would you like?; **¿me pones más patatas?** could I have some more potatoes?
12 (*Esp*) (= *conectar por teléfono*) to put through; **¿me pone con el Sr. García, por favor?** could you put me through to Mr García, please?; **en seguida le pongo** I'll put you through; **te pongo con Pedro** (*al mismo teléfono*) I'll put you on to Pedro; (*a distinto teléfono*) I'll put you through to Pedro
13 (*Esp*) (= *exhibir*) **¿qué ponen en el cine?** what's on at the cinema (*esp Brit*) *o* movie theater (*EEUU*)?; **¿ponen alguna película esta noche?** is there a film (*esp Brit*) *o* movie (*esp EEUU*) on tonight?
14 (= *enviar*) [+ *telegrama*] to send
15 (= *escribir*) to put; **¿qué pongo en la carta?** what shall I put in the letter?; **¿te has acordado de ~ el remite?** did you remember to put the return address on it?
16 (*Esp*) (= *decir, estar escrito*) to say; **¿qué pone aquí?** what does it say here?
17 (= *imponer*) [+ *examen, trabajo*] to give, set; **nos pone mucho trabajo** he gives *o* sets us a lot of work; **me han puesto una multa** I've been fined, I've been given a fine
18 (= *oponer*) [+ *inconvenientes*] to raise; **nos han puesto muchos problemas** they've put a lot of obstacles in our way; **le pone peros a todo** he's always finding fault with everything

19 (= *aportar, contribuir*) [+ *dinero*] **he puesto 25 euros de mi bolsillo** I put in 25 euros out of my own pocket; **yo pongo la bebida y vosotros el postre** I'll get the drink and you can get the dessert; **puso todos sus ahorros en aquel negocio** he put all his savings into that business
20 (= *llamar*) to call; **¿qué nombre** *o* **cómo le van a ~?** what are they going to call him?, what name are they giving him?
21 (= *calificar*) **te puso muy bien ante el jefe** she was very nice about you to the boss; **me han puesto muy bien esa película** I've heard that film (*esp Brit*) *o* movie (*esp EEUU*) is very good; **¡cómo te han puesto!** (= *te han criticado*) they had a real go at you!*; (= *te han alabado*) they were really nice about you!
22 (= *suponer*) **pongamos 120** let's say 120; **pongamos que ganas la lotería** suppose *o* supposing you win the lottery; ✦ MODISMO **~le*: ponle 20 minutos caminando** I reckon it's 20 minutes' walk*
23 ~ **a algn a** (+ INFIN): **nada más llegar nos pusieron a barrer** no sooner had we arrived than we were set to sweeping the floor; **puso a sus hijos a trabajar** she sent her children out to work
24 (*en trabajo*) ~ **a algn de**: **puso a su hija de sirvienta** she got her daughter a job as a servant; **lo han puesto de dependiente en una tienda** they got him a job as a shop assistant (*Brit*) *o* sales clerk (*EEUU*)
25 [*gallina*] [+ *huevos*] to lay
Ⓑ VERBO INTRANSITIVO [*aves*] to lay (eggs)
Ⓒ **ponerse** VERBO PRONOMINAL
1 (= *colocarse, situarse*) (*de pie*) to stand; (*sentado*) to sit; (*echado*) to lie; **se puso delante de la ventana** he stood in front of the window; **se ponía a mi lado en clase** he used to sit next to me in class; **póngase de lado** lie on your side; ~**se cómodo** to make o.s. comfortable; **ponte en mi lugar** put yourself in my place; **todos se pusieron de** *o* **en pie** everyone stood up; **se puso de rodillas** she knelt down
2 [+ *ropa, calzado, joyas*] to put on; **ponte las zapatillas** put your slippers on; **no sé qué ~me** I don't know what to wear
3 (= *aplicarse, administrarse*) **ponte más perfume** put some more perfume on; **te pones demasiado maquillaje** you wear too much make-up; **se puso un supositorio** he used a suppository
4 [*sol*] to set
5 (= *volverse*) (+ ADJ, ADV) ~**se enfermo/gordo** to get ill/fat; **se puso hecho una furia** he got absolutely furious; **¡no te pongas así!** don't be like that!; **¡qué guapa te has puesto!** you look lovely!; **en el agua se pone verde** it turns green in water
6 (*Esp*) (*al teléfono*) **dile que se ponga** tell him to come to *o* on the phone; **¿se puede ~ María, por favor?** could I speak to María, please?
7 (= *empezar*) ~**se a hacer algo** to start *o* begin to do sth, start *o* begin doing sth; **se va a ~ a llover** it's going to start raining; ~**se con algo: ahora me pongo con los deberes** I'm going to start on my homework now
8 (= *llenarse*) ~**se de algo: ¡cómo te has puesto de barro!** you're all covered in mud!; **nos hemos puesto bien de comida** we ate our fill
9 (*Esp*) (= *llegar*) ~**se en** to get to, reach; **se puso en Madrid en dos horas** he got to *o* reached Madrid in two hours
10 (= *emplearse*) **me puse a servir** I went into service; ~**se de conserje** to take a job as a janitor
11 ~**se bien con algn** to get on good terms with sb; (*pey*) to get in with sb; ~**se mal con algn** to get on the wrong side of sb
12 (**) (= *drogarse*) to get high**
13 (= *parecer*) **se me pone que ...** (*SAm*) (= *me parece*) it seems to me that ...

poney ['poni] SM (*pl* ~**s**) (*Esp*) pony

ponga *etc ver* **poner**

poni SM pony

ponible ADJ wearable

poniente Ⓐ ADJ west, western Ⓑ SM **1** (= *oeste*) west **2** (= *viento*) west wind

ponqué SM (*Col, Méx*) cake

pontevedrés ADJ of/from Pontevedra

pontificado SM papacy, pontificate

pontificar /1g/ VI to pontificate

pontífice SM pope, pontiff; **el Sumo Pontífice** the Supreme Pontiff

pontificio ADJ papal, pontifical

pontón SM **1** (= *barco*) pontoon; **puente de pontones** pontoon bridge **2** (= *puente*) bridge of planks **3** [*de hidroavión*] float

pony ['poni] SM (*pl* ~**s**) pony

ponzoña SF poison, venom

ponzoñoso ADJ [*ataque*] venomous, poisonous; [*propaganda*] poisonous; [*costumbre, idea*] pernicious

pop ADJ, SM (*Mús*) pop

popa SF stern; **a** ~ astern, abaft

pope SM **1** (*Rel*) priest of the Orthodox Church **2** (***) (= *líder*) guru, spiritual leader; (= *ídolo*) idol

popelín SM, **popelina** SF poplin

popof* ADJ INV (*Méx*), **popoff*** ADJ INV (*Méx*) posh*

popote SM (*Méx*) drinking straw

populachero ADJ **1** (= *plebeyo*) common, vulgar; (= *chabacano*) cheap **2** [*discurso, política*] rabble-rousing; [*político*] demagogic (*frm*), who plays to the gallery

populacho SM (= *capa social*) plebs* *pl* (*pey*); (= *multitud*) mob

popular ADJ **1** (= *del pueblo*) [*cultura, levantamiento*] popular; [*tradiciones*] popular, folk *antes de s*; [*lenguaje*] popular, colloquial; **el tribunal** ~ the people's court **2** (= *muy conocido*) popular; **un actor muy** ~ a very popular actor

popularidad SF popularity

popularizar /1f/ **Ⓐ** VT to popularize **Ⓑ** **popularizarse** VPR to become popular

populista ADJ, SMF populist

póquer SM poker

poquísimo ADJ very little; **poquísimos** very few

poquito PRON **1** (*como demostrativo*) **un** ~ a little bit (**de** of); (*después de v*) a little, a bit **2 a ~s** bit by bit, little by little; **se añade la leche** ~ **a poco** o **de a** ~ (*LAm*) the milk is added a little at a time o gradually

---

por

por PREPOSICIÓN

1 (*causa*)

1.1 (+ SUSTANTIVO) because of; **tuvo que suspenderse** ~ **el mal tiempo** it had to be cancelled because of the weather; **nos encontramos** ~ **casualidad** we met by chance; **lo hago** ~ **gusto** I do it because I like to; **fue** ~ **necesidad** it was out of necessity; ~ **temor a** for fear of

1.2 (+ INFIN) **no aprobó** ~ **no haber estudiado** he didn't pass because he hadn't studied; ~ **venir tarde se perdió la mitad** he missed half of it because he arrived late; **me castigaron** ~ **mentir** I was punished for lying

1.3 (+ ADJ) **le expulsaron** ~ **revoltoso** they expelled him for being a troublemaker; **lo dejó** ~ **imposible** he gave it up as (being) impossible

2 (*objetivo*)

2.1 (+ SUSTANTIVO) for; **trabajar** ~ **dinero** to work for money; **daría lo que fuera** ~ **un poco de tranquilidad** I'd give anything for a bit of peace and quiet; **brindemos** ~ **nuestro futuro** let's drink to our future

2.2 (+ INFIN) **lo hizo** ~ **complacerle** he did it to please her; ~ **no llegar tarde** so as not to arrive late, in order not to be late; **hablar** ~ **hablar** to talk for the sake of talking

◆ **estar por** +INFIN (*LAm*) (= *a punto de*) to be about to + *infin*

◆ **ir (a) por algo/algn** (= *en busca de*) to go and get sth/sb; **voy a** ~ **él** (*a buscarlo*) I'll go and get him; (*a atacarlo*) I'm going to get him; **sólo van a** ~ **las pelas*** they're only in it for the money; **¡a** ~ **ellos!** get them!; ◆ MODISMO **ir a** ~ **todas** to really go for it

3 (= *en favor, defensa de*) for; **hazlo** ~ **mí** do it for me, do it for my sake; **luchar** ~ **la patria** to fight for one's country

4 (*elección*) **su amor** ~ **la pintura** his love of painting; **está loca** ~ **ti** she's crazy about you; **no sabía** ~ **cuál decidirme** I couldn't decide which to choose

5 (*evidencia*) judging by, judging from; ~ **lo que dicen** judging by o from what they say; ~ **la cara que pone no debe de gustarle** judging by o from his face I don't think he likes it

6 (*medio*) ~ **su propia mano** by his own hand; **la conozco** ~ **mi hermano** I know her through my brother; ~ **correo** by post (*esp Brit*) o mail (*esp EEUU*); ~ **mar** by sea; **hablar** ~ **señas** to use sign language

7 (*agente*) by; **"dirigido** ~**"** "directed by"; **fueron apresados** ~ **la policía** they were captured by the police

8 (*modo*) by; **me agarró** ~ **el brazo** he grabbed me by the arm; **buscaron casa** ~ **casa** they searched house by house; **están dispuestos** ~ **tamaños** they are arranged according to size o by size; ~ **orden alfabético** in alphabetical order

9 (*lugar*) **se va** ~ **ahí** it's that way; **¿** ~ **dónde?** which way?; **ir a Bilbao** ~ **Santander** to go to Bilbao via Santander; **cruzar la frontera** ~ **Canfranc** to cross the border at Canfranc; **pasar** ~ **Madrid** to go through Madrid; **se asomaron** ~ **la ventana** they leaned out of the window; **iban cantando** ~ **la calle** they were walking along the street singing; **paseábamos** ~ **la playa** we were walking along the beach; ~ **todas partes** everywhere; ~ **todo el país** throughout the country; **viajar** ~ **el mundo** to travel (around) the world

10 (*aproximación*) **busca** ~ **ahí** look over there; **viven** ~ **esta zona** they live around here; ~ **aquí cerca** near o around here; **aquello ocurrió** ~ **abril** it happened around April; **está** ~ **el norte** it's somewhere up north

11 (*tiempo*) **se levanta** ~ **la mañana temprano** she gets up early in the morning; **la mañana siempre tengo mucho trabajo** I always have a lot of work in o during the morning; **no sale** ~ **la noche** he doesn't go out at night

12 (*duración*) for; **será** ~ **poco tiempo** it won't be for long; **se quedarán** ~ **dos semanas** they will stay for two weeks

13 (*sustitución, intercambio*) (= *a cambio de*) for; (= *en lugar de*) instead of; **lo vendí** ~ **15 dólares** I sold it for 15 dollars; **me dieron 13 francos** ~ **una libra** I got 13 francs to the pound; **hoy doy yo la clase** ~ **él** today I'm giving the class for him o in his place; **ha puesto B** ~ **V** he has put B instead of V

14 (*representación*) **hablo** ~ **todos** I speak on behalf of o for everyone; **interceder** ~ **algn** to intercede on sb's behalf, intercede for sb

15 (*distribución*) **diez dólares** ~ **hora** ten dollars an hour; **80km** ~ **hora** 80km per o an hour; **tres dólares** ~ **persona** three dollars each, three dollars per person

16 (*en multiplicaciones*) **cinco** ~ **tres, quince** five times three is fifteen, five threes are fifteen; **mide seis metros de alto** ~ **cuatro de ancho** it is six metres high by four wide

17 (= *en cuanto a*) ~ **mí no hay inconveniente** that's fine as o so far as I'm concerned; ~ **mí, como si te mueres de hambre** you can starve for all I care; **si** ~ **mi fuera, tú estarías trabajando** if it were o was down to me, you'd be working

18 (= *como*) **tomar a algn** ~ **esposo/esposa** to take sb to be one's husband/wife; **le dan** ~ **muerto** they have given him up for dead; **le tienen** ~ **tonto** they think he's stupid

19 (*concesión*) (+ SUBJUN) ~ **(muy) difícil que sea** however hard it is o may be; ~ **mucho que lo quisieran** however much they would like to, much as they would like to; ~ **más que lo intente** no matter how o however hard I try, try as I might

20 (*acción inacabada*) (+ INFIN) **quedan platos** ~ **lavar** there are still some dishes to do; **aún me quedan tres páginas** ~ **traducir** I still have three pages left to translate

21 (*en preguntas*)

◆ **por qué** why; **¿** ~ **qué no vienes conmigo?** why don't you come with me?; **no tengo** ~ **qué ir** there's no reason why I should go

◆ **¿por?*** why (do you ask)?

porcelana SF **1** (= *material*) porcelain; (= *loza*) china, chinaware, porcelain **2** (= *objeto*) **estantes llenos de ~s** shelves full of china o chinaware o porcelain

porcentaje SM percentage; **un elevado** ~ **de algo** a high percentage o proportion of sth; **el** ~ **de defunciones** the death rate; **trabajar a ~** to work on a percentage basis

porcentual ADJ percentage *antes de s*

porche SM **1** [*de casa*] porch **2** (= *soportal*) arcade

porcino Ⓐ ADJ pig *antes de s*, porcine (*frm*); **ganado ~** pigs *pl* Ⓑ SM **carne de ~** pork

porción SF (*gen*) portion; (*en reparto*) share; (*de chocolate, pastel*) piece; **quesitos en porciones** cheese portions

pordiosero/a SM/F beggar

porfa* EXCL please

porfiado Ⓐ ADJ (= *terco*) stubborn, obstinate; (= *insistente*) persistent Ⓑ SM (*Perú*) (= *muñeco*) roly-poly doll, tumbler (toy)

porfiar /1c/ VI to persist, insist; **~ en algo** to persist in sth

pormenor SM detail, particular

pormenorizado ADJ detailed

pormenorizar /1f/ Ⓐ VT **1** (= *describir*) to describe in detail **2** (= *detallar*) to detail, set out in detail Ⓑ VI to go into detail

porno* Ⓐ ADJ INV porn*, porno* Ⓑ SM porn*

pornografía SF pornography

pornográfico ADJ pornographic

poro¹ SM (*Anat*) pore

poro² SM (*Chi, Méx*) (= *puerro*) leek

pororó SM (*RPl*) popcorn

porosidad SF porousness, porosity

poroso ADJ porous

poroto SM **1** (*CS*) (= *judía*) bean; ✦ MODISMO **ganarse los ~s** to earn one's daily bread ➤ **poroto verde** (*Chi*) green bean, runner bean **2** ✦ MODISMO **anotarse un ~** (*CS**) to score a point

porque CONJ because; **no pudo ir ~ estaba enferma** she couldn't go because she was ill; **porque sí** just because

porqué SM reason (**de** for); **el ~ de su actitud** the reason for her attitude; **no me interesan los ~s** I'm not interested in the whys and wherefores

porquería SF **1** (= *suciedad*) dirt, muck*; **estar hecho una ~** to be covered in dirt *o* muck*.
2 (= *guarrada*) **no hagas ~s con la comida** don't make such a mess with your food
3 (= *indecencia*) **estas ~s no deberían salir por la tele** that filth *o* smut shouldn't be shown on TV; **decir ~s** to say filthy things
4 (= *cosa de poca calidad*) junk*, garbage*, rubbish (*esp Brit**); **comer ~s** to eat junk*; **la novela es una ~** the novel is just garbage *o* (*esp Brit*) rubbish*
5 (= *poco dinero*) pittance; **me han pagado una ~** they paid me a pittance
6 de ~ (*SAm**) (= *condenado*) lousy*

porqueriza SF pigsty (*esp Brit*), pigpen (*EEUU*)

porra SF **1** [*de policía*] truncheon (*Brit*), billy club (*EEUU*) **2** (*Téc*) large hammer **3** (*Culin*) *large club-shaped fritter* **4** (*) (= *nariz*) conk (*Brit**), hooter (*Brit**), schnozzle (*esp EEUU***) **5** (= *juego*) sweep, sweepstake **6** (**) (*en exclamaciones*) **¡porras!** (*Esp*) (= *¡maldición!*) damn!**; (= *¡mentira!*) rubbish! (*esp Brit*), baloney! (*esp EEUU*); **¡una ~!** (*Esp*) no way!*; **¡a la ~!** to hell with it!**; **mandar a algn a la ~** to tell sb to go to hell**; **¡qué coche ni que ~s!** car my foot!* **7** (*Méx*) (= *seguidores*) (*Dep, Mús*) fans *pl*

porrada* SF (*Esp*) **una ~ de** loads of*; **hace una ~ de tiempo** ages ago

porrazo SM **1** (= *golpe*) thump, blow; (= *caída*) bump; **me di un ~ contra la puerta** I banged myself on the door **2** ✦ MODISMOS **de ~** (*Perú*) in one go; **de golpe y ~** suddenly

porrillo*: a ~ ADV **tiene ropa a ~** he's got loads of clothes*; **gana dinero a ~** he earns loads of money*

porrista (*Col, Méx*) Ⓐ SMF (= *seguidor*) fan Ⓑ SF (= *animadora*) cheerleader

porro* SM **1** (*Esp*) joint* **2** (*Méx*) (= *policía*) *plain-clothes police officer who infiltrates universities and student demonstrations*

porrón SM **1** (= *recipiente*) *jar with a long spout for drinking* *from* **2** (*Esp*) **un ~ de*** loads of*; **ese libro me gustó un ~*** that book is the business* **3** (*Arg*) [*de cerveza*] bottle of beer **4** (*CS*) (= *pimiento*) green pepper; (= *puerro*) leek

portaaviones SM INV aircraft carrier

portabebés SM INV baby carrier

portación SF (*LAm*) **por ~ de armas** for carrying weapons

portada SF **1** (= *primera plana*) [*de libro*] title page, frontispiece (*frm*); [*de periódico*] front page **2** (= *cubierta*) [*de revista, libro*] cover; [*de disco*] sleeve (*esp Brit*), jacket (*EEUU*) **3** (*Arquit*) (= *fachada*) façade; (= *pórtico*) porch, doorway

portadocumentos SM INV document holder; (*LAm*) briefcase

portador(a) SM/F **1** [*de cheque, carta*] bearer **2** (*Med*) [*de germen, virus*] carrier

portaequipajes SM INV **1** (*en coche*) (= *maletero*) boot (*Brit*), trunk (*EEUU*); (= *baca*) roof-rack **2** (*en autocar*) (*sobre el asiento*) luggage rack; (= *compartimento aparte*) boot (*Brit*), trunk (*EEUU*)

portaesquíes SM INV, **portaesquís** SM INV ski rack

portaestandarte SMF standard bearer

portafolio SM, **portafolios** SM INV briefcase, attaché case

portal SM **1** [*de edificio*] (= *vestíbulo*) hallway; (= *puerta*) front door; **la llave del ~** the front door key; **un vecino de su ~** a neighbour who lives in the same block **2** [*de casa*] hall, vestibule (*frm*) **3** (*Rel*) ➤ **portal de Belén** (= *representación navideña*) Nativity scene; **el ~ de Belén** (*Biblia*) the stable at Bethlehem **4** [*de muralla*] gate **5** (*Internet*) portal **6 portales** (= *soportales*) arcade *sing*

portalámparas SM INV (light)bulb socket

portaligas SM INV suspender belt (*Brit*), garter belt (*EEUU*)

portalón SM **1** (*Arquit*) large gate, imposing entrance **2** (*Náut*) gangway

portamaletas SM INV **1** (*Aut*) (= *baca*) roof rack; (*Chi*) (= *maletero*) boot (*Brit*), trunk (*EEUU*) **2** (*en autocar*) (*sobre el asiento*) luggage rack; (= *compartimento aparte*) boot (*Brit*), trunk (*EEUU*)

portaminas SM INV propelling pencil

portamonedas SM INV purse (*Brit*), coin purse (*EEUU*)

portaobjeto SM, **portaobjetos** SM INV microscope slide

portapapeles SM INV (*Inform*) clipboard

portar /1a/ Ⓐ VT [+ *bolsa, documentación*] to carry; [+ *arma*] to carry, bear (*frm*) Ⓑ **portarse** VPR **1** (= *comportarse*) to behave, conduct o.s. (*frm*); **~se bien** to behave well; **~se mal** to misbehave, behave badly **2** (= *distinguirse*) to show up well, come through creditably **3** (= *comportarse bien*) to behave well

portarretratos SM INV photo frame, picture frame

portátil Ⓐ ADJ portable Ⓑ SM portable, portable computer

portaviones SM INV aircraft carrier

portavoz Ⓐ SMF spokesman/spokeswoman, spokesperson Ⓑ SM (*pey*) (= *periódico, emisora*) mouthpiece

portazo SM slam; **cerrar la puerta de un ~** to slam the door (shut); **dar** *o* **pegar un ~** to slam the door

porte SM **1** (*Com*) (= *acto*) carriage, transport (*esp Brit*), transportation (*esp EEUU*); (= *costos*) carriage, delivery charges ➤ **porte debido** freight C.O.D. ➤ **porte pagado** carriage paid, post-paid, postage paid **2** [*de persona*] bearing, demeanour, demeanor (*EEUU*); **de ~ distinguido** with a distinguished bearing *o* air

porteador(a) SM/F porter

portear /1a/ VT to carry, transport

portento SM (= *prodigio*) marvel, wonder; (= *genio*) genius, wizard; **¡qué ~ de memoria!** what a prodigious memory!, what an amazing memory!

portentoso ADJ marvellous, marvelous (*EEUU*), extraordinary

porteño ADJ of/from Buenos Aires

portería SF 1 (= *conserjería*) caretaker's office (*Brit*), janitor's office (*esp EEUU*) 2 (*Dep*) (= *meta*) goal

portero/a Ⓐ SM/F 1 [*de edificio*] caretaker (*Brit*), (apartment house) manager (*EEUU*) 2 (*en hotel*) doorman, porter (*Brit*) 3 (*Dep*) goalkeeper Ⓑ SM ➤ **portero automático, portero electrónico** entry phone

portezuela SF door

pórtico SM 1 [*de iglesia, monumento*] portico ➤ **pórtico de entrada** gateway 2 [*de tiendas*] arcade

portillo SM (= *abertura*) gap, opening; (= *puerta falsa*) side entrance

portón SM 1 (= *puerta grande*) large door 2 (= *puerta principal*) main door 3 (*en cerca*) gate

portorriqueño/a ADJ, SM/F Puerto Rican

portuario ADJ (= *del puerto*) port *antes de s*, harbour *antes de s*, harbor *antes de s* (*EEUU*); (= *del muelle*) dock *antes de s*; **trabajador ~** docker (*Brit*), longshoreman (*EEUU*)

Portugal SM Portugal

portugués/esa Ⓐ ADJ, SM/F Portuguese Ⓑ SM (*Ling*) Portuguese

porvenir SM future; **labrarse un ~** to carve out a future for o.s.; **un hombre sin ~** a man with no prospects *o* future; **leer el ~ a algn** to tell sb's fortune

pos SM **en ~ de** (*liter*) after, in pursuit of; **ir en ~ de algo/algn** to chase (after) sth/sb, pursue sth/sb

posada SF 1 (= *hospedaje*) shelter, lodging; **dar ~ a algn** to give shelter to sb, take sb in 2 (= *lugar*) (*para comer*) inn; (*para dormir*) boarding house

posaderas* SFPL backside* *sing*, butt *sing* (*esp EEUU***), buttocks

posadero/a SM/F innkeeper

posar /1a/ Ⓐ VT [+ *carga*] to lay down, put down; [+ *mano*] to place, lay; **posó la mirada en el horizonte** his gaze rested on the horizon, his eyes came to rest on the horizon Ⓑ VI (*Arte*) to sit, pose Ⓒ **posarse** VPR 1 [*pájaro*] to perch, sit, alight; [*insecto*] to alight; [*avión*] to land 2 [*líquido, polvo*] to settle

posavasos SM INV (*de corcho, madera, cerámica*) coaster; (*de cartón*) beer mat

pose SF 1 (*para foto, cuadro*) pose 2 (*pey*) (= *afectación*) affectation, pose; (= *postura afectada*) affected pose

poseedor(a) SM/F 1 (= *dueño*) owner, possessor (*frm*) 2 [*de puesto, récord*] holder

poseer /2e/ VT 1 [+ *bienes*] to own; [+ *fortuna*] to own, have; [+ *talento, cultura*] to have 2 [+ *ventaja*] to have, enjoy; [+ *puesto, récord*] to hold 3 (*sexualmente*) to possess, have

poseído/a Ⓐ ADJ possessed Ⓑ SM/F **gritar como un ~** to scream like one possessed

posesión SF 1 (= *propiedad*) possession; [*de un puesto*] tenure, occupation; **dar ~ a algn** to hand over to sb; **él está en ~ de las cartas** he is in possession of the letters; **está en ~ del récord** he holds the record; **tomar ~ de algo** to take possession of sth, take sth over; **tomar ~ de un cargo** to take up a post 2 (= *cosa poseída*) possession; (= *finca*) estate

posesionar /1a/ Ⓐ VT **~ a algn de algo** to hand sth over to sb Ⓑ **posesionarse** VPR **~se de algo** to take possession of sth, take sth over

posesivo ADJ, SM possessive

poseso/a ADJ, SM/F = **poseído**

posestructuralismo SM post-structuralism

posestructuralista ADJ, SMF post-structuralist

posgrado SM **curso de ~** postgraduate course

posgraduado/a Ⓐ ADJ postgraduate (*Brit*), graduate (*esp EEUU*) Ⓑ SM/F (= *persona*) postgraduate (*Brit*), graduate student (*EEUU*)

posguerra SF postwar period; **los años de la ~** the postwar years

posibilidad SF 1 (= *oportunidad*) chance, possibility; **no tenemos ninguna ~** we don't have the slightest chance, we don't stand a chance; **este chico tiene ~es** this boy has got

potential; **¿tienes ~ de aprobar el examen?** do you have any chance of passing the exam?

2 (= *alternativa*) possibility; **hay dos ~es: operación o radioterapia** there are two alternatives *o* possibilities: an operation or radiotherapy

3 **posibilidades** (= *recursos*) means; **un deportivo no está dentro de mis ~es** a sports car is beyond my means *o* out of my price range; **vive por encima de sus ~es** he lives above his means

posibilista Ⓐ ADJ optimistic, positive Ⓑ SMF optimist, positive thinker

posibilitar /1a/ VT [+ *acuerdo, acceso*] to make possible; [+ *idea, plan*] to make feasible; **~ que algn haga algo** to allow sb to do sth, make it possible for sb to do sth

posible Ⓐ ADJ 1 [*opción, solución*] possible; **un ~ comprador** a possible *o* potential buyer; **hemos hecho todas las concesiones ~s** we have made all possible concessions *o* all the concessions we can; **hacer algo ~** to make sth possible; **entra dentro de lo ~** it is within the bounds of possibility; **en la medida de lo ~** as far as possible, insofar as possible (*frm*); **haremos todo lo ~ por evitarlo** we shall do everything possible *o* all we can to avoid it

2 **es ~** (= *probable, permitido*) it is possible; (= *realizable*) it is feasible; —**¿crees que vendrá? —es ~** "do you think he'll come?" — "possibly *o* he might *o* it's possible"; **es ~ hacer algo** it is possible to do sth; **no me fue ~ llegar a tiempo** I was unable to get there in time; **es ~ que** (+ SUBJUN): **es muy ~ que vuelva tarde** it's quite possible that I'll be back late, I may well be back late; **a o de ser ~** if possible; **si es ~** if possible; **le ruego que, si le es ~, acuda a la reunión** please come to the meeting if you possibly can Ⓑ ADV **lo más ... ~** as ... as possible; **lo más pronto ~** as soon as possible Ⓒ **posibles** SMPL (*Esp*) means; **una familia de ~s** a well-to-do family

posiblemente ADV possibly; **~ tengamos que mudarnos** we might have to move, it's possible that we'll have to move

posición SF 1 (= *postura*) position; **en ~ vertical** in an upright position; **estar en ~ de firme** (*Mil*) to be at attention 2 (= *lugar*) position; **la ~ de los jugadores en el terreno de juego** the position of the players on the pitch 3 (= *categoría*) position, standing 4 (= *punto de vista*) position, stance 5 (*en competición, liga*) place, position; **terminó en primera ~** he finished first *o* in first place; **perder posiciones** to lose ground

posicionamiento SM (= *acción*) positioning; (= *postura*) stance, attitude

posimpresionismo SM post-impressionism

posimpresionista ADJ, SMF post-impressionist

posindustrial ADJ post-industrial

positiva SF (*Fot*) positive, print

positivado SM (*Fot*) printing

positivamente ADV positively

positivismo SM positivism

positivo Ⓐ ADJ 1 (= *afirmativo, beneficioso*) positive; **el conductor dio ~** the driver tested positive 2 (*Mat*) positive, plus 3 [*idea*] constructive; **es ~ que ...** it is good that ..., it is encouraging that ... Ⓑ SM 1 (*Ling*) positive 2 (*Fot*) positive, print

posmodernismo SM postmodernism

posmoderno/a Ⓐ ADJ postmodern Ⓑ SM/F postmodernist

posnatal ADJ postnatal

poso SM [*de vino*] sediment, dregs *pl*, lees *pl*; [*de café*] dregs *pl*, grounds *pl* ➤ **posos de té** tea leaves

posología SF dosage

posoperatorio Ⓐ ADJ post-operative Ⓑ SM post-operative period

posparto Ⓐ ADJ postnatal Ⓑ SM postnatal period, postpartum (*frm*)

posponer /2q/ VT to postpone

posta SF 1 (†) (= *caballos*) relay 2 (*LAm Dep*) (= *carrera*) relay (race); (= *etapa*) leg 3 (*Caza*) (= *munición*) slug, pellet 4 (*Chi Med*) emergency medical centre o (*EEUU*) center 5 ✦ MODISMO **a ~** (*Esp*) on purpose, deliberately

postal Ⓐ ADJ postal; **giro ~** postal order (*Brit*), money order (*EEUU*) Ⓑ SF postcard

postdata SF postscript

postdoctoral ADJ post-doctoral

poste SM 1 (= *palo*) post, pole; (*Dep*) post, upright ➤ **poste del tendido eléctrico** electricity pylon ➤ **poste telegráfico** telegraph pole (*Brit*), telephone pole (*EEUU*) 2 ➤ **poste restante** (*LAm*) poste restante (*esp Brit*), general delivery (*EEUU*)

postelectoral ADJ post-electoral

postemilla SF (*LAm*) gumboil

póster SM (*pl* ~**es** o ~**s**) poster

postergación SF postponement

postergar /1h/ VT 1 (= *aplazar*) to defer, postpone; (= *retrasar*) to delay 2 (= *relegar*) (*en el trato*) to disregard, neglect; (*en ascenso*) to pass over, ignore

posteridad SF posterity

posterior ADJ 1 [*lugar*] back, rear; [*motor*] rear-mounted 2 (*en tiempo*) later, subsequent; **ser ~ a algo** to be later than sth 3 (*en orden*) later, following

posteriori *ver* **a posteriori**

posterioridad SF **con ~** subsequently, later; **con ~ a algo** subsequent to sth, after sth

posteriormente ADV later, subsequently, afterwards

postgrado SM = **posgrado**

postgraduado/a ADJ, SM/F = **posgraduado**

postigo SM 1 (*en ventana*) shutter 2 (†) (*en puerta*) wicket (gate)

postín SM (*Esp*) 1 (= *lujo*) elegance; **de ~** posh* 2 (= *jactancia*) **darse ~** to show off

postizo Ⓐ ADJ [*dientes, sonrisa, bigote*] false; [*cuello de camisa*] detachable Ⓑ SM [*de pelo*] hairpiece, switch

postoperatorio ADJ, SM = **posoperatorio**

postor SM bidder; **al mejor ~** to the highest bidder

postparto ADJ, SM = **posparto**

postración SF prostration

postrado ADJ **~ en la cama** (*temporalmente*) confined to bed; (*por invalidez*) bed-ridden

postrarse /1a/ VPR to prostrate o.s.

postre Ⓐ SM dessert, pudding; **¿qué hay de ~?** what's for dessert?; ✦ MODISMO **llegar para los ~s** to come very late Ⓑ SF ✦ MODISMO **a la ~** when all is said and done, at the end of the day

postrer ADJ = **postrero**

postrero ADJ last

postrimerías SFPL final stages, closing stages; **en las ~ del siglo** in the last few years of the century, at the end o close of the century

postulación SF 1 (*Rel*) postulancy 2 (= *colecta*) collection 3 (*CS*) (= *solicitud*) application 4 (*LAm Pol*) nomination, candidature

postulado SM (= *supuesto*) assumption, postulate (*frm*); (= *proposición*) proposition

postulante SMF 1 (*Rel*) postulant, candidate 2 (*en colecta*) collector 3 (*CS*) (*para un trabajo*) applicant 4 (*LAm Pol*) candidate

postular /1a/ Ⓐ VT 1 (= *defender*) [+ *teoría*] to postulate 2 (*en colecta*) to collect (for charity) 3 (*LAm Pol*) [+ *candidato*] to nominate Ⓑ VI 1 (*en colecta*) to collect (for charity) 2 (*CS*) (= *solicitar*) to apply (**para** for) Ⓒ **postularse** VPR (*LAm Pol*) to stand

póstumo ADJ posthumous

postura SF 1 [*del cuerpo*] position ➤ **postura del loto** lotus position 2 (= *actitud*) stance, position; **una ~ poco razonable** an unreasonable stance o position; **tomar ~** to take a stand 3 (*en una subasta*) bid

postural ADJ postural

post-venta ADJ INV, **posventa** ADJ INV after-sales *antes de s*

pota SF (*Esp*) 1 (= *calamar*) cuttlefish 2 **echar la(s) ~(s)**** to puke**, throw up*

potabilizar /1f/ VT **~ el agua** to make the water drinkable

potable ADJ 1 (= *bebible*) drinkable; **agua ~** drinking water 2 (*) (= *aceptable*) good enough, passable

potaje SM *vegetable and pulse stew*

potasio SM potassium

pote SM 1 (= *tarro*) jar; (= *olla*) pot ➤ **pote gallego** Galician stew 2 (*Esp**) (= *trago*) drink; **tomar unos ~s** to have a few drinks

potear* /1a/ VI (*Esp*) to have a few drinks

potencia SF 1 (= *capacidad*) power ➤ **potencia hidráulica** hydraulic power ➤ **potencia muscular** muscular power, muscular strength 2 (*Mec*) power 3 (*Pol*) power; **las grandes ~s** the great powers ➤ **potencia mundial** world power 4 (*Mat*) power; **elevado a la quinta ~** raised to the power of five 5 **en ~** potential, in the making; **es una guerra civil en ~** it is a civil war in the making

potenciación SF = **potenciamiento**

potenciador Ⓐ ADJ **ser ~ de algo** to stimulate sth Ⓑ SM ➤ **potenciador del sabor** flavour enhancer

potencial Ⓐ ADJ potential Ⓑ SM 1 (= *capacidad*) potential 2 (*Ling*) conditional

potenciamiento SM 1 [*de turismo, artes, producto*] promotion 2 [*de economía, producción, cooperación*] boosting, strengthening

potenciar /1b/ VT 1 [+ *turismo, artes, producto*] to favour, favor (*EEUU*), foster, promote 2 (= *fortalecer*) to boost, strengthen

potentado/a SM/F 1 (*en la industria*) tycoon, magnate 2 (= *poderoso*) big shot*

potente ADJ powerful

potestad SF authority, jurisdiction; **patria ~** paternal authority

potestativo ADJ optional, facultative

potingue* SM 1 (= *brebaje*) concoction, brew 2 (= *crema*) face cream

potito SM (*Esp*) jar of baby food

poto* SM (*And*) 1 (= *culo*) backside*, bum (*Brit**), butt (*EEUU***) 2 (= *fondo*) lower end

potra SF 1 (*Zool*) filly 2 (*) (= *suerte*) luck; **tener ~** to be jammy*

potranco/a SM/F colt/filly, young horse/mare

potrero SM (*LAm*) 1 (= *pastizal*) pasture; (= *cercado*) paddock 2 (*LAm*) (= *llanura*) open grassland

potrillo SM 1 (= *caballo*) colt 2 (*Chi*) (= *copa*) tall glass

potro SM 1 (*Zool*) colt 2 (*Dep*) (vaulting) horse 3 [*de tortura*] rack

poyo SM (*para sentarse*) stone bench; [*de ventana*] stone ledge

poza SF (*gen*) puddle, pool; [*de río*] backwater, pool

pozo SM 1 [*de agua*] well; ✦ MODISMOS **ser un ~ de sabiduría** to be a fount of wisdom; **ser un ~ sin fondo** to be a bottomless pit ➤ **pozo artesiano** artesian well ➤ **pozo ciego** cesspool ➤ **pozo de petróleo** oil well ➤ **pozo negro** cesspool ➤ **pozo séptico** septic tank 2 [*de río*] deep part 3 (*Min*) shaft 4 (*LAm*) (= *fondo común*) pool, kitty; (*en lotería, apuestas*) pool; **llevarse el ~** to win the (rollover) jackpot

PP SM ABR (*Esp Pol*) = **Partido Popular**

práctica SF 1 [*de actividad*] practice; **aprender con la ~** to learn by practice; **llevar algo a la ~** ◊ **poner algo en ~** to put sth into practice; **en la ~** in practice ➤ **práctica de riesgo** high-risk practice 2 **prácticas** (= *aprendizaje*) (*gen*) practice *sing*, training *sing*; [*de laboratorio*] experiments; **contrato en ~s** (*Esp*) work experience contract; **período de ~s** (*Esp*) (practical) training period ➤ **prácticas de tiro** target practice *sing* ➤ **prácticas en empresa** (*Esp*) work experience *sing*, internship *sing* (*EEUU*)

practicable ADJ **1** (= *factible*) practicable, workable, feasible **2** [*camino*] passable, usable

prácticamente ADV practically

practicante Ⓐ ADJ (*Rel*) practising, practicing (*EEUU*) **Ⓑ** SMF (*Med*) medical assistant, nurse (*specializing in giving injections, taking blood pressure, etc*)

practicar /1g/ **Ⓐ** VT **1** [+ *habilidad, virtud*] to practise, practice (*EEUU*), exercise **2** [+ *actividad, profesión*] to practise, practice (*EEUU*); [+ *deporte*] to play **3** [+ *operación quirúrgica*] to carry out, perform (*frm*); [+ *detención, incisión*] to make **4** [+ *hoyo*] to cut, make **Ⓑ** VI (*en deporte, juego*) to practise, practice (*EEUU*); (*en profesión*) to do one's training *o* practice

práctico Ⓐ ADJ **1** (= *útil*) (*gen*) practical; [*herramienta*] handy; [*ropa*] sensible, practical **2** (= *no teórico*) [*estudio, formación*] practical **3** (= *pragmático*) practical; **sé ~ y búscate un trabajo que dé dinero** be practical *o* sensible and find a job with money **Ⓑ** SM (*Náut*) pilot (*in a port*)

pradera SF (= *prado*) meadow, meadowland; (*de Canadá, EEUU*) prairie; **unas extensas ~s** extensive grasslands

prado SM (= *campo*) meadow, field; (= *pastizal*) pasture

Praga SF Prague

pragmático ADJ pragmatic

pragmatismo SM pragmatism

preacuerdo SM preliminary agreement, outline *o* draft agreement

prealerta SF standby, yellow alert

preámbulo SM [*de libro, discurso*] introduction; [*de ley, constitución*] preamble; **sin más ~s** without further ado, without preamble

preautonómico ADJ (*Esp Pol*) *before the creation of the autonomous regional governments*

preaviso SM forewarning, early warning

prebenda SF **1** (*Rel*) (= *renta*) prebend **2** (= *gaje*) perk*; **las ~s del cargo** the perks of the job*

preboste SM bigwig*

precalentamiento SM (*Dep*) warm-up; (*Aut*) warming up

precalentar /1j/ **Ⓐ** VT [+ *horno*] to preheat; (*Dep*) to warm up **Ⓑ** **precalentarse** VPR (*Dep*) to warm up

precampaña SF (*tb ~ electoral*) run-up to the election campaign

precariedad SF **1** [*de empleo, salud, situación*] precariousness **2** [*de recursos, medios*] scarcity

precario Ⓐ ADJ [*salud*] precarious; [*situación*] precarious, difficult; [*economía, democracia*] unstable; [*vivienda*] poor, inferior; [*medios*] unpredictable, reduced **Ⓑ** SM precarious state; **vivir en ~** to live from hand to mouth, scrape a living

precaución SF **1** (= *medida*) precaution; **tomar precauciones** to take precautions; **extremar las precauciones** to be extra careful **2** (= *cautela*) **ir con ~** to proceed with caution; **lo hicimos por ~** we did it to be on the safe side, we did it as a precautionary measure *o* as a precaution

precaverse /2a/ VPR to be on one's guard, take precautions (**contra** against); **~ de algo** to be on one's guard against sth, beware of sth

precavido ADJ cautious; **✦** REFRÁN **hombre ~ vale por dos** forewarned is forearmed

precedente Ⓐ ADJ preceding, previous, foregoing (*frm*) **Ⓑ** SM precedent; **establecer** *o* **sentar un ~** to set a precedent; **sin ~(s)** unprecedented, without precedent; **por primera vez y sin que sirva de ~, voy a seguir tu consejo** just this once, I'll follow your advice

preceder /2a/ VT **~ a algo/algn** to precede sth/sb; **le precedía un coche** he was preceded by a car; **los años que precedieron a la Guerra Civil** the years leading up to the Civil War, the years preceding the Civil War

preceptivo ADJ compulsory, obligatory, mandatory

precepto SM (= *regla*) precept; (= *mandato*) order, rule; **día** *o* **fiesta de ~** (*Rel*) holy day of obligation

preceptor/a SM/F (private) tutor

preces SFPL prayers, supplications

preciado ADJ [*posesión*] prized; [*amigo*] valued, esteemed

preciarse /1b/ VPR **~ de algo** to pride o.s. on sth; **~ de hacer algo** to pride o.s. on doing sth

> Recuérdese que las preposiciones en inglés rigen gerundio y no infinitivo, de ahí **to pride o.s. on doing sth**.

precintado Ⓐ ADJ [*paquete*] sealed, presealed; [*calle, zona*] sealed off **Ⓑ** SM [*de paquete*] sealing; [*de calle, zona*] sealing off

precintar /1a/ VT [+ *paquete*] to seal, preseal; [+ *calle, zona*] to seal off

precinto SM seal

precio SM **1** (= *importe*) [*de producto*] price; [*de viaje*] fare; (*en hotel*) rate, charge; **¿qué ~ tiene?** how much is it?; **a ~ de saldo** at a knockdown price; **a o por un ~ simbólico** for a nominal *o* token sum; **✦** MODISMOS **poner ~ a la cabeza de algn** to put a price on sb's head; **no tener ~** to be priceless ➤ **precio al contado** cash ➤ **precio al detalle**, **precio al por menor** retail price ➤ **precio de compra** purchase price ➤ **precio de coste** (*Esp*), **precio de costo** cost-price ➤ **precio de fábrica** ex works price ➤ **precio de ocasión** bargain price ➤ **precio de salida** starting price ➤ **precio de venta al público** retail price ➤ **precios al consumo** retail prices **2** (= *coste, sacrificio*) **pagó un ~ muy alto por su libertad** he paid a very high price for his freedom; **lo hará a cualquier ~** he'll do it whatever the cost *o* at any price; **evítelo a cualquier ~** avoid it at all costs

preciosidad SF (= *objeto*) beautiful thing; **es una ~** it's beautiful; **¡oye, ~!** hey, beautiful!

preciosismo SM preciosity

precioso ADJ **1** (= *valioso*) precious, valuable **2** (= *hermoso*) lovely, beautiful

preciosura SF (*LAm*) = **preciosidad**

precipicio SM cliff, precipice

precipitación SF **1** (*al hacer algo*) (= *prisa*) haste; (= *imprudencia*) rashness; **con ~** hastily, precipitately (*frm*) **2** (*Meteo*) rainfall, precipitation (*frm*); **precipitaciones abundantes** heavy rainfall **3** (*Quím*) precipitation

precipitadamente ADV [*huir, lanzarse*] headlong; [*irse*] very suddenly; [*actuar*] rashly, precipitately (*frm*); **escribí una nota ~** I dashed off a note

precipitado Ⓐ ADJ [*huida*] headlong; [*partida*] hasty, sudden; [*conducta*] hasty, rash **Ⓑ** SM (*Quím*) precipitate

precipitar /1a/ **Ⓐ** VT **1** (= *arrojar*) to hurl down, throw (**desde** from) **2** (= *apresurar*) to hasten, precipitate (*frm*); **aquello precipitó su salida** that affair hastened *o* (*frm*) precipitated his departure; **no precipitemos los acontecimientos** let's not rush things **3** (*Quím*) to precipitate **Ⓑ** **precipitarse** VPR **1** (= *arrojarse*) to throw o.s., hurl o.s. (**desde** from); **~se sobre algo** [*pájaro*] to swoop down on sth; [*animal*] to pounce on sth; **~se sobre algn** to throw *o* hurl o.s. on sb **2** (= *correr*) to rush, dash; **~se a hacer algo** to rush to do sth; **~se hacia la salida** to rush towards the exit **3** (= *actuar sin reflexión*) to act hastily; **no te precipites** don't rush into things

precisado ADJ **verse ~ a hacer algo** to be forced *o* obliged to do sth

precisamente ADV **1** (= *con precisión*) precisely **2** (= *exactamente*) precisely, exactly; **~ por eso** for that very reason, precisely because of that; **~ estamos hablando de eso** we're just talking about that; **yo no soy un experto ~** I'm not exactly an expert; **no es eso ~** it's not quite that

precisar /1a/ **Ⓐ** VT **1** (= *necesitar*) to need, require; **no precisa lavado** it needs no washing, it doesn't require washing; **"se precisan mensajeros"** "messengers required", "messengers wanted" **2** (= *especificar*) to specify; **no precisó**

a qué hora llegaría he didn't specify when he would arrive; **¿puedes ~ un poco más?** can you be a little more specific? ⓑ VI ~ **de algo** to need *o* require sth

precisión SF precision, accuracy, preciseness; **instrumento de** ~ precision instrument

preciso ⓐ ADJ **1** (= *exacto*) precise; **una descripción precisa** a precise description; **un reloj muy** ~ a very precise *o* accurate watch
2 (= *justo*) **en aquel ~ momento** at that precise *o* very moment
3 (= *necesario*) necessary; **cuando sea** ~ when it becomes necessary; **si es** ~ **iré yo mismo** I'll go by myself if necessary; **es ~ tener coche** it is essential to have a car; **es ~ que lo hagas** you must do it; **no es ~ que vengas** there's no need for you to come
4 [*estilo, lenguaje*] concise
ⓑ ADV (*Col*) (*para confirmar*) ~ **que viene cuando yo no estoy** he's bound to come when I'm not there

preclaro ADJ illustrious

precocidad SF precociousness, precocity

precocinado ADJ pre-cooked; **platos ~s** ready meals, pre-cooked meals

precolombino ADJ pre-Columbian

preconcebido ADJ preconceived; **idea preconcebida** preconceived idea, preconception

preconciliar ADJ preconciliar, before Vatican II

preconizar /1f/ VT **1** (= *elogiar*) to praise **2** (= *recomendar*) to advocate

precordillera SF (*SAm*) Andean foothills *pl*

precoz ADJ [*envejecimiento, calvicie, eyaculación*] premature; [*diagnóstico, pronóstico*] early; [*niño*] precocious

precursor(a) SM/F precursor, forerunner

predador SM predator

predecesor(a) SM/F predecessor

predecir /3o/ VT to predict, forecast

predestinación SF predestination

predestinado ADJ predestined; **estar ~ a hacer algo** to be predestined to do sth

predestinar /1a/ VT to predestine

predeterminar /1a/ VT to predetermine

prédica SF (= *sermón*) sermon; **~s** preaching

predicado SM predicate

predicador/a SM/F preacher

predicamento SM **1** (= *prestigio*) standing, prestige; **no goza ahora de tanto ~** it has less prestige now, it is not so well thought of now **2** (*LAm*) (= *situación difícil*) predicament

predicar /1g/ VT, VI to preach; **~ con el ejemplo** to practise what one preaches

predicativo ADJ predicative

predicción SF [*de catástrofe, hecho futuro*] prediction; [*del tiempo*] forecast

predilección SF predilection; **tener ~ por algo** to have a predilection for sth

predilecto ADJ favourite, favorite (*EEUU*); **fue nombrado hijo ~ de Madrid** he was named one of Madrid's honorary citizens

predio SM (*LAm*) (= *finca*) property, estate; (= *local*) premises *pl*; **~s** land *sing*

predisponer /2q/ VT (= *inclinar*) to predispose; (*con prejuicios*) to prejudice, bias (**contra** against)

predisposición SF (= *tendencia*) predisposition (**a** to); (= *prejuicio*) prejudice, bias (**contra** against)

predispuesto ADJ predisposed; **ser ~ a los catarros** to have a tendency to get colds; **estar ~ contra algn** to be prejudiced against sb

predominante ADJ [*papel, poder*] predominant; [*opinión, ideología, viento*] prevailing

predominar /1a/ VI [*papel, poder*] to predominate, dominate; [*opinión, ideología, viento*] to prevail

predominio SM predominance

preelectoral ADJ pre-election *antes de s*

preeminencia SF pre-eminence

preeminente ADJ pre-eminent

preescolar ⓐ ADJ preschool; **educación ~** preschool education, nursery education ⓑ SM (= *escuela*) nursery school, nursery

preestablecido ADJ pre-established

preestreno SM preview

preexistente ADJ pre-existing, pre-existent

prefabricado ⓐ ADJ prefabricated ⓑ SM prefabricated building, prefab*

prefacio SM preface, foreword

prefecto SM prefect

prefectura SF prefecture

preferencia SF **1** (= *prioridad*) preference; **tendrán ~ los que no lleguen al salario mínimo** preference will be given to those earning less than the minimum wage; **tienen ~ los vehículos que vienen por la derecha** vehicles coming from the right have priority; **localidad de ~** reserved seat; **tratamiento de ~** preferential treatment
2 (= *predilección*) preference; **tiene una clara ~ por la hija mayor** his eldest daughter is his clear favourite

preferencial ADJ preferential

preferente ADJ **1** [*trato*] (= *especial*) preferential; (= *prioritario*) priority *antes de s*; [*lugar*] prominent; [*derecho*] prior; (*Fin*) [*acción*] preference *antes de s* **2 clase ~** (*Aer*) club class

preferible ADJ preferable (**a** to)

preferido/a ⓐ ADJ favourite, favorite (*EEUU*) ⓑ SM/F favourite, favorite (*EEUU*); **yo era la preferida de mi madre** I was my mother's favourite *o* (*EEUU*) favorite

preferir /3i/ VT to prefer; **~ el té al café** to prefer tea to coffee; **¿cuál prefieres?** which do you prefer?; **¿qué prefieres (tomar)?** what will you have?; **prefiero ir a pie** I prefer to walk, I'd rather walk

prefijar /1a/ VT to fix beforehand, prearrange

prefijo SM **1** (*Ling*) prefix **2** (*Telec*) (dialling) code, STD code (*Brit*), area code (*EEUU*)

preformateado ADJ preformatted

pregón SM (= *proclama*) proclamation, announcement (*by town crier*); (*Com*) street cry, vendor's cry ➤ **pregón de las fiestas** local festival opening speech

pregonar /1a/ VT [+ *inocencia propia, interés*] to proclaim, announce; [+ *secreto*] to disclose, reveal; [+ *mercancía*] to hawk; [+ *méritos*] to proclaim (for all to hear); **no estaría bien que lo fueras pregonando por ahí** you shouldn't go spreading it around

pregonero/a SM/F **1** (*municipal*) town crier **2** [*de fiestas*] *person who makes the opening speech*

pregrabar /1a/ VT to pre-record

pregunta SF question; **hacer una ~** to ask *o* put a question; **"preguntas frecuentes"** "FAQs", "frequently asked questions" ➤ **pregunta capciosa** trick question

preguntar /1a/ ⓐ VT to ask; **~ algo a algn** to ask sb sth; **pregúntale si quiere venir** ask him if he wants to come, ask him whether he wants to come or not ⓑ VI to ask, inquire; **~ por algn: si te preguntan por mí** if they ask about me; **hay alguien al teléfono que pregunta por el jefe** there's someone on the phone asking for the boss; **~ por la salud de algn** to ask after sb's health ⓒ **preguntarse** VPR to wonder; **me pregunto si vale la pena** I wonder if it's worthwhile

preguntón* ADJ inquisitive

prehistoria SF prehistory

prehistórico ADJ prehistoric

preinscripción SF (*para cursar estudios*) pre-enrolment, pre-enrollment (*EEUU*); (*para congreso, cursillo*) provisional booking

preinstalación SF **~ de radio** radio fitted as standard; **~ de aire acondicionado** air conditioning pre-installed

preinstalado ADJ [*software*] pre-installed

prejubilación SF early retirement

prejubilar VT to force to take early retirement

prejuiciado ADJ (*LAm*) prejudiced (**contra** against)

prejuicio SM prejudice, bias (**contra** against); **no tienen ~s contra los españoles** they are not prejudiced against Spaniards

prejuzgar /1h/ VT to prejudge

prelado SM prelate

prelatura SF prelature

prelavado SM prewash

preliminar Ⓐ ADJ [*estudio, resultado*] preliminary; **fase ~** (*Dep*) qualifying round(s) Ⓑ SM o SF (*LAm Dep*) qualifier

preludiar /1b/ VT to herald

preludio SM prelude

premamá ADJ (*Esp*) **vestido (de) ~** maternity dress

prematrimonial ADJ premarital, before marriage

prematuro/a Ⓐ ADJ premature; **es ~ hablar de detalles** it's too early to talk about details, it would be rather premature to talk about details Ⓑ SM/F premature baby

premeditación SF premeditation

premeditado ADJ [*acto, crimen, tiro*] premeditated; [*ironía*] deliberate; [*negligencia*] wilful; [*insulto*] calculated

premeditar /1a/ VT to premeditate

premenstrual ADJ premenstrual

premiación SF (*LAm*) **1** (= *acción*) **no estoy de acuerdo con su ~** I don't think the award should go to him **2** (= *ceremonia*) (*Escol*) prize-giving

premiado/a Ⓐ ADJ [*novela*] prizewinning; [*número, boleto*] winning; **tu billete resultó o salió ~ con 60 millones** your ticket won 60 million Ⓑ SM/F prizewinner

premiar /1b/ VT **1** (= *dar un premio a*) to award a prize to; **fue premiado el director italiano** the Italian director received an award **2** (= *recompensar*) to reward (**con** with)

premier [pre'mjer] SMF prime minister, premier

premiere [pre'mjer] SF premiere

premio Ⓐ SM **1** (*en competición*) prize; **Gran Premio de Fórmula Uno** Formula One Grand Prix ► **premio de consolación, premio de consuelo** (*CS*) consolation prize ► **premio gordo** jackpot **2** (= *recompensa*) reward; **como ~ a sus servicios** as a reward for her services Ⓑ SMF (= *persona galardonada*) **el actual ~ Cervantes** the current Cervantes Prize winner

premisa SF premise

premonición SF premonition

premonitorio ADJ premonitory (*frm*), warning *antes de s*

premunirse /3a/ VPR (*LAm*) **~ de algo** to equip o.s. with; **llegaron premunidos de herramientas** they came equipped with tools

premura SF **1** (= *prisa*) haste, urgency **2** (= *aprieto*) pressure; **con ~ de tiempo** under pressure of time, with very little time

prenatal ADJ antenatal, prenatal

prenavideño ADJ pre-Christmas *antes de s*

prenda SF **1** (*tb* **~ de vestir**) garment, article of clothing; **~s de punto** knitwear *sing* **2** (= *garantía*) pledge; **dejar algo en ~** (*por dinero*) to pawn sth; (*como garantía*) to leave sth as security; ✦ MODISMO **no soltar ~** to give nothing away; **no dolerle ~s a algn: a mí no me duelen ~s** I don't mind saying nice things about others, it doesn't worry me that I'm not as good as others **3** (= *juego*) forfeit; **pagar ~** to pay a forfeit **4** (***) (*apelativo cariñoso*) darling

prendarse /1a/ VPR **~ de algo** to be captivated by sth, be enchanted with sth; **~ de algn** to fall in love with sb

prendedor SM clasp, brooch, broach (*EEUU*)

prender /2a/ Ⓐ VT **1** [+ *persona*] (= *capturar*) to catch, capture; (= *detener*) to arrest **2** (*Cos*) (= *sujetar*) to fasten; (*con alfiler*) to pin, attach (**en** to); **~ el pelo con horquillas** to pin one's hair with grips **3** (*esp LAm*) [+ *fuego, horno, vela, cigarrillo*] to light; [+ *cerilla*] to strike; [+ *luz, TV*] to switch on Ⓑ VI **1** [*fuego*] to catch; **sus ideas prendieron fácilmente**

en la juventud his ideas soon caught on with the young **2** [*planta*] to take, take root Ⓒ **prenderse** VPR to catch fire

prendido ADJ **quedar ~** (= *enganchado*) to be caught (fast), be stuck; (= *cautivado*) to be captivated

prensa SF **1** (= *publicaciones*) **la ~** the press, the (news)papers; ✦ MODISMO **tener mala ~** to have o get a bad press ► **la prensa amarilla** the gutter press (*Brit*), the scandal sheets (*EEUU*) ► **la prensa del corazón** periodicals specializing in real-life romance stories, glossies* ► **prensa roja** (*CS*) sensationalist press specializing in crime stories **2** (= *máquina*) (*Mec, Dep*) press; (*Tip*) printing press

---

PRENSA DEL CORAZÓN

The **prensa del corazón** is the generic term given in Spain to weekly or fortnightly magazines specializing in society gossip and the social lives of the rich and famous. The pioneer was **¡Hola!** which first appeared in 1944 (**Hello!** magazine is the English-language version), while other popular titles include **Pronto**, **Lecturas**, **Semana** and **Diez Minutos**. They constitute a highly profitable sector of the market, occupying six of the top ten places in magazine sales.

---

prensado Ⓐ ADJ compressed Ⓑ SM pressing

prensar /1a/ VT to press

preñado ADJ **1** [*mujer, animal*] pregnant **2** **~ de algo** pregnant with sth, full of sth **3** [*muro*] bulging, sagging

preñar /1a/ VT [+ *mujer*] to get pregnant; (*Zool*) to impregnate, fertilize

preñez SF pregnancy

preocupación SF worry, concern

preocupado ADJ worried, concerned (**por** about)

preocupante ADJ worrying (*esp Brit*), worrisome (*esp EEUU*)

preocupar /1a/ Ⓐ VT (= *inquietar*) to worry; (= *molestar*) to bother; **esto me preocupa muchísimo** I'm extremely worried about this, this worries me very much; **no le preocupa el qué dirán** he's not bothered about what people may say Ⓑ **preocuparse** VPR **1** (= *inquietarse*) to worry (**de, por** about); **¡no se preocupe!** (*para calmar a algn*) don't worry!; (*para que algn no haga algo*) don't bother!; **no se preocupa en lo más mínimo** he doesn't care in the least **2** (= *ocuparse*) to concern o.s. (**de** about); **tú preocúpate de que todo esté listo** you see to it that everything is ready

preolímpico ADJ **torneo ~** Olympic qualifying tournament

prepagado ADJ [*sobre*] pre-paid

prepago SM prepayment; **tarjeta de ~** prepayment card

preparación SF **1** (= *realización*) preparation; **tiempo de ~: 30 minutos** preparation time: 30 minutes; **un plato de fácil ~** an easy dish to make; **estar en ~** to be in preparation **2** (*antes de hacer algo*) **¿cuánto tiempo dedicas a la ~ de un examen?** how long do you spend studying for o preparing an exam?; **clases de ~ al parto** ante-natal classes **3** (= *formación*) (= *estudios*) education; (*profesional*) training ► **preparación física** (= *entrenamiento*) training; (= *estado*) physical condition

preparado Ⓐ ADJ **1** (= *dispuesto*) [*persona*] prepared, ready; **¡~s, listos, ya!** (*gen*) ready, steady, go!; (*Dep*) on your marks, get set, go!; **no estoy ~ mentalmente para la entrevista** I am not mentally prepared for the interview **2** (*Culin*) (= *listo para servir*) ready to serve; (= *precocinado*) ready cooked **3** (*Educ*) (*con estudios*) educated; (*como salida profesional*) trained; (*con título*) qualified Ⓑ SM (*Farm*) preparation

preparador(a) SM/F **1** [*de deportista*] trainer, coach; [*de opositor*] private tutor ► **preparador(a) físico/a** fitness trainer **2** [*de caballo*] trainer

preparar /1a/ Ⓐ VT **1** (= *dejar listo*) [+ *comida*] to make, prepare; [+ *habitación, casa*] to prepare, get ready; [+ *compuesto, derivado*] (*Quím*) to prepare, make up; **¿te preparo un café?** shall I make you a coffee?

2 (= *organizar*) [+ *acción, viaje*] to prepare; [+ *ejemplar, revista*] to prepare, work on; **tengo una sorpresa preparada para ti** I've got a surprise for you
3 [+ *persona*] (*para un partido*) to train, coach; (*para examen, oposición*) to coach, tutor
4 [+ *examen, prueba*] to study for, prepare for
Ⓑ prepararse VPR **1** (= *disponerse*) to get ready; **~se a hacer algo** to get ready to do sth; **~se para** to get ready for, prepare for
2 (= *estudiar*) [+ *discurso*] to prepare; [+ *examen*] to prepare for, study for
3 (= *formarse, entrenarse*) to prepare
4 (= *aproximarse*) [*problemas, tormenta*] to loom; **se prepara una reestructuración ministerial** a cabinet reshuffle is imminent *o* afoot *o* looming

preparativo Ⓐ ADJ preparatory, preliminary
Ⓑ preparativos SMPL preparations

preparatorio ADJ [*curso, trabajo, material*] preparatory; [*diseño, dibujo, boceto*] preliminary; **ejercicios ~s** preliminary exercises, warm-up exercises

pre-Pirineo SM Pyrenean foothills

preponderancia SF preponderance

preponderante ADJ predominant, preponderant (*frm*)

preposición SF preposition

preposicional ADJ prepositional

prepotencia SF high-handedness; **nunca me habían tratado con tanta ~** I had never been treated in such a high-handed manner *o* with such arrogance

prepotente ADJ [*actitud*] high-handed; **un ministro fatuo y ~** a conceited and arrogant minister

prepucio SM foreskin, prepuce (*frm*)

prerrequisito SM prerequisite

prerrogativa SF prerogative

prerrománico ADJ pre-romanesque

presa SF **1** (= *animal apresado*) (*por cazador*) catch; (*por otro animal*) prey; **ave de ~** bird of prey; **huyó ~ del pánico** he fled in panic; **la desesperación hizo ~ en los soldados** the soldiers were seized with despair; **ser ~ de algo** to be a prey to sth **2** (*en un río*) (= *dique*) dam; (= *represa*) weir, barrage **3** (*esp LAm*) [*de pollo*] piece

presagiar /1b/ VT to betoken, forebode, presage

presagio SM omen, portent

presbiteriano/a ADJ, SM/F Presbyterian

presbítero/a SM/F priest

prescindible ADJ dispensable

prescindir /3a/ VI **~ de 1** (= *renunciar a*) to do without, go without; **no puede ~ de su secretaria** he can't do without his secretary **2** (= *omitir*) to dispense with; **prescindamos de los detalles inútiles** let's dispense with *o* skip the unnecessary details

prescribir /3a/ (*pp* **prescrito**) **Ⓐ** VT (= *recetar*) to prescribe
Ⓑ VI [*plazo*] to expire, run out

prescripción SF (*Med*) prescription; **por ~ facultativa** on the doctor's orders

prescriptivo ADJ prescriptive

prescrito ADJ prescribed

preselección SF **1** (*Dep*) (= *acción*) seeding; (= *equipo*) squad, team **2** [*de candidatos, participantes*] shortlist, shortlisting

preseleccionar /1a/ VT **1** [+ *candidatos*] to shortlist
2 (*Dep*) to seed

presencia SF **1** (*al estar*) presence; **en ~ de algn** in the presence of sb, in sb's presence **2** (= *aspecto*) appearance; **tener buena ~** to look smart ➤ **presencia de ánimo** presence of mind

presencial ADJ **testigo ~** eyewitness

presenciar /1b/ VT (= *asistir a*) to be present at, attend; (= *ver*) to witness, see

presentable ADJ presentable

presentación SF **1** (*entre personas que no se conocen*) introduction

2 (= *introducción*) [*de personaje, proyecto*] presentation; [*de producto*] launch, presentation; [*de campaña*] launch
➤ **presentación en público** first public appearance, debut
➤ **presentación en sociedad** coming out, debut
3 (= *entrega*) submission; **el plazo de ~ de solicitudes está ya cerrado** applications are no longer being accepted, the closing date for applications is now past
4 (= *muestra*) presentation; **previa ~ de su carné de socio** on presentation of your membership card
5 (= *aspecto*) [*de persona*] appearance; [*de comida, producto, trabajo*] presentation

presentador(a) SM/F **1** [*de acto*] host/hostess, presenter (*esp Brit*) **2** (*TV, Radio*) [*de informativo*] presenter (*esp Brit*), anchorman/anchorwoman (*EEUU*); [*de programa de variedades, concurso*] host/hostess, presenter (*esp Brit*)

presentar /1a/ **Ⓐ** VT **1** (= *enseñar, exponer*) (*gen*) to present; [+ *moción, candidato*] to propose, put forward; [+ *pruebas, informe*] to submit; [+ *documento, pasaporte*] to show; **~ una propuesta** to make *o* present a proposal
2 (= *entregar*) [+ *trabajo, dimisión*] to hand in
3 (= *exponer al público*) [+ *producto, disco, libro*] to launch; **presentó su obra en la Galería Mons** she showed her work at the Mons Gallery
4 (*en espectáculo*) [+ *obra*] to perform; [+ *actor, actriz*] to present, feature
5 (*TV*) [+ *programa*] to present, host; [+ *noticias*] to present, read
6 (= *tener*) [+ *ventajas*] to have; [+ *señal, síntoma*] to show; **el cadáver presentaba varios impactos de bala** the body had several bullet wounds
7 [+ *persona*] to introduce; **me presentó a sus padres** he introduced me to his parents; **te presento a Carlos** this is Carlos; **a ver si te presento a mi amiga Jacinta** you must meet my friend Jacinta; **ser presentada en sociedad** to come out, make one's debut
8 (= *ofrecer*) [+ *disculpa*] to offer, make; **presentó sus respetos** she paid her respects
9 (*Mil*) **~ armas** to present arms; **~ batalla** (*lit*) to draw up in battle array; (*fig*) to offer resistance
Ⓑ presentarse VPR **1** (= *aparecer*) to turn up; **se ~on sin avisar** they turned up unexpectedly
2 (= *comparecer*) **tendrá que ~se ante el juez cada semana** he'll have to report to the judge once a week; **hay que ~se el lunes por la mañana en la oficina del paro** we have to go to the Job Centre on Monday morning; **~se voluntario** to volunteer
3 (= *hacerse conocer*) to introduce o.s. (**a** to); **antes de nada, me voy a ~** first of all, let me introduce myself
4 [*candidato*] to run, stand; **~se a** [+ *puesto*] to apply for; [+ *examen*] to sit, enter for; [+ *concurso*] to enter; **he decidido no ~me a las elecciones** I've decided not to stand *o* run in the elections
5 (= *surgir*) [*problema*] to arise, come up; [*oportunidad*] to present itself, arise; **el futuro no se presenta optimista** the future isn't looking too good

presente Ⓐ ADJ **1** (*en el espacio*) **el objeto del ~ trabajo** the purpose of this essay; **los firmantes del ~ escrito** we the undersigned; **el público ~** those present in the audience; **—¡Miguel García! —¡presente!** "Miguel García!" — "here!"; **un problema siempre ~** an ever-present problem; **estar ~** to be present; **hacer ~ algo a algn** (*frm*) to inform sb of sth; **hacerse ~** to manifest o.s.; **tener algo ~** to bear sth in mind
2 [*año, mes, temporada*] current; [*momento*] present; **el día 28 del ~ mes** the 28th of this month
3 (*CS*) (*en sobre*) **"presente"** "by hand"
Ⓑ SMF **los/las ~s** those present
Ⓒ SM **1** (*tb momento ~*) present; **hay que vivir el ~** you have to live in the present
2 (*Ling*) present, present tense ➤ **presente de indicativo** present indicative ➤ **presente de subjuntivo** present subjunctive
3 (= *regalo*) present, gift
Ⓓ SF (*frm*) **le comunico por la ~ que ...** I hereby inform you that ... (*frm*)

presentimiento SM premonition, presentiment; **tener un mal ~** to have a sense of foreboding

presentir /3i/ VT to feel, be aware of; **presiento que ... I**

have a feeling that ..., I feel that ...

preservar /1a/ VT 1 (= *proteger*) to protect (**contra** against; **de** from) 2 (*LAm*) (= *conservar*) to maintain, preserve

preservativo SM 1 (= *anticonceptivo*) condom, contraceptive sheath (*frm*) 2 (*And*) (= *conservante*) preservative

presidencia SF [*de nación*] presidency; [*de comité*] chairmanship; **ocupar la ~ de** [+ *empresa*] to be the president of; [+ *comité*] to be the chairman of

presidenciable ❶ ADJ **ministro ~** minister who has the makings of a president ❷ SMF possible candidate *o* contender for the presidency

presidencial ADJ presidential

presidente/a SM/F (SF *tb* **presidente**) 1 (*Pol, Com*) [*de país, asociación*] president; [*de comité, reunión*] chair, chairperson, chairman/chairwoman; (*Esp Pol*) (*tb* **Presidente del Gobierno**) prime minister; [*de la cámara*] speaker; **candidato a ~** (*Pol*) presidential candidate 2 (*Jur*) (= *magistrado*) presiding magistrate; (= *juez*) presiding judge

presidiario/a SM/F convict

presidio SM prison; **un año de ~** a year in prison

presidir /3a/ ❶ VT 1 [+ *gobierno*] to preside over, be president of; [+ *reunión*] to chair, be chairman of 2 (= *dominar*) **los temores presidieron la jornada de ayer** fear dominated *o* held sway the whole day yesterday ❷ VI (*en gobierno*) to hold the presidency; (*en ceremonia*) to preside; (*en reunión*) to be the chair

presilla SF [*de hilo, tela*] loop; [*de metal*] eye

presión SF (*Meteo, Fís, Téc*) pressure; (*con la mano*) press, squeeze; **olla a ~** pressure cooker; **reactor de agua a ~** pressurized water reactor; **indicador/medidor de ~** pressure gauge; **hacer ~ sobre algo** to press (on) sth ➤ **presión arterial** blood pressure ➤ **presión atmosférica** atmospheric pressure, air pressure ➤ **presión sanguínea** blood pressure 2 (= *influencia*) pressure; **ejercer** *o* **hacer ~ para que se haga algo** to press for sth to be done; (*Pol*) to lobby for sth to be done; **hacer algo bajo ~** to do sth under pressure ➤ **presión fiscal, presión impositiva** tax burden

presionar /1a/ ❶ VT 1 [+ *botón, tecla*] to press 2 [+ *persona*] to pressure, pressurize, put pressure on; **~ a algn para que haga algo** to pressure *o* pressurize sb into doing sth, put pressure on sb to do sth ❷ VI to press

preso/a ❶ ADJ **llevar ~ a algn** to take sb prisoner; **estuvo ~ durante tres años** he was in prison for three years; **la cárcel donde estuvo ~** the prison where he served his sentence ❷ SM/F (= *prisionero*) prisoner ➤ **preso/a común** ordinary prisoner ➤ **preso/a de conciencia** prisoner of conscience ➤ **preso/a político/a** political prisoner

prestación SF 1 (= *subsidio*) benefit ➤ **prestación por desempleo** unemployment benefit (*Brit*), unemployment compensation (*EEUU*) ➤ **prestaciones sociales** social security benefits (*Brit*), welfare benefits (*EEUU*) 2 (= *acción*) **se limitaron a la ~ de ayuda técnica** they limited themselves to giving technical aid; **le agradecemos la ~ de sus servicios** we are grateful for the services rendered ➤ **prestaciones sanitarias** health services ➤ **prestación social sustitutoria** community service (*alternative to national service*) 3 **prestaciones** (*Téc, Inform*) features, facilities; (*Aut*) (= *equipamiento*) features; (= *rendimiento*) performance *sing*

prestado ADJ (*gen*) borrowed; (*en biblioteca*) on loan; **de ~: fue a la boda de ~** he went to the wedding in borrowed clothes; **tuvo que vivir un tiempo de ~** he had to live at other people's expense for a while; **dejar algo ~** to lend sth; **pedir algo ~** (= *tomar prestado*) to borrow sth; (= *preguntar*) to ask to borrow sth; **tomar algo ~** to borrow sth

prestamista SMF [*de dinero*] moneylender; [*de empeños*] pawnbroker

préstamo SM 1 (= *acción*) (*de prestar*) lending; (*de pedir prestado*) borrowing; **en ~** on loan 2 (= *dinero prestado*) loan; **conceder un ~** to grant a loan; **pedir un ~** to ask for a loan ➤ **préstamo bancario** bank loan ➤ **préstamo**

hipotecario mortgage (loan), real-estate loan (*EEUU*) 3 (*Ling*) loanword

prestancia SF (= *elegancia*) elegance, poise; (= *excelencia*) excellence, distinction

prestar /1a/ ❶ VT 1 (= *dejar prestado*) to lend; **¿me puedes ~ el coche?** can I borrow your car?, can you lend me your car? 2 (*LAm*) (= *pedir prestado*) to borrow (**a** from) 3 (= *dedicar*) [+ *esfuerzo*] to devote; [+ *apoyo, auxilio, ayuda*] to give; **le agradecemos los servicios prestados** we thank you for the services rendered; **la embajada también prestó su colaboración** the embassy also cooperated; **~ atención a algn/algo** to pay attention to sb/sth; **no podía ~ crédito a mis oídos** I couldn't believe my ears; **~ declaración** (*ante la policía*) to make a statement; (*en un juicio*) to give evidence, testify; **~ juramento** (*gen*) to take the oath, be sworn in 4 (*frm*) (= *aportar*) **los jóvenes prestaban alegría a la fiesta** the young people brought good cheer to *o* brightened up the party; **el color azul le prestaba un encanto especial a la habitación** the blue colour gave *o* lent a special charm to the room ❷ **prestarse** VPR 1 **~se a** [*persona*] 1.1 (= *aceptar*) to accept; **no se ~á a participar en ese tipo de juego** he will never agree to be involved in that kind of game 1.2 (= *ofrecerse*) to volunteer to; **se prestó a echarnos una mano si hacía falta** he volunteered to give us a hand if we needed it 2 (= *dar lugar a*) **~se a algo: sus palabras se ~on a confusión** his words were misinterpreted; **ese argumento se presta a discusión** that argument is open to debate 3 (= *servir*) **~se para algo** to be suitable for sth; **se presta para cualquier uso** it is suitable for any purpose

presteza SF promptness, alacrity (*frm*); **con ~** speedily, promptly, with alacrity (*frm*)

prestidigitación SF conjuring, sleight of hand, prestidigitation (*frm*)

prestidigitador(a) SM/F conjurer, prestidigitator (*frm*)

prestigiar /1b/ VT to give prestige to

prestigiado ADJ (*Chi*) prestigious

prestigio SM prestige; **de ~** prestigious

prestigioso ADJ prestigious, famous

presto ❶ ADJ 1 (= *listo*) ready (**para** for; **a** to) 2 (*Mús*) presto ❷ ADV quickly, swiftly

presumible ADJ presumable, probable; **es ~ la existencia de restos más antiguos** we can assume the existence of older remains, we can assume that older remains exist

presumido ADJ (= *creído*) conceited; (= *coqueto*) vain

presumir /3a/ ❶ VI (= *alardear*) to give o.s. airs, show off; (= *envanecerse*) to be conceited; **lo hizo para ~ ante sus amistades** he did it to show off in front of his friends; **~ de listo** to think o.s. very smart ❷ VT (= *suponer*) to presume; **según cabe ~** as may be presumed, presumably

presunción SF 1 (= *suposición*) supposition, presumption; **el principio de ~ de inocencia** the principle that one is presumed innocent until proven guilty 2 (= *vanidad*) conceit, presumptuousness

presuntamente ADV supposedly, allegedly

presunto ADJ (*gen*) supposed, presumed; [*criminal*] suspected, alleged; **Gómez, ~ implicado en ...** Gómez, allegedly involved in ...

presuntuoso ADJ conceited, presumptuous

presuponer /2q/ VT to presuppose, assume

presupuestal ADJ (*Méx*) = **presupuestario**

presupuestar /1a/ VT [+ *gastos*] to budget for; **su costo está presupuestado en 16 millones** its cost is estimated at 16 million

presupuestario ADJ budget *antes de s*, budgetary

presupuesto SM 1 (*Fin*) budget; **~ de ventas** sales budget ➤ **los Presupuestos Generales (del Estado)** the national budget 2 (*para obra, encargo*) estimate; **pedir ~** to ask for an estimate

presuroso ADJ (= *rápido*) quick, speedy; (= *precipitado*) hasty; [*paso*] quick, brisk; **entró ~** he rushed in

pretemporada SF (*Dep*) pre-season

pretencioso ADJ **1** (= *con pretensiones*) pretentious, presumptuous; (= *fanfarrón*) showy **2** (*LAm*) (= *presumido*) vain

pretender /2a/ VT **1** (= *aspirar a*) **¿qué pretende usted?** what are you after?, what do you hope to achieve?; ~ **el trono** to pretend to the throne; ~ **hacer algo: pretendió convencerme** he tried to convince me; **pretendo sacar algo de provecho** I intend to get something out of it; **¿qué pretende usted decir con eso?** what do you mean by that?; **no pretendo ser rico** I've no aspirations to be rich; ~ **que** (+ SUBJUN) to expect that ... **2** (*frm*) (= *afirmar*) to claim **3** (†) (= *cortejar*) to woo, court

pretendido ADJ supposed, alleged

pretendiente/a Ⓐ SM/F (= *aspirante*) (*a cargo*) candidate, applicant (**a** for); (*al trono*) pretender (**a** to) **Ⓑ** SM (†) [*de una mujer*] suitor

pretensado ADJ prestressed

pretensión SF **1** (= *intención*) aim; (= *aspiración*) aspiration; **un libro sin más ~ que divertir** a book which only aims to entertain **2 pretensiones** (*pey*) **tiene pretensiones intelectuales** he likes to think of himself as an intellectual; **una simple chaqueta sin pretensiones** a simple jacket, nothing fancy

pretensor SM **cinturón con ~** inertia-reel seat belt

pretérito Ⓐ ADJ **1** (*Ling*) past **2** (= *pasado*) past, former **Ⓑ** SM (*Ling*) (*tb* ~ **indefinido**) preterite, past historic ➤ **pretérito imperfecto** imperfect ➤ **pretérito perfecto** present perfect

pretextar /1a/ VT to use as an excuse; ~ **que ...** to claim that ..., use as an excuse the fact that ...

pretexto SM pretext; **con el ~ de que ...** on the pretext that ...; **bajo ningún ~** under no circumstances

pretil SM (= *muro*) parapet; (= *barandilla*) handrail, railing

pretoriano ADJ **guardia pretoriana** praetorian guard

prevalecer /2d/ VI to prevail (**sobre** against, over)

prevaricación SF (*Jur*) perversion of the course of justice, corrupt practice

prevaricar /1g/ VI to pervert the course of justice, be guilty of corrupt practice

prevención SF **1** [*de accidente, enfermedad*] prevention; **en ~ de algo** in order to prevent sth; **medidas de ~** emergency measures, contingency plans **2** (= *medida*) precautionary measure, precaution

prevenido ADJ **1 ser ~** (= *cuidadoso*) to be cautious; (= *previsor*) to be far-sighted **2 estar ~** (= *advertido*) to be forewarned, be on one's guard (**contra** against)

prevenir /3r/ VT **1** (= *evitar*) to prevent; **hay accidentes que no se pueden ~** some accidents cannot be prevented; ✦ REFRÁN **más vale ~ que curar** prevention is better than cure, better safe than sorry **2** (= *advertir*) to warn; ~ **a algn** to warn sb, put sb on his guard (**contra, de** against, about) **Ⓑ prevenirse** VPR (= *prepararse*) ~**se contra algo** to take precautions against sth, prepare for sth

preventiva SF (*Méx*) amber light

preventivo ADJ [*medida*] preventive, precautionary; (*Med*) preventive

prever /2u/ VT **1** (= *adivinar*) to foresee; (= *predecir*) to predict, forecast; ~ **que ...** to anticipate that ..., expect that ...; **ya lo preveía** I expected as much; **se prevé un descenso de precios** a drop in prices is predicted *o* forecast **2** (= *proyectar*) to plan; **tenemos previsto atravesar el desierto** we are planning to cross the desert; **un embarazo no previsto** an unplanned pregnancy; **no teníamos previsto nada para eso** we had not made any allowance for that **3** (= *establecer*) to provide for, establish; **la ley prevé que ...** the law provides *o* stipulates that ...

previamente ADV previously

previo Ⓐ ADJ **1** [*experiencia, programa, conocimiento*] previous; [*examen*] preliminary; [*compromiso, autorización*] prior; **sin ~ aviso** without prior warning **2** ~ **a** before, prior

to **Ⓑ** PREP (= *tras*) ~ **acuerdo de todas las partes afectadas** subject to the agreement of all interested parties; ~ **pago de los derechos** on payment of the fees; **"previa cita"** "by appointment only", "appointment required"

previsible ADJ foreseeable, predictable

previsión SF **1** (*como cualidad*) foresight, far-sightedness **2** (= *acto*) precaution, precautionary measure; **en ~ de algo** (= *como precaución*) as a precaution against sth; (= *esperando*) in anticipation of sth **3** (= *pronóstico*) forecast; **las previsiones del plan quinquenal** the forecasts of the five-year plan

previsivo ADJ (*Col, Méx, Ven*) = **previsor**

previsor ADJ [*medida, política*] far-sighted; **seguro que tiene comida, es muy ~a** she's bound to have something to eat, she thinks of everything

previsto ADJ [*resultado*] predicted, anticipated; **la reunión prevista para el día 20** the meeting planned for the 20th; **empezó a la hora prevista** it started on time; **todo salió según lo ~** everything went as planned *o* (according) to plan

PRI SM ABR (*Méx Pol*) = **Partido Revolucionario Institucional**

prieta SF (*Chi*) black pudding

prieto ADJ **1** (= *apretado*) [*nudo*] tight; **de carnes prietas** firm-bodied **2** (*esp Méx*) dark

priísta ADJ (*Méx Pol*) of or pertaining to the PRI party

prima SF **1** [*de seguro*] premium **2** (= *gratificación*) bonus ➤ **prima de peligrosidad** danger money ➤ **prima de productividad** productivity bonus; *ver tb* **primo**

primacía SF (= *superioridad*) primacy, first place; (= *supremacía*) supremacy; **tener la ~ sobre algo** to be superior to sth

primado SM (*Rel*) primate

primar /1a/ **Ⓐ** VI (= *predominar*) **en el acuerdo bilateral prima la cooperación militar** military cooperation is key to the bilateral agreement; **en sus diseños prima la elegancia** elegance is the keynote in his designs; ~ **sobre algo** to take precedence over sth, have priority over sth **Ⓑ** VT (*Dep*) to give a bonus to

primaria SF **1** (*Educ*) primary education (*esp Brit*), elementary education (*esp EEUU*) **2** (*Pol*) (*tb* ~**s**) primary election(s)

primario ADJ [*color*] primary; [*sector, escuela*] primary (*esp Brit*), elementary (*esp EEUU*); [*instinto, necesidad*] basic

primate SM (*Zool*) primate

primavera SF **1** (= *estación*) spring; **en ~** in spring, in springtime; ✦ REFRÁN **la ~ la sangre altera** spring is in the air **2** (*liter*) (= *esplendor*) **está en la ~ de la vida** he is in the prime of life **3 primaveras** (*liter*) (= *años*) summers (*liter*); **tenía quince ~s** she was a girl of fifteen summers (*liter*) **4** (*Bot*) primrose

primaveral ADJ spring *antes de s*, springlike

primer ADJ *ver* **primero**

primera SF **1** (*Aut*) first gear, bottom gear; **meter (la) ~** to change into first gear **2** (*en viajes*) first class **3 a la ~** (= *primera ocasión*) [*acertar*] first time; **saqué el carnet de conducir a la ~** I got my driving licence (*Brit*) *o* driver's license (*EEUU*) at the first attempt; **dijo sí a la ~** he said yes straight away **4** ✦ MODISMOS **de ~** (= *excelente*) excellent, brilliant*; **aquí vendemos un jamón de ~** here we sell the finest quality ham; **a la(s) ~(s) de cambio** (= *sin avisar*) without warning; (= *tras la primera dificultad*) at the first sign of trouble; *ver tb* **primero**

primerizo/a Ⓐ ADJ (= *novato*) green, inexperienced **Ⓑ** SM/F (= *principiante*) beginner **Ⓒ** SF (*Med*) first time mother

primero Ⓐ ADJ (*antes de sm sing* **primer**) **1** (*numeral*) **1.1** (*en el espacio*) [*página, planta*] first; [*fila*] front, first; **una foto en primera página** a front-page photo, a photo on the front page; **las primeras páginas del libro** the first few pages of the book **1.2** (*en el tiempo*) [*día, semana, fase*] first; [*época, poemas*] early; [*síntoma*] first, early; **no es la primera**

vez it is not the first time; **sus dos primeras novelas** his first two novels; **la primera época de Picasso** Picasso's early period; **en los ~s años del siglo** in the early years of the century; **a primera hora (de la mañana)** first thing in the morning; **a primeras horas de la tarde de ayer** early yesterday afternoon; **en primer lugar** (*dentro de un orden*) first of all; (*para dar énfasis*) in the first place; *ver tb* **sexto** 2 (= *principal*) [*deber, objetivo*] main, primary; **lo ~ es que te pongas bueno** the main thing is that you get well; **productos de primera calidad** top quality products; **artículos de primera necesidad** basic essentials, staple items; **primer actor** leading man; **primera actriz** leading lady; **~s auxilios** first aid; **de primera categoría** first-class; **primer ministro** prime minister; **primer violín** (= *concertino*) leader (*Brit*), concertmaster (*EEUU*); (*de sección*) first violin; ✦ MODISMO **lo ~ es lo ~** first things first
Ⓑ PRON first; **soy el ~ de la lista** I'm top of the list, I'm first on the list; **quedó entre los diez ~s** he was in *o* among the first ten; **es la primera de la clase** she is the best in the class, she is top of the class; **llegar el ~** to be the first to arrive
Ⓒ SM 1 (*tb* **primer plato**) first course, starter (*esp Brit*) 2 **a ~s (de mes)** at the beginning of the month
Ⓓ ADV first; **~ iremos a comprar** first, we'll do the shopping; **~ está la obligación y después la diversión** business before pleasure; **estar ~** (*en una cola*) to be first; (*en importancia*) to come first; *ver tb* **primera**

primicia SF (= *novedad*) novelty; (= *estreno*) first appearance ➤ **primicia informativa** scoop

primigenio ADJ primitive, original

primitiva SF **la ~** (*Esp**) = **lotería primitiva**; *ver* **lotería**

primitivo ADJ 1 [*arte, pueblo*] primitive; **el hombre ~** primitive man 2 (= *original*) first, original; **devolver algo a su estado ~** to restore sth to its original state

primo/a Ⓐ ADJ 1 [*número*] prime 2 [*materia*] raw **Ⓑ** SM/F 1 (= *pariente*) cousin ➤ **primo/a carnal, primo/a hermano/a** first cousin; ✦ MODISMO **ser ~s hermanos** (*referido a cosas*) to be extraordinarily alike 2 (*Esp**) (= *incauto*) dupe, sucker*; ✦ MODISMO **hacer el ~** to be taken for a sucker*, be taken for a ride*; *ver tb* **prima**

primogénito/a ADJ, SM/F first-born

primor SM 1 (= *delicadeza*) delicacy 2 (= *maestría*) care, skill; **hecho con ~** done most skilfully *o* (*EEUU*) skillfully, delicately made 3 (= *objeto primoroso*) fine thing, lovely thing; **hace ~es con la aguja** she makes lovely things with her needlework; **hijos que son un ~** delightful children, charming children

primordial ADJ fundamental, essential; **esto es ~** this is top priority; **es ~ saberlo** it is essential to know it

primoroso ADJ (= *delicado*) exquisite, fine; (= *esmerado*) neat, skilful, skillful (*EEUU*)

prímula SF primrose

princesa SF princess

principado SM principality

principal Ⓐ ADJ 1 (= *más importante*) (*gen*) principal, main; [*crítico, adversario*] foremost; **lo ~ es que el problema se ha solucionado** the main thing is the problem has been solved 2 [*persona, autoridad*] illustrious **Ⓑ** SM 1 (*Fin*) principal, capital 2 (*Teat*) dress circle

príncipe SM prince; **el ~ de Asturias** the heir to the Spanish throne ➤ **príncipe azul** Prince Charming, knight in shining armour ➤ **príncipe de Gales** Prince of Wales ➤ **príncipe heredero** crown prince

principesco ADJ princely

principiante/a Ⓐ ADJ [*actor, fotógrafo, jugador*] inexperienced; **conductor ~** learner driver **Ⓑ** SM/F (= *novato*) beginner, novice; (= *aprendiz*) learner

principiar /1b/ VT to begin

principio SM 1 (= *comienzo*) beginning; **al ~** at first, in the beginning; **a ~s del verano** at the beginning of the summer, early in the summer; **desde el ~** from the first, from the outset; **desde el ~ hasta el fin** from start to finish, from beginning to end; **en un ~** at first, to start with 2 **principios** (= *nociones*) rudiments, first notions;

"Principios de física" "Introduction to Physics", "Outline of Physics"
3 (= *norma*) principle; **persona de ~s** man of principles; **en ~** in principle; **por ~** on principle; **sin ~s** unprincipled 4 (*Quím*) element, constituent ➤ **principio activo** active ingredient

pringado/a* SM/F (*Esp*) 1 (= *sin suerte*) unlucky person; (= *infeliz*) poor devil, wretch; **el ~ del grupo** the odd man out, the loser 2 (= *tonto*) fool, idiot

pringar /1h/ **Ⓐ** VT 1 (*Culin*) [+ *pan*] to dip, dunk; [+ *asado*] to baste 2 (= *ensuciar*) to dirty, soil (with grease) 3 (*) (= *implicar*) **~ a algn en un asunto** to involve sb in a matter 4 **~la**** (= *meter la pata*) to drop a brick*, make a boob*; **~la(s)**** (= *morir*) to kick the bucket*, snuff it* **Ⓑ** pringarse VPR 1 (= *ensuciarse*) to get covered (**con, de** with, in) 2 (*) (= *involucrarse*) to get mixed up (**en** in); **o nos pringamos todos, o ninguno** either we all carry the can or none of us does*

pringoso ADJ (= *grasiento*) greasy; (= *pegajoso*) sticky

pringue SM *o* SF 1 (= *grasa*) grease, dripping 2 (= *suciedad*) dirt 3 (*) (= *molestia*) nuisance

prior(a) SM/F prior/prioress

priorato SM (*Rel*) priory

priori *ver* **a priori**

prioridad SF (= *precedencia*) priority; (*Aut*) (*tb* **~ de paso**) right of way, priority

prioritario ADJ priority *antes de s*; **un proyecto de carácter ~** a plan with top priority, a (top) priority plan

priorizar /1f/ VT to give priority to, treat as a priority, prioritize

prisa SF hurry, haste; **voy con mucha ~** I'm in a great hurry; **a ~** quickly, hurriedly; **a toda ~** as quickly as possible; **correr ~** (*Esp*) to be urgent; **¿te corre ~?** are you in a hurry?; **darse ~** to hurry, hurry up; **¡date ~!** hurry (up)!, come along!; **meter ~ a algn** to make sb get a move on, make sb hurry up; **tener ~** to be in a hurry; ✦ MODISMO **sin ~ pero sin pausa** slow but steady

prisco SM (*CS*) apricot, *sort of peach*

prisión SF 1 (= *cárcel*) prison; **~ de alta *o* máxima seguridad** top-security prison 2 (= *encarcelamiento*) imprisonment; **cinco años de ~** five years' imprisonment, prison sentence of five years ➤ **prisión domiciliaria** house-arrest ➤ **prisión mayor** *sentence of more than six years and a day* ➤ **prisión menor** *sentence of less than six years and a day* ➤ **prisión preventiva** preventive detention; **el juez ha decretado la ~ preventiva** the judge remanded him in custody

prisionero/a SM/F prisoner; **hacer ~ a algn** to take sb prisoner ➤ **prisionero/a de guerra** prisoner of war

prisma SM 1 (*Fís, Ópt*) prism 2 (= *punto de vista*) point of view, angle

prismáticos SMPL binoculars, field glasses

prístino ADJ pristine, original

priva* SF (*Esp*) **la ~** the booze*, the drink

privacidad SF privacy

privación SF 1 (= *acto*) deprivation, deprival; **sufrir ~ de libertad** to suffer loss of liberty 2 **privaciones** (= *miserias*) hardship *sing*, privations

privada SF (*Méx*) private road (*with security control*)

privado ADJ 1 (= *confidencial*) private; **en ~** privately, in private 2 (*Col, Méx*) (= *inconsciente*) unconscious

privar¹ /1a/ **Ⓐ** VT 1 (= *quitar*) **~ a algn de algo** to deprive sb of sth, take sth away from sb; **nos vimos privados de su compañía** we found ourselves deprived of her company 2 (*Col, Méx*) (= *dejar inconsciente*) **lo privó de un golpe** he knocked him out **Ⓑ** VI 1 (*) (= *gustar mucho*) **las motos me privan** I'm mad about motorbikes* 2 (*Esp**) (= *estar de moda*) to be in fashion, be all the rage* **Ⓒ** privarse VPR 1 **~se de algo** (= *abstenerse*) to deprive o.s. of sth; (= *renunciar*) to give sth up, forgo sth; **no se privan de nada** they don't want for anything, they lack nothing 2 (*Col, Méx*) (= *desmayarse*) to faint

privar²* /1a/ (*Esp*) VI to booze*

privativo ADJ 1 (= *exclusivo*) exclusive; **esa función es privativa del presidente** that function is the president's alone 2 (*Jur*) **una pena privativa de libertad** a prison sentence

privatización SF privatization

privatizar /1f/ VT to privatize

prive** SM = **priva**

privilegiado/a Ⓐ ADJ [*vida, posición, persona*] privileged; [*clima, inteligencia, memoria*] exceptional Ⓑ SM/F privileged person; **los ~s** the privileged

privilegiar /1b/ VT (= *favorecer*) to favour, favor (*EEUU*); (= *dar privilegio*) to grant a privilege to

privilegio SM privilege; **disfrutar** o **gozar de un ~** to enjoy a privilege; **conceder un ~** to grant a privilege

pro Ⓐ SM **en ~ de** (= *en nombre de*) on behalf of; (= *en favor de*) in favour of; **los ~s y los contras** the pros and cons, for and against; **de ~** (= *bueno*) worthy; (= *verdadero*) real, true; **hombre de ~** worthy man, honest man Ⓑ PREP for, on behalf of; **asociación ~ ciegos** association for (aid to) the blind

proa SF (*Náut*) bow, prow; (*Aer*) nose; **en la ~** in the bows; **poner la ~ a** (*Náut*) to head for, set a course for

probabilidad SF 1 (= *capacidad de suceder*) likelihood, probability; **con pocas ~es de lluvia** with little likelihood of rain 2 (= *oportunidad*) chance, prospect; **hay pocas ~es de que venga** there is little prospect of his coming; **tenemos grandes ~es de ganar** we've got a good chance of winning

probable ADJ probable, likely; **es ~ que ...** it is probable o likely that ...; **es ~ que no venga** he probably won't come

probablemente ADV probably

probado ADJ 1 (= *demostrado*) proven; **un sistema de probada eficacia** a system of proven efficiency; **es un hecho ~ que ...** it has been proved that ... 2 (= *analizado*) tested; **productos de probada calidad** tried and tested products

probador SM changing room, fitting room

probar /1l/ Ⓐ VT 1 (= *demostrar*) [+ *eficacia, inocencia, teoría*] to prove; **¿cómo puedes ~ que no estabas allí?** how can you prove that you weren't there?
2 (= *poner a prueba*) [+ *sustancia, vacuna, persona*] to test; [+ *método*] to try; [+ *aparato, arma*] to test, try out; [+ *actor, músico*] to audition; **te dan diez días para ~ el ordenador** they give you a ten-day trial period for the computer, they give you ten days to try out the the the computer
3 (= *catar*) to try, taste; **prueba un poco** try o taste a bit; **yo el vino no lo pruebo** I never touch o drink wine; **llevamos horas sin ~ bocado** it's hours since we've had a bite to eat
4 [+ *ropa*] (*hecha a medida*) to fit; (*de confección*) to try on Ⓑ VI (= *intentar*) to try, have a go; **déjame que pruebe yo** let me try, let me have a go; **¿has probado con este bolígrafo?** have you tried this pen?; **~ a hacer algo** to try doing sth Ⓒ **probarse** VPR [+ *ropa, zapatos*] to try on

probeta Ⓐ SF test tube Ⓑ ADJ INV test-tube *antes de s*; **bebé ~** test-tube baby

probidad SF integrity, honesty

problema SM (*tb Mat*) problem; **el ~ del paro** the problem of unemployment; **el ~ es que no tengo tiempo** the problem is I don't have time; **¿tienes ~s de dinero?** do you have any money worries o financial problems?; **este coche nunca me ha dado ~s** this car has never given me any trouble; **no quiero ~s** I don't want any trouble; **hacerse ~s** (*LAm*) to worry

problemática SF problems *pl*, questions *pl*

problemático ADJ problematic

procacidad SF 1 [*de persona*] insolence, impudence 2 [*de comentario, chiste*] indecency, obscenity

procaz ADJ 1 [*persona*] insolent, impudent 2 [*comentario, chiste*] indecent, obscene

procedencia SF 1 (= *origen*) source, origin 2 [*de tren, avión*] point of departure; [*de barco*] port of origin 3 (*Jur*) propriety, legitimacy 4 (= *conveniencia*) properness

procedente ADJ 1 **~ de** from; **llegó a Madrid ~ de Colombia** he arrived in Madrid from Colombia 2 (= *conveniente*) proper, fitting 3 (*Jur*) proper; **procedimiento ~** proper procedure

proceder /2a/ Ⓐ VI 1 (= *provenir*) **~ de** to come from, originate in
2 (= *obrar*) to proceed, behave; **conviene ~ con cuidado** it is best to go carefully, it would be best to proceed with caution; **~ contra algn** (*Jur*) to take proceedings against sb
3 (= *pasar*) **~ a** to proceed to; **procedieron a la detención de los sospechosos** they proceeded to arrest the suspects
4 (= *ser correcto*) to be right (and proper), be fitting; **no procede obrar así** it is not right to act like that; **luego, si procede, ...** then, if appropriate, ...; **táchese lo que no proceda** cross out what does not apply
Ⓑ SM (= *conducta*) behaviour, behavior (*EEUU*); (= *línea de acción*) course of action

procedimiento SM (= *sistema*) process; (= *método*) means, method; (= *trámites*) procedure; (*Jur*) proceedings; **por un ~ deductivo** by a deductive process

proceloso ADJ (*liter*) stormy, tempestuous

prócer SM 1 (= *persona eminente*) worthy, notable; (*esp LAm Pol*) famous son, famous citizen; **~ de las letras** literary figure, eminent writer 2 (= *líder*) great man, leader; (*LAm*) leader of the independence movement

procesado¹ Ⓐ ADJ [*alimento*] processed Ⓑ SM (*Téc*) processing

procesado²/a ADJ, SM/F accused

procesador SM processor ➤ **procesador de textos** word processor

procesal ADJ [*derecho, obligación*] procedural; [*gasto, costas*] legal

procesamiento SM 1 (*Jur*) (*gen*) prosecution; (= *juicio*) trial 2 (*Inform*) processing ➤ **procesamiento de datos** data processing ➤ **procesamiento de textos** word processing 3 (*Téc*) processing

procesar /1a/ VT 1 (= *juzgar*) [*juez*] to try, put on trial; [*estado, acusación*] to prosecute, put on trial 2 (*Téc, Inform*) to process

procesión SF 1 (*Rel*) procession 2 (= *hilera*) stream; **una ~ de mendigos/hormigas** a never-ending stream of beggars/ants; ✦ MODISMO **la ~ va por dentro** he keeps his troubles o problems to himself

proceso SM 1 (= *desarrollo, tb Anat, Quím*) process ➤ **proceso de paz** peace process ➤ **proceso de selección** selection process ➤ **proceso mental** mental process 2 (*Med*) **un ~ gastroenterítico** an attack of gastroenteritis; **un ~ gripal** a bout of flu 3 (*Jur*) (= *juicio*) trial; (= *pleito*) lawsuit, proceedings *pl*; **abrir o entablar ~** to bring a suit (**a** against) 4 (*Inform*) processing ➤ **proceso de textos** word processing ➤ **proceso electrónico de datos** electronic data processing

proclama SF 1 (*Pol*) (= *bando*) proclamation; (= *discurso*) address 2 **proclamas** (= *amonestaciones*) banns

proclamación SF proclamation

proclamar /1a/ Ⓐ VT to proclaim; **~ a algn algo** to proclaim sb sth; ✦ MODISMO **~ algo a los cuatro vientos** to shout sth from the rooftops Ⓑ **proclamarse** VPR **~se campeón** to become champion, win the championship; **~se rey** to proclaim o.s. king

proclive ADJ inclined, prone (**a** to)

proclividad SF proclivity (*frm*), inclination

procreación SF procreation (*frm*), breeding

procrear /1a/ VT, VI to procreate (*frm*), breed

procura SF (*LAm*) **en ~ de** in search of; **andar en ~ de algo** to be trying to get sth

procurador(a) SM/F 1 (*Jur*) (= *abogado*) attorney, solicitor ➤ **procurador(a) general** attorney general 2 (= *apoderado*) proxy 3 (*tb ~ en Cortes*) (*Pol, Hist*) deputy, *member of Spanish parliament under Franco*; (*actualmente*) *member of a regional parliament*

procurar /1a/ Ⓐ VT 1 (= *intentar*) **~ hacer algo** to try to do sth, endeavour o (*EEUU*) endeavor to do sth; **procura que no**

te vean don't let them see you, take care not to let them see you **2** (= *conseguir*) to obtain; **esto nos ~á grandes beneficios** this will bring us great benefits ⓑ **procurarse** VPR **~se algo** to secure sth

prodigar /1h/ Ⓐ VT to lavish, give lavishly; **nos prodigó sus atenciones** he was very generous in his kindnesses to us; **~ algo a algn** to lavish sb with sth, lavish sth on sb ⓑ **prodigarse** VPR **~se en: se ~on en alabanzas** they were lavish with *o* in their praise

prodigio Ⓐ SM **1** (= *cosa*) wonder; **este nuevo chip es un ~ electrónico** this new chip is an electronic wonder *o* marvel **2** (= *persona*) prodigy **3** (*Rel*) miracle ⓑ ADJ INV **niño ~** child prodigy

prodigioso ADJ prodigious, marvellous, marvelous (*EEUU*)

pródigo ADJ **1** (= *exuberante*) bountiful; **un discurso ~ en citas bíblicas** a discourse rich in biblical quotations; **la pródiga naturaleza** bountiful nature **2** (= *generoso*) lavish, generous (**de** with) **3** (= *derrochador*) prodigal, wasteful; **hijo ~** prodigal son

producción SF **1** (*Com*) (= *acción*) production; (= *cantidad*) output; **en fase de ~** in the production phase ➤ **producción en cadena** production-line assembly ➤ **producción en serie** mass production **2** (*Literat, Mús*) output; **la ~ poética de Lorca** Lorca's poetic output **3** (*Cine, Teat, TV*) production

producir /3n/ Ⓐ VT **1** [+ *cereales, fruta, petróleo*] to produce **2** (= *fabricar*) [+ *aceite, coche*] to produce, make; [+ *electricidad, energía*] to produce, generate; **~ algo en serie** to mass-produce sth **3** [+ *cambio, efecto, herida, daños*] to cause; **un fallo en los frenos produjo el accidente** the accident was caused by brake failure; **tanto ruido me produce dolor de cabeza** all this noise is giving me a headache; **el polvo me produce alergia** I'm allergic to dust; **¿qué impresión te produjo?** what impression did it make on you?; **~ alegría a algn** to make sb happy; **~ tristeza a algn** to make sb sad **4** (*Fin*) [+ *interés*] to yield; [+ *beneficio*] to yield, generate **5** (= *crear*) [+ *novela, cuadro*] to produce **6** (*Cine, TV*) to produce ⓑ **producirse** VPR **1** (= *ocurrir*) [*cambio, efecto*] to take place; [*accidente, explosión, terremoto*] to occur; [*guerra, incendio, revolución*] to break out; **a no ser que se produzca un cambio** unless there is a change, unless a change takes place; **se desconoce a qué hora se produjo la muerte** the time of death is unknown **2** (= *provocarse*) [+ *herida, fractura*] **se produjo varias heridas con una cuchilla** he inflicted wounds on himself with a razor blade; **él mismo se produjo la muerte** he caused his own death

productividad SF productivity

productivo ADJ [*tierra, fábrica, encuentro*] productive; [*negocio*] profitable

producto SM **1** (= *artículo*) product; **nuestra gama de ~s cosméticos** our range of cosmetic products; **~s de primera necesidad** staple items, staple products, basic necessities; **"consuma productos españoles"** "buy Spanish goods"; **los ~s del campo** country produce ➤ **productos agrícolas** agricultural produce *sing*, farm produce *sing* ➤ **productos alimenticios** foodstuffs ➤ **productos de belleza** beauty products ➤ **productos de consumo** consumer goods ➤ **producto derivado** by-product; **~s derivados de la leche** dairy products, dairy produce *sing*; **~s derivados del petróleo** oil products ➤ **productos de desecho** waste products ➤ **producto químico** chemical product, chemical **2** (= *resultado*) result, product; **es ~ de años de investigación** it's the result *o* product of years of research **3** (*Fin*) (= *beneficio*) yield, profit ➤ **producto interior bruto** gross domestic product ➤ **producto nacional bruto** gross national product **4** (*Mat*) product

productor(a¹) Ⓐ ADJ **1** (*Com, Agr*) producing; **países ~es de petróleo** oil producing countries; **las naciones ~as** producer nations **2** (*Cine, TV, Mús*) production *antes de s*; **la compañía ~a** the production company ⓑ SM/F **1** (*Com*) producer; (*Agr*) producer, grower **2** (*Cine, TV*) producer

productora² SF (*Cine, TV*) production company

produje, produzco *etc ver* **producir**

proemio SM preface, introduction

proeza SF exploit, feat, heroic deed

profanación SF desecration

profanar /1a/ VT [+ *tumba, templo*] to desecrate, defile; **~ la memoria de algn** to blacken the memory of sb

profano/a Ⓐ ADJ **1** (= *laico*) profane, secular **2** (= *irrespetuoso*) irreverent **3** (= *no experto*) **soy ~ en la materia** I don't know anything about the subject ⓑ SM/F (= *inexperto*) layman/laywoman

profe* SMF teacher

profecía SF prophecy

proferir /3i/ VT [+ *palabra, sonido, maldición*] to utter; [+ *insulto*] to hurl, let fly

profesar /1a/ Ⓐ VT [+ *religión*] to profess; [+ *admiración, creencia*] to profess, declare ⓑ VI (*Rel*) to take vows

profesión SF **1** (= *ocupación*) profession; (*en formulario*) occupation; **abogado de ~** a lawyer by profession ➤ **profesión liberal** liberal profession **2** [*de fe*] profession, declaration

profesional Ⓐ ADJ professional ⓑ SMF professional; **un ~ del diseño** a professional designer

profesionalidad SF, **profesionalismo** SM professionalism

profesionalizar /1f/ Ⓐ VT to professionalize ⓑ **profesionalizarse** VPR to become professional, turn professional

profesionista SMF (*Méx*) professional

profesor(a) SM/F **1** (= *enseñante*) (*gen*) teacher; (= *instructor*) instructor ➤ **profesor(a) de autoescuela** driving instructor ➤ **profesor(a) particular** private tutor **2** (*Escol*) teacher ➤ **profesor(a) de educación física** P.E. teacher ➤ **profesor(a) de instituto** secondary teacher **3** (*Univ*) lecturer (*Brit*), professor (*EEUU*); **es ~ de griego** he is a lecturer in Greek (*Brit*), he lectures in Greek (*Brit*), he is a professor of Greek (*EEUU*) ➤ **profesor(a) adjunto/a** assistant lecturer (*Brit*), assistant professor (*EEUU*)

profesorado SM teaching staff, faculty (*EEUU*)

profeta SM prophet

profético ADJ prophetic

profetizar /1f/ VT to prophesy

profiláctico Ⓐ ADJ prophylactic ⓑ SM (= *condón*) condom, sheath (*frm*), prophylactic (*frm*)

profilaxis SF INV prophylaxis

prófugo SM (= *fugitivo*) fugitive; (= *desertor*) deserter

profundamente ADV **1** [*creer, meditar, desconfiar*] deeply, profoundly; [*dormir*] deeply, soundly **2** [*religioso, afectado*] deeply, profoundly; [*dividido*] deeply; [*conservador*] extremely

profundidad SF **1** (= *hondura*) depth; **tener una ~ de 30cm** to be 30cm deep; **¿qué ~ tiene?** how deep is it?; **la poca ~ del río** the shallowness of the river; **la ~ de la crisis** the severity of the crisis **2** **las ~es del océano** the depths of the ocean **3** (= *meticulosidad*) depth, profundity; **investigación en ~** in-depth investigation; **reforma en ~** radical *o* far-reaching reform

profundizar /1f/ Ⓐ VI **~ en algo** to go more deeply into sth; **no voy a ~ en este tema** I'm not going to go any more deeply into this topic ⓑ VT to deepen

profundo ADJ **1** (= *hondo*) deep; **poco ~** shallow **2** (= *intenso*) [*suspiro, voz, respiración*] deep; [*nota*] low, deep; [*sueño*] deep, sound; [*misterio, pensador*] profound; **siento un ~ respeto hacia él** I have great *o* a deep respect for him; **conocedor ~ del arte** expert in the art **3** **en la Francia profunda** in the French heartland

profusión SF **1** (= *abundancia*) profusion **2** (= *prodigalidad*) wealth; **con ~ de detalles** with a wealth of detail

profuso ADJ (= *abundante*) profuse; (= *pródigo*) lavish, extravagant

progenie SF progeny (*frm*), offspring, brood (*pey*)

progenitor(a) SM/F (= *antepasado*) ancestor; (= *padre*) father/mother; **progenitores** parents

programa SM 1 (*de curso, actividades, TV, Radio*) programme, program (*EEUU*); ~ **de gimnasia** exercise plan *o* regime ➤ **programa coloquio** talk *o* (*Brit*) chat show ➤ **programa concurso** game show ➤ **programa debate** TV debate ➤ **programa de estudios** curriculum, syllabus ➤ **programa doble** (*Cine*) double bill ➤ **programa electoral** electoral programme, electoral program (*EEUU*), election manifesto 2 (*Inform*) program 3 (*RPl**) (*amoroso*) pick-up

programación SF 1 (*Inform*) programming, programing (*EEUU*) 2 (*Radio, TV*) programme planning; (*en periódico*) programme guide, viewing guide; **ha habido ciertos cambios en la** ~ there have been a few changes to the schedule ➤ **programación abierta** uncoded programmes *pl*, non-scrambled programmes *pl* ➤ **programación codificada** scrambled programmes *pl*

> En inglés americano se usa **program** en lugar de **programme**.

programador(a) SM/F programmer

programar /1a/ VT 1 [+ *actividades, vacaciones*] (= *planear*) to plan; (*detalladamente*) to draw up a programme *o* (*EEUU*) program for 2 [+ *ordenador*] to program; [+ *vídeo*] to programme, program (*EEUU*) 3 (*TV, Radio*) to show 4 (*Ferro*) to schedule, timetable 5 [+ *futuro*] to shape, mould, mold (*EEUU*), determine

programático ADJ programmatical

progre* Ⓐ ADJ leftish, liberal Ⓑ SMF lefty*, liberal

progresar /1a/ VI to progress, make progress

progresión SF progression ➤ **progresión aritmética** arithmetic progression ➤ **progresión geométrica** geometric progression

progresista ADJ, SMF progressive

progresivo ADJ (= *que avanza*) progressive; (= *paulatino*) gradual; (= *continuo*) continuous; (*Ling*) continuous

progreso SM (= *mejora*) progress; (= *avance*) advance; **hacer ~s** to progress, make progress

prohibición SF 1 (= *veto*) ban (**de** on), prohibition (**de** of); **levantar la ~ de algo** to remove *o* lift the ban on sth 2 [*de exportaciones, venta*] embargo (**de** on)

prohibicionismo SM prohibitionism

prohibir /3a/ VT 1 (= *vedar*) [+ *venta, consumo, publicidad, prueba nuclear*] to ban, prohibit; **la ley lo prohíbe** it is banned by law; **~ la caza de ballenas** to put a ban on whaling, ban whaling; **queda terminantemente prohibido** it is strictly forbidden
2 (= *no permitir*) **~ algo a algn: prohibieron el acceso a la prensa** the press were banned; **el médico me ha prohibido los dulces** the doctor says I'm not allowed (to eat) sweet things, the doctor has banned me from eating sweet things; **me prohibió entrar en su casa** he banned me from his house, he forbade me to enter his house; **te prohíbo que me hables así** I forbid you to talk to me like that; **le tenían prohibido salir de casa** he was not allowed out
3 (*en letreros*) **"prohibida la entrada a menores de 18 años"** "no (admission to) under-18s"; **"prohibido el paso a toda persona ajena a la obra"** "no unauthorized entry", "authorized personnel only"; **"prohibido fumar"** "no smoking"

prohibitivo ADJ prohibitive

prohombre SM outstanding man, great man

prójimo SM fellow man, fellow creature; **el dinero del ~** other people's money; **amar al ~** to love one's neighbour *o* (*EEUU*) neighbor

prolapso SM prolapse

prole SF (= *descendencia*) offspring; (*pey, hum*) brood (*pey, hum*), spawn (*pey*)

prolegómeno SM preface, introduction; **los ~s del partido** (= *comienzo*) the early stages of the match; (= *ceremonias*) the pre-match ceremonies

proletariado SM proletariat

proletario/a Ⓐ ADJ proletarian Ⓑ SM/F proletarian (*frm*), worker

proliferación SF proliferation

proliferar /1a/ VI to proliferate

prolífico ADJ prolific

prolijo ADJ 1 (= *extenso*) prolix (*frm*); (= *largo*) long-winded; (= *pesado*) tedious; (= *muy minucioso*) excessively meticulous 2 (*RPl*) (= *pulcro*) smart, neat

prologar /1h/ VT to write an introduction to

prólogo SM 1 (= *introducción*) introduction (**de** to); **un texto con ~ y notas de ...** a text edited by ... 2 (*primer capítulo*) prologue, prolog (*EEUU*) (**de** to) 3 (= *principio*) prelude (**de** to)

prolongación SF 1 (= *acto*) prolongation, extension 2 [*de carretera*] extension 3 (*Elec*) extension

prolongado ADJ [*reunión, viaje*] lengthy; **no se recomienda su uso** ~ not suitable for prolonged use

prolongar /1h/ Ⓐ VT 1 (= *alargar*) (*gen*) to prolong, extend; [+ *tubería*] to make longer, extend; [+ *reunión*] to prolong 2 (*Mat*) [+ *línea*] to produce Ⓑ **prolongarse** VPR to extend, go on; **la fiesta se prolongó hasta la madrugada** the party went on until the early hours

promediar /1b/ VT 1 (*Mat*) to work out the average of, average (out) 2 (= *tener un promedio de*) to average

promedio SM average; **el ~ de asistencia diaria** the average daily attendance; **para aprobar hace falta sacar un cinco de ~** you need an average of five to pass

promesa Ⓐ SF 1 (= *ofrecimiento*) (*gen*) promise; (*con compromiso formal*) pledge; **cumplir una ~** to keep a promise; **faltar a una ~** to break a promise, go back on one's word ➤ **promesa de matrimonio** promise of marriage 2 (= *persona*) **la joven ~ del deporte español** the bright hope of Spanish sport Ⓑ ADJ INV **jugador ~** promising player

promesero/a SM/F (*And*) pilgrim

prometedor ADJ promising

prometer /2a/ Ⓐ VT 1 (= *dar palabra*) to promise; **¡te lo prometo!** I promise!; **prometió llevarnos a la ópera** he promised to take us to the opera
2 (*) (= *asegurar*) to assure; **te prometo que se acordará de mí** I can assure you he will remember me
3 (= *augurar*) to promise; **esto promete ser interesante** this promises to be interesting
4 (*Rel*) **~ hacer algo** to take a vow to do sth Ⓑ VI (= *tener porvenir*) to have promise, show promise Ⓒ **prometerse** VPR 1 **~se algo** to expect sth, promise o.s. sth; ✦ MODISMO **prometérselas muy felices** (*Esp*) to have high hopes
2 [*novios*] to get engaged; **~se con algn** to get engaged to sb

prometido/a Ⓐ ADJ 1 [*ayuda, favor*] promised; ✦ REFRÁN **lo ~ es deuda** a promise is a promise, you can't break a promise 2 [*persona*] engaged; **estar ~ con algn** to be engaged to sb Ⓑ SM/F (= *novio*) fiancé/fiancée

prominencia SF 1 (= *abultamiento*) bump, protuberance; [*del terreno*] rise 2 (*esp LAm*) (= *importancia*) prominence

prominente ADJ 1 [*mentón, tripa*] prominent 2 (= *importante*) prominent

promiscuidad SF promiscuity

promiscuo ADJ promiscuous

promoción SF 1 [*de producto, oferta*] promotion; **está en ~** it's on (special) offer 2 (= *año*) class, year; **estaba en mi ~** he was from my class *o* year, he was the same class *o* year as me 3 (= *ascenso*) promotion

promocional ADJ promotional

promocionar /1a/ VT 1 [+ *producto, artista*] to promote 2 [+ *empleado*] to promote

promontorio SM (= *altura*) promontory; (*en la costa*) promontory, headland

promotor(a) SM/F (*gen*) promoter; [*de disturbios*] instigator, prime mover ➤ **promotor(a) de ventas** sales promoter ➤ **promotor(a) inmobiliario/a** property developer

promotora SF property development company

promover /2h/ VT 1 (= *impulsar*) [+ *proceso, plan, intereses, desarrollo*] to promote; [+ *debate, conflicto*] to provoke 2 (= *ascender*) [+ *persona, equipo*] to promote (**a** to)

promulgación SF 1 (= *anuncio*) announcement 2 [*de ley*] enactment

promulgar /1h/ VT 1 (= *anunciar*) to announce 2 [+ *ley*] to enact, pass

pronombre SM pronoun

pronominal ADJ pronominal

pronosticar /1g/ VT to forecast; **pronosticó un aumento de la inflación** he forecast *o* predicted an increase in inflation

pronóstico SM 1 (= *predicción*) (*gen*) prediction, forecast; (*en carreras*) tip ➤ **pronóstico del tiempo** weather forecast 2 (*Med*) prognosis; **de ~ leve** slight, not serious; **su ~ es reservado** (*por falta de datos*) his condition is uncertain; (*por posibilidad de agravamiento*) his condition is unstable

prontamente ADV promptly

prontitud SF quickness, promptness; **respondió con ~** he replied promptly

pronto Ⓐ ADV 1 (= *dentro de poco*) soon; **el tren estará ~ aquí** the train will be here soon; **~ hará diez años que nos casamos** it will soon be ten years since we got married; **cuanto más ~ mejor** the sooner the better; **¡hasta ~!** see you soon!; **lo más ~ posible** as soon as possible 2 (*Esp*) (= *temprano*) early; **acostarse ~** to go to bed early; **levantarse ~** to get up early 3 (= *rápidamente*) quickly; **se hizo famoso muy ~** he became famous very quickly; **¡venid aquí, ~!** come here, right now *o* quickly!; ✦ MODISMO **se dice (muy) ~*** (*algo difícil*) it's easier said than done; (*algo sorprendente*) it's quite a thought 4 (*otras locuciones*) **al ~** at first; **de ~** (= *repentinamente*) suddenly; (= *inesperadamente*) unexpectedly; (*Col, RPl*) (= *a lo mejor*) maybe, perhaps; **por de** *o* **lo ~** (= *por ahora*) for now, for the moment; (= *en primer lugar*) for a start, for one thing; **tan ~ se ríe, tan ~ llora** one minute he's laughing, the next he's crying; **te llamaré tan ~ como sepa algo** I'll call you as soon as I hear anything Ⓑ ADJ (*frm*) [*regreso, solución, mejoría*] swift; [*respuesta*] prompt; [*servicio, persona*] quick Ⓒ SM (*Esp**) (= *arrebato*) **le dio un ~ y se largó** he left on a sudden impulse; **tiene unos ~s muy malos** he gets ratty all of a sudden*

prontuario SM 1 (= *libro*) handbook, manual, compendium 2 (*CS Jur*) criminal record

pronunciación SF pronunciation

pronunciado ADJ [*acento*] pronounced, strong; [*curva*] sharp; [*facciones*] marked, noticeable; [*pendiente*] steep; [*tendencia*] marked, noticeable

pronunciamiento SM military revolt, military uprising

pronunciar /1b/ Ⓐ VT 1 (*Ling*) [+ *palabra, idioma*] to pronounce; [+ *sonido*] to make, utter 2 (= *decir*) [+ *discurso*] to make, deliver; [+ *brindis*] to propose; **~ unas palabras de elogio** to say a few words of tribute 3 (*Jur*) [+ *sentencia*] to pass, pronounce Ⓑ **pronunciarse** VPR 1 (= *expresarse*) to declare o.s., state one's opinion; **~se a favor de algo** to pronounce in favour *o* (*EEUU*) favor of sth, declare o.s. in favour *o* (*EEUU*) favor of sth; **un 20% no se pronunció** 20% expressed no opinion 2 (*Pol, Mil*) (= *rebelarse*) to revolt, rise 3 (= *acentuarse*) to become (more) pronounced

propagación SF 1 (= *extensión*) [*de enfermedad, infección, fuego*] spreading; [*de ruido*] spreading, diffusion (*frm*); [*de ideas*] spreading, dissemination (*frm*) 2 (*Biol*) propagation

propaganda SF 1 (*Pol*) propaganda ➤ **propaganda electoral** electoral propaganda 2 (*Com*) (= *publicidad*) advertising; **hacer ~ de algo** to advertise sth 3 (= *panfletos, octavillas*) advertising leaflets *pl*

propagandista SMF propagandist

propagandístico ADJ 1 (*Pol*) propaganda *antes de s* 2 (*Com*) advertising *antes de s*

propagar /1h/ Ⓐ VT 1 (= *extender*) [+ *ideas*] to spread, disseminate; [+ *rumor, enfermedad, fuego*] spread 2 (*Biol*) to propagate Ⓑ **propagarse** VPR 1 [*ideas, rumores, enfermedad, fuego*] to spread 2 (*Biol*) to propagate

propalar /1a/ VT to divulge, disclose

propano SM propane

propasarse /1a/ VPR (= *excederse*) to go too far, overstep the bounds; (*sexualmente*) to take liberties

propelente SM propellent

propender /2a/ VI **~ a algo** to tend towards sth, incline to sth; **~ a hacer algo** to tend to do sth, have a tendency to do sth

propensión SF inclination, tendency (**a** to); (*Med*) tendency

propenso ADJ **~ a** prone to

propiamente ADV 1 (*tb ~ dicho* o *hablando*) strictly speaking 2 (= *auténticamente*) really, exactly

propiciar /1b/ VT (= *favorecer*) to favour, favor (*EEUU*); (= *crear condiciones*) to create a favourable *o* (*EEUU*) favorable atmosphere for; (= *provocar*) to cause, give rise to

propiciatorio ADJ **víctima propiciatoria** scapegoat

propicio ADJ [*momento, condiciones*] favourable, favorable (*EEUU*)

propiedad SF 1 (= *pertenencia*) possession, ownership; **es ~ del municipio** it is the property of the town, it belongs to the council, it's council property; **una finca de la ~ del marqués** an estate belonging to the marquis; **tener un piso en ~** to own a flat (*esp Brit*) *o* an apartment (*esp EEUU*); **ceder algo a algn en ~** to transfer to sb the full rights (of ownership) over sth, transfer sth completely to sb ➤ **propiedad privada** private ownership 2 (= *objeto poseído*) property; **una ~** a property ➤ **propiedad particular** private property 3 (*Quím, Med*) property 4 (= *característica*) property, attribute 5 (= *adecuación*) propriety; **hablar con ~** to speak properly *o* correctly 6 (*Com*) (= *derechos*) right, rights *pl*; **"es propiedad"** "copyright" ➤ **propiedad industrial** patent rights *pl* ➤ **propiedad intelectual, propiedad literaria** copyright

propietario/a Ⓐ ADJ **la inmobiliaria propietaria de la casa** the property company which owns the house Ⓑ SM/F (*gen*) owner, proprietor/proprietress; [*de casa alquilada*] landlord/landlady; [*de tierras*] landowner; **es ~ de una cadena de restaurantes** he owns a chain of restaurants

propina SF (*en restaurante, bar*) tip, gratuity (*frm*); [*de los niños*] pocket money (*Brit*), allowance (*esp EEUU*); **me dieron mil pesetas de ~** they gave me a thousand-peseta tip

propinar /1a/ VT [+ *golpe*] to strike, deal; [+ *azotes, paliza*] to give

propio Ⓐ ADJ 1 (*uso enfático*) 1.1 (*con posesivos*) own; **lo vi con mis ~s ojos** I saw it with my own eyes 1.2 (= *mismo*) **la solicitud debe ser firmada por el ~ interesado** the application must be signed by the applicant himself; **hacer lo ~** to do the same, follow suit 2 (*indicando posesión*) own; **¿tiene coche ~?** do you have your own car?; **en defensa propia** in self-defence; **hablo en nombre ~ y en el de mis compañeros** I speak for myself and my colleagues 3 (= *característico*) **~ de algo/algn** typical of sth/sb; **ese gesto era muy ~ de él** that gesture was very like him *o* very typical of him 4 (= *adecuado*) suitable; **recibieron al rey con los honores que le son ~s** they received the king with the honours which are his due *o* with all suitable honours Ⓑ **~s y extraños** SMPL all and sundry

proponer /2q/ (*pp propuesto*) Ⓐ VT 1 (= *sugerir*) [+ *idea, proyecto*] to suggest, propose; [+ *candidato*] to propose, put forward; [+ *brindis, moción de censura*] to propose; [+ *teoría*] to put forward, propound (*frm*); **te voy a ~ un trato** I'll make you a deal *o* a proposition; **~ a algn hacer algo** to suggest to sb that they should do sth; **yo propongo que lo paguemos a medias** I suggest we go halves on it

2 (= *recomendar*) ~ **a algn para** [+ *cargo*] to nominate sb for, propose sb as; [+ *premio*] to nominate sb for
3 (= *plantear*) [+ *problema*] (*gen*) to pose; (*Mat*) to set
Ⓑ **proponerse** VPR ~**se algo** to put one's mind to sth; ~**se hacer algo** (*con intención*) to mean to do sth, intend to do sth; (*con empeño*) to be determined to do sth, be intent on doing sth; **sin proponérselo** unintentionally

proporción SF **1** (*gen*) proportion; (*Mat*) ratio; **está en ~ con los gastos** it is in proportion to the expenses
2 proporciones [*de objeto*] proportions; [*de plan, escándalo*] scope; **una máquina de proporciones gigantescas** a machine of huge size *o* proportions; **se desconocen las proporciones del desastre** the size *o* extent *o* scope of the disaster is unknown; **guarda bien las proporciones** it remains in proportion

proporcionado ADJ **1 bien ~** [*persona, cara*] well-proportioned; [*talle*] shapely **2** (= *en proporción*) proportionate (**a** to)

proporcional ADJ proportional (**a** to)

proporcionar /1a/ VT to supply, provide; ~ **dinero a algn** to supply sb with money

proposición SF **1** (= *sugerencia, oferta*) proposal; **¿cuál es tu ~?** what do you propose?, what is your proposal *o* proposition? ➤ **proposición de ley** bill ➤ **proposición de matrimonio** marriage proposal, proposal of marriage ➤ **proposiciones deshonestas** indecent proposals, indecent suggestions **2** (*Ling*) clause **3** (*Fil, Mat*) proposition

propósito SM **1** (= *intención*) purpose; **para lograr este ~** with this in mind, for this purpose; **no veo ~ de enmienda en su comportamiento** I don't see him mending his ways *o* turning over a new leaf; **buenos ~s** (*para el futuro*) good intentions; (*para el año nuevo*) resolutions; **hacer(se) el) ~ de hacer algo** to resolve to do sth, decide to do sth; **sin ~** [*caminar, moverse*] aimlessly; [*actuar*] unintentionally; **tener (el) ~ de hacer algo** to intend *o* mean to do sth, be one's intention to do sth
2 a ~ **2.1** (*como adjetivo*) suitable, right (**para** for) **2.2** (*como adverbio*) on purpose, deliberately; **no lo hice a ~** I didn't do it on purpose *o* deliberately; **me he comprado un traje a ~ para la boda** I've bought a dress especially for the wedding; **venir a ~** (= *venir expresamente*) to come especially; (= *ser adecuado*) [*comentario, observación*] to be well-timed; [*dinero*] to come in handy **2.3** (= *por cierto*) by the way; **a ~, ¿qué vais a hacer en Semana Santa?** by the way, what are you doing at Easter? **2.4 a ~ de** (*después de verbo*) about; (*uso independiente*) talking of, à propos of; **a ~ de dinero, ¿cuándo me vas a pagar?** now you mention it *o* talking of money, when are you going to pay me?; **¿a ~ de qué me dices eso ahora?** why do you say that now?

propuesta SF **1** (= *sugerencia*) proposal; **a ~ de algn** at the proposal *o* suggestion of sb; **rechazar una ~** to reject a proposal, turn down a proposal **2** (= *recomendación*) (*para un cargo*) candidature; (*para un premio*) nomination **3** (= *proyecto*) design; **concurso de ~s** design competition

propuesto PP *de* **proponer**

propugnar /1a/ VT (= *proponer*) to advocate, propose, suggest; (= *apoyar*) to defend, support

propulsar /1a/ VT **1** [+ *vehículo*] to drive, propel; [+ *avión, cohete*] to propel **2** [+ *actividad, cambio*] to promote, encourage

propulsión SF propulsion; **con ~ a chorro** jet-propelled

propulsor(a) Ⓐ ADJ **1** [*motor*] jet *antes de s* **2** [*medidas*] driving Ⓑ SM (*Téc*) (= *combustible*) propellent, fuel; (= *motor*) motor, engine Ⓒ SM/F (= *persona*) promoter

propuse *etc ver* **proponer**

prorrata SF share, quota, prorate (*EEUU*); **a ~** proportionately, pro rata

prorratear /1a/ VT to share out, distribute proportionately, prorate (*EEUU*)

prórroga SF (= *plazo extra*) extension; (*Dep*) extra time (*Brit*), overtime (*EEUU*); (*Mil*) deferment; (*Jur*) stay (of execution), respite

prorrogable ADJ which can be extended

prorrogar /1h/ VT [+ *período, contrato*] to extend; [+ *decisión*] to defer, postpone; [+ *sesión*] to prorogue, adjourn; (*Mil*) to defer; (*Jur*) to grant a stay of execution to

prorrumpir /3a/ VI to burst forth, break out; **la multitud prorrumpió en aplausos** the crowd burst (out) into applause; ~ **en gritos** to start shouting; ~ **en lágrimas** to burst into tears

prosa SF **1** (*Literat*) prose; **poema en ~** prose poem ➤ **prosa poética** prose poetry **2** (= *prosaísmo*) prosaic nature, ordinariness; **la ~ de la vida** the ordinariness of life **3** (*And, CAm*) (= *afectación*) pomposity, affectation

prosaico ADJ [*tono, lenguaje*] prosaic; [*explicación*] mundane, prosaic; [*ambición, objetivo*] mundane

prosapia SF lineage, ancestry

proscenio SM proscenium

proscribir /3a/ VT **1** (= *prohibir*) (*gen*) to prohibit, ban; [+ *partido*] to proscribe, outlaw; [+ *criminal*] to outlaw **2** (= *desterrar*) to banish, exile

proscrito/a, proscripto/a (*RPl*) Ⓐ PP *de* **proscribir** Ⓑ ADJ **1** (= *prohibido*) (*gen*) banned, prohibited; [*actividad*] outlawed, proscribed **2** (= *desterrado*) exiled Ⓒ SM/F (= *exiliado*) exile; (= *bandido*) outlaw

prosecución SF continuation

proseguir /3d, 3k/ Ⓐ VT [+ *charla, reunión*] to continue, carry on; [+ *demanda*] to go on with, press; [+ *investigación, estudio*] to pursue Ⓑ VI to continue, go on; **¡por favor, prosiga!** please go on! *o* continue!; **prosiguió con el cuento** he went on with the story; ~ **en** *o* **con una actitud** to continue in one's attitude, maintain one's attitude

proselitismo SM proselytism

prosélito/a SM/F convert, proselyte (*frm*)

prosista SMF prose writer

prosodia SF prosody

prosopopeya SF **1** (= *personificación*) personification, prosopopoeia (*frm*) **2** (= *pomposidad*) pomposity, affectation

prospección SF **1** (= *exploración*) exploration (**de** for); ➤ **prospección de mercados** market research **2** (*Min*) prospecting (**de** for); ➤ **prospección de petróleo** prospecting for oil, drilling for oil

prospecto SM [*de medicamento*] directions for use; [*de empresa*] prospectus

prosperar /1a/ VI [*industria*] to prosper, thrive; [*idea, proyecto*] to prosper

prosperidad SF prosperity

próspero ADJ prosperous, thriving; **feliz Navidad y ~ Año Nuevo** Happy Christmas and a prosperous new year

próstata SF prostate

prosternarse /1a/ VPR to prostrate o.s.

prostíbulo SM brothel

prostitución SF prostitution

prostituir /3g/ Ⓐ VT to prostitute Ⓑ **prostituirse** VPR **1** (*en sentido sexual*) (*por primera vez*) to become a prostitute; (*como profesión*) to work as a prostitute **2** (= *corromperse*) to prostitute o.s.

prostituto/a SM/F male prostitute/prostitute

protagonismo SM (= *papel*) leading role; (= *importancia*) prominence; **afán de ~** urge to be in the limelight

protagonista SMF **1** (*en hecho real*) main figure; **los ~s del conflicto** the main figures in the dispute **2** [*de obra literaria*] main character, protagonist (*frm*); [*de película, serie*] main character, lead

protagonizar /1f/ VT **1** (*Cine, Teat*) to play the lead in; **una película protagonizada por Greta Garbo** a film (*esp Brit*) *o* movie (*esp EEUU*) starring Greta Garbo **2** [+ *proceso, rebelión*] to lead; [+ *manifestación, protesta*] to be involved in; [+ *escándalo*] to be caught up in, be involved in; [+ *derrota, victoria*] to figure in, be involved in

protección SF protection ➤ **protección civil** civil defence *o* (*EEUU*) defense ➤ **protección de datos** data protection

proteccionismo SM protectionism

proteccionista Ⓐ ADJ [*medida*] protectionist; [*arancel*] protective Ⓑ SMF protectionist

protector(a) Ⓐ ADJ 1 (= *defensivo*) protecting, protective; **cubierta ~a** protective cover; **medidas ~as de la industria** measures to protect industry, protective measures towards industry; **crema ~a** barrier cream 2 [*tono*] patronizing Ⓑ SM/F (= *defensor*) (*gen*) protector; [*de artista*] patron; [*de la tradición*] guardian Ⓒ SM ➤ **protector bucal** (*Boxeo*) gum shield ➤ **protector de pantalla** (*Inform*) screen saver ➤ **protector solar** sun protection

protectorado SM protectorate

proteger /2c/ Ⓐ VT to protect (**contra, de** against, from); **sus padres la protegen demasiado** her parents are overprotective towards her Ⓑ **protegerse** VPR **~se de** o **contra algo** to protect o.s. from o against sth; **~se de las miradas indiscretas** to shield o.s. from prying eyes

protegido/a Ⓐ ADJ 1 [*especie*] protected 2 [*vivienda*] subsidised Ⓑ SM/F protégé, protégée

proteína SF protein

proteínico ADJ protein *antes de s*

protésico/a Ⓐ ADJ prosthetic Ⓑ SM/F prosthetist, limb-fitter ➤ **protésico/a dental** dental technician

prótesis SF INV (*Med*) (*gen*) prosthesis; (= *brazo, pierna*) artificial limb ➤ **prótesis de cadera** artificial hip; **le han puesto una ~ de cadera** she's had a hip replacement ➤ **prótesis de mama** breast implant ➤ **prótesis dental** dental prosthesis

protesta SF 1 (= *queja*) protest; **una manifestación de ~ contra la nueva ley** a protest demonstration against the new law; **en señal de ~ contra** o **por algo** in protest against sth 2 (*Méx*) (= *promesa*) promise; (= *juramento*) oath

protestante ADJ, SMF Protestant

protestantismo SM Protestantism

protestar /1a/ Ⓐ VI 1 (= *quejarse*) to complain; **~on contra la subida de la gasolina** they complained o (*frm*) protested against the rise in the price of petrol 2 (*Jur*) **¡protesto, Su Señoría!** objection, Your Honour o (*esp EEUU*) Honor! Ⓑ VT [+ *letra, pagaré*] to protest, note; **un cheque protestado por falta de fondos** a cheque referred to drawer

protestón/ona* Ⓐ ADJ perpetually moaning, whingeing (*pey**) Ⓑ SM/F perpetual moaner, whinger (*pey**)

protocolario ADJ 1 (= *ceremonial*) required by protocol, established by protocol 2 (= *formulario*) ceremonial, formal

protocolo SM 1 (*Pol, Inform*) protocol 2 (= *reglas ceremoniales*) protocol, convention; **sin ~s** informal(ly), without formalities

protón SM proton

prototipo SM (= *arquetipo*) prototype; (= *modelo*) model

protuberancia SF protuberance

provecho SM benefit; **de ~** [*negocio*] profitable; [*actividad*] useful; [*persona*] worthy, honest; **¡buen ~!** enjoy your meal!; **en ~ de** to the benefit of; **en ~ propio** for one's own benefit, to one's own advantage; **sacar ~ de algo** to benefit from sth, profit by o from sth

provechoso ADJ (= *beneficioso*) beneficial, useful; (= *rentable*) profitable

proveedor(a) SM/F (= *abastecedor*) supplier, purveyor; (= *distribuidor*) dealer; **consulte a su ~ habitual** consult your usual dealer; ➤ **proveedor de servicios de Internet** Internet service provider, ISP

proveer /2e/ (*pp* **provisto, proveído**) Ⓐ VT 1 (= *suministrar*) to supply, furnish (**de** with) 2 [+ *vacante*] to fill 3 (*Jur*) to decree Ⓑ VI **~ a** to provide for Ⓒ **proveerse** VPR **~se de algo** to provide o.s. with sth

proveniente ADJ **~ de** from

provenir /3r/ VI **~ de** to come from

provenzal ADJ, SM Provençal

proverbial ADJ proverbial

proverbio SM proverb

providencia SF 1 (*Rel*) **la (Divina) Providencia** (Divine) Providence 2 (*Jur*) ruling, decision

providencial ADJ providential

provincia SF 1 (= *distrito*) province; (*Esp Admin*) ≈ county; **la capital de la ~** the provincial capital 2 **provincias, una ciudad de ~s** a country town, a provincial town; **una gira por ~s** a tour of the provinces

PROVINCIA

Spain is divided into 55 administrative **provincias**, including the islands and territories in North Africa. Each one has a **capital de provincia** which generally has the same name as the province itself. **Provincias** are grouped by geography, history and culture into **comunidades autónomas**. ⇨ COMUNIDAD AUTÓNOMA

provincial ADJ provincial, ≈ county *antes de s*

provinciano/a Ⓐ ADJ 1 (= *rural*) country *antes de s* 2 (= *paleto*) provincial Ⓑ SM/F provincial country dweller

proviniente ADJ = **proveniente**

provisión SF 1 (= *acto*) provision; **concurso para la ~ de 84 plazas de profesorado** competition to fill 84 teaching jobs 2 (= *abastecimiento*) provision, supply 3 **provisiones** (= *alimentos*) provisions, supplies 4 (*Fin*) ➤ **provisión de fondos** financial cover

provisional ADJ provisional

provisorio ADJ (*esp LAm*) provisional

provisto PP *de* **proveer**; **~ de algo** [*persona*] provided with sth, supplied with sth; [*automóvil, máquina*] equipped with sth

provocación SF provocation

provocador(a) Ⓐ ADJ provocative; **agente ~** agent provocateur Ⓑ SM/F trouble-maker

provocar /1g/ Ⓐ VT 1 (= *causar*) [+ *protesta, explosión*] to cause, spark off; [+ *fuego*] to cause, start (deliberately); [+ *cambio*] to bring about, lead to; [+ *proceso*] to promote; **~ risa a algn** to make sb laugh; **incendio provocado** arson 2 [+ *parto*] to induce, bring on 3 [+ *persona*] (*gen*) to provoke; (= *incitar*) to rouse, stir up (to anger); (= *tentar*) to tempt, invite; **¡no me provoques!** don't start me! 4 (*sexualmente*) to arouse Ⓑ VI (*Col, Perú, Ven*) **¿te provoca un café?** would you like a coffee?, do you fancy a coffee?

provocativo ADJ 1 (= *provocador*) [*mirada, vestido*] provocative; [*risa, gesto*] inviting, provocative 2 (*Col, Perú, Ven*) (= *apetecible*) tempting

proxeneta SMF pimp, procurer/procuress

próximamente ADV shortly, soon

proximidad SF nearness, closeness; **en las ~es de Madrid** in the vicinity of Madrid

próximo/a ADJ 1 (= *cercano*) [*lugar*] near, close; [*pariente*] close; **un lugar ~ a la costa** a place near the coast; **vivimos muy ~s** we live very close by; **en fecha próxima** soon, at an early date; **estar ~ a algo** to be close to sth, be near sth 2 (= *siguiente*) next; **el mes ~** next month; **el ~ 5 de junio** on June 5th next; **se bajarán en la próxima parada** they will get off at the next stop

proyección SF 1 [*de imagen*] projection; [*de luz*] casting, throwing 2 (*Cine*) screening 3 (= *alcance*) hold, influence; **un intelectual con gran ~ social** a very influential intellectual; **un artista de una gran ~ internacional** an internationally renowned artist

proyectar /1a/ VT 1 (= *planear*) **~ hacer algo** to plan to do sth 2 (*Arquit*) to plan; (*Mec*) to design 3 (*Cine, Fot*) to project, screen 4 [+ *luz*] to cast, project; [+ *sombra*] to cast 5 (= *dirigir*) [+ *objeto*] to hurl, throw; [+ *chorro, líquido*] to shoot out 6 (*Mat*) to project

proyectil SM projectile, missile

proyectista SMF 1 (= *diseñador*) designer 2 (*Cine*) projectionist

proyecto SM 1 (= *intención*) plan; **tener algo en ~** to be planning sth; **tener ~s para algo** to have plans for sth 2 (= *trabajo*) project; (= *diseño*) plan, design ➤ **proyecto de**

fin de carrera (*Univ*) (*práctico*) final-year project; (*teórico*) final-year dissertation ➤ **proyecto de ley** (*Pol*) bill ➤ **proyecto piloto** pilot scheme **3** (*Fin*) detailed estimate

proyector SM **1** (*Cine*) projector ➤ **proyector de diapositivas** slide projector **2** (= *foco de luz*) (*Teat*) spotlight; (*para monumentos*) floodlight; (*Mil*) searchlight

prudencia SF (= *cuidado*) care, caution; (= *cordura*) wisdom, prudence; **actuar con ~** to be careful o cautious; **extremar la ~** to proceed with extreme caution

prudencial ADJ **1** (= *adecuado*) prudential; (= *sensato*) sensible; **tras un intervalo ~** after a decent interval, after a reasonable time **2** [*cantidad, distancia*] roughly correct

prudente ADJ sensible, prudent; **es una conductora muy ~** she's a very careful driver; **manténgase a una distancia ~ del vehículo delantero** keep a safe distance from the car in front

prueba SF **1** (= *demostración*) proof; **eso es la ~ de que él lo hizo** this proves that he did it, this is the proof that he did it; **es ~ de que tiene buena salud** that proves o shows he's in good health; **sin dar la menor ~ de ello** without giving the faintest sign of it; **ser buena ~ de algo** to be clear proof of sth; **como** o **en ~ de** in proof of; **a las ~s me remito** (I'll let) the facts speak for themselves **2** (*Jur*) piece of evidence; **~s** evidence *sing*; **por falta de ~s** for lack of evidence ➤ **pruebas documentales** documentary evidence *sing* **3** (= *examen*) (*Escol, Univ, Med*) test; [*de actor*] (*Cine*) screen test; (*Teat*) audition; **se tendrán que hacer la ~ del sida** they'll have to be tested for AIDS; ✦ MODISMO **ser la ~ de fuego de algo** to be an acid test of sth ➤ **prueba de acceso** entrance test, entrance examination ➤ **prueba de alcoholemia** Breathalyzer® test ➤ **prueba de(l) embarazo** pregnancy test ➤ **prueba de nivel** placement test ➤ **prueba de paternidad** paternity test ➤ **prueba nuclear** nuclear test **4** (= *ensayo*) **haz la ~** try it; **a prueba** (*Téc*) on trial; (*Com*) on approval, on trial; **poner a ~ la paciencia de algn** to try sb's patience; **poner a ~ los nervios de algn** to test sb's nerves; **período de ~** [*de persona*] probationary period; [*de producto*] trial period; **piloto de ~s** test pilot; **vuelo de ~s** test flight; **estar en (fase de) ~s** to be on trial; **emitir en ~s** (*TV*) to broadcast test transmissions **5 a ~ de: a ~ de agua** waterproof; **a ~ de bala(s)** bulletproof; **a ~ de bomba(s)** (*lit*) bombproof, shellproof; **un método a ~ de bombas** a surefire method; **es de una honestidad a ~ de bomba** he's completely honest **6** (*Dep*) (= *disciplina*) event; (= *carrera*) race; **la ~ de los cien metros lisos** o (*LAm*) **planos** the hundred metres ➤ **prueba clasificatoria** heat ➤ **prueba contrarreloj** time trial ➤ **prueba de resistencia** endurance test ➤ **prueba de vallas** hurdles, hurdles race ➤ **prueba por equipos** (*Ciclismo*) team trial **7** (*Cos*) fitting; **sala de ~s** fitting room **8** **pruebas** (*Tip*) proofs; **corrector de ~s** proofreader

prurito SM **1** (*Med*) (= *picor*) itching, pruritus (*frm*) **2** (= *anhelo*) itch, urge; **por un ~ de exactitud** out of an excessive desire for accuracy, because of his eagerness to get everything just right

psicoanálisis SM INV psychoanalysis

psicoanalista SMF psychoanalyst

psicoanalítico ADJ psychoanalytic, psychoanalytical

psicoanalizar /1f/ VT to psychoanalyse

psicodélico ADJ psychedelic

psicolingüística SF psycholinguistics *sing*

psicología SF psychology

psicológico ADJ psychological

psicólogo/a SM/F psychologist

psicomotricidad SF psychomotor activity

psicópata SMF psychopath

psicosis SF INV psychosis

psicosomático ADJ psychosomatic

psicotécnico ADJ **test ~** ◇ **prueba psicotécnica** response test

psicoterapeuta SMF psychotherapist

psicoterapia SF psychotherapy

psicótico/a ADJ, SM/F psychotic

psique SF psyche

psiquiatra SMF psychiatrist

psiquiatría SF psychiatry

psiquiátrico Ⓐ ADJ psychiatric Ⓑ SM mental hospital

psíquico ADJ psychic, psychical

PSOE [pe'soe] SM ABR (*Esp*) = **Partido Socialista Obrero Español**

psoriasis SF INV psoriasis

PSS SF ABR = **prestación social sustitutoria**

ptas ABR = **pesetas**

pts ABR = **pesetas**

púa SF **1** (= *pincho*) (*Bot, Zool*) prickle, spine; [*de erizo*] quill; [*de peine*] tooth; [*de tenedor*] prong, tine; [*de alambre*] barb; (*LAm*) [*de gallo de pelea*] spur **2** (*para guitarra*) plectrum, pick; (*RPl*) [*de tocadiscos*] needle

puaf* EXCL yuck!*

pub [pub, paβ] SM (*pl* **pubs** [pub, paβ]) *late night music bar*

púber ADJ, SMF adolescent

pubertad SF puberty

púbico ADJ pubic

pubis SM INV pubis

publicación SF publication

publicar /1g/ VT **1** (*Com*) [+ *libro, artículo*] to publish; [+ *disco, grabación*] to issue **2** (= *difundir*) (*gen*) to publicize; [+ *secreto*] to make public, divulge

publicidad SF **1** (*Com*) advertising; **hacer ~ de** to advertise **2** (= *divulgación*) publicity; **dar ~ a algo** to give publicity to sth

publicista SMF publicist

publicitario/a Ⓐ ADJ advertising *antes de s*, publicity *antes de s* Ⓑ SM/F advertising agent, advertising executive

público Ⓐ ADJ **1** (= *de los ciudadanos, del Estado*) [*transporte, organismo, gasto*] public; **colegio ~** state school (*Brit*), public school (*EEUU*); **la vía pública** the street, the public highway (*frm*) **2** (= *no íntimo*) [*acto, escándalo*] public; **hacer algo ~** to make sth public Ⓑ SM **1** (= *audiencia*) (*Mús, Teat*) audience; (*Dep, Taur*) spectators *pl*, crowd; **había poco ~ en la sala** there weren't many people in the audience; **"apta para todos los públicos"** "certificate U" (*Brit*), "G movie" (*EEUU*); **en ~** [*actuar, hablar*] in public; [*actuación, presentación, aparición*] public; **el gran ~** (*gen*) the general public ➤ **público infantil** children's audience **2** (= *seguidores*) [*de periódico, escritor*] readers *pl*, readership; [*de cantante*] fans *pl* **3** [*de oficina, banco, museo*] **nuestros precios están expuestos al ~** our prices are displayed publicly; **a las dos cerramos al ~** we close (to the public) at two o'clock; **"horario de atención al público"** (*en bancos*) "hours of business"; (*en tiendas*) "opening hours"

publirreportaje SM advertising feature

pucará SF (*LAm*) pre-Columbian fort

pucha* SF (*SAm*) **¡(la) ~!** (*con sorpresa*) well I'm damned!; (*con irritación*) drat!

puchero SM **1** (= *olla*) cooking pot **2** (= *guiso*) stew **3** (*) (= *mueca*) pout; **hacer ~s** to pout, screw up one's face

pucho* SM (*LAm*) **1** (= *colilla*) fag end* **2** (= *cigarrillo*) fag* **3** (= *resto*) scrap, left-over(s) *pl* **4 a ~s** in dribs and drabs

pude *etc ver* **poder**

pudibundo ADJ prudish

púdico ADJ (= *recatado*) modest; (= *casto*) chaste

pudiendo *ver* **poder**

pudiente ADJ wealthy, well-to-do; **las gentes menos ~s** the less well-off; **las clases ~s** the upper classes

pudín SM pudding

pudo *etc ver* **poder**

pudor SM 1 (= *recato*) modesty; (= *vergüenza*) (sense of) shame, (sense of) decency; **con ~** modestly, discreetly; **lo dijo sin ningún ~** she said it without embarrassment 2 (= *castidad*) chastity, virtue; **atentado al ~** indecent assault

pudoroso ADJ (= *recatado*) modest; (= *casto*) chaste, virtuous

pudrir /3a/ Ⓐ VT 1 (= *descomponer*) to rot, decay 2 (*RPl**) (= *molestar*) to upset; (= *aburrir*) to bore stiff* Ⓑ **pudrirse** VPR 1 [*comida*] to rot, decay 2 [*persona*] to rot, languish; **¡ahí o así te pudras!*** you can rot for all I care! 3 (*RPl**) (*de aburrimiento*) to get bored stiff*

pueblerino/a Ⓐ ADJ [*carácter, ambiente*] small-town *antes de s*; [*persona*] rustic, provincial Ⓑ SM/F (= *aldeano*) rustic, country person; (*pey*) country bumpkin*, hick (*EEUU**)

pueblo SM 1 (*Pol*) people, nation; **la voluntad del ~** the people's will ➤ **pueblo elegido** chosen people 2 (= *plebe*) common people *pl*, lower orders *pl*; **el ~ llano** the common people 3 (= *localidad pequeña*) (*gen*) small town; (*en el campo*) country town; (*de pocos habitantes*) village; **ser de ~** (*gen*) to be a country person, be from the countryside; (*pey*) to be a country bumpkin*, be a country hick (*EEUU**)

puedo *etc ver* **poder**

puente Ⓐ SM 1 (*Arquit*) bridge; ✦ MODISMO **tender un ~** ✧ **tender ~s** to build bridges ➤ **puente aéreo** (*de servicio frecuente*) shuttle service; (*en crisis*) airlift ➤ **puente colgante** suspension bridge ➤ **puente levadizo** drawbridge 2 [*de gafas, entre dientes*] bridge 3 (*Elec*) **hacer un ~ a un coche** to hot-wire a car 4 (*Náut*) (*tb* **~ de mando**) bridge; (= *cubierta*) deck 5 (*entre fiestas*) long weekend; **hacer ~** to take a long weekend Ⓑ ADJ INV **curso ~** intermediate course (*between two degrees*)

HACER PUENTE

When a public holiday falls on a Tuesday or Thursday it is common practice for employers to make the Monday or Friday a holiday as well and to give everyone a four-day weekend. This is known as **hacer puente**. When a named public holiday such as the **Día de la Constitución** in Spain falls on a Tuesday or a Thursday, people refer to the whole holiday period as e.g. the **puente de la Constitución**.

---

puenting ['pwentin] SM bungee jumping (*from a bridge*)

puerco/a Ⓐ SM/F 1 (= *cerdo*) pig/sow, hog/sow (*EEUU*) ➤ **puerco espín** porcupine 2 (*) (= *sinvergüenza*) pig*; (= *canalla*) swine*, rotter (*Brit*†*) Ⓑ ADJ 1 (= *asqueroso*) dirty, filthy 2 (= *repugnante*) nasty, disgusting 3 (= *grosero*) coarse 4 (= *mezquino*) rotten*, mean

puericultor(a) SM/F (*en guardería*) nursery nurse; (= *enfermera*) paediatric o (*EEUU*) pediatric nurse; (= *médico*) paediatrician, pediatrician (*EEUU*)

puericultura SF (*gen*) childcare; (= *especialidad*) paediatrics *sing*, pediatrics *sing* (*EEUU*)

pueril ADJ childish, puerile (*frm*)

puerro SM leek

puerta SF 1 [*de casa, vehículo, armario*] door; [*de jardín, ciudad*] gate; **llaman a la ~** there's somebody at the door; **un coche de dos ~s** a two-door car; **le esperé a la ~ de la escuela** I waited for him outside the entrance to the school; **Susana me acompañó a la ~** Susana saw me out ➤ **puerta corredera** sliding door ➤ **puerta de artistas** stage door ➤ **puerta de servicio** tradesman's entrance ➤ **puerta principal** [*de casa*] front door; [*de edificio público*] main entrance ➤ **puerta trasera** back door 2 (*locuciones*) **de ~s abiertas: jornada de ~s abiertas** open day (*Brit*), open house (*EEUU*); **a ~ cerrada** (*gen*) behind closed doors; (*Jur*) in camera; **de ~ en ~** from door to door; ✦ MODISMOS **a las ~s de: a las ~s de la muerte** at death's

door; **ya a las ~s de la primavera** with spring just around the corner; **dejar la ~ abierta a algo** to leave the way open to sth; **abrir la ~ a algo** to open the door to sth; **de ~s afuera: lo que pasa de ~s afuera** (= *fuera de casa*) what happens outside of this home; (= *en el extranjero*) what happens abroad; **cerrar todas las ~s a algn** to close off all avenues to sb; **coger la ~** (*Esp**) to leave; **dar con la ~ en las narices a algn** to slam the door in sb's face; **por la ~ grande: entrar por la ~ grande** to make a grand entrance; **salir por la ~ grande** [*torero*] to make a triumphant exit; **si me voy, lo haré por la ~ grande** if I leave, I'll leave with my head held high; **querer poner ~s al campo** to try to stem the tide 3 (*Aer*) gate ➤ **puerta de embarque** boarding gate 4 (*Dep*) goal; **un disparo o remate a ~** a shot at goal; **sacar de ~** to take a goal kick

puertaventana SF shutter

puerto SM 1 (*para embarcaciones*) port, harbour, harbor (*EEUU*); **entrar a o tomar ~** to enter (into) port; ✦ MODISMO **llegar a buen ~** to get over a difficulty, come through safely ➤ **puerto de mar** seaport ➤ **puerto deportivo** marina, yachting harbour o (*EEUU*) harbor ➤ **puerto franco, puerto libre** free port ➤ **puerto pesquero** fishing port 2 (*tb* **~ de montaña**) pass 3 (*Inform*) port ➤ **puerto de expansión** expansion port ➤ **puerto de serie** serial port ➤ **puerto USB** USB port

Puerto Rico SM Puerto Rico

puertorriqueño/a ADJ, SM/F Puerto Rican

pues CONJ 1 (*con valor consecutivo*) then; **—tengo sueño —¡~ vete a la cama!** "I'm tired" — "then go to bed!"; **llegó, ~, con dos horas de retraso** so he arrived two hours late 2 (*con valor enfático*) well; **~ no voy** well I'm not going; **¡~ claro!** yes, of course! 3 (*indicando duda*) **~ no sé** well, I don't know 4 (*frm*) (*con valor causal*) since, for; **cómpralo, ~ lo necesitas** buy it, since you need it

puesta SF 1 (= *acción*) ➤ **puesta al día** updating ➤ **puesta a punto** fine tuning ➤ **puesta de largo** coming-out (in society) ➤ **puesta de sol** sunset ➤ **puesta en común** idea-sharing session ➤ **puesta en escena** staging ➤ **puesta en marcha** (= *acto*) starting; (= *dispositivo*) self-starter ➤ **puesta en práctica** putting into effect, implementation 2 [*de huevos*] egg-laying; **una ~ anual de 300 huevos** an annual lay o output of 300 eggs

puestero/a SM/F 1 (*LAm*) (*en mercado*) stallholder, market vendor 2 (*CS Agr*) farm overseer

puesto Ⓐ PP *de* **poner** Ⓑ ADJ 1 **con el sombrero ~** with one's hat on, wearing a hat; **salieron del país con lo ~** they left the country with nothing but the clothes they were wearing 2 [*persona*] **bien ~ o ✧ muy ~** well dressed, smartly turned out 3 **ir ~*** (= *estar drogado*) to be high*; (= *estar borracho*) to be plastered*, be soused (*EEUU**) 4 (*Esp*) (= *informado*) **no está muy ~ en este tema** he's not very well up on this subject 5 **estar ~** (*Méx**) (= *dispuesto*) to be willing, be prepared; (*Chi**) (= *borracho*) to be plastered*, be soused (*EEUU**) Ⓒ SM 1 (= *lugar*) place; (= *posición*) position; **ocupa el tercer ~ en la liga** it is in third place in the league; **ceder el ~ a algn** to give up one's place to sb; **sabe estar en su ~** he knows his place ➤ **puesto de honor** leading position 2 (= *empleo*) post, position, job; **se crearán 200 ~s de trabajo** 200 new jobs will be created 3 [*de policía, soldado*] post ➤ **puesto de control** checkpoint ➤ **puesto de observación** observation post ➤ **puesto de socorro** first-aid post ➤ **puesto de vigilancia** (= *garita*) guard post; (= *torre*) watchtower ➤ **puesto fronterizo** border post 4 (*Com*) (*en mercado*) stall; (*en feria de muestras*) stand, booth ➤ **puesto de periódicos** newspaper stand Ⓓ **~ que** CONJ since, as

puf¹ EXCL ugh!

puf² SM (*pl* **~s**) pouffe

pufo** SM (*Esp*) 1 (= *trampa*) trick, swindle 2 (= *deuda*) debt

púgil SM boxer

pugilístico ADJ boxing *antes de s*

pugilato SM 1 (= *boxeo*) boxing 2 (= *disputa*) conflict

pugna SF struggle, conflict; **entrar en ~ con algn** to clash with sb, come into conflict with sb; **estar en ~ con algn** to clash with sb, conflict with sb

pugnar /1a/ VI 1 (= *luchar*) to fight (**por** for); **~ en defensa de algo** to fight in defence of sth 2 (= *esforzarse*) to struggle, strive; **~ por hacer algo** to struggle o strive to do sth; **~ con** [+ *opinión, idea*] to clash with, conflict with; [+ *persona*] to battle it out with

puja SF (*Esp*) (*en subasta*) bidding

pujante ADJ (= *fuerte*) strong, vigorous; (= *potente*) powerful; (= *poderoso económicamente*) booming

pujanza SF [*de grupo, país*] power, strength; [*de idioma, industria, economía*] strength

pujar /1a/ VI 1 (*Esp*) (*en subasta*) to bid, bid up 2 (= *esforzarse*) to struggle, strain; **~ por hacer algo** to struggle to do sth 3 (*CAm, Méx***) (= *quejarse*) to moan, whinge*

pulcritud SF neatness, tidiness

pulcro ADJ (= *ordenado*) neat, tidy; (= *elegante*) smartly dressed

pulga SF flea; ✦ MODISMOS **buscar las ~s a algn*** to tease sb, needle sb*; **tener malas ~s*** to be short-tempered, be bad-tempered

pulgada SF inch

pulgar SM thumb

pulgón SM plant louse

pulgoso ADJ, **pulguiento** ADJ (*And, RPl*) flea-ridden, verminous

pulido ADJ 1 [*madera, metal*] polished 2 [*estilo, lenguaje*] refined, polished

pulidora SF polishing machine

pulimentado SM polishing

pulimentar /1a/ VT to polish

pulir /3a/ Ⓐ VT 1 [+ *cristal, metal, suelo*] to polish 2 (= *perfeccionar*) to polish 3 [+ *persona*] **nadie ha logrado ~lo** nobody has managed to polish his manners; **en este colegio ~án su educación** they will finish off o round off her education at this school 4 (**) (= *birlar*) to pinch* Ⓑ **pulirse** VPR 1 (= *refinarse*) to acquire polish 2 (*) (= *gastar*) to go through, get through

pulla SF cutting remark, wounding remark

pulmón SM lung; **a pleno ~** [*respirar*] deeply; [*gritar*] at the top of one's lungs ➤ **pulmón de acero** iron lung

pulmonar ADJ pulmonary (*frm*), lung *antes de s*

pulmonía SF pneumonia

pulóver SM (*pl* **pulovers**) 1 (*LAm*) (*con mangas*) pullover 2 (*Ven*) (= *chaleco*) tank top

pulpa SF 1 [*de fruta, planta*] pulp ➤ **pulpa de madera** wood pulp ➤ **pulpa de papel** paper pulp 2 (*LAm*) (= *carne*) meat off the bone, fillet

pulpejo SM fleshy part, soft part

pulpería SF (*LAm*) general store, food store

pulpero/a SM/F (*LAm*) storekeeper, grocer

púlpito SM pulpit

pulpo SM octopus; ✦ MODISMO **ser como un ~** to be all arms

pulque SM pulque

pulquear /1a/ (*Méx*) Ⓐ VI to drink pulque Ⓑ **pulquearse** VPR to get drunk on pulque

pulquería SF (*Méx*) bar

pulsación SF 1 (= *latido*) beat 2 [*de tecla*] keystroke

pulsar /1a/ VT 1 [+ *botón*] to press; [+ *tecla*] to strike, touch, tap; (*Mús*) to play 2 [+ *opinión*] to sound out

pulsear /1a/ VI (*CS*) 1 (= *echar un pulso*) to arm-wrestle 2 (= *apuntar*) to take aim

pulsera SF bracelet, wristlet; **reloj de ~** wristwatch

pulso SM 1 (*Med*) pulse; **tomar el ~ a algn** to take sb's pulse, feel sb's pulse; **tomar el ~ a la opinión pública** to sound out public opinion 2 (= *seguridad en la mano*) **tener buen ~** to have a steady hand; **tener mal ~** to have an unsteady hand; **le tiembla el ~** his hand is shaking 3 **a ~: levantar algo a ~** to lift sth with one hand; **dibujo (hecho) a ~** freehand drawing; ✦ MODISMO **ganar(se) algo a ~** (= *con esfuerzo*) to get sth through one's own hard work; (= *con dificultad*) to get sth the hard way 4 (= *pelea*) **echar un ~** to arm-wrestle; **echar un ~ a algn** (= *contender*) to have a trial of strength with sb; (= *desafiar*) to challenge sb

pulular /1a/ VI to swarm (**por** around)

pulverizador SM [*de colonia, ambientador*] spray; [*de pintura*] spray gun ➤ **pulverizador nasal** nasal inhaler

pulverizar /1f/ VT 1 [+ *sólido*] to pulverize 2 [+ *líquido*] to spray 3 [+ *enemigo, ciudad*] to pulverize, smash; [+ *rival, oponente*] to hammer, thrash; **pulverizó el récord** she smashed the record

pum EXCL (*en disparo*) bang!; ✦ MODISMO **ni ~** not a thing

puma SM puma (*esp Brit*), cougar (*esp EEUU*)

puna SF (*And*) 1 (*Geog*) (= *altiplano*) puna; (= *páramo*) bleak upland 2 (= *soroche*) mountain sickness

punción SF puncture

pundonor SM (= *dignidad*) self-respect, amour propre; (= *honra*) honour, honor (*EEUU*)

punga* Ⓐ SF (*CS*) thieving, nicking** Ⓑ SMF (*CS*) pickpocket, thief

punible ADJ punishable

púnico ADJ, SM (*Ling*) Punic

punitivo ADJ punitive

punki ['punki] ADJ, SMF punk

punta Ⓐ SF 1 (= *extremo*) [*de dedo, lengua, pincel*] tip; [*de ciudad*] side; [*de mesa*] end; [*de pañuelo*] corner; **la ~ de los dedos** the fingertips, the tips of one's fingers; **de ~ a cabo** o **de ~ a punta** from one end to the other; ✦ MODISMOS **la ~ del iceberg** the tip of the iceberg; **tener algo en la ~ de la lengua** to have sth on the tip of one's tongue; **ir de ~ en blanco** to be all dressed up, be dressed up to the nines; **poner a algn los pelos de ~** to make sb's hair stand on end; **a ~ pala** (*Esp**): **había gente a ~ pala** there were loads of people*

2 (= *extremo puntiagudo*) [*de cuchillo, tijeras, lápiz*] point; [*de flecha*] tip; **un rotulador de ~ fina** a felt-tip pen with a fine point; **un cuchillo con ~** a pointed knife; **una estrella de cinco ~s** a five-pointed star; **de ~: tenía todo el pelo de ~** her hair was all on end; **unos zapatos de ~** a pair of pointed shoes; **acabado en ~** pointed; **a ~ de pistola** at gunpoint; **sacar ~ a** [+ *lápiz*] to sharpen; (*Esp*) [+ *comentario, opinión*] to twist ➤ **punta de lanza** spearhead

3 (= *cantidad pequeña*) (*lit*) bit; (*fig*) touch; **una puntita de sal** a pinch of salt

4 (= *clavo*) tack

5 (*Geog*) (= *cabo*) point; (= *promontorio*) headland

6 (= *asta*) [*de toro*] horn; [*de ciervo*] point, tine

7 (*Ftbl*) **juega en la ~** he plays up front

8 **puntas** [*del pelo*] ends; **quiero cortarme las ~s** I'd like a trim, I'd like to have my hair trimmed ➤ **puntas de espárrago** asparagus tips ➤ **puntas de solomillo** *finest cuts of pork*

9 (*CS, Méx*) **una ~ de algo** a lot of sth; **son todos una ~ de ladrones** they are all a bunch of thieves

Ⓑ ADJ INV peak; **horas ~** [*de electricidad, teléfono*] peak times; **la hora ~** [*del tráfico*] the rush hour; **tecnología ~**

latest technology, leading edge technology

puntada SF **1** (*Cos*) stitch **2** (*CS*) (= *dolor*) stitch, sharp pain **3** (*Méx*) witty remark, witticism

puntaje SM (*LAm*) (*en partido*) score; (*en examen*) mark, grade (*EEUU*)

puntal SM (*Arquit*) prop, support; (*Agr*) prop; (*Téc*) strut

puntapié SM kick; **pegar un ~ a algn** to give sb a kick

puntazo* SM **fue un ~** (*Esp*) it went down really well*

puntear /1a/ VT **1** (*con puntos*) (= *motear*) to dot, cover o mark with dots; (= *pintar*) to stipple; (= *jaspear*) to fleck **2** (*Mús*) [+ *guitarra*] to pluck; [+ *violín*] to play pizzicato **3** (*LAm*) [+ *carrera, etapa*] to head, lead

punteo SM plucking

puntera SF (= *punta*) toe; (= *refuerzo*) toecap

puntería SF **1** (*al apuntar*) aim, aiming **2** (= *destreza*) marksmanship; **tener buena ~** to be a good shot; **tener mala ~** to be a bad shot

puntero ④ ADJ (= *primero*) top, leading; (= *moderno*) up-to-date **⑧** SM **1** (*para señalar*) pointer ➤ **puntero luminoso** light pen **2** (*LAm*) (= *equipo*) leading team **3** (*Col, CS Ftbl*) (= *jugador*) winger

puntiagudo ADJ sharp, sharp-pointed

puntilla SF **1** (*Cos*) lace edging **2** (*Taur*) *short dagger for giving the coup de grâce*; ✦ MODISMOS **dar la ~ a algo/algn** to finish sth/sb off; **aquello fue la ~** that was the last straw **3 de ~s ◇ en ~** (*LAm*) on tiptoe; **andar de ~s** to walk on tiptoe

puntillismo SM pointillism

puntilloso ADJ (= *detallista*) punctilious; (= *susceptible*) touchy, sensitive

punto SM **1** (= *topo*) (*en un diseño*) dot, spot; (*en plumaje*) spot, speckle; (*en carta, dominó*) spot, pip; **línea de ~s** dotted line ➤ **punto negro** (= *espinilla*) blackhead **2** (= *signo*) (*en la i*) dot; (*de puntuación*) full stop (*Brit*), period (*EEUU*); **dos ~s** colon; ✦ MODISMOS **con ~s y comas** down to the last detail; **poner los ~s sobre las íes** to dot the i's and cross the t's; **le puso los ~s sobre las íes** she corrected him, she drew attention to his inaccuracies; **y ~:** ¡**lo digo yo y ~!** I'm telling you so and that's that! ➤ **punto final** full stop (*Brit*), period (*EEUU*); (*fig*) end; **poner ~ final a la discusión** to put an end to the argument, draw a line under the argument ➤ **puntos suspensivos** (*gen*) suspension points; (*en dictado*) dot, dot, dot ➤ **punto y aparte** (*en dictado*) full stop, new paragraph (*Brit*), period, new paragraph (*EEUU*) ➤ **punto y coma** semicolon ➤ **punto y seguido** (*en dictado*) full stop (no new paragraph) (*Brit*), period (no new paragraph) (*EEUU*) **3** (*Dep*) point; **están empatados a ~s** they are level on points; **ganar** o **vencer por ~s** to win on points; ✦ MODISMOS **perder (muchos) ~s** to lose (a lot of) prestige **4** (= *tema*) (*gen*) point; (*en programa de actividades*) item; **contestar ~ por ~** to answer point by point **5** (= *labor*) (*Esp*) knitting; (= *tejido*) knitted fabric, knit; **prendas de ~** knitwear *sing*; **hacer ~** to knit ➤ **punto del derecho** plain knitting ➤ **punto del revés** purl **6** (*Cos, Med*) (= *puntada*) stitch; [*de media*] loose stitch ➤ **punto de sutura** stitch **7** (= *lugar*) (*gen*) spot, place; (*Geog, Mat*) point; [*de proceso*] point, stage; (*en el tiempo*) point, moment; **al llegar a este ~** at this point o stage ➤ **punto cardinal** cardinal point; **los cuatro ~s cardinales** the four points of the compass ➤ **punto clave** key point ➤ **punto débil** weak point o spot ➤ **punto de ebullición** boiling-point ➤ **punto de encuentro** meeting point ➤ **punto de inflexión** turning point ➤ **punto de información** information centre ➤ **punto de luz** light ➤ **punto de mira** [*de rifle*] sight; (= *objetivo*) aim, objective; (= *punto de vista*) point of view ➤ **punto de partida** starting point ➤ **punto de referencia** point of reference ➤ **punto de venta** point of sale; **está presente en 3.000 ~s de venta** it's available at 3,000 outlets ➤ **punto de vista** point of view, viewpoint ➤ **punto flaco** weak point, weak spot ➤ **punto muerto** (*Mec*) dead centre; (*Aut*) neutral (gear); (= *estancamiento*) deadlock, stalemate ➤ **punto negro** (*en la piel*) blackhead; (*Aut*) (accident) black spot; (*fig*) blemish

8 (*otras locuciones*) **a punto** ready; **está a ~** it's ready; **con sus cámaras a ~ para disparar** with their cameras at the ready; **llegar a ~** to come just at the right moment; **poner un motor a ~** to tune an engine; **al ~** (*Esp*) at once, immediately; **a ~ de:** **a ~ de caramelo** caramelized; **batir las claras a ~ de nieve** beat the egg whites until stiff o until they form stiff peaks; **estar a ~ de hacer algo** to be on the point of doing sth, be about to do sth; **estábamos a ~ de salir cuando llamaste** we were about to go out when you phoned; **estuve a ~ de llamarte** I almost called you; **a las siete en ~** at seven o'clock sharp o on the dot; **en su ~** [*carne*] done to a turn; [*fruta*] just ripe; **la tensión había llegado hasta tal ~ que ...** the tension had reached such a pitch that ...; ✦ MODISMOS **coger** o **pillar un buen ~** (*Esp***) (*con alcohol*) to get merry*; (*con drogas*) to get high*; **coger** o **pillar el ~ a algn**** to work sb out; **dar el ~ a algn** (*Esp***): **si me da el ~, voy** if I feel like it, I'll go; **si le da el ~ es capaz de cualquier cosa** if he gets it into his head he can do anything; **de todo ~** (*Esp*) completely, absolutely

puntocom ADJ INV, SF INV, **punto.com** ADJ INV, SF INV dotcom, dot.com

puntuable ADJ **una prueba ~ para el campeonato** a race which counts towards o scores in the championship

puntuación SF **1** (*Ling, Tip*) punctuation **2** (= *puntos*) mark(s) (*pl*), grade (*EEUU*); (*Dep*) score **3** (= *acción*) (*Escol*) marking, grading (*EEUU*); (*Dep*) scoring

puntual ④ ADJ **1** [*persona, llegada*] punctual **2** (= *detallado*) [*informe*] detailed; [*cálculo*] exact, accurate **3** (= *aislado*) **se trata de casos muy ~es** they are very isolated cases **⑧** ADV (= *a tiempo*) **nunca llega ~** he's never on time

puntualidad SF punctuality; **pagar con ~** to pay promptly

puntualizar /1f/ VT [+ *detalles*] to specify; **quisiera ~ que ...** I'd like to make it clear that ...; —**no es así— puntualizó** "that's not the case," he stressed

puntualmente ADV [*llegar*] punctually; [*pagar*] promptly

puntuar /1e/ **④** VT **1** (*Ling, Tip*) to punctuate **2** (= *evaluar*) [+ *clase, estilo*] to evaluate, assess; [+ *examen*] to mark, grade (*EEUU*) **⑧** VI **1** (= *valer*) to count; **eso no puntúa** that doesn't count **2** (= *marcar*) to score

puntudo ADJ (*And, RPl*) (= *puntiagudo*) pointed; (= *afilado*) sharp

punzada SF **1** (*Med*) (= *punto*) stitch; (= *dolor*) twinge (of pain), shooting pain **2** [*de pena, remordimiento*] pang, twinge

punzante ADJ **1** [*dolor*] shooting, stabbing **2** [*instrumento*] sharp **3** [*comentario*] biting, caustic

punzar /1f/ VT (= *pinchar*) to puncture, prick, pierce; (*Téc*) to punch; (= *perforar*) to perforate

punzón SM (= *buril*) burin; (*Téc*) punch; (*Tip*) bodkin

puñado SM handful; **a ~s** by handfuls, in plenty

puñal SM dagger

puñalada SF (= *herida*) stab, wound, knife wound; ✦ MODISMO **coser a ~s** to stab repeatedly, carve up*

puñeta*** (*Esp*) **④** SF ¡**no me vengas con ~s!** give me peace!, stop your whining!; ¡**qué coche ni que ~s!** car my arse (*Brit*) o ass (*EEUU*)!***; ✦ MODISMOS **irse a hacer ~s** to go to hell*; **hacer la ~ a algn** to screw sb around*** **⑧** EXCL ¡**~s!** ◇ ¡**qué ~s!** (*indicando enojo*) shit!***, hell!*

puñetazo SM punch; **a ~s** with one's fists

puñetero** ADJ (*Esp*) damned*

puño SM **1** (*Anat*) fist; **con el** o **a ~ cerrado** with one's clenched fist; ✦ MODISMOS **mentiras como ~s** whopping great lies*; **de ~ y letra del poeta** in the poet's own handwriting; **tener a algn (metido) en un ~** to have sb under one's thumb **2** [*de camisa, chaqueta*] cuff **3** [*de espada*] hilt; [*de herramienta*] handle, haft, grip

pupa* SF **1** (= *ampolla*) blister; (*en los labios*) cold sore (*esp Brit*), fever blister (*EEUU*) **2** (*Esp*) (*en lenguaje infantil*) pain; **hacer ~ a algn** to hurt sb; **hacerse ~** to get hurt

pupila SF pupil

pupilo/a SM/F **1** (*en pensión*) boarder **2** (*Jur*) ward

pupitre SM desk

pupurrí SM pot-pourri

purasangre SMF (*pl* ~**s**) thoroughbred

puré SM (*Culin*) purée, (thick) soup; ~ **de patatas** mashed potatoes *pl*; ~ **de verduras** thick vegetable soup; ✦ MODISMO **estar hecho** ~* to be knackered*

pureza SF purity

purga SF 1 (*Med*) purge, purgative 2 (*Pol*) purge

purgación SF purging

purgante ADJ, SM purgative

purgar /1h/ VT 1 (*Med*) to purge 2 (*Pol*) (= *depurar*) to expel 3 [+ *pecado*] to purge, expiate; [+ *delito*] to pay for; [+ *pasiones*] to purge 4 (*Mec*) [+ *depósito, tubería*] to drain; [+ *radiador*] to bleed, drain; [+ *frenos*] to bleed

purgatorio SM purgatory

puridad SF **en** ~ (= *claramente*) plainly, directly; (= *estrictamente*) strictly speaking

purificación SF purification

purificador Ⓐ ADJ purifying Ⓑ SM ➤ **purificador de agua** water filter ➤ **purificador de aire** air purifier, air filter

purificar /1g/ VT [+ *agua, raza*] to purify; [+ *pulmones*] to cleanse

purista SMF purist

puritanismo SM puritanism

puritano/a Ⓐ ADJ 1 (*Rel*) Puritan 2 [*actitud, tradición*] puritanical, puritan Ⓑ SM/F 1 (*Rel*) Puritan 2 (*fig*) puritan

puro Ⓐ ADJ 1 (= *sin mezcla*) [*color, lenguaje*] pure; [*aire*] clean; [*oro*] solid 2 (*con valor enfático*) pure, simple; **de** ~ **aburrimiento** out of sheer boredom; **por pura casualidad** by sheer chance; ✦ MODISMO ~ **y duro**: **fue un timo** ~ **y duro** it was a straightforward *o* downright swindle 3 (= *casto*) pure, chaste 4 (*LAm*) (= *uno solo*) only, just; **me queda una pura porción** I have just one portion left Ⓑ ADV **de** ~ **cansado** out of sheer tiredness; **no se le ve el color de** ~ **sucio** it's so dirty you can't tell what colour it is Ⓒ SM 1 (*tb* **cigarro** ~) cigar ➤ **puro habano** Havana cigar 2 ✦ MODISMO **meter un** ~ **a algn** (*Esp**) (*gen*) to throw the book at sb*; (*Mil*) to put sb on a charge

púrpura SF purple

purpúreo ADJ purple

purpurina SF (*gen*) metallic paint; (*para decoración, maquillaje*) glitter

pus SM pus

puse *etc ver* **poner**

pusilánime ADJ fainthearted, pusillanimous

pústula SF pustule

put [pʊt] SM (*pl* ~**s** [pʊt]) (*Golf*) putt

puta* SF 1 (= *prostituta*) whore, prostitute; **casa de** ~**s** brothel; **ir(se) de** ~**s** to go whoring 2 **¡la** ~**!** (*expresando sorpresa*) well I'm damned!; ✦ MODISMO **pasarlas** ~**s** to have a shitty time*, have a rotten time*; *ver tb* **puto**

putada** SF (= *mala pasada*) dirty trick; **¡es una** ~**!** it's a real bugger!**

putativo ADJ putative (*frm*), supposed

puteado** ADJ (*Esp*) **nos tienen** ~**s** they're really screwing us around**

putear /1a/ Ⓐ VT (**) 1 (*Esp*) (= *fastidiar*) to mess around*, bugger about (*Brit***) 2 (*LAm*) (= *insultar*) to lay into* Ⓑ VI (*) 1 (= *ir de putas*) to go whoring 2 (= *ser prostituta*) to be on the game*

puticlub* [putɾˈklu] SM (*Esp hum*) pick up joint**

puto** Ⓐ ADJ (*Esp*) bloody*, bloody awful*; **no me hizo ni** ~ **caso** she completely bloody ignored me**; **no tengo ni un** ~ **duro** I'm absolutely skint*; **¡ni puta idea!** I've no bloody idea!*; ✦ MODISMO **de puta madre** (= *bueno*) terrific*, smashing*; (*uso adverbial*) marvellously*; **cocina de puta madre** she's a bloody marvellous cook** Ⓑ SM male prostitute; *ver tb* **puta**

putrefacción SF rotting, putrefaction; **basura en** ~ rotting rubbish (*esp Brit*) *o* garbage (*EEUU*); **en avanzado estado de** ~ in an advanced estate of decomposition

putrefacto ADJ (= *podrido*) rotten, putrid; (= *descompuesto*) decayed

pútrido ADJ putrid, rotten

puya SF 1 (= *vara*) (*gen*) goad, pointed stick; (*Taur*) point of the picador's lance 2 (= *sarcasmo*) gibe, barbed comment

puyar /1a/ VT (*Col*) to jab, prick

puyazo SM 1 (*Taur*) jab with the lance 2 (= *palabras*) gibe, barbed comment

puzle [ˈpuθle] SM, **puzzle** [ˈpuθle] SM puzzle

PVC SM ABR (= **polyvinyl-chloride**) PVC

PVP SM ABR (= **precio de venta al público**) RRP

PYME SF ABR, **pyme** SF ABR = **Pequeña y Mediana Empresa**

Qq

Q, q [ku] SF (= *letra*) Q, q

QED ABR (= **quod erat demonstrandum**) QED

q.e.p.d. ABR (= **que en paz descanse**) RIP

qm ABR (= **quintal(es) métrico(s)**)

qts. ABR (= **quilates**) c

quantum [ˈkwantum] SM (*pl* **quanta** [ˈkwanta]) (*Fís*) quantum

quark SM (*pl* **~s**) quark

quásar SM quasar

que[1] PRON REL **1** (*refiriéndose a personas*) **1.1** (*como sujeto*) who, that; **el hombre ~ vino ayer** the man who *o* that came yesterday; **hable con alguien ~ entienda de esto** talk to someone who knows about this **1.2** (*como complemento: a menudo se omite*) that; **el hombre ~ vi en la calle** the man (that) I saw in the street
2 (*refiriéndose a cosas*) **2.1** (*como sujeto*) that, which; **la novela ~ ganó el premio** the novel that *o* which won the award **2.2** (*como complemento: a menudo se omite*) that, which; **el coche ~ compré** the car (that *o* which) I bought; **el libro del ~ te hablé** the book (that *o* which) I spoke to you about; **el día ~ ella nació** the day (when *o* that) she was born
3 él/la/los/las — *ver* **el 8**
4 lo — *ver* **lo**[1] **3**

que[2] CONJ **1** (*en subordinada sustantiva: a menudo se omite*) **1.1** (+ INDIC) that; **dijo ~ vendría** he said (that) he'd come; **estoy seguro de ~ lloverá** I am sure (that) it will rain **1.2** (+ SUBJUN) that; **no sabía ~ tuviera coche** I didn't know (that) he had a car; **me alegro de ~ hayan ganado** I am glad (that) they have won; **es una pena ~ no tengamos más tiempo** it's a pity that we haven't got more time; **espero ~ os sea útil** I hope you'll find it useful; **quieren ~ les esperes** they want you to wait for them **1.3** **decir ~ sí** to say yes
2 (*en comparaciones*) **eres igual ~ mi padre** you're just like my father; **más ~** more than; **ganas más ~ yo** you earn more than me; **es más alto ~ tú** he's taller than you; **menos ~ tú** less than; **yo ~ tú** if I were you
3 (*expresando resultado*) (*a menudo se omite*) that; **es tan grande ~ no lo puedo levantar** it's so big (that) I can't lift it; **tengo una sed ~ me muero** I'm dying of thirst
4 (*expresando causa*) **llévate un paraguas, ~ está lloviendo** take an umbrella, it's raining; **no lo derroches, ~ es muy caro** don't waste it, it's very expensive; **¡vamos, ~ cierro!** come on now, I'm closing!; **¡cuidado, ~ te caes!** careful or you'll fall!, mind *o* take care you don't fall!
5 (*expresando reiteración o insistencia*) **siguió toca ~ toca** he kept on playing; **estuvieron habla ~ habla toda la noche** they talked and talked all night; **¡~ sí!: —es verde —¡~ no! —¡~ sí!** "it's green" — "no it isn't!" — "yes it is!"; **—no funciona —~ sí** "it doesn't work" — "yes it does"
6 (*sin antecedente expreso*) **6.1** (*expresando mandato*) **¡~ lo haga él!** let him do it!, he can do it himself!; **¡~ entre!** send him in!, let him come in! **6.2** (*expresando deseo*) **¡~ te mejores!** get well soon!; **¡~ os guste la obra!** enjoy the play! **6.3** (*expresando sorpresa*) **¡~ no estabas allí?** (are you telling me) you weren't there?
7 el ~ (+ SUBJUN) (= *el hecho de que*) the fact that; **el ~ viva en Vitoria no es ningún problema** the fact that he lives in Vitoria isn't a problem

qué Ⓐ PRON **1** (*interrogativo*) **¿qué?** what?; **¿~ has dicho?** what did you say?; **¿a ~ has venido?** why have you come?, what have you come for?; **¿con ~ lo vas a pagar?** how are you going to pay for it?, what are you going to pay with?; **¿de ~ lo conoces?** how do you know him?, where do you know him from?; **¿en ~ lo notas?** how can you tell?; **no sé ~ quiere decir** I don't know what it means; **¿~ tan grande es?** (*LAm*) how big is it?; **¿~ más?** (*gen*) what else?; (*en tienda*) anything else?; **¿para ~?: ¿para ~ lo quiere?** why does he want it?, what does he want it for?; **¿para ~, si nunca me hace caso?** what's the point? he never listens to me anyway; **¿por ~?** why?; **¿~ tal?** how are things?; **¿~ tal**

estás? how are you?; **¿~ tal el trabajo?** how's work?; **¿~ tanto?** (*LAm*) how much?; **¿y ~?** so what?; **¿y a mí ~?** so what?, what has that got to do with me?
2 (*exclamativo*) **¡~ de gente había!** what a lot of people there were!; **¡~ de cosas te diría!** what a lot I'd have to say to you!; **¡~ va!: ¡~ va!, no me parece caro** no, I don't think it's expensive at all!; **¿aquí, corrupción? ¡~ va!** corruption? come off it!
Ⓑ ADJ **1** (*interrogativo*) **¿~ día del mes es hoy?** what's today's date?, what's the date today?; **¿~ camisa le regalarías?** which shirt would you give him?; **dime ~ libro buscas** tell me which book you are looking for; **—¿has encontrado mi lápiz? —¿~ lápiz?** "have you found my pencil?" — "what pencil?"; **¿~ edad tiene?** how old is he?, what age is he?; **¿de ~ tamaño es?** how big is it?, what size is it?
2 (*exclamativo*) **¡~ día más espléndido!** what a glorious day!, what's the date today?; **¡~ casualidad!** what a coincidence!; **¡~ asco!** how revolting!; **¡~ maravilla!** how wonderful!; **¡~ maravilla de casa!** what a wonderful house!
Ⓒ ADV **¡~ bonito!** isn't it pretty!, how pretty it is!; **¡~ boba eres!** you're so silly!; **¡~ mala suerte!** what rotten luck!; **¡~ bien canta!** she sings so well!, she's such a good singer!

quebracho SM quebracho, quebracho tree

quebrada SF **1** (= *hondonada*) ravine, gorge **2** (*SAm*) (= *arroyo*) brook, mountain stream

quebradero SM ➤ **quebradero de cabeza** headache, worry

quebradizo ADJ fragile, brittle

quebrado Ⓐ ADJ **1** [*objeto*] broken; [*terreno*] rough, uneven; [*línea*] irregular, zigzag **2** (*Fin*) bankrupt Ⓑ SM **1** (*Mat*) fraction **2** (*Fin*) bankrupt

quebradora* SF (*CAm*) **la ~** dengue fever

quebradura SF (*LAm Med*) [*de hueso*] fracture, break; [*de órgano*] rupture

quebrantahuesos SM INV bearded vulture

quebrantar /1a/ VT [+ *resistencia*] to weaken, break; [+ *salud, posición*] to destroy, undermine; [+ *persona*] to break; [+ *cimientos, furia, moral*] to weaken

quebranto SM **1** (= *perjuicio*) damage, harm **2** [*de persona*] (= *agotamiento*) exhaustion; (= *mala salud*) broken health; (*Ven*) (= *fiebre*) slight temperature, slight fever (*EEUU*) **3** (= *aflicción*) sorrow, affliction

quebrar /1j/ Ⓐ VT **1** (= *romper*) to break **2** (*Méx**) (= *matar*) to bump off*, waste* Ⓑ VI **1** (*Fin*) to fail, go bankrupt **2 ~ con algn** (*CAm*) to break with sb Ⓒ **quebrarse** VPR to break

quebrazón SF (*LAm*) smashing, shattering

quechua Ⓐ ADJ Quechua, Quechuan Ⓑ SMF Quechua(n) Indian Ⓒ SM (*Ling*) Quechua

---

QUECHUA

Quechua, the language spoken by the Incas, is the most widely spoken indigenous language in South America, with some 13 million speakers in the Andean region. The first Quechua grammar was compiled by a Spanish missionary in 1560, as part of a linguistic policy intended to aid the process of evangelization. In 1975 Peru made Quechua an official state language. From Quechua come words such as llama, condor and puma.

---

queda SF **toque de ~** curfew

quedado* ADJ **1** (*Chi*) (= *lerdo*) slow, backward **2** (*Ven*) (= *aletargado*) slow

quedar /1a/

Ⓐ VERBO INTRANSITIVO
Ⓑ VERBO PRONOMINAL

Para expresiones como **quedarse tan ancho, quedarse con las ganas, quedarse helado, quedarse parado** *etc, ver la entrada correspondiente a la otra palabra.*

quedar Ⓐ VERBO INTRANSITIVO
1 (*indicando lugar*) to be; **queda a 6km de aquí** it's 6km from here; **¿por dónde queda Correos?** where's the post office?
2 (*indicando posición*) **quedó el penúltimo** he was second last; **~ atrás: no quieren ~ atrás en la carrera espacial** they don't want to be left behind *o* fall behind in the space race; **la crisis ha quedado atrás** the crisis is behind us
3 (*indicando resultado*)
3.1 (*con adjetivos, adverbios, locuciones preposicionales, participios*) **el autobús quedó destrozado** the bus was wrecked; **te ha quedado muy bonita la cocina** you've made a great job of the kitchen; **quedó paralítico tras el accidente** the accident left him paralysed; **la cara le ha quedado desfigurada** her face has been disfigured; **al final quedamos como amigos** we were still friends afterwards; **~ ciego** to go blind; **~ viuda/viudo** to be widowed, lose one's husband/wife
3.2 ~ en algo: ¿en qué quedó la conversación? how did the conversation end?; **al final todo quedó en un susto** it gave us a scare but it turned out all right in the end
3.3 ~ sin: miles de personas han quedado sin hogar thousands of people have been left homeless; **el proyecto quedó sin realizar** the project was never carried out
4 (*en el trato, al hablar*) **ha quedado como un canalla** he has shown himself to be a rotter; **~ bien: regalando flores siempre queda uno bien** taking flowers always makes a good impression; **sólo lo ha hecho por ~ bien** he only did it to make himself look good; **~ mal: nos hiciste ~ mal haciendo esas preguntas** you made us look bad by asking those questions; **no quiero ~ mal con ellos** I don't want to get on the wrong side of them; **~ en ridículo: ha quedado en ridículo** he ended up looking a fool
5 (= *permanecer*) to stay; **quedo a la espera de sus noticias** (*en carta*) I look forward to hearing from you
6 (= *haber todavía*) to be left; **¿queda algo de la cena?** is there any dinner left?; **no quedaba nadie en el autobús** there was nobody left on the bus; **de la ciudad sólo queda el castillo** all that remains *o* is left of the city is the castle; **si a ocho le quito dos, quedan seis** if I take two from eight, I'm left with *o* it leaves six; **~le a algn: no nos queda mucho dinero** we don't have much money left; **~ a deber algo** to owe sth; **quedan pocos días para la fiesta** the party is only a few days away; **nos quedan 12km para llegar a Lugo** we've still got 12km to go to Lugo; **~ por hacer: nos queda por pagar la luz** we still have to pay the electricity bill; **queda por limpiar la cocina** the kitchen still needs cleaning;
✦ MODISMO **que no quede** (*Esp*): **por mí que no quede, yo he ayudado en lo que he podido** it won't be for want of trying on my part, I helped as much as I could; **por probar que no quede** there's no harm in trying; **tú por ser amable que no quede** nobody could accuse you of not being nice
7 (*Educ*) [*asignatura*] **me han quedado las matemáticas** I failed mathematics
8 (*ropa*)
8.1 (= *ser la talla*) to fit; **¿qué tal (de grande) te queda el vestido?** does the dress fit you?; **me queda pequeño** it's too small for me; **no me queda** (*Col, Méx*) it doesn't fit me
8.2 (= *sentar*) to suit; **no te queda bien ese vestido** that dress doesn't suit you; **no queda bien así** it doesn't look right like that
9 ~ en (= *acordar*): **¿quedamos en eso, entonces?** we'll do that, then, all right?; **~ en** *o* (*LAm*) **de hacer algo** to agree to do sth; **quedamos en vernos mañana** we arranged to meet tomorrow; **~ en que** to agree that; **¿en qué quedamos? ¿lo compras o no?** so what's it to be then? are you going to buy it or not?

10 (= *citarse*) to arrange to meet; **habíamos quedado, pero no se presentó** we had arranged to meet, but he didn't turn up; **¿quedamos a las cuatro?** shall we meet at four?; **¿cómo quedamos?** where shall we meet and what time?; **~ con algn** to arrange to meet sb; **¿quedamos con ella en la parada?** shall we meet her at the bus stop?
Ⓑ quedarse VERBO PRONOMINAL
1 (= *permanecer, estar*)
1.1 (*gen*) to stay; **ve tú, yo me quedo** you go, I'll stay; **me quedé en casa** I stayed at home; **salieron de trabajar a las cinco, pero yo me quedé hasta las ocho** they left work at five, but I stayed behind until eight; **~se atrás** (= *atrasarse*) to fall behind, be left behind; (= *en posición retrasada*) to stay up behind
1.2 (+ GERUND) **me quedé estudiando hasta que cerraron la biblioteca** I carried on *o* stayed working in the library until it closed; **me quedé viendo la tele hasta muy tarde** I stayed up late watching TV
2 (*indicando resultado*)
2.1 (*con adjetivos, locuciones preposicionales*) **me estoy quedando sordo** I'm going deaf; **se ha quedado viudo** he has been widowed, he has lost his wife; **se me ha quedado pequeña esta camisa** (*Esp*) I've outgrown this shirt
2.2 ~se sin: nos hemos quedado sin café we've run out of coffee; **~se sin empleo** to lose one's job; **al final nos quedamos sin ver el concierto** we didn't get to see the concert in the end
3 (= *conservar*) (*gen*) to keep; (= *comprar*) to take; **quédatela como recuerdo** keep it as a memento; **me la quedo** I'll take it; **~se con** (= *retener*) to keep; (= *comprar*) to take; (= *preferir*) to go for, take; **se quedó con mi pluma** he kept my pen; **me quedo con este paraguas** I'll take this umbrella; **entre A y B, me quedo con B** given a choice between A and B, I'd go for *o* take B; **~se con hambre** to be still hungry
4 (= *retener en la memoria*) **no se le quedan las cosas** he can't remember things; **lo siento, no me quedé con su nombre** sorry, I can't quite remember your name
5 (*And, Col* = *olvidarse*) **se me ~on las llaves** I forgot the keys
6 (*Esp*) **~se con algn*** (= *engañar*) to con sb*; (= *tomar el pelo a*) to take the mickey out of sb*, pull sb's leg*; **¿te estás quedando conmigo?** are you trying to kid me?*

quedo Ⓐ ADJ **1** (= *inmóvil*) still **2** (= *tranquilo*) [*voz*] quiet, gentle; [*paso*] soft **Ⓑ** ADV softly, gently

quehacer SM job, task; **~es domésticos** housework *sing*, household chores; **agobiado de ~** overburdened with work

queimada SF *traditional Galician hot drink made with flamed "orujo", sugar and lemon*

queja SF **1** (= *reclamación*) **tener ~ de algn** to have a complaint to make about sb; **estoy harto de tus ~s** I'm tired of your complaining **2** (= *gemido*) moan, groan

quejarse /1a/ VPR **1** (= *reclamar*) (*gen*) to complain (**de** about, of); (*refunfuñando*) to grumble; **~ de que** to complain (about the fact) that; **✦** MODISMO **~ de vicio*** to be always complaining **2** (= *gemir*) to moan, groan

quejica* (*Esp*) **Ⓐ** ADJ moaning **Ⓑ** SMF moaner, grumbler

quejido SM moan, groan

quejón/ona* **Ⓐ** ADJ moaning **Ⓑ** SM/F moaner, grumbler

quejoso/a **Ⓐ** ADJ [*persona*] complaining; [*tono*] plaintive **Ⓑ** SM/F (*Méx*) **los ~s** the complainers

quejumbroso ADJ = **quejoso A**

quema SF **1** (= *incendio*) fire; (= *combustión*) burning; (*LAm Agr*) burning-off (of scrub); **✦** MODISMO **salvarse de la ~: fue el único atleta español que se salvó de la ~** he was the only athlete to escape the carnage **2** (*Arg*) (= *vertedero*) rubbish dump (*esp Brit*), garbage dump (*EEUU*)

quemado Ⓐ ADJ **1** (*por fuego, sol*) burned, burnt; **esto sabe a ~** this tastes burned *o* burnt; **aquí huele a ~** there's a smell of burning in here
2 (= *desprestigiado*) **un político ya ~** a political has-been; **ya está ~ como futbolista** he's had it as a football player*; **un artista ~ por salir demasiado en televisión** an artist who

has become overexposed through being on television too much
3 (*) (= *harto*) sick and tired*; **la vecina me tiene ~** I've had it up to here with the woman next door*, I'm sick and tired of the woman next door*; **estar ~ con algo** to be sick and tired of sth*
4 (*LAm*) (= *bronceado*) tanned
5 (*Chi**) (= *falto de suerte*) unlucky
B quemados SMPL (= *heridos*) burn victims

quemador SM burner

quemadura SF (*por fuego, sol*) burn; (*por líquido hirviendo*) scald; **una ~ de cigarro** a cigarette burn; **~ de primer/segundo grado** first-/second-degree burn
➤ **quemaduras de sol, quemaduras solares** sunburn *sing*

quemar /1a/ **A** VT **1** (= *hacer arder*) **1.1** [*fuego, sol*] [+ *papeles, mueble, arroz*] to burn; [+ *edificio*] to burn down; [+ *coche*] to set fire to; **he quemado la camisa con la plancha** I scorched *o* burned my shirt with the iron; **los guerrilleros ~on varias aldeas** the guerrillas set fire to *o* burned several villages **1.2** [*líquido hirviendo*] to scald; [*ácido, frío, helada*] to burn; **la pomada parece que te quema el brazo** the cream makes your arm burn
2 (= *dar sensación de calor*) [*radiador, especia picante*] to burn; **el radiador me está quemando la espalda** the radiator is burning my back
3 [+ *fusible*] to blow
4 (= *gastar*) [+ *calorías*] to burn, burn up; [+ *energías*] to burn off; [+ *fortuna*] to squander; [+ *dinero*] to blow*, squander; ✦ MODISMO **~ etapas** to rush ahead with things
5 (*) (= *fastidiar*) to bug*, get*; **lo que más me quemó** what bugged* me *o* got* me most
6 (= *desgastar*) [+ *político, gobierno*] to destroy, be the ruin of; **tanto aparecer en televisión va a ~ su carrera** all these TV appearances will damage his career
7 (*RPI*) **~ a algn** to make a fool of sb
B VI [*comida, líquido, metal*] to be boiling (hot); [*mejillas*] to be burning; **ya no quema** it's not too hot now; **¡cómo quema el sol!** the sun's really scorching (hot)!
C quemarse VPR **1** [*persona*] (*con fuego*) to burn o.s.; (*con el sol*) to get burned; **me quemé la lengua con la sopa** I burned my tongue on the soup; **~se a lo bonzo** to set fire to o.s.
2 (= *arder*) [*cuadros, papeles*] to get burned; [*edificio*] to burn down; [*comida*] to burn; **se está quemando la cortina** the curtain is getting burned; **se me ha quemado la cena** I've burned the dinner, the dinner has burned; **se han quemado 100 hectáreas en el incendio** 100 hectares have been destroyed in the fire
3 (= *desprestigiarse*) (*en TV*) to become overexposed; **tantos años y aún no se ha quemado** so many years working and he's still going strong
4 (*en juego, adivinanzas*) **caliente, caliente ... ¡que te quemas!** (you're getting) warm, warmer ... you're really hot *o* you're boiling!

quemarropa: a ~ ADV point-blank

quemazón SF **1** (= *sensación*) burning **2** (*LAm*) (= *incendio*) fire

quena SF Indian flute

quepis SM INV (*esp LAm Mil*) kepi, *round military cap*

quepo *etc ver* **caber**

queque SM (*And, CAm, Ven*) cake (*of various kinds*)

querella SF **1** (*Jur*) lawsuit; **interponer** *o* **presentar una ~ contra algn** to bring a lawsuit *o* an action against sb
2 (= *disputa*) dispute; **sus viejas ~s** their old disputes; **antiguas ~s familiares** old family feuds

querellante SMF (*Jur*) plaintiff

querellarse /1a/ VPR (*Jur*) to file a complaint, bring an action (**contra** against)

querencia SF **1** (= *instinto*) homing instinct **2** (= *terruño*) favourite haunt, home ground

querendón* ADJ (*LAm*) affectionate, loving

---

querer /2t/

A VERBO TRANSITIVO   **C** VERBO PRONOMINAL
B VERBO INTRANSITIVO   **D** SUSTANTIVO MASCULINO

Para la expresión **querer decir**, *ver la entrada correspondiente a la otra palabra.*

---

querer A VERBO TRANSITIVO
1 (*a una persona*) (= *amar*) to love; (= *apreciar*) to like; **¡te quiero!** I love you!; **la quiero con locura** I'm madly in love with her; **en la oficina lo quieren mucho** he is well liked at the office; **~ bien a algn** to want the best for sb; **hacerse ~ por algn** to endear o.s. to sb; **~ mal a algn** to wish sb ill; ✦ MODISMO **¡por lo que más quieras!** (*rogando*) by all that's sacred!; (*regañando*) for Heaven's sake!
2 (= *desear*)
2.1 [+ *objeto*] to want; **¿cuál quieres?** which one do you want?; **hace lo que quiere** she does what she wants *o* as she pleases; **se lo di, pero no lo quiso** I gave it to him, but he didn't want (to take) it; **¡lo que quieras!** as you wish!, have it your own way!; **¿quieres un café?** would you like some coffee?; **~ pelea** to be looking for trouble
2.2 (+ INFIN) to want; **~ hacer algo** to want to do sth; **quiere ser ingeniero** he wants to be an engineer; **¿qué quieres comer hoy?** what would you like for dinner today?; **no quiso pagar** he refused to pay, he wouldn't pay
2.3 **~ que algn haga algo** to want sb to do sth; **no quiero que vayas** I don't want you to go; **el destino quiso que volvieran a verse** fate decreed that they should see each other again; **¿qué quieres que te diga?** what can I say?; **¡qué más quisiera yo!** if only I could!; **¡qué más quisiera yo que ver juntos a mis hijos!** what more could I wish for *o* want than to see my children together?
3 (= *tener intención de*) (+ INFIN) **no quería hacerte daño** I didn't mean to hurt you; **quiso hacerlo pero no pudo** he tried to do it but he couldn't
4 (*pidiendo algo*) **quería dos kilos de patatas, por favor** I'd like two kilos of potatoes, please, could I have two kilos of potatoes, please?; **¿querría participar en nuestra oferta?** would you like to take advantage of our offer?; **¿cuánto quieren por el coche?** what are they asking for the car?, how much do they want for the car?
5 (= *requerir*) **¿para qué me querrá?** I wonder what he wants me for, what can he want me for?
6 (*uso impersonal*) **quiere llover** it looks like rain
B VERBO INTRANSITIVO
1 (= *desear*) **¿quieres?** (*ofreciendo algo*) do you want some?, would you like some?; **lo hago porque quiero** I do it because I want to; **como usted quiera** as you wish; **ven cuando quieras** come whenever you like; ✦ MODISMOS **como quiere: tiene tanto dinero que vive como quiere** he's so rich he can live as he pleases; **quiera o no** ◇ **quiera que no** whether he *etc* likes it or not; ✦ REFRÁN **~ es poder** where there's a will there's a way
2 (= *tener intención*) **lo hizo queriendo** he did it deliberately *o* on purpose; **lo hizo sin ~** he didn't mean to do it, he did it inadvertently
3 **como quiera que** *ver* **comoquiera**; **donde quiera que** *ver* **dondequiera**
C quererse VERBO PRONOMINAL (*recíproco*) **nos queremos** we love each other
D SUSTANTIVO MASCULINO love; **cosas del ~** affairs of the heart

querida SF mistress

querido/a A ADJ **1** (= *amado*) **nuestra querida patria** our beloved country; **sus seres ~s** his loved ones; **~s hermanos** (*Rel*) dearly beloved **2** (*en cartas*) dear **B** SM/F (*uso apelativo*) darling; **¡sí, ~!** yes, darling!

querosén SM, **querosene** SM (*LAm*), **queroseno** SM kerosene, paraffin (*Brit*)

querubín SM cherub

quesadilla SF (*Méx, CAm*) cheese tortilla

quesera SF cheese dish; *ver tb* **quesero**

quesería SF **1** (= *tienda*) cheese shop, dairy **2** (= *fábrica*) cheese factory

quesero/a Ⓐ ADJ **la industria quesera** the cheese industry Ⓑ SM/F cheesemaker; *ver tb* **quesera**

queso SM 1 (= *alimento*) cheese; ✦ MODISMO **dárselas a algn con ~*** to take sb in* ➤ **queso azul** blue cheese ➤ **queso crema** (*LAm*) cream cheese ➤ **queso de bola** Edam ➤ **queso de oveja** sheep's cheese ➤ **queso fundido** processed cheese, process cheese (*EEUU*) ➤ **queso rallado** grated cheese 2 **quesos**** (= *pies*) plates*, feet

quetzal SM 1 (= *moneda*) monetary unit of Guatemala 2 (= *ave*) quetzal

quevedos SMPL pince-nez

quichua Ⓐ ADJ Quechua, Quechuan Ⓑ SMF Quechua(n) Indian Ⓒ SM (*Ling*) Quechua; ⊅ *QUECHUA*

quicio SM doorjamb; ✦ MODISMO **sacar a algn de ~** to drive sb up the wall*

quid SM gist, crux; **el ~ de la cuestión** the crux of the matter

quiebra SF 1 (*Fin*) bankruptcy; **declararse en ~** to declare o.s. bankrupt 2 (= *deterioro*) breakdown; **la ~ de los valores tradicionales** the breakdown of traditional values

quiebro SM (*Taur*) dodge, swerve

quien PRON REL 1 (*con antecedente*) **1.1** (*como sujeto*) who; **hablé con mi abogado, ~ me dio la razón** I spoke to my solicitor, who said I was right; **él es ~ se ocupa de estos asuntos** he is the one who deals with these things **1.2** (*como complemento*) who, whom (*frm*); **su profesor, a ~ está dedicado el libro** his teacher, who the book is dedicated to, his teacher, to whom the book is dedicated (*frm*); **el pintor a ~ describe en su libro** the painter he describes in his book, the painter whom he describes in his book 2 (*como indefinido*) **2.1** (+ SUBJUN) **para ~ sepa poco del tema** for anyone who knows little about the subject; **~es no estén de acuerdo** anyone who doesn't agree; **pregúntale a ~ quieras** ask anyone *o* whoever you like; **"a quien corresponda"** "to whom it may concern" **2.2** (+ INDIC) **~ más se quejaba era él** the person who complained most was him, he was the one that *o* who complained the most; **yo hablo con ~ quiero** I'll speak to who I like; **lo dijo como ~ anuncia una gran noticia** he said it like someone announcing some really important news; **hay ~ no piensa lo mismo** there are some *o* those who do not think the same; **¡no hay ~ te entienda!** there's no understanding you! **2.3** ✦ MODISMOS **~ más, ~ menos: ~ más, ~ menos tiene un amigo que ha estudiado en el extranjero** most of us have a friend who has studied abroad; **~ más, ~ menos, todos hemos tenido miedo a la oscuridad de pequeños** all of us, to some extent, have been afraid of the dark as children; **como ~ dice** so to speak; **como ~ no quiere la cosa: se acercó, como ~ no quiere la cosa** he casually moved closer to us; **era capaz de beberse una botella, como ~ no quiere la cosa** he was quite capable of drinking a whole bottle, just like that *o* as if it were nothing; **como ~ oye llover: y él, como ~ oye llover** but it was like water off a duck's back; **no ser ~: él no es quién para decirme lo que tengo que hacer** it's not for him to tell me what to do

quién PRON 1 (*interrogativo*) (*como sujeto*) who; (*como complemento*) whom; **no sé ~ lo dijo primero** I don't know who said it first; **¿~ era?** who was it?; **¿a ~ se lo diste?** who did you give it to?; **¿con ~ estabas anoche?** who were you with last night?; **¿de ~ es la bufanda esa?** whose scarf is that?; **¿~ de ustedes lo reconoce?** which of you recognizes it? 2 (*exclamativo*) **¡~ sabe!** who knows!; **¡~ pudiese!** if only I could!; **¡~ lo hubiera dicho!** who would have thought it!

quienquiera PRON INDEF (*pl* **quienesquiera**) whoever; **~ que sea el responsable** whoever is responsible

quiera *etc ver* **querer**

quieto ADJ (= *parado*) still; (= *inmóvil*) motionless; **¡quieto!** (*al perro*) down boy!; (*a un niño*) keep still!, stop fidgeting!; (= *sé bueno*) behave yourself!; **dejar algo ~** to leave sth alone; **¡estate ~!** keep still!

⚠ **quieto** ≠ *quiet*

quietud SF [*de persona, noche*] stillness, quietude (*frm*); [*de situación*] calm

quijada SF jaw, jawbone

quijote SM quixotic person, dreamer, do-gooder*

quijotesco ADJ quixotic

quil. ABR = **quilates** c

quilate SM carat; **oro de 18 ~s** 18 carat gold

quilla SF (*Náut*) keel

quillango SM (*RPl*) blanket of furs, fur blanket

quilombo** SM (*And, RPl*) 1 (= *burdel*) brothel 2 (= *lío*) mess

quiltro* SM (*Chi*) mongrel

quimera SF illusion, chimera

quimérico ADJ [*plan, proyecto, idea*] fanciful; [*esperanza*] impossible

química SF chemistry

químico/a Ⓐ ADJ chemical Ⓑ SM/F chemist

quimioterapia SF chemotherapy

quimono SM kimono

quina SF quinine, Peruvian bark; ✦ MODISMO **ser más malo que la ~** (*Esp**) to be a little horror

quincalla SF 1 (= *ferretería*) hardware, ironmongery (*Brit*) 2 (= *baratija*) trinket

quince ADJ, PRON, SM (*cardinal*) fifteen; (*ordinal, en la fecha*) fifteenth; **~ días** a fortnight; *ver tb* **seis**

quinceañero/a SM/F fifteen-year-old; (*en general*) teenager

quinceavo ADJ, PRON fifteenth; *ver tb* **sexto**

quincena SF fortnight (*Brit*), two weeks; **la segunda ~ de enero** the second half of January, the last two weeks in January

quincenal ADJ fortnightly (*Brit*), bimonthly (*EEUU*)

quincenalmente ADV fortnightly (*Brit*), once a fortnight (*esp Brit*), semimonthly (*EEUU*)

quincha SF (*SAm*) wall or roof etc made of rushes and mud

quincuagésimo ADJ, PRON fiftieth; *ver tb* **sexto**

quiniela SF (*Esp*) 1 (= *boleto*) pools coupon (*Brit*), sports lottery ticket (*EEUU*); **echar la ~** to hand in one's coupon (*Brit*) *o* ticket (*EEUU*) 2 (= *juego*) football pool(s) (*Brit*), sports lottery (*EEUU*); **jugar a la ~** *o* **a las ~s** to do the (football) pools (*Brit*), play the sports lottery (*EEUU*) ➤ **quiniela hípica** horse-racing totalizator

---

QUINIELA

The **quiniela** is the Spanish equivalent of the football pools and coupons are available from **estancos**. Players can predict a home win (1), a draw (X) or an away win (2) for most premier and first division matches. 12 or more correct forecasts wins a prize, the size of which varies from week to week depending on the takings or **recaudación**. There is also a version for horse racing, the **quiniela hípica**, although most betting on horses is done at the racecourse. ⊅ ESTANCO

---

quinielista SMF (*Esp*) pools punter (*Brit*), sports lottery gambler (*EEUU*)

quinielístico ADJ (*Esp*) pools *antes de s* (*Brit*), sports lottery *antes de s* (*EEUU*)

quinientos ADJ, PRON, SM (*cardinal*) five hundred; (*ordinal*) five hundredth; ✦ MODISMO **volvió a las (mil) quinientas*** he got back at some ungodly hour; *ver tb* **seiscientos**

quinina SF quinine

quino SM cinchona, cinchona tree

quinqué SM oil lamp

quinquenal ADJ quinquennial; **plan ~** five-year plan

quinqui* SM small-time delinquent

quinta SF 1 (= *casa de campo*) villa, country house 2 (*Esp Mil*) draft, call-up; **ser de la (misma) ~ de algn** to be the same age as sb; **la ~ de 1998** the 1998 call-up, the class called up in 1998

quintaescencia SF quintessence

quintal SM 100lb ➤ **quintal métrico** ≈ 100kg

quinteto SM quintet

quintillizo/a SM/F quintuplet

Quintín SM ✦ MODISMO **se armó la de San ~*** all hell broke loose*; **se va a armar la de San ~** there will be an almighty row*

quinto Ⓐ ADJ, PRON fifth; *ver tb* **sexto** Ⓑ SM **1** (*Esp Mil*) conscript, draftee (*EEUU*), national serviceman **2** (*Méx*) (= *moneda*) nickel; ✦ MODISMOS **estar sin ~*** to be (flat) broke*; **ni un ~*** not a penny

quintuplicar /1g/ Ⓐ VT to quintuple Ⓑ **quintuplicarse** VPR to quintuple; **el número de casos se ha quintuplicado** the number of cases has increased fivefold, there has been a fivefold increase in the number of cases

quíntuple SMF (*Chi, Ven*) quintuplet

quíntuplo Ⓐ ADJ quintuple, fivefold Ⓑ SM quintuple; **25 es el ~ de cinco** 25 is five times more than five

quiosco SM [*de venta*] kiosk, stand; (= *pabellón*) summerhouse, pavilion ➤ **quiosco de música** bandstand

quiosquero/a SM/F owner of a news-stand, newspaper seller

quiqui*** SM (*Esp*) screw***

quiquiriquí SM cock-a-doodle-doo

quirófano SM operating theatre (*Brit*), operating room (*EEUU*)

quiromancia SF palmistry

quiromasaje SM massage

quiropráctica SF chiropractic

quirúrgico ADJ surgical; **sin intervención quirúrgica** without surgery

quise *etc ver* **querer**

quisque* SM, **quisqui*** SM **cada** *o* **todo ~** (absolutely) everyone, every man-Jack

quisquilla SF shrimp

quisquilloso ADJ (= *susceptible*) touchy, oversensitive; (= *perfeccionista*) pernickety*, persnickety (*EEUU**), choosy, fussy

quiste SM cyst ➤ **quiste ovárico** ovarian cyst ➤ **quiste sebáceo** sebaceous cyst

quita SF **de ~ y pon** detachable

quitaesmalte SM nail-polish *o* nail-varnish remover

quitamanchas SM INV stain remover

quitanieves SM INV snowplough, snowplow (*EEUU*)

quitar /1a/ Ⓐ VT **1** (= *sacar*) (*gen*) to remove; [+ *ropa, zapatos*] to take off; [+ *póster, estantes*] to take down; **le ~on las vendas** they took her bandages off, they removed her bandages; **~on las banderas** they took the flags down, they removed the flags; **quita eso de allí** get that away from there; **~ la mesa** to clear the table; ✦ MODISMOS **~ de en medio a algn** to get rid of sb; **no ~le ojo a algn** not to take one's eyes off sb

2 (= *arrebatar*) (*gen*) to take away; (*para robar*) to take,

steal; [+ *vida*] to take; **me ~on la licencia** I had my licence taken away; **le ~on la cartera en el tren** someone took his wallet on the train, he had his wallet stolen on the train; **~ el sitio a algn** to steal sb's place

3 (= *eliminar*) [+ *mancha*] to remove, get rid of; [+ *dolor*] to relieve, stop; [+ *felicidad, ilusión*] to take away; [+ *preocupaciones, temores*] to allay; **me quitó las ganas de comer** it spoiled my appetite; **trataba de ~me esa idea de la cabeza** she tried to make me change my mind; **~ el hambre a algn** (= *apetito*) to spoil sb's appetite; (= *necesidad de comer*) to stop sb feeling hungry; **~ la sed a algn** to quench sb's thirst; **~ el sueño: el café me quita el sueño** coffee stops me sleeping; **ese asunto no me quita el sueño** I'm not losing any sleep over that matter

4 (= *restar*) **no le quiero ~ méritos** I don't want to detract from him; **me quita mucho tiempo** it takes up a lot of my time; **~ importancia a algo** to play sth down; **quitando tres o cuatro, van a ir todos** except for three or four (people), everybody is going

5 (*Esp, Méx*) (= *apartar*) **~ a algn del tabaco/de las drogas** to get sb off cigarettes/drugs

6 (= *impedir*) **~ a algn de hacer algo** to stop *o* prevent sb (from) doing sth

7 (*Mat*) to take away, subtract

Ⓑ VI **¡quita!, ¡quita de ahí!** (*Esp*) (= *¡aparta!*) get out of the way!; (= *¡qué va!*) get away!, come off it!; ✦ MODISMOS **eso no quita: eso no quita que eche de menos a mi mujer** that doesn't mean I don't miss my wife; **ni quito ni pongo** (= *soy imparcial*) I'm neutral, I'm not saying one thing or the other; (= *no cuento*) I have no say

Ⓒ **quitarse** VPR **1** (= *apartarse*) **¡quítate de ahí!** ✧ **¡quítate de en medio!** get out of the way!; **¡quítate de mi vista!** get out of my sight!

2 (= *desaparecer*) [*dolor*] to go, go away; [*mancha*] to come out; **esa mancha no se quita** that stain won't come out

3 (= *acabarse*) **se me quitan las ganas de ir** I don't feel like going now; **se me ~on las ganas de viajar** I no longer felt like travelling

4 (= *sacarse*) [+ *ropa, zapatos*] to take off; [+ *barba*] to shave; [+ *lentillas*] to take out; **~se años: te has quitado diez años (de encima)** you look ten years younger; **no te quites años** don't lie about your age; **~se algo/a algn de encima** to get rid of sth/sb; **¡no me la puedo ~ de encima!** I can't get rid of her!; **¡qué peso nos hemos quitado de encima!** what a relief!, that's a real weight off our minds!

5 **~se de** (= *dejar*) **~se del tabaco** to give up smoking

quite SM (*Taur*) distracting manoeuvre *o* (*EEUU*) maneuver; **estar al ~** to be always ready to help *o* be at hand; **hacer el ~ a algn/algo** (*And*) to avoid sb/sth

quiteño/a Ⓐ ADJ of *o* from Quito Ⓑ SM/F native *o* inhabitant of Quito; **los ~s** the people of Quito

Quito SM Quito

quiubo* EXCL (*Chi, Méx*) how's it going?

quizá ADV, **quizás** ADV perhaps, maybe; **~ llegue mañana** if we're lucky, perhaps it will arrive tomorrow; **~ no** maybe not

quórum ['kworum] SM (*pl* **~s** ['kworum]) quorum

Rr

R, r ['ere] SF (= *letra*) R, r

rabadilla SF **1** (*Anat*) coccyx **2** (*Culin*) [*de pollo*] parson's nose (*Brit**), pope's nose (*EEUU**)

rábano SM radish; **me importa un ~*** I don't care *o* give two hoots* ➤ **rábano picante** horseradish

rabia SF **1** (*Med*) rabies **2** (= *ira*) fury, anger; **me da ~** it makes me mad *o* infuriates me; **¡qué ~!** (= *ira*) isn't it infuriating!; (= *pena*) what a pity!; ✦ MODISMO **es fea con ~** she's as ugly as sin* **3** (= *antipatía*) **tener ~ a algn** to have a grudge against sb, have it in for sb*

rabiar /1b/ VI **1** (*) (= *sufrir*) (*de dolor*) to be in great pain; **estaba rabiando de las muelas** she had a raging toothache **2** (*) (= *encolerizarse*) **hacer ~ a algn** to infuriate sb, make sb see red; ✦ MODISMO **a ~*: me gusta a ~** I just love it; **está que rabia** he's hopping mad*, he's furious **3** (*Med*) to have rabies, be rabid

rabieta SF tantrum; **agarrar(se)** *o* **coger(se) una ~** to throw a tantrum, fly into a rage

rabillo SM **1** (*Bot*) leaf stalk **2** (= *punta*) tip; **mirar por el ~ del ojo** to look out of the corner of one's eye

rabino SM rabbi

rabioso ADJ **1** (= *furioso*) [*persona*] furious; [*aficionado*] rabid, fervent; **de rabiosa actualidad** highly topical **2** [*dolor*] terrible **3** (*Med*) rabid

rabo SM **1** (*Zool*) tail; ✦ MODISMO **con el ~ entre las piernas** with one's tail between one's legs ➤ **rabo de buey** oxtail **2** (***) (= *pene*) cock***, dick***

rabón ADJ **1** [*animal*] (= *de rabo pequeño*) short-tailed; (= *sin rabo*) tailless **2** (*LAm*) (= *pequeño*) short, small

rabona SF **hacer (la) ~** (*Escol*) to play truant, skip school, play hookey (*esp EEUU**)

racanear* /1a/ VI to be stingy*

rácano/a* Ⓐ ADJ stingy*, mean (*esp Brit*) Ⓑ SM/F scrooge*, cheapskate*

racha SF **1** (*Meteo*) gust of wind **2** (= *período*) string, series; **buena ~** run of good luck; **mala ~** run of bad luck; ✦ MODISMO **a ~s** by fits and starts

racheado ADJ gusty, squally

racial ADJ racial, race *antes de s*

racimo SM bunch, cluster; **un ~ de uvas** a bunch of grapes

raciocinio SM **1** (= *facultad*) reason **2** (= *razonamiento*) reasoning

ración SF **1** (*Mat*) ratio **2** (= *porción*) portion, helping; (*Mil*) ration; **una ~ de albóndigas** a portion *o* plate of meatballs

racional ADJ **1** (*Mat, Fil*) rational **2** (= *razonable*) reasonable, sensible

racionalista ADJ, SMF rationalist

racionalizar /1f/ VT **1** (*Psic, Fil*) to rationalize **2** (*Com*) to streamline, rationalize (*euf*)

racionamiento SM rationing

racionar /1a/ VT to ration

racismo SM racism

racista ADJ, SMF racist

radar SM (= *sistema*) radar; (= *estación*) radar station

radiación SF radiation ➤ **radiación solar** solar radiation ➤ **radiación ultravioleta** ultraviolet radiation

radiactividad SF radioactivity

radiactivo ADJ radioactive

radiado ADJ radio *antes de s*; **en una entrevista radiada** in a radio interview

radiador SM radiator

radial ADJ **1** (*Mec*) radial **2** (*LAm Rad*) radio *antes de s* **3** (*Aut*) **carretera ~** radial trunk road, *trunk road leading from periphery of a country to its centre*

radiante ADJ **1** (*Fís*) radiant **2** [*persona*] radiant;

estaba ~ she was radiant (**de** with)

radiar /1b/ VT **1** (*Fís*) to radiate **2** (*Rad*) to broadcast **3** (*Med*) to treat with radiation

radicado ADJ **~ en** based in

radical Ⓐ ADJ, SMF radical Ⓑ SM **1** (*Ling*) root **2** (*Mat*) square-root sign **3** (*Quím*) radical

radicalismo SM radicalism

radicalización SF [*de pensamiento*] increasing radicalism, radicalization (*frm*); [*de posturas, política*] toughening, radicalization (*frm*); [*de conflicto*] intensification

radicar /1g/ Ⓐ VI **1** [*dificultad, problema*] **~ en** to lie in **2** (*frm*) (= *localizarse*) to be, be situated, lie Ⓑ **radicarse** VPR to establish o.s. (**en** in)

radio¹ SM **1** (*Mat*) radius; **en un ~ de 10km** within a radius of 10km ➤ **radio de acción** [*de autoridad*] jurisdiction, extent of one's authority; (*Aer*) range ➤ **radio de giro** turning circle **2** [*de rueda*] spoke **3** (*Quím*) radium **4** (*Anat*) radius **5** (= *mensaje*) wireless message **6** (*LAm*) = **radio² 2**

radio² SF **1** (= *sistema*) radio; **hablar por ~** to talk on the radio ➤ **radio macuto*: enterarse de algo por ~ macuto** to hear sth on the grapevine ➤ **radio pirata** (= *sistema*) pirate radio; (= *emisora*) pirate radio station **2** (= *aparato*) radio, radio set

radioactividad SF radioactivity

radioactivo ADJ radioactive

radioaficionado/a SM/F radio ham*, amateur radio enthusiast

radiocasete SM radio cassette, radio-cassette player

radiodespertador SM clock radio, radio alarm

radiodifusión SF broadcasting

radiodifusora SF (*LAm*) radio station

radioemisora SF radio station

radioescucha SMF listener

radiofaro SM radio beacon

radiofónico ADJ radio *antes de s*

radiografía SF **1** (= *técnica*) radiography, X-ray photography **2 una ~** an X-ray, a radiograph (*frm*)

radiografiar /1c/ VT to X-ray

radiólogo/a SM/F radiologist

radionovela SF radio serial

radiopatrulla SM patrol car

radiotaxi SM radio cab, radio taxi

radioteléfono SM radiotelephone

radiotelescopio SM radio telescope

radioterapia SF radiotherapy

radiotransmisión SF (= *acto*) transmission, broadcasting; (= *programa*) transmission, broadcast

radioyente SMF listener

radón SM radon

RAE SF ABR = **Real Academia Española**

raer /2y/ VT (= *rascar*) to scrape; (= *quitar*) to scrape off

ráfaga SF **1** (*Meteo*) gust **2** [*de tiros*] burst **3** [*de intuición, luz*] flash

rafia SF raffia

rafting ['raftin] SM white-water rafting

raglán ADJ INV **manga ~** raglan sleeve

raid [raid] SM (*pl* **raids** [raid]) **1** (= *incursión*) [*de soldados*] raid; [*de policías*] police raid **2** (*esp Méx Aut*) ride, lift (*esp Brit*); **pedir ~** to hitch a ride *o* (*esp Brit*) lift

raído ADJ [*paño*] frayed, threadbare; [*ropa, persona*] shabby

raigambre SF (*a veces* SM) (= *tradición*) tradition; (= *antecedentes*) antecedents *pl*, history

rail SM, **raíl** SM rail

raíz SF 1 [*de planta*] root; **echar raíces** [*planta*] to take root; [*persona*] to put down roots; ✦ MODISMO **de ~: arrancar algo de ~** to root sth out completely; **cortar un problema de ~** to nip a problem in the bud 2 [*de diente, pelo*] root 3 (*Mat*) ➤ **raíz cuadrada** square root ➤ **raíz cúbica** cube root 4 (= *origen*) root; **la ~ del problema** the root of the problem 5 **a ~ de** as a result of 6 (*Ling*) root 7 (*Inform*) root

raja SF 1 (*en la piel*) gash; (*en muro*) chink; (*en porcelana, cristal, madera*) crack 2 [*de melón, sandía*] slice

rajá SM rajah

rajado/a* SM/F coward, chicken*

rajar /1a/ ❶ VT 1 [+ *papel, tejido*] to tear, rip; [+ *neumático, rueda*] to slash; [+ *vidrio, cerámica*] to crack 2 (*) (= *acuchillar*) to cut up* 3 (*RPl**) (= *echar*) to kick out*; (*de trabajo*) to fire* 4 (*And***) [+ *alumno*] to flunk*, fail ❷ VI 1 (*) (= *criticar*) **~ de algn** to slag sb off** 2 (*RPl**) (= *irse*) **rajen de acá** push off* 3 **salir rajando** (*RPl**) to rush out ❸ **rajarse** VPR 1 [*papel, tejido*] to tear, rip; [*vidrio, cerámica*] to crack; [*neumático*] to get ripped 2 (*) (= *echarse atrás*) to back out*

rajatabla: a ~ ADV (= *estrictamente*) strictly, rigorously; (= *exactamente*) exactly

rajón/ona ❶ ADJ (*CAm, Méx*) (= *cobarde*) cowardly ❷ SM/F 1 (*CAm, Méx*) (= *remolón*) quitter 2 (*And, Méx*) (= *chismoso*) gossip, telltale, tattletale (*EEUU*)

ralea SF (*pey*) kind, sort; **de esa ~** of that sort *o* (*liter*) ilk; **gente de baja ~** riffraff, common people

ralear /1a/ VI to become thin, become sparse

ralentí SM 1 (*Cine*) slow motion 2 (*Aut*) **estar al ~** ◇ **funcionar al ~** to be ticking over

ralentizar /1f/ VT, VI to slow down

rallador SM grater

ralladura SF **~ de limón** grated lemon rind

rallar /1a/ VT to grate

rally ['rrali] (*pl ~s*) SM, **rallye** SM ['rrali] rally

ralo ADJ [*pelo*] thin, sparse; [*bosque*] sparse

rama SF 1 [*de árbol*] branch; **en ~: algodón en ~** raw cotton; **canela en ~** cinnamon sticks *pl*; ✦ MODISMO **andarse** *o* **irse por las ~s: se va por las ~s** he goes off on tangents; **no te vayas por las ~s** stick to the point 2 [*de ciencia, familia, organización*] branch

ramada SF (*LAm*) *shelter or covering made of branches*

ramadán SM, **Ramadán** SM Ramadan

ramaje SM branches *pl*

ramal SM 1 (= *cabo*) strand; (*para el caballo*) halter 2 (= *desvío*) (*Aut*) branch; (*Ferro*) branch line

ramalazo SM [*de depresión, locura*] fit; ✦ MODISMO **tener ~** to be effeminate

rambla SF 1 (= *avenida*) boulevard, avenue 2 (= *arroyo*) watercourse 3 (*LAm*) (= *paseo marítimo*) esplanade, promenade

ramera SF whore, prostitute

ramificación SF ramification

ramificarse /1g/ VPR to branch, branch out, ramify (*frm*)

ramillete SM 1 [*de flores*] bouquet, bunch 2 (= *conjunto selecto*) choice bunch, select group

ramo SM 1 [*de flores*] bouquet, bunch 2 (*Com*) (= *sector*) field, section, department

rampa SF ramp ➤ **rampa de acceso** entrance ramp ➤ **rampa de lanzamiento** launch(ing) ramp

rampante ADJ rampant

ramplón ADJ common, coarse

ramplonería SF commonness, coarseness

rana SF 1 (*Zool*) frog; ✦ MODISMOS **cuando las ~s críen pelo** when pigs fly, when pigs learn to fly; **salir ~** to turn out badly, be a big disappointment 2 (= *juego*) *game of throwing coins into the mouth of an iron frog*

ranchera SF 1 (*Mús*) *Mexican folk song* 2 (= *coche*)

station wagon; *ver tb* **ranchero**

ranchería SF 1 (*LAm*) = **rancherío** 2 (*Carib*) (= *chabolas*) shantytown

rancherío SM (*LAm*) settlement

ranchero/a ❶ ADJ (*Méx*) (= *tímido*) shy ❷ SM/F 1 (*LAm*) (= *jefe de rancho*) rancher 2 (*Méx*) (= *campesino*) peasant, country person; *ver tb* **ranchera**

rancho SM 1 (*Méx*) (= *granja*) ranch, small farm 2 (*LAm*) (= *choza*) hut 3 (*Carib*) (= *chabola*) shanty, shack; **~s** (*And, Carib*) shanty town 4 (*Mil*) mess, communal meal; (*pey*) (= *comida*) bad food, grub*; ✦ MODISMO **hacer ~ aparte** to set up on one's own, go one's own way

rancio ADJ 1 [*vino*] old, mellow; [*mantequilla, tocino*] rancid 2 [*linaje*] ancient; [*tradición*] very ancient, time-honoured, time-honored (*EEUU*); (*pey*) antiquated, old-fashioned

ranglan ADJ INV, **ranglán** ADJ INV = **raglán**

rango SM (= *categoría*) rank; (= *prestigio*) standing, status; **de alto ~** of high standing, of some status

ranita SM Babygro®, rompers *pl*, romper suit

ránking ['raŋkin] SM (*pl ~s* ['raŋkin]) 1 (= *clasificación*) ranking 2 (*LAm Mús*) top twenty, hit parade

ranura SF (= *hendedura*) groove; (*para monedas*) slot ➤ **ranura de expansión** (*Inform*) expansion slot

rap SM rap, rap music; **hacer ~** to rap

rapado/a ❶ ADJ [*pelo*] close-cropped ❷ SM/F (= *persona*) skinhead

rapapolvo* SM (*Esp*) telling-off*, ticking-off (*Brit**); **echar un ~ a algn** to give sb a telling-off *o* (*Brit*) ticking-off*

rapar /1a/ ❶ VT [+ *pelo*] to crop; [+ *barba*] to shave ❷ **raparse** VPR (*tb* **~se la cabeza**) to shave one's head

rapaz¹ ❶ ADJ 1 (*Orn*) of prey 2 (= *avaricioso*) rapacious, greedy; (= *inclinado al robo*) thieving ❷ SF bird of prey

rapaz²(a)†† SM/F (*Esp hum*) boy/girl, lad/lass

rape¹ SM **al ~** cut close

rape² SM (*Zool*) monkfish

rapé SM snuff

rapel SM, **rápel** SM = **rappel**

rapero/a* ❶ ADJ rap *antes de s* ❷ SM/F rapper

rápidamente ADV fast, quickly

rapidez SF speed; **con ~** quickly

rápido ❶ ADJ fast, quick ❷ ADV quickly; **¡y ~, eh!** and make it snappy!* ❸ SM 1 (*Ferro*) express 2 **rápidos** (*en río*) rapids

rapiña SF robbery, robbery with violence

rapiñar /1a/ VT to steal

raposa SF vixen

raposo SM fox

rappel SM abseiling (*Brit*), rappelling (*EEUU*); **hacer ~** to abseil (*Brit*), rappel (*EEUU*)

rappelar /1a/ VI to abseil (*Brit*), rappel (*EEUU*)

rapsodia SF rhapsody

raptar /1a/ VT to kidnap, abduct

rapto SM 1 (= *secuestro*) kidnapping, kidnaping (*EEUU*), abduction 2 (= *impulso*) sudden impulse; **en un ~ de celos** in a sudden fit of jealousy

raptor(a) SM/F kidnapper

raqueta SF [*de tenis, bádminton*] racket; [*de ping pong*] bat ➤ **raqueta de nieve** snowshoe

raquítico ADJ 1 (*Med*) rachitic 2 [*cantidad, sueldo*] paltry, miserly 3 [*árbol*] stunted

raquitismo SM rickets *pl*

raramente ADV rarely, seldom

rareza SF 1 (= *cualidad*) rarity 2 (= *objeto*) rarity 3 (= *rasgo singular*) oddity, peculiarity; **tiene sus ~s** he has his peculiarities, he has his little ways

raro ADJ 1 (= *extraño*) strange, odd; **¡qué ~!** ◇ **¡qué cosa más rara!** how (very) strange!, how (very) odd! 2 (= *poco común*) rare; **una especie muy rara** a very rare species; **rara**

vez nos visita he rarely visits us **3** (*Fís*) rare, rarefied

ras SM **a ~ de** level with, flush with; **volar a ~ de tierra** to fly (almost) at ground level

rasante ⒶADJ low; **tiro ~** low shot; **vuelo ~** low-level flight **ⒷSM** slope; **cambio de ~** (*Aut*) brow of a hill

rasar /1a/ VT to skim, graze; **la bala pasó rasando su sombrero** the bullet grazed his hat

rasca¹ ** SF **1** (*Esp*) (= *frío*) cold; **¡menuda ~ hace!** it's freezing! **2** (*And, Cam, Carib*) (= *borrachera*) drunkenness

rasca²* ADJ (*CS*) [*objeto*] cheap, trashy; [*lugar*] grotty

rascacielos SM INV skyscraper

rascar /1g/ **Ⓐ** VT **1** (*con uñas*) to scratch **2** (*antes de pintar*) [+ *puerta, pared*] to scrape; [+ *pintura*] to scrape off **3** (*hum*) [+ *instrumento*] to scrape, scratch *o* saw away at **ⒷVI** (*Col*) (= *picar*) to itch **Ⓒ rascarse** VPR to scratch o.s.; **~se la espalda** to scratch one's back; ✦ MODISMO **~se la barriga** to take it easy

rasquetear /1a/ VT **1** (*SAm*) [+ *superficie*] to scrape **2** (*CS*) [+ *caballo*] to brush down

rasero SM strickle; **doble ~** double standards *pl*; ✦ MODISMO **medir dos cosas con el mismo ~** to treat two things alike

rasgado ADJ **1** [*ojos*] almond-shaped; [*boca*] wide, big **2** (*And*) (= *generoso*) generous

rasgadura SF tear, rip

rasgar /1h/ VT **1** [+ *tejido, piel*] to tear, rip; [+ *papel*] to tear up, tear to pieces **2** = **rasguear**

rasgo SM **1** (*Anat*) feature **2** (= *peculiaridad*) characteristic, feature ➤ **rasgos distintivos** distinctive features **3** (*con pluma*) stroke, flourish; **~s** characteristics (*of one's handwriting*); ✦ MODISMO **a grandes ~s** broadly speaking

rasgón SM tear, rip

rasguear /1a/ VT to strum

rasguño SM scratch; **salir sin un ~** to come out of it without a scratch

raso ⒶADJ 1 [*campo, terreno*] (= *llano*) flat, level; (= *sin árboles*) clear, open **2** [*cielo*] clear; **está ~** the sky is clear **3** [*contenido*] level; **una cucharada rasa** a level spoonful **4** [*pelota, vuelo*] very low, almost at ground level **ⒷSM 1** (*Cos*) satin **2** (= *campo abierto*) **dormir al ~** to sleep out in the open

raspa SF **1** [*de cebada*] beard **2** [*de pescado*] backbone **3** (*Mús*) popular Mexican dance

raspado ⒶADJ (*) **un aprobado ~** a bare pass **ⒷSM 1** (*Med*) D and C, dilation and curettage **2** (*Col*) (= *helado*) ice lolly (*Brit*), Popsicle® (*EEUU*)

raspadura SF scrape, scraping, rasping

raspar /1a/ **Ⓐ** VT **1** [+ *pintura*] to scrape off; [+ *superficie*] to scrape **2** [+ *piel*] to scratch **3** [+ *texto*] to scratch out; **han raspado la firma** they have scratched out the signature **ⒷVI** [*manos, tejido, licor*] to be rough

raspón SM scratch, graze

rasposo ADJ **1** [*sabor*] sharp, rough **2** (*CS*) (= *raído*) scruffy, threadbare **3** (*CS**) (= *de mala calidad*) cheap, trashy; [+ *bar, hotel*] grotty*

rasta ADJ, SMF Rasta

rastra SF **1** (*Agr*) (= *rastrillo*) rake; (= *grada*) harrow **2 a ~s: tuvo que sacarme a ~s** she had to drag me out; **llevaba la bolsa a ~s** she was dragging the bag along behind her; **el herido fue a ~s hasta la puerta** the injured man crawled to the door **3** (*Pesca*) trawl; **pescar a la ~** to trawl

rastreador(a) Ⓐ SM/F (= *persona*) tracker **ⒷSM** (*Náut*) (*tb* **barco ~**) trawler ➤ **rastreador de minas** minesweeper

rastrear /1a/ **Ⓐ** VT **1** (= *buscar*) to track, trail; [+ *satélite*] to track; [+ *río*] to drag; **~ el monte** to comb the woods **2** (*Pesca*) to trawl **ⒷVI 1** (*Agr*) to rake, harrow **2** (*Pesca*) to trawl **3** (*Aer*) to skim the ground, fly very low

rastreo SM **1** (*en agua*) dredging, dragging; (*Pesca*) trawling **2** [*de satélite*] tracking

rastrero ADJ **1** [*conducta*] mean, despicable; [*persona*] cringing; [*método*] low; [*disculpa*] abject, humble

2 (*Bot*) creeping

rastrillar /1a/ VT (*Agr*) to rake; (= *recoger*) to rake up; (= *alisar*) to rake smooth

rastrillo SM **1** (*Agr*) rake **2** (*Méx*) (= *para afeitarse*) (safety) razor

rastro SM **1** (= *pista*) trail; (= *olor*) scent **2** (= *señal*) trace; **desaparecer sin dejar ~** to vanish without trace **3** (*Esp*) (= *mercadillo*) flea market; **el Rastro** *fleamarket in Madrid* **4** (*Méx*) (= *matadero*) slaughterhouse, abattoir (*Brit*)

rastrojo SM stubble

rasurado SM shave

rasurador SM, **rasuradora** SF (*Méx*) electric shaver, electric razor

rasurar /1a/ **Ⓐ** VT **1** (*esp Méx*) (= *afeitar*) to shave **2** (*Téc*) to scrape **Ⓑ rasurarse** VPR (*esp Méx*) to shave

rata Ⓐ SF rat; ✦ MODISMO **hacerse la ~** (*RPl**) to play truant, skip school, play hookey (*EEUU**) **Ⓑ** SMF (*) miser, stingy devil*

ratero/a SM/F (= *ladrón*) thief, petty thief; (= *carterista*) pickpocket

raticida SM rat poison

ratificación SF ratification

ratificar /1g/ VT [+ *tratado*] to ratify; [+ *noticia*] to confirm; [+ *opinión*] to support

ratio SM (*a veces* SF) ratio

rato SM **1** (= *espacio de tiempo*) **1.1** (*uso incontable*) **lleva bastante ~ hablando** he's been talking for quite a while *o* for quite some time; **al ~** shortly afterwards, shortly after, a short while later; **hace ~** a while ago, some time ago; **mucho ~** a long time; ✦ MODISMO **para ~: tenemos carretera para ~** we still have quite a way to go; **aún queda presidente para ~** the president will still be around for some time to come **1.2** (*uso contable*) **durante el ~ que estuve esperando** during the short time I was waiting; **en esos ~s me olvido de todo** at such moments I forget about everything; **a ~s** at times; **a ~s perdidos** in one's spare moments; **todo el ~** the whole time, all the time **1.3 un ~** a (short) while; **dentro de un ~** in a (short) while; **todavía tardará un ~ en salir** it'll still be a while before he comes out; **me quedaré un ~ más** I'll stay a bit longer; **cuando tengas un ~** when you have a spare moment; **no regresó hasta pasado un ~** he didn't come back for a while; **dar un mal ~ a algn** to give sb a hard time; **pasar un buen/ mal ~** to have a good/bad time; **pasar el ~** to pass the time ➤ **ratos libres** spare time, free time

2 (*) **un ~** (= *Esp*) (*uso adverbial*) (= *bastante*): **es un ~ listo** he's pretty smart*; **sabe un ~ largo de matemáticas** she knows quite a lot about maths (*Brit*) *o* math (*EEUU*)

ratón SM **1** (*Zool, Inform*) mouse ➤ **ratón de biblioteca** bookworm ➤ **ratón óptico** optical mouse **2** (*Ven**) (= *resaca*) hangover

ratonera SF **1** (= *trampa*) mousetrap **2** (= *agujero*) mouse hole

raudal SM **1** (= *torrente*) torrent, flood **2 a ~es** in abundance, in great numbers

raudo ADJ (*liter*) swift

raya¹ SF **1** (= *línea*) line; (*en tela, diseño*) stripe; **a ~s** striped; ✦ MODISMOS **mantener a ~ a algn** to keep sb at bay; **pasarse de la ~** to overstep the mark, go too far; **poner a ~ a** to check, hold back; **tener a ~** (= *impedir el avance*) to keep off, keep at bay; (= *controlar*) to keep in check, keep under control ➤ **raya diplomática** (*en tejido*) pinstripe **2** (= *marca*) (*en una superficie*) scratch, mark **3** (*en el pelo*) parting (*Brit*), part (*EEUU*); **hacerse la ~** to part one's hair **4** (*en el pantalón*) crease **5** (*Tip*) line, dash; (*en morse*) dash **6** (**) (= *droga*) fix*, dose

raya² SF (= *pez*) ray, skate

rayado ADJ **1** [*papel*] ruled, lined; [*tela, diseño*] striped **2** [*disco, mueble*] scratched **3** (*CS**) (= *loco*) cracked*, crazy

rayano ADJ **~ en** bordering on

rayar /1a/ **Ⓐ** VT **1** (= *trazar líneas en*) to rule, draw lines on

2 (= *garabatear*) to scribble on **3** [+ *disco, mueble*] to scratch **4** (*Méx*) (= *pagar*) to pay **Ⓑ** VI **1 ~ en** (= *asemejarse*) to border on, verge on; **esto raya en lo increíble** this verges on the incredible **2** (= *arañar*) to scratch **3 al ~ el alba** (*liter*) at break of day, at first light **4** (*Méx*) (= *cobrar*) to be paid **Ⓒ rayarse** VPR **1** [*objeto*] to get scratched **2** (*CS**) (= *enloquecer*) to go crazy

rayo SM **1** [*de luz*] ray, beam ➤ **rayo de luna** moonbeam ➤ **rayo de sol** sunbeam, ray of sunlight ➤ **rayo láser** laser beam ➤ **rayos gamma** gamma rays ➤ **rayos infrarrojos** infrared rays ➤ **rayos ultravioleta** ultraviolet rays ➤ **rayos X** X-rays

2 (*Meteo*) lightning, flash of lightning; **cayó un ~ en la torre** the tower was struck by lightning;
✦ MODISMOS **saber a ~s** (*Esp**) to taste awful; **como un ~** like lightning, like a shot; **pasar como un ~** to rush past, flash past; **echar ~s y centellas** to rage, fume; **¡que lo parta un ~!*** damn him!*; **¡que me parta un ~ si lo sé!** I'm damned if I know!*
3 (*como exclamativo*) **¡~s!*** dammit!*; **¿qué ~s es eso?*** what in hell's name is that?*
4 (*LAm*) [*de rueda*] spoke

rayón SM rayon

rayuela SF (= *juego de adultos*) pitch-and-toss; (*RPI*) (= *juego de niños*) hopscotch

raza SF **1** (= *grupo étnico*) [*de persona*] race; [*de animal*] breed; **de (pura) ~** [*caballo*] thoroughbred; [*perro*] pedigree **2** (= *estirpe*) stock

razia SF raid

razón SF **1** (= *verdad*) **con ~ o sin ella** rightly or wrongly; **dar la ~ a algn** (= *estar de acuerdo*) to agree that sb is right; (= *apoyar*) to side with sb; **quitar la ~ a algn** to say sb is wrong; **tener ~** to be right; **no tener ~** to be wrong **2** (= *facultad*) reason; **entrar en ~** to see sense, listen to reason; **perder la ~** to go out of one's mind; **desde que tengo uso de ~** for as long as I can remember
3 (= *motivo*) reason; **no atiende a razones** he won't listen to reason; **con ~** with good reason; **están hartos con toda la ~ (del mundo)** they're fed up and they have good reason to be, they're fed up and rightly so; **¡con ~!** naturally!; **~ de más para ayudarlas** all the more reason to help them ➤ **razón de ser** raison d'être ➤ **razones de Estado** reasons of State
4 (= *información*) **"razón: Princesa 4"** "inquiries to 4 Princesa Street", "for further details apply to 4 Princesa Street"; **dar ~ de algo/algn** to give information about sth/sb
5 (*Mat*) ratio; **en ~ directa con** in direct ratio to; **a ~ de**: **a ~ de cinco a siete** in the ratio of five to seven; **lo devolverán a ~ de mil dólares mensuales** they will pay it back at a rate of a thousand dollars a month
6 (*Com*) ➤ **razón social** trade name, firm's name

razonable ADJ reasonable

razonado ADJ **1** (= *fundado en razones*) reasoned **2** [*cuenta*] itemized, detailed

razonamiento SM reasoning

razonar /1a/ **Ⓐ** VT **1** (= *argumentar*) to reason, argue **2** [+ *problema*] to reason out **Ⓑ** VI **1** (= *argumentar*) to reason, argue **2** (= *hablar*) to talk, talk together

razzia SF raid

RDSI SF ABR (= **Red Digital de Servicios Integrados**) ISDN

re SM (*Mús*) D ➤ **re mayor** D major

reabastecer /2d/ **Ⓐ** VT (*de combustible*) to refuel; (*de víveres*) to resupply **Ⓑ reabastecerse** VPR (*de combustible*) to refuel; (*de víveres*) to restock

reacción SF **1** (*Fís, Quím*) reaction (**a, ante** to) **2** (= *respuesta*) response (**a** to); ➤ **reacción en cadena** chain reaction **3** (*Téc*) **avión a o de ~** jet plane; **propulsión por ~** jet propulsion **4** (*Pol*) **la ~** the reactionaries *pl*

reaccionar /1a/ VI (*tb Fís, Quím*) to react (**a, ante** to)

reaccionario/a ADJ, SM/F reactionary

reacio ADJ reluctant; **ser ~ a** to resist, resist the idea of; **ser ~ a hacer algo** to be reluctant *o* unwilling to do sth

reacondicionar /1a/ VT [+ *motor*] to recondition; [+ *empresa, organización*] to reorganize, restructure

reactivar /1a/ VT to reactivate

reactor SM **1** (*Fís*) reactor ➤ **reactor nuclear** nuclear reactor **2** (*Aer*) (= *motor*) jet engine; (= *avión*) jet plane

readmisión SF readmission

readmitir /3a/ VT to readmit

reafirmación SF reaffirmation

reafirmar /1a/ VT to reaffirm, reassert

reagrupación SF regrouping

reagrupar /1a/ **Ⓐ** VT to regroup **Ⓑ reagruparse** VPR to regroup

reajustar /1a/ **Ⓐ** VT **1** (= *volver a ajustar*) to readjust **2** (*Pol*) to reshuffle **Ⓑ reajustarse** VPR to readjust

reajuste SM **1** (= *acción*) readjustment **2** (*Pol*) reshuffle ➤ **reajuste ministerial** cabinet reshuffle

real¹ ADJ (= *verdadero*) real

real² **Ⓐ** ADJ **1** (= *de la realeza*) royal; **la familia ~** the royal family; **porque no me da la ~ gana*** because I don't damn well feel like it**
2 (†) (= *espléndido*) grand, splendid **Ⓑ** SM **1** (= *de la feria*) fairground
2 (*Fin*) real (*sub-unit of currency in various Latin American states and unit of currency in Brazil*)

REAL ACADEMIA ESPAÑOLA

The **Real Academia Española (RAE)** was created in 1713 to protect the purity of the Spanish language. There are 46 members appointed for life from among Spain's most celebrated writers and linguists. It works in collaboration with the 21 other Spanish language academies, which represent all the countries where Spanish is a native language.
See also www.rae.es

---

realce SM **1** (= *esplendor*) lustre, luster (*EEUU*); **dar ~ a** to add lustre *o* (*EEUU*) luster to, enhance **2** (*Téc*) embossing

realeza SF royalty

realidad SF reality; **la dura ~** the harsh reality; **atengámonos a la ~** let's stick to the facts; **en ~** in fact, actually; **la ~ es que ...** the fact (of the matter) is that ... ➤ **realidad virtual** virtual reality

realismo SM realism ➤ **realismo mágico** magical realism ➤ **realismo social** social realism ➤ **realismo sucio** dirty realism

---

REALISMO MÁGICO

Realismo mágico, which derives from a term coined by the Cuban writer Alejo Carpentier in 1949, **lo real maravilloso**, refers to a primarily Latin American literary genre in which the writer combines elements of the fantastic and realistic in a conscious effort to reconcile tradition with modernity and American-Indian and Black oral culture with European literary writing. The most celebrated magical realist writer is Colombian Nobel prize winner Gabriel García Márquez.

---

realista **Ⓐ** ADJ realistic **Ⓑ** SMF realist

realizable ADJ **1** [*propósito*] attainable; [*proyecto*] practical, feasible **2** (*Fin*) [*activo*] realizable

realización SF **1** (= *acción*) **tras la ~ de su primer vuelo** after making his first flight **2** (*Cine, TV*) production **3** (*Fin*) realization **4** (*LAm*) (= *liquidación*) clearance sale

realizado ADJ **sentirse ~** to feel fulfilled

realizador(a) SM/F (*Cine, TV*) producer

realizar /1f/ **Ⓐ** VT **1** (= *hacer*) [+ *viaje, vuelo, compra*] to make; [+ *expedición*] to carry out, go on; [+ *labor, tarea*] to do **2** [+ *sueño*] to fulfil, fulfill (*EEUU*), realize **3** (*Fin*) [+ *activo*] to realize; [+ *ganancias*] to realize **Ⓑ realizarse** VPR **1** [*sueño*] to come true; [*esperanzas*] to materialize; [*proyecto*] to be carried out **2** [*persona*] to fulfil o.s., fulfill o.s. (*EEUU*); **~se como persona** to achieve personal fulfilment *o* (*EEUU*) fulfillment, fulfil o (EEUU) fulfill o.s. as a person

realmente ADV **1** (= *verdaderamente*) really **2** (= *de hecho*) really, actually

realojar /1a/ VT to rehouse

realquilar /1a/ VT to sublet

realzar /1f/ VT **1** (= *dar más importancia a*) to enhance, heighten, add to **2** (*Téc*) to emboss, raise **3** (*Arte*) to highlight

reanimación SF (= *restablecimiento*) revival; [*de un enfermo, accidentado*] resuscitation

reanimar /1a/ **Ⓐ** VT **1** (= *dar fuerzas a*) to revive **2** [+ *enfermo, accidentado*] to revive **3** (= *dar ánimo a*) to cheer up **Ⓑ reanimarse** VPR to revive

reanudación SF renewal, resumption

reanudar /1a/ **Ⓐ** VT [+ *diálogo, viaje*] to resume; **~on su amistad tras una larga separación** they resumed their friendship after a long separation, they took up their friendship again after a long separation **Ⓑ reanudarse** VPR to resume; **las clases se ~án el lunes** classes will resume on Monday

reaparecer /2d/ VI (= *volver a aparecer*) to reappear; [*síntomas*] to recur

reaparición SF (= *nueva aparición*) reappearance; [*de síntomas*] recurrence

reapertura SF reopening

rearme SM rearmament

reaseguro SM reinsurance

reata SF **1** (= *cuerda*) rope; (*Méx*) (= *lazo*) rope, lasso **2** (= *caballos*) string, string of horses, pack train

reavivar /1a/ VT to revive

rebaja SF **1** (= *descuento*) reduction, discount; **¿me puede hacer alguna ~?** could you give me a discount?; **los artículos de ~** sales goods **2** [*de impuestos, tarifas, condena*] reduction **3 rebajas** (*en comercios*) sales; **"rebajas"** "sale"; **están de ~s en Harrods** Harrods have a sale, Harrods are having a sale

rebajar /1a/ **Ⓐ** VT **1** (= *reducir*) **1.1** (*en dinero*) [+ *impuesto, coste, precio*] to reduce, cut, lower; **¿nos han rebajado algo?** have they taken something off?, have they given us a reduction o discount?; **hemos rebajado todos nuestros artículos** we have reduced all our stock **1.2** (*en tiempo*) [+ *condena, castigo*] to reduce; [+ *edad, límite*] to lower; **rebajó la plusmarca mundial en 1,2 segundos** he took 1.2 seconds off the world record **1.3** (*en cantidad*) [+ *nivel, temperatura*] to reduce, lower; [+ *luz, tensión, intensidad*] to reduce; [+ *peso*] to lose; [+ *dolor*] to ease, alleviate **2** (= *diluir*) [+ *líquido*] to dilute; [+ *pintura*] to thin; [+ *color*] to tone down; [+ *droga*] to cut, adulterate **3** (= *bajar la altura de*) [+ *terreno*] to lower, lower the level of; [+ *tejado*] to lower; [+ *puerta*] to rabbet **4** (= *humillar*) to humiliate, put down **Ⓑ rebajarse** VPR **~se a hacer algo** to lower o.s. to do sth, stoop to do sth; **~se ante algn** to humble o.s. before sb

rebalsarse /1a/ VPR (*CS*) to overflow

rebanada SF slice

rebanar /1a/ VT [+ *pan*] to slice; (*) [+ *pierna*] to slice off

rebañar /1a/ VT to scrape up

rebaño SM **1** [*de ovejas*] flock; [*de cabras*] herd **2** [*de personas*] (*tb Rel*) flock

rebasar /1a/ VT **1** [+ *límite*] to pass, go beyond; [+ *límite de tiempo*] to exceed; (*en cualidad, cantidad*) to exceed, surpass; (*en carrera, progreso*) to overtake, leave behind **2** (*esp Méx Aut*) to overtake (*esp Brit*), pass (*EEUU*); (*Náut*) to sail past

rebatinga SF (*CAm, Méx*) = **rebatiña**

rebatiña SF scramble, rush; **andar a la ~ de algo** to scramble for sth, fight over sth

rebatir /3a/ VT to reject, refute

rebato SM (*Mil*) surprise attack; **llamar o tocar a ~** to sound the alarm

rebeca SF (*Esp*) cardigan

rebeco SM chamois, ibex

rebelarse /1a/ VPR to rebel (**contra** against)

rebelde **Ⓐ** ADJ **1** (= *que se rebela*) rebellious **2** [*niño*] unruly; [*resfriado*] persistent; [*mancha*] stubborn; [*pelo*] unmanageable **Ⓑ** SMF rebel

rebeldía SF **1** (= *cualidad*) rebelliousness; (= *desafío*) defiance, disobedience; **estar en plena ~** to be in open revolt **2** (*Jur*) default; **caer en ~** to be in default; **fue juzgado en ~** he was judged by o in default

rebelión SF rebellion

rebenque SM (*LAm*) whip, riding crop

reblandecer /2d/ **Ⓐ** VT to soften **Ⓑ reblandecerse** VPR to go soft

rebobinar /1a/ VT to rewind

reborde SM (= *saliente*) ledge; (*Téc*) flange, rim

rebosante ADJ **~ de** brimming with, overflowing with

rebosar /1a/ **Ⓐ** VI **1** [*líquido, recipiente*] to overflow; **el grupo llenó la sala a ~** the group filled the room to overflowing **2** **~ de algo** to overflow with sth, be brimming with sth; **~ de salud** to be radiant with health **Ⓑ** VT to abound in; **su rostro rebosaba salud** he was the picture of health

rebotar /1a/ **Ⓐ** VI [*pelota*] to bounce; [*bala*] to ricochet, glance (**de** off) **Ⓑ rebotarse** (*) VPR to get cheesed off*; **~se con algn** to have a dig at sb*, have a go at sb*

rebote SM bounce, rebound; **de ~** (= *en el segundo bote*) on the rebound; (= *indirectamente*) indirectly

rebotica SF back room

rebozar /1f/ VT to dip in batter

rebozo SM **1** (= *mantilla*) muffler, wrap; (*LAm*) (= *chal*) shawl **2** (*frm*) **sin ~** openly, frankly

rebrote SM new outbreak, reappearance

rebujo SM mass, knot, tangle

rebullir /3a/ VT to stir up

rebuscado ADJ [*estilo*] affected; [*palabra*] recherché

rebuscar /1g/ VI to search carefully

rebuznar /1a/ VI to bray

rebuzno SM bray, braying

recabar /1a/ VT to manage to get (**de** from); **~ fondos** to raise funds

recadero/a SM/F (= *mensajero*) messenger; (= *repartidor*) errand boy/girl

recado SM **1** (= *mensaje*) message; **dejar ~** to leave a message; **mandar ~** to send word **2** (= *compra, encargo*) errand; **salir a hacer un ~** to go out on an errand; **chico de los ~s** messenger, errand boy **3** (*LAm*) (= *montura*) saddle and trappings

recaer /2n/ VI **1** (*Med*) to suffer a relapse, relapse **2** **~ en** o **sobre** [*elección*] to fall on, fall to; [*premio*] to go to; [*sospecha*] to fall on; [*legado*] to pass to

recaída SF relapse

recalcar /1g/ VT to stress, emphasize; **~ algo a algn** to stress the importance of sth to sb; **~ a algn que ...** to tell sb emphatically that ...

recalcitrante ADJ recalcitrant

recalentado ADJ warmed-up

recalentamiento SM overheating ➤ **recalentamiento del planeta** global warming

recalentar /1j/ **Ⓐ** VT **1** (= *demasiado*) to overheat **2** [+ *comida*] to warm up, reheat **Ⓑ recalentarse** VPR to get too hot

recalificación SF reassessment

recámara SF **1** (= *cuarto*) side room; (= *vestidor*) dressing room; (*esp Méx*) (= *dormitorio*) bedroom **2** [*de fusil*] breech, chamber

recamarera SF (*esp Méx*) chambermaid, maid

recambiar /1b/ VT to change over

recambio SM (*Mec*) spare; [*de pluma*] refill; **piezas de ~** spares, spare parts

recapacitar /1a/ VI to reconsider, think again

recapitulación SF recapitulation, summing-up

recapitular /1a/ VT, VI to recapitulate, sum up

recargable ADJ rechargeable

recargado ADJ (= *sobrecargado*) overloaded; [*estilo, diseño*] overelaborate

recargar /1h/ VT **1** [+ *encendedor, bolígrafo*] to refill; [+ *batería, pila*] to recharge; [+ *arma*] to reload **2** (= *cargar demasiado*) to clutter **3** (*Fin*) **recargan el 10% si ...** there is a 10% surcharge if ...

recargo SM extra charge, surcharge

recatado ADJ **1** (= *modesto*) modest, demure **2** (= *prudente*) cautious, circumspect

recato SM **1** (= *modestia*) modesty **2** (= *cautela*) caution, circumspection; **sin ~** openly

recauchar /1a/ VT = **recauchutar**

recauchutado SM (*Esp*) **1** [*de neumático*] retread **2** (= *proceso*) retreading, remoulding, remolding (*EEUU*)

recauchutar /1a/ VT [+ *neumático*] to retread, remould, remold (*EEUU*)

recaudación SF **1** (= *acción*) collection ➤ **recaudación de fondos** fundraising **2** (= *cantidad*) takings *pl*; (*Dep*) gate, gate money; ⧫ QUINIELA

recaudador(a) SM/F ➤ **recaudador(a) de impuestos** tax collector

recaudar /1a/ VT **1** [+ *fondos*] to raise **2** [+ *impuestos*] to collect

recaudo SM **a buen ~** in a safe place

recelar /1a/ **Ⓐ** VT ~ **que ...** to suspect that ..., fear that ... **Ⓑ** VI ~ **de** to be suspicious of; ~ **de hacer algo** to be wary of doing sth

> Recuérdese que las preposiciones en inglés rigen gerundio y no infinitivo, de ahí **to be wary of doing sth.**

recelo SM (= *suspicacia*) suspicion; (= *temor*) misgiving, apprehension; (= *desconfianza*) distrust, mistrust

receloso ADJ (= *suspicaz*) suspicious; (= *desconfiado*) distrustful; (= *temeroso*) apprehensive

recensión SF review

recepción SF **1** (= *acogida*) reception **2** (*Radio*) reception **3** (= *ceremonia*) reception **4** [*de hotel*] reception, reception desk

recepcionista SMF (hotel) receptionist

receptáculo SM (*frm*) receptacle

receptividad SF receptivity

receptivo ADJ receptive

receptor(a) **Ⓐ** SM (*Elec, Rad, TV*) receiver ➤ **receptor de televisión** television set **Ⓑ** SM/F **1** (*Med*) recipient ➤ **receptor(a) universal** universal recipient **2** (*en béisbol*) catcher; (*en fútbol americano*) receiver **3** (*Ling*) recipient

recesión SF recession

recesivo ADJ **1** (*Biol*) recessive **2** (*Econ*) recession *antes de s*, recessionary

receso SM **1** (*LAm Parl*) recess **2** (*Econ*) ➤ **receso económico** downturn in the economy

receta SF **1** (*Culin*) recipe (**de** for) **2** (*Med*) prescription

recetar /1a/ VT to prescribe

recetario SM collection of recipes, recipe book

rechazar /1f/ VT **1** [+ *acusación, idea*] to reject; [+ *oferta*] to turn down, refuse **2** [+ *persona*] to push away; [+ *ataque*] to repel, beat off; [+ *enemigo*] to drive back **3** (*Med*) [+ *órgano*] to reject

rechazo SM **1** (= *negativa*) refusal; ~ **frontal** [*de propuesta*] outright rejection; [*de oferta*] flat refusal **2** (*Med*) rejection **3** (= *desaire*) rebuff

rechifla SF **1** (= *silbido*) whistling; (= *abucheo*) booing; (*Teat*) catcall **2** (= *burla*) mockery

rechinar /1a/ VI [*madera, puerta*] to creak; [*máquina*] to

clank; [*metal seco*] to grate; [*motor*] to grind, whirr; [*dientes*] to grind, gnash; **hacer ~ los dientes** to grind one's teeth

rechistar /1a/ VI to complain; **se fue a la cama sin ~** he went to bed without (a word of) complaint; **nadie se atrevió a ~** nobody dared complain

rechoncho ADJ thickset, stocky

rechupete: **de ~*** **Ⓐ** ADJ [*comida*] delicious, scrumptious* **Ⓑ** ADV splendidly, jolly well*; **pasarlo de ~** to have a fantastic time*; **el examen me ha salido de ~** the exam went like a dream for me

recibí SM "received with thanks"

recibidor SM hall

recibimiento SM welcome, reception

recibir /3a/ **Ⓐ** VT **1** [+ *dinero, apoyo, llamada, noticias*] to receive, get; [+ *ayuda, homenaje*] to receive; **¿recibiste mi carta?** did you get my letter?; **estamos a la espera de ~ más mercancía** we're waiting for some new stock to arrive; **recibió el premio a la mejor película extranjera** it won the prize for best foreign film; **no reciben bien el Canal 8** the reception is not very good on Channel 8; **"mensaje recibido"** (*Radio*) "message received"; ~ **asistencia médica** to receive medical assistance, be given medical assistance; ~ **el calificativo de** to be labelled (as); ~ **el nombre de** (*frm*) (= *llamarse*) to be called; (*al nacer*) to be named **2** (= *sufrir*) [+ *susto*] to get; ~ **un disparo** to be shot; ~ **un golpe** to be hit, be struck **3** [+ *persona*] **3.1** (= *acoger*) to welcome; **para ~ a los invitados** to welcome the guests; **nos recibieron con gran alegría** they gave us a very warm welcome; **ir a ~ a algn** to meet sb; **salieron a ~los al jardín** they received them in the garden; ✦ MODISMO ~ **a algn con los brazos abiertos** to welcome sb with open arms **3.2** (*para reunión, entrevista*) (*gen*) to see; (*formalmente*) to receive; **el doctor lo ~á enseguida** the doctor will see you in a moment; **no se les permite ~ visitas** they are not allowed visits **4** (*Taur*) ~ **al toro** to meet the bull's charge **5** (= *aceptar*) [+ *propuesta, sugerencia*] to receive **6** (*en correspondencia*) **recibe un fuerte abrazo de tus padres** lots of love from Mum and Dad; **reciba un saludo de ...** yours sincerely ... **7** [+ *peso*] to bear **Ⓑ** VI **1** (*frm*) (*en casa*) (= *tener invitados*) to entertain; (= *tener visitas*) to receive visitors; **la baronesa sólo puede ~ los lunes** the baroness is only at home on Mondays, the baroness can only receive visitors on Mondays **2** [*médico*] to see patients **Ⓒ** **recibirse** VPR (*LAm Univ*) to graduate; **~se de** to qualify as

recibo SM **1** (= *factura*) bill, account; ~ **de la luz** electricity bill **2** (*de haber pagado*) receipt; **acusar ~ (de algo)** to acknowledge receipt (of sth) **3** ✦ MODISMO **ser de ~: no es de ~ que ...** it is unacceptable that ...

reciclable ADJ recyclable

reciclado **Ⓐ** ADJ recycled **Ⓑ** SM (*Téc*) recycling; [*de persona*] retraining

reciclaje SM, **reciclamiento** SM [*de papel, vidrio*] recycling; [*de profesional*] retraining

reciclar /1a/ **Ⓐ** VT [+ *papel, vidrio*] to recycle; [+ *profesional*] to retrain **Ⓑ** **reciclarse** VPR [*profesional*] to retrain

recidiva SF (*esp RPl*) relapse

recién ADV **1** (*antepuesto a participio*) newly; ~ **casado** newly married; **los ~ casados** the newlyweds; ~ **hecho** newly-made; **los ~ llegados** (*a un lugar*) the newcomers; (*a una reunión*) the latecomers; **el ~ nacido** the newborn; **un ~ nacido** a newborn child **2** (*SAm*) (= *hace un momento*) ~ **llegó** he's just arrived; ~ **lo había planchado** I had just ironed it **3** (*SAm*) (= *sólo*) ~ **ayer me llamó para avisarme** he didn't phone me to let me know until yesterday; ~ **ahora puedo decir que me siento mejor** only just now I can say I feel better

reciente ADJ recent; **un descubrimiento muy ~** a very recent discovery

recinto SM (= *cercado*) enclosure; (= *área*) area, place; (= *zona delimitada*) precincts *pl*; **dentro del ~ universitario**

on the university campus ➤ **recinto ferial** exhibition site ➤ **recinto penitenciario** prison grounds *pl*

recio Ⓐ ADJ **1** [*persona*] strong, tough; [*cuerda*] thick, strong; [*prueba*] tough, demanding, severe **2** [*voz*] loud **Ⓑ** ADV loudly

recipiente Ⓐ SMF (= *persona*) recipient **Ⓑ** SM (= *vaso*) container

recíproco ADJ reciprocal

recital SM [*de música*] recital; [*de literatura*] reading ➤ **recital de poesía** poetry reading

recitar /1a/ VT to recite

reclamación SF **1** (= *queja*) complaint; **formular** *o* **presentar una** ~ to make *o* lodge a complaint **2** (= *reivindicación*) claim ➤ **reclamación salarial** wage claim

reclamar /1a/ **Ⓐ** VT **1** [+ *herencia, tierras*] to claim; [+ *derechos*] to demand; **reclama su parte de los beneficios** he is claiming his share of the profits; **~on su presencia ante el tribunal** they demanded he appear before the court **2** [+ *atención, solución*] to demand; **esto reclama toda nuestra atención** this demands our full attention **Ⓑ** VI (= *quejarse*) to complain

reclame SM *o* SF (*LAm*) advertisement

reclamo SM **1** (*Orn*) call; (*Caza*) decoy, lure; **acudir al** ~ to answer the call **2** (= *anuncio*) advertisement; (= *aliciente*) lure, attraction ➤ **reclamo publicitario** advertising ploy **3** (*LAm*) (= *protesta*) complaint

reclinable ADJ **asiento** ~ reclining seat

reclinar /1a/ **Ⓐ** VT to lean, recline, rest (**contra** against; **sobre** on) **Ⓑ** **reclinarse** VPR to lean back

reclinatorio SM prie-dieu

recluir /3g/ **Ⓐ** VT (= *encerrar*) to shut away; (*Jur*) (= *encarcelar*) to imprison **Ⓑ** **recluirse** VPR to shut o.s. away

reclusión SF **1** (= *encarcelamiento*) imprisonment, confinement **2** (= *encierro voluntario*) seclusion

recluso/a Ⓐ ADJ imprisoned; **población reclusa** prison population **Ⓑ** SM/F inmate, prisoner

recluta SMF recruit

reclutamiento SM recruitment

reclutar /1a/ VT to recruit

recobrar /1a/ **Ⓐ** VT [+ *salud*] to recover, get back; [+ *ciudad*] to recapture; [+ *amistad*] to win back; ~ **las fuerzas** to get one's strength back; ~ **el conocimiento** to regain consciousness, come to **Ⓑ** **recobrarse** VPR **1** (= *recuperarse*) to recover **2** (*frm*) (= *volver en sí*) to regain consciousness, come to

recochinearse* /1a/ VPR (*Esp*) ~ **de algn** to take the mickey out of sb*

recochineo* SM (*Esp*) mickey-taking*

recocido ADJ overcooked

recodo SM bend, turn

recogecables SM INV automatic cable retractor

recogedor SM dustpan

recogepelotas SMF INV ball boy/ball girl

recoger /2c/ **Ⓐ** VT **1** (= *levantar*) [+ *objeto caído*] to pick up; [+ *objetos dispersos*] to gather (up), gather together; **recogió la ropa del suelo** she gathered the clothes up off the floor **2** (= *recolectar*) [+ *datos, información*] to gather, collect; [+ *dinero, firmas*] to collect; [+ *correo, basura*] to collect, pick up; **a las diez recogen la basura** the rubbish gets collected at ten o'clock **3** (= *ordenar*) [+ *objetos*] to clear up, clear away; [+ *casa, habitación*] to tidy up, straighten up; ~ **la mesa** to clear the table **4** (= *guardar*) [+ *ropa lavada*] to take in, get in; [+ *herramientas*] to put away **5** (= *ir a buscar*) [+ *persona*] to pick up, fetch, collect; [+ *billetes, paquete*] to collect, pick up **6** (*Agr*) to harvest, gather in, take in; [+ *fruta, guisantes*] to pick; [+ *flores*] to pick, gather **7** (= *reducir, ajustar*) [+ *cuerda, vela*] to take in; [+ *alas*] to fold; [+ *falda*] to gather up, lift up; [+ *mangas*] to roll up

8 (= *almacenar*) [+ *polvo*] to gather; [+ *líquido*] to absorb, take up; (*en recipiente*) to collect **9** (= *mostrar*) to show; **la imagen recoge uno de los momentos más dramáticos** the picture shows *o* captures one of the most dramatic moments; **vocablos no recogidos en el diccionario** words not included in the dictionary **10** [+ *demandas, reivindicaciones*] to take into account **11** (= *recibir*) **ahora empieza a ~ los frutos de su esfuerzo** she's beginning to reap the reward(s) of her efforts **12** (= *retirar*) [+ *periódico, libro*] to seize; [+ *moneda*] to call in **13** (= *dar asilo a*) to take in, shelter **Ⓑ** VI (= *ordenar*) to tidy up, straighten up; (*al cerrar, terminar*) to clear up **Ⓒ** **recogerse** VPR **1** (= *retirarse*) to withdraw, retire; (*a casa*) to go home **2** [+ *falda*] to gather up, lift up; [+ *mangas, pantalones*] to roll up; ~**se el pelo** to put one's hair up; **se recogió el pelo en un moño** she put her hair up in a bun **3** (= *refugiarse*) to take shelter

recogida SF **1** [*de basura, correo*] collection ➤ **recogida de basuras** refuse collection, garbage collection (*EEUU*) ➤ **recogida de equipajes** (*Aer*) baggage reclaim **2** (*Agr*) harvest

recogido ADJ **1** [*vida*] quiet; [*lugar*] secluded; [*persona*] reserved, retiring **2** (= *apretado*) bunched up, tight

recogimiento SM **1** (= *estado*) absorption; **vivir con** ~ to live in seclusion, live in peace and quiet **2** (*Rel*) recollection

recolección SF (*Agr*) (= *acto*) harvesting; (= *época*) harvest time

recolectar /1a/ VT = **recoger A2, A6**

recolector(a) SM/F (*Agr*) picker

recoleto ADJ **1** [*persona*] quiet, retiring **2** [*calle*] quiet

recomendable ADJ advisable; **poco** ~ inadvisable

recomendación SF **1** (= *consejo*) recommendation **2** (*para un trabajo*) **carta de** ~ letter of introduction *o* recommendation; **tiene buenas recomendaciones** he is strongly recommended

recomendado ADJ (*Col, Uru*) registered

recomendar /1j/ VT **1** (= *aconsejar*) to recommend; ~ **a algn que haga algo** to recommend *o* advise sb to do sth; **le recomiendo esta novela** I recommend this novel to you **2** (*para un trabajo*) **lo ~on para el puesto** he was recommended for the job

recompensa SF **1** (*por un servicio*) reward, recompense; **como** *o* **en** ~ **por los servicios prestados** (in return) for services rendered **2** (*por daño, perjuicio*) compensation (**de** for)

recompensar /1a/ VT **1** [+ *servicio*] to reward, recompense; **"se recompensará"** "reward offered" **2** [+ *daño, perjuicio*] to compensate

recomponer /2q/ VT **1** (= *arreglar*) to mend, repair **2** (*Tip*) to reset

reconciliación SF reconciliation

reconciliar /1b/ **Ⓐ** VT to reconcile **Ⓑ** **reconciliarse** VPR to become reconciled, be reconciled

reconcomerse /2a/ VPR to bear a secret grudge, harbour *o* (*EEUU*) harbor resentment

recóndito ADJ recondite; **en lo más** ~ **de** in the depths of; **en lo más** ~ **del corazón** in one's heart of hearts

reconfortante ADJ (= *que conforta*) comforting; (= *que anima*) cheering

reconfortar /1a/ VT (= *confortar*) to comfort; (= *animar*) to cheer, encourage

reconocer /2d/ **Ⓐ** VT **1** (= *conocer*) to recognize; **lo reconocí por la voz** I knew *o* recognized him by his voice **2** (= *identificar*) to identify **3** (= *aceptar*) [+ *gobierno, hijo*] to recognize **4** (= *admitir*) to admit; **reconozco que no existen pruebas** I admit that there is no evidence **5** (*Med*) [+ *paciente*] to examine **6** [+ *terreno*] to survey; (*Mil*) to reconnoitre, spy out **Ⓑ** **reconocerse** VPR **se ha reconocido**

culpable he has admitted his guilt

reconocible ADJ recognizable

reconocido ADJ recognized

reconocimiento SM **1** (= *aprobación*) recognition; **en ~ a** ◇ **como ~ por** in recognition of **2** (= *registro*) search, searching; (= *inspección*) inspection, examination **3** (*Mil*) reconnaissance; **vuelo de ~** reconnaissance flight **4** (*Med*) examination, checkup ➤ **reconocimiento médico** medical (examination) **5** (*Inform*) ➤ **reconocimiento de la voz** speech recognition ➤ **reconocimiento óptico de caracteres** optical character recognition

reconquista SF reconquest, recapture; **la Reconquista** the Reconquest (*of Spain*)

RECONQUISTA

The term **Reconquista** refers to the eight centuries during which the Christian kings of the Spanish kingdoms gradually reclaimed their country from the Moors, who had invaded the Iberian Peninsula in 711. It is generally accepted that the reconquest began in 718 and ended in 1492, when Ferdinand and Isabella, the **Reyes Católicos**, retook Granada, the last Muslim stronghold. The final years of the **Reconquista** were a time of great intolerance with Arabs and Jews being forcibly converted to Christianity, after which they were known as **conversos**. Those refusing to be converted were expelled in 1492.

reconquistar /1a/ VT **1** (*Mil*) [+ *terreno*] to regain, reconquer; [+ *ciudad*] to recapture **2** [+ *estima*] to recover, win back

reconsiderar /1a/ VT to reconsider

reconstituir /3g/ VT (= *rehacer*) to reconstitute; [+ *crimen, escena*] to reconstruct

reconstituyente SM tonic

reconstrucción SF reconstruction

reconstruir /3g/ VT to reconstruct

reconvenir /3r/ VT **1** (*frm*) (= *reprender*) to reprimand **2** (*Jur*) to counterclaim

reconversión SF (= *reestructuración*) restructuring, reorganization ➤ **reconversión industrial** industrial rationalization

recopa SF cup-winners' cup

recopilación SF **1** (= *recolección*) compilation; (= *resumen*) summary ➤ **recopilación de datos** (*Inform*) data collection **2** (*Jur*) code

recopilar /1a/ VT **1** (= *reunir*) to compile; (= *resumir*) to summarize **2** [+ *leyes*] to codify

récord, record ['rekor] Ⓐ ADJ INV record; **cifras ~** record numbers; **en un tiempo ~** in record time Ⓑ SM (*pl* **récords, records** ['rekor]) record; **batir el ~** to break the record

recordar /1l/ Ⓐ VT **1** (= *acordarse de*) to remember; **no lo recuerdo** I can't remember, I don't remember; **creo ~ que ...** I seem to remember o recall that ...; **~ haber hecho algo** to remember doing o having done sth; **~ que ...** to remember that ...
2 (= *traer a la memoria*) to remind; **¿a qué te recuerda esa foto?** what does that photo remind you of?; **el poema recuerda a García Lorca** the poem is reminiscent of García Lorca; **~ algo a algn** to remind sb of sth; **te recuerdo que son las tres** let me remind you that it's three o'clock; **recuérdame que ponga la lavadora** remind me to put the washing (machine) on
Ⓑ VI to remember; **no recuerdo** I can't o don't remember; **si mal no recuerdo** if my memory serves me right o correctly, if I remember rightly o correctly; **que yo recuerde** as far as I can remember, as I recall (*frm*)
Ⓒ **recordarse** VPR (*Chi*) to remember; **~se de algo** to remember sth

⚠ **recordar** ≠ **record**

recordatorio SM **1** (= *tarjeta*) [*de fallecimiento*] in memoriam card; [*de primera comunión*] First Communion card **2** (= *aviso*) reminder

recorrer /2a/ VT **1** [+ *ciudad, país*] to travel around; **recorrimos Francia en moto** we travelled around France on a motorbike; **~ una ciudad a pie** to walk round a city, do a city on foot **2** [+ *trayecto*] to cover, do; **ese día recorrimos 100 kilómetros** we covered o did 100 kilometres that day

recorrido SM **1** (= *viaje*) run, journey; **hicimos un ~ por los pueblos de Andalucía** we travelled round o we did a tour of the villages of Andalusia; **durante todo el ~** throughout the journey; **el ~ del primer día fue de 450km** we covered 450km on the first day
2 (= *distancia*) **de corto ~** (*Aer*) short-haul; **de largo ~** (*Aer*) long-haul; **tren de largo ~** intercity train
3 (= *ruta*) route; **hicieron un ~ diferente** they took a different route; **este es el ~ más largo** this is the longest route o way
4 [*de émbolo*] stroke
5 (*Golf*) round
6 (*Hípica*) **un ~ sin penalizaciones** a clear round

recortable SM cut-out

recortar /1a/ Ⓐ VT **1** [+ *pelo*] to trim; [+ *exceso, sobras*] to cut away, cut off **2** [+ *figura, papel*] to cut out **3** [+ *presupuesto*] to cut, reduce; [+ *plantilla*] to cut, cut back; [+ *víveres*] to cut down Ⓑ **recortarse** VPR to stand out, be silhouetted (**en, sobre** against)

recorte SM **1** (= *acción*) cutting, trimming **2** [*del pelo*] trim **3** (*para economizar*) cut; **un ~ de gastos** a cut o cutback in spending ➤ **recortes de personal** staff cutbacks ➤ **recorte presupuestario** spending cut **4** [*de periódico, revista*] clipping, cutting (*Brit*); **álbum de ~s** scrapbook

recostable ADJ **~ asiento** reclining seat

recostado ADJ reclining; **estar ~** to be lying down

recostar /1l/ Ⓐ VT to lean (**en** on) Ⓑ **recostarse** VPR (= *reclinarse*) to lie back, recline (*frm*); (= *tumbarse*) to lie down

recoveco SM **1** [*de calle*] turn, bend **2** (= *rincón*) odd corner; **todos los ~s** every corner o every nook and cranny **3** **recovecos** (= *complejidades*) ins and outs

recreación SF (= *esparcimiento*) recreation; (= *diversión*) amusement

recrear /1a/ Ⓐ VT **1** (= *crear de nuevo*) to recreate **2** (= *divertir*) to amuse, entertain Ⓑ **recrearse** VPR to enjoy o.s.; **se recrea viendo los infortunios de otros** he takes pleasure in o gloats over others' misfortunes

recreativo ADJ Ⓐ ADJ recreational Ⓑ SM games arcade

recreo SM **1** (= *esparcimiento*) recreation **2** (*Escol*) break (*Brit*), playtime, recess (*EEUU*)

recriminación SF recrimination

recriminar /1a/ VT to reproach

recrudecer /2d/ Ⓐ VT to worsen Ⓑ **recrudecerse** VPR (= *intensificarse*) to intensify; (= *empeorar*) to intensify, worsen; (= *aumentar*) to recrudesce, break out again

recrudecimiento SM new outbreak, flare-up

recta SF **1** (= *línea*) straight line **2** (*Dep*) straight ➤ **recta de llegada, recta final** home straight

rectal ADJ rectal

rectangular ADJ rectangular

rectángulo Ⓐ ADJ [*triángulo*] right-angled Ⓑ SM rectangle, oblong

rectificación SF correction

rectificar /1g/ VT **1** (= *corregir*) to rectify, correct; **—no, eran cuatro, —rectificó** "no," he said, correcting himself, "there were four" **2** (= *cambiar*) [+ *cálculo*] to correct; [+ *conducta*] to change, reform **3** (*Culin*) **~ de sal si hace falta** add salt to taste

rectilíneo ADJ straight, rectilinear

rectitud SF rectitude, honesty

recto Ⓐ ADJ **1** (= *derecho*) straight; (= *vertical*) upright **2** **ángulo ~** right angle **3** [*persona*] (= *honrado*) honest, upright; (= *estricto*) strict; [*juez*] fair, impartial **4** [*sentido*] proper ⓑ ADV **siga todo** ~ go straight on ⓒ SM (*Anat*) rectum

rector(a) ⓐ ADJ [*entidad*] governing; [*idea, principio*] guiding, governing ⓑ SM/F **1** (*Univ*) ≈ vice-chancellor, rector, president (*EEUU*) **2** [*de colegio*] principal

rectorado SM **1** (= *cargo*) vice-chancellorship, presidency (*EEUU*) **2** (= *oficina*) ≈ vice-chancellor's office, president's office (*EEUU*)

recua SF mule train, train of pack animals

recuadro SM box

recubrir /3a/ (*pp* recubierto) VT (= *cubrir*) to cover (**con, de** with); (= *pintar*) to coat (**con, de** with)

recuento SM (= *acto*) recount; (= *inventario*) inventory; **hacer el** ~ **de** to count up, reckon up

recuerdo SM **1** (= *memoria*) memory; **guardar un feliz** ~ **de algn** to have happy memories of sb **2** (= *regalo*) souvenir, memento; **"recuerdo de Mallorca"** "a souvenir from Majorca"; **toma esto como** ~ take this as a keepsake ➤ **recuerdo de familia** family heirloom **3 recuerdos** (= *saludos*) regards; **¡~s a tu madre!** give my regards to your mother!; **te manda muchos ~s** he sends you his warmest regards

recular /1a/ VI [*animal, vehículo*] to move backwards, go back; [*fusil*] to recoil

recuperación SF **1** (= *vuelta a la normalidad*) [*de economía, divisa*] recovery; [*de enfermo, paciente*] recovery, recuperation (*más frm*) **2** (= *reutilización*) [*de edificio*] restoration; [*de tierras*] reclamation; [*de chatarra, vidrio*] salvage; [*de algo perdido, olvidado*] revival **3** [*de dinero, joyas*] recovery; (*Com*) [*de costes, pérdidas*] recovery, recoupment (*frm*) **4** (*Esp Educ*) (= *examen*) retake, resit (*Brit*); **examen de** ~ retake, resit (*Brit*)

recuperar /1a/ ⓐ VT **1** (= *recobrar*) **1.1** [+ *bienes*] to recover; [+ *costes, pérdidas, inversión*] to recoup, recover **1.2** [+ *credibilidad, poder, libertad, control*] to regain; [+ *fuerzas*] to get back, regain; **el país comienza a** ~ **la normalidad** the country is beginning to return to normality; **el dólar recupera posiciones** the dollar is recovering **1.3** [+ *clase, día*] to make up; **esta clase tendremos que** ~**la** we'll have to make up this class **1.4** (*Inform*) to retrieve **2** (= *reutilizar*) **2.1** [+ *edificio*] to restore; [+ *tierras*] to reclaim; [+ *chatarra, vidrio*] to salvage **2.2** (*del olvido*) [+ *artista, obra*] to revive; [+ *tradiciones*] to restore, revive **3** (*Educ*) [+ *asignatura*] to retake, resit (*Brit*) ⓑ **recuperarse** VPR **1** [*enfermo*] to recover; ~**se de** [+ *operación, enfermedad, crisis, viaje*] to recover from **2** (*Com*) [*economía, mercado, divisa*] to recover

recurrente ADJ recurrent

recurrir /3a/ ⓐ VI **1** ~ **a** [+ *medio, violencia*] to resort to; [+ *persona*] to turn to **2** (*Jur*) to appeal (**a** to; **contra** against) ⓑ VT (*Jur*) to appeal against

recurso SM **1** (= *medio*) **una mujer de** ~**s** a resourceful woman; **como último** ~ as a last resort **2** (*Jur*) appeal; **interponer** ~ **contra algn** to lodge an appeal against sb ➤ **recurso de apelación** appeal to the Supreme Court **3 recursos** (= *bienes*) resources ➤ **recursos económicos** economic resources ➤ **recursos energéticos** energy resources ➤ **recursos humanos** human resources ➤ **recursos naturales** natural resources

recusación SF **1** (= *rechazo*) rejection **2** (*Jur*) challenge

recusar /1a/ VT **1** (= *rechazar*) to reject, refuse **2** (*Jur*) to challenge, challenge the authority of

red SF **1** (*para pescar*) (*tb Dep*) net; [*del pelo*] hairnet **2** [*de cosas relacionadas*] network; [*de agua, suministro eléctrico*] mains, main (*EEUU*), supply system; **la Red** (*Internet*) the Net ➤ **red de comunicaciones** communications network ➤ **Red Digital de Servicios Integrados** Integrated Services Digital Network ➤ **red ferroviaria** railway network, railway system ➤ **red local** (*Inform*) local network, local area network ➤ **red viaria** road network **3** (= *trampa*) snare, trap

redacción SF **1** (= *acción*) writing; **la** ~ **del texto me llevó dos horas** it took me two hours to write the text **2** (= *expresión*) wording **3** (*Escol*) essay, composition

4 (*Prensa*) (= *oficina*) newspaper office; (= *personas*) editorial staff

redactar /1a/ ⓐ VT **1** [+ *carta, noticia, artículo*] to write; [+ *acuerdo, contrato*] to draw up **2** (*Prensa*) [+ *periódico*] to edit ⓑ VI to write; **redacta muy mal** he writes very badly

redactor(a) SM/F **1** (*en periódico*) editor **2** (= *escritor*) writer, drafter

redada SF raid

redaño SM **1** (*Anat*) mesentery **2 redaños*** (= *valor*) guts*

rededor: **al** ~ ◇ **en** ~ = **alrededor**

redefinir /3a/ VT to redefine

redención SF (*Rel*) redemption; (*Fin frm*) repayment, redemption (*frm*)

redentor(a) ⓐ ADJ redeeming ⓑ SM/F redeemer ⓒ SM **Redentor** Redeemer, Saviour, Savior (*EEUU*)

redescubrir /3a/ (*pp* redescubierto) VT to rediscover

redicho* ADJ affected

redil SM sheepfold

redimir /3a/ VT **1** (*Rel*) to redeem **2** (*Fin frm*) to redeem (*frm*), repay **3** (*+ cautivo*) to ransom, redeem (*frm*); [+ *esclavo*] to redeem (*frm*)

redistribuir /3g/ VT to redistribute

rédito SM return, interest

redoblado ADJ [*fuerzas*] renewed

redoblar /1a/ ⓐ VT (= *aumentar*) to redouble ⓑ VI (*Mús*) to play a roll on the drum

redoble SM [*de tambor*] drumroll

redoma SF **1** (= *frasco*) flask, phial **2** (*Ven Aut*) roundabout (*Brit*), traffic circle (*EEUU*)

redomado ADJ **1** [*mentiroso, estafador*] inveterate **2** (= *taimado*) sly, artful

redonda SF **1** (*Mús*) semibreve (*Brit*), whole note (*EEUU*) **2** (*Tip*) roman **3 a la** ~: **en muchas millas a la** ~ for many miles around

redondear /1a/ VT **1** (= *hacer redondo*) to round off **2** (= *completar*) to round off; ~ **un negocio** to close a deal **3** [+ *cifra*] (*tomando un valor superior*) to round up; (*tomando un valor inferior*) to round down

redondel SM **1** (= *círculo*) ring, circle **2** (*Taur*) bullring, arena

redondo ⓐ ADJ **1** [*forma*] round; **tiene la cara redonda** he has a round face; ✦ MODISMO **caer** ~ (*al suelo*) to collapse in a heap; (*dormido*) to go out like a light **2** [*cantidad, cifra*] round; **en números** ~**s** in round numbers, in round figures **3** (*) (= *perfecto*) **todo salió** ~ it all went well brilliantly (well); **será un negocio** ~ it will be a really good deal ⓑ SM **1 en** ~: **girar en** ~ to turn right round; **negarse en** ~ to refuse flatly **2** (*Culin*) rump steak

reducción SF **1** (= *disminución*) **1.1** [*de cantidad, precios, consumo, tamaño*] reduction; **una** ~ **del gasto público** a cut *o* reduction in public spending **1.2** [*de tiempo*] reduction; **los sindicatos piden la** ~ **de la jornada laboral** they unions are calling for a shorter working day (*Brit*) *o* workday (*EEUU*) **2** (*Mat*) (= *conversión*) [*de unidades, medidas*] conversion; [*de ecuaciones*] reduction **3** [*de rebeldes*] defeat **4** (*Med*) setting, reduction (*frm*) **5** (*Chi*) [*de indígenas*] reservation

reducido ADJ [*grupo, número*] small; [*ingresos, recursos*] limited; [*tarifa, precio*] reduced; [*espacio*] confined; **una sala de dimensiones reducidas** a small-sized room; **a precios ~s** at reduced prices; **todo quedó** ~ **a un malentendido** everything boiled down to a misunderstanding

reducidor(a) SM/F (*SAm*) fence*, receiver (*of stolen goods*)

reducir /3n/ ⓐ VT **1** (= *disminuir*) **1.1** (*en cantidad*) [+ *gastos, inflación, precio*] to reduce, bring down; cut; [+ *tensión, ansiedad*] to reduce; [+ *riesgo*] to reduce, lessen; **el autobús redujo su velocidad** the bus reduced speed, the bus slowed down; **conviene** ~ **el consumo de grasas** it is advisable to cut down on fatty foods; **el banco redujo su beneficio un 12%** the bank saw its profits fall by 12%; ~ **algo en algo** to reduce sth by sth, cut sth by sth; ~ **a la mínima expresión** to reduce to the bare minimum; ~ **algo al mínimo** to reduce *o* cut sth to the minimum; ~ **algo a la**

mitad to cut sth by half **1.2** (en tiempo) [+ jornada laboral] to reduce, shorten; [+ sentencia] to reduce **1.3** (en tamaño) [+ copia] to reduce; [+ discurso, artículo] to cut down, shorten
2 (= convertir) ~ **algo a algo** [+ cantidad, medida] to convert sth into sth; [+ fracción, ecuación] to reduce sth into sth; ✦ MODISMO ~ **algo al absurdo** to expose the absurdity of sth
3 (= someter) [+ ladrón, fugitivo, loco] to overpower; [+ alborotadores] to subdue; [+ fortaleza] to subdue, reduce (frm)
4 (Med) [+ hueso, hernia] to set, reduce (frm)
5 (Quím) to reduce
Ⓑ VI (Aut) to change down (Brit), shift down (EEUU)
Ⓒ **reducirse** VPR **1** (= disminuir) [inflación, población, beneficios] to fall; [color] to become less intense, decrease; [salsa] to reduce; **el número de accidentes se ha reducido en un 16,5%** the number of accidents has fallen by 16.5%; **sus gastos se redujeron a la mitad** their expenses were cut o reduced by half
2 (= limitarse) ~**se a** **2.1** (en cantidad) **el mobiliario se reduce a unas pocas mesas y sillas** the furniture amounts to no more than o is simply a few tables and chairs; **sus ingresos se reducen a ...** his income is limited o consists only of ... **2.2** (en extensión) **el problema se reduce a una pura cuestión económica** the problem comes down to o boils down to simple economics, the problem is simply a question of economics **2.3** [persona] to limit o.s. to; **se vieron reducidos a pedir limosna** they were reduced to begging for alms

reducto SM [de ideología, rebeldes] stronghold, redoubt

reduje etc ver **reducir**

redundancia SF redundancy; **valga la** ~ forgive the repetition

redundante ADJ redundant, superfluous

redundar /1a/ VI ~ **en** to redound to (frm); ~ **en beneficio de algn** to benefit sb, be to sb's advantage

reedición SF reissue, reprint, reprinting

reeditar /1a/ VT to reissue, reprint

reeducar /1g/ VT to re-educate

reelección SF re-election

reelegir /3c, 3k/ VT to re-elect

reembolsable ADJ refundable, repayable

reembolsar /1a/ Ⓐ VT **1** (+ persona) to reimburse; [+ dinero] to repay, pay back; [+ depósito] to refund, return
Ⓑ **reembolsarse** VPR to reimburse o.s.; ~**se una cantidad** to recover a sum

reembolso SM [de gastos] reimbursement; [de depósito] refund; **enviar algo contra** ~ to send sth cash on delivery

reemisor SM booster station

reemplazar /1f/ VT **1** [+ modelo, pieza] to replace; ~ **a algo/algn** to replace sth/sb; ~ **algo con** o **por algo** to replace sth with sth **2** [+ persona] **2.1** (= ocupar el lugar de) (gen) to replace; (brevemente) to stand in for; **tras el descanso, Pérez reemplazó a Carlos** Pérez came on for Carlos after half-time, Carlos was substituted by Pérez after half-time **2.2** (= poner en lugar de) to replace; ~ **a algn con** o **por algn** to replace sb with sb

reemplazo Ⓐ SMF (= persona sustituta) replacement
Ⓑ SM **1** (= sustitución) replacement; **vino en** ~ **del profesor de física** he came to replace the physics teacher, he came as the replacement for the physics teacher **2** (Esp Mil) intake of conscripts; **los soldados pertenecientes al último** ~ **de 1994** soldiers recruited in the last call-up o draft of 1994; **soldados de** ~ conscripts, draftees (EEUU)

reemprender /2a/ VT to resume

reencarnación SF reincarnation

reencarnar /1a/ Ⓐ VT to reincarnate Ⓑ **reencarnarse** VPR to be reincarnated (**en** as)

reencauchar /1a/ VT (Col) = **recauchutar**

reencontrarse /1l/ VPR to meet again

reencuentro SM reunion

reengancharse /1a/ VPR to re-enlist

reenviar /1c/ VT (a nuevo domicilio) to forward; (a diferente dirección) to redirect; (al remitente) to return

reequilibrar /1a/ VT **1** (Pol) to restabilize **2** [+ peso, carga] to rebalance

reescribir /3a/ VT to rewrite

reestrenar /1a/ VT (Teat) to revive, put on again; (Cine) to re-release

reestreno SM (Teat) revival; (Cine) re-release

reestructuración SF restructuring, reorganizing

reestructurar /1a/ VT to restructure, reorganize

reevaluar /1e/ VT to reappraise

refacción SF **1** (SAm) (= arreglo) refurbishment, repair **2 refacciones** (Méx) (= repuestos) spares, spare parts

refaccionar /1a/ (SAm) VT to refurbish, repair

refajo[+] SM **1** (= prenda) underskirt **2** (Col) (= bebida) shandy

refanfinflar* /1a/ VT (Esp) **me la refanfinfla** I couldn't give a damn*

refectorio SM refectory

referencia SF **1** (= mención) reference; **con** ~ **a** with reference to; **hacer** ~ **a** to refer to, allude to **2** (= informe) account, report; **me han dado buenas** ~**s de ella** I have had good reports of her

referendo SM referendum

referéndum SM (pl ~**s**) referendum

referente ADJ ~ **a** relating to, about, concerning

referí SMF (LAm) referee, umpire

referir /3i/ Ⓐ VT **1** (= contar) to tell, recount; ~ **que ...** to say that ..., tell how ... **2** (= dirigir) ~ **al lector a un apéndice** to refer the reader to an appendix **3** (= relacionar) to refer, relate **4** ~ **a** (Fin) to convert into Ⓑ **referirse** VPR ~**se a** to refer to; **no me refiero a ti** I'm not referring to you; **¿a qué te refieres?** what exactly do you mean?; **por lo que se refiere a eso** as for that, as regards that, as far as that is concerned

refilón: **de** ~ ADV obliquely, on the slant; **el sol da de** ~ the sun falls on the slant; **mirar a algn de** ~ to look out of the corner of one's eye at sb

refinado ADJ refined

refinamiento SM refinement

refinar /1a/ VT (Téc) to refine **2** (= perfeccionar) [+ sistema] to refine, perfect; [+ estilo] to polish

refinería SF refinery ➤ **refinería de petróleo** oil refinery

reflectante ADJ reflective

reflector SM **1** (Elec) spotlight; (Aer, Mil) searchlight **2** (= cuerpo que refleja) reflector

reflejar /1a/ Ⓐ VT **1** [+ imagen, luz] to reflect **2** (= manifestar) to reflect; **la novela refleja la problemática social de la época** the novel reflects the social problems of the time; **su expresión reflejaba inquietud** you could see the worry in her face, she wore a worried expression (on her face) Ⓑ **reflejarse** VPR **1** [imagen, luz] to be reflected **2** (= manifestarse) **el temor se reflejaba en su rostro** fear was written on his face

reflejo Ⓐ ADJ **1** [luz] reflected **2** [movimiento] reflex Ⓑ SM **1** (= imagen) reflection **2** (= índice) reflection; **este es un** ~ **de la inquietud del pueblo** this reflects o is a reflection of people's unease **3** (Anat) reflex; (= acción) reflex action; **tener buenos** ~**s** to have good reflexes; **perder** ~**s** (fig) to lose one's touch **4 reflejos** (= brillo) gleam sing, glint sing **5 reflejos** (en el pelo) highlights **6** (= tinte para el pelo) rinse

reflejoterapia SF reflexology

reflex, réflex Ⓐ ADJ INV SLR, reflex Ⓑ SF SLR camera

reflexión SF **1** (Fís) reflection **2** (= consideración) reflection, thought; **sin** ~ without thinking

reflexionar /1a/ Ⓐ VI (= considerar) to reflect (**sobre** on); (antes de actuar) to think, pause; **¡reflexione!** you think about it!, think for a moment! Ⓑ VT to reflect on, think about

reflexivo ADJ **1** [verbo] reflexive **2** [persona] thoughtful, reflective

reflexología SF reflexology

reflexoterapia SF reflex therapy

reflotar /1a/ VT [+ *empresa, negocio*] to relaunch, re-establish; [+ *barco*] to refloat

reflujo SM ebb, ebb tide

refocilarse /1a/ VPR 1 (= *divertirse*) ~ **con algo** to enjoy sth hugely, take great delight in sth 2 (= *alegrarse*) to cheer up no end

reforestación SF reforestation

reforestar /1a/ VT to reforest

reforma SF 1 (= *modificación*) reform; **~s políticas** political reforms; **la Reforma** (*Rel*) the Reformation; (*Méx Pol*) *19th century reform movement* ➤ **reforma educativa** education reform 2 **reformas** (*en edificio, local*) alterations; **cerrado por ~s** closed for refurbishment, closed for alterations 3 (*Cos*) alteration

reformar /1a/ ⒶVT 1 [+ *edificio*] to renovate 2 [+ *ley, sistema*] to reform 3 [+ *persona*] to reform 4 (*Cos*) to alter Ⓑ **reformarse** VPR [*persona*] to reform, mend one's ways

reformatear /1a/ VT (*Inform*) to reformat

reformatorio SM reformatory

reformista Ⓐ ADJ reforming Ⓑ SMF reformist, reformer

reforzado ADJ reinforced

reforzar /1f, 1l/ VT 1 (*Arquit, Carpintería*) to reinforce 2 (= *fortalecer*) to reinforce, strengthen 3 (*Mil*) to reinforce 4 [+ *dosis*] to increase

refracción SF refraction

refractar /1a/ VT to refract

refractario ADJ 1 (*Téc*) fireproof, heat-resistant; (*Culin*) ovenproof 2 **ser ~ a la reforma** to be resistant *o* opposed to reform

refrán SM proverb, saying; **como dice el ~** as the saying goes

refranero SM collection of proverbs

refregar /1h, 1j/ VT 1 (= *frotar*) to rub, rub hard; (= *limpiar*) to scrub 2 (*fig*) (= *restregar*) ~ **algo a algn** *o* **en las narices de algn** to rub sth in to sb, harp on about sth to sb

refrenar /1a/ VT 1 [+ *caballo*] to rein back 2 [+ *pasiones, ánimos*] to restrain, hold in check

refrendar /1a/ VT 1 [+ *documento*] to countersign; [+ *decisión, nominación*] to endorse 2 [+ *pasaporte*] to stamp

refrescante ADJ refreshing, cooling

refrescar /1g/ ⒶVT 1 (= *enfriar*) to cool, cool down 2 [+ *conocimiento*] to brush up, polish up; ~ **la memoria a algn** to refresh sb's memory Ⓑ VI 1 (*Meteo*) to get cooler, cool down 2 [*bebida*] to be refreshing Ⓒ **refrescarse** VPR (*lavándose*) to freshen up; (*con una bebida*) to refresh o.s.; (*dejar de pasar calor*) to cool off

refresco SM soft drink ➤ **refresco de cola** cola

refriega SF (*de poca importancia*) scuffle; (*violenta*) brawl

refrigeración SF [*de comida*] refrigeration; (*Mec*) cooling; [*de casa*] air conditioning

refrigerador SM 1 (= *frigorífico*) refrigerator, fridge (*esp Brit*) 2 (*para el aire acondicionado*) cooling unit, cooling system

refrigerar /1a/ VT (= *enfriar*) to chill, refrigerate; (*Téc*) to refrigerate; (*Mec*) to cool; [+ *sala*] to air-condition

refrigerio SM (= *comida*) snack; (= *bebida*) cooling drink

refrito SM (*Literat*) rehash, revised version

refuerzo SM 1 (= *reforzamiento*) reinforcement 2 (*Téc*) support 3 **refuerzos** (*Mil*) reinforcements 4 (= *ayuda*) aid

refugiado/a ADJ, SM/F refugee

refugiarse /1b/ VPR (= *acogerse a un refugio*) to take refuge; (= *cobijarse*) to shelter (**en** in)

refugio SM 1 (= *sitio*) refuge, shelter ➤ **refugio antiaéreo** air-raid shelter ➤ **refugio antinuclear, refugio atómico** fallout shelter ➤ **refugio de montaña** mountain hut ➤ **refugio nuclear** fallout shelter ➤ **refugio subterráneo** (*Mil*) underground shelter, dugout 2 (*Esp Aut*) street island

refulgente ADJ (*frm*) brilliant, refulgent (*frm o liter*)

refulgir /3c/ VI (*frm*) to shine, shine brightly

refundir /3a/ ⒶVT 1 (*Téc*) to recast 2 [+ *obra*] to adapt, rewrite 3 (*And, CAm, Méx*) (= *perder*) to lose, mislay Ⓑ **refundirse** VPR (*And, CAm, Méx*) to get lost, be mislaid

refunfuñar /1a/ VI to grumble

refunfuñón/ona* Ⓐ ADJ grumpy Ⓑ SM/F grouch*

refutar /1a/ VT to refute

regadera SF 1 (*para plantas*) watering can; ✦ MODISMO **estar como una ~** (*Esp**) to be crazy 2 (*Col, Méx*) shower

regadío SM **de ~** irrigated; **tierra de ~** irrigated land; **cultivo de ~** crop that grows on irrigated land

regalado ADJ 1 (= *cómodo*) (*pey*) **una vida regalada** an easy life, a soft life 2 (= *gratis*) free; **a ese precio está ~** they're practically giving it away; **no lo quiero ni ~** I wouldn't have it if you were giving it away

regalar /1a/ ⒶVT 1 (= *dar*) to give, give as a present; ~ **algo a algn** to give sb sth; **me regaló un CD** she gave me a CD as a present 2 (*frm*) (= *agasajar*) **lo ~on con toda clase de atenciones** they lavished attention on him Ⓑ **regalarse** VPR (= *darse gusto*) to indulge o.s., pamper o.s.

regalía SF 1 (= *privilegio*) privilege, prerogative 2 **regalías** [*del rey*] royal prerogatives

regaliz SM liquorice, licorice (*EEUU*)

regalo SM 1 (= *obsequio*) present, gift; **hacer un ~ a algn** to give sb a present *o* gift; **de ~: dan estos libros de ~** they're giving these books away; **estuche de ~** presentation case ➤ **regalo de boda** wedding present ➤ **regalo de cumpleaños** birthday present 2 (= *deleite, placer*) pleasure; [*de comida*] treat, delicacy; **es un ~ para el oído** it's a treat to listen to; **un ~ del cielo** a godsend

regalón ADJ 1 (= *comodón*) comfort-loving 2 [*vida*] (= *de lujo*) of luxury; (*pey*) (= *fácil*) soft, easy

regalonear /1a/ (*CS*) ⒶVT (= *mimar*) to spoil, pamper Ⓑ VI (= *dejarse mimar*) to allow o.s. to be pampered

regañada* SF (*And, CAm, Méx*) = **regaño**

regañadientes: a ~ ADV unwillingly, reluctantly

regañar /1a/ ⒶVT to scold, tell off* Ⓑ VI 1 [*persona*] to grumble, grouse* 2 [*dos personas*] to fall out, quarrel

regañina SF = **regaño**

regaño SM scolding, telling-off*

regañón ADJ (= *gruñón*) grumbling; [*mujer*] nagging

regar /1h, 1j/ VT 1 [+ *planta*] to water; [+ *campo, terreno*] to irrigate; [+ *calle*] to hose down 2 (*Culin*) **~on la cena con Rioja** they washed the meal down with some Rioja 3 (*Geog*) [*río*] to water; [*mar*] to wash 4 (= *esparcir*) to sprinkle, scatter

regata SF (*Náut*) (= *una carrera*) race, boat race; (= *varias carreras*) regatta

regate SM swerve, dodge; (*Dep*) dribble

regatear¹ /1a/ VI (*Náut*) to race

regatear² /1a/ ⒶVI 1 (*Com*) to haggle, bargain 2 (*Dep*) to dribble Ⓑ VT 1 (*Com*) [+ *precio*] to haggle over, bargain over 2 (= *economizar*) to be stingy *o* (*esp Brit*) mean with; **no hemos regateado esfuerzos para terminarlo** we have spared no effort to finish it

regateo SM (*Com*) haggling, bargaining; (*Dep*) piece of dribbling

regato SM pool

regazo SM lap

regencia SF regency

regeneración SF regeneration

regenerar /1a/ VT to regenerate

regentar /1a/ VT [+ *hotel, negocio*] to run, manage; [+ *destinos*] to guide, preside over

regente ADJ, SMF regent

regicida SMF regicide

regicidio SM regicide

regidor(a) Ⓐ ADJ [*principio*] governing, ruling Ⓑ SM/F

(*Teat*) stage manager; (*TV*) floor manager **⊙** SM (*Hist*) alderman

régimen SM (*pl* **regímenes**) **1** (*Pol*) régime; **antiguo ~** ancien régime **2** (*Med*) (*tb ~* **alimenticio**) diet; **estar a ~** to be on a diet; **ponerse a ~** to go on a diet; **hacer ~** to be on a diet ➤ **régimen de adelgazamiento** diet, slimming diet **3** (= *reglas*) rules *pl*, set of rules; **prisión de ~ abierto** minimum security prison, open prison (*Brit*); **he cambiado de ~ de vida** I have changed my whole way of life; **alojamiento en ~ de pensión completa** (accommodation *o* (*EEUU*) accommodations with) full board ➤ **régimen tributario** tax system

regimiento SM **1** (*Mil*) regiment **2** (*) (= *multitud*) crowd

regio ⊙ ADJ **1** (= *real*) royal, regal **2** (*And, CS**) (= *genial*) great*, terrific* **⊙** EXCL (*And, CS**) great!*, fine!

región SF **1** (*Geog, Pol*) region; (= *área*) area, part **2** (*Anat*) region

regional ADJ regional

regionalismo SM regionalism

regir /*3c, 3k*/ **⊙** VT **1** [+ *país*] to rule, govern; [+ *colegio*] to run; [+ *empresa*] to manage, run **2** (*Econ, Jur*) to govern **3** (*Ling*) to take **⊙** VI **1** (= *estar en vigor*) [*ley, precio*] to be in force; [*condición*] to prevail, obtain **2** (*frm*) (*con mes, año*) **el mes que rige** the present month, the current month **3** (= *funcionar*) to work **4** (*) (= *estar cuerdo*) **no ~** to have a screw loose*, not be all there* **⊙** *regirse* VPR **-se por** to be ruled by, be guided by, go by

registrar /*1a*/ **⊙** VT **1** [+ *equipaje, lugar, persona*] to search; **lo hemos registrado todo de arriba abajo** we have searched the whole place from top to bottom; **✦** MODISMO **¡a mí que me registren!*** search me!* **2** (= *anotar en registro*) to register, record **3** [+ *temperatura*] to record, register; [+ *temblor*] to register **4** (*Mús*) to record **5** (*Méx*) [+ *correo*] to register **⊙** *registrarse* VPR **1** (= *apuntarse*) to register **2** (= *ocurrir*) **hoy se han registrado las temperaturas más altas del año** the highest temperatures this year were recorded today

registro SM **1** (= *acción*) registration, recording **2** (= *libro*) register; (*Inform*) record ➤ **registro de la propiedad inmobiliaria** land registry ➤ **registro mercantil** business register **3** (= *lista*) list, record; (= *apunte*) note **4** (= *entrada*) entry **5** (= *oficina*) registry, record office ➤ **registro civil** ≈ registry office (*esp Brit*), ≈ county clerk's office (*EEUU*) ➤ **registro de la propiedad** (= *oficina*) land registry, land registry office ➤ **registro de patentes y marcas** patent office **6** (= *búsqueda*) search; (= *inspección*) inspection ➤ **registro domiciliario** house search **7** (*Mús*) (= *grabación*) recording; (= *timbre*) [*de la voz*] register; [*del órgano*] stop; [*del piano*] pedal; **✦** MODISMO **tocar todos los ~s** to pull out all the stops **8** (*Téc*) manhole **9** (*Ling*) register **10** (*Dep*) (= *marca*) personal best; (= *récord*) record

regla SF **1** (= *instrumento*) ruler ➤ **regla de cálculo** slide rule **2** (= *norma*) rule; **en ~** in order; **no tenía los papeles en ~** his papers were not in order; **por ~ general** generally, as a rule ➤ **regla de tres** rule of three ➤ **reglas del juego** rules of the game ➤ **reglas de oro** golden rules **3** (= *menstruación*) period **4** (*Rel*) rule, order

reglable ADJ adjustable

reglaje SM **1** (*Mec*) adjustment; [*de neumáticos*] alignment **2** (*Mil*) correction (of aim)

reglamentación SF **1** (= *acción*) regulation **2** (= *reglas*) regulations *pl*, rules *pl*

reglamentar /*1a*/ VT to regulate

reglamentario ADJ [*uniforme*] regulation *antes de s*; **en el traje ~** in the regulation dress; **en la forma reglamentaria** in the properly established way

reglamento SM (= *reglas*) rules *pl*, regulations *pl*; (*municipal*) by-law; [*de profesión*] code of conduct; **pistola**

de ~ standard issue pistol ➤ **reglamento del tráfico** highway code

regleta SF space

regocijar /*1a*/ **⊙** VT to gladden, delight; **la noticia regocijó a la familia** the news delighted the family, the news filled the family with joy **⊙** *regocijarse* VPR to rejoice, be glad; **se regocija de la mala suerte de otros** he delights in somebody else's misfortunes

regocijo SM (*frm*) (= *alegría*) joy, happiness; (= *júbilo*) delight, elation

regodearse /*1a*/ VPR **~ con** *o* **en algo** to gloat over sth

regodeo SM delight

regordete ADJ [*persona*] chubby, plump; [*manos*] fat

regresar /*1a*/ **⊙** VI (= *venir*) to return, come back; (= *irse*) to return, go back **⊙** VT (*LAm*) to give back, return **⊙** *regresarse* VPR (*LAm*) = **A**

regresión SF **1** (= *acción*) (*tb Psic*) regression **2** (= *retroceso*) [*de productividad*] fall, decrease; [*de actividad cultural*] decline ➤ **regresión demográfica** population decline, fall in population

regresivo ADJ regressive, backward

regreso SM return; **viaje de ~** return trip; **emprender el ~ a** to return to, go/come back to; **de ~ a casa** on the way home

reguero SM **1** (= *señal*) trail; **✦** MODISMO **como un ~ de pólvora** like wildfire **2** (*Agr*) irrigation ditch

regulable ADJ adjustable

regulación SF **1** (*con reglas*) regulation; (*Mec*) adjustment ➤ **regulación del tráfico** traffic control **2** (*euf*) ➤ **regulación de empleo** redundancy

regulador SM (*Mec*) regulator, throttle; (*Radio*) control, button

regular[1] ADJ **1** (= *uniforme*) regular; **a intervalos ~es** at regular intervals **2** (= *mediano*) medium, average; **de tamaño ~** medium-sized, average-sized **3** (= *común*) ordinary; **por lo ~** as a rule, generally **4** (= *no muy bueno*) so-so, not too bad; **me gusta ~** I don't like it much, I'm not really into it*

regular[2] /*1a*/ VT **1** (= *ajustar*) to regulate, control; [*ley*] to govern; [+ *tráfico, precio*] to control **2** (*Mec*) to adjust, regulate

regularidad SF regularity; **con ~** regularly

regularizar /*1f*/ VT (= *ajustar, legalizar*) to regularize; (= *acomodar*) to standardize, bring into line

regurgitar /*1a*/ VT to regurgitate

regusto SM aftertaste

rehabilitación SF **1** [*de enfermo, delincuente*] rehabilitation **2** (*en cargo*) reinstatement **3** [*de edificio*] restoration

rehabilitar /*1a*/ VT **1** [+ *persona*] to rehabilitate; (*en cargo*) to reinstate **2** (*Arquit*) to restore, renovate

rehacer /*2r*/ **⊙** VT [+ *trabajo*] to do again, redo; **no ha podido ~ su vida** he hasn't been able to piece his life together again *o* rebuild his life **⊙** *rehacerse* VPR **~se de algo** to get over sth, recover from sth

rehén SMF hostage

rehilete SM **1** (= *flecha*) dart; (*Taur*) banderilla **2** (*Dep*) (= *volante*) shuttlecock **3** (*Méx*) (= *juguete infantil*) windmill, pinwheel (*EEUU*)

rehogar /*1h*/ VT to sauté, toss in oil

rehuir /*3g*/ VT to avoid

rehusar /*1a*/ **⊙** VT to refuse; **~ hacer algo** to refuse to do sth **⊙** VI to refuse

reilón ADJ (*Ven*) (= *que se ríe*) giggly; (= *alegre*) merry

reimplantar /*1a*/ VT to re-establish, reintroduce

reimpresión SF reprint, reprinting

reimprimir /*3a*/ VT to reprint

reina ⊙ SF **1** (= *monarca*) queen ➤ **reina de la fiesta** carnival queen **2** (*Ajedrez*) queen **3** (*Zool*) queen **⊙** ADJ INV **la prueba ~** the main event

reinado SM reign; **bajo el ~ de** in the reign of

reinante ADJ 1 (= *soberano*) reigning 2 (= *que prevalece*) prevailing

reinar /1a/ VI 1 [*rey, reina*] to reign, rule 2 [*caos, confusión, paz*] to reign; **reina una confusión total** total confusion reigns, there is total confusion; **entre la población reinaba el descontento** there was widespread discontent among the population

reincidente SMF recidivist, persistent offender

reineta Ⓐ ADJ **manzana** ~ pippin Ⓑ SF pippin

reincidir /3a/ VI (= *recaer*) to relapse (**en** into); [*criminal*] to reoffend; [*pecador*] to backslide

reincorporación SF 1 [*de trabajador*] (*tras descanso, vacaciones*) return; (*tras despido*) reinstatement 2 [*de colonia, territorio*] reincorporation

reincorporar /1a/ Ⓐ VT 1 [+ *colonia, territorio*] to reincorporate 2 [+ *trabajador*] to reinstate Ⓑ **reincorporarse** VPR **~se a algo** to rejoin sth; **~se al trabajo** (*tras vacaciones, descanso*) to return to work; (*tras despido*) to be reinstated

reingresar /1a/ VI **~ en** to re-enter

reinicializar /1f/ VT (*Inform*) to reset, reboot

reiniciar /1b/ VT to begin again

reino SM kingdom ➤ **reino animal** animal kingdom ➤ **el Reino Unido** the United Kingdom ➤ **reino vegetal** plant kingdom

reinserción SF ➤ **reinserción en la sociedad, reinserción social** social rehabilitation, assimilation into society

reinsertar /1a/ Ⓐ VT to rehabilitate, assimilate into society Ⓑ **reinsertarse** VPR **~se en la sociedad** to resume an ordinary social life

reinstalar /1a/ VT 1 [+ *aparato*] to reinstall 2 (*en un puesto*) to reinstate

reintegración SF 1 (*a cargo*) reinstatement (**a** in) 2 (*Fin*) refund, repayment

reintegrar /1a/ Ⓐ VT 1 (= *restituir, reconstituir*) to reintegrate 2 [+ *persona*] to reinstate (**a** in) 3 (*frm*) [+ *dinero*] to pay back; **~ a algn una cantidad** to refund *o* pay back a sum to sb; **le han reintegrado todos sus gastos** he has been reimbursed for all his expenses Ⓑ **reintegrarse** VPR **~se a** to return to

reintegro SM 1 (*frm*) refund, reimbursement; (*en banco*) withdrawal 2 [*de lotería*] return of one's stake

reintroducir /3n/ VT to reintroduce

reinventar /1a/ VT to reinvent

reinvertir /3i/ VT to reinvest

reír /3l/ Ⓐ VI to laugh; **no me hagas ~** don't make me laugh; **echarse a ~** to burst out laughing Ⓑ VT to laugh at; **todos le ríen los chistes** everybody laughs at his jokes Ⓒ **reírse** VPR to laugh; **~se con algo/algn: todos se ríen con sus chistes** everybody laughs at his jokes; **siempre nos reímos con él** we always have a good laugh with him; **~se de algn/algo** to laugh at sb/sth

reiteración SF (*frm*) reiteration (*frm*), repetition

reiterado ADJ (*frm*) repeated

reiterar /1a/ VT (*frm*) to reiterate (*frm*), repeat

reiterativo ADJ (*frm*) reiterative

reivindicación SF 1 (= *reclamación*) demand; **las reivindicaciones de los sindicatos** the union's demands ➤ **reivindicación salarial** pay claim, wage claim 2 [*de asesinato, crimen*] **se produjo la ~ del atentado** responsibility for the attack has been claimed 3 (= *desagravio*) **una lucha por la ~ de la memoria de Galileo** a fight to vindicate Galileo's memory

reivindicar /1g/ VT 1 (= *reclamar*) [+ *derechos, condiciones, independencia*] to demand; [+ *herencia*] to claim 2 [+ *asesinato, crimen*] to claim responsibility for 3 [+ *reputación*] to vindicate Ⓑ **reivindicarse** VPR (*LAm*) to vindicate o.s.

reivindicativo ADJ [*movimiento, acto*] protest *antes de s*

reja SF 1 [*de ventana*] bars *pl*, grille; [*de cercado*] railing;

✦ MODISMO **entre ~s** behind bars 2 (*Agr*) ➤ **reja del arado** ploughshare, plowshare (*EEUU*)

rejego* ADJ (*Méx*) wild, rebellious

rejilla SF 1 [*de caño, alcantarilla*] grating, grille; [*de equipaje*] luggage rack; [*de horno*] shelf; [*de ventilador*] vent 2 (*en muebles*) wickerwork; **silla de ~** wicker chair

rejo SM 1 (= *punta*) spike 2 [*de insecto*] sting 3 (*Col*) (= *látigo*) whip

rejoneador(a) SM/F (*Taur*) *mounted bullfighter who uses the lance*

rejonear /1a/ (*Taur*) Ⓐ VT [+ *toro*] to wound with the lance Ⓑ VI to fight the bull on horseback with the lance

rejuntar /1a/ VT (*Méx*) to round up

rejuvenecedor ADJ rejuvenating

rejuvenecer /2d/ Ⓐ VT to rejuvenate Ⓑ VI to be rejuvenated

relación SF 1 (= *vínculo*) connection; **guardar** *o* **tener ~ con algo** [*suceso*] to be connected with sth, be related to sth; [*persona*] to be connected with sth; **no guardar ~ (alguna) con algo** (= *no parecerse*) to bear no relation (whatsoever) to sth; (= *no estar relacionado*) to have no connection *o* relation (at all) with sth; **¿tiene alguna ~ con esa empresa?** do you have any connection with that company? ➤ **relación calidad/precio** value for money; **tener buena ~ calidad/precio** to be good value for money 2 **con ~ a ⬦ en ~ a** *o* **con** (= *comparado con*) compared to, compared with; (= *en lo referente a*) with regard to, in connection with 3 (= *entre personas*) 3.1 (*en el momento presente*) relations *pl*; **estar en** *o* **mantener buenas relaciones con** [+ *persona*] to be on good terms with; [+ *organización*] to have good relations with; **romper las relaciones con** [+ *país, organización*] to break off relations with; [+ *familiar, amigo*] to break off all contact with 3.2 (*de larga duración*) relationship; **tenía una ~ de amistad con algunos de sus alumnos** he had a friendly relationship with some of his students; **tu ~ de pareja** your relationship with your partner; **llevan varios meses de relaciones** they've been seeing each other for some months ➤ **relaciones comerciales** trade relations ➤ **relaciones diplomáticas** diplomatic relations ➤ **relaciones laborales** labour relations, labor relations (*EEUU*) ➤ **relaciones públicas** (= *actividad*) public relations, PR; (= *profesional*) public relations officer, PR officer 4 (*tb* **~ sexual**) (= *acto*) sex; (= *trato*) sexual relationship; **mantener** *o* **tener relaciones sexuales con algn** (*de forma esporádica*) to have sex with sb; (*de forma continuada*) to be in a sexual relationship with sb ➤ **relaciones prematrimoniales** premarital sex, sex before marriage 5 (= *referencia*) **hacer ~ a algo** to refer to sth 6 **relaciones** (= *personas conocidas*) acquaintances; (= *enchufes*) contacts, connections; **tener (buenas) relaciones** to be well connected, have good contacts *o* connections 7 (*Mat*) (= *proporción*) ratio 8 (*frm*) (= *narración*) account; **hacer una ~ de algo** to give an account of sth 9 (= *lista*) list; **el usuario dispone de una ~ de sus llamadas** the customer receives a breakdown of calls made

relacionado ADJ 1 [*acontecimiento, tema, problema*] related; **~ con algo** related to sth 2 [*persona*] **una persona bien relacionada** a well-connected person; **~ con algn/algo** connected with sb/sth, linked to sb/sth

relacionar /1a/ Ⓐ VT 1 (= *asociar*) to connect (**con** with) 2 (= *enumerar*) to list Ⓑ **relacionarse** VPR 1 [*persona*] **un hombre que sabe ~se** a man who mixes with the right people; **~se con algn** to mix with sb 2 [*sucesos, temas*] to be connected, be related; **~se con algo** to be related to sth

relajación SF relaxation

relajado ADJ relaxed

relajante Ⓐ ADJ 1 [*ejercicio, actividad*] relaxing 2 (*Med*) sedative 3 (*CS*) [*comida*] sickly sweet Ⓑ SM sedative

relajar /1a/ Ⓐ VT 1 (= *sosegar*) to relax 2 (*moralmente*) to weaken, corrupt 3 (*Carib*) (= *hacer mofa de*) to mock, deride 4 (*RPl*) (= *insultar*) to lay into* Ⓑ **relajarse** VPR

1 (= *distenderse*) to relax **2** [*moralidad*] to become lax

relajo* SM **1** (*LAm*) (= *desorden*) rumpus*, ruckus*; **armar (un)** ~ to kick up a rumpus *o* ruckus* **2** (= *relajación*) relaxation

relamerse /2a/ VPR **1** [*animal*] to lick its chops; [*persona*] to lick one's lips **2** (*fig*) ~ **con algo** to relish the prospect of sth; (*pey*) to gloat over the prospect of sth

relamido ADJ **1** (= *afectado*) affected **2** (= *remilgado*) prim and proper

relámpago ᴀ SM (= *rayo*) flash of lightning; **ayer hubo ~s** there was lightning yesterday; ✦ MODISMO **como un ~** as quick as lightning, in a flash **ᴃ** ADJ INV **visita ~** lightning visit; **viaje ~** lightning trip

relampaguear /1a/ VI **relampagueó toda la noche** there was lightning all night

relanzamiento SM relaunch, relaunching

relanzar /1f/ VT to relaunch

relatar /1a/ VT to relate, tell

relatividad SF relativity

relativizar /1f/ VT to play down, diminish the importance of

relativo ᴀ ADJ **1** (= *no absoluto*) relative; **una humedad relativa del 60%** a relative humidity of 60%; **un problema de una importancia muy relativa** a relatively unimportant problem **2** (= *referente*) ~ **a algo** relating to sth; **en lo ~ a la educación ...** as regards education ..., with regard to education ... **3** (*Ling*) relative **ᴃ** SM relative

relato SM (= *narración*) story, tale; (= *informe*) account, report

relax [re'las] SM (*Esp*) **1** (= *distensión*) relaxation **2** **"relax"** (*euf*) (*anuncio*) "personal services"

releer /2e/ VT to reread

relegar /1h/ VT to relegate; ~ **algo al olvido** to consign sth to oblivion

relente SM night dew

relevante ADJ **1** (= *importante*) significant **2** (= *pertinente*) relevant

relevar /1a/ VT **1** (*Mil*) [+ *guardia*] to relieve; [+ *colega*] to replace, substitute for; ~ **la guardia** to relieve the guard **2** (= *destituir*) ~ **a algn de un cargo** to remove sb from office; **ser relevado de su mando** to be relieved of one's command **3** (= *dispensar*) ~ **a algn de una obligación** to relieve sb of a duty, free sb from an obligation; ~ **a algn de hacer algo** to free sb from the obligation to do sth **4** (*Téc*) to emboss

relevo SM **1** (= *acto*) relief, change; (= *personas*) relief; **tomar el** ~ to take over; ~ **de la guardia** changing of the guard **2** **relevos** (*Dep*) relay *sing*, relay race *sing*; **100 metros ~s** 100 metre relay

relicario SM **1** (*Rel*) shrine, reliquary **2** (= *medallón*) locket

relieve SM **1** (*Arte, Téc*) relief; **bajo** ~ bas-relief; **en** ~ in relief **2** (*Geog*) **un país de** ~ **montañoso** a mountainous country **3** (= *importancia*) importance; **un personaje de** ~ an important *o* prominent figure; **dar** ~ **a algo** to lend importance to sth; **poner algo de** ~ to highlight sth

religión SF religion

religiosidad SF **1** (= *devoción*) piety, religiousness, religiosity **2** (= *puntualidad*) religiousness

religioso/a ᴀ ADJ religious **ᴃ** SM/F monk/nun, member of a religious order

relinchar /1a/ VI to neigh, snort

reliquia SF **1** (*Rel*) relic **2** **reliquias** (= *restos*) relics, remains; (= *vestigios*) traces, vestiges ➤ **reliquia de familia** family heirloom

rellano SM landing

rellena SF (*Col, Méx*) black pudding (*esp Brit*), blood sausage (*EEUU*)

rellenar /1a/ VT **1** (= *volver a llenar*) to refill, replenish; (*Aer*) to refuel **2** (= *llenar hasta arriba*) to fill up **3** [+ *formulario*] to fill out, fill in (*esp Brit*); [+ *espacios*] to fill out, fill in (*esp Brit*) **4** (*Culin*) to stuff (**de** with) **5** (*Cos*) to pad

relleno ᴀ ADJ **1** (*Culin*) stuffed (**de** with) **2** (= *gordito*) [*persona*] plump; [*cara*] full **ᴃ** SM **1** (*Culin*) (*para dulces*) filling; (*para carnes*) stuffing **2** (*en un escrito*) **frases de** ~ padding **3** (*Arquit*) plaster filling **4** (*Cos*) padding

reloj [re'lo] SM (*grande*) clock; [*de pulsera*] watch; **contra (el)** ~ against the clock; ✦ MODISMO **como un** ~ like clockwork ➤ **reloj de arena** hourglass, sandglass ➤ **reloj de cuco** cuckoo clock ➤ **reloj de fichar** time clock ➤ **reloj de pie** grandfather clock ➤ **reloj de pulsera** wristwatch ➤ **reloj de sol** sundial ➤ **reloj despertador** alarm clock

relojería SF **1** (= *tienda*) watchmaker's **2** (= *arte*) watchmaking, clockmaking; **bomba de** ~ time bomb; **mecanismo de** ~ timing device

relojero/a SM/F (*de relojes de pulsera*) watchmaker; (*de relojes de pared*) clockmaker

reluciente ADJ (= *brillante*) shining, brilliant; [*joyas*] glittering, sparkling

relucir /3f/ VI (= *brillar*) to shine; [*joyas*] to glitter, sparkle; ✦ MODISMO **sacar algo a** ~ to bring sth up, mention sth

relumbrar /1a/ VI (= *brillar*) to dazzle; (= *deslumbrar*) to glare

relumbrón SM flashiness, ostentation; **joyas de** ~ flashy jewellery *o* (*EEUU*) jewelry

remachar /1a/ VT **1** (*Téc*) [+ *metales*] to rivet; [+ *clavo*] to clinch **2** [+ *aspecto, asunto, punto*] **quisiera** ~ **este punto** I would like to stress this point

remache SM **1** (*Téc*) rivet **2** (= *acción*) [*de metal*] riveting; [*de clavo*] clinching

remador(a) SM/F rower

remanente ᴀ ADJ **1** (*Com*) [*de producto*] surplus **2** (*Fís*) remanent **ᴃ** SM (= *lo que queda*) remainder; (*Com*) [*de producto*] surplus

remangar /1h/ VT = **arremangar**

remansarse /1a/ VPR to form a pool

remanso SM **1** (*en río*) pool **2** (= *lugar*) quiet place; **un ~ de paz** an oasis of peace

remar /1a/ VI to row; ~ **en seco** to go on a rowing machine

remarcar /1g/ VT **1** (= *subrayar*) to emphasize, underline **2** (= *observar*) to notice, observe **3** (= *señalar*) to point out

rematadamente ADV terribly, hopelessly; ~ **mal** terribly *o* hopelessly bad; **es** ~ **tonto** he's utterly stupid

rematado ADJ hopeless, complete; **es un loco** ~ he's a raving lunatic

rematador(a) SM/F **1** (*Dep*) goal scorer **2** (*And, CS*) auctioneer

rematar /1a/ **ᴀ** VT **1** (= *matar*) to finish off **2** (= *terminar*) [+ *discurso, actuación*] to round off, conclude; [+ *trabajo*] to finish off; [+ *bebida, comida*] to finish up, finish off; **remató el concierto cantando su último éxito** she rounded off the concert by singing her latest hit **3** (*Tenis*) to smash; (*Ftbl*) (*con el pie*) to shoot; (*con la cabeza*) to head; **remató el centro (de cabeza)** he met the cross (with a header); **remató la jugada** he finished off the move **4** (*Cos*) to cast off **5** (*Arquit*) to top, crown **6** (*LAm Com*) (= *subastar*) to auction; (= *liquidar*) to sell off cheap **ᴃ** VI **1** (= *terminar*) to end, finish off **2** ~ **en** to end in **3** (*Tenis*) to smash; (*Ftbl*) (*con el pie*) to shoot; (*con la cabeza*) to head; ~ **de cabeza** to head the ball towards goal

remate SM **1** (= *cabo*) end; (= *punta*) tip, point **2** (= *toque final*) **como** ~ **al concierto hizo un bis** to round off the concert he played an encore; ✦ MODISMOS **poner** ~ **a algo** to cap sth; **de** ~**: está loco de** ~ he's stark raving mad*; **para** ~**:** to crown it all, top it all **3** (*Ftbl*) (*con el pie*) shot; (*tb* ~ **de cabeza**) header **4** (*LAm Com*) (= *subasta*) auction

rematista SMF (*And, Carib*) auctioneer

remedar /1a/ VT (= *imitar*) to imitate, copy; (*para burlarse*) to ape, mimic

remediar /1b/ VT **1** (= *solucionar*) to remedy; **llorando no remedias nada** you're not going to solve anything by crying, crying won't solve anything **2** (= *evitar*) **no puedo ~lo** I can't help it **3** [+ *necesidades*] to meet, help with

remedio SM **1** (= *alternativa*) choice, alternative; **no tengo más ~ que ir** I've got no alternative *o* choice but to go; **¡qué ~!** I've got no choice!; **¿qué ~ me queda?** what else can I do?, what choice have I got?
2 (= *solución*) **Juan no tiene ~** Juan's a hopeless case, Juan's beyond redemption; **como último ~** as a last resort; **es un tonto sin ~** he's hopelessly stupid, he's so stupid he's beyond redemption; **poner ~ a algo** to remedy sth, correct sth
3 (*Med*) cure, remedy; **un ~ contra** *o* **para la tos** a cough remedy; ✦ MODISMO **es peor el ~ que la enfermedad** the solution is worse than the problem ➤ **remedio casero** home remedy

remedo SM (= *imitación*) imitation, copy; (*pey*) parody

rememorar /1a/ VT to recall

remendar /1j/ VT [+ *ropa*] to darn, mend; (*con parche*) to patch

remendón/ona Ⓐ ADJ **zapatero ~** cobbler Ⓑ SM/F cobbler

remera SF (*RPl*) (= *camiseta*) T-shirt

remero/a Ⓐ SM/F oarsman/oarswoman, rower Ⓑ SM (= *máquina*) rowing machine

remesa SF [*de dinero*] remittance; [*de bienes*] shipment

remeter /2a/ VPR to tuck in

remezón SM (*SAm*) earth tremor, slight earthquake

remiendo SM [*de ropa*] mend, darn; (= *parche*) patch; **echar** *o* **hacer un ~ a algo** (= *coser*) to darn sth; (= *poner un parche*) to patch sth, put a patch on sth

remilgado ADJ **1** (= *melindroso*) finicky, fussy, particular **2** (= *mojigato*) prudish, prim

remilgo SM **1** (= *melindre*) fussiness; **él no le hace ~s a ninguna clase de trabajo** he won't turn up his nose at any kind of work **2** (= *mojigatería*) prudery, primness

remilgoso ADJ (*LAm*) = **remilgado**

reminiscencia SF reminiscence

remirado ADJ fussy, pernickety*, persnickety (*EEUU**)

remise SM **auto de ~** (*Arg*) hire car (*Brit*), rental car (*EEUU*)

remisión SF **1** (= *envío*) sending; (*esp LAm Com*) shipment, consignment **2** (*al lector*) reference (**a** to) **3** (*Rel*) forgiveness, remission

remiso ADJ **estar** *o* **mostrarse ~ a hacer algo** to be reluctant to do sth, be unwilling to do sth

remite SM sender

remitente SMF sender

remitido SM paid insert

remitir /3a/ Ⓐ VT **1** (= *enviar*) to send; [+ *dinero*] to remit, send; (*Com*) to ship, send **2** [+ *lector*] to refer (**a** to) **3** ~ **una decisión a algn** to refer a decision to sb **4** (*Rel*) to forgive, pardon Ⓑ VI (= *disminuir*) to slacken, let up Ⓒ **remitirse** VPR **a las pruebas me remito** look at the facts (of the matter)

remo SM **1** (= *pala*) oar; **cruzar un río a ~** to row across a river **2** (*Dep*) rowing; **practicar el ~** to row

remoción SF (*LAm*) removal

remodelación SF **1** (*Arquit*) remodelling, remodeling (*EEUU*) **2** [*de organización*] restructuring; (*Pol*) reshuffle

remodelar /1a/ VT **1** (*Arquit*) to remodel **2** (*Pol*) to reshuffle; [+ *organización*] to restructure

remojar /1a/ VT **1** [+ *legumbres, prenda*] to soak, steep (**en** in); [+ *galleta*] to dip (**en** in, into) **2** (*) (= *celebrar bebiendo*) **¡este triunfo habrá que ~lo!** this victory calls for a drink!

remojo SM **poner algo a** *o* **en ~** to leave sth to soak

remojón SM **darse un ~*** to go in for a dip

remolacha SF beetroot (*Brit*), beet (*EEUU*) ➤ **remolacha azucarera** sugar beet

remolcador SM **1** (*Náut*) tug **2** (*Aut*) breakdown lorry (*Brit*), tow truck (*EEUU*)

remolcar /1g/ VT **1** (*Náut*) to tug **2** (*Aut*) to tow

remoler /2h/ VI (*And**) to live it up*

remolino SM **1** [*de agua*] (*pequeño*) swirl, eddy; (*grande*) whirlpool **2** [*de aire*] (*pequeño*) eddy; (*grande*) whirlwind; [*de humo, polvo*] whirl, cloud **3** [*de pelo*] cowlick **4** (*CS*) (= *juguete*) windmill, pinwheel (*EEUU*)

remolón/ona* Ⓐ ADJ (= *vago*) lazy Ⓑ SM/F (= *vago*) slacker, shirker **2** (= *disimulado*) **hacerse el ~** to pretend not to notice

remolonear /1a/ VI to slack, shirk

remolque SM **1** [*de camión*] trailer, semitrailer (*EEUU*); (= *caravana*) caravan (*Brit*), trailer (*EEUU*); (*Náut*) ship on tow **2** (= *acción*) towing; **a ~** on tow; **llevar un coche a ~** to tow a car; **ir a ~ de algn** to go along with sb

remontar /1a/ Ⓐ VT **1** [+ *río*] to go up; [+ *obstáculo*] to negotiate, get over **2** [+ *zapato*] to mend, repair Ⓑ **remontarse** VPR **1** [*avión, pájaro*] to rise, soar; [*edificio*] to soar, tower **2** (*en tiempo*) ~**se a** to go back to; **tenemos que ~nos al siglo XV** we must go back to the 15th century

remonte SM ski lift

rémora SF **1** (*Zool*) remora **2** (*frm*) (= *obstáculo*) hindrance

remorder /2h/ VI **me remuerde haberle tratado así** I have a guilty conscience about treating him like that; **no me remuerde la conciencia** I don't have any qualms about it

remordimiento SM (*tb* ~**s**) remorse, regret; **tener ~s** to feel remorse, suffer pangs of conscience

remoto ADJ **1** [*época*] far-off, distant **2** [*país*] faraway, distant **3** [*posibilidad*] remote; **no tengo ni la más remota idea** I haven't the faintest *o* remotest idea

remover /2h/ VT **1** [+ *tierra*] to turn over, dig up; [+ *objetos*] to move round; [+ *fuego, brasas*] to poke, stir; [+ *sopa*] to stir; [+ *ensalada*] to toss; [+ *cóctel*] to shake; ~ **el pasado** to stir up the past; ~ **un asunto** to go into a matter; ✦ MODISMOS ~ **cielo y tierra** ◇ ~ **Roma con Santiago** to move heaven and earth **2** (= *quitar*) to remove **3** (*esp LAm frm*) (= *cesar*) to dismiss

remozar /1f/ Ⓐ VT [+ *persona*] to rejuvenate; [+ *aspecto*] to brighten up; [+ *organización*] to give a new look to, give a face-lift to; [+ *edificio, fachada*] to renovate Ⓑ **remozarse** VPR to be rejuvenated; **la encuentro muy remozada** she looks so much younger

remuneración SF remuneration

remunerado ADJ **trabajo mal ~** badly-paid job

remunerar /1a/ VT to remunerate

renacentista ADJ Renaissance *antes de s*

renacer /2d/ VI **1** (= *volver a nacer*) to be reborn; (*Bot*) to reappear, come up again **2** (= *reavivar*) to revive; **hacer ~** to revive; **hoy me siento ~** today I feel like a new person *o* as if I've come to life again; **sentían ~ la esperanza** they felt new hope

renacimiento SM rebirth, revival; **el Renacimiento** the Renaissance

renacuajo SM **1** (*Zool*) tadpole **2** (*) (= *niño*) shrimp

renal ADJ renal, kidney *antes de s*

rencilla SF quarrel; ~**s** arguments, bickering *sing*

renco ADJ lame

rencor SM (= *amargura*) rancour, rancor (*EEUU*), bitterness; (= *resentimiento*) ill feeling, resentment; **guardar ~** to bear malice, harbour *o* (*EEUU*) harbor a grudge (**a** against)

rencoroso ADJ spiteful

rendición SF surrender

rendido ADJ **1** (= *cansado*) exhausted, worn-out **2** (= *enamorado*) devoted

rendidor ADJ (*LAm*) **1** [*día*] productive **2** [*producto*] **las lentejas son muy ~as** with lentils, a little goes a long way

rendija SF crack, cleft

rendimiento SM **1** [*de máquina*] (= *capacidad*) capacity; (= *producción*) output; **el ~ del motor** the performance of the engine; **funcionar a pleno ~** to work all-out, work at full throttle **2** [*de persona*] performance, achievement; **tiene muy bajo ~ escolar** he's not doing very well *o* achieving much academically **3** (*Fin*) yield, profit, profits *pl* ➤ **rendimiento del capital** return on capital

rendir /3k/ Ⓐ VT 1 (= *producir*) to produce; [+ *beneficios*] to yield; [+ *producto, total*] to produce; [+ *interés*] to bear 2 (= *cansar*) to exhaust, tire out; **la rindió el sueño** she was overcome by sleep 3 ~ **homenaje a** to pay tribute to; ~ **culto a** to worship 4 ~ **examen** (CS) to sit *o* take an exam Ⓑ VI 1 (= *dar resultados*) **el negocio no rinde** the business is not profitable *o* doesn't pay; **este año ha rendido poco** it has done poorly this year; **trabajo, pero no rindo** I work hard but without much to show for it 2 [*arroz, detergente*] to go a long way Ⓒ **rendirse** VPR (*a la fuerza, persuasión*) to yield (**a** to); (*Mil*) to surrender; (= *entregarse*) to give o.s. up; ~**se a la evidencia** to bow before the evidence; **¡me rindo!** I give in!

renegado/a SM/F (= *traidor*) renegade; (*Rel*) apostate; (*Pol*) rebel

renegar /1h, 1j/ Ⓐ VI 1 ~ **de** [+ *fe*] to renounce; [+ *familia*] to disown 2 (= *maldecir*) to curse, swear; (= *blasfemar*) to blaspheme 3 (= *refunfuñar*) to complain (**de** about) 4 (*LAm*) (= *enojarse*) to get angry, get upset Ⓑ VT **negar y ~ algo** to deny sth vigorously

renegociar /1b/ VT to renegotiate

renegrido ADJ very black, very dark

RENFE SF ABR, **Renfe** SF ABR = **Red Nacional de los Ferrocarriles Españoles**

renglón SM line, line of writing; ✦ MODISMO **a ~ seguido** immediately after

rengo ADJ (*LAm*) lame

renguear /1a/ VI (*LAm*) to limp, hobble

renguera SF (*LAm*) limp, limping

reno SM reindeer

renombrado ADJ renowned, famous

renombre SM renown, fame; **de ~** renowned, famous

renovable ADJ renewable

renovación SF 1 [*de contrato, pasaporte, suscripción*] renewal 2 [*de edificio*] renovation; **subvenciones para la ~ de los sistemas informáticos** subsidies for updating *o* upgrading computer systems 3 [*de partido, asamblea*] reform

renovado ADJ renewed, redoubled

renovador(a) ADJ, SM/F (*Pol*) reformist

renovar /1l/ Ⓐ VT 1 [+ *contrato, pasaporte, suscripción*] to renew 2 (= *mejorar*) [+ *edificio*] to renovate; [+ *sistemas tecnológicos*] to update, upgrade 3 [+ *muebles*] to change 4 [+ *partido, asamblea*] to reform 5 (= *reanudar*) [+ *ataques*] to renew; [+ *conversaciones*] to resume Ⓑ **renovarse** VPR 1 (= *reanudarse*) **se han renovado los ataques** there have been renewed attacks, the attacks have resumed 2 [*persona*] ~**se o morir** adapt or perish

renquear /1a/ VI 1 (= *cojear*) to limp, hobble 2 (*) (= *ir tirando*) to get by, just about manage 3 [*motor*] to splutter

renta SF 1 (= *ingresos*) income; (= *ganancia*) interest, return; **vivir de (las) ~s** to live on one's private income; **título de ~ fija** fixed-interest bond ➤ **renta gravable** taxable income ➤ **renta nacional** national income ➤ **renta vitalicia** annuity 2 (*esp LAm*) (= *alquiler*) rent

rentabilidad SF profitability

rentabilizar /1f/ VT (= *hacer rentable*) to make profitable, make more profitable; (= *sacar provecho de*) to exploit to the full; (*pey*) to cash in on

rentable ADJ profitable; **no ~** unprofitable

rentar /1a/ VT 1 (= *producir*) to produce, yield 2 (*esp Méx*) [+ *casa*] [*inquilino*] to rent; [*propietario*] to let, rent out; [+ *coche, bicicleta*] to rent, hire (*esp Brit*)

rentero/a SM/F tenant farmer

rentista SMF rentier

renuente ADJ 1 (*frm*) [*persona*] reluctant, unwilling 2 [*materia*] awkward, difficult

renuncia SF 1 (*a derecho, trono*) renunciation; **han hecho pública la ~ a sus exigencias/planes** they announced that they have abandoned *o* dropped their claims/plans

2 (= *dimisión*) resignation 3 (= *abnegación*) renunciation

renunciar /1b/ VI 1 ~ **a** [+ *derecho, trono, violencia*] to renounce; [+ *exigencia, plan*] to abandon, drop 2 (= *dimitir*) to resign

reñido ADJ 1 [*batalla, concurso*] hard-fought, close 2 (= *enfadado*) **estar ~ con algn** to have fallen out with sb, be on bad terms with sb 3 (= *en contradicción*) **está ~ con el principio de igualdad** it goes against *o* is contrary to the principle of equality

reñir /3h, 3k/ Ⓐ VT (= *regañar*) to scold; (= *reprender*) to tell off*, reprimand (**por** for) Ⓑ VI 1 (= *enfadarse*) to fall out, quarrel; **ha reñido con su novio** she's fallen out with her boyfriend 2 (= *discutir*) to quarrel; **se pasan la vida riñendo** they spend their whole time quarrelling *o* (*EEUU*) quarreling

reo SMF culprit, offender; (*Jur*) accused, defendant

reoca * SF **es la ~** (*Esp*) (= *bueno*) it's the tops*; (= *malo*) it's the pits*

reojo: de ~ ADV **mirar a algn de ~** to look at sb out of the corner of one's eye

reorganización SF reorganization

reorganizar /1f/ Ⓐ VT to reorganize Ⓑ **reorganizarse** VPR to reorganize

reorientación SF [*de negocio, economía*] reorientation; [*de recursos*] redeployment

reorientar /1a/ VT [+ *economía*] to reorientate; [+ *dirección, costumbre*] to change; [+ *recursos*] to redeploy

repanchigarse * /1h/ VPR to lounge, sprawl, loll (back)

reparación SF 1 (= *arreglo*) repair 2 (= *desagravio*) reparation

reparador ADJ [*sueño*] refreshing; [*comida*] fortifying, restorative

reparadora SF (*tb* ~ **de calzados**) (*Chi, Méx*) shoe repairer's

reparar /1a/ Ⓐ VT 1 (= *arreglar*) to repair, mend, fix 2 [+ *ofensa*] to make amends for; [+ *daño, pérdida*] to make good 3 ~ **fuerzas** to get one's strength back Ⓑ VI 1 ~ **en** (= *darse cuenta de*) to observe, notice; **no reparó en la diferencia** he didn't notice the difference 2 ~ **en** (= *considerar*) to consider; **no ~ en las dificultades** not to consider the problems; **sin ~ en gastos** regardless of the cost; **no ~ en nada** to stop at nothing 3 (*Méx*) [*caballo*] to rear, buck

reparo SM 1 (= *escrúpulo*) scruple, qualm; **no tuvo ~ en hacerlo** he had no qualms about doing it, he did not hesitate to do it 2 (= *objeción*) objection; **poner ~s** to raise objections (**a** to) 3 (*Esgrima*) parry 4 (*Méx*) **dar un ~** [*caballo*] to rear up

repartición SF 1 (= *distribución*) distribution; (= *división*) sharing out, division 2 (*CS Admin*) government department

repartidor(a) SM/F (= *distribuidor*) distributor; (*Com*) deliveryman/deliverywoman ➤ **repartidor(a) de periódicos** paperboy/papergirl ➤ **repartidor(a) de pizzas** pizza delivery boy/girl

repartimiento SM (= *distribución*) distribution; (= *división*) division

repartir /3a/ Ⓐ VT 1 (= *dividir entre varios*) to divide (up), share (out); ~ **dividendos** to share the profits; **los estudiantes están repartidos en cuatro grupos** the students are divided into four groups; **el premio está muy repartido** the prize is shared among many; **"se reparte a domicilio"** "home delivery (service)" 2 (= *distribuir, dar*) [+ *correo, periódicos*] to deliver; [+ *folletos, premios*] to give out, hand out; [+ *naipes*] to deal; **repartieron golpes a todo el que se les acercaba** they lashed out at anyone who came near them 3 (= *esparcir*) **hay guarniciones repartidas por todo el país** there are garrisons dotted about *o* spread about *o* distributed all over the country Ⓑ **repartirse** VPR **se repartieron el botín** they divided (up) *o* shared (out) the spoils among themselves

reparto SM 1 (= *partición*) sharing out ➤ **reparto de beneficios** profit sharing 2 (= *entrega*) [*de correo, periódicos*] delivery; **"reparto a domicilio"** "home delivery (service)";

vamos a efectuar el ~ de premios we are going to give out the prizes **3** (*Cine, Teat*) cast

repasador SM (*Col, CS*) tea towel (*Brit*), dish towel (*EEUU*)

repasar /1a/ VT **1** (= *revisar*) [+ *cuenta*] to check; [+ *lección, apuntes*] to go over (again), revise (*Brit*), review (*EEUU*); (*añadiendo correcciones*) to go over, double-check **2** (*Mec*) (= *arreglar*) to check, overhaul **3** (= *planchar*) to iron **4** (*Cos*) (= *coser*) to sew, sew up **5** (*CS*) [+ *mueble*] to dust

repaso SM **1** (= *revisión*) revision (*Brit*), reviewing (*EEUU*); **ejercicios de** ~ revision exercises (*Brit*), review exercises (*EEUU*); **dale un ~ a esta lección** revise (*Brit*) o review (*EEUU*) this lesson; **los técnicos daban el último ~ a la nave** the technicians were giving the ship a final check; **le di un último ~ a la carta antes de enviarla** I read through the letter again before sending it **2** (*Cos*) (= *arreglo*) **tengo que darle un ~ a esta falda** I have to mend this skirt

repatear* /1a/ VT **ese tipo me repatea** that guy gets on my wick**

repatingarse* /1h/ VPR to lounge, sprawl, loll (back)

repatriación SF repatriation

repatriado/a 🅐 ADJ repatriated **🅑** SM/F repatriate

repatriar /1b/ VT to repatriate

repecho SM steep slope

repelar /1a/ VT (*Méx*) ~ **por algo** to complain about sth

repelente 🅐 ADJ **1** (= *repulsivo*) repellent, repulsive **2** (*) (= *sabelotodo*) **es** ~ he's a know-all (*Brit*) o know-it-all (*EEUU*) **🅑** SM repellent, insect repellent

repeler /2a/ **🅐** VT **1** [+ *enemigo*] to repel, repulse, drive back **2** (= *rechazar*) **este tejido repele el agua** this material is water-resistant **🅑** VI (= *repugnar*) to repel, disgust; **me repele su actitud** I find his attitude repellent **🅒** repelerse VPR (*uso recíproco*) to repel (each other)

repelús* SM **me da** ~ it gives me the willies* o shivers

repensar /1j/ VT to rethink, reconsider

repente SM **1** (= *movimiento*) sudden movement, start; (*fig*) (= *impulso*) sudden impulse ➤ **repente de ira** fit of anger **2 de** ~ (= *de pronto*) suddenly; (= *inesperadamente*) unexpectedly; (*CS*) (= *a lo mejor*) perhaps **3** (*Méx Med*) fit

repentino ADJ (= *súbito*) sudden; (= *imprevisto*) unexpected; [*curva, vuelta*] sharp

repera* SF (*Esp*) **es la** ~ it's the tops*

repercusión SF repercussion; **de amplia** o **de ancha** ~ far-reaching, with profound effects

repercutir /3a/ VI ~ **en** to have repercussions on, affect

repertorio SM **1** (= *lista*) list, index; (= *catálogo*) catalogue, catalog (*EEUU*) **2** (*Teat, Mús*) repertoire

repesca SF **1** (*Escol*) repeat, repeat exam **2** (*Dep*) play-off, play-off for third place

repetición SF (= *acción*) repetition; (= *reaparición*) recurrence

repetido ADJ **1** (= *reiterado*) repeated **2** (= *numeroso*) numerous; **repetidas veces** repeatedly, over and over again **3** [*sello*] duplicate

repetidor SM (*Radio, TV*) booster, booster station

repetir /3k/ **🅐** VT **1** (= *reiterar*) to repeat; (= *rehacer*) to do again; **le repito que es imposible** I repeat that it is impossible; ~ **el postre** to have a second helping o seconds* of dessert; ~ **un curso** to repeat a year **🅑** VI **1** (= *servirse de nuevo*) to have a second helping **2** [*ajo, pepino, chorizo*] **el pepino repite mucho** cucumber keeps repeating on you **🅒** repetirse VPR **1** [*persona*] to repeat o.s. **2** [*suceso*] to recur; **¡ojalá no se repita esto!** I hope this won't happen again!

repetitivo ADJ repetitive

repicar /1g/ VT to ring

repipi* ADJ (= *afectado*) affected; (= *esnob*) la-di-dah*; **es una niña** ~ she's a little madam

repique SM ringing, pealing

repiquetear /1a/ **🅐** VT **1** [+ *campanas*] to ring **2** [+ *tambor*] to tap, beat rapidly **🅑** VI **1** (*Mús*) to peal, ring out **2** [*máquina*] to clatter

repisa SF shelf; **la** ~ **de la chimenea** the mantelpiece

replanteamiento SM rethink, reconsideration

replantear /1a/ **🅐** VT to raise again, reopen **🅑** replantearse VPR ~ **se algo** to rethink o reconsider sth, think again about sth

replegar /1h, 1j/ **🅐** VT **1** (= *plegar*) to fold over; (*de nuevo*) to fold again, refold **2** [+ *tren de aterrizaje*] to retract, draw up **🅑** replegarse VPR (*Mil*) to withdraw, fall back

repleto ADJ **1** (= *lleno*) full up; ~ **de** full of, crammed with **2 estar** ~ [*persona*] to be full up

réplica SF **1** (*frm*) (= *respuesta*) answer; (*Jur*) replication; **derecho de** ~ right of reply; **~s** backchat *sing* **2** (*Arte*) replica, copy

replicar /1g/ **🅐** VT to answer, retort **🅑** VI to argue, answer back; **¡no repliques!** don't answer back!

repliegue SM (*Mil*) withdrawal, retreat

repoblación SF [*de personas*] repopulation; [*de peces*] restocking; [*de árboles*] reafforestation

repoblar /1l/ VT [+ *país*] to repopulate; [+ *río*] to restock; (*con árboles*) to plant trees on

repollita SF (*Col*), **repollito** SM ➤ **repollito de Bruselas** (*CS*) Brussels sprout

repollo SM cabbage

reponer /2q/ (*pp* **repuesto**) **🅐** VT **1** [+ *productos, surtido*] to replenish **2** (= *devolver*) [+ *objeto dañado*] to replace, pay for; ~ **el dinero robado** to pay back the stolen money **3** (= *recuperar*) ~ **fuerzas** to get one's strength back **4** (*Teat*) to revive, put on again; (*TV*) to re-run, repeat (*Brit*) **🅑** reponerse VPR to recover; ~ **se de** to recover from, get over

reportaje SM **1** (*Prensa*) feature; (*TV*) documentary **2** (*LAm*) (= *entrevista*) interview; **hacer un** ~ **a algn** to interview sb

reportar /1a/ (*frm*) **🅐** VT **1** (= *producir*) to give, bring; **esto le habrá reportado algún beneficio** this will have brought him some benefit **2** (*LAm*) (= *denunciar*) to report **🅑** reportarse VPR (*LAm*) (= *presentarse*) to report

reporte SM (*LAm*) to report

reportear /1a/ VT (*LAm*) to report, report on

reportero/a SM/F reporter ➤ **reportero/a gráfico/a** news photographer, press photographer

reposacabezas SM INV headrest

reposado ADJ (= *tranquilo*) quiet; (= *lento*) unhurried, calm

reposar /1a/ **🅐** VI **1** (= *descansar*) to rest **2** (= *apoyarse*) to lie, rest; **su mano reposaba sobre mi hombro** her hand lay o rested on my shoulder; **la columna reposa sobre una base circular** the column is resting o sitting on a circular base **3** [*restos mortales*] to lie, rest **4** (*Culin*) **dejar** ~ **algo** to let sth stand **🅑** VT **1** (= *apoyar*) to lay, rest **2** ~ **la comida** to let one's food settle o go down

reposición SF **1** (= *recambio*) replacement **2** (*Teat*) revival; (*TV*) re-run, repeat (*Brit*)

reposo SM rest, repose (*frm* o *liter*); **estar en** ~ to be resting; **guardar** ~ to rest, stay in bed

repostar /1a/ **🅐** VT ~ **combustible** o **gasolina** (*Aer*) to refuel; (*Aut*) to fill up, fill up with petrol (*Brit*) o gas (*EEUU*) **🅑** VI to refuel

repostería SF cakes and pastries *pl*

reprender /2a/ VT to reprimand, tell off*; [+ *niño*] to scold

represa SF (= *presa*) dam; (= *lago artificial*) lake, pool

represalia SF reprisal; **como** ~ **por** in reprisal for; **tomar ~s** to retaliate, take reprisals (**contra** against)

representación SF **1** [*de concepto, idea, imagen*] representation **2** [*de país, pueblo, organización*] (= *acto*) representation; (= *delegación*) delegation; **en** ~ **de: ir en** ~ **de la empresa** to go as a representative of the company; **habló en** ~ **de todos** she spoke on behalf of everyone **3** (*Teat*) (= *función*) performance; (= *montaje*) production **4** (*Com*) representation; **tener la** ~ **exclusiva de un producto** to be sole agent for a product, have sole agency of a product (*frm*)

representado/a SM/F client

representante SMF **1** [*de organización, país, en parlamento*] representative; **uno de los máximos ~s del surrealismo** one of the greatest exponents *o* representatives of surrealism **2** (*Com*) representative **3** [*de artista, deportista*] agent

representar /1a/ **Ⓐ** VT **1** (= *actuar en nombre de*) [+ *país, votantes*] to represent; [+ *cliente, acusado*] to act for, represent; **el príncipe representó al rey en la ceremonia** the prince attended the ceremony on behalf of the king *o* representing the king **2** (= *simbolizar*) to symbolize, represent **3** (= *reproducir*) to depict; **nuevas formas de ~ el mundo** new ways of representing *o* portraying *o* depicting the world **4** (= *equivaler a*) [+ *porcentaje, mejora, peligro*] to represent; [+ *amenaza*] to pose, represent; **los bantúes representan el 70% de los habitantes de Suráfrica** the Bantu account for *o* represent 70% of the inhabitants of South Africa; **no sabes lo mucho que representa este trabajo para él** you don't know how much this job means to him **5** (= *requerir*) [+ *trabajo, esfuerzo, sacrificio*] to involve **6** (*Teat*) [+ *obra*] to perform; [+ *papel*] to play **7** (= *aparentar*) [+ *edad*] to look **Ⓑ representarse** VPR to imagine

representativo ADJ **1** (= *simbólico, característico*) representative **2** (*Pol*) representative

represión SF **1** [*de deseos, impulsos*] repression **2** [*de rebelión*] suppression

represivo ADJ, **represor** ADJ repressive

reprimenda SF reprimand, rebuke

reprimido/a **Ⓐ** ADJ repressed **Ⓑ** SM/F repressed person

reprimir /3a/ **Ⓐ** VT **1** [+ *deseos, impulsos*] to repress **2** [+ *rebelión*] to suppress **3** [+ *bostezo*] to suppress; [+ *risa*] to hold in, hold back **Ⓑ reprimirse** VPR **~se de hacer algo** to stop o.s. (from) doing sth

reprise[1] SF (*esp LAm Teat*) revival

reprise[2] [re'pris] SM (*a veces* SF) (*Aut*) acceleration

reprobable ADJ reprehensible

reprobación SF reproval, reprobation

reprobar /1l/ **Ⓐ** VT **1** (= *desaprobar*) to reprove, condemn **2** (*LAm Escol*) [+ *materia, alumno*] to fail **Ⓑ** VT (*LAm*) to fail

réprobo ADJ (*frm*) reprehensible

reprochar /1a/ **Ⓐ** VT to reproach; **~ algo a algn** to reproach sb for sth **Ⓑ reprocharse** VPR to reproach o.s.; **no tienes nada que ~te** you have nothing to reproach yourself for

reproche SM reproach

reproducción SF reproduction ➤ **reproducción asistida** assisted reproduction

reproducir /3n/ **Ⓐ** VT **1** (= *volver a producir*) to reproduce **2** (*Biol*) to reproduce, breed **3** (= *copiar*) to reproduce **Ⓑ reproducirse** VPR **1** (*Biol*) to reproduce, breed **2** [*condiciones*] to be reproduced; [*suceso*] to happen again, recur; **se le han reproducido los síntomas** the symptoms have reappeared *o* recurred

reproductor **Ⓐ** ADJ [*órgano, sistema*] reproductive **Ⓑ** SM ➤ **reproductor de CD** CD player

reprografía SF reprography

reptar /1a/ VI to creep, crawl

reptil **Ⓐ** ADJ reptilian **Ⓑ** SM reptile

república SF republic ➤ **república bananera** banana republic ➤ **República Dominicana** Dominican Republic

republicano/a ADJ, SM/F republican; ⮡ *GUERRA CIVIL ESPAÑOLA*

repudiar /1b/ VT **1** [+ *violencia*] to repudiate **2** (= *no reconocer*) to disown

repudio SM repudiation

repuesto **Ⓐ** PP *de* **reponer** **Ⓑ** SM **1** (*Aut, Mec*) spare, spare part; **rueda de ~** spare wheel (*esp Brit*), spare tire (*EEUU*) **2** [*de pluma*] refill

repugnancia SF **1** (= *asco*) disgust, repugnance; (= *aversión*) aversion (**hacia, por** to) **2** (*moral*) repugnance

repugnante ADJ disgusting, revolting

repugnar /1a/ **Ⓐ** VT to disgust, revolt; **ese olor me repugna** that smell is disgusting; **me repugna mirarlo** it disgusts *o* sickens me to watch it **Ⓑ** VI to be disgusting, be revolting

repujado ADJ embossed

repujar /1a/ VT to emboss, work in relief

repulsa SF [*de atentado*] condemnation; [*de oferta, persona*] rejection

repulsión SF **1** (= *aversión*) repulsion, disgust **2** (*Fís*) repulsion

repulsivo ADJ disgusting, revolting

repuntar /1a/ VI **1** [*economía*] to pick up **2** [*marea*] to turn

repunte SM (= *mejora*) upturn; [*de mar*] turn of the tide; **un ~ económico** an economic upturn

reputación SF reputation

reputar /1a/ VT (*frm*) to deem, consider

requebrar /1j/ VT (*liter*) (= *halagar*) to flatter, compliment; (= *flirtear*) to flirt with

requemar /1a/ **Ⓐ** VT (= *quemar*) to scorch; (*Culin*) to burn **Ⓑ requemarse** VPR (= *quemarse*) to get scorched; (= *secarse*) to get parched, dry up; [*comida*] to burn

requerimiento SM **1** (= *petición*) request **2** (= *notificación*) notification

requerir /3i/ **Ⓐ** VT **1** (= *necesitar*) to need, require; **esto requiere cierto cuidado** this requires some care; **"se requiere dominio del inglés"** "good command of English required" **2** (*frm*) (= *solicitar*) to request, ask; **~ a algn que haga algo** to request *o* ask sb to do sth **3** (*frm*) (= *llamar*) to send for, summon (*frm*) **4** (††) **~ de amores** to court, woo **Ⓑ** VI **~ de** (*esp LAm*) to need, require

requesón SM cottage cheese

requete...* PREF extremely ...; **una chica ~guapa** a really attractive girl; **me parece ~bién** it seems absolutely splendid to me

requiebro SM (*liter*) compliment, flirtatious remark

réquiem SM (*pl* ~**s**) requiem

requintar /1a/ VT (*Méx*) to tighten

requisa SF **1** (= *inspección*) inspection **2** (*esp LAm*) (= *confiscación*) seizure, confiscation **3** (*LAm*) (= *registro*) search

requisar /1a/ VT **1** (= *confiscar*) to seize, confiscate **2** (*LAm*) (= *registrar*) to search **3** (*Col*) [+ *persona*] to search

requisito SM requirement, requisite; **cumplir los ~s** to fulfil *o* (*EEUU*) fulfill the requirements ➤ **requisito previo** prerequisite

requisitoria SF **1** (*Jur*) (= *citación*) summons; (= *orden*) writ **2** (*LAm*) (= *interrogatorio*) examination, interrogation

res SF **1** (= *animal*) beast, animal; **100 ~es** 100 animals, 100 head of cattle **2** (*Méx*) (= *carne*) beef

resabiado ADJ [*persona*] knowing, crafty; [*caballo*] vicious

resabido ADJ [*persona*] pretentious, pedantic

resabio SM **1** (= *gusto*) unpleasant aftertaste; **tener ~s de** (*fig*) to smack of **2** (= *costumbre*) bad habit

resaca SF **1** [*de mar*] undertow, undercurrent **2** [*de borrachera*] hangover; **tener ~** to have a hangover, be hung over **3** (*CS*) (*en playa*) line of driftwood and rubbish (*esp Brit*) *o* garbage (*EEUU*) **4** (*CS**) (= *personas*) dregs *pl* of society

resacoso* ADJ hung over

resaltante ADJ (*LAm*) outstanding

resaltar /1a/ **Ⓐ** VI **1** (= *destacarse*) to stand out; **lo escribí en mayúsculas para que ~a** I wrote it in capitals to make it stand out; **entre sus cualidades resalta su elegancia** her most striking quality is her elegance; **hacer ~ algo** to set sth off; (*fig*) to highlight sth **2** (= *sobresalir*) to jut out, project **Ⓑ** VT to highlight

resarcimiento SM (= *pago*) repayment; (= *compensación*) compensation

resarcir /3b/ **Ⓐ** VT (= *pagar*) to repay; (= *compensar*) to indemnify, compensate; **~ a algn de una cantidad** to repay sb a sum; **~ a algn de una pérdida** to compensate sb for a loss Ⓑ **resarcirse** VPR **~se de** to make up for

resbalada SF (*LAm*) slip

resbaladilla SF (*Méx*) slide, chute

resbaladizo ADJ slippery

resbalar /1a/ Ⓐ VI 1 (*al andar*) to slip (**en, sobre** on); (*Aut*) to skid; **le resbalaban las lágrimas por las mejillas** tears were trickling down her cheeks 2 (= *equivocarse*) to slip up, make a slip 3 (*) (= *ser indiferente*) **me resbala** it leaves me cold; **las críticas le resbalan** criticism runs off him like water off a duck's back Ⓑ **resbalarse** VPR to slip

resbalón SM slip; **dar** o **pegar un ~** to slip up

resbaloso ADJ (*LAm*) slippery

rescatar /1a/ VT 1 (*de incendio, naufragio*) to save, rescue 2 [+ *cautivo*] to rescue, free; [+ *pueblo*] to recapture, recover

rescate SM 1 (*en incendio, naufragio*) rescue; **operaciones de ~** rescue operations 2 [*de cautivo*] rescue, freeing; [*de pueblo*] recapture, recovery 3 (= *dinero*) ransom

rescindir /3a/ VT to cancel, rescind

rescisión SF cancellation

rescoldo SM 1 (= *brasa*) embers *pl*, hot ashes *pl* 2 (= *recelo*) doubt, scruple

resecar¹ /1g/ Ⓐ VT to dry (out) Ⓑ **resecarse** VPR to dry (out)

resecar² /1g/ VT (*Med*) to remove

reseco ADJ very dry, too dry

resentido/a Ⓐ ADJ 1 (= *disgustado*) resentful; **aún está ~ porque no lo felicitaste** he still feels resentful that you didn't congratulate him 2 (= *dolorido*) painful Ⓑ SM/F **es un ~** he has a chip on his shoulder, he is resentful

resentimiento SM (= *rencor*) resentment; (= *amargura*) bitterness

resentirse /3i/ VPR 1 (= *estar resentido*) **~ con** o **por algo** to resent sth, feel bitter about sth 2 (= *debilitarse*) to be weakened, suffer; **los cimientos se resintieron con el terremoto** the foundations were weakened by the earthquake; **sin que se resienta el dólar** without the dollar being affected 3 (= *sentir*) **~ de** to suffer from; **todavía me resiento del golpe** I can still feel the effects of the injury

reseña SF 1 (= *resumen*) outline, summary; [*de libro*] review 2 (= *descripción*) brief description

reseñar /1a/ VT 1 (= *resumir*) to write up, write a summary of 2 [+ *libro*] to review

resero SM (*LAm*) (= *vaquero*) cowboy, herdsman

reserva Ⓐ SF 1 (= *provisiones*) [*de minerales, armamentos, vitaminas*] reserve; [*de agua*] supply; [*de productos ya almacenados*] stock; **acumularon grandes ~s de carbón para el invierno** they built up large stocks of coal for the winter; **~s de víveres** food supplies; **de ~** [*precio, jugador, fondo*] reserve *antes de s*; [*zapatos, muda*] spare 2 (= *Econ*) reserve; **las ~s de divisas** currency reserves ➤ **reservas de oro** gold reserves 3 (= *solicitud*) (*en hotel, avión*) reservation; (*en teatro, restaurante*) reservation, booking; **hacer ~s por teléfono** to make a telephone reservation o booking, book by phone 4 (= *territorio protegido*) reserve ➤ **reserva de indios** Indian reservation ➤ **reserva natural** nature reserve 5 (*Mil*) **pasar a la ~** to join the reserve ➤ **reserva activa** active reserve 6 (*Dep*) **estar en la ~** to be a reserve 7 (*Aut*) reserve tank 8 (= *recelo*) reservation; **contestó con ciertas ~s** she answered with some reservation; **nos apoyaron sin ~s** they gave us their unreserved support 9 [*de carácter*] (= *inhibición*) reserve; (= *discreción*) discretion 10 (= *secreto*) confidence; **se ruega absoluta ~** your strictest confidence is requested Ⓑ SMF (*Dep*) reserve; **el banquillo de los ~s** the reserves' bench Ⓒ SM (= *vino*) vintage wine (*that has been aged for a minimum of three years*)

reservación SF (*LAm*) reservation

reservadamente ADV in confidence

reservado Ⓐ ADJ 1 [*actitud, persona*] (= *poco comunicativo*) reserved; (= *discreto*) discreet 2 (= *confidencial*) [*asunto, documento*] confidential Ⓑ SM 1 (= *habitación aparte*) (*en restaurante*) private room; (*en tren*) reserved compartment 2 (*CS*) (= *vino*) vintage wine

reservar /1a/ Ⓐ VT 1 [+ *asiento, habitación, mesa*] to reserve, book; [+ *billete, entrada*] to book 2 (= *guardar*) to keep, keep in reserve, set aside; **lo reserva para el final** he's keeping it till last Ⓑ **reservarse** VPR 1 (*para luego*) to save o.s. (**para** for) 2 (= *encubrir*) to conceal; (= *callar*) to keep to o.s.; **prefiero ~me los detalles** I prefer not to reveal the details

reservista SMF reservist

resfriado Ⓐ ADJ **estar ~** to have a cold Ⓑ SM cold

resfriarse /1c/ VPR to catch a cold

resfrío SM (*SAm*) cold

resguardar /1a/ Ⓐ VT to protect, shield (**de** from) Ⓑ **resguardarse** VPR to take shelter (**de** from)

resguardo SM 1 [*de compra*] slip, receipt; [*de cheque*] stub 2 (= *protección*) defence, defense (*EEUU*), protection

residencia SF 1 (= *casa*) residence; (= *hotel*) guest house, boarding house; **segunda ~** second home ➤ **residencia canina** dogs' home, kennels *sing y pl*, kennel ➤ **residencia de ancianos** residential home, old people's home ➤ **residencia de estudiantes** hall of residence (*esp Brit*), dormitory (*EEUU*) ➤ **residencia sanitaria** hospital ➤ **residencia universitaria** hall of residence (*esp Brit*), dormitory (*EEUU*) 2 (= *domicilio*) residence; **fijó su ~ en Barcelona** he took up residence in Barcelona; **con ~ en Bogotá** resident in Bogotá 3 (= *estancia*) residence; **permiso de ~** residence permit

residencial Ⓐ ADJ residential Ⓑ SF (*CS*) boarding house, small hotel

residente ADJ, SMF resident; **no ~** non-resident

residir /3a/ VI 1 (= *vivir*) to reside, live 2 **~ en** (= *radicar en*) to reside in, lie in; (= *consistir en*) to consist in; **la dificultad reside en que ...** the difficulty resides in o lies in the fact that ...

residual ADJ residual, residuary; **aguas ~es** sewage *sing*

residuo SM 1 (= *parte que queda*) residue; (*Mat*) remainder; (*Quím*) residuum 2 **residuos** (= *materiales*) waste *sing*, waste products ➤ **residuos radiactivos** radioactive waste *sing* ➤ **residuos sólidos** solid waste *sing* ➤ **residuos tóxicos** toxic waste *sing*

resignación SF resignation

resignado ADJ resigned

resignarse /1a/ VPR to resign o.s. (**a, con** to); **~ a hacer algo** to resign o.s. to doing sth

> Recuérdese que las preposiciones en inglés rigen gerundio y no infinitivo, de ahí **to resign o.s. to doing sth**.

resina SF resin

resinoso ADJ resinous

resistencia SF 1 (= *oposición*) resistance; **la Resistencia** (*Hist*) the Resistance; **los acusaron de ~ a la autoridad** they were charged with resisting arrest; **ofrecer** u **oponer ~** to offer resistance, resist ➤ **resistencia pasiva** passive resistance 2 (= *aguante*) stamina; **una carrera de ~** an endurance race 3 (*a enfermedad, frío*) resistance 4 [*de materiales*] strength 5 (*Elec*) (= *cualidad*) resistance; (= *componente de circuito*) resistor; [*de plancha, secador*] element

resistente ADJ (= *gen*) resistant (**a** to); [*tela*] tough, hard-wearing (*esp Brit*); [*ropa*] strong; (*Bot*) hardy; **~ al calor** resistant to heat, heat-resistant; **~ al fuego** fireproof

resistir /3a/ Ⓐ VT 1 [+ *peso*] to bear, take, support; [+ *presión*] to take, withstand 2 [+ *ataque, tentación*] to resist; [+ *propuesta*] to resist, oppose, make a stand against 3 (= *tolerar*) to put up with, endure

Ⓑ VI **1** (= *oponer resistencia*) to resist **2** (= *durar*) to last (out), hold out **3** (= *soportar peso*) **¿~á la silla?** will the chair take it? **Ⓒ resistirse** VPR **1** = **B1** **2** (= *no estar dispuesto*) **~se a hacer algo** to be reluctant to do sth, resist doing sth

> Recuérdese que **resist** rige gerundio y no infinitivo:

no pude ~me a probar el pastel I couldn't resist trying the cake; **me resisto a creerlo** I find it hard to believe **3** [*materia, problema*] **se me resiste la química** I'm not very good at chemistry

resol SM glare of the sun

resolana SF (*LAm*) (= *resol*) glare of the sun; (= *sitio*) sunspot, suntrap

resollar /1l/ VI (= *respirar*) to breathe noisily; (= *jadear*) to puff and pant

resolución SF **1** (= *decisión*) decision; **tomar una ~** to take a decision **2** [*de problema*] (= *acción*) solving; (= *respuesta*) solution **3** [*de conflicto*] resolution **4** (= *determinación*) resolve, determination; **obrar con ~** to act with determination **5** [*de imagen*] **alta ~** high resolution; **baja ~** low resolution

resoluto ADJ determined

resolver /2h/ (*pp* **resuelto**) **Ⓐ** VT **1** (= *solucionar*) [+ *problema*] to solve; [+ *asunto*] to decide, settle; **crimen sin ~** unsolved crime **2** (= *decidirse por*) **~ hacer algo** to resolve to do sth **Ⓑ** VI to rule, decide; **~ a favor de algn** to rule o decide in sb's favour **Ⓒ resolverse** VPR **1** [*problema*] to resolve itself, work out **2** (= *decidir*) **~se a hacer algo** to resolve to do sth

resonancia SF **1** (= *reverberación*) resonance; (= *eco*) echo **2** (*Med*) (*tb* **~ magnética**) magnetic resonance imaging, MRI **3** (= *consecuencia*) wide impact, wide effect

resonar /1l/ VI to resound, ring (**de** with)

resondrar* /1a/ VT (*Per*) to tell off*, tick off (*Brit**)

resoplar /1a/ VI to puff

resoplido SM (*de cansancio*) puff, puffing; **dar ~s** [*persona*] to breathe heavily, puff; [*motor*] to chug, puff

resorte SM **1** (= *muelle*) spring **2** (= *medio*) means, expedient; **tocar todos los ~s** to use all one's influence, pull all the strings one can **3** (*Méx*) (= *gomita*) elastic

resortera SF (*Méx*) catapult (*Brit*), slingshot (*EEUU*)

respaldar /1a/ VT **1** (= *apoyar*) to back, support **2** [+ *documento*] to endorse **Ⓑ respaldarse** VPR **1** (= *apoyarse*) **~se con** o **en** to base one's arguments on **2** (= *reclinarse*) to lean back (**contra** against; **en** on)

respaldo SM **1** [*de silla*] back; [*de cama*] head **2** [*de documento*] (= *dorso*) back; (= *cosa escrita*) endorsement **3** (= *apoyo*) support, backing

respectar /1a/ VT **por lo que respecta a** as for, with regard to

respectivamente ADV respectively

respectivo ADJ **1** (= *correspondiente*) respective **2 en lo ~ a** as regards, with regard to

respecto SM **al ~** on this matter; **a ese ~** in that respect; **no sé nada al ~** I know nothing about it; (**con**) **~ a ◊ ~ de** with regard to, in relation to; (**con**) **~ a mí** as for me

respetable **Ⓐ** ADJ respectable **Ⓑ** SM **el ~** (*Teat hum*) the audience, the public

respetar /1a/ **Ⓐ** VT **1** [+ *persona, derecho, opinión*] to respect; **hacerse ~** to win respect, earn respect; **"respeten las plantas"** "be careful of the plants" **2** (= *obedecer*) [+ *normas*] to observe; **no respetan los semáforos** they ignore the traffic lights, they do not observe the traffic lights **3** [+ *forma original*] to conserve **Ⓑ respetarse** VPR (*reflexivo*) to have self-respect, respect o.s.; (*mutuo*) to respect each other

respeto SM **1** (= *consideración*) respect; **~ a las personas mayores** respect for one's elders; **con el debido ~, creo que**

se equivoca with all due respect, I think you're wrong; **~ a** o **de sí mismo** self-respect; **¡un ~!** show some respect!; **faltar al ~ a algn** to be disrespectful to sb, be rude to sb; **guardar ~ a algn** to respect sb; **perder el ~ a algn** to lose one's respect for sb; **por ~ a algn** out of consideration for sb; **tener ~ a algn** to respect sb **2** (*) (= *miedo*) **volar me impone mucho ~** I'm very wary of flying; **les tengo mucho ~ a las tormentas** I'm fearful of thunderstorms

respetuoso ADJ respectful

respingado ADJ snub, turned-up

respingo SM start, jump; **dar un ~** to start, jump

respingón ADJ turned-up

respiración SF breathing; **ejercicios de ~** breathing o (*más frm*) respiration exercises; **llegué sin ~** I arrived breathless o out of breath; **contener la ~** to hold one's breath; **dejar a algn sin ~** to leave sb breathless, take sb's breath away ➤ **respiración artificial** artificial respiration ➤ **respiración asistida** artificial respiration (*by machine*); **está con ~ asistida** she is on a ventilator o respirator ➤ **respiración boca a boca** mouth-to-mouth resuscitation; **se le hizo la ~ boca a boca** he was given mouth-to-mouth resuscitation, he was given the kiss of life (*Brit*)

respiradero SM vent, valve

respirador SM (*tb* **~ artificial**) ventilator, (artificial) respirator

respirar /1a/ **Ⓐ** VI **1** (= *tomar aire*) to breathe; **respire hondo** take a deep breath, breathe deeply; **salí al balcón a ~ un poco** I went out to the balcony to get some air **2** (= *descansar*) **no me dejan ni tiempo para ~** they don't give me time to breathe; **sin ~** without a break, without respite **3** (= *sentir alivio*) to breathe again; **~ tranquilo** to breathe easily o freely (again) **4** (= *hablar*) **no respiró en toda la reunión** he didn't utter a word in the whole meeting **5** (= *ventilarse*) **5.1** [*fruta, vino*] to breathe **5.2** (*Aut*) **levanta el capó para que respire el motor** put the bonnet up to ventilate the engine **Ⓑ** VT **1** [+ *aire, oxígeno*] to breathe **2** (= *mostrar*) [+ *optimismo, felicidad*] to exude, radiate **3** (= *notar*) **se respiraba ya un ambiente prebélico** there was a sense of war in the air; **¿cuál es el clima que se respira en el país tras el atentado?** what is the feeling in the country following the bomb attack?

respiratorio ADJ [*insuficiencia, sistema, vías*] respiratory; [*problemas, dificultades*] breathing *antes de s*, respiratory

respiro SM **1** (= *respiración*) breath; **dio un ~ hondo** he took a deep breath; **lanzó un ~ de alivio** she breathed a sigh of relief **2** (= *descanso*) [*de trabajo, esfuerzo*] break, rest; [*de ataque, preocupación*] respite; **los clientes no nos dan un momento de ~** the customers don't give us a moment's peace; **tomarse un ~** to take a break, take a breather* **3** [*de enfermedad, preocupación*] relief **4** (= *prórroga*) extension; **acordaron conceder un ~ de seis meses** they agreed to an extension of six months o agreed to grant six months' grace

resplandecer /2d/ VI **1** (= *relucir*) to shine; [*joyas*] to sparkle, glitter **2** (*con sentimientos*) to shine; **~ de felicidad** to be radiant, shine with happiness

resplandeciente ADJ **1** (= *brillante*) shining; [*joyas*] sparkling, glittering **2** (*de alegría*) radiant (**de** with)

resplandor SM (= *brillantez*) brilliance, brightness; [*de joyas*] sparkle, glitter

responder /2a/ **Ⓐ** VI **1** (= *contestar*) (*a pregunta, llamada*) to answer; (*en diálogo, carta*) to reply; **~ a** [+ *pregunta*] to answer; [+ *carta*] to reply to, answer; [+ *críticas, peticiones*] to respond to, answer; **~ al nombre de** [*persona*] to go by the name of; [*animal*] to answer to the name of **2** (= *replicar*) to answer back **3** (= *reaccionar*) to respond; **los frenos no respondieron** the brakes didn't respond; **no respondió al tratamiento** he did not respond to the treatment **4** (= *rendir*) [*negocio*] to do well; [*máquina*] to perform well;

[*empleado*] to produce results
5 (= *satisfacer*) ~ **a** [+ *exigencias, necesidades*] to meet; [+ *expectativas*] to come up to
6 (= *corresponder*) ~ **a** [+ *idea, imagen, información*] to correspond to; [+ *descripción*] to answer, fit
7 (= *responsabilizarse*) **yo ya te avisé, así que no respondo** I warned you before, I'm not responsible; ~ **de** [+ *acto, consecuencia*] to answer for; [+ *seguridad, deuda*] to be responsible for; [+ *honestidad*] to vouch for; **yo no respondo de lo que pueda pasar** I cannot answer for the consequences
8 ~ **por algn** to vouch for sb
Ⓑ VT (= *contestar*) [+ *pregunta, llamada*] to answer; **me respondió que no sabía** she told me that *o* she replied that she didn't know; **le respondí que sí** I said yes

respondón* ADJ cheeky, lippy*, mouthy*

responsabilidad SF responsibility; (*Jur*) liability; **bajo mi ~** under my responsibility; **hay que exigir ~es al gobierno por los hechos** the government must be held accountable *o* responsible for what happened; **cargo de ~** position of responsibility ➤ **responsabilidad civil** public liability, public liability insurance

responsabilizar /1f/ Ⓐ VT to blame, hold responsible; ~ **a algn de algo** to hold sb responsible for sth, place the blame for sth on sb Ⓑ **responsabilizarse** VPR **no me responsabilizo de sus actos** I'm not responsible for her actions; ~**se de un atentado** to claim responsibility for an attack

responsable Ⓐ ADJ **1** (= *sensato*) responsible
2 (= *encargado*) responsible, in charge; **es ~ de la política municipal** she is responsible for *o* in charge of council policy
3 (= *culpable*) responsible; **el conductor ~ del accidente** the driver responsible for the accident; **el fabricante es ~ de los daños causados** the manufacturer is liable for the damage caused; **hacerse ~ de algo** to take responsibility for sth
Ⓑ SMF **1** (= *culpable*) **tú eres la ~ de lo ocurrido** you're responsible for what happened; **la policía busca a los ~s** the police are looking for the culprits
2 (= *encargado*) **el ~** the person in charge

responso SM *prayer for the dead*

respuesta SF **1** (= *contestación*) (*a pregunta, en examen, test*) answer; (*a carta, comentario*) reply; **preguntas y ~s** questions and answers **2** (= *reacción*) (*ante un estímulo, ataque*) response; (*a problema*) answer

resquebrajar /1a/ Ⓐ VT to crack, split Ⓑ **resquebrajarse** VPR to crack, split

resquemor SM **1** (= *resentimiento*) resentment, bitterness **2** (= *sospecha*) secret suspicion

resquicio SM **1** (= *abertura*) chink, crack **2** (= *oportunidad*) opening, opportunity; **un ~ de esperanza** a glimmer of hope ➤ **resquicio legal** legal loophole

resta SF (*Mat*) subtraction

restablecer /2d/ Ⓐ VT [+ *relaciones*] to re-establish; [+ *orden*] to restore Ⓑ **restablecerse** VPR (*Med*) to recover

restablecimiento SM **1** [*de relaciones*] re-establishment; [*de orden*] restoration **2** (*Med*) recovery

restallar /1a/ VI [*látigo*] to crack; [*lengua*] to click; **hacer ~ el látigo** to crack the whip

restallido SM [*de látigo*] crack; [*de lengua*] click

restante ADJ remaining; **lo ~** the rest, the remainder; **los ~s** the rest

restañar /1a/ VT (*liter*) ~ **las heridas** to heal the wounds

restar /1a/ Ⓐ VT **1** (*Mat*) to take away, subtract; **réstale 10 a 24** subtract 10 from 24, take away 10 from 24; **a esta cifra hay que ~le los gastos** you have to deduct *o* subtract the expenses from this figure **2** (= *quitar*) ~ **autoridad a algn** to take away authority from sb; **le restó importancia** he did not give it much importance **3** (*Dep*) [+ *pelota*] to return Ⓑ VI (*frm*) to remain, be left

restauración SF **1** (*Arte, Hist*) restoration; **la Restauración** (*Esp*) *the restoration of the Spanish monarchy (1873)*
2 (= *hostelería*) **la ~** the restaurant industry

restaurador(a) SM/F **1** (*Arte*) restorer **2** [*de hotel*] restaurateur, restaurant owner

restaurante SM restaurant

restaurar /1a/ VT to restore

restiramiento SM (*Méx*) ➤ **restiramiento facial** facelift

restitución SF **1** (= *devolución*) return
2 (= *restablecimiento*) restoration

restituir /3g/ VT **1** (= *devolver*) to return, give back (**a** to)
2 (= *restablecer*) to restore

resto SM **1** (*lo que queda*) rest; (*Mat*) remainder; **yo haré el ~** I'll do the rest; ✦ MODISMO **para los ~s*: yo me quedo aquí para los ~s** I'm staying here for good **2** restos [*de edificio, muralla*] remains; [*de comida*] leftovers, scraps; [*de avión, naufragio*] wreckage *sing* ➤ **restos de edición** remainders ➤ **restos de serie** leftovers, remainders ➤ **restos humanos** human remains ➤ **restos mortales** (mortal) remains **3** (*Dep*) (= *devolución*) return (of service); (= *jugador*) receiver

restorán SM (*LAm*) restaurant

restregar /1h, 1j/ VT (*con cepillo, estropajo*) to scrub; (*con trapo*) to rub, rub hard

restricción SF (= *limitación*) restriction, limitation; **sin ~ de** without restrictions as to; **hablar sin restricciones** to talk freely ➤ **restricciones presupuestarias** budgetary constraints

restrictivo ADJ restrictive

restringido ADJ restricted, limited

restringir /3c/ VT to restrict, limit (**a** to)

resucitar /1a/ Ⓐ VT **1** (*Rel*) to raise from the dead **2** [+ *idea, temor, fantasma*] to bring back, revive Ⓑ VI (*Rel*) to rise from the dead

resuello SM **1** (= *aliento*) breath; (= *respiración*) breathing; **sin ~** out of breath, out of puff* **2** (= *jadeo*) puff; (= *respiración ruidosa*) wheeze

resuelto Ⓐ PP *de* **resolver** Ⓑ ADJ (= *determinado*) resolute, resolved, determined; **estar ~ a algo** to be set on sth; **estar ~ a hacer algo** to be determined to do sth

resulta SF result; **de ~s de** as a result of

resultado SM **1** [*de elecciones, examen, competición*] result; [*de partido*] score, result **2** (= *efecto*) result; **dar ~** [*plan, método*] to succeed, be successful; [*tratamiento*] to produce results **3** (*Mat*) result

resultante Ⓐ ADJ resulting *antes de s*, resultant (*frm*) *antes de s*; ~ **de** resulting from Ⓑ SF (*Fís*) resultant

resultar /1a/ VI **1** (= *tener como resultado*) **1.1** (+ ADJ, SUSTANTIVO) to be; **el conductor resultó muerto** the driver was killed; **resultó ganador un escritor desconocido** the winner was an unknown writer **1.2** (+ INFIN) **resultó ser el padre de mi amigo** he turned out to be my friend's father **1.3** **resulta que** it turns out that; **al final resultó que era inocente** he proved *o* he turned out to be innocent in the end, in the end it turned out that he was innocent; **me gustaría ir, pero resulta que no tengo dinero** I'd like to go, but the thing is *o* the fact is that I haven't got any money **2** (= *salir*) to turn out, work out
3 (*frm*) (= *ser*) (+ ADJ) **3.1** (*uso impersonal*) **resulta difícil decidir si ...** it is hard to decide whether ...; **resulta más barato hacerlo así** it works out cheaper to do it this way **3.2** (*con complemento de persona*) **la casa nos resulta muy pequeña** the house is too small for us; **me resulta simpático** he seems like a nice guy to me **4** (*frm*) ~ **de** to be the result of, result from

resultón* ADJ attractive

resumen SM summary; **hacer un ~ de algo** to summarize sth; **en ~** (= *en conclusión*) to sum up; (= *brevemente*) in short

resumidero SM (*RPl*) = **sumidero**

resumir /3a/ Ⓐ VT (= *condensar*) to summarize; (= *cortar*) to abridge, shorten; (= *recapitular*) to sum up; **la situación se resume en pocas palabras** the situation can be summed up in a few words
Ⓑ VI **bueno, resumiendo, ...** so, to sum up, ..., so, in short, ...

© **resumirse** VPR **~se en** to boil *o* come down to

⚠ **resumir ≠ resume**

resurgimiento SM resurgence
resurgir /3c/ VI to reappear, revive
resurrección SF resurrection
retablo SM (*Arte*) altarpiece; (*Teat*) tableau
retacear /1a/ VT (*CS*) to skimp on; **nos retacean los recursos** our resources are skimped
retachar /1a/ VT, VI (*Méx*) to bounce
retaco SM midget
retacón* ADJ (*esp CS*) short, squat
retador(a) SM/F (*LAm Dep*) challenger
retaguardia SF (*Mil*) rearguard; **estar** *o* **ir a la** (*o* **en**) **~** to bring up the rear
retahíla SF (= *serie*) string, series; [*de injurias*] stream
retal SM remnant
retaliación SF (*LAm*) retaliation
retama SF, **retamo** SM (*LAm*) broom
retar /1a/ VT **1** (= *desafiar*) to challenge **2** (*CS**) (= *regañar*) to tell off
retardar /1a/ VT [+ *marcha*] to hold up; [+ *tren*] to delay, make late
retardo SM (*frm*) delay
retazo SM remnant, bit, piece; **retazos** snippets, bits and pieces
retén SM **1** (= *reserva*) reserve, store; **tener algo a ~** to have sth in reserve **2** (*Mil*) reserves *pl*, reinforcements *pl*; **hombre de ~** reserve; **estar de ~** to be on call **3** (*Ven*) (= *correccional*) remand home **4** (*Col, Méx*) (*en carretera*) checkpoint
retención SF **1** (= *contención*) (*tb Med*) retention **2** (*Fin*) (= *cantidad*) deduction; (= *acción*) stoppage ➤ **retención fiscal** deduction for tax purposes
retener /2k/ **©** VT **1** (= *no dejar marchar*) to keep; [*la policía*] to hold, detain; **lo retiene su familia** his family is what keeps him there; **retuvieron a los inmigrantes en la aduana** they held *o* detained the immigrants at customs; **una llamada de última hora me retuvo en la oficina** a last-minute phone call held me up *o* kept me back at the office **2** (= *conservar*) [+ *datos, información*] to withhold; [+ *pasaporte*] to retain **3** (= *memorizar*) to retain **4** (*Fin*) [+ *dinero*] to deduct **5** [+ *calor*] to retain; [+ *líquido*] to hold; **no puede ~ la orina** he can't hold his water **©** **retenerse** VPR to restrain o.s.
retentiva SF memory
reticencia SF **1** (= *renuencia*) unwillingness, reluctance **2** (= *reserva*) reticence
reticente ADJ **1** (= *reacio*) unwilling, reluctant; **estar** *o* **ser ~ a hacer algo** to be unwilling *o* reluctant to do sth **2** (= *con reserva*) reticent
retina SF retina
retintín SM **1** (= *tono*) sarcastic tone; **decir algo con ~** to say sth sarcastically **2** (= *tintineo*) tinkle, tinkling; [*de llaves*] jingle, jangle
retinto ADJ (*esp LAm*) very dark
retirada SF **1** (*Mil*) retreat, withdrawal; **batirse en ~** ◇ **emprender la ~** to retreat, beat a retreat **2** [*de dinero, embajador*] withdrawal **3** [*de vehículo, objeto*] removal
retirado ADJ **1** [*lugar*] remote **2** [*vida*] quiet **3** (= *jubilado*) retired
retirar /1a/ **©** VT **1** [+ *acusación, apoyo, subvención*] to withdraw; [+ *demanda*] to withdraw, take back; **~ la palabra a algn** to stop speaking to sb; **~ el saludo a algn** to stop saying hello to sb **2** (*del uso público*) [+ *moneda, sello*] to withdraw (from circulation); [+ *autobús, avión*] to withdraw (from service)

3 [+ *permiso, carnet, pasaporte*] to withdraw, take away **4** (*del banco*) [+ *dinero*] to withdraw **5** [+ *tropas*] to withdraw; [+ *embajador*] to recall, withdraw; [+ *atleta, caballo*] to withdraw, scratch **6** (= *quitar*) to take away, remove; **la camarera retiró las copas** the waitress took the glasses away **7** [+ *cabeza, cara*] to pull back, pull away; [+ *mano*] to draw back, withdraw **8** (= *jubilar*) to retire, pension off **©** **retirarse** VPR **1** (= *moverse*) to move back *o* away (**de** from); **retírate de la entrada** move back *o* away from the door; **~se ante un peligro** to shrink back from a danger **2** (= *irse*) **puede usted ~se** you may leave; **~se de las negociaciones** to withdraw from the negotiations; **se ~on del torneo** (*antes de empezar*) they withdrew from *o* pulled out of the tournament; (*una vez empezado*) they retired from *o* pulled out of the tournament; **¡no se retire!** (*al teléfono*) hold the line! **3** **~se (a su habitación)** to retire (to one's room *o* to bed) (*frm, liter*) **4** (*Mil*) to withdraw, retreat **5** (= *jubilarse*) to retire (**de** from)
retiro SM **1** (= *jubilación*) retirement **2** (= *pensión*) retirement pension, pension **3** (= *lugar*) quiet place, secluded spot; (*Rel*) retreat
reto SM **1** (= *desafío*) challenge **2** (*CS*) (= *reprimenda*) telling off, scolding
retobado ADJ (*LAm*) (= *rebelde*) rebellious; (= *terco*) obstinate
retobarse* /1a/ VPR (*LAm*) to get awkward, get bolshie (*Brit**)
retocar /1g/ **©** VT [+ *dibujo, foto*] to touch up **©** **retocarse** VPR (*Esp*) to freshen one's make-up
retomar /1a/ VT to take up again
retoñar /1a/ VI (*Bot*) to sprout, shoot
retoño SM **1** (*Bot*) sprout, shoot **2** (*) (= *niño*) kid*
retoque SM (= *acción*) touching-up; **dar los últimos ~s a algo** to put the finishing touches to sth
retorcer /2b, 2h/ **©** VT **1** [+ *brazo*] to twist; [+ *manos, ropa lavada*] to wring **2** [+ *argumento*] to turn, twist; [+ *sentido*] to twist **©** **retorcerse** VPR **1** [*cordel*] to get into knots, get tangled (up) *o* twisted **2** [*persona*] **~se de dolor** to writhe in pain; **~se de risa** to double up with laughter **3** **~ el bigote** to twirl one's moustache
retorcido ADJ **1** [*estilo*] involved **2** [*persona, mente*] devious
retorcijón SM (*LAm*) = **retortijón**
retorcimiento SM **1** [*de brazo*] twisting; [*de manos, ropa*] wringing **2** [*de estilo*] involved nature **3** [*de persona, mente*] deviousness
retórica SF rhetoric
retórico ADJ rhetorical
retornable ADJ returnable; **no ~** non-returnable
retornar /1a/ **©** VI (= *venir*) to return, come back; (= *irse*) to return, go back **©** VT **1** (= *devolver*) to return, give back **2** (= *reponer*) to replace, put back
retorno SM return; **viaje de ~** return journey; **operación ~** (*Sp*) *traffic control operation for the mass return home after holidays*
retortero* SM **andar al ~** to bustle about; **nos lleva** *o* **trae siempre al ~** she always has us running around after her
retortijón SM (*tb* **~ de tripas**) stomach cramp
retozar /1f/ VI to romp, frolic, frisk about
retozón ADJ **1** (= *juguetón*) playful, frisky **2** [*risa*] bubbling
retracción SF retraction
retractar /1a/ **©** VT to retract, withdraw **©** **retractarse** VPR to retract, recant; **me retracto** I take that back
retráctil ADJ **1** (*Aer*) retractable **2** (*Biol*) retractile
retraer /2o/ **©** VT [+ *uñas*] to draw in, retract **©** **retraerse** VPR to go into one's shell
retraído ADJ shy, reserved
retraimiento SM shyness, reserve

retransmisión SF (*TV, Radio*) **durante la ~** during the broadcast ➤ **retransmisión en diferido** delayed transmission ➤ **retransmisión en directo** live broadcast, live transmission

retransmitir /3a/ VT (*TV*) to show, broadcast; (*Radio*) to broadcast

retrasado/a Ⓐ ADJ **1** (*en una actividad*) **estar** o **ir ~** to be behind; **estar ~ en los pagos** to be behind in o with one's payments, be in arrears; **vamos ~s en la producción** we are lagging behind in the production **2** (*en el tiempo*) late **3** (*país, pueblo, sociedad*) backward **4** (*ideas, estilo*) outdated, outmoded **5** (*reloj*) slow **6** (*mentalmente*) mentally retarded Ⓑ SM/F (*tb ~/a mental*) mentally handicapped

retrasar /1a/ Ⓐ VT **1** (= *aplazar*) (+ *suceso, acción*) to postpone, put off; (+ *fecha*) to put back; **~ la edad de jubilación** to raise the retirement age **2** (= *retardar*) to delay, hold up; **varios problemas ~on la salida del avión** a number of problems delayed o held up the departure of the plane **3** (+ *reloj*) to put back; **esta noche tenemos que ~ los relojes** we have to put the clocks back tonight Ⓑ VI (*reloj*) to be slow Ⓒ **retrasarse** VPR **1** (*persona, vuelo*) to be late; **se han retrasado en el pago de los sueldos** they're late in paying the wages; **se han retrasado en el pago del alquiler** they're in arrears with the rent, they've fallen behind with the rent **2** (*acontecimiento, producción*) to be delayed, be held up **3** (= *quedarse atrás*) (*en los estudios*) to get behind, fall behind; (*andando*) to lag behind

retraso SM **1** (*de persona, vuelo*) delay; **perdona el ~** sorry for the delay; **ir con ~** to be running late; **llegar con ~** to be late, arrive late; **llegó con 25 minutos de ~** he was o arrived 25 minutes late; **llevo un ~ de seis semanas en mi trabajo** I'm six weeks behind with my work; **las obras se iniciaron con ~** the building work started late **2** (*en país, investigación*) backwardness **3** ➤ **retraso mental** mental deficiency

retratar /1a/ Ⓐ VT (*Arte*) to paint the portrait of; (*Fot*) to photograph, take a picture of **2** (= *representar*) to portray, depict, describe Ⓑ **retratarse** VPR (*en cuadro*) to have one's portrait painted; (*en fotografía*) to have one's photograph taken

retratista SMF (*Arte*) portrait painter; (*Fot*) photographer

retrato SM **1** (*Arte*) portrait; (*Fot*) photograph, portrait; ✦ MODISMO **ser el vivo ~ de algn** to be the spitting image of sb ➤ **retrato hablado** (*LAm*) Identikit picture **2** (= *descripción*) portrayal, depiction, description

retrato-robot SM (*pl* **retratos-robot**) (*Esp*) Identikit picture

retreta SF **1** (*Mil*) retreat **2** (*LAm*) (= *concierto*) open-air band concert

retrete SM lavatory (*esp Brit*), bathroom (*EEUU*)

retribución SF (= *pago*) pay, payment; (= *recompensa*) reward

retribuir /3g/ VT **1** (= *pagar*) to pay; (= *recompensar*) to reward **2** (*LAm*) (+ *favor*) to repay, return

retro* ADJ INV (*moda*) retro

retroactivo ADJ retroactive, retrospective; **ley con** o **de efecto ~** retroactive o retrospective law; **un aumento ~ desde abril** a rise (*Brit*) o raise (*esp EEUU*) backdated to April

retroalimentación SF feedback

retroceder /2a/ VI **1** (= *moverse*) to move back, go back; (*ejército*) to fall back, retreat; (*aguas*) to go down; **tienes que ~ a la primera casilla** you have to go back to the first square **2** (= *desistir*) to give up

retroceso SM **1** (= *movimiento*) backward movement; (*Mil*) retreat **2** (*de rifle*) recoil **3** (*Tip*) backspace

retrógrado ADJ (*ideas*) retrograde; (*persona*) conservative

retropropulsión SF jet propulsion

retroproyector SM overhead projector

retrospectiva SF **1** (*Arte*) retrospective, retrospective exhibition **2 en ~** with hindsight

retrospectivo ADJ retrospective; **escena retrospectiva** flashback; **mirada retrospectiva** look back (**a** at)

retrotraer /2o/ VT to carry back (in time), take back; **ahora podemos ~ su origen al siglo XI** now we can take its origin further back to the 11th century

retrovisor SM (*tb* **espejo ~**) driving mirror, rear-view mirror

retrucar /1g/ VI **1** (*CS*) (= *replicar*) to retort **2** (*Billar*) to kiss

retruécano SM pun, play on words

retumbar /1a/ VI **1** (*artillería*) to boom, thunder; (*trueno*) to roll, crash **2** (*voz, pasos*) to echo

reubicar /1g/ VT (+ *trabajador, empresa*) to relocate; (+ *comunidad, pueblo*) to resettle

reuma SM, **reúma** SM rheumatism

reumático ADJ rheumatic

reumatismo SM rheumatism

reunido ADJ (*Esp*) **estar ~** to be in a meeting

reunificación SF reunification

reunificar /1g/ VT to reunify

reunión SF **1** (*de trabajo*) meeting; (*social*) gathering ➤ **reunión de trabajo** business meeting **2** (= *gente reunida*) meeting

reunir /3a/ Ⓐ VT **1** (= *juntar*) to join, join together **2** (= *recolectar*) (+ *cosas dispersas*) to gather, gather together, get together; (+ *datos*) to collect, gather; (+ *recursos*) to pool; (+ *colección*) to assemble, make; (+ *dinero*) to collect; (+ *fondos*) to raise **3** (+ *personas*) to bring together, get together **4** (+ *cualidades*) to combine; (+ *condiciones*) to have, possess; **la casa no reúne las condiciones mínimas para vivir** the house doesn't meet the basic living standards; **creo ~ todos los requisitos** I think I meet o satisfy all the necessary requirements Ⓑ **reunirse** VPR (*en asamblea*) to meet, gather; (*socialmente*) to get together

reutilizable ADJ reusable

reutilizar /1f/ VT to reuse

reválida SF final examination

revalidar /1a/ VT (= *ratificar*) to confirm, ratify; **~ un título** (*Dep*) to regain a title

revalorización SF, **revaloración** SF (*de moneda*) revaluation; (*Fin*) reassessment

revalorizar /1f/ Ⓐ VT (+ *moneda*) to revalue; (*Fin*) to reassess Ⓑ **revalorizarse** VPR (*divisa*) to rise; (*mercancía*) to rise in value

revaluación SF revaluation

revaluar /1e/ VT to revalue

revancha SF **1** (= *venganza*) revenge; **tomarse la ~** to get one's revenge, get one's own back **2** (*Dep*) return match (*Brit*), rematch (*esp EEUU*); (*Boxeo*) return fight

revelación Ⓐ SF (*de algo oculto*) revelation; (*de un secreto*) disclosure; **fue una ~ para mí** it was a revelation to me Ⓑ ADJ INV **el coche ~ del año** the surprise car of the year

revelado SM developing

revelador Ⓐ ADJ revealing Ⓑ SM (*Fot*) developer

revelar /1a/ Ⓐ VT **1** (= *descubrir*) to reveal; **~ un secreto** to reveal o give away a secret **2** (*frm*) (= *evidenciar*) to reveal, show **3** (*Fot*) to develop Ⓑ **revelarse** VPR **~se como: se ha revelado como una gran pianista** she has turned out to be o shown herself to be a great pianist

revender /2a/ VT **1** (+ *entradas*) to resell, tout (*Brit*), scalp (*EEUU**) **2** (= *vender*) to retail

revenido ADJ stale

revenirse /3r/ VPR to go stale

reventa SF **1** (*de entradas*) touting (*Brit*), scalping (*EEUU**) **2** (= *venta al por menor*) resale

reventado* ADJ (= *cansado*) exhausted

reventar /1j/ Ⓐ VT **1** (*por presión*) (+ *globo, neumático, tubería, ampolla*) to burst; (+ *espinilla*) to squeeze; **tengo una cubierta reventada** I've got a puncture, I have a flat tyre

2 (*por una explosión*) [+ *puente, vehículo*] to blow up; [+ *cristales*] to shatter, blow out; **los ladrones ~on la caja fuerte** the robbers blew (open) the safe
3 (= *agotar*) [+ *caballo*] to ride into the ground
4 (*) (= *golpear*) **lo ~on a palos** they beat the living daylights out of him*; **te voy a ~ a patadas** I'm going to kick your face in*
5 (*) (= *hacer fracasar*) [+ *plan, espectáculo*] to wreck; [+ *asamblea, mitin, ceremonia*] to disrupt
6 (*) (= *fastidiar*) **me revienta que nos traten así** being treated like that really bugs me*
Ⓑ VI **1** (= *explotar*) [*globo, tubería, depósito*] to burst; [*neumático*] to burst, blow out; [*granada, proyectil*] to blow up; [*cristal*] to break, shatter; **hacer ~** [+ *neumático*] to burst; [+ *costuras*] to split
2 [*persona*] **2.1** (*por estar lleno*) **voy a ~** (*por comer*) I'm full to bursting; (*por ganas de orinar*) I'm bursting*
2.2 (*por enfado*) to explode **2.3** ~ **de: reventaba de ganas de contárselo todo** I was dying *o* bursting to tell him all about it; ~ **de ira** to be livid, be absolutely furious; ~ **de risa** to kill o.s. laughing, split one's sides (laughing)
2.4 (*) (= *morir*) to drop dead*
3 [*lugar*] **el teatro estaba a ~** the theatre was packed full, the theatre was full to bursting
Ⓒ reventarse VPR **1** (*por presión*) [*tubería*] to burst; [*pantalón, vestido*] to split
2 (*por explosión*) [*depósito, tanque*] to explode, blow up

reventón SM **1** (= *explosión*) [*de neumático*] blowout; [*de tubería*] burst **2** (*Méx*) (= *juerga*) rave-up*

reverberación SF **1** [*de luz*] play, reflexion **2** [*de sonido*] reverberation

reverberar /1a/ VI **1** [*luz*] to play, be reflected **2** [*sonido*] to reverberate

reverbero SM **1** [*de luz*] play, reflection **2** (*LAm*) (= *cocinilla*) small spirit stove

reverdecer /2d/ **Ⓐ** VI **1** (*Bot*) to grow green again **2** (= *renacer*) to come to life again, revive **Ⓑ** VT (= *reavivar*) to revive, reawaken

reverencia SF **1** (= *inclinación*) bow; **hacer una ~** to bow **2** (= *respeto*) reverence **3** (*Rel*) **Reverencia** (*tb* **Su Reverencia, Vuestra Reverencia**) Your Reverence

reverendo ADJ **1** (*Rel*) reverend **2** (*LAm**) (= *inmenso*) big, awful; **un ~ imbécil** a complete idiot

reversa SF (*LAm*) reverse; **meter ~** to go into reverse

reversible ADJ reversible

reverso SM (= *revés*) back, other side; [*de moneda*] reverse; **✦ MODISMO el ~ de la medalla** *o* **moneda** the other side of the coin

revertir /3i/ VI **1** [*posesión*] to revert (**a** to) **2** (= *venir a parar*) ~ **en** to end up as; ~ **en beneficio de** to benefit; ~ **en perjuicio de** to be to the detriment of

revés SM **1** (= *lado contrario*) **el ~** [*de papel, sello, mano, tela*] the back; [*de prenda*] the inside
2 al *o* **del ~** (*con sustantivo*) (= *lo de arriba abajo*) upside down; (= *lo de dentro fuera*) inside out; (= *lo de delante atrás*) back to front; **tienes el libro al ~** you are holding the book the wrong way round *o* upside down; **te has puesto la gorra del ~** you've put your cap on back to front; **has puesto los cables al ~** you've put the wires on the wrong way round; **llevas los zapatos al ~** you've got your shoes on the wrong feet; **volver al** *o* **del ~** [+ *prenda, objeto*] to turn the other way; [+ *argumento, situación*] to turn on its head
3 al ~ (*con verbo*) the other way round; (*como nexo*) on the contrary; **ponte al ~** turn the other way round; **Luis le dejó dinero a Gerardo, ¿o fue al ~?** Luis lent Gerardo some money, or was it the other way round?; **todo nos salió al ~** everything went wrong for us, nothing went right for us; **a mí no me produce ningún complejo, al ~, es un orgullo** I'm not embarrassed by it, on the contrary, I feel very proud; **al ~ de: fue al ~ de lo que dices** it was the opposite of what you say; **al ~ de lo que se cree, ...** contrary to popular belief, ...
4 (= *bofetada*) slap, backhand slap
5 (*Dep*) backhand
6 (= *contratiempo*) setback; **sufrir un ~** to suffer a setback

revestimiento SM (*Téc*) coating, covering; (= *forro*) lining; [*de carretera*] surface

revestir /3k/ **Ⓐ** VT **1** (= *recubrir*) [+ *pared, suelo*] to cover (**de, con** with); [+ *tubo*] to sheathe (**de, con** in); [+ *fachada*] to face (**de, con** with, in); **un armazón de acero revestido de hormigón** a steel frame clad in concrete
2 (*frm*) (= *presentar, tener*) **sus heridas no revisten importancia** his injuries are not serious
3 (*frm*) [+ *lenguaje, texto*] to lard (**de** with)
Ⓑ revestirse VPR (*frm*) ~ **de paciencia** to summon up all one's patience; **se revistió de valor y fue a hablarle** he summoned all his courage and went to speak to her

revirado ADJ (*CS*) **1** (= *revoltoso*) unruly, wild **2** (= *loco*) crazy

revisación SF (*CS*) medical examination

revisar /1a/ VT **1** [+ *texto*] to revise, look over, go through; [+ *edición*] to revise **2** [+ *cuenta*] to check; (*Fin*) to audit **3** (*Jur*) to review **4** [+ *teoría*] to reexamine, review **5** (*Mec*) to check, overhaul; (*Aut*) to service **6** (*CS, Méx*) (= *registrar*) to search; (= *examinar*) to examine

revisión SF **1** [*de teoría, método*] review, revision ➤ **revisión salarial** pay review **2** (*tb* ~ **médica**) checkup, medical examination **3** (*Mec*) check, overhaul; [*de ITV*] service

revisionista ADJ, SMF revisionist

revisor(a) **Ⓐ** SM/F ticket collector, inspector **Ⓑ** SM ➤ **revisor ortográfico** spellchecker, spelling checker

revista SF **1** [*de información general*] magazine; (*especializada*) journal, review ➤ **revista científica** scientific journal ➤ **revista del corazón** *magazine featuring celebrity gossip and real-life romance stories* **2** (= *sección*) section **3** (= *inspección*) inspection; (*Mil, Náut*) review, inspection; **pasar ~ a la tropa** to review *o* inspect the troops; **ahora pasaremos ~ a la actualidad deportiva** now we'll review today's sporting events **4** (*Teat*) variety show, revue

revistero SM magazine rack

revitalizar /1f/ VT to revitalize

revivir /3a/ **Ⓐ** VT **1** (= *recordar*) to revive memories of **2** (= *vivir de nuevo*) to relive, live again **Ⓑ** VI **1** (= *volver a vivir*) to revive, be revived **2** (= *renacer*) to come to life again

revocar /1g/ VT **1** [+ *decisión*] to revoke, reverse; [+ *orden*] to cancel **2** (*Arquit*) to plaster

revolcar /1g, 1l/ **Ⓐ** VT **1** [+ *persona*] to knock down, knock over; (*Taur*) to knock down and trample on **2** (*) [+ *adversario*] to wipe the floor with* **Ⓑ revolcarse** VPR [*persona*] to roll about; [*animal*] to wallow; (*) [*amantes*] to have a romp in the hay*; ~ **se de dolor** to writhe in pain

revolcón SM fall, tumble; **darse un ~ con algn** to have a roll in the hay with sb*

revolear /1a/ VT (*CS*) to twirl, spin

revolotear /1a/ VI [*pájaro*] to flutter, fly about; [*mariposa*] to flit (about)

revoloteo SM [*de pájaro*] fluttering; [*de mariposa*] flitting

revolqué *ver* **revolcar**

revoltijo SM (= *confusión*) jumble, confusion; (= *desorden*) mess

revoltoso/a **Ⓐ** ADJ (= *rebelde*) rebellious, unruly; [*niño*] naughty, unruly **Ⓑ** SM/F troublemaker, agitator

revolución SF **1** (*Téc*) revolution; **revoluciones por minuto** revolutions per minute **2** (*Pol*) revolution ➤ **revolución industrial** industrial revolution

revolucionar /1a/ VT **1** [+ *industria, moda*] to revolutionize **2** (*Pol*) to stir up, sow discontent among **3** [+ *persona*] to get excited

revolucionario/a ADJ, SM/F revolutionary

revolver /2h/ (*pp* **revuelto**) **Ⓐ** VT **1** [+ *líquido*] to stir **2** [+ *tierra*] to turn over, turn up, dig over **3** (= *desordenar*) to mix up, mess up **4 me revuelve el estómago** it turns my stomach **Ⓑ** VI ~ **en** to go through, rummage in, rummage about in; **¡deja de ~!** ◇ **¡no revuelvas!** (*a niño*) stop messing about with things!, stop fidgeting!

revolverse VPR 1 (*en cama*) to toss and turn; ~**se de dolor** to writhe in pain; **se me revuelve el estómago sólo de pensarlo** it turns my stomach just thinking about it 2 (= *enfrentarse*) ~**se contra algn** to turn on *o* against sb

revólver SM revolver

revoque SM (*Arquit*) 1 (= *acción*) plastering 2 (= *material*) plaster

revuelco SM fall, tumble

revuelo SM 1 [*de aves*] flutter, fluttering 2 (= *conmoción*) stir, commotion; **armar** *o* **levantar un gran** ~ to cause a great stir

revuelta SF 1 (*Pol*) disturbance, riot 2 (= *agitación*) commotion, disturbance

revuelto ⒶPP *de* revolver ⒷADJ 1 [*objetos*] mixed up, in disorder; [*agua*] cloudy, turbid; [*mar*] rough; [*tiempo*] unsettled; **todo estaba** ~ everything was in disorder *o* upside down; **los tiempos están** ~**s** these are troubled times; **tengo el pelo** ~ my hair's all untidy *o* in a mess; **tener el estómago** ~ to have an upset stomach, have a stomach upset 2 [*asunto*] complicated, involved ⒸSM (*Culin*) scrambled eggs with vegetables

revulsionar /1a/ VT (*frm*) ~ **a algn** to turn sb's stomach

revulsivo SM (= *acicate*) **el mal resultado electoral fue un** ~ **para la izquierda** the bad election results were a salutary lesson for the left

rey ⒶSM 1 (= *monarca*) king; **los Reyes** the King and Queen; ✦ MODISMOS **se cree el** ~ **del mambo** he really fancies himself*, he thinks he's the bee's knees*; **hablando del** ~ **de Roma** talk of the devil 2 **Reyes** (= *fecha*) Epiphany; **los Reyes Magos** the Magi, the Three Kings, the Three Wise Men; **¿qué te han traído los Reyes?** ≈ what did Father Christmas bring you? 3 (*en ajedrez, naipes*) king 4 (*uso apelativo*) pet*; (*más cariñoso*) love ⒷADJ INV **el deporte** ~ the king of sports

---

DÍA DE REYES

In the Spanish-speaking world, **los Reyes** or **el Día de Reyes** is the day when children and adults traditionally receive presents for the Christmas season. When they go to bed on January 5, children leave their shoes outside their bedroom doors or by their windows for the **Reyes Magos** (Wise Men) to leave presents beside. They may already have written letters to **SS.MM. los Reyes Magos de Oriente** with a list of what they would like. For **Reyes** it is traditional to eat **Roscón de Reyes**, a ring-shaped cake studded with frosted fruits and containing a little trinket or coin.

See also www.sgci.mec.es/au/navidad.htm

---

reyerta SF (*liter*) quarrel

reyezuelo SM 1 (= *monarca*) petty king, kinglet 2 (*Orn*) goldcrest

Reykiavik SM Reykjavik

rezagado/a ⒶADJ **quedar** ~ (= *quedar atrás*) to be left behind; (= *estar retrasado*) to be late, be behind; (*en pagos, progresos*) to fall behind ⒷSM/F (= *que llega tarde*) latecomer; (*Mil*) straggler

rezagarse /1h/ VPR to fall behind

rezago SM (*And, Méx*) unclaimed letters *pl*

rezar /1f/ ⒶVT [+ *oración*] to say ⒷVI 1 (*Rel*) to pray (**a** to) 2 [*texto*] to read, go; **reza así** it reads *o* goes as follows 3 ~ **con** (= *tener que ver con*) to concern, have to do with; **eso no reza conmigo** that has nothing to do with me

rezo SM 1 (= *oración*) prayer, prayers *pl* 2 (= *acto*) praying

rezongar /1h/ ⒶVT (*CAm, Uru*) (= *regañar*) to scold ⒷVI (= *gruñir*) to grumble

rezongo SM (*CAm, Uru*) scolding

rezongón ADJ grumbling, grouchy*, cantankerous

rezumar /1a/ ⒶVT to ooze, exude ⒷVI 1 [*contenido*] to ooze (out), seep (out), leak (out); [*recipiente*] to ooze, leak 2 [*orgullo, violencia*] to ooze Ⓒ **rezumarse** VPR 1 = **B1** 2 (= *traslucirse un hecho*) to leak out, become known

Rh ABR (= **Rhesus**) Rh; **soy Rh positivo** I'm rhesus positive

ría[1] SF estuary

ría[2] *ver* reír

riachuelo SM brook, stream

riada SF flood

ribeiro SM *young white wine from Galicia*

ribera SF [*de río, lago*] bank; [*del mar*] shore

ribereño/a ⒶADJ (= *de río*) riverside *antes de s*; (= *costero*) coastal ⒷSM/F (*de río*) riverside resident; (*de costa*) coastal resident

ribete SM 1 (*Cos*) border 2 (= *adorno*) addition, adornment 3 **ribetes** (= *toques*) **tiene sus** ~**s de pintor** he's got a bit of the painter about him

ribetear /1a/ VT to edge, border (**de** with)

riboflavina SF riboflavin

ricacho/a* SM/F, **ricachón/ona*** SM/F well-heeled man/woman*

ricamente ADV 1 (= *lujosamente*) richly 2 (= *estupendamente*) **viven muy** ~ **sin él** they manage very *o* perfectly well without him; **he dormido tan** ~ I've had such a good sleep

rico/a ⒶADJ 1 (= *adinerado*) rich, wealthy 2 [*suelo*] rich; ~ **de** *o* **en** rich in 3 (= *valioso*) valuable, precious; (= *lujoso*) [*tela*] fine, rich, sumptuous 4 (= *sabroso*) delicious, tasty 5 (*) (= *bonito*) cute, lovely; (*en oración directa*) **¡oye, ~!** (*iró*) hey *o* oy, watch it!*; **¡que no, ~!** (*Esp*) no way, mate!*; **¡qué ~ es el niño!** isn't the little one cute! ⒷSM/F rich person; **nuevo** ~ nouveau riche

rictus SM INV [*de desprecio*] sneer; [*de burla*] grin ➤ **rictus de amargura** bitter smile ➤ **rictus de dolor** wince of pain

ricura* SF **¡qué ~ de bebé!** what a gorgeous baby!; **¡oye, ~!** (*a una chica*) hey, gorgeous!

ridiculez SF 1 (= *dicho absurdo*) **¡qué ~!** how ridiculous!; **no digas más ridiculeces** don't be so ridiculous 2 (= *insignificancia*) **¿y no os habláis por una ~ así?** (do) you mean you've stopped talking to each other because of a silly little thing like that?; **¿sólo vas a comer esta ~?** is that all you're eating?

ridiculizar /1f/ VT to ridicule, deride

ridículo ⒶADJ ridiculous ⒷSM **hacer el** ~ to make a fool of oneself; **puso a Ana en** ~ **delante de todos** he made a fool of Ana in front of everyone, he showed Ana up in front of everyone; **no tiene sentido del** ~ he isn't afraid of making a fool of himself

riego SM 1 (= *aspersión*) watering; (= *irrigación*) irrigation ➤ **riego por aspersión** watering by spray, watering by sprinklers ➤ **riego por goteo** trickle irrigation 2 (*Anat*) ➤ **riego sanguíneo** blood flow, blood circulation

riel SM 1 (*Ferro*) rail 2 (*Téc*) ingot 3 [*de cortina*] rail

rielar /1a/ VI (*poét*) to shimmer (*liter*)

ríen *etc ver* reír

rienda SF rein; ✦ MODISMOS **aflojar las** ~**s** to let up; **llevar las** ~**s** to be in charge, be in control; **soltar las** ~**s** to let go; **a** ~ **suelta** without the least restraint; **dar** ~ **suelta a** to give free rein to; **dar** ~ **suelta a la imaginación** to let one's imagination run wild; **dar** ~ **suelta a algn** to give sb a free hand

riendo *ver* reír

riesgo SM risk (**de** of); **esta operación presenta mayores** ~**s** the risks are higher with this operation, this operation is riskier; **un** ~ **para la salud** a health hazard *o* risk; **grupos de** ~ risk groups; **de alto** ~ high-risk; **seguro a** *o* **contra todo** ~ fully comprehensive insurance policy; **a** ~ **de que me expulsen** at the risk of being expelled; **correr** ~**s** to take risks; **corres el** ~ **de que te despidan** you run the risk of being dismissed; ✦ MODISMO **por su cuenta y** ~ at one's own risk

riesgoso ADJ (*LAm*) risky, dangerous

rifa SF raffle

rifar /1a/ ⒶVT to raffle; ~ **algo con fines benéficos** to raffle sth for charity Ⓑ **rifarse** VPR ~**se algo/a algn*** to fight over sth/sb

rifirrafe* SM, **rifirirafe*** SM shindy*, row

rifle SM (= *arma*) rifle; (*Dep*) sporting rifle; (*Caza*) hunting gun ➤ **rifle de repetición** repeating rifle

rigidez SF **1** [*de material*] stiffness, rigidity; [*de pierna, tendón*] stiffness **2** (= *inflexibilidad*) [*de actitud*] inflexibility; [*de carácter*] strictness, inflexibility

rígido ADJ **1** (= *tieso*) rigid, stiff **2** [*actitud*] rigid, inflexible **3** (*moralmente*) strict, harsh

rigor SM **1** (= *severidad*) severity, harshness; (= *dureza*) toughness **2** (*Meteo*) harshness, severity; **los ~es del clima** the rigours *o* (*EEUU*) rigors of the climate **3** (= *exactitud*) rigour, rigor (*EEUU*); **con todo ~ científico** with scientific precision **4 ser de ~** to be de rigueur, be absolutely essential; **después de los saludos de ~** after the usual *o* customary greetings

riguroso ADJ **1** [*control, dieta, disciplina*] strict; [*actitud, castigo*] severe, harsh; [*medida*] tough; **iban de luto ~** they were wearing deep mourning; **exigen un cumplimiento ~ del acuerdo** they're demanding strict compliance with the agreement; **en ~ orden alfabético** in strict alphabetical order **2** [*invierno, clima*] harsh **3** [*método, estudio*] rigorous; **es fruto de una investigación rigurosa** it's the product of rigorous research; **un trabajo poco ~** a sloppy piece of work

rima SF **1** (= *consonancia*) rhyme ➤ **rima interna** internal rhyme **2** (= *composición*) **rimas** verse *sing*, poetry *sing*

rimar /1a/ VI to rhyme (**con** with)

rimbombante ADJ **1** (= *pomposo*) pompous, bombastic **2** (= *ostentoso*) showy, flashy **3** (= *resonante*) resounding, echoing

rímel SM, **rimmel** SM mascara

rin SM **1** (*Col, Méx Aut*) rim, wheel rim **2** (*Perú Telec*) metal phone token

rincón SM **1** (= *ángulo*) corner (*inside*) **2** (= *escondrijo*) corner, nook; **en un ~ de mi mente** somewhere in the back of my mind

rinconera SF (= *mesita*) corner table, corner unit; (= *armario*) corner cupboard, dresser

ring [rrin] SM (*esp LAm*) ring, boxing ring

rinitis SF INV ➤ **rinitis alérgica** hay fever

rinoceronte SM rhinoceros

riña SF (= *discusión*) quarrel, argument; (= *lucha*) fight, brawl

riñendo *etc ver* **reñir**

riñón SM (*Anat*) kidney; **me duelen los riñones** my lower back hurts; ✦ MODISMO **me costó un ~*** it cost me a fortune, it cost the earth

riñonera SF bum bag (*Brit*), fanny pack (*EEUU*)

río[1] **Ⓐ** SM **1** (= *corriente de agua*) river; **~ abajo** downstream; **~ arriba** upstream; ✦ REFRÁN **cuando el ~ suena, agua o piedras lleva** there's no smoke without fire **2** (= *torrente*) stream, torrent; **un ~ de gente** a stream of people, a flood of people **Ⓑ** ADJ INV (†) **novela ~** saga, roman fleuve

río[2], **rió** *etc ver* **reír**

Río de Janeiro SM Rio de Janeiro

Río de la Plata SM River Plate, Plata River (*EEUU*)

Rioja SF **La ~** La Rioja; *see also* www.larioja.org

rioja SM Rioja (wine)

riojano/a ADJ, SM/F Riojan

rioplatense ADJ of/from the River Plate region; **el español ~** River Plate Spanish

ripio SM **1** (= *palabras inútiles*) padding, empty words *pl*; (*en poesía*) trite verse **2** (*CS*) (= *grava*) gravel

riqueza SF **1** (= *bienes*) wealth; **la distribución de la ~** the distribution of wealth; **no le importaba nada toda su ~** all her riches meant nothing to her **2** (= *abundancia*) richness; **la ~ del suelo** the richness of the soil; **tiene una gran ~ de vocabulario** she has a very extensive *o* rich vocabulary

risa SF laugh; **hubo ~s** there was laughter; **dar ~**: **daba ~ la manera en que lo explicaba** it was so funny the way he

told it; **me dio la ~** I got (a fit of) the giggles; **de ~: no es cosa de ~** it's no laughing matter; **le pagan un sueldo de ~** they pay him a pittance, what they pay him is a joke; **entrar a algn la ~**: **me entró la ~** I got (a fit of) the giggles; **¡qué ~!** how funny!; **tomarse algo a ~** to treat sth as a joke; ✦ MODISMOS **desternillarse de ~** to split one's sides laughing, laugh one's head off; **morirse de ~** to die laughing, kill o.s. laughing; **mondarse o partirse o troncharse de ~** to split one's sides laughing, laugh one's head off ➤ **risa contagiosa** infectious laugh ➤ **risa floja**, **risa tonta**: **me dio o entró la ~ floja o tonta** I got (a fit of) the giggles

risco SM **1** (= *peñasco*) cliff, crag **2 riscos** (= *terreno*) rough parts

risible ADJ ludicrous, laughable

risotada SF guffaw, loud laugh

ristra SF string; **una ~ de ajos** a string of garlic

ristre SM **en ~** at the ready

risueño ADJ **1** [*cara*] smiling; **muy ~** with a big smile **2** [*temperamento*] cheerful

rítmico ADJ rhythmic, rhythmical

ritmo SM **1** (*Mús*) rhythm; **daban palmas al ~ de la música** they were clapping in time to the music; **marcaba el ~ con el pie** he kept time with his foot **2** (= *marcha*) pace; **lo haré a mi ~** I'll do it at my own pace ➤ **ritmo cardíaco** heart rate ➤ **ritmo de crecimiento**, **ritmo de expansión** growth rate ➤ **ritmo de vida**: **el tranquilo ~ de vida de los pueblos** the quiet pace of life in the villages; **no puedo llevar este ~ de vida** I can't keep up with this lifestyle

rito SM rite ➤ **rito iniciático** initiation rite

ritual Ⓐ ADJ ritual **Ⓑ** SM ritual

rival Ⓐ ADJ rival, competing **Ⓑ** SMF rival, competitor

rivalidad SF rivalry, competition

rivalizar /1f/ VI to compete, contend; **~ con** to rival, compete with

rizado ADJ **1** [*pelo*] curly **2** [*mar*] choppy

rizador SM curling iron, hair curler

rizapestañas SM INV eyelash curlers *pl*

rizar /1f/ **Ⓐ** VT **1** [+ *pelo*] to curl **2** [+ *mar*] to ripple, ruffle **Ⓑ rizarse** VPR **1** **~se el pelo** to perm one's hair, have one's hair permed **2** [*agua*] to ripple

rizo[1] SM **1** [*de pelo*] curl; ✦ MODISMO **rizar el ~** to split hairs **2 hacer el ~** (*Aer*) to loop the loop

rizo[2] SM (*Náut*) reef

RNE SF ABR = **Radio Nacional de España**

robalo SM, **róbalo** SM sea bass

robar /1a/ **Ⓐ** VT **1** [+ *objeto, dinero*] to steal; [+ *banco*] to rob; **¡nos han robado!** we've been robbed!; **~ algo a algn** to steal sth from sb; **el defensa le robó el balón** the defender stole the ball off him; **no quiero ~le su tiempo** I don't want to take up your time **2** (= *ocupar*) [+ *atención*] to steal, capture; [+ *tranquilidad*] to destroy, take away; [+ *vida*] to take, steal **3** (= *estafar*) to cheat, rob **4** [+ *naipes*] to take, draw **Ⓑ** VI **1** (= *quitar*) to steal; **entraron a ~ en mi casa** my house was burgled **2** (*Naipes*) to take a card, draw a card

roble SM (= *árbol*) oak tree; (= *madera*) oak

robledal SM oakwood

robo SM **1** [*de dinero, objetos*] theft; (*en vivienda*) burglary; (*en tienda, banco*) robbery ➤ **robo a mano armada** armed robbery **2** (= *estafa*) **¡esto es un ~!** this is daylight robbery!; **¿cinco mil por una camiseta? ¡vaya ~!** five thousand for a T-shirt? what a rip-off!*

robot [ro'βo] SM (*pl* **~s** [ro'βo]) (= *autómata, máquina*) robot; (*de cocina*) food processor

robótica SF robotics *sing*

robotizar /1f/ VT (= *automatizar*) to automate; (*fig*) [+ *persona*] to turn into a robot

robustecer /2d/ **Ⓐ** VT to strengthen **Ⓑ robustecerse** VPR

to grow stronger

robusto ADJ strong, tough, robust

roca SF rock

rocambolesco ADJ (= *raro*) odd, bizarre; [*estilo*] ornate, over-elaborate

roce SM **1** (= *acción*) rub, rubbing; (*Téc*) friction; (*Pol*) friction **2** (= *herida*) graze **3** (*) (= *contacto*) close contact; **tener ~ con algn** to be in close contact with sb, have a lot to do with sb **4** (= *problema*) brush; **tuvo algún ~ con la autoridad** he had a few brushes with the law **5** (*CS*) (= *modales*) manners *pl*; **¡qué falta de ~!** what bad manners!

rociador SM (*para rociar*) spray; (*Agr*) sprinkler

rociar /1c/ VT **1** [+ *agua*] to sprinkle, spray; [+ *balas*] to spray **2** (*Culin*) (= *acompañar*) **~ el plato con un vino de la tierra** to wash down the dish with a local wine

rocín SM hack, nag

rocío SM dew

rock ADJ, SM rock

rockero/a Ⓐ ADJ rock *antes de s*; **música rockera** rock music; **es muy ~** he's a real rock fan Ⓑ SM/F (= *músico*) rock musician; (= *aficionado*) rock fan

rococó ADJ, SM rococo

rocola SF jukebox

rocoso ADJ rocky

rocote SM (*SAm*), **rocoto** SM (*SAm*) pepper

rodaballo SM turbot

rodada SF (*CS*, *Méx*) (= *caída*) fall (from a horse)

rodado Ⓐ ADJ **1** [*tráfico*] vehicular **2** [*piedra*] rounded; **salir** *o* **venir ~** to go smoothly Ⓑ SM (*CS frm*) vehicle, wheeled vehicle

rodadura SF (*tb* **banda de ~**) tread

rodaja SF slice; **limón en ~s** sliced lemon

rodaje SM **1** (*Cine*) shooting, filming **2** (*Aut*) running-in (*Brit*), breaking in (*EEUU*); **"en rodaje"** "running in (*Brit*)", "breaking in (*EEUU*)" **3** (*Téc*) wheels *pl*, set of wheels **4** (= *inicio*) **período de ~** initial phase; **poner en ~** to launch **5** (= *experiencia*) experience

rodante ADJ rolling; **material ~** rolling stock

rodapié SM skirting board (*Brit*), baseboard (*EEUU*)

rodar /1l/ Ⓐ VI **1** (= *dar vueltas*) [*pelota*] to roll; [*rueda*] to go round, turn; **rodó escaleras abajo** he fell *o* rolled downstairs; ✦ MODISMOS **echarlo todo a ~** to mess it all up **2** (*) (= *deambular*) **tienen al niño rodando de guardería en guardería** they keep moving *o* shifting the kid about from nursery to nursery **3** (*Cine*) to shoot, film **4** (*) (= *existir todavía*) to be still going, still exist Ⓑ VT **1** [+ *vehículo*] to wheel, wheel along; [+ *coche nuevo*] to run in **2** (= *hacer rodar*) [+ *objeto*] to roll, roll along **3** (*Cine*) to shoot, film

rodear /1a/ Ⓐ VT **1** (= *poner alrededor de*) to encircle, enclose; **~on el terreno con una alambrada de púas** they surrounded the field with barbed wire, they put a barbed wire fence around the field; **le rodeó el cuello con los brazos** she threw her arms round his neck **2** (= *ponerse alrededor de*) to surround **3** (*LAm*) [+ *ganado*] to round up Ⓑ **rodearse** VPR **~se de** to surround o.s. with

rodeo SM **1** (= *ruta indirecta*) long way round, roundabout way; (= *desvío*) detour; **dar un ~** to make a detour **2** (*en discurso*) circumlocution; **andarse con ~s** to beat about the bush; **hablar sin ~s** to speak plainly **3** (*LAm Agr*) roundup **4** (*Dep*) rodeo

rodera SF rut, wheel track

rodete SM **1** [*de pelo*] bun **2** [*de cerradura*] ward

rodilla SF **1** (*Anat*) knee; **doblar** *o* **hincar la ~** (= *arrodillarse*) to kneel down; (= *ser servil*) to bow, humble o.s. (**ante** to); **ponerse de ~s** to kneel, kneel down **2** (*para llevar carga*) pad **3** (= *paño*) floor cloth, mop

rodillazo SM push with the knee; **dar un ~ a** to knee

rodillera SF (= *protección*) knee guard; (= *remiendo*) knee patch

rodillo SM (*Culin*) rolling pin; (*Tip*) ink roller; [*de máquina de escribir*] cylinder, roller; (*para pintura, césped*) roller ➤ **rodillo pastelero** rolling pin

rodio SM rhodium

rododendro SM rhododendron

Rodríguez SM **estar de ~** (*Esp**) to be left on one's own

roedor SM rodent

roer /2z/ VT **1** [+ *comida*] to gnaw; [+ *hueso*] to gnaw, pick **2** (= *corroer*) to corrode, eat away

rogar /1h, 1l/ Ⓐ VT (= *suplicar*) to beg; **démelo, se lo ruego** give it to me, I beg you; **"se ruega no fumar"** "please do not smoke" Ⓑ VI **1** (= *suplicar*) to beg, plead; **hacerse de ~** to play hard to get; **no se hace de ~** he doesn't have to be asked twice **2** (*Rel*) to pray

rogativa SF (*Rel*) rogation

rojez SF (*en la piel*) blotch

rojizo ADJ reddish

rojo/a Ⓐ ADJ **1** (*color*) red; ✦ MODISMOS **poner ~ a algn** to make sb blush; **ponerse ~** to turn red, blush; **ponerse ~ de ira** to go purple with rage **2** (*Pol*) red; (*Esp Hist*) Republican Ⓑ SM **1** (= *color*) red, red colour *o* (*EEUU*) color; **calentar al ~ vivo** to make red-hot; **el ambiente está al ~ vivo** the atmosphere is electric; **la emoción está al ~ vivo** excitement is at fever pitch; **un semáforo en ~** a red light **2** ➤ **rojo de labios** lipstick Ⓒ SM/F (*Pol*) (= *de izquierdas*) red; (*Esp Hist*) Republican

rol SM **1** (*Teat*) role, part **2** (= *función*) role; **juegos de ~** role-playing games **3** (*Náut*) muster

rolar /1a/ Ⓐ VT (*Méx*) to pass from hand to hand Ⓑ VI [*viento*] to veer round

rollizo ADJ (= *rechoncho*) plump; [*niño*] chubby; [*mujer*] plump, buxom

rollo Ⓐ SM **1** (= *cilindro*) [*de tela, papel, cuerda fina, cable fino*] roll; [*de cuerda gruesa, cable grueso*] coil; [*de película de cine*] reel; [*de pergamino*] scroll; **un ~ de papel higiénico** a roll of toilet paper; **regalamos un ~ color** we offer a free colour film **2** (*Culin*) **2.1** (*tb* **~ pastelero**) (*Esp*) rolling pin **2.2** [*de masa, relleno*] (pastry) roll ➤ **rollo de primavera** spring roll **3** (*) (= *michelín*) roll of fat, spare tyre* (*hum*) **4** (*Esp**) (*tb* **~ macabeo** *o* **patatero**) (= *explicación*) spiel*; (= *sermón*) lecture; (= *mentira*) yarn; **¡menudo ~ que tiene!** he's always waffling (on) about something!*; **¡vaya ~ patatero que me estás contando!** you're talking a load of old tosh! (*esp Brit***), you're talking a load of baloney! (*EEUU**); **perdona por el ~ que te he soltado** sorry if I have bored you to death with my story; ✦ MODISMOS **cortar el ~** to cut it short*, cut the crap***; **cortar el ~ a algn: ¡con lo bien que lo estábamos pasando! ¡nos has cortado el ~!** we were having a great time until you went and spoiled things! **5** (*) (= *aburrimiento*) **¡qué ~!** what a pain!**; **ser un ~** [*discurso, conferencia*] to be dead boring*; [*persona*] to be a bore*, be a pain* (*hum*); **lo de las lentillas es un ~** contact lenses are a real pain* **6** (**) (= *asunto*) thing; **no sabemos de qué va el ~** we don't know what it's all about *o* what's going on; **ir a su ~** to do one's own thing **7** (*Esp***) (= *ambiente*) scene*; **no me va el ~ de esta gente** I'm not into their scene* **8** (**) (= *sensación*) **buen/mal ~: en sus fiestas siempre hay buen ~** there's always a good atmosphere at his parties; **había muy buen ~ entre nosotros** we got on really well together; **¡qué mal ~!** what a pain!*; **me da buen/mal ~** I've got a good/nasty *o* bad feeling about it; **tener un buen/mal ~ con algn** to get on well/badly with sb **9** (*) (= *relación sentimental*) **tener un ~ (con algn)** to be involved (with sb) Ⓑ ADJ INV (*Esp, Méx**) boring; **esa película es muy ~** that film's dead boring*; **no seas ~** don't be a bore* *o* pain**

rolo/a* ADJ, SM/F = **bogotano**

Roma SF Rome; ✦ MODISMOS **revolver ~ con Santiago** to

leave no stone unturned; **hablando de ~ ...** talk of the devil ...

romana SF steelyard; *ver tb* **romano**

romance Ⓐ ADJ [*idioma*] Romance Ⓑ SM **1** (*Ling*) Romance language **2** (*Literat*) ballad **3** (= *amorío*) romance, love affair; (= *amante*) lover

romancero SM collection of ballads

romaní Ⓐ ADJ, SMF Romany Ⓑ SM (*Ling*) Romany

románico ADJ **1** [*idioma*] Romance **2** (*Arte, Arquit*) Romanesque; (*en Inglaterra*) Norman

romano/a Ⓐ ADJ, SM/F Roman Ⓑ SM (*Esp†*) cop*; *ver tb* **romana**

romanticismo SM romanticism

romántico/a ADJ, SM/F romantic

romanticón* ADJ [*persona*] sentimental, soppy*; [*película, novela*] slushy*, soppy*

rombo SM (*Mat*) rhombus; (*en diseño*) diamond, diamond shape

romboidal ADJ rhomboid

romboide SM rhomboid

romería SF pilgrimage; **ir en ~** to go on a pilgrimage

ROMERÍA

In Spain **romerías** are annual religious pilgrimages to chapels and shrines associated with particular saints or miracles of the Virgin. The pilgrims, called **romeros**, make their way on foot to the particular holy site, often covering long distances, and make offerings. Some **romerías** are large-scale events, one of the best known being the **Romería de la Virgen del Rocío** at Huelva in Andalusia, which involves spectacular processions of pilgrims in traditional Andalusian dress, some on horseback and some in brilliantly decorated wagons.

romero¹/a SM/F (= *peregrino*) pilgrim

romero² SM (*Bot*) rosemary

romo ADJ **1** (= *sin punta*) blunt; [*persona*] snub-nosed **2** (= *aburrido*) dull, lifeless

rompebolas*** SMF INV (*Arg*) pain in the arse (*Brit***) *o* ass (*EEUU***)

rompecabezas SM INV **1** (= *juego*) jigsaw, jigsaw puzzle **2** (= *algo complicado*) puzzle; (= *problema*) problem, headache

rompehielos SM INV icebreaker

rompeolas SM INV breakwater

romper /2a/ (*pp* **roto**) Ⓐ VT **1** (= *partir, destrozar*) **1.1** (*intencionadamente*) [+ *juguete, mueble, cuerda*] to break; [+ *rama*] to break, break off; [+ *vaso, jarrón, cristal*] to break, smash **1.2** (= *rasgar*) [+ *tela, vestido, papel*] to tear, rip **1.3** (*por el uso*) [+ *zapatos, ropa*] to wear out **1.4** [+ *barrera*] (*lit*) to break down, break through; (*fig*) to break down; **~ la barrera del sonido** to break the sound barrier **1.5** ✦ MODISMOS **~ aguas: todavía no ha roto aguas** her waters haven't broken yet; **~ la cara a algn*** to smash sb's face in*; **~ el hielo** to break the ice; **~ una lanza en favor de algn/algo** to stick up for sb/sth; **no haber roto un plato: se comporta como si no hubiera roto un plato en su vida** he behaves as if butter wouldn't melt in his mouth; **de rompe y rasga: es una mujer de rompe y rasga** she's not someone to mess with

2 (= *terminar*) [+ *equilibrio, silencio, maleficio, contrato*] to break; [+ *relaciones, amistad*] to break off; **~ la racha de algo** to break a run of sth; **~ el servicio a algn** (*Tenis*) to break sb's service

3 (*Mil*) [+ *línea, cerco*] to break, break through; **¡rompan filas!** fall out!

4 (*Agr*) [+ *tierra*] to break, break up

Ⓑ VI **1** [*olas*] to break

2 (= *salir*) [*diente*] to come through; [*capullo, flor*] to come out

3 [*alba, día*] to break; **al ~ el alba** at crack of dawn, at daybreak

4 (= *empezar*) **rompió a proferir insultos contra todo el mundo** he suddenly started hurling *o* to hurl insults at everyone; **al verme rompió a llorar** when he saw me he burst into tears; **cuando rompa el hervor** when it comes to the boil

5 (= *separarse*) [*pareja, novios*] to split up; **~ con** [+ *novio, amante*] to split up with, break up with; [+ *amigo, familia*] to fall out with; [+ *aliado*] to break off relations with; [+ *tradición, costumbre, pasado*] to break with; [+ *imagen, tópico, leyenda*] to break away from; **ha roto con su novio** she has broken *o* split up with her boyfriend

Ⓒ **romperse** VPR **1** (= *partirse, destrozarse*) **1.1** [*juguete, mueble, cuerda*] to break; [*plato, cristal*] to break, smash; **la rama se ha roto con el viento** the branch broke (off) in the wind; **se me rompió un dedo en el accidente** my finger got broken in the accident, I broke a finger in the accident **1.2** (*uso enfático*) **me he roto la muñeca jugando al tenis** I broke my wrist playing tennis; ✦ MODISMO **~se la cabeza*** (= *pensar mucho*) to rack one's brains; (= *preocuparse*) to kill o.s. worrying

2 (= *rasgarse*) [*tela, papel*] to tear, rip

3 (= *estropearse*) [*coche, motor*] to break down; [*televisor*] to break; **se ha roto la lavadora** the washing machine is broken, the washing machine has broken down

4 (*Ciclismo*) [*pelotón*] to break up

rompevientos SM INV **1** (*Arg, Méx*) (= *impermeable*) anorak **2** (*Arg*) (= *sudadera*) sweatshirt **3** (*Uru*) [*de lana*] sweater

rompiente SM **1** (= *escollo*) reef, shoal **2 rompientes** (= *olas*) breakers, surf *sing*

ron SM rum

roncar /1g/ VI **1** (*cuando se duerme*) to snore **2** (*Chi**) (= *ser mandón*) to be bossy *o* domineering

roncha SF **1** (*por enfermedad*) spot; **me salieron ~s** I came out in a rash **2** [*de mosquito, serpiente*] bite; [*de avispa, abeja*] sting

ronco ADJ [*persona*] hoarse; [*voz*] husky

ronda SF **1** [*de guardia*] beat; (= *personas*) watch, patrol, guard; **ir de ~** to do one's round ➤ **ronda nocturna** night patrol, night watch **2** (*Mús*) group of serenaders **3** [*de bebidas*] round; **pagar una ~** to pay for a round **4** [*de negociaciones, elecciones*] round **5** [*de cartas*] hand, game **6** (*en competición, concurso*) round; (*Golf*) round **7** (*Aut*) (*tb* **~ de circunvalación**) ring road (*Brit*), beltway (*EEUU*), bypass **8** (*CS*) [*de niños*] ring; **en ~** in a ring

rondalla SF band of street musicians

rondar /1a/ Ⓐ VT **1** [*policía, soldado*] to patrol **2** [+ *cifra, edad*] **el precio ronda los mil dólares** the price is in the region of a thousand dollars; **rondaba los 30 años** he was about 30 **3** (= *perseguir*) **la ronda a todas horas para que le preste dinero** he pesters her night and day to lend him money; **es una idea que me ronda la cabeza desde hace tiempo** it's an idea which I've had going round in my head for quite a while **4** (†) (= *cortejar*) to court

Ⓑ VI **1** [*policía, soldado*] to (be on) patrol **2** (= *deambular*) to prowl **3** [*pensamiento, idea*] **debes rechazar las dudas que te rondan por la cabeza** you must dispel the doubts that are besetting you **4** (†) [*enamorado, la tuna*] to serenade

rondín SM (*And*) night watchman

rondón: de ~ ADV unexpectedly; **entrar de ~** (= *sin aviso*) to rush in; (*en fiesta*) to gatecrash

ronquera SF hoarseness; **tener ~** to be hoarse

ronquido SM snore, snoring

ronronear /1a/ VI to purr

ronroneo SM purr

ronzal SM halter

roña SF **1** (= *mugre*) dirt, grime; (*en metal*) rust **2** (*) (= *tacañería*) stinginess, meanness (*esp Brit*) **3** (*Vet*) mange **4** (*And Med*) feigned illness

roñica* SMF skinflint

roñoso ADJ **1** (= *mugriento*) dirty, filthy; [*metal*] rusty

2 (*) (= *tacaño*) stingy, mean (*esp Brit*) **3** (*Vet*) mangy

ropa SF clothes *pl*; **voy a cambiarme de ~** I'm going to change (my clothes); **tender la ~** to hang out the washing; ✦ MODISMOS **hay ~ tendida** the walls have ears; **nadar y guardar la ~** to cover one's back ➤ **ropa blanca** (= *ropa interior*) underwear; (= *ropa de cama, manteles*) linen; (*para la lavadora*) whites *pl* ➤ **ropa de cama** bed linen ➤ **ropa de color** coloureds *pl*, coloreds *pl* (*EEUU*) ➤ **ropa de trabajo** work clothes *pl* ➤ **ropa interior** underwear ➤ **ropa sucia** dirty washing, dirty clothes *pl*, laundry

ropaje SM gown, robes *pl*; **ropajes** (*Rel*) vestments *pl*

ropero SM (= *guardarropa*) wardrobe; [*de ropa blanca*] linen cupboard (*Brit*), linen closet (*EEUU*)

roque¹ SM (*Ajedrez*) rook, castle

roque²* ADJ **estar ~** to be asleep; **quedarse ~** to fall asleep

roquedal SM rocky place

rosa Ⓐ SF (*Bot*) rose; **palo ~** rosewood; ✦ MODISMO **estar como una ~** to feel as fresh as a daisy; *ver tb* **color 5** Ⓑ SM (= *color*) pink; **de color ~** pink; (*fig*) rosy ➤ **rosa de los vientos, rosa náutica** compass, compass card, compass rose Ⓒ ADJ pink; **revista ~** magazine of sentimental stories

rosáceo ADJ = **rosado A**

rosado Ⓐ ADJ pink Ⓑ SM (= *vino*) rosé

rosal SM rose bush, rose tree

rosaleda SF rose bed, rose garden

rosario SM **1** (*Rel*) rosary; (= *sarta*) rosary beads *pl*, rosary; **rezar el ~** to say the rosary; ✦ REFRÁN **acabar como el ~ de la aurora** *o* **del alba** to end up in confusion, end with everybody falling out **2** (= *serie*) string, series; **un ~ de maldiciones** a string of curses

rosbif SM roast beef

rosca SF **1** [*de humo*] ring, spiral **2** (*Culin*) ring-shaped roll, ring-shaped pastry, ≈ doughnut; ✦ MODISMOS **hacer la ~ a algn*** to suck up *o* (*EEUU*) kiss up to sb*; **no comerse una ~*** (= *no ligar*) to get absolutely nowhere ➤ **rosca de Reyes** (*LAm*) = **roscón 3** [*de tornillo*] thread; [*de espiral*] turn; **pasarse de ~** [*tornillo*] to have a crossed thread; [*persona*] to go too far, overdo it **4** [*de grasa*] roll of fat **5** (*And, CS Pol*) ruling clique, oligarchy **6** (*Chi**) (= *discusión*) noisy argument; (= *jaleo*) uproar, commotion

rosco SM **1** (*Culin*) ring-shaped roll, ring-shaped pastry, ≈ doughnut; ✦ MODISMO **no comerse un ~*** (= *no ligar*) to get absolutely nowhere (**con** with) **2** (*) (= *nota*) zero, nought (*esp Brit*)

roscón SM (*tb* **~ de Reyes**) ring-shaped cake (*eaten on January 6th*)

rosedal SM (*CS*) = **rosaleda**

roseta SF **1** (*Bot*) small rose **2** (*Dep*) rosette **3** [*de regadera*] rose, nozzle **4 rosetas** [*de maíz*] popcorn *sing*

rosetón SM rose window

rosquete** SM (*And*) queer**, poof (*Brit***), fag (*EEUU***)

rosquilla SF **1** [*de humo*] ring **2** (*Culin*) ring-shaped pastry, doughnut; ✦ MODISMO **venderse como ~s** to sell like hot cakes

rosticería SF (*Méx, Chi*) roast chicken shop

rostizar /1a/ VT to spit-roast

rostro SM **1** (= *semblante*) countenance; (= *cara*) face **2** (*) (= *descaro*) nerve*, cheek*

rotación SF **1** (= *giro*) rotation **2** (*Agr*) ➤ **rotación de cultivos** crop rotation **3** (*Com*) [*de producción*] turnover

rotar /1a/ VT to rotate

rotativo Ⓐ ADJ (= *que gira*) rotary, revolving; [*prensa*] rotary Ⓑ SM **1** (*Tip*) rotary press **2** (*frm*) (= *periódico*) newspaper

rotería SF (*Chi**) common people *pl*, plebs* *pl*

rotisería SF (*CS*) delicatessen

roto/a Ⓐ PP *de* **romper**
Ⓑ ADJ **1** (= *partido, destrozado*) [*juguete, mueble, cristal,*

puerta] broken; **tengo la pierna rota** I've broken my leg, I've got a broken leg

2 (= *rasgado*) [*tela, papel*] torn

3 (= *estropeado*) [*lavadora, televisor*] broken; [*coche, motor*] broken down

4 [*zapato*] worn, worn-out

5 [*persona*] broken; [*vida*] shattered; **estar ~ de cansancio** to be exhausted, be worn-out

6 (*Chi**) (= *de clase baja*) common, low-class; (= *maleducado*) rude

Ⓒ SM/F **1** (*Perú, Bol**) Chilean, Chilean person

2 (*Chi**) **2.1** (= *pobre*) pleb* **2.2** (= *maleducado*) **esta rota no sabe comportarse a la mesa** she's so rude *o* such a pig**, she doesn't know how to behave at the dinner table

Ⓓ SM (*en pantalón, vestido*) hole; ✦ MODISMO **valer** *o* **servir lo mismo para un ~ que para un descosido** to serve a multitude of purposes

rotonda SF **1** (*Aut*) roundabout (*Brit*), traffic circle (*EEUU*) **2** (*Arquit*) rotunda, circular gallery

rotoso* ADJ **1** (*SAm*) (= *harapiento*) ragged, shabby **2** (*Chi**) (= *ordinario*) low-life, common

rótula SF **1** (*Anat*) kneecap **2** (*Mec*) ball-and-socket joint

rotulador SM felt tip pen

rotular /1a/ VT to label

rotulista SMF sign painter

rótulo SM **1** (= *letrero*) sign, notice; (= *cartel*) placard, poster ➤ **rótulo de salida** (*TV*) credits *pl* ➤ **rótulo luminoso** illuminated sign **2** (= *encabezamiento*) heading, title; (*en mapa*) lettering

rotundo ADJ **1** (= *terminante*) [*negativa*] flat; [*victoria*] clear, convincing; **me dio un "sí"** ~ he gave me an emphatic "yes" **2** (= *redondo*) round

rotura SF **1** [*de objeto*] **el seguro del coche cubre la ~ de cristales** the car insurance covers window breakage; **la casa está sin agua por una ~ en las tuberías** the house has no water because of a broken pipe; **en la fotografía puede apreciarse la ~ del muro** in the photograph you can see where the wall is broken *o* the break in the wall **2** (*Med*) **la ~ del hueso se produjo en el momento de la caída** the bone broke at the moment of the fall; **ingresó por ~ de cadera** he was admitted for a broken hip; **ha sufrido una ~ de ligamentos** he has torn ligaments **3** (*en tela*) tear, rip

roturar /1a/ VT (*Agr*) to break up, plough, plow (*EEUU*)

round ['raun] SM (*pl* **~s**) round

royalty SM (*pl* **royalties**) royalty

rozadura SF (= *marca*) mark of rubbing, chafing mark; (*en la piel*) abrasion, graze; [*de zapato*] sore patch

rozagante ADJ healthy-looking

rozamiento SM (= *fricción*) rubbing, chafing; (*Mec*) friction

rozar /1f/ Ⓐ VT **1** (= *tocar ligeramente*) **la rocé al pasar** I brushed past her; **estas botas me rozan los tobillos** these boots rub my ankles; **la pelota rozó el poste** the ball shaved *o* grazed the post

2 (= *acercarse a*) **debe estar rozando los 50** she must be getting on for 50; **es una cuestión que roza lo judicial** it's almost a judicial matter

Ⓑ VI **~ con algo**: **eso roza con la codicia** that's bordering *o* verging on greed

Ⓒ **rozarse** VPR **1** (= *tocarse ligeramente*) **se rozó conmigo al pasar** he brushed past me; **me rocé la rodilla con el muro** I grazed *o* scraped my knee on the wall

2 (*) (= *tratarse*) **~se con algn** to hobnob with sb*, rub shoulders with sb

3 (= *desgastarse*) [*cuello, puños*] to become frayed *o* worn

Rte. ABR = **remite, remitente**

RTVE SF ABR = **Radiotelevisión Española**

ruana SF (*And, Carib, Col*) poncho, ruana

Ruanda SF Rwanda

rubeola SF, **rubéola** SF German measles

rubí SM (= *piedra preciosa*) ruby; [*de reloj*] jewel

rubicundo ADJ 1 [*cara*] ruddy; [*persona*] ruddy-faced 2 (= *rojizo*) reddish

rubio/a Ⓐ ADJ 1 [*persona*] fair-haired, fair, blond/blonde; **~ ceniza** ash-blond; **~ platino** platinum-blonde 2 **tabaco ~** Virginia tobacco Ⓑ SM/F blond/blonde, fair-haired person ➤ **rubia de bote** peroxide blonde Ⓒ SM Virginia tobacco

rublo SM rouble

rubor SM 1 (*en cara*) blush, flush; **causar ~ a algn** to make sb blush 2 (= *timidez*) bashfulness 3 (*CS, Méx*) (= *colorete*) blusher

ruborizar /1f/ Ⓐ VT to cause to blush, make blush Ⓑ **ruborizarse** VPR to blush, redden (**de** at)

ruboroso ADJ (*frm*) **ser ~** to blush easily

rúbrica SF 1 (= *señal*) red mark 2 [*de la firma*] flourish 3 (= *título*) title, heading; **bajo la ~ de** under the heading of

rubricar /1g/ VT 1 (= *firmar*) to sign with a flourish; [+ *documento*] to initial 2 (= *concluir*) to sign and seal

rubro SM (*LAm*) 1 (= *título*) heading, title 2 (*Com*) (= *división*) heading; **el ~ alimentos** the budget for food 3 [*de cuenta*] heading

ruca SF *Araucanian Indian dwelling*

rucio/a Ⓐ ADJ 1 [*caballo*] grey, gray (*EEUU*); [*persona*] grey-haired, gray-haired (*EEUU*) 2 (*Chi**) (= *rubio*) fair, blond/blonde Ⓑ SM/F (*Chi**) (= *rubio*) blond/blonde, blond/blonde person

ruco* ADJ (*And, Méx*) old

rudeza SF coarseness

rudimentario ADJ rudimentary

rudimento SM 1 (*Anat*) rudiment 2 **rudimentos** (= *lo básico*) rudiments

rudo ADJ 1 (= *tosco*) coarse 2 [*golpe*] hard; **fue un ~ golpe para mí** it was a terrible blow for me 3 [*madera*] rough; (= *sin pulir*) unpolished 4 (*Mec*) [*pieza*] stiff

rueca SF distaff

rueda SF 1 (*Mec*) wheel; (= *neumático*) tyre, tire (*EEUU*); [*de mueble*] roller, castor; ✦ MODISMO **ir sobre ~s*** to go smoothly ➤ **rueda auxiliar** (*RPl*), **rueda de auxilio** (*RPl*) spare wheel (*esp Brit*), spare tire (*EEUU*) ➤ **rueda de la fortuna** wheel of fortune ➤ **rueda de molino** millwheel ➤ **rueda dentada** cog ➤ **rueda de recambio** spare wheel ➤ **rueda impresora** (*Inform*) print wheel 2 (= *círculo*) circle, ring ➤ **rueda de prensa** press conference ➤ **rueda de reconocimiento** identification parade 3 (= *rodaja*) slice, round

ruedo SM 1 (*Taur*) bullring, arena 2 (*Pol*) ring 3 [*de vestido*] hem

ruega *etc ver* **rogar**

ruego SM request; **a ~ de** at the request of; **"ruegos y preguntas"** (*en una conferencia*) "any other business"

rufián SM (= *gamberro*) hooligan; (= *canalla*) scoundrel

rugby ['rugbi] SM rugby

rugido SM roar

rugir /3c/ VI [*león*] to roar; [*tormenta, viento*] to roar, howl, rage; [*estómago*] to rumble; **~ de dolor** to roar o howl with pain

rugosidad SF roughness

rugoso ADJ 1 (= *áspero*) rough 2 (= *arrugado*) wrinkled, creased

ruibarbo SM rhubarb

ruido SM 1 (= *sonido*) noise; **no hagas tanto ~** don't make so much noise; **lejos del mundanal ~** (*hum o liter*) far from the madding crowd (*liter*); ✦ MODISMO **mucho ~ y pocas nueces** much ado about nothing ➤ **ruido de fondo** background noise 2 (= *escándalo*) **hacer o meter ~** to cause a stir

ruidoso ADJ 1 (= *estrepitoso*) noisy 2 [*noticia*] sensational

ruin ADJ 1 (= *vil*) [*persona*] contemptible, mean 2 [*trato*] (= *injusto*) mean, shabby; (= *cruel*) heartless, callous

3 (= *tacaño*) stingy, mean (*esp Brit*) 4 [*animal*] vicious

ruina SF 1 (*Fin*) ruin; **estaba al borde de la ~** he was on the brink of (financial) ruin; **la empresa lo llevó a la ~** his business ruined him (financially); **estar en la ~** to be ruined 2 [*de edificio*] collapse; **amenazar ~** to threaten to collapse, be about to fall down; **el castillo está en ~s** the castle is in ruins 3 [*de imperio*] fall, decline; [*de persona*] ruin, downfall; **el alcohol va a ser mi ~** alcohol will be the ruin of me, alcohol will be my downfall 4 **ruinas** ruins; **han descubierto unas ~s romanas** they have discovered some Roman ruins

ruindad SF 1 (= *cualidad*) meanness, lowness 2 (= *acto*) low act, mean act

ruinoso ADJ 1 (*Arquit*) ruinous; (= *destartalado*) tumbledown 2 (*Fin*) ruinous, disastrous

ruiseñor SM nightingale

rular* /1a/ VI 1 [*persona*] to wander around 2 [*máquina*] to work

rulemán SM (*CS*) ball-bearing, roller bearing

rulero SM (*And, CS*) hair curler, roller

ruleta SF roulette ➤ **ruleta rusa** Russian roulette

ruletear /1a/ VI (*CAm, Méx*) to drive a taxi, drive a cab

ruletero/a SM/F (*CAm, Méx*) taxi driver, cab driver

rulo SM 1 (= *rodillo*) roller 2 (*para el pelo*) curler 3 (*And, CS*) (= *rizo*) curl

ruma SF (*Chi*) heap, pile

Rumanía SF, **Rumania** SF Romania

rumano/a Ⓐ ADJ, SM/F Rumanian, Romanian Ⓑ SM (*Ling*) Rumanian, Romanian

rumba SF rumba

rumbear /1a/ VI 1 (*LAm*) (= *orientarse*) to find one's way, get one's bearings 2 (*Cub**) (= *ir de rumba*) to have a party 3 (*RPl**) (= *dirigirse*) **~ para** to head for, make one's way towards

rumbero ADJ (*Carib, Col*) party-going, fond of a good time

rumbo SM 1 (= *dirección*) (*Aer, Náut*) course; **perder el ~** (*Aer, Náut*) to go off course; **poner ~ a** to set a course for; **zarparon con ~ sur** they set a southerly course; **sin ~ (fijo)** [*pasear*] aimlessly; [*viajar*] with no fixed destination 2 (= *tendencia*) **los acontecimientos han tomado un nuevo ~** events have taken a new turn 3 (= *generosidad*) generosity, lavishness

rumboso* ADJ 1 [*persona*] generous 2 [*regalo*] lavish; [*boda, fiesta*] big, showy

rumiante ADJ, SM ruminant

rumiar /1b/ Ⓐ VI to chew the cud Ⓑ VT 1 (= *masticar*) to chew 2 [+ *asunto*] to chew over

rumor SM 1 (= *noticia vaga*) rumour, rumor (*EEUU*); **circula o corre el ~ de que ...** there's a rumour o (*EEUU*) rumor going round that ... 2 (= *murmullo*) murmur; [*de voces*] buzz

rumorearse /1a/ VPR, **rumorarse** /1a/ VPR (*Méx, Col*) **se rumorea que** it is rumoured o (*EEUU*) rumored that

rumoroso ADJ (*liter*) murmuring; [*arroyo*] babbling

runrún SM [*de voces*] murmur 2 (= *rumor*) rumour, rumor (*EEUU*), buzz* 3 [*de máquina*] whirr

runrunearse /1a/ VPR **se runrunea que ...** the rumour o (*EEUU*) rumor is that ...

rupestre ADJ rock *antes de s*; **pintura ~** cave painting; **planta ~** rock plant

rupia SF (= *moneda*) rupee

ruptura SF 1 [*de cable, cerco*] **tenemos que encontrar el punto de ~ del cable** we need to find the point where the cable broke; **la ofensiva de ~ del cerco de Sarajevo** the attack to break the siege of Sarajevo 2 (= *interrupción*) [*de pacto, contrato*] breaking; [*de relaciones, negociaciones*] breaking-off 3 (= *disolución*) break-up; **los motivos de su ~ matrimonial**

the reasons for the break-up of their marriage
4 (= *división*) split, rupture (*frm*)
5 (*con el pasado*) break
6 (*Tenis*) break; **seis puntos de** ~ six break points

rural Ⓐ ADJ rural Ⓑ SF (*RPl Aut*) estate car (*Brit*), station wagon (*EEUU*)

Rusia SF Russia

ruso/a Ⓐ ADJ Russian Ⓑ SM/F Russian; **los Rusos** the Russians, the people of Russia Ⓒ SM (*Ling*) Russian

rústica SF **libro en** ~ paperback (book); **edición (en)** ~

paperback edition; *ver tb* **rústico**

rústico/a Ⓐ ADJ **1** (= *del campo*) rustic, rural, country *antes de s* **2** (= *tosco*) coarse, uncouth; (= *grosero*) crude; (= *descortés*) unmannerly Ⓑ SM/F peasant, yokel, hillbilly (*EEUU*); *ver tb* **rústica**

ruta SF **1** [*de viaje*] route **2** (*RPl*) (= *carretera*) road

rutilante ADJ (*liter*) shining, sparkling, glowing

rutilar /1a/ VI (*liter*) to shine, sparkle

rutina SF routine; **por** ~ from force of habit ➤ **rutina diaria** daily routine

Ss

S, s ['ese] SF (= *letra*) S, s
S ABR **1** (= *sur*) S **2** (= *sobresaliente*) v.g.
S. ABR (*Rel*) (= **San, Santa, Santo**) St
s. ABR (= *siglo*) c
S.A. ABR (= **Sociedad Anónima**) ≈ PLC (*Brit*), ≈ Corp (*EEUU*), ≈ Inc. (*EEUU*)

sábado SM **1** (= *día de la semana*) Saturday; **el ~ pasado** last Saturday; **el ~ próximo** o **que viene** this o next Saturday; **el ~ que viene no, el otro** Saturday week, a week on Saturday, the Saturday after next; **el ~ por la mañana** (on) Saturday morning; **la noche del ~** (on) Saturday night; **un ~ sí y otro no** ◇ **cada dos ~s** every other o second Saturday; **no trabaja los ~s** he doesn't work on Saturdays; **vendrá el ~** he will come on Saturday ➤ **sábado inglés** (*CS*) non-working Saturday ➤ **Sábado Santo** Easter Saturday; ◇ *SEMANA SANTA*
2 (*Rel*) [*de los judíos*] Sabbath

> En inglés los días de la semana se escriben con mayúscula.

sabana SF savannah
sábana SF **1** [*de cama*] sheet; ✦ MODISMO **se le pegan las ~s** he oversleeps **2** (*Rel*) altar cloth
sabandija SF **1** (= *animal*) bug, creepy-crawly* **2** (*LAm**) (= *diablillo*) rascal
sabanear /1a/ VT **1** (*CAm*) (= *agarrar*) to catch **2** (*CAm*) (= *halagar*) to flatter
sabañón SM chilblain
sabático ADJ sabbatical
sabedor ADJ **ser ~ de algo** to know about sth
sabelotodo* SMF INV know-all (*Brit**), know-it-all (*EEUU**)
saber /2m/ Ⓐ VT **1** (= *tener conocimiento de*) **1.1** [+ *dato, información*] to know; **sé que me has mentido** I know you've lied to me; **lo sé** I know; **hacer ~ algo a algn** to inform sb of sth, let sb know about sth; **el motivo de esta carta es hacerle ~ que ...** I am writing to inform o advise you that ... **1.2** (*locuciones*) **a ~** namely; **dos planetas, a ~, Venus y Marte** two planets, namely Venus and Mars; **a ~ si realmente lo compró** I wonder whether he really did buy it; **cualquiera sabe si ...** it's anybody's guess whether ...; **lo dudo, pero nunca se sabe** I doubt it, but you never know; **para que lo sepas** let me tell you, for your information; **que yo sepa** as far as I know; **un no sé qué** a certain something; **¡quién sabe!** who knows!; **¡si lo sabré yo!** I should know!; **tú sabrás (lo que haces)** I suppose you know (what you're doing); **¿tú qué sabes?** what do you know about it?; **¡vete a ~!** God knows!; **vete tú a ~** your guess is as good as mine; **ya lo sabía yo** I thought as much; **¡yo qué sé!, ¡qué sé yo!** how should I know!, search me!*; ✦ MODISMOS **cada uno sabe dónde le aprieta el zapato** everyone knows their own weaknesses; **no sabía dónde meterse** he didn't know what to do with himself
2 (= *enterarse de*) to find out; **cuando lo supe** when I heard o found out about it
3 (= *tener noticias*) to hear; **no sabemos nada de él** we haven't heard from him
4 (= *tener destreza en*) **¿sabes ruso?** do you speak Russian?, can you speak Russian?

> Cuando **saber** va seguido de un infinitivo, suele traducirse por **can** si se refiere a una habilidad permanente y por **know how to** si se refiere a la capacidad de resolver un problema concreto:

~ hacer algo: Jaime sabe tocar el piano Jaime can play the piano; **¿sabes nadar?** can you swim?; **¿sabes cambiar una rueda?** do you know how to change a wheel?; **¿sabes ir?** do you know the way?; **todavía no sabe orientarse por la** ciudad he still doesn't know his way around town; **es una persona que sabe escuchar** she's a good listener
5 (*LAm*) **~ hacer algo** to be in the habit of doing sth

> Recuérdese que las preposiciones en inglés rigen gerundio y no infinitivo, de ahí **to be in the habit of doing sth.**

no sabe venir por aquí he doesn't usually come this way
Ⓑ VI **1** (= *tener conocimiento*) **~ de algo** to know of sth; **sabe mucho de ordenadores** he knows a lot about computers; **sé de un sitio muy bueno** I know of a very good place
2 (= *estar enterado*) to know; **un 5% no sabe, no contesta** there were 5% "don't knows"
3 (= *tener sabor*) to taste; **sabe un poco amargo** it tastes rather bitter; **~ a** to taste of; **esto sabe a queso** this tastes of cheese; **esto sabe a demonio(s)** this tastes awful; ✦ MODISMO **~ mal a algn: me supo muy mal lo que hicieron** I wasn't at all pleased about what they did; **no me sabe mal que un amigo me gaste bromas** I don't mind a friend playing jokes on me
Ⓒ **saberse** VPR **1** (*uso enfático*) **se lo sabe de memoria** she knows it by heart; ✦ MODISMO **se las sabe todas*** he knows every trick in the book*
2 (*uso impersonal*) **2.1** (= *ser conocido*) **ya se sabe que ...** it is known that ...; **no se saben las causas** the causes are not known o are unknown; **¿quién es usted, si se puede ~?** who are you, may I ask?; **nunca más se supo de ellos** they were never heard of again **2.2** (= *ser descubierto*) **se supo que ...** it was learnt o discovered that ...; **por fin se supo el secreto** finally the secret was revealed
Ⓓ SM knowledge, learning
sabidillo/a* SM/F know-all (*Brit**), know-it-all (*EEUU**)
sabido ADJ **es ~ que** it is well known that; **como es ~** as we all know
sabiduría SF wisdom ➤ **sabiduría popular** folklore
sabiendas: a ~ ADV knowingly; **a ~ de que ...** knowing full well that ...
sabihondo/a* ADJ, SM/F know-all (*Brit**), know-it-all (*EEUU**)
sabio/a Ⓐ ADJ **1** [*persona*] (= *docto*) learned; (= *juicioso*) wise **2** [*acción, decisión*] wise Ⓑ SM/F (= *docto*) learned man/learned woman; (= *experto*) scholar, expert
sablazo SM **1** (*con sable*) sabre slash, saber slash (*EEUU*)
2 (*) **dar** o **pegar un ~ a algn** (*en tienda, restaurante*) to rip sb off*; (*al pedir dinero*) to scrounge money off sb*
sable¹ SM (= *arma*) sabre, saber (*EEUU*), cutlass
sable² SM (*Heráldica*) sable
sablear* /1a/ VT **~ dinero a algn** to scrounge money off sb*
sabor SM taste, flavour, flavor (*EEUU*); **con ~ a queso** cheese-flavoured, cheese-flavored (*EEUU*); **tiene ~ a naranja** it tastes of orange, it's orange-flavoured o (*EEUU*) orange-flavored; ✦ MODISMO **le deja a uno mal/buen ~ de boca** it leaves a nasty/pleasant taste in the mouth ➤ **sabor local** local colour, local color (*EEUU*)
saborear /1a/ VT **1** [+ *comida*] to savour, savor (*EEUU*)
2 [+ *venganza, momento, triunfo, victoria*] to relish, savour, savor (*EEUU*); [+ *desgracia ajena*] to delight in
sabotaje SM sabotage
saboteador(a) SM/F saboteur
sabotear /1a/ VT to sabotage
sabré *etc ver* **saber**
sabrosear* /1a/ VI (*Ven*) to have fun
sabroso Ⓐ ADJ **1** [*comida*] tasty, delicious; (= *salado*) slightly salty **2** [*oferta*] substantial **3** [*broma, historia*] racy, daring **4** (*And, Carib, Méx*) (= *agradable*) pleasant **5** (*And, Ven**) [*mujer*] gorgeous*, tasty** **6** (*And**) [*persona*] (= *lleno de*

energía) lively **③** ADV (*And, Ven**) beautifully

sabrosón* ADJ **1** (*LAm*) (= *comida*) tasty, delicious
2 = **sabroso 4, 5**

sabueso ④ SM (*Zool*) bloodhound **③** SMF (= *detective*) sleuth*

saca SF big sack ➤ **saca de correo, saca de correos** mailbag

sacacorchos SM INV corkscrew

sacamuelas* SMF INV (*hum*) tooth-puller

sacaperras* (*Esp*) **④** SMF INV (= *persona*) con artist* **③** SM (= *cosa*) rip-off*

sacapuntas SM INV pencil sharpener

---

sacar /1g/

④ VERBO TRANSITIVO	**⑥** VERBO PRONOMINAL
③ VERBO INTRANSITIVO	

Para las expresiones **sacar adelante, sacar brillo, sacar los colores a algn, sacar faltas a algo, sacar algo en limpio, sacar provecho, sacar a relucir** *etc, ver la entrada correspondiente a la otra palabra.*

---

sacar ④ VERBO TRANSITIVO

1 (= *poner fuera*) to take out, get out; **sacó el revólver y disparó** he drew his revolver and fired, he took *o* got his revolver out and fired; **saca la basura, por favor** please put *o* take the rubbish (*esp Brit*) *o* garbage (*EEUU*) out; **~on a los rehenes por la ventana** they got the hostages out through the window; **~ a algn a <u>bailar</u>** to get sb up for a dance; **~ algo/a algn <u>de</u>: sacó toda su ropa del armario** she took all his clothes out of the wardrobe, she removed all his clothes from the wardrobe; **~ dinero del cajero** to take *o* get some money out of the machine; **~ un libro de la biblioteca** to get a book out of the library; **¡sacadme de aquí!** get me out of here!; **mañana sacan a dos terroristas de la cárcel** tomorrow two terrorists will be released from jail; **~ a <u>pasear</u> a algn** to take sb (out) for a walk;
✦ MODISMO **~ a algn de sí** to drive sb mad
2 (*de una persona*) [+ *diente*] to take out; **¡deja ese palo, que me vas a ~ un ojo!** stop playing with that stick, you're going to poke my eye out!; **~ <u>sangre</u> a algn** to take blood from sb
3 (*con partes del cuerpo*) to stick out; **~ la lengua a alguien** to stick one's tongue out at sb; **saca la mano si vas a aparcar** stick your hand out if you're going to park
4 (= *obtener*)
4.1 [+ *notas, diputados, puesto*] to get; **siempre saca buenas notas** he always gets good marks; **¿y tú qué sacas con denunciarlo a la policía?** and what do you get out of *o* gain from reporting him to the police?; **sacó un seis** (*con dados*) he threw a six; **sacó la plaza de enfermera** she got the nursing post; **ha sacado el pelo rubio de su abuela** she gets her blonde hair from her grandmother; **~ algo a algn** to get sth out of sb; **le ~on toda la información que necesitaban** they got all the information they needed from *o* out of him; **~ algo <u>de</u>** [+ *material, petróleo*] to extract sth from; **los datos están sacados de dos libros** the statistics are taken *o* come from two books; **¿de dónde has sacado esa idea?** where did you get that idea?; **¿qué conclusión se puede ~ de todo esto?** what conclusion can be drawn from all of this?
4.2 [+ *dinero*] **lo hago para ~ unas pesetas** I do it to make a bit of money; **sacó el premio gordo** he got *o* won the jackpot; **sacamos una ganancia de ...** we made a profit of ...
5 (= *comprar*) [+ *entradas*] to get; **yo ~é los billetes** I'll get the tickets
6 (= *lanzar*) [+ *modelo nuevo*] to bring out; [+ *libro*] to bring out, publish; [+ *disco*] to release; [+ *moda*] to create; **han sacado sus nuevos productos al mercado** they have brought out their new product range
7 (= *hacer* [+ *foto*] to take; [+ *copia*] to make; **te voy a ~ una foto** I'm going to take a photo of you
8 (= *resolver*) **no conseguí ~ el problema** I couldn't solve the problem
9 (= *mostrar*) **lo han sacado en el periódico** he was in the

paper; **no me sacó en la foto** he missed me out of the photo
10 (= *mencionar*) **no me saques ahora eso** don't come to me with that now
11 (*esp LAm*) (= *quitar*) [+ *ropa*] to take off; [+ *mancha*] to get out *o* off, remove (*frm*)
12 (= *aventajar en*) **al terminar la carrera le sacaba 10 metros al adversario** he finished the race 10 metres ahead of his rival; **le saca 10cm a su hermano** he is 10cm taller than his brother
13 (= *salvar*) to get out; **nos sacó de esa penosa situación** she got us out of that difficult situation
14 (*Ftbl*) **saca el balón Kiko** (*en saque de banda*) the throw-in is taken by Kiko; (*en falta*) Kiko takes the free kick; **~ una falta** to take a free kick
15 (*Cos*) [+ *prenda de vestir*] (= *ensanchar*) to let out; (= *alargar*) to let down
③ VERBO INTRANSITIVO
1 (*Tenis*) to serve
2 (*Ftbl*) (*en córner, tiro libre*) to take the kick; (*en saque de banda*) to take the throw-in
⑥ **sacarse** VERBO PRONOMINAL
1 (= *extraer*) [+ *objeto*] to take out; **se sacó la mano del bolsillo** he took his hand out of his pocket; **casi me saco un ojo** I almost poked my eye out; **se va a ~ una muela** she's going to have a tooth out; **~se sangre** to have a blood test done
2 (*esp LAm*) (= *quitarse*) **~se la ropa** to take one's clothes off
3 (= *conseguir*) to get; **~se unas pesetas** to make a bit of money; **~se el carnet de conducir** to get one's driving licence (*Brit*) *o* driver's license (*EEUU*), pass one's driving test; **~se el título de abogado** to qualify as a lawyer

sacarina SF saccharin, saccharine

sacerdocio SM priesthood

sacerdotal ADJ priestly

sacerdote SM priest; **sumo ~** high priest

sacerdotisa SF priestess

saciar /1b/ **④** VT **1** [+ *hambre*] to satisfy; [+ *sed*] to quench
2 [+ *deseos, curiosidad*] to satisfy; [+ *ambición*] to fulfil, fulfill (*EEUU*) **③** **saciarse** VPR **1** (*de comida, bebida*) to sate *o* satiate o.s. (**con, de** with) **2** (= *satisfacerse*) to be satisfied (**con, de** with)

saciedad SF **comer hasta la ~** to eat one's fill; **repetir hasta la ~** to repeat ad nauseam

saco[1] SM **1** (= *costal*) (*referido al contenedor*) bag, sack; (*referido al contenido*) bagful; ✦ MODISMOS **a ~s** by the ton; **caer en ~ roto** to fall on deaf ears; **entrar a ~*** to go for it*; **mandar a algn a tomar por ~** (*Esp****) to tell sb to get stuffed***; **ser un ~ de huesos** to be a bag of bones ➤ **saco de dormir** sleeping bag ➤ **saco terrero** sandbag **2** (*Anat*) sac ➤ **saco amniótico** amniotic sac **3** (*LAm*) (= *chaqueta*) jacket; ✦ REFRÁN **al que le venga el ~ que se lo ponga** if the cap fits, wear it

saco[2] SM (*Mil*) sack; **entrar a ~ en** to sack

SACRA SM ABR (*Arg*) = **Sindicato de Amas de Casa de la República Argentina**

SACRA

Founded in 1984, **SACRA**, or the **Sindicato de Amas de Casa de la República Argentina**, was the world's first trade union for housewives. One of its main aims has been to redefine housework as employment and to obtain for its members the salaries, pensions and health benefits traditionally associated with union membership. It has developed an educational programme designed to improve women's job opportunities, organized cheap holidays for housewives and obtained free medical treatment for its members. While union membership has allowed thousands of women to take part in public affairs, critics believe that the idea that housewives should have salaries simply reaffirms the stereotypical view that women function best in the home and, in the long run, may encourage non-participation outside.

sacralizar /1f/ VT to consecrate

sacramental ADJ (*Rel*) [*rito*] sacramental; [*palabras*] ritual

sacramento SM sacrament; **recibir los ~s** to receive the sacraments

sacrificado ADJ **1** [*profesión, vida*] demanding **2** [*persona*] self-sacrificing

sacrificar /1g/ **Ⓐ** VT **1** (*Rel*) to sacrifice (**a** to) **2** (= *matar*) [+ *ganado*] to slaughter; [+ *animal doméstico*] to put to sleep **Ⓑ sacrificarse** VPR to sacrifice o.s.

sacrificio SM **1** (*Rel*) sacrifice **2** [*de animal*] slaughter, slaughtering

sacrilegio SM sacrilege

sacrílego ADJ sacrilegious

sacristán SM verger, sexton, sacristan

sacristía SF vestry, sacristy

sacro ADJ [*arte, música*] sacred

sacrosanto ADJ sacrosanct

sacudida SF **1** (= *agitación*) shake, shaking; **dar una ~ a una alfombra** to beat a carpet; **avanzar dando ~s** to bump o jolt o lurch along **2** (= *movimiento brusco*) [*de cuerpo, rodilla*] jerk; [*de cabeza*] toss **3** [*de terremoto*] shock; [*de explosión*] blast ➤ **sacudida eléctrica** electric shock **4** (= *alteración brusca*) [*de situación*] violent change; (*Pol*) upheaval

sacudidor SM (*Méx*) feather duster

sacudir /3a/ **Ⓐ** VT **1** (= *agitar*) [+ *árbol, edificio, cabeza*] to shake; [+ *alfombra*] to beat; [+ *colchón*] to shake, shake the dust out of **2** (= *quitar*) [+ *tierra*] to shake off; **~ el polvo** (*esp CS, Méx*) to dust **3** (= *conmover*) to shake; **una tremenda emoción sacudió a la multitud** a great wave of excitement ran through the crowd **4** (***) (= *pegar*) **~ a algn** to belt sb* **Ⓑ** VI (*CS, Méx*) to dust **Ⓒ sacudirse** VPR (*uno mismo*) to shake o.s.; [+ *brazo, pelo*] to shake; **sacúdete la arena del pelo** shake the sand out of your hair; **el caballo se sacudía las moscas con la cola** the horse brushed off the flies with its tail

sacudón SM (*LAm*) **1** (= *sacudida*) violent shake **2** (= *terremoto*) quake

S.A. de C.V. ABR (*Méx*) (= **Sociedad Anónima de Capital Variable**) ≈ PLC (*Brit*), ≈ Corp (*EEUU*), ≈ Inc. (*EEUU*)

sádico/a Ⓐ ADJ sadistic **Ⓑ** SM/F sadist

sadismo SM sadism

sadoca** SMF = **sadomasoquista B**

sadomasoquismo SM sadomasochism

sadomasoquista Ⓐ ADJ sadomasochistic **Ⓑ** SMF sadomasochist

saeta SF **1** (*Mil*) arrow, dart **2** (*Mús*) *sacred song in flamenco style*

safado* ADJ (*Chi*) mad, crazy

safari SM safari

saga SF **1** (*Literat*) saga **2** (= *clan*) clan, dynasty

sagacidad SF (= *astucia*) shrewdness, cleverness; (= *perspicacia*) sagacity

sagaz ADJ (= *astuto*) shrewd, clever; (= *perspicaz*) sagacious

Sagitario SM (= *signo*) Sagittarius

sagitario SMF INV (= *persona*) Sagittarius; **soy ~** I'm Sagittarius

sagrado ADJ [*lugar, libro*] holy, sacred; [*deber*] sacred; **Sagradas Escrituras** Holy Scriptures; **Sagrada Familia** Holy Family

sagrario SM sacrarium

Sahara [sa'ara] SM, **Sáhara** ['saxara] SM (*Esp*) Sahara

saharaui [saxa'raui] ADJ Saharan

sahariana SF safari jacket

saibó SM (*Col, Ven*) sideboard

sainete SM one-act farce, one-act comedy

sajón/ona ADJ, SM/F Saxon

sal¹ SF **1** (*Culin, Quím*) salt ➤ **sal de cocina** kitchen salt, cooking salt ➤ **sal de fruta(s)** liver salts, fruit salts ➤ **sales aromáticas** smelling salts ➤ **sales de baño** bath salts ➤ **sal gorda** kitchen salt, cooking salt **2** [*de persona*] (= *gracia*) wit; (= *encanto*) charm; **tiene mucha ~** he's very amusing

sal² *ver* **salir**

sala SF **1** (*en casa, tb* ~ **de estar**) living room, sitting room, lounge; (= *cuarto grande*) hall; [*de castillo*] hall **2** (= *local público*) (*Teat, Mús*) auditorium; (*Jur*) court; (*Med*) ward; (*en cine*) screen ➤ **sala capitular** chapterhouse, meeting room ➤ **sala cinematográfica** cinema (*esp Brit*), movie theater (*EEUU*) ➤ **sala de conciertos** concert hall ➤ **sala de conferencias** (*gen*) conference hall; (*Univ*) lecture hall, lecture theatre, lecture theater (*EEUU*) ➤ **sala de embarque** departure lounge ➤ **sala de espera** (*Med, Ferro*) waiting room; (*Aer*) departure lounge ➤ **sala de fiestas** night club (*with cabaret*) ➤ **sala de juntas** (*Com*) boardroom ➤ **sala de lectura** reading room ➤ **sala de máquinas** (*Náut*) engine room ➤ **sala de profesores** staffroom

salacidad SF salaciousness, prurience

sala-cuna SF (*pl* **salas-cuna**) (*CS*) day-nursery

salado ADJ **1** (*Culin*) (= *con sal*) salt *antes de s*, salted; (= *con demasiada sal*) salty; (= *no dulce*) savoury; **agua salada** salt water; **está muy ~** it's very salty **2** [*persona*] (= *gracioso*) amusing; (= *encantador*) charming **3** (*LAm**) (= *desgraciado*) unlucky, unfortunate **4** (*CS**) (= *caro*) expensive **5** (*Méx**) (= *que trae mala suerte*) jinxed*

salamandra SF salamander

salamanquesa SF lizard, gecko

salame SM **1** (*CS Culin*) salami **2** (*RPl***) idiot, thickhead*

salar¹ SM (*And, CS*) salt flat, salt pan

salar² /1a/ **Ⓐ** VT (*Culin*) (*para poner salado*) to add salt to, put salt in; (*para conservar*) to salt **Ⓑ salarse** VPR (*CAm, Méx**) [*sorpresa, planes*] to go wrong, fall through

salarial ADJ wage *antes de s*; **reclamación ~** wage claim

salario SM wage, wages *pl*, pay, salary ➤ **salario base** basic wage ➤ **salario mínimo** minimum wage ➤ **salario mínimo interprofesional** (*Esp*) guaranteed minimum wage

salaz ADJ salacious, prurient

salazón SF **1** (= *acto*) salting **2** (*Culin*) (= *carne*) salted meat; (= *pescado*) salted fish

salchicha SF sausage

salchichón SM *salami-type sausage*

salchichonería SF (*Méx*) delicatessen (*specializing in cold meats*)

saldar /1a/ **Ⓐ** VT **1** (*Com*) [+ *cuenta*] to settle, pay; [+ *deuda*] to settle, pay off **2** [+ *diferencias*] to settle **3** [+ *existencias*] to clear, sell off **Ⓑ saldarse** VPR **~se con algo** to result in sth; **el accidente se ha saldado con cuatro muertos** the accident resulted in four deaths, four people died in the accident

saldo SM **1** [*de cuenta*] balance ➤ **saldo acreedor** credit balance ➤ **saldo a favor** credit balance ➤ **saldo deudor** debit balance ➤ **saldo negativo** debit balance, adverse balance ➤ **saldo positivo** credit balance **2** (= *liquidación*) sale; **precio de ~** sale price **3** (= *pago*) settlement, payment **4** [*de móvil*] credit; **no me queda saldo en el móvil** I haven't any credit left on my mobile **5** (= *resultado final*) **la manifestación acabó con un ~ de 20 personas heridas** a total of 20 people were injured in the demonstration; **el ~ oficial es de 28 muertos** the official toll is 28 dead

salero SM **1** [*de mesa*] salt cellar (*Brit*), salt shaker (*EEUU*) **2** [*de persona*] (= *ingenio*) wit; (= *encanto*) charm

saleroso* ADJ = **salado 2**

salga *etc ver* **salir**

salida SF **1** [*de un lugar*] **le prohibieron la ~ del país** he was forbidden to leave the country; **tras su ~ de la cárcel** when he came out of prison; **a la ~: te esperaremos a la ~** we'll wait for you on the way out; **sondeos realizados a la ~ de las urnas** exit polls; **dar ~ a: necesitaba dar ~ a su creatividad** he needed to give expression to o find an outlet for his creativity; **dio ~ a su indignación** he gave vent to his anger; **puerta de ~** exit door

2 (= *aparición*) **los fans esperaban su ~ al escenario** the fans were waiting for her to come (out) onto the stage; **precio de ~** [*de objeto subastado*] starting price; [*de acciones*] offer price ➤ **salida del sol** sunrise
3 (= *lugar*) [*de edificio*] exit, way out; [*de autopista*] exit, turn-off; **"salida"** (*encima de la puerta*) "exit"; (*en el pasillo*) "way out", "exit"; **una cueva sin ~** a cave with no way out; **tener ~ a algo: nuestro edificio tiene ~ a las dos calles** our building has access onto both streets; **un país que no tiene ~ al mar** a country with no access to the sea ➤ **salida de artistas** stage door ➤ **salida de emergencia** emergency exit ➤ **salida de incendios** fire exit
4 [*de avión, tren*] departure; **"salidas internacionales"** "international departures"; **"salidas nacionales"** "domestic departures"; **el autobús efectuará su ~ desde el andén número cuatro** the bus will depart from bay number four
5 (= *escapada*) [*de viaje*] trip; [*de excursión*] trip, outing; (*por la noche*) night out, evening out; **en mi primera ~ al extranjero** on my first trip abroad, on my first foreign trip; **es su primera ~ desde que dio a luz** it's the first time she's been out since she gave birth
6 (= *comienzo*) [*de carrera, desfile*] start; **acudieron a los puestos de ~** they took their starting positions; **dar la ~ to** give the starting signal
7 (*Teat*) (*al entrar en escena*) appearance; (*para recibir aplausos*) curtain call
8 (= *solución*) solution; **la única ~ está en la negociación** the only way out is through negotiation, the only solution is to negotiate; **no le quedaba otra ~ que la dimisión** she had no alternative *o* option but to resign
9 (*al hablar*) **tiene unas ~s que te mueres de risa** some of the things he comes out with are just hilarious ➤ **salida de bombero** (*Esp hum*) **¡vaya ~s de bombero que tuvo!** he dropped some real clangers!* ➤ **salida de tono: fue una ~ de tono** it was inappropriate *o* uncalled-for
10 (*Com*) [*de producto*] launch; **dar ~ a: dar ~ a los excedentes agrícolas** to find an outlet for surplus produce; **dimos ~ a nuestras existencias en dos meses** we sold off our stock in two months; **tener ~** to sell well
11 (*Fin*) (= *cargo*) debit entry; **entradas y ~s** income and expenditure
12 salidas (*en el trabajo*) openings, job opportunities; **esa carrera no tiene apenas ~s** there are very few openings *o* job opportunities for someone with that degree ➤ **salidas profesionales** job opportunities
13 (*Téc*) [*de aire, gas, vapor*] vent; [*de agua*] outlet

salido* ADJ (*Esp*) randy*, horny*
salidor ADJ (*LAm*) fond of going out a lot
saliente ❶ ADJ **1** (*Arquit*) projecting **2** [*rasgo*] prominent **3** (= *importante*) salient **4** [*sol*] rising ❷ SM (*Arquit*) projection
salina SF (= *mina*) salt mine
salino ADJ saline

salir /3q/

❶ VERBO INTRANSITIVO   ❷ VERBO PRONOMINAL

Para las expresiones **salir adelante, salir ganando, salir de viaje** *etc, ver la entrada correspondiente a la otra palabra.*

salir ❶ VERBO INTRANSITIVO
1 (= *partir*) [*persona*] to leave; [*tren, autobús, avión*] to leave, depart (*frm*); (*Náut*) to leave, sail; (*Inform*) to quit; **sale un tren cada dos horas** there is a train every two hours; **~ de** to leave; **¿a qué hora sales de la oficina?** what time do you leave the office?; **salgo de clase a las cinco** I finish school at five; **~ para** to set off for
2 (= *no entrar*) (= *ir fuera*) to go out; (= *venir fuera*) to come out; **salió a la calle a ver si venían** she went outside *o* she went out into the street to see if they were coming; **—¿está Juan? —no, me temo que ha salido** "is Juan in?" — "no, I'm afraid he's gone out"; **¿vas a ~ esta noche?** are you going out tonight?; **nunca he salido al extranjero** I've never been abroad; **los rehenes salieron por la ventana** the hostages got out through the window; **salió corriendo (del cuarto)** he ran out (of the room); **~ de: nos la encontramos**

al ~ del museo we bumped into her when we were coming out of the museum; **¿de dónde has salido?** where did you appear *o* spring from?; **~ de paseo** to go out for a walk; ✦ MODISMOS **de esta no salimos*** we'll never get out of this one*; **~ de pobre** to stop being poor
3 (*al mercado*) [*revista, libro, disco*] to come out; [*moda*] to come in; **acaba de ~ un disco suyo** an album of his has just come out *o* been released
4 (*en medios de comunicación*) **la noticia salió en el periódico de ayer** the news was *o* appeared in yesterday's paper; **~ por la televisión** to be *o* appear on TV
5 (= *surgir*) to come up; **en el debate no salió el tema del aborto** the subject of abortion didn't come up in the debate; **~ algo a algn: le ha salido novio/un trabajo** she's got herself a boyfriend/a job
6 (= *aparecer*) [*agua*] to come out; [*sol*] to come out; [*mancha*] to appear; **no sale agua del grifo** there's no water coming out of the tap (*Brit*) *o* faucet (*EEUU*); **me sale sangre** I'm bleeding
7 (= *nacer*) [*diente*] to come through; [*planta, sol*] to come up; [*pelo*] to grow; [*pollito*] to hatch; **ya le ha salido un diente al niño** the baby already has one tooth; **le han salido muchas espinillas** he's got a lot of blackheads; **nos levantamos antes de que saliera el sol** we got up before sunrise
8 (= *quitarse*) [*mancha*] to come out, come off
9 (= *costar*) to work out; **la calefacción de gas saldría más barata** gas heating would work out cheaper; **me salió por unos 1.000 pesos** it cost me about 1,000 pesos; **salimos a diez libras por persona** (*Esp*) it works out at £10 each
10 (= *resultar*) **¿cómo salió la representación?** how did the performance go?; **¿qué número ha salido premiado en la lotería?** what was the winning number in the lottery?; **salió alcalde por tres votos** he was elected mayor by three votes; **~ bien: el plan salió bien** the plan worked out well; **espero que todo salga bien** I hope everything works out all right; **¿salió bien la fiesta?** did the party go well?; **¿cómo te salió el examen?** how did your exam go?; **~ mal: los festejos salieron mal por la lluvia** the celebrations were spoiled by the rain; **¡qué mal me ha salido el dibujo!** oh dear! my drawing hasn't come out very well!
11 ~ algo a algn
11.1 (= *poder resolverse*) **este crucigrama no me sale** I can't do this crossword
11.2 (= *resultar natural*) **no me sale ser amable con ella** I find it difficult being nice to her
11.3 (= *poder recordarse*) **no me sale su apellido** I can't think of his name
12 ~ a [*calle*] to come out in, lead to; **esta calle sale a la plaza** this street comes out in *o* leads to the square
13 ~ a algn (= *parecerse*) to take after sb; **ha salido a su padre** he takes after his father
14 ~ con algn to go out with sb; **está saliendo con un compañero de clase** she's going out with one of her classmates
15 ~ con algo (*al hablar*) to come out with sth; **y ahora sale con esto** and now he comes out with this; **ahora me sale con que yo le debo dinero** and now he starts complaining that I owe him money
16 ~ de [*proceder*] to come from; **el aceite que sale de la aceituna** oil which comes from olives
17 ~ por algn (= *defender*) to come out in defence of sb, stick up for sb
18 (*Teat*) to come on; **sale vestido de policía** he comes on dressed as a policeman; **"sale el rey"** (*al escenario*) "enter the king"
19 (= *empezar*) (*Dep*) to start; (*Ajedrez*) to have first move; (*Naipes*) to lead
❷ **salirse** VERBO PRONOMINAL
1 (= *irse*) to leave; ✦ MODISMO **~se con la suya** to get one's way
2 (= *escaparse*) to escape (**de** from), get out (**de** of); **el tigre se salió de la jaula** the tiger escaped from the cage, the tiger got out of the cage
3 (= *filtrarse*) [*aire, líquido*] to leak (out); **se salía el aceite del motor** oil was leaking out of the engine
4 (= *rebosar*) to overflow; **el río se salió de su cauce** the river burst its banks; ✦ MODISMO **~se de madre** to lose one's self-control

5 (= *desviarse*) to come off; **nos salimos de la carretera** we came off the road; **~se de la vía** to jump the rails; **~se del tema** to get off the point
6 (= *desconectarse*) to come out; **se ha salido el enchufe** the plug has come out
7 (= *excederse*) **~se de lo normal** to go beyond what is normal; **~se de los límites** to go beyond the limits

salita SF sitting room

salitre SM **1** (= *sustancia salina*) saltpetre, saltpeter (*EEUU*), nitre **2** (*Chi*) (= *nitrato*) Chilean nitrate

saliva SF saliva; **✦** MODISMOS **gastar ~** to waste one's breath (**en** on); **tragar ~** to swallow one's feelings

salivar /1a/ VI **1** (= *segregar saliva*) to salivate **2** (*LAm*) (= *escupir*) to spit

salivazo SM gobbet of spit

salmantino ADJ of/from Salamanca, Salamancan

salmo SM psalm

salmodia SF **1** (*Rel*) psalmody **2** (*) (= *canturreo*) drone

salmón SM salmon

salmonela SF salmonella

salmonelosis SF INV salmonellosis, salmonella food-poisoning

salmonete SM red mullet

salmuera SF pickle, brine

salobre ADJ salt, salty; **agua ~** brackish water

salomónico ADJ **juicio ~** judgement of Solomon

salón SM **1** [*de casa*] living-room, lounge; **juego de ~** parlour game, parlor game (*EEUU*) ➤ **salón comedor** lounge-dining-room **2** [*de lugar público*] (*gen*) hall, assembly-room; (*Com*) show, trade fair, exhibition ➤ **salón de actos** assembly room ➤ **salón de baile** ballroom ➤ **salón de belleza** beauty parlour, beauty parlor (*EEUU*) ➤ **salón de fiestas** (*LAm*) function room ➤ **salón del automóvil** motor show, auto show (*EEUU*) ➤ **salón de plenos del Ayuntamiento** Council chamber ➤ **salón de sesiones** assembly hall ➤ **salón de té** tearoom

salpicadera SF (*Méx*) mudguard (*esp Brit*), fender (*EEUU*)

salpicadero SM (*Esp*) dashboard

salpicado ADJ **~ de** dotted with; **un paisaje ~ de granjas** a landscape dotted with farms

salpicadura SF **1** (= *acto*) splashing **2** (= *mancha*) splash

salpicar /1g/ VT **1** (= *manchar*) to splash (**de** with); (= *rociar*) to sprinkle (**de** with); **este asunto salpica al gobierno** the government has been tainted by this affair **2** [+ *conversación, discurso*] to sprinkle (**de** with)

salpicón SM ➤ **salpicón de marisco(s)** seafood salad

salpimentar /1a/ VT to season, add salt and pepper to

salsa[1] SF (*Culin*) (*gen*) sauce; [*de carne*] gravy; **✦** MODISMO **estar en su ~** to be in one's element ➤ **salsa de tomate** (*frito*) tomato sauce; (*esp Col*) ketchup

salsa[2] SF (*Mús*) salsa

salsamentaría SF (*Col*) delicatessen (*specializing in cold meats*)

salsera SF sauce boat

salsero ADJ (*Mús*) salsa-loving; **ritmo ~** salsa rhythm

saltador(a) SM/F (*Atletismo*) jumper; (*Natación*) diver ➤ **saltador(a) de altura** high-jumper ➤ **saltador(a) de longitud** long-jumper ➤ **saltador(a) de pértiga** pole-vaulter ➤ **saltador(a) de trampolín** trampolinist ➤ **saltador(a) de triple** triple jumper

saltamontes SM INV grasshopper

saltante ADJ (*Perú*) outstanding, noteworthy

saltar /1a/ **Ⓐ** VI **1** [*persona, animal*] (= *dar un salto*) (*tb Atletismo*) to jump; [*más lejos*] to leap; (*a la pata coja*) to hop; **~ de alegría** to jump with *o* for joy; **~ a la comba** to skip (*esp Brit*), jump rope (*EEUU*); **✦** MODISMO **está a la que salta** he never misses a trick*
2 (= *lanzarse*) **2.1** (*lit*) **~ al campo** *o* **al césped** (*Dep*) to come out on to the pitch; **~ al agua** to jump *o* dive into the water; **~ de la cama** to leap out of bed; **~ en paracaídas** to

parachute; **~ sobre algn** to jump *o* leap *o* pounce on sb; **~ a tierra** to leap ashore **2.2** (*fig*) **~ al mundo de la política** to go into politics, move into the political arena; **~ del último puesto al primero** to jump from last place to first; **~ a la fama** to win fame, be shot to fame
3 (= *salir disparado*) [*chispa*] to fly, fly out; [*líquido*] to shoot out, spurt out; [*corcho*] to pop out; [*resorte*] to break, go*; [*astilla*] to fly off; [*pelota*] to fly; **saltan chispas** sparks are flying; **está saltando el aceite** the oil is spitting; **el balón saltó por encima de la portería** the ball flew over the bar; **el asunto ha saltado a la prensa** the affair has reached the newspapers; **✦** MODISMO **salta a la vista** it's patently obvious, it hits you in the eye
4 (= *estallar*) [*cristal*] to shatter; [*recipiente*] to crack; **hacer ~ un edificio** to blow up a building; **el coche saltó por los aires** the car was blown up
5 (*Elec*) [*alarma*] to go off; [*plomos*] to blow
6 (*al hablar*) **6.1** (*de forma inesperada*) to say, pipe up*; **~ con una patochada** to come out with a ridiculous *o* foolish remark; **~ de una cosa a otra** to skip from one thing *o* subject to another, skip about **6.2** (*con ira*) to explode, blow up

Ⓑ VT **1** [+ *muro, obstáculo*] (*por encima*) to jump over, jump; (*llegando más lejos*) to leap, leap over; (*apoyándose con las manos*) to vault
2 (*CS Culin*) to sauté

Ⓒ **saltarse** VPR **1** (= *omitir*) [+ *párrafo, renglón*] to skip; **nos saltamos el desayuno** we skipped breakfast
2 (= *no hacer caso de*) **~se un semáforo** to go through a red light, jump the lights; **~se un stop** to disobey a stop sign; **~se todas las reglas** to break all the rules
3 (= *salirse*) [*pieza*] to come off, fly off; **se me ~on las lágrimas** I burst out crying

saltarín ADJ **1** (= *que salta*) [*cabra, cordero, niño*] frolicking; [*rana, pulga*] jumping, leaping **2** (= *inquieto*) restless

salteado ADJ **—¿has leído el libro? —sólo unas páginas salteadas** "have you read the book?" — "I just skipped through it"

salteador SM (*tb* **~ de caminos**) highwayman

saltear /1a/ **Ⓐ** VT (*Culin*) to sauté **Ⓑ** **saltearse** VPR (*RPI*) = **saltarse** C1

salterio SM **1** (*Rel*) psalter **2** (*Mús*) psaltery

saltimbanqui SM acrobat

salto SM **1** (= *acción*) (*gen*) jump; (*de mayor altura, distancia*) leap; (*al agua*) dive; **un gran ~ adelante en tecnología** a great leap forward in technology; **el pájaro avanzaba a saltitos** the bird hopped along; **dar un ~** [*persona, animal*] to jump; [*corazón*] to leap; **empezó a dar ~s para calentarse** he started jumping about to warm up; **me daba ~s el corazón** my heart was pounding; **el progreso da ~s imprevisibles** progress makes unpredictable leaps; **subió/bajó de un ~** he jumped up/down; **su ~ a la fama** his leap to fame, his springboard to fame; **pegar un ~** = **dar un salto**; **✦** MODISMOS **a ~ de mata: vivir a ~ de mata** (= *sin organización*) to lead a haphazard life; (= *sin seguridad*) to live from hand to mouth; **dar el ~** to make the leap *o* jump; **tirarse al ~** (*Chi**) to take a chance *o* risk ➤ **salto al vacío** leap in the dark ➤ **salto de agua** (*Geog*) waterfall ➤ **salto de cama** negligee
2 (*Atletismo*) jump; (*Natación*) dive; **las pruebas de ~s** the jump events; **triple ~** triple jump ➤ **salto alto** (*LAm*) high jump ➤ **salto con garrocha** (*LAm*), **salto con pértiga** pole vault ➤ **salto de altura** high jump ➤ **salto de esquí** ski-jump; **la Copa del Mundo de ~s de esquí** ski-jumping World Cup ➤ **salto de longitud** long jump ➤ **salto largo** (*LAm*) long jump ➤ **salto mortal** somersault

saltón ADJ **1** [*ojos*] bulging **2** (*And*) [*persona*] wary

salubre ADJ healthy, salubrious (*frm*)

salubridad SF healthiness, salubriousness (*frm*)

salud SF **1** (*Med*) health; **estar bien/mal de ~** to be in good/bad health; **mejorar de ~** to get better; **tener buena ~** ◇ **gozar de buena ~** to enjoy good health ➤ **salud ambiental** environmental health ➤ **salud mental** mental health, mental well-being ➤ **salud ocupacional** occupational health ➤ **salud pública** public health **2** (*en brindis*) **¡salud!** ◇ **¡a su salud!** cheers!, good health!; **beber a**

la ~ de algn to drink to the health of sb **3** (*al estornudar*) **¡salud!** bless you!

saludable ADJ (*Med*) healthy; **un aviso ~** a salutary warning

saludar /1a/ ㊐ VT **1** (*al encontrarse con algn*) (*con palabras*) to say hello to, greet (*frm*); (*con gestos*) to wave at, wave to; **entré a ~la** I went in to say hello to her; **me saludó dándome un beso** he greeted me with a kiss; **nos saludó con la mano** she waved to us; **la compañía en pleno salió a ~ al público** the whole company came out to take a bow; **salude de mi parte a su marido** give my regards to your husband **2** (*en carta*) **Le saluda atentamente** Yours faithfully (*Brit*), Sincerely yours (*EEUU*) **3** (*Mil*) to salute **4** [+ *noticia, suceso*] to hail, welcome ㊐ VI **1** (= *dirigir un saludo*) to say hello; **nunca saluda** she never says hello **2** (*Mil*) to salute ㊑ saludarse VPR to greet each other; **se ~on con un beso** they greeted each other with a kiss; **hace tiempo que no se saludan** they haven't been speaking for some time

saludo SM **1** (*al encontrarse con algn*) (= *palabra*) greeting; (= *gesto*) wave; **no contestó a mi ~** he didn't respond to my greeting; **nos dirigió un ~ con la mano** he gave us a wave, he waved to us; **~s a Ana de mi parte** say hello to Ana for me; (*más formal*) my regards to Ana; ✦ MODISMO **negar el ~ a algn** to cut sb dead, ignore sb, blank sb* **2** (*en carta*) **un ~ cariñoso a Gonzalo** warm regards to Gonzalo; **un ~ afectuoso** o **cordial** kind regards; **~s** best wishes **3** (*Mil*) salute

salva SF **1** [*de aplausos*] storm **2** (*Mil*) salute, salvo ➤ **salva de advertencia** warning shots *pl*

salvación SF (*Rel*) salvation ➤ **salvación eterna** eternal salvation

salvada SF **1** (*Perú*) (= *rescate*) rescue (**de** from) **2** (*Chi*) [*de accidente, peligro*] escape **3** (*CS Ftbl*) save

salvado SM bran

Salvador SM **1 el ~** (*Rel*) the Saviour, the Savior (*EEUU*) **2 El ~** (*Geog*) El Salvador

salvador(a) SM/F saviour, savior (*EEUU*)

salvadoreño/a ADJ, SM/F Salvadoran

salvaeslip SM (*pl* **~s**) panty liner

salvaguarda SF safeguard

salvaguardar /1a/ VT to safeguard

salvaguardia SF safeguard, defence, defense (*EEUU*)

salvajada SF savage deed, atrocity

salvaje ㊐ ADJ **1** [*planta, animal, tierra*] wild **2** (= *no autorizado*) [*huelga*] unofficial, wildcat; [*construcción*] unauthorized **3** [*pueblo, tribu*] savage **4** (= *brutal*) [*asesinato*] savage, brutal ㊐ SMF (*lit, fig*) savage

salvajismo SM savagery

salvamanteles SM INV table mat, hot pad (*EEUU*)

salvamento SM rescue; **operaciones de ~** rescue operations; **bote de ~** lifeboat

salvapantallas SM screen saver

salvar /1a/ ㊐ VT **1** (*de un peligro*) to save; **me salvó la vida** he saved my life; **me has salvado de tener que sentarme con ese pesado** you saved me (from) having to sit next to that old bore **2** (*Rel*) to save **3** (= *evitar*) [+ *dificultad, obstáculo*] to get round, overcome; [+ *montaña, río, barrera*] to cross; [+ *rápidos*] to shoot **4** (*frm*) [+ *distancia*] to cover **5 salvando** (= *exceptuando*): **salvando algún detalle** apart from a few minor details ㊐ salvarse VPR **1** (*de un peligro*) to escape; **pocos se ~on del naufragio** few escaped from o survived the shipwreck; **¡sálvese quien pueda!** every man for himself! **2** (*) (= *librarse*) **los considera incompetentes a todos, no se salva nadie** in his view they are all incompetent, without

exception; **Carlos es el único que se salva** Carlos is the one exception **3** (*Rel*) to be saved

salvataje SM (*CS*) rescue

salvavidas ㊐ SM INV (= *flotador*) lifebelt, life preserver (*EEUU*); (= *chaleco*) life jacket ㊐ ADJ INV **bote ~** lifeboat; **chaleco ~** life jacket

salvedad SF reservation, qualification; **con la ~ de que ...** with the proviso that ...; **me gustaría hacer una ~** I would like to qualify what you said o to make a qualification

salvia SF sage

salvo ㊐ ADJ safe ㊐ PREP except, except for, save; **~ aquellos que ya contamos** except (for) those we have already counted; **~ error u omisión** errors and omissions excepted ㊒ ADV **a ~** out of danger; **a ~ de** safe from; **para dejar a ~ su reputación** in order to safeguard his reputation; **ponerse a ~** to reach safety ㊓ CONJ **~ que** ◇ **~ si** unless; **iré ~ que me avises de lo contrario** I'll go unless you tell me otherwise

salvoconducto SM safe-conduct

samaritano/a SM/F Samaritan

samba SF samba

sambenito SM **le colgaron el ~ de cobarde** they branded him a coward

samotana* SF (*CAm*) row, uproar

sampablera* SF (*Ven*) quarrel, fight

San SM (*apócope de* **santo**) saint; **~ Juan** Saint John

sanar /1a/ ㊐ VT to cure ㊐ VI [*herida*] to heal; [*persona*] to recover

sanatorio SM sanatorium, sanitarium (*EEUU*) ➤ **sanatorio mental** psychiatric clinic, psychiatric hospital

sanción SF sanction ➤ **sanción disciplinaria** punishment, disciplinary measure ➤ **sanciones económicas** economic sanctions

sancionar /1a/ VT **1** (= *castigar*) (*gen*) to sanction; (*Jur*) penalize **2** (= *permitir*) to sanction

sancochar /1a/ VT (*LAm*) to parboil

sancocho SM (*LAm*) stew (of meat, yucca *etc*)

sandalia SF sandal

sándalo SM sandal, sandalwood

sandez SF stupid thing; **fue una ~ obrar así** it was a stupid thing to do; **decir sandeces** to talk nonsense

sandía SF watermelon

sandinista ADJ, SMF Sandinista

sánduche SM (*LAm*) sandwich

sandunga SF **1** (*) (= *encanto*) charm; (= *gracia*) wit **2** (*LAm*) (= *juerga*) binge*

sandunguero ADJ (= *encantador*) charming; (= *gracioso*) witty

sandwich ['saŋgwitʃ, 'sanwis] SM (*pl* **~s, ~es**) (*con pan de molde*) sandwich; (*LAm*) (*con panecillo*) roll

saneamiento SM **1** (= *limpieza*) [*de río, ciudad, alcantarillado*] clean-up; [*de terreno*] drainage; **materiales de ~** (*Esp*) sanitary fittings **2** [*de empresa*] restructuring; **el ~ de la economía** putting the economy back on a sound footing

sanear /1a/ VT **1** (= *limpiar*) [+ *río, ciudad, alcantarillado*] to clean up **2** [+ *empresa*] to restructure; **~ la economía** to put the economy back on a sound footing

sanfasón* SF (*RPl*), **sanfazón** SF (*LAm*) **a la ~** unceremoniously, informally; (*pey*) carelessly

sanfermines SMPL *festivities in celebration of San*

Fermín (Pamplona)

SANFERMINES

The **Sanfermines** is a week-long festival starting on July 7 in Pamplona (Navarre) to honour **San Fermín**, the town's patron saint. One of the main events is bullfighting. The bulls have to be led from their enclosure to the bullring early in the morning through the city's main streets; young men, dressed in traditional red berets, white shirts and trousers with red sashes round their waists, run through the streets leading the fast-moving bulls. This activity, known as the **encierro**, in which people risk serious injury and even death, was popularized by writers such as Ernest Hemingway and now attracts visitors from all over the world.

---

sangrante ADJ **1** [*encías, úlcera*] bleeding **2** [*batalla, guerra*] bloody **3** (= *indignante*) scandalous; **lo más ~ del caso es que ...** the most scandalous aspect of the affair was that ...

sangrar /1a/ ② VT **1** [+ *enfermo, vena*] to bleed **2** [+ *árbol, tubería, horno*] to tap **3** [+ *texto, línea*] to indent **4** (= *explotar*) **~ a algn** to bleed sb dry ③ VI to bleed; **me sangra la nariz** (*de forma espontánea*) I've got a nosebleed; (*a consecuencia de un golpe*) my nose is bleeding

sangre ② SF **1** (*Biol*) blood; **las enfermedades de la ~** blood diseases; **la tela es de color rojo ~** the fabric is a blood-red colour; **chupar la ~ a algn** (*lit*) to suck sb's blood; (*fig*) (= *explotar*) to bleed sb dry; (*Méx*) (= *hacer pasar mal rato*) to give sb a hard time, make sb's life a misery; **dar ~** to give blood; **echar ~** to bleed; **estuvo echando ~ por la nariz** (*de forma natural*) he had a nosebleed; (*a consecuencia de un golpe*) his nose was bleeding, he was bleeding from the nose; **hacer ~ a algn** to make sb bleed; **me pegó y me hizo ~** he hit me and I started bleeding *o* to bleed, he hit me and made me bleed; **hacerse ~: ¿te has hecho ~?** are you bleeding?; **me hice ~ en la rodilla** my knee started bleeding *o* to bleed; **salir ~ a algn: me está saliendo ~ de la herida** my cut is bleeding ▸ **sangre caliente: por sus venas corre ~ caliente** he is very hot-blooded; **de ~ caliente** [*animal*] warm-blooded *antes de s*; [*persona*] hot-blooded *antes de s* ▸ **sangre fría** coolness, sang-froid (*frm*); **era el que tenía más ~ fría a la hora de tomar decisiones** he was the coolest when it came to taking decisions; **la ~ fría del asesino** the murderer's cold-blooded nature; **lo asesinaron a ~ fría** they killed him in cold blood; **de ~ fría** [*animal*] cold-blooded *antes de s*; [*persona*] cool-headed *antes de s*; **mantener la ~ fría** to keep calm, keep one's cool **2** ✦ MODISMOS **arder la ~ a algn: me arde la ~ cada vez que me habla** each time he speaks to me it makes my blood boil; **beber la ~ a algn** (*Méx*) to give sb a hard time, make sb's life a misery; **hacer correr la ~** to shed blood; **dar su ~ por algo** to give one's life for sth, shed one's blood for sth (*frm*); **encender la ~ a algn** to make sb's blood boil; **a ~ y fuego** ruthlessly, by fire and sword (*liter*); **hacerse mala ~** to get annoyed; **helar la ~ a algn** to make sb's blood run cold; **hervir la ~ a algn: me hierve la ~ cuando nos tratan así** it really makes me mad *o* it makes my blood boil when they treat us like this; **tener la ~ de horchata** *o* (*Méx*) **atole** to be cold-hearted; **ser de ~ ligera** (*Méx*) ✧ **ser liviano de ~** (*Chi*) to be easy-going *o* good-natured; **andar con ~ en el ojo** (*CS**) to bear a grudge; **es de ~ pesada** (*Méx*) ✧ **es pesado de ~** (*Chi*) he's not a very nice person, he's not very good-natured; **no llegar la ~ al río: discutimos un poco pero no llegó la ~ al río** we argued a bit but it didn't come *o* amount to much; **sudar ~** to sweat blood; **no tener ~ en las venas** to be a cold fish **3** (= *linaje*) blood; **lleva ~ española en las venas** he has Spanish blood (in him); **somos hermanos de ~** we're blood brothers; ✦ MODISMO **llevar algo en la ~** to have sth in one's blood ▸ **sangre azul** blue blood; **ser de ~ azul** to belong to the aristocracy ③ ▸ **pura sangre** SM INV (= *caballo*) thoroughbred

sangría SF **1** (*Med*) bleeding, bloodletting **2** [*de recursos*] outflow, drain **3** (*Culin*) sangria **4** (*Tip, Inform*) indentation

sangriento ADJ **1** [*herida*] bleeding; [*arma, manos*] bloody,

bloodstained **2** [*batalla, guerra*] bloody

sangrón/ona* ② ADJ (*Méx*) annoying ③ SM/F pain (in the neck)*

sanguijuela SF leech

sanguinario ADJ bloodthirsty, cruel

sanguíneo ADJ blood *antes de s*; **vaso ~** blood vessel

sanguinolento ADJ **1** (= *con sangre*) [*flujo*] bloody; [*ojos*] bloodshot **2** (= *manchado de sangre*) bloodstained **3** (*Culin*) underdone, rare

sanidad SF **1** (= *cualidad*) health, healthiness **2** (*Admin*) health, public health; **(Ministerio de) Sanidad** Ministry of Health; **inspector de ~** health inspector ▸ **sanidad pública** public health (department)

sanitario/a ② ADJ [*condiciones*] sanitary; [*centro, medidas*] health *antes de s*; **control ~** public health inspection; **asistencia sanitaria** medical attention ③ SM **1** (*Col, Méx, Ven*) (= *wáter*) toilet (*Brit*), washroom (*EEUU*) **2 sanitarios** (= *aparatos de baño*) sanitary ware *sing*, bathroom fittings ⓒ SM/F (*Med*) (*gen*) health worker; (*en emergencias*) paramedic

sanjacobo SM *escalope with cheese filling*

San José SM (*Geog*) San José

San Juan SM (= *santo*) Saint John; (*Geog*) San Juan

SAN JUAN

The **Día de San Juan** on June 24 fuses Christian tradition with ancient summer solstice celebrations. In many areas, particularly near the sea, it is customary to light large bonfires on open ground on the night of June 23 and to burn an effigy, normally a large rag doll, at the stake. These **hogueras de San Juan**, which are accompanied by fireworks and music, draw crowds of people wanting to dance or simply to enjoy the summer evening, until the fire dies out in the small hours. Some legends credit this night with magical qualities and talk of ghostly apparitions.

San Marino SM San Marino

sano ADJ **1** (= *con salud*) [*persona*] healthy; [*órgano*] sound; ✦ MODISMO **cortar por lo ~** to take extreme measures, go right to the root of the problem **2** (= *beneficioso*) [*clima, dieta*] healthy; [*comida*] wholesome **3** (= *entero*) whole, intact; **~ y salvo** safe and sound; **no quedó plato ~ en toda la casa** there wasn't a plate in the house left unbroken **4** (= *sin vicios*) [*persona*] healthy; [*enseñanza, idea*] sound; [*deseo*] earnest, sincere; [*objetivo*] worthy

> ⚠ **sano** ≠ **sane**

San Salvador SM (*Geog*) San Salvador

sansalvadoreño ADJ of/from San Salvador

sánscrito ADJ, SM Sanskrit

sanseacabó* EXCL **y ~** and that's the end of it

santanderino ADJ of/from Santander

santero/a SM/F (*Carib*) *maker or seller of religious images, prints, etc*

Santiago SM St James ▸ **Santiago (de Chile)** Santiago (de Chile) ▸ **Santiago (de Compostela)** Santiago de Compostela

santiagués ADJ of/from Santiago de Compostela

santiaguino ADJ of/from Santiago (de Chile)

santiamén* SM **en un ~** in no time at all, in a flash

santidad SF [*de lugar*] holiness, sanctity; [*de persona*] saintliness; **su Santidad** His Holiness

santificar /1g/ VT [+ *persona*] to sanctify; [+ *lugar*] to consecrate; [+ *fiesta*] to keep; **santificado sea Tu Nombre** hallowed be Thy Name

santiguarse /1i/ VPR to cross o.s.

santísimo ② ADJ SUPERL holy, most holy ③ SM **el Santísimo** the Holy Sacrament

santo/a Ⓐ ADJ **1** (*Rel*) [*vida, persona*] holy; [*tierra*] consecrated; [*persona*] saintly; [*mártir*] blessed **2** (*enfático*) blessed; **todo el ~ día** the whole blessed day; **hacer su santa voluntad** to do as one jolly well pleases Ⓑ SM/F **1** (*Rel*) saint; **Santo Tomás** St Thomas ➤ **santo/a patrón/ona** patron saint

2 ✦ MODISMOS **¿a ~ de qué?** why on earth?*; **darse de ~s** (*Méx*) to count o.s. lucky; **¡por todos los ~s!** for pity's sake!; **no es ~ de mi devoción** he's not my cup of tea*; **se le fue el ~ al cielo** he forgot what he was about to say; **llegar y besar el ~** to pull it off at the first attempt; **fue llegar y besar el ~** it was as easy as pie*; **quedarse para vestir ~s** to be left on the shelf

3 (= *persona*) saint; **es un ~** he's a saint Ⓒ SM **1** (= *onomástica*) saint's day; **mañana es mi ~** tomorrow is my name day *o* saint's day **2** (*en libro*) picture **3** ➤ **santo y seña** (*Mil*) password

Santo Domingo SM Santo Domingo

santoral SM calendar of saints' days

santuario SM (= *templo*) sanctuary, shrine; (= *lugar sagrado*) sanctuary

santurrón/ona SM/F sanctimonious person

saña SF (= *furor*) rage; (= *crueldad*) cruelty; **con ~** viciously

sapo[1] SM (*Zool*) toad; ✦ MODISMO **echar ~s y culebras** to turn the air blue

sapo[2]**/a*** Ⓐ ADJ (*And, CAm, CS*) (= *astuto*) cunning, sly Ⓑ SM/F (*And, Ven*) (= *soplón*) informer, grass (*Brit**), fink (*EEUU**)

saque SM **1** (*Tenis*) service, serve; (*Rugby*) line-out; (*Ftbl*) (*para dar comienzo al partido*) kick-off ➤ **saque de banda** (*Ftbl*) throw-in ➤ **saque de esquina** (*Ftbl*) corner, corner kick ➤ **saque de honor** (*Esp*) guest appearance ➤ **saque de portería, saque de puerta** goal kick ➤ **saque de valla** (*CS*) goal kick ➤ **saque inicial** kick-off **2** (= *apetito*) **tener buen ~** to have a hearty appetite

saqué *etc ver* **sacar**

saquear /1a/ VT **1** (*Mil*) to sack **2** (= *robar*) to loot, plunder, pillage

saqueo SM **1** (*Mil*) sacking **2** (= *robo*) looting, plundering, pillaging

S.A.R. ABR (= **Su Alteza Real**) HRH

sarampión SM measles

sarao SM soirée, evening party

sarape SM (*CAm, Méx*) *brightly-coloured striped blanket*

sarcasmo SM sarcasm

sarcástico ADJ sarcastic

sarcófago SM sarcophagus

sarcoma SM sarcoma

sardana SF *Catalan dance and music*

sardina SF sardine; ✦ MODISMO **como ~s en lata** like sardines

sardinel SM (*Col*) **1** (= *acera*) pavement (*Brit*), sidewalk (*EEUU*) **2** (= *borde*) kerb (*Brit*), curb (*EEUU*)

sardinero ADJ sardine *antes de s*

sardónico ADJ sardonic, sarcastic

sargazo SM gulfweed

sargento SMF **1** (*Mil*) sergeant ➤ **sargento de primera** [*de tierra*] staff sergeant; [*de aire*] flight sergeant **2** (*pey**) (= *mandón*) bossy person

sari SM sari

sarmentoso ADJ **1** [*planta*] twining, climbing **2** (*Anat*) [*manos*] gnarled

sarmiento SM vine shoot

sarna SF (*Med*) scabies; (*Vet*) mange

sarnoso ADJ (*Med*) scabious; (*Vet*) mangy

sarpullido SM (*Med*) rash

sarraceno/a ADJ, SM/F Saracen

sarro SM (= *depósito*) (*en los dientes*) tartar, plaque; (*en la lengua*) fur; (*en una caldera*) scale

sarta SF string; **una ~ de mentiras** a pack of lies

sartén SF (*en LAm tb* SM) frying pan; ✦ MODISMO **tener la ~ por el mango** to have the upper hand

sastre/a Ⓐ SM/F tailor Ⓑ ADJ INV **traje ~** tailor-made suit

sastrería SF tailor's (shop)

Satán SM, **Satanás** SM Satan

satánico ADJ satanic

satanizar /1f/ VT to demonize

satélite Ⓐ SM satellite; **transmisión vía ~** satellite broadcasting ➤ **satélite artificial** artificial satellite ➤ **satélite de comunicaciones** communications satellite ➤ **satélite meteorológico** weather satellite Ⓑ ADJ INV [*ciudad, país*] satellite

satén SM, **satín** SM (*LAm*) satin

satinado ADJ glossy, shiny

satinar /1a/ VT to gloss, make glossy

sátira SF satire

satírico ADJ satiric, satirical

satirizar /1f/ VT to satirize

sátiro SM (*Literat*) satyr

satisfacción SF **1** (= *placer*) satisfaction **2** (*de ofensa*) satisfaction, redress

satisfacer /2r/ Ⓐ VT **1** (+ *persona*) to satisfy; **el resultado no me satisface** I'm not satisfied *o* happy with the result; **~ a algn de *o* por una ofensa** to give sb satisfaction for an offence **2** (= *compensar*) [+ *deuda*] to pay; [+ *necesidad*] to meet, satisfy; (*Com*) [+ *letra de cambio*] to honour, honor (*EEUU*) Ⓑ **satisfacerse** VPR to satisfy o.s., be satisfied

satisfactorio ADJ satisfactory

satisfecho ADJ **1** (= *complacido*) satisfied; **darse por ~ con algo** to declare o.s. satisfied with sth; **dejar ~s a todos** to satisfy everybody **2** (*después de comer*) **quedarse ~** to be full

saturación SF saturation

saturar /1a/ VT (*Fís, Quím*) to saturate; **~ el mercado** to flood the market; **estos aeropuertos son los más saturados** those airports are the most crowded *o* stretched; **¡estoy saturado de tanta televisión!** I can't take any more television!

Saturno SM Saturn

sauce SM willow ➤ **sauce llorón** weeping willow

saúco SM elder

saudí ADJ, SMF, **saudita** ADJ, SMF Saudi

sauna SF (SM *en LAm*) sauna

saurio SM saurian

savia SF sap

saxo SM sax

saxofón SM saxophone

saxofonista SMF saxophonist

sayo SM smock, tunic; ✦ REFRÁN **al que le venga el ~ que se lo ponga** (*LAm*) if the cap fits, wear it

sazón Ⓐ SF **1** (*de fruta*) ripeness; **en ~** ripe, ready (to eat); **fuera de ~** out of season **2** (*liter*) **a la ~** then, at that time **3** (= *sabor*) flavour, flavor (*EEUU*) Ⓑ SM (*Méx*) flavour, flavor (*EEUU*)

sazonado ADJ 1 [*plato*] seasoned 2 ~ **de** seasoned with, flavoured *o* (*EEUU*) flavored with

sazonar /1a/ VT (*Culin*) to season (**de** with)

schop [ʃop] SM (*Chi*) (= *vaso*) mug, tankard; (= *cerveza*) beer, draught *o* (*EEUU*) draft beer

Scotch® SM (*And*) Sellotape® (*Brit*), Scotch tape® (*EEUU*)

SE ABR (= **sudeste**) SE

se PRON PERS 1 (*complemento indirecto*) 1.1 (*a él*) him; (*a ella*) her; (*a ellos*) them; (*a usted, ustedes*) you; **voy a dárselo** I'll give it to him *o* her *o* them *o* you; **he hablado con mis padres y se lo he explicado** I've talked to my parents and explained it to them; **aquí tiene las flores, ¿se las envuelvo, señor?** here are your flowers, shall I wrap them for you, sir?; **no lo tenemos, pero se lo puedo encargar** we haven't got it, but I can order it for you 1.2 (*con doble complemento indirecto*) **dáselo a Enrique** give it to Enrique, **¿se lo has preguntado a tus padres?** have you asked your parents about it? 1.3 (*con partes del cuerpo, ropa*)

> Con partes del cuerpo o con prendas que se llevan puestas se usa el adjetivo posesivo:

Pablo se lavó los dientes Pablo cleaned his teeth; **Carmen no podía abrocharse el vestido** Carmen couldn't do up her dress; **han prometido no cortarse la barba** they have sworn not to cut their beards 1.4 (*uso enfático*) **se comió un pastel** he ate a cake; **no se esperaba eso** he didn't expect that

2 (*uso reflexivo*) 2.1 (*masculino*) himself; (*femenino*) herself; (*plural*) themselves; (*de usted*) yourself; (*de ustedes*) yourselves; (*sujeto no humano*) itself; **Marcos se ha cortado con un cristal** Marcos cut himself on a piece of broken glass; **Margarita se estaba preparando para salir** Margarita was getting (herself) ready to go up; **¿se ha hecho usted daño?** have you hurt yourself?; **se tiraron al suelo** they threw themselves to the ground; **la calefacción se apaga sola** the heating turns itself off automatically; **se está afeitando** he's shaving; **¡siéntese!** sit down 2.2 (*indefinido*) oneself; **mirarse en el espejo** to look at oneself in the mirror

3 (*como parte de un verbo pronominal*) **se durmió** he fell asleep; **se enfadó** he got annoyed; **se marchó** he left 4 (*uso recíproco*) each other, one another; **se escriben a menudo** they write to each other often; **se quieren** they love each other; **se miraron todos** they all looked at one another

5 (*uso impersonal*) 5.1 (*con sujeto indeterminado*) **se registraron nueve muertos** there were nine deaths, nine deaths were recorded; **no se sabe por qué** it is not known *o* people don't know why; **en esa zona se habla galés** Welsh is spoken in that area, people speak Welsh in that area 5.2 (*referido al hablante*) **no se oye bien** you can't hear very well; **es lo que pasa cuando se come tan deprisa** that's what happens when you eat so fast; **¿cómo se dice eso en inglés?** how do you say that in English?; **se admiten sugerencias** we welcome suggestions; **"véndese coche"** "car for sale"; **se avisa a los interesados que ...** those concerned are informed that ... 5.3 (*en recetas, instrucciones*) **se pelan las patatas** peel the potatoes; **"sírvase muy frío"** "serve chilled"; **"no se admiten visitas"** "no visitors"; **"se prohíbe fumar"** "no smoking"

sé *ver* **saber, ser**

S.E. ABR (= **Su Excelencia**) H.E.

sea *etc ver* **ser**

sebáceo ADJ sebaceous

sebo SM (= *grasa*) (*gen*) grease, fat; (*para velas*) tallow; (*Culin*) suet

seboso ADJ (= *grasiento*) greasy; (= *mugriento*) grimy

secadero SM drying place

secado SM drying ➤ **secado a mano** blow-dry

secador SM drier, dryer ➤ **secador de pelo** hairdrier, hairdryer

secadora SF (*para la ropa*) dryer, tumble dryer (*esp Brit*); (*CAm, Méx*) (*para el pelo*) hairdryer, hairdrier

secamente ADV [*contestar*] curtly; [*ordenar*] sharply; **se comportó muy ~ con nosotros** he was very short *o* curt with us

secano SM (*tb* **tierra de ~**) unirrigated land; **cultivo de ~** dry farming

secante[1] ADJ **papel ~** blotting paper

secante[2] SF (*Mat*) secant

secar /1g/ **Ⓐ** VT 1 (= *quitar la humedad*) (*con paño, toalla*) to dry; (*con fregona*) to mop up; (*con papel secante*) to blot; **me sequé las lágrimas** I dried my tears; **~ los platos** to dry the plates, dry up
2 (= *resecar*) [+ *planta, terreno*] to dry up; [+ *piel*] to dry out
3 (*Uru*) (= *fastidiar*) to annoy, vex
Ⓑ VI to dry; **lo he puesto a ~** I've left it to dry
Ⓒ secarse VPR 1 (*uso reflexivo*) 1.1 [*persona*] to dry o.s., get dry 1.2 [+ *manos, pelo*] to dry; [+ *lágrimas, sudor*] to dry, wipe; **~se la frente** to mop one's brow
2 (= *quedarse sin agua*) 2.1 [*ropa*] to dry, dry off; **hasta que no se seque el suelo** until the floor is dry *o* has dried 2.2 [*arroz, pasta*] to go dry; [*garganta*] to get dry; [*río, pozo*] to dry up, run dry; [*hierba, terreno*] to dry up; [*planta*] to wither

secarropas SF INV (*RPI*) tumble dryer, tumble drier

sección SF 1 (*Arquit, Mat*) section ➤ **sección longitudinal** longitudinal section ➤ **sección transversal** cross section 2 (= *parte*) (*gen*) section; [*de almacén, oficina*] department ➤ **sección deportiva** sports page, sports section 3 (*Mil*) section, platoon

seccional SF 1 (*RPI*) police station 2 (*Col*) branch office

seccionar /1a/ VT (= *dividir*) to section; (= *cortar*) to cut off

secesión SF secession

seco ADJ 1 (= *no húmedo*) dry; **tengo los labios ~s** my lips are dry; **las sábanas no están secas todavía** the sheets are still not dry; **es un calor ~** it's a dry heat; **"limpiar en seco"** "dry clean only"
2 (= *desecado*) [*flor, higo, pescado*] dried; [*hojas*] dead, dried; [*árbol*] dead; **estaban ~s todos los geranios** all the geraniums had dried up; **dame una cerveza, que estoy ~*** give me a beer, I'm really parched*
3 (= *no graso*) [*piel, pelo*] dry
4 (= *no dulce*) [*vino, licor*] dry
5 (= *flaco*) thin, skinny*
6 (= *no amable*) [*persona, carácter, respuesta*] curt; [*orden*] sharp; [*estilo*] dry; **estuvo muy ~ conmigo por teléfono** he was very curt *o* short with me on the phone
7 (= *sin resonancia*) [*tos*] dry; [*golpe, impacto*] sharp
8 **en ~** (= *bruscamente*) [*frenar*] sharply; **pararse en ~** to stop dead, stop suddenly
9 ✦ MODISMOS **a secas: no existe la libertad a secas** there's no such thing as freedom pure and simple; **Gerardo a secas para los amigos** just Gerardo to his friends; **nos alimentamos de pan a secas** we survived on nothing but bread; **dejar ~ a algn*** (= *matar*) to kill sb stone dead*; **lo dejó ~ de un tiro** he blew him away*; **ser ~ para algo** (*Chi**) to be a great one for sth*; **tener ~ a algn** (*Col, RPI*): **me tienen ~** I've had enough of them; **tomarse algo al ~** (*Chi*) to down sth in one

secoya SF redwood, sequoia

secreción SF secretion

secretaría SF 1 (= *oficina*) secretary's office 2 (= *cargo*) secretaryship 3 (*Méx*) (= *Ministerio*) ministry

secretariado SM (= *curso*) secretarial course

secretario/a SM/F 1 (= *administrativo*) secretary ➤ **secretario/a de dirección** executive secretary ➤ **secretario/a general** (*gen*) general secretary; (*Pol*) secretary general ➤ **secretario/a judicial** clerk of the court 2 (*Méx Pol*) minister, Minister of State, secretary of state (*EEUU*) ➤ **secretario/a de Estado** (*Esp*) junior minister, undersecretary (*EEUU*)

secreter SM writing desk

secretismo SM secrecy, excessive secrecy

secreto **Ⓐ** SM 1 (= *confidencia*) secret; **en ~** in secret, secretly; **guardar un ~** to keep a secret ➤ **secreto a voces**

open secret ➤ **secreto de confesión** (*Rel*) confessional secret ➤ **secreto de estado** state secret ➤ **secreto de sumario, secreto sumarial: debido al ~ del sumario** o **sumarial** because the matter is sub judice **2** (= *clave*) secret; **¿cuál es el ~ de su éxito?** what is the secret of her success? **3** (= *reserva*) secrecy; **lo han hecho con mucho ~** they have done it in great secrecy **B** ADJ secret; **todo es de lo más ~** it's all highly secret

secta SF sect

sectario ADJ sectarian

sectarismo SM sectarianism

sector SM **1** (*Econ, Geom*) sector; **el ~ turístico/del automóvil** the tourist/motor (*esp Brit*) o auto (*EEUU*) industry ➤ **sector industrial** (*Col*) industrial estate (*Brit*) o park (*EEUU*) ➤ **sector privado** private sector ➤ **sector público** public sector ➤ **sector terciario** tertiary sector, service industries *pl*, service sector **2** (= *sección*) [*de opinión*] section; [*de ciudad*] area, sector

sectorial ADJ sectorial

secuaz SMF (*pey*) henchman

secuela SF consequence

secuencia SF sequence

secuencial ADJ sequential

secuestrador(a) SM/F **1** [*de persona*] kidnapper **2** [*de avión*] hijacker

secuestrar /1a/ VT **1** [+ *persona*] to kidnap **2** [+ *avión*] to hijack **3** (*Jur*) to seize, confiscate

secuestro SM **1** [*de persona*] kidnapping, kidnaping (*EEUU*) **2** [*de avión*] hijack, hijacking **3** (*Jur*) [*de cargamento, contrabando*] seizure; [*de propiedad*] sequestration

secular ADJ **1** (*Rel*) secular, lay **2** [*tradición*] age-old, ancient

secularizar /1f/ VT to secularize

secundar /1a/ VT **1** [+ *moción*] to second; [+ *huelga*] to take part in, join **2** [+ *persona*] (*en un proyecto*) to support; (*para la votación*) to second

secundaria SF **1** (*esp LAm*) (= *enseñanza*) secondary education, high school education (*EEUU*) **2** (*Méx*) (= *colegio*) secondary school, high school (*EEUU*)

secundario ADJ (*gen*) secondary; [*carretera, efectos*] side *antes de s*; **actor** ~ supporting actor

secuoia SF (*LAm*), **secuoya** SF (*LAm*) = **secoya**

sed SF **1** (= *ganas de beber*) thirst; **tener (mucha)** ~ to be (very) thirsty **2** (= *ansia*) thirst, craving (**de** for); **tener ~ de** to thirst o be thirsty for, crave

seda SF silk; ✦ MODISMOS **como la ~** (*adj*) as smooth as silk; (*adv*) smoothly; **ir como la ~** to go like clockwork ➤ **seda dental** dental floss

sedal SM fishing line

sedán SM saloon (*Brit*), sedan (*EEUU*)

sedante ADJ, SM sedative

sedar /1a/ VT to sedate

sede SF **1** (= *residencia oficial*) [*de gobierno*] seat; [*de organización*] headquarters *pl*, central office; (*Dep*) venue ➤ **sede social** head office, central office **2** (*Rel*) see; **Santa Sede** Holy See

sedentario ADJ sedentary

sedicioso/a **A** ADJ seditious **B** SM/F rebel

sediento ADJ [*persona*] thirsty; [*campos*] parched; **~ de poder** power-hungry

sedimentación SF sedimentation

sedimento SM sediment, deposit

sedoso ADJ silky, silken

seducción SF **1** (= *acción*) seduction **2** (= *encanto*) seductiveness

seducir /3n/ VT **1** (*en sentido sexual*) to seduce **2** (= *cautivar*) to charm, captivate; **seduce a todos con su simpatía** she captivates everyone with her charm; **no me seduce la idea** I'm not taken with the idea

seductor(a) **A** ADJ **1** (*sexualmente*) seductive **2** (= *cautivador*) [*persona*] charming; [*idea*] tempting **B** SM/F seducer/seductress

sefardí, sefardita **A** ADJ Sephardic **B** SMF Sephardic Jew/Sephardic Jewess, Sephardi; **-es ◇ sefarditas** Sephardim

segador(a) SM/F (= *persona*) harvester, reaper

segadora SF (*Mec*) harvester

segadora-trilladora SF combine harvester

segar /1h, 1j/ VT **1** (*Agr*) [+ *mies*] to reap, cut **2** (= *acabar con*) [+ *esperanzas*] to ruin; **~ la juventud de algn** to cut sb off in his prime

seglar **A** ADJ secular, lay **B** SMF layman/laywoman; **los ~es** the laity

segmentación SF segmentation

segmentar /1a/ **A** VT **1** (= *cortar*) to segment **2** (= *dividir*) to divide up, separate out **B** **segmentarse** VPR to fragment, divide up

segmento SM (*Mat, Zool*) segment; (*Com, Fin*) sector, group

segoviano ADJ of/from Segovia

segregación SF **1** (= *separación*) segregation ➤ **segregación racial** racial segregation **2** (*Anat*) secretion

segregar /1h/ VT **1** (= *separar*) to segregate **2** (*Anat*) to secrete

seguida SF **en ~** right away; **en ~ voy** I'll be right there; **en ~ termino** I've nearly finished, I shan't be a minute

seguidamente ADV **~ les ofrecemos ...** next ..., and next ...; **dijo ~ que ...** he went on at once to say that ...

seguidilla SF (*Mús*) seguidilla (*dance and piece of music in a fast triple rhythm*)

seguido **A** ADJ **1 cinco días ~s** five days running, five days in a row; **llevo dos horas seguidas esperándote** I've been waiting for you for two whole o solid hours **2 ~ de algo/algn** followed by sth/sb **B** ADV **1** (= *directo*) straight on; **vaya todo ~** just keep going straight on **2** (*LAm*) (= *a menudo*) often; **nos vemos muy ~** we see each other very often

seguidor(a) SM/F (*gen*) follower; (*Dep*) supporter, fan*

seguimiento SM [*de proceso*] (*tb Med*) monitoring; **el ~ de la huelga** the support for the strike; **estación de ~** [*de satélite*] tracking station

seguir /3d, 3k/ **A** VT **1** [+ *persona, pista*] to follow; [+ *indicio*] to follow up; [+ *presa*] to chase, pursue; **ella llegó primero, seguida del embajador** she arrived first, followed by the ambassador; **nos están siguiendo** we're being followed; **la seguía con la mirada** his eyes followed her **2** (= *estar atento a*) [+ *programa de TV*] to watch, follow; [+ *programa de radio*] to listen to, follow; [+ *proceso, progreso*] to monitor, follow up; [+ *satélite*] to track; **~ los acontecimientos de cerca** to monitor events closely **3** (= *hacer caso de*) [+ *instrucciones, doctrina, líder*] to follow; **siguió el ejemplo de su padre** he followed his father's example; **~ los pasos de algn** to follow in sb's footsteps **4** [+ *rumbo, dirección*] to follow; **seguimos el curso del río** we followed the course of the river; **siga la flecha** follow the arrow; **~ su curso** [*enfermedad, justicia*] to take its course **5** (= *entender*) [+ *razonamiento*] to follow; **¿me sigues?** are you with me?

B VI **1** (= *continuar*) to go on, carry on; **¡siga!** (= *hable*) go on!, carry on; (*LAm*) (= *pase*) come in; **"sigue"** (*en carta*) P.T.O.; (*en libro*) continued; **la carretera sigue hasta el pueblo** the road goes on as far as the town; **siga por la carretera hasta el cruce** follow the road up to the crossroads; **~ por este camino** to carry on along this path **2 ~ adelante** [*persona*] to go on, carry on; [*acontecimiento*] to go ahead **3** (*en estado, situación*) to be still; **sigue enfermo** he's still ill; **¿cómo sigue?** how is he?; **seguimos sin teléfono** we still haven't got a phone; **sigo sin comprender** I still don't understand; **esas preguntas siguen sin respuesta** those questions remain unanswered **4 ~ haciendo algo** to go on doing sth, carry on doing sth;

siguió mirándola he went on *o* carried on looking at her; **sigo pensando lo mismo** I still think the same; **sigue lloviendo** it's still raining

5 (= *venir a continuación*) to follow, follow on; **lo que sigue es un resumen** what follows is a summary; **~ a algo: las horas que siguieron a la tragedia** the hours following *o* that followed the tragedy

según Ⓐ PREP **1** (= *de acuerdo con*) according to; **~ este mapa** according to this map; **~ las instrucciones** to act in accordance with one's instructions; **lo que dice** from what he says, going by what he says **2** (= *depende de*) depending on; **el dinero que tengamos** depending on what money we have

Ⓑ CONJ **1** (= *depende de*) depending on; **~ esté el tiempo** depending on the weather; **~ (que) vengan tres o cuatro** depending on whether three or four come **2** (*indicando manera*) as; **está ~ lo dejaste** it's just as you left it; **~ se entra, a la izquierda** to the left as you go in; **~ están las cosas, es mejor no intervenir** the way things are, it's better not to get involved; **~ parece** seemingly, apparently **3** (*indicando simultaneidad*) as; **lo vi ~ salía** I saw him as I was going out; **~ íbamos entrando** as we went in

Ⓒ ADV (*) **—¿lo vas a comprar? —según** "are you going to buy it?" — "it all depends"; **~ y como** ◇ **~ y conforme** it all depends

segunda SF **1** (*Aut*) second gear **2** (*Ferro*) second class **3 segundas** (= *doble sentido*) double meaning; **lo dijo con ~s** he really meant something else when he said it; *ver tb* **segundo**

segundero SM second hand (*of watch*)

segundo/a Ⓐ ADJ, PRON **1** (*numeral*) second; **en ~ lugar** (*en clasificación*) in second place; (*en discurso*) secondly ➤ **segundo/a de a bordo** (*Náut*) first mate; (*fig*) second in command; *ver tb* **sexto 2** (= *piso*) second floor (*Brit*), third floor (*EEUU*); *ver tb* **segunda** Ⓑ SM (= *medida de tiempo*) second

seguramente ADV **seguramente será tu hermana** it'll probably be your sister, I expect it'll be your sister; **~ llegarán mañana** they'll probably arrive tomorrow, I expect they'll arrive tomorrow

seguridad SF **1** (= *falta de riesgo*) safety; (*ante accidente, peligro*) safety; (*ante delito, atentado*) security; **para mayor ~ recomendamos el uso de la mascarilla** for safety's sake we recommend that you use a mask; **cinturón de ~** safety belt; **empresa de ~** security company **1.2** (*económica*) security; **hasta que no tenga trabajo no tendrá ~ económica** until he has a job he won't have any financial security **1.3** (*Mil, Pol*) security; **las fuerzas de ~ del Estado** state security forces ➤ **seguridad ciudadana** the security of the public from crime; **nos preocupa mucho la ~ ciudadana** we are very concerned about crime ➤ **seguridad en el trabajo** health and safety at work ➤ **seguridad social** (= *sistema de pensiones y paro*) social security (*Brit*), welfare (*EEUU*); (= *contribuciones*) national insurance; (= *sistema médico*) national health service ➤ **seguridad vial** road safety **2** (= *sensación*) (*de no tener peligro*) security; (*de confianza*) confidence, assurance; **la ~ que da tener unos buenos frenos** the security that good brakes give you; **habla con mucha ~** he speaks with great confidence *o* assurance ➤ **seguridad en uno mismo** self-confidence, self-assurance **3** (= *certeza*) certainty; **no hay ninguna ~ de que vaya a ocurrir** there's no certainty that that will happen; **con ~:** **no lo sabemos con ~** we don't know for sure *o* for certain; **tener la ~ de que ...** to be sure *o* certain that ...; **tengan ustedes la ~ de que ...** (you may) rest assured that ... (*frm*)

seguro Ⓐ ADJ **1** (= *sin peligro*) safe **1.1** [*refugio, método, vehículo*] safe **1.2** [*persona, objetos de valor*] safe; **el bebé se siente ~ cerca de su madre** the baby feels safe *o* secure close to its mother **2** (= *sujeto, estable*) secure; **la carga no parece muy segura** the load doesn't seem to be very securely attached *o* very secure **3** (= *definitivo*) [*fracaso, muerte*] certain; [*fecha*] definite; **su dimisión no es segura** her resignation is not certain; **lo más ~ es que no pueda ir** I almost certainly *o* most likely won't be able to go; **dar algo por ~: se da por ~ que se trataba de**

un secuestro there's little doubt that it was a kidnapping; **es ~ que: es ~ que el congreso se celebrará en Barcelona** the conference is definitely going to be held in Barcelona **4** (= *convencido*) sure; **—¿estás ~ de que era él? —sí, segurísimo** "are you sure it was him?" — "yes, positive"; **~ de algo** sure of sth; **no estoy ~ de poder ir** I'm not sure I'll be able to go **5** (*de uno mismo*) confident; **se muestra cada vez más ~ en el escenario** he is more and more sure of himself *o* confident on stage; **me noto más segura al andar** I feel more steady on my feet, I feel more confident walking now; **~ de sí mismo** self-confident, self-assured **6** (= *fiable*) [*fuente, cálculo, método*] reliable

Ⓑ ADV for sure, for certain; **no lo sabemos ~** we don't know for sure *o* certain; **—¿seguro que te interesa? —sí, seguro** "are you sure that you're interested?" — "yes, I'm sure"; **a buen ~** ◇ **de ~** certainly; **~ que algunos se alegrarán** some people will certainly be pleased, I'm sure that some people will be pleased; **~ que llueve mañana** it's sure to rain tomorrow; ✦ MODISMO **ir** *o* **jugar sobre ~** to play (it) safe

Ⓒ SM **1** (= *dispositivo*) **1.1** [*de puerta, lavadora*] lock; [*de arma de fuego*] safety catch; [*de pulsera*] clasp; **echar el ~ del coche** to lock the doors **1.2** (*CAm, Méx*) (= *imperdible*) safety pin **2** (*Com, Fin*) insurance; **¿tienes el ~ del coche?** have you got your car insurance documents with you?; **hacerse un ~** to take out insurance ➤ **seguro a todo riesgo** comprehensive insurance ➤ **seguro contra terceros** third-party insurance ➤ **seguro de daños a terceros** third-party insurance ➤ **seguro de enfermedad** health insurance ➤ **seguro de incendios** fire insurance ➤ **seguro de vida** life assurance (*Brit*), life insurance (*esp EEUU*) **3** (*) (= *sistema médico*) national health*

seibó SM (*Col, Ven*) sideboard

seis Ⓐ ADJ, PRON (*cardinal*) six; (*ordinal, en la fecha*) sixth; **~ mil** six thousand; **tiene ~ años** she is six (years old); **un niño de ~ años** a six-year-old (child), a child of six; **son las ~** it's six o'clock; **son las cinco menos ~ minutos** ◇ **son ~ minutos para las cinco** (*LAm*) it's six minutes to five; **nos fuimos los ~ a la playa** all six of us went to the beach; **somos ~ para comer** there six of us for dinner; **hoy es ~** today is the sixth; **llega el ~ de agosto** he arrives on August the sixth *o* (*Brit*) on the sixth of August; **vive en el ~** he lives at number six; **el ~ de corazones** the six of hearts Ⓑ SM **1** (= *número*) six; **el ~ es mi número de la suerte** six is my lucky number; **dos más cuatro son ~** two plus four are six **2** (*en aposición*) **planta ~** sixth floor; **le escribí el día ~** I wrote to him on the sixth; **en la página ~** on page six

seiscientos ADJ, PRON, SM (*cardinal*) six hundred; (*ordinal*) six hundredth; **~ soldados** six hundred soldiers; **~ cuarenta** six hundred and forty; **el año ~** the year six hundred; **en el ~** in the seventeenth century

seísmo SM (*Esp*) (= *terremoto*) earthquake; (= *temblor*) tremor

selección SF **1** (= *acción*) selection ➤ **selección natural** natural selection **2** (= *equipo*) ➤ **selección nacional** national team, national side (*Brit*)

seleccionador(a) SM/F (*Dep*) manager, coach (*EEUU*)

seleccionar /1a/ VT to select, pick, choose

selectividad SF (*Esp Univ*) entrance examination

selectivo ADJ selective

selecto ADJ [*vino, producto*] select; [*club*] exclusive

selector SM selector

selenizar /1f/ VI to land on the moon

self-service SM self-service restaurant

sellar /1a/ VT **1** [+ *documento oficial*] to seal; [+ *pasaporte, visado*] to stamp **2** (= *cerrar*) [+ *pacto, labios*] to seal; [+ *urna, entrada*] to seal up

sello SM **1** (*Correos*) stamp **2** (= *estampación*) (*personal, de rey*) seal; (*administrativo*) stamp, official stamp; (*LAm*) (*en reverso de moneda*) tails **3** (*Com*) brand; (*tb ~ discográfico*) record label; (*tb ~ editorial*) imprint **4** (= *marca*) (*tb ~ distintivo*) hallmark, stamp

selva SF **1** (= *jungla*) jungle ➤ **selva tropical** rainforest, tropical rainforest **2** (= *bosque*) forest ➤ **Selva Negra** Black Forest

selvático ADJ **1** (= *de la selva*) forest *antes de s* **2** (= *de la jungla*) jungle *antes de s*

semáforo SM **1** (*Aut*) traffic lights *pl* **2** (*Náut*) semaphore **3** (*Ferro*) signal

semana SF week; **un día entre** ~ one day during the week ➤ **semana laboral** working week (*esp Brit*), workweek (*EEUU*) ➤ **Semana Santa** Holy Week

SEMANA SANTA

In Spain celebrations for **Semana Santa** (Holy Week) are often spectacular. **Viernes Santo**, **Sábado Santo** and **Domingo de Resurrección** (Good Friday, Holy Saturday, Easter Sunday) are all national public holidays, with additional days being given as local holidays. There are long processions through the streets with **pasos** - religious floats and sculptures. Religious statues are carried along on the shoulders of the **cofrades**, members of the **cofradías** or lay brotherhoods that organize the processions. These are accompanied by **penitentes** and **nazarenos** generally wearing long hooded robes. Seville, Málaga and Valladolid are particularly well known for their spectacular Holy Week processions.

semanal ADJ weekly

semanario SM weekly, weekly magazine

semántica SF semantics *sing*

semántico ADJ semantic

semblante SM (*liter*) countenance (*liter*), face; (= *aspecto*) look; **mudar de** ~ to change colour *o* (*EEUU*) color

semblantear /1a/ VT (*CAm, Méx*) ~ **a algn** to look sb straight in the face, scrutinize sb's face

semblanza SF biographical sketch

sembradío SM (*Chi, Col*) sown field

sembrado SM sown field

sembrador(a) SM/F sower

sembrar /1j/ VT **1** (*Agr*) to sow (**de** with); ~ **un campo de nabos** to sow *o* plant a field with turnips **2** [+ *superficie*] to strew (**de** with) **3** (= *extender*) [+ *objetos*] to scatter, spread; [+ *noticia*] to spread; [+ *minas*] to lay; ~ **la discordia** to sow discord; ~ **el pánico** to spread panic, sow panic (*liter*)

sembrío SM (*Perú*) sown field

semejante ⓐ ADJ **1** (= *parecido*) similar; **ser ~s** to be alike *o* similar; ~ **a** like; **es** ~ **a ella en el carácter** she is like her in character **2** (*Mat*) similar **3** (*uso enfático*) such; **nunca hizo cosa** ~ he never did any such thing *o* anything of the sort; **¿se ha visto frescura ~?** did you ever see such cheek? ⓑ SM fellow man, fellow creature; **nuestros ~s** our fellow men

semejanza SF similarity, resemblance; **a** ~ **de** like, as

semejar /1a/ ⓐ VI to look like, resemble ⓑ **semejarse** VPR to look alike, resemble each other; **~se a** to look like, resemble

semen SM semen

semental SM stallion, stud horse

semestral ADJ [*reunión, examen, resultados*] half-yearly (*Brit*), semiannual (*EEUU*), six-monthly; [*informe, revista*] biannual

semestre SM (*gen*) period of six months; (*Univ*) semester; (*Fin*) half-yearly payment

semiautomático ADJ semiautomatic

semibreve SF semibreve (*Brit*), whole note (*EEUU*)

semicircular ADJ semicircular

semicírculo SM semicircle

semiconductor SM semiconductor

semiconsonante SF semiconsonant

semicorchea SF semiquaver (*Brit*), sixteenth (note) (*EEUU*)

semidesértico ADJ semidesert *antes de s*

semidesnatado ADJ (*Esp*) semi-skimmed

semidiós/osa SM/F demigod/demigoddess

semifinal SF semifinal

semifinalista SMF semifinalist

semifondo SM middle-distance race

semiinconsciente ADJ semiconscious, half-conscious

semilla SF **1** (*Bot*) seed; **uvas sin ~s** seedless grapes **2** (= *origen*) seed, source; **la** ~ **de la discordia** the seeds of discord

semillero SM seedbed, nursery; **un** ~ **de delincuencia** a hotbed of *o* a breeding ground for crime; **la decisión fue un** ~ **de disgustos** the decision caused a whole series of problems

seminal ADJ seminal

seminario SM **1** (*Rel*) seminary **2** (*Univ*) seminar

seminarista SMF seminarian

seminuevo ADJ nearly new, pre-owned (*EEUU*)

semiología SF semiology

semioscuridad SF half-darkness

semiótica SF semiotics *sing*

semiótico ADJ semiotic

semi-seco SM medium-dry

semita ⓐ ADJ Semitic ⓑ SMF Semite

semítico ADJ Semitic

semitono SM semitone

semivocal SF semivowel

sémola SF semolina

sempiterno ADJ (*lit*) eternal; (*fig*) never-ending

Sena SM Seine

senado SM senate; ⇨ *CORTES GENERALES*

senador(a) SM/F senator; ⇨ *CORTES GENERALES*

senatorial ADJ senatorial

sencillamente ADV simply

sencillez SF **1** [*de costumbre, estilo, ropa*] simplicity; **se viste con mucha** ~ she dresses very simply **2** [*de tema, problema*] simplicity, straightforwardness **3** (*en el trato*) naturalness

sencillo ⓐ ADJ **1** [*costumbre, estilo, ropa*] simple **2** [*asunto, problema*] simple, straightforward **3** (= *no afectado*) natural, unaffected **4** [*billete*] single ⓑ SM **1** (= *disco*) single **2** (*LAm*) (= *cambio*) small change

senda SF **1** (= *sendero*) path, track **2** (*para conseguir algo*) path **3** (*CS Aut*) lane

senderismo SM rambling, hill walking

senderista¹ SMF (*Dep*) rambler, hill walker

senderista² SMF (*Perú Pol*) member of Sendero Luminoso

sendero SM path, track ➤ **Sendero Luminoso** (*Perú Pol*) Shining Path guerrilla movement

sendos ADJ PL **les dio** ~ **golpes** he hit both of them, he gave each of them a beating; **recibieron** ~ **regalos** each one received a present

Senegal SM Senegal

senegalés/esa ADJ, SM/F Senegalese

senil ADJ senile

senilidad SF senility

senior, sénior ⓐ ADJ INV senior ⓑ SMF (*pl* ~**s** *o* **séniors**) senior

seno SM **1** (= *pecho*) breast; **dar el** ~ (*Ven*) to breastfeed **2** (= *centro*) **en el** ~ **de la familia** in the bosom of the family **3** (*liter*) (= *útero*) **lleva un niño en su** ~ she is with child (*liter*) ➤ **seno materno** womb **4** (*Mat*) sine **5** (*Anat*) ➤ **seno frontal** frontal sinus ➤ **seno maxilar** maxillary sinus

sensación SF **1** (= *percepción*) feeling, sensation; **tengo la** ~ **de que ...** ◇ **me da la** ~ **de que ...** I have a feeling that ... **2** (= *conmoción*) sensation; **causar** *o* **hacer** ~ to cause a sensation

sensacional ADJ sensational

sensacionalismo SM sensationalism

sensacionalista ADJ, SMF sensationalist

sensatez SF good sense; **con** ~ sensibly

sensato ADJ sensible

sensibilidad SF **1** (*al dolor, al frío*) feeling; **no tiene ~ en las piernas** he has no feeling in his legs **2** (= *emotividad*) sensitivity; ~ **afectiva** emotional sensitivity **3** (= *disposición*) feeling, sensitivity ➤ **sensibilidad artística** artistic feeling *o* sensitivity **4** [*de aparato, máquina*] sensitivity

sensibilizado ADJ **1** (= *alérgico*) sensitized **2** (*Fot*) sensitive

sensibilizar /1f/ VT **1** (= *concienciar*) ~ **a la opinión pública (sobre algo)** to raise public awareness (about sth) **2** (*Fot, Med*) to sensitize

sensible ADJ **1** (*al dolor, al frío*) sensitive (**a** to); **tiene la piel muy** ~ she has very sensitive skin; **es muy ~ a los cambios de temperatura** it's very sensitive to changes in temperature **2** (= *impresionable*) sensitive (**a** to); **es muy ~ y llora con facilidad** he is very sensitive and cries easily **3** (= *evidente*) [*cambio, mejoría, diferencia*] appreciable, noticeable; [*pérdida*] considerable **4** (*Téc, Fot*) sensitive (**a** to);

⚠ **sensible** ≠ *sensible*

sensiblemente ADV perceptibly, appreciably, noticeably

sensiblería SF sentimentality

sensitivo ADJ **1** [*órgano*] sense *antes de s* **2** [*animal*] sentient, capable of feeling

sensor SM sensor

sensorial ADJ sensory

sensual ADJ sensual, sensuous

sensualidad SF sensuality, sensuousness

sentada SF **1** (= *tiempo*) sitting; **de** *o* **en una** ~ at one sitting **2** (*Pol*) sit-in

sentadera SF **1** (*LAm*) (*para sentarse*) seat (*of a chair etc*) **2 sentaderas** (*CS**) (= *trasero*) backside* *sing*

sentado ADJ **1 estar** ~ to be sitting, be seated; **permanecer** ~ to remain seated; ✦ MODISMO **puedes esperar ~*** you've got another think coming* **2 dar por** ~ to take for granted; **di por ~ que estabas de acuerdo** I took it for granted that you were in agreement, I assumed you were in agreement **3 dejar ~**: **quiero dejar ~ que ...** I want to make it clear that ...

sentador ADJ (*CS*) flattering

sentar /1j/ ⒜ VT **1** [+ *persona*] to sit, seat **2** (= *establecer*) [+ *principio*] to establish; [+ *precedente*] to set; ~ **las bases de algo** to lay the foundations for sth ⒝ VI **1** (*en el aspecto*) to suit; **ese peinado le sienta horriblemente** that hairstyle doesn't suit her at all, that hairstyle looks awful on her **2** ~ **bien/mal a algn** [*comida*] to agree/disagree with sb; **un descanso le ~ía bien** he could do with a break **3** (= *agradar*) ~ **bien/mal** to go down well/badly; **le ha sentado mal que lo hayas hecho tú** he didn't like your doing it ⒞ **sentarse** VPR to sit, sit down, seat o.s. (*frm*); **¡siéntese!** (do) sit down, take a seat

sentencia SF **1** (*Jur*) sentence; **visto para** ~ ready for sentencing **2** (*Literat*) maxim

sentenciar /1b/ ⒜ VT to sentence (**a** to) ⒝ VI to pronounce o.s., give one's opinion

sentido ⒜ ADJ [*carta, palabras, declaración*] heartfelt; **una pérdida muy sentida** a deeply felt loss; **mi más ~ pésame** my deepest sympathy, my heartfelt condolences ⒝ SM **1** (*para sentir, percibir*) sense; **ha perdido el ~ del gusto** he has lost his sense of taste; **los cinco ~s** the five senses; **no tiene ~ del ritmo** he has no sense of rhythm; ✦ MODISMOS **poner los cinco ~s** to be on one's toes; **tener un sexto** ~ to have a sixth sense ➤ **sentido común**

common sense ➤ **sentido de la orientación** sense of direction ➤ **sentido del humor** sense of humour ➤ **sentido del ridículo**: **su ~ del ridículo le impidió hacerlo** he felt self-conscious *o* embarrassed so he didn't do it ➤ **sentido práctico**: **tener ~ práctico** to be practical **2** (= *significado*) meaning; **¿cuál es el ~ literal de esta palabra?** what is the literal meaning of this word?; **la vida sin ti no tendría** ~ without you life would have no meaning *o* would be meaningless; **doble** ~ double meaning; **sin** ~ [*palabras, comentario*] meaningless; **decía cosas sin** ~ he was talking nonsense **3** (= *lógica*) sense; **no le veo** ~ **a esta discusión** I can't see any sense *o* point in this argument; **sin** ~ [*crueldad, violencia*] senseless; [*debate*] pointless; **tener** ~ to make sense; **no tiene** ~ **que te disculpes ahora** it's pointless (you) apologizing now, there's no sense *o* point in (you) apologizing now **4** (= *conciencia*) consciousness; **lo encontré en el suelo sin** ~ I found him unconscious on the floor; **recobrar el** ~ to regain consciousness; ✦ MODISMO **quitar el ~ a algn** to take sb's breath away **5** (= *dirección*) direction; **en ~ contrario** in the opposite direction; **"sentido único"** "one way"; **en el ~ de las agujas del reloj** clockwise; **en ~ contrario al de las agujas del reloj** anticlockwise (*Brit*), counterclockwise (*EEUU*) **6** (*otras expresiones*) **en el buen ~ de la palabra** in the best *o* good sense of the word; **en cierto** ~ in a sense; **en ese ~** (*con nombre*) to that effect; (*con verbo*) in that sense, in that respect; **en ~ estricto** in the strict sense of the word *o* term; **en tal** ~ to that effect

sentimental ADJ **1** [*persona, objeto*] sentimental; [*mirada*] soulful; **ponerse** ~ to get sentimental **2** [*asunto, vida*] love *antes de s*; **aventura** ~ love affair

sentimentalismo SM sentimentality

sentimentaloide* ADJ sugary, over-sentimental

sentimiento SM **1** (= *emoción*) feeling ➤ **sentimiento de culpa** feeling of guilt, guilty feeling **2** (= *pena*) sorrow; **le acompaño en el** ~ please accept my condolences **3 sentimientos** (= *forma de sentir*) feelings

sentir /3i/ ⒜ VT **1** [+ *emoción, sensación, dolor*] to feel; **no siento la pierna** I can't feel my leg; **dejarse** ~ to be felt; **están empezando a dejarse** ~ **los efectos de la crisis** the effects of the crisis are beginning to be felt; **en octubre ya se deja** ~ **el frío** by October it's already starting to get cold; ~ **hambre/pena por algn** to feel pity for sb, feel sorry for sb; ~ **sed** to feel thirsty **2** (= *percibir*) to sense; **sintió la presencia de alguien en la oscuridad** he sensed a presence in the darkness **3** (*con otros sentidos*) **3.1** (= *oír*) to hear; **no la sentí entrar** I didn't hear her come in **3.2** (*esp LAm*) [+ *olor*] to smell; [+ *sabor*] to taste **4** [+ *música, poesía*] to have a feeling for **5** (= *lamentar*) to be sorry about, regret (*más frm*); **siento mucho lo que pasó** I'm really sorry about what happened; **siento no haber podido ir** I'm sorry I wasn't able to go; **siento informarle que ...** I'm sorry to tell you that ..., I regret to inform you that ... (*más frm*); **lo siento** I'm sorry; **lo siento muchísimo** ◊ **¡cuánto lo siento!** I'm so sorry; **siento mucho que pienses de esa forma** I'm very sorry that you feel that way ⒝ VI to feel; **ni oía ni sentía nada** he could neither hear nor feel anything; **el tiempo se me pasaba sin** ~ I didn't notice the time passing ⒞ **sentirse** VPR **1** (*en estado, situación*) to feel; **no me siento con ánimos para eso** I don't feel up to it; **se sentía observada** she felt she was being watched; **se sintió herido en su orgullo** his pride had been wounded; **~se mal** to feel ill **2** (*LAm*) (= *ofenderse*) to take offence; **no te sientas con él** don't be annoyed with him, don't take offence **3** (*Méx*) [*pared, hueso, vasija*] to crack ⒟ SM **1** (= *opinión*) feeling, opinion; **el ~ mayoritario** the feeling *o* opinion of the majority; **el ~ popular** popular feeling, popular opinion **2** (= *sentimiento*) feelings *pl*; ~ **religioso** religious sentiment *o* feeling

seña SF **1** (= *gesto*) sign; **hablar por ~s** (*gen*) to communicate using signs; [*sordos*] to use sign-language; **hacer una ~ a algn** to make a sign to sb, signal to sb **2 señas** (= *dirección*) address *sing*; **dar las ~s de algn** to give sb's address **3 señas** (= *indicios*): **dar ~s de algo** to show signs of sth; **por** o **para más ~s** to be precise ➤ **señas de identidad** identifying marks, distinguishing marks **4** (*Mil*) **santo y ~** password **5** (*RPI*) (= *depósito*) deposit

señal SF **1** [*de aviso*] (*gen*) signal; (= *letrero*) sign; **un silbido era la ~** a whistle was the signal; **dar la ~** o **para algo** to give the signal for sth; **hacer una ~ a algn** (*con un gesto cualquiera*) to gesture to sb; (*ya acordada*) to signal to sb ➤ **señal de alarma** (*ante un peligro*) warning signal; (= *síntoma*) warning sign; **la muerte de varias ovejas ha hecho sonar la ~ de alarma** the death of several sheep has set alarm bells ringing ➤ **la señal de la cruz** the sign of the cross ➤ **señal de salida** (*Dep*, *Ferro*) starting signal ➤ **señales de humo** smoke signals

2 (*Aut*) sign; **la ~ de stop** the stop sign ➤ **señal de peligro** warning sign ➤ **señal de tráfico** traffic sign, road sign ➤ **señal horizontal** road marking ➤ **señal vertical** road sign

3 (= *indicio*) sign; **es ~ de que las cosas van mejorando** it is a sign that things are improving; **~es de violencia** signs of violent treatment; **es buena ~** it's a good sign; **dar ~es de algo** to show signs of sth; **lleva más de un mes sin dar ~es de vida** there's been no sign of him for more than a month; **en ~ de algo** as a sign of sth; **en ~ de respeto** as a mark o sign of respect

4 (= *marca*) mark; **haz una ~ en los paquetes urgentes** put a mark on the express parcels, mark the express parcels **5** (*Med*) (= *síntoma*) symptom **6** (*Com*, *Fin*) (= *depósito*) deposit; **dejar una cantidad en ~** to leave a sum as a deposit **7** (*Radio*) signal; **se ha ido la ~** the signal has gone ➤ **señal horaria** time signal **8** (*Telec*) (*al teléfono*) tone; (*en contestador*) beep, tone ➤ **señal de comunicando** engaged tone (*Brit*), busy signal (*EEUU*) ➤ **señal de llamada** dialling tone (*Brit*), ringing (*Brit*) o ring (*EEUU*) tone ➤ **señal de ocupado** (*LAm*) engaged tone (*Brit*), busy signal (*EEUU*)

señalado ADJ **1** (= *especial*) [*día*] special; [*ocasión*, *acontecimiento*] special, momentous; **en una fecha tan señalada como hoy** on such a special o momentous day as today; **los rasgos más ~s de su poesía** the most notable features of his poetry **2** [*persona*] (*gen*) distinguished; (*pey*) notorious

señalar /1a/ Ⓐ VT **1** (= *indicar*) (*gen*) to show; (*con el dedo*) to point; **como señala el informe** as shown in the report; **la aguja señala el nivel del aceite** the needle shows the oil level; **es de mala educación ~ a la gente** it's rude to point (at people); **~ una falta** (*Dep*) to indicate a foul **2** (= *marcar*) to mark; **señala en rojo dónde están los fallos** mark the mistakes in red; **señaló las cajas con etiquetas** he labelled the boxes; **eso señaló el principio de la decadencia** that marked the start of the decline **3** (= *destacar*) to point out; **tenemos que ~ tres aspectos fundamentales** we have to point out three fundamental aspects **4** (= *designar*) [+ *fecha*, *precio*] to fix, settle; [+ *tarea*] to set; **en el momento señalado** at the given moment, at the appointed time; **todas las encuestas lo señalan como el candidato favorito** all the opinion polls point to him as the favourite candidate **5** (*Aut*) [+ *carretera*, *ruta*] to signpost **6** [+ *ganado*] to brand

Ⓑ **señalarse** VPR to distinguish o.s. (**como** as)

señalización SF **1** (= *acto*) (*Aut*) signposting, signing (*EEUU*) (*Ferro*) signalling, signaling (*EEUU*) **2** (= *conjunto de señales*) (*en carretera*) road signs *pl*; (*en edificio*) signposting

señalizar /1f/ Ⓐ VT **1** (*Aut*) [+ *ruta*, *carretera*] to signpost **2** (*Ferro*) to signal Ⓑ VI to signal, indicate (*esp Brit*)

señero ADJ unequalled, unequaled (*EEUU*), outstanding

señor(a) Ⓐ SM/F **1** (= *persona madura*) man o (*más frm*) gentleman/lady; **lo he comprado en la planta de ~as** I bought it in ladieswear ➤ **señora de compañía** companion **2** (= *dueño*) [*de tierras*] owner; [*de criado*, *esclavo*] master/ mistress; **¿está la ~a?** is the lady of the house in?

3 (= *fórmula de tratamiento*) **3.1** (*con apellido*) Mr/Mrs; **es para el ~ Serrano** it's for Mr Serrano; **el ~ y la ~a Durán** Mr and Mrs Durán; **los ~es Centeno y Sánchez** (*frm*) Messrs Centeno and Sánchez (*frm*); **los ~es (de) González** Mr and Mrs González **3.2** (*) (*con nombre de pila*) **buenos días, ~ Mariano** (*a Mariano Ruiz*) good morning, Mr Ruiz; **la ~a María es de mi pueblo** (*hablando de María Ruiz*) Mrs Ruiz is from my village **3.3** (*hablando directamente*) sir/madam; **¡oiga, ~a!** excuse me, madam!; **¡~as y ~es!** ladies and gentlemen! **3.4** (*con nombre de cargo o parentesco*) **el ~ alcalde** the mayor; **el ~ cura** the priest; **~ presidente** Mr President; **~ alcalde** Mr Mayor; **sí, ~ juez** yes, my Lord **3.5** (*frm*) (*en correspondencia*) **muy ~ mío** Dear Sir; **muy ~a mía** Dear Madam; **muy ~es nuestros** Dear Sirs; **~ director** (*en carta o periódico*) Dear Sir

4 (*uso enfático*) **pues sí ~, así es como pasó** yes indeed, that's how it happened; **¡no ~, ahora no te vas!** oh no, you're not going anywhere yet!; *ver tb* **señora**

Ⓑ SM **1** (*Hist*) lord ➤ **señor de la guerra** warlord ➤ **señor feudal** feudal lord

2 (*Rel*) **el Señor** the Lord

señora SF **1** (= *esposa*) wife; **la ~ de García** Mrs García **2** (*Rel*) **Nuestra Señora** Our Lady; *ver tb* **señor**

señoría SF **su** o **vuestra Señoría** your o his lordship/your o her ladyship

señorial ADJ noble, majestic, stately

señorita Ⓐ ADJ (*CS*) polite Ⓑ SF **1** (= *mujer soltera*) young lady ➤ **señorita de compañía** (*euf*) escort girl **2** (= *fórmula de tratamiento*) **2.1** (*con apellido*) Miss; **~ Pérez** Miss Pérez; **¿es usted señora o ~?** is it Mrs or Miss? **2.2** (*con nombre de pila*) **buenos días, ~ Rosa** (*a Rosa Pérez*) good morning, Miss Pérez **2.3** (*hablando directamente*) **¿puedo ayudarla en algo, ~?** can I help you, madam? **2.4** (*usado por criados*) **la ~ no está en casa** (*referido a Rosa Pérez*) Miss Pérez is not at home; **¿a qué hora desea la ~ que la despierte?** what time would you like me to wake you, Miss? **2.5** (*en correspondencia*) **estimada ~** (*a Rosa Pérez*) Dear Miss Pérez, Dear Ms Pérez **3** (*) (= *maestra*) teacher

señorito Ⓐ ADJ (*pey*) high and mighty*; **es muy señorita** she's too high and mighty* Ⓑ SM **1** (= *hijo de señor*) young gentleman; (*en lenguaje de criados*) master, young master **2** (*pey*) rich kid*

señuelo SM **1** (*Caza*) decoy **2** (*fig*) (= *cebo*) bait, lure

seo SF cathedral

sepa *etc ver* **saber**

separación SF **1** (= *división*) division; **la estantería sirve de ~ entre las dos zonas** the bookcase acts as a division between the two areas; **la línea de ~** the dividing line ➤ **separación de bienes** division of property ➤ **separación de poderes** separation of powers **2** (*entre cónyuges*, *amigos*) separation ➤ **separación legal**, **separación matrimonial** legal separation **3** (= *distancia entre objetos*) gap, space **4** [*de un cargo*] removal, dismissal

separado/a Ⓐ ADJ **1** (= *independiente*) separate; **en camas separadas** in separate beds; **tiene los ojos muy ~s** his eyes are very far apart; **por ~** separately **2** [*cónyuge*] separated; **es hija de padres ~s** her parents are separated Ⓑ SM/F **los ~s con hijos** separated people with children

separador SM **1** (*en carpeta*, *maletín*) divider **2** (*Col Aut*) central reservation (*Brit*), median strip (*EEUU*)

separar /1a/ Ⓐ VT **1** (= *apartar*) to separate; **la maestra nos separó para que no habláramos** the teacher split us up o separated us so that we wouldn't talk; **separe la parte de abajo del formulario** detach the bottom of the form; **~ algn/algo de algn/algo** to separate sb/sth from sb/sth; **al nacer se ~on de sus padres** they were taken (away) o separated from their parents at birth; **separa el sofá de la pared** move the sofa away from the wall; **separe la cazuela de la lumbre** take the pot off the heat; ✦ MODISMO **~ el grano de la paja** to separate the wheat from the chaff **2** (= *distanciar*) **nada conseguirá ~nos** nothing can come between us; **el trabajo la mantiene separada de su familia** work keeps her away from her family; **hasta que la muerte nos separe** till death us do part

3 (= *deslindar*) **el abismo que separa a los ricos de los pobres** the gulf between *o* separating (the) rich and (the) poor; **unas barreras de protección separaban el escenario de la plaza** there were crash barriers separating the stage from the rest of the square
4 (= *dividir*) to divide; **separa las palabras en sílabas** divide the words into syllables
5 (= *poner aparte*) **¿me puedes ~ un poco de tarta?** can you put aside some cake for me?
6 (= *destituir*) (*de un cargo*) to remove, dismiss
B separarse VPR **1** (*en el espacio*) to part; **caminaron hasta la plaza, donde se ~on** they walked as far as the square, where they went their separate ways *o* where they parted; **~se de algn/algo** to leave sb/sth; **consiguió ~se del pelotón** he managed to leave the pack behind; **no se separen del grupo** stay with the group; **no quiere ~se de sus libros** he doesn't want to part with his books
2 (*en una relación*) [*cónyuges*] to separate, split up; [*socios, pareja*] to split up; **~se de** [+ *cónyuge*] to separate from, split up with; [+ *socio, pareja*] to split up with
3 (= *desprenderse*) [*fragmento, trozo*] to detach itself (**de** from), come away; [*pedazos*] to come apart
4 (*Pol, Rel*) to break away; **cuando la Iglesia anglicana se separó de Roma** when the Anglican Church broke away *o* (*frm*) seceded from Rome

separata SF offprint

separatismo SM separatism

separatista ADJ, SMF separatist

separo SM (*Méx*) cell

sepelio SM burial, interment

sepia A ADJ, SM INV (= *color*) sepia **B** SF **1** (= *pez*) cuttlefish **2** (*Arte*) sepia

septentrional ADJ north, northern

septicemia SF septicaemia, septicemia (*EEUU*)

séptico ADJ septic

septiembre SM September; **llegará el (día) 11 de ~** he will arrive on September the 11th *o* (*Brit*) on the 11th of September; **en ~** in September; **en ~ del año pasado/del año que viene** last/next September; **a mediados de ~** in mid-September; **estamos a tres de ~** it's the third of September; **todos los años, en ~** every September

> En inglés los meses se escriben con mayúscula.

séptimo ADJ, PRON seventh; *ver tb* **sexto**

septuagésimo ADJ, PRON seventieth; *ver tb* **sexto**

sepulcral ADJ **1** (= *del sepulcro*) sepulchral; **la inscripción ~** the inscription on the tomb *o* grave **2** (= *sombrío*) [*silencio*] deathly

sepulcro SM (*esp Biblia*) tomb, grave, sepulchre, sepulcher (*EEUU*)

sepultar /1a/ VT to bury; **quedaron sepultados bajo la roca** they were buried under the rock

sepultura SF **1** (= *acción*) burial; **dar ~ a** to bury; **recibir ~** to be buried **2** (= *tumba*) grave, tomb

sepulturero SM gravedigger

seque *etc ver* **secar**

sequedad SF **1** (= *falta de humedad*) dryness **2** (*en contestación, carácter*) curtness

sequía SF drought

séquito SM retinue, entourage

---

ser /2v/

A VERBO INTRANSITIVO   **C** SUSTANTIVO MASCULINO
B VERBO AUXILIAR

---

ser A VERBO INTRANSITIVO
1 (*con función copulativa*)
1.1 (+ ADJ) to be; **es difícil** it's difficult; **es muy alto** he's very tall; **es pesimista** he's a pessimist; **somos seis** there are six of us; **me es imposible asistir** I'm unable to attend, it's impossible for me to attend; **—eres estúpida —no, no lo**

soy "you're stupid" — "no I'm not"; **¡~á posible!** I don't believe it!; **¡~ás burro!** you can be so stupid!
1.2 (+ SUSTANTIVO, PRONOMBRE) **el gran pintor que fue Goya** the great painter Goya; **hable con algún abogado que no sea Pérez** speak to some lawyer other than Pérez; **soy ingeniero** I'm an engineer; **¡hola, soy Pedro!** hello, it's Pedro; **soy yo** it's me; **es él quien debiera hacerlo** he's the one who should do it
◆ **ser de** (*indicando origen*) to be from; (*indicando composición*) to be made of; (*indicando pertenencia*) to belong to; **es de lana** it's made of wool, it's woollen; **el parque es del municipio** the park belongs to the council; **¿de quién es este lápiz?** whose pencil is this?, who does this pencil belong to?; **es de Joaquín** it's Joaquín's; **¿qué ~á de mí?** what will become of me?; **¿qué habrá sido de él?** what can have become of him?, what can have happened to him?; **es de creer que** presumably; **no es de creer que lo encarcelen** they probably won't put him in prison
◆ **ser para** (*indicando dirección, finalidad*) **las flores son para ti** the flowers are for you; **este cuchillo es para cortar pan** this knife is for cutting bread; **esas finuras no son para mí** such niceties are not for me
2 (= *existir*) to be; **~ o no ~** to be or not to be; **érase una vez una princesa ...** ◇ **érase que se era una princesa ...** once upon a time there was a princess ...
3 (= *tener lugar*) **la fiesta va a ~ en su casa** the party will be at her house; **el crimen fue en agosto** the crime took place in August; **✦** MODISMO **otra vez ~á** some other time
4 (*con horas del día, fecha, tiempo*) to be; **son las siete** it's seven o'clock; **hoy es cuatro de septiembre** today is the fourth of September (*Brit*) *o* (*EEUU*) September fourth; **es verano** it's summer; **era de noche** it was night time
5 (= *en cálculos*) to be; **tres y dos son cinco** three plus two is five; **—¿cuánto es? —son doscientas pesetas** "how much is it?" — "two hundred pesetas, please"
6 (*locuciones con infinitivo*) **a no ~ que** unless; **no vaya a ~ que ...**: **déjales tu teléfono, no vaya a ~ que se pierdan** give them your phone number in case they get lost; **anda despacio, no vaya a ~ que te caigas** walk slowly so you don't fall over
7 (*locuciones en indicativo*) **es más**: **creo que eso es así, es más, podría asegurártelo** I think that is the case, in fact I can assure you it is; **es que**: **—¿por qué no llamaste? —es que no pude** "why didn't you call?" — "because I couldn't"; **es que no quiero molestarle** it's just that I don't want to upset him; **¿es que no te enteras?** don't you understand, or what?; **¿cómo es que no llamaste?** how come you didn't call?
8 (*locuciones en subjuntivo*) **¡sea!** agreed!, all right!; **o sea** that is to say; **mis compañeros, o sea, Juan y Pedro** my colleagues, that is, Juan and Pedro; **o sea, que no vienes** so you're not coming; **no sea que** in case; **llévate el móvil no sea que llamen** take your cellphone *o* mobile phone (*Brit*) with you in case they call; **pon aquí las llaves, no sea que las pierdas** put the keys here so you don't lose them
B VERBO AUXILIAR (*en formas pasivas*) to be; **fue construido** it was built; **está siendo estudiado** it is being studied; **ha sido asaltada una joyería** there has been a raid on a jeweller's
C SUSTANTIVO MASCULINO
1 (= *ente*) being; **sus ~es queridos** her loved ones ➤ **ser humano** human being ➤ **Ser Supremo** Supreme Being ➤ **ser vivo** living creature
2 (= *esencia, alma*) being; **todo su ~** her whole being; **en lo más íntimo de su ~** deep within himself

sera SF pannier, basket

seráfico ADJ angelic, seraphic

serafín SM (*Rel*) seraph

Serbia SF Serbia

serbio/a A ADJ Serbian **B** SM/F Serb **C** SM (*Ling*) Serbian

serbocroata A ADJ, SMF Serbo-Croatian **B** SM (*Ling*) Serbo-Croat

serenar /1a/ **A** VT (*frm*) to calm **B serenarse** VPR
1 [*persona*] to calm down **2** [*mar*] to grow calm; [*tiempo*] to clear up, settle (down)

serenata SF serenade

serenidad SF calmness, serenity

sereno Ⓐ ADJ 1 [*persona*] calm, serene; [*cara, expresión*] serene 2 [*tiempo*] settled, fine; [*cielo*] cloudless, clear 3 [*ambiente*] calm, quiet; [*tarde, noche*] still, peaceful; [*aguas*] calm, still 4 (= *sobrio*) sober Ⓑ SM 1 (= *humedad*) night dew; **dormir al** ~ to sleep out in the open 2 (= *vigilante*) night watchman

serial SM (SF *en* CS) serial

serializar /1f/ VT to serialize

serie SF 1 (= *sucesión*) (*tb* Biol, Mat) series; **asesinatos en** ~ serial killings 2 (*Industria*) **de** ~ [*modelo, tamaño*] standard; **en** ~: **fabricación en** ~ mass production; **fabricar** *o* **producir en** ~ to mass-produce; **fuera de** ~ (= *extraordinario*) special, out of the ordinary 3 (= *conjunto*) [*de monedas, sellos*] series; [*de inyecciones*] course 4 (TV, Radio) (*en episodios sueltos*) series; (*en historia continua*) serial 5 (*Cine*) **película de** ~ Ⓑ B-movie 6 (*Dep*) qualifying heat

seriedad SF 1 (= *calidad personal*) seriousness; **hablar con** ~ to speak seriously *o* in earnest 2 (= *responsabilidad*) responsibility, sense of responsibility; **falta de** ~ lack of responsibility, irresponsibility 3 [*de enfermedad, crisis, problema*] seriousness 4 (= *fiabilidad*) reliability, trustworthiness

serigrafía SF silk-screen printing; **una** ~ a silk-screen print

serio ADJ 1 [*expresión, tono*] serious; **su padre es muy** ~ his father's a very serious person; **se quedó mirándome muy** ~ he looked at me very seriously, he stared gravely at me 2 **en** ~ seriously; **tomar un asunto en** ~ to take a matter seriously; **no hablaba en** ~ I wasn't serious; **¿lo dices en ~?** are you serious?, do you really mean it? 3 [*problema, enfermedad, pérdida*] serious 4 (= *fiable*) [*persona, empresa*] reliable; [*trato*] straight, honest; **es una persona poco seria** he's not very reliable; **no es** ~ **que ahora decidan echarse atrás** it's not very responsible of them to back out now 5 [*color*] serious, severe; **lleva un traje muy** ~ he's wearing a very formal suit 6 [*estudio, libro*] serious

sermón SM 1 (Rel) sermon 2 (*) (= *regañina*) lecture*

sermonear* /1a/ VT to lecture*

sernambí SM (And, Carib) inferior rubber

serón SM pannier, large basket

seropositivo ADJ (*gen*) seropositive; (*con VIH*) HIV-positive

serotonina SF serotonin

serpentear /1a/ VI [*camino*] to wind, twist and turn; [*río*] to wind, meander

serpentín SM coil

serpentina SF 1 (Min) serpentine 2 (= *papel*) streamer

serpiente SF snake, serpent ➤ **serpiente de cascabel** rattlesnake, rattler (EEUU*) ➤ **serpiente pitón** python

serranía SF mountains *pl*, mountainous area, hilly country

serrano ADJ 1 (Geog) mountain *antes de s*, hill *antes de s* 2 (*) [*cuerpo*] fine-looking

serrar /1j/ VT to saw up

serrería SF sawmill

serrín SM sawdust

serruchar /1a/ VT (*esp LAm*) to saw (up)

serrucho SM saw, handsaw

servicial ADJ helpful, obliging

servicio SM 1 (= *ayuda, atención*) 1.1 (*a empresa, país*) service; **lleva veinte años de** ~ **en la empresa** he has twenty years' service with the company; **un agente secreto al** ~ **de la Corona** a secret agent in the service of the Crown; **estar de** ~ to be on duty; **estar fuera** *o* **libre de** ~ to be off duty; **prestar sus ~s en** [*empleado*] to work at; [*militar*] to serve in 1.2 (*a cliente*) service; **el** ~ **no está incluido** service is not included; **a su** ~ at your service; **"servicio a domicilio"** "we deliver", "home delivery service" 1.3 [*de tren, autobús*] service ➤ **servicio de atención al cliente** customer service ➤ **servicio de inteligencia** intelligence service ➤ **servicio de limpieza** cleaning services *pl* ➤ **servicio de orden** (*en*

manifestación) stewards *pl*, marshals *pl* ➤ **servicio de transportes** (*para personas*) transport (*esp* Brit) *o* transportation (*esp* EEUU) system; (*para mercancías*) delivery service ➤ **servicio posventa** after-sales service ➤ **servicio secreto** secret service ➤ **servicios informativos** broadcasting services ➤ **servicios mínimos** minimum service *sing*, skeleton service *sing* ➤ **servicio social (sustitutorio)** community service (*performed in place of military service*) ➤ **servicios sociales** social services 2 (= *funcionamiento*) **estar en** ~ to be in service; **entrar en** ~ to come *o* go into service; **fuera de** ~ out of service; **poner en** ~ to put into service 3 (= *beneficio*) service; **hizo un gran** ~ **a su país** he did his country a great service; **es un abrigo viejo, pero me hace mucho** ~ it's an old coat, but I get a lot of use out of it; **hacer un flaco** ~ **a algn** to do sb a disservice 4 (Mil) (*tb* ~ **militar**) military service ➤ **servicio activo** active service 5 (*en un hospital*) department ➤ **servicio de urgencias** accident and emergency department (Brit), emergency department (EEUU) 6 **servicios** (Econ) public services; **el sector** ~**s** the public service sector 7 (= *retrete público*) toilet (Brit), restroom (EEUU), washroom (EEUU); **¿dónde están los** ~**s?** where are the toilets? (Brit), where is the restroom *o* washroom? (EEUU) 8 (*en la mesa*) 8.1 (*para cada comensal*) **un juego de café con seis** ~**s** a six-piece coffee set; **faltan dos** ~**s** we are two places *o* settings short 8.2 (= *juego*) set ➤ **servicio de café** coffee set, coffee service ➤ **servicio de mesa** dinner service (Brit), dinnerware set (EEUU) ➤ **servicio de té** tea set, tea service 9 (*tb* ~ **doméstico**) (= *personas*) servants *pl*; (= *actividad*) service, domestic service; **escalera de** ~ service staircase; **puerta de** ~ tradesman's entrance 10 (Tenis) serve, service 11 (Rel) service 12 (Fin) [*de una deuda*] servicing 13 (LAm) [*de un automóvil*] service

servidor(a) Ⓐ SM/F 1 (= *criado*) servant 2 (*como expresión cortés*) **—¿quién es la última de la cola? —servidora** "who's last in the queue (*esp* Brit) *o* line (EEUU)?" — "I am"; **—Francisco Ruiz —¡servidor!** (*frm*) "Francisco Ruiz" — "present! *o* at your service!" (*frm*); **"su seguro servidor"**[†] (*en cartas*) "Yours faithfully" (Brit *frm*), "Yours truly" (EEUU *frm*); **un** ~ (*hum*) yours truly* 3 (*) (CS) ➤ **servidor(a) del orden** police officer Ⓑ SM (Inform) server ➤ **servidor de correo** (Internet) mail server ➤ **servidor de red** network server

servidumbre SF 1 (= *criados*) staff, servants *pl* 2 (= *condición*) [*de criado*] servitude; [*de esclavo*] slavery 3 (Hist) (*tb* ~ **de la gleba**) serfdom 4 (Jur) ➤ **servidumbre de aguas** water rights *pl* ➤ **servidumbre de paso** rights *pl* of way

servil ADJ [*actitud, comportamiento*] servile, obsequious; [*trabajo*] menial

servilismo SM servility, obsequiousness (*frm*)

servilleta SF napkin, serviette (Brit)

servilletero SM napkin ring

servir /3k/ Ⓐ VT 1 [+ *amo, intereses, causa*] to serve; **¿en qué puedo ~le?** how can I help you?; ✦ MODISMO **para ~le**[†] at your service 2 (*en la mesa*) [+ *comida, comensal*] to serve; [+ *bebida*] to serve, pour; **¿me ayudas a ~ la mesa?** can you help me serve (the food)?; **la cena está servida** dinner's on the table, dinner is served (*frm*); **¿te sirvo un poco más?** would you like some more?, can I give you some more?; **había cinco criados para ~ la mesa** there were five servants waiting at *o* serving at table 3 (Com) [+ *pedido*] to process 4 (Tenis) to serve Ⓑ VI 1 (= *ser útil*) to be useful; **todavía puede** ~ it might still be useful; **este mismo me ~á** this one will do; **eso no sirve** that's no good *o* use; **ya no me sirve** it's no good *o* use to me now; ~ **para algo: puede** ~ **para limpiar el metal** it can be used for *o* it is suitable for cleaning metal; **¿para qué sirve?** what is it for?; **esta huelga no está sirviendo para**

nada this strike is not achieving anything; **no sirves para nada** you're completely useless; **yo no ~ía para médico** I'd be no good as a doctor

2 ~ de algo: la legislación italiana puede ~nos de guía we can use Italian law as a guide, Italian law can serve a guide; **~ de ejemplo a algn** to be an example to sb; **esa experiencia le ha servido de lección** that experience taught him a lesson; **por si sirve de algo** in case that's any use; **no sirve de nada quejarse** it's no good *o* use complaining, there's no point in complaining; **¿de qué sirve mentir?** what's the good *o* of lying?, what's the point in lying? **3** (*en el servicio doméstico*) to work as a servant; **ponerse a ~** to become a servant

4 [*camarero*] to serve

5 (*Mil*) to serve (*frm*)

6 (*Tenis*) to serve

7 (*Naipes*) (*tb ~ del palo*) to follow suit

❻ servirse VPR **1** (= *ponerse*) [+ *comida*] to help o.s. to; [+ *bebida*] to pour o.s., help o.s. to

2 (= *utilizar*) **~se de** [+ *herramienta, objeto*] to use, make use of; [+ *amistad, influencia*] to use

3 (*frm*) (= *hacer el favor de*) **~se hacer algo: sírvase volver por aquí mañana** (would you) please come back tomorrow

servodirección SF power steering

servofrenos SMPL power-assisted brakes

sésamo SM sesame; **¡ábrete ~!** open sesame!

sesear /1a/ VT *to pronounce c (before e, i) and z as s (a feature of Andalusian and LAm pronunciation)*

sesenta ADJ, PRON, SM (*cardinal*) sixty; (*ordinal*) sixtieth; *ver tb* **seis**

sesentón/ona ❶ ADJ sixty-year-old, sixtyish **❷** SM/F man/woman of about sixty, sixty-year-old

seseo SM *pronunciation of c (before e, i) and of z as s (a feature of Andalusian and LAm pronunciation)*

sesgado ADJ **1** (= *inclinado*) slanted, slanting, oblique **2** [*opinión, reportaje*] bias(s)ed, slanted

sesgar /1h/ VT **1** (= *inclinar*) to slant, place obliquely **2** (*Cos*) to cut on the bias **3** [+ *vida*] to cut short

sesgo SM **1** (= *inclinación*) **al ~** slanting **2** (*Cos*) bias; **al ~** on the bias **3** (= *dirección*) direction; **ha tomado otro ~** it has taken a new turn

sesión SF **1** (*Admin*) session ➤ **sesión parlamentaria** parliamentary session **2** (= *espacio de tiempo*) (*para retrato*) sitting; (*para tratamiento médico*) session ➤ **sesión de espiritismo** séance **3** (*Cine*) showing; (*Teat*) show, performance; **la segunda ~** the second showing ➤ **sesión continua** continuous showing **4** (*Inform*) session

seso SM **1** (*Anat*) brain **2** (= *inteligencia*) brains *pl*; **✦** MODISMOS **calentarse o devanarse los ~s** to rack one's brains; **eso le tiene sorbido el ~** he's crazy about it; **perder el ~** to go off one's head (**por** over) **3** sesos (*Culin*) brains

sestear /1a/ VI to take a siesta, have a nap

sesudo ADJ **1** (= *sensato*) sensible, wise **2** (= *inteligente*) brainy

set SM (*pl ~ o ~s*) (*Dep*) set

seta SF mushroom ➤ **seta venenosa** toadstool

setecientos ADJ, PRON, SM (*cardinal*) seven hundred; (*ordinal*) seven hundredth; *ver tb* **seiscientos**

setenta ADJ, PRON, SM (*cardinal*) seventy; (*ordinal*) seventieth; *ver tb* **seis**

setentón/ona ❶ ADJ seventy-year-old, seventyish **❷** SM/F man/woman of about seventy, seventy-year-old

setiembre SM = **septiembre**

seto SM hedge

seudónimo SM (*gen*) pseudonym; [*de escritor*] pen name, pseudonym

Seúl SM Seoul

severidad SF **1** (*en el trato*) severity **2** (= *austeridad*) sternness

severo ADJ **1** (= *riguroso*) [*persona*] severe, harsh; [*padre, profesor, disciplina*] strict; [*castigo, crítica*] harsh; [*estipulaciones*] stringent; [*condiciones*] harsh, stringent; **ser**

~ con algn to treat sb harshly **2** (= *duro*) [*invierno*] severe, hard; [*frío*] bitter **3** (= *austero*) [*vestido, moda*] severe; [*actitud*] stern

Sevilla SF Seville

sevillanas SFPL **1** (= *cante*) *popular Sevillian tune* **2** (= *baile*) *typical Sevillian dance*

sevillano/a ADJ, SM/F Sevillian

sexagenario/a ADJ, SM/F sexagenarian, sixty-year-old

sexagésimo ADJ, PRON sixtieth; *ver tb* **sexto**

sexismo SM sexism

sexista ADJ, SMF sexist

sexo SM **1** (*Biol*) sex; **el ~ opuesto** the opposite sex; **de ambos ~s** of both sexes; **✦** MODISMO **hablar del ~ de los ángeles** to indulge in pointless discussion ➤ **sexo oral** oral sex ➤ **sexo seguro** safe sex **2** (= *órgano sexual*) [*de hombre*] penis, sexual organs *pl* (*frm*); [*de mujer*] vagina, sexual organs *pl* (*frm*)

sexología SF sexology

sexólogo/a SM/F sexologist

sex shop ['sekʃop] SM (*a veces* SF) (*pl ~s*) sex shop

sextante SM sextant

sexteto SM sextet

sextillizo/a SM/F sextuplet

sexto ADJ, PRON **1** (*ordinal*) sixth; **Juan ~** John the sixth; **vigésimo ~** twenty-sixth; **en ~ lugar** in sixth place, sixth; **en el ~ (piso)** on the sixth floor **2** (*partitivo*) sixth; **una sexta parte** a sixth, a sixth part; **cinco ~s** five sixths

séxtuplo/a ADJ sixfold

sexual ADJ sexual, sex *antes de s*; **vida ~** sex life

sexualidad SF sexuality

sexy ADJ [*persona*] sexy; [*libro, escena*] erotic, titillating

s/f ABR (*Com*) = **su favor**

SGAE SF ABR = **Sociedad General de Autores de España**

sgte. ABR (= **siguiente**) foll., f

share [ʃear] SM (*TV*) audience share

shiatsu ['sjatsu] SM shiatsu

shock [ʃok] SM (*pl ~ o ~s* [ʃok]) shock; **~ postraumático** post-traumatic shock

shopping ['ʃopin] SM (*RPl*) shopping mall, shopping centre (*Brit*)

show [tʃo, ʃou] SM **1** (*Teat*) show **2** (***) (= *jaleo*) fuss, bother; **menudo ~ montó** he made a great song-and-dance about it

si¹ CONJ **1** (*uso condicional*) if; **si lo quieres, te lo doy** if you want it I'll give it to you; **si lo sé, no te lo digo** I wouldn't have told you, if I'd known; **si tuviera dinero** if I had any money; **si me lo hubiese pedido** if he had asked me for it; **si no** (*condición negativa*) if not; (*indicando alternativa*) otherwise, or (else); **si no estudias, no aprobarás** you won't pass if you don't study, you won't pass unless you study; **ponte crema porque si no, te quemarás** put some cream on, otherwise *o* or (else) you'll get sunburned; **llevo el paraguas por si (acaso) llueve** I've got my umbrella (just) in case it rains; **¿y si llueve?** what if it rains?; **¿y si se lo preguntamos?** why don't we ask her?

2 (*en interrogativas indirectas*) whether; **no sé si hacerlo o no** I don't know whether to do it or not; **me pregunto si vale la pena** I wonder whether *o* if it's worth it; **¿sabes si nos han pagado ya?** do you know if we've been paid yet?

3 (*uso concesivo*) **no sé de qué te quejas, si eres una belleza** I don't know what you're complaining about when you're so beautiful; **si bien** although

4 (*uso desiderativo*) **¡si fuera verdad!** if only it were true!, I wish it were true!; **¡si viniese pronto!** I wish he'd come!, if only he'd come!

5 (*indicando protesta*) but; **¡si no sabía que estabas allí!** but I didn't know you were there!

6 (*uso enfático*) **¡si serán hipócritas!** they're such hypocrites!, they're so hypocritical!; **¡si lo sabré yo!** "don't I know it!", "you're telling me!"

7 (*indicando sorpresa*) **¡pero si es el cartero!** why, it's the postman (*Brit*) *o* mailman (*EEUU*)!; **¡pero si eres tú! no te**

había reconocido oh, it's you, I didn't recognize you!

si² SM (*Mús*) B ➤ **si mayor** B major

sí¹ Ⓐ ADV **1** (*como respuesta*) yes; **—¿te gusta? —sí** "do you like it?" — "yes (I do)"; **¡ah, sí?** really?; **bueno, eso sí** yes, that's true

2 (*uso enfático*) **2.1** (*en oposición a una negación*) **él no quiere pero yo sí** he doesn't want to but I do; **no tiene hermanos, pero sí dos hermanas** he doesn't have any brothers but he does have two sisters; **—¿a que no eres capaz? —¿a que sí?** "I bet you can't" — "do you want a bet?"*; **—yo eso no me lo creo —¡que sí, hombre!** "I can't believe that" — "I'm telling you, it's true!"; **un sábado sí y otro no** every other Saturday **2.2** (*en oraciones afirmativas*) **ahí sí me duele** it definitely hurts there, that's where it hurts; **pero eso sí, el tabaco no les falta** but they're certainly never short of cigarettes; **¿a que sí, Luisa?** isn't that right, Luisa?; **sí que: pero nosotros sí que lo oímos** but WE certainly heard it; **sí que me lo dijo** (yes) he DID tell me; **eso sí que no: me piden que traicione a mis amigos y eso sí que no*** they're asking me to betray my friends and that's just not on*; **—¿puedo hacer unas fotos? —¡ah, no, eso sí que no!** "can I take some photos?" — "no, absolutely not!"; ✦ MODISMO **porque sí** (= *sin esfuerzo*) just like that; (= *sin razón*) just for the sake of it; **pues porque sí** (just) because!

3 (*en oraciones subordinadas*) **creo que sí** I think so; **—¿asistirá el presidente? —puede que sí** "will the president be there?" — "he might be"; **decir que sí** to say yes; **dijo que sí con la cabeza** he nodded in agreement **Ⓑ** SM **1** (= *consentimiento*) yes; **un sí rotundo** a definite yes; **dar el sí** (*a una propuesta*) to say yes; (*en la boda*) to say "I do"

2 síes (= *votos*) votes in favour

sí² PRON **1** (*uso reflexivo*) **1.1** (*de tercera persona*) (*referido a una persona*) himself/herself; (*referido a objeto, concepto*) itself; (*en plural*) themselves; **no lo podrá hacer por sí solo** he won't be able to do it on his own *o* by himself; **el producto en sí es inofensivo** the product itself is inoffensive; **sí mismo/a** (*referido a persona*) himself/herself; (*referido a objeto, concepto*) itself; (*uso impersonal*) yourself, oneself (*más frm*); **ha puesto lo mejor de sí mismo en ese proyecto** he has put his best into the project; **sí mismos/as** themselves **1.2** (*referido a usted*) (*en singular*) yourself; (*en plural*) yourselves; **sí mismo/a** yourself; **sí mismos/as** yourselves **1.3** ✦ MODISMOS **de por sí: el problema ya es bastante difícil de por sí** the problem is difficult enough in itself *o* as it is; **él, de por sí, ya tiene mal carácter** he's got a really bad temper at the best of times; **estar fuera de sí** to be beside o.s.; **empezó a dar gritos fuera de sí** he started shouting hysterically

2 entre sí: son idénticos entre sí they are identical to each other; **se repartieron la herencia entre sí** they shared (out) the inheritance among themselves; **las dos soluciones son incompatibles entre sí** the two solutions are mutually incompatible; **las dos ciudades distan entre sí 45km** the two cities are 45km apart

siamés/esa ADJ, SM/F Siamese

sibarita Ⓐ ADJ sybaritic, luxury-loving **Ⓑ** SMF sybarite, lover of luxury

sibaritismo SM sybaritism, love of luxury

Siberia SF Siberia

siberiano/a ADJ, SM/F Siberian

sibilante ADJ, SF sibilant

sibilino ADJ sibylline

sicario SM hired killer, hitman*

Sicilia SF Sicily

siciliano/a Ⓐ ADJ, SM/F Sicilian **Ⓑ** SM (= *dialecto*) Sicilian

sicomoro SM, **sicómoro** SM sycamore

sida SM ABR (= **síndrome de inmunodeficiencia adquirida**) AIDS

sidecar SM sidecar

sideral ADJ **1** (*Astron*) (= *de los astros*) astral; (= *del espacio exterior*) space *antes de s* **2** [*coste, precio*] astronomic

siderometalurgia SF iron and steel industry

siderometalúrgico ADJ iron and steel *antes de s*

siderurgia SF iron and steel industry

siderúrgico ADJ iron and steel *antes de s*

sidra SF cider, hard cider (*EEUU*)

sidrería SF cider bar

siega SF **1** (= *acción*) (= *cosechar*) reaping, harvesting **2** (= *época*) harvest, harvest time

siembra SF **1** (= *acción*) sowing **2** (= *época*) sowing time

siempre Ⓐ ADV **1** (*indicando frecuencia*) always; **está ~ lloviendo** it's always raining; **como** ~ as usual; **tú tan modesto como ~** (*iró*) modest as ever; **de ~** [*lugar, hora*] usual *antes de s*; **por favor, lo de ~** my usual, please; **protestan los de ~** it's the same people as usual protesting; **los mismos problemas de ~** the same old problems; **desde ~** always; **¡hasta ~!** farewell!; **para ~** forever, for good*; **por ~** (*liter*) for ever; **por ~ jamás** for ever and ever

2 (= *en todo caso*) always; ~ **puedes decir que no lo sabías** you can always say you didn't know

3 (*LAm**) (= *todavía*) still; **¿~ se va mañana?** are you still going tomorrow?

4 (*esp Méx*) (= *definitivamente*) certainly, definitely; ~ **no me caso este año** I'm certainly *o* definitely not getting married this year

5 (*Chi*) (= *de todas maneras*) still; **lo tenían rodeado y ~ se escapó** they had him surrounded but he still escaped **Ⓑ** CONJ **1** ~ **que** (= *cada vez que*) whenever; (= *a condición de que*) as long as, provided (that), providing (that); **voy ~ que puedo** I go whenever I can; ~ **que salgo llueve** every time *o* whenever I go out it rains; **riéguelas ~ que sea necesario** water them whenever necessary; ~ **que él esté de acuerdo** as long as he agrees, provided (that) *o* providing (that) he agrees

2 ~ **y cuando** as long as, provided (that), providing (that)

sien SF temple

siena ADJ, SM INV (= *color*) sienna

siento *etc* ver **sentar**, **sentir**

sierpe SF snake, serpent

sierra SF **1** (= *herramienta*) saw ➤ **sierra de marquetería** fretsaw, coping saw ➤ **sierra mecánica** power saw **2** (*Geog*) mountain range, sierra; **la ~** (= *zona*) the hills, the mountains

Sierra Leona SF Sierra Leone

siervo/a SM/F slave ➤ **siervo de Dios** servant of the Lord ➤ **siervo de la gleba** serf

siesta SF **1** (= *sueñecito*) siesta, nap; **dormir la** *o* **echarse una ~** to have an afternoon nap **2** (= *hora del día*) afternoon

siete Ⓐ ADJ, PRON (*cardinal*) seven; (*ordinal, en la fecha*) seventh; ✦ MODISMO **hablar más que ~** to talk nineteen to the dozen **Ⓑ** SM **1** (= *número*) seven; *ver tb* **seis 2** (= *roto*) **hacerse un ~ en la camisa** to tear one's shirt (*making an L-shaped tear*) **Ⓒ** SF (*CS**) **de la gran ~** terrible*, tremendous*; **hijo de la gran ~** bastard***, son of a bitch (*EEUU***)

sietemesino/a Ⓐ ADJ two months premature **Ⓑ** SM/F baby born two months premature

sífilis SF INV syphilis

sifilítico/a ADJ, SM/F syphilitic

sifón SM **1** (*Téc*) trap, U-bend **2** [*de agua*] siphon, syphon; **whisky con ~** whisky and soda **3** (*Col*) (= *cerveza*) draught beer, draft beer (*EEUU*)

sifrino ADJ (*Carib*) stuck-up*, full of airs and graces

sigilo SM (= *silencio*) stealth; (= *secreto*) secrecy; **con mucho ~** [*entrar, caminar*] very stealthily; [*reunirse, negociar*] amid great secrecy, with great secrecy

sigiloso ADJ stealthy

sigla SF symbol; **siglas** (*pronunciadas como una palabra*) acronym *sing*; (*pronunciadas individualmente*) abbreviation *sing*

siglo SM **1** (= *cien años*) century; **por los ~s de los ~s** world without end, for ever and ever ➤ **Siglo de las Luces** Age of Enlightenment ➤ **Siglo de Oro** (*Literat*) Golden Age **2** (= *largo tiempo*) **hace un ~** *o* **hace ~s que no lo veo** I haven't seen him for ages **3** (*Rel*) **el ~** the world

signatario/a ADJ, SM/F signatory

signatura SF **1** [*de biblioteca*] catalogue number, catalog number (*EEUU*), press mark **2** (*Mús, Tip*) signature

significación SF significance

significado SM meaning

significante SM (*Ling*) signifier

significar /1g/ **Ⓐ** VT **1** (= *querer decir*) [*palabra*] to mean; [*suceso*] to mean, signify **2** (= *representar*) **él no significa nada para mí** he means nothing to me; **~á la ruina de la empresa** it will mean the end for the company **Ⓑ significarse** VPR to become known, distinguish o.s. (**como** as)

significativo ADJ **1** [*cambio, detalle, desarrollo*] significant; **es ~ que ...** it is significant that ... **2** [*mirada*] meaningful

signo SM **1** (= *señal*) sign; **un ~ de los tiempos** a sign of the times ➤ **signo de admiración** exclamation mark (*Brit*), exclamation point (*EEUU*) ➤ **signo de interrogación** question mark ➤ **signo de la victoria** victory sign, V-sign ➤ **signo (de) más** plus sign ➤ **signo (de) menos** minus sign ➤ **signo igual** equal sign, equals sign (*Brit*) **2** (*tb* **~ del zodíaco**) star sign

sigo *etc ver* **seguir**

siguiente ADJ next, following; **el ~ vuelo** the next flight; **¡el ~, por favor!** next please!; **al día ~** the following *o* next day; **dijo lo ~** he said the following

sij ADJ, SMF (*pl* **~s**) Sikh

sílaba SF syllable

silábico ADJ syllabic

silbar /1a/ **Ⓐ** VT **1** [+ *melodía*] to whistle **2** [+ *orador, banda*] to whistle at **Ⓑ** VI to whistle

silbatina SF (*SAm*) whistling

silbato SM whistle

silbido SM **1** (*con los labios*) whistle, whistling; (*al respirar*) wheezing **2** (*en los oídos*) ringing **3** (= *abucheo*) hissing

silenciador SM [*de arma*] silencer; (*Aut*) silencer (*Brit*), muffler (*EEUU*)

silenciar /1b/ VT **1** [+ *suceso*] to hush up; [+ *hecho*] to keep silent about **2** [+ *persona*] to silence **3** [+ *motor*] to silence

silencio SM **1** (= *falta de ruido*) silence; **¡silencio!** silence!, quiet!; **un poco de ~, por favor** let's have a bit of quiet, please; **¡qué ~ hay aquí!** it's so quiet here!; **en ~** in silence; **la casa estaba en ~** the house was silent; **guardar ~** to keep silent, keep quiet; **guardar un minuto de ~** to observe a one-minute *o* a minute's silence ➤ **silencio administrativo** administrative silence **2** (*Mús*) rest

silencioso ADJ [*persona*] silent, quiet; [*máquina*] silent, noiseless

sílex SM silex, flint

sílfide SF sylph

silicato SM silicate

sílice SF silica

silicio SM, **silicón** SM (*Méx*) silicon

silicona SF silicone

silicosis SF INV silicosis

silla SF **1** (= *asiento*) seat, chair; ✦ MODISMO **calentar la ~** to stay too long, outstay one's welcome ➤ **silla de hamaca** (*LAm*) rocking chair ➤ **silla de manos** sedan chair ➤ **silla de paseo** (*para bebé*) pushchair (*Brit*), stroller (*EEUU*) ➤ **silla de ruedas** wheelchair ➤ **silla de tijera** folding chair ➤ **silla eléctrica** electric chair ➤ **silla giratoria** swivel chair ➤ **silla plegable** folding chair **2** (*tb* **~ de montar**) saddle

sillar SM block of stone, ashlar

sillería SF **1** (= *asientos*) chairs *pl*, set of chairs; (*Rel*) choir stalls *pl* **2** (= *taller*) chair-maker's workshop **3** (*Arquit*) masonry, ashlar work

sillín SM saddle

sillón SM armchair, easy chair ➤ **sillón de dentista** dentist's chair ➤ **sillón orejero** wing chair

silo SM silo

silogismo SM syllogism

silueta SF **1** (= *contorno*) silhouette; **se adivinaba una ~ detrás de la cortina** you could make out a silhouette *o* figure behind the curtain **2** (= *tipo*) figure; **un bañador que realza la ~** a swimsuit that shows off your figure

silvestre ADJ **1** (*Bot*) wild **2** (= *agreste*) rustic, rural

silvicultor(a) SM/F forestry expert

silvicultura SF forestry

sima SF abyss, chasm

simbiosis SF INV symbiosis

simbólico ADJ [*momento, papel*] symbolic; [*cantidad, gesto, pago, huelga*] token

simbolismo SM symbolism

simbolista ADJ, SMF symbolist

simbolizar /1f/ VT to symbolize

símbolo SM symbol

simbología SF symbols *pl*, system of symbols

simetría SF symmetry

simétrico ADJ symmetrical

simiente SF seed

simiesco ADJ simian

símil SM **1** (= *comparación*) comparison **2** (*Literat*) simile

similar ADJ similar (**a** to)

similitud SF similarity, resemblance

simio SM ape, simian (*frm*)

simpatía SF **1** (= *afecto*) **son muestras de ~ hacia** *o* **por la víctima** it's a show of sympathy towards the victim; **ganarse la ~ de todos** to win everybody's affection; **tener ~ a algn** ◇ **sentir ~ hacia** *o* **por algn** to like sb; **~s y antipatías** likes and dislikes **2** (= *cordialidad*) friendly nature, friendliness; **su ~ nos cautivó** we were charmed by her friendly nature *o* friendliness **3 simpatías** (*Pol*) sympathies **4** (*Fís, Med*) sympathy

simpático ADJ **1** [*persona*] nice, pleasant, likeable; [*ambiente*] congenial, pleasant; **estuvo muy simpática con todos** she was very nice to everybody; **los cubanos son muy ~s** Cubans are very nice *o* friendly people; **no le hemos caído muy ~s** she didn't really take to us, she didn't really like us; **me cae ~** I think he's nice, I like him; **siempre procura hacerse el ~** he's always trying to ingratiate himself **2** (*Anat, Med*) sympathetic

simpatizante SMF sympathizer (**de** with)

simpatizar /1f/ VI **1** [*dos personas*] to get on, get on well together; **pronto ~on** they soon became friends **2 ~ con algn** to get on well with sb, take to sb

simple **Ⓐ** ADJ **1** (= *sin adornos*) [*peinado, objeto*] simple; [*vestido, decoración*] plain **2** [*método*] simple, easy, straightforward **3** (*antes de sustantivo*) (= *mero*) mere; **por ~ descuido** through sheer carelessness; **somos ~s aficionados** we're just amateurs **4** (*antes de sustantivo*) (= *corriente*) ordinary; **es un ~ abogado** he's only *o* just a solicitor; **un ~ soldado** an ordinary soldier **5** [*persona*] (= *sin complicaciones*) simple; (= *crédulo*) gullible; (*pey*) (= *de pocas luces*) simple-minded **6** (*Ling, Quím*) simple **7** (*Bot*) single **Ⓑ** SMF (= *persona*) simpleton

simplemente ADV simply, just

simpleza SF **1** [*de persona*] (= *cualidad mental*) simpleness; (= *credulidad*) gullibility; (= *necedad*) simple-mindedness **2** (= *acto*) silly thing

simplicidad SF simplicity, simpleness

simplificación SF simplification

simplificar /1g/ VT to simplify

simplista ADJ simplistic

simposio SM symposium

simulación SF **1** (= *representación*) simulation **2** (= *fingimiento*) pretence, pretense (*EEUU*)

simulacro SM sham, pretence, pretense (*EEUU*) ➤ **simulacro de ataque** simulated attack, mock attack ➤ **simulacro de combate** mock battle ➤ **simulacro de incendio** fire practice, fire drill

simulador SM ➤ **simulador de vuelo** flight simulator

simular /1a/ VT **1** [+ *ataque, robo*] to simulate **2** (= *fingir*) to feign, sham

simultanear /1a/ VT ~ **dos cosas** to do two things simultaneously; ~ **A con B** to fit in A and B at the same time, combine A with B

simultáneo ADJ simultaneous

sin PREP **1** (+ SUSTANTIVO, PRONOMBRE) **1.1** (= *faltando*) without; **¿puedes abrirla ~ llave?** can you open it without a key?; **llevamos diez meses ~ noticias** it's been ten months since we've hadany news,we've been ten months without news; **parejas jóvenes, ~ hijos** young couples with no children; **un producto ~ disolventes** a solvent-free product; **un vestido ~ tirantes** a strapless dress; **un hombre ~ escrúpulos** an unscrupulous man; **estar ~ algo: estuvimos varias horas ~ luz** we had no electricity for several hours; **quedarse ~ algo** (= *terminarse*) to run out of sth; (= *perder*) to lose sth; **me he quedado ~ cerillas** I've run out of matches; **se ha quedado ~ trabajo** he's lost his job **1.2** (= *no incluyendo*) not including, excluding; **ese es el precio de la bañera ~ los grifos** that is the price of the bathtub *o* (*esp Brit*) bath, excluding *o* not including the taps **2** (+ INFIN) **2.1** (*indicando acción*) **se fueron ~ despedirse** they left without saying goodbye; **no me gusta estar ~ hacer nada** I don't like having nothing to do, I don't like doing nothing **2.2** (*indicando continuidad*) **son las doce y el cartero ~ venir** it's twelve o'clock and the postman (*Brit*) *o* mailman (*EEUU*) still hasn't come; **llevan mucho tiempo ~ hablarse** they haven't spoken to each other for a long time; **seguir ~: sigo ~ entender para qué sirven** I still don't understand what they are for **2.3** (*tras sustantivo pasivo*) **recibos ~ pagar** unpaid bills **3** ~ **que** (+ SUBJUN) without; **salieron ~ que nadie se diera cuenta** they left without anyone realizing; **no lo haré ~ que me lo pidan** I won't do it unless they ask me to

sinagoga SF synagogue

sinalefa SF elision

sincerarse /1a/ VPR ~ **con** to be honest with, level with

sinceridad SF sincerity; **respóndeme con ~** please answer honestly; **con toda ~, me parece un libro pésimo** to be quite honest *o* in all sincerity, I think it's a terrible book

sincero ADJ sincere; **es muy ~** he's very sincere; **ser ~ con algn** to be honest with sb; **si quieres que te sea ~** if you want my honest opinion; **reciba nuestro más ~ pésame** (*frm*) please accept our deepest sympathies *o* our heartfelt condolences

síncopa SF **1** (*Ling*) syncope **2** (*Mús*) syncopation

sincopar /1a/ VT to syncopate

síncope SM **1** (*Ling*) syncope **2** (*Med*) syncope (*frm*); **casi le da un ~** she nearly fainted

sincronía SF synchrony

sincrónico ADJ **1** [*sucesos*] simultaneous **2** (*Ling*) synchronic

sincronizar /1f/ VT to synchronize

sindicación SF **1** [*de obreros*] unionization **2** (*Prensa*) syndication **3** (*LAm Jur*) charge, accusation

sindical ADJ union *antes de s*, trade-union *antes de s* (*esp Brit*), labor union *antes de s* (*EEUU*)

sindicalista Ⓐ ADJ union *antes de s*, trade-union *antes de s* (*esp Brit*), labor union *antes de s* (*EEUU*) Ⓑ SMF union member, trade(s) unionist (*esp Brit*)

sindicar /1g/ Ⓐ VT **1** [+ *trabajadores*] to unionize **2** (*LAm*) to charge, accuse Ⓑ **sindicarse** VPR [*trabajador*] to join a trade(s) (*esp Brit*) *o* labor (*EEUU*) union; [*trabajadores*] to form a trade(s) (*esp Brit*) *o* labor (*EEUU*) union

sindicato SM **1** [*de trabajadores*] trade union (*esp Brit*), labor union (*EEUU*) ➤ **sindicato amarillo, sindicato charro** (*Méx*) *conservative union that is in the pocket of the management* **2** [*de negociantes*] syndicate

síndico SM [*de organización*] trustee; (*en bancarrota*) receiver, official receiver

síndrome SM syndrome ➤ **síndrome de abstinencia** withdrawal symptoms *pl* ➤ **síndrome de Down** Down's syndrom ➤ **síndrome de la clase turista** economy-class syndrome ➤ **síndrome de (la) falsa memoria** false memory syndrome ➤ **síndrome premenstrual** premenstrual syndrome, premenstrual tension ➤ **síndrome tóxico** poisoning

sine qua non ADJ **condición ~** sine qua non

sinergia SF synergy

sinfín SM **un ~ de** no end of, countless

sinfonía SF symphony

sinfónico ADJ symphonic; **orquesta sinfónica** symphony orchestra

Singapur SM Singapore

singladura SF **1** (*Náut*) (= *recorrido*) day's run; (= *día*) nautical day **2** (*Pol*) course, direction

single ['singel] SM **1** (*Mús*) single **2 singles** (*LAm Tenis*) singles

singular Ⓐ ADJ **1** (*Ling*) singular **2 combate ~** single combat **3** (= *destacado*) outstanding, exceptional **4** (= *raro*) singular, odd Ⓑ SM (*Ling*) singular; **en ~** in the singular

singularidad SF singularity, peculiarity

singularizar /1f/ Ⓐ VT to single out Ⓑ **singularizarse** VPR to distinguish o.s., stand out

siniestra SF left hand; **a mi ~** on my left

siniestrado/a Ⓐ ADJ damaged, wrecked, crashed; **la zona siniestrada** the disaster zone Ⓑ SM/F victim

siniestralidad SF accident rate

siniestro Ⓐ ADJ **1** [*intenciones, personaje*] sinister; [*mirada*] evil **2** (*liter*) (= *izquierdo*) left Ⓑ SM (= *desastre natural*) disaster; (= *accidente*) accident ➤ **siniestro marítimo** disaster at sea ➤ **siniestro total** total write-off

sinnúmero SM **un ~ de** no end of, countless

sino¹ SM fate, destiny

sino² CONJ **1** (= *pero*) but; **no son ocho ~ nueve** there are not eight but nine; **no sólo ..., sino ...** not only ..., but ... **2** (= *únicamente*) only; **¿quién ~ él se habría atrevido?** only he would have dared!; **no te pido ~ una cosa** I ask only *o* but one thing of you

sínodo SM synod

sinónimo Ⓐ ADJ synonymous (**de** with) Ⓑ SM synonym

sinopsis SF INV **1** (= *resumen*) synopsis **2** (*CS*) [*de película*] trailer

sinóptico ADJ synoptic, synoptical; **cuadro ~** diagram, chart

sinrazón SF wrong, injustice

sintáctico ADJ syntactic, syntactical

sintagma SM syntagma, syntagm

sintaxis SF INV syntax

síntesis SF INV **1** (= *resumen*) summary; **en ~** in short **2** (*Biol, Quím, Fil*) synthesis

sintético ADJ synthetic

sintetizador SM synthesizer

sintetizar /1f/ VT **1** (*Quím, Mús*) to synthesize **2** (= *resumir*) to summarize

sintiendo *etc ver* **sentir**

sintoísmo SM Shintoism

síntoma SM **1** (*Med*) symptom **2** (= *señal*) sign, indication

sintomático ADJ symptomatic

sintonía SF **1** (*Radio*) [*del dial*] tuning **2** (*Radio*) (= *melodía*) theme song, signature tune (*Brit*); **estén atentos a nuestra ~** stay tuned **3** (*entre personas*) **estar en ~ con algn** to be in tune with sb

sintonización SF tuning

sintonizador SM tuner

sintonizar /1f/ Ⓐ VT to tune to, tune in to Ⓑ VI ~ **con** to be in tune with, be on the same wavelength as

sinuoso ADJ **1** (= con curvas) [camino] winding, sinuous; [línea, raya] wavy; [rumbo] devious **2** [persona, actitud] devious

sinusitis SF INV sinusitis

sinvergüenza Ⓐ ADJ (= pillo) rotten; (= descarado) brazen, shameless **Ⓑ** SMF (= pillo) scoundrel, rogue; (= canalla) rotter*; (= insolente) cheeky devil

sionismo SM Zionism

sionista ADJ, SMF Zionist

síper SM (CAm, Méx, Ven) zip (Brit), zipper (EEUU)

siquiera Ⓐ ADV **1** (= al menos) at least; **una vez** – once at least, just once; ~ **come un poquito** at least eat a bit **2** (en frases negativas) **ni** – **me dio las gracias** he didn't even say thank you, he didn't so much as say thank you **Ⓑ** CONJ even if, even though; **ven** ~ **sea por pocos días** do come even if it's only for a few days

sirena SF **1** (Mit) siren, mermaid **2** [de ambulancia] siren

Siria SF Syria

sirimiri SM drizzle

sirio/a ADJ, SM/F Syrian

siroco SM sirocco

sirope SM (LAm) syrup

sirviendo etc ver **servir**

sirviente/a SM/F servant

sisa SF **1** (Esp) (= acto concreto) petty theft; (= acción en general) pilfering, petty thieving **2** (Cos) armhole

sisar /1a/ VT (Esp) to thieve, pilfer

sisear /1a/ VT, VI to hiss

siseo SM hiss, hissing

sísmico ADJ seismic

sismo SM (esp LAm) = **seísmo**

sismografía SF seismography

sismógrafo SM seismograph

sistema SM **1** (= conjunto ordenado) system ➤ **sistema educativo** education system ➤ **sistema impositivo** tax system ➤ **sistema inmunitario** immune system ➤ **sistema métrico** metric system ➤ **Sistema Monetario Europeo** European Monetary System ➤ **sistema montañoso** mountain range ➤ **sistema nervioso** nervous system ➤ **sistema operativo** operating system **2** (= método) method; **trabajar con** ~ to work systematically o methodically; **yo por** – **lo hago así** I make it a rule to do it this way, I've got into the habit of doing it this way

sistemático ADJ systematic

sistematizar /1f/ VT to systematize

sistémico ADJ systemic

sitial SM seat of honour

sitiar /1b/ VT **1** (= asediar) to besiege, lay siege to **2** (= acorralar) to corner, hem in

sitio SM **1** (= lugar) place; **un** ~ **tranquilo** a peaceful place o spot; **cambiar algo de** ~ to move sth; **cambiarse de** ~ **con algn** to change places with sb; **en cualquier** ~ anywhere; **no lo encuentro en ningún** ~ I can't find it anywhere; **en todos los** ~**s** everywhere; ✦ MODISMOS **así no vas a ningún** ~ you'll get nowhere like that; **poner a algn en su** ~ to put sb firmly in his place; **quedarse en el** ~ to die instantly, die on the spot **2** (= espacio) room, space; **hay** ~ **de sobra** there's plenty of room o space; **te he guardado un** ~ I've saved you a place; **¿has encontrado somewhere to park o aparcar?** have you found somewhere to park o a parking space?; **hacer** ~ **a algn** to make room for sb **3** (Mil) siege; **poner** ~ **a algo** to besiege sth **4** (= sitio web) site ➤ **sitio web** website **5** (Chi) (= solar) site, lot (EEUU) **6** (Méx) [de taxis] taxi rank (Brit), taxi stand (EEUU)

sito ADJ situated, located (**en** at, in)

situ: in ~ ADV on the spot, in situ

situación SF **1** (= circunstancias) situation; **¿qué harías en una** ~ **así?** what would you do in a situation like that?; **no estoy en** ~ **de desmentirlo** I'm not in a position to deny it ➤ **situación límite** extreme situation **2** (= emplazamiento) situation, location; **la casa tiene una** ~ **inmejorable** the house is in a superb location **3** (en la sociedad) position, standing

situado ADJ **1** (= colocado) situated, placed; **está** ~ **en …** it's situated in …; **la casa no está muy bien situada** the house isn't very well situated **2** (Fin) **estar (bien)** ~ to be financially secure

situar /1e/ **Ⓐ** VT **1** (= colocar) to place, put; (Mil) to post; [+ edificio, construcción] to site, locate; **esto la sitúa entre los mejores** this places o puts her among the best **2** (= señalar) to find, locate; **no supo** ~ **Grecia en el mapa** he couldn't find o locate Greece on the map **3** (†) (= invertir) to place, invest **Ⓑ situarse** VPR **1** (= colocarse) to position o.s.; **se ha situado muy bien en la empresa** he's got himself a very good position in the company **2** [novela, película] to be set **3** (en la sociedad) to do well for o.s.

siútico* ADJ (Chi) = **cursi**

skay [es'kai] SM imitation leather

S.L. ABR (= Sociedad Limitada) ≈ Ltd (Brit), ≈ Corp (EEUU)

slalom [ez'lalom] SM slalom

slip [ez'lip] SM (pl ~**s** [ez'lip]) **1** (= calzoncillos) underpants, pants (Brit), shorts (EEUU) **2** (= bañador) bathing trunks pl

slogan [ez'loɣan] SM = **eslogan**

SME SM ABR (= Sistema Monetario Europeo) EMS

SMI SM ABR = **salario mínimo interprofesional**

smiley SM smiley

smoking [ez'mokin] SM (pl ~**s** [ez'mokin]) dinner jacket (Brit), tuxedo (EEUU)

⚠ **smoking** ≠ **smoking**

SMS SM INV (= mensaje) text (message), SMS

s/n ABR = **sin número**

so¹ EXCL (para parar) whoa!

so² EXCL (como intensificador) **¡so burro!** you idiot!, you great oaf!

so³ PREP **so pena de** under penalty of; **so pretexto de** (frm) under pretext of

SO ABR (= suroeste) SW

s/o ABR (Com) = **su orden**

soba* SF hiding; **dar una** ~ **a algn** to wallop sb*

sobacal ADJ underarm antes de s

sobaco SM armpit

sobado ADJ **1** [ropa] worn, shabby **2** [libro] well-thumbed, dog-eared **3** [tema] well-worn; [chiste] old, corny*

sobaquera SF **1** (Cos) armhole **2** (*) (= mancha) stain

sobar /1a/ **Ⓐ** VT **1** (= toquetear) [+ tela] to finger, dirty (with one's fingers); [+ ropa] to rumple, mess up; [+ masa] to knead **2** (*) (= magrear) to grope*, paw* **3** (Perú) (= lisonjear) to flatter **4** (Col, Ven) [+ músculo] to massage, rub **Ⓑ** VI (Esp*) to kip*, sleep

soberanía SF sovereignty

soberano/a Ⓐ ADJ **1** (Pol) sovereign **2** (= supremo) supreme **3** (*) (= tremendo) real, really big; **una soberana paliza** a real walloping* **Ⓑ** SM/F sovereign; **los** ~**s** the king and queen, the royal couple

soberbia SF (= orgullo) pride; (= altanería) haughtiness, arrogance

soberbio ADJ **1** [persona] (= orgulloso) proud; (= altanero) haughty, arrogant **2** (= magnífico) magnificent, grand; **¡soberbio!** splendid!

sobornar /1a/ VT to bribe

soborno SM **1** (= pago) bribe **2** (= delito) bribery

sobra SF **1 de** ~: **aquí tengo de** ~ I've more than enough here; **tenemos comida de** ~ we've got more than enough food; **tengo tiempo de** ~ I've got plenty of time; **tuvo**

motivos de ~ he was more than justified; **lo sé de** ~ I know it only too well; **es de ~ conocido** it's common knowledge **2 sobras** [*de comida*] leftovers

sobradamente ADV **lo conozco** ~ I know him only too well; **con eso queda ~ satisfecho** he is more than satisfied with that; **es ~ sabido que ...** it is common knowledge that ...

sobrado ⓐ ADJ **1** (= *más que suficiente*) **motivo más que ~ para hacerlo** all the more reason to do it; **tuvo razones sobradas para ...** he had good reason to ...; **sobradas veces** repeatedly **2 estar ~ de algo** to have more than enough of sth **3** (And*) (= *engreído*) **ser ~** to be full of o.s. ⓑ ADV easily, comfortably ⓒ SM **1** (= *desván*) attic, garret **2 sobrados** (*Col*) (= *restos*) leftovers

sobrante ⓐ ADJ (= *excedente*) spare; (= *restante*) remaining ⓑ SM surplus, remainder

sobrar /1a/ VI **1** (= *quedar de más*) to remain, be left, be left over; **ha sobrado mucha comida** there's a lot of food left (over); **sobra uno** there's one too many, there's one left; **al terminar me sobraba medio metro** I had half a metre left over when I finished **2** (= *ser superfluo*) to be spare; **esta pieza sobra** this piece is spare; **este ejemplo sobra** this example is unnecessary **3** (= *ser más que suficiente*) to be more than enough; **con este dinero ~á** this money will be more than enough; **no es que sobre talento** it's not that there's a surplus of talent; **nos sobra tiempo** we have plenty of time; ✦ REFRÁN **más vale que sobre que no que falte** better too much than too little

sobrasada SF Majorcan sausage

sobre[1] SM **1** (*para cartas*) envelope **2** [*de azúcar*] sachet, packet; [*de sopa*] packet (*Brit*), package (*EEUU*) **3** (**) (= *cama*) bed; **meterse en el ~** to hit the sack*, hit the hay* **4** (*LAm*) (= *cartera*) clutch bag

sobre[2] PREP **1** (= *encima de*) on; **está ~ la mesa** it's on the table; **prestar juramento ~ la Biblia** to swear on the Bible; **varios policías se abalanzaron ~ él** several policemen jumped on *o* fell upon him; **la responsabilidad que recae ~ sus hombros** the responsibility which rests on *o* upon his shoulders; ✦ MODISMO **estar ~ algn** to keep constant watch over sb **2** (= *por encima de*) **2.1** [+ *lugar*] over; **volamos ~ Cádiz** we're flying over Cádiz; **se inclinó ~ la mesa** she leant over the table **2.2** (*con cantidades*) above; **500 metros ~ el nivel del mar** 500 metres *o* (*EEUU*) meters above sea level; **dos grados ~ cero** two degrees above cero **3** (*indicando superioridad*) over; **tiene muchas ventajas ~ los métodos convencionales** it has many advantages over conventional methods; **amaba la belleza ~ todas las cosas** he loved beauty above all things **4** (*indicando proporción*) out of, in; **tres ~ cien** three out of every hundred, three in a hundred; **una puntuación de tres ~ cinco** three (marks) out of five **5** (*Fin*) on; **un préstamo ~ una propiedad** a loan on a property; **un impuesto ~ algo** a tax on sth **6** (*Esp*) (= *aproximadamente*) about; **~ las seis** at about six o'clock **7** (= *acerca de*) about, on; **un libro ~ Tirso** a book about *o* on Tirso; **hablar ~ algo** to talk about sth **8** ~ **todo** (= *en primer lugar*) above all; (= *especialmente*) especially; ~ **todo, no perdamos la calma** above all, let's keep calm; ~ **todo me gusta éste** I especially like this one

sobreabundancia SF superabundance, overabundance

sobreactuar /1e/ VI to overact

sobrealimentar /1a/ VT **1** [+ *persona*] to overfeed **2** (*Mec*) to supercharge

sobrecalentar /1j/ VT to overheat

sobrecama SM *o* SF bedspread

sobrecapacidad SF overcapacity, excess capacity

sobrecarga SF (*lit*) overload; (*fig*) extra burden

sobrecargar /1h/ VT **1** (*con peso*) [+ *camión*] to overload; [+ *persona*] to weigh down, overburden (**de** with) **2** (*Elec*) to overload

sobrecargo SMF **1** (*Náut*) purser **2** (*Aer*) senior flight attendant

sobrecogedor ADJ **1** [*paisaje, silencio*] imposing, impressive **2** (= *horrible*) [*escena*] horrific

sobrecoger /2c/ ⓐ VT (= *sobresaltar*) to startle; (= *asustar*) to scare, frighten ⓑ **sobrecogerse** VPR **1** (= *sobresaltarse*) to be startled, start; (= *asustarse*) to get scared, be frightened **2** (= *quedar impresionado*) to be overawed (**de** by); **~se de emoción** to be overcome with emotion

sobrecontratar /1a/ VT, VI to overbook

sobrecubierta SF jacket, dust jacket

sobredimensionado ADJ excessively large, oversized

sobredosis SF INV overdose

sobreentender /2g/ ⓐ VT to understand ⓑ **sobreentenderse** VPR **se sobreentiende que ...** it is implied that ..., it goes without saying that ...

sobreescribir /3a/ VT to overwrite

sobreestimar /1a/ VT to overestimate

sobreexcitar /1a/ VT to overexcite

sobreexplotar /1a/ VT [+ *recursos*] to over-exploit, drain; [+ *trabajadores*] to exploit

sobreexponer /2q/ VT to overexpose

sobregirar /1a/ VT, VI to overdraw

sobregiro SM overdraft

sobrehilar /1a/ VT to whipstitch, overcast

sobrehumano ADJ superhuman

sobreimpresionar /1a/ VT to superimpose

sobrellevar /1a/ VT [+ *peso*] to carry, help to carry; [+ *desgracia, desastre, enfermedad*] to bear, endure

sobremanera ADV exceedingly; **me interesa** ~ I'm most interested in it

sobremesa SF **1** (= *después de comer*) **estar de** ~ to sit round the table after lunch/dinner; **programa de** ~ (*TV*) afternoon programme; **un cigarro de** ~ an after-lunch/dinner cigar; **hablaremos de eso en la** ~ we'll talk about that after lunch/dinner **2 lámpara de** ~ table lamp; **ordenador de** ~ desktop computer

sobrenatural ADJ supernatural

sobrenombre SM nickname

sobrepaga SF extra pay, bonus

sobrepasar /1a/ ⓐ VT [+ *límite, esperanzas*] to exceed; [+ *rival, récord*] to beat; [+ *pista de aterrizaje*] to overshoot ⓑ **sobrepasarse** VPR = **propasarse**

sobrepeso SM [*de paquete, persona*] excess weight; [*de camión*] extra load

sobreponer /2q/ (*pp* **sobrepuesto**) ⓐ VT to superimpose ⓑ **sobreponerse** VPR to control o.s., pull o.s. together; **~se a un susto** to get over a fright

sobreprima SF extra premium

sobreproducción SF overproduction

sobreprotección SF over-protection

sobrepujar /1a/ VT to outbid

sobresaliente ⓐ ADJ (*Educ*) first class ⓑ SMF (*Teat*) understudy ⓒ SM (= *nota*) ≈ A

sobresalir /3q/ VI **1** (*Arquit*) to project, overhang, jut out **2** (= *destacar*) (*por altura, mérito*) to stand out

sobresaltar /1a/ ⓐ VT to startle, frighten ⓑ **sobresaltarse** VPR to start, be startled (**con, de** at)

sobresalto SM (= *sorpresa*) start; (= *susto*) fright, scare; (= *conmoción*) sudden shock

sobreseer /2e/ VT ~ **una causa** (*Jur*) to dismiss a case

sobreseimiento SM stay (of proceedings)

sobresueldo SM bonus, extra pay

sobretasa SF surcharge

sobretensión SF (*Elec*) surge

sobretiempo SM (*And*) overtime

sobretodo SM (= *abrigo*) overcoat

sobrevalorar /1a/ VT [+ *dinero, moneda*] to overvalue; [+ *persona*] to overrate

sobrevenir /3r/ VI to occur (unexpectedly)

sobreventa SF (*tb* ~ **de billetes**) overbooking

sobreviviente ADJ, SMF = **superviviente**

sobrevivir /3a/ VI (= *quedar vivo*) to survive; **sobrevivir a** [+ *accidente*] to survive; [+ *persona*] to survive, outlive

sobrevolar /1l/ VT to fly over

sobriedad SF 1 [*de estilo, color, decoración*] sobriety; **vestía con** ~ he was soberly dressed 2 (= *moderación*) moderation

sobrino/a SM/F nephew/niece; **mis ~s** (= *varones*) my nephews; **mis ~s** (= *varones y hembras*) my nieces and nephews

sobrio ADJ 1 (= *no borracho*) sober 2 [*color, estilo, decoración*] sober 3 (= *moderado*) [*vida*] frugal; **ser ~ con la bebida** to drink in moderation

sobros SMPL (*CAm*) leftovers, scraps

soca SF (*Col, Méx*) [*de arroz*] young shoots; [*de tabaco*] top leaf

socaire SM 1 (*Náut*) lee; **al** ~ to leeward 2 **al** ~ **de algo** under the protection of sth

socarrón ADJ [*persona, comentario, tono*] sarcastic; [*humor*] snide

socarronería SF [*de persona, comentario, tono*] sarcasm; [*de humor*] snide humour, snide humor (*EEUU*)

sócate SM (*Ven*) socket, lampholder

socavar /1a/ VT to undermine

socavón SM (*en la calle*) hole; (= *galería*) gallery, tunnel; (= *hueco*) hollow

sociable ADJ [*persona*] sociable, friendly; [*animal*] social, gregarious

social ADJ 1 (= *de la sociedad*) social 2 (*Com, Fin*) company *antes de s*, company's

socialdemocracia SF social democracy

socialdemócrata Ⓐ ADJ social democrat, social-democratic Ⓑ SMF social democrat

socialismo SM socialism

socialista ADJ, SMF socialist

sociedad SF 1 (*Sociol*) society; **la** ~ **de consumo** the consumer society; **la** ~ **del ocio** the leisure society; **en la** ~ **actual** in contemporary society
2 (= *asociación*) society, association ➤ **sociedad gastronómica** dining club ➤ **sociedad protectora de animales** society for the protection of animals ➤ **sociedad secreta** secret society
3 (*Com, Fin*) (= *empresa*) (*gen*) company; [*de socios*] partnership ➤ **sociedad anónima** ≈ limited liability company (*Brit*), ≈ corporation (*EEUU*) ➤ **Sociedad Anónima** (*en nombres de empresa*) ≈ PLC (*Brit*), ≈ Incorporated (*EEUU*) ➤ **sociedad comanditaria** limited partnership ➤ **sociedad en comandita** limited partnership ➤ **sociedad limitada** limited company (*esp Brit*), private limited company (*esp Brit*), corporation (*EEUU*) ➤ **sociedad mercantil** trading company
4 **alta** *o* **buena** ~ high society; **presentarse en** ~ to come out, make one's debut; **notas de** ~ gossip column, society news column

socio/a SM/F 1 [*de club*] member; **hacerse** ~ **de** to become a member of, join ➤ **socio/a de número** full member ➤ **socio/a honorario/a** honorary member 2 (*Com, Fin*) partner ➤ **socio capitalista** sleeping partner (*Brit*), silent partner (*EEUU*) 3 (*) (= *amigo*) buddy, mate (*Brit**)

sociocultural ADJ sociocultural

socioeconómico ADJ socioeconomic

sociolingüística SF sociolinguistics *sing*

sociología SF sociology

sociológico ADJ sociological

sociólogo/a SM/F sociologist

socorrer /2a/ VT ~ **a algn** to help sb, come to sb's aid

socorrido ADJ 1 (= *útil*) handy; **un** ~ **primer plato** a common starter (*Brit*) *o* appetizer (*EEUU*) 2 [*ejemplo, método*] hackneyed, well-worn

socorrismo SM life-saving

socorrista SMF lifeguard, life-saver

socorro SM help, aid, assistance; **¡socorro!** help!; **trabajos de** ~ relief *o* aid work *sing*; **pedir** ~ to ask for help

socrático ADJ Socratic

soda SF 1 (*Quím*) soda 2 (= *bebida*) soda water

sódico ADJ sodium *antes de s*

sodio SM sodium

sodomía SF sodomy

sodomizar /1f/ VT to sodomize

soez ADJ dirty, crude, coarse

sofá SM sofa, settee

sofá-cama SM (*pl* **sofás-cama**) sofa bed, studio couch

sófero ADJ (*Perú*) huge

Sofía SF (*Geog*) Sofia

sofisma SM sophism

sofista SMF sophist

sofisticación SF sophistication

sofisticado ADJ sophisticated

soflama SF fiery speech, harangue

sofocado ADJ **estar** ~ (= *sin aire*) to be out of breath; (= *ahogándose*) to feel stifled; (= *abochornado*) to be hot and bothered

sofocante ADJ stifling, suffocating

sofocar /1g/ Ⓐ VT 1 (= *ahogar*) [*calor*] to stifle; [*fuego, humo*] to suffocate 2 (= *apagar*) [+ *incendio*] to smother, put out; [+ *rebelión*] to crush, put down; [+ *epidemia*] to stamp out Ⓑ **sofocarse** VPR 1 (= *ahogarse*) (*por el esfuerzo*) to get out of breath; (*por el calor*) to suffocate 2 (= *sonrojarse*) to blush 3 (= *avergonzarse*) to get embarrassed 4 (= *enojarse*) to get angry, get upset

sofoco SM 1 (*por el calor*) stifling sensation; (*por la menopausia*) hot flush (*Brit*), hot flash (*EEUU*) 2 (= *azoro*) embarrassment; **pasar un** ~ to have an embarrassing time 3 (= *ira*) anger, indignation

sofocón* SM **llevarse un** ~ to get upset

sofreír /3l/ (*pp* **sofrito**) VT to fry lightly

sofrito Ⓐ PP *de* **sofreír** Ⓑ SM *fried onion, garlic and tomato used as a base for cooking sauces and dishes*

sofrología SF sleep therapy

software ['sofwer] SM software

soga SF rope; ✦ MODISMO **estar con la** ~ **al cuello** to be in deep water

sois *ver* **ser**

soja SF soya

sojuzgar /1h/ VT (= *vencer*) to conquer; (= *subyugar*) to subjugate

sol[1] SM 1 (= *astro*) sun; **al ponerse el** ~ at sunset; **al salir el** ~ at sunrise; **de** ~ **a** ~ from dawn to dusk; ✦ MODISMOS **arrimarse al** ~ **que más calienta** to keep in with the right people; **ser un** ~ to be a darling ➤ **sol naciente** rising sun ➤ **sol poniente** setting sun ➤ **sol y sombra** (*Esp*) brandy and anisette
2 (= *luz solar*) sun, sunshine; **entra mucho** ~ **en el comedor** the dining room gets a lot of sun *o* sunshine; **nueve horas de** ~ nine hours of sunshine; **hay** *o* **hace** ~ it is sunny, the sun is shining; **un día de** ~ a sunny day; **estar al** ~ to be in

the sun; **tomar el ~** to sunbathe; ✦ MODISMOS **hacía un ~ de justicia** the sun was blazing down; **no me deja ni a ~ ni a sombra** he doesn't give me a moment's peace
3 (*uso apelativo*) darling, pet*
4 (*Taur*) **localidades de ~** the cheapest seats in a bullring in the direct sunlight
5 (*Perú Fin*) sol, *former monetary unit of Peru*

sol² SM (*Mús*) G ➤ **sol mayor** G major

solamente ADV = **solo**2

solana SF sunny spot, suntrap

solanas* ADJ INV (*Esp*) alone, all on one's own

solapa SF [*de chaqueta*] lapel; [*de sobre, libro, bolsillo*] flap

solapado ADJ sly, underhand

solapar /1a/ Ⓐ VT to overlap Ⓑ **solaparse** VPR to overlap

solar¹ SM **1** (= *terreno*) (*gen*) site, lot (*EEUU*); (*en obras*) building site **2** (= *casa solariega*) ancestral home, family seat **3** (*Perú*) (= *edificio*) tenement building **4** (*Col, Ven*) (= *patio*) back yard

solar² ADJ solar, sun *antes de s*; **rayos ~es** solar rays

solariego ADJ **casa solariega** family seat, ancestral home

solario SM, **solárium** SM solarium

solas: **a ~** ADV alone, by oneself

solaz SM (= *descanso*) recreation, relaxation; (= *consuelo*) solace

solazar /1f/ Ⓐ VT (= *divertir*) to amuse, provide relaxation for; (= *consolar*) to console, comfort Ⓑ **solazarse** VPR to enjoy o.s., relax

soldada SF pay

soldadera SF (*Méx*) camp follower

soldadesca SF army rabble

soldadito SM ➤ **soldadito de plomo** tin soldier

soldado SMF soldier ➤ **soldado de marina** marine ➤ **soldado raso** private

soldador(a) Ⓐ SM/F (= *persona*) welder Ⓑ SM (*Téc*) soldering iron

soldadura SF **1** (= *acción*) (*con estaño*) soldering; (*sin estaño*) welding ➤ **soldadura autógena** welding **2** (= *junta*) (*con estaño*) solder; (*sin estaño*) welded seam, weld

soldar /1l/ Ⓐ VT (*con estaño*) to solder; (*fundiendo*) to weld Ⓑ **soldarse** VPR [*huesos*] to knit, knit together

soleado ADJ sunny

solecismo SM solecism

soledad SF (*voluntaria*) solitude; (*involuntaria*) loneliness, lonesomeness (*EEUU*); **en la ~ de su habitación** in the solitude of his room; **tengo miedo a la ~** I have a fear of loneliness; **la ~ me deprime** being alone makes me feel depressed

solemne ADJ **1** (= *serio*) solemn **2** (*) (= *enorme*) [*mentira*] downright; [*tontería*] utter; [*error*] complete, terrible

solemnidad SF **1** solemnity; **pobre de ~** miserably poor, penniless **2 solemnidades** (= *formalismos*) formalities

soler /2h; *defectivo*/ VI **1** (*en presente*) **suele pasar por aquí** he usually comes this way; **como se suele hacer por estas fechas** as is normal o customary at this time of the year **2** (*en pasado*) **solíamos ir todos los años a la playa** we used to go to the beach every year

solera SF **1** (= *tradición*) tradition; **vino de ~** vintage wine; **es un barrio con ~** it's a district full of traditional character **2** (*Chi*) [*de acera*] kerb (*Brit*), curb (*EEUU*) **3** (*CS*) (= *vestido*) sun dress

solfa SF **1** (*Mús*) sol-fa; ✦ MODISMO **poner algo/a algn en ~** to hold sth/sb up to ridicule **2** (*) (= *paliza*) thrashing

solfear /1a/ VT to sol-fa (*EEUU*), sing to sol-fa

solfeo SM musical theory

solicitado ADJ **estar muy ~** to be in great demand, be much sought after

solicitante SMF applicant

solicitar /1a/ VT [+ *permiso, apoyo*] to ask for, seek; [+ *datos, información*] to ask for, request (*más frm*); [+ *empleo, puesto*] to apply for; [+ *votos, opiniones*] to canvass

solícito ADJ (= *diligente*) solicitous (**por** about, for); (= *atento*) attentive; (= *servicial*) obliging

solicitud SF **1** (= *petición*) (*gen*) request; (*para puesto, beca, permiso*) application ➤ **solicitud de extradición** request o application for extradition **2** (= *impreso*) application form **3** (*frm*) (= *atención*) **atendió con ~ nuestras reclamaciones** he was very solicitous in dealing with our complaints

solidaridad SF solidarity

solidario ADJ **1** (= *humanitario*) caring; **un mundo poco ~** an uncaring world, a world where it's every man for himself; **un acto ~** an act of solidarity; **ser ~ con algo/algn** to show solidarity with sth/sb; **hacerse ~ con algo/algn** to declare one's solidarity with sth/sb **2** (*Jur*) [*compromiso*] mutually binding, shared in common; [*firmante, participante*] jointly liable

solidarizarse /1f/ VPR **~ con** to declare one's support for

solidez SF solidity

solidificar /1g/ Ⓐ VT to solidify, harden Ⓑ **solidificarse** VPR to solidify, harden

sólido Ⓐ ADJ **1** [*objeto*] solid; [*zapatos*] stout, strong; [*color*] fast **2** [*argumento*] solid, sound; [*base, principio*] sound Ⓑ SM solid

soliloquio SM soliloquy, monologue

solista SMF soloist

solitaria SF tapeworm

solitario Ⓐ ADJ **1** [*persona, vida*] solitary, lonely, lonesome (*EEUU*) **2** [*lugar*] lonely, desolate; **a esa hora la calle está solitaria** at that hour the street is deserted o empty Ⓑ SM **1** (*Naipes*) patience (*Brit*), solitaire (*esp EEUU*) **2** (= *diamante*) solitaire **3 en ~** alone, on one's own; **vuelta al mundo en ~** solo trip around the world

soliviantado ADJ rebellious

soliviantar /1a/ VT to stir up, rouse, rouse to revolt

sollozar /1f/ VI to sob

sollozo SM sob; **decir algo entre ~s** to sob sth

solo¹ Ⓐ ADJ **1** (= *sin compañía*) alone, on one's own; **iré ~** I'll go alone o on my own; **dejar ~ a algn** to leave sb alone; **me quedé ~** I was left alone; **habla ~** he talks to himself; ✦ MODISMOS **estar más ~ que la una*** to be all on one's own; **es tonto como él ~** he's as stupid as they come; **lo hace como él ~** he does it as no one else can; **se queda ~ contando mentiras** he's as good a liar as you'll find; ✦ REFRÁN **más vale estar ~ que mal acompañado** it's better to be on your own than in bad company
2 (= *solitario*) lonely; **me siento muy ~** I feel very lonely
3 (= *único*) **su sola preocupación** his one o only concern; **con esta sola condición** on this one condition; **no hubo ni una sola objeción** there was not a single objection
4 [*whisky, vodka, ron*] straight, neat (*Brit*); (*Esp*) [*café, té*] black; **tendremos que comer pan ~** we shall have to eat plain bread
Ⓑ SM **1** (*Mús*) solo; **un ~ de guitarra** a guitar solo
2 (*Esp*) (= *café*) black coffee

> Para expresar que alguien está **solo** porque no hay nadie más se utiliza el adjetivo **alone**, p.ej., "Me dejaron solo", *I was left alone*. **Lonely**, en cambio, se utiliza para expresar que alguien se siente solo, p.ej., "A veces me siento solo", *I sometimes feel lonely*.

solo² ADV, **sólo** ADV only; **sólo quiero verlo** I only o just want to see it; **es ~ un teniente** he's only a lieutenant, he's a mere lieutenant; **no ~ A sino también B** not only A but also B; **~ con apretar un botón** at the touch of a button; **ven aunque ~ sea para media hora** come even if it's just for half an hour; **tan ~** only, just; **me parece bien ~ que no tengo tiempo** that's fine, only o but I don't have the time

solomillo SM sirloin steak

solsticio SM solstice ➤ **solsticio de invierno** winter solstice ➤ **solsticio de verano** summer solstice

soltar /1l/ Ⓐ VT **1** (= *dejar de agarrar*) to let go of; **¡suéltenme!** let go of me!, let me go!; **no sueltes la cuerda** don't let go of the rope

2 [+ *amarras*] to cast off; [+ *nudo, cinturón*] (= *quitar*) to untie, undo; (= *aflojar*) to loosen; **ve soltando cuerda mientras bajas** pay the rope out gradually as you descend **3** (*Aut*) [+ *embrague*] to let out, release, disengage (*frm*); [+ *freno*] to release **4** (= *dejar libre*) [+ *preso, animal*] to release, set free **5** (= *emitir*) [+ *gas, olor*] to give off; [+ *grito*] to let out; **~ una carcajada** to burst out laughing; **~ un estornudo** to sneeze; **~ un suspiro** to sigh **6** (= *asestar*) **~ un golpe** to deal a blow; **le soltó un puñetazo** she hit him **7** (*al hablar*) [+ *indirecta*] to drop; **les volvió a ~ el mismo sermón** he gave them the lecture all over again; **¡suéltalo ya!** out with it!, spit it out!* **8** (*) (= *perder*) [+ *puesto, privilegio*] to give up; [+ *dinero*] to cough up* **9** [*serpiente*] [+ *piel*] to shed **B** **soltarse** VPR **1** (= *liberarse*) [*animal*] to break loose; [*prisionero*] to break free **2** (= *desprenderse*) to come off; (= *aflojarse*) to come loose, work loose; **~se el pelo** to let one's hair down **3** (= *deshacerse*) [*cordón, nudo*] to come undone, come untied **4** (= *desenvolverse*) (*con idioma*) to become fluent; **~se a andar/hablar** to start walking/talking

soltería SF (*gen*) single state, unmarried state; [*de hombre*] bachelorhood; [*de mujer*] spinsterhood

soltero/a **A** ADJ single, unmarried; **madre soltera** single *o* unmarried mother **B** SM/F single *o* unmarried man/woman, bachelor/spinster; **apellido de soltera** maiden name; **la señora de García, Rodríguez de soltera** Mrs García, née Rodríguez

solterón/ona SM/F (= *hombre*) confirmed bachelor; (= *mujer*) spinster; (*pey*) old maid

soltura SF ease; **habla árabe con ~** he speaks Arabic fluently

soluble ADJ **1** (*Quím*) soluble; **~ en agua** water-soluble, soluble in water **2** [*problema*] solvable

solución SF **1** (*Quím*) solution **2** (= *respuesta*) [*de problema*] solution, answer (**a** to); [*de crucigrama, pregunta*] answer (**de** to) **3** ➤ **solución de continuidad** break in continuity, interruption

solucionar /1a/ VT **1** [+ *problema*] to solve; **un problema sin ~** an unsolved problem **2** (= *decidir*) to resolve, settle

solvencia SF **1** (*Fin*) solvency **2** (= *fiabilidad*) reliability; **fuentes de toda ~** completely reliable sources ➤ **solvencia moral** good character; **de toda ~ moral** completely trustworthy

solventar /1a/ VT **1** [+ *deuda*] to settle, pay **2** [+ *dificultad*] to resolve; [+ *asunto*] to settle

solvente **A** ADJ **1** (*Fin*) solvent, free of debt **2** [*fuente*] reliable **B** SM (*Quím*) solvent

somalí ADJ, SMF Somali

Somalia SF Somalia

somanta* SF beating, thrashing

somático ADJ somatic

sombra SF **1** (*proyectada por un objeto*) shadow; **sólo vi una ~** I only saw a shadow; **Juan se ha convertido en tu ~** Juan follows you round like your shadow; **hacer ~** to cast a shadow; **no quiere que otros le hagan ~** he doesn't want to be overshadowed by anybody else; **medró a la ~ del presidente** she flourished under the protection of the president; ✦ MODISMO **no se fía ni de su ~** he doesn't trust a soul ➤ **sombra de ojos** eyeshadow ➤ **sombras chinescas** shadow play *sing*, pantomime *sing* **2** (= *zona sin sol*) shade; **siéntate a la ~** sit in the shade; **luz y ~** light and shade; **se sentó a la ~ del olivo** she sat in the shade of the olive tree; ✦ MODISMOS **a la ~*** (= *en prisión*) inside*, in the nick (*Brit**); **permanecer** *o* **quedarse en la ~** to stay in the background, remain on the sidelines **3** (= *rastro*) shadow; **sin ~ de duda** without a shadow of a doubt; **no es ni ~ de lo que era** he's a shadow of his former self **4** (= *suerte*) luck; **¡qué mala ~!** how unlucky!, what bad luck!

5 (= *gracia*) **tiene muy buena ~ para contar chistes** he's got a knack *o* gift for telling jokes, he's very funny telling jokes; **tener mala ~** to have a bad sense of humour **6** (= *mancha*) stain, blot; **es una ~ en su carácter** it is a stain *o* blot on his character **7** (*Arte*) shade

sombreado SM shading

sombrerera SF **1** (= *caja*) hatbox **2** (*Perú*) (= *perchero*) hat stand

sombrerero/a SM/F (*de hombre*) hatter; (*de mujer*) milliner

sombrero SM hat; ✦ MODISMO **quitarse el ~ ante algo** to take off one's hat to sth ➤ **sombrero de copa** top hat ➤ **sombrero de jipijapa** Panama hat ➤ **sombrero de tres picos** cocked hat, three-cornered hat

sombrilla SF (*gen*) parasol, sunshade; (*Col*) [*de mujer*] lady's umbrella

sombrío ADJ **1** (= *con sombra*) shaded **2** (= *triste*) [*lugar*] sombre, somber (*EEUU*), gloomy, dismal; [*persona, perspectiva*] gloomy

somero ADJ **1** (= *poco detallado*) superficial, summary (*frm*) **2** (= *a poca profundidad*) shallow

someter /2a/ **A** VT **1** (= *dominar*) [+ *territorio, población*] to subjugate; [+ *rebeldes*] to subdue, put down; [+ *asaltante*] to overpower, overcome **2** (= *subordinar*) **sometió sus intereses a los de su pueblo** he put the interests of the people before his own, he subordinated his interests to those of the people (*frm*); **~ su opinión a la de otros** to put the opinion of others above one's own **3** **~ a** **3.1** (= *exponer*) [+ *represión, tortura, interrogatorio*] to subject to; **hay que ~ a examen todas las ideas establecidas** all established ideas should be subjected to scrutiny; **lo tiene sometido a su entera voluntad** he is entirely subject to her will; **~ algo/a algn a una prueba** to put sth/sb to the test; **la princesa sometió a sus pretendientes a una prueba** the princess made her suitors undergo a test; **~ algo a votación** to put sth to the vote **3.2** (= *entregar*) to submit sth to; **~á el acuerdo a la aprobación de los ministros** he will submit the agreement for the approval of the ministers **B** **someterse** VPR **1** (= *aceptar*) **~se a** [+ *disciplina, autoridad*] to submit to; [+ *normas*] to comply with; **me someto a la voluntad de Dios** I submit to God's will; **~se a la mayoría** to give way to the majority; **~se a la opinión de algn** to bow to sb's opinion **2** (= *exponerse*) **~se a** [+ *desprecio, humillación*] to subject o.s. to; [+ *operación, prueba, tratamiento*] to undergo

sometimiento SM **1** (= *dominación*) [*de un pueblo*] subjugation; **han conseguido el ~ de los rebeldes** they have managed to subdue the rebels **2** (= *sumisión*) **2.1** (*por la fuerza*) subjection (**a** to) **2.2** (*voluntariamente*) (*a la autoridad*) submission (**a** to); (*a la ley*) compliance (**a** with) **3** (= *entrega*) [*de propuesta*] submission (**a** to)

somier [so'mjer] SM (*pl* **~s, ~es**) (*sin concretar tipo*) bed base; [*de muelles*] springs *pl*; [*de láminas de madera*] slats *pl*

somnífero SM sleeping pill

somnolencia SF sleepiness, drowsiness

somnoliento ADJ sleepy, drowsy

somos *ver* **ser**

son[1] SM **1** (= *sonido*) sound; **al ~ de** to the sound of; **a los ~es de la marcha nupcial** to the strains of the wedding march **2** **en ~ de**: **en ~ de paz** in peace; **no vienen en ~ de protesta** they haven't come with the idea of complaining **3** (*Mús*) Afro-Cuban dance and tune

son[2] *ver* **ser**

sonado ADJ **1** (= *comentado*) [*éxito, noticia*] much talked-about; [*escándalo, estafa*] notorious; **ha sido un divorcio muy ~** their divorce has caused a great stir, it has been a much talked-about divorce; **hacer una que sea sonada*** to kick up a stink* **2** (*) (= *chiflado*) **estar ~** to be crazy; (*Boxeo*) to be punch drunk

sonaja SF, **sonajas** SFPL rattle

sonajero SM rattle

sonambulismo SM sleepwalking, somnambulism (*frm*)

sonámbulo/a SM/F sleepwalker, somnambulist (*frm*)

sonar¹ /1l/ Ⓐ VI **1** (= *producir sonido*) **1.1** [*campana, teléfono, timbre*] to ring; [*aparato electrónico*] to beep, bleep; **el reloj de la iglesia no sonó** the church clock did not chime; **hacer ~** [+ *alarma, sirena*] to sound; [+ *campanilla, timbre*] to ring; [+ *trompeta, flauta*] to play; **haz ~ el claxon** blow *o* beep the horn **1.2** [*alarma, despertador, sirena*] to go off **1.3** [*máquina, aparato*] to make a noise; [*música*] to play; **¡cómo suena este frigorífico!** what a noise this refrigerator makes!; **~on tres disparos** three shots were heard; **empezó a ~ el himno nacional** the national anthem started to play; **le sonaban las tripas** his stomach was rumbling
2 (*Ling*) [*fonema, letra*] to be pronounced; [*frase, palabra*] to sound; **escríbelo tal como suena** write it as it sounds
3 (= *parecer por el sonido*) to sound; **cantan en inglés y suenan muy bien** they sing in English and they sound very good; **ese título suena bien** that sounds like a good title; **~ a** to sound like; **eso me suena a excusa** that sounds like an excuse to me; **~ a hueco** to sound hollow; ✦ MODISMOS **así como suena** just like that; **me suena a chino** it sounds double Dutch to me
4 (= *ser conocido*) to sound familiar, ring a bell*; **¿no te suena el nombre?** isn't the name familiar?, doesn't the name sound familiar *o* ring a bell?
5 (= *mencionarse*) **su nombre suena constantemente en relación con este asunto** her name is always coming up *o* being mentioned in connection with this affair
6 (*And, CS**) (= *fracasar*) to come to grief*; **ahora sí que sonamos** now we're really in trouble
7 (*CS**) (= *morirse*) to kick the bucket*, peg out*
8 (*CS**) **hacer ~** (*gen*) to wreck; [+ *dinero*] to blow*; **hacer ~ a algn** (= *derrotar*) to thrash sb*; (= *castigar*) to do sb**; (*en examen*) to fail, flunk (*EEUU**)
Ⓑ VT **1** [+ *campanilla*] to ring; [+ *trompeta*] to play; [+ *alarma, sirena*] to sound
2 ~ la nariz a algn to blow sb's nose
3 (*Méx, Ven**) (= *pegar*) to clobber*
4 (*Méx, Ven**) (= *ganar*) to thrash*
Ⓒ **sonarse** VPR (*tb* **~se los mocos** *o* **la nariz**) to blow one's nose

sonar² SM, **sónar** SM sonar

sonata SF sonata

sonda SF **1** (*Med*) (*para explorar*) probe; (*para drenaje*) catheter **2** (*Náut*) lead ➤ **sonda acústica** echo sounder ➤ **sonda espacial** space probe **3** (*Téc*) bore, drill

sondar /1a/ VT **1** (*Med*) (= *explorar*) to probe; (= *drenar*) to catheterize **2** (*Náut*) to sound, take soundings of **3** (*Téc*) to bore, bore into, drill **4** [+ *terreno*] to explore

sondear /1a/ VT **1** [+ *persona, intenciones*] to sound out; **~ a la opinión pública** to sound out public opinion; **~ el terreno** to spy out the land, see how the land lies
2 = **sondar 2, 3, 4**

sondeo SM **1** (= *encuesta*) poll; **~ realizado a la salida de las urnas** exit poll ➤ **sondeo de opinión** opinion poll **2** (*Náut*) sounding **3** (*Téc*) drilling

sónico ADJ sonic, sound *antes de s*

sonido SM sound

soniquete SM = **sonsonete**

sonoridad SF sonority

sonorizar /1f/ VT **1** [+ *local*] to install a sound system in **2** (*Ling*) to voice

sonoro ADJ **1** [*cavidad*] resonant; [*voz*] rich, sonorous; [*cueva*] echoing; [*beso*] loud **2** (*Ling*) voiced **3** [*banda, efectos*] sound *antes de s*

sonotone SM hearing aid

sonreír /3l/ Ⓐ VI **1** [*persona*] to smile; **~ a algn** to smile at sb **2** (= *favorecer*) **le sonríe la fortuna** fortune smiles (up)on him Ⓑ **sonreírse** VPR to smile

sonría *etc ver* **sonreír**

sonriente ADJ smiling

sonrisa SF smile; **~ amarga** wry smile; **~ forzada** forced smile; **no perder la ~** to keep smiling; **una ~ de oreja a oreja** an ear-to-ear grin

sonrojar /1a/ Ⓐ VT **~ a algn** to make sb blush Ⓑ **sonrojarse** VPR to blush (**de** at)

sonrojo SM blush

sonrosado ADJ rosy, pink

sonsacar /1g/ VT **~ a algn** to pump sb for information; **~ un secreto a algn** to worm a secret out of sb

sonsera SF (*LAm*), **sonsería** SF (*LAm*) = **zoncera**

sonso/a* ADJ, SM/F (*LAm*) = **zonzo**

sonsonete SM monotonous delivery, singsong, singsong voice

soñado ADJ **1** (= *ideal*) [*casa*] dream *antes de s* **2** (= *deseado*) dreamed-of; **llegó el ~ día del armisticio** the dreamed-of armistice day dawned **3** (*Col, CS**) (= *divino*) gorgeous; **un traje de novia ~** a gorgeous wedding dress

soñador(a) Ⓐ ADJ [*ojos, mirada*] dreamy; **siempre he sido un poco ~a** I've always been a a bit of a dreamer Ⓑ SM/F dreamer

soñar /1l/ Ⓐ VT **1** (*durmiendo*) **1.1** [+ *ensueño*] to dream; **no recuerdo lo que soñé anoche** I can't remember what I dreamed about last night; **soñé que me había perdido en la selva** I dreamed that I had got lost in the jungle **1.2** (*Méx*) [+ *persona*] to dream about
2 (= *imaginar*) to dream; **más dinero del que jamás habían soñado** more money than they ever dreamed of *o* dreamed possible; ✦ MODISMOS **¡ni ~lo!*** no chance!*; **¡ni lo sueñes!** in your dreams!, dream on!*
Ⓑ VI **1** (*durmiendo*) to dream; **~ con algo** to dream about sth; **"que sueñes con los angelitos"** "sweet dreams"; **~ en voz alta** to talk in one's sleep
2 (= *fantasear*) to dream; **deja ya de ~ y ponte a trabajar** stop daydreaming *o* dreaming and get on with some work; **~ con algo** to dream of sth; **~ con hacer algo** to dream of doing sth

---

Recuérdese que las preposiciones en inglés rigen gerundio y no infinitivo, de ahí **to dream of doing sth**.

~ despierto to daydream

soñoliento ADJ sleepy, drowsy

sopa SF soup; ✦ MODISMOS **hasta en la ~: los encontramos hasta en la ~** they're everywhere, they're ten a penny; **andar a** *o* **vivir a** *o* **comer la ~ boba** to scrounge one's meals ➤ **sopa de letras** word search, word search game ➤ **sopa de sobre** packet soup (*esp Brit*), instant soup ➤ **sopas de leche** bread and milk

sopapo SM slap, smack

sopear /1a/ VT (*Chi, Méx*) [+ *salsa, jugo*] to mop up

sopera SF soup tureen

sopero ADJ [*plato, cuchara*] soup *antes de s*

sopesar /1a/ VT to weigh up

sopetón* SM **de ~** suddenly, unexpectedly

soplagaitas* SMF INV idiot, twit*

soplamocos* SM INV punch, slap

soplapollas* ** SMF INV (*Esp*) berk*, wanker***, prick***

soplar /1a/ Ⓐ VI **1** (= *echar aire sobre*) [+ *superficie, sopa, fuego*] to blow on; [+ *vela*] to blow out; [+ *polvo*] to blow away, blow off; [+ *globo*] to blow up; [+ *vidrio*] to blow
2 (*) (= *decir confidencialmente*) **~ la respuesta a algn** to whisper the answer to sb
3 (*) (= *delatar*) to split on*
4 (*) (= *birlar*) to pinch*
5 (*) (= *cobrar*) to charge, sting*; **¿cuánto te ~on?** how much did they sting you for?*
6 (*) [+ *golpe*] **le sopló un buen mamporro** she whacked *o* clouted him one*
Ⓑ VI **1** [*persona, viento*] to blow; **¡sopla!*** (*indicando sorpresa*) well I'm blowed!*
2 (*) (= *delatar*) to split*, squeal*
3 (*) [*beber*] to drink, booze
Ⓒ **soplarse** (*) VPR **1** (= *devorar*) **~se un pastel** to wolf (down) a cake; **se sopla un litro entero** he knocks back a whole litre*
2 (*Méx, Perú*) (= *aguantar*) [+ *sermón, película*] to sit through;

~se a algn to put up with sb

soplete SM **1** (*para soldar*) blowtorch, blowlamp (*Brit*) ➤ **soplete soldador** welding torch **2** (*CS*) (*para pintar*) spray gun

soplido SM strong puff, blast

soplo SM **1** [*de aire*] (*con la boca*) blow, puff; (*por el viento*) puff, gust; ✦ MODISMO **como** o **en un ~: la semana pasó como** o **en un ~** the week flew by, the week was over in no time **2** (*Téc*) blast **3** (*) tip-off; **dar el ~** to squeal* **4** ➤ **soplo cardíaco** heart murmur

soplón/ona* SM/F (*en el colegio*) telltale; (*de la policía*) grass (*Brit**), fink (*EEUU**)

soponcio* SM **1** (= *desmayo*) **nos va a dar un ~** we're all going to pass out **2** (*por impresión*) fit; **le dio un ~** she had a fit

sopor SM **1** (*Med*) drowsiness **2** (= *letargo*) torpor

soporífero, soporífico Ⓐ ADJ soporific Ⓑ SM **1** (= *pastilla*) sleeping pill **2** (= *bebida*) sleeping draught o (*EEUU*) draft

soportable ADJ bearable

soportal SM **1** [*de casa*] porch **2 soportales** (*en una calle*) arcade *sing*, colonnade *sing*

soportar /1a/ Ⓐ VT **1** (= *resistir*) [+ *peso*] to support; [+ *presión*] to resist, withstand; **cuatro pilares soportan la bóveda** the vault is supported by four pillars; **las vigas soportan el peso del techo** the beams bear o carry the weight of the ceiling **2** (= *aguantar*) [+ *dolor, contratiempo, clima*] to bear; [+ *persona*] to put up with; **no soporto a ese imbécil** I can't stand that idiot

> Recuérdese que **stand** rige que el verbo que le siga inmediatamente aparezca en gerundio y no en infinitivo:

no soporta que la critiquen she can't stand being criticized Ⓑ **soportarse** VPR **no se soportan** they can't stand each other

soporte SM **1** (= *apoyo*) [*de puente*] support; [*de repisa*] bracket **2** (= *pedestal*) base, stand **3** [*de persona*] support **4** (*Inform*) medium ➤ **soporte físico** hardware ➤ **soporte lógico** software

soprano SMF soprano

soquete SM **1** (*CS*) ankle sock (*Brit*), anklet (*EEUU*) **2** (*Col, RPl**) (= *tonto*) idiot **3** (*Chi*) (*para bombilla*) bulb holder, socket, lampholder

sor SF Sister; **Sor María** Sister Mary

sorber /2a/ VT **1** (= *beber*) (*poco a poco*) to sip; (*chupando*) to suck up; **~ por una paja** to drink through a straw **2** [*esponja, papel secante*] to soak up, absorb **3** [+ *palabras*] to drink in

sorbete SM sorbet (*Brit*), sherbet (*EEUU*)

sorbo SM (*al beber*) (= *trago pequeño*) sip; (= *trago grande*) gulp, swallow; **beber a ~s** to sip; **de un ~** in one gulp

sordera SF deafness

sordidez SF **1** (= *suciedad*) sordidness, squalor **2** (= *inmoralidad*) sordidness

sórdido ADJ **1** (= *sucio*) dirty, squalid **2** (= *inmoral*) sordid

sordina SF **1** (*Mús*) mute **2 con ~** on the quiet, surreptitiously

sordo/a Ⓐ ADJ [*persona*] deaf; **quedarse ~** to go deaf; **se mostró ~ a sus súplicas** he was deaf to her entreaties, her entreaties fell on deaf ears; ✦ MODISMO **~ como una tapia** as deaf as a post **2** (= *insonoro*) [*ruido*] dull, muffled; [*dolor*] dull **3** (*Ling*) voiceless Ⓑ SM/F deaf person; **hacerse el ~** to pretend not to hear, turn a deaf ear

sordomudo/a Ⓐ ADJ deaf and dumb Ⓑ SM/F deaf-mute

soriano ADJ of/from Soria

soriasis SF INV psoriasis

sorna SF **1** (= *malicia*) sarcasm **2** (= *tono burlón*) sarcastic tone; **con ~** sarcastically, mockingly

sorocharse /1a/ VPR (*And*) = **asorocharse**

soroche SM (*And*) mountain sickness, altitude sickness

sorprendente ADJ surprising

sorprender /2a/ Ⓐ VT **1** (= *asombrar*) to surprise; **no me ~ía que ...** I wouldn't be surprised if ... **2** (= *coger desprevenido*) to catch; (*Mil*) to surprise; **lo sorprendieron robando** they caught him stealing **3** [+ *conversación*] to overhear; [+ *secreto*] to find out, discover Ⓑ VI to be surprising Ⓒ **sorprenderse** VPR to be surprised

sorprendido ADJ surprised

sorpresa Ⓐ SF **1** (= *asombro*) surprise; **ante** o **para mí ~** to my surprise; **con gran ~ mía** much to my surprise; **dar una ~ a algn** to surprise sb; **llevarse una ~** to get a surprise **2** (= *regalo*) surprise Ⓑ ADJ INV surprise *antes de s*; **ataque ~** surprise attack; **sobres ~** lucky dip bags (*Brit*), grab bags (*EEUU*); **visita ~** unannounced visit, surprise visit

sorpresivo ADJ (*esp LAm*) (= *asombroso*) surprising; (= *imprevisto*) unexpected

sortear /1a/ Ⓐ VT **1** (= *decidir al azar*) to draw lots for **2** (= *rifar*) (*gen*) to raffle; (*Dep*) to toss up for **3** (= *evitar*) [+ *obstáculo*] to dodge, avoid; **el esquiador sorteó las banderas con habilidad** the skier swerved skilfully round the flags; **aquí hay que ~ el tráfico** you have to weave in and out of the traffic here **4** (= *librarse de*) [+ *dificultad*] to avoid, get round; [+ *pregunta*] to handle, deal with, deal with skilfully o (*EEUU*) skillfully
Ⓑ VI **1** (*en sorteo*) to draw lots **2** (*con moneda*) to toss, toss up

sorteo SM (*en lotería*) draw; (= *rifa*) raffle; (*Dep*) toss; **el ganador se decidirá mediante ~** lots will be drawn to decide the winner; ➪ *EL GORDO*

sortija SF ring ➤ **sortija de compromiso**, **sortija de pedida** engagement ring

sortilegio SM **1** (= *hechizo*) spell, charm **2** (= *hechicería*) sorcery

sos (*esp Arg, CAm*) = **sois**; *ver* **ser**

sosa SF soda ➤ **sosa cáustica** caustic soda

sosco SM (*And*) bit, piece

sosegado ADJ **1** [*apariencia, vida*] calm, peaceful **2** [*persona*] calm, serene

sosegar /1h, 1j/ Ⓐ VT to calm Ⓑ **sosegarse** VPR to calm down

sosiego SM **1** [*de lugar, ambiente*] (= *tranquilidad*) calm, calmness, tranquility; (= *quietud*) peacefulness **2** [*de persona*] calmness, serenity

soslayar /1a/ VT [+ *dificultad*] to get round; [+ *pregunta*] to avoid, dodge, sidestep; [+ *encuentro*] to avoid

soslayo: al o **de ~** ADV obliquely, sideways; **mirada de ~** sidelong glance; **mirar de ~** (*lit*) to look out of the corner of one's eye (at); (*fig*) to look askance (at)

soso ADJ **1** (*Culin*) (= *insípido*) tasteless, insipid; (= *sin sal*) unsalted; **estas patatas están sosas** these potatoes are unsalted o need more salt **2** (= *aburrido, inexpresivo*) dull, uninteresting

sospecha SF suspicion

sospechar /1a/ Ⓐ VT to suspect Ⓑ VI **~ de algn** to suspect sb, be suspicious of sb

sospechoso/a Ⓐ ADJ [*comportamiento*] suspicious; **tipos ~s** suspicious-looking types; **todos son ~s** everybody is under suspicion; **es ~ de asesinato** he is suspected of murder Ⓑ SM/F suspect

sostén SM **1** (*Arquit*) support, prop **2** (= *prenda femenina*) bra, brassiere **3** (= *alimento*) sustenance **4** (= *apoyo*) support; **el único ~ de su familia** the sole support of his family

sostener /2k/ Ⓐ VT **1** (= *aguantar*) **1.1** (*en las manos, los brazos*) to hold **1.2** (*en pie*) [+ *construcción, edificio, techo*] to hold up, support; **las piernas apenas me sostenían** my legs could barely hold me up o support me **1.3** [+ *peso, carga*] to bear, carry, sustain (*frm*) **2** (= *proporcionar apoyo a*) **2.1** (*económicamente*) [+ *familia*] to support; **para ~ al club** to keep the club going **2.2** (= *alimentar*) to support, sustain (*frm*)

2.3 (*moralmente*) to support; **una mayoría capaz de ~ al Gobierno** a majority large enough to keep *o* support the government in power; **sólo lo sostiene el cariño de sus hijos** the love of his children is all that keeps him going **3** (= *mantener*) **3.1** [+ *opinión*] to hold; **siempre he sostenido lo contrario** I've always held the opposite opinion; **para ~ esa afirmación** to back up *o* support that statement; **como sostiene el juez** as the judge maintains *o* holds; **~ que** to maintain *o* hold that **3.2** [+ *situación*] to maintain, keep up; **~ la mirada de algn** to hold sb's gaze **4** (= *tener*) [+ *conversación, enfrentamiento, polémica*] to have; [+ *reunión, audiencia*] to hold **5** (*Mús*) [+ *nota*] to hold, sustain **Ⓑ sostenerse** VPR **1** (= *aguantarse*) to stand; **la escultura se sostiene sobre cuatro columnas** the sculpture stands on four columns; **no se me sostiene el peinado** my hair won't stay up; **~se en pie** [*persona*] to stand upright, stand on one's feet; [*edificio*] to stand **2** (= *sustentarse*) **2.1** (*económicamente*) [*persona*] to support o.s.; [*empresa*] to keep going **2.2** (*con alimentos*) **~se a base de algo** to live on sth, survive on sth **3** (= *resistir*) **~se en el poder** to maintain o.s. in power

sostenible ADJ sustainable

sostenido Ⓐ ADJ **1** (= *continuo*) sustained **2** (*Mús*) sharp; **do ~** C sharp **Ⓑ** SM (*Mús*) sharp

sostenimiento SM **1** (= *sujeción*) support **2** (= *conservación*) **una política de ~ de precios** a policy of maintaining price levels **3** (= *apoyo*) (*financiero*) maintenance; (*con alimentos*) sustenance

sota SF (*Naipes*) jack, knave (*esp Brit*)

sotana SF (*Rel*) cassock, soutane

sótano SM (*habitable*) basement; (*como almacén*) cellar

sotavento SM (*Náut*) lee, leeward; **a ~** to leeward

soterrado ADJ buried, hidden

soterrar /1j/ VT **1** (= *enterrar*) to bury **2** (= *esconder*) to hide away, bury

soto SM (= *matorral*) thicket; (= *arboleda*) grove, copse

sotobosque SM undergrowth (*Brit*), underbrush (*EEUU*)

soufflé [su'fle] SM soufflé

soul ADJ INV, SM (*Mús*) soul

souvenir [suβe'nir] SM (*pl* **~s**) souvenir

soviet SM soviet

soviético/a Ⓐ ADJ Soviet *antes de s* **Ⓑ** SM/F **los ~s** the Soviets, the Russians

soy *ver* **ser**

soya SF (*LAm*) soya (*Brit*), soy (*EEUU*)

speed* [es'piδ] SM (= *droga*) speed

spleen [es'plin] SM = **esplín**

sport [es'por] SM **chaqueta (de) ~** sports jacket, sports coat (*EEUU*); **ropa de ~** casual wear; **vestir de ~** to dress casually

spot [es'pot] SM (*pl* **~s**) (*tb* **~ publicitario**) commercial, ad*

spray [es'prai] SM (*pl* **~s**) spray, aerosol

sprint [es'prin] SM (*pl* **~s** [es'prin]) (*Dep*) sprint

sprínter [es'printer] SMF sprinter

squash [es'kwas] SM squash

Sr. ABR (= **Señor**) Mr; ⇨ *DON/DOÑA*

Sra. ABR (= **Señora**) Mrs, Ms; ⇨ *DON/DOÑA*

> La forma **Sra** se traduce por **Mrs** si se quiere especificar que la mujer está casada. De no ser así se utiliza **Ms**.

S.R.C. ABR (= **se ruega contestación**) RSVP

Sres. ABR (= **Señores**) Messrs

Sri Lanka SM Sri Lanka

Srs. ABR (= **Señores**) Messrs

Srta. ABR (= **Señorita**) Miss, Ms; ⇨ *DON/DOÑA*

> La forma **Srta** se traduce por **Miss** si se quiere especificar que la mujer no está casada. De no ser así se utiliza **Ms**.

S.S. ABR **1** (*Rel*) (= **Su Santidad**) HH **2** = **Seguridad Social 3** = **Su Señoría**

SS.MM. ABR (= **Sus Majestades**) HRHs

SSS SM ABR = **servicio social sustitutorio**

Sta. ABR (= **Santa**) St

stand [es'tan] SM (*pl* **~s** [es'tan]) stand

standard ADJ, SM, **stándard** ADJ, SM [es'tandar] = **estándar**

standing [es'tandin] SM standing; **de alto ~** [*ejecutivo*] top; [*piso*] luxury

starter [es'tarter] (*pl* **~s**) SM **1** (*Aut*) (= *aire*) choke; (*LAm*) (= *arranque*) self-starter, starter motor **2** (*LAm Equitación*) (= *persona*) starter; (= *puerta*) starting gate

statu quo SM status quo

step [es'tep] SM step (aerobics)

Sto. ABR (= **Santo**) St

stock [es'tok] SM (*pl* **~s** [es'tok]) stock, supply

stop [es'top] SM (= *señal*) stop sign, halt sign

su ADJ POSES **1** (*sing*) (= *de él*) his; (= *de ella*) her; (= *de usted*) your; (= *de animal, cosa*) its; (*impersonal*) one's; **dígame su número de teléfono** give me your telephone number; **un oso y su cachorro** a bear and its cub; **uno tiene que mirar por su negocio** one has to look after one's own business **2** (*pl*) (= *de ustedes*) your; (= *de ellos, de ellas*) their **3** (*uso enfático*) **su dinero le habrá costado** it must have cost her a pretty penny; **una casa de muñecas con sus cortinitas y todo** a doll's house with little curtains and everything

suave ADJ **1** (= *liso*) [*piel, pasta*] smooth; [*superficie*] smooth, even **2** (= *no fuerte*) [*color, movimiento, brisa, reprimenda*] gentle; [*clima, sabor*] mild; [*operación mecánica*] smooth, easy; [*melodía, voz*] soft, sweet; [*olor*] slight **3** [*persona, personalidad*] gentle, sweet **4** (*Méx**) (= *estupendo*) great*, fabulous*; **¡suave!** great idea!*, right on! (*EEUU**)

suavemente ADV [*golpear, llover*] gently; [*entrar*] softly; [*mover, deslizar*] smoothly

suavidad SF **1** (= *lisura*) [*de piel*] smoothness; [*de superficie*] smoothness, evenness **2** (= *moderación*) [*de color, movimiento, brisa, reprimenda*] gentleness; [*de clima, sabor, olor*] mildness; [*de melodía, voz*] softness, sweetness

suavizante SM (*para ropa*) softener, fabric softener; (*para pelo*) conditioner

suavizar /1f/ **Ⓐ** VT **1** (= *alisar*) to smooth out, smooth down **2** (= *ablandar*) (*gen*) to soften; [+ *carácter*] to mellow; [+ *severidad, dureza*] to temper; [+ *medida*] to relax **3** (= *quitar fuerza a*) [+ *navaja*] to strop; [+ *pendiente*] to ease, make more gentle; [+ *color*] to tone down; [+ *tono*] to soften **Ⓑ suavizarse** VPR to soften

subacuático ADJ underwater

subalimentación SF undernourishment

subalpino ADJ subalpine

subalquilar /1a/ VT to sublet

subalterno/a Ⓐ ADJ [*personal*] auxiliary; [*importancia*] secondary **Ⓑ** SM/F **1** (= *subordinado*) subordinate **2** (*Taur*) assistant bullfighter

subarrendar /1j/ VT to sublet, sublease

subarrendatario/a SM/F subtenant

subarriendo SM subtenancy, sublease

subasta SF **1** (= *venta*) auction, sale by auction; **poner en** *o* **sacar a pública ~** to put up for auction, sell at auction **2** (= *contrato de obras*) tender, tendering

subastador(a) SM/F auctioneer

subastar /1a/ VT to auction, sell at auction

subatómico ADJ subatomic

subcampeón/ona SM/F runner-up

subcampeonato SM (= *posición*) runner-up position, second place

subcomisario/a SM/F deputy superintendent

subcomité SM subcommittee

subconjunto SM subset

subconsciente Ⓐ ADJ subconscious Ⓑ SM **el ~** the subconscious ➤ **subconsciente colectivo** collective subconscious

subcontrata SF subcontract

subcontratar /1a/ VT to subcontract

subcontratista SMF subcontractor

subcultura SF subculture

subcutáneo ADJ subcutaneous

subdesarrollado ADJ underdeveloped

subdesarrollo SM underdevelopment

subdirección SF section, subdepartment

subdirector(a) SM/F [*de organización*] deputy director; [*de colegio*] deputy head

subdirectorio SM subdirectory

súbdito/a ADJ, SM/F subject

subdividir /3a/ Ⓐ VT to subdivide Ⓑ **subdividirse** VPR to subdivide

subdivisible ADJ subdivisible

subdivisión SF subdivision

subempleo SM underemployment

subespecie SF subspecies

subestación SF substation

subestimar /1a/ VT [+ *capacidad, enemigo*] to underestimate, underrate; [+ *objeto, propiedad*] to undervalue

subexponer /2q/ VT to underexpose

subexposición SF underexposure

subfusil SM automatic rifle

subgénero SM 1 (*Literat*) minor genre 2 (*Zool*) subspecies

subida SF 1 (= *ascensión*) [*de montaña, cuesta*] ascent; **es una ~ difícil** it's a tough ascent *o* climb; **a la ~ tuvimos que parar varias veces** we had to stop several times on the way up 2 (= *pendiente*) slope, hill 3 (= *aumento*) rise, increase ➤ **subida salarial** pay rise (*Brit*) *o* raise (*EEUU*), wage increase 4 (*) [*de drogas*] high*

subido ADJ [*color*] bright, intense; [*olor*] strong; **un chiste ~ de tono** a risqué joke

subíndice SM subscript

subir /3a/ Ⓐ VT 1 (= *levantar*) [+ *pierna, brazo, objeto*] to lift, lift up, raise; [+ *calcetines, pantalones, persianas*] to pull up
2 (= *poner arriba*) (*llevando*) to take up; (*trayendo*) to bring up; **¿me ayudas a ~ las maletas?** can you help me to take up the cases?; **lo subimos a un taxi** we put him in a taxi
3 (= *ascender*) [+ *calle, cuesta, montaña*] (= *ir arriba*) to go up; (= *venir arriba*) to come up; **subió las escaleras de dos en dos** she went up the stairs two at a time; **tenía problemas para ~ las escaleras** he had difficulty getting up *o* climbing the stairs
4 (= *aumentar*) [+ *precio, tarifa, salario*] to put up, raise, increase; [+ *artículo en venta*] to put up the price of; **van a ~ la gasolina** they are going to put up *o* increase the price of petrol (*Brit*) *o* gasoline (*EEUU*)
5 (= *elevar*) [+ *volumen, televisión, radio*] to turn up; [+ *voz*] to raise
Ⓑ VI 1 (= *ir arriba*) to go up; (= *venir arriba*) to come up; (*en un monte, en el aire*) to climb; **suba al tercer piso** go up to the third floor; **sube, que te voy a enseñar unos discos** come up, I've got some records to show you; **tuvimos que ~ andando** we had to walk up
2 (*en autobús, avión, tren, bicicleta, moto, caballo*) to get on; (*en coche, taxi*) to get in; **~ a un autobús/avión/tren** to get on(to) a bus/plane/train; **~ a un coche** to get in(to) a car; **~ a una bicicleta/un caballo** to get on(to) a bike/a horse
3 (*en el escalafón*) to be promoted (**a** to); **~ a primera división** to go up *o* be promoted to the First Division
4 (= *aumentar*) [*precio, valor, fiebre*] to go up, rise; [*temperatura*] to rise; **la gasolina ha vuelto a ~** (the price of) petrol (*Brit*) *o* gasoline (*EEUU*) has gone up again
5 (= *aumentar de nivel*) [*río, mercurio*] to rise; [*marea*] to come in
6 [*cantidad*] **~ a** to come to, total

Ⓒ **subirse** VPR 1 (*en autobús, avión, tren, moto, caballo*) to get on; (*en coche, taxi*) to get in; (*en bicicleta*) to get on, climb on; **~se a un autobús/avión/tren** to get on(to) a bus/plane/train; **~se a un coche** to get in(to) a car; **~se a una bicicleta/un caballo** to get on(to) a bike/a horse
2 (= *trepar*) (*a árbol, tejado*) to climb; ✦ MODISMO **~se por las paredes** to hit the roof; **están que se suben por las paredes** they're hopping mad
3 (*con ropa*) **~se los calcetines** to pull up one's socks; **~se la cremallera (de algo)** to zip (sth) up
4 **subírse a algn: el vino/el dinero se le ha subido a la cabeza** the wine/money has gone to his head

súbito ADJ 1 [*cambio, acción*] (= *repentino*) sudden; (= *imprevisto*) unexpected 2 **de ~** suddenly, unexpectedly

subjefatura SF local headquarters, local police headquarters

subjetividad SF subjectivity

subjetivo ADJ subjective

subjuntivo SM subjunctive

sublevación SF revolt, uprising

sublevar /1a/ Ⓐ VT 1 (= *amotinar*) to rouse to revolt 2 (= *indignar*) to infuriate Ⓑ **sublevarse** VPR to revolt, rise, rise up

sublimación SF sublimation

sublimar /1a/ VT 1 [+ *deseos*] to sublimate 2 (*Quím*) to sublimate

sublime ADJ sublime

subliminal ADJ subliminal

subliteratura SF third-rate literature, pulp writing

submarinismo SM (*como deporte*) scuba diving; (*para pescar*) underwater fishing

submarinista SMF scuba diver

submarino Ⓐ ADJ underwater, submarine; **pesca submarina** underwater fishing Ⓑ SM 1 (*Náut*) submarine 2 (*RPl*) (= *bebida*) hot milk containing a piece of chocolate

submundo SM underworld

subnormal Ⓐ ADJ 1 (*Med*) subnormal, mentally handicapped 2 (*pey**) nuts*, mental* Ⓑ SMF 1 (*Med*) subnormal person, mentally handicapped person 2 (*pey**) nutcase*, blockhead*

suboficial SMF non-commissioned officer, NCO

subordinado/a Ⓐ ADJ subordinate (**a** to) Ⓑ SM/F subordinate

subordinar /1a/ Ⓐ VT to subordinate Ⓑ **subordinarse** VPR **~se a** to subordinate o.s. to

subproducto SM by-product

subprograma SM subprogram

subrayado Ⓐ ADJ (*con línea*) underlined 2 (*en cursiva*) italicized, in italics Ⓑ SM 1 (*con línea*) underlining 2 (*en cursiva*) italics *pl*; **el ~ es mío** my italics, the italics are mine

subrayar /1a/ VT 1 [+ *texto, frase*] (*con línea*) to underline; (*en cursiva*) to italicize, put in italics 2 (= *recalcar*) to underline, emphasize

subrepticio ADJ surreptitious

subrogar /1h, 1l/ VT to substitute, replace

subsahariano ADJ sub-Saharan

subsanar /1a/ VT [+ *perjuicio, defecto*] to repair, make good; [+ *error*] to rectify, put right; [+ *deficiencia*] to make up for; [+ *dificultad, obstáculo*] to get round, overcome

subsecretario/a SM/F undersecretary, assistant secretary

subsector SM subsection, subsector

subsidiario ADJ subsidiary

subsidio SM subsidy ➤ **subsidio de desempleo** unemployment benefit (*Brit*), unemployment compensation (*EEUU*) ➤ **subsidio de enfermedad** sickness benefit, sick pay ➤ **subsidio de vejez** old age pension (*Brit*), social security (benefit) (*EEUU*) ➤ **subsidio familiar** ≈ family credit (*Brit*), ≈ welfare (*EEUU*)

subsiguiente ADJ subsequent

subsistema SM subsystem

subsistencia SF subsistence

subsistir /3a/ VI (= *malvivir*) to subsist, live (**con, de** on); (= *perdurar*) to survive, endure; **sin ayuda económica no podrá ~ el colegio** the school will not be able to survive without financial aid

subsuelo SM 1 [*de tierra*] subsoil 2 [*de edificio*] (CS) basement

subte* SM (*Arg*) underground (*Brit*), tube (*Brit*), subway (*EEUU*)

subteniente/a SM/F sub-lieutentant, second lieutenant

subterfugio SM subterfuge

subterráneo Ⓐ ADJ underground, subterranean Ⓑ SM 1 (= *túnel*) underground passage 2 (*Arg*) (= *metro*) underground (*Brit*), subway (*EEUU*)

subtexto SM subtext

subtitular /1a/ VT to subtitle

subtítulo SM subtitle

subtropical ADJ subtropical

suburbano Ⓐ ADJ suburban Ⓑ SM (= *tren*) suburban train

suburbio SM 1 (= *afueras*) suburb, outlying area 2 (= *barrio bajo*) working-class district

subvalorar /1a/ VT (= *no valorar*) to undervalue, underrate; (= *subestimar*) to underestimate

subvención SF subsidy, subvention, grant

subvencionar /1a/ VT to subsidize

subversión SF subversion

subversivo ADJ subversive

subvertir /3i/ VI to subvert

subyacente ADJ underlying

subyacer /2x/ VI ~ **a algo** to underlie sth, lie behind sth

subyugar /1h/ VT 1 (= *dominar*) [+ *país*] to subjugate, subdue; [+ *enemigo*] to overpower; [+ *voluntad*] to dominate, gain control over 2 (= *hechizar*) to captivate, charm

succión SF suction

succionar /1a/ VT 1 (= *sorber*) to suck 2 (*Téc*) to absorb, soak up

sucedáneo SM substitute

suceder /2a/ Ⓐ VI 1 (= *ocurrir*) to happen; **no le había sucedido eso nunca** that had never happened to him before; **¿qué sucede?** what's going on?; **lo que sucede es que ...** the fact *o* the trouble is that ... 2 (= *seguir*) ~ **a algo** to follow sth; **al invierno sucede la primavera** spring follows winter Ⓑ VT [+ *persona*] to succeed; ~ **a algn en un puesto** to succeed sb in a post Ⓒ **sucederse** VPR to follow one another

sucesión SF 1 (*al trono, en un puesto*) succession (**a** to) 2 (= *secuencia*) sequence, series; **una ~ de acontecimientos** a succession *o* series of events 3 (= *herencia*) inheritance; **derechos de ~** death duty 4 (= *hijos*) issue, offspring; **morir sin ~** to die without issue

sucesivamente ADV successively; **y así ~** and so on

sucesivo ADJ (= *subsiguiente*) successive; (= *consecutivo*) consecutive; **tres días ~s** three days running, three consecutive days; **en lo ~** (= *en el futuro*) henceforth (*frm o liter*), in future; (= *desde entonces*) thereafter, thenceforth (*frm o liter*)

suceso SM (= *acontecimiento*) event; (= *incidente*) incident; **los ~s de la última decada** the events of the last decade; **el ~ ocurrió sobre las tres de la tarde** the incident happened at around three in the afternoon; **acudieron rápidamente al lugar del ~** they rushed to the scene; **sección de ~s** (*Prensa*) (section of) accident and crime reports

⚠ **suceso** ≠ *success*

sucesor(a) SM/F 1 (*al trono, a un puesto*) successor 2 (= *heredero*) heir/heiress

sucesorio ADJ [*lucha, derechos, crisis*] succession *antes de s*; [*impuesto*] inheritance *antes de s*; **tercero en la línea sucesoria** third in (the) line of succession

suciedad SF 1 (= *porquería*) dirt; **un detergente que elimina la ~** a detergent that banishes dirt 2 (= *falta de limpieza*) dirtiness

sucinto ADJ succinct, concise

sucio Ⓐ ADJ 1 (= *manchado*) [*cara, ropa, suelo*] dirty; **tienes las manos sucísimas** your hands are filthy; **hazlo primero en ~** make a rough draft first, do it in rough first 2 [*color*] dirty 3 (= *fácil de manchar*) **los pantalones blancos son muy ~s** white trousers (*Brit*) *o* pants (*EEUU*) show the dirt, white trousers (*Brit*) *o* pants (*EEUU*) get dirty very easily 4 (= *obsceno*) dirty, filthy 5 (= *deshonesto*) [*jugada*] foul, dirty; [*táctica*] dirty; [*negocio*] shady 6 [*lengua*] coated, furred Ⓑ ADV **jugar ~** to play dirty Ⓒ SM (*Ven*) (= *mancha*) dirty mark

sucre SM sucre (*standard monetary unit of Ecuador*)

suculento ADJ (= *sabroso*) tasty, rich; (= *jugoso*) succulent

sucumbir /3a/ VI to succumb (**a** to)

sucursal SF (= *oficina local*) branch, branch office; (= *filial*) subsidiary

sudaca* ADJ, SMF (*Esp pey*) South American

sudadera SF sweatshirt

sudado SM (*Perú*) stew

Sudáfrica SF South Africa

sudafricano/a ADJ, SM/F South African

Sudamérica SF South America

sudamericano/a ADJ, SM/F South American

Sudán SM Sudan

sudanés/esa ADJ, SM/F Sudanese

sudar /1a/ Ⓐ VI 1 (= *transpirar*) to sweat; ✦ MODISMO ~ **a chorros*** ◇ ~ **a mares*** to sweat buckets* 2 (= *exudar*) [*recipiente*] to ooze; [*pared*] to sweat Ⓑ VT 1 (= *transpirar*) to sweat; ✦ MODISMO ~ **la gota gorda** to sweat buckets* 2 (= *mojar*) [+ *ropa, prenda*] to make sweaty; ✦ MODISMOS ~ **la camiseta** to sweat blood; **me la suda** (*Esp****) it bores the pants off me* 3 (*) (= *conseguir con esfuerzo*) **ha sudado el premio** he really went flat out to get that prize

sudario SM shroud

sudeste SM = **sureste**

sudista Ⓐ ADJ southern Ⓑ SMF Southerner

sudoeste = **suroeste**

sudor SM 1 (= *transpiración*) sweat; **con el ~ de su frente** by the sweat of one's brow; **estar bañado en ~** to be dripping with sweat 2 (*tb* ~**es**) (= *esfuerzo*) toil *sing*, labour *sing*, labor *sing* (*EEUU*)

sudoración SF sweating

sudoroso ADJ sweaty

Suecia SF Sweden

sueco/a Ⓐ ADJ Swedish Ⓑ SM/F Swede; ✦ MODISMO **hacerse el ~*** to act dumb Ⓒ SM (*Ling*) Swedish

suegro/a SM/F father-in-law/mother-in-law; **suegros** parents-in-law, in-laws

suela SF (= *base*) sole; (= *trozo de cuero*) piece of strong leather; ✦ MODISMO **no llegar a algn a la ~ del zapato: Juan no le llega a la ~ del zapato a Pablo** Juan can't hold a candle to Pablo

suelazo SM (*SAm*) heavy fall, nasty bump

sueldo SM (= *paga*) (*gen*) pay; (*mensual*) salary; (*semanal*) wages *pl*; **asesino a ~** hired killer, contract killer ➤ **sueldo base** basic salary

suelo SM 1 (*en el exterior*) (= *tierra*) ground; **caer al ~** to fall to the ground, fall over; ✦ MODISMOS **por los ~s: los precios están por los ~s** prices are at rock bottom; **esos géneros están por los ~s** those goods are dirt cheap; **tengo el ánimo por los ~s** I feel really low; **arrastrar *o* poner *o* tirar por los ~s** [+ *persona*] to slate, slag off*; [+ *novela, película*] to pan*, slam*, rubbish (*Brit**) ➤ **suelo natal, suelo patrio**

native land, native soil
2 (*en edificio*) (= *superficie*) floor; (= *revestimiento*) flooring
3 (= *terreno*) soil, land ➤ **suelo edificable** building land
4 [*de pan, vasija*] bottom

suelte *etc ver* **soltar**

suelto Ⓐ ADJ **1** (= *libre*) (*gen*) free; [*criminal*] free, out; [*animal*] loose; **el bandido anda ~** the bandit's on the loose **2** (= *desatado*) [*cordones*] undone, untied; [*cabo, hoja, tornillo*] loose; **el arroz tiene que quedar ~** rice shouldn't stick together
3 **dinero ~** loose change
4 [*prenda de vestir*] loose, loose-fitting; **iba con el pelo ~** she had her hair down *o* loose
5 [*vientre*] loose
6 (= *separado*) [*trozo, pieza*] separate, detached; [*ejemplar, volumen*] individual, odd; [*calcetín*] odd; **no se venden ~s** they are not sold singly *o* separately
7 (*Com*) (= *de forma individual*) loose
8 [*movimiento*] (= *libre*) free, easy; (= *ágil*) quick
9 (= *fluido*) [*estilo*] fluent; [*conversación*] easy, easy-flowing; **está muy ~ en inglés** he is very good at *o* fluent in English
Ⓑ SM (= *cambio*) loose change, small change

suene *etc ver* **sonar**

sueña *etc ver* **soñar**

sueño SM **1** (= *estado*) sleep; **conciliar el ~** to get to sleep; **echarse un ~** to have a nap; **en** *o* **entre ~s**: **hablaste entre ~s** you talked in your sleep; **tener el ~ ligero** to be a light sleeper; **tener el ~ pesado** to be a heavy sleeper ➤ **sueño eterno** eternal rest
2 (= *ganas de dormir*) **tienes cara de ~** you look sleepy; **tengo ~ atrasado** I haven't caught up on sleep, I haven't had much sleep lately; **caerse de ~** to be asleep on one's feet; **dar ~:** **su conversación me da ~** his conversation sends me to sleep; **la televisión me da ~** television makes me sleepy; **estar muerto de ~** to be asleep on one's feet, be so tired one can hardly stand; **quitar el ~ a algn** to keep sb awake; **ya se me ha quitado el ~** I'm not sleepy any more; **tener ~** to be sleepy, be tired; ✦ MODISMO **perder el ~ por algo** to lose sleep over sth
3 (= *imagen soñada*) dream; **¿sabes interpretar los ~s?** do you know how to interpret dreams?; **¡que tengas dulces ~s!** sweet dreams!; ✦ MODISMO **¡ni en ~s!** no chance!*; **eso no te lo crees tú ni en ~s** don't give me that!**; **no pienso volver a hablarle ni en ~s** there's no way I'd ever talk to him again ➤ **sueño húmedo** wet dream
4 (= *ilusión*) dream; **la casa de sus ~s** the house of her dreams, her dream home; **estas vacaciones son como un ~** these holidays are like a dream come true; **mi ~ dorado** my greatest dream ➤ **el sueño americano** the American Dream

suero SM **1** (*Med*) (*de la sangre, para inmunizar*) serum; (*tb* **~ fisiológico**) saline solution **2** [*de leche*] whey

suerte SF **1** (= *fortuna*) luck; **con un poco de ~** with a bit of luck; **¡suerte!** ◇ **¡buena suerte!** good luck!; **dar ~** to bring good luck; **este número me da ~** this is my lucky number; **día de ~** lucky day; **un hombre de ~** a lucky man; **estar de ~** to be in luck; **mala ~** bad luck; **¡qué mala ~!** how unlucky!, what bad luck!; **por ~** luckily, fortunately; **probar ~** to try one's luck; **tener ~** to be lucky; **¡que tengas ~!** good luck!, the best of luck!; **tuvo la ~ de que el autobús saliera con retraso** he was lucky that the bus left late, luckily for him his bus left late; **traer ~** to be lucky, bring good luck; **trae mala ~** it's bad luck, it's unlucky
2 (= *destino*) fate; **estar resignado a su ~** to be resigned to one's fate; **los abandonaron a su ~** they left them to their fate; **correr la misma ~ que algn** to suffer the same fate as sb
3 (= *azar*) chance; **lo echaron a ~s** (*con cerillas, papeletas*) they drew lots; (*con moneda*) they tossed (a coin); **tocar en ~ a algn**: **al equipo español le tocó en ~ enfrentarse a Turquía** as chance had it, the Spanish team were drawn to play against Turkey; **¡vaya marido que me ha tocado en ~!** what a husband I ended up with!; ✦ MODISMO **la ~ está echada** the die is cast
4 (= *clase*) sort, kind; **hubo toda ~ de comentarios** there were all sorts *o* kinds of remarks; **con toda ~ de detalles** in great detail

5 (*Taur*) stage of the bullfight

suertero* ADJ (*Méx*), **suertudo*** ADJ (*esp LAm*) lucky, jammy*

suéter SM sweater

suficiencia SF **1** (= *competencia*) competence; **demostrar su ~** to prove one's competence, show one's capabilities **2** (= *satisfacción de sí mismo*) smugness, self-satisfaction

suficiente Ⓐ ADJ **1** (= *bastante*) enough; **ahora no llevo ~ dinero (como) para pagarte** I don't have enough money on me at the moment to pay you **2** (= *de sí mismo*) smug, self-satisfied Ⓑ SM (*Escol*) ≈ C, pass mark, passing grade (*EEUU*)

suficientemente ADV sufficiently; **no era ~ grande** it wasn't big enough *o* sufficiently big

sufijo SM suffix

suflé SM soufflé

sufragar /1h/ Ⓐ VT [+ *gastos*] to meet, defray; [+ *proyecto*] to pay for, defray the costs of Ⓑ VI (*LAm*) to vote (**por** for)

sufragio SM **1** (= *voto*) vote; **los ~s emitidos a favor del candidato** the votes cast for the candidate **2** (= *derecho al voto*) suffrage ➤ **sufragio universal** universal suffrage

sufragista Ⓐ ADJ, SMF suffragist Ⓑ SF (*Hist*) suffragette

sufrido ADJ **1** [*persona*] (= *fuerte*) tough; [*paciente*] long-suffering, patient **2** [*tela*] hard wearing, tough; [*color*] that does not show the dirt, that wears well

sufrimiento SM suffering

sufrir /3a/ Ⓐ VI to suffer; **hacer ~ a algn** to make sb suffer; **~ de algo** to suffer from sth Ⓑ VT **1** (= *tener*) [+ *accidente*] to have, suffer; [+ *consecuencias, revés*] to suffer; [+ *cambio*] to undergo; [+ *intervención quirúrgica*] to have, undergo; [+ *pérdida*] to suffer, sustain; **sufrió un ataque al corazón** he had a heart attack **2** (= *soportar*) to bear, stand; **no puede ~ que la imiten** she can't bear *o* stand people imitating her

sugerencia SF suggestion; **hacer una ~** to make a suggestion

sugerente ADJ **1** (= *que hace pensar*) [*exposición, obra*] thought-provoking; [*lenguaje*] evocative **2** (= *seductor*) [*mirada, gesto, voz*] suggestive; [*ropa, iluminación*] seductive

sugerir /3i/ VT **1** (= *proponer*) to suggest; **¿tú qué me sugieres?** what do you suggest?; **~ hacer algo** to suggest doing sth; **yo sugiero empezar más temprano** I suggest that we begin earlier, I suggest beginning earlier; **~ a algn que** (+ SUBJUN): **me ha sugerido que escriba una novela** he has suggested that I write a novel *o* that I should write a novel **2** (= *insinuar*) to hint at, suggest
3 (= *indicar*) to suggest; **como el título podría ~** as the title might suggest
4 (= *evocar*) **la idea que nos sugiere este nuevo producto** the idea conveyed by this new product

sugestión SF **1** (= *convencimiento*) **sus problemas no son más que pura ~** his problems are all in his mind; **poderes de ~** hypnotic powers **2** (= *insinuación*) suggestion

sugestionable ADJ impressionable, suggestible

sugestionar /1a/ Ⓐ VT to influence; **es probable que se haya dejado ~ por ...** he may have allowed himself to be influenced by ... Ⓑ **sugestionarse** VPR to indulge in auto-suggestion; **~se con algo** to talk o.s. into sth

sugestivo ADJ **1** (= *que invita a pensar*) stimulating, thought-provoking **2** (= *atractivo*) attractive

sugiera *etc ver* **sugerir**

suiche SM (*Col, Ven*) switch

suicida Ⓐ ADJ [*conductor*] suicidal; [*comando*] suicide Ⓑ SMF **1** (= *que ha intentado suicidarse*) suicidal case; (= *muerto*) suicide victim; **es un ~ conduciendo** he's a maniac behind the wheel

suicidarse /1a/ VPR to commit suicide, kill o.s.

suicidio SM suicide

sui géneris ADJ INV individual, idiosyncratic

suite [swit] SF **1** (*en hotel*) suite **2** (*Mús*) suite

Suiza SF Switzerland

suizo¹/a ADJ, SM/F Swiss

suizo² SM (*Culin*) sugared bun

sujeción SF (= *dominación*) subjection (**a** to); **con ~ a** subject to

sujetador SM bra, brassiere (*frm*)

sujetalibros SM INV book-end

sujetapapeles SM INV paper clip

sujetar /1a/ **Ⓐ** VT **1** (= *agarrar*) to hold; **dos policías lo sujetaban contra la pared** two policemen pinned *o* held him against the wall **2** (= *afianzar*) **hay que ~ bien a los niños dentro del coche** children should be properly strapped in *o* properly secured when travelling by car; **~ algo a**: **se sujeta a la pared por medio de argollas** it is fixed *o* attached *o* secured to the wall through rings; **~ algo con**: **~ algo con clavos** to nail sth down; **~ algo con grapas** to staple sth; **~ algo con tornillos** to screw sth down; **sujetó las facturas con un clip** she clipped the invoices together **3** (= *contener*) [+ *rebelde*] to subdue, conquer; [+ *rival, animal enfurecido*] to keep down; **sus padres no lo pueden ~** his parents can't control him; **vive sin ataduras que la sujeten** she has nothing to tie her down, she has no ties to bind her **Ⓑ sujetarse** VPR **1** (= *agarrarse*) **1.1** [+ *pelo, sombrero*] to hold; **salió sujetándose los pantalones** he came out holding his trousers (*Brit*) *o* pants (*EEUU*) up **1.2** **~se a algo** to hold on to sth **2** (= *someterse*) **~se a** [+ *normas, reglas*] to abide by; [+ *autoridad*] to submit to

sujeto **Ⓐ** ADJ **1** (= *fijo*) fastened, secure; **¿está sujeta la cuerda?** is the rope fastened securely?, is the rope secure?; **los espejos estaban ~s a la pared** the mirrors were fastened *o* fixed to the wall **2** (= *dependiente*) **~ a algo** subject to sth; **la programación podría estar sujeta a cambios** the programme could be subject to changes **Ⓑ** SM **1** (*) (= *tipo*) character* **2** (*Med, Fil, Ling*) subject **3** (*Fin*) ➤ **sujeto pasivo** taxpayer

sulfatar /1a/ VT to fertilize, fertilize with sulphate

sulfato SM sulphate, sulfate (*EEUU*) ➤ **sulfato potásico** potassium sulphate *o* (*EEUU*) sulfate

sulfurar /1a/ **Ⓐ** VT **1** (*Quím*) to sulphurate, sulfurate (*EEUU*) **2** (*) (= *sacar de quicio a*) to rile* **Ⓑ sulfurarse** (*) VPR (= *enojarse*) to get riled*, see red, blow up*

sulfúrico ADJ sulphuric, sulfuric (*EEUU*)

sulfuro SM sulphide, sulfide (*EEUU*)

sultán/ana SM/F sultan/sultana

suma SF **1** (*Mat*) (= *acción*) addition, adding, adding up; (= *cantidad*) total, sum; (= *dinero*) sum; **¿cuánto es la ~ de todos los gastos?** what are the total expenses?; **una ~ de dinero** a sum of money; **hacer ~s** to add up, do addition **2** (= *resumen*) **en ~** in short

sumamente ADV extremely, exceedingly, highly

sumar /1a/ **Ⓐ** VT **1** (*Mat*) to add (together) **2** (= *totalizar*) to add up to, come to; **la cuenta suma seis dólares** the bill (*Brit*) *o* check (*EEUU*) adds up *o* comes to six dollars **Ⓑ** VI to add up; **suma y sigue** (*Contabilidad*) carried forward **Ⓒ sumarse** VPR **~se a algo** to join sth; **~se a una protesta** to join in a protest

sumarial ADJ summary

sumario **Ⓐ** ADJ **1** (= *breve*) brief, concise **2** (*Jur*) summary **Ⓑ** SM **1** (*en revista*) contents *pl* **2** (*Jur*) indictment; **abrir** *o* **instruir un ~** to institute legal proceedings, present *o* issue an indictment (*esp EEUU*)

sumarísimo ADJ summary

sumergible **Ⓐ** ADJ [*nave*] submersible; [*reloj*] waterproof **Ⓑ** SM submarine

sumergido ADJ **economía sumergida** black economy

sumergir /3c/ **Ⓐ** VT (*completamente*) to immerse; (*parcialmente*) to dip (**en** in) **Ⓑ sumergirse** VPR **1** (= *hundirse*) [*objeto, persona*] to sink beneath the surface; [*submarino*] to dive **2** (*en un ambiente*) **~se en** to immerse o.s. in

sumersión SF submersion

sumidero SM drain

sumido ADJ **~ en su trabajo** immersed *o* buried in one's

work; **~ en mis pensamientos** lost in thought

suministrador(a) SM/F supplier

suministrar /1a/ VT [+ *géneros, información*] to supply, provide; [+ *persona*] to supply; **me ha suministrado muchos datos** he has given me a lot of information, he has provided *o* supplied me with a lot of information

suministro SM **1** (= *provisión*) supply; **~s** (*Mil*) supplies ➤ **suministro de agua** water supply **2** (= *acción*) supplying, provision

sumir /3a/ **Ⓐ** VT **1** (= *hundir*) (*gen*) to sink, plunge; [*mar, olas*] to swallow up, suck down **2** (= *abismar*) to plunge (**en** into); **el desastre lo sumió en la tristeza** the disaster filled him with sadness **3** (*Col, Méx*) (= *abollar*) to dent **Ⓑ sumirse** VPR **1** (= *hundirse*) to sink **2** **~se en el estudio** to throw o.s. into one's studies; **~se en la tristeza** to be filled with sadness **3** (*Col, Méx*) (= *abollarse*) to get dented

sumisión SF **1** (= *acción*) submission **2** (= *docilidad*) submissiveness

sumiso ADJ submissive

súmmum SM height

sumo¹ ADJ **1** (= *supremo*) great, supreme; **con suma destreza** with consummate skill **2** [*rango*] high, highest; **~ sacerdote** high priest; **la suma autoridad** the supreme authority **3** **a lo ~** at (the) most

sumo² SM (*Dep*) sumo, sumo wrestling

suní ADJ, SMF, **sunita** ADJ, SMF Sunni

suntuosidad SF sumptuousness, magnificence

suntuoso ADJ sumptuous, magnificent

supe *etc ver* **saber**

supeditar /1a/ **Ⓐ** VT to subordinate (**a** to) **Ⓑ supeditarse** VPR **~se a** (= *subordinarse*) to be subject to; (= *ceder*) to give in to

súper* **Ⓐ** ADJ super* **Ⓑ** SM supermarket

superable ADJ [*dificultad*] surmountable, that can be overcome; **un obstáculo difícilmente ~** an obstacle not easily overcome

superabundancia SF superabundance, overabundance

superación SF **1** (= *acto*) overcoming, surmounting **2** (= *mejora*) improvement

superar /1a/ **Ⓐ** VT **1** (= *aventajar*) [+ *contrincante, adversario*] to overcome; [+ *límite*] to go beyond; [+ *récord, marca*] to break; **las ventas han superado con creces nuestras expectativas** sales have far exceeded our expectations; **las temperaturas han superado los 20 grados** temperatures have risen (to) above 20 degrees; **~ a algn en algo**: **superó al adversario en cuatro puntos** she beat her opponent by four points; **nos superaban en número** they outnumbered us; **nos supera a todos en inteligencia** she's cleverer than all of us **2** (= *pasar con éxito*) [+ *dificultad, obstáculo*] to overcome; [+ *enfermedad, crisis*] to get over; **aún no ha superado el divorcio de sus padres** he still hasn't got over his parents' divorce **3** [+ *etapa*] to get past; **el equipo francés no superó la primera ronda** the French team did not get past the first round **4** [+ *prueba, examen*] to pass **Ⓑ superarse** VPR to excel o.s.; **¡te has superado!** you've excelled yourself!; **un atleta que siempre intenta ~se** an athlete who is always trying to do better

superávit SM (*pl* **~s**) surplus

superbloque SM (*Ven*) giant block of flats (*Brit*) *o* apartment building (*EEUU*)

superbombardero SM superbomber

superchería SF fraud, trick, swindle

superconductor **Ⓐ** ADJ superconductive **Ⓑ** SM superconductor

supercuerda SF (*Fís*) superstring

superdotado/a **Ⓐ** ADJ extremely gifted **Ⓑ** SM/F extremely gifted person

superego SM superego

superempleo SM overemployment

superestructura SF superstructure

superficial ADJ **1** [*herida*] superficial, skin *antes de s* **2** [*interés*] superficial; [*mirada*] brief, perfunctory; [*carácter*] shallow

superficie SF **1** [*de cuerpo, líquido*] surface; **la ~ terrestre** the earth's surface; **ruta de ~** surface route **➤ superficie de rodadura** (*Aut*) tread **2** (*en medidas*) area; **una ~ de 200 hectáreas** an area of 200 hectares **3** (= *aspecto externo*) surface; **es un comentario inofensivo en la ~** it's a harmless comment on the surface **4** (*Com*) **gran ~** hypermarket, superstore

superfino ADJ superfine

superfluo ADJ superfluous

superhéroe SM superhero

superhombre SM superman

superintendente SMF (= *supervisor*) supervisor, superintendent; (= *capataz*) overseer

superior[1] **A** ADJ **1** (= *más alto*) [*estante, línea*] top *antes de s*; [*labio, mandíbula*] upper; **en la parte ~ de la página** at the top of the page **2** (= *mejor*) superior, better; **ser ~ a algo** to be superior to sth, be better than sth **3** (= *excelente*) **una moqueta de calidad ~** a superior quality *o* top-quality carpet **4** [*cantidad*] **cualquier número ~ a doce** any number above *o* higher than twelve; **nos son muy ~es en número** they greatly outnumber us **5** (*en categoría*) [*animal, especie*] higher; **una casta ~** a higher caste; **tiene un cargo ~ al tuyo** he has a higher-ranking post than yours **6** (*Educ*) [*curso, nivel*] advanced; [*enseñanza*] higher **B** SM (*en rango*) superior

superior[2]**/a** (*Rel*) **A** ADJ superior **B** SM/F superior/mother superior

superioridad SF superiority; **con aire de ~** condescendingly, patronizingly

superlativo ADJ, SM superlative

superlujo SM **hotel de ~** super-luxury hotel

supermercado SM supermarket

supermujer SF superwoman

supernova SF supernova

supernumerario/a ADJ, SM/F supernumerary

superpoblación SF [*de país, región*] overpopulation; [*de barrio*] overcrowding

superpoblado ADJ [*país, región*] overpopulated; [*barrio*] overcrowded, congested

superponer /2q/ VT **1** (= *colocar encima*) to superimpose, put on top **2 ~ una cosa a otra** (*fig*) to give preference to one thing over another, put one thing before another

superpotencia SF superpower, great power

superproducción SF overproduction

supersónico ADJ supersonic

superstición SF superstition

supersticioso ADJ superstitious

supertalla SF special size

superventas* SM INV best seller; **lista de ~** (*Mús*) charts *pl*

supervigilancia SF (*And*) supervision

supervisar /1a/ VT to supervise

supervisión SF supervision

supervisor(a) SM/F supervisor

supervivencia SF survival

superviviente **A** ADJ surviving **B** SMF survivor

supervivir /3a/ VI to survive

supino ADJ, SM supine

súpito ADJ **1** (*Col, Méx*) (= *atónito*) dumbfounded **2** (*Méx**) (= *dormido*) asleep

suplantar /1a/ VT **1** (= *sustituir*) to supplant, take the place of **2** (*fraudulentamente*) to impersonate, pass o.s. off as **3** (*CS*) (*en un cargo*) to stand in for

suplementario ADJ [*ingresos, vitaminas, información*] supplementary; **tren ~** extra *o* relief train; **tiempo ~** overtime

suplemento SM **1** (= *recargo*) (*al pagar*) supplement; (*Ferro*) excess fare **2** (= *revista*) supplement **➤ suplemento dominical** Sunday supplement

suplencia SF substitution, replacement

suplente **A** ADJ substitute, deputy; **maestro ~** supply teacher (*Brit*), substitute teacher (*EEUU*) **B** SMF (= *sustituto*) substitute, deputy; (= *jugador, deportista*) reserve; (= *profesor*) supply teacher; (= *médico*) locum; (*Teat*) understudy

supletorio **A** ADJ [*cama, sillón*] extra; [*medida*] stopgap *antes de s*; **teléfono ~** extension **B** SM (= *teléfono*) extension

súplica SF (= *ruego*) request; (= *petición*) supplication, entreaty, plea; (*Jur*) (= *instancia*) petition; **~s** entreaties, pleading *sing*

suplicar /1g/ VT to beg, implore; **~ a algn no hacer algo** to beg *o* implore sb not to do sth; **te suplico que te quedes** I beg you to stay

suplicio SM **1** (= *tortura*) torture; (*Hist*) (= *ejecución*) punishment, execution **2** (= *tormento*) torment, torture

suplir /3a/ VT **1** (= *compensar*) [+ *necesidad*] to fulfil, fulfill (*EEUU*); [+ *omisión*] to make good; [+ *falta*] to make good, make up for **2** (= *sustituir*) to replace, substitute; **~ a uno con otro** to replace one with another, substitute one for another

supo *etc ver* **saber**

supondré *etc ver* **suponer**

suponer /2q/ (*pp* **supuesto**) **A** VT **1** (= *imaginar*) to imagine; **ya puedes ~ lo que pasó** you can guess *o* imagine what happened; **le pagaron, supongamos, diez millones** he was paid, say, ten million; **es de ~ : es de ~ que haya protestas** I would imagine there will be protests, presumably there will be protests; **están muy apenados, como es de ~** they are very upset, as you would expect; **como era de ~, llegaron tarde** as was to be expected, they arrived late; **~ que** (*intentando adivinar*) to imagine that, suppose that, guess that*; (*como hipótesis*) to suppose that; (*dando por sentado*) to assume that, presume that; **supongo que necesitaréis un descanso** I guess* *o* imagine *o* suppose you'll need a break; **supón que tuvieras mucho dinero** suppose *o* supposing you had a lot of money; **supongo que no habrá problemas** I don't suppose there will be any problems; **suponiendo que todo salga según lo previsto** assuming *o* presuming everything goes according to plan **2** (= *atribuir*) (*con objeto indirecto de persona*) **os suponía informados de este asunto** I assumed *o* presumed you had been informed about this matter; **el equipo no mostró la calidad que se le suponía** the team did not show the talent expected of them *o* they had been credited with **3** (= *implicar*) to mean; **la mudanza no nos supondrá grandes gastos** the move won't mean *o* involve a lot of expense for us; **nuestra amistad supone mucho para mí** our friendship means a great deal to me **B** **suponerse** VPR to imagine; **el viaje resultó justo como me suponía** the trip turned out just as I had imagined; **ya me lo suponía** I thought so; **suponte que os pasa algo** suppose *o* supposing something happens to you **C** SM **si te ofrecen el puesto, es un ~, ¿lo aceptarías?** supposing *o* suppose they were to offer you the job, would you accept?; **supongamos, es sólo un ~, que eso sea verdad** let us suppose, for the sake of argument, that it is true

suponga *etc ver* **suponer**

suposición SF assumption

supositorio SM suppository

supranacional ADJ supranational

supremacía SF supremacy

supremo ADJ supreme

supresión SF [*de rebelión, crítica*] suppression; [*de costumbre, derecho, institución*] abolition; [*de dificultad, obstáculo*] removal, elimination; [*de detalle, pasaje*] deletion

suprimir /3a/ VT [+ *rebelión, crítica*] to suppress; [+ *costumbre, derecho, institución*] to abolish; [+ *dificultad, obstáculo*] to remove, eliminate; [+ *detalle, pasaje*] to delete, cut out, omit; ~ **la grasa de la dieta** to cut out *o* eliminate fat from one's diet

supuesto Ⓐ PP *de* **suponer** Ⓑ ADJ 1 (= *falso*) [*nombre*] assumed, false 2 (= *no demostrado*) supposed; **en el ~ informe policial** in the supposed police report 3 **¡por ~!** of course!; **por ~ que iré** of course I'll go 4 **dar algo por ~** to take sth for granted Ⓒ SM (= *hipótesis*) assumption; **en el ~ de que no venga** assuming that he doesn't come

supuración SF suppuration

supurar /1a/ VI to suppurate, fester

supuse *etc ver* **suponer**

sur Ⓐ ADJ [*región, orilla*] southern; [*costa*] south; [*dirección, rumbo*] southerly; [*viento*] south, southerly; **en la zona ~ de la ciudad** in the south *o* in the southern part of the city; **en la zona ~ de Inglaterra** in the south of England, in southern England; **en la costa ~** on the south coast; **íbamos en dirección ~** we were going south *o* in a southerly direction Ⓑ SM 1 (= *punto cardinal*) **el Sur** the South, the south 2 [*de región, país*] south; **el ~ del país** the south of the country; **de norte a ~** from north to south; **Toledo está al ~ de Madrid** Toledo is south of *o* to the south of Madrid; **vivía en el ~ de la isla** he lived in the south of the island; **las ciudades del ~ de España** cities in the south of *o* in southern Spain; **viajábamos hacia el ~** we were travelling south; **vientos del ~** south *o* southerly winds; **en la parte del ~** in the southern part 3 (*Meteo*) (*tb* **viento del ~**) south wind

Suráfrica SF = **Sudáfrica**

surafricano/a ADJ, SM/F = **sudafricano**

Suramérica SF = **Sudamérica**

suramericano/a ADJ, SM/F = **sudamericano**

surazo SM (*CS*) strong southerly wind

surcar /1g/ VT [+ *tierra*] to plough through, plow through (*EEUU*), furrow; [+ *superficie*] to score, groove; **una superficie surcada de ...** a surface lined *o* criss-crossed with ...; **los barcos que surcan los mares** (*liter*) the ships which ply the seas

surco SM 1 (*Agr*) furrow 2 (= *ranura*) (*en metal*) groove, score; (*en disco*) groove 3 (*Anat*) wrinkle 4 (*en agua*) track, wake

surcoreano/a ADJ, SM/F South Korean

sureño/a Ⓐ ADJ southern Ⓑ SM/F southerner

surero SM (*And*) cold southerly wind

sureste Ⓐ ADJ [*región*] southeast, southeastern; [*dirección, rumbo*] southeasterly; [*viento*] southeast, southeasterly Ⓑ SM 1 [*de región, país*] southeast 2 (*Meteo*) (*tb* **viento del ~**) southeast wind; *ver tb* **sur**

surf SM surfing

surfing SM **hacer ~** to surf, go surfing

surfista SMF surfer

surgir /3c/ VI 1 (= *aparecer*) (*gen*) to arise, emerge, appear; [*líquido*] to spout, spout out, spurt; [*barco*] (*en la niebla*) to loom up; [*persona*] to appear unexpectedly 2 [*dificultad*] to arise, come up, crop up

surja *etc ver* **surgir**

suroeste Ⓐ ADJ [*región*] southwest, southwestern; [*dirección, rumbo*] southwesterly; [*viento*] southwest, southwesterly Ⓑ SM 1 [*de región, país*] southwest 2 (*Meteo*) (*tb* **viento del ~**) southwest wind; *ver tb* **sur**

surrealismo SM surrealism

surrealista Ⓐ ADJ surrealist, surrealistic Ⓑ SMF surrealist

surtido Ⓐ ADJ 1 (= *variado*) assorted; **pasteles ~s** assorted cakes 2 (= *provisto*) **estar bien ~ de** to be well supplied with, have good stocks of Ⓑ SM selection, assortment, range

surtidor SM 1 (= *chorro*) jet, spout; (= *fuente*) fountain 2 ➤ **surtidor de gasolina** (= *aparato*) petrol pump (*Brit*), gas pump (*EEUU*); (= *lugar*) petrol station (*Brit*), gas station (*EEUU*)

surtir /3a/ Ⓐ VT 1 (= *suministrar*) to supply; ~ **a algn de combustible** to supply sb with fuel 2 (= *tener*) *ver* **efecto 1** Ⓑ **surtirse** VPR ~**se de** to provide o.s. with

susceptibilidad SF 1 [*de persona*] susceptibility (**a** to) 2 **susceptibilidades** sensibilities

susceptible ADJ 1 ~ **de** capable of; ~ **de mejora(r)** capable of improvement; ~ **de sufrir daño** liable to suffer damage 2 [*persona*] susceptible; ~ **a las críticas** sensitive to criticism

suscitar /1a/ VT [+ *rebelión*] to stir up; [+ *escándalo, conflicto*] to cause, provoke; [+ *discusión*] to start; [+ *duda, problema*] to raise; [+ *interés, sospechas*] to arouse

suscribir /3a/ (*pp* **suscrito**) Ⓐ VT 1 [+ *contrato, memoria*] to sign 2 (= *reafirmar*) [+ *promesa*] to make; [+ *opinión*] to subscribe to, endorse 3 (*Fin*) [+ *acciones*] to take out an option on; [+ *seguro*] to underwrite 4 ~ **a algn a una revista** to take out a subscription to a magazine for sb Ⓑ **suscribirse** VPR to subscribe (**a** to); ~**se a una revista** to take out a subscription for a magazine

suscripción SF subscription

suscriptor(a) SM/F subscriber

susodicho ADJ above-mentioned

suspender /2a/ Ⓐ VT 1 (= *colgar*) to hang, hang up, suspend (**de** from) 2 (= *interrumpir*) [+ *pago, trabajo*] to stop, suspend; [+ *reunión, sesión*] to adjourn; [+ *línea, servicio*] to discontinue; [+ *plan, viaje*] to call off, cancel; ~ **a algn de empleo y sueldo** to suspend sb (from work) without pay; ~ **la emisión de un programa** to cancel the showing of a programme; **ha suspendido su visita hasta la semana que viene** he's postponed his visit until next week; **el partido se suspendió a causa de la lluvia** the game was rained off 3 (*Esp*) [+ *asignatura*] to fail; **lo han suspendido en química** he's failed Chemistry 4 (*LAm*) [+ *alumno*] to suspend Ⓑ VI (*Esp*) to fail

suspense SM suspense; **novela/película de ~** thriller

suspensión SF 1 (*Aut, Mec*) suspension 2 [*de campeonato*] suspension; [*de sesión*] adjournment; [*de servicios*] stoppage; **¿a qué se ha debido la ~ del campeonato?** why was the championship suspended? ➤ **suspensión de empleo y sueldo** suspension without pay ➤ **suspensión de hostilidades** cessation of hostilities ➤ **suspensión de pagos** suspension of payments 3 (*LAm*) [*de alumno*] suspension

suspensivo ADJ **puntos ~s** dots, suspension points

suspenso Ⓐ ADJ (*Esp*) [*candidato*] failed Ⓑ SM 1 (*Esp Escol*) (= *asignatura*) fail, failure; **tengo un ~ en inglés** I failed English 2 **estar en** *o* **quedar en ~**: **la reunión ha quedado en ~ hasta el jueves** they've adjourned the meeting until next Thursday; **el juicio está en ~ hasta que se encuentre un nuevo juez** the trial has been suspended until a new judge can be found 3 (*LAm*) (= *misterio*) suspense; **una novela/película de ~** a thriller

suspensores SMPL 1 (*Chi*) (= *prenda*) braces (*Brit*), suspenders (*EEUU*) 2 (*Perú, RPl Dep*) athletic support *sing*, jockstrap *sing*

suspensorio SM athletic support, jockstrap

suspicacia SF suspicion, mistrust

suspicaz ADJ suspicious, distrustful

suspirar /1a/ VI to sigh; ~ **por** (= *anhelar*) to long for

suspiro SM sigh; **exhalar el último ~** to breathe one's last

sustancia SF 1 (= *materia*) substance 2 (= *esencia*) substance; **en ~** in substance, in essence; **sin ~** [*teoría, discurso*] lacking in substance; [*persona*] shallow, superficial 3 [*de alimento*] substance

sustancial ADJ substantial, significant

sustancioso ADJ [*discurso*] that gives food for thought; [*comida*] solid, substantial; [*ganancias*] healthy, fat (*pey*)

sustantivar /1a/ VT to nominalize

sustantivo SM noun, substantive

sustentación SF 1 (= *manutención*) maintenance

2 (= *apoyo*) support **3** (*Aer*) lift

sustentar /1a/ ❹ VT **1** (= *sujetar*) to hold up, support, bear the weight of **2** (= *alimentar*) to sustain, nourish **3** [+ *familia, hijos*] to support, maintain **4** [+ *esperanzas*] to sustain, keep alive **5** [+ *idea, teoría*] to maintain, uphold ❺ **sustentarse** VPR **~se con** to sustain o.s. with, subsist on; **~se de esperanzas** to live on hopes

sustento SM **1** (= *apoyo*) support **2** (= *alimento*) sustenance **3** (= *manutención*) maintenance; **ganarse el ~** to earn one's living, earn a livelihood

sustitución SF substitution (**por** for), replacement (**por** by)

sustituir /3g/ VT **1** (= *poner en lugar de*) to replace, substitute; **~ A por B** to replace A by *o* with B, substitute B for A **2** (= *tomar el lugar de*) (*gen*) to replace; (*temporalmente*) to stand in for; **lo sustituí como secretario de la asociación** I replaced him as club secretary; **¿me puedes ~ un par de semanas?** can you stand in for me for a couple of weeks?

sustitutivo ADJ substitute

sustituto/a SM/F (*temporal*) substitute, stand-in; (*para siempre*) replacement; **soy el ~ del profesor de inglés** I'm standing in for the English teacher

sustitutorio ADJ substitute, replacement *antes de s*

susto SM fright, scare; **¡qué ~!** what a fright!; **dar un ~ a algn** to give sb a fright *o* scare; **darse** *o* **llevarse** *o* **pegarse un ~*** to have a fright, get scared (*EEUU*); ✦ MODISMO **no ganar para ~s*: este año no ganamos para ~s** it's been one setback after another this year

sustracción SF **1** (= *resta*) subtraction, taking away; (= *descuento*) deduction **2** (= *hurto*) theft

sustraer /2p/ ❹ VT **1** (= *llevarse*) to remove, take away **2** (*Mat*) (= *restar*) to subtract, take away **3** (= *robar*) to steal ❺ **sustraerse** VPR **~se a** to avoid

sustrato SM substratum

susurrar /1a/ ❹ VT to whisper ❺ VI **1** [*persona*] to whisper; **~ al oído de algn** to whisper to sb, whisper in sb's ear **2** (= *sonar*) [*viento*] to whisper; [*arroyo*] to murmur; [*hojas*] to rustle

susurro SM **1** (= *murmullo*) whisper **2** (= *sonido*) [*de viento*] whisper; [*de arroyo*] murmur; [*de hojas*] rustle

sutil ADJ **1** [*diferencia*] subtle **2** (= *afinado*) [*inteligencia, persona*] sharp, keen; [*comentario*] subtle **3** (= *delicado*) [*hilo, hebra*] fine; [*tela*] delicate, thin, light; [*atmósfera*] thin; [*olor*] subtle, delicate; [*brisa*] gentle

sutileza SF subtlety

sutura SF suture

suturar /1a/ VT to suture

suyo/a ❹ ADJ POSES **1** (= *de él*) his; (= *de ella*) her; (= *de ellos, ellas*) their; **no es amigo ~** he is not a friend of his/ hers *etc*; **no es culpa suya** it's not his/her *etc* fault, it's no fault of his/hers *etc*; **eso es muy ~** that's just like him, that's typical of him
2 (= *de usted, ustedes*) your; **¿es ~ esto?** is this yours? ❺ PRON POSES (= *de él*) his; (= *de ella*) hers; (= *de usted, ustedes*) yours; (*de animal, cosa*) its; (= *de uno mismo*) one's own; (= *de ellos, ellas*) theirs; **este libro es el ~** this book is his/hers *etc*; **los ~s** (= *familia*) one's family *o* relations; (= *partidarios*) one's own people *o* supporters; **Suyo afectísimo** Yours faithfully *o* sincerely (*Brit*), Yours truly (*EEUU*); ✦ MODISMOS **lo ~** (= *mucho*): **aguantar lo ~** to put up with a lot; **él pesa lo ~** he's really heavy, he's a fair weight; **ir a lo ~** to go one's own way; (*pey*) to go one's own sweet way, think only of o.s.; **hacer de las suyas** to get up to one's old tricks; **salirse con la suya** (*en una decisión*) to get one's own way; (*en una discusión*) to carry one's point

> **Suyo** se traduce por **his**, **hers**, **theirs** *o* **yours** (dependiendo de si hablamos de "él/ella", "ellos/ellas" *o* "usted/ustedes"), cuando nos referimos a las posesiones de alguien: "Este libro es (el) suyo", *This book is his*. En cambio, se traduce por **of his/hers**, etc., cuando significa "uno de sus": "un primo suyo", *a cousin of his*.

switch [switʃ] SM (*esp Méx*) **1** (*Elec*) switch **2** (*Aut*) ignition (switch)

Tt

T, t [te] SF (= *letra*) T, t

taba SF (= *hueso*) ankle bone; (= *juego*) jacks

tabacal SM (= *plantación*) tobacco plantation; (= *terreno*) tobacco field

tabacalera SF cigarette factory

tabacalero ADJ tobacco *antes de s*

tabaco SM 1 (= *producto*) tobacco; (= *planta*) tobacco plant ➤ **tabaco de hebra** loose tobacco ➤ **tabaco de liar** rolling tobacco ➤ **tabaco de mascar** chewing tobacco ➤ **tabaco de pipa** pipe tobacco ➤ **tabaco negro** dark tobacco ➤ **tabaco rubio** Virginia tobacco 2 (*Esp*) (= *cigarrillos*) cigarettes *pl*; **¿tienes ~?** have you any cigarettes? 3 (*Col*) (= *puro*) cigar

tabalear /1a/ VI to drum, tap

tabanco SM 1 (*CAm*) (= *desván*) attic 2 (*Méx*) (= *puesto*) stall

tábano SM horsefly, gadfly

tabaquera SF 1 (= *bolsa*) tobacco pouch 2 (= *estuche*) (*para puros*) cigar case; (*para cigarrillos*) cigarette case; (*para rapé*) snuffbox; *ver tb* **tabaquero**

tabaquero/a Ⓐ ADJ tobacco *antes de s* Ⓑ SM/F (= *tendero*) tobacconist (*Brit*), tobacco dealer (*EEUU*); (= *mayorista*) tobacco merchant; (= *cultivador*) tobacco grower; *ver tb* **tabaquera**

tabaquismo SM smoking habit

tabarra* SF nuisance, bore; **dar la ~** to be a nuisance, be a pain in the neck*; **dar la ~ a algn** to pester sb

taberna SF bar, pub (*Brit*); (*Hist*) tavern

tabernáculo SM tabernacle

tabicar /1g/ VT 1 [+ *puerta, ventana*] (*con ladrillos*) to brick up; (*con madera*) to board up 2 [+ *habitación*] to partition off

tabique SM 1 (= *pared*) thin wall; (*entre habitaciones*) partition (wall) ➤ **tabique nasal** nasal septum 2 (*Méx*) (= *ladrillo*) brick

tabla SF 1 (= *pieza*) [de madera] plank, board; (*Arte*) panel; ✦ MODISMO **hacer ~ rasa** to make a clean sweep; **hacer ~ rasa de algo** to completely disregard sth, ride roughshod over sth ➤ **tabla de cocina** chopping board (*Brit*), cutting board (*EEUU*) ➤ **tabla de lavar** washboard ➤ **tabla de picar** chopping board (*Brit*), cutting board (*EEUU*) ➤ **tabla de planchar** ironing board ➤ **tabla de quesos** cheeseboard ➤ **tabla de salvación** (*fig*) last resort, only hope ➤ **tabla de surf** surfboard ➤ **tabla de windsurf** windsurfing board 2 **tablas** 2.1 (*Taur*) barrier *sing* 2.2 (*Teat*) stage *sing*; ✦ MODISMOS **coger ~s** (*en teatro*) to gain acting experience; (*fig*) to get the hang of it; **tener (muchas) ~s** [*actor*] to have a good stage presence; [*político*] to be an old hand 3 **tablas** (*Ajedrez*) draw *sing*, (*fig*) stalemate *sing*; **hacer ~s** ◇ **quedar en ~s** (*lit*) to draw; (*fig*) to reach stalemate, be deadlocked 4 [de falda] box pleat, broad pleat 5 (= *lista*) (*Mat*) table; (*en libro*) table; (*Dep*) (*tb ~ clasificatoria*) table, (league) table; (*Inform*) array ➤ **tabla de abdominales** abdominal routine ➤ **tabla de ejercicios, tabla de gimnasia** exercise routine, set of exercises ➤ **tabla de logaritmos** table of logarithms ➤ **tabla de materias** table of contents ➤ **tabla de multiplicar** multiplication table

tablado SM stage

tablao SM (= *espectáculo*) flamenco show; (= *escenario*) dance floor (*for flamenco dancing*); (= *local*) flamenco venue

tablear /1a/ VT 1 [+ *madera*] to cut into boards *o* planks 2 [+ *terreno*] (= *dividir*) to divide up into plots; (= *nivelar*) to level off

tablero SM 1 (= *panel*) [de madera] board; (*para anuncios*) notice board (*Brit*), bulletin board (*EEUU*); (= *pizarra*) blackboard, chalkboard (*EEUU*); [de mesa] top; [de mármol] slab; (*Elec*) switchboard ➤ **tablero de gráficos** (*Inform*) graph pad ➤ **tablero de instrumentos, tablero de mandos** instrument panel 2 (*para juegos*) board ➤ **tablero de ajedrez** chessboard

tableta SF [de chocolate] bar, slab; (*Med*) tablet

tablilla SF 1 (= *tabla*) small board; (*Med*) splint 2 (*Méx*) [de chocolate] bar

tablón SM (= *tabla*) plank; (= *viga*) beam ➤ **tablón de anuncios** notice board (*Brit*), bulletin board (*EEUU*)

tabú Ⓐ ADJ INV taboo Ⓑ SM (*pl ~s, ~es*) taboo

tabulador SM tab, tabulator

tabular Ⓐ /1a/ VT to tabulate Ⓑ ADJ tabular

taburete SM stool

TAC SF/M ABR (= **tomografía axial computerizada**) CAT

tacañería SF stinginess, meanness (*esp Brit*)

tacaño ADJ stingy, mean (*esp Brit*)

tacar /1g/ VT (*And*) to shoot at sb

tacatá* SM, **tacataca** SM [de bebé] baby walker; [de anciano] walking frame, Zimmer frame®

tacha¹ SF (*Téc*) large tack, stud

tacha² SF blemish; **sin ~** [vida, reputación] unblemished; [estilo, conducta] faultless; [lealtad] absolute; **una persona sin ~** a person who is beyond reproach

tachadura SF (= *tachón*) crossing-out, erasure (*frm*); (= *corrección*) correction

tachar /1a/ VT 1 (= *suprimir*) to cross out; (= *corregir*) to correct; **~ a algn de una lista** to cross *o* take sb off a list 2 **~ a algn de** to brand sb (as); **~ a algn de incapaz** to brand sb (as) incompetent

tachero/a* SM/F (*RPl*) taxi driver

tacho SM 1 (*CS*) (= *cubo*) bucket, pail; (= *olla*) pan 2 (*And, CS*) (*para papeles*) wastepaper basket, wastebasket (*EEUU*); ✦ MODISMO **irse al ~** (*CS**) to be ruined, fail ➤ **tacho de la basura** dustbin (*Brit*), rubbish bin (*Brit*), trash *o* garbage can (*EEUU*) 3 (*RPl**) (= *taxi*) taxi, cab

tachón¹ SM 1 (*Téc*) ornamental stud, boss 2 (*Ven Cos*) pleat

tachón² SM (= *tachadura*) crossing-out, deletion (*frm*); **escribe con letra clara y sin tachones** write clearly and avoid crossing things out

tachonado ADJ **~ de estrellas** star-studded, star-spangled

tachonar /1a/ VT to stud

tachuela SF 1 (*en cinturón, ropa*) stud 2 (= *clavo*) (tin) tack 3 (*Chi, Méx, Ven**) (= *persona*) short stocky person

tácito ADJ 1 (*gen*) tacit; [acuerdo] unspoken, tacit; [ley] unwritten 2 (*Ling*) understood

taciturno ADJ (= *callado*) taciturn, silent; (= *malhumorado*) sullen, moody; (= *triste*) glum

taco SM 1 (= *pieza*) (*para tornillo*) Rawlplug®; (= *tapón*) plug, stopper; [de bota de fútbol] stud; (*para fusil*) wad, wadding; (= *tarugo*) wooden peg 2 (*Billar*) cue 3 (*de papeles*) (*para escribir*) pad; [de billetes, cupones] book; [de cheque] stub; (= *calendario*) tear-off calendar 4 (*Esp*) [de jamón, queso] cube 5 (*Esp**) (= *palabrota*) rude word, swearword; **dice muchos ~s** he swears a lot 6 (*Esp***) (= *lío*) mess; **armarse *o* hacerse un ~** to get into a mess, get mixed *o* muddled up 7 (*Esp***) (= *año*) year; **tener 16 ~s** to be 16 (years old) 8 (*CS, Perú*) (= *tacón*) heel 9 (*Méx Culin*) taco, filled rolled tortilla; (*) (= *bocado*) snack, bite; ✦ MODISMO **darse ~** (*CAm, Méx**) to give o.s. airs 10 (*Chi*) (= *obstrucción*) blockage, obstruction; (*) (= *atasco*) traffic jam

tacón SM heel; **nunca llevo tacones** I never wear high heels; **zapatos de ~ (alto)** high-heeled shoes ➤ **tacón (de) aguja** stiletto heel

taconazo SM (= *patada*) kick (with one's heel); (= *golpecito*) heel tap; **dar un ~** to click one's heels

taconear /1a/ VI **1** (= caminar) to walk clicking o tapping one's heels **2** (= dar golpecitos) to tap with one's heels; (Mil) to click one's heels

taconeo SM **1** (al andar) **podíamos oír el ~ de sus zapatos** we could hear her shoe heels clicking about **2** (= golpecitos) tapping with one's heels; (Mil) heel-clicking

táctica SF **1** (= estrategia) tactic; **una nueva ~** a new tactic, new tactics; **el equipo cambió de ~** the team changed tactics **2** (= jugada) move; (fig) gambit

táctico/a Ⓐ ADJ tactical Ⓑ SM/F tactician

táctil ADJ tactile

tacto SM **1** (= sentido) (sense of) touch; (= acción) touch; **ser áspero al ~** to be rough to the touch; **conoce las monedas por el ~** she identifies coins by touch **2** (= cualidad) feel **3** (= diplomacia) tact; **tener ~** to be tactful

tacuche* SM (Méx) suit

TAE SF ABR (= tasa anual efectiva o equivalente) APR

tae kwon do SM, **tae-kwon-do** SM taekwondo, tae-kwon-do

tafetán SM **1** (= tela) taffeta **2** (tb ~ **adhesivo**, ~ **inglés**) sticking plaster (Brit), Band-Aid® (EEUU) **3 tafetanes** (= banderas) flags; (= galas) frills, buttons and bows

tafilete SM morocco leather

tagalo/a Ⓐ ADJ, SM/F Tagalog Ⓑ SM (Ling) Tagalog

tahona SF (= panadería) bakery, bakehouse; (= molino) flour mill

tahúr SMF (= jugador) gambler; (pey) cardsharp, cheat

taiga SF taiga

taguara SF (Ven) cheap restaurant

tailandés/esa Ⓐ ADJ, SM/F Thai Ⓑ SM (Ling) Thai

Tailandia SF Thailand

taimado ADJ **1** (= astuto) sly, crafty **2** (= hosco) sullen

taita* SM (And, CAm, Méx, Ven) (= papá) dad*, daddy*; (Chi) (= tratamiento) respectful term of address used to an older man

Taiwán SM Taiwan

tajada SF **1** (Culin) slice **2** (*) (= beneficio) rake-off*; **sacar ~** to get one's share, take one's cut*; **sacaron buena ~ de ello** they did well out of it **3** (Esp*) (= borrachera) **coger** o **pillar una ~** to get plastered*

tajamar SM **1** (Náut) stem; [de puente] cutwater **2** (CAm, CS) (= muro) mole

tajante ADJ [negativa] emphatic; [órdenes] strict; [crítica, distinción] sharp; [comentario] incisive; **contestó con un "no"** he answered with an emphatic "no"; **hacer afirmaciones ~s** to make categorical statements; **fueron ~s en su condena** they were categorical in their condemnation

tajear* /1a/ VT (LAm) to slash

Tajo SM Tagus

tajo SM **1** (= corte) cut, slash; **cortar algo de un ~** to slice sth off **2** (Geog) (= corte) cut, cleft; (= escarpa) steep cliff, sheer drop **3** (Esp*) (= trabajo) work **4** (Culin) (= tabla) chopping block

tal Ⓐ ADJ **1** (en relación con algo ya mencionado) such; **nunca he hecho ~ cosa** I never did any such thing o anything of the sort; **hace diez años,** o **día como hoy** on the same day ten years ago, ten years ago today; **el ~ cura** this priest (we were talking about), this priest person (pey) **2** (indicando extrañeza o exageración) such; **con ~ atrevimiento** with such a cheek, so cheekily; **~ era su fuerza** he was so strong **3** (indicando indeterminación) **se aloja en ~ o cual hotel** he is staying at such-and-such a hotel; **~ día, a ~ hora** on such-and-such a day, at such-and-such a time; **un ~ García** one García, a man called García or something (pey) Ⓑ PRON **1** (= persona indeterminada) **el ~** this man I mentioned; **y como ~, ...** and as such, ...; ✦ MODISMO **son ~ para cual** they're two of a kind **2** (= cosa indeterminada) **me dijo que sí ~ y que si cual** he said this, that and the other; **y ~** (Esp*): **fuimos al cine y ~**

we went to the pictures and stuff*; **estábamos charlando y ~** we were just chatting and so on

Ⓒ ADV **1** (en comparaciones) **~ como: estaba ~ como lo dejé** it was just as I had left it; **~ y como están las cosas, no creo que sea buena idea** as things are o given the current state of affairs, I don't think it would be a good idea; **~ cual: déjalo ~ cual** leave it just as it is; **después de tantos años sigue ~ cual** she hasn't changed after all these years; **se enteró de la noticia y se quedó ~ cual** when he heard the news he didn't bat an eyelid

2 (en preguntas) **¿qué ~?** how's things?, how are you?; **¿qué ~ estás?** how are you?; **¿qué ~ estoy con este vestido?** how do I look in this dress?; **¿qué ~ has dormido?** how did you sleep?; **¿qué ~ si lo compramos?** why don't we buy it?, suppose we buy it?

3 ~ vez perhaps, maybe; **~ vez me pase por tu casa mañana** I may drop in at your place tomorrow

4 con ~ de: hace lo que sea con ~ de llamar la atención he'll do anything to attract attention; **no importa el frío con ~ de ir bien abrigado** the cold doesn't matter as long as o if you're well wrapped up; **con ~ de que** provided (that), as long as

tala SF [de árboles] felling, cutting down; (= destrucción) havoc

talacha SF, **talache** SM (Méx) **1** (= reparación) tyre repair, tire repair (EEUU) **2** (*) (= trabajo) work; **tiene a alguien que le hace la ~** he's got someone to do all the hard work o donkey-work* for him **3** (= herramienta) mattock

taladradora SF pneumatic drill, jackhammer (EEUU)

taladrar /1a/ VT **1** [+ pared] to drill a hole/holes in, drill; [+ billete, documento] to punch **2** [ruido, mirada, dolor] to pierce; **un ruido que taladra los oídos** an ear-splitting noise; **me taladró con la mirada** she fixed me with a piercing gaze

taladro SM **1** (= herramienta) drill ➤ **taladro mecánico** power drill ➤ **taladro neumático** pneumatic drill **2** (= agujero) drill hole

talaje SM (Chi) **1** (= pasto) pasture **2** (= pastoreo) grazing

tálamo SM (liter) marriage bed

talante SM **1** (= carácter) **un hombre de ~ liberal** a liberal-minded man **2** (= humor) mood; **estar de buen ~** to be in a good mood; **estar de mal ~** to be in a bad mood **3** (= disposición) **hacer algo de buen ~** to do sth willingly

talar /1a/ VT to fell, cut down

talco SM (Quím) talc; (tb **polvos de ~**) talcum powder

talega SF **1** (= bolsa) sack, bag **2 talegas** (Méx***) balls***

talego SM **1** (= saco) long sack, big sack; (Col) (= bolsa) bag **2** (Esp**) (= cárcel) nick (Brit*), can (EEUU**), jail **3** (Esp**) (= billete) 1,000 pesetas

talento SM **1** (= inteligencia) **una mujer de enorme ~** a woman of enormous talent **2** (= aptitud) talent; **sus hijos tienen ~ para la música** their children have a talent for music **3** (= prodigio) talent; **su hijo es un auténtico ~** her son is a really gifted o talented boy

talentoso ADJ talented, gifted

Talgo SM ABR (Esp) inter-city express train

talibán/ana Ⓐ ADJ Taliban antes de s Ⓑ SM/F (= persona) member of the Taliban Ⓒ SM (= régimen) Taliban

talión SM **la ley del ~** an eye for an eye

talismán SM talisman

talla¹ SF **1** [de ropa] size; **¿de qué ~ es este vestido?** what size is this dress? **2** (= altura) height; **dar la ~** (lit) to be tall enough; (fig) to measure up **3** (= categoría, nivel) stature; **hay pocos políticos de la ~ de este ministro** there are few politicians of the stature of this minister **4** (Arte) (= escultura) sculpture ➤ **talla en madera** woodwork, wood carving **5** = **tallado** B

talla²* SF (Chi) (= broma) joke

tallado Ⓐ ADJ [madera] carved; [piedra] sculpted; [metal] engraved Ⓑ SM (en madera) carving; (en piedra) sculpting

tallador(a) SM/F **1** (= persona) [de madera] carver; [de piedra] sculptor; [de diamantes] cutter; [de metal] engraver ➤ **tallador(a) de madera** woodworker, wood carver **2** (LAm

Naipes) dealer, banker

tallar /1a/ **Ⓐ** VT **1** [+ *madera*] to carve, work; [+ *piedra*] to sculpt; [+ *diamante*] to cut; [+ *metal*] to engrave **2** [+ *persona*] to measure (the height of) **3** (*Naipes*) to deal **4** (*Méx*) (= *friccionar*) to rub; (= *fregar*) [+ *olla, sartén*] to scrub **Ⓑ** VI **1** (*Naipes*) to deal **2** (*Col*) (= *apretar*) [*ropa, zapatos*] to be too tight for me; **esta camisa me talla** this shirt is too tight for me **Ⓖ tallarse** VPR (*Méx*) (= *frotarse*) to rub o.s.; (*para limpiarse*) to scrub o.s.

tallarín SM noodle

talle SM **1** (= *cintura*) waist; **un vestido de ~ bajo** a dress with a low waist **2** (= *medidas*) waist and chest measurements *pl*; (*RPl*) (= *talla*) size, fitting **3** (= *tipo*) [*de mujer*] figure; [*de hombre*] build, physique; **de ~ esbelto** slim; **tiene buen ~** she has a good figure

taller SM (*Téc, Educ, Teat*) workshop; (= *fábrica*) factory, mill; (*Aut*) garage, repair shop; (*Arte*) studio; (*Cos*) workroom ➤ **taller de coches** car repair shop, garage (*for repairs*) ➤ **taller de montaje** assembly shop ➤ **taller de reparaciones** repair shop ➤ **taller de teatro** theatre workshop, drama workshop ➤ **taller de trabajo** (*en congreso, curso*) workshop ➤ **talleres gráficos** printing works ➤ **taller mecánico** garage (*for repairs*) ➤ **taller ocupacional** occupational therapy workshop

tallo SM [*de flor*] stem, stalk; [*de hierba*] blade

talludito* ADJ mature, middle-aged; **el actor es ~ ya para este papel** the actor is getting on a bit now for this role; **Sofía Loren, que está ya talludita** Sofia Loren, who is no longer as young as she was

Talmud SM Talmud

talón SM **1** [*de pie, calcetín, zapato*] heel; ♦ MODISMO **pisar los talones a algn** to be hard on sb's heels ➤ **talón de Aquiles** Achilles heel **2** (*Esp*) (= *cheque*) cheque

En inglés americano se usa **check** en lugar de **cheque**.

un ~ a favor de Luis González a cheque made out to *o* made payable to Luis González ➤ **talón al portador** bearer cheque, cheque payable to the bearer ➤ **talón en blanco** blank cheque ➤ **talón sin fondos** bad cheque

talonario SM [*de cheques*] cheque book, check book (*EEUU*); [*de recibos*] receipt book; [*de billetes*] book of tickets; [*de recetas*] prescription pad

talonear /1a/ **Ⓐ** VT **1** (*LAm*) [+ *caballo*] to spur along, dig one's heels into **2** (*Dep*) to heel **Ⓑ** VI (*Méx*) [*prostituta*] to walk the streets, ply her trade

talonera SF heel-pad

talquera SF talcum powder container; (*con borla*) compact

talud SM (*en terreno*) slope, bank; (*Geol*) talus

tamal SM (*LAm*) tamale

tamaño Ⓐ SM size; **son del mismo ~ ◇ tienen el mismo ~** they are the same size; **¿de qué ~ es?** how big is it?, what size is it?; **un ordenador del ~ de un libro** a computer the size of a book; **una foto ~ carnet** a passport-size photo; **de ~ natural** full-size, life-size ➤ **tamaño de bolsillo** pocket-size ➤ **tamaño familiar** family-size **Ⓑ** ADJ such, such a; **tamaña humillación** such humiliation *o* shame; **~ error** such a mistake

tamarindo SM **1** (*Bot*) tamarind **2** (*Méx***) traffic cop*

tamarisco SM, **tamariz** SM tamarisk

tambache SM (*Méx*) [*de ropa*] bundle of clothes; (= *bulto*) big package

tambaleante ADJ **1** [*persona*] staggering; [*paso*] unsteady; [*mueble*] unsteady, wobbly; [*vehículo*] swaying **2** [*economía, democracia*] shaky; [*régimen*] tottering

tambalear /1a/ **Ⓐ** VT to shake, rock **Ⓑ tambalearse** VPR **1** [*persona*] to stagger; [*vehículo*] to lurch, sway; [*mueble*] to wobble; **ir tambaleándose** to stagger along **2** [*gobierno*] to totter

tambaleo SM [*de persona*] staggering; [*de vehículo*] swaying; [*de mueble*] wobble

también ADV **1** (= *además*) also, too, as well; **hablaron ~ de otros temas** they also discussed other matters, they discussed other matters too *o* as well; **Italia tomará ~ parte en la competición** ITALY will take part in the competition too *o* as well; **—estoy cansado —yo ~** "I'm tired" — "so am I" *o* "me too*"; **ácido ascórbico, ~ conocido como vitamina C** ascorbic acid, also known as vitamin C **2** (*uso enfático*) **tuvimos mala suerte, aunque ~ es cierto que nos faltaba preparación** we were certainly unlucky but (then again) we were also underprepared *o* we were underprepared too *o* as well

tambo SM **1** (*And Hist*) (= *taberna*) wayside inn, country inn **2** (*RPl*) (= *granja*) (small) dairy farm **3** (*RPl*) (= *corral*) milking yard **4** (*Méx*) (= *recipiente*) bucket; **el ~ de la basura** the rubbish bin (*Brit*), the garbage *o* trash can (*EEUU*) **5** (*Méx**) (= *cárcel*) nick (*Brit**), can (*EEUU**), jail

tambor SM **1** (*Mús*) (= *instrumento*) drum; (= *persona*) drummer; ♦ MODISMO **venir *o* salir a ~ batiente** to come out with flying colours ➤ **tambor mayor** drum major **2** [*de lavadora, freno*] drum ➤ **tambor del freno** brake drum **3** (*Anat*) ➤ **tambor del oído** eardrum **4** [*de detergente*] drum **5** (*Cos*) (= *bastidor*) tambour **6** (*LAm*) (= *recipiente*) drum **7** (*Méx*) (*para la cama*) springs *pl*

tamboril SM small drum

tamborilear /1a/ VI **1** (*Mús*) to drum **2** [*lluvia*] to patter, drum

tamborileo SM **1** (*con los dedos*) drumming **2** [*de lluvia*] patter, pattering

tamborilero/a SM/F drummer

Támesis SM Thames

tamiz SM sieve

tamizado Ⓐ ADJ [*harina, información*] sifted; [*luz*] filtered **Ⓑ** SM sifting

tamizar /1f/ VT [+ *harina, azúcar*] to sift, sieve; [+ *datos, información*] to sift through; [+ *luz*] to filter; [+ *rayos*] to filter out

tampoco ADV **1** not ...either, neither, nor; **yo no lo compré ~** I didn't buy it either; **ni Ana ni Cristóbal ~** neither Ana nor Cristóbal; **—yo no voy —yo ~** "I'm not going" — "nor am I *o* neither am I *o* me neither"; **—yo no fui —yo ~** "I didn't go" — "nor did I *o* neither did I *o* me neither" **2** (*uso enfático*) **~ nos vamos a enfadar ahora por eso** we're not going to fall out over that, are we?; **bueno, ~ es como para ponerse a llorar** it's not as if it's anything to cry about

tampón SM **1** (*Med*) tampon **2** (*para entintar*) ink pad

tan ADV **1** (*tras verbo*) so; **estaba ~ cansado que me quedé dormido** I was so tired I fell asleep; **¡no es ~ difícil!** it's not so difficult!

2 (*tras sustantivo*) such; **no es una idea ~ buena** it's not such a good idea

3 (*en exclamaciones*) **¡qué regalo ~ bonito!** what a beautiful present!; **¡que cosa ~ rara!** how strange!

4 (*en comparaciones*) **es ~ feo como yo** he's as ugly as me **5** ~ **sólo** only; **hace ~ sólo unas semanas** only a few weeks ago

6 ~ **siquiera** = **siquiera A**

7 (*LAm*) **qué ~** how; **¿qué ~ grande es?** how big is it?

tanatorio SM *official building for funerals containing chapels of rest*

tanda SF **1** (= *grupo*) [*de cosas, personas*] batch; [*de golpes*] series; [*de inyecciones*] course, series; **por ~s** in batches ➤ **tanda de avisos** (*LAm*) commercial break, ad break* ➤ **tanda de penaltis** series of penalties, penalty shoot-out **2** (*Billar*) game; (*Béisbol*) innings *pl* **3** (*CAm, Méx*) (= *espectáculo*) show, performance

tándem SM (= *bicicleta*) tandem; (*Pol*) duo, team; **en ~** (*Elec*) tandem; (*fig*) in tandem, jointly, in association

tanga SM (SF *en LAm*) tanga, G-string

tangencial ADJ tangential

tangente SF tangent; ♦ MODISMO **salirse por la ~** (= *hacer una digresión*) to go off at a tangent; (= *esquivar una pregunta*) to dodge the issue

Tánger SM Tangier(s)

tangible ADJ (*lit*) tangible; (*fig*) tangible, concrete

tango SM tango

tanguero/a SM/F, **tanguista** SMF tango dancer

tánico ADJ tannic; **ácido ~** tannic acid

tanino SM tannin

tano/a SM/F (*RPl pey*) Italian, wop*** (*pey*)

tanque SM 1 (= *depósito*) tank, reservoir; (*Aut*) tanker
2 (*Mil*) tank

tanqueta SF small tank, armoured *o* (*EEUU*) armored car

tantán SM (= *tambor*) tomtom; (= *gong*) gong

tantear /1a/ **Ⓐ** VT 1 (*con la mano*) to feel; **tanteó la mesilla en busca del reloj** he felt for the watch on the bedside table
2 (= *probar*) to test, try out; (= *sondear*) to probe; [+ *intenciones, persona*] to sound out; ✦ MODISMO **~ el terreno** to test the water, get the lie of the land
3 (= *calcular*) [+ *tela, cantidad*] to make a rough estimate of; [+ *peso*] to feel, get the feel of; [+ *situación*] to weigh up; [+ *problema*] to consider
4 (*Dep*) to keep the score of
Ⓑ VI 1 (*Dep*) to score, keep (the) score
2 (= *ir a tientas*) to grope, feel one's way

tanteo SM 1 (= *cálculo*) rough estimate; (= *consideración*) weighing up; **a** *o* **por ~** by guesswork 2 (= *prueba*) test, testing, trial; [*de sondeo*] sounding out; **al ~** by trial and error 3 (*Dep*) score; **un ~ de 9-7** a score of 9-7

tantito* (*Méx*) **Ⓐ** ADJ a bit of, a little **Ⓑ** ADV a bit, a little; **~ antes** a bit *o* little earlier

tanto Ⓐ ADJ 1 (*indicando gran cantidad*) (*en singular*) so much; (*en plural*) so many; **ahora no bebo tanta leche** I don't drink so *o* as much milk now; **tiene ~ dinero que no sabe qué hacer con él** he has so much money he doesn't know what to do with it; **¡tuve tanta suerte!** I was so lucky!; **~ ... como** (*en singular*) as much ... as; (*en plural*) as many ... as; **~ gusto** how do you do?, pleased to meet you
2 (*indicando cantidad indeterminada*) **había cuarenta y ~s invitados** there were forty-odd guests; **hay otros ~s candidatos** there are as many more candidates, there's the same number of candidates again
Ⓑ PRON 1 (= *gran cantidad*) (*en singular*) so much; (*en plural*) so many; **no necesitamos tantas** we don't need so many; **vinieron ~s que no cabían en la sala** so many people came that they wouldn't all fit into the room; **~ como** (*en singular*) as much as; (*en plural*) as many as; **es uno de ~s** he's nothing special
2 (= *cantidad indeterminada*) **nació en el mil novecientos cuarenta y ~s** she was born in nineteen forty-something *o* some time in the forties; ✦ MODISMO **las tantas (de la madrugada** *o* **de la noche): el tren llegó a las tantas** the train arrived really late *o* in the middle of the night; **deben de ser las tantas** it must be pretty late
3 (*otras locuciones*) **entre ~** meanwhile; **mientras ~** meanwhile; **no es para ~** (*por quejarse*) it's not as bad as all that; (*por enfadarse*) there's no need to get like that about it; **por lo ~** so, therefore; **no nos desviamos ni ~ así** we didn't deviate even by this much; **no le tengo ni ~ así de lástima** I haven't a scrap of pity for him; **¡y ~!** (*Esp*): **—¿necesitarás un descanso? —¡y ~!** "do you need a break?" — "you bet I do!"
Ⓒ ADV 1 (*con verbos*) (*indicando duración, cantidad*) so much; (*indicando frecuencia*) so often; **se preocupa ~ que no puede dormir** he gets so worried that he can't sleep, he worries so much that he can't sleep; **estoy cansada de ~ andar** I'm tired after all this walking; **no deberías trabajar ~** you shouldn't work so hard; **¡no corras ~!** don't run so fast!; **ahora no la veo ~** I don't see so *o* as much of her now, I don't see her so often now; **él gasta ~ como yo** he spends as much as I do *o* as me; **tú como yo** both you and I; **~ si viene como si no** whether he comes or not; **~ es así que** so much so that; **qué ~** (*LAm*) how much
2 (*con adjetivos, adverbios*) **los dos son ya mayores, aunque su mujer no ~** the two of them are elderly, although his wife less so; **es difícil, pero ~ como eso no creo** it's difficult, but not that difficult; **es ~ más difícil** it is all the more difficult; **~ mejor** so much the better; **~ peor** so much the worse; ✦ MODISMO **¡ni ~ ni tan calvo!** there's no need to exaggerate!
3 (*en locuciones conjuntivas*) **en ~** as (being); **estoy en contra de las leyes en ~ sistema represivo** I am against laws as (being) a repressive system; **en ~ que** (= *mientras que*) while; (= *como*) as
Ⓓ SM 1 (= *cantidad*) **me paga un ~ fijo cada semana** he pays me a fixed amount each week; **las máquinas costaron otro ~** the machines cost as much again *o* the same again
➤ **tanto alzado** fixed price ➤ **tanto por ciento** percentage
2 (= *punto*) (*Ftbl, Hockey*) goal; (*Baloncesto, Tenis*) point; **marcó dos ~s** he scored twice ➤ **tanto a favor** goal for, point for ➤ **tanto del honor** consolation goal ➤ **tanto en contra** goal against, point against
3 **estar al ~** to be up to date; **estar al ~ de los acontecimientos** to be fully abreast of events; **mantener a algn al ~ de algo** to keep sb informed about sth; **poner a algn al ~ de algo** to put sb in the picture about sth
4 **un ~** (*como adv*) rather; **estoy un ~ cansado** I'm rather tired

Tanzania SF Tanzania

tañer /2f/ VT [+ *instrumento de cuerda*] to play; [+ *campana*] to ring

tañido SM (*Mús*) sound; [*de campana*] ringing

tapa SF [*de caja, olla, piano*] lid; [*de frasco*] top; [*de depósito de gasolina*] cap; ✦ MODISMO **levantarse la ~ de los sesos** to blow one's brains out ➤ **tapa de registro** manhole cover, inspection cover 2 [*de libro*] cover; **libro de ~s duras** hardback 3 [*de zapato*] heelplate 4 (*Esp*) [*de comida*] snack (*consumed in a bar with drinks*); **ir de ~s = ir de tapeo**; *ver* **tapeo**

tapabarros SM INV (*Chi, Perú*) mudguard (*esp Brit*), fender (*EEUU*)

tapacubos SM INV hubcap

tapadera SF 1 [*de olla*] lid; [*de tarro de plástico*] top, cap
2 [*de organización*] cover, front, front organization (**de** for); [*de espía*] cover

tapadillo: **de ~** ADV secretly, stealthily

tapado ADJ 1 (*And*) (= *vago*) lazy, slack; (= *ignorante*) ignorant 2 (*Ven*) **ser ~ para algo** to be useless at sth

tapar /1a/ **Ⓐ** VT 1 (= *cubrir*) (*gen*) to cover; (*más deliberada o completamente*) to cover up; **un velo le tapaba parte de la cara** part of her face was covered by a veil; **le ~on los ojos y se lo llevaron** he was blindfolded and taken away
2 (= *cerrar*) [+ *olla, tarro*] to put the lid on; [+ *botella*] (*gen*) to put the top on; (*con corcho*) to put the cork on
3 [+ *tubo, túnel, agujero, ranura*] (= *obstruir*) block up; (= *rellenar*) to fill, fill in
4 (= *abrigar*) (*con ropa*) to wrap up; (*en la cama*) to cover up
5 (= *ocultar*) [+ *objeto*] to hide; [+ *vista*] to block; [+ *hecho, escándalo*] to cover up
6 (*Chi, Méx, And*) [+ *diente*] to fill
Ⓑ **taparse** VPR 1 (= *cubrirse*) (*gen*) to cover o.s.; (= *envolverse*) to wrap (o.s.) up
2 **~se los oídos/ojos** to cover one's ears/eyes
3 [*cañería, excusado*] (*LAm*) to get blocked

taparrabos SM INV loincloth

tapatío (*Méx*) ADJ of/from Guadalajara

tapear /1a/ VI (*Esp*) = **ir de tapeo**; *ver* **tapeo**

tapeo SM (*Esp*) **ir de ~** to go round the bars (*drinking and eating snacks*); **bar de ~** tapas bar

tapete SM (= *mantel*) tablecloth (*usually lace or embroidered*); (= *paño*) runner; (*Col, Méx*) (= *alfombra*) rug; (*tb ~ verde*) (*Naipes*) card table; ✦ MODISMOS **estar sobre el ~** to be under discussion; **poner un asunto sobre el ~** to put a matter up for discussion

tapia SF (*gen*) wall; [*de jardín*] garden wall

tapiar /1b/ VT 1 [+ *jardín, terreno*] to wall in 2 [+ *puerta, ventana*] (*con ladrillos*) to brick up; (*con tablas*) to board up

tapicería SF 1 [*de coche, muebles*] upholstery 2 (= *arte*) tapestry making

tapicero/a SM/F [*de muebles*] upholsterer

tapioca SF tapioca

tapir SM tapir

tapisca SF (*CAm, Méx*) maize harvest (*Brit*), corn harvest (*EEUU*)

tapiz SM [*de pared*] tapestry; [*de suelo*] carpet ➤ **tapiz de empapelar** (*Méx*) wallpaper

tapizar /1f/ VT [+ *muebles*] to upholster, cover; [+ *coche*] to upholster; [+ *pared*] to cover with fabric

tapón SM 1 [*de botella*] (*gen*) cap, top; [*de corcho*] cork; [*de vidrio*] stopper ➤ **tapón de rosca** screw top 2 (*en los oídos*) (*para el ruido*) earplug; [*de cera*] plug 3 [*de lavabo*] plug 4 (*Baloncesto*) block 5 (*Aut*) (= *atasco*) traffic jam 6 (*) (= *persona*) chubby person 7 (*CS Elec*) fuse

taponar /1a/ **Ⓐ** VT [+ *tubería, puerta, carretera*] to block; [+ *agujero*] to plug, block; (*Dep*) to block, stop; (*Med*) to tampon **Ⓑ taponarse** VPR [*nariz, oídos*] to get blocked up

taponazo SM (*LAm Ftbl*) shot

tapujo* SM (= *engaño*) deceit, dodge; (= *secreto*) secrecy; (= *subterfugio*) subterfuge, dodge*; **andar con ~s** to be involved in some shady business*; **sin ~s** (= *claramente*) honestly, openly; (= *sin rodeos*) without beating about the bush

taquear /1a/ VI 1 (*Perú*) to play billiards (*Brit*) *o* pool (*EEUU*) 2 (*Méx*) (= *comer tacos*) to have a snack of tacos

taquería SF (*Méx*) taco stall, taco bar

taquicardia SF abnormally rapid heartbeat, tachycardia

taquigrafía SF shorthand, stenography (*EEUU*)

taquígrafo/a SM/F shorthand writer, stenographer (*EEUU*); ✦ MODISMO **con luz y ~s** openly

taquilla SF 1 (*para billetes, entradas*) (= *sala*) ticket office, booking office (*Brit*); (= *ventanilla*) ticket window; [*de teatro, cine*] box office; **éxito de ~** box-office success, box-office hit 2 (= *recaudación*) (*Teat*) takings *pl* (*Brit*), take (*EEUU*); (*Dep*) gate money, proceeds *pl* 3 (= *armario*) locker

taquillero/a **Ⓐ** ADJ popular, successful (at the box office); **ser ~** to be good (for the) box office, be a draw, be popular **Ⓑ** SM/F clerk, ticket clerk

taquimecanografía SF shorthand typing

taquito SM (*Esp*) [*de jamón*] small cube

tara SF 1 (= *peso*) tare 2 (= *defecto*) defect, blemish

taracea SF inlay, marquetry

tarado/a **Ⓐ** ADJ 1 (*Com*) defective, imperfect 2 [*persona*] crippled 3 (*) (= *idiota*) stupid; (= *loco*) crazy, nuts* **Ⓑ** SM/F (*) (= *idiota*) cretin*, moron*

tarambana SMF, **tarambanas** SMF INV (= *casquivano*) harebrained person; (= *estrafalario*) crackpot*

tarántula SF tarantula

tarar /1a/ VT (*Com*) to tare

tararear /1a/ VT, VI to hum

tararí* **Ⓐ** ADJ (*Esp*) crazy **Ⓑ** EXCL no way!*, you must be joking!

tarasca SF 1 (= *monstruo*) carnival dragon, monster 2 (*) (= *mujer*) old hag, old bag* 3 (*Chi*) (= *boca*) big mouth

tardado ADJ (*Méx*) slow, time-consuming

tardanza SF 1 (= *demora*) delay 2 (= *lentitud*) slowness

tardar /1a/ **Ⓐ** VT **he tardado un poco por la lluvia** I'm a bit late because of the rain; **¿cuánto se tarda?** how long does it take?; **aquí tardan mucho en servirte** the service is very slow here, they take a long time to serve you here; **tardó mucho en repararlo** he took a long time to repair it **Ⓑ** VI **no tardes** don't be long; **~ en hacer algo: tardó en llegar** it took a while to arrive; **tarda en hacer efecto** it takes a while to take effect, it doesn't take effect immediately; **a más** at the latest **Ⓒ** **tardarse** VPR (*Méx*) to be long, take a long time; **no me tardo** I won't be long, I won't take long

tarde **Ⓐ** ADV (*gen*) late; (= *demasiado tarde*) too late; **llegar ~** to be late, arrive late; **ya es ~ para quejarse** it's too late to complain now; **se hace ~** it's getting late; **de ~ en ~** from time to time; **más ~** later; **~ o temprano** sooner or later **Ⓑ** SF (= *primeras horas*) afternoon; (= *últimas horas*) evening; **a las siete de la ~** at seven in the evening; **¡buenas ~s!** good afternoon!/good evening!; **en la ~** (*LAm*) ◇ **por la ~** in the afternoon/evening; **el domingo por la ~** on Sunday afternoon/evening

tardío ADJ [*periodo, producto*] late

tardo ADJ 1 (= *lento*) slow, sluggish 2 (= *torpe*) dull, dense

tarea SF 1 (= *trabajo*) task, job; **es una ~ poco grata** it's a thankless task; **todavía me queda mucha ~** I've still got a lot left to do ➤ **tareas domésticas** housework *sing*, household chores 2 (*tb* **~s**) [*de colegial*] homework *sing*

tarifa SF 1 (= *precio fijado*) [*de suministros*] rate; [*de transportes*] fare ➤ **tarifa nocturna** (*Telec*) cheap rate ➤ **tarifa plana** unmetered access ➤ **tarifa postal** postal rate ➤ **tarifa reducida** (*Transportes*) reduced fare 2 (= *lista de precios*) price list 3 (= *arancel*) tariff ➤ **tarifa aduanera** customs tariff

tarima SF 1 (= *plataforma*) platform; (= *estrado*) dais; (= *soporte*) stand 2 (= *suelo*) flooring

tarjar /1a/ VT (*And, CS*) (= *tachar*) to cross out

tarjeta SF card; **pagar con ~** to pay by (credit) card ➤ **tarjeta amarilla** (*Dep*) yellow card ➤ **tarjeta de circuitos** (*Inform*) circuit board ➤ **tarjeta de crédito** credit card ➤ **tarjeta de embarque** boarding pass ➤ **tarjeta de expansión** expansion card ➤ **tarjeta de felicitación** greetings card, greeting card (*EEUU*) ➤ **tarjeta de fidelidad** loyalty card ➤ **tarjeta de gráficos** graphics card ➤ **tarjeta de identidad** identity card ➤ **tarjeta de memoria** memory card ➤ **tarjeta de Navidad** Christmas card ➤ **tarjeta de presentación** business card ➤ **tarjeta de sonido** sound card ➤ **tarjeta de video** (*LAm*), **tarjeta de vídeo** (*Sp*) video card ➤ **tarjeta de visita** business card, visiting card ➤ **tarjeta gráfica** (*Inform*) graphics card ➤ **tarjeta monedero** electronic purse *o* wallet ➤ **tarjeta postal** postcard ➤ **tarjeta roja** (*Dep*) red card ➤ **tarjeta SIM** SIM card ➤ **tarjeta telefónica** phonecard

tarot SM tarot

tarraconense ADJ of/from Tarragona

tarrina SF [*de helado, margarina*] tub

tarro SM 1 (= *recipiente*) [*de vidrio*] jar; [*de porcelana*] pot; (*Chi*) [*de metal*] can, tin (*esp Brit*); (*Méx, Ven*) (= *taza*) mug; (= *jarra*) tankard 2 (*Esp**) (= *cabeza*) nut*, noggin (*EEUU**); ✦ MODISMOS **comer el ~ a algn** (= *engañar*) to put one over on sb*; (= *lavar el cerebro*) to brainwash sb; **comerse el ~** to rack one's brains, think hard

tarso SM tarsus

tarta SF 1 (= *pastel*) cake; (*con base de hojaldre*) tart ➤ **tarta de cumpleaños** birthday cake ➤ **tarta de manzana** apple tart ➤ **tarta de queso** cheesecake ➤ **tarta nupcial** wedding cake 2 (= *gráfico*) pie chart

tartaja* **Ⓐ** ADJ INV stammering, tongue-tied **Ⓑ** SMF INV stammerer

tartajear /1a/ VT to stammer

tartamudear /1a/ VI to stutter, stammer

tartamudeo SM stutter(ing), stammer(ing)

tartamudez SF stutter, stammer

tartamudo/a **Ⓐ** ADJ stuttering, stammering **Ⓑ** SM/F stutterer, stammerer

tartán SM tartan

tartana SF 1 (= *carruaje*) trap 2 (*Esp**) (= *coche viejo*) banger (*Brit**), clunker (*EEUU**)

tartárico ADJ tartaric; **ácido ~** tartaric acid

tártaro ADJ, SM tartar

tartera SF (= *fiambrera*) lunch box; (*para horno*) cake tin (*Brit*), cake pan (*EEUU*)

tarugo **Ⓐ** ADJ (*) stupid **Ⓑ** SM 1 (= *pedazo de madera*) lump, chunk; (= *clavija*) wooden peg; (= *tapón*) plug, stopper; (= *adoquín*) wooden paving block 2 (= *pan*) chunk of stale bread 3 (*) (= *imbécil*) chump*, blockhead*

tarumba* ADJ **volver ~ a algn** to confuse sb, get sb all mixed up; **volverse ~** to get all mixed up, get completely confused; **esa chica me tiene ~** I'm crazy about that girl

tasa SF 1 (= *precio*) rate ➤ **tasa de aeropuerto** airport tax ➤ **tasas académicas** tuition fees ➤ **tasas judiciales** legal fees 2 (= *índice*) rate ➤ **tasa de crecimiento** growth rate ➤ **tasa de interés** interest rate ➤ **tasa de mortalidad** death rate, mortality rate ➤ **tasa de natalidad** birth rate 3 (= *tasación*) valuation, appraisal (*EEUU*) 4 (= *medida, regla*) measure; **sin ~** boundless, limitless; **gastar sin ~** to spend like there's no tomorrow

tasación SF valuation, appraisal (*EEUU*); ~ **de un edificio** valuation of a building

tasador(a) SM/F valuer (*Brit*), appraiser (*EEUU*)

tasajear /1a/ VT (*Méx, Perú*) to cut, slash

tasar /1a/ VT **1** (= *valorar*) to value **2** [+ *trabajo*] to rate (**en** at) **3** (= *restringir*) to limit, put a limit on, restrict; (= *racionar*) to ration

tasca SF bar, pub (*Brit*); **ir de -'s** to go on a pub crawl (*Brit**), go bar hopping (*EEUU**)

tata* Ⓐ SM (*LAm*) (= *padre*) dad*, daddy*; (= *abuelo*) grandad* Ⓑ SF (*Esp*) (= *niñera*) nanny; (= *chacha*) maid

tatarabuelo/a SM/F great-great-grandfather/-mother; **mis ~s** my great-great-grandparents

tataranieto/a SM/F great-great-grandson/-daughter; **sus ~s** his great-great-grandchildren

ta-te-ti SM (*RPl*) noughts and crosses *sing* (*Brit*), tic tac toe (*EEUU*)

tatuaje SM **1** (= *dibujo*) tattoo **2** (= *acto*) tattooing

tatuar /1d/ VT to tattoo

taumaturgo SM miracle worker

taurino ADJ bullfighting *antes de s*; **el mundo ~** the bullfighting business; **una revista taurina** a bullfighting magazine

Tauro SM (= *signo*) Taurus

tauro SMF INV (= *persona*) Taurus; **soy ~** I'm Taurus

tauromaquia SF (art of) bullfighting, tauromachy (*frm*)

tautología SF tautology

tautológico ADJ tautological

taxativo ADJ **1** (= *restringido*) limited, restricted; [*sentido*] specific **2** (= *tajante*) sharp, emphatic

taxi SM taxi, cab; **fuimos en ~** we went by taxi ➤ **taxi colectivo** (*Col*) minibus

taxidermia SF taxidermy

taxímetro SM **1** (= *aparato*) taximeter, clock **2** (*Arg*) (= *vehículo*) taxi

taxista SMF taxi driver, cab driver (*EEUU*)

taxonomía SF taxonomy

Tayikistán SM Tadzhikistan

taza SF **1** (= *recipiente*) cup; (= *contenido*) cupful ➤ **taza de café** (= *café*) cup of coffee; (= *recipiente*) coffee cup **2** [*de fuente*] basin, bowl; [*de lavabo*] bowl; [*de retrete*] pan, bowl ➤ **taza del wáter** toilet bowl

tazón SM (= *cuenco*) bowl; (= *jarra*) mug

te¹ SF *name of the letter t*

te² PRON PERS **1** (*como complemento directo*) you; **ayer te vi en el centro** I saw you in the city centre yesterday **2** (*como complemento indirecto*) you; **te he traído esto** I've brought you this, I've brought this for you; **¿te han arreglado el ordenador?** have they fixed your computer (for you)? **3** (*con partes del cuerpo, ropa*)

Con partes del cuerpo o con prendas que se llevan puestas se usa el adjetivo posesivo:

¿te duelen los pies? do your feet hurt?; **¿te has puesto el abrigo?** have you put your coat on?
4 (*uso enfático*) **te lo comiste todo** you ate it all up; **se te ha parado el reloj** your watch has stopped
5 (*uso reflexivo o pronominal*) **¿te has lavado?** have you washed?; **¿te levantas temprano?** do you get up early?; **tienes que defenderte** you have to defend yourself; **te equivocas** you're wrong; **¿te has hecho daño?** have you hurt yourself?
6 (*uso impersonal*) **aquí siempre te intentan timar** they always try to cheat you here

té SM **1** (= *bebida*) tea **2** (*LAm*) (= *reunión*) tea-party ➤ **té canasta** *tea-party, often in aid of charity, where canasta is played*

tea SF (= *antorcha*) torch; (= *astilla*) firelighter; ✦ MODISMO **arder como una ~** to go up like a torch

teatral ADJ **1** [*grupo, temporada*] theatre *antes de s*, theater *antes de s* (*EEUU*); [*asociación, formación*] dramatic; **obra ~** play **2** (= *aparatoso*) [*persona*] theatrical; [*gesto, palabras*] dramatic, theatrical; (*pey*) histrionic, stagey

teatrero/a* Ⓐ ADJ **1** (= *exagerado*) theatrical **2** (= *aficionado*) **ser muy ~** to be a great theatre-goer Ⓑ SM/F **1** (= *aficionado*) theatre-goer **2** (= *profesional*) theatre-worker

teatro SM

En inglés americano se suele emplear **theater** en lugar de **theatre**.

1 (*gen*) theatre; (= *escenario*) stage ➤ **teatro de calle** street theatre ➤ **teatro del absurdo** theatre of the absurd ➤ **teatro de la ópera** opera house ➤ **teatro de títeres** puppet theatre ➤ **teatro de variedades** variety theatre, music hall (*esp Brit*), vaudeville theater (*EEUU*)
2 (*Literat*) (= *género*) drama; (= *obras de teatro*) plays *pl*; **el ~ del siglo XVIII** 18th century theatre *o* drama; **el ~ de Cervantes** Cervantes's plays
3 [*de suceso*] scene; (*Mil*) theatre ➤ **teatro de operaciones** theatre of operations
4 (= *exageración*) **hacer ~** (= *alborotar*) to make a fuss; (= *exagerar*) to exaggerate; **tiene mucho ~** he's always so melodramatic

tebeo SM (*Esp*) (children's) comic (*esp Brit*), comic book (*EEUU*); ✦ MODISMO **está más visto que el ~** that's old hat

teca SF teak

techado SM (= *tejado*) roof; (= *cubierta*) covering; **bajo ~** under cover, indoors

techar /1a/ VT to roof (in *o* over)

techo SM **1** (*interior*) ceiling; (*exterior, Aut*) roof; **bajo ~** indoors; **bajo el mismo ~** under the same roof; **los sin ~** the homeless ➤ **techo corredizo, techo solar** (*Aut*) sunroof **2** (= *límite, tope*) ceiling, limit; (*Fin*) ceiling; **ha tocado ~** it has reached its upper limit, it has peaked ➤ **techo de cristal** glass ceiling **3** (*Aer*) ceiling

techumbre SF roof

tecla SF (*Inform, Mús, Tip*) key; ✦ MODISMOS **dar en la ~*** (= *acertar*) to get it right; (= *aprender*) to get the hang of it; **no le queda ninguna otra ~ por tocar** there's nothing else left for him to try ➤ **tecla de edición** edit key ➤ **tecla de función** function key

teclado SM (*tb Inform*) keyboard, keys *pl*; [*de órgano*] keyboard, manual ➤ **teclado numérico** (*Inform*) numeric keypad

tecleado SM typing

teclear /1a/ Ⓐ VT (*gen*) to key in, type in; (*en cajero automático*) to enter Ⓑ VI (*en máquina de escribir, ordenador*) to type; (*en el piano*) to play

tecleo SM **1** (= *tecleado*) typing, keying **2** (*Mús*) playing

teclista SMF (*Inform*) keyboard operator, key-boarder; (*Mús*) keyboard player

técnica SF **1** (= *método*) technique **2** (= *tecnología*) technology **3** (= *destreza*) skill; *ver tb* **técnico**

tecnicismo SM **1** (= *carácter técnico*) technical nature **2** (*Ling*) technical term

técnico/a Ⓐ ADJ technical Ⓑ SM/F **1** (*en fábrica, laboratorio*) technician ➤ **técnico/a de laboratorio** laboratory technician, lab technician* ➤ **técnico/a de mantenimiento** maintenance engineer ➤ **técnico/a de sonido** sound technician, sound engineer (*esp Brit*) ➤ **técnico/a informático/a** computer programmer **2** (= *experto*) expert, specialist **3** (*Dep*) trainer, coach; *ver tb* **técnica**

tecnicolor® SM Technicolor®

tecnología SF technology; **alta ~** high technology; **nuevas ~s** new technologies ➤ **tecnología Bluetooth®** Bluetooth® technology ➤ **tecnología inalámbrica** wireless technology ➤ **tecnología punta** leading-edge technology

tecnológico ADJ technological

tecnólogo/a SM/F technologist

tecolote SM **1** (*CAm, Méx*) (= *búho*) owl **2** (*Méx**) (= *policía*) policeman, cop*

tecorral SM (*Méx*) stone wall

tectónica SF tectonics *sing*

tedio SM (= *aburrimiento*) boredom, tedium; (= *vaciedad*) sense of emptiness

tedioso ADJ tedious

Teherán SM Teheran

teja SF (roof) tile; ✦ MODISMOS **de ~s abajo** in this world, in the natural way of things; **de ~s arriba** in the next world; **pagar a toca ~** (*Esp**) to pay on the nail

tejado SM (tiled) roof

tejano/a Ⓐ ADJ, SM/F Texan Ⓑ **tejanos** SMPL (= *vaqueros*) jeans, denims

tejar /1a/ VT to tile, roof with tiles

tejaván SM (*Méx*) (= *cobertizo*) shed; (= *galería*) gallery; (= *choza*) rustic dwelling

tejedor(a) SM/F (= *persona*) weaver

tejedora SF (= *máquina*) (*de hacer punto*) knitting machine; (*de tejer*) loom

tejemaneje* SM **1** (= *intriga*) intrigue; (= *chanchullo*) shady deal*; **los políticos y sus ~s** politicians and their shady deals* **2** (= *actividad*) bustle; (= *bulla*) fuss; **se trae un tremendo ~** he's making a tremendous fuss

tejer /2a/ Ⓐ VT **1** [+ *tela*] to weave; [+ *tela de araña*] to spin, make; [+ *capullo*] to spin **2** (= *hacer punto*) to knit; (= *hacer ganchillo*) to crochet; (= *coser*) to sew **3** [+ *complot*] to hatch; [+ *plan*] to devise; [+ *mentira*] to fabricate; [+ *cambio*] to bring about little by little Ⓑ VI **1** (*en telar*) to weave **2** (= *hacer punto*) to knit; (= *hacer ganchillo*) to crochet

tejido SM **1** (= *tela*) fabric, material; **el ~ social** the social fabric ➤ **tejido de punto** knitted fabric **2** (*LAm*) (= *labor*) knitting **3** (*Anat*) tissue ➤ **tejido conjuntivo** connective tissue **4** (= *trama*) weave; (= *textura*) texture; **un ~ de intrigas** a web of intrigue

tejo[1] SM **1** (= *aro*) ring, quoit; ✦ MODISMO **echar** o **tirar los ~s a algn*** to make a play for sb **2** (= *juego*) hopscotch

tejo[2] SM (*Bot*) yew (tree)

tejón SM badger

tel. ABR (= *teléfono*) tel.

tela SF **1** (= *tejido*) cloth, fabric; (= *trozo*) piece of cloth; **un libro en ~** a clothbound book; ✦ MODISMO **poner en ~ de juicio** to (call into) question, cast doubt on ➤ **tela asfáltica** roofing felt ➤ **tela de araña** spider's web ➤ **tela de saco** sackcloth ➤ **tela metálica** wire netting **2** (*Arte*) (= *lienzo*) canvas, painting **3** (*Anat*) membrane **4** (*Bot*) skin ➤ **tela de cebolla** onion skin **5** (*Esp***) (= *dinero*) dough*, cash* **6** (*And*) (= *tortilla*) thin maize pancake **7** (*tb ~ marinera*) (*Esp**) **el asunto tiene ~ (marinera)** it's a complicated matter, there's a lot to it; **—ya va por el quinto marido —¡tiene ~ (marinera)!** "she's already on her fifth husband" — "that takes some beating!"*; **hay ~ para rato** there's lots to talk about **8** (*enfático*) **~ de****: **es ~ de guapa** she's dead o really gorgeous*

telar SM **1** (= *máquina*) loom; **telares** (= *fábrica*) textile mill *sing* **2** (*Teat*) gridiron

telaraña SF cobweb, spider's web

tele* SF TV, telly (*Brit**)

teleadicto/a* SM/F telly addict*

telebanco SM cash dispenser (*Brit*), ATM (*EEUU*)

telebasura* SF junk TV

telecabina SF (o SM) cable car

telediario SM (television) news *sing*, TV news *sing*

telecomedia SF TV comedy show

telecompra SF TV shopping

telecomunicación SF telecommunication

teleconferencia SF (= *reunión*) teleconference; (= *sistema*) teleconferencing

teledifusión SF telecast

teledirigido ADJ remote-controlled, radio-controlled

teleférico SM cable railway, aerial tramway (*EEUU*); (*para esquiadores*) ski lift

telefilm SM, **telefilme** SM TV film (*esp Brit*), TV movie (*esp EEUU*)

telefonazo* SM phone call; **te daré un ~** I'll give you a call o (*esp Brit*) ring

telefonear /1a/ VT, VI to telephone, phone (up)

telefonía SF telephony; **red de ~ móvil** cellular phone network, mobile phone network (*Brit*) ➤ **telefonía celular** cellular telephone system ➤ **telefonía fija** landline phones *pl*

telefónico ADJ telephone *antes de s*, telephonic; **llamada telefónica** telephone call

telefonista SMF (telephone) operator, telephonist

teléfono SM **1** (*Telec*) (= *aparato*) telephone, phone; (= *número*) telephone number, phone number; **coger el ~** ◇ **contestar al ~** to answer the phone; **está hablando por ~** he's on the phone; **llamar a algn por ~** to phone sb (up), ring sb up (*esp Brit*); **te llaman por** o **al ~** there's someone on the phone for you ➤ **teléfono celular** (*esp LAm*) cellular phone, mobile (phone) (*Brit*) ➤ **teléfono de tarjeta** card phone ➤ **teléfono inalámbrico** cordless (tele)phone ➤ **teléfono móvil** (*Esp*) mobile (phone) ➤ **teléfono particular** home telephone number ➤ **teléfono rojo** (*Pol*) hotline ➤ **teléfono sin hilos** cordless (tele)phone ➤ **teléfono wap** WAP(-enabled) phone **2** [*de ducha*] shower head

telegrafía SF telegraphy

telegrafiar /1c/ VT, VI to telegraph

telegráfico ADJ telegraphic, telegraph *antes de s*

telégrafo SM telegraph ➤ **telégrafo óptico** semaphore

telegrama SM telegram; **poner un ~ a algn** to send sb a telegram

telele* SM fit, queer turn; **le dio un ~** it gave him quite a turn

telemando SM remote control

telemanía SF TV addiction

telemarketing SM, **telemárketing** SM telesales *pl*

telemática SF data transmission, telematics *sing*

telemático ADJ telematic

telenoticias SFPL television news *sing*, TV news *sing*

telenovela SF soap (opera), TV serial

teleobjetivo SM telephoto lens, zoom lens

teleología SF teleology

teleoperador(a) SM/F telemarketing phone operator

telepatía SF telepathy

telepático ADJ telepathic

telequinesia SF telekinesis

telerrealidad SF reality TV

telescópico ADJ telescopic

telescopio SM telescope

teleserie SF TV series

telesilla SM o SF chair lift, ski lift

telespectador(a) SM/F viewer

telesquí SM ski lift

teletaxi SM radio cab, radio taxi

teletexto SM teletext

teletipo SM teletype, teleprinter

teletrabajador(a) SM/F teleworker

teletrabajo SM teleworking

televendedor(a) SM/F telesales person

televenta SF, **televentas** SFPL telesales

televidente SMF viewer

televisar /1a/ VT to televise

televisión SF television; **hacer ~** to work in television; **salir en** o **por ~** to be on television; **ver (la) ~** to watch television ➤ **televisión digital** digital TV ➤ **televisión en color** colour o (EEUU) color television ➤ **televisión por cable** cable television ➤ **televisión por satélite** satellite television

televisivo ADJ television antes de s; **serie televisiva** television series

televisor SM television set

télex SM INV telex

telón SM (Teat) curtain ➤ **telón de acero** (Esp Pol) Iron Curtain ➤ **telón de seguridad** safety curtain

telonero/a Ⓐ ADJ (Mús) [grupo] support antes de s Ⓑ SM/F (Mús) support band, support act; (Teat) first turn, curtain-raiser

telúrico ADJ 1 (= de la Tierra) **movimiento ~** earthquake 2 [fuerzas, corrientes] telluric

tema SM 1 (= asunto) subject; **es un ~ recurrente en su obra** it is a recurring theme in his work; **tienen ~ para rato** they have plenty to talk about; **cambiar de ~** to change the subject ➤ **tema de actualidad** topical issue ➤ **tema de conversación** talking point 2 (Ling) [de palabra] stem; [de oración] theme 3 (Mús) theme

temario SM 1 (Univ) (= temas) list of topics; (= programa) programme, program (EEUU); (= asignaturas) syllabus 2 [de oposiciones] set of topics

temática SF 1 (= conjunto de temas) subjects pl 2 (= tema) [de obra, película] subject matter

temático ADJ 1 [acuerdo, trato] thematic; **parque ~** theme park 2 (Ling) stem antes de s

temblar /1j/ VI 1 [persona] (por miedo) to tremble, shake; (por frío) to shiver; **~ de miedo** to tremble o shake with fright; **~ de frío** to shiver with cold; **echarse a ~** to get frightened; **tiemblo de pensar en lo que pueda ocurrir** I shudder to think what may happen 2 [edificio] to shake, shudder; [tierra] to shake

tembleque* SM violent shaking, shaking fit; **le entró un ~** he got the shakes, he began to shake violently

temblor SM 1 [de miedo] trembling, shaking; [de frío, fiebre] shivering; **le entró un ~ violento** he began to shake violently; **los ~es son síntomas de fiebre** shivering is a symptom of fever 2 (tb **~ de tierra**) (earth) tremor

tembloroso ADJ 1 [persona] (por miedo) shaking, trembling; (por frío) shivering; **con voz temblorosa** in a tremulous o shaky voice 2 [llama] flickering

temer /2a/ Ⓐ VT [+ persona, castigo, consecuencias] to be afraid of, fear; **~ a Dios** to fear God; **~ hacer algo** to be afraid of doing sth

> Recuérdese que las preposiciones en inglés rigen gerundio y no infinitivo, de ahí **to be afraid of doing sth.**

~ que to be afraid (that), fear (that); **teme que no vaya a volver** she's afraid o she fears (that) he might not come back

Ⓑ VI to be afraid; **no temas** don't be afraid; **~ por algo** to fear for sth

Ⓒ **temerse** VPR **ya me lo temía, es el carburador** it's the carburettor, I thought as much o I was afraid it might be; **se temen lo peor** they fear the worst; **mucho me temo que ya no lo encontrarás** I'm very much afraid (that) you won't find it now, I very much suspect (that) you won't find it now; **me temo que no** I'm afraid not

temerario ADJ 1 [persona, acto] (= imprudente) rash, reckless; (= audaz) bold 2 [juicio] hasty, rash

temeridad SF 1 (= imprudencia) rashness; (= audacia) boldness; (= prisa) hastiness 2 (= acto) rash act, folly

temeroso ADJ 1 (= con temor) fearful, frightened 2 **~ de Dios** God-fearing, full of the fear of God

temible ADJ fearsome, frightful; [adversario] fearsome, redoubtable

temor SM (= miedo) fear; **~ a** fear of; **por ~ a equivocarme** for fear of making a mistake; **sin ~ a** without fear of ➤ **temor de Dios** fear of God

témpano SM (tb **~ de hielo**) ice floe; **quedarse como un ~*** to be chilled to the bone

témpera SM tempera

temperamental ADJ temperamental

temperamento SM 1 (= manera de ser) temperament, nature; **tiene un ~ muy equilibrado** he has a very balanced temperament; **es una mujer de ~ emprendedor** she is a woman with an enterprising nature 2 (= genio) temperament; **tener ~** to be temperamental

temperante* (Méx) Ⓐ ADJ teetotal Ⓑ SMF teetotaller, abstainer

temperar /1a/ Ⓐ VT to temper Ⓑ VI (Col, Ven) to have a change of air, have a change of climate

temperatura SF temperature; **a ~ ambiente** at room temperature; **descenso/aumento de las ~s** fall/rise in temperature; **tomar la ~ a algn** to take sb's temperature

tempestad SF storm; **levantar una ~ de protestas** to raise a storm of protest ➤ **tempestad de arena** sandstorm ➤ **tempestad de nieve** snowstorm

tempestuoso ADJ stormy

templado Ⓐ ADJ 1 [líquido, comida] lukewarm; [clima] mild, temperate; (Geog) [zona] temperate 2 (= moderado) moderate, restrained; (al comer) frugal; (al beber) of sober habits, abstemious; **nervios ~s** nerves of steel 3 (Mús) well-tuned Ⓑ SM (Téc) tempering, hardening

templanza SF 1 (= virtud) temperance 2 (Meteo) mildness

templar /1a/ Ⓐ VT 1 [+ comida] (= calentar) to warm up; (= enfriar) to cool down 2 [+ clima] to make mild; [+ calor] to reduce 3 (= moderar) to moderate; [+ ánimos] to calm; [+ cólera] to restrain, control 4 (Quím) [+ solución] to dilute 5 [+ acero] to temper, harden 6 (Mús) to tune (up) Ⓑ VI (= refrescar) to get cooler; (= hacer más calor) to get warmer, get milder Ⓒ **templarse** VPR 1 [agua, ambiente] (= calentarse) to warm up, get warm; (= enfriarse) to cool down 2 [persona] to be moderate, act with restraint

templario SM Templar

temple SM 1 (Téc) (= proceso) tempering; (= efecto) temper 2 (Mús) tuning 3 (= humor) mood; **estar de mal ~** to be in a bad mood

templete SM 1 (en parque) pavilion, kiosk ➤ **templete de música** bandstand 2 (= templo) small temple; (= santuario) shrine; (= nicho) niche

templo SM 1 (= edificio de culto) temple; ✦ MODISMOS **como un ~*** (= enorme) huge, enormous; (= excelente) first-rate, excellent; **una verdad como un ~** a glaring truth 2 (= iglesia) church ➤ **templo metodista** Methodist church o chapel ➤ **templo protestante** Protestant church

templón* SM (Ven) pull, tug

tempo SM tempo

temporada SF 1 (= periodo determinado) season; **en plena ~** at the height of the season; **estar fuera de ~** to be out of season ➤ **temporada alta** high season ➤ **temporada baja** low season ➤ **temporada de esquí** ski season 2 (= periodo indeterminado) period; **llevan una ~ de peleas continuas** they've been going through a phase o period of constant squabbling; **nos vamos a pasar una temporada al campo** we're going to spend some time in the country; — **¿tienes mucho trabajo? —va a o por ~s** "have you got a lot of work?" — "it's a bit on and off o it goes in phases"*

temporal Ⓐ ADJ 1 (= provisional) temporary; [trabajo] temporary, casual; (en turismo, agricultura) seasonal 2 (Anat) temporal Ⓑ SM 1 (= tormenta) storm; (= mal tiempo) spell of rough weather; ✦ MODISMO **capear el ~** to weather the storm, ride out the storm ➤ **temporal de agua, temporal de lluvia** (= tormenta) rainstorm; (= período lluvioso) rainy weather, prolonged rain 2 (Anat) temporal bone

temporalero/a SM/F (*Méx*) *wet-season agricultural worker*

temporario ADJ (*LAm*) (= *provisional*) temporary; (*en turismo, agricultura*) seasonal

témporas SFPL ember days

temporero/a **Ⓐ** ADJ [*obrero*] (= *eventual*) temporary, casual; (= *de temporada*) seasonal **Ⓑ** SM/F (= *eventual*) casual worker; (= *de temporada*) seasonal worker

temporizador **Ⓐ** ADJ **mecanismo** ~ timing device **Ⓑ** SM timer, timing device

tempranero ADJ **1** [*fruta*] early **2** [*persona*] **ser** ~ to be an early riser

temprano **Ⓐ** ADJ early; **a una edad temprana** at an early age **Ⓑ** ADV early; **ayer me acosté** ~ I went to bed early yesterday; **aún es** ~ **para conocer los resultados** it's too soon to know the results yet

ten *ver* **tener**

tenacidad SF **1** (= *perseverancia*) tenacity **2** (= *persistencia*) [*de dolor*] persistence; [*de mancha*] stubbornness; [*de creencia*] strength, stubbornness (*pey*); [*de resistencia*] tenacity **3** [*de material*] toughness, resilience

tenacillas SFPL (*para azúcar*) sugar tongs; (*para cabello*) curling tongs, curling irons (*EEUU*); (*Med*) tweezers, forceps

tenaz ADJ **1** [*persona*] (= *perseverante*) tenacious, persistent **2** (= *persistente*) [*dolor*] persistent; [*mancha*] stubborn; [*creencia*] firm, stubborn (*pey*); [*resistencia*] tenacious **3** [*material*] tough, durable, resistant **4** (*Col**) (= *difícil*) [*examen, problema*] tough

tenazas SFPL (*Téc*) pliers, pincers; [*de cocina, para el fuego*] tongs; (*Med*) forceps

tenca SF (= *pez*) tench

tendal* SM **1** (*And, CAm*) (*para café*) *sunny place for drying coffee* **2** (*RPl*) [*de cosas diseminadas*] **siempre deja este** ~ **de ropa** he always leaves his clothes scattered over the floor like this

tendalada* SF (*Chi*) *a lot of scattered objects or people*; **una** ~ **de** a lot of, loads of*

tendedero SM (= *lugar*) drying place; (= *cuerda*) clothes line, washing line; (= *armazón*) clothes horse

tendencia SF tendency, trend; **tengo** ~ **a engordar** I have a tendency o I tend to put on weight ➤ **tendencia al alza** upward trend ➤ **tendencia bajista** downward trend

tendencioso ADJ tendentious

tender /2g/ **Ⓐ** VT **1** (= *extender*) [+ *herido, paciente*] to lay; [+ *mantel*] to spread; (*Naipes*) to lay down **2** (= *colgar*) [+ *ropa*] to hang out; [+ *cuerda*] to stretch **3** (= *acercar*) [+ *lápiz, libro*] to hold out; **me tendió la mano** he stretched o held out his hand to me **4** [+ *trampa*] to set, lay **5** (= *construir*) [+ *puente, ferrocarril*] to build; [+ *cable, vía*] to lay **6** (*LAm*) ~ **la cama** to make the bed; ~ **la mesa** to set o (*esp Brit*) lay the table **7** [+ *arco*] to draw **Ⓑ** VI **1** ~ **a hacer algo** to tend to do sth **2** ~ **a algo** to tend to o towards sth; **tiende al egocentrismo** she tends to self-centredness; **la inflación tiende al alza** the trend is for inflation to go up **Ⓒ** **tenderse** VPR **1** (= *acostarse*) to lie down, stretch (o.s.) out **2** [*caballo*] to run at full gallop

tenderete SM **1** (*en mercado*) (= *puesto*) (market) stall; (= *carretón*) barrow (*Brit*), pushcart (*EEUU*); **montar un** ~ to set up a stall **2** (= *géneros*) display of goods for sale **3** (*para ropa lavada*) = **tendedero**

tendero/a SM/F (*gen*) shopkeeper (*Brit*), storekeeper (*EEUU*); [*de comestibles*] grocer

tendido **Ⓐ** ADJ **1** [*persona*] lying, lying down; **estaba tendida en el suelo** she was lying on the ground **2** [*galope*] fast **Ⓑ** SM **1** (= *ropa lavada*) washing, clothes *pl* (*tb* ~**s**) (*hung out to dry*) **2** (*Taur*) front rows of seats **3** [*de cable*] (*por tierra*) laying; (*por el aire*) hanging; [*de vía*] laying **4** (= *cables*) wires *pl* ➤ **tendido de alta tensión** high

voltage power line ➤ **tendido eléctrico** power line, overhead cables *pl*, overhead lines *pl* **5** (*And, Méx*) (= *ropa de cama*) bedclothes *pl* **6** (*Méx**) (= *cadáver*) corpse

tendinitis SF INV tendinitis, tendonitis

tendón SM tendon, sinew ➤ **tendón de Aquiles** Achilles' tendon

tendonitis SF INV tendinitis, tendonitis

tendré *etc ver* **tener**

tenebroso ADJ **1** (= *oscuro*) dark, gloomy **2** [*perspectiva*] gloomy, black **3** (*pey*) [*complot, pasado*] sinister **4** [*estilo*] obscure

tenedor(a) **Ⓐ** SM/F (*Com, Fin*) holder, bearer ➤ **tenedor(a) de acciones** shareholder ➤ **tenedor(a) de libros** book-keeper **Ⓑ** SM [*de mesa*] fork; **restaurante de cinco** ~**es** ≈ five-star restaurant

tenencia SF **1** (= *posesión*) [*de vivienda*] tenancy, occupancy; [*de propiedad*] possession; ~ **de drogas** possession of drugs; ~ **ilícita de armas** illegal possession of weapons **2** [*de cargo*] tenure ➤ **tenencia asegurada** security of tenure **3** (= *puesto*) ~ **de alcaldía** post of deputy mayor **4** (*Méx*) (= *impuesto*) road tax

---

tener /2k/

Ⓐ VERBO TRANSITIVO	**Ⓒ** VERBO PRONOMINAL
Ⓑ VERBO AUXILIAR	

Para las expresiones como **tener cuidado**, **tener ganas**, **tener suerte**, **tener de particular**, **tener en cuenta** *etc, ver la entrada correspondiente a la otra palabra.*

---

tener **Ⓐ** VERBO TRANSITIVO

El uso de **got** con el verbo **have** es más frecuente en inglés británico, pero sólo se usa en el presente.

---

1 (= *poseer, disponer de*) to have, have got; **¿tienes un bolígrafo?** do you have o have you got a pen?; **ahora no tengo tiempo** I don't have o I haven't got time now **2** (*referido a aspecto*) to have, have got; **tiene el pelo rubio** he has blond hair, he's got blond hair; **tenía el pelo mojado** his hair was wet **3** (*referido a edad*) to be; **tiene siete años** he's seven (years old); **¿cuántos años tienes?** how old are you? **4** (*referido a ocupaciones*) to have, have got; **el lunes tenemos una reunión** we're having a meeting on Monday, we've got a meeting on Monday; **mañana tengo una fiesta** I'm going to a party tomorrow **5** (= *parir*) to have; **va a** ~ **un niño** she's going to have a baby **6** (= *medir*) to be; ~ **5cm de ancho** to be 5cm wide **7** (= *sentir*) (+ SUSTANTIVO) to be + *adj*; ~ **hambre/sed/calor/frío** to be hungry/thirsty/hot/cold; **no tengas tantos celos** don't be so jealous; **le tengo mucho cariño** I'm very fond of him **8** (= *padecer, sufrir*) to have; **han tenido un accidente** they have had an accident; **tengo fiebre** I have o I've got a (high) temperature **9** (= *sostener*) to hold; **tenme el vaso un momento, por favor** hold my glass for me for a moment, please; **¡ten!** ◇ **¡aquí tienes!** here you are! **10** (= *recibir*) to have; **aún no he tenido carta** I haven't had a letter yet; **¿has tenido noticias suyas?** have you heard from her? **11** (= *pensar, considerar*) ~ **a bien hacer algo** to see fit to do sth; ~ **a algn en algo**: **te tendrán en más estima** they will hold you in higher esteem; ~ **a algn por** (+ ADJ) to consider sb (to be) + *adj*; **le tengo por poco honrado** I consider him (to be) rather dishonest; **ten por seguro que ...** rest assured that ... **12**

◆ **tener algo que** + INFIN: **tengo trabajo que hacer** I have o I've got work to do; **eso no tiene nada que ver** that has o that's got nothing to do with it **13** (*locuciones*) **ya saben dónde me tienen** you always know where you can find me; **¡ahí lo tienes!** there you are!, there you have it!; **~ algo de** (+ ADJ): **de bueno no tiene nada** there's nothing good about it; **no tiene nada de particular** it's nothing special; **¿qué tiene de malo?** what's wrong with that?; **~lo difícil** to find it difficult; **~lo fácil** to have it easy; ✦ MODISMOS **¿(conque) ésas tenemos?** so that's the game, is it?, so it's like that, is it?; **no ~las todas consigo** (= *dudar*) to be dubious *o* unsure; (= *desconfiar*) to be uneasy, be wary; **~ todas las de perder** to be fighting a losing battle, look like losing

Ⓑ VERBO AUXILIAR **1**
◆ **tener que** + INFIN **1.1** *(indicando obligación)* **tengo que comprarlo** I have to *o* I've got to buy it, I must buy it; **tuvo que devolver todo el dinero** he had to pay all the money back; **tiene que ser así** it has to be this way
1.2 *(indicando suposición, probabilidad)* **¡tienes que estar cansadísima!** you must be really tired!; **tiene que dolerte mucho ¿no?** it must hurt a lot, mustn't it?
1.3 *(en reproches)* **¡tendrías que haberlo dicho antes!** you should have said so before!; **¡tú tenías que ser!** it would be you!, it had to be you!
1.4 *(en sugerencias, recomendaciones)* **tendrías que comer más** you should eat more
2 (+ PARTICIPIO) **tenía puesto el sombrero** he had his hat on; **nos tenían preparada una sorpresa** they had prepared a surprise for us; **tenía pensado llamarte** I had been thinking of phoning you
3 (+ ADJ) **procura ~ contentos a todos** he tries to keep everybody happy
4 *(esp Méx)* (= *llevar*) **tienen tres meses de no cobrar** they haven't been paid for three months, it's three months since they've been paid; **tengo cuatro años aquí** I've been here for four years
Ⓒ tenerse VERBO PRONOMINAL
1 (= *sostenerse*) **~se firme** *(lit)* to stand upright; *(fig)* to stand firm; **~se de** *o* **en pie** to stand up; **no se tiene en pie** he can hardly stand; **estoy que no me tengo de sueño** I'm falling asleep on my feet, I'm about to drop
2 (= *considerarse*) **se tiene por muy listo** he thinks himself very clever, he thinks he's very clever

tenga, tengo *ver* **tener**

tenia SF tapeworm

tenida SF *(Chi)* outfit

teniente SMF (SF *a veces* **tenienta**) **1** *(Mil)* lieutenant, first lieutenant *(EEUU)* ➤ **teniente coronel** lieutenant colonel ➤ **teniente general** lieutenant general **2** (= *ayudante*) deputy, assistant ➤ **teniente de alcalde** deputy mayor

tenis SM INV **1** (= *deporte*) tennis ➤ **tenis de mesa** table tennis **2** (= *zapato*) tennis shoe, plimsoll

tenista SMF tennis player

tenor[1] SM *(Mús)* tenor

tenor[2] SM (= *sentido*) meaning, sense; **el ~ de esta declaración** the tenor of this statement; **a ~ de** (= *según*) according to; *(Jur)* in accordance with

tensar /1a/ **Ⓐ** VT [+ *cable, cuerda*] to tighten, tauten; [+ *músculo*] to tense; [+ *arco*] to draw; [+ *relaciones*] to strain **Ⓑ tensarse** VPR [*relaciones*] to become strained

tensión SF **1** [*de cable, cuerda*] tension, tautness **2** [*de músculos*] tension; **con los músculos en ~** with one's muscles all tensed up **3** *(Med)* blood pressure; **tener la ~ alta** to have high blood pressure; **tomarse la ~** to have one's blood pressure taken ➤ **tensión arterial** blood pressure **4** *(Elec)* [*voltaje*] tension, voltage; **alta ~** high tension **5** [*de gas*] pressure **6** (= *estrés*) strain, stress; **estar en ~** to be tense ➤ **tensión nerviosa** nervous strain, nervous tension ➤ **tensión premenstrual** premenstrual tension, PMT **7** *(en situación)* tension, tenseness; **hubo momentos de gran ~** there were some very tense moments ➤ **tensión racial** racial tension

tenso ADJ **1** (= *tirante*) tense, taut **2** [*persona, situación*] tense; [*relaciones*] strained

tensor Ⓐ SM *(Téc)* guy, strut; *(Anat)* tensor; [*de cuello*] stiffener; *(Dep)* chest expander **Ⓑ** ADJ tensile

tentación SF **1** (= *impulso*) temptation; **resistir (a) la ~** to resist temptation; **vencer la ~** to overcome temptation **2** (*) (= *cosa tentadora*) **las gambas son mi ~** I can't resist prawns; **¡eres mi ~!** you'll be the ruin of me!

tentáculo SM tentacle

tentado ADJ **estuve ~ de decírselo** I was tempted to tell him

tentador(a) Ⓐ ADJ tempting **Ⓑ** SM/F tempter/temptress

tentar /1j/ **Ⓐ** VT **1** (= *seducir*) to tempt; **me tentó con una copita de anís** she tempted me with a glass of anisette; **no me tienta nada la idea** I can't say I fancy the idea* **2** (= *palpar*) to feel; *(Med)* to probe **3** (= *probar*) to test, try (out) **Ⓑ tentarse** (*) VPR *(CS)* to give in (to temptation)

tentativa SF (= *intento*) attempt; *(Jur)* criminal attempt ➤ **tentativa de robo** attempted robbery

tentempié* SM snack, bite

tenue ADJ **1** [*tela, velo*] thin, fine **2** [*olor, sonido, línea*] faint; [*neblina, lluvia*] light; [*aire*] thin **3** [*razón*] tenuous, insubstantial; [*relación*] tenuous **4** [*estilo*] simple, plain

teñido SM dying

teñir /3h, 3k/ **Ⓐ** VT **1** [+ *pelo, ropa*] to dye; **~ una prenda de azul** to dye a garment blue **2** (= *manchar*) to stain; **teñido de sangre** stained with blood **3** (= *matizar*) to tinge (**de** with) **4** *(Arte)* [+ *color*] to darken **Ⓑ teñirse** VPR **1** **~se el pelo** to dye one's hair **2** **el mar se tiñó de negro** *(liter)* the sea darkened

teocracia SF theocracy

teologal ADJ **las virtudes ~es** the three Christian virtues *(faith, hope and charity)*

teología SF theology

teológico ADJ theological

teólogo/a SM/F theologian, theologist

teorema SM theorem

teoría SF theory; **en ~** in theory, theoretically ➤ **teoría de conjuntos** set theory ➤ **teoría de la relatividad** theory of relativity

teóricamente ADV theoretically, in theory

teórico/a Ⓐ ADJ theoretic(al); **examen ~** theory (exam) **Ⓑ** SM/F theoretician, theorist

teorizar /1f/ VI to theorize

tepalcate SM *(Méx)* **1** (= *fragmento*) shard, piece of broken pottery **2** (= *cacharro*) piece of junk

tepetate SM *(Méx)* limestone

tequesquite SM *(Méx) salt made by evaporation from salt lakes*

tequila SM tequila

terapeuta SMF therapist

terapéutica SF therapeutics *sing*

terapéutico ADJ therapeutic(al)

terapia SF therapy ➤ **terapia de choque** shock therapy ➤ **terapia de grupo** group therapy ➤ **terapia intensiva** *(Méx, RPl)* intensive care ➤ **terapia ocupacional** occupational therapy

tercer ADJ *ver* **tercero**

tercera SF **1** *(Mús)* third **2** *(Aut)* third (gear) **3** (= *clase*) third class; *ver tb* **tercero**

tercermundista Ⓐ ADJ third-world *antes de s*; *(pey)* *(fig)* backward **Ⓑ** SM third-world country

tercero/a Ⓐ PRON, ADJ *(antes de sm sing* **tercer**) *(numeral)* third; **la tercera vez** the third time; **terceras personas** third parties; **tercer grado (penitenciario)** *lowest category within the prison system which allows day release privileges*; **Tercer Mundo** Third World; ✦ MODISMO **a la tercera va la vencida** third time lucky; *ver tb* **sexto, edad 1 Ⓑ** SM/F **1** (= *árbitro*) mediator, arbitrator; *(Jur)* third party ➤ **tercero en discordia** third party **2** *(pey)* (= *alcahuete*) procurer/procuress, go-between; *ver tb* **tercera**

terceto SM **1** *(Mús)* trio **2** *(Literat)* tercet, triplet

terciado ADJ **1** *(Esp)* *(en tamaño)* **una merluza terciada** a medium-sized hake **2** *(Esp)* (= *usado*) **está ~ ya** [*botella*] it's a third finished **3** **llevar algo ~** [+ *bolso, arma*] to wear sth crosswise *o* across one's chest *etc*; **con el sombrero** ~ with his hat at a rakish angle

terciar /1b/ **Ⓐ** VT 1 (*Mat*) (= *dividir entre tres*) to divide into three
2 (= *inclinar*) to slant, slope; [+ *arma*] to wear (diagonally) across one's chest; [+ *sombrero*] to tilt, wear on the slant 3 (*Méx*) (= *mezclar*) to mix, blend
Ⓑ VI 1 (= *mediar*) to mediate; ~ **entre dos rivales** to mediate between two rivals; **yo ~é con el jefe** I'll have a word with the boss
2 (= *participar*) ~ **en algo** to take part in sth, join in sth
Ⓒ **terciarse** VPR (*Esp*) **si se tercia, él también sabe hacerlo** if it comes to that, he knows how to do it too; **si se tercia una buena oportunidad** if a good chance presents itself *o* comes up

terciario ADJ tertiary

tercio SM 1 (= *tercera parte*) third; **dos ~s** two thirds 2 (*Taur*) stage, part (*of the bullfight*); **cambiar de** ~ (*Taur*) to enter the next stage (*of the bullfight*); (= *cambiar de tema*) to change the subject 3 (*Mil, Hist*) regiment, corps ➤ **tercio extranjero** foreign legion 4 **hacer buen ~ a algn** ➤ (= *hacer favor*) to do sb a service; (= *ser útil*) to serve sb well, be useful to sb; **hacer mal ~ a algn** to do sb a bad turn 5 (*Carib*) (= *hombre*) fellow, guy*

terciopelo SM velvet

terco ADJ stubborn, obstinate; ✦ MODISMO ~ **como una mula** as stubborn as a mule

tergal® SM Terylene® (*Brit*), Dacron® (*EEUU*)

tergiversación SF distortion

tergiversar /1a/ VT to distort, twist (the sense of)

termal ADJ thermal

termas SFPL (= *baños*) thermal baths; (= *manantiales*) thermal springs, hot springs

térmica[1] SF (= *corriente*) thermal, hot-air current

térmica[2] SF (*tb* **central** ~) power station

térmico ADJ thermic, heat *antes de s*; [*cristal*] heated

terminación SF 1 (= *finalización*) ending, termination; **la fecha prevista para la ~ de las obras** the date work was due to be finished 2 (*Ling*) ending, termination 3 (*CS Téc*) (= *acabado*) finish, finishing 4 ➤ **terminaciones nerviosas** nerve endings

terminado **Ⓐ** SM (*Téc*) finish, finishing **Ⓑ** ADJ (= *acabado*) finished; **bien** ~ well finished

terminal **Ⓐ** ADJ 1 (= *final*) [*enfermedad, estación*] terminal; **un enfermo en fase** ~ a terminal patient; **los enfermos ~es** the terminally ill 2 (*Bot*) [*hoja, rama*] terminal **Ⓑ** SM (*a veces* SF) (*Elec, Inform*) terminal ➤ **terminal informático** computer terminal **Ⓒ** SF (*a veces* SM) (*Aer, Náut*) terminal; [*de autobuses, trenes*] terminus ➤ **terminal de carga** freight terminal

terminante ADJ [*respuesta*] categorical, conclusive; [*negativa*] flat, outright; [*prohibición*] strict; [*decisión*] final

terminantemente ADV [*responder*] categorically, conclusively; [*negar*] flatly; [*prohibir*] strictly; **queda ~ prohibido fumar en clase** smoking during lectures is strictly forbidden

terminar /1a/ **Ⓐ** VT to finish; **he terminado el libro** I've finished the book; **quiso ~ sus días al lado del mar** she wanted to end her days by the sea
Ⓑ VI 1 [*persona*] 1.1 (*en una acción, un trabajo*) to finish; **¿todavía no has terminado?** haven't you finished yet?; ~ **de hacer algo** to finish doing sth, stop doing sth; **cuando termine de hablar** when he finishes *o* stops speaking; **terminaba de salir del baño** she had just got out of the bath; **no me cae mal, pero no termina de convencerme** I don't dislike him, but I'm not too sure about him either 1.2 (*de una forma determinada*) to end up; **terminé rendido** I ended up exhausted; **~on peleándose** they ended up fighting 1.3 ~ **con**: **han terminado con todas las provisiones** they've finished off all the supplies; **un cáncer terminó con su vida** cancer killed him; **he terminado con Andrés** I've broken up with *o* finished with Andrés; **¡estos niños van a ~ conmigo!** these children will be the death of me! 1.4 ~ **por hacer algo** to end up doing sth; **seguro que**

~á por dimitir I bet he ends up resigning
2 [*obra, acto*] to end; **la ceremonia terminó con un baile** the ceremony ended with a dance; **estoy deseando que termine este año** I can't wait for this year to be over *o* to end
3 [*objeto, palabra*] ~ **en algo** to end in sth
4 (*Inform*) to quit
Ⓒ **terminarse** VPR 1 [*obra, acto*] to end
2 [*comida, gasolina, carrete*] to run out; **se nos ha terminado el café** we've run out of coffee
3 (*enfático*) to finish; **me terminé el libro en dos días** I finished the book in two days; **termínate la copa y vámonos** finish your drink and let's go, drink up and let's go

término SM 1 (= *fin*) end, conclusion (*frm*); **al ~ del partido/del debate** at the end *o* (*frm*) conclusion of the match/of the debate; **dar ~ a** [+ *situación*] to end; [+ *labor*] to complete; **llegar a ~** [*negociación, proyecto*] to be completed, come to a conclusion; [*embarazo*] to go to (full) term; **llevar algo a ~** to bring sth to a conclusion; **poner ~ a algo** to put an end to sth
2 (= *lugar*) **primer** ~ [*de imagen*] foreground; **en primer ~** in the foreground; **de ahí se deduce, en primer ~, que ...** thus we may deduce, firstly, that ...; **segundo** ~ middle distance; **con la recesión el problema pasó a un segundo ~** with the recession the problem took second place; **en último** ~ (= *en último lugar*) ultimately; (= *si no hay otro remedio*) as a last resort; **la decisión, en último ~, es suya** ultimately, the decision is his; **la causa fue, en último ~, la crisis económica** the cause was, in the final *o* last analysis, the economic crisis; **en último ~ puedes dormir en el sofá** if the worst comes to the worst, you can always sleep on the sofa ➤ **término medio** (= *punto medio*) happy medium; (= *solución intermedia*) compromise, middle way; **como** *o* **por ~ medio** on average
3 (*Ling*) [*palabra, expresión*] term
4 **términos** 4.1 (= *palabras*) terms; **en ~s de productividad** in terms of productivity; **en ~s generales** in general terms, generally speaking; **en ~s reales** in real terms
4.2 (= *condiciones*) [*de contrato, acuerdo, tregua*] terms; **estar en buenos ~s con algn** to be on good terms with sb
5 (*Mat, Fil*) [*de fracción, ecuación*] term; ✦ MODISMO **invertir los ~s** to reverse the roles
6 (= *límite*) [*de terreno*] boundary, limit; (= *en carretera*) boundary stone ➤ **término municipal** municipal district, municipal area
7 (= *plazo*) period, term (*frm*); **en el ~ de diez días** within a period *o* (*frm*) term of ten days
8 (*Col, Méx*) (*en restaurante*) —**¿qué ~ quiere la carne?** —**término medio, por favor** "how would you like the meat?" — "medium, please"

terminología SF terminology

terminológico ADJ terminological

termita SF, **térmite** SF termite

termo SM (= *frasco*) Thermos flask®

termoaislante ADJ heat-insulating

termodinámica SF thermodynamics *sing*

termómetro SM thermometer

termonuclear ADJ thermonuclear

termostato SM thermostat

terna SF short list (*of three candidates*)

ternario ADJ ternary

ternera SF 1 (*Agr*) (heifer) calf 2 (*Culin*) veal

ternero SM (*Agr*) calf

ternilla SF cartilage

terno SM 1 (= *grupo de tres*) set of three, group of three; (= *trío*) trio 2 (= *traje*) three-piece suit; (*LAm*) suit

ternura SF (= *sentimiento*) tenderness; (= *cariño*) affection, fondness; **miró a los niños con ~** she looked fondly *o* tenderly at the children

terquedad SF 1 (= *obstinación*) stubbornness, obstinacy 2 (= *dureza*) hardness, toughness

terracota SF terracotta

terrado SM (= *tejado*) flat roof; (= *terraza*) terrace

terral SM (*And, Méx*) cloud of dust

Terranova SF Newfoundland

terraplén SM 1 (*en carretera, ferrocarril*) embankment 2 (*Agr*) terrace 3 (= *cuesta*) slope

terráqueo/a Ⓐ ADJ earth *antes de s*, terrestrial (*frm*); **globo** ~ globe Ⓑ SM/F earthling

terrario SM terrarium

terrateniente SMF landowner

terraza SF 1 (*Arquit*) (= *balcón*) balcony; (= *azotea*) flat roof, terrace 2 (= *café*) pavement café (*Brit*), sidewalk café (*EEUU*); **nos sentamos en la ~ de un café** we sat outside a cafe 3 (*Agr*) terrace

terrazo SM terrazzo

terregal SM (*Méx*) (= *tierra*) loose earth, dusty soil; (= *polvareda*) cloud of dust

terremoto SM earthquake

terrenal ADJ worldly; **la vida** ~ worldly life, earthly life

terreno Ⓐ ADJ 1 (*Rel*) [*bienes*] earthly; **esta vida terrena** this earthly life (*liter*) 2 (*Biol, Geol*) terrestrial Ⓑ SM 1 (= *extensión de tierra*) (*gen*) land; (= *parcela*) piece of land, plot of land; **30 hectáreas de** ~ 30 hectares of land; **es ~ municipal** it is council land; **nos hemos comprado un ~ en las afueras** we've bought a piece of land *o* plot of land *o* some land on the outskirts of the city; **el ~ que antes ocupaba la fábrica** the site the factory used to be on 2 (*explicando sus características*) [*en relieve*] ground, terrain; [*en composición*] soil, land; **un ~ pedregoso** stony ground *o* terrain; **estamos sobre un ~ arenoso** we're on sandy soil *o* land; **vehículos todo** ~ all-terrain vehicles 3 (= *campo de acción*) [*de estudio*] field; [*de actividad*] sphere, field; **se ha avanzado poco en este** ~ little progress has been made in this area 4 ✦ MODISMOS **ceder** ~ to give ground (**a, ante** to); **pisar ~ firme** to be on safe *o* firm *o* solid ground; **ganar** ~ to gain ground; **perder** ~ to lose ground; **saber** *o* **conocer el ~ que se pisa** to be on familiar ground; **preparar el** ~ to pave the way; **sobre el** ~ on the ground; **analizarán la situación sobre el** ~ they will analyse the situation on the ground; **resolveremos el problema sobre el** ~ we will solve the problem as we go along; ~ **abonado**: **es** ~ **abonado para el vicio** it is a breeding ground for vice; **dichas tendencias han encontrado el** ~ **abonado entre la juventud** these trends have found a fertile breeding ground amongst the young 5 (*Dep*) **empataron en su** ~ they drew at home; **perdieron en su propio** ~ they lost on their home ground (*Brit*) *o* field (*EEUU*) ➤ **terreno de juego** pitch, field

terrestre ADJ 1 (= *de la Tierra*) **la atmósfera** ~ the earth's atmosphere; **la superficie** ~ the surface of the earth, the earth's surface 2 (= *ni de aire ni de agua*) [*fuerzas, tropas*] ground *antes de s*, land *antes de s*; [*minas, frontera*] land *antes de s*; [*transporte*] land *antes de s*, terrestrial (*frm*); [*ofensiva*] (= *no aérea*) ground *antes de s*; (= *no por mar*) land *antes de s* 3 (*Téc, TV*) terrestrial 4 [*animal, vegetación*] land *antes de s*, terrestrial (*frm*) 5 (*Rel*) earthly

terrible ADJ terrible, awful

terrícola SMF earthling

territorial ADJ (= *de territorio*) territorial; (= *de región*) regional

territorio SM territory; **en todo el ~ nacional** in the whole country

terrón SM 1 [*de tierra*] clod, lump 2 [*de azúcar*] lump; **azúcar en ~es** lump sugar

terror SM terror; **película de** ~ horror film (*esp Brit*) *o* movie (*esp EEUU*); **me da** ~ **pensar que tengo que hablar con él** the thought of having to speak to him terrifies me, it terrifies me to think I have to speak to him ➤ **terrores nocturnos** nightmares

terrorífico ADJ terrifying, frightening

terrorismo SM terrorism

terrorista ADJ, SMF terrorist

terruño SM (= *parcela de tierra*) plot, piece of ground; (= *tierra nativa*) native soil, home (ground); **apego al** ~ attachment to one's native soil

terso ADJ 1 (= *liso*) smooth; (= *brillante*) shiny, glossy; **piel tersa** smooth skin, soft skin 2 [*estilo*] polished, smooth

tersura SF 1 (= *suavidad*) smoothness; (= *brillo*) shine, glossiness 2 [*de estilo, lenguaje*] smoothness, flow

tertulia SF social gathering, regular informal gathering ➤ **tertulia literaria** literary circle, literary gathering ➤ **tertulia radiofónica** radio talk show

tertuliano/a SM/F 1 (= *contertulio*) member of a social gathering 2 (*Radio, TV*) talk show guest

tesauro SM thesaurus

tesina SF dissertation, minor thesis

tesis SF INV 1 (*Univ*) thesis ➤ **tesis doctoral** doctoral thesis, doctoral dissertation (*EEUU*), PhD thesis 2 (*Fil*) thesis 3 (= *teoría*) **su** ~ **es insostenible** his theory is untenable; **las ~ de la defensa** the defence's arguments

tesitura SF 1 (= *mental*) attitude, frame of mind 2 (*Mús*) tessitura

tesón SM tenacity, persistence; **resistir con** ~ to resist tenaciously

tesonero ADJ (*LAm*) tenacious, persistent

tesorería SF 1 (= *cargo*) treasurership, office of treasurer 2 (= *oficina*) treasury 3 (= *activo disponible*) liquid assets *pl*

tesorero/a SM/F treasurer

tesoro SM 1 (*de mucho valor*) treasure; **valer un** ~ to be worth a fortune; **tenemos una cocinera que es todo un** ~ we have a cook who is a real treasure, we have a real gem of a cook 2 (*en oración directa*) darling; **¡sí, ~!** yes, my darling! 3 **el Tesoro** (*tb* **el Tesoro Público**) the Exchequer, the Treasury

test [tes] SM (*pl* ~**s** [tes]) test; **examen tipo** ~ multiple-choice exam ➤ **test de embarazo** pregnancy test

testa SF head

testador(a) SM/F testator/testatrix

testaferro SM front man

testamentario/a Ⓐ ADJ testamentary Ⓑ SM/F executor/executrix

testamento SM 1 (*Jur*) will, testament; **hacer** ~ to make one's will 2 (*Biblia*) **Antiguo Testamento** Old Testament; **Nuevo Testamento** New Testament

testar /1a/ VI to make a will

testarudo ADJ stubborn, pigheaded

testículo SM testicle

testificar /1g/ Ⓐ VT (= *atestiguar*) to attest; (*en juicio*) to testify to, give evidence of Ⓑ VI (*en juicio*) to testify, give evidence; ~ **de** (= *atestiguar*) to attest; (= *dar testimonio*) to testify to, give evidence of

testigo Ⓐ SMF 1 (*Jur*) witness; [*de boda, contrato*] witness; **citar a algn como** ~ to call sb as a witness ➤ **testigo de cargo** witness for the prosecution ➤ **testigo de descargo** witness for the defence ➤ **testigo ocular, testigo presencial** eyewitness 2 (= *espectador*) witness; **declaró un** ~ **del accidente** a person who had witnessed the accident gave evidence; **tú eres** ~ **de que nunca le he pegado** you can testify to *o* vouch for the fact that I have never hit him; **pongo al cielo por** ~ as God is my witness 3 (*Rel*) ➤ **testigo de Jehová** Jehovah's witness Ⓑ SM 1 (*Dep*) (*en relevos*) baton 2 (*Aut*) ~ **luminoso** warning light

testimonial ADJ token, nominal

testimoniar /1b/ Ⓐ VT (= *testificar*) to testify to, bear witness to; (= *mostrar*) to show, demonstrate Ⓑ VI to testify, bear witness

testimonio SM 1 (*Jur*) (= *declaración*) testimony, evidence; (= *afidávit*) affidavit; **dar** ~ to testify (**de** to), give evidence (**de** of); **falso** ~ perjury, false testimony 2 (= *prueba*) proof; (= *indicación*) evidence; **los fósiles son** ~ **de ello** fossils are evidence of this; **las calles nos dan** ~ **de**

su pasado árabe the streets bear witness to its Arab past

testosterona SF testosterone

teta SF 1 (*) (= *mama*) breast, tit***, boob**; **dar (la) ~ a** to suckle, breast-feed; **niño de ~** baby at the breast 2 [*de biberón*] teat (*Brit*), nipple (*EEUU*)

tétano SM, **tétanos** SM INV tetanus

tetera SF (*para té*) teapot; (*Méx*) (*para hervir agua*) kettle

tetero SM (*Col, Ven*) feeding bottle (*esp Brit*), nursing bottle (*EEUU*)

tetilla SF 1 [*de hombre*] nipple 2 [*de biberón*] teat (*Brit*), nipple (*EEUU*)

tetina SF teat (*Brit*), nipple (*EEUU*)

tetona* ADJ busty*

tetrabrik® SM INV, **tetra brik**® SM INV Tetra-Pak®, carton

tetraedro SM tetrahedron

tetrapléjico ADJ tetraplegic

tétrico ADJ [*ambiente, habitación, lugar*] gloomy, dismal; [*humor, pensamiento, cuento, relato*] gloomy, pessimistic; [*luz*] dim, wan

teutón/ona Ⓐ ADJ Teutonic Ⓑ SM/F Teuton

teutónico ADJ Teutonic

textil Ⓐ ADJ 1 [*industria*] textile 2 [*playa*] non-nudist Ⓑ **textiles** SMPL (= *tejidos*) textiles Ⓒ SF textile company

texto SM text; **libro de ~** textbook

textual ADJ 1 (= *de un texto*) textual; **cita** = quotation 2 (= *exacto*) exact; (= *literal*) literal; **son sus palabras ~es** those are his exact words

textualmente ADV 1 (*Literat*) textually 2 (= *exactamente*) exactly; (= *literalmente*) literally, word for word; **dice ... que ...** he says — and I quote — that ...

textura SF texture

tez SF (= *piel*) complexion, skin; (= *color*) colouring, coloring (*EEUU*)

tezontle SM (*Méx*) volcanic rock (*for building*)

Tfno. ABR, **tfno.** ABR (= *teléfono*) Tel., tel.

ti PRON PERS you; **es para ti** it's for you; **¿a ti te gusta el jazz?** do you like jazz?; **sólo piensas en ti (mismo)** you only think of yourself

tianguis SM INV (*CAm, Méx*) (open-air) market

tiara SF tiara

tiarrón/ona* SM/F big guy*/big girl

Tíbet SM **El ~** Tibet

tibetano/a Ⓐ ADJ, SM/F Tibetan Ⓑ SM (*Ling*) Tibetan

tibia SF tibia

tibieza SF 1 [*de líquidos*] lukewarmness, tepidness 2 [*de creencias*] half-heartedness; [*de persona*] lukewarmness, lack of enthusiasm

tibio ADJ 1 [*comida, líquido*] lukewarm, tepid 2 [*creencia*] half-hearted; [*persona*] lukewarm; [*recibimiento*] cool, unenthusiastic; **estar ~ con algn** to be cool to sb, behave distantly towards sb; ✦ MODISMO **poner ~ a algn***
(= *insultar*) to hurl abuse at sb, give sb a verbal battering; (*por detrás*) to say dreadful things about sb

tiburón SM 1 (*Zool*) shark 2 (*) (= *persona sin escrúpulos*) shark* 3 (*Bolsa*) raider

tic SM (*pl* **~s**) 1 (= *sonido*) click; [*de reloj*] tick 2 (*Med*) tic ➤ **tic nervioso** nervous tic

tícket ['tike] SM (*pl* **~s** ['tike]) (= *billete*) ticket; [*de compra*] receipt

tico/a* ADJ, SM/F (*CAm*) Costa Rican

tictac SM [*de reloj*] tick, ticking; [*de corazón*] beat; **hacer ~** [*reloj*] to tick; [*corazón*] to beat

tiempo SM 1 (*indicando duración*) time; **no tengo ~** I haven't got time; **tómate el ~ que quieras** take as long as you want; **hace bastante ~ que lo compré** I bought it quite a while ago; **¿cuánto ~ se va a quedar?** how long is he staying for?; **¿cuánto ~ hace de eso?** how long ago was that?; **¿cuánto ~ hace que vives aquí?** how long have you

been living here?; **¡cuánto ~ sin verte!** I haven't seen you for ages!; **más ~: necesito más ~ para pensármelo** I need more time *o* longer to think about it; **no puede quedarse más ~** he can't stay any longer; **mucho ~: has tardado mucho ~** you took a long time; **al poco ~ de** soon after ➤ **tiempo libre** spare time, free time ➤ **tiempo real** (*Inform*) real time
2 (*otras locuciones*) **a tiempo** in time; **llegamos a ~ de ver las noticias** we got there in time to watch the news; **todavía estáis a ~ de cambiar de idea** it's still not too late for you to change your minds; **el avión llegó a ~** the plane arrived on time; **cada cierto ~** every so often; **a ~ completo** full-time; **con ~: llegamos con ~ de darnos un paseo** we arrived in time to have a walk; **si me lo dices con ~** if you tell me beforehand; **con el ~:** eventually; **dar ~: ¿crees que te dará ~?** do you think you'll have (enough) time?; **dale ~** give him time; **fuera de ~** at the wrong time; **ganar ~** to save time; **hacer ~** to while away the time; **matar el ~** to kill time; **a ~ parcial** part-time; **de un** *o* **algún ~ a esta parte** for some time (past); **pasar el ~** to pass time; **perder el ~** to waste time; **estás perdiendo el ~** you're wasting your time; **¡rápido, no perdamos (el) ~!** quick, there's no time to lose!; **sacar ~ para hacer algo** to find the time to do sth; **tener ~ para algo** to have time for sth; ✦ MODISMOS **el ~ apremia** time presses; **dar ~ al ~** to let matters take their course; ✦ REFRÁN **el ~ es oro** time is precious
3 (= *momento*) time; **al mismo ~** ✧ **a un ~** at the same time; **al (mismo) ~ que** at the (same) time as; **cada cosa a su ~** everything in good time; **llegamos antes de ~** we arrived early; **ha nacido antes de ~** he was born prematurely, he was premature; **a su debido ~** in due course
4 (= *época*) time; **durante un ~ vivimos en Valencia** we lived in Valencia for a time *o* while; **en mis ~s** in my day; **en los buenos ~s** in the good old days; **en estos ~s que corren** these days; **en otros ~s** formerly; **en los últimos ~s** recently, lately, in recent times; **a través de los ~s** through the ages ➤ **tiempos modernos** modern times
5 (= *edad*) age; **¿cuánto** *o* **qué ~ tiene el niño?** how old is the baby?
6 (*Dep*) half; **primer ~** first half; **segundo ~** second half ➤ **tiempo muerto** (*lit*) time-out; (*fig*) breather
7 (*Mús*) [*de compás*] tempo, time; [*de sinfonía*] movement
8 (*Ling*) tense; **en ~ presente** in the present tense ➤ **tiempo simple** simple tense
9 (*Meteo*) weather; **hace buen ~** the weather is good; **¿qué ~ hace ahí?** what's the weather like there?; **¿quiere el agua fría o del ~?** would you like the water chilled or at room temperature?; **prefiero la fruta del ~** I prefer fruit that's in season; ✦ REFRÁN **a mal ~, buena cara** one must try to put a brave face on it
10 (*Mec*) cycle; **motor de dos ~s** two-stroke engine

tienda SF 1 (*Com*) shop (*esp Brit*), store (*EEUU*); **ir de ~s** to go shopping ➤ **tienda de abarrotes** (*CAm, And, Méx*), **tienda de comestibles** grocer's (shop) (*esp Brit*), grocery (*EEUU*) ➤ **tienda de departamentos** (*Méx*) department store ➤ **tienda de regalos** gift shop ➤ **tienda de ultramarinos** grocer's (shop) (*esp Brit*), grocery (*EEUU*) 2 (*tb ~ de campaña*) tent; **montar la ~** to pitch the tent

tienta SF 1 **a ~s** gropingly, blindly; **andar a ~s** (*lit*) to grope one's way along, feel one's way; (*fig*) to feel one's way; **buscar algo a ~s** to grope around for sth 2 (*Taur*) trial, test

tiento SM 1 (= *diplomacia*) tact; (= *prudencia*) care; **ir con ~** to go carefully 2 (*Esp*) (= *toque*) feel(ing), touch 3 (*) (= *propuesta*) pass* 4 (*Esp**) (= *trago*) swig*; **dar un ~ a** take a swig (**a** from)

tierno ADJ 1 [*blando*] [*carne*] tender; [*pan*] fresh 2 [*brote*] tender 3 (= *afectuoso*) [*persona*] tender, affectionate; [*mirada, sonrisa*] tender 4 (= *joven*) tender; **en su más tierna infancia** in his tenderest youth

tierra SF 1 **la Tierra** the earth, the Earth
2 (= *superficie*) 2.1 (*fuera del agua*) land; **¡~ a la vista!** land ahoy!; **~ adentro** inland; **por ~** overland, by land; **atravesar un país por ~** to go overland *o* by land across a country; **por ~ y por mar** by land and by sea; **tomar ~** to reach port, get in 2.2 (= *no aire*) (*desde el aire*) ground; (*desde el espacio*) earth; **un ataque por ~ y aire** a ground and air attack; **tocar ~** to touch down; **tomar ~** to land ➤ **tierra**

firme (= *no aire*) solid ground; (= *no agua*) land
3 (= *suelo*) ground; **caer a ~** to fall down; **caer por ~**
[*persona*] to fall to the ground; [*argumento, teoría*] to fall
apart; **echarse a ~** to throw o.s. on *o* to the ground;
✦ MODISMOS **echar** *o* **tirar por ~** [+ *trabajo, organización*] to
ruin, destroy; [+ *expectativas, sueños*] to shatter; [+ *teoría,
tesis*] to demolish; **poner ~ de por medio** to get away as
quickly as possible; **¡~, trágame!** I want to die! (*iró*)
4 (= *material*) (*gen*) earth; (= *polvo*) dust; (= *barro*) mud;
(*para jardinería, cultivo*) soil; **viviendas con suelo de ~**
houses with earth *o* dirt floors; **un saco de ~** a bag of soil;
jugarán en pistas de ~ they'll play on clay courts;
✦ MODISMOS **estar bajo ~** to be dead and buried; **echar ~ a**
o **sobre algo** (= *ocultar*) to hush up sth; (= *olvidar*) to put
sth behind one; **echar ~ a algn** (*Méx, Chi**) to sling *o* throw
mud at sb; (*Col*) to make sb look bad
5 (*Agr*) land; **trabajar la ~** to work the land; **heredó unas ~s
cerca del río** he inherited some land near the river ➤ **tierra
baldía** wasteland ➤ **tierra de cultivo** arable land
6 (= *división territorial*) **6.1** (= *lugar de origen*) **en mi ~ no se
usa esa expresión** we don't use that expression where I
come from; **todo refugiado siente nostalgia de su ~** every
refugee feels homesick for *o* misses his native land
homeland; **de la ~** (*vino, queso*) local, locally produced;
[*fruta, verduras*] locally grown **6.2** (*en plural*) **sus viajes por
~s de Castilla** his travels through the lands of Castile; **no
es de estas ~s** he's not from these parts, he's not from this
part of the world ➤ **Tierra del Fuego** Tierra del Fuego
➤ **tierra de nadie** no-man's-land ➤ **tierra natal** native land
➤ **tierra prometida** promised land ➤ **Tierra Santa** Holy
Land
7 (*Elec*) earth (*Brit*), ground (*EEUU*); **conectar un aparato a ~**
to earth (*Brit*) *o* ground (*EEUU*) an appliance

tierral SM (*And, Méx*) = **terral**

tierrero SM (*Col, Ven*) cloud of dust

tieso ADJ **1** (= *rígido*) stiff; (= *erguido*) erect; (= *derecho*)
straight; (*Col*) (= *duro*) [*carne*] tough; [*pan*] hard; **con las
orejas tiesas** with its ears pricked; **ponte tieso** stand up
straight; ✦ MODISMOS **dejar ~ a algn*** (= *matar*) to do sb in*;
(= *sorprender*) to amaze sb, leave sb speechless; **quedarse ~***
(= *morirse*) to snuff it*, peg out*; (= *sorprenderse*) to be left
speechless
2 (= *poco amable*) (*en conducta*) stiff; (*en actitud*) rigid
3 (*) (= *orgulloso*) proud; (= *presumido*) conceited, stuck-
up*; (= *pagado de sí mismo*) smug
4 (*Col*) (= *valiente*) **ser ~** to have guts*

tiesto SM **1** (= *maceta*) flowerpot **2** (= *cascote*) shard, piece
broken of pottery **3** (*Chi*) (= *palangana*) basin

tifoideo ADJ **fiebre tifoidea** typhoid

tifón SM **1** (= *huracán*) typhoon **2** (= *tromba*) waterspout

tifus SM INV typhus

tigre SM **1** (*Zool*) tiger; (*LAm*) jaguar ➤ **tigre de Bengala**
Bengal tiger **2** (*Esp***) (= *wáter*) bog (*Brit***), loo (*Brit**), john
(*EEUU***); **esto huele a ~** this stinks, this smells foul

tigresa SF **1** (= *animal*) tigress **2** (= *mujer cruel*) shrew;
(= *mujer fatal*) vamp*

tijera SF **1** (*tb ~s*) [*de costura*] scissors *pl*; (*para jardín*)
shears *pl*, clippers *pl*; **unas ~s** a pair of scissors;
✦ MODISMOS **darle a la ~** (*RPl**) to bitch*; **estar/ser cortados
por la misma ~** (*LAm**) to be all the same, be all as bad as
each other ➤ **tijeras de coser** sewing scissors ➤ **tijeras de
podar** pruning shears, secateurs (*Brit*) **2** [*de bicicleta*] fork
3 de ~ folding; **silla de ~** (= *con respaldo*) folding chair;
(= *banqueta*) folding stool, camp stool; **escalera de ~** steps,
stepladder

tijereta SF **1** (= *insecto*) earwig **2** (*Bot*) vine tendril **3** (*Dep*)
scissor(s) kick, overhead kick

tijeretada SF, **tijeretazo** SM snip, snick

tila SF **1** (= *planta*) lime tree **2** (= *infusión*) lime flower tea

tildar /1a/ VT **1** (= *acusar*) **~ a algn de racista** to brand sb
(as) a racist; **lo ~on de vago** they dismissed him as lazy,
they called him lazy **2** (*Tip*) (*gen*) to put an accent on;
(*sobre la n*) to put a tilde over

tilde SF **1** (*ortográfica*) (= *acento*) (*gen*) accent; (*sobre la n*)
tilde **2** (= *mancha*) blemish; (= *defecto*) defect, flaw

tiliches* SMPL (*CAm, Méx*) (= *pertenencias*) belongings;
(= *baratijas*) trinkets; (= *trastos*) junk *sing*

tilín SM [*de campanilla*] tinkle, ting-a-ling; ✦ MODISMOS
hacer ~ a algn*: **me hace ~** [*persona*] I fancy him*; [*cosa*] I
like it, I go for it*; **no me hace ~** [*cosa*] it doesn't do
anything for me; **en un ~** (*Col, Ven**) in a flash

tilo SM **1** (= *planta*) lime tree **2** (*Chi*) (= *infusión*) lime flower
tea

timador(a) SM/F swindler, trickster

timar /1a/ VT to swindle, con*; **¡me han timado!** I've been
conned!*

timba SF **1** (*en juego de azar*) hand **2** (= *garito*) gambling
den

timbal SM small drum, kettledrum; **~es** timpani

timbrado ADJ **voz bien timbrada** well-toned voice

timbrar /1a/ **Ⓐ** VT **1** [+ *documento*] to stamp **2** [+ *carta*] to
postmark, frank **Ⓑ** VI (*Col*) to ring the bell

timbre SM **1** (*Elec*) bell; **tocar el ~** to ring the bell ➤ **timbre
de alarma** alarm bell **2** (*Mús*) timbre **3** (*Com, Fin*) (= *sello*)
fiscal stamp, revenue stamp; (= *renta*) stamp duty (*Brit*),
revenue stamp (*EEUU*) **4** (*Méx*) [*de correos*] (postage) stamp

timidez SF shyness, timidity

tímido ADJ shy, timid

timo SM swindle, con trick*; **dar un ~ a algn** to swindle sb,
con sb*; **¡es un ~!** it's a rip-off!*

timón SM **1** (*Aer, Náut*) rudder; (= *mando, control*) helm;
poner el ~ a babor to turn to port, port the helm;
✦ MODISMO **coger** *o* **empuñar el ~** to take the helm, take
charge **2** [*de carruaje*] pole; [*de arado*] beam **3** (*And*)
(= *volante*) steering wheel; (*Perú*) (= *manillar*) handlebars *pl*

timonear /1a/ **Ⓐ** VT (*LAm*) (= *dirigir*) to direct, manage;
(= *guiar*) to guide **Ⓑ** VI to steer; (*And Aut*) to drive

timonel SMF (*Náut*) steersman/steerswoman, helmsman/
helmswoman; (*en barca de remo*) cox

timorato ADJ **1** (= *tímido*) lily-livered, spineless
2 (= *mojigato*) sanctimonious, prudish **3** (= *que teme a Dios*)
God-fearing

tímpano SM **1** (*Anat*) tympanum, eardrum **2** (*Arquit*)
tympanum **3** (*Mús*) small drum, kettledrum

tina SF (= *recipiente*) tub, vat; (*para bañarse*) bath(tub)

tinaco SM (*Méx*) water tank

tinaja SF large earthenware jar

tincada SF (*And*) hunch

tincar* /1g/ VI (*And*) **1** (= *presentir*) **me tinca que ...** it seems
to me that ..., I have a feeling that ... **2** (= *apetecer*) **me
tinca** I like it; **no me tinca** I don't fancy the idea*
3 (= *parecer bien*) to look good to; **este restaurante me tinca**
this restaurant looks good to me, I like the look of this
restaurant

tinglado SM **1** (= *tablado*) platform; (= *cobertizo*) shed
2 (*) (= *sistema*) set-up; **montar el ~** to get going, set up in
business **3** (= *intriga*) plot, intrigue **4** (= *follón*) mess

tinieblas SFPL **1** (= *oscuridad*) dark(ness) *sing*
2 (= *confusión*) confusion *sing*; (= *ignorancia*) ignorance *sing*

tino SM **1** (*Mil*) (= *puntería*) (accurate) aim;
✦ MODISMO **coger el ~** to get the feel *o* hang of it
2 (= *tacto*) tact; (= *juicio*) good judgement; **sin ~** foolishly;
obrar con mucho ~ to act very wisely **3** (= *moderación*)
moderation; **sin ~** immoderately

tinta SF **1** (*para escribir*) ink; ✦ MODISMOS **saber algo de
buena ~** to know sth on good authority; **sudar ~*** to slog,
slave one's guts out* ➤ **tinta china** Indian ink, India ink
(*EEUU*) ➤ **tinta invisible** invisible ink **2** [*de pulpo, calamar*]
ink; **calamares en su ~** squid in their own ink **3** (*Arte*)
(= *color*) colour, color (*EEUU*); **tintas** (*liter*) shades, hues;
✦ MODISMOS **cargar las ~s** to exaggerate; **medias ~s**
(= *medidas*) half measures; (= *ideas*) half-baked ideas;
(= *respuestas*) inadequate answers

tintar /1a/ VT to dye

tinte SM **1** (= *acto*) dyeing **2** (= *producto*) dye, dyestuff;
(*para madera*) stain **3** (*Esp*) (= *tintorería*) dry cleaner's
4 (= *tendencia*) hint

tinterillo SM (*And*) shyster lawyer*

tintero SM inkpot, ink bottle (*EEUU*); ✦ MODISMO **dejarse algo en el ~** (= *olvidar*) to forget about sth; (= *no mencionar*) to leave sth unsaid

tintín SM [*de campanilla*] tinkle, tinkling; [*de cadena, llaves*] jingle; [*de copas, tazas*] clink, chink

tintinear /1a/ VI [*campanilla*] to tinkle; [*cadena, llaves*] to jingle; [*copas, tazas*] to clink, chink

tintineo SM = **tintín**

tinto Ⓐ ADJ [*vino*] red Ⓑ SM 1 (= *vino*) red wine; **un ~** a (glass of) red wine 2 (*Col*) (= *café*) black coffee

tintorería SF dry cleaner's

tintorro* SM cheap red wine, red plonk (*Brit**)

tintura SF 1 (*Quím*) dye, dyestuff; (*Téc*) stain 2 (*Farm*) tincture

tiña SF 1 (*Med*) ringworm 2 (= *tacañería*) stinginess, meanness (*esp Brit*)

tiñoso/a ADJ 1 (*Med*) scabby, mangy 2 (= *tacaño*) stingy, mean (*esp Brit*)

tío/a SM/F 1 (= *pariente*) uncle/aunt; **mis ~s** (= *sólo hombres*) my uncles; (= *hombres y mujeres*) my uncle(s) and aunt(s); **el ~ Sam** Uncle Sam; ✦ MODISMOS **¡no hay tu tía!*** nothing doing!; **¡cuéntaselo a tu tía!*** pull the other one!* ➤ **tío/a abuelo/a** great-uncle/great-aunt 2 (*Esp**) (= *hombre*) guy*, bloke*; (= *mujer*) woman; (= *chica*) girl; **¿quién es ese ~?** who's that guy *o* bloke?*; **los ~s** guys*, blokes*; **las tías** women; **¡qué ~!** **¡no ha perdido un solo partido!** the guy's incredible, he hasn't lost a single match!* ➤ **tío/a bueno/a** hunk*/stunner*; **¡tía buena!** hello gorgeous!*

tiovivo SM (*Esp*) merry-go-round, roundabout (*Brit*), carousel (*EEUU*)

tipazo* SM 1 (= *buen cuerpo*) [*de hombre*] good build; [*de mujer*] good figure 2 (= *hombre*) tall chap*, big guy*

tipear /1a/ VT, VI (*LAm*) to type

tipejo/a* SM/F (*raro*) oddball*, queer fish*; (*despreciable*) nasty character

típico ADJ 1 (= *característico*) typical; **es muy ~ de él** it's typical of him 2 (= *pintoresco*) full of local colour *o* (*EEUU*) color; (= *tradicional*) traditional; (= *regional*) regional; [*costumbre*] typical; **baile ~** regional dance, national dance

tipificar /1g/ VT 1 (= *clasificar*) to class, consider (**como** as) 2 (= *ser típico de*) to typify, characterize

tiple Ⓐ SM 1 (*Mús*) (= *cantante*) treble, boy soprano 2 (= *voz*) soprano Ⓑ SF (= *cantante*) soprano

tipo¹/a SM/F (*) (= *individuo*) (= *hombre*) guy*, bloke (*Brit**); (= *mujer*) chick**, bird (*Brit***), dame (*EEUU**); **¿quién es ese ~?** who's that guy *o* (*Brit*) bloke?*

tipo² Ⓐ SM 1 (= *clase*) type, kind, sort; **un nuevo ~ de bicicleta** a new type of bicycle; **tuvimos todo ~ de problemas** we had all sorts *o* kinds of problems 2 (*Bot, Literat, Zool*) type 3 (*Com, Fin*) rate ➤ **tipo de cambio** exchange rate ➤ **tipo de interés** interest rate ➤ **tipo impositivo** tax rate 4 (= *figura, cuerpo*) [*de hombre*] build; [*de mujer*] figure; **tiene el ~ de su padre** he has his father's build; **tener buen ~** [*hombre*] to be well built; [*mujer*] to have a good figure; ✦ MODISMOS **aguantar** *o* **mantener el ~** (*Esp*) to keep one's composure; **jugarse el ~** (*Esp*) to risk one's neck 5 (*Tip*) type ➤ **tipo de letra** typeface Ⓑ ADJ INV 1 (= *similar a*) **un sombrero ~ Bogart** a Bogart-style hat; **una foto ~ carné** a passport-size photo 2 (= *típico*) average, typical; **dos conductores ~** two average *o* typical drivers; **lengua ~** standard language Ⓒ ADV (*CS*) **me fui ~ nueve** I left at about nine

tipografía SF 1 (= *arte*) typography 2 (= *taller*) printing works, printing press

tipográfico ADJ typographical, printing *antes de s*

tipógrafo/a SM/F printer

tipología SF typology

tíquet ['tike] SM (*pl ~s* ['tike]) 1 (= *recibo de compra*) receipt 2 (= *billete*) ticket

tiquete SM (*Col*) = **tíquet**

tiquismiquis* Ⓐ SMF INV (= *persona*) fusspot (*Brit**), fussbudget (*EEUU**) Ⓑ SMPL (= *escrúpulos*) silly scruples; (= *detalles*) fussy details; (= *quejas*) silly *o* trivial objections

tira¹ Ⓐ SF 1 [*de tela*] strip; [*de zapato*] strap; **cortar algo en ~s** to cut sth into strips ➤ **tira cómica** comic strip ➤ **tira publicitaria** flysheet, advertising leaflet 2 ✦ MODISMO **la ~***: **me gusta la ~** I love it; **de eso hace la ~** that was ages ago; **estoy aquí desde hace la ~ de tiempo** I've been here for absolutely ages Ⓑ SM ➤ **tira y afloja** (= *negociaciones*) hard bargaining; (= *concesiones*) give and take, mutual concessions *pl*

tira² Ⓐ SMF (*Méx, Chi**) (plainclothes) cop*, detective; (*Perú, RPl***) undercover cop* Ⓑ SF (*CAm, Méx**) **la ~** the cops* *pl*

tirabuzón SM 1 (= *rizo*) curl, ringlet 2 (= *sacacorchos*) corkscrew

tirachinas SM INV catapult (*Brit*), slingshot (*EEUU*)

tirada SF 1 [*de dados, dardos*] throw; **en la primera ~ hizo diez puntos** he scored ten points in the first throw; **de una ~** in one go; **leyó la novela de una ~** he read the novel straight through in one go 2 (= *distancia*) distance; **aún nos queda una buena ~** we've still got a long way to go 3 (*Tip*) (= *ejemplares impresos*) print run; (= *ejemplares vendidos*) circulation 4 (*Méx**) (= *intención*) aim; **mi ~ era regresar mañana pero ...** I was going to go back tomorrow but ...

tirado/a Ⓐ ADJ 1 (= *tumbado*) **estar ~** to be lying; **siempre está ~ en el sofá** he's always lying on the sofa; **los juguetes estaban ~s por toda la habitación** the toys were lying *o* strewn all over the room 2 (*) (= *barato*) **estar ~** to be dirt-cheap* 3 (*) (= *fácil*) **estar ~** to be dead easy *o* a cinch* 4 (*) **dejar ~ a algn** to leave sb in the lurch; **quedarse ~** to be left in the lurch Ⓑ SM/F (*) no-hoper*

tirador(a) Ⓐ SM/F (= *persona*) marksman/markswoman, shooter; **es un buen ~** he's a good shot Ⓑ SM 1 [*de cajón*] handle; [*de puerta*] knob 2 [*de campanilla*] bell pull 3 (= *tirachinas*) catapult (*Brit*), slingshot (*EEUU*) 4 (*RPl*) [*de vestido*] strap 5 **tiradores** (*Arg, Bol*) [*de pantalón*] braces (*Brit*), suspenders (*EEUU*)

tiraje (*Tip*) = **tirada 3**

tiralíneas SM INV drawing pen, ruling pen

tiranía SF tyranny

tiránico ADJ (*gen*) tyrannical; [*amor*] possessive, domineering; [*atracción*] irresistible, all-powerful

tiranizar /1f/ VT (= *oprimir*) to tyrannize; (= *gobernar*) to rule despotically; (= *dominar*) to domineer

tirano/a Ⓐ ADJ (= *tiránico*) tyrannical, despotic; (= *dominante*) domineering Ⓑ SM/F tyrant, despot

tirantas SFPL (*Col*) braces (*Brit*), suspenders (*EEUU*)

tirante Ⓐ ADJ 1 [+ *soga*] tight, taut; (= *tensado*) tensed, drawn tight 2 [*relaciones, situación*] tense, strained Ⓑ SM [*de vestido*] shoulder strap; **tirantes** [*de pantalones*] braces (*Brit*), suspenders (*EEUU*); **vestido sin ~s** strapless dress

tirantez SF 1 (*Téc*) tightness, tension 2 [*de relaciones, situación*] tension, strain

---

tirar /1a/

Ⓐ VERBO TRANSITIVO	Ⓒ VERBO PRONOMINAL
Ⓑ VERBO INTRANSITIVO	

Para las expresiones como **tirar de la lengua**, **tirar de la manta**, **tirar por la borda**, **tirar por tierra** *etc, ver la entrada correspondiente a la otra palabra.*

tirar Ⓐ VERBO TRANSITIVO
1 (= *lanzar*) to throw; **~ algo a algn** (*para que lo coja*) to throw sth to sb; (*para hacer daño*) to throw sth at sb
2 (= *derribar*) [+ *edificio*] to pull down; [+ *jarrón, silla, estatua*] to knock over; [+ *pared, verja*] to knock down; **la moto la tiró al suelo** the motorbike knocked her over; **¡abre, o tiro la puerta abajo!** open up, or I'll break the door down!
3 (= *dejar caer*) to drop; **tropezó y tiró la bandeja** she tripped and dropped the tray

4 (= *desechar*) to throw away; **no tires las sobras, que se las voy a dar al perro** don't throw away the leftovers, I'll give them to the dog; **tira las sobras a la basura** throw the leftovers in the bin (*esp Brit*) *o* garbage can (*EEUU*)
5 (= *malgastar*) [+ *dinero*] to waste; [+ *fortuna*] to squander
6 (= *disparar*) [+ *tiro*] to fire; [+ *flecha*] to shoot; [+ *cohete*] to launch, fire
7 [+ *foto*] to take
8 (= *dar, pegar*) **deja ya de ~ patadas** stop kicking; **la mula le tiró una coz** the mule kicked him *o* gave him a kick
9 (*Tip*) (= *imprimir*) to print, run off
10 (= *trazar*) [+ *línea*] to draw, trace
11 (*LAm*) = **B 1**
B VERBO INTRANSITIVO
1 (*haciendo fuerza*)
1.1 (= *traer hacia sí*) to pull; **¡tira un poco más fuerte!** pull a bit harder!; **~ de** [+ *soga, cuerda*] to pull; **tire de ese cabo** pull that end; **~ de la cadena (del wáter)** to flush the toilet, pull the chain; **"tirar"** (*en puerta*) "pull"
1.2 (= *llevar tras sí*) **~ de** to pull; **un burro tiraba de la carreta** a donkey was pulling the cart along, the cart was drawn by a donkey
2 (*) (= *atraer*) **no le tira el estudio** studying does not appeal to him, studying holds no attraction for him; **la patria tira siempre** one's native land always exerts a powerful pull
3 (= *estar tirante*) [*ropa*] to be tight; **este vestido tira un poco de aquí** this dress is a bit tight here; **me tira de sisa** it's tight round my armpits
4 (= *usar*) **~ de** [+ *espada, navaja*] to draw
5 (= *disparar*) to shoot; **¡no tires!** don't shoot!; **~ al blanco** to aim; **~ a matar** to shoot to kill
6 (*Dep*) (*con balón*) to shoot; (*con fichas, cartas*) to go, play; **¡tira!** shoot!; **tira tú ahora** it's your go now; **~ al arco** (*LAm*) ◇ **~ a puerta** (*Esp*) to shoot at goal
7 (*) (= *arreglárselas*) to get by; **podemos ~ con menos dinero** we can get by on less money; **ir tirando** to get by, manage; **—¿qué tal esa salud? —vamos tirando** "how's your health?" — "we're getting by"
8 (= *funcionar*) [*motor*] to pull; [*chimenea, puro*] to draw, pull
9 (*Esp*) (= *ir*) to go; **tire usted adelante** go straight on; **¡tira de una vez!** get on with it!, go on, then!; **~ a la derecha** to turn right
10 (*) (= *durar*) to last; **esos zapatos ~án todavía otro invierno** those shoes will last another winter yet
11 (*seguido*) *de preposición*
◆ **tirar a** (= *tender*) **tiene el pelo rubio tirando a rojizo** he has reddish blond hair; **es mediocre tirando a malo** it's middling to bad, it's mediocre verging on bad
◆ **tirar para** (= *aspirar a ser*) **la pequeña tira para actriz** the little girl has ambitions of becoming an actress
12 (*LAm***) (*sexualmente*) to screw***
C **tirarse** VERBO PRONOMINAL
1 (= *lanzarse*) to throw o.s.; **~se al suelo** to throw o.s. to the ground; **~se por una ventana** to jump from *o* out of a window, throw o.s. out of a window; **~se al agua** (*gen*) to plunge into the water; (*de cabeza*) *o* plunge into the water; **~se en paracaídas** to parachute (down); (*en emergencia*) to bale out; **~se sobre algn** to rush at sb, spring on sb
2 (*) (= *pasar*) to spend; **se tiró dos horas arreglándolo** he spent two hours fixing it
3 (= *expeler*) **~se un eructo*** to burp*, belch, break wind; **~se un pedo*** to fart**
4 **~se a algn*** (*sexualmente*) to screw sb***, lay sb**
5 (*Col, RPI*) (= *tumbarse*) to lie down; ◆ MODISMO **tirárselas de algo*: el tipo ese que se las tira de periodista** that guy who likes to think he's a journalist*; **se las tira de víctima** he acts the victim

tirita SF (*Esp*) (sticking) plaster (*Brit*), Band-aid® (*EEUU*)

tiritar /1a/ VI **1** (*de frío, miedo*) to shiver (**de** with) **2** (*Esp**) **esta botella ha quedado tiritando** there isn't much left of this bottle

tiritón **A** SM shiver **B** ADJ (*LAm**) shivery

tiritona SF shivering (fit)

tiro SM **1** (= *disparo*) shot; **lo mataron de un ~ o a tiros** they shot him dead; **se oyeron varios ~s a lo lejos** gunfire was heard *o* shots were heard in the distance; **pegar un ~ a algn**

to shoot sb; **¡que le peguen cuatro ~s!** he ought to be shot!; **se pegó un ~** he shot himself; ◆ MODISMOS **al ~** (*esp Chi**) at once, right away; **de a ~** (*Méx**) completely; **estar a ~ de hacer algo** (*Col**) to be about to do sth, be on the point of doing sth; **a ~ fijo*** for sure; **esperar a ver por dónde van los ~s** to wait and see which way the wind is blowing; **ir de ~s largos** to be all dressed up, wear one's Sunday best; **ni a ~s*: no lo haría ni a ~s** I wouldn't do it for love or money; **a ~ de piedra** a stone's throw away; **sentar como un ~*: me sienta como un ~** [*obligación*] it's a real pain*; [*ropa, peinado*] it looks really awful *o* terrible on me*; [*comida*] it really doesn't agree with me ➤ **tiro al blanco** target practice ➤ **tiro al plato** trap shooting, clay pigeon shooting ➤ **tiro con arco** archery ➤ **tiro de gracia** coup de grâce
2 (= *alcance*) range; **estar a ~** to be within range; **tener algo a ~** to be within one's reach, have within one's reach; **a ~ de fusil** within shooting distance
3 (*Dep*) (= *lanzamiento*) shot; **parar un ~** to stop a shot ➤ **tiro a gol** shot at goal ➤ **tiro de castigo** (*Méx*) penalty kick ➤ **tiro de esquina** (*Col*) corner (kick) ➤ **tiro libre** (*en fútbol*) free kick; (*en baloncesto*) free throw
4 [*de animales*] team; **animal de ~** draught *o* (*EEUU*) draft animal
5 [*de pantalón*] distance between crotch and waist; **el pantalón me va corto de ~** the trousers (*Brit*) *o* pants (*EEUU*) are too tight around my crotch
6 (*Arquit*) (*en escalera*) flight of stairs; [*de chimenea*] draught, draft (*EEUU*)
7 (*Min*) (= *pozo*) shaft ➤ **tiro de mina** mineshaft
8 (*Méx Tip*) = **tirada 3**

tiroides **A** ADJ INV thyroid **B** SM INV (*a veces* SF INV) thyroid (gland)

tirón SM **1** (= *acción*) pull, tug; **dar un ~ a algo** to give sth a pull *o* tug, pull *o* tug at sth; **me dio un ~ del jersey** she pulled *o* tugged at my sweater; **le dio un ~ de pelo** she pulled his hair; **dar un ~ de orejas a algn** (*lit*) to pull *o* tug sb's ear; (*fig*) to tell sb off; ◆ MODISMO **aguantar el ~** to ride out *o* weather the storm
2 (*en músculo, tendón*) **sufrió un ~ en la pantorrilla** he pulled a calf muscle ➤ **tirón muscular** pulled muscle
3 (= *robo*) bag-snatching
4 ◆ MODISMO **de un ~: leyó la novela de un ~** he read the novel straight through in one go; **se lo bebió de un ~** he drank it down in one go; **trabajan diez horas de un ~** they work ten hours at a stretch; **he dormido toda la noche de un ~** I slept right through the night

tironear /1a/ (*LAm*) **A** VT to pull (at), tug (at) **B** VI **~ de algo** to pull at sth, tug (at) sth

tirotear /1a/ **A** VT (= *disparar*) to shoot at, fire on; (= *matar*) to shoot, shoot down **B** **tirotearse** VPR to exchange shots

tiroteo SM (= *tiros*) shooting, exchange of shots; (= *escaramuza*) skirmish; (= *batalla*) gunfight; (*con policía*) shoot-out

tirria* SF dislike; **tener ~ a algn** to dislike sb, have a grudge against sb

tisana SF tisane, herbal tea

tísico/a **A** ADJ consumptive, tubercular **B** SM/F consumptive

tisis SF INV consumption, tuberculosis

tisú SM (*pl* **~s**) lamé

titán SM titan, giant; **una tarea de titanes** a titanic task

titánico ADJ titanic

titanio SM titanium

títere **A** SM **1** (= *marioneta*) puppet; ◆ MODISMO **no dejar ~ con cabeza** (= *cambiar*) to turn everything upside down; (= *romper*) to break up everything in sight; (= *criticar*) to spare no one **2** **títeres** (= *espectáculo*) puppet show *sing*; (= *arte*) puppetry *sing* **3** (= *persona*) puppet, tool **B** ADJ INV **gobierno ~** puppet government

titilar /1a/ VI [*luz, estrella*] to twinkle; [*párpado*] to flutter, tremble

titipuchal* SM (*Méx*) **un ~** loads* *pl*, masses* *pl*

titiritero/a SM/F **1** (= *que maneja marionetas*) puppeteer **2** (= *acróbata*) acrobat; (= *malabarista*) juggler; (= *artista de circo*) circus artist

tito/a* SM/F (*Esp*) uncle/ auntie*

titubeante ADJ **1** (= *que vacila*) hesitant **2** (= *que balbucea*) stuttering **3** [*discurso, voz*] halting

titubear /1a/ VI **1** (= *vacilar*) to hesitate, vacillate; **respondió sin ~** he answered without hesitation **2** (= *balbucear*) to stutter

titubeo SM **1** (= *vacilación*) hesitation, vacillation **2** (= *balbuceo*) stuttering

titulación SF (*Univ*) degrees and diplomas *pl*; **"se necesita titulación universitaria"** "university degree required"

titulado/a Ⓐ ADJ **1** [*libro*] entitled **2** [*persona*] with a degree, qualified; **~ en ingeniería** with a degree in engineering Ⓑ SM/F graduate

titular Ⓐ ADJ **jugador ~** regular first-team player; **profesor ~** *teacher assigned to a particular post in the state education system*
Ⓑ SMF **1** [*de puesto*] holder, incumbent; (*Rel*) incumbent **2** [*de cuenta, pasaporte*] holder; [*de coche, vivienda*] owner **3** (*Dep*) regular first-team player; (*LAm*) captain
Ⓒ SM (*Prensa*) headline; **los ~es** (*Radio, TV*) the (news) headlines
Ⓓ VT /1a/ [+ *libro, película*] to title, entitle; **¿cómo vas a ~ el trabajo?** what title are you going to give the essay?
Ⓔ **titularse** VPR **1** [*novela, poema*] **¿cómo se titula el libro?** what's the title of the book?, what's the book called? **2** (*Univ*) to graduate; **~se en algo** to graduate in sth

titularidad SF **1** (= *propiedad*) ownership; **empresa de ~ pública** publicly-owned company **2** (*de un cargo*) tenure; **durante la ~ de Bush** during Bush's period of office **3** (*Dep*) first place, first-team place, top spot

título SM **1** [*de libro, película*] title; (*Jur*) heading **2** [*de campeón*] title **3** (*Educ*) (= *diploma*) certificate; (= *licenciatura*) degree; (= *calificación*) qualification; **tener los ~s para un puesto** to have the qualifications for a job ➤ **título universitario** university degree **4** (= *dignidad*) title; (= *persona*) titled person ➤ **título de nobleza** title of nobility **5** **a ~ de** (= *a modo de*) by way of; (= *en calidad de*) in the capacity of; **a ~ de ejemplo, ...** by way of example, ..., for example, ...; **el dinero fue a ~ de préstamo** the money was by way of (being) a loan; **ya ha comenzado a funcionar a ~ experimental** it is already being used on an experimental basis; **a ~ particular** o **personal** in a personal capacity, in an unofficial capacity; **a ~ póstumo** posthumously **6** (*de bienes*) title ➤ **título de propiedad** title deed **7** (*Fin*) (= *bono*) bond **8** (= *derecho*) right; **con justo ~** rightly

tiza SF (*para escribir, de billar*) chalk; **una ~** a piece of chalk

tiznajo* SM = **tiznón**

tiznar /1a/ Ⓐ VT **1** (= *ennegrecer*) to blacken, black; (= *manchar*) to smudge, stain (**de** with) **2** [+ *reputación*] to stain, tarnish; [+ *nombre, carácter*] to defame, blacken Ⓑ **tiznarse** VPR **1 ~se la cara con hollín** to blacken one's face with soot **2** (= *mancharse*) to get smudged, get soiled

tizne SM (= *hollín*) soot; (= *mancha*) smut

tiznón SM [*de hollín*] speck of soot, smut; (= *mancha*) smudge

tizón SM **1** (= *madera*) firebrand; ✦ MODISMO **negro como un ~** as black as coal **2** (*Bot*) smut **3** (= *deshonra*) stain, blemish

tlapalería SF (*Méx*) hardware store, ironmonger's (shop) (*Brit*)

TNT SM ABR (= **trinitrotolueno**) TNT

toalla SF towel; ✦ MODISMO **arrojar** o **tirar la ~** to throw in the towel ➤ **toalla de baño** bath towel ➤ **toalla de playa** beach towel   .

toallero SM towel rail

tobillera SF ankle support

tobillo SM ankle

tobogán SM **1** (*en parque*) slide; (*en piscina*) chute, slide **2** (*para nieve*) toboggan, sledge (*Brit*), sled (*EEUU*) **3** [*de feria*] switchback

toc ADV **¡toc, toc!** (*en puerta*) rat-a-tat!, knock, knock!

toca SF **1** [*de monja*] cornet, wimple **2** (*Hist*) (= *tocado*) headdress; (= *sombrero sin ala*) toque; (= *gorrito*) bonnet

tocadiscos SM INV record player, phonograph (*EEUU*)

tocado¹ ADJ **estar ~** (*Dep*) to be injured; ✦ MODISMO **estar ~ de la cabeza** to be weak in the head

tocado² Ⓐ ADJ **~ con un sombrero** wearing a hat Ⓑ SM **1** (= *prenda*) headdress **2** (= *peinado*) coiffure, hairdo

tocador SM **1** (= *mueble*) dressing table; **jabón de ~** toilet soap; **juego de ~** toilet set **2** (= *cuarto*) boudoir, dressing room ➤ **tocador de señoras** ladies' room

tocador(a) SM/F (*Mús*) player

tocamientos SMPL (sexual) molestation *sing*

tocante ADJ **~ a** regarding, with regard to, about; **en lo ~ a** so far as ... is concerned, as regards

tocar /1g/ Ⓐ VT **1** (*gen*) to touch; (*para examinar*) to feel; **¡no me toques!** don't touch me!; **que nadie toque mis papeles** don't let anyone touch my papers; **tócale la frente, la tiene muy caliente** feel his forehead, it's very hot; **el delantero tocó la pelota con la mano** the forward handled (the ball); ✦ MODISMO **~ madera** to touch wood (*Brit*), knock on wood (*EEUU*)
2 (= *estar en contacto con*) to touch; **la mesa está tocando la pared** the table is touching the wall; **ponte ahí, tocando la pared** stand up against the wall over there; **~ tierra** to touch down, land
3 (= *hacer sonar*) [+ *piano, violín, trompeta*] to play; [+ *campana, timbre*] to ring; [+ *tambor*] to beat; [+ *silbato*] to blow; [+ *disco*] to play; **~ la bocina** o **el claxon** to sound o (*esp Brit*) hoot one's horn
4 [+ *tema*] to refer to, touch on; **no tocó para nada esa cuestión** he didn't refer to o touch on that matter at all; **prefiero no ~ lo relacionado con el trabajo** I'd prefer not to talk about work
5 (= *afectar*) to concern; **esa cuestión me toca de cerca** that issue closely concerns me; **por lo que a mí me toca** so far as I am concerned
6 (*Esp*) (= *estar emparentado con*) to be related to
7 (= *conmover*) to touch; **las imágenes me ~on en lo más profundo** the pictures moved o touched me deeply; **me has tocado el amor propio** you've wounded my pride
8 (*Dep*) to hit
9 (*Náut*) **hacía varios días que no tocábamos puerto** it was several days since we had called at o put in at a port
Ⓑ VI **1** (*Mús*) to play; **toca en un grupo de rock** he's in o he plays in a rock group
2 (= *sonar*) **en cuanto toque el timbre** when the bell rings; **~ a muerto** to toll the death knell
3 (= *llamar*) **~ a una puerta** to knock on o at a door
4 (= *corresponder*) **no toca hacerlo hasta el mes que viene** it's not due to be done until next month; **~ a algn: les tocó un dólar a cada uno** they got a dollar each; **me ha tocado el peor asiento** I ended up with o got the worst seat; **le tocó la lotería** he won the lottery; **¿a quién le toca?** whose turn is it?; **~ a algn hacer algo: nos toca pagar a nosotros** it's our turn to pay; **siempre me toca fregar a mí** I'm always the one who has to do the dishes; ✦ MODISMO **¡a pagar tocan!** it's time to pay up!
5 (= *rayar*) **~ en algo** to border on sth, verge on sth
6 (= *chocar*) **~ con algo** to touch sth
7 **~ a su fin** to be drawing to a close
Ⓒ **tocarse** VPR **1** (*uso reflexivo*) **no te toques los granos** don't pick your spots; **está todo el día tocándose la barba** he's always playing with his beard
2 (*uso recíproco*) to touch; **los cables no deben ~se** the wires should not be touching

tocata SF (*Mús*) toccata

tocateja: a ~* ADV (*Esp*) on the nail*

tocayo/a SM/F **1** [*de nombre*] namesake; **es mi ~** he's my namesake; **somos ~s** we have the same name **2** (= *amigo*) friend

toche* ADJ (*Ven*) stupid

tocho* SM big fat book, tome

tocinillo SM ➤ **tocinillo de cielo** *pudding made with egg yolk and syrup*

tocino SM **1** (= *grasa*) salted fresh lard; (*con vetas de carne*) salt pork; [*de panceta*] bacon **2** ➤ **tocino de cielo** = **tocinillo de cielo**; *ver* **tocinillo**

tocología SF obstetrics *sing*

tocólogo/a SM/F obstetrician

tocón¹/ona* SM/F groper*; **es un ~** he's got wandering hands*

tocón² ADJ (*And*) (= *sin rabo*) tailless; (*Carib*) (= *sin cuernos*) hornless

tocuyo SM (*SAm*) coarse cotton cloth

todavía ADV **1** (*temporal*) (*en oraciones afirmativas*) still; (*en oraciones negativas*) yet, still; **está nevando ~** it is still snowing; **—¿has acabado? —todavía no** "have you finished?" — "not yet"; **~ no se ha ido** she hasn't gone yet, she still hasn't gone; **~ en 1970** as late as 1970 **2** (= *incluso*) even; **es ~ más inteligente que su hermano** he's even more intelligent than his brother, he's more intelligent still than his brother **3** (*) (= *encima*) **has aprobado sin estudiar y ~ te quejas** you passed without doing any work and (yet) you're still complaining

---

Todavía se traduce por **still** en oraciones afirmativas e interrogativas: "Todavía tienen hambre", *They're still hungry*; "¿Todavía te duele?", *Is it still hurting?* Se traduce por **yet** en oraciones negativas e interrogativas negativas: "El doctor no ha llegado todavía", *The doctor hasn't arrived yet*; "¿Todavía no han llamado?", *Haven't they phoned yet?* En este último caso, puede utilizarse también **still** si se quiere dar mayor énfasis: "Y todavía no me has devuelto el libro", *You still haven't given me the book back*.

---

todero/a* SM/F (*Col, Ven*) jack of all trades

todo Ⓐ ADJ **1** (*en singular*) (= *en su totalidad*) all; **no he dormido en toda la noche** I haven't slept all night; **ha viajado por ~ el mundo** he has travelled throughout *o* all over the world; **lo sabe ~ Madrid** all Madrid knows it; **en toda España no hay más que cinco** there are only five in the whole of Spain; **~ lo que usted necesite** everything *o* whatever you need; **con ~ lo listo que es, no es capaz de resolver esto** clever as he is *o* for all his intelligence, he can't solve this problem; **~ lo demás** all the rest; **a ~ con toda prisa** in all haste, with all speed; **a toda velocidad** at full speed; ✦ MODISMO **a ~ esto** (= *entretanto*) meanwhile; (= *a propósito*) by the way **2** (*en plural*) **2.1** (*en un conjunto*) all; **~s los libros** all the books; **~s vosotros** all of you **2.2** (= *cada*) every; **~s los días** every day; **habrá un turno para ~s y cada uno de los participantes** each and every one of the participants will have their turn **3** (*con valor enfático*) **es ~ un hombre** he's every inch a man, he's a real man; **es ~ un héroe** he's a real hero; **soy ~ oídos** I'm all ears; **puede ser ~ lo sencillo que usted quiera** it can be as simple as you wish; **~ lo contrario** quite the opposite **4** (= *del todo*) **lleva una falda toda rota** she's wearing a skirt that's all torn; **vaya ~ seguido** go straight on *o* ahead Ⓑ PRON **1** (*en singular*) **se lo comió ~** he ate it all; **lo han vendido ~** they've sold the lot, they've sold it all; **lo sabemos ~** we know everything; **~ o nada** all or nothing; **y luego ~ son sonrisas** and then it's all smiles; **~ el que quiera ...** everyone *o* anyone who wants to ... ➤ **todo a cien** SM (*Esp*) *shop where everything costs 100 pesetas*, ≈ dollar store (*EEUU*) **2** (*en plural*) (= *cosas*) all (of them); (= *personas*) everybody, everyone; **el más bonito de ~s** the prettiest of all; **~s estaban de acuerdo** everybody *o* everyone agreed; **~s los que quieran venir** all those who want to come, anyone who wants to come **3** (*locuciones con preposición*) **ante ~** first of all, in the first place; **con ~:** **con ~ y con eso llegamos una hora tarde** we still arrived an hour late, nevertheless we arrived an hour late; **de ~:** **lo llamaron de ~** they called him every name under the sun; **nos pasó de ~** everything possible

happened to us, you name it, it happened to us; **del ~** wholly, entirely; **no es del ~ malo** it is not wholly *o* all bad; **no es del ~ verdad** it is not entirely true; **después de ~** after all; ✦ MODISMOS **estar en ~** to be on the ball*; **ir a por todas** to give it one's all Ⓒ SM **el ~** the whole; **como** *o* **en un ~** as a whole

todopoderoso Ⓐ ADJ almighty, all-powerful Ⓑ SM **el Todopoderoso** the Almighty

todoterreno Ⓐ SM INV (*tb* **coche ~, vehículo ~**) four-wheel drive ve(*Brit*)hicle, all-terrain vehicle Ⓑ ADJ INV (= *versátil*) multi-purpose; (= *adaptable*) adaptable

toga SF (*Hist*) toga; (*Jur*) robe, gown; (*Univ*) gown

toilette [tua'le] SM (*CS*) toilet (*Brit*), lavatory (*esp Brit*), washroom (*EEUU*)

Tokio SM Tokyo

tolda SF (*Col*) (= *tienda de campaña*) tent; (= *mosquitero*) mosquito net

toldería SF (*And, CS*) Indian village, camp of Indian huts

toldo SM **1** (*en tienda, balcón*) awning; (*en la playa*) sunshade; (*para fiesta*) marquee, garden tent (*EEUU*); (*para tapar*) tarpaulin **2** (*And, CS*) (= *choza*) Indian hut

toledano ADJ Toledan, of/from Toledo

tolerable ADJ tolerable

tolerado ADJ tolerated; **película tolerada (para menores)** a film (*esp Brit*) *o* movie (*esp EEUU*) suitable for children

tolerancia SF **1** (= *respeto*) tolerance; [*de ideas*] toleration ➤ **tolerancia cero** zero tolerance **2** (*Med, Téc*) tolerance

tolerante ADJ tolerant

tolerar /1a/ VT **1** (= *consentir*) to tolerate; **no se puede ~ esto** this cannot be tolerated; **no tolera que digan eso** he won't allow them to say that; **su madre le tolera demasiado** his mother lets him get away with too much **2** (= *aguantar*) to bear, put up with; **su estómago no tolera los huevos** eggs don't agree with him **3** (*Med, Téc*) to tolerate

toletole SM (*And, CS*) row, uproar

tolteca Ⓐ ADJ Toltec Ⓑ SMF Toltec

toma Ⓐ SF **1** (*Téc*) (*de agua, gas*) (= *entrada*) inlet; (= *salida*) outlet ➤ **toma de aire** air inlet, air intake ➤ **toma de antena** (*Radio, TV*) aerial socket (*Brit*), antenna outlet (*EEUU*) ➤ **toma de corriente** wall socket, power point (*Brit*) ➤ **toma de tierra** earth (wire) (*Brit*), ground (wire) (*EEUU*) **2** (*Cine, TV*) shot; **¡escena primera, tercera ~!** scene one, take three! **3** (= *ingestión*) [*de jarabe, medicina*] dose; [*de bebé*] feed **4** (*Mil*) (= *captura*) taking, capture; **la ~ de Granada** the taking *o* capture of Granada **5** (*LAm*) (= *acequia*) irrigation channel **6** ➤ **toma de conciencia** realization ➤ **toma de contacto** initial contact ➤ **toma de decisiones** decision-making, decision-taking ➤ **toma de posesión: mañana tendrá lugar la ~ de posesión del nuevo presidente** the new president will take office tomorrow ➤ **toma de tierra** (*Aer*) landing, touchdown Ⓑ SM ➤ **toma y daca** give and take

tomado ADJ **1** [*voz*] hoarse **2 estar ~** (*LAm**) (= *borracho*) to be drunk

tomador(a) SM/F **1** (*Com*) [*de bono, cheque*] drawee; [*de seguro*] policy holder **2** (*LAm**) (= *borracho*) drunkard

tomadura SF ➤ **tomadura de pelo** (= *guasa*) leg-pull*; (= *mofa*) mockery; (= *timo*) con*, rip-off*

---

tomar /1a/

Ⓐ VERBO TRANSITIVO	Ⓒ VERBO PRONOMINAL
Ⓑ VERBO INTRANSITIVO	

Para las expresiones **tomar impulso, tomar tierra** *etc, ver la entrada correspondiente a la otra palabra.*

---

tomar Ⓐ VERBO TRANSITIVO
1 (= *asir, agarrar*) to take; **si no tienes bolígrafo toma éste**

take this pen if you haven't got one; **la tomó de la mano** he took her by the hand; **lo toma o lo deja** take it or leave it; **¡toma!** here (you are)!
2 (= *ingerir, consumir*) [+ *comida*] to eat, have; [+ *bebida*] to drink, have; [+ *medicina*] to take; **si tienes hambre podemos ~ algo** if you're hungry we can get something to eat; **tomas demasiado café** you drink too much coffee; **tomamos unas cervezas** we had a few beers; **¿qué quieres ~?** what would you like?, what will you have?; **~ el pecho** to feed at the breast, breastfeed
3 [+ *tren, avión, taxi*] to take
4 (*Cine, Fot, TV*) to take
5 (= *apuntar*) [+ *notas, apuntes*] to take; [+ *discurso*] to take down; **nunca toma apuntes en clase** he never takes notes in class; **tomo nota de todo lo que me has dicho** I have taken note of everything you have told me
6 (= *medir*) [+ *temperatura, pulso*] to take; **tengo que ir a que me tomen la tensión** I have to go and have my blood pressure taken
7 (= *adoptar*) [+ *decisión, precauciones*] to take
8 (= *adquirir*) **la situación está tomando mal cariz** the situation is beginning to look ugly; **el proyecto ya está tomando forma** the project is taking shape
9 (= *empezar a sentir*) **le han tomado mucho cariño** they have become very fond of him; **les tomé asco a los caracoles** I went off snails; ♦ MODISMO **-la o tenerla tomada con algn*** to have (got) it in for sb*
10 (= *disfrutar de*) [+ *baño, ducha*] to have, take; **~ el aire o el fresco** to get some fresh air; **~ sol** (*Méx, CS*) **o el sol** to sunbathe
11 (*Mil*) (= *capturar*) to take, capture; (= *ocupar*) to occupy
12 (= *ocupar*) to take; **traducirlo me ha tomado tres horas** it took me three hours to translate it
13 (= *entender, interpretar*) to take; **lo tomó como una ofensa** he took offence at it, he was offended by it; **lo han tomado a broma** they haven't taken it seriously, they are treating it as a joke; **no lo tomes en serio** don't take it seriously
14
♦ **tomar a algn por** (= *confundir*) **~ a algn por policía** to take sb for a policeman, think that sb is a policeman; **~ a algn por loco** to think sb mad; **¿por quién me toma?** what do you take me for?, who do you think I am?
Ⓑ VERBO INTRANSITIVO
1 (*Bot*) [*planta*] to take (root); [*injerto*] to take
2 (*LAm*) (= *ir*) **~ a la derecha** to turn right
3 (*LAm*) (= *beber*) to drink
4 (*Esp**) (*exclamaciones*) **¡toma! menuda suerte has tenido** well, of all the luck!, can you believe it? what luck!; **¡toma! pues yo también lo sé hacer** hey! I know how to do that too; ♦ MODISMO **¡toma ya!: ¡toma ya, vaya golazo!** look at that, what a fantastic goal!
Ⓒ **tomarse** VERBO PRONOMINAL
1 [+ *vacaciones, libertades*] to take; **me he tomado la libertad de leer tu informe** I have taken the liberty of reading your report; **no se ~on la molestia de informarnos** they didn't bother o take the trouble to let us know
2 (= *ingerir*) [+ *bebida*] to drink, have; [+ *comida*] to eat, have; [+ *medicina*] to take; **se tomó tres cervezas** he drank o had three beers; **me tomé un bocadillo** I ate o had a sandwich
3 (= *medirse*) [+ *pulso, temperatura*] to take
4 (= *entender, interpretar*) to take; **no te lo tomes así** don't take it that way; **no te lo tomes tan a mal** don't take it so badly, don't take it so much to heart; **se lo toma todo muy en serio** he takes it all very seriously

tomatal SM tomato bed, tomato field

tomatazo SM **recibió un montón de ~s** he was pelted with tomatoes

tomate SM **1** (= *verdura*) tomato; ♦ MODISMO **ponerse como un ~** to turn as red as a beetroot (*Brit*) o beet (*EEUU*;) **2** (*) (*en calcetín, media*) hole **3** (*Esp**) (= *jaleo*) fuss, row; (= *pelea*) set-to*; **al final de la noche hubo ~** there was a fight at the end of the evening

tomatera SF **1** (= *planta*) tomato plant **2** (*Chi**) (= *juerga*) drunken spree

tomavistas SM INV cine camera (*Brit*), movie camera (*EEUU*)

tombo** SM (*Col, Ven*) fuzz**, police

tómbola SF tombola

tomillo SM thyme

tomo¹ SM volume; **en tres ~s** in three volumes

tomo² SM (= *bulto*) bulk, size; ♦ MODISMO **de ~ y lomo*** utter, out-and-out

ton SM **sin ~ ni son** (= *sin motivo*) for no particular reason; (= *sin lógica*) without rhyme or reason

tonada SF **1** (= *melodía*) tune; (= *canción*) song, air **2** (*LAm*) (= *acento*) accent

tonadilla SF little tune, ditty

tonal ADJ tonal

tonalidad SF **1** (*Mús*) tonality; (*Radio*) tone **2** (*Arte*) (= *tono*) shade; (= *colores*) colour scheme, color scheme (*EEUU*)

tonel SM **1** (= *barril*) barrel, cask **2** (*) (= *persona*) fat lump*

tonelada SF ton

tonelaje SM tonnage

tongo¹ SM (*Dep*) (= *trampa*) fixing; **¡hay ~!** it's been fixed!, it's been rigged!; **hubo ~ en las elecciones** the elections were rigged

tongo² SM (*And*) (= *sombrero*) bowler hat (*esp Brit*), derby (*EEUU*)

tónica SF **1** (= *bebida*) tonic, tonic water **2** (= *tendencia*) tone, trend, tendency

tónico Ⓐ ADJ **1** (*Mús*) [+ *nota*] tonic **2** (*Ling*) [+ *sílaba*] tonic *antes de s*, stressed **3** (*Med*) (= *estimulante*) tonic, stimulating Ⓑ SM tonic

tonificador ADJ, **tonificante** ADJ invigorating, stimulating

tonificar /1g/ VT [+ *músculos, piel*] to tone up; [+ *ánimo*] to invigorate

tonillo SM **1** (*especial*) (sarcastic) tone of voice **2** (*monótono*) monotonous tone of voice, monotonous drone **3** (*regional*) accent

tono SM **1** [*de sonido*] tone ➤ **tono de discado** (*CS*), **tono de marcar** (*Telec*) dialling tone (*Brit*), dial tone (*EEUU*) ➤ **tono de voz** tone of voice; **lo noté por el ~ de su voz** I could tell from his tone of voice; **—ya me he dado cuenta —dijo, alzando el ~ de voz** "I can see that," he said, raising his voice
2 [*de palabras, discusión, escrito*] tone; **le molestó el ~ de mi carta** she was upset by the tone of my letter; **¡cómo hablas en ese ~ a tu padre!** how dare you speak to your father in that tone (of voice)!; **contestó con ~ de enfado** she replied angrily; **bajar el ~** to soften one's tone; **cambiar de ~** to change one's tone; **fuera de ~** [*respuesta, comentario, actitud*] uncalled for; **subir de ~** [*discusión, conversación*] to grow o become heated; [*conflicto*] to intensify; [*quejas*] to grow louder; **las voces empezaron a subir de ~** they began to raise their voices; **chistes subidos de ~** racy jokes
3 a ~ matching; **estar a ~ con algo** [*color*] to match sth; [*diseño, comentarios*] to be in keeping with sth; **una escena final divertida, muy a ~ con el resto de la película** an amusing final scene, very much in keeping with the rest of the film; **una ideología más a ~ con los tiempos** an ideology more in tune with the times; **ponerse a ~** (= *prepararse físicamente*) to get (o.s.) into shape; (= *animarse*) to perk o.s. up*
4 (= *clase, distinción*) **es de mal ~ hablar de esos temas** it is bad form to talk about such matters, it's (simply) not done to talk about such things; ♦ MODISMO **darse ~** to put on airs
5 [*de color*] shade, tone; **en ~s grises y azules** in shades of grey and blue, in grey and blue tones; **~s pastel** pastel shades, pastel tones
6 (*Anat, Med*) tone ➤ **tono muscular** muscle tone
7 (*Mús*) (= *intervalo*) tone; (= *tonalidad*) key; (= *altura*) pitch
8 (*Mús*) (= *diapasón*) tuning fork; (= *corredera*) slide

tonsura SF tonsure

tontear* /1a/ VI **1** (= *hacer el tonto*) to fool about, act the fool **2** (= *decir tonterías*) to talk nonsense **3** (*amorosamente*) to flirt

tontera SF (*LAm*) = **tontería**

tontería SF **1** (= *dicho*) **eso son ~s** ◊ **eso es una ~** that's nonsense *o* rubbish (*esp Brit*) *o* garbage (*esp EEUU*); **decir ~s** to talk nonsense *o* rubbish (*esp Brit*) *o* garbage (*esp EEUU*); **¡qué ~ acabas de decir!** that was a silly thing to say!; **lo que has dicho no es ninguna ~** what you've just said isn't such a bad idea
2 (= *acto*) **ha sido una ~ el negarte a verle** it was silly of you to refuse to see him; **hacer una ~** to do a silly thing *o* something silly
3 (= *insignificancia*) silly little thing; **cualquier ~ le afecta** he gets upset over any silly little thing *o* the slightest thing; **lo vendió por una ~** he sold it for next to nothing
4 (= *remilgo*) **Juanito tiene mucha ~ a la hora de comer** Juanito is so picky about his food
5 (= *cualidad*) silliness, foolishness

tonto/a Ⓐ ADJ **1** [*persona*] **1.1** (= *bobo*) (*dicho con afecto*) silly; (*dicho con enfado*) stupid; **¿tú te has creído que yo soy ~?** ◊ **¿me tomas por ~?** do you think I'm stupid?; ✦ MODISMO **es ~ del bote** *o* **de capirote** *o* **de remate** he's a total *o* complete idiot* **1.2** (= *poco inteligente*) stupid; **¡y parecía ~!** and we thought he was stupid!; ✦ MODISMOS **y a lo ~, a lo ~, se le pasó la mitad del día** and before he knew it, half the day had slipped by; **hacer ~ a algn** (*Chi**) to trick sb; **a tontas y a locas: no quiero que actúes/hables a tontas y a locas** don't just do/say the first thing that comes into your head **1.3** (= *insolente*) silly; **¡si te pones ~ no te vuelvo a traer a la playa!** if you start being silly I won't take you to the beach again! **1.4** (= *torpe*) **me quedé como ~ después del golpe** I felt dazed after the knock; **hoy se me olvida todo, estoy como ~** I keep forgetting things today, I'm out of it* **1.5** (= *presumido*) stuck-up* **1.6** (*Med*) imbecile
2 [*risa, frase, accidente*] silly; **me entró la risa tonta** I started giggling
Ⓑ SM/F idiot; **el ~ del pueblo** the village idiot; ✦ MODISMOS **hacer el ~** (*a propósito*) to act the fool, play the fool; (*sin querer*) to be a fool; **hacerse el ~** to act dumb

tontorrón/ona* SM/F dimwit*

toñeco/a* Ⓐ ADJ (*Ven*) spoilt Ⓑ SM/F spoilt brat*

topacio SM topaz

topar /1a/ Ⓐ VI **1** (= *encontrar*) **~ con** [+ *persona*] to run into, come across, bump into; [+ *objeto*] to find, come across **2** (= *chocar*) **~ contra** to run into, hit; **~ con un obstáculo** to run into an obstacle, hit an obstacle
Ⓑ VT **1** (*Zool*) to butt, horn **2** [+ *persona*] to run into, come across, bump into; [+ *objeto*] to find, come across
Ⓒ **toparse** VPR **~se con** [+ *persona*] to run into, come across, bump into; [+ *objeto*] to find, come across

tope¹ Ⓐ ADJ INV (= *máximo*) maximum, top; **fecha ~** closing date, deadline
Ⓑ SM **1** (= *límite*) limit; ✦ MODISMOS **estar a ~** *o* **hasta el ~** *o* **hasta los ~s***: **el teatro estaba (lleno) a ~** the theatre was packed*; **el contenedor está hasta los ~s** the container is overloaded; **voy a estar a ~ de trabajo** (*Esp*) I'm going to be up to my eyes *o* neck in work*; **ir a ~** (*Esp**) to go flat out*; **vivir a ~** (*Esp**) to live life to the full
2 (*And*) (= *cumbre*) peak, summit
Ⓒ ADV (*Esp***) (= *muy*) **es ~ enrollada** she's mega-cool*; **es ~ guay** it's well cool*

tope² SM (= *objeto*) stop, check; [*de tren*] buffer; [*de coche*] bumper (*Brit*), fender (*EEUU*); [*de puerta*] doorstop, wedge; [*de revólver*] catch; (*Méx*) (*en una calle*) speed bump

topetazo SM, **topetón** SM bump, bang

tópico Ⓐ ADJ **1** (*Med*) local; **de uso ~** for external use **2** (= *trillado*) commonplace, trite Ⓑ SM **1** (= *lugar común*) commonplace, cliché **2** (*LAm*) (= *tema*) topic, subject

top-less SM, **topless** SM (*en playa, piscina*) topless bathing; (*en club*) topless entertainment; **ir en** *o* **hacer ~** to go topless

top-model SMF (*pl* **~s**) supermodel

topo SM **1** (*Zool*) mole **2** (= *torpe*) clumsy person, blunderer **3** (= *espía*) mole **4** (*Esp*) (= *lunar*) polka dot **5** (*Col**) (= *pendiente*) earring

topocho/a* Ⓐ ADJ (*Ven*) dumpy (*pey**) Ⓑ SM/F (*Ven*) kid* Ⓒ SM baby banana

topografía SF topography

topógrafo/a SM/F topographer

toponimia SF **1** (= *nombres*) toponymy (*frm*), place names *pl* **2** (= *estudio*) study of place names

topónimo SM place name

toque SM **1** (= *golpecito*) tap; **el jefe tuvo que darle un ~ de atención por llegar tarde** the boss had to pull him up for being late; **te van a dar un ~ si sigues portándote mal*** you'll get a telling-off if you keep behaving badly
2 (= *sonido*) [*de campana*] chime, ring; [*de reloj*] stroke; [*de timbre*] ring; [*de tambor*] beat; **al ~ de las doce** on the stroke of twelve; **dar un ~ a algn** (*por teléfono*) to give sb a bell* ➤ **toque de diana** reveille ➤ **toque de difuntos** death knell ➤ **toque de oración** call to prayer ➤ **toque de queda** curfew
3 (= *detalle*) touch; **el ~ personal** the personal touch; **faltan algunos ~s para completarlo** it still needs a few touches to finish it off; **dar el último** *o* **los últimos ~s a algo** to put the finishing touch *o* touches to sth
4 (*Arte*) [*de color, brillo*] touch ➤ **toque de luz** highlight
5 (*Méx***) [*de marihuana*] joint*, spliff**
6 (*Méx**) (= *descarga eléctrica*) (electric) shock

toquetear* /1a/ VT **1** (= *manosear*) to handle, finger **2** (= *acariciar*) to fondle, feel up*, touch up*

toqueteo* SM **1** (= *manoseo*) handling, fingering **2** (= *caricias*) fondling, touching up*

toquilla SF (= *chal*) knitted shawl; (*para la cabeza*) headscarf

torácico ADJ thoracic

tórax SM thorax; **radiografía de ~** chest X-ray

torbellino SM **1** [*de viento*] whirlwind; [*de polvo*] dust cloud **2** [*de cosas*] whirl

torcedura SF **1** (*gen*) twist(ing); (*Med*) sprain, strain **2** (= *vino*) weak wine

torcer /2b, 2h/ Ⓐ VT **1** (= *retorcer*) [+ *dedo, muñeca, tronco*] to twist; [+ *tobillo*] to twist, sprain; [+ *madera*] to warp; [+ *soga*] to plait (*esp Brit*), braid (*EEUU*); **torció la cabeza para mirarla** he turned (his head) to look at her
2 ~ el gesto to scowl; **~ los ojos** *o* **la vista** to squint
3 [+ *ropa*] to wring
4 (= *cambiar*) [+ *rumbo*] to change; [+ *voluntad*] to bend; [+ *pensamientos*] to turn; [+ *significado*] to distort, twist; **el conflicto ha torcido el curso de los acontecimientos** the conflict has changed the course of events
5 (= *pervertir*) [+ *persona*] to lead astray
Ⓑ VI (= *girar*) [*camino, vehículo, viajero*] to turn; **~ a la derecha/izquierda** to turn right/left
Ⓒ **torcerse** VPR **1** (= *retorcerse*) to twist; (= *doblarse*) to bend; **me torcí el tobillo** I twisted *o* sprained my ankle
2 (= *ladearse*) **gira el volante que te estás torciendo** turn the steering wheel, you're not driving straight; **usa papel rayado para no ~se escribiendo** use ruled paper so you write straight
3 (= *ir mal*) [*persona*] to go astray, go off the rails; [*proyecto*] to go off the rails; [*proceso, acontecimientos*] to take a strange turn

torcido ADJ [*nariz, línea*] crooked; **el cuadro está ~** the picture is not straight, the picture is crooked; **llevaba el sombrero algo ~** he had his hat on not quite straight

tordo Ⓐ ADJ dappled, dapple-grey Ⓑ SM (= *ave*) thrush; (*RPl*) starling

torear /1a/ Ⓐ VT **1** [+ *toro*] to fight, play **2** (= *evitar*) to dodge, avoid **3** (= *burlarse*) to tease; ✦ MODISMO **a mí no me torea nadie!** (*Esp*) nobody messes me around!* **4** (*LAm**) (= *provocar*) to torment Ⓑ VI to fight (bulls); **no volverá a ~** he will never fight again; **el muchacho quiere ~** the boy wants to be a bullfighter

toreo SM (art of) bullfighting

torera SF (= *chaqueta*) short tight jacket; ✦ MODISMOS **saltarse algo a la ~**: **saltarse un deber a la ~** to neglect one's duty; **saltarse una ley a la ~** to flout a law

torero/a SM/F bullfighter

toril SM bullpen

tormenta SF **1** (*Meteo*) storm; ✦ MODISMO **una ~ en un**

vaso de agua a storm in a teacup (*Brit*), a tempest in a teapot (*EEUU*) ➤ **tormenta de arena** sandstorm ➤ **tormenta de nieve** snowstorm 2 (= *discusión*) storm; (= *trastorno*) upheaval, turmoil; **desencadenó una ~ de pasiones** it unleashed a storm of passions

tormento SM (= *tortura*) torture; (*fig*) torture, torment; (= *angustia*) anguish, agony; **dar ~ a** to torment; (*fig*) to torment, plague; **darse ~** to torment o.s.; **estos zapatos son un ~** these shoes are agony

tormentoso ADJ stormy

torna SF (= *vuelta*) return; ✦ MODISMO **cambiar las ~s** to turn the tables

tornado SM tornado

tornar /1a/ **Ⓐ** VI (*liter*) to return, go back; **~ a hacer algo** to do sth again **Ⓑ** **tornarse** VPR 1 (= *regresar*) to return 2 (= *convertirse*) to become, turn

tornasol SM 1 (*Bot*) sunflower 2 (*Quím*) litmus 3 (*fig*) sheen, iridescence

torneado **Ⓐ** ADJ 1 (*Téc*) turned (*on a lathe*) 2 [*brazo*] shapely, delicately curved; [*figura*] pleasingly rounded **Ⓑ** SM turning

tornear /1a/ VT to turn (*on a lathe*)

torneo SM 1 (*Dep*) tournament, competition ➤ **torneo de tenis** tennis tournament ➤ **torneo por equipos** team tournament 2 (*Hist*) joust

tornero/a SM/F machinist, turner

tornillo SM (*en punta*) screw; (*para tuerca*) bolt; ✦ MODISMOS **apretar los ~s a algn** to apply pressure on sb, put the screws on sb*; **le falta un ~*** he has a screw loose*

torniquete SM 1 (= *barra giratoria*) turnstile 2 (*Med*) tourniquet

torno SM 1 (*para levantar pesos*) winch, windlass; (*para tensar*) winding drum 2 (*para tornear*) lathe ➤ **torno de alfarero** potter's wheel ➤ **torno de tornero** turning lathe 3 **en ~ a: se reunieron en ~ a él** they gathered round him; **la conversación giraba en ~ a las elecciones** the conversation revolved o centred around the election

toro SM 1 (*Zool*) bull; ✦ MODISMO **agarrar al ~ por las astas** (*LAm*) ◇ **coger el ~ por los cuernos** (*Esp*) to take the bull by the horns ➤ **toro bravo**, **toro de lidia** fighting bull 2 (= *hombre*) strong man, he-man*, tough guy* 3 **los ~s** (= *corrida*) bullfight *sing*; (= *toreo*) bullfighting; **ir a los ~s** to go to the bullfight; **no me gustan los ~s** I don't like bullfighting; ✦ MODISMO **ver los ~s desde la barrera** to stand on the sidelines, remain uncommitted

toronja SF grapefruit, pomelo (*EEUU*)

torpe ADJ 1 (= *poco ágil*) [*persona*] clumsy; [*movimiento*] ungainly 2 (= *necio*) dim, slow; **soy muy ~ para la informática** I'm very dim o slow when it comes to computers 3 (= *con poco tacto*) clumsy

torpedear /1a/ VT (*Mil*) to torpedo; **~ a algn con preguntas** to bombard sb with questions

torpedo SM torpedo

torpeza SF 1 (= *falta de agilidad*) [*de persona*] clumsiness; [*de movimientos*] ungainliness 2 (= *falta de inteligencia*) dimness, slowness 3 (= *falta de tacto*) **fue una ~ por mi parte decírselo** it was stupid o clumsy of me to tell him 4 (= *tontería*) **cometer una ~** to do sth stupid

torpor SM torpor

torre SF 1 (*Arquit*) tower; [*de oficinas, viviendas*] high-rise, tower block (*Brit*); (*Radio*) mast, tower; [*de electricidad*] pylon; [*de pozo de petróleo*] derrick ➤ **torre de alta tensión**, **torre de conducción eléctrica** electricity pylon ➤ **Torre de Babel** Tower of Babel ➤ **torre de marfil** ivory tower 2 (*Ajedrez*) rook, castle 3 (*Aer, Mil, Náut*) turret; (*Mil*) watchtower ➤ **torre de control** (*Aer*) control tower ➤ **torre del homenaje** keep ➤ **torre de observación** observation tower, watchtower ➤ **torre de perforación** drilling rig

torrefacto ADJ high roast

torreja SF 1 (*Perú*) (*fried*) slices of fruit and vegetables 2 (*Chi*) slice

torrencial ADJ torrential

torrente SM 1 (= *río*) torrent ➤ **torrente de sangre**, **torrente sanguíneo** bloodstream 2 [*de palabras*] torrent, rush; [*de insultos*] stream, torrent; [*de lágrimas*] flood; [*de gente*] stream ➤ **torrente de voz** powerful voice

torrentoso ADJ (*LAm*) [*río*] torrential, rushing

torreón SM [*de castillo*] tower; [*de casa*] turret

torreta SF 1 (*Aer, Mil, Náut*) turret; [*de submarino*] conning tower 2 (*Elec*) pylon, mast

tórrido ADJ torrid

torrija SF bread soaked in milk and fried in batter with honey or sugar and wine, eaten especially at Easter

torsión SF 1 (= *torcedura*) twist, twisting 2 (*Mec*) torsion, torque

torso SM (*Anat*) torso; (*Arte*) head and shoulders

torta SF 1 (*) (= *bofetada*) thump; (= *puñetazo*) punch, sock*; (= *caída*) fall; (= *choque*) crash; **liarse a ~s** to get involved in a punch-up 2 (*esp LAm*) (= *pastel*) cake; (*con base de masa quebrada*) tart, flan; (= *crepe*) pancake; (*Méx*) sandwich; ✦ MODISMO **no entendió ni ~** he didn't understand a word of it

tortazo* SM (= *bofetada*) slap, sock*; (= *golpe*) thump; **pegarse un ~** to get a knock

tortícolis SF INV stiff neck; **me levanté con ~** I got up with a stiff neck o a crick in my neck

tortilla SF 1 [*de huevo*] omelette; ✦ MODISMOS **dar la vuelta a la ~** to turn the tables; **volverse la ~: se ha vuelto la ~** now the boot is on the other foot, it's a different story now; **se le volvió la ~** it came out all wrong for him, it all blew up in his face ➤ **tortilla de patatas**, **tortilla española** Spanish potato omelette ➤ **tortilla francesa** (*Esp*) plain omelette 2 [*de maíz*] flat maize pancake, tortilla

tortillera* SF (= *lesbiana*) dyke***, lesbian

tortita SF pancake

tórtola SF turtledove

tórtolo SM 1 (= *ave*) (male) turtledove 2 (*) (= *amante*) lovebird, loverboy; **tórtolos** pair of lovers, lovebirds

tortuga SF [*de tierra*] tortoise; (*tb* **~ marina**) turtle (*Brit*), sea turtle (*EEUU*); ✦ MODISMO **a paso de ~** at a snail's pace

tortuguismo SM (*Méx*) go-slow (*Brit*), slowdown (*EEUU*)

tortuoso ADJ 1 [*camino*] winding, full of twists and turns 2 [*conducta*] devious

tortura SF torture

torturar /1a/ VT to torture

torvo ADJ grim, fierce

tos SF cough; **acceso de ~** coughing fit; **tiene ~** he's got a cough ➤ **tos convulsa**, **tos ferina** whooping cough

tosco ADJ coarse, rough, crude

toser /2a/ **Ⓐ** VI to cough **Ⓑ** VT ✦ MODISMO **no hay quien le tosa** (*Esp*): **no hay quien le tosa a la hora de cocinar** he's in a class by himself when it comes to cooking; **cuando se pone así no hay quien le tosa** no one gets in his way when he's in that mood

tosquedad SF coarseness, roughness, crudeness

tostada SF 1 [*de pan*] piece of toast; **~s** toast *sing*; ✦ MODISMO **olerse la ~** to smell a rat 2 (*Méx*) (= *tortilla*) fried tortilla

tostado **Ⓐ** ADJ 1 (*Culin*) toasted 2 [*color*] dark brown, ochre; [*persona*] tanned 3 (*Ven**) (= *loco*) crazy **Ⓑ** SM 1 (= *acción*) [*de pan*] toasting; [*de café*] roasting 2 (= *bronceado*) tan

tostador SM [*de pan*] toaster; [*de café*] roaster ➤ **tostador de pan** electric toaster

tostadora SF toaster

tostar /1l/ **Ⓐ** VT 1 [+ *pan*] to toast; [+ *café*] to roast 2 (= *broncear*) to tan **Ⓑ** **tostarse** VPR (*tb* **~se al sol**) to tan, get brown

tostón SM 1 (*Esp**) (= *lata*) bore, nuisance; (= *discurso*) long boring speech; (= *cuento*) tedious tale; **dar el ~** (= *aburrir*) to be a bore; (= *fastidiar*) to be a nuisance 2 (*Esp*) (*para la sopa*) crouton 3 (= *cochinillo*) roast sucking pig 4 (*Ven*) (= *plátano*) fried plantain 5 (*Méx**) (= *moneda*) 50-cent piece

total Ⓐ ADJ **1** (= *absoluto*) [*éxito, fracaso*] total; **una revisión ~ de su teoría** a complete revision of his theory; **una calamidad ~** a total disaster
2 [*importe, suma*] total
3 (*Esp**) (= *excelente*) smashing*, brilliant*, awesome (*EEUU**)
Ⓑ ADV **1** (= *resumiendo*) in short, all in all; (= *así que*) so; **~ que** to cut a long story short, the upshot of it all was that ...; **~, que no fuimos** so we didn't go after all; **~, que vas a hacer lo que quieras** basically then you're going to do as you please
2 (= *al fin y al cabo*) at the end of the day; **~, ¿qué más te da?** at the end of the day, what do you care?; **~, usted manda** well, you're the boss after all
Ⓒ SM (= *suma total*) total; (= *totalidad*) whole; **el ~ de la población** the whole (of the) population; **en ~** in all

totalidad SF whole; **la práctica ~ de los votantes** nearly all the voters; **quieren publicar el informe en su ~** they want to publish the report in its entirety

totalitario ADJ totalitarian

totalitarismo SM totalitarianism

totalizar /1f/ Ⓐ VT to totalize, add up Ⓑ VI to add up to, total

totalmente ADV totally, completely; **estoy ~ de acuerdo** I totally *o* completely agree; **—¿estás seguro? —totalmente** "are you sure?" — "absolutely"

totogol SM (*Col*) football pools *pl* (*Brit*), sports lottery (*EEUU*)

totopo SM (*CAm, Méx*) crisp tortilla

totora SF (*And*) large reed

touroperador(a) SM/F tour operator

toxicidad SF toxicity

tóxico Ⓐ ADJ toxic, poisonous Ⓑ SM poison, toxin

toxicología SF toxicology

toxicomanía SF drug-addiction

toxicómano/a Ⓐ ADJ addicted to drugs Ⓑ SM/F drug addict

toxina SF toxin

tozudez SF stubbornness, obstinacy

tozudo ADJ stubborn, obstinate

traba SF **1** (= *unión*) bond, tie; (*Mec*) clasp, clamp; [*de caballo*] hobble; (*Chi*) hair slide; (*RPl*) [*de corbata*] tie pin
2 (= *estorbo*) obstacle, hindrance; **sin ~s** unrestrained, free; **poner ~s a** to restrain, obstruct; **ponerse ~s** to make difficulties for o.s.

trabado ADJ (= *unido*) joined; [*discurso*] coherent, well constructed

trabajado ADJ **1** (= *elaborado*) carefully worked; **bien ~** well made, elaborately fashioned **2** [*persona*] (= *cansado*) worn out, weary from overwork

trabajador(a) Ⓐ ADJ hard-working, industrious Ⓑ SM/F worker ➤ **trabajador(a) autónomo/a** self-employed person ➤ **trabajador(a) social** social worker

trabajar /1a/ Ⓐ VI **1** [*persona*] to work; **no trabajes tanto** don't work so hard; **ese actor trabaja muy bien** that actor's very good; **~ de algo** to work as sth; **~ en algo**: **¿en qué trabajas?** what's your job?; **¿ha trabajado antes en diseño gráfico?** do you have any previous work experience in graphic design?; **trabajan en una compañía aérea** they work for an airline; **~ por horas** to work by the hour; **~ jornada completa** to work full-time; **~ media jornada** to work half-days; **estamos trabajando por conseguir nuestros derechos** we are working towards getting our rights; **~ a tiempo parcial** to work part-time; ✦ MODISMOS **~ como una mula** to work like a Trojan; **~ como un condenado** *o* **un negro** to work like a slave
2 (= *funcionar*) [*fábrica*] to work; [*máquina*] to run, work; **para que el cerebro trabaje** for the brain to work (properly); **el tiempo trabaja a nuestro favor** time is on our side; **hacer ~**: **si quiere hacer ~ su dinero** if you want to make your money work for you
3 [*tierra, árbol*] to bear, yield
Ⓑ VT **1** [+ *tierra, cuero, madera*] to work; [+ *masa*] to knead; [+ *ingredientes*] to mix in

2 [+ *detalle, proyecto*] to work on; [+ *mente*] to exercise; **hay que ~ un poco más los números musicales** we need to do a bit more work on the musical numbers
3 (*Com*) (= *vender*) to sell; **nosotros no trabajamos esa marca** we don't sell *o* stock that brand
Ⓒ **trabajarse** VPR [+ *persona, asunto*] to work on; **se está trabajando a su tía para sacarle los ahorros** he's working on his aunt in order to get hold of her savings; **tienes que ~te el ascenso un poco más** you need to work a bit harder on getting that promotion

trabajo SM **1** (= *labor*) work; **tengo mucho ~** I have a lot of work; **me queda ~ para una hora** I have an hour's work left; **¡buen ~!** good work!; **tiene una enorme capacidad de ~** she's a very willing worker; **planchar la ropa es el ~ que menos me gusta** the ironing is the job I like least; **a veces le sale algún que otro trabajillo** he gets odd jobs now and then; **el ~ de la casa** the housework; **ropa de ~** work clothes; **estar sin ~** to be unemployed; **quedarse sin ~** to find o.s. out of work, lose one's job; ✦ MODISMO **es un ~ de chinos*** it's a fiddly job that takes a lot of patience
➤ **trabajo de campo** field work ➤ **trabajo en equipo** teamwork ➤ **trabajo por turnos** shiftwork ➤ **trabajos forzados** hard labour *sing*, hard labor *sing* (*EEUU*) ➤ **trabajos manuales** (*Escol*) handicrafts ➤ **trabajo social** social work ➤ **trabajo sucio** dirty work
2 (*tb* **puesto de ~**) job

> **Trabajo** se traduce tanto por **work** como por **job**, pero **work** es un sustantivo incontable y **job** es contable:

estoy buscando ~ I'm looking for a job; **estoy buscando ~ work; le han ofrecido un ~ en el banco** he's been offered a job at the bank; **no encuentro ~** I can't find work *o* a job ➤ **trabajo fijo** permanent job
3 (*tb* **lugar de ~**) work; **vivo cerca de mi ~** I live near work *o* near my workplace; **está en el ~** she's at work; **ir al ~** to go to work
4 (= *esfuerzo*) **lo hizo con mucho ~** it cost him a lot of effort to do it; **ahorrarse el ~** to save o.s. the trouble; **costar ~**: **le cuesta ~ hacerlo** he finds it hard to do; **me cuesta ~ decir que no** I find it hard to say no; **dar ~**: **reparar la casa nos ha dado mucho ~** it was hard work *o* a real job repairing the house; **los niños pequeños dan mucho ~** small children are a lot of work; **tomarse el ~ de hacer algo** to take the trouble to do sth
5 (= *obra*) (*Arte, Literat*) work; (*Educ*) essay; [*de investigación*] study
6 (= *mano de obra*) labour, labor (*EEUU*)

trabajoso ADJ (= *difícil*) hard, laborious; (= *doloroso*) painful

trabalenguas SM INV tongue twister

trabar /1a/ Ⓐ VT **1** [+ *puerta, ventana*] (*para que quede cerrada*) to wedge shut; (*para que quede abierta*) to wedge open
2 [+ *salsa, líquido*] to thicken
3 (*Carpintería*) to join; (*Constr*) to point
4 (= *comenzar*) [+ *conversación, debate*] to start (up), strike up; [+ *batalla*] to join; **~ amistad** to strike up a friendship
5 (= *enlazar*) **una serie de razonamientos muy bien trabados** a tightly woven *o* very well constructed argument
6 (= *obstaculizar*) to hold back
7 [+ *caballo*] to hobble
8 [+ *sierra*] to set
Ⓑ VI **1** [*planta*] to take
2 [*ancla, garfio*] to grip
Ⓒ **trabarse** VPR **1** (= *enredarse*) to get tangled up; **se le traba la lengua** he gets tongue-tied
2 (= *involucrarse*) **~se en una discusión** to get involved in an argument

trabazón SF **1** (*Téc*) joining, assembly **2** [*de líquido*] consistency **3** (= *coherencia*) coherence

trabilla SF (= *tira*) small strap; (= *broche*) clasp; [*de cinturón*] belt loop; (= *puntada*) dropped stitch

trabucar /1g/ Ⓐ VT (= *confundir*) to confuse; (= *desordenar*) to mix up, mess up Ⓑ **trabucarse** VPR to get all mixed up

trabuco SM (*tb* ~ **naranjero**) blunderbuss

traca SF [*de fuegos artificiales*] string of fireworks; (= *ruido fuerte*) row, racket

trácala SF (*Carib, Méx*) (= *trampa*) trick, ruse

tracalada* SF (*Chi, Ven*) **una ~ de** a load of*; **a ~s** by the hundred

tracción SF traction, drive ➤ **tracción a las cuatro ruedas** four-wheel drive ➤ **tracción delantera** front-wheel drive ➤ **tracción trasera** rear-wheel drive

tractor SM tractor

tractorista SMF tractor driver

tradición SF tradition

tradicional ADJ traditional

tradicionalista ADJ, SMF traditionalist

tradicionalmente ADV traditionally

tráding ['tradin] Ⓐ ADJ **empresa ~** trading company Ⓑ SF trading company

traducción SF translation (**a** into; **de** from); ➤ **traducción asistida por ordenador** computer-assisted translation ➤ **traducción automática** automatic translation, machine translation ➤ **traducción directa** *translation into one's own language* ➤ **traducción simultánea** simultaneous translation

traducir /3n/ Ⓐ VT to translate (**a** into; **de** from) Ⓑ **traducirse** VPR **~se en** (= *significar*) to mean in practice; (= *suponer*) to entail, result in

traductor(a) SM/F translator ➤ **traductor(a) jurado/a, traductor(a) público/a** (*RPl*) official translator

traer /2o/ Ⓐ VT **1** (= *transportar*) to bring; **el muchacho que trae los periódicos** the lad who delivers *o* brings the newspapers; **¿nos trae la cuenta, por favor?** can we have the bill, please?; **trae, ya lo arreglo yo** give it to me, I'll fix it; **¿me puedes ~ mañana a la oficina?** can you bring me to work *o* give me a lift to work tomorrow?; **¿qué la trae por aquí?** what brings you here?; **~ un hijo al mundo** to bring a child into the world; ✦ MODISMO **como su madre** *o* **como Dios lo trajo al mundo** as naked as the day he was born, in his birthday suit
2 (= *llevar encima*) [+ *ropa*] to wear; [+ *objeto*] to carry; **¿qué traes en esa bolsa?** what have you got in that bag?, what are you carrying in that bag?
3 [*periódico, revista*] **¿trae alguna noticia interesante?** is there any interesting news?
4 (= *causar*) [+ *suerte, paz, beneficios*] to bring; [+ *recuerdos*] to bring back; [+ *consecuencias*] to have; **te ~á buena suerte** it'll bring you good luck; **la recesión trajo consigo un aumento del paro** the recession brought with it *o* brought about an increase in unemployment
5 (= *tener*) (+ ADJ) **la ausencia de noticias me trae muy inquieto** the lack of news is making me very anxious; **el juego lo trae perdido** gambling is his ruin
6 ✦ MODISMOS **me trae sin cuidado** I couldn't care less*; **me la trae floja** (*Esp***) I couldn't give a damn**; **~ de cabeza a algn: este caso trae de cabeza a la policía local** this case is proving to be a headache for local police; **~la con algn** (*Méx*) to have it in for sb*; **llevar o ~ a mal ~ a algn** [*persona*] to give sb nothing but trouble; [*problema*] to be the bane of sb's life; **~ y llevar a algn** (= *molestar*) to pester sb; (= *chismorrear*) to gossip about sb
Ⓑ **traerse** VPR **1** (= *tramar*) to be up to; **esos dos se traen algún manejo sucio** the two of them are up to something shady
2 (*uso enfático*) to bring; **me he traído la cámara** I've brought the camera, I've brought the camera with me
3 ✦ MODISMO **se las trae*: es un problema que se las trae** it's a real nightmare of a problem; **tiene un padre que se las trae** her father is impossible, her father is a real nightmare

traído ADJ ✦ MODISMO **~ y llevado: el tan ~ y llevado tema del papel de la familia hoy día** the overworked *o* time-worn subject of the role of the family today; **el tan ~ y llevado oro de Moscú** the much talked-about Moscow gold

trafagar /1h/ VI to bustle about

traficante SMF dealer (**en** in); ➤ **traficante de armas** arms

dealer ➤ **traficante de drogas** drug dealer ➤ **traficante de esclavos** slave trader

traficar /1g/ VI to deal (**con** with; **en** in); (*pey*) to traffic (**en** in)

tráfico SM **1** (*Aut, Ferro*) traffic; **accidente de ~** road accident, traffic accident; **cortar el ~** to interrupt traffic ➤ **tráfico de mercancías** goods traffic ➤ **tráfico rodado** road traffic, vehicular traffic **2** (*Esp*) (*tb* **Dirección General de Tráfico**) *public department in charge of controlling traffic* **3** (= *negocio*) trade; (*pey*) traffic (**en** in); ➤ **tráfico de drogas, tráfico de estupefacientes** drug traffic ➤ **tráfico de influencias** peddling of political favours *o* (*EEUU*) favors

tragaderas SFPL **1** (= *garganta*) throat *sing*, gullet *sing* **2** (= *credulidad*) gullibility *sing*; (= *tolerancia*) tolerance *sing*; **tener buenas ~** (= *ser crédulo*) to be gullible; (= *ser permisivo*) to be very easy-going, be prepared to put up with a lot

tragaldabas* SMF INV (*Esp*) glutton, pig*, hog (*EEUU*)

tragaluz SM skylight

traganíqueles* SM INV (*Col*) = **tragaperras**

tragaperras SF INV (*gen*) slot machine; (*en bar*) fruit-machine, one-armed bandit

tragar /1h/ Ⓐ VT **1** [+ *comida, bebida*] to swallow; **le molesta la garganta al ~ saliva** her throat bothers her when she swallows hard
2 (= *absorber*) to soak up
3 (*) (= *gastar*) to use
4 (*) (= *aguantar*) [+ *insultos, reprimenda*] to put up with; **le ha hecho ~ mucho a su mujer** his wife has had to put up with a lot; **no puedo ~ a tu hermano** I can't stand your brother
5 (*Esp**) (= *creer*) to swallow*, fall for*
Ⓑ VI **1** (*) (= *engullir*) **tu hijo traga que da gusto** your son really enjoys *o* loves his food
2 (*Esp**) (= *creer*) to swallow*, fall for*; **—¿han tragado? —no, no se han creído nada** "did they swallow it *o* fall for it?" — "no, they didn't believe a word"*
3 (*RPl**) [*estudiante*] to swot (*Brit**), grind away (*EEUU*)
Ⓒ **tragarse** VPR **1** [+ *comida, bebida*] to swallow; **se lo tragó entero** he swallowed it whole
2 (= *absorber*) [*arena, tierra*] to soak up; [*mar, abismo*] to swallow up, engulf
3 (= *aguantar*) [+ *insultos, reprimenda*] to put up with; **siempre tengo que ~me los problemas de los demás** I always have to sit and listen to other people's problems; **pone la tele y se traga todo lo que le echen** he puts the TV on and watches anything that's on
4 (*) (= *creer*) to swallow*, fall for*; **se ~á todo lo que se le diga** he'll swallow *o* fall for whatever he's told*
5 (= *reprimir*) **~se las lágrimas** to hold back one's tears; **~se el orgullo** to swallow one's pride

tragedia SF tragedy

trágico Ⓐ ADJ tragic(al); **lo ~ es que ...** the tragedy of it is that ..., the tragic thing about it is that ... Ⓑ SM tragedian

tragicomedia SF tragicomedy

trago SM **1** (*de un líquido*) drink; **un traguito de agua** a sip of water; **no vendría mal un ~ de vino** a drop of wine would not come amiss; **echar un ~** to have a drink, have a swig*; **beber algo de un ~** to drink sth in one gulp **2** (*LAm*) (= *bebida alcohólica*) drink; **¡échame un ~!** give me a drink! **3** (= *experiencia*) **mal ~** ◇ **~ amargo: fue un ~ amargo** it was a cruel blow; **nos quedaba todavía el ~ más amargo** the worst of it was still to come

tragón/ona Ⓐ ADJ greedy Ⓑ SM/F glutton; **es un ~** he's very greedy, he's a greedy pig*

traición SF **1** (= *deslealtad*) betrayal; (= *alevosía*) treachery; **una ~ a** a betrayal; **cometer una ~ contra algn** to betray sb; **matar a algn a ~** to kill sb treacherously **2** (*Jur*) treason; **alta ~** high treason

traicionar /1a/ VT to betray

traicionero ADJ treacherous

traidor(a) Ⓐ ADJ [*persona*] treacherous; [*acto*] treasonable Ⓑ SM/F traitor/traitress; (*Teat*) villain

traiga *etc ver* **traer**

trailer SM (*pl* ~s), **tráiler** SM (*pl* ~s) **1** (*Esp Cine*) trailer **2** (= *caravana*) caravan (*Brit*), trailer (*EEUU*); [*de camión*] trailer, semi-trailer (*EEUU*)

trainera SF [*de pesca*] small fishing boat (*used for trawling*); [*de remo*] *rowing boat used for racing*

traje¹ *ver* **traer**

traje² SM (*de dos piezas*) suit; (= *vestido*) dress; (*típico*) dress, costume; **~ hecho a la medida** made-to-measure suit; **un policía en ~ de calle** a plain-clothes policeman ➤ **traje de baño** bathing costume, swimsuit, swimming costume ➤ **traje de chaqueta** suit ➤ **traje de época** period costume ➤ **traje de etiqueta** dress suit, dinner dress ➤ **traje de luces** bullfighter's costume ➤ **traje de noche** evening dress ➤ **traje de novia** wedding dress, bridal gown ➤ **traje de paisano** (*Esp*) civilian clothes; (*de policía*) plain clothes ➤ **traje largo** evening gown ➤ **traje regional** regional costume, regional dress

trajeado ADJ **ir bien ~** to be well dressed, be well turned out

trajera *etc ver* **traer**

traje-sastre SM (*pl* **trajes-sastre**) suit, tailor-made suit

trajín* SM coming and going, bustle, commotion; (= *jaleo*) fuss

trajinado ADJ [*tema*] well-worked, overworked, trite

trajinar /1a/ VI (= *ajetrearse*) to bustle about; (= *viajar*) to travel around a lot; (= *moverse mucho*) to be on the go, keep on the move

tralla SF (= *cuerda*) whipcord, whiplash; (= *látigo*) lash, whip

trallazo SM [*de látigo*] (= *ruido*) crack of a whip; (= *golpe*) lash

trama SF **1** [*de un tejido*] weft, woof **2** [*de historia*] plot **3** (= *conjura*) plot, scheme, intrigue **4** (*Tip*) shaded area

tramador ADJ (*Col*) exciting

tramar /1a/ VT **1** (= *tejer*) to weave **2** [+ *engaño, enredo*] to plan, plot; [+ *complot*] to lay, hatch; **están tramando algo** they're up to sth; **algo se está tramando** there's something going on, there's something afoot **3** (*Col*) (= *atraer*) to grip; **me tramó desde el principio** I was gripped from the start

tramitación SF **~ de divorcio** divorce proceedings *pl*; **~ de visado** visa application

tramitar /1a/ VT [+ *pasaporte, permiso*] to process; [+ *crédito*] to negotiate; **ya están tramitando su divorcio** they have started divorce proceedings

trámite SM **1** (= *fase*) step, stage; **tuvimos que hacer muchos ~s antes de abrir el negocio** we had a lot of paperwork to do before we could start the business; **estoy harto de tantos ~s** I'm fed up with all this red tape *o* form-filling **2** (= *formalidad*) formality; **este examen es puro ~** this exam is purely a formality **3** (= *proceso*) procedure; **para acortar los ~s lo hacemos así** to make the procedure shorter we do it this way; **se limita a resolver asuntos de ~** he is dealing only with routine business matters; **el proyecto de ley está en ~ parlamentario** the bill is going through parliament ➤ **trámites judiciales** court proceedings

tramo SM **1** [*de carretera*] section, stretch; [*de puente*] span; [*de escalera*] flight **2** [*de tiempo*] period

tramontana SF north wind

tramoya SF **1** (*Teat*) piece of stage machinery **2** (= *enredo*) plot, scheme; (= *estafa*) trick, swindle

tramoyista SMF **1** (*Teat*) stagehand, scene shifter **2** (= *estafador*) swindler, trickster; (= *intrigante*) schemer

trampa SF **1** (*para cazar*) trap; (= *lazo*) snare ➤ **trampa mortal** death trap **2** (= *engaño*) trap; **no vayas, es una ~** don't go, it's a trap; **aquí hay ~** there's a catch here; **caer en la ~** to fall into the trap; **tender una ~ a algn** to set *o* lay a trap for sb; ✦ MODISMO **ni ~ ni cartón** (*Esp*): **este contrato no tiene ni ~ ni cartón** there's no hidden catch in this contract **3** (*en el juego*) **¡eso es ~!** that's cheating!; **hacer ~(s)** to cheat **4** (= *puerta*) trapdoor

trampear /1a/ ❹ VT (*en el juego*) to cheat ❺ VI **1** (= *hacer trampa*) to cheat; (= *conseguir dinero*) to get money by false pretences **2** (= *ir tirando*) to manage, get by

trampero/a SM/F trapper

trampilla SF trap, hatchway

trampolín SM **1** (*Dep*) (*en piscina*) springboard, diving board; (*en gimnasia*) trampoline; [*de esquí*] ski-jump **2** (*para conseguir algo*) springboard

tramposo/a ❹ ADJ crooked, tricky; **ser ~** to be a cheat ❺ SM/F **1** (*en el juego*) cheat; (= *estafador*) crook*, shyster (*EEUU*), swindler **2** (*Fin*) bad payer

tranca SF **1** [*de puerta, ventana*] bar; ✦ MODISMO **a ~s y barrancas** with great difficulty, overcoming many obstacles **2** (= *garrote*) cudgel, club **3** (*esp LAm**) (= *borrachera*) **tener una ~** to be drunk **4** (*Carib Aut*) traffic jam

trancar /1g/ VT **1** [+ *puerta, ventana*] to bar **2** (*Ven*) (= *obstaculizar*) to block

trancazo SM **1** (= *golpe*) blow, bang (with a stick) **2** (*Esp**) (= *gripe*) heavy cold

trance SM **1** (= *momento difícil*) **estamos pasando por un mal ~** we're going through a difficult period *o* patch; **aún no ha logrado superar el ~** he still hasn't managed to get over what he's been through; **estar en ~ de muerte** to be at death's door; **estar en ~ de hacer algo** to be on the point of doing sth; **último ~** last *o* dying moments ➤ **trance mortal** last *o* dying moments *pl* **2** [*de médium*] trance; (*Rel*) trance, ecstasy; **estar en ~** to be in a trance

tranco SM stride, big step; **andar a ~s** to walk with long strides, take big steps; **en dos ~s** (*lit*) in a couple of strides; (*fig*) in a couple of ticks

tranque SM (*CS*) reservoir

tranquera SF (*LAm*) cattle gate

tranquilamente ADV **1** (= *plácidamente*) peacefully **2** (= *sin prisa*) **fuimos paseando ~ hasta el pueblo** we took a leisurely stroll into the village; **piénsalo ~ antes de responder** take your time and think about it before you answer **3** (*con aplomo*) calmly; **háblale ~** speak to him calmly **4** (= *sin preocupación*) **le puedo contar todos mis secretos ~** I can tell her all my secrets with no worries; **se puede ver ~ tres películas seguidas** he's quite capable of watching three films in a row **5** (= *con descaro*) **y se fue ~ sin pagar** and he went off, cool as you please *o* like, without paying

tranquilidad SF **1** (= *placidez*) peace; **¡qué ~ se respira en el campo!** the countryside is so peaceful!; **si no hay ~ no puedo estudiar** I can't study without peace and quiet **2** (= *falta de prisa*) **llévatelo a casa y léelo con ~** take it home and read it at your leisure **3** (= *aplomo*) calm; **respondió con ~** he answered calmly **4** (= *falta de preocupación*) **para mayor ~ llama a tus padres** call your parents, to put your mind at rest; **¡qué ~! ya se han acabado los exámenes** what a relief, the exams are over at last!; **puedes decírmelo con total ~, no se lo contaré a nadie** you're quite safe telling me, I won't tell anyone **5** (= *descaro*) **dijo con toda ~ que no pensaba pagar** she said quite calmly *o* as cool as you please *o* like that she didn't intend to pay

tranquilizador ADJ [*música*] soothing; [*hecho*] reassuring

tranquilizante ❹ ADJ = **tranquilizador** ❺ SM (*Med*) tranquillizer, tranquilizer (*EEUU*)

tranquilizar /1f/ ❹ VT to calm down; **el árbitro intentó ~ a los jugadores** the referee tried to calm the players down; **las palabras del médico me ~on** the doctor's words reassured me; **¿por qué no llamas a tu madre para ~la?** why don't you call your mother to put her mind at rest? ❺ **tranquilizarse** VPR to calm down; **¡tranquilícese!** calm down!; **se tranquilizó al saber que habían llegado bien** she stopped worrying when she found out that they had arrived safely

tranquilla SF latch, pin

tranquillo* SM (*Esp*) knack; **coger el ~ a algo** to get the hang of sth, get the knack of sth

tranquilo Ⓐ ADJ **1** (= *plácido*) [*sitio, momento*] quiet, peaceful; [*mar*] calm
2 (= *sosegado*) calm
3 (= *sin preocupación*) **¡estad ~s que yo me encargo de todo** don't worry, I'll look after everything; **¡deja ya ~ al pobre chico!** leave the poor boy alone!; **¡~, no merece la pena enfadarse!** calm down! there's no point getting annoyed; **¡eh, ~, sin empujar!** hey, easy does it! no pushing!; **tener la conciencia tranquila** to have a clear conscience
4 (= *descarado*) **se quedó tan ~** he didn't bat an eyelid Ⓑ ADV (*Méx**) easily; **son ~ unos 2.000 km** it's easily 2,000 km, it's 2,000 km, easy*

tranquiza SF (*Méx*) beating

transacción SF (*Com*) transaction; (= *acuerdo*) deal, bargain ➤ **transacción comercial** business deal

transandino ADJ trans-Andean

transar /1a/ Ⓐ VT **1** (*LAm Bolsa*) [+ *acciones, valores*] to trade **2** (*CS*) (= *comerciar*) to trade **3** (*RPl**) (= *comprar*) [+ *droga*] to buy **4** (*Méx**) (= *engañar*) to con* Ⓑ VI **1** (*LAm*) (= *ceder*) to give way; **~ en algo** to agree to sth **2** (*esp Chi*) (= *negociar*) to reach a deal **3** (*RPl**) (*con droga*) to deal*

transatlántico Ⓐ ADJ transatlantic; [*travesía*] Atlantic; **los países ~s** the countries on the other side of the Atlantic Ⓑ SM (= *barco*) (ocean) liner

transbordador SM (*Náut*) ferry; (*Aer*) shuttle ➤ **transbordador espacial** space shuttle

transbordar /1a/ Ⓐ VT (*gen*) to transfer; (*Náut*) to transship Ⓑ VI (*Ferro*) to change

transbordo SM **1** (*Ferro*) [*de pasajeros*] change; **hacer ~** to change (**en** at) **2** [*de equipajes*] transfer

transcribir /3a/ (*pp* **transcrito**) VT (= *copiar*) to transcribe; (*de alfabeto distinto*) to transliterate

transcripción SF (= *copia*) transcription; [*de alfabeto distinto*] transliteration

transcurrir /3a/ VI **1** [*tiempo*] to pass, elapse; **han transcurrido siete años** seven years have passed **2** [*acto, celebración*] to pass, go

transcurso SM passing, lapse, course; **~ del tiempo** course of time, passing of time; **en el ~ de ocho días** in the course *o* space of a week; **en el ~ de los años** over the years

transeúnte SMF passer-by; **~s** passers-by

transexual ADJ, SMF transsexual

transferencia SF **1** (*Jur, Dep*) transfer ➤ **transferencia bancaria** banker's order, bank transfer **2** (*Psic*) transference

transferir /3i/ VT to transfer

transfiguración SF transfiguration

transfigurar /1a/ VT to transfigure (**en** into)

transformación SF **1** (= *cambio*) transformation, change (**en** into) **2** (*Culin*) processing **3** (*Rugby*) conversion

transformador SM (*Elec*) transformer

transformar /1a/ Ⓐ VT **1** (= *convertir*) **~ algo en algo** to turn sth into sth **2** (= *cambiar*) to transform **3** (*Rugby*) to convert Ⓑ **transformarse** VPR **1** (= *convertirse*) **~se en algo** to turn into sth; **la rana se transformó en príncipe** the frog turned into a prince **2** (= *cambiar*) **cuando sonríe se le transforma la cara** her face is transformed when she smiles; **desde que dejó de beber se ha transformado** since he stopped drinking he's a changed man

transformismo SM **1** (*Biol*) evolution, transmutation **2** (*sexual*) transvestism

transformista SMF **1** (*Teat*) quick-change artist(e) **2** (*sexual*) transvestite

tránsfuga SMF (*Pol*) [*de partido*] turncoat; [*de nación*] defector

transfundir /3a/ VT **1** [+ *líquidos*] to transfuse **2** [+ *noticias*] to tell, spread

transfusión SF transfusion ➤ **transfusión de sangre, transfusión sanguínea** blood transfusion

transgénico ADJ genetically modified, GM *antes de s*

transgredir /3a/ VT, VI to transgress

transgresión SF transgression

transgresor(a) SM/F transgressor

transiberiano ADJ trans-Siberian

transición SF transition (**a** to; **de** from); **período de ~** transitional period; **la ~** (*Esp Pol*) the transition (*to democracy after Franco's death*)

transido ADJ **~ de dolor** racked with pain

transigente ADJ **1** (= *que cede*) accommodating **2** (= *tolerante*) tolerant

transigir /3c/ VI **1** (= *ceder*) to give way, make concessions **2** (= *tolerar*) **~ con algo** to tolerate sth

transistor SM transistor

transistorizado ADJ transistorized

transitar /1a/ VI [*vehículo*] to travel; [*peatón*] to go, walk; **calle transitada** busy street; **~ por** to go along, pass along

transitable ADJ passable

transitivo ADJ transitive

tránsito SM **1** (= *paso*) transit, passage, movement; **"se prohíbe el tránsito"** "no thoroughfare"; **en ~** in transit **2** (*esp LAm*) (= *tráfico*) traffic; **calle de mucho ~** busy street; **horas de máximo ~** rush hour *sing*, peak (traffic) hours ➤ **tránsito rodado** vehicular traffic **3** (= *muerte*) passing, death

transitorio ADJ **1** (= *provisional*) [*medida*] provisional, temporary; [*período*] transitional, of transition **2** (= *pasajero*) transitory

transliteración SF transliteration

translúcido ADJ translucent

transmigración SF migration, transmigration

transmisible ADJ transmissible; (*Med*) contagious

transmisión SF **1** (= *acto*) transmission; (*Jur*) transfer ➤ **transmisión de dominio** transfer of ownership **2** (*Mec*) transmission **3** (*Elec*) transmission; (*Radio, TV*) transmission, broadcast(ing) ➤ **transmisión de datos** data transmission ➤ **transmisión en diferido** recorded programme *o* (*EEUU*) program, repeat broadcast ➤ **transmisión en directo** live broadcast ➤ **transmisión por satélite** satellite broadcasting **4 transmisiones** (*Mil*) signals (corps)

transmisor Ⓐ ADJ transmitting; **aparato ~** ◇ **estación ~a** transmitter Ⓑ SM transmitter

transmisor-receptor SM transceiver; (*portátil*) walkie-talkie

transmitir /3a/ Ⓐ VT **1** (*Radio, TV*) [+ *señal, sonido*] to transmit; [+ *programa*] to broadcast **2** [+ *bienes, saludos, recados*] to pass on **3** [+ *enfermedad, gérmenes*] to give, pass on **4** (*Jur*) to transfer (**a** to) Ⓑ VI (*Radio, TV*) to broadcast

transmutación SF transmutation

transmutar /1a/ VT to transmute (**en** into)

transoceánico ADJ transoceanic

transparencia SF **1** [*de cristal, agua*] transparency **2** (= *claridad*) openness, transparency ➤ **transparencia fiscal** *o* tax transparency ➤ **transparencia informativa** information transparency *o* disclosure **3** (*Fot*) slide, transparency

transparentar /1a/ Ⓐ VT (= *dejar ver*) to reveal, allow to be seen; [+ *emoción*] to reveal, betray Ⓑ **transparentarse** VPR **1** [*vidrio, agua*] to be transparent, be clear; [*objeto, ropa*] to show through; **se te transparenta el sujetador** your bra is showing through, you can see your bra through that **2** (*) [*ropa gastada*] to become threadbare

transparente Ⓐ ADJ **1** [*agua, cristal*] transparent, clear; [*aire*] clear; [*vestido*] see-through **2** [*persona*] transparent; [*intenciones, motivos*] clear, transparent **3** [*gestión, contabilidad*] open, transparent Ⓑ SM (= *pantalla*) blind, shade

transpiración SF **1** (= *sudor*) perspiration **2** (*Bot*) transpiration

transpirar /1a/ VI **1** (= *sudar*) to perspire **2** [*líquido*] to seep through, ooze out; (*Bot*) to transpire

transponer /2q/ (*pp* **transpuesto**) Ⓐ VT **1** (*gen*) to transpose; (= *cambiar de sitio*) to switch over, move about **2** (= *trasplantar*) to transplant Ⓑ VI (= *desaparecer*) to disappear from view; (= *ir más allá*) to go beyond, get past; [*sol*] to go down **⊙ transponerse** VPR **1** (= *cambiarse*) to change places **2** (= *esconderse*) to hide (behind); [*sol*] to go down **3** (= *dormirse*) to doze (off)

transportable ADJ transportable; **fácilmente ~** easily carried, easily transported

transportador SM transporter

transportar /1a/ **Ⓐ** VT **1** [+ *tropas, mercancías*] (*gen*) to transport; (*en barco*) to ship **2** (*Elec*) [+ *corriente*] to transmit **3** (*Mús*) to transpose **Ⓑ transportarse** VPR (= *extasiarse*) to be transported, be enraptured

transporte SM **1** [*de pasajeros, tropas*] transport (*esp Brit*), transportation (*EEUU*); [*de mercancías*] transport (*esp Brit*), transportation (*EEUU*), carriage; **se me va el sueldo en ~** all my wages go on transport ➤ **transporte de mercancías** goods transport (*esp Brit*), freight transportation (*esp EEUU*) ➤ **transporte escolar** school buses *pl* ➤ **transporte por carretera** road transport, road haulage ➤ **transporte público** public transport (*esp Brit*), public transportation (*EEUU*) **2** (*Náut*) transport, troopship **3** (= *éxtasis*) transport

transportista Ⓐ SMF (*Aut*) haulier, hauler (*EEUU*), haulage contractor **Ⓑ** SM (*Aer*) carrier

transposición SF transposition

transpuesto ADJ **quedarse ~** to doze off

transvasar /1a/ VT = **trasvasar**

transversal Ⓐ ADJ transverse, cross; (= *oblicuo*) oblique; **calle ~** cross street **Ⓑ** SF **una ~ de la Gran Vía** a street crossing *o* which cuts across the Gran Vía

tranvía SM (= *coche*) tram (*Brit*), streetcar (*EEUU*); (= *sistema*) tramway; (*Esp Ferro*) local train

tranza* (*Méx*) **Ⓐ** SMF con man* **Ⓑ** ADJ [*comerciante*] crooked, dodgy*; [*policía, juez*] crooked, bent* **Ⓒ** SF fiddle*

tranzar /1f/ VT (*Méx*) = **transar 4**

trapajoso ADJ **1** (= *andrajoso*) shabby, ragged **2** [*pronunciación*] defective, incorrect

trapeador SM (*LAm*) mop

trapear /1a/ VT (*LAm*) to mop

trapecio SM **1** (*en gimnasia, circo*) trapeze **2** (*Mat*) trapezium, trapezoid (*EEUU*)

trapecista SMF trapeze artist(e)

trapero/a Ⓐ SM/F ragman/ragwoman **Ⓑ** SM (*LAm*) floor cloth

trapichear* /1a/ **Ⓐ** VI (= *hacer trampa*) to be on the fiddle*; (= *tramar*) to plot, scheme; (= *andar en malos pasos*) to be mixed up in something shady* **Ⓑ** VT to deal in, trade in

trapicheo* SM fiddle*, shady deal*; **trapicheos** (= *trampas*) fiddles*, shady dealing* *sing*; (= *intrigas*) plots, schemes, tricks

trapichero/a* SM/F small-time dealer

trapío* SM **1** (= *encanto*) charm; (= *garbo*) elegance, graceful way of moving; **tener buen ~** to have a fine presence, carry o.s. elegantly, move well *o* gracefully; (*fig*) to have real class **2** [*de toro*] fine appearance

trapo SM **1** (= *paño para limpiar*) (*gen*) cloth; (*usado, raído*) rag; **un ~ húmedo** a damp cloth; **pasar un ~ por** [+ *suelo*] to give a wipe over *o* down; [+ *muebles*] to dust ➤ **trapo de cocina** (*para secar los platos*) tea towel (*Brit*), dish towel (*EEUU*); (*para limpiar*) dish cloth ➤ **trapo del polvo** duster, dust cloth (*EEUU*)
2 (= *trozo de tela*) (*gen*) piece of material; (*usado, raído*) rag, piece of rag; ✦ MODISMO **tener manos de ~** to be a butterfingers
3 trapos* (= *ropa*) clothes; **gasta una barbaridad en ~s** she spends a fortune on clothes
4 (*Náut*) (= *vela*) canvas, sails *pl*; **a todo ~** under full sail
5 (*Taur**) cape
6 ✦ MODISMOS **como un ~***: **dejar a algn como un ~** to tear sb to shreds*; **poner a algn como un ~** to lay into sb*, slag sb off**; **a todo ~*** (= *muy rápido*) at full speed, flat out*; (= *a toda potencia*) full blast, at full blast; (*LAm*) (= *a todo lujo*) in style ➤ **trapos sucios: no quieren que salgan a la luz los ~s sucios** they don't want the skeletons in the

cupboard (*Brit*) *o* closet (*EEUU*) to come out; **en la cena sacaron los ~s sucios (a relucir** *o* (*Esp*) **a la luz)** everyone at the dinner party washed their dirty linen in public

tráquea SF trachea, windpipe

traqueotomía SF tracheotomy, tracheostomy

traquetear /1a/ VI **1** (*con ruido*) [*vehículo*] to rattle, jolt; [*cohete*] to crackle, bang; [*ametralladora*] to rattle, clatter **2** (*CS, Méx**) [*persona*] to bustle about

traqueteo SM **1** [*de vehículo*] rattle, rattling, jolting; [*de cohete*] crackle, bang; [*de ametralladora*] rattle **2** (*CS, Méx**) [*de persona*] coming and going

tras PREP **1** (= *después de*) after; **día ~ día** day after day; **uno ~ otro** one after another *o* the other **2** (= *detrás de*) behind; **estaba oculto ~ las cortinas** he was hidden behind the curtains; **andar** *o* **estar ~ algo** to be after sth; **anda ~ un puesto en la administración pública** he's after a job in the civil service; **correr** *o* **ir ~ algn** to chase (after) sb

trascendencia SF **1** (= *importancia*) importance, significance; (= *consecuencias*) implications *pl*, consequences *pl*; **un encuentro sin ~** an inconsequential meeting; **la matanza no ha tenido ~ informativa** the killing did not make the headlines **2** (*Fil*) transcendence

trascendental ADJ, **trascendente** ADJ **1** (= *importante*) significant, important; (= *esencial*) vital **2** (*Fil*) transcendental

trascender /2g/ **Ⓐ** VI **1** (= *conocerse*) to leak out, get out; **por fin ha trascendido la noticia** the news has leaked *o* got out at last **2** (= *propagarse*) **~ a algo** to extend to sth; **su influencia trasciende a los países más remotos** his influence extends to the most remote countries **3** (= *ir más allá*) **~ de algo** to transcend sth, go beyond sth **4** (*Fil*) to transcend **Ⓑ** VT to transcend, go beyond

trascendido SM (*CS*) leak

trasegar /1h, 1j/ VT **1** (= *cambiar de sitio*) to move about, switch round; [+ *puestos*] to reshuffle **2** [+ *vino*] (*para la mesa*) to decant; (*en bodega*) to rack, pour into another container *o* bottle

trasero Ⓐ ADJ [*puerta*] back; [*asiento*] back, rear; **la parte trasera del edificio** the back *o* rear of the building; **rueda trasera** back wheel, rear wheel **Ⓑ** SM **1** (*) [*de persona*] bottom, behind **2** (*Zool*) hindquarters *pl*

trasfondo SM (*gen*) background; [*de crítica*] undertone, undercurrent

trasgo SM **1** (= *duende*) goblin, imp **2** (= *niño*) imp

trashumancia SF, **trashumación** SF seasonal migration, transhumance (*frm*)

trashumante ADJ migrating, on the move to new pastures

trasiego SM **1** (= *cambio de sitio*) move, switch; [*de puestos*] reshuffle; [*de vino*] (*para la mesa*) decanting; (*en bodega*) racking **2** (= *trastorno*) upset **3** (= *ir y venir*) coming and going

traslación SF **1** (*Astron*) movement, passage **2** (= *copia*) copy; (= *acción*) copy(ing) **3** (= *metáfora*) metaphor; (= *uso figurado*) figurative use

trasladar /1a/ **Ⓐ** VT **1** [+ *empleado, preso*] to transfer, move; [+ *muebles, tienda, oficina*] to move; **han trasladado la oficina a otra ciudad** they have moved the office to another city, they have relocated to another city **2** (= *aplazar*) [+ *evento*] to postpone (**a** until); [+ *reunión*] to adjourn (**a** until) **3** (= *traducir*) to translate (**a** into); **~ una novela a la pantalla** to transfer a novel to the screen **Ⓑ trasladarse** VPR **1** (= *desplazarse*) to travel; **los que se trasladan al trabajo en coche** those who travel to work by car; **después de la ceremonia nos trasladamos al hotel** after the ceremony we moved on *o* went to the hotel **2** (= *mudarse*) to move (**a** to); **nos hemos trasladado a un local más céntrico** we've moved to more central premises

traslado SM **1** [*de muebles*] removal (*Brit*), moving (*esp EEUU*); [*de oficina, residencia*] move **2** [*de empleado, preso*] transfer **3** (*Jur*) notification; **dar ~ a algn de una orden** to give sb a copy of an order

traslucir /3f/ **Ⓐ** VT (= *mostrar*) to show; (= *revelar*) to

reveal, betray **B** VI **dejar ~ algo** to suggest sth
C **traslucirse** VPR **1** (= *ser transparente*) to be translucent, be transparent **2** (= *ser visible*) to show through **3** (= *inferirse*) to reveal itself, be revealed; (= *ser obvio*) to be plain to see

trasluz SM **al ~: mirar algo al ~** to look at sth against the light

trasmano SM **a ~** (= *apartado*) out of the way; **me pilla a ~** it's out of my way, it's not on my way

trasmundo SM hidden world, secret world

trasnochado ADJ **1** (= *obsoleto*) outmoded **2** (= *ojeroso*) haggard, run-down

trasnochador/a **A** ADJ **son muy ~es** they go to bed very late, they keep very late hours **B** SM/F night bird, night owl

trasnochar /1a/ **A** VI (= *acostarse tarde*) to stay up late, go to bed late; (= *no acostarse*) to stay up all night; (= *ir de juerga*) to have a night out, have a night on the tiles **B** VT [+ *problema*] to sleep on **C** **trasnocharse** VPR (*Col, Méx, Perú**) = **trasnochar** A

traspapelar /1a/ **A** VT to lose, mislay **B** **traspapelarse** VPR to get mislaid

traspasar /1a/ VT **1** (= *penetrar*) to pierce, go through, penetrate; [*líquido*] to go/come through, soak through; **la bala le traspasó el pulmón** the bullet pierced his lung **2** [*dolor*] to pierce, go right through; **un ruido que traspasa el oído** an ear-splitting noise **3** [+ *calle*] to cross over **4** [+ *límites*] to go beyond, overstep; **~ la barrera del sonido** to break the sound barrier **5** [+ *propiedad*] (= *transferir*) to transfer; (= *vender*) to sell, make over; (*Jur*) to convey; **"se traspasa negocio"** "business for sale" **6** (*Dep*) [+ *jugador*] to transfer (*Brit*), trade (*EEUU*) **7** (*Pol*) [+ *poderes, competencias*] to devolve

traspaso SM **1** (= *venta*) transfer, sale; (*Jur*) conveyance **2** (= *propiedad*) property transferred; (*Jur*) property being conveyed **3** (*Dep*) (= *acción*) transfer (*Brit*), trade (*EEUU*); (= *pago*) transfer fee (*Brit*), trade o trading fee (*EEUU*) **4** (*Esp Pol*) ➤ **traspaso de competencias** transfer of powers

traspatio SM (*LAm*) backyard

traspié SM **1** (= *tropezón*) trip, stumble; **dar un ~** to trip, stumble **2** (= *error*) blunder, slip

trasplantar /1a/ VT to transplant

trasplante SM **1** (*Med*) transplant, transplantation ➤ **trasplante de corazón** heart transplant ➤ **trasplante de órganos** organ transplant **2** (*Bot*) transplanting

traspuesto ADJ **quedarse ~** to doze off

traspunte SMF prompt, prompter

trasquilar /1a/ VT **1** [+ *oveja*] to shear; [+ *pelo, persona*] to crop **2** (*) (= *cortar*) to cut (down)

trasquilón SM **¡menudo ~ que le han dado!** what a mess they've made of his hair!; **cortado a trasquilones** unevenly cut

trastabillar /1a/ VI (*esp LAm*) to stagger, stumble

trastabillón SM (*LAm*) stumble, trip

trastada* SF **1** (= *travesura*) prank, mischief **2** (= *mala pasada*) dirty trick

trastazo* SM bump, bang, thump; **darse o pegarse un ~** (*lit*) to get a knock; (*fig*) to come a cropper*

traste¹ SM **1** (*Mús*) [*de guitarra*] fret **2** ✦ MODISMOS **dar al ~ con algo** to spoil sth, mess sth up; **irse al ~** to fall through, be ruined

traste² SM **1** (*CAm, Méx, Ven*) [*de cocina*] **lavar los ~s** to do the dishes **2** (*CS**) (= *trasero*) bottom, backside*

trastear /1a/ **A** VT (= *mover*) to move around; (= *revolver*) to disarrange, mess up **B** VI **1** (= *mover objetos*) to move things around; **~ con o en** (= *buscar*) to rummage among; (= *manosear*) to fiddle with; (= *desordenar*) to mess up, disarrange **2** (*Col*) (= *trasladar*) to move **C** **trastearse** VPR to move

trastero SM lumber room

trastienda SF **1** [*de tienda*] back room **2** ✦ MODISMO **tiene mucha ~** he's a sly one

trasto SM **1** (= *cosa inútil*) piece of junk; ✦ MODISMO **tirarse los ~s a la cabeza** to have a blazing row ➤ **trastos viejos** junk *sing*, rubbish *sing* (*esp Brit*), garbage *sing* (*EEUU*) **2** **trastos** (*Esp**) gear *sing*, tackle *sing*; **liar los ~s** to pack up and go **3** (*Esp**) (= *persona inútil*) good-for-nothing, dead loss*

trastocar /1g, 1l/ VT = **trastrocar**

trastornado ADJ [*persona*] disturbed; [*mente*] disturbed, unhinged

trastornar /1a/ **A** VT **1** (= *perturbar*) [+ *persona*] to drive crazy, mentally disturb; [+ *mente*] to disturb, unhinge; **esa chica lo ha trastornado** that girl is driving him crazy, he's lost his head over that girl **2** (= *alterar*) [+ *persona*] to upset, trouble, disturb; [+ *ideas*] to confuse, upset; [+ *proyecto*] to upset; [+ *sentidos*] to daze, mess up; [+ *nervios*] to shatter; [+ *orden público*] to disturb **B** **trastornarse** VPR **1** [*persona*] to go out of one's mind, become deranged o disturbed **2** [*proyectos*] to fall through, be ruined

trastorno SM **1** (= *molestia*) inconvenience, trouble **2** (*Pol*) disturbance, upheaval **3** (*Med*) upset, disorder ➤ **trastorno de personalidad** personality disorder ➤ **trastorno digestivo** stomach upset ➤ **trastorno mental** mental disorder

trastrocar /1g, 1l/ VT **1** [+ *objetos*] to switch over, change round; [+ *orden*] to reverse, invert **2** [+ *palabras*] to change, transform

trasudar /1a/ VI [*atleta*] to sweat lightly; [*cosa*] to seep

trasunto SM **1** (= *copia*) copy, transcription **2** (= *semejanza*) image, likeness; (= *copia exacta*) carbon copy

trasvasar /1a/ VT **1** [+ *líquido*] to pour into another container, transfer; [+ *vino*] to decant **2** [+ *río*] to divert

trasvase SM (= *paso*) [*de vino*] pouring, decanting; [*de río*] diversion

trata SF ➤ **trata de blancas** trade of white women for prostitution ➤ **trata de esclavos** slave trade

tratable ADJ **1** (= *amable*) friendly, sociable **2** [*enfermedad*] treatable

tratado SM **1** (*Com*) agreement; (*Pol*) treaty, pact ➤ **Tratado de Adhesión** Treaty of Accession (*to EU*) ➤ **tratado de paz** peace treaty **2** (= *libro*) treatise; **un ~ de física** a treatise on physics

tratamiento SM **1** [*de objeto, material, tema*] treatment; [*de problema*] handling, treatment **2** (*Med*) treatment; **un ~ con rayos X** an X-ray treatment ➤ **tratamiento médico** medical treatment **3** (*Inform*) processing ➤ **tratamiento de datos** data processing ➤ **tratamiento de la información** information processing ➤ **tratamiento de textos** word processing **4** [*de persona*] treatment; **el ~ que recibí** the way I was treated, the treatment I received **5** (= *título*) title, style (*of address*); **dar ~ a algn** to give sb his full title

tratante SMF dealer, trader (**en** in)

tratar /1a/ **A** VT **1** [+ *persona, animal, objeto*] to treat; **la vida la ha tratado muy bien** life has been very kind to her, life has treated her very well; **este asunto debe ser tratado con cuidado** this matter should be handled carefully; ✦ MODISMO **~ a algn a patadas** to treat sb like dirt **2** (= *llamar*) **¿cómo lo tenemos que ~ cuando nos hable?** how should we address him when he speaks to us?; **~ a algn de tú/usted** to address sb as "tú"/"usted" **3** (= *relacionarse con*) **~ a algn: ya no lo trato** I no longer have any dealings with him; **me cae bien, pero no la he tratado mucho** I like her, but I haven't had a lot to do with her **4** (*Med*) [+ *paciente, enfermedad*] to treat; **¿qué médico te está tratando?** which doctor is treating you? **5** [+ *tejido, madera, residuos*] to treat **6** (= *hablar de*) [+ *tema*] to deal with; [+ *acuerdo, paz*] to negotiate **7** (*Inform*) to process **B** VI **1 ~ de** [*libro*] to be about, deal with; [*personas*] to talk about, discuss

2 (= *intentar*) ~ **de hacer algo** to try to do sth; ~ **de que**: ~**é de que ésta sea la última vez** I'll try to make sure that this is the last time; **trata por todos los medios de que el trabajo esté acabado para mañana** try and do whatever you can to make sure that the job is done by tomorrow

3 (= *relacionarse*) ~ **con algn: trato con todo tipo de gente** I deal with all sorts of people; **para ~ con animales hay que tener mucha paciencia** you have to be very patient when dealing with animals

4 (*Com*) ~ **con** o **en algo** to deal in sth; **trataban con** o **en pieles** they dealt in furs, they were involved in the fur trade

◉ tratarse VPR **1** (= *cuidarse*) to look after o.s.

2 (= *relacionarse*) ~**se con algn** to have dealings with sb **3** (= *hablarse*) to address each other; **¿cómo nos tenemos que ~?** how should we address each other?; **no se tratan desde hace tiempo** they haven't been speaking (to each other) for some time; **¿aquí nos tratamos de tú o de usted?** are we on "tú" or "usted" terms here?

4 ~**se de algo 4.1** (= *ser acerca de*) to be about sth; **¿de qué se trata?** what's it about? **4.2** (= *ser cuestión de*) **se trata de aplazarlo un mes** it's a question of putting it off for a month; **se trata sencillamente de que rellenéis este formulario** all you have to do is fill out this form **4.3** (= *ser*) **ahora bien, tratándose de ti ...** now, seeing as it's you ...; **si no se trata más que de eso** if there's no more to it than that, if that's all it is

tratativas SFPL (*CS*) negotiations

trato SM **1** (= *acuerdo*) deal; **¡~ hecho!** it's a deal!; **cerrar un ~** to close o clinch a deal; **hacer un ~** to do a deal **2** (= *relación*) **no quiero ~ con él** I want nothing to do with him; **tener ~ carnal** o **sexual con algn** to have sexual relations with sb

3 *tratos* (= *negociaciones*) negotiations; **entrar en ~s con algn** to enter into negotiations o discussions with sb; **estar en ~s con algn** to be in negotiations with sb, be negotiating with sb

4 (= *tratamiento*) treatment; **daba muy mal ~ a sus empleados** he treated his employees very badly; **malos ~s** physical abuse *sing* ➤ **trato de favor, trato preferente** preferential treatment

5 (= *manera de ser*) manner; **es una persona de ~ agradable** he has a pleasant manner; **de fácil ~** easy to get on with **6** (*forma de cortesía*) **no sé qué ~ darle, si de tú o de usted** I don't know whether to address him as "tú" or as "usted"; **dar a algn el ~ debido** to give sb his proper title

trauma SM **1** (= *shock*) trauma **2** (= *lesión*) injury

traumático ADJ traumatic

traumatismo SM traumatism

traumatizar /1f/ VT (*Med, Psic*) to traumatize; (*fig*) to shock, affect profoundly

traumatología SF (= *ciencia*) orthopaedics, orthopedics (*EEUU*); (= *sección*) orthopaedic o (*EEUU*) orthopedic department

traumatólogo/a SM/F traumatologist

travelling ['traβelin] SM (*pl* ~**(s)** ['traβelin]), **travelín** SM (*Cine*) (= *aparato*) dolly, travelling platform; (= *movimiento*) tracking shot

través SM **1 a ~ de** across; (= *por medio de*) through; **fuimos a ~ del bosque** we went through the woods; **lo sé a ~ de un amigo** I heard about it through a friend **2 al ~** across, crossways; **de ~** across, crossways; (= *oblicuamente*) obliquely; (= *de lado*) sideways

travesaño SM (*Arquit*) crossbeam; (*Dep*) crossbar

travesera SF (*Mús*) flute

travesía SF **1** (= *viaje*) (*Náut*) crossing, voyage; (*Aer*) crossing; (= *distancia*) distance travelled, distance to be crossed ➤ **travesía del desierto** (*fig*) period in the wilderness **2** (*Esp*) (= *calle*) side street; [*de pueblo*] *road that passes through a village*

travesti SMF, **travestí** SMF (= *transformista*) transvestite; (= *artista*) drag artist

travestido/a ⒶADJ disguised, in disguise ⒷSM/F = **travesti**

travestismo SM transvestism

travesura SF prank, lark; **son ~s de niños** they're just childish pranks

traviesa SF crossbeam

travieso ADJ naughty, mischievous

trayecto SM **1** (= *distancia*) distance **2** (= *viaje*) journey; **comeremos durante el ~** we'll eat during the journey o on the way; **final del ~** end of the line **3** [*de bala*] trajectory

trayectoria SF **1** (= *camino*) trajectory, path ➤ **trayectoria de vuelo** flight path **2** (= *desarrollo*) development, path; **la ~ actual del partido** the party's present line; **la ~ poética de Garcilaso** Garcilaso's poetic development ➤ **trayectoria profesional** career

trayendo *etc ver* **traer**

traza SF **1** (= *aspecto*) appearance; **por** o **según las ~s** judging by appearances; **esto lleva** o **tiene ~s de no acabar nunca** this looks as though it will never end **2** [*de edificio*] plan, design; [*de ciudad*] layout **3** (= *habilidad*) skill, ability

trazado SM **1** [*de carretera*] route **2** [*de edificio*] plan, design; [*de ciudad*] layout

trazador(a) ⒶADJ (*Mil, Fís*) tracer *antes de s*; **bala ~a** tracer bullet ⒷSM/F (= *persona*) planner, designer ⒸSM **1** (*Fís*) tracer **2** (*Inform*) ➤ **trazador de gráficos, trazador gráfico** plotter

trazar /1f/ VT **1** (= *dibujar*) [+ *línea*] to draw, trace; (*Arte*) to sketch, outline; (*Arquit, Téc*) to plan, design **2** [+ *fronteras, límites*] to mark out; [+ *itinerario*] to plot; [+ *desarrollo, política*] to lay down, mark out

trazo SM **1** (= *línea*) stroke, line ➤ **trazo de lápiz** pencil line, pencil stroke ➤ **trazo discontinuo** broken line **2** (= *esbozo*) sketch, outline **3** *trazos* [*de cara*] lines, features; **de ~s enérgicos** vigorous-looking; **de ~s indecisos** with an indecisive look about him

trébol SM **1** (*Bot*) clover **2** (*Arquit*) trefoil **3** *tréboles* (*Naipes*) clubs

trece ADJ, PRON, SM (*cardinal*) thirteen; (*ordinal, en la fecha*) thirteenth; ✦ MODISMO **mantenerse en sus ~** to stand one's ground, stick to one's guns; *ver* **seis**

trecho SM **1** (= *tramo*) stretch; (= *distancia*) way, distance; (= *tiempo*) while; **andar un buen ~** to walk a good way; **a ~s** (= *en parte*) in parts, here and there; (= *cada tanto*) intermittently, by fits and starts; **de ~ en ~** every so often, at intervals **2** (*) (= *trozo*) bit, part; **queda un buen ~ que hacer** there's still quite a bit to do; **he terminado ese ~** I've finished that bit

tregua SF **1** (*Mil*) truce **2** (= *descanso*) lull, respite; **sin ~** without respite; **no dar ~** to give no respite

treinta ADJ, PRON, SM (*cardinal*) thirty; (*ordinal, en la fecha*) thirtieth; *ver tb* **seis**

treintañero/a Ⓐ ADJ, SM/F thirtysomething*

treintena SF (about) thirty

tremebundo ADJ (= *terrible*) terrible, frightening; (= *amenazador*) threatening; (= *violento*) fierce, savage

tremenda SF **tomarse algo a la ~** to make a great fuss about sth, take sth too seriously

tremendismo SM **1** [*de noticia*] stark reality **2** (*Arte*) use of realism to shock

tremendo ADJ **1** (*) (= *grandísimo*) tremendous; **le dio una paliza tremenda** he gave him a tremendous beating; **un error ~** a terrible mistake; **me llevé un disgusto ~** I was terribly upset **2** (= *terrible*) terrible, horrific **3** (*) (= *divertido*) **es ~, ¿eh?** he's something else, isn't he?* **4** (*) (= *travieso*) **esta niña es tremenda** this girl is a (little) terror

trementina SF turpentine

trémulo ADJ [*voz*] tremulous, shaky, quavering; [*mano*] trembling; [*luz*] flickering

tren SM **1** (*Ferro*) train; **cambiar de ~** to change trains, change train; **subirse a** o **tomar** o **coger un ~** to catch a train; **ir en ~** to go by train; ✦ MODISMOS **estar como un ~** (*Esp**) to be hot stuff*, be a bit of all right*; **para parar un ~***: **tenemos libros para parar un ~** we've got books coming out of our ears*; **recibimos cartas para parar un ~** we got more letters than you could possibly imagine; **perder el ~ de algo: perdimos el ~ de la revolución científica** when it came to the scientific revolution, we missed the boat; **subirse al ~ de algo: no han sabido subirse al ~ de la reconversión económica** they failed to take the road to economic restructuring ➤ **tren correo** mail train ➤ **tren de alta velocidad** high-speed train ➤ **tren de carga** goods train, freight train (*EEUU*) ➤ **tren de carretera** articulated vehicle ➤ **tren de cercanías** suburban train, local train ➤ **tren de largo recorrido** long-distance train ➤ **tren de mercancías** goods train, freight train (*EEUU*) ➤ **tren de pasajeros** passenger train ➤ **tren directo** through train ➤ **tren expreso** express, express train

2 (= *ritmo*) **ir a buen ~** to go at a good speed; **forzar el ~** to force the pace; ✦ MODISMO **vivir a todo ~** to live in style ➤ **tren de vida** lifestyle

3 (*Mec*) set (*of gears, wheels*) ➤ **tren de aterrizaje** (*Aer*) undercarriage, landing gear ➤ **tren de lavado** (*Aut*) car wash

4 (*Mil*) convoy

5 en ~ de (*LAm*) in the process of; **estamos en ~ de realizarlo** we are in the process of doing it

trenca SF (*Esp*) duffle-coat

tren-cremallera SM (*pl* **trenes-cremallera**) funicular (railway)

trenza SF [*de pelo*] plait (*esp Brit*), braid (*EEUU*); (*Cos*) braid; [*de pajas, cintas*] plait (*esp Brit*), braid (*EEUU*); [*de hilos*] twist

trenzado ADJ [*pelo*] plaited (*esp Brit*), braided (*EEUU*); (*Cos*) braided; (= *entrelazado*) intertwined, twisted together

trenzar /1f/ **Ⓐ** VT [+ *cabello*] to plait (*esp Brit*), braid (*EEUU*); [+ *pajas, cintas*] to plait (*esp Brit*), braid (*EEUU*); (*Cos*) to braid; [+ *hilo*] to weave, twist (together) **Ⓑ trenzarse** VPR **1** (*LAm*) (= *enzarzarse*) to get involved; **~se a golpes** to come to blows **2** (*RPl*) (= *pelear*) to fight

trepa* SMF (= *arribista*) social climber; (= *cobista*) creep*

trepador(a) **Ⓐ** ADJ [*planta*] climbing; [*rosa*] rambling **Ⓑ** SM/F (*) (= *persona*) social climber **Ⓒ** SM (*Bot*) climber; (= *rosa*) rambler

trepadora SF (*Bot*) climber, rambler

trepanación SF trepanation

trepar /1a/ **Ⓐ** VI **1** [*persona, animal*] to climb; **~ a un árbol** to climb (up) a tree **2** (*Bot*) to climb (**por** up) **Ⓑ** VT **~ puestos** to climb the ladder

trepidante ADJ [*ritmo*] frenetic, frantic; [*ruido*] intolerable, ear-splitting; [*frío*] extreme

trepidar /1a/ VI **1** (= *temblar*) to shake, vibrate **2** (*Chi*) (= *vacilar*) to hesitate, waver

tres ADJ, PRON, SM (*cardinal*) three; (*ordinal, en la fecha*) third; ✦ MODISMOS **de ~ al cuarto** cheap, poor quality; **ni a la de ~** on no account, not by a long shot; **no ver ~ en un burro** to be as blind as a bat ➤ **tres en raya** noughts and crosses *sing* (*Brit*), tic tac toe (*EEUU*); *ver tb* **seis**

trescientos ADJ, PRON, SM (*cardinal*) three hundred; (*ordinal*) three hundredth; *ver tb* **seiscientos**

tresillo SM **1** (= *sofá*) three-piece suite **2** (*Mús*) triplet

treta SF (= *truco*) trick; (= *ardid*) ruse, stratagem; (*Com*) stunt, gimmick ➤ **treta publicitaria** advertising gimmick

tríada SF triad

trial **Ⓐ** SM (*Dep*) trial **Ⓑ** SF trial motorcycle

triangular **Ⓐ** ADJ triangular **Ⓑ** /1a/ VT to triangulate

triángulo SM triangle ➤ **triángulo amoroso** love triangle ➤ **triángulo de aviso** warning triangle ➤ **triángulo de las Bermudas** Bermuda Triangle

triatlón SM triathlon

tribal ADJ tribal

tribu SF tribe

tribulación SF tribulation

tribuna SF **1** [*de orador*] platform, rostrum; (*en mitin*) platform **2** (*Dep*) stand, grandstand ➤ **tribuna cubierta** covered stand ➤ **tribuna de invitados** visitors gallery ➤ **tribuna de prensa** (*Dep*) press box; (*Parl*) press gallery

tribunal SM **1** (*Jur*) (= *lugar*) court; (= *conjunto de jueces*)

court, bench; **llevar a algn ante los ~es** to take sb to court ➤ **Tribunal Constitucional** constitutional court ➤ **Tribunal de la Haya** International Court of Justice ➤ **tribunal de primera instancia** court of first instance ➤ **tribunal popular** jury ➤ **Tribunal Supremo** High Court (*Brit*), Supreme Court (*EEUU*) ➤ **tribunal (tutelar) de menores** juvenile court **2** (*Univ*) (= *examinadores*) board of examiners **3** (*Pol*) (= *comisión investigadora*) tribunal

tribuno SM tribune

tributación SF **1** (= *pago*) payment **2** (= *impuesto*) taxation

tributar /1a/ **Ⓐ** VT **1** (*Fin*) to pay **2** [+ *homenaje, respeto*] to pay; [+ *recibimiento*] to give **Ⓑ** VI (= *pagar impuestos*) to pay taxes

tributario **Ⓐ** ADJ **1** (*Geog, Pol*) tributary *antes de s* **2** (*Fin*) tax, taxation *antes de s*; **sistema ~** tax system **Ⓑ** SM tributary

tributo SM **1** (= *homenaje*) tribute; **rendir ~** to pay tribute **2** (*Fin*) (= *impuesto*) tax

triceps SMPL triceps

triciclo SM tricycle

tricolor **Ⓐ** ADJ tricolour, tricolor (*EEUU*), three-coloured, three-colored (*EEUU*); **bandera ~** tricolour **Ⓑ** SF tricolour, tricolor (*EEUU*)

tricornio SM three-cornered hat

tricota SF (*RPl*) (*sin botones*) sweater; (*con botones*) cardigan

tricotar /1a/ VT, VI (*Esp*) to knit

tricotosa SF (*Esp*) knitting machine

tridente SM trident

tridimensional ADJ three-dimensional

trienal ADJ triennial

trienio SM **1** (= *período*) period of three years, triennium (*frm*) **2** (= *pago*) *monthly bonus for each three-year period worked with the same employer*

trifásico ADJ (*Elec*) three-phase, triphase

trifulca* SF row, shindy*

trigal SM wheat field

trigésimo ADJ, PRON thirtieth; *ver tb* **sexto**

trigo SM **1** (= *cereal*) wheat; **de ~ entero** wholemeal (*Brit*), wholewheat (*esp EEUU*); **no ser ~ limpio** to be dishonest ➤ **trigo candeal** bread wheat ➤ **trigo duro** hard wheat, durum wheat **2 trigos** (= *campo*) wheat *sing*, wheat field(s)

trigonometría SF trigonometry

trigueño ADJ [*cabello*] dark blond, corn-coloured; [*rostro*] olive-skinned, golden-brown

triguero ADJ wheat *antes de s*

trilateral ADJ trilateral, three-sided

trilla SF threshing

trillado ADJ **1** (*Agr*) threshed **2** [*camino*] well-trodden **3** [*tema*] (= *gastado*) well-worn, hackneyed; (= *conocido*) well-known

trilladora SF threshing machine

trillar /1a/ VT **1** (*Agr*) to thresh **2** [+ *tema*] to overuse

trillizo/a SM/F triplet

trillo SM threshing machine

trillón SM quintillion

trilogía SF trilogy

trimestral ADJ quarterly, three-monthly; (*Univ*) term *antes de s*

trimestre SM **1** (= *período*) (*gen*) quarter, period of three months; (*Univ*) term **2** (*Fin*) (= *pago*) quarterly payment

trinar /1a/ VI **1** (*Orn*) to sing, warble, trill; (*Mús*) to trill **2** (*) (= *enfadarse*) to fume, be angry; **está que trina** he's hopping mad*

trinca SF group of three, set of three, threesome

trincar¹ /1g/ VT **1** (= *atar*) to tie up, bind; (*Náut*) to lash **2** (= *inmovilizar*) to pinion, hold by the arms **3** (*) (= *detener*) to nick*

trincar²* /1g/ VT, VI (= *beber*) to drink

trinchador SM **1** (= *cuchillo*) carving knife, carver **2** (*Méx*) (= *mueble*) sideboard

trinchante SM **1** (= *cuchillo*) carving knife, carver; (= *tenedor*) meat fork, carving-fork **2** (*RPl*) (= *mueble*) sideboard

trinchar /1a/ VT to carve, cut up

trinche SM (*Méx*) fork

trinchera SF **1** (= *zanja*) ditch; (*Mil*) trench; (*Ferro*) cutting **2** (= *abrigo*) trench coat

trineo SM (*pequeño*) sledge (*Brit*), sled (*EEUU*); (*grande*) sleigh

Trinidad SF **1** (*Rel*) Trinity **2** (*Geog*) Trinidad

trino SM (*Orn*) warble, trill; (*Mús*) trill

trinquete SM **1** (*Mec*) pawl, catch; [*de rueda dentada*] ratchet **2** (*Méx*) (= *trampa*) cheating; (= *fraude*) fraud

trío SM trio

tripa SF **1** (= *intestino*) intestine, gut; (= *vísceras*) guts*, insides*, innards*; **me duele la ~** I have a stomach ache; **quitar las ~s a un pez** to gut a fish; **◆ MODISMOS hacer el ~s corazón** to pluck up courage; **echar ~s** (= *vomitar*) to retch, vomit violently; **revolver a algn las ~s** to turn sb's stomach **2** (*Esp**) (= *barriga*) **2.1** (*gen*) belly, tummy*; **echar ~** to put on weight, start to get a paunch **2.2** [*de embarazada*] bulge **3 las ~s*** (= *mecanismo*) the insides*, the works; (= *piezas*) the parts

tripartito ADJ tripartite

tripi** SM (*Esp*) LSD, dose of LSD

triple Ⓐ ADJ triple; (*de tres capas*) with three layers; **~ salto** triple jump Ⓑ SM **1 el ~: es el ~ de lo que era** it is three times what it was *o* as big as it was **2** (*Dep*) (= *salto*) triple jump; (*en baloncesto*) three-point basket Ⓒ SF **➤ triple vírica** triple vaccine

triplicado ADJ triplicate; **por ~** in triplicate

triplicar /1g/ Ⓐ VT to treble, triple; **las pérdidas triplican las ganancias** losses are three times bigger *o* more than the profits Ⓑ **triplicarse** VPR to treble, triple

triplo SM = **triple B1**

trípode SM tripod

Trípoli SM Tripoli

tripón/ona* Ⓐ ADJ fat, potbellied Ⓑ SM/F (*Ven*) little boy, little girl; **los tripones** the kids*

tríptico SM **1** (*Arte*) triptych **2** (= *folleto*) three-page leaflet

triptongo SM triphthong

tripulación SF crew

tripulado ADJ **vuelo ~** manned flight; **~ por** manned by, crewed by

tripulante SMF [*de barco, avión*] crew member; **tripulantes** crew *sing*

tripular /1a/ VT **1** [+ *barco, avión*] to crew **2** (*Aut*) to drive

triquiñuela SF trick, dodge; **saber las ~s del oficio** to know the tricks of the trade, know all the dodges

tris SM INV **1** (= *estallido*) crack; (*al rasgarse*) rip, tearing noise **2 ◆ MODISMO en un ~** in a trice; **recogimos la mesa en un ~** we cleared the table in no time; **estar en un ~ de hacer algo** to be within an inch of doing sth

trisílabo Ⓐ ADJ trisyllabic, three-syllabled Ⓑ SM trisyllable

triste ADJ **1** [*persona*] (= *entristecido*) sad; (= *desgraciado*) miserable; [*carácter*] gloomy, melancholy; **poner ~ a algn** to make sb sad, make sb unhappy, make sb miserable **2** (= *entristecedor*) [*noticia, canción*] sad; [*paisaje*] dismal, desolate; [*cuarto*] gloomy; **es ~ verlo así** it is sad to see him like that **3** (*) (= *mustio*) [*flor*] withered **4** (= *insignificante*) miserable; **me dieron un ~ trozo de pan para comer** they gave me a miserable piece of bread for lunch; **hizo un ~ papel** he cut a sorry figure

tristeza SF sadness, sorrow

tristón ADJ (= *triste*) sad, downhearted; (= *pesimista*) pessimistic, gloomy

tritón SM (*Zool*) newt

trituración SF grinding, crushing, trituration (*frm*)

triturador SM, **trituradora** SF (*Téc*) grinder, crushing machine; (*Culin*) mincer (*Brit*), meat grinder (*EEUU*)

triturar /1a/ VT to grind, crush, triturate (*frm*)

triunfador(a) Ⓐ ADJ [*ejército*] triumphant, victorious; [*equipo, concursante*] winning, victorious Ⓑ SM/F winner; **es un ~ nato** he's a born winner

triunfal ADJ **1** [*arco, marcha*] triumphal **2** [*grito, sonrisa, recibimiento*] triumphant

triunfalismo SM (= *optimismo*) euphoria, excessive optimism; (= *petulancia*) smugness, over-confidence, triumphalism; **lo digo sin ~s** I say it without wishing to gloat

triunfalista ADJ (= *optimista*) euphoric, excessively optimistic; (= *petulante*) smug, over-confident, triumphalist

triunfante ADJ **1** (= *victorioso*) triumphant; **salir ~** to come out the winner, emerge victorious **2** (= *jubiloso*) jubilant, exultant

triunfar /1a/ VI **1** (= *ganar, vencer*) to triumph, win; **los socialistas ~on en las elecciones** the socialists triumphed in *o* won the elections; **~ en un concurso** to win a competition; **al final triunfó el amor** in the end love conquered all **2** (= *tener éxito*) to be successful, succeed; **~ en la vida** to succeed *o* be successful in life **3** (*Naipes*) [*jugador*] to play a trump; **triunfan corazones** hearts are trumps

triunfo SM **1** (= *victoria*) win, victory; (= *éxito*) victory, success; **adjudicarse el ~** to win **2** (*Naipes*) trump; **seis sin ~s** six no-trumps; **palo del ~** trump suit

triunvirato SM triumvirate

trivial ADJ trivial, trite

trivialidad SF **1** (= *cualidad*) triviality, triteness **2** (= *asunto*) trivial matter; (= *dicho*) trite remark; **~es** trivia, trivialities; **decir ~es** to talk in platitudes

trivialización SF trivializing, minimizing (the importance of), playing-down

trivializar /1f/ VT to trivialize, minimize (the importance of), play down

triza SF bit, shred; **hacer algo ~s** (= *rasgar*) to tear sth to shreds; (= *hacer pedazos*) to smash sth to bits; **hacer ~s a algn** (= *cansar*) to wear sb out; (= *aplastar*) to flatten sb, crush sb; **estar hecho ~s** [*persona*] to be shattered*

trocar /1g, 1l/ Ⓐ VT **1** (= *canjear*) barter, to exchange **2** (= *cambiar*) to change; **~ la alegría en tristeza** to change gaiety into sadness **3** (= *confundir*) to mix up, confuse Ⓑ **trocarse** VPR **1** (= *transformarse*) **~se en** become, turn into **2** (= *confundirse*) to get mixed up

trocear /1a/ VT to cut up, cut into pieces

trocha SF (*LAm Ferro*) gauge, gage (*EEUU*) **➤ trocha normal** standard gauge

troche: a ~ y moche ADV [*correr*] helter-skelter, pell-mell; [*desparramar*] all over the place; [*distribuir*] haphazardly; **gastar dinero a ~ y moche** to spend money like water

trofeo SM trophy

troglodita SMF **1** (= *cavernícola*) cave dweller, troglodyte **2** (= *bruto*) brute, oaf

trola* SF (*Esp*) fib, lie

trolebús SM trolley bus

tromba SF whirlwind; **entrar en ~** to come in in a torrent, come rushing in **➤ tromba de agua** violent downpour

trombo SM clot, thrombus (*frm*)

trombón Ⓐ SM (= *instrumento*) trombone **➤ trombón de varas** slide trombone Ⓑ SMF (= *músico*) trombonist

trombonista SMF trombonist

trombosis SF INV thrombosis **➤ trombosis cerebral** brain haemorrhage, cerebral haemorrhage

trompa Ⓐ SF **1** (*Mús*) horn **2** (= *juguete*) spinning top **3** (*Zool*) [*de elefante*] trunk; [*de insecto*] proboscis **4** (*Esp**) (= *nariz*) snout**, hooter**; (*SAm*) (= *labios*) lips *pl*, kisser**; **poner ~** to look grumpy*, be sour-faced **5** (*Anat*) tube,

duct; **ligadura de ~s** tubal ligation ➤ **trompa de Eustaquio** Eustachian tube ➤ **trompa de Falopio** Fallopian tube
6 (*Esp**) (= *borrachera*) **cogerse** *o* **agarrarse una ~** to get tight* **B** SMF (*Mús*) horn player

trompada* SF (*SAm*) punch, thump

trompazo SM bump, bang

trompear /1a/ (*LAm*) **A** VT to punch, thump **B** **trompearse** VPR to fight

trompeta A SF trumpet **B** SMF (*Mús*) trumper player; (*Mil*) trumpeter

trompetazo SM (*Mús*) trumpet blast; (*fig*) blast, blare

trompetilla SF **1** (*tb ~ acústica*) ear trumpet **2** (*Ven**) (= *ruido*) raspberry*

trompetista SMF trumpet player

trompicar /1g/ **A** VT (= *hacer tropezar*) to trip up **B** VI (= *tropezar*) to trip

trompicón SM (= *tropiezo*) trip, stumble; ✦ MODISMO **a trompicones** in fits and starts

trompo SM **1** (= *juguete*) spinning top; ✦ MODISMO **ponerse como un ~*** to stuff o.s.*, eat to bursting point **2** (*Aut*) 180 degree turn *o* skid

trompudo ADJ (*LAm*) thick-lipped, blubber-lipped

trona SF high chair

tronado ADJ **1** (= *viejo*) old, useless **2** (*) **estar ~** (= *loco*) to be potty*

tronar /1l/ **A** VI **1** (*Meteo*) to thunder; ✦ MODISMO **por lo que pueda ~** just in case, to be on the safe side **2** [*cañones*] to boom, thunder **3** (*) (= *enfurecerse*) to rave, rage; **~ contra** to spout forth against, rage *o* thunder against **4** (*Méx*) (*en relación*) to fall out; (*en negocio, examen*) to fail **B** VT **1** (*CAm, Méx**) (= *fusilar*) to shoot **2** (*Méx*) [+ *examen*] to fail, flunk (*EEUU**); **la tronó*** he blew it**

troncal ADJ **línea ~** main (trunk) line; **materia ~** core subject

tronchante* ADJ hilarious, killingly funny

tronchar /1a/ **A** VT **1** (= *talar*) to fell, chop down; (= *cortar*) to cut up, cut off; (= *hender*) to split, crack, shatter **2** [+ *vida*] to cut short; [+ *esperanzas*] to dash **B** **troncharse** VPR **1** (*) *tb* **~se de risa** to split one's sides laughing **2** [*árbol*] to fall down, split

troncho SM stem, stalk

tronco SM **1** [*de árbol*] trunk; (= *leño*) log; ✦ MODISMO **dormir como un ~** to sleep like a log ➤ **tronco de Navidad** (*Culin*) yule log **2** (*Anat*) trunk **3** (= *estirpe*) stock

tronco/a* **A** SM/F (*Esp*) (= *tío*) guy (*EEUU**); (= *tía*) bird (*Brit**), chick (*EEUU***) **B** SM (*Esp*) (= *amigo*) (*en oración directa*) pal*, mate (*Brit**)

tronera SF **1** (*Mil*) (= *aspillera*) loophole, embrasure; (*Arquit*) small window **2** (*Billar*) pocket **3** (*Col, Ven*) (= *agujero*) big hole

tronido SM **1** (*Meteo*) thunderclap; **~s** thunder *sing*, booming *sing* **2** (= *explosión*) loud report, bang, detonation

tronío SM lavish expenditure, extravagance

trono SM (= *asiento*) throne; (= *símbolo*) crown; **heredar el ~** to inherit the crown; **subir al ~** to ascend the throne, come to the throne

tropa SF **1** (*Mil*) (= *soldados rasos*) rank and file, ordinary soldiers *pl*; (= *ejército*) army; **las ~s** the troops ➤ **tropas de asalto, tropa de choque** storm troops **2** (= *multitud*) crowd, troop; (*pey*) mob, troop **3** (*CS*) [*de ganado*] herd

tropecientos* ADJ PL umpteen*

tropel SM mob, crowd; **acudir en ~** to crowd in, come en masse

tropezar /1f, 1j/ **A** VI **1** (*con los pies*) to trip, stumble; **tropezó y por poco se cae** he tripped *o* stumbled and nearly fell; **he tropezado con el escalón** I tripped on the step
2 (= *chocar*) **~ con** *o* **contra algo** to bump into sth **3** (= *enfrentarse*) **~ con algo** to run into sth, encounter sth **4** (= *encontrarse*) **~ con algn** to bump into sb, run into sb **5** (= *cometer un error*) to err, make a mistake **B** **tropezarse** VPR [*dos personas*] to bump *o* run into each

other; **nos tropezamos casi cada día por la calle** we bump *o* run into each other practically every day in the street; **~se con algn** to bump *o* run into sb

tropezón SM **1** (= *traspié*) trip, stumble; **dar un ~** to trip, stumble; **hablar a tropezones** to speak jerkily, speak falteringly **2** (= *equivocación*) slip, blunder; (*moral*) lapse **3 tropezones** (*Culin*) small pieces of food added to soup

tropical ADJ tropical

trópico SM tropic; **los ~s** the tropics ➤ **trópico de Cáncer** Tropic of Cancer ➤ **trópico de Capricornio** Tropic of Capricorn

tropiezo SM **1** (= *error*) slip, blunder; (*moral*) moral lapse **2** (= *revés*) (*gen*) setback; (*en el amor*) disappointment in love

tropo SM trope

troquel SM die

troquelar /1a/ VT **1** [+ *cuero, cartón*] to die-cut; [+ *moneda, medalla*] to strike; [+ *metal*] to die-cast **2** (= *perforar*) to punch

trotaconventos SF INV go-between, procuress

trotamundos SMF INV globetrotter

trotar /1a/ VI **1** [*caballo*] to trot **2** (*) (= *viajar*) to travel about, chase around here and there

trote SM **1** [*de caballo*] trot; **ir al ~** to trot, go at a trot; ✦ MODISMO **irse al ~** to go off in a hurry **2** (*) (= *uso*) **de mucho ~** tough, hard-wearing (*esp Brit*); **una chaqueta para todo ~** a jacket for everyday wear **3** (*) (= *ajetreo*) bustle; **el abuelo ya no está para esos ~s** grandad is not up to that sort of thing any more

trotskismo SM Trotskyism

trova SF ballad

trovador SM troubadour

Troya SF Troy; ✦ MODISMOS **¡aquí fue ~!** you should have heard the fuss!; **¡arda ~!** press on regardless!, never mind the consequences!

troyano/a ADJ, SM/F Trojan

trozar /1f/ VT (*LAm*) to cut up, cut into pieces

trozo SM **1** (= *pedazo*) piece, bit; **un ~ de madera** a piece of wood; **a ~s** in bits **2** (*Literat, Mús*) passage; **~s escogidos** selected passages, selections

trucaje SM **1** (*Cine*) trick photography **2** (*en el juego*) rigging, fixing

trucar* /1g/ VT **1** [+ *resultado*] to fix, rig; [+ *baraja*] to tamper with; **las cartas estaban trucadas** (*fig*) the dice were loaded against us **2** (*Aut*) [+ *motor*] to soup up*

trucha SF trout

truco SM **1** (= *ardid*) trick, dodge; (*Cine*) trick effect, piece of trick photography; **coger el ~ a algn** to see how sb works a trick, catch on to sb's little game **2** (= *habilidad*) knack; **coger el ~** to get the knack, get the hang of it*, catch on

truculencia SF gruesomeness

truculento ADJ gruesome, horrifying

trueno SM **un ~** a clap of thunder, a thunderclap; **~s** thunder *sing*

trueque SM exchange; (*Com*) barter; **a ~ de** in exchange for

trufa SF truffle

trufado ADJ stuffed with truffles

trufar /1a/ VT to stuff with truffles

truhán SM **1** (= *pillo*) rogue, crook*, shyster (*EEUU*); (= *estafador*) swindler; (= *charlatán*) mountebank **2** (*Hist*) jester, buffoon

truísmo SM truism

trulla SF crowd, throng

truncado ADJ (= *reducido*) truncated, shortened; (= *incompleto*) incomplete

truncar /1g/ VT **1** (= *acortar*) [+ *texto*] to truncate, shorten; [+ *cita*] to mutilate **2** [+ *carrera, vida*] to cut short; [+ *esperanzas*] to dash; [+ *proyecto*] to ruin; [+ *desarrollo*] to stunt, check

trusa SF **1** (*And*) (= *calzoncillos*) underpants *pl* ➤ **trusa de baño** trunks *pl*, swimming trunks *pl* (*Brit*) **2** (*RPl*) (= *faja*) girdle

trust [trus] SM (*pl* **~s** [trus]) (*Fin*) trust, cartel

tu ADJ POSES your; **han venido tu tía y tus primos** your aunt and your cousins have come; **hágase tu voluntad** (*Rel*) thy will be done

tú PRON PERS **1** you; **es mucho más alto que tú** he is much taller than you (are); **en el partido se mantuvo el tú a tú** the game was between equals, the game was an equal struggle; **hablar** o **llamar** o **tratar a algn de tú** to use the "tú" form of address **2** (*) (*uso vocativo*) **¡tú! ven aquí** you! come here; **¡tú cállate!** shut up, you!

tuareg ADJ, SMF (*pl* **~** o **~s**) Tuareg

tubérculo SM **1** (*Bot*) tuber; (= *patata*) potato **2** (*Anat, Med*) tubercle

tuberculosis SF tuberculosis

tuberculoso/a Ⓐ ADJ tuberculous, tubercular Ⓑ SM/F tuberculosis patient

tubería SF **1** (= *tubo*) pipe **2** (= *conjunto de tubos*) pipes *pl*, piping

tubo SM **1** (= *conducto*) tube ➤ **tubo capilar** capillary ➤ **tubo de desagüe** (*interior*) waste pipe; (*exterior*) drainpipe ➤ **tubo de ensayo** test tube ➤ **tubo de escape** exhaust (pipe) ➤ **tubo de imagen** television tube ➤ **tubo de rayos catódicos** cathode-ray tube ➤ **tubo de respiración** breathing tube ➤ **tubo digestivo** alimentary canal ➤ **tubo fluorescente** fluorescent tube **2** (= *tubería*) pipe **3** ✦ MODISMO **por un ~** (*Esp**) loads*; **gastó por un ~** he spent a fortune* **4** (*RPl*) [*de teléfono*] handset, earpiece

tubular Ⓐ ADJ tubular Ⓑ SM (= *prenda*) roll-on

tucán SM, **tucano** SM (*LAm*) toucan

tuco SM (*CS, Perú*) (= *salsa*) pasta sauce; [*de tomate*] tomato sauce

tuerca SF nut; ✦ MODISMO **apretar las ~s a algn** to tighten the screws on sb

tuerto/a Ⓐ ADJ (= *con un ojo*) one-eyed; (= *ciego en un ojo*) blind in one eye Ⓑ SM/F (= *persona*) one-eyed person; person who is blind in one eye

tueste SM roasting

tuétano SM marrow (*Brit*), squash (*EEUU*); ✦ MODISMO **hasta los ~s** through and through, utterly; **mojarse hasta los ~s** to get soaked to the skin

tufo SM **1** (= *emanación*) fumes *pl* **2** (= *hedor*) (*gen*) stink; [*de cuarto*] fug

tugurio SM **1** (= *cafetucho*) den, joint**; (= *chabola*) hovel, slum, shack; (= *cuartucho*) poky little room **2** **tugurios** (*And*) shanty town *sing*

tul SM tulle, net

tulipa SF lampshade

tulipán SM tulip

tullido/a Ⓐ ADJ (= *lisiado*) crippled; (= *paralizado*) paralysed Ⓑ SM/F cripple

tullir /3h/ VT **1** (= *lisiar*) to cripple, maim; (= *paralizar*) to paralyse

tumba SF tomb, grave; ✦ MODISMOS **hablar a ~ abierta** to speak openly; **llevar a algn a la ~** to carry sb off; **ser (como) una ~** to keep one's mouth shut, not breathe a word to anyone

tumbaburros * SM INV (*Méx*) dictionary

tumbar /1a/ Ⓐ VT **1** (= *derribar*) [+ *persona*] to knock down, knock over; [+ *puerta*] (*a golpes*) to batter down; (*a patadas*) to kick down o in; [*viento*] to blow down; **lo ~on a golpes** they punched him to the ground **2** (**) (= *matar*) to do in** **3** (*) [*olor*] to knock back*; **un olor que te tumba*** an overpowering smell, a smell which knocks you back* **4** (= *impresionar*) to amaze, overwhelm Ⓑ **tumbarse** VPR **1** (= *acostarse*) to lie down; **estar tumbado** to lie, be lying down **2** [*trigo*] to go flat

tumbo SM **1** (= *sacudida*) shake, jolt; ✦ MODISMO **dando ~s** with all sorts of difficulties **2** (= *caída*) fall, tumble; **dar un ~** to fall, shake

tumbona SF (*Esp*) [*de jardín*] lounger; [*de playa*] deckchair, beach chair (*EEUU*)

tumefacción SF swelling

tumefacto ADJ swollen

tumor SM tumour, tumor (*EEUU*), growth ➤ **tumor benigno** benign tumour o (*EEUU*) tumor ➤ **tumor cerebral** brain tumour o (*EEUU*) tumor ➤ **tumor maligno** malignant growth o tumour o (*EEUU*) tumor

túmulo SM tumulus, burial mound

tumulto SM turmoil, tumult; (*Pol*) (= *motín*) riot, disturbance

tumultuoso ADJ tumultuous; (*pey*) riotous, disorderly

tuna¹ SF (*Bot*) prickly pear

tuna² SF (*Esp Mús*) (*tb ~ estudiantina*) student music group

---

TUNA

Tunas, also known as **estudiantinas**, are groups of students dressed in 17th century costumes who play guitars, lutes and tambourines and go serenading through the streets. They also make impromptu appearances at weddings and parties singing traditional Spanish songs, often of a bawdy nature, in exchange for drinks or some money.
See also http://tuna.upv.es

---

tunante SM rogue, villain; **¡tunante!** you villain!; (*a un niño*) you young scamp!

tunda SF **1** (= *paliza*) beating, thrashing **2 darse una ~** to wear o.s. out

tundra SF tundra

tunecino/a ADJ, SM/F Tunisian

túnel SM **1** (= *conducto*) tunnel ➤ **túnel aerodinámico** wind tunnel ➤ **túnel de lavado** car wash ➤ **túnel del Canal de la Mancha** Channel Tunnel ➤ **túnel del tiempo** time warp ➤ **túnel de pruebas aerodinámicas** wind tunnel **2** (= *crisis*) bad time

Túnez SM (= *país*) Tunisia; (= *ciudad*) Tunis

tungsteno SM tungsten

túnica SF **1** (*Hist*) tunic; [*de monje*] robe **2** (*Anat, Bot*) tunic

tuno/a (*Esp*) Ⓐ SM/F (= *pícaro*) rogue, villain; **el muy ~** the old rogue Ⓑ SM (*Mús*) *member of a student music group*

tuntún: **al ~** ADV thoughtlessly, any old how

tupamaro/a ADJ, SM/F (*Hist, Pol*) Tupamaro

tupé SM **1** (= *mechón*) quiff **2** (= *peluca*) toupée, hairpiece **3** (*) (= *caradura*) nerve*, cheek*

tupí Ⓐ SMF Tupi (Indian) Ⓑ SM (*Ling*) Tupi; ⊃ GUARANÍ

tupido Ⓐ ADJ **1** (= *denso*) thick; (= *impenetrable*) impenetrable; [*tela*] close-woven **2** (= *torpe*) dim*, dense* Ⓑ ADV (*Méx, CS*) hard

tupí-guaraní Ⓐ ADJ Tupi-Guarani Ⓑ SM (*Ling*) Tupi-Guarani; ⊃ GUARANÍ

turba¹ SF (= *combustible*) peat

turba² SF (= *muchedumbre*) crowd, throng; (*en movimiento*) swarm; (*pey*) mob

turbación SF **1** (= *alteración*) disturbance **2** (= *inquietud*) alarm, worry; (= *perplejidad*) bewilderment, confusion **3** (= *vergüenza*) embarrassment

turbado ADJ **1** (= *alterado*) disturbed **2** (= *inquieto*) alarmed, worried; (= *perplejo*) bewildered **3** (= *avergonzado*) embarrassed

turbador ADJ (= *inquietante*) disturbing, alarming; (= *vergonzoso*) embarrassing

turbante SM turban

turbar /1a/ Ⓐ VT **1** [+ *silencio, reposo, orden*] to disturb; **nada turbó la buena marcha de las negociaciones** nothing hindered o disturbed the smooth progress of the negotiations **2** [+ *agua*] to disturb, stir up **3** (= *alterar*) **la noticia turbó su ánimo** the news troubled his mind, the news perturbed him **4** (= *avergonzar*) to embarrass

turbarse VPR **1** (= *alterarse*) **al reconocer a su agresor se turbó enormemente** she was deeply disturbed when she recognized her attacker **2** (= *avergonzarse*) to get embarrassed

turbina SF turbine ➤ **turbina de gas** gas turbine ➤ **turbina eólica** wind turbine

turbio Ⓐ ADJ **1** [*agua*] cloudy, muddy, turbid (*frm*) **2** [*vista*] dim, blurred; [*mente, pensamientos*] disturbed; [*tema*] unclear, confused **3** [*período*] turbulent, unsettled **4** [*negocio*] shady*; [*método*] dubious Ⓑ ADV **ver ~** not to see clearly, have blurred vision

turbión SM **1** (*Meteo*) (= *aguacero*) heavy shower, downpour **2** (= *aluvión*) shower, torrent

turbo Ⓐ SM (*Mec*) turbo, turbocharger; (= *coche*) turbocharged car Ⓑ ADJ INV turbo *antes de s*

turboalimentado ADJ turbocharged

turbodiesel ADJ INV, SM turbo diesel

turbopropulsor, turborreactor Ⓐ SM turbojet (aeroplane (*Brit*) *o* airplane (*EEUU*)) Ⓑ ADJ INV turbojet *antes de s*

turbulencia SF **1** (*Meteo*) turbulence **2** [*de río, aguas*] turbulence

turbulento ADJ **1** [*río, aguas*] turbulent **2** [*período*] troubled, turbulent; [*reunión*] stormy **3** [*carácter*] restless

turco/a Ⓐ ADJ Turkish Ⓑ SM/F **1** (= *de Turquía*) Turk **2** (*LAm pey*) *immigrant from the Middle East* Ⓒ SM (*Ling*) Turkish

turcochipriota ADJ, SMF Turkish-Cypriot

turgencia SF turgidity

turgente ADJ, **túrgido** ADJ turgid, swollen

turismo SM **1** (= *actividad*) tourism; (= *industria*) tourist industry *o* trade ➤ **turismo cultural** cultural tourism ➤ **turismo de calidad** quality tourism ➤ **turismo ecológico** eco-tourism ➤ **turismo rural** country holidays *pl*, green tourism; **promover el ~ rural** to promote tourism in rural areas; **casas de ~ rural** ≈ holiday cottages ➤ **turismo sexual** sex tourism **2** (*Aut*) car, private car

turista SMF (*gen*) tourist; (= *visitante*) sightseer; **clase ~** economy class, tourist class

turístico ADJ tourist *antes de s*

túrmix® SM *o* SF mixer, blender

turnar /1a/ Ⓐ VI to take turns Ⓑ **turnarse** VPR to take turns; **se turnan para usarlo** they take it in turns to use it

turné SM tour, trip

turno SM **1** (= *vez*) turn; (*en juegos*) turn, go; **es tu ~** it's your turn; **por ~s** in turns, by turns; **estuvo con su querida de ~** he was with his lover of the moment; **el tonto de ~** the inevitable idiot ➤ **turno de preguntas** round of questions **2** [*de trabajo*] shift; **hago el ~ de tarde** I do the afternoon shift; **trabajo por ~s** shiftwork; **trabajar por ~s** to work shifts, do shiftwork ➤ **turno de día** day shift ➤ **turno de noche** night shift

turolense ADJ of/from Teruel

turquesa Ⓐ ADJ, SM (= *color*) turquoise Ⓑ SF (= *piedra*) turquoise

Turquía SF Turkey

turrón SM ≈ nougat

turulato* ADJ stunned, flabbergasted; **se quedó ~ con la noticia** he was stunned by the news

tururú* Ⓐ ADJ (= *loco*) **estar ~** to be crazy Ⓑ EXCL no way!*, you're joking!

tusa SF **1** (*And, CAm, Carib*) [*de maíz*] (= *mazorca*) cob of maize, corncob; (*sin grano*) corn husk, maize husk **2** (*Chi*) (= *crin*) horse's mane

tusar /1a/ VT (*Col, CS, Ven*) (= *esquilar*) to cut, clip, shear; (= *cortar*) to cut roughly, cut badly

tute SM *card game similar to bezique*; ✦ MODISMO **darse un ~** to work extra hard

tutear /1a/ Ⓐ VT **~ a algn** (*lit*) to address sb as "tú" (*2nd person sing*); (*fig*) to be on familiar terms with sb Ⓑ **tutearse** VPR **se tutean desde siempre** they have always addressed each other as "tú", they have always been on familiar terms

tutela SF **1** (*Jur*) guardianship; **bajo ~** in ward; **estar bajo ~ jurídica** [*niño*] to be a ward of court **2** (= *protección*) tutelage, protection; **estar bajo la ~ de** (= *amparo*) to be under the protection of; (= *auspicios*) to be under the auspices of

tutelaje SM (*LAm*) = **tutela**

tutelar Ⓐ ADJ tutelary; **ángel ~** guardian angel Ⓑ /1a/ VT to protect, guard

tuteo SM use of (the familiar) "tú", addressing a person as "tú"; **se ha extendido mucho el ~** the use of "tú" has greatly increased

tutiplén†*: a ~ (*Esp*) ADV [*dar*] freely; [*repartir*] haphazardly, indiscriminately; [*comer*] hugely, to excess

tutor(a) SM/F **1** (*Jur*) guardian **2** (*Univ*) tutor ➤ **tutor(a) de curso** (*Escol*) form master/mistress

tutoría SF **1** (*Jur*) guardianship **2** (*Univ*) tutorial (class), section (of a course) (*EEUU*)

tutú SM tutu

tuve *etc ver* **tener**

tuyo/a Ⓐ ADJ POSES yours; **¿es ~ este abrigo?** is this coat yours?; **cualquier amigo ~** any friend of yours Ⓑ PRON POSES **1** (*gen*) yours; **este es el ~** this one's yours; **mis amigos y los ~s** my friends and yours; **¡adelante, ésta es la tuya!** go on, now's your chance!; **¿ya estás haciendo de las tuyas?** are you up to your tricks again?; **lo ~: he puesto lo ~ en esta caja** I've put your things in this box; **sé que lo ~ con Ana acabó hace tiempo** I know that you and Ana finished a while ago; **la informática no es lo ~** computers are not your thing **2 los ~s** (= *tus familiares*) your folks*, your family

> **Tuyo** se traduce por **yours** cuando hace referencia a las posesiones de alguien: "Es (el) tuyo", *It's yours*. En cambio, se traduce por **of yours** cuando significa "uno de tus": "un amigo tuyo", *a friend of yours*.

TV SF ABR (= **televisión**) TV

TVE SF ABR = **Televisión Española**

tweed [twi] SM tweed

txistulari SM (Basque) flute player

Uu

U, u[^1] [u] SF (= *letra*) U, u; **doble U** (*Méx*) W; **curva en U** hairpin bend

u[^2] CONJ (*used instead of "o" before o-, ho-*) or; **siete u ocho** seven or eight

ubérrimo ADJ exceptionally fertile

ubicación SF (*esp LAm*) situation, location

ubicado ADJ (*esp LAm*) **1** (= *situado*) situated, located; **bien ~** well situated *o* located, in a desirable location **2** (*en un trabajo*) working

ubicar /1g/ **Ⓐ** VT **1** (*LAm*) (= *colocar*) to place, locate, site **2** (*esp Lam*) (= *encontrar*) to find, locate; **no supo ~ Madrid en el mapa** he was unable to find *o* locate Madrid on the map; **no hemos podido ~ al jefe** we have been unable to find *o* locate the boss, we have been unable to track down the boss

Ⓑ ubicarse VPR **1** (= *estar situado*) **el museo se ubica en el centro de la ciudad** the museum is located *o* situated in the city centre *o* (*EEUU*) center

2 (= *orientarse*) to find one's way around; **a pesar del mapa no consigo ~me** even though I have a map I can't find my way around; **¿te ubicas ahora?** have you got (*esp Brit*) *o* do you have (*esp EEUU*) your bearings now?

3 (*LAm**) (= *colocarse*) to get a job

ubicuidad SF ubiquity; **el don de la ~** the gift for being everywhere at once

ubre SF udder

UCD SF ABR (*Esp*) = **Unión de Centro Democrático**

UCI SF ABR (= **Unidad de Cuidados Intensivos**) ICU, intensive care unit

Ucrania SF Ukraine

ucraniano/a ADJ, SM/F, **ucranio/a** ADJ, SM/F Ukrainian

Ud. PRON ABR = **usted**

Uds. PRON ABR = **ustedes**

UE SF ABR (= **Unión Europea**) EU

UEFA SF ABR (= **Unión Europea de Fútbol Asociación**) UEFA

UEM SF ABR (= **unión económica y monetaria**) EMU

UEO SF ABR (= **Unión Europea Occidental**) WEU

UF SF ABR (*Chi*) (= **Unidad de Fomento**) *changing monetary unit in a fixed dollar system*

uf EXCL (*cansancio*) phew!

ufanarse /1a/ VPR to boast; **~ con** *o* **de algo** to boast of sth, pride o.s. on sth

ufano ADJ (= *orgulloso*) proud; (= *satisfecho*) smug; **iba muy ~ en el nuevo coche** he was going along so proudly in his new car

ufología SF ufology, study of unidentified flying objects

Uganda SF Uganda

ugandés/esa ADJ, SM/F Ugandan

UGT SF ABR (*Esp*) = **Unión General de Trabajadores**

ujier SM (*en un tribunal*) usher; (= *conserje*) doorkeeper, attendant

úlcera SF ulcer, sore ➤ **úlcera de decúbito** bedsore

ulcerar /1a/ **Ⓐ** VT to make sore, ulcerate **Ⓑ ulcerarse** VPR to ulcerate

ulpo SM (*Chi, Perú*) *cold drink made with roasted flour*

últimamente ADV lately, recently

ultimar /1a/ VT **1** (= *terminar*) [+ *detalles, acuerdo*] to finalize; [+ *proyecto, obra*] to put the finishing *o* final touches to; **están ultimando los preparativos para la boda** they are making the final preparations for the wedding **2** (*LAm frm*) (= *matar*) to kill, murder

ultimato SM, **ultimátum** SM (*pl* **ultimátums**) ultimatum

último/a **Ⓐ** ADJ **1** (= *final*) last; **el ~ día del mes** the last day of the month; **las últimas Navidades que pasamos allí** the last Christmas we spent there; **a lo ~*** in the end; **por ~** finally, lastly; **por última vez** for the last time

2 (= *más reciente*) **2.1** (*en una serie*) [*ejemplar, moda, novedad*] latest; [*elecciones, período*] last; **este coche es el ~ modelo** this car is the latest model; **¿has leído el ~ número de la revista?** have you read the latest issue of the magazine?; **las últimas noticias** the latest news; **durante la última década** in *o* over the last decade; **en las últimas horas** in the last few hours; **los ~s libros que he leído** the last few books that I have read; **ahora ~** (*Chi*) recently; **no es de ahora ~** it is not a recent thing; **en los ~s años** in *o* over the last few years, in recent years; **en los ~s tiempos** lately **2.2** (*entre dos*) latter; **de los dos, éste ~ es el mejor** of the two, the latter is the better

3 (*en el espacio*) **3.1** (= *más al fondo*) back; **un asiento en la última fila** a seat in the back row **3.2** (= *más alto*) top; **viven en el ~ piso** they live on the top floor **3.3** (= *más bajo*) bottom, last; **el equipo en última posición** the team in last *o* bottom place **3.4** (= *más lejano*) most remote, furthest; **las noticias llegan hasta el ~ rincón del país** news gets to the most remote *o* the furthest parts of the country

4 (= *extremo*) [*recurso*] last; [*fin*] ultimate; **en ~ caso, iría yo** as a last resort *o* if all else fails, I would go

5 (= *definitivo*) **es mi última oferta** that's my final offer; **✦** MODISMO **decir la última palabra** to have the last word

6 lo ~* 6.1 (= *lo más moderno*) the latest thing; **lo ~ en teléfonos móviles** the latest thing in mobile phones; **lo ~ en tecnología ofimática** the latest (in) office technology **6.2** (= *lo peor*) the limit; **pedirme eso encima ya es lo ~** for him to ask that of me as well really is the limit

Ⓑ SM/F **1 el ~** the last, the last one; **llegó la última** she arrived last; **ser el ~ en hacer algo** to be the last (one) to do sth; **✦** MODISMOS **reírse el ~** to have the last laugh; **a la última: estar a la última** (*en moda*) to be very trendy*; **está a la última en ordenadores** he's really up-to-date on computers; **siempre va vestida a la última** she's always wearing the latest thing; **estar en las últimas*** (= *a punto de morir*) to be at death's door, be on one's last legs*; (= *sin dinero*) to be down to one's last penny *o* (*EEUU*) cent; **en últimas** (*Col*) as a last resort

2 (*) **¿a qué no sabes la última de Irene?** do you know the latest about Irene?

3 (*Esp*) **a últimos de mes** towards the end of the month **Ⓒ** ADV (*CS*) in the last position, in the last place

ultra **Ⓐ** ADJ INV extreme right-wing **Ⓑ** SMF extreme right-winger

ultracongelar /1a/ VT (*Esp*) to deep-freeze

ultracorrección SF hypercorrection

ultraderecha SF extreme right, extreme right-wing

ultraderechista **Ⓐ** ADJ extreme right(-wing) **Ⓑ** SMF extreme right-winger

ultrafino ADJ ultrafine

ultrajante ADJ (= *ofensivo*) offensive; (= *injurioso*) insulting

ultrajar /1a/ VT (= *ofender*) to offend; (= *injuriar*) to insult, abuse

ultraje SM (= *injuria*) insult; (= *atrocidad*) outrage

ultraligero SM ultralight (aircraft), microlight (aircraft) (*Brit*)

ultramar SM **de** *o* **en ~** overseas, abroad; **los países de ~** foreign countries; **productos venidos de ~** goods from abroad

ultramarinos SM INV (*tb* **tienda de ~**) grocer's (shop) (*esp Brit*), grocery (*EEUU*)

ultramoderno ADJ ultramodern

ultramontano ADJ, SM ultramontane

ultranza SF **a ~ 1** (*como adjetivo*) (*Pol*) out-and-out, extreme; **un nacionalista a ~** a rabid nationalist **2** (*como adverbio*) **defender algo a ~** to defend sth to the last

ultrasur SMF INV *extremist fan of Real Madrid FC*

ultratumba SF **la vida de ~** life beyond the grave, life after death; **una voz de ~** a ghostly voice

ultravioleta ADJ INV ultraviolet

[^1]: U, u superscript 1
[^2]: u superscript 2

ulular /1a/ VI [*animal, viento*] to howl, shriek; [*búho*] to hoot, screech

umbilical ADJ umbilical; **cordón ~** umbilical cord

umbral SM threshold; **estar en los ~es de algo** to be on the threshold *o* verge of sth ➤ **umbral de la pobreza** poverty line

umbrío ADJ shady

UME SF ABR (= **Unión Monetaria Europea**) EMU

un(a)¹ Ⓐ ART INDEF **1** (*en singular*) (*refiriéndose a algo no conocido o de forma imprecisa*) a; (*antes de vocal o de h*) an; (*dando mayor énfasis, con expresiones temporales*) one; **una silla** a chair; **un paraguas** an umbrella; **hay una cosa que me gustaría saber** there is one thing I would like to know; **una mañana me llamó** he called me one morning

2 (*en plural*) **2.1** (*uso indefinido*) (= *algunos*) some; (= *pocos*) a few; **fui con unos amigos** I went with some friends; **unas horas más tarde** a few hours later; **tiene unas piernas muy largas** she has very long legs **2.2** (*con objetos a pares*) **me he comprado unos zapatos de tacón** I've bought some high-heels; **necesito unas tijeras** I need a pair of scissors **2.3** (*con cantidades, cifras*) about, around; **había unas 20 personas** there were about *o* around 20 people, there were some 20 people

3 (*enfático*) **¡se dio un golpe!** he banged himself really hard!; **¡había una gente más rara!** there were some real weirdos there!*

Ⓑ ADJ (*numeral*) one; **sólo quiero una hoja** I only want one sheet; **una excursión de un día** a one-day trip, a day trip; **tardamos una mañana entera** it took us a whole morning; *ver tb* **uno**

una² PRON **1 es la ~** (= *hora*) it's one o'clock; **¡a la ~, a las dos, a las tres!** (*antes de empezar algo*) one, two, three!; (*en subasta*) going, going, gone!; (*Dep*) ready, steady (*esp Brit*) *o* set (*esp EEUU*), go!; ✦ MODISMOS **~ de dos** either one thing or the other; **todos a ~** all together

2 (*enfático*) **armar ~** to kick up a fuss *o* storm; **¡te voy a dar ~ que verás!** I'll give you something to cry about!; **hacerle ~ a algn** to play a dirty trick on sb; **¡había ~ de gente!** what a crowd there was!; ✦ MODISMO **no dar ~** not to get a single thing right

unánime ADJ unanimous

unanimidad SF unanimity; **por ~** unanimously

unción SF (*Rel*) unction

uncir /3b/ VT to yoke

undécimo ADJ, PRON eleventh; *ver tb* **sexto**

UNED SF ABR (*Esp*) (= **Universidad Nacional de Educación a Distancia**) ≈ OU

UNESCO SF ABR (= **United Nations Educational, Scientific and Cultural Organization**) UNESCO

ungir /3c/ VT **1** (*Med*) to put ointment on, rub with ointment **2** (*Rel*) to anoint **3** (*Chi frm*) (= *nombrar*) **fue ungido candidato/presidente** he was officially chosen as candidate/president

ungüento SM ointment, unguent

únicamente ADV only, solely

UNICEF SM ABR (= **United Nations International Children's Emergency Fund**) UNICEF

único ADJ **1** (= *solo*) only; **fue el ~ sobreviviente** he was the sole *o* only survivor; **sistema de partido ~** one-party *o* single-party system; **es lo ~ que nos faltaba** (*iró*) that's all we needed **2** (= *singular*) unique; **este ejemplar es ~** this specimen is unique; **como pianista es única** as a pianist she is in a class of her own; **¡eres ~! sólo a ti se te podía ocurrir algo así** you're amazing! only you could think of something like that

unicornio SM unicorn

unidad SF **1** (= *cohesión*) unity; **falta de ~ en la familia** lack of family unity

2 (*Com, Mat*) unit; **precio por ~** unit price; **cien pesetas la ~** one hundred pesetas each; **se venden en cajas de seis ~es** they are sold in boxes of six ➤ **unidad de cuenta europea** European currency unit ➤ **unidad de medida** unit of measurement

3 (*Med, Téc*) unit ➤ **unidad coronaria** coronary unit

➤ **unidad de cuidados intensivos** intensive care unit ➤ **unidad de quemados** burns unit ➤ **unidad de terapia intensiva** (*Arg, Méx*), **unidad de tratamiento intensivo** (*Chi*), **unidad de vigilancia intensiva** intensive care unit ➤ **unidad móvil** outside broadcast unit

4 (= *vagón*) coach, wagon

5 (= *avión*) aircraft

6 (*Mil*) unit

unidimensional ADJ one-dimensional

unidireccional ADJ **calle ~** one-way street

unido ADJ [*amigos, familiares*] close; **una familia muy unida** a very close *o* very close-knit family; **está muy unida a su madre** she's very close to her mother; **mantenerse ~s** to keep together, stick together, stay together

unifamiliar ADJ single-family

unificar /1g/ VT **1** (= *unir*) to unite, unify **2** (= *hacer uniforme*) to standardize

uniformado ADJ uniformed

uniformar /1a/ VT (= *hacer uniforme*) to make uniform; (*Téc*) to standardize

uniforme Ⓐ ADJ [*movimiento, sistema*] uniform; [*superficie*] level, even, smooth; [*velocidad*] steady, uniform Ⓑ SM uniform

uniformidad SF (*gen*) uniformity; [*de acabado*] evenness, smoothness; [*de velocidad*] steadiness

unilateral ADJ unilateral, one-sided

unión SF **1** (= *acción*) [*de empresas*] merger; **mediante la ~ de sus apellidos** by joining together *o* combining their surnames; **solicitaron su ~ a la OTAN** they applied to join NATO; **en ~ con** *o* **de** (= *acompañado de*) together with, along with; (= *en asociación con*) in association with, together with

2 (= *cualidad*) unity; **por falta de ~** through lack of unity; ✦ REFRÁN **la ~ hace la fuerza** united we stand

3 (= *organización*) ➤ **Unión Europea** European Union ➤ **Unión General de Trabajadores** (*Esp*) *socialist union confederation* ➤ **unión libre** cohabitation ➤ **Unión Monetaria (Europea)** (European) Monetary Union

4 (*Mec*) joint

unipartidismo SM one-party system

unipersonal ADJ single, individual

unir /3a/ Ⓐ VT **1** (= *acercar*) **1.1** [+ *grupos, tendencias, pueblos*] to unite; **es la persona perfecta para ~ al partido** he is the ideal person to unite the party **1.2** [*sentimientos*] to unite; **los une el mismo amor a la verdad** they are united in their love of the truth; **nos une el interés por la ciencia** we share an interest in science; **me une a él una estrecha amistad** I have a very close friendship with him **1.3** [*lazos*] to link, bind; **los lazos que unen ambos países** the ties that bind *o* link both countries

2 (= *atar*) [*contrato*] to bind; **con el periódico me unía un mero contrato** I was bound to the newspaper by nothing more than a simple contract; **~ a dos personas en matrimonio** to join together two people in matrimony

3 (= *asociar, agrupar*) to combine; **uniendo los dos nombres resulta un nuevo concepto** a new concept is created by combining the two nouns; **ha logrado ~ su nombre al de los grandes deportistas** he has won a place among the great sporting names *o* among the great names in sport(s)

4 (= *conectar*) [*carretera, vuelo, ferrocarril*] to link (**con** with); **la carretera une las dos poblaciones** the road links the two towns

5 [+ *objetos, piezas*] (*gen*) to join, join together; (*con pegamento, celo*) to stick together

6 (*Culin*) [+ *líquidos*] to mix; [+ *salsa*] to blend

7 (*Com*) [+ *compañías, intereses*] to merge

Ⓑ **unirse** VPR **1** (= *cooperar*) (*para proyectos importantes*) to join together, come together, unite; (*en cuestiones puntuales*) to join forces; **si nos unimos todos, seremos más fuertes** if we all join together *o* come together *o* unite, we will be stronger; **ambas empresas se han unido para distribuir sus productos en Asia** the two companies have joined forces to distribute their products in Asia

2 (= *formar una unidad*) [*empresas, instituciones*] to merge; **~se en matrimonio** to be joined in matrimony (*frm*), marry

3 ~se a 3.1 [+ *movimiento, organización, expedición*] to join; [+ *propuesta, iniciativa*] to support; **se unieron al resto del grupo en París** they joined the rest of the group in Paris; **me uno a esta propuesta** I support this proposal
3.2 [*problemas, características, estilos*] **a este atraso económico se une un paro estructural** this economic underdevelopment is compounded by structural unemployment; **a la maravillosa cocina se une un servicio muy eficiente** the wonderful cooking is complemented by very efficient service
4 ~se to join together with, combine with
5 [*líneas, caminos*] to meet

unisex ADJ INV unisex

unísono SM **al ~** in unison

unitario ADJ (*Pol*) unitary; (*Rel*) Unitarian

universal ADJ (= *general*) universal; (= *mundial*) world, world-wide; **historia ~** world history; **de fama ~** internationally *o* world famous

universalizar /1f/ VT to universalize

universidad SF university ➤ **Universidad a Distancia** ≈ Open University ➤ **universidad laboral** technical college (*Brit*), technical school *o* institute (*EEUU*)

universitario/a ⓐ ADJ university *antes de s* **ⓑ** SM/F (= *estudiante*) (university) student; (= *licenciado*) university graduate

universo SM **1** (= *cosmos*) universe **2** (= *conjunto*) world; **el ~ poético de Lorca** Lorca's poetic world

unívoco ADJ [*palabra, término*] univocal, monosemous; [*correspondencia*] one-to-one

uno/a ⓐ PRON **1** (*uso como numeral*) one; **queda sólo ~** there's only one left; **el ~ de mayo** (*Esp*) May the first, the first of May (*Brit*); **dos maletas grandes y una más pequeña** two large suitcases and a smaller one; **~ a ~** one by one; **de ~ en ~** one by one; **~ tras otro** one after another, one after the other; **~ por ~** one by one; ✦ MODISMOS **una y no más** that's the last time I'm doing that; **lo ~ por lo otro** the one cancels out the other; **es todo ~ ◇ es ~ y lo mismo** it's all the same
2 (*uso indefinido*) (= *persona*) **2.1** (*en singular*) somebody, someone; **ha venido una que dice que te conoce** somebody *o* someone came who says she knows you; **más de ~: más de ~ estaría encantado con esto** most people would be more than happy with this; **para mí es ~ de tantos** as far as I'm concerned he's just one of many *o* a very ordinary guy
2.2 (*en plural*) **llegaron ~s y se sentaron** some people arrived and sat down; **~s que estaban allí protestaron** some (of those) who were there protested; **~s y otros** all of them
3 (*uso impersonal*) you, one (*frm*); **~ puede equivocarse** you *o* (*frm*) one can make a mistake; **~ no es perfecto** I'm not perfect, one isn't perfect (*frm*); **~ mismo** yourself, oneself
4 (*uso recíproco*) **el ~ al otro** each other; **~s a otros** each other, one another
ⓑ SM **1** (= *número*) (*cardinal*) one; (*ordinal*) first; **el ~ es mi número de la suerte** one is my lucky number; ✦ MODISMO **hacer del ~** (*Méx, Perú**) to have a pee*
2 (*en aposición*) **planta ~** first floor; **la fila ~** the first row, the front row; *ver tb* **un, seis**

untar /1a/ **ⓐ** VT **1** (= *cubrir*) **~ el pan con mantequilla** to spread butter on one's bread **2** (= *engrasar*) to grease; **~ un molde con aceite** to grease a baking dish with oil **3** (*) (= *sobornar*) to bribe, grease the palm of **ⓑ** **untarse** VPR **1** (= *ensuciarse*) **~se con** *o* **de** to smear o.s. with; **te has untado las manos de crema** you've got cream all over your hands **2** (*) (*fraudulentamente*) to have sticky fingers*

unto SM **1** (= *ungüento*) ointment **2** (= *grasa*) grease, animal fat

untuoso ADJ [*producto*] creamy; [*crema*] rich

uña SF **1** (*Anat*) [*de la mano*] nail, fingernail; [*del pie*] toenail; (*Zool*) claw; ✦ MODISMOS **ser ~ y carne** to be inseparable; **estar de ~s con algn** to be at daggers drawn with sb; **defender algo con ~s y dientes** to defend sth tooth and nail; **dejarse las ~s: se dejó las ~s en ese trabajo** he wore his fingers to the bone at that job; **enseñar** *o* **mostrar** *o* **sacar las ~s** to show one's claws; **ser largo de ~s** to be light-fingered; **rascarse con las propias ~s** to look out

for o.s. **2** (= *pezuña*) hoof **3** (*Méx*) (= *púa*) plectrum

uñalarga SMF (*Perú*) thief

uñero SM **1** (= *inflamación*) whitlow **2** (= *uña encarnada*) ingrowing toenail (*Brit*), ingrown toenail (*EEUU*) **3** [*de libro*] thumb index

uñeta SF (*CS*) plectrum

uperización SF UHT treatment

uperizado ADJ **leche uperizada** UHT milk

Urales SMPL (*tb* **Montes ~**) Urals

uralita® SF *corrugated asbestos and cement roofing material*

uranio SM uranium

Urano SM Uranus

urbanidad SF courtesy, politeness, urbanity (*frm*)

urbanismo SM town planning

urbanista SMF town planner

urbanístico ADJ [*problemas*] town-planning *antes de s*; [*plan, entorno*] urban, city *antes de s*

urbanita SMF townie*

urbanización SF **1** (= *acto*) urbanization **2** (*Esp*) (= *colonia, barrio*) housing estate (*Brit*), housing development (*EEUU*)

urbanizar /1f/ VT to develop, build on, urbanize

urbano ADJ urban, town *antes de s*, city *antes de s*

urbe SF large city, metropolis

urdimbre SF **1** [*de tela*] warp **2** (= *intriga*) scheme, intrigue

urdir /3a/ VT **1** [+ *tela*] to warp **2** (= *tramar*) to plot

urea SF urea

uréter SM ureter

uretra SF urethra

urgencia SF **1** (= *apresuramiento*) urgency; **pedir algo con ~** to request sth urgently; **asuntos de ~** urgent *o* pressing matters **2** (= *emergencia*) (*Med*) emergency; **medida de ~** emergency measure; **"urgencias"** "accident & emergency (*Brit*)", "emergency room (*EEUU*)"; **tuvimos que ir a ~s** we had to go to casualty (*Brit*) *o* to the emergency room (*EEUU*)

urgente ADJ [*mensaje, trabajo*] urgent; [*asunto*] urgent, pressing; **carta ~** special delivery letter; **pedido ~** rush order

urgentemente ADV urgently

urgir /3c/ VI to be urgent *o* pressing; **me urge la respuesta** I need a reply urgently *o* as soon as possible; **me urge terminarlo** I must finish it as soon as I can; **"úrgeme vender: dos gatos ..."** "must be sold: two cats ..."

úrico ADJ uric

urinario ⓐ ADJ urinary **ⓑ** SM urinal, public lavatory

urna SF **1** (= *vasija*) urn; [*de cristal*] glass case **2** (*Pol*) (*tb* **~ electoral**) ballot box; **acudir a las ~s** to vote, go to the polls **3** (*Chi, Ven*) (= *ataúd*) (*euf*) coffin, casket (*EEUU*)

urogallo SM capercaillie

urología SF urology

urólogo/a SM/F urologist

urraca SF magpie

URSS [urs] SF ABR (*Hist*) (= **Unión de Repúblicas Socialistas Soviéticas**) USSR

urticaria SF urticaria, nettle rash

urubú SM (*CS*) black vulture

Uruguay SM (*tb* **el ~**) Uruguay

uruguayo/a ADJ, SM/F Uruguayan

usado ADJ **1** (= *no nuevo*) [*coche*] second-hand, used; [*televisor, ropa*] second-hand; [*sello, billete*] used **2** (= *gastado*) [*ropa, disco*] worn-out; **un diccionario muy ~** a well-thumbed dictionary

usanza SF usage, custom; **a ~ india ◇ a ~ de los indios** according to Indian custom

usar /1a/ **ⓐ** VT **1** (= *utilizar*) to use; **la maleta está sin ~** the suitcase has never been used; **no olvide ~ el cinturón de seguridad** don't forget to wear your seat belt; **~ algo/a algn como** to use sth/sb as; **lo ~on como conejillo de indias** they used

him as a guinea pig; **de ~ y tirar** [*envase, producto*] disposable
2 (= *llevar*) [+ *ropa, perfume*] to wear; **esa falda está sin ~** this skirt has not been worn; **¿qué número usa?** what size do you take?
3 (= *soler*) **~ hacer algo** to be in the habit of doing sth

> Recuérdese que las preposiciones en inglés rigen gerundio y no infinitivo, de ahí **to be in the habit of doing sth**.

B VI **~ de** [+ *derecho, poder*] to exercise
C **usarse** VPR to be worn; **la chistera ya no se usa** top hats are not worn nowadays, no one wears top hats nowadays

Usbekistán SM Uzbekistan

usía PRON PERS Your Lordship/Your Ladyship

usina SF **1** (*LAm*) large factory, plant **2** (*RPl*) [*de electricidad*] power plant

uslero SM rolling-pin

uso SM **1** (= *utilización*) use; **un mango gastado por el ~** a handle worn through use; **no está permitido el ~ del claxon** you cannot honk *o* (*esp Brit*) hoot your horn; **el ~ y abuso de un producto/una expresión** the excessive use of a product/an expression; **términos de ~ común** terms in common use *o* usage; **un analgésico de ~ corriente** a commonly used painkiller; **jeringuillas de un solo ~** disposable syringes; **estar en ~** to be in use; **tratamientos actualmente en ~** treatments currently being used *o* currently in use; **un termino aún hoy en ~** a term still used today; **hacer ~ de** [+ *derecho, privilegio, poder*] to exercise; [+ *armas, fuerza*] to use; **hacer ~ de la palabra** to speak
➤ **uso de razón: desde que tuvo ~ de razón** (*lit*) since he reached the age of reason; (*fig*) for as long as he could remember
2 (= *aplicación*) use; **tiene innumerables ~s industriales** it has countless uses in industry
3 (= *costumbre*) custom; **los ~s sociales** the social customs
4 al ~: **los tópicos al ~** the usual clichés; **ésta no es una guía de turismo al ~** this is not the usual kind of travel guide, this is not a travel guide in the usual sense of the word; **por emplear el tecnicismo al ~** to use the current technical jargon

usted PRON PERS **1** (*en singular*) you (*polite or formal address*); **esto es para ~** this is for you; **—muchas gracias —a ~** "thank you very much" — "thank YOU"; **mi coche y el de ~** my car and yours; **hablar o llamar o tratar de ~ a algn** to use the "usted" form with sb, address sb using the "usted" form; **no me hables de ~** you don't need to use the "usted" form with me
2 ustedes you (*polite or formal plural in Spain, normal plural elsewhere*); **gracias a todos ~es podremos pagarlo** thanks to all of you we shall be able to pay it; **a ver, niños ¿~es qué quieren para cenar?** (*esp LAm*) right, what do you children want for tea?

usual ADJ usual, customary

usuario/a SM/F user

usufructo SM usufruct, use

usura SF usury

usurero/a SM/F usurer

usurpar /1a/ VT [+ *poder, trono*] to usurp; [+ *tierras*] to seize

utensilio SM (= *herramienta*) tool, implement; (*Culin*) utensil ➤ **utensilios de cirujano** surgeon's instruments ➤ **utensilios de pesca** fishing tackle

uterino ADJ uterine

útero SM womb, uterus ➤ **útero de alquiler** surrogate motherhood

UTI ABR = **Unidad de Terapia Intensiva** (*Chi*), = **Unidad de Tratamiento Intensivo** (*Arg, Méx*) ICU, intensive care unit

útil **A** ADJ **1** (= *de utilidad*) useful; **es muy ~ saber conducir** it is very useful to be able to drive; **¿en qué puedo serle ~?** can I help you?, what can I do for you? **2 ~ para el servicio** (*Mil*) [*persona*] fit for military service; [*vehículo*] operational
B **útiles** SMPL tools, equipment *sing* ➤ **útiles de labranza** agricultural implements ➤ **útiles de pesca** fishing tackle ➤ **útiles escolares** (*LAm*) school equipment *sing*

utilería SF (*LAm*) props *pl*

utilero/a SM/F (*LAm Teat*) property manager, props man/woman

utilidad SF **1** (*gen*) usefulness; **la ~ de tu invento** the usefulness of your invention; **un método de gran ~** a very useful method; **ya le encontraremos alguna ~** we'll find some use for it; **un servicio de ~ pública** a public service; **sacar la máxima ~ a algo** to use sth to the full, make full use of sth **2** (*LAm Com, Fin*) profit **3** (*Inform*) utility

utilitario SM small car, compact car

utilitarismo SM utilitarianism

utilizable ADJ (= *que puede usarse*) usable, serviceable; (= *disponible*) available for use, ready to use

utilización SF use, utilization (*frm*)

utilizar /1f/ VT **1** (= *usar*) to use, make use of, utilize (*frm*) **2** (= *explotar*) [+ *recursos*] to harness

utillaje SM tools *pl*, equipment

utopía SF Utopia; **es una ~** it's like Utopia

utópico ADJ Utopian

UVA ABR (= *ultravioleta*) UV, UVA

uva SF grape; **las doce ~s** twelve grapes eaten at midnight on New Year's Eve; ⋄ *NOCHEVIEJA*; **tener muy mala ~** (*Esp**) to be a mean so-and-so*, be a nasty piece of work (*Brit**) ➤ **uva blanca** green grape, white grape ➤ **uva negra** black grape ➤ **uva pasa** raisin

uve SF (*Esp*) (name of the letter) V ➤ **uve doble** (name of the letter) W

UVI SF ABR (*Esp*) (= **Unidad de Vigilancia Intensiva**) ICU, intensive care unit ➤ **UVI móvil** mobile intensive care unit

uxoricidio SM uxoricide

V, v ['uβe] (*Esp, Méx*), [be'korta] (*LAm*), [be'tʃika] (*Méx*) SF (= *letra*)
V, v

v ABR (*Elec*) (= **voltio(s)**) V

V. ABR 1 = **Usted** 2 = **Véase**

v. ABR = **ver, véase**

va *ver* **ir**

vaca SF 1 (= *animal*) cow; **el mal** o **la enfermedad de las ~s locas** mad cow disease; ✦ MODISMOS **(los años de) las ~s flacas** the lean years; **(los años de) las ~s gordas** the fat years, the boom years; **hacer(se) la ~** (*Perú**) to play truant, play hooky (*EEUU*); **hacer una ~** (*CS, Méx**) (= *colecta*) to make a collection, have a whip-round (*esp Brit**); **ponerse como una ~*** to get as fat as a pig* ➤ **vaca lechera** dairy cow ➤ **vaca marina** sea cow, manatee 2 (*Culin*) (*tb* **carne de ~**) beef 3 (*Méx**) (*en apuesta*) pool

vacacional ADJ holiday *antes de s*, vacation *antes de s*; **período ~** holiday period

vacacionar /1a/ VT (*Méx*) to spend one's holidays (*esp Brit*) o vacation (*EEUU*)

vacaciones SFPL holiday(s) (*esp Brit*), vacation *sing* (*EEUU*); **estar de ~** to be (away) on holiday (*esp Brit*) o vacation (*EEUU*); **irse** o **marcharse de ~** to go (away) on holiday (*esp Brit*) o vacation (*EEUU*), go off on holiday (*esp Brit*) o vacation (*EEUU*)

vacacionista SMF (*Méx*) holidaymaker (*Brit*), vacationer (*EEUU*)

vacante Ⓐ ADJ (*gen*) vacant; [*silla*] empty, unoccupied; [*puesto*] unfilled Ⓑ SF vacancy

vacar /1g/ VI (*gen*) to fall vacant, become vacant; [*puesto*] to remain unfilled

vaciado SM 1 [*de escultura*] cast, mould(ing), mold(ing) (*EEUU*) 2 [*de piscina, estanque*] emptying

vaciar /1c/ Ⓐ VT 1 [+ *recipiente, contenido*] to empty; [+ *radiador*] to drain; (= *beber*) to drink up 2 [+ *madera, piedra*] to hollow out; [+ *estatua*] to cast Ⓑ VI [*río*] to flow, empty (**en** into) Ⓒ **vaciarse** VPR [*bañera, depósito*] to empty

vacilación SF hesitation, vacillation

vacilante ADJ 1 [*mano, paso*] unsteady; [*voz*] faltering, halting; [*memoria*] uncertain; [*mueble*] wobbly, tottery 2 [*persona*] hesitant 3 [*luz*] flickering

vacilar /1a/ Ⓐ VI 1 (= *dudar*) to hesitate, waver; **sin ~** unhesitatingly; **~ en hacer algo** to hesitate to do sth 2 (*por falta de estabilidad*) [*mueble*] to be unsteady, wobble; [*persona*] (*al andar*) to totter, reel; (*al hablar*) to falter 3 [*luz*] to flicker 4 (*) (= *guasearse*) **~ con algn** to tease sb, take the mickey out of sb (*Brit**) 5 (*) (= *divertirse*) to have fun, mess around*; (= *ir de juerga*) to go on a spree 6 (*Esp**) (= *presumir*) to talk big*, show off, swank* Ⓑ VT (*) to take the mickey out of (*Brit**), make fun of

vacile* SM (= *guasa*) teasing; **estar de ~** to tease

vacilón/ona* Ⓐ ADJ teasing, jokey; **estar ~** to be in a jokey mood Ⓑ SM/F tease, joker Ⓒ SM (*CAm, Col, Méx*) (= *juerga*) party; (= *diversión*) fun; **andar de ~** to be out on the town

vacío Ⓐ ADJ 1 (*gen*) empty; [*puesto, local*] vacant, empty; **nunca bebo cerveza con el estómago ~** I never drink beer on an empty stomach; **Madrid queda ~ en agosto** Madrid is empty o deserted in August; **volver de ~** (*Esp*) [*persona*] to come back empty-handed; [*vehículo*] to come back empty; ✦ MODISMO **irse con las manos vacías** to leave empty-handed 2 (= *superficial*) [*persona*] shallow; [*conversación*] meaningless; **un discurso ~ de contenido** a speech empty o devoid of any content 3 (= *sin sentido*) [*existencia*] empty, meaningless Ⓑ SM 1 (*Fís*) vacuum; **envasado al ~** vacuum-packed 2 (= *hueco*) (empty) space, gap; **tener un ~ en el estómago** to have an empty stomach; ✦ MODISMO **hacer el ~ a algn** to give sb the silent treatment, send sb to Coventry (*Brit*) 3 (= *abismo*) **el ~** the void, space; **saltó al ~** he jumped into space o the void; **se arrojó al ~ desde un quinto piso** he threw himself out of a fifth-floor window; ✦ MODISMO **caer en el ~** to fall on deaf ears 4 (= *falta de sentido*) void; **el ~ existencial** the existential void; **su muerte dejó un ~ en nuestras vidas** his death left a void in our lives; **una sensación de ~** a feeling of emptiness 5 (*Jur, Pol*) ➤ **vacío de poder** power vacuum

vacuna SF vaccine; **poner una ~ a algn** to vaccinate sb

vacunar /1a/ Ⓐ VT 1 (*Med*) to vaccinate (**contra** against) 2 (*ante adversidad, dolor*) (= *preparar*) to prepare; **estar vacunado contra algo** to be immune to sth Ⓑ **vacunarse** VPR to be o get vaccinated

vacuno Ⓐ ADJ bovine, cow *antes de s*; **ganado ~** cattle Ⓑ SM (= *ganado*) cattle *pl*; **carne de ~** beef

vacuo ADJ vacuous (*frm*)

vadear /1a/ VT [+ *río*] (= *atravesar*) to ford; (*a pie*) to wade across; [+ *agua*] to wade through

vademécum SM (*pl* **~s**) vade mecum

vado SM 1 [*de río*] ford 2 (*Esp Aut*) garage entrance; **"vado permanente"** "garage entrance", "keep clear"

vagabundear /1a/ VI to wander, rove

vagabundeo SM wandering, roving

vagabundería SF (*Ven*) abuse

vagabundo/a Ⓐ ADJ [*persona*] wandering, roving; [*perro*] stray Ⓑ SM/F 1 (= *persona errante*) wanderer, rover 2 (= *pordiosero*) tramp, bum (*EEUU*), vagabond (*frm*); (*pey*) vagrant

vagamente ADV vaguely

vagancia SF laziness, idleness

vagar /1h/ VI to wander (about), roam

vagido SM cry (*of new-born baby*)

vagina SF vagina

vaginal ADJ vaginal

vaginitis SF INV vaginitis

vago/a Ⓐ ADJ 1 [*persona*] lazy, slack 2 [*ojo*] lazy 3 [*recuerdo, explicación*] vague; (*Arte, Fot*) blurred, ill-defined Ⓑ SM/F idler, lazybones*; **hacer el ~** to loaf around

vagón SM (*Ferro*) coach, carriage (*Brit*), passenger car (*EEUU*) ➤ **vagón cisterna** tanker, tank wagon ➤ **vagón de ganado** cattle truck (*esp Brit*), stock car (*EEUU*) ➤ **vagón de primera** first-class carriage (*Brit*) o passenger car (*EEUU*) ➤ **vagón restaurante** dining car

vagoneta SF pick-up truck

vaguada SF watercourse, stream bed

vaguear /1a/ VI to laze around

vaguedad SF 1 (= *ambigüedad*) vagueness 2 (= *comentario*) vague remark; **hablar sin ~es** to get straight to the point

vaguería SF laziness, idleness, slackness

vahído SM dizzy spell

vaho SM 1 (*vapor*) steam, vapour, vapor (*EEUU*); (*en cristal*) mist, condensation 2 **vahos** (*Med*) inhalation *sing*

vaina SF 1 [*de espada*] sheath, scabbard; [*de útil*] sheath, case 2 [*de garbanzo, guisante*] pod 3 **vainas** (= *judías*) green beans 4 (*Col, Perú, Ven**) (= *pega*) problem, snag; (= *molestia*) nuisance, bore; (= *cosa*) thing; **¡qué ~!** what a nuisance!, what a pain!*; ✦ MODISMOS **de ~** (*Ven**): **de ~ no perdí el avión** I nearly missed the plane; **no vayas ni de ~** don't even think of going; **echar una ~ a algn** (*Ven**) to mess sb around*; **echar ~(s)** (*Ven**) (= *bromear*) to have a laugh*; (= *causar problemas*) to make a nuisance of o.s.

vainica SF (*Cos*) hemstitch

vainilla SF vanilla

vais *ver* **ir**

vaivén SM **1** (= *balanceo*) swaying; (= *acción de mecerse*) rocking; [*de columpio*] swinging; (= *ir y venir*) to-ing and fro-ing; [*de pistón*] backward and forward motion **2** [*de la suerte*] change of fortune **3** *vaivenes* (= *altibajos*) ups and downs, vicissitudes (*frm*)

vajilla SF (*gen*) dishes *pl*; (= *juego*) service, set

valdré *etc ver* **valer**

vale¹ Ⓐ SM (= *cupón*) voucher, chit; (= *pagaré*) promissory note (*frm*), IOU*; (= *recibo*) receipt ➤ **vale de comida** luncheon voucher (*Brit*), luncheon coupon (*EEUU*) ➤ **vale de compra** voucher ➤ **vale de descuento** discount voucher *o* coupon ➤ **vale de regalo** gift voucher (*Brit*), gift certificate (*EEUU*) **Ⓑ** SMF = **valedor 2**

vale²* EXCL (*Esp*) OK, sure

valedero ADJ valid

valedor(a) SM/F **1** (= *protector*) protector, guardian **2** (*Méx*) (= *amigo*) pal*, buddy (*EEUU*)

Valencia SF Valencia; *see also* www.gva.es

valencia SF (*Quím*) valency (*esp Brit*), valence (*EEUU*)

valenciana SF (*Méx*) trouser turn-up (*Brit*), pants cuff (*EEUU*)

valenciano ADJ of/from Valencia

valentía SF bravery, courage

---

valer /2p/

Ⓐ VERBO TRANSITIVO	**Ⓒ** VERBO PRONOMINAL
Ⓑ VERBO INTRANSITIVO	

valer *ver tb* **pena Ⓐ** VERBO TRANSITIVO
1 (= *costar*) to cost; **este libro vale cinco dólares** this book costs five dollars; **¿cuánto vale?** ✧ **¿qué vale?** how much is it?, how much does it cost?; **ésas valen (a) dos euros el kilo** those are two euros a kilo
2 (= *tener un valor de*) to be worth; **el terreno vale más que la casa** the land is worth more than the house;
✦ MODISMOS **no vale un higo** *o* **un pimiento** (*Esp**) it's not worth a brass farthing (*Brit*) *o* a wooden nickel (*EEUU*), **vale lo que pesa (en oro)** it's worth its weight in gold
3 (= *ser causa de*) [+ *premio*] to win; [+ *críticas, amenazas*] to earn; **la final que le valió la copa del mundo** the final in which he won the world cup; **esa tontería le valió un rapapolvo** that piece of stupidity got *o* earned him an earful *o* (*Brit*) a telling-off
4 (*Mat*) (= *equivaler a*) to equal; **en ese caso X vale 9** in that case X equals 9
5 (= *proteger*) **¡válgame (Dios)!** oh, my God!, God help me!
Ⓑ VERBO INTRANSITIVO
1 (= *costar*) **este coche vale muy caro** this car is very expensive *o* costs a lot of money; **¿vale mucho?** is it very expensive?
2 (= *tener valía*) **vale mucho como intérprete** he's an excellent *o* first-rate interpreter; **su última novela no vale gran cosa** his latest novel is not much good *o* (*esp Brit*) is not up to much; **hacer ~: hizo ~ sus derechos** he asserted his rights; **hacerse ~** to assert o.s.; **~ por** (= *equivaler a*) to be worth; **cuatro fichas azules valen por una negra** four blue counters equal *o* are worth one black one
3 (= *servir*)
3.1 [*herramienta, objeto*] to be useful; **todavía puede ~** it might still be useful; **este mismo valdrá** this one will do; **eso no vale** that's no good *o* use; **ya no me vale** it's no good *o* use to me now; **~ para algo: este trozo no me vale para hacer la cortina** this piece won't do to make the curtain
3.2 (*Esp*) [*ropa*] **este sombrero me vale aún** I can still wear *o* use this hat; **me vale la ropa de mi hermana** my sister's clothes do for* *o* fit me as well; **a mi hijo no le vale la ropa del año pasado** the clothes my son wore last year are too small for him now
3.3 [*situación*] **no le vale ser hijo del ministro** being the minister's son is no use to him; **no le valdrán excusas** excuses won't help him *o* do him any good
3.4 [*persona*] **yo no valdría para enfermera** I'd be no good as a nurse; **no vales para nada** you're hopeless *o* useless,

you're a dead loss (*Brit**)
4 (= *ser válido*) [*documento*] to be valid; [*moneda, billete*] to be legal tender; **es una teoría que no vale ya** it is a theory which no longer holds; **valga la expresión** for want of a better way of putting it; **—¡pero querido! —¡no hay querido que valga!** "but darling!" — "don't darling me!"*
5 más vale: más vale así it's better this way; **¡más te vale!** you'd better!; **más vale que me vaya** I'd *o* I had better go; **más vale que te lleves el abrigo** you'd *o* you had better take your coat; **✦** REFRÁN **más vale tarde que nunca** better late than never
6 (*Esp*) (= *ser suficiente*) to be enough; **dos terrones valen para endulzarlo** two lumps are enough to sweeten it; **¡vale ya!** that's enough!; **no, así ya vale** no, it's OK like that
7 (*) (= *estar permitido*) to be allowed; **no vale empujar** pushing's not allowed; **¡eso no vale!** (= *no es justo*) that's not on! (*Brit**), that's not kosher! (*esp EEUU**)
8 (*Méx**) (= *no tener valor*) to be no use; (= *estropearse*) to get ruined
9 (*Méx**) (= *no importar*) **~ algo a algn: lo que él diga me vale** I don't care what he says; **me vale madre** I couldn't care less*, I don't give a damn!**
Ⓒ valerse VERBO PRONOMINAL
1 ~se de (= *utilizar*) [+ *herramienta, objeto*] to use, make use of; (= *aprovecharse de*) [+ *amistad, influencia*] to use; **se valió de su cargo para conseguir la información** she used her position to obtain the information
2 (= *arreglárselas*) **todavía se vale** she can still do things for herself; **no se vale solo ✧ no puede ~se por sí mismo** he can't take care of himself *o* manage on his own
3 (*esp Méx*) (= *estar permitido*) to be allowed

valeriana SF valerian

valeroso ADJ brave, valiant

valga *etc ver* **valer**

valía SF worth, value; **de gran ~** [*objeto*] very valuable, of great worth; [*persona*] worthy, estimable

validar /1a/ VT to validate

validez SF validity; **dar ~ a** to validate

valido SM (*Hist*) (royal) favourite, (royal) favorite (*EEUU*)

válido ADJ valid (**hasta** until)

valiente Ⓐ ADJ **1** [*persona, acción, decisión*] brave, courageous **2** (*iró*) (*antes de s*) fine; **¡~ amigo estás tú hecho!** a fine friend *o* some friend you are!* **Ⓑ** SMF brave man/woman

valija SF **1** (*RPl*) suitcase **2** ➤ **valija diplomática** diplomatic bag (*Brit*), diplomatic pouch (*EEUU*)

valioso ADJ valuable

valkiria SF Valkyrie

valla SF (= *cercado*) fence; (*Dep*) hurdle ➤ **valla de contención** crush barrier ➤ **valla de seguridad** barrier ➤ **valla publicitaria** hoarding (*Brit*), billboard (*EEUU*)

vallar /1a/ VT to fence in

valle Ⓐ SM (*Geog*) valley ➤ **valle de lágrimas** (*liter*) vale of tears (*liter*) **Ⓑ** ADJ INV off-peak

vallisoletano ADJ of/from Valladolid

valona SF (*Méx*) **hacer una** *o* **la ~ a algn** to put in a word for sb

valor SM **1** (*Com, Fin*) value; **¿cuál es el ~ real de ese cuadro?** what's this painting worth in real terms?, what's the real value of this painting?; **un documento de gran ~** a very valuable document, a document of great value; **objetos de incalculable ~** priceless objects; **el contrato fue declarado nulo y sin ~** the contract was declared null and void; **el ~ del cheque no es correcto** the amount on the cheque *o* (*EEUU*) check is not correct; **de ~** [*joya, obra*] valuable; **objetos de ~** valuables; **por ~ de** to the value of; **un cheque por ~ de ...** a cheque *o* (*EEUU*) check for the sum of *o* to the value of ...; **ha habido pérdidas por ~ de 30 millones** there have been losses of 30 million ➤ **valor adquisitivo** purchasing power ➤ **valor nominal** nominal value ➤ **valor según balance** book value
2 (= *importancia*) **una pintura de gran ~ artístico** a painting of great artistic merit *o* value; **este anillo tiene un gran ~ para mí** this ring means a great deal to me, this ring is very valuable to me; **dar ~ a algo: lo que le da ~ musical a este trabajo es su originalidad** it is the originality of this

work that gives it its musical worth o value; **no le di ~ a sus palabras** I didn't attach any importance to what he said; **quitar ~ a algo** to minimize the importance of sth ➤ **valor alimenticio** nutritional value, food value ➤ **valor nutritivo** nutritional value ➤ **valor sentimental** sentimental value
3 valores 3.1 (= *principios*) values **3.2** (*Fin*) (= *títulos*) securities, stocks, bonds
➤ **valores en cartera** holdings
4 (= *persona famosa*) star; **uno de los nuevos ~es del cine cubano** one of the rising stars of Cuban cinema
5 (= *validez*) validity; **este documento ya no tiene ~** this document is no longer valid
6 (*en una escala*) level; **~es superiores a los normales** higher than normal levels
7 (*Mat, Mús*) value
8 (= *coraje*) bravery, courage; **no tuve ~ para decírselo** I didn't have the courage to tell her; **armarse de ~** to pluck up (the) courage
9 (*) (= *descaro*) nerve*

valoración SF **1** [*de joya, obra de arte*] valuation **2** [*de daños, pérdidas*] (= *acción*) assessment; (= *resultado*) estimate **3** [*de actuación, situación*] assessment; **hacer una ~ de algo** to make an assessment of sth, assess sth

valorar /1a/ VT **1** (= *tasar*) [+ *joya, obra de arte*] to value (**en** at); [+ *daños, pérdidas*] to assess (**en** at); **un cuadro valorado en dos millones** a painting valued at two million; **las pérdidas fueron valoradas en miles de millones** the damage has been estimated o assessed at thousands of millions **2** (= *apreciar*) [+ *cualidad*] to value, appreciate; **un trabajo no valorado por la sociedad** it is a job which is not valued o appreciated by society; **los resultados han sido valorados negativamente** the results were judged negatively; **los jóvenes valoran muy poco a los políticos** young people have a very poor opinion of politicians; **"se valorarán los conocimientos de inglés"** "knowledge of English an advantage"

valorización SF **1** (= *tasación*) = **valoración 1, 2 2** (*LAm*) (= *aumento*) increase in value

valorizar /1f/ **ⓐ** VT (= *tasar*) = **valorar 1 ⓑ valorizarse** VPR (*LAm*) to increase in value

vals (*pl ~es*) SM waltz

valuar /1e/ VT = **valorar**

valva SF (*Bot, Zool*) valve

válvula SF valve ➤ **válvula de escape** (*Mec*) exhaust valve; (*fig*) safety valve

vamos *ver* **ir**

vampiresa SF (*Cine*) vamp, femme fatale

vampiro SM vampire

van *ver* **ir**

vanagloria SF vainglory

vanagloriarse /1b/ VPR to boast (**de** of); **~ de hacer algo** to boast of doing sth

---

Recuérdese que las preposiciones en inglés rigen gerundio y no infinitivo, de ahí **to boast of doing sth.**

---

vandálico ADJ [*acto, comportamiento*] loutish

vandalismo SM vandalism

vándalo/a ⓐ ADJ loutish **ⓑ** SM/F **1** (= *salvaje*) vandal **2** (*Hist*) Vandal

vanguardia SF vanguard; **un pintor de ~** an avant-garde painter; **ir a la** o **en ~** to be in the vanguard

vanguardista ADJ [*moda, estilo*] avant-garde; [*tecnología*] revolutionary; **un coche de tecnología ~** a car at the cutting edge of technology

vanidad SF **1** (= *presunción*) vanity; **halagar la ~ de algn** to play up to sb's vanity **2** (*Rel*) vanity

vanidoso ADJ (*en el aspecto físico*) vain; (= *arrogante*) conceited

vano ⓐ ADJ **1** (= *infundado*) [*ilusión, esperanza*] empty, vain; [*temor, sospecha*] groundless **2** (= *inútil*) [*intento*] vain, futile; **sus esfuerzos fueron ~s** their efforts were in vain; **en**

~ in vain; no en ~ se le considera el mejor nadador not for nothing is he held to be the best swimmer **3** (= *vacío*) [*promesa, palabras*] empty **ⓑ** SM (*Arquit*) space, opening

vapor SM **1** (*gen*) vapour, vapor (*EEUU*); (*Téc*) [*de agua*] steam; **verduras al ~** steamed vegetables; **a todo ~** (*lit, fig*) at full steam ➤ **vapor de agua** water vapour o (*EEUU*) vapor **2** (*Náut*) steamship, steamer

vaporizador SM vaporizer

vaporizar /1f/ **ⓐ** VT [+ *agua*] to vaporize; [+ *perfume*] to spray **ⓑ vaporizarse** VPR to vaporize

vaporoso ADJ sheer, diaphanous

vapulear /1a/ VT **1** (*como castigo*) to beat, thrash; (*en pelea*) to beat up **2** (= *criticar*) to slate (*Brit**), slam (*EEUU****) **3** (*en deportes*) to thrash*

vapuleo SM **1** (= *paliza*) beating, thrashing **2** (= *crítica*) slating* **3** (*en deporte*) thrashing*

vaquería SF dairy

vaqueriza SF (= *establo*) cowshed; (= *corral*) cattle yard

vaquero/a ⓐ ADJ (= *de los pastores*) cowboy *antes de s*; [*tela, falda*] denim *antes de s*; **pantalones ~s** jeans **ⓑ** SM/F **1** [*de ganado*] cowboy/cowgirl **2** (*Perú**) (= *estudiante*) truant, skiver (*Brit**) **ⓒ vaqueros** SMPL (= *pantalones*) jeans

vaqueta SF (*Col, CS*) cowhide, leather

vaquetón* ADJ (*Méx*) barefaced, brazen

vaquilla SF **1** (= *ternera*) heifer **2 vaquillas** (= *reses*) young calves; (= *fiesta*) (*tb* **corrida de ~s**) *bullfight with young bulls*

vaquillona SF (*CS, Perú*) heifer

vara SF **1** (= *palo*) stick, pole; (*Mec*) rod, bar; ✦ MODISMO **medir las cosas con la misma ~** to judge things by the same standards ➤ **vara de medir** yardstick **2** (*Pol*) (= *insignia*) staff of office **3** (*esp LAm Mat*) ≈ yard (= *0.836 metres, = 2.8 feet*) **4** (*Taur*) (= *lanza*) lance, pike **5** ✦ MODISMO **dar la ~ a*** to annoy, bother

varadero SM dry dock

varado ADJ **1** (*Náut*) (*en la playa*) beached; (*en un banco de arena*) grounded **2** (*LAm*) (= *aislado*) stranded; **~s por la nieve** cut off by the snow **3** (*Chi*) (= *sin trabajo*) out of work; (*CAm, Col, Méx*) (= *sin dinero*) broke*

varazón SF (*LAm*) **la ~ de peces que ese produjo** the fish that were washed up o ashore; **cuando ocurrió la ~ de la ballena** when the whale was beached

varapalo SM (= *regañina*) dressing-down*

varar /1a/ **ⓐ** VT to beach, run aground **ⓑ** VI to run aground **ⓒ vararse** VPR to run aground

varear /1a/ VT **1** [+ *frutas*] to knock down (*with poles*); [+ *alfombra*] to beat **2** (*RPl*) [+ *caballo*] to exercise, train

variable ADJ, SF variable

variación SF (*gen, Mús*) variation; (*Meteo*) change; **sin ~** unchanged

variado ADJ (*gen*) varied; (= *surtido*) assorted

variante SF **1** [*de palabra, texto*] variant **2** (*Aut*) diversion **3** (*en quiniela*) *draw or away win*

variar /1c/ **ⓐ** VT **1** (= *cambiar*) to change, alter; **han variado el enfoque de la revista** they have changed o altered the magazine's focus **2** (= *dar variedad a*) to vary; **intento ~ el menú** I try to vary the menu **ⓑ** VI **1** (= *cambiar*) to vary; **~ de opinión** to change one's mind; **~ de tamaño** to vary in size; **para ~** (*iró*) (just) for a change **2** (= *ser diferente*) to be different, differ; **esto varía de lo que dijo antes** this is different o this differs from what he said earlier **ⓒ variarse** VPR (*RPl**) to show off

varicela SF chickenpox

varicoso ADJ varicose

variedad SF **1** (= *diversidad*) variety **2** (*Biol*) variety **3 variedades** (*Teat*) variety show *sing*; **teatro de ~es** variety theatre, music hall (*esp Brit*), vaudeville theater (*EEUU*)

varilla SF **1** [*de metal*] rod; [*de faja, abanico, paraguas*] rib; [*de rueda*] spoke; [*de corsé*] rib, stay; [*de gafas*] sidepiece, earpiece 2 (*Méx*) (*en mercería*) haberdashery

variopinto ADJ [*objetos, regalos*] diverse, miscellaneous; [*gente, público*] very mixed

varios Ⓐ ADJ motley; (= *muchos*) several, a number of; **hay varias posibilidades** there are several *o* a number of *o* various possibilities; **los inconvenientes son ~** there are several drawbacks Ⓑ PRON some

varita SF (*tb ~ mágica*) magic wand

variz (*pl* **varices** *o* **várices**) SF **tener varices** to have varicose veins

varón Ⓐ ADJ male; **hijo ~** son, boy Ⓑ SM (= *niño*) boy; (= *hombre*) man, male; **tuvo cuatro hijos, todos varones** she had four children, all boys

varonera* SF (*RPl*) tomboy

varonil ADJ 1 (= *viril*) manly, virile 2 [*mujer*] mannish

Varsovia SF Warsaw

vas *etc ver* **ir**

vasallaje SM (*Hist*) vassalage

vasallo SM vassal

vasco/a Ⓐ ADJ Basque Ⓑ SM/F Basque; **los ~s** the Basques Ⓒ SM (*Ling*) Basque

vascófono/a Ⓐ ADJ Basque-speaking Ⓑ SM/F Basque speaker

vascofrancés ADJ French Basque

vascohablante Ⓐ ADJ Basque-speaking Ⓑ SMF Basque speaker

vascongado/a ADJ, SM/F = **vasco**

vascuence SM (*Ling*) Basque

vascular ADJ vascular

vasectomía SF vasectomy

vaselina SF Vaseline®, petroleum jelly

vasija SF pot, dish

vaso SM 1 (*para beber*) (*gen*) glass; **un ~ de papel** a paper cup; ◆ MODISMO **ahogarse en un ~ de agua** to make a mountain out of a molehill ➤ **vaso de vino** (= *recipiente*) wineglass; (= *contenido*) glass of wine 2 (= *cantidad*) glass, glassful 3 (= *recipiente*) (*Archeol*) vase, urn ➤ **vasos comunicantes** communicating vessels 4 (*Anat*) vessel ➤ **vaso sanguíneo** blood vessel

⚠ **vaso** ≠ **vase**

vástago SM 1 (*Bot*) shoot 2 (= *hijo, descendiente*) offspring, descendant

vasto ADJ vast, huge

váter SM lavatory, WC (*Brit*), restroom (*EEUU*)

Vaticano SM **El ~** The Vatican

vaticano ADJ (*gen*) Vatican; (= *papal*) papal

vaticinar /1a/ VT (= *predecir*) to predict; (= *pronosticar*) to forecast

vaticinio SM (= *predicción*) prediction; (= *pronóstico*) forecast

vatio SM watt

vaya *etc ver* **ir**

Vd. ABR = **usted**

Vda. ABR = **viuda**

Vds. ABR = **ustedes**

ve[1] *ver* **ir, ver**

ve[2] SF ➤ **ve chica** (*Méx*), **ve corta** (*LAm*) *name of the letter V*

vea *etc ver* **ver**

vecinal ADJ local

vecindad SF, **vecindario** SM neighbourhood, neighborhood (*EEUU*)

vecino/a Ⓐ ADJ 1 (= *cercano*) neighbouring, neighboring (*EEUU*); **un pueblo ~** a nearby *o* neighbouring *o* (*EEUU*) neighboring village 2 (= *contiguo*) **vive en el edificio ~** he lives in the house next door; **el garaje ~ al mío** the garage next to mine; **las**

dos fincas son vecinas the two properties adjoin 3 (*frm*) (= *parecido*) similar Ⓑ SM/F 1 [*de edificio, calle*] neighbour, neighbor (*EEUU*); **somos ~s** we are neighbours *o* (*EEUU*) neighbors 2 (= *habitante*) [*de un pueblo*] inhabitant; [*de un barrio*] resident; **un pueblo de 800 ~s** a village of 800 inhabitants; **asociación de ~s** residents' association

vector SM vector

veda SF 1 (= *prohibición*) prohibition 2 (= *temporada*) close season, closed season

vedado SM private preserve ➤ **vedado de caza** game reserve

vedar /1a/ VT to prohibit, ban

vedette [be'ðet] SF (= *principal*) star; (*de menor importancia*) starlet

vega SF 1 (= *terreno*) fertile plain, rich lowland 2 (*Chi*) (= *mercado*) market

vegetación SF 1 (= *plantas*) vegetation 2 **vegetaciones** (*Med*) adenoids

vegetal Ⓐ ADJ [*aceite, productos*] vegetable *antes de s*; **patología ~** plant pathology Ⓑ SM 1 (= *planta*) plant, vegetable 2 (= *persona inmóvil*) vegetable

vegetar /1a/ VI 1 (*Bot*) to grow 2 [*persona*] to vegetate

vegetariano/a ADJ, SM/F vegetarian

vegetativo ADJ vegetative

vehemencia SF vehemence

vehemente ADJ vehement

vehículo SM 1 (*Aut*) vehicle ➤ **vehículo a motor** motor vehicle ➤ **vehículo espacial** spacecraft 2 [*de modas, ideas*] vehicle (**de** for)

veinte ADJ, PRON, SM (*cardinal*) twenty; (*ordinal, en la fecha*) twentieth; **el siglo ~** the twentieth century; *ver tb* **seis**

veinteañero/a, veintiañero/a Ⓐ ADJ twentyish, about twenty Ⓑ SM/F person of about twenty, person in his/her twenties; **un grupo de veinteañeras** a group of twenty-somethings*

veintena SF **una ~** about twenty

veintitantos ADJ PL twenty-odd; **tiene ~ años** he's in his twenties, he's twenty-something*, he's twenty-odd*

veintiuna SF (*Naipes*) pontoon (*Brit*), twenty-one (*EEUU*)

vejación SF, **vejamen** SM humiliation

vejatorio ADJ humiliating, degrading

vejestorio SM (*pey*) old dodderer*, old crock*

vejete* SM old boy*

vejez SF old age

vejiga SF bladder ➤ **vejiga natatoria** air bladder, swim bladder

vela[1] SF 1 [*de cera*] candle; ◆ MODISMOS **estar a dos ~s*** (= *sin enterarse*) to be in the dark; (= *sin dinero*) to be broke*; **¿quién te dio ~ en este entierro?** who asked you to butt in? 2 (= *vigilia*) **estar en ~** to be unable to get to sleep; **pasar la noche en ~** to have a sleepless night 3 (*) (= *moco*) bogey (*Brit**), booger (*EEUU**)

vela[2] SF (*Náut*) sail; (= *deporte*) sailing; **barco de ~** sailing ship ➤ **vela mayor** mainsail

velada SF (evening) party, soirée ➤ **velada musical** musical evening

velado ADJ (*gen, tb fig*) veiled; (*Fot*) fogged, blurred; [*sonido*] muffled

velador(a) Ⓐ SM/F (*Méx*) guard, watchman Ⓑ SM 1 (= *mesa*) pedestal table; (*SAm*) (= *mesita*) bedside table, night table (*EEUU*) 2 (*Col, RPl*) (= *lámpara*) night light

veladora SF 1 (*Méx, RPl*) (= *lámpara*) table lamp, bedside lamp 2 (*LAm*) (= *vela*) candle

velamen SM sails *pl*, canvas

velar[1] /1a/ Ⓐ VT 1 [+ *enfermo*] to sit up with; [+ *muerto*] to keep vigil over 2 (*Mil*) to watch, keep watch over Ⓑ VI 1 (†) (= *despierto*) to stay awake 2 **~ por algo/algn** to take care of sth/sb

velar[2] /1a/ Ⓐ VT (*Fot*) to fog Ⓑ **velarse** VPR (*Fot*) to fog

velar³ ADJ (*Ling*) velar

velatorio SM wake

veleidad SF **1** (= *cualidad*) fickleness **2 veleidades** (*esp RPl*) (= *humos, pretensiones*) airs and graces

velero SM **1** (*Náut*) (*grande*) sailing ship; (*pequeño*) sailing boat (*Brit*), sailboat (*EEUU*) **2** (*Aer*) glider

veleta Ⓐ SF [*para el viento*] weather vane, weathercock; (*Pesca*) float Ⓑ SMF (= *persona*) fickle person

vello SM (*Anat*) fuzz, soft hair; (*Bot*) down; (*en frutas*) bloom, velvet ➤ **vello facial** facial hair

vellocino SM fleece

vellosidad SF (= *pelusa*) downiness; (= *pelo fuerte*) hairiness

velloso ADJ (= *con pelusa*) downy; (*más fuerte*) hairy

velludo ADJ hairy

velo SM **1** [*de tul, gasa*] veil; **corramos un tupido ~ sobre esto** let us draw a discreet veil over this **2** [*de silencio, misterio*] shroud **3** (*Anat*) ➤ **velo del paladar** soft palate, velum

velocidad SF **1** (*gen*) speed; **de alta ~** high-speed; **a toda ~** at full speed, at top speed; **¿a qué ~?** how fast?, at what speed?; **¿a qué ~ ibas?** what speed were you doing?; **cobrar ~** to pick up *o* gather speed; **disminuir/moderar la ~** to slow down ➤ **velocidad de crucero** cruising speed ➤ **velocidad del sonido** speed of sound ➤ **velocidad de obturación, velocidad de obturador** shutter speed **2** (*Mec*) gear, speed; **segunda/tercera/cuarta ~** second/third/fourth gear

velocímetro SM speedometer

velocípedo SM velocipede

velocista SMF sprinter

velódromo SM cycle track

velomotor SM moped

velorio SM funeral wake

veloz ADJ [*tren, coche, barco*] fast; [*movimiento*] quick, swift

ven *ver* **venir**

vena SF **1** (*Anat*) vein; **abrirse** *o* **cortarse las ~s** to slit one's wrists ➤ **vena yugular** jugular vein **2** (*Min*) vein, seam **3** (*en piedra, madera*) grain **4** (*) [*de humor, ánimo*] mood; **estar en ~ to be in the mood (para** for); ✦ MODISMO **dar a algn la ~: cuando le da la ~** when he gets the urge **5** (= *talento*) talent, promise; **tiene ~ de pintor** he has the makings of a painter

venado SM **1** (= *ciervo*) deer; (*macho*) stag; ✦ MODISMO **pintar ~** (*Méx*) to make o.s. scarce* **2** (*Culin*) venison

venal ADJ (*frm*) (= *sobornable*) venal (*frm*), corrupt

vencedor(a) Ⓐ ADJ [*equipo, partido*] winning, victorious (*frm*); [*general, país*] victorious Ⓑ SM/F (= *ganador*) [*de competición, elecciones*] winner; [*de guerra*] victor

vencejo SM swift

vencer /2b/ Ⓐ VT **1** (= *derrotar*) [+ *enemigo, rival*] to defeat, beat; [+ *enfermedad, dolor*] to beat, overcome **2** (= *controlar*) [+ *miedo, tentación*] to overcome; [+ *pasión*] to control **3** (= *prevalecer*) [*miedo, sueño*] to overcome; **por fin lo venció el sueño** sleep finally overcame him; **me venció el pánico** panic got the better of me *o* I was overcome with panic **4** (*Dep*) [+ *obstáculo*] to overcome; [+ *prueba*] to complete; [+ *distancia*] to do, complete; [+ *montaña*] to conquer; **vencieron los 15km en dos horas** they did *o* completed the 15km in two hours **5** (= *hacer ceder*) [+ *soporte, rama*] to break; **el peso de los libros ha vencido el estante** the shelf gave way under the weight of the books, the weight of the books broke the shelf

Ⓑ VI **1** (*en batalla, partido, elecciones*) to win; **¡venceremos!** we shall win *o* overcome!; **dejarse ~ (por)** to give in(to); **no te dejes ~ por las dificultades** don't give up in the face of difficulties, don't let difficulties get the better of you **2** (*liter*) [*amor, pasión*] to triumph, be triumphant

3 (*Com*) [*documento, póliza, pasaporte*] to expire; [*inversión*] to mature; **el plazo para pagar el alquiler vence mañana** the deadline for paying the rent is tomorrow, the rent is due tomorrow; **el plazo para la entrega de solicitudes vence mañana** the closing date for applications is tomorrow

Ⓒ **vencerse** VPR **1** (= *ceder*) [*muelle, estante, soporte*] to give way; **la mesa se vence hacia un lado** the table leans to one side **2** (*LAm*) (= *caducar*) [*pasaporte, permiso*] to expire; **cómetelo antes de que se venza** eat it before the use-by date; **se venció el plazo** the time's up

vencido/a Ⓐ ADJ **1** (= *derrotado*) [*ejército, general*] defeated; [*equipo, jugador*] losing; **darse por ~** to give up, give in **2** (= *combado*) [*tabla, viga de madera*] sagging **3** (*Com*) [*intereses, deuda*] due, payable; **le pagan por meses ~s** he is paid at the end of the month **4** (*LAm*) [*boleto, permiso*] out of date; [*medicamento, alimento*] past its use-by date Ⓑ SM/F (*Dep*) loser; **los ~s** (*Dep*) the losers; (*Mil*) the defeated, the vanquished (*frm*)

vencimiento SM [*de plazo, contrato*] expiry, expiration (*frm*); [*de inversión, préstamo*] expiry date, date of expiration (*frm*); [*de deuda*] maturity; **con ~ el 1 de marzo** expiring on 1st March

venda SF bandage ➤ **venda elástica** elastic bandage

vendaje SM dressing, bandaging

vendar /1a/ VT [+ *herida*] to bandage, dress; [+ *ojos*] to cover, blindfold

vendaval SM gale, strong wind

vendedor(a) Ⓐ ADJ selling Ⓑ SM/F (*gen*) seller, vendor; (*en tienda*) sales assistant, shop assistant (*Brit*), sales clerk (*EEUU*); [*de empresa*] sales representative, salesman/saleswoman ➤ **vendedor(a) ambulante** hawker, pedlar, peddler (*EEUU*)

vender /2a/ Ⓐ VT **1** [+ *producto*] to sell; **lo vendieron por 5.000 pesetas** they sold it for 5,000 pesetas; **se vende en supermercados** it is sold in supermarkets; **se vendían a 1.200 pesetas en el mercado** they were selling at *o* for 1,200 pesetas in the market; **"se vende coche"** "car for sale"; **~ al contado** to sell for cash; **~ al por mayor** to sell wholesale; **~ al por menor** to sell retail **2** (= *traicionar*) [+ *amigo*] to betray, sell out*; [+ *cómplice*] to shop* Ⓑ VI to sell

Ⓒ **venderse** VPR **1** (= *hacerse publicidad*) to sell o.s.; (= *dejarse corromper*) to sell out; (= *dejarse sobornar*) to accept a bribe; **"se vende"** "for sale"; **es buen político, pero no sabe ~se** he's a good politician but he doesn't know how to sell himself; ✦ MODISMO **~se caro** to play hard to get

vendido ADJ ✦ MODISMO **ir** *o* **estar ~ a algo/algn*** to be at the mercy of sth/sb

vendimia SF grape harvest, wine harvest

vendimiador(a) SM/F vintager

vendimiar /1b/ VT to harvest, pick

vendré *etc ver* **venir**

venduta SF (*Col*) public sale

Venecia SF Venice

veneciano ADJ of/from Venice

veneno SM (*gen*) poison; [*de serpiente*] venom

venenoso ADJ [*animal*] poisonous, venomous; [*planta, sustancia*] poisonous; [*palabras, lengua*] venomous

venera SF (*Zool*) scallop; (= *concha*) scallop shell; ↪ *CAMINO DE SANTIAGO*

venerable ADJ venerable

veneración SF (*gen*) worship; (*Rel*) veneration

venerar /1a/ VT (*gen*) to worship, revere; (*Rel*) to venerate

venéreo ADJ venereal

venero SM **1** (*Min*) lode, seam **2** (= *fuente*) spring

venezolano/a Ⓐ ADJ Venezuelan Ⓑ SM/F Venezuelan; **los ~s** the Venezuelans

Venezuela SF Venezuela

venga *etc ver* **venir**

vengador(a) Ⓐ ADJ avenging Ⓑ SM/F avenger

venganza SF revenge, vengeance; **mintió por** ~ she lied out of revenge o vengeance

vengar /1h/ Ⓐ VT to avenge Ⓑ **vengarse** VPR to take revenge, get one's revenge; **~se de algn** to take revenge on sb; **~se de una ofensa** to take revenge for an offence

vengativo ADJ [persona, espíritu] vengeful, vindictive; [acto] retaliatory

vengo etc ver **venir**

venia SF 1 (= permiso) permission, consent; **con su** ~ by your leave, with your permission 2 (RPI Mil) salute 3 (Col, CS) (= reverencia) bow; **hacer una** ~ to bow; (Teat, Mús) to take a bow

venial ADJ venial

venida SF (= llegada) arrival; (LAm) (= vuelta) return

venidero ADJ coming, future; **en lo** ~ in (the) future; **los ~s** posterity, future generations

venir /3r/

Ⓐ VERBO INTRANSITIVO   Ⓑ VERBO PRONOMINAL

Para las expresiones **venir al caso**, **venir de lejos**, **venir a menos**, **venir de perlas**, **venirse abajo**, **venirse encima** etc, ver la entrada correspondiente a la otra palabra.

venir Ⓐ VERBO INTRANSITIVO
1 (a un lugar) to come; **¡ven acá** o **aquí!** come (over) here!; **~ a** (+ INFIN): **vinieron a verme al hospital** they came to see me in hospital (Brit) o in the hospital (EEUU); **¿a qué vienen tantos llantos?** what's all this crying about?; **¿y ahora a qué vienes?** what do you want now?; **hacer ~ a algn: lo hicieron ~ desde Londres** they had him come (all the way) from London; **hicieron ~ al médico** they sent for the doctor, they called out the doctor; **~ a** (a) **por algn/algo** to come for sb/sth; **han venido (a) por el coche** they've come to pick up the car, they've come for the car; ✦ MODISMO **~ a algn con: no me vengas con historias** don't give me any of your stories
2 (= volver) **¡enseguida** o **ahora vengo!** I'll be right back!*; **cuando vinimos del supermercado** when we got back from the supermarket
3 (= estar) to be; **la noticia venía en el periódico** the news was in the paper; **viene en la página 47** it's on page 47; **el texto viene en castellano** the text is (written) in Spanish; **viene en varios colores** it comes in several colours o (EEUU) colors
4 (= ocurrir) to come; **ahora viene lo mejor del libro** this is the best part of the book, the best part of the book is coming up now; **lo veía** ~ I could see it coming; ✦ MODISMOS **(estar) a verlas** ~ to wait and see what happens; **venga lo que venga** come what may; **~ rodado** to go smoothly; ✦ REFRÁN **las desgracias nunca vienen solas** it never rains but it pours
5
✦ **venir de** (= provenir) to come from; **esta palabra viene del árabe** this word comes from the Arabic; **esta especia viene de oriente** this spice comes from the East; **la fortuna le viene de su padre** his fortune comes from his father
6 (= sobrevenir) **de repente le vinieron muchos problemas** a lot of problems suddenly cropped up; **le vino la idea de salir** he had the idea of going out; **me vinieron ganas de llorar** I felt like crying; ✦ MODISMO **como te** o **le venga en gana** just as you wish
7 (= quedar) **la falda me viene ancha** the skirt is too loose (for me); **el abrigo te viene algo pequeño** the coat is rather small on o for you; **~ bien: ¿te viene bien el sábado?** is Saturday all right for you?; **hoy no me viene bien** today is not convenient for me; **me vendría bien una copita** I could do with a drink*; **~ mal: mañana me viene mal** tomorrow is inconvenient; **no me vendría mal un descanso** I could do with a rest
8
✦ **por venir** (= futuro) **las generaciones por** ~ future generations, generations to come; **lo peor está por** ~ the worst is yet o still to come
✦ **que viene** (= próximo) next; **el mes que viene** next

month; **lo estudiaremos el curso que viene** we'll be studying it next year
✦ **venga a** (con sentido reiterativo) **yo no tenía dinero y el niño venga a pedir chucherías** I didn't have any money and my boy was always o forever asking for little treats; **los periodistas venga a preguntas** the journalists wouldn't stop asking questions
9 (como auxiliar)
9.1 **~ a** (+ INFIN): **viene a llenar un gran vacío** it fills a big gap; **vino a parar** o **dar a la cárcel** he ended up in jail; **~ a ser: viene a ser 84 en total** it comes to 84 all together; **viene a ser lo mismo** it comes to o amounts to the same thing
9.2 (+ GERUNDIO) **eso lo vengo diciendo desde hace tiempo** that's what I've been saying all along
9.3 (+ PARTICIPIO) **vengo cansado** I'm tired; **venía hecho polvo*** he was bushed o (Brit) shattered*
10
✦ **¡venga!** (Esp*) **¡venga, vámonos!** come on, let's go!; **¡venga, una canción!** let's have a song!; **préstame diez euros, venga** go on o come on, lend me ten euros; **—¡hasta luego! —¡venga!** "see you later!" —"OK!"; **¡venga ya!** (animando) come on!; (con incredulidad) you're kidding!*
Ⓑ **venirse** VERBO PRONOMINAL
1 (= llegar) to come; **el niño se vino solo** the child came here all on his own
2 (= volver) to come back; **se vino de la fiesta porque estaba aburrido** he came back from the party because he was bored
3 (= convenirse) **lo que se ha venido en llamar ...** what we have come to call ...

venta SF 1 (Com) sale; **han prohibido la ~ de armas** the sale of arms has been banned; **estar a la ~** to be on sale; **poner algo a la ~** to put sth on o up for sale; **salir a la ~** to go on sale; **de ~ únicamente en farmacias** available only at chemists (Brit) o drugstores (EEUU); **estar en ~** to be (up) for sale, be on the market; **"en venta"** "on sale" ➤ **venta a domicilio** door-to-door selling ➤ **venta al contado** cash sale ➤ **venta al detalle** retail ➤ **venta al por mayor** wholesale ➤ **venta al por menor** retail ➤ **venta a plazos** hire purchase (Brit), installment plan (EEUU) ➤ **venta callejera** street selling ➤ **venta de garaje** (esp Méx) garage sale ➤ **venta por catálogo** mail-order selling
2 (†) (= posada) country inn

ventaja SF 1 (= beneficio) advantage; **tiene la ~ de que está cerca de casa** it has the advantage of being close to home; **llevar ~ a algn** to have the advantage over sb, be ahead of sb, be one up on sb 2 (Dep) (en carrera) start, advantage; (Tenis) advantage; **me dio una ~ de cuatro metros** ⬦ **me dio cuatro metros de** ~ he gave me a four metre start; **llevar ~** (en carrera) to be leading o ahead

ventajista, ventajero/a (LAm) Ⓐ ADJ opportunistic Ⓑ SMF, SM/F (LAm) opportunist

ventajoso ADJ 1 (gen) advantageous; (Fin) profitable 2 (Col) = **ventajista** A

ventana SF 1 (Constr) window; **doble ~** double-glazed window 2 [de nariz] nostril 3 (Inform) window

ventanal SM large window

ventanilla SF 1 [de vehículo] window 2 (en cine, teatro) box office; (en oficina) window; **para abonar en cuenta pase por ~** please make deposits at the cash desk (Brit) o cashier's desk (EEUU)

ventarrón SM gale, strong wind

ventilación SF ventilation; **sin ~** unventilated

ventilador SM 1 (= aparato) fan 2 (= abertura) air vent, ventilator

ventilar /1a/ Ⓐ VT 1 (= airear) [+ cuarto] to air, ventilate; [+ ropa] to air 2 (*) (= resolver) [+ asunto, problema] to sort (out)* 3 (= hacer público) [+ intimidades, secreto] to air Ⓑ **ventilarse** VPR 1 (= airearse) [ropa] to air; **abre la ventana para que se ventile la habitación** open the window to air o ventilate the room 2 (Esp*) [+ comida, bebida, trabajo] to polish off* 3 (*) (= matar) **~se a algn** to do sb in*

ventisca SF blizzard, snowstorm

ventisquero SM (= acumulación) snowdrift; (= lugar) snowfield

ventolera SF **1** (= *ráfaga*) gust of wind, blast **2** (*) (= *capricho*) whim, wild idea; **le dio la ~ de comprarlo** he had a sudden notion to buy it

ventolina SF (*CS*) sudden gust of wind

ventosa SF **1** (*Zool*) sucker **2** (*Med*) cupping glass **3** (*Téc*) suction pad

ventosear /1a/ VI to break wind

ventosidad SF wind, flatulence (*frm*)

ventoso ADJ windy

ventrículo SM ventricle

ventrílocuo/a SM/F ventriloquist

ventura SF **1** (= *dicha*) happiness **2** (= *suerte*) luck, (good) fortune; **por su mala ~** as bad luck would have it; **por ~** (*frm*) (= *por suerte*) fortunately; (= *por casualidad*) by (any) chance; **echar la buena ~ a algn** to tell sb's fortune; **probar ~** to try one's luck

venturoso ADJ lucky, fortunate

ventuta SF (*Col*) garage sale

Venus Ⓐ SF (*Mit*) Venus Ⓑ SM (*Astron*) Venus

veo-veo SM (= *juego*) I spy (with my little eye)

---

ver /2u/

Ⓐ VERBO TRANSITIVO	Ⓒ VERBO PRONOMINAL
Ⓑ VERBO INTRANSITIVO	Ⓓ SUSTANTIVO MASCULINO

Para las expresiones **ver visiones, no ver tres en un burro** *etc, ver el sustantivo.*

ver Ⓐ VERBO TRANSITIVO
1 = (*percibir*)
1.1 [+ *persona, objeto*] to see; **te vi en el parque** I saw you in the park; **desde aquí lo ~ás mejor** you can see it better from here; **lo he visto con mis propios ojos** I saw it with my own eyes; **los vi paseando por el parque** I saw them walking in the park; **la vi bajar la escalera** I saw her come downstairs; **me acuerdo como si la estuviera viendo** I remember it as if I were seeing it now, I remember it as if it were yesterday; **¡vieran qué casa!** (*LAm*) ◇ **¡hubieran visto qué casa!** (*LAm*) you should have seen the house!; **dejarse ~: este año Pedro no se ha dejado ~ por aquí** we haven't seen much of Pedro this year; ✦ MODISMOS **no veo ni jota** I can't see a thing; **si te he visto no me acuerdo: le pedí que me ayudara, pero si te he visto no me acuerdo** I asked him to help me but he (just) wasn't interested *o* (*esp Brit*) didn't want to know; **~ algn/algo venir: eso ya lo veía venir** well, you could see it coming; **ya te veo venir** I know what you're after
1.2 (+ INFIN) **eso lo he visto hacer aquí muchas veces** I have often seen that done here
1.3 (+ ADJ) **te veo muy triste** you look very sad; **esta casa la veo pequeña para tanta gente** I think this house is too small for so many people
2 (= *mirar*) [+ *televisión, programa, partido*] to watch; **es (digno) de ~** it's worth seeing; ✦ MODISMO **no poder (ni) ~ a algn: no lo puedo (ni) ~** I can't stand him
3 (*en saludos*) **¡cuánto tiempo sin ~te!** I haven't seen you for ages!; **¡hasta más ~!** see you again!
4 (= *visitar*) to see; **ayer fui a ~ a tu hermano** I went to see your brother yesterday; **tendré que ir a ~ al abogado** I shall have to go to *o* and see my lawyer
5 (= *imaginar*) to see, imagine; **lo estoy viendo de almirante** I can just see *o* imagine him as an admiral
6 (= *vivir*) to live through; **yo he visto dos guerras mundiales** I have lived through two world wars
7 (= *examinar*) to look at; **este tema lo ~emos en la próxima clase** we'll be looking at this subject in the next lesson
8 (= *comprobar*) to see; **¡~ás como al final te caerás!** you'll fall, you just wait and see!; **habrá que ~: habrá que ~ lo que les habrá contado** we'll have to see what he's told them; **voy a ~ si está en su despacho** I'll see if he's in his office
9 (= *notar*) to see; **no veo la diferencia** I can't see the difference; **ya veo que tendré que hacerlo yo solo** I can see I'll have to do it myself; **—gana más de 2.000 euros al mes**

—**¡ya ves!** she earns more than 2,000 euros a month — you see!; **dejarse ~: los efectos de la crisis se dejaron ~ meses después** the effects of the crisis were felt months later; **echar de ~ algo** to notice sth; **hacerse ~** (*RPl**) to show off; **por lo que veo** from what I can see
10 (= *entender*) to see; **¿no ves que ...?** don't *o* can't you see that ...?; **no veo muy claro para qué lo quiere** I can't really see what he wants it for; **hacer ~ algo a algn** to point sth out to sb
11 (= *encontrar*) to see; **no le veo solución al conflicto** I can't see a solution to the conflict
12 (*Jur*) [+ *pleito*] to hear, try
13
✦ **tener que ver: ¿y eso qué tiene que ~?** what's that got to do with it?; **yo no tuve nada que ~ en la venta del terreno** I had nothing to do with the sale of the land
14
✦ **a ver: a ~ niños, ¿cuál es la capital de Francia?** now, children, what is the capital of France?; **a ~ ...** let's have a look ..., let's see ...; **a ~ ese niño, que no se quede solo** don't leave that child on his own; **a ~ qué dicen las noticias sobre el robo** let's see if there's anything about the robbery on the news; **¡a ~, no queda más remedio!** well, I haven't got much choice!; **¡a ~!** (*CAm, Col*) (*al teléfono*) hello?; **a ~ si ...: a ~ si acabas pronto** see if you can finish this off quickly; **¡a ~ si te crees que no lo sé!** surely you don't think I don't know about it!
Ⓑ VERBO INTRANSITIVO
1 (= *percibir*) to see; **no veo muy bien con el ojo derecho** I can't see very well with my right eye; **como ~emos más adelante** as we shall see later; **eso está por ~** that remains to be seen; ✦ MODISMOS **que no veo*: ¡tengo un hambre que no veo!** I'm famished!; **que no veas*: un coche que no veas** an amazing car; **~ y callar: no digas nada, tú sólo ~ y callar** you'd better keep your mouth shut about this; **~ para creer** seeing is believing
2 (= *comprobar*) to see; **no sé, voy a ~** I don't know, I'll go and see; **ya veo** so I see
3 (= *entender*) to see; **¿ves?, así es más fácil** you see? it's much easier like this; **a mi modo de ~** as I see it, the way I see it
4 **~ de hacer algo** to see about doing sth, try to do sth

Recuérdese que las preposiciones en inglés rigen gerundio y no infinitivo, de ahí **to see about doing sth.**

5 (*otras locuciones*) **estar** *o* **quedar en ~emos** (*LAm*): **eso está en ~emos** it's not certain yet; **¡hay que ~!: ¡hay que ~ lo que te pareces a tu madre!** gosh! how like your mother you are *o* look!; **¡hay que ~ lo que ha cambiado la ciudad!** it's incredible *o* you wouldn't believe how much the town has changed!; **¡para que veas!: ha aprobado todo las asignaturas, ¡para que veas!** she passed all her exams, how about that!; **no sólo no perdí, sino que arrasé, ¡para que veas!** not only did I not lose, but I won by a mile, so there!; **vamos a ~ ... let's see ...**, let me see ...; **¿por qué no me llamaste, vamos a ~?** why didn't you call me, I'd like to know?; **ya veremos** we'll see
Ⓒ **verse** VERBO PRONOMINAL
1 (*reflexivo*) to see o.s.; **no quiere ~se en el espejo** she doesn't want to see herself in the mirror; **se vio reflejado en el espejo** he saw his reflection in the mirror
2 (*recíproco*) (= *saludarse, visitarse*) to see each other; (= *citarse*) to meet; **ahora apenas nos vemos** we hardly see (anything of) each other nowadays; **¡luego nos vemos!** see you later!; **quedamos en ~nos en la estación** we arranged to meet at the station; **~se con algn** to see sb
3 (= *percibirse*) **desde aquí no se ve** you can't see it from here; **se le veía mucho en el parque** he was often to be seen in the park; **se le veían las bragas** you could see her panties; **¿cuándo se vio nada igual?** have you ever seen anything like it!; **es digno de ~se** it's worth seeing; **¡habráse visto!*** of all the nerve!*, well I like that!; **eso ya se ~á** that remains to be seen
4 (= *mirar*) **véase la página 9** see page 9
5 (= *notarse*) **ya se ve** I can see that; **se ve que no tiene idea** he obviously doesn't have a clue; **se ve que sí** so it seems
6 (= *imaginarse*) to see o.s., imagine o.s.; **yo ya me veía en la**

cárcel I could see myself going to jail
7 (*LAm**) (= *parecer*) to look; **se ve más joven sin barba** he looks younger without his beard
8 (= *estar, encontrarse*) to find o.s., be; **~se en un apuro** to find o.s. *o* be in a jam*
9
◆ **vérselas: me las vi y me las deseé para hacerlo*** it was a real sweat to get it done*, it was a tough job to get it done*; **vérselas con algn: tendrá que vérselas con mi abogado** he'll have my lawyer to deal with
Ⓓ SUSTANTIVO MASCULINO **de buen** ~ good-looking

vera SF [*de río*] bank; **a la ~ del camino** beside the road, at the roadside; **a mi ~** beside me

veracidad SF truthfulness, veracity (*frm*)

veranda SF veranda(h)

veraneante SMF holiday-maker (*Brit*), (summer) vacationer (*EEUU*)

veranear /1a/ VI to spend the summer (holiday) (*esp Brit*), spend the summer (vacation) (*EEUU*); **veranean en Jaca** they go to Jaca for the summer; **es un buen sitio para ~** it's a nice place for a summer holiday (*esp Brit*) *o* vacation (*EEUU*)

veraneo SM summer holiday (*esp Brit*), summer vacation (*EEUU*); **lugar de ~** summer resort, holiday resort; **estar de ~** to be away on (one's summer) holiday (*esp Brit*) *o* vacation (*EEUU*)

veraniego ADJ summer *antes de s*

veranillo SM ➤ **veranillo de San Juan** (*SAm*) (*en junio*) ≈ Indian summer ➤ **veranillo de San Martín** (*Esp*) (*en noviembre*) ≈ Indian summer

verano SM **1** (= *estación*) summer **2** (*en regiones ecuatoriales*) dry season

veras SFPL **de ~** really, truly; **¿de ~?** really?, is that so?; **lo siento de ~** I am truly sorry; **esto va de ~** this is serious; **esta vez va de ~** this time it's the real thing*

veraz ADJ truthful

verbal ADJ (*gen*) verbal; [*mensaje*] oral

verbena SF **1** (= *fiesta*) fair; (= *baile*) open-air dance **2** (*Bot*) verbena

verbenero ADJ **cohetes ~s** fiesta rockets; **persona verbenera** party animal*

verbigracia ADV for example, e.g.

verbo SM **1** (*Ling*) verb ➤ **verbo auxiliar** auxiliary verb ➤ **verbo defectivo** defective verb ➤ **verbo intransitivo** intransitive verb ➤ **verbo reflexivo** reflexive verb ➤ **verbo transitivo** transitive verb **2** **el Verbo** (*Rel*) the Word

verborrea SF verbosity, verbal diarrhoea *o* (*EEUU*) diarrhea*

verboso ADJ verbose, wordy

verdad SF **1** (= *veracidad*) truth; **la pura ~** the plain truth; **hay una parte de ~ en todo esto** there is some truth *o* an element of truth in all this; **decir la ~** to tell the truth; **a decir ~ ◇ si te digo la ~** to be honest, to tell you the truth; ◆ MODISMOS **ir con la ~ por delante** to be completely open about things
2 de ~ (*como adj*) real; (*como adv*) really; **¿son de ~ estas balas?** are those real bullets?; **ése sí que es un torero de ~** he's what I call a real bullfighter; — **vendré a ayudarte —¿de ~?** "I'll come and help you" — "really?" *o* "will you?"; **de ~ que no me importa** I really don't mind, I don't mind, honestly *o* really
3 es ~ it's true; **eso no es ~** that's not true; **¿es ~ que ...?** is it true that ...?; **bien es ~ que** of course; **si bien es ~ que** although, even though
4 (*) (*para enfatizar*) **la ~ es que no me gusta mucho** to be honest I don't like it much, I don't really like it much
5 (*para corroborar algo*) **estás cansado ¿verdad?** *o* **¿no es ~?** you're tired, aren't you?; **no os gustó ¿verdad?** you didn't like it, did you?; **¿~ que sí fuimos?** we went, didn't we?, we did go, didn't we?; **¿~ que has sido tú?** it was you, wasn't it?
6 (= *afirmación verdadera*) truth; **las ~es a medias** half-truths; ◆ MODISMOS **ser una ~ de Perogrullo** to be patently obvious; **ser una ~ como un puño*** to be the bitter *o* painful truth; **ser una ~ como un templo** to be the plain truth; **decirle cuatro ~es a algn** to give sb a piece of one's mind*

verdaderamente ADV **1** (= *de verdad*) really; **es ~ una pena** it really is a shame **2** (*con adjetivo*) really, truly; **es ~ triste** it's really *o* truly sad; **un hombre ~ bueno** a really *o* truly good man **3** (*para confirmar*) indeed; **y ~, el sitio no es nada especial** and indeed, the place is nothing special

verdadero ADJ **1** (= *auténtico*) [*caso, joya, motivo, nombre*] real; [*historia, versión*] true; [*testimonio*] truthful **2** (*para enfatizar*) real; **es un ~ héroe** he's a real hero

verde Ⓐ ADJ **1** (*color*) green; ◆ MODISMOS **estar ~ de envidia** (*CS*) to be green with envy; **poner ~ a algn** (*Esp, Méx**) (*a sus espaldas*) to run sb down*; (*delante*) to give sb a piece of one's mind
2 [*zona, espacio*] green
3 [*fruta, verdura*] green, unripe; [*madera*] unseasoned
4 (*) (= *sin experiencia*) green*; **está muy ~*** he's very green*
5 (*) [*chiste, canción*] smutty*, blue*, dirty; **viejo ~** dirty old man*
6 (*Pol*) Green
Ⓑ SM **1** (= *color*) green ➤ **verde botella** bottle green ➤ **verde esmeralda** emerald green ➤ **verde lima** lime green ➤ **verde manzana** apple green
2 (= *hierba*) grass; (= *follaje*) greenery; **sentarse en el ~** to sit on the grass
Ⓒ SMF (*Pol*) Green

verdear /1a/ VI **1** (= *tener color*) to look green **2** (= *volverse verde*) to go green, turn green

verdolaga SF purslane

verdor SM greenness

verdoso ADJ greenish

verdugo SM **1** (= *ejecutor*) executioner; (*en la horca*) hangman **2** (= *tirano*) cruel master, tyrant **3** (= *látigo*) lash **4** (*Bot*) shoot **5** (= *pasamontañas*) balaclava

verdulera[1] SF (*pey*) fishwife

verdulero/a[2] SM/F greengrocer (*esp Brit*), vegetable merchant (*EEUU*)

verdura SF **1** (*Culin*) greens *pl*, (green) vegetables *pl*; **sopa de ~(s)** vegetable soup **2** (= *color*) greenness

vereda SF **1** (= *senda*) path, lane; ◆ MODISMOS **entrar en ~** to toe the line; **hacer entrar en ~ a algn** ◇ **meter en ~ a algn** to bring sb into line **2** (*CS, Perú*) (= *acera*) pavement (*Brit*), sidewalk (*EEUU*) **3** (*Col*) (= *zona*) section of a village

veredicto SM verdict

verga SF **1** (= *vara*) rod, stick; (*Náut*) yard(arm), spar **2** (*Zool*) penis; (***) [*de hombre*] prick***, cock***

vergel SM (*liter*) (= *jardín*) garden (*Brit*), yard (*EEUU*); (= *huerto*) orchard

vergonzante ADJ shameful

vergonzoso ADJ **1** [*persona*] bashful, shy **2** [*acto*] shameful, disgraceful

vergüenza SF **1** (= *azoramiento*) embarrassment; **casi me muero de ~** I almost died of embarrassment; **¡qué ~!** how embarrassing!; **me da ~ decírselo** I feel too embarrassed to tell him; **sentir ~ ajena** to feel embarrassed for sb
2 (= *dignidad*) shame, sense of shame; **¡~ debería darte!** you should be ashamed!, shame on you!; **¡qué poca ~ tienes!** you've got no shame!, you're utterly shameless
3 (= *escándalo*) disgrace; **es una ~ que esté tan sucio** it's a disgrace *o* it's disgraceful that it should be so dirty
4 vergüenzas (*euf, **) (= *genitales*) privates

vericuetos SMPL **1** (= *terreno escarpado*) rough track *sing* **2** (= *complejidades*) **los ~ del sistema fiscal** the intricacies of the tax system

verídico ADJ truthful, true

verificación SF (= *inspección*) inspection, check; (*Mec*) testing; [*de hechos*] verification

verificar /1a/ VT (= *inspeccionar*) to inspect, check; (*Mec*) to test; [+ *hechos*] to verify, establish

verificativo SM (*Méx frm*) **tener ~** to take place

verismo SM (= *realismo*) realism, truthfulness; (*Arte, Literat*) verism

verja SF (= *puerta*) iron gate; (= *cerca*) railings *pl*; (= *reja*) grating, grille

vermut [ber'mu] SM (*pl* ~**s**) **1** (= *bebida*) vermouth **2** (*CS Cine*) (early evening) matinee

vernáculo ADJ vernacular

verónica SF **1** (*Bot*) veronica, speedwell **2** (*Taur*) *a kind of pass with the cape*

verosímil ADJ (= *probable*) likely, probable; (= *creíble*) credible

verraco Ⓐ ADJ (*Col**) **1** (= *estupendo*) fantastic* **2** (= *valiente*) brave, plucky* Ⓑ SM boar

verruga SF **1** (*en cara, espalda*) wart; (*en manos, pies*) verruca **2** (*Bot*) wart

versado ADJ ~ **en** (= *conocedor*) versed in, conversant with; (= *experto*) expert in, skilled in

versalitas SFPL (*Tip*) small capitals

versar /1a/ VI ~ **sobre** to deal with, be about

versátil ADJ **1** (= *adaptable*) versatile **2** (= *inconstante*) fickle, changeable

versatilidad SF **1** (= *adaptabilidad*) versatility **2** (= *inconstancia*) fickleness

versículo SM verse

versificar /1g/ VT to versify

versión SF (*gen*) version; (= *canción*) cover version; (= *traducción*) translation; **película en ~ original** original version

verso SM (= *línea*) line, verse line; (= *poema*) poem; (= *género*) verse; **teatro en ~** verse drama; **hacer ~s** to write poetry; ✦ MODISMO **hacer el ~ a algn** (*RPl**) to feed sb a line*, sweet-talk sb* ➤ **verso libre** free verse

versus PREP versus, against

vértebra SF vertebra

vertebrado ADJ, SM vertebrate

vertebral ADJ vertebral; **columna ~** spinal column, spine

vertebrar /1a/ VT to provide the backbone of, be the essential structure of

vertedero SM rubbish tip (*Brit*), garbage dump (*EEUU*)

verter /2g/ Ⓐ VT **1** [+ *contenido*] to pour (out), empty (out); (*sin querer*) to spill, pour; [+ *lágrimas, luz, sangre*] to shed; [+ *basura, residuos*] to dump, tip (*Brit*) **2** [+ *recipiente*] (= *vaciar*) to empty (out); (*sin querer*) to upset **3** (*Ling*) to translate (**a** into) Ⓑ VI [*río*] to flow, run (**a** into)

vertical Ⓐ ADJ [*línea, plano*] vertical; [*postura, piano*] upright Ⓑ SF **1** (*Téc, Mat*) vertical line, vertical; **descender en ~** to descend vertically; **elevarse en ~** to rise vertically **2** (*Dep*) **hacer la ~** to do a handstand

vértice SM **1** [*de cono, pirámide*] apex, vertex; [*de ángulo*] vertex **2** (*Anat*) crown (of the head)

vertido SM **1** (= *acto*) (*accidental*) spillage; (*deliberado*) dumping **2 vertidos** (= *residuos*) waste *sing*; ~**s tóxicos** toxic waste *sing*

vertiente SF **1** [*de montaña, tejado*] slope **2** (= *aspecto*) side, aspect; **la ~ ética de la cuestión** the ethical side *o* aspect of the issue; **el curso tiene una ~ filosófica** the course has a philosophical dimension **3** (*CS*) (= *manantial*) spring

vertiginoso ADJ **1** (= *que causa vértigo*) giddy, dizzy, vertiginous (*frm*) **2** [*velocidad*] dizzy, excessive; [*alza*] very rapid

vértigo SM **1** (*por la altura*) vertigo; **mirar hacia abajo me da ~** looking down makes me (feel) dizzy; **no subo porque tengo ~** I'm not going up because I'm afraid of heights **2** (= *frenesí*) frenzy; **el ~ de la vida en la ciudad** the frenzy of city life **3 de ~***: **una velocidad de ~** breakneck speed; **es de ~ cómo crece la ciudad** it's astonishing how quickly the city is growing

vesícula SF **1** (*tb* ~ **biliar**) gall-bladder **2** (= *de líquido*) vesicle

vespa® SF Vespa®, scooter, motor-scooter

vespertina SF (*Col*) (early evening) cinema matinee

vespertino Ⓐ ADJ evening *antes de s* Ⓑ SM **1** (= *periódico*) evening paper **2** (*Chi Educ*) night school

vespino SM small motorcycle

vesre* SM (*Arg*), **vesrre*** SM (*Arg*) back slang

vestíbulo SM [*de casa, hotel*] vestibule (*frm*), lobby, hall; (*Teat*) foyer

vestido Ⓐ ADJ dressed; **ir bien ~** to be well-dressed; **¿cómo iba vestida?** what was she wearing?; ~ **con algo** wearing sth, dressed in sth; ~ **de algo** wearing sth, dressed in sth; **siempre va ~ de negro** he always wears black; **verte vestida de blanco** to see you all in white; **ir ~ de verano** to wear summer clothes Ⓑ SM **1** (= *prenda*) [*de mujer*] dress; (*Col*) [*de hombre*] suit ➤ **vestido de noche** evening dress ➤ **vestido de novia** wedding dress, bridal gown **2** (= *vestimenta*) clothes *pl*; **la historia del ~** the history of costume

vestidor SM (*en casa*) dressing room; (*Chi, Méx Dep*) changing room (*Brit*), locker room (*EEUU*)

vestiduras SFPL (*Rel*) vestments; ✦ MODISMO **rasgarse las ~** to tear one's hair

vestier SM (*Col*) = **vestidor**

vestigio SM **1** (= *señal*) trace, vestige **2 vestigios** (= *ruinas*) remains, relics

vestimenta SF clothing; (*pey*) stuff*, gear**

vestir /3k/ Ⓐ VT **1** (= *poner la ropa a*) [+ *niño , muñeca*] to dress **2** (= *disfrazar*) to dress up **3** (= *proporcionar la ropa*) [*persona*] to clothe; [*institución, Estado*] to pay for one's clothing **4** (= *llevar puesto*) to wear **5** (= *revestir*) [+ *sillón*] to cover, upholster; [+ *pared*] to cover, decorate Ⓑ VI **1** (= *llevar ropa*) to dress; **siempre viste a la última moda** she always dresses in *o* wears the latest fashions; **¿todavía estás sin ~?** aren't you dressed yet?, haven't you got dressed yet?; ~ **bien** to dress well; ~ **mal** to dress badly; ~ **de**: **le gusta ~ de gris** he likes to wear grey; ~ **de sport** to dress casually; ✦ MODISMO **el mismo que viste y calza**† the very same **2** (= *ser elegante*) [*traje, color*] to be elegant; **el negro viste mucho** black is very elegant; **lo que viste es viajar al Caribe*** the Caribbean is the trendy *o* the in place to go*; **de ~** [*ropa, zapatos*] smart (*esp Brit*), sharp (*esp EEUU*); [*traje*] formal; **ese traje es de mucho ~** that suit's too dressy* *o* formal Ⓒ **vestirse** VPR **1** (= *ponerse la ropa*) to get dressed; **me vestí con lo primero que encontré** I put on the first thing I picked up; **¿cómo te vas a ~?** what are you going to wear?; ~**se de algo** to wear sth; ~**se de fiesta** *o* **de gala** [*persona*] to get (all) dressed up; [*ciudad*] to be (all) decked out; ~**se de largo** (*para fiesta, recepción*) to wear an evening dress **2** (= *disfrazarse*) ~**se de algo** to dress up as sth; **me vestí de marinero** I dressed up as a sailor **3** (= *comprar la ropa*) to buy one's clothes **4** (*liter*) (= *cubrirse*) ~**se de algo** to be covered in sth; **toda la ciudad amaneció vestida de blanco** the day dawned on a city entirely covered in white Ⓓ SM (= *forma de vestir*) **su elegancia en el ~** the smart (*esp Brit*) *o* sharp (*esp EEUU*) way she dresses

vestón SM (*CS*) jacket

vestuario SM **1** (= *ropa*) wardrobe; (*Teat*) wardrobe, costumes *pl* **2** (= *cuarto*) (*Teat*) dressing room; (*Dep*) changing room

veta SF (*Min*) seam, vein; [*de madera*] grain; (*en piedra, carne*) streak, stripe

vetar /1a/ VT (*gen*) to veto; [+ *socio*] to blackball

veteado Ⓐ ADJ [*mármol*] veined; [*madera*] grained; [*tocino*] streaky Ⓑ SM [*del mármol*] veining; [*de la madera*] graining

veteranía SF (= *servicio*) long service; (= *antigüedad*) seniority

veterano/a Ⓐ ADJ (*Mil*) veteran; **es veterana en el oficio** she's an old hand* Ⓑ SM/F (*Mil*) veteran; (*fig*) old hand*

veterinaria SF veterinary medicine, veterinary science

veterinario/a SM/F veterinary surgeon (*Brit*), vet (*esp Brit*), veterinarian (*EEUU*)

veto SM veto

vetusto ADJ ancient, very old; (*iró*) hoary

vez SF **1** (= *ocasión*) time; **por esta ~** this time, this once; **la próxima ~** next time; **hablaban todos <u>a la</u> ~** they were all talking at once *o* at the same time; **¿has estado <u>alguna</u> ~ en Londres?** have you ever been to London?; **alguna que otra ~** occasionally, now and then; <u>**toda ~ que** ...</u> since ..., given that ...; **¿cuándo lo viste por última ~?** when was the last time you saw him?, when did you see him last? **2** (*indicando frecuencia*) **lo he hecho cien veces** I've done it hundreds *o* lots of times*; **¿cuántas veces al año?** how many times a year?; **<u>a veces</u> ◇ <u>algunas</u> veces** sometimes, at times; **de ~ <u>en cuando</u>** now and again, from time to time, occasionally; **¿cuántas veces?** how often?, how many times?; **<u>dos</u> veces** twice; **<u>en</u> ... veces: se fríen las patatas en dos veces** fry the potatoes in two batches; **<u>muchas</u> veces** often; **<u>otra</u> ~** again; **<u>pocas</u> veces** seldom, rarely; **<u>rara</u> ~ ◇ <u>raras</u> veces** seldom, rarely; **<u>una</u> ~** once; **érase *o* había una ~ una princesa ...** once upon a time there was a princess ...; **una y otra ~** time and (time) again; **<u>varias</u> veces** several times **3** (*otras expresiones*) **de una ~** (= *en una sola ocasión*) in one go (*esp Brit*) *o* shot (*EEUU*); (= *definitivamente*) once and for all*; **¡dilo de una ~!** just say it!; **<u>en</u> ~ de** instead of; **hacer las veces de** to serve as; **una ~ <u>que</u>** once; **una ~ que se hayan marchado todos** once they've all left; **de una ~ para <u>siempre</u> ◇ de una ~ por <u>todas</u>** once and for all*, for good; **a su ~** in turn **4** (*Esp*) (= *turno*) turn, go; **cuando le llegue la ~** when his turn comes; **<u>ceder</u> la ~** (= *gen*) to give up one's turn; (*en cola*) to give up one's place; **pedir la ~** to ask who's last in the queue (*esp Brit*) *o* line (*esp EEUU*); **quitar la ~ a algn** to push in in front of sb

vía Ⓐ SF **1** (= *ruta, camino*) **¡dejen la ~ libre!** please make way!; ➤ **vía de abastecimiento** supply route ➤ **vía de acceso** access road ➤ **vía de agua** leak ➤ **vía de comunicación** communication route ➤ **vía de escape** escape route, way out ➤ **Vía Láctea** Milky Way ➤ **vía libre: el gobierno ha dado *o* dejado ~ libre al proyecto** the government has given the go-ahead to the project; **eso es dar *o* dejar la ~ libre a la corrupción** that's leaving the way open for corruption ➤ **vía pública** public highway, thoroughfare **2** (*Transportes, Correos*) ➤ **vía aérea** airway; **por ~ aérea** [*viaje*] by air; [*envío postal*] (by) airmail ➤ **vía fluvial** waterway ➤ **vía marítima** sea route, seaway; **por ~ marítima** by sea ➤ **vía terrestre** overland route; **por ~ terrestre** [*viaje*] overland, by land; [*envío postal*] (by) surface mail **3** (*Ferro*) (= *raíl*) track, line; (= *andén*) platform; **cuando cruzaba la ~** when he was crossing the track *o* line; **el tren está estacionado en la ~ ocho** the train is (standing) at platform eight ➤ **vía ancha** broad gauge ➤ **vía estrecha** narrow gauge ➤ **vía férrea** railway (*esp Brit*), railroad (*EEUU*) ➤ **vía muerta** (*Ferro*) siding; **el proceso ha entrado en una ~ muerta** the process has come to a dead end **4** (*Anat*) tract *sing* ➤ **vías respiratorias** respiratory tract *sing* ➤ **vías urinarias** urinary tract *sing* **5** (*Med*) **por ~ oral** orally; **por ~ tópica** topically, externally; **por ~ interna** internally **6** (= *medio, canal*) **por la ~ de la violencia** through violence *o* by using violence; **por ~ arbitral** by (process of) arbitration; **por ~ oficial** through official channels **7** **en ~s de: un país en ~s de desarrollo** a developing country; **una especie en ~s de extinción** an endangered species; **el asunto está en ~s de solución** the matter is on its way to being solved **8** (*Rel*) way ➤ **Vía Crucis** Way of the Cross, Stations of the Cross *pl*
Ⓑ PREP via; **un vuelo a Nueva York ~ Londres** a flight to New York via London; **retransmisión ~ satélite** satellite broadcast

viabilidad SF viability, feasibility

viable ADJ viable, feasible

viacrucis SM INV **1** (*Rel*) Way of the Cross, Stations *pl* of the Cross* **2** (= *problemas*) load of disasters, heap of troubles

viada SF (*Méx, Perú*) speed

viaducto SM viaduct

viajante SMF (*tb* **~ de comercio**) commercial traveller, traveling salesman (*EEUU*)

viajar /1a/ VI (= *hacer viajes*) to travel; **~ en coche/autobús** to go by car/bus

viaje¹ SM **1** (= *desplazamiento*) (*gen*) trip; (*por mar, el espacio*) voyage; **es su primer ~ al extranjero** it's her first trip abroad; **¡buen ~!** have a good trip!; **un ~ en barco** a boat trip; **los ~s** (= *actividad*) travelling, traveling (*EEUU*), travel; **tras dos años de ~s por África** after two years' travel in Africa; **se fue de ~ a Perú** she went on a trip to Peru; **estar de ~** to be away; **salir de ~** to go away ➤ **viaje de estudios** field trip ➤ **viaje de fin de curso** end-of-year trip ➤ **viaje de ida** outward journey ➤ **viaje de ida y vuelta**, **viaje redondo** (*Méx*) return trip, round trip ➤ **viaje de negocios** business trip ➤ **viaje de novios** honeymoon ➤ **viaje organizado** package tour **2** (= *trayecto*) journey; **es un ~ muy largo** it's a very long journey **3** (= *carga*) load; **un ~ de leña** a load of wood **4** (*) [*de droga*] trip* **5** (= *vez*) **de un ~** all in one go (*esp Brit*) *o* shot (*EEUU*)

viaje²* SM (= *tajo*) slash (*with a razor*); (= *puñalada*) stab; (= *golpe*) bash*

viajero/a Ⓐ ADJ [*persona*] travelling, traveling (*EEUU*); (*Zool*) migratory Ⓑ SM/F (*gen*) traveller, traveler (*EEUU*); (= *pasajero*) passenger

vial ADJ road *antes de s*

vianda SF **1** (*tb* **~s**) (= *comida*) food **2** (*CS*) (= *fiambrera*) lunchbox, dinner pail (*EEUU*)

viandante SMF (= *peatón*) pedestrian; (= *paseante*) passer-by

viario ADJ road *antes de s*

viático SM (*Rel*) viaticum

víbora SF (*Zool*) viper; ✦ MODISMO **ser una ~** to have a sharp tongue ➤ **víbora de cascabel** (*esp Méx*) rattlesnake

vibración SF **1** (= *temblor*) vibration **2 vibraciones*** (*entre personas*) vibrations, vibes*

vibrador SM vibrator

vibrante ADJ **1** (= *que vibra*) vibrating **2** (*Ling*) rolled, trilled **3** [*voz*] ringing; **~ de** ringing with, vibrant with

vibrar /1a/ VI to vibrate

vicaría SF vicarage; ✦ MODISMO **pasar por la ~*** to tie the knot*, get hitched**

vicario SM (*Rel*) ➤ **Vicario de Cristo** Vicar of Christ ➤ **vicario general** vicar general

vicealmirante SMF vice-admiral

vicecampeón/ona SM/F runner-up

vicecónsul SMF vice-consul

vicelendakari SMF, **vicelehendakari** SMF *vice-president of the Basque autonomous government*

vicepresidente/a SM/F (*Pol*) vice-president; [*de comité, empresa*] vice-chairman

viceversa ADV vice versa

vichar /1a/ VT (*esp CS*) (= *mirar*) to observe; (= *espiar*) to spy on

viciado ADJ **1** [*aire*] foul, stale **2** [*costumbres, texto*] corrupt, contaminated

viciar /1b/ Ⓐ VT **1** (= *corromper*) to corrupt, pervert **2** (*Jur*) to nullify, invalidate **3** [+ *texto*] to corrupt **4** [+ *droga, producto*] to adulterate; [+ *aire*] to pollute **5** [+ *objeto*] to bend, twist; [+ *madera*] to warp Ⓑ **viciarse** VPR **1** (= *corromperse*) to become corrupted **2** [*objeto*] to warp, lose its shape **3** [*aire, agua*] to be/become polluted

vicio SM **1** (= *corrupción*) vice **2** (= *mala costumbre*) bad habit, vice; **quejarse de ~** to complain for no reason at all **3** (= *defecto*) defect, blemish; (*Jur*) error; (*Ling*) mistake **4** [*de superficie*] warp **5 de ~** (*Esp**) (= *estupendo*) great, super*

vicioso/a Ⓐ ADJ **1** (= *depravado*) dissolute, depraved

2 (*Mec*) faulty, defective **Ⓑ** SM/F **1** (= *depravado*) dissolute person, depraved person **2** (= *adicto*) addict; **soy un ~ del fútbol** I am hooked on football*, I am a football fanatic *o* addict*

vicisitud SF (= *suceso*) vicissitude (*liter*); (= *desgracia*) accident, mishap

víctima SF (*gen*) victim; [*de accidente*] casualty; **fue ~ de una estafa** she was the victim of a swindle; **no hay que lamentar ~s del accidente** there were no casualties in the accident; **falleció ~ de un ataque cardiaco** he died of *o* from a heart attack

victimar /1a/ VT (*LAm frm*) to kill

victimario/a SM/F (*LAm frm*) killer, murderer

victimismo SM *tendency to see oneself as being victimized*

victoria SF victory; (*Dep*) win, victory; ✦ MODISMO **cantar ~** to claim victory

victorioso ADJ victorious

vicuña SF vicuna

vid SF vine

vida SF **1** (= *existencia*) life; **toda mi ~** all my life; **¿qué es de tu ~?** what's new?, how's life?; **salir con ~** to escape *o* come out alive; **en ~ de mi marido** when my husband was alive, during my husband's lifetime; **¡en la *o* mi ~!** never (in all my life)!; **~ o muerte: una operación a ~ o muerte** a life-or-death operation; **es una cuestión de ~ o muerte** it's a matter of life and death; **la otra ~** the next life; **perder la ~** to lose one's life; **de por ~** for life; **quitar la ~ a algn** to take sb's life; **quitarse la ~** to take one's own life; **sin ~** lifeless; **encontró en el suelo el cuerpo sin ~ de su marido** she found her husband's lifeless body on the floor; **toda la ~: un amigo de toda la ~** a lifelong friend; **ya no hay trabajos para toda la ~** there are no jobs for life nowadays ➤ **vida eterna** everlasting life ➤ **vida íntima** private life ➤ **vida nocturna** nightlife ➤ **vida privada** private life ➤ **vida sentimental** love-life
2 (= *forma de vivir*) life; **llevan una ~ muy tranquila** they lead a very quiet life; **mujer de ~ alegre** loose woman; **la ~ cotidiana** everyday life; **doble ~** double life; **hacer ~ marital** to live together (as man and wife); **hacer una ~ normal** to lead a normal life; **no hacer ~ social** to have no social life; **hay que dejarles hacer su ~** you must let them live their own life ➤ **vida de perros, vida perra** dog's life, wretched life
3 (= *sustento*) **la ~ está muy cara** the cost of living is very high; **tienen la ~ resuelta** they are set up for life; **coste de la ~** cost of living; **ganarse la ~** to earn *o* make one's living
4 [*de objeto*] **la ~ de estos edificios es breve** the life of these buildings is short; **la media de ~ de un televisor** the average lifespan of a television set
5 ✦ MODISMOS **amargar la ~ a algn** to make sb's life a misery; **así es la ~** that's life, such is life; **dar ~ a algn: la mujer que me dio la ~** the woman who brought me into the world; **dar ~ a un personaje** to play a part; **darse buena ~ o la ~ padre** to live the life of Riley*; **estar encantado de la ~** to be delighted; **¡esto es ~!** this is the life!; **meterse en ~s ajenas** to pry into other people's affairs, meddle in other people's affairs; **¡hijo de mi ~!** my dear child!; **la ~ y milagros de algn** sb's life story; **pasarse la ~: se pasa la ~ quejándose** he's forever complaining; **pasar a mejor ~** (*euf*) to pass away, go to a better place; **pegarse la gran ~ o la ~ padre** to live the life of Riley*; **tener siete ~s (como los gatos)** (*hum*) to have nine lives
6 (= *vitalidad*) **lleno de ~** [*ojos*] lively; [*persona*] full of life; **sus ojos sin ~** his lifeless eyes; **dar ~ a: la música le da ~ a estas imágenes** the music brings these images to life; **dar ~ a una fiesta** to liven up a party
7 (*apelativo cariñoso*) **¡vida!** ◇ **¡~ mía!** my love!, my darling!
8 (*euf*) (= *prostitución*) **una mujer de ~** a loose woman; **echarse a la ~** to start walking the streets

vidente **Ⓐ** ADJ sighted **Ⓑ** SMF **1** (= *no ciego*) sighted person **2** (= *clarividente*) clairvoyant(e); (= *profeta*) seer, viewer

vídeo SM, **video** SM (*LAm*) (= *sistema*) video; (= *aparato*) video (recorder); **cinta de ~** videotape; **película de ~** video film (*esp Brit*) *o* movie (*esp EEUU*); **grabar en ~** to video, (video)tape

videocámara SF (*gen*) video camera; (*doméstica*) camcorder

videocasete SM video cassette

videocassette SF video cassette

videoclip SM (*pl* **~s**) videoclip, video

videoclub SM (*pl* **~s** *o* **~es**) video shop (*esp Brit*), video store (*esp EEUU*)

videoconferencia SF videoconference, teleconference

videoedición SF video editing

videojuego SM video game

videoteca SF video library

videoteléfono SM videophone

vidilla * SF **dar ~ a algo** to spice sth up, liven sth up; **dar ~ a algn** to liven sb up

vidorra * SF, **vidorria** * (*Uru*) SF good life, easy life; **pegarse la ~** (= *sin trabajar*) to live the life of Riley*; (= *divirtiéndose*) to live it up*

vidriado ADJ glazed

vidriar /1b/ **Ⓐ** VT to glaze **Ⓑ** **vidriarse** VPR [*objeto*] to become glazed; [*ojos*] to glaze over

vidriera SF **1** (= *puerta*) glass door; (= *ventana*) glass window; (*tb* **~ de colores**) stained glass window **2** (*LAm*) (= *escaparate*) shop window (*esp Brit*), store window (*EEUU*)

vidrio SM (= *material*) glass; (*LAm*) [*de ventana*] windowpane; **~s rotos** broken glass *sing*; ✦ MODISMOS **ahí los ~s** (*Méx**) see you there!*; **pagar los ~s rotos** to carry the can (*Brit**), be the whipping boy

vidrioso ADJ **1** [*material*] glassy **2** [*ojo*] glassy; [*expresión*] glazed **3** [*asunto*] delicate

vidurria SF (*RPl, Ven*) = **vidorra**

vieira SF scallop

vieja * SF (*Col, Méx*) (= *mujer*) woman; *ver tb* **viejo**

viejito/a * SM/F (*LAm*) **1** (= *anciano*) old person **2** (= *amigo*) friend

viejo/a **Ⓐ** ADJ **1** (= *de mucha edad*) old; **hacerse *o* ponerse ~** to grow old, get old; **de ~ me gustaría vivir junto al mar** when I'm old, I'd like to live by the sea
2 (= *envejecido*) old; **está muy ~ para la edad que tiene** he looks very old for his age
3 (= *usado*) old; **ropa vieja** old clothes *pl*; **librería de ~** secondhand bookshop (*esp Brit*) *o* bookstore (*esp EEUU*); **zapatero de ~** cobbler; ✦ MODISMO **se cae de ~** it's falling to pieces
4 (= *antiguo*) old; **un ~ amigo** an old friend; **viejas costumbres** old customs; **mi padre es de la vieja escuela** my father is of the old school
Ⓑ SM/F **1** (= *persona mayor*) old man/old woman; **los ~s** the elderly, old people ➤ **Viejo Pascuero** (*Chi*) Father Christmas
2 (*) (= *padre, madre*) old man/woman*; **mis ~s** my parents, my folks*
3 (*Méx**) (= *esposo, esposa*) old man/woman*
4 (*LAm**) (*en oración directa*) (= *querido*) darling; (= *amigo*) pal*, mate (*Brit**), buddy (*EEUU**); *ver tb* **vieja**

Viena SF Vienna

viene *etc ver* **venir**

vienés/esa ADJ, SM/F Viennese

viento SM **1** (*Meteo*) wind; **corre *o* hay *o* hace *o* sopla (mucho) ~** it is (very) windy; **~ en popa** following wind; ✦ MODISMOS **correr malos ~s para algo** to be the wrong moment for sth; **contra ~ y marea** at all costs, come what may; **gritar algo a los cuatro ~s** to shout sth from the rooftops, tell all and sundry about sth; **echar a algn con ~ fresco** * to throw sb out*; **ir ~ en popa** to go splendidly, go great guns*; [*negocio*] to prosper; **tomarse los ~s** (*RPl**) to beat it**; **lo mandé a tomar ~** * I sent him packing ➤ **viento de cola** tail wind ➤ **viento huracanado** hurricane force wind, violent wind ➤ **viento racheado** gusty wind, squally wind ➤ **vientos alisios** trade winds
2 (*Mús*) wind
3 (*Camping*) guy rope, guy

vientre SM **1** (= *estómago*) belly; **bajo ~** lower abdomen

2 (= *matriz*) womb **3** (= *intestino*) bowels *pl*; **hacer de ~** to have a bowel movement, move one's bowels **4** [*de recipiente*] belly

viernes SM INV Friday ➤ **Viernes Santo** Good Friday; *ver tb* **sábado**; ⇨ *SEMANA SANTA*

> En inglés los días de la semana se escriben con mayúscula.

Vietnam SM Vietnam

vietnamita Ⓐ ADJ, SMF Vietnamese Ⓑ SM (*Ling*) Vietnamese

viga SF [*de madera*] beam, rafter; [*de metal*] girder ➤ **viga maestra** main beam ➤ **viga transversal** crossbeam

vigencia SF (= *validez*) validity, applicability; [*de contrato*] term, life; **estar en ~** to be in force, be valid; **perder ~** to go out of use, be no longer applicable; **tener ~** to be valid, apply

vigente ADJ [*ley, reglamento*] current, in force; [*tarifa*] current; **según la normativa ~** according to the regulations currently in force; **una costumbre aún ~** a custom which still prevails

vigésimo ADJ, PRON twentieth; *ver tb* **sexto**

vigía Ⓐ SMF lookout, watchman; **los ~s** (*Náut*) the watch Ⓑ SF watchtower

vigilancia SF **1** (= *custodia*) vigilance; **burlaron la ~ de sus guardianes** they evaded the watchful eye of their guards; **tener bajo ~** [+ *paciente*] to keep under observation; [+ *prisionero*] to keep under surveillance **2** (= *servicio*) security

vigilante Ⓐ ADJ vigilant, watchful Ⓑ SMF (*en tienda*) store detective; [*de museo*] curator; (*en piscina*) attendant ➤ **vigilante jurado** armed security guard ➤ **vigilante nocturno** night watchman

vigilar /1a/ Ⓐ VT **1** [+ *niño, equipaje, máquina*] to keep an eye on, watch; **vigila el arroz para que no se pegue** keep an eye on the rice to make sure it doesn't stick **2** [+ *presos*] to guard; [+ *frontera*] to guard, police; **vigilaban de cerca al sospechoso** they kept a close watch on the suspect Ⓑ VI to keep watch

vigilia SF **1** (= *vela*) wakefulness; **pasar la noche de ~** to stay awake all night **2** (*Rel*) vigil; (= *abstinencia*) abstinence

vigor SM **1** (= *fuerza*) vigour, vigor (*EEUU*); **con ~** vigorously **2** (= *vigencia*) **en ~** [*norma*] in force; [*tarifa, horario*] valid, applicable; **entrar en ~** to take effect, come into force

vigorizar /1f/ VT to invigorate

vigoroso ADJ (*gen*) vigorous; [*esfuerzo*] strenuous

vigueta SF joist, small beam

VIH SM ABR (= **virus de inmunodeficiencia humana**) HIV

vihuela SF (*Hist*) *early form of the guitar*

vikingo/a SM/F Viking

vil ADJ [*persona*] low, villainous; [*acto*] vile, rotten; [*conducta*] despicable, mean; **el ~ metal** filthy lucre

vileza SF **1** (= *cualidad*) vileness **2** (= *acción*) vile act, base deed

vilipendiar /1b/ VT **1** (= *denunciar*) to vilify, revile **2** (= *despreciar*) to despise, scorn

villa SF **1** (= *pueblo*) town; **la Villa (y Corte)** (*Esp*) Madrid ➤ **villa miseria** (*Arg*) shantytown ➤ **villa olímpica** Olympic village **2** (= *casa*) villa

Villadiego SM ✦ MODISMO **tomar las de ~*** to beat it quick*

villancico SM (Christmas) carol

villano/a Ⓐ ADJ **1** (*Hist*) (= *campesino*) peasant *antes de s* **2** (= *vil*) villainous, base Ⓑ SM/F **1** (*Hist*) serf, villein **2** (= *canalla*) rat*, scumbag**; (*Cine*) villain

villero/a SM/F (*Arg*) shantytown dweller

villorrio SM one-horse town, dump*

vilo ADV **en ~** (= *intranquilo*) on tenterhooks; **estar con el alma en ~** to be left in suspense, be on tenterhooks; **tener a algn en ~** to keep sb in suspense, keep sb waiting

vinagre SM vinegar

vinagrera SF **1** (= *botella*) vinegar bottle **2 vinagreras** (= *juego*) cruet stand *sing* **3** (*And Med*) heartburn, acidity

vinagreta SF (*tb* **salsa ~**) vinaigrette, French dressing

vinatería SF wine shop (*esp Brit*), wine store (*esp EEUU*)

vinatero/a SM/F wine merchant, vintner

vincha SF (*SAm*) hairband

vinculación SF **1** (= *relación*) bond, link **2** (*Jur*) entail

vincular /1a/ VT **1** (= *relacionar*) to link, bind (**a** to); **~ su suerte a la de otro** to make one's fate dependent on sb else's; **están estrechamente vinculados entre sí** they are closely bound together **2** (*Jur*) to entail

vínculo SM **1** (= *relación, lazo*) link, bond; **los ~s de la amistad** the bonds of friendship ➤ **vínculo de parentesco** family ties *pl*, ties *pl* of blood **2** (*Jur*) entail

vindicación SF **1** (= *defensa*) vindication **2** (= *venganza*) revenge, vengeance

vindicar /1g/ VT **1** [+ *persona, reputación*] to vindicate; [+ *derecho*] to regain, win back **2** (= *vengar*) to avenge

vine *etc ver* **venir**

vinería SF (*LAm*) wine shop

vinícola ADJ [*industria*] wine *antes de s*; [*región*] wine-growing *antes de s*, wine-making *antes de s*

vinicultor(a) SM/F wine grower

vinicultura SF wine growing, wine production

vinilo SM, **vinil** SM (*Méx*) vinyl

vino SM **1** (= *bebida*) wine ➤ **vino añejo** mature wine ➤ **vino blanco** white wine ➤ **vino de aguja** sparkling wine ➤ **vino de la casa** house wine ➤ **vino del año** new wine, wine for early drinking ➤ **vino de mesa** table wine ➤ **vino de reserva** reserve ➤ **vino de solera** vintage wine ➤ **vino espumoso** sparkling wine ➤ **vino peleón** cheap wine, plonk (*Brit**), jug wine (*EEUU*) ➤ **vino rosado** rosé (wine) ➤ **vino tinto** red wine **2** (= *recepción*) drinks *pl*, reception; **después de la conferencia hubo un ~** there were drinks after the lecture ➤ **vino de honor** official reception

viña SF vineyard

viñador(a) SM/F (= *propietario*) wine grower; (= *trabajador*) vineyard worker

viñatero/a SM/F (*And, CS*) wine grower

viñedo SM vineyard

viñeta SF **1** [*de tira cómica*] picture; (*en periódico, revista*) cartoon **2** (*en libro*) vignette

viola SF (*Mús*) viola

violáceo ADJ violet

violación SF **1** (*sexual*) rape **2** (= *incumplimiento*) [*de ley*] infringement; [*de acuerdo, principio*] violation, breach **3** [*de derecho, territorio*] violation ➤ **violación de domicilio** (*Arg, Méx, Ven*) housebreaking

violador(a) SM/F [*de persona*] rapist; [*de acuerdo, derecho*] violator, offender (**de** against)

violar /1a/ VT **1** [+ *persona*] to rape **2** [+ *ley*] to break, infringe (*frm*); [+ *acuerdo, principio*] to violate, breach **3** [+ *derecho, territorio*] to violate **4** (= *profanar*) to violate

violencia SF (*gen*) violence; (= *fuerza*) force; **hacer algo con ~** to do sth violently; **usar la ~ para abrir una caja** to force open a box ➤ **violencia doméstica** domestic violence

violentar /1a/ Ⓐ VT **1** [+ *puerta, cerradura*] to force **2** [+ *persona*] to embarrass **3** [+ *sentido*] to distort, twist Ⓑ **violentarse** VPR to get embarrassed

violentismo SM (*Chi*) political violence

violento ADJ **1** [*acto, deporte, persona*] violent **2** (= *incómodo*) awkward, uncomfortable; **me fue muy ~ verlo llorar** seeing him cry made me feel very awkward *o* uncomfortable

violeta SM, SF, ADJ INV violet

violín Ⓐ SM **1** (= *instrumento*) violin; ✦ MODISMOS **meter ~ en bolsa** (*RPl**) to stay (well) out of it; **pintar un ~** (*Méx**) to make a rude sign; **tocar el ~** (*Chi, Ven**) to play gooseberry

(*Brit*), be a third wheel (*EEUU*) **2** (*Ven**) (= *mal olor*) BO*, body odour Ⓑ SMF (= *persona*) violinist; **primer ~** (= *concertino*) leader; [*de sección*] first violin

violinista SMF violinist, fiddler*

violón SM double bass

violoncelista SMF cellist

violoncelo SM cello

violonchelista SMF cellist

violonchelo SM cello

vip* SM (*pl* **-s**) VIP

viperino ADJ viperish; **lengua viperina** wicked tongue

virador SM (*Fot*) toner

viraje SM **1** (= *giro*) (*Náut*) tack; [*de coche*] turn; (*repentino*) swerve **2** (*Pol*) (= *cambio*) abrupt switch, volte-face; [*de votos*] swing **3** (*Fot*) toning

viral ADJ viral

virar /1a/ Ⓐ VT **1** (*Náut*) to put about, turn **2** (*Fot*) to tone **3** (*LAm*) (= *dar vuelta a*) to turn Ⓑ VI (*Náut*) to tack, go about; [*vehículo*] to turn; (*con violencia*) to swerve

virgen (*pl* **vírgenes**) Ⓐ ADJ [*persona*] virgin; [*cinta*] blank; [*película*] unexposed Ⓑ SMF virgin; (*Rel*) **la Virgen** the Virgin; **la Santísima Virgen** the Blessed Virgin; ✦ MODISMOS **aparecerse la Virgen a algn***: **se le apareció la Virgen** he got his big chance, he struck lucky (*esp Brit**), he lucked out (*EEUU**); **es un viva la Virgen** (*Esp**) he doesn't give a damn** *o* a hoot*

virginal ADJ virginal

virginidad SF virginity

Virgo SM (= *signo*) Virgo

virgo Ⓐ SM (= *virginidad*) virginity Ⓑ SMF INV (*Astron*) (= *persona*) Virgo; **soy ~** I'm Virgo

virguería* SF (*Esp*) **es una ~** it's wonderful; **hacer ~s** to work wonders

virguero* ADJ (*Esp*) (= *bueno*) super*, smashing*; (= *hábil*) clever, smart

vírico ADJ viral, virus *antes de s*

viril ADJ virile, manly

virilidad SF virility, manliness

virolo* ADJ (*Ven*) cross-eyed

virreinato SM viceroyalty

virrey SM viceroy

virtual ADJ **1** (= *potencial*) virtual; [*ganador, presidente*] likely, probable; **son ya los ~es campeones 2** they are virtually assured of the championship **2** (*Inform, Fís*) virtual

virtud SF **1** (= *calidad*) virtue ➤ **virtud cardinal** cardinal virtue **2** (= *capacidad*) ability, power; **en ~ de** by virtue of, by reason of; **tener la ~ de ...** (+ INFIN) to have the virtue of ... + *ger*, have the power to ... + *infin*; **~es curativas** healing power *sing*, healing properties

virtuosismo SM virtuosity

virtuoso/a Ⓐ ADJ virtuous Ⓑ SM/F virtuoso

viruela SF **1** (= *enfermedad*) smallpox **2 viruelas** (= *marcas*) pockmarks; **picado de ~s** pockmarked ➤ **viruelas locas** chickenpox *sing*

virulé: **a la ~*** ADJ (*Esp*) (= *estropeado*) damaged; (= *torcido*) bent, twisted; **ojo a la ~** shiner*

virulencia SF virulence

virulento ADJ virulent

virus SM INV virus ➤ **virus de inmunodeficiencia humana** human immunodeficiency virus ➤ **virus informático** computer virus

viruta SF shaving

visado SM, **visa** (*LAm*) SF visa

visaje SM (wry) face, grimace

vis a vis Ⓐ ADV face to face Ⓑ SM (= *reunión*) face to face (meeting); (*en la cárcel*) private visit

visceral ADJ **1** (*Anat*) visceral **2** (= *profundo*) visceral, deep-rooted; **reacción ~** gut reaction

visceralmente ADV deeply, viscerally (*frm*)

vísceras SFPL viscera *pl*, entrails

viscosa SF viscose

viscosidad SF viscosity

viscoso ADJ (*gen*) viscous; [*secreción*] slimy

visera SF [*de gorra*] peak; [*de jockey, tenista*] eyeshade; [*de casco*] visor

visibilidad SF visibility

visible ADJ **1** (= *que se ve*) visible; **es ~ a simple vista** it's visible to the naked eye, it can be seen with the naked eye **2** (= *evidente*) **dio muestras de ~ disgusto** he was visibly upset **3** (= *decente*) decent, presentable; **¿estás ~?** are you decent *o* presentable?

visigodo/a Ⓐ ADJ Visigothic Ⓑ SM/F Visigoth

visigótico ADJ Visigothic

visillo SM lace curtain, net curtain

visión SF **1** (*Anat*) vision, (eye)sight **2** (*Rel*) vision; **ver visiones** to be seeing things, suffer delusions **3** (= *vista*) view; **un político con ~ de futuro** a farsighted politician ➤ **visión de conjunto** complete picture, overall view **4** (= *punto de vista*) view; **su ~ del problema** his view of the problem

visionar /1a/ VT (*TV*) to view, see; (*por adelantado*) to preview

visionario/a ADJ, SM/F visionary

visir SM vizier

visita SF **1** (= *acción*) visit; (*breve*) call; **horas de ~** visiting hours; **estar de ~ en un lugar** to be on a visit to a place; **ir de ~** to go visiting; **hacer una ~ a** to visit, pay a visit to ➤ **visita de cortesía**, **visita de cumplido** formal visit, courtesy call ➤ **visita guiada** (*LAm*) guided tour ➤ **visita oficial** official visit **2** (= *persona*) visitor, caller; **hoy tenemos ~** we have visitors today; **"no se admiten visitas"** "no visitors"

visitador(a) SM/F ➤ **visitador(a) médico/a** medical representative ➤ **visitador(a) social** (*SAm*) social worker

visitante SMF visitor

visitar /1a/ VT (*gen*) to visit; (*brevemente*) to call on

vislumbrar /1a/ VT **1** [+ *paisaje, figura*] to glimpse, catch a glimpse of **2** [+ *solución*] to glimpse, begin to see

viso SM **1** [*de metal*] gleam, glint **2** (= *aspecto*) **una crisis sin ~s de solución** a seemingly insoluble crisis; **no tenía ~s de acabar** it seemed that it was never going to finish **3 visos** [*de tela*] sheen *sing*, gloss *sing*

visón SM mink

visor SM **1** (*en avión*) bombsight; (*Mil*) sight **2** (*Fot*) (*tb ~ de imagen*) viewfinder

víspera SF eve, day before; **la ~ de ◊ en ~s de** on the eve of (*tb fig*); **estar en ~s de hacer algo** to be on the point *o* verge of doing sth

vista SF **1** (= *visión*) sight, eyesight; **el coche desapareció de mi ~** the car disappeared from sight; **hasta donde alcanza la ~** as far as the eye can see; **tener buena/mala ~** to have good/bad eyesight; ✦ MODISMO **hacer la ~ gorda** to turn a blind eye, pretend not to notice ➤ **vista cansada** (*por defecto*) longsightedness; (*por agotamiento*) eyestrain ➤ **vista de águila**, **vista de lince** eagle eye; **tener ~ de águila** *o* **de lince** to have eyes like a hawk

2 (= *ojos*) **2.1** (= *órgano*) eyes *pl*; **tiene un problema en la ~** she has something wrong with her eyes; **a la altura de la ~** at eye level; **torcer la ~** to squint **2.2** (= *mirada*) **no apartar la ~ de algo** to keep one's eyes glued to sth; **bajar la ~** to look down, lower one's gaze; **buscar algo con la ~** to look around for sth; **con la ~ puesta en las elecciones** with a view to the elections; **¡quítate de mi ~!** get out of my sight!; **volver la ~ atrás** to look back; ✦ MODISMOS **comerse** *o* **devorar a algn con la ~** (*con deseo*) to devour sb with one's eyes; (*con ira*) to look daggers at sb*; **perder algo de ~** to lose sight of sth; **no perder a algn de ~** to keep sb in sight

3 (= *perspicacia*) foresight; **tuvieron ~ para comprar las acciones** they showed foresight in buying the shares; **ha tenido mucha ~ con la casa** he was very far-sighted about the house

4 (= *panorama*) view; **la ~ desde el castillo** the view from the castle; **con ~s a: una habitación con ~s al mar** a room with a sea view, a room overlooking the sea
5 (*otras expresiones*) **a ... años/días ~: pagadero a 30 días ~** payable within 30 days; **a dos años ~ de la exposición** (= *antes*) two years before the exhibition; (= *después*) two years after the exhibition; **a la ~** in sight *o* view; **la parte que quedaba a la ~** the part that was visible *o* in view; **no tengo ningún proyecto a la ~** I have no plans in sight; **a la ~ está (que ...)** it's obvious (that ...), you can see for yourself (that ...); **a la ~ de todos** in full view (of everyone); **los resultados están a la ~ de todos** the results are there for everyone to see; **a la ~ de sus informes** in the light of *o* in view of his reports; **con ~s a** with a view to; **con ~s a una solución del problema** with a view to solving the problem; **han modernizado el estadio con ~s al Mundial** they have modernized the stadium ahead of the World Cup; **de ~** by sight; **conocer a algn de ~** to know sb by sight; **en ~ de** in view of; **en ~ de que ...** in view of the fact that ...; **¡hasta la ~!** see you!, so long!; **observar algo a ~ de pájaro** to get a bird's-eye view of sth; **a primera ~** at first sight, on the face of it; **a simple ~** (= *sin ayuda de aparatos*) to the naked eye; (= *por la primera impresión*) at first sight
6 (*Jur*) hearing ➤ **vista oral** first hearing

vistazo SM look, glance; **de un ~** at a glance; **echar** *o* **pegar un ~ a*** to glance at, have a (quick) look at

visto¹ *ver* **vestir**

visto² ⒶPP *de* **ver**
ⒷADJ **1** (= *conocido*) **ese color está muy ~** you see that colour *o* (*EEUU*) color all over the place, everyone is wearing that colour *o* (*EEUU*) color; **ese chiste ya está más que ~** that joke is as old as the hills; **ser lo nunca ~** to be unheard of; ✦ MODISMO **más ~ que el tebeo** (*Esp*) as old as the hills
2 (= *considerado*) **estar bien/mal ~** [*comportamiento*] to be the done thing/be frowned upon; [*persona*] to be well/badly thought of
3 (= *expuesto*) [*ladrillo*] bare, exposed; [*viga*] exposed
4 (*Jur*) **~ para sentencia** adjourned for sentencing
5 (*en locuciones*) **está ~ que ...** it is clear *o* obvious that ...; **por lo ~** apparently; ✦ MODISMOS **ni ~ ni oído** like lightning; **~ y no ~: cogió el bolso y salió corriendo, fue ~ y no ~** he grabbed the bag and ran out, one minute he was there and the next minute he was gone; **en un ~ y no ~** in a flash
6 **~ que** since; **~ que no nos hacían caso nos fuimos** since they took no notice of us we left
ⒸSM ➤ **visto bueno** approval, go-ahead*; **dar el ~ bueno a algo** to give sth one's approval, give sth the go-ahead*

vistosidad SF (*gen*) brightness; [*de feria, ballet*] spectacular nature

vistoso ADJ [*ropa*] bright, colourful, colorful (*EEUU*); [*partido*] spectacular

visual ⒶADJ visual; **campo ~** field of vision ⒷSF **1** (= *línea*) line of sight **2** (*) (= *vistazo*) look, glance

visualización SF visualization

visualizador SM (*Inform*) display screen, VDU

vital ADJ **1** (= *de la vida*) [*fuerza*] life *antes de s*; [*espacio*] living **2** (= *fundamental*) vital; **de ~ importancia** vitally important **3** (= *enérgico*) vital, full of vitality **4** (*Anat*) vital; **órganos ~es** vital organs

vitalicio ADJ life *antes de s*, for life; **cargo ~** post held for life; **pensión vitalicia** life pension

vitalidad SF vitality

vitalismo SM **1** (*Fil*) vitalism **2** [*de persona*] vitality

vitalista ADJ **1** (*Fil*) vitalist **2** [*persona*] vital, full of life

vitalizante ADJ revitalizing

vitamina SF vitamin

vitaminado ADJ with added vitamins

vitamínico ADJ vitamin *antes de s*

vitela SF vellum

vitícola ADJ [*industria*] grape *antes de s*, vine *antes de s*; [*región*] grape-producing, vine-producing

viticultor(a) SM/F vine grower

viticultura SF vine growing, viticulture (*frm*)

vitola SF cigar band

vítor SM cheer

vitorear /1a/ VT to cheer

vitoriano ADJ of/from Vitoria

vítreo ADJ **1** [*ojos*] glassy **2** (*Geol, Min*) vitreous

vitrificar /1g/ VT to vitrify

vitrina SF **1** [*de tienda*] glass case, showcase; (*en casa*) display cabinet **2** (*LAm*) (= *escaparate*) shop window (*esp Brit*), store window (*EEUU*)

vitrinear* /1a/ VT (*And*) to go window-shopping

vitro ADJ, ADV *ver* **in vitro**

vitrocerámica SF **placa de ~** glass-ceramic hob

vitrola SF (*SAm*) gramophone, phonograph (*EEUU*)

vituallas SFPL provisions *pl*, victuals *pl*

vituperar /1a/ VT to condemn, censure, vituperate against (*frm*)

vituperio SM condemnation, censure, vituperation (*frm*)

viuda¹ SF ➤ **viuda negra** (= *araña*) black widow (spider); *ver tb* **viudo**

viudedad SF **1** [*de mujer*] widowhood; [*de hombre*] widowerhood **2** (*Fin*) widow's pension

viudez SF [*de mujer*] widowhood; [*de hombre*] widowerhood

viudo/a² ⒶADJ widowed ⒷSM/F widower/widow; *ver tb* **viuda**

viva SM cheer

vivac SM (*pl* **~s**) bivouac

vivacidad SF (= *personalidad*) liveliness, vivacity; (= *inteligencia*) sharpness; [*de colores*] brightness

vivalavirgen* (*Esp*) ⒶADJ INV happy-go-lucky* ⒷSMF INV happy-go-lucky person*

vivamente ADV [*describir, recordar*] vividly; [*sentir*] acutely, intensely; **se lo deseo ~** I sincerely hope he gets it

vivar /1a/ VT (*LAm*) to cheer

vivaracho ADJ **1** [*persona*] vivacious **2** [*ojos*] bright, lively, twinkling **3** (*Méx*) sharp, sly

vivencia SF experience

víveres SMPL provisions; (*esp Mil*) stores, supplies

vivero SM **1** [*de plantas*] nursery **2** (*para peces*) ➤ **vivero de ostras** oyster bed **3** (*fig*) breeding ground; (*pey*) hotbed; **es un ~ de discordias** it's a hotbed of discord

viveza SF [*de ritmo*] liveliness; [*de imagen*] vividness; [*de mente, movimiento*] sharpness, quickness; [*de sensación*] intensity, acuteness; [*de emoción*] strength, depth ➤ **viveza criolla** native wit; (*pey*) low cunning (*pey*)

vívido ADJ (= *experimentado*) **los años ~s en Brasil** the years we lived in Brazil; **la crisis vivida por el gobierno** the crisis the government went through *o* experienced

vívido ADJ vivid, graphic

vividor ⒶADJ opportunistic ⒷSM (= *aprovechado*) hustler; (= *sibarita*) bon viveur*

vivienda SF **1** (= *alojamiento*) housing; **el problema de la ~** the housing problem **2** (= *casa*) house, home; (= *piso*) flat (*esp Brit*), apartment (*EEUU*); **segunda ~** second home; **bloque de ~s** block of flats (*Brit*), apartment block (*EEUU*) ➤ **vivienda de renta limitada** controlled rent housing ➤ **viviendas de interés social** (*Méx, Perú*), **viviendas de protección oficial** state-subsidized housing

viviente ADJ living

vivificar /1g/ VT to revitalize

vivíparo ADJ viviparous

vivir /3a/ ⒶVI **1** (= *estar vivo*) to live; **mientras yo viva** as long as I live; **todavía vive** he's still alive
2 (= *pasar la vida*) to live; **sólo vive para la música** music is her whole life, she only lives for music; **ahora ya puedes ~ tranquila** now you can relax; **vivieron felices y comieron perdices** they lived happily ever after; **en este país se vive**

bien people live well in this country, people have a good life in this country; **no dejar ~ a algn: los dolores no me dejan ~** the pain never lets up; **los celos no la dejan ~** she is eaten up with jealousy; **saber ~** to know how to live;
◆ MODISMOS **~ del cuento** to live on *o* by one's wits; **~ para ver** you live and learn
3 (= *habitar*) to live; **en esa casa no vive nadie** nobody lives in that house
4 (= *subsistir*) **la fotografía no me da para ~** I can't make *o* earn a living from photography, photography doesn't give me enough to live on; **~ de algo** to live on sth; **vive de la caridad** he lives on charity; **yo vivo de mi trabajo** I work for a living; **vive de ilusiones** he lives in a dream world; **~ al día** to live from day to day; **~ de las rentas** (*lit*) to have a private income; **publicó un libro hace años y desde entonces vive de las rentas** years ago he published a book and he's lived off it *o* lived on the strength of it ever since
5 (= *durar*) [*recuerdo*] to live, live on
6 (*como exclamación*) **¡viva!** hurray!; **¡viva el rey!** long live the king!; **¡vivan los novios!** (here's) to the bride and groom!
Ⓑ VT **1** (= *experimentar*) [+ *guerra, período difícil*] to live through, go through; **la época que nos ha tocado ~** the age in which we happen to live; **a ~ la vida** to live life to the full *o* get the most out of life
2 (= *sentir*) to experience; **parece que estoy viviendo ese momento otra vez** it's as if I were *o* was experiencing that moment all over again
Ⓒ SM **gente de mal ~** undesirable people

vivito ADJ **estar ~ y coleando** to be alive and kicking

vivo/a Ⓐ ADJ **1** (= *con vida*) (*tras sustantivo*) living; (*tras verbo*) alive; **los seres ~s** living beings; **lo quemaron ~** he was burned alive; **"se busca vivo o muerto"** "wanted, dead or alive"; **venden los cebos ~s** they sell live bait; **tenía la piel en carne viva** his skin was raw
2 (*TV, Radio*) **en ~** (= *en directo*) live; (= *en persona*) in person; **un espectáculo con música en ~** a live music show, a show with live music
3 (= *intenso*) [*descripción*] vivid, graphic; [*imaginación, mirada, ritmo*] lively; [*color*] bright; [*sensación*] acute; [*genio*] fiery; [*ingenio*] ready; [*inteligencia*] sharp, keen; **su recuerdo siempre seguirá ~ entre nosotros** her memory will always be with us, her memory will live on in our minds;
◆ MODISMO **ser la viva imagen** *o* **el ~ retrato de algn** to be the spitting image of sb
4 [*persona*] (= *listo*) clever; (= *astuto*) sharp
Ⓑ SM/F **1** (*) (= *aprovechado*) **es un ~** he's a clever one*, he's a sly one*
2 los ~s the living

vizacha SF (*LAm*) viscacha

vizcaíno ADJ of/from Biscay

vizconde(sa) SM/F viscount/viscountess

V.O. ABR (*Cine*) = **versión original**

vocablo SM (*frm*) word, term

vocabulario SM vocabulary

vocación SF vocation, calling

vocacional Ⓐ ADJ vocational **Ⓑ** SF (*Méx Educ*) technical college

vocal Ⓐ ADJ [*cuerdas*] vocal **Ⓑ** SMF [*de comité, tribunal*] member; (= *portavoz*) chairperson **Ⓒ** SF (*Ling*) vowel

vocalía SF committee

vocálico ADJ vocalic, vowel *antes de s*

vocalista SMF vocalist, singer

vocalizar /1f/ VI to vocalize

vocativo SM vocative

voceador SM **1** (= *pregonero*) town crier **2** (*Col, Méx*) [*de periódicos*] news vendor, newspaper seller

vocear /1a/ **Ⓐ** VT **1** [+ *mercancías*] to cry **2** (= *llamar*) to call loudly to, shout to **3** [+ *secreto*] to shout to all and sundry, shout from the rooftops **Ⓑ** VI to yell, bawl

vocería SF (*LAm*) position of spokesperson

vocerío SM shouting

vocero/a SM/F (*esp LAm*) spokesman/spokeswoman, spokesperson

vociferar /1a/ VI to vociferate (*frm*)

vocinglero ADJ loud-mouthed

vodevil SM music hall, variety, vaudeville (*EEUU*)

vodka SM vodka

vol. ABR (= *volumen*) vol.

volada SF **1** (*RPl, Ven*) (= *oportunidad*) **aprovechar la ~** to sieze the opportunity **2** (= *escapada*) **pegarse una ~** (*Col**) [*preso*] to escape; [*alumno*] to skive off (*Brit**), play hooky (*EEUU**); [*novios*] to run away **3 de ~** (*Méx**) quickly; **pasó de ~ por aquí** he popped in here*; **se tomó la cerveza de ~ y se fue** he knocked back the beer and went*; **en una ~** (*Col**) in next to no time

volado Ⓐ ADJ **1 estar ~*** (= *loco*) to be crazy*; (= *drogado*) to be high* **2** (*Chi**) (= *despistado*) absent-minded **3** (*Col, Ven**) (*de genio*) quick-tempered **Ⓑ** SM **1** (*Méx*) (*con una moneda*) **echar un ~** to toss a coin **2** (*Carib, RPl Cos*) flounce **Ⓒ** ADV (*And, CAm, Méx*) in a rush, hastily; **ir ~** to go off in a hurry

volador Ⓐ ADJ flying *antes de s* **Ⓑ** SM **1** (= *pez*) flying fish **2** (= *cohete*) rocket

voladura SF blowing up

volandas ADV **en ~** (= *por el aire*) through the air; (*) (= *con rapidez*) like lightning

volantazo SM (*Aut*) sharp turn

volante Ⓐ ADJ **1** (= *volador*) flying **2** (= *itinerante*) [*estudio, sede*] travelling, traveling (*EEUU*) **Ⓑ** SM **1** (*Aut*) steering wheel; **ir al ~** to be at the wheel, be driving **2** (*Téc*) (*en motor*) flywheel; (*en reloj*) balance wheel **3** (*LAm*) [*de propaganda*] pamphlet **4** (*Esp Med*) referral note **5** (*Bádminton*) shuttlecock **6** (*Cos*) flounce **Ⓒ** SMF (*Chi*) **1** (*Ftbl*) (= *jugador*) winger **2** (= *conductor*) racing driver

volantín SM (*Chi*) (= *cometa*) kite; (*Perú*) (= *voltereta*) somersault

volar /1l/ **Ⓐ** VI **1** (= *en el aire*) [*avión, pájaro, persona*] to fly; **los papeles salieron volando por la ventana** the papers blew out of the window; **el balón pasó volando por encima de nosotros** the ball flew over our heads; **echar a ~** [+ *pájaro*] to set free, let go; [+ *globo, cometa*] to fly; [+ *noticia*] to spread; **echarse a ~** [*pájaro*] (*por primera vez*) to (begin to) fly; (= *levantar el vuelo*) to take off; **dejar ~ la imaginación** to let one's imagination run riot
2 hacer ~ algo/a algn to blow sth/sb up; **hacer ~ algo en pedazos** to blow sth to pieces *o* to smithereens
3 volando: me preparó la cena volando he made my dinner in double-quick time*; **pasó volando en la moto** he whizzed *o* sped past on his motorbike; **me voy volando al banco** I must rush to the bank
4 (= *pasar rápido*) [*noticia*] to travel fast; [*tiempo*] to fly; [*días, semanas, meses*] to fly by; **¡cómo vuela el tiempo!** (how) time flies!
5 (*) (= *desaparecer*) [*objeto, persona*] to go, disappear; **cuando me di cuenta, el bolso ya había volado** before I knew it, the bag was gone *o* had gone *o* had disappeared; **el tabaco parece que vuela en esta casa** cigarettes seem to sprout legs in this house*
Ⓑ VT **1** (= *hacer volar*) [+ *cometa, globo*] to fly; (*Caza*) [+ *pájaro*] to flush out
2 (= *hacer explotar*) [+ *edificio, vehículo*] to blow up; [+ *caja fuerte*] to blow (open); **le ~on la cabeza de un disparo** they blew his head off with one shot
3 (*Chi, Méx, Ven**) (= *robar*) to pinch*, nick (*Brit**)
Ⓒ **volarse** VPR **1** (= *irse por el aire*) [*papel, paraguas*] to blow away; [*globo*] to fly away, fly off; [*sombrero*] to blow off; **con el viento se me ha volado el paraguas** the wind has blown my umbrella away
2 (*) (= *escaparse*) [*persona*] to run off
3 (*LAm**) (= *desaparecer*) to go, disappear
4 (*LAm**) (= *enfadarse*) to lose one's temper, blow up*

volátil ADJ volatile

volatilidad SF volatility

volatilizar /1f/ **Ⓐ** VT (*Quím*) to volatilize **Ⓑ** **volatilizarse** VPR **1** (*Quím*) to volatilize **2** (= *esfumarse*) to vanish into thin air

volatín SM acrobatics *pl*

volcán SM volcano; ✦ MODISMO **estar sobre un ~** to be sitting on top of a powder keg

volcánico ADJ volcanic

volcar /1g, 1l/ Ⓐ VT [+ *recipiente, vaso*] to upset, knock over; [+ *contenido*] to empty out, tip out; [+ *carga*] to dump; [+ *coche, camión*] to overturn; [+ *barco*] to overturn, capsize
Ⓑ VI [*coche, camión*] to overturn
Ⓒ **volcarse** VPR 1 (= *voltearse*) [*recipiente*] to be upset, get overturned; [*contenido*] to tip over; [*coche, camión*] to overturn; [*barco*] to capsize
2 (= *desvivirse*) to bend over backwards*, go out of one's way; **~se por complacer a algn** to bend over backwards to satisfy sb*
3 (= *entregarse*) **~se en una actividad** to throw o.s. into an activity

volea SF volley

volear /1a/ VT, VI to volley

voleibol SM volleyball

voleiplaya SM beach ball, beach volleyball

volibol SM (*Col, Méx*) volleyball

voleo SM 1 ✦ MODISMOS **sembrar a ~** to scatter the seed; **repartir algo a o al ~** to distribute sth haphazardly 2 (*) (= *golpe*) punch, bash*

volición SF volition

volitivo ADJ volitional, volitive

volován SM vol-au-vent

volqueta SF, **volquete** SM dumper, dump truck

voltaico ADJ voltaic

voltaje SM voltage

volteada SF (*RPl Agr*) roundup

voltear /1a/ Ⓐ VT 1 (*esp LAm*) (= *volver al revés*) to turn over, turn upside down; (= *dar la vuelta a*) to turn round; (= *lanzar al aire*) to toss 2 (*esp CS, Méx*) (= *volcar*) to knock, knock over 3 [+ *campanas*] to peal Ⓑ **voltearse** VPR (*LAm*) 1 (= *darse la vuelta*) to turn around; (*Pol*) (= *cambiar de lado*) to change sides; **~se contra algn** to turn against sb 2 (*Méx*) (= *volcarse*) to overturn, tip over

voltereta SF (*hacia delante*) somersault; (*hacia los lados*) cartwheel; (*por caída*) roll, tumble ➤ **voltereta lateral** cartwheel

voltímetro SM voltmeter

voltio SM 1 (*Fís*) volt 2 (*) (= *vuelta, paseo*) stroll; **darse un ~** to go for *o* take a stroll

voluble ADJ (= *inconstante*) fickle, changeable

volumen SM (*pl* **volúmenes**) 1 [*de cuerpo*] volume; **cajas de gran ~** large *o* bulky boxes 2 [*de sonido*] volume; **puso la radio a todo ~** he turned the radio up full blast 3 (*Com*) volume ➤ **volumen de negocios, volumen de operaciones** turnover 4 (= *tomo*) volume 5 [*de cabello*] body

voluminoso ADJ (*gen*) voluminous; [*paquete*] bulky

voluntad SF 1 (= *capacidad decisoria*) will; **por ~ propia** of one's own volition *o* free will
2 (= *deseo*) wish; **no lo dije con ~ de ofenderle** I did not say it with any wish to offend you, I had no desire to offend you; **última ~** last wish; (*Jur*) last will and testament; **lo hizo contra mi ~** he did it against my will; **por causas ajenas a mi ~** for reasons beyond my control; **hace siempre su santa ~** he always does exactly as he pleases ➤ **voluntad popular** will of the people
3 (= *determinación*) (*tb* **fuerza de ~**) willpower; **tiene mucha ~** he has a lot of willpower *o* a strong will ➤ **voluntad de hierro, voluntad férrea** iron will
4 (= *disposición*) will; **buena ~: con un poco de buena ~** with a bit of good will; **lo sugerí con buena ~** I suggested it with the best of intentions, I suggested it in good faith; **los hombres de buena ~** (*Rel*) men of goodwill; **mala ~: hay muy mala ~ contra el presidente** there is a lot of ill will against the president; ✦ MODISMO **ganar(se) la ~ de algn** to win sb over

5 **~** at will; **se puede beber a ~** you can drink as much as you like
6 **la ~** (*Esp*) (= *dinero*): **un mendigo le pidió la ~** a beggar asked him if he could spare some money; **—¿cuánto es? —la ~** "how much is it?" — "as much as you think it's worth"
7 (†) **tener ~ a algn** to be fond of sb, feel affection for sb

voluntariado SM (= *trabajo*) voluntary work; (= *trabajadores*) voluntary workers *pl*

voluntariamente ADV voluntarily

voluntario/a Ⓐ ADJ voluntary Ⓑ SM/F volunteer; **ofrecerse ~** to volunteer (**para** for)

voluntarioso ADJ 1 (= *dedicado*) dedicated, willing 2 (= *terco*) headstrong, wilful, willful (*EEUU*)

voluptuosidad SF voluptuousness

voluptuoso/a Ⓐ ADJ voluptuous Ⓑ SM/F voluptuary

voluta SF 1 (*Arquit*) scroll, volute 2 [*de humo*] spiral, column

volver /2h/ (*pp* **vuelto**) Ⓐ VT 1 (= *dar la vuelta a*) [+ *cabeza*] to turn; [+ *colchón, tortilla, enfermo*] to turn over; [+ *jersey, calcetín*] to turn inside out; [+ *página*] to turn, turn over; **~ la espalda** to turn away; **me volvió la espalda** he turned his back on me; **~ la esquina** to go around *o* turn the corner
2 (= *cambiar la orientación de*) to turn; **volvió el arma contra sí mismo** he turned the gun on himself; **~ la vista atrás** to look back
3 (+ ADJ) to make; **el ácido lo vuelve azul** the acid turns it blue; **vuelve fieras a los hombres** it turns men into wild beasts; **~ loco a algn** to drive sb mad
Ⓑ VI 1 (= *regresar*) (*a donde se está*) to come back, return; (*a donde se estaba*) to go back, return (**a** to; **de** from); **déjalas aquí y luego vuelves a por ellas** leave them here and come back for them later; **no he vuelto por allí** I've never gone back there; **volvió muy cansado** he got back very tired; **volviendo a lo que decía ...** going back *o* returning to what I was saying ...; **~ atrás** to go back, turn back
2 **~ a hacer algo** to do sth again; **~ a empezar** to start (over) again; **me he vuelto a equivocar** I've made a mistake again, I've made another mistake; **volvió a casarse** she remarried, she (got) married again; **volví a poner en marcha el motor** I restarted the engine
3 **~ en sí** to come to, come around, come round (*Brit*)
4 (*Méx*) (= *vomitar*) to be sick (*Brit*), vomit
Ⓒ **volverse** VPR 1 (= *darse la vuelta*) 1.1 [*persona*] to turn, turn around; **se volvió para mirarlo** he turned (around) to look at it; **~se atrás** (*en camino*) to turn back; (*en decisión*) to back out; (*en negociaciones*) to withdraw 1.2 [*objeto*] (*boca abajo*) to turn upside down; (*de dentro afuera*) to turn inside out; ✦ MODISMO **~se (en) contra (de) algn** to turn against sb
2 (= *regresar*) to turn back, go back; **empezó a llover y nos volvimos** it started to rain and we turned back; **vuélvete a buscarlo** go back and look for it
3 (+ ADJ) **se ha vuelto muy cariñoso** he's become very affectionate; **~se loco** to go mad

vomitar /1a/ Ⓐ VT 1 (= *devolver*) to vomit, bring up; **~ sangre** to cough up blood 2 [+ *humo, llamas*] to belch, belch forth; [+ *lava*] to spew; [+ *injurias*] to hurl (**contra** at) Ⓑ VI to vomit, be sick; **eso me da ganas de ~** (*fig*) that makes me sick

vomitivo Ⓐ ADJ 1 (*Med*) emetic 2 (*fig*) disgusting; [*chiste*] sick-making, repulsive Ⓑ SM (*Med*) emetic

vómito SM 1 (= *acto*) vomiting, being sick 2 (= *materia*) vomit

voracidad SF voracity, voraciousness

vorágine SF [*de mar, río*] whirlpool, vortex, maelstrom (*frm*); [*de odio, destrucción, confusión*] maelstrom; [*de actividad, publicidad*] whirl

voraz ADJ 1 (= *devorador*) voracious, ravenous 2 [*fuego*] raging, fierce

vórtice SM 1 (= *remolino*) [*de agua*] whirlpool, vortex; [*de viento*] whirlwind 2 [*de ciclón*] eye

vos* PRON PERS 1 (*esp RPl**) you *sing* 2 (††) you, ye††

vosear /1a/ VT (*esp RPl*) to address as "vos"

voseo SM (*esp RPl*) *addressing a person as "vos", the familiar usage*

vosotros/as PRON (*Esp*) **1** (*sujeto*) you (*familiar form of address*); **vendréis conmigo** you'll come with me; **hacedlo ~ mismos** do it yourselves **2** (*después de prep, en comparaciones*) you; **lo han hecho mejor que vosotras** they've done it better than you; **¿no pedís nada para ~?** aren't you going to ask for anything for yourselves?

votación SF (= *acto*) voting; (= *votos*) ballot, vote; **por popular** by popular vote; **por ~ secreta** by secret ballot; **someter algo a ~** to put sth to the vote, take a vote on sth ➤ **votación a mano alzada** show of hands

votante Ⓐ ADJ voting Ⓑ SMF voter

votar /1a/ Ⓐ VT [+ *candidato, partido*] to vote for; [+ *moción, proyecto de ley*] (= *decidir*) to put to the vote; (= *aprobar*) to pass, approve (*by vote*); **Pérez fue el más votado** Pérez received the highest number of votes, Pérez got most votes Ⓑ VI to vote (**por** for)

voto SM **1** (*Pol*) vote; **hubo 13 ~s a favor y 11 en contra** there were 13 votes for and 11 against ➤ **voto en blanco** blank vote ➤ **voto nulo** spoiled ballot paper ➤ **voto por correo** postal vote, absentee ballot (*EEUU*)
2 (*Rel*) (= *promesa*) vow ➤ **voto de castidad** vow of chastity ➤ **voto de obediencia** vow of obedience ➤ **voto de pobreza** vow of poverty ➤ **voto de silencio** vow of silence ➤ **votos monásticos** monastic vows
3 *votos* (= *deseos*) wishes; **hacer ~s por el restablecimiento de algn** to wish sb a quick recovery, hope that sb will get well soon

vox populi ADJ **ser ~** to become common knowledge

voy *ver* **ir**

voyeur [boˈjer] SM voyeur

vóytelas EXCL (*Méx*) wow!*

voz SF **1** (= *sonido humano*) voice; **con la ~ entrecortada** *o* **empañada** in a voice choked with emotion; **en ~ alta** (= *de forma audible*) aloud, out loud; (= *con tono potente*) loudly; **soñar en ~ alta** to think aloud *o* out loud; **en ~ baja** in a low voice, in a whisper; **está empezando a cambiar la ~** his voice is beginning to break; **forzar la ~** to strain one's voice; **a media ~** in a whisper; **perder la ~** *o* ◆ **quedarse sin ~** (*temporalmente*) to lose one's voice; (*definitivamente*) to lose the power of speech; **tener la ~ tomada** to be hoarse; **de viva ~** (= *en alto*) aloud; (= *oralmente*) personally *o* in person; ✦ MODISMO **decir algo a ~ en cuello** *o* **a ~ en grito** to shout sth at the top of one's voice ➤ **voz en off** (*TV, Cine*) voice-over
2 (*Mús*) **2.1** (= *sonido*) [*de instrumento*] sound
2.2 (= *persona*) voice; **canción a cuatro voces** song for four voices, four-part song; **cantar a dos voces** to sing a duet; **llevar la ~ cantante** (*en un grupo de pop, rock*) to be the lead singer; (*en un concierto clásico*) to be the lead soprano/tenor *etc*; (= *mandar*) to call the tune **2.3** (= *habilidad*) voice; **tiene muy buena ~** she has a very good voice
3 (= *aviso*) voice; **la ~ de la conciencia** the promptings *o* voice of conscience; **dar la ~ de alarma** to raise the alarm; **dar una ~ a algn** to give sb a shout* *o* call ➤ **voz de mando** (*Mil*) command; **llevar la ~ de mando** to be the boss
4 (= *rumor*) rumour, rumor (*EEUU*); **circula** *o* **corre la ~ de que ...** there is a rumour *o* (*EEUU*) rumor going round that ..., the word is that ...; **hacer circular** *o* **correr la ~ de que ...** to spread the rumour *o* (*EEUU*) rumor *o* word that ...
5 (*Pol*) (= *opinión*) voice; **la ~ del pueblo** the voice of the people; **tener ~ y voto** to have full voting rights; **miembro con ~ y voto** full member; **nosotros no tenemos ni ~ ni voto** we have no say whatsoever
6 *voces* (= *gritos*) shouting *sing*; **se oían voces a lo lejos** there was shouting in the distance; **a voces: discutir a voces** to argue noisily *o* loudly; **estuve llamando a voces** I called out *o* shouted; **su boda es un secreto a voces** their marriage is a well-known secret; **dar** *o* **pegar voces** to shout; ✦ MODISMO **dar cuatro voces a algn** to take sb to task
7 (*en el juego*) call
8 (*Ling*) **8.1** (= *vocablo*) word **8.2** [*del verbo*] voice ➤ **voz activa** active voice ➤ **voz pasiva** passive voice

vozarrón SM booming voice

vs. ABR (= *versus*) vs

vudú SM voodoo

vuela *etc ver* **volar**

vuelapluma: a ~ ADV quickly, without much thought

vuelco SM upset, spill; **dar un ~** [*coche*] to overturn; [*barco*] to capsize; **mi corazón dio un ~** my heart missed a beat

vuelo[1] *ver* **volar**

vuelo[2] SM **1** [*de ave, avión*] flight; **durante el ~** during the flight; **alzar** *o* **levantar el ~** (= *echar a volar*) to fly off; (= *marcharse*) to dash off; (= *independizarse*) to leave the nest; **remontar el ~** [*ave*] to soar (up) into the sky, take the sky; [*economía*] to take off; ✦ MODISMOS **captar** *o* **cazar** *o* **coger algo al ~** to be quick to understand sth; **cazarlas al ~** to be quick on the uptake*; **cortar los ~s a algn** to clip sb's wings; **no se oía ni el ~ de una mosca** you could have heard a pin drop; **a ~ de pájaro** (*LAm*): **hacer un cálculo a ~ de pájaro** to make a rough estimate; **leer algo a ~ de pájaro** to skim through sth; **de altos ~s** [*plan*] important ➤ **vuelo chárter** charter flight ➤ **vuelo de reconocimiento** reconnaissance flight ➤ **vuelo directo** direct flight, non-stop flight ➤ **vuelo en picado** dive ➤ **vuelo espacial** space flight ➤ **vuelo nacional** domestic flight ➤ **vuelo rasante** low-level flying ➤ **vuelo regular** scheduled flight ➤ **vuelo sin escalas** non-stop flight ➤ **vuelo sin motor** gliding; [*ejecutivo*] high-flying
2 [*de falda, capa*] **el ~ de la falda** the spread *o* swirl of the skirt; **falda de mucho ~** full *o* wide skirt
3 (*Chi*) (= *adorno*) flounce

vuelta SF **1** (= *giro*) **dar media ~** (*Aut*) to do a U-turn; (*Mil*) to do an about-turn (*esp Brit*) *o* an about-face (*EEUU*); (= *volver*) to turn round and go back ➤ **vuelta al ruedo** (*Taur*) circuit of the ring made by a triumphant bullfighter; **dar la ~ al ruedo** to go around the ring ➤ **vuelta atrás** backward step ➤ **vuelta de campana: el coche dio una ~ de campana en el aire** the car turned right over in mid-air ➤ **vuelta de tuerca** turn of the screw
◆ **dar la vuelta** (= *volverse*) to turn around; **dar la ~ a** [+ *llave, manivela*] to turn; [+ *página*] to turn (over); **dar la ~ al mundo** to go around the world
◆ **dar vueltas: el coche dio dos ~s y cayó boca abajo** the car turned over twice and landed upside down; **dar ~s sobre un eje** to turn on *o* spin around an axis; **he estado dando ~s en la cama toda la noche** I've been tossing and turning (in bed) all night; **el avión dio ~s y más ~s antes de aterrizar** the plane circled around and around before landing; **he tenido que dar muchas ~s para encontrarlo** I had to go all over the place to find it; **dar ~s alrededor de un planeta** to go *o* revolve around a planet
◆ **dar vueltas a algo: el cinturón le daba dos ~s a la cintura** the belt went twice around her waist; **le dimos tres ~s al parque corriendo** we ran three times around the park
◆ **dar vueltas a algn: me da ~s la cabeza** my head is spinning; **todo me daba ~s** everything was going *o* spinning round
◆ **darse la vuelta** (*de pie*) to turn round; (*tumbado*) to turn over
2 (= *otro lado*) [*de hoja*] back, other side; [*de tela*] wrong side; **lo escribió a la ~ del sobre** he wrote it on the back of the envelope; **dar la ~ a** ◆ **dar ~ a** (*CS*) [+ *disco*] to turn over; **dale la ~ al jersey** (= *ponlo del derecho*) turn the sweater the right way out; (= *ponlo del revés*) turn the sweater inside out; **dale la ~ al vaso** (= *ponlo boca arriba*) turn the glass the right way up; (= *ponlo boca abajo*) turn the glass upside down; **a la ~ de la esquina** around the corner
3 (= *regreso*) **3.1** (= *acción*) **¿para cuándo tenéis prevista la ~?** when do you expect to be back?; **este acuerdo supone una ~ a la normalidad** the agreement means that things should get back to normal; **"vuelta al colegio"** "back to school"; **a ~ de correo** by return (of post (*esp Brit*) *o* mail (*esp EEUU*)); **de ~** on the way back; **de ~, iremos a verlos** we'll go and see them on the way back; **de ~ al trabajo** back to work; **estar de ~** (*lit*) to be back; **el público ya está de ~ de todo** the public has seen it all before
3.2 (*en transportes*) **cerrar la ~** to specify the return date;

billete de ida y ~ return (*esp Brit*) *o* round-trip (*EEUU*) ticket; **el viaje de ~** the return journey
4 (= *paseo*) (*a pie*) stroll; (*en coche, bicicleta*) ride; **dar una ~: dimos una ~ por el parque** we went for a stroll in the park; **me voy a dar una ~** I'm going out for a while; **salieron a dar una ~ en la bici** they went out for a ride on their bikes; **date una ~ por esta zona** take a walk around here
5 (*en camino, ruta*) **una carretera con muchas ~s** a road with lots of bends *o* twists and turns in it; **el camino da muchas ~s** the road twists and turns; **por este camino se da mucha más ~** it's much further this way, this is a much longer way around
6 (*a un circuito, pista*) lap; (*Golf*) round; **di tres ~s a la pista** I did three laps of the track
7 (*Ciclismo*) tour ➤ **vuelta ciclista** cycle tour; **la ~ ciclista a España** the Tour of Spain
8 (= *ronda*) [*de elección, torneo, bebidas*] round
9 (*Esp*) (= *dinero suelto*) (*tb* **~s**) change; **quédese con la ~** keep the change
10 (= *cambio*) **las ~s de la vida** the ups and downs of life; **este acontecimiento dio la ~ a las negociaciones** this event changed the direction of the talks completely
11 (= *transcurso*) **a la ~ de tres años** after three years
12 (*Cos*) [*de puntos*] row; [*de pantalón*] turn-up (*Brit*), cuff (*EEUU*)
13 (*Perú, RPl*) (= *vez*) time; **hay tallarines otra ~** it's noodles again; **de ~** again, once more
14 ✦ MODISMOS **a ~s con algo: ¡ya estamos otra vez a ~s con la guerra!** not the war again!; **siempre están a ~s con lo mismo** they're always going on about the same thing; **buscar las ~s a algn** to try to catch sb out; **dar cien (mil) ~s a algn*: te da cien (mil) ~s** she can run rings around you, she's miles better than you; **dar la ~ a algn** (*CAm**) to con sb*; **dar ~s a algo: darle ~s a un asunto** to think a matter over; **no le des más ~s a lo que dijo** stop worrying about what he said; **no tiene ~ de hoja: esto es así y no tiene más ~ de hoja** that's how it is and that's all there is to it; **poner a algn de ~ y media*** (= *insultar*) to lay into sb; (= *reprender*) to give sb a dressing-down*; **sacar la ~ a algo/algn** (*Chi, Méx**) to avoid sth/sb; **dar la ~ a la tortilla** ✧ **dar ~ a la tortilla** (*CS*) to change things completely

vuelto 🅐 PP *de* **volver 🅑** SM (*LAm*) change

vuelva *etc ver* **volver**

vuestro/a (*Esp*) 🅐 ADJ POSES your (*familiar form of address*);

(*después de sustantivo*) of yours; **~ perro** your dog; **~s hijos** your children; **un amigo ~** a friend of yours
🅑 PRON POSES yours (*familiar form of address*); **es ~** it's yours; **éste es el ~** this one's yours; **la vuestra está en la cocina** yours is in the kitchen; **mis amigos y los ~s** my friends and yours; **lo ~: lo ~ también le pertenece a ella** what is yours also belongs to her; **he puesto lo ~ en la caja** I have put your things in the box; **¿ya se han enterado de lo ~?** do they know about you two yet?; **los ~s** (= *vuestra familia*) your folks*; (= *vuestro equipo*) your guys*, your side; **es (uno) de los ~s** he's one of you

---

Vuestro se traduce por **yours** y nunca va precedido de artículo, cuando se refiere a las posesiones de alguien: "Es (el) vuestro", *It's yours*. En cambio, se traduce por **of yours** cuando significa "uno de vuestros": "un compañero vuestro", *a colleague of yours*.

---

vulcanizadora SF (*Chi, Méx*) tyre *o* (*EEUU*) tire repair shop

vulcanizar /1f/ VT to vulcanize

Vulcano SM Vulcan

vulcanología SF vulcanology

vulgar ADJ **1** (= *no refinado*) [*lengua, gusto, vestido*] vulgar; [*modales, rasgos*] coarse **2** (= *común, corriente*) [*persona, físico*] ordinary, common; [*suceso, vida*] ordinary, everyday; **~ y corriente** ordinary **3** (= *no técnico*) common

vulgaridad SF **1** (= *cualidad*) vulgarity, coarseness **2** (= *frase*) vulgar *o* coarse expression

vulgarismo SM vulgarism

vulgarización SF popularization; **obra de ~** popular work

vulgarmente ADV commonly, popularly

Vulgata SF Vulgate

vulgo SM common people; (*pey*) lower orders *pl*, common herd

vulnerable ADJ vulnerable (**a** to)

vulneración SF infringement, contravention

vulnerar /1a/ VT **1** (= *perjudicar*) [+ *fama*] to damage, harm; [+ *costumbre, derechos*] to interfere with, affect seriously **2** (*Jur*) to violate, break

vulva SF vulva

Ww

W, w ['uβe 'doβle, (*LAm*) 'doβle be] SF (= *letra*) W, w

W ABR, **w** ABR (= *vatio*) W

walki-talki [walki'talki] SM walkie-talkie

Walkman® ['wolman] SM Walkman®

walquiria [bal'kirja] SF Valkyrie

wat SM, **watt** SM [bat, wat] (*pl* **wats**, **watts**) watt

wáter ['bater (*Esp*), '(g)water (*LAm*)] SM (= *taza*) toilet, lavatory; (= *lugar*) toilet (*Brit*), rest room (*EEUU*)

waterpolista [waterpo'lista] SMF water polo player

waterpolo [water'polo] SM water polo

web [web] SM o SF (= *página*) website; (= *red*) (World Wide) Web; ➤ **web site** web site

webcam [web'kam] SF webcam

webmaster ['webmaster, web'master] SMF webmaster

welter SM, **wélter** SM ['belter] welterweight

western ['western] SM western

whiskería SF, **wisquería** SF [wiske'ria, gwiske'ria] bar (*specializing in whisk(e)y*)

whisky SM, **whiskey** SM ['wiski, 'gwiski] whisky (*Brit*), whiskey (*EEUU*, *Irl*) ➤ **whisky de malta** malt whisky (*Brit*) o whiskey (*EEUU*, *Irl*)

windsurf ['winsurf] SM windsurfing; **hacer ~** to go windsurfing

windsurfista [winsur'fista] SMF windsurfer

wolfram ['bolfram] SM, **wolframio** [bol'framjo] SM wolfram

Xx

X, **x** ['ekis] SF (= *letra*) X, x

xantofila SF xanthophyll

xenófilo/a Ⓐ ADJ xenophilic Ⓑ SM/F xenophile

xenofobia SF xenophobia

xenófobo/a Ⓐ ADJ xenophobic Ⓑ SM/F xenophobe

xenón SM xenon

xerocopia SF photocopy

xerocopiar /1b/ VT to photocopy

xerófito ADJ xerophytic

xerografía SF xerography

xerografiar /1b/ VT to xerograph

xilófono SM xylophone

xilografía SF 1 (= *arte*) xylography 2 (= *impresión*) xylograph, wood engraving

Xto. ABR = **Cristo**

Xunta SF *Galician autonomous government*

Yy

Y, y [i'ɣrjeɣa] SF (= *letra*) Y, y

y CONJ **1** (*uso copulativo*) and; **fuimos a Málaga y a Granada** we went to Malaga and Granada; **una isla exótica y de gran belleza** an exotic, tremendously beautiful island; **treinta y uno** thirty-one
2 (*al comienzo de una pregunta*) **a mí no me apetece ir, ¿y a ti?** I don't feel like going, what about you?; **—id vosotros —¿y tú, qué vas a hacer?** "you go" — "but what are you going to do?"; **—he decidido dejar de estudiar —¿y eso?** "I've decided to stop studying" — "why's that then?"; **¿y qué?** (*con desinterés, desprecio*) so (what)?; (*con interés*) and?
3 (*uso adversativo*) **¡él viviendo en una mansión y su hermano en la calle!** he's living in a mansion while his brother is on the streets!; **¿dices que no quieres tarta y te la comes entera?** you say you don't want any cake and then you eat a whole one?
4 (*esp LAm*) (*en repetición*) **estuvo llora y llora** he was crying and crying
5 (*esp RPl*) (*en respuestas*) **—lo lamento mucho —y bueno, habrá que aceptarlo** "I'm very sorry" — "well, we just have to accept it"

ya Ⓐ ADV **1** (*con acción pasada*) already; **lo hemos visto ya** we've seen it already; **¿ya has terminado?** have you finished already?; **¿ya habías estado antes en Valencia?** had you been to Valencia before?; **ya me lo suponía** I thought as much; **ya en el siglo X** as early as the tenth century
2 (*con verbo en presente*) **2.1** (*con una acción esperada*) **ya es hora de irnos** it's time for us to go now; **ya está aquí** he's here already; **ya viene el autobús** here's the bus; **ya puedes irte** you can go now **2.2** (*expresando sorpresa*) **¿ya te vas?** are you leaving already? **2.3** (= *ahora*) now; **lo quiero ya** I want it (right) now; **¡ya voy!** coming!; **desde ya (mismo)** right now *o* away; **una estrategia que empiezo a poner en marcha desde ya mismo** a strategy which I will start to adopt as of now *o* as of this very moment; **ya mismo** (*esp LAm**) at once
3 (*con acción futura*) **ya te llegará el turno a ti** you'll get your turn; **ya lo arreglarán** it'll get fixed sometime; **ya veremos** we'll see (about that)
4 ya no no more, no longer; **ya no vive aquí** he doesn't live here any more, he no longer lives here; **ya no lo volverás a ver** you won't see it any more
5 (*expresando que se ha entendido o se recuerda algo*) **ya entiendo** I see; **¡ya lo sé!** I know!; **¡ah, ya!** oh yes, of course!
6 (*expresando acuerdo o incredulidad*) **ya, pero ...** yes, but ...; **¡ya, ya!** (*iró*) yes, yes!, oh, yes!, oh, sure!; **ya, y luego viste un burro volando ¿no?** (*iró*) sure, and pigs might fly!
7 (*con valor enfático*) **pues ya está lejos ¿eh?** it must be quite some way away!; **¿que no se ha casado? ya lo creo que sí** you say she hasn't got married? I think you'll find she has; **es más pobre que Haití, que ya es decir** it's poorer than Haiti, and that's saying something; **¡murió con 104 años, que ya es decir!** she was 104 when she died, which is no mean achievement!; **pues si él no viene, ya me dirás qué hacemos** you tell me what we'll do if he doesn't come; **¡ya está!** that's it; **¡ya me gustaría a mí poder viajar!** I wouldn't mind being able to travel either!; **¡ya era hora!** about time too!; **¡ya podían haber avisado de que venían!** they could have said they were coming!; **¡ya puedes ir preparando el dinero!** you'd better start getting the money ready!
Ⓑ CONJ **1** (*uso distributivo*) **ya ... ya ...** whether ... or ...; **ya por una razón, ya por otra** whether for one reason or another; **no ya ... sino ...** not only ... but ...
2 ya que (seeing) as, since; **ya que no viene, iremos nosotros** (seeing) as *o* since she's not coming, we'll go

yacaré SM (*LAm*) alligator

yacente ADJ reclining, recumbent

yacer /2x/ VI to lie; **aquí yace Pedro Núñez** here lies Pedro Núñez

yacimiento SM (*Geol*) bed, deposit; (*arqueológico*) site
➤ **yacimiento petrolífero** oilfield

yagua SF (*Ven*) royal palm

yagual SM (*CAm, Méx*) padded ring (*for carrying loads on the head*)

yaguareté SM (*And, RPl*) jaguar

yak [jak] SM (*pl ~s*) yak

Yakarta SF Jakarta

yámbico ADJ iambic

yanacón/ona SM/F (*And Hist*) (= *aparcero*) Indian tenant farmer, Indian sharecropper; (= *criado*) Indian servant

yanqui* Ⓐ ADJ Yankee* Ⓑ SMF Yank*, Yankee*

yanquilandia SF (*pey*) the USA

yantar†† /1a/ VI to eat

yapa* SF (*CS, Perú*) extra bit; **dar algo de ~** (*lit*) to throw in a bit *o* a little extra for free; (*fig*) to add sth for good measure

yarará SF (*And, CS*) rattlesnake

yarda SF yard

yate SM yacht

yaya SF (*Chi, Perú*) pain; **hacerse ~** to get hurt; **tengo una ~ en la rodilla** my knee hurts

yayo/a* SM/F grandpa/grandma*

yazca *etc ver* **yacer**

yedra SF ivy

yegua SF **1** (= *animal*) mare **2** (*RPl**) (*usado como insulto*) old bag* **3** (*Chi**) (= *puta*) whore (*pey*); (= *torpe*) idiot

yeísmo SM *pronunciation of Spanish "ll" as "y"*

yelmo SM helmet

yema SF **1** [*del huevo*] yolk **2** (*Bot*) leaf bud **3** (*Anat*) (*tb ~ del dedo*) fingertip **4** (*Culin*) sweet made with egg yolk and sugar

Yemen SM ~ Yemen

yemení ADJ, SMF, **yemenita** ADJ, SMF Yemeni

yen SM (*pl ~s o ~es*) yen

yendo *ver* **ir**

yerba SF **1** = **hierba 2** ~ **mate** maté **3** (*) (= *marihuana*) grass**

yerbatero/a (*SAm*) Ⓐ ADJ maté *antes de s* Ⓑ SM/F (= *herbolario*) herbalist; (= *curandero*) quack doctor

yerga *etc ver* **erguir**

yermar /1a/ VT to lay waste

yermo ADJ (= *inhabitado*) uninhabited; (= *estéril*) barren

yerno SM son-in-law

yerre *etc ver* **errar**

yerro SM error, mistake

yerto ADJ stiff, rigid

yesca SF (= *materia inflamable*) tinder; (*CS*) (= *piedra*) flint

yesería SF plastering, plasterwork

yeso SM **1** (*Arquit*) plaster **2** (*Med*) plaster **3** (*Geol*) gypsum

yesquero SM (*Col, RPl*) cigarette lighter

yeta* SF (*RPl*) bad luck

yeti SM yeti

yetudo* ADJ (*RPl*) jinxed

ye-yé†* ADJ groovy*, trendy; **música ~** sixties pop music

yídish SM, **yíddish** SM ['jidiʃ] Yiddish

yihad [ji'ad] SM jihad

yira** SF (*RPl*) hooker*

yirar** /1a/ VI (*RPl*) to be on the game*

yo Ⓐ PRON PERS **1** (*sujeto*) I; **Carlos y yo no fuimos** Carlos and I didn't go; **¡y tú que confiaba en ti!** and to think that I trusted you!; **yo que tú** if I were you; **soy yo** it's me; **yo no** not me; **lo hice yo misma** I did it myself
2 (*en comparaciones, después de prep*) me; **es más delgada que yo** she is thinner than me *o* than I am; **que esto quede entre tú y yo** this is between you and me; **nos lo**

comeremos entre tú y yo we'll eat it between us Ⓑ SM (*Psic*) **el yo** the self, the ego

yodado ADJ iodized, with added iodine

yodo SM iodine

yoga SM yoga

yogui SM yogi

yogur SM yogurt; **mal ~** (*euf*) = **mala leche ➤ yogur descremado, yogur desnatado** low-fat yogurt

yogurtera SF yogurt-maker

yonque* SM (*Méx*) scrap metal; **estar para el ~** to be ready for the scrap heap

yonqui* SMF junkie*

yoyó SM (*pl* **~s**), **yo-yo** SM (*pl* **yo-yos**) yo-yo

yuca SF (*ornamental*) yucca; (*comestible*) manioc root, cassava

yudo SM judo

yugo SM yoke

Yugoslavia SF, **Yugoeslavia** SF (*Hist*) Yugoslavia

yugoslavo/a, yugoeslavo/a (*Hist*) Ⓐ ADJ Yugoslavian Ⓑ SM/F Yugoslav

yugular ADJ jugular; ✦ MODISMO **lanzarse a la ~** to go for the jugular

yuju EXCL yipee!

yungas SFPL (*Bol, Perú*) hot tropical valleys

yunque SM anvil

yunta SF **1** [*de bueyes*] yoke, team (of oxen) **2** (*Chi*) [*de personas*] pair; **hacer ~ con algn** to join forces with sb

yuppie ['jupi] ADJ, SMF yuppie

yute SM jute

yuxtaponer /2q/ VT to juxtapose

yuxtaposición SF juxtaposition

yuyo SM **1** (*RPl*) (*silvestre*) weed **2** (*Perú, RPl*) (*medicinal*) herb

Zz

Z, z ['θeta, (*esp LAm*) 'seta] SF (= *letra*) Z, z

zacate SM (*CAm, Méx*) **1** (= *hierba*) grass; (= *heno*) hay, fodder; (= *paja*) straw, thatch **2** (= *estropajo*) scouring pad, scourer

zafacoca* SF (*LAm*) (= *pelea*) brawl; (*Chi*) (= *alboroto*) commotion

zafado/a Ⓐ ADJ **1** (*LAm*) (= *loco*) mad, crazy **2** (*SAm*) (= *descarado*) cheeky (*Brit**), cute (*EEUU**) Ⓑ SM/F **1** (*LAm*) (= *loco*) crazy, daft (*Brit**) **2** (*SAm*) (= *descarado*) shameless, brazen

zafadura SF (*LAm*) dislocation

zafar /1a/ Ⓐ VT (*Carib*) to untie Ⓑ **zafarse** VPR **1** (= *escaparse*) to escape, run away; (= *soltarse*) to break loose **2** **~se de** to get out of, wriggle out of **3** (*LAm*) (= *dislocarse*) **~se un brazo** to dislocate one's arm

zafarrancho SM (*Náut*) clearing for action ➤ **zafarrancho de combate** call to action stations

zafio ADJ coarse, uncouth

zafiro SM sapphire

zafra SF **1** (*LAm*) (= *cosecha*) sugar harvest **2** (*Arg*) (= *esquila*) (sheep-)shearing

zaga SF **a la ~** behind, in the rear; **Juan ha quedado muy a la ~ de Pedro** Juan is well behind Pedro; **Ana no le va a la ~ a Rosa** Ana is every bit as good as Rosa

zagal(a) SM/F (= *joven*) boy/girl, lad/lass; (= *pastor*) shepherd/shepherdess

zaguán SM hallway, entrance hall

zaguero/a SM/F (*Ftbl*) defender; (*Rugby*) full back

zaherir /3i/ VT to wound, hurt

zahorí SMF dowser

zaino ADJ [*caballo*] chestnut; [*vaca*] black

Zaire SM Zaire

zaireño/a ADJ, SM/F Zairean

zalamería SF (*tb* ~**s**) flattery; **no me vengas con ~s** stop trying to butter me up*

zalamero/a Ⓐ ADJ flattering Ⓑ SM/F flatterer

zamarra SF (= *piel*) sheepskin; (= *chaqueta*) sheepskin jacket

zamarro SM **1** (= *piel*) sheepskin; (= *chaqueta*) sheepskin jacket **2** **zamarros** (*Col*) (= *pantalones*) chaps

zamba SF *Argentinian handkerchief dance*; *ver tb* **zambo**

Zambia SF Zambia

zambo/a Ⓐ ADJ (*) knock-kneed Ⓑ SM/F (*LAm*) person of mixed race (*esp of black and Indian parentage*); *ver tb* **zamba**

zambomba Ⓐ SF *kind of rustic drum* Ⓑ EXCL (*) wow!

zambullida SF dive, plunge

zambullirse /3h/ VPR (*en el agua*) to dive (**en** into); (*debajo del agua*) to duck (**en** under)

zamorano ADJ of/from Zamora

zampar* /1a/ Ⓐ VT **1** (*LAm*) (= *poner*) **lo zampó en el suelo** he flung it onto the floor **2** (*LAm*) (= *pegar*) **~ una torta a algn** to wallop sb* Ⓑ VI (*Esp*) to gobble Ⓒ **zamparse** VPR **1** (*LAm*) = *lanzarse*) to jump, leap **2** (= *comerse*) **~se algo** to wolf sth down

zamuro SM (*Ven*) turkey vulture, turkey buzzard (*EEUU*)

zanahoria Ⓐ SF carrot Ⓑ SMF (*) **1** (*RPl*) (= *imbécil*) idiot, nitwit* **2** (*Ven*) (= *anticuado*) old fogey*

zanahorio* ADJ (*Col*) (= *mojigato*) strait-laced; (= *anticuado*) unhip*

zanca SF shank

zancada SF stride; **alejarse a grandes ~s** to stride away

zancadilla SF (*para derribar a algn*) trip; (= *trampa*) trick; **poner la ~ a algn** (*lit*) to trip sb up; (*fig*) to pull the rug from under sb, put the skids under sb (*Brit**)

zancajo SM heel

zanco SM stilt

zancón ADJ (*Méx, Ven*) [*vestido*] too short

zancudo Ⓐ ADJ long-legged Ⓑ SM (*LAm*) mosquito

zanfona SF hurdy-gurdy

zanganear* /1a/ VI to idle, loaf about

zángano/a Ⓐ SM/F (*) idler, slacker Ⓑ SM (= *insecto*) drone

zanja SF (= *fosa*) ditch; (= *hoyo*) pit

zanjar /1a/ VT [+ *conflicto*] to resolve, clear up; [+ *discusión*] to settle

zanjón SM (*Chi*) gully, ravine

Zanzíbar SM Zanzibar

zapa SF **1** (= *pala*) spade **2** (*Mil*) sap, trench

zapador SM sapper

zapallito SM (*CS*) (*tb* ~ **italiano**) courgette (*Brit*), zucchini (*EEUU*)

zapallo SM (*CS, Perú, Ven*) gourd, pumpkin

zapapico SM pick, pickaxe, pickax (*EEUU*)

zapata SF shoe ➤ **zapata de freno(s)** brake shoe

zapatazo SM (= *golpe*) blow with a shoe; (= *caída, ruido*) thud

zapateado SM **1** (= *claqué*) tap dance **2** (= *baile típico español*) zapateado

zapatear /1a/ VI (= *dar golpecitos*) to tap one's feet; (= *bailar*) to tap-dance

zapateo SM tapping ➤ **zapateo americano** (*RPl*) tap dancing

zapatería SF (= *tienda*) shoe shop (*esp Brit*), shoe store (*EEUU*); (= *fábrica*) shoe factory, footwear factory

zapatero/a Ⓐ ADJ [*industria*] shoemaking *antes de s* Ⓑ SM/F shoemaker ➤ **zapatero remendón** cobbler Ⓒ SM (= *mueble*) shoe rack

zapatilla SF **1** (*para casa*) slipper; (*Dep*) training shoe, trainer (*Brit*), sneaker (*esp EEUU*) ➤ **zapatillas de ballet** ballet shoes ➤ **zapatillas de deporte** training shoes, trainers (*Brit*), sneakers (*EEUU*) ➤ **zapatillas de tenis** tennis shoes **2** (*Méx*) [*de mujer*] (lady's/woman's) shoe **3** (*Mec*) washer

zapatista ADJ, SMF Zapatista

zapato SM shoe; ✦ MODISMO **saber dónde aprieta el ~** to know the score* ➤ **zapatos de cordones** lace-up shoes ➤ **zapatos de golf** golf shoes ➤ **zapatos de goma** (*Ven*) tennis shoes ➤ **zapatos de tacón** high-heeled shoes ➤ **zapatos de tacón de aguja** stilettos

zapatón SM (*Col*) (= *chanclo*) overshoe, galosh; (*Chi*) (= *zapato con cordones*) lace-up shoe

zape EXCL shoo!

zapear /1a/ Ⓐ VI (*TV*) to channel-hop Ⓑ VT (*Perú*) (= *espiar*) to spy on, watch

zapeo SM channel-hopping

zaperoco* SM (*Carib*) muddle, mess

zapote SM (*CAm, Méx*) (= *planta*) sapodilla, sapota; (= *fruta*) sapodilla plum, sapota

zapoteca ADJ, SMF Zapotec

zapping ['θapin] SM channel-hopping; **hacer ~** to channel-hop

zar SM tsar, czar (*esp EEUU*)

zarabanda SF **1** (*Hist*) sarabande **2** (= *movimiento*) rush, whirl **3** (*Méx*) (= *paliza*) beating

zaragozano ADJ of/from Saragossa

zarandajas* SFPL trifles

zarandear /1a/ Ⓐ VT (= *sacudir*) to shake; (= *empujar*) to jostle, push around Ⓑ **zarandearse** VPR to shake

zarandeo SM shaking

zarape SM (*CAm, Méx*) brightly-coloured striped blanket

zarcillo SM (*Ven*) earring

zarina SF czarina, tsarina

zarista ADJ, SMF czarist, tsarist

zarpa SF [*de león, tigre*] paw; (*) [*de persona*] paw, mitt; **echar la ~ a algo** to get one's hands on sth

zarpar /1a/ VI to weigh anchor, set sail

zarpazo SM **1** [*de animal*] **el gato me dio un ~** the cat scratched me; **el oso me dio un ~** the bear hit me with its paw **2** (= *desgracia*) blow

zarrapastroso ADJ [*persona*] scruffy; [*ropa*] shabby

zarza SF bramble, blackberry (bush)

zarzal SM bramble patch

zarzamora SF blackberry

zarzaparrilla SF sarsaparilla

zarzo SM (*Col*) attic; ✦ MODISMO **ser como caído del ~** to be naive

zarzuela 1 SF *Spanish light opera*
2 ➤ **zarzuela de mariscos** (*Esp*) seafood casserole
3 (**Palacio de**) **la Zarzuela** *royal palace in Madrid*

ZARZUELA

Zarzuelas, named after the Zarzuela Palace where they were first performed in the 17th century for the entertainment of Philip IV, are a kind of Spanish comic folk opera. They are usually in three acts, and their chief ingredients include stock characters, traditional scenes and a mixture of dialogue, music and traditional song. After a decline in popularity in the 18th century, interest in this very Spanish genre was rekindled as part of the 19th century revival of Spanish nationalism.

---

zas EXCL bang!, crash!

zascandil* SM (*Esp*) ne'er-do-well

zascandilear /1a/ VI (*Esp*) to buzz around uselessly, fuss around

zen ADJ INV, SM Zen

zeta SF the (name of the) letter z

zigoto SM zygote

zigzag SM (*pl* ~**ues** *o* ~**s**) zigzag

zigzaguear /1a/ VI to zigzag

Zimbabue SM, **Zimbabwe** SM Zimbabwe

zinc SM zinc

zíngaro/a ADJ, SM/F = **cíngaro**

zíper SM (*CAm, Méx, Ven*) zip (*Brit*), zipper (*EEUU*)

zipizape* SM (*Esp*) set-to*, rumpus*

zócalo SM **1** (*Arquit*) (= *pedestal*) plinth, base **2** [*de pared*] skirting board (*Brit*), baseboard (*EEUU*) **3** (*Méx*) (= *plaza*) main square

zoco¹ ADJ (*Col*) left-handed

zoco² SM (*Arab*) market, souk

zodiaco SM, **zodíaco** SM zodiac

zombi SMF zombie

zona SF **1** (*en país, región*) area; **las ~s más ricas/remotas/deprimidas del país** the richest/remotest/most depressed areas *o* parts of the country; **comimos en uno de los restaurantes típicos de la ~** we ate in a typical local restaurant; **~ montañosa** *o* **de montaña** mountainous area, mountainous region; **~s rurales** rural areas ➤ **zona catastrófica** disaster area ➤ **zona cero** Ground Zero ➤ **zona de combate** combat zone ➤ **zona de exclusión (aérea)** (air) exclusion zone ➤ **zona de guerra** war zone ➤ **zona de influencia** area of influence ➤ **zona de libre comercio** free-trade zone, free-trade area ➤ **zona euro** Eurozone ➤ **zona franca** duty-free zone ➤ **zona fronteriza** (*gen*) border area; (*Mil*) border zone ➤ **zona húmeda** wetland ➤ **zona militar** military zone, military area ➤ **zona roja** (*Esp Hist*) Republican territory
2 (*en ciudad*) area; **¿dónde está la ~ de copas?** where do people go out to drink? ➤ **zona azul** (*Esp Aut*) restricted parking zone ➤ **zona centro** centre, center (*EEUU*); **los aparcamientos de la ~ centro** city-centre car parks (*Brit*), downtown parking lots (*EEUU*) ➤ **zona comercial** (*para negocios en general*) commercial district; (*sólo de tiendas*) shopping area ➤ **zona peatonal** pedestrian precinct ➤ **zona residencial** residential area ➤ **zona roja** (*LAm*) red-light district ➤ **zona rosa** (*Méx*) *partly pedestrianized zone, so called because of its pink paving stones* ➤ **zona verde** green space
3 (*en edificio, recinto*) area; **~ de no fumadores** no smoking area ➤ **zona de castigo** (*Dep*) sin bin ➤ **zona de penumbra** (*lit*) shaded area; (*fig*) area of secrecy ➤ **zona oscura: las ~s oscuras de la personalidad** the hidden areas of the personality; **las ~s oscuras de la política** the shady *o* murky areas of politics ➤ **zona técnica** technical area
4 (*Geog*) zone ➤ **zona glacial** glacial zone ➤ **zona templada** temperate zone ➤ **zona tórrida** torrid zone
5 (*Anat, Med*) area; **sentí un dolor por la ~ del hombro** I felt a pain around my shoulder ➤ **zona erógena** erogenous zone ➤ **zona lumbar** lumbar region
6 (*Baloncesto*) free-zone lane

zoncear /1a/ VI (*LAm*) to behave stupidly

zoncera SF **1** (*LAm*) (= *cualidad*) silliness, stupidity **2** (*RPI*) (= *insignificancia*) mere trifle; **costar una ~** to cost next to nothing; **comer una ~** to have a bite to eat

zonzo/a (*LAm*) Ⓐ ADJ silly, stupid Ⓑ SM/F idiot

zoo SM zoo

zoofilia SF bestiality

zoología SF zoology

zoológico Ⓐ ADJ zoological Ⓑ SM zoo

zoólogo/a SM/F zoologist

zoom [θum] SM zoom lens

zopenco/a Ⓐ ADJ dull, stupid Ⓑ SM/F blockhead*

zopilote SM (*CAm, Méx*) vulture

zoquete Ⓐ ADJ thick (*Brit**), dumb (*esp EEUU**) Ⓑ SMF blockhead*

zorongo SM (*Mús*) *popular song and dance of Andalusia*

zorra Ⓐ SF **1** (= *animal*) vixen **2** (**) (= *prostituta*) slut** Ⓑ ADJ (*Esp***) bloody (*Brit***), frigging***; **no tengo ni ~ idea** I haven't a bloody clue (*Brit***), I don't have a frigging*** *o* damn** clue (*esp EEUU*); *ver tb* **zorro**

zorrería SF foxiness, craftiness, sly trick

zorrillo SM (*LAm*), **zorrino** SM (*CS*) skunk

zorro Ⓐ ADJ foxy, crafty Ⓑ SM **1** (= *animal*) fox ➤ **zorro gris** grey fox **2** (= *persona*) crafty old fox; ✦ MODISMO **estar hecho unos ~s*** [*habitación*] to be in an awful state; [*persona*] to be done in; *ver tb* **zorra**

zorzal SM thrush

zote* Ⓐ ADJ dim, stupid Ⓑ SMF dimwit*

zozobra SF worry, anxiety

zozobrar /1a/ VI **1** [*barco*] (= *hundirse*) to founder, sink; (= *volcar*) to capsize, overturn **2** (= *fracasar*) [*plan*] to fail, founder; [*negocio*] to be ruined

zueco SM clog, wooden shoe

zulo SM (*Esp*) cache

zulú ADJ, SMF Zulu

zumba SF (*LAm**) beating

zumbado* ADJ (*Esp*) **estar ~** to be crazy

zumbador SM buzzer

zumbar /1a/ Ⓐ VI **1** (= *sonar*) [*insecto*] to buzz; [*máquina*] to hum, whirr; **me zumban los oídos** my ears are ringing, I have a buzzing in my ears; ✦ MODISMO **le estarán zumbando los oídos** his ears must be burning
2 ✦ MODISMO **salir zumbando*** to zoom off; **tengo que salir zumbando para no perder el tren** I must rush so I don't miss the train Ⓑ VT **1** (= *burlar*) to tease **2** (= *golpear*) to beat, hit **3** (= *tirar*) to chuck*

zumbido SM [*de insecto*] buzz(ing); [*de máquina*] hum(ming), whirr(ing) ➤ **zumbido de oídos** buzzing in the ears, ringing in the ears

zumbón ADJ [*persona*] waggish, funny; [*tono*] teasing

zumo SM juice ➤ **zumo de naranja** orange juice

zurcir /3b/ VT to darn, mend; **¡que te zurzan!*** get lost!*

zurdo/a Ⓐ ADJ [*mano*] left; [*persona*] left-handed Ⓑ SM/F (*gen*) left-handed person; (*Tenis*) left-hander

zurear /1a/ VI to coo

zurito SM small glass (*of beer*)

zurra* SF hiding*

zurrapas SFPL dregs

zurrar* /1a/ VT to wallop*, give a hiding (to)*

zurriagazo* SM lash, stroke

zurrón SM pouch, bag

zurullo* SM turd***

zutano/a SM/F (Mr *etc*) So-and-so; **si se casa fulano con zutana** if Mr X marries Miss Y

SPANISH IN ACTION

CONTENTS

SPANISH IN ACTION

▼ LIKES, DISLIKES AND PREFERENCES

► Asking people what they like

¿**Te gusta** el yogur de fresa?	do you like …?
¿**Cuál de** las tres camisas **te gusta más**?	which of … do you like best?
¿**Te gustaría** viajar a otra época?	would you like to …?
De las dos posibilidades, ¿**cuál prefiere**?	which do you prefer?
¿**Prefieres** salir ahora **o** después de comer?	would you prefer … or …?

► Saying what you like

Me ha gustado mucho el regalo que me has enviado	I was delighted with
A mí los turistas que vienen por aquí **me caen (muy) bien**	I (really) like
La verdad es que el chocolate **me vuelve loco** or **me chifla**	I'm mad or nuts about
Me encanta el mar	I love
Soy muy aficionado a la danza contemporánea	I'm very keen on

► Saying what you dislike

No me gusta comer fuera de casa	I don't like
No me gusta nada que me mientan	I really dislike
Me molesta que me miren	it annoys me that
Mi vecina **me cae muy mal** or **no me cae nada bien**	I don't like … at all
Le tengo manía a ese chico	I can't stand
No soporto or **No aguanto que** me hagan esperar	I can't stand or I can´t bear
Lo que más me fastidia es que suban tanto el volumen	what really annoys me is when
Detesto cualquier tipo de violencia	I hate
Me horrorizan las corridas de toros	I really hate

► Saying what you prefer

Prefiero la lectura **a** la televisión	I prefer … to
Prefiero que vengas ahora **a que** lo hagas más tarde	I'd rather you … than
Es mejor or **preferible** hablar en el idioma del cliente	it's better to
Nos vendría mejor or **Nos convendría más** el lunes	… would suit us better

► Expressing indifference

Me da igual or **Me da lo mismo** vivir aquí **que** allí	it's all the same to me whether … or
Me es (completamente) indiferente que venga **o** no	it makes (absolutely) no difference to me whether … or
¿Vendrás también mañana? – **Como quieras**	if you like
Si no lo veo hoy **no importa** or **no pasa nada**	it doesn't matter (in the slightest) if

▼ OPINIONS

► Asking for someone's opinion

¿**Qué piensas de** su actitud?	what do you think of …?
¿**Qué te parece** mi trabajo?	what do you think of …?
¿**Crees que** le gustará el regalo?	do you think that …?
¿**Piensas que** se puede estudiar en estas condiciones?	do you think that …?
¿**Qué opinas de** la exportación de animales vivos?	what do you think of …?
En tu opinión, ¿cuáles son los derechos de los animales?	in your opinion

► Expressing your opinion

Creo or **Pienso** or **Me parece que** le va a encantar tu visita	I think that
En mi opinión or **A mi juicio**, fue un error no haberlo contratado antes	in my opinion or to my mind

A mis padres, **imagino que** *or* **supongo que** también les gustará	*I imagine* or *suppose that*
Yo considero que eso no es perjudicial para el sistema	*it is my belief that*
Lo que es yo, no lo veo necesario	*personally*
Estoy totalmente seguro de que nos lo van a devolver	*I'm quite sure that*
Estoy convencido de que no es culpa suya	*I'm convinced that*
Si quieres que te diga la verdad, no me gusta nada	*to tell you the truth*
Tengo la impresión de que algo marcha mal	*I have the impression that*
Me da que no va a venir	*I suspect that*
Me da la sensación de que no va a dar resultado	*I have a (funny) feeling that*

► Replying without giving an opinion

No sé qué decirte	*I don't know what to say*
No sabría decir	*I couldn't say*
Depende	*it depends*
No puedo opinar sobre ese tema	*I can't express an opinion on*

▼ AGREEMENT

► Agreeing with a statement

¡Claro que sí! *or* **¡Naturalmente!** ¡Ya lo creo que iré!	*of course*
¡Exacto! Ahí está la raíz del problema	*exactly*
Tienes (toda la) razón	*You're (quite) right*
Yo pienso lo mismo (que tú) *or* **Estoy de acuerdo (contigo)**	*I agree (with you)*
Por supuesto que no hay derecho a que nos traten así	*of course*
En eso tienes *or* **te doy toda la razón**, son muy jóvenes	*you are quite right there*
Es cierto que es un tema que nunca se ha tomado en serio	*it is true that*
Admito que estaba equivocado	*I admit that*
Los dos **somos del mismo parecer** *or* **de la misma opinión**	*are of the same opinion*
En eso coincido totalmente contigo	*I entirely agree with you there*

► Agreeing to a proposal

¡Me apunto!	*count me in!*
¡Vale! *or* **¡Perfecto!** Nos vemos a las cuatro	*fine*
De acuerdo, publicaremos el artículo en el próximo número	*agreed*
Me parece una idea estupenda	*I think it's a great idea*
Estamos conformes con el precio que piden	*we agree to*
Estamos dispuestos a aceptar sus condiciones	*we are willing to*

► Agreeing to a request

¿Que si puedo ayudaros? **¡Por supuesto que sí!**	*of course I will*
¡No faltaría más! *or* **¡Claro!**, por supuesto que lo haré	*of course*
Estaré encantado de participar en ese intercambio	*I'll be delighted to*
No tengo ningún inconveniente en que vengan ellos	*I have no objection to*

▼ DISAGREEMENT

► Disagreeing with what someone has said

¡Qué va! *or* **¡Pero qué dices, hombre!**, 1000 por lo menos	*no way!* or *you must be joking!*
¡No digas tonterías!	*don't talk rubbish!*
Yo no lo veo así	*that's not how I see it*
En eso te equivocas *or* **estás equivocado**	*you're wrong there*
No estoy de acuerdo contigo en ese punto	*I disagree with you on*
No estamos de acuerdo con lo que dices	*we don't agree with*
Yo opino de manera distinta	*I see it differently*
No comparto tu opinión al respecto	*I do not share your view*

► Disagreeing with what someone proposes

¡De ninguna manera!	*no way!*
Me parece una idea descabellada mudarse ahora	*I think it would be madness to*
Me niego a votar sin estar debidamente informado	*I refuse to*
No lo veo muy claro	*I'm not sure*
No me hace mucha gracia levantarme tan temprano	*I'm not keen on (the idea of)*
Me temo que no me será posible aceptar tu oferta	*I'm afraid I shall not be able to*

► Refusing a request

¡Ni hablar!	*no chance!*
¡Ni pensarlo!	*it's out of the question!*
¡Ni lo sueñes!	*not on your life!*
No puede ser. Se ha acabado el plazo de demanda	*it's impossible*
Me gustaría, pero no voy a poder	*I'd like to, but I can't*

▼ APPROVAL

Y si quieren ir, **pues muy bien** *or* **estupendo, que** vayan	*fine or great*
¡Así se hace!	*well done!*
Me parece perfecto. Podemos empezar cuando quieras	*that seems fine to me*
¡Buena idea! Yo también me voy a bañar	*good idea!*
Has hecho bien en decírmelo	*you were right to*
Me parece muy bien que lo veas positivamente	*I think it's great that*
Me alegro mucho de que des un paso tan importante	*I'm so pleased that*
Estoy muy contento con el rendimiento de los jugadores	*I'm very pleased with*
Me parece una idea excelente que aceptes ese trabajo	*I think it's excellent that*
Será un placer colaborar con ustedes	*I shall be delighted to*

▼ DISAPPROVAL

Pero **¿qué dices?** ¿que nadie vino al concierto?	*what are you on about?*
¡Menuda ocurrencia!	*what a ridiculous idea!*
Es una lástima que ese niño sea tan maleducado	*it's a shame that*
Me parece fatal que la gente fume	*I think it's awful that*
Lo que me parece mal es que no me hayas dicho nada	*what I think is wrong is that*
No deberías haber hablado así	*you should not have*
Me ha decepcionado lo que ha dicho	*I'm disappointed by*
No estoy dispuesto a tolerar tales afirmaciones	*I'm not prepared to put up with*
No estamos conformes con tu versión de los hechos	*we are not happy with*

▼ APOLOGIES

► Apologizing

¡Perdón!	*sorry!*
Perdona por lo que dije	*I'm sorry about*
Perdona que no avisara con tiempo suficiente	*I'm sorry*
Pido perdón a la familia **por** lo que hicimos	*I ask … to forgive*
Lo lamento, a veces me cuesta reprimirme	*I'm very sorry*
Lamentamos profundamente que haya ocurrido esto	*we are very sorry that*
Perdonen las molestias	*sorry for any inconvenience*
Disculpen si les he causado alguna molestia	*I apologize if*

► Apologizing for being unable to do something

Lo siento, pero no consigo acordarme	*I'm sorry*
Siento mucho no haber podido conseguir la información	*I'm so sorry that I wasn't able to*
Siento comunicarle que me es totalmente imposible	*I regret to have to tell you that*
Desgraciadamente *or* **Lamentablemente, nos es imposible** aceptarlo	*unfortunately, we are unable to*

► Admitting responsibility

Es culpa mía or **Yo tengo la culpa**	*it's my fault*
Reconozco or **Admito que estaba equivocado**	*I admit (that) I was wrong*
Me responsabilizo plenamente de lo ocurrido	*I take full responsibility for*

► Disclaiming responsibility

De verdad que **no lo hice a posta**	*I didn't do it on purpose*
Ha sido sin querer	*it was an accident*
Lo dijeron sin mala intención	*they didn't mean any harm*
Lo hice sin darme cuenta	*I did it without thinking*
No era mi intención ofenderte, hablaba en broma	*I didn't mean to offend you*
Espero que comprendas lo difícil de nuestra situación	*I hope you will understand*

► Replying to an apology

No pasa nada or **No te preocupes**, ya compraré otro	*don't worry about it*
No importa, ya lo sabíamos	*it doesn't matter*
No es ninguna molestia	*it's no trouble*
El retraso **no tiene (ninguna) importancia**	*doesn't matter (at all)*

▼ EXPLANATIONS

Tuvimos que marcharnos **porque** se puso a llover	*because*
Como tardabas en llegar, decidimos irnos	*as*
Las plantas se han marchitado **por** exceso de riego	*due to*
Tiene ahorros **gracias a** una herencia que recibió	*thanks to*
Con la nevada que ha caído no ha venido el cartero	*what with*
Es que no consigo acordarme	*it's just that*
Ha tenido muy mala suerte. **Por eso** le tengo tanta lástima	*that's why*
En vista de que or **Dado que** no llegaban, decidimos entrar	*seeing that* or *given that*
Debido al mal tiempo, decidieron cancelar la regata	*owing to*
El problema es grave, **ya que** han disminuido las ventas	*for*
Recomiendo ir pronto, **puesto que** or **pues** habrá mucha gente	*since*
Se cansa mucho **a causa de** su enfermedad	*because of*
El hotel estaba lleno. **Por ese motivo** hubo que cambiar la fecha	*for that reason*
Dimitió **por razones de** salud	*for … reasons*
No había autobuses **a** or **como consecuencia de** la huelga	*as a result of*
Los problemas de la zona **se deben a** una mala gestión	*are due to*
El valor de su poesía **radica en** la fuerza de las metáforas	*lies in*
La película me aburrió **tanto** or **de tal manera que** me dormí	*so much that*
No quería ir sin comer nada, **así que** piqué unas aceitunas	*so*
Llamé antes de salir, **de modo que** sabían que íbamos para allá	*so that*

▼ COMPARISONS

► Contrasting facts

La gente cena muy tarde, **comparado con** el Reino Unido	*compared with*
En comparación con mi país, el clima **no es tan** lluvioso aquí	*in comparison with … is not so*
A mí me gusta el cine, **mientras que** ella prefiere el teatro	*while*

► Comparing similar things or facts

Su programa político **es igual que** el de la oposición	*is the same as*
Recibimos **casi tantos** turistas **como** en Grecia	*almost as many … as*
El paisaje es **tan** bello **como** lo describió el poeta	*as … as*
Ambos coches valen **exactamente lo mismo**	*exactly the same*
Ha vuelto a suceder **lo mismo que** hace unos años	*the same thing as*
Los dos hermanos **se parecen mucho** físicamente	*are very alike*
Tu hijo **se parece mucho a** ti	*is very like*

El clima de aquí **es muy parecido a** or **similar al** de mi país — *is very similar to*

> ► Comparing dissimilar things or facts

Los pros **son (muchos) más que** los contras — *there are (far) more ... than*
Aquí se la aprecia **(muchísimo) menos que** en el extranjero — *(far) less than*
Es **aún más** nacionalista que su hermano — *even more ... than*
Es **más** inteligente **de lo que** parece — *more ... than*
Este vino **es muy superior al** otro — *is vastly superior to*
Un coche nuevo contamina **bastante menos que** uno viejo — *considerably less than*
No es lo mismo ponerse a dieta **que** volverse anoréxico — *is not the same as*
Esa canción ya **no** suena **tanto como** el año pasado — *not ... as much as*
Este premio **no es tan** importante **como** el anterior — *is not as ... as*
No se parece en nada a su padre — *he's not at all like*
Un modelo **se diferencia** or **se distingue del** otro **por** el color — *the difference between ... and ... is*

La realidad **es muy diferente** or **distinta de** lo que pensábamos — *is very different from*
Me encuentro **muchísimo mejor que** antes — *much better than*
Este hotel es **mucho peor que** el del año pasado — *much worse than*

▼ INCREASING AND DECREASING

Estos juegos **tienen cada vez más aceptación entre** los niños — *are becoming more and more popular with*

Las desigualdades **son cada vez mayores** — *are becoming greater and greater*
A decir verdad, **cada vez** escribo **menos** — *... less and less*
Cuanto más madura un vino, **más** añejo es su sabor — *the more ..., the more*

▼ OFFERS

¿**Te ayudo**? — *can I help (you)?*
¿**Cierro** la ventana? — *shall I close ...?*
¿**Quieres que** vaya a recoger al niño al colegio? — *would you like me to ...?*
¿**Necesitas ayuda**? — *do you need any help?*
¿**Me dejas que te eche una mano con** los preparativos? — *can I lend (you) a hand with ...?*
Déjame que te ayude — *let me help you*
Si quieres, te acompaño — *if you like*
Estoy dispuesto a hacer todo lo que sea necesario — *I'm ready to*

▼ REQUESTS

¿**Me traes** un vaso de agua? — *would you fetch me ...?*
¿**Me dejas** tu chaqueta? — *can I borrow ...?*
¿**Quieres** or **Te importa(ría)** cambiarme el turno? — *would you mind ...?*
¿**Te puedo pedir un favor**? — *can I ask you a favour?*
¿**Puedes hacerme el favor de** decírselo tú? — *would you mind ...?*
Por favor, házmelo cuanto antes — *please can you do it for me*
¿**Podrías decirme** qué pone en ese cartel, **por favor**? — *could you tell me ..., please?*
Haz el favor de no poner los pies en el asiento — *please don't*
Nos vendría bien saberlo mañana, antes de la reunión — *it would be good if we could*
Preferiría que no lo utilizaras a partir de las ocho — *I would rather you didn't*
Vuelva a llamar en cinco minutos, **si es tan amable** — *if you don't mind*
Le agradecería que me ayudara a resolver el problema — *I'd be grateful if you would*
Tenga la amabilidad de presentarse en nuestras oficinas — *please*
Le quedaría muy agradecido si pudiera enviarme información — *I would be obliged if*

▼ SUGGESTIONS

> ► Making suggestions

¿**Te apetece que vayamos** a verlo esta tarde? — *do you fancy going ...?*
¿**Y si** organizáramos una fiesta para darle una sorpresa? — *what if ...?*

¿Te parece bien que la invitemos a la fiesta?	*do you think we should …?*
¿Qué te parece decírselo por carta?	*how about …?*
¿No crees que sería mejor hacerlo ahora?	*mightn't it be better to …?*
Lo que podríamos hacer es hablar con él	*what we could do is*
Si te parece bien, podemos enviártelo por correo urgente	*if you agree, we could*
Propongo que busquemos ayuda profesional	*I suggest that*
Lo mejor sería no hacer ningún caso de los rumores	*the best thing to do would be*
Quizás habría que ser un poco más firmes con ellos	*perhaps you/we should*
Convendría que recurriera a un especialista	*you would do well to*
Le sugeriría que llamara antes por teléfono	*I would advise you to*
Sería conveniente que acudieran a un abogado	*it would be advisable for … to*
En su caso **sería muy poco aconsejable** salir del país	*it would be very inadvisable to*
Si me permite una sugerencia, creo que debería aplazarse	*if I may make a suggestion*

▶ Asking for suggestions

¿Alguna idea?	*any ideas?*
¿Tú qué dices? *or* **¿Cómo lo ves?**	*what do you think?*
¿Tú qué harías?	*what would you do?*
¿Qué hacemos ahora?	*what shall we do now?*
¿A ti qué te parece que podemos hacer ahora?	*what do you think we can …?*
Si se te ocurre algo	*if you have any ideas*

▼ ADVICE

▶ Asking for advice

¿Tú qué me aconsejas?	*what would you advise me to do?*
¿Tú qué harías (si estuvieras) en mi lugar?	*what would you do if you were me?*
¿Qué me aconsejarías que hiciera?	*what would you advise me to …?*
¿Qué restaurante **me recomiendas**?	*which … would you recommend?*

▶ Giving advice

Yo que tú *or* **Yo en tu lugar** no haría nada por ahora	*if I were you*
Hay que tomarse las cosas con más calma	*you must*
Deberías mostrarte más abierto y sincero en tu relación	*you should*
¿Por qué no la llamas por teléfono?	*why not …?*
¿Y si fueras a su casa y le pidieras perdón?	*what if …?*
Yo te aconsejaría un cambio de aires	*I'd recommend*
Harías bien en visitar a un especialista	*you would do well to*
Más vale *or* **Sería mejor no** decir nada por el momento	*it would be better/best not to*
Mi consejo es que les digas la verdad	*my advice would be to*
Yo te diría que fueras *or* **Te recomiendo que** seas prudente	*I would advise you to*
No sería mala idea enviarlo todo por correo electrónico	*it wouldn't be a bad idea to*
Lo que habría que hacer es consultarlo con un experto	*what we/you ought to do is*
Lo mejor que puedes hacer es pedir más información	*the best thing you can do is*

▶ Warnings

Les advierto que no vamos a dar ninguna información	*I should warn you that*
No te fíes de lo que te digan	*don't trust*
No te olvides de cerrar la puerta al salir	*don't forget to*
Corremos el riesgo de perder toda credibilidad	*we run the risk of*
Sería cosa de locos *or* **una locura** pagar tal cantidad	*it would be madness to*

▼ INTENTIONS AND DESIRES

▶ Asking what someone intends to do

¿Qué piensas hacer?	*what do you intend to do?*
¿Qué vas a hacer con las plantas estas vacaciones?	*what are you going to do …?*

SPANISH IN ACTION

¿**Qué planes tienes** para la familia?   *what plans have you got …?*
¿**Qué intentas hacer**?   *what are you trying to do?*

▶ Saying what you intend to do

Voy a tomar el tren de las siete   *I'm going to*
Pienso marcharme cuando haya acabado el trabajo   *I intend to*
Haremos los preparativos para la fiesta la noche antes   *we shall*
Tengo la intención de buscar un nuevo trabajo   *I plan to*
Tenemos previsto or **pensado** casarnos durante las vacaciones   *we are planning to*
Estoy decidido or **resuelto a** conseguir ese trabajo como sea   *I'm determined to*

▶ Saying what you would like

Me gustaría or **Querría que** me prestaras mayor atención   *I would* or *should like … to*
Me encantaría poder trabajar con un director como él   *I'd love to be able to*
Ojalá no lloviera tanto para poder salir más a menudo   *if only it didn't rain*
Esperemos que todo salga bien   *let's hope that*
Es de esperar que la propuesta sea aceptada por todos   *hopefully*
Quisiera dedicar una canción a mi hija, que hoy cumple años   *I should like to*

▶ Saying what you don't intend or don't want to do

No quiero que vayas a pensar otra cosa   *I don't want you to*
No pienso hacerle caso   *I do not intend to*
Me niego (rotundamente) a entrar en la polémica   *I (categorically) refuse to*
No desearíamos causarles molestias   *we would not wish to*

▼ OBLIGATIONS

▶ Saying what someone must do

Tenemos que levantarnos a primera hora de la mañana   *we have to*
No me queda or **No tengo más remedio que** decirlo   *I have no option but to*
En nombre del gobierno **debo** hacer la siguiente declaración   *I must*
Las circunstancias políticas **me obligaron a** emigrar   *forced me to*
Estamos obligados a or **Tenemos la obligación de** acatar la ley   *we have a duty to*
En verano **hay que** or **es preciso** proteger la piel contra el sol   *you must* or *have to*
Es obligatorio que figure en el envase la fecha de caducidad   *it is compulsory for … to*
Es esencial or **imprescindible** or **indispensable** leerlo   *it is essential to*
Es un país donde **se exige que** todo el mundo lleve el DNI   *is required to*

▶ Asking if you are obliged to do something

¿**(De verdad) tengo que** or **es obligatorio** pagar para entrar?   *do I (really) have to …?*
¿**Qué debo hacer para** hacerme socio?   *what must I do to …?*
¿**Se necesita** carnet de conducir?   *do I need …?*

▶ Saying what someone is not obliged to do

Los ciudadanos europeos **no necesitan** un permiso de trabajo   *do not need*
No hace falta or **no es necesario que** lo hagas **si no quieres**   *you needn't … if you don´t want to*
No estás obligado a contestar si no quieres   *you're not obliged to*
No tienes por qué aceptar una oferta que no te interesa   *there is no reason for you to*
No es obligatorio llevar el pasaporte   *it is not compulsory to*

▶ Saying what someone must not do

No se puede or **No puedes** fumar **hasta que no** seas adulto   *you cannot … until*
No me hables más del tema   *don't say any more*
No te permito que me hables de ese modo   *I won't have you*
Te prohíbo que se lo digas a nadie   *I forbid you to*

SPANISH IN ACTION

Está prohibido pisar el césped en los parques	*you are not allowed to*

▼ PERMISSION

► Asking for permission

¿**Puedo** pasar?	*may I …?*
¿**Me dejas que** lo use yo antes?	*will you let me …?*
¿**Se puede** aparcar aquí?	*can I …?*
¿**Te importa si** subo la tele un poco?	*do you mind if I …?*
¿**Podría** hacerte unas preguntas?	*could I …?*
¿**Te molesta que** abra la ventana?	*do you mind if I …?*
¿**Tendrían inconveniente en que** tomáramos unas fotos?	*would you mind if …?*

► Giving permission

¡**Naturalmente** *or* **Claro que** puedes ir!	*of course*
Puedes llamar por teléfono, si te conviene mejor	*you can (always)*
Haz lo que quieras	*do what you like*
No tengo ningún inconveniente en responder	*I don't have any objection to*

► Refusing permission

¿Es que piensas que te voy a dejar el coche? ¡**Ni pensarlo**!	*no way!*
No puedo dejarte ir de excursión con este tiempo tan malo	*I can't let you*
No se puede fumar aquí	*you can't*
Lo siento, pero no está permitido el acceso a menores de edad	*I'm sorry, but … aren't allowed in*
Te prohíbo (terminantemente) que hables así delante de mí	*I absolutely forbid you to*

► Saying that permission is granted

La dejan acostarse a la hora que quiera	*she's allowed to*
Me dijo que podía venir cuando quisiera	*she said I could*
Nuestros padres **nos dieron permiso para** hacer una fiesta	*gave us permission to*
En este país el consumo de alcohol **está permitido**	*is allowed*

► Saying that permission is refused

No me dejan participar en la carrera por problemas de salud	*I'm not allowed to*
Me han denegado la beca de estudios que necesitaba	*I've been refused*
No me está permitido *or* **Tengo prohibido** hablar con la prensa	*I'm not allowed to*
No estoy autorizado a hacer declaraciones	*I'm not authorized to*

▼ CERTAINTY, PROBABILITY, POSSIBILITY AND CAPABILITY

► Certainty

Seguro que no está en casa	*I'm sure*
Está claro que no tienen intención de votar	*it is obvious that*
Estoy segura de que ésa es la fecha del examen	*I'm sure that*
Estamos convencidos de que su coche ha sido robado	*we are convinced that*
Es obvio que *or* **evidente que** será todo un éxito	*it is clear that*
Por supuesto que siempre va a haber alguien que se crea eso	*of course*
Será, casi con toda *or* **total seguridad**, este domingo	*it will almost certainly be*
Sin lugar a dudas *or* **Sin duda alguna**, se trata de una estafa	*without a doubt*

► Probability

Aquí en este barrio **es fácil que** te atraquen	*you are quite likely to be*
Seguramente se ha retrasado por el camino	*… probably …*
Debe (de) haberse olvidado de su compromiso	*he must have*
Lo más seguro *or* **probable es que** ésa no fuera su intención	*… almost certainly …*

USEFUL SENTENCES

Es muy posible or **probable que** lleguemos a la hora prevista	... may well
Posiblemente or **Probablemente** se trate de una falsa alarma	... (very) probably ...
Parece ser que han decidido no publicar la noticia	it seems that
No me sorprendería que su equipo ganara la copa	I shouldn't be surprised if
Hay muchas posibilidades de que lo consigamos	it is very likely that
Todavía tiene muchas posibilidades de aprobar el examen	he still has a good chance of

▶ Possibility

Igual tengo suerte y apruebo	I may
A lo mejor hago escala en Tenerife de camino a Montevideo	maybe
Quizá(s) or **Tal vez** tengamos que volver antes de lo previsto	perhaps
Puede que la situación se convierta en irreversible	... may
Dicho grupo **podría ser** el autor del robo	could be

▶ Capability

¿**Sabes** escribir a máquina?	can you ...?
¿**Sabes** usar el nuevo procesador de textos?	do you know how to ...?
Hablo (el) francés y **entiendo** (el) italiano	I can speak ... I can understand
Puedo invertir hasta trece millones en las obras	I can
Tengo sólo **conocimientos básicos de** mecánica	a basic knowledge of

▼ DOUBT, IMPROBABILITY, IMPOSSIBILITY AND INCAPABILITY

▶ Doubt

No sé si debemos discutir ese tema ahora	I don't know if
No estoy seguro de que or **No tengo muy claro que** sea lo mejor	I'm not sure if ...
No es seguro que el viaje de vuelta sea en el mismo tren	... won't necessarily be
No está claro quién va a salir ganando de todo esto	it isn't clear who
Me pregunto si realmente merece la pena trabajar fuera	I wonder if
Dudo que vuelva a haber otra oferta similar	I doubt if
No se sabe con certeza si es una enfermedad hereditaria	no one knows for certain whether

▶ Improbability

Es difícil que el actual campeón participe este año	... is unlikely to
Dudo mucho que el cambio implique una mejora de la calidad	I very much doubt whether
No parece que vaya a hacer buen tiempo	it doesn't look as if
Me extrañaría or **Me sorprendería (mucho) que** fuera ella	I should be (very) surprised if
Es (muy) poco probable que aumente el número de turistas	... is (very) unlikely to
Tiene muy pocas posibilidades de ascender de puesto	he doesn't have much chance of

▶ Impossibility

No, no estuve en París. ¡**Qué más quisiera yo**!	chance would be a fine thing!
A estas horas **no puede ser** or **no es posible que sea** el cartero	it can't be
Es totalmente or **completamente imposible que** fuera él	it can't possibly
No existe ninguna posibilidad de que construyan un museo	there isn't the slightest chance of
Me es imposible llamarla hasta mañana	I can't

▶ Incapability

No veo nada desde aquí	I can't see anything
No sé cómo explicar lo que vi	I can't explain
Apenas se podía uno mover entre tanta gente	you could hardly
Soy (totalmente) incapaz de hablar en público	I am (quite) incapable of
No sirvo para este trabajo	I'm not cut out for

▼ STANDARD LETTER OPENINGS AND ENDINGS

► Personal letters

(fairly formal)

Estimado señor (García)*
Estimado colega

Reciba un respetuoso saludo de
Un cordial saludo

(fairly informal)

Querida Marta
Queridos amigos
Queridísimo Antonio

Con (mucho) cariño
(Recibe) un fuerte abrazo de
Afectuosamente

the abbreviated forms **Sr., **Sra.**, **Srta.** can be used before the surname*

► Formal letters to a firm or institution

Muy señor(es) mío(s) *(esp Sp)*
Estimado(s) señor(es)
De nuestra consideración: *(LAm)*

Le(s) saluda atentamente
Atentamente

▼ STARTING A PERSONAL LETTER

Muchas gracias por la carta.   *Thank you for your letter.*
Me alegró mucho recibir noticias tuyas.   *It was lovely to hear from you.*
Perdona que no te haya escrito antes, pero …   *Sorry I haven't written sooner but …*

▼ ENDING A PERSONAL LETTER

Recuerdos a *or* **para …**   *Give my regards to …*
Saluda de mi parte a … *or* **Saludos para …**   *Give my love to …*
Julia te manda recuerdos.   *Julia sends her best wishes.*
Escríbe(me) pronto.   *Write soon.*

▼ STARTING A FORMAL LETTER

En respuesta a su (atenta) carta de fecha …   *In reply to your letter of …*
En relación *or* **referencia a …**   *With reference to …*
Agradecemos su (atenta) carta de …   *Thank you for your letter of …*
Nos complace comunicarle/anunciarle que …   *We are pleased to inform you that …*
Lamentamos tener que comunicarle *or* **anunciarle que …**   *We regret to inform you …*
Me dirijo a usted para *or* **El objeto de mi carta es …**   *I am writing to you to …*
Le agradecería (que) me enviara …   *I would be grateful if you would send me …*

Les ruego (que) me envíen …   *Please send me …*

▼ ENDING A FORMAL LETTER

Muchas gracias de antemano por su colaboración.   *Thanking you in advance for your help.*

Si desea más información no dude en ponerse en contacto conmigo.   *If you require any further information, please do not hesitate to contact me.*

(Sin otro particular,) Quedo a la espera de sus noticias/ de su respuesta.   *I look forward to hearing from you.*

SPANISH IN ACTION

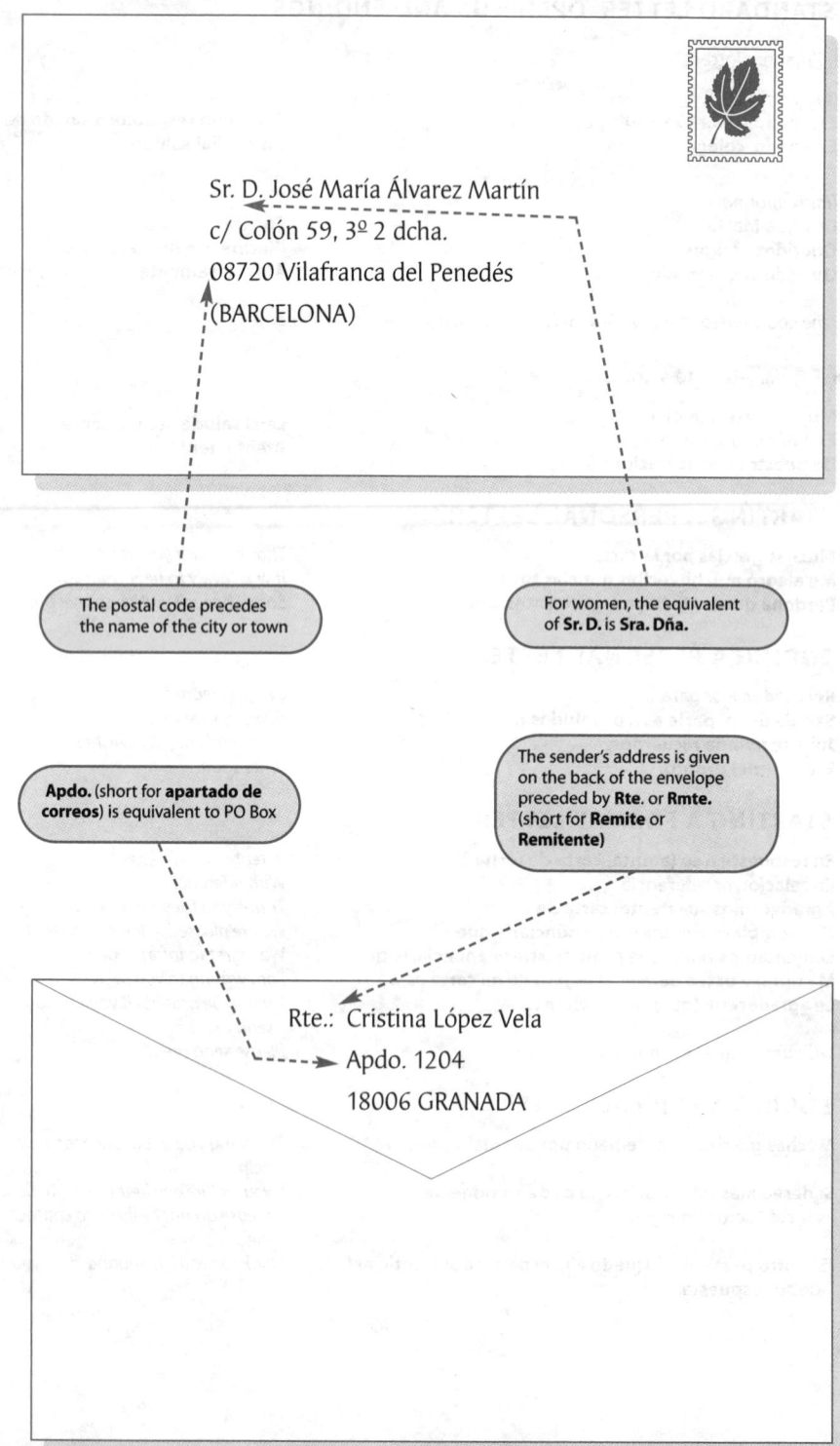

Sr. D. José María Álvarez Martín
c/ Colón 59, 3º 2 dcha.
08720 Vilafranca del Penedés
(BARCELONA)

The postal code precedes the name of the city or town

For women, the equivalent of **Sr. D.** is **Sra. Dña.**

Apdo. (short for **apartado de correos**) is equivalent to PO Box

The sender's address is given on the back of the envelope preceded by **Rte**. or **Rmte.** (short for **Remite** or **Remitente**)

Rte.: Cristina López Vela
Apdo. 1204
18006 GRANADA

SPANISH IN ACTION

▼ INFORMAL THANK-YOU LETTER

In personal letters, the place and date are combined and the address omitted

Manchester, 5 de septiembre de 2001

Queridos amigos:

Muchísimas gracias por vuestra maravillosa y cálida acogida durante mi estancia en vuestra casa este verano. Fue una experiencia que jamás podré olvidar. Gracias a vuestra amabilidad y dedicación, tuve la oportunidad de conocer otra cultura y otras gentes que desconocía por completo. Me hizo mucha ilusión, ya que siempre había deseado conocer vuestro país. Además, he tenido la suerte de hacer buenas amistades allí.

Note the use of the colon

Espero poder volver a veros muy pronto ya que os echo mucho de menos. Sabéis de sobra que estáis todos invitados a venir a mi casa cuando queráis, así que espero que pronto me hagáis una visita. Seguro que os gustará el lugar donde vivo.

Muchos besos y abrazos a todos. Sois maravillosos,

Mike

PD stands for posdata and is equivalent to PS

PD: Os mando una foto de recuerdo. Espero que os guste.

▼ FORMAL LETTER OF COMPLAINT

SÁNCHEZ & HIJOS S.L.
Avda. de América, 144 - 42003 Oviedo
Tel: 954 48 22 94 - Fax: 954 34 00 45

28 de febrero de 2002

El Buen Vino S.A.
Ronda de la Victoria, s/n
17890 BILBAO

Note the use of the colon

Muy señores míos:

El objeto de nuestra carta no es otro que constatar nuestro malestar por la demora en la entrega de la partida de vinos embotellados del pasado 25 de febrero. Estamos muy preocupados porque este mismo hecho ya ha tenido lugar en repetidas ocasiones. Como consecuencia, esto ha provocado que determinadas pequeñas y medianas empresas se vean en la situación de no poder hacer frente a la gran demanda recibida por parte de los consumidores. Como representante de estas entidades y particulares, solicitamos se tomen las medidas pertinentes para, en un futuro, evitar estas lamentables situaciones que de mediar un mínimo de prevención se habrían evitado.

Tenemos constancia de su apretada lista de envíos en la que han de satisfacer a una gran cantidad de clientes. No obstante, nos veremos obligados a cambiar de proveedor en el caso de que no mejore la actual situación en la que nos encontramos.

Sin otro particular, quedamos a la espera de sus noticias.

Atentamente,

F.R.L.

Francisco Romero Lucas
Representante Comercial

SPANISH IN ACTION

▼ FAXED BOOKING

FAX **Auto Express S.A.**

| Avda. de las Angustias, 19 | 23012 - MÁLAGA |
| Fax 947 45 34 20 | Tel. 947 34 56 81 |

DE:	Marta Arteaga Sánchez, Secretaria
PARA:	Marcos Fernández Arroyo, Departamento de Servicio al Cliente, Hotel Oasis
FECHA:	25/03/2001
ASUNTO:	Detalles de la Reserva
NÚMERO DE PÁGINAS:	3

Como acordamos anteriormente por teléfono, quisiera confirmar la reserva realizada el pasado martes a nombre de nuestra compañía. A continuación adjunto una lista con los nombres de todas las personas que van a alojarse en el hotel. Quisiera recordarle que la estancia es en régimen de pensión completa así como que la fecha de llegada será el 4 de abril con salida el día 9. Asimismo, la forma de pago se realizará a través de transferencia bancaria con gastos a nuestro cargo (enviaré el comprobante por fax más adelante).

Si tiene alguna pregunta, no dude en llamarme o bien envíeme un fax (ver número en la parte superior) e intentaré responderle lo antes posible.

Un cordial saludo,

Marta Arteaga

▼ JOB APPLICATION

> The name and address of the sender are given at the top and those of the addressee below

José Arteaga Pérez
Plaza San Agustín 45, 3º A
34012 ZARAGOZA

19 de marzo de 2001

Sr. Director Adjunto
SEINFOTEC, Servicios informáticos tecnológicos
Plaza Cardenal Martín s/n
46005 BARCELONA

Muy señor mío:

Me dirijo a usted para solicitar el puesto de técnico informático anunciado en EL MUNDO el 16 de este mes.

Como podrá comprobar en la copia del currículum vitae que adjunto, tengo considerable experiencia en el sector técnico al haber realizado numerosas prácticas durante estos últimos años, además de participar en importantes proyectos junto con otros técnicos de la zona, sin duda de gran utilidad para un puesto como el que se oferta.

Asimismo, adjunto toda la documentación justificativa que se exige.

Quedo a su disposición para cualquier aclaración que necesite y le agradezco la atención prestada.

Atentamente,

José A P

SPANISH IN ACTION

▼ CURRICULUM VITAE

CURRICULUM VITAE

Datos Personales

Nombre y apellidos:	Carmen Moreno Gil
Fecha de nacimiento:	22 de enero de 1977
Lugar de nacimiento:	Madrid
D.N.I:	98.576.789-H
Domicilio:	c/ Antonio Machado 45, 3º izda.
CP-Población:	14001 Córdoba
Teléfono particular:	953 482375 **Teléfono móvil**: 932445221
Estado civil:	soltera
Dirección electrónica:	cmorenogil@canal15.es

Datos Académicos

2000 – 2001	Master en Traducción e Interpretación, Universidad de Stirling, Escocia
1994 – 1999	Licenciatura en Filología Inglesa, Facultad de Filosofía y Letras, Universidad de Córdoba

Otros Cursos y Seminarios

Sept. 1999 – Mar. 2000	CAP (Curso de Aptitud Pedagógica), Universidad de Córdoba
Diciembre 1999	Curso sobre "Nuevas Tendencias en Traducción", Centro de Estudios de la Universidad de Sevilla
Julio 1998	Seminario sobre "Lingüística Cognitiva", Departamento de Filosofía y Letras, Universidad de Málaga

Datos Profesionales

Sept. 1999 – Mar. 2000	Profesora de inglés en prácticas, Instituto "Las Carmelitas", Córdoba
Oct. 1998 – Jul. 1999	Ayudante Colaboradora e Investigadora Bibliotecaria, Departamento de Filologías Extranjeras, Universidad de Córdoba

Otros Datos de Interés

Idiomas:	Inglés, nivel proficiency (hablado y escrito)
	Francés y alemán, nivel avanzado (buen conocimiento)
Informática:	Conocimientos avanzados a nivel de usuario: Internet, Windows, MS-DOS, Procesadores de Texto: Word Perfect, Microsoft Word, así como Hojas de Cálculo: Excel, Lotus 123 y Bases de Datos: Dbase, Access
Aficiones:	Leer, viajar, natación, voleibol
Carnet de Conducir:	A-2 y B-1
Vehículo propio	
Disponibilidad para viajar	

Referencias

Kent A. Martin, Catedrático de la Universidad de Stirling, Escocia
Tel. 00 88 0140 5432; e-mail: kentmartin@hs.ac.uk
Jesús Márquez González, Director del Departamento de Estudios Británicos, Universidad de Córdoba
Tel. 912 463752; e-mail: fl1jmg@ucor.es

Para:	martalaborda@tntnet.arg
Cc:	anapeinado@bit.es
Asunto:	Hola Luis!!
Fecha:	Lunes, 14 Marzo 2002 11:10:53 pm

> In Spanish, when telling someone your e-mail address, you say: "ana peinado arroba bit punto es"

Hola Luis:

¿Qué tal estás? Espero que tus exámenes de ingreso para la Facultad de Medicina hayan ido bien y que pronto sepas los resultados para poder ir a celebrarlo. Yo por mi parte estoy muy liado con el trabajo porque empieza el nuevo curso académico y el papeleo se acumula. Además, tengo que asistir al Congreso que se imparte el próximo día 25 para presentar la ponencia que ya te comenté en el último e-mail.

Perdona que no te pueda contar más pero es que tengo que atender una reunión en unos minutos. Te mando en archivo adjunto las fotos de las vacaciones de verano. Espero que te gusten.

Estaremos en contacto. Un fuerte abrazo,

Pepe

PD: saludos a María y a los niños.

Fotos.jpg

Para:	clientes@atat.es
Cc:	
Asunto:	Nuevo Servicio de Traducción
Fecha:	Lunes, 5 de abril 2002 13:04:45

Estimados amigos:

Ponemos en conocimiento de nuestros distinguidos clientes y amigos que a partir del día de la fecha, EINSTEIN, empresa filial de ATAT, ya no sólo atenderá aquellas traducciones de tipo general, sino también se encargará de traducciones técnicas y científicas (inglés, francés, español y alemán) que tengan a bien encomendarles.

Para satisfacer dicha demanda, Einstein cuenta con la colaboración de profesionales titulados con una amplia y probada experiencia en el campo de la traducción.

Gracias por la confianza que les merecen nuestros servicios.

Atentamente,

Belén Herrero

Para más información, contacte con nosotros en info.ref@atat.es o bien, visite nuestra página web en www.atat.es

> Note that in mobile-phone messages accents and upside-down punctuation are often omitted

HI wapal Dnd estas?
Vienes l cine x l nxe, x fa?
MIML. Bboo. Miguel :-)

Lo siento. Xam mñn.
No puedo salir. TBL.
Bboo. Ana :-(

▼ USEFUL INTERNET AND E-MAIL VOCABULARY

un archivo	a file	hacer doble clic en	to double-click on
un archivo adjunto	an attachment	una hoja de cálculo	a spreadsheet
atrás/adelante	back/forward	un icono	an icon
una barra de desplazamiento vertical	a scroll bar	"inicio"	"home"
		un/una internauta	an Internet user
una barra de herramientas	a toolbar	Internet (m or f)	the Internet
borrar	to delete	mandar un e-mail a alguien	to e-mail someone
un buscador	a search engine	marcar	to highlight
buscar	to search	la memoria	memory
una carpeta	a folder	un mensaje de texto	a text message
un chat	a chat room	un navegador	a browser
el ciberespacio	cyberspace	navegar por Internet or la Red	to surf the Net
el comercio electrónico	e-commerce	una orden	a command
conectado/desconectado	on-line/off-line	una página de inicio	a homepage
estar conectado	to be on-line	una página web	a web page
una contraseña	a password	la pantalla	the screen
una copia de seguridad	a backup	la papelera de reciclaje	the wastebasket
copiar	to copy	pegar	to paste
el correo ordinario	snail mail	preguntas frecuentes	FAQs (frequently asked questions)
el correo basura	spam, junk e-mail		
cortar y pegar	to cut and paste	un proveedor (de servicios) de Internet	an ISP (Internet Service Provider)
descargar	to download		
una dirección de Internet	a web address	una puntocom	a dotcom
una dirección electrónica	an e-mail address	la Red	the Net
un directorio	a directory	un salvapantallas	a screen saver
un e-mail	an e-mail	un servidor	a server
un emoticón	a smiley	un sitio web	a website
un enlace	a link	un smiley	a smiley
un favorito	a bookmark	un SMS	a text message
grupos de noticias	newsgroups	sugerencias de búsqueda	search tips
guardar como	to save as	la or el Web	the Web
guardar un archivo	to save a file		
hacer clic en	to click on		

▼ ABBREVIATIONS SOMETIMES USED IN TEXT MESSAGES AND E-MAILS

+t = súmate or apúntate	**ma** = mamá	**sbs?** = ¿sabes?
+ trd = más tarde	**mñn** = mañana	**spro** = espero
1mnt = un momento or un minuto	**MQ?** = ¿me quieres?	**s q** = es que
	msj = mensaje	**srt!** = ¡suerte!
2 = tú	**mxo** = mucho	**STLD** = si tú lo dices
a2 = adiós	**n l** = en el/en la	**tb** = también
bboo = besos	**NLS** = no lo sé	**TBL** = te veo luego
dko = discoteca	**NPH** = no puedo hablar	**t q** = te quiero
dnd? = ¿dónde?	**NS#** = no sé el número	**TQI** = tengo que irme
d nxe = de noche	**NT1D** = no tengo un duro	**vac** = vacaciones
eys = ellos	**pa** = papá	**vns?** = ¿vienes?
find = finde, fin de semana	**PDT** = paso de ti/piérdete	**wpa** = guapa
gnl = genial	**prf** = profe, profesor	**x** = por
h lgo or **HL** = hasta luego	**pqñ** = pequeño	**xa** = para
hr = hora	**q acc?** or **q hcs?** = ¿qué haces?	**xam** = examen
kls = clase	**qdms?** = ¿quedamos?	**xdon** = perdón
kyat = cállate	**qirsir?** = ¿quieres ir?	**x fa** = porfa, por favor
l = el/la/al/a la	**QT1BD** = que tengas un buen día	**xo** = pero
LAP = lo antes posible	**q tl?** = ¿qué tal?	**xq** = porque
M1ML = mándame un mensaje luego	**q t psa?** = ¿qué te pasa?	**xq?** = ¿por qué?
	salu2 = saludos	**ymam** = llámame

In text-message abbreviations, lower-case letters are commonly used as abbreviations of individual words while upper-case letters are often reserved for expressions or else for emphasis. So saying, usage varies.
K/k *is often substituted for* **Q/q**, *especially among young people.*

SPANISH IN ACTION

▶ Different types of call

llamada local or **metropolitana/llamada interprovincial/ llamada internacional**	local call/national call/international call
Quisiera hacer una llamada a cobro revertido a Londres	I want to make a reverse-charge call to a London number (Brit) or I want to call a London number collect (US)
¿Me podrían avisar por teléfono mañana por la mañana a las 7:30?	I'd like a wake-up call for … tomorrow morning

▶ Getting a number

¿Qué hay que hacer para obtener línea externa?	How do I make an outside call?
¿Me puede decir el número de Europost? **La dirección es …**	Could you give me the number of …? The address is …
¿Cuál es el prefijo de León?	What is the code for … ?

▶ When your number answers

¿Me pone con la extensión or (RPL) **el interno** or (Chi, Peru) **el anexo** 615?	Can you give me extension … ?
Por favor, ¿podría hablar con Carlos García? or **Quisiera hablar con** Carlos García, **por favor**	Could I speak to … please?
¿Es usted la Sra. Reyes?	Is that …?
Volveré a llamar dentro de media hora	I'll call back in …
¿Puede decirle que me llame cuando vuelva?	Could you ask him to call me when he gets back?

▶ The switchboard operator speaks

Le pongo or **Le paso**	I'm putting you through now
Hay una llamada desde Tokio **para** la Sra. Martínez	I have a call from … for …
Perdone la demora or **Siento haberle hecho esperar**	Sorry to keep you waiting
No cuelgue or **No se retire, por favor**	Please hold (the line)
No contesta	There's no reply
Comunica or **Está comunicando**	The line is engaged (Brit) or busy (US)

▶ Answering the telephone

¿Diga? or **¿Dígame?** or **¿Sí?** (Sp), **¿Aló?** (LAm), **¿Hola?** (SC), **¿Bueno?** (Mex)	Hello?
—¿Eres Ana? —**Sí, soy yo**	Speaking
¿Quién es? or **¿Con quién hablo?**	Who's speaking?
¿De parte de quién?	Who shall I say is calling?
¿Quiere dejar algún recado?	Would you like to leave a message?

▶ In case of difficulty

No consigo comunicar	I can't get through
No les funciona el teléfono	Their phone is out of order
Se ha cortado (la línea)	We were cut off
Debo (de) haberme equivocado de número	I must have dialled the wrong number
Se oye muy mal	This is a very bad line

When giving telephone numbers, where possible, Spanish speakers normally read out the numbers in tens:

959 48 32 94 - **nueve - cinco - nueve, cuarenta y ocho, treinta y dos, noventa y cuatro**
96 510 25 93 - **noventa y seis, quinientos diez** or **cinco - diez, veinticinco, noventa y tres**

We have outlined here those areas and words which most frequently cause students problems when working with Spanish.

▼ Translation

Beware of translating word for word. While this may sometimes be possible, very often it is not. The following illustrate the need for care:

▶ English phrasal verbs, i.e. verbs followed by an <u>adverb</u> or a <u>preposition</u> (e.g. *to run away, to fall over*) are usually translated by one word in Spanish

to run <u>away</u>	to fall <u>down</u>	to give <u>in</u>
huir	**caerse**	**ceder**

▶ English verbal constructions often contain a <u>preposition</u> where none exists in Spanish, and vice versa

to look <u>at</u>	to listen <u>to</u>	to use
mirar	**escuchar**	**servirse** <u>de</u>

▶ A word which is singular in English may be plural in Spanish, or vice versa

a holiday	his/her pyjamas	my trousers
unas vacaciones	**su pijama**	**mi pantalón**

▼ Tips relating to specific words and constructions

and

Remember to give **e** instead of **y** before words beginning with **i** or **hi** (but not **hie**) as well as before the letter **y** used on its own:

Spain and Italy	grapes and figs	words ending in S and Y
España e Italia	**uvas e higos**	**palabras terminadas en S e Y**

be: ser and estar

To be is generally translated by either **ser** or **estar**. These are not interchangeable.

▼ ser is used:

▶ When saying what something is made of or when explaining the origins of someone or something

The walls are made of brick	My mother is from Granada
Las paredes son de ladrillo	**Mi madre es de Granada**

▶ When you want to say that something belongs to someone

It's Miguel's house
La casa es de Miguel

▶ With a noun, pronoun or infinitive following the verb

Javier is a policeman	It's me, Enrique	It's all a matter of putting your mind to it
Javier es policía	**Soy yo, Enrique**	**Todo es proponérselo**

▶ To talk about times or days

It's half past three	Tomorrow is Saturday
Son las tres y media	**Mañana es sábado**

▶ To form the passive – a construction used less in Spanish than in English

This play was written by Lorca
Esta obra fue escrita por Lorca

▶ When you want to say where an event is taking or took place

The 1992 Olympics were in Barcelona
Los Juegos Olímpicos de 1992 fueron en Barcelona

SPANISH IN ACTION

▼ **estar** is used:

▶ When you want to indicate where someone or something (other than an event) is

The meal is on the table	We are in Madrid
La comida está en la mesa	**Estamos en Madrid**

▶ To form <u>continuous tenses</u> with the present participle

We are learning a great deal
Estamos aprendiendo mucho

▼ **ser and estar with adjectives**

ser + <u>adjective</u> expresses a permanent or inherent quality

estar + <u>adjective</u> expresses a temporary state or quality

▼ Thus **ser** is used:

▶ With adjectives seen as permanent or inherent

His parents are Italian	My brother is tall	María is intelligent
Sus padres son italianos	**Mi hermano es alto**	**María es inteligente**

▼ **estar** is used:

▶ With an adjective or adjectival phrase describing the current state of someone or something, a state which could change

I'm in a bad mood today	I'm very well	His friend is ill
Hoy estoy de mal humor	**Estoy muy bien**	**Su amigo está enfermo**

▼ Some adjectives can be used with both **ser** and **estar**, but with a different meaning

His sister is very young	She looks very young in that dress
Su hermana es muy joven	**Está muy joven con ese vestido**
They are very rich	The meal was very nice
Son muy ricos	**La comida estaba muy rica**
Travelling is tiring/boring	I'm tired/bored
Viajar es cansado/aburrido	**Estoy cansado/aburrido**
The idea is a good one	The paella was very good
La idea es buena	**La paella estaba muy buena**

NOTE: Only use **estar bueno** of food or to describe someone as desirable or fanciable.

▼ **ser and estar with past participles**

ser + <u>past participle</u> describes an action (passive use)

estar + <u>past participle</u> (used as an adjective) describes a state

Compare the following:

The agreement was soon broken	The window was broken
El acuerdo fue roto al poco tiempo	**La ventana estaba rota**
It was painted around 1925	The floor is painted a dark colour
Fue pintado hacia 1925	**El suelo está pintado de color oscuro**

can/be able

▶ The physical ability to do something is expressed by **poder**

I can't go out with you
No puedo salir contigo

▶ If you mean <u>to know how to</u>, use **saber**

Can you swim?
¿Sabes nadar?

▶ *Can* + a verb of seeing or hearing etc is usually not translated in Spanish

I can't see anything	Can't you hear me?
No veo nada	**¿Es que no me oyes?**

come

Use **ir** not **venir** when talking about joining or accompanying someone somewhere else:

I'm coming	I'll come and pick you up at 4	Shall I come with you?
Ya voy	**Iré a recogerte a las 4**	**¿Voy contigo?**

could

▶ Be careful to distinguish between *could* referring to the past, *could* hypothesizing and *could* in requests

I couldn't phone because I had no change	He could be charming when he wanted to be
No pude llamar porque no tenía suelto	**Podía ser encantador cuando quería**
You could learn to sew if you tried	He could have helped us if he'd wanted to
Podrías aprender a coser si lo intentaras or **intentases**	**Nos podría haber ayudado** or **Habría podido ayudarnos si hubiera querido**
It could be true	Could you pass me the salt please?
Podría ser verdad or **Puede que sea verdad**	**¿Podrías** or **puedes pasarme la sal por favor?**

▶ Use **saber** rather than **poder** when *could* means <u>knew how to</u>

She could read when she was three	I thought you could drive
Sabía leer a los tres años	**Pensaba que sabías conducir**

▶ *Could* + <u>a verb of seeing or hearing etc</u> is not translated in Spanish

I couldn't see what Giles was doing	He could hear her shouting
No veía lo que estaba haciendo Giles	**La oía gritar**

for

▼ **para** and **por** contrasted

▶ Use **para** to translate *for* + <u>recipient</u>, <u>destination</u> or <u>purpose</u>

There's a letter for you	He left for Bilbao this morning	It's not for eating
Hay una carta para ti	**Salió para Bilbao esta mañana**	**No es para comer**

▶ Use **para** when talking about <u>dates</u> or <u>deadlines</u>

The meeting was fixed for 10th January
La reunión quedó fijada para el 10 de enero

▶ Use **por** to translate *for* + <u>reason</u> or when it means <u>for the sake /benefit of</u> or indicates <u>exchange</u>

I was punished for lying	Do it for me	I'd give anything for a bit of peace
Me castigaron por mentir	**Hazlo por mí**	**Daría lo que fuera por un poco de tranquilidad**

good

Use **bien** rather than **bueno** when making general comments on a situation:

It's very good that you're saving	You've written a book, which is good
Está muy bien que ahorres dinero	**Has escrito un libro, lo que está bien**

have/look for

▶ When translating *have/look for* + *a* + <u>noun</u>, don't translate the *a* if it's normal only to *have* or *look for* one of the noun

Has he got a girlfriend?	I haven't got a washing machine	I'm looking for a flat
¿Tiene novia?	**No tengo lavadora**	**Estoy buscando piso**

▶ Do translate the *a* if the person or thing is qualified

He has a Spanish girlfriend	He's looking for a little flat
Tiene una novia española	**Busca un piso pequeño**

if

▶ Use **si** + present indicative to translate *if* + present in English

Don't do it if you don't want to	If you go on overeating, you'll get fat
No lo hagas si no quieres	**Si sigues comiendo tanto, vas a engordar**

▶ Use **si** + past subjunctive to translate *if* + past in English for remote or uncertain possibilities and hypotheses

If we won the lottery, we would never have to work again	What would you do if I weren't here?
Si nos tocara or **tocase la lotería, no tendríamos que trabajar nunca más**	**¿Qué harías si yo no estuviera** or **estuviese aquí?**

If Paula hadn't lost her ticket, she would have left today
Si Paula no hubiera or **hubiese perdido el billete, habría salido hoy**

▶ Alternatively, instead of a clause with **si**, you can often use **de (no) haber** + past participle

If Paula hadn't lost her ticket, she would have left today
De no haber perdido Paula el billete, habría salido hoy

-ing

▶ *to be …-ing* can be translated by the less common **estar** + present participle if the action really is/was in progress at the time; if not, other constructions must be used

I understand what you are going through
Entiendo lo que estás pasando

▶ *to be …-ing* is often translated by a simple verb

What are you doing?	He's going to miss the train	He was joking
¿Qué haces?	**Va a perder el tren**	**Hablaba en broma**

BUT: use the past participle when talking about the physical position of someone or something:

She is sitting over there	He was lying on the ground
Está sentada allí	**Estaba tendido en el suelo**

▼ *-ing* can also be translated by:

▶ an infinitive

I like going to the cinema	I've heard her singing	before going out
Me gusta ir al cine	**La he oído cantar**	**antes de salir**

▶ a perfect infinitive

After opening the box, María …
Después de haber abierto la caja, María …

▶ a present participle

Being shyer than me, Antonio …
Siendo más tímido que yo, Antonio …

▶ a noun

SPANISH IN ACTION

Skiing keeps me fit
El esquí me mantiene en forma

may

▶ If you are expressing **possibility**, use either **poder** + <u>infinitive</u> or **puede (ser)** + <u>subjunctive</u>

He may still change his mind
Todavía puede cambiar de opinión

She may not know
Puede (ser) que no lo sepa

▶ To express <u>permission</u>, use **poder**

May I go?
¿Puedo irme?

You may sit down
Puede sentarse

must

▶ If you are expressing an <u>assumption</u>, **deber de** is often used, though **de** can be omitted

He must have lied
Ha debido (de) mentir

He must like it
Debe (de) gustarle

▶ When *must* expresses <u>obligation</u>, there are three main translations: **tener que**, **deber** and **hay que** (*impersonal*)

We must leave early tomorrow
Tenemos que salir temprano mañana

You must listen to what they tell you
Debes escuchar lo que te dicen

I must visit them
Debo visitarlos

We (You *etc*) must work harder
Hay que trabajar más

or

Remember to give **u** instead of **o** before words beginning with **o** or **ho**:

for one reason or another
por un motivo u otro

Personal a

When the direct object of a verb (other than **tener**) is a specific person or pet, **a** must be placed before it:

They loved their children dearly
Querían mucho a sus hijos

The boy was looking at his dog in astonishment
El niño miraba a su perro con asombro

should

▶ *Should* relating to <u>duty</u> or <u>advisability</u> can usually be translated using **deber** in the conditional, though other tenses of **deber** are often possible too, as are constructions using **tener que**

He should behave better
Debería comportarse mejor

What do you think I should do?
¿Qué crees que debería hacer?

Do you think we should go?
¿Crees que deberíamos ir?

You shouldn't have asked Lee to help
No deberías haber pedido *or* **No habrías debido pedir ayuda a Lee**

▶ When *should* is used to express an <u>assumption</u>, **deber (de)** is often used

Linda should be in Paris by now
Linda debería (de) estar ya en París

They should have finished by now
Deberían (de) haber terminado ya

▶ When *should* is used with the same meaning as <u>would</u> ('d), it can usually be translated using the <u>conditional</u> of the relevant verb

We should like to go to Madrid first
Nos gustaría ir a Madrid primero

I should have liked to say hello to him
Me habría gustado saludarlo

SPANISH IN ACTION

▶ But, use the <u>present</u> for translating phrases like *I should think* or *I should imagine*

> I should imagine you won't want to see her again
> **Me imagino que no querrás volver a verla**

wear

▶ Don't translate the *a* in sentences like *he wasn't wearing a coat, was she wearing a hat?* if the number of such items is not significant since people normally only wear one at a time

> He wasn't wearing a coat
> **No llevaba abrigo**
>
> Was he wearing a hat?
> **¿Llevaba sombrero?**

▶ Do translate the *a* if the garment, item of jewellery etc is qualified

> Queen Sofía is wearing a long dress
> **Doña Sofía lleva un vestido largo**

will

▶ *will* is often translated using the Spanish <u>future tense</u> or, when expressing intention, by **ir a** + <u>infinitive</u>

> I think Diego will be there
> **Creo que Diego estará allí**
>
> We'll be having lunch late
> **Vamos a comer tarde**

▶ But remember to use the <u>subjunctive</u> in subordinate clauses after expressions of doubt or fear as well as after verbs of saying, believing and thinking used negatively

> I doubt whether she will have time to read it
> **Dudo que tenga tiempo de leerlo**
>
> I'm not saying that they won't be very happy, but …
> **No digo que no vayan a ser felices, pero …**

▶ Translate *will* in requests using the <u>present tense</u> of the main verb

> Will you give me a piece of paper?
> **¿Me das un papel?**

▶ Use the <u>present tense</u> of **querer** to express <u>willingness</u> or <u>desire</u>

> He won't help me
> **No quiere ayudarme**
>
> Will you marry me?
> **¿Quieres casarte conmigo?**

would

▶ When talking hypothetically or when reporting what someone said or thought, you can generally translate *would* using the <u>conditional tense</u>

> He would do anything for his children
> **Haría cualquier cosa por sus hijos**
>
> He said he would do it
> **Dijo que lo haría**

▶ But remember to use the <u>subjunctive</u> in subordinate clauses after expressions of doubt or fear as well as after verbs of saying, believing and thinking used negatively

> He doubted whether he would ever see her again
> **Dudaba que volviera** or **volviese a verla**
>
> No one believed that he would do it
> **Nadie creía que lo hiciera** or **hiciese**
>
> She was afraid that he wouldn't have time to finish it
> **Temía que él no tuviera** or **tuviese tiempo de terminarlo**

▶ To talk about <u>willingness</u> in the past, use the <u>preterite</u> or <u>imperfect</u> of **querer**

> They wouldn't come
> **No quisieron** or **querían venir**

▶ To refer to a repeated or habitual action in the past, use either the <u>imperfect tense</u> of the verb, or the <u>imperfect</u> of **soler** + <u>infinitive</u>

> She would watch them for hours on end
> **Las miraba hora tras hora**
>
> Latterly he would eat very little
> **Últimamente solía comer muy poco**

► Cardinal Numbers

0	cero	15	quince	30	treinta
1	uno (un, una)*	16	dieciséis	31	treinta y uno (un, una)*
2	dos	17	diecisiete	42	cuarenta y dos
3	tres	18	dieciocho	54	cincuenta y cuatro
4	cuatro	19	diecinueve	65	sesenta y cinco
5	cinco	20	veinte	76	setenta y seis
6	seis	21	veintiuno (-ún, -una)*	88	ochenta y ocho
7	siete	22	veintidós	99	noventa y nueve
8	ocho	23	veintitrés	100	cien (ciento)**
9	nueve	24	veinticuatro	101	ciento uno (un, una)*
10	diez	25	veinticinco	212	doscientos/as doce
11	once	26	veintiséis	540	quinientos/as cuarenta
12	doce	27	veintisiete	680	seiscientos/as ochenta
13	trece	28	veintiocho	730	setecientos/as treinta
14	catorce	29	veintinueve	990	novecientos/as noventa

1.000	mil	100.000	cien mil
1.001	mil (y) uno (un, una)*	1.000.000	un millón
2.000	dos mil	1.000.000.000	mil millones
3.500	tres mil quinientos/as	1.000.000.000.000	un billón

NOTE: A full stop, not a comma, separates thousands and millions.

► Ordinal Numbers

1º, 1er/1ª	primero (primer, primera)***	13º/13ª	decimotercero/a or decimotercio/a
2º/2ª	segundo/a	14º/14ª	decimocuarto/a
3º, 3er/3ª	tercero (tercer, tercera)***	15º/15ª	decimoquinto/a
4º/4ª	cuarto/a	16º/16ª	decimosexto/a
5º/5ª	quinto/a	17º/17ª	decimoséptimo/a
6º/6ª	sexto/a	18º/18ª	decimoctavo/a
7º/7ª	séptimo/a	19º/19ª	decimonoveno/a or decimonono/a
8º/8ª	octavo/a	20º/20ª	vigésimo/a
9º/9ª	noveno/a	21º/21ª	vigésimo primero/a
10º/10ª	décimo/a	30º/30ª	trigésimo/a
11º/11ª	undécimo/a	100º/100ª	centésimo/a
12º/12ª	duodécimo/a	1000º/1000ª	milésimo/a

NOTE: In Spanish the ordinal numbers from 1 to 10 are commonly used; those from 11 to 20 rather less; and above 21 cardinal numbers tend to be used instead, although **milésimo** and **centésimo** are very common.

► Fractions and percentages

½	medio/a	0,5	cero coma cinco
⅓	un tercio, una tercera parte	3,5	tres coma cinco
¼	un cuarto, una cuarta parte	6,89	seis coma ochenta y nueve
¹/₁₀	un décimo, una décima parte	10%	un diez por cien(to)
⅔	dos tercios	100%	un cien por cien(to)

NOTE: A comma, not a full stop, is used to show decimal places.

* **Uno** (+ **treinta y uno** etc) agrees in gender (but not number) with its noun: *treinta y una personas*; the masculine form is shortened to **un** before a noun: *treinta y un caballos*.

** **Ciento** is used in compound numbers, except when it multiplies: *ciento diez*, but *cien mil*. **Cien** is used before nouns: *cien hombres, cien casas*.

*** **Primero** and **tercero** are shortened to **primer** and **tercer** when they directly precede a masculine singular noun: *en el primer capítulo*, but *los primeros coches en llegar*.

SPANISH IN ACTION

¿Qué hora es?   *What time is it?*

Es la una

Es la una y cuarto

Son las dos menos diez

Son las tres y media

Son las seis menos veinte

Son las ocho menos cuarto

Son las nueve

Son las doce

▶ Asking the time

¿Qué hora tienes?	*What time do you make it?*
¿Me dices la hora?	*Can you tell me the time?*
¿Tienes hora?	*Do you have the time (on you)?*

▶ Telling the time

Yo tengo las dos y veinte	*I make it twenty past two*
Serán las once	*It must be about eleven*
Son las tres en punto	*It's three o'clock exactly*
Son las cinco y pico	*It's just gone five o'clock*
Falta (un) poco para las cuatro	*It's nearly four o'clock*

▶ What time?

¿A qué hora empieza?	*What time does it start?*
A medianoche	*At midnight*
Dentro de veinte minutos	*In twenty minutes*
A eso de las ocho	*At around eight o'clock*
Sale a las siete y media	*It leaves at 7.30*

▶ Night and day

las doce de la noche	*midnight*
las tres de la madrugada	*three am*
las seis de la mañana	*six am*
las doce del mediodía	*midday*
las siete de la tarde	*seven pm*
las once de la noche	*eleven pm*

► The days of the week

lunes	*Monday*
martes	*Tuesday*
miércoles	*Wednesday*
jueves	*Thursday*
viernes	*Friday*
sábado	*Saturday*
domingo	*Sunday*

► The months of the year

enero	*January*
febrero	*February*
marzo	*March*
abril	*April*
mayo	*May*
junio	*June*
julio	*July*
agosto	*August*
septiembre	*September*
octubre	*October*
noviembre	*November*
diciembre	*December*

NOTE: in Spanish, the days of the week and months of the year always begin with a small letter.

► The seasons

primavera	*spring*
verano	*summer*
otoño	*autumn*
invierno	*winter*

► Talking about the date

¿Qué día es hoy?	*What day is it today?*
Es sábado or **Estamos a sábado**	*It's Saturday*
1/24 de octubre de 2002	*1st/24th October 2002*

► When?

hoy/ayer/mañana	*today/yesterday/tomorrow*
pasado mañana	*the day after tomorrow*
antes de ayer	*the day before yesterday*
el día siguiente	*the next* or *following day*
ayer por la tarde	*yesterday afternoon/evening*
mañana por la mañana	*tomorrow morning*
los sábados	*on Saturdays*
el domingo que viene	*next Sunday*
el martes pasado	*last Tuesday*
una vez por semana/mes	*once a week/month*
hace una semana	*a week ago*
el año pasado	*last year*
dentro de dos días	*in two days' time*
hace quince días	*a fortnight ago*
a principios de año	*at the beginning of the year*
a mediados de mayo	*in the middle of May*
a finales de mes	*at the end of the month*
a más tardar	*at the latest*
lo más pronto	*at the earliest*
no más tarde de	*no later than*
en 1999	*in 1999*
en el siglo diecinueve	*in the nineteenth century*
en los años noventa	*in the (nineteen) nineties*
en el año dos mil	*in the year two thousand*
44 a. de C.	*44 BC*
14 d. de C.	*14 AD*

SPANISH IN ACTION

INFINITIVE	PRESENT INDICATIVE	PRESENT SUBJUNCTIVE	PRETERITE
[1a] cantar (regular: see table at end of list) Gerund: *cantando*			
[1b] cambiar **i** of the stem is not stressed and the verb is regular Gerund: *cambiando*	cambio cambias cambia cambiamos cambiáis cambian	cambie cambies cambie cambiemos cambiéis cambien	cambié cambiaste cambió cambiamos cambiasteis cambiaron
[1c] enviar **i** of the stem stressed in parts of the present tenses Gerund: *enviando*	envío envías envía enviamos enviáis envían	envíe envíes envíe enviemos enviéis envíen	envié enviaste envió enviamos enviasteis enviaron
[1d] evacuar **u** of the stem is not stressed and the verb is regular Gerund: *evacuando*	evacuo evacuas evacua evacuamos evacuáis evacuan	evacue evacues evacue evacuemos evacuéis evacuen	evacué evacuaste evacuó evacuamos evacuasteis evacuaron
[1e] situar **u** of the stem stressed in parts of the present tenses Gerund: *situando*	sitúo sitúas sitúa situamos situáis sitúan	sitúe sitúes sitúe situemos situéis sitúen	situé situaste situó situamos situasteis situaron
[1f] cruzar Stem consonant **z** written **c** before **e** Gerund: *cruzando*	cruzo cruzas cruza cruzamos cruzáis cruzan	cruce cruces cruce crucemos crucéis crucen	crucé cruzaste cruzó cruzamos cruzasteis cruzaron
[1g] picar Stem consonant **c** written **qu** before **e** Gerund: *picando*	pico picas pica picamos picáis pican	pique piques pique piquemos piquéis piquen	piqué picaste picó picamos picasteis picaron
[1h] pagar Stem consonant **g** written **gu** (with **u** silent) before **e** Gerund: *pagando*	pago pagas paga pagamos pagáis pagan	pague pagues pague paguemos paguéis paguen	pagué pagaste pagó pagamos pagasteis pagaron
[1i] averiguar **u** of the stem written **ü** (so that it is pronounced) before **e** Gerund: *averiguando*	averiguo averiguas averigua averiguamos averiguáis averiguan	averigüe averigües averigüe averigüemos averigüéis averigüen	averigüé averiguaste averiguó averiguamos averiguasteis averiguaron
[1j] cerrar Stem vowel **e** becomes **ie** when stressed Gerund: *cerrando*	cierro cierras cierra cerramos cerráis cierran	cierre cierres cierre cerremos cerréis cierren	cerré cerraste cerró cerramos cerrasteis cerraron

INFINITIVE	PRESENT INDICATIVE	PRESENT SUBJUNCTIVE	PRETERITE
[1l] contar Stem vowel **o** becomes **ue** when stressed Gerund: *contando*	cuento cuentas cuenta contamos contáis cuentan	cuente cuentes cuente contemos contéis cuenten	conté contaste contó contamos contasteis contaron
[1m] agorar As [1l], but diphthong written **üe** (so that the **u** is pronounced) Gerund: *agorando*	agüero agüeras agüera agoramos agoráis agüeran	agüere agüeres agüere agoremos agoréis agüeren	agoré agoraste agoró agoramos agorasteis agoraron
[1n] jugar Stem vowel **u** becomes **ue** when stressed; stem consonant **g** written **gu** (with **u** silent) before **e** Gerund: *jugando*	juego juegas juega jugamos jugáis juegan	juegue juegues juegue juguemos juguéis jueguen	jugué jugaste jugó jugamos jugasteis jugaron
[1o] estar Irregular. Imperative: *está (tú)* Gerund: *estando*	estoy estás está estamos estáis están	esté estés esté estemos estéis estén	estuve estuviste estuvo estuvimos estuvisteis estuvieron
[1p] andar Irregular. Gerund: *andando*	ando andas anda andamos andáis andan	ande andes ande andemos andéis anden	anduve anduviste anduvo anduvimos anduvisteis anduvieron
[1q] dar Irregular. Gerund: *dando*	doy das da damos dais dan	dé des dé demos deis den	di diste dio dimos disteis dieron
[2a] temer (regular: see table at end of list)			
[2b] vencer Stem consonant **c** written **z** before **a** and **o** Gerund: *venciendo*	venzo vences vence vencemos vencéis vencen	venza venzas venza venzamos venzáis venzan	vencí venciste venció vencimos vencisteis vencieron
[2c] coger Stem consonant **g** written **j** before **a** and **o** Gerund: *cogiendo*	cojo coges coge cogemos cogéis cogen	coja cojas coja cojamos cojáis cojan	cogí cogiste cogió cogimos cogisteis cogieron
[2d] conocer Stem consonant **c** becomes **zc** before **a** and **o** Gerund: *conociendo*	conozco conoces conoce conocemos conocéis conocen	conozca conozcas conozca conozcamos conozcáis conozcan	conocí conociste conoció conocimos conocisteis conocieron

SPANISH IN ACTION

INFINITIVE	PRESENT INDICATIVE	PRESENT SUBJUNCTIVE	PRETERITE
[2e] leer Unstressed **i** between vowels is written **y** Past Participle: *leído* Gerund: *leyendo*	leo lees lee leemos leéis leen	lea leas lea leamos leáis lean	leí leíste leyó leímos leísteis leyeron
[2f] tañer Unstressed **i** after **ñ** (and also after **ll**) is omitted Gerund: *tañendo*	taño tañes tañe tañemos tañéis tañen	taña tañas taña tañamos tañáis tañan	tañí tañiste tañó tañimos tañisteis tañeron
[2g] perder Stem vowel **e** becomes **ie** when stressed Gerund: *perdiendo*	p**ie**rdo p**ie**rdes p**ie**rde perdemos perdéis p**ie**rden	p**ie**rda p**ie**rdas p**ie**rda perdamos perdáis p**ie**rdan	perdí perdiste perdió perdimos perdisteis perdieron
[2h] mover Stem vowel **o** becomes **ue** when stressed Gerund: *moviendo*	m**ue**vo m**ue**ves m**ue**ve movemos movéis m**ue**ven	m**ue**va m**ue**vas m**ue**va movamos mováis m**ue**van	moví moviste movió movimos movisteis movieron
[2i] oler As [2h], but diphthong is written **hue-** at the start of the word Gerund: *oliendo*	**hue**lo **hue**les **hue**le olemos oléis **hue**len	**hue**la **hue**las **hue**la olamos oláis **hue**lan	olí oliste olió olimos olisteis olieron
[2j] haber (see table at end of list)			
[2k] tener Irregular. Future: *tendré* Imperative: *ten (tú)* Gerund: *teniendo*	tengo tienes tiene tenemos tenéis tienen	tenga tengas tenga tengamos tengáis tengan	tuve tuviste tuvo tuvimos tuvisteis tuvieron
[2l] caber Irregular. Future: *cabré* Gerund: *cabiendo*	quepo cabes cabe cabemos cabéis caben	quepa quepas quepa quepamos quepáis quepan	cupe cupiste cupo cupimos cupisteis cupieron
[2m] saber Irregular. Future: *sabré* Gerund: *sabiendo*	sé sabes sabe sabemos sabéis saben	sepa sepas sepa sepamos sepáis sepan	supe supiste supo supimos supisteis supieron
[2n] caer Unstressed **i** between vowels written **y**, as [2e] Past Participle: *caído* Gerund: *cayendo*	caigo caes cae caemos caéis caen	caiga caigas caiga caigamos caigáis caigan	caí caíste cayó caímos caísteis cayeron

SPANISH IN ACTION

INFINITIVE	PRESENT INDICATIVE	PRESENT SUBJUNCTIVE	PRETERITE
[2o] **traer** Irregular. Past Participle: *traído* Gerund: *trayendo*	traigo traes trae traemos traéis traen	traiga traigas traiga traigamos traigáis traigan	traje trajiste trajo trajimos trajisteis trajeron
[2p] **valer** Irregular. Future: *valdré* Gerund: *valiendo*	valgo vales vale valemos valéis valen	valga valgas valga valgamos valgáis valgan	valí valiste valió valimos valisteis valieron
[2q] **poner** Irregular. Future: *pondré* Past Participle: *puesto* Imperative: *pon (tú)* Gerund: *poniendo*	pongo pones pone ponemos ponéis ponen	ponga pongas ponga pongamos pongáis pongan	puse pusiste puso pusimos pusisteis pusieron
[2r] **hacer** Irregular. Future: *haré* Past Participle: *hecho* Imperative: *haz (tú)* Gerund: *haciendo*	hago haces hace hacemos hacéis hacen	haga hagas haga hagamos hagáis hagan	hice hiciste hizo hicimos hicisteis hicieron
[2s] **poder** Irregular. In present tenses like [2h] Future: *podré* Gerund: *pudiendo*	puedo puedes puede podemos podéis pueden	pueda puedas pueda podamos podáis puedan	pude pudiste pudo pudimos pudisteis pudieron
[2t] **querer** Irregular. In present tenses like [2g] Future: *querré* Gerund: *queriendo*	quiero quieres quiere queremos queréis quieren	quiera quieras quiera queramos queráis quieran	quise quisiste quiso quisimos quisisteis quisieron
[2u] **ver** Irregular. Imperfect: *veía* Past Participle: *visto* Gerund: *viendo*	veo ves ve vemos veis ven	vea veas vea veamos veáis vean	vi viste vio vimos visteis vieron

[2v]   **ser** (see table at end of list)

[2w]   **placer.** Exclusively 3rd person singular. Irregular forms: Present subj. *plazca*; Preterite *plació* (less commonly *plugo*); Imperfect subj. I *placiera*, II *placiese* (less commonly *plugiera*, *plugiese*).

[2x]   **yacer.** Archaic. Irregular forms: Present indic. *yazco* (less commonly *yazgo* or *yago*), *yaces* etc; Present subj. *yazca* (less commonly *yazga*), *yazcas* etc; Imperative *yace (tú)* (less commonly *yaz*).

[2y]   **raer.** Present indic. usually *raigo*, *raes* etc (like *caer* [2n]), but *rayo* occasionally found; Present subj. usually *raiga*, *raigas* etc (also like *caer*), but *raya*, *rayas* etc occasionally found.

[2z]   **roer.** Alternative forms in present tenses: Indicative, *roo*, *roigo* or *royo*; *roes*, *roe* etc. Subjunctive, *roa*, *roiga* or *roya*. First persons usually avoided because of the uncertainty. The gerund is *royendo*.

INFINITIVE	PRESENT INDICATIVE	PRESENT SUBJUNCTIVE	PRETERITE
[3a] **partir** (regular: see table at end of list)			
[3b] **esparcir** Stem consonant **c** written **z** before **a** and **o** Gerund: *esparciendo*	esparzo esparces esparce esparcimos esparcís esparcen	esparza esparzas esparza esparzamos esparzáis esparzan	esparcí esparciste esparció esparcimos esparcisteis esparcieron
[3c] **dirigir** Stem consonant **g** written **j** before **a** and **o** Gerund: *dirigiendo*	dirijo diriges dirige dirigimos dirigís dirigen	dirija dirijas dirija dirijamos dirijáis dirijan	dirigí dirigiste dirigió dirigimos dirigisteis dirigieron
[3d] **distinguir** **u** after the stem consonant **g** omitted before **a** and **o** Gerund: *distinguiendo*	distingo distingues distingue distinguimos distinguís distinguen	distinga distingas distinga distingamos distingáis distingan	distinguí distinguiste distinguió distinguimos distinguisteis distinguieron
[3e] **delinquir** Stem consonant **qu** written **c** before **a** and **o** Gerund: *delinquiendo*	delinco delinques delinque delinquimos delinquís delinquen	delinca delincas delinca delincamos delincáis delincan	delinquí delinquiste delinquió delinquimos delinquisteis delinquieron
[3f] **lucir** Stem consonant **c** becomes **zc** before **a** and **o** Gerund: *luciendo*	luzco luces luce lucimos lucís lucen	luzca luzcas luzca luzcamos luzcáis luzcan	lucí luciste lució lucimos lucisteis lucieron
[3g] **huir** A **y** is inserted before endings not beginning with **i** Gerund: *huyendo*	huyo huyes huye huimos huís huyen	huya huyas huya huyamos huyáis huyan	huí huiste huyó huimos huisteis huyeron
[3h] **gruñir** Unstressed **i** after **ñ** (and also after **ch** and **ll**) omitted Gerund: *gruñendo*	gruño gruñes gruñe gruñimos gruñís gruñen	gruña gruñas gruña gruñamos gruñáis gruñan	gruñí gruñiste gruñó gruñimos gruñisteis gruñeron
[3i] **sentir** The stem vowel **e** becomes **ie** when stressed; **e** becomes **i** in 3rd persons of Preterite, 1st and 2nd persons pl. of Present Subjunctive. Gerund: *sintiendo* In *adquirir* the stem vowel **i** becomes **ie** when stressed	siento sientes siente sentimos sentís sienten	sienta sientas sienta sintamos sintáis sientan	sentí sentiste sintió sentimos sentisteis sintieron
[3j] **dormir** The stem vowel **o** becomes **ue** when stressed; **o** becomes **u** in 3rd persons of Preterite, 1st and 2nd persons pl. of Present Subjunctive. Gerund: *durmiendo*	duermo duermes duerme dormimos dormís duermen	duerma duermas duerma durmamos durmáis duerman	dormí dormiste durmió dormimos dormisteis durmieron

INFINITIVE	PRESENT INDICATIVE	PRESENT SUBJUNCTIVE	PRETERITE
[3k] pedir The stem vowel **e** becomes **i** when stressed, and in 3rd persons of Preterite, 1st and 2nd persons pl. of Present Subjunctive. Gerund: *pidiendo*	pido pides pide pedimos pedís piden	pida pidas pida pidamos pidáis pidan	pedí pediste pidió pedimos pedisteis pidieron
[3l] reír Irregular. Past Participle: *reído* Gerund: *riendo* Imperative: *ríe (tú)*	río ríes ríe reímos reís ríen	ría rías ría riamos riáis rían	reí reíste rió reímos reísteis rieron
[3m] erguir Irregular. Gerund: *irguiendo* Imperative: *yergue (tú)* and less commonly *irgue (tú)*	yergo yergues yergue erguimos erguís yerguen	yerga yergas yerga yergamos yergáis yergan	erguí erguiste irguió erguimos erguisteis irguieron
[3n] reducir The stem consonant **c** becomes **zc** before **a** and **o** as [3f]; irregular preterite in **-uj-** Gerund: *reduciendo*	reduzco reduces reduce reducimos reducís reducen	reduzca reduzcas reduzca reduzcamos reduzcáis reduzcan	reduje redujiste redujo redujimos redujisteis redujeron
[3o] decir Irregular. Future: *diré* Past Participle: *dicho* Gerund: *diciendo* Imperative: *di (tú)*	digo dices dice decimos decís dicen	diga digas diga digamos digáis digan	dije dijiste dijo dijimos dijisteis dijeron
[3p] oír Irregular. Unstressed **i** between vowels becomes **y** Past Participle: *oído* Gerund: *oyendo*	oigo oyes oye oímos oís oyen	oiga oigas oiga oigamos oigáis oigan	oí oíste oyó oímos oísteis oyeron
[3q] salir Irregular. Future: *saldré* Imperative: *sal (tú)* Gerund: *saliendo*	salgo sales sale salimos salís salen	salga salgas salga salgamos salgáis salgan	salí saliste salió salimos salisteis salieron
[3r] venir Irregular. Future: *vendré* Gerund: *viniendo* Imperative: *ven (tú)*	vengo vienes viene venimos venís vienen	venga vengas venga vengamos vengáis vengan	vine viniste vino vinimos vinisteis vinieron
[3s] ir Irregular. Imperfect: *iba* Gerund: *yendo* Imperative: *ve (tú), id (vosotros)*	voy vas va vamos vais van	vaya vayas vaya vayamos vayáis vayan	fui fuiste fue fuimos fuisteis fueron

SPANISH IN ACTION

[1a] **cantar** (regular verb)	[2a] **temer** (regular verb)	[3a] **partir** (regular verb)	[2j] **haber**	[2v] **ser**
Gerund cantando	*Gerund* temiendo	*Gerund* partiendo	*Gerund* habiendo	*Gerund* siendo
Past Participle cantado	*Past Participle* temido	*Past Participle* partido	*Past Participle* habido	*Past Participle* sido
Imperative canta (tú) cantad (vosotros)	*Imperative* teme (tú) temed (vosotros)	*Imperative* parte (tú) partid (vosotros)		*Imperative* sé (tú) sed (vosotros)

INDICATIVE	**INDICATIVE**	**INDICATIVE**	**INDICATIVE**	**INDICATIVE**
Present canto cantas canta cantamos cantáis cantan	*Present* temo temes teme tememos teméis temen	*Present* parto partes parte partimos partís parten	*Present* he has ha hemos habéis han	*Present* soy eres es somos sois son
Imperfect cantaba cantabas cantaba cantábamos cantabais cantaban	*Imperfect* temía temías temía temíamos temíais temían	*Imperfect* partía partías partía partíamos partíais partían	*Imperfect* había habías había habíamos habíais habían	*Imperfect* era eras era éramos erais eran
Preterite canté cantaste cantó cantamos cantasteis cantaron	*Preterite* temí temiste temió temimos temisteis temieron	*Preterite* partí partiste partió partimos partisteis partieron	*Preterite* hube hubiste hubo hubimos hubisteis hubieron	*Preterite* fui fuiste fue fuimos fuisteis fueron
Future cantaré cantarás cantará cantaremos cantaréis cantarán	*Future* temeré temerás temerá temeremos temeréis temerán	*Future* partiré partirás partirá partiremos partiréis partirán	*Future* habré habrás habrá habremos habréis habrán	*Future* seré serás será seremos seréis serán
Conditional cantaría cantarías cantaría cantaríamos cantaríais cantarían	*Conditional* temería temerías temería temeríamos temeríais temerían	*Conditional* partiría partirías partiría partiríamos partiríais partirían	*Conditional* habría habrías habría habríamos habríais habrían	*Conditional* sería serías sería seríamos seríais serían

SUBJUNCTIVE	**SUBJUNCTIVE**	**SUBJUNCTIVE**	**SUBJUNCTIVE**	**SUBJUNCTIVE**
Present cante cantes cante cantemos cantéis canten	*Present* tema temas tema temamos temáis teman	*Present* parta partas parta partamos partáis partan	*Present* haya hayas haya hayamos hayáis hayan	*Present* sea seas sea seamos seáis sean
Imperfect cantara/-ase cantaras/-ases cantara/-ase cantáramos/-ásemos cantarais/-aseis cantaran/-asen	*Imperfect* temiera/-iese temieras/-ieses temiera/-iese temiéramos/-iésemos temierais/-ieseis temieran/-iesen	*Imperfect* partiera/-iese partieras/-ieses partiera/-iese partiéramos/-iésemos partierais/-ieseis partieran/-iesen	*Imperfect* hubiera/-iese hubieras/-ieses hubiera/-iese hubiéramos/-iésemos hubierais/-ieseis hubieran/-iesen	*Imperfect* fuera/-ese fueras/-eses fuera/-ese fuéramos/-ésemos fuerais/-eseis fueran/-esen

INGLÉS ACTIVO

ÍNDICE

▼ **GUSTOS Y PREFERENCIAS**

▶ Para preguntarle a alguien sus preferencias

Do you like chips?	¿te gustan …?
Do you like swimming?	¿te gusta …?
Would you like to come with us?	¿te gustaría …?
What's your favourite film?	¿cuál es tu … preferida?
Which of the two colours **do you prefer**?	¿cuál de los dos … prefieres?
What would you rather do?	¿qué preferirías …?

▶ Para expresar gustos

I like cooking	me gusta
I love travelling	me encanta
I'm very keen on gardening	me gusta mucho
I'm very fond of my grandmother	quiero mucho a
I really enjoyed the film	me gustó mucho
I don't mind being on my own	no me importa
There's nothing better than a nice cup of tea	no hay nada mejor que

▶ Para decir lo que a uno no le gusta

I don't like football	no me gusta
I don't like his attitude **at all**	no me gusta nada
I hate shopping	odio
What I hate most is waiting for buses	lo que más odio
I can't stand o **can't bear** the thought of seeing him	no soporto
I'm not keen on seafood	no me entusiasma
Rock climbing **doesn't appeal to me**	no me atrae
I've gone off chocolate	ya no me gusta
I've completely **gone off the idea of** going	ya no tengo ganas de

▶ Para decir lo que uno prefiere

I like the blue T-shirt **better than** the white one	me gusta … más que
What I like best about Barcelona **is** the atmosphere	lo que más me gusta de … es
My favourite city **is** Paris	mi … preferida es
I prefer red wine **to** white	prefiero … a
I'd prefer to wait o **I'd rather** wait	prefiero
I'd prefer not to o **I'd rather not** talk about it	prefiero no

▶ Para expresar indiferencia

I don't care	me da igual
It's all the same to me	me da exactamente igual
I don't mind at all	me da exactamente lo mismo
It doesn't matter	no importa
I have no preference	no tengo preferencias

▼ **OPINIONES**

▶ Para pedir la opinión de alguien

What do you think of the new Managing Director?	¿qué te parece … ?
What's your opinion on the subject?	¿qué opinas sobre …?
What do you think about the monarchy?	¿qué piensas de …?
What should he do, **in your opinion**?	en tu opinión
Do you have any thoughts on the matter?	¿tienes alguna opinión sobre …?
What are your views on this issue?	¿cuál es tu opinión sobre …?

INGLÉS ACTIVO

▶ Para expresar una opinión propia

You're right	*tienes razón*
He was right/wrong to resign	*hizo bien/mal en*
Personally, I believe that education is a right	*yo personalmente creo que*
I'm sure he doesn't mean it	*estoy seguro de que*
I feel that we ought to be being more proactive	*creo que*
I think you should be more responsible	*creo que*
I think you are mistaken	*creo que*
I'm convinced that he did it	*estoy convencido de que*
In my opinion, eight years as President is quite enough	*en mi opinión*
I dare say she will be there already	*me figuro que*
To my mind, it should not be legalized	*en mi opinión*
In my view, he should not have done it	*en mi opinión*
As far as I'm concerned, Barnes had it coming to him	*en lo que a mí respecta*
If you ask me, there's something strange going on	*para mí que*

▶ Para responder sin expresar una opinión

It depends	*depende*
It all depends on what you mean	*todo depende de*
It depends on your point of view	*depende de tu punto de vista*
I'd rather not comment on it	*preferiría no pronunciarme sobre*
I don't know anything about it	*no sé nada sobre*
I've never thought about it	*nunca lo he pensado*

▼ ACUERDO

▶ Para mostrarse en acuerdo con lo que se ha dicho

I agree	*estoy de acuerdo*
I quite agree	*estoy totalmente de acuerdo*
I totally agree with you	*estoy totalmente de acuerdo contigo*
I agree up to a point	*estoy de acuerdo hasta cierto punto*
I couldn't agree with you more	*estoy totalmente de acuerdo contigo*
We are in complete agreement on this	*estamos totalmente de acuerdo*
I share your doubts about the proposal	*yo también tengo mis dudas sobre*
You were right to leave	*hiciste bien en*
I have no objection to this being done	*no tengo inconveniente en que*
What a good idea!	*¡qué buena idea!*
It's a great idea	*es una idea estupenda*
I'll be happy to organize it for you	*estaré encantado de*
We should be delighted to accept your offer	*… con mucho gusto*

▼ DESACUERDO

▶ Para mostrarse en desacuerdo con lo que se ha dicho

I disagree	*no estoy de acuerdo*
I cannot agree with you on this point	*no estoy de acuerdo contigo*
It's not true to say that people care less about poverty	*no es cierto que*
We must agree to differ on this point	*habrá que aceptar que nunca nos pondremos de acuerdo*
You are wrong to criticize	*te equivocas al*
I entirely reject his claims	*rechazo totalmente*
I totally disagree with the previous two callers	*no estoy en absoluto de acuerdo con*

FRASES ÚTILES

I don't share that point of view	*no comparto ese punto de vista*
I won't hear of it	*no quiero ni oír hablar de ello*
I don't think much of this idea	*no me convence mucho*
I wouldn't dream of doing a thing like that	*no se me ocurriría hacer*
I just couldn't do something like that	*es que no podría*
It's quite out of the question	*no puede ser*
I won't agree to any such plan	*no voy a apoyar*
I'm afraid you are mistaken	*creo or me temo que está usted equivocado*
I am afraid I must refuse	*lo siento pero he de negarme*

▼ APROBACIÓN Y DESAPROBACIÓN

▶ Aprobación

I couldn't have put it better myself	*yo no lo hubiera dicho mejor*
It's just the job!	*¡perfecto!*
This is exactly what I had in mind	*es justo lo que yo tenía pensado*
You were right to consult me first	*hiciste bien en*
I'm in favour of higher taxation	*estoy a favor de*
I'd certainly go along with that	*estoy totalmente de acuerdo*
What an excellent idea!	*¡qué idea tan estupenda!*
I think it's a great idea	*creo que es una idea estupenda*
I have a very high opinion of their new teaching methods	*tengo muy buena opinión de*
I think very highly of the people who have been leading thus far	*… me merecen muy buena opinión*
People **rightly believe** that it's time for a change	*cree, y con razón, que*

▶ Desaprobación

I don't think much of what this government has done so far	*no tengo muy buena opinión de*
I've had enough of this	*… (ya) me tiene harto*
I can't bear o **stand** people who smoke in restaurants	*no soporto*
I think he was quite wrong to repeat what I said	*creo que hizo muy mal en*
We are opposed to nuclear testing	*nos oponemos a*
I am against animal experiments	*estoy en contra de*
You shouldn't have spoken to him like that	*no deberías haber*
I strongly disapprove of such behaviour	*desapruebo totalmente*
I'm disappointed by his attitude	*me decepciona*
I'm disappointed in him	*me decepciona*
It's a pity that you don't like her	*es una pena que*
It's a most regrettable situation	*es … muy de lamentar*

▼ DISCULPAS

▶ Para disculparse

Sorry	*lo siento*
I'm really sorry but we won't be able to come tonight	*de verdad lo siento pero*
Sorry to disturb you	*siento*
I do apologize for what happened	*pido disculpas (por)*
I'm afraid I may be late	*quizá(s) llegue tarde*
Please forgive me for behaving so badly	*perdóname por*
Please accept our apologies	*les rogamos acepten nuestras disculpas*

▶ Para aceptar responsabilidad de algo

It's my fault	*es culpa mía*
I shouldn't have lost my temper	*no debería haber*
If only I hadn't lost the keys	*ojalá no hubiera*

It was a mistake to come here — *fue un error*
I take full responsibility for what happened — *me hago plenamente responsable de*

▶ Para expresar lo que se lamenta

It's a shame that you should feel like that — *es una pena que*
I'm sorry, but that's the way it is — *lo siento*
I'm afraid I can't help you very much — *(me temo que) no puedo*
I have no other option but to resign — *no tengo más remedio que*
We very much regret that we have been unable to agree — *lamentamos mucho*
We regret to inform you that the post of Editor has now been filled — *lamentamos tener que informarle que*

▶ Para rechazar toda responsabilidad

It wasn't my fault — *no fue culpa mía*
I didn't do it on purpose — *no lo hice a propósito*
I didn't mean to upset you — *no era mi intención*
I had no choice o **option** — *no me quedaba otro remedio*
I had nothing to do with it — *no tuve nada que ver con ello*
We are unhappy with 1.5%, but under the circumstances **we have no alternative but to** accept — *no nos queda otra alternativa que*

▼ EXPLICACIONES

▶ Para dar las razones de algo

I didn't have any lunch **because** I wasn't hungry — *porque*
I was held up **because of** the traffic — *por*
They have backed down **as a result of** public pressure — *como consecuencia de*
We were not allowed out **for** security **reasons** — *por razones de*
They are facing higher costs **owing to** rising inflation — *debido a*
The match was called off **due to** bad weather — *debido a*
Thanks to their efforts, productivity has increased — *gracias a*
People have died **for lack of** proper medical attention — *por falta de*
I refused to leave **out of** stubbornness — *por*
The court had ordered his release, **on the grounds that** he had already been acquitted of most of the charges — *basándose en que*
It was a cigarette end that **caused** the fire — *provocó*
He was very tired **as** he had been up since 4 am — *como*
Since you've been so kind, I really can't refuse — *ya que*
I couldn't find you, **so** I left — *así que*
What the Party said was taken to be right, **therefore** anyone who disagreed must be wrong — *por lo tanto*
Seeing that you're here, you might as well stay — *en vista de que*
Given the scale of the problem, any help is welcome — *dada*
Given that she's only young, she's done very well — *dado que*

▶ Consecuencias

I've got a meeting in half an hour, **so** we'll have to hurry — *así que*
I put the oven on too hot, **with the result that** everything was burned to a frazzle — *y el resultado fue que*
I need to find a babysitter **so that** we can go out tonight — *para que*
We didn't send out the invitations in time, **consequently** nobody turned up — *y por consiguiente*
Voting in the elections **has resulted in** an overall win for the Democrats — *ha tenido como resultado*
He doesn't listen. **That's why** people think he's stupid — *por eso*

INGLÉS ACTIVO

▼ COMPARACIONES

► Para destacar el parecido

This dessert **is like** a soufflé	*es como*
Her work **is comparable to** anything by the other students	*es comparable a*
People **compare him to** Robert Redford	*lo compara con*
The immune system **can be compared to** a complicated electronic network	*se puede comparar con*
The impact was **equivalent to** a bomb exploding	*equivalente a*
Pay **corresponds to** levels of productivity	*corresponde a*
She **reminds me of** my old headmistress	*me recuerda a*
She and her son **were very alike**	*había un gran parecido entre … y*
The new computerized system costs **much the same as** a more conventional one	*prácticamente lo mismo que*
A nectarine? **It's the same as** a peach without the furry skin	*es lo mismo que*

► Para destacar el contraste

How do the new candidates rate **as compared to** previous ones?	*comparados con*
If you compare today's team **to** that of the 1980s, you will find few similarities	*si comparas … con*
Compared to previous years, investment has fallen sharply	*comparado con*
The streets are narrow **compared with** British ones	*comparadas con*
You can't compare new methods **with** traditional ones	*no se pueden comparar … con*
The bomb was small **in** o **by comparison with** those often used nowadays	*en comparación con*
No catastrophe **can compare to** Chernobyl	*no hay … que se pueda comparar a*
T**here's no comparison between** the photos I take **and** those of a professional	*no hay comparación entre … y*
In contrast to the rest of the world, Asia is not experiencing a recession	*en contraste con*
Only 30% of the females died **as opposed to** 57% of the males	*frente a*
Whereas burglars used to make off only with video recorders, they now also empty the fridge	*mientras que*
The two leaders **differ in** their approach	*difieren en*
Real ale is **better than** lager	*mejor que*
While some people like to go out on Saturday night, others prefer to stay in and watch TV	*mientras que*
My old chair **was nowhere near as** comfortable **as** my new one	*no era ni mucho menos tan … como*
We may be twins, but **we have nothing in common**	*no tenemos nada en común*

▼ PETICIONES

I'd like two lagers and a packet of crisps, **please**	*¿me pone …?*
Could you give me a hand with this?	*¿puedes …?*
Can you pass on the message **to** Eddie?	*¿le pasas … a …?*
Would you mind looking after Hannah tomorrow?	*¿te importaría …?*
If you wouldn't mind just waiting here a moment	*si hace el favor de*
Would you be so kind as to show me the way out?	*¿podría hacer el favor de …?*
Do you mind if I smoke?	*¿te importa que …?*
Could I borrow the car on Sunday?	*¿me dejas …?*
Let me know if you need any help	*si … dímelo*
I'd be most grateful if you could spare me some time	*le agradecería que*
I should be grateful if you could increase my credit limit	*le agredecería que*

▼ PROPUESTAS

I could pick you up on my way home, if you like	*si quieres*
Can I give you a hand with that?	*¿te echo una mano …?*
How would you like to go and live in California?	*¿qué te parecería …?*
How about a nice hot bath/a gin and tonic?	*¿qué tal …?*
What would you say to a trip up to town next week?	*¿qué te parece si …?*
It would be nice if you could come too	*estaría bien que*
Do you want me to come and pick you up?	*¿quieres que …?*
Would you like to watch a video?	*¿te gustaría …?*
Would you like me **to** babysit for you?	*¿quieres que …?*

▼ CONSEJOS Y SUGERENCIAS

▶ Para pedir consejo

What would you do **if you were me**?	*en mi lugar*
I don't know any of these wines – **what would you recommend?**	*¿cuál me recomiendas?*
Do you think I ought to tell the truth?	*¿crees que debería …?*
What do you think?	*¿tú qué crees?*
What would you advise me to do?	*¿qué me aconsejas que haga?*
What would you advise under the circumstances?	*¿qué me aconsejas …?*
Have you any idea how I should go about this?	*¿se te ocurre cómo …?*
I'm not sure what to do. **What do you suggest?**	*¿qué sugieres tú?*

▶ Para aconsejar

A word of advice: always read the instructions first	*un consejo*
A useful tip: pour salt on wine spills	*un consejo*
It might be better to think it over before doing anything	*quizá(s) sería mejor*
You'd be as well to tell him now	*más te valdría*
What if you try ignoring her?	*¿y si …?*
Why don't you come with us?	*¿por qué no …?*
You could try again next year	*puedes*
What you need is a change of scene	*lo que necesitas es*
Suppose o **Supposing you** took your holiday now?	*¿y si …?*
How would you feel about going back to work?	*¿qué te parecería …?*
You'd better take some extra cash	*es mejor que*
If I were you, I'd be moving on	*yo que tú, me pondría a*
Take my advice and don't rush into anything	*hazme caso*
I think you ought to o **should** seek professional advice	*creo que deberías*
Perhaps you should speak to your boss about it	*a lo mejor deberías*
It would be better to wait and see what happens	*sería mejor*
Perhaps it would be as well to change the locks	*quizá(s) lo mejor sería*
It might be a good idea to tell her about this	*sería una buena idea*
I suggest that you go to bed and try to sleep	*te aconsejo que*

▶ Para hacer una advertencia

I don't think you should get involved	*creo que no deberías*
I should warn you that he can be very awkward	*te advierto que*
Watch you don't trip over your shoelaces	*cuidado no*
Make sure that o **See that** you don't miss your bus	*ten cuidado no vayas a*
Whatever you do, don't drink the local schnapps	*no se te ocurra*

▼ INTENCIONES Y DESEOS

▶ Para preguntar a alguien lo que piensa hacer

Will you take the job?	*¿vas a …?*
What are you going to do when you leave school?	*¿qué vas a hacer …?*
What will you do when she finds out?	*¿qué vas a hacer …?*

INGLÉS ACTIVO

FRASES ÚTILES

What will you do if you can't find a job?	¿qué vas a hacer si …?
Are you planning on staying long?	¿tienes pensado …?
Are you planning to come back?	¿tienes pensado …?
What do you intend doing o **to do**?	¿qué piensas hacer?
Did you mean to tell him about it?	¿tenías intención de …?
Are you thinking of going on holiday this year?	¿tienes pensado …?

▶ Para expresar las propias intenciones

I'm thinking of retiring next year	estoy pensando en
I'm hoping to go and see her when I'm in Paris	espero
I was planning to visit her later this month	había pensado
I aim to reach Africa in three months	pretendo
I am going to sell the car as soon as possible	voy a
I intend to put the house on the market	tengo la intención de
The council **intends to** build a new shopping centre here	tiene intención de
I've made up my mind to o **I've decided to** sell	he decidido
I have no intention of accepting the post	no tengo intención de

▶ Para expresar lo que se desea hacer

I'd like to work in publishing	me gustaría
I want to work abroad when I leave college	quiero
We want her to be an architect when she grows up	queremos que
I'd have liked to be an actress	me habría gustado
I hope to find a job in advertising	espero
It's my dream to travel round the world	mi sueño es
I'm dying to see him	me muero de ganas de

▼ OBLIGACIÓN

You've got to o **You have to** be back before midnight	tienes que
You must be eighteen before you can apply	tienes que
You really should talk to him about it	tendrías que
You ought to phone him	tienes que
You need to have a valid passport if you want to go abroad	hay que
I must try to see her	debo
He was forced to ask his family for a loan	se vio obligado a
Men **are forced to** hide their emotions	se sienten obligados a
We were obliged to take off our shoes before entering	nos obligaron a
It is essential to know what the career options are	es esencial
School **is compulsory** up to the age of 16	es obligatorio
We have no alternative o **option but to** fight	no nos queda otro remedio más que
I had no choice but to refuse	no tuve más remedio que
Lots of women **have to** work, **they have no** (**other**) option	tienen que … no les queda otro remedio
Three passport photos **are required**	se necesitan
I don't have to o **I haven't got to** work late tonight	no tengo que
You don't have to o **You needn't** go there if you don't want to	no hace falta que
You are not allowed to sit the exam more than twice	no puedes
You mustn't show this document to anyone	no debes
You're not supposed to o **meant to** use this room unless	no puedes
Smoking **is prohibited** o **is not permitted** in the lounge	está prohibido

▼ PERMISO

▶ Para pedir permiso

Can I o **Could I borrow** your car this afternoon?	¿me dejas …?
Can I use the telephone, please?	¿puedo …?

Are we allowed to smoke in here?	*¿podemos …?*
Would it be all right if I arrived on Monday instead?	*¿te importaría que …?*
We leave tomorrow. **Is that all right by you?**	*¿te parece bien?*
Do you mind if I come to the meeting next week?	*¿te importa que …?*

► Para dar permiso

You can have anything you want	*puedes*
You are allowed to visit the palace on certain days	*se puede*
They allowed everyone **to leave**	*dejaron salir*
I've nothing against her going there with us	*no me opongo a que*
I don't mind if you read my letter	*no me importa que*
I don't mind	*me da igual*
That's fine by me	*me parece bien*
Yes, by all means	*sí, por supuesto*

► Para denegar permiso

No. **You can't** swim here	*no puedes*
You mustn't go anywhere near the research lab	*no puedes*
You're not allowed to go swimming on your own	*no puedes*
I'm afraid **it's not allowed**	*no está permitido*
You mustn't enter the premises without permission	*no puede*
We can't allow the marriage **to take place**	*no podemos permitir que*
I absolutely forbid you to go	*te prohíbo terminantemente que*
Smoking **is strictly forbidden** at all times	*está terminantemente prohibido*

▼ CERTEZA, PROBABILIDAD Y POSIBILIDAD

► Certeza

Undoubtedly, there will be problems	*sin duda*
He is, **without doubt**, the worst referee I've ever seen	*sin duda*
It's quite true that I was in the building at the time	*es totalmente cierto que*
She has **obviously** changed her mind	*obviamente*
She **was bound to** find out	*era de esperar que*
I'm sure o **certain** (**that**) he'll keep his word	*estoy seguro de que*
I'm positive o **convinced** (**that**) it was your mother I saw	*estoy convencido de que*
We now know for certain o **for sure that** the exam papers were stolen and copied	*sabemos ya con seguridad que*
There is no doubt that the talks will be long and difficult	*no hay ninguna duda de que*

► Probabilidad

I'll **probably** go next week	*seguramente*
You'll **very probably** be met at the airport by one of our men	*es muy probable que*
It's highly probable that there will be a recession	*es muy probable que*
It seems highly likely that they had met before	*parece muy probable que*
It's very likely that you will get withdrawal symptoms	*lo más seguro es que*
He must have forgotten to turn off the lights	*debe de haber*
The cheque **should** reach you by Saturday	*debería*
It's quite possible that we could adapt our equipment	*es bastante posible que*
It looks as though o **as if** it might rain	*parece que*
It sounds like o **as though** the deal is off	*parece que*

► Posibilidad

It's possible	*es posible*
Possibly	*posiblemente*

INGLÉS ACTIVO

The situation **could** change	*podría*
In a few months everything **may** have changed	*puede que*
Perhaps I am mistaken	*quizá(s)*
Britain **could perhaps** play a more positive role in developing policy	*podría quizá(s)*
It is possible that psychological factors play some unknown role in the healing process	*es posible que*
It should be possible to repair it	*seguramente se puede*
It is not inconceivable that the economy is already in recession	*cabe la posibilidad de que*
It may be that the battle will have to be fought over again	*puede ser que*

▼ INCERTIDUMBRE, IMPROBABILIDAD E IMPOSIBILIDAD

► Incertidumbre

I'm not sure it's useful	*no estoy seguro de que*
I'm not sure o **certain that** I really know the answer	*no estoy seguro de que*
We can't say for sure what time we'll arrive	*no podemos decir con seguridad*
Will he come? **I doubt it**	*lo dudo*
I have my doubts about his guilt	*tengo mis dudas sobre*
I doubt (whether) he'll have any problems getting here	*dudo que*
It's doubtful whether the match will take place	*no es seguro que*
I doubt if he knows where it came from	*dudo que*
I'm wondering if I should offer to help?	*no sé si*

► Improbabilidad

He **probably** won't come	*seguramente*
You have **probably not** yet seen the report in question	*seguramente no*
I'd be surprised if she knew anything about it	*me sorprendería que*
It's unlikely that we'll stay in touch	*es bastante improbable que*
It's very doubtful whether the expedition will succeed	*es bastante dudoso que*
In the unlikely event that the room was bugged, the music would drown out their conversation	*si se diera el caso poco probable de que*

► Imposibilidad

It's impossible	*es imposible*
There can be no changes in the schedule	*no puede haber*
I couldn't possibly invite George and not his wife	*¿cómo voy a …?*
There is no possibility of a ceasefire	*no hay posibilidades de*
There's no chance of him buying a round of drinks	*no … ni por casualidad*
There is no question of us getting this finished on time	*es imposible que*
The idea of trying to govern twelve nations from one centre **is unthinkable**	*es impensable*

INGLÉS ACTIVO

▼ FÓRMULAS DE ENCABEZAMIENTO Y DESPEDIDA

▶ Cuando se escribe a conocidos y amigos

Dear Mr and Mrs Roberts
Dear Kate and Jeremy
Dear Aunt Jane and Uncle Alan
Dear Tommy

Yours (bastante formal)
With best wishes
Love from
Lots of love from (muy informal)

▶ En correspondencia de carácter formal

Dear Sirs
Dear Sir
Dear Madam
Dear Sir or Madam

Yours faithfully (Brit)
Sincerely (yours) (US)
Respectfully yours (US)

Dear Professor Meldrum
Dear Ms Gilmour

Yours sincerely (Brit)
Sincerely (yours) (US)

▼ COMIENZO DE UNA CARTA A CONOCIDOS O AMIGOS

Thank you so much for your letter.	Muchísimas gracias por tu carta.
It was lovely to hear from you.	Me alegró mucho recibir noticias tuyas.
Sorry I haven't written sooner but …	Perdona que no (te) haya escrito antes, pero …

▼ FINAL DE UNA CARTA A CONOCIDOS O AMIGOS

Give my regards to …	Recuerdos a o para …
Give my love to …	Saluda de mi parte a … o Saludos para …
Julia sends her best wishes.	Julia te manda recuerdos.
Write soon.	Escribe o Escríbeme pronto.

▼ COMIENZO DE UNA CARTA DE CARÁCTER FORMAL

In reply to your letter of …	En respuesta a su (atenta) carta de fecha …
With reference to …	En relación o referencia a …
Thank you for your letter of …	Agradecemos su (atenta) carta de …
We are pleased to inform you that …	Nos complace comunicarle o anunciarle que …
We regret to inform you that …	Lamentamos (tener que) comunicarle(s) o anunciarle(s) que …
I am writing to you to …	Me dirijo a usted para … o El objeto de mi carta es …
I would be grateful if you would send me …	Le agradecería (que) me enviara …
Please send me …	Les ruego (que) me envíen …

▼ FINAL DE UNA CARTA DE CARÁCTER FORMAL

Thanking you in advance for your help	Muchas gracias de antemano por su colaboración
If you require any further information, please do not hesitate to contact me	Si desea más información, no dude en ponerse en contacto conmigo
I look forward to hearing from you	Quedo a la espera de sus noticias/de su respuesta

▼ DIFERENCIAS EN LA FORMA DE ESCRIBIR LA FECHA EN INGLÉS

En inglés **británico**, se puede utilizar cualquiera de las siguientes fórmulas:

6th March   **6 March**   **March 6th**   **March 6**

En cambio, en inglés **americano**, sólo se utilizan las siguientes:

March 6th   **March 6**

Con el fin de evitar confusión, se recomienda no escribir la fecha de esta manera: **12.03.02**, ya que en inglés británico se leería como **12 de marzo de 2002** mientras que en inglés americano se leería como **3 de diciembre de 2002**.

INGLÉS ACTIVO

CORRESPONDENCIA

▼ DIRECCIONES BRITÁNICAS

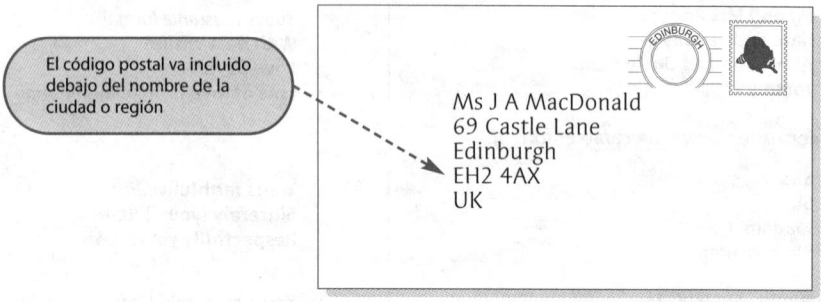

El código postal va incluido debajo del nombre de la ciudad o región

Ms J A MacDonald
69 Castle Lane
Edinburgh
EH2 4AX
UK

Si se escribe la dirección del remitente, como suele ocurrir cuando se envía correspondencia al extranjero, ésta debe aparecer en el remite, precedida por la palabra **sender** o **from**:

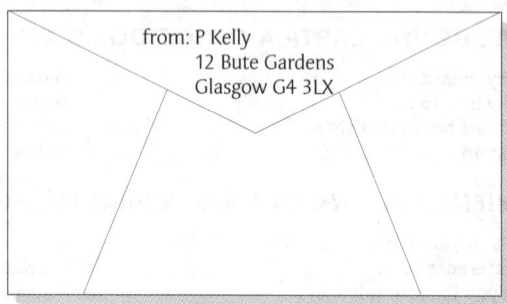

from: P Kelly
12 Bute Gardens
Glasgow G4 3LX

▼ DIRECCIONES ESTADOUNIDENSES

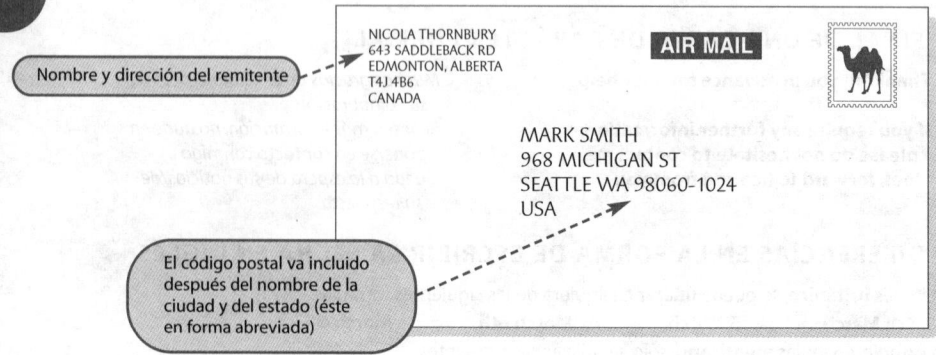

Nombre y dirección del remitente

NICOLA THORNBURY
643 SADDLEBACK RD
EDMONTON, ALBERTA
T4J 4B6
CANADA

AIR MAIL

MARK SMITH
968 MICHIGAN ST
SEATTLE WA 98060-1024
USA

El código postal va incluido después del nombre de la ciudad y del estado (éste en forma abreviada)

INGLÉS ACTIVO

▼ CARTA DE AGRADECIMIENTO INFORMAL

Dirección del remitente

85 Hamilton Drive
Glasgow
G12 9EQ

4 August 2001

Se puede usar coma, o, sobre todo en el caso de cartas escritas a máquina, omitir el signo de puntuación después del saludo

Dear Richard and Jenny,

As you can see, I'm now in Glasgow and wishing I were back with you and the children.

I really enjoyed my month with you and only wish it could have been longer. Thank you so much for making me feel part of the family and for taking me on all those wonderful trips.

Glasgow looks very attractive from what I've seen of it and Mr and Mrs Duncan seem nice. I'm not sure how I'm going to manage with the children, though; they're terribly naughty and keep telling me that the last au pair only lasted a week!

How are all of you? I hope you're enjoying the summer and the lovely weather we're having.

Take care of yourselves.

With lots of love,

Anna

XXX

Nota: Las Xs equivalen a besos. En inglés norteamericano, también se puede emplear el símbolo O, equivalente a abrazo

Omitir la coma en la despedida si se ha hecho lo propio en el saludo inicial

▼ CARTA DE RECLAMACIÓN FORMAL

Dirección del remitente

39 Hill Street
Snuffleborough
SN55 1PQ

Nombre y dirección del destinatario

The Manager
Vine2Wine
6-8 Queens Road
Snuffleborough
SN19 6ZZ

Cuando no se sabe si el destinatario es hombre o mujer se debe usar esta fórmula

10 August 2001

Dear Sir or Madam

En cartas escritas a máquina, se suele omitir la coma después del saludo

It is with much regret that I am writing to tell you that my wife and I will be taking our custom elsewhere owing to the poor service received at your shop.

On 18 July 2001, I placed an order for six cases of champagne for my daughter's wedding on 3 August. I was told that they would be available for collection on 1 August.

When I returned on 1 August, however, the assistant told me that there was no record of my order on file and that a new order would not arrive until 5 August. When I explained that this would be too late, he offered me some inferior wine instead. When I declined, he told me to take it or leave it.

Fortunately for us, staff at nearby *Wine Lines* were infinitely more helpful; thanks to them and their special next-day delivery, our guests were able to toast the happy couple in genuine champagne.

Las cartas que empiezan con **Dear Sir or Madam**, **Dear Sir** y **Dear Madam**, normalmente acaban con **Yours faithfully** en inglés británico y con **Sincerely (yours)** o **Respectfully yours** en inglés norteamericano, seguido de la firma

Yours faithfully

Thomas Henderson

Thomas Henderson

Omitir la coma en la depedida si se ha hecho lo propio en el saludo inicial

▼ CARTA EN INGLÉS NORTEAMERICANO (FORMAL)

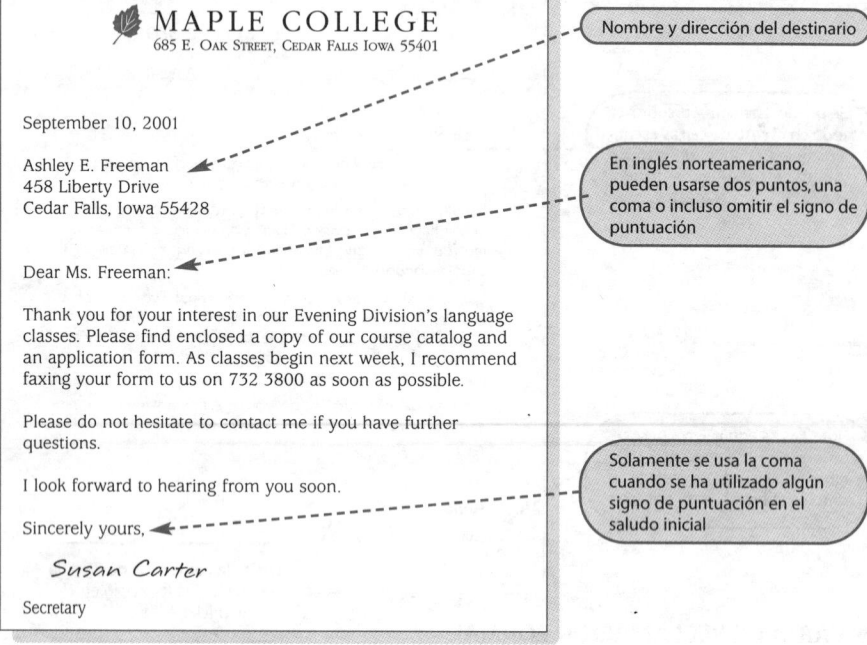

🍁 **MAPLE COLLEGE**
685 E. Oak Street, Cedar Falls Iowa 55401

September 10, 2001

Ashley E. Freeman
458 Liberty Drive
Cedar Falls, Iowa 55428

Dear Ms. Freeman:

Thank you for your interest in our Evening Division's language classes. Please find enclosed a copy of our course catalog and an application form. As classes begin next week, I recommend faxing your form to us on 732 3800 as soon as possible.

Please do not hesitate to contact me if you have further questions.

I look forward to hearing from you soon.

Sincerely yours,

Susan Carter

Secretary

> Nombre y dirección del destinario

> En inglés norteamericano, pueden usarse dos puntos, una coma o incluso omitir el signo de puntuación

> Solamente se usa la coma cuando se ha utilizado algún signo de puntuación en el saludo inicial

▼ RESERVA DE HOTEL POR FAX

FAX Marsham Engineering Ltd, 180–182 Stockton Road, Middlesbrough TS1 4ZZ

TO: Mr M. Quayle (Manager), Tower View Hotel, Douglas, Isle of Man
FAX NUMBER: 01624 444333

FROM: Linda Evans (PA to Martin Broomhill, Assistant Managing Director)
FAX NUMBER: 01642 369 666

DATE: 2 April 2002
SUBJECT: Reservations 1-8 August 2002 (Engineering World Conference)
NUMBER OF PAGES (including this one): one

Dear Mr Quayle

We should like to reserve six single rooms with ensuite facilities for one week from 1 to 7 August 2002 for members of staff attending the above-mentioned conference. I understand from the *Stupendous Stay* hotel guide that your rates would be £90 per person per night, inclusive of breakfast.

I should be very grateful if you could let me know as soon as possible whether or not you have rooms available for these dates and, if so, if you could confirm your rates.

I look forward to hearing from you.

Yours sincerely

Linda Evans

IF YOU HAVE ANY PROBLEMS RECEIVING THIS MESSAGE,
PLEASE TELEPHONE LINDA EVANS ON 01642 369 662

> **Yours sincerely** se utiliza en inglés británico en correspondencia de carácter formal dirigida a una persona si previamente se ha incluido su nombre en el saludo inicial. Su equivalente en inglés norteamericano es **Sincerely** o **Sincerely yours.**

INGLÉS ACTIVO

▼ CURRICULUM VITAE BRITÁNICO

CURRICULUM VITAE

Personal Details

Name:	Nicola Clare Thornbury	**Mobile Phone:**	07999 543 123
Address:	46 Greenbank Road	**Email:**	nct101@hotmail.com
	Newcastle upon Tyne	**Date of Birth:**	23 April 1977
	NE6 6AZ	**Nationality:**	British
Home Tel:	0191 444 6161	**Marital Status:**	single

Qualifications

1999	BA Hons German with French (Upper Second Division), Tyne University, Newcastle upon Tyne
1995	4 A Levels (French A, Spanish A, Physics B, Chemistry B)
1994	1 AS Level (Mathematics B)
1993	10 GCSEs including English and Mathematics

Employment history

September 2001 – present	Trainee manager, Hotel Organica, Newcastle upon Tyne
September 1999 – July 2000	Call centre worker at Cutting-Edge Computers, Glasgow, dealing with orders from Germany and Austria
June – August 1995	Summer job as receptionist at Hotel Organica, Newcastle upon Tyne

Skills

Fully computer literate (Word for Windows, Excel)
Clean driving licence since 1996

Interests

Travel (have travelled extensively throughout Europe and North America)
Amateur Dramatics

Referees

Douglas Johnson (Team Leader), Cutting-Edge Computers, Maryhill Road, Glasgow, G22 9QQ
Dr Brian Flowers, German Dept, Tyne University, Newcastle upon Tyne, NE3 4AZ

▼ CURRICULUM VITAE NORTEAMERICANO

RÉSUMÉ

ASHLEY ELIZABETH FREEMAN

458 Liberty Drive
Cedar Falls
Iowa
55428
USA
Tel: (723) 1678 9502

JOB OBJECTIVE

To find employment in the field of Social Work, especially addiction recovery.

WORK EXPERIENCE

Internship at Cedar Falls Veterans' Hospital. Provided counseling to recovering drug addicts.
Teacher's assistant in the Head Start Day Care Program, Cedar Falls.
Volunteer tutor for GED program at Waterloo Community Center (Iowa). Helped 30 students earn their High School Diploma over a year's period.

EDUCATION

BA in Sociology and Psychology, University of Iowa. Graduated *magna cum laude.*
High School Diploma, Waterloo, Iowa. Graduated *cum laude.*

OTHER DETAILS

Member of Amnesty International and Sociology Honor Society.
Hobbies include kick boxing, electric guitar, and learning Spanish.

REFERENCES AVAILABLE UPON REQUEST

INGLÉS ACTIVO

49

From:	Carol Lawson (New Products Coordinator) <Carol.Lawson@sureinsure.co.uk>
To:	Sales Reps <sales.reps@sureinsure.co.uk>
Subject:	Training Course
Date:	Tues 2 April 2002 08:55:07

As most of you will be aware, our training week has had to be put back to 22 - 26 April, owing to recent events affecting the whole of the insurance industry.

Arrangements will be as before as regards venue (i.e. Coronation Hotel, Barchester Square, Norwich), and the course will begin at 11.30 am on the 22nd, giving you plenty of time to check in.

Please ensure you have read the attached agenda and documents beforehand, so that you can raise any questions you may have.

Regards

Carol

📄 agenda.doc

En inglés la dirección de correo se lee así:
Carol dot Lawson at sureinsure dot co dot U K

From:	Jessica <jess@conspan.net>
To:	peter.oxleigh@crow.ac.uk
Subject:	party time
Date:	Wed, 3 April 2002 14:35:21

Hi Peter

How's life? I hope you're enjoying freshers' week.

Did you get your computer problems sorted out? It was lousy luck getting that virus and losing so much data; I guess you won't be opening any unsolicited e-mail from now on.

Anyway, the reason I'm e-mailing is that I'm having a party on Saturday 13 April, and I wondered if you could come.

Pls say yes!

Love

Jessica

PS I really enjoyed that book you sent me :-)

THX FOR THE MSG. XLNT NEWS! CU AT THE WKEND THEN. LOL JAMES

JUST TO LET U KNOW! CAN'T MAKE IT 2 THE MATCH ON SAT. NJOY YOURSELVES.

▼ INTERNET Y CORREO ELECTRÓNICO

an attachment	un archivo adjunto
back/forward	atrás/adelante
a backup	una copia de seguridad
a bookmark	un marcador o un favorito
a browser	un navegador
a chat room	un chat
to click on	hacer clic en
a command	una orden
to copy	copiar
to cut and paste	cortar y pegar
cyberspace	ciberespacio
to delete	borrar
a directory	un directorio
a dotcom	una puntocom
to double-click on	hacer doble clic en
to download	descargar o bajar
downloadable	descargable
e-commerce	el comercio electrónico
an e-mail	un e-mail
an e-mail address	una dirección electrónica
to e-mail someone	mandar un e-mail a alguien
FAQs (frequently asked questions)	preguntas frecuentes
a file	un archivo
a folder	una carpeta
to highlight	marcar
"home"	"inicio"
a homepage	una página de inicio
an icon	un icono
the Internet	Internet
an Internet user	un/una internauta
an ISP (Internet Service Provider)	un proveedor (de servicios) de Internet
a link	un enlace
memory	memoria
the Net	la Red
newsgroups	grupos de noticias
on-line/off-line	conectado/desconectado
to be on-line	estar conectado
a password	una contraseña
to save a file	guardar un archivo
to save as	guardar como
the screen	la pantalla
a screen saver	un salvapantallas
a scroll bar	una barra de desplazamiento vertical
to search	buscar
a search engine	un buscador
search tips	sugerencias de búsqueda
a server	un servidor
a smiley	un smiley
snail mail	correo ordinario
spam	correo basura
a spreadsheet	una hoja de cálculo
to surf the Net	navegar por Internet o la Red
a text message	un mensaje de texto
text messaging	mensajes de texto
a toolbar	una barra de herramientas
the wastebasket	la papelera de reciclaje
the Web	la o el Web
a web address	una dirección de Internet
a web page	una página web
a website	un sitio web

▼ ABREVIATURAS EN MENSAJES DE TEXTO Y CORREO ELECTRÓNICO

2 = to
2DAY = today
2MORO = tomorrow
2NITE = tonight
2U = to you
4 = for
AFAIK = as far as I know
ASAP = as soon as possible
B = be
B4 = before
BCNU = be seeing you
BRB = be right back
BTDT = been there done that
BTW = by the way
CID = consider it done
COZ = because
CU = see you
EZ = easy
FWIW = for what it's worth
FYI = for your information
GAL = get a life
GBTM = get back to me
GR8 = great

GTG = got to go
H8 = hate
HTH = hope this helps
IMHO = in my humble opinion
IMO = in my opinion
IOU = I owe you
L8R = later
LOL = laugh out loud/lots of love
LV = love
M8 = mate
MSG = message
MYOB = mind your own business
NE = any
NE1 = anyone
NJOY = enjoy
NO1 = no one
NP = no problem
NRN = no reply necessary
OIC = oh I see
OTT = over the top
PLS = please
PPL = people
R = are

RN = right now
RU = are you
RUOK = are you ok
S/O = someone
S/TH = something
SUM1 = someone
THX = thanks
TMB = text me back
TTFN = ta ta or bye for now
TTYL = talk to you later
TXT = text
TYVM = thank you very much
U = you
V = very
WAN2 = want to
WBS = write back soon
WIV = with
XLNT = excellent
WKND = weekend
W/O = without
WUD = what are you doing
Y = why
YR = your

INGLÉS ACTIVO

▶ Diferentes tipos de llamadas

local call/national call/international call	*llamada local o metropolitana/ llamada interprovincial/llamada internacional*
I want to make a reverse-charge call to a London **number** *(Brit)* o **I want to call a** London **number collect** *(US)*	*Quisiera hacer una llamada a cobro revertido a*
I'd like a wake-up call for 7:30 **tomorrow morning**	*¿me podrían avisar por teléfono mañana por la mañana a …?*

▶ Para obtener un número

How do I make an outside call?	*¿Qué hay que hacer para obtener línea externa?*
Can you give me the number of Europost, 20 Duke Street, Whitby?	*¿Me puede decir el número de …? La dirección es …*
What is the code for Exeter?	*¿Cuál es el prefijo de …?*

▶ Cuando contestan

Can you give me o **Could I have extension** 516, **please**?	*¿Me pone con la extensión o (RPL) el interno o (Chi, Peru) el anexo … por favor?*
Could I speak to Mr Swinton, **please**?	*Por favor, ¿podría hablar con …?*
Is that Mrs King?	*¿Es usted …?*
I'll call you back in half an hour	*Volveré a llamar dentro de*
Could you ask him to call me when he gets back?	*¿Puede decirle que me llame cuando vuelva?*

▶ Contesta la centralita/el conmutador

I'm putting you through now	*Le pongo o Le paso*
I have a call from Tokyo **for** Mrs Thomas	*Hay una llamada desde … para*
Sorry to keep you waiting	*Perdone la demora o Siento haberle hecho esperar*
Please hold (the line)	*No cuelgue o No se retire, por favor*
There's no reply	*No contesta*
The line is engaged *(Brit)* o **busy** *(US)*	*Comunica o Está comunicando*

▶ Para contestar al teléfono

Hello?	*¿Diga? o ¿Dígame? o ¿Sí? (Sp), ¿Aló? (LAm), ¿Hola? (SC), ¿Bueno? (Mex)*
Yes, it's Mark **speaking**	*Sí, soy*
"Is that Ana?" – **"Speaking"**	*Sí, soy yo*
Who's speaking?	*¿Quién es? o ¿Con quién hablo?*
Who shall I say is calling?	*¿De parte de quién?*
Would you like to leave a message?	*¿Quiere dejar algún recado?*

▶ En caso de dificultad

I can't get through	*No consigo comunicar*
Their phone is out of order	*No les funciona el teléfono*
We were cut off	*Se ha cortado (la línea)*
I must have dialled the wrong number	*Debo (de) haberme equivocado de número*
This is a very bad line	*Se oye muy mal*

*Por regla general, para indicar el número de teléfono, en inglés se leen los dígitos de uno en uno, aunque si se repite el dígito, con frecuencia se emplean las palabras **double** o **triple** (seguidas del dígito repetido). Ha de tenerse en cuenta que en inglés británico, por regla general, se lee el dígito <u>cero</u> como la letra **O** del alfabeto, mientras que en inglés americano, se lee como el número **cero (zero)**:*
01924 323 644 - **O** *(Brit)* o **zero** *(US)* - **one - nine - two - four, three - two - three, six - double four**

En esta sección se van a tratar algunos de los problemas más frecuentes que surgen a la hora de traducir al inglés y se darán algunos consejos prácticos para resolverlos.

▼ La traducción directa

Un error muy frecuente consiste en traducir palabra por palabra, lo que genera textos no sólo poco naturales, sino a veces incluso incorrectos. Se van a dar algunos ejemplos que muestran la falta de correspondencia entre los dos idiomas:

► Muchos verbos españoles se traducen por un verbo seguido de <u>adverbio</u> o <u>preposición</u>

huir	ceder	mirar
to run <u>away</u>	**to give <u>in</u>**	**to look <u>at</u>**

► En cambio, algunos verbos españoles que necesitan ir seguidos de preposición, a menudo se traducen al inglés por verbos <u>sin preposición</u>

casarse <u>con</u>	olvidarse <u>de</u>	subirse <u>a</u>
to marry	**to forget**	**to climb**

► Muchas palabras que en español se usan en singular, en inglés lo hacen en plural, y viceversa

su aspecto	su pijama es rosa	me gustan las tostadas calientes
her looks	**her pyjamas are pink**	**I like hot toast**

► Otra construcción que no corresponde palabra por palabra es la forma de expresar la posesión, que en inglés se realiza por medio de la construcción <u>poseedor</u>+ **'s** + <u>objeto poseído</u>. En caso de que el poseedor sea un sustantivo plural ya acabado en **-s**, solamente se le añadiría el símbolo apóstrofo.

la habitación de mi hermano	los amigos de mis hermanos	la habitación de los niños
my brother<u>'s</u> room	**my brothers<u>'</u> friends**	**the children<u>'s</u> room**

▼ Problemas específicos de traducción de palabras y construcciones españolas al inglés

aburrido

Se emplea **bored** cuando se refiere al hecho de <u>estar</u> aburrido, es decir, de sentir aburrimiento, y **boring** para algo que <u>produce</u> aburrimiento:

Si estás aburrida podrías ayudarme con esto	¡Qué novela más aburrida!
If you're bored you could help me with this	**What a boring novel!**

algo, alguien, alguno

► En frases afirmativas o interrogativas que expresan algún tipo de ofrecimiento o petición y cuya respuesta se espera que sea positiva, los pronombres y adjetivos indefinidos se suelen traducir por **some** o por alguna de sus formas compuestas

He leído algunos libros sobre el tema	Alguien llama a la puerta
I've read some books on the subject	**There is someone knocking at the door**
He comprado algo para ti	Tienes muchos libros. ¿Me dejas alguno?
I've bought something for you	**You've got a lot of books. Can I borrow some?**

► En el resto de las frases interrogativas, empléese **any** o alguna de sus formas compuestas

¿Se te ocurre alguna otra idea?	¿Hay algún sitio donde podamos escondernos?
Do you have any other ideas?	**Is there anywhere we can hide?**

artículo – su uso en generalizaciones

Cuando el sustantivo se utiliza en plural en sentido general, o bien cuando se trata de sustantivos incontables que expresan un concepto general, en inglés no se usa el artículo:

<u>Las</u> faldas son más cortas este año	<u>La</u> leche contiene mucho calcio
Skirts are shorter this year	**Milk contains a lot of calcium**

INGLÉS ACTIVO

bastante

Para traducir *bastante*, **enough** se coloca <u>delante de</u> los <u>sustantivos</u>, pero <u>detrás de</u> los <u>adjetivos</u> o <u>adverbios</u>:

¿Queda bastante vino?
Is there enough wine left?

No estamos trabajando lo bastante rápido
We aren't working fast enough

cada

Cada se traduce por **each** cuando se quiere individualizar, cuando se quiere dar importancia a los elementos dentro del grupo, o bien cuando se habla sólo de dos cosas o personas. Se traduce por **every** cuando se está generalizando o en expresiones temporales:

Quiero tener una charla con cada uno de vosotros
I want to have a chat with each (one) of you

Cada vez que viene nos trae un regalo
Every time he comes he brings us a present

cansado

Cansado se traduce por **tired** para referirse al hecho de <u>estar</u> cansado, y por **tiring** para algo que <u>produce</u> cansancio:

Estoy cansado de trabajar
I'm tired of working

Conducir 140 km todos los días es muy cansado
Driving 140 km every day is very tiring

casa

▶ A la hora de traducir expresiones como *ir a casa, volver a casa, venir a casa*, hay que tener en cuenta que **home** sigue directamente al verbo sin ninguna preposición

Quiero irme a casa
I want to go home

No puede volver a casa
He can't go back home

▶ Sin embargo, se coloca **to** cuando **home** viene calificado

Quiere volver a su antigua casa
She wants to return to her former home

concordancia

▶ Recuérdese que en inglés la tercera persona del singular de los verbos en presente añade normalmente la desinencia **s**. Si el verbo acaba en **o, s, sh, ch** o **x**, se le añade **es**, y si acaba en <u>consonante</u> + **y**, se cambia la **y** por **i** y se le añade **es**

Vivo en Londres pero mi hijo vive en Francia
I live in London but my son lives in France
Él se esfuerza mucho pero su hermana ni lo intenta
He tries hard but his sister doesn't try at all

▶ Al traducir algunas palabras referidas a grupos de personas, tales como *familia, tripulación, gobierno, grupo, equipo, policía*, etc, hay que tener en cuenta que el verbo puede ir en singular o plural, con la excepción de **people** (*gente*), que lleva el verbo siempre en plural

Mi familia vive en Granada
My family live/lives in Granada

La gente de aquí es muy simpática
People here are very friendly

decir

▶ Por regla general, *decir* se traduce por **say** en estilo directo. Normalmente no lleva un complemento de persona pero si se menciona a quién se está dirigiendo el hablante, el complemento de persona tiene que ir precedido por la preposición **to**

—Ya son las tres, —dije   —¡Qué tiempo más malo! —Eso fue lo único que me dijo
"It's already three o'clock," I said   **"What awful weather!" That was all he said to me**

▸ *Decir* se traduce por **tell** cuando se informa o se ordena hacer algo y lleva un objeto de persona <u>sin</u> la preposición **to**

Me dijo que tenía una entrevista de trabajo   ¡Te he dicho que no lo toques!
He told me he had a job interview   **I've told you not to touch it!**

▸ Si *decir* va acompañado de un calificativo, a menudo se puede traducir al inglés por otros verbos que no sean **say** o **tell**

—Lo he perdido todo, —<u>dijo entre sollozos</u>   <u>Dijo con voz ronca</u> algo sobre necesitar un médico

"I've lost everything," she <u>sobbed</u>   **He <u>croaked</u> something about needing a doctor**

dejar

Dejar con el sentido de <u>prestar</u> se puede traducir por **borrow** o **lend**. **Borrow** se usa cuando el sujeto es quien pide (significa <u>tomar prestado</u>) y **lend** cuando el sujeto es quien da (significa <u>dejar prestado</u>). **Borrow** y **lend** no se utilizan normalmente con objetos que no pueden trasladarse de un sitio a otro:

¿Me dejas tus botas de esquiar?   Nos ha dejado su chalet para este fin de semana
Can I borrow your o   **He's letting us use his villa this weekend**
Can you lend me your ski boots?

demasiado

Demasiado se traduce por **too**, **too much** y **too many**. Se traduce por **too** cuando va delante de <u>adjetivos</u> y <u>adverbios</u>, por **too much** cuando describe o se refiere a <u>nombres incontables</u> y cuando complementa al <u>verbo</u>, y por **too many** cuando describe o se refiere a <u>nombres contables en plural</u>:

Hace demasiado calor   Hablas demasiado deprisa
It's too hot   **You talk too quickly**
Le he echado demasiada agua a las patatas   Creo que he comido demasiado
I've put too much water in the potatoes   **I think I've eaten too much**
Aquí se producen demasiados accidentes de tráfico
There are too many car accidents here

depender

Depender de se traduce por **to depend on**, <u>nunca</u> por **depend of**:

Todo depende de lo que quieras decir
It all depends on what you mean

desde

▸ *Desde (que)* se traduce por **since** siempre que se especifique a partir de cuándo comenzó una acción o un estado que sigue desarrollándose en el presente o en el momento en que se habla

Dijo que no la había visto desde el verano   Llevamos viviendo aquí desde 1999
He said he hadn't seen her since the summer*   **We've been living here since 1999***

▸ *Desde* se traduce por **from** cuando simplemente indica el momento en el que comenzó la acción, cuando la oración indica el final de la acción o implica, de algún modo, que ésta ya ha terminado

Y desde aquel día el rey no volvió a hablar del asunto
And from that day on(wards), the king never spoke about the subject again

▸ También se emplea **from** en la construcción *desde ... hasta*

Trabajamos desde las nueve de la mañana hasta las cinco de la tarde
We work from nine in the morning until o **to five in the afternoon**

INGLÉS ACTIVO

GUÍA PRÁCTICA DE TRADUCCIÓN

▶ *Desde hace* y *desde hacía* se traducen por **for**, ya que van seguidos de una cantidad de tiempo, mientras que *desde cuándo* se traduce por **how long**

> Estoy esperando desde hace más de una hora
> **I have been waiting for over an hour***

> ¿Desde cuándo os conocéis?
> **How long have you known each other?***

* en todas estas estructuras se emplea el <u>pretérito perfecto</u> y el <u>pluscuamperfecto</u> ya que implican acciones o estados que comenzaron en un punto y que continúan en el presente o en el momento en que se habla.

durante

▶ Si *durante* hace referencia a cuándo ocurre la acción, se traduce por **during**

> Se conocieron durante la guerra
> **They met during the war**

> El tráfico es peor durante el verano
> **The traffic is worse during the summer**

▶ Si se trata de una acción progresiva o que se repite durante todo el período de tiempo que se indica, es preferible traducir *durante* por **over**

> La situación ha empeorado durante los últimos años
> **The situation has worsened over the last few years**

▶ Si se refiere a la duración de la acción, *durante* suele traducirse por **for**

> Fue periodista durante cuatro años
> **He was a journalist for four years**

> La habían estado explotando durante años
> **They had been exploiting her for years**

en

Como preposición de lugar, *en* se traduce normalmente por **on**, **in** o **at**. La elección de una de estas tres preposiciones depende a menudo de cómo percibe el hablante la relación espacial. He aquí unas líneas generales:

▶ Se traduce por **on** cuando *en* equivale a <u>encima de</u> o cuando se refiere a algo que se percibe como una superficie o línea, como por ejemplo una mesa, una carretera, etc

> Estaban tumbados en la playa
> **They were lying on the beach**

> un pueblo en la costa oeste
> **a village on the west coast**

> I saw him on TV
> **Lo vi en la tele**

▶ Se traduce por **in** cuando equivale a <u>dentro de</u> o cuando se refiere a un espacio que se percibe como limitado

> Tus gafas están en mi bolso
> **Your glasses are in my bag**

> Lo leí en un libro
> **I read it in a book**

▶ Se traduce por **at** para referirse a un edificio cuando se habla de la actividad que normalmente se realiza en él o cuando *en* indica un lugar concreto. También se traduce por **at** cuando en la dirección incluimos el número o el nombre de la casa

> Comimos en el restaurante nuevo
> **We had lunch at the new restaurant**

> Vivimos en la calle Cervantes número 3
> **We live at number 3, Cervantes Street**

esperar (transitivo)

▶ *Esperar* se traduce por **hope** cuando se desea que algo suceda, pero no se está seguro de si tendrá lugar o no

> Espero que no se enfade mucho conmigo
> **I hope (that) she won't be very annoyed with me**

▶ *Esperar* se traduce por **expect** cuando se está bastante seguro de que algo va a suceder o bien cuando hay una razón lógica para que algo suceda

> Espero aprobar porque el examen fue muy fácil
> **I expect I'll pass because the exam was very easy**

> Está esperando un niño
> **She's expecting a baby**

INGLÉS ACTIVO

▶ Se traduce por **wait for** cuando *esperar* se refiere al hecho de aguardar la llegada de alguien o de un suceso

> Hice el examen hace dos meses y todavía estoy esperando los resultados
> **I took the exam two months ago and I'm still waiting for the results**

explicar

Cuando *explicar* lleva objeto directo e indirecto, el orden en inglés es por regla general el siguiente: **explain** + <u>objeto directo</u> + **to** + <u>objeto indirecto</u>. Sin embargo, si el objeto directo es una construcción más compleja, en inglés se sigue el mismo orden que en español, sin olvidar el uso de la preposición **to**:

> ¿Puedes explicarme eso?
> **Can you explain that to me?**

> ¿Puedes explicarme por qué llegaste tarde?
> **Can you explain to me why you were late?**

formas impersonales

En muchas ocasiones la forma impersonal se expresa en inglés mediante la voz pasiva:

> Lo anunciaron ayer
> **It <u>was announced</u> yesterday**

> A menudo se dice que ...
> **It <u>is</u> often <u>said</u> that ...**

hacer

Para describir el tiempo que hace, el inglés utiliza el verbo **be**:

> ¿Qué tiempo hace?
> **What is the weather like?**

> Hace frío/sol/viento
> **It is cold/sunny/windy**

hay, había y hubo

La forma impersonal *hay* se traduce por **there is** o **there are**, según se refiera a una o más personas o cosas:

> Hay un supermercado en la esquina
> **There is a supermarket on the corner**

> En Toledo hay muchos lugares que visitar
> **There are lots of places to visit in Toledo**

De igual modo, *había* y *hubo* se traducen por **there was** o **there were** cuando se refiere a una o más personas o cosas.

infinitivos

En los siguientes casos, el <u>infinitivo</u> se traduce al inglés por la forma **-ing**:

▶ detrás de preposiciones

> antes de verla
> **before seeing her**

> sin olvidar nada
> **without forgetting anything**

▶ en construcciones del tipo <u>ver/oír a algn hacer</u> cuando la acción del infinitivo está incompleta. En el caso de que la acción está completa, se suele usar el infinitivo

> Los veo venir
> **I can see them coming**

> *PERO*: He oído entrar a alguien
> **I heard someone come in**

▶ detrás de otros muchos verbos

> Me gusta ir al cine
> **I like going to the cinema**

> ¡Deja de hablar!
> **Stop talking!**

▶ cuando el infinitivo se refiere a algún deporte o actividad

> Esquiar, nadar y leer son sus actividades favoritas
> **Skiing, swimming and reading are her favourite pastimes**

INGLÉS ACTIVO

INGLÉS ACTIVO

ir, venir

Aunque *ir* y **go**, por regla general, dan una idea de movimiento en dirección opuesta al hablante, y *venir* y **come** implican que hay un movimiento en dirección al hablante, tenemos que distinguir algunos casos en los que hay diferencias entre los dos idiomas:

▶ En español no se suele describir el movimiento de una acción desde el punto de vista de la otra persona, mientras que en inglés sí. Por ejemplo, si alguien nos llama, respondemos

> Ya voy
> **I'm coming**

▶ Igualmente, si se está acordando algo por teléfono, por carta, o en una conversación, en inglés se emplea **come**

> Iré a recogerte a las cuatro   ¿Voy contigo?
> **I'll come and pick you up at four**   **Shall I come with you?**

llegar

A la hora de traducir *llegar a*, se emplea **arrive in** cuando va acompañado de nombres de países, ciudades, pueblos, etc y se emplea **arrive at** cuando se refiere a lugares más pequeños, como aeropuertos, estaciones, etc. La expresión *llegar a casa* es una excepción, ya que se traduce por **arrive** *o* **get home**, es decir, va sin preposición:

> Esperamos llegar a Italia el día 2 de junio   Llegamos al aeropuerto con 4 horas de retraso
> **We expect to arrive in Italy on June 2**   **We arrived at the airport 4 hours late**
> Llegué a casa completamente agotado
> **I arrived home completely exhausted**

Recuérdese que *llegar a* nunca se traduce por **arrive to**.

no

Cuando este adverbio de negación se encuentra en el interior de la frase, se traduce al inglés por **not** (con frecuencia contraído como **n't** detrás de verbos modales, auxiliares y el verbo **be**). Sin embargo, como respuesta se traduce por **no**:

> No asomarse a la ventana   No es español   —¿Te gusta el pescado? —No
> **Do not** *o* **Don't lean out**   **He's not** *o* **He isn't Spanish**   **"Do you like fish?" – "No(, I don't)"**

olvidar

▶ Por regla general, si no se menciona el lugar donde se ha olvidado el objeto, *olvidar* se traduce por **forget** *o* **leave behind**

> He olvidado la cartera   No olvides el pasaporte
> **I've forgotten my wallet** *o*   **Don't forget your passport** *o*
> **I've left my wallet behind**   **Don't leave your passport behind**

▶ Si se menciona el lugar donde se ha olvidado el objeto, *olvidar* se traduce por **leave**

> He olvidado la cartera en el restaurante
> **I've left my wallet in the restaurant**

pasar

Pasar se traduce por **spend** cuando tiene un uso transitivo y se quiere indicar un período de tiempo concreto, seguido de la actividad, que en ese tiempo se desarrolla, o del lugar. En cambio, cuando se describe la forma en que se pasa el tiempo mediante un adjetivo, se debe emplear en inglés la construcción **have** + (**a**) + <u>adjetivo</u> + <u>sustantivo</u>:

> Me pasé la tarde aquí/escribiendo cartas   Pasamos un rato estupendo jugando al squash
> **I spent the evening here/writing letters**   **We had a fantastic time playing squash**

preferir

▸ Por regla general, *preferir* se traduce por **prefer** cuando se generaliza y si va seguido de un verbo, se emplea la forma -**ing**

Prefiero los gatos a los perros
I prefer cats to dogs

Prefiere trabajar en casa que en la oficina
She prefers working at home to working at the office

▸ No obstante, cuando se quiere indicar una preferencia en una ocasión concreta, **prefer** va seguido de infinitivo con **to**

Me ofrecí ayudar a James pero él prefirió hacerlo solo
I offered to help but James preferred to do it alone

▸ Para traducir *preferiría* + infinitivo, se debe utilizar en inglés la construcción **would rather** + infinitivo sin **to** o **would prefer** + infinitivo con **to**

—¿Vamos al cine? —Preferiría quedarme en casa
"Shall we go to the cinema?" – "I'd rather stay o **I'd prefer to stay at home"**

▸ Para traducir *preferiría que* + sujeto + verbo, se debe utilizar alguna de las siguientes construcciones: **would rather** + sujeto + verbo en pasado, **would prefer it if** + sujeto + verbo en pasado o bien **would prefer** + objeto + infinitivo con **to**

Preferiría que él me llamara
I'd rather he phoned me o **I'd prefer it if he phoned me** o **I'd prefer him to phone me**

pronombres sujeto

▸ Por regla general, cuando funciona como sujeto, el uso del pronombre es obligatorio en inglés

Es difícil
It is difficult

Estoy leyendo
I am reading

Sabe leer y escribir
She can read and write

▸ Hay que recordar que, cuando van precedidos de preposición, en inglés hay que utilizar los pronombres objeto

Nos fuimos del bar sin él/ella
We left the bar without him/her

vacaciones

En inglés británico, *vacaciones* se puede traducir tanto por **holiday** como por **holidays**, cuando se habla de un período de tiempo sin colegio o trabajo. En cambio, se traduce sólo por **holiday** cuando se habla de un viaje en particular:

Dónde pasaste las vacaciones?
Where did you spend your holiday(s)?

El año pasado pasamos unas vacaciones maravillosas en Mallorca
We had a lovely holiday in Majorca last year

En el segundo ejemplo, **holiday** funciona como sustantivo contable. Cuando se trata de más de un viaje, se añade una **s**. La expresión *estar de vacaciones* se traduce por **to be on holiday** y en este caso **holiday** no acepta el plural

verbos reflexivos

En construcciones del tipo *lavarse las manos*, *cortarse el pelo*, etc, que emplean verbos reflexivos, en inglés es necesario usar los posesivos que acompañan al complemento:

Va a lavarse las manos
She's going to wash her hands

Ayer me corté el pelo
I had my hair cut yesterday

INGLÉS ACTIVO

INGLÉS ACTIVO

► Los Números Cardinales

0	zero, nought*	12	twelve	30	thirty	
1	one	13	thirteen	31	thirty-one	
2	two	14	fourteen	40	forty	
3	three	15	fifteen	50	fifty	
4	four	16	sixteen	60	sixty	
5	five	17	seventeen	70	seventy	
6	six	18	eighteen	80	eighty	
7	seven	19	nineteen	90	ninety	
8	eight	20	twenty	100	one o a hundred	
9	nine	21	twenty-one	101	one o a hundred and one	
10	ten	22	twenty-two	212	two hundred and twelve	
11	eleven	23	twenty-three	999	nine hundred and ninety-nine	

1,000	one o a thousand	100,000	one o a hundred thousand
1,001	one o a thousand and one	1,000,000	one o a million
2,500	two thousand five hundred	1,000,000,000	one o a billion

NOTA: en inglés los miles y millones se separan con una coma y no con un punto.

► Los Números Ordinales

1st	first	19th	nineteenth
2nd	second	20th	twentieth
3rd	third	21st	twenty-first
4th	fourth	22nd	twenty-second
5th	fifth	23rd	twenty-third
6th	sixth	30th	thirtieth
7th	seventh	31st	thirty-first
8th	eighth	40th	fortieth
9th	ninth	50th	fiftieth
10th	tenth	60th	sixtieth
11th	eleventh	70th	seventieth
12th	twelfth	80th	eightieth
13th	thirteenth	90th	ninetieth
14th	fourteenth	100th	hundredth
15th	fifteenth	101st	hundred and first
16th	sixteenth	1000th	thousandth
17th	seventeenth	1,000,000th	millionth
18th	eighteenth	1,000,000,000th	billionth

► Las Fracciones y Porcentajes

½	a half	0.5	zero point five o nought* point five
⅓	a third, one third	3.5	three point five
¼	a quarter, one quarter	6.89	six point eight nine
¹/₁₀	a tenth, one tenth	10%	ten per cent
⅔	two thirds	100%	one o a hundred percent

NOTA: en inglés se separan los decimales con un punto y no con una coma.

* **Nought** se emplea sobre todo en inglés británico.

What time is it?

¿Qué hora es?

It's one o'clock

It's (a) quarter past one
o It's one fifteen

It's ten to two

It's half past three

It's twenty to six

It's (a) quarter to eight

It's nine o'clock

It's twelve o'clock

▶ Cómo preguntar la hora

What time do you make it?	*¿Qué hora tienes?*
Can you tell me the time?	*¿Me dices la hora?*
Do you have the time (on you)?	*¿Tienes hora?*

▶ Cómo contestar

I make it 2.20 *o* **twenty past two**	*Yo tengo las dos y veinte*
It must be about eleven	*Serán las once*
It's three o'clock exactly	*Son las tres en punto*
It's just gone five o'clock	*Son las cinco y pico*
It's nearly four o'clock	*Falta (un) poco para las cuatro*

▶ ¿A qué hora?

What time does it start?	*¿A qué hora empieza?*
At midnight	*A medianoche*
In twenty minutes	*Dentro de veinte minutos*
At around eight o'clock	*A eso de las ocho*
It leaves at seven thirty	*Sale a las siete y media*

▶ Día y noche

in the morning	*por la mañana*
in the afternoon	*por la tarde*
in the evening	*por la tarde*
at night	*por la noche*
noon *o* **midday**	*las doce del mediodía*
midnight	*medianoche*

INGLÉS ACTIVO

INGLÉS ACTIVO

► Los días de la semana

Monday	*lunes*
Tuesday	*martes*
Wednesday	*miércoles*
Thursday	*jueves*
Friday	*viernes*
Saturday	*sábado*
Sunday	*domingo*

► Los meses del año

January	*enero*
February	*febrero*
March	*marzo*
April	*abril*
May	*mayo*
June	*junio*
July	*julio*
August	*agosto*
September	*septiembre*
October	*octubre*
November	*noviembre*
December	*diciembre*

Nota: en inglés, los días de la semana y los meses del año siempre se escriben con mayúscula.

► Las estaciones

spring	*primavera*
summer	*verano*
autumn	*otoño*
winter	*invierno*

► Cómo expresar la fecha

What day is it today?	*¿Qué día es hoy?*
It's Saturday	*Es sábado o Estamos a sábado*
1st/24th October 2002	*1/24 de octubre de 2002*
Ver también **CORRESPONDENCIA**, *p.45*	

► ¿Cuándo?

today/yesterday/tomorrow	*hoy/ayer/mañana*
the day after tomorrow	*pasado mañana*
the day before yesterday	*antes de ayer*
the next o **following day**	*el día siguiente*
yesterday afternoon/evening	*ayer por la tarde*
last night	*ayer por la noche*
tomorrow morning	*mañana por la mañana*
on Saturday	*el sábado*
on Saturdays	*los sábados*
next Sunday	*el domingo que viene*
last Tuesday	*el martes pasado*
once a week/month	*una vez por semana/mes*
a week ago	*hace una semana*
last year	*el año pasado*
in two days	*dentro de/en dos días*
a fortnight ago	*hace quince días*
at the beginning of the year	*a principios de año*
in the middle of o **halfway through May**	*a mediados de mayo*
at the end of the month	*a finales de mes*
at the latest	*a más tardar*
at the earliest	*lo más pronto*
no later than	*no más tarde de*
in 1999	*en 1999*
in the nineteenth century	*en el siglo diecinueve*
in the (nineteen) nineties	*en los años noventa*
in the year two thousand	*en el año dos mil*
44 BC	*44 a. de C.*
14 AD	*14 d. de C.*

INFINITIVO	PRETÉRITO	PARTICIPIO DE PASADO	INFINITIVO	PRETÉRITO	PARTICIPIO DE PASADO
arise	arose	arisen	feel	felt	felt
awake	awoke o awaked	awoken o awaked	fight	fought	fought
be	was, were	been	find	found	found
bear	bore	(llevado) borne, (nacido) born	flee	fled	fled
			fling	flung	flung
beat	beat	beaten	fly	flew	flown
become	became	become	forbid	forbad(e)	forbidden
begin	began	begun	forget	forgot	forgotten
bend	bent	bent	forsake	forsook	forsaken
beseech	besought	besought	freeze	froze	frozen
bet	bet	bet	get	got	got, (US) gotten
bid (ordenar)	bade	bidden	give	gave	given
(licitar etc)	bid	bid	go	went	gone
bind	bound	bound	grind	ground	ground
bite	bit	bitten	grow	grew	grown
bleed	bled	bled	hang	hung, (ahorcar) hanged	hung, (ahorcar) hanged
blow	blew	blown			
break	broke	broken	have	had	had
breed	bred	bred	hear	heard	heard
bring	brought	brought	heave	heaved, (Naut) hove	heaved, (Naut) hove
build	built	built			
burn	burned o burnt	burned o burnt	hew	hewed	hewed o hewn
burst	burst	burst	hide	hid	hidden
buy	bought	bought	hit	hit	hit
can	could	–	hold	held	held
cast	cast	cast	hurt	hurt	hurt
catch	caught	caught	keep	kept	kept
choose	chose	chosen	kneel	knelt	knelt
cling	clung	clung	know	knew	known
come	came	come	lay	laid	laid
cost	cost	cost	lead	led	led
creep	crept	crept	lean	leaned o leant	leaned o leant
cut	cut	cut	leap	leaped o leapt	leaped o leapt
deal	dealt	dealt	learn	learned o learnt	learned o learnt
dig	dug	dug	leave	left	left
do	did	done	lend	lent	lent
draw	drew	drawn	let	let	let
dream	dreamed o dreamt	dreamed o dreamt	lie	lay	lain
drink	drank	drunk	light	lit o lighted	lit o lighted
drive	drove	driven	lose	lost	lost
dwell	dwelt	dwelt	make	made	made
eat	ate	eaten	may	might	–
fall	fell	fallen	mean	meant	meant
feed	fed	fed	meet	met	met

INGLÉS ACTIVO

63

VERBOS IRREGULARES

INFINITIVO	PRETÉRITO	PARTICIPIO DE PASADO	INFINITIVO	PRETÉRITO	PARTICIPIO DE PASADO
mow	mowed	mown o mowed	spill	spilled o spilt	spilled o spilt
pay	paid	paid	spin	spun	spun
put	put	put	spit	spat	spat
quit	quit o quitted	quit o quitted	split	split	split
read [riːd]	read [red]	read [red]	spoil	spoiled o spoilt	spoiled o spoilt
rid	rid	rid	spread	spread	spread
ride	rode	ridden	spring	sprang	sprung
ring	rang	rung,l	stand	stood	stood
rise	rose	risen	steal	stole	stolen
run	ran	run	stick	stuck	stuck
saw	sawed	sawed o sawn	sting	stung	stung
say	said	said	stink	stank	stunk
see	saw	seen	stride	strode	stridden
seek	sought	sought	strike	struck	struck
sell	sold	sold	string	strung	strung
send	sent	sent	strive	strove	striven
set	set	set	swear	swore	sworn
sew	sewed	sewn	sweep	swept	swept
shake	shook	shaken	swell	swelled	swollen
shave	shaved	shaved o shaven	swim	swam	swum
shear	sheared	sheared o shorn	swing	swung	swung
shed	shed	shed	take	took	taken
shine	shone	shone	teach	taught	taught
shoe	shod	shod	tear	tore	torn
shoot	shot	shot	tell	told	told
show	showed	shown	think	thought	thought
shrink	shrank	shrunk	throw	threw	thrown
shut	shut	shut	thrust	thrust	thrust
sing	sang	sung	tread	trod	trodden
sink	sank	sunk	wake	woke o waked	woken o waked
sit	sat	sat	wear	wore	worn
slay	slew	slain	weave	wove	woven
sleep	slept	slept	weep	wept	wept
slide	slid	slid	win	won	won
sling	slung	slung	wind	wound	wound
slink	slunk	slunk	wring	wrung	wrung
slit	slit	slit	write	wrote	written
smell	smelled o smelt	smelled o smelt			
smite	smote	smitten			
sow	sowed	sown			
speak	spoke	spoken			
speed	sped o speeded	sped o speeded			
spell	spelled o spelt	spelled o spelt			
spend	spent	spent			

ENGLISH-SPANISH DICTIONARY

DICCIONARIO INGLÉS-ESPAÑOL

A, a¹ [eɪ] **Ⓐ** N **1** (= *letter*) A, a *f*; **A for Andrew** A de Antonio **2** (*Mus*) **A** la *m* **3** (*Scol*) sobresaliente *m* **Ⓑ** CPD ➤ **A level** ABBR (*Brit Scol*) (= **Advanced level**) ≈ bachillerato *m* ➤ **A road** (*Brit*) ≈ carretera *f* nacional ➤ **A to Z**® (*Brit*) (= *map book*) callejero *m*

a² [eɪ, ə] INDEF ART (*before vowel or silent h* **an**) **1** un(a) *m/f*; (+ *fem noun starting with stressed* **a** *or* **ha**) un; **a book** un libro; **an apple** una manzana; **a soul** un alma; **he is an engineer** es ingeniero; **he's a brilliant scientist** es un excelente científico; **have you got a passport?** ¿tiene usted pasaporte?; **I haven't got a car** no tengo coche; **she's looking for a secretary** busca secretaria; **she has a daughter** tiene una hija; **they have a lovely house** tienen una casa preciosa; **you don't stand a chance** no tienes posibilidad alguna; **without a doubt** sin duda; **Patrick, a lecturer at Glasgow University, says that ...** Patrick, profesor de la Universidad de Glasgow, dice que ...; **the Duero, a Spanish river** el Duero, un río español **2** (= *a certain*) un(a) tal; **a Mr Smith called to see you** vino a verte un tal señor Smith **3** (= *each, per*) por; **two apples a head** dos manzanas por persona; **£80 a week** 80 libras por semana; **50 kilometres an hour** 50 kilómetros por hora; **30 pence a kilo** 30 peniques el kilo; **once a week/three times a month** una vez a la semana/tres veces al mes **4** (*in expressions*) **half an hour** media hora; **what an idiot!** ¡qué idiota!; **a hundred pounds** cien libras

A. ABBR (= **answer**) R.

A3 [ˈeɪˈθriː] ADJ **A3 paper** papel *m* tamaño A3, doble folio *m*

A4 [ˈeɪˈfɔːʳ] ADJ **A4 paper** papel *m* tamaño A4, papel *m* tamaño folio, folios *mpl*

AA N ABBR **1** = **Alcoholics Anonymous** A.A. **2** (*Brit*) (= **Automobile Association**) *servicio de asistencia para averías en carretera*, ≈ RACE *m* (*Sp*) **3** (*US Univ*) = **Associate in Arts**

AAA N ABBR (*US*) (= **American Automobile Association**) *servicio de asistencia para averías en carretera*, ≈ RACE *m* (*Sp*)

A&E [ˌeɪənˈdiː] N ABBR (*Brit*) (= **Accident and Emergency**) ≈ Urgencias *fpl*

AB ABBR **1** (*US*) (= **Bachelor of Arts**) Lic. en Fil. y Let. **2** (*Canada*) = **Alberta**

aback [əˈbæk] ADV **to be taken ~** quedarse desconcertado, sorprenderse; **I was quite taken ~ by the news** la noticia me causó desconcierto *or* me dejó desconcertado

abacus [ˈæbəkəs] N ábaco *m*

abandon [əˈbændən] VT **1** (= *desert*) [+ *car, family*] abandonar, dejar; **~ ship!** ¡abandonen el barco! **2** (= *give up*) [+ *plan, attempt*] renunciar a; [+ *game*] anular

abandoned [əˈbændənd] ADJ (= *deserted*) abandonado

abase [əˈbeɪs] VT **to ~ o.s.** rebajarse (**so far as to** hasta el punto de + *infin*)

abashed [əˈbæʃt] ADJ (= *shy*) tímido, retraído; (= *ashamed*) avergonzado

abate [əˈbeɪt] VI [*wind, storm*] amainar; [*fever*] bajar; [*flood*] retirarse, bajar; [*noise*] disminuir; [*anger*] aplacarse; [*pain, symptoms*] remitir; [*enthusiasm*] moderarse

abatement [əˈbeɪtmənt] N [*of wind, storm*] amaine *m*; [*of fever, flood*] bajada *f*; (*Jur*) [*of noise, pollution*] (= *elimination*) eliminación *f*; (= *reduction*) disminución *f*, moderación *f*

abattoir [ˈæbətwɑːʳ] N (*Brit*) matadero *m*

abbey [ˈæbɪ] N abadía *f*

abbot [ˈæbət] N abad *m*

abbr., abbrev. ABBR = **abbreviation, abbreviated**

abbreviate [əˈbriːvɪeɪt] VT abreviar

abbreviation [əˌbriːvɪˈeɪʃən] N abreviatura *f*

ABC [ˈeɪbiːˈsiː] **Ⓐ** N (= *alphabet*) abecé *m*; **the ~ of Politics** (*as title*) el Abecé de la Política; **✦** IDIOM **it's as easy** *or* **simple as ~*** es coser y cantar*, es facilísimo

Ⓑ ABBR (*US*) = **American Broadcasting Company**

abdicate [ˈæbdɪkeɪt] **Ⓐ** VT **1** [+ *throne*] abdicar **2** [+ *responsibility, right*] renunciar a **Ⓑ** VI abdicar (**in favour of** en, en favor de)

abdication [ˌæbdɪˈkeɪʃən] N **1** [*of monarch*] abdicación *f* **2** [*of responsibility, right*] renuncia *f* (**of** a)

abdomen [ˈæbdəmən, (*Med*) æbˈdəʊmən] N abdomen *m*, vientre *m*

abdominal [æbˈdɒmɪnl] **Ⓐ** ADJ abdominal **Ⓑ** **abdominals** NPL abdominales *mpl*

abduct [æbˈdʌkt] VT raptar, secuestrar

abduction [æbˈdʌkʃən] N rapto *m*, secuestro *m*

abductor [æbˈdʌktəʳ] N raptor(a) *m/f*, secuestrador(a) *m/f*

aberrant [əˈberənt] ADJ [*behaviour*] anormal

aberration [ˌæbəˈreɪʃən] N aberración *f*

abet [əˈbet] VT [+ *criminal*] incitar; [+ *crime*] instigar; **to ~ sb in a crime** ser cómplice de algn en un delito

abeyance [əˈbeɪəns] N **to be in ~** estar en desuso; **to fall into ~** caer en desuso

abhor [əbˈhɔːʳ] VT aborrecer, abominar

abhorrence [əbˈhɒrəns] N aborrecimiento *m*, repugnancia *f*; **violence fills me with ~** aborrezco la violencia

abhorrent [əbˈhɒrənt] ADJ aborrecible, detestable

abide [əˈbaɪd] VT (*neg only*) aguantar, soportar; **I can't ~ him** no lo aguanto *or* soporto, no lo puedo ver; **I can't ~ a coward** aborrezco los cobardes
➤ **abide by** VI + PREP [+ *rules*] atenerse a; [+ *promise*] cumplir con; [+ *decision*] respetar, atenerse a

abiding [əˈbaɪdɪŋ] ADJ permanente, perdurable

ability [əˈbɪlɪtɪ] N **1** (= *capacity*) aptitud *f*, capacidad *f*; **his ~ in French** su aptitud para el francés; **to the best of my ~** lo mejor que pueda *or* sepa; **~ to pay** solvencia *f*, recursos *mpl* **2** (= *talent*) talento *m*; **abilities** talento *msing*, dotes *fpl*

abject [ˈæbdʒekt] ADJ **1** (= *wretched*) [*condition*] deplorable; [*state*] lamentable; **England's ~ performance in the World Cup** la pésima actuación de Inglaterra en el Mundial **2** (= *grovelling*) sumiso; **he sounded ~** su tono era sumiso y arrepentido **3** (*as intensifier*) [*misery, failure*] absoluto; [*cowardice*] abyecto; **to live in ~ poverty** vivir en la miseria más absoluta

ablaze [əˈbleɪz] ADV (= *on fire*) en llamas, ardiendo; **the garden was ~ with colour** el jardín resplandecía de color

able [ˈeɪbl] ADJ **1 to be ~ to do sth** (*of acquired skills*) saber hacer algo; (*other contexts*) poder hacer algo **2** (= *capable*) [*person*] capaz; [*piece of work*] sólido

able-bodied [ˈeɪblˈbɒdɪd] ADJ sano

ably [ˈeɪblɪ] ADV hábilmente, con mucha habilidad

abnegate [ˈæbnɪgeɪt] VT (*frm*) [+ *responsibility*] eludir, rehuir; **to ~ one's rights** renunciar a sus derechos

abnormal [æbˈnɔːməl] ADJ anormal

abnormality [ˌæbnɔːˈmælɪtɪ] N anormalidad *f*

abnormally [æbˈnɔːməlɪ] ADV de modo anormal, anormalmente

aboard [əˈbɔːd] **Ⓐ** ADV a bordo; **to go ~** embarcar, subir a bordo **Ⓑ** PREP **~ the ship** a bordo del barco; **~ the train** en el tren

abode [əˈbəʊd] N (*also* **place of ~**) domicilio *m*; **of no fixed ~** sin domicilio fijo

abolish [əˈbɒlɪʃ] VT abolir, suprimir

abolition [ˌæbəʊˈlɪʃən] N abolición *f*, supresión *f*

A-bomb† [ˈeɪbɒm] N ABBR (= **atom(ic) bomb**) bomba *f* atómica

abominable [əˈbɒmɪnəbl] ADJ abominable, detestable
➤ **the abominable snowman** el abominable hombre de las nieves

abominably [əˈbɒmɪnəblɪ] ADV abominablemente, pésimamente

abomination [ə,bɒmɪˈneɪʃən] N escándalo *m*

aboriginal [,æbəˈrɪdʒənl] ADJ, N aborigen *mf*, indígena *mf*

Aborigine [,æbəˈrɪdʒɪnɪ] N aborigen *mf* australiano/a

abort [əˈbɔːt] **Ⓐ** VI **1** (*Med*) abortar **2** (*Comput*) abandonar **3** (= *fail*) fracasar, malograrse **Ⓑ** VT **1** (*Med*) abortar **2** (= *abandon*) [+ *mission, operation*] suspender; [+ *deal, agreement*] anular; [+ *plan*] abandonar; [+ *landing, takeoff*] abortar **3** (= *cause to fail*) malograr **4** (*Comput*) abandonar

abortion [əˈbɔːʃən] N (*Med*) (= *termination*) aborto *m* (provocado); **to have an ~** hacerse un aborto, abortar (*no de forma espontánea*) ➤ **abortion clinic** clínica *f* donde se practican abortos

abortive [əˈbɔːtɪv] ADJ **1** (= *failed*) [*attempt, plan*] fracasado, frustrado **2** (*Med*) [*method, medicine*] abortivo

abound [əˈbaʊnd] VI abundar; **to ~ in** *or* **with** estar lleno de, abundar en

about [əˈbaʊt]

> When **about** is an element in a phrasal verb, eg **bring about, come about**, look up the verb.

Ⓐ ADV **1** (= *approximately*) más o menos, alrededor de; **~ £20** unas 20 libras, 20 libras más o menos; **~ seven years ago** hace unos siete años; **at ~ two o'clock** a eso de las dos, sobre las dos; **it's ~ two o'clock** son las dos, más o menos; **he must be ~ 40** tendrá alrededor de 40 años; **that's ~ it** eso es (, más o menos); **it's just ~ finished** está casi terminado; **it's ~ time you stopped** ya es hora de que lo dejes **2** (*esp Brit*) (*place*) **is anyone ~?** ¿hay alguien?; **is Mr Brown ~?** ¿está por aquí el Sr. Brown?; **to be (up and) ~ again** (*after illness*) estar levantado; **there's a lot of measles ~** hay mucho sarampión, está dando el sarampión; **he must be ~ somewhere** debe de andar por aquí **3 to be ~ to do sth** estar a punto de *or* (*LAm*) por hacer algo **Ⓑ** PREP **1** (= *relating to*) de, acerca de, sobre; **a book ~ gardening** un libro de jardinería, un libro sobre (la) jardinería; **I can tell you nothing ~ him** no le puedo decir nada acerca de él; **I'm phoning ~ tomorrow's meeting** llamo por la reunión de mañana; **~ the other night ...** respecto a la otra noche ...; **there's nothing I can do ~ it** no puedo hacer nada al respecto; **how** *or* **what ~ this one?** ¿qué te parece éste?; **how** *or* **what ~ coming with us?** ¿por qué no vienes con nosotros?; **how** *or* **what ~ it?** (= *what do you say?*) ¿qué te parece?; (= *what of it?*) ¿y qué?; **what ~ me?** y yo, ¿qué?; **what's that book ~?** ¿de qué trata ese libro?; **what did she talk ~?** ¿de qué habló?; **"I want to talk to you" — "what ~?"** —quiero hablar contigo —¿(acerca) de qué? **2** (= *particular to*) **there's something ~ him (that I like)** tiene un no sé qué (que me gusta); **there's something odd ~ it** aquí hay algo raro **3** (= *doing*) **and while I'm ~ it I'll talk to your father** y de paso hablaré con tu padre; **you've been a long time ~ it** has tardado bastante en hacerlo **4** (= *around*) **to do jobs ~ the house** hacer arreglos en la casa; **I had no money ~ me** no llevaba dinero encima; **he looked ~ him** miró a su alrededor; **somewhere ~ here** por aquí cerca

about-face [ə,baʊtˈfeɪs] N = **about-turn**

about-turn [ə,baʊtˈtɜːn] N **1** (*Mil*) media vuelta *f* **2** (*esp Brit*) (*fig*) cambio *m* radical de postura, giro *m* (brusco)

above [əˈbʌv]

> When **above** is an element in a phrasal verb, eg **get above**, look up the verb.

Ⓐ ADV **1** (= *overhead*) arriba; **seen from ~** visto desde arriba; **the flat ~** el piso de arriba **2** (*in status*) **orders from ~** órdenes *fpl* superiores *or* de arriba **3** (*in text*) (más) arriba; **see ~** véase (más) arriba; **as I said ~** como ya he dicho **4** (= *more*) **boys of five and ~** los niños mayores de cinco años; **seats are available at £5 and ~** las entradas cuestan a partir de cinco libras **Ⓑ** PREP **1** (= *higher than, over*) encima de; **there was a picture ~ the fireplace** había un cuadro encima de la chimenea; **2,000 metres ~ sea level** 2.000 metros sobre el nivel del mar **2** (= *upstream of*) **the Thames ~ London** el Támesis más arriba de Londres **3** (*of rank*) **he is ~ me in rank** tiene una categoría superior a la mía, tiene un rango superior al mío; **~ all** sobre todo; **he was, ~ all else, a musician** era, ante todo, un músico **4** (= *morally superior to*) **he's ~ that sort of thing** está muy por encima de esas cosas; **he's not ~ a bit of blackmail** es capaz hasta del chantaje; **to get ~ o.s.** (*Brit*) pasarse (de listo) **5** (*numbers*) **she can't count ~ ten** no sabe contar más allá de diez; **children ~ seven years of age** los niños mayores de siete años; **temperatures ~ 40 degrees** temperaturas por encima de los 40 grados; **temperatures well ~ normal** temperaturas muy superiores a las normales **Ⓒ** ADJ [*fact, place*] sobredicho, arriba mencionado; [*photo, illustration*] de arriba **Ⓓ** N **the ~ is a photo of ...** lo anterior *or* lo que se ve arriba es una foto de ...

above-board [əˈbʌvˈbɔːd] ADJ legítimo, honrado

above-mentioned [əˈbʌvˈmenʃənd] ADJ [*fact, point, place*] sobredicho, arriba mencionado; [*person*] susodicho

abrasion [əˈbreɪʒən] N abrasión *f*, escoriación *f*

abrasive [əˈbreɪsɪv] ADJ **1** [*substance, surface*] abrasivo **2** [*personality*] displicente, brusco

abrasively [əˈbreɪsɪvlɪ] ADV [*say, reply*] ásperamente, con tono áspero *or* desabrido

abreast [əˈbrest] ADV **1** (= *side by side*) **to march four ~** marchar en columna de cuatro en fondo **2** (= *aware of*) **to be/keep ~ of sth** estar/mantenerse al corriente de algo; **to keep ~ of the news** mantenerse al día *or* al corriente

abridge [əˈbrɪdʒ] VT [+ *book*] resumir, compendiar

abroad [əˈbrɔːd] ADV (= *in foreign country*) en el extranjero; **to live ~** vivir en el extranjero; **to go ~** ir al extranjero

abrupt [əˈbrʌpt] ADJ **1** (= *sudden*) [*change, rise*] brusco; [*departure*] repentino; [*resignation, dismissal*] repentino, súbito; **to come to an ~ end** terminar de repente **2** (= *brusque*) [*person*] brusco, cortante; [*comment, reply*] cortante **3** (= *steep*) [*hillside, precipice*] abrupto, escarpado

abruptly [əˈbrʌptlɪ] ADV **1** (= *suddenly*) [*stop, end, leave*] bruscamente, repentinamente **2** (= *brusquely*) [*say, ask*] bruscamente **3** (= *steeply*) abruptamente

abruptness [əˈbrʌptnɪs] N **1** (= *suddenness*) lo repentino **2** (= *brusqueness*) brusquedad *f* **3** (= *steepness*) lo escarpado

ABS N ABBR = **antilock braking system** ABS *m*

abscess [ˈæbsɪs] N absceso *m*

abscond [əbˈskɒnd] VI fugarse; (*with funds*) huir

abseil [ˈæbseɪl] VI (*Brit*) hacer rappel, bajar en la cuerda; **he ~ed down the rock** hizo rappel roca abajo

abseiling [ˈæbseɪlɪŋ] N (*Brit Sport*) rappel *m*

absence [ˈæbsəns] N [*of person*] ausencia *f*; [*of thing*] falta *f*; **in the ~ of** [+ *person*] en ausencia de; [+ *thing*] a falta de

absent Ⓐ [ˈæbsənt] ADJ **1** (= *not present*) [*person, thing*] ausente; **to be ~** faltar (**from** a); **to go ~ without leave** ausentarse sin permiso; **a spirit of compromise was noticeably ~ from the meeting** en la reunión la voluntad de llegar a un acuerdo brilló por su ausencia **2** (= *absent-minded*) ausente, distraído **Ⓑ** [æbˈsent] VT **to ~ o.s.** ausentarse (**from** de)

absentee [,æbsənˈtiː] N (*from school, work*) ausente *mf* ➤ **absentee ballot** (*US*) voto *m* por correo ➤ **absentee landlord** propietario/a *m/f* absentista (*Sp*) *or* ausentista (*LAm*) ➤ **absentee rate** nivel *m* de absentismo (*Sp*) *or* ausentismo (*LAm*)

absenteeism [,æbsənˈtiːɪzəm] N absentismo *m* (*Sp*), ausentismo *m* (*LAm*)

absently [ˈæbsəntlɪ] ADV distraídamente

absent-minded [ˈæbsəntˈmaɪndɪd] ADJ (*momentarily*)

distraído, ausente; (*habitually*) despistado, distraído

absent-mindedly [ˈæbsənt'maɪndɪdlɪ] ADV distraídamente

absent-mindedness [ˈæbsənt'maɪndɪdnɪs] N (*momentary*) distracción *f*; (*habitual*) despiste *m*

absolute [ˈæbsəluːt] **Ⓐ** ADJ **1** (= *complete*) [*certainty, confidence, majority, need*] absoluto; [*support*] incondicional, total; [*refusal*] rotundo; [*proof*] irrefutable; [*denial*] rotundo, categórico; [*right*] incuestionable; **the divorce was made ~** concedieron el divorcio por sentencia firme; **it was the ~ truth, I promise** era la pura verdad, se lo prometo; **~ veto** veto *m* total
2 (= *unlimited*) [*power, monarch*] absoluto
3 (= *not relative*) [*value*] absoluto; **in ~ terms** en términos absolutos
4 (*as intensifier*) [*liar, villain*] redomado; **the party was an ~ disaster** la fiesta fue un completo desastre; **it's an ~ disgrace** es una auténtica vergüenza; **it's the ~ end!** ¡es el colmo!; **the man's an ~ idiot** es completamente idiota; **it's ~ rubbish!** ¡es puro disparate!
Ⓑ N (*Philos*) **the ~** lo absoluto

absolutely [ˈæbsəluːtlɪ] ADV **1** (= *completely*) [*clear, impossible, alone, untrue*] completamente, totalmente; [*hilarious, beautiful, wonderful*] realmente; [*exhausted, horrible*] totalmente; [*necessary*] absolutamente; **it's ~ boiling in here!** ¡aquí dentro hace un calor infernal!; **he's ~ delighted at being a father again** está contentísimo de volver a ser padre; **the food was ~ disgusting** la comida era verdaderamente asquerosa; **punctuality is ~ essential** la puntualidad es de vital importancia; **it's ~ freezing in here!** ¡aquí dentro hace un frío que pela!; **to be ~ right** tener toda la razón; **are you ~ sure?** ¿estás completamente seguro?; **it's ~ true** es la pura verdad, es totalmente cierto
2 (= *unconditionally*) [*refuse, deny*] rotundamente; [*believe*] firmemente; **I agree ~** estoy totalmente de acuerdo
3 (***) (= *certainly*) desde luego; **"it's worrying, isn't it?"** — **"absolutely"** —es preocupante ¿verdad? —desde luego; **"does this affect your attitude to your work?"** — **"~ not"** —¿afecta esto a su actitud hacia el trabajo? —no, en absoluto

absolution [ˌæbsə'luːʃən] N (*Rel*) absolución *f*; **to give ~ to sb** dar la absolución a algn, absolver a algn

absolve [əb'zɒlv] VT absolver (**from** de)

absorb [əb'zɔːb] VT **1** [+ *liquid*] absorber; [+ *heat, sound, shock, vibrations, radiation*] amortiguar **2** (*fig*) [+ *information*] asimilar; [+ *time, energy*] ocupar, absorber **3** (= *engross*) **to be ~ed in** estar absorto en, estar ensimismado con

absorbent [əb'zɔːbənt] ADJ absorbente ➤ **absorbent cotton** (*US*) algodón *m* hidrófilo

absorbing [əb'zɔːbɪŋ] ADJ (= *fascinating*) apasionante; (= *engrossing*) absorbente; **I find history very ~** me apasiona la historia, encuentro la historia apasionante

absorption [əb'zɔːpʃən] N absorción *f*

abstain [əb'steɪn] VI abstenerse (**from** de)

abstemious [əb'stiːmɪəs] ADJ abstemio

abstention [əb'stenʃən] N abstención *f*

abstinence [ˈæbstɪnəns] N abstinencia *f* (**from** de)

abstract **Ⓐ** [ˈæbstrækt] ADJ abstracto **Ⓑ** [ˈæbstrækt] N **1** (= *summary*) resumen *m*, sumario *m* **2** (*Art*) pintura *f* abstracta **3 in the ~** en abstracto **Ⓒ** [æb'strækt] VT (= *remove*) quitar; (*Chem*) extraer **Ⓓ** [ˈæbstrækt] CPD ➤ **abstract art** arte *m* abstracto ➤ **abstract noun** nombre *m* abstracto

abstractedly [æb'stræktɪdlɪ] ADV **she listened ~** escuchaba distraída

abstraction [æb'strækʃən] N **1** (= *act*) abstracción *f* **2** (= *absent-mindedness*) distraimiento *m*, ensimismamiento *m*

abstruse [æb'struːs] ADJ recóndito, abstruso

absurd [əb'sɜːd] **Ⓐ** ADJ [*idea, plan*] absurdo; [*appearance*] ridículo; **don't be ~!** ¡no digas tonterías!; **how ~!** ¡qué ridículo! **Ⓑ** N **the ~** el absurdo

absurdity [əb'sɜːdɪtɪ] N **1** (= *quality*) lo absurdo **2** (= *act of madness*) locura *f*, disparate *m*; **it would be an ~ to try** sería una locura *or* un disparate intentarlo

absurdly [əb'sɜːdlɪ] ADV absurdamente, ridículamente

ABTA [ˈæbtə] N ABBR (= **Association of British Travel Agents**) ≈ AEDAVE *f*

abundance [ə'bʌndəns] N abundancia *f*; **in ~** en abundancia, en cantidad, en grandes cantidades

abundant [ə'bʌndənt] ADJ abundante

abundantly [ə'bʌndəntlɪ] ADV abundantemente; **he made it ~ clear to me that ...** me dejó meridianamente claro que ...

abuse **Ⓐ** [ə'bjuːs] N **1** (= *insults*) insultos *mpl* **2** (= *misuse*) abuso *m*; **~ of trust/power** abuso de confianza/poder; **open to ~** abierto al abuso **Ⓑ** [ə'bjuːz] VT **1** (= *insult*) insultar, injuriar **2** (= *mistreat*) [+ *child*] (*physically*) maltratar; (*sexually*) abusar de **3** (= *misuse*) [+ *position, privilege*] abusar de

abusive [əb'juːsɪv] ADJ **1** (= *offensive*) ofensivo, insultante; **to become ~** ponerse grosero **2** (*physically*) [*person*] que maltrata; [*relationship*] de malos tratos **3** (*sexually*) [*person*] que abusa (*sexually*); [*relationship*] de abuso sexual **4** [*practice*] abusivo

abysmal [ə'bɪzməl] ADJ **1** (= *very bad*) [*result, performance*] pésimo **2** (= *very great*) [*ignorance*] abismal

abyss [ə'bɪs] N abismo *m*

AC N ABBR (= **alternating current**) C.A. *f*

a/c ABBR **1** (= **account**) c/, c.ᵗᵃ **2** (*US*) (= **account current**) c/c

academic [ˌækə'demɪk] **Ⓐ** ADJ **1** (*Scol, Univ*) [*ability, qualifications, achievement*] académico; **the ~ world** el mundo académico; **~ journal** revista *f* dirigida a académicos; **~ staff** profesorado *m*, personal *m* docente **2** (= *scholarly*) **an exam for ~ children** un examen para niños intelectualmente dotados **3** (= *theoretical*) [*question*] (puramente) teórico, sin interés práctico; [*debate*] (puramente) teórico; **it is of ~ interest only** sólo tiene interés teórico **Ⓑ** N académico/a *m/f*, profesor(a) *m/f* universitario/a **Ⓒ** CPD ➤ **academic advisor** (*US*) jefe *mf* de estudios ➤ **academic year** (*Univ*) año *m* académico; (*Scol*) año *m* escolar

academy [ə'kædəmɪ] **Ⓐ** N **1** (= *private college*) academia *f*; **~ of music** conservatorio *m* **2** (= *learned society*) academia *f*; **the Spanish Academy** la Real Academia Española **Ⓑ** CPD ➤ **Academy Award** (*Cine*) galardón *m* de la Academia de Hollywood, Oscar *m*

ACAS [ˈeɪkæs] N ABBR (*Brit*) (= **Advisory Conciliation and Arbitration Service**) ≈ IMAC *m*

accede [æk'siːd] VI **to ~ to 1** [+ *request*] acceder a; [+ *suggestion*] aceptar **2** [+ *office, post*] tomar posesión de; [+ *throne*] acceder a, subir a

accelerate [æk'seləreɪt] **Ⓐ** VT acelerar, apresurar; **~d program** (*US Univ*) curso *m* intensivo **Ⓑ** VI acelerar

acceleration [ækˌselə'reɪʃən] N aceleración *f*

accelerator [æk'seləreɪtəʳ] N acelerador *m*

accent **Ⓐ** [ˈæksənt] N **1** (*written*) acento *m*; **written ~** acento *m* ortográfico **2** (= *pronunciation*) acento *m*; **he has a French ~** tiene acento francés **3** (= *emphasis*) **to put the ~ on** subrayar (la importancia de), recalcar **Ⓑ** [æk'sent] VT acentuar

accentuate [æk'sentjʊeɪt] VT **1** [+ *syllable, word*] acentuar **2** [+ *need, difference etc*] recalcar, subrayar; [+ *colour, feature*] realzar

accept [ək'sept] **Ⓐ** VT **1** [+ *gift, invitation, apology, offer*] aceptar **2** [*machine*] [+ *coin*] admitir **3** (*Comm*) [+ *cheque, orders*] aceptar **4** (= *acknowledge*) reconocer, admitir; [+ *person*] admitir, acoger; **it is ~ed that ...** se reconoce or admite que ...; **to ~ responsibility for sth** asumir la responsabilidad de algo; **he was ~ed as one of us** se le admitió or acogió como a uno de nosotros **Ⓑ** VI aceptar, asentir

acceptable [ək'septəbl] ADJ [*behaviour, plan, offer*] aceptable; [*gift*] grato

acceptance [ək'septəns] N **1** (*of gift, invitation, apology*) aceptación *f* **2** (= *approval*) aprobación *f*, acogida *f*; **to meet with general ~** tener una buena acogida general

accepted [ək'sɛptɪd] ADJ [*fact, idea, practice*] reconocido, establecido

access ['æksɛs] Ⓐ N **1** (= *entry etc*) acceso *m*; **to gain ~ (to)** (*lit*) lograr entrar (en); **to give ~ to a room** comunicar con *or* dar acceso a una habitación; **to have ~ to sb** tener libre acceso a algn **2** (*in divorce*) derecho *m* de visita **3** (*Comput*) acceso *m* Ⓑ VT (*Comput*) [+ *file*] conseguir acceso a Ⓒ CPD ➤ **access road** vía *f* de acceso

accessible [æk'sɛsəbl] ADJ accesible

accession [æk'sɛʃən] N (*frm*) **1** (= *elevation*) (*to office, post*) entrada *f* en posesión (**to** de); [*of king, queen*] subida *f*, ascenso *m* (**to the throne** al trono) **2** (= *consent*) (*to treaty*) accesión *f*, adherencia *f* (**to** a) **3** (= *entry, admission*) entrada *f* (**to** en)

accessory [æk'sɛsərɪ] N **1 accessories** accesorios *mpl* **2** (*Jur*) cómplice *mf* (**to** de); **~ after the fact** cómplice *mf* encubridor(a); **~ before the fact** cómplice *mf*

accident ['æksɪdənt] Ⓐ N **1** (= *mishap*) accidente *m*; **to have an ~** tener *or* sufrir un accidente; ✦ IDIOM **it's an ~ waiting to happen** es un peligro en potencia; ✦ PROV **~s will happen** son cosas que pasan **2** (= *unforeseen event*) casualidad *f*; **by ~** (= *by chance*) por *or* de casualidad; (= *unintentionally*) sin querer, involuntariamente; **more by ~ than design** más por casualidad que por intención; **I'm sorry, it was an ~** lo siento, lo hice sin querer; **it's no ~ that ...** no es casualidad *or* casual que ... Ⓑ CPD ➤ **Accident and Emergency Department** (*Brit*) Urgencias *fpl*

accidental [æksɪ'dɛntl] ADJ **1** (= *by chance*) casual, fortuito; **~ death** muerte *f* por accidente **2** (= *unintentional*) imprevisto; **I didn't do it deliberately, it was ~** no lo hice adrede, fue sin querer

accidentally [æksɪ'dɛntəlɪ] ADV **1** (= *by chance*) por casualidad **2** (= *unintentionally*) sin querer, involuntariamente; ✦ IDIOM **~ on purpose*** sin querer y no tan sin querer

accident-prone ['æksɪdənt,prəʊn] ADJ susceptible a los accidentes

acclaim [ə'kleɪm] Ⓐ VT aclamar, alabar Ⓑ N (= *praise*) alabanza *f*, aclamación *f*; **the book met with great ~** el libro tuvo una extraordinaria acogida, el libro recibió encendidos elogios

acclamation [æklə'meɪʃən] N aclamación *f*

acclimatize [ə'klaɪmətaɪz], **acclimate** (*US*) [ə'klaɪmət] Ⓐ VT aclimatar (**to** a); **to ~ o.s.** aclimatarse (**to** a) Ⓑ VI aclimatarse (**to** a)

accolade ['ækəleɪd] N (= *praise*) elogio *m* entusiasta; (= *honour*) honor *m*; (= *award*) galardón *m*, premio *m*

accommodate [ə'kɒmədeɪt] VT **1** (= *put up*) alojar, hospedar; **can you ~ four people in July?** ¿tiene usted habitaciones para cuatro personas en julio? **2** (= *have space for*) tener cabida para

accommodating [ə'kɒmədeɪtɪŋ] ADJ complaciente

accommodation [ə,kɒmə'deɪʃən] N **1** (*also US* **~s**) (= *lodging*) alojamiento *msing*; (= *rooms*) habitaciones *fpl*; **to book ~ in a hotel** reservar (una) habitación en un hotel **2** (= *space*) lugar *m*, cabida *f* **3** (= *agreement*) acuerdo *m*

accompaniment [ə'kʌmpənɪmənt] N acompañamiento *m*

accompanist [ə'kʌmpənɪst] N (*Mus*) acompañante/a *m/f*

accompany [ə'kʌmpənɪ] VT acompañar; **to be accompanied by sb** ir acompañado de algn; **~ing letter** carta *f* adjunta; **to ~ o.s. on the piano** acompañarse al piano

accomplice [ə'kʌmplɪs] N cómplice *mf*

accomplish [ə'kʌmplɪʃ] VT **1** (= *achieve*) efectuar, lograr; [+ *task, mission*] llevar a cabo; [+ *purpose, one's design*] realizar **2** (= *finish*) terminar, concluir

accomplished [ə'kʌmplɪʃt] ADJ [*pianist etc*] experto, consumado; [*performance*] logrado

accomplishment [ə'kʌmplɪʃmənt] N **1** (= *achievement*) logro *m* **2** (= *completion, fulfilment*) realización *f* **3** (= *skill*) talento *m*; **accomplishments** talento *msing*, dotes *fpl*

accord [ə'kɔːd] Ⓐ N **1** (= *agreement, treaty*) acuerdo *m* **2** (*in expressions*) **to be in ~** estar de acuerdo, estar en armonía (**with** con); **with one ~** de *or* por común acuerdo; **of his/her own ~** espontáneamente, (de) motu proprio Ⓑ VT [+ *welcome, praise*] dar (**to** a); [+ *honour*] conceder (**to** a)

accordance [ə'kɔːdəns] N **in ~ with** conforme a, de acuerdo con

according [ə'kɔːdɪŋ] ADV **~ to** según; (= *in accordance with*) conforme a, de acuerdo con; **~ to him ...** según él ...; **~ to what he told me** según me dijo; **it went ~ to plan** salió conforme a *or* de acuerdo con nuestros *etc* planes; **classified ~ to size** clasificado por *or* según tamaños; **to play the game ~ to the rules** jugar siguiendo las reglas

accordingly [ə'kɔːdɪŋlɪ] ADV **1** (= *correspondingly*) **it is a difficult job and he should be paid ~** es un trabajo difícil y debería recibir un pago acorde; **to act ~** actuar en consecuencia **2** (= *therefore*) por consiguiente, por lo tanto

accordion [ə'kɔːdɪən] N acordeón *m*

accordionist [ə'kɔːdɪənɪst] N acordeonista *mf*

accost [ə'kɒst] VT abordar; **he ~ed me in the street** me abordó en la calle, se dirigió a mí en la calle

account [ə'kaʊnt] Ⓐ N **1** (= *bank account*) cuenta *f* (bancaria); (*at shop*) cuenta *f*; (= *invoice*) factura *f*; **they have the Blotto ~** (*Advertising*) ellos hacen la publicidad de Blotto; **cash or ~?** ¿en metálico o a cuenta?; **to charge sth to sb's ~** cargar algo en cuenta a algn; **to close an ~** liquidar una cuenta; **payment on ~** pago a cuenta; **to buy sth on ~** comprar algo a cuenta; **to get £50 on ~** recibir 50 libras anticipadas; **to put £50 down on ~** cargar 50 libras a la cuenta; **~ payable** cuenta por pagar; **to settle an ~** liquidar una cuenta; **to settle ~s (with)** (*fig*) ajustar cuentas (con)
2 accounts (= *calculations*) cuentas *fpl*; (*Brit*) (= *department*) (sección *f* de) contabilidad *f*; **to keep the ~s** llevar las cuentas
3 (= *report*) informe *m*; **by/according to her own ~** por lo que dice ella; **by all ~s** a decir de todos, según se dice; **to give an ~ of** dar cuenta de, informar sobre
4 (= *consideration*) consideración *f*; **on no ~** ⬦ **not on any ~** de ninguna manera, bajo ningún concepto; **on his ~** por él, en su nombre; **on his own ~** por cuenta propia; **on ~ of** (= *because of*) a causa de; (*esp US**) (= *because*) porque, debido a que; **to take ~ of sth** ⬦ **take sth into ~** tener algo en cuenta *or* consideración, tener algo presente
5 (= *importance*) importancia *f*; **of little ~** de poca importancia; **to be of no ~** no tener importancia
6 (= *explanation*) **to bring** *or* **call sb to ~** pedir cuentas a algn; **to give a good ~ of o.s.** (= *perform well*) tener una buena actuación; (= *make good impression*) causar buena impresión; **to be held to ~ for sth** ser obligado a rendir cuentas por algo
7 (= *benefit*) **to put** *or* **turn sth to (good) ~** aprovechar algo, sacar provecho de algo
Ⓑ CPD ➤ **account holder** titular *mf* de cuenta ➤ **account number** número *m* de cuenta ➤ **accounts department** (*Brit*) sección *f* de contabilidad
➤ **account for** VI + PREP **1** (= *explain*) explicar, justificar; **how do you ~ for it?** ¿cómo lo explica *or* justifica usted?; **I cannot ~ for it** no me lo explico; ✦ IDIOM **there's no ~ing for taste(s)** sobre gustos no hay nada escrito **2** (= *give reckoning of*) [+ *actions, expenditure*] dar cuenta de, responder de; **many are still not ~ed for** aún se desconoce la suerte que han corrido muchas personas **3** (≈ *represent*) representar, suponer; **children ~ for 5% of the audience** los niños representan *or* suponen el 5 por ciento de la audiencia

accountability [ə,kaʊntə'bɪlətɪ] N responsabilidad *f*

accountable [ə'kaʊntəbl] ADJ responsable (**for** de; **to** ante)

accountancy [ə'kaʊntənsɪ] N contabilidad *f*

accountant [ə'kaʊntənt] N contable *mf* (*Sp*), contador(a) *m/f* (*LAm*)

accounting [ə'kaʊntɪŋ] N contabilidad *f* ➤ **accounting department** (*US*) sección *f* de contabilidad ➤ **accounting period** periodo *m* contable, ejercicio *m* financiero

accoutrements [ə'kuːtrəmənts], **accouterments** (*US*)

[əˈkuːtəmənts] NPL equipo *msing*, avíos *mpl*

accredit [əˈkredɪt] VT **1** (= *credit*) atribuir (**to** a) **2** (= *recognize*) [+ *qualification*] reconocer (oficialmente); [+ *representative, body*] autorizar, acreditar **3** (= *appoint*) acreditar

accreditation [ə,kredɪˈteɪʃən] N reconocimiento *m* (oficial); (*US*) habilitación *f* de enseñanza ➤ **accreditation officer** (*US Scol*) inspector(a) *m/f* de enseñanza

accredited [əˈkredɪtɪd] ADJ autorizado

accrue [əˈkruː] **Ⓐ** VI acumularse; **to ~ to** corresponder a **Ⓑ** VT acumular

accrued interest [ə,kruːdˈɪntrɪst] N interés *m* acumulado

accumulate [əˈkjuːmjʊleɪt] **Ⓐ** VT acumular **Ⓑ** VI acumularse

accumulation [ə,kjuːmjʊˈleɪʃən] N **1** (= *amassing*) acumulación *f*, acopio *m* **2** (= *mass*) montón *m*

accuracy [ˈækjʊrəsɪ] N [*of measurement, figures, clock*] exactitud *f*; [*of instrument*] precisión *f*; [*of translation, copy, words, description*] fidelidad *f*, exactitud *f*; [*of forecast*] lo acertado; [*of aim, shot*] lo certero

accurate [ˈækjʊrɪt] ADJ [*number, measurement, figure, calculation*] exacto; [*instrument, scales*] preciso; [*translation, copy, information, description, memory*] fiel, exacto; [*observation, answer, forecast*] acertado; [*instructions*] preciso; [*shot, aim*] certero; [*missile*] de gran precisión; [*typist*] que no comete errores; **it was his father or, to be ~, his stepfather** era su padre o, para ser exacto, su padrastro; **the scales are ~ to half a gram** la balanza tiene un margen de error de sólo medio gramo

accurately [ˈækjʊrɪtlɪ] ADV [*measure, predict*] con exactitud; [*calculate*] exactamente; [*reflect, translate, copy, draw*] fielmente, exactamente; [*inform, describe*] fielmente, con exactitud; [*shoot, aim*] certeramente

accusation [,ækjʊˈzeɪʃən] N acusación *f*

accusative [əˈkjuːzətɪv] N (*also* ~ *case*) acusativo *m*

accusatory [əˈkjuːzətərɪ] ADJ [*remark*] acusatorio; [*glance, gesture, manner*] acusador

accuse [əˈkjuːz] VT acusar (**of** de)

accused [əˈkjuːzd] N **the** ~ (*sing*) el/la acusado/a; (*plural*) los/las acusados/as

accuser [əˈkjuːzəʳ] N acusador(a) *m/f*

accusing [əˈkjuːzɪŋ] ADJ [*look, eyes*] acusador; **in an** ~ **voice** en tono acusador

accusingly [əˈkjuːzɪŋlɪ] ADV [*say*] en tono acusador

accustom [əˈkʌstəm] VT acostumbrar, habituar (**to** a); **to ~ sb to (doing) sth** acostumbrar a algn a (hacer) algo; **to be ~ed to (doing) sth** estar acostumbrado a (hacer) algo

accustomed [əˈkʌstəmd] ADJ acostumbrado, usual

AC/DC [eɪsiːˈdiːsiː] N ABBR (= **alternating current/direct current**) CA/CC

ace [eɪs] **Ⓐ** N **1** (*Cards*) as *m*; ✦ IDIOMS **to keep an ~ up one's sleeve** ◇ **have an ~ in the hole** (*US**) guardar un triunfo en la mano, guardarse un as en la manga; **to hold all the ~s** tener la sartén por el mango **2** (*Tennis*) ace *m* **3** (= *pilot, racing driver etc*) as *m*; **he's ~s** (*US**) es fenomenal* **Ⓑ** ADJ (*) estupendo*, de aúpa*; ~ **player** as *m* **Ⓒ** CPD ➤ **Ace Bandage®** (*US*) venda *f* elástica

acerbic [əˈsɜːbɪk] ADJ **1** [*taste*] acre, acerbo **2** (*fig*) mordaz, cáustico

acetate [ˈæsɪteɪt] N acetato *m*

acetic [əˈsiːtɪk] ADJ acético ➤ **acetic acid** ácido *m* acético

acetone [ˈæsɪtəʊn] N acetona *f*

ache [eɪk] **Ⓐ** N (= *pain*) dolor *m*; **I have an ~ in my side** me duele el costado; ✦ IDIOM **with an ~ in one's heart** con mucho pesar **Ⓑ** VI **1** (= *hurt*) doler; **I'm aching all over** me duele todo **2** (*fig*) **my heart ~s for you** lo siento en el alma **3** (= *yearn*) desear, suspirar (**for** por); **I am aching to see you again** me muero por volver a verte

achieve [əˈtʃiːv] VT (= *reach*) conseguir, alcanzar; (= *complete*) llevar a cabo; (= *accomplish*) realizar; **he will never ~ anything** él no hará nunca nada; **what do you hope to ~ by that?** ¿qué esperas lograr con eso?

achievement [əˈtʃiːvmənt] N **1** (= *act*) realización *f*, consecución *f* **2** (= *thing achieved*) logro *m*, éxito *m*; **that's quite an ~** es todo un logro *or* éxito, es toda una hazaña **3** (*Scol*) **the level of ~** el nivel de rendimiento escolar

achiever [əˈtʃiːvəʳ] N (*also* **high ~**) *persona que desarrolla al máximo su potencial o que llega muy alto*

Achilles [əˈkɪliːz] N Aquiles ➤ **Achilles heel** talón *m* de Aquiles ➤ **Achilles tendon** tendón *m* de Aquiles

aching [ˈeɪkɪŋ] ADJ [*tooth, feet*] dolorido, que duele; **with an ~ heart** con mucho pesar

acid [ˈæsɪd] **Ⓐ** N ácido *m* **Ⓑ** ADJ (= *sharp, bitter*) ácido (*also Chem*); [*remark, tone*] mordaz; [*voice*] agrio, mordaz **Ⓒ** CPD ➤ **acid drops** (*Brit*) caramelos *mpl* ácidos ➤ **acid house party** fiesta *f* acid ➤ **acid rain** lluvia *f* ácida ➤ **the acid test** (*fig*) la prueba de fuego, la prueba decisiva

acidic [əˈsɪdɪk] ADJ ácido

acidity [əˈsɪdɪtɪ] N acidez *f*

acknowledge [əkˈnɒlɪdʒ] VT **1** (= *admit*) reconocer; [+ *claim, truth*] admitir; [+ *crime*] confesarse culpable de; **I ~ that ...** reconozco que ...; **to ~ defeat** darse por vencido; **to ~ sb as leader** reconocer a algn como jefe **2** [+ *favour, gift*] agradecer, dar las gracias por; [+ *letter*] acusar recibo de **3** (= *greet*) saludar; [+ *person*] saludar; [+ *greeting*] contestar a

acknowledged [əkˈnɒlɪdʒd] ADJ **an ~ expert** un experto reconocido como tal; **a generally ~ fact** un hecho generalmente reconocido

acknowledgement [əkˈnɒlɪdʒmənt] **Ⓐ** N **1** (= *admission*) admisión *f*; (= *recognition*) reconocimiento *m* **2** [*of letter etc*] acuse *m* de recibo **3** [*of greeting*] contestación *f* **4 acknowledgements** (*in book*) menciones *fpl* **Ⓑ** CPD ➤ **acknowledgement slip** (*Comm*) acuse *m* de recibo

ACLU N ABBR (*US*) = **American Civil Liberties Union**

acme [ˈækmɪ] N colmo *m*, cima *f*

acne [ˈæknɪ] N acné *m or f*

acolyte [ˈækəlaɪt] N acólito *m*

acorn [ˈeɪkɔːn] N bellota *f*

acoustic [əˈkuːstɪk] ADJ acústico ➤ **acoustic guitar** guitarra *f* acústica

acoustics [əˈkuːstɪks] N acústica *f*

acquaint [əˈkweɪnt] VT **1** (= *inform*) **to ~ sb with sth** informar a algn de *or* sobre algo; **to ~ o.s. with sth** informarse sobre algo **2** (= *know*) **to be ~ed with** [+ *person*] conocer; [+ *fact*] saber; **to be ~ed** conocerse

acquaintance [əˈkweɪntəns] N (= *person*) conocido/a *m/f*; **to make sb's ~** conocer a algn

acquiesce [,ækwɪˈes] VI consentir (**in** en), conformarse (**in** con)

acquiescence [,ækwɪˈesns] N aquiescencia *f* (**in** a, en), consentimiento *m* (**in** para)

acquiescent [,ækwɪˈesnt] ADJ conforme, aquiescente

acquire [əˈkwaɪəʳ] VT [+ *possessions*] (= *get*) adquirir, obtener; (= *manage to get*) conseguir; [+ *habit, reputation, native language*] adquirir; [+ *foreign language*] aprender; [+ *company*] adquirir; **where did you ~ that?** ¿dónde conseguiste eso?; **to ~ a name for honesty** ganarse fama de honrado

acquired [əˈkwaɪəd] ADJ adquirido

acquisition [,ækwɪˈzɪʃən] N adquisición *f*

acquisitive [əˈkwɪzɪtɪv] ADJ codicioso

acquit [əˈkwɪt] VT **1** (*Jur*) absolver, exculpar (**of** de); **he was ~ted on all charges** lo absolvieron de todas las acusaciones **2 to ~ o.s.: how did he ~ himself?** ¿cómo se desenvolvió?; **to ~ o.s. well** defenderse bien

acquittal [əˈkwɪtl] N absolución *f*, exculpación *f*

acre [ˈeɪkəʳ] N acre *m* (*4.047 metros cuadrados*)

acreage [ˈeɪkərɪdʒ] N superficie *f* medida en acres, extensión *f* medida en acres

acrid [ˈækrɪd] ADJ acre, punzante

acrimonious [,ækrɪˈməʊnɪəs] ADJ [*argument, meeting, exchange*] reñido; [*divorce, break-up*] amargo

acrimony [ˈækrɪmənɪ] N acritud f, acrimonia f; **their first meeting ended in** ~ su primera reunión acabó en una disputa enconada

acrobat [ˈækrəbæt] N acróbata mf

acrobatic [ˌækrəʊˈbætɪk] ADJ acrobático

acrobatics [ˌækrəʊˈbætɪks] NPL acrobacia fsing

acronym [ˈækrənɪm] N sigla(s) f(pl), acrónimo m

across [əˈkrɒs]

> When **across** is an element in a phrasal verb, eg **come across, run across**, look up the verb.

Ⓐ PREP **1** (= from one side to other of) a través de; **a long journey** ~ **the desert** un largo viaje a través del desierto; **to go** ~ **a bridge** atravesar or cruzar un puente; **to run** ~ **a road** cruzar una calle corriendo; **the bridge** ~ **the Tagus** el puente sobre el Tajo
2 (= on the other side of) al otro lado de; ~ **the street from our house** al otro lado de la calle enfrente de nuestra casa
3 (= crosswise over) a través de
Ⓑ ADV **1** (= from one side to the other) a través, al través; **don't go around, go** ~ no des la vuelta, ve al través; **shall I go** ~ **first?** ¿paso yo el primero?; **to swim** ~ atravesar a nado
2 (= opposite) **it's** ~ **from the Post Office** está enfrente de Correos; **he sat down** ~ **from her** se sentó frente a ella
3 (in measurements) **the lake is 12km** ~ el lago tiene 12km de ancho; **the plate is 30cm** ~ el plato tiene un diámetro de 30cm
4 (= crossways) a través, en cruz, transversalmente

acrylic [əˈkrɪlɪk] ADJ acrílico

ACT N ABBR (= **American College Testing**) prueba de aptitud estándar que por lo general hacen los estudiantes que quieren entrar a la universidad por primera vez

act [ækt] **Ⓐ** N **1** (= deed) acto m, acción f; **to catch sb in the** ~ sorprender a algn en el acto; **I was in the** ~ **of writing to him** justamente le estaba escribiendo
2 (= law) ley f
3 (Theat) acto m; (in show) número m; ✦ IDIOMS **it's a hard** ~ **to follow** es muy difícil de igualar; **to get in on the** ~* introducirse en el asunto, lograr tomar parte; **to get one's** ~ **together*** organizarse, arreglárselas
4 (= pretence) cuento m, teatro m; **to put on an** ~ fingir, hacer teatro*
Ⓑ VT (Theat) [+ play] representar; [+ scene] interpretar; **to** ~ **the part of** hacer el papel de; ✦ IDIOM **to** ~ **the fool** hacerse el tonto
Ⓒ VI **1** (in film, play) actuar; (= be an actor) ser actor/actriz; (= do theatre) hacer teatro; (= do cinema) hacer cine; **who's** ~**ing in it?** ¿quién actúa?; **I** ~**ed in my youth** de joven fui actor; **he's only** ~**ing** (fig) lo está fingiendo (nada más)
2 (= behave) actuar, comportarse; **he is** ~**ing strangely** está actuando or se está comportando de una manera rara
3 (= take action) obrar, tomar medidas; **to** ~ **with caution** obrar con precaución; **now is the time to** ~ hay que ponerse en acción ahora mismo
4 (= work) **he was** ~**ing as ambassador** hacía de embajador; ~**ing in my capacity as chairman** en mi calidad de presidente; **to** ~ **for sb** representar a algn
5 (= function) **to** ~ **as sth** servir de algo; **it** ~**s as a deterrent** sirve para disuadir, sirve de disuasión; **it** ~**s as a safety valve** funciona como válvula de seguridad
6 (= take effect) [drug] surtir efecto, actuar
Ⓓ CPD ➤ **act of faith** acto m de fe ➤ **act of God** (caso m de) fuerza f mayor ➤ **Act of Parliament** ley f (aprobada por el Parlamento) ➤ **act of war** acción f de guerra
➤ **act on** VI + PREP [+ advice, suggestion] seguir; [+ order] obedecer
➤ **act out** VT + ADV representar
➤ **act up*** VI + ADV [person] portarse mal; [knee, back, injury] molestar, doler; [machine] fallar, estropearse
➤ **act upon** = **act on**

acting [ˈæktɪŋ] **Ⓐ** ADJ (gen) interino, suplente; [president] en funciones **Ⓑ** N (Theat) (= performance) interpretación f, actuación f; (= profession) profesión f de actor, teatro m; **what was his** ~ **like?** ¿qué tal hizo el papel?; **she has done**

some ~ tiene alguna experiencia como actriz

action [ˈækʃən] **Ⓐ** N **1** (= activity) **the time has come for** ~ ha llegado el momento de hacer algo or de actuar; **to put a plan into** ~ poner un plan en práctica or en marcha; **to be out of** ~ [machinery] no funcionar, estar averiado; **"out of action"** "no funciona", "fuera de servicio"; **the illness put him out of** ~ **for six months** la enfermedad lo dejó seis meses fuera de combate*; ~ **stations!** ¡a sus puestos!
2 (= steps) medidas fpl; **emergency** ~ medidas fpl de emergencia; **to take** ~ **against sb/sth** tomar medidas contra algn/algo; **their advice is to take no** ~ aconsejan no hacer nada
3 (= deed) acto m; **he wasn't responsible for his** ~**s** no era responsable de sus actos
4 (*) (= excitement) animación f, marcha* f; **they were hoping to find some** ~ esperaban encontrar algo de animación, esperaban encontrar algo de marcha*
5 (Mil) (= intervention) intervención f; (= engagement) contienda f, enfrentamiento m; **to go into** ~ [person, unit] entrar en acción or en combate; [army, battleship] entrar en acción; **wounded/killed in** ~ herido/muerto en acción (de guerra) or en combate; **to see** ~ luchar
6 (= effect) [of acid, drug, elements] efecto m
7 (Jur) (= measures) acción f judicial; (= lawsuit) proceso m judicial; **the police are not taking any** ~ la policía no va a emprender ninguna acción judicial; **to bring an** ~ **against sb** comenzar un proceso judicial contra algn
8 (Theat, Ciné) acción f; **action!** (Ciné) ¡acción!
Ⓑ CPD ➤ **action point** punto m a seguir ➤ **action replay** (Brit TV) repetición f (de la jugada)

action-packed [ˈækʃnpækt] ADJ [film, book] lleno de acción, con mucha acción; [holiday, life] muy movido

activate [ˈæktɪveɪt] VT activar

active [ˈæktɪv] **Ⓐ** ADJ **1** (= lively) [person, brain] activo; [imagination] vivo
2 (= busy) [life, day] de mucha actividad, muy movido
3 (= not passive) [member, population, vocabulary] activo; **guerrilla groups are** ~ **in the province** grupos de guerrilleros están luchando en la provincia; **to take an** ~ **interest in sth** interesarse vivamente por algo; **the government must take** ~ **steps to bring down inflation** el gobierno debe tomar medidas directas para bajar la inflación; **to be politically** ~ militar políticamente
4 (= not extinct) [volcano] en actividad
5 (Chem, Phys, Electronics) activo; **the** ~ **ingredient** el ingrediente activo
6 (Fin, Comm) [trading, market] activo
Ⓑ N (Gram) **the** ~ la voz activa
Ⓒ CPD ➤ **active service, active duty** (esp US) servicio m activo; **to be on** ~ **service** or **duty** estar en activo; **to die on** ~ **service** morir en acto de servicio ➤ **the active voice** la voz activa

actively [ˈæktɪvlɪ] ADV [encourage, campaign, support,] enérgicamente; [seek, consider] seriamente; **to be** ~ **involved in sth** tomar parte activa en algo, participar activamente en algo

activist [ˈæktɪvɪst] N activista mf

activity [ækˈtɪvɪtɪ] N actividad f ➤ **activity holiday** vacaciones con actividades ya programadas

actor [ˈæktər] N actor m, actriz f

actress [ˈæktrɪs] N actriz f

actual [ˈæktjʊəl] **Ⓐ** ADJ **1** (= real) real; **the** ~ **number is much higher than that** el número real es mucho más alto; **the film was based on** ~ **events** la película estaba basada en hechos reales; **let's take an** ~ **case/example** tomemos un caso/ejemplo concreto; **there is no** ~ **contract** no hay contrato propiamente dicho; **you met an** ~ **film star?** ¿has conocido a una estrella de cine de verdad?; **in** ~ **fact** en realidad; ~ **size** tamaño m real
2 (= precise) [amount, figure] exacto; [words] exacto, textual
Ⓑ CPD ➤ **actual bodily harm** daños mpl físicos, lesiones fpl corporales

> ⚠ actual ≠ *actual*

actuality [ˌæktjʊˈælɪtɪ] N realidad f; **in** ~ en realidad

actually [ˈæktjʊəlɪ] ADV **1** (= *really*) en realidad, realmente; **inflation has ~ fallen** la inflación de hecho ha bajado; **I never thought you'd ~ do it!** ¡jamás pensé que lo harías de verdad!
2 (*correcting, clarifying*) **that's not true, ~** bueno, eso no es cierto; **~, I don't know him at all** pues la verdad, no lo conozco de nada; **~, you were quite right** pues mira, de hecho tenías razón; **£50, ~** 50 libras para ser exactos **3** (= *exactly*) exactamente; **what did he ~ say?** ¿qué es lo que dijo exactamente?
4 (*for emphasis*) **we ~ caught a fish!** ¡incluso *or* hasta pescamos un pez!; **you only pay for the electricity you ~ use** sólo pagas la electricidad que consumes

⚠ **actually ≠ actualmente**

actuary [ˈæktjʊərɪ] N actuario/a *m/f* de seguros
acumen [ˈækjʊmen] N perspicacia *f*, tino *m*, agudeza *f*
acupuncture [ˈækjʊpʌŋktʃəʳ] N acupuntura *f*
acupuncturist [ˌækjʊˈpʌŋktʃərɪst] N acupuntor(a) *m/f*, acupunturista *mf*
acute [əˈkjuːt] ADJ **1** (= *intense*) [*crisis, problem*] grave; [*anxiety, joy*] profundo, intenso; [*pain*] agudo; [*discomfort*] fuerte; **the report has caused the government ~ embarrassment** el informe ha puesto en una situación de lo más embarazosa al gobierno; **to become ~** [*shortage, problem*] agravarse **2** (= *keen*) [*hearing*] fino, agudo; [*sense of smell*] fino **3** (= *shrewd*) agudo, perspicaz **4** [*illness, appendicitis, angle, accent*] agudo
acutely [əˈkjuːtlɪ] ADV [*feel, suffer*] intensamente; [*embarrassing, uncomfortable*] sumamente; **I am ~ aware that ...** me doy perfecta cuenta de que ..., me doy cuenta perfectamente de que ..., soy perfectamente consciente de que ...; **they were ~ aware of the difficulties involved** tenían plena consciencia de todas las dificultades que suponía
AD ADV ABBR (= **Anno Domini**) d. de C.
ad* [æd] N ABBR = **advertisement**
Adam [ˈædəm] N Adán; ✦ IDIOMS **I don't know him from ~*** no lo conozco en absoluto; **to be as old as ~** ser de tiempos de Maricastaña, ser más viejo que el mundo ➤ **Adam's apple** nuez *f* (de la garganta)
adamant [ˈædəmənt] ADJ firme, inflexible
adamantly [ˈædəməntlɪ] ADV [*refuse*] rotundamente, terminantemente; **to be ~ opposed to sth** oponerse terminantemente *or* firmemente a algo
adapt [əˈdæpt] Ⓐ VT **1** [+ *machine*] ajustar, adaptar; [+ *building*] remodelar; **to ~ o.s. to sth** adaptarse a algo, ajustarse a algo **2** [+ *text*] adaptar; **~ed for television** adaptado para la televisión Ⓑ VI adaptarse
adaptability [əˌdæptəˈbɪlɪtɪ] N adaptabilidad *f*, capacidad *f* para adaptarse *or* acomodarse
adaptable [əˈdæptəbl] ADJ adaptable; **he's very ~** se adapta *or* se acomoda con facilidad a las circunstancias
adaptation [ˌædæpˈteɪʃən] N (*Bio, etc*) adaptación *f*; [*of text*] versión *f*
adapter, adaptor [əˈdæptəʳ] N (*gen*) adaptador *m*; (*Brit Elec*) enchufe *m* múltiple, ladrón *m*
ADC N ABBR (= **aide-de-camp**) edecán *m*
ADD N ABBR = **Attention Deficit Disorder**
add [æd] Ⓐ VT **1** (*Math*) sumar **2** (= *join*) añadir, agregar (*esp LAm*) (**to** a); **"add salt to taste"** "añadir sal al gusto"; ✦ IDIOM **to ~ insult to injury** para colmo de males **3** (= *say further*) añadir, agregar; **he ~ed that ...** añadió que ..., agregó que ...; **there's nothing to ~** no hay nada (más) que añadir *o* decir Ⓑ VI (*Math*) sumar
➤ **add on** VT + ADV añadir
➤ **add to** VI + PREP aumentar, acrecentar; **then, to ~ to our troubles ...** luego, para colmo de desgracias ..., luego, para más desgracias ...
➤ **add together** VT + ADV sumar
➤ **add up** Ⓐ VT + ADV **1** [+ *figures*] sumar **2** [+ *benefits, advantages*] calcular Ⓑ VI + ADV **1** [*figures*] sumar **2** (= *make sense*) tener sentido; **it just doesn't ~ up** no tiene sentido; **it's all beginning to ~ up** la cosa empieza a aclararse

➤ **add up to** VI + PREP **1** (*Math*) sumar, ascender a; **it ~s up to 25** suma 25, asciende a 25 **2** (*fig*) (= *mean*) querer decir, venir a decir; **what all this ~s up to is ...** lo que significa *or* quiere decir todo esto es que ...; **it doesn't ~ up to much** es poca cosa, no tiene gran importancia
added [ˈædɪd] ADJ añadido, adicional; **~ to which ...** y además ..., por si fuera poco ... ➤ **added value** valor *m* añadido
adder [ˈædəʳ] N víbora *f*
addict [ˈædɪkt] N **1** (*addicted to drugs etc*) adicto/a *m/f* **2** (*) (= *enthusiast*) entusiasta *mf*
addicted [əˈdɪktɪd] ADJ (*lit*) adicto; **to be ~ to sth** ser adicto a algo (also *fig*); **to be ~ to drugs** ser drogadicto; **to be ~ to heroin** ser heroinómano; **to become ~ to** (*lit, fig*) enviciarse con
addiction [əˈdɪkʃən] N adicción *f* (**to** a); **his ~ to drugs** su adicción a las drogas, su drogodependencia
addictive [əˈdɪktɪv] ADJ [*drug*] que crea adicción, adictivo; [*personality*] propenso a las adicciones; **rock climbing is ~** el alpinismo es como una droga *or* es adictivo
addition [əˈdɪʃən] N **1** (*Math*) adición *f*, suma *f* **2** (= *inclusion*) adición *f*; **in ~** además; **in ~ to** además de **3** (= *acquisition*) adquisición *f*; **this is a welcome ~ to our books on agriculture** éste aumenta valiosamente nuestra colección de libros sobre agricultura; **an ~ to the family** un nuevo miembro de la familia
additional [əˈdɪʃənl] ADJ [*cost, payment*] adicional, extra; [*troops, men*] más; **it is an ~ reason to** (+ INFIN) es razón de más para + *infin*; **~ charge** cargo *m* adicional
additionally [əˈdɪʃənlɪ] ADV (= *moreover*) además
additive [ˈædɪtɪv] N aditivo *m*
additive-free [ˈædɪtɪvˈfriː] ADJ sin aditivos
addled [ˈædld] ADJ [*brain*] confuso, débil
add-on [ˈædɒn] Ⓐ N (*Comput*) componente *m or* dispositivo *m* adicional Ⓑ ADJ [*product, part*] adicional
address [əˈdres] Ⓐ N **1** [*of house*] dirección *f* (also *Comput*), señas *fpl*; **he isn't at this ~ any more** ya no vive aquí **2** (= *speech*) discurso *m* **3** (= *title*) **form of ~** tratamiento *m* Ⓑ VT **1** [+ *letter*] (= *direct*) dirigir (**to** a); (= *put address on*) poner la dirección en; **the letter was ~ed to the editor** la carta iba dirigida al director; **I ~ed it to your home** lo mandé a tu casa; **this is ~ed to you** esto viene a su nombre; **this letter is wrongly ~ed** esta carta lleva la dirección equivocada
2 [+ *people*] (= *speak to*) dirigirse a; (= *make a speech to*) pronunciar un discurso ante; **to ~ sb as "tú"** tratar a algn de "tú", tutear a algn **3** [+ *remarks*] dirigir; **please ~ your complaints to the manager** se ruega dirijan sus reclamaciones al director Ⓒ CPD ➤ **address book** librito *m* de direcciones, agenda *f*
addressee [ˌædreˈsiː] N destinatario/a *m/f*; (*Comm*) consignatario/a *m/f*
adenoids [ˈædɪnɔɪdz] NPL vegetaciones *fpl* (adenoideas)
adept Ⓐ [əˈdept] ADJ experto, hábil (**at, in** en); **to be ~ at sth/at doing sth** ser experto *or* maestro en algo/en hacer algo Ⓑ [ˈædept] N experto/a *m/f*, maestro/a *m/f*
adequate [ˈædɪkwɪt] ADJ **1** (= *sufficient*) [*funds*] suficiente; **one teaspoonful should be ~** una cucharadita bastará *or* será suficiente; **my income is quite ~ for my needs** mis ingresos cubren bien mis necesidades **2** (= *satisfactory*) [*diet*] equilibrado, apropiado; [*income, standard*] aceptable; [*housing, facilities*] adecuado, apropiado; [*explanation*] convincente; **this saw should be ~ for the job** este serrucho valdrá para ese trabajo **3** (= *passable*) [*performance, essay*] aceptable, pasable
adequately [ˈædɪkwɪtlɪ] ADV [*prepared, trained, protected*] suficientemente; [*punish*] de forma apropiada; **this has never been ~ explained** esto nunca se ha explicado con claridad; **he speaks the language ~** habla el idioma de forma aceptable
ADHD N ABBR = **Attention Deficit Hyperactivity Disorder**
adhere [ədˈhɪəʳ] VI (= *stick*) adherirse, pegarse (**to** a)

➤ **adhere to** VI + PREP [+ *policy*] adherirse a; [+ *rule*] observar

adherence [əd'hıərəns] N (*to policy*) adhesión *f* (**to** a); (*to rule*) observancia *f* (**to** de)

adherent [əd'hıərənt] N partidario/a *m/f*

adhesion [əd'hi:ʒən] N (*Med*) adhesión *f*; (*to road*) adherencia *f*; [*of glue*] adherencia *f*, adhesión *f*

adhesive [əd'hi:zɪv] Ⓐ ADJ adhesivo Ⓑ N adhesivo *m*, pegamento *m*

ad hoc [æd'hɒk] ADJ [*decision*] a propósito para el caso, adecuado; [*committee*] formado con fines específicos; **on an ~ basis** cuando hace/hacía etc falta

ad infinitum [ˌædɪnfɪ'naɪtəm] ADV hasta el infinito, ad infinitum; **it just carries on ~** es inacabable, es cosa de nunca acabar

adjacent [ə'dʒeɪsənt] ADJ contiguo; [*angle*] adyacente; **~ to** contiguo a

adjective ['ædʒektɪv] N adjetivo *m*

adjoin [ə'dʒɔɪn] Ⓐ VT estar contiguo a, lindar con, colindar con Ⓑ VI estar contiguo, colindar

adjoining [ə'dʒɔɪnɪŋ] ADJ contiguo, colindante; **the ~ house** la casa contigua, la casa de al lado; **two ~ countries** dos países vecinos, dos países colindantes (*more frm*); **in an ~ room** en un cuarto contiguo

adjourn [ə'dʒɜːn] Ⓐ VT (= *suspend*) suspender; (= *postpone*) aplazar; **to ~ a discussion for a week** aplazar un debate por una semana; **the court is ~ed** se levanta la sesión Ⓑ VI [*meeting*] aplazarse; (*Parl*) disolverse; **the court then ~ed** entonces el tribunal levantó la sesión; **let's ~ for lunch** (*meeting*) continuaremos la reunión después de comer; **they ~ed to the pub*** se trasladaron al bar

adjournment [ə'dʒɜːnmənt] N (= *period*) suspensión *f*; (= *postponement*) aplazamiento *m*

adjudicate [ə'dʒuːdɪkeɪt] Ⓐ VT [+ *contest*] arbitrar, hacer de árbitro en; [+ *claim*] decidir sobre Ⓑ VI arbitrar; **to ~ on a matter** arbitrar en un asunto

adjudication [əˌdʒuːdɪ'keɪʃən] N adjudicación *f*

adjudicator [ə'dʒuːdɪkeɪtəʳ] N juez *mf*, árbitro *mf*

adjunct ['ædʒʌŋkt] N adjunto/a *m/f*, accesorio/a *m/f*

adjust [ə'dʒʌst] Ⓐ VT [+ *height, temperature, speed, knob, dial*] regular; [+ *machine, engine, brakes, mirror, figures*] ajustar; [+ *wages, prices*] reajustar; **to ~ o.s. to a situation** adaptarse a una situación; **she ~ed her head scarf** se arregló la pañoleta Ⓑ VI [*person*] adaptarse; [*machine, device*] ajustarse; **to ~ to sth** acostumbrarse a algo

adjustable [ə'dʒʌstəbl] ADJ ajustable, regulable ➤ **adjustable spanner** llave *f* inglesa

adjusted [ə'dʒʌstɪd] ADJ **well ~** equilibrado

adjustment [ə'dʒʌstmənt] N 1 (= *regulation*) [*of temperature, height, knob, dial*] regulación *f*; [*of machine, engine, brakes*] ajuste *m* 2 (= *alteration*) modificación *f*, cambio *m*; **we can always make an ~** siempre podemos cambiarlo; **to make an ~ to one's plans** modificar sus planes 3 [*of figures*] ajuste *m*; [*of wages*] reajuste *m*

adjutant ['ædʒətənt] N ayudante *mf*

ad lib [æd'lɪb] Ⓐ ADV [*perform, speak*] improvisando; [*continue*] a voluntad, a discreción Ⓑ ADJ [*production, performance, speech*] improvisado Ⓒ VT, VI improvisar

admin* ['ædmɪn] N ABBR (*Brit*) (= **administration**) administración *f*

administer [əd'mɪnɪstəʳ] VT administrar

administrate [əd'mɪnɪstreɪt] VT administrar, dirigir

administration [ədˌmɪnɪs'treɪʃən] N (*gen*) administración *f*; (*esp US Pol*) (= *government*) gobierno *m*, administración *f*; **business ~** administración *f* de empresas; **the Bush ~** el gobierno de Bush, la administración de Bush

administrative [əd'mɪnɪstrətɪv] ADJ [*work, officer, system*] administrativo; [*costs, expenses*] de administración, administrativo; **~ staff** personal *m* de administración

administrator [əd'mɪnɪstreɪtəʳ] N administrador(a) *m/f*; (*Jur*) albacea *mf*

admirable ['ædmərəbl] ADJ admirable, digno de admiración

admirably ['ædmərəblɪ] ADV admirablemente, de una manera digna de admiración

admiral ['ædmərəl] N almirante *mf*

Admiralty ['ædmərəltɪ] N (*Brit*) Ministerio *m* de Marina, Almirantazgo *m*; **First Lord of the ~** Ministro *m* de Marina

admiration [ˌædmə'reɪʃən] N admiración *f*

admire [əd'maɪəʳ] VT admirar

admirer [əd'maɪərəʳ] N admirador(a) *m/f*

admiring [əd'maɪərɪŋ] ADJ [*look, glance, tone, voice*] (lleno) de admiración, admirativo; **his ~ fans** sus admiradores

admiringly [əd'maɪərɪŋlɪ] ADV [*say, describe*] con admiración; **he looked at her ~** le lanzó una mirada (llena) de admiración, la miró con admiración

admissible [əd'mɪsəbl] ADJ admisible, aceptable

admission [əd'mɪʃən] Ⓐ N 1 (*to building*) entrada *f*; **"admission free"** "entrada gratis"; **"no admission"** "prohibida la entrada", "se prohíbe la entrada" 2 (*to institution as member*) ingreso *m* (**to** en) 3 (= *acknowledgement*) confesión *f*, reconocimiento *m*; **it would be an ~ of defeat** sería un reconocimiento de la derrota, sería reconocer la derrota Ⓑ CPD ➤ **admission fee** cuota *f* de entrada

admit [əd'mɪt] VT 1 (= *allow to enter*) dejar entrar; [+ *patient*] ingresar; **"this ticket admits two"** "entrada para dos personas" 2 (= *acknowledge*) reconocer; [+ *crime*] confesar; **it is hard, I ~** es difícil, lo reconozco; **it must be ~ted that ...** hay que reconocer que ... ➤ **admit of** VI + PREP admitir ➤ **admit to** VI + PREP [+ *crime*] confesarse culpable de; **I ~ to feeling a bit ill** confieso que me siento algo mal

admittance [əd'mɪtəns] N entrada *f*; **"no admittance"** "se prohíbe la entrada", "prohibida la entrada"

admittedly [əd'mɪtɪdlɪ] ADV **it's only a theory, admittedly, but ...** reconozco que *or* es verdad que *or* de acuerdo que sólo es una teoría, pero ...; **admittedly, ...** hay que reconocer *or* admitir que, ..., es verdad que, ...

admonish [əd'mɒnɪʃ] VT reprender, amonestar (**for** por)

ad nauseam [æd'nɔːsɪæm] ADV hasta la saciedad

ado [ə'duː] N **without further** *or* **more ~** sin más (ni más *o* preámbulos); **much ~ about nothing** mucho ruido y pocas nueces

adolescence [ˌædə'lesns] N adolescencia *f*

adolescent [ˌædə'lesnt] ADJ, N adolescente *mf*

adopt [ə'dɒpt] VT 1 [+ *child*] adoptar 2 [+ *report*] aprobar; [+ *suggestion*] seguir, aceptar; (*Pol*) [+ *candidate*] elegir

adopted [ə'dɒptɪd] ADJ adoptivo, adoptado (*Mex*)

adoption [ə'dɒpʃən] N adopción *f*; **they have two children by ~** tienen dos hijos adoptivos; **country of ~** patria *f* adoptiva

adoptive [ə'dɒptɪv] ADJ adoptivo

adorable [ə'dɔːrəbl] ADJ adorable, encantador

adoration [ˌædɔː'reɪʃən] N adoración *f*

adore [ə'dɔːʳ] VT (= *love*) adorar; **I ~ your new flat** me encanta tu nuevo piso

adoring [ə'dɔːrɪŋ] ADJ [*look*] lleno de adoración; [*parent etc*] cariñoso

adoringly [ə'dɔːrɪŋlɪ] ADV con adoración

adorn [ə'dɔːn] VT adornar, embellecer

adornment [ə'dɔːnmənt] N 1 (= *act*) [*of body, person*] adorno *m*, embellecimiento *m*; [*of building, room*] decoración *f* 2 (= *object*) adorno *m*

adrenalin(e) [ə'drenəlɪn] N adrenalina *f*

Adriatic [ˌeɪdrɪ'ætɪk] ADJ, N **the ~ (Sea)** el (Mar) Adriático

adrift [ə'drɪft] ADV (*Naut*) a la deriva; **to come ~** (*Brit*) [*rope, wire*] soltarse

adroit [ə'drɔɪt] ADJ diestro, hábil

adulation [ˌædjʊ'leɪʃən] N adulación *f*

adult ['ædʌlt] Ⓐ ADJ [*person, animal*] adulto; [*film, book*] para adultos; **to be ~ about sth** comportarse como una persona adulta/como personas adultas con respecto a algo **B** N adulto/a *m/f*; **"adults only"** (*Cine*) "(autorizado) para mayores de 18 años" **C** CPD ➤ **adult education** educación *f* para adultos

adulterate [ə'dʌltəreɪt] VT adulterar

adulterous [ə'dʌltərəs] ADJ adúltero

adultery [ə'dʌltəri] N adulterio *m*

adulthood ['ædʌlthʊd] N adultez *f*, mayoría *f* de edad, edad *f* adulta

advance [əd'vɑːns] **A** N 1 [*of troops, etc*] avance *m* 2 (*in science, technology*) avance *m*, adelanto *m* 3 (= *initial payment*) anticipo *m*, adelanto *m*; **could you give me an ~?** ¿me podría dar un anticipo?; **any ~ on £15?** (*in auction*) ¿alguien ofrece más de 15 libras?, 15 libras ¿alguien da más?
4 **advances** (*amorous*) insinuaciones *fpl*
5 **in ~: a week in ~** con ocho días de antelación; **to book in ~** reservar con antelación; **the dish may be made in ~** el plato puede prepararse con anterioridad; **to arrive in ~ of sb** llegar antes que algn; **to pay in ~** pagar por adelantado
B VT 1 (= *further*) [+ *plan, knowledge, understanding*] potenciar; [+ *career*] promocionar; [+ *cause, claim*] promover
2 (= *put forward*) [+ *idea, theory*] proponer, sugerir; [+ *proposal*] presentar; [+ *opinion*] expresar
3 [+ *money*] (*as initial fee*) adelantar, anticipar; (*as early wages*) adelantar
C VI 1 (= *move forward*) avanzar; **the advancing army** el ejército que avanza; **to ~ on sth/sb** acercarse a algo/algn, avanzar hacia algo/algn
2 (= *progress*) [*science, technology*] progresar, adelantarse; [*work, society*] avanzar; **despite his advancing years** a pesar de su edad (avanzada)
D CPD ➤ **advance booking** reserva *f* anticipada, reserva *f* por anticipado; **"advance booking advisable"** "se recomienda que reserven por adelantado" ➤ **advance booking office** (*Brit*) taquilla *f* (de reservas *or* venta anticipada) ➤ **advance copy** [*of book*] ejemplar *m* de muestra ➤ **advance notice** aviso *m* previo ➤ **advance payment** anticipo *m* ➤ **advance warning** aviso *m* previo

advanced [əd'vɑːnst] **A** ADJ 1 (= *developed*) [*civilization, society*] avanzado 2 (= *not elementary*) [*course, level, studies*] avanzado, superior; [*student*] (de nivel) avanzado 3 (*in time*) [*stage*] avanzado **B** CPD ➤ **advanced gas-cooled reactor** reactor *m* avanzado refrigerado por gas ➤ **Advanced Level** (*Brit Scol frm*) ≈ bachillerato *m*

advancement [əd'vɑːnsmənt] N (= *furthering*) fomento *m*; (= *improvement*) progreso *m*; (*in rank*) ascenso *m*

advantage [əd'vɑːntɪdʒ] N 1 ventaja *f*; **"languages and shorthand an ~"** (*in job advert*) "serán méritos *or* se valorarán idiomas y taquigrafía"; **to have an ~ over sb** llevar ventaja a algn; **to take ~ of sb/sth** (*unfairly*) aprovecharse de algn/algo, sacar partido de algn/algo; **to take ~ of sb** (*sexually*) abusar de algn; **to take ~ of an opportunity** aprovechar una oportunidad; **it's to our ~** es ventajoso para nosotros; **to turn sth to (one's) ~** sacar buen partido de algo
2 (*Tennis*) **~ González** ventaja González

advantageous [ædvən'teɪdʒəs] ADJ [*offer, position*] ventajoso, provechoso; **to be ~ to sb** ser ventajoso *or* provechoso para algn, beneficiar a algn

advent ['ædvənt] **A** N 1 (= *arrival*) advenimiento *m* 2 (*Rel*) **Advent** Adviento *m* **B** CPD ➤ **Advent calendar** calendario *m* de Adviento

adventure [əd'ventʃər] N aventura *f* ➤ **adventure playground** (*Brit*) parque *m* infantil ➤ **adventure story** novela *f* de aventuras

adventurer [əd'ventʃərər] N aventurero/a *m/f*

adventurous [əd'ventʃərəs] ADJ [*person*] aventurero; [*style*] innovador, atrevido

adverb ['ædvɜːb] N adverbio *m*

adverbial [əd'vɜːbɪəl] ADJ adverbial

adversary ['ædvəsəri] N adversario/a *m/f*, contrario/a *m/f*

adverse ['ædvɜːs] ADJ adverso

adversely ['ædvɜːslɪ] ADV desfavorablemente, negativamente; **to affect ~** perjudicar

adversity [əd'vɜːsɪtɪ] N infortunio *m*, desgracia *f*; **in times of ~** en tiempos difíciles

advert* ['ædvɜːt] N ABBR (*Brit*) = **advertisement**

advertise ['ædvətaɪz] **A** VT (*Comm etc*) anunciar; **"as ~d on TV"** "anunciado en TV" **B** VI [*company*] hacer publicidad, hacer propaganda; (*in newspaper etc*) poner un anuncio; (*on TV*) hacer publicidad; **to ~ for** buscar por medio de anuncios

advertisement [əd'vɜːtɪsmənt] N anuncio *m* (**for** de); **it's not much of an ~ for the place** (*esp Brit**) no dice mucho en favor de la ciudad/del hotel *etc*

advertiser ['ædvətaɪzər] N anunciante *mf*

advertising ['ædvətaɪzɪŋ] N (= *business*) publicidad *f*; (= *advertisements*) anuncios *mpl*; **my brother's in ~** mi hermano se dedica a la publicidad ➤ **advertising agency** agencia *f* de publicidad ➤ **advertising campaign** campaña *f* publicitaria ➤ **advertising rates** tarifa *fsing* de anuncios

advice [əd'vaɪs] **A** N 1 (*gen*) consejos *mpl*; **he ignored my ~** ignoró mis consejos; **it was good ~** *or* **a good piece of ~** fue un buen consejo; **her doctor's ~ was to rest** el médico le aconsejó descansar; **let me give you some ~** permíteme que te dé un consejo, permíteme que te aconseje; **to take sb's ~** seguir el consejo *or* los consejos de algn, hacer caso a algn
2 (= *professional help*) asesoramiento *m*; **you need expert ~** necesitas el asesoramiento de un experto, necesitas hacerte asesorar por un experto; **to take legal ~** consultar a un abogado, asesorarse con un abogado
B CPD ➤ **advice column** (*gen*) consultorio *m*; (*agony aunt's*) consultorio *m* sentimental ➤ **advice columnist** (*US*) consultor(a) *m/f* sentimental ➤ **advice line** teléfono *m* de asistencia

advisable [əd'vaɪzəbl] ADJ aconsejable, conveniente

advise [əd'vaɪz] **A** VT 1 (= *give advice to*) aconsejar; (= *inform professionally*) asesorar
2 (= *recommend*) [+ *action*] aconsejar, recomendar; **I'd ~ leaving the car here** aconsejaría que dejáramos el coche aquí; **to ~ sb to do sth** aconsejar a algn que haga algo; **you would be well ~d to go** sería prudente que fueras, harías bien yendo *or* en ir
3 (= *inform*) **to ~ sb of sth** informar a algn de algo; (*officially*) notificar algo a algn
4 (= *warn*) advertir; **to ~ sb against doing sth** aconsejar a algn que no haga algo
B VI (= *make recommendations*) dar consejos; **I would ~ against it** yo te lo desaconsejaría, yo no te lo aconsejaría; **he ~d against going** nos aconsejó que no fuéramos

adviser, advisor [əd'vaɪzər] N (*in business, politics etc*) asesor(a) *m/f*, consejero/a *m/f*

advisory [əd'vaɪzərɪ] **A** ADJ [*body*] consultivo; **in an ~ capacity** como asesor(a) **B** N (*US*) nota *f* oficial, anuncio *m* público

advocate A ['ædvəkeɪt] VT (= *be in favour of*) abogar por, ser partidario de; **what do you ~?** ¿qué nos aconsejas?; **I ~ doing nothing** yo recomiendo no hacer nada **B** ['ædvəkɪt] N defensor(a) *m/f*, partidario/a *m/f*; (*Scot Jur*) abogado/a *m/f*; ⇨ *LAWYERS; QC/KC*

Aegean [iː'dʒiːən] ADJ, N **the ~ (Sea)** el (Mar) Egeo

aeon ['iːən] N eón *m*; **~s** (*fig*) siglos, una eternidad

aerate ['eəreɪt] VT [+ *liquid*] gasificar; [+ *blood*] oxigenar

aerial ['eərɪəl] **A** ADJ aéreo **B** N (*Brit Rad, TV*) antena *f* **C** CPD ➤ **aerial photograph** aerofoto *f*, fotografía *f* aérea

aerie ['eərɪ] N (*US*) = **eyrie**

aerobatics [ˌeərəʊ'bætɪks] NPL acrobacia *fsing* aérea

aerobics [eə'rəʊbɪks] NPL aerobic *msing*; **I do ~** hago aerobic

aerodynamic ['eərəʊdaɪ'næmɪk] ADJ aerodinámico

aerodynamics ['eərəʊdaɪ'næmɪks] N aerodinámica *fsing*

aeronautics [ˌeərə'nɔːtɪks] N aeronáutica *fsing*

aeroplane ['eərəpleɪn] N (*Brit*) avión *m*

aerosol ['eərəsɒl] N aerosol *m*, atomizador *m*

aerospace ['ɛərəʊspeɪs] ADJ aeroespacial ➤ **the aerospace industry** la industria aeroespacial

aesthete, esthete (US) ['i:sθi:t] N esteta *mf*

aesthetic, esthetic (US) [i:s'θetɪk] ADJ estético

aesthetically, esthetically (US) [i:s'θetɪkəlɪ] ADV estéticamente

aesthetics, esthetics (US) [i:s'θetɪks] N estética *fsing*

afar [ə'fɑːʳ] ADV (*liter*) lejos; **from ~** desde lejos

affable ['æfəbl] ADJ afable

affair [ə'fɛəʳ] N **1** (= *business*) asunto *m*; **that's my ~** eso es asunto mío *or* cosa mía, eso sólo me concierne a mí **2 affairs** (= *matters*) asuntos *mpl*; **you'll have to put your ~s in order** tendrás que aclarar tus asuntos **3** (= *event*) ocasión *f*; **it will be a big ~** será una ocasión importante, será todo un acontecimiento **4** (= *case*) caso *m*, asunto *m*; **the Watergate ~** el caso Watergate, el asunto (de) Watergate **5** (= *love affair*) aventura *f* (amorosa), affaire *m*, lío *m* (amoroso)*; **he had an ~ with a French girl** tuvo una aventura *or* un affaire con una (chica) francesa, tuvo un lío *or* estuvo liado con una (chica) francesa*; **they're having an ~** están liados

affect [ə'fekt] VT **1** (= *have effect on*) afectar; **this will ~ everybody** esto afectará a todos; **it did not ~ my decision** no influyó en mi decisión **2** (= *harm*) perjudicar **3** (= *move*) conmover, afectar **4** (= *feign*) **he ~ed indifference** afectó *or* aparentó indiferencia, fingió ser indiferente

affectation [æfek'teɪʃən] N afectación *f*, falta *f* de naturalidad

affected [ə'fektɪd] ADJ **1** (= *pretentious*) [*person, manner, accent*] afectado **2** (= *feigned*) [*remorse, enthusiasm*] fingido **3** (= *suffering effects*) [*area, region, part of body*] afectado

affection [ə'fekʃən] N afecto *m* (**for** a; **towards** hacia), cariño *m*

affectionate [ə'fekʃənɪt] ADJ **1** (= *showing affection*) cariñoso, afectuoso **2** (*in letter endings*) **with ~ greetings** cariñosamente, afectuosamente; **your ~ nephew** abrazos de tu sobrino

affectionately [ə'fekʃənɪtlɪ] ADV afectuosamente, cariñosamente

affidavit [æfɪ'deɪvɪt] N declaración *f* jurada, afidávit *m*

affiliate Ⓐ [ə'fɪlɪeɪt] VI afiliarse (**to, with** a) **Ⓑ** [ə'fɪlɪɪt] N (= *organization*) filial *f*; (= *person*) afiliado/a *m/f*

affiliated [ə'fɪlɪeɪtɪd] ADJ [*member, society*] afiliado (**to, with** a); **~ company** empresa *f* filial *or* subsidiaria

affinity [ə'fɪnɪtɪ] N afinidad *f*; **A has certain affinities with B** entre A y B existe cierta afinidad

affirm [ə'fɜːm] VT afirmar

affirmation [æfə'meɪʃən] N afirmación *f*

affirmative [ə'fɜːmətɪv] **Ⓐ** ADJ afirmativo **Ⓑ** N **to answer in the ~** dar una respuesta afirmativa, contestar afirmativamente **Ⓒ** CPD ➤ **affirmative action** (US Pol) medidas *fpl* a favor de las minorías

affix Ⓐ [ə'fɪks] VT [+ *signature*] poner, añadir; [+ *stamp*] poner, pegar; [+ *seal*] imprimir **Ⓑ** N ['æfɪks] (Ling) afijo *m*

afflict [ə'flɪkt] VT afligir

affliction [ə'flɪkʃən] N **1** (= *suffering*) aflicción *f*, congoja *f* **2** (*bodily*) mal *m*; **the ~s of old age** los achaques de la vejez **3** (= *misfortune*) desgracia *f*, infortunio *m*

affluence ['æflʊəns] N riqueza *f*, opulencia *f*; **to live in ~** vivir con lujo

affluent ['æflʊənt] ADJ acaudalado, rico; **the ~ society** la sociedad de la abundancia *o* de consumo

afford [ə'fɔːd] VT **1** (= *pay for*) **we can ~ it** podemos permitírnoslo; **we can't ~ such things** no podemos permitirnos tales cosas, tales cosas no están a nuestro alcance; **we can't ~ to go on holiday** no podemos permitirnos el lujo de ir de vacaciones; **how much can you ~?** ¿cuánto puedes gastar(te)? **2** (= *spare, risk*) **I can't ~ the time** no tengo tiempo; **I can't ~ to be idle** no puedo permitirme el lujo de no hacer nada;

an opportunity you cannot ~ to miss una ocasión que no puedes desperdiciar **3** (*frm*) [+ *opportunity*] proporcionar, dar

affordable [ə'fɔːdəbl] ADJ [*price*] razonable; [*purchase*] posible

affray [ə'freɪ] N (*frm*) refriega *f*, reyerta *f*

affront [ə'frʌnt] **Ⓐ** N afrenta *f*, ofensa *f*; **to be an ~ to** afrentar a **Ⓑ** VT ofender, afrentar; **to be ~ed** ofenderse

Afghan ['æfgæn] ADJ, N afgano/a *m/f*

Afghanistan [æf'gænɪstæn] N Afganistán *m*

aficionado [ə,fɪsjə'nɑːdəʊ] N aficionado/a *m/f*

afield [ə'fiːld] ADV **far ~** muy lejos; **countries further ~** países más lejanos; **you'll have to go further ~ for that** para eso hará falta buscar más lejos

AFL-CIO N ABBR (US) = **American Federation of Labor and Congress of Industrial Organizations**

afloat [ə'fləʊt] ADJ a flote; **to stay ~** (*lit, fig*) mantenerse a flote

afoot [ə'fʊt] ADV **there is something ~** algo se está tramando

aforementioned [ə,fɔː'menʃənd], **aforenamed** ə'fɔː'neɪmd], **aforesaid** [ə'fɔː'sed] ADJ susodicho, mencionado

afraid [ə'freɪd] ADJ **1** (= *frightened*) **to be ~** tener miedo; **don't be ~** no tengas miedo; **I was ~ that nobody would believe me** tenía miedo de que nadie me creyera, temía que nadie me creyera; **I was ~ to ask** me daba miedo preguntar, tenía miedo de preguntar; **to be ~ for sth/sb** temer por algo/algn; **she suddenly looked ~** de repente parecía asustada; **to be ~ of sth/sb** tener miedo de *or* a algo/algn; **he was ~ of losing his job** tenía miedo de perder su trabajo, temía perder su trabajo (*more frm*); **she's ~ of flying** le da miedo volar; **I'm ~ of dogs** los perros me dan miedo, les tengo miedo a los perros; **you have nothing to be ~ of** no tienes nada que temer; **he's not ~ of hard work** el trabajo duro no le asusta; **I was ~ of that** me lo temía **2** (= *sorry*) **I'm ~ he's out** lo siento, pero no está; **it's a bit stuffy in here, I'm ~** me temo que el ambiente está muy cargado aquí dentro; **I'm ~ not** me temo que no *or* no, lo siento; **I'm ~ so** me temo que sí *or* sí, lo siento

afresh [ə'freʃ] ADV de nuevo, otra vez; **to start ~** volver a empezar

Africa ['æfrɪkə] N África *f*; **sub-Saharan ~** el África subsahariana

> Use **el/un** not **la/una** before feminine nouns beginning with stressed **a** or **ha** like **África**.

African ['æfrɪkən] ADJ, N africano/a *m/f*

African-American [,æfrɪkənə'merɪkən] ADJ, N afroamericano/a *m/f*

Afrikaans [,æfrɪ'kɑːns] N afrikaans *m*

Afrikaner [æfrɪ'kɑːnəʳ] ADJ, N afrikaner *mf*

Afro ['æfrəʊ] N (*also* ~ **hairstyle**) peinado *m* afro

Afro-American [,æfrəʊə'merɪkən] ADJ, N afroamericano/a *m/f*

Afro-Caribbean [,æfrəʊkærɪ'biːən] ADJ, N afrocaribeño/a *m/f*

aft [ɑːft] ADV en popa; **to go ~** ir a popa

after ['ɑːftəʳ]

> When **after** is an element in a phrasal verb, eg **ask after**, **look after**, **take after**, look up the verb.

Ⓐ PREP **1** (*in time*) después de; **soon ~ eating it** poco después de comerlo; **I'll have a shower ~ you** me ducharé después que tú; **it was twenty ~ three** (US) eran las tres y veinte **2** (*in position, order*) detrás de, tras; **day ~ day** día tras día; **one ~ the other** uno tras otro; **~ you!** ¡pase usted!, ¡usted primero!; **~ you with the salt** pásame la sal cuando acabes; **our biggest customer ~ the US** nuestro mayor cliente después de Estados Unidos **3** (= *behind*) **close the door ~ you** cierra la puerta al salir *or* cuando salgas; **I'm tired of cleaning up ~ you** estoy cansado

de ir detrás de ti limpiándolo todo
4 (= *seeking*) **the police are ~ him** la policía lo está buscando *or* está detrás de él; **they're all ~ the same thing** todos van a por lo mismo; **what is he ~?** ¿qué pretende?
5 (*Brit*) (= *in honour of*) **he was named ~ Churchill** se le llamó así por Churchill
6 (= *in view of*) después de; **all I've done for you** después de *or* con todo lo que he hecho por ti; **he can't go back ~ what he's done** después de lo que ha hecho no puede volver; **~ all** después de todo
Ⓑ ADV (= *afterward*) después; **for weeks ~** durante varias semanas después; **long ~** mucho tiempo después; **soon ~** poco después
Ⓒ CONJ después de que; **we ate ~ they'd gone** comimos después de que ellos se marcharan; **I went out ~ I'd eaten** salí después de comer; **we'll eat ~ you've gone** comeremos cuando te hayas ido

afterbirth [ˈɑːftəbɜːθ] N secundinas *fpl*, placenta *f*

aftercare [ˈɑːftəkeəʳ] N asistencia *f* postoperatoria

after-effect [ˈɑːftərɪfekt] N consecuencia *f*; **after-effects** [*of treatment*] efectos *mpl* secundarios; [*of illness, operation, accident*] secuelas *fpl*

afterlife [ˈɑːftəlaɪf] N vida *f* de ultratumba

aftermath [ˈɑːftəmæθ] N consecuencias *fpl*, secuelas *fpl*; **in the ~ of the war** en el periodo de posguerra

afternoon [ˈɑːftəˈnuːn] N tarde *f*; **good ~!** ¡buenas tardes!; **in the ~** por la tarde ➤ **afternoon tea** (*Brit*) ≈ merienda *f*

afters* [ˈɑːftəz] NPL (*Brit*) postre *msing*; **what's for ~?** ¿qué hay de postre?

after-sales [ˈɑːftəseɪlz] CPD ➤ **after-sales service**, **after-sales support** servicio *m* posventa, asistencia *f* posventa

aftershave [ˈɑːftəʃeɪv] N (*also* **~ lotion**) aftershave *m inv*, loción *f* para después del afeitado

aftershock [ˈɑːftəʃɒk] N [*of earthquake*] réplica *f*

after-sun [ˈɑːftəsʌn] ADJ [*lotion, cream*] para después del sol

aftertaste [ˈɑːftəteɪst] N (*lit, fig*) regusto *m*, dejo *m*

afterthought [ˈɑːftəθɔːt] N ocurrencia *f* tardía, idea *f* adicional, idea *f* de última hora; **as an ~** por si acaso

afterward [ˈɑːftəwəd], **afterwards** (*esp Brit*) [ˈɑːftəwədz] ADV después, más tarde; **~ we all helped with the washing up** después *or* luego *or* más tarde todos ayudamos a fregar los platos; **I realized ~ that he was right** después *or* luego me di cuenta de que él tenía razón; **immediately ~** inmediatamente después, acto seguido; **shortly *or* soon ~** poco después, al poco (rato)

again [əˈgen] ADV **1** (= *once more*) otra vez, de nuevo

Note: **again** is often translated by **volver a** + INFIN:

try ~ inténtalo otra vez *or* de nuevo, vuelve a intentarlo; **he climbed up ~** volvió a subir; **would you do it all ~?** ¿lo volverías a hacer?; **come ~ soon** vuelve pronto; **what was that joke ~?** ¿cómo era el chiste aquel (que contaste)?; **I've told you ~ and ~** te lo he dicho una y otra vez *or* mil veces; **I won't do it ever ~** no lo haré nunca más; **as many ~** otros tantos; **as much ~** otro tanto; **never ~!** ¡nunca más!; **oh no, not ~!** ¡Dios mío, otra vez!, ¡otra vez no!; **now and ~** de vez en cuando; **to say sth ~** repetir algo
2 (= *besides, moreover*) **~, it may not be true** por otra parte, puede no ser verdad; **and again ...** ⬦ **then again ...** (= *on the other hand*) por otra parte ...; (= *moreover*) además ...; **these are different ~** también éstos son distintos

against [əˈgenst]

When **against** is an element in a phrasal verb, eg **go against**, **run up against**, look up the verb.

PREP **1** (= *in opposition to*) [+ *person*] contra, en contra de; [+ *plan*] en contra de; **what have you got ~ me?** ¿qué tiene usted en contra mía?, ¿qué tiene usted contra mí?; **he was ~ it** estaba en contra, se opuso a ello; **he was ~ going** estaba en contra de ir; **it's ~ the law** la ley lo prohíbe, es

ilegal; **it's ~ the rules** no lo permiten las reglas; **luck was ~ him** la suerte le era contraria; **to stand ~ sb** (*Pol*) presentarse en contra de algn; ✦ IDIOM **to be up ~ it** estar en un aprieto
2 (= *in contact with*) contra; **he leant the ladder ~ the wall** apoyó la escalera contra la pared
3 (= *in front of*) **the light ~** contra la luz, a contrasol; **the hills stood out ~ the sunset** las colinas se destacaban sobre la puesta del sol
4 (*in comparisons*) **(as) ~** contra, en contraste con
5 (= *for*) **refund available ~ this voucher** se devuelve el precio al presentar este comprobante

age [eɪdʒ] **Ⓐ** N **1** [*of person, animal, building*] edad *f*; **what ~ is she?** ¿qué edad tiene?, ¿cuántos años tiene?; **when I was your ~** cuando tenía tu edad; **I have a daughter the same ~ as you** tengo una hija de tu edad *or* de tu misma edad; **he's twice your ~** te dobla en edad; **he's half your ~** lo doblas en edad; **act your ~!** ¡compórtate de acuerdo con tu edad!, ¡no seas niño!; **people of all ~s** gente de todas las edades; **at my ~** a mi edad; **at the ~ of 11** a los 11 años, a la edad de 11 años; **from an early ~** desde muy pequeño; **60 is no ~ at all** 60 años no son nada; **he is five years of ~** tiene cinco años (de edad)
2 (= *adulthood*) **to be of ~** ser mayor de edad; **to come of ~** llegar a *or* alcanzar la mayoría de edad; **to be under ~** ser menor de edad
3 (= *time*) **wine improves with ~** el vino mejora con el paso del tiempo
4 (= *era*) era *f*; **this is the ~ of the car** ésta es la era del automóvil
5 (*) (= *long time*) **we waited an ~ *or* for ~s** esperamos una eternidad; **it's ~s *or* an ~ since I saw him** hace siglos *or* un siglo que no lo veo
Ⓑ VT [+ *person*] envejecer; [+ *wine*] añejar
Ⓒ VI [*person*] envejecer; [*wine*] añejarse; **he has ~d a lot** ha envejecido mucho; **she has ~d well** se conserva bien para la edad que tiene, le sientan bien los años
Ⓓ CPD ➤ **age bracket**, **age group** grupo *m* de edad, grupo *m* etario (*more frm*); **the 40 to 50 ~ group** el grupo de edades comprendidas entre los 40 y 50 años ➤ **age limit** límite *m* de edad, edad *f* mínima/máxima

aged **Ⓐ** ADJ **1** [ˈeɪdʒɪd] (= *old*) viejo, anciano **2** [eɪdʒd] **~ 15** de 15 años (de edad), que tiene 15 años **Ⓑ** [ˈeɪdʒɪd] NPL **the ~** los ancianos *mpl*

ageing [ˈeɪdʒɪŋ] **Ⓐ** ADJ [*person*] anciano, envejecido; [*machinery, vehicle*] anticuado, viejo **Ⓑ** N envejecimiento *m*, el envejecer, senescencia *f*

ageism [ˈeɪdʒɪzəm] N discriminación *f* por razón de edad

ageless [ˈeɪdʒlɪs] ADJ (= *eternal*) eterno; (= *always young*) siempre *or* eternamente joven

agency [ˈeɪdʒənsɪ] N **1** (= *office*) agencia *f* **2** (= *branch*) delegación *f* **3** (= *department*) organismo *m*

agenda [əˈdʒendə] N **1** (*at meeting*) orden *m* del día; **on the ~** en el orden del día **2** (*fig*) **environmental issues are high on the party's ~** los asuntos medioambientales ocupan un lugar prominente en el programa político del partido; **to have one's own ~** tener sus propias prioridades; **to set the ~** marcar la pauta

agent [ˈeɪdʒənt] N **1** (*for company, sports personality, actor*) agente *mf*, representante *mf*; (*Jur*) apoderado/a *m/f*; (*Pol*) delegado/a *m/f*; (*undercover*) agente *mf*; **his father acts as his ~** su padre actúa como su representante **2** (*Chem*) agente *m*; **chemical ~** agente *m* químico

age-old [ˈeɪdʒəʊld] ADJ multisecular, antiquísimo

agglomeration [əˌglɒməˈreɪʃən] N aglomeración *f*

aggravate [ˈægrəveɪt] VT **1** (= *make worse*) agravar **2** (*) (= *annoy*) irritar, sacar de quicio

aggravating [ˈægrəveɪtɪŋ] ADJ **1** (*Jur*) agravante **2** (*) (= *annoying*) molesto; **he's an ~ child** es un niño molesto; **it's very ~** es para volverse loco

aggravation [ˌægrəˈveɪʃən] N **1** (= *exacerbation*) agravación *f*, empeoramiento *m* **2** (*) (= *annoyance*) irritación *f*

aggregate **Ⓐ** [ˈægrɪgɪt] N **1** (= *total*) conjunto *m*; **on ~** (*Brit*) en conjunto **2** (*Geol, Constr*) agregado *m* **Ⓑ** [ˈægrɪgɪt] ADJ total, global **Ⓒ** [ˈægrɪgeɪt] VT juntar, sumar

aggression [ə'greʃən] N **1** (= *behaviour*) agresión *f*; **an act of** ~ un acto de agresión **2** (= *feeling*) agresividad *f*; ~ **is not a solely masculine trait** la agresividad no es una característica únicamente masculina

aggressive [ə'gresɪv] ADJ **1** (= *belligerent*) agresivo **2** (= *assertive*) [*salesman, company*] enérgico, agresivo; [*player*] agresivo; ~ **marketing techniques** técnicas *fpl* de marketing agresivas

aggressively [ə'gresɪvlɪ] ADV **1** (= *belligerently*) [*behave, react*] agresivamente, de manera agresiva; [*say*] con mucha agresividad **2** (= *assertively*) [*trade, sell*] enérgicamente, con empuje; [*play*] agresivamente

aggressiveness [ə'gresɪvnɪs] N (= *belligerence*) agresividad *f*; (= *assertiveness*) empuje *m*

aggressor [ə'gresəʳ] N agresor(a) *m/f*

aggrieved [ə'griːvd] ADJ ofendido; **the** ~ **husband** el marido ofendido; **in an** ~ **tone** en un tono de queja; **he was much** ~ se ofendió mucho; **to feel** ~ ofenderse, resentirse (**at** por)

aggro* ['ægrəʊ] N (*Brit*) **1** (= *hassle*) líos *mpl*, problemas *mpl*; **I'm not going, it's too much** ~ no voy, es mucha lata* **2** (= *violence*) agresividad *f*, violencia *f*

aghast [ə'gɑːst] ADJ horrorizado, pasmado (**at** ante); **to be** ~ **at** horrorizarse *or* sobrecogerse ante

agile ['ædʒaɪl] ADJ ágil

agility [ə'dʒɪlɪtɪ] N agilidad *f*

aging ['eɪdʒɪŋ] ADJ, N = **ageing**

agitate ['ædʒɪteɪt] Ⓐ VT **1** (= *upset*) inquietar, perturbar **2** (= *shake*) agitar Ⓑ VI (*Pol*) **to** ~ **for/against** hacer campaña en pro de/en contra de

agitated ['ædʒɪteɪtɪd] ADJ inquieto, perturbado

agitation [ˌædʒɪ'teɪʃən] N **1** (*mental*) inquietud *f*, perturbación *f* **2** (*Pol*) agitación *f*

agitator ['ædʒɪteɪtəʳ] N (*Pol*) agitador(a) *m/f*

AGM N ABBR (*Brit*) (= **annual general meeting**) junta *f* anual

agnostic [æg'nɒstɪk] ADJ, N agnóstico/a *m/f*

ago [ə'gəʊ] ADV **long** ~ hace mucho tiempo; **not long** ~ no hace mucho (tiempo); **how long** ~ **was it?** ¿hace cuánto tiempo?, ¿cuánto tiempo hace?; **a week** ~ hace una semana; **a little while** ~ hace poco; **just a moment** ~ hace un momento nada más; **as long** ~ **as 1978** ya en 1978

agog [ə'gɒg] ADJ **the country was** ~ el país estaba emocionadísimo; **he was** ~ **to hear the news** tenía enorme curiosidad por saber las noticias

agonize ['ægənaɪz] VI **to** ~ **over a decision** estar angustiado ante una decisión

agonizing ['ægənaɪzɪŋ] ADJ [*pain*] atroz, muy agudo; [*indecision, suspense*] angustioso; [*moment*] de angustia; [*reappraisal*] agonizante, doloroso

agony ['ægənɪ] N **1** (*physical*) dolor *m* agudo; **I was in** ~ sufría dolores horrorosos **2** (*mental*) angustia *f*; **to suffer agonies of doubt** estar atormentado por las dudas; **to be in an** ~ **of impatience** impacientarse mucho; **it was** ~**!*** ¡fue fatal!* Ⓑ CPD ➤ **agony aunt*** (*Brit*) columnista *f* del consultorio sentimental ➤ **agony column*** (*Brit*) consultorio *m* sentimental ➤ **agony uncle*** (*Brit*) columnista *m* del consultorio sentimental

agoraphobia [ˌægərə'fəʊbɪə] N agorafobia *f*

agree [ə'griː] Ⓐ VI **1** (= *consent*) consentir; **eventually he** ~**d** por fin consintió; **you'll never get him to** ~ no lograrás nunca su consentimiento; **to** ~ **to sth** consentir en *or* aceptar algo **2** (= *be in agreement*) estar de acuerdo; (= *come to an agreement*) ponerse de acuerdo; **I** ~ estoy de acuerdo, estoy conforme; **I quite** ~ estoy completamente de acuerdo; **to** ~ **about** *or* **on sth** (= *be in agreement*) estar de acuerdo sobre *or* en algo; (= *come to an agreement*) ponerse de acuerdo sobre algo; **to** ~ **with** [+ *person*] estar de acuerdo *or* coincidir con; [+ *policy*] estar de acuerdo con, aprobar **3** (= *accord, coincide*) concordar (**with** con); **these statements do not** ~ (**with each other**) estas declaraciones no concuerdan **4** **to** ~ **with** (= *approve of*) aprobar; **I don't** ~ **with women**

playing football no apruebo que las mujeres jueguen al fútbol **5 to** ~ **with** (= *be beneficial to*): **garlic/this heat doesn't** ~ **with me** el ajo/este calor no me sienta bien **6** (*Gram*) concordar (**with** con)
Ⓑ VT **1** (= *consent*) **to** ~ **to do sth** consentir en *or* aceptar hacer algo **2** (= *be in agreement, come to an agreement*) **"it's impossible," she** ~**d** —es imposible —asintió; **to** ~ **that** estar de acuerdo en que; **it was** ~**d that ...** se acordó que ...; **it was** ~**d to** (+ INFIN) se acordó + *infin*; **we** ~**d to meet up later** quedamos en vernos después; **to** ~ **to disagree** *or* **differ** estar en desacuerdo amistoso **3** (= *admit*) reconocer; **I** ~ **that it was foolish** reconozco que era insensato **4** [+ *plan, statement etc*] aceptar, llegar a un acuerdo sobre; [+ *price*] convenir; **"salary to be agreed"** "sueldo a convenir"; **at a date to be** ~**d** en una fecha (que queda) por determinar *or* concertar

agreeable [ə'griːəbl] ADJ **1** (= *pleasing*) agradable; **she made a point of being** ~ **to them** se esforzó por ser agradable *or* simpática con ellos **2** (= *acceptable*) **is that** ~ **to you?** ¿está de acuerdo?, ¿está conforme?; **a solution that would be** ~ **to all** una solución satisfactoria para todos **3** (= *willing*) **get your secretary to do it if she is** ~ dáselo a tu secretaria para que lo haga si (a ella) no le importa

agreeably [ə'grɪəblɪ] ADV **they were** ~ **surprised to discover that ...** se llevaron una agradable sorpresa al descubrir que ...

agreed [ə'griːd] ADJ [*time, plan*] convenido; **as** ~ según lo convenido; **are we all** ~**?** ¿estamos todos de acuerdo?; **agreed!** ¡de acuerdo!, ¡conforme(s)!

agreement [ə'griːmənt] N **1** (= *understanding, arrangement*) acuerdo *m*; (= *consent*) consentimiento *m*; (= *treaty etc*) acuerdo *m*, pacto *m*; (*Comm*) contrato *m*; **to come to** *or* **reach an** ~ llegar a un acuerdo; **he nodded in** ~ asintió con la cabeza; **to be in** ~ **with** estar de acuerdo con **2** (*Gram*) concordancia *f*

agribusiness ['ægrɪˌbɪznɪs] N agroindustria *f*, industria *f* agropecuaria

agricultural [ˌægrɪ'kʌltʃərəl] ADJ agrícola ➤ **agricultural college** escuela *f* de agricultura

agriculture ['ægrɪkʌltʃəʳ] N agricultura *f*

agrochemical [ˌægrəʊ'kemɪkəl] Ⓐ ADJ agroquímico Ⓑ N (producto *m*) agroquímico *m*

aground [ə'graʊnd] ADV **to run** ~ encallar

ahead [ə'hed] ADV **1** (*in space, order*) delante; **to be** ~ (*in*

> When **ahead** is an element in a phrasal verb, eg **go ahead**, look up the verb.

race) llevar la delantera, ir (por) delante, ir ganando; (*fig*) llevar la ventaja, ir a la cabeza; **to go on** ~ ir adelante; **this put Barcelona three points** ~ esto dio al Barcelona tres puntos de ventaja; **to send sb** ~ enviar a algn por delante **2** (*in time*) (= *before*) antes; [*book*] con anticipación; **in the months** ~ en los próximos meses; **there's trouble** ~ han de sobrevenir disgustos, ya se prevén dificultades; **to look** ~ (*fig*) anticipar; **to plan** ~ planificar por adelantado *or* con anticipación; **to think** ~ pensar en el futuro **3** ~ **of 3.1** (*in space, order*) delante de; **there were three people** ~ **of us** había tres personas delante de nosotros; **to be** ~ **of sb** (*in race, competition*) llevar ventaja a algn **3.2** (*in time*) **you'll get there** ~ **of us** llegarás antes que nosotros; **he's two hours** ~ **of the next competitor** lleva dos horas de ventaja sobre el rival más próximo; **share prices rose** ~ **of the annual report** la cotización subió en anticipación del informe anual; **we are three months** ~ **of schedule** llevamos tres meses de adelanto sobre la fecha prevista; **to arrive** ~ **of time** llegar antes de la hora prevista; **the plane is** ~ **of its time** el avión llega antes de su hora prevista; **to be** ~ **of one's time** anticiparse a su época

ahold [ə'həʊld] N (*esp US*) **1 to get** ~ **of sb** (= *get in touch with*) contactar con algn; (= *find*) localizar a algn; **to get** ~

of sth (= *obtain*) conseguir *or* obtener algo **2 to get ~ of o.s.** controlarse

ahoy [əˈhɔɪ] EXCL **ship ~!** ¡barco a la vista!; **~ there!** ¡ah del barco!

AI N ABBR **1** (= **Amnesty International**) AI *f* **2** (= **artificial intelligence**) IA *f* **3** = **artificial insemination**

aid [eɪd] Ⓐ N **1** (= *assistance*) ayuda *f*; **with the ~ of** con la ayuda de; **to come/go to sb's ~** (*lit*) acudir en ayuda de algn; (*in argument*) salir en defensa de algn; **a charity performance in ~ of the blind** (*esp Brit*) una representación benéfica a beneficio de los ciegos; **what's all this in ~ of?** (*esp Brit**) ¿a qué viene todo esto?
2 (*economic, medical*) ayuda *f*; **to give ~** prestar ayuda
3 (= *book, tool*) ayuda *f*; **the book is an invaluable ~ to teachers** el libro es una ayuda valiosísima para los profesores
4 (= *person*) asistente *mf*
Ⓑ VT **1** [+ *progress, process, recovery*] (= *speed up*) acelerar; (= *contribute to*) contribuir a
2 [+ *person*] ayudar; **to ~ sb to do sth** ayudar a algn a hacer algo; **to ~ and abet sb** ser cómplice de algn
Ⓒ VI ayudar
Ⓓ CPD ➤ **aid agency** organismo *m* de ayuda ➤ **aid package** dotación *f* de ayuda ➤ **aid station** (*US*) puesto *m* de socorro ➤ **aid worker** cooperante *mf*

aide [eɪd] N **1** (*Mil*) edecán *m* **2** (*Pol*) ayudante *mf*

AIDS, Aids [eɪdz] N ABBR (= **Acquired Immune Deficiency Syndrome**) SIDA *m*, sida *m* ➤ **AIDS campaign** campaña *f* anti-sida ➤ **AIDS clinic** sidatorio *m* (*LAm*), clínica *f* para enfermos de sida (*Sp*) ➤ **AIDS sufferer** enfermo/a *m/f* de sida ➤ **AIDS test** prueba *f* del sida

AIDS-related [ˈeɪdzrɪˌleɪtɪd] ADJ relacionado con el SIDA

ailing [ˈeɪlɪŋ] ADJ [*person*] enfermo, achacoso; [*industry, economy*] debilitado

ailment [ˈeɪlmənt] N enfermedad *f*, achaque *m*

aim [eɪm] Ⓐ N **1** (= *purpose, object*) objetivo *m*, propósito *m*; **to achieve one's ~s** conseguir sus propósitos *or* lo que se propone; **with the ~ of doing sth** con miras a hacer algo, con la intención de hacer algo
2 (*with gun, arrow*) puntería *f*; **to have a good/poor ~** tener buena/mala puntería; **to take ~** apuntar (**at** a)
Ⓑ VT [+ *gun, missile*] apuntar; [+ *camera*] dirigir, enfocar; **he ~ed the pistol at me** me apuntó con la pistola; **missiles ~ed at the capital** misiles apuntando a la capital; **he ~ed a kick at my shins** intentó darme una patada en las espinillas; **this advertising is ~ed at children** esta campaña va dirigida a los niños; **talks ~ed at ending the war** conversaciones *or* negociaciones encaminadas a la finalización de la guerra
Ⓒ VI **1** (*with weapon*) apuntar; **I ~ed at his forehead** le apunté a *or* en la frente
2 (= *aspire*) **to ~ to do sth** ponerse como objetivo hacer algo; **we must ~ at reducing inflation** debemos aspirar a *or* dirigir nuestros esfuerzos a reducir la inflación; **it will give you something to ~ for** así tendrás algo a lo que aspirar
3 (= *intend*) **to ~ to do sth** [*person*] proponerse *or* pretender hacer algo

aimless [ˈeɪmlɪs] ADJ [*way of life, pursuit*] sin sentido, sin propósito; [*person*] sin objeto, sin propósito

aimlessly [ˈeɪmlɪslɪ] ADV [*wander, drift, walk*] sin rumbo (fijo); [*chat, talk*] por hablar; [*live*] sin propósito

ain't** [eɪnt] (*dial*) = **am not, is not, are not, has not, have not**; *see* **be, have**

air [ɛəʳ] Ⓐ N **1** (*lit*) aire *m*; **I need some ~!** ¡necesito un poco de aire!; **by ~** [*travel*] en avión; [*send*] por avión, por vía aérea; **(seen) from the ~** desde el aire; **to get some (fresh) ~** tomar un poco el aire; **spring is in the ~** ya se siente la primavera en el ambiente; **our plans are up in the ~** nuestros planes están en el aire; **there's something in the ~** se respira algo en el ambiente; **we let the ~ out of his tyres** le desinflamos las ruedas; **in the open ~** al aire libre
2 (*Rad, TV*) **off ~** fuera de antena; **to go off (the) ~** [*broadcaster, station*] cerrar la emisión; [*programme*] finalizar; **to be on (the) ~** [*programme, person*] estar en el aire; [*station*] emitir, estar en el aire; **to go on (the) ~** salir al aire
3 (= *appearance, manner*) aire *m*; **he looked at me with an ~**

of surprise me miró con aire de sorpresa, me miró algo sorprendido; **to give o.s. ~s ◊ put on ~s** darse aires (de importancia); **~s and graces** afectación *fsing*
4 (*Mus*) aire *m*
Ⓑ VT **1** (= *ventilate*) [+ *room*] ventilar, airear; [+ *clothes, bed*] airear, orear
2 (= *make public*) [+ *idea, grievance*] airear, hacer público
3 (*US Rad, TV*) [+ *programme*] emitir
4 (*US*) (= *transport*) transportar por avión, aerotransportar
Ⓒ VI **1** [*clothes*] airearse, orearse
2 (*US TV, Rad*) [*programme*] emitirse
Ⓓ CPD ➤ **air ambulance** (= *plane*) avión *m* sanitario, avión *m* ambulancia; (= *helicopter*) helicóptero *m* sanitario, helicóptero *m* ambulancia ➤ **air bag** airbag *m*, bolsa *f* de aire ➤ **air base** base *f* aérea ➤ **air bed** colchón *m* inflable ➤ **air bubble** burbuja *f* de aire ➤ **air carrier** aerolínea *f* ➤ **air conditioning** aire *m* acondicionado, climatización *f*; **a cinema with ~ conditioning** un cine climatizado ➤ **air fare** precio *m* del billete (*Sp*) *or* pasaje *m* (*LAm*) de avión ➤ **air force** fuerzas *fpl* aéreas, ejército *m* del aire ➤ **Air Force One** (*US*) avión *m* presidencial ➤ **air freight** (= *transport, charge*) flete *m* aéreo; (= *goods*) carga *f* aérea; **to send sth by ~ freight** transportar algo por avión ➤ **air freshener** ambientador *m* ➤ **air gun** (= *pistol*) pistola *f* de aire (comprimido); (= *rifle*) escopeta *f* de aire (comprimido) ➤ **air hostess** (*Brit*) azafata *f*, aeromoza *f* (*LAm*), cabinera *f* (*Col*) ➤ **air lane** pasillo *m* aéreo, corredor *m* aéreo ➤ **air letter** aerograma *m* ➤ **air mattress** colchón *m* inflable ➤ **air miles** puntos *mpl* (acumulables para viajar) ➤ **air pocket** bolsa *f* de aire, bache *m* ➤ **air pressure** presión *f* atmosférica ➤ **air rage** síndrome *m* del pasajero alborotado ➤ **air raid** ataque *m* aéreo ➤ **air rifle** escopeta *f* de aire (comprimido) ➤ **air show** exhibición *f* de acrobacia aérea ➤ **air space** espacio *m* aéreo ➤ **air steward** auxiliar *m* de vuelo ➤ **air stewardess** auxiliar *f* de vuelo, azafata *f* ➤ **air strike** ataque *m* aéreo ➤ **air terminal** (*esp Brit*) terminal *f* (de aeropuerto) ➤ **air time** (*Rad, TV*) tiempo *m* en antena ➤ **air traffic** tráfico *m* aéreo ➤ **air traffic control** control *m* del tráfico aéreo ➤ **air traffic controller** controlador(a) *m/f* aéreo/a ➤ **air travel** viajes *mpl* en avión

airborne [ˈɛəbɔːn] ADJ **1** [*aircraft*] volando, en el aire; **we shall soon be ~** el avión despegará pronto **2** (*Mil*) aerotransportado **3** [*virus, germ*] transmitido por el aire

air-conditioned [ˈɛəkənˌdɪʃənd] ADJ [*room, hotel*] climatizado, con aire acondicionado

air-cooled [ˈɛəkuːld] ADJ refrigerado por aire

aircraft [ˈɛəkrɑːft] N (*pl inv*) avión *m* ➤ **aircraft carrier** porta(a)viones *m inv* ➤ **the aircraft industry** la industria aeronáutica

aircrew [ˈɛəkruː] N tripulación *f* del avión

airdrop [ˈɛədrɒp] N entrega *f* por paracaídas

airfield [ˈɛəfiːld] N campo *m* de aviación

airing [ˈɛərɪŋ] N **to give sth an ~** [+ *linen, room, issue, matter*] ventilar algo; [+ *idea*] airear algo, someter algo a discusión ➤ **airing cupboard** (*Brit*) armario *m* para oreo

airless [ˈɛəlɪs] ADJ [*room*] mal ventilado; [*day*] sin viento

airlift [ˈɛəlɪft] Ⓐ N puente *m* aéreo Ⓑ VT aerotransportar, transportar por avión

airline [ˈɛəlaɪn] N línea *f* aérea ➤ **airline pilot** piloto *mf* de compañía aérea

airliner [ˈɛəlaɪnəʳ] N avión *m* de pasajeros

airlock [ˈɛəlɒk] N **1** (*in pipe*) burbuja *f* de aire **2** (*in spacecraft etc*) cámara *f* estanca, compartimiento *m* estanco

airmail [ˈɛəmeɪl] N correo *m* aéreo; **to send a letter (by) ~** mandar una carta por correo aéreo *or* por avión ➤ **airmail letter** carta *f* por correo aéreo ➤ **airmail paper** papel *m* para avión ➤ **airmail sticker** etiqueta *f* de correo aéreo

airplane [ˈɛəpleɪn] N (*US*) = **aeroplane**

airport [ˈɛəpɔːt] N aeropuerto *m*

air-raid [ˈɛəreɪd] CPD ➤ **air-raid shelter** refugio *m* antiaéreo ➤ **air-raid warden** *vigilante que se encarga de dar la voz de alarma en caso de ataque aéreo* ➤ **air-raid warning** alarma *f* antiaérea

air-sea rescue [ˈɛəsiːˈreskjuː] N rescate *m* aeronaval

airship [ˈɛəʃɪp] N dirigible *m*

airsick [ˈɛəsɪk] ADJ **to be ~** estar mareado (en avión); **to get ~** marearse (en avión)

airspeed [ˈɛəspiːd] N velocidad *f* aérea

airstrip [ˈɛəstrɪp] N pista *f* de aterrizaje

airtight [ˈɛətaɪt] ADJ [*container, seal*] hermético; [*case, argument*] sin fisuras, irrefutable

air-to-air [ˌɛətəˈɛəʳ] ADJ aire-aire

air-to-ground [ˌɛətəˈɡraʊnd], **air-to-surface** [ˌɛətəˈsɜːfɪs] ADJ [*missile*] aire-superficie, aire-tierra

airworthy [ˈɛəwɜːðɪ] ADJ en condiciones de volar, en condiciones de vuelo

airy [ˈɛərɪ] ADJ (*compar* **airier**; *superl* **airiest**) **1** [*room, building*] (= *spacious*) espacioso, amplio; (= *well ventilated*) bien ventilado **2** [*fabric, clothing*] ligero

airy-fairy* [ˌɛərɪˈfɛərɪ] ADJ (*Brit*) [*ideas, principles*] superficial, vacío; [*plan, promises*] vano, fantasioso; [*person*] insustancial

aisle [aɪl] N (*Rel*) nave *f* (lateral); (*in theatre, plane, train, supermarket*) pasillo *m*; **~ seat** asiento *m* de pasillo;
◆ IDIOM **to walk up** *or* **down the ~ with sb** llevar al altar a algn

ajar [əˈdʒɑːʳ] ADV entreabierto

AK ABBR (*US*) = **Alaska**

AKA, aka ABBR (= *also known as*) alias

akimbo [əˈkɪmbəʊ] ADV **with arms ~** en jarras

akin [əˈkɪn] ADJ parecido (**to** a), semejante (**to** a)

AL, Ala. ABBR (*US*) = **Alabama**

alabaster [ˈæləbɑːstəʳ] Ⓐ N alabastro *m* Ⓑ ADJ alabastrino

à la carte [ˌæˈlæˈkɑːt] ADV a la carta

alacrity [əˈlækrɪtɪ] N (*frm*) prontitud *f*, presteza *f*; **with ~** con prontitud *or* presteza

alarm [əˈlɑːm] Ⓐ N **1** (= *warning, bell*) alarma *f*; (= *signal*) señal *f* de alarma; **to raise the ~** dar la alarma **2** (= *fear*) alarma *f*, sobresalto *m*; **there was general ~** cundió la alarma general; **there was some ~ at this** esto produjo cierta inquietud; **to cry out in ~** gritar alarmado **3** (*also* **~ clock**) despertador *m*
Ⓑ VT alarmar; **to be ~ed at** asustarse de; **don't be ~ed** no te asustes, no te inquietes
Ⓒ CPD ► **alarm bell** timbre *m* de alarma; **the court's decision has set ~ bells ringing in government** la decisión del tribunal ha hecho cundir la alarma entre el gobierno ► **alarm call** llamada *f* de aviso (para despertar); **I'd like an ~ call for six a.m., please** llámenme *or* despiértenme a las seis, por favor ► **alarm clock** despertador *m* ► **alarm signal** señal *f* de alarma ► **alarm system** sistema *m* de alarma

alarmed [əˈlɑːmd] ADJ sobresaltado, asustado

alarming [əˈlɑːmɪŋ] ADJ alarmante

alarmingly [əˈlɑːmɪŋlɪ] ADV de modo alarmante; **~ high numbers** cifras *fpl* alarmantes

alarmist [əˈlɑːmɪst] ADJ, N alarmista *mf*

alas [əˈlæs] EXCL ¡ay (de mí)!; **~, it is not so** desafortunadamente, no es así

Alas. ABBR (*US*) = **Alaska**

Albania [ælˈbeɪnɪə] N Albania *f*

Albanian [ælˈbeɪnɪən] ADJ, N albanés/esa *m/f*

albatross [ˈælbətrɒs] N albatros *m inv*

albeit [ɔːlˈbiːɪt] CONJ aunque

albino [ælˈbiːnəʊ] ADJ, N albino/a *m/f*

album [ˈælbəm] N álbum *m* ► **album cover** portada *f* de disco

albumen, albumin [ˈælbjʊmɪn] N (= *egg white*) clara *f* de huevo; (*Bot*) albumen *m*; (*Chem*) albúmina *f*

alchemy [ˈælkɪmɪ] N alquimia *f*

alcohol [ˈælkəhɒl] N alcohol *m*

alcohol-free [ˈælkəhɒlˌfriː] ADJ sin alcohol

alcoholic [ˌælkəˈhɒlɪk] Ⓐ ADJ alcohólico Ⓑ N alcohólico/a *m/f*, alcoholizado/a *m/f*

alcoholism [ˈælkəhɒlɪzəm] N alcoholismo *m*

alcopop [ˈælkəʊpɒp] N (*Brit*) *combinado de refresco y alcohol que se vende ya embotellado*

alcove [ˈælkəʊv] N nicho *m*, hueco *m*

⚠ **alcove** ≠ *alcoba*

alderman [ˈɔːldəmən] N (*pl* **aldermen**) concejal(a) *m/f* (*de categoría superior*)

ale [eɪl] N cerveza *f*

alert [əˈlɜːt] Ⓐ ADJ **1** (= *mentally acute*) [*person*] espabilado, despierto; [*expression*] vivo **2** (= *vigilant*) alerta *inv*, atento; **we must stay ~** hay que estar atentos **3** (= *aware*) **to be ~ to sth** ser consciente *or* estar al tanto de algo Ⓑ N alerta *f*; **to be on the ~** estar alerta Ⓒ VT alertar, poner sobre aviso (**to** de)

alfalfa [ælˈfælfə] N alfalfa *f*

alfresco [ælˈfreskəʊ] ADJ, ADV al aire libre

alga [ˈælɡə] N (*pl* **~e** [ˈældʒiː]) alga *f*

Use **el/un** not **la/una** before feminine nouns beginning with stressed **a** or **ha** like **alga**.

algebra [ˈældʒɪbrə] N álgebra *f*

Use **el/un** not **la/una** before feminine nouns beginning with stressed **a** or **ha** like **álgebra**.

Algeria [ælˈdʒɪərɪə] N Argelia *f*

Algerian [ælˈdʒɪərɪən] ADJ, N argelino/a *m/f*

Algiers [ælˈdʒɪəz] N Argel *m*

algorithm [ˈælɡərɪðəm] N algoritmo *m*

alias [ˈeɪlɪəs] Ⓐ N alias *m inv* Ⓑ ADV alias

alibi [ˈælɪbaɪ] N (*for suspect*) coartada *f*; (*) (= *excuse*) excusa *f*, pretexto *m*

alien [ˈeɪlɪən] Ⓐ ADJ **1** (= *foreign*) extranjero **2** (= *extraterrestrial*) alienígena, extraterrestre **3** (= *unfamiliar*) extraño, ajeno; **~ to** ajeno a Ⓑ N **1** (= *foreigner*) extranjero/a *m/f* **2** (= *extraterrestrial*) alienígena *mf*, extraterrestre *mf*

alienate [ˈeɪlɪəneɪt] VT (= *offend*) ofender; (= *make o.s. unpopular with*) ganarse la antipatía de; (*Psych, Pol*) alienar, enajenar; **to ~ sb from** alejar a algn de; **to ~ o.s. from sb** alejarse *or* apartarse de algn

alienation [ˌeɪlɪəˈneɪʃən] N **1** (*Psych, Pol*) alienación *f*, enajenación *f* **2** (= *estrangement*) [*of friend*] alejamiento *m*

alight[1] [əˈlaɪt] ADJ (*lit*) **to be ~** [*building*] estar ardiendo; [*fire*] estar encendido; [*lamp*] estar encendido *or* (*LAm*) prendido; **to set sth ~** pegar fuego a algo, incendiar algo

alight[2] [əˈlaɪt] VI **1** (*from vehicle*) bajar, apearse (**from** de) **2** (*on branch, etc*) [*bird, insect*] posarse (**on** sobre)

align [əˈlaɪn] VT alinear; **to ~ o.s. with** ponerse del lado de

alignment [əˈlaɪnmənt] N alineación *f*; **to be in ~** estar alineados, estar en línea recta; **to be out of ~ (with)** no estar alineado (con)

alike [əˈlaɪk] Ⓐ ADJ **they are very ~** son muy parecidos, se parecen mucho; **you're all ~!** ¡sois todos iguales!, ¡todos son iguales! (*esp LAm*); **to look ~** parecerse Ⓑ ADV **1** (= *in the same way*) del mismo modo, igual **2** (= *both, equally*) **men and women ~** tanto los hombres como las mujeres

alimentary [ˌælɪˈmentərɪ] ADJ alimenticio ► **alimentary canal** tubo *m* digestivo

alimony [ˈælɪmənɪ] N pensión *f* alimenticia

alive [əˈlaɪv] ADJ **1** (= *living*) vivo; **to be ~** estar vivo, vivir; **to be still ~** vivir todavía; [*dying person*] estar todavía con vida; **to bring a story ~** dar vida a una historia, animar una historia; **the scene came ~ as she described it** la escena cobraba vida al describirla ella; **we were being eaten ~ by mosquitoes** los mosquitos nos comían vivos; **to keep sb ~** conservar a algn con vida; **to keep a tradition ~** mantener viva una tradición; **he managed to stay ~ on fruit**

logró sobrevivir comiendo frutas
2 (= *lively*) activo, enérgico
3 ~ **with** [+ *insects*] lleno de, hormigueante de

alkali ['ælkəlaɪ] N álcali *m*

alkaline ['ælkəlaɪn] ADJ alcalino

---

all

Ⓐ ADJECTIVE	**Ⓓ** NOUN
Ⓑ PRONOUN	**Ⓔ** COMPOUNDS
Ⓒ ADVERB	

When **all** *is part of a set combination, eg* **in all probability**, *look up the noun. Note that* **all right** *has an entry to itself.*

---

all [ɔ:l] **Ⓐ** ADJECTIVE
1 todo; ~ **my life** toda mi vida; ~ **men** todos los hombres; ~ **the others went home** todos los demás se fueron a casa; **it rained** ~ **day** llovió todo el día, llovió el día entero; *BUT* **I'll take** ~ **three (of them)** me llevo los tres; **40% of** ~ **marriages** el 40% de los matrimonios; **it would have to rain today, of** ~ **days!** ¡tenía que llover hoy justamente!; **they chose him, of** ~ **people** lo eligieron a él, como si no hubiera otros
✦ **all that: it's not as bad as** ~ **that** no es para tanto; ~ **that is irrelevant now** todo eso ya no importa
✦ **and all that** y cosas así, y otras cosas por el estilo
✦ **of all the ...: of** ~ **the luck!** ¡vaya suerte!; **of** ~ **the tactless things to say!** ¡qué falta de tacto!
2 (= *any*) **it has been proved beyond** ~ **doubt** se ha probado sin que quepa la menor duda; **the town had changed beyond** ~ **recognition** la ciudad había cambiado hasta hacerse irreconocible
Ⓑ PRONOUN
1 (*singular*)
1.1 (= *everything*) todo; **we did** ~ **we could to stop him** hicimos todo lo posible para/por detenerlo; **it was** ~ **I could do not to laugh** apenas pude contener la risa; ~ **of it** todo; **I didn't read** ~ **of it** no lo leí todo *or* entero; **not** ~ **of it was true** no todo era cierto; **I do** ~ **of the work** yo hago todo el trabajo; **it took him** ~ **of three hours** (= *at least*) le llevó tres horas enteras; (*iro*) le llevó ni más ni menos que tres horas; **is** **that** ~? ¿eso es todo?, ¿nada más?; **that's** ~ eso es todo, nada más
1.2 (= *the only thing*) ~ **I can tell you is ...** todo lo que *or* lo único que puedo decirte es ...; ~ **I want is to sleep** lo único que quiero es dormir; **that was** ~ **that we managed to salvage from the fire** eso fue todo lo que conseguimos rescatar del incendio; ~ **that matters is that you're safe** lo único que importa es que estás a salvo
2 (*plural*) todos/as *mpl/fpl*; **they** ~ **came with their husbands** todas vinieron con sus maridos; **the pears? I'm afraid I've eaten them** ~ ¿las peras? me temo que me las he comido todas; **this concerns** ~ **of you** esto les afecta a todos ustedes; **his was the worst performance of** ~ la suya fue la peor actuación de todas; ~ **who** **knew him loved him** todos los que lo conocieron le querían
3 (*in scores*) **the score is two** ~ van empatados a dos, el marcador es de empate a dos; **to draw two** ~ empatar a dos; **it's thirty** ~ (*Tennis*) treinta iguales
4 (*in set structures*)
✦ **above all** sobre todo
✦ **after all** después de todo
✦ **all but:** ~ **but seven** todos menos siete
✦ **all in all** en general; ~ **in** ~, **things turned out quite well** en general, las cosas salieron bastante bien; **we thought,** ~ **in** ~, **it wasn't a bad idea** pensamos que, mirándolo bien, no era una mala idea
✦ **all told** en total
✦ **for all I know: for** ~ **I know he could be dead** puede que hasta esté muerto, no lo sé
✦ **if (...) at all: I'll go tomorrow if I go at** ~ si es que voy, iré mañana; **I'd like to see him today, if (it's) at** ~ **possible** me gustaría verlo hoy, si es del todo posible; **they won't attempt it, if they have any sense at** ~ si tienen el más mínimo sentido común, no lo intentarán
✦ **in all: 50 men in** ~ 50 hombres en total

✦ **it all: he ate it** ~ se lo comió todo; **it** ~ **happened so quickly** sucedió todo tan rápido
✦ **it's all or nothing** es todo o nada
✦ **most of all** sobre todo, más que nada
✦ **no ... at all: I have no regrets at** ~ no me arrepiento en absoluto; **it makes no difference at** ~ da exactamente igual
✦ **not ... at all: I don't feel at** ~ **well** no me siento nada bien; **she wasn't at** ~ **apologetic** no se disculpó para nada; **I'm not at** ~ **tired** no estoy cansado en lo más mínimo *or* en absoluto; **it was not at** ~ **nice** no fue nada agradable; **he didn't cry at** ~ no lloró en ningún momento
✦ **not at all!** (*answer to thanks*) ¡de nada!, ¡no hay de qué!; **"are you disappointed?" — "not at** ~**"** —¿estás defraudado? —en absoluto
Ⓒ ADVERB
1 = *entirely* todo

Make **todo** agree with the person or thing described:

she's ~ **wet** está toda mojada; **he was** ~ **covered in blood** estaba completamente cubierto de sangre; **the children were** ~ **alone** los niños estaban completamente solos; **there were insects** ~ **around us** había insectos por todas partes; **I did it** ~ **by myself** lo hice completamente solo; **she was dressed** ~ **in black** iba vestida completamente de negro

---

2 (*in set structures*)
✦ **all along:** ~ **along the street** a lo largo de toda la calle, por toda la calle; **this is what I feared** ~ **along** esto es lo que estaba temiendo desde el primer momento *or* el principio
✦ **all but** (= *nearly*) casi; **he** ~ **but died** casi se muere, por poco se muere
✦ **all for sth: to be** ~ **for sth** estar completamente a favor de algo; **I'm** ~ **for it** estoy completamente a favor
✦ **all in** (= *all inclusive*) (*Brit*) todo incluido; (*) (= *exhausted*) hecho polvo*
✦ **all out: to go** ~ **out** (= *spare no expense*) tirar la casa por la ventana; (*Sport*) emplearse a fondo; **to go** ~ **out for the prize** volcarse por conseguir el premio
✦ **all over:** ~ **over the world** por todo el mundo; **you've got mud** ~ **over your shoes** tienes los zapatos cubiertos de barro; **I spilled coffee** ~ **over my shirt** se me cayó el café encima y me manché toda la camisa; **they were** ~ **over him*** le recibieron con el mayor entusiasmo; **I ache** ~ **over** me duele (por) todo el cuerpo; **that's him** ~ **over*** eso es muy típico de él
✦ **all the more ...: considering his age, it's** ~ **the more remarkable that he succeeded** teniendo en cuenta su edad, es aún más extraordinario que lo haya logrado; **she valued her freedom,** ~ **the more so because she had fought so hard for it** valoraba mucho su libertad, tanto más cuanto que había luchado tanto por conseguirla
✦ **all too ...: it's** ~ **too true** lamentablemente es cierto; **the evening passed** ~ **too quickly** la tarde pasó demasiado rápido
✦ **all up with: it's** ~ **up with him** está acabado
✦ **all very ...: that's** ~ **very well but ...** todo eso está muy bien, pero ...
✦ **not all that ...: it isn't** ~ **that far** no está tan lejos
Ⓓ NOUN (= *utmost*) **I decided to give it my** ~ decidí echarle el resto; **he puts his** ~ **into every game** se entrega por completo en cada partido
Ⓔ COMPOUNDS ➤ **the all clear** (= *signal*) el cese de la alarma, el fin de la alarma; (*fig*) el visto bueno, luz verde; ~ **clear!** ¡fin de la alerta!; **to be given the** ~ **clear** (*to do sth*) recibir el visto bueno, recibir luz verde; (*by doctor*) recibir el alta médica *or* definitiva ➤ **All Saints' Day** día *m* de Todos los Santos

Allah ['ælə] N Alá *m*

all-around ['ɔ:lə'raʊnd] ADJ (*US*) = **all-round**

allay [ə'leɪ] VT [+ *fears*] aquietar, calmar; [+ *doubts*] despejar

allegation [ælɪ'geɪʃən] N alegato *m*

allege [ə'ledʒ] VT **1** (*with verb/clause*) afirmar (**that** que); **she is** ~**d to have stolen money from a cash box** se afirma que robó dinero del que había en una caja; **he is** ~**d to be wealthy** según se dice es rico **2** (*with noun*) alegar; **he**

absented himself alleging illness se ausentó alegando estar enfermo

alleged [ə'ledʒd] ADJ [*crime, thief, victim, author*] presunto; [*fact, reason*] supuesto

allegedly [ə'ledʒɪdlɪ] ADV presuntamente, supuestamente; **the crimes he had ~ committed** los crímenes que presuntamente *or* supuestamente había cometido; **his van ~ struck two people** según se afirma *or* supuestamente, su furgoneta atropelló a dos personas; **~ illegal immigrants** inmigrantes presuntamente ilegales

allegiance [ə'liːdʒəns] N lealtad *f*

allegory ['ælɪgərɪ] N alegoría *f*

allergic [ə'lɜːdʒɪk] ADJ alérgico (**to** a)

allergy ['ælədʒɪ] N alergia *f* (**to** a)

alleviate [ə'liːvɪeɪt] VT aliviar, mitigar

alley ['ælɪ] Ⓐ N **1** (*between buildings*) callejón *m*, callejuela *f*; (*in garden, park*) paseo *m*; ✦ IDIOM **it's right up my ~** (*US**) esto es lo que me va, esto es lo mío **2** (*US Tennis*) banda *f* lateral para dobles Ⓑ CPD ▸ **alley cat** gato/a *m/f* callejero/a

alleyway ['ælɪweɪ] N **alley A1**

alliance [ə'laɪəns] N alianza *f*; **to enter into an ~ with** aliarse con

allied ['ælaɪd] ADJ **1** (*Mil, Pol*) [*troops, countries, parties*] aliado **2** (= *associated*) [*subjects, products, industries*] relacionado, afín; **~ to sth** relacionado con algo, afín a algo

alligator ['ælɪgeɪtə'] N caimán *m*

all-important ['ɔːlɪm'pɔːtənt] ADJ de primera *or* de suma importancia

all-in ['ɔːlɪn] ADJ (*Brit*) [*price*] global, con todo incluido; [*insurance policy*] contra todo riesgo

all-inclusive ['ɔːlɪn'kluːsɪv] ADJ [*price*] con todo incluido; **~ insurance policy** póliza *f* de seguro contra todo riesgo

alliteration [ə,lɪtə'reɪʃən] N aliteración *f*

all-night ['ɔːlnaɪt] ADJ [*café, garage*] abierto toda la noche; [*vigil, party*] que dura toda la noche

allocate ['æləkeɪt] VT **1** (= *allot*) asignar (**to** a) **2** (= *distribute*) repartir (**among** entre)

allocation [,ælə'keɪʃən] N **1** (= *allotting*) asignación *f* **2** (= *distribution*) reparto *m* **3** (= *share, amount*) ración *f*, cuota *f*

allot [ə'lɒt] VT **1** (= *assign*) [+ *task, share, time*] asignar (**to** a); **we finished in the time ~ted** terminamos en el tiempo previsto **2** (= *distribute*) repartir, distribuir

allotment [ə'lɒtmənt] N (*Brit*) (= *land*) parcela *f*

all-out ['ɔːl'aut] ADJ [*effort*] supremo; [*attack*] con máxima fuerza; ~ **strike** huelga *f* general; ~ **war** guerra *f* total

allow [ə'lau] VT **1** (= *permit*) permitir; **smoking is not ~ed** no está permitido fumar; **"no dogs allowed"** "no se admiten perros"; ~ **me!** ¡permítame!; **to ~ sb to do sth** dejar *or* (*more frm*) permitir a algn hacer algo, dejar *or* (*more frm*) permitir que algn haga algo; ~ **the mixture to cool** deje enfriar la mezcla; **to ~ o.s. to be persuaded** dejarse convencer; **he was ~ed home after hospital treatment** le permitieron *or* le dejaron irse a casa tras recibir tratamiento en el hospital; **to ~ sb in/out/past** permitir *or* dejar a algn entrar/salir/pasar, permitir *or* dejar a algn que entre/salga/pase; **they made holes in the box to ~ air in** hicieron unos agujeros en la caja para que entrara el aire; **he is not ~ed visitors** no le permiten visitas **2** (= *reckon on*) dejar; ~ (**yourself**) **three hours for the journey** deja *or* calcula tres horas para el viaje; **how much should I ~ for expenses?** ¿cuánto debo prever para los gastos?; **please ~ 28 days for delivery** lo recibirá en su casa en un plazo de 28 días **3** (= *grant*) [+ *money*] asignar; [+ *time*] dar **4** (*Jur*) [+ *claim, appeal*] admitir, aceptar **5** (*Sport*) [+ *goal*] conceder

▸ **allow for** VI + PREP tener en cuenta; ~ **for delays on some roads** tengan en cuenta que puede haber retenciones en algunas carreteras; **we have to ~ for that possibility** debemos tener presente esa posibilidad

allowable [ə'lauəbl] ADJ [*expense*] deducible; ~ **against tax** desgravable

allowance [ə'lauəns] N **1** (*from state*) prestación *f*; (*from ex-husband, benefactor*) pensión *f*; (*from parents*) dinero mensual/semanal *etc*; (*from fund*) asignación *f*; (*esp US*) (= *pocket money*) dinero *m* de bolsillo **2** (= *discount*) descuento *m*, rebaja *f*; **tax ~** (*Brit*) desgravación *f* fiscal **3** (= *concession*) concesión *f*; **one must make ~s** hay que hacer concesiones; **to make ~(s) for sb** ser comprensivo con algn, disculpar a algn; **to make ~(s) for the weather** tener en cuenta el tiempo

alloy ['ælɔɪ] N (= *metal*) aleación *f*; (*fig*) mezcla *f*

all-party ['ɔːl'pɑːtɪ] ADJ [*group, talks*] multipartidista

all-points bulletin [,ɔːlpɔɪnts'bʊlɪtɪn] N (*US*) boletín difundido por la policía para la búsqueda y captura de un sospechoso

all-powerful ['ɔːl'pauəfəl] ADJ omnipotente, todopoderoso

all-purpose ['ɔːl'pɜːpəs] ADJ [*tool, cleaner*] multiuso *inv*, universal; [*vehicle, flour, wine*] para todo uso

all right [,ɔːl'raɪt] Ⓐ ADJ **1** (= *satisfactory*) **the film was ~** la película no estuvo mal; **yes, that's ~** sí, de acuerdo; **are you ~?** ¿estás bien?; **it's ~** (= *it's fine*) todo está bien; (= *passable*) no está mal; (= *don't worry*) no te preocupes; **it's ~ by me** yo, de acuerdo, lo que es por mí, no hay problema; **it's ~ for you!** a ti ¿qué te puede importar?; **it's ~ for some!** ¡los hay con suerte!; **it's ~ for you to smile** tú bien puedes sonreír; **is it ~ for me to go at four?** ¿puedo marcharme a las cuatro?; **is it ~ for me to take the dog?** ¿se me permite llevar al perro?; **is that ~ with you?** ¿te parece bien?; **it's ~ with me** yo, de acuerdo, lo que es por mí, no hay problema **2** (= *safe, well*) bien; **I'm/I feel ~ now** ya estoy bien; **she's ~ again now** está mejor, se ha repuesto ya **3** (= *well-provided*) **we're ~ for the rest of our lives** no tendremos problemas económicos el resto de nuestra(s) vida(s); **are you ~ for cigarettes?** ¿tienes suficiente tabaco? **4** (= *available*) **are you ~ for Tuesday?** ¿te viene bien el martes? Ⓑ ADV **1** (= *satisfactorily, without difficulty*) bien; **everything turned out ~** todo salió bien; **he's doing ~ for himself*** no le van nada mal las cosas **2** (*) (= *without doubt*) **he complained ~!** ¡ya lo creo que se quejó!; **you'll get your money back ~** se te devolverá tu dinero, eso es seguro Ⓒ EXCL (*in approval*) ¡bueno!, ¡muy bien!; (*in agreement*) ¡de acuerdo!, ¡vale! (*Sp*), ¡okey! (*esp LAm*); (*changing subject*) bueno

all-round ['ɔːl'raund] ADJ [*success etc*] completo; [*improvement*] general, en todos los aspectos; [*view*] amplio

all-rounder ['ɔːl'raundə'] N (*Brit*) persona *f* con capacidad para todo

allspice ['ɔːlspaɪs] N pimienta *f* inglesa, pimienta *f* de Jamaica

all-terrain vehicle [,ɔːltəreɪn'viːɪkl] N (vehículo *m*) todo terreno

all-time ['ɔːl'taɪm] ADJ de todos los tiempos; **an ~ record** un récord nunca igualado; **exports have reached an ~ high** las exportaciones han alcanzado cifras nunca antes conocidas; **the pound is at an ~ low** la libra ha caído a su punto más bajo

allude [ə'luːd] VI **to ~ to** aludir a, referirse a

allure [ə'ljuə'] N atractivo *m*, encanto *m*

alluring [ə'ljuərɪŋ] ADJ seductor, atrayente

allusion [ə'luːʒən] N alusión *f*, referencia *f*

alluvial [ə'luːvɪəl] ADJ aluvial

ally Ⓐ ['ælaɪ] N aliado/a *m/f*; **the Allies** los Aliados Ⓑ [ə'laɪ] VT **to ~ o.s. with** aliarse con, hacer *or* formar alianza con

all-year-round ['ɔːl,jɪə'raund] ADJ [*sport*] que se practica todo el año; [*resort*] abierto todo el año

almanac ['ɔːlmənæk] N almanaque *m*

almighty [ɔːl'maɪtɪ] Ⓐ ADJ **1** (= *omnipotent*) todopoderoso **2** (*) (= *tremendous*) tremendo, de mil demonios* Ⓑ N **the Almighty** el Todopoderoso

almond ['ɑːmənd] Ⓐ N (= *nut*) almendra *f*; (= *tree*) almendro *m* Ⓑ ADJ **an ~ taste** un sabor a almendra Ⓒ CPD de almendra(s) ➤ **almond tree** almendro *m*

almost ['ɔːlməʊst] ADV casi; **it's ~ finished/ready** casi está terminado/listo; **it's ~ midnight** ya es casi medianoche; **he ~ certainly will win** casi seguro que gana; **he ~ fell** casi se cae, por poco no se cae; **I had ~ forgotten about it** casi lo olvido, por poco lo olvido; **we're ~ there** estamos a punto de llegar, ya nos falta poco para llegar

alms [ɑːmz] NPL limosna *fsing*

aloft [ə'lɒft] ADV (*liter*) (= *above*) en alto; (= *upward*) hacia arriba

alone [ə'ləʊn] Ⓐ ADJ **1** (= *by oneself*) solo; **all ~** (completamente) solo; **they are not ~ in their belief** no son los únicos que lo creen, no son sólo ellos los que lo creen; **to leave sb ~** dejar solo a algn **2** (= *undisturbed*) **to leave sb ~** dejar a algn en paz; **to leave sth ~** no tocar algo; **why can't he leave things ~?** ¿por qué no puede dejar las cosas como están?; **you'd better leave** *or* **let well ~** mejor no te metas en ese asunto **3** (*as conj*) **let ~: he can't read, let ~ write** no sabe leer y aún menos escribir
Ⓑ ADV solamente, sólo; **you and you ~ can make that decision** tú y solamente *or* sólo tú puedes tomar esa decisión, eres el único que puede tomar esa decisión; **the travel ~ cost £600** solamente *or* sólo el viaje costó 600 libras; **I decided to go it ~*** (= *do it unaided*) decidí hacerlo solo, decidí hacerlo por mi cuenta; (= *start a company*) decidí establecerme por mi cuenta

along [ə'lɒŋ]

> When **along** is an element in a phrasal verb, eg **get along, play along, string along,** look up the verb.

Ⓐ PREP por, a lo largo de; **to walk ~ the street** andar por la calle; **the trees ~ the path** los árboles a lo largo del camino; **all ~ the street** todo lo largo de la calle; **the shop is ~ here** la tienda está por aquí; **somewhere ~ the way** *or* **the line someone made a mistake** en un momento determinado alguien cometió un error
Ⓑ ADV **1** (= *forward*) **move ~ there!** ¡circulen, por favor! **2** (= *with you, us etc*) **bring him ~ if you like** tráelo, si quieres; **are you coming ~?** ¿tú vienes también? **3** (= *here, there*) **I'll be ~ in a moment** ahora voy **4** (*in set expressions*) **all ~** desde el principio; **~ with** junto con

alongside [ə'lɒŋ'saɪd] Ⓐ PREP al lado de; **the car stopped ~ me** el coche se paró a mi lado; **they have to work ~ each other** tienen que trabajar juntos; **how can these systems work ~ each other?** ¿cómo funcionar en colaboración? Ⓑ ADV (*Naut*) de costado; **to come ~** atracar

aloof [ə'luːf] ADJ (*person, manner*) distante

aloofness [ə'luːfnɪs] N actitud *f* distante

aloud [ə'laʊd] ADV en voz alta

alphabet ['ælfəbet] N alfabeto *m*

alphabetical [,ælfə'betɪkəl] ADJ alfabético; **in ~ order** en *or* por orden alfabético

alphabetically [,ælfə'betɪkəlɪ] ADV alfabéticamente, en *or* por orden alfabético

alpine ['ælpaɪn] Ⓐ ADJ alpino Ⓑ N planta *f* alpestre

Alps [ælps] NPL **the ~** los Alpes

Al Qaeda [æl'kaɪdə] N Al Qaeda *m o f*

already [ɔːl'redɪ] ADV ya; **Liz had ~ gone** Liz ya se había ido

alright [,ɔːl'raɪt] = **all right**

Alsatian [æl'seɪʃən] Ⓐ ADJ alsaciano Ⓑ N **1** (= *person*) alsaciano/a *m/f* **2** (*Brit*) (= *dog*) (perro *m*) pastor *m* alemán, perro *m* lobo

also ['ɔːlsəʊ] ADV también; **her cousin ~ came** su primo también vino; **~, I must explain that ...** además debo aclarar que ...

also-ran ['ɔːlsəʊræn] N (*Sport*) caballo *m* perdedor; (*) (= *person*) nulidad *f*

altar ['ɒltəʳ] N altar *m* ➤ **altar boy** acólito *m*, monaguillo *m*

alter ['ɒltəʳ] Ⓐ VT **1** (= *change*) [+ *text*] modificar, cambiar;

[+ *painting, speech*] retocar; [+ *opinion, course*] cambiar de; (*Sew*) arreglar; **then that ~s things** entonces la cosa cambia **2** (= *falsify*) [+ *evidence*] falsificar; [+ *document*] alterar **3** (*US*) (= *castrate*) castrar Ⓑ VI cambiar

alteration [,ɒltə'reɪʃən] N (= *change*) (*to text*) modificación *f*, cambio *m*; (*to painting, speech etc*) retoque *m*; (*Sew*) arreglo *m*; **to make ~s to** [+ *building, text*] hacer modificaciones en; [+ *dress*] hacer arreglos a

altercation [,ɒltə'keɪʃən] N altercado *m*

alter ego ['æltər'iːgəʊ] N álter ego *m*

alternate Ⓐ [ɒl'tɜːnɪt] ADJ **1** (= *alternating*) alterno; **let's read ~ lines** vamos a leer cada uno un renglón **2** (= *every second*) **on ~ days** cada dos días, un día sí y otro no; **he lives ~ months in Brussels and London** vive un mes en Bruselas y uno en Londres; **to write on ~ lines** escribir en renglones alternos **3** (*US*) = **alternative A**
Ⓑ [ɒl'tɜːnɪt] N (*US*) suplente *mf*
Ⓒ ['ɒltɜːneɪt] VI alternar; **the temperatures ~ between very hot and extremely cold** las temperaturas oscilan entre un calor y un frío intensos
Ⓓ ['ɒltɜːneɪt] VT alternar

alternately [ɒl'tɜːnɪtlɪ] ADV **the meetings took place ~ in France and Germany** las reuniones se celebraron una vez en Francia y la siguiente en Alemania; **I lived ~ with my mother and my grandmother** vivía unas veces con mi madre y otras con mi abuela

alternating ['ɒltɜːneɪtɪŋ] ADJ alterno ➤ **alternating current** corriente *f* alterna

alternative [ɒl'tɜːnətɪv] Ⓐ ADJ alternativo, otro Ⓑ N alternativa *f*; **there are several ~s** hay varias alternativas *or* posibilidades; **what ~s are there?** ¿qué alternativas *or* opciones hay?; **I have no ~** no tengo más remedio, no me queda otra alternativa *or* opción; **you have no ~ but to go** no tienes más alternativa *or* opción *or* remedio que ir Ⓒ CPD ➤ **alternative medicine** medicina *f* alternativa

alternatively [ɒl'tɜːnətɪvlɪ] ADV **~, you can use household bleach** si no, puede usar lejía doméstica; **we could go on to the next village, or, ~, we could camp here** podemos ir hasta el siguiente pueblo, o podemos acampar aquí

alternator ['ɒltɜːneɪtəʳ] N alternador *m*

although [ɔːl'ðəʊ] CONJ aunque

altitude ['æltɪtjuːd] N altitud *f*, altura *f* ➤ **altitude sickness** mal *m* de altura, soroche *m* (*LAm*)

alto ['æltəʊ] Ⓐ N (= *instrument, male singer*) alto *m*; (= *female singer*) contralto *f* Ⓑ ADJ [*instrument*] alto; [*part*] de alto, para alto Ⓒ CPD ➤ **alto saxophone** saxofón *m* alto

altogether [,ɔːltə'geðəʳ] ADV **1** (= *in all*) en total; **how much is that ~?** ¿cuánto es en total?; **~ it was rather unpleasant** en general fue muy desagradable **2** (= *entirely*) [*stop, disappear*] por completo, del todo; [*different, impossible*] totalmente; [*wonderful*] realmente; **I'm not ~ happy with your work** no estoy del todo satisfecho con tu trabajo; **Asia was another matter ~** lo de Asia era un tema totalmente diferente; **"do you believe him?" — "not ~"** —¿le crees? — no del todo

altruism ['æltruɪzəm] N altruismo *m*

altruistic [,æltru'ɪstɪk] ADJ altruista

aluminium [,ælju'mɪnɪəm], **aluminum** (*US*) [ə'luːmɪnəm] N aluminio *m* ➤ **aluminium foil** papel *m* de aluminio, aluminio *m* doméstico

alumnus [ə'lʌmnəs] N (*pl* **alumni** [ə'lʌmnaɪ]), **alumna** [ə'lʌmnə] N (*pl* **alumnae** [ə'lʌmniː]) (*esp US*) graduado/a *m/f*

always ['ɔːlweɪz] ADV siempre; **as ~** como siempre; **nearly ~** casi siempre; **he's ~ late** siempre llega tarde; **you can ~ go by train** también puedes ir en tren

Alzheimer's (disease) ['æltshaɪməz(dɪ,ziːz)] N (enfermedad *f* de) Alzheimer *m*

AM N ABBR **1** (= **amplitude modulation**) A.M. *f* **2** (*Welsh Pol*) (= **Assembly Member**) parlamentario/a *m/f*

am¹ [æm] 1ST PERS SING PRESENT *of* **be**

am² [eɪ'em] ADV ABBR (= **ante meridiem**) de la mañana; **at four am** a las cuatro de la mañana

AMA N ABBR (US) = **American Medical Association**

amalgam [ə'mælgəm] N amalgama f (**of** de)

amalgamate [ə'mælgəmeɪt] Ⓐ VT [+ texts] amalgamar; [+ companies] fusionar Ⓑ VI [organizations] amalgamarse, unirse; [companies] fusionarse

amalgamation [ə,mælgə'meɪʃən] N amalgamiento m; [of companies] fusión f

amass [ə'mæs] VT [+ wealth, information] acumular

amateur ['æmətəʳ] Ⓐ N 1 (= non-professional) amateur mf; (= hobbyist) aficionado/a m/f 2 (pej) chapucero/a m/f Ⓑ ADJ 1 (= not professional) [athlete, actor, production] amateur; [club, competition] para amateurs, para aficionados; ~ **athletics/photography** atletismo/fotografía para amateurs; **an ~ photographer** un aficionado a la fotografía, un fotógrafo aficionado; **an ~ detective** un detective aficionado 2 (pej) [production, performance] de aficionados, chapucero Ⓒ CPD ➤ **amateur dramatics** SING teatro m amateur, teatro m de aficionados

amateurish ['æmətərɪʃ] ADJ poco profesional, inexperto

amaze [ə'meɪz] VT pasmar, asombrar; **to be ~d (at)** quedarse pasmado (ante)

amazed [ə'meɪzd] ADJ [glance, expression] asombrado, atónito, lleno de estupor

amazement [ə'meɪzmənt] N asombro m; **to my ~** para mi gran asombro or sorpresa; **they looked on in ~** miraron asombrados

amazing [ə'meɪzɪŋ] ADJ 1 (= astonishing) asombroso 2 (= wonderful) extraordinario

amazingly [ə'meɪzɪŋlɪ] ADV 1 (= astonishingly) asombrosamente; **it was ~ easy** asombraba lo fácil que era, era asombrosamente fácil; **~ enough** por increíble que parezca, aunque parece mentira 2 (= wonderfully) extraordinariamente

Amazon ['æməzən] Ⓐ N 1 (= river) **the ~** el Amazonas 2 (Myth) amazona f Ⓑ CPD ➤ **Amazon basin** cuenca f del Amazonas ➤ **Amazon rain forest** selva f del Amazonas or amazónica

Amazonian [æmə'zəʊnɪən] ADJ amazónico

ambassador [æm'bæsədəʳ] N embajador(a) m/f; **the Spanish ~** el embajador de España

amber ['æmbəʳ] Ⓐ N ámbar m; **at ~** (Brit Aut) en ámbar Ⓑ ADJ 1 [jewellery] de ámbar; [colour] ambarino 2 (Brit Aut) **~ light** luz f ámbar

ambidextrous [æmbɪ'dekstrəs] ADJ ambidiestro, ambidextro

ambience ['æmbɪəns] N ambiente m, atmósfera f

ambiguity [æmbɪ'gjʊɪtɪ] N ambigüedad f

ambiguous [æm'bɪgjʊəs] ADJ ambiguo

ambiguously [æm'bɪgjʊəslɪ] ADV ambiguamente, de forma ambigua

ambition [æm'bɪʃən] N ambición f; **to have an ~ to be a doctor** ambicionar ser médico

ambitious [æm'bɪʃəs] ADJ ambicioso; **perhaps you're being too ~** quizá estés intentando abarcar demasiado

ambivalent [æm'bɪvələnt] ADJ ambivalente

amble ['æmbl] VI [person] andar sin prisa; [horse] amblar, ir a paso de andadura; **to ~ along** andar sin prisa, pasearse despacio; **he ~d up to me** se me acercó a paso lento

ambulance ['æmbjʊləns] N ambulancia f ➤ **ambulance driver, ambulance man** (Brit) conductor/a m/f de ambulancia, ambulanciero m

ambush ['æmbʊʃ] Ⓐ N emboscada f; **to set** or **lay an ~ for** tender una emboscada a; **to lie in ~ for sb** estar esperando a algn (tras haber preparado una emboscada) Ⓑ VT cazar por sorpresa, agarrar por sorpresa (LAm); **to be ~ed** caer en una emboscada, ser cazado por sorpresa

ameba [ə'miːbə] N (US) = **amoeba**

amen ['ɑː'men] EXCL amén; **~ to that** así sea, ojalá sea así

amenable [ə'miːnəbl] ADJ (= responsive) **~ to argument**

flexible, que se deja convencer; **~ to discipline** sumiso, dispuesto a dejarse disciplinar; **~ to reason** dispuesto a entrar en razón; **I'd like to visit you at home if you're ~** me gustaría hacerle una visita a su casa, si le parece bien

amend [ə'mend] VT [+ law] enmendar; [+ text, wording] corregir

amendment [ə'mendmənt] N 1 (to law) enmienda f (**to** a) 2 (to text) corrección f

amends [ə'mendz] NPL **to make ~ (to sb) for sth** (= apologize) dar satisfacción (a algn) por algo; (= compensate) compensar (a algn) por algo

amenities [ə'miːnɪtɪz] NPL **a house with all ~** una casa con todas las comodidades or todo confort; **the hotel has very good ~** el hotel tiene excelentes servicios e instalaciones; **the town has many ~** la ciudad ofrece gran variedad de servicios; **we are trying to improve the city's ~** nos esforzamos por mejorar las instalaciones de la ciudad

America [ə'merɪkə] N (= USA) Estados mpl Unidos; (= continent) América f

American [ə'merɪkən] Ⓐ ADJ (= of USA) norteamericano, estadounidense; [continent] americano Ⓑ N 1 (= person) (from USA) norteamericano/a m/f, americano/a m/f; (from continent) americano/a m/f 2 (= language) (*) inglés m americano Ⓒ CPD ➤ **American Dream** sueño m americano ➤ **American English** inglés m americano ➤ **American football** (Brit) fútbol m americano ➤ **American Indian** (Brit) amerindio/a m/f ➤ **American plan** (US) (in hotel) (habitación f con) pensión f completa

---

AMERICAN DREAM

El término **American Dream**, (el sueño americano), se refiere a los valores y creencias que para muchos estadounidenses son característicos de su modo de entender la vida como nación y que encuentran su materialización en la Declaración de Independencia de 1776. Con este término se pone especial énfasis en el individualismo, la importancia de trabajar duro, el hecho de que todos podemos mejorar y que la libertad y la justicia han de ser universales. Para muchos el sueño americano era una oportunidad para hacer fortuna.

El término también se usa de forma irónica para referirse al contraste entre estos ideales y las actitudes materialistas que caracterizan a la sociedad estadounidense actual.

Americanism [ə'merɪkənɪzəm] N americanismo m

Americanize [ə'merɪkənaɪz] VT americanizar; **to become ~d** americanizarse

Amerindian [æmə'rɪndɪən] ADJ, N amerindio/a m/f

amethyst ['æmɪθɪst] N amatista f

AmEx® ['æmeks] N ABBR (US) = **American Express**

Amex ['æmeks] N ABBR (US) = **American Stock Exchange**

amiable ['eɪmɪəbl] ADJ amable, afable

amiably ['eɪmɪəblɪ] ADV amablemente, afablemente

amicable ['æmɪkəbl] ADJ amistoso, amigable; **to reach an ~ settlement** llegar a un acuerdo amistoso

amicably ['æmɪkəblɪ] ADV amistosamente, amigablemente

amid [ə'mɪd] PREP en medio de, entre

amidst [ə'mɪdst] PREP en medio de, entre

amiss [ə'mɪs] Ⓐ ADJ **there's something ~** pasa algo Ⓑ ADV **don't take it ~, will you?** no lo tomes a mal, no te vayas a ofender; **a lick of paint wouldn't go** or **come ~** (Brit) una mano de pintura no vendría mal

ammo* ['æməʊ] N ABBR = **ammunition**

ammonia [ə'məʊnɪə] N amoníaco m; **liquid ~** amoníaco m líquido

ammunition [æmjʊ'nɪʃən] N 1 (lit) munición f 2 (fig) argumentos mpl

amnesia [æmˈniːzɪə] N amnesia f

amnesty [ˈæmnɪstɪ] Ⓐ N amnistía f; **to grant an ~ to** amnistiar (a), conceder una amnistía a Ⓑ VT amnistiar

Amnesty International [ˌæmnɪstɪntəˈnæʃnəl] N Amnistía f Internacional

amoeba [əˈmiːbə] N (pl **~s**, **~e** [əˈmiːbiː]) ameba f, amiba f

amok [əˈmɒk] ADV **to run ~** enloquecerse, desbocarse

among(st) [əˈmʌŋ(st)] PREP entre, en medio de; **one can say that ~ friends** eso se puede decir entre amigos; **they quarrelled** or (US) **quarreled ~ themselves** riñeron entre sí; **share it ~ yourselves** repártanlo entre ustedes

amoral [eɪˈmɒrəl] ADJ amoral

amorous [ˈæmərəs] ADJ [person, look] apasionado; **he made ~ advances to his secretary** se le insinuó a su secretaria

amorphous [əˈmɔːfəs] ADJ amorfo

amount [əˈmaʊnt] N **1** (= quantity) cantidad f; **the total ~** el total, la cantidad total; **any ~ of** cualquier cantidad de; **we have had any ~ of trouble** hemos tenido un sinnúmero de problemas; **no ~ of arguing will help** es totalmente inútil discutir **2** (= sum of money) cantidad f, suma f **3** (= total value) valor m; **a bill for the ~ of** una cuenta por importe or valor de; **debts to** or (US) **in the ~ of £100** deudas fpl por valor de 100 libras
➤ **amount to** VI + PREP **1** (= add up to) [sums, figures, debts] sumar, ascender a **2** (= be equivalent to) equivaler a, significar; **it ~s to the same thing** es igual, viene a ser lo mismo **3** (= be worth) **it doesn't ~ to much** apenas es significativo, viene a ser poca cosa; **he'll never ~ to much** nunca dejará de ser nadie

amp [æmp] N **1** (= ampere) amperio m; **a 13-~ plug** un enchufe de 13 amperios **2** (*) (= amplifier) ampli* m, amplificador m

ampere, ampère [ˈæmpɛəʳ] N amperio m

ampersand [ˈæmpəsænd] N el signo & (= and)

amphetamine [æmˈfetəmiːn] N anfetamina f

amphibian [æmˈfɪbɪən] N anfibio m

amphibious [æmˈfɪbɪəs] ADJ [animal, vehicle] anfibio

amphitheatre, amphitheater (US) [ˈæmfɪˌθɪətəʳ] N anfiteatro m

ample [ˈæmpl] ADJ (compar **~r**; superl **~st**) **1** (= plentiful, more than sufficient) **1.1 to be ~** ser más que suficiente; **one cupful of rice is ~ for two people** una taza de arroz es más que suficiente para dos personas **1.2** (before noun) [evidence, proof, resources] abundante; [time, space] de sobra; **she has ~ means** tiene medios más que suficientes; **there'll be ~ opportunity to relax** habrá oportunidades de sobra para relajarse **2** (= generous) [garment] amplio, grande; [portion, bosom] generoso

amplifier [ˈæmplɪfaɪəʳ] N amplificador m

amplify [ˈæmplɪfaɪ] VT **1** [+ sound] amplificar; (Rad) aumentar **2** [+ statement etc] desarrollar; **he refused to ~ his remarks** se negó a hacer más comentarios

amply [ˈæmplɪ] ADV ampliamente, suficientemente

ampoule, ampule (US) [ˈæmpuːl] N ampolla f

amputate [ˈæmpjʊteɪt] VT amputar

amputation [ˌæmpjʊˈteɪʃən] N amputación f

amputee [ˌæmpjʊˈtiː] N persona cuya pierna o cuyo brazo ha sido amputada/o

Amsterdam [ˌæmstəˈdæm] N Amsterdam m

Amtrak [ˈæmtræk] N (US) empresa nacional de ferrocarriles de los EEUU

amuck [əˈmʌk] ADV = **amok**

amuse [əˈmjuːz] VT **1** (= cause mirth to) divertir; **to be ~d at** or **by** divertirse con **2** (= entertain) distraer, entretener; **to keep sb ~d** entretener a algn; **to ~ o.s.** distraerse; **run along and ~ yourselves** marchaos y a pasarlo bien

amusement [əˈmjuːzmənt] Ⓐ N **1** (= mirth) **with a look of ~** con mirada risueña; **there was general ~ at this** al oír esto se rieron todos; **much to my ~** con gran regocijo mío **2** (= entertainment) distracción f, diversión f **3 amusements** (in fairground) atracciones f; (in amusement arcade)

máquinas fpl electrónicas, máquinas fpl tragaperras Ⓑ CPD
➤ **amusement arcade** (Brit) sala f de juegos recreativos
➤ **amusement park** (esp US) parque m de atracciones

amusing [əˈmjuːzɪŋ] ADJ **1** (= funny) gracioso, divertido; **I didn't find it ~** no le vi la gracia **2** (= entertaining) entretenido

an [æn, ən, n] INDEF ART see **a**

anabolic [ˌænəˈbɒlɪk] ADJ anabólico ➤ **anabolic steroid** esteroide m anabolizante

anachronism [əˈnækrənɪzəm] N anacronismo m

anaemia, anemia (US) [əˈniːmɪə] N anemia f

anaemic, anemic (US) [əˈniːmɪk] ADJ anémico

anaerobic [ˌænɛəˈrəʊbɪk] ADJ anaerobio

anaesthetic, anesthetic (US) [ˌænɪsˈθetɪk] Ⓐ N anestésico m; **local/general ~** anestesia f local/general; **to give sb an ~** anestesiar a algn Ⓑ ADJ anestésico

anaesthetist, anesthetist (US) [æˈniːsθɪtɪst] N anestesista mf

anaesthetize, anesthetize (US) [æˈniːsθɪtaɪz] VT anestesiar

anagram [ˈænəgræm] N anagrama m

anal [ˈeɪnəl] ADJ anal

analgesic [ˌænælˈdʒiːsɪk] Ⓐ ADJ analgésico Ⓑ N analgésico m

analog [ˈænəlɒg] N, ADJ = **analogue**

analogous [əˈnæləgəs] ADJ análogo (**to, with** a)

analogue, analog (esp US) [ˈænəlɒg] Ⓐ N análogo m Ⓑ ADJ analógico Ⓒ CPD ➤ **analogue computer** ordenador m analógico (Sp), computadora f analógica (LAm)

analogy [əˈnælədʒɪ] N analogía f; (= similarity) semejanza f; **by ~ (with)** por analogía (con)

analyse, analyze (US) [ˈænəlaɪz] VT **1** (= study) analizar **2** (= psychoanalyse) psicoanalizar

analysis [əˈnælɪsɪs] N (pl **analyses** [əˈnælɪsiːz]) **1** (= study) análisis m inv; **in the final ~** a fin de cuentas **2** (Psych) psicoanálisis m

analyst [ˈænəlɪst] N **1** (Chem etc) analista mf **2** (Psych) psicoanalista mf

analytic [ˌænəˈlɪtɪk] ADJ (esp US) = **analytical**

analytical [ˌænəˈlɪtɪkəl] ADJ analítico

analyze [ˈænəlaɪz] VT (US) = **analyse**

anarchic [æˈnɑːkɪk] ADJ anárquico

anarchical [æˈnɑːkɪkə(l)] ADJ = **anarchic**

anarchist [ˈænəkɪst] ADJ, N anarquista mf

anarchy [ˈænəkɪ] N anarquía f

anathema [əˈnæθɪmə] N **1** (Rel) anatema m **2** (fig) **he is ~ to me** no lo puedo ver, para mí es inaguantable; **the idea is ~ to her** para ella la idea es una abominación, la idea le resulta odiosa

anatomical [ˌænəˈtɒmɪkəl] ADJ anatómico

anatomy [əˈnætəmɪ] N anatomía f

ANC N ABBR (= **African National Congress**) CNA m

ancestor [ˈænsɪstəʳ] N antepasado/a m/f

ancestral [ænˈsestrəl] ADJ ancestral ➤ **ancestral home** casa f solariega

ancestry [ˈænsɪstrɪ] N ascendencia f, linaje m

anchor [ˈæŋkəʳ] Ⓐ N **1** (Naut) ancla f

Use **el/un** not **la/una** before feminine nouns beginning with stressed **a** or **ha** like **ancla**.

a rusty ~ un ancla oxidada; **to drop ~** echar anclas **2** (US TV, Rad) presentador(a) m/f Ⓑ VT **1** (Naut) anclar **2** (fig) sujetar (**to** a), afianzar (**to** en) Ⓒ VI anclar

anchorman [ˈæŋkəmæn] N (pl **anchormen**) (TV, Rad) presentador m

anchorwoman [ˈæŋkəˌwʊmən] N (pl **anchorwomen**) (TV, Rad) presentadora f

anchovy ['æntʃəvɪ] N (*live, fresh*) boquerón *m*; (*salted, tinned*) anchoa *f*

ancient ['eɪnʃənt] ADJ 1 (= *old, classical*) antiguo; ~ **Greek** griego *m* antiguo; ~ **history** historia *f* antigua 2 (*hum**) [*person*] viejo, anciano; [*clothing, object*] antiquísimo, de los tiempos de Maricastaña*

ancillary [æn'sɪlərɪ] ADJ [*staff, workers*] auxiliar

and [ænd, ənd, nd, ən] CONJ 1 y; (*before i-, hi- but not hie-*) e; **you ~ me** tú y yo; **French ~ English** francés e inglés; **and?** ¿y?, ¿y qué más?; ~ **how!*** ¡y (no veas) cómo!; **and/or** y/o 2 (*with compar adj*) **better ~ better** cada vez mejor; **more ~ more difficult** cada vez más difícil 3 (*in numbers*) **one ~ a half** uno y medio; **a hundred ~ one** ciento uno; **two hundred ~ ten** doscientos diez; **ten dollars ~ 50 cents** diez dólares y *or* con 50 centavos 4 (*negative sense*) ni; **without shoes ~ socks** sin zapatos ni calcetines 5 (*repetition, continuation*) **he talked ~ talked** habló sin parar *or* (*LAm*) cesar; **I rang ~ rang** llamé muchas veces 6 (*before infin*) **try ~ do it** trata de hacerlo; **wait ~ see** espera y verás; **come ~ see me** ven a verme 7 (*implying a distinction*) **there are lawyers ~ lawyers** hay abogados y abogados 8 (*implying a conditional*) **one move ~ you're dead!** ¡como te muevas disparo!, ¡un solo movimiento y disparo!

Andalusia [ændə'luːzɪə] N Andalucía *f*

Andalusian [ændə'luːzɪən] ADJ, N andaluz(a) *m/f*

Andean ['ændɪən] ADJ andino

Andes ['ændiːz] NPL **the ~** los Andes

Andorra [æn'dɔːrə] N Andorra *f*

Andorran [æn'dɔːrən] ADJ, N andorrano/a *m/f*

androgynous [æn'drɒdʒɪnəs] ADJ andrógino

android ['ændrɔɪd] N androide *m*

anecdote ['ænɪkdəʊt] N anécdota *f*

anemia [ə'niːmɪə] N (*US*) = **anaemia**

anemic [ə'niːmɪk] ADJ (*US*) = **anaemic**

anemone [ə'nemənɪ] N anémona *f*

anesthesiologist [ænɪsˌθiːzɪ'ɒlədʒɪst] N (*US*) anestesista *mf*

anesthetic [ænɪs'θetɪk] ADJ, N (*US*) = **anaesthetic**

anesthetist [æ'niːsθɪtɪst] N (*US*) = **anaesthetist**

anesthetize [æ'niːsθɪtaɪz] VT (*US*) = **anaesthetize**

anew [ə'njuː] ADV (*liter*) de nuevo, otra vez; **to begin ~** comenzar de nuevo, volver a empezar

angel ['eɪndʒəl] N 1 (*Rel*) ángel *m* 2 (*) (= *person*) **she's an ~** es un ángel; **be an ~ and give me a cigarette** ¿me das un pitillo, amor?

angelic [æn'dʒelɪk] ADJ angélico

anger ['æŋgəʳ] ❶ N ira *f*; **red with ~** rojo de ira; **words spoken in ~** palabras pronunciadas en un momento de enfado (*Sp*) *or* enojo (*LAm*) ❷ VT enfadar (*Sp*), enojar (*LAm*)

angina [æn'dʒaɪnə] N angina *f* (de pecho)

angle¹ [æŋgl] ❶ N 1 (*Math, Geom, etc*) ángulo *m*; **at an 80 degree ~** con un ángulo de 80 grados; **he wore his hat at an ~** llevaba el sombrero ladeado; **hold the knife at an ~** coge el cuchillo inclinado; **cut the bread at an ~** corte el pan en diagonal; **to be at an ~ to sth** formar ángulo con algo 2 (= *point of view*) punto *m* de vista; **from the parents' ~** desde el punto de vista *or* la perspectiva de los padres 3 (= *focus*) perspectiva *f*, ángulo *m*; **to look at sth from a different ~** enfocar algo desde otra perspectiva *or* desde otro ángulo ❷ VT [+ *object*] orientar; [+ *shot*] sesgar, ladear ❸ CPD ➤ **angle bracket** (= *support*) escuadra *f*; (*Typ*) corchete *m* agudo

angle² [æŋgl] VI 1 (= *fish*) pescar (con caña); **to ~ for trout** pescar truchas 2 (*fig*) **to ~ for sth** (*gen*) andar buscando algo; (*for votes, job*) andar a la caza de algo; **he's just angling for sympathy** sólo anda buscando compasión

Anglepoise® ['æŋglpɔɪz] N (*Brit*) (*also* ~ **lamp**) lámpara *f* de estudio

angler ['æŋgləʳ] N pescador(a) *m/f* (de caña)

Anglican ['æŋglɪkən] ADJ, N anglicano/a *m/f*

anglicism ['æŋglɪsɪzəm] N anglicismo *m*, inglesismo *m*

anglicize ['æŋglɪsaɪz] VT dar forma inglesa a, anglicanizar

angling ['æŋglɪŋ] N pesca *f* con caña

Anglo- ['æŋgləʊ] PREF anglo...; ~**Spanish** angloespañol; **an ~French project** un proyecto anglofrancés

Anglo-Saxon ['æŋgləʊ'sæksən] ❶ ADJ anglosajón ❷ N 1 (= *person*) anglosajón/ona *m/f* 2 (*Ling*) anglosajón *m*

Angola [æŋ'gəʊlə] N Angola *f*

Angolan [æŋ'gəʊlən] ADJ, N angoleño/a *m/f*

angora [æŋ'gɔːrə] ❶ N angora *f* ❷ ADJ de angora

angrily ['æŋgrɪlɪ] ADV [*react, speak*] con ira; **"I tried!" he said ~** —¡lo intenté! —dijo enfadado *or* (*LAm*) enojado

angry ['æŋgrɪ] ADJ (*compar* **angrier**; *superl* **angriest**) 1 (= *cross*) [*person*] enfadado (*Sp*), enojado (*LAm*); [*voice*] de enfado (*Sp*), de enojo (*LAm*); [*letter, reply, scene*] airado; **you won't be ~, will you?** no te vas a enfadar (*Sp*) *or* (*LAm*) enojar ¿verdad?; **to be ~ about** *or* **at sth** estar enfadado (*Sp*) *or* (*LAm*) enojado por algo; **he was very ~ about** *or* **at being dismissed** estaba furioso porque lo habían despedido; **to get ~** enfadarse (*Sp*), enojarse (*LAm*); **she gave me an ~ look** me miró con cara de enfado (*Sp*) *or* enojo (*LAm*); **this sort of thing makes me ~** estas cosas me sacan de quicio* 2 [*wound, rash*] inflamado

angst [æŋst] N angustia *f*

anguish ['æŋgwɪʃ] N angustia *f*

anguished ['æŋgwɪʃt] ADJ angustiado

angular ['æŋgjʊləʳ] ADJ [*shape, lines*] angular; [*face, features*] anguloso

animal ['ænɪməl] ❶ N 1 (= *not plant*) animal *m* 2 (*pej**) (= *person*) animal* *mf*, bestia* *mf*; **you ~!** ¡animal!*, ¡bestia!* ❷ ADJ animal ❸ CPD ➤ **animal fats** grasas *fpl* de animal ➤ **the animal kingdom** el reino animal ➤ **animal liberationist** miembro *mf* del Frente de Liberación de los Animales ➤ **animal rights movement** movimiento *m* pro derechos de los animales

animate ❶ ['ænɪmɪt] ADJ vivo ❷ ['ænɪmeɪt] VT animar, estimular

animated ['ænɪmeɪtɪd] ADJ [*person, discussion*] animado; **to become ~** animarse ➤ **animated cartoon** dibujos *mpl* animados

animation [ænɪ'meɪʃən] N 1 (= *liveliness*) vivacidad *f*, animación *f* 2 (*Cine*) (= *process*) animación *f*; (= *film*) película *f* de animación, dibujos *mpl* animados

animator ['ænɪmeɪtəʳ] N (*Cine*) animador(a) *m/f*

animosity [ænɪ'mɒsɪtɪ] N animosidad *f*, rencor *m*

aniseed ['ænɪsiːd] N (= *flavour*) anís *m*; (= *seed*) grano *m* de anís

Ankara ['æŋkərə] N Ankara *f*

ankle ['æŋkl] N tobillo *m* ➤ **ankle sock** (*Brit*) calcetín *m* tobillero

ankle-deep ['æŋkl'diːp] ADV **to be ~ in water** estar metido hasta los tobillos en el agua; **the water is only ~** el agua llega a los tobillos nada más

annals ['ænəlz] NPL anales *mpl*

annex Ⓐ [ə'neks] VT [+ *territory*] anexar, anexionar (**to** a) Ⓑ ['æneks] N (*US*) = **annexe**

annexation [ænek'seɪʃən] N anexión *f*

annexe ['æneks] N **1** (= *building*) edificio *m* anexo **2** (= *document*) anexo *m*

annihilate [ə'naɪəleɪt] VT aniquilar

annihilation [ə,naɪə'leɪʃən] N aniquilación *f*, aniquilamiento *m*

anniversary [ænɪ'vɜːsərɪ] N aniversario *m*; **wedding ~** aniversario *m* de bodas

Anno Domini ['ænəʊ'dɒmɪnaɪ] N (*frm*) ~ **43** el año 43 después de Jesucristo; **the third century ~** el siglo tercero después de Cristo

annotate ['ænəʊteɪt] VT anotar, comentar

annotation [ænəʊ'teɪʃən] N (= *act*) anotación *f*; (= *instance*) anotación *f*, apunte *m*

announce [ə'naʊns] VT **1** (*gen*) anunciar; **we regret to ~ the death of ...** lamentamos tener que anunciar la muerte de ... **2** (= *declare*) declarar; **he ~d that he wasn't going** declaró que no iba

announcement [ə'naʊnsmənt] N (*gen*) anuncio *m*; (= *declaration*) declaración *f*; **~ of birth** (aviso *m*) natalicio *m*; **~ of death** (nota *f*) necrológica *f*

announcer [ə'naʊnsə[r]] N **1** (*TV, Rad*) locutor(a) *m/f* **2** (*at airport etc*) el or la que hace anuncios

annoy [ə'nɔɪ] VT molestar, fastidiar; **to be ~ed about sth/ with sb** estar enfadado (*Sp*) or molesto por algo/con algn; **to get ~ed** enfadarse (*Sp*), enojarse (*LAm*)

annoyance [ə'nɔɪəns] N **1** (= *displeasure*) irritación *f*; (= *anger*) enfado *m* (*Sp*), enojo *m* (*LAm*); **to my ~ I find that ...** con gran disgusto mío descubro que ... **2** (= *annoying thing*) molestia *f*

annoying [ə'nɔɪɪŋ] ADJ [*habit, noise*] molesto, irritante; [*person*] irritante, pesado; **the ~ thing about it is that ...** lo que más me fastidia del asunto es que ...; **how ~!** ¡qué fastidio!; **it's ~ to have to wait** es un fastidio tener que esperar

annual ['ænjʊəl] Ⓐ ADJ anual Ⓑ N **1** (= *publication*) anuario *m*; (= *children's comic book*) cómic para niños que se publica en forma de libro normalmente por Navidad **2** (*Bot*) planta *f* anual Ⓒ CPD ➤ **annual general meeting** (*Brit*) junta *f* general anual ➤ **annual income** ingresos *mpl* anuales ➤ **annual report** informe *m* anual

annually ['ænjʊəlɪ] ADV anualmente, cada año; **£500 ~** 500 libras al año

annuity [ə'njuːɪtɪ] N renta *f* vitalicia

annul [ə'nʌl] VT anular

annulment [ə'nʌlmənt] N anulación *f*

Annunciation [ə,nʌnsɪ'eɪʃən] N Anunciación *f*

anode ['ænəʊd] N ánodo *m*

anodyne ['ænəʊdaɪn] ADJ anodino

anoint [ə'nɔɪnt] VT **1** (*with oil etc*) ungir (**with** de) **2** (*fig*) (= *nominate*) designar, nombrar

anomalous [ə'nɒmələs] ADJ anómalo

anomaly [ə'nɒməlɪ] N anomalía *f*

anon¹ [ə'nɒn] ADV luego, dentro de poco; **I'll see you ~** nos veremos luego

anon² [ə'nɒn] ABBR = **anonymous**

anonymity [ænə'nɪmɪtɪ] N anonimato *m*; **to preserve one's ~** permanecer en el anonimato

anonymous [ə'nɒnɪməs] ADJ (*gen*) anónimo; [*ballot*] secreto; **he received an ~ letter** recibió un anónimo; **to remain ~** permanecer en el anonimato

anonymously [ə'nɒnɪməslɪ] ADV [*send, give, speak*] anónimamente, de manera anónima; [*live*] en el anonimato; [*publish*] de forma anónima, sin el nombre del autor

anorak ['ænəræk] N (= *coat*) anorak *m*

anorexia [ænə'reksɪə] N anorexia *f* ➤ **anorexia nervosa** anorexia *f* nerviosa

anorexic [ænə'reksɪk] ADJ, N anoréxico/a *m/f*

another [ə'nʌðə[r]] Ⓐ ADJ otro; **would you like ~ beer?** ¿quieres otra cerveza?; **have ~ one** toma or coge otro; **we need ~ two men** necesitamos dos hombres más, necesitamos otros dos hombres; **not ~ minute!** ¡ni un minuto más!; **without ~ word** sin decir ni una palabra más; **I've discovered yet ~ problem** he descubierto otro problema más; **do it ~ time** hazlo en otra ocasión; **that's quite ~ matter** eso es otra cosa totalmente distinta, eso es otro cantar Ⓑ PRON otro/a *m/f*; **in one form or ~** de una forma u otra; **what with one thing and ~** entre una cosa y otra

ANSI ['ænsɪ] N ABBR (*US*) = **American National Standards Institute**

answer ['ɑːnsə[r]] Ⓐ N **1** (= *reply*) respuesta *f*, contestación *f*; **he has an ~ for everything** tiene respuesta or contestación para todo; **I never got an ~ to my question** nunca me respondieron or contestaron (a) la pregunta; **in ~ to your question** en or como respuesta a su pregunta, para responder or contestar (a) su pregunta; **to know all the ~s** (*fig*) tener respuesta para todo, saberlo todo; **there's no ~** (*Telec*) no contestan; **I knocked but there was no ~** llamé a la puerta pero no hubo respuesta or no abrieron; **there's no ~ to that** no existe una respuesta para eso; **it was the ~ to my prayers** fue la solución a todos mis problemas **2** (= *solution*) solución *f*; **we have the ~ to your problem** tenemos la solución a su problema **3** (= *equivalent*) **Belgium's ~ to Sylvester Stallone** el Sylvester Stallone belga **4** (*in exam, quiz*) **4.1** (= *correct response*) (*to question*) respuesta *f*; (*to problem*) solución *f* **4.2** (= *individual response*) respuesta *f*
Ⓑ VT [+ *person*] contestar a, responder a; [+ *question*] contestar (a), responder (a); [+ *letter*] contestar (a); **to ~ your question, I did see him** contestando or respondiendo a tu pregunta, (te diré que) sí lo vi; **two men ~ing the description of the suspects** dos hombres que respondían a la descripción de los sospechosos; **to ~ the door** (ir a) abrir la puerta, atender la puerta (*LAm*); **our prayers have been ~ed** nuestras súplicas han sido escuchadas; **to ~ the telephone** contestar al teléfono
Ⓒ VI contestar, responder; **the doorbell rang but I didn't ~** sonó el timbre pero no abrí
Ⓓ CPD ➤ **answer paper** hoja *f* de respuestas
➤ **answer back** VI + ADV **1** (= *be cheeky*) (*on one occasion*) replicar, contestar; (*habitually*) ser respondón/ona; **don't ~ back!** ¡no repliques! **2** (= *defend o.s.*) defenderse (*contra las críticas*)
➤ **answer for** VI + PREP **1** (= *take responsibility for*) [+ *actions, consequences*] responder de; **he's got a lot to ~ for** tiene la culpa de muchas cosas **2** (= *reply for*) responder por
➤ **answer to** VI + PREP **1** (= *be accountable to*) **to ~ to sb** responder ante algn; **I ~ to nobody** no tengo que dar cuentas a nadie **2** (= *be called*) **the dog ~s to the name of Kim** el perro atiende por Kim **3** (= *fit*) [+ *description*] responder a

answerable ['ɑːnsərəbl] ADJ (= *accountable*) responsable (**to sb/for sth** ante algn/de algo); **he's not ~ to anyone** no tiene que dar cuentas a nadie

answering ['ɑːnsərɪŋ] CPD ➤ **answering machine** contestador *m* (automático) ➤ **answering service** (*live*) servicio *m* telefónico de contestación; (*with answerphone*) servicio *m* de contestador automático

answerphone ['ɑːnsəfəʊn] N (*esp Brit*) contestador *m* (automático)

ant [ænt] N hormiga *f*

antacid [ænt'æsɪd] N antiácido *m*

antagonism [æn'tægənɪzəm] N (*towards sb*) hostilidad *f*; (*between people*) rivalidad *f*, antagonismo *m*

antagonist [æn'tægənɪst] N antagonista *mf*, adversario/a *m/f*

antagonistic [æn,tægə'nɪstɪk] ADJ hostil, antagonista

antagonize [æn'tægənaɪz] VT **I don't want to ~ him** no quiero contrariarlo; **he managed to ~ everybody** logró ponerse a malas con todos, logró suscitar el antagonismo de todos

Antarctic [ænt'ɑːktɪk] **Ⓐ** ADJ antártico **Ⓑ** N **the ~ (Ocean)** el (Océano) Antártico

Antarctica [ænt'ɑːktɪkə] N Antártida *f*

ante ['æntɪ] N ✦ IDIOM **to up the ~*** elevar las demandas

anteater ['ænt,iːtəʳ] N oso *m* hormiguero

antecedent [,æntɪ'siːdənt] N antecedente *m*

antedate ['æntɪdeɪt] VT (= *precede*) preceder, ser anterior a

antelope ['æntɪləʊp] N antílope *m*

antenatal ['æntɪ'neɪtl] ADJ prenatal; **~ exercises** ejercicios *mpl* para mujeres embarazadas ➤ **antenatal clinic** clínica *f* prenatal

antenna [æn'tenə] N **1** (*Rad, TV*) antena *f* **2** (*pl* **~e** [æn'teniː]) (*of animal*) antena *f*

anterior [æn'tɪərɪəʳ] ADJ anterior (**to** a)

anteroom ['æntɪrʊm] N antesala *f*

anthem ['ænθəm] N himno *m*

anthill ['ænthɪl] N hormiguero *m*

anthology [æn'θɒlədʒɪ] N antología *f*

anthracite ['ænθrəsaɪt] N antracita *f*

anthrax ['ænθræks] N ántrax *m*

anthropologist [ænθrə'pɒlədʒɪst] N antropólogo/a *m/f*

anthropology [ænθrə'pɒlədʒɪ] N antropología *f*

anti-abortionist [æntɪə'bɔːʃənɪst] N antiabortista *mf*

anti-aircraft ['æntɪ'eəkrɑːft] ADJ antiaéreo

anti-ballistic ['æntɪbə'lɪstɪk] ADJ antibalístico

antibiotic ['æntɪbaɪ'ɒtɪk] **Ⓐ** N antibiótico *m* **Ⓑ** ADJ antibiótico

antibody ['æntɪ,bɒdɪ] N anticuerpo *m*

Antichrist ['æntɪkraɪst] N Anticristo *m*

anticipate [æn'tɪsɪpeɪt] VT **1** (= *expect*) [+ *trouble, pleasure*] esperar, contar con; **this is worse than I ~d** esto es peor de lo que esperaba; **as ~d** según se esperaba, como esperábamos **2** (= *foresee*) [+ *event, profit*] prever; [+ *question, objection, wishes*] anticipar **3** (= *forestall*) [+ *person*] anticiparse a, adelantarse a; [+ *event*] anticiparse a, prevenir

anticipation [æn,tɪsɪ'peɪʃən] N **1** (= *expectation*) expectativa *f*; **in ~** (= *ahead of time*) de antemano; **in ~ of a fine week** esperando una semana de buen tiempo; **I bought it in ~ of her visit** lo compré en previsión de su visita; **thanking you in ~** en espera de sus noticias; **we waited in great ~** esperábamos con gran ilusión **2** (= *foresight*) previsión *f*, anticipación *f*

anticlimax ['æntɪ'klaɪmæks] N (= *disappointment*) decepción *f*; **what an ~!** ¡qué decepción!

anticlockwise ['æntɪ'klɒkwaɪz] (*Brit*) ADJ, ADV en sentido contrario al de las agujas del reloj

antics ['æntɪks] NPL (*of clown*) payasadas *fpl*; (*of child, animal*) gracias *fpl*; (= *pranks*) travesuras *fpl*; **he's up to his old ~ again** ya está haciendo de las suyas otra vez

anticyclone ['æntɪ'saɪkləʊn] N anticiclón *m*

anti-dandruff [æntɪ'dændrəf] ADJ anticaspa *inv*

antidepressant [æntɪdɪ'presnt] **Ⓐ** ADJ antidepresivo **Ⓑ** N antidepresivo *m*

antidote ['æntɪdəʊt] N (*Med*) antídoto *m* (**for, to** contra); (*fig*) remedio *m* (**for, to** contra, para)

anti-Establishment ['æntɪɪs'tæblɪʃmənt] ADJ en contra del sistema

antifreeze ['æntɪ'friːz] N anticongelante *m*

anti-globalization ['æntɪ,gləʊbəlaɪ'zeɪʃən] N antiglobalización *f*; **~ protesters** manifestantes *mfpl* antiglobalización

anti-hero ['æntɪ,hɪərəʊ] N (*pl* **antiheroes**) antihéroe *m*

antihistamine [æntɪ'hɪstəmɪn] N antihistamínico *m*

anti-inflationary [æntɪɪn'fleɪʃnərɪ] ADJ antiinflacionista

antimatter ['æntɪ,mætəʳ] N antimateria *f*

antinuclear ['æntɪ'njuːklɪəʳ] ADJ antinuclear

antipathy [æn'tɪpəθɪ] N antipatía *f* (**between** entre; **towards, to** hacia)

anti-perspirant [æntɪ'pɜːspərənt] **Ⓐ** ADJ antitranspirante **Ⓑ** N antitranspirante *m*

Antipodean, antipodean [æn,tɪpə'diːən] **Ⓐ** ADJ de las antípodas; (*Brit hum*) (= *Australian*) australiano **Ⓑ** N habitante *mf* de las antípodas; (*Brit hum*) (= *Australian*) australiano/a *m/f*

Antipodes [æn'tɪpədiːz] NPL (*Brit*): **the ~** Australia *f* (y Nueva Zelanda *f*)

antiquarian [,æntɪ'kweərɪən] ADJ anticuario ➤ **antiquarian bookseller** librero/a *m/f* de viejo ➤ **antiquarian bookshop** librería *f* de viejo

antiquated ['æntɪkweɪtɪd] ADJ (*pej*) anticuado

antique [æn'tiːk] **Ⓐ** ADJ **1** [*furniture, vase*] de época; [*bracelet*] antiguo **2** (*pej*) anticuado **Ⓑ** N antigüedad *f* **Ⓒ** CPD ➤ **antique dealer** anticuario/a *m/f* ➤ **antique shop** (*esp Brit*), **antique store** (*US*) tienda *f* de antigüedades

antiquity [æn'tɪkwɪtɪ] N **1** (= *ancient times*) antigüedad *f*; **of great ~** muy antiguo; **in ~** en la antigüedad, en el mundo antiguo **2 antiquities** antigüedades *fpl*

anti-rust ['æntɪ'rʌst] ADJ antioxidante

anti-semitic ['æntɪsɪ'mɪtɪk] ADJ antisemita

anti-semitism ['æntɪ'semɪtɪzəm] N antisemitismo *m*

antiseptic [,æntɪ'septɪk] **Ⓐ** ADJ antiséptico **Ⓑ** N antiséptico *m*

antisocial ['æntɪ'səʊʃəl] ADJ (= *offensive*) antisocial; (= *unsociable*) insociable

antistatic ['æntɪ'stætɪk] ADJ antiestático

anti-terrorist ['æntɪ'terərɪst] ADJ antiterrorista

anti-theft device [,æntɪ'θeftdɪ,vaɪs] N sistema *m* antirrobo, mecanismo *m* antirrobo

antithesis [æn'tɪθɪsɪs] N (*pl* **antitheses** [æn'tɪθɪsiːz]) antítesis *f inv*

anti-trust ['æntɪ'trʌst] ADJ (*US*) antimonopolista

antlers ['æntləz] NPL cornamenta *fsing*

antonym ['æntənɪm] N antónimo *m*

Antwerp ['æntwɜːp] N Amberes *m*

anus ['eɪnəs] N ano *m*

anvil ['ænvɪl] N yunque *m*

anxiety [æŋ'zaɪətɪ] N **1** (= *concern*) preocupación *f*, inquietud *f*; **he expressed his anxieties about the future** expresó su preocupación *or* inquietud por el futuro; **it is a great ~ to me** me preocupa mucho **2** (= *keenness*) ansia *f* (**to do sth** de hacer algo);

> Use **el/un** not **la/una** before feminine nouns beginning with stressed **a** or **ha** like **ansia**.

in his ~ to leave, he forgot his case estaba tan ansioso por irse que olvidó su maleta **3** (*Med, Psych*) ansiedad *f*, angustia *f*

anxious ['æŋkʃəs] ADJ **1** (= *worried*) [*person*] preocupado, inquieto; [*expression*] de preocupación, de inquietud; [*face, eyes*] angustiado; **to be ~ about sth** estar preocupado por algo; **he was ~ about starting his new job** le preocupaba empezar en el nuevo trabajo

2 (= *worrying*) [*situation, wait*] angustioso; [*hours, days*] lleno de ansiedad, angustioso

3 (= *keen*) **he's ~ that nothing should go wrong** no quiere que exista el más mínimo riesgo de que algo salga mal, no quiere de ninguna manera que nada vaya mal; **she is ~ to see you before you go** tiene muchas ganas de verte antes de que te vayas; **he is ~ for results** está deseoso de *or* ansioso por ver resultados; **he was ~ for her to leave** estaba impaciente por que ella se marchara, tenía muchas ganas de que ella se marchara

4 (*Med, Psych*) [*feeling*] de angustia; [*person*] que padece de ansiedad; **to be ~** tener ansiedad

anxiously ['æŋkʃəslɪ] ADV **1** (= *worriedly*) [*look, wait*] con preocupación, con inquietud; **"am I boring you?" she said, ~** —¿te aburro? —dijo con ansiedad

2 (= *keenly, eagerly*) ansiosamente, con ansiedad

---

any

ⓐ ADJECTIVE   **ⓒ** ADVERB
ⓑ PRONOUN

---

any ['enɪ] **ⓐ** ADJECTIVE
1 (*in questions*)

> When **any** modifies an uncountable noun in questions it is usually not translated:

have you got ~ money? ¿tienes dinero?; **is there ~ sugar?** ¿hay azúcar?

> When **any** modifies a plural noun in questions it is often not translated. However, if a low number is expected in response, **algún/alguna** + singular noun is used:

are there ~ tickets left? ¿quedan entradas?; **do you speak ~ foreign languages?** ¿hablas algún idioma extranjero?; **do you have ~ questions?** ¿alguna pregunta?
2 (*with negative, implied negative*)

> When **any** modifies an uncountable noun it is usually not translated:

I haven't got ~ money no tengo dinero; **I have hardly ~ money left** casi no me queda dinero

> When the translation is countable, **ningún/ninguna** + singular noun can be used:

you haven't got ~ excuse no tienes ninguna excusa; **we got him home without ~ problem** lo llevamos a casa sin ningún problema

> When **any** modifies a plural noun, it is either left untranslated or, for greater emphasis, translated using **ningún/ninguna** + singular noun:

he hasn't got ~ friends no tiene amigos; **I can't see ~ cows** no veo ninguna vaca
3 (*in conditional constructions*)

> **Any** +plural noun is often translated using **algún/alguna** + a singular noun:

if there are ~ tickets left si queda alguna entrada; *BUT* **if he had ~ decency he would apologize** si tuviera un poco de decencia, se disculparía
4 (= *no matter which*) cualquier; **~ teacher will tell you** te lo dirá cualquier profesor; **wear ~ hat (you like)** ponte el sombrero que quieras; **he's not just ~ violinist** no es un violinista cualquiera; **bring me ~ old book** tráeme un libro cualquiera; **take ~ one you like** tome cualquiera, tome el que quiera; **it's much like ~ other seaside resort** es muy parecido a cualquier otro sitio costero; **come at ~ time** ven cuando quieras; **~ person who breaks the rules will be punished** se castigará a toda persona que no acate las reglas
5 (*in set expressions*)
✦ **any amount of: they'll spend ~ amount of money to get it** se gastarán lo que haga falta para conseguirlo
✦ **any number of: there must be ~ number of people in my position** debe de haber gran cantidad de personas en mi situación; **I've told you ~ number of times** te lo he dicho montones de veces
ⓑ PRONOUN

1 (*in questions*)

> When **any** refers to an uncountable noun in questions it is usually not translated:

I fancy some soup, have we got ~? me apetece sopa, ¿tenemos?

> When **any** refers to a plural noun in questions it is often translated using **alguno/alguna** in the singular:

I need a stamp, have you got ~? necesito un sello, ¿tienes alguno?; **do ~ of you know the answer?** ¿sabe alguno (de ustedes) la respuesta?
2 (*with negative, implied negative*)

> When **any** refers to an uncountable noun it is usually not translated:

"can I have some cake?" — **"we haven't (got) ~"** —¿me das un poco de pastel? —no tenemos

> When **any** refers to a plural noun, it is either left untranslated or, for greater emphasis, translated using **ningún/ninguna** in the singular:

"did you buy the oranges?" — **"no, there weren't ~"** ¿compraste (las) naranjas? —no, no había *or* no tenían; **she has two brothers but I haven't got ~** tiene dos hermanos pero yo no tengo ninguno; **I don't believe ~ of them has done it** no creo que lo haya hecho ninguno de ellos; *BUT* **he hasn't done ~ of his homework** no ha hecho nada de deberes
3 (*in conditional constructions*) **if ~ of you knows how to drive** si alguno de vosotros sabe conducir; **few, if ~, survived** pocos, si alguno, sobrevivió
4 (= *no matter which*) cualquiera; **~ of those books will do** cualquiera de esos libros servirá
ⓒ ADVERB
1 (*in questions*) **would you like ~ more soup?** ¿quieres más sopa?; **is he ~ better?** ¿está (algo) mejor?
2 (*with negative*) **don't wait ~ longer** no esperes más (tiempo); **I don't love him ~ more** ya no le quiero; **I couldn't do that ~ more than I could fly** yo puedo hacer eso tanto como volar
3 (*esp US**) (= *at all*) **it doesn't help us ~** eso no nos ayuda para nada
anybody ['enɪbɒdɪ] PRON **1** (*in questions, conditional constructions*) alguien; **is there ~ else I can talk to?** ¿hay alguien más con quien pueda hablar?; **if ~ calls, I'm not in** si llama alguien, no estoy; **if ~ can do it, he can** si alguien lo puede hacer, es él
2 (*with negative, implied negative*) nadie; **I can't see ~** no veo a nadie; **she doesn't like ~ contradicting her** no le gusta que nadie la contradiga; **I didn't ask ~ else** no se lo pregunté a nadie más; **there was hardly ~ there** casi no había nadie
3 (= *no matter who*) cualquiera; **~ will tell you the same** cualquiera te diría lo mismo, todos te dirán lo mismo; **it's ~'s race** esta carrera la podría ganar cualquiera; **it would have defeated ~ but Jane** habría desanimado a cualquiera *or* a todos menos a Jane; **~ else would have laughed** cualquier otro se hubiera reído; **that's ~'s guess!** ¡quién sabe!; **I'm not going to marry just ~** yo no me caso con cualquiera; **bring ~ you like** trae a quien quieras; **~ who** *or* **that wants to go back should go now** si alguno quiere volver, que lo haga ahora; **~ who invests in this** todo el que invierta en esto; **~ with any sense would know that!** ¡cualquiera con (algo de) sentido común sabría eso!
4 (= *person of importance*) alguien; **she knows everybody who's ~** conoce a toda la gente importante
anyhow ['enɪhaʊ] ADV **1** = **anyway 2** (*) (= *carelessly, haphazardly*) de cualquier modo, de cualquier manera
anyone ['enɪwʌn] PRON = **anybody**
anyplace* ['enɪpleɪs] PRON (*US*) = **anywhere**

anything ['enɪθɪŋ] PRON **1** (*in questions, conditional constructions*) algo, alguna cosa; **would you like ~ to eat?** ¿quieres algo *or* alguna cosa de comer?; **are you doing ~ tonight?** ¿haces algo *or* alguna cosa esta noche?, ¿tienes algún plan para esta noche?; **is there ~ more boring than ...?** ¿puede haber algo más aburrido que ...?; **did you see ~ interesting?** ¿viste algo de interés?; **if ~ should happen to me** si algo me ocurriera; **think before you say ~** piensa antes de decir nada; **~ else?** (*in shop etc*) ¿algo más?, ¿alguna cosa más?; **if ~ it's much better** es mucho mejor si cabe; **if ~ it's larger** si acaso, es algo más grande **2** (*with negative, implied negative*) nada; **I can't see ~** no veo nada; **can't ~ be done?** ¿no se puede hacer nada?; **I didn't see ~ interesting** no vi nada de interés; **we can't do ~ else** no podemos hacer otra cosa, no podemos hacer nada más; **hardly ~** casi nada; **I don't think there's ~ more annoying than ...** no creo que haya nada más irritante que ...; ✦ IDIOM **not for ~ in the world** por nada del mundo **3** (*no matter what*) cualquier cosa; **~ could happen** puede pasar cualquier cosa; **they'll eat ~** comen de todo, comen cualquier cosa (*pej*); **he will give you ~ (that) you ask for** te dará lo que pidas; **~ but that** todo menos eso; **"~ but!"** —¡nada de eso!; **it was ~ but pleasant** fue cualquier cosa menos agradable, era de todo menos agradable; **their friendship was more important than ~ else** su amistad era más importante que todo lo demás; **she wanted more than ~ else to be an actress** ella quería ser actriz por encima de todo; **he did it more out of pity than ~ else** más que nada lo hizo por compasión; **I'm not buying just ~** yo no compro cualquier cosa; **sing ~ you like** canta lo que quieras, canta cualquier cosa **4** (*in guesses, estimates*) **he must have ~ between 15 and 20 apple trees** debe de tener entre 15 y 20 manzanos; **it could take ~ up to three months** podría llevar hasta tres meses **5** (*in set expressions*) **as much as ~: I'm in it for the publicity as much as ~** más que nada estoy en esto por la publicidad; **he ran like ~*** corrió hasta más no poder, corrió como loco*; **did she say who she was or ~?** ¿dijo quién era ella o algo por el estilo?; **he's not a minister or ~** no es ministro ni nada por el estilo

anyway ['enɪweɪ], **anyways*** (*US*) ['enɪweɪz] ADV **1** (= *in any event, regardless*) de todas formas, de todos modos; **~, you're here** de todas formas *or* de todos modos, estás aquí; **who needs men ~?** de todas formas *or* de todos modos, ¿quién necesita a los hombres?; **I shall go ~** iré de todas formas *or* de todos modos **2** (= *at least*) al menos; **it's not a good idea, I don't think so ~** no es buena idea, al menos eso es lo que yo pienso **3** (= *incidentally*) por cierto; **why are you going ~?** por cierto ¿por qué te vas? **4** (*continuing what has been said*) en fin; **~, as I was saying ...** en fin, como decía antes ...

anywhere ['enɪweə*] ❹ ADV **1** (*in questions*) (*location*) en alguna parte, en algún lugar *or* sitio; (*direction*) a alguna parte, a algún lugar *or* sitio; **have you seen my coat ~?** ¿has visto mi abrigo en *or* por alguna parte?, ¿has visto mi abrigo por algún sitio?; **did you visit ~ else?** ¿visitasteis algún otro sitio? **2** (*with negatives, implied negatives*) (*location*) por *or* en ninguna parte, por *or* en ningún sitio; (*direction*) a ninguna parte, a ningún sitio; **I can't find it ~** no lo encuentro por *or* en ninguna parte, no lo encuentro por *or* en ningún sitio; **I'm not going ~** no voy a ninguna parte, no voy a ningún sitio; **we didn't go ~ special** no fuimos a ningún sitio especial; **it's not available ~ else** no lo tienen en ningún otro sitio, no lo tienen en ninguna otra parte; **it isn't ~ near Castroforte** está bastante lejos de Castroforte; **the house isn't ~ near big enough*** la casa no es ni por asomo lo bastante grande; **it isn't ~ near enough*** (*sum of money*) con eso no hay suficiente ni mucho menos; ✦ IDIOM **that won't get you ~*** así no conseguirás nada, así no vas a ninguna parte **3** (*in affirmative sentences*) en cualquier parte; **put the books down ~** pon los libros en cualquier parte *or* donde sea; **~ you go you'll see the same** dondequiera que vayas verás lo mismo, verás lo mismo en cualquier parte a donde vayas; **sit ~ you like** siéntate donde quieras; **she could have been ~ between 30 and 50 years old** podría

haber tenido desde 30 hasta 50 años; **~ between 200 and 300** entre 200 y 300; **~ in the world** en cualquier parte del mundo **⑬** PRON **we haven't found ~ else to live** no hemos encontrado ningún otro sitio para vivir; **it's miles from ~** está completamente aislado; **a flight to ~ in the world** un vuelo a cualquier parte del mundo

AOB ABBR (= **any other business**) ruegos *mpl* y preguntas

aorta [eɪ'ɔ:tə] N aorta *f*

apace [ə'peɪs] ADV aprisa, rápidamente

apart [ə'pɑ:t]

> When **apart** is an element in a phrasal verb, eg **fall apart**, **tear apart**, look up the verb.

ADV **1** (= *separated*) **it was the first time we had been ~** era la primera vez que estábamos separados; **with one's feet ~** con los pies separados; **the two towns are 15km ~** los dos pueblos están a 15km (de distancia) el uno del otro; **their birthdays are two days ~** sus cumpleaños se separan por dos días; **to keep ~** separar, mantener aislado (**from** de); **they have been living ~ for six months** viven separados desde hace seis meses; **the house stands somewhat ~** la casa está algo aislada; **he stood ~ from the others** se mantuvo apartado de los otros; **I can't tell them ~** no puedo distinguir el uno del otro **2** (= *in pieces*) **to come** *or* **fall ~** romperse, deshacerse; **to take sth ~** desmontar algo **3** (= *aside*) **joking ~ ...** en serio ...; **these problems ~ ...** aparte de estos problemas ..., estos problemas aparte ... **4** **~ from 4.1** (= *excluding*) aparte de; **~ from the fact that ...** aparte del hecho de que ... **4.2** (= *except for*) **he ate everything ~ from the meat** comió todo menos *or* excepto la carne; **they all voted against ~ from John** todos votaron en contra menos John *or* aparte de John

apartheid [ə'pɑ:teɪt] N apartheid *m*

apartment [ə'pɑ:tmənt] N (*esp US*) piso *m*, departamento *m* (*LAm*) ➤ **apartment building** (*US*), **apartment house** (*US*) edificio *m* de apartamentos

apathetic [ˌæpə'θetɪk] ADJ apático

apathy ['æpəθɪ] N apatía *f*, indiferencia *f*

APB N ABBR (*US*) (= **all points bulletin**) *frase usada por la policía por* "*descubrir y aprehender*"

ape [eɪp] ❹ N mono *m*, simio *m*, antropoide *mf* ⑬ VT imitar, remedar

aperitif [əˌperɪ'ti:f] N aperitivo *m*

aperture ['æpətʃə*] N **1** (= *crack*) rendija *f*, resquicio *m* **2** (*Phot*) abertura *f*

APEX ['eɪpeks] N ABBR = **Advance Purchase Excursion** [*ticket, fare*] APEX

apex ['eɪpeks] N **1** (*Math*) vértice *m* **2** (*fig*) cumbre *f*, cima *f*

aphid ['eɪfɪd] N áfido *m*

aphorism ['æfərɪzəm] N aforismo *m*

aphrodisiac [ˌæfrə'dɪzɪæk] ❹ ADJ afrodisíaco ⑬ N afrodisíaco *m*

apiece [ə'pi:s] ADV cada uno/a

aplenty [ə'plentɪ] ADV (*liter*) **there was food ~** había comida abundante, había abundancia de comida

aplomb [ə'plɒm] N aplomo *m*

Apocalypse [ə'pɒkəlɪps] N Apocalipsis *m*

apocalyptic [əˌpɒkə'lɪptɪk] ADJ apocalíptico

apocryphal [ə'pɒkrɪfəl] ADJ apócrifo

apolitical [ˌeɪpə'lɪtɪkəl] ADJ apolítico

apologetic [əˌpɒlə'dʒetɪk] ADJ [*look, smile, letter*] de disculpa; **he was very ~** se deshizo en disculpas; **to be ~ about sth** disculparse por algo

apologetically [əˌpɒlə'dʒetɪkəlɪ] ADV **he smiled ~** sonrió como pidiendo disculpas; **"it's my fault," he said ~** —es culpa mía —dijo en tono de disculpa

apologize [ə'pɒlədʒaɪz] VI disculparse, pedir perdón; (*for absence etc*) presentar las excusas; **to ~ to sb (for sth)**

disculparse con algn (por algo)

apology [ə'pɒlədʒɪ] N **1** (= *expression of regret*) disculpa *f*; **letter of** ~ carta *f* de disculpa; **to make an** ~ disculparse, presentar sus excusas (**for** por); **I make no** ~ **for being blunt** no tengo ningún reparo en serle franco; **please accept my apologies** le ruego me disculpe **2** (*pej*) **this** ~ **for a system** esta farsa del sistema

⚠ **apology ≠ *apología***

apoplectic [ˌæpə'plektɪk] ADJ **1** (*Med*) apoplético **2** (*) (= *angry*) furioso; **to get** ~ enfurecerse

apoplexy ['æpəpleksɪ] N **1** (*Med*) apoplejía *f* **2** (= *anger*) cólera *f*, ira *f*

apostle [ə'pɒsl] N apóstol *m*

apostolic [ˌæpəs'tɒlɪk] ADJ apostólico

apostrophe [ə'pɒstrəfɪ] N apóstrofo *m*

apotheosis [əˌpɒθɪ'əʊsɪs] N (*pl* **apotheoses** [əˌpɒθɪ'əʊsiːz]) apoteosis *f*

appal, appall (*US*) [ə'pɔːl] VT horrorizar; **everyone was** ~**led** se horrorizaron todos; **I was** ~**led by the news** me horrorizó la noticia

appalling [ə'pɔːlɪŋ] ADJ [*sight, behaviour, weather, mistake, smell*] espantoso; [*suffering, crime, conditions*] atroz, espantoso; **he has** ~ **taste in clothes** tiene un gusto pésimo para la ropa

appallingly [ə'pɔːlɪŋlɪ] ADV **1** (= *badly*) [*sing, play*] pésimamente; [*treat*] espantosamente mal, terriblemente mal; [*suffer*] horriblemente, terriblemente; **he had behaved** ~ se había portado fatal *or* terriblemente mal **2** (= *extremely*) [*difficult, selfish, ignorant*] terriblemente; **the film was** ~ **bad** la película era pésima

apparatus [ˌæpə'reɪtəs] (*pl* ~, ~**es**) N **1** (*Anat, Mech*) aparato *m*; (= *set of instruments*) equipo *m*; **the** ~ (*Gymnastics*) los aparatos **2** (= *system*) sistema *m*, aparato *m*

apparel [ə'pærəl] N (*Brit†*) (= *attire*) atuendo *m*; (*US*) (= *clothing*) ropa *f*

apparent [ə'pærənt] ADJ **1** (= *clear*) claro; **it is** ~ **that ...** está claro que ...; **it was** ~ **to me that there were problems** veía claro *or* me resultaba obvio que había problemas; **for no** ~ **reason** sin motivo aparente **2** (= *seeming*) [*success, contradiction, interest*] aparente

apparently [ə'pærəntlɪ] ADV **1** (= *it appears*) por lo visto, según parece; **apparently not** por lo visto no, parece que no **2** (= *seemingly, on the surface*) aparentemente; **an** ~ **harmless question** una pregunta aparentemente inocente

apparition [ˌæpə'rɪʃən] N aparición *f*

appeal [ə'piːl] Ⓐ N **1** (= *call*) llamamiento *m*, llamado *m* (*LAm*); (= *request*) petición *f*, solicitud *f*; (= *entreaty*) súplica *f*; **he made an** ~ **for calm** hizo un llamamiento a la calma; **our** ~ **for volunteers** la petición *or* solicitud que hicimos de voluntarios; **an** ~ **on behalf of a charity** una petición de ayuda para una organización benéfica; **they launched a £5 million** ~ **for cancer research** realizaron una campaña para la recaudación de 5 millones de libras para la lucha contra el cáncer
2 (*Jur*) apelación *f*, recurso *m* (de apelación)
3 (= *attraction*) atractivo *m*, encanto *m*; **the idea held little** ~ la idea no le resultaba muy atrayente
Ⓑ VI **1 to** ~ **for** (= *call publicly for*) [+ *peace, tolerance, unity, calm*] hacer un llamamiento a; (= *request*) solicitar, pedir; **the police have** ~**ed to the public for information** la policía ha hecho un llamamiento al público pidiendo información; **to** ~ **for funds** solicitar *or* pedir fondos; **he** ~**ed for silence** rogó silencio
2 (= *call upon*) **to** ~ **to sb's finer feelings/sb's generosity** apelar a los sentimientos nobles/la generosidad de algn
3 (*Jur*) apelar; **to** ~ **against** [+ *sentence, ruling*] apelar contra *or* de, recurrir (contra); **they have** ~**ed to the Supreme Court to stop her extradition** han apelado *or* recurrido al Tribunal Supremo para detener su proceso de extradición
4 (= *be attractive*) **to** ~ **to sb** [*idea, activity*] atraer a algn, resultar atrayente a algn
Ⓒ VT (*US Jur*) **to** ~ **a decision/verdict** apelar contra *or* de una

decisión/un veredicto, recurrir (contra) una decisión/un veredicto
Ⓓ CPD ➤ **appeal court** tribunal *m* de apelación

appealing [ə'piːlɪŋ] ADJ [*idea*] atractivo, atrayente; **the book is especially** ~ **to the younger reader** el libro es de especial interés para el lector joven

appear [ə'pɪəʳ] VI **1** (= *arrive, become visible*) [*person, graffiti, spot, crack, symptom*] aparecer; [*ghost*] aparecerse; **he** ~**ed from nowhere** salió *or* apareció de la nada; **where did you** ~ **from?** ¿de dónde has salido?; **to** ~ **in public** aparecer en público; **to** ~ **to sb** (*as vision*) aparecerse a algn
2 (*Theat, TV*) salir; **she** ~**ed in "Fuenteovejuna"** hizo *or* tenía un papel *or* salió en "Fuenteovejuna"; **to** ~ **on television** salir en *or* por televisión
3 (*Jur*) **3.1** [*defendant*] comparecer; **to** ~ **before sb** comparecer ante algn; **to** ~ **in court** comparecer ante el tribunal *or* los tribunales **3.2** [*lawyer*] **to** ~ **for** *or* **on behalf of sb** representar a algn
4 (= *be published*) salir, publicarse
5 (= *seem*) parecer; **he** ~**s tired** parece cansado; **there** ~**s to be a mistake** parece que hay un error; **it** ~**s not** ✧ **it would** ~ **not** parece que no; **she** ~**ed not to notice** no pareció darse cuenta; **"so it would** ~**"** —eso parece; **she got the job, or so it would** ~ le dieron el trabajo, según parece

appearance [ə'pɪərəns] N **1** (= *act of showing o.s.*) aparición *f*; **to make an** ~ aparecer, dejarse ver; **to make a personal** ~ aparecer en persona
2 (*Theat, TV*) aparición *f*; **to make one's first** ~ hacer su primera aparición, debutar; **his** ~ **in "Don Mendo"** su actuación en "Don Mendo"; **cast in order of** ~ personajes *mpl* en orden de aparición en escena
3 (*Jur*) comparecencia *f*
4 [*of book etc*] publicación *f*
5 (= *look*) aspecto *m*; **she takes great care over her** ~ cuida mucho su aspecto; **he had the** ~ **of an executive** parecía ejecutivo, tenía aspecto de ejecutivo; **in** ~ de aspecto
6 appearances apariencias *fpl*; ~**s can be deceptive** las apariencias engañan; **to all** ~**s** al parecer; **to judge by** ~**s, ...** a juzgar por las apariencias, ...; **to keep up** ~**s** guardar las apariencias; **for** ~**s' sake** para guardar las apariencias

appease [ə'piːz] VT [+ *person*] apaciguar; [+ *hunger*] saciar

appeasement [ə'piːzmənt] N apaciguamiento *m*; (*Pol*) contemporización *f*, entreguismo *m*

appellate court [ə'pelɪtkɔːt] N (*US*) tribunal *m* de apelación

append [ə'pend] (*frm*) VT **1** (= *add*) [+ *signature*] añadir; [+ *note*] agregar, añadir **2** (= *attach*) adjuntar **3** (*Comput*) anexionar (al final)

appendage [ə'pendɪdʒ] N apéndice *m*

appendicitis [əˌpendɪ'saɪtɪs] N apendicitis *f inv*; **to have** ~ tener apendicitis

appendix [ə'pendɪks] N (*pl* ~**es**, **appendices** [ə'pendɪsiːz]) apéndice *m*

appetite ['æpɪtaɪt] N **1** (*for food*) apetito *m*; **to have a good** ~ tener buen apetito; **to have no** ~ no tener apetito **2** (*fig*) deseo *m*, anhelo *m* (**for** de); **they had no** ~ **for further fighting** ya no les apetecía seguir luchando, no tenían más ganas de luchar

appetizer ['æpɪtaɪzəʳ] N (= *drink*) aperitivo *m*; (= *food*) aperitivo *m*, tapas *fpl* (*Sp*), botanas *fpl* (*Mex*), bocaditos *mpl* (*Per*); (*US*) (= *first course*) entrada *f*

appetizing ['æpɪtaɪzɪŋ] ADJ apetitoso

applaud [ə'plɔːd] VT, VI aplaudir

applause [ə'plɔːz] N aplausos *mpl*; **a round of** ~ **for Peter!** ¡un aplauso para Peter!

apple ['æpl] N (= *fruit*) manzana *f*; (= *tree*) manzano *m*; ✦ IDIOMS **the Big Apple** (*US**) la Gran Manzana, Nueva York *f*; **the** ~ **of sb's eye** la niña de los ojos de algn ➤ **apple core** corazón *m* de manzana ➤ **apple pie** pastel *m* de manzana, pay *m* de manzana (*LAm*) ➤ **apple sauce** compota *f* de manzana ➤ **apple tree** manzano *m*

applecart ['æplkɑːt] N ✦ IDIOM **to upset the** ~ echarlo todo a rodar, desbaratar los planes

applet ['æplɪt] N (*Comput*) applet *m*

appliance [ə'plaɪəns] N **1** (= *device*) aparato *m*; **electrical ~** (= *household appliance*) (aparato *m*) electrodoméstico *m* **2** (= *application*) aplicación *f*

applicable [ə'plɪkəbl] ADJ aplicable, pertinente (**to** a); **delete what is not ~** táchese lo que no proceda

applicant ['æplɪkənt] N **1** (*for post etc*) aspirante *mf*, candidato/a *m/f* (**for a post** a un puesto) **2** (*for money, assistance*) solicitante *mf* **3** (*Jur*) suplicante *mf*

application [æplɪ'keɪʃən] **Ⓐ** N **1** (*of ointment etc*) aplicación *f* **2** (= *request*) solicitud *f*, petición *f* (**for** de); **to submit one's ~** presentar su solicitud; **to make an ~ for** solicitar; **to make an ~ to** dirigirse a; **prices on ~** los precios, a solicitud; **details may be had on ~ to the office** los detalles pueden obtenerse mediante solicitud a nuestra oficina **3** (= *diligence*) aplicación *f* **Ⓑ** CPD ➤ **application form** solicitud *f* ➤ **applications package** paquete *m* de programas de aplicación ➤ **application(s) program** programa *m* de aplicación *or* aplicaciones ➤ **application(s) software** paquete *m* de aplicación *or* aplicaciones

applicator ['æplɪkeɪtəʳ] N aplicador *m*

applied [ə'plaɪd] ADJ aplicado

apply [ə'plaɪ] **Ⓐ** VT **1** (+ *ointment, paint etc*] aplicar (**to** a) **2** (= *impose*) [+ *rule, law*] aplicar, emplear **3** (= *use*) **to ~ the brakes** frenar; **to ~ pressure on sth** ejercer presión sobre algo **4** (= *dedicate*) **to ~ one's mind to a problem** dedicarse a resolver un problema; **to ~ o.s. to a task** dedicarse a *or* aplicarse en una tarea **Ⓑ** VI **1** (= *be relevant*) ser aplicable, ser pertinente; **cross out what does not ~** táchese lo que no proceda; **to ~ to** (= *be applicable to*) ser aplicable a, referirse a **2** (*for job, audition*) presentarse; **"please apply at the office"** "diríjanse a la oficina"; **to ~ to sb** dirigirse a algn, acudir a algn; **to ~ for** [+ *scholarship, grant, assistance*] solicitar, pedir; [+ *job*] solicitar, presentarse a; **"patent applied for"** "patente en trámite"; **to ~ to sb for sth** solicitar algo a algn

appoint [ə'pɔɪnt] VT **1** (= *nominate*) nombrar (**to** a); **they ~ed him chairman** le nombraron presidente **2** (*frm*) [+ *time, place*] fijar, señalar (**for** para); **at the ~ed time** a la hora señalada

⚠ **appoint ≠ apuntar**

appointment [ə'pɔɪntmənt] N **1** (*with client, bank manager etc*) cita *f*; **I have an ~ at ten** tengo cita a las diez; **to keep an ~** acudir a una cita; **to make an ~ (with sb)** concertar una cita (con algn); **to make an ~ for three o'clock** pedir (una) cita para las tres; **to meet sb by ~** reunirse con algn mediante cita previa **2** (*with dentist, doctor, hairdresser etc*) hora *f*; **I have an ~ at ten** tengo hora a las diez; **to make an ~ (with sb)** pedir hora (con algn); **to make an ~ for three o'clock** pedir hora para las tres **3** (*to a job*) nombramiento *m* (**to** para); (= *job*) puesto *m*, empleo *m*; **"appointments (vacant)"** "ofertas de empleo"

apportion [ə'pɔːʃən] VT [+ *resources etc*] repartir, distribuir; [+ *blame*] asignar

apposite ['æpəzɪt] ADJ apropiado (**to** para)

appraisal [ə'preɪzl] N **1** (= *valuation*) tasación *f*, valoración *f* **2** (*of worth, importance*) estimación *f*, apreciación *f*; (*of situation, employee*) evaluación *f*

appraise [ə'preɪz] VT **1** (= *value*) [+ *property, jewellery*] tasar, valorar **2** (= *assess*) [+ *worth, importance*] estimar, apreciar; [+ *situation*] evaluar; [+ *staff*] evaluar

appraiser [ə'preɪzəʳ] N (*US Comm, Fin*) tasador(a) *m/f*

appreciable [ə'priːʃəbl] ADJ **1** (= *noticeable*) apreciable **2** (= *large*) importante, considerable

appreciably [ə'priːʃəblɪ] ADV sensiblemente, perceptiblemente; **the weather had turned ~ colder** el tiempo se había vuelto bastante más frío

appreciate [ə'priːʃɪeɪt] **Ⓐ** VT **1** (= *be grateful for*) agradecer;

we should much ~ it if ... agradeceríamos mucho que ... + *subjun* **2** (= *value, esteem*) apreciar, valorar; **he does not ~ music** no sabe apreciar *or* valorar la música **3** (= *understand*) comprender; **yes, I ~ that** sí, lo comprendo **Ⓑ** VI [*property etc*] revalorizarse, aumentar(se) en valor

appreciation [ə,priːʃɪ'eɪʃən] N **1** (= *understanding*) comprensión *f*; [*of art etc*] aprecio *m*; **you have no ~ of art** no sabes apreciar el arte, no entiendes de arte **2** (= *gratitude*) gratitud *f*, agradecimiento *m*; **as a token of my ~** en señal de mi gratitud *or* agradecimiento **3** (= *report*) informe *m*; (*Literat*) crítica *f*, comentario *m* **4** (= *rise in value*) revalorización *f*, aumento *m* en valor

appreciative [ə'priːʃɪətɪv] ADJ **1** (= *grateful*) [*person*] agradecido; [*smile*] de agradecimiento; [*look*] lleno de agradecimiento **2** (= *admiring*) [*person*] apreciativo; [*comment*] elogioso; [*look, whistle*] de admiración; **to be ~ of** [+ *art, music, good food*] saber apreciar **3** (= *aware*) **to be ~ of** [+ *danger, risk*] ser capaz de apreciar

appreciatively [ə'priːʃɪətɪvlɪ] ADV **the audience clapped** *or* **applauded ~** el público aplaudió agradecido; **she smiled ~** sonrió con admiración, sonrió agradecida

apprehend [æprɪ'hend] VT (= *arrest*) detener, aprehender

apprehension [æprɪ'henʃən] N (= *fear*) aprensión *f*, temor *m*

apprehensive [æprɪ'hensɪv] ADJ inquieto; **to be ~ about sth** estar inquieto por algo

apprehensively [æprɪ'hensɪvlɪ] ADV con aprensión, con temor

apprentice [ə'prentɪs] **Ⓐ** N aprendiz(a) *m/f* **Ⓑ** VT **to ~ sb to** colocar a algn de aprendiz con; **to be ~d to** estar de aprendiz con **Ⓒ** CPD ➤ **apprentice electrician** aprendiz(a) *m/f* de electricista

apprenticeship [ə'prentɪʃɪp] N aprendizaje *m*

apprise [ə'praɪz] VT (*frm*) **to ~ sb of sth** informar a algn de algo

approach [ə'prəʊtʃ] **Ⓐ** VT **1** (= *near*) [+ *place*] acercarse a, aproximarse a; [+ *person*] abordar, dirigirse a; **it was ~ing midnight** era casi medianoche; **he's ~ing 50** se acerca a los 50 **2** (*with request etc*) dirigirse a; (= *speak to*) hablar con **3** (= *tackle*) [+ *subject, problem, job*] abordar; **it all depends on how we ~ it** depende de cómo lo enfoquemos **Ⓑ** VI acercarse **Ⓒ** N **1** (= *act*) acercamiento *m*, aproximación *f*; **at the ~ of night** al caer la noche **2** (*to problem, subject*) enfoque *m*, planteamiento *m*; **a new ~ to maths** un nuevo enfoque *or* planteamiento sobre las matemáticas; **I don't like your ~ to this matter** no me gusta tu modo de enfocar esta cuestión; **we must think of a new ~** tenemos que idear otro método; **why don't we try a different ~?** ¿por qué no probamos de otra manera? **3** (= *offer*) oferta *f*, propuesta *f*; (= *proposal*) proposición *f*, propuesta *f* **4** (= *access*) acceso *m*; (= *road*) vía *f* de acceso, entrada *f* **Ⓓ** CPD ➤ **approach road** vía *f* de acceso, entrada *f*

approachable [ə'prəʊtʃəbl] ADJ accesible

approaching [ə'prəʊtʃɪŋ] ADJ (*gen*) próximo, venidero; [*car, vehicle*] que se acerca en dirección opuesta, que viene en dirección contraria

approbation [æprə'beɪʃən] N aprobación *f*

appropriate Ⓐ [ə'prəʊprɪt] ADJ [*time, place, method, response*] apropiado, adecuado; [*moment*] oportuno, apropiado, adecuado; [*authority, department*] competente, correspondiente; **it is ~ that ...** resulta apropiado *or* adecuado que ...; **it may be ~ to discuss this with your solicitor** quizá sería conveniente que discutiera esto con su abogado; **the most ~ person to present the award** la persona más indicada *or* más adecuada para presentar el premio; **to take ~ action** tomar las medidas apropiadas *or* adecuadas *or* pertinentes; **choose A, B or C as ~** elija A, B o C según corresponda; **it would not be ~ for me to discuss individual cases** no sería apropiado que comentara casos concretos **Ⓑ** [ə'prəʊprɪeɪt] VT **1** (= *steal*) apropiarse de

2 (= *set aside*) [+ *funds*] asignar, destinar (**for** a)

appropriately [əˈprəʊprɪɪtlɪ] ADV [*dress*] apropiadamente; [*respond*] apropiadamente, adecuadamente; [*act*] debidamente; **it's entitled, ~ enough, "Art for the Nation"** se titula, muy apropiadamente, "Arte para la Nación"

appropriation [ə,prəʊprɪˈeɪʃən] N apropiación *f*

approval [əˈpruːvəl] N (= *consent*) aprobación *f*, visto *m* bueno; **to meet with sb's ~** obtener la aprobación de algn; **on ~** (*Comm*) a prueba

approve [əˈpruːv] **Ⓐ** VT [+ *plan, decision, legislation*] aprobar; [+ *drug, medicine, method*] autorizar **Ⓑ** VI **1** (= *be in favour*) **I think she'll ~** creo que estará de acuerdo, creo que le parecerá bien **2** (= *give authorization*) dar su aprobación ➤ **approve of** VI + PREP **to ~ of sth: not everyone ~s of the festival** no todo el mundo está de acuerdo con la celebración del festival; **he doesn't ~ of drinking** no le parece bien *or* no le gusta que se beba alcohol; **to ~ of sb: they don't ~ of my fiancé** no les parece bien mi novio

approving [əˈpruːvɪŋ] ADJ aprobatorio, de aprobación

approvingly [əˈpruːvɪŋlɪ] ADV con aprobación; **he nodded ~** hizo un gesto de aprobación con la cabeza

approx [əˈprɒks] ABBR (= **approximately**) aprox.

approximate **Ⓐ** [əˈprɒksmɪt] ADJ aproximado **Ⓑ** [əˈprɒksmeɪt] VI **to ~ to** aproximarse a, acercarse a

approximately [əˈprɒksmɪtlɪ] ADV aproximadamente, más o menos

approximation [ə,prɒksɪˈmeɪʃən] N aproximación *f*

APR, apr N ABBR (= **annual(ized) percentage rate**) TAE *f*

Apr. ABBR (= **April**) ab., abr.

apricot [ˈeɪprɪkɒt] N **1** (= *fruit*) albaricoque *m*, chabacano *m* (*Mex*), damasco *m* (*LAm*) **2** (= *tree*) albaricoquero *m*, chabacano *m* (*Mex*), damasco *m* (*LAm*)

April [ˈeɪprəl] N abril *m* ➤ **April Fool** (= *trick*) ≈ inocentada *f*; **~ Fool!** ≈ ¡inocente! ➤ **April Fools' Day** ≈ día *m* de los (Santos) Inocentes (*en el Reino Unido y los EEUU, el 1 de abril*) ➤ **April showers** lluvias *fpl* de abril; *see* **July**

APRIL FOOLS' DAY

El 1 de abril es **April Fools' Day** en la tradición anglosajona. En ese día se les gastan bromas a los desprevenidos, quienes reciben la denominación de **April Fool** (inocente), y tanto la prensa escrita como la televisión difunden alguna historia falsa con la que sumarse al espíritu del día.

apron [ˈeɪprən] N delantal *m* ➤ **apron strings: he's tied to his mother's ~ strings** está pegado a las faldas de su madre

apropos [,æprəˈpəʊ] ADV a propósito; **~ of** a propósito de

apse [æps] N ábside *m*

apt [æpt] ADJ (*compar* **-er**; *superl* **-est**) **1** (= *suitable*) [*name, title, etc*] acertado, apropiado **2** (= *liable*) **to be ~ to do sth** tener tendencia a hacer algo, tender a hacer algo; **I am ~ to be out on Mondays** los lunes no suelo estar

aptitude [ˈæptɪtjuːd] N aptitud *f*, talento *m*; **to have an ~ for sth** tener aptitud(es) *or* talento para algo ➤ **aptitude test** prueba *f* de aptitud

aptly [ˈæptlɪ] ADV [*describe, remark*] acertadamente; **an ~ named plant** una planta con un nombre muy acertado *or* apropiado

aquaerobics [,ækweɪˈrəʊbɪks] NSING aquaerobic *m*

aqualung [ˈækwəlʌŋ] N escafandra *f* autónoma

aquamarine [,ækwəməˈriːn] ADJ (de color) verde mar *inv*

aquarium [əˈkwɛərɪəm] N acuario *m*

Aquarius [əˈkwɛərɪəs] N **1** (= *sign, constellation*) Acuario *m* **2** (= *person*) acuario *mf inv*; **she's (an) ~** es acuario

aquatic [əˈkwætɪk] ADJ acuático

aqueduct [ˈækwɪdʌkt] N acueducto *m*

aquiline [ˈækwɪlaɪn] ADJ **an ~ nose** una nariz aguileña *or* aquilina

AR ABBR (*US*) = **Arkansas**

Arab [ˈærəb] ADJ, N árabe *mf*

Arabian [əˈreɪbɪən] ADJ árabe, arábigo ➤ **the Arabian Desert** el desierto Arábigo ➤ **the Arabian Gulf** el golfo Arábigo ➤ **The Arabian Nights** Las mil y una noches ➤ **the Arabian Sea** el mar de Omán

Arabic [ˈærəbɪk] **Ⓐ** ADJ árabe **Ⓑ** N (*Ling*) árabe *m* **Ⓒ** CPD ➤ **Arabic numerals** numeración *fsing* arábiga

arable [ˈærəbl] ADJ cultivable, arable (*esp LAm*); **~ farming** agricultura *f*; **~ land** tierra *f* de cultivo *or* cultivable

Aragon [ˈærəgən] N Aragón *m*

arbiter [ˈɑːbɪtəʳ] N árbitro/a *m/f*; **to be an ~ of taste** ser un árbitro del buen gusto

arbitrarily [ˈɑːbɪtrərɪlɪ] ADV arbitrariamente

arbitrary [ˈɑːbɪtrərɪ] ADJ arbitrario

arbitrate [ˈɑːbɪtreɪt] **Ⓐ** VT resolver, juzgar **Ⓑ** VI arbitrar, mediar (**between** entre)

arbitration [,ɑːbɪˈtreɪʃən] N arbitraje *m*; **they went to ~** recurrieron al arbitraje

arbitrator [ˈɑːbɪtreɪtəʳ] N árbitro/a *m/f*, mediador(a) *m/f*

arbour, arbor (*US*) [ˈɑːbəʳ] N cenador *m*, pérgola *f*

arc [ɑːk] **Ⓐ** N arco *m* **Ⓑ** VI arquearse, formar un arco

arcade [ɑːˈkeɪd] **Ⓐ** N **1** (= *shopping precinct*) galería *f* comercial; (*round public square*) soportales *mpl*, pórtico *m*; (= *series of arches*) arcada *f* **2** (*Brit*) (*also* amusement ~) sala *f* de juegos, salón *m* de juegos **Ⓑ** CPD ➤ **arcade game** videojuego *m*

arcane [ɑːˈkeɪn] ADJ arcano

arch¹ [ɑːtʃ] **Ⓐ** N **1** (*Archit*) arco *m*; (= *vault*) bóveda *f* **2** [*of foot*] puente *m* **Ⓑ** VT [+ *back, body etc*] arquear; **to ~ one's eyebrows** arquear las cejas

arch² [ɑːtʃ] ADJ **1** (= *superior*) [*look*] de superioridad; [*remark*] en tono de superioridad **2** (= *mischievous*) malicioso

arch³ [ɑːtʃ] ADJ (= *great*) **an ~ criminal** un consumado delincuente; **an ~ hypocrite** un consumado hipócrita, un hipócrita de primer orden

archaeological, archeological (*US*) [,ɑːkɪəˈlɒdʒɪkəl] ADJ arqueológico

archaeologist, archeologist (*US*) [,ɑːkɪˈɒlədʒɪst] N arqueólogo/a *m/f*

archaeology, archeology (*US*) [,ɑːkɪˈɒlədʒɪ] N arqueología *f*

archaic [ɑːˈkeɪɪk] ADJ arcaico

archangel [ˈɑːk,eɪndʒəl] N arcángel *m*

archbishop [ˈɑːtʃˈbɪʃəp] N arzobispo *m*

arched [ɑːtʃt] ADJ [*roof, window, doorway*] abovedado; [*bridge*] con arcos, con arcadas; [*brow*] arqueado

arch-enemy [ˈɑːtʃˈenɪmɪ] N archienemigo/a *m/f*

archeology *etc* [,ɑːkɪˈɒlədʒɪ] N (*US*) = **archaeology** *etc*

archer [ˈɑːtʃəʳ] N arquero/a *m/f*

archery [ˈɑːtʃərɪ] N tiro *m* con arco

archetypal [ˈɑːkɪˈtaɪpl] ADJ arquetípico

archetype [ˈɑːkɪtaɪp] N arquetipo *m*

archipelago [,ɑːkɪˈpelɪgəʊ] N archipiélago *m*

architect [ˈɑːkɪtekt] N arquitecto/a *m/f*

architectural [,ɑːkɪˈtektʃərəl] ADJ arquitectónico

architecture [ˈɑːkɪtektʃəʳ] N arquitectura *f*

archive [ˈɑːkaɪv] **Ⓐ** N archivo *m* **Ⓑ** VT archivar **Ⓒ** CPD ➤ **archive material** material *m* de archivo

archivist [ˈɑːkɪvɪst] N archivero/a *m/f*, archivista *mf* (*LAm*)

archly [ˈɑːtʃlɪ] ADV **1** (= *in a superior way*) con aire de superioridad **2** (= *mischievously*) maliciosamente

archway [ˈɑːtʃweɪ] N (= *passage*) pasaje *m* abovedado; (= *arch*) arco *m*

arctic [ˈɑːktɪk] **Ⓐ** ADJ **1** (*Geog*) ártico **2** (*fig*) glacial, gélido **Ⓑ** N **the Arctic** el Ártico **Ⓒ** CPD ➤ **the Arctic Circle** el Círculo Polar Ártico ➤ **the Arctic Ocean** el Océano Ártico

ardent [ˈɑːdənt] ADJ [*supporter, opponent*] apasionado, ferviente; [*feminist, nationalist*] acérrimo; [*lover*] apasionado

ardently [ˈɑːdntlɪ] ADV [*support, defend, desire*] ardientemente, fervientemente; [*speak*] con vehemencia; [*kiss*] apasionadamente

ardour, ardor (*US*) [ˈɑːdəʳ] N **1** (*romantic*) ardor *m*, pasión *f* **2** (*for sth*) (= *love*) pasión *f*; (= *fervour, eagerness*) fervor *m*, ardor *m*

arduous [ˈɑːdjʊəs] ADJ [*work, task*] arduo; [*climb, journey*] arduo, penoso; [*conditions*] riguroso, duro

are [ɑːʳ] PRESENT (*2nd pers sing, 1st, 2nd, 3rd pers pl*) *of* **be**

area [ˈɛərɪə] Ⓐ N

> Remember to use **el/un** not **la/una** before feminine nouns beginning with stressed **a** or **ha** like **área**, a common translation of **area**.

1 (= *surface*) superficie *f*, extensión *f*, área *f* **2** (= *region*) [*of country*] zona *f*, región *f*; [*of city*] zona *f*; (*Admin, Pol*) zona *f*, área *f*; **the London** ~ la zona *or* el área de Londres; **rural/urban ~s** zonas *fpl* rurales/urbanas **3** (= *extent, patch*) zona *f*; **the blast caused damage over a wide** ~ la explosión causó daños en una extensa zona **4** (= *space*) **dining** ~ comedor *m*; **play** ~ zona *f* recreativa **5** (*also* **penalty** ~) área *f* de penalti, área *f* de castigo **6** (= *sphere*) [*of knowledge*] campo *m*, terreno *m*; [*of responsibility*] esfera *f*
Ⓑ CPD ➤ **area code** (*US Telec*) prefijo *m* (local), código *m* territorial ➤ **area manager** jefe/a *m/f* de zona

arena [əˈriːnə] N **1** (= *stadium*) estadio *m* **2** (= *circus*) pista *f* **3** (*Bullfighting*) (= *building*) plaza *f*; (= *pit*) ruedo *m* **4** (*fig*) **the political** ~ el ruedo político

aren't [ɑːnt] = **are not**; *see* **be**

Argentina [ˌɑːdʒənˈtiːnə] N Argentina *f*

Argentine [ˈɑːdʒəntaɪn] Ⓐ ADJ argentino Ⓑ N **1** (= *person*) argentino/a *m/f* **2 the** ~ la Argentina

Argentinian [ˌɑːdʒənˈtɪnɪən] ADJ, N argentino/a *m/f*

arguable [ˈɑːgjʊəbl] ADJ discutible; **it is ~ whether ...** no está probado que ...; **it is ~ that ...** se puede decir que ...

arguably [ˈɑːgjʊəblɪ] ADV **he is ~ the best player in the world** se podría mantener que es el mejor jugador del mundo

argue [ˈɑːgjuː] Ⓐ VI **1** (= *disagree*) discutir; (= *fight*) pelearse; **his parents were always arguing** sus padres estaban siempre discutiendo *or* peleándose; **to ~ with sb about sth** discutir *or* pelearse con algn por algo; **you can't ~ with that** eso es indiscutible; **I didn't dare ~** no me atreví a llevar la contraria; **just get in and don't ~!** ¡entra y no discutas! **2** (= *reason*) **he ~s well** presenta sus argumentos de modo convincente, razona bien; **to ~ against sth** dar razones en contra de algo; **to ~ against doing sth** dar razones para que no se haga algo; **to ~ in favour of sth** abogar por algo Ⓑ VT **1** (= *debate*) discutir; **I won't ~ that point** no voy a discutir ese punto; **a well ~d case** un argumento bien expuesto; **to ~ the case for sth** abogar en favor de algo **2** (= *maintain*) sostener; **to ~ that** sostener que; **it could be ~d that ...** se podría decir que ...

argument [ˈɑːgjʊmənt] N **1** (= *disagreement*) discusión *f*; (= *fight*) pelea *f*; **to have an ~ (with sb)** discutir (con algn); (*more heatedly*) pelearse (con algn); **we had an ~ about money** tuvimos una discusión *or* discutimos por razones de dinero **2** (= *debate*) polémica *f*; **there is some ~ as to whether or not it's possible** hay bastante polémica sobre si es posible o no; **the conclusion is open to ~** la conclusión se presta a discusión *or* es discutible **3** (= *case*) argumento *m*, razones *fpl*; **there is a strong ~ for doing nothing** existen argumentos *or* razones de peso para *or* en favor de no hacer nada; **an ~ could be made for government intervention** se podrían alegar razones para la intervención del gobierno; **you've only heard one side of the ~** tú sólo conoces una cara del asunto **4** (= *reasoning*) razonamiento *m*; **if you take this ~ one step**

further si llevas el razonamiento un poco más allá; **his ~ is that ...** él sostiene que ...

argumentative [ˌɑːgjʊˈmentətɪv] ADJ amigo de las discusiones, discutidor

aria [ˈɑːrɪə] N aria *f*; **a baroque ~** un aria barroca

> Use **el/un** not **la/una** before feminine nouns beginning with stressed **a** or **ha** like **aria**:

arid [ˈærɪd] ADJ árido

aridity [əˈrɪdɪtɪ] N (*lit, fig*) aridez *f*

Aries [ˈɛəriːz] N **1** (= *sign, constellation*) Aries *m* **2** (= *person*) aries *mf inv*; **I'm (an)** ~ soy aries

arise [əˈraɪz] (*pt* **arose**; *pp* ~**n** [əˈrɪzn]) VI **1** (= *occur*) surgir, presentarse; **should the need** ~ de ser necesario; **should the occasion** ~ si se presenta la ocasión; **the question does not** ~ no hay tal problema, la cuestión no viene al caso **2** (= *result*) surgir; **there are problems arising from his attitude** surgen problemas a raíz de su actitud

aristocracy [ˌærɪsˈtɒkrəsɪ] N aristocracia *f*

aristocrat [ˈærɪstəkræt] N aristócrata *mf*

aristocratic [ˌærɪstəˈkrætɪk] ADJ aristocrático

arithmetic Ⓐ [əˈrɪθmətɪk] N aritmética *f* Ⓑ [ˌærɪθˈmetɪk] ADJ aritmético; ~ **progression** progresión *f* aritmética

Ariz. ABBR (*US*) = **Arizona**

ark [ɑːk] N arca *f*; **Noah's Ark** el Arca *f* de Noé; ✦ IDIOM **it's out of the Ark*** viene del año de la nana*

> Use **el/un** not **la/una** before feminine nouns beginning with stressed **a** or **ha** like **arca**.

Ark. ABBR (*US*) = **Arkansas**

arm¹ [ɑːm] N **1** (*Anat*) brazo *m*; **with one's ~s folded** con los brazos cruzados; **to hold sth/sb in one's ~s** coger algo/a algn en brazos; **he walked arm in arm with his wife** iba cogido del brazo de su mujer; **they were walking along ~ in** ~ iban cogidos del brazo; **to put one's ~(s) around sb** abrazar a algn; **within ~'s reach** al alcance de la mano; **to take sb's** ~ coger a algn del brazo; **to take sb in one's ~s** tomar a algn en sus brazos; ✦ IDIOMS **to cost an ~ and a leg*** costar un ojo de la cara*; **to keep sb at ~'s length** mantener las distancias con algn; **to welcome sth/sb with open ~s** recibir algo/a algn con los brazos abiertos; **I'd give my right ~ to own it** daría mi brazo derecho por que fuera mío **2** [*of chair, river, crane*] brazo *m*; [*of coat*] manga *f* **3** [*of organization, company, also Mil*] (= *division*) división *f*; (= *section*) sección *f*; (*Pol*) brazo *m*

arm² [ɑːm] Ⓐ N **1 arms** (= *weapons*) armas *fpl*; **to take up ~s (against sth/sb)** tomar las armas (contra algo/algn); ✦ IDIOM **to be up in ~s about sth: environmental groups are up in ~s about the plan** los grupos ecologistas se oponen al plan enfurecidamente **2 arms** (= *coat of arms*) escudo *msing* de armas, blasón *msing* Ⓑ VT [+ *person, ship, nation*] armar, proveer de armas; [+ *missile*] equipar; **to ~ o.s. with sth** (*lit*) armarse de *or* con algo; (*fig*) armarse de algo Ⓒ CPD ➤ **arms control** control *m* de armamento(s) ➤ **arms dealer** traficante *mf* de armas ➤ **arms manufacturer** fabricante *mf* de armas ➤ **the arms race** la carrera armamentística, la carrera de armamentos ➤ **arms trade** tráfico *m* de armas

Armageddon [ˌɑːməˈgedn] N (*Bible*) la batalla de Armagedón; (*fig*) la guerra del fin del mundo

armaments [ˈɑːməmənts] NPL armamento *msing*

armband [ˈɑːmbænd] N (*made of cloth*) brazalete *m*; (*esp Brit*) (= *float*) flotador (*para los brazos*)

armchair [ˈɑːmtʃɛəʳ] N sillón *m*

armed [ɑːmd] ADJ armado; **the ~ forces** las fuerzas armadas; ~ **robbery** robo *m* a mano armada; ~ **with sth** (*lit,* *fig*) armado de *or* con algo; ✦ IDIOM ~ **to the teeth** armado hasta los dientes

Armenia [ɑːˈmiːnɪə] N Armenia *f*

Armenian [ɑːˈmiːnɪən] ADJ, N armenio/a *m/f*

armful [ˈɑːmfʊl] N brazada *f*

armhole [ˈɑːmhəʊl] N sobaquera *f*, sisa *f*

armistice [ˈɑːmɪstɪs] N armisticio *m*

armour, armor (US) [ˈɑːməʳ] N (*Mil, Zool, fig*) armadura *f*; (= *steel plates*) blindaje *m*

armoured, armored (US) [ˈɑːməd] ADJ acorazado, blindado; ~ **car** carro *m* blindado

armour-plated, armor-plated (US) [ˈɑːməˈpleɪtɪd] ADJ blindado

armoury, armory (US) [ˈɑːmərɪ] N **1** (= *arsenal*) (*lit, fig*) arsenal *m* **2** (US) (= *arms factory*) fábrica *f* de armas

armpit [ˈɑːmpɪt] N sobaco *m*, axila *f*

armrest [ˈɑːmrest] N (*of chair*) brazo *m*; (*in bus, plane, etc*) apoyo *m* para el brazo, apoyabrazos *m inv*

arm-wrestling [ˈɑːmˌreslɪŋ] N pulso *m*, pulseada *f* (*Cono Sur*)

army [ˈɑːmɪ] N ejército *m*; **to be in the** ~ ser militar; **to join the** ~ alistarse ➤ **army chaplain** capellán *m* castrense ➤ **army doctor** médico/a *m/f* militar ➤ **army life** vida *f* militar ➤ **army surplus** excedentes *mpl* del ejército

aroma [əˈrəʊmə] N aroma *m* (**of** de, a)

aromatherapy [əˈrəʊməˈθerəpɪ] N aromaterapia *f*

aromatic [ˌærəʊˈmætɪk] ADJ aromático

arose [əˈrəʊz] PT *of* **arise**

around [əˈraʊnd]

> When **around** is an element in a phrasal verb, eg **look around, move around,** look up the verb.

Ⓐ ADV alrededor, en los alrededores; **is he** ~? ¿está por aquí?; **there's a lot of flu** ~ hay mucha gripe en el ambiente; **all** ~ por todos lados; **she's been** ~* (= *travelled*) ha viajado mucho, ha visto mucho mundo; (*pej*) (= *experienced*) se las sabe todas; ~ **here** por aquí; **is there a chemist's** ~ **here?** ¿hay alguna farmacia por aquí?; **for miles** ~ en muchas millas a la redonda; **he must be somewhere** ~ debe de estar por aquí
Ⓑ PREP **1** alrededor de; **she ignored the people** ~ **her** ignoró a la gente que estaba a su alrededor; **to wander** ~ **the town** pasearse por la ciudad; **there were books all** ~ **the house** había libros en todas partes de la casa *or* por toda la casa; **to go** ~ **the world** dar la vuelta al mundo
2 (= *approximately*) aproximadamente, alrededor de; **it costs** ~ **£100** cuesta alrededor de *or* aproximadamente 100 libras; ~ **50** 50 más o menos; **he must be** ~ **50** debe (de) tener unos 50 años; ~ **1950** alrededor de 1950, hacia 1950; ~ **two o'clock** a eso de las dos

arouse [əˈraʊz] VT **1** (*frm*) (*from sleep*) despertar
2 [+ *suspicion, curiosity, interest*] despertar, suscitar
3 (*sexually*) excitar

arpeggio [ɑːˈpedʒɪəʊ] N arpegio *m*

arr. ABBR = **arrives, arrival**

arrange [əˈreɪndʒ] **Ⓐ** VT **1** (= *put into order*) [+ *books, thoughts*] ordenar; [+ *hair, flowers*] arreglar; **to** ~ **one's affairs** poner sus asuntos en orden
2 (= *place*) [+ *furniture, chairs*] disponer, colocar
3 (= *plan*) planear, fijar; [+ *meeting, party*] organizar; [+ *schedule, programme*] acordar; **everything is** ~**d** todo está arreglado; **"to be** ~**d"** "por determinar"; **it was** ~**d that ...** se quedó en que ...; **have you anything** ~**d for tomorrow?** ¿tienes planes para mañana?, ¿tienes algún compromiso mañana?; **I've** ~**d a surprise for tonight** he preparado una sorpresa para esta noche; **to** ~ **a time for** fijar una hora para; **what did you** ~ **with him?** ¿en qué quedaste con él?
4 (*Mus*) adaptar, hacer los arreglos de
Ⓑ VI **to** ~ **to do sth** quedar en hacer algo; **I** ~**d to meet him at the cafe** quedé en verlo *or* quedé con él en el café; **to** ~ **with sb to** (+ INFIN) ponerse de acuerdo con algn para que

+ *subjun*; **can you** ~ **for him to replace you?** ¿puedes arreglarlo para que te sustituya?

arranged [əˈreɪndʒd] ADJ [*marriage*] concertado (por los padres)

arrangement [əˈreɪndʒmənt] N **1** (= *order*) orden *m*; [*of furniture, etc*] disposición *f*
2 (*Mus*) arreglo *m*
3 (= *agreement*) acuerdo *m*; **prices by** ~ precios a convenir; **larger orders by** ~ los pedidos de mayor cantidad previo acuerdo; **by** ~ **with Covent Garden** con permiso de Covent Garden; **to come to an** ~ **(with sb)** llegar a un acuerdo (con algn)
4 (= *plan*) plan *m*
5 arrangements (= *plans*) planes *mpl*; (= *preparations*) preparativos *mpl*; **what are the** ~**s for your holiday?** ¿qué plan *or* planes tienes para las vacaciones?; **all the** ~**s are made** todo está arreglado; **Pamela is in charge of the travel** ~**s** Pamela se encarga de los preparativos para el viaje

array [əˈreɪ] N **1** (*Mil*) formación *f*, orden *m*; **in battle** ~ en orden *or* formación de batalla **2** (= *collection*) colección *f*; (= *series*) serie *f*; **a fine** ~ **of flowers** un bello conjunto de flores; **a great** ~ **of hats** una magnífica colección de sombreros

arrears [əˈrɪəz] NPL atrasos *mpl*; **rent** ~ atrasos *mpl* de alquiler; **to be in** ~ (*with rent*) ir atrasado en los pagos; **to get into** ~ atrasarse en los pagos; **to pay one month in** ~ pagar con un mes de retraso *or* a mes vencido

arrest [əˈrest] **Ⓐ** N [*of person*] detención *f*; [*of goods*] secuestro *m*; **to make an** ~ hacer una detención; **to be under** ~ estar detenido; **to put sb under** ~ detener *or* arrestar a algn **Ⓑ** VT **1** [+ *criminal*] detener, arrestar **2** [+ *attention*] atraer **3** [+ *progress, decay etc*] (= *halt*) detener, parar; (= *hinder*) obstaculizar **Ⓒ** CPD ➤ **arrest warrant** orden *f* de detención

arresting [əˈrestɪŋ] ADJ llamativo, que llama la atención

arrival [əˈraɪvəl] **Ⓐ** N **1** [*of person, letter etc*] llegada *f*, arribo *m* (*esp LAm*); **"Arrivals"** (*Aer*) "Llegadas"; **on** ~ al llegar; **he was dead on** ~ ingresó cadáver **2** (= *person*) **Jim was the first** ~ **at the party** Jim fue el primero en llegar a la fiesta; **a new** ~ (= *newcomer*) un recién llegado; (= *baby*) un recién nacido **Ⓑ** CPD ➤ **arrivals board, arrival board** (US) panel *m* de llegadas ➤ **arrivals hall** (*Aer*) sala *f* de llegadas

arrive [əˈraɪv] VI (*gen*) llegar, arribar (*esp LAm*); [*baby*] nacer, llegar; **to** ~ **(up)on the scene** entrar en escena
➤ **arrive at** VI + PREP [+ *decision, solution*] llegar a; [+ *perfection*] lograr, alcanzar; **how did you** ~ **at this figure?** ¿cómo has llegado a esta cifra?; **we finally** ~**d at a price** por fin convenimos (en) un precio

arrogance [ˈærəgəns] N arrogancia *f*, prepotencia *f* (*esp LAm*)

arrogant [ˈærəgənt] ADJ arrogante, prepotente (*esp LAm*)

arrogantly [ˈærəgəntlɪ] ADV con arrogancia, con prepotencia (*esp LAm*)

arrow [ˈærəʊ] N flecha *f*

arse*** [ɑːs] N (*Brit*) culo** *m*

arsehole*** [ˈɑːsheʊl] N (*Brit*) **1** (= *person*) gilipollas *mf inv* (*Sp****), pendejo/a *m/f* (*LAm**), huevón/ona *m/f* (*And, Ven**) **2** (*Anat*) culo** *m*

arsenal [ˈɑːsɪnl] N arsenal *m*

arsenic [ˈɑːsnɪk] N arsénico *m*

arson [ˈɑːsn] N incendio *m* premeditado

arsonist [ˈɑːsənɪst] N incendiario/a *m/f*, pirómano/a *m/f*

art [ɑːt] **Ⓐ** N **1** (= *painting, sculpture, etc*) arte *m*; **the** ~**s** la cultura, el mundo de la cultura; **work of** ~ obra *f* de arte; **the** ~ **of embroidery** el arte del bordado
2 (*Univ*) **Arts** Filosofía *fsing* y Letras; **Faculty of Arts** Facultad *f* de Filosofía y Letras
Ⓑ CPD ➤ **art collection** colección *f* de arte ➤ **art college** escuela *f* de Bellas Artes ➤ **art dealer** marchante *mf* ➤ **art deco** art decó *m* ➤ **art exhibition** exposición *f* de arte ➤ **art form** medio *m* de expresión artística ➤ **art gallery** (*state-owned*) museo *m* (de arte); (*private*) galería *f* de arte ➤ **art nouveau** modernismo *m* ➤ **arts and crafts** artesanías *fpl* ➤ **art school** escuela *f* de Bellas Artes ➤ **Arts Council** (*Brit*) *institución pública encargada de la promoción de la*

cultura y de las actividades artísticas ➤ **Arts degree** licenciatura *f* en Letras ➤ **Arts student** estudiante *mf* de Letras ➤ **art student** estudiante *mf* de Bellas Artes

artefact, artifact *(esp US)* ['ɑːtɪfækt] N *(= object)* artefacto *m*

arterial [ɑː'tɪərɪəl] ADJ *[blood]* arterial; **~ road** arteria *f*

arteriosclerosis [ɑː'tɪərɪəʊsklɪə'rəʊsɪs] N arteriosclerosis *f inv*

artery ['ɑːtərɪ] N arteria *f*

art-house ['ɑːthaʊs] ADJ de autor, de arte y ensayo

arthritic [ɑː'θrɪtɪk] ADJ artrítico

arthritis [ɑː'θraɪtɪs] N artritis *f inv*

artichoke ['ɑːtɪtʃəʊk] N alcachofa *f*, alcaucil *m*

article ['ɑːtɪkl] **Ⓐ** N **1** *(= item, product)* artículo *m*; *(= object)* objeto *m*, cosa *f*; **~s of clothing** prendas *fpl* de vestir **2** *(in newspaper etc)* artículo *m* **3** *(Gram)* artículo *m* **4** *(Admin, Jur)* artículo *m*, cláusula *f* **Ⓑ** VT *(Brit)*: **to be ~d to sb** estar de aprendiz con algn

articulate Ⓐ [ɑː'tɪkjʊlɪt] ADJ *[speech, account]* articulado; **she's very ~** se expresa muy bien; **he's not very ~** le cuesta expresarse **Ⓑ** [ɑː'tɪkjʊleɪt] VT **1** *(= express)* expresar **2** *(= pronounce)* articular

articulated lorry [ɑː'tɪkjʊleɪtɪd'lɒrɪ] N *(Brit)* camión *m* articulado

articulation [ɑː'tɪkjʊ'leɪʃən] N **1** *(= expression)* [*of thoughts, feelings*] expresión *f* **2** *(= pronunciation)* [*of word, sentence*] articulación *f* **3** *(Anat)* articulación *f*

artifact ['ɑːtɪfækt] N *(esp US)* = **artefact**

artifice ['ɑːtɪfɪs] N **1** *(= cunning)* habilidad *f*, ingenio *m* **2** *(= trick)* artificio *m*, ardid *m*; *(= strategem)* estratagema *f*

artificial [ˌɑːtɪ'fɪʃəl] ADJ **1** *(= synthetic)* [*light, flower, leg*] artificial; [*leather*] sintético; [*jewel*] de imitación **2** [*person, manner*] artificial, afectado; [*smile*] forzado

artificiality [ˌɑːtɪfɪʃɪ'ælɪtɪ] N artificialidad *f*; [*of person, manner*] artificialidad *f*, afectación *f*, falta *f* de naturalidad

artificially [ˌɑːtɪ'fɪʃəlɪ] ADV artificialmente; *(fig)* con afectación

artillery [ɑː'tɪlərɪ] N artillería *f*

artisan ['ɑːtɪzæn] N artesano/a *m/f*

artist ['ɑːtɪst] N artista *mf*

artiste [ɑː'tiːst] N *(esp Brit Theat)* artista *mf* (del espectáculo); *(Mus)* intérprete *mf*

artistic [ɑː'tɪstɪk] ADJ artístico; **to be ~** [*person*] tener dotes artísticas ➤ **artistic director** director(a) *m/f* artístico/a

artistically [ɑː'tɪstɪkəlɪ] ADV [*arranged, presented*] con mucho arte, artísticamente; **to be ~ inclined** tener dotes artísticas; **artistically, ...** desde el punto de vista artístico, ...

artistry ['ɑːtɪstrɪ] N arte *m*, habilidad *f*

artless ['ɑːtlɪs] ADJ **1** *(= straightforward)* [*beauty*] natural; [*person, smile, comment*] ingenuo, sin malicia; [*book, story, film*] sencillo, sin artificios **2** *(= naïve)* simple

artsy* ['ɑːtsɪ] *(esp US)* = **arty**

artsy-fartsy** ['ɑːtsɪ'fɑːtsɪ] ADJ *(US)* = **arty-farty**

artwork ['ɑːtwɜːk] N material *m* gráfico

arty* ['ɑːtɪ] ADJ [*style*] con pretensiones artísticas, seudoartístico; [*clothing*] afectado, extravagante; [*person*] de gusto muy afectado, que se las da de muy artista

arty-farty** ['ɑːtɪ'fɑːtɪ] ADJ pretencioso, con pretensiones artísticas

as	
Ⓐ CONJUNCTION	**Ⓒ** ADVERB
Ⓑ PREPOSITION	

For set combinations in which **as** *is not the first word, eg* **such ... as, the same ... as, dressed as**, *look up the other word.*

as [æz, əz] **Ⓐ** CONJUNCTION

1 *(in time clauses)*

You can usually use **cuando** when the **as** clause simply tells you when an event happened:

(= when) cuando; **as I was passing the house** cuando pasaba por delante de la casa

Alternatively, use **al** + INFINITIVE:

he came in as I was leaving entró al salir yo *or* cuando yo salía; **he tripped as he was coming out of the bank** tropezó al salir *or* cuando salía del banco

Translate **as** using **mientras** for longer actions which are happening at the same time:

(= while) mientras; **as we walked, we talked about the future** mientras caminábamos, hablábamos del futuro

In the context of two closely linked actions involving parallel development, translate **as** using **a medida que** or **conforme**. Alternatively, use **según va** *etc* + GERUND:

as he got older he got deafer a medida que *or* conforme envejeció se fue volviendo más sordo, según fue envejeciendo se fue volviendo más sordo

2 *(in reason clauses)*

When **as** means **since** or **because**, you can generally use **como**, provided you put it at the beginning of the sentence. Alternatively, use the more formal **puesto que** either at the beginning of the sentence or between the clauses or **ya que** especially between the clauses:

como; *(more frm)* puesto que, ya que; **as you're here, I'll tell you** como estás aquí *or* puesto que estás aquí, te lo diré; **he couldn't come as he had an appointment** no pudo asistir porque *or* puesto que *or* ya que tenía un compromiso **3** *(describing way, manner)* como; **leave things as they are** dejad las cosas como están; **I'm okay as I am** estoy bien tal como estoy; **the village, situated as it is near a motorway, ...** el pueblo, situado como está cerca de una autopista, ...; **as I was saying ...** como iba diciendo ...; **her door is the first as you go up** su puerta es la primera según se sube; **she is very gifted, as is her brother** tiene mucho talento, al igual que su hermano; **you'll have it by noon as <u>agreed</u>** lo tendrá antes del mediodía, tal como acordamos; **it's not bad, as hotels <u>go</u>** no está mal, en comparación con otros hoteles; **as often <u>happens</u>** como suele ocurrir; **as you <u>know</u>** como sabe; **do as you <u>wish</u>** haga lo que quiera **4** *(= though)* aunque; **tired as he was, he went to the party** aunque estaba cansado, asistió a la fiesta; **unlikely as it may seem ...** por imposible que parezca ... **5** *(in set structures)*

✦ **as if** *or* **as though** como si; **he looked as if** *or* **as though he was ill** parecía como si estuviera enfermo; **it isn't as if** *or* **as though he were poor** no es que sea pobre, que digamos; **as if she knew!** ¡como si ella lo supiera!; **don't tell her, will you? — as if!*** —no se lo dirás, ¿verdad? —¡tú qué crees?; **did he finally own up? — as if!*** —¿al final ha confesado? —¿tú qué crees?

✦ **as if to: the little dog nodded his head, as if to agree** el perrito movió la cabeza, como asintiendo

✦ **as in: it's spelled with V as in Valencia** se escribe con V de Valencia

✦ **as it is: as it is, it doesn't make much difference** en realidad, casi da lo mismo; **as it is we can do nothing** en la práctica *or* tal y como están las cosas no podemos hacer nada; **I've got quite enough to do as it is** tengo ya bastante trabajo

✦ **as it were** por así decirlo

Ⓑ PREPOSITION

1 *(= while)* **she was often ill as a child** de pequeña se ponía enferma con frecuencia

2 (= *in the capacity of*) como; **he succeeded as a politician** tuvo éxito como político; **I don't think much of him as an actor** como actor, no me gusta mucho; **he was there as adviser** estaba allí en calidad de asesor; **he works as a waiter** trabaja de camarero
ⓒ ADVERB
1 (*in comparisons*)
✦ **as ... as** tan ... como; **I am as tall as him** soy tan alto como él; **this tree can grow as tall as 50 feet** este árbol puede llegar a medir 50 pies de alto; **as big as a house** (tan) grande como una casa; **he was writing as long ago as 1945** en 1945 ya escribía; **she doesn't walk as quickly** or **as fast as me** no camina tan rápido como yo; **walk as fast as you can** camina lo más rápido que puedas; **he ate as quickly as possible** comió lo más rápido posible; **it was still being done by hand as recently as 1960** en 1960 todavía seguía haciéndose a mano; **is it as big as all that?** ¿es de verdad tan grande?
✦ **as little as**: **by saving as little as ten pounds a month** ahorrando tan sólo diez libras al mes
✦ **as many ... as** tantos/as ... como
✦ **as much ... as** tanto/a ... como
✦ **half/twice/three times as ...**: **it's half as expensive** es la mitad de caro; **it's twice as expensive** es el doble de caro; **it's three times as expensive** es tres veces más caro; **her coat cost twice as much as mine** su abrigo costó el doble que el mío
✦ **without as** or **so much as**: **she gave me back the book without as** or **so much as an apology** me devolvió el libro sin pedirme siquiera una disculpa
2 (*in set structures*)
✦ **as for** en cuanto a; **as for that ...** en cuanto a esto ...
✦ **as from** (*Brit*): **as from tomorrow** a partir de mañana
✦ **as of**: **as of yesterday/now** a partir de ayer/ahora
✦ **as to**: **as to that I can't say** en lo que a eso se refiere, no lo sé; **as to her mother ...** en cuanto a su madre ...; **to question sb as to his intentions** preguntar a algn sus intenciones
✦ **as yet** hasta ahora, hasta el momento

a.s.a.p.* ADV ABBR (= **as soon as possible**) lo antes posible, lo más pronto posible

asbestos [æz'bestəs] N amianto *m*, asbesto *m*

asbestosis [ˌæzbes'təʊsɪs] N asbestosis *f inv*

ascend [ə'send] **ⓐ** VT (*frm*) [+ *stairs*] subir; [+ *mountain*] subir a; [+ *throne*] ascender a, subir a **ⓑ** VI (= *rise*) subir, ascender; (= *slope up*) elevarse

ascendancy [ə'sendənsɪ] N ascendiente *m*, dominio *m*

ascendant [ə'sendənt] N **to be in the ~** estar en auge, ir ganando predominio

Ascension [ə'senʃən] N Ascensión *f* ➤ **Ascension Day** día *m* de la Ascensión

ascension [ə'senʃən] N ascensión *f*

ascent [ə'sent] N **1** (= *climb, way up*) subida *f*; (*in plane*) ascenso *m* (*also fig*) **2** (= *slope*) pendiente *f*, cuesta *f*

ascertain [ˌæsə'teɪn] VT determinar, establecer (**that** que)

ascetic [ə'setɪk] **ⓐ** ADJ ascético **ⓑ** N asceta *mf*

asceticism [ə'setɪsɪzəm] N ascetismo *m*

ASCII ['æski:] N ABBR (= **American Standard Code for Information Interchange**) ASCII *m* ➤ **ASCII file** fichero *m* ASCII

ascribe [ə'skraɪb] VT **to ~ sth to sb/sth** atribuir algo a algn/algo

ASE N ABBR (*US*) = **American Stock Exchange**

ASEAN N ABBR = **Association of South-East Asian Nations**

aseptic [eɪ'septɪk] ADJ aséptico

asexual [eɪ'seksjʊəl] ADJ asexual

ash¹ [æʃ] N **1** (*also* **~ tree**) fresno *m* **2** (= *wood*) (madera *f* de) fresno *m*

ash² [æʃ] N (*from fire, cigarette*) ceniza *f*; **~es** (*gen, mortal remains*) cenizas *fpl*; **to reduce sth to ~es** reducir algo a cenizas ➤ **ash bin, ash can** (*US*) cubo *m* or (*LAm*) bote *m* or (*LAm*) tarro *m* de la basura ➤ **Ash Wednesday** miércoles *m inv* de Ceniza

ashamed [ə'ʃeɪmd] ADJ **1** (= *remorseful*) avergonzado, apenado (*LAm*); **he was ~ about what had happened** estaba avergonzado or (*LAm*) apenado por lo que había pasado; **she was ~ about having been so nasty** estaba avergonzada or (*LAm*) apenada de haber sido tan cruel; **you ought to be ~ of yourself!** ¡debería darte vergüenza or (*LAm*) pena!, ¡no te da vergüenza or (*LAm*) pena!
2 (= *embarrassed*) **I was ~ to ask for money** me daba vergüenza or (*LAm*) pena pedir dinero; **I was too ~ to tell anyone** me sentía demasiado avergonzado or (*LAm*) estaba demasiado apenado como para decírselo a nadie; **it's nothing to be ~ of** no hay por qué avergonzarse or (*LAm*) apenarse

ash blond(e) [æʃ'blɒnd] ADJ, N rubio/a *m/f* ceniza

ashen ['æʃn] ADJ (= *greyish*) ceniciento; (= *pale*) pálido

ashore [ə'ʃɔːʳ] ADV (= *on land*) **to be ~** estar en tierra; **to go/come ~** desembarcar

ashtray ['æʃtreɪ] N cenicero *m*

Asia ['eɪʃə] N Asia

> Use **el/un** not **la/una**, before feminine nouns beginning with stressed **a** or **ha** like **Asia**.

Asian ['eɪʃn] ADJ, N asiático/a *m/f*

Asiatic [ˌeɪsɪ'ætɪk] ADJ, N asiático/a *m/f*

aside [ə'saɪd]

> When **aside** is an element in a phrasal verb, eg **brush aside, cast aside, put aside, stand aside**, look up the verb.

ⓐ ADV **1** (= *to one side*) a un lado; **to cast ~** desechar, echar a un lado; **to step ~** hacerse a un lado; **joking ~** bromas aparte **2** **~ from** aparte de **ⓑ** N (*Theat*) aparte *m*

ask

ⓐ TRANSITIVE VERB	**ⓒ** PHRASAL VERBS
ⓑ INTRANSITIVE VERB	

ask [ɑːsk] **ⓐ** TRANSITIVE VERB
1 (= *inquire*) preguntar; **"how is Frank?" he ~ed** —¿cómo está Frank? —preguntó; **I ~ed him his name/the time** le pregunté su nombre/la hora; **did you ~ him about the job?** ¿le has preguntado por el trabajo?; (*in more detail*) ¿le has preguntado acerca del trabajo?; **don't ~ me!*** ¡yo qué sé!*, ¡qué sé yo! (*esp LAm**); **I ~ you!*** (*despairing*) ¿te lo puedes creer?; **~ him if he has seen her** pregúntale si la ha visto; **if you ~ me, I think she's crazy** para mí que está loca; **to ~ (sb) a question** hacer una pregunta (a algn); **I ~ed the teacher what to do next** le pregunté al profesor lo que tenía que hacer después; **~ her why she didn't come** pregúntale por qué no vino
2 (= *request*) pedir; **to ~ to do sth: I ~ed to see the director** pedí ver al director; **to ~ sb to do sth** pedir a algn que haga algo; **how much are they ~ing for the car?** ¿cuánto piden por el coche?; **that's ~ing the impossible** eso es pedir lo imposible; **it's not a lot to ~** no es mucho pedir
3 (= *invite*) invitar; **to ~ sb to dinner** invitar a algn a cenar
ⓑ INTRANSITIVE VERB
1 (= *inquire*) preguntar; **~ about our reduced rates for students** pregunta por or infórmate sobre nuestros descuentos para estudiantes; **he was ~ing about the Vikings** preguntaba acerca de or sobre los vikingos; **I was only ~ing** era sólo una pregunta
2 (= *make request*) **if you need anything, just ~** si quieres algo no tienes más que pedirlo; **the ~ing price** el precio que se pide/pedía *etc*
ⓒ PHRASAL VERBS
➤ **ask after** VI + PREP preguntar por
➤ **ask along** VT + ADV invitar; **~ him along if you like** si quieres, dile que venga, invítale si quieres
➤ **ask around** VT + ADV invitar (a casa)
➤ **ask back** VT + ADV (*for second visit*) volver a invitar; (*on reciprocal visit*) devolver la invitación a; **she ~ed me back**

to her house after the show me invitó a su casa después del espectáculo
➤ **ask for** ⒶVI + PREP **1** (= *request*) pedir, solicitar (*more frm*) **2** (= *look for*) **to ~ for sb** preguntar por algn **3** (*in idiomatic phrases*) **he is all I could ~ for in a son** tiene todo lo que podría pedirle a un hijo; **he ~ed for it!** ¡él se lo ha buscado!; **it's just ~ing for trouble** eso no es otra cosa que buscarse problemas ⒷVT + PREP **to ~ sb for sth** pedir algo a algn
➤ **ask in** VT + ADV invitar a entrar, invitar a pasar; **to ~ sb in for a drink** invitar a algn a que pase a tomar algo
➤ **ask out** VT + ADV invitar a salir; **he ~ed her out to dinner** la invitó (a salir) a cenar
➤ **ask over** VT + ADV invitar (a casa)
➤ **ask round** VT + ADV (*Brit*) = **ask around**

askance [əˈskɑːns] ADV **to look ~ at sb** mirar a algn con recelo *or* desconfianza; **to look ~ at sth** ver algo con recelo *or* desconfianza

askew [əˈskjuː] ADJ torcido; **the picture is ~** el cuadro está torcido

asking price [ˈɑːskɪŋpraɪs] N precio *m* inicial

asleep [əˈsliːp] ADJ **1** (= *not awake*) dormido; **to be ~** estar dormido; **to be fast** *or* **sound ~** estar profundamente dormido; **to fall ~** dormirse, quedarse dormido **2** (= *numb*) adormecido; **my foot's ~** se me ha (quedado) dormido el pie

ASLEF [ˈæzlef] N ABBR (*Brit*) = **Associated Society of Locomotive Engineers and Firemen**

AS level [eɪˈeslevl] N (*Brit*) *título intermedio entre los GCSEs y los A levels*

asp [æsp] N áspid(e) *m*

asparagus [əsˈpærəgəs] N (= *plant*) espárrago *m*; (= *food*) espárragos *mpl* ➤ **asparagus tips** puntas *fpl* de espárrago

ASPCA N ABBR (*US*) = **American Society for the Prevention of Cruelty to Animals**

aspect [ˈæspekt] N aspecto *m*; **to study all ~s of a question** estudiar un asunto bajo todos sus aspectos; **seen from this ~** desde este punto de vista; **a house with a northerly ~** una casa orientada hacia el norte

aspersions [sˈpɜːʃənz] NPL **to cast ~ on sb** difamar *or* calumniar a algn

asphalt [ˈæsfælt] N **1** (= *material*) asfalto *m* **2** (= *surface, ground*) pista *f* asfaltada, recinto *m* asfaltado

asphyxia [æsˈfɪksɪə] N asfixia *f*

asphyxiate [æsˈfɪksɪeɪt] VT asfixiar

asphyxiation [æsˌfɪksɪˈeɪʃən] N asfixia *f*

aspic [ˈæspɪk] N gelatina *f* (*de carne etc*)

aspirate Ⓐ [ˈæspərɪt] ADJ aspirado Ⓑ [ˈæspəreɪt] VT aspirar; **~d H** H *f* aspirada

aspiration [ˌæspəˈreɪʃən] N aspiración *f*

aspire [əsˈpaɪəʳ] VI **to ~ to sth** aspirar a algo; **we can't ~ to that** no aspiramos a tanto, nuestras pretensiones son más modestas; **to ~ to do sth** aspirar a hacer algo, ambicionar hacer algo

aspirin [ˈæsprɪn] N (*pl ~ or ~s*) aspirina *f*

aspiring [əsˈpaɪərɪŋ] ADJ (= *ambitious*) ambicioso; (= *budding*) en potencia, en ciernes

ass[1] [æs] N **1** (= *animal*) asno *m*, burro *m* **2** (*) (= *fool*) imbécil *mf*

ass[2]*** [æs] (*US*) N (= *behind*) culo** *m*

assail [əˈseɪl] VT (= *attack*) atacar; **he was ~ed by critics** los críticos se le echaron encima; **they ~ed her with questions** la asaltaron *or* bombardearon a preguntas; **he was ~ed by doubts** le asaltaban las dudas

assailant [əˈseɪlənt] N asaltante *mf*, agresor(a) *m/f*

assassin [əˈsæsɪn] N asesino/a *m/f*

assassinate [əˈsæsɪneɪt] VT asesinar

assassination [əˌsæsɪˈneɪʃən] N asesinato *m*

assault [əˈsɔːlt] Ⓐ N **1** (*Mil, fig*) asalto *m*, ataque *m* (**on** a); **to make** *or* **mount an ~ on** asaltar **2** (*Jur*) agresión *f*; **~ and battery** (*Jur*) lesiones *fpl* Ⓑ VT **1** (*Mil*) asaltar, atacar **2** (*Jur*) asaltar, agredir; (*sexually*) agredir sexualmente; (= *rape*)

violar Ⓒ CPD ➤ **assault course** (*Brit*) pista *f* americana

assemble [əˈsembl] Ⓐ VT **1** [+ *people, team, collection*] reunir; [+ *facts, evidence, ideas*] recopilar; (*Parl*) convocar **2** [+ *device, furniture*] armar, montar Ⓑ VI reunirse

assembly [əˈsemblɪ] Ⓐ N **1** (= *meeting*) reunión *f*, asamblea *f*; (= *people present*) concurrencia *f*, asistentes *mpl*; **the right of ~** el derecho de reunión **2** (*Pol*) asamblea *f*; **the Assembly** (*US*) la Asamblea **3** (*Brit Scol*) reunión *f* general de todos los alumnos **4** (*Tech*) montaje *m*, ensamblaje *m* Ⓑ CPD ➤ **assembly line** cadena *f* de montaje ➤ **assembly plant** fábrica *f* de montaje

assent [əˈsent] Ⓐ N (= *agreement*) asentimiento *m*, consentimiento *m*; (= *approval*) aprobación *f* Ⓑ VI asentir (**to** a), consentir (**to** en)

assert [əˈsɜːt] VT **1** (= *declare*) afirmar, aseverar; [+ *innocence*] afirmar **2** (= *insist on*) [+ *rights*] hacer valer **3** (= *establish*) [+ *authority*] imponer; **to ~ o.s.** imponerse

assertion [əˈsɜːʃən] N afirmación *f*, aseveración *f*

assertive [əˈsɜːtɪv] ADJ [*manner, tone*] firme y enérgico; [*behaviour*] enérgico; **you were very ~ in that meeting** te mostraste muy firme y enérgico en esa reunión; **slowly she began to become more ~** poco a poco empezó a mostrarse más segura de sí misma *or* empezó a hacerse valer más

assertiveness [əˈsɜːtɪvnɪs] N firmeza *f*

assess [əˈses] VT **1** (= *evaluate*) [+ *damage, property, situation*] valorar **2** (= *calculate*) [+ *value, amount*] calcular (**at** en); [+ *income*] gravar **3** (*Univ, Scol, Ind*) evaluar

assessment [əˈsesmənt] N **1** (= *evaluation*) [*of damage, property*] valoración *f*, tasación *f*; (= *judgment*) juicio *m*, valoración *f* **2** (*Fin, Tax*) **tax ~** cálculo *m* de los ingresos, estimación *f* de la base impositiva **3** (*Univ, Scol, Ind*) (= *appraisal*) evaluación *f*

asset [ˈæset] Ⓐ N **1** (= *advantage*) ventaja *f*; **she is a great ~ to the department** es una persona valiosísima en el departamento **2** (*Fin etc*) bien *m*; (= *book-keeping item*) partida *f* del activo; **~s** (*on accounts*) haberes *mpl*, activo *msing*; **personal ~s** bienes *mpl* personales; **~s and liabilities** activo *msing* y pasivo *msing* Ⓑ CPD ➤ **asset stripper** *especulador que compra empresas en crisis para vender sus bienes* ➤ **asset stripping** *acaparamiento de activos con vistas a su venta y a la liquidación de la empresa*

asshole* [ˈæshəʊl] (*esp US*) N **1** (*Anat*) culo** *m* **2** (= *person*) gilipollas*** *mf inv*, pendejo/a *m/f* (*LAm**), huevón/ona *m/f* (*And, Ven**)

assiduous [əˈsɪdjʊəs] ADJ diligente

assiduously [əˈsɪdjʊəslɪ] ADV diligentemente

assign [əˈsaɪn] VT (= *allot*) [+ *task*] asignar; [+ *room*] destinar; [+ *date*] señalar, fijar (**for** para); [+ *person*] destinar; **to ~ sb to sth** destinar a algn a algo

assignation [ˌæsɪgˈneɪʃən] N [*of lovers*] cita *f* secreta

assignment [əˈsaɪnmənt] N **1** (= *mission*) misión *f*; (= *task*) tarea *f*; **to be on (an) ~** estar cumpliendo una misión **2** (*Scol, Univ*) trabajo *m* **3** (= *allocation*) asignación *f*

assimilate [əˈsɪmɪleɪt] Ⓐ VT asimilar Ⓑ VI asimilarse

assimilation [əˌsɪmɪˈleɪʃən] N asimilación *f*

assist [əˈsɪst] Ⓐ VT [+ *person*] ayudar; [+ *development, growth etc*] fomentar, estimular; **to ~ sb to do sth** ayudar a algn a hacer algo; **we ~ed him to his car** le ayudamos a llegar a su coche Ⓑ VI ayudar; **to ~ in sth** ayudar en algo; **to ~ in doing sth** ayudar a hacer algo

assistance [əˈsɪstəns] N ayuda *f*, auxilio *m*; **to be of ~ to** ayudar a, prestar ayuda a; **can I be of any ~?** ¿puedo ayudarle?, ¿le puedo servir en algo?; **to come to sb's ~** acudir en ayuda *or* auxilio de algn

assistant [əˈsɪstənt] N ayudante *mf*; (= *language assistant*) lector(a) *m/f* ➤ **assistant manager** subdirector(a) *m/f* ➤ **assistant referee** (*Ftbl*) asistente *mf*

assizes [əˈsaɪzɪz] NPL (*Brit*) (*formerly*) sesiones *fpl* jurídicas (regionales)

associate Ⓐ [əˈsəʊʃɪɪt] ADJ [*company*] asociado Ⓑ [əˈsəʊʃɪɪt] N (= *colleague*) colega *mf*; **Fred Bloggs and Associates** Fred Bloggs y Asociados Ⓒ [əˈsəʊʃɪeɪt] VT **1** (*mentally*) [+ *ideas, things, people*] asociar,

relacionar (**with** con)
2 (= *link*) vincular, asociar; **high blood pressure is ~d with heart disease** se vincula *or* asocia la tensión alta con las enfermedades coronarias
Ⓓ [əˈsəʊʃɪeɪt] VI **to ~ with sb** relacionarse con algn, tratar con algn
Ⓔ [əˈsəʊʃɪɪt] CPD ➤ **associate degree** (*US*) licenciatura *f*
➤ **associate member** [*of society*] miembro *mf* no numerario/a; [*of professional body*] colegiado/a *m/f*; [*of learned body*] miembro *mf* correspondiente

association [ə,səʊsɪˈeɪʃən] **Ⓐ** N **1** (= *act, partnership*) asociación *f*; **in ~ with** conjuntamente con
2 (= *organization*) sociedad *f*, asociación *f* **3** (= *connection*) conexión *f*; **~ of ideas** asociación *f* de ideas; **the name has unpleasant ~s** el nombre trae recuerdos desagradables; **the town has historic ~s** la ciudad posee connotaciones históricas **Ⓑ** CPD ➤ **association football** (*Brit*) fútbol *m*

assorted [əˈsɔːtɪd] ADJ surtido; **~ cakes** pasteles surtidos; **he dined with ~ ministers** cenó con diversos ministros

assortment [əˈsɔːtmənt] N **1** (*Comm*) surtido *m*
2 (= *mixture*) mezcla *f*; (= *collection*) colección *f*; **there was a strange ~ of guests** había una extraña mezcla de invitados

assuage [əˈsweɪdʒ] VT (*liter*) [+ *feelings, anger*] aplacar; [+ *pain*] calmar, aliviar; [+ *passion*] mitigar, suavizar; [+ *desire*] satisfacer; [+ *appetite*] satisfacer, saciar; **he was not easily ~d** no resultaba fácil apaciguarlo *or* sosegarlo

assume [əˈsjuːm] VT **1** (= *suppose*) suponer; **we may therefore ~ that ...** así, es de suponer que ...; **let us ~ that ...** pongamos por caso *or* supongamos que ...; **assuming that ...** suponiendo que ..., en el supuesto de que ...; **you are assuming a lot** supones demasiado, eso es mucho suponer; **you resigned, I ~** dimitiste, me imagino **2** (= *take on, take over*) [+ *power, control, responsibility*] asumir; [+ *authority*] (*unjustly*) apropiarse, arrogarse **3** (= *adopt*) [+ *name, attitude, look of surprise*] adoptar; [+ *air*] darse

assumption [əˈsʌmpʃən] **Ⓐ** N **1** (= *supposition*) suposición *f*, supuesto *m*; **on the ~ that** suponiendo que, poniendo por caso que **2** [*of power, responsibility*] asunción *f* **Ⓑ** CPD ➤ **Assumption Day** Día *m* de la Asunción

assurance [əˈʃʊərəns] N **1** (= *guarantee*) garantía *f*, promesa *f*; **I give you my ~ that ...** le puedo asegurar que ...
2 (= *certainty*) certeza *f*, seguridad *f* **3** (= *confidence*) confianza *f*; (= *self-confidence*) seguridad *f*, aplomo *m* **4** (*Brit*) (= *insurance*) seguro *m*

assure [əˈʃʊəʳ] VT asegurar; **you may rest ~d that ...** tenga la (plena) seguridad de que ...

AST N ABBR (*US, Canada*) = **Atlantic Standard Time**

asterisk [ˈæstərɪsk] N asterisco *m*

asteroid [ˈæstərɔɪd] N asteroide *m*

asthma [ˈæsmə] N asma *f*

> Use **el/un** not **la/una** before feminine nouns beginning with stressed **a** or **ha** like **asma**.

asthmatic [æsˈmætɪk] ADJ, N asmático/a *m/f*

astigmatism [æsˈtɪɡmətɪzəm] N astigmatismo *m*

astonish [əˈstɒnɪʃ] VT asombrar, pasmar; **you ~ me!** (*iro*) ¡no me digas!, ¡vaya sorpresa!

astonished [əˈstɒnɪʃt] ADJ estupefacto, pasmado; **to be ~** asombrarse (**at** de); **I am ~ that ...** me asombra que ... + *subjun*

astonishing [əˈstɒnɪʃɪŋ] ADJ [*achievement, coincidence, news*] asombroso, pasmoso; **I find it ~ that ...** me asombra *or* pasma que ... + *subjun*, me parece increíble que ... + *subjun*

astonishingly [əˈstɒnɪʃɪŋlɪ] ADV asombrosamente; **it was ~ easy** asombraba lo fácil que era, era asombrosamente fácil; **an ~ beautiful young woman** una joven de una belleza asombrosa; **~, he was right** por increíble que parezca, tenía razón

astonishment [əˈstɒnɪʃmənt] N asombro *m*; (*stronger*) estupefacción *f*; **to my ~** para mi asombro *or* sorpresa

astound [əˈstaʊnd] VT asombrar, pasmar

astounded [əˈstaʊndɪd] ADJ pasmado, estupefacto

astounding [əˈstaʊndɪŋ] ADJ asombroso, pasmoso; **I find it ~ that ...** me asombra *or* pasma que ... + *subjun*

astral [ˈæstrəl] ADJ astral

astray [əˈstreɪ] ADV **to go ~** (= *get lost*) extraviarse; (*morally*) ir por mal camino; **to lead sb ~** llevar a algn por mal camino

astride [əˈstraɪd] **Ⓐ** ADV a horcajadas **Ⓑ** PREP [+ *horse, fence*] a horcajadas sobre

astringent [əˈstrɪndʒənt] **Ⓐ** ADJ **1** (*Med*) astringente **2** (*fig*) adusto, austero **Ⓑ** N (*Med*) astringente *m*

astrologer [əˈstrɒlədʒəʳ] N astrólogo/a *m/f*

astrology [əˈstrɒlədʒɪ] N astrología *f*

astronaut [ˈæstrənɔːt] N astronauta *mf*

astronomer [əˈstrɒnəməʳ] N astrónomo/a *m/f*

astronomical [æstrəˈnɒmɪkəl] ADJ astronómico

astronomically [æstrəˈnɒmɪkəlɪ] ADV [*rise, increase*] astronómicamente, exageradamente; **lobster is ~ expensive** la langosta está a precios astronómicos

astronomy [əˈstrɒnəmɪ] N astronomía *f*

astrophysics [ˈæstrəʊˈfɪzɪks] NSING astrofísica *f*

Astroturf® [ˈæstrəʊtɜːʃ] N césped *m* artificial

Asturias [æˈstʊərɪæs] N Asturias *f*

astute [əsˈtjuːt] ADJ astuto; **that was very ~ of you** en eso has sido muy listo

asunder [əˈsʌndəʳ] ADV **to tear ~** (*liter*) hacer pedazos

asylum [əˈsaɪləm] N (= *refuge*) asilo *m*; (= *mental hospital*) manicomio *m*; **political ~** asilo *m* político ➤ **asylum seeker** solicitante *mf* de asilo

asymmetrical [ˌeɪsɪˈmetrɪkəl], **asymmetric** [ˌeɪsɪˈmetrɪk] ADJ asimétrico ➤ **asymmetrical bars** barras *fpl* asimétricas

at [æt] PREP

> When **at** is an element in a phrasal verb, eg **look at**, look up the verb.

1 (*position*) en; **at the party/lecture** en la fiesta/conferencia; **at the hairdresser's/supermarket** en la peluquería/el supermercado; **at the office** en la oficina; **at school** en la escuela, en el colegio; **at table** en la mesa; **at John's** en casa de Juan; ✦ IDIOMS **where it's at***: **Glasgow's where it's at*** en Glasgow sí que hay ambiente *or* (*Sp*) marcha**; **where we're at**: **I'll just run through where we're at** te voy a poner al tanto *or* al corriente de cuál es la situación; **my room's at the back/front of the house** mi dormitorio está en la parte de atrás/parte delantera de la casa; **the dress fastens at the back/front** el vestido se abrocha por detrás/por delante; **at the bottom of the stairs** al pie de las escaleras; **to stand at the door** estar de pie *or* (*LAm*) parado en la puerta; **at the top** (*gen*) en lo alto; (*of mountain*) en la cumbre; **to be at the window** estar junto a la ventana
2 (*esp Internet*) (= *name of @ symbol*) arroba *f*
3 (= *towards*) hacia; **the car was coming straight at us** el coche venía directo hacia nosotros
4 (*time, age*) a; **at four o'clock** a las cuatro; **at 16** (*age*) a los 16 años; **at lunchtime** a la hora de la comida, a la hora de almorzar; **at an early age** de pequeño; **at Christmas** por *or* en Navidades; **at Easter** en Semana Santa; **at the moment** en este momento; **at night** de noche, por la noche; **at a time like this** en un momento como éste; **at my time of life** con los años que tengo
5 (*rate*) a; **at 50p a kilo** a 50 peniques el kilo; **at 50p each** (a) 50 peniques cada uno; **two at a time** de dos en dos; **to go at 100km an hour** ir a 100km por hora
6 (*activity*) **he's good at games** se le dan bien los deportes; **at it**: **while you're at it*** (= *doing it*) de paso; (= *by the way*) a propósito; **she's at it again*** otra vez con las mismas; **I could tell she'd been at the whisky** se notaba que le había estado dando al whisky*; **at war** en guerra; **to be at work** (= *working*) estar trabajando; (= *in the office*) estar en la oficina
7 (*manner*) **acting at its best** una actuación de antología; **at peace** en paz; **at a run** corriendo, a la carrera; **at full speed** a toda velocidad

8 (*cause*) **to awaken at the least sound** despertarse al menor ruido; **at her cries** al escuchar sus gritos; **at my request** a petición mía; **at his suggestion** a sugerencia suya

ate [et, eɪt] PT *of* **eat**

atheism ['eɪθɪɪzəm] N ateísmo *m*

atheist ['eɪθɪɪst] N ateo/a *m/f*

Athens ['æθɪnz] N Atenas *f*

athlete ['æθliːt] N atleta *mf* ➤ **athlete's foot** (*Med*) pie *m* de atleta

athletic [æθ'letɪk] ADJ [*club, association, event*] de atletismo; [*person, body*] atlético

athletics [æθ'letɪks] NSING (*Brit*) atletismo *m*; (*US*) deportes *mpl*

Atlantic [ət'læntɪk] **Ⓐ** ADJ atlántico **Ⓑ** N **the ~ (Ocean)** el (Océano) Atlántico

atlas ['ætləs] N (= *world atlas*) atlas *m inv*; (= *road atlas*) guía *f* de carreteras

ATM N ABBR (*US*) (= **Automated Teller Machine**) cajero *m* automático

atmosphere ['ætməsfɪəʳ] N atmósfera *f*; (*fig*) ambiente *m*

atmospheric [ætməs'ferɪk] ADJ (*Met, Phys*) atmosférico; [*music, film, book*] evocador

atoll ['ætɒl] N atolón *m*

atom ['ætəm] N (*Phys*) átomo *m*; **there is not an ~ of truth in it** eso no tiene ni pizca de verdad; **to smash sth to ~s** hacer algo añicos ➤ **atom bomb** bomba *f* atómica

atomic [ə'tɒmɪk] ADJ atómico

atomizer ['ætəmaɪzəʳ] N atomizador *m*, pulverizador *m*

atone [ə'təʊn] VI **to ~ for** expiar

atonement [ə'təʊnmənt] N expiación *f*; **to make ~ for** enmendar, desagraviar

atrocious [ə'trəʊʃəs] ADJ **1** (= *shocking*) [*crime, treatment*] atroz **2** (*) (= *very bad*) [*film, food, spelling*] pésimo, espantoso; [*weather*] espantoso

atrociously [ə'trəʊʃəslɪ] ADV **1** (= *shockingly*) [*treat*] atrozmente; **he was ~ bad-tempered** tenía un genio atroz **2** (*) (= *badly*) [*sing, spell, behave*] pésimamente, espantosamente

atrocity [ə'trɒsɪtɪ] N atrocidad *f*

atrophy ['ætrəfɪ] **Ⓐ** N (*Med*) atrofia *f* **Ⓑ** VI atrofiarse

attach [ə'tætʃ] VT **1** (= *fasten*) sujetar; (= *stick*) pegar; (= *tie*) atar, amarrar (*LAm*); (*with pin etc*) prender; (= *join up*) [+ *trailer etc*] acoplar; (= *put on*) [+ *seal*] poner **2** (*in letter*) adjuntar; **the ~ed letter** la carta adjunta; **please find ~ed details of ...** les adjuntamos detalles de ... **3** (= *attribute*) [+ *importance, value*] dar, atribuir (**to** a) **4** (= *connect*) **to ~ conditions (to sth)** imponer condiciones (a algo); **to be ~ed to an embassy** estar agregado a una embajada **5** (*emotionally*) **they are very ~ed (to each other)** se quieren mucho; **to become ~ed to sb** encariñarse con algn

attaché [ə'tæʃeɪ] N agregado/a *m/f* ➤ **attaché case** maletín *m*

attachment [ə'tætʃmənt] N **1** (= *accessory*) accesorio *m*, dispositivo *m* **2** (*Comput*) archivo *m* adjunto, documento *m* adjunto

attack [ə'tæk] **Ⓐ** N **1** (*Mil, Sport, fig*) ataque *m* (**on** a, contra, sobre); (= *assault*) atentado *m*, agresión *f*; **to leave o.s. open to ~** dejarse expuesto a un ataque; **to be/come under ~** ser atacado; ✦ PROV **~ is the best form of defence** la mejor defensa es el ataque *or* un buen ataque **2** (*Med*) (*gen*) ataque *m*; (= *fit*) acceso *m*, crisis *f inv*; **an ~ of pneumonia** una pulmonía; **an ~ of nerves** un ataque de nervios, una crisis nerviosa **Ⓑ** VT **1** (*Mil, Sport, Med, fig*) atacar; (= *assault*) agredir **2** (= *tackle*) [+ *job, problem*] enfrentarse con; (= *combat*) combatir **Ⓒ** VI atacar

attacker [ə'tækəʳ] N agresor(a) *m/f*, atacante *mf*

attain [ə'teɪn] VT [+ *knowledge, happiness, goal, aim*] lograr; [+ *age, rank*] llegar a, alcanzar; (= *get hold of*) conseguir

attainable [ə'teɪnəbl] ADJ alcanzable

attainment [ə'teɪnmənt] N **1** (= *achieving*) [*of knowledge, happiness, goal, aim*] logro *m*; [*of independence, freedom*] conquista *f*, consecución *f* **2** (= *accomplishment*) logro *m*

attempt [ə'tempt] **Ⓐ** N **1** (= *try*) intento *m*; **at the first ~** en el primer intento; **this is my first ~** es la primera vez que lo intento; **we had to give up the ~** tuvimos que renunciar a la empresa; **it was a good ~** fue un esfuerzo digno de alabanza; **to make an ~ to do sth** hacer una tentativa de hacer algo, intentar hacer algo; **he made no ~ to help** ni siquiera intentó ayudar; **he made two ~s at it** lo intentó dos veces **2** (= *attack*) atentado *m*; **to make an ~ on sb's life** atentar contra la vida de algn **Ⓑ** VT [+ *task*] tratar de realizar, intentar realizar; [+ *exam question*] tratar de responder a, intentar responder a; **to ~ suicide** tratar de suicidarse, intentar suicidarse; **to ~ to do sth** tratar de *or* intentar *or* procurar hacer algo; **~ed murder** tentativa *f* de asesinato, intento *m* de asesinato

attend [ə'tend] **Ⓐ** VT **1** (= *be present at*) [+ *meeting etc*] asistir a, acudir a; (*regularly*) [+ *school, church*] ir a **2** (= *wait upon*) [*waiter*] servir, atender; [*servant, helper*] ocuparse de; (*Med*) atender, asistir; (= *accompany*) acompañar **Ⓑ** VI (= *be present*) asistir, acudir ➤ **attend to** VI + PREP **1** (= *deal with*) [+ *task, business*] ocuparse de, atender; (*Comm*) [+ *order*] tramitar; **to ~ to one's work** ocuparse de su trabajo **2** (= *give help to*) servir a; **to ~ to a customer** atender a un(a) cliente; **are you being ~ed to?** (*in shop*) ¿le atienden?

attendance [ə'tendəns] **Ⓐ** N **1** (= *presence*) asistencia *f* (**at** a); **is my ~ necessary?** ¿debo asistir?, ¿es preciso que asista yo? **2** (= *those present*) concurrencia *f*; **a large ~** una numerosa concurrencia; **what was the ~ at the meeting?** ¿cuántos asistieron a la reunión? **3** (*Med*) asistencia *f* **Ⓑ** CPD ➤ **attendance fee** honorarios *mpl* por asistencia ➤ **attendance sheet** hoja *f* de asistencia

attendant [ə'tendənt] **Ⓐ** N (*in car park, museum*) guarda *mf*, celador(a) *m/f*; (*at wedding etc*) acompañante *mf* **Ⓑ** ADJ (*frm*) (= *associated*) relacionado, concomitante; **old age and its ~ ills** la vejez y los achaques correspondientes

attention [ə'tenʃən] **Ⓐ** N **1** atención *f*; **(your) ~ please!** ¡atención por favor!; **to attract sb's ~** llamar la atención de algn; **to call** *or* **draw sb's ~ to sth** hacer notar algo a algn; **it has come to my ~ that ...** me he enterado de que ...; **for the ~ of Mr. Jones** a la atención del Sr. Jones; **to pay ~ (to)** prestar atención (a); **he paid no ~ (to that)** no hizo caso (de eso) **2** (*Mil*) **~!** ¡firme(s)!; **to stand to ~** estar firme(s) **3 attentions** [*of would-be suitor, media*] atenciones *fpl* **Ⓑ** CPD ➤ **Attention Deficit Disorder** síndrome *m* de déficit de atención ➤ **attention span** capacidad *f* de concentración

attention-seeking [ə'tenʃənˌsiːkɪŋ] ADJ que busca *or* intenta llamar la atención

attentive [ə'tentɪv] ADJ **1** (= *alert*) [*audience, pupil*] atento; **you have to be ~ to the customers' needs** tienes que estar pendiente de *or* prestar atención a las necesidades de los clientes **2** (= *considerate, polite*) atento (**to** con)

attentively [ə'tentɪvlɪ] ADV atentamente

attenuate [ə'tenjʊeɪt] VT atenuar

attest [ə'test] **Ⓐ** VT atestiguar; [+ *signature*] legalizar; **to ~ that ...** atestiguar que ... **Ⓑ** VI **to ~ to** dar fe de, dar testimonio de

attic ['ætɪk] N desván *m*, altillo *m* (*LAm*), entretecho *m* (*LAm*)

attire [ə'taɪəʳ] (*frm*) **Ⓐ** N traje *m*, vestido *m*; (*hum*) atavío *m* **Ⓑ** VT vestir (**in** de); (*hum*) ataviar (**in** de)

attitude ['ætɪtjuːd] N **1** (= *way of behaving*) actitud *f*; **I don't like your ~** no me gusta tu actitud; **his ~ towards me has changed** su actitud con respecto a mí ha cambiado; **if that's your ~** si te pones en ese plan; **what's your ~ to this?** ¿cuál es tu postura a este respeto? **2** (*) (= *spirit*) **women with ~** mujeres *fpl* con carácter, mujeres *f* con personalidad

attorney [ə'tɜːnɪ] N (*US*) abogado/a *m/f* ➤ **Attorney General** (*US*) ≈ ministro/a *m/f* de justicia, ≈ procurador(a) *m/f* general (*LAm*); (*Brit*) ≈ fiscal *mf* general del Estado

attract [ə'trækt] VT (*gen*) atraer; [+ *attention*] llamar; **to be ~ed to sb** sentirse atraído por algn

attraction [ə'trækʃən] N **1** (*between people, also Phys*) atracción *f*; **I felt an instant ~ towards him** inmediatamente me sentí atraída por él **2** (= *attractive feature*) encanto *m*, atractivo *m*; (= *inducement*) aliciente *m*; **the main ~ at the party was Cindy** Cindy era el principal atractivo que tenía la fiesta

attractive [ə'træktɪv] ADJ (*gen*) atractivo; [*name*] bonito; [*sound*] agradable; [*option, plan, prospect*] atrayente; **to find sb ~** encontrar atractivo a algn; **the idea was ~ to her** la idea la atraía

attractively [ə'træktɪvlɪ] ADV [*smile, laugh*] de manera atrayente; [*arranged, presented*] de manera atractiva

attributable [ə'trɪbjʊtəbl] ADJ **~ to** atribuible a

attribute Ⓐ [ˈætrɪbjuːt] N atributo *m* Ⓑ [ə'trɪbjuːt] VT (*gen, Literat, Art*) atribuir (**to** a); [+ *blame*] atribuir, achacar (**to** a); **to what would you ~ this?** ¿a qué atribuyes *or* achacas tú esto?

attributive [ə'trɪbjʊtɪv] ADJ atributivo

attrition [ə'trɪʃən] N **1** (= *wearing away*) desgaste *m*; **war of ~** guerra *f* de desgaste **2** (*esp US Ind, Univ*) amortización *f* de puestos

attune [ə'tjuːn] VT **to be ~d to sth** (= *sensitive to*) estar sensibilizado a algo; (= *in keeping with*) estar acorde con algo

atypical [eɪ'tɪpɪkəl] ADJ atípico

aubergine [ˈəʊbəʒiːn] N (*Brit*) berenjena *f*

auburn [ˈɔːbən] ADJ [*hair*] color castaño rojizo *inv*

auction [ˈɔːkʃən] Ⓐ N subasta *f*, remate *m* (*LAm*); **to put up for ~** subastar, poner en pública subasta Ⓑ VT (*also ~ off*) subastar, rematar (*LAm*) Ⓒ CPD ➤ **auction house** casa *f* de subastas ➤ **auction room** sala *f* de subastas ➤ **auction sale** subasta *f*, remate *m* (*LAm*)

auctioneer [ɔːkʃə'nɪəʳ] N subastador(a) *m/f*, rematador(a) *m/f*

audacious [ɔː'deɪʃəs] ADJ **1** (= *bold*) audaz, osado **2** (= *impudent*) atrevido, descarado

audacity [ɔː'dæsɪtɪ] N **1** (= *boldness*) audacia *f*, osadía *f* **2** (= *impudence*) atrevimiento *m*, descaro *m*; **to have the ~ to do sth** tener el descaro de hacer algo

audible [ˈɔːdɪbl] ADJ audible; **his voice was scarcely ~** apenas se podía oír su voz, su voz era apenas perceptible

audibly [ˈɔːdɪblɪ] ADV de forma audible

audience [ˈɔːdɪəns] Ⓐ N **1** (= *gathering*) público *m*; (*in theatre etc*) público *m*, auditorio *m*; **there was a big ~** asistió un gran público; **TV ~s** telespectadores *mpl* **2** (= *interview*) audiencia *f* (**with** con); **to have an ~ with** tener audiencia con, ser recibido en audiencia por Ⓑ CPD ➤ **audience participation** participación *f* del público ➤ **audience rating** índice *m* de audiencia

audio [ˈɔːdɪəʊ] Ⓐ ADJ de audio Ⓑ N audio *m* Ⓒ CPD ➤ **audio book** audiolibro *m* ➤ **audio cassette** cassette *f*, cinta *f* de audio ➤ **audio equipment** equipo *m* de audio

audiotape [ˈɔːdɪəʊteɪp] Ⓐ N **1** (= *tape*) cinta *f* de audio **2** (*US*) (= *recording*) grabación *f* (en cinta) Ⓑ VT (*US*) grabar (en cinta)

audiotypist [ˈɔːdɪəʊˌtaɪpɪst] N mecanógrafo/a *m/f* de dictáfono

audiovisual [ɔːdɪəʊ'vɪzjʊəl] ADJ audiovisual

audit [ˈɔːdɪt] Ⓐ N auditoría *f*, revisión *f* de cuentas Ⓑ VT **1** (*Fin*) auditar, realizar una auditoría de, revisar **2** (*US Univ*) **to ~ a course** asistir a un curso como oyente

audition [ɔː'dɪʃən] Ⓐ N (*Theat, Cine, TV*) prueba *f*, audición *f*; **to give sb an ~** (*Theat*) hacer una prueba a algn, ofrecer una audición a algn Ⓑ VI **he ~ed for the part** hizo una prueba *or* audición para el papel Ⓒ VT hacer una prueba *or* audición a; **he was ~ed for the part** le hicieron una prueba *or* audición para el papel

auditor [ˈɔːdɪtəʳ] N **1** (*Comm, Fin*) auditor(a) *m/f*; **~'s report** informe *m* de auditoría **2** (*US Univ*) oyente *mf*, estudiante *mf* libre

auditorium [ɔːdɪ'tɔːrɪəm] N (*pl* **~s** *or* **auditoria** [ɔːdɪ'tɔːrɪə]) auditorio *m*, sala *f*

Aug. ABBR (= **August**) ag.

augment [ɔːg'ment] Ⓐ VT aumentar Ⓑ VI aumentar(se)

au gratin [əʊ'grætæn] ADJ (*Culin*) gratinado

augur [ˈɔːgəʳ] VI **it ~s well/ill** es un buen/mal augurio (**for** para); **it ~s no good** esto no promete nada bueno

August [ˈɔːgəst] N agosto *m*; *see* **July**

august [ɔː'gʌst] ADJ augusto

aunt [ɑːnt] N tía *f*; **my ~ and uncle** mis tíos *mpl*; **Aunt Julia phoned** ha llamado la tía Julia

auntie*, **aunty*** [ˈɑːntɪ] N tía *f*

au pair [əʊ'peəʳ] Ⓐ N (*pl* **~s**) au pair *mf* Ⓑ VI **to ~ (for sb)** hacer de au pair (para algn)

aura [ˈɔːrə] N aura *f*, halo *m*; (*Rel*) aureola *f*

> Use **el/un** not **la/una** before feminine nouns beginning with stressed **a** or **ha** like **aura**.

aural [ˈɔːrəl] ADJ del oído; **~ exam** examen *m* de comprensión oral

aurora borealis [ɔː'rɔːrəbɔːrɪ'eɪlɪs] N aurora *f* boreal

auspices [ˈɔːspɪsɪz] NPL **under the ~ of** bajo los auspicios de

auspicious [ɔːs'pɪʃəs] ADJ (*frm*) [*day, time*] propicio; [*sign*] de buen augurio; [*occasion, moment*] feliz; **to make an ~ start** comenzar felizmente *or* con buenos auspicios

Aussie* [ˈɒzɪ] = **Australian**

austere [ɒs'tɪəʳ] ADJ austero, severo

austerity [ɒs'terɪtɪ] N austeridad *f*

Australasia [ɒːstrə'leɪzɪə] N Australasia *f*

Australia [ɒs'treɪlɪə] N Australia *f*; *ver tb* **www.gov.au**

Australian [ɒs'treɪlɪən] ADJ, N australiano/a *m/f*

Austria [ˈɒstrɪə] N Austria *f*

Austrian [ˈɒstrɪən] ADJ, N austriaco/a *m/f*

authentic [ɔː'θentɪk] ADJ auténtico

authenticate [ɔː'θentɪkeɪt] VT autentificar, autenticar

authenticity [ɔːθen'tɪsɪtɪ] N **1** (= *genuineness*) [*of text, painting*] autenticidad *f* **2** (= *realistic quality*) [*of decor, furniture*] realismo *m*

author [ˈɔːθəʳ] N (= *writer*) autor(a) *m/f*

authoritarian [ɔːθɒrɪ'teərɪən] ADJ, N autoritario/a *m/f*

authoritative [ɔː'θɒrɪtətɪv] ADJ **1** (= *reliable*) [*account, book, writer, professor*] de gran autoridad, acreditado; [*source, statement, information, study*] autorizado **2** (= *commanding*) autoritario

authority [ɔː'θɒrɪtɪ] N **1** (= *power*) autoridad *f*; **those in ~** los que tienen la autoridad; **who is in ~ here?** ¿quién manda aquí?
2 (= *authorization*) **to give sb the ~ to do sth** autorizar a algn a hacer algo, autorizar a algn para que haga algo; **to have ~ to do sth** tener autoridad *or* estar autorizado para hacer algo; **on one's own ~** por su propia autoridad; **to do sth without ~** hacer algo sin tener autorización
3 (= *official body*) autoridad *f*; **the customs authorities** las autoridades aduaneras; **to apply to the proper authorities** dirigirse a la autoridad competente
4 (= *expert*) autoridad *f*; **he's an ~ (on)** es una autoridad (en)
5 (= *expert opinion*) autoridad *f*; **on the ~ of Plato** con la autoridad de Platón; **I have it on good ~ that ...** sé de buena fuente que ...

authorization [ɔːθəraɪ'zeɪʃən] N autorización *f*

authorize [ˈɔːθəraɪz] VT (= *empower*) autorizar; (= *approve*) aprobar; **to ~ sb to do sth** autorizar a algn a hacer algo; **to be ~d to do sth** estar autorizado para hacer algo, tener autorización para hacer algo

authorized [ˈɔːθəraɪzd] ADJ autorizado; **~ agent** agente *mf* oficial; **~ biography** biografía *f* oficial

authorship [ˈɔːθəʃɪp] N [*of book etc*] autoría *f*; **of unknown**

~ de autor desconocido, anónimo

autism [ˈɔːtɪzəm] N autismo *m*

autistic [ɔːˈtɪstɪk] ADJ autista

auto [ˈɔːtəʊ] N (*US*) coche *m*, automóvil *m*, carro *m* (*LAm*) ➤ **auto repair** reparación *f* de automóviles ➤ **Auto Show** Salón *m* del Automóvil ➤ **auto worker** trabajador(a) *m/f* de la industria automovilística *or* del automóvil

autobank [ˈɔːtəʊbæŋk] N cajero *m* automático

autobiographical [ˈɔːtəʊˌbaɪəˈɡræfɪkəl] ADJ autobiográfico

autobiography [ˌɔːtəʊbaɪˈɒɡrəfɪ] N autobiografía *f*

autocratic [ˌɔːtəˈkrætɪk] ADJ autocrático

autocue [ˈɔːtəʊkjuː] N (*Brit TV*) autocue *m*, chuleta* *f*

autograph [ˈɔːtəɡrɑːf] Ⓐ N autógrafo *m* Ⓑ VT (= *sign*) firmar; [+ *book, photo*] dedicar Ⓒ CPD ➤ **autograph album** álbum *m* de autógrafos ➤ **autograph hunter** cazador(a) *m/f* de autógrafos

automat [ˈɔːtəmæt] N (*US*) restaurante *m* de autoservicio

automata [ɔːˈtɒmətə] NPL *of* **automaton**

automated [ˈɔːtəˌmeɪtɪd] ADJ automatizado ➤ **automated teller** cajero *m* automático

automatic [ˌɔːtəˈmætɪk] Ⓐ ADJ automático Ⓑ N (= *pistol*) pistola *f* automática; (= *car*) coche *m* automático; (= *washing machine*) lavadora *f* Ⓒ CPD ➤ **automatic data processing** (*Comput*) proceso *m* automático de datos

automatically [ˌɔːtəˈmætɪkəlɪ] ADV automáticamente

automation [ˌɔːtəˈmeɪʃən] N automatización *f*

automaton [ɔːˈtɒmətən] N (*pl* **~s** *or* **automata**) autómata *m*

automobile [ˈɔːtəməbiːl] (*US*) N coche *m*, automóvil *m*, carro *m* (*LAm*) ➤ **automobile industry** industria *f* del automóvil

automotive [ɔːtəˈməʊtɪv] ADJ automotor (*f*: automotora, automotriz)

autonomous [ɔːˈtɒnəməs] ADJ autónomo

autonomy [ɔːˈtɒnəmɪ] N autonomía *f*

autopilot [ˈɔːtəʊpaɪlət] N (*Aer*) piloto *m* automático; **to be on ~** (*fig*) ir como un/una autómata

autopsy [ˈɔːtɒpsɪ] N autopsia *f*

auto-timer [ˈɔːtəʊˌtaɪməʳ] N programador *m* automático

autumn [ˈɔːtəm] N (*esp Brit*) otoño *m*; **in ~** en otoño; **in early/ late ~** a principios/a finales del otoño

autumnal [ɔːˈtʌmnəl] ADJ otoñal, de(l) otoño

auxiliary [ɔːɡˈzɪlɪərɪ] Ⓐ ADJ auxiliar Ⓑ N **1** (*Med*) ayudante *mf* **2** (*also* **~ verb**) verbo *m* auxiliar

Av. ABBR (= **Avenue**) Av., Avda.

avail [əˈveɪl] (*liter*) Ⓐ N **it is of no ~** es inútil; **to be of little ~** ser de poco provecho; **to no ~** en vano Ⓑ VT **to ~ o.s. of** aprovechar(se de), valerse de

availability [əˌveɪləˈbɪlɪtɪ] N [*of goods, tickets*] disponibilidad *f*; **..., subject to ~** [*goods*] ..., siempre que haya existencias; **this depends on your ~ for work** esto depende de si estás disponible para trabajar

available [əˈveɪləbl] ADJ **1** [*object, service*] **1.1** (*with verb*) **to be ~**: **application forms are ~ here** las solicitudes se pueden conseguir aquí; **it's ~ in other colours** también viene en otros colores; **this item is not ~ at the moment** no disponemos de *or* no tenemos este artículo en este momento; **to become ~**: **new treatments are becoming ~** están apareciendo nuevos tratamientos; **a place has become ~ on the course** ha quedado una plaza libre en el curso; **~ for sth/sb**: **a car park is ~ for the use of customers** hay un aparcamiento a disposición de los clientes; **there are three boats ~ for hire** hay tres botes que se pueden alquilar; **the guide is ~ from all good bookshops** la guía se puede encontrar en todas las buenas librerías; **tickets are ~ from the box office** las entradas están a la venta en taquilla; **to make sth ~ to sb** [+ *resources*] poner algo a la disposición de algn **1.2** (*with noun*) disponible; **we did what we could in the time ~** hicimos lo que pudimos en el tiempo disponible *or* del que disponíamos; **he tried every ~ means to find her** hizo todo lo posible para encontrarla;

I'd like a seat on the first ~ flight quiero una plaza en el primer vuelo que haya **2** [*person*] libre; **are you ~ next Thursday?** ¿estás libre el jueves que viene?; **I'm ~ on this number** me puedes localizar en este número; **counsellors are ~ to talk to anyone who needs advice** los asesores están a la disposición de *or* están disponibles para hablar con cualquiera que necesite consejo; **there's no-one ~ to take your call** no hay nadie que pueda atender a su llamada; **the Minister is not ~ for comment** el Ministro no se dispone a hacer comentarios; **to make o.s. ~: he made himself ~ in case anybody had any questions** se puso a disposición de cualquiera que tuviese preguntas

avalanche [ˈævəlɑːnʃ] N avalancha *f*

avant-garde [ˈævɒŋˈɡɑːd] Ⓐ ADJ vanguardista, de vanguardia Ⓑ N vanguardia *f*

avarice [ˈævərɪs] N avaricia *f*

avaricious [ˌævəˈrɪʃəs] ADJ avaro

Ave ABBR (= **avenue**) Av., Avda.

avenge [əˈvendʒ] VT vengar; **to ~ o.s.** vengarse (**on sb** en algn)

avenue [ˈævənjuː] N (= *road*) avenida *f*, paseo *m*; **to explore every ~** explorar todas las vías *or* todos los caminos

average [ˈævərɪdʒ] Ⓐ ADJ **1** (*Math, Statistics*) [*age, wage, price, speed*] medio, promedio *inv* **2** (= *normal, typical*) medio; **of ~ ability** de capacidad media; **of ~ height** de estatura mediana *or* media; **he's not your ~ footballer*** no es el típico futbolista **3** (= *mediocre*) mediocre Ⓑ N media *f*, promedio *m*; **to do an ~ of 150kph** hacer una media *or* un promedio de 150kph; **above ~** superior a la media *or* al promedio, por encima de la media *or* del promedio; **below ~** inferior a la media *or* al promedio, por debajo de la media *or* del promedio; **on ~** como promedio, por término medio Ⓒ VT **1** (= *calculate average of*) calcular la media de, calcular el promedio de **2** (= *reach an average of*) **pay increases are averaging 9.75%** los aumentos de sueldo son, como media *or* promedio, del 9,75%; **the sales ~ 200 copies a week** el promedio de ventas es de unos 200 ejemplares a la semana; **the temperature ~d 13 degrees over the month** la temperatura media *or* promedio fue de unos 13 grados a lo largo del mes, la temperatura alcanzó una media *or* un promedio de unos 13 grados a lo largo del mes; **he ~d 140kph all the way** hizo un promedio *or* una media de 140kph en todo el recorrido ➤ **average out** Ⓐ VT + ADV calcular la media de, calcular el promedio de Ⓑ VI + ADV **it ~s out at 50p a glass** sale a un promedio *or* una media de 50 peniques el vaso; **our working hours ~ out at eight a day** trabajamos un promedio *or* una media de ocho horas al día

averse [əˈvɜːs] ADJ **to be ~ to sth** sentir repugnancia por algo; **to be ~ to doing sth** ser reacio a hacer algo; **I'm not ~ to an occasional drink** no me opongo a tomar una copa de vez en cuando

aversion [əˈvɜːʃən] N (= *dislike*) aversión *f* (**to, for** hacia); **I have an ~ to garlic** el ajo me repugna, tengo aversión por el ajo; **I have an ~ to him** me repugna, le tengo aversión

avert [əˈvɜːt] VT **1** (= *turn away*) [+ *eyes, thoughts*] apartar (**from** de); [+ *suspicion*] desviar (**from** de); [+ *possibility*] evitar **2** (= *prevent*) [+ *accident, danger etc*] prevenir

aviary [ˈeɪvɪərɪ] N pajarera *f*

aviation [ˌeɪvɪˈeɪʃən] N aviación *f* ➤ **aviation fuel** queroseno *m*, querosén *m* (*LAm*), combustible *m* utilizado en la aviación ➤ **aviation industry** industria *f* de la aviación

avid [ˈævɪd] ADJ [*collector, viewer, reader*] ávido; [*supporter, fan*] ferviente

avidly [ˈævɪdlɪ] ADV ávidamente, con avidez

avocado [ˌævəˈkɑːdəʊ] N (*pl* **~s**) (*also Brit* **~ pear**) aguacate *m*, palta *f* (*And, SC*)

avoid [əˈvɔɪd] VT evitar; [+ *duty*] eludir; **are you trying to ~**

me? ¿me estás evitando *or* esquivando?; **this way we ~ London** por esta ruta evitamos pasar por Londres; **to ~ sb's eye** esquivar la mirada de algn; **to ~ doing sth** evitar hacer algo

avoidable [əˈvɔɪdəbl] ADJ evitable

avoidance [əˈvɔɪdəns] N **the ~ of fatty foods** el evitar los alimentos grasos; **you can improve your health by the ~ of stress** uno puede mejorar su salud evitando el estrés

avowed [əˈvaʊd] ADJ declarado

AWACS [eɪˈwæks] N ABBR (= **Airborne Warning and Control System**) AWACS *m*

await [əˈweɪt] VT esperar, aguardar

awake [əˈweɪk] (*pt* **awoke** *or* **~d**; *pp* **awoken** *or* **~d**) **Ⓐ** ADJ despierto; **to be ~** estar despierto; **I was still only half ~** aún estaba medio dormido; **coffee keeps me ~** (= *keeps me alert*) el café me mantiene despierto; (= *stops me sleeping*) el café me desvela; **the noise kept me ~** el ruido no me dejó dormir; **I found it difficult to stay ~** me costaba mantenerme despierto, me costaba no dormirme; **I'm not going to stay ~ all night worrying about that** no voy a pasarme toda la noche en vela preocupándome por eso; **wide ~** totalmente despierto **Ⓑ** VT **1** (= *wake up*) despertar
2 (= *arouse*) [+ *suspicion, curiosity*] despertar; [+ *memories*] reavivar, resucitar **Ⓒ** VI **1** (*liter*) (= *wake up*) despertar; **he awoke to find himself in hospital** al despertar(se) vio que se hallaba en el hospital; **I awoke from a deep sleep** desperté de un sueño profundo
2 (= *become aware*) **she awoke to the fact that ...** se dio cuenta de que ...; **he finally awoke to his responsibilities** finalmente tomó conciencia de sus responsabilidades

awaken [əˈweɪkən] VT, VI = **awake B, C**

awakening [əˈweɪknɪŋ] N despertar *m*; **he got a rude ~** tuvo una desagradable sorpresa

award [əˈwɔːd] **Ⓐ** N **1** (= *prize*) premio *m*; (*Mil*) (= *medal*) condecoración *f*
2 (*Jur*) (= *sum of money*) (*punitive*) sanción *f*; (= *damages*) concesión *f*; **a record ~ for sexual harassment** una sanción récord por acoso sexual **Ⓑ** VT **1** [+ *prize, medal*] conceder, otorgar
2 (*Jur*) [+ *damages*] adjudicar
3 (*Sport*) **to ~ a penalty (against sb)** pitar *or* señalar (un) penalti (contra algn); **to ~ sb a penalty** conceder un penalti a algn **Ⓒ** CPD ➤ **award(s) ceremony** ceremonia *f* de entrega de premios ➤ **award winner** premiado/a *m/f*, galardonado/a *m/f*

award-winning [əˈwɔːdˌwɪnɪŋ] ADJ premiado, galardonado

aware [əˈwɛəʳ] ADJ **1** (= *cognizant*) **to be ~ that ...** saber que ..., ser consciente de que ...; **I am fully ~ that ...** tengo plena conciencia de que ...; **we are ~ of what is happening** somos conscientes de lo que ocurre; **not that I am ~ (of)** que yo sepa, no; **to become ~ of** enterarse de
2 (= *knowledgeable*) **politically ~** con conciencia política; **socially ~** sensibilizado con los temas sociales

awareness [əˈwɛənɪs] N conciencia *f*, conocimiento *m*

awash [əˈwɒʃ] ADJ inundado (**with** de)

away [əˈweɪ]

When **away** is an element in a phrasal verb, eg **die away**, **get away**, look up the verb.

Ⓐ ADV **1** (= *at or to a distance*) **far ~** lejos; **~ in the distance** a lo lejos; **it's ten miles ~ (from here)** está a diez millas (de aquí); **~ from the noise** lejos del ruido; **~ back in 1066** allá en 1066
2 (= *absent*) **to be ~ (from home)** estar fuera, estar ausente; **she's ~ today** hoy está fuera; **he's ~ for a week** está fuera una semana; **he's ~ in Bognor** está en Bognor; **she was ~ before I could shout** se fue antes de que yo pudiese gritar; **~ with you!*** (= *go away!*) ¡vete!, ¡fuera de aquí!; (*expressing disbelief*) ¡venga ya!, ¡anda ya!; (*joking*) ¡no digas bobadas ya!
3 (*Sport*) fuera (de casa); **to play ~** (*Sport*) jugar fuera;

Chelsea are ~ to Everton on Saturday el Chelsea juega fuera, en campo del Everton, el sábado
4 (*as intensifier*) sin parar; **he was working ~ in the garden** estaba trabajando sin parar en el jardín **Ⓑ** ADJ **the ~ team** el equipo de fuera; **~ match** partido *m* fuera de casa; **~ win** victoria *f* fuera de casa

awe [ɔː] N (= *fear*) pavor *m*; (= *wonder*) asombro *m*; (= *reverence*) temor *m* reverencial; **to be in ~ of** tener temor reverencial a

awe-inspiring [ˈɔːɪnˌspaɪərɪŋ] ADJ = **awesome 1**

awesome [ˈɔːsəm] ADJ **1** (= *impressive*) impresionante
2 (= *huge*) [*task, responsibility*] abrumador **3** (*esp US**) (= *excellent*) formidable

awe-struck [ˈɔːstrʌk] ADJ pasmado, atemorizado

awful [ˈɔːfəl] **Ⓐ** ADJ **1** (= *dreadful*) [*weather*] horrible, espantoso; [*clothes, crime*] horroroso, espantoso; [*smell, dilemma, suspicion*] terrible; **you are ~!** (= *wicked*) ¡qué malo eres!, ¡qué mala idea tienes!; **to feel ~** (= *embarrassed, guilty*) sentirse fatal; (= *ill*) encontrarse *or* sentirse fatal; **how ~!** ¡qué horror!
2 (= *bad, poor*) **his English is ~** habla inglés fatal
3 (= *awesome*) imponente, tremendo
4 (*) (*as intensifier*) **there were an ~ lot of people** había un montón de gente*; **it's an ~ nuisance** es una molestia terrible; **it seems an ~ waste** parece un desperdicio terrible **Ⓑ** ADV (*) **ten years is an ~ long time** diez años es un montón de tiempo*

awfully* [ˈɔːflɪ] ADV **he's ~ nice** es majísimo; **it's ~ hard** *or* **difficult** es terriblemente difícil; **she works ~ hard** trabaja durísimo; **it was ~ hot** hacía un calor espantoso; **that's ~ good of you** es muy amable de su parte; **I'm ~ sorry** lo siento muchísimo

awhile [əˈwaɪl] (*esp US*) ADV un rato, algún tiempo; **not yet ~** todavía no

awkward [ˈɔːkwəd] ADJ **1** (= *difficult*) [*moment, time*] malo; [*shape*] incómodo, poco práctico; [*corner*] peligroso; [*age*] difícil; **have I called at an ~ moment?** ¿he llamado en mal momento?; **it would be ~ to postpone my trip again** sería difícil volver a aplazar mi viaje; **he's being ~ about it** está poniendo inconvenientes; **he's an ~ customer*** es un tipo difícil*, es un sujeto de cuidado*; **Thursday is ~ for me** el jueves no me viene bien; **to make things ~ for sb** poner las cosas difíciles a algn, crear dificultades a algn
2 (= *uncomfortable*) [*silence*] embarazoso; [*problem, question, situation, subject*] delicado; **to feel ~** sentirse incómodo; **I felt ~ about asking her for a rise** me resultaba violento pedirle un aumento de sueldo; **there was an ~ moment when ...** hubo un momento violento *or* embarazoso cuando ...
3 (= *clumsy*) [*person, gesture, movement*] torpe; [*phrasing*] poco elegante, torpe

awkwardly [ˈɔːkwədlɪ] ADV **1** (= *uncomfortably*) [*say, shake hands*] embarazosamente **2** (= *clumsily*) [*move, walk, dance*] torpemente, con torpeza; [*translate*] con poca fluidez; **he expresses himself ~** se expresa mal, le cuesta expresarse

awkwardness [ˈɔːkwədnɪs] N **1** (= *difficult nature*) [*of problem*] lo delicado; [*of situation*] lo delicado, lo violento; [*of person*] falta *f* de colaboración; [*of shape, design*] lo incómodo, lo poco práctico **2** (= *embarrassment, discomfort*) embarazo *m* **3** (= *clumsiness*) torpeza *f*

awl [ɔːl] N lezna *f*

awning [ˈɔːnɪŋ] N toldo *m*

awoke [əˈwəʊk] PT *of* **awake**

awoken [əˈwəʊkən] PP *of* **awake**

AWOL [ˈeɪwɒl] ABBR (= **absent without leave**) ausente sin permiso; **to go ~** ausentarse sin permiso

awry [əˈraɪ] ADV **to be ~** estar de través, estar al sesgo, estar mal puesto; **with his hat on ~** con el sombrero torcido *or* ladeado; **to go ~** salir mal, fracasar

axe, **ax** (*US*) [æks] **Ⓐ** N (= *tool*) hacha *f*

Use **el/un** not **la/una** before feminine nouns beginning with stressed **a** or **ha** like **hacha**.

a prehistoric ~ un hacha prehistórica; ✦ IDIOMS **I have no ~ to grind** no tengo ningún interés personal; **to get** *or* **be given the ~** [*employee*] ser despedido; [*project*] ser cancelado Ⓑ VT [+ *budget*] recortar; [+ *project, service*] cancelar; [+ *jobs*] reducir; [+ *staff*] despedir

axes ['æksiːz] NPL *of* **axis**

axiom ['æksɪəm] N axioma *m*

axiomatic [ˌæksɪə'mætɪk] ADJ axiomático

axis ['æksɪs] N (*pl* **axes**) eje *m*

axle ['æksl] N eje *m*, árbol *m*, flecha *f* (*Mex*)

ayatollah [aɪə'tɒlə] N ayatolá *m*, ayatollah *m*

aye [aɪ] Ⓐ ADV (*esp Scot*) sí Ⓑ N sí *m*; **the ~s have it** se ha aprobado la moción; **there were 50 ~s and three noes** votaron 50 a favor y tres en contra

AYH N ABBR (*US*) = **American Youth Hostels**

AZ ABBR (*US*) = **Arizona**

azalea [ə'zeɪlɪə] N azalea *f*

Azerbaijan [ˌæzəbaɪ'dʒɑːn] N Azerbaiyán *m*

Azeri [ə'zeərɪ] ADJ, N azerí *mf*

Azores [ə'zɔːz] NPL Azores *fpl*

AZT N ABBR (= **azidothymidine**) AZT *m*

Aztec ['æztek] ADJ, N azteca *mf*

Bb

B, b [biː] **Ⓐ** N **1** (= *letter*) B *f*, b *f*; **B for Birmingham** B de Burgos **2** (*Mus*) B si *m* **3** (*Scol*) notable *m* **Ⓑ** CPD ➤ **B road** (*Brit*) ≈ carretera *f* comarcal *or* secundaria

b. ABBR (= **born**) n.

B2B ABBR = **business to business**

BA N ABBR (= **Bachelor of Arts**) Lic. en Fil. y Let.

babble ['bæbl] **Ⓐ** N [*of baby*] balbuceo *m*; [*of stream, voices*] murmullo *m* **Ⓑ** VI (= *talk too much*) parlotear*; (= *gossip*) chismorrear*, cotillear (*Sp**); [*baby*] balbucear; [*stream*] murmurar; **he was babbling on about his holidays** hablaba sin parar sus vacaciones, no paraba de hablar de sus vacaciones **Ⓒ** VT decir balbuceando

babe [beɪb] N (*esp US**) (= *girl*) chica *f*; (*in direct address*) nena* *f*

baboon [bəˈbuːn] N babuino *m*

baby ['beɪbɪ] **Ⓐ** N **1** (= *infant*) bebé *mf*, bebe/a *m/f* (*Arg*), guagua *f* (*And*); (= *small child*) niño/a *m/f*; **she's having a ~ in May** va a tener un niño en mayo; **she's having the ~ in hospital** va a dar a luz en el hospital; **the ~ of the family** el benjamín/la benjamina; **don't be such a ~!** ¡no seas niño/niña!; **the new system was his** ~ el nuevo sistema fue obra suya; ✦ IDIOMS **I was left holding the ~** (*Brit**) me tocó cargar con el muerto; **to throw out the ~ with the bathwater** actuar con exceso de celo, pasarse* **2** (*) (= *darling*) cariño *m* **Ⓑ** ADJ **1** (= *young*) ~ **hedgehog** cría *f* de erizo; ~ **rabbit** conejito *m* **2** (= *small*) pequeño; ~ **sweetcorn** mazorca *f* pequeña **Ⓒ** CPD (= *for a baby*) de niño ➤ **baby bed** (*US*) cuna *f* ➤ **baby blues*** depresión *fsing* posparto ➤ **baby boom** explosión *f* demográfica, boom *m* de natalidad ➤ **baby boomer** baby boomer *mf*, *persona nacida en una época de explosión demográfica, esp. entre los años 1945-55* ➤ **baby boy** nene *m* ➤ **baby brother** hermanito *m* ➤ **baby buggy** (*Brit*) (= *pushchair*) sillita *f* de paseo; (= *US*) = **baby carriage** ➤ **baby carriage** (*US*) cochecito *m* (de bebé) ➤ **baby clothes** ropita *fsing* de niño ➤ **baby food(s)** comida *f* para bebés, potitos *mpl* (*Sp**) ➤ **baby girl** nena *f* ➤ **baby grand** piano *m* de media cola ➤ **baby minder** niñera *f* ➤ **baby seat** (*Aut*) sillita *f* or asiento *m* de seguridad para bebés ➤ **baby shower** (*US*) *fiesta con entrega de regalos a la madre y al recién nacido* ➤ **baby sister** hermanita *f* ➤ **baby talk** habla *f* infantil ➤ **baby tender** (*US*) babysitter *mf*, canguro *mf* (*Sp*) ➤ **baby tooth*** diente *m* de leche ➤ **baby wipe** toallita *f* húmeda

babyish ['beɪbɪʃ] ADJ infantil

baby-sit ['beɪbɪsɪt] (*pt*, *pp* **baby-sat**) VI cuidar niños, hacer de babysitter *or* (*Sp*) canguro

baby-sitter ['beɪbɪˌsɪtə'] N babysitter *mf*, canguro *mf* (*Sp*)

baccalaureate [ˌbækəˈlɔːrɪɪt] N bachillerato *m*

bachelor ['bætʃələ'] **Ⓐ** N **1** (= *unmarried man*) soltero *m* **2** (*Univ*) **Bachelor of Arts/Science** (= *degree*) licenciatura *f* en Filosofía y Letras/Ciencias; (*Brit*) (= *person*) licenciado/a *m/f* en Filosofía y Letras/Ciencias **Ⓑ** CPD ➤ **bachelor flat** piso *m* (*esp Sp*) *or* departamento *m* (*LAm*) de soltero **bachelor girl** (*US*) soltera *f* ➤ **bachelor's degree** licenciatura *f*; *ver tb* www.education.org.uk

back [bæk] **Ⓐ** NOUN
1 (= *part of body*) [*of person*] espalda *f*; [*of animal*] lomo *m*; **to carry sth/sb on one's ~** llevar algo/a algn a la espalda; **he was lying on his ~** estaba tumbado boca arriba; **to have one's ~ to sth/sb** estar de espaldas a algo/algn; **sitting ~ to ~** sentados espalda con espalda; ✦ IDIOMS **behind sb's ~** a espaldas de algn; **to get off sb's ~*** dejar a algn en paz; **to get sb's ~ up*** poner negro a algn*, mosquear a algn**; **to be on sb's ~*** estar encima de algn; **on the ~ of sth** a consecuencia de algo; **to put one's ~ into doing sth*** hacer algo con ahínco, emplearse a fondo en hacer algo; **to put sb's ~ up*** poner negro a algn*, mosquear a algn**; **I was glad to see the ~ of him** (*Brit**) me alegró deshacerme de él; **as soon as your ~ is turned ...** en cuanto te descuidas ...; **to have one's ~ to the wall** estar entre la espada y la pared **2** (= *reverse side*) [*of cheque, envelope*] dorso *m*, revés *m*; [*of hand*] dorso *m*; [*of head*] parte *f* de atrás, parte *f* posterior (*more frm*); [*of dress*] espalda *f*; [*of medal*] reverso *m*; **the ~ of the neck** la nuca; ✦ IDIOM **to know sth like the ~ of one's hand** conocer algo como la palma de la mano **3** (= *rear*) [*of room, hall*] fondo *m*; [*of chair*] respaldo *m*; [*of car*] parte *f* trasera, parte *f* de atrás; [*of book*] (= *back cover*) tapa *f* posterior; (= *spine*) lomo *m*; **at the ~ (of)** [+ *building*] en la parte de atrás (de); [+ *cupboard, hall, stage*] en el fondo (de); **he's at the ~ of all this trouble** él está detrás de todo este lío*; **this idea had been at the ~ of his mind for several days** esta idea le había estado varios días rondándole la cabeza; ~ **to front** (*esp Brit*) al revés; **I'll sit in the** ~ yo me sentaré detrás; **in ~ of the house** (*US*) detrás de la casa **4** (*Sport*) (= *defender*) defensa *mf*
Ⓑ ADVERB
1 (*in space*) atrás; **stand ~!** ¡atrás!; **keep ~!** (= *out of danger*) ¡quédate ahí atrás!; (= *don't come near me*) ¡no te acerques!; **meanwhile, ~ in London** mientras, en Londres; ~ **and forth** de acá para allá
2 (*in time*) **some months ~** hace unos meses; ~ **in the 12th century** allá en el siglo XII; **it all started ~ in 1980** todo empezó ya en 1980; **I saw her ~ in August** la vi el agosto pasado
3 (= *returned*) **to be ~:** **he's not ~ yet** aún no ha vuelto, aún no está de vuelta; ~ **30 kilometres there and** ~ 30 kilómetros ida y vuelta; **you can go there and ~ in a day** puedes ir y volver en un día; **full satisfaction or your money** ~ si no está totalmente satisfecho, le devolvemos el dinero; **everything is ~ to normal** todo ha vuelto a la normalidad
Ⓒ TRANSITIVE VERB
1 (= *reverse*) [+ *vehicle*] dar marcha atrás a; **he ~ed the car into a wall** dio marcha atrás y chocó con un muro; **she ~ed the car into the garage** entró el coche en el garaje dando marcha atrás
2 (= *support*) [+ *plan, person*] apoyar
3 (= *finance*) [+ *person, enterprise*] financiar
4 (*Mus*) [+ *singer*] acompañar
5 (= *bet on*) [+ *horse*] apostar por
Ⓓ INTRANSITIVE VERB (= *reverse*) (*in car*) dar marcha atrás; (= *step backwards*) echarse hacia atrás, retroceder; **she ~ed into me** (*in car*) dio marcha atrás y chocó conmigo
Ⓔ ADJECTIVE
1 (= *rear*) [*leg, pocket, wheel*] de atrás, trasero; **the ~ row** la última fila
2 (= *previous, overdue*) [*rent, tax, issue*] atrasado
Ⓕ COMPOUNDS ➤ **back alley** callejuela *f* (*que recorre la parte de atrás de una hilera de casas*) ➤ **back burner** ✦ IDIOM **to put sth on the ~ burner** posponer algo, dejar algo para más tarde ➤ **the back country** (*US*) zona rural con muy baja densidad de población ➤ **back door** puerta *f* trasera; ✦ IDIOM **to do sth by the ~ door** hacer algo de forma encubierta ➤ **back number** número *m* atrasado ➤ **back pain** dolor *m* de espalda, dolor *m* lumbar ➤ **back pay** atrasos *mpl* ➤ **back road** carretera *f* comarcal, carretera *f* secundaria ➤ **back seat** asiento *m* trasero, asiento *m* de atrás; ✦ IDIOM **to take a ~ seat** mantenerse en un segundo plano ➤ **back street** callejuela *f*; **the ~ streets** (*quiet*) las calles tranquilas, las calles apartadas del centro; (*poor*) las calles de los barrios bajos ➤ **back tooth** muela *f*
Ⓖ PHRASAL VERBS
➤ **back away** VI + ADV **1** (= *move*) retroceder (**from** ante)

2 (*from promise, pledge, statement*) echarse atrás, dar marcha atrás (**from** en)
➤ **back down** VI + ADV echarse atrás, dar marcha atrás (**on sth** en algo)
➤ **back off** VI + ADV (= *stop exerting pressure*) echarse atrás, dar marcha atrás (**from** en); ~ **off!** ¡déjame en paz!, ¡déjame estar!
➤ **back on to** VI + PREP **the house ~s on to the golf course** por atrás la casa da al campo de golf
➤ **back out** **Ⓐ** VI + ADV **1** (*lit*) [*vehicle, driver*] salir marcha atrás (**of** de) **2** (*fig*) [*person*] (*of team*) retirarse (**of** de); (*of deal, duty*) echarse atrás (**of** en) **Ⓑ** VT + ADV [+ *vehicle*] sacar marcha atrás
➤ **back up** **Ⓐ** VT + ADV **1** (= *support*) [+ *person*] apoyar, respaldar **2** (= *confirm*) [+ *claim, theory*] respaldar **3** (= *reverse*) [+ *car*] dar marcha atrás a, hacer retroceder **4** (*Comput*) [+ *file*] hacer una copia de seguridad de **5** (= *delay*) **the traffic was ~ed up for two miles** había una caravana (de tráfico) de dos millas, había dos millas de retenciones (de tráfico) **Ⓑ** VI + ADV **traffic is ~ing up for miles** hay varias millas de retenciones (de tráfico) *or* una caravana (de tráfico) de varias millas

backache [ˈbækeɪk] N dolor *m* de espalda
backbench [ˈbækbentʃ] ADJ (*Brit*) [*MP*] que no ostenta ningún cargo oficial
backbencher [ˌbækˈbentʃəʳ] N (*Brit Parl*) diputado sin cargo oficial en el gobierno o la oposición

---
BACKBENCHER

Se conoce como **backbencher** al parlamentario británico que no se sienta en los escaños (**benches**) de las primeras filas de la Cámara de los Comunes (**House of Commons**) junto al líder de su partido, por no pertenecer al gobierno o a su equivalente en la oposición. Al no ser titulares de ningún cargo, les resulta más fácil hablar o votar en contra de la política oficial del partido. Se les conoce también colectivamente como los **backbenches**.
Ver tb www.parliament.uk

---

backbenches [ˌbækˈbentʃəz] NPL (*Brit Parl*) escaños de los diputados sin cargo oficial en el gobierno o la oposición
backbiting [ˈbækbaɪtɪŋ] N murmuración *f*
backbone [ˈbækbəʊn] N (*Anat*) columna *f* vertebral, espina *f* dorsal; (= *courage*) agallas *fpl*; **the ~ of the organization** el pilar de la organización
back-breaking [ˈbækbreɪkɪŋ] ADJ matador
backdate [ˈbækˈdeɪt] VT [+ *cheque*] poner fecha anterior a, antedatar; [+ *pay rise*] dar efecto retroactivo a; **a pay rise ~d to April** un aumento salarial con efecto retroactivo desde abril
backdrop [ˈbækdrɒp] N telón *m* de fondo (*also fig*)
backer [ˈbækəʳ] N (= *guarantor*) fiador(a) *m/f*; (= *financier*) promotor(a) *m/f*, patrocinador(a) *m/f*; (*Pol*) (= *supporter*) partidario/a *m/f*
backfire [ˈbækˈfaɪəʳ] VI [*vehicle*] petardear; **their plan ~d** les salió el tiro por la culata*
backgammon [ˈbækˌgæmən] N backgammon *m*
background [ˈbækgraʊnd] **Ⓐ** N **1** [*of picture*] fondo *m*; **on a red ~** sobre un fondo rojo; **in the ~** (*lit*) al *or* en el fondo; (*fig*) en segundo plano, en la sombra **2** [*of person*] formación *f*, educación *f*; **he comes from a wealthy ~** proviene de una familia acaudalada **3** [*of situation, event*] antecedentes *mpl* **Ⓑ** CPD [*music, noise*] de fondo
➤ **background reading** lecturas *fpl* de fondo, lecturas *fpl* preparatorias
backhand [ˈbækhænd] N (*also ~ shot*) revés *m*
backhanded [ˈbækˈhændɪd] ADJ [*compliment*] ambiguo, equívoco
backhander* [ˈbækˈhændəʳ] N (*Brit*) (= *bribe*) soborno *m*, mordida *f* (*CAm, Mex*), coima *f* (*And, SC*)
backing [ˈbækɪŋ] **Ⓐ** N **1** (= *support*) apoyo *m*; (*Comm*) respaldo *m* (financiero) **2** (*Mus*) acompañamiento *m*

3 (= *protective layer*) refuerzo *m* **Ⓑ** CPD ➤ **backing group** (*Mus*) grupo *m* de acompañamiento
backlash [ˈbæklæʃ] N (*Pol*) reacción *f* violenta
backlog [ˈbæklɒg] N **because of the ~ (of work)** por el trabajo acumulado *or* atrasado; **because of the ~ (of orders)** por el volumen de pedidos pendientes
backpack [ˈbækpæk] N mochila *f*
backpacker [ˈbækˌpækəʳ] N mochilero/a *m/f*
backpacking [ˈbækˌpækɪŋ] N **to go ~** hacer excursionismo de mochila
back-pedal [ˈbækˈpedl] VI (= *backtrack*) echarse atrás, dar marcha atrás
back-seat driver [ˌbæksiːˈtdraɪvəʳ] N *pasajero que siempre está dando consejos al conductor*
backside* [ˈbækˈsaɪd] N trasero* *m*
backslash [ˈbækslæʃ] N (*Typ*) barra *f* inversa
backslide [ˈbækˈslaɪd] (*pt, pp* **backslid**) VI reincidir, recaer
backstage [ˈbækˈsteɪdʒ] ADV entre bastidores; **to go ~** ir a los camarines
backstreet [ˈbækstriːt] ADJ [*hotel, shop*] de barrio
➤ **backstreet abortion** aborto *m* clandestino
backstroke [ˈbækstrəʊk] N espalda *f*; **the 100 metres ~** los 100 metros espalda
back-to-back [ˈbæktəˈbæk] **Ⓐ** ADJ **~ houses** (*Brit*) casas *fpl* adosadas (*por la parte trasera*) **Ⓑ** ADV **they showed two episodes ~** echaron dos capítulos seguidos
backtrack [ˈbæktræk] VI (*on promise, decision*) echarse atrás, dar marcha atrás (**on** en)
backup [ˈbækʌp] **Ⓐ** N **1** (= *support*) apoyo *m* **2** (*Comput*) copia *f* de seguridad **3** (*US*) [*of traffic*] embotellamiento *m* **Ⓑ** CPD [*train, plane*] suplementario; (*Comput*) [*copy, disk, file*] de seguridad ➤ **backup lights** (*US*) luces *fpl* de marcha atrás
backward [ˈbækwəd] **Ⓐ** ADJ **1** [*motion, glance*] hacia atrás **2** [*pupil, country*] atrasado **Ⓑ** ADV (*also ~s*) **1** [*look*] atrás, hacia atrás; [*move*] hacia atrás; **this is a step ~** (*fig*) esto supone un paso atrás **2** (= *in reverse*) al revés; ✦ IDIOM **to know sth ~** (*Brit**) ✧ **to know sth ~ and forward** (*US**) saberse algo al dedillo *or* de pe a pa
backward-looking [ˈbækwədˌlʊkɪŋ] ADJ retrógrado
backwards [ˈbækwədz] ADV (*esp Brit*) = **backward B**
backwater [ˈbækwɔːtəʳ] N [*of river*] remanso *m*; (*fig*) lugar *m* atrasado
backyard [ˈbækˈjɑːd] N (*Brit*) patio *m* trasero; (*US*) jardín *m* trasero; **in one's own ~** en su misma puerta, delante de sus narices*
bacon [ˈbeɪkən] N beicon *m* (*Sp*), tocino *m* (*LAm*), panceta *f* (*Arg*); **~ and eggs** huevos *mpl* con tocino; ✦ IDIOMS **to bring home the ~*** (= *earn living*) ganarse las habichuelas*; **to save sb's ~*** salvar el pellejo a algn*
bacteriology [bækˌtɪərɪˈɒlədʒɪ] N bacteriología *f*
bacterium [bækˈtɪərɪəm] N (*pl* **bacteria** [bækˈtɪərɪə]) bacteria *f*
bad [bæd] **Ⓐ** ADJ (*compar* **worse**; *superl* **worst**)

The commonest translation of **bad** is **malo**, which must be shortened to **mal** before a masculine singular noun.

---

1 malo; **I've had a ~ day at work** he tenido un mal día en el trabajo; **his handwriting is ~** tiene mala letra; **you ~ boy!** ¡qué niño más malo eres!; **I was ~ at sports** era muy malo para los deportes; **business is ~** el negocio va mal; **he was a ~ driver** conducía mal; **I feel ~ about hurting his feelings** me sabe mal haber herido sus sentimientos; **smoking is ~ for you** fumar es malo *or* perjudicial para la salud, fumar perjudica la salud; **~ light stopped play** se suspendió el partido debido a la falta de luz; **it'll look ~ if we don't go** quedará mal que no vayamos; **he wasn't ~--looking** no estaba mal; **this wine's not ~ at all** este vino no está nada mal; **you've come at a ~ time** vienes en un mal momento; **it's too ~ you couldn't get tickets** es una pena *or* una lástima que no hayas podido conseguir entradas; **if you don't like it, (that's) too ~!** si no te gusta, ¡peor para ti!; **the**

plane was diverted due to ~ **weather** el avión fue desviado debido al mal tiempo; **a ~ word** una palabrota; ✦ IDIOM **to go from ~ to worse** ir de mal en peor
2 (= *serious, severe*) [*accident, mistake*] grave; [*headache*] fuerte; **she's got a ~ cold** está muy resfriada, tiene un resfriado fuerte; **the traffic was ~ today** hoy había mucho tráfico
3 (= *ailing*) **he has a ~ back** está mal de la espalda; **I feel ~** me siento mal; **the economy is in a ~ way** (*Brit*) la economía va mal
4 (= *rotten*) [*food*] podrido; [*milk*] cortado; [*tooth*] picado; **to go ~** pasarse, estropearse
5 (*Fin*) [*cheque*] sin fondos; **a ~ debt** una deuda incobrable
Ⓑ **to take the ~ with the good** aceptar tanto lo bueno como lo malo
Ⓒ ADV (*) (= *badly*) **you can tell she's got it ~** (= *is in love with him*) se nota que está colada por él*; **he's hurt ~** está malherido; **to need sth real ~** necesitar algo desesperadamente; **she took it ~** se lo tomó a mal
Ⓓ CPD ➤ **bad guy*** (*esp US*) malo *m* ➤ **bad hair day*** (= *bad day*) día *m* en el que todo sale al revés, mal día *m*; **I'm having a bad hair day** hoy todo me está saliendo al revés

baddy*, **baddie*** ['bædɪ] N malo/a *m*

bade [bæd] PT of **bid**

badge [bædʒ] N (= *emblem*) insignia *f*; (*sewn on coat*) distintivo *m*; (*Brit*) (*metal*) chapa *f*

badger ['bædʒə*] Ⓐ N tejón *m* Ⓑ VT acosar, atormentar (**for** para obtener); **stop ~ing me!** ¡deja ya de fastidiarme!

badly ['bædlɪ] ADV **1** (= *poorly*) mal; **he did ~ in his exams** los exámenes le fueron mal; **made/written** mal hecho/escrito; **"how did he take it?" — "badly"** —¿qué tal se lo tomó? —fatal
2 (= *seriously*) gravemente; **he was ~ injured** estaba gravemente herido; **the building was ~ damaged in the explosion** en la explosión el edificio resultó muy dañado
3 (= *very much*) **~ needed medical supplies** medicamentos que se necesitan desesperadamente; **he ~ needs help** necesita ayuda a toda costa; **we ~ need another assistant** nos hace muchísima falta otro ayudante; **they ~ wanted a child** estaban desesperados por tener un niño; **to be ~ mistaken** estar muy equivocado
4 to be ~ off (= *poor*) andar *or* estar mal de dinero; **we are ~ off for coal** andamos mal de carbón

bad-mannered ['bæd'mænəd] ADJ maleducado, grosero

badminton ['bædmɪntən] N bádminton *m*

badmouth* ['bæd,mavθ] VT hablar pestes de*

bad-tempered ['bæd'tempəd] ADJ [*person*] (*temporarily*) de mal humor; (*permanently*) de mal genio, de mal carácter

baffle ['bæfl] VT (= *perplex*) desconcertar; **the police are ~d** la policía está desconcertada *or* perpleja

baffling ['bæflɪŋ] ADJ incomprensible, desconcertante; [*crime*] misterioso

bag [bæg] Ⓐ N **1** (*paper, plastic*) bolsa *f*; (= *handbag*) bolso *m*, cartera *f* (*LAm*); (= *suitcase*) maleta *f*, valija *f* (*LAm*), veliz *m* (*Mex*); (*carried over shoulder*) zurrón *m*, mochila *f*; **bags** (= *luggage*) equipaje *msing*; **~s under one's eyes** ojeras *fpl*; ✦ IDIOMS **to be left holding the ~** (*US**) cargar con el muerto*; **it's in the ~*** es cosa segura, está en el bote (*Sp**); **it's not his ~** (*US**) no es lo suyo
2 (*Brit**) **~s of** (= *lots of*) un montón de; **we've ~s of time** tenemos tiempo de sobra
3 old ~* (= *woman*) bruja* *f*
Ⓑ VT **1** (*also ~ up*) meter en una bolsa/en bolsas
2 (*Hunting*) cazar
3 (*) (= *take*) pillar*, hacerse con; (*Brit*) (= *reserve*) reservarse
Ⓒ CPD ➤ **bag lady*** indigente *f* vagabunda ➤ **bag snatcher** ladrón/a *m/f* de bolsos

baggage ['bægɪdʒ] N equipaje *m*; (*Psych*) bagaje *m*
➤ **baggage allowance** límite *m* de equipaje ➤ **baggage (check)room** (*US*) consigna *f* ➤ **baggage handler** despachador(a) *m/f* de equipaje ➤ **baggage (re)claim** recogida *f* de equipaje

baggy ['bægɪ] ADJ (*compar* **baggier**; *superl* **baggiest**) ancho

Baghdad [,bæg'dæd] N Bagdad *m*

bagpipes ['bægpaɪps] NPL gaita *fsing*

Bahamas [bə'hɑːməz] NPL **the ~** las Bahamas

Bahrain [bɑː'reɪn] N Bahrein *m*

bail [beɪl] Ⓐ N fianza *f*; **to be released on ~** ser puesto en libertad bajo fianza; **to go ~ for sb** pagar la fianza de algn Ⓑ VT poner en libertad bajo fianza Ⓒ CPD ➤ **bail bond** (*US*) fianza *f*
➤ **bail out** Ⓐ VT + ADV [+ *water*] achicar; [+ *ship*] achicar *or* sacar el agua de Ⓑ VI + ADV (*Aer*) lanzarse *or* tirarse en paracaídas

bailiff ['beɪlɪf] N alguacil *m*

bait [beɪt] Ⓐ N cebo *m*; (*fig*) anzuelo *m*, cebo *m*; ✦ IDIOM **he didn't take** *or* (*esp Brit*) **rise to the ~** no picó Ⓑ VT **1** [+ *hook, trap*] cebar **2** (= *torment*) atormentar

bake [beɪk] Ⓐ VT **1** [+ *food*] cocer (al horno); [+ *bricks*] cocer; **to ~ one's own bread** hacer el pan en casa; **to ~ a cake** hacer un pastel; **~d beans** (*Brit*) judías *fpl* en salsa de tomate; (*US*) (*with meat*) judías *fpl* en salsa de tomate con tocino; **~d potato** patata *f* (*Sp*) *or* papa *f* (*LAm*) al horno
2 (= *harden*) endurecer Ⓑ VI (*lit*) hacer pasteles/pan *etc* al horno; **we were baking in the heat** nos asábamos de calor

baker ['beɪkə*] N [*of bread*] panadero/a *m/f*; [*of cakes*] pastelero/a *m/f*; **~'s (shop)** panadería *f*; (= *cakeshop*) pastelería *f*

bakery ['beɪkərɪ] N panadería *f*; (= *cakeshop*) pastelería *f*

baking ['beɪkɪŋ] Ⓐ N **she does the ~ on Mondays** los lunes hace el pan/los pasteles *etc*
Ⓑ ADJ, ADV (*) **it's ~ (hot) in here** esto es un horno; **a ~ hot day** un día de calor asfixiante
Ⓒ CPD ➤ **baking chocolate** (*US*) chocolate *m* fondant ➤ **baking dish** fuente *f* para el horno ➤ **baking mitt** (*US*) guante *m* para el horno, manopla *f* para el horno ➤ **baking pan** (*US*) molde *m* (para el horno) ➤ **baking powder** Royal® *m*, levadura *f* en polvo (*Sp*) ➤ **baking sheet** bandeja *f* de horno ➤ **baking soda** bicarbonato *m* de soda ➤ **baking tin** (*Brit*) molde *m* (para el horno) ➤ **baking tray** (*Brit*) bandeja *f* de horno

balaclava [,bælə'klɑːvə] N pasamontañas *m inv*

balance ['bæləns] Ⓐ N **1** (= *equilibrium*) equilibrio *m*; **to keep/lose one's ~** mantener/perder el equilibrio; **to throw sb off ~** (*fig*) desconcertar a algn; **on ~** teniendo *or* tomando en cuenta todos los factores, una vez considerados todos los factores (*frm*); **~ of power/nature** equilibrio *m* de poder/de la naturaleza; **to strike a ~** conseguir *or* establecer un equilibrio
2 (= *scales*) balanza *f*; ✦ IDIOM **to hang in the ~** estar pendiente de un hilo
3 (= *bank balance, balance of account*) saldo *m*; **~ carried forward** balance *m* a cuenta nueva; **closing ~** saldo *m* de cierre; **credit/debit ~** saldo *m* acreedor/deudor; **~ due** saldo *m* deudor; **~ outstanding** saldo *m* pendiente
4 (= *remainder*) resto *m*
5 (*Audio*) balance *m*
Ⓑ VT **1** (= *place in equilibrium*) [+ *weight, wheel*] equilibrar; **he ~d the glass on top of the books** puso el vaso en equilibrio sobre los libros
2 (= *compare*) comparar, sopesar; (= *make up for*) compensar; **this increase must be ~d against the rate of inflation** hay que sopesar este aumento y la tasa de inflación
3 (*Comm*) **to ~ the books** hacer balance, hacer cuadrar las cuentas; **to ~ the budget** nivelar el presupuesto
Ⓒ VI **1** (= *keep equilibrium*) mantener el equilibrio, mantenerse en equilibrio
2 (*Comm*) [*accounts*] cuadrar
Ⓓ CPD ➤ **balance of payments** balanza *f* de pagos ➤ **balance of power** (*Mil, Comm*) equilibrio *m* de poder; (*Phys*) equilibrio *m* de fuerzas ➤ **balance of trade** balanza *f* de comercio ➤ **balance sheet** balance *m*, hoja *f* de balance

balanced ['bælənst] ADJ equilibrado

balcony ['bælkənɪ] N balcón *m*; (*large*) terraza *f*; (*interior, Theat*) galería *f*; **first/second ~** (*US Theat*) primer/segundo piso *m*

bald [bɔːld] Ⓐ ADJ (*compar* **~er**; *superl* **~est**) **1** (= *hairless*) [*person, head*] calvo; (= *shaven*) pelado; **to go ~** quedarse calvo; ✦ IDIOM **(as) ~ as an egg** *or* **a coot** más calvo que una bola de billar **2** [*tyre*] desgastado, gastado; [*lawn*] pelado
3 [*statement*] directo, sin rodeos; [*style*] escueto

Ⓑ CPD ➤ **bald eagle** águila *f* de cabeza blanca

> Use **el/un** not **la/una** before feminine nouns beginning with stressed **a** or **ha** like **águila**.

➤ **bald patch** calva *f*

baldness ['bɔːldnɪs] N **1** [*of person*] calvicie *f* **2** [*of tyre*] desgaste *m* **3** [*of statement*] lo directo; [*of style*] lo escueto

bale [beɪl] N [*of cloth*] bala *f*; [*of hay*] fardo *m*, bala *f*
➤ **bale out** VT + ADV = **bail out** A

Balearics [ˌbælɪ'ærɪks] NPL **the ~** las Baleares

baleful ['beɪlfʊl] ADJ [*influence, presence*] funesto, siniestro; [*look, stare*] torvo, hosco

balk [bɔːk] VI **to ~ at doing sth** resistirse a hacer algo

Balkan ['bɔːlkən] Ⓐ ADJ balcánico Ⓑ N **the ~s** los Balcanes

ball [bɔːl] Ⓐ N **1** (*Tennis, Cricket, Golf*) pelota *f*; (*Ftbl*) balón *m*; (= *sphere*) bola *f*; **to play ~ (with sb)** (*lit*) jugar a la pelota (con algn); (*fig*) cooperar (con algn); ✦ IDIOMS **that's the way the ~ bounces** (*US**) así es la vida, así son las cosas; **the ~ is in your court** te corresponde a ti dar el siguiente paso; **to keep one's eye on the ~** no perder de vista lo principal; **to be on the ~** estar al tanto, ser muy despabilado; **to start/ keep the ~ rolling** poner/mantener la cosa en marcha; **the whole ~ of wax** (*US**) toda la historia*
2 (*Mil*) bala *f*; **~ and chain** (*lit*) grillete *m* con bola; (*fig*) atadura *f*
3 [*of wool*] ovillo *m*
4 (*Anat*) [*of foot*] pulpejo *m*; [*of thumb*] base *f*
5 (***) (= *testicle*) cojón*** *m*, huevo*** *m*
6 balls (= *courage*) cojones*** *mpl*, pelotas*** *fpl*; (*Brit*) (= *nonsense*) pavadas* *fpl*, huevadas *fpl* (*And, Chi****)
7 (= *dance*) baile *m* de etiqueta; ✦ IDIOM **we had a ~*** lo pasamos en grande*
Ⓑ CPD ➤ **ball bearing** cojinete *m* de bolas, balero *m* (*Mex*), rulemán *m* (*SC*) ➤ **ball boy** recogedor *m* de pelotas ➤ **ball game** (*US*) partido *m* de béisbol; ✦ IDIOMS **this is a different ~ game*** esto es otro cantar*, esto es algo muy distinto; **it's a whole new ~ game*** las cosas han cambiado totalmente ➤ **ball girl** recogedora *f* de pelotas

ballad ['bæləd] N balada *f*; (*Spanish*) romance *m*, corrido *m* (*Mex*)

ballast ['bæləst] N lastre *m*

ballcock ['bɔːlkɒk] N llave *f* de bola, llave *f* de flotador

ballerina [ˌbælə'riːnə] N bailarina *f* (de ballet)

ballet ['bæleɪ] N ballet *m* ➤ **ballet dancer** bailarín/ina *m/f* (de ballet) ➤ **ballet school** escuela *f* de ballet ➤ **ballet shoes** zapatillas *fpl* de ballet

ballistic [bə'lɪstɪk] ADJ balístico; ✦ IDIOM **to go ~*** subirse por las paredes*

balloon [bə'luːn] Ⓐ N globo *m*; (*in cartoons*) bocadillo *m*; ✦ IDIOMS **that went down like a lead ~*** eso cayó muy mal, eso cayo fatal*; **then the ~ went up** luego se armó la gorda* Ⓑ VI **1** [*injury*] hincharse (como un tomate) **2** (*also* **to ~ out**) [*sail*] hincharse como un globo; [*skirt*] inflarse

balloonist [bə'luːnɪst] N ascensionista *mf*, aeronauta *mf*

ballot ['bælət] Ⓐ N (= *voting*) votación *f*; (= *paper*) papeleta *f* (de voto); **on the first ~** a la primera votación; **to vote by secret ~** votar en secreto Ⓑ VT **to ~ the members on a strike** someter la huelga a votación entre los miembros Ⓒ CPD ➤ **ballot box** urna *f* ➤ **ballot paper** papeleta *f* (de voto) ➤ **ballot rigging, ballot box stuffing** (*US*) fraude *m* electoral, pucherazo* *m*

ballpark ['bɔːlpɑːk] Ⓐ N **1** (*US*) estadio *m* de béisbol **2** ✦ IDIOM **it's in the same ~** está en la misma categoría Ⓑ CPD ➤ **ballpark estimate** cálculo *m* aproximado ➤ **ballpark figure** cifra *f* aproximada

ballplayer ['bɔːl,pleɪə'] N (*US*) jugador(a) *m/f* de béisbol

ballpoint (pen) ['bɔːlpɔɪnt('pen)] N bolígrafo *m*, birome *m* or *f* (*SC*)

ballroom ['bɔːlrʊm] N salón *m* de baile, sala *f* de baile ➤ **ballroom dancing** baile *m* de salón

balm [bɑːm] N bálsamo *m*

balmy ['bɑːmɪ] ADJ (*compar* **balmier**; *superl* **balmiest**) [*breeze, air*] suave, cálido

baloney* [bə'ləʊnɪ] N (*esp US*) tonterías *fpl*, chorradas *fpl* (*Sp**)

balsam ['bɔːlsəm] N bálsamo *m*

Baltic ['bɔːltɪk] Ⓐ ADJ báltico; **the ~ states** los estados bálticos; **one of the ~ ports** uno de los puertos del mar Báltico Ⓑ N **the ~ (Sea)** el (mar) Báltico

balustrade [ˌbæləs'treɪd] N balaustrada *f*, barandilla *f*

bamboo [bæm'buː] N bambú *m* ➤ **bamboo shoots** brotes *mpl* de bambú

bamboozle* [bæm'buːzl] VT enredar, engatusar

ban [bæn] Ⓐ N prohibición *f* (**on** de); **to put a ~ on sth** prohibir algo Ⓑ VT [+ *activity, book*] prohibir; **he was ~ned from the club** le prohibieron la entrada en el club; **he was ~ned from driving** le retiraron el carnet de conducir; **the bullfighter was ~ned for three months** al torero le prohibieron torear durante tres meses

banal [bə'nɑːl] ADJ banal

banana [bə'nɑːnə] N plátano *m*, banana *f* (*LAm*); ✦ IDIOM **to go ~s** perder la chaveta* (**over** por); ➤ **banana peel** (*US*) piel *f* de plátano ➤ **banana republic** república *f* bananera ➤ **banana skin** (*Brit*) piel *f* de plátano ➤ **banana tree** platanero *m*, banano *m* (*LAm*)

band [bænd] Ⓐ N **1** (= *instrumentalists*) orquesta *f*, conjunto *m*; (= *brass band*) banda *f*; (= *pop group*) grupo *m*; ✦ IDIOM **then the ~ played** (*US**) y se armó la gorda* **2** (= *gang*) cuadrilla *f*, grupo *m*; (*pej*) pandilla *f* **3** (= *strip*) [*of material*] faja *f*, tira *f*; (= *ribbon*) cinta *f*; (= *edging*) franja *f*; (= *stripe*) raya *f* **4** (= *ring*) anillo *m*, sortija *f* (*LAm*) **5** (*Rad*) banda *f* **6** (*Brit*) [*of statistics, tax etc*] banda *f* Ⓑ VT (*Brit*) dividir en bandas
➤ **band together** VI + ADV juntarse, asociarse; (*pej*) apandillarse

bandage ['bændɪdʒ] Ⓐ N venda *f* Ⓑ VT (*also* **to ~ up**) vendar

Band-Aid® ['bændeɪd] N (*esp US*) tirita *f* (*Sp*), curita *f* (*LAm*)

bandan(n)a [bæn'dænə] N pañuelo *m*

B & B N ABBR (= **bed and breakfast**) alojamiento y desayuno

bandit ['bændɪt] N bandido *m*

bandleader ['bændˌliːdə'] N líder *mf* de banda

bandstand ['bændstænd] N (*esp Brit*) (*with roof*) quiosco *m* de música; (*esp US*) (= *raised platform*) tarima *f*

bandwagon ['bænd,wægən] N ✦ IDIOM **to jump** or **climb on the ~** subirse al carro or al tren

bandy ['bændɪ] VT cambiar, intercambiar
➤ **bandy about, bandy around** VT + ADV **the story was bandied about that ...** se rumoreaba que ...

bandy-legged [ˌbændɪ'legd] ADJ estevado

bane [beɪn] N plaga *f*, azote *m*; **it's the ~ of my life** me amarga la vida

bang [bæŋ] Ⓐ N (= *noise*) [*of explosion*] estallido *m*; [*of door*] portazo *m*; **the door closed with a ~** la puerta se cerró de golpe; ✦ IDIOMS **it went with a ~*** fue todo un éxito; **to get more ~ for one's buck** (*esp US**) llevarse más por el mismo precio
Ⓑ ADV **1 to go ~** hacer ¡pum!, estallar; **~ go our holidays*** adiós las vacaciones
2 (*) (= *right*) justo, exactamente; **~ in the middle** justo en (el) medio; **~ on!** ¡acertado!; **the answer was ~ on** (*Brit*) la respuesta dio en el blanco; **~ on time** (*Brit*) a la hora justa
Ⓒ VT (= *strike*) golpear; **to ~ one's head (on sth)** dar con la cabeza (contra algo); **he ~ed himself against the wall** se dio contra la pared; **to ~ one's fist on the table** dar un puñetazo en la mesa; **to ~ the door** dar un portazo
Ⓓ VI (= *explode*) explotar, estallar; (= *slam*) [*door*] cerrarse de golpe; **to ~ at** or **on sth** dar golpes en algo
Ⓔ EXCL [*of gunshot*] ¡pum!; [*of blow*] ¡zas!
➤ **bang on*** VI + ADV (*Brit*): **to ~ on about sth** dar la tabarra con algo*
➤ **bang up**** VT + ADV (*Brit*) meter en chirona**; **he'll be ~ed up for ten years** pasará diez años en chirona**

banger* ['bæŋə'] (*Brit*) N **1** (= *sausage*) salchicha *f*

2 (= *firework*) petardo *m* **3** (= *car*) armatoste* *m*, cacharro* *m*

Bangladeshi [ˌbæŋɡləˈdeʃɪ] ADJ, N bangladesí *mf*

bangle [ˈbæŋɡl] N brazalete *m*, pulsera *f*

bangs [bæŋz] NPL (*US*) (= *fringe*) flequillo *msing*

banish [ˈbænɪʃ] VT [+ *person*] expulsar, desterrar; [+ *thought, fear*] desterrar, apartar (**from** de)

banisters [ˈbænɪstəz] NPL barandilla *fsing*, pasamanos *msing inv*

banjo [ˈbændʒəʊ] N (*pl* ~**es** *or* ~**s**) banjo *m*

bank¹ [bæŋk] Ⓐ N [*of river*] orilla *f*; (= *small hill*) loma *f*; (= *embankment*) terraplén *m*; [*of phones*] equipo *m*, batería *f* Ⓑ VT (*also* ~ **up**) [+ *earth, sand*] amontonar, apilar; [+ *fire*] alimentar (*con mucha leña o carbón*) Ⓒ VI (*Aer*) ladearse

bank² [bæŋk] Ⓐ N (*Fin*) banco *m*; (*in games*) banca *f* Ⓑ VT [+ *money*] depositar en un/el banco, ingresar (*Sp*) Ⓒ VI **we ~ with Lloyds** tenemos la cuenta en el banco Lloyds Ⓓ CPD [*account, loan, transfer, giro*] bancario ➤ **bank balance** saldo *m* ➤ **bank book** libreta *f* (de depósitos); (*in savings bank*) cartilla *f* ➤ **bank card** tarjeta *f* de crédito, tarjeta *f* de banco ➤ **bank charges** (*Brit*) comisión *fsing* ➤ **bank clerk** (*Brit*) empleado/a *m/f* de banco ➤ **bank draft** letra *f* de cambio ➤ **bank holiday** (*Brit*) fiesta *f*, día *m* festivo, (día *m*) feriado *m* (*LAm*) ➤ **bank manager** director(a) *m/f* de banco ➤ **bank rate** tipo *m* de interés bancario ➤ **bank robber** ladrón *m* de banco ➤ **bank run** (*US*) asedio *m* de un banco ➤ **bank statement** estado *m* de cuenta ➤ **bank on** VI + PREP contar con

---

BANK HOLIDAY

El término **bank holiday** se aplica en el Reino Unido a todo día festivo oficial en el que cierran bancos y comercios, que siempre cae en lunes. Los más destacados coinciden con Navidad, Semana Santa, finales de mayo y finales de agosto. Al contrario que en los pases de tradición católica, no se celebran las festividades dedicadas a los santos.
Ver tb www.dti.gov.uk/er/bankhol.htm

---

banker [ˈbæŋkə*] N banquero/a *m/f* ➤ **banker's draft** letra *f* de cambio ➤ **banker's order** (*Brit*) orden *f* bancaria

banking [ˈbæŋkɪŋ] Ⓐ N (*Comm, Fin*) banca *f* Ⓑ CPD bancario ➤ **banking hours** horas *fpl* bancarias

banknote [ˈbæŋknəʊt] N billete *m* de banco

bankroll [ˈbæŋkrəʊl] (*esp US*) Ⓐ N recursos *mpl* económicos Ⓑ VT financiar

bankrupt [ˈbæŋkrʌpt] Ⓐ ADJ en quiebra; **to be ~** estar en quiebra; **to go ~** ir a la bancarrota, quebrar Ⓑ N quebrado/a *m/f* Ⓒ VT llevar a la quiebra

bankruptcy [ˈbæŋkrəptsɪ] N quiebra *f*

banned substance [ˌbændˈsʌbstəns] N sustancia *f* prohibida

banner [ˈbænə*] N (= *flag*) bandera *f*; (= *placard*) pancarta *f* ➤ **banner headlines** grandes titulares *mpl*

bannisters [ˈbænɪstəz] N = **banisters**

banns [bænz] NPL amonestaciones *fpl*; **to call the ~** correr las amonestaciones

banquet [ˈbæŋkwɪt] N banquete *m*

banqueting hall [ˈbæŋkwɪtɪŋˌhɔːl] N comedor *m* de gala, sala *f* de banquetes

bantam [ˈbæntəm] N gallina *f* bántam

bantamweight [ˈbæntəmweɪt] N peso *m* gallo

banter [ˈbæntə*] Ⓐ N bromas *fpl*, guasa *f* Ⓑ VI bromear

bap [bæp] N (*Brit*) bollo *m* pequeño de pan

baptism [ˈbæptɪzəm] N (*in general*) bautismo *m*; (= *ceremony*) bautizo *m*; ~ **of fire** bautismo *m* de fuego

Baptist [ˈbæptɪst] N baptista *mf*, bautista *mf*; **St John the ~** San Juan Bautista ➤ **Baptist church** Iglesia *f* Bautista

baptize [bæpˈtaɪz] VT bautizar

bar¹ [bɑː*] Ⓐ N **1** (= *piece*) [*of wood, metal*] barra *f*; [*of soap*] pastilla *f*; [*of chocolate*] tableta *f*

2 (= *lever*) palanca *f*; [*of window, cage*] reja *f*; (*on door*) tranca *f*; (*on electric fire*) (*Brit*) resistencia *f*; **behind ~s** entre rejas; **to put sb behind ~s** encarcelar a algn

3 (= *hindrance*) obstáculo *m* (**to** para)

4 (= *ban*) prohibición *f* (**on** de)

5 (= *pub*) bar *m*, cantina *f* (*esp LAm*); (= *counter*) barra *f*, mostrador *m*

6 (*Jur*) **the Bar** (= *people*) el colegio de abogados; (= *profession*) la abogacía, la Barra (*Mex*); **the prisoner at the ~** el/la acusado/a; **to be called** *or* (*US*) **admitted to the Bar** recibirse de abogado, ingresar en la abogacía

7 (*Brit Mus*) (= *measure, rhythm*) compás *m*

8 (*Ftbl*) larguero *m*

Ⓑ VT **1** (= *obstruct*) [+ *way*] obstruir

2 (= *prevent*) [+ *progress*] impedir

3 (= *exclude*) excluir (**from** de); (= *ban*) prohibir; **to be ~red from a club** ser excluido de un club; **to ~ sb from doing sth** prohibir a algn hacer algo

4 (= *fasten*) [+ *door, window*] atrancar

Ⓒ CPD ➤ **bar billiards** (*esp Brit*) billar *m* americano ➤ **bar chart** (*esp Brit*) cuadro *m* de barras ➤ **bar code** código *m* de barras ➤ **bar girl** * (*US*) camarera *f* de barra ➤ **bar graph** (*esp US*) gráfico *m* de barras

bar² [bɑː*] PREP salvo, con excepción de; ~ **none** sin excepción

Barbadian [bɑːˈbeɪdɪən] Ⓐ ADJ de Barbados Ⓑ N nativo/a *m/f* de Barbados, habitante *mf* de Barbados

barbaric [bɑːˈbærɪk] ADJ bárbaro

barbarous [ˈbɑːbərəs] ADJ bárbaro

barbecue [ˈbɑːbɪkjuː] Ⓐ N (= *grill*) barbacoa *f*; (= *party*) parrillada *f*, barbacoa *f*, asado *m* (*LAm*) Ⓑ VT asar a la parrilla Ⓒ CPD ➤ **barbecue sauce** salsa *f* picante

barbed [bɑːbd] Ⓐ ADJ **1** [*arrow*] armado de lengüetas **2** (*fig*) [*criticism*] incisivo, mordaz Ⓑ CPD ➤ **barbed wire** alambre *m* de espino, alambre *m* de púas ➤ **barbed-wire fence** alambrada *f* (de espino)

barber [ˈbɑːbə*] N peluquero *m*, barbero *m* ➤ **barber shop** (*US*), **barber's (shop)** (*Brit*) peluquería *f*, barbería *f*

barbiturate [bɑːˈbɪtjʊrɪt] N barbitúrico *m*

bard [bɑːd] N (*liter*) bardo *m*, vate *m*

bare [bɛə*] Ⓐ ADJ (*compar* ~**r**; *superl* ~**st**) **1** (= *uncovered*) [*body, skin, person*] desnudo; [*head*] descubierto; [*feet*] descalzo; [*landscape*] pelado; [*tree*] sin hojas; [*ground*] árido, sin vegetación; [*floorboards*] sin alfombrar; (*Elec*) [*wire*] pelado, sin protección; **in one's ~ feet** descalzo; **he killed the lion with his ~ hands** mató al león sólo con las manos, mató al león sin armas; ~ **patch** (*on lawn, carpet*) calva *f*

2 (= *empty, unadorned*) [*cupboard, larder*] vacío; [*room*] desnudo; [*wall*] desnudo; [*statement*] escueto

3 (= *meagre*) [*majority*] escaso; **the ~ minimum** lo justo, lo indispensable; ✦ IDIOM **the ~ bones** lo esencial

4 (= *mere*) **the match lasted a ~ 18 minutes** el partido duró apenas 18 minutos

Ⓑ VT **to ~ one's head** descubrirse; **to ~ one's soul to sb** abrir el corazón a algn; **the dog ~d its teeth** el perro enseñó *or* mostró los dientes

bareback [ˈbɛəbæk] ADV a pelo, sin silla

barefaced [ˈbɛəfeɪst] ADJ descarado

barefoot(ed) [ˈbɛəˈfʊt(ɪd)] ADJ, ADV descalzo

bareheaded [ˈbɛəˈhedɪd] ADJ con la cabeza descubierta

bare-legged [ˈbɛəˈlegɪd] ADJ con las piernas descubiertas

barely [ˈbɛəlɪ] ADV apenas

bargain [ˈbɑːɡɪn] Ⓐ N **1** (= *agreement*) trato *m*; (= *transaction*) negocio *m*; **it's a ~!** ¡trato hecho!, ¡de acuerdo!; **into** *or* (*US*) **in the ~** para colmo; **you drive a hard ~** sabes regatear; **to make** *or* **strike a ~** cerrar un trato; **I'll make a ~ with you** hagamos un trato

2 (= *cheap thing*) ganga *f*; **it's a real ~** es una verdadera ganga; ~**s** artículos *mpl* de ocasión, oportunidades *fpl* Ⓑ VI **1** (= *negotiate*) negociar (**about** sobre; **with** con; **for** para obtener)

2 (= *haggle*) regatear

Ⓒ CPD [*article*] de ocasión ➤ **bargain basement**, **bargain counter** sección *f* de ofertas *or* oportunidades ➤ **bargain**

hunter cazador(a) *m/f* de ofertas *or* oportunidades ➤ **bargain price** precio *m* de ganga

bargaining ['bɑːɡɪnɪŋ] N (= *negotiation*) negociación *f*; (= *haggling*) regateo *m* ➤ **bargaining power** poder *m* de negociación ➤ **bargaining table** mesa *f* de negociaciones

barge [bɑːdʒ] Ⓐ N barcaza *f*; (*ceremonial*) falúa *f* Ⓑ VI **to ~ past sb** apartar a algn de un empujón; **to ~ into** [+ *person*] chocar contra; [+ *room*] irrumpir en Ⓒ CPD ➤ **barge pole** ✦ IDIOM **I wouldn't touch it with a ~ pole** (*Brit**) yo no lo querría ni regalado
➤ **barge in** VI + ADV (= *enter*) irrumpir; (= *interrupt*) meterse

baritone ['bærɪtəʊn] N barítono *m*

bark[1] [bɑːk] N [*of tree*] corteza *f*

bark[2] [bɑːk] Ⓐ N [*of dog*] ladrido *m*; ✦ IDIOM **his ~ is worse than his bite** perro ladrador, poco mordedor Ⓑ VI **1** [*dog*] ladrar (**at** a); ✦ IDIOM **to be ~ing up the wrong tree** ir muy descaminado **2** (= *speak sharply*) vociferar (**at** a) Ⓒ VT (*also ~ out*) [+ *order*] escupir, gritar

barking ['bɑːkɪŋ] Ⓐ N [*of dog*] ladrido *m* Ⓑ ADJ, ADV **~ (mad)** (*Brit**) chiflado*, como una regadera*

barley ['bɑːlɪ] N cebada *f* ➤ **barley sugar** azúcar *m* cande ➤ **barley water** (*esp Brit*) hordiate *m*

barmaid ['bɑːmeɪd] N (*esp Brit*) camarera *f*, moza *f* (*LAm*)

barman ['bɑːmən] N (*esp Brit*) (*pl* **barmen**) barman *m*, camarero *m*

Bar Mitzvah, bar mitzvah [bɑːˈmɪtsvə] N Bar Mitzvah *m*

barmy* ['bɑːmɪ] ADJ (*compar* **barmier**; *superl* **barmiest**) (*Brit*) chiflado*, chalado*

barn [bɑːn] N granero *m*; (= *raised barn*) troje *f*; (*US*) (*for horses*) cuadra *f*; (*US*) (*for cattle*) establo *m* ➤ **barn dance** baile *m* campesino ➤ **barn owl** lechuza *f*

barnacle ['bɑːnəkl] N percebe *m*

barometer [bəˈrɒmɪtə*] N barómetro *m*

baron ['bærən] N barón *m*; (*fig*) magnate *m*

baroness ['bærənɪs] N baronesa *f*

baronet ['bærənɪt] N baronet *m*

baroque [bəˈrɒk] Ⓐ ADJ barroco Ⓑ N barroco *m*

barracks ['bærəks] NPL cuartel *msing*; **confined to ~** arrestado en cuartel

barrage ['bærɑːʒ] Ⓐ N **1** (*Mil*) cortina *f* de fuego; **a ~ of questions** una lluvia de preguntas **2** (= *dam*) presa *f* Ⓑ CPD ➤ **barrage balloon** globo *m* de barrera

barrel ['bærəl] Ⓐ N **1** (*gen*) barril *m*, tonel *m*; [*of oil*] barril *m*; ✦ IDIOM **to have sb over a ~*** tener a algn con el agua al cuello* **2** [*of gun, pen*] cañón *m* Ⓑ CPD ➤ **barrel organ** organillo *m*

barren ['bærən] ADJ [*soil*] árido; [*plant, woman*] estéril

barricade [ˌbærɪˈkeɪd] Ⓐ N barricada *f* Ⓑ VT cerrar con barricadas; **to ~ o.s. in a house** hacerse fuerte en una casa

barrier ['bærɪə*] N **1** (*lit*) (*gen*) barrera *f*; (*also* **crash ~**) valla *f* protectora **2** (*fig*) barrera *f*, obstáculo *m* (**to** para) Ⓑ CPD ➤ **barrier cream** crema *f* protectora ➤ **barrier method** método *m* (de) barrera

barring ['bɑːrɪŋ] PREP excepto, salvo; **we shall be there ~ anything unforeseen** iremos a menos que suceda algo imprevisto

barrister ['bærɪstə*] N (*Brit*) abogado/a *m/f*

bar-room ['bɑːˌrʊm] N (*US*) bar *m*, taberna *f* ➤ **bar-room brawl** pelea *f* de taberna

barrow ['bærəʊ] N (= *wheelbarrow*) carretilla *f*; (*Brit*) (= *market stall*) carreta *f*

bartender ['bɑːtendə*] N (*esp US*) barman *m*, camarero *m*

barter ['bɑːtə*] Ⓐ N trueque *m* Ⓑ VT **to ~ sth (for sth)** trocar *or* cambiar algo (por algo) Ⓒ VI **to ~ with sb (for sth)** negociar con algn (por algo)

base[1] [beɪs] Ⓐ N **1** (= *bottom*) [*of wall*] base *f*; [*of column*] base *f*, pie *m*; [*of vase, lamp*] pie *m*
2 (= *basis, starting point*) base *f* (*also Math*)
3 (= *place*) [*of organization, company*] sede *f*; (= *residence*) lugar *m* de residencia; (= *workplace, military camp*) base *f*
4 (*Baseball*) base *f*; **to reach first ~** llegar a la primera base;

(*fig*) alcanzar la primera meta; ✦ IDIOMS **to touch ~ with sb** ponerse en contacto con algn; **to touch** *or* **cover all (the) ~s** (*esp US*) abarcarlo todo; **to be off ~** (*US**): **he's way off ~** está totalmente equivocado
Ⓑ VT **1** (= *post, locate*) **to ~ sb at/in** (*Mil*) estacionar a algn en; **the job is ~d in London** el trabajo tiene su base en Londres; **where are you ~d now?** ¿dónde estás ahora?
2 (= *found*) **to ~ sth on** basar *or* fundar algo en; **to be ~d on** basarse *or* fundarse en
Ⓒ CPD ➤ **base camp** campo *m* base ➤ **base lending rate** tipo *m* de interés base ➤ **base rate** (*Brit*) tipo *m* de interés base

base[2] [beɪs] (*compar* **~r**; *superl* **~st**) ADJ **1** [*action, motive*] vil, bajo **2** [*metal*] bajo de ley

baseball ['beɪsbɔːl] N (= *sport*) béisbol *m*; (= *ball*) pelota *f* de béisbol ➤ **baseball cap** gorra *f* de béisbol ➤ **baseball player** jugador(a) *m/f* de béisbol

baseboard ['beɪsbɔːd] N (*US*) rodapié *m*, zócalo *m*

baseline ['beɪslaɪn] N **1** (*Tennis*) línea *f* de saque, línea *f* de fondo **2** (*Survey*) línea *f* de base **3** (*fig*) (*on scale*) punto *m* de referencia

basement ['beɪsmənt] N sótano *m*

bases ['beɪsiːz] NPL *of* **basis**

bash* [bæʃ] Ⓐ N **1** (= *knock*) porrazo* *m*, golpe *m* **2** (*Brit*) (= *try*) **I'll have a ~ (at it)** lo intentaré **3** (= *party*) fiesta *f*, juerga *f* Ⓑ VT [+ *table, door*] golpear; [+ *person*] pegar
➤ **bash in*** VT + ADV **to ~ sb's head in** romper la crisma a algn*
➤ **bash up*** VT + ADV (*Brit*) [+ *car*] estrellar; [+ *person*] pegar una paliza a

bashful ['bæʃfʊl] ADJ tímido, vergonzoso

BASIC ['beɪsɪk] N ABBR (*Comput*) (= **Beginner's All-purpose Symbolic Instruction Code**) BASIC *m*

basic ['beɪsɪk] Ⓐ ADJ **1** (= *fundamental*) básico; **~ French** francés *m* básico *or* elemental; **a ~ right** un derecho fundamental; **~ to sth** básico *or* fundamental para algo **2** [*salary, working hours*] base
3 (= *rudimentary*) [*equipment, furniture*] rudimentario; [*cooking*] muy sencillo, muy poco elaborado; **the hotel was extremely ~** el hotel era sumamente sencillo
Ⓑ **basics** NPL **~s such as bread and milk** alimentos básicos como el pan y la leche; **they had forgotten everything and we had to go back to (the) ~s** lo habían olvidado todo y tuvimos que volver a empezar por los principios; **to get down to (the) ~s** ir a lo importante
Ⓒ CPD ➤ **basic airman** (*US*) soldado *m* raso de la fuerzas aéreas ➤ **basic wage** salario *m* base

basically ['beɪsɪklɪ] ADV básicamente, fundamentalmente; **it's ~ simple** en el fondo es sencillo

basil ['bæzl] N albahaca *f*

basilica [bəˈzɪlɪkə] N basílica *f*

basin ['beɪsn] N **1** (= *washbasin*) palangana *f*; (*in bathroom*) lavabo *m* **2** (*for mixing*) bol *m*, cuenco *m* **3** (*Geog*) cuenca *f*

basis ['beɪsɪs] N (*pl* **bases**) base *f*; **on the ~ of what you've said** en base a lo que ha dicho

bask [bɑːsk] VI **to ~ in the sun** tomar el sol

basket ['bɑːskɪt] Ⓐ N **1** cesto *m*, cesta *f*; [*of balloon*] barquilla *f* **2** (*Basketball*) canasta *f*; **to score a ~** encestar, meter una canasta Ⓑ CPD ➤ **basket case*** chalado/a* *m/f*, majareta *mf* (*Sp**)

basketball ['bɑːskɪtbɔːl] N baloncesto *m* ➤ **basketball player** jugador(a) *m/f* de baloncesto

Basque [bæsk] Ⓐ ADJ vasco Ⓑ N **1** (= *person*) vasco/a *m/f* **2** (*Ling*) euskera *m*, vascuence *m* Ⓒ CPD ➤ **the Basque Country** el País Vasco, Euskadi *f* ➤ **the Basque Provinces** las Vascongadas

bass[1] [beɪs] (*Mus*) Ⓐ ADJ bajo Ⓑ N (= *voice, singer, guitar*) bajo *m*; (= *double bass*) contrabajo *m* Ⓒ CPD ➤ **bass clef** clave *f* de fa ➤ **bass drum** bombo *m* ➤ **bass guitar** bajo *m*

bass[2] [bæs] (*pl* **~**) N (= *fish*) róbalo *m*

bassoon [bəˈsuːn] N bajón *m*, fagot *m*

bastard ['bɑːstəd] N **1** (= *illegitimate child*) bastardo/a *m/f* **2** (****) (= *nasty person*) cabrón/ona*** *m/f*, hijo/a *m/f* de puta***, hijo/a *m/f* de la chingada (*Mex****); **this job is a real ~** este trabajo es muy jodido***

baste [beɪst] VT pringar

bastion ['bæstɪən] N baluarte *m*

bat¹ [bæt] N (= *animal*) murciélago *m*; **old ~**** (= *old woman*) bruja* *f*; ✦ IDIOM **to go like a ~ out of hell*** ir como alma que lleva el diablo, ir a toda hostia (*Sp**)

bat² [bæt] Ⓐ N (*in ball games*) paleta *f*, pala *f*; (*in cricket, baseball*) bate *m*; ✦ IDIOMS **off one's own ~** (*Brit**) por cuenta propia; **right off the ~** (*US**) de repente Ⓑ VI (*Sport*) batear Ⓒ VT (*) (= *hit*) golpear, apalear; **to ~ sth around** (*US**) (= *discuss*) discutir acerca de algo

bat³ [bæt] VT **he didn't ~ an eyelid** (*Brit*) or **an eye** (*US*) ni pestañeó; **without ~ting an eyelid** (*Brit*) or **an eye** (*US*) sin pestañear, sin inmutarse

batch [bætʃ] N [*of goods*] lote *m*, remesa *f*; [*of people*] grupo *m*; [*of bread*] hornada *f*

bated ['beɪtɪd] ADJ **with ~ breath** sin respirar

bath [bɑːθ] Ⓐ N (*pl* **~s** [bɑːðz]) **1** (*esp Brit*) (*also* **~tub**) bañera *f*, tina *f* (*LAm*), bañadera *f* (*SC*) **2** (= *act*) baño *m*; **to have a ~** darse un baño, bañarse; **to give sb a ~** dar un baño a algn, bañar a algn **3** (*Chem, Phot*) baño *m* **4** (*Brit*) (= *swimming pool*) piscina *fsing*, alberca *fsing* (*Mex*), pileta *fsing* (*SC*) Ⓑ VT (*Brit*) bañar, dar un baño a Ⓒ VI (*Brit*) bañarse Ⓓ CPD [*salts, towel*] de baño

bathe [beɪð] Ⓐ N (*Brit*) (= *swim*) baño *m*; **to go for a ~** ir a bañarse Ⓑ VT **1** [+ *wound etc*] lavar **2** (*esp US*) (= *bath*) bañar **3 ~d in light** bañado de luz; **~d in tears/sweat** bañado en lágrimas/sudor Ⓒ VI (*Brit*) (= *swim*) bañarse; (*US*) (= *have bath*) bañarse

bather ['beɪðəʳ] N (*esp Brit*) bañista *mf*

bathing ['beɪðɪŋ] N el bañarse ➤ **bathing cap** gorro *m* de baño ➤ **bathing costume** (*Brit*), **bathing suit** traje *m* de baño, bañador *m*, malla *f* (*SC*) ➤ **bathing trunks** bañador *msing* (*de hombre*)

bathmat ['bɑːθmæt] N alfombra *f* de baño

bathrobe ['bɑːθrəʊb] N albornoz *m*

bathroom ['bɑːθrʊm] N cuarto *m* de baño; (*esp US*) (= *toilet*) servicio *m*, baño *m* (*esp LAm*); **to go to** or **use the ~** ir al servicio ➤ **bathroom cabinet** armario *m* de aseo ➤ **bathroom scales** báscula *fsing* de baño

bathtub ['bɑːθtʌb] N (*esp US*) bañera *f*, tina *f* (*LAm*), bañadera *f* (*SC*)

baton ['bætən] N (*Mus*) batuta *f*; (*Mil*) bastón *m*; (*Brit*) [*of policeman*] porra *f*; (*in race*) testigo *m*; ✦ IDIOM **to pick up the ~** recoger el testigo ➤ **baton charge** (*Brit*) carga *f* con bastones

batsman ['bætsmən] N (*pl* **batsmen**) (*Cricket*) bateador *m*

battalion [bə'tælɪən] N batallón *m*

batter¹ ['bætəʳ] N (*Culin*) mezcla *f* para rebozar; **in ~** rebozado

batter² ['bætəʳ] Ⓐ N (*Baseball, Cricket*) bateador(a) *m/f* Ⓑ VT [+ *person*] apalear; [+ *wife, baby*] maltratar; [*wind, waves*] azotar; (*Mil*) cañonear, bombardear

battered ['bætəd] ADJ (= *bruised*) magullado; [*hat*] estropeado; [*car*] abollado; [*wife, baby*] maltratado

battering ['bætərɪŋ] N (= *blows*) paliza *f*; (*Mil*) bombardeo *m*; **the ~ of the waves** el golpear de las olas; **he got a ~ from the critics** los críticos fueron muy duros con él, los críticos lo pusieron como un trapo* ➤ **battering ram** ariete *m*

battery ['bætərɪ] Ⓐ N **1** (*dry*) pila *f*; (*wet*) batería *f* **2** (*Mil*) batería *f* **3** (= *series*) [*of tests*] serie *f*; [*of lights*] batería *f*, equipo *m*; [*of questions*] descarga *f*, sarta *f* **4** (= *assault*) violencia *f*, agresión *f* Ⓑ CPD ➤ **battery charger** (*Elec*) cargador *m* de baterías ➤ **battery farm** (*Brit*) granja *f* (*avícola*) de cría intensiva ➤ **battery farming** (*Brit*) cría *f* (*avícola*) intensiva ➤ **battery hen** (*Brit*) gallina *f* de criadero

battery-operated [,bætərɪ'ɒpəreɪtɪd] ADJ a pilas

battle ['bætl] Ⓐ N **1** (*Mil*) batalla *f*; **to fight a ~** luchar **2** (*fig*) lucha *f* (**for control of** por el control de; **to control** por controlar); **a ~ of wills/wits** un duelo de voluntades/ ingenio; **to do ~ for** luchar por

Ⓑ VI luchar (**against** contra; **for** por; **to do** por hacer) Ⓒ VT (*esp US*) luchar contra, librar batalla contra Ⓓ CPD ➤ **battle cruiser** crucero *m* de batalla ➤ **battle cry** (*Mil*) grito *m* de combate; (*fig*) lema *m*, consigna *f* ➤ **battle dress** traje *m* de campaña ➤ **battle royal** batalla *f* campal ➤ **battle out** VT + ADV **to ~ it out** enfrentarse

battlefield ['bætlfiːld], **battleground** ['bætlgraʊnd] N campo *m* de batalla

battlements ['bætlmənts] NPL almenas *fpl*

battleship ['bætlʃɪp] N **1** (*Mil*) acorazado *m* **2 battleships** (= *game*) los barquitos (*juego*)

batty** ['bætɪ] ADJ (*compar* **battier**; *superl* **battiest**) (*esp Brit*) chiflado*, chalado*

baulk [bɔːlk] VI = **balk**

Bavaria [bə'veərɪə] N Baviera *f*

bawdy ['bɔːdɪ] ADJ (*compar* **bawdier**; *superl* **bawdiest**) subido de tono, verde*, colorado (*Mex**)

bawl [bɔːl] VI (= *cry*) berrear; (= *shout*) chillar; **to ~ at sb** gritar a algn

bay¹ [beɪ] N (*Geog*) bahía *f*; (*small*) abra *f*; (*very large*) golfo *m*; **the Bay of Biscay** el Golfo de Vizcaya

> Use **el/un** not **la/una** before feminine nouns beginning with stressed **a** or **ha** like **abra**.

bay² [beɪ] N **1** (*between two walls*) crujía *f*; (*also* **~ window**) ventana *f* salediza **2** (*for parking*) parking *m*, área *f* de aparcamiento or (*LAm*) estacionamiento; (*for loading*) área *f* de carga

> Use **el/un** not **la/una** before feminine nouns beginning with stressed **a** or **ha** like **área**.

bay³ [beɪ] Ⓐ ADJ [*horse*] bayo Ⓑ N caballo *m* bayo

bay⁴ [beɪ] N (*Bot*) laurel *m* ➤ **bay leaf** (hoja *f* de) laurel *m* ➤ **bay rum** ron *m* de laurel, ron *m* de malagueta

bay⁵ [beɪ] Ⓐ VI [*dog*] aullar (**at** a); ✦ IDIOMS **to ~ for blood** (*Brit*) clamar venganza; **to ~ for sb's blood** (*Brit*) pedir la cabeza de algn Ⓑ N **1** (= *bark*) aullido *m* **2 at ~** (*Hunting*) acorralado (also fig); **to keep** or **hold sth/sb at ~** (*fig*) mantener algo/a algn a raya

bayonet ['beɪənɪt] Ⓐ N bayoneta *f* Ⓑ VT herir/matar con la bayoneta Ⓒ CPD ➤ **bayonet bulb** bombilla *f* or (*LAm*) foco *m* de bayoneta ➤ **bayonet charge** carga *f* a la bayoneta

bazaar [bə'zɑːʳ] N bazar *m*

bazooka [bə'zuːkə] N bazuca *f*

BBC N ABBR = **British Broadcasting Corporation**; **the ~** la BBC; *ver tb* www.bbc.co.uk

BBQ N ABBR = **barbecue**

BC Ⓐ ADV ABBR (= **Before Christ**) a. de C., a.C., A.C. Ⓑ N ABBR (*Canada*) = **British Columbia**

---

be

Ⓐ INTRANSITIVE VERB	Ⓒ AUXILIARY VERB
Ⓑ IMPERSONAL VERB	Ⓓ MODAL VERB

be [biː] (*present* **am, is, are**; *pt* **was, were**; *pp* **been**) Ⓐ INTRANSITIVE VERB

1 (*linking nouns, noun phrases, pronouns*) ser; **he's a pianist** es pianista; **two and two are four** dos y dos son cuatro; **she's his sister** es su hermana; **it's me!** ¡soy yo!; **if I were you ...** yo en tu lugar ..., yo que tú ...*

2 (*characteristics seen as inherent*) ser; **it's blue** es azul; **he is boring** es aburrido; **if I were rich** si fuera rico

> Use **estar** with past participles used as adjectives describing the results of an action or process:

it's broken está roto; **he's dead** está muerto

3 (*changeable or temporary state*) estar; **it's dirty** está sucio;

she's bored/ill está aburrida/enferma; **how are you?** ¿cómo estás?, ¿qué tal estás?

> In certain expressions where English uses **be** + ADJECTIVE to describe feelings, Spanish uses **tener** with a noun:

I'm cold/hot tengo frío/calor; **my feet are cold** tengo los pies fríos; **I'm hungry/thirsty** tengo hambre/sed
4 (*age*) **"how old is she?"** — **"she's nine"** —¿cuántos años tiene? —tiene nueve años; **she will be two tomorrow** mañana cumple dos años; **when I'm old** cuando sea viejo
5 (= *take place*) ser; **the service will be at St John's Church** la misa será en la iglesia de San Juan
6 (= *be situated*) estar; **where is the Town Hall?** ¿dónde está *or* queda el ayuntamiento?; **it's 5km to the village** el pueblo está *or* queda a 5km; **here you are (,take it)** aquí tienes, (tómalo)
7 (= *exist*) haber; **there is/are** hay; **there must be an explanation** debe de haber una explicación; *BUT* **there are three of us** somos tres; **after the shop there's the bus station** después de la tienda está la estación de autobuses
8 (= *cost*) **how much is it?** ¿cuánto es?; (*when paying*) **how much do I owe you?** ¿cuánto le debo?; **how much was it?** ¿cuánto costó?; **the book is £20** el libro vale *or* cuesta 20 libras
9 (= *visit*) **has the postman been?** ¿ha venido el cartero?; **he has been and gone** vino y se fue; **I have been to see my aunt** he ido a ver a mi tía; **have you ever been to Glasgow?** ¿has estado en Glasgow alguna vez?
10 (*in noun compounds*) **mother to be** futura madre *or* mamá *f*; **my wife to be** mi futura esposa
11 (*in set expressions*)
✦ **be that as it may** sea como fuere
✦ **what is it to you?*** ¿a ti qué te importa?
B IMPERSONAL VERB
1 (*weather*) hacer; **it's hot/cold** hace calor/frío; **it's fine** hace buen tiempo
2 (*time, date*) ser; **it's eight o'clock** son las ocho; **what's the date (today)?** ¿qué fecha es hoy?; **it's the 3rd of May** ✧ **it's May 3rd** es el 3 de mayo; **it's Monday today** hoy es lunes

> but note the following alternatives with **estar**:

it's the 3rd of May ✧ **it's May 3rd** estamos a 3 de mayo; **it's Monday today** hoy estamos a lunes
3 (*asking and giving opinion*) ser; **is it certain that ...?** ¿es verdad *or* cierto que ...?; **it is easy to make a mistake** es fácil cometer un error; *BUT* **it's not clear whether ...** no está claro si ...; **it would be wrong for us to do that** no estaría bien que nosotros hiciésemos eso
4 (*emphatic*) ser; **it's me who does all the work** soy yo quien hace todo el trabajo
5 (*in set expressions*) **if it hadn't been for you** *or* (*frm*) **had it not been for you ...** si no hubiera sido por ti *or* de no haber sido por ti ...
C AUXILIARY VERB
1 (*passive*) ser; **the house was destroyed by an earthquake** la casa fue destruida por un terremoto

> The passive is not used as often in Spanish as in English, active and reflexive constructions often being preferred:

the box had been opened habían abierto la caja; **these cars are made in Spain** estos coches se fabrican en España; **it is said that ...** dicen que ..., se dice que ...; **he was killed by a terrorist** lo mató un terrorista; **she was killed in a car crash** murió en un accidente de coche; **what's to be done?** ¿qué hay que hacer?
2 (*forming continuous*) estar; **it's raining** está lloviendo; **what are you doing?** ¿qué estás haciendo?, ¿qué haces?

> Use the present simple to talk about planned future events and the **ir a** construction to talk about intention:

they're coming tomorrow vienen mañana; **will you be seeing her tomorrow?** ¿la verás *or* la vas a ver mañana?

> The imperfect tense can be used for continuous action in the past:

he was driving too fast conducía demasiado rápido
3 (*in question tags*) **he's handsome, isn't he?** es guapo, ¿verdad? *or* ¿no? *or* ¿no es cierto?; **she wasn't happy, was she?** no era feliz, ¿verdad?; **so he's back again, is he?** así que ha vuelto, ¿eh?; **you're not ill, are you?** ¿no estarás enfermo?
4 (*in tag responses*) **"I'm worried"** — **"so am I"** —estoy preocupado —yo también; **"I'm not ready"** — **"neither am I"** —no estoy listo —yo tampoco; **"you're tired"** — **"no, I'm not!"** —estás cansado —no, ¡qué va!; **"you're not eating enough"** — **"yes I am"** —no comes lo suficiente —que sí; **"they're getting married"** — **"oh, are they?"** (*showing surprise*) —se casan —¿ah, sí? *or* —¡no me digas!; **"he's always late, isn't he?"** — **"yes, he is"** —siempre llega tarde, ¿verdad? —(pues) sí; **"is it what you expected?"** — **"no, it isn't"** —¿es esto lo que esperabas? —(pues) no
5 (*verb substitute*) **he's older than you are** es mayor que tú; **he isn't as happy as he was** no está tan contento como antes
D MODAL VERB (*with infinitive construction*) **1** (= *must, have to*) **you're to put on your shoes** tienes que ponerte los zapatos; **he's not to open it** no debe abrirlo, que no lo abra; **I am to do it** he de hacerlo yo, soy yo el que debe hacerlo
2 (= *should*) deber; **am I to understand that ...?** ¿debo entender que ...?; **he was to have come yesterday** tenía que *or* debía haber venido ayer; **he is to be congratulated on his work** debemos felicitarlo por su trabajo
3 (= *will*) **they are to be married in the summer** se casarán en el verano
4 (= *can*) **these birds are to be found all over the world** estos pájaros se encuentran por todo el mundo; **you weren't to know** no tenías por qué saberlo
5 (*expressing destiny*) **this was to have serious repercussions** esto iba a tener serias repercusiones; **they were never to return** jamás regresaron; **it was not to be** no quiso el destino que así fuera
6 (*in conditional sentences*) **you must work harder if you are to succeed** debes esforzarte más si quieres triunfar; **if it were to snow ...** si nevase *or* nevara ...

beach [biːtʃ] **A** N playa *f* **B** VT [+ *whale*] embarrancar, encallar **C** CPD ► **beach ball** balón *m* de playa ► **beach buggy** buggy *m* ► **beach chair** (*US*) tumbona *f*, perezosa *f* (*LAm*) ► **beach hut** caseta *f* de playa ► **beach towel** toalla *f* de playa ► **beach umbrella** sombrilla *f*

beachcomber [ˈbiːtʃˌkəʊməʳ] N raquero/a *m/f*

beachwear [ˈbiːtʃwɛəʳ] N ropa *f* de playa

beacon [ˈbiːkən] N (*in port*) faro *m*; (*on aerodrome*) baliza *f*, aerofaro *m*; (*Rad*) radiofaro *m*; (= *fire*) almenara *f*

bead [biːd] N **1** (*gen*) cuenta *f*; [*of glass*] abalorio *m*; **beads** (= *necklace*) collar *msing* **2** [*of dew, sweat*] gota *f*

beady [ˈbiːdɪ] ADJ ~ **eyes** ojos *mpl* pequeños y brillantes

beagle [ˈbiːgl] N beagle *m*

beak [biːk] N [*of bird*] pico *m*; (*) (= *nose*) napia* *f*

beaker [ˈbiːkəʳ] N **1** (*Brit*) (*plastic*) vaso *m* (de plástico duro); (*US*) (= *glass*) vaso *m*; (= *mug*) jarrita *f* (para beber) **2** (*Chem*) vaso *m* de precipitación

be-all [ˈbiːɔːl] N (*also* ~ **and end-all**) único objeto *m*, única cosa *f* que importa; **money is not the** ~ el dinero no es lo único que importa

beam [biːm] **A** N **1** [*of light, laser*] rayo *m*; **to drive on full** (*Brit*) *or* **high** (*US*) ~ conducir con luz de carretera *or* con luces largas **2** (*Archit*) viga *f*, travesaño *m* **3** (*Sport*) barra *f* fija **B** VT **1** (= *transmit*) [+ *signal*] emitir **2** (= *smile*) **she ~ed her thanks at me** me lanzó una mirada de agradecimiento **C** VI **1** (= *shine*) brillar **2** (= *smile*) sonreír satisfecho; **~ing with pride** radiante de orgullo

beaming [ˈbiːmɪŋ] ADJ sonriente, radiante

bean [biːn] **A** N **1** (*gen*) frijol *m*, alubia *f* (*Sp*); (*broad,* *haricot*) haba *f*; (*green*) habichuela *f*, judía *f* verde (*Sp*), ejote *m* (*Mex*), poroto *m* verde (*Chi*); (*coffee*) grano *m*; ✦ IDIOMS **to be full of ~s** (*Brit**) estar lleno de vida; **I haven't a ~** (*Brit**) estoy pelado*, no tengo un duro (*Sp**), no tengo un peso (*LAm**); **he doesn't know ~s about it** (*US**) no sabe ni papa de eso*, no tiene ni zorra idea (*Sp**) **2** (*US**) (= *head, brain*) coco* *m* **ⓒ** CPD ➤ **bean curd** tofu *m*

beanbag ['biːnbæg] N (*for throwing*) *saquito que se usa para realizar ejercicios gimnásticos*; (*for sitting on*) puf *m* de saco, *asiento en forma de bolsa rellena de bolitas de poliestireno*

beanpole ['biːnpəʊl] N emparrado *m*; ✦ IDIOM **he's a real ~*** está como un espárrago*

beanshoots ['biːnʃuːts], **beansprouts** ['biːnspraʊts] NPL brotes *mpl* de soja

bear¹ [beəʳ] **Ⓐ** N **1** (= *animal*) oso/a *m/f*; **the Great/Little Bear** la Osa Mayor/Menor; ✦ IDIOMS **to be like a ~ with a sore head*** estar de un humor de perros*; **to be loaded for ~** (*US**) estar dispuesto para el ataque **2** (*also* **teddy ~**) osito *m* de peluche **3** (*Fin*) (= *pessimistic trader*) bajista *mf* **ⓒ** CPD ➤ **bear cub** osezno *m* ➤ **bear hug** fuerte abrazo *m* ➤ **bear market** (*Fin*) mercado *m* bajista

bear² [beəʳ] (*pt* **bore**; *pp* **borne**) **Ⓐ** VT **1** (= *support*) [+ *weight*] aguantar, sostener **2** (= *take on*) [+ *cost*] correr con, pagar; **the government ~s some responsibility for this crisis** el gobierno tiene parte de responsabilidad en esta crisis; **he bore no responsibility for what had happened** no era responsable de lo que había pasado; **to ~ the burden of** soportar la carga de **3** (= *endure*) [+ *pain, suspense*] soportar, aguantar; **I can't ~ him** no lo puedo ver, no lo soporto *or* aguanto; **he can't ~ seeing** *or* **to see her suffer** no soporta verla sufrir; **I can't ~ to look** no puedo mirar; **it doesn't ~ thinking about*** da horror sólo pensarlo **4** (= *bring*) [+ *news, gift*] traer **5** (= *carry*) llevar, portar (*liter*) **6** (= *have*) [+ *date, message, title*] llevar; [+ *mark*] conservar **7** (= *stand up to*) [+ *examination*] resistir; **her story won't ~ scrutiny** su historia no resistirá un análisis **8** (= *produce*) [+ *interest*] devengar; **her hard work bore fruit** sus esfuerzos dieron fruto; **she bore him a son** le dio un hijo **ⓑ** VI **1** (= *move*) **to ~ (to the) right/left** torcer *or* girar a la derecha/izquierda **2 to ~ on sth** (= *relate to*) guardar relación con algo, tener que ver con algo; (= *influence*) influir en algo ➤ **bear down** VI + ADV (= *come closer*) **to ~ down on sth/sb** echarse encima a algo/algn ➤ **bear out** VT + ADV [+ *story*] confirmar, corroborar; **Jane will ~ me out** Jane confirmará *or* corroborará lo que he dicho ➤ **bear up*** VI + ADV **how are you ~ing up?** ¿qué tal ese ánimo?; **"how are you?" — "~ing up!"** —¿qué tal? —¡voy aguantando! ➤ **bear with** VI + PREP tener paciencia con; **if you'll ~ with me, I'll explain** si esperas un poco, te explico

bearable ['beərəbl] ADJ soportable

beard [bɪəd] N barba *f*; **to have a ~** llevar barba

bearded ['bɪədɪd] ADJ con barba; (*heavily*) barbudo

bearer ['beərəʳ] N [*of letter, news, cheque*] portador(a) *m/f*; [*of credentials, office, passport*] titular *mf*; (*also* **pallbearer**) portador/a *m/f* del féretro; (*also* **stretcher-~**) camillero/a *m/f*; **I hate to be the ~ of bad news** siento traer malas noticias

bearing ['beərɪŋ] N **1** (= *relevance*) relación *f*; **this has no ~ on the matter** esto no tiene relación *or* no tiene nada que ver con el asunto; **this has a direct ~ on our future** esto influye directamente en nuestro futuro **2 to get one's ~s** orientarse; **to lose one's ~s** desorientarse **3** (= *posture*) porte *m*; (= *behaviour*) comportamiento *m*, modales *mpl* **4** (*Mech*) cojinete *m*

beast [biːst] N **1** (= *animal*) bestia *f*; **~ of burden** bestia *f* de carga; **the king of the ~s** el rey de los animales; **this is quite a different ~** eso es otra cosa **2** (*) (= *person*) bestia* *mf*

beastly†* ['biːstlɪ] ADJ (*compar* **beastlier**; *superl* **beastliest**) (= *horrid*) **that was a ~ thing to do** eso sí que fue cruel; **you**

were ~ to me te portaste muy mal conmigo; **where's that ~ book?** ¿dónde está el maldito libro ese?

beat [biːt] (*vb: pt ~; pp* **~en**) **Ⓐ** N **1** [*of drum*] redoble *m*; [*of heart*] latido *m*; **her heart missed** *or* **skipped a ~** le dio un vuelco el corazón; **the ~ of wings** el batir de alas **2** (*Mus*) (= *rhythm*) compás *m*, ritmo *m*; (= *tempo*) tiempo *m* **3** (= *route*) [*of policeman*] ronda *f*; **we need more officers on the ~** deberíamos tener más agentes haciendo la ronda **ⓑ** VT **1** (= *strike, thrash*) [+ *surface*] golpear, dar golpes en; [+ *drum*] tocar; [+ *carpet*] sacudir; [+ *metal, eggs, cream*] batir; (*Hunting*) batir; ✦ IDIOM **~ it!*** ¡lárgate!* **2** (= *beat up*) [+ *person*] pegar; **he was badly ~en** le habían dado una buena paliza; **to ~ sb to death** matar a algn a golpes *or* de una paliza **3** (= *flap*) [+ *wings*] batir **4** (*Mus*) **to ~ time** marcar el compás **5** (= *defeat*) [+ *team, adversary*] ganar a; [+ *problem, inflation*] superar; **Arsenal ~ Leeds 5-1** el Arsenal ganó 5-1 contra el Leeds, el Arsenal derrotó al Leeds 5-1; **she doesn't know when she's ~en** no sabe reconocer que ha perdido; **our prices cannot be ~en** nuestros precios son imbatibles *or* inigualables; **"how did he escape?" — "(it) ~s me!"*** —¿cómo escapó? —¡no me lo explico! *or* —¡(no tengo) ni idea!; ✦ IDIOM **if you can't ~ them, join them** si no puedes con ellos, únete a ellos **6** (= *better*) [+ *record*] batir; **it ~s sitting at home doing nothing*** es mejor que estar en casa sin hacer nada; **you can't ~ a nice cup of tea*** no hay nada mejor que una buena taza de té; **coffee ~s tea any day*** el café da cien vueltas al té; **that ~s everything!*** ¡eso es el colmo!; **can you ~ it or that?*** ¿has visto cosa igual? **7** (= *pre-empt*) adelantarse; **if we leave early, we can ~ the rush hour** si salimos temprano, nos evitamos la hora punta; **I'll ~ you to that tree** ¿a que llego antes que tú a aquel árbol?, te echo una carrera hasta aquel árbol; **I ~ him to it** me adelanté **ⓒ** VI **1** (= *hit*) **to ~ on** *or* **against** *or* **at sth** [*rain, waves*] azotar algo; [*person*] dar golpes en algo, golpear algo **2** (= *rhythmically*) [*heart*] latir; [*drum*] redoblar; [*wings*] batir **3** (*Hunting*) batir; ✦ IDIOM **to ~ about the bush** andarse con rodeos **Ⓓ** ADJ (*) **1** (= *exhausted*) rendido, molido* **2** (= *defeated*) **the problem has me ~** me doy por vencido con este problema ➤ **beat back** VT + ADV **1** (= *fight off*) [+ *attack*] rechazar **2** (= *force back*) hacer retroceder ➤ **beat down Ⓐ** VT + ADV **1** [+ *door*] derribar a golpes **2** [+ *seller*] **he tried to ~ me down on the price** intentó que le rebajase el precio, intentó que se lo dejase más barato; **I ~ him down to £20** conseguí que me lo rebajara a 20 libras **ⓑ** VI + ADV [*sun*] caer a plomo; [*rain*] caer con fuerza ➤ **beat off** VT + ADV **they ~ off competition from other companies to win the contract** derrotaron a otras compañías que competían por conseguir el contrato; **England won 4-1, ~ing off challenges from the US and France** Inglaterra ganó 4-1 frente al reto que suponían EE.UU. y Francia ➤ **beat out** VT + ADV **1** [+ *flames*] apagar (a golpes); [+ *dent*] quitar (a golpes) **2** (*Mus*) marcar **3** (*US*) [+ *person*] derrotar ➤ **beat up** VT + ADV [+ *person*] dar una paliza a, pegar ➤ **beat up on** VI + PREP (*US**) (= *hit*) dar una paliza a, pegar; (= *bully*) intimidar; (= *criticize*) arremeter contra

beaten ['biːtn] **Ⓐ** PP *of* **beat** **ⓑ** ADJ **1** [*metal, earth*] batido; ✦ IDIOM **off the ~ track** (= *isolated*) apartado, retirado; (= *unfrequented*) fuera de los lugares donde va todo el mundo **2** (= *defeated*) [*person*] derrotado

beaten-up* ['biːtnʌp] ADJ [*car*] hecho un cacharro*

beater ['biːtəʳ] N **1** (*for cooking*) batidora *f* **2** (*Hunting*) ojeador(a) *m/f*, batidor(a) *m/f*

beating ['biːtɪŋ] N **1** (= *striking*) [*of drum*] redoble *m*; [*of heart*] latido *m*, pulsación *f*; **the ~ of wings** el batir de alas; **the ~ of the rain/the waves** el batir *or* el azote de la lluvia/ las olas **2** (= *punishment*) paliza *f*, golpiza *f* (*LAm*); **to get a ~** recibir una paliza; **to give sb a ~** dar una paliza a algn **3** (= *bettering*) **that score will take some ~** será difícil superar esa puntuación

beat-up* ['biːtʌp] ADJ hecho polvo*, de perras*

beautician [bjuːˈtɪʃən] N esteticista *mf*

beautiful [ˈbjuːtɪfəl] ADJ hermoso, bello, lindo (*esp LAm*); **what a ~ house!** ¡qué casa más preciosa!

beautifully [ˈbjuːtɪflɪ] ADV (= *wonderfully*) maravillosamente; (= *perfectly*) perfectamente

beautify [ˈbjuːtɪfaɪ] VT embellecer

beauty [ˈbjuːtɪ] Ⓐ N (= *quality*) belleza *f*, hermosura *f*; (= *person, thing*) belleza *f*, preciosidad *f*; **the ~ of it is that ...** lo mejor de esto es que ...; **that's the ~ of it** eso es lo que tiene de bueno; **it's a ~** es una preciosidad; ✦ PROVS **~ is in the eye of the beholder** todo es según el cristal con que se mira; **~ is only skin-deep** la belleza no lo es todo, la belleza es algo sólo superficial Ⓑ CPD [*competition, product*] de belleza ➤ **beauty parlour**, **beauty parlor** (*US*) salón *m* de belleza ➤ **beauty queen** reina *f* de la belleza ➤ **beauty shop** (*US*) = **beauty parlour** ➤ **beauty sleep** (*hum*): **I need my ~ sleep** necesito dormir mis horas (para luego estar bien) ➤ **beauty spot** (= *mole*) lunar *m*; (*in country*) lugar *m* pintoresco

beaver [ˈbiːvəʳ] N castor *m* ➤ **beaver away*** VI + ADV trabajar con empeño

became [bɪˈkeɪm] PT *of* **become**

because [bɪˈkɒz] CONJ **1** porque; **I came ~ you asked me to** vine porque me lo pediste; **~ he was ill he couldn't go** no pudo ir por estar enfermo; **just ~ he has two cars ...** sólo porque tiene dos coches ... **2 ~ of** por; **many families break up ~ of a lack of money** muchas familias se deshacen por falta de dinero

beck [bek] N ✦ IDIOM **to be at the ~ and call of** estar siempre a disposición de

beckon [ˈbekən] Ⓐ VT llamar con señas, hacer señas a; **he ~ed me in/over** me hizo señas para que entrara/me acercara Ⓑ VI **1 to ~ to sb** llamar a algn con señas, hacer señas a algn **2** [*bright lights, fame*] ejercer su atracción

become [bɪˈkʌm] (*pt* **became**; *pp* **~**) Ⓐ VI **1** (= *grow to be*)

> **Become** + ADJECTIVE is often translated by a specific verb. Otherwise, use **ponerse** to talk about temporary but normal changes:

ponerse; **this is becoming difficult** esto se está poniendo difícil; **to ~ ill** ponerse enfermo, enfermar

---

> Use **volverse** to refer to sudden, longer-lasting and unpredictable changes, particularly those affecting the mind:

volverse; **she has ~ very impatient in the last few years** se ha vuelto muy impaciente estos últimos años; **he's ~ very affectionate** se ha vuelto muy cariñoso

---

> Use **quedar(se)** especially when talking about changes that are permanent, involve deterioration and are due to external circumstances. Their onset may or may not be sudden:

quedar(se); **he became blind/deaf** (se) quedó ciego/sordo

> Use **hacerse** for states resulting from effort or from a gradual, cumulative process:

hacerse; **to ~ famous** hacerse famoso; **the pain became unbearable** el dolor se hizo insoportable

---

> Use **llegar a ser** to suggest reaching a peak:

llegar a ser; **the heat became stifling** el calor llegó a ser agobiante; **to become accustomed to sth** acostumbrarse a algo; **it became known that ...** se supo que ..., llegó a saberse que ...; **she became pregnant** (se) quedó embarazada

2 (= *turn into*) convertirse en, transformarse en

3 (= *acquire position of*) (*through study*) hacerse; (*by promotion etc*) llegar a ser; **to ~ a doctor** hacerse médico; **to ~ a father** convertirse en padre; **he became king in 1911** subió al trono en 1911 Ⓑ IMPERS VB **what has ~ of him?** ¿qué ha sido de él?; **whatever can have ~ of that book?** ¿dónde estará ese libro? Ⓒ VT (= *look nice on*) favorecer, sentar bien; **that thought does not ~ you** ese pensamiento es indigno de ti

becoming† [bɪˈkʌmɪŋ] ADJ **1** [*hairstyle, hat*] favorecedor, sentador (*LAm*); **that dress is very ~** ese vestido es muy favorecedor, ese vestido te sienta muy bien **2** (= *suitable*) [*conduct, language*] apropiado

BEd [biːˈed] N ABBR = **Bachelor of Education**

bed [bed] Ⓐ N **1** (= *furniture*) cama *f*; **to get into ~** meterse en la cama; **to get into ~ with sb** (*Pol etc*) aliarse con algn; **could you give me a ~ for the night?** ¿me puede hospedar *or* alojar esta noche?; **to go to ~** acostarse; **to go to ~ with sb** acostarse con algn; **I was in ~** estaba en la cama; **to make the ~** hacer la cama; **to put a child to ~** acostar a un niño; **to stay in ~** (*because ill*) guardar cama; (*because lazy*) quedarse en la cama; **to take to one's ~** irse a la cama; ✦ IDIOMS **to get out of ~ (on) the wrong side** (*Brit*) ◇ **get up (on) the wrong side of the ~** (*US*) levantarse con el pie izquierdo **2** [*of animal*] lecho *m* **3** [*of river*] cauce *m*, lecho *m*; [*of sea*] fondo *m* **4** (*for plants, flowers*) arriate *m*; ✦ IDIOM **his life's no ~ of roses** su vida no es un lecho de rosas **5** (= *layer*) [*of coal, ore*] estrato *m*, capa *f*; (*Culin*) base *f* Ⓑ CPD ➤ **bed and breakfast** pensión *f* (con desayuno) ➤ **bed bath: they gave her a ~ bath** la lavaron en la cama ➤ **bed jacket** mañanita *f* ➤ **bed linen** (*Brit*) ropa *f* de cama ➤ **bed rest** reposo *m* en cama ➤ **bed settee** sofá-cama *m* ➤ **bed down** VI + ADV acostarse

bedbug [ˈbedbʌg] N chinche *m or f*

bedclothes [ˈbedkləʊðz] NPL ropa *fsing* de cama

bedding [ˈbedɪŋ] N ropa *f* de cama; (*for animal*) cama *f* ➤ **bedding plant** planta *f* de parterre

bedevil [bɪˈdevəl] VT **to be ~led** *or* (*US*) **~ed by problems** [*project*] estar plagado de problemas; **the team has been ~led** *or* (*US*) **~ed by injuries** el equipo ha sufrido muchas lesiones

bedfellow [ˈbedfeləʊ] N **they make strange ~s** forman una extraña pareja

bedlam [ˈbedləm] N (= *uproar*) alboroto *m*; **it was absolute ~** era una locura total

bedpan [ˈbedpæn] N bacinilla *f* (de cama), cuña *f*

bedpost [ˈbedpəʊst] N columna *f or* pilar *m* de cama

bedraggled [bɪˈdrægld] ADJ [*person*] desaliñado; [*hair, feathers, fur*] enmarañado; [*flowers*] mustio

bedridden [ˈbedrɪdn] ADJ postrado en la cama

bedrock [ˈbedrɒk] N (*Geol*) lecho *m* de roca; (*fig*) lo fundamental, base *f*

bedroll [ˈbedrəʊl] N petate *m*

bedroom [ˈbedrʊm] N habitación *f*, dormitorio *m*, recámara *f* (*CAm, Mex*) ➤ **bedroom slippers** pantuflas *fpl*, zapatillas *fpl* (*Sp*) ➤ **bedroom suburb** (*US*) ciudad *f* dormitorio

-bedroomed [ˈbedrʊmd] ADJ (*ending in compounds*) **three-bedroomed flat** piso *m or* (*LAm*) departamento *m* de tres dormitorios

bedside [ˈbedsaɪd] N cabecera *f* ➤ **bedside lamp** lámpara *f* de noche ➤ **bedside manner: to have a good ~ manner** tener mucho tacto con los enfermos ➤ **bedside table** mesilla *f* de noche

bedsit* [ˈbedsɪt], **bedsitter** [ˈbedˈsɪtəʳ] N (*Brit*) *habitación amueblada, cuyo alquiler incluye cocina y baño comunes*

bedsocks [ˈbedsɒks] NPL calcetines *mpl* de cama

bedsore [ˈbedsɔːʳ] N úlcera *f* de decúbito

bedspread [ˈbedspred] N colcha *f*, cubrecama *m*

bedtime [ˈbedtaɪm] N hora *f* de acostarse; **it's past your ~** ya deberías estar acostado; **ten o'clock is my usual ~** normalmente me voy a la cama a las diez; **¡bedtime!** ¡a la cama! ➤ **bedtime story** cuento *m* (*para dormir a un niño*)

bed-wetting ['bedwetɪŋ] N incontinencia *f* nocturna, enuresis *f* (*frm*)

bee [biː] N **1** (= *insect*) abeja *f*; ✦ IDIOMS **to have a ~ in one's bonnet about sth** tener algo metido entre ceja y ceja; **he thinks he's the ~'s knees*** se cree la mar de listo/de elegante *etc** **2** (*esp US*) círculo *m* social

beech [biːtʃ] N (*also* ~ **tree**) haya *f*

> Use **el/un** not **la/una** before feminine nouns beginning with stressed **a** or **ha** like **haya**.

beef [biːf] Ⓐ N **1** (= *meat*) carne *f* de vaca *or* (*LAm*) de res **2** (*esp US**) (= *complaint*) queja *f* Ⓑ VI (***) (= *complain*) quejarse (**about** de) Ⓒ CPD ➤ **beef cattle** ganado *m* vacuno ➤ **beef tea** caldo *m* de carne (*para enfermos*) ➤ **beef up*** VT + ADV [+ *essay, speech*] reforzar, fortalecer

beefburger ['biːf,bɜːgəʳ] N hamburguesa *f*

beefeater ['biːf,iːtəʳ] N (*Brit*) alabardero *m* de la Torre de Londres

beehive ['biːhaɪv] N colmena *f*

beekeeping ['biːˌkiːpɪŋ] N apicultura *f*

beeline ['biːlaɪn] N ✦ IDIOM **to make a ~ for sth/sb** ir directo *or* derecho a algo/algn

been [biːn] PP *of* **be**

beep [biːp] Ⓐ N (*Brit*) pitido *m*; (*on answering machine*) señal Ⓑ VI sonar Ⓒ VT [+ *horn*] tocar

beeper ['biːpəʳ] N buscapersonas *m inv*, busca *m inv* (*Sp**), bipper *m* (*LAm**)

beer [bɪəʳ] N cerveza *f*; ✦ IDIOM **life isn't all ~ and skittles** (*Brit*) la vida no es un lecho de rosas, la vida no es todo Jauja*** ➤ **beer belly*** panza* *f* (*de beber cerveza*) ➤ **beer can** bote *m or* lata *f* de cerveza ➤ **beer garden** (*Brit*) terraza *f* de verano, jardín *m* (de un bar) ➤ **beer glass** jarra *f* de cerveza

beermat ['bɪəmæt] N posavasos *m inv*

beeswax ['biːzwæks] N cera *f* de abejas

beet [biːt] N **1** (= *crop*) remolacha *f* forrajera **2** (*US*) = **beetroot**

beetle ['biːtl] N escarabajo *m*

beetroot ['biːtruːt] N (*Brit*) remolacha *f*, betabel *m* (*Mex*), betarraga *f* (*Chi, Bol*)

befall [bɪˈfɔːl] (*pt* **befell**; *pp* ~**en**) (*liter*) VT acontecer a, suceder a

befit [bɪˈfɪt] VT corresponder a

before [bɪˈfɔːʳ]

> When **before** is an element in a phrasal verb, eg **go before**, look up the verb.

Ⓐ PREP **1** (*in time, order, rank*) antes de; **~ Christ** antes de Cristo; **the week ~ last** hace dos semanas; **~ long** (*in future*) antes de poco; (*in past*) poco después; **~ going, would you …** antes de marcharte, quieres …; **income ~ tax** renta *f* bruta *or* antes de impuestos; **profits ~ tax** beneficios *mpl* antes de impuestos

2 (= *in front of*) delante de; (= *in the presence of*) ante, delante de, en presencia de

3 (= *facing*) **the question ~ us** el asunto que tenemos que discutir; **the problem ~ us is …** el problema que se nos plantea es …; **a new life lay ~ him** una vida nueva se abría ante él

Ⓑ ADV antes; **why didn't you say so ~?** ¿por qué no lo has dicho antes?; **a moment ~** un momento antes; **have you been to Spain ~?** ¿has estado ya en España?, ¿es la primera vez que vienes a España?; **I had been to León a couple of times ~** ya había estado (antes) en León un par de veces; **the day ~** el día anterior; **that chapter and the one ~** ese capítulo y el anterior

Ⓒ CONJ antes de que; **I'll ask Matt about it ~ he goes away on holiday** se lo preguntaré a Matt antes de que se vaya de vacaciones; **we reached home ~ the storm broke** llegamos a

casa antes de que empezara la tormenta; **give me a ring ~ you leave the office** llámame antes de salir de la oficina

beforehand [bɪˈfɔːhænd] ADV de antemano, con antelación

befriend [bɪˈfrend] VT entablar amistad con, hacerse amigo de

beg [beg] Ⓐ VT **1** (= *implore*) rogar, suplicar; **I ~ you!** ¡te lo suplico!; **to ~ forgiveness** suplicar *or* implorar perdón; **to ~ sb for sth** suplicar algo a algn; **he ~ged me to help him** me suplicó que le ayudara; **I ~ to differ** siento tener que disentir; ✦ IDIOM **to ~ the question** evadir la cuestión **2** [*beggar*] [+ *food, money*] pedir Ⓑ VI **1 to ~ for** [+ *forgiveness, mercy*] implorar **2** [*beggar*] mendigar, pedir limosna; **there's some cake going ~ging*** queda un poco de tarta, ¿no la quiere nadie?

began [bɪˈgæn] PT *of* **begin**

beggar ['begəʳ] Ⓐ N mendigo/a *m/f*, pordiosero/a *m/f*; ✦ PROV ~**s can't be choosers** a buen hambre no hay pan duro Ⓑ VT **1** (= *ruin*) arruinar **2 it ~s description** es imposible describirlo; **it ~s belief** resulta totalmente inverosímil

begging ['begɪŋ] N mendicidad *f* ➤ **begging bowl** platillo *m* para limosnas ➤ **begging letter** *carta en la que se pide dinero*

begin [bɪˈgɪn] (*pt* **began**; *pp* **begun**) Ⓐ VT **1** (= *start*) empezar, comenzar; **to ~ doing sth** ✧ **~ to do sth** empezar a hacer algo; **I can't ~ to thank you** no encuentro palabras para agradecerle; **it doesn't ~ to compare with …** no puede ni compararse con …; **this skirt began life as an evening dress** esta falda empezó siendo un traje de noche **2** (= *undertake*) emprender; (= *set in motion*) iniciar Ⓑ VI **1** (= *start*) empezar, comenzar; **the teacher began by writing on the board** el profesor empezó escribiendo en la pizarra; **let me ~ by saying …** quiero comenzar diciendo …; ~**ning from Monday** a partir del lunes; **to ~ with sth** comenzar con *or* por algo; **to ~ with, I'd like to know …** en primer lugar, quisiera saber …; **to ~ with there were only two of us** al principio sólo éramos dos **2** (= *originate*) [*river*] nacer; [*rumour*] originarse

beginner [bɪˈgɪnəʳ] N principiante *mf*

beginning [bɪˈgɪnɪŋ] N **1** [*of speech, book, film etc*] principio *m*, comienzo *m*; **at the ~ of** al principio de; **at the ~ of the century** a principios de siglo; **right from the ~** desde el principio; **from ~ to end** de principio a fin, desde el principio hasta el final; **in the ~** al principio **2** (= *origin*) origen *m*; **from humble ~s** de orígenes modestos

begrudge [bɪˈgrʌdʒ] VT **1** (= *envy*) **to ~ sb sth** envidiar algo a algn **2** (= *give reluctantly*) dar de mala gana; **I don't ~ all the money I've spent** no me duele todo el dinero que he gastado

beguiling [bɪˈgaɪlɪŋ] ADJ seductor, persuasivo

begun [bɪˈgʌn] PP *of* **begin**

behalf [bɪˈhɑːf] N **on** *or* (*US*) **in ~ of** (= *representing*) en nombre de, de parte de; (= *for the benefit of*) en beneficio de; **I interceded on his ~** intercedí por él; **don't worry on my ~** no te preocupes por mí

behave [bɪˈheɪv] VI **1** [*person*] portarse (**to, towards** con), comportarse; **he ~d like an idiot** se comportó como un idiota; **to ~ (o.s.)** portarse bien; ~ **(yourself)!** ¡compórtate!, ¡pórtate bien! **2** (*Mech etc*) (= *work*) funcionar

behaviour, behavior (*US*) [bɪˈheɪvjəʳ] N [*of person*] conducta *f*, comportamiento *m*; **to be on one's best ~** comportarse lo mejor posible

behavioural, behavioral (*US*) [bɪˈheɪvjərəl] ADJ [*problems, changes*] conductual

behead [bɪˈhed] VT decapitar

beheld [bɪˈheld] PT, PP *of* **behold**

behind [bɪˈhaɪnd] Ⓐ PREP **1** (= *to the rear of*) detrás de;

> When **behind** is an element in a phrasal verb, eg **fall behind**, **stay behind**, look up the verb.

look ~ you! ¡cuidado atrás!; **it's all ~ us now** todo eso ha

quedado ya atrás; **she has four novels ~ her** tiene cuatro novelas en el haber
2 (= *responsible for*) detrás de; **what's ~ all this?** ¿qué hay detrás de todo esto?
3 (= *less advanced than*) **Cox is nine points ~ Jay** Cox tiene nueve puntos menos que Jay; **we're well ~ them in technology** nos dejan muy atrás en tecnología, estamos muy a la zaga de ellos en tecnología
4 (= *supporting*) **his family is ~ him** tiene el apoyo de su familia
B ADV **1** (= *in or at the rear*) detrás, atrás; **to come from ~** venir desde atrás; **to attack sb from ~** atacar a algn por la espalda
2 (= *behind schedule*) **to be ~ with one's work** estar atrasado en el trabajo; **to be ~ with the rent** tener atrasos de alquiler
3 (= *less advanced*) **Pepe won with Paco only two strokes ~** ganó Pepe con Paco a sólo dos golpes de distancia
C N (*) (= *bottom*) trasero *m*

behold [bɪˈhəʊld] (*pt, pp* **beheld**) VT (*liter*) contemplar; **behold!** ¡mire!

beige [beɪʒ] **A** ADJ (color) beige *inv* **B** N beige *m*

Beijing [ˈbeɪˈdʒɪŋ] N Pekín *m*

being [ˈbiːɪŋ] N **1** (= *existence*) existencia *f*; **to come into ~** nacer **2** (= *creature*) ser *m*

Belarus [belaˈrʊs] N Bielorrusia *f*

Belarussian [ˌbelaˈrʌʃən] ADJ bielorruso

belated [bɪˈleɪtɪd] ADJ tardío, atrasado

belatedly [bɪˈleɪtɪdlɪ] ADV con retraso

belch [beltʃ] **A** N eructo *m* **B** VI eructar **C** VT (*also ~ out*) [+ *smoke, flames*] arrojar, vomitar

beleaguered [bɪˈliːɡəd] ADJ **1** [*city*] asediado **2** (*fig*) [*person, economy, government*] acosado

belfry [ˈbelfrɪ] N campanario *m*

Belgian [ˈbeldʒən] ADJ, N belga *mf*

Belgium [ˈbeldʒəm] N Bélgica *f*

Belgrade [belˈɡreɪd] N Belgrado *m*

belie [bɪˈlaɪ] VT [+ *hopes*] defraudar; [+ *words*] contradecir, desmentir

belief [bɪˈliːf] N **1** (= *doctrine*) creencia *f*; (= *trust*) confianza *f*; (= *opinion*) opinión *f*; **it is my ~ that ...** estoy convencido de que ...; **I did it in the ~ that ...** lo hice creyendo que ...; **contrary to popular ~ ...** al contrario de lo que muchos creen ...; **a man of strong ~s** un hombre de firmes convicciones **2** (= *faith*) fe *f*

believable [bɪˈliːvəbl] ADJ creíble, verosímil

believe [bɪˈliːv] **A** VT creer; **I ~ so** creo que sí; **he is ~d to be abroad** se cree que está en el extranjero; **don't you ~ it!** ¡no te lo creas!; **~ it or not, she bought it** aunque parezca mentira, lo compró; **it was hot, ~ (you) me!*** hacía calor, ¡y cómo!; **I couldn't ~ my eyes*** no podía dar crédito a mis ojos; **I would never have ~d it of him** jamás le hubiera creído capaz de eso
B VI creer; **to ~ in God** creer en Dios; **I don't ~ in corporal punishment** no soy partidario del castigo corporal; **we don't ~ in drugs** no aprobamos el uso de las drogas

believer [bɪˈliːvəʳ] N **1** (*Rel*) creyente *mf*, fiel *mf*
2 (= *advocate*) partidario/a *m/f*; **to be a great ~ in ...** ser muy partidario de ...

belittle [bɪˈlɪtl] VT (= *demean*) menospreciar; (= *minimize*) quitar importancia a, minimizar

Belize [beˈliːz] N Belice *m*

bell [bel] N (= *church bell*) campana *f*; (= *handbell*) campanilla *f*; (= *doorbell, electric bell*) timbre *m*; (*for cow*) cencerro *m*; (*on toy, dress, collar*) cascabel *m*; ◆ IDIOMS **I'll give you a ~** (*Brit*) te llamaré; **he was saved by the ~** se salvó por los pelos* ► **bell bottoms** pantalones *mpl* acampanados **bell jar** fanal *m*, campana *f* de cristal (*esp Sp*), campana *f* de vidrio (*esp LAm*) ► **bell pepper** (*esp US*) pimiento *m*, pimentón *m* (*LAm*) ► **bell ringer** campanero/a *m/f*; (*as hobby*) campanólogo/a *m/f* ► **bells and whistles*** (*esp Comput*) elementos *mpl* accesorios; (*pej*) florituras *fpl* ► **bell tower** campanario *m*

bell-bottomed [ˈbelˈbɒtəmd] ADJ acampanado

bellboy [ˈbelbɔɪ] N botones *m inv*

bellhop [ˈbelhɒp] N (*US*) botones *m inv*

belligerence [bɪˈlɪdʒərəns] N agresividad *f*

belligerent [bɪˈlɪdʒərənt] ADJ beligerante

bellow [ˈbeləʊ] **A** N [*of animal*] bramido *m*; [*of person*] rugido *m* **B** VI [*animal*] bramar; [*person*] rugir **C** VT (*also ~ out*) [+ *order, song*] gritar

bellows [ˈbeləʊz] NPL fuelle *msing*; **a pair of ~** un fuelle

belly [ˈbelɪ] N barriga* *f*, guata *f* (*Chi**) ► **belly button*** ombligo *m* ► **belly dance** danza *f* del vientre ► **belly dancer** danzarina *f* del vientre ► **belly flop** panzazo* *m* ► **belly laugh** carcajada *f* (grosera)

bellyache* [ˈbelɪeɪk] **A** N (= *pain*) dolor *m* de barriga*
B VI (= *complain*) renegar, echar pestes* (**at** de)

belly-up* [belɪˈʌp] ADV **to go ~** [*company, scheme*] irse al garete*, irse al traste

belong [bɪˈlɒŋ] VI **1 to ~ to** (= *be owned by*) pertenecer a; [+ *party*] estar afiliado a, ser miembro de; [+ *club*] ser socio de; [+ *church*] pertenecer a; **who does this ~ to?** ¿a quién pertenece esto?, ¿de quién es esto?; **the handwriting ~s to a male** la letra es de hombre
2 (= *be appropriate*) **we truly ~ together** estamos verdaderamente hechos el uno para el otro; **those ideas ~ in the Middle Ages** esas ideas son de la Edad Media
3 (= *fit in*) **I feel I ~ here** aquí me siento en casa; **I don't ~ here** éste no es mi sitio; **he feels the need to ~** siente la necesidad de ser parte de algún grupo
4 (= *live*) **it ~s on the shelf** va en el estante; **go back home where you ~** vuelve a casa, que es donde está tu sitio

belongings [bɪˈlɒŋɪŋz] NPL pertenencias *fpl*

Belorussian [ˌbeləʊˈrʌʃən] ADJ = **Belarussian**

beloved [bɪˈlʌvɪd] ADJ, N querido/a *m/f*

below [bɪˈləʊ] **A** PREP **1** (= *under*) debajo de, bajo; **the room ~ this is my study** la habitación que está debajo de ésta es mi estudio; **her skirt reaches well ~ her knees** la falda le llega muy por debajo de las rodillas; **their readership has dropped to ~ 18,000** el número de lectores que tenían ha descendido por debajo de los 18.000; **to be ~ sb in rank** ser inferior a algn en rango; **~ average** inferior al promedio, inferior a *or* por debajo de la media; **~ (the) ground** bajo tierra; **temperatures ~ normal** temperaturas inferiores a las normales; **~ sea level** por debajo del nivel del mar; **it was five degrees ~ zero** hacía cinco grados bajo cero
2 (= *downstream of*) más abajo de
B ADV **1** (= *beneath*) abajo; **the flat ~** el piso de abajo; **they live two floors ~** viven dos pisos más abajo; **her name was written ~** su nombre estaba escrito debajo; **down ~** abajo; **far ~** mucho más abajo
2 (*in document*) **see ~** véase más abajo
3 (*Naut*) (*also ~ deck*) abajo; **to go ~** bajar

belt [belt] **A** N **1** (= *garment*) cinturón *m*, fajo *m* (*Mex*); (= *seat belt*) cinturón *m* de seguridad; ◆ IDIOMS **that was below the ~** ese fue un golpe bajo; **it was a ~-and-braces job*** se tomaron todas las precauciones posibles; **to tighten one's ~** apretarse el cinturón; **he has three novels under his ~** tiene tres novelas en su haber
2 (= *conveyor belt etc*) correa *f*, cinta *f*
3 (= *zone*) zona *f*; **industrial ~** cinturón *m* industrial
B VT (*) (= *thrash*) zurrar (con correa); **he ~ed me one** (= *slap*) me dio una torta*; (= *punch*) me dio un mamporro*
C VI (*Brit**) (= *rush*) **he ~ed down the street** salió pitando por la calle abajo*
► **belt out*** VT + ADV [+ *song*] cantar a pleno pulmón
► **belt up** VI + ADV **1** (= *do up seat belt*) abrocharse el cinturón **2** (*Brit***) **~ up!** ¡cállate la boca!**

beltway [ˈbeltweɪ] N (*US*) carretera *f* de circunvalación

bemoan [bɪˈməʊn] VT lamentar

bemused [bɪˈmjuːzd] ADJ aturdido, confuso

bench [bentʃ] N **1** (= *seat, workbench*) banco *m*; (*Sport*) banquillo *m*; **the Bench** (*Jur*) la magistratura; **to be on the Bench** (*Jur*) ser juez, ser magistrado; (*Sport*) estar en el banquillo **2 benches** (*Brit Parl*) **on the Labour/Tory ~es** en los escaños laboristas/conservadores; ⇨ *BACKBENCHER, FRONT BENCH*

benchmark ['bentʃmɑːk] N cota *f* ➤ **benchmark price** precio *m* de referencia

bend [bend] (*vb: pt, pp* **bent**) **Ⓐ** N **1** (*gen*) curva *f*; (*in pipe*) ángulo *m*; (= *corner*) recodo *m*; **"dangerous bend"** "curva peligrosa"; ✦ IDIOMS **to go round the ~** (*Brit**) volverse loco; **to drive sb round the ~** (*Brit**) volver loco a algn*
2 the ~s (*Med*) la enfermedad de descompresión
Ⓑ VT **1** (= *make curved*) [+ *wire*] curvar, doblar; (= *cause to sag*) combar; [+ *arm, knee*] doblar; **to ~ the rules for sb** adaptar las normas a beneficio de algn; ✦ IDIOM **to ~ sb's ear*** marear a algn*
2 (= *incline*) [+ *body, head*] inclinar
Ⓒ VI **1** [*branch, knee*] doblarse; [*wire*] torcerse; [*road, river*] torcer (**to the left** a la izquierda)
2 [*person*] (= *stoop*) inclinarse, doblarse
➤ **bend down** VI + ADV agacharse
➤ **bend over** VI + ADV inclinarse; ✦ IDIOM **to ~ over backwards (to do sth)** hacer lo imposible (por hacer algo)

beneath [bɪ'niːθ] **Ⓐ** PREP **1** (= *below*) debajo de, bajo
2 (*fig*) inferior a, por debajo de; **it would be ~ him to do such a thing** hacer tal cosa sería indigno de él; **she married ~ her** se casó con un hombre de clase inferior; **~ contempt** despreciable **Ⓑ** ADV abajo, debajo

benefactor ['benɪfæktəʳ] N bienhechor(a) *m/f*, benefactor(a) *m/f*

beneficial [benɪ'fɪʃəl] ADJ beneficioso; **~ to the health** beneficioso para la salud; **the change will be ~ to you** el cambio te resultará beneficioso

beneficiary [benɪ'fɪʃərɪ] N beneficiario/a *m/f*

benefit ['benɪfɪt] **Ⓐ** N **1** (= *advantage*) beneficio *m*, provecho *m*; **to give sb the ~ of the doubt** dar a algn el beneficio de la duda; **for the ~ of one's health** en beneficio de la salud; **I'll try it on for you** lo probaré en tu honor; **to have the ~ of** tener la ventaja de; **to be of ~ to sb** beneficiar a algn; **without ~ of** sin la ayuda de
2 (*Admin*) (= *money*) ayuda *f*; (*also* **unemployment ~**) subsidio *m* de desempleo; **to be on ~(s)** recibir una ayuda del Estado
Ⓑ VI beneficiar(se), sacar provecho (**by/from** de) **Ⓒ** VT beneficiar
Ⓓ CPD ➤ **benefit association** (*esp US*) sociedad *f* de beneficencia ➤ **benefit match** partido *m* con fines benéficos ➤ **benefit performance** función *f* benéfica

benevolent [bɪ'nevələnt] **Ⓐ** ADJ **1** (= *kind*) benévolo, benevolente **2** (*Brit*) (= *charitable*) [*organization, society*] benéfica, de beneficencia **Ⓑ** CPD ➤ **benevolent fund** (*Brit*) fondos *mpl* benéficos

Bengal [beŋ'gɔːl] N Bengala *f*

Bengali [beŋ'gɔːlɪ] **Ⓐ** ADJ bengalí **Ⓑ** N (= *person*) bengalí *mf*; (*Ling*) bengalí *m*

benign [bɪ'naɪn] ADJ **1** (= *kind*) [*person, view*] benevolente; [*smile, gesture*] benévolo, benevolente **2** (= *favourable*) [*substance, influence*] benéfico; [*conditions*] favorable; [*climate*] benigno **3** (*Med*) [*tumour, growth*] benigno

bent [bent] **Ⓐ** PT, PP *of* **bend** **Ⓑ** ADJ **1** [*wire, pipe*] doblado; (= *twisted*) torcido **2** (*Brit***) (= *dishonest*) pringado (*Sp**), chueco (*LAm**), corrupto **3** (*pej***) (= *homosexual*) del otro bando*, invertido **4 to be ~ on doing sth** (= *determined*) estar resuelto a *or* empeñado en hacer algo **Ⓒ** N (= *inclination*) inclinación *f*; (= *aptitude*) facilidad *f*

bequeath [bɪ'kwiːð] VT legar

bequest [bɪ'kwest] N legado *m*

bereaved [bɪ'riːvd] ADJ afligido; **the ~** los familiares del difunto/de la difunta

bereavement [bɪ'riːvmənt] N (= *loss*) pérdida *f*; (= *mourning*) duelo *m*; (= *sorrow*) pesar *m*

bereft [bɪ'reft] ADJ (*frm*) **to be ~ of** (= *not have to hand*) estar desprovisto de; (= *not possess*) estar falto de; (= *be robbed*) ser despojado de

beret ['bereɪ] N boina *f*

Bering Sea ['berɪŋ'siː] N mar *m* de Bering

berk** [bɜːk] N (*Brit*) imbécil* *mf*, gilipollas *mf inv* (*Sp****),

pendejo/a *m/f* (*LAm**), huevón/ona *m/f* (*And, Ven***)

Berlin [bɜː'lɪn] **Ⓐ** N Berlín *m* **Ⓑ** CPD berlinés ➤ **the Berlin Wall** el Muro de Berlín

Berliner [bɜː'lɪnəʳ] N berlinés/esa *m/f*

berm [bɜːm] N (*US*) arcén *m*

Bermuda [bɜː'mjuːdə] N las Bermudas ➤ **Bermuda shorts** bermudas *fpl* ➤ **the Bermuda Triangle** el triángulo de las Bermudas

Bern [bɜːn] N Berna *f*

berry ['berɪ] N baya *f*

berserk [bə'sɜːk] ADJ desquiciado; **to drive sb ~** desquiciar a algn; **to go ~** perder los estribos, ponerse hecho una furia*

berth [bɜːθ] **Ⓐ** N **1** (= *cabin*) camarote *m*; (= *bunk*) litera *f* **2** (= *mooring*) amarradero *m*; ✦ IDIOM **to give sb a wide ~** evitar el encuentro con algn **Ⓑ** VI, VT (*Naut*) atracar

beseech [bɪ'siːtʃ] VT (*pt, pp* **besought**) **to ~ sb to do sth** suplicar a algn que haga algo

beset [bɪ'set] (*pt, pp* **~**) VT [+ *person*] acosar; **he was ~ with** *or* **by fears** le acosaban los temores; **a policy ~ with dangers** una política plagada de peligros

beside [bɪ'saɪd] PREP **1** (= *at the side of*) al lado de, junto a; (= *near*) cerca de; **to be ~ o.s.** (*with anger*) estar fuera de sí; (*with joy*) estar loco de alegría; **that's ~ the point** eso no tiene nada que ver con el asunto, eso no viene al caso
2 (= *compared with*) comparado con **3** (= *in addition to*) además de, aparte de; (= *apart from*) aparte de

besides [bɪ'saɪdz] **Ⓐ** ADV **1** (= *in addition*) además; **and much more ~** y mucho más todavía **2** (= *anyway*) además **Ⓑ** PREP (= *in addition to*) además de, aparte de; (= *apart from*) aparte de

besiege [bɪ'siːdʒ] VT asediar; **we were ~d with questions** nos asediaron con preguntas

besotted [bɪ'sɒtɪd] ADJ **he is ~ with her** anda loco por ella

besought [bɪ'sɔːt] PT, PP *of* **beseech**

bespectacled [bɪ'spektɪkld] ADJ con gafas

bespoke [bɪ'spəʊk] ADJ (*Brit*) [*garment*] hecho a la medida; [*tailor*] que confecciona a la medida

best [best] **Ⓐ** ADJ SUPERL *of* **good** mejor; **the ~ pupil in the class** el mejor alumno de la clase; **the ~ one of all** el/la mejor de todos; **"~ before June 20"** "consumir preferentemente antes del 20 de junio"; **to know what is ~ for sb** saber lo que más le conviene a algn; **may the ~ man win!** ¡que gane el mejor!; **for the ~ part of the year** durante la mayor parte del año; **the ~ thing to do is ...** lo mejor que se puede hacer es ...
Ⓑ ADV SUPERL *of* **well** mejor; **she did ~ of all in the test** hizo el test mejor que nadie; **as ~ I could** lo mejor que pude; **you had ~ leave now** lo mejor es que te vayas ahora; **I had ~ go** más vale que vaya
Ⓒ N (= *utmost*) mejor; **all the ~!** (*as farewell*) ¡que tengas suerte!; **at ~** en el mejor de los casos; **he wasn't at his ~** no estaba en plena forma; **at the ~ of times** en las mejores circunstancias; **to do one's ~** hacer todo lo posible (**to do sth**) hacer todo lo posible (para *or* por hacer algo); **it's all for the ~** todo conduce al bien a la larga; **to be the ~ of friends** ser muy amigos; **let's hope for the ~** esperemos lo mejor; **to look one's ~** tener un aspecto inmejorable; **to make the ~ of it** sacar el mayor partido posible; **the ~ of it is that ...** lo mejor del caso es que ...; **to play (the) ~ of three** jugar al mejor de tres; **to the ~ of my knowledge** que yo sepa; **I'll do it to the ~ of my ability** lo haré lo mejor que pueda; **she can dance with the ~ of them** sabe bailar como la que más; ✦ IDIOMS **to have the ~ of both worlds** tenerlo todo; **to make the ~ of a bad job** sacar el mejor partido posible **Ⓓ** CPD ➤ **best man** padrino *m* de boda

bestial ['bestɪəl] ADJ bestial

bestow [bɪ'stəʊ] VT [+ *title, honour*] conferir (**on** a); [+ *affections*] ofrecer (**on** a)

bestseller ['best'seləʳ] N best-seller *m*, éxito *m* de ventas

best-selling ['best'selɪŋ] ADJ **our ~ line** nuestro producto de mayor venta; **for years it was our ~ car** durante años fue el coche que más se vendió

bet [bet] (*pt, pp* ~) **Ⓐ** VI **1** (= *place bet*) apostar; **to ~ on sth/ sb** apostar a *or* por algo/por algn

2 (= *be certain*) **I wouldn't ~ on it!** ¡no estés tan seguro!; **"are you going?" — "you ~!"*** —¿vas a ir? —¡hombre, claro! *or* (*LAm*) —¡cómo no!; **I'll ~*** ya me lo imagino

Ⓑ VT **1** (= *stake*) [+ *money*] apostar, jugar; **to ~ £10 on a horse** apostar diez libras a *or* por un caballo, jugar diez libras a un caballo; **he ~ them that/he ~ them £500 that they would lose** hizo una apuesta con ellos/les apostó *or* jugó 500 libras a que perdían

2 (*) (= *predict*) apostar, jugarse; **I ~ you anything he won't come** te apuesto *or* me juego lo que quieras a que no viene; **you can ~ your bottom dollar** *or* **your life that ...*** te apuesto lo que quieras a que ...; **"I ~ I can jump over that stream" — "I ~ you can't!"** —¡a que puedo saltar ese arroyo! —¡a que no!; **"it wasn't easy" — "I ~ it wasn't"** —no fue fácil —ya me imagino que no; **"did you tell him off?" — "you ~ your life I did!"** —¿le reñiste? —¡ya lo creo!

Ⓒ N **1** (= *stake*) apuesta *f*; **place your ~s!** ¡hagan sus apuestas!; **to take ~s** aceptar apuestas; **I had a ~ on that horse** había apostado por ese caballo; **(do you) want a ~?*** ¿qué te apuestas *or* juegas?

2 (= *prediction*) **it's a fair ~ that interest rates will go up** es muy posible que los tipos de interés van a subir

3 (*) (= *option*) **your best** *or* **safest ~ is to keep quiet about it** lo mejor que puedes hacer es no decir nada; **these companies are a safe ~ for investors** estas compañías no presentan ningún riesgo para los inversores

Bethlehem ['beθlɪhem] N Belén *m*

betray [bɪ'treɪ] VT **1** (= *be disloyal to*) traicionar **2** (= *inform on*) delatar; **to ~ sb to the enemy** entregar a algn al enemigo **3** (= *reveal*) [+ *ignorance, fear*] delatar, revelar; **his accent ~s him** su acento lo delata

betrayal [bɪ'treɪəl] N [*of person, country*] traición *f*; [*of secret, plot*] revelación *f*; **a ~ of trust** un abuso de confianza

betrothed [bɪ'trəʊðd] ADJ, N INV (*esp hum*) prometido/a *m/f*

better¹ ['betəʳ] **Ⓐ** ADJ COMPAR *of* **good, well²** mejor; **he is ~ than you** es mejor que tú; **he's much ~** (*Med*) está mucho mejor; **that's ~!** ¡eso es!; **it is ~ to** (+ INFIN) es mejor + *infin*, más vale + *infin*; **~ and** ~ cada vez mejor; **she is ~ at dancing than her sister** se le da mejor bailar a ella que a su hermana; **to get ~** mejorar; (*Med*) mejorar(se), reponerse; **he's no ~ than a thief** no es más que un ladrón; **it lasted the ~ part of a year** duró la mayor parte del año; **it would be ~ to go now** sería mejor *or* valdría más que nos fuéramos ahora

Ⓑ ADV COMPAR *of* **well²** mejor; **all the ~!** ¡tanto mejor!; **I feel all the ~ for having confided in someone** me siento mucho mejor después de haberme confiado a alguien; **he was all the ~ for it** le hizo mucho bien; **I had ~ go** más vale que me vaya, mejor me vaya (*esp LAm*); **at his age he ought to know** ~ a la edad que tiene debería tener más juicio; **they are ~ off than we are** están mejor de dinero que nosotros; **you'd be ~ off staying where you are** te convendría más quedarte; **so much the ~!** ¡tanto mejor!; **~ still** mejor aún; **to think ~ of it** cambiar de parecer

Ⓒ N **1 the ~** el/la mejor; **it's a change for the ~** es una mejora; **to get the ~ of** (= *beat*) vencer, quedar por encima de; **for ~ or worse** para bien o mal

2 my ~s mis superiores

Ⓓ VT (*gen*) mejorar; [+ *record, score*] superar; **to ~ o.s.** (*financially*) mejorar su posición; (*culturally, educationally*) superarse

better² ['betəʳ] N (= *gambler*) apostador(a) *m/f*

betting ['betɪŋ] **Ⓐ** ADJ **I'm not a ~ man** no me gusta hacer apuestas **Ⓑ** N **what's the ~ he won't come back?** ¿qué te apuestas a que no vuelve? **Ⓒ** CPD ➤ **betting shop** (*Brit*) casa *f* de apuestas

between [bɪ'twiːn] **Ⓐ** PREP entre; **~ you and me** *or* **ourselves** entre nosotros; **we only had £5 ~ us** teníamos sólo cinco libras entre todos; **we did it ~ the two of us** lo hicimos entre los dos; **the shops are shut ~ two and four o'clock** las tiendas cierran de dos a cuatro; **~ now and May** de ahora a mayo **Ⓑ** ADV (*also* **in ~**) (*time*) mientras tanto; (*place*) en medio, entre medio

bevelled beveled (*US*) ['bevəld] ADJ biselado

beverage ['bevərɪdʒ] N bebida *f*

bevy ['bevɪ] N grupo *m*

bewail [bɪ'weɪl] VT lamentar

beware [bɪ'weəʳ] VI **to ~ of sth/sb** tener cuidado con algo/ algn; **"beware of the dog!"** "¡cuidado con el perro!"; **"beware of pickpockets!"** "¡ojo con los carteristas!"; **"beware of imitations!"** "desconfíe de las imitaciones"

bewilder [bɪ'wɪldəʳ] VT desconcertar, dejar perplejo

bewildered [bɪ'wɪldəd] ADJ [*person*] desconcertado, perplejo; **he gave me a ~ look** me miró perplejo

bewildering [bɪ'wɪldərɪŋ] ADJ desconcertante

bewitch [bɪ'wɪtʃ] VT (= *cast a spell on*) hechizar; (= *seduce*) seducir, cautivar; (= *enchant*) encantar

bewitching [bɪ'wɪtʃɪŋ] ADJ cautivador

beyond [bɪ'jɒnd] **Ⓐ** PREP **1** (= *further than*) más allá de; (= *on the other side of*) al otro lado de; **you can't go ~ the barrier** no se puede cruzar la barrera; **~ the convent walls** tras los muros del convento

2 (*fig*) **that job was ~ him** ese trabajo era demasiado para él *or* era superior a sus fuerzas; **it's ~ belief** es increíble; **what he has done is ~ my comprehension** lo que ha hecho me resulta incomprensible; **that's ~ a joke** eso es el colmo; **it's ~ me why ...*** no alcanzo a ver por qué ...; **~ repair** irreparable

3 (= *apart from*) aparte de

Ⓑ ADV (*in distance*) más allá; (= *afterward*) después

Ⓒ N **✦** IDIOM **to live in** *or* **at the back of ~*** vivir en el quinto pino, vivir en el quinto infierno*

b/f, b/fwd ABBR = **brought forward**

Bhutan [buː'tɑːn] N Bután *m*

biannual [baɪ'ænjʊəl] ADJ semestral

bias ['baɪəs] **Ⓐ** N **1** (= *inclination*) propensión *f*, predisposición *f* (**to, towards** a); **a course with a practical ~** un curso orientado a la práctica; **a right-wing ~** una tendencia derechista

2 (= *prejudice*) prejuicio *m* (**against** contra), parcialidad *f*

3 [*of material*] sesgo *m*, bies *m*

Ⓑ VT influir en; **to ~ sb against sth** predisponer a algn en contra de algo; **to be ~(s)ed against** tener prejuicio contra; **to be ~(s)ed in favour of** estar predispuesto a *or* en favor de **Ⓒ** CPD ➤ **bias binding** bies *m*, ribete *m* al bies

bias(s)ed ['baɪəst] ADJ parcial

bib [bɪb] N (*for child*) babero *m*; (*on dungarees*) peto *m*

Bible ['baɪbl] N Biblia *f* ➤ **the Bible Belt** (*US*) los estados ultraprotestantes de EEUU ➤ **Bible school** (*US*) escuela *f* de enseñanza de la Biblia ➤ **Bible story** historia *f* de la Biblia ➤ **Bible study** estudio *m* de la Biblia

biblical ['bɪblɪkəl] ADJ bíblico

bibliography [bɪblɪ'ɒgrəfɪ] N bibliografía *f*

bicarbonate of soda [baɪkɑːbənɪtəv'səʊdə] N bicarbonato *m* de soda

bicentenary [baɪsen'tiːnərɪ] N (*Brit*) bicentenario *m*

bicentennial [baɪsen'tenɪəl] N (*US*) bicentenario *m*

biceps ['baɪseps] N bíceps *m inv*

bicker ['bɪkəʳ] VI discutir, reñir

bickering ['bɪkərɪŋ] N riñas *fpl*, discusiones *fpl*

bicycle ['baɪsɪkl] **Ⓐ** N bicicleta *f* **Ⓑ** CPD [*chain, pump*] de bicicleta ➤ **bicycle clip** pinza *f* para ir en bicicleta ➤ **bicycle lane** carril *m* para ciclistas ➤ **bicycle shed** cobertizo *m* para bicicletas

bid [bɪd] **Ⓐ** N **1** (*at auction*) oferta *f*, puja *f* (*Sp*); (*Fin*) oferta *f*; **the highest ~** la mejor oferta

2 (= *attempt*) tentativa *f*, intento *m*; **in a ~ to** en un intento de; **to make a ~ for freedom/power** hacer un intento para conseguir la libertad/el poder

3 (*Cards*) marca *f*; **no ~** paso

Ⓑ VT **1** (*pt, pp* ~) (*at auction etc*) ofrecer; **to ~ £10 for** ofrecer diez libras por

2 (*pt* **bade**; *pp* **~den**) ['bɪdn]) **2.1 to ~ sb good morning** dar los buenos días a algn **2.2** (†) (= *order*) mandar; **to ~ sb (to) do sth** mandar a algn hacer algo

Ⓒ VI (*pt, pp* ~) **1** (*at auction*) **to ~ (for)** hacer una oferta

(por), pujar (por) (*Sp*); **to ~ against sb** hacer una oferta contra algn, pujar contra algn (*Sp*)
2 (= *try*) **to ~ for power** intentar alcanzar el poder
3 (*Cards*) marcar, declarar
D CPD ➤ **bid price** precio *m* de oferta

bidder ['bɪdəʳ] N (*gen*) postor(a) *m/f*; (*Cards*) declarante *mf*; **the highest ~** el/la mejor postor(a)

bidding ['bɪdɪŋ] N **1** (*at auction*) **the ~ opened at £5** la primera oferta *or* (*Sp*) puja fue de cinco libras **2** (*Cards*) declaración *f*; **to open the ~** abrir la declaración **3** (= *order*) **to do sb's ~** cumplir las órdenes *or* el mandato de algn; **they did it at her ~** lo hicieron cumpliendo sus órdenes

bide [baɪd] VT **to ~ one's time** esperar la hora propicia

bidet ['biːdeɪ] N bidet *m*, bidé *m*

biennial [baɪ'enɪəl] **A** ADJ bienal **B** N (= *plant*) planta *f* bienal

bifocals ['baɪ'fəʊktələ] N gafas *fpl* bifocales

big [bɪg] **A** ADJ (*compar* ~**ger**; *superl* ~**gest**)

> The commonest translation of **big** is **grande**, which must be shortened to **gran** before a singular noun.

1 (*in size*) [*house, book, city*] grande; **a ~ car** un coche grande; **how ~ is the wardrobe?** ¿cómo es de grande el armario?; **he was a ~ man** era un hombre corpulento; **the ~ city** la gran ciudad; **to get** *or* **grow ~(ger)** crecer
2 (= *significant, serious*) [*change, problem*] grande; **it's a ~ problem** es un gran problema; **the ~gest problem at the moment is unemployment** el mayor problema de hoy día es el desempleo; **the ~ question is ...** la gran pregunta es ...
3 (= *important*) [*company, bank*] importante, grande; **this is her ~ day** hoy es su gran día, hoy es un día muy importante para ella; **to be ~ in publishing/plastics** ser muy conocido en el mundo editorial/la industria del plástico
4 (*) (*in age*) [*girl, boy*] grande; **~ boys don't cry** los niños grandes no lloran; **you're a ~ girl now!** ¡ahora ya eres mayorcita!; **my ~ brother/sister** mi hermano/a mayor
5 (*) (*as intensifier*) **he's a ~ liar** es un mentiroso de marca mayor
6 (*in phrases*) **what's the ~ hurry?*** ¿a qué viene tanta prisa *or* (*LAm*) tanto apuro?; **what's the ~ idea?*** ¿a qué viene eso?; **to earn ~ money** ganar mucho dinero; **me and my ~ mouth!*** ¡quién me manda decir nada!; **Mr Big*** el número uno; (**that's**) **~ of you!** (*iro*) ¡qué generosidad la tuya!; **a ~ one** (*US**) un billete de mil dólares; **we're onto something ~!** ¡hemos dado con algo gordo!; **I think boxing will take off in a ~ way here*** pienso que el boxeo va a tener una aceptación bestísima aquí; **the ~ wide world** el ancho mundo; ✦ IDIOM **you're getting too ~ for your boots!*** se te están subiendo mucho los humos
B ADV (*) **to make it ~** triunfar; **to talk ~** darse mucha importancia, fanfarronear; **to think ~** planear a lo grande, ser ambicioso
C CPD ➤ **the Big Apple** la Gran Manzana ➤ **the big bang** el big bang, la gran explosión ➤ **big business** (= *companies*) las grandes empresas; **tourism is ~ business in Thailand** el turismo es un gran negocio en Tailandia ➤ **the big cats** los grandes felinos ➤ **big dipper** (*Brit*) (*at fair*) montaña *f* rusa; **the Big Dipper** (*US Astron*) la Osa Mayor ➤ **big end** (*Aut*) cabeza *f* de biela ➤ **big fish*** (= *person*) pez *m* gordo* ➤ **big game hunting** caza *f* mayor ➤ **the big hand** la aguja grande ➤ **The Big Issue** (*Brit*) *revista vendida por personas sin hogar* ≈ La Farola (*Sp*) ➤ **big name*** figura *f* importante ➤ **big noise***, **big shot*** pez *m* gordo* ➤ **the big time*** el estrellato, el éxito; **to make the ~ time** alcanzar el éxito, triunfar ➤ **big toe** dedo *m* gordo (del pie) ➤ **big top** (= *circus*) circo *m*; (= *main tent*) carpa *f* principal ➤ **big wheel** (*Brit*) (*at fair*) noria *f* (*Sp*), rueda de la fortuna (*Mex*), rueda gigante (*Chi*); (= *person*) personaje *m*, pez *m* gordo*

bigamist ['bɪgəmɪst] N bígamo/a *m/f*

bigamous ['bɪgəməs] ADJ bígamo

bigamy ['bɪgəmɪ] N bigamia *f*

biggish ['bɪgɪʃ] ADJ bastante grande

big-headed* ['bɪg'hedɪd] ADJ creído*, engreído

big-hearted ['bɪg'hɑːtɪd] ADJ generoso

bigot ['bɪgət] N intolerante *mf*

bigoted ['bɪgətɪd] ADJ intolerante

bigotry ['bɪgətrɪ] N intolerancia *f*

big-ticket ['bɪg,tɪkɪt] ADJ (*US*) **~ item** compra *f* importante

big-time* ['bɪg'taɪm] **A** ADJ **~ football/politics** fútbol *m*/política *f* de alto nivel; **a ~ politician/actor** un político/actor de primera línea **B** ADV **he has tasted success ~** ha conocido el éxito con mayúsculas*; **they screwed (things) up ~** metieron la pata bien hondo*

bigwig* ['bɪgwɪg] N gerifalte *mf*, pez *m* gordo*

bike* [baɪk] **A** N (= *bicycle*) bici *f*; (= *motorcycle*) moto *f*; **on your ~!** (*Brit**) ¡largo de aquí!*, ¡andando!* **B** VI ir en bici; **I ~d 10km** hice 10km en bici **C** CPD ➤ **bike lane** carril-bici *m* ➤ **bike rack** (*on floor, ground*) aparcamiento *m* para bicicletas; (*on car roof*) portabicicletas *m inv* ➤ **bike shed** cobertizo *m* para bicicletas

biker* ['baɪkəʳ] N motociclista *mf*

bikeway ['baɪkweɪ] N (*US*) ruta *f* para ciclistas, senda *f* para ciclistas

bikini [bɪ'kiːnɪ] N bikini *m or* (*Arg*) *f* ➤ **bikini bottom(s)** parte *f* de abajo del bikini, braga *f* del bikini ➤ **bikini top** parte *f* de arriba del bikini

bilateral [baɪ'lætərəl] ADJ bilateral

bile [baɪl] N (*Med*) bilis *f*; (= *anger*) mal genio *m*, displicencia *f*

bilingual [baɪ'lɪŋgwəl] ADJ bilingüe

bilious ['bɪlɪəs] ADJ bilioso; **to feel ~** sentirse revuelto

Bill [bɪl] N (*Brit***) **the (Old) ~** la poli*, la pasma (*Sp***)

bill¹ [bɪl] **A** N **1** (*Brit*) (*in restaurant, hotel etc*) cuenta *f*, adición *f* (*RPl*); **can we have the ~, please?** ¿nos trae la cuenta, por favor?; ✦ IDIOM **to foot the ~ (for sth)** correr con los gastos (de algo), pagar (algo)
2 (= *invoice*) factura *f*; **the ~ for the gas** la factura del gas
3 (*Parl*) proyecto *m* de ley
4 (*US*) (= *note*) billete *m*; **a 5-dollar ~** un billete de 5 dólares
5 (= *notice*) cartel *m*
6 (*Theat*) programa *m*; **to top the ~** ser la atracción principal, encabezar el reparto; ✦ IDIOM **that fits the ~** eso cumple los requisitos
B VT **1** (*Comm*) **to ~ sb for sth** extender *or* pasar a algn la factura de algo
2 (*Theat*) anunciar, presentar; **he is ~ed to appear next week** figura en el programa de la semana que viene
C CPD ➤ **bill of exchange** letra *f* de cambio ➤ **bill of fare** carta *f*, menú *m* ➤ **bill of health the doctor gave him a clean ~ of health** el médico le aseguró que estaba perfectamente ➤ **bill of rights** declaración *f* de derechos ➤ **bill of sale** escritura *f* de venta

bill² [bɪl] **A** N (*of bird*) pico *m* **B** VI **to ~ and coo** [*birds*] arrullarse; [*lovers*] arrullarse, hacerse arrumacos

billboard ['bɪlbɔːd] N cartelera *f*

billet ['bɪlɪt] (*Mil*) **A** N alojamiento *m* **B** VT **to ~ sb (on sb)** alojar a algn (en casa de algn)

billfold ['bɪlfəʊld] N (*US*) billetero *m*, cartera *f*

billiard ['bɪljəd] CPD ➤ **billiard ball** bola *f* de billar ➤ **billiard cue** taco *m* (de billar) ➤ **billiard table** mesa *f* de billar

billiards ['bɪljədz] NSING billar *msing*

billing ['bɪlɪŋ] N **to get top ~** ser la atracción principal, encabezar el reparto

billion ['bɪlɪən] NUMBER (= *thousand million*) mil millones *mpl*; **three ~ dollars** tres mil millones de dólares; **I've told you a ~ times*** te lo he dicho infinidad de veces

billionaire [bɪlɪə'neəʳ] N billonario/a *m/f*

billow ['bɪləʊ] VI [*smoke*] salir en nubes; [*sail*] ondear

billy ['bɪlɪ] N (*US*) (*also ~ club*) porra *f*

billy goat ['bɪlɪgəʊt] N macho *m* cabrío

bimbo* ['bɪmbəʊ] N tía *f* buena sin coco (*Sp**), *mujer guapa y tonta*

bin [bɪn] **Ⓐ** N **1** (*for bread*) panera *f*; (*for coal*) carbonera *f* **2** (*esp Brit*) (= *rubbish bin, dustbin*) cubo *m* de la basura, tarro *m* de la basura (*LAm*); (= *litter bin*) papelera *f* **Ⓑ** VT (*Brit**) tirar **Ⓒ** CPD ➤ **bin bag** (*esp Brit*) bolsa *f* de basura ➤ **bin liner** (*esp Brit*) bolsa *f* de basura

binary ['baɪnərɪ] ADJ binario

bind [baɪnd] (*pt, pp* **bound**) **Ⓐ** VT **1** (= *tie together*) atar; (= *tie down, make fast*) sujetar; (*fig*) (= *link*) unir (**to** a) **2** [+ *wound, arm etc*] vendar; [+ *bandage*] enrollar; [+ *book*] encuadernar **3** (= *oblige*) **to ~ sb to sth/to do sth** obligar a algn a cumplir con algo/a hacer algo **4** (*Culin*) unir, trabar **Ⓑ** N (*Brit**) (= *nuisance*) lata* *f*; **it's a ~** es una lata* ➤ **bind over** VT + ADV (*Brit Jur*) **to ~ sb over for six months** conceder a algn la libertad bajo fianza durante seis meses; **to ~ sb over to keep the peace** exigir a algn legalmente que no reincida ➤ **bind together** VT + ADV (*lit*) atar; (*fig*) unir ➤ **bind up** VT + ADV [+ *wound*] vendar **2 to be bound up with** estar estrechamente ligado *or* vinculado a

binder ['baɪndə'] N (= *file*) carpeta *f*

binding ['baɪndɪŋ] **Ⓐ** N **1** [*of book*] encuadernación *f* **2** (*Sew*) ribete *m* **3** (*on skis*) ataduras *fpl* **Ⓑ** ADJ [*agreement, contract*] vinculante; [*promise*] que hay que cumplir; **to be ~ on sb** ser obligatorio para algn

binge* [bɪndʒ] **Ⓐ** N [*of drinking*] borrachera *f*; [*of eating*] comilona* *f*, atracón* *m*; **to go on a ~** ir de juerga; **to have a ~** darse una comilona*, darse un atracón* **Ⓑ** VI (*gen*) cometer excesos, excederse; (*eating*) cometer excesos en la comida, comer demasiado; **to ~ on chocolate** darse un atracón *or* ponerse hasta arriba de chocolate*

bingo ['bɪŋgəʊ] **Ⓐ** N bingo *m* **Ⓑ** EXCL ¡premio! **Ⓒ** CPD ➤ **bingo hall** bingo *m*

binoculars [bɪ'nɒkjʊləz] NPL (*gen*) gemelos *mpl*, prismáticos *mpl*; (*Mil*) anteojo *m* de campaña

biochemist ['baɪəʊ'kemɪst] N bioquímico/a *m/f*

biochemistry ['baɪəʊ'kemɪstrɪ] N bioquímica *f*

biodegradable [,baɪədɪ'greɪdəbl] ADJ biodegradable

biodiversity [,baɪədaɪ'vɜːsɪtɪ] N biodiversidad *f*

biographer [baɪ'ɒgrəfə'] N biógrafo/a *m/f*

biographic [,baɪə'græfɪk] ADJ = **biographical**

biographical [,baɪə'græfɪkəl] ADJ biográfico

biography [baɪ'ɒgrəfɪ] N biografía *f*

biological [,baɪə'lɒdʒɪkəl] ADJ biológico ➤ **biological clock** reloj *m* biológico ➤ **biological warfare** guerra *f* biológica

biologist [baɪ'ɒlədʒɪst] N biólogo/a *m/f*

biology [baɪ'ɒlədʒɪ] N biología *f*

biophysics [,baɪəʊ'fɪzɪks] NSING biofísica *f*

biopic* ['baɪəʊ,pɪk] N biografía *f* cinematográfica

biopsy ['baɪɒpsɪ] N biopsia *f*

biosphere ['baɪə,sfɪə'] N biosfera *f*

biotechnology [,baɪəʊtek'nɒlədʒɪ] N biotecnología *f*

bioterrorism [,baɪəʊ'terərɪzm] N bioterrorismo *m*

bioterrorist [,baɪəʊ'terərɪst] N bioterrorista *mf*

bipartisan [,baɪ'pɑːtɪzæn] ADJ bipartidario

biped ['baɪped] N bípedo *m*

birch [bɜːtʃ] **Ⓐ** N (= *tree, wood*) abedul *m*; (*for whipping*) vara *f* **Ⓑ** VT (= *punish*) castigar con la vara **Ⓒ** CPD ➤ **birch tree** abedul *m*

bird [bɜːd] **Ⓐ** N **1** (*small*) pájaro *m*; (*large*) ave *f*

Use **el/un** not **la/una** before feminine nouns beginning with stressed **a** or **ha** like **ave**.

✦ IDIOMS **the ~s and the bees: they haven't yet told her about the ~s and the bees** todavía no le han explicado las cosas de la vida; **the ~ has flown** el pájaro ha volado; **to give sb the ~** (*US*) hacer un gesto grosero con el dedo; **to kill two ~s with one stone** matar dos pájaros de un tiro; **a little ~ told me*** (*hum*) me lo dijo un pajarito; ✦ PROVS **~s of a feather flock together** Dios los cría y ellos se juntan; **a ~ in**

the hand is worth two in the bush más vale pájaro en mano que ciento volando **2** (*Brit***) (= *girl*) chica *f*, pollita *f*, niña *f* (*LAm*) **Ⓑ** CPD ➤ **bird bath** pila *f* para pájaros ➤ **bird brain*** casquivano/a *m/f* ➤ **bird dog** (*US*) perro *m* de caza ➤ **bird flu** gripe *f* aviar ➤ **bird of prey** ave *f* de rapiña ➤ **bird sanctuary** reserva *f* de pájaros ➤ **bird's nest** nido *m* de pájaro ➤ **bird table** mesita de jardín para poner comida a los pájaros

birdcage ['bɜːdkeɪdʒ] N jaula *f* de pájaro; (*large, outdoor*) pajarera *f*

bird's-eye view [,bɜːdzaɪ'vjuː] N vista *f* de pájaro

bird-watcher ['bɜːdwɒtʃə'] N observador(a) *m/f* de aves

bird-watching ['bɜːd,wɒtʃɪŋ] N observación *f* de aves; **to go ~** realizar observación de aves

Biro ® ['baɪrəʊ] N (*Brit*) bolígrafo *m*, birome *f* (*SC*)

birth [bɜːθ] **Ⓐ** N (*gen*) nacimiento *m*; (= *Med*) parto *m*; (*fig*) nacimiento *m*, surgimiento *m*; **at ~** al nacer; **French by ~** francés de nacimiento; **of humble ~** de origen humilde; **place of ~** lugar *m* de nacimiento; **to give ~ to** (*lit*) dar a luz a; (*fig*) dar origen a ➤ **birth certificate** partida *f* de nacimiento ➤ **birth control** control *m* de la natalidad; **method of ~ control** método *m* anticonceptivo ➤ **birth control pill** píldora *f* anticonceptiva ➤ **birth mother** madre *f* biológica ➤ **birth rate** tasa *f* or índice *m* de natalidad

birthdate ['bɜːθdeɪt] N fecha *f* de nacimiento

birthday ['bɜːθdeɪ] **Ⓐ** N cumpleaños *m inv*; **happy ~!** ¡feliz cumpleaños!; **on my 21st ~** el día en que cumplo/cumplí 21 años **Ⓑ** CPD [*card, cake, party, present*] de cumpleaños ➤ **birthday suit*: in one's ~ suit** (*hum*) en cueros*

birthmark ['bɜːθmɑːk] N antojo *m*, marca *f* de nacimiento

birthplace ['bɜːθpleɪs] N lugar *m* de nacimiento

Biscay ['bɪskeɪ] N Vizcaya *f*

biscuit ['bɪskɪt] N **1** (*Brit*) (= *cookie*) galleta *f*; ✦ IDIOM **that takes the ~!**** ¡eso es el colmo!* **2** (*US*) (= *cake*) magdalena *f*

bisect [baɪ'sekt] VT bisecar

bisexual [baɪ'seksjʊəl] ADJ, N bisexual *mf*

bishop ['bɪʃəp] N (*Rel*) obispo *m*; (*Chess*) alfil *m*

bison ['baɪsən] N (*pl ~ or ~s*) bisonte *m*

bistro ['biːstrəʊ] N bistro(t) *m*

bit¹ [bɪt] **Ⓐ** N **1** (= *piece*) trozo *m*, pedazo *m*; **in ~s** (= *broken*) hecho pedazos; (= *dismantled*) desmontado, desarmado; **~s and pieces** (= *items*) cosas *fpl*; (= *possessions*) cosas *fpl*, trastos* *mpl*; **to come to ~s** (= *break*) hacerse pedazos; (= *be dismantled*) desmontarse, desarmarse; ✦ IDIOM **to love sb to ~s*** querer un montón a algn* **2 a ~ of** (= *some*) un poco de; **he's a ~ of all right*** ése está buenísimo *or* para comérselo*; **he's a ~ of a liar** es bastante *or* un poco mentiroso; **quite a ~ of** bastante; **I've been seeing quite a ~ of her** la he estado viendo bastante; **it was a ~ of a shock** fue un golpe bastante duro **3** (*adverbial uses*) **a ~** un poco; **a ~ bigger** un poco más grande; **a ~ later** poco después, un poco más tarde; **~ by ~** poco a poco; **our performance was every ~ as good as theirs** nuestra actuación fue tan buena como la suya en todos los aspectos; **a good ~ bigger/cheaper** bastante más grande/barato; **would you like a little ~ more?** ¿quieres un poquito más?; **I'm not a ~ surprised** no me sorprende lo más mínimo *or* en absoluto; **not a ~ of it** qué va*, en absoluto; **he's quite a ~ older than me** es bastante mayor que yo; **I've had a ~ too much to eat** me he pasado un poco comiendo, he comido un poco más de la cuenta **4** (= *part*) parte *f*; **he'd just got to the exciting ~** acababa de llegar a la parte emocionante **5** (*Brit**) (= *role*) **we must all do our ~** todos debemos aportar nuestro granito de arena; **I've done my ~** yo he hecho mi parte *or* lo que me tocaba **6** (= *moment*) rato *m*, momento *m*; **I'll see you in a ~** te veo dentro de un momento *or* dentro de un ratito; **I waited quite a ~** esperé bastante tiempo *or* un buen rato **7** (= *coin*) (*Brit*) moneda *f*; (*US*) (= *12 cents*) doce centavos y medio; **two ~s** (*US*) 25 centavos **8** (*Comput*) bit *m* **Ⓑ** CPD ➤ **bit part** (*Cine, Theat*) papel *m* de poca importancia, papel *m* pequeño

bit² [bɪt] N **1** (*of drill*) broca *f* **2** (*for horse*) freno *m*, bocado *m*; ✦ IDIOM **once she gets the ~ between her teeth, there's no stopping her** una vez que se pone en marcha no hay quien la pare

bit³ [bɪt] PT *of* **bite**

bitch [bɪtʃ] Ⓐ N **1** (= *dog*) perra *f* **2** (******) (= *woman*) bruja* *f* **3** (******) **life's a ~** esta vida es un asco* *or* una mierda** **4** (*esp US**) (= *complaint*) queja *f* Ⓑ VI (*) quejarse (**about** de)

bitchy* [ˈbɪtʃɪ] ADJ (*compar* **bitchier**; *superl* **bitchiest**) [*person*] malicioso; [*remark*] malintencionado, de mala leche (*Sp**); **to be ~ to sb** ser malicioso con algn

bite [baɪt] (*vb: pt* **bit**; *pp* **bitten**) Ⓐ N **1** (= *nip*) mordisco *m*; (= *wound*) [*of dog, snake etc*] mordedura *f*; [*of insect*] picadura *f*; (= *toothmark*) dentellada *f*; **the dog took a ~ at him** el perro intentó morderlo **2** (*) [*of food*] bocado *m*; **do you fancy a ~ (to eat)?** ¿te apetece algo (de comer)?; **to take a ~ out of** [+ *apple etc*] dar un mordisco a; (*esp US*) [+ *savings, budget*] llevarse un pellizco de; ✦ IDIOM **he wants another** *or* **a second ~ at the cherry** quiere otra oportunidad, quiere probar otra vez **3** (*Fishing*) **are you getting any ~s?** ¿están picando? **4** (*fig*) (= *punch*) mordacidad *f*; (*Culin*) fuerza *f*; **a novel with ~** una novela mordaz

Ⓑ VT **1** [*dog, person, snake*] morder; [*insect, fish*] picar; **to ~ one's nails** comerse *or* morderse las uñas; ✦ IDIOMS **to ~ the bullet** enfrentarse al toro; **to ~ the dust** (= *die*) morder el polvo; (= *fail*) venirse abajo; **it's the old story of biting the hand that feeds you** ya sabes "cría cuervos (y te sacarán los ojos)"; **to ~ one's lip** *or* **tongue** morderse la lengua; ✦ PROV **once bitten twice shy** el gato escaldado del agua fría huye **2** [*acid*] corroer; (*Mech*) asir, trabar

Ⓒ VI **1** [*dog, person, snake*] morder; [*insect, fish*] picar **2** [*cuts, inflation etc*] hacerse sentir; **the strike is beginning to ~** la huelga empieza a hacer mella

➤ **bite back** VT + ADV [+ *words*] dejar sin decir, tragarse*

➤ **bite off** VT + ADV arrancar con los dientes; ✦ IDIOMS **to ~ sb's head off** echar una bronca a algn*; **to ~ off more than one can chew** abarcar demasiado

bite-size(d)* [ˈbaɪtˌsaɪz(d)] ADJ **1** (*lit*) [*food*] cortado en dados; **~ pieces of ham** dados *mpl or* (*Sp*) taquitos *mpl* de jamón **2** [*information*] en cantidades digeribles, en pequeñas dosis

biting [ˈbaɪtɪŋ] ADJ [*cold, wind*] cortante; [*criticism*] mordaz

bitten [ˈbɪtn] PP *of* **bite**

bitter [ˈbɪtə²] Ⓐ ADJ **1** (*in taste*) [*drink, medicine*] amargo; ✦ IDIOM **a ~ pill to swallow** un trago amargo **2** (= *deep, fierce*) [*disappointment, protest*] amargo; [*enemy, hatred*] implacable; [*battle*] encarnizado; [*struggle*] enconado; **to carry on to the ~ end** continuar hasta el final (cueste lo que cueste) **3** (= *resentful*) [*person*] amargado, resentido; **to feel ~ about sth** estar amargar *or* resentido por algo **4** (= *icy*) [*weather, winter*] gélido, glacial; [*wind*] cortante, gélido; **it's ~ today** hoy hace un frío gélido *or* glacial Ⓑ N (*Brit*) (= *beer*) cerveza *f* amarga Ⓒ CPD ➤ **bitter lemon** refresco *m* de limón

bitterly [ˈbɪtəlɪ] ADV **1** (= *deeply*) [*regret, resent, weep*] amargamente; [*oppose*] implacablemente; [*fight*] a muerte; [*resentful, jealous, ashamed*] muy; **I was ~ disappointed** sufrí una terrible *or* amarga decepción, quedé terriblemente decepcionado **2** (= *resentfully*) [*say, reply*] con rencor; [*speak, think*] amargamente, con rencor; [*complain*] amargamente **3** (= *icily*) **it's ~ cold** hace un frío gélido *or* glacial; **a ~ cold day** un día gélido *or* glacial

bitterness [ˈbɪtənɪs] N **1** (= *taste*) amargor *m* **2** (= *depth*) [*of struggle*] lo enconado; [*of hatred*] lo implacable **3** (= *resentment*) amargura *f*, rencor *m*

bittersweet [ˈbɪtəswiːt] ADJ (*lit, fig*) agridulce

biweekly [baɪˈwiːklɪ] (*US*) Ⓐ ADJ quincenal Ⓑ ADV quincenalmente, cada quince días

bizarre [bɪˈzɑːʳ] ADJ (= *strange*) extraño, raro; [*dress, appearance*] estrafalario

blab* [blæb] VI (*to police etc*) cantar*

black [blæk] Ⓐ ADJ (*compar* **~er**; *superl* **~est**) **1** (*in colour*) negro; **~ man/woman** negro/a *m*; **~ and white photo** foto *f* en blanco y negro; **his face was ~ and blue** tenía la cara amoratada; **with a face as ~ as thunder** con cara de pocos amigos **2** (= *dark*) oscuro, tenebroso **3** (= *dirty*) sucio; (*with smoke*) negro, ennegrecido **4** (*fig*) [*day, event*] negro, funesto, aciago; [*outlook*] negro; [*forecast*] pesimista; [*look*] ceñudo, de desaprobación; **a ~ day on the roads** una jornada negra en las carreteras; **he is not as ~ as he is painted** no es tan malo como lo pintan; **things look pretty ~** la situación es desconsoladora; **things were looking ~ for him** la situación se le presentaba muy difícil

Ⓑ N **1** (= *colour*) negro *m*, color *m* negro; ✦ IDIOMS **I should like it in ~ and white** quisiera tenerlo por escrito; **to stay in the ~** (*Fin*) estar en números negros **2** (= *person*) negro/a *m/f*

Ⓒ VT **to ~ sb's eye** poner a algn el ojo amoratado, poner a algn el ojo a la funerala (*Sp**)

Ⓓ CPD ➤ **black box** caja *f* negra ➤ **black coffee** café *m* solo, tinto *m* (*Col*); (*large*) café *m* americano ➤ **black comedy** comedia *f* negra ➤ **Black Death** peste *f* negra ➤ **black economy** (*Brit*) economía *f* negra ➤ **black eye** ojo *m* amoratado, ojo *m* a la funerala (*Sp**) ➤ **Black Forest gâteau** pastel *m* de chocolate, nata y guindas ➤ **black hole** agujero *m* negro ➤ **black humour** humor *m* negro ➤ **black ice** hielo *m* invisible en la carretera ➤ **black magic** magia *f* negra ➤ **black mark** (*fig*) nota *f* adversa, punto *m* negativo ➤ **black market** mercado *m* negro, estraperlo *m* (*Sp*) ➤ **black marketeer** estraperlista *mf* (*Sp*) ➤ **black pepper** pimienta *f* negra ➤ **black pudding** (*esp Brit*) morcilla *f*, moronga *f* (*Mex*) ➤ **Black Sea** Mar *m* Negro ➤ **black sheep (of the family)** oveja *f* negra ➤ **(accident) black spot** (*Brit*) punto *m* negro ➤ **black tie** corbata *f* de lazo, corbata *f* de smoking; **"~ tie"** (*on invitation*) "de etiqueta" ➤ **black tie dinner** cena *f* de etiqueta ➤ **black widow (spider)** viuda *f* negra

➤ **black out** Ⓐ VI + ADV (= *faint*) desmayarse, perder el conocimiento Ⓑ VT + ADV **the storm ~ed out the city** la tormenta causó un apagón en la ciudad

blackberry [ˈblækbərɪ] N (= *fruit*) zarzamora *f*, mora *f*; (= *plant*) zarza *f*

blackbird [ˈblækbɜːd] N mirlo *m*

blackboard [ˈblækbɔːd] N (*Brit*) pizarra *f*, encerado *m*

blackcurrant [ˌblækˈkʌrənt] N (= *fruit*) grosella *f* negra; (= *bush*) grosellero *m* negro, casis *f inv*

blacken [ˈblækən] VT **1** ennegrecer; (*by fire*) calcinar; [+ *face*] tiznar de negro **2** [+ *reputation*] manchar

blackhead [ˈblækhed] N espinilla *f*

blackleg [ˈblækleg] N (*Brit*) esquirol *mf*

blacklist [ˈblæklɪst] Ⓐ N lista *f* negra Ⓑ VT poner en la lista negra

blackmail [ˈblækmeɪl] Ⓐ N chantaje *m*; **it's sheer ~!** ¡es un chantaje! Ⓑ VT chantajear; **to ~ sb into doing sth** chantajear a algn para que haga algo; **he was ~ed into it** lo hizo obligado por el chantaje

blackmailer [ˈblækmeɪləʳ] N chantajista *mf*

blackout [ˈblækaʊt] N **1** (*Elec*) apagón *m* **2** (*Med*) desmayo *m* **3** (*of news*) bloqueo *m* informativo, apagón *m* informativo

blacksmith [ˈblæksmɪθ] N herrero/a *m/f*; **~'s** herrería *f*

blacktop [ˈblæktɒp] (*US*) Ⓐ N asfalto *m* Ⓑ VT asfaltar

bladder [ˈblædəʳ] N vejiga *f*

blade [bleɪd] N [*of knife*] (= *cutting edge*) filo *m*; (= *flat part*) hoja *f*; [*of skate*] cuchilla *f*; [*of propeller*] paleta *f*; [*of oar*] pala *f*; [*of wiper*] rasqueta *f*; [*of grass*] brizna *f*

Blairite [ˈblɛəraɪt] N, ADJ (*Brit Pol*) blairista *mf*

blame [bleɪm] Ⓐ N (= *responsibility*) culpa *f*; **to lay the ~ (for sth) on sb** echar a algn la culpa (de algo) Ⓑ VT **1** (= *hold responsible*) culpar, echar la culpa a; **to ~ sb (for sth)** echar a algn la culpa (de algo), culpar a algn (de algo); **to ~ sth on sb** culpar de algo a algn; **to be to ~ (for)** tener la culpa (de); **you have only yourself to ~** la culpa la tienes tú **2** (= *reproach*) censurar; **and I don't ~ him** y con toda la razón, y lo comprendo perfectamente

blameless [ˈbleɪmlɪs] ADJ (= *innocent*) inocente; (= *irreproachable*) intachable

blanch [blɑːntʃ] **Ⓐ** VI palidecer **Ⓑ** VT (*Culin*) blanquear; (= *boil*) escaldar; **~ed almonds** almendras *fpl* peladas

blancmange [bləˈmɒnʒ] N (*Brit*) crema *f* (de vainilla *etc*)

bland [blænd] ADJ (*compar* **~er**; *superl* **~est**) **1** (= *dull*) [*food, taste*] soso, insípido; [*smile, expression*] insulso; [*music, book, film*] soso, anodino; [*statement*] anodino **2** (= *mild*) [*person, action*] suave, afable; [*diet*] blando

blank [blæŋk] **Ⓐ** ADJ [*paper, space*] en blanco; [*tape*] virgen, sin grabar; [*expression, look*] vacío, vago; **the screen went ~** se fue la imagen de la pantalla; **my mind went ~** se me quedó la mente en blanco
Ⓑ N **1** (= *void*) vacío *m*; (*on form*) espacio *m* en blanco; **my mind was a complete ~** no pude recordar nada; **✦** IDIOM **to draw a ~** no llegar a ninguna parte
2 (*Mil*) cartucho *m* de fogueo; **to fire ~s** usar municiones de fogueo
Ⓒ CPD ➤ **blank cartridge** cartucho *m* de fogueo ➤ **blank cheque, blank check** (*US*) cheque *m* en blanco; **✦** IDIOM **to give sb a ~ cheque** dar carta blanca a algn (**to do sth** para hacer algo); ➤ **blank verse** verso *m* blanco *or* suelto
➤ **blank out** VT + ADV [+ *feeling, thought*] desechar

blanket [ˈblæŋkɪt] **Ⓐ** N manta *f*, frazada *f* (*LAm*), cobija *f* (*LAm*); [*of snow*] manto *m* **Ⓑ** ADJ [*statement, agreement*] general; [*ban*] global; [*coverage*] exhaustivo

blankly [ˈblæŋklɪ] ADV **he looked at me ~** me miró sin comprender

blare [bleəʳ] **Ⓐ** N estruendo *m* **Ⓑ** VT (*also* **~ out**) emitir a todo volumen; **a radio was blaring out the news** una radio emitía las noticias a todo volumen **Ⓒ** VI (*also* **~ out**) sonar a todo volumen, resonar

blarney* [ˈblɑːnɪ] N labia* *f*

blasé [ˈblɑːzeɪ] ADJ [*attitude*] indiferente; **she's very ~ about the risks involved** le traen sin cuidado los riesgos que el asunto conlleva; **he's won so many Oscars he's become ~ about it** ha ganado tantos oscars que ya está de vuelta de ello *or* le da igual

blaspheme [blæsˈfiːm] VI blasfemar

blasphemous [ˈblæsfɪməs] ADJ blasfemo

blasphemy [ˈblæsfɪmɪ] N blasfemia *f*

blast [blɑːst] **Ⓐ** N **1** [*of air, steam, wind*] ráfaga *f*; [*of sand, water*] chorro *m*; (**at**) **full ~** a toda marcha
2 (= *sound*) [*of whistle etc*] toque *m*; [*of bomb*] explosión *f*
3 (= *shock wave*) sacudida *f*, onda *f* expansiva
Ⓑ VT **1** (= *tear apart*) (*with explosives*) volar; (*Mil*) bombardear; **to ~ open** abrir con carga explosiva
2 (= *shoot*) pegar un tiro a, abrir fuego contra
3 (= *criticize*) [+ *person*] emprenderla con; [+ *film, novel, report*] poner por los suelos
4 (= *send out*) [+ *air, water*] lanzar
Ⓒ EXCL (*Brit***) ~ (**it)!** ¡maldita sea!*
Ⓓ CPD ➤ **blast furnace** alto horno *m*
➤ **blast off** VI + ADV [*spacecraft*] despegar
➤ **blast out Ⓐ** VT + ADV [*DJ*] [+ *tune*] tocar a todo volumen **Ⓑ** VI + ADV [*music, siren*] sonar a todo volumen, resonar

blasted** [ˈblɑːstɪd] ADJ (= *wretched*) condenado*, maldito*

blast-off [ˈblɑːstɒf] N [*of spacecraft*] despegue *m*

blatant [ˈbleɪtənt] ADJ [*injustice, lie*] flagrante; [*bully, coward, thief, liar*] descarado

blatantly [ˈbleɪtəntlɪ] ADV [*sexist, racist*] descaradamente; [*unfair*] descaradamente, obviamente; [*encourage, disregard*] descaradamente, abiertamente; **its faults are ~ obvious** sus defectos saltan a la vista; **it's ~ obvious that ...** es a todas luces evidente que ...

blaze¹ [bleɪz] **Ⓐ** N **1** (= *fire*) (*in hearth*) fuego *m*; (= *flare-up*) llamarada *f*; [*of buildings*] incendio *m*; (= *glow*) [*of fire, sun*] resplandor *m* **2 a ~ of colour** un derroche de color; **in a ~ of publicity** en medio de un gran despliegue publicitario **Ⓑ** VI [*fire*] arder; [*eyes*] centellear; [*light*] brillar

blaze² [bleɪz] VT **✦** IDIOM **to ~ a trail** abrir camino

blazer [ˈbleɪzəʳ] N (= *jacket*) chaqueta *f* de sport, blazer *m*

blazing [ˈbleɪzɪŋ] ADJ **1** [*building*] en llamas; [*fire*] llameante; [*sun*] abrasador, ardiente **2** (*Brit**) [*row, anger*] violento

bleach [bliːtʃ] **Ⓐ** N lejía *f* **Ⓑ** VT [+ *clothes*] blanquear; [+ *hair*] aclarar, decolorar

bleachers [ˈbliːtʃəz] NPL (*US*) gradas *fpl*

bleak [bliːk] ADJ (*compar* **~er**; *superl* **~est**) [*landscape*] desolado, inhóspito; [*weather*] desapacible, crudo; [*future*] sombrío; **things look rather ~ for him** las cosas no se le presentan muy alentadoras

bleary [ˈblɪərɪ] ADJ (*compar* **blearier**; *superl* **bleariest**) (*with tears, sleep*) lloroso; (= *tired*) agotado

bleat [bliːt] **Ⓐ** N balido *m* **Ⓑ** VI [*sheep, goat*] balar; (*) (= *complain*) quejarse (**about** de), gimotear

bled [bled] PT, PP of **bleed**

bleed [bliːd] (*pt, pp* **bled**) **Ⓐ** VI sangrar; **his nose is ~ing** le sangra la nariz; **to ~ to death** morir desangrado; **my heart ~s for him** (*iro*) ¡qué pena me da! **Ⓑ** VT (*Med*) sangrar; [+ *brakes, radiator*] desaguar, sangrar; **✦** IDIOM **to ~ sb dry** *or* **white** chupar la sangre a algn

bleeding [ˈbliːdɪŋ] N desangramiento *m*, hemorragia *f*

bleep [bliːp] **Ⓐ** N (*esp Brit*) pitido *m* **Ⓑ** VI (*esp Brit*) emitir pitidos **Ⓒ** VT (*) (*in hospital etc*) llamar por el buscapersonas *or* (*Sp*) busca *or* (*LAm**) bipper

bleeper [ˈbliːpəʳ] N buscapersonas *m inv*, busca *m inv* (*Sp**), bipper *m* (*LAm**)

blemish [ˈblemɪʃ] N (*on fruit*) mancha *f*; (*on complexion*) imperfección *f*; (*on reputation*) tacha *f*

blend [blend] **Ⓐ** N mezcla *f* **Ⓑ** VT mezclar **Ⓒ** VI (= *harmonize*) armonizar (**with** con); **to ~ in with** armonizarse con; **to ~ into** [*colour*] fundirse con

blender [ˈblendəʳ] N batidora *f*

bless [bles] VT bendecir; **~ you!** (*thanking*) ¡qué cielo eres!; (*after sneezing*) ¡Jesús!; **and Paul, ~ him, had no idea that ...*** y Paul, el pobre, no tenía ni idea de que ...; **to ~ o.s.** santiguarse

blessed [ˈblesɪd] ADJ **1** (= *holy*) bendito, santo; (= *beatified*) beato; **the Blessed Virgin** la Santísima Virgen **2** (*Brit***) (= *wretched*) santo*, dichoso*

blessing [ˈblesɪŋ] N **1** (*Rel*) bendición *f* **2** (= *advantage*) beneficio *m*; **✦** IDIOMS **to count one's ~s** agradecer lo que se tiene; **you can count your ~s that ...** tienes que estar agradecido de que ...; **it's a ~ in disguise** no hay mal que por bien no venga

blew [bluː] PT of **blow²**

blight [blaɪt] **Ⓐ** N [*of plants, cereals, fruit*] roya *f*; (*fig*) plaga *f* **Ⓑ** VT (= *ruin*) arruinar

blimey** [ˈblaɪmɪ] EXCL (*Brit*) ¡caray!

blind [blaɪnd] **Ⓐ** ADJ (*lit, fig*) ciego; **a ~ man** un (hombre) ciego; **to go ~** quedar(se) ciego; **~ in one eye** tuerto; **to be ~ to sth** no (poder) ver algo; **✦** IDIOMS (**as**) **~ as a bat*** más ciego que un topo; **to turn a ~ eye (to sth)** hacer la vista gorda (con algo); **✦** PROV **love is ~** el amor es ciego
2 (= *irrational*) [*rage, panic, faith*] ciego
3 (*Brit*) **a ~ bit of sth: he didn't take a ~ bit of notice** no hizo ni caso; **it isn't a ~ bit of use** no sirve absolutamente para nada
Ⓑ N **the ~** los ciegos; **✦** IDIOM **it's a case of the ~ leading the ~** es como un ciego llevando a otro ciego
2 (= *shade*) persiana *f*
Ⓒ ADV [*fly, land*] guiándose sólo por los instrumentos; **he swore ~ that ...** juró y perjuró que ...; **to be ~ drunk** (*Brit**) estar más borracho que una cuba*
Ⓓ VT **1** (= *render sightless*) dejar ciego, cegar; (*fig*) cegar; **to be ~ed in an accident** quedar ciego después de un accidente; **to be ~ed by anger/hate** estar cegado por la ira/el odio, estar ciego de ira/odio; **her love ~ed her to his faults** su amor no le dejaba ver sus faltas
2 (= *dazzle*) [*sun, light*] deslumbrar, cegar; **to ~ sb with science** deslumbrar a algn con conocimientos
Ⓔ CPD ➤ **blind alley** callejón *m* sin salida ➤ **blind corner** curva *f* sin visibilidad ➤ **blind date** cita *f* a ciegas; **to go on a ~ date with sb** tener una cita a ciegas con algn ➤ **blind man's buff** gallina *f* ciega ➤ **blind spot** (*Aut*) ángulo *m* muerto; (*Med*) punto *m* ciego; **I have a ~ spot about computers** los ordenadores no son mi punto fuerte

blindfold [ˈblaɪndfəʊld] **Ⓐ** ADJ con los ojos vendados

B N venda *f* **C** VT vendar los ojos a

blinding ['blaɪndɪŋ] ADJ [*light, glare*] cegador, deslumbrante; **I've got a ~ headache** tengo un dolor de cabeza que no veo

blindly ['blaɪndlɪ] ADV [*grope, stumble*] a ciegas, a tientas; [*follow, accept, obey*] ciegamente

blindness ['blaɪndnɪs] N ceguera *f*

blink [blɪŋk] **A** N [*of eyes*] parpadeo *m*; ✦ IDIOMS **in the ~ of an eye** en un abrir y cerrar de ojos; **to be on the ~*** [*TV etc*] estar averiado **B** VT **to ~ one's eyes** parpadear, pestañear **C** VI [*person, eyes*] parpadear, pestañear; [*light*] parpadear

blinkered ['blɪŋkəd] ADJ (*Brit*) [*horse*] con anteojeras; [*person*] estrecho de miras; [*view*] miope, estrecho

blinking* ['blɪŋkɪŋ] ADJ (*Brit*) maldito; **you ~ idiot!** ¡imbécil!*

blip [blɪp] N (= *aberration*) irregularidad *f* momentánea; **this is just a ~** es un problema pasajero

bliss [blɪs] N (*Rel*) dicha *f*; (*) (*fig*) éxtasis *m*, arrobamiento *m*; **the concert was ~!** ¡el concierto fue una gloria!; **what ~!** ¡qué gustazo!*

blissful ['blɪsfəl] ADJ **1** (= *happy*) dichoso **2** (*) (= *wonderful*) maravilloso, estupendo

blissfully ['blɪsfəlɪ] ADV [*sigh, lounge*] con felicidad; **~ happy** sumamente feliz; **~ ignorant** feliz en la ignorancia

blister ['blɪstə⁰] **A** N (*on skin*) ampolla *f*; (*on paintwork*) burbuja *f* **B** VI [*skin*] ampollarse; [*paintwork*] formar burbujas

blistering ['blɪstərɪŋ] ADJ [*heat*] abrasador; [*criticism*] feroz, devastador; [*pace*] frenético

blithe [blaɪð] ADJ (*liter*) alegre

blithely ['blaɪðlɪ] ADV [*go on, ignore*] alegremente

blitz [blɪts] **A** N **1** (*Aer*) bombardeo *m* aéreo; **the Blitz** el bombardeo alemán de Gran Bretaña en 1940 y 1941 **2** (*) (*fig*) campaña *f* (**on** contra); **I'm going to have a ~ on ironing** voy a atacar la plancha*, voy a ponerme a planchar a todo meter **B** VT (*Mil*) bombardear

blizzard ['blɪzəd] N ventisca *f*

bloated ['bləʊtɪd] ADJ hinchado

blob [blɒb] N (= *drop*) gota *f*; (= *stain*) mancha *f*

bloc [blɒk] N bloque *m*; **en ~** en bloque

block [blɒk] **A** N **1** (= *chunk*) [*of stone*] bloque *m*; [*of wood*] zoquete *m*, tarugo *m*; (*butcher's, executioner's*) tajo *m*; (= *toy*) cubo *m*; [*of brake*] zapata *f*
2 (= *batch*) [*of tickets, stamps*] serie *f*; **~ of seats** grupo *m* de asientos
3 (= *group of buildings*) manzana *f*, cuadra *f* (*LAm*); **to walk around the ~** dar la vuelta a la manzana; **~ of flats** (*Brit*) bloque *m* de pisos (*Sp*), edificio *m* de departamentos (*LAm*)
4 (= *blockage*) (*in pipe*) atasco *m*; (*Med*) bloqueo *m*; **writer's ~** bloqueo *m* de escritor; **to have a mental ~** tener un bloqueo mental
5 (= *writing pad*) bloc *m*
6 (*Sport*) (**starting**) **~s** tacos *mpl* de salida
7 (*) ✦ IDIOM **to knock sb's ~ off*** romper la crisma a algn*
B VT (*gen*) bloquear; [+ *traffic, progress*] estorbar, impedir; [+ *pipe*] obstruir; **to ~ sb's way** cerrar el paso a algn; **he stopped in the doorway, ~ing her view** se paró en la entrada, tapándole la vista; **am I ~ing your view?** ¿te estoy tapando?; **my nose is ~ed** tengo la nariz taponada
C CPD ➤ **block and tackle** aparejo *m* de poleas ➤ **block booking** reserva *f* en bloque ➤ **block capitals** (letras *fpl*) mayúsculas *fpl*; **in ~ capitals** en mayúsculas, en letra *or* caracteres de imprenta ➤ **block grant** subvención *f* en bloque ➤ **block letters** = **block capitals** ➤ **block release** (*Brit Educ*) exención *f* por estudios ➤ **block vote** voto *m* por representación
➤ **block off** VT + ADV [+ *road*] cortar; (*accidentally*) bloquear
➤ **block out** VT + ADV **1** [+ *thought, idea*] apartar de la mente, borrar de la mente **2** (= *obscure*) [+ *light*] tapar
➤ **block up** VT + ADV **1** (= *obstruct*) [+ *pipe*] atascar; **my nose is all ~ed up** tengo la nariz taponada **2** (= *fill in*) [+ *gap*] cerrar

blockade [blɒ'keɪd] N (*Mil, Ind*) bloqueo *m*

blockage ['blɒkɪdʒ] N (*Med*) obstrucción *f*; (*in pipe*) atasco *m*

blockbuster* ['blɒkbʌstə⁰] N (= *film*) exitazo* *m*, gran éxito *m* de taquilla; (= *book*) exitazo* *m*, best-seller *m*

bloke* [bləʊk] N (*Brit*) tipo* *m*, tío *m* (*Sp**)

blond(e) [blɒnd] **A** ADJ (*compar* **blonder**; *superl* **blondest**) rubio, güero (*CAm, Mex*), catire (*Carib*) **B** N rubio/a *m/f*, güero/a *m/f* (*CAm, Mex*), catire/a *m/f* (*Carib*) **C** CPD ➤ **blond(e) bombshell*** rubia *f* explosiva*

blood [blʌd] **A** N sangre *f*; **acting was in his ~** llevaba la profesión de actor en la sangre; **of noble/royal ~** de sangre noble/real; **new** *or* **young ~** savia *f* nueva; ✦ IDIOMS **to be after sb's ~** tenérsela jurada a algn*; **bad ~** hostilidad *f*; **it makes my ~ boil** me saca de quicio*, hace que me hierva la sangre; **in cold ~** a sangre fría; **to have ~ on one's hands** tener las manos manchadas de sangre; **the look in his eyes made her ~ run cold** su mirada hizo que se le helara la sangre (en las venas); **to get ~ out of a stone** sacar agua de las piedras; **to sweat ~** sudar tinta *or* sangre*; ✦ PROV **~ is thicker than water** la sangre tira
B CPD (*bank, brother, donor, transfusion*) de sangre ➤ **blood and guts: a ~ and guts film** una película sangrienta *or* violenta ➤ **blood cell** glóbulo *m* ➤ **blood clot** coágulo *m* de sangre ➤ **blood count** hemograma *m*, recuento *m* sanguíneo, recuento *m* globular ➤ **blood group** grupo *m* sanguíneo ➤ **blood heat** temperatura *f* del cuerpo ➤ **blood money** dinero *m* manchado de sangre, (*en pago por asesinato*); (*as compensation*) indemnización que se paga a la familia de alguien que ha sido asesinado ➤ **blood orange** naranja *f* sanguina ➤ **blood poisoning** septicemia *f*, envenenamiento *m* de la sangre ➤ **blood pressure** tensión *f* arterial, presión *f* arterial, presión *f* sanguínea; **to have high/low ~ pressure** tener la tensión alta/baja, tener hipertensión/hipotensión; **to take sb's ~ pressure** tomar la tensión a algn ➤ **blood pudding** morcilla *f* ➤ **blood relation she is no ~ relation to him** ella y él no son de la misma sangre, ella y él no son (parientes) cosanguíneos (*frm*) ➤ **blood sausage** (*US*) morcilla *f* ➤ **blood sport** deporte en el que se matan animales ➤ **blood sugar (level)** nivel *m* de azúcar en la sangre ➤ **blood supply** riego *m* sanguíneo ➤ **blood test** análisis *m inv* de sangre ➤ **blood vessel** vaso *m* sanguíneo

bloodbath ['blʌdbɑːθ] N carnicería *f*, baño *m* de sangre

bloodcurdling ['blʌdkɜːdlɪŋ] ADJ espeluznante

bloodhound ['blʌdhaʊnd] N sabueso *m*

bloodless ['blʌdlɪs] ADJ **1** (= *pale*) pálido; (*due to blood loss*) exangüe **2** [*revolution, coup*] incruento, sin derramamiento de sangre

blood-red ['blʌd'red] ADJ [*fabric, paint, car*] (de color) rojo sangre; [*sky, sunset*] de un rojo encendido

bloodshed ['blʌdʃed] N derramamiento *m* de sangre

bloodshot ['blʌdʃɒt] ADJ [*eye*] (*from crying, lack of sleep*) rojo, enrojecido; (*from anger*) inyectado en sangre

bloodstained ['blʌdsteɪnd] ADJ manchado de sangre

bloodstream ['blʌdstriːm] N **the ~** la corriente sanguínea, el flujo sanguíneo

bloodthirsty ['blʌdθɜːstɪ] ADJ (*compar* **bloodthirstier**; *superl* **bloodthirstiest**) (= *brutal*) sanguinario

bloody ['blʌdɪ] **A** ADJ (*compar* **bloodier**; *superl* **bloodiest**) **1** (= *bloodstained*) [*hands, dress*] ensangrentado, manchado de sangre; (= *cruel*) [*battle*] sangriento, cruento (*frm*); **to give sb a ~ nose** romper la nariz a algn
2 (*Brit***) **you ~ idiot!** ¡maldito imbécil!*; **~ hell!** ¡maldita sea!*, ¡joder! (*Sp****)
B ADV (*Brit***) **not ~ likely!** ¡ni hablar!, ¡ni de coña! (*Sp****); **he can ~ well do it himself!** ¡que lo haga él, leche!** *or* coño!***; **it's a ~ awful place** es un sitio asqueroso, es un sitio de mierda***
C CPD ➤ **Bloody Mary** bloody mary *m*

bloody-minded* ['blʌdɪ'maɪndɪd] ADJ (*Brit*) **1** (= *stubborn*) terco, empecinado **2** (= *awkward*) atravesado, difícil; **you're just being ~** son ganas de ser atravesado *or* difícil, son ganas de fastidiar

bloom [bluːm] Ⓐ N (= *flower*) flor *f*; **in ~** en flor; **in full ~** en plena floración; **to come into ~** florecer Ⓑ VI [*flower*] abrirse; [*tree*] florecer; [*economy, industry*] prosperar

blooming ['bluːmɪŋ] ADJ **1** [*tree*] floreciente, en flor **2** (= *flourishing*) radiante; **to be ~ with health** estar rebosante de *or* rebosar salud **3** (*Brit**) maldito*

blooper* ['bluːpəʳ] N planchazo *m*, metedura *f* de pata

blossom ['blɒsəm] Ⓐ N (= *collective*) flores *fpl*; (= *single*) flor *f*; **in ~** en flor Ⓑ VI [*tree*] florecer; (*fig*) florecer, llegar a su apogeo; **it ~ed into love** se transformó en amor

blot [blɒt] Ⓐ N [*of ink*] borrón *m*, mancha *f*; (*on reputation*) tacha *f*, mancha *f*; **the chimney is a ~ on the landscape** la chimenea afea el paisaje Ⓑ VT (*with ink*) manchar; ✦ IDIOM **to ~ one's copybook** (*Brit*) manchar su reputación **2** (*with blotter*) secar
➤ **blot out** VT + ADV [+ *view*] tapar, ocultar

blotch [blɒtʃ] N mancha *f*

blotchy ['blɒtʃɪ] ADJ (*compar* **blotchier**; *superl* **blotchiest**) manchado, lleno de manchas

blotter ['blɒtəʳ] N **1** (= *blotting paper*) secante *m* **2** (*US*) (= *notebook*) registro *m*

blotting paper ['blɒtɪŋˌpeɪpəʳ] N papel *m* secante

blouse [blaʊz] N (= *shirt*) blusa *f*; (*US Mil*) guerrera *f*

blow¹ [bləʊ] N **1** (= *hit*) golpe *m*; (= *slap*) bofetada *f*; **a ~ with a hammer** un martillazo; **at one ~** de un solo golpe; **to come to ~s** (*lit, fig*) llegar a las manos; ✦ IDIOMS **to cushion the ~** disminuir los efectos (*de un desastre etc*); **to strike a ~ for freedom** dar un paso más hacia la libertad **2** (= *setback*) golpe *m*; **that's a ~!** ¡qué lástima!

blow² [bləʊ] (*pt* **blew**; *pp* **~n**) Ⓐ VT **1** (= *move*) [+ *leaves, papers*] hacer volar; **the wind blew the ship towards the coast** el viento llevó *or* empujó el barco hacia la costa; **it's ~ing a gale** hace muchísimo viento; **the wind blew the door shut** el viento cerró la puerta de golpe **2** [+ *trumpet, whistle*] tocar, sonar; [+ *glass*] soplar; **to ~ bubbles** (*soap*) hacer pompas; (*gum*) hacer globos; **to ~ sb a kiss** enviar *or* tirar un beso a algn; **to ~ one's nose** sonarse (la nariz); **to ~ smoke in sb's face/eyes** (*lit*) echar el humo en la cara/los ojos a algn; (*fig*) (*US*) engañar a algn; ✦ IDIOMS **to ~ one's own trumpet** *or* (*US*) **horn** darse bombo*; **to ~ the whistle on sth/sb** dar la voz de alarma sobre algo/algn **3** (= *burn out, explode*) [+ *fuse*] fundir, quemar; [+ *tyre*] reventar; [+ *safe*] volar; ✦ IDIOMS **to ~ sb's mind*** dejar alucinado a algn*; **to ~ one's top** ◇ **~ one's cork** *or* **stack** (*US*) reventar, estallar **4** (= *spoil, ruin*) **to ~ one's chance of doing sth*** echar a perder *or* desperdiciar la oportunidad de hacer algo; **to ~ sb's cover** desenmascarar a algn; **now you've ~n it!*** ¡ahora sí que la has pifiado!*; **to ~ one's lines*** perder el hilo, olvidar el papel **5 to ~ money on sth*** malgastar dinero en algo **6** (*esp Brit**) (= *damn*) **~ the expense!** ¡al cuerno el gasto!* Ⓑ VI **1** [*wind*] soplar; **to ~ on one's fingers** soplarse los dedos; **to ~ on one's soup** enfriar la sopa soplando **2** [*leaves etc*] volar; **the door blew open/shut** se abrió/cerró la puerta con el viento **3** (= *make sound*) [*trumpet, siren*] sonar **4** [*fuse*] fundirse, quemarse; [*tyre*] reventar Ⓒ CPD ➤ **blow drier** secador *m* de pelo ➤ **blow job*** **to give sb a ~ job** mamársela *or* chupársela a algn***
➤ **blow away** Ⓐ VI + ADV [*hat*] salir volando, volarse Ⓑ VT + ADV **1** [*wind*] [+ *leaves, rubbish*] hacer volar **2** (**) (= *kill*) liquidar* **3** (**) (= *surprise*) dejar alucinado*
➤ **blow down** Ⓐ VT + ADV derribar Ⓑ VI + ADV venirse abajo
➤ **blow off** VI + ADV [*hat*] salir volando, volarse
➤ **blow out** Ⓐ VT + ADV **1** [+ *candle*] apagar (con un soplo); **the storm had ~n itself out** la tormenta se había calmado **2 to ~ sb's brains out*** pegar un tiro a algn, levantar *or* volar la tapa de los sesos a algn* Ⓑ VI + ADV **1** [*candle*] apagarse **2** [*tyre*] reventar
➤ **blow over** Ⓐ VT + ADV derribar, tumbar Ⓑ VI + ADV **1** [*tree etc*] caer **2** [*storm*] pasar **3** [*dispute*] olvidarse
➤ **blow up** Ⓐ VT + ADV **1** [+ *bridge etc*] volar **2** [+ *tyre etc*] inflar, hinchar (*Sp*) **3** [+ *photo*] ampliar **4** (= *exaggerate*) exagerar Ⓑ VI + ADV **1** [*explosive*] estallar, explotar;

[*container*] estallar, reventar **2** [*storm*] levantarse **3** [*row*] estallar **4** (*) (= *lose temper*) salirse de sus casillas*

blow-by-blow [ˌbləʊbaɪˈbləʊ] ADJ **a ~ account** una narración pormenorizada

blow-dry ['bləʊˌdraɪ] N **I'd like a cut and ~** quisiera un corte y secado a mano

blowlamp ['bləʊlæmp] N (*Brit*) soplete *m*

blown [bləʊn] PP *of* **blow²**

blow-out ['bləʊaʊt] N **1** (*Aut*) reventón *m*, pinchazo *m*, ponchada *f* (*Mex*) **2** (**) (= *meal*) comilona* *f*, atracón* *m*

blowtorch ['bləʊtɔːtʃ] N soplete *m*

blow-up ['bləʊʌp] N (*Phot*) ampliación *f*

blubber¹ ['blʌbəʳ] N [*of whale, seal*] grasa *f*

blubber²* ['blʌbəʳ] VI (= *weep*) lloriquear

bludgeon ['blʌdʒən] VT (*lit*) aporrear; **to ~ sb into doing sth** (*fig*) coaccionar *or* forzar a algn a hacer algo

blue [bluː] Ⓐ ADJ (*compar* **~r**; *superl* **~st**) **1** azul; **~ with cold** amoratado de frío; ✦ IDIOMS **once in a ~ moon** de Pascuas a Ramos; **you can shout till you're ~ in the face*** puedes gritar hasta que no puedas más
2 (*) (= *obscene*) verde, colorado (*LAm*); [*film*] porno *inv*
3 (*) (= *sad*) triste, deprimido
Ⓑ N **1** (= *colour*) azul *m*; ✦ IDIOM **to come out of the ~** [*money, good news*] venir como cosa llovida del cielo, bajar del cielo; [*bad news*] caer como una bomba; **he said out of the ~** dijo de repente, dijo inesperadamente
2 blues (*Mus*) blues *m*; (= *feeling*) melancolía *f*, tristeza *f*; **he's got the ~s** está deprimido
Ⓒ CPD ➤ **blue blood** sangre *f* azul ➤ **blue book** (*US Scol*) cuaderno *m* de exámenes ➤ **blue cheese** queso *m* de pasta verde ➤ **blue jeans** tejanos *mpl*, vaqueros *mpl*

bluebell ['bluːbel] N campánula *f* azul

blueberry ['bluːbərɪ] N arándano *m*

bluebottle ['bluːˌbɒtl] N moscarda *f*

blue-chip ['bluːtʃɪp] ADJ [*company*] de primera (categoría); [*investment*] asegurado ➤ **blue-chip securities** fianzas *fpl* fiables

blue-collar ['bluːˌkɒləʳ] ADJ [*job*] manual ➤ **blue-collar worker** obrero/a *m/f*, trabajador(a) *m/f* manual

blue-eyed ['bluːˌaɪd] ADJ de ojos azules ➤ **blue-eyed boy** (*fig*) consentido *m*, niño *m* mimado

blueprint ['bluːprɪnt] N (= *plan*) proyecto *m*, anteproyecto *m*; (= *drawing*) cianotipo *m*

blue-sky ['bluːskaɪ] ADJ **we need to do some ~ thinking** tenemos que ponernos a pensar sin ningún tipo de límite

bluetit ['bluːtɪt] N herrerillo *m* (común)

Bluetooth® ['bluːtuːθ] ADJ **~ technology** tecnología *f* Bluetooth®

bluff¹ [blʌf] ADJ [*person*] franco, directo

bluff² [blʌf] Ⓐ N (= *act of bluffing*) farol *m*, bluff *m*; ✦ IDIOM **to call sb's ~** poner a algn en evidencia Ⓑ VT **to ~ it out by ...** salvar la situación haciendo creer que ... Ⓒ VI farolear, tirarse un farol (*Sp**)

blunder ['blʌndəʳ] Ⓐ N metedura *f* de pata*, plancha *f* (*Sp**); **to make a ~** meter la pata*, tirarse una plancha (*Sp**) Ⓑ VI **1** (= *err*) cometer un grave error, meter la pata* **2** (= *move clumsily*) **to ~ about** andar dando tumbos; **to ~ into sth** (*lit*) tropezar con algo; (*fig*) caer *or* meterse en algo

blunt [blʌnt] Ⓐ ADJ **1** [*edge*] desafilado; [*point*] despuntado **2** [*manner, person*] directo, franco; [*statement*] terminante; **I will be ~ with you** voy a hablarte con franqueza; **he was very ~ with me** no se mordió la lengua conmigo Ⓑ VT [+ *blade, knife*] desafilar; [+ *pencil*] despuntar

bluntly ['blʌntlɪ] ADV francamente, directamente

bluntness ['blʌntnɪs] N **1** [*of blade*] falta *f* de filo, lo poco afilado **2** (= *outspokenness*) franqueza *f*

blur [blɜːʳ] Ⓐ N (= *shape*) contorno *m* borroso; **everything is a ~ when I take off my glasses** todo se vuelve borroso cuando me quito las gafas *or* (*LAm*) los lentes; **my mind was a ~** todo se volvió borroso en mi mente Ⓑ VT [+ *writing*] borrar, hacer borroso; [+ *outline*] desdibujar; **my eyes were ~red with tears** las lágrimas me enturbiaban la vista

C VI desdibujarse, volverse borroso

blurb [blɜːb] N propaganda f

blurred [blɜːd] ADJ **1** [outline] borroso, poco nítido; **a ~ photo** una foto movida or desenfocada **2** [memory] borroso; **to be/become ~** (gen) estar/volverse borroso; **class distinctions are becoming ~** las diferencias de clase se están difuminando

blurt [blɜːt] VT **to ~ out** [+ secret] dejar escapar; [+ whole story] contar de buenas a primeras

blush [blʌʃ] **A** N **1** (from embarrassment) rubor m, sonrojo m **2** (US) (= make-up) colorete m **B** VI ruborizarse, sonrojarse (**at** por; **with** de); **to make sb ~** hacer que algn se ruborice or se sonroje; **I ~ even to think about it** me avergüenzo de sólo pensarlo

blusher [ˈblʌʃəʳ] N colorete m

bluster [ˈblʌstəʳ] **A** N fanfarronadas fpl, bravatas fpl **B** VT **to ~ it out** defenderse echando bravatas, baladronear

blustery [ˈblʌstəri] ADJ [wind] tempestuoso; [day] de mucho viento

Blu-Tack® [ˈbluːtæk] N Blu-Tack® m

BMX N ABBR (= **bicycle motocross**) ciclocross m ➤ **BMX bike** bicicleta f de ciclocross

BO N ABBR (Brit) (= **body odour**) olor m a sudor

boa [ˈbəʊə] N **1** (also = **constrictor**) boa f **2** (= garment) boa f (de plumas)

boar [bɔːʳ] N (= male pig) cerdo m, verraco m

board [bɔːd] **A** N **1** [of wood] tabla f, tablón m; (for chess etc) tablero m; (= notice board) tablón m; (= card) cartón m; **✦** IDIOMS **above ~** legítimo; **across the ~: an increase across the ~** un aumento global or general; **to go by the ~** (= go wrong) ir al traste; (= be abandoned) abandonarse **2** (= meals) comida f; **full ~** pensión f completa; **half ~** media pensión f; **~ and lodging** (Brit) casa f y comida **3** (Naut, Aer) **on ~** a bordo; **to go ~** embarcarse, subir a bordo; **✦** IDIOM **to take sth on ~** adoptar algo, asimilar algo **4** (= group of officials) junta f, consejo m **5** (gas, water etc) comisión f **B** VT [+ ship, plane] subir a bordo de, embarcarse en; [+ enemy ship] abordar; [+ bus, train] subir a **C** VI **1** (= lodge) **to ~ with** hospedarse en casa de **2** (Aer) **flight 101 is now ~** pasajeros del vuelo 101 acudan a las puertas de embarque **D** CPD ➤ **board game** juego m de tablero ➤ **board meeting** reunión f de la junta directiva or del consejo de administración ➤ **board of directors** junta f directiva, consejo m de administración ➤ **board of governors** (Brit Scol) consejo m (de un colegio, instituto etc) ➤ **board of inquiry** comisión f investigadora ➤ **Board of Trade** (US) Cámara de Comercio ➤ **board up** VT + ADV [+ door, window] entablar

boarder [ˈbɔːdəʳ] N (in house) huésped(a) m/f; (Brit Scol) interno/a m/f

boarding [ˈbɔːdɪŋ] CPD ➤ **boarding card** (Naut, Aer) tarjeta f de embarque, pase m de embarque (LAm) ➤ **boarding house** pensión f, casa f de huéspedes, residencial f (SC) ➤ **boarding school** internado m

boardroom [ˈbɔːdrʊm] N sala f de juntas

boardwalk [ˈbɔːdwɔːk] N (US) paseo m marítimo entablado

boast [bəʊst] **A** N alarde m; **it is his ~ that ...** se jacta de que ... **B** VT ostentar, jactarse de **C** VI presumir, alardear; **he ~s about his strength** presume de fuerte; **that's nothing to ~ about** eso no es motivo para vanagloriarse

boastful [ˈbəʊstfəl] ADJ jactancioso, fanfarrón

boat [bəʊt] N (gen) barco m; (= large ship) buque m, navío m; (small) barca f; (= rowing boat) barca f, bote m (de remo); (= racing eight, ship's boat) bote m; **to go by ~** ir en barco; **✦** IDIOMS **to push the ~ out** (Brit*) tirar la casa por la ventana*; **we're all in the same ~*** estamos todos en la misma situación ➤ **boat deck** cubierta f de botes ➤ **boat train** tren m que enlaza con el barco

boatbuilder [ˈbəʊtˌbɪldəʳ] N constructor(a) m/f de barcos; **~'s (yard)** astillero m

boater [ˈbəʊtəʳ] N (= hat) canotié m

boathouse [ˈbəʊthaʊs] N cobertizo m para botes

boating [ˈbəʊtɪŋ] N **to go ~** ir a dar un paseo en barca ➤ **boating trip** paseo m en barca

boatyard [ˈbəʊtjɑːd] N astillero m

Bob [bɒb] N **✦** IDIOM **~'s your uncle!** (Brit*) ¡y se acabó!, ¡y listo!

bob¹ [bɒb] **A** N (= curtsy) reverencia f; [of head] sacudida f, meneo m **B** VI **to ~ to sb** hacer una reverencia a algn ➤ **bob up** VI + ADV (= appear) surgir, presentarse; **to ~ up and down** [cork] subir y bajar; [boat] cabecear; [person] levantarse y sentarse repetidas veces

bob² [bɒb] **A** N (= hairstyle) pelo m a lo garçon **B** VT [+ hair] cortar a lo garçon

bob³* [bɒb] N (pl bob) (Brit) (formerly) (= shilling) chelín m; **✦** IDIOMS **he's not short of a few ~** está forrado*; **that must be worth a ~ or two** eso tiene que valer un buen pico* or un dineral

bob⁴ [bɒb] N (= bobsleigh) bob m, bobsleigh m

bobbin [ˈbɒbɪn] N (Tech) carrete m, bobina f; [of cotton] canilla f

bobble [ˈbɒbl] **A** N **1** (Brit) (on hat) borla f **2** (US*) (= mistake) pifia* f **B** VT (US*) (= handle ineptly) pifiarla con* **C** CPD ➤ **bobble hat** (Brit) gorro m con borla

bobby* [ˈbɒbɪ] **A** N (Brit†) (= policeman) poli* m **B** CPD ➤ **bobby pin** (US) horquilla f, clipe m

bobcat [ˈbɒbkæt] N (US) lince m

bobsled (esp US) [ˈbɒbsled], **bobsleigh** (Brit) [ˈbɒbsleɪ] N bob m, bobsleigh m

bode [bəʊd] VI (liter) **it ~s well/ill** es de buen/mal agüero

bodice [ˈbɒdɪs] N [of dress] canesú m

bodily [ˈbɒdɪlɪ] **A** ADJ [comfort] físico; [fluid] corporal, del cuerpo; **~ functions** funciones fpl fisiológicas; **~ needs** necesidades fpl corporales; **grievous ~ harm** daños mpl físicos graves, lesiones fpl corporales graves **B** ADV **to lift sb ~** levantar a algn totalmente

body [ˈbɒdɪ] **A** N **1** [of person, animal] cuerpo m, tronco m; **✦** IDIOM **her salary hardly keeps ~ and soul together** apenas se gana para vivir **2** (= corpse) cadáver m **3** (= external structure) armazón m or f, casco m; (Aut) (also **~work**) carrocería f **4** (= core) [of argument] meollo m; **the main ~ of his speech** la parte principal or el meollo de su discurso **5** (= mass, collection) [of information, literature] conjunto m, grueso m; [of people] grupo m; [of water] masa f; **in a ~** todos juntos, en masa; **the ~ politic** (frm) el estado **6** (= organization) organismo m, órgano m **7** [of wine] cuerpo m; [of hair] volumen m, cuerpo m **8** (Astron, Chem) cuerpo m **9** = **body stocking** **B** CPD ➤ **body armour, body armor** (US) equipo de protección corporal ➤ **body bag** bolsa f para restos humanos ➤ **body blow** (fig) golpe m duro, revés m ➤ **body clock** reloj m biológico ➤ **body count** (US) (= casualties) número m or balance m de las víctimas; **to do a ~ count** [of those present] hacer un recuento de la asistencia; [of dead] hacer un recuento de los muertos ➤ **body double** (Cine, TV) doble mf ➤ **body fat** grasa f corporal, grasa f (del cuerpo) ➤ **body language** lenguaje m corporal, lenguaje m del cuerpo ➤ **body lotion** loción f corporal ➤ **body odour, body odor** (US) olor m corporal ➤ **body repairs** (Aut) reparación f de la carrocería ➤ **body search** registro m de la persona ➤ **body (repair) shop** (Aut) taller m de reparaciones (de carrocería) ➤ **body stocking** body m, bodi m ➤ **body swerve** (Sport) finta f, regate m ➤ **body temperature** temperatura f corporal ➤ **body warmer** chaleco m acolchado ➤ **body weight** peso m (del cuerpo)

bodybuilder [ˈbɒdɪˌbɪldəʳ] N culturista mf

bodybuilding [ˈbɒdɪˌbɪldɪŋ] N culturismo m

bodyguard [ˈbɒdɪgɑːd] N (= one person) guardaespaldas mf inv, guarura mf (Mex); (= group) escolta f, guardia f personal

bodywork [ˈbɒdɪwɜːk] N (Aut) carrocería f

boffin* ['bɒfɪn] N (Brit) cerebrito* mf

bog [bɒg] N **1** (= swamp) pantano m, ciénaga f **2** (Brit**) (= toilet) retrete m, meadero** m

boggle* ['bɒgl] VI **the mind ~s!** ¡me quedo helado! or muerto!*, ¡yo alucino!*

boggy ['bɒgɪ] ADJ (compar **boggier**; superl **boggiest**) pantanoso

bog-standard* ['bɒg'stændəd] ADJ (Brit) normalito*, común y corriente

bogus ['bəʊgəs] ADJ [claim] falso, fraudulento; [interest] fingido; [doctor, policeman] falso

Bohemian [bəʊ'hiːmɪən] ADJ, N bohemio/a m/f

boil¹ [bɔɪl] N (= swelling) divieso m, furúnculo m, chupón m (And), postema f (Mex)

boil² [bɔɪl] VI **1** (lit) hervir; **the kettle's ~ing** el agua de la tetera está hirviendo; **to ~ dry** quedarse sin caldo/agua **2** (fig) **it makes me ~** me hace rabiar; **to ~ with rage** estar furioso
ⒷVT [+ liquid] hervir; [+ vegetables, meat] cocer; [+ egg] pasar por agua; **to ~ the kettle** poner el agua a hervir
ⒸN **to be on the ~** (lit) estar hirviendo; [situation] estar a punto de estallar; **to bring to the** or (US) **a ~** calentar hasta que hierva, llevar a ebullición; **to come to the** or (US) **a ~** comenzar a hervir; (fig) entrar en ebullición
➤ **boil down** ⒶVT + ADV [+ sauce etc] reducir por cocción; (fig) reducir a forma más sencilla ⒷVI **it all ~ed down to money** todo se reducía a una cuestión de dinero
➤ **boil over** VI + ADV **1** [liquid] irse, rebosar **2** (fig) desbordarse

boiled [bɔɪld] ADJ hervido ➤ **boiled egg** huevo m pasado por agua, huevo m a la copa (And, SC) ➤ **boiled potatoes** patatas fpl cocidas al agua ➤ **boiled sweet** (Brit) caramelo m con sabor a frutas

boiler ['bɔɪləʳ] N (for central heating) caldera f; (in ship, engine) calderas fpl ➤ **boiler room** sala f de calderas ➤ **boiler suit** (Brit) mono m, overol m (LAm), mameluco m (SC)

boiling ['bɔɪlɪŋ] Ⓐ ADJ **1** (gen) hirviendo **2** (*) (also used as adv) **I'm ~ (hot)** estoy asado*; **it's ~ (hot) in here** aquí hace un calor terrible; **a ~ hot day** un día asfixiante de calor **3** (*) (= angry) echando chispas* Ⓑ CPD ➤ **boiling point** punto m de ebullición

boisterous ['bɔɪstərəs] ADJ [child, game] bullicioso, alborotado; [party] bullicioso, muy animado

bold [bəʊld] Ⓐ ADJ (compar **-er**; superl **-est**) **1** (= brave) atrevido, audaz **2** (= forward) atrevido, descarado; ✦ IDIOM **(as) ~ as brass** más fresco que una lechuga* **3** (= striking) [colour, clothes, design] llamativo; [brush stroke, handwriting, move] enérgico **4** (Typ) [letters] en negrita Ⓑ N (Typ) negrita f Ⓒ CPD ➤ **bold type** negrita f

boldly ['bəʊldlɪ] ADV **1** (= bravely) [speak, behave] audazmente; **you must act ~ and confidently** debes actuar con audacia y seguridad en ti mismo **2** (= forwardly) [stare, announce, claim] descaradamente, con atrevimiento **3** (= strikingly) **a ~ patterned fabric** una tela con un estampado llamativo

boldness ['bəʊldnɪs] N **1** (= daring) audacia f **2** (= forwardness) atrevimiento m, descaro m **3** (= striking quality) [of design, colours, clothes] lo llamativo; [of lines, strokes] lo enérgico

Bolivia [bə'lɪvɪə] N Bolivia f

Bolivian [bə'lɪvɪən] ADJ, N boliviano/a m/f

bollard ['bɒləd] N (Brit) (= post) baliza f; (Naut) noray m, bolardo m

bollocking*** ['bɒləkɪŋ] N (Brit) **to give sb a ~** echar una bronca a algn*, poner a algn como un trapo*

bollocks*** ['bɒləks] (Brit) Ⓐ NPL cojones*** mpl Ⓑ N (= nonsense) pavadas* fpl, huevadas fpl (And, Chi***)

bolshie*, bolshy* (Brit) ['bɒlʃɪ] Ⓐ N (Pol) bolchevique mf Ⓑ ADJ (Pol) bolchevique; (fig) rebelde, protestón

bolster ['bəʊlstəʳ] Ⓐ N cabezal m, almohadón m (con forma cilíndrica) Ⓑ VT (also ~ up) reforzar; [+ morale] levantar

bolt [bəʊlt] Ⓐ N **1** (on door, gun) cerrojo m; [of lock]

pestillo m; (for nut) perno m, tornillo m **2** [of lightning] rayo m, relámpago m; ✦ IDIOM **it came like a ~ from the blue** cayó como una bomba Ⓑ ADV **~ upright** rígido, muy erguido; **to sit ~ upright** (= change position) incorporarse de golpe Ⓒ VT **1** [+ door] echar el cerrojo a; **to ~ two things together** unir dos cosas con pernos **2** (also ~ **down**) [+ food] engullir Ⓓ VI **1** (= escape) escaparse, huir; [horse] desbocarse **2** (= rush) echar a correr Ⓔ CPD ➤ **bolt hole** (Brit) refugio m

bomb [bɒm] Ⓐ N bomba f; ✦ IDIOMS **to go like a ~** (Brit*): **it went like a ~** [party, event] resultó fenomenal*, fue un éxito; **this car goes like a ~** este coche va como un bólido*; **to cost a ~** (Brit*) costar un ojo de la cara*; **to make a ~** (Brit*) ganarse un fortunón* Ⓑ VT bombardear Ⓒ VI (US*) (= fail) fracasar; **the show ~ed** el espectáculo fracasó Ⓓ CPD ➤ **bomb disposal** desactivación f or neutralización f de bombas ➤ **bomb disposal expert** artificiero/a m/f, experto/a m/f en desactivar bombas ➤ **bomb scare** amenaza f de bomba ➤ **bomb shelter** refugio m antiaéreo ➤ **bomb site** lugar m en el que ha estallado una bomba ➤ **bomb out** VT + ADV [+ house] volar; **the family was ~ed out** (by terrorists) a la familia les volaron la casa; (by planes) a la familia les bombardearon la casa

bombard [bɒm'bɑːd] VT (Mil) bombardear (with con); **I was ~ed with questions** me acosaron or bombardearon a preguntas

bombardment [bɒm'bɑːdmənt] N bombardeo m

bombastic [bɒm'bæstɪk] ADJ [language, manner, style] ampuloso, rimbombante; [person] pomposo

bomber ['bɒməʳ] Ⓐ N **1** (= aircraft) bombardero m **2** (= person) terrorista mf que coloca bombas Ⓑ CPD ➤ **bomber command** jefatura f de bombardeo ➤ **bomber jacket** chaqueta f or (Sp) cazadora f (tipo aviador)

bombing ['bɒmɪŋ] N bombardeo m

bombshell ['bɒmʃel] N (= news etc) bomba f; **it fell like a ~** cayó como una bomba

bona fide ['bəʊnə'faɪdɪ] ADJ (= genuine) auténtico; (= legal) legal

bonanza [bə'nænzə] N (in profits) bonanza f

bond [bɒnd] Ⓐ N **1** (= link) lazo m, vínculo m **2** (Fin) bono m **3** (Chem) enlace m **4** bonds (= chains) cadenas fpl Ⓑ VT **1** (= stick) unir, pegar **2** (emotionally) unir Ⓒ VI **1** (= stick) adherirse (with a) **2** (emotionally) establecer lazos or vínculos afectivos (with con)

bondage ['bɒndɪdʒ] N **1** (= enslavement) esclavitud f, cautiverio m **2** (= sexual practice) bondage m

bone [bəʊn] Ⓐ N [of human, animal] hueso m; [of fish] espina f; ✦ IDIOMS **chilled** or **frozen to the ~** congelado de frío; **close to the ~** [joke] subido de tono; **to cut costs to the ~** reducir los gastos al mínimo; **~ of contention** manzana f de la discordia; **I feel it in my ~s** tengo esa corazonada, me da en la nariz (Sp*); **he made no ~s about it** no se anduvo con rodeos; **he won't make old ~s** no llegará a viejo; **I have a ~ to pick with you** tenemos una cuenta que ajustar; **to work one's fingers to the ~** trabajar como un esclavo Ⓑ VT [+ meat] deshuesar; [+ fish] quitar las espinas a Ⓒ CPD ➤ **bone china** porcelana f fina ➤ **bone marrow** médula f ósea

bone-dry [ˌbəʊn'draɪ] ADJ completamente seco

bone-idle* [ˌbəʊn'aɪdl] ADJ gandul, holgazán, flojo (LAm)

boneless ['bəʊnlɪs] ADJ [fish] sin espinas; [ham, chicken] deshuesado; [meat] sin hueso

bonfire ['bɒnfaɪəʳ] N (for celebration) hoguera f; (for rubbish) fogata f ➤ **Bonfire Night** (Brit) fiesta que se celebra en la noche de cinco de noviembre en toda Gran Bretaña

bonk [bɒŋk] VI (Brit**) echarse un polvo***, follar (Sp***)

bonkers** ['bɒŋkəz] ADJ (esp Brit) **to be ~** estar chalado*, estar como una cabra*; **to go ~** perder la chaveta*

bonnet ['bɒnɪt] N **1** (baby's) gorro m; (woman's) gorra f;

(*esp Scot*) (*man's*) gorra *f* escocesa **2** (*Brit*) (*on car*) capó *m*, cofre *m* (*Mex*)

bonny ['bɒnɪ] ADJ (*compar* **bonnier**; *superl* **bonniest**) (*esp Scot*) [*child*] hermoso, lindo (*esp LAm*)

bonsai ['bɒnsaɪ] N bonsai *m*

bonus ['bəʊnəs] N (*on wages*) prima *f*, bonificación *f*; (*fig*) ventaja *f* ➤ **bonus point** (*in game, quiz*) punto *m* extra ➤ **bonus scheme** plan *m* de incentivos ➤ **bonus shares** acciones *fpl* gratuitas

bony ['bəʊnɪ] ADJ (*compar* **bonier**; *superl* **boniest**) **1** [*fish*] espinoso, lleno de espinas **2** (= *like bone*) óseo **3** (= *thin*) [*person*] flaco, delgado

boo [buː] Ⓐ N rechifla *f*, abucheo *m*; ✦ IDIOM **he wouldn't say ~ to a goose*** es incapaz de matar una mosca Ⓑ EXCL ¡uh! Ⓒ VT abuchear, silbar Ⓓ VI silbar

boob [buːb] Ⓐ N **1** (*Brit**) (= *mistake*) metedura *f* de pata*; **to make a ~** meter la pata* **2** (**) (= *breast*) teta* *f* Ⓑ VI (*Brit**) meter la pata* Ⓒ CPD ➤ **boob tube*** (*Brit*) (= *garment*) camiseta-tubo *f*; (*US*) (= *TV set*) televisor *m*

booboo* ['buːbuː] N metedura *f* de pata*

booby-trap ['buːbɪtræp] Ⓐ N trampa *f* Ⓑ VT **the house had been ~ped** habían puesto una trampa explosiva en la casa

book [bʊk] Ⓐ N **1** (= *publication*) libro *m*; **a ~ on politics** un libro de política; ✦ IDIOMS **by the ~** según las reglas; **in my ~** tal como yo lo veo, a mi modo de ver; **to bring sb to ~** pedir cuentas a algn; **to be in sb's good/bad ~s: I'm in his bad ~s at the moment** en este momento estoy en su lista negra; **I was trying to get back in her good ~s** estaba intentando volver a congraciarme con ella; **I can read him like a ~** (= *I'm not deceived*) a mí no me engaña **2** (*also* **notebook**) libreta *f*, librito *m*; (*also* **exercise ~**) cuaderno *m* **3** (*also* **telephone ~**) guía *f* **4** (= *set*) [*of tickets, cheques*] talonario *m*; [*of matches*] estuche *m*; [*of stamps*] librito *m* **5** (*Comm*) **the ~s** las cuentas, la contabilidad; **to keep the ~s** llevar las cuentas *or* los libros *or* la contabilidad **6** **books** (= *register of members*) registro *msing*; **they had less than 30 members on their ~s** tenían menos de 30 miembros en el registro **7** (*also* **statute ~**) código *m*; ✦ IDIOM **to throw the ~ at sb** castigar severamente a algn Ⓑ VT **1** (= *reserve*) [+ *ticket, room, table, flight*] reservar; **have you ~ed your holiday yet?** ¿ya has reservado las vacaciones?; **all the restaurants are fully ~ed** todos los restaurantes están llenos **2** (= *arrange*) **I've ~ed an appointment with the dentist** he pedido hora con el dentista; **can we ~ a time to meet soon?** ¿podemos quedar un día de éstos? **3** (= *engage*) [+ *performer, artiste*] contratar **4** (*) (= *take name of*) [+ *player*] amonestar; (= *fine*) multar, poner una multa a; (= *charge*) acusar **5** (= *note down*) [+ *order*] anotar Ⓒ VI hacer una reserva, reservar; **to ~ into a hotel** hacer una reserva *or* reservar en un hotel Ⓓ CPD ➤ **book club** club *m* del libro, club *m* de lectores ➤ **book token** vale *m* para libros, cheque *m* regalo para libros ➤ **book value** valor *m* contable
➤ **book in** (*Brit*) Ⓐ VI + ADV (= *record arrival*) registrarse; (= *reserve a room*) reservar habitación Ⓑ VT + ADV **they're ~ed in at the White Swan** tienen reservada una habitación en el White Swan; **I've ~ed you in with Dr Stuart for four o'clock** te he conseguido hora con el Dr. Stuart para las cuatro
➤ **book up** VT + ADV (*esp Brit*) **1** [+ *holiday*] hacer reserva de **2 to be ~ed up: the hotel is ~ed up** el hotel está completo, todas las habitaciones del hotel están reservadas; **all the flights were ~ed up** todos los vuelos estaban completos, no quedaban plazas en ningún vuelo; **I'm ~ed up all next week** la semana que viene tengo un programa muy apretado

bookable ['bʊkəbl] ADJ (*esp Brit*) **1** [*seat*] que se puede reservar **2** (*Sport*) [*offence*] sujeto a tarjeta amarilla

bookcase ['bʊkkeɪs] N librería *f*, estantería *f*, librero *m* (*Mex*)

bookie* ['bʊkɪ] N corredor(a) *m/f* de apuestas

booking ['bʊkɪŋ] Ⓐ N **1** (= *reservation*) reserva *f*; **to make a ~** hacer una reserva; **telephone ~** reserva *f* por teléfono **2** (= *engagement*) **the band has a ~ next week** han contratado al grupo para la semana que viene Ⓑ CPD ➤ **booking clerk** (*US*) taquillero/a *m/f* ➤ **booking fee** suplemento *m* por hacer la reserva ➤ **booking form** formulario *m* de reserva ➤ **booking office** (*Brit Theat*) taquilla *f*

bookkeeper ['bʊk,kiːpə'] N contable *mf* (*Sp*), tenedor(a) *m/f* de libros, contador(a) *m/f* (*LAm*)

bookkeeping ['bʊk,kiːpɪŋ] N contabilidad *f*, teneduría *f* de libros

booklet ['bʊklɪt] N folleto *m*

bookmaker ['bʊkmeɪkə'] N corredor *m* de apuestas

bookmark ['bʊkmɑːk] Ⓐ N **1** (*for book*) marcador *m*, señalador *m* **2** (*Internet*) favorito *m*, marcador *m* Ⓑ VT (*Internet*) marcar como sitio favorito, agregar a favoritos

bookseller ['bʊk,selə'] N librero/a *m/f*; **a ~'s** una librería

bookshelf ['bʊkʃelf] N (*pl* **bookshelves**) estante *m* (para libros); **bookshelves** estantería *fsing*

bookshop ['bʊkʃɒp] N (*esp Brit*) librería *f*

bookstall ['bʊkstɔːl] N (*at station*) quiosco *m* (de libros); (*at fair*) puesto *m* de libros

bookstore ['bʊkstɔː'] N (*esp US*) librería *f*

bookworm ['bʊkwɜːm] N ratón *m* de biblioteca*

boom[1] [buːm] N **1** (*Naut*) botalón *m*, botavara *f* **2** (*across harbour*) barrera *f* **3** [*of crane*] aguilón *m*; [*of microphone*] jirafa *f*

boom[2] [buːm] Ⓐ N [*of guns*] estruendo *m*, estampido *m*; [*of thunder*] retumbo *m*, trueno *m* Ⓑ VI [*voice, radio*] (*also* **~ out**) resonar, retumbar; [*gun*] tronar, retumbar Ⓒ VT (*also* **~ out**) tronar Ⓓ CPD ➤ **boom box*** (*US*) radiocasete *m* portátil (*muy grande*)

boom[3] [buːm] Ⓐ N (*in an industry*) auge *m*, boom *m*; (= *period of growth*) expansión *f* Ⓑ VI [*prices*] estar en alza; [*commodity*] tener mucha demanda; [*industry, town*] gozar de un boom, estar en auge; **business is ~ing** el negocio está en auge Ⓒ CPD ➤ **boom town** ciudad *f* beneficiaria del auge

boomerang ['buːməræŋ] N bumerang *m*

boon [buːn] N (= *blessing*) gran ayuda *f*; **it would be a ~ if he went** nos ayudaría muchísimo que él fuera

boondocks* ['buːndɒks] NPL (*US*) **out in the ~** en el quinto pino

boorish ['bʊərɪʃ] ADJ grosero

boost [buːst] Ⓐ N **1** (= *encouragement*) estímulo *m*, aliento *m*; **to give a ~ to** estimular, alentar **2** (= *upward thrust*) (*to rocket*) impulso *m*, propulsión *f* Ⓑ VT **1** (= *increase*) [+ *sales, production*] fomentar, incrementar; [+ *confidence, hopes*] estimular **2** (*Comm*) [+ *product*] promover, hacer publicidad de **3** (*Elec*) [+ *voltage*] elevar; [+ *radio signal*] potenciar **4** (*Space*) propulsar, lanzar

booster ['buːstə'] N (*TV, Rad*) repetidor *m*; (*Elec*) elevador *m* de tensión; (*Space*) (*also* **~ rocket**) cohete *m* secundario; (*Aer*) impulsor *m*, impulsador *m*; (*Med*) dosis *f inv* de refuerzo *or* recuerdo; (*US*) (= *supporter*) fan *mf*; **the project's ~s** (*US*) los defensores del proyecto

boot[1] [buːt] Ⓐ N **1** bota *f*; ✦ IDIOMS **now the ~ is on the other foot** (*Brit*) ahora se ha dado vuelta a la tortilla; **to give sb the ~*** despedir a algn, poner a algn en la calle*; **to put the ~ in** (*Brit**) meter caña* **2** (*Brit Aut*) maletero *m*, baúl *m* (*SC*), maletera *f* (*And, Chi*), cajuela *f* (*Mex*) **3** (*US*) (*also* **Denver ~**) cepo *m* Ⓑ VT **1** (*) (= *kick*) dar un puntapié a; **to ~ sb out*** poner a algn de patitas en la calle* **2** (*Comput*) (*also* **~ up**) cebar, inicializar **3** (*US*) [+ *car*] poner un cepo en Ⓒ VI (*Comput*) (*also* **~ up**) cebar, inicializar Ⓓ CPD ➤ **boot camp** (*in army*) campamento *m* militar; (= *prison*) prisión civil con régimen militar ➤ **boot polish** betún *m*

boot² [buːt] **to ~** ADV (*liter*) además, por añadidura

bootblack ['buːtblæk] N limpiabotas *mf inv*, bolero/a *m/f* (*Mex*), embolador(a) *m/f* (*Col*)

bootee [buːˈtiː] N bota *f* de lana

booth [buːð] N **1** (*Telec, interpreter's, voting*) cabina *f* **2** (*US*) (*at exhibition*) caseta *f*, stand *m*

bootleg ['buːtleg] **Ⓐ** ADJ [*alcohol*] de contrabando; [*tape, edition*] pirata *inv* **Ⓑ** VT [+ *tape etc*] grabar y vender ilegalmente

bootlegger ['buːtˌlegəʳ] N [*of alcohol*] contrabandista *mf*; [*of tapes, recordings*] productor/a *m/f* de copias pirata

booty ['buːtɪ] N botín *m*

booze* [buːz] **Ⓐ** N bebida *f*; **to go on the ~** darse a la bebida **Ⓑ** VI empinar el codo*

boozer** ['buːzəʳ] N **1** (= *person*) bebedor(a) *m/f*, tomador(a) *m/f* (*LAm*) **2** (*Brit*) (= *pub*) bar *m*

booze-up** ['buːzˌʌp] N (*Brit*) *reunión social donde se bebe mucho alcohol*

border ['bɔːdəʳ] **Ⓐ** N **1** (= *edge*) (*as decoration*) borde *m*, margen *m*; (*as boundary*) límite *m*; (*in garden*) arriate *m*, parterre *m* **2** (= *frontier*) frontera *f* **Ⓑ** VT (= *adjoin*) bordear, lindar con; **it is ~ed on the north by ...** linda al norte con ... **Ⓒ** CPD [*area, dispute, town*] fronterizo; [*guard*] de la frontera **➤ border patrol** (*US*) patrulla *f* de fronteras **➤ border post** puesto *m* fronterizo
➤ border (up)on VI + PREP **1** [+ *area, country*] lindar con, limitar con **2** (= *come near to being*) rayar en

borderline ['bɔːdəlaɪn] N límite *m*, línea *f* divisoria; **on the ~** (*between classes*) a medio camino; (*in exam*) en el límite **➤ borderline case** caso *m* dudoso

bore¹ [bɔːʳ] PT *of* **bear²**

bore² [bɔːʳ] **Ⓐ** N **1** (= *person*) pesado/a *m/f*, pelmazo/a* *m/f*; **what a ~ he is!** ¡qué hombre más pesado!, ¡es más pesado que el plomo!* **2** (= *event, task*) lata* *f*; **it's such a ~** es una lata*, es un rollo (*Sp**) **Ⓑ** VT aburrir; **to be/get ~d** aburrirse; **he's ~d to death** *or* **tears** ◇ **he's ~d stiff** está aburrido como una ostra*, está muerto de aburrimiento; **to be ~d with** estar aburrido *or* harto de

bore³ [bɔːʳ] **Ⓐ** N **1** (= *tool*) taladro *m*, barrena *f* **2** (*Geol*) sonda *f*; (*also* **~ hole**) perforación *f* **3** [*of gun*] calibre *m*; **a 12-~ shotgun** una escopeta del calibre 12 **Ⓑ** VT [+ *hole, tunnel*] hacer, perforar

boredom ['bɔːdəm] N aburrimiento *m*

boring ['bɔːrɪŋ] ADJ aburrido, pesado; **she's so ~** es muy aburrida *or* pesada

born [bɔːn] **Ⓐ** ADJ nacido; **to be ~** (*lit*) nacer; [*idea*] surgir, nacer; **I was ~ in 1990** nací en 1990; **he wasn't ~ yesterday!*** ¡no se chupa el dedo!* **Ⓑ** ADJ [*actor, leader*] nato; **he is a ~ liar** es mentiroso por naturaleza; **he's a Londoner ~ and bred** ha nacido y se ha criado en Londres, es un londinense de pura cepa; **in all my ~ days** en mi vida

-born [bɔːn] ADJ (*ending in compounds*) **British-born** británico de nacimiento

born-again ['bɔːnəˌgen] ADJ renacido, vuelto a nacer

borne [bɔːn] PP *of* **bear²**

-borne [bɔːn] ADJ (*ending in compounds*) llevado por, traído por

Borneo ['bɔːnɪəʊ] N Borneo *m*

borough ['bʌrə] N municipio *m*; (*in London, New York*) distrito *m*

borrow ['bɒrəʊ] VT pedir prestado (**from** a), tomar prestado; [+ *idea*] adoptar, apropiarse; [+ *word*] tomar (**from** de); **may I ~ your car?** ¿me prestas el coche?

borrower ['bɒrəʊəʳ] N [*of money*] prestatario/a *m/f*; (*in library*) usuario/a *m/f*

borrowing ['bɒrəʊɪŋ] N préstamo(s) *m(pl)* (**from** de)

borstal ['bɔːstl] N (*Brit*) correccional *m* de menores

Bosnia ['bɒznɪə] N Bosnia *f*

Bosnian ['bɒznɪən] ADJ, N bosnio/a *m/f*

bosom ['bʊzəm] N seno *m*, pecho *m*; **in the ~ of the family**

en el seno de la familia **➤ bosom friend** amigo/a *m/f* íntimo/a

boss [bɒs] **Ⓐ** N (*gen*) jefe/a *m/f*; (= *owner, employer*) patrón/ona *m/f*; (= *manager*) gerente *mf*; (= *foreman*) capataz *m*; [*of gang*] cerebro *m*; (*US Pol*) cacique *m*; **OK, you're the ~** de acuerdo, tú mandas **Ⓑ** VT mangonear*, dar órdenes a **Ⓒ** ADJ (*US**) chulo*
➤ boss around*, boss about (*Brit**) VT + ADV mangonear*, dar órdenes a

bossy ['bɒsɪ] ADJ (*compar* **bossier**; *superl* **bossiest**) mandón

botanic [bəˈtænɪk], **botanical** [bəˈtænɪkəl] ADJ botánico

botanist ['bɒtənɪst] N botánico/a *m/f*, botanista *mf*

botany ['bɒtənɪ] N botánica *f*

botch* [bɒtʃ] **Ⓐ** N (= *crude repair*) chapuza* *f* **Ⓑ** VT (*also* **~ up**) hacer una chapuza de*; **a ~ed job** una chapuza*

both [bəʊθ] **Ⓐ** ADJ los/las dos, ambos/as; **~ (the) boys** ambos *or* los dos chicos **Ⓑ** PRON los/las dos *mpl/fpl*, ambos/as *mpl/fpl*; **~ of them** los dos, ambos; **~ of us** nosotros dos, los dos; **we ~ went** fuimos los dos **Ⓒ** ADV a la vez; **she was ~ laughing and crying** reía y lloraba a la vez; **the book is ~ interesting and depressing** el libro es interesante y deprimente a la vez; **he ~ plays and sings** canta y además toca; **~ you and I saw it** lo vimos tanto tú como yo, lo vimos los dos

bother ['bɒðəʳ] **Ⓐ** N **1** (= *nuisance*) molestia *f*, lata* *f* **2** (= *problems*) problemas *mpl*; **I found the street without any ~** encontré la calle sin problemas; **he had a spot of ~ with the police** (*Brit**) tuvo un pequeño problema con la policía **3** (= *trouble*) molestia *f*; **it's no ~** no es ninguna molestia **Ⓑ** VT **1** (= *worry*) preocupar; (= *annoy*) molestar, fastidiar; **his leg ~s him** le duele la pierna **2** (= *inconvenience*) molestar; (= *pester*) dar la lata a*; **I'm sorry to ~ you** perdona la molestia **3** (*esp Brit*) **be ~ed: I can't be ~ed (to go)** me da pereza (ir), no tengo ganas (de ir), me da flojera (ir) (*LAm*); **"shall we stay in or go out?" — "I'm not ~ed"** —¿salimos o nos quedamos? —me da igual **Ⓒ** VI molestarse (**to do** en hacer), tomarse la molestia (**to do** de hacer); **~ about/with** molestarse *or* preocuparse por; **don't ~** no te molestes, no te preocupes; **he didn't even ~ to write** ni siquiera se molestó en escribir **Ⓓ** EXCL (*) ¡porras!*

Botswana [bɒˈtswɑːnə] N Botsuana *f*

bottle ['bɒtl] **Ⓐ** N **1** (*gen*) botella *f*; (*empty*) envase *m*; [*of ink, scent*] frasco *m*; (*baby's*) biberón *m*; ✦ IDIOM **to take to the ~*** darse a la bebida **2** (*Brit**) (= *courage*) **it takes a lot of ~ to ...** hay que tener muchas agallas para ...*; **to lose one's ~** rajarse* **Ⓑ** VT [+ *wine*] embotellar; [+ *fruit*] envasar, enfrascar **Ⓒ** CPD **➤ bottle bank** contenedor *m* de vidrio **➤ bottle opener** abrebotellas *m inv*, destapador *m* (*LAm*) **➤ bottle party** *fiesta a la que cada invitado contribuye con una botella*
➤ bottle up VT + ADV [+ *emotion*] reprimir, contener

bottled ['bɒtld] ADJ **~ beer** cerveza *f* de botella; **~ gas** gas *m* de bombona; **~ water** agua *f* embotellada

---

Use **el/un** not **la/una** before feminine nouns beginning with stressed **a** or **ha** like **agua**.

---

bottle-feed ['bɒtlˌfiːd] VT criar con biberón

bottle-green ['bɒtlˈgriːn] **Ⓐ** ADJ verde botella *inv* **Ⓑ** N verde *m* botella

bottleneck ['bɒtlnek] N (*on road*) embotellamiento *m*, atasco *m*; (*fig*) obstáculo *m*

bottom ['bɒtəm] **Ⓐ** N **1** [*of box, cup, sea, river, garden*] fondo *m*; [*of stairs, page, mountain, tree*] pie *m*; [*of foot*] planta *f*; [*of shoe*] suela *f*; [*of ship*] quilla *f*, casco *m*; **at the ~ of** [+ *page, hill, ladder*] al pie de; [+ *road*] al fondo de; **to be at the ~ of the list/class** ser el último de la lista/clase; **at ~** en el fondo; **the ~ has fallen out of the market** el mercado se ha venido abajo; **the ~ fell** *or* **dropped out of his world** se le vino el mundo abajo; **on the ~ (of)** (= *underside*) [+ *box, case etc*] en la parte inferior (de); [+ *sea, lake etc*] en el fondo (de); **~s up!*** ¡salud!; ✦ IDIOMS **he's at the ~ of it** él

está detrás de esto; **to get to the ~ of sth** llegar al fondo de algo; **from the ~ of my heart** de todo corazón
2 (= *buttocks*) trasero *m*
3 (*also* **~s**) [*of tracksuit, pyjamas*] pantalón *m*, parte *f* de abajo; [*of bikini*] braga *f*, parte *f* de abajo
Ⓑ ADJ (= *lowest*) más bajo; (= *last*) último
Ⓒ CPD ➤ **bottom gear** primera *f* (marcha) ➤ **bottom half** parte *f* de abajo, mitad *f* inferior ➤ **bottom line** (= *minimum*) mínimo *m* aceptable; (= *essential point*) lo fundamental; **the ~ line is he has to go** a fin de cuentas tenemos que despedirlo
➤ **bottom out** VI + ADV [*figures etc*] tocar fondo

bottomless ['bɒtəmlɪs] ADJ [*pit*] sin fondo, insondable; [*supply*] interminable

botulism ['bɒtjʊlɪzəm] N botulismo *m*

bough [baʊ] N rama *f*

bought [bɔːt] PT, PP *of* **buy**

bouillon cube [buːˈjɑːnˌkjuːb] N (*US*) cubito *m* de caldo

boulder ['bəʊldəʳ] N canto *m* rodado

boulevard ['buːləvɑːd] N bulevar *m*, zócalo *m* (*Mex*)

bounce [baʊns] **Ⓐ** N **1** [*of ball*] rebote *m*; [*of hair, mattress*] elasticidad *f* **2** (= *energy*) energía *f*, dinamismo *m* **Ⓑ** VT **1** [*ball*] hacer rebotar; **to ~ one's ideas off sb** exponer las ideas a algn para que dé su opinión **2** (*) [+ *cheque*] rechazar **3** (*Brit*) **I will not be ~d into it** no lo voy a hacer bajo presión, no voy a dejar que me presionen para hacerlo **Ⓒ** VI **1** [*ball*] rebotar **2** (*) [*cheque*] ser rechazado **3** (= *bound*) dar saltos
➤ **bounce back** VI + ADV recuperarse

bouncer* ['baʊnsəʳ] N gorila* *m*

bouncing ['baʊnsɪŋ] ADJ **~ baby** niño/a *m/f* sanote

bound[1] [baʊnd] **Ⓐ** N **bounds** (= *limits*) límite *m*sing; **his ambition knows no ~s** su ambición no tiene límites; **out of ~s** zona *f* prohibida; **it's out of ~s to civilians** los civiles tienen la entrada prohibida; **it is within the ~s of possibility** cabe dentro de los límites de lo posible **Ⓑ** VT limitar, rodear; **on one side it is ~ed by the park** por un lado limita *or* linda con el parque

bound[2] [baʊnd] **Ⓐ** N (= *jump*) salto *m*; **at a ~ ◇ in one ~** de un salto **Ⓑ** VI [*person, animal*] saltar; [*ball*] (re)botar; **he ~ed out of bed** se levantó de la cama de un salto

bound[3] [baʊnd] **Ⓐ** PT, PP *of* **bind**
Ⓑ ADJ **1** (= *tied*) [*prisoner*] atado; **~ hand and foot** atado de pies y manos; **the problems are ~ together** existe una estrecha relación entre los problemas
2 (= *sure*) **we are ~ to win** seguro que ganamos, estamos seguros de ganar; **he's ~ to come** es seguro que vendrá, no puede dejar de venir; **it's ~ to happen** tiene forzosamente que ocurrir
3 (= *obliged*) obligado; **I'm ~ to say that ...** me siento obligado a decir que ..., siento el deber de decir que ...; **I feel ~ to tell you that ...** me veo en la necesidad de decirte que ...

bound[4] [baʊnd] ADJ **~ for** [*train, plane*] con destino a; [*ship*] con rumbo a; **he's ~ for London** se dirige a Londres

boundary ['baʊndərɪ] N **1** (= *border*) límite *m* **2** (*Cricket*) banda *f*

boundless ['baʊndlɪs] ADJ ilimitado, sin límite

bounty ['baʊntɪ] **Ⓐ** N **1** (= *generosity*) generosidad *f*, munificencia *f* **2** (= *reward*) recompensa *f*; (*Mil*) premio *m* de enganche **Ⓑ** CPD ➤ **bounty hunter** cazarrecompensas *mf inv*

bouquet [bʊˈkeɪ] N **1** [*of flowers*] ramo *m*, ramillete *m* **2** [*of wine*] buqué *m*

Bourbon ['bʊəbən] (*Hist*) **Ⓐ** N Borbón *m* **Ⓑ** ADJ borbónico

bourbon ['bɜːbən] N (*US*) whisky *m* americano, bourbon *m*

bourgeois ['bʊəʒwɑː] ADJ, N burgués/esa *m/f*

bourgeoisie [ˌbʊəʒwɑːˈziː] N burguesía *f*

bout [baʊt] N **1** [*of illness*] ataque *m*; [*of work*] tanda *f* **2** (= *boxing match*) combate *m*, encuentro *m*

boutique [buːˈtiːk] N boutique *f*, tienda *f* de ropa

bow[1] [bəʊ] **Ⓐ** N **1** (= *weapon, also Mus*) arco *m*; **~ and**

arrow arco *m* y flechas **2** (= *knot*) lazo *m*; **to tie a ~** hacer un lazo **Ⓑ** CPD ➤ **bow legs** piernas *fpl* arqueadas ➤ **bow tie** pajarita *f* (*Sp*), corbata *f* de moño (*LAm*) ➤ **bow window** mirador *m*, ventana *f* saledizza

bow[2] [baʊ] **Ⓐ** N (= *greeting*) reverencia *f*; **to make a ~** inclinarse (**to** delante de), hacer una reverencia (**to** a); **to take a ~** salir a agradecer los aplausos, salir a saludar **Ⓑ** VT (= *lower*) [+ *head*] inclinar, bajar **Ⓒ** VI **1** (*in greeting*) inclinarse (**to** delante de), hacer una reverencia (**to** a) **2** (= *bend*) [*branch etc*] arquearse, doblarse **3** (= *yield*) inclinarse *or* ceder (**to** ante); **to ~ to the inevitable** resignarse a lo inevitable
➤ **bow down** VI + ADV (*lit, fig*) doblegarse
➤ **bow out** VI + ADV retirarse, despedirse

bow[3] [baʊ] N (*also* **~s**) proa *f*; **on the port/starboard ~** a babor/estribor ➤ **bow doors** portón *m*sing de proa

bowel ['baʊəl] N intestino *m*; **bowels** intestinos *mpl*, vientre *m*sing; (*fig*) entrañas *fpl* ➤ **bowel movement** evacuación *f* (del vientre)

bowl[1] [bəʊl] N **1** (*for soup*) plato *m* sopero; (*for washing up*) palangana *f*, barreño *m*; (*for salad*) fuente *f*, ensaladera *f*; (= *large cup*) tazón *m*, cuenco *m*; [*of lavatory*] taza *f*; [*of spoon*] cuenco *m* **2** (*US*) (= *stadium*) estadio *m*

bowl[2] [bəʊl] **Ⓐ** N **1** (= *ball*) bola *f*, bocha *f* **2** **~s** (= *tenpin bowling*) bolos *mpl*, boliche *m*; (*Brit*) (*on green*) bochas *fpl* **Ⓑ** VT (*Cricket*) [+ *ball*] lanzar, arrojar; (*also* **~ out**) [+ *batsman*] eliminar **Ⓒ** VI **1** (*Cricket*) lanzar **2 to go ~ing** (*tenpin*) ir a jugar a los bolos *or* al boliche; (*Brit*) (*on green*) ir a jugar a las bochas

bow-legged ['bəʊˈlegɪd] ADJ [*person*] estevado, que tiene las piernas en arco

bowler[1] ['bəʊləʳ] N **1** (*Cricket, Rounders etc*) lanzador(a) *m/f* **2** (*esp US*) (= *bowls player*) jugador(a) *m/f* de bolos

bowler[2] ['bəʊləʳ] N (*Brit*) (*also* **~ hat**) bombín *m*, sombrero hongo *m*

bowling ['bəʊlɪŋ] **Ⓐ** N **1** (*also* **tenpin ~**) bolos *mpl*, boliche *m* **2** (*on green*) bochas *fpl* **3** (*Cricket*) lanzamiento *m* **Ⓑ** CPD ➤ **bowling alley** bolera *f*, boliche *m* ➤ **bowling green** campo *m* de bochas

box[1] [bɒks] **Ⓐ** N **1** (*gen*) caja *f*; (= *large*) cajón *m*; (*for jewels*) estuche *m*
2 (*in theatre, stadium*) palco *m*
3 the ~ (*esp Brit**) (= *television*) la tele*
4 (*on form to be filled in*) casilla *f*; (*surrounding table, diagram*) recuadro *m*
5 (*Sport*) (= *protection*) protector *m*; (*Ftbl**) (= *penalty area*) área *f*

> Use **el/un** not **la/una** before feminine nouns beginning with stressed **a** or **ha** like **área**.

6 (*also* **post-office ~**) apartado *m* de correos, casilla *f* de correo (*LAm*)
Ⓑ VT poner en una caja
Ⓒ CPD ➤ **box file** archivador *m*, archivo *m* ➤ **box junction** (*Brit*) cruce *m* con parrilla ➤ **box kite** cometa en forma de cubo, abierto por dos lados ➤ **box lunch** (*US*) bocadillos *o* comida preparada para llevar al colegio, a la oficina, a una excursión etc ➤ **box number** apartado *m* de correos, casilla *f* de correo (*LAm*) ➤ **box office** taquilla *f*, boletería *f* (*LAm*) ➤ **box seat** (*US*) asiento *m* de palco
➤ **box in** VT + ADV [+ *car*] encajonar; **to get ~ed in** (*Sport*) encontrarse tapado; **to feel ~ed in** sentirse acorralado

box[2] [bɒks] **Ⓐ** VT **to ~ sb's ears** guantear a algn, dar un mamporro a algn* **Ⓑ** VI boxear

box[3] [bɒks] N (*Bot*) boj *m*

boxcar ['bɒkskɑːʳ] N (*US Rail*) furgón *m*

boxer ['bɒksəʳ] N (= *person*) boxeador(a) *m/f*; (= *dog*) bóxer *mf* ➤ **boxer shorts** calzones *mpl*

boxing ['bɒksɪŋ] N boxeo *m*, box *m* (*LAm*) ➤ **Boxing Day** (*Brit*) día *m* de San Esteban (*26 de diciembre*) ➤ **boxing gloves** guantes *mpl* de boxeo *or* (*SC*) box ➤ **boxing match** combate *m* de boxeo *or* (*SC*) box ➤ **boxing ring**

cuadrilátero *m*, ring *m*

box-office ['bɒksɒfɪs] ADJ taquillero ➤ **box-office success** éxito *m* de taquilla

boxroom ['bɒksrʊm] N (*Brit*) trastero *m*

boy [bɔɪ] N (= *small*) niño *m*; (= *young man*) muchacho *m*, chico *m*, joven *m* (*LAm*); (= *son*) hijo *m*; **he's out with the ~s** ha salido con los amigos ➤ **boy band** (*Brit*) grupo de música pop masculino ➤ **boy scout** (muchacho *m* or niño *m*) explorador *m*

boycott ['bɔɪkɒt] Ⓐ N boicot *m* Ⓑ VT boicotear

boyfriend ['bɔɪfrend] N amigo *m*; (= *fiancé etc*) novio *m*, pololo *m* (*Chi**)

boyhood ['bɔɪhʊd] N niñez *f*; (*as teenager*) adolescencia *f*

boyish ['bɔɪɪʃ] ADJ [*appearance, manner*] juvenil; (= *tomboyish*) (*of girl*) de muchacho, de chico; (*of small girl*) de niño

bozo** ['bəʊzəʊ] N (*esp US*) imbécil* *mf*

bra [brɑ:] N sostén *m*, sujetador *m*, corpiño *m* (*Arg*)

brace [breɪs] Ⓐ N **1** (*Constr*) (= *strengthening piece*) abrazadera *f*, refuerzo *m*; (= *tool*) berbiquí *m* **2** (*Typ*) corchete *m* **3** (*pl inv*) (= *pair*) par *m* **4** (*also ~s*) (*for teeth*) corrector *msing*, aparato *msing* **5 braces** (*Brit*) (*for trousers*) tirantes *mpl*, suspensores *mpl* (*LAm*) Ⓑ VT (= *strengthen*) **to ~ o.s.** prepararse (*para resistir una sacudida etc*); (*fig*) fortalecer su ánimo; **to ~ o.s. for** prepararse para

bracelet ['breɪslɪt] N pulsera *f*, brazalete *m*

bracing ['breɪsɪŋ] ADJ [*air, activity*] vigorizante

bracken ['brækən] N helecho *m*

bracket ['brækɪt] Ⓐ N **1** (= *support*) soporte *m*; (= *angle bracket*) escuadra *f*; (*Archit*) ménsula *f*, repisa *f* **2** (*Typ*) (*usu pl*) (*round*) (*Brit*) paréntesis *m inv*; (*also* **square ~**) corchete *m*; (*angled*) corchete *m* (*agudo*); (*curly*) corchete *m*, llave *f*; **in ~s** (*Brit*) entre paréntesis **3** (= *group*) clase *f*, categoría *f* Ⓑ VT **1** (*Constr*) (= *join by brackets*) asegurar con soportes/ escuadras **2** (*Typ*) poner entre paréntesis/corchetes **3** (*also ~ together*) agrupar (**with** con), poner juntos

brackish ['brækɪʃ] ADJ [*water*] salobre

brag [bræg] Ⓐ VI jactarse, fanfarronear (**about, of** de; **that** de que) Ⓑ N (= *boast*) fanfarronada *f*, bravata *f*

braid [breɪd] Ⓐ N **1** (*on dress, uniform*) galón *m* **2** (*esp US*) [*of hair etc*] trenza *f* Ⓑ VT (*esp US*) [*+ hair, etc*] trenzar, hacer trenzas en

Braille [breɪl] N Braille *m*

brain [breɪn] Ⓐ N **1** cerebro *m*; ✦ IDIOMS **to get one's ~ into gear*** poner la mente a carburar*; **on the ~: he's got politics on the ~** tiene la política metida en la cabeza **2 brains** (*Anat, Culin*) sesos *mpl*; (*) (= *intelligence*) inteligencia *fsing*, cabeza *fsing*; **he's got ~s** es muy listo, tiene mucha cabeza; **he's the ~s of the family** es el listo de la familia Ⓑ VT (**) romper la crisma a* Ⓒ CPD ➤ **brain damage** lesión *f* cerebral *or* medular ➤ **brain death** muerte *f* clínica *or* cerebral ➤ **brain drain** fuga *f* de cerebros ➤ **brain scan** exploración *f* cerebral mediante escáner ➤ **brain teaser** rompecabezas *m inv* ➤ **brain tumour, brain tumor** (*US*) tumor *m* cerebral

brainchild ['breɪntʃaɪld] N parto *m* del ingenio, invento *m*

brain-dead ['breɪn,ded] ADJ (*Med*) clínicamente muerto; (*) (= *stupid*) subnormal*, tarado*

brainless ['breɪnlɪs] ADJ estúpido, tonto

brainstorm ['breɪnstɔ:m] Ⓐ N **1** (*Brit*) (= *aberration*) ataque *m* de locura, frenesí *m* **2** (*US*) (= *good idea*) idea *f* luminosa*, idea *f* genial* Ⓑ VI hacer una puesta en común de ideas y sugerencias

brainstorming ['breɪnstɔ:mɪŋ] N puesta *f* en común, brainstorming *m*

brainwash ['breɪnwɒʃ] VT lavar el cerebro a; **to ~ sb into doing sth** convencer a algn para que haga algo

brainwave ['breɪnweɪv] N **1** (*Brit**) (= *good idea*) idea *f* luminosa*, idea *f* genial* **2 brainwaves** (*Med*) ondas *fpl* cerebrales

brainy* ['breɪnɪ] ADJ (*compar* **brainier**; *superl* **brainiest**) listo, inteligente

braise [breɪz] VT cocer a fuego lento, estofar

brake [breɪk] Ⓐ N freno *m*; **to put the ~s on** (*Aut*) frenar; (*fig*) poner freno a Ⓑ VI, VT frenar Ⓒ CPD ➤ **brake block** pastilla *f* de frenos ➤ **brake fluid** líquido *m* de frenos ➤ **brake light** luz *f* de freno ➤ **brake pad** pastilla *f* de frenos ➤ **brake pedal** pedal *m* de freno

bramble ['bræmbl] N zarza *f*

bran [bræn] N salvado *m* ➤ **bran tub** (*Brit*) sorteo *m* de regalos

branch [brɑ:ntʃ] Ⓐ N **1** [*of tree, family, science*] rama *f*; [*of industry*] ramo *m*; [*of government, police*] sección *f* **2** [*of company, bank*] sucursal *f* **3** (*in road, railway, pipe*) ramal *m*; [*of river*] brazo *m* Ⓑ VI [*road etc*] bifurcarse Ⓒ CPD ➤ **branch line** ramal *m*, línea *f* secundaria ➤ **branch office** sucursal *f* ➤ **branch off** VI + ADV **a small road ~es off to the right** hay una carretera pequeña que sale hacia la derecha; **we ~ed off before reaching Madrid** tomamos un desvío antes de llegar a Madrid ➤ **branch out** VI + ADV extenderse

brand [brænd] Ⓐ N **1** (*Comm*) marca *f* (de fábrica) **2** (*Agr*) (= *mark*) marca *f*; (= *iron*) hierro *m* de marcar **3** (= *burning wood*) tizón *m*, tea *f* Ⓑ VT **1** [*+ cattle*] marcar (con hierro candente) **2** (*fig*) **to be ~ed as a liar** ser tildado de mentiroso **3 ~ed goods** (*Brit*) artículos *mpl* de marca Ⓒ CPD ➤ **brand image** imagen *f* de marca ➤ **brand name** nombre *m* de marca

brandish ['brændɪʃ] VT [*+ weapon*] blandir

brand-name goods [,brændneɪm'gʊdz] NPL (*US*) artículos *mpl* de marca

brand-new ['bænd'nju:] ADJ [*car, motorbike*] salido de fábrica, flamante; [*house, sofa*] completamente nuevo; [*TV series*] nuevo

brandy ['brændɪ] N coñac *m*, brandy *m*

brash [bræʃ] ADJ (*compar* **~er**; *superl* **~est**) (= *over-confident*) presuntuoso

brass [brɑ:s] Ⓐ N (= *metal*) latón *m*; **the ~** (*Mus*) los metales Ⓑ CPD (= *made of brass*) (hecho) de latón ➤ **brass band** banda *f* de metal ➤ **brass knuckles** (*US*) puño *msing* de hierro ➤ **brass neck*** cara(dura)* *f*, valor *m* ➤ **brass rubbing** (= *art, object*) calco *m* de plancha sepulcral (de latón) ➤ **the brass section** (*Mus*) los metales ➤ **brass tacks** ✦ IDIOM **to get down to ~ tacks*** ir al grano*

brat* [bræt] N mocoso/a* *m/f*

bravado [brə'vɑ:dəʊ] N bravatas *fpl*, baladronadas *fpl*; **out of sheer ~** de puro bravucón

brave [breɪv] Ⓐ ADJ (*compar* **~r**; *superl* **~st**) valiente, valeroso; **be ~!** ¡sé valiente!; ✦ IDIOM **as ~ as a lion** más fiero que un león Ⓑ N (= *Native American*) guerrero *m* Ⓒ VT [*+ weather*] afrontar, hacer frente a; [*+ death*] desafiar

bravely ['breɪvlɪ] ADV valientemente, con valor; **she smiled ~** sonrió valiente *or* valientemente

bravery ['breɪvərɪ] N valentía *f*, valor *m*

bravo ['brɑ:'vəʊ] EXCL ¡bravo!, ¡olé!

brawl [brɔ:l] Ⓐ N pelea *f*, reyerta *f* Ⓑ VI pelear, pegarse

brawn [brɔ:n] N **1** (= *strength*) fuerza *f* muscular **2** (*Brit*) (= *meat dish*) carne *f* en gelatina

brawny ['brɔ:nɪ] ADJ (*compar* **brawnier**; *superl* **brawniest**) fornido, musculoso

bray [breɪ] **Ⓐ** N [of ass] rebuzno m; (= laugh) carcajada f **Ⓑ** VI [ass] rebuznar

brazen ['breɪzn] **Ⓐ** ADJ descarado **Ⓑ** VT **to ~ it out** echar cara (a la situación)

brazier ['breɪzɪəʳ] N (for heating) brasero m; (US) (= grill) barbacoa f

Brazil [brə'zɪl] N Brasil m ➤ **Brazil nut** nuez f del Brasil

Brazilian [brə'zɪlɪən] ADJ, N brasileño/a m/f

breach [briːtʃ] **Ⓐ** N **1** (= violation) [of law] violación f, infracción f **2** (in wall, also Mil) brecha f **3** (= estrangement) ruptura f **Ⓑ** VT **1** [+ defences, wall] abrir brecha en **2 to ~ security** infringir las medidas de seguridad **Ⓒ** CPD ➤ **breach of confidence** abuso m de confianza ➤ **breach of contract** incumplimiento m de contrato ➤ **breach of security** violación f de seguridad ➤ **breach of the peace** perturbación f del orden público

bread [bred] **Ⓐ** N **1** (= food) pan m; **~ and butter** pan m con mantequilla; ✦ IDIOM **to know which side one's ~ is buttered (on)** saber dónde aprieta el zapato **2** (**) (= money) pasta* f, lana f (LAm*), plata f (LAm*) **Ⓑ** CPD ➤ **bread bin** panera f

bread-and-butter ['bredən'bʌtəʳ] ADJ [issues, needs] básico, primario

breadboard ['bredbɔːd] N tabla f para cortar el pan

breadbox ['bredbɒks] N (US) panera f

breadcrumbs ['bredkrʌmz] NPL pan m sing rallado; **fish in ~** pescado m empanado

breadknife ['brednaɪf] N (pl **breadknives**) cuchillo m para cortar pan

breadline ['bredlaɪn] N (US) cola f del pan; ✦ IDIOM **on the ~** (Brit) en la miseria

breadth [bretθ] N **1** (= width) anchura f, ancho m; **to be two metres in ~** tener dos metros de ancho **2** [of experience, knowledge] amplitud f

breadwinner ['bred,wɪnəʳ] N sostén m de la familia

break [breɪk] (vb: pt **broke**; pp **broken**) **Ⓐ** N **1** (= fracture) rotura f; (in bone) fractura f; (in relationship) ruptura f; **to make a ~ with** romper con **2** (= gap) (in wall etc) abertura f, brecha f; **a ~ in the clouds** un claro entre las nubes **3** (= pause) (in conversation) interrupción f, pausa f; (in journey) descanso m, pausa f; (= stop) parada f; (= holiday) vacaciones fpl; (= rest) descanso m; (= tea break) descanso m para tomar el té; (Brit Scol) recreo m; **give me a ~!** ¡dame un respiro!; (impatient) ¡déjame, anda!; **to have** or **take a ~** descansar, tomarse un descanso; **to take a weekend ~** hacer una escapada de fin de semana; **with a ~ in her voice** con la voz entrecortada; **a ~ in the weather** un cambio del tiempo; **without a ~** sin descanso or descansar **4** (*) (= chance) oportunidad f; **to give sb a ~** dar una oportunidad a algn **5** (= break-out) fuga f; **to make a ~ for it** tratar de fugarse **6 at ~ of day** al amanecer **7** (Tennis) ruptura f; **two ~s of service** dos servicios rotos **8** (Billiards, Snooker) tacada f, serie f **Ⓑ** VT **1** (= smash) [+ glass etc] romper; [+ branch, stick] romper, quebrar (LAm); **I'm not going to ~ my back to finish it today** no me voy a matar para terminarlo hoy; **the ship broke its back** el barco se partió por la mitad; **to ~ one's leg** romperse la pierna; ✦ IDIOMS **to ~ the back of sth** (Brit*) (= do the difficult part) hacer la peor parte de algo; (= do the main part) hacer lo más gordo de algo*, hacer la mayor parte de algo; **to ~ sb's heart** romper or partir el corazón a algn; **to ~ the ice** romper el hielo **2** (= surpass) [+ record] batir, superar **3** (= fail to observe) [+ law, rule] violar, quebrantar; **he broke his word/promise** faltó a su palabra/promesa **4** (= weaken, destroy) [+ spirits] quebrantar, quebrar (LAm); [+ strike] romper, quebrar (LAm); [+ habit] perder; [+ person (morally)] abatir, vencer **5** (= interrupt) [+ silence, spell] romper; [+ journey] interrumpir; [+ electrical circuit] cortar, interrumpir **6** (= soften) [+ fall] amortiguar **7** (= disclose) [+ news] comunicar (**to** a)

8 (= leave) **to ~ camp** levantar el campamento; **to ~ cover** salir al descubierto; **to ~ ranks** romper filas **Ⓒ** VI **1** (= smash) [window, glass] romperse **2** (= be fractured) [chair] romperse, partirse; [branch, twig] romperse, quebrarse (LAm); (fig) [heart] romperse, partirse **3** (= stop working) [machine] estropearse **4** (= arrive) [dawn, day] apuntar, rayar; [news] darse a conocer; [story] revelarse; [storm] estallar **5** (= give way) [spirits] quebrantarse; [weather] cambiar; [boy's voice] mudarse **6** (= pause) **let's ~ for lunch** vamos a hacer un descanso para comer **7 to ~ free** (from chains, ropes etc) soltarse; (fig) liberarse; **to ~ loose** desatarse, escaparse **8 to ~ even** llegar a cubrir los gastos **9** (Billiards, Snooker) abrir el juego **Ⓓ** CPD ➤ **break dancing** break m

➤ **break away** VI + ADV **1** [piece] desprenderse, separarse **2** (Ftbl etc) escapar, despegarse **3 to ~ away from** [+ guard] evadirse de; [+ group] separarse de
➤ **break down Ⓐ** VT + ADV **1** (= destroy) [+ door] echar abajo, derribar; [+ resistance] vencer, acabar con; [+ suspicion] disipar **2** (= analyse) [+ figures] analizar, desglosar; [+ substance] descomponer **Ⓑ** VI + ADV [machine] estropearse, malograrse (Per), descomponerse (LAm); [vehicle] averiarse, descomponerse (LAm); [person] (under pressure) derrumbarse; (from emotion) romper or echarse a llorar; [health] quebrantarse; [talks] fracasar; [chemicals, waste] descomponerse
➤ **break in Ⓐ** VT + ADV [+ horse] domar, amansar; [+ recruit] formar; [+ shoes] domar, acostumbrarse a **Ⓑ** VI + ADV **1** [burglar] forzar la entrada **2** (= interrupt) interrumpir
➤ **break into** VI + PREP **1** [+ house] entrar a robar en, allanar (Sp); [+ safe] forzar; **to ~ into a new market** introducirse en un mercado nuevo **2** (= start) echar a, romper a; **to ~ into a run** echar or empezar a correr; **to ~ into song** ponerse a cantar
➤ **break off Ⓐ** VT + ADV **1** [+ piece] partir **2** [+ engagement, talks] romper **Ⓑ** VI + ADV **1** [piece of rock, ice, handle] desprenderse; [twig] desgajarse **2** (= pause) interrumpirse, pararse
➤ **break out Ⓐ** VI + ADV **1** [prisoners] fugarse, escaparse **2** (= start) [fire, war, epidemic] estallar; [discussion, fighting, argument] producirse **3** (Physiol) **he broke out in a rash** le salió un sarpullido; **he broke out in a sweat** quedó cubierto de sudor **Ⓑ** VT + ADV [+ champagne] descorchar
➤ **break through Ⓐ** VI + ADV [sun] salir **Ⓑ** VI + PREP [+ defences, barrier] atravesar
➤ **break up Ⓐ** VT + ADV **1** [+ crowd] dispersar, disolver; [+ meeting, organization] disolver; [+ gang] desarticular; [+ marriage] deshacer; [+ estate] parcelar; [+ industry] desconcentrar; [+ fight] intervenir en; **~ it up!** ¡basta ya! **2** (US*) (= cause to laugh) hacer reír a carcajadas **Ⓑ** VI + ADV **1** [ship] hacerse pedazos; [ice] deshacerse **2** (= separate) [partnership] deshacerse, disolverse; [marriage] deshacerse; [couple] separarse; [crowd, clouds] dispersarse **3** (Brit Scol) [pupils] empezar las vacaciones; [session] levantarse, terminar; **school ~s up tomorrow** las clases terminan mañana **4** (US*) (= laugh) reír a carcajadas

breakable ['breɪkəbl] **Ⓐ** ADJ (= brittle) quebradizo; (= fragile) frágil **Ⓑ** N **breakables** objetos mpl frágiles

breakage ['breɪkɪdʒ] N (= act of breaking) rotura f; (= thing broken) destrozo m

breakaway ['breɪkəweɪ] ADJ [group etc] disidente ➤ **breakaway state** estado m independizado

breakdown ['breɪkdaʊn] **Ⓐ** N **1** (= failure) [of system, electricity] fallo m (Sp), falla f (LAm); [of negotiations, marriage] fracaso m; [of vehicle, machine] avería f, descompostura f (LAm); [of talks] ruptura f **2** (Med) colapso m, crisis f inv nerviosa **3** (= analysis) [of numbers] análisis m inv, desglose m; (Chem) descomposición f; (= report) informe m detallado **Ⓑ** CPD ➤ **breakdown service** (Brit) servicio m de asistencia en carretera ➤ **breakdown truck, breakdown van** (Brit) (camión m) grúa f

breaker ['breɪkəʳ] N (= wave) ola f grande

breakfast ['brekfəst] **Ⓐ** N desayuno m; **to have ~** desayunar **Ⓑ** VI desayunar; **to ~ on eggs** desayunar huevos

ⓒ CPD ➤ **breakfast cereal** cereales *mpl* para el desayuno ➤ **breakfast TV** tele(visión) *f* matinal

break-in ['breɪkˌɪn] N robo *m* (con allanamiento de morada)

breaking ['breɪkɪŋ] CPD ➤ **breaking and entering** violación *f* de domicilio, allanamiento *m* de morada ➤ **breaking news** noticia *fsing* de última hora ➤ **breaking point** (*lit*) punto *m* de máxima tensión tolerable; [*of person*] límite *m*; **to reach ~ point** llegar al límite

break-out ['breɪkaʊt] N fuga *f*, evasión *f*

breakthrough ['breɪkθruː] N adelanto *m* muy importante

break-up ['breɪkʌp] N [*of partnership*] disolución *f*; [*of couple*] separación *f*

breakwater ['breɪkˌwɔːtə'] N rompeolas *m inv*

breast [brest] N (= *chest*) pecho *m*; [*of woman*] seno *m*, pecho *m*; (*Culin*) [*of bird*] pechuga *f*; ✦ IDIOM **to make a clean ~ of it** confesarlo todo, descargar la conciencia ➤ **breast cancer** cáncer *m* de mama ➤ **breast milk** leche *f* materna ➤ **breast pocket** bolsillo *m* de pecho

breast-feed ['brestfiːd] (*pt, pp* **breast-fed**) VT amamantar, criar a los pechos

breast-feeding ['brestˌfiːdɪŋ] N amamantamiento *m*, cría *f* a los pechos

breaststroke ['breststrəʊk] N braza *f* de pecho; **to swim** or **do the ~** nadar a la braza

breath [breθ] **ⓐ** N 1 (*lit*) (= *respiration*) aliento *m*; **to have bad ~** tener mal aliento; **to get one's ~ back** recobrar el aliento *or* la respiración; **to hold one's ~** (*lit*) contener la respiración; **the whole world is holding its ~** el mundo entero está en vilo; **"he said he would be here"** — **"well, I wouldn't hold your ~"** —dijo que vendría —sí, pues yo lo esperaría sentado*; **to be/get out of ~** estar/quedar sin aliento; **without pausing for ~** sin detenerse ni un momento para recobrar el aliento *or* la respiración; **in the same** or **next ~** acto seguido; **he took a deep ~** respiró hondo; **to take one's ~ away** dejar a uno sin habla; **he muttered something under his ~** dijo algo entre dientes *or* en voz baja 2 (= *puff*) soplo *m*; **we went out for a ~ of fresh air** salimos a tomar el (aire) fresco **ⓑ** CPD ➤ **breath test** (*Aut*) prueba *f* de la alcoholemia, prueba *f* del alcohol

breathalyse, breathalyze ['breθəlaɪz] VT someter a la prueba de la alcoholemia *or* del alcohol

Breathalyser®, **Breathalyzer**® ['breθəlaɪzə'] N alcoholímetro *m* ➤ **Breathalyser test** prueba *f* de la alcoholemia, prueba *f* del alcohol

breathe [briːð] **ⓐ** VT 1 [+ *air*] respirar; ✦ IDIOMS **to ~ new life into sth** infundir nueva vida a algo; **to ~ one's last** exhalar el último suspiro 2 (= *utter*) **to ~ a sigh** suspirar, dar un suspiro; **I won't ~ a word** no diré nada *or* palabra **ⓑ** VI [*person, animal*] respirar; (*noisily*) resollar; [*wine*] respirar; [*fabric, garment*] transpirar, dejar pasar el aire; **now we can ~ again** ahora podemos respirar tranquilos ➤ **breathe in** VT + ADV, VI + ADV aspirar ➤ **breathe out** **ⓐ** VT + ADV exhalar **ⓑ** VI + ADV espirar

breather* ['briːðə'] N respiro *m*, descanso *m*; **to take a ~** tomarse un respiro *or* descanso

breathing ['briːðɪŋ] N respiración *f* ➤ **breathing space** respiro *m*

breathless ['breθlɪs] ADJ **he arrived ~** llegó sin aliento, llegó jadeando; **she was ~ with excitement** la emoción la había dejado sin aliento; **it leaves you ~** corta la respiración; **at a ~ pace** a un ritmo acelerado

breathlessness ['breθlɪsnɪs] N falta *f* de aliento, dificultad *f* al respirar

breathtaking ['breθˌteɪkɪŋ] ADJ [*sight*] imponente, impresionante; [*speed*] vertiginoso

breath-test ['breθtest] VT someter a la prueba de la alcoholemia *or* del alcohol

bred [bred] PT, PP *of* **breed**

-bred [bred] ADJ (*ending in compounds*) criado, educado; **well-bred** bien educado, formal

breed [briːd] (*vb: pt, pp* **bred**) **ⓐ** N raza *f* **ⓑ** VT [+ *animals*] criar; [+ *hate, suspicion*] crear, engendrar **ⓒ** VI [*animals*] reproducirse, procrear

breeder ['briːdə'] N (= *person*) criador(a) *m/f*

breeding ['briːdɪŋ] **ⓐ** N 1 (*Bio*) reproducción *f*; [*of stock*] cría *f* 2 (*also* **good ~**) educación *f*, crianza *f* **ⓑ** CPD ➤ **breeding ground** (*fig*) caldo *m* de cultivo (**of, for** de, para); ➤ **breeding season** época *f* de reproducción

breeze [briːz] N (= *wind*) brisa *f*; ✦ IDIOMS **it's a ~*** es coser y cantar*; **to do sth in a ~** (*US**) hacer algo con los ojos cerrados **ⓑ** VI **to ~ in** entrar como si nada; **to ~ through sth*** hacer algo con los ojos cerrados

breeze-block ['briːzblɒk] N (*Brit*) bovedilla *f*

breezy ['briːzɪ] ADJ (*compar* **breezier**; *superl* **breeziest**) 1 [*day, weather*] de viento 2 [*manner*] (= *cheerful*) animado, alegre; (= *nonchalant*) despreocupado

brevity ['brevɪtɪ] N (= *shortness*) brevedad *f*; (= *conciseness*) concisión *f*; ✦ PROV **~ is the soul of wit** lo bueno si breve dos veces bueno

brew [bruː] **ⓐ** N [*of beer*] variedad *f* (de cerveza); [*of tea, herbs*] infusión *f* **ⓑ** VT [+ *beer*] elaborar; [+ *tea*] hacer, preparar **ⓒ** VI 1 [*beer*] elaborarse; [*tea*] hacerse 2 [*storm*] avecinarse; **there's trouble ~ing** algo se está tramando

brewer ['bruːə'] N cervecero/a *m/f*

brewery ['bruːərɪ] N cervecería *f*, fábrica *f* de cerveza

bribe [braɪb] **ⓐ** N soborno *m*, mordida *f* (*CAm, Mex**), coima *f* (*And, SC**); **to take a ~** dejarse sobornar (**from** por) **ⓑ** VT sobornar, comprar*; **to ~ sb to do sth** sobornar a algn para que haga algo

bribery ['braɪbərɪ] N soborno *m*, mordida *f* (*CAm, Mex**), coima *f* (*And, SC**)

brick [brɪk] **ⓐ** N 1 (*Constr*) ladrillo *m*, tabique *m* (*Mex*); **~s and mortar** construcción *f*, edificios *mpl* 2 (*Brit*) (= *toy*) cubo *m* **ⓑ** CPD ➤ **brick wall** pared *f* de ladrillos; ✦ IDIOM **to beat one's head against a ~ wall** esforzarse en balde

brick-built ['brɪkbɪlt] ADJ construido de ladrillos

bricklayer ['brɪkˌleɪə'] N albañil *mf*

brickwork ['brɪkwɜːk] N enladrillado *m*, ladrillos *mpl*

bridal ['braɪdl] ADJ nupcial

bride [braɪd] N novia *f*; **the ~ and groom** los novios

bridegroom ['braɪdgrʊm] N novio *m*

bridesmaid ['braɪdzmeɪd] N ≈ dama *f* de honor

bride-to-be [ˌbraɪdtə'biː] (*pl* **brides-to-be**) N novia *f* (antes de casarse); **his ~** su futura esposa

bridge¹ [brɪdʒ] **ⓐ** N 1 (*gen*) puente *m* (*also Mus*) 2 (*Naut*) puente *m* de mando 3 [*of nose*] caballete *m*; [*of spectacles, false teeth*] puente *m* **ⓑ** VT **to ~ a gap** llenar un vacío **ⓒ** CPD ➤ **bridge building** (= *reconciliation*) restablecimiento *m* de relaciones

bridge² [brɪdʒ] N (*Cards*) bridge *m*

bridging loan ['brɪdʒɪŋˌləʊn] N (*Brit*) crédito *m* puente

bridle ['braɪdl] **ⓐ** N brida *f*, freno *m* **ⓑ** VT (= *put bridle on*) [+ *horse*] poner la brida a **ⓒ** VI picarse, ofenderse (**at** por) **ⓓ** CPD ➤ **bridle path** camino *m* de herradura

brief [briːf] **ⓐ** ADJ (*compar* **~er**; *superl* **~est**) 1 (= *short*) [*visit, period, career*] breve, corto; [*glimpse, moment*] breve 2 (= *concise*) breve; **in ~** en resumen, en suma 3 (= *skimpy*) [*shorts etc*] diminuto, breve **ⓑ** N 1 (*Jur*) escrito *m*; ✦ IDIOM **I hold no ~ for those who ...** no soy partidario de los que ..., no abogo por los que ... 2 (= *instructions, remit*) instrucciones *fpl* 3 **briefs** (*man's*) calzoncillos *mpl*, slip *m*, calzones *mpl* (*LAm*); (*woman's*) bragas *fpl* (*Sp*), calzones *mpl* (*LAm*) **ⓒ** VT 1 (*Jur, Mil*) (= *instruct*) dar instrucciones a 2 (= *inform, prepare*) informar (**on** sobre)

briefcase ['briːfkeɪs] N cartera *f*, maletín *m*

briefing ['briːfɪŋ] N sesión *f* informativa; (*written*) informe *m*

briefly ['briːflɪ] ADV 1 [*speak, reply, pause*] brevemente; **she visited us ~** nos hizo una breve *or* corta visita; **I wondered ~ if he were lying** por un momento me pregunté si no estaría mintiendo

2 (= *in brief*) en pocas palabras, en resumen

brigade [brɪˈɡeɪd] N (*Mil*) brigada *f*; (*fire etc*) cuerpo *m*

brigadier [ˌbrɪɡəˈdɪəʳ] N general *mf* de brigada

bright [braɪt] Ⓐ ADJ (*compar* ~**er**; *superl* ~**est**) **1** [*light, sun, reflection*] brillante, luminoso; [*star, metal, eyes*] brillante; [*fire*] luminoso; [*uniform, bird, flower*] lleno de colorido; [*colour*] fuerte, vivo
2 (= *sunny*) [*day, weather*] radiante, soleado; [*room, house*] luminoso, con mucha luz; **a ~, sunny day** un día de sol radiante; **the outlook is ~er tomorrow** (*Met*) la previsión meteorológica para mañana es que hará mejor tiempo
3 (= *cheerful*) [*person*] alegre, animado; [*face, expression, smile*] radiante; ✦ IDIOM **to look on the ~ side** ver el lado positivo de las cosas
4 (= *clever*) [*person*] listo, inteligente; [*idea*] brillante, genial
5 (= *promising*) [*future*] brillante, prometedor; [*outlook, prospects, start*] prometedor
Ⓑ ADV **to get up ~ and early** levantarse tempranito
Ⓒ CPD ➤ **bright lights he was attracted by the ~ lights of the big city** (*fig*) se sentía atraído por las luces de neón de la gran ciudad ➤ **bright spark*** (*Brit iro*) listo/a *m/f*

brighten [ˈbraɪtn] (*also* ~ **up**) Ⓐ VT **1** (= *make lighter*) [+ *room*] dar más luz a, iluminar más **2** (= *make more cheerful*) [+ *room*] alegrar Ⓑ VI **1** [*person*] animarse, alegrarse **2** [*weather*] despejarse; [*prospects*] mejorar

brightly [ˈbraɪtlɪ] ADV **1** (= *brilliantly*) [*shine*] intensamente, con intensidad; [*burn*] con intensidad; ~ **lit** intensamente iluminado **2** (= *vividly*) ~ **coloured flowers** flores *fpl* de colores vivos; ~ **patterned shawls** mantones *mpl* con unos diseños llamativos **3** (= *cheerily*) [*smile, say*] alegremente

brightness [ˈbraɪtnɪs] Ⓐ N **1** [*of light, sun, eyes, metal*] brillo *m*, resplandor *m*; [*of colour*] viveza *f* **2** (= *cheerfulness*) alegría *f*, animación *f* **3** (= *cleverness*) inteligencia *f* Ⓑ CPD ➤ **brightness control** botón *m* de ajuste del brillo

brilliance [ˈbrɪljəns] N **1** [*of light*] resplandor *m*, brillo *m*; [*of colour*] luminosidad *f* **2** (= *cleverness*) brillantez *f*, genialidad *f*

brilliant [ˈbrɪljənt] ADJ **1** [*sunshine*] resplandeciente, radiante; [*light*] brillante; [*colour*] brillante, luminoso
2 (= *clever*) [*person, idea, mind*] brillante, genial
3 (= *outstanding*) [*career, future*] brillante; [*success, victory*] rotundo **4** (*esp Brit**) (= *wonderful*) [*book, film, restaurant*] genial*, buenísimo; **we had a ~ time in Spain** lo pasamos fenomenal *or* genial en España*; **she's ~ with children** se le dan fenomenal los niños*; **brilliant!** ¡fantástico!, ¡genial!*

brilliantly [ˈbrɪljəntlɪ] ADV **1** (= *brightly*) [*shine*] intensamente, con intensidad **2** (= *superbly*) [*play, perform, act*] brillantemente; [*written, executed*] con brillantez; **the strategy worked ~** la estrategia funcionó a la perfección

Brillo pad ® [ˈbrɪləʊˌpæd] N estropajo *m* de aluminio

brim [brɪm] Ⓐ N [*of cup*] borde *m*; [*of hat*] ala *f*

> Use **el/un** not **la/una** before feminine nouns beginning with stressed **a** or **ha** like **ala**.

Ⓑ VI (*also* ~ **over**) rebosar, desbordarse (**with** de)

brimful [ˈbrɪmˈfʊl] ADJ lleno hasta el borde

brine [braɪn] N (*for preserving*) salmuera *f*

bring [brɪŋ] (*pt, pp* **brought**) VT **1** [+ *news, luck etc*] traer; [+ *person*] llevar, conducir; ~ **it over here** tráelo para acá; ~ **it closer** acércalo; **to ~ sth to an end** terminar con algo
2 (= *cause*) traer; **to ~ pressure to bear (on)** ejercer presión (sobre); **it brought tears to her eyes** hizo que se le llenaran los ojos de lágrimas; **he brought it upon himself** se lo buscó él mismo
3 (*Jur*) [+ *charge*] hacer, formular; [+ *suit*] entablar
4 (= *yield*) [+ *profit etc*] dar, producir
5 (= *induce*) **to ~ o.s. to do sth: he couldn't ~ himself to tell her** no se sentía con el valor suficiente para decírselo
➤ **bring about** VT + ADV [+ *change*] provocar; [+ *crisis, death, war*] ocasionar, provocar
➤ **bring along** VT + ADV traer consigo, llevar consigo
➤ **bring around** VT + ADV **1** (= *persuade*) convencer
2 (= *steer*) [+ *conversation*] llevar, dirigir **3** [+ *unconscious*

person] hacer volver en sí, reanimar
➤ **bring back** VT + ADV (*lit*) [+ *person*] traer de vuelta; [+ *thing borrowed*] devolver; [+ *monarchy etc*] restaurar; (*to life*) devolver la vida a; **she brought a friend back for coffee** trajo a una amiga a casa para tomar café; **it ~s back memories** trae recuerdos
➤ **bring down** VT + ADV [+ *prices*] bajar; [+ *opponent*] derribar; [+ *government*] derrocar; (*Mil, Hunting*) abatir, derribar
➤ **bring forward** VT + ADV **1** [+ *evidence, idea*] presentar **2** [+ *date, meeting*] adelantar **3** (*Bookkeeping*) pasar a otra cuenta; **brought forward** saldo *m* anterior
➤ **bring in** VT + ADV **1** [+ *person*] hacer entrar, hacer pasar; [+ *object*] traer; [+ *heavy object*] entrar; [+ *harvest*] recoger; [+ *suspect*] detener, llevar a la comisaría; ~ **him in!** ¡que entre!, ¡que pase!; **to ~ in the police** pedir la intervención de la policía **2** (= *yield*) [+ *income*] producir, proporcionar; [+ *wages*] sacar **3** (= *introduce*) [+ *fashion, custom*] introducir; (*Pol*) [+ *bill*] presentar, introducir; **to ~ in a verdict** (*Jur*) pronunciar un veredicto **4** (= *attract*) atraer
➤ **bring off** VT + ADV [+ *plan*] lograr, conseguir; [+ *success*] obtener; **he didn't ~ it off*** no le salió*
➤ **bring on** VT + ADV [+ *illness, quarrel*] producir, causar; [+ *crops*] hacer crecer *or* madurar; [+ *flowers*] hacer florecer; [+ *performer*] presentar; [+ *player*] sacar (de la reserva), hacer salir
➤ **bring out** VT + ADV **1** (= *take out*) sacar **2** (= *introduce*) [+ *product, model*] sacar, lanzar al mercado; [+ *book*] publicar, sacar **3** (= *reveal*) [+ *colour, meaning*] realzar **4** (= *develop*) [+ *quality*] sacar a la luz, despertar; **to ~ out the best in sb** sacar a la luz lo mejor que hay en algn **5** (= *give confidence to*) [+ *person*] ayudar a adquirir confianza
➤ **bring round** VT + ADV (*Brit*) = **bring around**
➤ **bring together** VT + ADV reunir; (= *reconcile*) reconciliar
➤ **bring up** VT + ADV **1** (= *carry*) subir; [+ *person*] hacer subir **2** (= *rear*) [+ *child*] criar, educar; **a well brought up child** un niño bien educado; **he was brought up to believe that ...** lo educaron en la creencia de que ... **3** [+ *subject*] sacar a colación, sacar a relucir; (*in meeting*) plantar **4** (= *vomit*) devolver, vomitar **5 to ~ sb up short** parar a algn en seco **6 to ~ up the rear** (*Mil*) cerrar la marcha

bring-and-buy sale [ˌbrɪŋənˈdbaɪseɪl] N (*Brit*) mercadillo *m* benéfico

brink [brɪŋk] N (*lit, fig*) borde *m*; **on the ~ of sth** al borde de algo; **to be on the ~ of doing sth** estar a punto de hacer algo

brisk [brɪsk] ADJ (*compar* ~**er**; *superl* ~**est**) [*walk*] enérgico; [*person, voice, movement*] enérgico, dinámico; [*manner*] brusco; [*trade*] activo; **at a ~ pace** con paso brioso *or* enérgico; **business is ~** el negocio lleva un buen ritmo

brisket [ˈbrɪskɪt] N carne *f* de pecho (para asar)

bristle [ˈbrɪsl] Ⓐ N [*of brush, on animal*] cerda *f*; [*of beard*] ~(**s**) barba *f sing* (incipiente) Ⓑ VI **1** [*hair*] erizarse, ponerse de punta; **to ~ with** (= *be riddled with*) estar plagado de; **he was bristling with anger** temblaba de rabia *or* cólera **2** (*react angrily*) resentirse (**at** de)

bristly [ˈbrɪslɪ] ADJ (*compar* **bristlier**; *superl* **bristliest**) [*beard, hair*] erizado; **to have a ~ chin** tener la barba crecida

Brit* [brɪt] N británico/a *m/f*

Britain [ˈbrɪtən] N (*also* **Great ~**) Gran Bretaña *f*; (= *UK*) el Reino Unido

Se denomina **Great Britain** a la isla que comprende Inglaterra, Escocia y Gales. Administrativamente, el término también incluye las islas menores cercanas, a excepción de la Isla de Man (**Isle of Man**) y las Islas del Canal de la Mancha (**Channel Islands**).

British Isles es el término geográfico que abarca Gran Bretaña, Irlanda, la Isla de Man y las Islas del Canal.

United Kingdom (of Great Britain and Northern Ireland), o **UK**, es la unidad política que comprende Gran Bretaña e Irlanda del Norte.

El término **Britain** se utiliza para referirse al Reino Unido, y en algunas ocasiones también a la isla, a Gran Bretaña.

British ['brɪtɪʃ] **A** ADJ (*gen*) británico; ✦ IDIOM **the best of ~ (luck)!*** ¡y un cuerno!*
B NPL **the ~** los británicos
C CPD ➤ **British Council** Consejo *m* Británico ➤ **the British Isles** las Islas Británicas ➤ **British Summer Time** *hora de verano en Gran Bretaña*

BRITISH COUNCIL

El **British Council** se creó en 1935 para fomentar la cultura británica en el extranjero y actualmente tiene delegaciones en más de 100 países. Sus principales cometidos son la organización de actividades culturales, tales como exposiciones y conferencias, con el fin de dar a conocer el arte, la ciencia y la literatura del país, así como la enseñanza del inglés, además de ayudar a aquellos que desean estudiar en el Reino Unido. *Ver tb* www.education.org.uk

Briton ['brɪtən] N británico/a *m/f*

brittle ['brɪtl] ADJ (*compar* **~r**; *superl* **~st**) quebradizo

broach [brəʊtʃ] VT [+ *subject*] abordar, sacar a colación

broad [brɔːd] **A** ADJ (*compar* **~er**; *superl* **~est**) **1** (= *wide*) [*road*] ancho, amplio; [*shoulders*] ancho; [*smile*] de oreja a oreja; ✦ IDIOM **it's as ~ as it's long*** lo mismo da
2 (= *general, extensive*) [*outline, objectives, view*] general; **to be in ~ agreement** estar de acuerdo en líneas generales
3 (= *wide-ranging*) [*education, syllabus*] amplio; [*range, spectrum*] amplio, extenso
4 (= *unsubtle*) [*hint*] claro
5 (= *strong*) [*accent*] cerrado
6 in ~ daylight en plena luz del día
B N **1** (*US**) tipa* *f*, tía *f* (*Sp**)
2 the (Norfolk) Broads *área de estuarios en Norfolk*
C CPD ➤ **broad bean** (*esp Brit*) haba *f* gruesa

Use **el/un** not **la/una** before feminine nouns beginning with stressed **a** or **ha** like **haba**.

➤ **broad jump** (*US*) salto *m* de longitud

broadband ['brɔːdbænd] N banda *f* ancha ➤ **broadband access** acceso *m* de banda ancha

broad-based ['brɔːd'beɪst] ADJ que cuenta con una base amplia; **a ~ coalition** una coalición que representa gran diversidad de intereses

broadcast ['brɔːdkɑːst] (*vb*: *pt, pp* **~**) **A** N (*Rad, TV*) emisión *f*, programa *m* **B** VT **1** (*TV*) transmitir; (*Rad*) emitir, radiar **2** (*fig*) [+ *news, rumour*] divulgar, difundir **C** VI (*TV, Rad*) [*station*] transmitir, emitir
D CPD ➤ **broadcast media** medios *mpl* de radiodifusión y teledifusión

broadcaster ['brɔːdkɑːstəʳ] N (*Rad, TV*) locutor(a) *m/f*

broadcasting ['brɔːdkɑːstɪŋ] N (*TV*) teledifusión *f*, transmisión *f*; (*Rad*) radiodifusión *f* ➤ **broadcasting station** emisora *f*

broaden ['brɔːdn] **A** VT [+ *road*] ensanchar; [+ *horizons, outlook*] ampliar; **travel ~s the mind** los viajes son muy educativos **B** VI (*also* ~ **out**) ensancharse

broadly ['brɔːdlɪ] ADV **1** (= *by and large*) [*agree, accept*] en líneas generales; ~ **similar** parecido en líneas generales; ~ **speaking** en general, hablando en términos generales **2** (= *widely*) [*smile, grin*] abiertamente, de oreja a oreja

broad-minded ['brɔːd'maɪndɪd] ADJ tolerante, de miras amplias

broadsheet ['brɔːdʃiːt] N periódico *m* de gran formato

BROADSHEETS AND TABLOIDS

En el Reino Unido hay dos tipos de periódicos, los **broadsheets** y los **tabloids**. Los primeros son de tamaño más grande y contienen más noticias políticas y culturales, por lo que también son conocidos como **quality press**. Entre ellos se encuentran **The Daily Telegraph, The Times, The Guardian** y **The Independent**. Los llamados **tabloids** son de tamaño más pequeño, con grandes titulares, muchas fotografías y una clara preferencia por las noticias del corazón o los escándalos, por lo que también reciben el nombre de **gutter press**. Entre los más conocidos destacan **The Sun, The Daily Mirror, The Daily Express, The Daily Mail** y **The Daily Star**.

En Estados Unidos, el término **standard-sized newspapers** es el equivalente a **broadsheet**, cuyo representante más conocido es la edición nacional del **New York Times**. Entre los principales **tabloids** destacan el **New York Daily News** y el **Chicago Sun-Times**.

broad-shouldered ['brɔːd'ʃəʊldəd] ADJ ancho de espaldas

brocade [brə'keɪd] N brocado *m*

broccoli ['brɒkəlɪ] N brécol *m*, brócoli *m*

brochure ['brəʊʃəʳ] N folleto *m*

brogue¹ [brəʊg] N (= *shoe*) zapato *m* grueso de cuero

brogue² [brəʊg] N (= *accent*) acento *m* regional (*sobre todo irlandés*)

broil [brɔɪl] VT (*US Culin*) asar a la parrilla

broiler ['brɔɪləʳ] N **1** (= *chicken*) pollo *m* para asar **2** (*US*) (= *grill*) parrilla *f*, grill *m*

broiling ['brɔɪlɪŋ] ADJ (*US*) [*sun*] achicharrante

broke [brəʊk] **A** PT *of* **break** **B** ADJ **1** (*) (*incorrect usage*) (= *broken*) estropeado; ✦ IDIOM **if it ain't ~, don't fix it** no hay que complicar las cosas *or* complicarse la vida sin necesidad **2** (*) (= *penniless*) pelado*; **I'm ~** estoy pelado*, estoy sin un duro (*Sp**), estoy sin un peso (*LAm**);
✦ IDIOM **to go for ~** jugarse el todo por el todo

broken ['brəʊkən] **A** PP *of* **break**
B ADJ **1** [*object*] roto, quebrado (*LAm*); [*bone*] roto, fracturado; [*skin*] cortado
2 (= *not working*) [*machine*] estropeado, averiado
3 (= *ruined*) [*health, spirit*] quebrantado; [*heart*] roto, destrozado; **to die of a ~ heart** morir de pena; **a ~ man** un hombre deshecho; ✦ IDIOM **a ~ reed** una persona quemada
4 (= *interrupted*) [*line*] quebrado; [*voice*] entrecortado; [*sleep*] interrumpido; [*cloud*] fragmentario; **he speaks ~ English** chapurrea el inglés; **she had a ~ night** durmió mal, despertándose a cada momento
5 (= *failed*) [*marriage*] deshecho; **a ~ home** una familia dividida
6 [*promise*] roto, quebrantado

broken-down ['brəʊkən'daʊn] ADJ [*machine, car*] averiado, estropeado, descompuesto (*Mex*); [*house*] destartalado, desvencijado

broken-hearted ['brəʊkən'hɑːtɪd] ADJ con el corazón destrozado *or* partido

broker ['brəʊkəʳ] **A** N (*Comm*) agente *mf*; (= *stockbroker*) corredor(a) *m/f* de bolsa, bolsista *mf* **B** VT [+ *deal, agreement*] negociar

brolly* ['brɒlɪ] N (*Brit*) paraguas *m inv*

bronchitis [brɒŋ'kaɪtɪs] N bronquitis *f*

brontosaurus [,brɒntə'sɔːrəs] N brontosaurio *m*

Bronx cheer* [,brɒŋks'tʃɪəʳ] N (*US*) pedorreta** *f*

bronze [brɒnz] **A** N (= *metal, sculpture*) bronce *m* **B** ADJ (= *made of bronze*) de bronce; (= *bronze-coloured*) color de bronce **C** CPD ➤ **the Bronze Age** la Edad de Bronce
➤ **bronze medal** medalla *f* de bronce ➤ **bronze medallist** medallero/a *m/f* de bronce

bronzed [brɒnzd] ADJ [*person*] bronceado

brooch [brəʊtʃ] N prendedor *m*, broche *m*

brood [bruːd] Ⓐ N (*gen*) cría *f*, camada *f*; [*of chicks*] nidada *f*; (*hum*) [*of children*] prole *f* Ⓑ VI **1** [*bird*] empollar **2** [*person*] ponerse melancólico; **to ~ on** *or* **over** dar vueltas a

broody [bruːdɪ] ADJ (*compar* **broodier**; *superl* **broodiest**) **1** [*hen*] clueca; (*) [*woman*] con ganas de tener hijos **2** (= *pensive*) triste, melancólico

brook [brʊk] N arroyo *m*

broom [bruːm, brʊm] Ⓐ N **1** (= *brush*) escoba *f*; ✦ PROV **a new ~ sweeps clean** escoba nueva barre bien **2** (*Bot*) retama *f*, hiniesta *f* Ⓑ CPD ➤ **broom closet** (*US*), **broom cupboard** (*Brit*) armario *m* de los artículos de limpieza

broomstick [brʊmstɪk] N palo *m* de escoba

Bros. ABBR (= **Brothers**) Hnos.

broth [brɒθ] N caldo *m*

brothel [brɒθl] N burdel *m*, prostíbulo *m*

brother [brʌðəʳ] N (*gen, Rel*) hermano *m*; (*Trade Union etc*) compañero *m*

brotherhood [brʌðəhʊd] N **1** (= *fraternity*) fraternidad *f* **2** (= *group*) hermandad *f*

brother-in-law [brʌðərɪnlɔː] N (*pl* **brothers-in-law**) cuñado *m*, hermano *m* político

brotherly [brʌðəlɪ] ADJ fraterno, fraternal

brought [brɔːt] PT, PP *of* **bring**

brow [braʊ] N **1** (= *forehead*) frente *f*; (*also* **eyebrow**) ceja *f* **2** [*of hill*] cumbre *f*, cima *f*; [*of cliff*] borde *m*

browbeat [braʊbiːt] (*pt* **~**; *pp* **-en**) VT intimidar, convencer con amenazas; **to ~ sb into doing sth** intimidar a algn para que haga algo

brown [braʊn] Ⓐ ADJ (*compar* **~er**; *superl* **~est**) **1** (*gen*) marrón, color café (*LAm*); [*hair*] castaño; [*leather*] marrón **2** (= *tanned*) bronceado, moreno (*Sp*); [*skin*] moreno; **to go ~** ponerse moreno, broncearse; ✦ IDIOM **as ~ as a berry** bronceadísimo, muy moreno (*Sp*) Ⓑ N marrón *m*, color *m* café (*LAm*); [*of eyes, hair*] castaño *m* Ⓒ VI [*leaves etc*] volverse de color marrón; [*skin*] broncearse, ponerse moreno (*Sp*); (*Culin*) dorarse Ⓓ CPD ➤ **brown ale** cerveza *f* oscura *or* negra ➤ **brown bear** oso *m* pardo ➤ **brown bread** pan *m* negro, pan *m* moreno (*Sp*) ➤ **brown goods** (productos *mpl* de) línea *f or* gama *f* marrón ➤ **brown owl** autillo *m* ➤ **brown paper** papel *m* de estraza ➤ **brown rice** arroz *m* integral ➤ **brown sauce** (*Brit*) *salsa de condimento, con sabor agridulce* ➤ **brown sugar** azúcar *m* moreno

brownfield [braʊnfiːld] ADJ [*site, land*] urbanizado con anterioridad

brownie [braʊnɪ] N **1** (*also* **Brownie Guide**) niña *f* exploradora; ✦ IDIOM **to earn** *or* **win Brownie points** (*hum*) apuntarse tantos a favor, hacer méritos **2** (*esp US*) (= *cookie*) pastelillo *m* de chocolate y nueces

brown-nose** [braʊn,nəʊz] (*US*) Ⓐ N lameculos*** *mf inv* Ⓑ VT lamer el culo a***

brownstone [braʊnstəʊn] N (*US*) (casa *f* construida con) piedra *f* caliza de color rojizo

browse [braʊz] Ⓐ VI **1** (*in shop*) echar una ojeada, curiosear; **to spend an hour browsing in a bookshop** pasar una hora hojeando los libros en una librería **2** (*Internet*) navegar por Internet Ⓑ VT **to ~ the Internet** navegar por Internet Ⓒ N **to have a ~ (around)** = **browse A1**

browser [braʊzəʳ] N **1** (*in shop*) persona que entra a una tienda a curiosear **2** (*Internet*) navegador *m*

bruise [bruːz] Ⓐ N (*on person*) cardenal *m*, moretón *m* (*esp LAm*); (*on fruit*) maca *f*, magulladura *f* Ⓑ VT **1** [+ *leg etc*] magullar, amoratar; [+ *fruit*] magullar, dañar **2** (*fig*) [+ *feelings*] herir Ⓒ VI **I ~ easily** me salen cardenales *or* moretones con facilidad

bruising [bruːzɪŋ] ADJ [*experience*] doloroso, penoso; [*match*] durísimo, violento

brunch [brʌntʃ] N desayuno-almuerzo *m*

brunette [bruːnet] N morena *f*, morocha *f* (*LAm*), prieta *f* (*Mex*)

brunt [brʌnt] N **to bear the ~ of sth** aguantar lo más recio *or* duro de algo; **the ~ of the work** la mayor parte del trabajo

brush [brʌʃ] Ⓐ N **1** (*gen*) cepillo *m*; (= *sweeping brush*) cepillo *m*, escobilla *f*; (= *scrubbing brush*) cepillo *m* de cerda; (= *shaving brush, decorator's*) brocha *f*; (= *artist's*) pincel *m*; **shoe ~** cepillo *m* para zapatos **2** (= *act of brushing*) **give your coat a ~** cepíllate el abrigo; **let's give it a ~** vamos a pasar el cepillo **3** (= *tail*) [*of fox*] rabo *m*, hopo *m* **4** (= *skirmish*) roce *m*; **to have a ~ with the police** tener un roce con la policía **5** (= *light touch*) toque *m* **6** (= *undergrowth*) maleza *f*, broza *f* Ⓑ VT **1** (= *clean*) [+ *floor*] cepillar; [+ *clothes, hair*] cepillar; **to ~ one's shoes** limpiarse los zapatos; **to ~ one's teeth** lavarse los dientes, cepillarse los dientes **2** (= *touch lightly*) rozar
➤ **brush aside** VT + ADV no hacer caso de, dejar a un lado
➤ **brush off** Ⓐ VT + ADV **1** [+ *mud*] quitar (con cepillo *or* la mano etc) **2** (= *dismiss*) no hacer caso de Ⓑ VI + ADV **the mud ~es off easily** el barro sale *or* se quita fácilmente
➤ **brush up** VT + ADV **1** [+ *crumbs*] recoger **2** (= *improve, revise*) (*also* **~ up on**) repasar, refrescar

brushed [brʌʃt] ADJ [*nylon, denim etc*] afelpado

brush-off* [brʌʃɒf] N **to give sb the ~** mandar a algn a paseo*, zafarse de algn

brush-up [brʌʃʌp] N **to have a wash and ~** lavarse y arreglarse

brushwood [brʌʃwʊd] N maleza *f*, monte *m* bajo

brusque [bruːsk] ADJ (*compar* **~r**; *superl* **~st**) [*comment, manner etc*] brusco, áspero; [*person*] brusco; **he was very ~ with me** me trató con poca cortesía *or* con aspereza

Brussels [brʌslz] N Bruselas *f* ➤ **Brussels sprout** col *f* de Bruselas

brutal [bruːtl] ADJ [*person, murder, attack*] brutal; [*tone, remark*] cruel; **the government's ~ treatment of political prisoners** la brutalidad *or* la crueldad con la que el gobierno trata a los prisioneros políticos

brutality [bruːtælɪtɪ] N [*of person*] brutalidad *f*; [*of murder*] salvajismo *m*, crueldad *f*

brutalize [bruːtəlaɪz] VT brutalizar

brutally [bruːtəlɪ] ADV **1** (= *savagely*) [*attack, murder, suppress*] de manera brutal, brutalmente **2** (= *starkly*) [*say, reply, expose*] crudamente, descarnadamente; **let me be ~ frank with you** voy a serte tremendamente franco; **the talks had been ~ frank** las conversaciones habían sido francas y crudas

brute [bruːt] Ⓐ N (= *animal*) bestia *f*; (= *person*) bruto/a *m/f*, bestia *mf*; **you ~!** ¡bestia!, ¡animal!* Ⓑ ADJ [*force*] bruto

brutish [bruːtɪʃ] ADJ bruto

BS N ABBR **1** (= **British Standard**) *norma de calidad* **2** (*US*) = **Bachelor of Science 3** (*esp US***) = **bullshit**

BSc N ABBR = **Bachelor of Science**

BSE N ABBR (= **bovine spongiform encephalopathy**) EEB, encefalopatía *f* espongiforme bovina

BST N ABBR (*Brit*) = **British Summer Time**

BTW* ABBR (= **by the way**) por cierto

bubble [bʌbl] Ⓐ N (*in liquid*) burbuja *f*; (*in paint*) ampolla *f*; (= *soap bubble*) pompa *f*; (*in cartoon*) bocadillo *m*, globo *m*; **to blow ~s** (*with soap*) hacer pompas; (*with bubble gum*) hacer globos; **the ~ burst** (*fig*) se deshizo la burbuja Ⓑ VI burbujear Ⓒ CPD ➤ **bubble and squeak** (*Brit*) *carne picada frita con patatas y col* ➤ **bubble bath** gel *m* de baño ➤ **bubble gum** chicle *m* (de globo) ➤ **bubble memory** (*Comput*) memoria *f* de burbuja ➤ **bubble wrap** envoltorio *m* de plástico con burbujas
➤ **bubble over** VI + ADV [*boiling liquid*] derramarse; (*fig*) (*with happiness etc*) rebosar (**with** de)
➤ **bubble up** VI + ADV burbujear, borbotear

bubblejet printer [bʌbldʒet'prɪntəʳ] N impresora *f* de inyección de burbujas

bubbly [bʌblɪ] Ⓐ ADJ (*compar* **bubblier**; *superl* **bubbliest**) (*lit*) burbujeante, con burbujas; (*) [*person*] lleno de vida,

dicharachero ③ N (*) champaña *m*, champán *m*

buccaneer [ˌbʌkəˈnɪəʳ] N (*Hist*) bucanero *m*; (*Brit*) (*fig*) emprendedor(a) *m/f*

Bucharest [ˌbuːkəˈrest] N Bucarest *m*

buck [bʌk] ④ N 1 (= *male*) [*of deer*] ciervo *m* (macho); [*of rabbit*] conejo *m* (macho); (= *antelope*) antílope *m* 2 (*US**) (= *dollar*) dólar *m*; **to make a ~** hacer dinero; **to make a fast** *or* **quick ~** hacer dinero fácil 3 ✦ IDIOMS **to pass the ~*** escurrir el bulto*, pasar la pelota*; **the ~ stops here** yo soy el responsable/nosotros somos los responsables ⑧ ADJ (= *male*) macho ⓒ ADV **~ naked** (*US**) en cueros* ⓓ VI 1 [*horse*] corcovear 2 **to ~ against** [+ *rules, authority*] rebelarse contra ⓔ VT **to ~ the market** ir en contra del mercado; **to ~ the system** rebelarse contra el sistema; **to ~ the trend** ir en contra de la tendencia ⓕ CPD ➤ **buck private** (*US*) soldado *mf* raso ➤ **buck rabbit** conejo *m* (macho) ➤ **buck sergeant** (*US*) sargento *mf* chusquero ➤ **buck's fizz** sangría hecha con champán u otro vino espumoso y zumo de naranja ➤ **buck teeth** dientes *mpl* salientes ➤ **buck up*** (*Brit*) ⑧ VI + ADV animarse, levantar el ánimo; **~ up!** ¡ánimo! ⑧ VT + ADV 1 (= *cheer up*) animar, dar ánimos a 2 **you'll have to ~ your ideas up** tendrás que moverte, tendrás que ponerte a trabajar en serio

bucket [ˈbʌkɪt] ④ N cubo *m*, balde *m* (*LAm*); (*child's*) cubito *m*; **a ~ of water** un cubo *or* (*LAm*) un balde de agua; ✦ IDIOMS **to rain ~s*** llover a cántaros; **to weep ~s*** llorar a mares ⑧ (*Brit*) **the rain is ~ing down*** ◇ **it's ~ing (down)*** está lloviendo a cántaros ⓒ CPD ➤ **bucket shop** (*Brit*) (*for air tickets*) agencia *f* de viajes que vende barato

buckle [ˈbʌkl] ④ N hebilla *f* ⑧ VT 1 [+ *shoe, belt*] abrochar 2 (= *warp*) [+ *wheel, girder*] combar, torcer ⓒ VI [*wheel, girder*] combarse, torcerse; [*knees*] doblarse ➤ **buckle down** VI + ADV ponerse a trabajar; **to ~ down to a task** dedicarse en serio a una tarea

buckskin [ˈbʌkskɪn] N (cuero *m* de) ante *m*

buckwheat [ˈbʌkwiːt] N alforfón *m*, trigo *m* sarraceno

bud¹ [bʌd] ④ N [*of flower*] capullo *m*; (*on tree, plant*) brote *m*, yema *f*; **in ~** [*tree*] en brote ⑧ VI brotar, echar brotes

bud²* [bʌd] N (*US*) = **buddy**

Buddha [ˈbʊdə] N Buda *m*

Buddhism [ˈbʊdɪzəm] N budismo *m*

Buddhist [ˈbʊdɪst] ADJ, N budista *mf*

budding [ˈbʌdɪŋ] ADJ [*talent*] en ciernes

buddy [ˈbʌdɪ] N (*esp US*) amigo *m*, amigote* *m*, compadre *m* (*LAm*), cuate *m* (*Mex**), pata *m* (*Per**); (*in direct address*) hermano* *m*, macho *m* (*Sp**)

budge [bʌdʒ] ④ VI (= *move*) moverse; (= *give in*) ceder, rendirse; ✦ IDIOM **he won't ~ an inch** no cede lo más mínimo ⑧ VT (= *move*) mover, hacer que se mueva; ✦ IDIOM **I couldn't ~ him an inch** no lo pude convencer

budgerigar [ˈbʌdʒərɪgaːʳ] N periquito *m*

budget [ˈbʌdʒɪt] ④ N presupuesto *m*; **the Budget** (*Brit*) los Presupuestos Generales del Estado; **my ~ won't run to steak** mi presupuesto no me permite comprar bistec ⑧ VI planear el presupuesto ⓒ VT [+ *sum*] asignar; **~ed costs** costos *mpl* presupuestados ⓓ CPD [*holiday, prices*] económico ➤ **Budget Day** (*Brit*) día *m* de la presentación de los Presupuestos Generales del Estado ➤ **budget deficit** déficit *m* presupuestario

budgie* [ˈbʌdʒɪ] N periquito *m*

Buenos Aires [ˌbwenəsˈaɪərɪz] ④ N Buenos Aires *msing* ⑧ ADJ bonaerense, porteño (*Arg**)

buff¹ [bʌf] ④ ADJ de color de ante ⑧ N piel *f* de ante; **in the ~*** en cueros* ⓒ VT (*also* **~ up**) lustrar, pulir

buff²* [bʌf] N (= *enthusiast*) aficionado/a *m/f*, entusiasta *mf*; **film ~** cinéfilo/a *m/f*

buffalo [ˈbʌfələʊ] N (*pl* **~** *or* **-es**) 1 búfalo *m* 2 (*esp US*) (= *bison*) bisonte *m*

buffer [ˈbʌfəʳ] ④ N (*Brit Rail*) (*on carriage*) tope *m*; (*in*

station) parachoques *m inv*, amortiguador *m* (de choques); (*US Aut*) parachoques *m inv*; (*Comput*) memoria *f* intermedia; ✦ IDIOM **the plan suddenly hit the ~s** el plan frenó de golpe ⑧ VT (*fig*) (= *protect*) proteger ⓒ CPD ➤ **buffer state** estado *m* tapón ➤ **buffer zone** zona *f* parachoques

buffet [ˈbʌfɪt]¹ VT (= *hit*) [*sea, wind*] zarandear

buffet² [ˈbʊfeɪ] N (= *café*) cantina *f*, cafetería *f*; (= *meal*) buffet *m* (libre), comida *f* buffet ➤ **buffet car** (*Brit*) coche-restaurante *m* ➤ **buffet lunch** almuerzo *m* buffet

buffoon [bəˈfuːn] N bufón *m*, payaso *m*

bug [bʌg] ④ N 1 (*) (= *any insect*) bicho *m* 2 (= *bedbug*) chinche *mf* 3 (*) (= *germ*) microbio *m*; (= *virus*) virus *m inv*; **there's a ~ going around** hay un virus que corre por ahí; **I've got the travel ~** me ha picado el gusanillo de los viajes 4 (*) (= *hidden microphone*) micrófono *m* oculto 5 (*esp US**) (= *defect, snag*) traba *f*, pega *f* 6 (*Comput*) virus *m inv* 7 (*US**) (= *enthusiast*) aficionado/a *m/f*, entusiasta *mf* ⑧ VT 1 (*) [+ *telephone*] intervenir, pinchar*; **do you think this room is ~ged?** ¿crees que en esta habitación hay un micro oculto? 2 (*) (= *annoy*) molestar; **don't ~ me!** ¡deja de molestar(me) *or* fastidiar!; **what's ~ging you?** ¿qué mosca te ha picado?*

bugbear [ˈbʌgbɛəʳ] N pesadilla *f*

bugger*** [ˈbʌgəʳ] (*Brit*) ④ N (= *person*) hijo/a *m/f* de puta**, gilipollas *mf* (*Sp***); **that silly ~** ese cabrón**, ese gilipollas (*Sp***); **some poor ~** algún desgraciado* ⑧ EXCL **bugger!** ¡mierda!*** ➤ **bugger off***** VI + ADV (*Brit*) largarse*; **~ off!** ¡vete a la mierda!*** ➤ **bugger up***** VT + ADV (*Brit*) joder***

buggery [ˈbʌgərɪ] N sodomía *f*

buggy [ˈbʌgɪ] N (*also* **baby ~**) (*Brit*) (= *pushchair*) sillita *f* de paseo; (*US*) (= *pram*) cochecito *m* (de niño)

bugle [ˈbjuːgl] N corneta *f*, clarín *m*

build [bɪld] (*vb*: *pt, pp* **built**) ④ N complexión *f*; **of powerful ~** de complexión fuerte, fornido ⑧ VT 1 [+ *house*] construir, hacer; [+ *ship*] construir; [+ *nest*] hacer; [+ *fire*] preparar; **built to last** hecho para durar 2 [+ *empire, organization*] levantar; [+ *relationship*] establecer; [+ *trust, confidence*] cimentar; [+ *self-confidence*] desarrollar ⓒ VI 1 (*Constr*) edificar, construir 2 (= *increase*) [*pressure, speed*] aumentar; [*excitement*] crecer ➤ **build in** VT + ADV [+ *safeguards*] incluir, incorporar ➤ **build on** ④ VT + ADV (= *add*) añadir; **to ~ a garage on to a house** añadir un garaje a una casa; **the house has a garage built on to it** la casa tiene un garaje anexo ⑧ VI + PREP (*fig*) **now we have a base to ~ on** ahora tenemos una base sobre la que podemos construir ➤ **build up** ④ VT + ADV 1 [+ *area, town*] urbanizar 2 (= *establish*) [+ *business, firm*] levantar; [+ *reputation*] labrarse; [+ *impression*] crear; **to ~ up a lead** tomar la delantera; **he had built up a picture in his mind of what she was like** se había formado una imagen mental de cómo era ella 3 (= *increase*) [+ *stocks etc*] acumular; [+ *sales, numbers*] incrementar; **to ~ up one's strength** fortalecerse; **to ~ up one's hopes** hacerse ilusiones ⑧ VI + ADV (= *increase*) [*pressure, sound, speed*] aumentar; [*excitement*] crecer; (*Fin*) [*interest*] acumularse

builder [ˈbɪldəʳ] N (= *business person*) constructor(a) *m/f*; (= *worker*) albañil *mf*; (= *contractor*) contratista *mf*

building [ˈbɪldɪŋ] ④ N 1 (= *house, office etc*) edificio *m* 2 (= *activity*) construcción *f* ⑧ CPD ➤ **building block** (= *toy*) bloque *m* de construcción; (*fig*) elemento *m* esencial, componente *m* básico ➤ **building contractor** contratista *mf* de construcciones ➤ **the building industry** la industria de la construcción ➤ **building materials** material *msing* de construcción ➤ **building site** obra *f* ➤ **building society** (*Brit*) sociedad *f* de crédito hipotecario ➤ **the building trade** la industria de la construcción

build-up [ˈbɪldʌp] N 1 [*of pressure, tension, traffic*] aumento *m*; [*of gas*] acumulación *f*, concentración *f*; [*of forces*] concentración *f* 2 (= *publicity*) propaganda *f*

built [bɪlt] **Ⓐ** PT, PP *of* **build Ⓑ** ADJ **heavily/slightly ~** [*person*] fornido/menudo

-built [bɪlt] ADJ (*ending in compounds*) **American-built** de construcción americana

built-in ['bɪlt'ɪn] ADJ [*wardrobe, mirror*] empotrado; (*as integral part of*) incorporado

built-up ['bɪlt'ʌp] N ~ **area** zona *f* urbanizada; (*Aut*) núcleo *m* de población

bulb [bʌlb] N **1** (*Bot*) bulbo *m*, camote *m* (*Mex*); [*of garlic*] cabeza *f* **2** (*Elec*) bombilla *f*, bombillo *m* (*LAm*), foco *m* (*LAm*)

bulbous ['bʌlbəs] ADJ bulboso

Bulgaria [bʌl'geərɪə] N Bulgaria *f*

Bulgarian [bʌl'geərɪən] **Ⓐ** ADJ búlgaro **Ⓑ** N **1** (= *person*) búlgaro/a *m/f* **2** (*Ling*) búlgaro *m*

bulge [bʌldʒ] **Ⓐ** N **1** (*in surface*) abombamiento *m*, protuberancia *f*; (*in pocket*) bulto *m* **Ⓑ** VI [*pocket*] estar abultado; [*eyes*] saltarse

bulging ['bʌldʒɪŋ] ADJ [*pocket*] muy lleno; [*suitcase*] que está para reventar; [*eyes*] saltón

bulimia [bjuːˈlɪmɪə] N bulimia *f*

bulimic [bjuːˈlɪmɪk] ADJ, N bulímico/a *m/f*

bulk [bʌlk] **Ⓐ** N **1** (= *size*) [*of thing*] bulto *m*; [*of person*] corpulencia *f*, masa *f* **2** (= *main part*) **the ~ of** la mayoría de; **the ~ of the work** la mayor parte del trabajo **3** (*Comm*) **to buy in ~** (= *in quantity*) comprar al por mayor; **in ~** (= *not prepacked*) suelto, a granel **Ⓑ** CPD ➤ **bulk buying** compra *f* al por mayor ➤ **bulk carrier** (buque *m*) granelero *m* ➤ **bulk purchase** compra *f* al por mayor

bulkhead ['bʌlkhed] N mamparo *m*

bulky ['bʌlkɪ] ADJ (*compar* **bulkier**; *superl* **bulkiest**) [*parcel*] abultado; [*person*] corpulento

bull¹ [bʊl] **Ⓐ** N **1** (= *farm animal*) toro *m*; ✦ IDIOMS **like a ~ in a china shop** como un elefante en una cristalería; **to take the ~ by the horns** coger *or* (*LAm*) agarrar el toro por los cuernos
2 (= *male*) [*of elephant, seal*] macho *m*
3 (******) (= *nonsense*) sandeces* *fpl*, chorradas *fpl* (*Sp**) **Ⓑ** ADJ (= *male*) macho
Ⓒ VT (*Fin*) **to ~ the market** hacer subir el mercado comprando acciones especulativamente
Ⓓ CPD ➤ **bull bars** (*Aut*) defensa *fsing* (delantera *or* frontal) ➤ **bull calf** becerro *m* ➤ **bull market** (*Fin*) mercado *m* en alza *or* alcista ➤ **bull terrier** bulterrier *m*

bull² [bʊl] N (*Rel*) bula *f*

bulldog ['bʊldɒg] N dogo *m*, buldog *m* ➤ **bulldog clip** (*Brit*) pinza *f*

bulldoze ['bʊldəuz] VT **1** [+ *site*] nivelar (con motoniveladora); [+ *building*] arrasar (con motoniveladora) **2** (*fig*) [+ *opposition*] arrollar; **I was ~d into doing it** me forzaron a hacerlo; **the government ~d the bill through parliament** el gobierno hizo presiones para que se aprobara el proyecto de ley en el parlamento

bulldozer ['bʊldəuzə'] N motoniveladora *f*, bulldozer *m*

bullet ['bʊlɪt] N bala *f* ➤ **bullet hole** agujero *m* de bala ➤ **bullet train** tren *m* de gran velocidad (*japonés*) ➤ **bullet wound** balazo *m*

bulletin ['bʊlɪtɪn] N (= *statement*) comunicado *m*, parte *m*; (= *journal*) boletín *m* ➤ **bulletin board** (*on wall*) (*US*) tablón *m* de anuncios; (*Comput*) tablero *m* de noticias

bulletproof ['bʊlɪtpruːf] CPD ➤ **bulletproof glass** vidrio *m* antibalas *or* a prueba de balas ➤ **bulletproof vest** chaleco *m* antibalas *or* a prueba de balas

bullfight ['bʊlfaɪt] N corrida *f* (de toros)

bullfighting ['bʊlfaɪtɪŋ] N toreo *m*, tauromaquia *f*; **I hate ~** odio los toros

bullhorn ['bʊlhɔːn] N (*US*) megáfono *m*

bullion ['bʊljən] N oro *m*/plata *f* en barras *or* en lingotes

bullock ['bʊlək] N buey *m*

bullring ['bʊlrɪŋ] N plaza *f* de toros

bull's-eye ['bʊlzaɪ] N [*of target*] blanco *m*; **to hit the ~** ✧ **score a ~** (*lit, fig*) dar en el blanco

bullshit*** ['bʊlʃɪt] **Ⓐ** N sandeces* *fpl*, chorradas *fpl* (*Sp**) **Ⓑ** VI decir sandeces*, decir chorradas (*Sp**) **Ⓒ** VT **don't ~ me now** no me vengas ahora con sandeces *or* chorradas*

bully¹ ['bʊlɪ] **Ⓐ** N (= *person*) matón/ona *m/f*, peleón/ona *m/f* **Ⓑ** VT intimidar; **to ~ sb into doing sth** intimidar a algn para que haga algo

bully²* ['bʊlɪ] EXCL ~ **for you!** ¡bravo!

bully-boy* ['bʊlɪbɔɪ] N matón *m*, esbirro *m*

bullying ['bʊlɪɪŋ] **Ⓐ** ADJ [*attitude*] amedrentador, propio de matón **Ⓑ** N intimidación *f*, abuso *m*

bum¹* [bʌm] N (*Brit Anat*) culo* *m*; ✦ IDIOM **to put ~s on seats** llenar el teatro *or* cine etc ➤ **bum bag** (*Brit*) riñonera *f*

bum²* [bʌm] **Ⓐ** N (*esp US*) (= *idler*) holgazán/ana *m/f*, vago/a *m/f*; (= *tramp*) vagabundo/a *m/f*; (= *scrounger*) gorrón/ona* *m/f*, garronero/a *m/f* (*RPl*); (*as term of general disapproval*) vago/a *m/f* **Ⓑ** ADJ (= *worthless*) sin ningún valor **Ⓒ** VT [+ *money, food*] gorrear*; **he ~med a cigarette off me** me gorreó un pitillo* **Ⓓ** CPD ➤ **bum deal: I knew I was getting a ~ deal** sabía que se estaban aprovechando de mí ➤ **bum rap** acusación *f* falsa

bumblebee ['bʌmblbiː] N abejorro *m*

bumbling ['bʌmblɪŋ] ADJ inepto, inútil

bumf* [bʌmf] N (*Brit pej*) papeleo* *m*, papeles *mpl*

bummer** ['bʌmə'] N (= *nuisance*) latazo* *m*; (= *disaster*) desastre *m*; **what a ~!** ¡vaya desastre!

bump [bʌmp] **Ⓐ** N **1** (= *blow, noise*) choque *m*, topetazo *m*; (= *jolt of vehicle*) sacudida *f*; (*Aer*) rebote *m*; (*in falling*) batacazo *m*; ✦ IDIOM **to come down to earth with a ~** volver a la realidad de un golpe
2 (*on object*) (= *large dent*) bollo *m*; (= *small dent*) abolladura *f*; (*on road etc*) bache *m*; (*on skin*) (= *swelling*) chichón *m*, hinchazón *f*
Ⓑ VT [+ *car*] chocar contra *or* con; **to ~ one's head** darse un golpe en la cabeza; **to ~ one's head on a door** dar con la cabeza contra una puerta
Ⓒ VI **to ~ along** avanzar dando sacudidas
➤ **bump into** VI + PREP **1** (= *collide with*) chocar contra *or* con, dar con *or* contra **2** (*) (= *meet*) tropezar con, toparse con; **fancy ~ing into you!** ¡qué casualidad encontrarte aquí!
➤ **bump off*** VT + ADV (= *kill*) liquidar*
➤ **bump up*** VT + ADV [+ *price*] subir, aumentar

bumper¹ ['bʌmpə'] N (*Brit*) parachoques *m inv*; **traffic is ~ to ~ as far as the airport** hay una caravana que llega hasta el aeropuerto ➤ **bumper car** (*US*) auto *m* de choque

bumper² ['bʌmpə'] ADJ [*crop, harvest*] abundante ➤ **bumper issue** edición *f* especial

bumph* [bʌmf] N (*Brit pej*) papeleo* *m*, papeles *mpl*

bumptious ['bʌmpʃəs] ADJ engreído, presuntuoso

bumpy ['bʌmpɪ] ADJ (*compar* **bumpier**; *superl* **bumpiest**) [*surface*] desigual; [*road*] lleno de baches; [*journey, flight*] agitado, con mucho traqueteo

bun [bʌn] N **1** (*Culin*) bollo *m* **2** (= *hairstyle*) moño *m*; **to wear one's hair in a ~** recogerse el pelo en un moño **3** **buns** (*US***) (= *bottom*) trasero* *msing*

bunch [bʌntʃ] N **1** [*of flowers*] ramo *m*; (*small*) ramillete *m*; [*of bananas, grapes*] racimo *m*; [*of keys*] manojo *m*; **the best** *or* **pick of the ~*** (*fig*) el/la mejor de todos; **to wear one's hair in ~es** (*Brit*) llevar coletas **2** (*) (= *set of people*) grupo *m*, pandilla *f*; **they're an odd ~** son gente rara; ✦ IDIOM **the best of a bad ~** entre malos, los mejores **3** (*US**) **a ~ of** (= *several, many*) un montón de **4 thanks a ~!** (*iro*) ¡hombre, pues te lo agradezco!, ¡gracias mil!
➤ **bunch together Ⓐ** VT + ADV agrupar, juntar **Ⓑ** VI + ADV [*people*] agruparse, apiñarse

bundle ['bʌndl] **Ⓐ** N **1** [*of clothes, rags*] bulto *m*, fardo *m*, lío *m*; [*of sticks*] haz *m*; [*of papers*] legajo *m*; ~ **of joy** (= *baby*) bebé *mf*; **he's a ~ of nerves** es un manojo de nervios; **he's not exactly a ~ of laughs** no es muy divertido que digamos
2 (**) (= *money*) **it cost a ~** costó un dineral; **to make a ~** ganarse un dineral*, ganarse un pastón (*Sp***)
3 (*Comput*) paquete *m*
Ⓑ VT **1** (*also* ~ **up**) [+ *clothes*] atar en un bulto

2 (= *put hastily*) **the body was ~d into the car** metieron el cadáver en el coche a la carrera
⊙ CPD ► **bundled software** (*Comput*) paquete *m* de software
► **bundle off** VT + ADV [+ *person*] despachar

bung [bʌŋ] **Ⓐ** N **1** [*of cask*] tapón *m* **2** (*Brit**) (= *bribe*) soborno *m* **Ⓑ** VT (*Brit*) **1** (*also* ~ **up**) [+ *pipe, hole*] tapar, taponar; **to be ~ed up** [*sink, pipe*] estar atascado, estar obstruido; **my nose is ~ed up*** tengo la nariz tapada **2** (**) (= *throw*) echar; (= *put*) poner, meter; ~ **it over** échalo para acá

bungalow [ˈbʌŋɡələʊ] N chalé *m*, bungalow *m*

bungee jumping [ˈbʌndʒiːˈdʒʌmpɪŋ] N bungee *m*, banyi *m*; (*from bridge*) puenting *m*, puentismo *m*; **to go ~** hacer bungee *or* banyi; (*from bridge*) hacer puenting *or* puentismo

bungle [ˈbʌŋɡl] VT echar a perder; **the police ~d the arrest** la detención no salió bien por culpa de la policía, la policía metió la pata al realizar la detención; **a ~d job** una chapuza*; **to ~ it** hacer una chapuza*, amolarlo (*Mex**)

bungling [ˈbʌŋɡlɪŋ] ADJ torpe, desmañado

bunion [ˈbʌnjən] N juanete *m*

bunk¹ [bʌŋk] N (= *Rail, Naut*) litera *f* ► **bunk bed** litera *f*

bunk²* [bʌŋk] N (*Brit*) **to do a ~** largarse*, escaquearse (*Sp**) ► **bunk off*** (*Brit*) **Ⓐ** VI + ADV (*also* ~ **off school**) hacer novillos *or* rabona; (= *run off*) escaparse, escurrir el bulto*; (= *get out of task*) zafarse, quitarse de en medio, escaquearse (*Sp***) **Ⓑ** VI + PREP **to ~ off school** hacer novillos *or* rabona

bunk³* [bʌŋk] N (= *nonsense*) bobadas* *fpl*

bunker [ˈbʌŋkəʳ] N **1** (= *coal bunker*) carbonera *f* **2** (*Mil*) refugio *m* antiaéreo/antinuclear, búnker *m* **3** (*Golf*) búnker *m*

bunny [ˈbʌnɪ] **Ⓐ** N **1** (*also* ~ **rabbit***) conejito *m* **2** (*US**) (= *pretty girl*) bombón* *m*, tía *f* buena (*Sp**) **Ⓑ** CPD ► **bunny girl** conejita *f*

bunting¹ [ˈbʌntɪŋ] N (= *bird*) escribano *m*

bunting² [ˈbʌntɪŋ] N (= *flags*) banderitas *fpl*, empavesado *m*

buoy [bɔɪ, (*US*) ˈbuːɪ] N boya *f*
► **buoy up** VT + ADV [+ *spirits etc*] levantar; [+ *person*] animar, alentar

buoyancy [ˈbɔɪənsɪ] N **1** [*of ship, object*] capacidad *f* para flotar, flotabilidad *f* **2** [*of market, prices*] tendencia *f* al alza **3** (= *optimism*) optimismo *m*

buoyant [ˈbɔɪənt] ADJ **1** [*ship, object*] flotante, boyante (*Tech*) **2** [*market, prices*] con tendencia al alza **3** [*mood, person*] optimista

burble [ˈbɜːbl] VI **1** [*baby*] hacer gorgoritos; [*stream*] burbujear **2** (*pej*) (= *talk*) farfullar

burden [ˈbɜːdn] **Ⓐ** N **1** (= *load*) carga *f*; (= *weight*) peso *m* **2** [*of taxes, years*] peso *m*, carga *f*; **to be a ~ to sb** ser una carga para algn; **the ~ of proof lies with him** le corresponde a él probar que es verdad lo que dice **Ⓑ** VT cargar (**with** con)

bureau [ˈbjʊərəʊ] **Ⓐ** N (*pl* ~**x**) **1** (= *agency*) agencia *f*, oficina *f* **2** (*US*) (= *government department*) departamento *m* **3** (*Brit*) (= *desk*) buró *m*, escritorio *m* **4** (*US*) (= *chest of drawers*) cómoda *f* **Ⓑ** CPD ► **bureau de change** [ˌbjʊərəʊdəˈʃɒndʒ] caja *f* de cambio ► **Bureau of Indian affairs** (*US*) Departamento *m* de Asuntos Indios

bureaucracy [bjʊəˈrɒkrəsɪ] N burocracia *f*

bureaucrat [ˈbjʊərəkræt] N burócrata *mf*

bureaucratic [ˌbjʊərəˈkrætɪk] ADJ burocrático

bureaux [ˈbjʊərəʊz] NPL *of* **bureau**

burgeon [ˈbɜːdʒən] VI [*trade etc*] florecer

burger [ˈbɜːɡəʳ] N hamburguesa *f*

burglar [ˈbɜːɡləʳ] N ladrón/ona *m/f* ► **burglar alarm** alarma *f* antirrobo

burglarize [ˈbɜːɡləraɪz] VT (*US*) robar en, desvalijar

burglary [ˈbɜːɡlərɪ] N robo *m* (*en una casa*), allanamiento *m* de morada (*Jur*)

burgle [ˈbɜːɡl] VT (*Brit*) robar en, desvalijar

burgundy [ˈbɜːɡəndɪ] ADJ (= *colour*) granate *inv*

burial [ˈberɪəl] N entierro *m* ► **burial ground** cementerio *m*, camposanto *m*, panteón *m* (*LAm*)

burlap [ˈbɜːlæp] N (*esp US*) arpillera *f*

burlesque [bɜːˈlesk] **Ⓐ** ADJ burlesco **Ⓑ** N **1** (= *parody*) parodia *f* **2** (*US Theat*) revista *f* de estriptís **Ⓒ** VT parodiar **Ⓓ** CPD ► **burlesque show** (*US*) revista *f* de estriptís

burly [ˈbɜːlɪ] ADJ (*compar* **burlier**; *superl* **burliest**) fornido, fuerte

Burma [ˈbɜːmə] N Birmania *f*

Burmese [bɜːˈmiːz] ADJ, N birmano/a *m/f*

burn¹ [bɜːn] (*vb: pt, pp* ~**ed**, ~**t**) **Ⓐ** N (*Med*) quemadura *f* **Ⓑ** VT **1** (*gen*) quemar; [+ *house, building*] incendiar; [+ *corpse*] incinerar; [+ *mouth, tongue*] quemar, escaldar; **to ~ a hole in sth** hacer un agujero en algo quemándolo; **to ~ sth to ashes** reducir algo a cenizas; **to be ~ed alive** ser quemado vivo; **to be ~t to death** morir abrasado; **to ~ one's hand** quemarse la mano; **I've ~t myself!** ¡me he quemado!, ¡me quemé! (*LAm*); **I've ~t the toast** se me ha quemado la tostada; ✦ IDIOMS **to ~ one's bridges** *or* (*Brit*) **boats** quemar las naves; **to ~ the candle at both ends** hacer de la noche día; **to get one's fingers ~ed** pillarse los dedos; **money ~s a hole in his pocket** el dinero le quema las manos
2 [*sun*] [+ *person, skin*] quemar
3 [+ *fuel*] consumir, usar
Ⓒ VI **1** [*fire, building*] arder, quemarse; [*meat, pastry*] quemarse
2 [*skin*] (*in sun*) quemarse, tostarse
3 [*light, gas*] estar encendido
4 (*fig*) **to be ~ing to do sth** desear ardientemente hacer algo
► **burn down Ⓐ** VT + ADV [+ *building*] incendiar **Ⓑ** VI + ADV **1** [*house*] incendiarse **2** [*candle, fire*] apagarse
► **burn out Ⓐ** VT + ADV **the fire had ~t itself out** (*in hearth*) el fuego se había apagado; [*forest fire*] el incendio se había extinguido; **he's ~t himself out** (*fig*) está quemado **Ⓑ** VI + ADV [*candle, fire*] apagarse
► **burn up Ⓐ** VI + ADV [*rocket*] desintegrarse **Ⓑ** VT + ADV [+ *calories, energy*] quemar

burn² [bɜːn] N (*Scot*) (= *stream*) arroyo *m*, riachuelo *m*

burner [ˈbɜːnəʳ] N (*on cooker*) quemador *m*

burning [ˈbɜːnɪŋ] **Ⓐ** N **1** (= *singeing*) **there's a smell of ~** huele a quemado; **I can smell ~** huelo a quemado
2 [*of building*] quema *f*
Ⓑ ADJ **1** (= *on fire*) [*building, forest*] en llamas; [*coals, flame*] ardiente; [*candle*] encendido
2 (= *hot*) [*sun*] abrasador, ardiente; [*sand*] ardiente; [*desert*] infernal; [*face, skin*] ardiendo; [*thirst, fever*] abrasador; [*sensation*] de ardor, de escozor; **with a ~ face** (*through embarrassment, shame*) con la cara ardiendo de vergüenza
3 (= *intense*) [*desire, passion, eyes*] ardiente; [*ambition*] que quema; [*question, topic*] candente
Ⓒ ADV ~ **hot: his forehead was ~ hot** su frente estaba ardiendo

burnish [ˈbɜːnɪʃ] VT [+ *metal*] bruñir

BURNS NIGHT

En la noche del 25 de enero, **Burns Night**, se celebra el aniversario del nacimiento del poeta escocés Robert Burns (1759-1796). Los escoceses de todo el mundo se reúnen para celebrar su vida y obra haciendo una cena en su honor (**Burns Supper**), en la que, al son de la gaita, se sirve **haggis** (asaduras de cordero, avena y especias cocidas en las tripas del animal) con patatas y puré de nabos. Después de la cena se cantan canciones de Burns, se leen sus poemas y se hacen discursos de carácter festivo relacionados con ellos.

burnt [bɜːnt] **Ⓐ** PT, PP *of* **burn** **Ⓑ** ADJ quemado

burp* [bɜːp] **Ⓐ** N eructo *m* **Ⓑ** VI eructar **Ⓒ** VT [+ *baby*] hacer eructar

burqa ['bɜːkə] N burqa *m*, burka *m*

burrow ['bʌrəʊ] **Ⓐ** N (*gen*) madriguera *f*; [*of rabbit*] conejera *f* **Ⓑ** VT [+ *hole*] cavar **Ⓒ** VI hacer una madriguera

bursar ['bɜːsəʳ] N (*Univ*) tesorero/a *m/f*; [*of school*] administrador(a) *m/f*

bursary ['bɜːsərɪ] N (*Brit*) beca *f*

burst [bɜːst] (*vb: pt, pp ~*) **Ⓐ** N **1** (*in pipe*) reventón *m* **2** [*of shell etc*] estallido *m*, explosión *f*; [*of shots*] ráfaga *f*; **a ~ of activity** un arranque repentino de actividad; **a ~ of applause** una salva de aplausos; **he put on a ~ of speed** aceleró bruscamente

Ⓑ ADJ **a ~ blood vessel** un derrame; **a ~ pipe** una tubería reventada; **a ~ tyre** or (*US*) **tire** un neumático reventado, una llanta pinchada (*LAm*)

Ⓒ VT [+ *pipe, balloon, bag, bubble*] reventar; [+ *banks, dam*] romper; **the river has ~ its banks** el río se ha desbordado; **to ~ open a door** abrir una puerta de golpe

Ⓓ VI [*pipe, balloon, tyre, boil, bubble*] reventar(se); [*dam*] romperse; [*shell*] explotar, estallar; [*storm*] desatarse, desencadenarse; (*fig*) [*heart*] partirse; **~ing at the seams** lleno a reventar; **I'm ~ing for the loo** (*Brit**) estoy que reviento*, tengo que ir al wáter; **to ~ into tears** echarse a llorar; **the door ~ open** la puerta se abrió de golpe; **I was ~ing to tell you** reventaba de ganas de decírtelo; **to be ~ing with pride** no caber dentro de sí de orgullo

➤ **burst in** VI + ADV entrar violentamente

➤ **burst out** VI + ADV **1 to ~ out of a room** salir repentinamente de un cuarto **2 to ~ out laughing** echarse a reír

Burundi [bəˈrʊndɪ] N Burundi *m*

bury ['berɪ] VT **1** [+ *body, treasure*] enterrar; **to be buried alive** ser enterrado vivo; **buried by an avalanche** sepultado por una avalancha; **he wanted to be buried at sea** quería que su cadáver fuera arrojado al mar; **✦** IDIOMS **to ~ the hatchet ◇ ~ the tomahawk** (*US*) enterrar el hacha de guerra **2** (= *conceal*) **he buried his face in his hands** escondió la cara entre las manos **3** (= *engross*) **she buried herself in her book** se ensimismó en la lectura, se enfrascó en el libro **4** (= *plunge*) [+ *claws, knife*] clavar (**in** en)

bus [bʌs] (*pl* **~es** or (*US*) **~ses**) **Ⓐ** N **1** (= *city bus*) autobús *m*, colectivo *m* (*Arg*), micro *f* (*Chi*), micro *m* (*SC*), carrito *m* (*por puesto*) (*Ven*), camión *m* (*Mex, CAm*), ómnibus *m* (*Per, Uruguay*); (= *coach*) autobús *m*, autocar *m* (*Sp*), ómnibus *m* (*Arg*), camión *m* (*Mex, CAm*), pullman *m* (*SC*), flota *f* (*Bol, Col*); **to come/go by ~** venir/ir en autobús *etc* **2** (*Comput*) bus *m*

Ⓑ VT transportar en autobús *etc*; **the children are ~sed to school** los niños van al colegio en autobús

Ⓒ VI ir en autobús *etc*

Ⓓ CPD [*ticket, driver*] de autobús *etc*; [*station, service, lane*] de autobuses *etc* ➤ **bus conductor** cobrador(a) *m/f* ➤ **bus depot** cochera *f* (*Sp*) or garaje *m* (*LAm*) de autobuses *etc* ➤ **bus route** recorrido *m* del autobús *etc*; **the house is on a ~ route** pasa un autobús por delante de la casa ➤ **bus shelter** marquesina *f* de autobús *etc* ➤ **bus stop** parada *f*, paradero *m* (*LAm*)

busboy ['bʌsbɔɪ] N (*US*) ayudante *m* de camarero

busby ['bʌzbɪ] N (*Brit*) gorro *m* alto de piel negra

bush [bʊʃ] **Ⓐ** N **1** (= *shrub*) arbusto *m*, mata *f*; (= *thicket*) (*also* **~es**) matorral *m*; **✦** IDIOM **to beat about the ~** andarse con rodeos or por las ramas **2** (*in Africa, Australia*) **the ~** el monte **Ⓑ** CPD ➤ **bush baby** lemúrido *m* ➤ **bush fire** incendio *m* de monte

bushed* [bʊʃt] ADJ agotado, hecho polvo*

bushy ['bʊʃɪ] ADJ (*compar* **bushier**; *superl* **bushiest**) [*plant*] parecido a un arbusto; [*hair*] espeso, tupido; [*beard, eyebrows*] poblado

bushy-tailed [ˌbʊʃɪˈteɪld] ADJ **✦** IDIOM **bright-eyed and ~** rebosante de energía y entusiasmo

busily ['bɪzɪlɪ] ADV afanosamente; **he was ~ engaged in painting it** lo estaba pintando afanosamente; **everyone was ~ writing** todos escribían con ahínco

business ['bɪznɪs] **Ⓐ** N **1** (= *commerce*) negocios *mpl*, comercio *m*; **~ is good at the moment** el negocio va bien por el momento; **to do ~ with** negociar con; **he's in ~ se**

dedica al comercio; **to go into ~** dedicarse al comercio; **the shop is losing ~** la tienda está perdiendo clientela; **he means ~** habla en serio; **I'm here on ~** estoy (en viaje) de negocios; **to go out of ~** quebrar; **to put sb out of ~** hacer que algn quiebre; **to set up in ~ as** montar un negocio de; **to set sb up in ~** montar un negocio a algn; **to get down to ~** ir al grano; **✦** IDIOM **now we're in ~*** ya caminamos

2 (= *firm*) negocio *m*, empresa *f*; **it's a family ~** es una empresa familiar

3 (= *trade, profession*) oficio *m*, ocupación *f*; **what ~ are you in?** ¿a qué se dedica usted?

4 (= *task, duty, concern*) asunto *m*, responsabilidad *f*; **to send sb about his ~** echar a algn con cajas destempladas; **I have ~ with the minister** tengo asuntos que tratar con el ministro; **what ~ have you to intervene?** ¿con qué derecho interviene usted?; **we are not in the ~ of subsidizing scroungers** no tenemos por costumbre costearles la vida a los gorrones; **that's my ~** eso es cosa mía; **I will make it my ~ to tell him** yo me encargaré de decírselo; **it's no ~ of mine** yo no tengo nada que ver con eso, no es cosa mía; **you had no ~ doing that** no tenías derecho a hacerlo; **they're working away like nobody's ~** están trabajando como locos; **it's none of his ~** no es asunto suyo; **none of your ~!*** ¡y a ti qué te importa!, ¡no te metas!*; **any other ~** (*on agenda*) ruegos *mpl* y preguntas

5 (*) (= *matter*) asunto *m*, cuestión *f*; **finding a flat can be quite a ~ about** encontrar piso or (*LAm*) un departamento puede ser muy difícil; **did you hear about that ~ yesterday?** ¿te contaron algo de lo que pasó ayer?

Ⓑ CPD ➤ **business address** dirección *f* comercial or profesional ➤ **business administration** (*as course*) administración *f* de empresas ➤ **business card** tarjeta *f* de visita ➤ **business class** (*Aer*) clase *f* preferente ➤ **business expenses** gastos *mpl* (comerciales) ➤ **business hours** horas *fpl* de oficina ➤ **business lunch** comida *f* de negocios ➤ **business management** dirección *f* empresarial ➤ **business people** empresarios *mpl*, gente *f* de negocios ➤ **business plan** plan *m* de empresa ➤ **business premises** local *msing* comercial ➤ **business sense** cabeza *f* para los negocios ➤ **business Spanish** español *m* comercial ➤ **(Faculty of) Business Studies** (Facultad *f* de) Ciencias *fpl* Empresariales ➤ **business trip** viaje *m* de negocios

businesslike ['bɪznɪslaɪk] ADJ formal, serio

businessman ['bɪznɪsmæn] N (*pl* **businessmen**) hombre *m* de negocios; (= *trader*) empresario *m*

businesswoman ['bɪznɪswʊmən] N (*pl* **businesswomen**) mujer *f* de negocios; (= *trader*) empresaria *f*

busing ['bʌsɪŋ] N (*US*) transporte *m* escolar

busk [bʌsk] VI (*Brit*) tocar música (en la calle)

busker ['bʌskəʳ] N (*Brit*) músico/a *m/f* callejero/a

bussing ['bʌsɪŋ] N = **busing**

bust¹ [bʌst] **Ⓐ** N **1** (*Art*) busto *m* **2** (= *bosom*) pecho *m* **Ⓑ** CPD ➤ **bust measurement** talla *f* de pecho

bust² [bʌst] **Ⓐ** ADJ **1** (*) (= *broken*) estropeado, escacharrado (*Sp**); **New York or ~!*** ¡o Nueva York o nada! **2** (*) (= *bankrupt*) **to go ~** [*business*] quebrar, irse a pique*; [*person*] arruinarse **Ⓑ** VT **1** (*) (= *break*) destrozar, escacharrar (*Sp**) **2** (*Police***) (= *arrest*) agarrar, trincar (*Sp**); (= *raid*) hacer una redada en **3** (*esp US**) (= *demote*) [+ *police officer*] degradar

➤ **bust up*** **Ⓐ** VT + ADV [+ *marriage, friendship*] romper **Ⓑ** VI + ADV [*friends*] reñir, pelearse; **to ~ up with sb** (= *quarrel*) reñir or pelearse con algn; (= *break up*) romper con algn

bustle¹ ['bʌsl] **Ⓐ** N (= *activity*) ajetreo *m*, bullicio *m*; (= *haste*) prisa *f* **Ⓑ** VI (*also* ~ **about**) ir y venir; **to ~ in/out** entrar/salir afanosamente; **bustling with activity** rebosante de actividad

bustle² ['bʌsl] N (*Hist*) [*of dress*] polisón *m*

bustling ['bʌslɪŋ] ADJ [*street*] animado, lleno de movimiento

bust-up* ['bʌstʌp] N (= *quarrel*) riña *f*, bronca* *f*; (= *break-up*) ruptura *f*

busty* ['bʌstɪ] ADJ tetuda*

busy ['bɪzɪ] **Ⓐ** ADJ (*compar* **busier**; *superl* **busiest**) **1** [*person*] ocupado; **are you ~?** ¿está ocupado?; **to be ~ doing sth**

estar ocupado haciendo algo; **to be ~ on/with** estar ocupado en/con; **let's get ~!** ¡a trabajar!; **to keep ~** mantenerse ocupado; **to keep sb ~** ocupar a algn **2** [*day, time*] activo, ajetreado
3 [*place, town*] concurrido; [*scene*] animado, lleno de movimiento
4 [*telephone, line*] comunicando, ocupado
Ⓑ VT **to ~ o.s. with/doing sth** ocuparse con/en hacer algo **Ⓒ** CPD ► **Busy Lizzie** alegría *f* de la casa ► **busy signal** (*esp US*) señal *f* de comunicado, tono *m* (de) ocupado

busybody ['bɪzɪbɒdɪ] N entrometido/a *m/f*

but [bʌt] **Ⓐ** CONJ **1** (*contrasting*) pero; **I want to go ~ I can't afford it** quiero ir, pero no tengo el dinero
2 (*in direct contradiction*) sino; **he's not Spanish ~ Italian** no es español sino italiano
3 (*as linker*) **~ then you must be my cousin!** ¡entonces tú debes de ser mi primo!
Ⓑ ADV sólo, solamente, no más que; **she's ~ a child** no es más que una niña; **you can ~ try** con intentar no se pierde nada; **if I could ~ speak to him** si solamente pudiese hablar con él; **one cannot ~ admire him** no se puede sino admirarlo; **had I ~ known** de haberlo sabido (yo), si lo hubiera sabido
Ⓒ PREP (= *except*) menos, excepto, salvo; **anything ~ that** cualquier cosa menos eso; **~ for you** si no fuera por ti; **there is nothing for it ~ to pay up** no hay más remedio que pagar; **who ~ she could have said something like that?** ¿quién sino ella podría haber dicho semejante cosa?
Ⓓ N **no ~s about it!** ¡no hay pero que valga!

butane ['bjuːteɪn] N butano *m*; (*US*) (*for camping*) camping gas *m* ► **butane gas** gas *m* butano

butch** [bʊtʃ] ADJ [*woman*] marimacho; [*man*] macho

butcher ['bʊtʃəʳ] **Ⓐ** N (*gen, also fig*) carnicero/a *m/f*; **~'s (shop)** carnicería *f*; **at the ~'s** en la carnicería; ✦ IDIOM **let's have a ~'s** (*Brit***) déjame verlo; ⇨ *RHYMING SLANG* **Ⓑ** VT [+ *animal*] matar; (*fig*) hacer una carnicería con, masacrar

butchery ['bʊtʃərɪ] N (= *violence*) matanza *f*, carnicería *f*; (= *trade*) carnicería *f*

butler ['bʌtləʳ] N mayordomo *m*

butt¹ [bʌt] N (= *barrel*) tonel *m*; (*for rain*) tina *f*, aljibe *m*

butt² [bʌt] N **1** (*also* **~-end**) cabo *m*, extremo *m*; [*of gun*] culata *f*; [*of cigar*] colilla *f* **2** (*US**) (= *cigarette*) colilla *f* **3** (*esp US***) (= *bottom*) trasero* *m*, culo** *m*; ✦ IDIOM **to work one's ~ off** romperse los cuernos*

butt³ [bʌt] N (= *target*) blanco *m*; **she's the ~ of his jokes** ella es el blanco de sus bromas

butt⁴ [bʌt] VT [*goat*] topetar; [*person*] dar un cabezazo a; **to ~ one's head against** dar un cabezazo contra
► **butt in** VI + ADV (= *interrupt*) interrumpir; (= *meddle*) meterse

butter ['bʌtəʳ] **Ⓐ** N mantequilla *f*, manteca *f* (*Arg*); ✦ IDIOM **~ wouldn't melt in his mouth** es una mosquita muerta* **Ⓑ** VT [+ *bread*] untar con mantequilla **Ⓒ** CPD [*knife, icing*] de mantequilla ► **butter bean** *tipo de frijol blanco o judía blanca* ► **butter dish** mantequera *f*
► **butter up*** VT + ADV (*Brit*) dar jabón a*

butterball* ['bʌtəbɔːl] N (*US*) gordo/a *m/f*

buttercup ['bʌtəkʌp] N ranúnculo *m*

butterfingers* ['bʌtəˌfɪŋgəz] N manazas* *mf*; **~!** ¡premio!

butterfly ['bʌtəflaɪ] **Ⓐ** N **1** (= *insect*) mariposa *f*; ✦ IDIOM **to have butterflies (in one's stomach)** tener cosquillas en el estómago **2** (*Swimming*) mariposa *f* **Ⓑ** CPD ► **butterfly stroke** braza *f* de mariposa

buttermilk ['bʌtəmɪlk] N suero *m* de leche, suero *m* de manteca

buttocks ['bʌtəks] NPL nalgas *fpl*

button ['bʌtn] **Ⓐ** N **1** (*on garment, machine*) botón *m*; **on the ~*** [*arrive*] en punto; (= *exactly*) exacto **2** (*US*) (= *badge*) insignia *f* **Ⓑ** VT (*also* **~ up**) abrochar, abotonar; ✦ IDIOM **to ~ one's lip*** no decir ni mu* **Ⓒ** CPD ► **button mushroom** champiñón *m* pequeño

buttoned-up* ['bʌtnd,ʌp] ADJ [*person*] reservado

buttonhole ['bʌtnhəʊl] **Ⓐ** N **1** [*of garment*] ojal *m* **2** (*Brit*)

(= *flower*) *flor que se lleva en el ojal* **Ⓑ** VT enganchar; **I was ~d by Brian** Brian me enganchó y no me dejaba irme

buttress ['bʌtrɪs] **Ⓐ** N **1** (*Archit*) contrafuerte *m* **2** (*fig*) apoyo *m*, sostén *m* **Ⓑ** VT **1** (*Archit*) apuntalar **2** (*fig*) reforzar, apoyar

buxom ['bʌksəm] ADJ con mucho pecho

buy [baɪ] (*vb: pt, pp* **bought**) **Ⓐ** N compra *f*; **a good/bad ~** una buena/mala compra; **this month's best ~** la mejor oferta del mes
Ⓑ VT **1** (= *purchase*) comprar; **to ~ sth for sb** ◇ **~ sb sth** comprar algo a algn; **I bought it from my brother** se lo compré a mi hermano; **I bought it from the shop on the corner** lo compré en la tienda de la esquina; **you can ~ them cheaper at the supermarket** en el supermercado los venden más baratos **2** (*) (= *believe*) creer, tragar; **all right, I'll ~ it** bueno, te creo
► **buy in** VT + ADV (*Brit*) [+ *food*] proveerse *or* abastecerse de
► **buy into** VI + PREP **1** [+ *company*] comprar acciones de **2** (*) [+ *idea*] apoyar
► **buy off*** VT + ADV (= *bribe*) sobornar, comprar*
► **buy out** VT + ADV [+ *business, partner*] comprar su parte de
► **buy up** VT + ADV [+ *property*] acaparar; [+ *stock*] comprar todas las existencias de

buyer ['baɪəʳ] N comprador(a) *m/f* ► **buyer's market** mercado *m* favorable al comprador

buy-out ['baɪaʊt] N compra *f* de la totalidad de las acciones; **management ~** compra *f* de acciones por los gerentes; **workers' ~** compra *f* de una empresa por los trabajadores

buzz [bʌz] **Ⓐ** N **1** [*of insect, device*] zumbido *m*; [*of conversation*] rumor *m*
2 (*) (= *telephone call*) llamada *f* (telefónica), telefonazo* *m*; **to give sb a ~** dar un telefonazo *or* (*Sp*) un toque a algn*
3 (*) (= *thrill*) **to get a ~ from sth** gozar con algo
Ⓑ VT (*) (= *call by buzzer*) llamar por el interfono; (*US Telec*) dar un telefonazo *or* (*Sp*) un toque a*
Ⓒ VI [*insect, crowd*] zumbar; **my head is ~ing** me zumba la cabeza; **the school ~ed with the news** todo el colegio comentaba la noticia
Ⓓ CPD (= *trendy*) [*phrase, topic*] de moda
► **buzz around***, **buzz about*** VI + ADV [*person*] trajinar
► **buzz off**** VI + ADV (*esp Brit*) largarse*; **~ off!** ¡largo de aquí!*

buzzard ['bʌzəd] N (*Brit*) águila *f* ratonera; (*US*) buitre *m*, gallinazo *m* (*LAm*), zopilote *m* (*CAm, Mex*)

> Use **el/un** not **la/una** before feminine nouns beginning with stressed **a** or **ha** like **águila**.

buzzer ['bʌzəʳ] N (= *intercom*) portero *m* automático, interfono *m*; (*on cooker, timer*) timbre *m*

buzzsaw ['bʌzsɔː] N (*US*) sierra *f* circular

buzzword* ['bʌzwɜːd] N palabra *f* que está de moda, cliché *m*

b/w ABBR (= **black and white**) b/n

by

Ⓐ PREPOSITION	**Ⓑ** ADVERB

> When **by** is the second element in a phrasal verb, eg **go by**, **stand by**, look up the verb. When it is part of a set combination, eg **by chance**, **by half**, look up the other word.

by [baɪ] **Ⓐ** PREPOSITION
1 (= *close to*) al lado de, junto a; **the house by the church** la casa que está al lado de *or* junto a la iglesia; **come and sit by me** ven y siéntate a mi lado *or* junto a mí; *BUT* **a holiday by the sea** unas vacaciones en la costa
2 (= *via*) por; **I went by Dover** fui por Dover
3 (= *past*) por delante de; **we drove by the cathedral** pasamos con el coche por delante de la catedral
4 (= *during*) **by day/night** de día/noche
5 (= *not later than*) **can you finish it by tomorrow?** ¿puedes

terminarlo para mañana?; **applications must be submitted by April 21** las solicitudes deben presentarse antes del 21 de abril; **by the time I got there it was too late** cuando llegué ya era demasiado tarde
6 (= *already on/in etc*) **by tomorrow/Tuesday, I'll be in France** mañana/el martes ya estaré en Francia; **by yesterday it was clear that ...** ayer ya se veía claro que ...; **by 30 September we had spent £500** a 30 de septiembre habíamos gastado 500 libras; **by 1998 the number of people out of work had doubled** en 1998 el número de desempleados se había duplicado
7 (*indicating amount or rate*) **to reduce sth by a third** reducir algo en una tercera parte; **letters were arriving by the sackload** las cartas llegaban a montones; **it's getting bigger by the minute/day** cada minuto/día que pasa se hace más grande; **to sell sth by the dozen/kilo** vender algo por docenas/por kilos; **we get paid by the hour** nos pagan por horas; **little by little** poco a poco; **one by one** uno tras otro, uno a uno; **two by two** de dos en dos
8 (*indicating agent, cause*) por; **the thieves were caught by the police** los ladrones fueron capturados por la policía, la policía capturó a los ladrones; *BUT* **surrounded by enemies** rodeado de enemigos; **a painting by Picasso** un cuadro de Picasso
9 (*indicating transport, method, etc*) **by air** [*travel*] en avión; [*send*] por avión, por vía aérea; **by bus/car/train** en autobús/coche/tren; **to pay by cheque** pagar con cheque; **made by hand** hecho a mano; **by land** por tierra; **by sea** por mar
10 (*with gerund*) **by working hard** a fuerza de mucho trabajar, trabajando mucho; **he ended by saying that ...** terminó diciendo que ...
11 (= *according to*) según; **by my watch it's five o'clock** según mi reloj son las cinco; **it's all right by me** por mí no hay problema *or* está bien; **if that's okay by you** si no tienes inconveniente
12 (*measuring difference*) **she missed the plane by a few minutes** perdió el avión por unos minutos; **we beat them to Joe's house by five minutes** llegamos a casa de Joe cinco minutos antes que ellos; **broader by a metre** un metro más ancho
13 (*in measurements*) **a room three metres by four** una habitación de tres metros por cuatro
14 by oneself solo
15 (*in oaths*) por; **I swear by Almighty God** juro por Dios

Todopoderoso
B ADVERB
1 (= *past*) **she rushed by without stopping** pasó a toda prisa, sin pararse
2 (*in set expressions*) **by and by**: **I'll be with you by and by** enseguida estoy contigo; **by and by we heard voices** al poco rato oímos unas voces; **by and large** en general, por lo general

bye¹* [baɪ] EXCL adiós, hasta luego, chao *or* chau (*esp LAm*)
bye² [baɪ] N **by the ~** por cierto, a propósito
bye-bye* [ˌbaɪ'baɪ] EXCL adiós, hasta luego, chao *or* chau (*esp LAm*)
by-election [ˈbaɪɪˌlekʃən] N elección *f* parcial

BY-ELECTION

Se denomina **by-election** en el Reino Unido y otros pases de la **Commonwealth** a las elecciones convocadas con carácter excepcional cuando un escaño queda desierto por fallecimiento o dimisión de un parlamentario (**Member of Parliament**). Dichas elecciones tienen lugar únicamente en el área electoral representada por el citado parlamentario, su **constituency**.

---

bygone [ˈbaɪɡɒn] **A** ADJ [*days, times*] pasado **B** N
✦ IDIOM **to let ~s be ~s** olvidar el pasado; **let ~s be ~s** lo pasado, pasado está
by-law [ˈbaɪlɔː] N ordenanza *f* municipal
bypass [ˈbaɪpɑːs] **A** N **1** (= *road*) circunvalación *f*, carretera *f* de circunvalación **2** (*Med*) (operación *f* de) by-pass *m*; **a heart ~** un by-pass de corazón **B** VT **1** [+ *town*] evitar entrar en **2** (*fig*) [+ *person, difficulty*] evitar **C** CPD
➤ **bypass operation** (operación *f* de) by-pass *m*
by-product [ˈbaɪˌprɒdəkt] N (*Chem etc*) subproducto *m*, derivado *m*; (*fig*) consecuencia *f*, resultado *m*
bystander [ˈbaɪˌstændəʳ] N (= *spectator*) espectador(a) *m/f*; (= *witness*) testigo *mf*
byte [baɪt] N (*Comput*) byte *m*, octeto *m*
byway [ˈbaɪweɪ] N camino *m* poco frecuentado

Cc

C¹, c¹ [siː] N **1** (= *letter*) C, c *f*; **C for Charlie** C de Carmen **2** (*Mus*) **C** do *m*

C² ABBR = **Celsius, Centigrade**

c² ABBR **1** (*US*) (= **cent**) c **2** (= **century**) s. **3** (= **circa**) h.

c. ABBR (= **chapter**) cap., c., c/

CA N ABBR **1** = **Central America 2** (*US*) = **California**

CAA N ABBR **1** (*Brit*) = **Civil Aviation Authority 2** (*US*) = **Civil Aeronautics Authority**

CAB N ABBR (*Brit*) = **Citizens' Advice Bureau**

cab [kæb] **Ⓐ** N **1** (= *taxi*) taxi *m*, colectivo *m* (*LAm*) **2** [*of lorry*] cabina *f* **Ⓑ** CPD ➤ **cab driver** taxista *mf*

cabaret [ˈkæbəreɪ] N cabaret *m*

cabbage [ˈkæbɪdʒ] N col *f*, repollo *m*

cabbie*, cabby* [ˈkæbɪ] N taxista *mf*

cabin [ˈkæbɪn] **Ⓐ** N **1** (= *hut*) cabaña *f* **2** (*on boat*) camarote *m* **3** (*on plane*) cabina *f* **Ⓑ** CPD ➤ **cabin crew** tripulación *f* de pilotaje ➤ **cabin cruiser** yate *m* de crucero (a motor)

cabinet [ˈkæbɪnɪt] **Ⓐ** N **1** (= *cupboard*) armario *m*; (*for display*) vitrina *f*; (*for medicine*) botiquín *m*; (*for TV*) caja *f* **2** (*Pol*) (*also* **Cabinet**) consejo *m* de ministros, gabinete *m* ministerial **Ⓑ** CPD ➤ **cabinet meeting** consejo *m* de ministros ➤ **cabinet minister** ministro/a *m/f* (del Gabinete)

cabinetmaker [ˈkæbɪnɪtˌmeɪkəʳ] N ebanista *mf*

cable [ˈkeɪbl] **Ⓐ** N cable *m* **Ⓑ** VT [+ *news, money*] mandar por cable, cablegrafiar; [+ *person*] mandar un cable a **Ⓒ** CPD ➤ **cable car** (*suspended*) teleférico *m*; (*on rail*) funicular *m* ➤ **cable railway** (*suspended*) teleférico *m*; (*with rail*) funicular *m* aéreo ➤ **cable television** televisión *f* por cable

cache [kæʃ] N **1** [*of contraband, arms, explosives*] alijo *m* **2** (*also* **~ memory**) (*Comput*) (memoria *f*) cache *m or f*

cackle [ˈkækl] **Ⓐ** N **1** [*of hen*] cacareo *m* **2** (= *laugh*) risa *f* aguda **Ⓑ** VI **1** [*hen*] cacarear **2** [*person*] reírse a carcajada limpia, carcajearse

cacophony [kæˈkɒfənɪ] N cacofonía *f*

cactus [ˈkæktəs] (*pl* **~es** *or* **cacti** [ˈkæktaɪ]) N cacto *m*, cactus *m inv*

CAD N ABBR (= **computer-aided design**) DAO *m*, DAC *m* (*LAm*)

cad†* [kæd] N canalla *m*, sinvergüenza *m*

cadaver [kəˈdeɪvəʳ, kəˈdævəʳ] N (*esp US*) cadáver *m*

CADCAM [ˈkædˌkæm] N ABBR = **computer-aided design and manufacture**

caddie, caddy¹ [ˈkædɪ] N (*Golf*) caddie *mf*

caddy² [ˈkædɪ] N **1** (*also* **tea ~**) cajita *f* para té **2** (*US*) (= *shopping trolley*) carrito *m* de la compra

cadence [ˈkeɪdəns] N [*of voice*] cadencia *f*; (= *rhythm*) ritmo *m*, cadencia *f*

cadet [kəˈdet] N cadete *m* ➤ **cadet school** escuela *f* en la que se ofrece instrucción militar

cadge* [kædʒ] VT (*Brit*) [+ *money, cigarette etc*] sablear*, gorronear (*Sp**) (**from** a); **could I ~ a lift from you?** ¿me puedes llevar?, ¿me das un aventón? (*Mex*)

cadmium [ˈkædmɪəm] N cadmio *m*

CAE N ABBR (= **computer-aided engineering**) IAO *f*, IAC *f* (*LAm*)

Caesar [ˈsiːzəʳ] N César

Caesarean, Cesarean (*US*) [siːˈzɛərɪən] N (*also* **~ operation** *or* **section**) (operación *f* de) cesárea *f*

café [ˈkæfeɪ] N café *m* ➤ **café society** la gente de moda

cafeteria [ˌkæfɪˈtɪərɪə] N (restaurante *m* de) autoservicio *m*; (*in factory, office*) cafetería *f*, comedor *m*

caffein(e) [ˈkæfiːn] N cafeína *f*

cage [keɪdʒ] **Ⓐ** N jaula *f* **Ⓑ** VT enjaular; **~(d) bird** pájaro *m* de jaula

cagey [ˈkeɪdʒɪ] (*compar* **cagier**; *superl* **cagiest**) ADJ (= *reserved*) reservado; (= *cautious*) cauteloso; **he was very ~ about it** en eso se anduvo con mucha reserva; **Ian was ~ about his plans** Ian mantenía sus planes celosamente en secreto

cagoule [kəˈguːl] N chubasquero *m*; (*without zip*) canguro *m*

cahoots* [kəˈhuːts] NPL ✦ IDIOM **to be in ~ with sb** estar conchabado con algn*

cairn [kɛən] N montón *m* de piedras colocadas como señal

Cairo [ˈkaɪərəʊ] N El Cairo

cajole [kəˈdʒəʊl] VT engatusar; **to ~ sb into doing sth** engatusar a algn para que haga algo

Cajun [ˈkeɪdʒən] **Ⓐ** ADJ cajún; **~ cookery** cocina *f* tipo cajún **Ⓑ** N **1** (= *person*) cajún *mf* **2** (*Ling*) cajún *m*

cake [keɪk] **Ⓐ** N **1** (*large*) tarta *f*, pastel *m*, torta *f* (*LAm*); (*small*) pastel *m*, queque *m* (*LAm*); (*sponge, plain*) bizcocho *m*, pan *m* dulce; ✦ IDIOMS **he wants to have his ~ and eat it** quiere nadar y guardar la ropa; **to go** *or* **sell like hot ~s*** venderse como rosquillas; **it's a piece of ~*** es pan comido, está tirado* **2** (= *bar*) [*of soap*] pastilla *f* **Ⓑ** VT **~d with mud** embarrado, cubierto de barro seco **Ⓒ** VI [*blood*] coagularse; [*mud*] endurecerse **Ⓓ** CPD ➤ **cake mix** polvos *mpl* para hacer pasteles ➤ **cake pan** (*US*) molde *m* para pastel ➤ **cake shop** pastelería *f* ➤ **cake tin** (*for storing*) caja *f* de pastel; (*Brit*) (*for baking*) molde *m* para pastel

Cal. ABBR (*US*) = **California**

cal. [kæl] N ABBR = **calorie**

calamine [ˈkæləmaɪn] N (*also* **~ lotion**) (loción *f* de) calamina *f*

calamitous [kəˈlæmɪtəs] ADJ calamitoso, desastroso

calamity [kəˈlæmɪtɪ] N calamidad *f*, desastre *m*

calcify [ˈkælsɪfaɪ] **Ⓐ** VT calcificar **Ⓑ** VI calcificarse

calcium [ˈkælsɪəm] N calcio *m*

calculate [ˈkælkjʊleɪt] **Ⓐ** VT calcular; **his words were ~d to cause pain** había planeado expresamente sus palabras para hacer daño; **a move ~d to improve his popularity** una operación diseñada *or* pensada para darle mayor popularidad **Ⓑ** VI (*Math*) calcular, hacer cálculos ➤ **calculate on** VI + PREP contar con

calculated [ˈkælkjʊleɪtɪd] ADJ [*insult, action*] deliberado, intencionado; [*risk*] calculado

calculating [ˈkælkjʊleɪtɪŋ] ADJ calculador

calculation [ˌkælkjʊˈleɪʃən] N cálculo *m*; **to make a ~** realizar un cálculo

calculator [ˈkælkjʊleɪtəʳ] N calculadora *f*

calculus [ˈkælkjʊləs] N cálculo *m*

calendar [ˈkæləndəʳ] N calendario *m*; **the sporting ~** el año *or* calendario deportivo ➤ **calendar month** mes *m* civil ➤ **calendar year** año *m* civil

calf¹ [kɑːf] N (*pl* **calves**) **1** (= *young cow*) becerro/a *m/f*, ternero/a *m/f*; (= *young seal, elephant etc*) cría *f*; (= *young whale*) ballenato *m* **2** (*also* **~skin**) piel *f* de becerro

calf² [kɑːf] N (*pl* **calves**) [*of leg*] pantorrilla *f*, canilla *f* (*esp LAm*)

caliber [ˈkælɪbəʳ] N (*US*) = **calibre**

calibrate [ˈkælɪbreɪt] VT calibrar

calibre, caliber (*US*) [ˈkælɪbəʳ] N calibre *m*

calico [ˈkælɪkəʊ] N calicó *m*, percal *m*

Calif. ABBR = **California**

California [ˌkælɪˈfɔːnɪə] N California *f*

Californian [ˌkælɪˈfɔːnɪən] ADJ, N californiano/a *m/f*

calipers [ˈkælɪpəz] NPL (*US*) = **callipers**

calisthenics [ˌkælɪsˈθenɪks] NSING (US) = **callisthenics**

call [kɔːl] **Ⓐ** N **1** (= to attract attention) llamada f, llamado m (LAm); (= shout) grito m; [of bird] canto m, reclamo m **2** (Telec) llamada f; **to make a ~** llamar (por teléfono), hacer una llamada, telefonear (esp LAm); **please give me a ~ at seven** (in hotel) despiérteme a las siete, por favor **3** (= appeal, invitation) llamamiento m, llamado (LAm); (for flight) anuncio m; **there were ~s for the Minister's resignation** hubo quienes pidieron la dimisión del ministro; **to be on ~** estar de guardia **4** (= lure) llamada f; **to answer the ~ of nature** (euph) hacer sus necesidades fisiológicas **5** (= visit) visita f **6** (= need) motivo m; **there is no ~ for alarm** no tienen por qué asustarse **7** (= demand) demanda f (**for** de); **there isn't much ~ for these now** hay poca demanda de éstos ahora **Ⓑ** VT **1** (= shout out) [+ name, person] llamar, gritar **2** (= summon) [+ doctor, taxi] llamar; [+ meeting, election, strike] convocar; **to ~ sb as a witness** citar a algn como testigo **3** (Telec) llamar (por teléfono); **don't ~ us, we'll ~ you** no se moleste en llamar, nosotros le llamaremos **4** (= announce) [+ flight] anunciar **5** (= waken) despertar, llamar **6** (= name, describe) llamar; **to be ~ed** llamarse; **I'm ~ed Peter** me llamo Peter; **what are you ~ed?** ¿cómo te llamas?; **are you ~ing me a liar?** ¿me está diciendo que soy un mentiroso?, ¿me está llamando mentiroso? **7** (= consider) **I ~ it an insult** para mí eso es un insulto; **let's ~ it £50** quedamos en 50 libras; **what time do you ~ this?** ¿qué hora crees que es?; **~ yourself a friend?** ¿y tú dices que eres un amigo?; **✦ IDIOM let's ~ it a day*** ya basta por hoy **8** (US Sport) [+ game] suspender **Ⓒ** VI **1** (= shout) [person] llamar; (= sing) [bird] cantar; **did you ~?** ¿me llamaste? **2** (Telec) **who's ~ing?** ¿de parte de quién?, ¿quién (le) llama? **3** (= visit) **please ~ again** gracias por su visita **Ⓓ** CPD ➤ **call centre, call center** (US) servicio m de atención telefónica, central f telefónica (para atención al cliente, telemárketing, etc) ➤ **call girl** prostituta f (que concierta citas por teléfono) ➤ **call sign** (Rad) (señal f de) llamada f
➤ **call away** VT + ADV **he was ~ed away** tuvo que salir or marcharse (**from** de); **to be ~ed away on business** tener que ausentarse por razones de trabajo or asuntos de negocios
➤ **call back Ⓐ** VT + ADV **1** (= phone again) volver a llamar a; (= return phonecall) devolver la llamada a **2** (= recall) hacer volver **Ⓑ** VI + ADV **1** (= phone again) volver a llamar; (= return phonecall) devolver la llamada **2** (= return) volver, regresar
➤ **call for** VI + PREP **1** (= summon) pedir; **to ~ for help** pedir auxilio **2** (= demand) [+ courage, action] exigir, requerir; **this ~s for a celebration!** ¡esto hay que celebrarlo! **3** (= collect) [+ person] pasar a buscar; [+ goods] recoger
➤ **call in Ⓐ** VT + ADV **1** (= summon) hacer entrar; [+ doctor, expert, police] llamar a **2** (= withdraw) [+ faulty goods, currency] retirar; [+ book, loan] pedir la devolución de **Ⓑ** VI + ADV venir, pasar; **to ~ in on sb** pasar a ver a algn; **~ in any time** ven cuando quieras, pasa por aquí cuando quieras
➤ **call off** VT + ADV [+ meeting, race] cancelar, suspender; [+ deal] anular; [+ search] abandonar, dar por terminado; [+ dog] llamar (para que no ataque)
➤ **call on** VI + PREP **1** (= visit) pasar a ver **2** (also ~ **upon**) **2.1** (= appeal to) **to ~ on sb for help** pedir ayuda a algn, acudir a algn pidiendo ayuda; **to ~ on sb to do sth** (= appeal to) apelar a algn para que haga algo; (= demand) exigir a algn que haga algo **2.2** (= invite to speak) ceder or pasar la palabra a; **I now ~ on Mr Brown to speak** cedo la palabra al Sr. Brown
➤ **call out Ⓐ** VT + ADV **1** [+ name] gritar **2** [+ doctor, rescue services] llamar; [+ troops] hacer intervenir **Ⓑ** VI + ADV gritar
➤ **call round** VI + ADV pasar por casa; **I'll ~ round in the morning** pasaré por ahí por la mañana; **to ~ round to see sb** ir de visita a casa de algn
➤ **call up** VT + ADV **1** (Brit Mil) llamar para el servicio militar **2** (= phone) llamar (por teléfono) **3** [+ memories] traer a la memoria
➤ **call upon** VI + PREP = **call on 2**

callbox [ˈkɔːlbɒks] N (Brit) cabina f (telefónica)

caller [ˈkɔːləʳ] N **1** (= visitor) visita f **2** (Brit Telec) persona f que llama

calligraphy [kəˈlɪɡrəfɪ] N caligrafía f

call-in [ˈkɔːlɪn] N (also ~ **program**) (US) (programa m) coloquio m (por teléfono)

calling [ˈkɔːlɪŋ] N (= vocation) vocación f, profesión f
➤ **calling card** (esp US) tarjeta f de visita comercial

callipers, calipers (US) [ˈkælɪpəz] NPL (Med) soporte msing ortopédico; (Math) calibrador msing

callisthenics, calisthenics (US) [ˌkælɪsˈθenɪks] NSING calistenia f

callous [ˈkæləs] ADJ [person, remark] insensible, cruel; [treatment, murder, crime, attack] despiadado, cruel

calloused [ˈkæləsd] ADJ encallecido, calloso

callously [ˈkæləslɪ] ADV despiadadamente, cruelmente

callousness [ˈkæləsnɪs] N insensibilidad f, crueldad f

callow [ˈkæləʊ] ADJ imberbe, bisoño

call-up [ˈkɔːlʌp] N (Mil) llamada f al servicio militar; [of reserves] movilización f ➤ **call-up papers** notificación fsing de llamada a filas

calm [kɑːm] **Ⓐ** ADJ (compar ~**er**; superl ~**est**) **1** [person, voice, place] tranquilo; **to grow ~** tranquilizarse, calmarse; **to keep ~** mantener la calma; **keep ~!** ¡tranquilo(s)!, ¡calma! **2** [sea, water, weather] en calma **Ⓑ** N calma f, tranquilidad f **Ⓒ** VT (also ~ **down**) [+ person] calmar, tranquilizar; **to ~ o.s.** calmarse, tranquilizarse
➤ **calm down Ⓐ** VI + ADV [person] tranquilizarse, calmarse; **~ down!** ¡tranquilízate!, ¡cálmate! **Ⓑ** VT + ADV = **calm C**

calming [ˈkɑːmɪŋ] ADJ tranquilizante, calmante

calmly [ˈkɑːmlɪ] ADV [walk] tranquilamente; [speak, discuss, reply] con calma, tranquilamente; [react, think] con calma

calmness [ˈkɑːmnɪs] N [of person, voice] calma f, tranquilidad f; [of weather, sea] calma f

Calor gas ® [ˈkæləˌɡæs] N (Brit) butano m

calorie [ˈkælərɪ] N caloría f

calorific [ˌkæləˈrɪfɪk] ADJ calorífico

calumny [ˈkæləmnɪ] N calumnia f

calve [kɑːv] VI parir

calves [kɑːvz] NPL of **calf**[1,2]

Calvinist [ˈkælvɪnɪst] ADJ, N calvinista mf

CAM [kæm] N ABBR (= **computer-aided manufacture**) FAO f

camaraderie [ˌkæməˈrɑːdərɪ] N compañerismo m

camber [ˈkæmbəʳ] N (in road) combadura f

Cambodia [kæmˈbəʊdɪə] N Camboya f

Cambodian [kæmˈbəʊdɪən] ADJ, N camboyano/a m/f

camcorder [ˈkæmkɔːdəʳ] N videocámara f, filmadora f (LAm)

came [keɪm] PT of **come**

camel [ˈkæməl] **Ⓐ** N **1** (= animal) camello m **2** (= colour) color m camello **Ⓑ** CPD ➤ **camel coat, camel-hair coat, camel's hair coat** (US) abrigo m de pelo de camello

camellia [kəˈmiːlɪə] N camelia f

cameo [ˈkæmɪəʊ] N **1** (= jewellery) camafeo m **2** (Cine) (also ~ **role**) papel m de estrella invitada

camera [ˈkæmərə] N (Phot) cámara f, máquina f fotográfica; (Cine, TV) cámara f; **on ~** delante de la cámara, en cámara; **to be on ~** estar enfocado ➤ **camera crew** equipo m de cámara

cameraman [ˈkæmərəmæn] N (pl **cameramen**) cámara mf, operador(a) m/f

camera-shy [ˈkæmərəˌʃaɪ] ADJ **to be ~** cohibirse en presencia de la cámara

camerawork [ˈkæmərəˌwɜːk] N manejo m de la cámara

Cameroon, Cameroun [ˌkæməˈruːn] N Camerún m

camisole [ˈkæmɪsəʊl] N camisola f

camomile ['kæməmaɪl] N camomila f ➤ **camomile tea** manzanilla f

camouflage ['kæməflɑːʒ] Ⓐ N camuflaje m Ⓑ VT camuflar

camp[1] [kæmp] Ⓐ N 1 (= *collection of tents*) campamento m; (= *organized site*) camping m; **to pitch ~** poner or montar el campamento, acampar 2 (*Pol etc*) bando m, facción f; ✦ IDIOM **to have a foot in both ~s** tener intereses en ambos bandos Ⓑ VI acampar; **to go ~ing** ir de camping, ir de acampada Ⓒ CPD ➤ **camp bed** (*Brit*) cama f de campaña, cama f plegable, catre m (*LAm*) ➤ **camp site** camping m ➤ **camp stove** hornillo m de camping
➤ **camp out** VI + ADV pasar la noche al aire libre

camp[2] [kæmp] Ⓐ ADJ 1 (= *affected*) amanerado, afectado 2 (= *effeminate*) afeminado Ⓑ VT **to ~ it up*** parodiarse a sí mismo

campaign [kæm'peɪn] Ⓐ N campaña f; **the ~ for human rights** la campaña pro derechos humanos or en pro de los derechos humanos Ⓑ VI hacer campaña; **to ~ for/against** hacer campaña a favor de/en contra de

campaigner [kæm'peɪnəʳ] N defensor(a) m/f, partidario/a m/f (**for sth** de algo); **a ~ against sth** un(a) luchador(a) contra algo

camper ['kæmpəʳ] N 1 (*in holiday camp*) veraneante mf 2 (*also ~ van*) caravana f, autocaravana f

camphor ['kæmfəʳ] N alcanfor m

camping ['kæmpɪŋ] N camping m ➤ **Camping gas®** (*Brit*) (= *gas*) gas m butano; (*US*) (= *stove*) camping gas® m ➤ **camping site** camping m ➤ **camping van** caravana f, autocaravana f

campus ['kæmpəs] N (*Univ*) campus m inv

camshaft ['kæmʃɑːft] N árbol m de levas

can[1] [kæn] MODAL AUX VB (*neg* **~not**, **~'t**; *cond*, *pt* **could**) 1 (= *be able to*) poder; **I ~'t or cannot go any further** no puedo seguir; **he couldn't concentrate because of the noise** no se podía concentrar a causa del ruido; **I'll tell you all I ~** te diré todo lo que pueda; **he will do all he ~ to help you** hará lo posible por ayudarte; **they couldn't help it** ellos no tienen la culpa
2 (= *know how to*) saber; **he ~'t swim** no sabe nadar; **~ you speak Italian?** ¿sabes (hablar) italiano?; **his wife couldn't drive** su mujer no sabía conducir
3 (= *may*) poder; **~ I use your telephone?** ¿puedo usar su teléfono?; **~ I have your name?** ¿me dice su nombre?; **could I have a word with you?** ¿podría hablar contigo un momento?; **~'t I come too?** ¿puedo ir también?
4 (*with verbs of perception: not translated*) **I ~ hear it** lo oigo; **I couldn't see it anywhere** no lo veía en ninguna parte; **I ~'t understand why** no comprendo por qué
5 (*expressing disbelief*) **that cannot be!** ¡eso no puede ser!, ¡es imposible!; **he ~'t have said that** no puede haber dicho eso; **they ~'t have left already!** ¡no es posible que ya se han ido!; **how could you lie to me?** ¿cómo pudiste mentirme?; **you ~'t be serious!** ¿lo dices en serio?; **it ~'t be true!** ¡no puede ser!; **what ~ he want?** ¿qué querrá?
6 (*expressing possibility, suggestion*) **he could be in the library** puede que esté en la biblioteca; **you could try telephoning his office** ¿por qué no le llamas a su despacho?; **you could have told me!** ¡podías habérmelo dicho!; **it could have been a wolf** podía ser un lobo
7 (= *want to*) **I'm so happy I could cry** soy tan feliz que me dan ganas de gritar or que me voy a echar a llorar; **I could have cried** me daban ganas de llorar; **I could scream!** ¡es para volverse loco!
8 (= *be occasionally capable of*) **she ~ be very annoying** a veces te pone negro; **it ~ get very cold here** aquí puede llegar a hacer mucho frío
9 (*in comparisons*) **I'm doing it as well as I ~** lo hago lo mejor que puedo; **as big as big ~ be** lo más grande posible; **she was as happy as could be** estaba de lo más feliz
10 **could do with: I could do with a drink!** ¡qué bien me vendría una copa!; **we could do with a bigger house** nos convendría una casa más grande

can[2] [kæn] Ⓐ N 1 [*of food, drink*] bote m, lata f; (*for oil,*

water etc) bidón m; ✦ IDIOMS **a ~ of worms*** un asunto peliagudo; **to open a ~ of worms*** abrir la caja de Pandora 2 (*esp US*) (= *garbage can*) cubo m or (*LAm*) bote m or tarro m de la basura 3 (*Cine*) [*of film*] lata f; ✦ IDIOM **it's in the ~*** está listo 4 (*US***) (= *prison*) chirona* f; (= *toilet*) wáter m Ⓑ VT 1 [+ *food*] enlatar, envasar; ✦ IDIOM **~ it!** (*US***) ¡cállate! 2 (*US**) (= *dismiss*) despedir Ⓒ CPD ➤ **can opener** abrelatas m inv

Canada ['kænədə] N Canadá m; *ver tb* http://canada.gc.ca

Canadian [kə'neɪdɪən] ADJ, N canadiense mf

canal [kə'næl] N 1 (= *watercourse*) canal m 2 (*Anat*) tubo m

Canaries [kə'nɛərɪz] NPL **the ~** las Canarias

canary [kə'nɛərɪ] N canario m ➤ **the Canary Islands** las Islas Canarias ➤ **canary yellow** amarillo m canario

Canberra ['kænbərə] N Canberra f

cancel ['kænsəl] Ⓐ VT 1 [+ *reservation, order*] anular, cancelar; [+ *room*] anular la reserva de; [+ *holiday, party, plans*] cancelar; [+ *flight, train, performance*] suspender, cancelar 2 (= *mark, frank*) [+ *stamp*] matar; [+ *cheque*] anular Ⓑ VI [*tourist etc*] cancelar la reserva/el vuelo *etc* Ⓒ CPD ➤ **cancel key** tecla f de anulación
➤ **cancel out** Ⓐ VT + ADV anular; (*fig*) contrarrestar, compensar; **they ~ each other out** (*Math*) se anulan mutuamente; (*fig*) se contrarrestan, una cosa compensa la otra Ⓑ VI + ADV (*Math*) anularse

cancellation [ˌkænsə'leɪʃən] N [*of reservation, order*] anulación f, cancelación f; [*of room*] anulación f de reserva; [*of holiday, party, plans*] cancelación f; [*of flight, train, performance*] suspensión f, cancelación f
➤ **cancellation fee** tarifa f por cancelación

Cancer ['kænsəʳ] N 1 (= *sign, constellation, also Geog*) Cáncer m 2 (= *person*) cáncer mf inv; **I'm (a) ~** soy cáncer

cancer ['kænsəʳ] N (*Med*) cáncer m ➤ **cancer patient** enfermo/a m/f de cáncer ➤ **cancer research** investigación f del cáncer ➤ **cancer specialist** cancerólogo/a m/f, oncólogo/a m/f

cancerous ['kænsərəs] ADJ canceroso

candelabra [ˌkændɪ'lɑːbrə] N candelabro m

candid ['kændɪd] ADJ franco, sincero; **to be quite ~ ...** hablando con franqueza ...

⚠ candid ≠ cándido

candidacy ['kændɪdəsɪ] N candidatura f

candidate ['kændɪdeɪt] N (*for job*) aspirante mf (**for** a), solicitante mf (**for** de); (*for election, examination*) candidato/a m/f (**for** a)

candidature ['kændɪdətʃəʳ] N (*Brit*) candidatura f

candidly ['kændɪdlɪ] ADV francamente, con franqueza

candied ['kændɪd] ADJ azucarado ➤ **candied peel** piel f almibarada

candle ['kændl] N vela f, candela f; (*in church*) cirio m; ✦ IDIOM **you can't hold a ~ to him** no le llegas ni a la suela de los zapatos

candlelight ['kændllaɪt] N luz f de una vela; **by ~** a la luz de las velas/una vela

candlelit ['kændllɪt] ADJ alumbrado por velas; **a ~ dinner for two** una cena para dos con velas

candlestick ['kændlstɪk] N (*single*) candelero m; (*low, with handle*) palmatoria f; (*for two candles or more*) candelabro m

can-do* [ˌkæn'duː] ADJ (*US*) dinámico

candour, candor (*US*) ['kændəʳ] N franqueza f, sinceridad f

candy ['kændɪ] Ⓐ N (*US*) golosinas fpl, caramelos mpl, dulces mpl Ⓑ VT [+ *fruit*] escarchar Ⓒ CPD ➤ **candy bar** (*US*) barrita f de caramelo; (*chocolate*) chocolatina f ➤ **candy floss** (*Brit*) algodón m de azúcar ➤ **candy store** (*US*) confitería f, bombonería f

candy-striped ['kændɪˌstraɪpt] ADJ a rayas de colores

cane [keɪn] Ⓐ N 1 (*Bot*) caña f; (*for baskets, chairs etc*) mimbre *m* **2** (*for walking*) bastón *m*; (*for punishment*) vara *f*, palmeta *f*; **to get the** ~ (*Scol*) ser castigado con la vara *or* palmeta ⓑ VT [+ *pupil*] castigar con la vara *or* palmeta ⓒ CPD ➤ **cane sugar** azúcar *m* de caña

canine ['kænaɪn] ⓐ ADJ canino ⓑ N (*also* ~ **tooth**) colmillo *m*, diente *m* canino

canister ['kænɪstəʳ] N (*for tea, coffee*) lata *f*, bote *m*; [*of gas*] bombona *f*; (*for film*) lata *f*

cannabis ['kænəbɪs] N (= *plant*) cáñamo *m* (índico); (= *drug*) cannabis *m* ➤ **cannabis resin** resina *f* de hachís

canned [kænd] ⓐ PT, PP *of* **can²** ⓑ ADJ **1** (*US*) [*food*] enlatado, en lata **2** (*) [*music*] grabado, enlatado; ~ **laughter** (*TV, Rad*) risas *fpl* grabadas

cannelloni [ˌkænɪ'ləʊnɪ] NPL canelones *mpl*

cannibal ['kænɪbəl] N caníbal *mf*, antropófago/a *m/f*

cannibalism ['kænɪbəlɪzəm] N canibalismo *m*

cannibalize ['kænɪbəlaɪz] VT [+ *car etc*] desguazar, desmontar

canning factory ['kænɪŋˌfæktərɪ] N fábrica *f* de conservas

cannon ['kænən] N cañón *m* ➤ **cannon fodder** carne *f* de cañón

cannonball ['kænənbɔːl] N bala *f* de cañón

cannot ['kænɒt] NEG *of* **can¹**

canny ['kænɪ] ADJ (*compar* **cannier**; *superl* **canniest**) astuto

canoe [kə'nuː] ⓐ N (*gen*) canoa *f*; (*Sport*) piragua *f* ⓑ VI ir en canoa

canoeing [kə'nuːɪŋ] N piragüismo *m*

canoeist [kə'nuːɪst] N piragüista *mf*

canon ['kænən] (= *priest*) canónigo *m* ➤ **canon law** derecho *m* canónico

canonize ['kænənaɪz] VT canonizar

canoodle* [kə'nuːdl] VI besuquearse*

canopy ['kænəpɪ] N **1** (= *outside shop*) toldo *m* **2** (*above bed, throne*) dosel *m*

cant [kænt] N hipocresía(s) *f(pl)*

can't [kɑːnt] NEG = **cannot**; *see* **can¹**

cantankerous [kæn'tæŋkərəs] ADJ cascarrabias *inv*, gruñón

canteen [kæn'tiːn] N **1** (= *restaurant*) cantina *f*, comedor *m* **2** (= *bottle*) cantimplora *f* **3** (*Brit*) **a** ~ **of cutlery** un juego de cubiertos

canter ['kæntəʳ] ⓐ N medio galope *m*; **to go for a** ~ ir a dar un paseo a caballo ⓑ VI ir a medio galope

Canterbury ['kæntəbərɪ] N Cantórbery *m*

cantilever ['kæntɪliːvəʳ] N viga *f* voladiza ➤ **cantilever bridge** puente *m* voladizo

Cantonese [ˌkæntə'niːz] ⓐ ADJ cantonés ⓑ N **1** (= *person*) cantonés/esa *m/f* **2** (*Ling*) cantonés *m*

Canuck* [kə'nʊk] N (*US pej*) canuck *mf*

Canute [kə'njuːt] N Canuto

canvas ['kænvəs] N (= *cloth*) lona *f*; (*Art*) lienzo *m*; **under** ~ en tienda de campaña, en carpa (*LAm*) ➤ **canvas shoes** zapatos *mpl* de lona; (*rope-soled*) alpargatas *fpl*

canvass ['kænvəs] ⓐ VT **1** (*Pol*) [+ *district*] hacer campaña en; [+ *voters*] solicitar el voto de; [+ *votes*] solicitar **2** (*US*) (= *scrutinize*) [+ *votes*] escudriñar **3** (= *survey*) sondear ⓑ VI [*campaigner*] solicitar votos, hacer campaña (**for** a favor de)

canvasser, canvaser (*US*) ['kænvəsəʳ] N (= *campaigner*) *persona que hace campaña electoral para un partido en una zona concreta*

canvassing ['kænvəsɪŋ] N **to go out** ~ salir a solicitar votos

canyon ['kænjən] N cañón *m*

CAP N ABBR (*Pol*) (= **Common Agricultural Policy**) PAC *f*

cap [kæp] ⓐ N **1** (= *hat*) gorra *f*; (*for swimming*) gorro *m* de baño **2** (*Brit Sport*) **he's an England** ~ forma parte de la selección nacional inglesa, juega con la selección nacional inglesa **3** (= *lid*) [*of bottle*] tapón *m*; (*made of metal*) chapa *f*, tapón *m*; [*of pen*] capuchón *m* **4** [*of tooth*] funda *f* **5** (= *radiator/petrol cap*) tapón *m* **6** (*Brit*) (= *contraceptive*) diafragma *m* ⓑ VT **1** [+ *tooth*] enfundar **2** (= *surpass*) **and to** ~ **it all, he ...** y para colmo, él ... **3** (= *limit*) [+ *expenditure*] restringir **4** (*Brit Sport*) [+ *player*] seleccionar (para el equipo nacional), incluir en la selección nacional

cap. ABBR (*Typ*) (= **capital (letter)**) may.

capability [ˌkeɪpə'bɪlɪtɪ] N (= *competence*) competencia *f*; (= *ability*) capacidad *f*; **to have the** ~ **to do sth** tener capacidad para hacer algo; **within/beyond one's capabilities** dentro de/más allá de sus posibilidades

capable ['keɪpəbl] ADJ (= *competent*) competente, capaz; ~ **of** capaz de; **sports cars** ~ **of reaching 150mph** coches deportivos que pueden alcanzar *or* que son capaces de alcanzar las 150 millas por hora

capably ['keɪpəblɪ] ADV competentemente

capacitor [kə'pæsɪtəʳ] N capacitor *m*

capacity [kə'pæsɪtɪ] ⓐ N **1** [*of container etc*] capacidad *f*; (= *seating*) cabida *f*, aforo *m*; **filled to** ~ al completo **2** (= *position*) calidad *f*; **in my** ~ **as Chairman** en mi calidad de presidente; **I've worked for them in various capacities** he trabajado para ellos desempeñando distintas funciones **3** (= *aptitude*) capacidad *f*, aptitud *f* **4** (= *output*) rendimiento *m*; **to work at full** ~ [*machine, factory*] funcionar a pleno rendimiento ⓑ CPD ➤ **capacity audience, capacity crowd** lleno *m*; **there was a** ~ **audience in the theatre** hubo un lleno en el teatro

cape¹ [keɪp] N (*Geog*) cabo *m*; **the Cape** (*also* **Cape Province**) la provincia del Cabo; (*also* **the Cape of Good Hope**) el Cabo de Buena Esperanza ➤ **Cape Town** El Cabo, Ciudad *f* del Cabo

cape² [keɪp] N (= *garment*) capa *f*; [*of policeman, cyclist*] chubasquero *m*; (*Bullfighting*) capote *m*

caper¹ ['keɪpəʳ] N (*for eating*) alcaparra *f*

caper² ['keɪpəʳ] ⓐ N **1** [*of horse*] cabriola *f* **2** (= *escapade*) travesura *f*; (*) (= *business*) lío *m*, embrollo *m* ⓑ VI [*horse*] hacer cabriolas; **to** ~ **about** brincar, juguetear

capful ['kæpfʊl] N tapón *m*; **one** ~ **to four litres of water** un tapón por cada cuatro litros de agua

capillary [kə'pɪlərɪ] ⓐ ADJ capilar ⓑ N capilar *m*

capital ['kæpɪtl] ⓐ ADJ **1** (*Jur*) capital **2** (= *essential*) capital, primordial **3** [*letter*] mayúsculo; **he's Conservative with a** ~ **C** es conservador con mayúscula ⓑ N **1** (*also* ~ **letter**) mayúscula *f*; ~**s** (*large*) mayúsculas *fpl*, versales *fpl*; (*small*) versalitas *fpl* **2** (*also* ~ **city**) capital *f* **3** (*Fin*) capital *m*; ✦ IDIOM **to make** ~ **out of sth** sacar provecho de algo ⓒ CPD ➤ **capital assets** activo *msing* fijo ➤ **capital city** capital *f* ➤ **capital expenditure** inversión *f* de capital ➤ **capital gains tax** impuesto *m* sobre las plusvalías ➤ **capital goods** bienes *mpl* de equipo ➤ **capital offence, capital offense** (*US*) delito *m* capital ➤ **capital punishment** pena *f* de muerte, pena *f* capital

capitalism ['kæpɪtəlɪzəm] N capitalismo *m*

capitalist ['kæpɪtəlɪst] ADJ, N capitalista *mf*

capitalize [kə'pɪtəlaɪz] VI **to** ~ **on** sacar provecho de, aprovechar

Capitol ['kæpɪtɒl] N (US) Capitolio m

capitulate [kə'pɪtjʊleɪt] VI capitular

capitulation [kə,pɪtjʊ'leɪʃən] N capitulación f, rendición f

capon ['keɪpən] N capón m

cappuccino [,kæpə'tʃiːnəʊ] N capuchino m

caprice [kə'priːs] N capricho m

capricious [kə'prɪʃəs] ADJ caprichoso, antojadizo

Capricorn ['kæprɪkɔːn] N 1 (= sign, constellation, also Geog) Capricornio m 2 (= person) capricornio mf inv; **she's (a) ~** es capricornio

caps [kæps] NPL ABBR (= **capitals, capital letters**) may.

capsicum ['kæpsɪkəm] N pimiento m

capsize [kæp'saɪz] VT, VI volcar

capstan ['kæpstən] N cabrestante m

capsule ['kæpsjuːl] N cápsula f

Capt. ABBR = **Captain**

captain ['kæptɪn] Ⓐ N (Mil, Naut, Sport) capitán/ana m/f; (Aer) comandante mf; (US Police) comisario/a m/f de distrito; **~ of industry** magnate mf de la industria, gran industrial mf Ⓑ VT [+ team] capitanear

captaincy ['kæptənsɪ] N capitanía f

caption ['kæpʃən] N (= heading) título m, titular m; (on photo, cartoon) leyenda f, pie m; (in film) subtítulo m

captivate ['kæptɪveɪt] VT encantar, cautivar

captive ['kæptɪv] Ⓐ ADJ cautivo; **he had a ~ audience** tenía cautivada a la audiencia, la gente no tenía más remedio que escucharle Ⓑ N prisionero/a m/f, cautivo/a m/f; **to take sb** ~ hacer prisionero a algn; **to hold sb** ~ tener or mantener prisionero a algn

captivity [kæp'tɪvɪtɪ] N cautiverio m, cautividad f

captor ['kæptə'] N captor(a) m/f, apresador(a) m/f

capture ['kæptʃə'] Ⓐ N 1 (of animal, escapee) captura f, apresamiento m; (of city) toma f, conquista f 2 (Comput) captura f, recogida f Ⓑ VT 1 (+ animal, escapee) capturar, apresar; (+ city) tomar, conquistar; (+ market) conquistar, acaparar 2 (= attract) (+ interest) captar; (+ imagination) cautivar; (+ attention) llamar 3 (= convey, evoke) captar, reflejar; **to ~ sth on film** captar algo con la cámara

car [kɑː'] Ⓐ N 1 (= automobile) coche m, automóvil m (more frm), carro m (LAm), auto m (SC); **by** ~ en coche 2 (esp US) (of train) vagón m, coche m 3 (= tramcar) tranvía m, carro m (Chi) 4 (of cable railway) coche m Ⓑ CPD ➤ **car accident** accidente m de coche or (LAm) carro etc ➤ **car bomb** (gen) coche-bomba m; (magnetic) bomba f lapa ➤ **car boot sale** (Brit) mercadillo m (en el que se exponen las mercancías en el maletero del coche) ➤ **car chase** persecución f en coche ➤ **car ferry** transbordador m para coches, ferry m (LAm) ➤ **car hire** alquiler m de coches ➤ **car hire firm** empresa f de alquiler de coches ➤ **car industry** industria f del automóvil ➤ **car insurance** seguro m de automóvil ➤ **car journey** viaje m en coche ➤ **car park** (Brit) parking m, aparcamiento m (Sp), estacionamiento m (esp LAm) ➤ **car phone** teléfono m móvil (de coche) (Sp), celular m (de coche) (LAm) ➤ **car pool** [of organization] flota f de coches or automóviles etc, parque m móvil; (= sharing) uso m compartido de coches ➤ **car rental = car hire** ➤ **car sickness** mareo m al ir en coche; **to suffer ~ sickness**

marearse (en coche) ➤ **car wash** tren m or túnel m de lavado (de coches)➤ **car worker** trabajador(a) m/f de la industria del automóvil

Caracas [kə'rækəs] N Caracas m

carafe [kə'ræf] N garrafa f

caramel ['kærəməl] N caramelo m ➤ **caramel cream** flan m

carat ['kærət] N quilate m; **24-~ gold** oro m de 24 quilates

caravan ['kærəvæn] Ⓐ N 1 (Brit Aut) caravana f, remolque m, tráiler m (LAm); (gipsies') carromato m 2 (in desert) caravana f Ⓑ VI (Brit): **to go ~ning** ir de vacaciones en una caravana Ⓒ CPD ➤ **caravan site** (Brit) camping m para caravanas

caraway ['kærəweɪ] N alcaravea f ➤ **caraway seeds** carvis mpl

carbohydrate ['kɑːbəʊ'haɪdreɪt] N (Chem) hidrato m de carbono; (= starch in food) fécula f

carbolic [kɑː'bɒlɪk] N (also ~ **acid**) ácido m carbólico or fénico; (also ~ **soap**) jabón m con fenol

carbon ['kɑːbən] Ⓐ N 1 (Chem) carbono m 2 (Elec) carbón m 3 (= carbon paper) papel m de calco, papel m carbón, papel m carbónico (SC) Ⓑ CPD ➤ **carbon copy** copia f hecha con papel de carbón; (fig) vivo retrato m ➤ **carbon credit** crédito m de carbono ➤ **carbon dating** datación f utilizando carbono 14 ➤ **carbon dioxide** bióxido m de carbono ➤ **carbon fibre** fibra f de carbono ➤ **carbon monoxide** monóxido m de carbono ➤ **carbon paper** papel m de calco, papel m carbón, papel m carbónico (SC)

carbonated ['kɑːbəneɪtɪd] ADJ [water] con gas; **~ drink** bebida f gaseosa

carbuncle ['kɑːbʌŋkl] N (Med) carbunc(l)o m

carburettor, carburetor (US) [,kɑːbjʊ'retə', kɑːbə'retə'] N carburador m

carcass, carcase ['kɑːkəs] N 1 [of animal] res f muerta; (= corpse) cadáver m 2 [of building, vehicle] carcasa f, armazón m or f

carcinogen [kɑː'sɪnədʒen] N carcinógeno m

carcinogenic [,kɑːsɪnə'dʒenɪk] ADJ cancerígeno, carcinógeno

carcinoma [,kɑːsɪ'nəʊmə] N carcinoma m

card [kɑːd] Ⓐ N 1 (= greetings card, visiting card) tarjeta f; (= membership card, press card) carnet m, carné m; (= index card) ficha f 2 (= playing card) carta f, naipe m; **a pack of ~s** una baraja; **to play ~s** jugar a las cartas or los naipes 3 (= thin cardboard) cartulina f 4 ✦ IDIOMS **to play** or **keep one's ~s close to one's chest** or (US) **close to the vest** no soltar prenda; **to have a ~ up one's sleeve** guardarse una carta bajo la manga; **to hold all the ~s** tener los triunfos en la mano; **to lay one's ~s on the table** poner las cartas sobre la mesa or boca arriba; **it's on** or (US) **in the ~s es** probable; **it's quite on** or (US) **in the ~s that ...** es perfectamente posible que ... + subjun; **to play one's ~s right** jugar bien sus cartas Ⓑ VT (US*): **to ~ sb** verificar los papeles de identidad de algn Ⓒ CPD ➤ **card game** juego m de naipes or cartas ➤ **card index** fichero m ➤ **card phone** (Brit) teléfono m de tarjeta ➤ **card sharp(er)** fullero/a m/f, tahur m ➤ **card table** mesa f de juego ➤ **card trick** truco m de cartas

cardamom ['kɑːdəməm] N cardamomo m

cardboard ['kɑːdbɔːd] N cartón *m*; (*thin*) cartulina *f* ➤ **cardboard box** caja *f* de cartón ➤ **cardboard city*** *área en la que los vagabundos duermen a la intemperie*

card-carrying member [,kɑːd,kærɪɪŋ'membə'] N miembro *mf* con carnet

cardholder ['kɑːd,həʊldə'] N [*of political party, organization*] miembro *mf* con carnet; [*of credit card*] titular *mf* (de tarjeta de crédito)

cardiac ['kɑːdiæk] ADJ cardíaco ➤ **cardiac arrest** paro *m* cardíaco

cardie* ['kɑːdɪ] N ABBR (*Brit*) = **cardigan**

cardigan ['kɑːdɪɡən] N chaqueta *f* (de punto)

cardinal ['kɑːdɪnl] **Ⓐ** ADJ cardinal; **a ~ rule** una regla primordial *or* fundamental **Ⓑ** N (*Rel*) cardenal *m* **Ⓒ** CPD ➤ **cardinal number** número *m* cardinal ➤ **cardinal sin** pecado *m* capital

card-index [,kɑːd'ɪndeks] VT fichar, catalogar

cardiologist [,kɑːdɪ'ɒlədʒɪst] N cardiólogo/a *m/f*

cardiology [,kɑːdɪ'ɒlədʒɪ] N cardiología *f*

care [kɛə'] **Ⓐ** N **1** (= *carefulness*) cuidado *m*, atención *f*; **to take ~** tener cuidado; **take ~!** (*as warning*) ¡cuidado!, ¡ten cuidado!; (*as good wishes*) ¡cuídate!; **to take ~ to** (+ INFIN) cuidar de que + *subjun*, asegurarse de que + *subjun*; **take ~ not to drop it!** ¡cuidado no lo vayas a dejar caer!, ¡procura no soltarlo!; **convicted of driving without due ~ and attention** declarado culpable de conducir sin la debida precaución

2 (= *charge*) cargo *m*, cuidado *m*; (*Med*) asistencia *f*, atención *f* médica; **the parcel was left in my ~** dejaron el paquete a mi cargo *or* cuidado; **the child was taken into ~** pusieron al niño en un centro de protección de menores; **Mr López ~ of** *or* (*US*) **in ~ of Mr. Jones** (*on letter*) Sr. Jones, para (entregar a) Sr. López; **to take ~ of** (= *take charge of*) encargarse de, ocuparse de; (= *look after*) cuidar a; **I'll take ~ of him!** ¡yo me encargo de él!; **I'll take ~ of this** [+ *bill*] esto corre de mi cuenta

3 (= *anxiety*) preocupación *f*, inquietud *f*; **he has many ~s** hay muchas cosas que le preocupan; **he hasn't a ~ in the world** no le preocupa nada

Ⓑ VI (= *be concerned*) preocuparse (**about** por), interesarse (**about** por); **I don't ~** no me importa, me da igual *or* lo mismo; **for all I ~, you can go** por mí, te puedes ir; **that's all he ~s about** es lo único que le interesa; **to ~ deeply about** [+ *person*] querer mucho a; [+ *thing*] interesarse mucho por; **who ~s?** ¿qué me importa?, ¿y qué?

Ⓒ VT **1** (= *be concerned*) **I don't ~ what you think** no me importa tu opinión; **I couldn't** (*Brit*) *or* **I could** (*US*) **~ less what people say** me importa un bledo lo que diga la gente **2** (= *like*) **to ~ to: I shouldn't ~ to meet him** no me gustaría conocerlo; **if you ~ to** si quieres; **would you ~ to take a walk?** ¿te apetece dar un paseo?

Ⓓ CPD ➤ **care giver** (*esp US*) *persona que cuida de un incapacitado* ➤ **care home** hogar *m* de acogida ➤ **care label** (*on garment*) etiqueta *f* de instrucciones de lavado ➤ **care worker** asistente *mf* social, cuidador(a) *m/f*

➤ **care for** VI + PREP **1** (= *look after*) [+ *people*] cuidar; [+ *things*] cuidar de; **well ~d for** (bien) cuidado **2** (= *like*) sentir cariño por; **I don't much ~ for him** no me resulta simpático; **I don't ~ for coffee** no me gusta el café; **would you ~ for a drink?** ¿te apetece una copa?

career [kə'rɪə'] **Ⓐ** N (= *occupation*) profesión *f*; (= *working life*) carrera *f* profesional; **he made a ~ (for himself) in advertising** se dedicó a la publicidad, desarrolló su carrera profesional en el campo de la publicidad

Ⓑ VI correr a toda velocidad; **to ~ down the street** correr calle abajo

Ⓒ CPD [*diplomat, soldier*] de carrera; [*criminal*] profesional ➤ **career girl** mujer *f* de carrera ➤ **career guidance** (*US*) orientación *f* profesional ➤ **career move** cambio *m* (en la trayectoria) profesional; **a good/bad ~ move** una buena/mala decisión para la trayectoria profesional ➤ **career prospects** perspectivas *fpl* profesionales ➤ **careers advisor** (*Brit*), **careers counselor** (*US*) *encargado de la orientación profesional de los estudiantes* ➤ **careers guidance** (*Brit*) orientación *f* profesional ➤ **careers office** oficina *f* de guía vocacional ➤ **career woman** mujer *f* de carrera

careerist [kə'rɪərɪst] N ambicioso/a *m/f*, arribista *mf*

carefree ['kɛəfriː] ADJ despreocupado, alegre

careful ['kɛəfʊl] ADJ **1** (= *cautious*) prudente, cauteloso; **he's a ~ driver** es un conductor prudente, conduce con prudencia *or* cuidado; **to be ~** tener cuidado; **(be) ~!** ¡(ten) cuidado!; **she's very ~ about what she eats** pone mucho cuidado en *or* es muy prudente con lo que come; **be ~ that he doesn't hear you** procura que no te oiga, ten cuidado de que no te oiga; **he was ~ to point out that ...** se cuidó de señalar que ...; **be ~ not to drop it** ✧ **be ~ (that) you don't drop it** procura que no se caiga, ten cuidado de que no se te caiga; **you can't be too ~** todas las precauciones son pocas; **be ~ what you say to him** (ten) cuidado con lo que le dices; **be ~ with the glasses** cuidado con los vasos; **he's very ~ with his money** es muy ahorrador; (*pej*) es muy tacaño

2 (= *painstaking*) cuidadoso, esmerado; **after ~ consideration of all the relevant facts** después de considerar todos los datos cuidadosamente; **after weeks of ~ preparation** después de semanas de cuidadosos *or* intensos preparativos

carefully ['kɛəfəlɪ] ADV [*drive, step*] con cuidado, con prudencia; [*choose*] con cuidado, cuidadosamente; [*listen*] atentamente; **she ~ avoided looking at him** tuvo cuidado de no mirarlo; **think ~ before you answer** piénsalo bien antes de contestar; **to go** *or* **tread ~** (*lit, fig*) andar con cuidado

careless ['kɛəlɪs] ADJ (= *negligent*) [*person*] descuidado; **~ driving** conducción *f* negligente; **~ driver** conductor(a) *m/f* negligente; **a ~ mistake** un descuido; **it was ~ of her to do that** no fue muy prudente de *or* por su parte hacer eso; **how ~ of me!** ¡qué descuido!; **you shouldn't be so ~ with money** deberías tener más cuidado con el dinero, deberías mirar más el dinero

carelessly ['kɛəlɪslɪ] ADV **1** (= *negligently*) [*write, leave, handle*] sin cuidado, sin la debida atención; [*drive*] imprudentemente, con negligencia **2** (= *casually*) [*say, reply*] a la ligera; [*drop, toss*] despreocupadamente

carelessness ['kɛəlɪsnɪs] N **1** (= *negligence*) falta *f* de atención, falta *f* de cuidado **2** (= *casualness*) despreocupación *f*

carer ['kɛərə'] N (*Brit*) (*professional*) cuidador(a) *m/f* (de atención domiciliaria); (= *relative, friend*) persona que cuida de un incapacitado

caress [kə'res] **Ⓐ** N caricia *f* **Ⓑ** VT acariciar

caretaker ['kɛə,teɪkə'] **Ⓐ** N **1** (*Brit*) [*of school, flats*] portero/a *m/f*, conserje *mf* **2** (*US*) (= *care giver*) cuidador(a) *m/f* (de atención domiciliaria) **Ⓑ** CPD ➤ **caretaker government** gobierno *m* de transición ➤ **caretaker manager** (*Sport*) entrenador(a) *m/f* provisional *or* suplente

careworn ['kɛəwɔːn] ADJ [*person*] agobiado; [*face, frown*] preocupado, lleno de ansiedad

carfare ['kɑːfɛə'] N (*US*) precio *m* (del billete (*Sp*) *or* boleto (*LAm*)), pasaje *m*

cargo ['kɑːgəʊ] N (*pl* ~**es** *or* (*esp US*) ~**s**) cargamento *m*, carga *f* ➤ **cargo plane** avión *m* de carga

Caribbean [,kærɪ'biːən] **Ⓐ** ADJ caribe; **the ~ Sea** el mar Caribe **Ⓑ** N **the ~** el caribe

caribou ['kærɪbuː] N (*pl* ~) caribú *m*

caricature ['kærɪkətjʊə'] VT caricaturizar

caricaturist [,kærɪkə'tjʊərɪst] N caricaturista *mf*

caring ['kɛərɪŋ] ADJ afectuoso, bondadoso; **the ~ professions** (*Brit*) las profesiones humanitarias; **the ~ society** la sociedad humanitaria

Carlist ['kɑːlɪst] ADJ, N carlista *mf*

carnage ['kɑːnɪdʒ] N matanza *f*, carnicería *f*

carnal ['kɑːnl] ADJ carnal

carnation [kɑː'neɪʃən] N clavel *m*

carnival ['kɑːnɪvəl] N (= *festival*) carnaval *m*; (*US*) (= *fair*) parque *m* de atracciones

carnivore ['kɑːnɪvɔː'] N carnívoro/a *m/f*

carnivorous [kɑː'nɪvərəs] ADJ carnívoro

carol ['kærəl] N (*also* **Christmas ~**) villancico *m*

carouse [kə'raʊz] VI ir de juerga *or* jarana

carousel [,kæru:'sel] N **1** (*US*) (= *merry-go-round*) caballitos *mpl*, carrusel *m* (*esp LAm*), calesita(s) *f(pl)* (*And, SC*) **2** (*Phot*) proyector *m* de diapositivas (*con magazine circular*) **3** (*at airport*) cinta *f* de equipajes

carp¹ [kɑ:p] N (*pl ~ or ~s*) (= *fish*) carpa *f*

carp² [kɑ:p] VI quejarse, poner pegas; **to ~ at** criticar

carpenter ['kɑ:pɪntəʳ] N carpintero/a *m/f*

carpentry ['kɑ:pɪntrɪ] N carpintería *f*

carpet ['kɑ:pɪt] Ⓐ N alfombra *f*; (*small*) tapete *m*; (*fitted*) moqueta *f* Ⓑ VT [+ *floor*] (*wall to wall*) enmoquetar (*Sp*), alfombrar (*LAm*); (*with individual rugs*) alfombrar (**with** de) Ⓒ CPD ➤ **carpet bag** (*US*) maletín *m*, morral *m* ➤ **carpet bombing** bombardeo *m* de arrasamiento ➤ **carpet slippers** zapatillas *fpl* ➤ **carpet sweeper** escoba *f* mecánica ➤ **carpet tile** loseta *f*

carpetbagger ['kɑ:pɪt,bægəʳ] N **1** (*US Pol*) aventurero/a *m/f* político/a **2** (*Fin*) oportunista *que trata de sacar beneficio de una operación de conversión de una sociedad de crédito hipotecario en entidad bancaria*

carport ['kɑ:pɔ:t] N cochera *f*

carriage ['kærɪdʒ] Ⓐ N **1** (*Brit Rail*) vagón *m*, coche *m* **2** (*horse-drawn*) coche *m*, carruaje *m* **3** (= *bearing*) [*of person*] porte *m* **4** (*Brit Comm*) (= *transport*) transporte *m*, flete *m*; (= *cost*) porte *m*, flete *m*; **~ paid** portes pagados Ⓑ CPD ➤ **carriage clock** reloj *m* de mesa

carriageway ['kærɪdʒweɪ] N (*Brit*) calzada *f*

carrier ['kærɪəʳ] Ⓐ N **1** (*Comm*) (= *person*) transportista *mf*; (= *company*) empresa *f* de transportes **2** (= *airline*) aerotransportista *m*, aerolínea *f* **3** [*of disease*] portador(a) *m/f* **4** (*on cycle*) cesta *f* Ⓑ CPD ➤ **carrier bag** (*Brit*) bolsa *f* (de papel *or* plástico) ➤ **carrier pigeon** paloma *f* mensajera

carrion ['kærɪən] N carroña *f* ➤ **carrion crow** corneja *f* negra

carrot ['kærət] N zanahoria *f*; ✦ IDIOM **to offer sb a ~** ofrecer un incentivo a algn ➤ **carrot cake** pastel *m* de zanahoria

carrot-and-stick ['kærətənd'stɪk] ADJ **a ~ policy** la política del palo y la zanahoria

carry ['kærɪ] Ⓐ VT **1** (= *take*) llevar; **to ~ sth around with one** llevar algo consigo; **it's too heavy to ~** pesa mucho para llevarlo encima *or* para cargar con ello; ✦ IDIOM **as fast as his legs could ~ him** tan rápido como le permitían sus piernas, a todo correr **2** (= *have on one's person*) [+ *money, documents*] llevar (encima); **he always carries a gun** siempre lleva pistola (encima) **3** (= *transport*) [+ *goods*] transportar; [+ *passengers, message*] llevar; **the wind carried the sound to him** el viento llevó el sonido hasta él **4** (= *stock*) [+ *goods*] tener, tratar en **5** (*Med*) [+ *disease*] ser portador de **6** (= *involve*) [+ *responsibility*] conllevar; [+ *authority*] revestir; **the offence carries a £50 fine** la infracción será penalizada con una multa de 50 libras; **a crime which carries the death penalty** un delito que lleva aparejada la pena de muerte; ✦ IDIOM **(to be left) to ~ the can** (*Brit**) pagar el pato **7** (= *have*) [+ *guarantee*] tener, llevar; [+ *warning*] llevar **8** [*newspaper etc*] [+ *story*] traer, imprimir **9** **to ~ sth too far** (*fig*) llevar algo demasiado lejos **10** (*Math*) [+ *figure*] llevarse; (*Fin*) [+ *interest*] llevar **11** (= *approve*) [+ *motion*] aprobar **12** (= *win*) [+ *election, point, seat*] ganar; **the bill was carried by 302 votes to 197** el proyecto de ley salió adelante por 302 votos frente a 197; ✦ IDIOMS **to ~ the day** triunfar; **to ~ all** *or* **everything before one** arrasar con todo **13** (= *hold*) **he carries himself like a soldier** tiene el porte de un soldado **14** (= *be pregnant with*) estar encinta Ⓑ VI [*sound*] oírse

➤ **carry away** VT + ADV **1** (*lit*) llevarse **2 to get carried away by sth** entusiasmarse con algo

➤ **carry forward** VT + ADV (*Math, Fin*) pasar a la página/

columna siguiente; **carried forward** suma y sigue

➤ **carry off** VT + ADV **1** (*lit*) llevarse **2** (= *seize, win*) [+ *prize*] alzarse con, arramblar con; [+ *election*] ganar; **he carried it off very well** salió muy airoso de la situación

➤ **carry on** Ⓐ VT + ADV [+ *tradition*] seguir, continuar; [+ *conversation*] mantener; [+ *business, trade*] llevar (adelante) Ⓑ VI + ADV **1** (= *continue*) continuar, seguir; **if you ~ on like that** si sigues así; **~ on!** ¡siga!; (*in talking*) ¡prosigue!; **to ~ on doing sth** seguir haciendo algo **2** (*) (= *make a fuss*) armarla*, montar un número (*Sp**); **to ~ on about sth** machacar sobre algo **3** (*) (= *have an affair*) tener un lío* (**with sb** con algn)

➤ **carry out** VT + ADV **1** (= *accomplish*) [+ *plan*] llevar a cabo; [+ *threat, promise, order*] cumplir **2** (= *perform, implement*) realizar, llevar a cabo; **to ~ out repairs** hacer reparaciones

➤ **carry through** VT + ADV **1** (= *accomplish*) [+ *task*] llevar a término **2** (= *sustain*) [+ *person*] sostener

carryall ['kærɪɔ:l] N (*US*) bolsa *f* de viaje

carrycot ['kærɪkɒt] N (*Brit*) cuna *f* portátil, capazo *m*

carry-on* ['kærɪɒn] N jaleo* *m*, lío* *m*, follón *m* (*Sp**)

carry-out ['kærɪ,aʊt] Ⓐ ADJ [*meal*] para llevar Ⓑ N (= *food*) comida *f* para llevar; (= *drink*) bebida *f* para llevar

car-sick ['kɑ:,sɪk] ADJ **to be/get ~** marearse (en el coche)

cart [kɑ:t] Ⓐ N **1** (*horse-drawn*) carro *m*; (*heavy*) carretón *m*; (= *hand cart*) carretilla *f*, carro *m* de mano; (*US*) (*for shopping*) carrito *m*; (*US*) (*motorized*) cochecito *m*; ✦ IDIOM **to put the ~ before the horse** empezar la casa por el tejado Ⓑ VT (*) llevar, acarrear; **I had to ~ his books about all day** tuve que cargar con sus libros todo el día

➤ **cart away***, **cart off*** VT + ADV llevarse

carte blanche [,kɑ:t'blɑ:ntʃ] N carta *f* blanca; **to give sb ~ (to do sth)** dar carta blanca a algn (para hacer algo)

cartel [kɑ:'tel] N cártel *m*

carthorse ['kɑ:thɔ:s] N caballo *m* de tiro

cartilage ['kɑ:tɪlɪdʒ] N cartílago *m*

cartography [kɑ:'tɒgrəfɪ] N cartografía *f*

carton ['kɑ:tən] N (*for milk*) envase *m* de cartón, caja *f*; (*for ice-cream*) vaso *m*; (*for yogurt*) tarrina *f*; (*for cigarettes*) cartón *m*

cartoon [kɑ:'tu:n] Ⓐ N **1** (*in newspaper etc*) viñeta *f*, chiste *m*; (= *comic strip*) historieta *f* **2** (*Art*) (= *sketch for fresco etc*) cartón *m* **3** (*Cine, TV*) dibujos *mpl* animados Ⓑ CPD ➤ **cartoon strip** (*esp Brit*) tira *f* cómica

cartoonist [kɑ:'tu:nɪst] N dibujante *mf*

cartridge ['kɑ:trɪdʒ] N cartucho *m*; (*for pen*) recambio *m* ➤ **cartridge belt** cartuchera *f*, canana *f* ➤ **cartridge paper** papel *m* de dibujo

cartwheel ['kɑ:twi:l] N (= *wheel*) rueda *f* de carro; **to turn a ~** dar una voltereta lateral, hacer la rueda

carve [kɑ:v] Ⓐ VT [+ *meat*] trinchar; [+ *stone, wood*] tallar, esculpir; [+ *name on tree etc*] grabar Ⓑ VI (*Culin*) trinchar la carne

➤ **carve out** VT + ADV [+ *statue, figure*] esculpir; **to ~ out a career for o.s.** abrirse camino

➤ **carve up** VT + ADV **1** [+ *meat*] trinchar **2** (*fig*) [+ *country*] repartirse

carvery ['kɑ:vərɪ] N restaurante *m* que se especializa en asados

carve-up* ['kɑ:v,ʌp] N división *f*, repartimiento *m*

carving ['kɑ:vɪŋ] N (= *act*) tallado *m*; (= *ornament*) talla *f*, escultura *f* ➤ **carving knife** cuchillo *m* de trinchar, trinchante *m*

cascade [kæs'keɪd] Ⓐ N (= *waterfall*) cascada *f*, salto *m* de agua; [*of sparks*] cascada *f*; [*of letters*] aluvión *m* Ⓑ VI caer en cascada

case¹ [keɪs] Ⓐ N **1** (*Brit*) (= *suitcase*) maleta *f*, valija *f* (*SC*), veliz *m* (*Mex*); [*of whisky, wine*] caja *f*; (*for jewellery*) joyero *m*, estuche *m*; (*for camera, guitar, gun*) funda *f*; (*for spectacles*) (*soft*) funda *f*; (*hard*) estuche *m*; (= *display case*) vitrina *f* **2** (*Typ*) **lower ~** minúscula *f*; **upper ~** mayúscula *f* Ⓑ VT **to ~ the joint*** estudiar el terreno para un robo

case² [keɪs] Ⓐ N **1** (= *matter*) (*gen, Med*) caso *m*; **it's a sad ~** es un caso triste; **as the ~ may be** según el caso; **it's a ~**

for the police éste es asunto para la policía, esto es cosa de la policía; **it's a ~ of ...** se trata de ...; **we're on the ~*** (fig) estamos en ello; **a ~ in point** un ejemplo al respecto or que hace al caso
2 (Jur) caso m, proceso m; (= particular dispute) causa f, pleito m; (= argument) argumento m, razón f; **the Dreyfus ~** el caso de Dreyfus; (more loosely) el asunto Dreyfus; **there's a strong ~ for reform** hay buenos fundamentos para exigir una reforma; **there's a ~ for saying that ...** puede decirse razonablemente que ...; **the ~ for the defence/prosecution** la defensa/la acusación; **to have a good ~** tener buenos argumentos or buenas razones; **to make (out) a ~ for sth** dar razones para algo, presentar argumentos en favor de algo; **to state one's ~** presentar sus argumentos, exponer su caso
3 (with "in") (just) **in ~** por si acaso, por si las moscas*; **in ~ he comes** por si viene, (en) caso de que venga; **in your ~** en tu caso; **in any ~** de todas formas, en cualquier caso, en todo caso; **in most ~s** en la mayoría de los casos; **in ~ of emergency** en caso de emergencia; **in that ~** en ese caso
4 (Gram) caso m
B CPD ➤ **case history** (Med) historial m médico or clínico ➤ **case law** jurisprudencia f ➤ **case study** estudio m de casos

case-sensitive ['keɪs,sensɪtɪv] ADJ (Comput) capaz de distinguir mayúsculas de minúsculas

casework ['keɪswɜːk] N trabajo m social individualizado

caseworker ['keɪs,wɜːkəʳ] N asistente mf social

cash [kæʃ] **A** N (= coins, notes) (dinero m en) efectivo m, metálico m; **to pay (in) ~** pagar al contado or en efectivo; **~ on delivery** envío m or entrega f contra reembolso; **~ down** al contado; **~ in hand** efectivo en caja; **I haven't any ~ on me*** no llevo dinero encima
B VT [+ cheque] cobrar, hacer efectivo; **to ~ sb a cheque** cambiar a algn un cheque
C CPD ➤ **cash advance** adelanto m ➤ **cash box** caja f para el dinero, alcancía f ➤ **cash card** (Brit) tarjeta f de cajero automático ➤ **cash crop** cultivo m comercial ➤ **cash desk** (Brit) caja f ➤ **cash discount** descuento m por pago al contado ➤ **cash dispenser** (Brit) cajero m automático ➤ **cash flow** flujo m de caja, movimiento m de efectivo; **~-flow problems** problemas mpl de cash-flow ➤ **cash machine** cajero m automático ➤ **cash offer** oferta f de pago al contado ➤ **cash payment** pago m al contado ➤ **cash price** precio m al contado ➤ **cash prize** premio m en metálico ➤ **cash register** caja f registradora ➤ **cash sale** venta f al contado ➤ **cash in** VT + ADV [+ investment, insurance policy] cobrar ➤ **cash in on*** VI + PREP sacar partido or provecho de ➤ **cash up** VI + ADV (Brit) contar el dinero recaudado

cash-and-carry ['kæʃən'kærɪ] N autoservicio m mayorista

cashback ['kæʃbæk] N **1** (= discount) devolución f **2** (at supermarket etc) retirada de dinero en efectivo de un establecimiento donde se ha pagado con tarjeta; también dinero retirado

cashbook ['kæʃbʊk] N libro m de caja

cashew [kæ'ʃuː] N (also ~ **nut**) anacardo m

cashier [kæ'ʃɪəʳ] N cajero/a m/f ➤ **cashier's check** (US) cheque m bancario ➤ **cashier's desk** (US) caja f

cashmere [kæʃ'mɪəʳ] **A** N cachemir m, cachemira f **B** CPD de cachemir, de cachemira

cashpoint ['kæʃpɔɪnt] N (Brit) (also ~ **machine**) cajero m automático

casing ['keɪsɪŋ] N (= cover) cubierta f; [of boiler] revestimiento m; [of cylinder] camisa f; [of window] marco m

casino [kə'siːnəʊ] N casino m

cask [kɑːsk] N (for wine) cuba f; (large) tonel m

casket ['kɑːskɪt] N (for jewels) estuche m, cofre m; (US) (= coffin) ataúd m

Caspian Sea ['kæspɪən,siː] N mar m Caspio

cassava [kə'sɑːvə] N mandioca f

casserole ['kæsərəʊl] **A** N (= utensil) cacerola f, cazuela f; (= food) guiso m, cazuela f **B** VT hacer un guiso de

cassette [kæ'set] N cas(s)ette m ➤ **cassette deck** platina f, pletina f ➤ **cassette player** cas(s)ette m ➤ **cassette**

recorder cas(s)ette m

cassock ['kæsək] N sotana f

cast [kɑːst] (vb: pt, pp ~) **A** N **1** [of play] reparto m **2** (for broken limb) escayola f (Sp), yeso m (LAm); **leg in a ~** pierna f escayolada (Sp) or enyesada (LAm) **3** (= impression, figure, mould) molde m; **to take a ~ of sth** hacer un molde de algo
B VT **1** (= throw) echar, lanzar; [+ net, anchor etc] echar; [+ shadow] proyectar; [+ light] arrojar (on sobre); [+ blame, spell] echar; **to ~ doubt on sth** poner algo en duda; **to ~ one's eyes over sth** echar una mirada a algo; **to ~ lots** echar a suertes; **to ~ one's vote** votar, dar su voto **2** (Theat) [+ part, play] hacer el reparto de; **to ~ an actor in the part of** dar a un actor el papel de **3** [+ metal] fundir; [+ statue, clay] moldear, vaciar
C VI (Fishing) lanzar, arrojar
D CPD ➤ **cast iron** hierro m fundido or colado ➤ **cast aside** VT + ADV descartar, desechar ➤ **cast down** VT + ADV **to be ~ down** estar deprimido ➤ **cast off A** VI + ADV **1** (Naut) soltar amarras **2** (Knitting) cerrar **B** VT + ADV **1** [+ burden] deshacerse de, quitarse de encima **2** (Knitting) [+ stitch] cerrar ➤ **cast on** VT + ADV, VI + ADV (Knitting) montar

castanets [,kæstə'nets] NPL castañuelas fpl

castaway ['kɑːstəweɪ] N náufrago/a m/f

caste [kɑːst] N casta f ➤ **caste mark** marca f de casta

caster ['kɑːstəʳ] **A** N (= wheel) ruedecilla f **B** CPD ➤ **caster sugar** (Brit) azúcar m extrafino, azúcar m lustre

castigate ['kæstɪgeɪt] VT reprobar, censurar

Castile [kæs'tiːl] N Castilla f

Castilian [kæs'tɪlɪən] **A** ADJ castellano **B** N **1** (= person) castellano/a m/f **2** (Ling) castellano m

casting vote [,kɑːstɪŋ'vəʊt] N voto m decisivo, voto m de calidad

cast-iron ['kɑːst,aɪən] ADJ **1** (lit) (hecho) de hierro fundido **2** (fig) [case] irrebatible; [excuse] frente a la que no se puede decir nada

castle ['kɑːsl] N (= building) castillo m; (Chess) torre f

cast-off ['kɑːstɒf] (Brit) **A** ADJ [clothing] de desecho, en desuso **B** N cast-offs: **he gave me some of his ~s** me dio alguna ropa que él ya no quería

castor ['kɑːstəʳ] N (= wheel) ruedecilla f ➤ **castor oil** aceite m de ricino

castrate [kæs'treɪt] VT castrar

casual ['kæʒjʊəl] ADJ **1** (= chance) [meeting, encounter] fortuito; **a ~ glance** una ojeada; **to the ~ observer** para el observador accidental; **a ~ remark** un comentario hecho a la ligera
2 (= offhand) [attitude] despreocupado, poco serio; [manner] informal; [tone] informal, poco serio; **he tried to appear/sound ~** intentó parecer/sonar relajado; **he was very ~ about it** no le dio mucha importancia
3 (= informal) [discussion] informal; [clothing] de sport, informal
4 (= occasional) esporádico; **he's just a ~ acquaintance** es un conocido nada más; **~ sex** relaciones fpl sexuales promiscuas
5 (= temporary) [labour, work, employment] eventual; **on a ~ basis** temporalmente, eventualmente; **~ worker** (in office, factory) trabajador(a) m/f eventual; (on farm) trabajador(a) m/f temporero/a, jornalero/a m/f

⚠ **casual** ≠ *casual*

casually ['kæʒjʊəlɪ] ADV **1** (= offhandedly) [walk, lean] con aire despreocupado, despreocupadamente; [look] despreocupadamente; [mention, say, ask] de pasada
2 (= informally) de manera informal, informalmente

⚠ **casually** ≠ *casualmente*

casualness ['kæʒjʊəlnɪs] N **1** (= offhandedness) despreocupación f **2** (= informality) informalidad f, naturalidad f

casualty ['kæʒjʊəltɪ] **A** N (Mil) (dead) baja f; (wounded) herido/a m/f; **there were heavy casualties** hubo muchas bajas **2** (in an accident) (dead) víctima f; (injured) herido/a m/f **3 Casualty** (Brit) (= A & E) Urgencias fpl **B** CPD ➤ **casualty ward** (Brit) sala f de urgencias

CAT [kæt] N ABBR (= **computerized axial tomography**) TAC m or f ➤ **CAT scan** escáner m TAC; **I'm going to have a ~ scan** me van a hacer un (escáner) TAC

cat [kæt] **A** N (domestic) gato/a m/f; (= lion etc) felino/a m/f; ✦ IDIOMS **to let the ~ out of the bag** irse de la lengua; **the ~'s out of the bag** se ha descubierto todo el pastel; **to look like the ~ that ate the canary** or (Brit) **that got the cream** estar más ancho que largo, no caber en sí de satisfacción; **he looked like something the ~ had dragged in*** estaba hecho un desastre; **to fight like ~ and dog** llevarse como el perro y el gato; **not to have a ~ in hell's chance*** no tener la más mínima posibilidad; **to play ~ and mouse with sb** jugar al gato y ratón con algn; **that's put the ~ among the pigeons!** (Brit) ¡eso ha puesto a los perros en danza!, ¡ya se armó la gorda!*; **there isn't room to swing a ~** aquí no cabe un alfiler; **(has the) ~ got your tongue?*** ¿te ha comido la lengua el gato?; **he thinks he's the ~'s whiskers** (Brit*) or **meow** (US*) se cree la mar de listo; ✦ PROV **when the ~'s away, the mice will play** cuando el gato no está, bailan los ratones **B** CPD ➤ **cat basket** (for carrying) cesto m para llevar al gato ➤ **cat burglar** (ladrón/ona m/f) balconero/a m/f ➤ **cat flap** gatera f ➤ **cat food** comida f para gatos ➤ **cat litter** arena f higiénica (para gatos)

cataclysm ['kætəklɪzəm] N cataclismo m

catacombs ['kætəku:mz] NPL catacumbas fpl

Catalan ['kætələn] **A** ADJ catalán **B** N **1** (= person) catalán/ana m/f **2** (Ling) catalán m

catalogue, catalog (US) ['kætəlɒg] **A** N catálogo m; **a whole ~ of complaints** toda una serie de quejas **B** VT catalogar, poner en un catálogo

Catalonia [,kætə'ləʊnɪə] N Cataluña f

catalyst ['kætəlɪst] N catalizador m

catalytic converter [,kætəlɪtɪkkən'vɜːtəʳ] N catalizador m

catamaran [,kætəmə'ræn] N catamarán m

catapult ['kætəpʌlt] **A** N **1** (Brit) tirador m, tirachinas m inv **2** (Aer, Mil) catapulta f **B** VT catapultar

cataract ['kætərækt] N catarata f

catarrh [kə'taːʳ] N catarro m

catastrophe [kə'tæstrəfɪ] N catástrofe f

catastrophic [,kætə'strɒfɪk] ADJ catastrófico

catatonic [,kætə'tɒnɪk] ADJ, N catatónico/a m/f

catcall ['kætkɔːl] **A** N silbido m **B** VI silbar

catch [kætʃ] (vb: pt, pp **caught**) **A** N **1** [of ball etc] cogida f, parada f; (= several fish) pesca f; (= one fish) presa f, pesca f, captura f; **good ~!** ¡la cogiste! ¡bien hecho!, ¡bien agarrada! (LAm) **2** (= fastener) cierre m; (Brit) (on door) pestillo m; (on box, window) cerradura f; (= small flange) fiador m **3** (= trick) trampa f; (= snag) pega f; **where's the ~?** ¿cuál es la trampa?; **the ~ is that ...** la dificultad es que ... **4 with a ~ in one's voice** con la voz entrecortada **B** VT **1** (= grasp) asir; [+ ball] coger, agarrar (LAm); [+ fish] pescar; [+ thief] coger, atrapar; **~!** ¡cógelo!, ¡toma!; **to ~ sb's attention** or **eye** llamar la atención a algn; ✦ IDIOM **to be caught like a rat in a trap** estar atrapado como un ratón **2** (= take by surprise) pillar or coger or (LAm) tomar de sorpresa; **to ~ sb doing sth** sorprender or pillar a algn haciendo algo; **to ~ o.s. doing sth** sorprenderse a sí mismo haciendo algo; **you won't ~ me doing that** yo sería incapaz de hacer eso, nunca me verás haciendo eso; **they caught him in the act** le pillaron con las manos en la masa or in fraganti; **we won't get caught like that again** no volveremos a caer en esta trampa; **he got caught in the rain** la lluvia lo pilló desprevenido; **you've caught me at a bad moment** me has pillado en un mal momento **3** (= get hold of) ver; **(I'll) ~ you later!*** ¡nos vemos! **4** [+ bus, train etc] coger, tomar (LAm) **5** (= hear) oír; (= understand) comprender, entender

6 (= see, hear, visit) [+ TV programme, film] ver; [+ radio programme] oír, escuchar; [+ exhibition, concert] ir a; **to ~ the post** llegar antes de la recogida del correo **7** [+ disease] coger, pillar, contagiarse de; **to ~ (a) cold** resfriarse **8** (= capture) [+ atmosphere, expression] saber captar, plasmar **9** (= trap) **I caught my fingers in the door** me pillé los dedos en la puerta; **I caught my jacket on that nail** mi chaqueta se enganchó en ese clavo **10** (= hit) **the punch caught him on the arm** recibió el puñetazo en el brazo; **I caught my head on that beam** me di con la cabeza en esa viga **11** (= receive) **this room ~es the morning sun** este cuarto recibe el sol de la mañana; **her brooch caught the light** su broche reflejaba la luz **12 to ~ one's breath** contener la respiración **13** (Brit): **you'll ~ it!*** ¡las vas a pagar!, ¡te va a costar caro! **C** VI **1** (= hook) engancharse (on en); (= tangle) enredarse; **her dress caught in the door** se pilló el vestido con la puerta; **her dress caught on a nail** se le enganchó el vestido en un clavo **2** [fire, wood] prender, encenderse **D** CPD ➤ **catch phrase** muletilla f, frase f de moda ➤ **catch question** pregunta f capciosa, pregunta f de pega ➤ **a catch-22 situation** un callejón sin salida, un círculo vicioso

➤ **catch on** VI **1** (= become popular) cuajar, tener éxito; **it never really caught on** no logró establecerse de verdad **2** (= understand) caer en la cuenta; (= get the knack) coger el truco; **to ~ on to** comprender

➤ **catch out** VT + ADV (esp Brit) (with trick question) hundir; **to ~ sb out** sorprender or pillar a algn; **we were caught out by the rise in the dollar** la subida del dólar nos cogió desprevenidos

➤ **catch up** **A** VT + ADV **1 to ~ sb up** alcanzar a algn **2** (= enmesh) **we were caught up in the traffic** nos vimos bloqueados por el tráfico **B** VI + ADV **to ~ up (on** or **with one's work)** ponerse al día (en el trabajo); **the police finally caught up with him in Vienna** al final la policía dio con él or lo localizó en Viena; **the truth has finally caught up with him** ya no le queda más remedio que enfrentarse a la verdad

catch-all ['kætʃɔːl] N algo que sirve para todo

catching ['kætʃɪŋ] ADJ contagioso

catchment area ['kætʃmənt,ɛərɪə] N (Brit) zona f de captación

catchy ['kætʃɪ] ADJ (compar **catchier**; superl **catchiest**) [tune, slogan] pegadizo (Sp), pegajoso (LAm); [name, title] fácil de recordar, con gancho

catechism ['kætɪkɪzəm] N (= instruction) catequesis f inv, catequismo m; (= book) catecismo m

categorical [,kætɪ'gɒrɪkəl] ADJ (gen) categórico, terminante; [refusal] rotundo

categorically [,kætɪ'gɒrɪkəlɪ] ADV [state etc] de modo terminante; [refuse] rotundamente

categorize ['kætɪgəraɪz] VT clasificar; **to ~ sth as** calificar algo de, clasificar algo como

category ['kætɪgərɪ] N categoría f

cater ['keɪtəʳ] VI **to ~ for** or (US) **to sb's needs** atender las necesidades de algn; **to ~ for** or (US) **to all tastes** atender a todos los gustos; **this magazine ~s for** or (US) **to the under-21's** esta revista está dirigida a gente por debajo de los 21 años

caterer ['keɪtərəʳ] N proveedor(a) m/f de catering

catering ['keɪtərɪŋ] N servicio m de comidas; **who did the ~?** ¿quién se encargó del servicio de comidas?; **a career in ~** una carrera en la hostelería ➤ **catering industry** hostelería f, restauración f

caterpillar ['kætəpɪləʳ] N oruga f ➤ **Caterpillar track®** rodado m de oruga ➤ **Caterpillar tractor®** tractor m de oruga

catfish ['kætfɪʃ] N (pl ~) siluro m, bagre m

cathartic [kə'θaːtɪk] ADJ catártico

cathedral [kə'θiːdrəl] N catedral f

catherine wheel ['kæθərɪn,wiːl] N girándula f

catheter ['kæθɪtəʳ] N catéter m

cathode ['kæθəʊd] N cátodo m ➤ **cathode ray tube** tubo m de rayos catódicos

catholic ['kæθəlɪk] **🅐** ADJ católico; **the Catholic Church** la Iglesia Católica **🅑** N católico/a m/f

Catholicism [kə'θɒlɪsɪzəm] N catolicismo m

catkin ['kætkɪn] N amento m, candelilla f

catnap* ['kætnæp] N siestecita f, sueñecito m; **to have a ~** echarse una siestecita or un sueñecito

Cat's-eye® ['kæts,aɪ] N (Brit) cataforo m

catsuit ['kætsuːt] N traje m de gato

catsup ['kætsəp] N (US) catsup m, salsa f de tomate

cattle ['kætl] NPL ganado msing ➤ **cattle breeder** criador(a) m/f de ganado ➤ **cattle grid** (Brit), **cattle guard** (US) rejilla f de retención (de ganado) ➤ **cattle market** mercado m de ganado (also fig) ➤ **cattle shed** establo m ➤ **cattle show** feria f de ganado ➤ **cattle truck** (esp Brit) camión m de ganado

catty* ['kætɪ] ADJ (compar **cattier**; superl **cattiest**) malicioso

catwalk ['kætwɔːk] N pasarela f

Caucasian [kɔː'keɪzɪən] ADJ, N caucásico/a m/f

caught [kɔːt] PT, PP of **catch**

cauldron ['kɔːldrən] N caldera f, calderón m

cauliflower ['kɒlɪflaʊəʳ] N coliflor f ➤ **cauliflower cheese** coliflor f con queso ➤ **cauliflower ear** oreja f deformada por los golpes

causality [kɔː'zælɪtɪ] N causalidad f

cause [kɔːz] **🅐** N 1 (= origin) causa f; (= reason) motivo m, razón f; **to be the ~ of** ser causa de; **~ and effect** (relación de) causa y efecto; **with good ~** con razón; **there's no ~ for alarm** no hay por qué inquietarse; **you have ~ to be worried** usted tiene motivo para estar preocupado 2 (= purpose) causa f; **it's all in a good ~** se está haciendo por una buena causa; **in the ~ of justice** por la justicia; **to take up sb's ~** apoyar la campaña de algn **🅑** VT causar; **I don't want to ~ you any inconvenience** no quisiera causarle ninguna molestia; **to ~ sb to do sth** hacer que algn haga algo

cause célèbre [,kɔːzseɪ'lebr] N pleito m or caso m célebre

causeway ['kɔːzweɪ] N calzada f or carretera f elevada; (in sea) arrecife m

caustic ['kɔːstɪk] ADJ (Chem) cáustico; [remark] mordaz, sarcástico ➤ **caustic soda** sosa f cáustica

cauterize ['kɔːtəraɪz] VT cauterizar

caution ['kɔːʃən] **🅐** N 1 (= care) cautela f, prudencia f; **"caution!"** (Aut) "¡cuidado!", "¡precaución!" 2 (= warning) advertencia f, aviso m; (Brit Police) amonestación f **🅑** VT **to ~ sb** (Brit Police) amonestar a algn; **to ~ sb against doing sth** advertir a algn que no haga algo

cautious ['kɔːʃəs] ADJ cauteloso, prudente

cautiously ['kɔːʃəslɪ] ADV cautelosamente, con cautela; **~ optimistic** moderadamente or prudentemente optimista

cautiousness ['kɔːʃəsnɪs] N cautela f, prudencia f

cavalier [,kævə'lɪəʳ] **🅐** N (Brit Hist) partidario del Rey en la Guerra Civil inglesa (1641-49) **🅑** ADJ desdeñoso

cavalry ['kævəlrɪ] N caballería f

cave [keɪv] N cueva f, caverna f ➤ **cave dweller** cavernícola mf, troglodita mf ➤ **cave painting** pintura f rupestre
▶ **cave in** VI + ADV 1 [ceiling] derrumbarse, desplomarse; [ground] hundirse 2 (*) (= submit) ceder, rendirse

caveat ['kæviæt] N advertencia f

caveman ['keɪvmæn] N (pl **cavemen**) hombre m de las cavernas, cavernícola m, troglodita m

caver ['keɪvəʳ] N espeleólogo/a m/f

cavern ['kævən] N caverna f

cavernous ['kævənəs] ADJ [eyes, cheeks] hundido; [pit, darkness] cavernoso

caviar(e) ['kævɪɑːʳ] N caviar m

caving ['keɪvɪŋ] N espeleología f; **to go ~** hacer espeleología; (on specific occasion) ir en una expedición espeleológica

cavity ['kævɪtɪ] N cavidad f; (in tooth) caries f inv ➤ **cavity wall** (Brit) pared f con cámara de aire, doble pared f ➤ **cavity wall insulation** (Brit) aislamiento m con cámara de aire

cavort [kə'vɔːt] VI (= jump about) dar or hacer cabriolas, dar brincos; (fig) divertirse ruidosamente

caw [kɔː] VI graznar

cayenne ['keɪen] N (also ~ **pepper**) pimentón m picante

CB N ABBR (= **Citizens' Band Radio**) BC f

CBE N ABBR (= **Commander (of the Order) of the British Empire**) título honorífico británico

CBI N ABBR (= **Confederation of British Industry**) ≈ CEOE (Sp); ver tb **www.cbi.org.uk**

CC ABBR (= **cubic centimetre(s)**) c.c., cm^3

CCTV N ABBR = **closed-circuit television**

CD N ABBR (= **compact disc**) CD m

CDC N ABBR (US) = **Centers for Disease Control and Prevention**

CD-I® N ABBR (= **compact disc interactive**) CD-I m

Cdr. ABBR (Brit) (= **commander**) Cdte.

CD-ROM [,siːdiː'rɒm] N ABBR (= **compact disc read-only memory**) CD-ROM m ➤ **CD-ROM drive** CD-ROM m, unidad f de CD-ROM

CDT N ABBR 1 (US) = **Central Daylight Time** 2 (Brit Scol) = **Craft, Design and Technology**

CDTV N ABBR = **compact disc television**

CDV, CD-video N ABBR = **compact disc video**

cease [siːs] **🅐** VT (= stop) cesar, parar; (= suspend) suspender; (= end) terminar; **to ~ doing sth** cesar de hacer algo; **to ~ trading** cerrar **🅑** VI cesar

ceasefire [,siːs'faɪəʳ] N alto m el fuego, cese m de hostilidades

ceaseless ['siːslɪs] ADJ incesante, continuo

cedar ['siːdəʳ] N cedro m

cede [siːd] VT ceder (**to** a)

cedilla [sɪ'dɪlə] N cedilla f

ceilidh ['keɪlɪ] N baile con música y danzas tradicionales escocesas o irlandesas

ceiling ['siːlɪŋ] N 1 (of room) techo m 2 (= upper limit) límite m, tope m; **to put a ~ on** fijar el límite de

celeb* [sɪ'leb] N famoso/a m/f

celebrate ['selɪbreɪt] **🅐** VT 1 (+ birthday, special occasion) celebrar; (with a party) festejar 2 (+ mass) celebrar, decir; (+ marriage) celebrar **🅑** VI divertirse, festejar

celebrated ['selɪbreɪtɪd] ADJ célebre, famoso

celebration [,selɪ'breɪʃən] N 1 (= act) celebración f; **in ~ of** para celebrar 2 (= party) fiesta f; **we must have a ~** hay que celebrarlo, hay que hacer una fiesta; **the jubilee ~s** los festejos or las celebraciones del sesenta aniversario

celebratory [,selɪ'breɪtərɪ] ADJ de celebración; **let's have a ~ dinner** vamos a ofrecer una cena para celebrarlo

celebrity [sɪ'lebrɪtɪ] N celebridad f

celeriac [sə'lerɪæk] N apio-nabo m

celery ['selərɪ] N apio m; **stick of ~** tallo m de apio

celestial [sɪ'lestɪəl] ADJ celestial

celibacy ['selɪbəsɪ] N celibato m

celibate ['selɪbɪt] ADJ célibe

cell [sel] N 1 (= room) celda f 2 (Bio, Pol) célula f 3 (Elec) pila f

cellar ['seləʳ] N sótano m; (for wine) bodega f

cellist ['tʃelɪst] N violoncelista mf, violonchelista mf

cellmate ['selmeɪt] N compañero/a m/f de celda

cello ['tʃeləʊ] N violoncelo m, violonchelo m

Cellophane® ['seləfeɪn] N celofán m

cellphone ['sel,fəʊn] N = **cellular phone**

cellular ['seljʊləʳ] ADJ celular ➤ **cellular phone** teléfono m celular

cellulite ['seljʊlaɪt] N celulitis f

celluloid ['seljʊlɔɪd] N celuloide m; **on ~** (Cine) en el celuloide, en el cine

cellulose ['seljʊləʊs] N celulosa f

Celsius ['selsɪəs] ADJ Celsius, centígrado; **20 degrees ~** 20 grados centígrados

Celt [kelt, selt] N celta mf

Celtic ['keltɪk, 'seltɪk] ADJ celta, céltico

cement [sə'ment] Ⓐ N cemento m Ⓑ VT 1 (Constr) cementar, cubrir de cemento 2 (fig) cimentar Ⓒ CPD ➤ **cement mixer** hormigonera f

cemetery ['semɪtrɪ] N cementerio m

cenotaph ['senətɑːf] N cenotafio m

censor ['sensə'] Ⓐ N censor(a) m/f Ⓑ VT censurar

censorship ['sensəʃɪp] N censura f

censure ['senʃə'] Ⓐ N censura f Ⓑ VT censurar

census ['sensəs] N (pl ~es) censo m; **to take a ~ of** levantar el censo de

cent [sent] N (= division of Euro) céntimo m; (= division of dollar) centavo m; **I haven't a ~** (US*) no tengo ni un céntimo or (LAm) ni un peso

centenarian [ˌsentɪ'neərɪən] ADJ, N centenario/a m/f

centenary [sen'tiːnərɪ] N (esp Brit) centenario m

centennial [sen'tenɪəl] Ⓐ ADJ centenario Ⓑ N (esp US) centenario m

center etc ['sentə'] (US) = **centre** etc

centigrade ['sentɪgreɪd] ADJ centígrado; **30 degrees ~** 30 grados centígrados

centilitre, centiliter (US) ['sentɪˌliːtə'] N centilitro m

centimetre, centimeter (US) ['sentɪˌmiːtə'] N centímetro m

centipede ['sentɪpiːd] N ciempiés m inv

central ['sentrəl] Ⓐ ADJ 1 (= in the middle) central 2 (= near the centre of town) [house, office, location] céntrico; **his flat is very ~** su piso está muy céntrico; **it's in ~ London** está en el centro de Londres 3 (= principal) [figure, problem, idea] central, fundamental; [role] fundamental; [aim] principal; **it is ~ to the plot of the film** es fundamental en el argumento de la película; **it is ~ to our policy** es un punto clave de nuestra política 4 (Admin, Pol) [committee, planning, control etc] central Ⓑ CPD ➤ **Central African Republic** República f Centroafricana ➤ **Central America** Centroamérica f, América f Central ➤ **Central Daylight Time** (US) horario m de verano de la zona central (de Estados Unidos) ➤ **Central Europe** Europa f Central ➤ **central government** gobierno m central ➤ **central heating** calefacción f central ➤ **central locking** (Aut) cierre m centralizado ➤ **central reservation** (Brit Aut) mediana f ➤ **Central Standard Time** (US) horario m de la zona central (de Estados Unidos)

Central European [ˌsentrəljʊərə'piːən] Ⓐ N centroeuropeo/a m/f Ⓑ ADJ centroeuropeo, de Europa Central

centralize ['sentrəlaɪz] VT centralizar

centrally ['sentrəlɪ] ADV [positioned, located] en el centro, en un sitio céntrico; **~ heated** con calefacción central

centre, center (US) ['sentə'] Ⓐ N (gen) centro m; [of chocolate] relleno m; **the man at the ~ of the controversy** el hombre sobre el que gira la polémica Ⓑ VT 1 (= place in centre) centrar 2 (Sport) [+ ball] pasar al centro, centrar 3 (= concentrate) concentrar (**on** en) Ⓒ VI **to ~ around/in/on** concentrarse en; [hopes etc] cifrarse en Ⓓ CPD ➤ **centre court** (Tennis) pista f central ➤ **centre forward** (delantero/a m/f) centro mf ➤ **centre half** medio mf centro ➤ **centre party** (Pol) partido m centrista ➤ **centre spread** (Brit Press) páginas fpl centrales ➤ **centre stage** (Theat) centro m del escenario; ✦ IDIOM **to take ~ stage** adquirir protagonismo, pasar a un primer plano

centrefold, centerfold (US) ['sentəˌfəʊld] N póster m central, encarte m central

centrepiece, centerpiece (US) ['sentəpiːs] N centro m de mesa; (fig) atracción f principal

centrifugal [sen'trɪfjʊgəl] ADJ centrífugo

centrifuge ['sentrɪfjuːʒ] N centrifugadora f

centurion [sen'tjʊərɪən] N centurión m

century ['sentjʊrɪ] N 1 siglo m; **in the twentieth ~** en el siglo veinte 2 (Cricket) cien puntos mpl, cien carreras fpl

CEO N ABBR = **Chief Executive Officer**

ceramic [sɪ'ræmɪk] ADJ de cerámica

ceramics [sɪ'ræmɪks] Ⓐ NSING (= art) cerámica fsing Ⓑ NPL (= objects) cerámicas fpl

cereal ['sɪərɪəl] Ⓐ ADJ cereal Ⓑ N (= crop) cereal m; (= breakfast cereal) cereales mpl

cerebral palsy [ˌserɪbrəl'pɔːlzɪ] N parálisis f cerebral

ceremonial [ˌserɪ'məʊnɪəl] ADJ [rite] ceremonial; [dress] de ceremonia, de gala

ceremony ['serɪmənɪ] N ceremonia f; **let's not stand on ~** dejémonos de ceremonias or cumplidos

cert* [sɜːt] N (Brit): **it's a (dead) ~** es cosa segura

cert. ABBR = **certificate**

certain ['sɜːtən] ADJ 1 (= convinced) **to be ~** [person] estar seguro (**about** de; **that** de que); **to feel ~ that** estar seguro de que 2 (= definite, sure) [defeat, death, winner] seguro; [cure] definitivo; [fact] cierto, seguro; **I can't say for ~** no puedo decirlo con seguridad or a ciencia cierta; **we don't know for ~ what caused the accident** no sabemos con seguridad or a ciencia cierta lo que causó el accidente; **he's up to something, that's for ~** trama algo, de eso no hay duda or eso es seguro; **he has been there four times to my ~ knowledge** me consta que or sé con certeza que ha estado allí cuatro veces; **to make ~ that** asegurarse de que; **one thing is ~ ...** una cosa es segura ...; **it is ~ that ...** es seguro que ... 3 (+ INFIN) **he is ~ to be there** (es) seguro que estará allí; **the plans are almost ~ to go ahead** los planes se llevarán a cabo casi con toda seguridad 4 (= particular) cierto; **on a ~ day in May** cierto día de mayo; **a ~ Mr/Mrs Smith** un tal señor/una tal señora Smith; **of a ~ age** de cierta edad; **a ~ number of** un cierto número de; **a ~ person told me that ...** cierta persona me dijo que ...; **she has a ~ something** tiene algo, tiene un no sé qué; **at ~ times of the month/year** en ciertos días del mes/ciertas épocas del año 5 (= slight) cierto; **to a ~ extent** hasta cierto punto

certainly ['sɜːtənlɪ] ADV 1 (= undoubtedly) con toda certeza, sin duda alguna; **your answer is almost ~ right** casi seguro que or casi con seguridad tu respuesta está bien; **it is ~ true that ...** desde luego es verdad or cierto que ... 2 (= definitely) **something should ~ be done about that** está claro que deberían hacer algo al respecto; **I will ~ get it finished by tomorrow** lo termino para mañana seguro; **I shall ~ be there** no faltaré, seguro que estaré; **I would ~ like to try** desde luego (que) me gustaría probar 3 (in answer to questions, requests) **"could you give me a lift?" — "certainly!"** —¿me podrías llevar? —¡claro (que sí)! or ¡por supuesto! or ¡faltaría más!; **~ madam!** ¡con mucho gusto, señora!, ¡por supuesto, señora!; **"wouldn't you agree?" — "oh, ~"** —¿estás de acuerdo? —sí, desde luego; **"had you forgotten?" — "~ not"** —¿se le había olvidado? —por supuesto que no or claro que no; **"will you accept his offer?" — "~ not!"** —¿vas a aceptar su oferta? —¡qué va! or ¡de ninguna manera! 4 (= granted) **~, she has potential, but ...** desde luego tiene or no hay duda de que tiene posibilidades, pero ...

certainty ['sɜːtəntɪ] N 1 (= conviction) certeza f, seguridad f 2 (= sure fact) **faced with the ~ of disaster** ante la seguridad or lo inevitable del desastre; **we know for a ~ that ...** sabemos a ciencia cierta que ...; **it's a ~** es cosa segura

certifiable [ˌsɜːtɪ'faɪəbl] ADJ demente

certificate [sə'tɪfɪkɪt] N certificado m; (Univ) diploma m, título m; **birth/marriage ~** partida f de nacimiento/matrimonio

certified ['sɜ:tɪfaɪd] **A** ADJ **1** [*translation*] confirmado, jurado; [*cheque*] certificado **2** [*person*] (*in profession*) titulado, diplomado; (= *declared insane*) demente **B** CPD ➤ **certified copy** copia *f* compulsada ➤ **certified mail** (*US*) correo *m* certificado ➤ **certified public accountant** (*US*) contable *mf* diplomado/a

certify ['sɜ:tɪfaɪ] VT **1** (= *confirm*) certificar; **to ~ that ...** declarar que ... **2** (*Med*) **to ~ sb (insane)** certificar que algn no está en posesión de sus facultades mentales

cervical ['sɜ:vɪkəl, sə'vaɪkəl] ADJ cervical ➤ **cervical cancer** cáncer *m* cervical *or* del cuello del útero ➤ **cervical smear** (*Brit*) frotis *m* cervical, citología *f*

cervix ['sɜ:vɪks] N cuello *m* del útero

cessation [se'seɪʃən] N cese *m*, suspensión *f*

cesspit ['sespɪt], **cesspool** ['sespu:l] N pozo *m* negro

cf ABBR (= *confer, compare*) cfr., cf.

CFC N ABBR (= *chlorofluorocarbon*) CFC *m*

ch. ABBR (= *chapter*) cap., c., c/

c.h. ABBR (= *central heating*) cal. cen.

Chad [tʃæd] N Chad *m*

chador ['tʃædəʳ] N chador *m*

chafe [tʃeɪf] **A** N **1** (= *rub against*) rozar, raspar **B** VI (*fig*) impacientarse *or* irritarse (**at** por)

chaff [tʃɑ:f] N cascarilla *f*, ahechaduras *fpl*; (*fig*) paja *f*

chaffinch ['tʃæfɪntʃ] N pinzón *m* (vulgar)

chagrin ['ʃægrɪn] N disgusto *m*; **to my ~** con gran disgusto mío

chain [tʃeɪn] **A** N **1** (*lit*) cadena *f*; **in ~s** encadenado; **to pull the ~** (*of lavatory*) tirar de la cadena **2** (*fig*) **~ of mountains** cordillera *f*; **~ of shops** cadena *f* de tiendas; **~ of events** serie *f* de acontecimientos **B** VT (*also* = **up**) encadenar; **he was ~ed to the wall** estaba encadenado a la pared **C** CPD ➤ **chain gang** (*US*) cadena *f* de presidiarios ➤ **chain letter** carta *f* que circula en cadena ➤ **chain mail** cota *f* de malla ➤ **chain reaction** reacción *f* en cadena ➤ **chain smoker** fumador(a) *m/f* empedernido/a ➤ **chain store** tienda *f* que pertenece a una cadena

chainsaw ['tʃeɪnsɔ:] N sierra *f* de cadena

chain-smoke ['tʃeɪnˌsməʊk] VI fumar un pitillo tras otro

chair [tʃeəʳ] **A** N **1** (*gen*) silla *f*; (= *armchair*) sillón *m*, butaca *f*; (= *wheelchair*) silla *f* (de ruedas) **2** (*Univ*) cátedra *f* **3** (= *chairperson*) presidente/a *m/f*; **to be in/take the ~** presidir **4** (*US*) **the ~** (= *electric chair*) la silla eléctrica **B** VT [+ *meeting*] presidir

chairlift ['tʃeəlɪft] N telesilla *m or f*, teleférico *m*

chairman ['tʃeəmən] N (*pl* **chairmen**) presidente/a *m/f*

chairmanship ['tʃeəmənʃɪp] N presidencia *f*

chairperson ['tʃeəˌpɜ:sn] N presidente/a *m/f*

chairwoman ['tʃeəˌwʊmən] N (*pl* **chairwomen**) presidenta *f*

chalet ['ʃæleɪ] N chalet *m*, chalé *m*

chalice ['tʃælɪs] N cáliz *m*

chalk [tʃɔ:k] N (*Geol*) creta *f*; (*for writing*) tiza *f*, gis *m* (*Mex*); **a (piece of) ~** una tiza, un gis (*Mex*); ✦ IDIOMS **to be as different as ~ and cheese** (*Brit*) ser como el día y la noche; **by a long ~** (*Brit**) de lejos; **not by a long ~** (*Brit**) ni con mucho, ni mucho menos
➤ **chalk up** VT + ADV [+ *success, victory*] apuntarse

chalkboard ['tʃɔ:kbɔ:d] N (*US*) pizarra *f*

challenge ['tʃælɪndʒ] **A** N **1** (*to game, fight etc*) desafío *m*, reto *m*; [*of sentry*] alto *m*; **to issue a ~ to sb** desafiar a algn; **to rise to the ~** ponerse a la altura de las circunstancias; **to take up a ~** aceptar un desafío *or* un reto **2** (= *bid*) (*for leadership etc*) intento *m* (**for** por) **3** (= *task*) desafío *m*, reto *m*; **this task is a great ~** esta tarea representa un gran desafío *or* reto; **the ~ of the 21st century** el desafío *or* reto del siglo XXI **B** VT **1** (*to duel*) desafiar, retar; [*sentry*] dar el alto a; **to ~ sb to do sth** desafiar *or* retar a algn a que haga algo **2** (= *dispute*) [+ *fact, point*] poner en duda **3** [+ *jury, juror*] recusar

-challenged ['tʃælɪndʒd] ADJ (*ending in compounds*) (*gen hum*) **vertically-challenged** no muy alto; **intellectually-challenged** no muy listo

challenger ['tʃælɪndʒəʳ] N (*gen*) desafiador(a) *m/f*; (= *competitor*) aspirante *mf*; (= *opponent*) contrincante *mf*

challenging ['tʃælɪndʒɪŋ] ADJ [*job, task*] que supone un desafío *or* un reto; [*book*] estimulante, provocador; [*remark, look, tone*] desafiante

chamber ['tʃeɪmbəʳ] N cámara *f*; **the Upper/Lower Chamber** (*Pol*) la Cámara Alta/Baja; **chambers** (*Brit*) [*of judge*] despacho *msing*; [*of barrister*] bufete *msing* ➤ **chamber music** música *f* de cámara ➤ **chamber of commerce** cámara *f* de comercio ➤ **chamber orchestra** orquesta *f* de cámara ➤ **chamber pot** orinal *m*

chambermaid ['tʃeɪmbəmeɪd] N camarera *f*

chameleon [kə'mi:lɪən] N camaleón *m*

chamois N **1** ['ʃæmwɑ:] (= *animal*) gamuza *f* **2** ['ʃæmɪ] (*also* ~ **leather**) gamuza *f*

chamomile ['kæməmaɪl] N = **camomile**

champ¹ [tʃæmp] VI ✦ IDIOM **to be ~ing at the bit (to do sth)** estar impaciente (por hacer algo)

champ²* [tʃæmp] N campeón/ona *m/f*

champagne [ʃæm'peɪn] N champán *m*, champaña *m or f* ➤ **champagne glass** copa *f* de champán

champion ['tʃæmpɪən] **A** N campeón/ona *m/f*; [*of cause*] defensor(a) *m/f*, paladín *m*; **world ~** campeón *m* mundial **B** ADJ **a ~ athlete** un campeón de atletismo **C** VT defender, abogar por

championship ['tʃæmpɪənʃɪp] N campeonato *m*

chance [tʃɑ:ns] **A** N **1** (= *fate*) azar *m*; (= *coincidence*) casualidad *f*; **by ~/by any ~** por casualidad; **to leave nothing to ~** no dejar nada al azar, no dejar ningún cabo suelto
2 (= *opportunity*) oportunidad *f*, ocasión *f*; **~ would be a fine thing!*** ¡ojalá!, ¡ya quisiera yo!; **you'll never get another ~ like this** nunca se te presentará otra oportunidad *or* ocasión como ésta; **all those eligible will get a ~ to vote** todas las personas que cumplan los requisitos podrán votar; **he didn't give me a ~ to say anything** no me dio (la) oportunidad de decir nada; **it's the ~ of a lifetime** es la oportunidad de mi/tu/su *etc* vida; **she's gone out, now's your ~!** ha salido, ¡ésta es tu oportunidad!; **to give sb a second ~** dar a algn una segunda oportunidad
3 (= *possibility*) posibilidad *f*; **it has a one in 11,000 ~ (of winning)** tiene una posibilidad entre 11.000 (de ganar); **the ~s are that ...** lo más probable es que ... + *subjun*; **to have a good ~ of success** tener bastantes posibilidades de éxito; **to be in with a ~** (*Brit**) tener posibilidades; **I had very little ~ of winning** tenía muy pocas posibilidades de ganar; **no ~!*** (*refusing*) ¡ni hablar!*; (*dismissing a possibility*) ¡qué va!*; **they don't stand a ~ (of winning)** no tienen ninguna posibilidad *or* posibilidad alguna (de ganar)
4 (= *risk*) riesgo *m*; **I'll take that ~** correré ese riesgo, me arriesgaré **B** VT **1** (= *run the risk of*) **to ~ it*** jugársela, arriesgarse; ✦ IDIOM **to ~ one's arm** *or* **one's luck** probar suerte **2** (*frm*) (= *happen*) **to ~ to do sth** hacer algo por casualidad **C** CPD ➤ **chance meeting** encuentro *m* fortuito *or* casual ➤ **chance remark** comentario *m* casual
➤ **chance upon** VI + PREP tropezar(se) con

chancel ['tʃɑ:nsəl] N coro *m* y presbiterio

chancellor ['tʃɑ:nsələʳ] N (*Pol*) canciller *mf*; (*Univ*) rector(a) *m/f* honorario/a ➤ **Chancellor of the Exchequer** (*Brit*) Ministro/a *m/f or* (*LAm*) Secretario/a *m/f* de Economía y Hacienda; *ver tb* www.hm-treasury.gov.uk

chancy* ['tʃɑ:nsɪ] ADJ (*compar* **chancier**; *superl* **chanciest**) arriesgado

chandelier [ˌʃændə'lɪəʳ] N araña *f* (de luces)

change [tʃeɪndʒ] **A** N **1** (*gen*) cambio *m*; (= *transformation*) transformación *f*; (= *alteration*) modificación *f*; (= *variation*) variación *f*; **~ of address** cambio *m* de domicilio; **a ~ for the better** un cambio para bien; **a ~ of clothes** ropa *f* para cambiarse; (= *underclothes*) una muda; **just for a ~** para variar; **he's had a ~ of heart** ha cambiado de idea; **a ~ in**

policy un cambio de política; **the ~ of life** la menopausia; **~ of ownership** cambio *m* de dueño; **to resist ~** resistirse a los cambios; **~ of scene** cambio *m* de aires; **a ~ for the worse** un cambio para mal; ✦ PROV **a ~ is as good as a rest** un cambio de aires da fuerzas para seguir
2 (= *small coins*) cambio *m*, suelto *m*, sencillo *m*, feria *f* (*Mex**); (= *money returned*) cambio *m*, vuelta *f* (*Sp*), vuelto *m* (*LAm*); **can you give me ~ for one pound?** ¿tiene cambio de una libra?, ¿puede cambiarme una moneda de una libra?; **keep the ~** quédese con el cambio *or* la vuelta (*Sp*) *or* el vuelto (*LAm*)
B VT **1** (*by substitution*) [+ *address, colour, job*] cambiar de; **to ~ one's clothes/name** cambiarse de ropa/nombre; **to ~ trains/planes (at)** hacer transbordo (en), cambiar de tren/avión (en); **to ~ gear** (*Brit Aut*) cambiar de marcha; **to get ~d** cambiarse; **to ~ hands** cambiar de mano *or* de dueño; **to ~ one's mind** cambiar de opinión *or* idea; **to ~ places** cambiar de sitio; **let's ~ the subject** cambiemos de tema
2 (= *exchange*) cambiar (**for** por)
3 (= *alter*) [+ *person*] cambiar; (= *transform*) transformar (**into** en)
4 [+ *money*] cambiar (**into** en)
5 (= *put fresh nappy on*) [+ *baby*] cambiar (el pañal de)
C VI **1** (= *alter*) cambiar; **you've ~d!** ¡cómo has cambiado!, ¡pareces otro!
2 (= *be transformed*) transformarse (**into** en)
3 (= *change clothes*) cambiarse; **she ~d into an old skirt** se cambió y se puso una falda vieja
4 (= *change trains*) hacer transbordo, cambiar de tren; (= *change buses*) hacer transbordo, cambiar de autobús; **all ~!** ¡fin de trayecto!
D CPD ➤ **change machine** máquina *f* de cambio ➤ **change purse** (*US*) monedero *m*
➤ **change down** VI + ADV (*Brit Aut*) cambiar a una velocidad inferior
➤ **change over** **A** VI + ADV (*from sth to sth*) cambiar (**to** a); [*players etc*] cambiar(se) **B** VT + ADV cambiar
➤ **change up** VI + ADV (*Brit Aut*) cambiar a una velocidad superior

changeable ['tʃeɪndʒəbl] ADJ [*situation, weather*] variable; [*person*] voluble, inconstante

changeover ['tʃeɪndʒ,əʊvəʳ] N cambio *m*

changing ['tʃeɪndʒɪŋ] **A** ADJ cambiante; **a ~ world** un mundo en perpetua evolución **B** N **the ~ of the Guard** el cambio *or* relevo de la Guardia **C** CPD ➤ **changing room** (*Brit*) vestuario *m*

channel ['tʃænl] **A** N (= *watercourse, TV channel*) canal *m*; (= *strait*) estrecho *m*; [*of communication*] vía *f*; **the (English) Channel** el Canal (de la Mancha); **green/red ~** (*Customs*) pasillo *m* verde/rojo; **to go through the usual ~s** seguir las vías normales **B** VT [+ *interest, energies*] encauzar, dirigir (**into** a) **C** CPD ➤ **the Channel Islands** las Islas Anglonormandas, las Islas del Canal de la Mancha ➤ **the Channel Tunnel** el túnel del Canal de la Mancha

channel-hop ['tʃænlhɒp] (*Brit*), **channel-surf** ['tʃænlsɜ:f] (*US*) VI hacer zapping

channel-hopping ['tʃænlhɒpɪŋ] (*Brit*), **channel-surfing** ['tʃænlsɜ:fɪŋ] (*US*) N zapping *m*

chant [tʃɑːnt] **A** N (*Mus, Rel*) canto *m*; [*of crowd*] grito *m*, consigna *f* **B** VT (*Mus, Rel*) cantar; [+ *slogan*] gritar (rítmicamente), corear **C** VI (*Mus, Rel*) cantar; (*at demonstration etc*) gritar (rítmicamente)

chaos ['keɪɒs] N caos *m*

chaotic [keɪ'ɒtɪk] ADJ caótico

chap* [tʃæp] N (*Brit*) (= *man*) tipo* *m*, tío *m* (*Sp**); **he's a nice ~** es buen chico, es buena persona

chap. ABBR (= **chapter**) cap., c., c/

chapel ['tʃæpəl] N (= *part of church, castle, university etc*) capilla *f*; (= *nonconformist church*) templo *m*

chaperon(e) ['ʃæpərəʊn] **A** N acompañante *f* (de señoritas), carabina *mf* (*Sp**) **B** VT acompañar a, hacer de carabina a (*Sp**)

chaplain ['tʃæplɪn] N capellán *m*

chapped [tʃæpt] ADJ agrietado

chapter ['tʃæptəʳ] N [*of book*] capítulo *m*; **he can quote you ~ and verse** él te lo puede citar textualmente

char [tʃɑːʳ] **A** VT carbonizar **B** VI carbonizarse

character ['kærɪktəʳ] **A** N **1** [*of thing*] carácter *m*, naturaleza *f*; [*of person*] carácter *m*, personalidad *f*; **a man of good ~** un hombre de buena reputación; **it was completely out of ~ (for him)** no era nada típico de él
2 (*in novel, play*) (= *person*) personaje *m*; (= *role*) papel *m*; **chief ~** protagonista *mf*
3 (*) (= *person*) tipo/a* *m/f*, individuo/a *m/f*; **he's quite a ~** es todo un personaje
4 (*Comput, Typ, Bio*) carácter *m*
B CPD ➤ **character actor** actor/actriz *m/f* de carácter ➤ **character assassination** difamación *f* ➤ **character reference** informe *m*, referencia *f*

characteristic [,kærɪktə'rɪstɪk] **A** ADJ característico (**of** de) **B** N característica *f*

characteristically [,kærɪktə'rɪstɪkəlɪ] ADV característicamente, de modo característico; **he was in ~ jovial mood** como es típico de él, estaba de muy buen talante

characterization [,kærɪktəraɪ'zeɪʃən] N caracterización *f*

characterize ['kærɪktəraɪz] VT (= *be characteristic of*) caracterizar; (= *describe*) calificar (**as** de)

charade [ʃə'rɑːd] N **1** (= *farce*) payasada *f*, farsa *f*
2 charades (= *game*) charada *fsing*

charcoal ['tʃɑːkəʊl] N carbón *m* vegetal; (*Art*) carboncillo *m* ➤ **charcoal drawing** dibujo *m* al carbón *or* al carboncillo

charcoal-grey [,tʃɑːkəʊl'greɪ] ADJ gris marengo *inv*

---

charge

A NOUN	**C** INTRANSITIVE VERB
B TRANSITIVE VERB	**D** COMPOUNDS

charge [tʃɑːdʒ] **A** NOUN
1 (= *accusation*) (*Jur*) cargo *m*, acusación *f* (*also fig*); **the ~s were dropped** retiraron los cargos *or* la acusación; **what is the ~?** ¿de qué se me acusa?; **to bring a ~ against sb** formular *or* presentar cargos contra algn; **he was arrested on a ~ of murder** *or* **a murder ~** lo detuvieron bajo acusación de asesinato
2 (= *fee*) precio *m*; (*professional*) honorarios *mpl*; **charges** (*Telec*) tarifa *f*; **~ for admission** precio *m* de entrada; **is there a ~?** ¿hay que pagar (algo)?; **there's no ~** es gratis; **extra ~** recargo *m*, suplemento *m*; **free of ~** gratis; **to make a ~ for (doing) sth** cobrar por (hacer) algo; **for a small ~, we can ...** por una pequeña cantidad, podemos ...
3 (*US*) (= *charge account*) **cash or ~?** ¿al contado o a crédito?
4 (= *responsibility*) **the patients under her ~** los pacientes a su cargo
✦ **in charge: the person in ~** el/la encargado/a; **who is in ~ here?** ¿quién es el encargado aquí?; **to be in ~ of** [+ *department, operation*] estar al frente *or* al cargo de; **he's in ~ of the shop when I'm out** se encarga de la tienda cuando yo no estoy; **it is illegal for anyone under 16 to be left in ~ of young children** es ilegal dejar a niños pequeños a cargo *or* al cuidado de alguien menor de 16 años; **to put sb in ~** [+ *department, operation*] poner a algn al frente *or* al cargo de; **to put sb in ~ of doing sth** encargar a algn que haga algo ✦ **to take charge** (*of firm, project*) hacerse cargo (**of** de)
5 (*electrical*) carga *f*
6 (= *explosive*) carga *f*
7 (= *attack*) (*by people, army*) carga *f*, ataque *m*; (*by bull*) embestida *f*
B TRANSITIVE VERB
1 (= *accuse*) acusar (**with** de); **to find sb guilty/not guilty as ~d** declarar a algn culpable/inocente de los delitos que se le imputan; **to ~ that** (*US*) alegar que
2 (= *ask for*) [+ *price*] cobrar; **what are they charging for the work?** ¿cuánto cobran *or* piden por el trabajo?; **to ~ 3% commission** cobrar un 3% de comisión
3 (= *record as debt*) **to ~ sth (up) to sb** cargar algo en la cuenta de algn
4 (= *attack*) [*person, army*] cargar contra, atacar
5 (*Elec*) (*also ~ up*) [+ *battery*] cargar
6 (= *order*) **to ~ sb to do sth** ordenar a algn hacer *or* que haga algo
7 (*US*) (*in library*) **to ~ a book** [*reader*] rellenar la ficha del préstamo; [*librarian*] registrar un libro como prestado

© INTRANSITIVE VERB
1 (= *ask for a fee*) cobrar
2 (= *attack*) [*person, army*] atacar; [*bull*] embestir; **charge!** ¡a la carga!; **he ~d into the room** irrumpió en la habitación
3 (*Elec*) (*also* **~ up**) [*battery*] cargarse
① COMPOUNDS ➤ **charge account** (*US*) cuenta *f* de crédito
➤ **charge card** (*Brit Comm*) tarjeta *f* (de) cliente; (*US*) (= *credit card*) tarjeta *f* de crédito

chargeable ['tʃɑːdʒəbl] ADJ **1** (*Jur*) [*offence*] imputable
2 (= *payable*) **to be ~ to** [+ *person*] correr a cargo de; [+ *account*] cargarse a

chargé d'affaires ['ʃɑːʒeɪdæ'feəʳ] (*pl* **chargés d'affaires**) N encargado *m* de negocios

charger ['tʃɑːdʒəʳ] N **1** (*Elec*) cargador *m* **2** (= *warhorse*) corcel *m*, caballo *m* de guerra

char-grilled [,tʃɑː'grɪld] ADJ (*Brit*) a la brasa

chariot ['tʃærɪət] N carro *m* (*romano, de guerra etc*)

charisma [kæ'rɪzmə] N carisma *m*

charismatic [,kærɪz'mætɪk] ADJ carismático

charitable ['tʃærɪtəbl] ADJ **1** [*organization, donation*] benéfico **2** (= *kindly*) [*person, deed, gesture*] benévolo, caritativo; [*remark, view*] comprensivo

charity ['tʃærɪtɪ] **①** N **1** (= *benevolence*) caridad *f*; (= *alms*) limosnas *fpl*; **out of ~** por caridad; **to live on ~** vivir de la caridad; ✦ PROV **~ begins at home** la caridad bien entendida empieza por uno mismo
2 (= *organization*) organización *f* benéfica; **all proceeds go to ~** todo lo recaudado se destinará a obras benéficas
③ CPD ➤ **charity shop** (*Brit*) tienda de artículos de segunda mano que dedica su recaudación a causas benéficas

charlady ['tʃɑːleɪdɪ] N (*Brit*) mujer *f* de la limpieza, asistenta *f*

charlatan ['ʃɑːlətən] N charlatán/tana *m/f*

charm [tʃɑːm] **①** N **1** (= *attractiveness*) encanto *m*, atractivo *m*; (= *pleasantness*) simpatía *f*; **he has great ~** es verdaderamente encantador, tiene un fuerte atractivo
2 (= *magic spell*) hechizo *m*; (*recited*) ensalmo *m*; **it worked like a ~** funcionó a las mil maravillas **3** (= *object*) dije *m*, amuleto *m* **③** VT encantar; **to lead a ~ed life** (*Brit*) tener suerte en todo **④** CPD ➤ **charm bracelet** pulsera *f* amuleto, pulsera *f* de dijes

charmer ['tʃɑːməʳ] N persona *f* encantadora

charming ['tʃɑːmɪŋ] ADJ [*place*] encantador; [*person*] encantador, simpático

chart [tʃɑːt] **①** N **1** (= *table*) tabla *f*, cuadro *m*; (= *graph*) gráfica *f*, gráfico *m*; (*showing weather*) mapa *m*; (*navigational*) carta *f* (de navegación); **weather ~** mapa meteorológico
2 (*Mus*) **the ~s*** la lista de éxitos; **to be in the ~s*** estar en la lista de éxitos **③** VT [+ *course*] trazar; [+ *sales, growth, etc*] hacer una gráfica de, representar gráficamente; [+ *progress*] (= *follow*) seguir; (= *reflect*) reflejar

charter ['tʃɑːtəʳ] **①** N [*of city*] fuero *m*; [*of organization*] estatutos *mpl* **③** VT [+ *bus*] alquilar; [+ *ship, plane*] fletar
④ CPD ➤ **charter flight** vuelo *m* chárter ➤ **charter plane** avión *m* chárter

chartered accountant [,tʃɑːtəd'kaʊntənt] N (*Brit, Canada*) censor(a) *m/f* jurado/a de cuentas, contador(a) *m/f* público/a (*LAm*)

charwoman ['tʃɑːwʊmən] N (*pl* **charwomen**) (*Brit*) mujer *f* de la limpieza, asistenta *f*

chary ['tʃɛərɪ] ADJ (*compar* **charier**; *superl* **chariest**) cauteloso; **he's ~ of getting involved** evita inmiscuirse

chase [tʃeɪs] **①** N persecución *f*; **a car ~** una persecución en coche; **to give ~** dar caza a, perseguir **③** VT perseguir
④ VI **to ~ after sb** correr tras algn
➤ **chase away, chase off** VT + ADV ahuyentar
➤ **chase up** VT + ADV [+ *information*] recabar, tratar de localizar; [+ *matter*] investigar; **I'll ~ it up for you** investigaré lo que está pasando con lo tuyo; **to ~ up debts** reclamar el cobro de las deudas; **I'll ~ him up about it** se lo voy a recordar

chaser ['tʃeɪsəʳ] N *bebida tomada inmediatamente después de otra distinta, p.ej., una copita de licor después de una cerveza*

chasm ['kæzəm] N sima *f*

chassis ['ʃæsɪ] N (*pl* **~**) chasis *m inv*

chaste [tʃeɪst] ADJ casto

chastened ['tʃeɪsnd] ADJ (*by experience*) escarmentado; [*tone*] sumiso; **they seemed much ~** parecían haberse arrepentido

chastening ['tʃeɪsnɪŋ] ADJ [*experience*] aleccionador

chastise [tʃæs'taɪz] VT (= *scold*) regañar; (= *punish*) castigar

chastity ['tʃæstɪtɪ] N castidad *f*

chat [tʃæt] **①** N charla *f*, plática *f* (*CAm*); **to have a ~ with** (*gen*) charlar con, platicar con (*CAm*); (*more serious*) hablar con **③** VI charlar, platicar (*CAm*) (**with, to** con); (*Internet*) chatear **④** CPD ➤ **chat room** (*Internet*) chat *m*, canal *m* de charla, grupo *m* de discusión ➤ **chat show** (*Brit*) programa *m* de entrevistas
➤ **chat up*** VT + ADV (*Brit*) tratar de ligar con*

chatline ['tʃætlaɪn] N (*Brit*) *servicio telefónico que permite a los que llaman conversar unos con otros sobre distintos temas*

chatter ['tʃætəʳ] **①** N (*gen*) charla *f*; (*excessive*) cháchara *f*, cotorreo *m*; [*of birds, monkeys*] parloteo *m* **③** VI [*person*] (*gen*) charlar; (*excessively*) estar de cháchara, cotorrear; [*birds, monkeys*] parlotear; **her teeth were ~ing** le castañeteaban los dientes

chatterbox* ['tʃætəbɒks], **chatterer** ['tʃætərəʳ] N charlatán/ana* *m/f*, parlanchín/ina* *m/f*, platicón/ona *m/f* (*Mex**)

chatty ['tʃætɪ] ADJ (*compar* **chattier**; *superl* **chattiest**) [*person*] hablador; [*letter*] afectuoso y lleno de noticias; [*style*] informal

chat-up line ['tʃætʌp,laɪn] N (*Brit*): **a good ~** una buena frase para entrarle a algn*

chauffeur ['ʃəʊfəʳ] **①** N chófer *mf* (*Sp*), chofer *mf* (*LAm*)
③ VT **I had to ~ him all over town** (*iro*) tuve que hacer de chófer (*Sp*) *or* chofer (*LAm*) y llevarle de una punta a otra de la ciudad **④** VI hacer de chófer (*Sp*) *or* chofer (*LAm*) (**for** para)

chauvinism ['ʃəʊvɪnɪzəm] N (= *male chauvinism*) machismo *m*; (= *nationalism*) chovinismo *m*, patriotería *f*

chauvinist ['ʃəʊvɪnɪst] **①** ADJ (= *male chauvinist*) machista; (= *nationalist*) chovinista, patriotero **③** N (= *male chauvinist*) machista *m*; (= *nationalist*) chovinista *mf*, patriotero/a *m/f*

chauvinistic [,ʃəʊvɪ'nɪstɪk] ADJ (= *male chauvinist*) machista; (= *nationalist*) chovinista, patriotero

cheap [tʃiːp] **①** ADJ (*compar* **~er**; *superl* **~est**)
1 (= *inexpensive*) [*goods, labour, shop*] barato; [*imports*] a bajo precio; [*loan, credit*] a bajo interés; **it's ten pence ~er** es diez peniques más barato; **buying is ~er than renting** sale más económico *or* barato comprar que alquilar; **dresses at ridiculously ~ prices** vestidos a unos precios regalados; **~ rate** tarifa *f* reducida
2 (= *poor-quality*) [*product*] barato, corriente
3 (= *vulgar, mean*) [*joke*] ordinario, chabacano; [*behaviour, tactics*] rastrero; [*remark, question*] de mal gusto; [*sensationalism*] barato; [*promises*] fácil; **a ~ trick** una mala pasada
4 (= *not deserving respect*) bajo, indigno; **to feel ~** sentirse humillado; **to look ~** parecer ordinario, tener un aspecto ordinario
③ ADV [*buy, sell*] barato; **it's going ~** se vende barato; **quality doesn't come ~** la calidad tiene un precio
④ N **on the ~*** [*decorate, travel*] en plan barato*; **to do sth on the ~** hacer algo en plan barato*; **to buy** *or* **get sth on the ~** comprar algo por poco dinero *or* a bajo precio

cheapen ['tʃiːpən] VT (= *debase*) [+ *sb's name, work*] degradar; **to ~ o.s.** hacer cosas indignas, rebajarse

cheaply ['tʃiːplɪ] ADV [*buy, sell*] barato, a bajo precio; [*produce goods*] a bajo precio; [*live, eat*] con poco dinero

cheapo* ['tʃiːpəʊ] ADJ baratejo

cheapskate* ['tʃiːpskeɪt] N tacaño/a *m/f*, roñoso/a* *m/f*

cheat [tʃiːt] **①** N **1** (= *person*) tramposo/a *m/f*; (*at cards*) tramposo/a *m/f*, fullero/a *m/f* **2** (= *fraud*) estafa *f*, fraude *m*; (= *trick*) trampa *f* **③** VT (= *swindle*) estafar, timar; (= *trick*) engañar; **to ~ sb out of sth** estafar algo a algn; **to feel ~ed**

sentirse defraudado **⊙** VI hacer trampa(s); (*in exam*) copiar ➤ **cheat on** VI + PREP engañar

cheating ['tʃiːtɪŋ] N trampa *f*; (*at cards*) trampas *fpl*, fullerías *fpl*; **that's ~** eso es trampa; **no ~!** ¡sin hacer trampas!

Chechen ['tʃetʃən] ADJ, N checheno/a *m/f*

Chechnya [tʃɪtʃ'njaː] N Chechenia *f*

check [tʃek] **④** N **1** (= *inspection*) control *m*, inspección *f*, chequeo *m*; (*Mech*) revisión *f*; **to keep a ~ on sth/sb** controlar algo/a algn, vigilar algo/a algn; **to run** *or* **make a ~ on sth** comprobar *or* revisar algo **2** (= *restraint*) **to hold** *or* **keep sth in ~** tener algo controlado *or* bajo control; **to hold** *or* **keep sb in ~** controlar a algn, mantener a algn a raya; **~s and balances** (*US Pol*) *mecanismo de equilibrio de poderes* **3** (*Chess*) jaque *m*; **~!** ¡jaque! **to be in ~** estar (en) jaque **4** (= *square*) cuadro *m*; (= *fabric*) tela *f* a *or* de cuadros **5** (*US*) **5.1** (= *bill*) cuenta *f* **5.2** (= *form of payment*) = **cheque 5.3** (= *tick*) marca *f*, señal *f*; **~!** ¡de acuerdo!, ¡vale! (*Sp**) **5.4** (= *tag, ticket*) resguardo *m*

⑤ VT **1** (= *examine*) [+ *ticket, passport*] controlar, revisar; [+ *merchandise, premises*] inspeccionar, controlar; [+ *tyres, oil*] revisar, comprobar; [+ *temperature, pressure*] controlar; **he stopped to ~ his map** se detuvo para leer *or* mirar el mapa; **~ each item for flaws** compruebe todos los artículos para ver que no tengan defectos **2** (= *confirm, verify*) [+ *facts, figures*] comprobar; **~ that he's gone before you do it** asegúrate de que *or* comprueba que se ha ido antes de hacerlo; **to ~ sth against sth** comparar *or* cotejar algo con algo **3** (= *hold back*) [+ *attack, advance, progress*] detener, frenar; **to ~ o.s.** contenerse, refrenarse **4** (*US*) **4.1** (= *tick*) marcar, señalar **4.2** [+ *luggage*] (*at airport*) facturar, chequear (*LAm*); [+ *clothes, property*] (*in cloakroom*) dejar (en el guardarropa)

⊙ VI **1** (= *confirm*) comprobar, chequear (*esp LAm*); **I'll need to ~ with the manager** lo tendré que consultar con el encargado **2** (= *examine*) **they ~ed for broken bones** lo examinaron para ver si tenía algún hueso roto; **~ periodically for wear and tear** compruebe periódicamente el deterioro **3** (= *hesitate*) pararse en seco, pararse de repente **4** (*US*) (= *agree*) concordar (**with** con)

⑩ CPD ➤ **check mark** (*US*) marca *f*, señal *f* ➤ **check suit** traje *m* a *or* de cuadros

➤ **check in ④** VI + ADV **1** (*at airport*) facturar *or* (*LAm*) chequear (el equipaje); (*at hotel*) registrarse; (*at clinic, hospital*) ingresar **2** (*US*) (= *communicate*) **he ~s in with us by phone every week** se pone en contacto con nosotros *or* nos llama por teléfono todas las semanas **⑤** VT + ADV [+ *luggage*] facturar, chequear (*LAm*); [+ *person*] (*at hotel*) registrar; (*at airport*) facturar el equipaje de

➤ **check off** VT + ADV (*esp US*) (= *check*) comprobar; (= *cross off*) tachar

➤ **check on** VI + ADV [+ *information, time etc*] verificar; **to ~ on sb** investigar a algn

➤ **check out ④** VI + ADV **1** (*of hotel*) (pagar y) marcharse (**of** de) **2** (= *agree*) cuadrar; **their credentials ~ out** sus credenciales cuadran **⑤** VT + ADV **1** (= *investigate*) investigar **2** (= *confirm*) [+ *facts, statement*] comprobar, verificar **3** (*) (= *look at*) mirar

➤ **check over** VT + ADV revisar, escudriñar

➤ **check up** VT + ADV **can you ~ up what time the film starts?** ¿puedes confirmar *or* mirar a qué hora empieza la película?

➤ **check up on** VI + PREP **1** (= *confirm*) [+ *story*] comprobar, verificar **2** (= *investigate*) **we've ~ed up on you and it seems you are telling the truth** hemos hecho indagaciones *or* averiguaciones sobre usted y parece que nos está diciendo la verdad; **I'm sure he knew I was ~ing up on him** estoy seguro de que sabía que lo estaba espiando *or* vigilando

checkbook ['tʃekbʊk] N (*US*) = **chequebook**

checked [tʃekt] ADJ a cuadros, de cuadros

checkerboard ['tʃekəbɔːd] N (*US*) tablero *m* de damas

checkered ['tʃekəd] ADJ (*esp US*) = **chequered**

checkers ['tʃekəz] NPL (*US*) damas *fpl*

check-in ['tʃekɪn] N (*also* **~ desk**) mostrador *m* de facturación ➤ **check-in time: your ~ time is an hour before departure** la facturación es una hora antes de la salida

checking account ['tʃekɪŋˌkaʊnt] N (*US*) cuenta *f* corriente

checklist ['tʃeklɪst] N lista *f* de control (*con la que se coteja algo*)

checkmate ['tʃekmeɪt] N (*in chess*) mate *m*, jaque *m* mate; (*fig*) callejón *m* sin salida; **~!** ¡jaque mate!

checkout ['tʃekaʊt] N (*in supermarket*) caja *f* ➤ **checkout girl** cajera *f* (de supermercado) ➤ **checkout time** hora *f* a la que hay que dejar libre la habitación

checkpoint ['tʃekpɔɪnt] N (punto *m* de) control *m*, retén *m* (*LAm*)

checkroom ['tʃekrʊm] N (*US*) guardarropa *m*; (*Rail*) consigna *f*

checkup ['tʃekʌp] N (*at doctor's*) reconocimiento *m* general, chequeo *m*; (*at dentist's*) revisión *f*

cheddar ['tʃedə'] N (*also* **~ cheese**) queso *m* cheddar

cheek [tʃiːk] N **1** (*Anat*) mejilla *f*, carrillo *m*; (= *buttock*) nalga *f*; **they were dancing ~ to ~** bailaban muy apretados **2** (*) (= *impudence*) descaro *m*, cara* *f*, frescura *f*; **what a ~!** ¡qué cara!*, ¡qué caradura!*, ¡qué frescura!; **to have the ~ to do sth** tener la cara de hacer algo

cheekbone ['tʃiːkbəʊn] N pómulo *m*

cheekily* ['tʃiːkɪlɪ] ADV (*Brit*) descaradamente, con frescura

cheeky ['tʃiːkɪ] ADJ (*Brit*) (*compar* **cheekier**; *superl* **cheekiest**) [*person*] descarado, fresco; [*question*] indiscreto, descarado

cheep [tʃiːp] **④** N [*of bird*] pío *m* **⑤** VI piar

cheer [tʃɪə'] **④** N **1** (= *ovation*) ovación *f*, aclamación *f*; (= *hurrah*) vítor *m*, viva *m*; **there were loud ~s at this** hubo una fuerte ovación en este momento; **three ~s for the president!** ¡viva el presidente!, ¡tres hurras por el presidente! **2** (= *comfort*) consuelo *m* **⑤** EXCL **~s!** (= *toast*) ¡salud!; (*Brit**) (= *thank you*) ¡gracias!; (*Brit**) (= *goodbye*) ¡hasta luego! **⊙** VT **1** (= *applaud*) [+ *winner etc*] aclamar, vitorear **2** (*also* **~ up**) alegrar, animar **⑩** VI dar vivas, dar vítores

➤ **cheer on** VT + ADV animar (*con aplausos or gritos*)

➤ **cheer up ④** VI + ADV animarse, alegrarse; **~ up!** ¡anímate!, ¡ánimo! **⑤** VT + ADV alegrar, animar

cheerful ['tʃɪəfʊl] ADJ [*person, expression, atmosphere*] alegre, jovial; [*occasion*] feliz; [*colour*] alegre, vivo; [*news, prospect, outlook*] alentador; **to be ~ about sth** alegrarse de *or* por algo

cheerfully ['tʃɪəfʊlɪ] ADV **1** [*smile, say, greet*] alegremente, jovialmente **2** (= *blithely*) [*ignore*] alegremente, tranquilamente **3** (= *gladly*) **I could ~ strangle him** con mucho gusto lo estrangularía

cheerfulness ['tʃɪəfʊlnɪs] N alegría *f*, jovialidad *f*

cheerily ['tʃɪərɪlɪ] ADV alegremente, jovialmente

cheering ['tʃɪərɪŋ] **④** ADJ [*news*] bueno, esperanzador; [*prospect*] alentador **⑤** N ovaciones *fpl*, vítores *mpl*

cheerio* ['tʃɪərɪ'əʊ] EXCL (*Brit*) ¡hasta luego!, ¡chau! (*LAm*)

cheerleader ['tʃɪəˌliːdə'] N (*esp US*) animador(a) *m/f*

cheerless ['tʃɪəlɪs] ADJ triste, sombrío

cheery ['tʃɪərɪ] ADJ (*compar* **cheerier**; *superl* **cheeriest**) [*person*] alegre, jovial; [*room, atmosphere*] acogedor

cheese [tʃiːz] **④** N queso *m*; **say ~!** (*Phot*) ¡a ver, una sonrisa! **⑤** VT (*Brit***) **I'm ~d off with this** estoy hasta las narices de esto* **⊙** CPD ➤ **cheese sauce** salsa *f* de queso, ≈ salsa *f* Mornay

cheeseboard ['tʃiːzbɔːd] N tabla *f* de quesos

cheeseburger ['tʃiːzˌbɜːgə'] N hamburguesa *f* con queso

cheesecake ['tʃiːzkeɪk] N tarta *f* or (*LAm*) pay *m* de queso

cheesecloth ['tʃiːzklɒθ] N estopilla *f*

cheetah ['tʃiːtə] N guepardo *m*

chef [ʃef] N cocinero/a *m/f* jefe/a, chef *m*

chemical ['kemɪkəl] **④** ADJ químico **⑤** N sustancia *f* química, producto *m* químico **⊙** CPD ➤ **chemical engineer** ingeniero/a *m/f* químico/a ➤ **chemical engineering**

ingeniería *f* química ➤ **chemical warfare** guerra *f* química ➤ **chemical weapon** arma *f* química

> Use **el/un** not **la/una** before feminine nouns beginning with stressed **a** or **ha** like **arma**.

chemically ['kemɪkəlɪ] ADV químicamente

chemist ['kemɪst] N (= *scientist*) químico/a *m/f*; (*Brit*) (= *pharmacist*) farmacéutico/a *m/f* ➤ **chemist's (shop)** (*Brit*) farmacia *f*; **all-night ~'s** farmacia *f* de turno *or* de guardia

chemistry ['kemɪstrɪ] N química *f*; **the ~ between them is right** están muy compenetrados ➤ **chemistry laboratory** laboratorio *m* de química ➤ **chemistry set** juego *m* de química

chemo* ['kiːməʊ] N = **chemotherapy** quimio *f*

chemotherapy ['kiːməʊ'θerəpɪ] N quimioterapia *f*

cheque, check (*US*) [tʃek] N cheque *m*, talón *m* (bancario) (*Sp*); **a ~ for £20** un cheque por *or* de 20 libras; **to pay by ~** pagar con cheque; **bad ~** cheque *m* sin fondos *or* sin provisión ➤ **cheque card** (*also* ~ **guarantee card**) (*Brit*) tarjeta *f* de identificación bancaria

chequebook, checkbook (*US*) ['tʃekbʊk] N talonario *m* de cheques, chequera *f* (*LAm*); ~ **journalism** periodismo *m* a golpe de talonario

chequered, checkered (*esp US*) ['tʃekəd] ADJ **1** (= *varied*) **a ~ career** una carrera accidentada *or* llena de altibajos **2** (= *checked*) a cuadros, de cuadros

cherish ['tʃerɪʃ] VT [+ *person*] querer, apreciar; [+ *hope*] abrigar, acariciar; [+ *memory*] conservar

cherished ['tʃerɪʃt] ADJ [*memory*] precioso, entrañable; [*possession*] preciado

cherry ['tʃerɪ] **Ⓐ** N (= *fruit*) cereza *f*; (= *tree, wood*) cerezo *m* **Ⓑ** CPD [*pie, jam*] de cereza ➤ **cherry brandy** aguardiente *m* de cerezas ➤ **cherry orchard** cerezal *m* ➤ **cherry red** rojo *m* cereza ➤ **cherry tree** cerezo *m*

cherry-pick ['tʃerɪpɪk] VT escoger cuidadosamente, seleccionar cuidadosamente

cherry-red [,tʃerɪ'red] ADJ (de) color rojo cereza

cherub ['tʃerəb] N querubín *m*

chervil ['tʃɜːvɪl] N perifollo *m*

Cheshire cat ['tʃeʃə'kæt] N ✦ IDIOM **to grin like a ~** sonreír de oreja a oreja

chess [tʃes] N ajedrez *m* ➤ **chess player** jugador(a) *m/f* de ajedrez, ajedrecista *mf* ➤ **chess set** (juego *m* de) ajedrez *m*

chessboard ['tʃesbɔːd] N tablero *m* de ajedrez

chessman ['tʃesmæn] N (*pl* **chessmen**) pieza *f* de ajedrez

chest [tʃest] **Ⓐ** N **1** (*Anat*) pecho *m*; **to have ~ trouble** tener problemas respiratorios, padecer de los bronquios; ✦ IDIOM **to get sth off one's ~*** desahogarse **2** (= *box*) cofre *m*, arca *f*

> Use **el/un** not **la/una** before feminine nouns beginning with stressed **a** or **ha** like **arca**.

Ⓑ CPD [*pain*] de pecho ➤ **chest freezer** congelador *m* de arcón ➤ **chest infection** infección *f* de las vías respiratorias ➤ **chest of drawers** cómoda *f* ➤ **chest size** [*of person*] anchura *f* de pecho; [*of clothes*] talla *f* (*de chaqueta etc*) ➤ **chest specialist** especialista *mf* de las vías respiratorias ➤ **chest X-ray** radiografía *f* torácica

chestnut ['tʃesnʌt] **Ⓐ** N **1** (= *fruit*) castaña *f*; (= *tree, colour*) castaño *m* **2** (= *horse*) caballo *m* castaño **3** (*) (= *story*) **not that old ~!** ¡ya estamos con la misma historia de siempre! **Ⓑ** ADJ (*also* ~ **brown**) [*hair*] (de color) castaño *inv* **Ⓒ** CPD ➤ **chestnut tree** castaño *m*

chesty* ['tʃestɪ] ADJ (*compar* **chestier**; *superl* **chestiest**) (*Brit*) [*cough*] de pecho; **you sound a bit ~** por la voz parece que tienes el pecho cargado *or* congestionado

chew [tʃuː] VT, VI mascar, masticar ➤ **chew on** VI + PREP (= *consider*) considerar, rumiar; (= *reflect on*) dar vueltas a ➤ **chew over*** VT + ADV (= *consider*) considerar, rumiar;

(= *reflect on*) dar vueltas a ➤ **chew up** VT + ADV [+ *food*] masticar bien

chewing gum ['tʃuːɪŋɡʌm] N chicle *m*, goma *f* de mascar

chewy ['tʃuːɪ] ADJ (*compar* **chewier**; *superl* **chewiest**) [*meat*] fibroso, correoso; [*sweet*] masticable

chic [ʃiːk] **Ⓐ** ADJ elegante **Ⓑ** N chic *m*, elegancia *f*

Chicano [tʃɪ'kɑːnəʊ] ADJ, N (*US*) chicano/a *m/f*

chick [tʃɪk] N (= *baby bird*) pajarito *m*; (= *baby hen*) pollito *m*, polluelo *m*; (**) (= *woman*) chica *f*, chavala *f* (*Sp*)

chicken ['tʃɪkɪn] N (= *hen*) gallina *f*; (= *cock*) pollo *m*; (*as food*) pollo *m*; (= *coward*) gallina *mf*; **to be ~*** dejarse intimidar, acobardarse; **it's a ~ and egg situation** es aquello de la gallina y el huevo; **the ~s are coming home to roost** ahora se ven las consecuencias; ✦ PROV **don't count your ~s before they're hatched** no hagas las cuentas de la lechera ➤ **chicken farmer** avicultor(a) *m/f* ➤ **chicken feed** (*lit*) pienso *m* para gallinas; **it's ~ feed to him** para él es una bagatela ➤ **chicken run** corral *m* ➤ **chicken wire** tela *f* metálica, alambrada *f* ➤ **chicken out*** VI + ADV rajarse; **he ~ed out of the audition/ of asking her to dinner** se rajó y no se presentó a la prueba/ y no la invitó a cenar

chickenpox ['tʃɪkɪnpɒks] N varicela *f*

chickpea ['tʃɪkpiː] N garbanzo *m*

chicory ['tʃɪkərɪ] N (*in coffee*) achicoria *f*; (*as salad*) escarola *f*

chide [tʃaɪd] VT reprender

chief [tʃiːf] **Ⓐ** ADJ (= *main*) principal; (*in rank*) jefe **Ⓑ** N [*of organization*] jefe/a *m/f*; [*of tribe*] jefe/a *m/f*, cacique *m*; (*) (= *boss*) jefe/a *m/f*, patrón(ona) *m/f* **Ⓒ** CPD ➤ **chief constable** (*Brit*) jefe/a *m/f* de policía ➤ **chief executive (officer)** [*of company*] director(a) *m/f* general ➤ **chief inspector** (*Brit Police*) inspector(a) *m/f* jefe ➤ **chief justice** (*US*) presidente/a *m/f* del Tribunal Supremo ➤ **Chief of Staff** Jefe *m* del Estado Mayor ➤ **chief superintendent** (*Brit*) comisario/a *m/f* jefe/a

chiefly ['tʃiːflɪ] ADV principalmente, sobre todo

chieftain ['tʃiːftən] N jefe/a *m/f*, cacique *m* (*LAm*)

chiffon ['ʃɪfɒn] **Ⓐ** N gasa *f* **Ⓑ** ADJ de gasa

chilblain ['tʃɪlbleɪn] N sabañón *m*

child [tʃaɪld] N (*pl* **-ren**) niño/a *m/f*; (= *son/daughter*) hijo/a *m/f*; **I have known him since he was a ~** lo conozco desde niño; ✦ IDIOM **it's ~'s play** es un juego de niños ➤ **child abuse** (*with violence*) malos tratos *mpl* a niños; (*sexual*) abuso *m* sexual de niños ➤ **child abuser** (*with violence*) persona que maltrata a un niño; (*sexual*) persona que abusa sexualmente de un niño ➤ **child benefit** (*Brit*) subsidio *m* familiar (por hijos) ➤ **child labour**, **child labor** (*US*) trabajo *m* de menores ➤ **child prodigy** niño/a *m/f* prodigio ➤ **children's home** centro *m* de acogida de menores ➤ **children's literature** literatura *f* infantil

childbearing ['tʃaɪld,beərɪŋ] ADJ **women of ~ age** las mujeres en edad de tener hijos

childbirth ['tʃaɪldbɜːθ] N parto *m*

childcare ['tʃaɪldkeəʳ] N cuidado *m* de los niños ➤ **childcare facilities** guarderías *fpl* ➤ **childcare provider** cuidador(a) *m/f* de niños

childhood ['tʃaɪldhʊd] N niñez *f*, infancia *f*

childish ['tʃaɪldɪʃ] ADJ infantil, pueril; **don't be ~!** ¡no seas niño!

childishly ['tʃaɪldɪʃlɪ] ADV de modo infantil *or* pueril, como un niño; **she behaved ~** se portó como una niña

childless ['tʃaɪldlɪs] ADJ sin hijos

childlike ['tʃaɪldlaɪk] ADJ de niño

childminder ['tʃaɪld,maɪndəʳ] N (*Brit*) cuidador(a) *m/f* de niños

children ['tʃɪldrən] NPL *of* **child**

Chile ['tʃɪlɪ] N Chile *m*

Chilean ['tʃɪlɪən] ADJ, N chileno/a *m/f*

chili ['tʃɪlɪ] N (*pl* **-es**) (*also* ~ **pepper**) chile *m*, ají *m* (*SC*), guindilla *f* (*Sp*); ~ **con carne** chile con carne; ~ **powder** chile *m* en polvo

chill [tʃɪl] **Ⓐ** N (= *coldness*) frío *m*; (= *head cold*) resfriado *m*; (= *mild fever*) escalofrío *m*; **there's a ~ in the air** hace fresco; **to catch a ~** resfriarse; **it sent a ~ down my spine** me dió escalofríos **Ⓑ** ADJ [*wind*] frío **Ⓒ** VT [+ *wine*] enfriar; [+ *food*] refrigerar; **serve ~ed** sírvase bien frío
➤ **chill out*** VI + ADV (*esp US*) tranquilizarse, relajarse; **~ out, man!** ¡tranqui tronco!*

chilli ['tʃɪlɪ] N = **chili**

chilling ['tʃɪlɪŋ] ADJ escalofriante

chilly ['tʃɪlɪ] ADJ (*compar* **chillier**; *superl* **chilliest**) **1** (= *cold*) [*weather, day*] frío; **to feel ~** [*person*] tener frío; **it's ~ today** hace fresquito hoy **2** (= *unfriendly*) frío

chime [tʃaɪm] **Ⓐ** N **1** (= *sound*) [*of church bells*] repique *m*; [*of clock*] campanada *f* **2 chimes** (= *set*) juego *msing* de campanas, carillón *msing* **Ⓑ** VI repicar, sonar; **the clock ~d six** el reloj dio las seis
➤ **chime in*** VI + ADV (= *butt in*) meter baza; (= *say*) decir; **to ~ in with** meter baza hablando de

chimney ['tʃɪmnɪ] N chimenea *f* ➤ **chimney breast** (*Brit*) campana *f* de chimenea ➤ **chimney pot** cañón *m* de chimenea ➤ **chimney stack** (*Brit*) fuste *m* de chimenea ➤ **chimney sweep** deshollinador(a) *m/f*

chimp* [tʃɪmp] N chimpancé *m*

chimpanzee [ˌtʃɪmpæn'ziː] N chimpancé *m*

chin [tʃɪn] **Ⓐ** N barbilla *f*, mentón *m*; **(keep your) ~ up!** ¡no te desanimes!, ¡ánimo! **Ⓑ** VI (*US**) charlar

China ['tʃaɪnə] N China *f* ➤ **China Sea** Mar *m* de China ➤ **China tea** té *m* de China

china ['tʃaɪnə] **Ⓐ** N (= *crockery*) loza *f*, vajilla *f*; (= *fine china*) porcelana *f* **Ⓑ** CPD [*cup, plate etc*] de porcelana ➤ **china cabinet** vitrina *f* de la porcelana ➤ **china clay** caolín *m*

Chinatown ['tʃaɪnətaʊn] N barrio *m* chino

Chinese [ˌtʃaɪ'niːz] **Ⓐ** ADJ chino **Ⓑ** N **1** (*also* **~ man/woman**) chino/a *m/f*; **the ~** los chinos **2** (*Ling*) chino *m* **Ⓒ** CPD ➤ **Chinese chequers** damas *fpl* chinas ➤ **Chinese lantern** farolillo *m* chino ➤ **Chinese leaves** col *fsing* china

chink¹ [tʃɪŋk] N (= *slit*) grieta *f*, hendidura *f*; **a ~ of light** un hilo de luz; ✦ IDIOM **it's the ~ in his armour** es su punto débil *or* su talón de Aquiles

chink² [tʃɪŋk] **Ⓐ** N (= *sound*) sonido *m* metálico, tintineo *m* **Ⓑ** VT [+ *metal*] hacer sonar; [+ *glass*] hacer tintinear **Ⓒ** VI [*metal*] sonar; [*glass*] tintinear

chintz [tʃɪnts] N cretona *f*

chip [tʃɪp] **Ⓐ** N **1** (= *piece*) pedacito *m*; (= *splinter*) [*of glass, wood*] astilla *f*; (= *stone*) lasca *f*; ✦ IDIOMS **he's a ~ off the old block** de tal palo tal astilla; **to have a ~ on one's shoulder** ser un resentido
2 chips (*Brit*) (= *French fries*) patatas *fpl* fritas (*Sp*), papas *fpl* fritas (*LAm*); (*US*) (= *crisps*) patatas *fpl* (*Sp*) *or* papas *fpl* (*LAm*) (fritas) de bolsa, chips *mpl*
3 (*on rim of vessel*) desportilladura *f*
4 (*Gambling*) ficha *f*; ✦ IDIOMS **he's had his ~s*** se le acabó la suerte; **when the ~s are down** cuando llega el momento de la verdad
5 (*Comput*) chip *m*
6 (*Golf*) chip *m*
Ⓑ VT [+ *pottery*] desconchar, desportillar; [+ *paint*] desconchar
Ⓒ VI [*pottery*] desconcharse, desportillarse; [*paint, varnish*] desconcharse
Ⓓ CPD ➤ **chip shop** (*Brit**) pescadería *f* (*donde se vende principalmente pescado rebozado y patatas fritas*)
➤ **chip away Ⓐ** VT + ADV [+ *paint, varnish*] desconchar **Ⓑ** VI + ADV [*paint, varnish*] desconcharse; **to ~ away at** [+ *lands*] ir usurpando; [+ *authority*] ir minando *or* debilitando
➤ **chip in*** VI + ADV **1** (= *contribute*) contribuir (**with** con); (= *share costs*) compartir los gastos **2** (= *interrupt*) interrumpir (**with** diciendo)

chipboard ['tʃɪpbɔːd] N madera *f* aglomerada, aglomerado *m*

chipmunk ['tʃɪpmʌŋk] N ardilla *f* listada

chippings ['tʃɪpɪŋz] NPL gravilla *fsing*; **"loose chippings"** "gravilla suelta"

chippy* ['tʃɪpɪ] N (*Brit*) *tienda que vende pescado frito con patatas fritas*

chiropodist [kɪ'rɒpədɪst] N (*Brit*) podólogo/a *m/f*, pedicuro/a *m/f*

chiropody [kɪ'rɒpədɪ] N (*Brit*) podología *f*, pedicura *f*

chiropractor ['kaɪrəʊˌpræktə'] N quiropráctico *m*

chirp [tʃɜːp] VI [*birds*] piar, gorjear; [*crickets*] chirriar, cantar

chirpy* ['tʃɜːpɪ] ADJ (*compar* **chirpier**; *superl* **chirpiest**) alegre, animado

chisel ['tʃɪzl] (*vb: pt, pp* **~led** *or* (*US*) **~ed**) **Ⓐ** N (*for wood*) formón *m*, escoplo *m*; (*for stone*) cincel *m* **Ⓑ** VT [+ *stone*] cincelar; (= *carve*) tallar, labrar

chit¹ [tʃɪt] N (= *note*) vale *m*

chit² [tʃɪt] N **a ~ of a girl** una muchachita no muy crecida

chitchat ['tʃɪttʃæt] N (= *gossip*) chismes *mpl*, habladurías *fpl*; **it was just ~** sólo estuvimos dándole al palique

chivalrous ['ʃɪvəlrəs] ADJ caballeroso

chivalry ['ʃɪvəlrɪ] N (= *courteousness*) caballerosidad *f*; (*in medieval times*) caballería *f*

chives [tʃaɪvz] NPL cebollinos *mpl*

chivvy* ['tʃɪvɪ] VT (*Brit*): **to ~ sb into doing sth** no dejar en paz a algn hasta que hace algo

chloride ['klɔːraɪd] N cloruro *m*

chlorinate ['klɒrɪneɪt] VT clorar, tratar con cloro

chlorine ['klɔːriːn] N cloro *m*

chlorofluorocarbon [ˌklɔːrəˌflʊərəʊ'kɑːbən] N clorofluorocarbono *m*

chloroform ['klɒrəfɔːm] N cloroformo *m*

chlorophyll ['klɒrəfɪl] N clorofila *f*

choc-ice ['tʃɒkaɪs] N (*Brit*) helado *m* cubierto de chocolate

chock [tʃɒk] **Ⓐ** N calzo *m*, cuña *f* **Ⓑ** VT calzar, poner un calzo *or* una cuña a

chock-a-block* ['tʃɒkə'blɒk] ADJ (*esp Brit*) de bote en bote, hasta los topes; **~ of** *or* **with** atestado de, totalmente lleno de

chocolate ['tʃɒklɪt] **Ⓐ** N chocolate *m*; (= *sweet*) bombón *m*; **a box of ~s** una caja de bombones **Ⓑ** ADJ (*also* **~ brown**) (de color) chocolate **Ⓒ** CPD [*biscuit, cake, egg*] de chocolate ➤ **chocolate éclair** relámpago *m* de chocolate

chocolate-box ['tʃɒklɪtbɒks] ADJ (*Brit*) [*look, picture*] de postal de Navidad

choice [tʃɔɪs] **Ⓐ** ADJ (= *selected*) selecto, escogido; (= *high quality*) de primera calidad
Ⓑ N **1** (= *act of choosing*) elección *f*, selección *f*; **it's your ~** ♢ **the ~ is yours** usted elige; **I did it from ~** lo hice de buena gana; **to make one's ~** elegir; **take your ~!** ¡elija usted!, ¡escoja usted!
2 (= *thing chosen*) preferencia *f*, elección *f*; **this book would be my ~** este libro es el que yo escogería
3 (= *variety*) surtido *m*; **we have a wide ~** (*Comm*) tenemos un gran surtido; **you have a wide ~** tienes muchas posibilidades
4 (= *option*) opción *f*, alternativa *f*; **he gave me two ~s** me dio a elegir entre dos opciones; **to have no ~** no tener alternativa, no tener opción; **he had no ~ but to go** no tuvo más remedio que ir

choir ['kwaɪə'] N (*Mus*) coro *m*, coral *f* ➤ **choir school** escuela primaria para niños cantores ➤ **choir stall** silla *f* de coro

choirboy ['kwaɪəbɔɪ] N niño *m* de coro

choke [tʃəʊk] **Ⓐ** VI [*person*] ahogarse, asfixiarse; **to ~ to death** morir asfixiado; **to ~ on a fishbone** atragantarse con una espina **Ⓑ** VT **1** [+ *person*] ahogar, asfixiar; **in a voice ~d with emotion** con una voz ahogada *or* sofocada por la emoción **2** [+ *pipe etc*] atascar, obstruir; **a canal ~d with weeds** un canal atascado por las hierbas; **a street ~d with traffic** una calle congestionada por el tráfico **Ⓒ** N (*Aut*) (e)stárter *m*, chok(e) *m* (*LAm*)
➤ **choke back** VT + ADV [+ *tears*] tragarse; [+ *feelings*] ahogar

choker ['tʃəʊkə'] N (= *necklace*) gargantilla *f*

cholera ['kɒlərə] N cólera *m*

cholesterol [kə'lestərɒl] N colesterol m

choose [tʃuːz] (pt **chose**; pp **chosen**) Ⓐ VT 1 (gen) elegir, escoger; (= select) [+ team] seleccionar; [+ candidate] elegir; **he was chosen as leader** fue elegido líder; **there is nothing to ~ between them** (Brit) vale tanto el uno como el otro, no veo la diferencia entre ellos
2 (= opt) **to ~ to do sth** optar por hacer algo; **if I don't ~ to** si no quiero
Ⓑ VI elegir, escoger; **to ~ between** elegir entre; **there are several to ~ from** hay varios entre los que elegir; **when I ~** cuando me parezca*, cuando me dé la gana (Sp**)

choosey, choosy ['tʃuːzɪ] ADJ (compar **choosier**; superl **choosiest**) exigente; **I'm ~ about who I go out with** yo no salgo con un cualquiera; **in his position he can't be ~** su posición no le permite darse el lujo de escoger

chop¹ [tʃɒp] Ⓐ N 1 (= blow) golpe m cortante; (= cut) tajo m 2 (Culin) chuleta f 3 (Brit*) **to get the ~** [+ project] ser rechazado or desechado; [person] ser despedido Ⓑ VT 1 [+ wood] cortar, talar; [+ meat, vegetables] picar 2 (Sport) [+ ball] cortar
➤ **chop down** VT + ADV [+ tree] talar
➤ **chop off** VT + ADV cortar de un tajo; **they ~ped off his head** le cortaron la cabeza
➤ **chop up** VT + ADV (gen) desmenuzar; [+ meat] picar

chop² [tʃɒp] VI (Brit*): **to ~ and change** cambiar constantemente de opinión

chopper ['tʃɒpəʳ] N 1 [of butcher] tajadera f, cuchilla f 2 (*) (= helicopter) helicóptero m; (Brit) (= bicycle) bicicleta de manillar alto y asiento alargado; (US) (= motorbike) motocicleta de manillar alto y asiento alargado

chopping board ['tʃɒpɪŋ,bɔːd] N (Brit) tajo m, tabla f de cortar

choppy ['tʃɒpɪ] ADJ (compar **choppier**; superl **choppiest**) [sea, weather] picado, agitado

chopsticks ['tʃɒpstɪks] NPL palillos mpl

choral ['kɔːrəl] ADJ coral ➤ **choral society** orfeón m

chord [kɔːd] N 1 (Mus) acorde m; ✦ IDIOM **to strike a ~ with sb** sonar a algn 2 (Math, Anat) cuerda f

chore [tʃɔːʳ] N faena f, tarea f; (pej) tarea f rutinaria; **to do the (household) ~s** hacer los quehaceres domésticos

choreographer [,kɒrɪ'ɒɡrəfəʳ] N coreógrafo/a m/f

choreography [,kɒrɪ'ɒɡrəfɪ] N coreografía f

chorister ['kɒrɪstəʳ] N corista mf

chortle ['tʃɔːtl] Ⓐ N risa f alegre Ⓑ VI reírse alegremente; **to ~ over sth** reírse satisfecho por algo

chorus ['kɔːrəs] Ⓐ N (pl **-es**) 1 [of singers, play] coro m; (in musical) conjunto m; **in ~** a coro 2 (= refrain) estribillo m; **to join in the ~** unirse en el estribillo Ⓑ VT contestar a coro Ⓒ CPD ➤ **chorus girl** corista f ➤ **chorus line** línea f de coro

chose [tʃəʊz] PT of **choose**

chosen ['tʃəʊzn] Ⓐ PP of **choose** Ⓑ ADJ **the ~ few** la minoría privilegiada; **the Chosen (People)** el pueblo elegido; **their ~ representative** el representante que han elegido

chow¹ [tʃaʊ] N (= dog) chow-chow m, perro m chino

chow²* [tʃaʊ] N (US) (= food) comida f

chowder ['tʃaʊdəʳ] N sopa f de pescado

Christ [kraɪst] Ⓐ N Cristo m Ⓑ EXCL **~!*** ¡hostia(s)! (Sp***), ¡carajo! (LAm***)

christen ['krɪsn] VT 1 (Rel) bautizar 2 (= name) bautizar con el nombre de 3 (*) (= use for first time) estrenar

christening ['krɪsnɪŋ] N bautizo m, bautismo m

Christian ['krɪstɪən] ADJ, N cristiano/a m/f ➤ **Christian Democrat** democratacristiano/a m/f, democristiano/a m/f ➤ **Christian Democrat(ic) Party** partido m democratacristiano, partido m democristiano ➤ **Christian name** nombre m de pila ➤ **Christian Science** Ciencia f Cristiana ➤ **Christian Scientist** Científico/a m/f Cristiano/a

Christianity [,krɪstɪ'ænɪtɪ] N cristianismo m

Christmas ['krɪsməs] Ⓐ N Navidad f; (= season) Navidades fpl; **at ~** en Navidad, por Navidades; **happy** or **merry ~!** ¡Feliz Navidad!, ¡Felices Pascuas!

Ⓑ CPD [decorations, festivities] de Navidad, navideño ➤ **Christmas box** (Brit) aguinaldo m ➤ **Christmas cake** pastel m de Navidad, tarta f de Navidad ➤ **Christmas card** crismas m inv, tarjeta f de Navidad ➤ **Christmas carol** villancico m ➤ **Christmas Day** día m de Navidad ➤ **Christmas dinner** comida f de Navidad ➤ **Christmas Eve** Nochebuena f ➤ **Christmas party** fiesta f de Navidad ➤ **Christmas present** regalo m de Navidad ➤ **Christmas pudding** (esp Brit) pudin m de Navidad ➤ **Christmas stocking** calcetines en los que se colocan los regalos de Navidad ➤ **Christmas time** Navidades fpl, Pascua f de Navidad ➤ **Christmas tree** árbol m de Navidad

chromatic [krə'mætɪk] ADJ cromático

chrome [krəʊm] N cromo m

chromium ['krəʊmɪəm] N cromo m

chromosome ['krəʊməsəʊm] N cromosoma m

chronic ['krɒnɪk] Ⓐ ADJ 1 [invalid, disease] crónico 2 (= inveterate) [smoker] empedernido; [liar] incorregible 3 (Brit*) [weather, person] horrible, malísimo Ⓑ CPD ➤ **Chronic Fatigue Syndrome** síndrome m de fatiga crónica

chronically ['krɒnɪkəlɪ] ADV **to be ~ sick** sufrir una enfermedad crónica

chronicle ['krɒnɪkl] Ⓐ N crónica f; **Chronicles** (Bible) Crónicas fpl Ⓑ VT hacer una crónica de

chronological [,krɒnə'lɒdʒɪkəl] ADJ cronológico; **in ~ order** por orden cronológico

chronologically [,krɒnə'lɒdʒɪkəlɪ] ADV por orden cronológico

chronology [krə'nɒlədʒɪ] N cronología f

chrysalis ['krɪsəlɪs] N (pl **-es**) crisálida f

chrysanthemum [krɪ'sænθəməm] N crisantemo m

chubby ['tʃʌbɪ] ADJ (compar **chubbier**; superl **chubbiest**) [baby, hands] rechoncho, regordete; [face, cheeks] mofletudo

chuck [tʃʌk] VT 1 (*) (= throw) tirar, echar 2 (* also = **away**) tirar, botar (LAm); [+ money] tirar; [+ chance] desperdiciar 3 (*) [+ job, boyfriend, girlfriend] dejar, dejar plantado*
➤ **chuck in** VT + ADV (Brit*) [+ job] dejar, dejar plantado*
➤ **chuck out** VT + ADV [+ rubbish] tirar, botar (LAm); [+ person] echar (fuera); [+ employee] despedir, dar el pasaporte a*
➤ **chuck up** Ⓐ VT + ADV (Brit*) [+ job] dejar, dejar plantado* Ⓑ VI + ADV (US**) (= vomit) arrojar*

chuckle ['tʃʌkl] Ⓐ N risita f, risa f sofocada; **we had a good ~ over that** nos reímos bastante con eso Ⓑ VI reírse entre dientes, soltar una risita; **to ~ at** or **over** reírse con

chuffed* [tʃʌft] ADJ (Brit) satisfecho, contento; **he was pretty ~ about it** estaba la mar de contento por eso

chug [tʃʌg] VI [steam engine] resoplar; [motor] traquetear; **the train ~ged past** pasó el tren resoplando
➤ **chug along** VI + ADV [car, train] ir renqueando; (fig) ir tirando

chum* [tʃʌm] N amiguete* m, colega mf, cuate mf (Mex*), pata mf (Per*); (= child) amiguito/a m/f; **to be great ~s** ser íntimos amigos

chump* [tʃʌmp] N (= idiot) tonto/a m/f; ✦ IDIOM **to be off one's ~** (Brit**) estar chiflado

chunk [tʃʌŋk] N [of bread, cheese etc] pedazo m, trozo m; (*) [of land, time] cantidad f considerable; **a sizeable ~ of their earnings** una buena parte del sueldo

chunky ['tʃʌŋkɪ] ADJ (compar **chunkier**; superl **chunkiest**) [person] fornido; [furniture] achaparrado; [knitwear] grueso, de lana gorda

church [tʃɜːtʃ] Ⓐ N 1 (= building) iglesia f
2 (= service) (Catholic) misa f; (Protestant) oficio m; **to go to ~** (gen) ir a la iglesia; (mass) ir a misa; **after ~** después de la misa/del oficio
3 (= institution) **the Church** la Iglesia
Ⓑ CPD [doctrine] de la Iglesia ➤ **church hall** salón m de actos de la parroquia ➤ **church music** música f sacra or religiosa ➤ **Church of England** Iglesia f anglicana ➤ **Church of Scotland** Iglesia f presbiteriana escocesa ➤ **church school** colegio m religioso ➤ **church service** oficio m,

servicio *m* religioso ➤ **church wedding they want a ~ wedding** quieren casarse por la iglesia

churchgoer [ˈtʃɜːˌtʃɡəʊəʳ] N fiel *mf*

churchyard [ˈtʃɜːtʃjɑːd] N cementerio *m*, campo *m* santo

churlish [ˈtʃɜːlɪʃ] ADJ (= *rude*) grosero, maleducado; (= *unfriendly*) poco amistoso, arisco; **it would be ~ not to thank him** sería muy grosero *or* maleducado no darle las gracias

churn [tʃɜːn] **A** N (*for butter*) mantequera *f*; (*Brit*) (*for milk*) lechera *f* **B** VT **1** [+ *butter*] batir *or* hacer en una mantequera **2** (*also* = **up**) [+ *sea, mud*] revolver, agitar **C** VI [*sea*] revolverse, agitarse; **her stomach was ~ing** se le revolvía el estómago
➤ **churn out** VT + ADV (*pej*) [+ *books, goods*] producir en serie, producir en masa

chute [ʃuːt] N **1** (*for rubbish*) vertedero *m* **2** (*Brit*) (*in playground, swimming pool*) tobogán *m*

chutney [ˈtʃʌtnɪ] N salsa *f* picante (de frutas y especias)

CIA N ABBR (*US*) (= **Central Intelligence Agency**) CIA *f*

cicada [sɪˈkɑːdə] N cigarra *f*

CID N ABBR (*Brit*) = **Criminal Investigation Department**

cider [ˈsaɪdəʳ] N sidra *f* ➤ **cider vinegar** vinagre *m* de sidra

cigar [sɪˈɡɑːʳ] N puro *m*, cigarro *m* ➤ **cigar lighter** (*Aut*) encendedor *m* de puro

cigarette [ˌsɪɡəˈret] N cigarrillo *m*, cigarro *m*; **he had a ~** (se) fumó un cigarrillo *or* cigarro ➤ **cigarette ash** ceniza *f* de cigarrillo ➤ **cigarette butt** colilla *f* ➤ **cigarette case** pitillera *f* ➤ **cigarette end** (*Brit*) colilla *f* ➤ **cigarette holder** boquilla *f* ➤ **cigarette lighter** encendedor *m*, mechero *m*; (*Aut*) encendedor *m* de puro ➤ **cigarette machine** máquina *f* de tabaco ➤ **cigarette paper** papel *m* de fumar

cigar-shaped [sɪˈɡɑːʃeɪpt] ADJ en forma de puro

ciggy* [ˈsɪɡɪ] N (*Brit*) = **cigarette**

CIM N ABBR (*Comput*) = **computer-integrated manufacturing**

cinch* [sɪntʃ] N **it's a ~** (= *easy thing*) está tirado, es pan comido; (*esp US*) (= *sure thing*) es cosa segura

cinder [ˈsɪndəʳ] N (= *ember*) carbonilla *f*; ✦ IDIOM **to be burned to a ~** (*Brit*) quedar carbonizado ➤ **cinder block** (*US*) bovedilla *f* ➤ **cinder track** pista *f* de ceniza

Cinderella [ˌsɪndəˈrelə] N Cenicienta *f*; **it's the ~ of the arts** es la hermana pobre de las artes

cine [ˈsɪnɪ] CPD (*Brit*) ➤ **cine camera** cámara *f* cinematográfica ➤ **cine film** película *f* de cine

cinema [ˈsɪnəmə] (*esp Brit*) N cine *m* ➤ **cinema complex** multicine *m*

cinema-going [ˈsɪnəməˌɡəʊɪŋ] (*esp Brit*) ADJ **the ~ public** el público aficionado al cine

cinnamon [ˈsɪnəmən] N canela *f*

cipher [ˈsaɪfəʳ] N **1** (= *secret writing*) cifra *f*, código *m* **2** (*fig*) **he's a mere ~** es un cero a la izquierda

circa [ˈsɜːkə] PREP hacia; **~ 1500** hacia (el año) 1500

circle [ˈsɜːkl] **A** N **1** (*gen*) círculo *m*; **to stand in a ~** formar un corro; ✦ IDIOMS **to come full ~** volver al punto de partida; **to go round in ~s*** dar vueltas sobre lo mismo, no avanzar
2 (= *set of people*) círculo *m*, grupo *m*; **in certain ~s** en ciertos medios; **in business ~s** en el mundo de los negocios
3 (*Brit Theat*) anfiteatro *m*
B VT **1** (= *surround*) cercar, rodear; (= *move round*) girar alrededor de, dar vueltas alrededor de; **the aircraft ~d the town twice** el avión dio dos vueltas sobre la ciudad
2 (= *draw round*) poner un círculo alrededor de, rodear con un círculo
C VI dar vueltas

circuit [ˈsɜːkɪt] **A** N **1** (= *route*) circuito *m* **2** (*esp Brit*) (= *sports track*) pista *f* **3** (*Aut, Elec*) circuito *m* **4** (*Sport*) (= *course*) recorrido *m*; (= *lap by runner*) vuelta *f* **5** (*Brit Jur*) distrito *m* **B** CPD ➤ **circuit board** tarjeta *f* de circuitos ➤ **circuit breaker** cortacircuitos *m inv* ➤ **circuit court** (*US*) tribunal *m* superior ➤ **circuit training** circuito *m* de entrenamiento

circuitous [sɜːˈkjʊɪtəs] ADJ [*route*] tortuoso, sinuoso; [*method*] tortuoso, solapado

circular [ˈsɜːkjʊləʳ] **A** ADJ circular, redondo; **~ motion** movimiento *m* circular; **~ tour** circuito *m* **B** N (= *letter*) circular *f*; (= *advertisement*) panfleto *m* **C** CPD ➤ **circular saw** (*Brit*) sierra *f* circular

circulate [ˈsɜːkjʊleɪt] **A** VI circular **B** VT hacer circular

circulation [ˌsɜːkjʊˈleɪʃən] N **1** (*gen*) circulación *f*; **he's back in ~*** se está dejando ver otra vez; **she has poor ~** (*Med*) tiene mala circulación **2** (= *number of papers*) tirada *f*

circumcise [ˈsɜːkəmsaɪz] VT circuncidar

circumcision [ˌsɜːkəmˈsɪʒən] N circuncisión *f*

circumference [səˈkʌmfərəns] N circunferencia *f*

circumflex [ˈsɜːkəmfleks] N circunflejo *m*

circumnavigate [ˌsɜːkəmˈnævɪɡeɪt] VT circunnavegar

circumscribe [ˈsɜːkəmskraɪb] VT (*lit*) circunscribir; (= *limit*) limitar, restringir

circumspect [ˈsɜːkəmspekt] ADJ circunspecto, prudente

circumstance [ˈsɜːkəmstəns] N circunstancia *f*; **in** *or* **under the ~s** en *or* dadas las circunstancias; **under no ~s** de ninguna manera, bajo ningún concepto; **a victim of ~** una víctima de las circunstancias

circumstantial [ˌsɜːkəmˈstænʃəl] ADJ **~ evidence** pruebas *fpl* circunstanciales

circumvent [ˌsɜːkəmˈvent] VT [+ *law, rule*] burlar

circus [ˈsɜːkəs] N (*pl* **~es**) **1** (= *entertainment*) circo *m* **2** (*Brit*) (*in place names*) plaza *f*, glorieta *f*

cirrhosis [sɪˈrəʊsɪs] N cirrosis *f*

CIS N ABBR (= **Commonwealth of Independent States**) CEI *f*

cissy* [ˈsɪsɪ] N mariquita* *m*

cistern [ˈsɪstən] N **1** (*esp Brit*) [*of WC*] cisterna *f* **2** (*US*) (*for rainwater*) tina *f* para recoger el agua de la lluvia

citadel [ˈsɪtədl] N ciudadela *f*

citation [saɪˈteɪʃən] N cita *f*; (*US Jur*) citación *f*; (*Mil*) mención *f*, citación *f*

cite [saɪt] VT citar

citizen [ˈsɪtɪzn] N [*of state*] ciudadano/a *m/f*, súbdito/a *m/f*; [*of city*] habitante *mf*, vecino/a *m/f* ➤ **Citizens' Advice Bureau** (*Brit*) *organización voluntaria británica que asesora legal o financieramente* ➤ **citizen's arrest** *arresto realizado por un ciudadano ordinario* ➤ **Citizens' Band** banda *f* ciudadana

citizenship [ˈsɪtɪznʃɪp] N ciudadanía *f*

citric acid [ˌsɪtrɪkˈæsɪd] N ácido *m* cítrico

citrus fruits [ˈsɪtrəsˌfruːtz] NPL cítricos *mpl*, agrios *mpl*

city [ˈsɪtɪ] **A** N ciudad *f*; **the City** (*Brit Fin*) *el centro financiero de Londres*
B CPD municipal, de la ciudad ➤ **city centre**, **city center** (*US*) centro *m* de la ciudad ➤ **city dweller** habitante *mf* de una ciudad ➤ **city hall** palacio *m* municipal; (*US*) ayuntamiento *m* ➤ **city limits** perímetro *msing* urbano ➤ **city news** (*Brit*) noticias *fpl* financieras; (*US*) noticias *fpl* de la ciudad ➤ **city planner** (*US*) urbanista *mf* ➤ **city planning** (*US*) urbanismo *m* ➤ **city technology college** (*Brit*) ≈ *centro m de formación profesional*

civic [ˈsɪvɪk] ADJ [*rights, duty*] cívico; [*authorities*] municipal ➤ **civic centre** (*Brit*) conjunto *m* de edificios municipales

civics [ˈsɪvɪks] NSING (*esp US*) educación *f* cívica

civil [ˈsɪvɪl] **A** ADJ **1** [*strife, aviation, ceremony, case*] civil; [*unrest*] social
2 (= *polite*) [*person*] cortés, atento; **to be ~ to sb** ser cortés *or* atento con algn; **that's very ~ of you** es usted muy amable
B CPD ➤ **Civil Aviation Authority** *organismo responsable de la aviación civil* ➤ **civil defence**, **civil defense** (*US*) defensa *f* civil ➤ **civil engineer** ingeniero/a *m/f* civil, ingeniero/a *m/f* de caminos (canales y puertos) (*Sp*) ➤ **civil engineering** ingeniería *f* civil, ingeniería *f* de caminos (canales y puertos) (*Sp*) ➤ **civil liberties** libertades *fpl* civiles ➤ **civil rights** derechos *mpl* civiles ➤ **civil rights movement** movimiento *m* pro derechos civiles ➤ **civil servant**

funcionario/a *m/f* (del Estado) ➤ **civil service**
administración *f* pública ➤ **civil war** guerra *f* civil; **the
American Civil War** la guerra de Secesión

civilian [sɪ'vɪlɪən] **Ⓐ** ADJ (= *non-military*) civil; **there were no
~ casualties** no hubo bajas entre la población civil **Ⓑ** N
civil *mf*

civility [sɪ'vɪlɪtɪ] N **1** (= *politeness*) cortesía *f*, amabilidad *f*
2 (*usu pl*) (= *polite remark*) cortesía *f*, cumplido *m*

civilization [ˌsɪvɪlaɪ'zeɪʃən] N civilización *f*

civilized ['sɪvɪlaɪzd] ADJ [*person*] (= *socially advanced,
refined*) civilizado; (= *well brought up*) educado; [*meal, place,
tastes*] refinado; **to become ~** civilizarse; **he never phones
at a ~ hour** nunca llama a una hora decente; **let's try and
be ~ about it** vamos a comportarnos como personas
civilizadas

civvies* ['sɪvɪz] NPL **in ~** vestido de paisano *or* civil

CJD N ABBR (= **Creutzfeldt-Jakob disease**) *enfermedad de
Creutzfeldt-Jakob*

cl ABBR (= **centilitre(s)**) cl

clad [klæd] ADJ vestido (**in** de)

claim [kleɪm] **Ⓐ** N **1** (= *demand*) (*for rights, wages*)
reivindicación *f*, demanda *f*; (*for damages, on insurance*)
reclamación *f*; (*for expenses, benefit*) solicitud *f*; (*Jur*)
demanda *f*; **pay** *or* **wage ~** reivindicación *f* salarial; **she lost
her ~ for damages** el tribunal rechazó su demanda de
daños y perjuicios; **to make a ~ (on one's insurance)**
reclamar (al seguro); **to put in a ~ (for sth)** (*for expenses*)
presentar una solicitud (de algo); (*on insurance*) reclamar
(algo); **there are many ~s on my time** tengo una agenda
muy apretada
2 (= *right*) (*to property, title, throne*) derecho *m*
3 (= *assertion*) afirmación *f*; **I make no ~ to be infallible** no
pretendo ser infalible
Ⓑ VT **1** (= *demand as due*) [+ *rights*] reivindicar; [+ *lost
property*] reclamar; [+ *allowance, benefit*] (= *apply for*)
solicitar; (= *receive*) cobrar; **if you wish to ~ expenses you
must provide receipts** si desea que se le reembolsen los
gastos debe presentar los recibos; **to ~ damages from sb**
demandar a algn por daños y perjuicios
2 (= *state title to*) [+ *territory*] reivindicar; [+ *victory*]
atribuirse; [+ *prize*] llevarse; [+ *throne*] reclamar; **so far no
one has ~ed responsibility for the bomb** hasta ahora nadie
ha reivindicado la colocación de la bomba
3 (= *assert*) **to ~ that** afirmar que; **he ~s to have seen her**
afirma haberla visto
4 (= *require*) [+ *attention*] requerir, exigir
5 (= *take*) [+ *life*] cobrarse; **the accident ~ed four lives** el
accidente se cobró cuatro vidas
Ⓒ VI (= *make demand*) presentar reclamación; **to ~ for sth**
reclamar (los gastos de) algo
Ⓓ CPD ➤ **claim form** (*for benefit*) (impreso *m* de) solicitud *f*;
(*for expenses*) impreso *m* de reembolso; (*Insurance*) impreso
m de reclamación ➤ **claims adjuster** (*US*) ajustador(a) *m/f*
de pérdidas, tasador(a) *m/f* de pérdidas

claimant ['kleɪmənt] N (*in court*) demandante *mf*; (*Brit*) [*of
benefit*] solicitante *mf*; (*to throne*) pretendiente *mf*

clairvoyant(e) [kleə'vɔɪənt] ADJ, N clarividente *mf*, vidente
mf

clam [klæm] N almeja *f* ➤ **clam chowder** (*US*) sopa *f* de
almejas
➤ **clam up*** VI + ADV cerrar el pico*, no decir ni pío

clamber ['klæmbə'] **Ⓐ** N subida *f* **Ⓑ** VI **to ~ over/up sth**
trepar sobre/a algo, subir gateando sobre/a algo

clammy ['klæmɪ] ADJ (*compar* **clammier**; *superl* **clammiest**)
(= *damp*) frío y húmedo; (= *sticky*) pegajoso

clamour, **clamor** (*US*) ['klæmə'] **Ⓐ** N clamor *m* **Ⓑ** VI
clamorear, vociferar; **to ~ for sth** clamar algo, pedir algo a
voces

clamp [klæmp] **Ⓐ** N (= *brace*) abrazadera *f*; (*on bench*)
cárcel *f*; (*Brit*) (*on parked car*) cepo *m* **Ⓑ** VT **1** (= *secure*) (*with
brace*) afianzar *or* sujetar con abrazadera; (*on bench*)
afianzar *or* sujetar con cárcel **2** (*Brit*) [+ *car*] poner un cepo en
➤ **clamp down** VI + ADV poner frenos (**on** a), tomar fuertes
medidas (**on** contra)

clampdown ['klæmpdaʊn] N restricción *f* (**on** de),
prohibición *f* (**on** en)

clan [klæn] N clan *m*

clandestine [klæn'destɪn] ADJ clandestino

clang [klæŋ] **Ⓐ** N ruido *m* metálico fuerte **Ⓑ** VI sonar
mucho, hacer estruendo; **the gate ~ed shut** la puerta se
cerró ruidosamente

clanger* ['klæŋə'] N (*Brit*) plancha *f* (*Sp**), metedura *f* *or*
(*LAm*) metida *f* de pata*; **✦** IDIOM **to drop a ~** meter la pata*,
tirarse una plancha (*Sp**)

clank [klæŋk] **Ⓐ** N sonido *m* metálico seco **Ⓑ** VI sonar;
the train went ~ing past el tren pasó con gran estruendo

clap[1] [klæp] **Ⓐ** N **1** (*on shoulder, of the hands*) palmada *f*; **a
~ of thunder** un trueno **2** (= *applause*) aplauso *m*; **to get a ~**
recibir un aplauso **Ⓑ** VT [+ *person, play, announcement*]
aplaudir; **to ~ one's hands** dar palmadas, batir las palmas;
to ~ sb on the back dar a algn una palmada en la espalda;
to ~ a hand over sb's mouth tapar la boca a algn con la
mano; **to ~ eyes on** clavar la vista en **Ⓒ** VI aplaudir

clap[2]** [klæp] N (= *disease*) **the ~** gonorrea *f*

clapped-out* [ˌklæpt'aʊt] ADJ (*Brit*) [*car, bus etc*]
desvencijado; [*person*] para el arrastre

clapper ['klæpə'] N **✦** IDIOM **to run like the ~s** (*Brit**) correr
como loco

clapping ['klæpɪŋ] N (= *applause*) aplausos *mpl*; (*to music*)
palmas *fpl*

claptrap* ['klæptræp] N burradas *fpl*, disparates *mpl*

claret ['klærət] N **1** (= *wine*) vino *m* de Burdeos **2** (= *colour*)
burdeos *m*

clarification [ˌklærɪfɪ'keɪʃən] N aclaración *f*

clarify ['klærɪfaɪ] VT aclarar, clarificar

clarinet [ˌklærɪ'net] N clarinete *m*

clarinettist [ˌklærɪ'netɪst] N clarinetista *mf*

clarity ['klærɪtɪ] N claridad *f*

clash [klæʃ] **Ⓐ** N **1** (= *noise*) estruendo *m*, fragor *m*; [*of
cymbals*] ruido *m* metálico
2 [*of armies, personalities*] choque *m*; [*of interests, opinions*]
conflicto *m*; **a ~ with the police** un choque *or* un
enfrentamiento con la policía; **a ~ of wills** un conflicto de
voluntades; **I've got a ~ of dates** me coinciden las fechas
Ⓑ VT [+ *cymbals, swords*] golpear
Ⓒ VI **1** [*personalities, interests*] oponerse, chocar; [*colours*]
desentonar; [*dates, events*] coincidir
2 (= *argue*) pelear; (*Mil*) encontrarse, enfrentarse (**with** con)

clasp [klɑːsp] **Ⓐ** N [*of brooch, necklace*] cierre *m*; [*of belt*]
broche *m* **Ⓑ** VT **1** (= *fasten*) abrochar **2** (= *take hold of*)
agarrar; **to ~ sb's hand** estrechar la mano de algn; **to ~
one's hands (together)** juntar las manos **3** (= *embrace*) **to ~
sb to one's bosom** estrechar a algn contra el pecho **Ⓒ** CPD
➤ **clasp knife** navaja *f*

class [klɑːs] **Ⓐ** N **1** (*gen, Scol, Bio, Sociol*) clase *f*; **the ~ of 89**
la promoción del 89; **ruling/middle/working ~** clase *f*
dirigente/media/obrera; **first ~** primera clase *f*; **lower ~es**
clase *fsing* baja; **upper ~** clase *f* alta
2 (= *category*) categoría *f*; **~ of degree** (*Brit Univ*) tipo de título
universitario según la nota con que se ha obtenido; **it's just not
in the same ~** no se puede comparar; **in a ~ of one's own**
sin par *or* igual
3 (= *style*) **to have ~** tener clase
Ⓑ VT clasificar; **to ~ sb as sth** clasificar a algn de algo
Ⓒ ADJ (= *classy*) [*player, actor*] de primera clase
Ⓓ CPD ➤ **class consciousness** conciencia *f* de clase ➤ **class
struggle** lucha *f* de clases ➤ **class system** sistema *m* de
clases sociales ➤ **class teacher** (*Brit*) tutor(a) *m/f*

class-conscious ['klɑːs'kɒnʃəs] ADJ con conciencia de
clase

classic ['klæsɪk] **Ⓐ** ADJ **1** (= *timeless, traditional*) clásico **2** (*)
(= *wonderful, memorable*) memorable; (= *funny*) genial*; **it
was ~** fue genial* **Ⓑ** N **1** (= *book, play*) clásico *m*; **that was a
~!*** ¡fue genial!* **2 classics** (*Univ*) clásicas *fpl*

classical ['klæsɪkəl] ADJ [*ballet, style, Greece*] clásico;
[*musician, recording*] de música clásica ➤ **classical music**
música *f* clásica

classically ['klæsɪkəlɪ] ADV [*educated, trained*] en la tradición clásica

classicist ['klæsɪsɪst] N clasicista *mf*

classification [ˌklæsɪfɪ'keɪʃən] N clasificación *f*

classified ['klæsɪfaɪd] **A** ADJ [*document, information*] confidencial, secreto **B** N **classifieds** (*also ~ advertisements*) anuncios *mpl* por palabras **C** CPD ➤ **classified section** (*Press*) sección *f* de anuncios por palabras

classify ['klæsɪfaɪ] VT **1** (= *sort*) clasificar (**in, into** en) **2** (= *restrict access to*) [+ *information*] clasificar como secreto

classless ['klɑːslɪs] ADJ [*society*] sin clases

classmate ['klɑːsmeɪt] N (*Brit*) compañero/a *m/f* de clase, condiscípulo/a *m/f*

classroom ['klɑːsrʊm] N aula *f*, clase *f* ➤ **classroom assistant** profesor(a) *m/f* de apoyo

> Use **el/un** not **la/una** before feminine nouns beginning with stressed **a** or **ha** like *aula*.

classy* ['klɑːsɪ] ADJ (*compar* **classier**; *superl* **classiest**) elegante, de buen tono

clatter ['klætəʳ] **A** N (= *loud noise*) estruendo *m*; [*of plates*] estrépito *m*; [*of hooves*] trápala *f* **B** VI [*metal object etc*] hacer estrépito, hacer estruendo; [*hooves*] trapalear; **to ~ in/out** entrar/salir estrepitosamente

clause [klɔːz] N (*Ling*) oración *f*; (*in contract, law*) cláusula *f*; (*in will*) disposición *f*

claustrophobia [ˌklɔːstrə'fəʊbɪə] N claustrofobia *f*

claustrophobic [ˌklɔːstrə'fəʊbɪk] ADJ claustrofóbico

claw [klɔː] **A** N **1** [*of cat, bird etc*] garra *f*; [*of lobster*] pinza *f*; ✦ IDIOMS **to get one's ~s into sb** (= *attack*) atacar con rencor a algn; (= *dominate*) dominar a algn; **to show one's ~s** sacar las uñas **2** (*Tech*) garfio *m*, gancho *m* **B** VT arañar ➤ **claw at** VI + PREP arañar ➤ **claw back** VT + ADV (*Brit*) volver a tomar, tomar otra vez para sí

clay [kleɪ] N arcilla *f*, barro *m* ➤ **clay court** pista *f* de tierra batida ➤ **clay pigeon** plato *m* de barro ➤ **clay pigeon shooting** tiro *m* al plato, tiro *m* al pichón ➤ **clay pipe** pipa *f* de cerámica

clean [kliːn] **A** ADJ (*compar* **~er**; *superl* **~est**) **1** (= *not dirty*) [*clothes, sheets, floor, face*] limpio; [*air, water*] limpio, puro; **the rain washed the streets ~** la lluvia limpió las calles; **to wipe sth ~** limpiar algo; ✦ IDIOMS **to make a ~ breast of it** confesarlo todo; **to come ~*** confesarlo todo; **to come ~ about sth*** confesar algo; **as ~ as a whistle** *or* **a new pin*** limpio como los chorros del oro, limpio como la patena **2** (= *fresh*) [*smell*] a limpio; [*taste*] refrescante **3** (= *new, unused*) [*sheet of paper, page*] en blanco, en limpio; **to make a ~ copy** hacer una copia en limpio **4** (= *pure*) [*joke*] inocente; [*life*] decente; **~ living** vida *f* sana **5** (= *smooth, even*) [*movement*] fluido; [*shot*] certero; [*cut*] limpio; [*sound*] nítido, claro; [*features, outline*] nítido, bien definido; **a ~ break with the totalitarian past** una ruptura radical con el pasado totalitario; **I need (to make) a ~ break with the past** necesito romper con el pasado totalmente **6** (= *fair*) [*fight, game*] limpio; [*player*] que juega limpio **7** (= *untarnished*) [*image, reputation*] bueno, impecable; **they gave him a ~ bill of health** le declararon en perfecto estado de salud; **a ~ driving licence** un carnet de conducir sin infracciones **8** (= *environmentally friendly*) [*machine, energy*] no contaminante **9** (**) (= *innocent*) **they can't touch me, I'm ~** no me pueden hacer nada, tengo las manos limpias* **10** (**) (= *not in possession of illegal goods*) **he's ~** no lleva nada encima; **his room was ~** no encontraron nada en su habitación **B** ADV **1** (*) (= *completely*) **he ~ forgot** lo olvidó por completo; **he got ~ away** se escapó sin dejar rastro; **it went ~ through the window** pasó limpiamente por la ventana **2** (= *fairly*) **to fight/play ~** luchar/jugar limpio **C** N limpieza *f*, aseo *m* (*LAm*); (= *wash*) lavado *m*; **to give**

sth a (good) ~ limpiar algo (bien); **to give sth a quick ~** dar una pasada (rápida) a algo **D** VT [+ *room, carpet, windows, shoes*] limpiar; [+ *vegetables, clothes*] lavar; [+ *blackboard*] borrar; [+ *wound, cut*] desinfectar; **to ~ one's teeth** lavarse los dientes **E** VI limpiar **F** CPD ➤ **clean sweep: to make a ~ sweep of sth** (*esp Sport*) arrasar con algo, barrer con algo ➤ **clean off** VT + ADV [+ *dirt, rust*] limpiar ➤ **clean out** VT + ADV **1** [+ *room, cupboard*] vaciar; **to ~ out a box** limpiar (el interior de) una caja **2** (*) (*fig*) **we were ~ed out** nos dejaron sin blanca ➤ **clean up** **A** VT + ADV **1** [+ *room, mess*] limpiar, asear; **to ~ o.s. up** lavarse, ponerse decente **2** (*fig*) [+ *city, television etc*] limpiar, quitar lo indecente de **B** VI + ADV **1** (= *tidy*) limpiar **2** (*) (= *make profit*) hacer mucho dinero (**on** con)

clean-cut ['kliːn'kʌt] ADJ [*person*] de buen parecer

cleaner ['kliːnəʳ] N **1** (= *man*) encargado *m* de la limpieza; (= *woman*) encargada *f* de la limpieza, asistenta *f*; **~'s (shop)** tintorería *f*, lavandería *f*; ✦ IDIOM **we'll take them to the ~'s*** les dejaremos sin blanca*, les dejaremos limpios* **2** (= *substance*) producto *m* de limpieza

cleaning ['kliːnɪŋ] N limpieza *f*, limpia *f* (*LAm*); **to do the ~** hacer la limpieza ➤ **cleaning fluid** líquido *m* de limpieza ➤ **cleaning lady** señora *f* de la limpieza

cleanliness ['klenlɪnɪs] N limpieza *f*

cleanly ['kliːnlɪ] ADV **1** (= *without polluting*) [*burn, operate*] de forma limpia, sin contaminar **2** (= *neatly*) [*cut, break*] limpiamente; [*hit, catch*] con habilidad, con destreza **3** (= *fairly*) [*play, fight*] limpiamente

clean-out ['kliːnaʊt] N limpieza *f*

cleanse [klenz] VT limpiar

cleanser ['klenzəʳ] N (= *detergent*) detergente *m*; (= *disinfectant*) desinfectante *m*; (= *cosmetic*) leche *f* or crema *f* limpiadora

clean-shaven ['kliːn'ʃeɪvn] ADJ sin barba ni bigote, totalmente afeitado; (= *smooth-faced*) lampiño

cleansing ['klenzɪŋ] **A** ADJ (*for complexion*) limpiador; (*fig*) purificador **B** N limpieza *f* **C** CPD ➤ **cleansing cream** crema *f* limpiadora ➤ **cleansing department** departamento *m* de limpieza ➤ **cleansing lotion** loción *f* limpiadora

clean-up ['kliːnʌp] N limpia *f*, limpieza *f*

clear [klɪəʳ] **A** ADJ (*compar* **~er**; *superl* **~est**) **1** (= *unambiguous*) [*meaning, explanation*] claro; **now let's get this ~ ...** vamos a dejar esto claro ...; **to make it ~ that ...** dejar claro *or* bien sentado que ...; **do I make myself ~?** ¿me explico bien? **2** (= *obvious*) [*motive, consequence*] claro; **it is (absolutely) ~ to me that ...** no me cabe (la menor) duda de que ...; **it's not ~ whether ...** no está claro sí ...; ✦ IDIOM **as ~ as crystal** más claro que el agua **3** (= *certain*) [*understanding, proof*] seguro, cierto; **I'm not very ~ about this** no tengo una idea muy clara de esto; **I'm not ~ whether ...** no tengo claro sí ... **4** (= *transparent*) [*water*] claro; [*glass*] transparente; **a ~ soup** una sopa clara **5** (= *bright*) [*light, colour*] claro; **~ blue eyes** ojos azul claro **6** (= *unsullied*) [*sky, weather, day*] despejado; [*complexion*] terso; **to have a ~ head** tener la cabeza despejada **7** (= *distinct*) [*photograph, outline*] claro, nítido; [*sound, impression, voice*] claro; ✦ IDIOM **as ~ as a bell: I could hear his voice as ~ as a bell** oía su voz como si estuviera a mi lado, oía su voz con toda claridad **8** (= *unobstructed*) [*road, space*] libre, despejado; **all ~!** ¡vía libre!, ¡adelante!; **to get a ~ look at sb/sth** poder ver algn/algo bien; **to be ~ of sth** (= *free of*) estar libre de algo; (= *away from*) estar lejos de algo **9** (= *untroubled*) [*conscience*] limpio, tranquilo **10** (*after deductions*) **a ~ profit** una ganancia neta **11** (= *decisive*) [*majority, winner*] absoluto; [*margin*] amplio **12** (= *without commitments*) [*day*] libre; [*diary*] despejado **B** ADV **1** (= *completely*) **he jumped ~ across the river** atravesó el río limpiamente de un salto **2** (= *free*) **to get ~ away** escaparse sin dejar rastro alguno; **when we get ~ of London** cuando estemos fuera de Londres; **keep ~ of the wall** no te acerques a la pared; **I**

decided to keep ~ of him decidí evitarle; **stand ~ of the doors!** ¡apártense de las puertas!
3 (*Brit Sport*) **to be seven seconds/points ~ of sb** estar siete segundos/puntos por delante de algn
4 (= *net*) **he'll get £250 ~** sacará 250 libras netas
⒞ N **to be in the ~** (= *free of suspicion*) quedar fuera de toda sospecha; (= *free of danger*) estar fuera de peligro
⒟ VT **1** (= *remove obstacles etc from*) [+ *place, surface, road, woodland*] despejar; [+ *court, hall*] desocupar, desalojar (de público *etc*); [+ *pipe*] desatascar; [+ *postbox*] recoger las cartas de; **to ~ one's head** despejar la cabeza; **to ~ sth of sth** despejar algo de algo; **to ~ a space for sth/sb** hacer sitio para algo/algn; **to ~ the table** recoger *or* quitar la mesa; **to ~ one's throat** carraspear, aclararse la voz; **to ~ the way for sth** dejar el camino libre para algo; **✦** IDIOM **to ~ the air** (= *clarify things*) aclarar las cosas; (= *ease tensions*) relajar el ambiente
2 (*Brit Sport*) [+ *ball*] despejar
3 (= *get over*) [+ *fence etc*] salvar, saltar por encima de; **the plane just ~ed the roof** el avión no tocó el tejado por poco, el avión pasó casi rozando el tejado
4 (= *declare innocent etc*) [+ *person*] absolver, probar la inocencia de; **he was ~ed of murder** fue absuelto de asesinato
5 (= *authorize*) **you will have to be ~ed by Security** será preciso que le acredite la Seguridad; **the plan will have to be ~ed with the director** el plan tendrá que ser aprobado por el director
6 **to ~ a cheque** *or* (*US*) **check** (= *accept*) aceptar *or* tramitar un cheque; (= *double-check*) compensar un cheque
7 (*Comm, Fin*) [+ *debt*] liquidar, saldar; [+ *goods etc*] liquidar; **he ~ed £50 on the deal** sacó 50 libras del negocio; **"half-price to clear"** "liquidación a mitad de precio"
8 (*Comput*) despejar
⒠ VI **1** (= *improve*) [*weather, sky*] despejarse; [*fog*] disiparse
2 [*cheque*] ser compensado
3 (*Sport*) despejar
⒡ CPD ➤ **clear round** ronda *f* sin penalizaciones
➤ **clear away** VT + ADV [+ *things, clothes etc*] quitar (de en medio); [+ *dishes*] retirar
➤ **clear off** VI + ADV (*Brit**) (= *leave*) largarse*, mandarse mudar (*LAm*); **~ off!** ¡lárgate!*, ¡fuera de aquí!
➤ **clear out ⒜** VT + ADV [+ *room*] ordenar y tirar los trastos de; [+ *cupboard*] vaciar; [+ *objects*] quitar; **he ~ed everyone out of the room** hizo salir a todo el mundo de la habitación; **he ~ed everything out of the room** despejó la habitación de cosas **⒝** VI + ADV = **clear off**
➤ **clear up ⒜** VT + ADV **1** (= *resolve*) [+ *matter, difficulty, doubt*] aclarar; [+ *mystery, crime*] resolver **2** (= *tidy*) [+ *room, books, toys*] ordenar **⒝** VI + ADV **1** [*weather*] despejarse
2 [*illness*] curarse **3** (= *tidy*) ponerlo todo en orden, ordenar

clearance ['klɪərəns] **⒜** N **1** (= *act of clearing*) [*of road etc*] despeje *m*; [*of land*] desmonte *m*, roza *f* **2** (= *height, width etc*) margen *m* (*de altura, anchura etc*) **3** (= *authorization*) (*by customs*) despacho *m* de aduana; (*by security*) acreditación *f*; [*of cheque*] tramitación *f*; **~ for take-off** (*Aer*) pista libre para despegar **4** (*Ftbl*) despeje *m* **⒝** CPD ➤ **clearance sale** liquidación *f*, realización *f* (*LAm*)

clear-cut ['klɪə'kʌt] ADJ [*case, decision, victory*] claro; [*statement*] sin ambages

clear-headed ['klɪə'hedɪd] ADJ lúcido, de mente despejada

clearing ['klɪərɪŋ] **⒜** N **1** (*in wood*) claro *m* **2** (*Fin*) liquidación *f* **⒝** CPD ➤ **clearing account** cuenta *f* de compensación ➤ **clearing bank** (*Brit*) banco *m* central ➤ **clearing house** cámara *f* de compensación

clearly ['klɪəlɪ] ADV **1** (= *unambiguously*) [*define, state, forbid*] claramente **2** (= *rationally*) [*think*] con claridad
3 (= *distinctly*) [*see, speak, hear*] claramente, con claridad; [*visible, marked*] claramente **4** (= *obviously*) evidentemente, obviamente; **he was ~ not convinced** estaba claro *or* era evidente que no estaba convencido

clear-out ['klɪəraʊt] N (*Brit*) (= *tidy*) **to have a good ~** limpiarlo todo, despejarlo todo

clear-sighted ['klɪə'saɪtɪd] ADJ clarividente, perspicaz

clear-up rate ['klɪərʌp,reɪt] N (*Brit Police*) *ratio de casos resueltos por número de denuncias*

---

cleat [kliːt] N (*US*) (*on sports shoes*) taco *m*

cleavage ['kliːvɪdʒ] N (*between breasts*) escote *m*

cleaver ['kliːvəʳ] N cuchilla *f* de carnicero

clef [klef] N (*Mus*) clave *f*

cleft [kleft] (*in rock*) grieta *f*, hendidura *f*; (*in chin*) partición *f* ➤ **cleft chin** barbilla *f* partida ➤ **cleft palate** fisura *f* del paladar ➤ **cleft stick** ✦ IDIOM **to be in a ~ stick** (*Brit*) estar entre la espada y la pared

clematis ['klemətɪs] N clemátide *f*

clemency ['klemənsɪ] N clemencia *f*

clementine ['kleməntaɪn] N clementina *f*

clench [klentʃ] VT [+ *teeth*] apretar; [+ *fist*] cerrar

clergy ['klɜːdʒɪ] NPL clero *msing*

clergyman ['klɜːdʒɪmən] N (*pl* **clergymen**) clérigo *m*, sacerdote *m*

cleric ['klerɪk] N eclesiástico *m*, clérigo *m*

clerical ['klerɪkəl] ADJ [*job*] de oficina; **~ error** error *m* de copia; **~ staff** personal *m* de oficina; **~ work** trabajo *m* de oficina; **~ worker** oficinista *mf*

clerk [klɑːk, (*US*) klɜːk] **⒜** N **1** (*Comm*) oficinista *mf*, empleado/a *m/f*; (*in civil service*) funcionario/a *m/f*; (*in bank*) empleado/a *m/f*; (*Jur*) escribano *m*; (*US*) (*in hotel*) recepcionista *mf* **2** (*US*) (= *shop assistant*) dependiente/a *m/f*, vendedor(a) *m/f* **⒝** VI (*US*) trabajar como dependiente

clever ['klevəʳ] ADJ (*compar* **~er**; *superl* **~est**) **1** (= *intelligent*) inteligente, listo; **~ girl!** ¡qué chica más lista!
2 (= *skilful*) [*craftsman, sportsman*] hábil, habilidoso; [*piece of work, action*] hábil, ingenioso; **he is very ~ with his hands** es muy mañoso, es muy hábil *or* habilidoso con las manos; **she is very ~ with cars** entiende de coches, tiene mano para los coches; **to be ~ at sth** tener aptitud para algo
3 (= *astute*) [*politician, lawyer, criminal, approach*] astuto; [*book, idea, trick, technique*] ingenioso; **don't get ~ (with me)!*** ¡no te hagas el listo (conmigo)!; **to be too ~ by half** (*Brit**) pasarse de listo

cleverly ['klevəlɪ] ADV **1** (= *intelligently*) [*deduce, work out*] de forma inteligente, con inteligencia **2** (= *skilfully*) hábilmente, ingeniosamente; **it is ~ designed** tiene un diseño ingenioso **3** (= *astutely*) [*avoid, plan, disguise*] astutamente, con maña

cleverness ['klevənɪs] N **1** (= *intelligence*) inteligencia *f*
2 (= *skill*) habilidad *f* **3** (= *ingenuity*) ingenio *m*
4 (= *astuteness*) [*of person*] astucia *f*, maña *f*; [*of trick, technique, plan*] lo ingenioso

clew [kluː] N (*US*) = **clue**

cliché ['kliːʃeɪ] N cliché *m*, tópico *m*

click [klɪk] **⒜** N [*of camera*] golpecito *m* seco, clic *m*; [*of heels*] taconeo *m*; [*of tongue*] chasquido *m*; [*of gun*] piñoneo *m*
⒝ VT [+ *tongue*] chasquear; (*Comput*) hacer clic en; **to ~ one's heels** dar un taconazo
⒞ VI **1** [*camera*] hacer clic; [*gun*] piñonear; **the door ~ed shut** la puerta se cerró con un golpecito seco
2 (*) (= *be understood*) quedar claro/a; **it didn't ~ with me until ...** no caí en la cuenta hasta (que) ...; **suddenly it all ~ed (into place)** de pronto, todo encajaba (en su sitio)
3 (*) (= *get on*) [*two people*] congeniar, gustarse inmediatamente
4 (*Comput*) hacer clic; **to ~ on an icon** hacer clic en un símbolo gráfico

clickable ['klɪkəbl] (*Comput*) cliqueable

client ['klaɪənt] N cliente/a *m/f*

clientele [ˌkliːɑ̃n'tel] N clientela *f*

cliff [klɪf] N (= *sea cliff*) acantilado *m*; [*of mountain*] risco *m*, precipicio *m*

cliffhanger ['klɪf,hæŋəʳ] N (= *film*) película *f* melodramática, película *f* de suspense; **the match was a real ~** el partido fue un suspense hasta el último momento

climactic [klaɪ'mæktɪk] ADJ culminante

climate ['klaɪmɪt] N clima *m*; (*fig*) ambiente *m*

climatic [klaɪ'mætɪk] ADJ climático

climax ['klaɪmæks] **⒜** N **1** (= *high point*) punto *m* culminante, apogeo *m*; [*of play*] clímax *m inv*; **to reach a ~** llegar a su punto álgido, alcanzar una cima de intensidad **2** (= *orgasm*) orgasmo *m* **Ⓑ** VI **1** (= *reach high point*) llegar a un *or* su clímax **2** (= *have orgasm*) tener un orgasmo

climb [klaɪm] **Ⓐ** N (*gen*) subida *f*, ascenso *m*; [*of mountain*] escalada *f*; (*fig*) ascenso *m* **Ⓑ** VT (*also ~ up*) [+ *wall, tree, ladder*] trepar por, subir a; [+ *staircase*] subir (por); [+ *mountain*] escalar **Ⓒ** VI **1** [*person, plant*] trepar, subir; **to ~ over a wall** franquear *or* saltar una tapia **2** [*road*] ascender; [*plane*] elevarse, remontar el vuelo; [*price, sun*] subir
➤ **climb down** **Ⓐ** VI + PREP [+ *tree*] bajar; [+ *cliff*] bajar por **Ⓑ** VI + ADV **1** [*person*] (*from tree etc*) bajar **2** (= *give in*) rendirse; (= *retract statement*) desdecirse, retractarse

climber ['klaɪmə'] N **1** (= *mountaineer*) montañista *mf*, alpinista *mf*, andinista *mf* (*LAm*) **2** (= *plant*) trepadora *f*, enredadera *f*

climbing ['klaɪmɪŋ] N (= *rock climbing*) montañismo *m*, alpinismo *m*, andinismo *m* (*LAm*); **to go ~** hacer montañismo *or* alpinismo, ir de escalada ➤ **climbing frame** (*Brit*) *estructura metálica en la cual los niños juegan trepando*

clinch [klɪntʃ] **Ⓐ** N **1** (*Boxing*) clinch *m* **2** (******) (= *embrace*) abrazo *m*; **in a ~** abrazados, agarrados (*LAm*) **Ⓑ** VT (= *settle decisively*) [+ *deal*] cerrar, firmar; [+ *argument*] remachar, terminar; [+ *agreement*] cerrar; **to ~ matters** para acabar de remacharlo; **that ~es it** está decidido, ni una palabra más

clincher* ['klɪntʃə'] N **that was the ~** eso fue el punto clave, eso fue el argumento irrebatible

cling [klɪŋ] (*pt, pp* **clung**) VI **1** (= *hold on*) (*to person*) pegarse (**to** a); (*affectionately*) agarrarse, aferrarse (**to** a); (*to rope*) agarrarse (**to** a, de); (*to belief, opinion*) aferrarse, seguir fiel (**to** a); **they clung to one another** no se desprendían de su abrazo **2** (= *stick*) [*clothes*] (*to skin*) pegarse (**to** a) **3** (= *stay close*) (*to friend, mother etc*) no separarse (**to** de)

Clingfilm ® ['klɪŋfɪlm] N (*Brit*) film *m* transparente (*para alimentos*)

clinging ['klɪŋɪŋ] **1** [*person*] pegajoso **2** [*dress*] ceñido

clingy* ['klɪŋɪ] ADJ [*person*] pegajoso

clinic ['klɪnɪk] N (*in NHS hospital*) consultorio *m*; (= *private hospital*) clínica *f*; (*for guidance*) consultorio *m*

clinical ['klɪnɪkəl] ADJ (*Med*) clínico; (= *unemotional*) frío ➤ **clinical depression** depresión *f* clínica ➤ **clinical psychologist** psicólogo/a *m/f* clínico/a ➤ **clinical trial** ensayo *m* clínico

clinician [klɪ'nɪʃən] N médico/a *m/f* de clínica

clink¹ [klɪŋk] **Ⓐ** N [*of coins*] tintín *m*, tintineo *m*; [*of glasses*] choque *m* **Ⓑ** VT hacer sonar, hacer tintinear; **to ~ glasses with sb** entrechocar la copa con algn **Ⓒ** VI [*coins*] tintinear

clink²** [klɪŋk] N (= *jail*) trena** *f*

clip¹ [klɪp] **Ⓐ** N **1** (*Cine*) secuencia *f* **2** (= *blow*) golpe *m*, cachete *m* **Ⓑ** VT **1** (= *cut*) cortar; (= *shorten*) acortar; [+ *hedge*] podar; (*Brit*) [+ *ticket*] picar; [+ *article from newspaper*] recortar; **✦** IDIOM **to ~ sb's wings** cortar las alas a algn **2** (= *hit*) golpear, dar un cachete a

clip² [klɪp] **Ⓐ** N (= *clamp*) grapa *f*; (= *paper clip*) sujetapapeles *m inv*, clip *m*, grampa *f* (*SC*); [*of pen*] sujetador *m*; (= *hair clip*) horquilla *f*, clip *m*; (= *brooch*) alfiler *m*, clip *m*, abrochador *m* (*LAm*); [*of cyclist*] pinza *f* **Ⓑ** VT sujetar
➤ **clip on** VT + ADV [+ *brooch*] prender, sujetar; [+ *document*] sujetar con un clip
➤ **clip together** VT + ADV unir

clipboard ['klɪp,bɔːd] N tablilla *f* con sujetapapeles, carpeta *f* sujetapapeles

clip-clop ['klɪp'klɒp] N *ruido de los cascos del caballo*

clip-on ['klɪpɒn] ADJ [*badge*] para prender, con prendedor; [*earrings*] de pinza

clipper ['klɪpə'] N (*Naut*) clíper *m*

clippers ['klɪpəz] NPL (*for hair*) maquinilla *fsing* (para el pelo); (*for nails*) cortaúñas *msing inv*; (*for hedge*) tijeras *fpl* de podar

clipping ['klɪpɪŋ] N (*from newspaper*) recorte *m*

clique [kliːk] N camarilla *f*

clitoris ['klɪtərɪs] N clítoris *m*

Cllr ABBR (*Brit*) = **Councillor**

cloak [kləʊk] **Ⓐ** N capa *f*, manto *m*; **under the ~ of darkness** al amparo de la oscuridad **Ⓑ** VT (= *hide*) encubrir, disimular

cloak-and-dagger ['kləʊkən'dægə'] ADJ clandestino; [*story*] de agentes secretos

cloakroom ['kləʊkrʊm] (*Brit*) **Ⓐ** N **1** (*for coats*) guardarropa *m*, ropero *m* **2** (= *toilet*) lavabo *m*, servicios *mpl*, baño *m* (*LAm*) **Ⓑ** CPD ➤ **cloakroom attendant** (*for coats*) encargado/a *m/f* del guardarropa ➤ **cloakroom ticket** resguardo *m* del guardarropa

clobber** ['klɒbə'] **Ⓐ** N (*Brit*) (= *gear*) bártulos* *mpl*, trastos *mpl* (*Sp**) **Ⓑ** VT **1** (= *defeat*) cascar* **2** (= *beat up*) dar una paliza a

clock [klɒk] **Ⓐ** N reloj *m*; [*of taxi*] taxímetro *m*; (*esp Brit*) (= *speedometer*) velocímetro *m*; (*esp Brit*) (= *milometer*) ≈ cuentakilómetros *m inv*; **you can't put the ~ back** (= *return to past*) no puedes volver al pasado; (= *stop progress*) no se puede detener el progreso; **to keep one's eyes on** *or* **watch the ~** mirar mucho el reloj (ansiando abandonar el trabajo); **to work against the ~** trabajar contra reloj; **the car has 30,000 miles on the ~** el coche tiene 30.000 millas; **round the ~** las veinticuatro horas del día
Ⓑ VT [+ *runner, time*] cronometrar; **we ~ed 80mph** alcanzamos una velocidad de 80 millas por hora
Ⓒ CPD ➤ **clock radio** radio-despertador *m* ➤ **clock repairer** relojero/a *m/f* ➤ **clock tower** torre *f* de reloj
➤ **clock in** VI + ADV (= *with card*) fichar, picar; (= *start work*) entrar a trabajar
➤ **clock off** VI + ADV = **clock out**
➤ **clock on** VI + ADV = **clock in**
➤ **clock out** VI + ADV (= *with card*) fichar *or* picar la salida; (= *leave work*) salir del trabajo
➤ **clock up** VT + ADV hacer; **he ~ed up 250 miles** hizo 250 millas

clockwise ['klɒkwaɪz] ADJ, ADV en el sentido de las agujas del reloj

clockwork ['klɒkwɜːk] **Ⓐ** N **to go like ~** funcionar como un reloj **Ⓑ** ADJ [*toy, train*] de cuerda

clod [klɒd] N [*of earth*] terrón *m*

clog [klɒg] **Ⓐ** N zueco *m*, chanclo *m* **Ⓑ** VT (*also ~ up*) atascar

cloister ['klɔɪstə'] N claustro *m*; **cloisters** soportales *mpl*

cloistered ['klɔɪstəd] ADJ **to lead a ~ life** llevar una vida de ermitaño

clone [kləʊn] **Ⓐ** N clon *m*; (*Comput*) clónico *m* **Ⓑ** VT clonar; **a ~d sheep** una oveja clónica

cloning ['kləʊnɪŋ] N clonación *f*, clonaje *m*

close¹ [kləʊs] **Ⓐ** ADJ **1** (= *near*) [*place*] cercano, próximo; [*contact*] directo; [*connection*] estrecho, íntimo; **where's the ~st service station?** ¿dónde está la gasolinera más cercana? *or* más próxima?; **to be ~ (to)** estar cerca (de); **the hotel is ~ to the station** el hotel está cerca de la estación; **she was ~ to tears** estaba a punto de llorar; **according to sources ~ to the police** según fuentes allegadas a la policía; **~ combat** lucha *f* cuerpo a cuerpo; **at ~ quarters** de cerca; **to come a ~ second** to sb/sth disputar la primera posición a algn/algo; **✦** IDIOM **it was a ~ shave*** se salvaron por un pelo *or* de milagro
2 (= *intimate*) [*relative*] cercano; [*friend*] íntimo; **I'm very ~ to my sister** estoy muy unida a mi hermana; **they're very ~ (to each other)** están muy unidos
3 (= *almost equal*) [*result, election, fight*] muy reñido; [*scores*] casi iguales
4 (= *exact, detailed*) [*examination, study*] detallado; [*investigation, questioning*] minucioso; [*surveillance, control*] estricto; **to pay ~ attention to sb/sth** prestar mucha atención a algn/algo; **to keep a ~ watch on sb** mantener a algn bajo estricta vigilancia
5 (= *not spread out*) [*handwriting, print*] compacto; [*texture, weave*] compacto, tupido; [*formation*] cerrado
6 (= *stuffy*) [*atmosphere, room*] sofocante, cargado; [*weather*]

pesado, bochornoso

7 (= *secretive*) reservado; (= *mean*) tacaño

B ADV (*compar* **~r**; *superl* **~st**) (= *near*) cerca; **he lives quite ~** vive bastante cerca; **I sat down ~ to the fire** me senté cerca de la chimenea; <u>come</u> **~r** acércate más; **to come ~ to** acercarse a; **we came very ~ to losing the match** estuvimos a punto de perder el partido, faltó poco para que perdiéramos el partido; **to** <u>follow</u> **~ behind** seguir muy de cerca; **to** <u>hold</u> **sb ~** abrazar fuertemente a algn; **to** <u>keep</u> **~ to the wall** ir arrimado a la pared; **he must be ~ on 50** debe andar cerca de los 50; **it's ~ on six o'clock** son casi las seis; <u>stay</u> **~ to me** no te alejes *or* separes de mí; **~** <u>together</u> juntos, cerca uno del otro; **to look at sth ~ up** mirar algo de cerca

C N recinto *m*

D CPD ➤ **close season** (*Hunting, Fishing*) veda *f*; (*Ftbl*) temporada *f* de descanso (*de la liga de fútbol*)

close² [kləʊz] **A** N (= *end*) final *m*, conclusión *f*; **at the ~** al final; **at the ~ of day** a la caída de la tarde; **to bring sth to a ~** terminar algo, concluir algo; **to draw to a ~** tocar a su fin, estar terminando

B VI **1** (= *shut*) [*shop*] cerrar; [*door, window*] cerrarse; **his eyes ~d** se le cerraron los ojos

2 (= *end*) terminar, terminarse, concluir; **shares ~d at 120p** al cierre las acciones estaban a 120 peniques

C VT **1** (= *shut*) cerrar; [+ *hole*] tapar; **"road closed"** "cerrado al paso"; **to ~ one's eyes** cerrar los ojos; **to ~ the gap between two things** llenar el hueco entre dos cosas; **~ your mouth when you're eating!** ¡no abras la boca comiendo!; **to ~ ranks** cerrar filas

2 (= *end*) [+ *discussion, meeting*] cerrar, poner fin a; [+ *ceremony*] clausurar, dar término a; [+ *bank account*] liquidar; [+ *account*] (*Comm*) saldar; [+ *bargain, deal*] cerrar
➤ **close down** **A** VI + ADV [*business*] cerrarse definitivamente; (*by order*) clausurarse; (*TV, Rad*) cerrar (la emisión) **B** VT + ADV cerrar definitivamente; (*by order*) clausurar
➤ **close in** VI + ADV [*hunters*] acercarse rodeando, rodear; [*night*] caer; [*darkness, fog*] cerrarse; **the days are closing in** los días son cada vez más cortos
➤ **close off** VT + ADV [+ *road*] cerrar al tráfico, cerrar al público; [+ *access*] bloquear
➤ **close up** **A** VI + ADV **1** (= *close*) [*flower*] cerrarse del todo; [*wound*] cicatrizarse **2** (= *move closer together*) juntarse; (*in queue*) ponerse más cerca, juntarse **B** VT + ADV [+ *building*] cerrar (del todo); [+ *pipe, opening*] tapar, obstruir; [+ *wound*] cerrar

close-cropped [ˈkləʊsˈkrɒpt] ADJ (cortado) al rape, rapado

closed [kləʊzd] ADJ (*gen*) cerrado; [*hearing, meeting*] a puerta cerrada; **behind ~ doors** a puerta cerrada; **to have a ~ mind** ser de miras estrechas, ser de mente cerrada; **sociology is a ~ book to me** la sociología es un misterio para mí ➤ **closed primary** (*US Pol*) elección primaria reservada a los miembros de un partido ➤ **closed season** (*Hunting, Fishing*) veda *f*; (*Ftbl, Rugby*) temporada *f* de descanso (*de la liga de fútbol*) ➤ **closed session** (*Jur*) sesión *f* a puerta cerrada ➤ **closed shop** (*Ind*) empresa *f* con todo el personal afiliado obligatoriamente a un solo sindicato

closed-circuit television [ˌkləʊzdsɜːkɪtˈtelɪvɪʒən] N televisión *f* por circuito cerrado

close-down [ˈkləʊzdaʊn] N cierre *m*

close-fitting [ˈkləʊsˈfɪtɪŋ] ADJ ceñido, ajustado

close-knit [ˈkləʊsnɪt] ADJ [*family*] muy unido

closely [ˈkləʊslɪ] ADV **1** (= *carefully*) [*look, examine*] atentamente, de cerca; **to watch ~** fijarse, prestar mucha atención; **to listen ~** escuchar con atención, escuchar atentamente; **a ~ guarded secret** un secreto celosamente guardado **2** (= *very much*) **to resemble sth/sb ~** parecerse mucho a algo/algn; **~ related/connected** estrechamente relacionado/unido; **~ contested** muy reñido

closeness [ˈkləʊsnɪs] N **1** (= *nearness*) proximidad *f* **2** [*of friendship*] intimidad *f* **3** [*of election*] lo muy reñido

close-run [ˈkləʊsˈrʌn] ADJ **~ race** carrera *f* muy reñida

closet [ˈklɒzɪt] **A** N **1** (= *toilet*) wáter *m*, lavabo *m* **2** (*US*) (= *cupboard*) armario *m*, placar(d) *m* (*LAm*); (*for clothes*)

ropero *m*; ✦ IDIOM **to come out of the ~** anunciarse públicamente **B** VT **to be ~ed with sb** estar encerrado con algn **C** ADJ [*fascist, racist*] secreto, no declarado

close-up [ˈkləʊsʌp] N primer plano *m*; **in ~** en primer plano ➤ **close-up lens** teleobjetivo *m*

closing [ˈkləʊzɪŋ] ADJ último, final; **~ speech** discurso *m* de clausura; **in the ~ stages** en las últimas etapas ➤ **closing date** fecha *f* tope, fecha *f* límite ➤ **closing down** cierre *m* ➤ **closing down sale** liquidación *f* por cierre ➤ **closing entry** (*in account*) asiento *m* de cierre ➤ **closing price** (*St Ex*) cotización *f* de cierre ➤ **closing time** (*Brit*) hora *f* de cerrar

closure [ˈkləʊʒəʳ] N **1** (= *close-down*) cierre *m* **2** (= *end*) fin *m*, conclusión *f* **3** (*Parl*) clausura *f*

clot [klɒt] **A** N **1** [*of blood*] coágulo *m*; (*Med*) embolia *f*; **~ on the brain** embolia *f* cerebral **2** (*Brit**) (= *fool*) bobo/a *m/f* **B** VI coagularse

cloth [klɒθ] **A** N **1** (= *material*) paño *m*, tela *f* **2** (*for cleaning*) trapo *m* **3** (= *tablecloth*) mantel *m* **4** (*Rel*) **the ~** el clero; **a man of the ~** un clérigo **B** CPD ➤ **cloth cap** (*Brit*) gorra *f* de paño

clothe [kləʊð] VT **1** vestir (**in, with** de) **2** (*fig*) cubrir, revestir (**in, with** de)

clothes [kləʊðz] NPL ropa *f*sing, vestidos *mpl*; **to put one's ~ on** vestirse, ponerse la ropa; **to take one's ~ off** quitarse la ropa, desvestirse ➤ **clothes brush** cepillo *m* de la ropa ➤ **clothes drier, clothes dryer** secadora *f* ➤ **clothes hanger** percha *f*, gancho *m* (*LAm*) ➤ **clothes horse** tendedero *m* plegable ➤ **clothes line** cuerda *f* para (tender) la ropa ➤ **clothes peg** (*Brit*), **clothes pin** (*US*) pinza *f* de la ropa ➤ **clothes shop** tienda *f* (de ropa)

clothing [ˈkləʊðɪŋ] N ropa *f*, vestimenta *f*; **article of ~** prenda *f* de vestir ➤ **clothing allowance** extra *m* para ropa de trabajo ➤ **clothing industry** industria *f* textil

clotted cream [ˌklɒtɪdˈkriːm] N (*Culin*) nata *f* (*Sp*) *or* crema *f* (*LAm*) cuajada

cloud [klaʊd] **A** N nube *f* (*also fig*); ✦ IDIOMS **to be under a ~** (= *under suspicion*) estar bajo sospecha; (= *resented*) estar desacreditado; **to have one's head in the ~s** estar en las nubes; **to be on ~ nine** estar en el séptimo cielo; ✦ PROV **every ~ has a silver lining** no hay mal que por bien no venga **B** VT **1** (= *make cloudy*) [+ *vision*] nublar; [+ *liquid*] enturbiar; [+ *mirror*] empañar **2** (= *confuse*) **to ~ the issue** complicar el asunto
➤ **cloud over** VI + ADV nublarse

cloudburst [ˈklaʊdbɜːst] N chaparrón *m*

cloud-cuckoo-land [ˌklaʊdˈkʊkuːˌlænd], **cloudland** (*US*) [ˈklaʊdlænd] N **to be in ~** estar en babia, estar con la cabeza en el aire (*LAm*)

cloudless [ˈklaʊdlɪs] ADJ sin nubes, despejado

cloudy [ˈklaʊdɪ] ADJ (*compar* **cloudier**; *superl* **cloudiest**) [*sky, day, weather*] nublado; [*liquid*] turbio; [*eyes, glass*] empañado; **it's ~ today** hoy está nublado

clout [klaʊt] **A** N **1** (= *blow*) tortazo *m* **2** (= *influence, power*) influencia *f*, peso *m*, palanca *f* (*LAm*) **B** VT dar un tortazo a

clove [kləʊv] N **1** (= *spice*) clavo *m* **2 ~ of garlic** diente *m* de ajo

cloven hoof [ˌkləʊvnˈhuːf] N pata *f* hendida

clover [ˈkləʊvəʳ] N trébol *m*; ✦ IDIOM **to be in ~*** vivir a cuerpo de rey

cloverleaf [ˈkləʊvəliːf] N (*pl* **cloverleaves**) hoja *f* de trébol

clown [klaʊn] **A** N payaso/a *m/f*, clown *mf* **B** VI (*also ~ about or around*) hacer el payaso

cloying [ˈklɔɪɪŋ] ADJ empalagoso

cloze test [ˈkləʊzˌtest] N *test consistente en rellenar los espacios en blanco de un texto*

club [klʌb] **A** N **1** (= *stick*) porra *f*, cachiporra *f* **2** (= *golf club*) palo *m* **3 clubs** (*Cards*) (*in conventional pack*) tréboles *mpl*; (*in Spanish pack*) bastos *mpl* **4** (= *association*) club *m*; (= *gaming club*) casino *m*; (= *building*) centro *m*, club *m*; **a tennis ~** un club de tenis;

join the ~! ¡ya somos dos!; **to be in the ~** (*hum*) estar en estado
5 (= *disco*) discoteca *f*
Ⓑ VT [+ *person*] aporrear, dar porrazos a; **to ~ sb to death** matar a algn a porrazos
Ⓒ VI **to ~ together** (*Brit*): **we all ~bed together to buy him a present** le compramos un regalo entre todos
Ⓓ CPD ➤ **club car** (*US Rail*) coche *m* club ➤ **club class** clase *f* club ➤ **club foot** pie *m* zopo ➤ **club sandwich** *bocadillo vegetal con pollo y beicon*

clubbing [ˈklʌbɪŋ] N **to go ~** ir a la discoteca

clubhouse [ˈklʌbhaʊs] N sede *f* de un club

cluck [klʌk] **Ⓐ** N [*of hen*] cloqueo *m* **Ⓑ** VI **1** [*hen*] cloquear **2** [*person*] chasquear con la lengua

clue, clew (*US*) [kluː] N (*in game, crime*) pista *f*; [*of crossword*] indicación *f*; **can you give me a ~?** ¿me das una pista?; **I haven't a ~*** no tengo ni idea

clued-up* [ˌkluːdˈʌp] ADJ (*Brit*): **clued up (on)** al tanto (de), al corriente (de)

clueless* [ˈkluːlɪs] ADJ despistado, que no tiene ni idea

clump¹ [klʌmp] N [*of trees, shrubs*] grupo *m*; [*of flowers, grass*] mata *f*; [*of earth*] terrón *m*

clump² [klʌmp] VI **to ~ about** caminar dando pisadas fuertes

clumsily [ˈklʌmzɪlɪ] ADV **1** (= *awkwardly*) [*walk, express, apologize*] con torpeza, torpemente **2** (= *roughly*) [*produced*] toscamente, chapuceramente

clumsiness [ˈklʌmzɪnɪs] N (= *awkwardness*) torpeza *f*; (= *tactlessness*) falta *f* de tacto

clumsy [ˈklʌmzɪ] ADJ (*compar* **clumsier**; *superl* **clumsiest**) [*person, movement, apology*] torpe; [*painting, forgery*] tosco, chapucero

clung [klʌŋ] PT, PP *of* **cling**

cluster [ˈklʌstəʳ] **Ⓐ** N [*of trees, houses, people*] grupo *m*; [*of flowers*] macizo *m*; [*of plants*] mata *f*; [*of fruit*] racimo *m*
Ⓑ VI **to ~ (around sb/sth)** apiñarse (en torno a algn/algo)
Ⓒ CPD ➤ **cluster bomb** bomba *f* de dispersión, bomba *f* de racimo

clutch [klʌtʃ] **Ⓐ** N **1** (*Aut*) embrague *m*, cloche *m* (*LAm*); (= *pedal*) (pedal *m* del) embrague *m or* (*LAm*) cloche *m*; **to let the ~ in** embragar; **to let the ~ out** desembragar **2** (= *grasp*) **to fall into sb's ~es** caer en las garras de algn; **to get sth out of sb's ~es** hacer que algn ceda la posesión *or* se desprenda de algo **3** (*US**) (= *crisis*) crisis *f inv*
Ⓑ VT (= *catch hold of*) asir, agarrar (*esp LAm*); (= *hold tightly*) apretar, agarrar
Ⓒ VI **to ~ at** tratar de agarrar; (*fig*) aferrarse a; ✦ IDIOM **to ~ at straws** aferrarse a cualquier esperanza

clutter [ˈklʌtəʳ] **Ⓐ** N desorden *m*, confusión *f*; **in a ~** en desorden, en un montón **Ⓑ** VT atestar; **to be ~ed up with sth** estar atestado de algo

cm ABBR = **centimetre(s)**) cm

CND N ABBR = **Campaign for Nuclear Disarmament**

CO N ABBR **1** (*Mil*) = **Commanding Officer 2** (*US*) = **Colorado**

Co. ABBR [kəʊ] (= *company*) Cía., S.A.; **Joe and ~*** Joe y compañía

c/o ABBR (= *care of*) c/d, a/c

coach [kəʊtʃ] **Ⓐ** N **1** (*Brit*) (= *bus*) autobús *m*, autocar *m* (*Sp*), coche *m* de línea (*Sp*), camión *m* (*Mex, CAm*), pullman *m* (*SC*), flota *f* (*Bol, Col*), (*Brit Rail*) coche *m*, vagón *m*
2 (*Sport*) entrenador(a) *m/f*; **the Spanish ~** el entrenador del equipo español
3 (= *tutor*) profesor(a) *m/f* particular
Ⓑ VT [+ *team*] entrenar, preparar; [+ *student*] enseñar, preparar; **to ~ sb for an exam** preparar a algn para un examen
Ⓒ CPD ➤ **coach driver** (*Brit*) conductor(a) *m/f* de autobús *etc* ➤ **coach station** (*Brit*) estación *f* de autobuses *etc* ➤ **coach tour** (*Brit*) gira *f or* viaje *m* en autobús *etc* ➤ **coach trip** (*Brit*) excursión *f* en autobús *etc*

coaching [ˈkəʊtʃɪŋ] N **1** (*Sport*) entrenamiento *m* **2** (= *tuition*) enseñanza *f* particular

coachload [ˈkəʊtʃləʊd] N (*Brit*) autobús *m* (lleno), autocar *m* (lleno) (*Sp*), camión *m* (*Mex, CAm*) (lleno), pullman *m* (*SC*) (lleno), flota *f* (*Bol, Col*) (llena); **they came by the ~** vinieron en masa

coagulate [kəʊˈægjʊleɪt] **Ⓐ** VT coagular **Ⓑ** VI coagularse

coal [kəʊl] N carbón *m*; (*soft*) hulla *f*; ✦ IDIOMS **to drag** or (*Brit*) **haul sb over the ~s** echarle una bronca a algn; **to take ~s to Newcastle** llevar leña al monte *or* agua al mar ➤ **coal bunker** carbonera *f* ➤ **coal cellar** carbonera *f* ➤ **coal dust** polvillo *m* de carbón, carbonilla *f* ➤ **coal fire** chimenea *f* de carbón ➤ **coal industry** industria *f* del carbón ➤ **coal merchant** carbonero *m* ➤ **coal mine** mina *f* de carbón ➤ **coal miner** minero/a *m/f* del carbón ➤ **coal mining** minería *f* del carbón ➤ **coal oil** (*US*) parafina *f* ➤ **coal scuttle** cubo *m* para carbón ➤ **coal shed** carbonera *f* ➤ **coal tar** alquitrán *m* mineral

coal-burning [ˈkəʊlˌbɜːnɪŋ] ADJ que quema carbón

coalface [ˈkəʊlfeɪs] N (*Brit*) frente *m* donde empieza la veta de carbón

coalfield [ˈkəʊlfiːld] N yacimiento *m* de carbón, cuenca *f* minera

coalition [ˌkəʊəˈlɪʃən] N coalición *f* ➤ **coalition government** gobierno *m* de coalición

coalman [ˈkəʊlmən] N (*pl* **coalmen**) carbonero *m*

coarse [kɔːs] **Ⓐ** ADJ (*compar* **~r**; *superl* **~st**) **1** (= *rough*) [*texture*] basto, áspero; [*sand*] grueso; [*skin*] áspero **2** (= *vulgar*) [*character, laugh, remark*] ordinario, tosco; [*joke*] verde **Ⓑ** CPD ➤ **coarse fishing** pesca *f* de agua dulce (*excluyendo salmón y trucha*)

coarsely [ˈkɔːslɪ] ADV [*laugh, say*] groseramente

coast [kəʊst] **Ⓐ** N (= *shore*) costa *f*; (= *coastline*) litoral *m*; ✦ IDIOM **the ~ is clear** no hay moros en la costa **Ⓑ** VI (*also* **~ along**) (*Aut*) ir en punto muerto; (*fig*) avanzar sin esfuerzo

coastal [ˈkəʊstəl] ADJ costero

coaster [ˈkəʊstəʳ] N posavasos *m inv*

coastguard [ˈkəʊstgɑːd] N (= *organization*) servicio *m* de guardacostas; (*Brit*) (= *person*) guardacostas *mf inv*

coastline [ˈkəʊstlaɪn] N litoral *m*

coat [kəʊt] **Ⓐ** N **1** abrigo *m*; (= *jacket*) chaqueta *f* (*Sp*), saco *m* (*LAm*); (*chemist's*) bata *f*; ✦ IDIOM **to cut one's ~ according to one's cloth** adaptarse a las circunstancias **2** (*animal's*) pelo *m*, pelaje *m*; (= *wool*) lana *f* **3** (= *layer*) capa *f*; **a ~ of paint** una mano de pintura **Ⓑ** VT cubrir, revestir (**with** de); (*with a liquid*) bañar (**with** en) **Ⓒ** CPD ➤ **coat hanger** percha *f*, gancho *m* (*LAm*) ➤ **coat of arms** escudo *m* (de armas) ➤ **coat tails** faldón *msing*

coating [ˈkəʊtɪŋ] N (*gen*) capa *f*, baño *m*; [*of paint*] mano *f*

coax [kəʊks] VT **to ~ sth out of sb** sonsacar algo a algn (engatusándolo); **to ~ sb into/out of doing sth** engatusar a algn para que haga/no haga algo

cob [kɒb] N (*Brit*) (= *loaf*) pan *m* redondo; (= *maize*) mazorca *f*

cobalt [ˈkəʊbɒlt] N cobalto *m*

cobble [ˈkɒbl] N adoquín *m*
➤ **cobble together** VT + ADV (= *gather together*) reunir; (= *make*) [+ *agreement*] redactar; [+ *essay, speech*] escribir; [+ *meal*] preparar

cobbled [ˈkɒbld] ADJ **~ street** calle *f* empedrada, calle *f* adoquinada

cobbler [ˈkɒbləʳ] N zapatero/a *m/f* (remendón/ona)

cobblestone [ˈkɒblstəʊn] N adoquín *m*

cobra [ˈkəʊbrə] N cobra *f*

cobweb [ˈkɒbweb] N telaraña *f*; ✦ IDIOM **to blow away the ~s** despejar la mente

cocaine [kəˈkeɪn] N cocaína *f* ➤ **cocaine addict** cocainómano/a *m/f* ➤ **cocaine addiction** adicción *f* a la cocaína

coccyx [ˈkɒksɪks] N cóccix *m inv*

cock [kɒk] **Ⓐ** N **1** (*esp Brit*) (= *rooster*) gallo *m*; (= *other male bird*) macho *m* **2** (***) (= *penis*) polla *f* (*Sp***), pinga *f* (*LAm***), pija *f* (*River Plate***) **3** ✦ IDIOM **to go off at half ~**

[*person*] precipitarse; [*plan*] ponerse en práctica sin la debida preparación **B** VT **1** [+ *gun*] amartillar; [+ *head*] ladear; ✦ IDIOM **to ~ a snook at sb/sth** (*Brit*) burlarse de algn/algo **2** (*also* ~ **up**) [+ *ears*] aguzar; **to keep one's ears ~ed** mantenerse alerta, aguzar el oído *or* la oreja **C** CPD [*bird*] macho
➤ **cock up*** VT + ADV (*Brit*) joder***

cock-a-doodle-doo ['kɒkədu:dl'du:] EXCL ¡quiquiriquí!

cockatoo [ˌkɒkə'tu:] N cacatúa *f*

cocked [kɒkt] ADJ ✦ IDIOM **to knock sth into a ~ hat** ser muy superior a algo

cockerel ['kɒkrəl] N (*esp Brit*) gallito *m*, gallo *m* joven

cockeyed ['kɒkaɪd] ADJ **1** (= *crooked*) torcido, chueco (*LAm*) **2** (= *absurd*) disparatado

cockfighting ['kɒkˌfaɪtɪŋ] N la pelea de gallos, peleas *fpl* de gallos

cockle ['kɒkl] N (*Zool*) berberecho *m*; ✦ IDIOM **to warm the ~s of sb's heart** llenar a algn de ternura

cockney ['kɒknɪ] **A** N **1** (= *person*) persona nacida en el este de Londres y especialmente de clase obrera **2** (= *dialect*) dialecto de esa zona **B** ADJ del este de Londres y especialmente de clase obrera; ⤷ *RHYMING SLANG*

COCKNEY

Se llama **cockneys** a las personas de la zona este de Londres conocida como **East End**, un barrio tradicionalmente obrero, aunque según la tradición un **cockney** auténtico ha de haber nacido dentro del área en la que se oye el repique de las campanas de la iglesia de **Mary-Le-Bow**, en la **City** londinense. Este término también hace referencia al dialecto que se habla en esta parte de Londres, aunque a veces también se aplica a cualquier acento de la clase trabajadora londinense. El actor Michael Caine es un **cockney** famoso. ⤷ RHYMING SLANG

---

cockpit ['kɒkpɪt] N cabina *f*

cockroach ['kɒkrəʊtʃ] N cucaracha *f*

cocksure ['kɒk'ʃʊə'] ADJ creído, engreído

cocktail ['kɒkteɪl] N (= *drink*) combinado *m*, cóctel *m*; **fruit ~** macedonia *f* de frutas; **prawn ~** cóctel *m* de gambas ➤ **cocktail cabinet** mueble-bar *m* ➤ **cocktail dress** vestido *m* de fiesta ➤ **cocktail party** cóctel *m* ➤ **cocktail sausage** salchichita *f* de aperitivo ➤ **cocktail shaker** coctelera *f*

cock-up* ['kɒkʌp] N (*Brit*) **what a ~!** ¡qué lío!, ¡qué desmadre!; **to make a ~ of sth** fastidiar algo, joder algo***; **there's been a ~ over my passport** ha habido un lío con mi pasaporte

cocky* ['kɒkɪ] ADJ (*compar* **cockier**; *superl* **cockiest**) creído

cocoa ['kəʊkəʊ] N (= *powder*) cacao *m*; (= *drink*) chocolate *m*; **a cup of ~** una taza de chocolate ➤ **cocoa bean** grano *m* de cacao

coconut ['kəʊkənʌt] N (= *nut*) coco *m*; (= *tree*) cocotero *m* ➤ **coconut matting** estera *f* de fibra de coco ➤ **coconut oil** aceite *m* de coco ➤ **coconut palm** cocotero *m* ➤ **coconut shy** tiro *m* al coco ➤ **coconut tree** cocotero *m*

cocoon [kə'ku:n] **A** N capullo *m* **B** VT envolver

COD ABBR **1** (*Brit*) (= **cash on delivery**) C.A.E. **2** (*US*) (= **collect on delivery**) C.A.E.

cod [kɒd] N (*pl* ~) bacalao *m*

coddle ['kɒdl] VT (*also* **mollycoddle**) consentir, mimar

code [kəʊd] **A** N **1** (= *cipher*) clave *f*, cifra *f*; **in ~** en clave, cifrado; **it's written in ~** está cifrado *or* escrito en clave **2** (*Telec*) prefijo *m*, código *m*; (*Comput*) código *m* **3** [*of laws*] código *m*; **~ of behaviour** código *m* de conducta; **~ of practice** código *m* profesional **B** CPD ➤ **code book** libro *m* de códigos ➤ **code name** alias *m inv*, nombre *m* en clave; (*Pol*) nombre *m* de guerra ➤ **code number** (*Tax*) ≈ número *m* de identificación fiscal ➤ **code word** palabra *f* en clave

coded ['kəʊdɪd] ADJ en cifra, en clave (*also fig*)

codeine ['kəʊdi:n] N codeína *f*

code-name ['kəʊdneɪm] VT **the operation was ~d Albert** la operación tenía el nombre en clave de Albert

codicil ['kɒdɪsɪl] N codicilo *m*

codify ['kəʊdɪfaɪ] VT codificar

cod-liver oil ['kɒdlɪvər'ɔɪl] N aceite *m* de hígado de bacalao

co-driver ['kəʊdraɪvə'] N copiloto *mf*

codswallop** ['kɒdzwɒləp] N (*Brit*) chorradas* *fpl*

coed* ['kəʊ'ed] **A** ADJ (*US*) mixto **B** N **1** (*Brit*) (= *school*) colegio *m* mixto **2** (*US†*) (= *student*) alumna *f* de un colegio mixto

coeducation ['kəʊˌedjʊ'keɪʃən] N enseñanza *f* mixta

coeducational ['kəʊˌedjʊ'keɪʃənl] ADJ mixto

coefficient [ˌkəʊɪ'fɪʃənt] N coeficiente *m*

coerce [kəʊ'ɜ:s] VT obligar, coaccionar; **to ~ sb into doing sth** obligar a algn a hacer algo, coaccionar a algn para que haga algo

coercion [kəʊ'ɜ:ʃən] N coacción *f*; **under ~** obligado a ello, a la fuerza

coexist ['kəʊɪg'zɪst] VI coexistir (**with** con)

coexistence ['kəʊɪg'zɪstəns] N coexistencia *f*

C of E [ˌsi:əv'i:] N ABBR = **Church of England**; **to be ~*** ser anglicano

coffee ['kɒfɪ] N café *m*; **a cup of ~** una taza de café, un café; **white ~** (*milky*) café *m* con leche; (*with dash of milk*) café *m* cortado; **black ~** (*small*) café *m* solo, tinto *m* (*Col*); (*large*) café *m* americano ➤ **coffee bar** café *m*, cafetería *f* ➤ **coffee bean** grano *m* de café ➤ **coffee break** descanso *m* (para tomar café) ➤ **coffee cake** (*Brit*) pastel *m* de café ➤ **coffee cup** taza *f* para café, tacita *f*, pocillo *m* (*LAm*) ➤ **coffee filter** filtro *m* de café ➤ **coffee grounds** *msing* de café ➤ **coffee machine** (*small*) máquina *f* de café, cafetera *f*; (= *vending machine*) máquina *f* expendedora de café ➤ **coffee maker** máquina *f* de hacer café, cafetera *f* ➤ **coffee mill** molinillo *m* de café ➤ **coffee morning** (*Brit*) tertulia *f* formada para tomar el café por la mañana ➤ **coffee plantation** cafetal *m* ➤ **coffee shop** café *m* ➤ **coffee spoon** cucharilla *f* de café ➤ **coffee table** mesita *f* para servir el café

coffee-coloured, coffee-colored (*US*) ['kɒfɪˌkʌləd] ADJ (de) color café

coffeepot ['kɒfɪpɒt] N cafetera *f*

coffer ['kɒfə'] N (= *chest*) cofre *m*, arca *f*; **coffers** (*fig*) tesoro *msing*, fondos *mpl*

> Use **el/un** not **la/una** before feminine nouns beginning with stressed **a** or **ha** like **arca**.

coffin ['kɒfɪn] N ataúd *m*

cog [kɒg] N diente *m* (de rueda dentada); ✦ IDIOM **just a ~ in the wheel** una pieza del mecanismo, nada más

cogent ['kəʊdʒənt] ADJ convincente, contundente

cogitate ['kɒdʒɪteɪt] VI meditar

cognac ['kɒnjæk] N coñac *m*

cohabit [kəʊ'hæbɪt] VI cohabitar (**with sb** con algn)

coherence [kəʊ'hɪərəns] N coherencia *f*

coherent [kəʊ'hɪərənt] ADJ coherente

coherently [kəʊ'hɪərəntlɪ] ADV coherentemente, de manera coherente, con coherencia

cohesive [kəʊ'hi:sɪv] ADJ cohesivo, unido

coil [kɔɪl] **A** N **1** (= *roll*) rollo *m*; (= *single loop*) vuelta *f*; [*of hair*] rizo *m*; [*of smoke*] espiral *f* **2** (= *contraceptive*) espiral *f*, DIU *m* **B** VT arrollar, enrollar; **to ~ sth up** enrollar algo **C** VI **to ~ up (into a ball)** hacerse un ovillo

coin [kɔɪn] **A** N moneda *f*; **a 20p ~** una moneda de 20 peniques; **to toss a ~** echar una moneda al aire, jugárselo a cara o cruz; ✦ IDIOM **to pay sb back in his own ~** (*Brit*) pagar a algn en *or* con la misma moneda **B** VT [+ *money*] acuñar; [+ *word*] inventar, acuñar; **to ~ a phrase** para decirlo así, si me permite la frase

coinage ['kɔɪnɪdʒ] N (= money) moneda f; (= system) sistema m monetario; [of word] invención f

coincide [ˌkəʊɪn'saɪd] VI coincidir (**with** con)

coincidence [kəʊ'ɪnsɪdəns] N coincidencia f, casualidad f

coincidental [kəʊˌɪnsɪ'dentl] ADJ fortuito

coin-operated ['kɔɪn'ɒpəreɪtɪd] ADJ que funciona con monedas

coitus ['kɔɪtəs] N coito m

Coke ®[kəʊk] N Coca-Cola® f

coke [kəʊk] N 1 (= fuel) coque m 2 (**) (= cocaine) coca f

Col. ABBR 1 (Mil) (= **Colonel**) Cnel., Cor. 2 (US) = **Colorado**

colander ['kʌləndəʳ] N colador m, escurridor m

cold [kəʊld] **Ⓐ** ADJ (compar ~**er**; superl ~**est**) 1 frío; **to be** ~ [person] tener frío; [thing] estar frío; **I'm** ~ tengo frío; **my hands are** ~ tengo las manos frías; **it was** ~ hacía frío; **to get** ~ [food, coffee] enfriarse; **your dinner's getting** ~ se te está enfriando la cena; **the nights are getting ~er** está haciendo más frío por las noches; **I'm getting** ~ me está entrando frío; **no, no, you're getting ~er** (in game) no, no, cada vez más frío; **to go** ~ [food, coffee] enfriarse; **your coffee's going** ~ se te está enfriando el café; **I went** ~ **at the very thought** sólo de pensarlo me entraron escalofríos; **the trail went** ~ **in Athens** las huellas desaparecieron en Atenas; ✦ IDIOMS **to leave sb** ~ dejar frío a algn; **to pour** ~ **water on sth** poner pegas or trabas a algo
2 (= hostile) [look, person] frío; **to give sb a** ~ **reception** recibir a algn con frialdad; **to give sb a ~ reception** acoger algo con frialdad; **to be** ~ **with sb** mostrarse frío con algn **Ⓑ** N 1 (= cold weather) frío m; **her hands were blue with** ~ tenía las manos moradas del frío; **come in out of the ~!** ¡entra, que hace frío!; **to feel the** ~ ser friolento or (Sp) friolero; ✦ IDIOM **to leave sb out in the** ~ dejar a algn al margen, dar a algn a un lado
2 (Med) resfriado m, catarro m, constipado m, resfrío m (LAm); **I've got a** ~ estoy resfriado or acatarrado or constipado; **to catch** or **get a** ~ resfriarse, constiparse; **to give sb a/one's** ~ contagiar or pegar un/el resfriado a algn **Ⓒ** CPD ➤ **cold calling** venta f en frío ➤ **cold cream** crema f hidratante ➤ **cold cuts** (US) fiambres fpl, embutidos mpl ➤ **cold fish** (= person) persona f seca ➤ **cold front** (Met) frente m frío ➤ **cold meats** fiambres fpl, embutidos mpl ➤ **cold snap** ola f de frío ➤ **cold sore** (esp Brit) herpes m inv labial, pupa* f ➤ **cold storage** conservación f en cámaras frigoríficas; ✦ IDIOM **to put sth into** ~ **storage** [+ project] aparcar algo* ➤ **cold store** (Brit) cámara f frigorífica ➤ **cold turkey*** mono* m, síndrome m de abstinencia; **to go** ~ **turkey** dejar la droga en seco ➤ **cold war** guerra f fría

cold-blooded ['kəʊld'blʌdɪd] ADJ (lit) de sangre fría; (fig) desalmado, despiadado

cold-hearted ['kəʊld'hɑːtɪd] ADJ insensible, cruel

coldly ['kəʊldlɪ] ADV fríamente, con frialdad

cold-shoulder ['kəʊld'ʃəʊldəʳ] VT volver la espalda a

coleslaw ['kəʊlslɔː] N ensalada de col, zanahoria, cebolla y mayonesa

colic ['kɒlɪk] N cólico m

collaborate [kə'læbəreɪt] VI colaborar (**with** con); **to** ~ **on sth** colaborar en algo

collaboration [kəˌlæbə'reɪʃən] N (gen) colaboración f; (with enemy) colaboracionismo m; **in** ~ en colaboración (**with** con)

collaborator [kə'læbəreɪtəʳ] N colaborador(a) m/f; (with enemy) colaboracionista mf

collage [kɒ'lɑːʒ] N collage m

collagen ['kɒlədʒən] N colágeno m

collapse [kə'læps] **Ⓐ** N (Med) colapso m; [of building, roof, floor] hundimiento m, desplome m; [of government] caída f; [of plans, scheme] fracaso m; (financial) ruina f; [of civilization, society] ocaso m; [of business] quiebra f; [of prices] hundimiento m, caída f **Ⓑ** VI 1 [person] (Med) sufrir un colapso; (with laughter) morirse (de risa); [building, roof, floor] hundirse, desplomarse; [civilization, society] desaparecer, extinguirse;

[government] caer; [scheme, deal] fracasar; [business] quebrar; [prices] hundirse, bajar repentinamente; **the bridge ~d during the storm** el puente se vino abajo durante la tormenta
2 (= fold down) plegarse, doblarse

collapsible [kə'læpsəbl] ADJ plegable

collar ['kɒləʳ] **Ⓐ** N 1 [of coat, shirt] cuello m; ✦ IDIOM **to get hot under the** ~ sulfurarse 2 (for dog, on pipe) collar m 3 (Med) collarín m **Ⓑ** VT (*) [+ person] abordar, acorralar; [+ object] (= get for o.s.) apropiarse **Ⓒ** CPD ➤ **collar size** medida f del cuello

collarbone ['kɒləbəʊn] N clavícula f

collate [kɒ'leɪt] VT cotejar

collateral [kɒ'lætərəl] N (Fin) garantía f subsidiaria ➤ **collateral damage** daños mpl colaterales

colleague ['kɒliːɡ] N colega mf

collect [kə'lekt] **Ⓐ** VT 1 (= assemble) reunir, juntar; [+ facts, documents] recopilar, reunir; (= collect in) recoger; **to** ~ **o.s.** or **one's thoughts** reponerse, recobrar el dominio de uno mismo; **the ~ed works of Shakespeare** las obras completas de Shakespeare
2 (as hobby) [+ stamps, valuables] coleccionar
3 (Brit) (= call for, pick up) [+ person] recoger, pasar por (LAm); [+ post, rubbish, ticket] recoger; [+ subscriptions, rent] cobrar; [+ taxes] recaudar; **I'll** ~ **you at eight** vengo a recogerte a las ocho
4 (= gather) [+ dust, water] acumular, retener **Ⓑ** VI 1 (= gather) [people] reunirse, congregarse; [water] estancarse; [dust] acumularse
2 (= collect money) hacer una colecta (**for** para); **to** ~ **for charity** recaudar or recolectar fondos con fines benéficos
3 (= pick up) ~ **on delivery** (US) contra reembolso **Ⓒ** ADV **to call** ~ (US Telec) llamar a cobro revertido **Ⓓ** CPD ➤ **collect call** (US) llamada f a cobro revertido

collection [kə'lekʃən] **Ⓐ** N 1 (= act) [of post, rubbish] recogida f; [of taxes] recaudación f 2 (= set) [of pictures, stamps] colección f 3 (= money) colecta f; **a** ~ **for charity** una colecta para obras benéficas; **a** ~ **for the poor** una colecta a beneficio de los pobres 4 (= group of people) grupo m **Ⓑ** CPD ➤ **collection plate** cepillo m, platillo m

collective [kə'lektɪv] **Ⓐ** N colectivo m **Ⓑ** ADJ colectivo **Ⓒ** CPD ➤ **collective bargaining** negociación f del convenio colectivo ➤ **collective farm** granja f colectiva

collector [kə'lektəʳ] N [of taxes] recaudador(a) m/f; [of stamps] coleccionista mf; **~'s item** pieza f de coleccionista

college ['kɒlɪdʒ] **Ⓐ** N 1 (= higher-education establishment) [of agriculture, technology] escuela f; [of music] conservatorio m; **to go to** ~ seguir estudios superiores
2 (within university) **2.1** (Brit) colegio m universitario, escuela f universitaria **2.2** (US) (= department) ≈ facultad f
3 (= school, body) colegio m **Ⓑ** CPD ➤ **College of Further Education** Escuela f de Formación Profesional

collide [kə'laɪd] VI chocar, colisionar (**with** con)

collie ['kɒlɪ] N perro *m* pastor escocés, collie *m*

colliery ['kɒlɪərɪ] N (*Brit*) mina *f* de carbón

collision [kə'lɪʒən] N choque *m*, colisión *f*; **to come into ~ with** chocar con, colisionar con ➤ **collision course: to be on a ~ course** ir camino del enfrentamiento

colloquial [kə'ləʊkwɪəl] ADJ coloquial, familiar

colloquialism [kə'ləʊkwɪəlɪzəm] N (= *word*) palabra *f* familiar; (= *expression*) expresión *f* familiar

collusion [kə'luːʒən] N confabulación *f*, connivencia *f*; **to be in ~ with** confabular *or* conspirar con

Colo. ABBR (*US*) = **Colorado**

cologne [kə'ləʊn] N (*also* **eau de ~**) agua *f* de colonia, colonia *f*

> Use **el/un** not **la/una** before feminine nouns beginning with stressed **a** or **ha** like **agua**.

Colombia [kə'lɒmbɪə] N Colombia *f*

Colombian [kə'lɒmbɪən] ADJ, N colombiano/a *m/f*

colon[1] ['kəʊlən] N (*Anat*) colon *m*

colon[2] ['kəʊlən] N (*Typ*) dos puntos *mpl*

colonel ['kɜːnl] N coronel *m*

colonial [kə'ləʊnɪəl] **Ⓐ** ADJ colonial; **the ~ power** el poder colonizador **Ⓑ** N colono *m*

colonize ['kɒlənaɪz] VT colonizar

colony ['kɒlənɪ] N colonia *f*

color *etc* ['kʌlər] (*US*) = **colour** *etc*

Colorado beetle [,kɒlə,rɑː'dəʊ'biːtl] N escarabajo *m* de la patata (*Sp*) *or* papa (*LAm*), dorífora *f*

colossal [kə'lɒsl] ADJ colosal, descomunal

colour, color (*US*) ['kʌlər] **Ⓐ** N **1** color *m*; **what ~ is it?** ¿de qué color es?; **they come in different ~s** los hay de varios colores; **it was green in ~** era de color verde; **in ~** (*TV, Cine*) en color; **the ~ drained from his face** palideció, se le fue el color de la cara; **people of ~** (*US*) personas *fpl* de color; ✦ IDIOMS **let's see the ~ of your money!** (*hum*) ¡a ver la pasta!*; **to be off ~** estar indispuesto
2 colours [*of country, team*] colores *mpl*; (= *flag*) bandera *fsing*; (*Mil*) estandarte *msing*; ✦ IDIOM **to show o.s. in one's true ~s** demostrar cómo se es de verdad
3 (= *authenticity, vividness*) color *m*, colorido *m*; **an article full of local ~** un artículo lleno de colorido local
Ⓑ VT **1** [+ *picture*] colorear; (*with crayons*) colorear; (*with paint*) pintar
2 (= *dye, tint*) teñir
3 (= *influence*) influir en
Ⓒ VI **1** (= *blush*) ponerse colorado, sonrojarse
2 (*with crayons*) [*child*] colorear
Ⓓ CPD [*film, photo*] en *or* (*LAm*) a color ➤ **colour bar** barrera *f* racial ➤ **colour blindness** daltonismo *m* ➤ **colour filter** filtro *m* de color ➤ **colour scheme** combinación *f* de colores ➤ **colour supplement** (*Brit*) suplemento *m* a color ➤ **colour television** televisión *f* en *or* (*LAm*) a color ➤ **colour in** VT + ADV (*with crayons*) colorear; (*with paint*) pintar

colourant, colorant (*US*) ['kʌlərənt] N colorante *m*

colour-blind, color-blind (*US*) ['kʌləblaɪnd] ADJ daltónico

colour-coded, color-coded (*US*) ['kʌlə'kəʊdɪd] ADJ con código de colores

coloured, colored (*US*) ['kʌləd] **Ⓐ** ADJ **1** [*pencils, glass, chalk, beads*] de colores **2** (= *biased*) parcial; **a highly ~ tale** una historia de lo más parcial **3** (†) (= *black*) [*person*] de color **4** (*in South Africa*) (de origen) mestizo **Ⓑ** N **1** (†) (= *black*) persona *f* de color **2** (*in South Africa*) mestizo/a *m/f* **3 coloureds** (= *clothes*) ropa *fsing* de color

-coloured, -colored (*US*) [,kʌləd] ADJ (*ending in compounds*) **coffee-coloured** (de) color café

colourfast, colorfast (*US*) ['kʌləfɑːst] ADJ no desteñible

colourful, colorful (*US*) ['kʌləfəl] ADJ **1** (= *bright*) [*display, image*] lleno de color, lleno de colorido; [*procession*] lleno de colorido; [*clothes, design*] de colores vivos
2 (= *picturesque*) [*character, history*] pintoresco; [*description, style*] colorista; [*scene*] vivo, animado **3** (*euph*) [*language*] subido de tono

colouring, coloring (*US*) ['kʌlərɪŋ] N (*gen*) colorido *m*; (= *substance*) colorante *m*; (= *complexion*) tez *f*; **"no artificial colouring"** "sin colores artificiales"; **food** ~ colorante *m* ➤ **colouring book** libro *m* (con dibujos) para colorear

colourless, colorless (*US*) ['kʌləlɪs] ADJ (*lit*) sin color, incoloro; [*person*] soso

colt [kəʊlt] N potro *m*

Columbus [kə'lʌmbəs] N Colón ➤ **Columbus Day** (*US*) Día *m* de la Raza

column ['kɒləm] N columna *f*

columnist ['kɒləmnɪst] N columnista *mf*, articulista *mf*

coma ['kəʊmə] N coma *m*; **in a ~** en (estado de) coma

comatose ['kəʊmətəʊs] ADJ comatoso

comb [kəʊm] **Ⓐ** N **1** (*for hair*) peine *m*; (*ornamental*) peineta *f*; **to run a ~ through one's hair** peinarse, pasarse un peine **2** [*of fowl*] cresta *f* **Ⓑ** VT **1** [+ *hair*] peinar; **to ~ one's hair** peinarse **2** (= *search*) registrar a fondo, peinar

combat ['kɒmbæt] **Ⓐ** N combate *m* **Ⓑ** VT combatir, luchar contra **Ⓒ** CPD ➤ **combat jacket** guerrera *f*

combatant ['kɒmbətənt] N combatiente *mf*

combination [,kɒmbɪ'neɪʃən] N (*gen*) combinación *f*; (= *mixture*) mezcla *f*; **a ~ of circumstances** un conjunto *or* una combinación de circunstancias ➤ **combination lock** cerradura *f* de combinación

combine **Ⓐ** [kəm'baɪn] VT **to ~ (with)** (*gen*) combinar (con); (= *make compatible*) compaginar (con); **it's difficult to ~ a career with a family** es difícil compaginar la profesión con la vida familiar **Ⓑ** [kəm'baɪn] VI **1** (= *join together*) combinarse, unirse; **to ~ with** aunarse con **2** (*Chem*) **to ~ (with)** combinarse (con), mezclarse (con) **Ⓒ** ['kɒmbaɪn] N **1** (*Comm*) asociación *f* **2** (*also* **~ harvester**) cosechadora *f*

combustible [kəm'bʌstɪbl] ADJ combustible

combustion [kəm'bʌstʃən] N combustión *f*

come [kʌm] (*pt* **came**; *pp* **~**) VI **1** (*gen*) venir; (= *arrive*) llegar; **we have ~ to help you** hemos venido a ayudarte; **the letter came this morning** la carta llegó esta mañana; **(I'm) coming!** ¡voy!, ¡ya voy!; **he came running/dashing** entró corriendo/volando *etc*; **the day/time will ~ when ...** ya llegará el día/la hora (en que) ...; **we'll ~ after you** te seguiremos; **~ and see us soon** (*Brit*) ven a vernos pronto; **it may ~ as a surprise to you ...** puede que te asombre *or* (*LAm*) extrañe ...; **it came as a shock to her** le afectó mucho; **to ~ for sth/sb** venir por *or* (*LAm*) pasar por algo/algn; **to ~ from** [*person*] ser de; [*word, custom*] venir de, proceder de, provenir de; **I ~ from Wigan** soy de Wigan; **where do you ~ from?** ¿de dónde eres?; **to ~ and go** ir y venir; **the pain ~s and goes** el dolor va y viene; **the picture ~s and goes** (*TV*) un momento tenemos imagen y al siguiente no; **we came to a village** llegamos a un pueblo; **to ~ to a decision** llegar a una decisión; **it came to me that ...** se me ocurrió que ...; **when it ~s to mathematics ...** en cuanto a *or* en lo que se refiere a las matemáticas ...; **I have ~ to like her** ha llegado a caerme bien; **when your turn ~s** cuando llegue tu turno; **they have ~ a long way** (*fig*) han llegado muy lejos; **~ with me** ven conmigo
2 (*in order*) venir; **May ~s before June** mayo viene antes de junio; **work ~s before pleasure** primero la obligación, luego la devoción; **the adjective ~s before the noun** el adjetivo precede al sustantivo; **he came third** llegó en tercer lugar
3 (= *happen*) **recovery came slowly** la recuperación fue lenta; **how does this chair ~ to be broken?** ¿cómo es que esta silla está rota?; **how ~?*** ¿cómo es eso?, ¿cómo así?, ¿por qué?; **how ~ you don't know?*** ¿cómo es que no lo sabes?; **no good will ~ of it** de eso no saldrá nada bueno; **nothing came of it** todo quedó en nada; **that's what ~s of being careless** eso es lo que pasa *or* ocurre por la falta de cuidado; **now I ~ to think of it** ahora que lo pienso, pensándolo bien; **no harm will ~ to him** no le pasará nada; **~ what may** pase lo que pase

4 (= *be available*) **those shoes ~ in two colours** esos zapatos vienen en dos colores

5 (**) (= *have orgasm*) correrse (*Sp****), acabar (*LAm****)

6 (*in phrases*) ~ **again?*** ¿cómo (dice)?; **he's as good as they ~** es bueno como él solo; **he's as stupid as they ~** es tonto de remate; **I like my tea just as it ~s** me gusta el té hecho de cualquier modo; **they don't ~ any better than that** mejores no los hay; **to ~ between two people** (= *interfere*) meterse *or* entrometerse entre dos personas; (= *separate*) separar a dos personas; **nothing can ~ between us** no hay nada que sea capaz de separarnos; **come, come!** ¡vamos!; **I don't know whether I'm coming or going** no sé lo que me hago; **he had it coming to him*** se lo tenía bien merecido; **if it ~s to it** llegado el caso; ~ **now!** ¡vamos!; **I could see it coming** lo veía venir; ~ **to that ...** si vamos a eso ...; **if it ~s to that** en tal caso, si llegamos a eso; **in (the) years to ~** en los años venideros

➤ **come about** VI + ADV suceder, ocurrir; **how did this ~ about?** ¿cómo ha sido esto?

➤ **come across** Ⓐ VI + PREP (= *meet*) dar con, topar con, encontrarse con Ⓑ VI + ADV **to ~ across well/badly** causar buena/mala impresión; **she ~s across as a nice girl** da la impresión de ser una chica simpática; **it didn't ~ across like that** no es ésa la impresión que nos produjo

➤ **come along** VI + ADV **1** ~ **along!** (*in friendly tone*) ¡vamos!, ¡venga!, ¡ándale! (*esp Mex*) ¡ándele! (*Mex*) (*impatiently*) ¡date prisa!, ¡apúrate! (*LAm*) **2** (= *join in*) **are you coming along?** ¿vienes?, ¿nos acompañas?; **you'll have to ~ along with me to the station** usted tendrá que acompañarme a la comisaría **3** (*Brit*) (= *progress*) ir; **how is the book coming along?** ¿qué tal va el libro?; **it's coming along nicely** va bien **4** (= *arrive*) presentarse

➤ **come apart** VI + ADV deshacerse, caer en pedazos

➤ **come around** VI + ADV **1** (= *visit*) ~ **around whenever you like** pasa por la casa cuando quieras; **he is coming around to see us tonight** viene *or* pasará a vernos esta noche **2** (= *occur regularly*) llegar; **I shall be glad when payday ~s around** ya estoy esperando el día de pago **3** (= *make detour*) desviarse **4** (= *change one's mind*) dejarse convencer; **she'll soon ~ around to my way of thinking** no tardará en darme la razón; **he came around to our view** adoptó nuestra opinión **5** (= *calm down*) tranquilizarse, calmarse; (= *cheer up*) animarse **6** (= *regain consciousness*) volver en sí

➤ **come away** VI + ADV **1** (= *leave*) marcharse, salir; ~ **away from there!** ¡sal *or* quítate de ahí! **2** (= *become detached*) separarse, desprenderse

➤ **come back** VI + ADV (= *return*) volver, regresar (*LAm*); **would you like to ~ back for a cup of tea?** ¿quieres volver a casa a tomar un té?; **it's all coming back to me** ahora sí me acuerdo

➤ **come by** Ⓐ VI + PREP (= *obtain*) conseguir, adquirir; **how did she ~ by that name?** ¿cómo adquirió ese nombre? Ⓑ VI + ADV (= *pass*) pasar; **next time you ~ by** la próxima vez que vengas por aquí

➤ **come down** Ⓐ VI + PREP bajar

Ⓑ VI + ADV **1** (= *descend*) [*person, prices, temperature*] bajar (**from** de; **to** a); [*rain*] caer; [*plane*] (= *land*) aterrizar; (= *crash*) estrellarse; **to ~ down in the world** (*esp Brit*) venir a menos; **to ~ down hard on sb** ser duro con algn; **so it ~s down to this** así que se reduce a esto; **if it ~s down to it, we'll have to move** si es necesario, tendremos que mudarnos; **to ~ down on sb's side** tomar partido por algn **2** (= *be transmitted*) [*heirloom*] pasar; [*tradition*] ser transmitido **3** [*building*] (= *be demolished*) ser derribado/a; (= *fall down*) derrumbarse

➤ **come down with** VI + PREP [+ *illness*] caer enfermo de, enfermar de

➤ **come forward** VI + ADV **1** (= *advance*) avanzar

2 (= *volunteer*) ofrecerse, presentarse; **to ~ forward with a suggestion** ofrecer una sugerencia **3** (= *respond*) responder

➤ **come in** Ⓐ VI + ADV [*person*] entrar; [*train, person in race*] llegar; [*tide*] crecer; ~ **in!** ¡pase!, ¡entre!, ¡siga! (*LAm*); **where do I ~ in?** y yo ¿qué hago?, y yo ¿qué pinto?; **they have no money coming in** no tienen ingresos *or* (*LAm*) entradas; **he came in last** (*in race*) llegó el último; **it will ~ in handy** vendrá bien; **to ~ in for criticism/praise** ser objeto de

críticas/elogios; **to ~ in on a deal** tomar parte en un negocio

➤ **come into** VI + PREP **1** (= *inherit*) [+ *legacy*] heredar **2** (= *be involved in*) tener que ver con, ser parte de; **melons don't ~ into it** los melones no tienen que ver, los melones no hacen al caso

➤ **come off** Ⓐ VI + ADV **1** [*button*] caerse; [*stain*] quitarse; **does this lid ~ off?** ¿se puede quitar esta tapa?

2 (= *take place, come to pass*) tener lugar, realizarse **3** (= *succeed*) tener éxito, dar resultados; **to ~ off well/badly** salir bien/mal **4** (= *acquit o.s.*) portarse; **to ~ off best** salir mejor parado, salir ganando

Ⓑ VI + PREP **1** (= *separate from*) **she came off her bike** se cayó de la bicicleta; **the car came off the road** el coche se salió de la carretera; **the label came off the bottle** la etiqueta se desprendió de la botella; ~ **off it!*** ¡vamos, anda!, ¡venga ya!

2 (= *give up*) dejar

➤ **come on** Ⓐ VI + ADV **1** ~ **on!** (*expressing encouragement*) ¡vamos!, ¡venga!, ¡ándale! (*esp Mex*), ¡ándele! (*Mex*); (*urging haste*) ¡date prisa!, ¡apúrate! (*LAm*)

2 (= *progress*) ir; **how is the book coming on?** ¿qué tal va el libro?; **it's coming on nicely** va bien **3** (= *start*) empezar; **winter is coming on now** ya está empezando el invierno; **I feel a cold coming on** creo que voy a coger un catarro **4** (*Theat*) salir a escena **5** [*light*] encenderse **6** (*US*) (*fig*) **he came on sincere** fingía ser sincero

Ⓑ VI + PREP [+ *object, person*] toparse con, encontrar

➤ **come on to** VI + PREP **1** (= *start discussing*) [+ *question, topic, issue*] pasar a; **I'll ~ on to that in a moment** de eso hablaré en seguida **2** (*esp US**) (*sexually*) tirar los tejos a*, insinuarse a

➤ **come out** VI + ADV **1** (= *emerge*) [*person, object, sun, magazine*] salir (**of** de); [*qualities*] mostrarse; [*news*] divulgarse, difundirse; [*scandal*] descubrirse, salir a la luz; [*film*] estrenarse; **he came out of it with credit** salió con honor

2 (= *open*) [*flower*] abrirse, florecer **3** (*into the open*) [*homosexual*] declararse; **to ~ out for/against sth** declararse en pro/en contra de algo **4** [*stain*] quitarse; [*dye*] desteñirse **5** (= *become covered with*) **he came out in a rash** le salió un sarpullido; **I came out in a sweat** empecé a sudar, me cubrí de sudor **6** (*in conversation*) **to ~ out with a remark** salir con un comentario; **you never know what he's going to ~ out with next!*** ¡nunca se sabe por dónde va a salir! **7** (= *turn out*) salir; **it all came out right** todo salió bien; **none of my photos came out** no salió ninguna de mis fotos; **it ~s out at £5 a head** sale a cinco libras por cabeza

➤ **come over** Ⓐ VI + ADV **1** (*lit*) venir, venirse; **they came over to England for a holiday** (se) vinieron a Inglaterra de vacaciones; **you'll soon ~ over to my way of thinking** ya me darás la razón

2 (*) (= *feel suddenly*) ponerse; **she came over quite ill** se puso bastante mala; **I came over all dizzy** me mareé **3** (= *give impression*) **to ~ over well/badly** causar buena/mala impresión; **to ~ over as** dar la impresión de ser, dar una imagen de

Ⓑ VI + PREP **I don't know what's ~ over him!** ¡no sé lo que le pasa!; **a feeling of weariness came over her** le invadió una sensación de cansancio

➤ **come round** VI + ADV (*Brit*) = **come around**

➤ **come through** Ⓐ VI + ADV **1** (= *survive*) sobrevivir; (= *recover*) recuperarse **2** [*telephone call*] llegar Ⓑ VI + PREP **1** (= *survive*) [+ *war, danger*] sobrevivir; (*uninjured*) salir ileso/a de; [+ *illness*] recuperarse de **2** (= *pass*) [+ *test*] superar

➤ **come to** Ⓐ VI + PREP [*amount*] ascender a, sumar; **how much does it ~ to?** ¿cuánto es en total?, ¿a cuánto asciende?; **it ~s to £15 altogether** en total son 15 libras; **what are we coming to?** ¿adónde va a parar todo esto? Ⓑ VI + ADV (= *regain consciousness*) recobrar el conocimiento

➤ **come under** VI + PREP **to ~ under the heading of** (= *be found under*) aparecer bajo el título de; (= *be responsibility of*) entrar dentro de la responsabilidad de, pertenecer a; **it**

~s **under the heading of vandalism** (*fig*) se puede clasificar de vandalismo; **he came under the teacher's influence** cayó bajo la influencia del profesor; **to ~ under attack** sufrir un ataque, verse atacado

➤ **come up Ⓐ** VI + ADV **1** (= *ascend*) [*person*] subir; [*sun*] salir; [*plant*] aparecer; **he has ~ up in the world** ha subido mucho en la escala social

2 (= *crop up*) [*difficulty*] surgir; [*matters for discussion*] plantearse, mencionarse; **to ~ up for sale** ponerse a la venta

3 (*Jur*) [*accused*] comparecer; [*lawsuit*] verse, presentarse; **his case ~s up tomorrow** su caso se verá mañana

4 (*Univ*) matricularse; **he came up to Oxford last year** (*Brit*) se matriculó en la universidad de Oxford el año pasado

Ⓑ VI + PREP subir; **to ~ up the stairs** subir las escaleras

➤ **come up against** VI + PREP [+ *problem*] tropezar con; [+ *enemy*] tener que habérselas con

➤ **come upon** VI + PREP topar(se) con, encontrar

➤ **come up to** VI + PREP **1** (= *reach*) llegar hasta

2 (= *approach*) acercarse a **3** (= *meet*) estar a la altura de, satisfacer; **it didn't ~ up to our expectations** no estuvo a la altura de lo que esperábamos; **the goods didn't ~ up to the required standard** la mercancía no satisfacía el nivel de calidad requerido

➤ **come up with** VI + PREP [+ *idea, plan*] proponer, sugerir; [+ *suggestion*] hacer; [+ *solution*] ofrecer, sugerir; [+ *money*] encontrar

comeback ['kʌmbæk] N **to make a ~** (*on stage*) volver a las tablas; (*on screen*) volver a los platós; **he is making a ~ to professional football** está listo para volver al fútbol profesional; **butter has made a ~ in the British diet** la mantequilla ha recobrado su importancia en la dieta británica

comedian [kə'miːdɪən] N humorista *mf*, cómico/a *m/f*

comedienne [kə,miːdɪ'en] N humorista *f*, cómica *f*

comedown ['kʌmdaʊn] N (*social*) pérdida *f* de estatus; (= *humiliation*) humillación *f*; **his new house is a bit of a ~** su nueva casa significa una cierta pérdida de estatus

comedy ['kɒmɪdɪ] N (*gen*) comedia *f*; (= *humour of situation*) comicidad *f*

come-on* ['kʌm,ɒn] N (= *enticement*) insinuación *f*, invitación *f*; **to give sb the ~** insinuársele a algn

comer ['kʌməʳ] N **the first ~** el primero/la primera en llegar; **he has defended his title against all ~s** ha defendido su título contra todos los contendientes

comet ['kɒmɪt] N cometa *m*

comeuppance [,kʌm'ʌpəns] N ✦ IDIOM **to get one's ~** llevarse su merecido

comfort ['kʌmfət] **Ⓐ** N **1** (= *solace*) consuelo *m*; **you're a great ~ to me** eres un gran consuelo para mí; **if it's any ~ to you** si te sirve de consuelo; **the exam is too close for ~** el examen está demasiado cerca para que me sienta tranquilo; **to take ~ from sth** consolarse con algo **2** (= *well-being*) confort *m*, comodidad *f*; (= *facility*) comodidad *f*

Ⓑ VT (= *give solace to*) consolar, confortar **Ⓒ** CPD

➤ **comfort station** (*US*) servicios *mpl*, aseos *mpl*, baño *m* (*LAm*)

comfortable ['kʌmfətəbl] ADJ **1** (*physically*) [*chair, shoes, position*] cómodo; [*room, house, hotel*] confortable, cómodo; **you don't look very ~** no pareces estar muy cómodo; **to make o.s. ~** ponerse cómodo

2 (*mentally, emotionally*) cómodo, a gusto; **to feel ~ with sb/ sth** sentirse cómodo *or* a gusto con algn/algo

3 (*financially*) [*income*] bueno, suficiente; [*life, lifestyle*] holgado

4 (= *easy*) [*lead, majority, margin*] amplio, holgado; **he was elected with a ~ majority** fue elegido por una amplia mayoría *or* una mayoría holgada; **to have a ~ win over sb** vencer a algn fácilmente

5 (*Med*) estable

comfortably ['kʌmfətəblɪ] ADV **1** [*sit, rest, lie*] cómodamente; **sitting ~** cómodamente sentado; **~ furnished** amueblado confortablemente **2** (*financially*) [*live*] holgadamente, con desahogo; **to be ~ off** vivir holgadamente *or* con desahogo, disfrutar de una posición acomodada *or* desahogada (*frm*) **3** (= *easily*) [*manage*] sin

problemas; [*win, defeat*] fácilmente, sin problemas; [*afford*] sin problemas, cómodamente

comforter ['kʌmfətəʳ] N (*baby's*) chupete *m*, chupón *m* (*LAm*) **2** (*US*) (*on bed*) edredón *m*

comforting ['kʌmfətɪŋ] ADJ (*gen*) consolador, (re)confortante; [*words*] de consuelo

comfy* ['kʌmfɪ] ADJ (*compar* **comfier**; *superl* **comfiest**) cómodo

comic ['kɒmɪk] **Ⓐ** ADJ cómico; (= *amusing*) gracioso, divertido **Ⓑ** N **1** (= *person*) cómico/a *m/f* **2** (*esp Brit*) (= *paper*) revista *f* de historietas, cómic *m* (*Sp*); (*children's*) revista *f* de historietas, tebeo *m* (*Sp*) **3** **comics** (*US*) (= *comic strip*) historieta *fsing*, tira *fsing* cómica **Ⓒ** CPD ➤ **comic book** (*esp US*) libro *m* de cómics ➤ **comic strip** historieta *f*, tira *f* cómica

comical ['kɒmɪkəl] ADJ cómico, gracioso

coming ['kʌmɪŋ] **Ⓐ** ADJ (= *approaching*) [*weeks, months, years*] próximo; **in the ~ weeks** en las próximas semanas **Ⓑ** N llegada *f*; **the ~ of spring** la llegada de la primavera; **the ~ of Christ** el advenimiento de Cristo; **the ~s and goings of the guests** las idas y venidas de los invitados **Ⓒ** CPD ➤ **coming of age** (llegada *f* a la) mayoría *f* de edad

comma ['kɒmə] N coma *f*

command [kə'mɑːnd] **Ⓐ** N **1** (= *order*) (*esp Mil*) orden *f*; (*Comput*) orden *f*, comando *m*; **he gave the ~ (to attack/ retreat)** dio la orden (de atacar/retirarse)

2 (= *control*) [*of army, ship*] mando *m*; **to be in ~ (of sth)** estar al mando (de algo); **who is in ~ here?** ¿quién manda aquí?; **second in ~** segundo *m*; **to take ~ of sth** asumir el mando de algo; **under the ~ of** bajo el mando de

3 (= *mastery*) dominio *m*; **his ~ of English** su dominio del inglés

Ⓑ VT **1** (= *order*) **to ~ sb to do sth** mandar *or* ordenar a algn que haga algo

2 (= *be in control of*) [+ *soldiers, army*] mandar, estar al mando de; [+ *ship*] comandar

3 (= *have at one's disposal*) disponer de, contar con

4 (= *deserve*) [+ *respect*] imponer

5 (= *overlook*) [+ *view*] tener, disfrutar de

Ⓒ CPD ➤ **command line** (*Comput*) orden *f*, comando *m*

commandant [,kɒmən'dænt] N comandante *mf*

commandeer [,kɒmən'dɪəʳ] VT requisar, expropiar

commander [kə'mɑːndəʳ] N (*Mil*) comandante *mf*; (*Naut*) capitán *m* de fragata

commander-in-chief [kə'mɑːndərɪn'tʃiːf] N (*pl* **commanders-in-chief**) jefe/a *m/f* supremo/a, comandante/a *m/f* en jefe

commanding [kə'mɑːndɪŋ] ADJ [*tone of voice*] autoritario, imperioso; [*lead*] abrumador; [*position*] dominante ➤ **commanding officer** comandante *mf*

commandment [kə'mɑːndmənt] N (*Bible*) mandamiento *m*; **the Ten Commandments** los diez mandamientos

commando [kə'mɑːndəʊ] N (*pl* **~s** *or* **~ es**) comando *m*

commemorate [kə'meməreɪt] VT conmemorar

commemoration [kə,memə'reɪʃən] **Ⓐ** N conmemoración *f*; **in ~ of** en conmemoración de **Ⓑ** ADJ [*service, ceremony*] de conmemoración

commemorative [kə'memərətɪv] ADJ conmemorativo

commence [kə'mens] VT, VI comenzar; **to ~ doing sth** comenzar a hacer algo

commencement [kə'mensmənt] N **1** (*frm*) (= *start*) comienzo *m*, principio *m* **2** (*US Univ*) (ceremonia *f* de) graduación *f*, (ceremonia *f* de) entrega *f* de diplomas

commend [kə'mend] VT **1** (= *praise*) elogiar; **to ~ sb for** *or* **on sth** elogiar a algn por algo; **to ~ sb for his action** elogiar la acción de algn; **her entry was highly ~ed** (*in competition*) su participación recibió una mención elogiosa *or* especial **2** (= *recommend*) recomendar; **it has little to ~ it** poco se puede decir en su favor **3** (= *entrust*) encomendar (**to** a)

commendable [kə'mendəbl] ADJ encomiable, loable

commendation [,kɒmen'deɪʃən] N **1** (= *praise*) elogio *m*, encomio *m*; (= *award*) mención *f* especial; (*Mil*) distinción *f*

commensurate [kə'menʃərɪt] ADJ **~ with** en proporción a, que corresponde a; **"salary commensurate with experience"** "sueldo según experiencia"

comment ['kɒment] **Ⓐ** N comentario *m*, observación *f*; **she made the ~ that ...** observó que ...; **he made no ~** no hizo ningún comentario; **"no comment"** "sin comentarios"; **to cause ~** provocar comentarios **Ⓑ** VI hacer observaciones o comentarios, comentar; **to ~ on** [+ *text*] comentar, hacer un comentario de **Ⓒ** VT observar; **to ~ that ...** observar que ...

commentary ['kɒməntərɪ] N (*gen*) comentario *m*; (*on sporting event*) crónica *f*; (*on text*) comentario *m* (de texto)

commentate ['kɒməntert] VI hacer la crónica, comentar

commentator ['kɒmənteɪtəʳ] N (*Rad, TV*) comentarista *mf*

commerce ['kɒmɜːs] N comercio *m*

commercial [kəˈmɜːʃəl] **Ⓐ** ADJ comercial **Ⓑ** N (*TV*) anuncio *m*, spot *m* publicitario **Ⓒ** CPD ➤ **commercial break** espacio *m* publicitario, pausa *f* publicitaria ➤ **commercial law** derecho *m* mercantil ➤ **commercial traveller, commercial traveler** (*US*) viajante *mf* (de comercio)

commercialize [kəˈmɜːʃəlaɪz] VT comercializar

commercially [kəˈmɜːʃəlɪ] ADV comercialmente; **it is not ~ available** no puede adquirirse en el mercado

commie* ['kɒmɪ] ADJ, N rojo/a *m/f*

commiserate [kəˈmɪzəreɪt] VI **friends called to ~ when they found out I hadn't got the job** cuando me rechazaron para el trabajo mis amigos me llamaron para decirme lo mucho que lo sentían; **"I know how you feel," he ~d** —sé cómo te sientes —le dijo a modo de consuelo

commission [kəˈmɪʃən] **Ⓐ** N **1** (= *committee*) comisión *f* **2** (*to artist, composer*) comisión *f* **3** (*on sale*) comisión *f*; **to sell things on ~** vender cosas a comisión; **I get 10% ~** me dan el 10 por ciento de comisión **4** (*Mil*) (= *position*) graduación *f* de oficial; (= *warrant*) nombramiento *m* **5** (= *use*) servicio *m*; **to put into ~** poner en servicio; **to be out of ~** estar fuera de servicio **Ⓑ** VT **1** [+ *artist etc*] hacer un encargo a; [+ *picture*] encargar, comisionar (*esp LAm*); **to ~ sb to do sth** encargar a algn que haga algo **2** (*Mil*) [+ *officer*] nombrar; **~ed officer** oficial *mf*

commissionaire [kə,mɪʃəˈnɛəʳ] N (*Brit*) portero *m*, conserje *m*

commissioner [kəˈmɪʃənəʳ] N (= *official*) comisario/a *m/f*; (= *member of commission*) comisionado/a *m/f*; **~ of police** inspector(a) *m/f* jefe de policía

commit [kəˈmɪt] **Ⓐ** VT **1** [+ *crime, sin, error*] cometer; **to ~ suicide** suicidarse **2** (= *consign*) [+ *resources*] asignar, destinar; [+ *troops*] enviar; **to ~ sb** (*to mental hospital*) internar a algn; **to ~ sth to memory** aprender algo de memoria; **to ~ sb for trial** (*Brit*) remitir a algn al tribunal; **to ~ sth to writing** poner algo por escrito **3** (= *pledge*) comprometer; **accepting this offer does not ~ you to anything** aceptar esta oferta no le compromete a nada; **we are deeply ~ted to this policy** creemos firmemente en esta política **4 to ~ o.s. (to doing sth)** comprometerse (a hacer algo) **Ⓑ** VI **to ~ to sb/sth** comprometerse con algn/a algo

commitment [kəˈmɪtmənt] N **1** (= *obligation*) obligación *f*; **he has heavy teaching ~s** tiene muchas obligaciones como profesor; **family ~s** obligaciones familiares **2** (= *pledge*) **to give a ~ to do sth** comprometerse a hacer algo **3** (= *devotion*) entrega *f*, devoción *f*

committed [kəˈmɪtɪd] ADJ comprometido

committee [kəˈmɪtɪ] N comité *m*, comisión *f*; **to be** or **sit on a ~** ser miembro de un comité ➤ **committee meeting** reunión *f* del comité ➤ **committee member** miembro *mf* del comité

commode [kəˈməud] N (*esp Brit*) silla *f* con orinal

commodity [kəˈmɒdɪtɪ] N (= *product*) artículo *m* (de consumo *or* de comercio), producto *m*, mercancía *f*, mercadería *f* (*LAm*) (*Fin, St Ex*) materia *f* prima ➤ **commodity markets** mercados *mpl* de materias primas

common ['kɒmən] **Ⓐ** ADJ **1** (= *ordinary*) común (*also Zool,*

Bot); **it is a ~ belief that ...** es una creencia extendida *or* generalizada que ...; **it's (just) ~ courtesy** es una cortesía elemental; **the ~ man** el hombre de la calle, el hombre medio; **the ~ people** la gente corriente; **it is ~ practice in the USA** es una práctica común en EE.UU.; **to have the ~ touch** saber tratar con la gente corriente; **✦** IDIOM **~ or garden** (*esp Brit**) común y corriente, normal y corriente **2** (= *shared*) [*cause, aim, language*] común; **by ~ agreement** *or* **consent** de común acuerdo; **for the ~ good** para el bien común, para el bien de todos; **~ ground** (*fig*) puntos *mpl* en común, puntos *mpl* de confluencia *or* acuerdo; **it is ~ knowledge that ...** es del dominio público que ...; **the desire for freedom is ~ to all people** todo el mundo comparte el deseo de la libertad **3** (= *vulgar*) [*person, behaviour, speech*] ordinario, basto; **✦** IDIOM **as ~ as muck** (*Brit**) de lo más ordinario, más basto que la lija (del cuatro) **Ⓑ** N (= *land*) campo *m* comunal, ejido *m*; **in ~: we have a lot in ~ (with other people)** tenemos mucho en común (con otra gente); **in ~ with many other companies ...** al igual que otras muchas empresas ... **Ⓒ** CPD ➤ **the Common Agricultural Policy** la Política Agrícola Común ➤ **common denominator** común denominador *m*; **lowest ~ denominator** mínimo común denominador *m* ➤ **Common Entrance** (*Brit Scol*) examen de acceso a un colegio de enseñanza privada ➤ **common land** propiedad *f* comunal ➤ **common law** (*established by custom*) derecho *m* consuetudinario; (*based on precedent*) jurisprudencia *f* ➤ **common room** (*esp Brit*) (*for students*) sala *f* de estudiantes; (*for teachers*) sala *f* de profesores ➤ **common sense** sentido *m* común

commoner ['kɒmənəʳ] N plebeyo/a *m/f*

common-law ['kɒmən,lɔː] ADJ [*marriage*] consensual; [*spouse*] en unión consensual

commonly ['kɒmənlɪ] ADV **1** (= *often*) [*called*] comúnmente; [*prescribed*] frecuentemente **2** (= *generally*) **the ~ held view** la opinión extendida *or* generalizada; **it is ~ believed that ...** es una creencia extendida *or* generalizada que ... **3** (= *vulgarly*) [*behave, speak*] ordinariamente, vulgarmente

commonness ['kɒmənnɪs] N **1** (= *frequency*) frecuencia *f* **2** (= *vulgarity*) ordinariez *f*

commonplace ['kɒmənpleɪs] **Ⓐ** ADJ (= *normal*) común, normal, corriente; (*pej*) vulgar, ordinario; **it is ~ to see this sort of thing** es frecuente *or* corriente ver este tipo de cosas **Ⓑ** N cosa *f* común y corriente

Commons ['kɒmənz] NPL (*Brit*): **the ~** (la Cámara de) los Comunes

commonsense ['kɒmən,sens] ADJ racional, lógico; **the ~ thing to do is ...** lo lógico es ...

Commonwealth ['kɒmənwelθ] N **the ~** la Comunidad Británica de Naciones

commotion [kəˈməuʃən] N (= *noise*) alboroto *m*; (= *activity*) jaleo *m*, tumulto *m*, confusión *f*; (*civil*) disturbio *m*; **to cause a ~** provocar *or* causar un alboroto; **to make a ~!** (= *noise*) armar un alboroto; (= *fuss*) armar un lío*; **what a ~!** ¡qué alboroto!

communal ['kɒmju:nl] ADJ [property, ownership] comunal; [living room, dining room, facilities] común

commune Ⓐ ['kɒmju:n] N comuna f Ⓑ [kə'mju:n] VI **1 to ~ with** estar en contacto con **2** (Rel) (esp US) comulgar

communicable [kə'mju:nɪkəbl] ADJ (gen) comunicable; [disease] transmisible

communicate [kə'mju:nɪkeɪt] Ⓐ VI (= speak) comunicarse (**with** con); **we ~ by telephone** estamos en contacto telefónico Ⓑ VT [+ thoughts, information] comunicar (**to sb** a algn)

communicating [kə'mju:nɪkeɪtɪŋ] ADJ **~ rooms** habitaciones fpl que se comunican

communication [kə,mju:nɪ'keɪʃən] Ⓐ N **1** (= contact) comunicación f; **to be in ~ with** estar en contacto con **2** (= message) mensaje m, comunicación f **3 communications** (= roads etc) comunicaciones fpl Ⓑ CPD ➤ **communication cord** (Brit) timbre m or palanca f de alarma ➤ **communication skills** habilidad fsing or aptitud fsing para comunicarse ➤ **communications satellite** satélite m de comunicaciones

communicative [kə'mju:nɪkətɪv] ADJ comunicativo

communion [kə'mju:nɪən] N comunión f; **to take ~** comulgar

communiqué [kə'mju:nɪkeɪ] N comunicado m

communism ['kɒmjʊnɪzəm] N comunismo m

communist ['kɒmjʊnɪst] ADJ, N comunista mf

community [kə'mju:nɪtɪ] Ⓐ N **1** (= people) comunidad f; **the local ~** el vecindario; **the black ~** la población negra; **the artistic ~** el mundillo artístico; **the English ~ in Rome** la colectividad or colonia inglesa de Roma **2 the Community** (= the EU) la Comunidad Ⓑ CPD **Community** (= EU) [+ policy, law] comunitaria ➤ **community centre, community center** (US) centro m social ➤ **community chest** (US) fondo m para beneficencia social ➤ **community college** (US) establecimiento docente de educación terciaria donde se realizan cursos de dos años ➤ **community service** trabajo m comunitario (prestado en lugar de cumplir una pena de prisión) ➤ **community worker** asistente mf social

commute [kə'mju:t] Ⓐ VI viajar diariamente (de la casa al trabajo); **I live in Brighton but I ~ to London** vivo en Brighton pero voy todos los días a trabajar a Londres Ⓑ VT [+ sentence] conmutar (**to** por) Ⓒ N (esp US) viaje m diario al trabajo

commuter [kə'mju:tə'] N persona que viaja cada día de su casa a su trabajo ➤ **commuter belt** (Brit) zona f de los barrios exteriores ➤ **commuter train** tren m de cercanías

compact Ⓐ [kəm'pækt] ADJ (= small) compacto; (= dense) apretado, sólido; [style] breve, conciso Ⓑ [kəm'pækt] VT comprimir (**into** en) Ⓒ ['kɒmpækt] N **1** (also **powder ~**) polvera f **2** (US Aut) (also **~ car**) utilitario m Ⓓ ['kɒmpækt] CPD ➤ **compact disc** disco m compacto, compact m ➤ **compact disc player** lector m de discos compactos

companion [kəm'pænjən] Ⓐ N **1** (= person) compañero/a m/f; (lady's) señora f de compañía; **travelling ~** compañero/a m/f de viaje **2** (= one of pair) compañero m, pareja f Ⓑ CPD ➤ **companion volume** tomo m complementario

companionable [kəm'pænjənəbl] ADJ sociable, amigable; **in ~ silence** en amigable silencio

companionship [kəm'pænjənʃɪp] N (= company) compañía f; (= friendship, friendliness) compañerismo m

company ['kʌmpənɪ] Ⓐ N **1** (= companionship) compañía f; **it's ~ for her** le hace compañía; **he's good/poor ~** es/no es muy agradable estar con él; **to keep sb ~** hacer compañía a algn; ✦ PROV **two's ~, three's a crowd** dos es compañía, tres es multitud **2** (= group, friends) **to get into bad ~** tener malas compañías; **to be in good ~** (fig) estar bien acompañado; **present ~ excepted** mejorando lo presente, salvando a los presentes **3** (= guests) visita f, invitados mpl; **we have ~** tenemos visita or invitados **4** (= firm) compañía f, empresa f; (= association) sociedad f; **Smith and Company** Smith y Compañía **5** (Mil) compañía f, unidad f; **ship's ~** tripulación f **6** (Theat) compañía f (de teatro) Ⓑ CPD ➤ **company car** coche m de la empresa ➤ **company director** director(a) m/f de empresa ➤ **company law** derecho m de compañías ➤ **company time: in ~ time** en horas de trabajo ➤ **company union** (US) sindicato m de empresa

comparable ['kɒmpərəbl] ADJ comparable (**to, with** a, con)

comparative [kəm'pærətɪv] Ⓐ ADJ **1** (= relative) [obscurity, ease etc] relativo **2** [study] comparativo, comparado Ⓑ N comparativo m

comparatively [kəm'pærətɪvlɪ] ADV (= relatively) relativamente

compare [kəm'pɛə'] Ⓐ VT (gen) comparar (**with, to** con, a); **Oxford is small ~d with London** Oxford es pequeño en comparación a or comparado con Londres; ✦ IDIOM **to ~ notes with sb** cambiar impresiones con algn Ⓑ VI **she can't ~ with you** no se la puede comparar contigo; **it doesn't ~ with yours** no se lo puede comparar al tuyo, no tiene comparación con el tuyo; **how do they ~?** ¿cuáles son sus cualidades respectivas?; **how do the prices ~?** ¿qué tal son los precios en comparación? Ⓒ N **beyond ~** incomparable, sin comparación, sin par

comparison [kəm'pærɪsn] N comparación f; **there's no ~ (between them)** no hay comparación (entre ellos), no se puede comparar (el uno con el otro); **in** or **by ~ (with)** en comparación (con)

compartment [kəm'pɑ:tmənt] N compartimiento m

compartmentalize [,kɒmpɑ:t'mentəlaɪz] VT dividir en categorías; (pej) aislar en compartimientos estancos, compartimentar

compass ['kʌmpəs] N **1** (Naut etc) brújula f **2** (Math) compás m; **a pair of ~es** un compás **3** (frm) (= range) alcance m; (= area) ámbito m

compassion [kəm'pæʃən] N compasión f; **to have ~ for** or **on sb** tener compasión por or de algn, compadecerse de algn

compassionate [kəm'pæʃənɪt] ADJ compasivo; **on ~ grounds** por compasión ➤ **compassionate leave** permiso m por motivos familiares

compatibility [kəm,pætə'bɪlɪtɪ] N compatibilidad f

compatible [kəm'pætɪbl] ADJ compatible; **an IBM-~ computer** un ordenador compatible con IBM

compatriot [kəm'pætrɪət] N compatriota mf

compel [kəm'pel] VT **1** (= oblige) obligar; **to ~ sb to do sth** obligar a algn a hacer algo; **I feel ~led to say that ...** me veo obligado a decir que ... **2** [+ respect, obedience] imponer

compelling [kəm'pelɪŋ] ADJ **1** [argument, evidence] convincente **2** [account, film, book] fascinante, apasionante

compellingly [kəm'pelɪŋlɪ] ADV de manera convincente, de modo convincente

compensate ['kɒmpənseɪt] Ⓐ VT **1** (gen) compensar, resarcir; (Jur, Insurance) indemnizar; **to ~ sb for sth** (gen) compensar or resarcir a algn por algo; (Jur, Insurance) indemnizar a algn por algo **2** (= reward) recompensar Ⓑ VI **to ~ for sth** compensar algo

compensation [,kɒmpən'seɪʃən] N compensación f; (for loss, damage) indemnización f, resarcimiento m; (= reward) recompensa f; **they got £2,000 ~** recibieron 2.000 libras de indemnización; **in ~ (for)** en compensación (por)

compere, compère (Brit) ['kɒmpeə'] Ⓐ N presentador(a) m/f, animador(a) m/f Ⓑ VT [+ show] presentar

compete [kəm'pi:t] VI (as rivals) competir (**against, with** con; **for** por); (= take part) tomar parte (**in** en), presentarse (**in** a); (Comm) competir (**for** por), hacer la competencia

competence ['kɒmpɪtəns], **competency** ['kɒmpɪtənsɪ] N **1** (= ability) competencia f, capacidad f **2** (= jurisdiction) competencia f

competent ['kɒmpɪtənt] ADJ **1** (= proficient) [person, pilot, nurse] competente, capaz; **to be ~ at sth** ser competente en algo; **to feel ~ to do sth** sentirse capacitado para hacer algo **2** (= satisfactory) [work, performance] aceptable; **he did a very ~ job** hizo su trabajo muy bien

competently ['kɒmpɪtəntlɪ] ADV competentemente, de forma muy competente

competing [kəm'piːtɪŋ] ADJ [product, bid, offer] rival; [interests] conflictivo

competition [ˌkɒmpɪ'tɪʃən] N 1 (= contest) concurso m; (Sport) competición f (Sp), competencia f (LAm); **to go in for a ~** inscribirse en or presentarse a un concurso 2 (Comm) competencia f; **unfair ~** competencia desleal 3 (= competing) competencia f, rivalidad f; **in ~ with** en competencia con

competitive [kəm'petɪtɪv] ADJ [person, sport, advantage, price] competitivo; [exam, selection] por concurso or oposiciones

competitively [kəm'petɪtɪvlɪ] ADV [think, behave] con espíritu competidor; [swim, run, play] a nivel de competición; **their products are ~ priced** sus productos tienen precios competitivos

competitiveness [kəm'petɪtɪvnɪs] N [of person] espíritu m competitivo, espíritu m de competencia; [of prices] competitividad f

competitor [kəm'petɪtə⁽ʳ⁾] N (= rival) competidor(a) m/f; (in contest) concursante mf; (Sport) competidor(a) m/f, participante mf; (eg for Civil Service post) opositor(a) m/f

compilation [ˌkɒmpɪ'leɪʃən] N [of list, catalogue] compilación f; [of information] recopilación f; (= document) compilación f ➤ **compilation album** álbum m recopilatorio

compile [kəm'paɪl] VT [+ list, catalogue, dictionary] compilar; [+ information] recopilar

complacent [kəm'pleɪsənt] ADJ [person] (demasiado) pagado de sí mismo; **we can't afford to be ~** no podemos confiarnos demasiado, no podemos dormirnos en los laureles

complain [kəm'pleɪn] VI 1 (= grumble) quejarse (**about, of** de; **to** a); **to ~ that** quejarse de que; **I can't ~** yo no me quejo 2 (formally) reclamar (**about** por; **to** ante) 3 (Med) **to ~ of** quejarse de

complaint [kəm'pleɪnt] Ⓐ N 1 (= grumble) queja f; (formal) reclamación f; (to police) denuncia f; **to make a ~** reclamar, formular una queja 2 (= cause) motivo m de queja 3 (= illness) mal m, dolencia f Ⓑ CPD ➤ **complaints book** libro m de reclamaciones

complement Ⓐ ['kɒmplɪmənt] N 1 (gen) complemento m; **to be a ~ to** complementar a 2 [of staff] dotación f, personal m; **the orchestra did not have its full ~ of brass** la orquesta no contaba con su sección de metales completa Ⓑ ['kɒmplɪment] VT complementar

complementary [ˌkɒmplɪ'mentərɪ] ADJ complementario ➤ **complementary medicine** medicina f complementaria

complete [kəm'pliːt] Ⓐ ADJ 1 (= whole) entero 2 (= finished) terminado 3 (= total) [control, lack] total, absoluto; [change] total; [surprise] auténtico; **in ~ agreement** totalmente de acuerdo, en completo acuerdo; **in ~ contrast to sth/sb** todo lo contrario que algo/algn; **he is the ~ opposite of me** no nos parecemos en nada; **to my ~ satisfaction** para mi completa or total satisfacción 4 (= full) [list, set, group] completo; **the Complete Works of Shakespeare** las Obras Completas de Shakespeare 5 (= all-round) [novelist, footballer] completo, perfecto 6 **~ with: a mansion ~ with swimming pool** una mansión con piscina y todo; **it comes ~ with instructions** viene con sus correspondientes instrucciones Ⓑ VT 1 (= make up) [+ set, collection, team] completar; [+ misfortune, happiness] colmar 2 (= finish) [+ work] terminar, acabar; [+ contract] cumplir, llevar a cabo; [+ prison sentence] cumplir; **the course takes three years to ~** se tarda tres años en hacer el curso 3 (= fill in) [+ form, questionnaire] rellenar

completely [kəm'pliːtlɪ] ADV completamente, totalmente; **~ and utterly ridiculous** total y absolutamente ridículo; **almost ~** casi completamente, casi por completo

completion [kəm'pliːʃən] N finalización f, terminación f, conclusión f; **to be nearing ~** estar a punto de finalizarse or terminarse or concluirse, estar llegando a su finalización or conclusión; **on ~ of contract** cuando se cumpla el contrato

➤ **completion date** (in house buying) fecha f de entrega (de llaves)

complex ['kɒmpleks] Ⓐ ADJ (= difficult) complejo, complicado; (= consisting of different parts) complejo Ⓑ N 1 (Psych) complejo m; **inferiority ~** complejo m de inferioridad; **he's got a ~ about his nose** está acomplejado por su nariz, su nariz lo acompleja 2 [of buildings] complejo m; **sports/shopping ~** complejo m deportivo/comercial; **housing ~** colonia f de viviendas, urbanización f (Sp)

complexion [kəm'plekʃən] N tez f, cutis m; (in terms of colour) tez f, piel f; **that puts a different ~ on it** eso le da otro cariz or aspecto

complexity [kəm'pleksɪtɪ] N complejidad f, lo complejo

compliance [kəm'plaɪəns] N (with rules etc) conformidad f; (= submissiveness) sumisión f (**with** a); **in ~ with** conforme a, en conformidad con

compliant [kəm'plaɪənt] ADJ sumiso

complicate ['kɒmplɪkeɪt] VT complicar

complicated ['kɒmplɪkeɪtɪd] ADJ complicado; **to get ~** complicarse

complication [ˌkɒmplɪ'keɪʃən] N complicación f

complicity [kəm'plɪsɪtɪ] N complicidad f (**in** en)

compliment Ⓐ ['kɒmplɪmənt] N 1 (praising sb/sth) halago m; (= courteous remark, respect) cumplido m; **to pay sb a ~** (= praise) halagar a algn; (courteous) hacer un cumplido a algn; **I take it as a ~ that ...** me halaga (el) que ...; **it was meant as a ~** lo dije con buena intención; **to return the ~** devolver el cumplido 2 **compliments** (= greetings) saludos mpl; **my ~s to the chef** mi enhorabuena al cocinero; **the ~s of the season** felicidades fpl; **"with compliments"** "con un atento saludo"; **with the ~s of the management** obsequio de la casa; **with the ~s of Mr Pearce** con un atento saludo del Sr. Pearce, de parte del Sr. Pearce Ⓑ ['kɒmplɪment] VT **to ~ sb on sth/on doing sth** felicitar a algn por algo/por haber hecho algo Ⓒ ['kɒmplɪmənt] CPD ➤ **compliment(s) slip** nota f de saludo, saluda m (Admin)

complimentary [ˌkɒmplɪ'mentərɪ] ADJ 1 [remark etc] elogioso; **he was very ~ about the play** habló de la obra en términos muy favorables 2 (= free) [book etc] de obsequio; **~ ticket** entrada f de regalo

comply [kəm'plaɪ] VI **to ~ with** [+ rules] cumplir; [+ laws] acatar; [+ orders] obedecer; [+ wishes, request] acceder a

component [kəm'pəʊnənt] Ⓐ ADJ componente; **its ~ parts** [of structure, device] las piezas que lo integran; [of organization, concept] las partes que lo integran Ⓑ N (= part) componente m; (Tech) pieza f Ⓒ CPD ➤ **components factory** fábrica f de componentes, maquiladora f (LAm)

compose [kəm'pəʊz] VT 1 [+ music] componer; [+ poetry, letter] escribir; **to be ~d of** constar de, componerse de 2 **to ~ o.s.** calmarse, serenarse

composed [kəm'pəʊzd] ADJ tranquilo, sereno

composer [kəm'pəʊzə⁽ʳ⁾] N compositor(a) m/f

composite ['kɒmpəzɪt] ADJ compuesto

composition [ˌkɒmpə'zɪʃən] N 1 (Mus) composición f; (Literat) redacción f 2 (Art) composición f

compos mentis ['kɒmpɒs'mentɪs] ADJ **to be ~** estar en su sano or entero juicio; (Jur) estar en pleno uso de sus facultades mentales

compost ['kɒmpɒst] N compost m, fertilizante m orgánico ➤ **compost heap** montón m de desechos para formar el compost

composure [kəm'pəʊʒə⁽ʳ⁾] N calma f, serenidad f; **to recover** or **regain one's ~** recobrar la calma

compound Ⓐ ['kɒmpaʊnd] N 1 (Chem) compuesto m 2 (= word) palabra f compuesta 3 (= place) recinto m (cercado) Ⓑ ['kɒmpaʊnd] ADJ 1 (Chem, Math) compuesto 2 [fracture] múltiple Ⓒ [kəm'paʊnd] VT [+ problem, difficulty] agravar Ⓓ ['kɒmpaʊnd] CPD ➤ **compound interest** interés m compuesto

comprehend [ˌkɒmprɪˈhend] VT, VI comprender
comprehensible [ˌkɒmprɪˈhensəbl] ADJ comprensible
comprehension [ˌkɒmprɪˈhenʃən] **Ⓐ** N
1 (= *understanding*) comprensión *f*; **it is beyond ~** es incomprensible **2** (*Scol*) prueba *f* de comprensión **Ⓑ** CPD ➤ **comprehension test** test *m* de comprensión
comprehensive [ˌkɒmprɪˈhensɪv] **Ⓐ** ADJ **1** [*list, guide, range*] completo; [*report, description, study*] exhaustivo; [*account, view*] de conjunto, integral; [*knowledge*] extenso; [*training*] completo, exhaustivo; [*victory, defeat*] aplastante
2 (*Brit Scol*) ~ **education** sistema de enseñanza secundaria que abarca a alumnos de todos los niveles de aptitud; ~ **school** instituto *m* (de segunda enseñanza)
3 [*insurance, policy, cover*] a todo riesgo
Ⓑ N (*Brit*) (*also* ~ **school**) instituto *m* (de segunda enseñanza)

COMPREHENSIVE SCHOOLS

La mayoría de las escuelas de educación secundaria en el Reino Unido se conocen como **comprehensive schools** y ofrecen una gran variedad de asignaturas para cubrir las necesidades educativas de alumnos con diferentes aptitudes. Fueron creadas en los años sesenta en un intento de fomentar la igualdad de oportunidades y acabar con la división tradicional entre los centros selectivos (**grammar schools**) de enseñanzas teóricas, y los centros o escuelas vocacionales (**secondary modern schools**).

comprehensively [ˌkɒmprɪˈhensɪvlɪ] ADV de forma exhaustiva
compress Ⓐ [kəmˈpres] VT (*gen*) comprimir; [+ *text*] condensar; **~ed air** aire *m* comprimido **Ⓑ** [ˈkɒmpres] N compresa *f*
compression [kəmˈpreʃən] N compresión *f*
comprise [kəmˈpraɪz] VT (= *include*) comprender; (= *be made up of*) constar de, consistir en
compromise [ˈkɒmprəmaɪz] **Ⓐ** N **1** (= *agreement*) arreglo *m*, solución *f* intermedia; **to reach a ~ (over sth)** llegar a un arreglo (sobre algo)
2 (= *giving in*) transigencia *f*; **there can be no ~ with treason** no transigimos con la traición
Ⓑ VI **1** (= *reach an agreement*) llegar a un arreglo; **so we ~d on seven** así que, ni para uno ni para otro, convinimos en siete
2 (= *give in*) transigir, contemporizar, transar (*LAm*); **to ~ with sb over sth** transigir con algn sobre algo; **to agree to ~ (with sb)** contemporizar (con algn); **in the end I agreed to ~** terminé accediendo (a lo que querían), terminamos llegando a un arreglo
Ⓒ VT **1** (= *endanger safety of*) poner en peligro
2 (= *bring under suspicion*) [+ *reputation, person*] comprometer; **to ~ o.s.** comprometerse
Ⓓ ADJ [*decision, solution*] intermedio
compulsion [kəmˈpʌlʃən] N **1** (= *urge*) compulsión *f*
2 (= *force*) **under ~** a la fuerza, bajo coacción; **you are under no ~** no tienes ninguna obligación
compulsive [kəmˈpʌlsɪv] ADJ compulsivo
compulsively [kəmˈpʌlsɪvlɪ] ADV compulsivamente
compulsory [kəmˈpʌlsərɪ] ADJ obligatorio
compunction [kəmˈpʌŋkʃən] N escrúpulo *m*
computation [ˌkɒmpjʊˈteɪʃən] N cómputo *m*, cálculo *m*
computer [kəmˈpjuːtəʳ] N ordenador *m* (*Sp*), computador *m* (*LAm*), computadora *f* (*LAm*); **the records have all been put on ~** todos los registros han entrado en (el) ordenador *or* (el) computador *or* (la) computadora; **she's in ~s** se dedica a la informática *or* (*LAm*) computación, trabaja en informática *or* (*LAm*) computación ➤ **computer crime** delito *m* informático ➤ **computer dating service** agencia *f* matrimonial por ordenador *or* (*LAm*) computador *or* computadora ➤ **computer expert** experto/a *m/f* en ordenadores *or* (*LAm*) computadores *or* computadoras ➤ **computer game** videojuego *m* ➤ **computer graphics**

gráficos *mpl* por ordenador *or* (*LAm*) computador *or* computadora ➤ **computer language** lenguaje *m* de ordenador *or* (*LAm*) computador *or* computadora ➤ **computer model** modelo *m* informático ➤ **computer operator** operador(a) *m/f* de ordenador *or* (*LAm*) computador *or* computadora ➤ **computer printout** impresión *f* (de ordenador *or* (*LAm*) computador *or* computadora) ➤ **computer program** programa *m* de ordenador *or* (*LAm*) computador *or* computadora ➤ **computer programmer** programador(a) *m/f* de ordenadores *or* (*LAm*) computadores *or* computadoras ➤ **computer programming** programación *f* de ordenadores *or* (*LAm*) computadores *or* computadoras ➤ **computer science** informática *f* ➤ **computer scientist** informático/a *m/f* ➤ **computer skills** conocimientos *mpl* de informática *or* (*LAm*) computación ➤ **computer studies** informática *fsing*, computación *fsing* (*LAm*) ➤ **computer user** usuario/a *m/f* de ordenador *or* (*LAm*) computador *or* computadora
computer-aided [kəmˌpjuːtəʳˈeɪdɪd], **computer-assisted** [kəmˌpjuːtərəˈsɪstɪd] ADJ asistido por ordenador *or* (*LAm*) computador *or* computadora
computer-generated [kəmˌpjuːtəˈdʒenəreɪtɪd] ADJ [*graphics, images*] realizado *or* creado por ordenador *or* (*LAm*) computador *or* computadora
computerization [kəmˌpjuːtəraɪˈzeɪʃən] N [*of organization, system*] informatización *f*; [*of data, records*] computerización *f*, computarización *f*, informatización *f*
computerize [kəmˈpjuːtəraɪz] VT [+ *system, accounts, organization*] informatizar; [+ *data, records*] computerizar, computarizar, informatizar; **we're ~d now** ahora estamos informatizados
computer-literate [kəmˌpjuːtəˈlɪtərɪt] ADJ **to be computer literate** saber cómo utilizar un ordenador *or* (*LAm*) un computador *or* una computadora
computing [kəmˈpjuːtɪŋ] N informática *f*, computación *f* (*LAm*)
comrade [ˈkɒmrɪd] N compañero/a *m/f*, camarada *mf*; (*Pol*) camarada *mf*
comradeship [ˈkɒmrɪdʃɪp] N compañerismo *m*, camaradería *f*
con¹* [kɒn] **Ⓐ** VT estafar, timar; **I've been ~ned!** ¡me han estafado!; **to ~ sb into doing sth** engañar a algn para que haga algo **Ⓑ** N estafa *f*, timo *m* **Ⓒ** CPD ➤ **con artist**, **con man** estafador(a) *m/f*, timador(a) *m/f* ➤ **con trick** timo *m*, estafa *f*
con² [kɒn] N (= *disadvantage*) contra *m*; **the pros and ~s** los pros y los contras
Con. ABBR (*Brit*) = **Conservative**
conc. ABBR (= **concessions**): **admission £5 (~ £4)** entrada: cinco libras (tarifa reducida: cuatro libras) (*para jubilados, parados, estudiantes, etc*)
concave [ˈkɒnkeɪv] ADJ cóncavo
conceal [kənˈsiːl] VT [+ *object, news*] ocultar; [+ *emotions, thoughts*] disimular; (*Jur*) encubrir
concealment [kənˈsiːlmənt] N [*of object*] ocultación *f*; [*of emotion*] disimulación *f*; (*Jur*) encubrimiento *m*
concede [kənˈsiːd] **Ⓐ** VT [+ *point, argument*] reconocer, conceder; [+ *game, territory*] ceder; **to ~ that** admitir que; **to ~ defeat** darse por vencido **Ⓑ** VI ceder, darse por vencido
conceit [kənˈsiːt] N vanidad *f*, presunción *f*, engreimiento *m*
conceited [kənˈsiːtɪd] ADJ vanidoso, engreído; **to be ~ about** envanecerse con *or* de *or* por
conceivable [kənˈsiːvəbl] ADJ imaginable, concebible
conceivably [kənˈsiːvəblɪ] ADV **you may ~ be right** es posible que tenga razón
conceive [kənˈsiːv] **Ⓐ** VT **1** [+ *child*] concebir **2** (= *think*) **I cannot ~ why** no entiendo porqué **Ⓑ** VI **1** (= *become pregnant*) concebir **2** (= *think*) **to ~ of sth** imaginar algo; **to ~ of doing sth** imaginarse haciendo algo
concentrate [ˈkɒnsəntreɪt] **Ⓐ** VT concentrar; **heavy industry is ~d in the north of the country** la industria

pesada se concentra en el norte del país
B VI **1** (= *pay attention*) concentrarse (**on** en)
2 (= *focus on*) **to ~ on sth** centrarse en algo; **the talks are expected to ~ on practical issues** se espera que las conversaciones se centren en cuestiones prácticas; **to ~ on doing sth** concentrarse or centrarse en hacer algo
3 (= *come together*) [*troops, crowd*] concentrarse, reunirse
C N (*Chem*) concentrado *m*

concentration [ˌkɒnsən'treɪʃən] N concentración *f*
➤ **concentration camp** campo *m* de concentración

concentric [kən'sentrɪk] ADJ concéntrico

concept ['kɒnsept] N concepto *m*; **have you any ~ of how hard it is?** ¿tienes idea de lo difícil que es?

conception [kən'sepʃən] N **1** [*of child, idea*] concepción *f*
2 (= *idea*) concepto *m*; **he has not the remotest ~ of ...** no tiene ni la menor idea de ...

concern [kən'sɜːn] **A** N **1** (= *business*) asunto *m*; **it's no ~ of yours** no es asunto tuyo; **what ~ is it of yours?** ¿qué tiene que ver contigo?
2 (= *anxiety*) preocupación *f*; **his health is giving cause for ~** su salud está dando motivo de preocupación
3 (= *interest, regard*) interés *m*; **my main ~ is ...** mi interés principal or lo que más me preocupa es ...; **it's of no ~ to me** me tiene sin cuidado, a mí no me importa; **out of ~ for the public's safety** por la seguridad pública
4 (= *firm*) negocio *m*, empresa *f*; **a going ~** un negocio próspero, una empresa próspera
B VT **1** (= *affect*) afectar, concernir
2 (= *interest, involve*) **please contact the department ~ed** póngase en contacto con la sección correspondiente; **it is best for all ~ed** es lo mejor para todas las partes interesadas; **as far as I am ~ed** por or en lo que a mí se refiere, por or en lo que a mí respecta; **I was just another student as far as he was ~ed** para él yo no era más que otra estudiante; **to ~ o.s. with sth**: **don't ~ yourself with things you can do nothing about** no te preocupes por cosas que están fuera de tu alcance; **those ~ed** los interesados; **to whom it may ~** a quien corresponda; **essential reading for anyone ~ed with children** lecturas fundamentales para cualquiera al que le interesen los niños
3 (= *be about*) **chapter two is ~ed with the civil war** el capítulo dos trata de la guerra civil
4 (= *worry*) preocupar; **it ~s me that ...** me preocupa el hecho de que ...

concerned [kən'sɜːnd] ADJ (= *worried*) preocupado; **to be ~ about sth/sb** estar preocupado por algo/algn; **to be ~ for sth/sb** estar preocupado por algo/algn; **he was ~ that he might have hurt her** le preocupaba que pudiera haberle hecho daño

concerning [kən'sɜːnɪŋ] PREP **1** (= *with regard to*) con respecto a, con relación a, en lo que se refiere a (*frm*)
2 (= *about*) sobre, acerca de; **theories ~ evolution** teorías sobre or acerca de la evolución; **something ~ his mother** algo que tenía que ver con su madre, algo relacionado con su madre

concert ['kɒnsət] N concierto *m*; **to give a ~** dar un concierto; **in ~ (with)** (*Mus*) en concierto (con) ➤ **concert hall** sala *f* de conciertos ➤ **concert pianist** pianista *mf* de concierto ➤ **concert tour** gira *f* de conciertos

concerted [kən'sɜːtɪd] ADJ [*campaign, attack*] coordinado, organizado; [*attempt*] coordinado, concertado; **to make a ~ effort (to do sth)** aunar or coordinar los esfuerzos (por hacer algo)

concertina [ˌkɒnsə'tiːnə] **A** N concertina *f* **B** VI **the vehicles ~ed into each other** los vehículos quedaron hechos un acordeón

concertmaster ['kɒnsət,mɑːstəʳ] N (*US*) primer violín *m*

concerto [kən'tʃɛətəʊ] N concierto *m*

concession [kən'seʃən] N concesión *f*; (*on tax*) desgravación *f*, exención *f*; **price ~** reducción *f*

concessionaire [kən,seʃə'nɛəʳ] N (*US*) concesionario/a *m/f*

concessionary [kən'seʃənərɪ] ADJ [*ticket, fare*] reducido

conciliation [kən,sɪlɪ'eɪʃən] N conciliación *f*

conciliatory [kən'sɪlɪətərɪ] ADJ conciliador

concise [kən'saɪs] ADJ conciso

concisely [kən'saɪslɪ] ADV concisamente, con concisión

conclave ['kɒnkleɪv] N cónclave *m*

conclude [kən'kluːd] **A** VT **1** (= *end*) acabar, concluir; **"to be concluded"** [*serial*] "terminará en el próximo episodio"
2 (= *finalize*) [+ *treaty*] concertar, pactar; [+ *deal*] cerrar
3 (= *infer*) concluir; **it was ~d that ...** se concluyó que ...; **what are we to ~ from that?** ¿que conclusión se saca de eso? **B** VI terminar, concluir; **he ~d by saying** terminó diciendo

concluding [kən'kluːdɪŋ] ADJ final

conclusion [kən'kluːʒən] N **1** (= *end*) conclusión *f*, término *m*; **in ~** para concluir or terminar, en conclusión; **to bring sth to a ~** concluir algo **2** (= *inference*) conclusión *f*; **to come to the ~ that** llegar a la conclusión de que; **to jump to ~s** sacar conclusiones precipitadas

conclusive [kən'kluːsɪv] ADJ concluyente

conclusively [kən'kluːsɪvlɪ] ADV concluyentemente

concoct [kən'kɒkt] VT [+ *food, drink*] confeccionar; [+ *lie, story*] inventar; [+ *plot*] tramar, fraguar

concoction [kən'kɒkʃən] N (= *food*) mezcla *f*, mejunje *m*; (= *drink*) brebaje *m*

concord ['kɒnkɔːd] N **1** (= *harmony*) concordia *f*
2 (= *treaty*) acuerdo *m*

concourse ['kɒnkɔːs] N **1** (*in building, station*) explanada *f*
2 [*of people*] concurrencia *f*

concrete ['kɒnkriːt] **A** ADJ **1** (= *not abstract*) concreto
2 (*Constr*) de hormigón or (*LAm*) concreto **B** N hormigón *m*, concreto *m* (*LAm*) **C** VT **to ~ a path** cubrir un sendero de hormigón **D** CPD ➤ **concrete jungle** jungla *f* de asfalto
➤ **concrete mixer** hormigonera *f* ➤ **concrete noun** nombre *m* concreto

concubine ['kɒnkjʊbaɪn] N concubina *f*

concur [kən'kɜːʳ] VI **1** (= *agree*) estar de acuerdo (**with** con)
2 (= *happen at the same time*) concurrir

concurrent [kən'kʌrənt] ADJ concurrente (**with** con)

concurrently [kən'kʌrəntlɪ] ADV al mismo tiempo, simultáneamente

concussed [kən'kʌst] ADJ **to be ~** sufrir una conmoción cerebral

concussion [kən'kʌʃən] N conmoción *f* cerebral

condemn [kən'dem] VT (= *sentence*) condenar; (= *censure*) condenar, censurar; [+ *building*] declarar en ruina; **to ~ sb to death** condenar a algn a muerte; **the ~ed cell** (*Brit*) la celda de los condenados a muerte; **the ~ed man** el reo de muerte

condemnation [ˌkɒndem'neɪʃən] N condena *f*, censura *f*

condemnatory [ˌkɒndem'neɪtərɪ] ADJ condenatorio

condensation [ˌkɒnden'seɪʃən] N **1** (= *vapour*) vaho *m*
2 (= *summary*) resumen *m*

condense [kən'dens] **A** VT **1** [+ *vapour*] condensar; **~d milk** leche *f* condensada **2** [+ *text*] abreviar, resumir **B** VI condensarse

condenser [kən'densəʳ] N condensador *m*

condescend [ˌkɒndɪ'send] VI **to ~ to sb** tratar a algn con condescendencia; **to ~ to do sth** dignarse (a) hacer algo, condescender a hacer algo

condescending [ˌkɒndɪ'sendɪŋ] ADJ [*attitude, tone, smile*] condescendiente; **he's very ~** tiene una actitud muy condescendiente, se cree muy superior; **to be ~ towards sb** tratar a algn con condescendencia

condiment ['kɒndɪmənt] N condimento *m*

condition [kən'dɪʃən] **A** N **1** (= *state*) condición *f*, estado *m*; **in good ~** en buenas condiciones, en buen estado; **to be in no ~ to do sth** no estar en condiciones de hacer algo; **to be out of ~** no estar en forma; **weather ~s** estado del tiempo; **working ~s** condiciones de trabajo
2 (= *stipulation*) condición *f*; **on ~ that** a condición de que; **on no ~** bajo ningún concepto; **I'll do it on one ~** lo haré, con una condición
3 (= *circumstance*) circunstancia *f*; **under existing ~s** en las circunstancias actuales

4 (= *disease*) enfermedad *f*, padecimiento *m*; **he has a heart ~** tiene una afección cardíaca
5 (*social*) clase *f*
Ⓑ VT **1** (= *make healthy*) [+ *hair*] condicionar
2 (= *determine*) determinar; **to be ~ed by** depender de
3 (*Psych*) condicionar

conditional [kənˈdɪʃənl] ADJ condicional; **~ offer** oferta *f* condicional; **~ tense/clause** tiempo *m*/oración *f* condicional; **to be ~ upon** depender de

conditionally [kənˈdɪʃnəlɪ] ADV condicionalmente, con reservas

conditioner [kənˈdɪʃənəʳ] N (*for hair*) suavizante *m*, acondicionador *m* (*LAm*), enjuague *m* (*LAm*); (*for skin*) crema *f* suavizante; (= *fabric conditioner*) suavizante *m*

conditioning [kənˈdɪʃənɪŋ] N condicionamiento *m*

condo [ˈkɒndəʊ] N (*US*) = **condominium**

condolence [kənˈdəʊləns] N pésame *m*; **to send one's ~s** dar el pésame; **please accept my ~s** le acompaño en el sentimiento

condom [ˈkɒndəm] N condón *m*, preservativo *m*

condominium [ˌkɒndəˈmɪnɪəm] N (*US*) (= *building*) bloque *m* de pisos, condominio *m* (*LAm*) (*en copropiedad con los que lo habitan*); (= *apartment*) piso *m* or apartamento *m* (*en propiedad*), condominio *m* (*LAm*)

condone [kənˈdəʊn] VT consentir, tolerar

conducive [kənˈdjuːsɪv] ADJ **~ to** conducente a

conduct Ⓐ [ˈkɒndʌkt] N comportamiento *m*, conducta *f*
Ⓑ [kənˈdʌkt] VT **1** (= *guide*) llevar, conducir; **~ed tour** visita *f* con guía **2** [+ *heat, electricity*] conducir **3** [+ *campaign*] dirigir, llevar; [+ *legal case*] presentar; (*Mus*) dirigir
4 (= *behave*) **to ~ o.s.** comportarse **Ⓒ** [kənˈdʌkt] VI (*Mus*) dirigir

conductivity [ˌkɒndʌkˈtɪvɪtɪ] N conductividad *f*

conductor [kənˈdʌktəʳ] N **1** (*Mus*) director(a) *m/f*; (*on bus*) cobrador(a) *m/f*; (*US Rail*) revisor(a) *m/f* **2** (*Phys*) [*of heat, electricity*] conductor *m*; (*also* **lightning ~**) pararrayos *m inv*

conduit [ˈkɒndɪt, ˈkɒndjʊɪt] N conducto *m*

cone [kəʊn] N **1** (*Math*) cono *m*; **traffic ~** cono *m* señalizador **2** (*Bot*) piña *f* **3** (*also* **ice cream ~**) cucurucho *m*

confectioner [kənˈfekʃənəʳ] N confitero/a *m/f*; **~'s (shop)** confitería *f*, dulcería *f* (*LAm*) ➤ **confectioners' sugar** (*US*) azúcar *m* glas(eado)

confectionery [kənˈfekʃənərɪ] N (= *sweets*) dulces *mpl*, golosinas *fpl*; (*Brit*) (= *cakes*) pasteles *mpl*

confederacy [kənˈfedərəsɪ] N (= *alliance*) confederación *f*; (= *plot*) complot *m*; **the Confederacy** (*US*) los Estados Confederados

confederate [kənˈfedərɪt] N **1** (= *accomplice*) cómplice *mf* **2** (*US Hist*) confederado/a *m/f*

confederation [kənˌfedəˈreɪʃən] N confederación *f*

confer [kənˈfɜːʳ] **Ⓐ** VT **to ~ sth on sb** [+ *honour*] conceder *or* otorgar algo a algn; [+ *title*] conferir *or* conceder algo a algn **Ⓑ** VI confenciar, estar en consultas; **to ~ with sb** consultar con algn

conference [ˈkɒnfərəns] N (= *discussion, meeting*) reunión *f*, conferencia *f*; (= *assembly*) asamblea *f*, congreso *m*; (*party political, academic*) congreso *m* ➤ **conference centre**, **conference center** (*US*) (= *building*) palacio *m* de congresos; (*in institution*) centro *m* de conferencias ➤ **conference hall** sala *f* de conferencias or congresos ➤ **conference member** congresista *mf* ➤ **conference room** sala *f* de conferencias ➤ **conference table** mesa *f* negociadora

confess [kənˈfes] **Ⓐ** VT [+ *crime, sin*] confesar; [+ *guilt, error*] confesar, reconocer; **to ~ that ...** confesar que ...; **to ~ one's guilt** confesar *or* reconocer ser culpable; **to ~ o.s. guilty of** [+ *sin, crime*] confesarse culpable de
Ⓑ VI **1** (= *admit*) confesar; **he ~ed to the murder** se confesó culpable del asesinato, confesó haber cometido el asesinato; **to ~ to having done sth** confesarse culpable de haber hecho algo; **I must ~, I like your car** debo reconocer que me gusta tu coche; **to ~ to a liking for sth** reconocerse aficionado a algo
2 (*Rel*) confesarse

confession [kənˈfeʃən] N **1** (= *act, document*) confesión *f*; **to make a ~** confesar, hacer una confesión **2** (*Rel*) **to go to ~** confesarse; **to hear sb's ~** confesar a algn

confessional [kənˈfeʃənl] N confesionario *m*

confessor [kənˈfesəʳ] N (= *priest*) confesor *m*; (= *spiritual adviser*) director *m* espiritual

confetti [kənˈfetiː] N confeti *m*

confidant [ˌkɒnfɪˈdænt] N confidente *m*

confidante [ˌkɒnfɪˈdænt] N confidenta *f*

confide [kənˈfaɪd] **Ⓐ** VT [+ *secret*] confiar; **he ~d to me that ...** me confió que ..., me dijo en confianza que ...
Ⓑ VI **to ~ in sb** confiarse a algn

confidence [ˈkɒnfɪdəns] **Ⓐ** N **1** (= *trust*) confianza *f*; **to have (every) ~ in sb** tener (entera) confianza en algn; **to have (every) ~ that** estar seguro de que; **a motion of no ~** moción *f* de censura; **to put one's ~ in sth/sb** confiar en algo/algn
2 (*also* **self-~**) confianza *f* (en sí mismo), seguridad *f* (en sí mismo)
3 (= *secrecy*) confianza *f*; **in ~** en confianza; **to take sb into one's ~** confiarse a algn
Ⓑ CPD ➤ **confidence man** (*US*) timador *m*, estafador *m* ➤ **confidence trick** (*esp Brit*), **confidence game** (*US*) timo *m*, estafa *f* ➤ **confidence trickster** timador(a) *m/f*, estafador(a) *m/f*

confident [ˈkɒnfɪdənt] ADJ [*person*] seguro, seguro de sí mismo; [*prediction*] hecho con seguridad *or* confianza; [*performance, smile, manner*] lleno de seguridad *or* confianza; **to be ~ that** estar seguro de que; **to be ~ of doing sth** confiar en hacer algo; **he is ~ of success** confía en obtener el éxito; **to be ~ about sth** tener confianza en algo; **to be in ~ mood** estar lleno de confianza

confidential [ˌkɒnfɪˈdenʃəl] ADJ [*information*] confidencial, secreto; [*tone of voice*] de confianza

confidentiality [ˌkɒnfɪˌdenʃɪˈælɪtɪ] N confidencialidad *f*

confidentially [ˌkɒnfɪˈdenʃəlɪ] ADV confidencialmente, en confianza

confidently [ˈkɒnfɪdəntlɪ] ADV [*predict, promise*] con seguridad, con confianza; [*smile, enter*] con seguridad; [*speak, reply*] con un tono de seguridad *or* confianza; **"sure," he said** —claro —dijo lleno de confianza

configuration [kənˌfɪgjʊˈreɪʃən] N configuración *f*

confine [kənˈfaɪn] VT **1** (= *imprison*) encerrar (**in, to** en); **to be ~d to bed** tener que guardar cama **2** (= *limit*) limitar; **to ~ o.s. to doing sth** limitarse a hacer algo; **please ~ yourself to the facts** por favor, limítese a los hechos; **the damage is ~d to this part** el daño afecta sólo a esta parte

confined [kənˈfaɪnd] ADJ [*space*] reducido

confinement [kənˈfaɪnmənt] N **1** (= *imprisonment*) prisión *f*, reclusión *f*; **to be in solitary ~** estar incomunicado **2** (*Med†*) parto *m*

confines [ˈkɒnfaɪnz] NPL confines *mpl*, límites *mpl*

confirm [kənˈfɜːm] VT confirmar

confirmation [ˌkɒnfəˈmeɪʃən] N confirmación *f*

confirmed [kənˈfɜːmd] ADJ [*bachelor, alcoholic*] empedernido; [*atheist*] inveterado, redomado

confiscate [ˈkɒnfɪskeɪt] VT confiscar, incautarse de

confiscation [ˌkɒnfɪsˈkeɪʃən] N confiscación *f*, incautación *f*

conflate [kənˈfleɪt] VT combinar

conflict Ⓐ [ˈkɒnflɪkt] N conflicto *m*; **in ~ with** en conflicto con; **~ of interests** conflicto *m* de intereses, incompatibilidad *f* (de intereses) **Ⓑ** [kənˈflɪkt] VI [*ideas, evidence, statements etc*] estar reñido (**with** con); [*interests*] estar en conflicto (**with** con); **that ~s with what he told me** eso contradice lo que me dijo

conflicting [kənˈflɪktɪŋ] ADJ [*reports, evidence*] contradictorio; [*interests*] opuesto

confluence [ˈkɒnflʊəns] N confluencia *f*

conform [kənˈfɔːm] VI (*to laws*) someterse (**to** a); (*to standards*) ajustarse (**to** a); (*socially*) adaptarse, amoldarse

conformist [kənˈfɔːmɪst] ADJ, N conformista *mf*

conformity [kənˈfɔːmɪtɪ] N conformidad f

confound [kənˈfaʊnd] VT pasmar, desconcertar

confront [kənˈfrʌnt] VT (= face squarely) hacer frente a; (= face defiantly) enfrentarse con; **to ~ sb with sth** confrontar a algn con algo; **to ~ sb with the facts** exponer delante de algn los hechos; **the problems which ~ us** los problemas con los que nos enfrentamos

confrontation [ˌkɒnfrənˈteɪʃən] N enfrentamiento m, confrontación f

confrontational [ˌkɒnfrənˈteɪʃənəl] ADJ confrontacional, agresivo

confuse [kənˈfjuːz] VT **1** (= perplex) confundir, desconcertar **2** (= mix up) confundir; **to ~ the issue** complicar el asunto

confused [kənˈfjuːzd] ADJ **1** [situation etc] confuso **2** (= perplexed) confuso, confundido, desconcertado; **to be ~** estar confuso or confundido; **to get ~** hacerse un lío; **his mind is ~** tiene la cabeza trastornada

confusing [kənˈfjuːzɪŋ] ADJ confuso; **it's all very ~** es muy difícil de entender

confusion [kənˈfjuːʒən] N **1** (= disorder) desorden m; **to be in ~** estar en desorden **2** (= perplexity) confusión f, desorientación f **3** (= commotion) confusión f

congeal [kənˈdʒiːl] VI coagularse, cuajarse

congenial [kənˈdʒiːnɪəl] ADJ [place, atmosphere] agradable; [person, company] simpático, agradable

congenital [kənˈdʒenɪtl] ADJ congénito

congested [kənˈdʒestɪd] ADJ **1** (with traffic) congestionado; (with people) atestado de gente **2** (Med) congestionado

congestion [kənˈdʒestʃən] **Ⓐ** N **1** [of traffic] congestión f; [of people] aglomeración f **2** (Med) congestión f **Ⓑ** CPD ➤ **congestion charge(s)** tasa fsing por congestión

conglomerate [kənˈglɒmərɪt] N conglomerado m

conglomeration [kənˌglɒməˈreɪʃən] N conglomeración f

Congo [ˈkɒŋgəʊ] N **the ~** el Congo

congratulate [kənˈgrætjʊleɪt] VT felicitar; **to ~ sb (on sth/ on doing sth)** felicitar a algn (por algo/por hacer algo)

congratulations [kənˌgrætjʊˈleɪʃənz] NPL felicitaciones fpl (on por); **~!** ¡enhorabuena!, ¡felicidades!; **~ on your new job!** ¡enhorabuena or felicidades por tu nuevo trabajo!

congregate [ˈkɒngrɪgeɪt] VI reunirse, congregarse

congregation [ˌkɒngrɪˈgeɪʃən] N **1** (Rel) fieles mpl, feligreses mpl **2** (= assembly) reunión f

congress [ˈkɒngres] N congreso m; **Congress** el Congreso

congressional [kɒŋˈgreʃənl] ADJ del congreso

congressman [ˈkɒŋgresmən] N (pl **congressmen**) (US) diputado m, miembro m del Congreso

congresswoman [ˈkɒŋgresˌwʊmən] N (pl **congresswomen**) (US) diputada f, miembro f del Congreso

conical [ˈkɒnɪkəl] ADJ cónico

conifer [ˈkɒnɪfəʳ] N conífera f

coniferous [kəˈnɪfərəs] ADJ conífero

conjecture [kənˈdʒektʃəʳ] **Ⓐ** N **it's only ~** son conjeturas, nada más **Ⓑ** VT, VI conjeturar

conjoined [kɒnˈdʒɔɪnd] ADJ: **conjoined twins** (gemelos/as mpl/fpl) siameses/as mpl/fpl

conjugal [ˈkɒndʒʊgəl] ADJ conyugal

conjugate [ˈkɒndʒʊgeɪt] **Ⓐ** VT conjugar **Ⓑ** VI conjugarse

conjugation [ˌkɒndʒʊˈgeɪʃən] N conjugación f

conjunction [kənˈdʒʌŋkʃən] N **1** (Gram) conjunción f **2 in ~ with** junto con, juntamente con

conjunctivitis [kənˌdʒʌŋktɪˈvaɪtɪs] N conjuntivitis f

conjure [ˈkʌndʒəʳ] VI hacer juegos de manos; **a name to ~ with** un personaje importante, una figura destacada ➤ **conjure up** VT + ADV **1** [+ rabbit etc] hacer aparecer **2** [+ memories, visions] evocar; [+ meal] preparar en un abrir y cerrar de ojos

conjurer, conjuror [ˈkʌndʒərəʳ] N ilusionista mf, prestidigitador(a) m/f

conjuring [ˈkʌndʒərɪŋ] N ilusionismo m, prestidigitación f ➤ **conjuring trick** juego m de manos

conker* [ˈkɒŋkəʳ] N (Brit) castaña f de Indias; **conkers** (= game) juego msing de las castañas

conk out* [ˌkɒŋkˈaʊt] VI + ADV **1** (= break down) averiarse, fastidiarse*, descomponerse (LAm) **2** (= die) estirar la pata*; (= fall asleep) dormir como un tronco*

Conn. ABBR (US) = **Connecticut**

connect [kəˈnekt] **Ⓐ** VT **1** (= join) conectar; [+ road, railway, airline] unir; [+ pipes, drains] empalmar (**to** a); **to ~ sth (up) to the mains** conectar algo a la red eléctrica **2** (= install) [+ cooker, telephone] conectar **3** (Telec) [+ caller] poner (Sp), comunicar (LAm) (**with** con); **please ~ me with Mr Lyons** póngame (Sp) or comuníqueme (LAm) con el Sr. Lyons, por favor; **"I am trying to ~ you"** "estoy intentando ponerle al habla" (Sp), "estoy tratando de comunicarlo con el número/la extensión/el Sr X etc" (LAm) **4** (= associate) vincular, asociar (**with** con) **Ⓑ** VI [trains, planes] enlazar (**with** con); [road, pipes, electricity] empalmar (**with** con)

connected [kəˈnektɪd] ADJ [concepts, events] relacionado; **to be ~ to** or **with** estar relacionado con; **are these matters ~?** ¿tienen alguna relación entre sí estas cuestiones?; **to be well ~** estar bien relacionado

connecting [kəˈnektɪŋ] ADJ [rooms etc] comunicado; **bedroom with ~ bathroom** habitación comunicada con el baño ➤ **connecting flight** vuelo m de enlace

connection, connexion [kəˈnekʃən] N **1** (Rail etc) enlace m; (Elec, Tech) conexión f, empalme m; (Telec) línea f, comunicación f; **we missed our ~** perdimos el enlace; **to make a ~** hacer enlace, empalmar; **our ~s with the town are poor** son malas nuestras comunicaciones con la ciudad; **there's a loose ~** hay un hilo suelto **2** (= relationship) relación f (**between** entre; **with** con); **in ~ with** en relación a, con respecto a; **there's no ~ between the two events** no hay ninguna relación or conexión entre los dos sucesos **3 connections** (= relatives) parientes mpl; (= business connections) relaciones fpl, contactos mpl; **you have to have ~s** hay que tener buenos contactos

connivance [kəˈnaɪvəns] N connivencia f (frm), complicidad f

connive [kəˈnaɪv] VI **1** (= conspire) confabularse; **to ~ with sb to do sth** confabularse con algn para hacer algo **2** (= turn a blind eye) hacer la vista gorda (**at** a)

conniving [kəˈnaɪvɪŋ] ADJ intrigante, mañoso

connoisseur [ˌkɒnəˈsɜːʳ] N conocedor(a) m/f, entendido/a m/f (**of** en)

connotation [ˌkɒnəʊˈteɪʃən] N connotación f

conquer [ˈkɒŋkəʳ] VT [+ territory, nation etc] conquistar; [+ fear, enemy] vencer

conqueror [ˈkɒŋkərəʳ] N conquistador(a) m/f

conquest [ˈkɒŋkwest] N conquista f

Cons. ABBR (Brit) = **Conservative**

conscience [ˈkɒnʃəns] N conciencia f; **in all ~** en conciencia; **to have a clear ~** tener la conciencia tranquila or limpia; **I have a guilty ~ (about it)** me remuerde la conciencia (por ello); **to have sth on one's ~** tener algo pesando sobre la conciencia, tener cargo or remordimiento de conciencia por algo

conscientious [ˌkɒnʃɪˈenʃəs] ADJ concienzudo ➤ **conscientious objector** objetor(a) m/f de conciencia

conscious ['kɒnʃəs] ADJ 1 (= *aware*) **to be ~ of sth/of doing sth** ser consciente de algo/de hacer algo; **to be ~ that** tener (plena) conciencia de que; **to become ~ of sth/that** darse cuenta de algo/de que; **politically ~** con conciencia política 2 (= *deliberate*) [*decision*] deliberado; [*error, irony, insult*] intencional, deliberado; **they made a ~ choice** *or* **decision not to have children** decidieron deliberadamente no tener hijos 3 (*Med*) consciente; **to be ~** estar consciente, tener conocimiento; **to be fully ~** estar totalmente consciente 4 (*Psych*) [*memory, thought*] consciente; **the ~ mind** la conciencia

-conscious [ˌkɒnʃəs] ADJ (*ending in compounds*) **security-conscious** consciente de los problemas relativos a la seguridad

consciously ['kɒnʃəslɪ] ADV 1 (= *deliberately*) conscientemente, deliberadamente 2 (= *with full awareness*) [*remember, think*] conscientemente; **to be ~ aware of sth** ser plenamente consciente de algo

consciousness ['kɒnʃəsnɪs] N 1 (= *awareness*) conciencia *f*, consciencia *f* (**of** de) 2 (*Med*) conocimiento *m*; **to lose ~** perder el conocimiento; **to regain ~** recobrar el conocimiento, volver en sí

conscript ❶ ['kɒnskrɪpt] N (*Brit*) recluta *mf*, conscripto/a *m/f* (*LAm*) ❷ [kən'skrɪpt] VT reclutar, llamar a filas

conscription [kən'skrɪpʃən] N servicio *m* militar obligatorio, conscripción *f* (*LAm*)

consecrate ['kɒnsɪkreɪt] VT consagrar

consecutive [kən'sekjʊtɪv] ADJ consecutivo; **on three ~ days** tres días consecutivos *or* seguidos

consecutively [kən'sekjʊtɪvlɪ] ADV consecutivamente

consensus [kən'sensəs] N consenso *m*; **the ~ of opinion** el consenso general

consent [kən'sent] ❶ N consentimiento *m*; **the age of ~** *edad en que a los adolescentes se los considera responsable de sus actos sexuales;* **by common ~** de *or* por común acuerdo ❷ VI **to ~ (to sth/to do sth)** consentir (en algo/en hacer algo); **between ~ing adults** entre personas de edad para consentir

consequence ['kɒnsɪkwəns] N 1 (= *result*) consecuencia *f*; **to take the ~s** aceptar las consecuencias; **in ~** por consiguiente, por lo tanto; **as a ~ of (which)** como consecuencia de (lo cual) 2 (= *importance*) importancia *f*, trascendencia *f*; **it is of no ~** no tiene importancia, es de poca trascendencia

consequent ['kɒnsɪkwənt] ADJ consiguiente

consequently ['kɒnsɪkwəntlɪ] ADV por consiguiente, por lo tanto

conservation [ˌkɒnsə'veɪʃən] N conservación *f*, protección *f* ➤ **conservation area** (*Brit*) (= *buildings*) zona *f* declarada patrimonio histórico-artístico; (= *nature reserve*) zona *f* protegida

conservationist [ˌkɒnsə'veɪʃənɪst] N conservacionista *mf*, ecologista *mf*

conservatism [kən'sɜ:vətɪzəm] N conservadurismo *m*

Conservative [kən'sɜ:vətɪv] (*Brit*) ❶ ADJ conservador; **~ Party** Partido *m* Conservador ❷ N conservador(a) *m/f*

conservative [kən'sɜ:vətɪv] ADJ 1 (= *conventional*) conservador 2 (= *cautious*) prudente, cauteloso

conservatory [kən'sɜ:vətrɪ] N invernadero *m*

conserve [kən'sɜ:v] VT [+ *environment, historic buildings*] conservar, preservar; [+ *moisture*] conservar; [+ *energy, water*] ahorrar, conservar; **to ~ one's energies** ahorrar (las) energías

consider [kən'sɪdə'] VT 1 (= *think about*) [+ *problem, possibility*] considerar, pensar en; **have you ever ~ed going by train?** ¿has pensado alguna vez (en) ir en tren?, ¿has considerado alguna vez ir en tren?; **he is being ~ed for the post** lo están considerando para el puesto; **we are ~ing the matter** estamos estudiando el asunto 2 (= *take into account*) tomar *or* tener en cuenta; **when one ~s that ...** cuando uno toma *or* tiene en cuenta que ... ; **all**

things **~ed** pensándolo bien 3 (= *think*) considerar; **I ~ that ...** considero que ...; **I ~ myself happy** me considero feliz; **to ~ sb to be intelligent** considerar a algn inteligente; **I ~ it an honour** lo considero un honor; **I ~ the matter closed** para mí el tema está cerrado; **~ yourself lucky!** ¡date por satisfecho!

considerable [kən'sɪdərəbl] ADJ considerable; **they achieved a ~ degree of success** tuvieron un éxito considerable; **we had ~ difficulty** tuvimos bastante dificultad; **I'd been living in England for a ~ time** llevaba bastante tiempo viviendo en Inglaterra; **to a ~ extent** en gran parte

considerably [kən'sɪdərəblɪ] ADV bastante, considerablemente

considerate [kən'sɪdərɪt] ADJ atento, considerado; **to be ~ towards** ser atento con

considerately [kən'sɪdərɪtlɪ] ADV con consideración

consideration [kənˌsɪdə'reɪʃən] N 1 (= *thought*) consideración *f*; **after due ~** tras (darle) la debida consideración; **in ~ of** en consideración a; **to take sth into ~** tener *or* tomar algo en cuenta *or* consideración; **the issue is under ~** la cuestión se está estudiando 2 (= *thoughtfulness*) consideración *f*; **out of ~ for sb/sb's feelings** por consideración a algn/los sentimientos de algn; **to show ~ for sb** respetar a algn 3 (= *factor*) factor *m*; **his age is an important ~** su edad es un factor importante; **that is a ~** eso debe tomarse en cuenta; **money is the main ~** el dinero es la consideración principal

considering [kən'sɪdərɪŋ] ❶ PREP teniendo en cuenta, en vista de; **~ the circumstances** teniendo en cuenta las circunstancias ❷ CONJ (*also* **~ that**) en vista de que, teniendo en cuenta que ❸ ADV después de todo, a fin de cuentas; **I got a good mark, ~** después de todo *or* a fin de cuentas, saqué buena nota

consign [kən'saɪn] VT 1 (*frm*) (= *commit, entrust*) confiar 2 (*Comm*) (= *send*) enviar, consignar

consignment [kən'saɪnmənt] N envío *m*, remesa *f* ➤ **consignment note** talón *m* de expedición

consist [kən'sɪst] VI **to ~ of** constar de, consistir en; **to ~ in sth/in doing sth** consistir en algo/en hacer algo

consistency [kən'sɪstənsɪ] N 1 (= *constancy*) [*of person, action, behaviour*] coherencia *f*, uniformidad *f*; [*of results*] la regularidad; **the manager was impressed by the ~ of her work** el jefe quedó impresionado por la calidad que caracterizaba todo su trabajo 2 (= *cohesion*) [*of argument*] coherencia *f*, lógica *f*; **their statements lack ~** sus declaraciones no concuerdan 3 (= *density*) [*of paste, mixture*] consistencia *f*

consistent [kən'sɪstənt] ADJ 1 (= *constant*) [*person, action, behaviour*] consecuente, coherente; [*results*] (muy) parecido, regular; [*work, performance*] de calidad constante 2 (= *cohesive*) [*argument*] coherente, lógico; **his actions are not ~ with his beliefs** sus actos no son consecuentes con sus ideas; **that is not ~ with what you told me** eso no encaja *or* no concuerda con lo que me dijiste

consistently [kən'sɪstəntlɪ] ADV 1 (= *regularly*) [*refuse, deny, oppose, support*] sistemáticamente; [*work, perform*] con un nivel de calidad constante; **the rate of inflation has been ~ low** el nivel de inflación se ha mantenido bajo; **he ~ achieved marks of over 90%** sus notas estaban habitualmente por encima del 90% 2 (= *logically*) [*argue, behave*] consecuentemente; **to act ~** obrar con consecuencia

consolation [ˌkɒnsə'leɪʃən] N consuelo *m*; **that's one ~** esto es un consuelo, por lo menos; **if it's any ~ to you** si te consuela de algún modo; **it is some ~ to know that ...** me reconforta saber que ... ➤ **consolation prize** premio *m* de consolación

console¹ [kən'səʊl] VT consolar (**sb for sth** a algn por algo)

console² ['kɒnsəʊl] N consola *f*

consolidate [kən'sɒlɪdeɪt] VT 1 (= *strengthen*) [+ *position, influence*] consolidar 2 (= *combine*) concentrar, fusionar

consommé [kən'sɒmeɪ] N consomé *m*, caldo *m*

consonant ['kɒnsənənt] N consonante *f*

consort ['kɒnsɔːt] Ⓐ N consorte *mf*; **prince ~** príncipe *m* consorte Ⓑ [kən'sɔːt] VI **to ~ with sb** asociarse con algn

consortium [kən'sɔːtɪəm] N (*pl* **consortia** [kən'sɔːtɪə]) consorcio *m*

conspicuous [kən'spɪkjʊəs] ADJ **1** [*clothes*] llamativo; [*person, behaviour*] que llama la atención; **to be ~ by one's absence** brillar por su ausencia; **to make o.s. ~** llamar la atención **2** (= *striking*) [*bravery*] destacado, manifiesto; [*success, failure*] rotundo; **a ~ lack of sth** una carencia manifiesta de algo

conspiracy [kən'spɪrəsɪ] N (= *activity*) conspiración *f*, conjuración *f*; (= *plot*) complot *m*, conjura *f* ➤ **conspiracy theory** teoría *f* de la conspiración

conspirator [kən'spɪrətəʳ] N conspirador(a) *m/f*

conspiratorial [kən,spɪrə'tɔːrɪəl] ADJ de conspirador

conspire [kən'spaɪəʳ] VI conspirar (**to do sth** para hacer algo)

constable ['kʌnstəbl] N (*Brit*) (*also* **police ~**) agente *mf* de policía, policía *mf*

constabulary [kən'stæbjʊlərɪ] N (*Brit*) policía *f*

constancy ['kɒnstənsɪ] N **1** (= *regularity*) [*of temperature etc*] constancia *f* **2** (= *faithfulness*) fidelidad *f*

constant ['kɒnstənt] Ⓐ ADJ **1** [*temperature, velocity*] constante **2** [*quarrels, interruptions, complaints*] constante, continuo; **to be in ~ pain** sufrir dolor continuamente Ⓑ N constante *f*

constantly ['kɒnstəntlɪ] ADV constantemente, continuamente

constellation [,kɒnstə'leɪʃən] N constelación *f*

consternation [,kɒnstə'neɪʃən] N consternación *f*

constipated ['kɒnstɪpeɪtɪd] ADJ estreñido

constipation [,kɒnstɪ'peɪʃən] N estreñimiento *m*

constituency [kən'stɪtjʊənsɪ] N (= *district*) distrito *m* electoral, circunscripción *f* electoral; (= *people*) electorado *m*

constituent [kən'stɪtjʊənt] Ⓐ N **1** (= *component*) constitutivo *m*, componente *m* **2** (= *voter*) elector(a) *m/f* Ⓑ ADJ [*part*] constitutivo, integrante

constitute ['kɒnstɪtjuːt] VT (= *amount to*) significar, constituir; (= *make up*) constituir, componer

constitution [,kɒnstɪ'tjuːʃən] N constitución *f*

constitutional [,kɒnstɪ'tjuːʃənl] ADJ constitucional ➤ **constitutional monarchy** monarquía *f* constitucional

constrain [kən'streɪn] VT obligar; **to feel/be ~ed to do sth** sentirse/verse obligado a hacer algo

constrained [kən'streɪnd] ADJ [*atmosphere*] constrictivo; [*voice, manner, smile*] constreñido

constraint [kən'streɪnt] N **1** (= *compulsion*) coacción *f*, fuerza *f*; **under ~** obligado (a ello) **2** (= *limit*) restricción *f*;

budgetary ~s restricciones presupuestarias **3** (= *restraint*) reserva *f*, cohibición *f*

constrict [kən'strɪkt] VT [+ *muscle*] oprimir; [+ *vein*] estrangular; [+ *movements*] restringir

constriction [kən'strɪkʃən] N (*gen*) constricción *f*; (*Med*) constricción, estrangulamiento *m*

construct Ⓐ [kən'strʌkt] VT construir Ⓑ ['kɒnstrʌkt] N construcción *f*

construction [kən'strʌkʃən] N construcción *f*; **under ~** en construcción ➤ **construction company** compañía *f* constructora ➤ **construction industry** industria *f* de la construcción ➤ **construction site** obra *f* **construction worker** obrero/a *m/f* de la construcción

constructive [kən'strʌktɪv] ADJ constructivo

constructively [kən'strʌktɪvlɪ] ADV constructivamente

construe [kən'struː] VT interpretar

consul ['kɒnsəl] N cónsul *mf*

consular ['kɒnsjʊləʳ] ADJ consular

consulate ['kɒnsjʊlɪt] N consulado *m*

consult [kən'sʌlt] Ⓐ VT consultar Ⓑ VI consultar; **to ~ together** reunirse para hacer consultas

consultancy [kən'sʌltənsɪ] N (*Comm*) consultoría *f*; (*Med*) puesto *m* de especialista ➤ **consultancy fees** (*Comm*) derechos *mpl* de asesoría

consultant [kən'sʌltənt] Ⓐ N **1** (*gen*) consultor(a) *m/f*, asesor(a) *m/f*; **to act as ~ to** asesorar **2** (*Brit Med*) especialista *mf* Ⓑ CPD ➤ **consultant paediatrician** especialista *mf* en pediatría

consultation [,kɒnsəl'teɪʃən] N (= *act*) consulta *f*; (= *meeting*) negociaciones *fpl*; **in ~ with** tras consultar a

consultative [kən'sʌltətɪv] ADJ consultivo

consulting [kən'sʌltɪŋ] CPD ➤ **consulting hours** (*Brit*) horas *fpl* de consulta ➤ **consulting room** (*Brit*) consultorio *m*, consulta *f*

consumables [kən'sjuːməblz] NPL bienes *mpl* consumibles, artículos *mpl* de consumo

consume [kən'sjuːm] VT **1** (= *eat*) consumir, comerse; (= *drink*) consumir, beber **2** (= *use*) [+ *resources, fuel*] consumir; [+ *space, time etc*] ocupar **3** (= *destroy*) (*by fire*) consumir; **to be ~d with envy/grief** estar muerto de envidia/pena

consumer [kən'sjuːməʳ] N consumidor(a) *m/f* ➤ **consumer demand** demanda *f* de consumo ➤ **consumer durables** (*Brit*) bienes *mpl* (de consumo) duraderos ➤ **consumer goods** bienes *mpl* de consumo ➤ **consumer price index** índice *m* de precios al consumo ➤ **consumer protection** protección *f* del consumidor ➤ **consumer research** estudios *mpl* de mercado ➤ **the consumer society** la sociedad de consumo

consumerism [kən'sjuːmərɪzəm] N consumismo *m*

consuming [kən'sjuːmɪŋ] ADJ [*passion*] dominante, avasallador

consummate Ⓐ [kən'sʌmɪt] ADJ consumado; [*skill*] sumo Ⓑ ['kɒnsʌmeɪt] VT consumar

consumption [kən'sʌmpʃən] N [*of food, fuel*] consumo *m*; **not fit for human ~** no apto para el consumo humano

cont. ABBR (= *continued*) sigue

contact ['kɒntækt] Ⓐ N **1** (= *connection*) contacto *m* (*also Elec*); **to come into ~ with** (= *touch*) tocar; (*violently*) chocar con **2** (= *communication*) comunicación *f*; **to be in ~ with sth/sb** estar en contacto con algo/algn; **to get in** *or* **make ~ with sb** ponerse en contacto con algn; **to lose ~ (with sb)** perder el contacto (con algn) **3** (= *personal connection*) relación *f*; (*pej*) enchufe *m*, cuña *f* (*LAm*), hueso *m* (*Mex**), muñeca *f* (*SC**); (= *intermediary*) contacto *m*; **business ~s** contactos *fpl* comerciales; **one of his business ~s** uno de sus colegas comerciales; **you have to have a ~ in the business** hay que tener un buen enchufe en el negocio; **he's got good ~s** tiene buenas relaciones Ⓑ VT (*gen*) contactar con, ponerse en contacto con; (*by telephone etc*) comunicar con; **where can we ~ you?** ¿cómo

podemos ponernos en contacto contigo?, ¿dónde podemos encontrarte?
Ⓒ CPD ➤ **contact lens** lente *f* or (*LAm*) lente *m* de contacto, lentilla *f* (*Sp*)

contagious [kən'teɪdʒəs] ADJ contagioso

contain [kən'teɪn] VT contener; **to ~ o.s.** contenerse

container [kən'teɪnəʳ] Ⓐ N **1** (= *box, jug etc*) recipiente *m*; (= *package, bottle*) envase *m* **2** (*for transport*) contenedor *m*, contáiner *m* Ⓑ CPD ➤ **container lorry** portacontenedores *m inv* ➤ **container port** puerto *m* para contenedores ➤ **container ship** portacontenedores *m inv*, buque *m* contenedor

contaminate [kən'tæmɪneɪt] VT contaminar; **to be ~d by** contaminarse con or de

contamination [kənˌtæmɪ'neɪʃən] N contaminación *f*

contemplate ['kɒntəmpleɪt] VT **1** (= *reflect upon*) considerar; **he ~d his future** estaba pensando or reflexionando sobre su futuro **2** (= *consider possibility of*) **we ~d a holiday in Spain** nos planteamos unas vacaciones en España; **he ~d suicide** pensó en suicidarse, contempló la posibilidad del suicidio; **to ~ doing sth** pensar en hacer algo **3** (= *look at*) contemplar

contemplation [ˌkɒntəm'pleɪʃən] N contemplación *f*, meditación *f*

contemplative [kən'templətɪv] ADJ contemplativo

contemporary [kən'tempərərɪ] Ⓐ ADJ contemporáneo (**with** de) Ⓑ N contemporáneo/a *m/f*

contempt [kən'tempt] N desprecio *m*, desdén *m*; **to hold sth/sb in ~** despreciar algo/a algn; **it's beneath ~** es más que despreciable ➤ **contempt of court** desacato *m* (a los tribunales)

contemptible [kən'temptəbl] ADJ despreciable, desdeñable

contemptuous [kən'temptjuəs] ADJ [*person*] desdeñoso (**of** con); [*gesture*] despectivo; **to be ~ of** desdeñar, menospreciar

contemptuously [kən'temptjuəslɪ] ADV desdeñosamente, con desprecio

contend [kən'tend] Ⓐ VT **to ~ that** afirmar que, sostener que Ⓑ VI **to ~ (with sb) for sth** competir (con algn) por algo; **we have many problems to ~ with** se nos plantean muchos problemas; **you'll have me to ~ with** tendrás que vértelas conmigo; **he has a lot to ~ with** tiene que enfrentarse a muchos problemas

contender [kən'tendəʳ] N (= *rival*) competidor(a) *m/f*; (= *candidate*) candidato (**for** para); (*Sport etc*) contendiente *mf* (**for** para)

content¹ [kən'tent] Ⓐ ADJ **1** (= *happy*) contento (**with** con); **to be ~** estar contento; **he is ~ to watch** se conforma or se contenta con mirar **2** (= *satisfied*) satisfecho (**with** con) Ⓑ VT (= *satisfy*) satisfacer; **to ~ o.s. with sth/with doing sth** contentarse or darse por contento con algo/con hacer algo

content² ['kɒntent] N **1 contents** [*of box, packet etc*] contenido *msing*; [*of book*] índice *msing* (de materias) **2** (= *subject matter, amount*) contenido *m*

contented [kən'tentɪd] ADJ satisfecho, contento

contentedly [kən'tentɪdlɪ] ADV con satisfacción, contentamente

contention [kən'tenʃən] N **1** (= *strife*) discusión *f*; (= *dissent*) disensión *f*; **teams in ~** equipos rivales; **he is in ~ for a place on the team** tiene posibilidades de conseguir un puesto en el equipo **2** (= *opinion*) opinión *f*, argumento *m*; **it is our ~ that ...** pretendemos que ..., sostenemos que ...

contentious [kən'tenʃəs] ADJ conflictivo, muy discutido

contentment [kən'tentmənt] N contento *m*, satisfacción *f*

contest Ⓐ ['kɒntest] N (= *struggle*) contienda *f*, lucha *f*; (*Boxing, Wrestling*) combate *m*; (= *competition, quiz*) concurso *m*; (*Sport*) competición *f* (*Sp*), competencia *f* (*LAm*); **beauty ~** concurso *m* de belleza; **a fishing ~** una competición (*Sp*) or competencia (*LAm*) de pesca Ⓑ [kən'test] VT [+ *argument, will etc*] impugnar, rebatir; (*esp Brit*) [+ *election, seat*] presentarse como candidato/a a;

[+ *legal suit*] defender; **the seat was not ~ed** no hubo disputa por el escaño, en las elecciones se presentó un solo candidato

⚠ **contest** ≠ **contestar**

contestant [kən'testənt] N (*in competition*) concursante *mf*; (*Sport etc*) contrincante *mf*, contendiente *mf*

context ['kɒntekst] N contexto *m*; **in/out of ~** en/fuera de contexto; **to put sth in ~** poner algo en su contexto

continent ['kɒntɪnənt] N **1** (*Geog*) continente *m* **2** (*Brit*) **the Continent** el continente europeo, Europa *f* (continental); **on the Continent** en Europa (continental)

continental [ˌkɒntɪ'nentl] Ⓐ ADJ continental Ⓑ N (*Brit*) europeo/a *m/f* (continental) Ⓒ CPD ➤ **continental breakfast** desayuno *m* estilo europeo

contingency [kən'tɪndʒənsɪ] N eventualidad *f*, contingencia *f*; **to provide for every ~** tener en cuenta cualquier eventualidad or contingencia ➤ **contingency funds** fondos *mpl* para imprevistos ➤ **contingency plans** medidas *fpl* para casos de emergencia

contingent [kən'tɪndʒənt] Ⓐ ADJ **to be ~ upon** depender de Ⓑ N (*Mil*) contingente *m*; (= *group*) representación *f*

continual [kən'tɪnjuəl] ADJ continuo, constante

continually [kən'tɪnjuəlɪ] ADV continuamente, constantemente

continuation [kənˌtɪnju'eɪʃən] N **1** (= *maintenance*) prosecución *f*; (= *resumption*) reanudación *f* **2** (= *sth continued*) prolongación *f*; (= *story, episode*) continuación *f*

continue [kən'tɪnjuː] Ⓐ VT **1** (= *carry on*) [+ *policy, tradition*] seguir
2 (= *resume*) [+ *story etc*] reanudar, continuar; **~d on page ten** sigue en la página diez; **to be ~d** continuará Ⓑ VI **1** (= *carry on*) continuar; **to ~ doing sth** or **to do sth** continuar or seguir haciendo algo; **to ~ on one's way** seguir su camino; **to ~ with sth** seguir con algo **2** (= *remain*) seguir; **to ~ in office** seguir en su puesto **3** (= *extend*) prolongarse, seguir; **the road ~s for two miles** la carretera se prolonga or sigue dos millas más

continuing [kən'tɪnjuɪŋ] ADJ [*argument*] irresoluto; [*correspondence*] continuado ➤ **continuing education** cursos de enseñanza para adultos

continuity [ˌkɒntɪ'njuːɪtɪ] N continuidad *f* ➤ **continuity man/girl** (*Cine*) secretario/a *m/f* de rodaje

continuous [kən'tɪnjuəs] ADJ continuo ➤ **continuous assessment** (*Brit*) evaluación *f* continua

continuously [kən'tɪnjuəslɪ] ADV continuamente

contort [kən'tɔːt] VT retorcer

contortion [kən'tɔːʃən] N contorsión *f*

contortionist [kən'tɔːʃənɪst] N contorsionista *mf*

contour ['kɒntuəʳ] N contorno *m* ➤ **contour line** curva *f* de nivel ➤ **contour map** plano *m* acotado

contraband ['kɒntrəbænd] Ⓐ N contrabando *m* Ⓑ ADJ de contrabando

contraception [ˌkɒntrə'sepʃən] N contracepción *f*, anticoncepción *f*

contraceptive [ˌkɒntrə'septɪv] Ⓐ ADJ anticonceptivo Ⓑ N anticonceptivo *m*, contraceptivo *m* Ⓒ CPD ➤ **contraceptive pill** píldora *f* anticonceptiva

contract Ⓐ ['kɒntrækt] N **1** (= *document*) contrato *m*; **by ~** por contrato; **to enter into a ~ (with sb) (to do sth/for sth)** firmar un contrato (con algn) (para hacer algo/de algo); **to put work out to ~** sacar una obra a contrato; **they are under ~ to X** tienen contrato con X, tienen obligaciones contractuales con X
2 (*fig*) **there's a ~ out on him** le han puesto precio Ⓑ [kən'trækt] VT **1** (= *acquire*) [+ *disease, debt*] contraer **2** [+ *worker*] contratar (**to do sth** para hacer algo) **3** (*Gram*) contraer Ⓒ [kən'trækt] VI **1** [*metal, muscles, face*] contraerse (*also Gram*)

2 (*Comm*) **to ~ (with sb) to do sth** comprometerse (con algn) por contrato a hacer algo

Ⓓ ['kɒntrækt] CPD ➤ **contract killer** asesino *m* a sueldo ➤ **contract killing** asesinato *m* pagado ➤ **contract work** trabajo *m* bajo contrato

➤ **contract in** VI + ADV tomar parte (**to** en)

➤ **contract out** Ⓐ VT + ADV **this work is ~ed out** este trabajo se hace fuera de la empresa con un contrato aparte Ⓑ VI + ADV (*Brit*) optar por no tomar parte (**of** en)

contraction [kən'trækʃən] N contracción *f*

contractor [kən'træktəʳ] N contratista *mf*

contractual [kən'træktʃʊəl] ADJ contractual

contradict [ˌkɒntrə'dɪkt] VT (= *be contrary to*) contradecir; (= *declare to be wrong*) desmentir; (= *argue with*) replicar, discutir; **don't ~ me!** ¡no me repliques!

contradiction [ˌkɒntrə'dɪkʃən] N contradicción *f*; **to be a ~ in terms** ser contradictorio

contradictory [ˌkɒntrə'dɪktərɪ] ADJ contradictorio

contraindication [ˌkɒntrəˌɪndrˈkeɪʃən] N contraindicación *f*

contralto [kən'træltəʊ] Ⓐ N (= *person*) contralto *f* Ⓑ CPD [*voice, part*] de contralto

contraption* [kən'træpʃən] N (= *gadget*) artilugio *m*, aparato *m*; (= *vehicle*) armatoste *m*

contrary¹ ['kɒntrərɪ] Ⓐ ADJ [*direction*] contrario; [*opinions*] opuesto; **~ to** en contra de, contrario a; **~ to what we thought** en contra de lo que pensábamos Ⓑ N contrario *m*; **on the ~** al contrario, todo lo contrario; **unless we hear to the ~** a no ser que nos digan lo contrario

contrary² [kən'treərɪ] ADJ (= *perverse*) terco

contrast Ⓐ ['kɒntrɑːst] N contraste *m*; **in ~ to** or **with** a diferencia de, en contraste con Ⓑ [kən'trɑːst] VT **to ~ with** comparar con, contrastar con Ⓒ [kən'trɑːst] VI **to ~ with** contrastar con, hacer contraste con

contrasting [kən'trɑːstɪŋ] ADJ [*opinion*] opuesto; [*colour*] que hace contraste

contravene [ˌkɒntrə'viːn] VT contravenir

contravention [ˌkɒntrə'venʃən] N contravención *f*

contribute [kən'trɪbjuːt] Ⓐ VT [+ *money, ideas*] contribuir con, aportar (*esp LAm*); [+ *article*] escribir; **she ~d £10 to the collection** contribuyó con diez libras a la colecta Ⓑ VI (*gen*) contribuir (**to** a); (*to newspaper*) colaborar (**to** en); (*to discussion*) intervenir (**to** en); **everyone ~d to the success of the play** todos contribuyeron al éxito de la obra

contribution [ˌkɒntrɪ'bjuːʃən] N (= *money*) contribución *f*, aporte *m* (*esp LAm*); (*to journal*) artículo *m*, colaboración *f*; (*to discussion*) intervención *f*, aportación *f*; (*to pension fund*) cuota *f*, cotización *f*

contributor [kən'trɪbjʊtəʳ] N [*of money*] persona *f* que contribuye; (*to journal*) colaborador(a) *m/f*

contributory [kən'trɪbjʊtərɪ] ADJ que contribuye, contribuyente

contrite ['kɒntraɪt] ADJ arrepentido

contrivance [kən'traɪvəns] N (= *machine, device*) artilugio *m*, aparato *m*; (= *invention*) invención *f*, invento *m*; (= *stratagem*) estratagema *f*

contrive [kən'traɪv] Ⓐ VT inventar, idear Ⓑ VI **to ~ to do sth** lograr hacer algo

contrived [kən'traɪvd] ADJ artificial

control [kən'trəʊl] Ⓐ N **1** control *m* (**over** sobre); **due to circumstances beyond our ~** debido a circunstancias ajenas a nuestra voluntad; **to gain ~ of** [+ *company, territory*] hacerse con el control de; **they have no ~ over their pupils** no pueden controlar a sus alumnos; **they are in complete ~ of the situation** tienen la situación totalmente controlada o dominada; **people feel more in ~ of their lives** la gente se siente más dueña de su vida, la gente siente que tiene mayor control de su vida; **to lose ~ (of o.s.)** perder el control (de uno mismo); **he lost ~ of the car** perdió el control del coche; **to be out of ~** estar fuera de control; **everything is under ~** todo está bajo control; **to bring a fire under ~** conseguir dominar or controlar un incendio; **to keep sth/sb under ~** mantener algo/a algn bajo control

2 (= *checkpoint*) control *m*; **an agreement to abolish border ~s** un acuerdo para eliminar los controles en las fronteras; **passport ~** control *m* de pasaportes

3 (= *restraint*) restricción *f*; **arms/birth ~** control *m* de armamentos/de la natalidad

4 (*Tech*) **4.1 controls** mandos *mpl*; **to be at the ~s** estar a (cargo de) los mandos **4.2** (= *knob, switch*) botón *m*

5 (*in experiment*) testigo *m*

6 (*Sport*) dominio *m*; **his ball ~ is very good** su dominio del balón es muy bueno, domina bien el balón

Ⓑ VT **1** (= *command, restrain*) [+ *country, crowd, child, disease*] controlar; [+ *fire, emotions, temper*] controlar, dominar; **to ~ o.s.** controlarse, dominarse; **to ~ the spread of malaria** contener la propagación de la malaria

2 (= *regulate*) [+ *activity, prices, expenditure*] controlar, regular; [+ *traffic*] dirigir

Ⓒ CPD ➤ **control column** palanca *f* de mando ➤ **control freak*: he's a total ~ freak** tiene la manía de controlarlo todo ➤ **control group** (*in experiment*) grupo *m* testigo ➤ **control key** tecla *f* de control ➤ **control panel** tablero *m* de control ➤ **control room** (*Mil, Naut*) sala *f* de mandos; (*Rad, TV*) sala *f* de control ➤ **control tower** torre *f* de control

controlled [kən'trəʊld] ADJ **1** (= *restrained*) [*emotion*] contenido; **she was very ~** tenía gran dominio de sí misma **2** (= *restricted*) [*drug, substance*] que se dispensa únicamente con receta médica **3** (= *regulated*) controlado; **~ explosion** explosión *f* controlada

controller [kən'trəʊləʳ] N (*Comm*) interventor(a) *m/f*; (*Aer*) controlador(a) *m/f*

controversial [ˌkɒntrə'vɜːʃəl] ADJ controvertido, polémico

controversy [kɒn'trɒvəsɪ] N controversia *f*, polémica *f*

conundrum [kə'nʌndrəm] N (= *riddle*) acertijo *m*, adivinanza *f*; (= *problem*) enigma *m*

conurbation [ˌkɒnɜː'beɪʃən] N (*Brit*) conurbación *f*

convalesce [ˌkɒnvə'les] VI convalecer

convalescence [ˌkɒnvə'lesəns] N convalecencia *f*

convalescent [ˌkɒnvə'lesənt] ADJ, N convaleciente *mf* ➤ **convalescent home** clínica *f* de reposo

convector [kən'vektəʳ] N (*also ~* **heater**) calentador *m* de convección

convene [kən'viːn] Ⓐ VT convocar Ⓑ VI reunirse

⚠ **convene ≠ convenir**

convenience [kən'viːnɪəns] Ⓐ N **1** (= *comfort*) comodidad *f*; (= *advantage*) ventaja *f*, provecho *m*; **at your earliest ~** tan pronto como le sea posible; **you can do it at your own ~** puede hacerlo cuando le venga mejor or (*LAm*) le convenga **2** (= *amenity*) comodidad *f*, confort *m*; *see also* **public** Ⓑ CPD ➤ **convenience foods** comidas *fpl* fáciles de preparar; (= *ready-cooked meals*) platos *mpl* preparados

convenient [kən'viːnɪənt] ADJ **1** (= *suitable*) conveniente; [*tool, device*] práctico, útil; [*size*] idóneo, cómodo; **would tomorrow be ~?** ¿le viene bien mañana?; **at a ~ moment** en un momento oportuno; **we looked for a ~ place to stop** buscamos un sitio apropiado para parar **2** (= *near*) bien situado, accesible; **the house is ~ for the shops** la casa está muy cerca de las tiendas; **the hotel is ~ for the airport** el hotel está bien situado con respecto al aeropuerto

conveniently [kən'viːnɪəntlɪ] ADV convenientemente; [*time*] oportunamente; **the house is ~ situated** la casa está en un sitio muy práctico; **he very ~ forgot to write it down** (*iro*) muy oportunamente, se olvidó de apuntarlo

convent ['kɒnvənt] N convento *m* ➤ **convent school** colegio *m* de monjas

convention [kən'venʃən] N **1** (= *custom*) convención *f* **2** (= *meeting*) asamblea *f*, congreso *m*

conventional [kən'venʃənl] ADJ [*behaviour, tastes, weapons, method*] convencional; [*person*] tradicional, convencional; [*belief, values*] tradicional; [*style, clothes*] clásico, tradicional; **~ medicine** la medicina tradicional or convencional; **in the ~ sense of the word** en el sentido generalmente aceptado de la palabra

converge [kən'vɜːdʒ] VI converger, convergir; **the crowd ~d on the square** la muchedumbre se dirigió a la plaza

convergence [kən'vɜːdʒəns] N convergencia *f*

conversant [kən'vɜːsənt] ADJ **~ with** versado en, familiarizado con; **to become ~ with** familiarizarse con

conversation [ˌkɒnvə'seɪʃən] N conversación *f*, plática *f* (*LAm*); **to have a ~ with sb** conversar *or* (*LAm*) platicar con algn; **what was your ~ about?** ¿de qué hablabas?; **I said it just to make ~** lo dije sólo por decir algo

conversational [ˌkɒnvə'seɪʃənl] ADJ [*style, tone*] familiar

conversationalist [ˌkɒnvə'seɪʃnəlɪst] N conversador(a) *m/f*; **to be a good ~** brillar en la conversación; **he's not much of a ~** no es muy buen conversador

converse¹ [kən'vɜːs] VI **to ~ (with sb) (about sth)** conversar *or* (*LAm*) platicar (con algn) (sobre algo)

converse² ['kɒnvɜːs] N (= *opposite*) inversa *f*; **but the ~ is true** pero la verdad es al revés

conversely [kɒn'vɜːslɪ] ADV a la inversa

conversion [kən'vɜːʃən] **Ⓐ** N **1** (*gen, Rel*) conversión *f* (**into** en; **to** a) **2** (= *house conversion*) reforma *f*, remodelación *f* **3** (*Rugby, US Football*) transformación *f* **Ⓑ** CPD **➤ conversion table** tabla *f* de equivalencias

convert **Ⓐ** ['kɒnvɜːt] N converso/a *m/f*; **to become a ~** convertirse, hacerse converso **Ⓑ** [kən'vɜːt] VT **1** [+ *house*] reformar, convertir (**into** en); [+ *currency*] convertir (**to, into** en); (*Rel*) convertir (**to** a); (*fig*) convencer (**to** a); **to ~ sth into** convertir algo en, transformar algo en **2** (*Rugby, US Football*) transformar **Ⓒ** [kən'vɜːt] VI convertirse (**to** a)

convertible [kən'vɜːtəbl] **Ⓐ** ADJ convertible **Ⓑ** N (= *car*) descapotable *m*

convex ['kɒnveks] ADJ convexo

convey [kən'veɪ] VT **1** (= *move*) [+ *goods, oil*] transportar, llevar; [+ *person*] conducir, acompañar (*LAm*) **2** (= *express*) [+ *thanks, congratulations*] comunicar; [+ *meaning, ideas*] expresar; **to ~ to sb that ...** comunicar a algn que ...

conveyance [kən'veɪəns] N (= *transport*) transporte *m*; (*Jur*) [*of property*] traspaso *m*

conveyancing [kən'veɪənsɪŋ] N (*Brit Jur*) preparación *f* de escrituras de traspaso

conveyor belt [kən'veɪəˌbelt] N cinta *f* transportadora

convict **Ⓐ** ['kɒnvɪkt] N (= *prisoner*) presidiario/a *m/f* **Ⓑ** [kən'vɪkt] VT declarar culpable (**of** de), condenar; **he was ~ed of drunken driving** fue condenado por conducir en estado de embriaguez; **a ~ed murderer** un asesino convicto y confeso

conviction [kən'vɪkʃən] N **1** (*Jur*) condena *f*; **to have no previous ~s** no tener antecedentes penales **2** (= *belief*) convicción *f*; **he said with ~** dijo con convicción; **without much ~** no muy convencido; **it is my ~ that ...** creo firmemente que ...

convince [kən'vɪns] VT convencer; **to ~ sb (that/of sth)** convencer a algn (de que/de algo); **I am not ~d** no estoy convencido, no me convence

convincing [kən'vɪnsɪŋ] ADJ convincente

convincingly [kən'vɪnsɪŋlɪ] ADV de forma convincente

convivial [kən'vɪvɪəl] ADJ [*person, company*] sociable, agradable; [*evening, atmosphere*] alegre, agradable

convoluted ['kɒnvəˌluːtɪd] ADJ [*argument*] enrevesado

convolution [ˌkɒnvə'luːʃən] N circunvolución *f*

convoy ['kɒnvɔɪ] N (= *procession*) convoy *m*; (= *escort*) escolta *f*; **in/under ~** en convoy

convulse [kən'vʌls] VT **to be ~d with laughter** desternillarse de risa; **to be ~d with pain** retorcerse de dolor

convulsion [kən'vʌlʃən] N (= *fit*) convulsión *f*; **to have ~s** tener convulsiones; **they were in ~s*** [*of laughter*] se desternillaban de risa

convulsive [kən'vʌlsɪv] ADJ [*movement*] convulsivo; [*laughter*] incontenible

coo [kuː] VI [*dove*] arrullar; [*baby*] hacer gorgoritos

cook [kʊk] **Ⓐ** N cocinero/a *m/f*; ✦ PROV **too many ~s spoil the broth** demasiadas cocineras estropean el caldo **Ⓑ** VT **1** (*Culin*) [+ *rice, vegetables*] cocinar; (= *boil*) cocer; (= *grill*) asar (a la parrilla); (= *fry*) freír; **to ~ a meal** preparar *or* hacer una comida **2** (*) (= *falsify*) [+ *accounts*] falsificar; ✦ IDIOM **to ~ the books** amañar las cuentas **Ⓒ** VI [*person*] cocinar; [*food*] cocinarse, cocerse; **can you ~?** ¿sabes cocinar?; ✦ IDIOM **what's ~ing?*** ¿qué pasa?
➤ cook up VT + ADV **1** (*Culin*) preparar **2** (*) [+ *excuse, story*] inventar; [+ *plan*] tramar

cookbook ['kʊkbʊk] N libro *m* de cocina

cooked [kʊkt] ADJ [*breakfast*] caliente **➤ cooked meats** fiambres *fpl*

cooker ['kʊkə'] N (*esp Brit*) cocina *f*, estufa *f* (*Col, Mex*); **gas/ electric ~** cocina *f* or (*Col, Mex*) estufa *f* de gas/eléctrica

cookery ['kʊkərɪ] N cocina *f* **➤ cookery book** (*Brit*) libro *m* de cocina

cookie ['kʊkɪ] N **1** (*US*) (= *biscuit*) galleta *f* **2** (*) (= *person*) **she's a smart ~** es una chica lista; **a tough ~** un tipo duro* **3** ✦ IDIOM **that's the way the ~ crumbles*** así es la vida **4** (*Internet*) cookie *f*

cooking ['kʊkɪŋ] **Ⓐ** N **1** (= *art*) cocina *f*; **to do the ~** cocinar, encargarse de cocinar **2** (= *process*) cocción *f* **Ⓑ** CPD [*utensils, salt*] de cocina; [*chocolate*] de hacer **➤ cooking apple** manzana *f* para cocer **➤ cooking salt** sal *f* de cocina **➤ cooking time** tiempo *m* de cocción

cookout ['kʊkaʊt] N (*US*) barbacoa *f*, comida *f* hecha al aire libre

cool [kuːl] **Ⓐ** ADJ (*compar* **~er**; *superl* **~est**) **1** (= *not hot*) [*room, skin, drink, dress, colour, blue*] fresco; **it's nice and ~ in here** aquí dentro hace fresquito *or* se está fresquito; **it's getting** *or* **turning ~er** está empezando a refrescar; **"keep in a cool place"** "guardar en (un) lugar fresco"
2 (= *calm*) [*person, manner, action, tone*] sereno; **to keep** *or* **stay ~** no perder la calma; **keep ~!** ¡tranquilo!
3 (*pej*) [*behaviour*] fresco, descarado; **he's a ~ customer*** es un fresco, es un caradura; ✦ IDIOM **to be as ~ as a cucumber*** (= *calm*) estar tan campante*; (= *cheeky*) tener más cara que espalda*
4 (= *unenthusiastic*) [*person, response*] frío; **a ~ welcome** *or* **reception** un recibimiento frío; **to be ~ towards** *or* **with sb** mostrarse frío con algn, tratar a algn con frialdad
5 (**) (= *trendy, stylish*) [*object, person*] enrollado (*Sp***), macanudo (*LAm***), padre (*Mex***)
6 (**) (= *acceptable*) **don't worry, it's ~** tranqui, no pasa nada*; **he's ~** es un tío enrollado (*Sp***), es un tipo bien (*LAm**)
Ⓑ N **1** (= *low temperature*) frescor *m*; **in the ~ of the evening** en el frescor de la tarde; **to keep sth in the ~** guardar algo en un lugar fresco
2 (= *calm*) **to keep/lose one's ~*** no perder/perder la calma **Ⓒ** VT [+ *room*] refrescar; [+ *wine, drink*] poner a enfriar; ✦ IDIOM **to ~ one's heels** esperar impaciente; **~ it!*** ¡tranquilo!
Ⓓ VI [*air, liquid*] enfriarse; [*weather*] refrescar; **by Monday tempers had ~ed** el lunes los ánimos se habían calmado **Ⓔ** CPD **➤ cool box** nevera *f* portátil
➤ cool down **Ⓐ** VT + ADV **1** (= *make colder*) enfriar **2** (= *make calmer*) calmar **Ⓑ** VI + ADV **1** (= *become colder*) [*object*] enfriarse; [*person*] refrescarse, tener menos calor **2** (= *become calmer*) [*person, situation*] calmarse
➤ cool off VI + ADV **1** (= *become calmer*) calmarse, apaciguarse; (= *lose enthusiasm*) perder (el) interés, enfriarse; (= *become less affectionate*) distanciarse, enfriarse

coolant ['kuːlənt] N (líquido *m*) refrigerante *m*

cooler ['kuːlə'] N **1** (= *cool box*) nevera *f* portátil **2** (**) (= *prison*) chirona* *f*, trena* *f*

cool-headed ['kuːlˈhedɪd] ADJ sereno, imperturbable

cooling ['kuːlɪŋ] ADJ refrescante **➤ cooling tower** torre *f* de refrigeración

cooling-off period [ˌkuːlɪŋˈɒfˌpɪərɪəd] N (*Ind*) plazo *m* de negociación; (*Comm*) plazo *m* de prueba

coolly ['kuːlɪ] ADV **1** (= *calmly*) con serenidad, con tranquilidad, con sangre fría **2** (*pej*) (= *audaciously*) descaradamente, con mucha frescura

3 (= *unenthusiastically*) fríamente, con frialdad

coolness ['ku:lnɪs] N **1** [*of water, air, weather*] frescor *m* **2** (= *calmness*) tranquilidad *f*, serenidad *f*; (*in battle, crisis*) sangre *f* fría **3** (*pej*) (= *audacity*) frescura *f*, descaro *m* **4** [*of welcome, person*] frialdad *f*

coop [ku:p] N gallinero *m*
➤ **coop up** VT + ADV encerrar

co-op* ['kəʊ,ɒp] N cooperativa *f*

cooperate [kəʊ'ɒpəreɪt] VI cooperar, colaborar; **to ~ with sb (in sth/to do sth)** cooperar con algn (en algo/para hacer algo)

cooperation [kəʊ,ɒpə'reɪʃən] N cooperación *f*, colaboración *f*

cooperative [kəʊ'ɒpərətɪv] **Ⓐ** ADJ **1** [*attitude*] colaborador, cooperador; [*person*] servicial, dispuesto a ayudar **2** [*farm etc*] cooperativo **Ⓑ** N cooperativa *f* **Ⓒ** CPD ➤ **cooperative society** (*Brit*) cooperativa *f*

co-opt [kəʊ'ɒpt] VT **to ~ sb (onto sth)** nombrar (como miembro) a algn (para algo)

coordinate Ⓐ [kəʊ'ɔ:dɪnɪt] N (*on map*) coordenada *f* **Ⓑ** [kəʊ'ɔ:dɪneɪt] VT [+ *movements, work*] coordinar; [+ *efforts*] aunar

coordination [kəʊ,ɔ:dɪ'neɪʃən] N coordinación *f*

coordinator [kəʊ'ɔ:dɪneɪtəʳ] N coordinador(a) *m/f*

co-ownership [,kəʊ'əʊnəʃɪp] N copropiedad *f*

cop* [kɒp] **Ⓐ** N **1** (= *policeman*) poli *m* (*Sp**), cana *m* (*SC**); **the ~s** la pasma (*Sp***), la cana (*SC***); **~s and robbers** policías y ladrones **2** (*Brit*) **it's not much** = no es gran cosa; **it's a fair ~!** ¡está bien! **Ⓑ** VT **1** (*Brit*) (= *catch*) **you'll ~ it!** ¡te la vas a ganar!; **I ~ped it from the headmaster** el director me puso como un trapo **2** (*US Jur*) **to ~ a plea** declararse culpable de un delito menor para obtener una sentencia más leve **Ⓒ** CPD ➤ **cop shop**** (*Brit*) comisaría *f*

cope [kəʊp] VI arreglárselas; **he's coping pretty well** se las está arreglando bastante bien; **we shall be able to ~ better next year** podremos arreglárnoslas mejor el año que viene; **how are you coping?** ¿cómo lo llevas?*; **he can't ~ any more** ya no puede más; **can you ~?** ¿tú puedes con esto?; **to ~ with** [+ *task, person*] poder con; [+ *situation*] enfrentarse con; [+ *difficulties, problems*] (= *tackle*) hacer frente a, abordar; (= *solve*) solucionar

Copenhagen [,kəʊpn'heɪgən] N Copenhague *m*

copier ['kɒpɪəʳ] N fotocopiadora *f*

co-pilot ['kəʊ'paɪlət] N copiloto *mf*

copious ['kəʊpɪəs] ADJ copioso, abundante

cop-out* ['kɒpaʊt] N evasión *f* de responsabilidad

copper ['kɒpəʳ] **Ⓐ** N **1** (= *metal*) cobre *m* **2** (*esp Brit**) (= *coin*) perra *f* (chica), centavo *m* (*LAm*); **it costs a few ~s** vale unos peniques **3** (*Brit*) = **cop A1 Ⓑ** ADJ (= *made of copper*) de cobre **Ⓒ** CPD ➤ **copper beech** haya *f* roja *or* de sangre

> Use **el/un** not **la/una** before feminine nouns beginning with stressed **a** or **ha** like **haya**.

copper-coloured, **copper-colored** (*US*) ['kɒpə,kʌləd] ADJ cobrizo

copperplate ['kɒpəpleɪt] N (*also* ~ **writing**) letra *f* inglesa

coppice ['kɒpɪs] N (*Brit*) soto *m*, bosquecillo *m*

co-production [,kəʊprə'dʌkʃən] N coproducción *f*

copse [kɒps] N soto *m*, bosquecillo *m*

copulate ['kɒpjʊleɪt] VI copular

copy ['kɒpɪ] **Ⓐ** N **1** (= *duplicate*) copia *f*; **to make a ~ of** hacer *or* sacar una copia de **2** [*of book, newspaper*] ejemplar *m*; [*of magazine*] número *m* **3** (= *written material*) **there's plenty of ~ here** tenemos aquí un material abundante; **to make good ~** ser una noticia de interés **Ⓑ** VT **1** (= *imitate*) copiar, imitar; (*Scol*) (= *cheat*) copiar **2** (= *make copy of*) (*gen*) sacar una copia de; (*in writing, Comput*) copiar; (= *photocopy*) fotocopiar **3** (= *send a copy to*) enviar una copia (**to** a)

copy editor editor(a) *m/f*, corrector(a) *m/f* de manuscritos ➤ **copy machine** fotocopiadora *f* ➤ **copy typist** mecanógrafo/a *m/f*

copybook ['kɒpɪbʊk] **Ⓐ** N cuaderno *m* de escritura; **✦** IDIOM **to blot one's ~** (*esp Brit*) manchar su reputación **Ⓑ** ADJ (*esp Brit*) perfecto

copycat* ['kɒpɪkæt] N imitador(a) *m/f* ➤ **copycat crime** crimen *m* que trata de emular a otros

copyright ['kɒpɪraɪt] N derechos *mpl* de autor, propriedad *f* literaria

copywriter ['kɒpɪ,raɪtəʳ] N escritor(a) *m/f* de material publicitario

coral ['kɒrəl] **Ⓐ** N coral *m* **Ⓑ** CPD de coral, coralino ➤ **coral island** isla *f* coralina ➤ **coral reef** arrecife *m* de coral

cord [kɔ:d] N **1** (= *thick string*) cuerda *f*; (*for pyjamas, curtains, of window*) cordón *m*; (*Elec*) cable *m* **2** (*also* **umbilical ~**) cordón *m* umbilical **3** (= *corduroy*) pana *f*; **cords** (= *trousers*) pantalones *mpl* de pana

cordial ['kɔ:dɪəl] **Ⓐ** ADJ cordial, afectuoso **Ⓑ** N **1** (*Brit*) (= *drink*) cordial *m* **2** (*US*) (= *liqueur*) licor *m*

cordite ['kɔ:daɪt] N cordita *f*

cordless ['kɔ:dlɪs] ADJ [*iron, kettle, tool*] sin cable; [*telephone*] inalámbrico, sin hilos

cordon ['kɔ:dn] **Ⓐ** N cordón *m* **Ⓑ** VT (*also* **to ~ off**) acordonar

corduroy ['kɔ:dərɔɪ] N pana *f*; **corduroys** pantalones *mpl* de pana

CORE [kɔ:ʳ] N ABBR (*US*) = **Congress of Racial Equality**

core [kɔ:ʳ] **Ⓐ** N **1** [*of fruit*] corazón *m*; [*of earth*] centro *m*, núcleo *m*; [*of cable, nuclear reactor*] núcleo *m* **2** [*of problem*] esencia *f*, meollo *m*; [*of group etc*] centro *m*; **a hard ~ of resistance** un núcleo *or* foco arraigado de resistencia; **English to the ~** inglés hasta los tuétanos; **rotten to the ~** corrompido hasta la médula **Ⓑ** VT [+ *fruit*] deshuesar **Ⓒ** CPD ➤ **core business** actividad *f* principal ➤ **core curriculum** asignaturas *fpl* comunes ➤ **core subject** asignatura *f* común

co-respondent ['kəʊrɪ'spɒndənt] N codemandado/a *m/f*

coriander [,kɒrɪ'ændəʳ] N culantro *m*, cilantro *m*

cork [kɔ:k] **Ⓐ** N **1** (= *substance*) corcho *m* **2** (= *stopper*) corcho *m*, tapón *m* **Ⓑ** VT (*also* ~ **up**) tapar con corcho, taponar **Ⓒ** ADJ de corcho

corkage ['kɔ:kɪdʒ] N precio que se cobra en un restaurante por abrir una botella traida de fuera

corked [kɔ:kt] ADJ con sabor a corcho

corkscrew ['kɔ:kskru:] N sacacorchos *m inv*

corm [kɔ:m] N bulbo *m*

cormorant ['kɔ:mərənt] N cormorán *m* (grande)

corn¹ [kɔ:n] N (*Brit*) (= *wheat*) trigo *m*; (*US*) (= *cereals*) cereales *mpl*; (*esp US*) (= *maize*) maíz *m*; (= *individual grains*) granos *mpl* ➤ **corn bread** (*US*) pan *m* de maíz ➤ **corn oil** aceite *m* de maíz ➤ **corn on the cob** mazorca *f* de maíz, choclo *m* (*And, SC*), elote *m* (*Mex*)

corn² [kɔ:n] N (*on foot*) callo *m*

cornea ['kɔ:nɪə] N córnea *f*

corned beef [,kɔ:nd'bi:f] N carne *f* de vaca en conserva

corner ['kɔ:nəʳ] **Ⓐ** N **1** (= *angle*) [*of object*] (*outer*) ángulo *m*, esquina *f*; (*inner*) rincón *m*; [*of mouth*] comisura *f*; [*of eye*] rabillo *m*; (= *bend in road*) curva *f*, recodo *m*; (*where two roads meet*) esquina *f*; **the ~ of a table/page** la esquina de una mesa/página; **in the ~ of the room** en un rincón de la habitación; **it's just around the ~** (*lit, fig*) está a la vuelta de la esquina; **to cut a ~** (*Aut*) tomar una curva muy cerrada; **out of the ~ of one's eye** con el rabillo del ojo; **to go round the ~** doblar la esquina; **to turn the ~** (*lit*) doblar la esquina; (*fig*) salir del apuro; **✦** IDIOMS **to cut ~s** (*Aut*) atajar; (= *save money, effort etc*) economizar (*en dinero, esfuerzos, tiempo etc*); **to be in a (tight) ~** estar en un aprieto **2** (*fig*) **every ~ of Europe** todos los rincones de Europa; **the four ~s of the world** las cinco partes del mundo **3** (*Ftbl*) córner *m*, saque *m* de esquina

Ⓑ VT **1** [+ *animal, fugitive*] acorralar, arrinconar; *(fig)* [+ *person*] abordar, detener **2** [+ *market*] acaparar **Ⓒ** VI *(Aut)* tomar las curvas **Ⓓ** CPD ➤ **corner seat** asiento *m* del rincón, rinconera *f* ➤ **corner shop** *(Brit)*, **corner store** *(US)* tienda *f* de la esquina, tienda *f* pequeña del barrio

cornerstone ['kɔ:nəstəʊn] N *(lit, fig)* piedra *f* angular

cornet ['kɔ:nɪt] N **1** *(Mus)* corneta *f* **2** *(Brit)* (= *ice cream*) cucurucho *m*

cornfield ['kɔ:nfi:ld] N *(Brit)* [*of wheat*] trigal *m*, campo *m* de trigo; *(US)* [*of maize*] maizal *m*, milpa *f*

cornflakes ['kɔ:nfleɪks] NPL copos *mpl* de maíz, cornflakes *mpl*; *(loosely)* cereales *mpl*

cornflour ['kɔ:nflaʊəʳ] N *(Brit)* harina *f* de maíz, maicena *f*

cornflower ['kɔ:nflaʊəʳ] N aciano *m*

cornice ['kɔ:nɪs] N cornisa *f*

Cornish ['kɔ:nɪʃ] **Ⓐ** ADJ de Cornualles **Ⓑ** N *(Ling)* córnico *m* **Ⓒ** CPD ➤ **Cornish pasty** *(Brit)* empanada *f* de Cornualles *(con cebolla, patata y carne)*

cornmeal ['kɔ:nmi:l] N harina *f* de maíz

cornstarch ['kɔ:nstɑ:tʃ] N *(US)* harina *f* de maíz, maicena *f*

cornucopia [,kɔ:njʊ'kəʊpɪə] N cuerno *m* de la abundancia

corny* ['kɔ:nɪ] ADJ *(compar* **cornier**; *superl* **corniest)** [*joke, story*] trillado, muy visto; [*film, play*] sensiblero, sentimental

corollary [kə'rɒlərɪ] N corolario *m*

coronary ['kɒrənərɪ] **Ⓐ** ADJ coronario **Ⓑ** N *(also ~* **thrombosis)** infarto *m*, trombosis *f* coronaria

coronation [,kɒrə'neɪʃən] N coronación *f*

coroner ['kɒrənəʳ] N juez *mf* de instrucción

coronet ['kɒrənɪt] N corona *f* (de marqués *etc*); (= *diadem*) diadema *f*

Corp ABBR **1** (= **Corporation**) ≈ S.A. **2** *(Mil)* = **Corporal**

corporal ['kɔ:pərəl] **Ⓐ** ADJ corporal **Ⓑ** N *(Mil)* cabo *m* **Ⓒ** CPD ➤ **corporal punishment** castigo *m* corporal

corporate ['kɔ:pərɪt] ADJ [*ownership, responsibility*] corporativo, colectivo; [*image, planning, identity, growth*] corporativo ➤ **corporate car** *(US)* coche *m* de la empresa

corporation [,kɔ:pə'reɪʃən] **Ⓐ** N **1** *(Brit Comm)* corporación *f*; *(US)* (= *limited company*) sociedad *f* anónima **2** [*of city*] ayuntamiento *m* **Ⓑ** CPD corporativo ➤ **corporation tax** *(Brit)* impuesto *m* sobre sociedades

corps [kɔ:ʳ] N *(pl ~* [kɔ:z]) *(Mil)* cuerpo *m* (de ejército) ➤ **corps de ballet** cuerpo *m* de baile

corpse [kɔ:ps] N cadáver *m*

corpulent ['kɔ:pjʊlənt] ADJ corpulento

corpuscle ['kɔ:pʌsl] N glóbulo *m*, corpúsculo *m*

corral [kə'rɑ:l] *(US)* **Ⓐ** N corral *m* **Ⓑ** VT acorralar

correct [kə'rekt] **Ⓐ** ADJ **1** (= *accurate*) correcto; **(that's) ~!** ¡correcto!, ¡exacto!; **your suspicions are ~** está en lo cierto con sus sospechas; **"correct fare only"** "importe exacto" **2 to be ~** [*person*] tener razón, estar en lo cierto; **am I ~ in saying that ...?** ¿me equivoco al decir que ...?, ¿estoy en lo cierto al decir que ...?; **it is ~ to say that ...** es acertado decir que ... **3** (= *appropriate*) [*method, weight, temperature*] apropiado, adecuado **4** (= *proper*) [*person, behaviour*] correcto; [*dress*] apropiado **Ⓑ** VT corregir; **me if I'm wrong, but ...** a lo mejor me equivoco, pero ...; **to ~ o.s.** corregirse

correcting fluid [kə,rektɪŋ'flu:ɪd] N corrector *m*

correction [kə'rekʃən] N **1** *(gen)* corrección *f*, rectificación *f*; *(on page)* tachadura *f* **2** *(esp US)* (= *punishment*) corrección *f*

correctly [kə'rektlɪ] ADV **1** [*answer, pronounce, behave*] correctamente; **if I remember ~** si mal no recuerdo; **if I understand you ~** si le he entendido bien **2** (= *appropriately*) **she refused, quite ~, to give in to his demands** se negó, con toda la razón, a ceder a sus exigencias

correctness [kə'rektnɪs] N **1** (= *accuracy*) [*of answer,

amount, term, calculation] exactitud *f* **2** (= *appropriateness*) [*of method, approach*] lo apropiado, lo adecuado **3** (= *decency*) [*of person, behaviour*] corrección *f*

correlate ['kɒrɪleɪt] **Ⓐ** VT establecer una correlación entre, correlacionar; **to ~ sth with sth** poner algo en correlación con algo **Ⓑ** VI tener correlación; **to ~ with** estar en correlación con

correlation [,kɒrɪ'leɪʃən] N correlación *f*

correspond [,kɒrɪs'pɒnd] VI **1** (= *agree*) corresponder **(with** con); (= *be equivalent*) equivaler **(to** a) **2** *(by letter)* mantener correspondencia **(with** con), escribirse

correspondence [,kɒrɪs'pɒndəns] **Ⓐ** N **1** (= *relation*) correspondencia *f*, conexión *f* **2** (= *letter-writing, letters*) correspondencia *f*; **to be in ~ with sb** mantener correspondencia con algn **Ⓑ** CPD ➤ **correspondence college** centro *m* de enseñanza por correspondencia ➤ **correspondence course** curso *m* por correspondencia

correspondent [,kɒrɪs'pɒndənt] N corresponsal *mf*; **I'm a hopeless ~** soy muy malo para escribir cartas

corresponding [,kɒrɪs'pɒndɪŋ] ADJ correspondiente

corridor ['kɒrɪdɔ:ʳ] N pasillo *m*, corredor *m*; **the ~s of power** los pasillos del poder

corroborate [kə'rɒbəreɪt] VT corroborar, confirmar

corrode [kə'rəʊd] **Ⓐ** VT corroer **Ⓑ** VI corroerse

corrosion [kə'rəʊʒən] N corrosión *f*

corrosive [kə'rəʊzɪv] ADJ corrosivo; *(fig)* destructivo

corrugated ['kɒrəgeɪtɪd] ADJ [*cardboard, paper*] ondulado ➤ **corrugated iron** hierro *m* ondulado, calamina *f* *(LAm)*

corrupt [kə'rʌpt] **Ⓐ** ADJ **1** (= *depraved*) pervertido, depravado **2** (= *dishonest*) corrompido, venal **3** *(Comput)* [*text, file*] corrompido **Ⓑ** VT **1** (= *deprave*) pervertir, corromper **2** [+ *language*] corromper; *(Comput)* [+ *text, file*] corromper **Ⓒ** CPD ➤ **corrupt practices** corrupción *f*sing

corruption [kə'rʌpʃən] N **1** (= *depravity*) perversión *f*, corrupción *f* **2** (= *dishonesty*) corrupción *f*, venalidad *f* **3** *(Comput)* [*of text, file*] corrupción *f*

corset ['kɔ:sɪt] N faja *f*; *(old style)* corsé *m*

Corsica ['kɔ:sɪkə] N Córcega *f*

Corsican ['kɔ:sɪkən] ADJ, N corso/a *m/f*

cortège [kɔ:'teɪʒ] N cortejo *m*

cortex ['kɔ:teks] N *(pl* **cortices** ['kɔ:tɪsi:z]) córtex *m*, corteza *f*

cortisone ['kɔ:tɪzəʊn] N cortisona *f*

COS ABBR (= **cash on shipment**) pago *m* al embarcar

cos¹ [kɒs] N *(Brit) (also ~* **lettuce)** lechuga *f* romana

cos²**, **'cos**** [kɒz] CONJ *(Brit)* = **because**

cosh [kɒʃ] *(Brit)* **Ⓐ** N porra *f*, cachiporra *f* **Ⓑ** VT aporrear

cosignatory ['kəʊ'sɪgnətərɪ] N cosignatario/a *m/f*

cosiness, coziness *(US)* ['kəʊzɪnɪs] N [*of room*] lo acogedor; (= *intimacy*) intimidad *f*

cosmetic [kɒz'metɪk] **Ⓐ** ADJ cosmético **Ⓑ** N cosmético *m* **Ⓒ** CPD ➤ **cosmetic surgery** cirugía *f* estética

cosmic ['kɒzmɪk] ADJ cósmico

cosmology [kɒz'mɒlədʒɪ] N cosmología *f*

cosmonaut ['kɒzmənɔ:t] N cosmonauta *mf*

cosmopolitan [,kɒzmə'pɒlɪtən] ADJ, N cosmopolita *mf*

cosmos ['kɒzmɒs] N cosmos *m*

cosset ['kɒsɪt] VT mimar, consentir

cost [kɒst] **Ⓐ** N **1** (= *expense*) costo *m*, coste *m* *(Sp)*; (= *amount paid, price*) precio *m*; **at ~** *(Comm)* a precio de costo *or* coste *(Sp)*; **at all ~s** ◇ **at any ~** ◇ **whatever the ~** *(fig)* cueste lo que cueste, a toda costa; **these solutions can be implemented at little ~** estas soluciones pueden ponerse en práctica a muy bajo costo *or* coste *(Sp)*; **at the ~ of his life/health** a costa de su vida/salud; **to my ~** *(fig)* a mis expensas **2 costs** *(legal)* costas *fpl*; *(commercial)* gastos *mpl* **Ⓑ** VT **1** *(pt, pp ~)* costar, valer; **how much does it ~?** ¿cuánto cuesta?, ¿cuánto vale?, ¿a cuánto está?; **it ~ £5** costó cinco libras; **what will it ~ to have it repaired?**

¿cuánto va a costar repararlo?; **it'll ~ you*** te va a salir caro; **it ~ him his life/job** le costó la vida/el trabajo; **whatever it ~s** (also fig) cueste lo que cueste; ✦ IDIOM **it ~s the earth*** cuesta un riñón, cuesta un ojo de la cara

2 (pt, pp **~ed**) (Comm) [+ articles for sale] calcular el costo or coste (Sp) de; [+ job] calcular el presupuesto de; **it has not been properly ~ed** no se ha calculado detalladamente el costo or coste (Sp)

⊙ CPD ➤ **cost analysis** análisis *m inv* de costos or costes (Sp) ➤ **cost control** control *m* de costos or costes (Sp) ➤ **cost of living** costo *m* or coste *m* (Sp) de la vida ➤ **cost price** (Brit) precio *m* de costo or coste (Sp); **at ~ price** a precio de costo or coste (Sp)

co-star ['kəʊstɑːʳ] **Ⓐ** N coprotagonista *mf*, coestrella *mf* **Ⓑ** VI **to ~ with sb** figurar con algn como protagonista **Ⓒ** VT **the film ~s A and B** la película presenta como protagonistas a A y B or está coprotagonizada por A y B

Costa Rica ['kɒstə'riːkə] N Costa Rica *f*

Costa Rican ['kɒstə'riːkən] ADJ, N costarricense *mf*

cost-benefit analysis [,kɒst,benəfɪt'næləsɪs] N análisis *m* coste-beneficio (Sp) or costo-beneficio (LAm)

cost-cutting ['kɒst,kʌtɪŋ] N recorte *m* de costes (Sp) or costos (LAm)

cost-effective [,kɒstɪ'fektɪv] ADJ rentable

cost-effectiveness [,kɒstɪ'fektɪvnɪs] N rentabilidad *f*, relación *f* coste-rendimiento (Sp) or costo-rendimiento (LAm)

costing ['kɒstɪŋ] N (esp Brit) cálculo *m* del coste (Sp), cálculo *m* del costo (LAm)

costly ['kɒstlɪ] ADJ (compar **costlier**; superl **costliest**) (= expensive) costoso; (= valuable) suntuoso

costume ['kɒstjuːm] **Ⓐ** N **1** (= fancy dress) disfraz *m*; (= lady's suit) traje *m* sastre; [of country] traje *m*; (also **bathing ~**) bañador *m*, traje *m* de baño **2 costumes** (Theat) vestuario *msing* **Ⓑ** CPD ➤ **costume drama** obra *f* dramática de época ➤ **costume jewellery** (Brit), **costume jewelry** (US) bisutería *f*, joyas *fpl* de fantasía

cosy, cozy (US) ['kəʊzɪ] **Ⓐ** ADJ (compar **cosier**; superl **cosiest**) **1** [room, atmosphere] acogedor **2** [chat] íntimo, personal **3** (pej) [arrangement, relationship] de lo más cómodo; [life] holgado **Ⓑ** N cubierta que se utiliza para mantener el té de una tetera, los huevos etc calientes

cot [kɒt] N (Brit) (for baby) cuna *f*; (US) (= folding bed) cama *f* plegable, catre* *m* ➤ **cot death** (Brit) muerte *f* en la cuna

cottage ['kɒtɪdʒ] N (= country house) casita *f* de campo, quinta *f* (LAm) ➤ **cottage cheese** requesón *m* ➤ **cottage hospital** (Brit) hospital *m* rural ➤ **cottage industry** industria *f* artesanal or casera ➤ **cottage loaf** (Brit) pan *m* casero ➤ **cottage pie** (Brit) pastel de carne cubierta de puré de patatas

cotton ['kɒtn] **Ⓐ** N (= cloth) algodón *m*; (= plant, industry etc) algodonero *m*; (Brit) (= thread) hilo *m* (de algodón); (US) (for cleaning, swabbing) algodón *m* hidrófilo **Ⓑ** CPD [shirt, dress] de algodón ➤ **cotton belt** (US Geog) zona *f* algodonera ➤ **cotton bud** (Brit) bastoncillo *m* de algodón ➤ **cotton candy** (US) algodón *m* (azucarado) ➤ **the cotton industry** la industria algodonera ➤ **cotton mill** fábrica *f* de algodón ➤ **cotton reel** carrete *m* de hilo, bobina *f* de hilo ➤ **cotton swab** (US) bastoncillo *m* de algodón ➤ **cotton wool** (Brit) algodón *m* hidrófilo ➤ **cotton on*** VI + ADV (Brit): **to ~ on (to sth)** caer en la cuenta (de algo)

couch [kaʊtʃ] **Ⓐ** N sofá *m*; (in doctor's surgery) camilla *f*; (psychiatrist's) diván *m* **Ⓑ** VT expresar; **~ed in jargon** redactado en jerigonza **Ⓒ** CPD ➤ **couch potato*** teleadicto/a *m/f*, persona *f* que se apalanca en el sofá

couchette [kuːˈʃet] N (esp Brit) litera *f*

cougar ['kuːgəʳ] N (esp US) puma *m*

cough [kɒf] **Ⓐ** N tos *f*; **to have a bad ~** tener mucha tos **Ⓑ** VI **1** (lit) toser **2** (**) (= confess) cantar* **Ⓒ** CPD ➤ **cough drop** pastilla *f* para la tos ➤ **cough mixture** (Brit) jarabe *m* para la tos ➤ **cough sweet** (Brit) caramelo *m* para la tos ➤ **cough up** VT + ADV **1** [+ blood, phlegm] (gen) escupir, arrojar; (Med) expectorar **2** (*) [+ money] soltar

could [kʊd] PT, COND of **can**[1]

couldn't ['kʊdnt] = **could not**; see **can**[1]

council ['kaʊnsl] **Ⓐ** N **1** (in local government) concejo *m* municipal; **city/town ~** ayuntamiento *m*; **you should write to the ~ about it** deberías escribir al ayuntamiento acerca de eso

2 (= committee) consejo *m*, junta *f*; (Rel) concilio *m* **Ⓑ** CPD ➤ **council estate** (Brit) barrio *m* de viviendas de protección oficial ➤ **council flat** (Brit) piso *m* or (LAm) departamento *m* de protección oficial ➤ **council house** (Brit) casa *f* de protección oficial ➤ **Council of Europe** Consejo *m* de Europa ➤ **council tax** (Brit) impuesto *municipal* ➤ **council tenant** (Brit) inquilino/a *m/f* (de una vivienda de protección oficial)

councillor, councilor (US) ['kaʊnsɪləʳ] N concejal(a) *m/f*

councilman ['kaʊnsɪlmən] N (pl **councilmen**) (US) concejal *m*

councilwoman ['kaʊnsl,wʊmən] N (pl **councilwomen**) (US) concejala *f*

counsel ['kaʊnsəl] **Ⓐ** N **1** (frm) (= advice) consejo *m*; **to keep one's own ~** guardar silencio **2** (Jur) (pl inv) abogado/a *m/f*; **~ for the defence** (Brit) abogado/a *m/f* defensor(a); **~ for the prosecution** (Brit) fiscal *mf* **Ⓑ** VT [+ person] (frm) (= advise) aconsejar; (Med etc) orientar; **to ~ sb to do sth** aconsejar a algn que haga algo

counselling, counseling (US) ['kaʊnsəlɪŋ] N (= advice) asesoramiento *m*; (Psych) asistencia *f* psicológica ➤ **counselling service** (gen) servicio *m* de orientación; (Psych) servicio *m* de asistencia psicológica

counsellor, counselor (US) ['kaʊnsələʳ] N **1** (Psych) consejero/a *m/f*; (= adviser) asesor(a) *m/f* **2** (US Scol) consejero/a *m/f*, asesor(a) *m/f* **3** (Irl, US Jur) (also **~-at-law**) abogado/a *m/f*

count[1] [kaʊnt] **Ⓐ** N **1** (= act of counting) recuento *m*; [of votes] escrutinio *m*, recuento *m*; (Boxing) cuenta *f*; **to keep/lose ~ (of sth)** llevar/perder la cuenta (de algo); **at the last ~** en el último recuento; **to be out for the ~** estar fuera de combate

2 (= total) recuento *m*; **the final ~** (in election) el último recuento; **hold the stretch for a ~ of ten, then relax** estírese y cuente hasta diez, luego relájese

3 (Jur) cargo *m*; **he was found guilty on all ~s** fue declarado culpable de todos los cargos

4 (= point) **you're wrong on both ~s** estás equivocado en los dos aspectos; **I think she deserves recognition on two ~s** creo que merece reconocimiento por dos motivos

Ⓑ VT **1** (= add up, check) contar; **she was ~ing the days until he came home** contaba los días que faltaban para su vuelta; **to ~ the cost of (doing) sth** (lit) reparar en el coste de (hacer) algo; (fig) reparar en las consecuencias de (hacer) algo

2 (= include) contar; **not ~ing the children** sin contar a los niños; **ten ~ing him** diez con él, diez contándolo a él

3 (= consider) considerar; **I ~ myself lucky** me considero feliz; **~ yourself lucky!** ¡date por satisfecho!

Ⓒ VI **1** (= add) contar; **to ~ to ten** contar hasta diez

2 (= be valid) valer, contar; **that doesn't ~** eso no vale, eso no cuenta; **every second ~s** cada segundo cuenta or es importante; **it will ~ against him** irá en su contra; **two children ~ as one adult** dos niños cuentan como un adulto; **ability ~s for little here** aquí la capacidad que se tenga sirve de muy poco

⒟ CPD ➤ **count noun** sustantivo *m* contable ➤ **count in*** VT + ADV incluir; **~ me in!** ¡yo me apunto!, ¡cuenta conmigo!; **to ~ sb in on sth** contar con algn para algo ➤ **count on** VI + PREP contar con; **we're ~ing on him** contamos con él; **I wouldn't ~ on it!** ¡no contaría con ello!; **he's ~ing on winning** cuenta con ganar; **he can be ~ed on to ruin everything** puedes contar con que or puedes estar seguro de que él lo estropeará todo ➤ **count out** VT + ADV **1** [+ money] ir contando; [+ small objects] contar (uno por uno) **2** (= exclude) descartar; **we can't ~ out the possibility that they'll attack** no podemos descartar la posibilidad de que ataquen **3** (*) **(you can) ~ me out of this!** ¡no cuentes conmigo para esto!, ¡déjame fuera de esto! ➤ **count toward(s)** VI + PREP contar para; **this work ~s**

toward(s) your final degree este trabajo cuenta para la nota final de la licenciatura
➤ **count up** VT + ADV contar
➤ **count upon** VI + PREP = **count on**

count² [kaʊnt] N (= *nobleman*) conde *m*

countable [ˈkaʊntəbl] ADJ contable ➤ **countable noun** nombre *m* contable

countdown [ˈkaʊntdaʊn] N cuenta *f* atrás, cuenta *f* regresiva (*LAm*)

countenance [ˈkaʊntɪnəns] Ⓐ N (*liter*) semblante *m*, rostro *m* Ⓑ VT (*frm*) **to ~ sth** consentir *or* permitir algo; **to ~ sb doing sth** permitir a algn que haga algo

counter¹ [ˈkaʊntəʳ] Ⓐ N 1 [*of shop*] mostrador *m*; [*of canteen*] barra *f*; (= *position in post office, bank*) ventanilla *f*; **you can buy it over the ~** (*Med*) esto se compra sin receta médica 2 (*in game*) ficha *f* 3 (= *device*) contador *m* Ⓑ CPD ➤ **counter staff** personal *m* de ventas

counter² [ˈkaʊntəʳ] Ⓐ ADV ~ **to** contrario a, en contra de; **to run ~ to** ir en sentido contrario a, ser contrario a Ⓑ VT [+ *blow*] responder a, parar; [+ *attack*] contestar a, hacer frente a; **to ~ sth with sth/by doing sth** contestar a algo con algo/haciendo algo Ⓒ VI **to ~ with** contestar *or* responder con

counteract [ˌkaʊntərˈækt] VT contrarrestar

counter-attack [ˈkaʊntərəˌtæk] Ⓐ N contraataque *m* Ⓑ VT, VI contraatacar

counterbalance [ˈkaʊntəˌbæləns] Ⓐ N contrapeso *m*; (*fig*) compensación *f* Ⓑ VT contrapesar; (*fig*) compensar

counterclaim [ˈkaʊntəkleɪm] N (*Jur*) contrademanda *f*

counterclockwise [ˈkaʊntəˈklɒkwaɪz] ADV (*US*) en sentido contrario al de las agujas del reloj

counter-espionage [ˈkaʊntərˈespɪənɑːʒ] N contraespionaje *m*

counterfeit [ˈkaʊntəfiːt] Ⓐ ADJ (= *false*) falsificado; [*note, coin*] falso Ⓑ N falsificación *f* Ⓒ VT falsificar

counterfoil [ˈkaʊntəfɔɪl] N (*Brit*) matriz *f* (*Sp*), talón *m* (*LAm*)

countermand [ˈkaʊntəmɑːnd] VT revocar, cancelar

counter-measure [ˈkaʊntəmeʒəʳ] N contramedida *f*

counter-offensive [ˈkaʊntərəˈfensɪv] N contraofensiva *f*

counterpart [ˈkaʊntəpɑːt] N (= *equivalent*) equivalente *m*; (= *person*) homólogo/a *m/f*

counter-productive [ˌkaʊntəprəˈdʌktɪv] ADJ contraproducente

countersign [ˈkaʊntəsaɪn] VT refrendar

countertenor [ˈkaʊntəˌtenəʳ] N contratenor *m*

countertop [ˈkaʊntətɒp] N (*US*) encimera *f*

countess [ˈkaʊntɪs] N condesa *f*

countless [ˈkaʊntlɪs] ADJ incontable, innumerable; **on ~ occasions** infinidad *f* de veces

country [ˈkʌntrɪ] Ⓐ N 1 (= *nation*) país *m*; (= *people*) pueblo *m*; **to go to the ~** (*Brit Pol*) convocar a elecciones generales
2 (= *native land*) patria *f*
3 (= *countryside*) campo *m*; **in the ~** en el campo
4 (= *terrain, land*) terreno *m*, tierra *f* Ⓑ CPD ➤ **country and western (music)** música *f* country, música *f* ranchera (*Mex*) ➤ **country club** club *m* campestre ➤ **country dancing** danza *f* folklórica ➤ **country folk** gente *f* del campo ➤ **country house** (*Brit*) casa *f* de campo, quinta *f*; (= *farm*) finca *f* (*esp LAm*), rancho *m* (*Mex*) ➤ **country road** camino *m* vecinal

countryman [ˈkʌntrɪmən] N (*pl* **countrymen**) 1 (= *rural dweller*) hombre *m* del campo, campesino *m* 2 (*also* **fellow-~**) compatriota *m*

countryside [ˈkʌntrɪsaɪd] N campo *m*

countrywide [ˌkʌntrɪˈwaɪd] ADJ nacional

countrywoman [ˈkʌntrɪˌwʊmən] N (*pl* **countrywomen**) 1 (= *rural dweller*) campesina *f* 2 (*also* **fellow-~**) compatriota *f*

county [ˈkaʊntɪ] N (*Brit*) condado *m*; (*US*) (= *subdivision of state*) comarca *f*, municipio *m* ➤ **county council, county commission** (*US*) ≈ diputación *f* provincial ➤ **county court**

(*Brit*) juzgado *m* de primera instancia ➤ **county road** (*US*) ≈ carretera *f* secundaria ➤ **county seat** (*US*), **county town** (*Brit*) capital *f* de condado

coup [kuː] N (*also* ~ **d'état**) golpe *m* (de estado); (= *triumph*) éxito *m* ➤ **coup de grace** golpe *m* de gracia

coupé (*Brit*) [ˈkuːpeɪ], **coupe** (*US*) [kuːp] N cupé *m*

couple [ˈkʌpl] Ⓐ N 1 (= *pair*) par *m*; **a ~ of** un par de
2 (= *partners*) pareja *f*; (= *married couple*) matrimonio *m*
3 (= *two or three*) **just a ~ of minutes** dos minutos nada más; **we had a ~ in a bar*** tomamos un par de copas en un bar Ⓑ VT (= *put together*) unir a, juntar (**with** con); **to ~ on** *or* **up (to)** (*Tech*) acoplar (a), enganchar (a); ~**d with** (= *together with*) junto con

couplet [ˈkʌplɪt] N pareado *m*

coupon [ˈkuːpɒn] N (*for price reduction or gifts*) vale *m*; (*for information, subscription*) cupón *m*; (= *football pools coupon*) boleto *m*

courage [ˈkʌrɪdʒ] N valor *m*, valentía *f*; **to have the ~ of one's convictions** obrar de acuerdo con su conciencia

courageous [kəˈreɪdʒəs] ADJ valiente, valeroso

courgette [kʊəˈʒet] N (*Brit*) calabacín *m*, calabacita *f*

courier [ˈkʊrɪəʳ] N (= *messenger*) mensajero/a *m/f*; (= *tourist guide*) guía *mf* de turismo

course [kɔːs] Ⓐ N 1 (= *route, direction*) [*of ship, plane*] rumbo *m*; [*of river*] curso *m*; [*of planet*] órbita *f*; **to change** (*lit*) cambiar de rumbo; **the government has changed ~ on Europe** el gobierno ha dado un nuevo rumbo *or* giro a su política con respecto a Europa; **to go off** ~ (*lit, fig*) desviarse de su rumbo; **the plane was 300 miles off** ~ el avión se había desviado 300 millas de su rumbo; **we are on ~ for victory** vamos bien encaminados para la victoria
2 (= *line of action*) **the best ~ would be to ...** lo mejor sería ...; **we have to decide on the best ~ of action** tenemos que decidir cuáles son las mejores medidas a tomar; **it's the only ~ left open to him** es la única opción que le queda
3 (= *process*) curso *m*; **in the ~ of the next few days** en el curso de los próximos días; **in the ~ of my work** en el cumplimiento de mi trabajo; **in the normal ~ of events** normalmente; **it changed the ~ of history** cambió el curso de la historia; **to let things take their ~** dejar que las cosas sigan su curso
4 **of ~** claro, desde luego, por supuesto, cómo no (*esp LAm*), sí pues (*SC*); **of ~! I should have known** ¡pero si está claro! me lo tenía que haber imaginado; **"can I have a drink?" — "of ~ you can"** —¿puedo tomar algo de beber? —claro *or* desde luego *or* por supuesto que sí; **I've read about her in the papers, of ~** por supuesto, la conozco de los periódicos; **of ~, I may be wrong** claro que puedo estar confundido; **of ~ not!** (*answering*) ¡claro que no!, ¡por supuesto que no!
5 (*Scol, Univ*) curso *m*; **to do a ~ in/on sth** hacer un curso de algo; **a ~ in business administration** un curso de administración de empresas; **short** ~ cursillo *m*
6 (*Med*) **she was put on a ~ of steroids** le pusieron un tratamiento a base de esteroides
7 (*Sport*) (= *distance*) recorrido *m*; (= *surface*) pista *f*; (= *racecourse*) hipódromo *m*; ✦ IDIOM **to stay the ~** no cejar, aguantar hasta el final
8 (*Culin*) plato *m*; **main** ~ plato *m* principal; **a three-~ meal** una comida de tres platos Ⓑ VI [*water, air*] correr; [*tears*] rodar; [*sweat*] caer Ⓒ CPD ➤ **course book** libro *m* de texto (*que se sigue en un curso determinado*) ➤ **course work** trabajos *mpl* (para clase)

court [kɔːt] Ⓐ N 1 (*Jur*) tribunal *m*, juzgado *m*, corte *f* (*esp LAm*); (= *officers and/or public*) tribunal *m*; **to take sb to ~ (over sth)** llevar a algn a los tribunales *or* ante el tribunal (por algo); **to settle (a case) out of** ~ llegar a un acuerdo las partes (sin ir a juicio)
2 (*Tennis*) pista *f*, cancha *f*
3 (*royal*) corte *f* Ⓑ VT 1 (= *woman*) pretender *or* cortejar a
2 [+ *death, disaster*] buscar, exponerse a Ⓒ VI (†) ser novios; **are you ~ing?** ¿tienes novio? Ⓓ CPD ➤ **court action she was threatened with ~ action** la amenazaron con llevarla a juicio, la amenazaron con presentar una demanda judicial contra ella ➤ **court case**

caso *m* judicial ➤ **court martial** (*pl* **~s martial** *or* **~ martials**) consejo *m* de guerra, tribunal *m* militar ➤ **court of appeal** tribunal *m* de apelación ➤ **court of law** tribunal *m* de justicia ➤ **court order** mandato *m* judicial ➤ **court shoe** (*Brit*) escarpín *m*

courteous [ˈkɜːtɪəs] ADJ cortés, atento

courtesy [ˈkɜːtɪsɪ] N (= *politeness*) cortesía *f*; (= *polite act*) atención *f*, gentileza *f*; **by ~ of** (por) cortesía de; **you might have had the ~ to tell me** podrías haber tenido la gentileza de decírmelo ➤ **courtesy call** visita *f* de cumplido ➤ **courtesy car** coche *m* de cortesía ➤ **courtesy card** (*US*) tarjeta *f* (de visita)

courthouse [ˈkɔːthaʊs] N (*esp US Jur*) palacio *m* de justicia

courtier [ˈkɔːtɪəʳ] N cortesano/a *m/f*

court-martial [ˈkɔːtˈmɑːʃəl] VT juzgar en consejo de guerra

courtship [ˈkɔːtʃɪp] N noviazgo *m*

courtyard [ˈkɔːtjɑːd] N patio *m*

cousin [ˈkʌzn] N primo/a *m/f*; **first ~** primo/a *m/f* carnal; **second ~** primo/a *m/f* segundo/a

cove [kəʊv] N (= *bay*) cala *f*, ensenada *f*; (*US*) (= *valley*) valle *m*

covenant [ˈkʌvɪnənt] **Ⓐ** N 1 (*legal*) pacto *m*, convenio *m*; (*also* **tax ~**) (*Brit*) *sistema de contribuciones caritativas con beneficios fiscales para el beneficiario* 2 **Covenant** (*Bible*) Alianza *f*

Coventry [ˈkɒvəntrɪ] N ✦ IDIOM **to send sb to ~** (*Brit*) hacer el vacío a algn

cover [ˈkʌvəʳ] **Ⓐ** N 1 [*of dish, saucepan*] tapa *f*, tapadera *f*; [*of furniture, typewriter*] funda *f*; [*of lens*] tapa *f*; (*on vehicle*) cubierta *f*
2 (= *bedspread*) cubrecama *m*, colcha *f*; (= *blanket*) manta *f*, frazada *f* (*LAm*), cobija *f* (*LAm*)
3 [*of magazine*] portada *f*; [*of book*] cubierta *f*, tapa *f*; **to read a book from ~ to ~** leer un libro de cabo a rabo
4 (*Comm*) **under separate ~** por separado
5 (= *shelter*) cobijo *m*, refugio *m*; (*for hiding*) escondite *m*; (= *covering fire*) cobertura *f*; **to break ~** salir al descubierto; **to run for ~** correr a cobijarse; (*fig*) ponerse a buen recaudo; **to take ~ (from)** (= *shelter*) protegerse *or* resguardarse (de); **under ~** a cubierto; (= *indoors*) bajo techo; **under ~ of darkness** al amparo de la oscuridad
6 (*Brit Fin, Insurance*) cobertura *f*; **full/fire ~** cobertura total/contra incendios
7 (*in espionage etc*) tapadera *f*; **to blow sb's ~*** (*accidentally*) poner a algn al descubierto; (*intentionally*) desenmascarar a algn
8 (*Brit frm*) (*at table*) cubierto *m*
Ⓑ VT 1 (*gen*) [*+ surface*] (*gen*) cubrir (**with** con); [*+ saucepan, hole, eyes, face*] tapar (**with** con); [*+ book*] forrar (**with** con); [*+ chair*] tapizar (**with** de, con); **to ~ one's face with one's hands** taparse la cara con las manos; **to be ~ed in *or* with snow/chocolate** estar cubierto de nieve/chocolate
2 (= *hide*) [*+ feelings, facts, mistakes*] ocultar; **to ~ (up) one's tracks** (*lit, fig*) borrar las huellas
3 (= *protect*) (*esp Mil, Sport*) cubrir; **the soldiers ~ed our retreat** los soldados nos cubrieron la retirada; **he only said that to ~ himself** lo dijo sólo para cubrirse; ✦ IDIOM **to ~ one's back*** cubrirse las espaldas
4 (= *point gun at*) **I've got you ~ed!** ¡te tengo a tiro!, ¡te estoy apuntando!
5 (*Insurance*) cubrir; **what does your travel insurance ~ you for?** ¿qué (cosas) cubre tu seguro de viaje?; **the house is ~ed against fire** la casa está asegurada contra incendios
6 (= *be sufficient for*) [*+ cost, expenses*] cubrir, sufragar; **£10 will ~ everything** con diez libras será suficiente
7 (= *deal with*) [*+ problem, area*] abarcar; [*+ points in discussion*] tratar, discutir
8 [*+ distance*] recorrer, cubrir; **we ~ed eight miles in one hour** recorrimos ocho millas en una hora; **to ~ a lot of ground** (*in travel, work*) recorrer mucho trecho; (= *deal with many subjects*) abarcar muchos temas
9 (= *report on*) cubrir; **all the newspapers ~ed the story** todos los periódicos cubrieron el caso; **he was sent to ~ the riots** lo enviaron para que hiciera un reportaje de los disturbios
Ⓒ VI **to ~ for sb** (*at work etc*) suplir a algn; (= *protect*) encubrir a algn

Ⓓ CPD ➤ **cover charge** (*in restaurant*) (precio *m* del) cubierto *m* ➤ **cover girl** modelo *f* de portada ➤ **cover letter** (*US*) carta *f* de explicación ➤ **cover note** (*Brit*) seguro *m* provisional ➤ **cover story** tapadera *f* ➤ **cover version** versión *f*
➤ **cover up Ⓐ** VT + ADV 1 [*+ child, object*] cubrir completamente, tapar 2 (= *hide*) [*+ facts*] ocultar; [*+ emotions*] disimular **Ⓑ** VI + ADV **to ~ up for sb** encubrir a algn

coverage [ˈkʌvərɪdʒ] N (*Press*) reportaje *m*; **to give full ~ to an event** (= *report widely*) dar amplia difusión a un suceso; (= *report in depth*) informar a fondo sobre un suceso

coveralls [ˈkʌvərɔːlz] NPL (*US*) mono *msing*

covering [ˈkʌvərɪŋ] **Ⓐ** N 1 (= *wrapping*) cubierta *f*, envoltura *f* 2 (= *layer*) capa *f*; **a ~ of snow/dust** una capa de nieve/polvo **Ⓑ** CPD ➤ **covering letter** (*Brit*) carta *f* de explicación

covert [ˈkʌvət] ADJ (*gen*) secreto, encubierto; [*glance*] furtivo, disimulado

cover-up [ˈkʌvərʌp] N encubrimiento *m*; **there's been a ~** están tratando de encubrir el asunto

covet [ˈkʌvɪt] VT codiciar

covetous [ˈkʌvɪtəs] ADJ [*person*] codicioso; [*glance*] ávido

cow¹ [kaʊ] **Ⓐ** N 1 (= *farm animal*) vaca *f*; (= *female of other species*) hembra *f*; ✦ IDIOM **till the ~s come home** hasta que las ranas críen pelo 2 (**) (= *woman*) estúpida* *f*, bruja** *f* **Ⓑ** CPD ➤ **cow town*** (*US*) pueblucho *m* de mala muerte

cow² [kaʊ] VT [*+ person*] intimidar, acobardar

coward [ˈkaʊəd] N cobarde *m/f*

cowardice [ˈkaʊədɪs], **cowardliness** [ˈkaʊədlɪnɪs] N cobardía *f*

cowardly [ˈkaʊədlɪ] ADJ cobarde

cowboy [ˈkaʊbɔɪ] **Ⓐ** N 1 vaquero *m*, gaucho *m* (*Arg*); (*Cine etc*) cowboy *m*; **~s and Indians** (= *game*) indios *mpl* y americanos 2 (*Brit* pej*) pillo/a* *m/f*, chorizo/a *m/f* (*Sp*) **Ⓑ** CPD ➤ **cowboy boots** botas *fpl* camperas ➤ **cowboy hat** sombrero *m* de cowboy

cower [ˈkaʊəʳ] VI encogerse (de miedo)

cowhide [ˈkaʊhaɪd] N cuero *m*

cowl [kaʊl] N (= *hood*) capucha *f*; (= *garment*) cogulla *f*; [*of chimney*] sombrerete *m*

cowpat [ˈkaʊpæt] N boñiga *f*

cowshed [ˈkaʊʃed] N establo *m*

cowslip [ˈkaʊslɪp] N (*Brit*) primavera *f*, prímula *f*

cox [kɒks] N timonel *mf*

coxswain [ˈkɒksn] N timonel *mf*

coy [kɔɪ] ADJ (*compar* **~er**; *superl* **~est**) 1 (= *demure*) tímido; (= *coquettish*) coqueta, coquetón 2 (= *evasive*) esquivo, reticente

coyote [kɔɪˈəʊtɪ] N coyote *m*

coziness [ˈkəʊzɪnɪs] N (*US*) = **cosiness**

cozy [ˈkəʊzɪ] ADJ (*US*) = **cosy**

CP N ABBR (= **Communist Party**) PC *m*

CPA N ABBR (*US*) = **Certified Public Accountant**

CPR N ABBR (= **cardiopulmonary resuscitation**) RCP *f*, reanimación *f* cardiopulmonar

CPU N ABBR (*Comput*) (= **central processing unit**) UPC *f*, UCP *f*

crab [kræb] **Ⓐ** N 1 (*Zool*) cangrejo *m*, jaiba *f* (*LAm*); **the Crab** (*Astron*) (la constelación de) Cáncer 2 **crabs** (*Med*) ladillas *fpl* **Ⓑ** CPD ➤ **crab apple** (= *fruit*) manzana *f* silvestre; (= *tree*) manzano *m* silvestre

crabby* [ˈkræbɪ] ADJ malhumorado, hosco

crack [kræk] **Ⓐ** N 1 (*in plate, glass*) raja *f*; (*in wall, ice, skin*) grieta *f* (*also fig*)
2 (= *slight opening*) rendija *f*; **I opened the door a ~** abrí un poquito la puerta
3 (= *noise*) [*of twigs*] crujido *m*; [*of whip*] chasquido *m*; [*of rifle*] estampido *m*, estallido *m*; ✦ IDIOM **to get a fair ~ of the whip** (*Brit*) tener la oportunidad de demostrar lo que uno vale

4 (= *blow*) golpe *m*
5 (*) (= *try*) **to have a ~ at sth** intentar algo
6 (*) (= *joke, insult*) comentario *m* burlón
7 (= *drug*) crack *m*
8 at the ~ of dawn al romper el alba
9 (*) (= *fun*) **it's good** ~ es muy divertido
Ⓑ ADJ [*team, sportsperson, troops*] de primera
Ⓒ VT **1** (= *break*) [+ *glass, pottery*] rajar; [+ *wood, ground, wall, skin*] agrietar, resquebrajar; [+ *ice*] resquebrajar; [+ *skin*] agrietar
2 (= *break open*) [+ *nut*] cascar; [+ *egg*] cascar, romper; [+ *safe*] forzar; [+ *drugs/spy ring*] desarticular; **to ~ (open) a bottle*** abrir una botella
3 (= *hit*) golpear; **he fell and ~ed his head on the pavement** se cayó y se golpeó la cabeza con la acera
4 (= *cause to sound*) [+ *whip*] chasquear, restallar; [+ *finger joints*] hacer crujir; ✦ IDIOM **to ~ the whip** apretar a algn las clavijas
5 (*) (= *tell*) **to ~ jokes** bromear, contar chistes
6 (= *solve*) [+ *problem, case*] resolver; [+ *code*] descifrar
Ⓓ VI **1** (= *break*) [*glass, pottery*] rajarse; [*wall, wood, ground*] agrietarse, resquebrajarse; [*ice*] resquebrajarse; [*skin*] agrietarse
2 [*voice*] (*with emotion*) quebrarse
3 (= *break down*) [*person*] desmoronarse, sufrir una crisis nerviosa
4 (= *make noise*) [*whip*] chasquear; [*wood, joints*] crujir
5 ✦ IDIOM **to get ~ing*** poner manos a la obra
Ⓔ CPD ➤ **crack cocaine** crack *m*
➤ **crack down** VI + ADV **to ~ down (on sth/sb)** tomar medidas enérgicas *or* duras (contra algo/algn)
➤ **crack on*** VI + ADV (*Brit*) ponerse en marcha, ponerse las pilas*
➤ **crack up*** **Ⓐ** VI + ADV **1** (*Psych*) [*person*] desmoronarse, sufrir una crisis nerviosa **2** (= *laugh*) troncharse de risa*
Ⓑ VT + ADV **the film's not all it's ~ed up to be** la película no es tan buena como se dice

crackdown [ˈkrækdaʊn] N campaña *f* (**on** contra), medidas *fpl* enérgicas (**on** contra)

cracked [krækt] ADJ **1** [*cup, plate*] rajado; [*wall, skin*] agrietado; [*lips*] cortado, agrietado **2** (*Brit**) (= *mad*) chiflado*, tarado*

cracker [ˈkrækəʳ] N **1** (= *firework*) buscapiés *m inv* **2** (*also* **Christmas ~**) sorpresa *f* (navideña) **3** (= *biscuit*) galleta *f* salada, cráquer *m* **4** (*Brit**) **a ~ of a game** un partido fenomenal*

crackers* [ˈkrækəz] ADJ (*Brit*) lelo, chiflado*

cracking* [ˈkrækɪŋ] (*Brit*) **Ⓐ** ADJ **at a ~ speed** a toda pastilla* **Ⓑ** ADV **her books are ~ good stuff** sus libros son superbuenos*

crackle [ˈkrækl] **Ⓐ** N (= *noise*) [*of twigs burning*] crepitación *f*, chisporroteo *m*; [*of frying*] chisporroteo *m*; (*on radio, telephone*) interferencia *f* **Ⓑ** VI [*burning twigs*] crepitar, chisporrotear; [*bacon*] chisporrotear; [*phone line*] tener interferencias

crackling [ˈkræklɪŋ] N **1** (*Culin*) chicharrones *mpl* **2** (= *sound*) chisporroteo *m*; (*on radio, telephone*) interferencias *fpl*

crackpot [ˈkrækpɒt] **Ⓐ** ADJ tonto **Ⓑ** N chiflado/a* *m/f*, excéntrico/a *m/f*

cradle [ˈkreɪdl] **Ⓐ** N cuna *f* **Ⓑ** VT [+ *child*] mecer, acunar; [+ *object*] abrazar **Ⓒ** CPD ➤ **cradle snatcher*: she's a ~ snatcher** le gusta ir detrás de los jovencitos, es una asalta cunas*

craft [krɑːft] **Ⓐ** N **1** (= *trade*) oficio *m* **2** (= *skill*) destreza *f*, habilidad *f* **3** (= *handicraft*) artesanía *f*; **arts and ~s** artesanías *fpl* **4** (= *cunning*) astucia *f*, maña *f* **5** (= *boat*) (*pl inv*) barco *m*, embarcación *f* **Ⓑ** VT hacer (a mano); **~ed** products productos *mpl* de artesanía **Ⓒ** CPD ➤ **craft, design and technology** (*Brit Scol*) diseño y pretecnología ➤ **craft fair** feria *f* de artesanía

craftsman [ˈkrɑːftsmən] N (*pl* **craftsmen**) artesano *m*

craftsmanship [ˈkrɑːftsmənʃɪp] N (= *skill*) destreza *f*, habilidad *f*; (= *workmanship*) trabajo *m*

craftswoman [ˈkrɑːftswʊmən] N (*pl* **craftswomen**) artesana *f*

crafty [ˈkrɑːftɪ] ADJ (*compar* **craftier**; *superl* **craftiest**)
1 [*person*] astuto, vivo; [*action*] hábil **2** [*gadget etc*] ingenioso

crag [kræg] N peñasco *m*, risco *m*

craggy [ˈkrægɪ] ADJ (*compar* **craggier**; *superl* **craggiest**) [*rock*] rocoso, escarpado; [*features*] hosco, arrugado

cram [kræm] **Ⓐ** VT **1** (= *stuff*) meter (**into** en); **we can't ~ any more in** es imposible meter más **2** (= *fill*) llenar a reventar (**with** de); **the hall is ~med** la sala está de bote en bote; **the room was ~med with furniture** la habitación estaba atestada de muebles
Ⓑ VI **1** [*people*] apelotonarse (**into** en); **seven of us ~med into the Mini** los siete nos metimos como pudimos en el Mini **2** [*pupil*] (*for exam*) matarse estudiando, empollar (*Sp**), matearse (*Chi**), clavarse (*Col**), zambutir (*Mex**), chancar (*Per**), tragar (*River Plate**)

cram-full [ˈkræmˈfʊl] ADJ atestado (**of** de)

cramp [kræmp] **Ⓐ** N calambre *m* **Ⓑ** VT ✦ IDIOM **to ~ sb's style** cortar las alas a algn

cramped [kræmpt] ADJ [*position*] encogido, incómodo; **to live in ~ conditions** vivir en la estrechez

crampon [ˈkræmpən] N crampón *m*

cranberry [ˈkrænbərɪ] N arándano *m* ➤ **cranberry sauce** salsa *f* de arándanos

crane [kreɪn] **Ⓐ** N **1** (= *bird*) grulla *f* **2** (= *machine*) grúa *f*
Ⓑ VT **to ~ one's neck** estirar el cuello **Ⓒ** CPD ➤ **crane driver, crane operator** operador(a) *m/f* de grúa

cranefly [ˈkreɪnflaɪ] N típula *f*

cranium [ˈkreɪnɪəm] N cráneo *m*

crank¹ [kræŋk] **Ⓐ** N manivela *f*, manubrio *m* **Ⓑ** VT [+ *engine*] hacer arrancar con la manivela

crank²* [kræŋk] N (*Brit*) (= *eccentric*) excéntrico/a *m/f*; (*US*) (= *irritable person*) ogro* *m*, cascarrabias* *mf inv*

crankshaft [ˈkræŋkʃɑːft] N cigüeñal *m*

cranky* [ˈkræŋkɪ] ADJ (*compar* **crankier**; *superl* **crankiest**) (*Brit*) (= *eccentric*) excéntrico; (*US*) (= *irritable*) malhumorado, enojón (*LAm*)

cranny [ˈkrænɪ] N grieta *f*

crap*** [kræp] **Ⓐ** N (= *faeces*) mierda*** *f*; (= *nonsense*) estupideces *fpl*, macanas* *fpl*, gilipolleces *fpl* (*Sp***), huevadas *fpl* (*Chi, And****), boludeces *fpl* (*SC****); **that's ~** eso son gilipolleces**, eso es una chorrada* **Ⓑ** ADJ [*joke, job*] pésimo; **the film was ~** la película era una mierda*** **Ⓒ** VI cagar***

crappy*** [ˈkræpɪ] ADJ chungo*

craps [kræps] NSING (*US*) (= *game*) dados *mpl*; **to shoot ~** jugar a los dados

crash [kræʃ] **Ⓐ** N **1** (= *noise*) estrépito *m*; (= *thunder*) estruendo *m*; (= *explosion*) estallido *m*
2 (= *accident*) (*Aut*) choque *m*; (*Aer*) accidente *m*; **to have a ~** (*Aut*) tener un accidente de coche, chocar con el coche; **to be in a car/plane ~** tener un accidente de coche/ aviación
3 [*of stock exchange*] crac *m*
Ⓑ VT [+ *car, aircraft etc*] estrellar (**into** contra)
Ⓒ VI **1** [*plane*] estrellarse, caer a tierra; [*two vehicles*] chocar; **to ~ into** chocar *or* estrellarse contra
2 (= *fall noisily*) caer con estrépito; (= *move noisily*) moverse de manera ruidosa
3 (*Fin*) [*business*] quebrar; [*stock exchange*] derrumbarse, sufrir una fuerte crisis; **when the stock market ~ed** cuando la bolsa se derrumbó
4 (*Comput*) bloquearse, colgarse (*Sp*)
Ⓓ EXCL ¡zas!, ¡pum!
Ⓔ CPD [*diet etc*] intensivo, acelerado ➤ **crash barrier** (*Brit Aut*) quitamiedos *m inv*; (*at stadium etc*) valla *f* protectora ➤ **crash course** curso *m* intensivo *or* acelerado ➤ **crash helmet** casco *m* protector ➤ **crash landing** aterrizaje *m* forzoso *or* de emergencia
➤ **crash out**** VI + ADV (= *sleep*) dormirse; (= *collapse*) caer redondo

crashing† [ˈkræʃɪŋ] ADJ **a ~ bore** una paliza*, un muermo (*Sp**)

crash-land [ˈkræʃlænd] **Ⓐ** VI aterrizar forzosamente **Ⓑ** VT poner forzosamente en tierra

crass [kræs] ADJ [*stupidity*] extremo; [*mistake*] craso; [*person, behaviour*] grosero, maleducado

crate [kreɪt] Ⓐ N cajón *m* de embalaje, jaula *f* Ⓑ VT (*also ~ up*) embalar (en cajones)

crater [ˈkreɪtəʳ] N cráter *m*

cravat [krəˈvæt] N pañuelo *m*

crave [kreɪv] VT [+ *food*] tener antojo de; [+ *affection, attention*] reclamar

craving [ˈkreɪvɪŋ] N (*for food etc*) antojo *m*; (*for affection, attention*) anhelo *m*, ansias *fpl*; **to get a ~ for sth** encapricharse por algo

crawfish [ˈkrɔːfɪʃ] N (*pl ~*) (*US*) = **crayfish**

crawl [krɔːl] Ⓐ N 1 (= *slow pace*) **the traffic went at a ~** la circulación avanzaba a paso de tortuga
2 (*Swimming*) crol *m*; **to do the ~** nadar a crol
Ⓑ VI 1 (= *drag o.s.*) arrastrarse; [*child*] andar a gatas, gatear; **to ~ in/out** meterse/salirse a gatas
2 (= *move slowly*) [*traffic*] avanzar lentamente, formar caravana
3 (*) (= *suck up*) **to ~ to sb** dar coba a algn*, hacer la pelota a algn*
4 **to be ~ing with vermin** estar plagado *or* cuajado de bichos; **the street was ~ing with police** la calle estaba plagada de policías

crayfish [ˈkreɪfɪʃ] N (*Brit*) (*pl ~*) (*freshwater*) cangrejo *m or* (*LAm*) jaiba *f* de río; (*saltwater*) cigala *f*

crayon [ˈkreɪən] N (*Art*) pastel *m*, lápiz *m* de tiza; (*child's*) lápiz *m* de color

craze [kreɪz] N (= *fashion*) moda *f* (**for** de); (= *fad*) manía *f* (**for** por); **it's the latest ~** es la última moda, es el último grito

crazed [kreɪzd] ADJ [*look, person*] loco, demente

crazy [ˈkreɪzɪ] Ⓐ ADJ (*compar* **crazier**; *superl* **craziest**)
1 (= *mad*) loco, chiflado*; **you were ~ to do it** fue una locura hacerlo; **you would be ~ to do that** tendrías que estar loco para hacer eso; **to drive sb ~** (*lit*) volver loco a algn; (= *infuriate*) sacar de quicio a algn; **to go ~** (= *mad*) volverse loco; (= *excited*) ponerse como loco; (= *angry*) ponerse como un energúmeno; **it was a ~ idea** fue una locura *or* un disparate, era una idea descabellada *or* disparatada; **everyone shouted like ~** todos gritaban como locos; **I've done some ~ things in my time** he hecho algunas locuras en mi vida
2 (*) (= *keen*) **to be ~ about sb** estar loco por algn; **they're ~ about football** el fútbol les vuelve locos; **I'm not ~ about it** no es que me vuelva loco, no me entusiasma
Ⓑ N (*US**) loco/a *m/f*
Ⓒ CPD ➤ **crazy bone** (*US*) hueso *m* del codo ➤ **crazy house*** (*US*) casa *f* de locos*, manicomio *m* ➤ **crazy paving** pavimento *m* de baldosas irregulares ➤ **crazy quilt** (*US*) edredón *m* de retazos

CRE N ABBR (*Brit*) = **Commission for Racial Equality**

creak [kriːk] Ⓐ N [*of wood, floorboard, shoe*] crujido *m*; [*of hinge*] chirrido *m* Ⓑ VI [*wood, floorboard, shoe*] crujir; [*hinge*] chirriar

creaky [ˈkriːkɪ] ADJ (*compar* **creakier**; *superl* **creakiest**) rechinador; (*fig*) poco sólido

cream [kriːm] Ⓐ N 1 (*on milk*) nata *f* (*Sp*), crema *f* (*LAm*)
2 (*for face, shoes etc*) crema *f*, pomada *f*; **shoe ~** betún *m*
3 (*fig*) flor *f* y nata, crema *f*; **the ~ of society** la flor y nata de la sociedad
Ⓑ ADJ 1 (= *cream-coloured*) color crema *inv*
2 (= *made with cream*) de nata (*Sp*) *or* crema (*LAm*)
Ⓒ VT [+ *butter*] batir; **~ed potatoes** puré *msing* de patatas (*Sp*) *or* papas (*LAm*)
Ⓓ CPD ➤ **cream cake** pastel *m* de nata (*Sp*) *or* crema (*LAm*)
➤ **cream cheese** queso *m* crema ➤ **cream cracker** (*Brit*) galleta *f* de soda ➤ **cream of tartar** crémor *m* tártaro
➤ **cream of tomato soup** sopa *f* de crema de tomate
➤ **cream of wheat** (*US*) sémola *f* ➤ **cream puff** petisú *m*, pastel *m* de nata (*Sp*) *or* crema (*LAm*) ➤ **cream soda** gaseosa *f* de vainilla ➤ **cream tea** (*Brit*) *merienda en cafetería que suele constar de té, bollos, mermelada y nata*

➤ **cream off*** VT + ADV separar lo mejor de

creamer [ˈkriːməʳ] N (*US*) jarrita *f* para la leche

creamery [ˈkriːmərɪ] N lechería *f*

creamy [ˈkriːmɪ] ADJ (*compar* **creamier**; *superl* **creamiest**) [*taste, texture*] cremoso; [*colour*] color crema *inv*

crease [kriːs] Ⓐ N 1 (= *fold*) raya *f*; (= *wrinkle*) arruga *f*
2 (*Cricket*) línea *f* de bateo Ⓑ VT [+ *paper*] doblar; (*esp several times*) plegar; [+ *clothes*] arrugar Ⓒ VI arrugarse
➤ **crease up*** (*Brit*) Ⓐ VT + ADV **he was ~d up (with laughter)** se tronchaba (de risa) Ⓑ VI + ADV troncharse (de risa)

create [kriːˈeɪt] Ⓐ VT (*gen*) crear; [+ *problem*] causar, crear Ⓑ VI (*Brit***) armar un lío*, montar un número (*Sp**)

creation [kriːˈeɪʃən] N creación *f*

creative [kriːˈeɪtɪv] ADJ creativo; **~ thinking** creatividad *f*
➤ **creative accounting** contabilidad *f* embellecida
➤ **creative writing** escritura *f* creativa

creativity [ˌkriːeɪˈtɪvɪtɪ] N creatividad *f*

creator [kriːˈeɪtəʳ] N creador(a) *m/f*

creature [ˈkriːtʃəʳ] N (*gen*) criatura *f*; (= *animal*) animal *m*; (= *insect etc*) bicho *m*; **poor ~!** ¡pobrecito!; **~ of habit** esclavo/a *m/f* de la costumbre ➤ **creature comforts** comodidades *fpl* (materiales)

crèche [kreɪʃ] N (*Brit*) guardería *f*

credence [ˈkriːdəns] N **to give ~ to** dar crédito a

credentials [krɪˈdenʃəlz] NPL (= *identifying papers*) credenciales *fpl*; (= *letters of reference*) referencias *fpl*

credibility [ˌkredəˈbɪlɪtɪ] N credibilidad *f* ➤ **credibility gap** falta *f* de credibilidad

credible [ˈkredɪbl] ADJ (*gen*) creíble, digno de crédito; [*person*] plausible; [*witness*] de integridad

credit [ˈkredɪt] Ⓐ N 1 (*Fin*) 1.1 (*esp Brit*) (*in bank account*) **his account is in ~** su cuenta tiene saldo positivo *or* está en números negros 1.2 (*for purchases*) crédito *m*; **they were refused ~** se les denegó un crédito; **is his ~ good?** ¿se le puede dar crédito sin riesgo?; **to buy sth on ~** comprar algo a crédito *or* a plazos 1.3 (*Accounting*) saldo *m* acreedor, saldo *m* positivo; **on the ~ side** (*lit*) en el haber; (*fig*) entre los aspectos positivos
2 (= *honour*) **he's a ~ to his family** es un orgullo para su familia, honra a su familia; **it does you ~** dice mucho a tu favor, te honra; **to his ~, I must point out that ...** debo decir en su favor que ...
3 (= *recognition*) mérito *m*; **they deserve ~ for not giving up** merecen que se les reconozca el mérito de no haberse rendido; **~ where ~'s due** a cada uno según sus méritos; **to get/take the ~ for (doing) sth** llevarse el mérito de (haber hecho) algo; **to give sb ~ for (doing) sth** reconocer a algn el mérito de (haber hecho) algo
4 (= *credence*) **he's a lot better than people give him ~ for** es bastante mejor que lo que la gente cree
5 **credits** (= *titles*) títulos *mpl* de crédito, créditos *mpl*; (= *achievements*) logros *mpl*
6 (*Univ*) (= *award*) crédito *m*
Ⓑ VT 1 (= *believe*) creer; **would you ~ it!** ¡parece mentira!
2 (= *attribute*) **I ~ed him with more sense** le creía más sensato; **~ me with some sense!** ¡no me tomes por idiota!
3 (*Comm*) [+ *money, interest*] abonar, ingresar; **the money was ~ed to his account** el dinero se abonó *or* se ingresó en su cuenta
Ⓒ CPD ➤ **credit balance** saldo *m* acreedor, saldo *m* positivo ➤ **credit card** tarjeta *f* de crédito ➤ **credit limit** límite *m* de crédito ➤ **credit note** (*Brit*) nota *f* de crédito
➤ **credit rating** clasificación *f* crediticia; (*fig*) credibilidad *f*
➤ **credit slip** (*US*) nota *f* de crédito ➤ **credit union** cooperativa *f* de crédito

creditable [ˈkredɪtəbl] ADJ loable, encomiable

creditor [ˈkredɪtəʳ] N acreedor(a) *m/f*

creditworthy [ˈkredɪtˌwɜːðɪ] ADJ solvente

credulity [krɪˈdjuːlɪtɪ] N credulidad *f*

credulous [ˈkredjʊləs] ADJ crédulo

creed [kriːd] N credo *m*

creek [kriːk] N (*esp Brit*) (= *inlet*) cala *f*, ensenada *f*; (*US*)

(= *stream*) riachuelo *m*; ✦ IDIOM **up the ~ (without a paddle)*** en un lío *or* (*LAm*) aprieto

creep [kriːp] (*pt, pp* **crept**) Ⓐ VI **1** [*animal*] deslizarse, arrastrarse; [*plant*] trepar
2 [*person*] (*stealthily*) avanzar sigilosamente; **to ~ in/out** entrar/salir sigilosamente; **to ~ about on tiptoe** andar a *or* de puntillas; **to ~ along** [*traffic*] avanzar a paso de tortuga; **to ~ up on sb** acercarse sigilosamente a algn
3 (*fig*) **it made my flesh ~** me puso la carne de gallina; **doubts began to ~ in** las dudas empezaron a aparecer; **an error crept in** se deslizó un error; **he felt old age ~ing up on him** sintió como la vida le ganaba años
Ⓑ N **1** (*) **what a ~!** (= *toady*) ¡qué lameculos es!*; **he's a ~** (= *odd person*) ¡qué tipo más raro!, ¡qué bicho!
2 it gives me the ~s* me da miedo, me da escalofríos

creeper [ˈkriːpəʳ] N **1** (= *plant*) enredadera *f* **2 creepers** (*US*) (*for baby*) pelele *m*sing

creeping [ˈkriːpɪŋ] ADJ progresivo ➤ **creeping inflation** inflación *f* progresiva

creepy* [ˈkriːpɪ] ADJ (*compar* **creepier**; *superl* **creepiest**) horripilante, escalofriante

creepy-crawly* [ˈkriːpɪˈkrɔːlɪ] N (*Brit*) bicho *m*

cremate [krɪˈmeɪt] VT incinerar

cremation [krɪˈmeɪʃən] N cremación *f*, incineración *f*

crematorium [ˌkreməˈtɔːrɪəm], **crematory** (*US*) [ˈkremə̩tɔːrɪ] N crematorio *m*

crème caramel [ˌkremkærəˈmel] N flan *m*

crème de la crème [ˈkremdəlɑːˈkrem] N **the ~** la crème de la crème, la flor y nata

crème fraîche [ˌkremˈfreʃ] N crema elaborada con nata agria

Creole [ˈkriːəʊl] Ⓐ ADJ criollo Ⓑ N **1** (= *person*) criollo/a *m/f* **2** (*Ling*) lengua *f* criolla

creosote [ˈkrɪəsəʊt] Ⓐ N creosota *f* Ⓑ VT echar creosota a

crepe, crêpe [kreɪp] N (= *fabric*) crespón *m* ➤ **crepe bandage** venda *f* de crespón ➤ **crepe paper** papel *m* crepé ➤ **crepe sole** suela *f* de crepé

crept [krept] PT, PP *of* **creep**

crescendo [krɪˈʃendəʊ] N crescendo *m*

crescent [ˈkresnt] Ⓐ ADJ creciente Ⓑ N (= *shape*) medialuna *f*; (*esp Brit*) (= *street*) calle en forma de semicírculo Ⓒ CPD ➤ **crescent moon** luna *f* creciente

cress [kres] N berro *m*

crest [krest] N **1** [*of bird, wave*] cresta *f*; [*of turkey*] moco *m*; [*of hill*] cima *f*, cumbre *f*; ✦ IDIOM **to be on the ~ of a wave** estar en la cresta de la ola **2** (*Heraldry*) blasón *m*

crestfallen [ˈkrestˌfɔːlən] ADJ cariacontecido

Crete [kriːt] N Creta *f*

cretin [ˈkretɪn] N cretino/a *m/f*

Creutzfeldt-Jakob disease [ˌkrɔɪtsfeltˈjækɒbdɪˌziːz] N enfermedad *f* de Creutzfeldt-Jakob

crevasse [krɪˈvæs] N grieta *f*

crevice [ˈkrevɪs] N grieta *f*, hendedura *f*

crew [kruː] Ⓐ N **1** (*Aer, Naut*) tripulación *f*; (*Navy*) dotación *f*; (*excluding officers*) marineros *mpl* rasos; **three of the ~** tres tripulantes **2** (*Cine, Rowing, gen*) (= *team*) equipo *m* **3** (= *gang*) pandilla *f*, banda *f* Ⓑ VI **to ~ for sb** hacer de tripulación para algn Ⓒ VT tripular Ⓓ CPD ➤ **crew cut** pelado *m* al rape

crewman [ˈkruːmən] N (*pl* **crewmen**) **1** (*Naut*) tripulante *m* **2** (*TV etc*) miembro *m* del equipo (*de cámara etc*)

crew-neck [ˈkruːnek] N cuello *m* de barco; (*also* **~ sweater**) suéter *m* con cuello de barco

crib [krɪb] Ⓐ N **1** (*Brit*) (*for infant*) pesebre *m*; (*US*) (*for toddler*) cuna *f*; (= *nativity scene*) Belén *m* **2** (*Brit Scol**) (= *piece of plagiarism*) plagio *m*; (*in exam*) chuleta* *f*; (= *translation*) traducción *f* Ⓑ VT (*Brit Scol**) plagiar, tomar (**from** de) Ⓒ VI (*Brit Scol**) usar una chuleta* Ⓓ CPD ➤ **crib death** (*US*) muerte *f* en la cuna

cribbage [ˈkrɪbɪdʒ] N *juego de cartas que se juega utilizando un tablero de puntuación*

crick [krɪk] Ⓐ N **to have a ~ in one's neck/back** tener tortícolis/lumbago Ⓑ VT **to ~ one's neck** hacerse daño en el cuello

cricket¹ [ˈkrɪkɪt] N (= *insect*) grillo *m*

cricket² [ˈkrɪkɪt] Ⓐ N (= *sport*) críquet *m*, crícket *m* Ⓑ ADJ [*match, ball, bat*] de críquet

cricketer [ˈkrɪkɪtəʳ] N criquetero/a *m/f*, jugador(a) *m/f* de críquet

crikey†** [ˈkraɪkɪ] EXCL (*Brit*) ¡caramba!

crime [kraɪm] Ⓐ N **1** (= *offence*) delito *m*; (*very serious*) crimen *m*; **it's a ~ to let that food go to waste** es un crimen echar a perder esa comida; **it's not a ~!** (*fig*) ¡no es para tanto! **2** (= *activity*) delincuencia *f*; **~ is rising** la delincuencia va en aumento; ✦ PROV **~ doesn't pay** el crimen no compensa Ⓑ CPD ➤ **crime of passion** crimen *m* pasional ➤ **crime prevention** prevención *f* del crimen ➤ **crime wave** ola *f* de crímenes *or* delitos ➤ **crime writer** autor(a) *m/f* de novelas policíacas

criminal [ˈkrɪmɪnl] Ⓐ N criminal *mf*
Ⓑ ADJ **1** (*Jur*) [*act, activity, behaviour*] delictivo; [*investigation, organization*] criminal; [*trial, case*] penal
2 (= *shameful*) **it would be ~ to throw them away** sería una barbaridad *or* un crimen tirarlos; **it was a ~ waste of resources** era un crimen desperdiciar recursos así
Ⓒ CPD ➤ **criminal court** juzgado *m* de lo penal ➤ **the criminal justice system** el sistema penal ➤ **criminal law** derecho *m* penal ➤ **criminal lawyer** penalista *mf*, abogado/a *m/f* criminalista ➤ **criminal record** antecedentes *mpl* penales; **to have a ~ record** tener antecedentes penales

criminology [ˌkrɪmɪˈnɒlədʒɪ] N criminología *f*

crimp [krɪmp] VT [+ *hair*] rizar, encrespar

crimson [ˈkrɪmzn] Ⓐ ADJ carmesí *inv* Ⓑ N carmesí *m*

cringe [krɪndʒ] VI (= *shrink back*) encogerse (**at** ante); **to ~ with embarrassment** morirse de vergüenza; **it makes me ~** me da horror

crinkle [ˈkrɪŋkl] Ⓐ N arruga *f* Ⓑ VI arrugarse

cripple [ˈkrɪpl] Ⓐ N (*lame*) cojo/a *m/f*, lisiado/a *m/f*; (*disabled*) minusválido/a *m/f*; **he's an emotional ~** tiene serios traumas Ⓑ VT **1** (*physically*) lisiar, mutilar **2** (*fig*) [+ *ship, plane*] inutilizar; [+ *production, exports*] paralizar

crippled [ˈkrɪpld] ADJ **1** (= *disabled*) minusválido; **he is ~ with arthritis** está paralizado por la artritis **2** (*fig*) [*plane, vehicle*] averiado; [*factory*] paralizado

crippling [ˈkrɪplɪŋ] ADJ [*disease*] que conduce a la parálisis; [*blow, defect*] muy grave, muy severo; [*taxes, debts*] abrumador, agobiante

crisis [ˈkraɪsɪs] N (*pl* **crises** [ˈkraɪsiːz]) crisis *f inv*; (*Med*) punto *m* crítico; **to come to a ~** entrar en crisis; **we've got a ~ on our hands** estamos enfrentándonos a una crisis ➤ **crisis management** gestión *f* de crisis

crisp [krɪsp] Ⓐ ADJ (*compar* **~er**; *superl* **~est**) **1** (= *crunchy*) [*lettuce, salad*] fresco; [*apple, snow, bacon, leaves*] crujiente; [*banknote*] nuevecito **2** (= *cold, clear*) [*day, morning*] frío y despejado **3** (= *sharp*) [*voice, sound*] bien definido, nítido; [*image*] nítido **4** (= *brisk*) [*tone, reply*] seco, tajante; [*statement, phrase*] escueto; **a ~ prose style** una prosa escueta Ⓑ N (*Brit*) (*also* **potato ~**) patata *f* frita (*Sp*) (*de bolsa*), papa *f* (frita) (*LAm*) (*de bolsa*)

crispbread [ˈkrɪspbred] N pan *m* tostado (escandinavo)

crispy [ˈkrɪspɪ] ADJ (*compar* **crispier**; *superl* **crispiest**) crujiente

criss-cross [ˈkrɪskrɒs] Ⓐ ADJ entrecruzado Ⓑ VI entrecruzarse Ⓒ VT entrecruzar

criterion [kraɪˈtɪərɪən] N (*pl* **criteria** [kraɪˈtɪərɪə]) criterio *m*

critic [ˈkrɪtɪk] N (= *reviewer*) crítico/a *m/f*; **he's a fierce ~ of the government** es muy crítico del gobierno

critical [ˈkrɪtɪkəl] Ⓐ ADJ **1** (= *important*) [*factor, element*] crítico; [*issue*] apremiante; [*problem*] muy serio; **it is ~ to understand what is happening** es de vital importancia entender lo que está ocurriendo
2 (= *decisive*) [*moment, stage*] crítico
3 (= *perilous, serious*) [*situation, state*] crítico
4 (*Med*) [*patient, condition, illness*] grave; **to be off the ~ list**

estar fuera de peligro
5 (= *fault-finding*) [*attitude, remark, report*] crítico; **he's too ~** siempre está criticando, critica demasiado; **to be ~ of sth/sb** criticar algo/a algn
6 (= *analytical*) [*person, reader, analysis*] crítico
7 (= *relating to critics*) **the film met with ~ acclaim** la película fue aplaudida por la crítica; **to be a ~ success** [*book, play etc*] ser un éxito de crítica
8 (*Phys, Nuclear Physics*) [*temperature, pressure*] crítico; **to go ~** empezar una reacción en cadena
Ⓑ CPD ➤ **critical mass** masa *f* crítica

critically ['krɪtɪkəlɪ] ADV **1** [*ill, injured*] gravemente, de gravedad; **~ important** crucial; **we are running ~ low on food supplies** nuestras provisiones de alimentos están quedando reducidas a unos niveles críticos
2 [*speak, say*] con desaprobación, en tono de crítica
3 [*study, examine, watch*] con ojo crítico, críticamente
4 (*by critics*) **the band's ~ acclaimed new album** el nuevo disco del grupo, aclamado por la crítica; **his first two books were ~ acclaimed** sus dos primeros libros tuvieron muy buena acogida por parte de la crítica

criticism ['krɪtɪsɪzəm] N crítica *f*

criticize ['krɪtɪsaɪz] VT, VI criticar

critique [krɪ'tiːk] N crítica *f*

croak [krəʊk] Ⓐ VI **1** [*raven*] graznar; [*frog*] croar, cantar; [*person*] carraspear **2** (*) (= *die*) estirar la pata**, espicharla* Ⓑ VT (= *say*) decir con voz ronca

croaky ['krəʊkɪ] ADJ [*voice*] ronco

Croat ['krəʊæt] N croata *mf*

Croatia [krəʊ'eɪʃə] N Croacia *f*

Croatian [krəʊ'eɪʃən] ADJ, N croata *mf*

crochet ['krəʊʃeɪ] Ⓐ N ganchillo *m*, croché *m* Ⓑ VT hacer de ganchillo, hacer en croché Ⓒ VI hacer ganchillo *or* croché Ⓓ CPD ➤ **crochet hook** aguja *f* de ganchillo

crock [krɒk] N **1** (= *earthenware pot*) vasija *f* de barro **2** (*Brit**) (*also* **old ~**) (= *person*) carcamal* *m*, vejete/a* *m/f*; (= *car etc*) cacharro* *m*

crockery ['krɒkərɪ] N (*Brit*) loza *f*, vajilla *f*

crocodile ['krɒkədaɪl] N cocodrilo *m*; **to walk in a ~** (*Brit*) andar en doble fila ➤ **crocodile tears** lágrimas *fpl* de cocodrilo

crocus ['krəʊkəs] N (*pl* **-es**) azafrán *m*

Croesus ['kriːsəs] N ✦ IDIOM **to be as rich as ~** nadar en la abundancia

croft [krɒft] N granja *f* pequeña

crofter ['krɒftə'] N arrendatario/a *m/f* de una granja pequeña

croissant ['kwæsɒŋ] N croissant *m*, cruasán *m*, medialuna *f* (*esp LAm*)

crone [krəʊn] N bruja *f*, vieja *f*

crony* ['krəʊnɪ] N compinche* *mf*, amigote/a* *mf*

crook [krʊk] Ⓐ N **1** (*shepherd's*) cayado *m*; (*bishop's*) báculo *m* **2** **the ~ of one's arm** el pliegue del codo **3** (*) (= *thief*) ladrón/ona *m/f*; (= *villain*) maleante *mf* Ⓑ VT [+ *finger*] doblar; **to ~ one's arm** empinar el codo Ⓒ ADJ (*Australia**) (= *ill*) mal

crooked ['krʊkɪd] ADJ **1** (= *not straight*) torcido, chueco (*LAm*); (= *bent over*) encorvado, doblado; [*smile*] torcido **2** (*) (= *dishonest*) [*deal*] sucio; [*means*] nada honrado; [*person*] nada honrado, criminal

croon [kruːn] VT, VI canturrear, cantar en voz baja

crop [krɒp] Ⓐ N **1** (= *species grown*) cultivo *m*; (= *produce*) [*of fruit, vegetables*] cosecha *f*; [*of cereals*] cereal *m*; (*fig*) montón *m* **2** (= *riding crop*) fusta *f*, látigo *m* de montar Ⓑ VT (= *cut*) [+ *hair*] cortar al rape; (= *eat*) [+ *grass*] pacer Ⓒ CPD ➤ **crop circle** círculo misterioso en los sembrados ➤ **crop sprayer** (= *device*) fumigadora *f* (de cultivos), sulfatadora *f*; (= *plane*) avión *m* fumigador
➤ **crop up** VI + ADV surgir, presentarse; **something must have ~ped up** habrán tenido algún problema, habrá pasado *or* surgido algo

cropper* ['krɒpə'] N ✦ IDIOM **to come a ~** (= *fall*) darse un

batacazo*, cazar la liebre*; (= *fail*) llevarse una buena plancha *or* un buen planchazo*

croquet ['krəʊkeɪ] N croquet *m*

croquette [krəʊ'ket] N croqueta *f*

cross [krɒs] Ⓐ N **1** (= *sign, decoration*) cruz *f*; **to sign with a ~** marcar con una cruz; **the Cross** la Cruz; ✦ IDIOM **we each have our ~ to bear** cada cual carga su cruz
2 (*Bio, Zool*) cruce *m*, cruzamiento *m*; (*fig*) mezcla *f*; **it's a ~ between a horse and a donkey** es un cruce *or* cruzamiento de caballo y burro; **the game is a ~ between squash and tennis** el juego es una mezcla de squash y tenis, el juego está a medio camino entre el squash y el tenis
3 (= *bias*) **cut on the ~** cortado al bies *or* al sesgo
4 (*Ftbl*) centro *m*, pase *m* cruzado
Ⓑ ADJ **1** (= *angry*) enfadado, enojado (*LAm*); (= *vexed*) molesto; **to get ~ with sb (about sth)** enfadarse *or* (*LAm*) enojarse con algn (por algo); **it makes me ~ when that happens** me da mucha rabia que pase eso
2 (= *diagonal etc*) transversal, oblicuo
Ⓒ VT **1** [+ *road, room, threshold, bridge*] cruzar; [+ *river, sea, desert*] cruzar, atravesar; **the bridge ~es the river here** el puente atraviesa el río por aquí; **it ~ed my mind that ...** se me ocurrió que ...; **they have clearly ~ed the boundary into terrorism** han traspasado con creces la frontera que los separaba del terrorismo; ✦ IDIOM **we'll ~ that bridge when we come to it** no anticipemos problemas
2 (*Brit*) (= *draw line across*) [+ *cheque*] cruzar
3 **to ~ o.s.** santiguarse; **~ my heart!** ¡te lo juro!
4 (= *place crosswise*) [+ *arms, legs*] cruzar; **keep your fingers ~ed for me!** ¡deséame suerte!; **there was a ~ed line** (*Telec*) había (un) cruce de líneas; ✦ IDIOMS **they got their lines ~ed** hubo un malentendido entre ellos; **to ~ swords with sb** cruzar la espada con algn
5 (= *thwart*) [+ *person*] contrariar, ir contra; **to be ~ed in love** sufrir un fracaso sentimental
6 [+ *animals, plants*] cruzar
Ⓓ VI **1** (= *go to other side*) **he ~ed from one side of the room to the other to speak to me** cruzó *or* atravesó la sala para hablar conmigo, fue hasta el otro lado de la sala para hablar conmigo; **to ~ from Newhaven to Dieppe** pasar *or* cruzar de Newhaven a Dieppe
2 [*roads, letters, people*] cruzarse
➤ **cross off** VT + ADV tachar
➤ **cross out** VT + ADV borrar
➤ **cross over** Ⓐ VI + ADV (= *cross the road*) cruzar; (= *change sides*) cambiar de chaqueta, ser un/una tránsfuga Ⓑ VI + PREP cruzar

crossbar ['krɒsbɑː'] N [*of bicycle*] barra *f*; [*of goalpost*] travesaño *m*, larguero *m*

cross-border ['krɒs'bɔːdə'] ADJ [*conflict*] fronterizo; [*trade*] internacional, transfronterizo

crossbow ['krɒsbəʊ] N ballesta *f*

crossbreed ['krɒsbriːd] Ⓐ N cruce *m*, híbrido *m* Ⓑ VT (*pt, pp* **crossbred**) cruzar

cross-Channel ferry [ˌkrɒs'tʃænl'ferɪ] N transbordador *m* que cruza el Canal de la Mancha

cross-check ['krɒstʃek] VT comprobar una vez más *or* por otro sistema, verificar

cross-country ['krɒs'kʌntrɪ] ADJ [*route, walk*] a campo traviesa ➤ **cross-country race** cross *m inv*, campo *m* a través ➤ **cross-country running** cross *m* ➤ **cross-country skiing** esquí *m* de fondo

cross-current ['krɒs'kʌrənt] N contracorriente *f*

cross-dress ['krɒsdres] VI travestirse

cross-examination ['krɒsɪgˌzæmɪ'neɪʃən] N (*Jur*) repreguntas *fpl*; (*fig*) interrogatorio *m*

cross-examine ['krɒsɪg'zæmɪn] VT (*Jur*) repreguntar; (*fig*) interrogar (severamente)

cross-eyed ['krɒsaɪd] ADJ bizco

cross-fertilize ['krɒs'fɜːtɪlaɪz] VT fecundar por fertilización cruzada

crossfire ['krɒsfaɪə'] N fuego *m* cruzado; **we were caught in the ~** quedamos atrapados en medio del tiroteo *or* en el fuego cruzado; (*fig*) nos veíamos atacados por ambos lados

crossing ['krɒsɪŋ] **Ⓐ** N **1** (*by sea*) travesía *f* **2** (= *road junction*) cruce *m*; (*Brit*) (= *pedestrian crossing*) paso *m* de peatones **Ⓑ** CPD ➤ **crossing guard** (*US*) *persona encargada de ayudar a los niños a cruzar la calle* ➤ **crossing point** paso *m*; (*at border*) paso *m* fronterizo

cross-legged ['krɒs'legd] ADV **to sit ~ on the floor** sentarse en el suelo con las piernas cruzadas

crossly ['krɒslɪ] ADV con enfado *or* (*LAm*) enojo; **"what do you mean?" he said ~** —¿qué quieres decir con eso? —dijo enfadado *or* (*LAm*) enojado

crossover ['krɒsəʊvə'] N (*Mus*) fusión *f*

cross-purposes ['krɒs'pɜ:pəsɪz] NPL **I think we're at ~** me temo que hemos tenido un malentendido; **we were talking at ~** hablábamos de cosas distintas

cross-question ['krɒs'kwestʃən] VT (*Jur*) repreguntar; (*fig*) interrogar

cross-reference ['krɒs'refərəns] **Ⓐ** N remisión *f* **Ⓑ** VT poner referencia cruzada a; **to ~ A to Q** hacer una remisión de A a Q, poner en A una nota que remite al usuario a Q

crossroads ['krɒsrəʊdz] NSING cruce *m*, encrucijada *f*; ✦ IDIOM **to be at a ~** estar en una encrucijada

cross-section ['krɒs'sekʃən] N [*of population*] muestra *f* (representativa)

crosswalk ['krɒs,wɔ:k] N (*US*) paso *m* de peatones

crosswind ['krɒswɪnd] N viento *m* de costado

crosswise ['krɒswaɪz] ADV transversalmente

crossword ['krɒswɜ:d] N (*also* ~ **puzzle**) crucigrama *m*

crotch [krɒtʃ] N entrepierna *f*

crotchet ['krɒtʃɪt] N (*Brit Mus*) negra *f*

crotchety ['krɒtʃɪtɪ] ADJ arisco, malhumorado

crouch [kraʊtʃ] VI (*also* ~ **down**) [*person*] agacharse, ponerse en cuclillas; [*animal*] agazaparse

croup [kru:p] N (*Med*) crup *m*

croupier ['kru:pɪeɪ] N crupier *mf*

crouton, croûton ['kru:tɒn] N cuscurro *m*, picatoste *m*

crow [krəʊ] **Ⓐ** N **1** (= *bird*) cuervo *m*; **as the ~ flies** en línea recta, a vuelo de pájaro; **stone the ~s!*** ¡caray!* **2** (= *noise*) [*of cock*] cacareo *m*; [*of baby, person*] grito *m*; **a ~ of delight** un gorjeo de placer **Ⓑ** VI **1** [*cock*] cacarear, cantar **2** [*child*] gorjear; (*fig*) jactarse, pavonearse; **it's nothing to ~ about** no hay motivo para sentirse satisfecho

crowbar ['krəʊbɑ:'] N palanca *f*

crowd [kraʊd] **Ⓐ** N **1** (= *mass*) multitud *f*, muchedumbre *f*; **she lost him in the ~** lo perdió de vista entre la multitud *or* la muchedumbre *or* el gentío; **~s of people** una multitud de gente; **there was quite a ~** había bastante gente **2** (= *spectators*) público *m*, espectadores *mpl*; **a ~ of 10,000 watched the parade** 10.000 espectadores presenciaron el desfile; **the match drew a big ~** el partido atrajo mucho público **3** (*) (= *social group*) gente *f*; **she got in with a nice ~** se juntó con (una) gente maja **4** (= *common people*) **she's just one of the ~** es del montón; **to follow the ~** dejarse llevar por los demás *or* por la corriente **Ⓑ** VT **1** (= *fill*) [+ *place*] atestar, llenar; **demonstrators ~ed the streets** los manifestantes atestaron *or* llenaron las calles; **new buildings ~ the narrow lanes of the old town** los nuevos edificios se apiñan en los estrechos callejones del casco viejo **2** (= *squeeze, force*) apiñar; **they ~ed the prisoners into trucks** apiñaron a los prisioneros en unos camiones **3** (= *press against*) empujar **4** (= *harass*) agobiar **Ⓒ** VI (= *gather together*) **to ~ in** entrar en tropel; **we all ~ed into her little flat** todos nos metimos en su pisito, abarrotándolo de gente; **thousands of people have ~ed into the capital** miles de personas han llegado en tropel a la capital; **to ~ around sth/sb** apiñarse alrededor de algo/algn **Ⓓ** CPD ➤ **crowd control** control *m* de masas ➤ **crowd**

scene (*Cine, Theat*) escena *f* multitudinaria ➤ **crowd out** VT + ADV atestar; **the bar was ~ed out** el bar estaba atestado (de gente)

crowded ['kraʊdɪd] ADJ [*room*] atestado (de gente), abarrotado (de gente); [*meeting, event*] muy concurrido; (= *busy*) [*day*] lleno de actividad; **they live in ~ conditions** viven hacinados; **the bar gets very ~ after nine o'clock** el bar se llena de gente a partir de las nueve; **the houses are ~ together** las casas están apiñadas

crowd-puller ['kraʊd,pʊlə'] N gran atracción *f*; **the show is bound to be a ~** no cabe duda de que este espectáculo atraerá a mucho público

crown [kraʊn] **Ⓐ** N **1** (= *headdress, monarchy*) corona *f* **2** (*Brit Jur*) **the Crown** ≈ el Estado **3** (= *top*) [*of hat*] copa *f*; [*of head*] coronilla *f*; [*of hill*] cumbre *f*, cima *f*; [*of tooth*] corona *f* **Ⓑ** VT **1** [+ *king etc*] coronar; **he was ~ed king** fue coronado rey; **all the ~ed heads of Europe** todos los monarcas europeos **2** (= *cap, round off*) coronar, rematar; **and to ~ it all it began to snow** y para colmo (de desgracias) *or* para remate empezó a nevar; **I wouldn't exactly say our efforts were ~ed with success** (*iro*) yo no me atrevería a decir que nuestros esfuerzos se vieron coronados por el éxito **3** [+ *tooth*] poner una corona en **Ⓒ** CPD ➤ **crown court** (*Brit Jur*) ≈ Audiencia *f* provincial ➤ **crown jewels** joyas *fpl* de la corona ➤ **crown prince** príncipe *m* heredero

crowning ['kraʊnɪŋ] ADJ [*achievement*] supremo, máximo; **the house's ~ glory is its garden** el máximo *or* mayor atractivo de la casa es el jardín

crow's-feet ['krəʊz'fi:t] NPL patas *fpl* de gallo

crow's-nest ['krəʊznest] N (*Naut*) cofa *f* de vigía

crucial ['kru:ʃəl] ADJ decisivo, crucial; **to play a ~ role in sth** desempeñar un papel decisivo *or* crucial en algo

crucially ['kru:ʃəlɪ] ADV [*depend*] de forma crucial; **to be ~ important** ser de crucial importancia

crucible ['kru:sɪbl] N crisol *m* (*also fig*)

crucifix ['kru:sɪfɪks] N crucifijo *m*

crucifixion [,kru:sɪ'fɪkʃən] N crucifixión *f*

crucify ['kru:sɪfaɪ] VT **1** (*lit*) crucificar **2** (*fig*) **he'll ~ me when he finds out!** ¡cuando se entere me mata!

crude [kru:d] **Ⓐ** ADJ (*compar* ~**r**; *superl* ~**st**) **1** (= *unprocessed*) [*oil*] crudo **2** (= *primitive*) [*device, method, hut*] rudimentario; [*drawing, piece of work*] tosco, burdo **3** (= *coarse*) [*person, language, joke*] grosero, ordinario **Ⓑ** N (*also* ~ **oil**) crudo *m*

crudely ['kru:dlɪ] ADV **1** (= *primitively*) [*carved, constructed, drawn*] toscamente, burdamente **2** (= *coarsely*) [*speak, behave, joke, gesture*] groseramente, ordinariamente; **to put it ~** hablando en plata*

cruel ['krʊəl] ADJ (*compar* ~**ler**; *superl* ~**lest**) cruel; ✦ PROV **you have to be ~ to be kind** quien bien te quiere te hará llorar

cruelty ['krʊəltɪ] N crueldad *f* (**to** con, hacia); **society for the prevention of ~ to animals** sociedad *f* protectora de animales

cruet ['kru:ɪt] N (*US*) (= *stand*) vinagreras *fpl*, alcuzas *fpl* (*Chi*)

cruise [kru:z] **Ⓐ** N crucero *m*; **to go on a ~** hacer un crucero **Ⓑ** VI **1** [*ship, fleet*] navegar; [*holidaymaker*] hacer un crucero; [*plane*] volar; **the car was cruising (along) at 80km/h** el coche marchaba plácidamente a una velocidad de 80km/h; **cruising speed** velocidad *f* de crucero **2** (*fig*) **to ~ to victory** vencer fácilmente **3** (*) (= *pick up men/women*) ir a ligar* **Ⓒ** VT [+ *streets*] circular por; **there were plenty of taxis cruising the streets** había muchos taxis circulando por la calle **Ⓓ** CPD ➤ **cruise missile** misil *m* de crucero

cruiser ['kru:zə'] N crucero *m*

crumb [krʌm] N miga *f*; **a ~ of comfort** algo de consuelo

crumble ['krʌmbl] **Ⓐ** VT [+ *bread*] desmigar, desmigajar **Ⓑ** VI **1** [*bread*] desmigarse, desmigajarse; [*building, plaster etc*] desmoronarse **2** [*hopes, power, self-confidence*] desmoronarse, venirse abajo; [*coalition*] venirse abajo, derrumbarse

crumbly ['krʌmblɪ] ADJ (*compar* **crumblier**; *superl* **crumbliest**) [*earth*] quebradizo; [*cheese*] que se desmenuza con facilidad; (*Culin*) [*mixture*] quebradizo; (*US*) [*pastry*] sobado

crummy* ['krʌmɪ] ADJ (*compar* **crummier**; *superl* **crummiest**) (= *bad*) miserable; [*hotel*] de mala muerte*****; **you can keep your ~ job** puede usted quedarse su empleo de pacotilla

crumpet ['krʌmpɪt] N (*esp Brit Culin*) ≈ bollo *m* blando para tostar

crumple ['krʌmpl] **Ⓐ** VT (*also* **~ up**) [+ *paper*] estrujar; [+ *clothes*] arrugar **Ⓑ** VI **1** [*material*] arrugarse; [*person*] (= *fall*) desplomarse; (= *lose one's nerve*) desmoronarse, venirse abajo; **his face ~d and he started to cry** se le descompuso el rostro y se echó a llorar **Ⓒ** CPD ➤ **crumple zone** (*Aut*) zona *f* de deformación absorbente

crunch [krʌntʃ] **Ⓐ** N crujido *m*; (*fig*) crisis *f*, punto *m* decisivo; ✦ IDIOMS **when it comes to the ~** cuando llega el momento de la verdad; **if it comes to the ~** si llega el momento **Ⓑ** VT (*with teeth*) mascar, ronzar; (*underfoot*) hacer crujir; (*fig*) [+ *numbers*] devorar **Ⓒ** VI [*gravel, snow, glass*] crujir; **the tyres ~ed on the gravel** la grava crujía bajo el peso de los neumáticos, los neumáticos hacían crujir la grava

crunchy ['krʌntʃɪ] ADJ (*compar* **crunchier**; *superl* **crunchiest**) crujiente

crusade [kruːˈseɪd] **Ⓐ** N cruzada *f*; (*fig*) campaña *f*, cruzada *f* **Ⓑ** VI **to ~ for/against sth** hacer una campaña en pro de/en contra de algo

crusader [kruːˈseɪdəʳ] N cruzado *m*; (*fig*) paladín *m*, campeón/ona *m/f*

crush [krʌʃ] **Ⓐ** N **1** (= *crowd*) aglomeración *f*, multitud *f*; [*of cars*] masa *f*; **there was an awful ~** hubo la mar de gente; **I lost my handbag in the ~** perdí el bolso en la aglomeración; **they died in the ~** murieron aplastados **2** (*) **to have a ~ on sb** estar enamorado de algn, perder la chaveta por algn* **Ⓑ** VT **1** (= *squash*) aplastar, apachurrar (*And, CAm*); (= *crumple*) [+ *paper*] estrujar; [+ *clothes*] arrugar; (= *grind, break up*) [+ *stones*] triturar, moler; [+ *grapes*] exprimir, prensar; [+ *garlic*] machacar; [+ *ice*] picar; [+ *scrap metal*] comprimir; **to ~ sth to a pulp** hacer papilla algo **2** [+ *enemy, opposition, resistance*] doblegar, aplastar; [+ *hopes*] defraudar **Ⓒ** VI [*clothes*] arrugarse; **can we all ~ in?** ¿habrá sitio para todos?

crushing ['krʌʃɪŋ] ADJ [*defeat, blow, reply*] aplastante; [*argument*] decisivo; [*burden*] agobiador

crust [krʌst] **Ⓐ** N [*of bread etc*] corteza *f*; (= *dry bread*) mendrugo *m*; [*of pie*] pasta *f*; (*on wound, sore*) costra *f*; (= *layer*) capa *f*; (*Geol*) corteza *f*; **the earth's ~** la corteza terrestre **Ⓑ** VT **boots ~ed with mud** botas con barro incrustado

crustacean [krʌsˈteɪʃən] N crustáceo *m*

crusty ['krʌstɪ] ADJ (*compar* **crustier**; *superl* **crustiest**) [*bread*] crujiente; [*loaf*] de corteza dura

crutch [krʌtʃ] N **1** (*Med*) muleta *f*; (*fig*) apoyo *m* **2** (*esp Brit*) = **crotch**

crux [krʌks] N **the ~ of the matter** lo esencial *or* el meollo *or* el quid del asunto

cry [kraɪ] **Ⓐ** N **1** (= *call, shout*) grito *m*; [*of street vendor*] pregón *m*; **to give a ~ of surprise** dar un grito de sorpresa; **a ~ for help** (*lit*) un grito de socorro *or* auxilio; (*fig*) una llamada de socorro *or* auxilio; **the newspapers are in full ~ over the scandal** la prensa ha puesto el grito en el cielo por el escándalo **2** (= *watchword*) lema *m*, slogan *m*; **"jobs, not bombs" was their ~** su grito de guerra fue —trabajo sí, bombas no **3** (= *weep*) **to have a ~** llorar; **she had a good ~** lloró largamente **Ⓑ** VI **1** (= *call out, shout*) gritar, llamar (en voz alta); **he**

cried (out) with pain dio un grito de dolor; **to ~ for help/ mercy** pedir socorro/clemencia a voces **2** (= *weep*) llorar; **he was ~ing for his mother** lloraba por su madre; **she was ~ing with rage** lloraba de rabia; **I laughed till I cried** terminé llorando de la risa; **I'll give him something to ~ about!*** le voy a dar de qué llorar; ✦ PROV **it's no good ~ing over spilt milk** a lo hecho, pecho **Ⓒ** VT **1** (= *call*) gritar; [+ *warning*] lanzar a gritos **2** **to ~ o.s. to sleep** llorar hasta dormirse ➤ **cry off*** VI + ADV (*Brit*) (= *back out*) rajarse* ➤ **cry out Ⓐ** VI + ADV (= *call out, shout*) lanzar un grito, echar un grito; **the system is ~ing out for reform** el sistema pide la reforma a gritos *or* necesita urgentemente reformarse; **for ~ing out loud!*** ¡por Dios! **Ⓑ** VT + ADV **1** (= *call*) gritar; [+ *warning*] lanzar a gritos **2** **to ~ one's eyes out** *or* **heart out** llorar a lágrima viva *or* a moco tendido

crybaby ['kraɪˌbeɪbɪ] N llorón/ona *m/f*

crying ['kraɪɪŋ] **Ⓐ** ADJ **1** [*child*] que llora; (= *whining*) llorón **2** (*) [*need*] urgente; **it's a ~ shame*** es una verdadera lástima; (= *outrage*) es una auténtica vergüenza **Ⓑ** N (= *weeping*) llanto *m*; (= *sobbing*) lloriqueo *m*

crypt [krɪpt] N cripta *f*

cryptic ['krɪptɪk] ADJ [*message, clue*] críptico; [*comment*] enigmático, críptico

crystal ['krɪstl] **Ⓐ** N cristal *m*; **quartz/rock ~** cristal *m* de roca **Ⓑ** CPD de cristal ➤ **crystal ball** bola *f* de cristal

crystal-clear ['krɪstl'klɪəʳ] ADJ (*lit*) [*water*] cristalino; (= *obvious*) evidente, más claro que el agua

crystallize ['krɪstəlaɪz] **Ⓐ** VI (*Chem*) cristalizarse **Ⓑ** VT (*Chem, also fig*) cristalizar; [+ *fruit*] escarchar

CS gas [ˌsiːˌesˈɡæs] N (*Brit*) gas *m* lacrimógeno

CT ABBR (*US*) = **Connecticut**

ct ABBR **1** (= *carat*) qts., quil. **2** = **cent**

Ct. ABBR (*US*) = **Connecticut**

CTC N ABBR = **City Technology College**

cub [kʌb] N **1** (= *animal*) cachorro *m*; **wolf/lion ~** cachorro *m* de lobo/león **2** (*also* **~ scout**) lobato *m*, niño *m* explorador

Cuba ['kjuːbə] N Cuba *f*

Cuban ['kjuːbən] ADJ, N cubano/a *m/f*

cubbyhole ['kʌbɪhəʊl] N (= *small room*) cuchitril *m*; (= *cupboard*) armario *m* pequeño; (= *pigeonhole*) casilla *f*

cube [kjuːb] **Ⓐ** N **1** (= *solid*) cubo *m*; [*of sugar*] terrón *m*; [*of ice*] cubito *m*; [*of cheese*] dado *m*, cubito *m* **2** (*Math*) **the ~ of four** cuatro (elevado) al cubo **Ⓑ** VT (*Math*) cubicar, elevar al cubo **Ⓒ** CPD ➤ **cube root** raíz *f* cúbica

cubic ['kjuːbɪk] ADJ cúbico ➤ **cubic capacity** capacidad *f* cúbica

cubicle ['kjuːbɪkəl] N (*in hospital, dormitory*) cubículo *m*; (*in swimming baths*) caseta *f*

cubism ['kjuːbɪzəm] N cubismo *m*

cuckold ['kʌkəld] N cornudo *m*

cuckoo ['kʊkuː] N cuco *m*, cuclillo *m* ➤ **cuckoo clock** reloj *m* de cuco, cucú *m*

cucumber ['kjuːkʌmbəʳ] N pepino *m*

cuddle ['kʌdl] **Ⓐ** N abrazo *m* **Ⓑ** VT abrazar, apapachar (*Mex**) **Ⓒ** VI abrazarse, estar abrazados; **to ~ up to sb** arrimarse a algn

cuddly ['kʌdlɪ] ADJ (*compar* **cuddlier**; *superl* **cuddliest**) [*person*] rico, tierno; [*animal*] cariñoso ➤ **cuddly toy** (muñeco *m* de) peluche *m*

cudgel ['kʌdʒəl] **Ⓐ** N porra *f*; ✦ IDIOM **to take up the ~s for sth/sb** salir a la defensa de algo/algn **Ⓑ** VT aporrear

cue [kjuː] N **1** (*Billiards*) taco *m* **2** (*Theat*) pie *m*, entrada *f*; **to give sb his ~** (*Theat*) dar el pie *or* la entrada a algn; **that gave me my ~** (*fig*) eso me sirvió de indicación; **right on ~** en el momento justo; ✦ IDIOM **to take one's ~ from sb** seguir el ejemplo de algn

cuff¹ [kʌf] **Ⓐ** N (= *blow*) bofetada *f* **Ⓑ** VT abofetear

cuff² [kʌf] N [*of sleeve*] puño *m*; (*US*) [*of trousers*] vuelta *f*;

cuffs* (= *handcuffs*) esposas *fpl*; ✦ IDIOM **off the ~** (*as adv*) de improviso; (*as adj*) improvisado

cufflinks ['kʌflɪŋks] NPL gemelos *mpl*, mancuernas *fpl* (*CAm, Mex*)

cuisine [kwɪ'ziːn] N cocina *f*

cul-de-sac ['kʌldəˈsæk] N (*pl* **culs-de-sac** *or* **~s**) (*Brit*) calle *f* sin salida, calle *f* cortada

culinary ['kʌlɪnərɪ] ADJ culinario

cull [kʌl] **Ⓐ** VT realizar una matanza selectiva de **Ⓑ** N matanza *f* selectiva

culminate ['kʌlmɪneɪt] VI **to ~ in** culminar en

culmination [ˌkʌlmɪ'neɪʃən] N culminación *f*, punto *m* culminante

culottes [kjuː'lɒts] NPL falda *fsing* pantalón

culpable ['kʌlpəbl] ADJ culpable ➤ **culpable homicide** homicidio *m* sin premeditación

culprit ['kʌlprɪt] N (*gen*) culpable *mf*; (*Jur*) acusado/a *m/f*)

cult [kʌlt] N culto *m* (of a) ➤ **cult figure** ídolo *m* ➤ **cult film, cult movie** película *f* de culto

cultivate ['kʌltɪveɪt] VT cultivar

cultivation [ˌkʌltɪ'veɪʃən] N cultivo *m*

cultural ['kʌltʃərəl] ADJ cultural

culture ['kʌltʃəʳ] **Ⓐ** N **1** (= *the arts, education*) cultura *f*; (= *civilization*) civilización *f*, cultura *f* **2** (*of tissue etc*) cultivo *m* **Ⓑ** VT [+ *tissue etc*] cultivar **Ⓒ** CPD ➤ **culture clash** choque *m* de culturas, choque *m* cultural ➤ **culture shock** choque *m* cultural

cultured ['kʌltʃəd] ADJ [*person*] culto, cultivado; [*tastes, voice*] refinado ➤ **cultured pearl** perla *f* cultivada

cum [kʌm] PREP con; **it's a sort of kitchen-cum-library** es algo así como cocina y biblioteca combinadas; **I was butler-cum-gardener to Lady Jane** yo fui mayordomo y jardinero a la vez en el servicio de Lady Jane

cu. m. ABBR (= **cubic metre(s), cubic meter(s)**) m³

cumbersome ['kʌmbəsəm] ADJ (= *bulky*) voluminoso, de mucho bulto; (= *awkward*) incómodo; **the machine was slow and ~ to use** la máquina resultaba lenta y aparatosa *or* lenta e incómoda (de manejar)

cumin ['kʌmɪn] N comino *m*

cummerbund ['kʌməbʌnd] N faja *f*

cumulative ['kjuːmjʊlətɪv] ADJ cumulativo

cunning ['kʌnɪŋ] **Ⓐ** ADJ **1** (= *sly*) taimado, vivo (*LAm*) **2** (= *clever*) [*person*] astuto, ingenioso; [*plan, scheme, device*] ingenioso **3** (*US**) (= *cute*) mono, precioso **Ⓑ** N (= *slyness*) astucia *f*; (= *cleverness*) ingenio *m*

cunt*** [kʌnt] N **1** (= *genitals*) coño*** *m*, concha *f* (*And, SC****) **2** (= *person*) hijo/a *m/f* de puta***

cup [kʌp] **Ⓐ** N (= *vessel, amount*) taza *f*; (= *prize*) copa *f*; [*of brassiere*] copa *f*; **a ~ of tea** una taza de té, un té; **coffee ~** tacita *f*, pocillo *m* (*LAm*); ✦ IDIOM **it's not everyone's ~ of tea*** no es del gusto de todos; **football isn't my ~ of tea** a mí el fútbol no me va **Ⓑ** VT **to ~ one's hands** (*for shouting*) formar bocina con las manos; (*for drinking*) ahuecar las manos **Ⓒ** CPD ➤ **cup final** final *m* de copa ➤ **cup tie** (*Brit*) partido *m* de copa

cupboard ['kʌbəd] N (*free-standing*) armario *m*; (*esp Brit*) (*built-in*) armario *m*, closet/clóset *m* (*LAm*), placar(d) *m* (*SC*) ➤ **cupboard love** (*Brit*) amor *m* interesado

cupcake ['kʌpkeɪk] N pastelito *m*

cupful ['kʌpfʊl] N taza *f*

Cupid ['kjuːpɪd] N Cupido *m*

cupidity [kjuː'pɪdɪtɪ] N (*frm*) codicia *f*

cupola ['kjuːpələ] N cúpula *f*

cuppa* ['kʌpə] N (*Brit*) taza *f* de té

curable ['kjʊərəbl] ADJ curable

curate ['kjʊərɪt] N (= *priest*) cura *m*; (= *assistant*) coadjutor *m*

curator [kjʊəˈreɪtəʳ] N [*of museum*] director(a) *m/f*; [*of museum department*] conservador(a) *m/f*)

curb [kɜːb] **Ⓐ** N **1** (= *check*) freno *m*; **to put a ~ on sth** (*esp Brit*) poner freno a algo, refrenar algo **2** (*US*) (*at edge of road*) = **kerb Ⓑ** VT (*fig*) [+ *temper, impatience etc*] dominar, refrenar; [+ *spending*] restringir; [+ *inflation*] poner freno a, frenar

curd [kɜːd] N cuajada *f* ➤ **curd cheese** requesón *m*

curdle ['kɜːdl] **Ⓐ** VT (= *cause to set*) cuajar; (= *cause to go bad*) cortar **Ⓑ** VI (= *set*) cuajarse; (= *go bad*) cortarse

cure [kjʊəʳ] **Ⓐ** N (= *remedy*) remedio *m*; (= *course of treatment*) cura *f*; (= *process of recovery*) curación *f*; **there is no known ~** no existe curación **Ⓑ** VT **1** [+ *disease, patient*] curar; [+ *poverty, injustice, evil*] remediar; **to ~ sb of a habit** quitar a algn un vicio **2** (= *preserve*) (*in salt*) salar; (*by smoking*) curar; (*by drying*) secar; [+ *animal hide*] curtir

cure-all ['kjʊərɔːl] N panacea *f*, curalotodo *m*

curfew ['kɜːfjuː] N toque *m* de queda

curio ['kjʊərɪəʊ] N curiosidad *f*

curiosity [ˌkjʊərɪ'ɒsɪtɪ] N curiosidad *f* (**about** por, acerca de); **out of ~** por curiosidad; ✦ PROV ➤ **killed the cat** la curiosidad mata al hombre

curious ['kjʊərɪəs] ADJ curioso; **it's ~ that she didn't say why** es curioso que no dijese por qué; **I'd be ~ to know** tengo curiosidad por saberlo

curiously ['kjʊərɪəslɪ] ADV **1** [*silent, reticent*] curiosamente; **~ enough, it's true** curiosamente *or* aunque parezca extraño, es cierto **2** [*ask, look*] con curiosidad

curl [kɜːl] **Ⓐ** N [*of hair*] rizo *m*; (= *ringlet*) bucle *m*, sortija *f* **Ⓑ** VT [+ *hair*] rizar; **she ~ed her lip in scorn** hizo una mueca de desprecio **Ⓒ** VI [*hair*] rizarse
➤ **curl up** VI + ADV [*cat, dog*] hacerse una pelota; [*person*] hacerse un ovillo, acurrucarse; [*paper, stale bread*] arrollarse; **she lay ~ed up on the bed** estaba acurrucada encima de la cama; **to ~ up into a ball** hacerse un ovillo; **to ~ up with a book** acurrucarse con un libro

curler ['kɜːləʳ] N rulo *m*, bigudí *m*, rulero *m* (*SC*)

curlew ['kɜːluː] N zarapito *m*

curling ['kɜːlɪŋ] N (*Sport*) curling *m* ➤ **curling tongs, curling irons** (*US*) tenacillas *fpl* de rizar

curly ['kɜːlɪ] ADJ (*compar* **curlier**; *superl* **curliest**) [*hair, eyelashes, lettuce*] rizado; [*writing*] de trazo ondulado, lleno de florituras

curly-haired [ˌkɜːlɪ'heəd], **curly-headed** [ˌkɜːlɪ'hedɪd] ADJ de pelo rizado

currant ['kʌrənt] N (= *dried grape*) pasa *f* de Corinto; (= *bush*) grosellero *m*; (= *fruit*) grosella *f* ➤ **currant bun** bollo *m* con pasas, pan *m* de pasas (*LAm*)

currency ['kʌrənsɪ] **Ⓐ** N **1** moneda *f*; **foreign ~** moneda *f* extranjera, divisas *fpl* **2** (= *acceptance*) aceptación *f*; **to gain ~** [*views, ideas*] darse a conocer, difundirse **Ⓑ** CPD ➤ **currency market** mercado *m* monetario, mercado *m* de divisas ➤ **currency unit** unidad *f* monetaria

current ['kʌrənt] **Ⓐ** ADJ [*fashion, tendency*] actual; [*price, word, use*] corriente; [*year, week*] presente, en curso; **the ~ issue of the magazine** el último número de la revista **Ⓑ** N corriente *f*; ✦ IDIOMS **to go against the ~** ir contra corriente; **to go with the ~** dejarse llevar por la corriente **Ⓒ** CPD ➤ **current account** (*Brit*) cuenta *f* corriente ➤ **current affairs, current events** temas *mpl* de actualidad

currently ['kʌrəntlɪ] ADV actualmente, en la actualidad

curriculum [kə'rɪkjʊləm] N (*pl* **~s** *or* **curricula** [kə'rɪkjʊlə]) [*of school*] plan *m* de estudios; [*of college/university course*] programa *m* de estudios ➤ **curriculum vitae** (*esp Brit*) curriculum *m* (vitae), historial *m* (profesional)

curried ['kʌrɪd] ADJ al curry

curry ['kʌrɪ] **Ⓐ** N curry *m* **Ⓑ** VT **1** (*Culin*) preparar con curry **2 to ~ favour** *or* (*US*) **favor with sb** tratar de ganar el favor de algn **Ⓒ** CPD ➤ **curry powder** curry *m* en polvo

curse [kɜːs] **Ⓐ** N **1** (= *spell*) maldición *f*; **to put a ~ on sb** maldecir a algn **2** (= *bane*) maldición *f*, azote *m* **3** (= *oath*) palabrota *f* **4 the ~*** (= *menstruation*) la regla **Ⓑ** VT [+ *luck, stupidity*] maldecir; [+ *person*] echar pestes de; **~ it!** ¡maldito sea!; **I ~ the day I met him** maldita sea la hora en que lo conocí; **to be ~d with** padecer, tener que soportar **Ⓒ** VI blasfemar, echar pestes, decir palabrotas

cursor ['kɜːsəʳ] N cursor *m*

cursory ['kɜːsərɪ] ADJ [*examination, inspection*] somero, superficial; [*nod*] brusco; **to give sth a ~ glance** mirar algo brevemente *or* de forma somera

curt [kɜːt] ADJ [*person, tone*] seco; [*nod*] brusco

curtail [kɜːˈteɪl] VT (= *restrict*) restringir; (= *cut short*) acortar, abreviar; (= *reduce*) reducir

curtailment [kɜːˈteɪlmənt] N (= *restriction*) restricción *f*; (= *shortening*) acortamiento *m*; (= *reduction*) reducción *f*

curtain ['kɜːtn] N (*gen, Mil*) cortina *f*; (= *lace, small etc*) visillo *m*, telón *m*; **to draw the ~s** (*together*) correr las cortinas; (*apart*) abrir las cortinas; ✦ IDIOM **to bring the ~ down on sth** poner punto final a algo ➤ **curtain call** (*Theat*) llamada *f* a escena ➤ **curtain hook** colgadero *m* de cortina ➤ **curtain ring** anilla *f* (de las cortinas) ➤ **curtain rod** barra *f* (de las cortinas)
➤ **curtain off** VT + ADV (= *separate*) separar con cortina; [+ *bed, area*] encerrar con cortina

curtain-raiser ['kɜːtnˌreɪzəʳ] N pieza *f* preliminar

curtsey, curtsy (*US*) ['kɜːtsɪ] Ⓐ N reverencia *f* Ⓑ VI hacer una reverencia (**to** a)

curvaceous* [kɜːˈveɪʃəs] ADJ curvilíneo

curvature ['kɜːvətʃəʳ] N **1** (*Math*) curvatura *f* **2 ~ of the spine** escoliosis *f inv*, desviación *f* de columna

curve [kɜːv] Ⓐ N curva *f* Ⓑ VI [*road, line etc*] torcerse, hacer curva; [*surface*] combarse; **a wide, curving staircase** una amplia escalera en curva

curved [kɜːvd] ADJ curvo, encorvado

cushion ['kʊʃən] Ⓐ N (*gen*) cojín *m*; [*of chair, for knees*] almohadilla *f*; [*of air, moss*] colchón *m* Ⓑ VT [+ *blow, fall*] amortiguar; **to ~ sb against sth** proteger a algn de algo Ⓒ CPD ➤ **cushion cover** funda *f* de cojín

cushy* ['kʊʃɪ] ADJ (*compar* **cushier**; *superl* **cushiest**) **a ~ job** un chollo*, un hueso (*Mex**); **to have a ~ life** tener la vida arreglada

cuss* [kʌs] (*US*) VT, VI = **curse C**

custard ['kʌstəd] N (*pouring*) ≈ natillas *fpl* (*utilizada como acompañante en algunos postres*); (*also* **egg ~**) flan *m*
➤ **custard cream** galleta *f* de crema ➤ **custard pie** pastel *m* de natillas; (= *missile*) torta *f* de crema ➤ **custard powder** polvos *mpl* para (hacer) natillas

custodial [kʌsˈtəʊdɪəl] ADJ (*Brit*) **~ sentence** condena *f* de prisión

custodian [kʌsˈtəʊdɪən] N (*gen*) custodio/a *m/f*, guardián/ana *m/f*; [*of museum etc*] conservador(a) *m/f*

custody ['kʌstədɪ] N [*of children*] custodia *f*; (= *police custody*) detención *f*; **to be in ~** estar detenido; **to take sb into ~** detener a algn; **in the ~ of** al cargo *or* cuidado de, bajo la custodia de

custom ['kʌstəm] N **1** (= *habit*) costumbre *f*; **social ~s** costumbres *fpl* sociales; **it is her ~ to go for a walk each evening** tiene la costumbre de *or* tiene por costumbre dar un paseo cada tarde, acostumbra *or* suele dar un paseo cada tarde **2** (*Brit Comm*) **to attract ~** atraer clientela; **the shop has lost a lot of ~** la tienda ha perdido muchos clientes

customary ['kʌstəmərɪ] ADJ [*place, time*] acostumbrado, de costumbre, habitual; [*wit, good humour etc*] acostumbrado, habitual; [*practice*] normal, habitual; **it's ~ to** (+ INFIN) es la costumbre + *infin*

custom-built ['kʌstəmˌbɪlt] ADJ hecho de encargo

customer ['kʌstəməʳ] N cliente *mf*; **he's an awkward ~** (*Brit**) es un tipo *or* (*Sp*) un tío difícil* ➤ **customer service department** departamento *m* de atención al cliente
➤ **customer services** (= *counter*) mostrador *m* de información y atención al cliente

customize ['kʌstəmaɪz] VT [+ *car*] adaptar al gusto del cliente, adaptar por encargo del cliente; [+ *product*] personalizar; **~d software** software *m* a medida del usuario

custom-made ['kʌstəmˈmeɪd] ADJ [*furniture, clothing*] a medida, hecho a medida; [*car*] hecho de encargo

customs ['kʌstəmz] NPL aduana *f sing*; **to go through ~** pasar por la aduana ➤ **Customs and Excise** (*Brit*) Aduanas *fpl* y Arbitrios ➤ **customs declaration** declaración *f*

aduanera ➤ **customs duty** derechos *mpl* de aduana
customs officer oficial *mf* de aduanas, vista *mf* (de aduanas), aduanero/a *m/f* ➤ **Customs Service** (*US*) aduana *f*, servicio *m* aduanero

cut [kʌt] (*vb*: *pt, pp* **~**) Ⓐ N **1** (*in skin*) corte *m*, cortadura *f*; (= *wound*) herida *f*; (= *slash*) tajo *m*; (*with knife*) cuchillada *f*; (*Med*) (= *incision*) corte *m*, incisión *f*; (*Cards*) corte *m*; **he had a ~ on his chin from shaving** se había hecho un corte *or* se había cortado en la barbilla al afeitarse; **he was treated for minor ~s and bruises** recibió asistencia médica por heridas y hematomas; ✦ IDIOMS **he's a ~ above the others** está por encima de los demás; **the ~ and thrust of politics** la esgrima política
2 (= *reduction*) (*in wages, prices, production*) rebaja *f*, reducción *f*; (*in expenditure, budget*) corte *m*, recorte *m*; (*in tax, interest rates*) bajada *f*, rebaja *f*; (*in staff, workforce*) reducción *f*, recorte *f*; **public spending ~s** recortes *mpl* presupuestarios; **wage ~s** rebajas *fpl* de sueldo; **to take a ~ in salary** aceptar una reducción de sueldo; **they made some ~s in the text** hicieron algunos cortes en el texto, suprimieron algunas cosas del texto
3 [*of clothes etc*] corte *m*
4 (= *haircut*) corte *m*, peinado *m*
5 [*of meat*] (= *part of animal*) corte *m* (de carne); (= *piece*) trozo *m*; (= *slice*) tajada *f*
6 (*) (= *share*) parte *f*, tajada *f*; **the salesman gets a ~ of 5%** el vendedor recibe su parte de 5%
7 (= *woodcut*) grabado *m*; (*US*) foto *f*, diagrama *m*, dibujo *m*
8 ~ and paste (*Comput*) opción *f* de cortar y pegar
Ⓑ VT **1** [+ *meat, bread, cards*] cortar; **to ~ one's finger** cortarse el dedo; **to ~ sb free** (*from wreckage*) liberar a algn; (*when tied up*) desatar *or* soltar a algn; **to ~ sth in half** cortar algo por la mitad; **to ~ sth open** abrir algo; **he ~ his head open** se abrió la cabeza; **to ~ sth (in)to pieces** cortar algo en pedazos; **to ~ sb's throat** degollar a algn; **he is ~ting his own throat** (*fig*) labra su propia ruina; **to ~ sth in two** cortar *or* partir algo en dos; ✦ IDIOMS **to ~ sb dead** (*Brit*) negar el saludo *or* (*LAm*) cortar a algn; **you could ~ the atmosphere with a knife** se mascaba *or* respiraba la tensión en el ambiente; **it ~ me to the quick** me tocó en lo vivo
2 (= *shape*) [+ *stone, glass, jewel*] tallar; [+ *key, hole*] hacer; [+ *channel*] abrir, excavar; [+ *engraving, record*] grabar
3 (= *clip, trim*) [+ *hedge, grass*] cortar; [+ *corn, hay*] segar; **to get one's hair ~** cortarse el pelo
4 (= *reduce*) [+ *wages, prices, production*] reducir, rebajar (**by 5%** en un 5 por cien); [+ *expenditure*] reducir, recortar; [+ *taxes, interest rates*] bajar, rebajar; [+ *staff, workforce*] reducir, recortar; [+ *speech, text*] acortar, hacer cortes en; [+ *film*] cortar, hacer cortes en; (= *delete*) [+ *passage*] suprimir, cortar; **she ~ two seconds off the record** mejoró *or* rebajó la plusmarca en dos segundos; **to ~ sth/sb short** interrumpir algo/a algn
5 (= *intersect with*) [*line*] cortar
6 (*esp US**) **to ~ classes** hacer novillos*, ausentarse de clase
7 (= *stop*) [+ *electricity supply*] cortar, interrumpir; **~ all this soft-soaping and tell me what you want*** deja ya de darme coba y dime qué quieres*
8 (= *succeed*) **he couldn't ~ it as a singer** como cantante no daba la talla
Ⓒ VI **1** [*person, knife*] cortar; **she ~ into the melon** cortó el melón; ✦ IDIOMS **it ~s both ways** tiene doble filo; **to ~ loose (from sth)** deshacerse (de algo)
2 (*Math etc*) [*lines*] cortarse
3 (= *hurry*) **I must ~ along now** tengo que marcharme ya; ✦ IDIOMS **to ~ and run*** largarse*, escaparse; **to ~ to the chase** (*esp US**) ir al grano, dejar de marear la perdiz*
4 (*Cine, TV*) (= *change scene*) cortar y pasar (**from** de; **to** a); **cut!** ¡corten!
5 (*Cards*) cortar
6 ~ and paste (*Comput*) cortar y pegar
Ⓓ ADJ [*flowers*] cortado; [*glass*] tallado; **~ price** a precio reducido, rebajado, de rebaja
➤ **cut across** VI + PREP **1** atajar por; **to ~ across a field** atajar por un campo **2** (*fig*) **this ~s across the usual categories** esto rebasa las categorías establecidas
➤ **cut away** VT + ADV cortar, eliminar
➤ **cut back** Ⓐ VT + ADV **1** [+ *plant*] podar **2** (= *reduce*) [+ *production, expenditure, staff*] reducir, recortar; **to ~ sth back by 50%** reducir algo en un 50 por ciento Ⓑ VI + ADV

economizar
➤ **cut down** Ⓐ VT + ADV **1** [+ *tree*] cortar, talar; [+ *enemy*] matar **2** [+ *consumption*] reducir; [+ *expenditure*] reducir, recortar; ✦ IDIOM **to ~ sb down to size** bajar los humos a algn Ⓑ VI + ADV **you're drinking too much, you really should ~ down** bebes demasiado, deberías moderarte un poco; **to ~ down on** [+ *food*] comer menos, reducir el consumo de; [+ *cigarettes*] fumar menos; [+ *alcohol*] beber menos; [+ *expenditure*] moderar, reducir; [+ *public services*] recortar, reducir
➤ **cut in** Ⓐ VI + ADV (*in conversation*) interrumpir; (*Aut*) meterse delante Ⓑ VT + ADV (*) **to ~ sb in (on sth)** incluir a algn (en algo)
➤ **cut into** VI + PREP **to ~ into one's holidays** interrumpir sus vacaciones; **we shall have to ~ into our savings** tendremos que usar una parte de los ahorros
➤ **cut off** VT + ADV **1** (*with scissors, knife*) cortar; (= *amputate*) amputar, quitar; **they ~ off his head** le cortaron la cabeza; ✦ IDIOM **to ~ off one's nose to spite one's face*** tirar piedras contra su propio tejado **2** (= *disconnect*) [+ *telephone, gas*] cortar, desconectar; **we've been ~ off** (*Telec*) nos han cortado la comunicación **3** (= *interrupt*) **to ~ sb off in the middle of a sentence** cortar *or* interrumpir a algn en mitad de una frase, no dejar terminar a algn; **to ~ off sb's supplies** cortar *or* interrumpir el suministro a algn **4** (= *isolate*) aislar; **I feel very ~ off** me siento muy aislado; **the village was ~ off for several days by the snow** la aldea quedó aislada *or* incomunicada por la nieve durante varios días; **to ~ o.s. off from sth/sb** aislarse de algo/algn; ✦ IDIOM **to ~ sb off without a penny** desheredar completamente a algn
➤ **cut out** Ⓐ VT + ADV **1** [+ *article, picture*] recortar; [+ *dress, skirt etc*] cortar; [+ *diseased part*] extirpar; ✦ IDIOMS **to be ~ out for sth/to do sth** estar hecho para ser algo/hacer algo; **he's not ~ out to be a poet** no tiene madera de poeta; **you'll have your work ~ out for you** te va a costar trabajo; **he had his work ~ out to finish it** tuvo que trabajar duro para terminarlo **2** (= *exclude*) [+ *unnecessary details*] eliminar, suprimir; [+ *light*] tapar; [+ *intermediary, middleman*] saltarse a, eliminar; **he ~ his nephew out of his will** borró de su testamento la mención del sobrino; **~ it out!*** ¡basta ya! **3** (= *give up*) [+ *fatty food*] dejar de comer; **to ~ out alcohol/cigarettes** dejar de beber/fumar Ⓑ VI + ADV [*car engine*] pararse; (*Elec*) cortarse, interrumpirse
➤ **cut through** VI + PREP **1** [+ *cable, wire, etc*] atravesar, traspasar **2** (= *take short cut via*) atajar por, cortar por **3** (= *circumvent*) saltarse, sortear
➤ **cut up** Ⓐ VT + ADV **1** [+ *food, paper, wood*] cortar en pedazos; [+ *meat*] picar **2** (*) **to be ~ up about sth** (*esp Brit*) (= *hurt*) estar muy afectado por algo; (= *annoyed*) estar muy molesto por algo Ⓑ VI + ADV ✦ IDIOM **to ~ up rough*** ponerse agresivo

cut-and-dried [ˌkʌtən'draɪd], **cut-and-dry** [ˌkʌtən'draɪ] ADJ [*answer*] concreto; [*situation, issue*] definido, claro

cutback ['kʌtbæk] N recorte *m*, reducción *f*

cute [kjuːt] ADJ **1** (= *sweet*) [*face, animal, baby*] lindo, precioso, mono*, rico*; [*person*] guapo **2** (*esp US*) (= *clever*) listo, vivo (*LAm*)

cut-glass ['kʌt'glɑːs] ADJ de vidrio tallado

cuticle ['kjuːtɪkl] N cutícula *f*

cutlery ['kʌtlərɪ] N (*Brit*) cubiertos *mpl*, cubertería *f*

cutlet ['kʌtlɪt] N chuleta *f*; **a veal ~** una chuleta de ternera

cut-off ['kʌtɒf] Ⓐ N **1** (*also* **~ point**) (= *limit*) límite *m* **2** (*US*) (= *short cut*) atajo *m* Ⓑ ADJ [*jeans*] cortado Ⓒ CPD ➤ **cut-off date** fecha *f* tope, fecha *f* límite

cut-out ['kʌtaʊt] N (= *figure*) recorte *m*, figura *f* recortada; (*child's*) (*for cutting out*) recortable *m*, diseño *m* para recortar

cut-price ['kʌtpraɪs] ADJ (*Brit*) [*goods*] a precio reducido, rebajado, de ocasión; [*shop*] saldo(s)

cutter ['kʌtə^r] N **1** (= *tool*) cortadora *f* **2** (= *boat*) cúter *m*

cut-throat ['kʌtθrəʊt] Ⓐ N asesino/a *m/f* Ⓑ ADJ [*competition*] feroz, encarnizado Ⓒ CPD ➤ **cut-throat razor** navaja *f* (de afeitar)

cutting ['kʌtɪŋ] Ⓐ N **1** [*from plant*] esqueje *m* **2** (*Brit*) (*from newspaper*) recorte *m*; (*Cine*) montaje *m* **3** (*Brit*) (*for road, railway*) desmonte *m*, zanja *f* Ⓑ ADJ [*edge, wind*] cortante; [*remark*] mordaz Ⓒ CPD ➤ **cutting board** (*US*) tajo *m*, tabla *f* de cortar ➤ **cutting edge** filo *m*; (*fig*) vanguardia *f* ➤ **cutting room** (*Cine*) sala *f* de montaje

cuttlefish ['kʌtlfɪʃ] N (*pl* ~) jibia *f*, sepia *f*

CV N ABBR (*esp Brit*) (= **curriculum vitae**) C.V. *m*

cyanide ['saɪənaɪd] N cianuro *m*

cybercafé ['saɪbəˌkæfeɪ] N cibercafé *m*

cybernetics [ˌsaɪbə'netɪks] NSING cibernética *f*

cyberspace ['saɪbəspeɪs] N ciberespacio *m*

cyberterrorism ['saɪbəˌterərɪzəm] N ciberterrorismo *m*

cyberterrorist ['saɪbəˌterərɪst] N ciberterrorista *mf*

cyclamen ['sɪkləmən] N ciclamen *m*

cycle ['saɪkl] Ⓐ N **1** (= *bicycle*) bicicleta *f* **2** [*of seasons, poems etc*] ciclo *m*; **life ~** ciclo *m* vital Ⓑ VI (= *travel*) ir en bicicleta; **I ~ to school** voy al colegio en bicicleta Ⓒ CPD ➤ **cycle lane, cycle path** (*Brit*) carril *m* de bicicleta, carril-bici *m* ➤ **cycle race** carrera *f* ciclista ➤ **cycle rack** soporte *m* para bicicletas; (*on car roof*) baca *f* para transportar bicicletas ➤ **cycle ride** paseo *m* en bicicleta; **to go for a ~ ride** ir a dar un paseo en bicicleta ➤ **cycle shed** cobertizo *m* para bicicletas ➤ **cycle track** (*in countryside*) ruta *f* para ciclistas, senda *f* para ciclistas; (*Sport*) pista *f* de ciclismo, velódromo *m*

cyclical ['saɪklɪkəl] ADJ cíclico

cycling ['saɪklɪŋ] N ciclismo *m*; **to go ~** ir *or* montar en bicicleta, hacer ciclismo ➤ **cycling holiday** vacaciones *fpl* en bicicleta ➤ **cycling shorts** culotes *mpl*, culotte(s) *m(pl)*

cyclist ['saɪklɪst] N ciclista *mf*

cyclone ['saɪkləʊn] N ciclón *m*

cygnet ['sɪgnɪt] N pollo *m* de cisne

cylinder ['sɪlɪndə^r] N cilindro *m*; **a six-~ engine** un motor de seis cilindros ➤ **cylinder head** culata *f* de cilindro ➤ **cylinder head gasket** junta *f* de culata

cylindrical [sɪ'lɪndrɪkəl] ADJ cilíndrico

cymbal ['sɪmbəl] N címbalo *m*, platillo *m*

cynic ['sɪnɪk] N cínico/a *m/f*

cynical ['sɪnɪkəl] ADJ cínico

cynically ['sɪnɪklɪ] ADV cínicamente, con cinismo

cynicism ['sɪnɪsɪzəm] N cinismo *m*

cypress ['saɪprɪs] N ciprés *m*

Cypriot ['sɪprɪət] ADJ, N chipriota *mf*

Cyprus ['saɪprəs] N Chipre *f*

Cyrillic [sɪ'rɪlɪk] Ⓐ ADJ cirílico Ⓑ N cirílico *m*

cyst [sɪst] N quiste *m*

cystic fibrosis [ˌsɪstɪkfaɪ'brəʊsɪs] N fibrosis *f* cística

cystitis [sɪs'taɪtɪs] N cistitis *f*

czar [zɑː^r] N zar *m*

czarina [zɑː'riːnə] N zarina *f*

Czech [tʃek] Ⓐ ADJ checo; **the ~ Republic** la República Checa Ⓑ N **1** (= *person*) checo/a *m/f* **2** (*Ling*) checo *m*

Czechoslovakia ['tʃekəʊsləˈvækɪə] N (*Hist*) Checoslovaquia *f*

Dd

D, d [di:] N **1** (= *letter*) D, d *f*; **D for David** D de Dolores **2** (*Mus*) **D** re *m*

d. ABBR (= **died**) m.

DA N ABBR (*US Jur*) = **District Attorney**

dab¹ [dæb] **Ⓐ** N (= *light stroke*) toquecito *m*; (= *small amount*) pizca *f*; [*of paint*] ligero brochazo *m*; [*of liquid*] gota *f* **Ⓑ** VT (*also ~ at*) (= *rub*) frotar ligeramente; **to ~ one's eyes** (= *dry*) secarse ligeramente los ojos; **to ~ sth on** (= *anoint o.s. with*) darse una ligera capa de algo, echarse un poco de algo; **I'll just ~ on some cologne** (*on you*) voy a echarte un poco de colonia

dab² [dæb] N (= *fish*) lenguado *m*

dab³* [dæb] ADJ ✦ IDIOM **to be a ~ hand at (doing) sth** (*Brit*) ser un hacha para (hacer) algo

dabble ['dæbl] VI **to ~ in sth** hacer algo/interesarse por algo superficialmente; **to ~ in politics** ser politiquero, politiquear; **to ~ in shares** jugar a la bolsa

dachshund ['dækshʊnd] N perro *m* salchicha

dad* [dæd] N papá *m*

daddy* ['dædɪ] N papá *m*

daddy-long-legs ['dædɪ'lɒŋlegz] N (*pl ~*) (*Brit*) típula *f*

daffodil ['dæfədɪl] N narciso *m*

daft* [dɑ:ft] ADJ (*compar* **~er**; *superl* **~est**) (*Brit*) [*person*] tonto, bobo, tarado (*SC**); [*idea, action, question*] tonto; **don't be ~** no seas tonto or bobo; **the ~ things some people do!** ¡hay que ver las estupideces que hace la gente!; **to be ~ about sb** estar loco por algn; **he's ~ about football** le apasiona el fútbol, el fútbol le vuelve loco; ✦ IDIOM **to be as ~ as a brush*** ser más tonto que Abundio*

dagger ['dægə'] N daga *f*, puñal *m*; ✦ IDIOMS **to be at ~s drawn (with sb)** (*Brit*) estar a matar (con algn); **to look ~s at sb** (*Brit*) fulminar a algn con la mirada

dahlia ['deɪlɪə] N dalia *f*

daily ['deɪlɪ] **Ⓐ** ADJ diario; **they are paid on a ~ basis** (= *by the day*) les pagan por días or por día trabajado; (= *every day*) les pagan cada día; **the ~ grind** la rutina diaria; **the ~ life of a primary school teacher** la vida cotidiana de un profesor de primaria; **we went about our ~ lives as if nothing had happened** continuamos con nuestra vida normal como si nada hubiera pasado; **incidents of this kind are a ~ occurrence** este tipo de incidentes ocurre diariamente or a diario **Ⓑ** ADV diariamente, a diario; **twice ~** dos veces al día **Ⓒ** N **1** (*also ~ newspaper*) diario *m*, periódico *m* **2** (*esp Brit**) (*also ~ help*) asistenta *f*, chacha* *f*

dainty ['deɪntɪ] ADJ (*compar* **daintier**; *superl* **daintiest**) delicado

dairy ['deərɪ] **Ⓐ** N **1** (= *shop*) lechería *f* **2** (*on farm*) vaquería *f* **Ⓑ** CPD [*products*] lácteo ➤ **dairy butter** mantequilla *f* casera ➤ **dairy cattle, dairy cows** vacas *fpl* lecheras ➤ **dairy farm** granja *f* de productos lácteos ➤ **dairy farming** industria *f* láctea ➤ **dairy herd** ganado *m* lechero ➤ **dairy ice cream** helado *m* de nata (*Sp*) or crema (*LAm*) ➤ **dairy produce** productos *mpl* lácteos

dais ['deɪɪs] N estrado *m*

daisy ['deɪzɪ] N margarita *f*; ✦ IDIOM **to be pushing up the daisies*** criar malvas* ➤ **daisy chain** (*esp Brit*) guirnalda *f* de margaritas

Dalai Lama ['dælaɪ'lɑːmə] N Dalai Lama *m*

dale [deɪl] N (*Brit*) valle *m*

dalliance ['dælɪəns] N (*esp hum*) escarceos *mpl*

dally ['dælɪ] VI tardar; **to ~ over sth** perder el tiempo con algo

Dalmatian [dæl'meɪʃən] ADJ, N dálmata *mf*

dalmatian [dæl'meɪʃən] N (= *dog*) perro *m* dálmata

dam [dæm] **Ⓐ** N (= *wall*) dique *m*, presa *f*; (= *reservoir*) presa *f*, embalse *m* **Ⓑ** VT poner un dique a, represar

damage ['dæmɪdʒ] **Ⓐ** N **1** (*gen*) daño *m*; (*to building, area*) daños *mpl*; (*visible, eg on car*) desperfectos *mpl*; **the bomb did a lot of ~** la bomba causó muchos daños; **not much ~ was caused to the car** el coche no sufrió grandes desperfectos **2** (*to chances, reputation etc*) perjuicio *m*, daño *m*; **the ~ is done** el daño ya está hecho; ✦ IDIOM **what's the ~?** (*hum**) ¿cuánto va a ser?, ¿qué se debe? **3 damages** (= *compensation*) daños *mpl* y perjuicios **Ⓑ** VT (*gen*) dañar; [+ *machine*] averiar, causar desperfectos en; [+ *health, chances, reputation*] perjudicar **Ⓒ** CPD ➤ **damage control operation** (*US*), **damage limitation exercise** (*Brit*) campaña *f* para minimizar los daños

damaging ['dæmɪdʒɪŋ] ADJ dañino; (*fig*) perjudicial (**to** para)

Damascus [də'mɑːskəs] N Damasco *m*

damask ['dæməsk] N damasco *m*

dame [deɪm] N **1** (*Brit*) **1.1 Dame** (= *title*) título equivalente a *"sir"*, *concedido a una mujer* **1.2** (*Theat*) *personaje de mujer anciana en las pantomimas británicas interpretado por un actor*; ⇨ PANTOMIME **2** (*US**) (= *woman*) tía* *f*, gachí *f* (*Sp***)

dammit** ['dæmɪt] EXCL ¡maldita sea!*

damn [dæm] **Ⓐ** VT **1** (*Rel*) condenar; ✦ IDIOM **to ~ sth/sb with faint praise** despachar algo/a algn con tímidos elogios **2** (**) (*in exclamations*) ~ **it!/you!** ¡maldita sea!/seas!*; **well I'll be ~ed!** ¡caramba!*, ¡vaya!*; **I'll be ~ed if I will!** ¡ni en broma!, ¡ni pensarlo! **Ⓑ** EXCL (**) ¡maldita sea!*, ¡caray!*, ¡me cago en la leche! (*Sp***), ¡carajo! (*LAm****) **Ⓒ** N (**) **I don't give a ~** me importa un pito or bledo* **Ⓓ** ADJ (**) maldito*, condenado*, fregado (*LAm**) **Ⓔ** ADV (**) **it's ~ hot/cold!** ¡vaya calor/frío que hace!, ¡hace un calor/frío del demonio!*; **he ~ near killed me** por poco me mata, casi me mata; **"did you tell him so?" — "~ right, I did!"** —¿eso le dijiste? —¡pues claro! or ¡ya lo creo!; **I should ~ well think so!** ¡hombre, eso espero!

damnation [dæm'neɪʃən] **Ⓐ** N perdición *f* **Ⓑ** EXCL (*) ¡maldición!

damned [dæmd] **Ⓐ** ADJ **1** [*soul*] condenado, maldito **2** (**) (= *darned*) maldito*, condenado*, fregado (*LAm**) **Ⓑ** ADV (**) muy, extraordinariamente **Ⓒ** N **the ~** las almas en pena

damnedest* ['dæmdɪst] N **to do one's ~ to succeed** hacer lo imposible para tener éxito

damning ['dæmɪŋ] ADJ [*evidence*] irrefutable

damp [dæmp] **Ⓐ** ADJ (*compar* **~er**; *superl* **~est**) húmedo; **it smells ~ in here** aquí huele a humedad or a húmedo; **a ~ patch** una mancha de humedad; ✦ IDIOM **to be a ~ squib** (*Brit*) **the concert was a bit of a ~ squib** el concierto fue decepcionante, nos llevamos un chasco con el concierto **Ⓑ** N humedad *f* **Ⓒ** CPD ➤ **damp course** (*Brit*) aislante *m* hidrófugo

dampen ['dæmpən] VT **1** (= *moisten*) humedecer **2** [+ *hopes*] frustrar; [+ *enthusiasm, zeal*] enfriar; **to ~ sb's spirits** desanimar or desalentar a algn

damper ['dæmpə'], **dampener** ['dæmpənə'] N ✦ IDIOM **to put a ~ on** [+ *celebration, party*] poner una nota de tristeza a; **to put a ~ on things*** aguar la fiesta

dampness ['dæmpnɪs] N humedad *f*

damp-proof ['dæmppru:f] **Ⓐ** ADJ hidrófugo, a prueba de humedad **Ⓑ** VT aislar contra la humedad

damsel† ['dæmzəl] N damisela *f*, doncella *f*; **a ~ in distress** (*hum*) una dama en apuros

damson ['dæmzən] N (= *fruit*) ciruela *f* damascena; (= *tree*) ciruelo *m* damasceno

dance [dɑ:ns] **Ⓐ** N (= *act, event*) baile *m*; (= *art*) danza *f*, baile *m* **Ⓑ** VT bailar **Ⓒ** VI bailar; (*artistically*) bailar, danzar; **shall we ~?** ¿quieres bailar?; **to ~ for joy** saltar or brincar de alegría ⓓ CPD [*class, teacher, music*] de baile ➤ **dance band** orquesta *f* de baile ➤ **dance floor** pista *f* de baile ➤ **dance hall** salón *m* de baile, sala *f* de fiestas ➤ **dance music** música *f* de baile

dancer ['dɑːnsəʳ] N bailarín/ina *m/f*; (*flamenco*) bailaor(a) *m/f*

dancing ['dɑːnsɪŋ] N baile *m* ➤ **dancing girl** bailarina *f* ➤ **dancing partner** pareja *f* de baile ➤ **dancing shoes** zapatos *mpl* de baile; (*for ballet*) zapatillas *fpl* de ballet

dandelion ['dændɪlaɪən] N diente *m* de león

dandruff ['dændrəf] N caspa *f* ➤ **dandruff shampoo** champú *m* anticaspa

dandy ['dændɪ] ⓐ N (*pej*) (= *man*) dandi *m*, petimetre *m* ⓑ ADJ (*USt**) excelente, chachi (*Sp**), macanudo (*LAm**); **fine and** ~ perfecto

Dane [deɪn] N danés/esa *m/f*

danger ['deɪndʒəʳ] N peligro *m*; **to be in** ~ estar en peligro, correr peligro; **to be in ~ of falling** correr el peligro *or* riesgo de caer; **there is a ~ of** hay peligro *or* riesgo de; **there was no ~ that he would be discovered** no había peligro de que lo descubrieran; **(to be) out of** ~ (estar) fuera de peligro; **to be a ~ to sth/sb/o.s.** ser un peligro para algo/algn/sí mismo; **"danger men at work"** "¡atención *or* ¡peligro obras!"; **"danger keep out"** "¡peligro de muerte! prohibido el acceso" ➤ **danger list: to be on the ~ list** estar grave ➤ **danger money** plus *m* de peligrosidad ➤ **danger signal** señal *f* de peligro ➤ **danger zone** área *f or* zona *f* de peligro

> Use **el/un** not **la/una** before feminine nouns beginning with stressed **a** or **ha** like **área**.

dangerous ['deɪndʒrəs] ADJ peligroso; **he was jailed for ~ driving** lo metieron en la cárcel por conducir con imprudencia temeraria

dangerously ['deɪndʒrəslɪ] ADV peligrosamente, de forma peligrosa; **to be ~ ill** estar gravemente enfermo; **I came ~ close to hitting him** faltó muy poco para que le pegara; **go on, live ~, have another glass!** (*hum*) venga, un día es un día, ¡tómate otra copa!

dangle ['dæŋgl] ⓐ VT 1 [+ *arm, leg*] colgar; [+ *object on string etc*] dejar colgado 2 (*fig*) **to ~ sth in front of** *or* **before sb** tentar a algn con algo ⓑ VI colgar, pender; ✦ IDIOM **to keep sb dangling** tener a algn pendiente

Danish ['deɪnɪʃ] ⓐ N 1 (*Ling*) danés *m* 2 **the ~** los daneses ⓑ ADJ danés, dinamarqués ⓒ CPD ➤ **Danish blue (cheese)** queso *m* azul danés ➤ **Danish pastry** bollo de masa de hojaldre con pasas, manzana o crema

dank [dæŋk] ADJ (*compar* **-er**; *superl* **-est**) húmedo y frío

Danube ['dænjuːb] N Danubio *m*

dapper ['dæpəʳ] ADJ pulcro

dappled ['dæpld] ADJ [*horse*] rodado

dare [dɛəʳ] ⓐ N (= *challenge*) reto *m*, desafío *m*; **I did it for a ~** me retaron, por eso lo hice ⓑ VT, MODAL AUX VB 1 (= *be so bold*) atreverse; **to ~ (to) do sth** atreverse a hacer algo; **I ~n't** no me atrevo; **I ~n't tell him** no me atrevo a decírselo; **how ~ you!** ¡cómo te atreves!, ¡qué cara!; **don't** *or* **just you ~!*** ¡ni se te ocurra! 2 **I ~ say that ...** no me sorprendería que ... + *subjun*; **I ~ say you're tired** supongo que estás cansado; **the programme was, ~ I say it, dull** me atrevería a decir que el programa fue aburrido 3 (= *challenge*) desafiar, retar; **to ~ sb to do sth** desafiar *or* retar a algn a hacer algo; **I ~ you!** ¡a que no te atreves!

daredevil ['dɛədevl] ADJ, N temerario/a *m/f*

daring ['dɛərɪŋ] ADJ [*plan, escape*] arriesgado; [*person*] atrevido, audaz; [*film, clothes*] atrevido

daringly ['dɛərɪŋlɪ] ADV atrevidamente, osadamente

dark [dɑːk] ⓐ ADJ (*compar* **~er**; *superl* **~est**) 1 (= *lacking light*) oscuro; (= *without lights*) a oscuras; **it was already ~ outside** ya había oscurecido, ya era de noche; **it gets ~ early in winter** en invierno oscurece pronto *or* se hace de noche pronto; **the ~ side of the moon** la cara oculta de la luna

2 (*in colour*) [*colour, clothes*] oscuro; [*complexion, hair*] moreno, prieto (*Mex*); **~ blue/red** azul/rojo oscuro; **he is tall and ~** es alto y moreno, es alto y prieto (*Mex*) 3 (= *gloomy*) [*day, period*] aciago; [*mood, thoughts*] sombrío; **these are ~ days for the steel industry** son días aciagos para la industria del acero 4 (= *mysterious*) oscuro; **~est Africa** lo más recóndito de África 5 (= *sinister*) [*secret, plan, threat*] siniestro; **I got some ~ looks from Janet** Janet me lanzaba miradas asesinas ⓑ N (= *darkness*) oscuridad *f*; (= *nightfall*) anochecer *m*; **he is afraid of the ~** le tiene miedo a la oscuridad; **why are you sitting in the ~?** ¿por qué estás sentado en lo oscuro?; **after ~** después del anochecer; **I want to leave before ~** quiero salir antes de que anochezca *or* antes del anochecer; ✦ IDIOMS **I'm still in the ~ (about it)*** aún no sé nada (de eso); **to keep sb in the ~ about sth*** mantener a algn desinformado de algo, ocultar algo a algn ⓒ CPD ➤ **the Dark Ages** (*lit*) la Alta Edad Media; (*fig*) la Edad Media ➤ **dark chocolate** chocolate *m* amargo, chocolate *m* negro ➤ **dark glasses** gafas *fpl* oscuras ➤ **dark horse** ✦ IDIOM **he's a ~ horse** es una incógnita, es un enigma

darken ['dɑːkən] ⓐ VT (*gen*) oscurecer; [+ *colour*] hacer más oscuro; **a ~ed room** un cuarto oscuro ⓑ VI [*room, landscape*] oscurecerse; [*sky*] (*at nightfall*) oscurecerse; (= *cloud over*) nublarse; [*colour*] ponerse más oscuro; [*face, future*] ensombrecerse

darkly ['dɑːklɪ] ADV (= *mysteriously*) enigmáticamente; (= *threateningly*) de manera amenazante; **the newspapers hinted ~ at conspiracies** los periódicos hacían enigmáticas referencias a conspiraciones; **"we'll see," he said ~** —ya veremos —dijo en tono amenazante

darkness ['dɑːknɪs] N 1 [*of complexion, hair, sky*] oscuridad *f*; **the house was in ~** la casa estaba a oscuras; **~ fell, and we returned home** cayó la noche y volvimos a casa 2 (= *evil*) el mal; **the forces of ~** las fuerzas del mal

darkroom ['dɑːkrʊm] N (*Phot*) cuarto *m* oscuro

dark-skinned [ˌdɑːkˈskɪnd] ADJ moreno, morocho (*LAm*)

darling ['dɑːlɪŋ] ⓐ N (*gen*) cariño *m*, querido/a *m/f*; **yes, ~** (*to woman*) sí, cariño *or* querida; **come here, ~** (*to child*) ven aquí, cielo; **be a ~ and ...*** sé bueno y ...; **she's a little ~** [*child*] es un encanto ⓑ ADJ 1 (= *beloved*) querido 2 (*) (= *lovely*) [*house, dress*] mono

darn¹ [dɑːn] ⓐ N zurcido *m*, zurcidura *f* ⓑ VT zurcir

darn²* [dɑːn] (*esp US*) ⓐ EXCL ~ **(it)!** ¡caray!* ⓑ ADJ = **darned A** ⓒ ADV = **darned B**

darned* [dɑːnd] (*esp US*) ⓐ ADJ condenado, maldito ⓑ ADV **free to do as you ~ well please** libre de hacer lo que te dé la real gana*; **we start working pretty ~ early** empezamos a trabajar mogollón *or* tela de pronto*

darning ['dɑːnɪŋ] N (= *action*) zurcido *m*; (= *items to be darned*) cosas *f* por zurcir ➤ **darning needle** aguja *f* de zurcir ➤ **darning wool** hilo *m* de zurcir

dart [dɑːt] ⓐ N 1 (= *movement*) **to make a ~ for** precipitarse hacia 2 (*Sport*) dardo *m*, rehilete *m*; **~s** (= *game*) dardos *mpl*; **to play ~s** jugar a los dardos 3 (= *weapon*) dardo *m*, flecha *f* 4 (*Sew*) pinza *f* ⓑ VI **to ~ in/out** entrar/salir como una flecha; **to ~ at** *or* **for sth** lanzarse *or* precipitarse hacia algo

dartboard ['dɑːtbɔːd] N diana *f*

Darwinism ['dɑːwɪnɪzəm] N darwinismo *m*

dash [dæʃ] ⓐ N 1 [*of liquid*] gota *f*, chorrito *m*; [*of salt, pepper*] pizca *f*; [*of colour*] toque *m* 2 (= *punctuation mark*) raya *f* 3 (= *rush*) carrera *f*; **there was a mad ~ for the exit** todos se precipitaron hacia la salida; **to make a ~ at** *or* **towards** precipitarse hacia; **we had to make a ~ for it** tuvimos que salir corriendo 4 (*US Sport*) **the 100-meter ~** los 100 metros lisos 5 ✦ IDIOM **to cut a ~** destacar 6 (*in car*) salpicadero *m* (*Sp*), tablero *m* de mandos (*LAm*) ⓑ VT [+ *hopes*] frustrar, defraudar; **to ~ sth to pieces** hacer añicos algo, estrellar algo ⓒ VI 1 (= *smash*) estrellarse; **the waves are ~ing against the**

rock las olas rompen contra la roca
2 (= *rush*) ir de prisa, precipitarse; **to ~ away/back** salir/volver corriendo; **to ~ in/out** entrar/salir disparado; **I must ~*** me voy corriendo
➤ **dash off** Ⓐ VI + ADV salir corriendo, marcharse apresuradamente Ⓑ VT + ADV hacer a la carrera

dashboard ['dæʃbɔːd] N salpicadero *m* (*Sp*), tablero *m* de mandos (*LAm*)

dashing† ['dæʃɪŋ] ADJ [*man*] gallardo, apuesto

DAT N ABBR = **digital audio tape**

data ['deɪtə] NPL (*with sing or pl vb*) datos *mpl* ➤ **data bank** banco *m* de datos ➤ **data collection** recogida *f* de datos, recopilación *f* de datos ➤ **data processing** (= *action*) procesamiento *m* de datos, proceso *m* de datos; (= *science*) informática *f* ➤ **data processor** procesador *m* de datos ➤ **data protection** protección *f* de datos ➤ **data transmission** transmisión *f* de datos, telemática *f*

database ['deɪtəbeɪs] N base *f* de datos

Datapost® ['deɪtəpəʊst] N (*Brit*) **by ~** por correo urgente

date¹ [deɪt] Ⓐ N **1** (= *day*) fecha *f*; **what's the ~ today?** ¿qué fecha es hoy?; **at some future ~** en alguna fecha futura; **at a later ~** en una fecha posterior; **to ~** hasta la fecha
2 (= *appointment*) cita *f*; **to have a ~ with sb** tener una cita con algn; **to make a ~ with sb** citarse *or* quedar con algn
3 (= *person*) pareja *f*, acompañante *mf*; **who's your ~ for tonight?** ¿con quién sales esta noche?
4 (= *concert etc*) actuación *f*
Ⓑ VT **1** [+ *letter*] fechar, poner fecha a
2 (= *establish age of*) [+ *object*] fechar, datar; **that really ~s you!** ¡eso demuestra lo viejo que eres!
3 (= *go out with*) salir con, pololear con (*Chi*)
Ⓒ VI **1** (= *show age*) pasar de moda
2 to ~ back to remontarse a; **to ~ from** datar de
3 (= *go out with sb*) **is she dating?** ¿sale con chicos?; **they've been dating for three months** llevan saliendo juntos tres meses
Ⓓ CPD ➤ **date of birth** fecha *f* de nacimiento ➤ **date rape** violación *f* durante una cita amorosa ➤ **date stamp** (*on library book, fresh food*) sello *m* de fecha; (= *postmark*) matasellos *m inv*

date² [deɪt] N (= *fruit*) dátil *m*; (*also* **~ palm**) palmera *f* datilera

dated ['deɪtɪd] ADJ pasado de moda, anticuado

dateline ['deɪtlaɪn] N línea *f* de cambio de fecha

dating ['deɪtɪŋ] N (*Archeol*) datación *f* ➤ **dating agency** agencia *f* de contactos

dative ['deɪtɪv] N (*also* **~ case**) dativo *m*

daub [dɔːb] Ⓐ N (= *smear*) mancha *f* Ⓑ VT (= *smear*) embadurnar; **to ~ a wall with paint** ◇ **~ paint onto a wall** embadurnar una pared de pintura

daughter ['dɔːtəʳ] N hija *f*

daughter-in-law ['dɔːtərɪnlɔː] N (*pl* **daughters-in-law**) nuera *f*, hija *f* política

daunt [dɔːnt] VT (= *inhibit*) amedrentar; (= *dishearten*) desmoralizar, desalentar; **nothing ~ed** sin dejarse amedrentar, sin inmutarse

daunting ['dɔːntɪŋ] ADJ (= *inhibiting*) abrumador, amedrentador; (= *disheartening*) desalentador, desmoralizante; **a ~ task** una tarea abrumadora

dauntless ['dɔːntlɪs] ADJ intrépido

dawdle ['dɔːdl] VI (*in walking*) andar muy despacio; (*over food, work*) entretenerse, demorarse

dawn [dɔːn] Ⓐ N **1** amanecer *m*; **at ~** al amanecer; **from ~ to dusk** de sol a sol **2** (*liter*) (= *beginning*) albores *mpl*; **the ~ of the radio age** los albores de la era de la radio Ⓑ VI [*day*] amanecer; **a new epoch has ~ed** ha nacido una época nueva; **it ~ed on me that ...** caí en la cuenta de que ..., empecé a comprender que ... Ⓒ CPD ➤ **dawn chorus** (*Brit*) canto *m* de los pájaros al amanecer ➤ **dawn raid** *redada efectuada en la madrugada*

day [deɪ] Ⓐ N **1** (*gen*) día *m*; **what ~ is it today?** ¿qué día es hoy?; **he works eight hours a ~** trabaja ocho horas al día;

twice a ~ dos veces al día; **the ~ after** el día siguiente; **the ~ after tomorrow** pasado mañana; **~ after ~** día tras día; **two ~s ago** hace dos días; **any ~** un día cualquiera; **any ~ now** cualquier día de éstos; **the ~ before** el día anterior; **the ~ before yesterday** anteayer; **the ~ before his birthday** la víspera de su cumpleaños; **two ~s before Christmas** dos días antes de Navidad; **by ~** de un día para otro, de día a día (*LAm*); **every ~** cada día, todos los días; **one fine ~** el día menos pensado; **on the following ~** al día siguiente; **for ~s on end** durante días; **from one ~ to the next** de un día a otro; **to live from ~ to ~** vivir al día; **~ in ~ out** un día sí y otro también; **everything will be all right on the ~** para el día en cuestión todo estará en orden; **the other ~** el otro día; **every other ~** un día sí y otro no; **some ~** un día; **one of these ~s** un día de éstos; **50 years ago to the ~** (hoy) hace exactamente 50 años; ✦ IDIOMS **he's fifty if he's a ~** (*esp Brit**) debe de tener cincuenta años mínimo; **to carry** *or* **win the ~** ganar la victoria; **to make sb's ~:** **it made my ~ to see him smile** me hizo feliz verlo sonreír; **that'll be the ~, when he offers to pay!*** ¡él nos invitará cuando las ranas críen pelo!
2 (= *daylight hours*) día *m*; **to work all ~** trabajar todo el día; **a ~ at the seaside** un día de playa; **to travel by ~** viajar de día; **it's a fine ~** hace buen tiempo hoy; **good ~!** ¡buenos días!; **to work ~s** trabajar de día; ✦ IDIOMS **it's all in a ~'s work** son gajes del oficio; **to call it a ~*** (*for good*) darse por vencido, abandonar; (*for today*) dejarlo por hoy
3 (= *working hours*) jornada *f*; **to work an eight-hour ~** trabajar una jornada de ocho horas; **paid by the ~** pagado por día; **a ~ off** un día libre; **to take a ~ off** darse un día libre
4 (= *period*) **during the early ~s of the strike** durante los primeros días de la huelga; **the happiest ~s of your life** los mejores días de su vida; **in those ~s** en aquellos tiempos; **in ~s to come** en días venideros; **in this ~ and age** hoy en día; **in my ~** en mis tiempos; **in Queen Victoria's ~** en la época de la reina Victoria; **these ~s** hoy en día; **those were the ~s, when ...** esa fue la buena época, cuando ...; **to this ~** hasta el día de hoy; **in his younger ~s** en su juventud
Ⓑ CPD ➤ **day bed** (*US*) meridiana *f* ➤ **day boy** (*Brit Scol*) externo *m* ➤ **day centre** (*Brit*) centro *m* de día ➤ **day girl** (*Brit Scol*) externa *f* ➤ **day job** trabajo *m* habitual, ocupación *f* habitual ➤ **day nursery** guardería *f* ➤ **day release course** (*Brit*) curso *m* de un día a la semana (para trabajadores) ➤ **day return (ticket)** (*Brit*) billete *m* (*Sp*) *or* boleto *m* (*LAm*) de ida y vuelta en el día ➤ **day school** colegio *m* sin internado ➤ **day shift** turno *m* de día ➤ **day trader** (*St Ex*) especulador(a) *m/f* a muy corto plazo ➤ **day trip** excursión *f* (de un día); **to go on a ~ trip to London** ir un día de excursión *or* (*LAm*) de paseo a Londres ➤ **day tripper** (*Brit*) excursionista *mf*

daybreak ['deɪbreɪk] N amanecer *m*; **at ~** al amanecer

daycare ['deɪkeəʳ] N (*for children*) servicio *m*(*pl*) de guardería; (*for elderly/disabled*) asistencia prestada a los ancianos/minusválidos durante el día ➤ **daycare centre**, **daycare center** (*US*) (*for children*) guardería *f*; (*for elderly, disabled*) centro *m* de día

daydream ['deɪdriːm] Ⓐ N ensueño *m*, ilusión *f* Ⓑ VI soñar despierto

daylight ['deɪlaɪt] N luz *f* (del día); **at ~** al amanecer; **in the ~** de día; **in broad ~** a plena luz del día, en pleno día; ✦ IDIOMS **I am beginning to see ~** (= *understand*) empiezo a ver las cosas claras; (= *approach the end of a job*) ya vislumbro el final; **to beat the (living) ~s out of sb*** dar una tremenda paliza a algn; **to scare the (living) ~s out of sb*** dar un susto de muerte a algn ➤ **daylight hours** horas *fpl* de luz ➤ **daylight robbery** (*Brit**) **it's ~ robbery!** ¡es un robo *or* una estafa!

daylight-saving time [ˌdeɪlaɪtˈseɪvɪŋˌtaɪm] N (*US*) horario *m* de verano

day-old ['deɪəʊld] ADJ [*chick*] de un día

dayroom ['deɪrʊm] N (*in hospital etc*) sala de estar para los internos

daytime ['deɪtaɪm] Ⓐ N día *m*; **in the ~** de día Ⓑ ADJ de día; **please give a ~ telephone number** por favor dé un teléfono de contacto durante el día **G** CPD ➤ **daytime TV** programación *f* televisiva de mañana y sobremesa

day-to-day ['deɪtə'deɪ] ADJ cotidiano, diario; **on a ~ basis** día por día, de día a día (*LAm*)

daze [deɪz] **A** N **to be in a ~** estar aturdido **B** VT 1 [*drug, blow*] atontar, aturdir 2 [*news*] aturdir, atolondrar

dazed [deɪzd] ADJ aturdido

dazzle ['dæzl] VT deslumbrar; **to be ~d by sth** (*fig*) quedar(se) deslumbrado por algo

dazzling ['dæzlɪŋ] ADJ deslumbrante

DBS N ABBR 1 = **direct broadcasting by satellite** 2 = **direct broadcasting satellite**

DC N ABBR 1 (= **direct current**) C.C. 2 (*US*) = **District of Columbia**

DCI N ABBR (*Brit*) = **Detective Chief Inspector**

DD N ABBR 1 = **Doctor of Divinity** 2 = **direct debit** 3 (*US*) = **dishonorable discharge**

D-day ['diːdeɪ] N (*Hist*) el día D, el día de la invasión aliada de Normandía (*6 de junio 1944*); (*fig*) día *m* D

DDT N ABBR (= **dichlorodiphenyltrichloroethane**) DDT *m*

DE ABBR (*US*) = **Delaware**

DEA N ABBR (*US*) (= **Drug Enforcement Administration**) *departamento para la lucha contra la droga*

deacon ['diːkən] N diácono *m*

deaconess ['diːkənes] N diaconisa *f*

deactivate [diːˈæktɪveɪt] VT desactivar

dead [ded] **A** ADJ 1 [*person, animal, plant*] muerto; [*leaf*] marchito, seco; **~ man** muerto *m*; **to be ~** estar muerto; **he's been ~ for two years** hace dos años que murió; **~ or alive** vivo o muerto; **to be ~ on arrival** llegar muerto, ingresar cadáver; **~ and buried** (*lit, fig*) muerto y bien muerto; **to drop (down) ~** caer muerto; ✦ IDIOMS **over my ~ body!*** ¡ni muerto!, ¡ni de chiste!; **as ~ as a dodo** *or* a **doornail** más muerto que mi abuela; **that issue is a ~ duck** esa cuestión ya no tiene interés; **to be ~ on one's feet** estar hecho migas *or* polvo*; **~ from the neck up*** bruto, imbécil, zoquete*; **to flog** *or* (*US*) **beat a ~ horse** machacar en hierro frío; **you're ~ meat!*** ¡te vas a enterar!, ¡vas a ver lo que es bueno!; **I wouldn't be seen ~ there** ni muerto ni vivo me verán allí; **to be ~ in the water** haberse ido al garete; **he was ~ to the world** estaba dormido como un tronco; ✦ PROV ~ **men tell no tales** los muertos no hablan

2 (= *inactive*) [*volcano, fire*] apagado; [*battery*] agotado; [*language, town, party*] muerto; **the line has gone ~** (*Telec*) la línea está cortada *or* muerta

3 **my fingers have gone ~** (= *numb*) se me han dormido los dedos; (*with cold*) se me han entumecido los dedos

4 (= *complete*) [*silence, calm*] total, completo; (= *exact*) [*centre*] justo; **a ~ cert*** una cosa segura; **to be a ~ loss** (*Brit*) [*person*] ser un inútil; [*thing*] ser una birria

B ADV 1 (*Brit*) (= *completely, exactly*) **he stopped ~** se paró en seco; **"drive slow"** (*Aut*) "reducir la marcha"; **to be ~ against sth** estar totalmente opuesto a algo; **~ ahead** todo seguido, todo derecho; **to be ~ beat*** estar hecho polvo; **~ certain*** completamente seguro; **~ drunk*** borracho perdido; **~ easy*** facilón, chupado**; **~ level: the scores are ~ level** van igualados en puntos; **to be ~ set on doing sth** estar decidido a hacer algo; **~ straight** todo seguido, todo derecho; **~ on time** a la hora exacta; **~ tired*** muerto (de cansancio)

2 ✦ IDIOM **to cut sb ~*** hacer el vacío a algn

C N 1 **the ~** los muertos *mpl*; **to come back** *or* **rise from the ~** resucitar

2 **at ~ of night** a altas horas de la noche; **in the ~ of winter** en pleno invierno

D CPD ➤ **dead end** (*lit, fig*) callejón *m* sin salida; **to come to a ~ end** (*fig*) llegar a un punto muerto ➤ **dead heat** (*Sport*) empate *m* ➤ **Dead Sea** Mar *m* Muerto ➤ **dead weight** peso *m* muerto

deadbeat* ['dedbiːt] N (*US*) haragán/ana *m/f*

deaden ['dedn] VT [+ *noise, shock*] amortiguar; [+ *feeling*] embotar; [+ *pain*] aliviar, calmar

dead-end ['ded'end] ADJ [*street*] sin salida; [*job*] sin

---

porvenir; **~ kids** (*US*) chicos *mpl* de la calle

deadline ['dedlaɪn] N (*Press, Comm*) fecha *f* tope; **to meet a ~** respetar un plazo; **we cannot meet the government's ~** no podemos terminarlo *etc* en el plazo señalado por el gobierno

deadlock ['dedlɒk] N punto *m* muerto; **to reach ~** llegar a un punto muerto, quedar estancado

deadly ['dedlɪ] **A** ADJ (*compar* **deadlier**; *superl* **deadliest**) 1 (= *lethal*) [*poison, disease, combination*] mortal; [*weapon, attack*] mortífero

2 (= *devastating*) **with ~ accuracy** (*Sport*) con precisión mortífera; (*Mil*) con precisión letal *or* mortal; **to be ~ enemies** ser enemigos mortales *or* a muerte; **there was ~ silence** se hizo un silencio sepulcral

3 (*) (= *boring*) aburridísimo

B ADV **~ dull** aburridísimo; **she thought he was joking but he was ~ serious** ella pensaba que bromeaba, pero lo decía completamente en serio

C CPD ➤ **deadly nightshade** belladona *f* ➤ **deadly sins the seven ~ sins** los siete pecados capitales

deadpan ['dedpæn] ADJ inexpresivo

deadwood ['ded,wʊd] N **to get rid of the ~** (*in organization*) eliminar al personal inútil

deaf [def] **A** ADJ (*compar* **~er**; *superl* **~est**) sordo; **~ in one ear** sordo de un oído; **~ to all appeals** sordo a todos los ruegos; ✦ IDIOMS **to be as ~ as a (door)post** estar más sordo que una tapia; **to turn a ~ ear to sth** hacer oídos sordos *or* no prestar oídos a algo; **to fall on ~ ears: the plea fell on ~ ears** el ruego cayó en saco roto **B** NPL **the deaf** los sordos *mpl* **C** CPD ➤ **deaf aid** audífono *m*, sonotone® *m*

deaf-and-dumb ['defən'dʌm] ADJ sordomudo

deafen ['defn] VT ensordecer

deafening ['defnɪŋ] ADJ ensordecedor

deaf-mute ['def'mjuːt] N sordomudo/a *m/f*

deafness ['defnɪs] N sordera *f*

deal[1] [diːl] (*vb: pt, pp* **dealt**) **A** N 1 (= *agreement*) acuerdo *m*, trato *m*; (= *transaction*) trato *m*, transacción *f*; **it's a ~!*** ¡trato hecho!; **arms ~** venta *f* de armas; **big ~!*** ¡vaya cosa!; **what's the big ~?*** ¿qué tiene eso de raro?; **this sort of thing happens every day, it's no big ~*** estas cosas pasan todos los días, no es nada del otro mundo; **to make a big ~ (out) of sth*** dar mucha *or* demasiada importancia a algo; **business ~** (*between companies, countries*) acuerdo *m or* trato *m* comercial; (*by individual*) negocio *m*; **to do a ~ with sb** hacer un trato con algn, llegar a un acuerdo con algn; **pay ~** acuerdo *m* salarial; ✦ IDIOM **it's a done ~** (*esp US*) es cosa hecha *or* segura, está atado y bien atado

2 (= *treatment*) trato *m*; **working women are not getting a fair ~** las mujeres que trabajan no están recibiendo un trato justo

3 (= *bargain*) ganga *f*; **they are offering good ~s on flights to Australia** tienen viajes a Australia a muy buen precio

4 (= *amount*) **a good** *or* **great ~ (of)** mucho; **a good** *or* **great ~ of money** mucho dinero; **there's a good ~ of truth in what you say** hay mucho de verdad en lo que dices; **she's a good ~ cleverer than her brother** es mucho *or* bastante más inteligente que su hermano; **"does he get out much?"** — **"not a great ~"** —¿sale mucho? —no mucho *or* demasiado; **she knew a great ~ about him** sabía muchas cosas sobre él

5 (*Cards*) reparto *m*; **whose ~ is it?** ¿a quién le toca dar *or* repartir?

B VT (*Cards*) dar, repartir; **the news dealt a severe blow to their hopes** la noticia fue un duro golpe para sus esperanzas

C VI (*Cards*) dar, repartir

➤ **deal in** VI + PREP [+ *goods*] comerciar con, negociar con; [+ *antiques, used cars*] dedicarse a la compraventa de; [+ *drugs*] traficar con; [+ *stocks, shares, currency*] operar con

➤ **deal out** VT + ADV [+ *playing cards*] repartir; [+ *punishment*] imponer

➤ **deal with** VI + PREP 1 (= *have dealings with*) tratar con; (= *do business with*) hacer negocio con, comerciar con

2 (= *attend to, tackle*) [+ *task*] ocuparse de, encargarse de; [+ *difficult person*] manejar, tratar; [+ *customer, order, application, complaint*] atender; [+ *problem*] (= *take on*) ocuparse de, encargarse de; (= *solve*) solucionar, resolver;

[+ *emotion*] superar; **she's not easy to ~ with** tiene un carácter difícil; **I'll ~ with your questions afterwards** contestaré (a) sus preguntas después; **have you dealt with that paperwork yet?** ¿has resuelto todo el papeleo ya?, ¿has terminado ya todo el papeleo?; **I'll ~ with you later!** ¡luego me encargaré de ti!; **anyone who disobeys will be severely dealt with** cualquiera que desobedezca será tratado con mucha severidad
3 (= *be about*) [*book, film*] tratar de

deal² [diːl] ADJ (= *wooden*) de pino

dealer ['diːləʳ] N **1** (= *seller*) comerciante *mf* (**in** de); (*in cattle, horses*) tratante *mf* (**in** de); (= *supplier*) distribuidor(a) *m/f*, proveedor(a) *m/f*; (*in cars*) concesionario/a *m/f*; **your local Honda** ~ su concesionario Honda más próximo; **he's a property** ~ se dedica a la compraventa de propiedades **2** (*Cards*) repartidor(a) *m/f* de cartas

dealership ['diːləʃɪp] N (*US*) representación *f*, concesión *f*

dealings ['diːlɪŋz] NPL **1** (= *relationship*) trato *msing*, relaciones *fpl*; **have you had any ~ with them?** ¿ha tratado con ellos alguna vez? **2** (*Comm, Fin*) negocios *mpl*; **he was accused of illegal share ~** lo acusaron de operar ilegalmente en la Bolsa

dealt [delt] PT, PP *of* **deal¹**

dean [diːn] N (*Rel*) deán *m*; (*Univ*) decano *m* ➤ **Dean's list** (*US Univ*) lista *f* de honor académica

dear [dɪəʳ] **Ⓐ** ADJ (*compar* **~er**; *superl* **~est**) **1** querido; **she's a very ~ friend of mine** es una amiga mía muy querida; **he's a ~ boy, but ...** es muy buena persona, pero ...; **what a ~ little necklace that is!** ¡qué bonita que es esa gargantilla!; **it's my ~est wish** es mi mayor deseo; **to hold sth** ~ apreciar algo; **his family life was very ~ to him** su familia era muy importante para él; **it is a subject ~ to her heart** es uno de sus temas preferidos
2 (*in letter writing*) **Dear Daddy** Querido papá; **Dear Peter** Estimado Peter; (*to closer friend*) Querido Peter; **Dear Mr and Mrs Smith** Estimados Sr. y Sra. Smith; **Dear Sir(s)** Estimado(s) señor(es), Muy señor(es) mío(s), De mi/nuestra consideración (*esp LAm*); **Dear Sir or Madam** Estimado/a señor/a
3 (*esp Brit**) (= *expensive*) [*product, shop, price*] caro
Ⓑ EXCL – **me! it's nearly one o'clock** ¡madre mía! es casi la una; **oh ~! we're going to be late** ¡vaya hombre! *or* ¡vaya por Dios! vamos a llegar tarde; **oh ~! look at the mess you're in** ¡ay, Dios mío! *or* ¡qué horror! ¡mira qué desastre vienes hecho!
Ⓒ N (*) (*as form of address*) cariño *m*; **would you be a ~ and pass me my book?** anda, sé bueno y pásame el libro; **(you) poor ~!** ¡pobrecito!
Ⓓ ADV [*sell, buy, pay*] caro

dearly ['dɪəlɪ] ADV **1** (= *very much*) mucho, de verdad; **I loved him ~** lo quería mucho *or* de verdad; **I should ~ love to go** me encantaría ir; **~ beloved** queridos *or* amados hermanos **2** (= *at great cost*) caro; **it cost him ~** le costó caro; **he paid ~ for his mistake** pagó caro su error

dearth [dɜːθ] N escasez *f*

death [deθ] **Ⓐ** N **1** muerte *f*, fallecimiento *m*; **it will be the ~ of him** acabará con su perdición; **you'll be the ~ of me!*** ¡vas a acabar conmigo!; **till ~ us do part** hasta que la muerte nos separe; **~ to traitors!** ¡muerte a los traidores!; **to fight/a fight to the ~** luchar/una lucha a muerte; **to put sb to ~** dar muerte a algn; **to sentence sb to ~** condenar a algn a muerte; ✦ IDIOMS **to catch one's ~ (of cold)** coger un catarro de muerte; **to be at ~'s door** estar a las puertas de la muerte; **to hold on like grim ~** estar firmemente agarrado; (*fig*) resistir con la mayor firmeza; **to look like ~ warmed up** *or* (*US*) **over*** estar muy demacrado, estar hecho una pena
2 to ~*: to be bored to ~ estar muerto de aburrimiento; **it frightens me to ~** me da un miedo espantoso; **I'm sick to ~ of it** estoy hasta la coronilla de ello
Ⓑ CPD ➤ **death blow** golpe *m* mortal ➤ **death camp** campo *m* de exterminio ➤ **death cell** (*Brit*) celda *f* de los condenados a muerte ➤ **death certificate** partida *f* de defunción ➤ **death duties** (*Brit*) impuesto *msing* de sucesiones ➤ **death knell** toque *m* de difuntos, doble *m*; **it sounded the ~ knell of the empire** anunció el fin *or*

presagió la caída del imperio ➤ **death penalty** pena *f* de muerte ➤ **death rate** tasa *f* de mortalidad, mortalidad *f* ➤ **death row** (*US*) celdas *fpl* de los condenados a muerte, corredor *m* de la muerte ➤ **death sentence** pena *f* de muerte ➤ **death squad** escuadrón *m* de la muerte ➤ **death threat** amenaza *f* de muerte ➤ **death throes** agonía *fsing* ➤ **death toll** número *m* de víctimas ➤ **death warrant** orden *f* de ejecución; ✦ IDIOM **to sign one's own ~ warrant** firmar su sentencia de muerte ➤ **death wish** ganas *fpl* de morir

deathbed ['deθbed] N lecho *m* de muerte; **on one's ~** en su lecho de muerte ➤ **deathbed confession** confesión *f* en el lecho de muerte

deathly ['deθlɪ] **Ⓐ** ADJ [*appearance, pallor*] cadavérico; [*silence*] sepulcral **Ⓑ** ADV **~ pale** pálido como un muerto

deathtrap ['deθtræp] N **to be a ~** ser un peligro *or* una trampa mortal

debacle, débâcle [deɪˈbɑːkl] N debacle *f*, desastre *m*

debar [dɪˈbɑːʳ] VT excluir; **to ~ sb from sth** excluir a algn de algo; **to ~ sb from doing sth** prohibir a algn hacer algo

debark [dɪˈbɑːk] VI (*US*) desembarcar

debarkation [diːbɑːˈkeɪʃən] N (*US*) desembarco *m*

debase [dɪˈbeɪs] VT [+ *language*] corromper; [+ *person, culture*] degradar; **to ~ o.s. (by doing sth)** degradarse (haciendo algo)

debasement [dɪˈbeɪsmənt] N [*of language*] corrupción *f*; [*of person, culture*] degradación *f*

debatable [dɪˈbeɪtəbl] ADJ discutible

debate [dɪˈbeɪt] **Ⓐ** VT [+ *topic, question, idea*] debatir, discutir; **we ~d whether to go or not** dudamos *or* nos planteamos si ir o no **Ⓑ** VI discutir, debatir; **to ~ with sb (about sth)** discutir con algn (sobre algo) **Ⓒ** N debate *m*, discusión *f*; **after much ~** después de mucho discutir; **that is open to ~** ése es un tema discutido

debating [dɪˈbeɪtɪŋ] N **~ is a difficult skill to learn** el saber debatir es una habilidad difícil de adquirir ➤ **debating society** círculo *m* de debates

debauched [dɪˈbɔːtʃt] ADJ depravado, libertino

debauchery [dɪˈbɔːtʃərɪ] N libertinaje *m*, depravación *f*

debenture [dɪˈbentʃəʳ] N (*Fin*) bono *m*, obligación *f* ➤ **debenture capital** capital *m* en obligaciones ➤ **debenture stock** obligaciones *fpl*

debilitate [dɪˈbɪlɪteɪt] VT debilitar

debilitating [dɪˈbɪlɪteɪtɪŋ] ADJ debilitante, que debilita

debit ['debɪt] **Ⓐ** N (*in the books of a business*) pasivo *m*; (*in a bank account*) debe *m*, débito *m*; (= *individual sum taken*) cargo *m* **Ⓑ** VT **to ~ an account with a sum** cargar una suma en cuenta; **to ~ sb's account with a sum** cargar una suma en la cuenta de algn **Ⓒ** CPD ➤ **debit balance** saldo *m* deudor ➤ **debit card** tarjeta *f* de débito ➤ **debit side: on the ~ side** (*fig*) entre las desventajas

debonair [ˌdebəˈneəʳ] ADJ (= *elegant*) gallardo; (= *courteous*) cortés; (= *cheerful*) alegre

debrief [ˌdiːˈbriːf] VT hacer dar parte

debriefing [ˌdiːˈbriːfɪŋ] N informe *m* sobre una operación *etc*

debris ['debriː] N [*of building, construction*] escombros *mpl*; [*of aeroplane*] restos *mpl*

debt [det] **Ⓐ** N **1** (= *money owed*) deuda *f*; **bad ~** deuda incobrable; **to be in ~ (to sb)** tener deudas *or* estar endeudado (con algn); **I am five pounds in ~** debo cinco libras (**to** a); **to get into ~** ◇ **run up ~s** contraer deudas; **to be out of ~** tener las deudas saldadas
2 (*fig*) **a ~ of gratitude/honour** una deuda de agradecimiento/honor; **to be in sb's ~** estar en deuda con algn
Ⓑ CPD ➤ **debt collection** cobro *m* de morosos ➤ **debt collector** cobrador(a) *m/f* de morosos ➤ **debt relief** alivio *m* de deuda ➤ **debt servicing** amortización *f* de la deuda

debtor ['detəʳ] N deudor(a) *f*

debug [ˌdiːˈbʌg] VT **1** (*Comput*) depurar, quitar los fallos a **2** (= *remove mikes from*) quitar los micrófonos ocultos de

debunk ['diːˈbʌŋk] VT desacreditar

debut, début ['deɪbuː] N debut *m*, presentación *f*; **to make one's ~** [*actor*] debutar, hacer su presentación

Dec. ABBR (= **December**) dic., dic.ᵉ, D.

dec. ABBR = **deceased**

decade ['dekeɪd] N década *f*, decenio *m*

decadence ['dekədəns] N decadencia *f*

decadent ['dekədənt] ADJ decadente

de-caff* ['diːkæf] N ABBR = **decaffeinated coffee**

decaffeinated [diːˈkæfɪneɪtɪd] ADJ descafeinado

decal [ˈdiːkæl] N (*US*) calcomanía *f*

decamp [dɪˈkæmp] VI **1** (*Mil*) levantar el campamento **2** (*) (= *make off*) escaparse; (= *move*) irse (**to** a)

decant [dɪˈkænt] VT [+ *wine etc*] decantar

decanter [dɪˈkæntəʳ] N licorera *f*

decapitate [dɪˈkæpɪteɪt] VT decapitar

decapitation [dɪˌkæpɪˈteɪʃən] N decapitación *f*

decathlon [dɪˈkæθlən] N decatlón *m*

decay [dɪˈkeɪ] Ⓐ N **1** [*of vegetation, food*] putrefacción *f*, descomposición *f*; [*of tooth*] caries *f*; [*of building*] desmoronamiento *m*, ruina *f* **2** [*of civilization*] decadencia *f* Ⓑ VI **1** [*leaves, food*] pudrirse, descomponerse; [*tooth*] cariarse; [*building*] desmoronarse **2** [*civilization*] decaer, estar en decadencia Ⓒ VT [+ *tooth*] cariar

decayed [dɪˈkeɪd] (*gen*) podrido; [*tooth*] cariado

decaying [dɪˈkeɪɪŋ] ADJ [*food, vegetation*] podrido; [*flesh*] en estado de descomposición, en descomposición; [*tooth*] cariado; [*building*] muy deteriorado, ruinoso

deceased [dɪˈsiːst] Ⓐ ADJ difunto Ⓑ N **the ~** el/la difunto/a

deceit [dɪˈsiːt] N (= *misleading*) engaño *m*; (= *fraud*) fraude *m*; (= *deceitfulness*) falsedad *f*

deceitful [dɪˈsiːtfʊl] ADJ [*person*] falso; [*child*] mentiroso; [*statement, behaviour*] engañoso

deceitfully [dɪˈsiːtfəlɪ] ADV engañosamente

deceive [dɪˈsiːv] VT engañar; **don't be ~d by appearances** no te dejes engañar por las apariencias; **let nobody be ~d by this** que nadie se llame a engaño por esto; **he thought his eyes were deceiving him** no creía lo que veían sus ojos; **to ~ o.s.** engañarse

decelerate [diːˈseləreɪt] VI desacelerar, decelerar

December [dɪˈsembəʳ] N diciembre *m*; *see* **July**

decency ['diːsənsɪ] N **1** (= *propriety*) decencia *f*, decoro *m*; **to have a sense of ~** tener sentido del decoro **2** (= *politeness*) educación *f*; **it is no more than common ~ to let him know** hay que avisarle, aunque sólo sea por una cuestión de educación **3** (= *kindness*) bondad *f*, amabilidad *f*; **he had the ~ to phone me** tuvo la amabilidad de llamarme

decent ['diːsənt] ADJ **1** (= *respectable*) [*person, house*] decente; [*clothes, behaviour, language*] decoroso, decente; **are you ~?** (*hum*) ¿estás visible? **2** (= *kind*) **he was very ~ to me** fue muy amable conmigo, se portó muy bien conmigo; **he's a ~ sort** es buena persona **3** (= *passable*) [*salary, meal*] adecuado, decente

decently ['diːsəntlɪ] ADV **1** (= *respectably*) decentemente, decorosamente **2** (= *kindly*) amablemente, con amabilidad

decentralization [diːˌsentrəlaɪˈzeɪʃən] N descentralización *f*

decentralize [diːˈsentrəlaɪz] VT descentralizar

deception [dɪˈsepʃən] N engaño *m*

⚠ **deception** ≠ **decepción**

deceptive [dɪˈseptɪv] ADJ engañoso

deceptively [dɪˈseptɪvlɪ] ADV **the village looks ~ near** el pueblo no está tan cerca como parece

decibel ['desɪbel] N decibelio *m*

decide [dɪˈsaɪd] Ⓐ VT decidir; **to ~ where to go/what to do** decidir adónde ir/qué hacer; **to ~ to do sth** decidir hacer algo; **it was ~d that** se decidió que; **that ~d me** eso me

convenció Ⓑ VI decidir, decidirse; **to ~ against sth** decidirse en contra de algo; **to ~ in favour of sth/sb** decidirse por algo/algn, decidir a favor de algo/algn
➤ **decide on** VI + PREP **to ~ on sth** decidirse por algo; **to ~ on doing sth** decidir hacer algo

decided [dɪˈsaɪdɪd] ADJ **1** (= *distinct*) [*difference, improvement*] indudable, marcado **2** (= *categorical*) [*opinion*] firme, categórico

decidedly [dɪˈsaɪdɪdlɪ] ADV (= *without doubt*) indudablemente, sin duda; (= *very, markedly*) decididamente

decider [dɪˈsaɪdəʳ] N (*Brit*) (= *game*) partido *m* decisivo; (= *replay*) partido *m* de desempate, desempate *m*; (= *goal*) gol *m* decisivo

deciding [dɪˈsaɪdɪŋ] ADJ decisivo

deciduous [dɪˈsɪdjʊəs] ADJ de hoja caduca

decilitre, deciliter (*US*) ['desɪˌliːtəʳ] N decilitro *m*

decimal ['desɪməl] Ⓐ ADJ decimal; **to three ~ places** con tres decimales Ⓑ N decimal *m* Ⓒ CPD ➤ **decimal point** ≈ coma *f* decimal, ≈ coma *f* de decimales ➤ **decimal system** sistema *m* métrico (decimal)

decimalization [ˌdesɪmələˈzeɪʃən] N conversión *f* al sistema métrico, decimalización *f*

decimate ['desɪmeɪt] VT diezmar

decipher [dɪˈsaɪfəʳ] VT descifrar

decision [dɪˈsɪʒən] N **1** (*gen*) decisión *f*; (*Jur*) fallo *m*; **to come to a ~** llegar a una decisión; **to make** *or* (*esp Brit*) **take a ~** tomar una decisión **2** (= *resoluteness*) resolución *f*, decisión *f*

decision-making [dɪˈsɪʒənˌmeɪkɪŋ] N **he's good at ~** es bueno tomando decisiones ➤ **decision-making process** proceso *m* decisorio

decisive [dɪˈsaɪsɪv] ADJ **1** [*victory, factor, influence*] decisivo, determinante **2** [*manner, reply, person*] decidido

decisively [dɪˈsaɪsɪvlɪ] ADV **1** (= *conclusively*) **to be ~ beaten** ser derrotado de modo decisivo **2** (= *resolutely*) con decisión, con resolución

deck [dek] Ⓐ N **1** (*Naut*) cubierta *f*; **to go up on ~** subir a la cubierta; **below ~** bajo cubierta; ✦ IDIOMS **to clear the ~s** despejar el terreno; **to hit the ~*** caer al suelo **2** [*of bus*] piso *m*; **top** *or* **upper ~** piso *m* de arriba **3** [*of cards*] baraja *f* Ⓑ VT **1** (*also* ~ **out**) [+ *room*] adornar, engalanar (**with** con); [+ *person*] ataviar, engalanar (**with** con); **all ~ed out** [*person*] de punta en blanco **2** (**) (= *knock down*) derribar de un golpe

deckchair ['dekˌtʃeəʳ] N tumbona *f* (*Sp*), perezosa *f* (*LAm*)

deckhand ['dekhænd] N marinero *m* de cubierta

declaim [dɪˈkleɪm] VT, VI declamar

declamatory [dɪˈklæmətərɪ] ADJ declamatorio

declaration [ˌdekləˈreɪʃən] N declaración *f* ➤ **the Declaration of Independence** la Declaración de Independencia (*de Estados Unidos*)

declare [dɪˈkleəʳ] VT **1** [+ *intentions, love*] declarar; [+ *dividend, result*] anunciar; **to ~ that** declarar que, manifestar que; **to ~ war** declarar la guerra (**on** a); **to ~ o.s.** declararse; **to ~ o.s. in favour of sth** pronunciarse *or* declararse a favor de algo **2** [+ *income*] declarar; **have you anything to ~?** ¿tiene usted algo que declarar?

declassify [diːˈklæsɪfaɪ] VT levantar el secreto oficial que pesa sobre

declension [dɪˈklenʃən] N declinación *f*

decline [dɪˈklaɪn] Ⓐ N **1** (*in numbers, sales*) descenso *m*, disminución *f* (**in** de); (*in support, interest*) disminución *f* (**in** de); **to be on the ~** ir disminuyendo **2** (= *deterioration*) decadencia *f*, declive *m*, deterioro *m*; (*in standards*) descenso *m*, declive *m*; (*Med*) debilitamiento *m* Ⓑ VT **1** (= *refuse*) rehusar, rechazar, declinar (*frm*); **to ~ to do sth** rehusar *or* (*frm*) declinar hacer algo **2** (*Gram*) declinar Ⓒ VI **1** (= *decrease*) disminuir; (= *deteriorate*) decaer; (*in health*) debilitarse, decaer; **to ~ in importance** ir perdiendo importancia **2** (= *refuse*) negarse, rehusar **3** (*Gram*) declinarse

declining [dɪˈklaɪnɪŋ] ADJ [*industry*] en decadencia; ~ **interest** pérdida *f* de interés

decode [ˈdiːˈkəʊd] VT descifrar; (*Ling, Comput, TV*) descodificar

decoder [diːˈkəʊdəʳ] N (*Comput, TV*) descodificador *m*

decommission [ˌdiːkəˈmɪʃən] VT [+ *power station*] desmantelar; [+ *aircraft, weapon*] desguazar, desmantelar

decompose [ˌdiːkəmˈpəʊz] VI descomponerse, pudrirse

decomposition [ˌdiːkɒmpəˈzɪʃən] N descomposición *f*, putrefacción *f*

decompress [ˌdiːkəmˈpres] VT descomprimir

decompression [ˌdiːkəmˈpreʃən] N descompresión *f*
➤ **decompression chamber** cámara *f* de descompresión
➤ **decompression sickness** aeroembolismo *m*, embolia *f* gaseosa

decongestant [ˌdiːkənˈdʒestənt] N anticongestivo *m*, descongestionante *m*

deconstruct [ˌdiːkənˈstrʌkt] VT deconstruir

deconstruction [ˌdiːkənˈstrʌkʃən] N deconstrucción *f*

decontaminate [ˌdiːkənˈtæmɪneɪt] VT descontaminar

decontamination [ˈdiːkənˌtæmɪˈneɪʃən] N descontaminación *f*

decontrol [ˌdiːkənˈtrəʊl] VT (*esp US*) liberalizar

décor [ˈdeɪkɔːʳ] N decoración *f*

decorate [ˈdekəreɪt] VT **1** (= *adorn*) decorar, adornar (**with** de) **2** [+ *room, house*] (= *paint*) pintar; (= *paper*) empapelar **3** (*with medal*) condecorar

decorating [ˈdekəreɪtɪŋ] N **I got someone in to do the ~** traje a una persona para que pintara/empapelara la casa

decoration [ˌdekəˈreɪʃən] N **1** (= *act*) decoración *f* **2** (= *ornament*) adorno *m* **3** (= *medal*) condecoración *f*

decorative [ˈdekərətɪv] ADJ (*in function*) de adorno, decorativo; (= *attractive*) hermoso, elegante

decorator [ˈdekəreɪtəʳ] N (*Brit*) (= *painter and decorator*) pintor *m* empapelador; (*US*) (= *interior decorator*) interiorista *mf*, decorador(a) *m/f*

decorous [ˈdekərəs] ADJ decoroso

decorum [dɪˈkɔːrəm] N decoro *m*

decoy [ˈdiːkɔɪ] N señuelo *m*, reclamo *m*

decrease Ⓐ [ˈdiːkriːs] N (*gen*) disminución *f*, reducción *f*; (*in wages*) descenso *m*, bajada *f*; (*in prices*) bajada *f*, disminución *f*; **a ~ in speed/strength** una reducción de velocidad/fuerza Ⓑ [diːˈkriːs] VT [+ *quantity, dose, speed*] disminuir, reducir; [+ *wages*] bajar, reducir Ⓒ [diːˈkriːs] VI disminuir; (*Knitting*) menguar; **to ~ by 10%** bajar *or* disminuir un 10%

decreasing [diːˈkriːsɪŋ] ADJ decreciente

decreasingly [diːˈkriːsɪŋlɪ] ADV decrecientemente

decree [dɪˈkriː] Ⓐ N decreto *m*; ~ **absolute/nisi** sentencia *f* definitiva/condicional de divorcio Ⓑ VT decretar

decrepit [dɪˈkrepɪt] ADJ [*building*] deteriorado, en mal estado; (*) [*person*] decrépito

decrepitude [dɪˈkrepɪtjuːd] N [*of building*] deterioro *m*, mal estado *m*

decriminalize [diːˈkrɪmɪnəlaɪz] VT despenalizar

decry [dɪˈkraɪ] VT (= *criticize*) criticar, censurar; (= *belittle*) menospreciar

dedicate [ˈdedɪkeɪt] VT **1** [+ *book*] dedicar (**to** a); [+ *church, monument*] dedicar, consagrar (**to** a); **to ~ one's life to (doing) sth** dedicar *or* consagrar su vida a (hacer) algo; **to ~ o.s. to (doing) sth** dedicarse *or* consagrarse a (hacer) algo **2** (*US*) (= *inaugurate*) inaugurar oficialmente

dedicated [ˈdedɪkeɪtɪd] ADJ **1** [*teacher, doctor*] entregado a su/mi *etc* trabajo; **a very ~ teacher** un maestro totalmente entregado a su trabajo; ~ **followers of classical music** devotos seguidores de la música clásica **2** (*Comput*) especializado, dedicado

dedication [ˌdedɪˈkeɪʃən] N **1** (= *act*) dedicación *f*, consagración *f* **2** (= *quality*) dedicación *f*, entrega *f*, devoción *f* **3** (*in book*) dedicatoria *f*

deduce [dɪˈdjuːs] VT deducir; **what do you ~ from that?** ¿qué conclusión sacas de eso?

deduct [dɪˈdʌkt] VT (*gen*) restar, descontar (**from** de); [+ *tax*] deducir (**from** de)

deductible [dɪˈdʌktəbl] ADJ (*gen*) deducible, descontable; (*for tax purposes*) desgravable, deducible

deduction [dɪˈdʌkʃən] N **1** (= *inference*) deducción *f*, conclusión *f* **2** (= *act of deducting*) deducción *f*; (= *amount deducted*) descuento *m*; **tax ~s** desgravaciones *fpl* fiscales, deducciones *fpl* fiscales

deductive [dɪˈdʌktɪv] ADJ deductivo

deed [diːd] Ⓐ N **1** (= *act*) acto *m*, acción *f*; **brave ~** hazaña *f*; **good ~** buena acción *f* **2** (= *document*) escritura *f* Ⓑ CPD
➤ **deed poll** (*Brit*) **to change one's name by ~ poll** cambiarse el apellido oficialmente

deejay* [ˈdiːdʒeɪ] N discjockey *mf*, pinchadiscos *mf inv* (*Sp**)

deem [diːm] VT (*frm*) juzgar, considerar; **she ~s it wise to ...** considera prudente ...

deep [diːp] Ⓐ ADJ (*compar* **~er**; *superl* **~est**) **1** (= *extending downward*) [*hole*] profundo, hondo; [*cut, wound, water*] profundo; [*pan, bowl, container*] hondo; **the water is two metres ~** el agua tiene una profundidad de dos metros; **they tramped through ~ snow** avanzaban con dificultad por una espesa capa de nieve; **he was waist-~ in water** el agua le llegaba a la cintura; ✦ IDIOM **to be in ~ water** estar hasta el cuello (de problemas)
2 (= *extending back*) [*shelf, cupboard*] hondo; [*border, hem*] ancho; **a cupboard a metre ~** un armario de un metro de fondo; **the spectators were standing six ~** los espectadores estaban de pie de seis en fondo
3 (= *immersed*) **to be ~ in debt** estar cargado de deudas; **to be ~ in thought/in a book** estar sumido *or* absorto en sus pensamientos/en la lectura
4 (= *low*) [*voice*] grave, profundo; [*note*] grave
5 (= *intense*) [*emotion, relaxation, concern*] profundo; [*recession*] grave; [*sigh*] profundo, hondo; **to take a ~ breath** respirar profundamente *or* hondo *or* a pleno pulmón; **she fell into a ~ sleep** se quedó profundamente dormida; **to be in ~ trouble** estar en grandes apuros
6 [*colour*] intenso, subido
7 (= *profound*) **it's too ~ for me** no lo entiendo, es demasiado complicado para mí; **they're adventure stories, they're not intended to be ~** son historias de aventuras, sin intención de ir más allá
Ⓑ ADV **1** (= *far down*) **don't go in too ~** no te metas muy hondo; **he thrust his hand ~ into his pocket** metió la mano hasta el fondo del bolsillo; **the company is sliding even ~ into the red** la empresa está cada vez más cargada de deudas; ~ **down he's a bit of a softie** en el fondo es un poco blandengue; **to go ~:** **his anger clearly went ~** la ira le había calado muy hondo; **I was in far too ~ to pull out now** estaba demasiado metido para echarme atrás ahora; **the roots of racial prejudice run ~** los prejuicios raciales están profundamente arraigados
2 (= *a long way inside*) ~ **in the forest** en lo hondo *or* profundo del bosque; **he gazed ~ into her eyes** la miró profundamente *or* a los ojos; ~ **in one's heart** en lo más profundo del corazón
Ⓒ N (*liter*) **the ~** el piélago *m*; **creatures of the ~** criaturas *fpl* de las profundidades
Ⓓ CPD ➤ **the deep end** (*in pool*) lo hondo, la parte honda; ✦ IDIOMS **to go off (at) the ~ end*** enfadarse, ponerse de morros*; **I was thrown in (at) the ~ end*** me echaron *or* arrojaron a los leones* ➤ **deep freeze(r)** congelador *m* ➤ **deep fryer** freidora *f* ➤ **the Deep South** los estados del sureste de EE.UU. ➤ **deep space** espacio *m* interplanetario ➤ **deep vein thrombosis** trombosis *f* venosa profunda

deepen [ˈdiːpən] Ⓐ VT [+ *hole*] hacer más profundo; [+ *understanding*] aumentar; [+ *love, friendship*] hacer más profundo *or* intenso, ahondar; [+ *crisis*] agudizar, acentuar Ⓑ VI [*voice*] hacerse más grave *or* profundo; [*emotion*] intensificarse; [*darkness*] hacerse más profundo; [*mystery, suspicion*] aumentar; [*understanding, love, friendship*] hacerse más profundo *or* intenso; [*crisis*] agudizarse, acentuarse

deepening [ˈdiːpənɪŋ] ADJ [*darkness, gloom, conflict,*

division] cada vez más profundo; [friendship] cada vez más profundo or intenso; [crisis] que se agudiza, que se acentúa

deep-fat fryer [ˌdiːpˌfætˈfraɪəʳ] N freidora f

deep-freeze [ˈdiːpˈfriːz] (pp **deep-froze**, pt **deep-frozen**) VT (at home) congelar; (in factory) ultracongelar

deep-fry [ˈdiːpˈfraɪ] VT freír en aceite abundante

deeply [ˈdiːplɪ] ADV **1** [dig] en profundidad; [drink] a grandes tragos; [sleep, regret] profundamente; [breathe, sigh] profundamente, hondo; [think] a ~ **held conviction** una convicción profunda **2** [sceptical, disappointed, shocked] sumamente; [concerned, troubled, grateful, religious] profundamente; [offensive, unhappy, depressed] terriblemente; **to be ~ in debt** estar lleno de deudas, estar cargado de deudas; ~ **embedded dirt** suciedad profundamente incrustado

deep-rooted [ˈdiːpˈruːtɪd] ADJ profundamente arraigado

deep-sea [ˈdiːpˈsiː] ADJ ➤ **deep-sea diver** buzo m ➤ **deep-sea diving** buceo m de altura ➤ **deep-sea fishing** pesca f de gran altura

deep-seated [ˈdiːpˈsiːtɪd] ADJ profundamente arraigado

deep-set [ˈdiːpˈset] ADJ [eyes] hundido

deep-six* [ˌdiːpˈsɪks] VT (US) (= throw out) tirar; (= kill) liquidar*

deer [dɪəʳ] N (pl ~) ciervo m, venado m (esp LAm); (= red deer) ciervo m común; (= roe deer) corzo m; (= fallow deer) gamo m

deerstalker [ˈdɪəˌstɔːkəʳ] N (= hat) gorro m de cazador

deface [dɪˈfeɪs] VT [+ wall, monument] llenar de pintadas; [+ work of art, poster, book] pintarrajear

de facto [deɪˈfæktəʊ] ADJ, ADV de facto, de hecho

defamation [ˌdefəˈmeɪʃən] N difamación f

defamatory [dɪˈfæmətərɪ] ADJ difamatorio

defame [dɪˈfeɪm] VT difamar, calumniar

default [dɪˈfɔːlt] Ⓐ N **1** (on contract) incumplimiento m (**on** de); (on payment) impago m (**on** de); **he won by** ~ ganó por incomparecencia de su adversario **2** (Comput) valor m por defecto Ⓑ VI **1** (= fail to pay) no pagar, faltar al pago; **to ~ on one's payments** no pagar los plazos **2** (Sport) (= not appear) no presentarse, no comparecer

defeat [dɪˈfiːt] Ⓐ N **1** [of army, team] derrota f; [of ambition, plan] fracaso m; [of bill, amendment] rechazo m; **eventually he admitted** ~ al final se dio por vencido Ⓑ VT **1** [+ army, team, opponent] vencer, derrotar; [+ plan, ambition] hacer fracasar, frustrar; [+ hopes] frustrar, defraudar; (Pol) [+ party] derrotar; [+ bill, amendment] rechazar **2** (= overcome) vencer; **the problem ~s me** el problema me supera

defeatism [dɪˈfiːtɪzəm] N derrotismo m

defeatist [dɪˈfiːtɪst] ADJ, N derrotista mf

defecate [ˈdefəkeɪt] VI defecar

defect Ⓐ [ˈdiːfekt] N defecto m Ⓑ [dɪˈfekt] VI (Pol) desertar; **to ~ (from a country)** huir (de un país)

defection [dɪˈfekʃən] N (Pol) deserción f, defección f

defective [dɪˈfektɪv] ADJ defectuoso

defector [dɪˈfektəʳ] N tránsfuga mf

defence, defense (US) [dɪˈfens] Ⓐ N defensa f; **as a ~ against** como defensa contra; **the case for the** ~ el argumento de la defensa; **counsel for the** ~ abogado/a m/f defensor(a); **Department of Defense** (US) Ministerio m de Defensa; **in his** ~ su en defensa; **what have you to say in your own ~?** ¿qué tiene usted que decir or alegar en defensa propia?; **in ~ of sth** en defensa de algo; **Ministry of Defence** (Brit) Ministerio m de Defensa Ⓑ CPD [policy, strategy, costs] de defensa ➤ **defence counsel** abogado/a m/f defensor(a) ➤ **defence mechanism** mecanismo m de defensa

defenceless, defenseless (US) [dɪˈfenslɪs] ADJ indefenso

defend [dɪˈfend] Ⓐ VT defender (**against** contra; **from** de); **to ~ o.s.** defenderse Ⓑ VI (Sport) jugar de defensa

defendant [dɪˈfendənt] N (civil) demandado/a m/f; (criminal) acusado/a m/f

defender [dɪˈfendəʳ] N defensor(a) m/f; (Sport) defensa mf

defending [dɪˈfendɪŋ] ADJ ~ **champion** campeón m vigente; ~ **counsel** abogado/a m/f defensor(a)

defense [dɪˈfens] N (US) = **defence**

defensive [dɪˈfensɪv] Ⓐ ADJ defensivo Ⓑ N **to be/go on the** ~ estar/ponerse a la defensiva

defensively [dɪˈfensɪvlɪ] ADV [say] en tono defensivo; [play] a la defensiva

defer[1] [dɪˈfɜːʳ] VT [+ meeting, business] posponer, diferir; [+ payment] aplazar, diferir, postergar (LAm)

defer[2] [dɪˈfɜːʳ] VI **to ~ to sth** deferir a algo (frm); **in this I ~ to you** a este respecto me someto a su opinión

deference [ˈdefərəns] N deferencia f, respeto m; **in ~ to sb** por deferencia or respeto a algn

deferential [ˌdefəˈrenʃəl] ADJ deferente, respetuoso

deferment [dɪˈfɜːmənt], **deferral** [dɪˈfɜːrəl] N aplazamiento m

defiance [dɪˈfaɪəns] N (= attitude) desafío m; (= resistance) resistencia f terca; **a gesture/an act of** ~ un gesto/acto desafiante; **in ~ of the law** desafiando a la ley

defiant [dɪˈfaɪənt] ADJ [person] atrevido, insolente; [tone, stare] desafiante, retador

defiantly [dɪˈfaɪəntlɪ] ADV [act] atrevidamente, insolentemente; [say, answer] en tono desafiante or retador, en son de reto

deficiency [dɪˈfɪʃənsɪ] N **1** (gen) deficiencia f; (= lack) falta f **2** (in system, plan, character etc) defecto m

deficient [dɪˈfɪʃənt] ADJ (gen) deficiente; (in quantity) insuficiente; (= incomplete) incompleto; (= defective) defectuoso; **to be ~ in sth** estar falto de algo

deficit [ˈdefɪsɪt] N déficit m; **the balance of payments is in ~** la balanza de pagos es deficitaria

defile [dɪˈfaɪl] VT [+ honour] manchar; [+ sacred thing, memory] profanar; [+ woman] deshonrar

definable [dɪˈfaɪnəbl] ADJ definible

define [dɪˈfaɪn] VT (= give definition for) definir (also Comput); (= characterize) caracterizar; (= delimit) determinar, delimitar; (= outline) destacar; **how would you ~ yourself politically?** ¿cómo se definiría políticamente?

definite [ˈdefɪnɪt] Ⓐ ADJ **1** (= fixed) [date, time, offer, plan] definitivo; [decision, agreement] final; **it is ~ that she will retire** ya es seguro or definitivo que se jubilará; **nothing ~** nada definitivo; **is that ~?** ¿es seguro?; **I don't intend to go, and that's ~** no pienso ir, y no voy a cambiar de idea **2** (= clear) [improvement, advantage] indudable; [feeling, impression] inequívoco; [increase] claro; **it's a ~ possibility** es una posibilidad clara **3** (= sure) seguro; **are you ~ about that?** ¿estás seguro de eso?; **I don't know for ~ yet** no lo sé seguro todavía; **I can't say for ~ yet** no puedo asegurarlo todavía **4** (= emphatic) [manner, tone] firme, terminante; [views, opinions] firme; **he was very ~ about it** lo dijo de forma categórica; **he was very ~ about wanting to resign** dijo categóricamente que quería dimitir Ⓑ CPD ➤ **definite article** artículo m definido

definitely [ˈdefɪnɪtlɪ] ADV **1** (= definitively) [agree, arrange, decide] definitivamente; [say] de forma definitiva **2** (= certainly) **something should ~ be done about that** decididamente, deberían hacer algo al respecto; **yes, we ~ do need a car** sí, está clarísimo que or sí, decididamente necesitamos un coche; **he is ~ leaving** es seguro que se va, definitivamente se va; **I'll ~ go** seguro que iré; **she ~ said two o'clock** estoy seguro de que dijo a las dos en punto; **it's ~ better** es sin duda mejor; **"do you think she'll pass?" — "definitely"** —¿crees que aprobará? —seguro or sin duda; **"will you accept his offer?" — "~ not!"** —¿vas a aceptar su oferta? —¡de ninguna manera!; **"can I go on my own?" — "~ not!"** —¿puedo ir solo? —¡ni hablar! **3** (= emphatically) [say, deny] terminantemente, categóricamente; [state] firmemente

definition [ˌdefɪˈnɪʃən] N [of word] definición f; [of powers, duties] delimitación f; **by ~** por definición

definitive [dɪˈfɪnɪtɪv] ADJ definitivo

definitively [dɪˈfɪnɪtɪvlɪ] ADV de manera definitiva, definitivamente

deflate [diːˈfleɪt] Ⓐ VT [+ *tyre*] desinflar, deshinchar; [+ *economy*] reducir la inflación de, deflactar; [+ *pompous person*] bajar los humos a Ⓑ VI [*tyre*] desinflarse, deshincharse

deflated [diːˈfleɪtɪd] ADJ **at this news he felt very ~** con esta noticia se desanimó por completo

deflation [diːˈfleɪʃən] N [*of tyre*] pérdida *f* de aire; (*Econ*) deflación *f*

deflationary [diːˈfleɪʃənərɪ] ADJ (*Econ*) deflacionario

deflect [dɪˈflekt] Ⓐ VT desviar (**from** de) Ⓑ VI desviarse

deflection [dɪˈflekʃən] N desvío *m*, desviación *f*

deforest [diːˈfɒrɪst] VT deforestar, despoblar de árboles

deforestation [diːˌfɒrəˈsteɪʃən] N deforestación *f*, despoblación *f* forestal

deform [dɪˈfɔːm] VT deformar

deformed [dɪˈfɔːmd] ADJ [*person, limb, body*] deforme; [*structure*] deformado

deformity [dɪˈfɔːmɪtɪ] N deformidad *f*

defraud [dɪˈfrɔːd] VT [+ *person, authorities*] estafar, defraudar; **to ~ sb of sth** estafar algo a algn

defray [dɪˈfreɪ] VT sufragar, costear; **to ~ sb's expenses** sufragar *or* costear los gastos de algn

defrock [diːˈfrɒk] VT apartar del sacerdocio

defrost [diːˈfrɒst] VT [+ *refrigerator, frozen food*] descongelar

deft [deft] ADJ (*compar* **~er**; *superl* **~est**) diestro, hábil

deftly [ˈdeftlɪ] ADV diestramente, con destreza, hábilmente

deftness [ˈdeftnɪs] N destreza *f*, habilidad *f*

defunct [dɪˈfʌŋkt] ADJ [*company, organization*] desaparecido, extinto; [*scheme*] paralizado, suspendido

defuse [diːˈfjuːz] VT [+ *bomb*] desactivar; [+ *tension*] calmar, apaciguar; [+ *situation*] reducir la tensión de

defy [dɪˈfaɪ] VT **1** (= *challenge*) [+ *person*] desafiar, retar; **I ~ you to do it** te desafío a hacerlo **2** (= *refuse to obey*) [+ *person*] desobedecer, enfrentarse a; [+ *order*] contravenir **3** (= *fly in the face of*) **it defies description** resulta imposible describirlo, es indescriptible

degenerate Ⓐ [dɪˈdʒenərɪt] ADJ, N degenerado/a *m/f* Ⓑ [dɪˈdʒenəreɪt] VI degenerar (**into** en)

degeneration [dɪˌdʒenəˈreɪʃən] N degeneración *f*

degradation [ˌdegrəˈdeɪʃən] N degradación *f*

degrade [dɪˈgreɪd] Ⓐ VT degradar; **to ~ o.s.** degradarse Ⓑ VI degradarse

degrading [dɪˈgreɪdɪŋ] ADJ degradante

degree [dɪˈgriː] Ⓐ N **1** (*gen, Geog, Math*) grado *m*; **ten ~s below freezing** diez grados bajo cero **2** (= *extent*) punto *m*, grado *m*; **to a certain ~** hasta cierto punto; **to such a ~ that ...** hasta tal punto que ...; **they have some ~ of freedom** tienen cierto grado de libertad; **with varying ~s of success** con mayor o menor éxito **3** (= *stage in scale*) grado *m*; **by ~s** poco a poco, gradualmente, por etapas; **first/second/third ~ burns** quemaduras *fpl* de primer/segundo/tercer grado; **first/ second ~ murder** homicidio *m* en primer/segundo grado **4** (*Univ*) título *m*; **first ~** licenciatura *f*; **higher ~** (= *doctorate*) doctorado *m*; (= *postgraduate course*) posgrado *m*; **she's got a ~ in English** es licenciada en filología inglesa; **to get a ~** sacar un título; **to take a ~ in** hacer la carrera de Ⓑ CPD ► **degree course** (*Brit*) licenciatura *f*

dehumanize [diːˈhjuːmənaɪz] VT deshumanizar

dehumidifier [ˌdiːhjuːˈmɪdɪfaɪəʳ] N deshumidificador *m*

dehydrate [diːˈhaɪdreɪt] VT deshidratar

dehydrated [ˌdiːhaɪˈdreɪtɪd] ADJ deshidratado

dehydration [ˌdiːhaɪˈdreɪʃən] N deshidratación *f*

de-ice [diːˈaɪs] VT descongelar

de-icer [ˈdiːˈaɪsəʳ] N descongelante *m*

de-icing [diːˈaɪsɪŋ] N descongelación *f*

deify [ˈdiːɪfaɪ] VT deificar

deign [deɪn] VT **to ~ to do sth** dignarse hacer algo

deity [ˈdiːɪtɪ] N deidad *f*; **the Deity** Dios *m*

déjà vu [ˌdeɪʒɑːˈvuː] N déjà vu *m*, *sensación de haber vivido algo antes*

dejected [dɪˈdʒektɪd] ADJ desanimado, abatido

dejectedly [dɪˈdʒektɪdlɪ] ADV [*sit, gaze*] con desánimo, desalentado; [*say*] con tono de abatimiento

dejection [dɪˈdʒekʃən] N desánimo *m*, abatimiento *m*

Del. ABBR (*US*) = **Delaware**

delay [dɪˈleɪ] Ⓐ N **1** (= *hold-up*) retraso *m*, demora *f*; (*to road traffic*) retención *f*, atasco *m*; **there will be ~s to traffic** habrá retenciones *or* atascos en las carreteras; **"delays possible until Dec 2005"** "posibles retenciones hasta diciembre de 2005" **2** (= *act of delaying*) retraso *m*, dilación *f*; **without ~** sin demora Ⓑ VT (= *hold up*) [+ *train, departure*] retrasar; [+ *start, opening*] retrasar, demorar; (= *postpone*) aplazar, demorar (*LAm*); (= *leave too long*) dejar para desmasiado tarde; (= *obstruct*) impedir; **the train was ~ed for two hours** el tren se retrasó dos horas; **if you are ~ed for any reason** si te retrasas por alguna razón; **what ~ed you?** ¿por qué has tardado tanto?; **we ~ed going out until Jane arrived** retrasamos la salida hasta que llegara Jane; **don't ~ booking the hotel** no tardes en reservar el hotel Ⓒ VI tardar, demorarse (*LAm*); **don't ~!** ¡no pierdas tiempo!

delayed-action [dɪˈleɪdˈækʃən] ADJ [*bomb*] de acción retardada

delaying [dɪˈleɪɪŋ] ADJ dilatorio ► **delaying tactics** tácticas *fpl* dilatorias

delectable [dɪˈlektəbl] ADJ delicioso

delectation [ˌdiːlekˈteɪʃən] N deleite *m*, delectación *f* (*frm*)

delegate Ⓐ [ˈdelɪgɪt] N delegado/a *m/f* (**to** en) Ⓑ [ˈdelɪgeɪt] VT [+ *task, power*] delegar (**to** en); **I was ~d to do it** me delegaron para hacerlo

delegation [ˌdelɪˈgeɪʃən] N delegación *f*

delete [dɪˈliːt] VT tachar, suprimir (**from** de); (*Comput*) borrar, suprimir; **"delete where inapplicable"** "táchese lo que no proceda" ► **delete key** tecla *f* de borrado, tecla *f* de supresión

deletion [dɪˈliːʃən] N supresión *f*, tachadura *f*; (*Comput*) borrado *m*, supresión *f*

deli* [ˈdelɪ] N = **delicatessen**

deliberate Ⓐ [dɪˈlɪbərɪt] ADJ **1** (= *intentional*) deliberado, premeditado **2** (= *unhurried*) pausado, lento Ⓑ [dɪˈlɪbəreɪt] VT [+ *issue, question*] (= *think about*) reflexionar sobre, deliberar sobre; (= *talk about*) deliberar sobre, discutir Ⓒ [dɪˈlɪbəreɪt] VI (= *think*) reflexionar, meditar (**on** sobre); (= *talk*) deliberar (**on** sobre)

deliberately [dɪˈlɪbərɪtlɪ] ADV **1** (= *on purpose*) a propósito, deliberadamente; [*rude, misleading*] deliberadamente **2** (= *slowly*) lentamente, pausadamente

deliberation [dɪˌlɪbəˈreɪʃən] N **1** (= *thought*) deliberación *f*, reflexión *f*; (= *discussion*) deliberación *f*, discusión *f*; **after due ~** después de pensarlo bien **2** (= *slowness*) pausa *f*, lentitud *f*

delicacy [ˈdelɪkəsɪ] N **1** (= *fineness*) [*of flavour, workmanship, instrument*] delicadeza *f* **2** (= *fragility*) fragilidad *f* **3** (= *awkwardness*) [*of situation, problem*] lo delicado; **a matter of some ~** un asunto algo delicado **4** (= *tact*) delicadeza *f* **5** (= *dish*) exquisitez *f*, manjar *m* exquisito

delicate [ˈdelɪkɪt] ADJ **1** (= *fine*) [*features, fabric, workmanship, instrument, flavour*] delicado; [*touch*] suave **2** (= *fragile*) [*china, balance*] frágil; [*person, health, skin*] delicado **3** (= *awkward*) [*situation, problem*] delicado, difícil

delicately [ˈdelɪkɪtlɪ] ADV **1** [*say, act*] con delicadeza, delicadamente **2** [*flavoured, scented, carved*] exquisitamente

delicatessen [ˌdelɪkəˈtesn] N ≈ charcutería *f*, ≈ rotisería *f* (*SC*), *tienda de alimentos selectos*

delicious [dɪˈlɪʃəs] ADJ [*food, taste, smell*] delicioso, exquisito, riquísimo; [*sensation*] delicioso

deliciously [dɪˈlɪʃəslɪ] ADV deliciosamente, exquisitamente

delight [dɪˈlaɪt] **Ⓐ** N **1** (= *feeling of joy*) deleite *m*, placer *m*; (= *jubilation*) regocijo *m*; **much to her ~, they lost** perdieron, con gran regocijo de su parte; **to take ~ in sth** disfrutar con algo, deleitarse con algo; **to take ~ in doing sth** disfrutar haciendo algo, deleitarse en hacer algo **2** (= *pleasurable thing*) encanto *m*; **one of the ~s of Majorca** uno de los encantos de Mallorca; **the book is sheer ~** el libro es una verdadera delicia *or* maravilla; **she is a ~ to teach** es un placer ser su maestra **Ⓑ** VT encantar, deleitar **Ⓒ** VI **to ~ in sth** disfrutar con algo, deleitarse con algo; **to ~ in doing sth** disfrutar haciendo algo, deleitarse en hacer algo

delighted [dɪˈlaɪtɪd] ADJ **delighted!** ¡encantado!; **I'd be ~** con (mucho) gusto; **to be ~ at/with sth** estar encantado con algo; **(I'm) ~ to meet you** (estoy) encantado de conocerlo, mucho gusto de conocerlo; **I was ~ to hear the news** me alegró mucho recibir la noticia

delightful [dɪˈlaɪtfʊl] ADJ [*person*] encantador; [*outfit*] precioso; [*food, breeze*] delicioso

delightfully [dɪˈlaɪtfəlɪ] ADV (*after vb*) maravillosamente; **the water was ~ cool** el agua estaba tan fresquita que daba gusto

delimit [diːˈlɪmɪt] VT delimitar

delineate [dɪˈlɪnɪeɪt] VT [+ *character*] describir, pintar; [+ *plans*] trazar

delinquency [dɪˈlɪŋkwənsɪ] N delincuencia *f*

delinquent [dɪˈlɪŋkwənt] ADJ, N delincuente *mf*

delirious [dɪˈlɪrɪəs] ADJ **1** (*Med*) delirante; **to be ~** delirar, desvariar **2** (*with happiness etc*) loco; **to be ~ with joy** estar loco de alegría

deliriously [dɪˈlɪrɪəslɪ] ADV **to be ~ happy** estar loco de alegría

delirium [dɪˈlɪrɪəm] N (*Med, fig*) delirio *m*

deliver [dɪˈlɪvəʳ] **Ⓐ** VT **1** (= *hand over*) [+ *goods*] entregar (**to** a); [+ *mail*] repartir; [+ *message*] llevar, comunicar; **✦ IDIOM to ~ the goods*** cumplir **2** (= *give*) [+ *speech, verdict*] pronunciar; [+ *lecture*] dar; **to ~ an ultimatum** dar un ultimátum **3** (= *throw*) [+ *blow, punch*] asestar, dar **4** [+ *baby*] asistir en el parto de **5** (*liter*) (= *save*) librar (**from** de) **Ⓑ** VI **1** (*Comm*) **"we deliver"** "(servicio de) entrega a domicilio" **2** (*) (*on promise*) cumplir lo prometido; **the match promised great things but didn't ~** el partido prometía mucho, pero no estuvo a la altura de lo que se esperaba

deliverance [dɪˈlɪvərəns] N (*liter*) liberación *f* (**from** de)

delivery [dɪˈlɪvərɪ] **Ⓐ** N **1** [*of goods*] entrega *f*; [*of mail*] reparto *m*; **allow 28 days for ~** la entrega se realizará en un plazo de 28 días; **the balance is payable on ~** el saldo pendiente se hará efectivo a la entrega; **to pay on ~** pagar contra entrega **2** [*of speaker*] presentación *f* oral, forma *f* de hablar en público **3** (= *birth*) parto *m*, alumbramiento *m* (*frm*) **Ⓑ** CPD [*date, order, time*] de entrega ➤ **delivery charge** gastos *mpl* de envío ➤ **delivery man** repartidor *m* ➤ **delivery note** nota *f* de entrega, albarán *m* (de entrega) ➤ **delivery service** servicio *m* de entrega a domicilio ➤ **delivery truck** (*US*), **delivery van** (*Brit*) furgoneta *f* de reparto, camioneta *f* de reparto

delouse [diːˈlaʊs] VT despiojar, espulgar

delta [ˈdeltə] N **1** (*Geog*) delta *m* **2** (= *letter*) delta *f*

delude [dɪˈluːd] VT engañar; **to ~ sb into thinking (that) ...** hacer creer a algn (que) ...; **to ~ o.s.** engañarse

deluded [dɪˈluːdɪd] ADJ iluso, engañado

deluge [ˈdeljuːdʒ] **Ⓐ** N [*of rain*] diluvio *m*; [*of floodwater*] inundación *f*; **a ~ of protests** una avalancha de protestas **Ⓑ** VT (*fig*) inundar (**with** de); **he was ~d with gifts** se vio inundado de regalos, le llovieron los regalos; **he was ~d**

with questions lo acribillaron a preguntas, le llovieron las preguntas

delusion [dɪˈluːʒən] N (= *false impression*) engaño *m*, error *m*; (= *hope*) ilusión *f*; (*Psych*) delirio *m*; **to labour under a ~** abrigar una falsa ilusión; **~s of grandeur** delirios *mpl* de grandeza

de luxe [dɪˈlʌks] ADJ de lujo

delve [delv] VI **to ~ into** [+ *pocket, cupboard*] hurgar en, rebuscar en; [+ *subject*] profundizar en, ahondar en; [+ *past*] hurgar en

Dem. (*US*) **Ⓐ** N ABBR = **Democrat Ⓑ** ADJ ABBR = **Democratic**

demagogue, demagog (*US*) [ˈdeməɡɒɡ] N demagogo/a *m/f*

demagogy [ˈdeməɡɒɡɪ] N demagogia *f*

demand [dɪˈmɑːnd] **Ⓐ** N **1** (= *request*) petición *f*, solicitud *f* (**for** de); **on ~** a libre disposición de todos, a petición; **abortion on ~** aborto *m* libre; **by popular ~** a petición del público **2** (= *urgent claim*) exigencia *f*; (*for payment*) aviso *m*, reclamación *f*; (*Pol, Ind*) reivindicación *f*; **the ~s of duty** las exigencias del deber; **final ~** (*for payment of bill*) último aviso *m*; **there are many ~s on my time** tengo muchas ocupaciones; **her children make great ~s on her time** sus hijos absorben gran parte de su tiempo **3** (*Comm*) demanda *f* (**for** de); **to be in great ~** tener mucha demanda; (*fig*) [*person*] estar muy solicitado, ser muy popular **Ⓑ** VT **1** (= *insist on*) exigir; (= *claim*) reclamar; **he ~ed to see my passport** insistió en *or* exigió ver mi pasaporte; **to ~ that** insistir en que; **"who are you?" he ~ed** —¿quién es usted? —preguntó **2** (= *require*) exigir, requerir

demanding [dɪˈmɑːndɪŋ] ADJ [*person*] exigente; [*part, role*] difícil; [*work*] (= *tiring*) agotador; **it's a very ~ job** es un trabajo que exige mucho

demarcate [ˈdiːmɑːkeɪt] VT demarcar

demean [dɪˈmiːn] VT degradar; **to ~ o.s.** rebajarse, degradarse

demeaning [dɪˈmiːnɪŋ] ADJ degradante

demeanour, demeanor (*US*) [dɪˈmiːnəʳ] N conducta *f*, comportamiento *m*; (= *bearing*) porte *m*

demented [dɪˈmentɪd] ADJ demente; (*fig*) loco

dementia [dɪˈmenʃɪə] N demencia *f*

demerara sugar [ˌdeməreərəˈʃʊɡəʳ] N (*Brit*) azúcar *m* moreno

demilitarize [ˈdiːˈmɪlɪtəraɪz] VT desmilitarizar

demise [dɪˈmaɪz] N (= *death*) fallecimiento *m*; [*of institution etc*] desaparición *f*

demist [diːˈmɪst] VT (*Aut*) desempañar

demister [diːˈmɪstəʳ] N (*Aut*) luneta *f* térmica, dispositivo *m* antivaho

demo* [ˈdeməʊ] N **1** (*Brit Pol*) manifestación *f*, mani* *f* **2** [*of machine, product*] demostración *f* **3** (*also* ~ **tape**) cinta *f* de demostración

demob* [ˈdiːˈmɒb] (*Brit*) **Ⓐ** N = **demobilization Ⓑ** VT = **demobilize**

demobilization [ˈdiːˌməʊbɪlaɪˈzeɪʃən] N desmovilización *f*

demobilize [diːˈməʊbɪlaɪz] VT desmovilizar

democracy [dɪˈmɒkrəsɪ] N democracia *f*

democrat [ˈdeməkræt] N **1** demócrata *mf* **2** (*US*) **Democrat** demócrata *mf*

democratic [ˌdeməˈkrætɪk] ADJ **1** [*society, election, ethos*] democrático **2** (*US*) **Democratic** demócrata; **the Democratic Party** el Partido Demócrata

democratically [ˌdeməˈkrætɪklɪ] ADV democráticamente

democratize [dɪˈmɒkrətaɪz] VT democratizar

demographic [ˌdeməˈɡræfɪk] ADJ demográfico

demography [dɪˈmɒɡrəfɪ] N demografía *f*

demolish [dɪˈmɒlɪʃ] VT [+ *building*] demoler, derribar, echar abajo; (*fig*) [+ *argument*] echar por tierra; [+ *opposition*] arrasar; (*hum*) [+ *cake*] zamparse*

demolition [ˌdeməˈlɪʃən] N demolición f, derribo m ➤ **demolition squad** equipo m de demolición

demon [ˈdiːmən] **A** N demonio m **B** ADJ **1 the ~ drink** el demonio de la bebida **2** (*) **he's a ~ squash-player** es un as del squash*, jugando al squash es fabuloso*

demonic [dɪˈmɒnɪk] ADJ demoníaco, demoniaco

demonstrable [ˈdemənstrəbl] ADJ demostrable

demonstrably [ˈdemənstrəblɪ] ADV manifiestamente

demonstrate [ˈdemənstreɪt] **A** VT **1** [+ theory] demostrar, probar; [+ method, product] hacer una demostración de; **to ~ that** demostrar que **2** (= display) [+ emotions] manifestar, expresar; [+ talent, ability] demostrar **B** VI (Pol) manifestarse (**against** en contra de; **in support of** en apoyo de; **in favour of** a favor de)

demonstration [ˌdemənˈstreɪʃən] N **1** (Pol) manifestación f; **to hold a ~** hacer una manifestación **2** (= illustration) demostración f **3** (= manifestation) muestra f, demostración f

demonstrative [dɪˈmɒnstrətɪv] ADJ **1** [person] expresivo; **not very ~** más bien reservado **2** (Gram) demostrativo

demonstrator [ˈdemənstreɪtəʳ] N **1** (Pol) manifestante mf **2** (in shop) demostrador(a) m/f

demoralize [dɪˈmɒrəlaɪz] VT desmoralizar

demoralizing [dɪˈmɒrəlaɪzɪŋ] ADJ desmoralizador

demote [dɪˈməʊt] VT rebajar de categoría; (Mil) degradar

demur [dɪˈmɜːʳ] VI objetar, poner reparos (**at** a)

demure [dɪˈmjʊəʳ] ADJ (= modest) recatado; (= coy) tímido y algo coqueto

demurely [dɪˈmjʊəlɪ] ADV (= modestly) recatadamente; (= coyly) con coqueta timidez

demutualize [diːˈmjuːtjʊəlaɪz] VI (Fin) dejar de ser una mutualidad

demystify [diːˈmɪstɪfaɪ] VT desmitificar

den [den] N **1** (animal's) guarida f; [of fox] madriguera f; **a ~ of iniquity** or **vice** un antro de vicio y perversión; **a ~ of thieves** una guarida de ladrones **2** (= room) estudio m, gabinete m

denationalize [diːˈnæʃnəlaɪz] VT desnacionalizar

denial [dɪˈnaɪəl] N **1** [of accusation, guilt] negación f; [of report, statement] desmentido m, mentís m inv; **the government issued an official ~** el gobierno lo desmintió oficialmente, el gobierno emitió un desmentido oficial; **to be in ~ about sth** no querer reconocer algo **2** (= refusal) [of request] denegación f; (= rejection) rechazo m

denier [ˈdeniəʳ] N denier m

denigrate [ˈdenɪɡreɪt] VT denigrar

denigration [ˌdenɪˈɡreɪʃən] N denigración f

denim [ˈdenɪm] N tela f vaquera; **denims** vaqueros mpl, bluyín msing (esp LAm) ➤ **denim jacket** chaqueta f vaquera, cazadora f vaquera, saco m de vaquero (LAm)

denizen [ˈdenɪzn] N (liter) morador(a) m/f, habitante mf

Denmark [ˈdenmɑːk] N Dinamarca f

denomination [dɪˌnɒmɪˈneɪʃən] N **1** (Rel) confesión f **2** [of coin] valor m

denominational [dɪˌnɒmɪˈneɪʃənl] ADJ confesional

denote [dɪˈnəʊt] VT denotar, indicar; [word] significar

denouement, dénouement [deɪˈnuːmɒn] N desenlace m

denounce [dɪˈnaʊns] VT (= accuse publicly) censurar, denunciar; (to police etc) denunciar

dense [dens] ADJ (compar ~r; superl ~st) **1** [forest, vegetation, fog, population] denso; [crowd] nutrido **2** [Phys) [liquid, substance] denso **3** (*) [person] corto de entendederas*, duro de mollera*

densely [ˈdenslɪ] ADV densamente; **~ populated** densamente poblado

density [ˈdensɪtɪ] N **1** [of forest, vegetation, fog, population] densidad f **2** (Phys) [of material, substance] densidad f; **single/double ~ disk** disco m de densidad sencilla/de doble densidad

dent [dent] **A** N (in metal) abolladura f; (in wood) muesca f, marca f; **to make a ~ in** [+ metal] abollar; [+ wood] hacer una muesca or marca en; **it's made a ~ in my savings*** se ha comido una buena parte de mis ahorros* **B** VT **1** [+ car, hat etc] abollar **2** [+ enthusiasm, confidence] hacer mella en; **his pride was somewhat ~ed** su orgullo resultó un tanto herido

dental [ˈdentl] ADJ dental ➤ **dental appointment** cita f con el dentista ➤ **dental floss** seda f dental, hilo m dental ➤ **dental nurse** auxiliar mf en odontología, enfermero/a m/f dental ➤ **dental surgeon** odontólogo/a m/f, dentista mf ➤ **dental surgery** clínica f dental, consultorio m dental, dentistería f (Ven) ➤ **dental technician** protésico/a m/f dental, mecánico/a m/f dental or dentista m (LAm)

dentist [ˈdentɪst] N dentista mf, odontólogo/a m/f; **at the ~'s** en el dentista ➤ **dentist's chair** silla f del dentista ➤ **dentist's surgery** (Brit), **dentist's office** (US) clínica f dental, consultorio m dental, dentistería f (Ven)

dentistry [ˈdentɪstrɪ] N odontología f, dentistería f (Ven)

dentures [ˈdentʃəz] NPL dentadura f sing postiza

denuclearize [diːˈnjuːklɪəraɪz] VT desnuclearizar; **a ~d zone** una zona desnuclearizada

denude [dɪˈnjuːd] VT **1** (Geol, Geog) denudar **2** (= strip) despojar (**of** de)

denunciation [dɪˌnʌnsɪˈeɪʃən] N denuncia f

Denver boot [ˌdenvəˈbuːt], **Denver clamp** [ˌdenvəˈklæmp] N (US) cepo m

deny [dɪˈnaɪ] VT **1** [+ charge] negar, rechazar; [+ report] desmentir; [+ possibility, truth of statement] negar; **to ~ having done sth** negar haber hecho algo; **to ~ that ...** negar que ...; **there's no ~ing it** no se puede negar, es innegable **2** (= refuse) [+ request] denegar; **to ~ sb sth** negar algo a algn, privar a algn de algo; **to ~ o.s. sth** privarse de algo

deodorant [diːˈəʊdərənt] N desodorante m

deodorize [diːˈəʊdəraɪz] VT desodorizar

dep. ABBR = **departs, departure** salida

depart [dɪˈpɑːt] VI [person] partir, irse, marcharse (**from** de); [train etc] salir (**at** a; **for** para; **from** de); **the train is about to ~** el tren está a punto de salir; **to ~ from** [+ custom, truth etc] apartarse de, desviarse de

departed [dɪˈpɑːtɪd] N(PL) (= singular) el/la difunto/a m/f; (plural) los/las difuntos/as mpl/fpl

department [dɪˈpɑːtmənt] **A** N **1** (gen) departamento m; (in shop) sección f; (Admin) sección f, oficina f; **the toy ~** la sección de juguetes; **the English ~** el departamento de inglés **2** [of government] ministerio m, secretaría f (Mex) **3** (*) **gardening is my wife's ~** del jardín se encarga mi mujer **B** CPD ➤ **department store** (grandes) almacenes mpl, tienda f por departamento (Carib)

departmental [ˌdiːpɑːtˈmentl] ADJ departamental ➤ **departmental manager** director(a) m/f de departamento ➤ **departmental meeting** reunión f de departamento, reunión f departamental

departure [dɪˈpɑːtʃəʳ] **A** N **1** [of person] partida f, marcha f (**from** de); [of train, plane] salida f (**from** de); **"Departures"** (Aer, Rail) "Salidas"; **point of ~** punto m de partida **2** (from custom, principle) desviación f (**from** de) **3** (= trend, course) **a new ~** un rumbo nuevo, una novedad **B** CPD ➤ **departure board** (Aer, Rail) tablón m de salidas, panel m de salidas ➤ **departure gate** (Aer) puerta f de embarque ➤ **departure lounge** (Aer) sala f de embarque ➤ **departure time** hora f de salida

depend [dɪˈpend] VI **1** (= rely) **to ~ (up)on** contar con; **you can ~ on me!** ¡cuenta conmigo!; **can we ~ on you to do it?** ¿podemos contar contigo para hacerlo?, ¿podemos confiar en que tú lo hagas?; **you can ~ on him to be late** ten por seguro que llegará tarde

2 (= be dependent) **to ~ (up)on** depender de; **he ~s on her for everything** depende de ella para todo; **your success ~s on how hard you work** tu éxito depende del trabajo que hagas; **it (all) ~s what you mean** depende de lo que quieras decir; **that ~s** eso depende

dependable [dɪˈpendəbl] ADJ [person] serio, formal, cumplidor; [machine] fiable

dependant [dɪˈpendənt] N *persona a cargo de algn*; **I have no ~s** no tengo cargas familiares; **how many ~s does he have?** ¿cuántas personas tiene a su cargo?

dependence [dɪˈpendəns] N dependencia f (**on** de); **drug ~** drogodependencia f (*frm*)

dependency [dɪˈpendənsɪ] **Ⓐ** N **1** (*Pol*) (= *territory*) posesión f, dominio m **2** (= *dependence*) dependencia f **Ⓑ** CPD ► **dependency culture** cultura f de dependencia

dependent [dɪˈpendənt] **Ⓐ** ADJ **he has no ~ relatives** no tiene cargas familiares, no tiene familiares a su cargo; **to be ~ on sth/sb** depender de algo/algn; **to be financially ~ on sb** depender económicamente de algn **Ⓑ** N (*esp US*) = **dependant**

depersonalize [diːˈpɜːsənəlaɪz] VT despersonalizar

depict [dɪˈpɪkt] VT (*in picture*) representar, pintar; (*in words*) describir

depiction [dɪˈpɪkʃən] N (*in picture*) representación f; (*in writing*) descripción f

depilatory [dɪˈpɪlətərɪ] N depilatorio m, crema f depilatoria

deplete [dɪˈpliːt] VT (= *reduce*) mermar; (= *exhaust totally*) agotar; **that holiday rather ~d our savings** esas vacaciones mermaron or redujeron bastante nuestros ahorros

depleted uranium [dɪˈpliːtɪdjʊəˈreɪnɪəm] N uranio m empobrecido

depletion [dɪˈpliːʃən] N (= *reduction*) reducción f, merma f; (= *exhaustion*) agotamiento m; **the ~ of the ozone layer** la rarefacción or destrucción de la capa de ozono

deplorable [dɪˈplɔːrəbl] ADJ **1** (= *disgraceful*) deplorable; **it is ~ that** es deplorable que + *subjun* **2** (= *very regrettable*) lamentable; **it would be ~ if** sería lamentable que + *subjun*

deplorably [dɪˈplɔːrəblɪ] ADV **1** (= *disgracefully*) deplorablemente **2** (= *regrettably*) lamentablemente

deplore [dɪˈplɔːʳ] VT **1** (= *find disgraceful*) deplorar **2** (= *regret*) lamentar

deploy [dɪˈplɔɪ] VT (*Mil*) desplegar; [+ *resources*] utilizar

deployment [dɪˈplɔɪmənt] N (*Mil*) despliegue m; [*of resources*] utilización f

depopulate [diːˈpɒpjʊleɪt] VT despoblar

depopulation [ˈdiːpɒpjʊˈleɪʃən] N despoblación f

deport [dɪˈpɔːt] VT deportar

deportation [ˌdiːpɔːˈteɪʃən] N deportación f ► **deportation order** orden f de deportación

deportment [dɪˈpɔːtmənt] N (= *behaviour*) conducta f, comportamiento m; (= *carriage*) porte m

depose [dɪˈpəʊz] VT [+ *ruler*] deponer, destituir

deposit [dɪˈpɒzɪt] **Ⓐ** N **1** (*in bank*) depósito m **2** (*on hire purchase, car*) depósito m, enganche m (*Mex*); (*on house*) desembolso m inicial, entrada f (*Sp*); (= *returnable security*) señal f, fianza f; **he paid a £2,000 ~ on the house** hizo un desembolso inicial de 2.000 libras para la casa, dio una entrada de 2.000 libras para la casa (*Sp*); **to lose one's ~** (*Brit Pol*) perder el depósito **3** (*Chem*) poso m, sedimento m **4** (*Geol*) [*of gas*] depósito m; [*of mineral*] yacimiento m **Ⓑ** VT **1** (= *put down*) depositar **2** (*in bank*) [+ *money*] depositar, ingresar (*Sp*) **Ⓒ** CPD ► **deposit account** (*Brit*) cuenta f de ahorros

deposition [ˌdiːpəˈzɪʃən] N **1** [*of ruler*] deposición f, destitución f **2** (*Jur*) declaración f, deposición f

depositor [dɪˈpɒzɪtəʳ] N depositante mf, impositor(a) m/f

depot [ˈdepəʊ] N (= *storehouse*) almacén m, depósito m; (*for vehicles*) parque m, cochera f; (*esp US*) (= *bus station*) terminal f; (*US Rail*) estación f; (*Mil*) depósito m

depravation [ˌdeprəˈveɪʃən] N depravación f

depraved [dɪˈpreɪvd] ADJ depravado

depravity [dɪˈprævɪtɪ] N depravación f

deprecating [ˈdeprɪkeɪtɪŋ] ADJ [*tone, attitude*] de desaprobación

depreciate [dɪˈpriːʃɪeɪt] **Ⓐ** VI depreciarse **Ⓑ** VT depreciar

depreciation [dɪˌpriːʃɪˈeɪʃən] N depreciación f

depress [dɪˈpres] VT **1** (= *make miserable*) deprimir, abatir; (= *discourage*) desalentar **2** (*Econ*) [+ *trade, price*] reducir **3** [+ *button, accelerator*] apretar; [+ *lever*] bajar

depressant [dɪˈpresnt] N depresivo m

depressed [dɪˈprest] ADJ **1** [*person*] deprimido, abatido (**about** por); **to get ~** deprimirse (**about** por) **2** [*market, economy, industry, area*] deprimido

depressing [dɪˈpresɪŋ] ADJ deprimente

depressingly [dɪˈpresɪŋlɪ] ADV [*say, reply*] tristemente; **it was a ~ familiar story** era una historia tan sabida or oída que resultaba deprimente

depression [dɪˈpreʃən] N **1** (= *dejection*) depresión f, abatimiento m **2** (*Econ*) depresión f, crisis f inv (económica) **3** (*Met*) depresión f

depressive [dɪˈpresɪv] ADJ, N depresivo/a m/f

depressurize [diːˈpreʃəˌraɪz] VT despresurizar

deprivation [ˌdeprɪˈveɪʃən] N (= *act*) privación f; (= *state*) necesidad f; **he lived a life of ~** vivía en la necesidad, vivió una vida llena de privaciones; **social ~** marginación f social

deprive [dɪˈpraɪv] VT **to ~ sb of sth** privar a algn de algo; **to ~ o.s. of sth** privarse de algo; **he was ~d of sleep/food for seven days** no le dejaron dormir/no le dieron de comer durante siete días; **the brain was ~d of oxygen** el cerebro no recibía su aporte de oxígeno

deprived [dɪˈpraɪvd] ADJ [*child, family*] necesitado, desventajado; [*area, district*] marginado; **she had a ~ childhood** tuvo una niñez llena de privaciones

Dept, dept ABBR (= **department**) Dep., Dpto.

depth [depθ] **Ⓐ** N **1** [*of water, hole, shelf*] profundidad f; [*of room, building*] fondo m; [*of colour, feelings*] intensidad f; [*of voice*] gravedad f, profundidad f; **at a ~ of three metres** a tres metros de profundidad; **the trench was two metres in ~** la zanja tenía dos metros de profundidad; **to study a subject in ~** estudiar un tema a fondo or en profundidad; **to get out of one's ~** (*lit*) perder pie; (*fig*) meterse en honduras, salirse de su terreno; **to be out of one's ~** (*lit*) no tocar fondo, no hacer pie; **he felt out of his ~ with these people** se sentía perdido entre esta gente **2 depths**: **in the ~s of the sea** en las profundidades del mar, en el fondo del mar; **to be in the ~s of despair** estar hundido en la desesperación; **in the ~s of winter** en lo más crudo del invierno; **it is deplorable that anyone should sink to such ~s** es deplorable que uno pueda caer tan bajo **Ⓑ** CPD ► **depth charge** carga f de profundidad

deputation [ˌdepjʊˈteɪʃən] N delegación f

deputize [ˈdepjʊtaɪz] VI **to ~ for sb** desempeñar las funciones de algn, sustituir a algn

deputy [ˈdepjʊtɪ] N (= *substitute*) suplente mf, sustituto/a m/f; (*Pol*) diputado/a m/f; (= *agent*) representante mf; (= *deputy sheriff*) ayudante mf del sheriff ► **deputy chairman** vicepresidente/a m/f ► **deputy director** director(a) m/f ► **deputy head** adjunto/a, subdirector(a) m/f ► **deputy manager** subdirector(a) m/f

derail [dɪˈreɪl] **Ⓐ** VT hacer descarrilar **Ⓑ** VI descarrilar

derailment [dɪˈreɪlmənt] N descarrilamiento m

deranged [dɪˈreɪndʒd] ADJ [*person*] loco, desquiciado; [*mind*] perturbado; **to be (mentally) ~** estar desquiciado, ser un perturbado mental

derby¹ [ˈdɑːbɪ, (*US*) ˈdɜːbɪ] N **1** (*Sport*) **local ~** derbi m **2 the Derby** (*Brit*) el Derby (*importante carrera de caballos en Inglaterra*)

derby² [ˈdɜːbɪ] N (*US*) (*also ~ hat*) sombrero m hongo, bombín m

deregulate [diːˈregjʊleɪt] VT desregular

deregulation [diːˌregjʊˈleɪʃən] N desregulación f

derelict [ˈderɪlɪkt] ADJ (= *abandoned*) abandonado; (= *ruined*) en ruinas

deride [dɪˈraɪd] VT ridiculizar, mofarse de

de rigueur [dərɪˈgɜːʳ] ADV de rigor

derision [dɪˈrɪʒən] N mofa f, burla f, irrisión f

derisively [dɪˈraɪsɪvlɪ] ADV burlonamente

derisory [dɪˈraɪsərɪ] ADJ irrisorio

derivation [ˌderɪ'veɪʃən] N derivación f

derivative [dɪ'rɪvətɪv] Ⓐ ADJ poco original Ⓑ N derivado m

derive [dɪ'raɪv] Ⓐ VT [+ comfort, pleasure] encontrar (**from** en); [+ profit] sacar, obtener (**from** de); **to be ~d from** [word] venir or proceder de Ⓑ VI **to ~ from** [word] proceder de, venir de; [view, notion] basarse en; [problem, power] provenir de

dermatitis [ˌdɜː'mətaɪtɪs] N dermatitis f inv

dermatologist [ˌdɜː'mə'tɒlədʒɪst] N dermatólogo/a m/f

dermatology [ˌdɜː'mə'tɒlədʒɪ] N dermatología f

derogatory [dɪ'rɒgətərɪ] ADJ despectivo

desalinate [diː'sælɪneɪt] VT desalinar

desalination [diːˌsælɪ'neɪʃən] N desalinización f ➤ **desalination plant** planta f desalinizadora

descale [diː'skeɪl] VT (Brit) desincrustar

descant ['deskænt] N (Mus) contrapunto m

descend [dɪ'send] Ⓐ VT **1** [+ stairs] descender, bajar **2 to be ~ed from sb** descender de algn Ⓑ VI **1** (= go down) descender, bajar (**from** de) **2 to ~ on** [fog, silence] caer sobre; [army, reporters, visitors] invadir **3** (= stoop) rebajarse; **I'd never ~ to that level** nunca me rebajaría a ese nivel **4** (= trace lineage) **to ~ from** descender de

descendant [dɪ'sendənt] N descendiente mf

descent [dɪ'sent] N **1** (= going down) descenso m, bajada f; (= slope) cuesta f, pendiente f **2** (= ancestry) ascendencia f; **of Italian ~** de ascendencia italiana

describe [dɪs'kraɪb] VT describir; **it's impossible to ~** es indescriptible; **she ~s herself as an executive** se define como una ejecutiva

description [dɪs'krɪpʃən] N descripción f; **do you know anyone of this ~?** ¿sabe de alguien que responda a esta descripción?; **beyond ~** indescriptible; **he carried a gun of some ~** llevaba un arma de algún tipo; **of every ~** de toda clase

descriptive [dɪs'krɪptɪv] ADJ descriptivo

desecrate ['desɪkreɪt] VT profanar

desecration [ˌdesɪ'kreɪʃən] N profanación f

desegregate [diː'segrəgeɪt] VT abolir la segregación de

desegregation ['diːˌsegrə'geɪʃən] N abolición f de la segregación

deselect [ˌdiːsɪ'lekt] VT no renovar la candidatura de, no reelegir como candidato

desensitize [diː'sensɪtaɪz] VT insensibilizar

desert¹ ['dezət] Ⓐ N desierto m Ⓑ CPD [climate, region] desértico; [tribe, people] del desierto ➤ **desert boots** botines mpl de ante ➤ **desert island** isla f desierta

desert² [dɪ'zɜːt] Ⓐ VT (Mil) desertar de; [+ person] abandonar; **his courage ~ed him** su valor le abandonó or se esfumó Ⓑ VI (Mil) desertar (**from** de; **to** a)

deserted [dɪ'zɜːtɪd] ADJ desierto

deserter [dɪ'zɜːtəʳ] N (Mil) desertor(a) m/f

desertion [dɪ'zɜːʃən] N (Mil) deserción f; [of spouse] abandono m

deserts [dɪ'zɜːts] NPL ✦ IDIOMS **to get one's just ~** llevarse su merecido; **to give sb his/her just ~** dar a algn su merecido

deserve [dɪ'zɜːv] VT merecer; **he ~s to win** merece ganar; **he got what he ~d** se llevó su merecido; **I thought I ~d better than that** opinaba que me tenían que haber tratado mejor

deservedly [dɪ'zɜːvɪdlɪ] ADV con razón, merecidamente; **and ~ so** y con razón

deserving [dɪ'zɜːvɪŋ] ADJ [cause] meritorio

desiccate ['desɪkeɪt] VT desecar

desiccated ['desɪkeɪtɪd] ADJ seco ➤ **desiccated coconut** coco rallado y seco

design [dɪ'zaɪn] Ⓐ N **1** (gen) diseño m; **industrial ~** diseño m industrial
2 (= intention) intención f, propósito m; **by ~** a propósito, adrede; **to have ~s on sth/sb** tener las miras puestas en algo/algn
Ⓑ VT **1** [+ building etc] diseñar, proyectar; [+ dress, hat] diseñar; [+ course] estructurar; **a well ~ed programme** un programa bien concebido
2 (= intend) **a product ~ed for sensitive skin** un producto creado para pieles delicadas; **a course ~ed for foreign students** un curso concebido or pensado para los estudiantes extranjeros; **clothes that are ~ed to appeal to young people** ropa que está diseñada para atraer a la juventud; **the strike was ~ed to cause maximum disruption** la huelga se planeó para causar el mayor trastorno posible
Ⓒ CPD ➤ **design fault** defecto m de diseño

designate ['dezɪgneɪt] VT (= appoint) nombrar, designar; (= indicate) señalar, indicar; **to ~ sb to do sth** nombrar or designar a algn para hacer algo; **I was ~d as their representative** me nombraron or designaron representante de su grupo; **some of the rooms were ~d as offices** destinaron algunas de las habitaciones a oficinas; **the woodland has been ~d (as) a bird sanctuary** el bosque ha sido declarado reserva ornitológica

designer [dɪ'zaɪnəʳ] N (gen) diseñador(a) m/f; (= fashion designer) diseñador(a) m/f de moda, modisto/a m/f; (in theatre) escenógrafo/a m/f ➤ **designer baby** bebé m de diseño ➤ **designer clothes** ropa fsing de diseño ➤ **designer drug** droga f de diseño, droga f de laboratorio ➤ **designer jeans** vaqueros mpl de marca ➤ **designer label** marca f de moda

desirability [dɪˌzaɪərə'bɪlɪtɪ] N [of plan] conveniencia f; [of person] atractivo m

desirable [dɪ'zaɪərəbl] ADJ [woman] deseable, atractiva; [offer] atrayente; [property] deseable; [action] conveniente, deseable

desire [dɪ'zaɪəʳ] Ⓐ N deseo m (**for** de; **to do sth** de hacer algo) Ⓑ VT desear (**to do sth** hacer algo)

desirous [dɪ'zaɪərəs] ADJ (frm) **to be ~ of sth** desear algo

desist [dɪ'zɪst] VI **to ~ from sth** desistir de algo; **to ~ from doing sth** dejar or desistir de hacer algo

desk [desk] Ⓐ N **1** (in office, study) escritorio m, mesa f de trabajo; (= bureau) escritorio m; (Scol) pupitre m **2** (in airport, hospital) mostrador m; (in shop, restaurant) (for payment) caja f; (in hotel) recepción f Ⓑ CPD ➤ **desk clerk** (US) recepcionista mf ➤ **desk diary** agenda f de escritorio ➤ **desk job** trabajo m de oficina ➤ **desk lamp** lámpara f de escritorio

desk-bound ['deskbaʊnd] ADJ sedentario

desktop ['desktɒp] ADJ [computer] de sobremesa, de escritorio ➤ **desktop publishing** autoedición f

desolate ['desəlɪt] ADJ [place] desolado, desierto; [outlook, future] desolador; [person] desolado, afligido

desolation [ˌdesə'leɪʃən] N **1** [of landscape] desolación f **2** [of person] desolación f, desconsuelo m **3** (= act) asolamiento m, arrasamiento m

despair [dɪs'pεəʳ] Ⓐ N desesperación f; **to be in ~** estar desesperado Ⓑ VI perder la esperanza, desesperarse; **we ~ed of ever seeing her again** perdimos la esperanza de volver a verla; **don't ~!** ¡ánimo!, ¡anímate!

despairing [dɪs'pεərɪŋ] ADJ [look, sigh] de desesperación; [parent, sufferer] desesperado

despairingly [dɪs'pεərɪŋlɪ] ADV desesperadamente

despatch [dɪs'pætʃ] N = dispatch

desperate ['despərɪt] ADJ **1** [person, act, attempt, situation] desesperado; **to feel ~** estar desesperado; **to be ~ for sth** necesitar algo urgentemente; **I'm ~ (for the lavatory)!*** me muero de ganas de ir al lavabo; **to get ~** desesperarse; **to be in ~ need of sth** necesitar algo urgentemente; **to do something ~** cometer una locura; **I was ~ to see her** estaba desesperada por verla, quería verla a toda costa, me moría por verla
2 (*) (= very bad) [book, film, meal] atroz, pésimo

desperately ['despərɪtlɪ] ADV **1** (= urgently, frantically) [say, look] desesperadamente, con desesperación; [try, struggle, look for] desesperadamente; [need, require] urgentemente, desesperadamente
2 (= horribly) [lonely, thin, poor, unhappy] terriblemente; **it's**

~ **cold** hace un frío terrible; ~ **ill** muy grave, gravemente enfermo; **to be ~ short of sth** andar escasísimo de algo; **my parents were ~ worried** mis padres estaban preocupadísimos
3 (*) (= *very much, very*) **I ~ wanted to become a film director** quería ser director de cine más que nada en el mundo *or* con todo el alma; **I'm not ~ keen on the idea*** la idea no me vuelve loco; **"do you want to have children?"** — **"not ~"*** —¿quieres tener hijos? —no estoy desesperado por tenerlos

desperation [ˌdespəˈreɪʃən] N desesperación *f*; **she drove him to ~** le llevó al borde de *or* le hizo caer en la desesperación; **in (sheer) ~** a la desesperada, de pura desesperación

despicable [dɪsˈpɪkəbl] ADJ vil, despreciable

despicably [dɪsˈpɪkəblɪ] ADV despreciablemente; [*behave*] de manera despreciable

despise [dɪsˈpaɪz] VT despreciar

despite [dɪsˈpaɪt] PREP a pesar de, pese a

despondency [dɪsˈpɒndənsɪ], **despondence** [dɪsˈpɒndəns] N abatimiento *m*, desaliento *m*, pesimismo *m*

despondent [dɪsˈpɒndənt] ADJ (= *dejected*) abatido, desanimado; (= *disheartened*) descorazonado; [*letter*] de tono triste, pesimista

despot [ˈdespɒt] N déspota *mf*

dessert [dɪˈzɜːt] N postre *m*; **what's for ~?** ¿qué hay de postre? ➤ **dessert plate** plato *m* de postre ➤ **dessert wine** vino *m* dulce (*para el postre*)

dessertspoon [dɪˈzɜːtspuːn] N cuchara *f* de postre

destabilization [diːˌsteɪbɪlaɪˈzeɪʃən] N desestabilización *f*

destabilize [diːˈsteɪbɪlaɪz] VT desestabilizar

destination [ˌdestɪˈneɪʃən] N destino *m*

destine [ˈdestɪn] VT destinar (**for, to** a)

destined [ˈdestɪnd] ADJ **1** (= *intended*) ~ **for** destinado a **2** (= *fated*) **to be ~ to do sth** estar destinado a hacer algo; **she was ~ for greater things** estaba destinada *or* predestinada a llegar lejos; **we were ~ never to meet again** el destino no quiso que nos volviéramos a encontrar **3** (= *travelling*) ~ **for London** con destino a Londres

destiny [ˈdestɪnɪ] N destino *m*

destitute [ˈdestɪtjuːt] ADJ indigente; **to be (utterly) ~** estar en la (más absoluta) miseria

destitution [ˌdestɪˈtjuːʃən] N indigencia *f*, miseria *f*

destroy [dɪsˈtrɔɪ] VT (*gen*) destruir, destrozar; (= *kill*) matar; [+ *pet*] sacrificar; [+ *vermin*] exterminar; [+ *relationship, hopes etc*] destrozar, acabar con; **the factory was ~ed by a fire** la fábrica quedó destrozada *or* fue arrasada por un incendio

destroyer [dɪsˈtrɔɪəʳ] N (*Naut*) destructor *m*

destruction [dɪsˈtrʌkʃən] N (*gen*) destrucción *f*; [*of person*] ruina *f*, perdición *f*

destructive [dɪsˈtrʌktɪv] ADJ [*weapon, person, behaviour, influence, emotion*] destructivo; [*effect*] destructor; [*child*] destrozón; **the ~ power of nuclear weapons** el poder destructivo *or* destructor de las armas nucleares

desultory [ˈdesəltərɪ] ADJ (*frm*) [*way of working etc*] poco metódico; [*applause*] poco entusiasta; [*gunfire*] intermitente, esporádico; **they made ~ conversation** entablaron sin ganas una conversación

det. ABBR = **detective**

detach [dɪˈtætʃ] VT (= *separate*) separar (**from** de); (= *unstick*) despegar; **to ~ o.s. from a situation** distanciarse de una situación

detachable [dɪˈtætʃəbl] ADJ [*collar, lining*] postizo, separable; [*parts*] desmontable, extraíble

detached [dɪˈtætʃt] **Ⓐ** ADJ **1** (= *separate*) separado, suelto; (*from friends, family*) distanciado; **to become ~** [*part, fragment*] desprenderse (**from** de); **she had become ~ from reality** había perdido contacto con la realidad **2** (= *impartial*) [*opinion*] objetivo, imparcial; (= *unemotional*) [*manner*] indiferente; **to take a ~ view of** considerar objetivamente **Ⓑ** CPD ➤ **detached house** (*esp Brit*) casa *f*

independiente, chalet *m* individual

detachment [dɪˈtætʃmənt] N **1** (= *impartiality*) objetividad *f*, imparcialidad *f* **2** (= *indifference*) indiferencia *f*

detail [ˈdiːteɪl] **Ⓐ** N (*gen*) detalle *m*; (*taken collectively*) detalles *mpl*; **in ~** en detalle, detalladamente; **to go into ~(s)** entrar en detalles, pormenorizar; **for further ~s contact J. Sims** para más información póngase en contacto con J. Sims; **the wonderful ~ of the painting** la maravillosa minuciosidad del cuadro; **attention to ~** minuciosidad *f* **Ⓑ** VT [+ *facts, story*] detallar

detailed [ˈdiːteɪld] ADJ [*knowledge, description, map, instructions*] detallado; [*examination, investigation*] minucioso, detenido; [*history*] pormenorizado

detain [dɪˈteɪn] VT **1** (= *arrest*) detener, arrestar **2** (= *keep waiting*) retener; **I was ~ed at the office** me entretuve *or* demoré en la oficina; **don't let me ~ you** no quiero entretenerla

detainee [ˌdiːteɪˈniː] N detenido/a *m/f*

detect [dɪˈtekt] VT (= *discover*) descubrir; (= *notice*) percibir, detectar; (*Tech*) detectar

detectable [dɪˈtektəbl] ADJ perceptible, detectable

detection [dɪˈtekʃən] N (= *discovery*) descubrimiento *m*; (= *perception*) percepción *f*; (*by detective*) investigación *f*; (*Tech*) detección *f*; **to escape ~** [*criminal*] no ser descubierto; [*mistake*] pasar desapercibido

detective [dɪˈtektɪv] N detective *mf* ➤ **detective constable** (*Brit*) ≈ agente *mf* (de policía) ➤ **detective inspector** (*Brit*) ≈ inspector(a) *m/f* (de policía) ➤ **detective sergeant** (*Brit*) ≈ oficial *mf* de policía ➤ **detective story** novela *f* policíaca ➤ **detective work** (*fig*) trabajo *m* detectivesco, trabajo *m* de investigación

detector [dɪˈtektəʳ] N detector *m*

détente [ˈdeɪtɑːnt] N distensión *f*

detention [dɪˈtenʃən] N [*of criminal*] detención *f*, arresto *m*; (*at school*) castigo *m*; **to get a ~** quedarse castigado después de clase ➤ **detention centre, detention center** (*US*) centro *m* de detención ➤ **detention home** (*US*) centro *m* de rehabilitación

deter [dɪˈtɜːʳ] VT (= *discourage*) desalentar; (= *dissuade*) disuadir; (= *prevent*) impedir; **don't let the weather ~ you** no desistas por el mal tiempo

detergent [dɪˈtɜːdʒənt] N detergente *m*

deteriorate [dɪˈtɪərɪəreɪt] VI [*work, situation, weather*] empeorar; [*health*] empeorar, deteriorarse; [*materials, building, relationship*] deteriorarse

deterioration [dɪˌtɪərɪəˈreɪʃən] N [*of work, situation*] empeoramiento *m* (**in, of** de); [*of health*] deterioro *m*, empeoramiento *m* (**in, of** de); [*of materials, building, relationship*] deterioro *m* (**in, of** de)

determination [dɪˌtɜːmɪˈneɪʃən] N **1** (= *resolve*) determinación *f*; **he set off with great ~** partió muy resuelto **2** (= *ascertaining*) [*of cause, position*] determinación *f*

determine [dɪˈtɜːmɪn] VT **1** (= *ascertain*) [+ *cause, meaning*] determinar **2** (= *fix*) [+ *price, date*] fijar, determinar; [+ *scope, limits, boundary*] definir, determinar **3** (= *be the deciding factor in*) [+ *fate, character*] determinar; **to be ~d by** depender de **4** (= *make determined*) **to ~ sb to do sth** hacer que algn se decida a hacer algo **5** (= *resolve*) **to ~ to do sth** decidir hacer algo, determinar hacer algo

determined [dɪˈtɜːmɪnd] ADJ [*person*] decidido, resuelto; [*effort*] resuelto, enérgico; **her refusal made me even more ~** su negativa sólo sirvió para que me decidiese aún más; **to be ~ that** estar decidido a que + *subjun*; **to be ~ to do sth** estar decidido *or* resuelto a hacer algo; **to make a ~ attempt to do sth** poner todo su empeño en hacer algo

determinedly [dɪˈtɜːmɪndlɪ] ADV [*say*] resueltamente; [*persevere*] con determinación

determining [dɪˈtɜːmɪnɪŋ] ADJ ~ **factor** factor *m* determinante

deterrent [dɪˈterənt] N elemento *m* disuasorio, elemento *m* disuasivo; **to act as a ~** servir de elemento disuasorio *or* disuasivo; **nuclear ~** fuerza *f* nuclear disuasoria *or* disuasiva; **these penalties are no ~ to criminals** estos castigos no disuaden a los criminales

detest [dɪ'test] VT detestar, aborrecer; **to ~ doing sth** detestar *or* odiar hacer algo

detestable [dɪ'testəbl] ADJ detestable, aborrecible

dethrone [diː'θrəʊn] VT destronar

detonate ['detəneɪt] Ⓐ VT hacer detonar Ⓑ VI detonar, estallar

detonation [ˌdetə'neɪʃən] N detonación *f*

detonator ['detəneɪtəʳ] N detonador *m*

detour ['diːtʊəʳ] Ⓐ N desvío *m*; **to make a ~** desviarse Ⓑ VT (*US*) desviar Ⓒ VI (*US*) desviarse

detox* ['diːtɒks] N desintoxicación *f*

detoxification [diːˌtɒksɪfɪ'keɪʃən] N desintoxicación *f* ➤ **detoxification centre, detoxification center** (*US*) centro *m* de desintoxicación ➤ **detoxification programme, detoxification program** (*US*) programa *f* de desintoxicación

detoxify [diː'tɒksɪfaɪ] VT [+ *alcoholic*] desintoxicar; [+ *chemical*] eliminar la toxicidad de

detract [dɪ'trækt] VI **to ~ from** [+ *value*] quitar mérito *or* valor a; [+ *reputation*] empañar

detractor [dɪ'træktəʳ] N detractor(a) *m/f*

detriment ['detrɪmənt] N detrimento *m*, perjuicio *m*; **to the ~ of** en detrimento *or* perjuicio de; **without ~ to** sin (causar) detrimento *or* perjuicio a

detrimental [ˌdetrɪ'mentl] ADJ perjudicial (**to** para)

deutschmark ['dɔɪtʃmɑːk] N marco *m* alemán

devaluation [ˌdiːvæljʊ'eɪʃən] N devaluación *f*

devalue [diː'væljuː] VT devaluar

devastate ['devəsteɪt] VT **1** (*lit*) [+ *place*] devastar, asolar; [+ *opponent, opposition*] aplastar, arrollar **2** (= *overwhelm*) [+ *person*] dejar desolado, dejar destrozado; **we were simply ~d** estábamos verdaderamente desolados *or* destrozados

devastating ['devəsteɪtɪŋ] ADJ **1** (= *destructive*) [*flood, storm, consequence, effect*] devastador; [*attack*] demoledor **2** (= *crushing*) [*blow, loss*] tremendo; [*argument, logic, defeat*] aplastante; [*news*] terrible; [*criticism, report*] demoledor; **a strike would be ~ to the economy** una huelga sería un golpe tremendo para la economía

devastation [ˌdevə'steɪʃən] N **1** (= *act*) devastación *f* **2** (= *state*) devastación *f*, destrozos *mpl*

develop [dɪ'veləp] Ⓐ VT **1** [+ *mind, body, argument, idea*] desarrollar **2** [+ *plan*] elaborar; [+ *process*] perfeccionar **3** [+ *interest, taste, habit*] adquirir; [+ *disease*] contraer; [+ *tendency*] coger, desarrollar; [+ *engine trouble*] empezar a tener; **she ~ed a liking for whisky** le cogió el gusto al whisky **4** (= *build on*) [+ *region*] desarrollar, fomentar; [+ *land*] urbanizar; [+ *site*] ampliar; **this land is to be ~ed** se va a construir en *or* urbanizar este terreno **5** (*Phot*) revelar; **to get a film ~ed** revelar un carrete Ⓑ VI **1** (= *change, mature*) desarrollarse; **to ~ into** convertirse *or* transformarse en **2** (= *come into being*) [*symptoms*] aparecer, mostrarse **3** (= *come about*) [*idea, plan, problem*] surgir

developed [dɪ'veləpt] ADJ [*country, world*] desarrollado

developer [dɪ'veləpəʳ] N (*also* **property ~**) promotor(a) *m/f* inmobiliario/a

developing [dɪ'veləpɪŋ] Ⓐ ADJ [*country*] en (vías de) desarrollo; [*crisis, storm*] que se avecina Ⓑ N (*Phot*) revelado *m*

development [dɪ'veləpmənt] N **1** (*gen*) desarrollo *m*; (= *unfolding*) evolución *f* **2** (= *change*) novedad *f*, cambio *m*; (= *event*) acontecimiento *m*; **there are no new ~s to report** no se registra ninguna novedad *or* ningún cambio **3** [*of resources*] explotación *f*; [*of land*] urbanización *f* **4** (= *area of new housing*) complejo *m* habitacional *or* residencial, urbanización *f* (*esp Sp*), fraccionamiento *m* (*Mex*)

deviance ['diːvɪəns], **deviancy** ['diːvɪənsɪ] N desviación *f*

deviant ['diːvɪənt] Ⓐ ADJ desviado Ⓑ N persona de conducta desviada

deviate ['diːvɪeɪt] VI desviarse (**from** de)

deviation [ˌdiːvɪ'eɪʃən] N desviación *f* (**from** de)

device [dɪ'vaɪs] N **1** (= *gadget*) aparato *m*; (= *mechanism*) mecanismo *m*, dispositivo *m*; (*explosive*) artefacto *m*; **nuclear ~** ingenio *m* nuclear **2** (= *scheme*) estratagema *f*, recurso *m*; **to leave sb to his own ~s** dejar a algn hacer lo que le dé la gana; (*to solve problem*) dejar que algn se las arregle solo

devil ['devl] N **1** (= *evil spirit*) demonio *m*, diablo *m*; **the Devil** el Diablo; **go to the ~!**** ¡vete al diablo!**, ¡vete a la porra! (*Sp**); ✦ IDIOMS **to play ~'s advocate** hacer de abogado del diablo; **to be between the ~ and the deep blue sea** estar entre la espada y la pared; **speak** *or* (*Brit*) **talk of the ~!*** hablando del rey de Roma (por la puerta asoma); ✦ PROVS **better the ~ you know** (*esp Brit*) vale más lo malo conocido que lo bueno por conocer; **the ~ finds work for idle hands** cuando el diablo no tiene que hacer con el rabo mata moscas **2** (*) (= *person*) demonio *m*; **poor ~** pobre diablo, pobrecito/a *m/f*; **go on, be a ~!** ¡anda, atrévete *or* lánzate!; **you little ~!** ¡qué diablillo *or* malo eres! **3** (*) (*as intensifier*) **it was the ~ of a job to do!** ¡menudo trabajo que (me) costó!; **we had the ~ of a job** *or* **the ~'s own job to find it** nos costó horrores encontrarlo; **how/ what/who the ~ ...?** ¿cómo/qué/quién demonios ...?; **there will be the ~ to pay** esto va a costar caro

devilish ['devlɪʃ] ADJ diabólico

devil-may-care ['devlmeɪ'keəʳ] ADJ despreocupado

devious ['diːvɪəs] ADJ [*means*] dudoso, artero; [*person*] taimado

deviousness ['diːvɪəsnɪs] N artería *f*

devise [dɪ'vaɪz] VT [+ *strategy*] concebir, idear; [+ *gadget*] inventar; [+ *plan*] elaborar; [+ *solution*] encontrar

devoid [dɪ'vɔɪd] ADJ **~ of** desprovisto de

devolution [ˌdiːvə'luːʃən] N (*Brit Pol*) descentralización *f*

devolve [dɪ'vɒlv] VT [+ *power*] delegar; [+ *government*] descentralizar

devote [dɪ'vəʊt] VT **to ~ sth to sth** dedicar algo a algo; **she ~d her life to finding a cure for the disease** dedicó *or* consagró su vida a encontrar una cura para la enfermedad; **to ~ o.s. to sth** dedicarse a algo

devoted [dɪ'vəʊtɪd] ADJ [*wife, husband, son*] abnegado; [*couple, family*] unido; [*friend*] leal, fiel; [*follower, admirer*] ferviente; **years of ~ service** años de dedicación y servicio; **they are ~ to one another** se adoran, sienten devoción el uno por el otro; **this chapter is ~ to politics** este capítulo está dedicado a la política

devotee [ˌdevəʊ'tiː] N **1** (*Rel*) devoto/a *m/f* **2** (= *enthusiast*) partidario/a *m/f* (**of** de)

devotion [dɪ'vəʊʃən] N (*to spouse, relative, football team, God*) devoción *f* (**to** por); (*to friend*) lealtad *f* (**to** a); (*to studies, duty, work, cause*) dedicación *f* (**to** a)

devour [dɪ'vaʊəʳ] VT [+ *food*] devorar; **to be ~ed with jealousy** morirse de envidia; **to be ~ed with curiosity** verse devorado *or* corroído por la curiosidad

devout [dɪ'vaʊt] ADJ **1** [*Christian, Muslim*] devoto; **she's a ~ Catholic** es muy católica **2** (= *fervent*) [*Communist*] convencido; **it was his ~ wish that his son should become a lawyer** deseaba de todo corazón que su hijo se hiciese abogado

dew [djuː] N rocío *m*

dewy-eyed ['djuːɹ'aɪd] ADJ ingenuo

dexterity [deks'terɪtɪ] N destreza *f*, habilidad *f*

dextrose ['dekstrəʊs] N dextrosa *f*

DfEE N ABBR (*Brit*) = **Department for Education and Employment**

DG N ABBR = **Director General** D.G. *mf*

DH N ABBR (*Brit*) = **Department of Health**

DI N ABBR **1** = **Donor Insemination 2** (*Brit Police*) = **Detective Inspector**

diabetes [ˌdaɪəˈbiːtiːz] NSING diabetes *f inv*

diabetic [ˌdaɪəˈbetɪk] **Ⓐ** ADJ [*patient*] diabético; [*chocolate*] para diabéticos **Ⓑ** N diabético/a *m/f*

diabolical [ˌdaɪəˈbɒlɪkəl] ADJ **1** [*laughter, plan, plot*] diabólico **2** (*) (= *very bad*) horrendo

diaeresis, dieresis (*US*) [daɪˈerɪsɪs] N (*pl* **diaereses** [daɪˈerɪsiːz]) diéresis *f inv*

diagnose [ˈdaɪəɡnəʊz] VT diagnosticar; **she was ~d with cancer** le diagnosticaron (un) cáncer

diagnosis [ˌdaɪəɡˈnəʊsɪs] N (*pl* **diagnoses** [ˌdaɪəɡˈnəʊsiːz]) diagnóstico *m*

diagonal [daɪˈæɡənl] **Ⓐ** ADJ diagonal **Ⓑ** N diagonal *f*

diagonally [daɪˈæɡənəlɪ] ADV [*cut, fold*] diagonalmente, en diagonal; **~ opposite** diagonalmente opuesto

diagram [ˈdaɪəɡræm] N (= *plan*) esquema *m*; (= *chart*) gráfica *f*; (*Math*) diagrama *m*

dial [ˈdaɪəl] **Ⓐ** N [*of clock*] esfera *f*, carátula *f* (*Mex*); [*of instrument*] esfera *f*, cuadrante *m*; [*of radio*] dial *m*; (*on dashboard*) cuadrante *m*; (= *tuner*) selector *m* **Ⓑ** VT (*Telec*) marcar, discar (*LAm*); **to ~ 999** (*Brit*) ✧ ~ **911** (*US*) llamar al teléfono de emergencia **Ⓒ** VI (*Telec*) marcar, discar (*LAm*) **Ⓓ** CPD ▸ **dial tone** (*US*) señal *f* de marcar, tono *m* de marcar

dialect [ˈdaɪəlekt] N dialecto *m*

dialectics [ˌdaɪəˈlektɪks] N dialéctica *f*

dialling, dialing (*US*) [ˈdaɪəlɪŋ] N marcación *f*, discado *m* (*LAm*) ▸ **dialling code** (*Brit*) prefijo *m* ▸ **dialling tone** (*Brit*) señal *f* de marcar, tono *m* de marcar

dialogue, dialog (*US*) [ˈdaɪəlɒɡ] N diálogo *m*

dialysis [daɪˈælɪsɪs] N (*pl* **dialyses** [daɪˈælɪsiːz]) diálisis *f inv*; **to be on ~** hacerse la diálisis ▸ **dialysis machine** máquina *f* de diálisis

diameter [daɪˈæmɪtəʳ] N diámetro *m*; **it is one metre in ~** tiene un diámetro de un metro, tiene un metro de diámetro

diametrically [ˌdaɪəˈmetrɪkəlɪ] ADV **~ opposed** diametralmente opuesto (**to** a)

diamond [ˈdaɪəmənd] **Ⓐ** N **1** (= *mineral*) diamante *m*; (= *jewel*) brillante *m*, diamante *m* **2** (= *shape*) rombo *m* **3** (*Cards*) diamante *m*; **the Queen of ~s** la dama *or* reina de diamantes **4** (*Baseball*) campo *m* de béisbol **Ⓑ** CPD ▸ **diamond mine** mina *f* de diamantes ▸ **diamond necklace** collar *m* de diamantes ▸ **diamond ring** anillo *m* de diamantes, sortija *f* de diamantes ▸ **diamond wedding** (**anniversary**) bodas *fpl* de diamante

diamond-shaped [ˈdaɪəməndˌʃeɪpt] ADJ de *or* en forma de rombo

diamorphine [ˌdaɪəˈmɔːfiːn] N diamorfina *f*

diaper [ˈdaɪəpəʳ] N (*US*) pañal *m* ▸ **diaper rash** irritación *f*; **to have ~ rash** estar escaldado

diaphragm [ˈdaɪəfræm] N diafragma *m*

diarrhoea, diarrhea (*US*) [ˌdaɪəˈriːə] N diarrea *f*

diary [ˈdaɪərɪ] N (= *journal*) diario *m*; (*esp Brit*) (*for engagements*) agenda *f*; **I keep a ~** tengo un diario

diatribe [ˈdaɪətraɪb] N diatriba *f* (**against** contra)

dice [daɪs] **Ⓐ** N (*pl* ~) (= *die*) dado *m*; **no ~!** (*US**) ¡ni hablar!, ¡nada de eso!; *see also* **die²** **1** **Ⓑ** VT [+ *vegetables*] cortar en cubitos **Ⓒ** VI **to ~ with death** jugar con la muerte

dicey* [ˈdaɪsɪ] ADJ (*compar* **dicier**; *superl* **diciest**) (*Brit*) (= *uncertain*) incierto, dudoso; (= *hazardous*) peligroso, arriesgado

dichotomy [daɪˈkɒtəmɪ] N dicotomía *f*

dick [dɪk] N **1** (*US**) (= *person*) sabueso *mf* **2** (***) (= *penis*) polla *f* (*Sp****), verga*** *f*

Dickensian [dɪˈkenzɪən] ADJ dickensiano

dickhead*** [ˈdɪkhed] N imbécil* *mf*, gilipollas *mf inv* (*Sp****)

Dictaphone® [ˈdɪktəfəʊn] N dictáfono® *m*

dictate [dɪkˈteɪt] **Ⓐ** [dɪkˈteɪt] VT **1** [+ *letter*] dictar **2** (= *order*) mandar; [+ *terms, conditions*] imponer **Ⓑ** [dɪkˈteɪt] VI dictar **Ⓒ** [ˈdɪkteɪt] N mandato *m*; **dictates** dictados *mpl*; **the ~s of conscience/reason** los dictados de la conciencia/razón

dictation [dɪkˈteɪʃən] N dictado *m*; **to take (a) ~** escribir al dictado

dictator [dɪkˈteɪtəʳ] N dictador(a) *m/f*

dictatorial [ˌdɪktəˈtɔːrɪəl] ADJ dictatorial

dictatorship [dɪkˈteɪtəʃɪp] N dictadura *f*

diction [ˈdɪkʃən] N dicción *f*

dictionary [ˈdɪkʃənrɪ] N diccionario *m*

did [dɪd] PT *of* **do¹**

didactic [daɪˈdæktɪk] ADJ didáctico

diddle* [ˈdɪdl] VT (*esp Brit*) estafar, timar; **to ~ sb out of sth** estafar algo a algn

didn't [ˈdɪdənt] = **did not**; *see* **do¹**

die¹ [daɪ] (*pres part* **dying**) **Ⓐ** VI **1** morir (**of, from** de); **to ~ of hunger** morir de hambre; **he ~d a hero** murió convertido en un héroe; **to ~ for one's country** morir por la patria; **her father was dying** su padre se moría *or* se estaba muriendo *or* estaba moribundo; **the secret ~d with her** se llevó el secreto a la tumba; **I nearly ~d!*** (*laughing*) ¡me moría de la risa!; (*with embarrassment*) ¡me moría de vergüenza!; (*with fear*) ¡casi me muero del susto!; ✦ IDIOM **a dress/house to ~ for*** un vestido/una casa para caerse de espaldas*, un vestido/una casa de ensueño; ✦ PROVS **never say ~*** no hay que darse por vencido; **old habits ~ hard** genio y figura hasta la sepultura **2** (= *end*) [*friendship, interest*] morir, desaparecer; [*light*] extinguirse; [*engine*] pararse, apagarse **3** (= *long*) **to be dying to do sth** morirse de ganas de hacer algo; **I'm dying for a cigarette** me muero de ganas de fumar un cigarrillo **Ⓑ** VT **to ~ a natural death** morir de muerte natural; **to ~ a violent death** tener una muerte violenta

▸ **die away** VI + ADV [*voice, sound*] irse apagando
▸ **die down** VI + ADV [*fire*] apagarse; [*wind, storm*] remitir, amainar; [*shelling*] disminuir; [*excitement, protests*] calmarse, apaciguarse
▸ **die off** VI + ADV [*plants, animals*] morirse, desaparecer
▸ **die out** VI + ADV [*custom*] desaparecer, caer en desuso; [*family, race, species*] extinguirse; (*US*) [*fire*] apagarse, extinguirse

die² [daɪ] N **1** (*pl* **dice**) dado *m*; ✦ IDIOM **the ~ is cast** la suerte está echada **2** (*pl* ~**s**) (= *stamp*) troquel *m*, cuño *m*; (= *mould*) matriz *f*, molde *m*

diehard [ˈdaɪhɑːd] **Ⓐ** ADJ acérrimo **Ⓑ** N intransigente *mf*

dieresis [daɪˈerɪsɪs] N (*pl* **diereses** [daɪˈerɪsiːz]) (*US*) = **diaeresis**

diesel [ˈdiːzəl] **Ⓐ** N **1** (= *fuel*) gasóleo *m*, gasoil *m* **2** (= *car, train*) vehículo *m* diesel **Ⓑ** CPD ▸ **diesel engine** motor *m* diesel ▸ **diesel fuel, diesel oil** gasóleo *m*, gasoil *m*

diet [ˈdaɪət] **Ⓐ** N **1** (= *usual food*) dieta *f*, alimentación *f* **2** (*for slimming*) régimen *m*, dieta *f*; **to be/go on a ~** estar/ponerse a régimen *or* dieta **Ⓑ** VI estar a régimen **Ⓒ** CPD [*soft drink*] light *inv*

dietary [ˈdaɪətərɪ] ADJ [*supplement*] dietético; [*needs, habits*] alimenticio; **~ fibre** fibra dietética

dietician [ˌdaɪˈtɪʃən] N dietista *mf*

differ [ˈdɪfəʳ] VI **1** (= *be dissimilar*) ser distinto, diferenciarse, diferir (*frm*) (**from** de) **2** (= *disagree*) [*people*] no estar de acuerdo, discrepar; [*texts, versions*] discrepar; **to ~ with sb (on** *or* **over** *or* **about sth)** no estar de acuerdo con algn (en algo), discrepar de algn (en algo); **I beg to ~** siento tener que disentir *or* discrepar, lamento estar en desacuerdo *or* no estar de acuerdo

difference [ˈdɪfrəns] N **1** (= *dissimilarity*) diferencia *f* (**between** entre); **the ~ in her is amazing!** ¡cuánto ha cambiado!; **that makes all the ~** eso cambia totalmente la cosa; **it makes no ~** da igual, da lo mismo; **it makes no ~ to me** me da igual *or* lo mismo; **what ~ does it make?** ¿qué más da?; **I'll pay the ~** yo pagaré la diferencia; **same ~*** lo mismo da*; **a car with a ~** un coche diferente *or* especial **2** (= *quarrel*) riña *f*; **a ~ of opinion** un desacuerdo

different [ˈdɪfrənt] ADJ **1** (= *not alike*) diferente, distinto

(from, to, (US) **than** de, a); **that's quite a ~ matter** eso es harina de otro costal; **I feel a ~ person** me siento otro **2** (= various) varios, distintos **3** (iro) (= distinctive) distinto, original; **"what do you think of my new hairstyle?"** — **"well ... it's certainly ~"** —¿qué te parece mi nuevo peinado? —pues ... desde luego es algo distinto or original

differential [ˌdɪfəˈrenʃəl] **Ⓐ** ADJ [rate, calculus, equation] diferencial **Ⓑ** N diferencial m

differentiate [ˌdɪfəˈrenʃieɪt] **Ⓐ** VT **1** (gen) diferenciar, distinguir (**from** de); **to ~ A from B** (= tell the difference) distinguir A de B; (= make the difference) diferenciar A de B **2** (Math) diferenciar **Ⓑ** VI distinguir (**between** entre)

differently [ˈdɪfrəntlɪ] ADV de modo distinto; **she wanted to do things ~** quería hacer las cosas de otro modo or de modo distinto

difficult [ˈdɪfɪkəlt] ADJ **1** (= hard) [task, book, question] difícil; [writer] complicado, complejo; **it is ~ to describe the feeling** es difícil describir la sensación; **these dogs are ~ to control** estos perros son difíciles de controlar; **many youngsters find it ~ to get work** a muchos jóvenes les resulta difícil encontrar trabajo; **it was ~ for him to leave her** le resultó difícil dejarla; **she is determined to make life ~ for him** está decidida a hacerle la vida imposible; **to put sb in a ~ position** poner a algn en una posición comprometida **2** (= awkward) [person, child, character] difícil

difficulty [ˈdɪfɪkəltɪ] N **1** (= hardness) dificultad f; **he has ~ (in) walking** tiene dificultades para andar, le resulta difícil andar; **I had no ~ finding the house** no tuve problemas para encontrar la casa, no me resultó difícil encontrar la casa; **with ~** con dificultad **2** (= problem) problema m, dificultad f; **to get into ~ or difficulties** [person] (gen) meterse en problemas or apuros; (while swimming) empezar a tener problemas; [ship] empezar a peligrar; **they are in financial difficulties** tienen problemas económicos, están pasando dificultades económicas; **to make difficulties for sb** crear problemas a algn

diffidence [ˈdɪfɪdəns] N falta f de confianza en sí mismo, timidez f

diffident [ˈdɪfɪdənt] ADJ que tiene poca confianza en sí mismo, tímido

diffidently [ˈdɪfɪdəntlɪ] ADV con poca confianza en sí mismo, tímidamente

diffuse [dɪˈfjuːz] **Ⓐ** VT [+ light, information, ideas] difundir; [+ heat] difundir, esparcir **Ⓑ** VI [heat, gas] difundirse, esparcirse

dig [dɪg] (vb: pt, pp **dug**) **Ⓐ** N **1** (Archeol) excavación f **2** (Brit) (= prod) (gen) empujón m; (with elbow) codazo m **3** (Brit*) (= taunt) indirecta f, pulla f; **to have a ~ at sb** lanzar una indirecta or una pulla a algn
Ⓑ VT **1** [+ hole] [person] cavar, excavar; [machine] excavar; [animal] cavar, escarbar; ✦ IDIOM **to ~ one's own grave** cavar su propia tumba
2 (= break up) [+ ground] remover; (= cultivate) [+ garden] cultivar, cavar en
3 (= thrust) **to ~ sth into sth** clavar algo en algo, hundir algo en algo
4 (= prod) empujar; (with elbow) dar un codazo a; **to ~ sb in the ribs** dar a algn un codazo en las costillas
5 (esp US†*) **5.1** (= enjoy) **I don't ~ jazz** no me gusta el jazz, el jazz no me dice nada; **I really ~ that** eso me chifla* **5.2** (= look at) **~ this!** ¡mira esto!
Ⓒ VI [person] (gen) cavar; (Archeol, Tech) excavar; [dog, pig] escarbar; **to ~ for gold** excavar en busca de oro; **he dug into his pockets for a coin** hurgó en los bolsillos para buscar una moneda; ✦ IDIOM **to ~ deep into one's pocket** rascarse el bolsillo
➤ **dig in Ⓐ** VI + ADV (*) (= eat) meter mano a la comida; **~ in!** ¡a comer! **Ⓑ** VT + ADV (= thrust) [+ nails, claws, knife] clavar, hundir; ✦ IDIOM **to ~ in one's heels** mantenerse en sus trece, empecinarse
➤ **dig into** VI + PREP **1** [+ sb's past] remover, hurgar en **2** [+ reserves] consumir, usar; **I had to ~ into my savings to pay for it** tuve que recurrir a or echar mano de mis ahorros

para pagarlo **3** (*) (= start) [+ food, meal] hincar el diente a, atacar
➤ **dig out** VT + ADV **1** [+ buried object] desenterrar, sacar; (from rubble) sacar (de entre los escombros) **2** (= search out) buscar
➤ **dig up** VT + ADV **1** [+ potatoes] sacar; [+ weeds] arrancar; [+ plant] desarraigar; [+ flowerbed] cavar en, remover la tierra de; [+ roadway] levantar; [+ treasure, body, artifacts] desenterrar **2** [+ information] desenterrar, sacar a la luz

digest [daɪˈdʒest] **Ⓐ** VT **1** [+ food] digerir **2** [+ information, news] asimilar, digerir **Ⓑ** VI digerir

digestible [dɪˈdʒestəbl] ADJ digerible

digestion [dɪˈdʒestʃən] N digestión f

digestive [dɪˈdʒestɪv] **Ⓐ** ADJ digestivo **Ⓑ** N (Brit) (also ~ biscuit) galleta f dulce integral, bizcocho m (LAm) **Ⓒ** CPD
➤ **digestive system** aparato m digestivo

digger [ˈdɪgəʳ] N (= machine) excavadora f

digit [ˈdɪdʒɪt] N **1** (Math) dígito m, cifra f **2** (= finger, toe) dedo m

digital [ˈdɪdʒɪtəl] ADJ dígital ➤ **digital television** televisión f digital

dignified [ˈdɪgnɪfaɪd] ADJ [person] de aspecto solemne, de aspecto digno; [manner, air] solemne, digno; [silence] decoroso

dignitary [ˈdɪgnɪtərɪ] N dignatario/a m/f

dignity [ˈdɪgnɪtɪ] N dignidad f; **doing the dishes would be beneath his ~** para él, lavar los platos sería rebajarse

digress [daɪˈgres] VI hacer una digresión; **but I ~** (often hum) pero me estoy apartando del tema

digression [daɪˈgreʃən] N digresión f

digs [dɪgz] NPL (Brit) alojamiento msing; **to be in ~** estar alojado, vivir en una pensión, estar de patrona*†

dike [daɪk] N = **dyke**

dilapidated [dɪˈlæpɪdeɪtɪd] ADJ [building] desmoronado, ruinoso; [vehicle] desvencijado

dilate [daɪˈleɪt] **Ⓐ** VI dilatarse **Ⓑ** VT dilatar; **her pupils were ~d** tenía las pupilas dilatadas

dilemma [daɪˈlemə] N dilema m; **to be in a ~** estar en or tener un dilema

dilettante [ˌdɪlɪˈtæntɪ] N (pl **~s** or **dilettanti** [ˌdɪlɪˈtæntiː]) diletante mf

diligence [ˈdɪlɪdʒəns] N diligencia f

diligent [ˈdɪlɪdʒənt] ADJ [person] diligente; [work, search] concienzudo

dill [dɪl] N eneldo m ➤ **dill pickle** (US) pepinillos mpl en vinagre al eneldo

dilly-dally* [ˈdɪlɪdælɪ] VI **1** (= loiter) entretenerse, demorarse **2** (= hesitate) andarse con titubeos

dilute [daɪˈluːt] **Ⓐ** VT diluir; **"dilute to taste"** "diluya a su gusto" **Ⓑ** ADJ diluido

dim [dɪm] **Ⓐ** ADJ (compar **~mer**; superl **~mest**) **1** (= not bright) [light] débil, tenue; [room] oscuro, poco iluminado; **she read the letter by the ~ light of a torch** leyó la carta con la ayuda de la débil or tenue luz de una linterna; **even in the ~ light the furniture looked dirty** incluso con la poca luz que había los muebles parecían sucios; ✦ IDIOM **to take a ~ view of sth*** ver algo con malos ojos
2 (= indistinct) [figure, outline] borroso; [memory] borroso, vago
3 (Brit*) (= unintelligent) corto, lerdo*; **he's a bit ~** es un poco corto, no tiene muchas luces
Ⓑ VT **1** [+ light] bajar, atenuar; [+ colours] apagar; **to ~ one's (head)lights** (US) poner las luces cortas or de cruce, poner las luces bajas (LAm)
2 (= diminish) [+ senses] debilitar
3 (= fade) [+ outline, memory] borrar
Ⓒ VI **1** [light] atenuarse, ir atenuándose; [colour] apagarse, ir apagándose
2 [outline, memory] hacerse borroso

dime [daɪm] N (Canada, US) moneda de diez centavos; **they're a ~ a dozen** son muy baratos; (fig) los hay a montones*
➤ **dime store** baratillo m, ≈ todo a cien m (Sp) (tienda que vende mercadería barata)

dimension [dɪˈmenʃən] N dimensión f
diminish [dɪˈmɪnɪʃ] **(A)** VT (gen) disminuir; [+ numbers, speed, strength] disminuir, reducir **(B)** VI disminuir
diminished [dɪˈmɪnɪʃt] ADJ [value] reducido; [ability] limitado; (Mus) [interval] disminuido ➤ **diminished responsibility** (Jur) responsabilidad f disminuida
diminutive [dɪˈmɪnjʊtɪv] **(A)** ADJ diminuto **(B)** N (Ling) diminutivo m
dimly [ˈdɪmlɪ] ADV **1** [shine, glow] débilmente, tenuemente; **~ lit** poco iluminado, iluminado con una luz tenue **2** (= vaguely) [remember, recollect] vagamente; **I was ~ aware that ...** era vagamente consciente de que ...
dimmer [ˈdɪmər] N **1** (also **~ switch**) regulador m de intensidad de luz **2** (US **~ switch**) interruptor m de las luces cortas or de cruce, interruptor m de las luces bajas (LAm)
dimple [ˈdɪmpl] N (in chin, cheek) hoyuelo m
dimwit* [ˈdɪmwɪt] N lerdo/a* m/f
dim-witted* [ˈdɪmˈwɪtɪd] ADJ lerdo*, corto de alcances
din [dɪn] N [of traffic, roadworks] estruendo m, estrépito m; [of voices, music] alboroto m, bulla* f
dine [daɪn] VI cenar; **to ~ on** or **off sth** cenar algo ➤ **dine out** VI + ADV cenar fuera
diner [ˈdaɪnər] N **1** (= person) comensal mf **2** (Rail) coche m comedor, vagón m restaurante, buffet m (Per) **3** (US) (gen) casa f de comidas, lonchería f (LAm); (= transport café) cafetería f de carretera
dinghy [ˈdɪŋgɪ] N (= rubber dinghy) lancha f neumática; (= sailing dinghy) bote m
dingo [ˈdɪŋgəʊ] N (pl **-es**) dingo m
dingy [ˈdɪndʒɪ] ADJ (compar **dingier**; superl **dingiest**) (= shabby) [furniture, decor] deslustrado, deslucido; (= gloomy) [town, house, room] sombrío, lóbrego; (= dirty) sucio
dining [ˈdaɪnɪŋ] CPD ➤ **dining car** coche m comedor, vagón m restaurante ➤ **dining hall** comedor m, refectorio m ➤ **dining room** comedor m ➤ **dining table** mesa f de comedor
dinner [ˈdɪnər] N (= supper) cena f; (= lunch) almuerzo m, comida f, lonche m (Mex); (= banquet) cena f de gala; **to have ~** (in the evening) cenar; (at midday) almorzar, comer; **we're having people to ~** tenemos invitados para or a cenar; **to go out to ~** salir a cenar (fuera) ➤ **dinner jacket** (Brit) esmoquin m, smoking m ➤ **dinner lady** empleada que da el servicio de comidas en las escuelas ➤ **dinner party** cena f (con invitados) ➤ **dinner plate** plato m llano ➤ **dinner service** (Brit) vajilla f ➤ **dinner table** (Brit) mesa f de comedor ➤ **dinner time** hora f de cenar/comer
dinnerware [ˈdɪnəweər] N (esp US) vajilla f ➤ **dinnerware set** (US) vajilla f
dinosaur [ˈdaɪnəsɔːr] N **1** (= reptile) dinosaurio m **2** (*) (= person) carcamal* mf; (= organization) reliquia f del pasado
dint [dɪnt] N **by ~ of** a fuerza de
diocese [ˈdaɪəsɪs] N diócesis f inv
diode [ˈdaɪəʊd] N diodo m
dioxide [daɪˈɒksaɪd] N dióxido m
dioxin [daɪˈɒksɪn] N dioxina f
DIP [dɪp] N ABBR (Comput) = **Dual-In-Line Package**
dip [dɪp] **(A)** N **1** (= swim) baño m, chapuzón m, zambullida f (LAm); **to go for a ~** ir a darse un baño or un chapuzón **2** (= slope) declive m, pendiente f; (= hollow) hondonada f, depresión f **3** (Culin) salsa f (para mojar) **4** (Agr) (for sheep) baño m de desinfección **(B)** VT **1** (into liquid) sumergir, bañar (**in, into** en); [+ pen] mojar (**in, into** en); [+ ladle, scoop] meter (**in, into** en); [+ sheep] bañar con desinfectante **2 to ~ one's (head)lights** (Brit) poner las luces cortas or de cruce, poner las luces bajas (LAm) **(C)** VI **1** [road] bajar en pendiente; [land] formar una hondonada

2 [bird, plane] bajar en picado (Sp) or en picada (LAm); [temperature] bajar; [sun] esconderse **3 to ~ into one's savings** echar mano de los ahorros **4 to ~ into a book** hojear un libro **(D)** CPD ➤ **dip switch** (Aut) interruptor m de las luces cortas or de cruce, interruptor m de las luces bajas (LAm)
Dip. ABBR = **Diploma**
diphtheria [dɪfˈθɪərɪə] N difteria f
diphthong [ˈdɪfθɒŋ] N diptongo m
diploma [dɪˈpləʊmə] N diploma m
diplomacy [dɪˈpləʊməsɪ] N diplomacia f
diplomat [ˈdɪpləmæt] N diplomático/a m/f
diplomatic [ˌdɪpləˈmætɪk] ADJ diplomático ➤ **diplomatic bag** (Brit) valija f diplomática ➤ **diplomatic immunity** inmunidad f diplomática ➤ **diplomatic pouch** (US) valija f diplomática ➤ **diplomatic service** servicio m diplomático
dipper [ˈdɪpər] N **big ~** (at fair) montaña f rusa; **the Big Dipper** (US Astron) la Osa Mayor
dipstick [ˈdɪpstɪk] N varilla f del aceite, cala f
dire [daɪər] ADJ (superl **~st**) **1** [consequences] nefasto, funesto; [situation] desesperado; [warning, prediction] alarmante; [poverty] extremo; **to be in ~ need of sth** necesitar algo desesperadamente; **to be in ~ straits** estar en un serio aprieto or apuro **2** (*) (= awful) [film, book] pésimo, malísimo
direct [daɪˈrekt] **(A)** ADJ **1** [route, flight, result, responsibility, descendant] directo; **"keep away from direct heat"** "no exponer directamente al calor"; **to make a ~ hit** dar en el blanco; **he's the ~ opposite** es exactamente el contrario **2** (= straightforward) [answer, refusal] claro, inequívoco; [manner, character] abierto, franco **(B)** ADV (= straight) [go, fly, pay] directamente; **we fly ~ to Santiago** volamos directo or directamente a Santiago **(C)** VT **1** [+ remark, gaze, attention] dirigir (**at, to** a) **2** (= give directions to) **can you ~ me to the station?** ¿me puede indicar cómo llegar a la estación? **3** (= control) [+ traffic, play, film] dirigir **4** (= instruct) **to ~ sb to do sth** mandar a algn hacer algo **(D)** CPD ➤ **direct debit** pago m a la orden ➤ **direct object** complemento m directo ➤ **direct speech** (esp Brit), **direct discourse** (US) estilo m directo
direction [daɪˈrekʃən] N **1** (= course) dirección f; **in the ~ of** hacia, en dirección a; **sense of ~** sentido m de la orientación; **in the opposite ~** en sentido contrario; **in all ~s** por todos lados; **they ran off in different ~s** salieron corriendo cada uno por su lado **2** (fig) (= purpose) orientación f; (= control) mando m; [of play, film] dirección f **3 directions** (= instructions) instrucciones fpl; (to a place) señas fpl; **~s for use** modo m de empleo, instrucciones fpl de uso
directive [dɪˈrektɪv] N directiva f
directly [dɪˈrektlɪ] **(A)** ADV **1** (= not in a roundabout way) [go, fly, look, pay, affect] directamente; **the two murders are not ~ related** or **linked** los dos asesinatos no están directamente relacionados; **to be ~ descended from sb** descender directamente de algn, descender de algn por línea directa **2** (= exactly) justo; **~ above/below sth/sb** justo encima de/ debajo de algo/algn; **~ opposite sth/sb** justo enfrente de algo/algn; **I hold you ~ responsible for this!** ¡te considero el responsable directo de esto! **3** (= immediately) inmediatamente; **~ after/before sth** inmediatamente después de/antes de algo **4** (= shortly) enseguida, de inmediato; **she will be here ~** vendrá enseguida or de inmediato **5** (= frankly) [speak, explain] con franqueza **(B)** CONJ (esp Brit) en cuanto; **he heard the door close he picked up the telephone** en cuanto oyó cerrarse la puerta cogió el teléfono; **~ you hear it, ...** en cuanto lo oigas, ...
directness [daɪˈrektnɪs] N [of person, speech] franqueza f
director [daɪˈrektər] N [of company] (= business executive) directivo/a m/f; (= board member) miembro mf del consejo de administración, consejero/a m/f; [of institution, department, play, film] director(a) m/f; (US Mus) director(a) m/f; **board of ~s** junta f directiva, consejo m de administración ➤ **director general** director(a) m/f general

➤ **Director of Public Prosecutions** (*Brit*) ≈ Fiscal *mf* General del Estado

directorship [dɪ'rektəʃɪp] N (= *post*) dirección *f*, cargo *m* de director; (= *term as director*) gerencia *f*, periodo *m* de gestión

directory [dɪ'rektərɪ] N (*also* **telephone ~**) guía *f* (telefónica); (= *street directory*) callejero *m*, guía *f* de calles; (*Comput*) directorio *m* ➤ **directory assistance** (*US*), **directory enquiries** (*Brit*) información *f* (telefónica)

dirge [dɜːdʒ] N canto *m* fúnebre, endecha *f*

dirt [dɜːt] **A** N **1** (= *filth*) suciedad *f*; ✦ IDIOMS **to dig up ~ on sb** sacar los trapos sucios de algn; **to treat sb like ~*** tratar a algn como si fuese basura, tratar a patadas a algn **2** (= *earth*) tierra *f*; (= *mud*) barro *m*, lodo *m* **3** (*) (= *obscenities*) porquerías *fpl*, cochinadas* *fpl*; **this book is nothing but ~** este libro está lleno de porquerías *or* cochinadas* **B** CPD ➤ **dirt farmer*** (*US*) pequeño granjero *m* (sin obreros) ➤ **dirt road** (*US*) camino *m* de tierra ➤ **dirt track** (*Sport*) pista *f* de ceniza; (= *road*) camino *m* de tierra

dirt-cheap* ['dɜːt'tʃiːp] ADJ tirado de precio*, baratísimo, regalado

dirty ['dɜːtɪ] **A** ADJ (*compar* **dirtier**; *superl* **dirtiest**) **1** [*hands, clothes, dishes, job*] sucio; **your hands are ~** tienes las manos sucias; **to get (o.s.) ~** ensuciarse; **to get sth ~** ensuciar algo; **to get one's hands ~** ensuciarse *or* mancharse las manos; **there was a ~ mark on his shirt** tenía una mancha en la camisa; ✦ IDIOM **to wash one's ~ linen** *or* (*US*) **air one's ~ laundry in public** sacar los trapos sucios a relucir **2** (= *dull*) [*grey, white*] sucio **3** (= *indecent*) [*story, joke*] verde, colorado (*Mex*); [*book*] cochino*, de guarrerías (*Sp**); [*magazine, film*] porno*; [*laugh*] lascivo; **to have a ~ mind** tener una mente pervertida, tener una mente guarra (*Sp**) **4** (*= *underhand*) sucio; **~ business** negocio *m* sucio; **~ money** dinero *m* sucio; **there are some ~ players in the team** algunos de los miembros del equipo juegan sucio; **a ~ trick** una mala pasada, una jugarreta*; **to play a ~ trick on sb** jugar una mala pasada a algn, hacer una jugarreta a algn*; **~ tricks** chanchullos *mpl*; **~ war** guerra *f* sucia; **he always gets other people to do his ~ work** siempre consigue que los demás le hagan el trabajo sucio **5** (*) (= *despicable*) asqueroso*, de mierda***; **you ~ rat!**** ¡canalla!**, ¡cerdo!** **6** (*) (= *angry*) **to give sb a ~ look** echar una mirada asesina a algn* **B** ADV **1** (= *unfairly*) **to fight ~** [*boxer*] no luchar limpiamente; **to play ~** [*footballer*] jugar sucio **2** (= *indecently*) **to talk ~** decir cochinadas*, decir guarrerías (*Sp**) **C** VT ensuciar **D** N ✦ IDIOM **to do the ~ on sb** (*Brit**) jugar una mala pasada a algn, hacer una jugarreta a algn* **E** CPD ➤ **dirty dog**†* tipo *m* asqueroso*, tío *m* guarro (*Sp**) ➤ **dirty old man** viejo *m* verde ➤ **dirty weekend*** (*Brit hum*) fin *m* de semana de lujuria ➤ **dirty word** palabrota *f*, lisura *f* (*And, SC*); **communism has become almost a ~ word** "comunismo" se ha convertido casi en una palabrota

dirty-minded [,dɜːtɪ'maɪndɪd] ADJ con la mente sucia

disability [,dɪsə'bɪlɪtɪ] **A** N **1** (= *state*) invalidez *f*, discapacidad *f*, minusvalía *f*; (= *handicap*) discapacidad *f*, minusvalía *f*; **people with a ~** los discapacitados, los minusválidos **2** (*fig*) desventaja *f* **B** CPD ➤ **disability allowance** subsidio *m* por incapacidad laboral

disable [dɪs'eɪbl] VT [+ *person*] dejar inválido; [+ *tank, gun, device*] inutilizar

disabled [dɪs'eɪbld] **A** ADJ [*person*] minusválido, discapacitado **B** NPL **the ~** los discapacitados, los minusválidos

disabuse [,dɪsə'bjuːz] VT desengañar (**of** de); **I was rapidly ~d of this notion** pronto me desengañé de esta idea, pronto salí del error

disadvantage [,dɪsəd'vɑːntɪdʒ] **A** N desventaja *f*, inconveniente *m*; **to be at a ~** estar en desventaja, estar en una situación desventajosa; **this put him at a ~** esto lo dejó en situación desventajosa **B** VT perjudicar

disadvantaged [,dɪsəd'vɑːntɪdʒd] **A** ADJ [*person*] perjudicado; **she comes from a ~ background** proviene de un entorno desfavorecido **B** NPL **the ~** los menos favorecidos, los marginados

disaffected [,dɪsə'fektɪd] ADJ desafecto (**towards** hacia)

disaffection [,dɪsə'fekʃən] N descontento *m*, desafección *f*

disagree [,dɪsə'griː] VI **1** (= *have different opinion*) no estar de acuerdo, estar en desacuerdo; **I ~ with you** no estoy de acuerdo contigo, no comparto tu opinión **2** (*esp Brit*) (= *disapprove*) **I ~ with bullfighting** yo no apruebo los toros, no me gustan los toros **3** (= *quarrel*) reñir, discutir (**with** con) **4** (= *not coincide*) [*accounts, versions*] diferir, no cuadrar (**with** con); **their findings ~** sus conclusiones difieren **5** (= *upset*) **to ~ with sb** [*climate, food*] sentar mal a algn; **onions ~ with me** las cebollas me sientan mal

disagreeable [,dɪsə'griːəbl] ADJ desagradable

disagreement [,dɪsə'griːmənt] N **1** (*with opinion*) desacuerdo *m*, disconformidad *f*; **the talks ended in ~** no se alcanzó un acuerdo *or* no hubo acuerdo en las conversaciones **2** (= *quarrel*) riña *f*, discusión *f* **3** (*between accounts, versions*) discrepancia *f* (**with** con)

disallow ['dɪsə'laʊ] VT **1** [+ *claim*] rechazar **2** (*Ftbl*) [+ *goal*] anular **3** (*Jur*) [+ *evidence*] desestimar, rechazar

disappear [,dɪsə'pɪəʳ] VI desaparecer; **he ~ed from view** desapareció de la vista; **to make sth ~** hacer desaparecer algo

disappearance [,dɪsə'pɪərəns] N desaparición *f*

disappoint [,dɪsə'pɔɪnt] VT defraudar, decepcionar, desilusionar

disappointed [,dɪsə'pɔɪntɪd] ADJ decepcionado, desilusionado; **she'll be terribly ~** se llevará una gran decepción *or* una desilusión muy grande; **she's ~ about** *or* **at having to give up her career** siente mucho tener que dejar su carrera; **I'm ~ in you** me has defraudado, me has decepcionado; **I was ~ that my mother was not there** me sentí defraudado porque mi madre no estaba allí, me decepcionó (el) que mi madre no estuviera allí; **we were ~ not to see her** sentimos mucho no verla; **they are ~ with the result** están decepcionados con el resultado, el resultado los ha decepcionado; **if you see him on stage you won't be ~** si lo ves actuar no te defraudará *or* decepcionará

disappointing [,dɪsə'pɔɪntɪŋ] ADJ decepcionante; **it's ~ that nobody wants to help** es decepcionante que nadie quiera ayudar; **the film/hotel was very ~** la película/el hotel fue una decepción; **how ~!** ¡qué decepción!, ¡qué desilusión!

disappointment [,dɪsə'pɔɪntmənt] N (= *feeling*) decepción *f*, desilusión *f*; **to our ~** para nuestra decepción, para nuestra gran desilusión; **he is a big ~ to us** nos ha decepcionado muchísimo; **the holiday was such a ~!** ¡las vacaciones fueron una decepción tan grande! *or* fueron tan decepcionantes!

disapproval [,dɪsə'pruːvəl] N desaprobación *f*

disapprove [,dɪsə'pruːv] VI **to ~ of sth** estar en contra de algo, desaprobar algo; **to ~ of sb** mirar mal a algn, no mirar con buenos ojos a algn; **I think he ~s of me** creo que me tiene poca simpatía; **your mother would ~** tu madre estaría en contra *or* lo desaprobaría

disapproving [,dɪsə'pruːvɪŋ] ADJ [*look, glance*] de desaprobación

disarm [dɪs'ɑːm] **A** VT **1** [+ *troops, attacker*] desarmar (*also fig*) **2** [+ *bomb*] desactivar **B** VI (*Mil*) desarmarse

disarmament [dɪs'ɑːməmənt] N desarme *m*

disarming [dɪs'ɑːmɪŋ] ADJ [*smile, modesty*] que desarma, encantador; [*frankness*] apabullante

disarray [,dɪsə'reɪ] N (*frm*) [*of house, flat*] desorden *m*; [*of clothes*] desaliño *m*; [*of institution, economy, government*] desorganización *f*; **to be in ~** [*house, flat, thoughts*] estar en desorden; [*clothes*] estar muy desarreglado *or* desaliñado; [*institution, economy, government*] estar sumido en el caos, estar totalmente desorganizado; **this threw our plans into ~**

esto dio al traste con nuestros planes

disassociate [ˌdɪsəˈsəʊʃɪˌeɪt] = **dissociate**

disaster [dɪˈzɑːstəʳ] N desastre *m* ➤ **disaster area** zona *f* catastrófica, zona *f* de desastre; **he's a walking ~ area** (*hum*) es un puro desastre ➤ **disaster fund** fondo *m* de ayuda para casos de desastre

disastrous [dɪˈzɑːstrəs] ADJ 1 (= *catastrophic*) [*decision, reforms*] desastroso, catastrófico; [*earthquake, flood*] catastrófico 2 (*) (= *unsuccessful*) desastroso; **his first movie was ~** su primera película fue desastrosa *or* un desastre

disband [dɪsˈbænd] Ⓐ VT [+ *army*] licenciar; [+ *organization*] disolver Ⓑ VI disolverse

disbelief [ˌdɪsbəˈliːf] N incredulidad *f*; **in ~ con** incredulidad

disbelieve [ˌdɪsbəˈliːv] VT [+ *person*] no creer a; [+ *story*] no creer

disc, disk (*US*) [dɪsk] N (*gen, also Anat*) disco *m*; (= *identity disc*) chapa *f* ➤ **disc brakes** (*Aut*) frenos *mpl* de disco ➤ **disc jockey** discjockey *mf*, pinchadiscos *mf inv* (*Sp**)

discard [dɪsˈkɑːd] VT [+ *unwanted thing*] deshacerse de; [+ *idea, plan*] desechar, descartar; [+ *clothing, person*] desembarazarse de

discern [dɪˈsɜːn] VT (= *make out*) distinguir; [+ *sb's intentions*] discernir

discernible [dɪˈsɜːnəbl] ADJ 1 (= *perceptible*) [*difference*] perceptible, apreciable; [*effect*] apreciable 2 (= *visible*) distinguible

discerning [dɪˈsɜːnɪŋ] ADJ [*person*] entendido, experto; **~ taste** muy buen gusto *m*

discernment [dɪˈsɜːnmənt] N (= *good judgment*) discernimiento *m*; (= *good taste*) buen gusto *m*

discharge Ⓐ [ˈdɪstʃɑːdʒ] N 1 [*of gun*] descarga *f*, disparo *m*
2 (= *release*) [*of patient*] alta *f*; [*of prisoner*] liberación *f*, puesta *f* en libertad; **he got his ~** (*Mil*) lo licenciaron

---

Use **el/un** not **la/una** before feminine nouns beginning with stressed **a** or **ha** like **alta**.

---

3 (= *dismissal*) [*of worker*] despido *m*; (*Mil*) baja *f*
4 (= *emission*) (*Elec*) descarga *f*; [*of liquid, waste*] vertido *m*; [*of gas, chemicals*] emisión *f*; (*Med*) secreción *f*, supuración *f*
5 (= *completion*) [*of duty*] ejercicio *m*, cumplimiento *m*
Ⓑ [dɪsˈtʃɑːdʒ] VT 1 (= *fire*) [+ *gun*] descargar, disparar
2 (= *release*) [+ *patient*] dar de alta, dar el alta a; [+ *prisoner*] liberar, poner en libertad
3 (= *dismiss*) [+ *employee*] despedir; [+ *soldier*] dar de baja del ejército
4 (= *emit*) [+ *liquid, waste*] verter; [+ *gas, chemicals*] emitir
5 (= *complete*) [+ *task, duty*] cumplir
6 (= *unload*) [+ *ship, cargo*] descargar

disciple [dɪˈsaɪpl] N discípulo/a *m/f*

disciplinarian [ˌdɪsɪplɪˈnɛərɪən] N **he was a strict ~** imponía una férrea disciplina (en el cumplimiento de las normas)

disciplinary [ˈdɪsɪplɪnərɪ] ADJ disciplinario

discipline [ˈdɪsɪplɪn] Ⓐ N disciplina *f* Ⓑ VT 1 (= *punish*) [+ *pupil, soldier*] castigar; [+ *employee*] sancionar
2 (= *control*) [+ *child*] disciplinar; **to ~ o.s. (to do sth)** disciplinarse (para hacer algo)

disclaim [dɪsˈkleɪm] VT [+ *statement*] desmentir, negar; [+ *responsibility*] negar; **he ~ed all knowledge of it** dijo que no sabía nada en absoluto de ello

disclaimer [dɪsˈkleɪməʳ] N (= *denial*) desmentido *m*; **to issue a ~** declarar descargo *or* limitación de responsabilidad

disclose [dɪsˈkləʊz] VT revelar

disclosure [dɪsˈkləʊʒəʳ] N revelación *f*

disco* [ˈdɪskəʊ] N ABBR (= **discotheque**) disco *f*, discoteca *f*

discolour, discolor (*US*) [dɪsˈkʌləʳ] Ⓐ VT (= *fade*) de(s)colorar; (= *stain*) manchar Ⓑ VI (= *lose colour*) de(s)colorarse; (= *run*) desteñir

discomfort [dɪsˈkʌmfət] N (*mental*) incomodidad *f*, turbación *f*; (*physical*) molestia *f*, malestar *m*; **the injury gave him some ~** la herida le causaba molestia

disconcert [ˌdɪskənˈsɜːt] VT desconcertar

disconcerting [ˌdɪskənˈsɜːtɪŋ] ADJ desconcertante

disconnect [ˌdɪskəˈnekt] VT 1 (*gen*) desconectar 2 (*Telec*) **I've been ~ed** (*for non-payment*) me han cortado el teléfono *or* la línea (por no pagar)

disconnected [ˌdɪskəˈnektɪd] ADJ (= *unrelated*) inconexo

disconsolate [dɪsˈkɒnsəlɪt] ADJ desconsolado

discontent [ˌdɪskənˈtent] N descontento *m*, malestar *m*

discontented [ˌdɪskənˈtentɪd] ADJ descontento (**with, about** con)

discontinue [ˌdɪskənˈtɪnjuː] VT [+ *production, payment*] suspender; [+ *practice*] abandonar; (*Comm*) [+ *product*] dejar de fabricar; (*Med*) [+ *treatment*] interrumpir, suspender; **"discontinued"** (*Comm*) "fin de serie"

discord [ˈdɪskɔːd] N discordia *f*

discordant [dɪsˈkɔːdənt] ADJ [*ideas, opinions*] discorde, opuesto; [*sound*] disonante

discotheque [ˈdɪskəʊtek] N discoteca *f*

discount Ⓐ [ˈdɪskaʊnt] N (*gen*) descuento *m*, rebaja *f*; **to give a 10% ~** dar un descuento del 10%; **to sell (sth) at a ~** vender (algo) con descuento *or* a precio reducido
Ⓑ [dɪsˈkaʊnt] VT 1 [+ *merchandise*] descontar, rebajar
2 (= *disregard*) [+ *report, rumour*] descartar Ⓒ [ˈdɪskaʊnt] CPD ➤ **discount store** (*US*) economato *m*

discourage [dɪsˈkʌrɪdʒ] VT 1 (= *dishearten*) desanimar, desalentar; **to get** *or* **become ~d** desanimarse, desalentarse
2 (= *deter*) [+ *tendency, relationship*] oponerse a
3 (= *dissuade*) **to ~ sb from doing sth** disuadir a algn de hacer algo; **I don't want to ~ you, but ...** no pretendo disuadirte *or* desanimarte, pero ...

discouragement [dɪsˈkʌrɪdʒmənt] N 1 (= *depression*) desánimo *m*, desaliento *m* 2 (= *dissuasion*) disuasión *f*
3 (= *deterrent*) impedimento *m*

discouraging [dɪsˈkʌrɪdʒɪŋ] ADJ desalentador

discourse Ⓐ [ˈdɪskɔːs] N 1 (= *talk*) conversación *f*, plática *f* (*LAm*) 2 (= *essay*) tratado *m* 3 (*Ling*) discurso *m* Ⓑ [dɪsˈkɔːs] VI **to ~ (up)on sth** disertar sobre algo

discourteous [dɪsˈkɜːtɪəs] ADJ descortés

discover [dɪsˈkʌvəʳ] VT 1 [+ *new country, species, talent*] descubrir; [+ *object*] (*after search*) encontrar, hallar
2 (= *notice*) darse cuenta de; **to ~ that** darse cuenta de que

discovery [dɪsˈkʌvərɪ] N descubrimiento *m*

discredit [dɪsˈkredɪt] Ⓐ N (= *dishonour*) descrédito *m*, deshonor *m*; **it was to the general's ~ that ...** fue un descrédito para el general que ...; **to bring ~ (up)on sth/sb** desacreditar algo/a algn, suponer un descrédito para algo/algn Ⓑ VT 1 (= *prove untrue*) [+ *theory*] rebatir, refutar
2 (= *cast doubt upon*) poner en duda 3 (= *sully reputation of*) [+ *family*] deshonrar, desacreditar; [+ *organization, profession*] desacreditar

discreet [dɪsˈkriːt] ADJ discreto; **at a ~ distance** a una distancia prudencial

discreetly [dɪsˈkriːtlɪ] ADV discretamente, con discreción

discrepancy [dɪsˈkrepənsɪ] N discrepancia *f* (**between** entre)

discrete [dɪsˈkriːt] ADJ específico, separado

discretion [dɪsˈkreʃən] N 1 (= *tact*) discreción *f*
2 (= *judgment*) criterio *m*, juicio *m*; **use your own ~** usa tu propio criterio *or* juicio; **at the ~ of the judge** a discreción *or* a criterio del juez

discretionary [dɪsˈkreʃənərɪ] ADJ discrecional

discriminate [dɪsˈkrɪmɪneɪt] VI 1 (= *show prejudice*) **to ~ against sb** discriminar a algn; **to ~ in favour of sb** discriminar positivamente a algn 2 (= *distinguish*) distinguir (**between** entre)

discriminating [dɪsˈkrɪmɪneɪtɪŋ] ADJ [*person*] entendido; [*taste*] refinado

discrimination [dɪsˌkrɪmɪˈneɪʃən] N 1 (= *prejudice*)

discriminación f (**against** de, contra; **in favour of** a favor de) **2** (= *good judgment*) buen criterio m, discernimiento m

discus ['dɪskəs] N (= *object*) disco m; **to throw the ~** lanzar el disco; **she won a gold medal in the ~** ganó la medalla de oro en la prueba de disco

discuss [dɪs'kʌs] VT **1** (= *talk about*) [+ *topic*] hablar de, discutir; [+ *person*] hablar de; [+ *problem, essay*] cambiar opiniones sobre, discutir **2** (*in exam question*) [+ *statement*] tratar, analizar

discussion [dɪs'kʌʃən] N discusión f; **we had a long ~ about it** hablamos largo y tendido de ello, tuvimos una larga discusión sobre ello; **it is under ~** se está discutiendo ➤ **discussion document** proposición f (para el debate) ➤ **discussion group** coloquio m

disdain [dɪs'deɪn] Ⓐ N desdén m, desprecio m Ⓑ VT desdeñar, despreciar

disdainful [dɪs'deɪnfʊl] ADJ [*look, expression, attitude*] desdeñoso, de desdén; **to be ~ towards sb** desdeñar or despreciar a algn, mostrar desdén or desprecio hacia algn

disease [dɪ'ziːz] N enfermedad f

diseased [dɪ'ziːzd] ADJ enfermo

disembark [ˌdɪsɪm'bɑːk] VT, VI desembarcar

disembodied [ˌdɪsɪm'bɒdɪd] ADJ incorpóreo

disembowel [ˌdɪsɪm'baʊəl] VT desentrañar, destripar

disenchanted [ˌdɪsɪn'tʃɑːntɪd] ADJ desencantado, desilusionado (**with** con)

disenfranchise [ˌdɪsɪn'fræntʃaɪz] VT privar del derecho de voto

disengage [ˌdɪsɪn'geɪdʒ] VT (= *free*) soltar; **she ~d her hand (from his)** soltó su mano (de la de él) con suavidad; **to ~ the clutch** desembragar, soltar el embrague

disfavour, disfavor (*US*) [dɪs'feɪvəʳ] N (= *disapproval*) desaprobación f; **to fall into ~** [*custom, practice*] caer en desuso; [*person*] caer en desgracia; [*pet, child*] estar castigado; **to look with ~ on sth** ver algo con malos ojos, desaprobar algo

disfigure [dɪs'fɪgəʳ] VT desfigurar

disgrace [dɪs'greɪs] Ⓐ N **1** (= *state of shame*) deshonra f, ignominia f; **to be in ~** [*adult*] estar totalmente desacreditado, haber caído en desgracia; [*pet, child*] estar castigado; **to bring ~ on** deshonrar **2** (= *shameful thing*) vergüenza f; **it's a ~** es una vergüenza; **you're a ~!** ¡lo tuyo es una vergüenza!; **to be a ~ to the school/family** ser una deshonra para la escuela/la familia Ⓑ VT [+ *family, country*] deshonrar; **he ~d himself** se deshonró

disgraceful [dɪs'greɪsfʊl] ADJ vergonzoso; **disgraceful!** ¡qué vergüenza!

disgracefully [dɪs'greɪsfəlɪ] ADV vergonzosamente

disgruntled [dɪs'grʌntld] ADJ (= *unhappy*) [*employee, staff, customer*] descontento; (= *bad-tempered*) contrariado, malhumorado

disguise [dɪs'gaɪz] Ⓐ N disfraz m; **to be in ~** estar disfrazado Ⓑ VT [+ *person*] disfrazar (**as** de); [+ *voice*] simular, cambiar; [+ *feelings*] ocultar, disimular; **to ~ o.s. as** disfrazarse de

disgust [dɪs'gʌst] Ⓐ N **1** (= *revulsion*) repugnancia f, asco m; **it fills me with ~** me da asco **2** (= *anger*) indignación f; **she left in ~** se marchó indignada Ⓑ VT dar asco a, repugnar; **you ~ me** me das asco

⚠️ **disgust** ≠ *disgustar*

disgusted [dɪs'gʌstɪd] ADJ [*viewer, reader, customer*] indignado; [*tone, voice*] de indignación; **I am ~ at the way we were treated** estoy indignado por la manera en que nos trataron

disgusting [dɪs'gʌstɪŋ] ADJ **1** (= *revolting*) [*habit, smell, food, place*] asqueroso, repugnante; [*person*] repugnante; **you're ~** me das asco, eres repugnante **2** (= *obscene*) [*book, film, photo*] repugnante, asqueroso; [*language*] indecente, cochino* **3** (= *disgraceful*) [*attitude, behaviour, manners*] vergonzoso **4** (*) (= *terrible*) [*weather*] asqueroso, de perros*

disgustingly [dɪs'gʌstɪŋlɪ] ADV asquerosamente; **it was ~**

dirty estaba asquerosamente sucio, estaba tan sucio que daba asco

dish [dɪʃ] Ⓐ N **1** (= *plate*) plato m; (= *serving dish*) fuente f; (= *food*) plato m, platillo m (*Mex*); **to wash** or **do the ~es** fregar los platos **2** (*TV*) antena f parabólica **3** (*) (= *girl, boy*) bombón* m Ⓑ CPD ➤ **dish aerial** (*Brit*), **dish antenna** (*US*) antena f parabólica ➤ **dish soap** (*US*) lavavajillas m inv ➤ **dish towel** (*US*) paño m de cocina, trapo m
➤ **dish out** VT + ADV [+ *food*] servir; [+ *money*] repartir; [+ *punishment*] infligir, impartir
➤ **dish up** Ⓐ VT + ADV **1** [+ *food*] servir **2** (= *present*) ofrecer Ⓑ VI + ADV servir

dishcloth ['dɪʃklɒθ] N (*pl* **~s** ['dɪʃklɒðz]) (*for washing*) bayeta f; (*for drying*) paño m (de cocina), trapo m

dishearten [dɪs'hɑːtn] VT desalentar, desanimar; **don't be ~ed!** ¡ánimo!, ¡no te desanimes!

disheartening [dɪs'hɑːtnɪŋ] ADJ desalentador

dishevelled, disheveled (*US*) [dɪ'ʃevəld] ADJ [*hair*] despeinado; [*clothes*] desarreglado, desaliñado

dishonest [dɪs'ɒnɪst] ADJ poco honrado, deshonesto

dishonestly [dɪs'ɒnɪstlɪ] ADV fraudulentamente, deshonestamente; **to act ~** obrar con poca honradez or de forma poco honrada

dishonesty [dɪs'ɒnɪstɪ] N falta f de honradez, deshonestidad f

dishonour, dishonor (*US*) [dɪs'ɒnəʳ] Ⓐ N deshonra f, deshonor m Ⓑ VT [+ *country, family*] deshonrar

dishonourable, dishonorable (*US*) [dɪs'ɒnərəbl] ADJ deshonroso ➤ **dishonorable discharge** (*US Mil*) baja f por conducta deshonrosa

dishrack ['dɪʃræk] N escurreplatos m inv, escurridor m

dishwasher ['dɪʃwɒʃəʳ] N (= *machine*) lavaplatos m inv, lavavajillas m inv

dishwashing liquid ['dɪʃwɒʃɪŋˌlɪkwɪd] N (*US*) lavavajillas m inv*

dishy* ['dɪʃɪ] ADJ (*compar* **dishier**; *superl* **dishiest**) (*Brit*) guapísimo; **he's/she's really ~** está buenísimo/a

disillusion [ˌdɪsɪ'luːʒən] Ⓐ N desilusión f; (*more intense*) desencanto m Ⓑ VT desilusionar; (*more intensely*) desencantar

disillusionment [ˌdɪsɪ'luːʒənmənt] N desilusión f; (*more intense*) desencanto m

disincentive [ˌdɪsɪn'sentɪv] N factor m desmotivador (**to** para)

disinclination [ˌdɪsɪnklɪ'neɪʃən] N poca disposición f (**to do sth** a hacer algo); **they showed a marked ~ to compromise** se mostraron manifiestamente reacios a comprometerse

disinclined ['dɪsɪn'klaɪnd] ADJ (*frm*) **to be ~ to do sth** estar poco dispuesto a hacer algo, ser reacio a hacer algo

disinfect [ˌdɪsɪn'fekt] VT desinfectar

disinfectant [ˌdɪsɪn'fektənt] N desinfectante m

disinformation [ˌdɪsɪnfə'meɪʃən] N desinformación f

disingenuous [ˌdɪsɪn'dʒenjʊəs] ADJ falso, poco sincero

disinherit ['dɪsɪn'herɪt] VT desheredar

disintegrate [dɪs'ɪntɪgreɪt] VI desintegrarse

disinterested [dɪs'ɪntrɪstɪd] ADJ (= *impartial*) desinteresado, imparcial

disjointed [dɪs'dʒɔɪntɪd] ADJ inconexo, deslavazado

disk [dɪsk] Ⓐ N **1** (*esp US*) (*gen, also Anat*) disco m; (= *identity disk*) chapa f **2** (*Comput*) disco m; **single-/double-sided ~** disco m de una cara/dos caras Ⓑ CPD ➤ **disk drive** unidad f de disco ➤ **disk space** espacio m disponible en disco

diskette [dɪs'ket] N disquete m, diskette m

dislike [dɪs'laɪk] Ⓐ N **1** (= *antipathy*) aversión f, antipatía f (**of** a, hacia); **to take a ~ to sb** coger or (*LAm*) tomar antipatía a algn
2 (= *thing disliked*) **likes and ~s** aficiones fpl y fobias or manías, cosas fpl que gustan y cosas que no Ⓑ VT [+ *person*] tener antipatía a; (*more intensely*) tener

aversión a; **I ~ her intensely** le tengo mucha antipatía *or* auténtica aversión; **it's not that I ~ him** no es que me caiga mal, no es que yo le tenga antipatía; **I ~ pop music** no me gusta la música pop

dislocate [ˈdɪsləʊkeɪt] VT dislocarse; **he ~d his shoulder** se dislocó el hombro

dislodge [dɪsˈlɒdʒ] VT **1** [+ *stone, obstruction*] sacar; [+ *party, ruler*] desbancar **2** (= *cause to fall*) hacer caer

disloyal [ˈdɪsˈlɔɪəl] ADJ desleal (**to** con)

dismal [ˈdɪzməl] ADJ **1** (= *gloomy, depressing*) [*weather*] deprimente; [*place*] sombrío, deprimente; [*day*] sombrío **2** (= *poor*) [*performance, condition*] pésimo; **my prospects of getting a job are ~/pretty ~** mis posibilidades de conseguir un trabajo son ínfimas/bastante escasas; **a ~ failure** un rotundo fracaso

dismantle [dɪsˈmæntl] VT [+ *machine*] desmontar, desarmar; [+ *system, organization*] desmantelar

dismay [dɪsˈmeɪ] **Ⓐ** N consternación *f*; **(much) to my ~** para (gran) consternación mía; **in ~** consternado **Ⓑ** VT consternar; **I am ~ed to hear that ...** me da pena *or* me produce consternación enterarme de que ...

dismember [dɪsˈmembəʳ] VT desmembrar

dismiss [dɪsˈmɪs] VT **1** [+ *worker*] despedir; [+ *official*] destituir; **to be ~ed from the service** (*Mil*) ser dado de baja, ser separado del servicio **2** (= *send away*) despachar; [+ *troops*] dar permiso para irse; **class ~ed!** eso es todo por hoy **3** (= *reject*) [+ *thought*] rechazar, apartar de sí; [+ *request*] rechazar; [+ *possibility*] descartar, desechar **4** (*Jur*) [+ *appeal*] desestimar, rechazar; **the case was ~ed** el tribunal absolvió al acusado

dismissal [dɪsˈmɪsəl] N **1** [*of worker*] despido *m*; [*of official*] destitución *f* **2** [*of suggestion, idea*] rechazo *m*

dismissive [dɪsˈmɪsɪv] ADJ [*gesture, wave, attitude*] despectivo, desdeñoso; **he was very ~ about it** parecía no tomar la cosa en serio

dismount [dɪsˈmaʊnt] VI desmontar

disobedience [ˌdɪsəˈbiːdɪəns] N desobediencia *f*

disobedient [ˌdɪsəˈbiːdɪənt] ADJ desobediente

disobey [ˈdɪsəˈbeɪ] VT, VI desobedecer

disorder [dɪsˈɔːdəʳ] N **1** (= *confusion*) desorden *m*; **to be in ~** estar en desorden **2** (= *rioting*) disturbios *mpl* **3** (*Med*) dolencia *f*, trastorno *m*; **mental ~** trastorno *m* mental

disorderly [dɪsˈɔːdəlɪ] ADJ [*room, queue*] desordenado; [*behaviour*] indisciplinado, turbulento; [*crowd*] indisciplinado, alborotado **➤ disorderly conduct** (*Jur*) alteración *f* del orden público

disorganized [dɪsˈɔːɡənaɪzd] ADJ desorganizado

disorient [dɪsˈɔːrɪent] VT desorientar

disorientate [dɪsˈɔːrɪənteɪt] VT desorientar

disown [dɪsˈəʊn] VT **1** [+ *son, wife*] desconocer, repudiar **2** (= *deny*) [+ *responsibility*] negar

disparaging [dɪsˈpærɪdʒɪŋ] ADJ [*remark*] despectivo; **to be ~ about sth/sb** menospreciar algo/a algn

disparate [ˈdɪspərɪt] ADJ dispar

disparity [dɪsˈpærɪtɪ] N disparidad *f*

dispassionate [dɪsˈpæʃnɪt] ADJ (= *unbiased*) imparcial; (= *unemotional*) [*voice, tone*] desapasionado

dispatch [dɪsˈpætʃ] **Ⓐ** N **1** [*of goods*] envío *m*, expedición *f* **2** (*in press*) reportaje *m*, informe *m* **Ⓑ** VT **1** [+ *letter, goods*] enviar, expedir; [+ *messenger, troops*] enviar **2** [+ *business*] despachar **3** [+ *duty*] ejercer, realizar **4** (*hum*) [+ *food*] despachar **5** (= *kill*) despachar **Ⓒ** CPD **➤ dispatch box** (*Brit*) cartera *f* **➤ dispatch rider** mensajero/a *m/f* (*con moto*)

dispel [dɪsˈpel] VT disipar

dispensable [dɪsˈpensəbl] ADJ prescindible

dispensary [dɪsˈpensərɪ] N (*gen*) dispensario *m*; (*in hospital*) farmacia *f*

dispensation [ˌdɪspenˈseɪʃən] N exención *f*

dispense [dɪsˈpens] VT [+ *food, money*] repartir; [+ *drug, prescription*] despachar; [+ *justice*] administrar; **this machine ~s coffee** esta máquina expende café

➤ dispense with VI + PREP **1** (= *do without*) prescindir de **2** (= *get rid of*) deshacerse de

dispenser [dɪsˈpensəʳ] N **1** (= *person*) farmacéutico/a *m/f* **2** (= *container*) (*for soap*) dosificador *m*; (= *machine*) distribuidor *m* automático, máquina *f* expendedora

dispensing chemist [dɪsˈpensɪŋˈkemɪst] N (= *shop*) farmacia *f*; (= *person*) farmacéutico/a *m/f*

dispersal [dɪsˈpɜːsəl] N dispersión *f*

disperse [dɪsˈpɜːs] **Ⓐ** VT dispersar **Ⓑ** VI [*crowd, army, troops*] dispersarse; [*mist*] disiparse

dispirited [dɪsˈpɪrɪtɪd] ADJ desanimado, desalentado

displace [dɪsˈpleɪs] VT **1** (= *force to leave home*) desplazar **2** (= *remove from office*) destituir **3** [+ *liquid*] desplazar

displacement [dɪsˈpleɪsmənt] N **1** (= *forced relocation*) desplazamiento *m* **2** (= *dismissal*) destitución *f* **3** [*of liquid*] desplazamiento *m*

display [dɪsˈpleɪ] **Ⓐ** N **1** (= *act of displaying*) [*of merchandise*] exposición *f*; (*in gallery, museum*) exposición *f*, exhibición *f*; [*of emotion, interest*] manifestación *f*, demostración *f*; [*of force*] despliegue *m*; **to be on ~** estar expuesto **2** (= *array*) [*of merchandise*] muestrario *m*, surtido *m*; (*in gallery, museum*) exposición *f*; **window ~** (*in shop*) escaparate *m* **3** (= *show*) (*Mil*) exhibición *f*, demostración *f*; **a firework(s) ~** fuegos *mpl* artificiales **4** (= *ostentation*) **the party made a ~ of unity** el partido se esforzó en dar una imagen de unidad **5** (*Comput*) (= *screen*) visualizador *m*; (= *act*) visualización *f* **Ⓑ** VT **1** [+ *goods, painting, exhibit*] exponer, exhibir; [+ *notice, results*] exponer, hacer público **2** [+ *emotion, ignorance*] mostrar, manifestar; [+ *courage*] demostrar, hacer gala de **3** (*Comput*) visualizar **Ⓒ** CPD **➤ display case** vitrina *f*

displease [dɪsˈpliːz] VT (= *annoy*) disgustar

displeased [dɪsˈpliːzd] ADJ **to be ~** estar disgustado (**at, with** con)

displeasure [dɪsˈpleʒəʳ] N disgusto *m*

disposable [dɪsˈpəʊzəbl] ADJ **1** [*nappy*] desechable, de usar y tirar; **~ goods** productos *mpl* desechables *or* no reutilizables **2** (= *available*) disponible; **~ assets** activos *mpl* disponibles; **~ income** renta *f* disponible

disposal [dɪsˈpəʊzəl] N **1** (= *sale, transfer*) [*of goods*] venta *f*; [*of property*] traspaso *m* **2** [*of waste*] eliminación *f*; **refuse ~** eliminación *f* de basuras **3** (= *availability for use*) disposición *f*; **to put sth at sb's ~** poner algo a disposición de algn; **to have sth at one's ~** tener algo a su disposición, disponer de algo

dispose [dɪsˈpəʊz] VT predisponer; **her behaviour did not ~ me to help her** su comportamiento no me predisponía a ayudarla *or* no hacía que me sintiese inclinado a ayudarla **➤ dispose of** VI + PREP **1** (= *get rid of*) [+ *evidence, body*] deshacerse de; [+ *rubbish*] tirar, botar (*LAm*) **2** (= *sell, transfer*) [+ *goods*] vender; [+ *property*] traspasar

disposed [dɪsˈpəʊzd] ADJ **to be ~ to do sth** estar dispuesto a hacer algo; **to be favourably ~ towards sth/sb** tener una disposición favorable hacia algo/algn

disposition [ˌdɪspəˈzɪʃən] N **1** (= *temperament*) carácter *m*, temperamento *m* **2** (= *inclination*) predisposición *f* (**to** a) **3** (= *arrangement*) disposición *f*, colocación *f*

dispossess [ˈdɪspəˈzes] VT [+ *tenant*] desahuciar; **to ~ sb of** desposeer *or* despojar a algn de

disproportion [ˌdɪsprəˈpɔːʃən] N desproporción *f*

disproportionate [ˌdɪsprəˈpɔːʃnɪt] ADJ desproporcionado (**to** en relación con)

disprove [dɪsˈpruːv] VT [+ *theory, argument*] refutar, rebatir; [+ *claim, allegation*] desmentir

dispute [dɪsˈpjuːt] **Ⓐ** N (= *quarrel*) disputa *f*, discusión *f*; (= *debate*) discusión *f*; (= *controversy*) polémica *f*, controversia *f*; (= *industrial dispute*) conflicto *m*; (*Jur*) contencioso *m*; **in** *or* **under ~** [*territory*] en litigio **Ⓑ** VT **1** [+ *statement, claim*] poner en duda; **I ~ that** lo dudo; **I do not ~ the fact that ...** no niego *or* no discuto que ...

2 (= *fight for*) **to ~ possession of a house with sb** tener un contencioso con algn sobre la posesión de una casa; **the final will be ~d between Agassi and Sampras** Agassi y Sampras se disputarán la final

disqualification [dɪsˌkwɒlɪfɪˈkeɪʃən] N **1** (= *act, effect*) inhabilitación *f*; (*Sport*) descalificación *f* **2** (= *thing that disqualifies*) impedimento *m*

disqualify [dɪsˈkwɒlɪfaɪ] VT **to ~ sb (from)** (= *incapacitate*) inhabilitar *or* incapacitar a algn (para); (*Sport*) descalificar a algn (para); **to ~ sb from driving** retirar el permiso de conducir a algn

disquieting [dɪsˈkwaɪətɪŋ] ADJ inquietante

disregard [ˈdɪsrɪˈɡɑːd] **Ⓐ** N (*for feelings, money, danger*) indiferencia *f* (**for** por, hacia); [*of law, rules*] desacato *m* (**of** a, de) **Ⓑ** VT [+ *remark, feelings*] hacer caso omiso de; [+ *authority, duty*] desatender

disrepair [ˈdɪsrɪˈpɛəʳ] N **in a state of ~** en mal estado; **to fall into ~** desmoronarse

disreputable [dɪsˈrepjʊtəbl] ADJ de mala fama

disrepute [ˈdɪsrɪˈpjuːt] N **to bring into ~** desprestigiar; **to fall into ~** desprestigiarse

disrespect [ˈdɪsrɪsˈpekt] N falta *f* de respeto; **I meant no ~** no quería ofenderle

disrespectful [ˌdɪsrɪsˈpektfʊl] ADJ irrespetuoso; **to be ~ to** *or* **towards sb** faltar al respeto a algn

disrupt [dɪsˈrʌpt] VT [+ *meeting, communications etc*] interrumpir; [+ *plans*] alterar, trastocar

disruption [dɪsˈrʌpʃən] N [*of meeting, communications*] interrupción *f*; [*of plans*] alteración *f*

disruptive [dɪsˈrʌptɪv] ADJ perjudicial

dissatisfaction [ˈdɪsˌsætɪsˈfækʃən] N insatisfacción *f* (**with** con)

dissatisfied [ˈdɪsˈsætɪsfaɪd] ADJ descontento, insatisfecho (**with** con); **everyone was ~ with the result** el resultado dejó descontento *or* insatisfecho a todo el mundo

dissect [dɪˈsekt] VT [+ *animal*] disecar; (*fig*) analizar minuciosamente

disseminate [dɪˈsemɪneɪt] VT divulgar, difundir

dissent [dɪˈsent] **Ⓐ** N disentimiento *m*, disconformidad *f*; (*Rel, Pol*) disidencia *f* **Ⓑ** VI disentir (**from** de), estar disconforme (**from** con); (*Rel*) disidir

dissenter [dɪˈsentəʳ] N disidente *mf*

dissenting [dɪˈsentɪŋ] ADJ [*voice*] discrepante

dissertation [ˌdɪsəˈteɪʃən] N disertación *f*; (*US Univ*) tesis *f inv*; (*Brit Univ*) tesina *f*

disservice [ˈdɪsˈsɜːvɪs] N perjuicio *m*; **to do sb a ~** perjudicar a algn

dissident [ˈdɪsɪdənt] ADJ, N disidente *mf*

dissimilar [ˈdɪˈsɪmɪləʳ] ADJ distinto, diferente (**to** de)

dissipate [ˈdɪsɪpeɪt] **Ⓐ** VT **1** [+ *fear, doubt*] disipar **2** [+ *efforts, fortune*] derrochar **Ⓑ** VI disiparse

dissociate [dɪˈsəʊʃɪeɪt] VT disociar (**from** de); **to ~ o.s. from sth/sb** disociarse *or* desligarse de algo/algn

dissolute [ˈdɪsəluːt] ADJ disoluto

dissolution [ˌdɪsəˈluːʃən] N disolución *f*

dissolve [dɪˈzɒlv] **Ⓐ** VT (*gen, Comm*) disolver **Ⓑ** VI disolverse; **it ~s in water** se disuelve en agua; **she ~d into tears** se deshizo en lágrimas

dissuade [dɪˈsweɪd] VT disuadir (**from** de); **to ~ sb from doing sth** disuadir a algn de hacer algo

distance [ˈdɪstəns] **Ⓐ** N distancia *f*; **we followed them at a ~** seguimos a distancia; **at a ~ of two metres** a dos metros de distancia; **from a ~** desde lejos; **to go the ~** (*Sport*) llegar hasta el final; **it's a good ~ (from here)** está muy *or* bastante lejos (de aquí); **to be within hearing ~** estar al alcance de la voz; **in the ~** a lo lejos; **to keep one's ~** (*lit*) mantenerse a distancia; (*fig*) guardar las distancias; **it's no ~** está cerquísima, está a nada de aquí; **it's only a short ~ away** está a poca distancia, está bastante cerca; **it is within walking ~** se puede ir andando; **what ~ is it from here to London?** ¿qué distancia hay de aquí a Londres?

Ⓑ VT **to ~ o.s.** distanciarse (**from sth** de algo) **Ⓒ** CPD ➤ **distance learning** enseñanza *f* a distancia, enseñanza *f* por correspondencia ➤ **distance race** carrera *f* de larga distancia

distant [ˈdɪstənt] ADJ **1** (*in space*) [*country, land*] distante, lejano; [*star, galaxy*] lejano, remoto **2** (*in time*) [*future, past, ancestor*] lejano; **in the not too or very ~ future** en un futuro no demasiado *or* no muy lejano; **a ~ memory** un recuerdo lejano; **in the ~ past** en un lejano pasado, en un pasado remoto **3** [*relative, cousin*] lejano **4** (= *aloof*) [*person, manner, voice*] distante **5** (= *removed*) **all this seems so ~ from the Spain of today** todo esto parece muy alejado de la realidad española de hoy, todo esto parece no tener nada que ver con la España de hoy **6** (= *distracted*) [*person, look*] ausente; **there was a ~ look in her eyes** tenía la mirada ausente *or* ida

distantly [ˈdɪstəntlɪ] ADV **1** (= *slightly*) ligeramente; **to be ~ related to sb** ser pariente lejano de algn **2** (= *coldly*) [*greet, say*] con frialdad, fríamente **3** (= *distractedly*) [*smile, nod*] distraídamente

distaste [ˈdɪsˈteɪst] N aversión *f* (**for** por, a); **she looked at his grubby clothes with ~** miró su ropa mugrienta con expresión de repugnancia

distasteful [dɪsˈteɪstfʊl] ADJ (*gen*) desagradable; [*task*] ingrato; **it is ~ to me to have to do this** no me resulta nada grato tener que hacer esto

distemper[1] [dɪsˈtempəʳ] N (= *paint*) temple *m*

distemper[2] [dɪsˈtempəʳ] N (= *disease*) moquillo *m*

distil, **distill** (*US*) [dɪsˈtɪl] VT destilar; **~led water** agua *f* destilada

> Use **el/un** not **la/una** before feminine nouns beginning with stressed **a** or **ha** like **agua**.

distillery [dɪsˈtɪlərɪ] N destilería *f*

distinct [dɪsˈtɪŋkt] ADJ **1** (= *different*) [*types, species, groups*] diferente, distinto (**from** a, de); **as ~ from** a diferencia de **2** (= *clear, definite*) [*shape, memory*] claro, definido; [*image, sound*] claro, nítido; [*increase, rise, fall*] marcado; [*advantage, disadvantage*] claro, obvio; [*lack*] evidente; **I had the ~ impression that ...** tuve la clara impresión de que ...; **there is a ~ possibility that ...** existe una clara posibilidad de que ... + *subjun*

distinction [dɪsˈtɪŋkʃən] N **1** distinción *f*; **to draw a ~ between** hacer una distinción entre; **a writer of ~** un escritor destacado **2** (*Univ, Scol*) sobresaliente *m*; **he got a ~ in English** le dieron un sobresaliente en inglés

distinctive [dɪsˈtɪŋktɪv] ADJ [*sound, colour, feature*] característico; [*flavour, smell, voice*] inconfundible, característico; [*plumage, fur*] distintivo, característico; [*style*] característico, particular; [*clothing, decor*] peculiar, particular; **what was most ~ about him was his extreme nervousness** lo que más le caracterizaba era su extremo nerviosismo

distinctly [dɪsˈtɪŋktlɪ] ADV **1** (= *clearly*) [*see, hear, remember*] claramente, perfectamente; [*promise*] definitivamente; [*prefer*] claramente; [*speak*] con claridad **2** (= *very*) [*odd*] verdaderamente; [*uncomfortable, nervous*] realmente; [*better*] marcadamente; **he is ~ lacking in imagination** carece totalmente de imaginación; **it is ~ possible that ...** bien podría ser que ... + *subjun*

distinguish [dɪsˈtɪŋɡwɪʃ] **Ⓐ** VT **1** (= *differentiate*) distinguir (**from** de); **to ~ o.s.** destacarse (**as** como) **2** (= *characterize*) caracterizar **3** (= *discern*) distinguir **Ⓑ** VI distinguir (**between** entre)

distinguishable [dɪsˈtɪŋɡwɪʃəbl] ADJ **1** (= *possible to differentiate*) distinguible; **the two types are easily ~** los dos tipos son fácilmente distinguibles *or* se pueden distinguir fácilmente; **this port is ~ by its deep red colour** este oporto se caracteriza por su color rojo oscuro; **the copy is barely ~ from the original** la copia apenas puede distinguirse del original **2** (= *discernible*) **to be clearly ~** [*landmark, shape*] distinguirse claramente *or* fácilmente

distinguished [dɪsˈtɪŋgwɪʃt] ADJ [*guest, appearance, career*] distinguido; [*professor, scholar, writer*] distinguido, eminente; **to look ~** tener un aspecto distinguido ➤ **distinguished service professor** (*US Univ*) profesor de universidad que ocupa una cátedra de prestigio

distinguishing [dɪsˈtɪŋgwɪʃɪŋ] ADJ distintivo; **~ features** [*of landscape, sb's work*] rasgos *mpl* característicos, características *fpl*; [*of animal*] rasgos *mpl* distintivos; **~ mark** marca *f* distintiva

distort [dɪsˈtɔːt] VT [+ *shape*] deformar; [+ *sound, image*] distorsionar; [+ *judgment*] distorsionar; [+ *truth*] tergiversar

distorted [dɪsˈtɔːtɪd] ADJ distorsionado; **he gave us a ~ version of the events** nos dio una versión distorsionada de los hechos

distortion [dɪsˈtɔːʃən] N [*of shape*] deformación *f*; [*of sound, image, events, facts*] distorsión *f*

distract [dɪsˈtrækt] VT **to ~ sb (from sth)** distraer a algn (de algo); **to ~ sb's attention (from sth)** desviar la atención de algn (de algo); **she is easily ~ed** se distrae fácilmente

distracted [dɪsˈtræktɪd] ADJ distraído

distracting [dɪsˈtræktɪŋ] ADJ que distrae la atención, molesto

distraction [dɪsˈtrækʃən] N **1** (= *interruption*) distracción *f* **2** (= *entertainment*) diversión *f* **3** (= *distress, anxiety*) aturdimiento *m*; **to drive sb to ~** volver loco a algn

distraught [dɪsˈtrɔːt] ADJ afligido, alterado (*LAm*)

distress [dɪsˈtres] **Ⓐ** N **1** (= *pain*) dolor *m*; (= *anguish*) angustia *f*, aflicción *f*; **to be in great ~** estar sufriendo mucho **2** (= *danger*) peligro *m*; **to be in ~** [*ship*] estar en peligro **3** (= *poverty*) miseria *f*; **to be in financial ~** pasar apuros económicos **Ⓑ** VT (*physically*) doler; (*mentally*) afligir, angustiar; (*Med*) agotar, fatigar **Ⓒ** CPD ➤ **distress rocket** cohete *m* de señales ➤ **distress signal** señal *f* de socorro

distressed [dɪsˈtrest] ADJ afligido, angustiado; **I am very ~ at the news** estoy muy afligido por la noticia; **I was ~ to hear that ...** estaba muy afectado cuando me enteré de que ...

distressing [dɪsˈtresɪŋ] ADJ [*situation, experience*] angustioso, doloroso; [*poverty, inadequacy*] acuciante

distribute [dɪsˈtrɪbjuːt] VT (= *share out*) repartir; (*Comm*) [+ *goods*] distribuir

distribution [ˌdɪstrɪˈbjuːʃən] N [*of wealth, population, goods*] distribución *f*; (= *sharing out*) reparto *m* ➤ **distribution network** red *f* de distribución

distributor [dɪsˈtrɪbjʊtəʳ] N **1** (= *firm*) compañía *f* distribuidora, distribuidora *f*; (*Cine*) distribuidora *f* **2** (*Aut*) distribuidor *m* (del encendido), delco® *m* (*Sp*)

district [ˈdɪstrɪkt] N [*of country*] región *f*, zona *f*; [*of town*] distrito *m*, barrio *m*; (= *administrative area*) (*gen, also Pol*) distrito *m* ➤ **district attorney** (*US*) fiscal *mf* (de distrito) ➤ **district commissioner** (*Brit*) jefe/a *m/f* de policía de distrito ➤ **district council** (*Brit*) municipio *m* ➤ **district court** (*US*) tribunal *m* de distrito ➤ **district manager** representante *mf* regional ➤ **district nurse** (*Brit*) enfermero/a de la Seguridad Social encargado/a de una zona determinada

distrust [dɪsˈtrʌst] **Ⓐ** N desconfianza *f* (**of** en), recelo *m* (**of** de) **Ⓑ** VT desconfiar de, recelar de

distrustful [dɪsˈtrʌstfʊl] ADJ desconfiado, receloso

disturb [dɪsˈtɜːb] VT **1** (= *bother*) molestar; **"please do not disturb"** "se ruega no molestar"; **sorry to ~ you** perdona la molestia; **try not to ~ Joseph, he's asleep** intenta no despertar a Joseph, está durmiendo **2** (= *interrupt*) [+ *order, balance*] alterar; [+ *meeting, sleep*] interrumpir; [+ *silence*] romper; **they ~ed a burglar breaking into their house** sorprendieron a un ladrón que estaba intentando entrar en su casa **3** (= *worry*) preocupar; (= *upset*) afectar **4** (= *disarrange*) [+ *papers*] desordenar; [+ *water, sediment*] agitar; **the police asked if anything had been ~ed** la policía preguntó si había algo fuera de su sitio

disturbance [dɪsˈtɜːbəns] N **1** (*social, political*) disturbio *m*; (*in house, street*) alboroto *m*; (= *fight*) altercado *m*, bronca *f* (*LAm*); **to cause a ~** armar alboroto **2** (= *interruption*) interrupción *f* (**to** de)

disturbed [dɪsˈtɜːbd] ADJ **1** (= *worried*) preocupado,

angustiado; (= *upset*) afectado **2** [*childhood, adolescence*] problemático; **children from ~ backgrounds** niños que proceden de hogares con problemas **3** (= *mentally ill*) [*person, mind*] trastornado; [*behaviour*] desequilibrado; **to be emotionally/mentally ~** tener trastornos afectivos/ mentales **4** (= *interrupted*) [*sleep*] interrumpido; **to have a ~ night** dormir mal

disturbing [dɪsˈtɜːbɪŋ] ADJ [*influence, thought*] perturbador; [*incident*] inquietante, preocupante; **it is ~ that ...** es inquietante que ...

disuse [ˈdɪsˈjuːs] N desuso *m*; **to fall into ~** caer en desuso

disused [ˈdɪsˈjuːzd] ADJ abandonado

ditch [dɪtʃ] **Ⓐ** N (*gen*) zanja *f*; (*at roadside*) cuneta *f*; (= *irrigation channel*) acequia *f*; (*as defence*) foso *m* **Ⓑ** VT (***) (= *get rid of*) [+ *car*] deshacerse de; [+ *person*] dejar plantado*; **to ~ a plane** hacer un amaraje forzoso

dither [ˈdɪðəʳ] **Ⓐ** N **to be in a ~** (= *be nervous*) estar muy nervioso; (= *hesitate*) no saber qué hacer, vacilar **Ⓑ** VI (= *be nervous*) estar nervioso; (= *hesitate*) no saber qué hacer, vacilar; **to ~ over a decision** vacilar al tomar una decisión

ditto [ˈdɪtəʊ] N ídem, lo mismo

ditty [ˈdɪtɪ] N cancioncilla *f*

diuretic [ˌdaɪjʊˈretɪk] **Ⓐ** ADJ diurético **Ⓑ** N diurético *m*

divan [dɪˈvæn] N diván *m*; (*Brit*) (*also* **~ bed**) cama *f* turca

dive [daɪv] **Ⓐ** N **1** (*into water*) salto *m* de cabeza (al agua), zambullida *f*, clavado *m* (*CAm, Mex*); (*by deep-sea diver, submarine*) inmersión *f* **2** (*Aer*) picado *m* (*Sp*), picada *f* (*LAm*) **3** (= *leap*) **to make a ~ for sth** lanzarse *or* abalanzarse sobre algo **4** (= *fall*) **his reputation has taken a ~*** su reputación ha caído en picado (*Sp*) *or* en picada (*LAm*) **5** (*pej**) (= *club etc*) garito *m* **Ⓑ** VI **1** [*swimmer*] (*from board, rock*) tirarse, zambullirse, dar un clavado (*CAm, Mex*), clavarse (*CAm, Mex*); (*underwater*) bucear; [*submarine*] sumergirse; **to ~ into the water** tirarse al agua, zambullirse **2** (*Aer*) bajar en picado (*Sp*) *or* en picada (*LAm*) **3** (= *leap*) **the goalkeeper ~d for the ball** el portero se lanzó a parar el balón; **to ~ for cover** precipitarse en busca de cobijo; **he ~d into the crowd** se metió entre la muchedumbre; **to ~ into one's pocket** meter la mano en el bolsillo **4** (= *fall*) [*prices etc*] bajar de golpe, caer en picado (*Sp*) *or* en picada (*LAm*)

dive-bomb [ˈdaɪvbɒm] VT bombardear en picado (*Sp*) *or* en picada (*LAm*)

diver [ˈdaɪvəʳ] N **1** (= *swimmer*) saltador(a) *m/f*, clavadista *mf* (*LAm*); (= *deep-sea diver*) submarinista *mf*, buzo *m*; (*sub-aqua*) escafandrista *mf* **2** (= *bird*) colimbo *m*

diverge [daɪˈvɜːdʒ] VI [*opinions*] divergir (**from** de); [*roads*] bifurcarse

divergence [daɪˈvɜːdʒəns] N divergencia *f*

divergent [daɪˈvɜːdʒənt] ADJ divergente

diverse [daɪˈvɜːs] ADJ diverso, variado

diversification [daɪˌvɜːsɪfɪˈkeɪʃən] N diversificación *f*

diversify [daɪˈvɜːsɪfaɪ] **Ⓐ** VT diversificar **Ⓑ** VI diversificarse, ampliar el campo de acción

diversion [daɪˈvɜːʃən] N **1** (*Brit*) [*of traffic*] desviación *f*, desvío *m*; **"Diversion"** "Desvío" **2** (= *distraction*) **to create a ~** (*gen*) distraer; (*Mil*) producir una diversión **3** (= *pastime*) diversión *f*

diversionary [daɪˈvɜːʃnərɪ] ADJ de diversión

diversity [daɪˈvɜːsɪtɪ] N [*of opinions etc*] diversidad *f*

divert [daɪˈvɜːt] VT **1** (*Brit*) [+ *traffic, train etc*] desviar **2** (= *amuse*) divertir, entretener

divest[1] [daɪˈvest] VT **to ~ sb of sth** despojar a algn de algo

divest[2] [daɪˈvest] VT, VI (*US Fin*) desinvertir

divide [dɪˈvaɪd] **Ⓐ** VT **1** (= *separate*) separar (**from** de) **2** (*also* **~ up**) [+ *money, work, kingdom*] dividir, repartir (**among, between** entre); [+ *sweets*] repartir (**among, between** entre); [+ *apple, orange, cake*] partir, dividir (**among, between** entre; **into** en); **they ~d it among themselves** se lo repartieron entre sí

3 (*Math*) dividir; **48 ~d by eight is six** 48 dividido entre *or* por ocho es seis; **~ six into 36** divide 36 entre *or* por seis
4 [+ *friends, political parties*] dividir
Ⓑ VI **1** [*road, river*] bifurcarse
2 (*also ~ up*) [*cells, people*] dividirse; **~ and rule** divide y vencerás
3 (*Math*) dividir
Ⓒ N (= *gap*) división *f*

divided [dɪˈvaɪdɪd] ADJ [*nation, government, society, opinion*] dividido; **to have ~ loyalties** sufrir un conflicto de lealtades; **opinions are ~ on** *or* **over that** las opiniones respecto a eso están muy divididas ➤ **divided highway** (*US*) autovía *f* ➤ **divided skirt** (*US*) falda *f* pantalón

dividend [ˈdɪvɪdend] N dividendo *m*

dividers [dɪˈvaɪdəz] NPL compás *msing* de puntas

dividing [dɪˈvaɪdɪŋ] ADJ [*wall, fence*] divisorio ➤ **dividing line** línea *f* divisoria

divine¹ [dɪˈvaɪn] ADJ (*Rel*) divino; (*) (= *wonderful*) divino, maravilloso ➤ **divine right** derecho *m* divino

divine² [dɪˈvaɪn] VT adivinar

diving [ˈdaɪvɪŋ] N (*underwater*) submarinismo *m*, buceo *m*; (*from board*) salto *m* de trampolín, clavado *m* (*CAm, Mex*); (*from side of pool*) salto *m*, zambullida *f* ➤ **diving board** trampolín *m* ➤ **diving suit** escafandra *f*, traje *m* de buceo

divinity [dɪˈvɪnɪtɪ] N **1** (= *deity, quality*) divinidad *f* **2** (*as study*) teología *f*

divisible [dɪˈvɪzəbl] ADJ divisible

division [dɪˈvɪʒən] **Ⓐ** N **1** división *f*; **~ of labour** (*Brit*) *or* **labor** (*US*) división *f* del trabajo **2** (*Comm*) (= *department*) sección *f* **3** (*Ftbl, Mil, Police*) división *f* **4** (= *conflict, discord*) discordia *f* **Ⓑ** CPD ➤ **division sign** signo *m* de división

divisive [dɪˈvaɪsɪv] ADJ divisivo, causante de divisiones

divorce [dɪˈvɔːs] **Ⓐ** N **1** (*Jur*) divorcio *m*; **to get a ~** divorciarse (**from** de) **2** (*fig*) separación *f* (**from** de) **Ⓑ** VT **1** (*Jur*) divorciarse de; **to get ~d** divorciarse **2** (*fig*) separar; **to ~ sth from sth** separar algo de algo **Ⓒ** VI divorciarse

divorced [dɪˈvɔːst] ADJ divorciado

divorcee [dɪˌvɔːˈsiː] N divorciado/a *m/f*

divulge [daɪˈvʌldʒ] VT divulgar, revelar

Dixie [ˈdɪksɪ] N *el sur de los Estados Unidos*

DIY N ABBR (*Brit*) (= **do-it-yourself**) bricolaje *m*

dizziness [ˈdɪzɪnɪs] N (*gen*) mareo *m*; (*caused by height*) vértigo *m*; **to have an attack of ~** tener *or* sufrir un mareo

dizzy [ˈdɪzɪ] ADJ (*compar* **dizzier**; *superl* **dizziest**) **1** (= *giddy*) [*person*] mareado; **to feel ~** (*because ill, drunk etc*) estar mareado, marearse; **if I look down I feel ~** si miro hacia abajo me da vértigo; **you're making me ~** me estás mareando; **she had a ~ spell** tuvo *or* le dio un mareo; **to be ~ with success** estar borracho de éxito **2** (*fig*) [*pace, speed*] vertiginoso **3** (*) (= *scatterbrained*) atolondrado

DJ Ⓐ N ABBR (= **disc-jockey**) discjockey *mf*, pinchadiscos *mf* (*Sp**) **Ⓑ** ABBR (*Brit*) (= **dinner jacket**) smoking *m*

Djakarta [dʒəˈkɑːtə] N Yakarta *f*

Djibouti [dʒɪˈbuːtɪ] N Yibuti *m*

DM, D-mark [ˈdiːmɑːk] ABBR (= **Deutschmark**) DM

dm ABBR (= **decimetre(s)**) dm

DMus ABBR **= Doctor of Music**

DNA N ABBR (= **deoxyribonucleic acid**) ADN *m* ➤ **DNA fingerprinting, DNA profiling** identificación *f* mediante el análisis del ADN ➤ **DNA test** prueba *f* del ADN

do

Ⓐ TRANSITIVE VERB	**Ⓓ** NOUN
Ⓑ INTRANSITIVE VERB	**Ⓔ** PHRASAL VERBS
Ⓒ AUXILIARY VERB	

do¹ [duː] (*3rd pers sing present* **does**; *pt* **did**; *pp* **done**)
Ⓐ TRANSITIVE VERB
1 hacer; **I've got nothing to do** no tengo nada que hacer; **he does nothing but complain** no hace más que quejarse; **to do sth again** volver a hacer algo, hacer algo de nuevo;

what's he ever done for me? ¿qué ha hecho él por mí?; **what can I do for you?** ¿en qué puedo servirle?, ¿qué se le ofrece? (*LAm*); **could you do something for me?** ¿me podrías hacer un favor?; **what are we going to do for money?** ¿de dónde vamos a sacar dinero?; **that dress doesn't do a lot for you*** este vestido no te queda muy bien; **the new measures will do a lot for small businesses** las nuevas medidas serán de gran ayuda para las pequeñas empresas; **if you do anything to him I'll kill you** si le haces algo te mato; **what have you done with my slippers?** ¿dónde has puesto mis zapatillas?; **what am I going to do with you?** ¿qué voy a hacer contigo?
2 (= *carry out*) [+ *work, essay, crossword*] hacer

Some **do** + noun combinations require a more specific Spanish verb:

to do the cooking cocinar; **to do the dishes** lavar los platos; **he did a drawing of her** la dibujó, hizo un dibujo de ella; **to do one's duty (by sb)** cumplir con su deber (con algn); **to do the ironing** planchar

3 (= *arrange, prepare*) [+ *vegetables*] preparar; [+ *room*] hacer, arreglar; [+ *flowers*] arreglar
4 (= *spend*) pasar; **he did six years (in jail)** pasó seis años en la cárcel; **I did five years as a policeman** fui policía durante cinco años
5 (= *finish*) **I've only done three pages** sólo he hecho tres páginas; **now you've (gone and) done it!*** ¡ahora sí que la has hecho buena!*; **that does it!*** ¡es el colmo!
6 (*esp Brit*) (= *offer, make available*) **we only do one make of gloves** sólo tenemos una marca de guantes
7 (= *study*) [+ *university course, option*] hacer, estudiar
8 (*Theat*) [+ *play*] representar, poner; [+ *part*] hacer
9 (= *mimic*) [+ *person*] imitar
10 (*Aut, Rail etc*) [+ *speed*] ir a; **we've done 200km already** ya hemos hecho 200km
11 (*) (= *visit*) [+ *city, museum*] visitar, recorrer
12 (*) (= *be suitable, sufficient for*) **will a kilo do you?** ¿le va bien un kilo?; **that'll do me nicely** (= *be suitable*) eso me vendrá muy bien; (= *suffice*) con eso me basta
13 (*) (= *cheat*) estafar, timar; (= *rob*) robar; **I've been done!** ¡me han estafado *or* timado!
14 (*) (= *prosecute*) procesar; (= *fine*) multar; **she was done for shoplifting** la procesaron por robar en una tienda; **he was done for speeding** le multaron por exceso de velocidad
15 to do drugs* estar metido en la droga, drogarse
Ⓑ INTRANSITIVE VERB
1 (= *act*) hacer; **do as I do** haz como yo; **he did right** hizo lo correcto; **do as you think** best haga lo que mejor le parezca; **do as you are told!** ¡haz lo que te digo!; **you would do well to take his advice** harías bien en seguir su consejo
2 (= *get on*) **he did badly in the exam** le fue mal en el examen; **you can do better than that** (*essay, drawing*) puedes hacerlo mejor; **how are you doing?*** ¿qué tal?, ¿cómo te va?; **how did you do in the audition?** ¿qué tal *or* cómo te fue en la audición?; **he's doing well at school** le va bien en el colegio; **the patient is doing well** el paciente está respondiendo bien
✦ how do you do? ¡mucho gusto!, ¡encantado!, gusto en conocerlo (*LAm*)
3 (= *be suitable*) **it doesn't do to upset her** cuidado con ofenderla; **will this one do?** ¿te parece bien éste?; **this room will do** esta habitación ya me va bien; **will tomorrow do?** ¿iría bien mañana?; **it's not exactly what I wanted, but it will** *or* **it'll do** no es exactamente lo que quería pero servirá; **this coat will do as a blanket** este abrigo servirá de manta; **that will have to do** tendremos que conformarnos con eso; **you can't go on your own, that would never do!** no podemos consentir que vayas sola, ¡eso no puede ser!
4 (= *be sufficient*) bastar; **three bottles of wine should do** bastará con tres botellas de vino; **will £20 do?** ¿bastarán 20 libras?, ¿tendrás bastante con 20 libras?; **that'll do** (= *be enough*) con eso basta; **that will do!** ¡basta ya!
5 (*) (= *happen*) **"could you lend me £50?" — "nothing doing!"** —¿me podrías prestar 50 libras? —¡de ninguna manera! *or* —¡ni hablar!
6 (*) (= *finish*) (*in past tenses only*) terminar, acabar; **have**

you done? ¿ya has terminado *or* acabado?; **I've done with travelling** ya no voy a viajar más, he renunciado a los viajes; **I've done with all that nonsense** ya no tengo nada que ver *or* ya he terminado con todas esas tonterías

C AUXILIARY VERB

> There is no equivalent in Spanish to the use of **do** in questions, negative statements and negative commands.

1 (*in questions*) **do you understand?** ¿comprendes?, ¿entiendes?; **where does he live?** ¿dónde vive?; **didn't you like it?** ¿no te gustó?

2 (*negation*) **I don't understand** no entiendo *or* comprendo; **don't worry!** ¡no te preocupes!; **she didn't go** no fue

3 (*for emphasis*) **DO sit down** (*esp Brit*) siéntese, por favor, tome asiento, por favor (*frm*); **she DOES look lovely in that dress** está preciosa con este vestido; **I DO hope so** así lo espero; **but I DO like it!** ¡sí que me gusta!, ¡por supuesto que me gusta!; **but I DID do it** pero sí que lo hice

4 (*with inversion*) **rarely does it happen that ...** rara vez ocurre que ...; **not once did they offer to pay** no se ofrecieron a pagar ni una sola vez

5 (*verb substitute*) **you speak better than I do** tú hablas mejor que yo; **"did you fix the car?" — "I did"** —¿arreglaste el coche? —sí; **"I love it" — "so do I"** —me encanta —a mí también; **I don't like sport and neither does he** no me gusta el deporte ni a él tampoco; **you didn't see him but I did** tú no lo viste pero yo sí; **she always says she'll come but she never does** siempre que vendrá pero nunca viene; **"he borrowed the car" — "oh he did, did he?"** —pidió el coche prestado —¿ah sí? ¡no me digas!; **I like this colour, don't you?** me gusta este color, ¿a ti no?; **"do you speak English?" — "yes, I do/no I don't"** —¿habla usted inglés? —sí, hablo inglés/no, no hablo inglés; **"may I come in?" — "(please) do!"** —¿se puede pasar? —¡pasa (por favor)!; **"who made this mess?" — "I did"** —¿quién lo ha desordenado todo? —fui yo; **"shall I ring her again?" — "no, don't!"** —¿la llamo otra vez? —¡no, no la llames!

6 (*in question tags*) **he lives here, doesn't he?** vive aquí, ¿verdad? *or* ¿no es cierto? *or* ¿no?; **I don't know him, do I?** no lo conozco, ¿verdad?; **it doesn't matter, does it?** no importa, ¿no?

D NOUN

1 (*Brit**) (= *party*) fiesta *f*; (= *formal gathering*) reunión *f*

2 (*in phrases*) **the dos and don'ts** of buying a house lo que debe y lo que no debe hacerse al comprar una casa

E PHRASAL VERBS

➤ **do away with** VI + PREP **1** [+ *nuclear weapons*] eliminar, acabar con; [+ *injustice, exploitation, system*] acabar con; [+ *capital punishment*] abolir **2** (*) (= *kill*) matar, liquidar*; **to do away with o.s.** matarse, suicidarse

➤ **do down*** VT + ADV (*Brit*) (= *denigrate*) menospreciar; **to do o.s. down** subestimarse

➤ **do for*** VI + PREP **I thought we were done for** (= *dead*) pensaba que nos íbamos a matar; **as a politician he's done for** como político está acabado; **they've seen him, he's done for!** lo han visto, ¡está perdido!; **I'm done for** (= *exhausted*) estoy molido* *or* rendido

➤ **do in**** VT + ADV **1** (= *kill*) liquidar* **2** (= *exhaust*) reventar*, hacer polvo*; **he's absolutely done in** está molido* *or* rendido, está totalmente reventado*, está hecho polvo* **3** (= *ruin*) [+ *back*] hacerse daño en, fastidiar (*Sp**)

➤ **do out of** VT + PREP **he has done me out of thousands of pounds*** me quedé sin miles de libras por su culpa; **he did her out of a job** le quitó el trabajo, se quedó sin el trabajo por su culpa

➤ **do over** VT + ADV **1** (*US**) (= *repeat*) volver a hacer, hacer de nuevo **2** (= *redecorate*) volver a pintar/empapelar **3** (*Brit**) (= *beat up*) dar una paliza a* **4** (*Brit**) (= *ransack*) [+ *place*] saquear; [+ *house, shop*] desvalijar

➤ **do up** VT + ADV **1** (= *fasten*) [+ *shoes, shoelaces*] atar; [+ *dress*] (*gen*) abrochar; (*with zip*) cerrar *or* subir la cremallera de; [+ *buttons, coat, necklace*] abrochar; [+ *zip*] cerrar, subir **2** (= *wrap up*) [+ *parcel*] envolver **3** (*Brit*) (= *renovate*) [+ *house*] reformar, hacer reformas en **4** (*) (= *dress up*) **she was all done up in her best clothes** iba de

---

punta en blanco*

➤ **do with** VI + PREP **1** (= *need*) **I could do with some help/a beer** no me vendría mal un poco de ayuda/una cerveza; **we could have done with you there** nos hiciste mucha falta; **you could do with a bath** te vendría bien un baño

2 (= *have connection with*) **it is to do with her application** es respecto a su solicitud; **it is nothing to do with me** no tiene nada que ver conmigo; **that has nothing to do with you!** ¡eso no tiene nada que ver contigo!; **that has nothing to do with it!** ¡eso no tiene nada que ver!

3 (*) **I can't be doing with his finicky eating habits** no soporto sus manías a la hora de comer

➤ **do without** VI + PREP **I can't do without my computer** yo no puedo pasar sin el ordenador; **you can't do without money** no se puede vivir sin dinero; **"I haven't brought my gym kit" — "you'll have to do without then!"** —no he traído mi equipo de gimnasia —pues vas a tener que apañártelas sin él; **I can do without your advice** no necesito tus consejos; **this bus strike is something I could do without*** esta huelga de autobuses es lo último que me faltaba

do² [dəʊ] N (*Mus*) do *m*

do. ABBR = **ditto** ídem, íd., lo mismo

doable*, do-able* ['duːəbl] ADJ **do you think it is ~?** ¿crees que es posible llevarlo a cabo?

d.o.b. ABBR = **date of birth**

Doberman ['dəʊbəmən] N (*also* ~ **pinscher**) dóberman *m*

doc [dɒk] N (*esp US**) = **doctor**

docile ['dəʊsaɪl] ADJ dócil, sumiso

dock¹ [dɒk] **A** N (*Naut*) dársena *f*, muelle *m*; **docks** muelles *mpl*, puerto *msing*; **to be in ~** estar en puerto **B** VT [+ *ship*] atracar; [+ *spacecraft*] acoplar **C** VI **1** (*Naut*) atracar; (*loosely*) llegar **2** [*spacecraft*] acoplarse (**with** a)

dock² [dɒk] N (*in court*) banquillo *m* de los acusados

dock³ [dɒk] N (= *plant*) acedera *f*, ramaza *f*

dock⁴ [dɒk] VT **to ~ sb's pay** descontar dinero del sueldo a algn; **I've been ~ed £20** me han descontado 20 libras

docker ['dɒkər] N (*Brit*) estibador *m*

docket ['dɒkɪt] N **1** (= *label*) etiqueta *f*, marbete *m*; (*esp Brit*) (= *certificate*) resguardo *m*, certificado *m*; (= *bill*) factura *f* **2** (*US Jur*) lista *f* de casos pendientes

dockyard ['dɒkjɑːd] N astillero *m*

doctor ['dɒktər] **A** N **1** (*Med*) médico/a *m/f*; **to go to the ~'s** ir al médico; **Doctor Brown** el doctor Brown; **✦** IDIOM **it was just what the ~ ordered*** fue mano de santo **2** (*Univ*) doctor(a) *m/f* (**of** en) **B** VT [+ *food, drink*] adulterar; [+ *document*] manipular **C** CPD ➤ **doctor's excuse** (*US*), **doctor's note** (*Brit*) baja *f* (médica)

doctorate ['dɒktərɪt] N doctorado *m*; *ver tb* www.education.org.uk

doctrinal [dɒk'traɪnl] ADJ doctrinal

doctrine ['dɒktrɪn] N doctrina *f*

docudrama ['dɒkjʊˌdrɑːmə] N docudrama *m*

document **A** ['dɒkjʊmənt] N documento *m* **B** ['dɒkjʊment] VT documentar

documentary [ˌdɒkjʊ'mentərɪ] **A** ADJ documental; ~ **evidence** pruebas documentales **B** N (*Cine, TV*) documental *m*

documentation [ˌdɒkjʊmen'teɪʃən] N documentación *f*

docu-soap ['dɒkjʊsəʊp] N (*TV*) *serie documental sobre la vida de personas reales*

DOD N ABBR (*US*) = **Department of Defense**

doddering ['dɒdərɪŋ], **doddery** ['dɒdərɪ] ADJ renqueante, chocho (*pej*)

doddle* ['dɒdl] N (*Brit*) **it's a ~** es pan comido*, está chupado

dodge [dɒdʒ] **A** N (*Brit**) (= *trick*) truco *m* **B** VT (= *elude*) [+ *blow, ball*] esquivar; [+ *pursuer*] dar esquinazo a; [+ *acquaintance, problem*] evitar; [+ *tax*] evadir; [+ *responsibility, duty, job*] eludir; **to ~ the issue** eludir el tema **C** VI (*gen*) escabullirse; (*Boxing*) hacer una finta; **to ~ out of the way** echarse a un lado; **to ~ behind a tree** ocultarse tras un árbol

dodgems ['dɒdʒəmz] N (*esp Brit*) **the ~** los coches de choque

dodgy* ['dɒdʒɪ] ADJ (*compar* **dodgier**; *superl* **dodgiest**) (*Brit*) **1** (= *dishonest*) [*person*] de poco fiar, poco fiable; [*business, deal, district*] oscuro, chungo (*Sp***); [*practice*] dudoso **2** (= *uncertain*) [*plan*] arriesgado; [*weather*] inestable; **the clutch is a bit ~** el embrague no anda muy bien; **to have a ~ back** tener la espalda fastidiada, estar fastidiado de la espalda

DOE N ABBR **1** (*Brit*) = **Department of the Environment 2** (*US*) = **Department of Energy**

doe [dəʊ] N (= *deer*) cierva *f*, gama *f*; (= *rabbit*) coneja *f*; (= *hare*) liebre *f*

does [dʌz] 3RD PERS SING *of* **do** [1]

doesn't ['dʌznt] = **does not**; *see* **do**[1]

dog [dɒg] **A** N **1** perro/a *m/f*; **the ~s** (*Brit**) (= *greyhounds*) las carreras de galgos; ✦ IDIOMS **it's ~ eat ~ in this place** aquí se despedazan unos a otros; **to go to the ~s*** [*person*] echarse a perder; [*nation, country*] ir a la ruina; **it's a ~'s life** es una vida de perros; **to be a ~ in the manger** (*Brit*) ser como el perro del hortelano; **to put on the ~** (*US**) vestirse de punta en blanco; **to be top ~** ser el gallo del lugar, triunfar; ✦ PROVS **every ~ has its day** a cada cerdo le llega su San Martín; **let sleeping ~s lie** más vale no meneallo **2** (= *male animal*) macho *m* **3** (**) (= *unattractive girl*) callo *m* (malayo)* **B** VT **he was ~ged by ill luck** le perseguía la mala suerte **C** CPD ➤ **dog basket** cesto *m* del perro ➤ **dog biscuit** galleta *f* de perro ➤ **dog breeder** criador(a) *m/f* de perros ➤ **dog collar** collar *m* de perro; (*) (*clergyman's*) gola *f*, alzacuello(s) *m inv* ➤ **dog food** comida *f* para perros ➤ **dog handler** adiestrador(a) *m/f* de perros ➤ **dog paddle** braza *f* de perro (*forma de nadar*) ➤ **dog's breakfast, dog's dinner** embrollo *m* ➤ **dog show** exposición *f* canina ➤ **dog tag** (*US Mil*) placa *f* de identificación

dog-eared ['dɒgɪəd] ADJ sobado, muy manoseado

dogfight ['dɒgfaɪt] N (*Aer*) combate *m* aéreo (reñido y confuso); (*) (= *squabble*) trifulca *f*, refriega *f*

dogged ['dɒgɪd] ADJ (= *obstinate*) porfiado, terco; (= *tenacious*) tenaz

doggerel ['dɒgərəl] N coplas *fpl* de ciego, malos versos *mpl*

doggy*, doggie* ['dɒgɪ] N (*baby talk*) perrito *m* ➤ **doggy bag** bolsita *f* con los restos de la comida (*en restaurante*) ➤ **doggy paddle** braza *f* de perro

doggy-paddle ['dɒgɪ,pædl] VI nadar como los perros

doghouse ['dɒghaʊs] N **1** (*US*) caseta *f* del perro **2** ✦ IDIOM **to be in the ~*** estar castigado

dogma ['dɒgmə] N dogma *m*

dogmatic [dɒg'mætɪk] ADJ dogmático

do-gooder* ['duː'gʊdə'] N (*pej*) hacedor(a) *m/f* de buenas obras

dog-paddle ['dɒg,pædl] VI nadar como los perros

dogsbody* ['dɒgzbɒdɪ] N (*Brit*) burro *m* de carga

dog-tired* ['dɒg'taɪəd] ADJ rendido*, hecho polvo*

doily ['dɔɪlɪ] N blonda *f*

doing ['duːɪŋ] N **1 this is your ~** esto es cosa tuya; **it was none of my ~** yo no he tenido nada que ver; **it will take a lot of** *or* **some ~** va a ser muy difícil hacerlo, costará mucho hacerlo **2** (*Brit*) **doings** (= *activities*) actividades *fpl*; (= *actions*) acciones *fpl*; (= *happenings*) sucesos *mpl*

do-it-yourself ['duːɪtjə'self] N bricolaje *m* ➤ **do-it-yourself enthusiast, do-it-yourself expert** aficionado/a *m/f* al bricolaje ➤ **do-it-yourself kit** modelo *m* para armar

Dolby® ['dɒlbɪ] N Dolby® *m*

doldrums ['dɒldrəmz] NPL ✦ IDIOM **to be in the ~** [*person*] estar abatido; [*business*] estar estancado; (*St Ex*) estar en calma

dole* [dəʊl] N (*Brit*) subsidio *m* de desempleo *or* (*Sp*) paro; **to be on the ~** estar cobrando el subsidio de desempleo, estar en el paro (*Sp*) ➤ **dole queue** cola *f* de desempleados, cola *f* del paro (*Sp*), cola *f* de cesantes (*Chi*); **to join the ~ queue** (*fig*) aumentar el número de desempleados *o* (*Chi*) cesantes, apuntarse al paro (*Sp*)
➤ **dole out** VT + ADV repartir, distribuir

doll [dɒl] **A** N **1** (= *toy*) muñeca *f* **2** (*esp US†**) (= *girl*) muñeca *f*, preciosidad *f* **B** CPD ➤ **doll's house** casa *f* de muñecas

dollar ['dɒlə'] N dólar *m*; ✦ IDIOMS **you can bet your bottom ~ that ...** te apuesto lo que quieras a que ...; **it's ~s to doughnuts that ...** (*US**) es tan cierto como hay Dios que ...* ➤ **dollar bill** billete *m* de un dólar ➤ **dollar sign** signo *m* del dólar

dollop ['dɒləp] N [*of jam, ketchup etc*] pegote *m*

dolphin ['dɒlfɪn] N delfín *m*

domain [də'meɪn] **A** N **1** (= *lands etc*) dominio *m*, propiedad *f* **2** (*Internet*) dominio *m* **3** (*fig*) campo *m*, competencia *f*; **the matter is now in the public ~** el asunto es ya del dominio público **B** CPD ➤ **domain name** (*Internet*) nombre *m* de dominio

dome [dəʊm] N cúpula *f*

domed [dəʊmd] ADJ [*roof*] abovedado; [*forehead*] en forma de huevo

domestic [də'mestɪk] **A** ADJ **1** (= *household*) [*activities, duty, life, animal*] doméstico; [*harmony, quarrel*] familiar; [*violence*] en el hogar; **for ~ use** para uso doméstico **2** (= *home-loving*) casero, hogareño **3** (= *internal*) [*industry, news, economy, politics*] nacional; [*market, consumption, policy*] nacional, interior; [*affairs, problems, flight*] nacional, interno **B** N doméstico/a *m/f*, empleado/a *m/f* doméstico/a **C** CPD ➤ **domestic appliance** aparato *m* doméstico, aparato *m* de uso doméstico ➤ **domestic science** (*esp Brit†*) economía *f* doméstica, hogar *m* (*Sp*) ➤ **domestic staff** (*in hospital, institution*) personal *m* de servicio; (*in private household*) servicio *m* doméstico

domesticated [də'mestɪkeɪtɪd] ADJ [*animal*] domesticado; [*person*] casero, hogareño

dominance ['dɒmɪnəns] N **1** (= *supremacy*) [*of person*] dominio *m* (**over** sobre); [*of class, nation*] dominio *m*, dominación *f* (**over** sobre) **2** (= *predominance*) predominio *m* **3** (*Bio, Ecol*) [*of gene, species, male*] dominancia *f*

dominant ['dɒmɪnənt] ADJ **1** [*person, role, gene, species*] dominante (*also Mus*) **2** [*feature, theme*] predominante

dominate ['dɒmɪneɪt] VT, VI dominar

domination [,dɒmɪ'neɪʃən] N (= *act of dominating*) dominación *f*; (= *control*) dominio *m*

domineering [,dɒmɪ'nɪərɪŋ] ADJ dominante, autoritario

Dominica [,dɒmɪ'niːkə] N Dominica *f*

Dominican [də'mɪnɪkən] **A** ADJ, N dominicano/a *m/f* **B** CPD ➤ **Dominican Republic** República *f* Dominicana

dominion [də'mɪnɪən] N dominio *m*; **to hold** *or* **have ~ over sb** ejercer dominio sobre algn

domino ['dɒmɪnəʊ] N (*pl* **~es**) (= *piece*) ficha *f* de dominó; **~es** (= *game*) dominó *msing*; **to play ~es** jugar al dominó, jugar dominó (*LAm*) ➤ **domino effect** (*Pol*) reacción *f* en cadena

don[1] [dɒn] N (*Brit Univ*) catedrático/a *m/f*

don[2] [dɒn] VT (*liter*) [+ *garment*] ponerse, ataviarse con

donate [dəʊ'neɪt] VT donar

donation [dəʊ'neɪʃən] N **1** (= *act*) donación *f* **2** (= *gift*) donativo *m*, donación *f*

done [dʌn] **A** PP *of* **do**[1] **B** ADJ **1** (= *finished*) terminado, acabado; **the job's ~** el trabajo está terminado *or* acabado; **why don't you tell him and have ~ with it?** ¿por qué no se lo dices y acabas de una vez?; ✦ PROV **what's ~ cannot be undone** a lo hecho, pecho **2** (= *accepted*) **it's just not ~!** ¡eso no se hace! **3** (*in exclamations*) **done!** (= *agreed*) ¡trato hecho!; **well ~!** ¡muy bien!, ¡bravo! **4** (*Culin*) **the vegetables are ~** la verdura está cocida *or* hecha; **I like my steak well ~** me gusta el filete muy hecho

5 (*) (= *exhausted*) agotado, hecho polvo*

donkey ['dɒŋkɪ] N burro *m*; **female** ~ burra *f*; ✦ IDIOM **I haven't seen him for ~'s years** (*Brit**) hace siglos que no lo veo ➤ **donkey jacket** (*Brit*) chaqueta *f* de lanilla de trabajo ➤ **donkey work*** (*Brit*) trabajo *m* pesado

donor ['dəʊnəʳ] N donante *mf* ➤ **donor card** carnet *m* de donante ➤ **donor organ** órgano *m* donado

don't [dəʊnt] **Ⓐ** AUX VB = **do not**; *see* **do¹** **Ⓑ** CPD ➤ **the don't knows** los que no saben

donut ['dəʊnʌt] N (*esp US*) donut® *m*, dona *f* (*LAm*)

doodle ['duːdl] **Ⓐ** N garabato *m* **Ⓑ** VI hacer garabatos

doom [duːm] **Ⓐ** N (= *fate*) destino *m* funesto; (= *death*) muerte *f*; **it's all ~ and gloom here** aquí reina el catastrofismo **Ⓑ** VT condenar (**to** a); **~ed to failure** condenado al fracaso

door [dɔːʳ] N puerta *f*; **he stopped <u>at</u> the ~ of his office** se detuvo a *or* en la puerta de su oficina; **to pay at the ~** pagar a la entrada *or* al entrar; **she lived a few ~s <u>down</u> from me** ella vivía unas cuantas puertas más abajo (de mí); **to be <u>on</u> the ~** [*of nightclub*] hacer de portero, estar en la puerta; **<u>out</u> of ~s** al aire libre; **to <u>see</u> sb to the ~** acompañar a algn a la puerta; **to <u>show</u> sb the ~** decir a algn dónde está la puerta; **to <u>shut</u> the ~ in sb's face** cerrar la puerta a algn en las narices*, dar a algn con la puerta en las narices*; **(from) ~ <u>to</u> ~** de puerta en puerta; ✦ IDIOM **to lay the blame for sth at sb's ~** echar la culpa de algo a algn; **behind closed ~s** a puerta cerrada; **to open the ~ to sth** abrir la(s) puerta(s) a algo; **this could open the ~ to a flood of claims for compensation** esto podría dar pie a una avalancha de reclamaciones de indemnización; ✦ PROV **as one ~ shuts, another opens** cuando una puerta se cierra, otra se abre ➤ **door chain** cadena *f* (de seguridad) de la puerta ➤ **door handle** (*gen*) picaporte *m*; [*of car*] manija *f* ➤ **door key** llave *f* (de la puerta) ➤ **door knocker** aldaba *f*, llamador *m*

doorbell ['dɔːbel] N timbre *m*

doorknob ['dɔːnɒb] N pomo *m* de la puerta, manilla *f* (*LAm*)

doorman ['dɔːmən] N (*pl* **doormen**) [*of hotel, block of flats*] portero/a *m/f*, conserje *mf*; (*at nightclub etc*) portero/a *m/f*

doormat ['dɔːmæt] N felpudo *m*, estera *f*

doorstep ['dɔːstep] N (= *threshold*) umbral *m*; (= *step*) peldaño *m* de la puerta; **we don't want an airport on our ~** no queremos un aeropuerto aquí tan cerca

door-to-door ['dɔːtədɔːʳ] ADJ [*selling*] a domicilio ➤ **door-to-door salesman** vendedor *m* a domicilio

doorway ['dɔːweɪ] N [*of house*] entrada *f*, puerta *f*; [*of block of flats, building*] portal *m*

dope [dəʊp] **Ⓐ** N (*) (= *drugs*) drogas *fpl*; (= *cannabis*) chocolate* *m*, mota *f* (*LAm*); (*Sport*) estimulantes *mpl*; **to do ~** (*esp US*) drogarse **Ⓑ** VT [+ *horse, person*] drogar; [+ *food, drink*] adulterar con drogas **Ⓒ** CPD ➤ **dope test** prueba *f* antidoping, control *m* antidoping

dopey* ['dəʊpɪ] ADJ (*compar* **dopier**; *superl* **dopiest**) (= *drugged*) drogado, colocado (*Sp*); (= *fuddled*) atontado; (= *stupid*) corto*

doping ['dəʊpɪŋ] N (*Sport*) dopaje *m*, doping *m*

dork* ['dɔːk] N (*esp US*) pazguato/a *m/f*

dormant ['dɔːmənt] ADJ [*volcano*] inactivo; (*Bio, Bot*) durmiente; [*energy*] latente

dormer ['dɔːməʳ] N (*also* ~ **window**) buhardilla *f*, lucerna *f*

dormice ['dɔːmaɪs] NPL *of* **dormouse**

dormitory ['dɔːmɪtrɪ] **Ⓐ** N **1** (= *bedroom*) dormitorio *m* **2** (*US*) (= *hall of residence*) residencia *f* **Ⓑ** CPD ➤ **dormitory suburb** (*Brit*) barrio *m* dormitorio ➤ **dormitory town** (*Brit*) ciudad *f* dormitorio

Dormobile® ['dɔːməbiːl] N (*Brit*) combi *f*

dormouse ['dɔːmaʊs] N (*pl* **dormice**) lirón *m*

DOS [dɒs] N ABBR = **disk operating system**

dosage ['dəʊsɪdʒ] N [*of medicine*] dosificación *f*; (*on medication instructions*) posología *f*; (= *amount*) dosis *f inv*

dose [dəʊs] N **1** [*of medicine*] dosis *f inv*; **in small ~s** en

pequeñas dosis *or* cantidades **2** (*) [*of flu*] ataque *m*

dosh* [dɒʃ] N (*Brit*) guita* *f*, pasta *f* (*Sp**), plata *f* (*LAm**), lana *f* (*LAm**)

doss* [dɒs] (*Brit*) **Ⓐ** N (= *easy task*) **he thought the course would be a** ~ pensó que el curso sería pan comido* **Ⓑ** VI **1** (*also* ~ **down**) echarse a dormir **2 to ~ around** gandulear, no hacer nada

dosser* ['dɒsəʳ] N (*Brit*) vagabundo/a *m/f*, pobre *mf*

dosshouse* ['dɒshaʊs] N (*Brit*) pensión *f* de mala muerte

dossier ['dɒsɪeɪ] N (*gen*) informe *m*, dossier *m*; (*Admin*) expediente *m* (**on** sobre)

DOT N ABBR (*US*) = **Department of Transportation**

dot [dɒt] **Ⓐ** N punto *m*; **dot, dot, dot** (*Typ*) puntos suspensivos; **at seven o'clock on the ~** a las siete en punto; **to pay on the ~** pagar puntualmente; ✦ IDIOM **since the year ~** (*Brit**) desde los tiempos de Maricastaña **Ⓑ** VT **1** [+ *letter*] poner el punto sobre; ✦ IDIOM **to ~ the i's and cross the t's** poner los puntos sobre las íes **2** (= *scatter*) esparcir, desparramar; **they are ~ted about the country** están esparcidos por todo el país **3** (= *speckle*) puntear, motear, salpicar de puntos; **~ted with flowers** salpicado de flores

dotcom, dot.com [dɒt'kɒm] N puntocom *f*

dote on [dəʊt'ɒn] VI + PREP adorar, chochear por

doting ['dəʊtɪŋ] ADJ (= *loving*) **her ~ parents** sus padres, que la adoran

dotted line [dɒtɪd'laɪn] N línea *f* de puntos; **"tear along the dotted line"** "cortar por la línea de puntos"; ✦ IDIOM **to sign on the ~** firmar

dotty* ['dɒtɪ] ADJ (*compar* **dottier**; *superl* **dottiest**) (*Brit*) [*person*] chiflado*; [*idea, scheme*] estrafalario, disparatado

double ['dʌbl] **Ⓐ** ADJ **1** (= *twice*) doble; **it is ~ what it was** es el doble de lo que era; **he's ~ your age** te dobla la edad; **~ the amount of money** el doble de dinero; **~ the size** doble de grande

2 (= *extra-big*) doble; **a ~ helping/whisky** una porción/un whisky doble

3 (= *two, dual*) **it is spelt with a ~ "m"** se escribe con dos emes; **that's B E ~ L** es B, E, doble L; **~ five two six (5526)** (*Telec*) cincuenta y cinco, veintiséis, cinco, cinco, dos, seis; **throw a ~ six to commence play** para empezar el juego tiene que sacar un seis doble al tirar los dados; **to lead a ~ life** llevar una doble vida; **it serves a ~ purpose** sirve un doble propósito

Ⓑ ADV **1** (= *twice as much*) [*cost, pay*] el doble; **he earns ~ what I earn** gana el doble que yo; **to see ~** ver doble

2 (= *in half*) por la mitad; **the blanket had been folded ~** habían doblado la manta por la mitad; **to be bent ~ with pain** retorcerse de dolor

Ⓒ N **1** (= *drink, throw of dice*) doble *m*; **~ or quits** doble o nada

2 (= *double room*) habitación *f* doble

3 (= *lookalike, stand-in*) doble *mf*

4 (*in expressions*) **at the ~** a la carrera, corriendo; **they ate their food at the ~** comieron a la carrera, comieron corriendo; **get into bed, at the ~!** ¡a la cama corriendo!; **on the ~*** ya mismo; **we'd better go on the ~** mejor vamos ya mismo

5 doubles (*Tennis, Badminton*) dobles *mpl*; **to play ~s** jugar dobles; **a game of mixed/ladies' ~s** un partido de dobles mixtos/femininos

Ⓓ VT **1** (= *increase twofold*) [+ *money, quantity, profits*] doblar, duplicar; [+ *price, salary, bet*] doblar; [+ *efforts*] redoblar; **think of a number and ~ it** piensa en un número y multiplícalo por dos *or* duplícalo

2 (*also* ~ **over**) [+ *paper, blanket*] doblar

Ⓔ VI **1** (= *become twice as great*) [*quantity*] doblarse, duplicarse; **these figures have ~d since last year** estas cifras se han duplicado desde el año pasado

2 (= *have two functions*) **to ~ <u>as</u> sth** hacer las veces de algo; **he ~d as Hamlet's father** también hizo el papel del padre de Hamlet

Ⓕ CPD ➤ **double agent** doble agente *mf* ➤ **double bass** contrabajo *m* ➤ **double bed** cama *f* de matrimonio ➤ **double bend** (*Aut*) curva *f* en S ➤ **double bill** (*Cine*) programa *m* doble ➤ **double boiler** (*US*) cazos *mpl* para hervir al baño María ➤ **double booking** (= *booking for two*) reserva *f* para dos; (= *over-booking*) doble reserva *f* ➤ **double chin** papada *f* ➤ **double cream** (*Brit*) nata *f* (para montar) (*Sp*), doble crema *f* (*Mex*), crema *f* doble (*LAm*) ➤ **double dealer** traidor(a) *m/f* ➤ **double density disk** (*Comput*) disco *m* de doble densidad ➤ **double doors** puerta *fsing* de dos hojas ➤ **double Dutch*** (*Brit*) chino* *m*; **it's ~ Dutch to me*** para mí es chino* ➤ **double entry** partida *f* doble ➤ **double figures: to be into ~ figures** rebasar la decena, pasar de diez; **only three batsmen reached ~ figures** sólo tres bateadores marcaron más de diez tantos ➤ **double first** (*Univ*) título universitario británico con nota de sobresaliente en dos especialidades ➤ **double glazing** (*esp Brit*) doble ventana *f*, doble acristalamiento *m* (*Sp*) ➤ **double jeopardy** (*US Jur*) procesamiento *m* por segunda vez ➤ **double meaning** doble sentido *m* ➤ **double room** habitación *f* doble ➤ **double saucepan** (*Brit*) cazos *mpl* para hervir al baño María ➤ **double standard: to have ~ standards** ✧ **have a ~ standard** aplicar una regla para unos y otra para otros ➤ **double take: to do a ~ take** (= *look twice*) tener que mirar dos veces ➤ **double talk** lenguaje *m* con doble sentido ➤ **double time** (*Ind, Comm*) tarifa *f* doble; **we earn ~ time on Sundays** los domingos nos pagan el doble ➤ **double vision** doble visión *f*, diplopía *f* ➤ **double windows** ventanas *fpl* dobles ➤ **double yellow lines** (*Aut*) línea doble amarilla de prohibido aparcar, ≈ línea *fsing* amarilla continua

➤ **double back** VI + ADV [*person*] volver sobre sus pasos; **to ~ back on itself** [*road*] volver sobre sí mismo ➤ **double up** Ⓐ VT + ADV **to be ~d up with pain** retorcerse de dolor Ⓑ VI + ADV **1** (= *bend over*) doblarse; **he ~d up with laughter** se partió de la risa **2** (= *share room*) compartir (una habitación)

double-barrelled ['dʌbl̩ˌbærəld] ADJ **1** [*gun*] de dos cañones **2** (*Brit*) [*surname*] compuesto

double-book [ˌdʌbl̩'bʊk] VT **the room had been ~ed** habían reservado la habitación para dos personas/parejas *etc* distintas

double-breasted ['dʌbl̩'brestɪd] ADJ cruzado, con botonadura doble

double-check ['dʌbl̩'tʃek] Ⓐ VT volver a comprobar; **to ~ that ...** volver a comprobar que ...:, asegurarse bien de que ... Ⓑ VI volver a comprobar, asegurarse bien; **to ~ with sb** confirmarlo con algn

double-click ['dʌbl̩ˌklɪk] VI (*Comput*) hacer doble clic (**on** en)

double-cross* ['dʌbl̩'krɒs] Ⓐ VT traicionar, engañar Ⓑ N engaño *m*, trampa *f*, traición *f*

double-decker ['dʌbl̩'dekəʳ] N (*esp Brit*) (*also ~* **bus**) autobús *m* de dos pisos

double-edged ['dʌbl̩'edʒd] ADJ [*remark*] con segundas; ✦ IDIOM **it's a ~ sword** es un arma de doble filo

double entendre ['duːblɑ̃ː'tɑ̃ːndr] N (*esp Brit*) equívoco *m*, frase *f* ambigua

double-park [ˌdʌbl̩'pɑːk] VI aparcar en doble fila, estacionar en doble fila

double-quick [ˌdʌbl̩'kwɪk] ADV rapidísimamente, en un santiamén

doubly ['dʌblɪ] ADV **1** (= *twice as*) [*important, difficult, dangerous*] doblemente; **you'll have to be ~ careful from now on** a partir de ahora tienes que tener el doble de cuidado; **he has to work ~ hard** tiene que trabajar el doble **2** (= *in two ways*) por partida doble; **Fran was ~ mistaken** Fran estaba equivocada por partida doble

doubt [daʊt] Ⓐ N duda *f*; **there is some ~ about it** sobre esto existen dudas; **to cast ~ on** poner en duda; **to have one's ~s about sth** tener sus dudas acerca de algo; **to be in ~** [*person*] tener dudas, dudar; [*sb's honesty*] ser dudoso; **she was in ~ whether to ...** dudaba si ...; **the matter is still in some ~** el caso sigue siendo dudoso; **in ~** en caso de duda; **no ~!** ¡sin duda!; **no ~ he will come** seguro que viene; **there is no ~ that** es indudable que, no cabe duda de que; **I have no ~ that it is true** no me cabe duda de que es verdad; **without (a) ~** sin duda (alguna)

Ⓑ VT **1** [+ *truth of statement etc*] dudar; **I ~ it very much** lo

dudo mucho; **I never ~ed you** nunca tuve dudas acerca de ti **2** (= *be uncertain*) **to ~ whether** *or* **if** dudar si; **I don't ~ that he will come** no dudo que vaya a venir Ⓒ VI dudar; **~ing Thomas** incrédulo/a *m/f*, escéptico/a *m/f*

doubtful ['daʊtfʊl] ADJ **1** (= *uncertain*) [*result, success, future*] incierto, dudoso **2** (= *unconvinced*) [*expression*] de duda; **I'm a bit ~** no estoy convencido del todo; **to be ~ about sth** tener dudas sobre algo; **he still looked ~** no parecía aún convencido; **to be ~ that** dudar que + *subjun*; **"all right then," he said in a ~ tone** —bueno, vale —dijo con un tono de duda en la voz; **I am ~ whether we should accept the offer** dudo si deberíamos aceptar la oferta o no **3** (= *unlikely, questionable*) dudoso; **in ~ taste** de dudoso gusto; **it is ~ that/whether** es poco probable que + *subjun*

doubtfully ['daʊtfəlɪ] ADV sin estar convencido; **Ralph looked at him ~** Ralph lo miró muy poco convencido

doubtless ['daʊtlɪs] ADV sin duda, seguramente

dough [dəʊ] N **1** (*Culin*) masa *f*, pasta *f* **2** (**) (= *money*) guita* *f*, pasta *f* (*Sp**), plata *f* (*LAm**), lana *f* (*LAm**)

doughnut ['dəʊnʌt] N (*Brit*) donut® *m*, dona *f* (*LAm*)

dour ['dʊəʳ] ADJ adusto, arisco

douse [daʊs] VT (= *soak*) mojar (**with** con); [+ *flames, light*] apagar

dove¹ [dʌv] N (= *bird*) paloma *f*; (*Pol*) pacifista *mf*

dove² [dəʊv] (*US*) PT *of* **dive**

Dover sole [ˌdəʊvəˈsəʊl] N lenguado *m*

dowager ['daʊədʒəʳ] N viuda *f* de un noble ➤ **dowager duchess** duquesa *f* viuda

dowdy ['daʊdɪ] ADJ (*compar* **dowdier**; *superl* **dowdiest**) [*person*] anticuado, trasnochado; [*clothes*] trasnochado, pasado de moda

Dow Jones index [ˌdaʊdʒəʊnzˈɪndeks] N índice *m* Dow Jones

down¹ [daʊn]

When **down** is an element in a phrasal verb, eg **back down, play down**, look up the verb.

Ⓐ ADV **1** (= *downwards*) abajo, hacia abajo; (= *to the ground*) a tierra; **face ~** boca abajo; **to fall ~** caerse; **I ran all the way ~** bajé toda la distancia corriendo **2** (*static position*) abajo; (= *on the ground*) por tierra, en tierra; **to be ~** (*Aer*) haber aterrizado, estar en tierra; [*person*] (*having fallen*) haber caído, estar en tierra; **I'll be ~ in a minute** ahora bajo; **he isn't ~ yet** todavía no ha bajado; **the blinds are ~** están bajadas las persianas; **the telephone lines are ~** las líneas de teléfono están cortadas; **~ below** allá abajo; **~ by the river** abajo en la ribera; **~ here** aquí (abajo); **~ there** allí (abajo) **3** (*Geog*) **he came ~ from Glasgow to London** ha bajado *or* venido de Glasgow a Londres; **he lives ~ South** vive en el sur; **to go ~ to Southampton** ir *or* bajar a Southampton; **~ under** (*Brit**) en Australia o en Nueva Zelanda **4** (= *named in writing*) **you're ~ for the next race** estás inscrito para la próxima carrera; **you're ~ for Tuesday** te hemos apuntado para el martes **5** (= *reduced*) **his temperature is ~** le ha bajado la temperatura; **the price of meat is ~** ha bajado el precio de la carne; **the tyres are ~** los neumáticos están desinflados; **England are two goals ~** Inglaterra está perdiendo por dos tantos; **I'm ~ to my last cigarette** me queda un cigarrillo nada más **6** (*indicating a series or succession*) **from the biggest ~ to the smallest** desde el más grande hasta el más pequeño **7** (= *ill*) **I've been ~ with flu** he estado con gripe **8** **~ to** (= *up to*) **it's ~ to him** le toca a él, le incumbe a él; **it's all ~ to us now** ahora nosotros somos los únicos responsables **9** (*as deposit*) **to pay £50 ~** pagar un depósito de 50 libras, hacer un desembolso inicial de 50 libras **10** (*in exclamations*) **down!** ¡abajo!; (*to dog*) ¡quieto!; **~ with traitors!** ¡abajo los traidores!

11 (= *completed etc*) **one ~, five** <u>to go</u> uno menos, ya sólo quedan cinco
12 (*esp US*) **to be ~** <u>on</u> **sb** tener manía *or* inquina a algn*
Ⓑ PREP **1** (*indicating movement*) **to go ~ the road/hill** ir calle/cuesta abajo; **he's gone ~ the pub** (*Brit**) se ha ido al bar; **he ran his finger ~ the list** pasó el dedo por la lista; **the rain was running ~ the trunk** la lluvia corría por el tronco
2 (= *at a lower point on*) **he lives ~ the street (from us)** vive en esta calle, más abajo de nosotros; **~ the ages** a través de los siglos; **~ river** río abajo (**from** de)
Ⓒ ADJ **1** (= *depressed*) deprimido
2 (= *not functioning*) **the computer is ~** el ordenador no funciona
3 (*Brit*) [*train, line*] de bajada
Ⓓ VT **(*)** [+ *food*] devorar; [+ *drink*] beberse (de un trago), tragarse; [+ *opponent*] tirar al suelo, echar al suelo; [+ *plane*] derribar, abatir; ✦ IDIOM **to ~ tools** (*Brit*) declararse en huelga
Ⓔ CPD ➤ **down payment** (*Fin*) (= *initial payment*) entrada *f*; (= *deposit*) desembolso *m* inicial

down² [daʊn] N (= *feathers*) plumón *m*, flojel *m*

down-and-out ['daʊnən,aʊt] **Ⓐ** N indigente *mf*, vagabundo/a *m/f* **Ⓑ** ADJ **to be ~** no tener donde caerse muerto, estar sin un cuarto

downbeat ['daʊn,bi:t] ADJ pesimista, deprimido

downcast ['daʊnkɑ:st] ADJ (= *sad*) abatido; [*eyes*] bajo, alicaído

downer* ['daʊnəʳ] N **1** (= *tranquilizer*) tranquilizante *m*
2 (= *depressing experience*) experiencia *f* deprimente

downfall ['daʊnfɔ:l] N **1** (= *collapse*) caída *f* **2** (= *ruin*) perdición *f*, ruina *f*; **it will be his ~** será su perdición

downgrade [daʊn'greɪd] VT [+ *job, hotel*] bajar de categoría; **he's been ~d to assistant manager** le han bajado a ayudante de dirección

downhearted ['daʊn'hɑ:tɪd] ADJ descorazonado; **don't be ~** no te dejes desanimar

downhill ['daʊn'hɪl] **Ⓐ** ADV cuesta abajo; **to go ~** [*road*] bajar; [*car*] ir cuesta abajo; (*fig*) [*person*] ir cuesta abajo; [*industry*] estar en declive, estar de capa caída; [*company*] ir de mal en peor **Ⓑ** ADJ [*skiing*] de descenso; **it was ~ all the way after that** (= *it got easier*) a partir de entonces la cosa fue más fácil; (= *it got worse*) a partir de entonces la cosa fue de mal en peor

Downing Street ['daʊnɪŋ,stri:t] N Downing Street (*calle de Londres en que están las residencias oficiales del ministro de Hacienda y del primer ministro británicos*)

DOWNING STREET

Downing Street es la calle de Londres, cerrada al público, donde se encuentran las residencias oficiales del Primer Ministro (**Prime Minister**) y del Ministro de Economía y Hacienda (**Chancellor of the Exchequer**), normalmente en los números 10 y 11 respectivamente. Los términos **Downing Street, Number Ten**, o **Ten Downing Street** se usan a menudo en los medios de comunicación para referirse al Primer Ministro o al Gobierno. Ver tb <u>www.number-10.gov.uk</u>

---

down-in-the-mouth ['daʊnɪnðə'maʊθ] ADJ decaído, deprimido

download [,daʊn'ləʊd] VT (*Comput*) descargar

downloadable [,daʊn'ləʊdəbl] ADJ (*Comput*) descargable

downmarket [,daʊn'mɑ:kɪt] **Ⓐ** ADJ [*product*] para el sector popular del mercado **Ⓑ** ADV **to go ~** buscar clientela en el sector popular

downpour ['daʊnpɔ:ʳ] N aguacero *m*, chaparrón *m*, chubasco *m* (*LAm*)

downright ['daʊnraɪt] **Ⓐ** ADJ [*nonsense, lie*] patente, manifiesto; [*refusal*] categórico **Ⓑ** ADV [*rude, angry*] realmente

downside ['daʊnsaɪd] N pega *f*, desventaja *f*, lo malo (**of** de)

downsize [,daʊn'saɪz] **Ⓐ** VT hacer recortes de personal en

Ⓑ VI reducir (el) personal

downspout ['daʊnspaʊt] N (*US*) tubo *m* de desagüe, cañería *f*

Down's Syndrome ['daʊnz,sɪndrəʊm] N síndrome *m* de Down; **a ~ child** un niño con síndrome de Down

downstairs ['daʊn'steəz] **Ⓐ** ADJ (= *on the ground floor*) de la planta baja; (= *on the floor underneath*) del piso de abajo; **a ~ window** una ventana de la planta baja **Ⓑ** ADV (= *on the ground floor*) en la planta baja, abajo; **to fall ~** caer por las escaleras; **to come/go ~** bajar la escalera **Ⓒ** N **the ~** la planta baja

downstream ['daʊn'stri:m] ADV río abajo (**from** de); **to go ~** ir río abajo

downtime ['daʊn,taɪm] N (*esp US*) tiempo *m* de inactividad, tiempo *m* muerto

down-to-earth ['daʊntʊ'ɜ:θ] ADJ (= *natural*) natural, llano; (= *practical*) práctico, realista

downtown ['daʊn'taʊn] (*esp US*) **Ⓐ** ADV (= *in the centre*) en el centro; (= *to the centre*) al centro **Ⓑ** ADJ **~ San Francisco** el centro de San Francisco

downtrodden ['daʊn,trɒdn] ADJ [*person*] oprimido, pisoteado

downward ['daʊnwəd] **Ⓐ** ADJ [*curve, movement*] descendente; [*slope*] hacia abajo **Ⓑ** ADV hacia abajo

downwards ['daʊnwədz] ADV (*esp Brit*) = **downward B**

dowry ['daʊrɪ] N dote *f*

doz. ABBR (= **dozen**) doc.

doze [dəʊz] **Ⓐ** N sueñecito *m*, siestecita *f*; **to have a ~** (*after meal*) echar una siestecita **Ⓑ** VI dormitar
➤ **doze off** VI + ADV dormirse

dozen ['dʌzn] N docena *f*; **80p a ~** 80 peniques la docena; **a ~ eggs** una docena de huevos; **~s of times/people** cantidad de veces/gente

dozy ['dəʊzɪ] ADJ (*compar* **dozier**; *superl* **doziest**)
1 (= *sleepy*) amodorrado, soñoliento **2** (*Brit**) (= *stupid*) corto*, lerdo*

DP N ABBR = **data processing**

DPh ABBR = **Doctor of Philosophy**

DPhil [,di:'fɪl] N ABBR = **Doctor of Philosophy**

dpi N ABBR (*Comput*) (= **dots per inch**) ppp *mpl*

DPM N ABBR = **Diploma in Psychological Medicine**

DPP N ABBR (*Brit*) = **Director of Public Prosecutions**

dpt ABBR (= **department**) dto.

Dr, Dr. ABBR **1** (= **Doctor**) Dr(a). **2** = **debtor 3** = **Drive**

drab [dræb] ADJ (*compar* **~ber**; *superl* **~best**) [*colour*] apagado; [*life*] monótono, gris

draft [drɑ:ft] **Ⓐ** N **1** (*written*) borrador *m* (*also Comput*); (= *drawing*) boceto *m* **2** (*Comm*) (*also banker's ~*) letra *f* de cambio, giro *m* **3** **the ~** (*US Mil*) (= *conscription*) la llamada a filas, el servicio militar **4** (*US*) = **draught Ⓑ** VT
1 [+ *document*] (= *write*) redactar; [+ *first attempt*] hacer un borrador de **2** (*Mil*) (*for specific duty*) destacar; (= *send*) mandar (**to** a); (*US Mil*) (= *conscript*) reclutar, llamar al servicio militar; (*fig*) forzar, obligar **Ⓒ** CPD ➤ **draft dodger** (*US*) prófugo *m*

draftsman ['drɑ:ftsmən] N (*pl* **draftsmen**) (*US*) = **draughtsman**

draftsmanship ['drɑ:ftsmənʃɪp] N (*US*) = **draughtsmanship**

draftswoman ['drɑ:fts,wʊmən] N (*pl* **draftswomen**) (*US*) = **draughtswoman**

drafty ['drɑ:ftɪ] ADJ (*US*) = **draughty**

drag [dræg] **Ⓐ** N **1** (*Aer*) (= *resistance*) resistencia *f* aerodinámica
2 (*) (= *boring thing*) lata* *f*, rollo *m* (*Sp**); **what a ~!** ¡qué lata!*, ¡qué rollo! (*Sp**); **she's a real ~!** ¡qué tía más pesada!*
3 (*) (*on cigarette*) chupada *f*, calada *f* (*Sp*)
4 (= *women's clothes*) **he was wearing ~** iba vestido de mujer, iba travestido; **a man in ~** un hombre vestido de mujer, un hombre travestido
5 the main ~ (*US**) la avenida principal
Ⓑ VT **1** (= *pull, trail*) arrastrar; **he ~ged her out of the car** la

sacó del coche a rastras; **I don't want to ~ the children round the supermarket** no quiero ir tirando de los niños por el supermercado; **I don't want to get ~ged into your argument** no quiero que me mezcléis en vuestra discusión; **we had to ~ the truth out of him** tuvimos que sacarle la verdad a la fuerza; ✦ IDIOM **to ~ one's feet** *or* **heels** (= *hold things up*) dar largas (al asunto)
2 (= *dredge, search*) [+ *sea bed, river*] dragar
ⓒ VI [*time*] pasar muy lentamente; [*film, play*] hacerse pesado; **the minutes ~ged by** los minutos pasaban muy lentamente *or* se alargaban sin fin
ⓓ CPD ➤ **drag and drop** (*Comput*) arrastrar y soltar *m*
➤ **drag artist** transformista *m*, travesti *m* ➤ **drag car** coche *m* trucado ➤ **drag queen*** drag-queen* *f*, reinona* *f*, travesti *m* ➤ **drag race** (*US Aut*) carrera de coches trucados de salida parada
➤ **drag about** VT + ADV = **drag around**
➤ **drag along** VT + ADV arrastrar
➤ **drag around** VT + ADV arrastrar de un lado a otro
➤ **drag away** VT + ADV **1** (*by force*) llevar a la fuerza **2** (*fig*) **I'm sorry to ~ you away from your meal** siento hacerte levantar de la mesa; **you can never ~ him away from the television** no hay forma de despegarlo* *or* apartarlo del televisor; **if you can ~ yourself away from the bar** si puedes despegarte del bar
➤ **drag down** VT + ADV **he could ~ down the entire party in this election** podría hacer fracasar a todo el partido en estas elecciones; **I'm not going to be ~ged down to your level** no me vas a arrastrar a tu mismo nivel
➤ **drag on** VI + ADV [*meeting, case*] alargarse; [*film, play*] hacerse pesadísimo; [*speech*] hacerse interminable
➤ **drag out** VT + ADV [+ *process*] alargar
➤ **drag up** VT + ADV **do you have to ~ that up again?** ¿otra vez tienes que sacar a relucir eso?; **this ~ged up painful memories for her** esto despertó en ella recuerdos dolorosos

draglift ['dræglɪft] N (*Ski*) arrastre *m*, remonte *m*

dragon ['dræɡən] N **1** (*Myth*) dragón *m* **2** (*) (= *woman*) bruja *f*

dragonfly ['dræɡənflaɪ] N libélula *f*, caballito *m* del diablo

drain [dreɪn] **ⓐ** N **1** (*in house*) desagüe *m*; (*in street*) boca *f* de alcantarilla, sumidero *m*; (*Agr*) zanja *f* de drenaje; **the ~s** el alcantarillado; ✦ IDIOM **to throw one's money down the ~*** tirar el dinero (por la ventana)
2 to be a ~ on [+ *energies, resources*] consumir, agotar; **they are a great ~ on our reserves** ellos se llevan gran parte de nuestras reservas
ⓑ VT **1** [+ *land, marshes, lake*] drenar, desecar; [+ *vegetables, last drops*] escurrir; [+ *glass, radiator etc*] vaciar
2 [+ *energies, resources*] consumir, agotar; **to feel ~ed (of energy)** sentirse agotado *or* sin fuerzas; **the country is being ~ed of wealth** al país lo están empobreciendo
ⓒ VI [*washed dishes, vegetables*] escurrir; [*liquid*] desaguar; [*stream*] desembocar (**into** en)
➤ **drain away** **ⓐ** VT + ADV [+ *liquid*] (*from vegetables etc*) escurrir; (*Med, Mech*) drenar
ⓑ VI + ADV [*liquid*] irse; [*strength*] agotarse
➤ **drain off** VT + ADV [+ *liquid*] (*from vegetables etc*) escurrir; (*Med, Mech*) drenar

drainage ['dreɪnɪdʒ] N **1** [*of land*] (*naturally*) desagüe *m*; (*artificially*) drenaje *m*; [*of lake*] desecación *f* **2** (= *sewage system*) alcantarillado *m*

drainboard (*US*) ['dreɪnbɔːd], **drainer** ['dreɪnə'], **draining board** (*esp Brit*) ['dreɪnɪŋ,bɔːd] N escurridero *m*

drainpipe ['dreɪnpaɪp] N tubo *m* de desagüe, cañería *f* ➤ **drainpipe trousers** (*Brit*) pantalones *mpl* de pitillo

drake [dreɪk] N pato *m* (macho)

DRAM, D-RAM ['diːræm] ABBR (*Comput*) = **dynamic random access memory**

drama ['drɑːmə] **ⓐ** N **1** (= *theatre*) teatro *m*; (= *play*) obra *f* dramática, drama *m* **2** (= *commotion*) drama *m* **ⓑ** CPD ➤ **drama critic** crítico/a *m/f* de teatro ➤ **drama school** escuela *f* de arte dramático

dramatic [drə'mætɪk] ADJ **1** (= *marked*) [*rise, decline, improvement*] espectacular; [*change*] radical, drástico; [*effect*] espectacular, dramático **2** (= *theatrical, spectacular*) [*entrance*] espectacular, teatral; [*escape*] espectacular;

[*decor*] de gran efecto, efectista; **with a ~ gesture** con gesto teatral **3** (*Theat*) [*works, film*] dramático, teatral; [*art*] dramático

dramatically [drə'mætɪkəlɪ] ADV **1** (= *markedly*) [*change*] radicalmente; [*rise, fall, improve*] espectacularmente; [*different*] radicalmente **2** (= *theatrically*) [*pause, sigh*] de forma teatral, con mucho teatro **3** (*Theat*) **~, it was very effective** desde el punto de vista dramático funcionó muy bien

dramatist ['dræmətɪst] N dramaturgo/a *m/f*

dramatize ['dræmətaɪz] VT **1** [+ *events*] dramatizar; (= *adapt*) [+ *novel*] adaptar a la televisión/al cine **2** (= *exaggerate*) dramatizar, exagerar

drank [dræŋk] PT *of* **drink**

drape [dreɪp] **ⓐ** VT [+ *object*] cubrir (**with** con, de); **~ this around your shoulders** ponte esto sobre los hombros; **he ~d a towel around himself** se cubrió con una toalla **ⓑ** **drapes** NPL (*US*) cortinas *fpl*

draper's ['dreɪpəz], **drapery** ['dreɪpərɪ] N (*Brit*) pañería *f*, mercería *f* (*LAm*)

drastic ['dræstɪk] ADJ [*measures, change, reduction*] drástico; [*effect*] notorio

drastically ['dræstɪkəlɪ] ADV drásticamente; **to be ~ reduced** sufrir una reducción drástica; **the plan went ~ wrong** el plan fracasó estrepitosamente

drat* [dræt] EXCL **drat!** ◇ **drat it!** ¡maldita sea!*, ¡mecachis! (*Sp**)

draught, draft (*US*) [drɑːft] **ⓐ** N **1** [*of air*] corriente *f* de aire; ✦ IDIOM **to feel the ~** pasar apuros (económicos) **2** (= *drink*) trago *m*; **at one ~** de un trago; **on ~** de barril **ⓑ** CPD ➤ **draught beer** cerveza *f* de barril ➤ **draught excluder** burlete *m*

draughtboard ['drɑːftbɔːd] N (*Brit*) tablero *m* de damas

draught-proof, draft-proof (*US*) ['drɑːftpruːf] ADJ a prueba de corrientes de aire

draughts [drɑːfts] NSING (*Brit*) juego *m* de damas; **to play ~** jugar a las damas

draughtsman, draftsman (*US*) ['drɑːftsmən] N (*pl* **draughtsmen**) **1** (*in drawing office*) delineante *mf*, dibujante *mf* **2** (*Brit*) (*in game*) dama *f*, pieza *f*

draughtsmanship, draftsmanship (*US*) ['drɑːftsmənʃɪp] N (= *skill*) arte *m* del delineante; (= *quality*) habilidad *f* para el dibujo

draughtswoman, draftswoman (*US*) ['drɑːfts,wʊmən] N (*pl* **draughtswomen**) dibujante *f*

draughty, drafty (*US*) ['drɑːftɪ] ADJ (*compar* **draughtier**; *superl* **draughtiest**) [*room*] con mucha corriente; [*street corner*] de mucho viento

draw [drɔː] (*vb: pt* **drew**; *pp* **~n**) **ⓐ** N **1** (= *lottery*) lotería *f*; (= *picking of ticket*) sorteo *m*; **the ~ takes place on Saturday** el sorteo es el sábado; **it's the luck of the ~** es la suerte **2** (*esp Brit*) (= *score*) empate *m*; **the match ended in a ~** el partido terminó en empate **3** (= *attraction*) atracción *f* **4 to be quick on the ~** (= *gunman*) ser rápido en sacar la pistola; (*fig*) ser muy avispado **ⓑ** VT **1** (= *pull*) [+ *bolt, curtains*] (*to close*) correr; (*to open*) descorrer; [+ *caravan, trailer*] tirar, jalar (*LAm*); **she drew him to one side** lo llevó a un lado; **she drew him towards her** lo atrajo hacia sí
2 (= *extract*) [+ *gun, sword, confession, tooth*] sacar; [+ *cheque*] girar; [+ *salary*] cobrar; [+ *number, prize*] sacarse; **it drew blood** le hizo sangre *or* (*more frm*) sangrar; **to ~ (a) breath** respirar; **to ~ comfort from sth** hallar consuelo en algo; **to ~ inspiration from sth** encontrar inspiración en algo; **to ~ lots** echar suertes; **to ~ a smile from sb** arrancar una sonrisa a algn
3 (= *attract*) [+ *attention, crowd, customer*] atraer; **to feel ~n to sb** simpatizar con algn; **he refuses to be ~n** (*esp Brit*) se niega a hablar de ello, se guarda de hacer comentario alguno
4 (= *cause*) [+ *laughter*] causar, provocar; [+ *applause*] despertar, motivar
5 (= *sketch*) [+ *scene, person*] dibujar; [+ *plan, line, circle, map*] trazar; **to ~ a picture** hacer un dibujo; **to ~ a picture**

of sb hacer un retrato de algn; ✦ IDIOM **I ~ the line at (doing) that** a (hacer) eso no llego
6 (= *formulate*) [+ *conclusion*] sacar (**from** de); **to ~ a comparison between A and B** comparar A con B; **to ~ a distinction** distinguir (**between** entre)
7 (*esp Brit*): **to ~ a match/game** empatar un partido; (*Chess*) entablar
⑤ VI **1** (= *move*) **he drew ahead of the other runners** se adelantó a los demás corredores; **to ~ to an end** llegar a su fin; **the train drew into the station** el tren entró en la estación; **the two horses drew level** los dos caballos se igualaron; **to ~ near** acercarse; **the car drew over to the kerb** el coche se acercó a la acera; **he drew to one side** se apartó; **to ~ towards** acercarse a
2 (*esp US*) (= *infuse*) [*tea*] reposar
3 (*esp Brit*) [*two teams, players*] empatar; (*Chess*) entablar; **we drew two all** empatamos a dos; **the teams drew for second place** los equipos empataron en segundo lugar
4 (= *sketch*) dibujar
➤ **draw aside** VT + ADV [+ *covering*] apartar; [+ *curtain*] descorrer; [+ *person*] apartar, llevar a un lado
➤ **draw away** VI + ADV apartarse, alejarse; (*in race*) dejar atrás a los otros; **to ~ away from the kerb** apartarse *or* alejarse de la acera
➤ **draw back ④** VT + ADV [+ *object, hand*] retirar; [+ *curtains*] descorrer **⑤** VI + ADV echarse atrás (**from** de)
➤ **draw in ④** VT + ADV **1** [*car*] detenerse, pararse (*LAm*); [*train*] entrar en la estación **2** (*Brit*) **the days are ~ing in** los días se van acortando *or* haciendo más cortos **⑥** VT + ADV [+ *breath, air*] aspirar; [+ *claws*] retraer; [+ *crowds*] atraer
➤ **draw on** VI + PREP [+ *source*] inspirarse en; [+ *resources*] usar, hacer uso de, explotar; [+ *experience*] recurrir a, servirse de; [+ *bank account*] retirar dinero de
➤ **draw out** ④ VT + ADV **1** (= *take out*) [+ *handkerchief, money*] sacar **2** (= *prolong*) [+ *meeting*] alargar **⑥** VI + ADV **1** [*train etc*] arrancar **2** [*days*] hacerse más largos
➤ **draw up ④** VT + ADV **1** [+ *will, contract*] redactar; [+ *report*] redactar, preparar; [+ *plan*] elaborar, trazar **2** (= *move*) [+ *chair*] acercar; [+ *troops*] ordenar, disponer; **to ~ o.s. up (to one's full height)** enderezarse, erguirse **⑥** VI + ADV [*vehicle*] detenerse, parar
➤ **draw upon** VI + PREP = **draw on**

drawback ['drɔ:bæk] N inconveniente *m*, desventaja *f*

drawbridge ['drɔ:brɪdʒ] N puente *m* levadizo

drawer[1] [drɔ:ʳ] N (*in desk, chest of drawers*) cajón *m*

drawer[2] ['drɔ:əʳ] N (*Comm*) girador(a) *m/f*, librador(a) *m/f*

drawing ['drɔ:ɪŋ] ④ N **1** (= *picture*) dibujo **m 2** (= *activity*) **I'm no good at ~** no sirvo para el dibujo, no se me da bien el dibujo **⑥** CPD ➤ **drawing board** mesa *f* de dibujo; ✦ IDIOM **back to the ~ board!** ¡a comenzar de nuevo! ➤ **drawing paper** papel *m* de dibujo ➤ **drawing pin** (*Brit*) chincheta *f* (*Sp*), chinche *m* or *f* (*LAm*) ➤ **drawing room** salón *m*, sala *f*

drawl [drɔ:l] ④ N voz *f* cansina; **a Southern ~** un acento del sur **⑥** VT decir alargando las palabras **⑥** VI hablar alargando las palabras

drawn [drɔ:n] ④ PP of **draw ⑥** ADJ **1** (*with tiredness*) demacrado, ojeroso; (*with pain*) macilento **2** [*game*] empatado **3 long ~ out** larguísimo, prolongado **4 with ~ sword** con la espada en la mano

drawstring ['drɔ:strɪŋ] N cordón *m*

dread [dred] ④ N terror *m*, pavor *m* **⑥** VT tener pavor a; **I ~ going to the dentist** me da pavor ir al dentista; **I ~ what may happen when he comes** me horroriza lo que pueda pasar cuando venga; **I ~ to think of it*** ¡sólo pensarlo me da horror!; **the ~ed exams** (*hum*) los muy temidos exámenes **⑥** ADJ espantoso

dreadful ['dredfʊl] ADJ [*news, accident, experience*] espantoso, terrible; **how ~!** ¡qué horror!; **I feel ~!** (= *ill*) ¡me encuentro muy mal!, ¡me encuentro fatal! (*Sp**); **I feel ~ about forgetting his birthday** me siento fatal por haber olvidado su cumpleaños*; **to look ~** (= *ill*) tener mala cara*; **I look ~ in this hat** estoy horrible con este sombrero, tengo una pinta horrorosa con este sombrero*; **that brown wallpaper looks ~** ese papel pintado marrón queda horroroso

dreadfully* ['dredfəlɪ] ADV **1** (= *very*) [*boring*] mortalmente, terriblemente; [*late, difficult*] increíblemente, muy; **I'm ~ sorry** lo siento muchísimo; **I felt something was ~ wrong** sentía que había pasado algo horrible **2** (= *very much*) [*suffer, miss*] muchísimo; [*hurt*] a rabiar **3** (= *badly*) [*behave, treat, sing*] muy mal, espantosamente, fatal (*Sp**)

dreadlocks ['dredlɒks] NPL *rizos de estilo rastafari*

dream [dri:m] (*vb: pt, pp* **~ed, ~t**) ④ N **1** (*while asleep*) sueño *m*; **a bad ~** una pesadilla; **to have a ~ about sth/sb** soñar con algo/algn; **to see sth in a ~** ver algo en sueños; **sweet ~s!** ¡que sueñes con los angelitos! **2** (= *daydream*) sueño *m*, ensueño *m*; **she goes about in a ~** siempre está en las nubes **3** (= *fantasy, ideal*) sueño *m*; **my ~ is to ...** el sueño de mi vida es ..., mi mayor ilusión es ...; **it was like a ~ come true** fue como un sueño hecho realidad; **the house/man of my ~s** mi casa/hombre ideal, la casa/el hombre de mis sueños; **never in my wildest ~s did I expect to win** ni en mis sueños más dorados hubiera podido imaginar que ganaría; **he lives in a ~ world** vive en un mundo de fantasía *or* de ensueño **4** (*) (= *marvel*) **it worked like a ~** funcionó de maravilla *or* a las mil maravillas; **that car goes like a ~** ese coche funciona de maravilla **⑥** VT **1** (*while asleep*) soñar; **I ~ed that I was being chased** soñé que me perseguían **2** (= *imagine*) soñar, imaginarse; **you must have ~ed it** lo habrás soñado, te lo habrás imaginado; **I never ~ed that she would accept** jamás soñé con que aceptaría, jamás imaginé que aceptaría **⑥** VI **1** (*while asleep*) soñar (**of, about** con) **2** (= *daydream*) estar en las nubes **3** (= *fantasize*) soñar (**of doing sth** con hacer algo); **something most of us only ~ of** *or* **about** algo que para la mayoría de nosotros no pasa de ser un sueño; **~ on!*** ¡ni en sueños!* **4** (= *imagine*) soñar, imaginarse; (*in neg context*) imaginarse; **who would ever ~ of a disaster like this?** ¿quién hubiera podido imaginarse una catástrofe así? **5** (= *consider*) **"will you ask them?" — "I wouldn't ~ of it!"** —¿les preguntarás? —¡ni pensarlo! *or* ¡ni en sueños!*; **I wouldn't ~ of doing such a thing** jamás se me ocurriría hacer tal cosa **⑩** CPD ➤ **dream house** (= *wonderful house*) casa *f* de ensueño; **my ~ house** la casa de mis sueños ➤ **dream ticket** (*Pol*) candidatos *mpl* ideales
➤ **dream up** VT + ADV [+ *plan*] trazar, idear; **only you could ~ up such a stupid idea** sólo a ti se te podría ocurrir una idea tan tonta

dreamer ['dri:məʳ] N soñador(a) *m/f*

dreamlike ['dri:mlaɪk] ADJ de ensueño, como de sueño

dreamt [dremt] PT, PP of **dream**

dreary ['drɪərɪ] ADJ (*compar* **drearier**; *superl* **dreariest**) [*landscape, weather*] gris, inhóspito; [*life, work*] monótono, aburrido; [*book, speech*] pesado

dredge [dredʒ] VT [+ *river, canal*] dragar
➤ **dredge up** VT + ADV sacar con draga; [+ *unpleasant facts*] sacar a la luz

dredger ['dredʒəʳ] N draga *f*

dregs [dregz] NPL [*of tea, coffee etc*] posos *mpl*, heces *fpl*; **the ~ of society** la escoria de la sociedad

drench [drentʃ] VT empapar (**with** de); **to get ~ed** empaparse; **he was ~ed to the skin** estaba empapado *or* calado hasta los huesos

dress [dres] ④ N **1** (= *frock*) vestido *m* **2** (= *clothing*) ropa *f*; **they were wearing traditional Nepalese ~** vestían el traje tradicional *or* típico de Nepal; **formal ~ will be required** el traje de etiqueta es de rigor **⑥** VT **1** (= *put clothes on*) vestir; **to get ~ed** vestirse **2** (*Culin*) [+ *salad*] aliñar, aderezar; [+ *meat, fish*] preparar y condimentar **3** [+ *wound*] vendar **⑥** VI (= *put on clothes*) vestirse; **they always ~ for dinner** siempre (se) ponen elegantes para cenar; **she ~es very well** viste muy bien, va muy bien vestida **⑩** CPD ➤ **dress circle** anfiteatro *m*, (*piso m*) principal *m*

➤ **dress code** *normas sobre la indumentaria* ➤ **dress designer** modisto/a *m/f* ➤ **dress parade** (*US Mil*) desfile *m* de gala ➤ **dress rehearsal** ensayo *m* general ➤ **dress sense** gusto *m* para vestir ➤ **dress shirt** camisa *f* de frac, camisa *f* de etiqueta

➤ **dress up** Ⓐ VI + ADV (*in smart clothes*) ponerse elegante; (*formally*) vestirse de etiqueta; (*in fancy dress*) disfrazarse Ⓑ VT + ADV (= *disguise*) disfrazar

dressed [drest] ADJ vestido; **to be smartly/casually ~** ir (vestido) elegante/informal *or* de sport; **~ as a man/woman** vestido de hombre/mujer; **to get ~** vestirse; **~ in black** vestido de negro; **to be ~ in a skirt/trousers** llevar falda/pantalones; ✦ IDIOM **to be ~ to kill*** ir despampanante*

dresser ['dresəʳ] N (*in kitchen*) aparador *m*; (*US*) (= *dressing table*) tocador *m*

dressing ['dresɪŋ] Ⓐ N 1 (= *bandage*) vendaje *m* 2 (= *salad dressing*) aliño *m* Ⓑ CPD ➤ **dressing case** neceser *m* ➤ **dressing gown** bata *f* ➤ **dressing room** (*Theat*) camerino *m*; (*Brit sport*) vestuario *m* ➤ **dressing table** tocador *m*

dressmaker ['dresmeɪkəʳ] N modista *f*, costurera *f*

dressmaking ['dresmeɪkɪŋ] N costura *f*, corte *m* y confección

drew [druː] PT *of* **draw**

dribble ['drɪbl] Ⓐ N (*of saliva*) babeo *m*; **a ~ of water** (= *thin stream*) un hilillo de agua; (= *drops*) gotas de agua Ⓑ VT 1 **he ~d his milk all down his chin** le chorreaba la leche por la barbilla 2 (*Ftbl*) regatear, driblar Ⓒ VI 1 (*baby*) babear; (*liquid*) gotear 2 (*Ftbl*) controlar el balón; **to ~ past sb** regatear *or* driblar a algn

dribs [drɪbz] NPL ✦ IDIOM **in ~ and drabs** poco a poco, con cuentagotas; **the money came in in ~ and drabs** el dinero fue llegando poco a poco *or* con cuentagotas; **the guests arrived in ~ and drabs** los invitados fueron llegando poco a poco

dried [draɪd] Ⓐ PT, PP *of* **dry** Ⓑ ADJ [*flowers, mushrooms, lentils*] seco; [*milk*] en polvo Ⓒ CPD ➤ **dried fruit(s)** frutas *fpl* pasas

dried-up [ˌdraɪd'ʌp] ADJ [*riverbed, stream, oasis*] seco

drier ['draɪəʳ] N = **dryer**

drift [drɪft] Ⓐ N 1 **the ~ to the city** el movimiento migratorio hacia la ciudad; **the ~ from the land** el éxodo rural, la despoblación del campo 2 (*) (= *meaning*) [*of questions*] significado *m*; **to catch sb's ~** seguir *or* entender a algn; **I don't get your ~** no te entiendo 3 (= *mass*) [*of snow*] ventisquero *m*; **continental ~** deriva *f* continental Ⓑ VI 1 (*in wind, current*) dejarse llevar, ir a la deriva; (= *be off course*) [*boat*] ir a la deriva; [*person*] vagar, ir a la deriva; **to ~ downstream** dejarse llevar río abajo; **he ~ed into marriage** se casó sin pensárselo; **to ~ from job to job** cambiar a menudo de trabajo sin propósito fijo 2 [*snow, sand*] amontonarse Ⓒ CPD ➤ **drift net** traína *f*

➤ **drift apart** VI + ADV irse separando poco a poco
➤ **drift off** VI + ADV (= *doze off*) dormirse, quedarse dormido

driftwood ['drɪftwʊd] N madera *f* de deriva

drill¹ [drɪl] Ⓐ N 1 (*for wood, metal*) taladradora *f*, taladro *m*; (= *bit*) broca *f*; (*Min*) (*for oil*) barrena *f*, perforadora *f*; (*dentist's*) fresa *f*; (*pneumatic*) martillo *m* neumático 2 (*Agr*) (= *machine*) sembradora *f* Ⓑ VT [+ *wood, road*] taladrar, perforar; [+ *tooth*] agujerear; [+ *oil well*] perforar; (*Agr*) sembrar con sembradora; **he ~ed a hole in the wall** hizo *or* taladró un agujero en la pared Ⓒ VI perforar (**for** en busca de)

drill² [drɪl] Ⓐ N (= *exercises*) (*Mil*) instrucción *f*; (*Scol*) ejercicios *mpl*; **you all know the ~*** todos sabéis lo que hay que hacer; **what's the ~?*** ¿qué es lo que tenemos que hacer? Ⓑ VT [+ *soldiers*] ejercitar; **to ~ pupils in grammar** hacer ejercicios de gramática con los alumnos; **to ~ good manners into a child** enseñar buenos modales a un niño; **I had it ~ed into me as a boy** me lo inculcaron de niño

drilling ['drɪlɪŋ] N (*for oil*) perforación *f* ➤ **drilling platform** plataforma *f* de perforación ➤ **drilling rig** torre *f* de perforación

drily ['draɪlɪ] ADV 1 (= *with dry humour*) **... he said ~** ... dijo con un humor cargado de ironía 2 (= *unemotionally*) secamente, con sequedad

drink [drɪŋk] (*vb: pt* **drank**; *pp* **drunk**) Ⓐ N 1 (= *liquid to drink*) bebida *f*; **there's food and ~ in the kitchen** hay comida y bebidas en la cocina, hay cosas de comer y de beber en la cocina; **cold ~s** (*non-alcoholic*) refrescos *mpl*; **to give sb a ~** dar algo de beber a algn; **can I have a ~?** ¿me podrías dar algo de beber *or* (*LAm*) tomar?; **I need a ~ of water** necesito un poco de agua 2 (= *glass of alcohol*) copa *f*, trago *m*; **to go (out) for a ~** salir a tomar algo *or* una copa; **they've asked us round for ~s** nos han invitado a su casa a tomar algo *or* unas copas; **to have a ~** tomar algo 3 (= *alcoholic liquor*) alcohol *m*, bebida *f*; **he's given up ~** ha dejado de beber, ha dejado el alcohol *or* la bebida; **he has a ~ problem** tiene problemas con el alcohol *or* la bebida; **to take to ~** darse a la bebida Ⓑ VT beber, tomar (*esp LAm*); **would you like something to ~?** ¿quieres tomar algo?; **in the end he drank himself to death** al final la bebida lo llevó a la tumba; **we drank ourselves into a stupor** bebimos hasta perder el sentido; **to ~ sb under the table*** dar cien vueltas a algn bebiendo; **to ~ a toast to sth/sb** brindar por algo/algn Ⓒ VI 1 (= *take liquid*) beber; **to ~ from the bottle** beber de la botella; **to ~ out of paper cups** beber en vasos de plástico 2 (= *take alcohol*) beber, tomar (*LAm*); **he doesn't ~** no bebe (alcohol), no toma (alcohol) (*esp LAm*); **don't ~ and drive** si bebes, no conduzcas; **to ~ to sth/sb** brindar por algo/algn; ✦ IDIOM **he ~s like a fish** bebe como una esponja

➤ **drink in** VT + ADV [+ *story, sight, atmosphere*] empaparse de; [+ *words*] estar pendiente de; **the children were ~ing it all in** a los niños no les escapaba nada
➤ **drink up** Ⓐ VT + ADV [+ *one's drink*] terminarse, terminar de beber, terminar de tomar (*LAm*) Ⓑ VI + ADV **up now, please!** ¡terminen(se) sus bebidas!

drinkable ['drɪŋkəbl] ADJ (= *not poisonous*) potable; (= *palatable*) aceptable, que se deja beber

drink-driver [ˌdrɪŋk'draɪvəʳ] N (*Brit*) conductor(a) *m/f* en estado de embriaguez

drink-driving ['drɪŋk'draɪvɪŋ] N (*Brit*) el conducir *or* (*LAm*) manejar en estado de embriaguez ➤ **drink-driving campaign** campaña *f* contra el alcohol en carretera

drinker ['drɪŋkəʳ] N bebedor(a) *m/f*; **he was a heavy ~** era un bebedor empedernido

drinking ['drɪŋkɪŋ] Ⓐ N 1 (= *taking liquid*) **my sore throat made ~ painful** al tener la garganta irritada me dolía mucho al beber 2 (*alcoholic*) **his ~ caused his marriage to break up** la bebida fue la causa de la ruptura de su matrimonio; **she had to put up with his ~** tuvo que aguantar sus borracheras Ⓑ CPD ➤ **drinking chocolate** chocolate *m* (*bebida*) ➤ **drinking companion** compañero/a *m/f* de copas ➤ **drinking fountain** fuente *f* (de agua potable) ➤ **drinking session** juerga *f*, farra *f* (*LAm**) ➤ **drinking trough** abrevadero *m*, camellón *m* ➤ **drinking water** agua *f* potable

> Use **el/un** not **la/una** before feminine nouns beginning with stressed **a** or **ha** like **agua**.

drinking-up time ['drɪŋkɪŋ'ʌpˌtaɪm] N *tiempo permitido para terminar las bebidas en el pub antes de cerrar*

drip [drɪp] Ⓐ N 1 (= *droplet*) gota *f* 2 (= *dripping sound*) goteo *m* 3 (*) (= *person*) soso/a *m/f* 4 (*Med*) gotero *m*, gota a gota *m inv*; **she is on a ~** tiene puesto un gotero *or* un gota a gota Ⓑ VT **her knee was ~ping blood** le salía mucha sangre de la rodilla; **you're ~ping paint all over the place** estás chorreando pintura por todas partes, lo estás poniendo todo perdido de pintura; **try not to ~ sauce onto the table cloth** procura que la salsa no gotee en el mantel Ⓒ VI [*tap, faucet*] gotear; **the rain was ~ping down the wall** las gotas de lluvia se deslizaban por la pared; **sweat was ~ping from his brow** le caían gotas de sudor de la frente

drip-dry ['drɪp'draɪ] ADJ inarrugable

dripping ['drɪpɪŋ] (*Brit*) **Ⓐ** N (= *fat*) pringue *m or f* **Ⓑ** ADJ
1 (= *soaking*) [*washing, coat*] que chorrea, que gotea;
[*person, hair*] empapado; **to be ~ wet*** estar empapado *or*
chorreando; **~ with blood** chorreando sangre; **to be ~ with
sweat** estar sudando a chorros, estar chorreando de sudor;
women ~ with diamonds mujeres cargadas de diamantes
2 [*tap, gutter*] que gotea

drive [draɪv] (*vb: pt* **drove**; *pp* **~n**) **Ⓐ** N **1** (= *outing*) vuelta *f*
en coche; paseo *m* en coche; (= *journey*) viaje *m* (en
coche); **to go for a ~** ir a dar una vuelta *or* un paseo en
coche; **it's only a short ~ from here** desde aquí se tarda
poco en coche; **one hour's ~ from London** a una hora en
coche de Londres; **it's a 50-mile ~** está a una distancia de
50 millas
2 (*in front of garage*) entrada *f*; (*to large house*) camino *m*
(de acceso), avenida *f*
3 (*Tennis*) golpe *m* directo, drive *m*; (*Golf*) drive *m*
4 (= *energy, motivation*) empuje *m*, dinamismo *m*; **to lack ~**
no tener empuje *or* dinamismo
5 (= *campaign*) campaña *f*; **a recruitment ~** una campaña
de reclutamiento; **a sales ~** una promoción de ventas; **the
~ towards industrialization** el camino hacia la
industrialización
6 (*Tech*) **four-wheel ~** tracción *f* en las cuatro ruedas; **front-
wheel/rear-wheel ~** tracción *f* delantera/trasera; **a left-hand/
right-hand ~ car** un coche con el volante a la izquierda/
derecha
7 (*Comput*) (*also* **disk ~**) unidad *f* de disco; **CD-ROM ~**
unidad *f* de CD-ROM
Ⓑ VT **1** (= *operate*) [+ *car, bus, train*] conducir, manejar
(*LAm*); [+ *racing car, speedboat*] pilotar; **he ~s a taxi** es
taxista; **he ~s a Mercedes** tiene un Mercedes
2 (= *take*) [+ *passenger*] llevar (en coche); **I'll ~ you home** te
llevo a tu casa
3 (= *power*) [+ *machine*] impulsar
4 (= *take*) **they ~ the cattle to new pastures** conducen el
ganado a otros pastos; **a strong wind was driving the clouds
across the sky** un viento fuerte arrastraba las nubes por el
cielo; **the gale drove the ship off course** el temporal hizo
que el barco perdiera su rumbo
5 (= *push, hammer*) [+ *nail, stake*] clavar (**into** en)
6 (= *force*) **competition has ~n prices down** la competencia
ha hecho que bajen los precios; **I was ~n to it** me vi
forzado a ello; **to ~ sb to despair** llevar a algn a la
desesperación; **his worries drove him to drink** sus
problemas le llevaron a la bebida; **it's enough to ~ you to
drink** (*hum*) te crispa los nervios; **to ~ sb mad** volver loco a
algn
7 (= *motivate*) empujar, mover; **to ~ sb to do sth** ◇ **~ sb
into doing sth** empujar *or* llevar a algn a hacer algo
8 (= *overwork*) **to ~ sb hard** hacer trabajar mucho a algn;
she is driving herself too hard se está exigiendo demasiado
9 (*Sport*) [+ *ball*] mandar
Ⓒ VI **1** (= *operate vehicle*) conducir, manejar (*LAm*); **can you
~?** ¿sabes conducir *or* (*LAm*) manejar?; **to ~ on the left**
circular por la izquierda
2 (= *go by car*) ir en coche; **next time we'll ~ there** la
próxima vez iremos en coche; **we've ~n 50 miles in the last
hour** hemos recorrido 80km en la última hora; **he ~s
around in an expensive car** va por ahí en un coche de esos
caros; **to ~ at 50km an hour** conducir a 50km por hora;
we'll ~ down in the car this weekend este fin de semana
bajaremos en coche; **he drove into a wall** chocó con un
muro; **to ~ to London** ir a Londres en coche
3 (= *handle*) conducirse, manejarse (*LAm*)
4 (= *beat*) **heavy rain drove against the window** la fuerte
lluvia azotaba la ventana
➤ **drive along Ⓐ** VT + ADV [*wind, current*] empujar **Ⓑ** VI
+ ADV [*vehicle*] circular; [*person*] conducir
➤ **drive at*** VI + PREP (= *intend, mean*) insinuar, dar a
entender; **what are you driving at?** ¿qué (es lo que) estás
insinuando *or* dando a entender?
➤ **drive away Ⓐ** VT + ADV **1** (= *chase away*) [+ *person*]
ahuyentar; [+ *cares*] alejar, quitarse de encima **2** (*in vehicle*)
llevarse (en coche) **Ⓑ** VI + ADV irse, marcharse (*en coche*);
[*vehicle*] partir
➤ **drive back Ⓐ** VT + ADV **1** (= *force back*) [+ *person, army*]

hacer retroceder **2** (*in vehicle*) llevar de vuelta (en coche)
Ⓑ VI + ADV volver (en coche)
➤ **drive off Ⓐ** VT + ADV (= *force back*) [+ *enemy*] ahuyentar;
(= *force out*) expulsar, echar **Ⓑ** VI + ADV irse, marcharse (en
coche); [*vehicle*] partir
➤ **drive on Ⓐ** VT + ADV [*person, vehicle*] (*after accident*) no
parar; (*after stopping*) seguir adelante; **~ on!** ¡siga! **Ⓑ** VT
+ ADV (= *incite, encourage*) empujar, mover; **it was the desire
to win that drove her on** era su deseo de ganar lo que la
empujaba *or* movía (a seguir)
➤ **drive on to** VI + PREP [+ *ferry*] embarcar en
➤ **drive out** VT + ADV (= *force out*) expulsar, echar; (= *force to
flee*) ahuyentar; **invading tribes drove them out** las tribus
invasoras los expulsaron de sus tierras; **it is said to ~ out
evil spirits** se dice que ahuyenta a los espíritus malignos
➤ **drive over Ⓐ** VT + ADV llevar en coche **Ⓑ** VI + PREP
aplastar **Ⓒ** VI + ADV (= *come*) venir en coche; (= *go*) ir en
coche; **we drove over to see them** fuimos a verlos (en
coche)
➤ **drive up Ⓐ** VT + ADV [+ *price*] hacer subir **Ⓑ** VI + ADV
[*person*] acercarse (en coche); [*vehicle*] pararse

drive-in ['draɪvɪn] (*esp US*) **Ⓐ** N (= *restaurant*) *restaurante
donde se sirve al cliente en su automóvil*; (*also* **~ cinema**)
autocine *m* **Ⓑ** ADJ *dispuesto para el uso del automovilista en
su coche*

drivel* ['drɪvl] N (= *nonsense*) tonterías *fpl*, chorradas* *fpl*,
babosadas *fpl* (*LAm**)

driven ['drɪvn] PP *of* **drive**

driver ['draɪvəʳ] **Ⓐ** N **1** [*of car, bus*] conductor(a) *m/f*,
chofer *mf* (*LAm*); (= *taxi driver*) taxista *mf*; (= *lorry driver*)
camionero/a *m/f*; (*Brit*) (= *train driver*) maquinista *mf*; **he's a
bus ~** es conductor de autobús; **she's an excellent ~**
conduce muy bien **2** (*Golf*) driver *m* **Ⓑ** CPD ➤ **driver's
license** (*US*) permiso *m* de conducir *or* (*LAm*) manejar,
carnet *m* de conducir *or* (*LAm*) manejar

drive-through, drive-thru (*esp US*) ['draɪvθruː] N = **drive-
in**

driveway ['draɪvweɪ] N entrada *f*

driving ['draɪvɪŋ] **Ⓐ** N (*Aut*) **his ~ was a bit erratic** su forma
de conducir *or* (*LAm*) manejar era bastante imprevisible; **we
share the ~** nos turnamos al volante; **why don't you let me
do the ~?** ¿por qué no me dejas conducir *or* (*LAm*) manejar
a mí?
Ⓑ ADJ [*force*] impulsor; [*rain*] torrencial; [*wind*] azotador
Ⓒ CPD ➤ **driving instructor** profesor(a) *m/f* de autoescuela
➤ **driving lesson** clase *f* de conducir *or* (*LAm*) manejar
➤ **driving licence** (*Brit*) permiso *m* de conducir *or* (*LAm*)
manejar, carnet *m* de conducir *or* (*LAm*) manejar ➤ **driving
mirror** retrovisor *m*, espejo *m* retrovisor ➤ **driving school**
autoescuela *f* ➤ **driving seat** asiento *m* del conductor;
✦ IDIOM **to be in the ~ seat** estar al mando; **he's in the ~
seat now** ahora él es quien manda ➤ **driving test** examen
m de conducir *or* (*LAm*) manejar

drizzle ['drɪzl] **Ⓐ** N llovizna *f*, garúa *f* (*LAm*) **Ⓑ** VI lloviznar

droll [drəʊl] ADJ gracioso, divertido

dromedary ['drɒmɪdərɪ] N dromedario *m*

drone [drəʊn] **Ⓐ** N **1** (= *male bee*) zángano *m* **2** (= *noise*)
[*of bees, engine*] zumbido *m*; [*of voice*] tono *m* monótono
Ⓑ VI [*bee, engine, aircraft*] zumbar; [*voice, person*] (*also* **~ on**)
hablar monótonamente

drool [druːl] VI (= *slobber*) babear; **she ~ed over the
kittens/her grandchildren** se le caía la baba con los gatitos/
sus nietos

droop [druːp] VI [*head*] inclinarse; [*shoulders*] encorvarse;
[*flower*] marchitarse

drop [drɒp] **Ⓐ** N **1** [*of liquid*] gota *f*; **we didn't have a ~ of
rain** no cayó ni una gota; **there's just a ~ left** queda sólo una
gota; ✦ IDIOM **a ~ in the ocean** una gota de agua en el mar
2 drops (*Med*) gotas *fpl*
3 (= *sweet*) pastilla *f*
4 (= *fall*) (*in price*) bajada *f*, caída *f*; (*in demand*)
disminución *f*, reducción *f*; **to take a ~ in salary** aceptar un
salario más bajo; **a ~ in temperature** una bajada de las
temperaturas; ✦ IDIOM **at the ~ of a hat** con cualquier
pretexto

5 (= *steep incline*) pendiente *f*; (= *fall*) caída *f*; **a ~ of ten metres** una caída de diez metros
6 (*of supplies, arms etc*) lanzamiento *m*; (*for secret mail*) escondrijo *m* (*para correo secreto*)
7 ✦ IDIOM **to have the ~ on sb** (*US**) llevar la delantera a algn, tener ventaja sobre algn
Ⓑ VT **1** (*deliberately*) [+ *object*] dejar caer; (= *release, let go of*) soltar; [+ *bomb, parachutist*] lanzar; [+ *anchor*] echar
2 (*accidentally*) **I ~ped the glass** se me cayó el vaso; **I've ~ped a stitch** (*Knitting*) se me escapó un punto
3 (= *lower*) [+ *eyes, price*] bajar
4 (*from car*) [+ *object, person*] dejar; **could you ~ me at the station?** ¿me puedes dejar en la estación?
5 [+ *remark, name, clue*] soltar; **to ~ (sb) a hint about sth** echar (a algn) una indirecta sobre algo; **to ~ sb a line** mandar unas líneas a algn
6 (= *omit*) (*from text*) suprimir; **to ~ one's aitches** no pronunciar las haches; **I've been ~ped from the team** me han sacado del equipo
7 [+ *boyfriend*] dejar, plantar; [+ *friend*] romper con; [+ *charges*] retirar; [+ *claim, plan*] renunciar a, abandonar; **we had to ~ what we were doing** tuvimos que dejar lo que estábamos haciendo; **I'm going to ~ chemistry** no voy a dar más química; **to ~ everything** soltarlo todo; ~ **it!*** (*subject*) ¡ya está bien!; **let's ~ the subject** cambiemos de tema
Ⓒ VI **1** (= *fall*) [*object, person*] caer(se); ~ **dead!*** ¡vete al cuerno!*; **I'm fit to ~*** estoy que no me tengo; **he let it ~ that ...** reveló que ...; **so we let the matter ~** así que dejamos el asunto
2 (= *decrease*) [*wind*] calmarse, amainar; [*temperature, price, voice*] bajar; [*numbers, crowd, demand*] disminuir
Ⓓ CPD ➤ **drop goal** drop *m* ➤ **drop kick** puntapié *m* de botepronto
➤ **drop behind** VI + ADV (*in race, competition*) quedarse atrás; (*in work etc*) rezagarse
➤ **drop by** VI + ADV pasar por casa, dejarse caer por casa; **do ~ by any time** ven a vernos cuando quieras
➤ **drop down** VI + ADV caerse; (= *crouch*) agacharse
➤ **drop in*** VI + ADV (= *visit*) pasar por casa, dejarse caer por casa; **do ~ in any time** ven a vernos cuando quieras; **to ~ in on sb** pasar por casa de algn
➤ **drop off Ⓐ** VI + ADV **1** (= *fall asleep*) dormirse **2** (= *decline*) [*sales, interest*] disminuir **3** [*part*] desprenderse, soltarse **Ⓑ** VT + ADV dejar; **could you ~ me off at the station?** ¿me puedes dejar en la estación?
➤ **drop out** VI + ADV [*contents*] derramarse, salirse; (*fig*) (*from competition*) retirarse; **to ~ out of a team** salirse de un equipo; **to ~ out of society/university** abandonar la sociedad/la universidad; **to ~ out of a race** abandonar una carrera; **he ~ped out of my life** desapareció de mi vida
➤ **drop round Ⓐ** VT + ADV **I'll ~ it round to you** pasaré por casa para dártelo **Ⓑ** VI + ADV = **drop by**

drop-dead** ['drɒpded] ADJ **a ~ gorgeous boy/girl** un chico/una chica que quita el hipo*

droplet ['drɒplɪt] N gotita *f*

drop-off ['drɒpɒf] N disminución *f*

dropout ['drɒpaʊt] N (*from society*) marginado/a *m/f*; (*from university*) estudiante *que abandona la universidad antes de graduarse*

droppings ['drɒpɪŋz] NPL excrementos *mpl*, caca* *f*

dross* [drɒs] N escoria *f*

drought [draʊt] N sequía *f*

drove[1] [drəʊv] PT *of* **drive**

drove[2] [drəʊv] N **~s of people** una multitud de gente; **they came in ~s** acudieron en tropel

drown [draʊn] **Ⓐ** VT **1** [+ *person, animal*] ahogar; **to ~ o.s.** ahogarse; ✦ IDIOM **like a ~ed rat** calado hasta los huesos **2** (*also* **~ out**) [+ *voice, sound, word*] ahogar; **his cries were ~ed by the noise of the waves** sus gritos se perdieron en el estruendo de las olas **Ⓑ** VI ahogarse, perecer ahogado

drowning ['draʊnɪŋ] N ahogo *m*

drowse [draʊz] VI dormitar; **to ~ off** adormilarse

drowsiness ['draʊzɪnɪs] N somnolencia *f*; **these tablets may cause ~** estas pastillas pueden producir somnolencia

drowsy ['draʊzɪ] ADJ (*compar* **drowsier**; *superl* **drowsiest**) (= *sleepy*) [*person*] adormilado, soñoliento; [*smile, look, voice*] soñoliento; **to be** *or* **feel ~** tener sueño *or* modorra, estar soñoliento *or* adormilado; (*because of medication*) tener somnolencia; **to become** *or* **grow ~** quedarse adormilado; **these tablets will make you ~** estas pastillas le producirán somnolencia

drudge [drʌdʒ] N (= *person*) esclavo/a *m/f*

drudgery ['drʌdʒərɪ] N trabajo *m* pesado

drug [drʌg] **Ⓐ** N (*Med*) medicamento *m*, fármaco *m*; (= *addictive substance*) droga *f*; (= *illegal substance*) droga *f*, narcótico *m*; **to take ~s** ◇ **be on ~s** (*illegal*) drogarse; **hard/soft ~s** drogas *fpl* duras/blandas
Ⓑ VT [+ *person*] drogar; [+ *wine*] echar una droga en
Ⓒ CPD ➤ **drug abuse** toxicomanía *f* ➤ **drug abuser** toxicómano/a *m/f* ➤ **drug addict** drogadicto/a *m/f* ➤ **drug addiction** drogadicción *f*, toxicomanía *f* ➤ **drug company** compañía *f* farmacéutica ➤ **drug(s) czar** fiscal *mf* antidroga ➤ **drug dealer** traficante *mf* de drogas ➤ **drug dependency** drogodependencia *f* ➤ **drug habit** adicción *f* (a las drogas) ➤ **drug peddler, drug pusher** traficante *mf* de drogas, camello* *mf* ➤ **drug smuggler** narcotraficante *mf* ➤ **drug squad** brigada *f* antidrogas, brigada *f* de estupefacientes ➤ **drugs ring** red *f* de narcotráfico ➤ **drug trafficking** narcotráfico *m*, tráfico *m* de drogas ➤ **drug user** consumidor(a) *m/f* de drogas, drogadicto/a *m/f*

druggist ['drʌgɪst] N (*US*) (= *person*) farmacéutico/a *m/f*; (*also* **~'s**) farmacia *f*

drug-related ['drʌgrɪˌleɪtɪd] ADJ relacionado con la droga ➤ **drug-related crime** drogodelincuencia *f*

drugstore ['drʌgstɔːr] N (*US*) tienda *de comestibles, periódicos y medicamentos*

drug-taking ['drʌgˌteɪkɪn] N consumo *m* de drogas

drum [drʌm] **Ⓐ** N **1** (*Mus*) tambor *m*; **to play (the) ~s** tocar la batería **2** (= *container*) (*for oil*) bidón *m*; (= *cylinder, machine part*) tambor *m* **3** (*also* **eardrum**) tímpano *m* **Ⓑ** VT **to ~ one's fingers on the table** tamborilear con los dedos sobre la mesa; **I had it ~med into me as a child** de niño me hicieron comprender eso a la fuerza *or* a fuerza de repetírmelo **Ⓒ** VI (*Mus*) tocar el tambor; (= *tap*) (*with fingers*) tamborilear
➤ **drum up** VT + ADV [+ *enthusiasm*] despertar; [+ *support*] movilizar; [+ *trade*] fomentar

drumkit ['drʌmkɪt] N batería *f*

drummer ['drʌmər] N (*in military band etc*) tambor *m*; (*in jazz/pop group*) batería *mf*

drumroll ['drʌmrəʊl] N redoble *m*

drumstick ['drʌmstɪk] N **1** (*Mus*) baqueta *f*, palillo *m* de tambor **2** (= *chicken leg*) muslo *m*

drunk [drʌŋk] **Ⓐ** PP *of* **drink**
Ⓑ ADJ (*compar* **~er**; *superl* **~est**) borracho, tomado (*LAm*); **he was arrested for being ~ and disorderly** lo detuvieron por embriaguez y alteración del orden público; **to get ~** emborracharse; **to get sb ~** emborrachar a algn; **to be ~ on whisky** estar borracho de whisky; **to get ~ on wine** emborracharse de vino; ✦ IDIOMS **to be as ~ as a lord** *or* **a skunk*** estar borracho como una cuba*; **to be ~ on** *or* **with success** estar ebrio de éxito
Ⓒ N borracho/a *m/f*
Ⓓ CPD ➤ **drunk driver** conductor(a) *m/f* en estado de embriaguez ➤ **drunk driving** el conducir en estado de embriaguez, el manejar en estado de embriaguez (*LAm*)

drunkard ['drʌŋkəd] N borracho/a *m/f*

drunken ['drʌŋkən] ADJ [*person*] borracho; [*brawl, orgy*] de borrachos; [*night, evening*] de borrachera; **a ~ old man** un viejo borracho; **a ~ party** una juerga; **in a ~ rage** en un ataque de furia provocado por el alcohol; **in a ~ stupor** flotando en los vapores del alcohol

drunkenness ['drʌŋkənnɪs] N (= *state*) borrachera *f*, embriaguez *f* (*more frm*); (= *habit, problem*) alcoholismo *m*

dry [draɪ] **Ⓐ** ADJ (*compar* **drier**; *superl* **driest**) **1** [*clothes, paint, weather, hair*] seco; [*climate*] árido, seco; **it was warm and ~ yesterday afternoon** ayer hizo una tarde cálida y seca; **wait till the glue is ~** espere a que la cola se seque; **her**

throat/mouth was ~ tenía la garganta/boca seca; **"keep in a dry place"** "mantener en un lugar seco"; ~ **bread** (without butter) pan m sin mantequilla; (stale) pan m seco; **there wasn't a ~ eye in the house** no había nadie que no estuviera llorando; **to get** ~ secarse; **on** ~ **land** en tierra firme; **to run** ~ [river, well] secarse; **to wipe sth** ~ secar algo (con un trapo); ✦ IDIOM **as** ~ **as a bone** más seco que una pasa
2 (*) (= thirsty) **to be** or **feel** ~ tener sed, estar seco*
3 (*) (= prohibiting alcohol) [country, state] seco
4 [humour, wit] mordaz; [laugh] sardónico
5 (= uninteresting) [lecture, subject, book] árido; [voice] seco; ✦ IDIOM **as** ~ **as dust** terriblemente árido
6 (= not sweet) [wine, sherry, cider] seco; **a ~ white wine** un vino blanco seco
Ⓑ N **the** ~ (Brit) lo seco; **such cars grip the road well, even in the** ~ estos coches se agarran bien al firme, incluso en seco; **come on into the** ~ métete aquí que no llueve
Ⓒ VT secar; **to** ~ **one's hands/eyes** secarse las manos/las lágrimas; **to** ~ **the dishes** secar los platos; **to** ~ **o.s.** secarse
Ⓓ VI secar; **leave it to** ~ déjalo que se seque; **would you rather wash or ~?** ¿prefieres lavar o secar?
Ⓔ CPD ➤ **dry cleaner's** tintorería f, tinte m (Sp) ➤ **dry cleaning** limpieza f en seco ➤ **dry dock** dique m seco ➤ **dry goods** (US) artículos mpl de confección ➤ **dry goods store** (US) mercería f ➤ **dry ice** nieve f carbónica ➤ **dry rot** putrefacción seca de la madera causada por un hongo ➤ **dry run** ensayo m ➤ **dry shampoo** champú m seco ➤ **dry ski slope** pista f artificial de esquí ➤ **dry stone wall** muro m seco
➤ **dry off** Ⓐ VI + ADV secarse Ⓑ VT + ADV secar
➤ **dry out** Ⓐ VI + ADV **1** (lit) secarse **2** (*) [alcoholic] seguir una cura de desintoxicación de alcohol Ⓑ VT + ADV **1** (lit) (= dry) [+ clothes, ground, food, skin] secar **2** (*) [+ alcoholic] curar del alcoholismo
➤ **dry up** VI + ADV **1** [river, well] secarse; [moisture] evaporarse, desaparecer; [source of supply] agotarse **2** (Brit) (= dry the dishes) secar los platos **3** (*) [speaker] quedarse en blanco; **~ up!** ¡cierra el pico!*

dry-clean ['draɪˈkliːn] VT limpiar en seco, lavar en seco; **"dry-clean only"** (on label) "limpiar or lavar en seco"

dryer ['draɪəʳ] N (for hair) secador m; (for clothes) secadora f; (= rack) tendedero m

drying-up ['draɪɪŋˈʌp] N (Brit) **to do the** ~ secar los platos

dryly ['draɪlɪ] ADV = **drily**

dryness ['draɪnɪs] N **1** [of hair, skin, climate] sequedad f **2** [of wit, humour] mordacidad f **3** [of wine, sherry, cider] lo seco **4** [of lecture, subject, book] aridez f

DS N ABBR (Brit Police) = **Detective Sergeant**

DSC N ABBR (Brit) (= Distinguished Service Cross) ≈ cruz f al mérito militar

DSc N ABBR (Univ) = **Doctor of Science**

DSM N ABBR (Brit) (= Distinguished Service Medal) ≈ medalla f al mérito militar

DSO N ABBR (Brit) = **Distinguished Service Order**

DST N ABBR (US) = **Daylight Saving Time**

DT N ABBR (Comput) = **data transmission**

DTI N ABBR (Brit Admin) = **Department of Trade and Industry**

DTP N ABBR = **desktop publishing**

DTs* NPL ABBR = **delirium tremens**

DU N ABBR = **depleted uranium**

dual ['djʊəl] ADJ doble ➤ **dual carriageway** (Brit) autovía f, carretera f de doble calzada ➤ **dual control** doble mando m ➤ **dual nationality** doble nacionalidad f ➤ **dual personality** doble personalidad f

dual-purpose ['djʊəlˈpɜːpəs] ADJ de doble uso

dub [dʌb] VT **1** (Cine) doblar; **the film was ~bed into Spanish** la película estaba doblada al español
2 (= nickname) apodar **3** [+ knight] armar caballero a

Dubai [duːˈbaɪ] N Dubai m

dubbing ['dʌbɪŋ] N (Cine) doblaje m ➤ **dubbing mixer** mezclador(a) m/f de sonido

dubious ['djuːbɪəs] ADJ **1** (= questionable) [reputation, claim,

privilege, taste] dudoso; [motive] sospechoso; [company, offer] poco fiable; [business deal, practice] sospechoso, turbio; [idea, measure] discutible; [compliment] equívoco; **to have the ~ honour/pleasure of doing sth** tener el dudoso honor/placer de hacer algo; **of ~ quality** de dudosa calidad
2 (= unsure) [look, smile] indeciso; **to be** ~ tener dudas or reservas; **I was ~ at first** al principio tenía mis dudas or reservas; **I am ~ that** or **whether the new law will achieve anything** tengo mis dudas or reservas sobre si la nueva ley va a lograr algo; **he looked/sounded** ~ parecía tener dudas or reservas, parecía dudar

Dublin ['dʌblɪn] N Dublín m ➤ **Dublin Bay prawn** cigala f

Dubliner ['dʌblɪnəʳ] N dublinés/esa m/f

duchess ['dʌtʃɪs] N duquesa f

duchy ['dʌtʃɪ] N ducado m (territorio)

duck [dʌk] Ⓐ N (= bird) pato m; (female) pata f; ✦ IDIOMS **to be a dead ~:** that **issue is a dead** ~ esa cuestión ya no tiene interés; **to take to sth like a ~ to water** sentirse como pez en el agua en or con algo, encontrarse en seguida en su elemento con algo
Ⓑ VT **1** (= plunge) [+ person, head] zambullir
2 to ~ one's head agachar la cabeza
3 [+ problem, question] eludir, esquivar
Ⓒ VI (also ~ **down**) agacharse, agachar la cabeza; (in fight) esquivar el golpe; (under water) sumergirse
Ⓓ CPD ➤ **duck pond** estanque m de patos
➤ **duck out*** VI + PREP escabullirse de

duck-billed platypus ['dʌkbɪldˈplætɪpəs] N ornitorrinco m

ducking ['dʌkɪŋ] N zambullida f; **to give sb a** ~ meter la cabeza en el agua a algn

duckling ['dʌklɪŋ] N patito m

duct [dʌkt] N **1** (for ventilation, liquid) conducto m **2** (Anat) conducto m, canal m

dud* [dʌd] Ⓐ ADJ [cheque] sin fondos; [merchandise] de tres al cuarto; [machine etc] estropeado; [shell, bomb] que no estalla Ⓑ N (= thing) filfa f; (= person) desastre m, inútil mf

dude* [djuːd] N (US) (= guy) tipo* m, tío m (Sp*); (= dandy) petimetre m ➤ **dude ranch** rancho m para turistas

due [djuː] Ⓐ ADJ **1** (= expected) **the train is ~ to arrive** or ~ **(in) at eight** el tren llega a las ocho, el tren tiene su hora de llegada a las ocho; **the train was ~ (in) ten minutes ago** el tren tenía que haber llegado hace diez minutos; **the results are ~ (in) today** está previsto que los resultados salgan hoy; **he is ~ back tomorrow** estará de vuelta mañana, está previsto que vuelva mañana; **when is the baby ~?** ¿cuándo se espera que nazca el niño?
2 (= owing) [sum, money] pagadero, pendiente; **it's ~ on the 30th** el plazo vence el día 30; **when is the rent ~?** ¿cuándo se paga el alquiler?, ¿cuándo hay que pagar el alquiler?; **I am ~ six days' leave** se me deben seis días de vacaciones; **I feel I'm about ~ a holiday!** ¡me parece que necesito unas vacaciones!; **to fall** ~ (Fin) vencer; **he is ~ for a rise/promotion** le corresponde un aumento de sueldo/un ascenso; **I have £50 ~ to me** me deben 50 libras; **our thanks are ~ to him** le estamos muy agradecidos; **they must be treated with the respect ~ to their age** deben ser tratados con el respeto que su edad merece
3 (= appropriate) [care, attention] debido; **to drive without ~ care and attention** (Jur) conducir or (LAm) manejar sin el cuidado y la atención debidos; **after ~ consideration** después de la debida consideración; **we'll let you know in ~ course** le avisaremos a su debido tiempo; **he has never received ~ credit for his achievements** nunca ha recibido el crédito que merece por sus logros; **with (all) ~ respect (to Mrs Fry)** con el debido respeto (hacia la señora Fry)
4 ~ to (= caused by) debido a; **~ to repairs, the garage will be closed next Saturday** esta gasolinera estará cerrada por obras el próximo sábado; **his death was ~ to natural causes** su muerte se debió a causas naturales; **what's it ~ to?** ¿a qué se debe?; **it is ~ to you that she is alive today** gracias a ti está todavía viva
Ⓑ ADV ~ **west of** justo hacia el oeste de; **to go ~ north** ir derecho hacia el norte
Ⓒ N **1** (= due credit) **to give him his ~, he did try hard** en honor a la verdad, se esforzó mucho

2 dues (= *fees*) cuota *f*sing
ⓓ CPD **➤ due date** [*of loan, debt*] fecha *f* de vencimiento

duel ['djʊəl] **ⓐ** N duelo *m*; **to fight a ~** batirse en duelo
ⓑ VI batirse en duelo

duet [dju:'et] N dúo *m*; **to sing/play a ~** cantar/tocar a dúo

duff• [dʌf] (*Brit*) ADJ (= *useless*) inútil; (= *poor quality*) de tres al cuarto
➤ duff up• VT + ADV (*Brit*) dar una paliza a

duffel bag ['dʌfəlbæg] N bolsa *f* de lona; (*Mil*) talego *m* (*para efectos de uso personal*)

duffel coat ['dʌfəlkəʊt] N abrigo *m* tres cuartos, trenca *f* (*Sp*), montgomery *m* (*SC*)

dug [dʌg] PT, PP *of* **dig**

dugout ['dʌgaʊt] N (*Mil*) refugio *m* subterráneo

DUI N ABBR (*US*) (= **driving under (the) influence (of alcohol)**) conducción *f* or (*LAm*) manejo *m* bajo los efectos del alcohol

duke [dju:k] N duque *m*

dull [dʌl] **ⓐ** ADJ (*compar* **~er**; *superl* **~est**) **1** (= *boring*) [*person, book, evening, job*] aburrido, pesado; [*place*] aburrido, soso; [*style, food*] soso; **deadly ~** terriblemente aburrido, aburridísimo; **there's never a ~ moment** no nos aburrimos nunca; **✦** IDIOM **as ~ as ditchwater** terriblemente aburrido **2** (= *not bright*) [*colour, metal, glow*] apagado, sin brillo; [*eyes*] apagado, sin brillo; [*hair, skin, complexion*] sin brillo; [*weather*] nublado; [*sky, day*] gris **3** (= *not sharp*) [*pain, feeling, sound*] sordo; **with a ~ thud** con un golpe sordo **4** (= *lethargic, withdrawn*) deprimido, desanimado **5** (= *slow-witted*) [*person, mind*] torpe; [*pupil*] lento
ⓑ VT [+ *senses, blade*] embotar; [+ *emotions*] enfriar; [+ *pain*] aliviar; [+ *sound*] amortiguar; [+ *mind, memory*] entorpecer; [+ *colour*] apagar; [+ *metal*] deslustrar, quitar el brillo de; [+ *sensitivity*] embrutecer; [+ *grief*] atenuar
ⓒ VI [*light*] amortiguarse; [*colour*] apagarse, perder intensidad; [*metal*] deslustrarse, perder brillo

dullness ['dʌlnɪs] N **1** [*of book, lecture, person, evening*] lo aburrido, pesadez *f* **2** [*of colour, metal, mirror*] falta *f* de brillo, lo opaco; [*of landscape*] monotonía *f*

duly ['dju:lɪ] ADV **1** (= *as expected*) [*arrive, land*] como estaba previsto; **the visitors were ~ impressed** los visitantes quedaron muy impresionados, como era de esperar **2** (= *properly*) [*elect, sign*] debidamente; **the point was ~ noted in the minutes** se tomó debida nota de ese punto

dumb [dʌm] ADJ (*compar* **~er**; *superl* **~est**) **1** (*Med*) mudo; (*with surprise etc*) sin habla; **she's deaf and ~** es sordomuda; **~ animals** animales *mpl* indefensos; **✦** IDIOM **to be struck ~** quedarse sin habla **2** (*esp US•*) (= *stupid*) tonto, bobo; **to act ~** hacerse el tonto; **he says some ~ things!** ¡dice cada tontería! *or* bobada!; **~ blonde** rubia *f* descerebrada *or* sin seso
➤ dumb down VT + ADV embrutecer, empobrecer intelectualmente

dumbbell ['dʌmbel] N pesa *f*

dumbfound [dʌm'faʊnd] VT dejar mudo; **we were ~ed** nos quedamos mudos de asombro

dummy ['dʌmɪ] **ⓐ** ADJ [*gun*] de juguete; [*ammunition*] de fogueo; [*container*] vacío **ⓑ** N **1** (*for clothes*) maniquí *m* **2** (*Brit*) (*for baby*) chupete *m* **3** (•) (= *idiot*) tonto/a *m/f*
ⓒ CPD **➤ dummy assault**, **dummy attack** simulacro *m* de ataque **➤ dummy run** (*Brit*) ensayo *m*, prueba *f*

dump [dʌmp] **ⓐ** N **1** (= *place for refuse*) vertedero *m*, basurero *m*, basural *m* (*LAm*), tiradero(s) *m(pl)* (*Mex*); (= *pile of rubbish*) montón *m* de basura; **a rubbish ~** un vertedero, un basurero **2** (*Mil*) depósito *m* **3** (*pej•*) (= *town*) poblacho *m*; (= *hotel etc*) cuchitril *m*; **it's a real ~!** ¡es una auténtica pocilga! **4** (*Comput*) vuelco *m* de memoria, volcado *m* de memoria **5** **✦** IDIOM **to be (down) in the ~s•** tener murria, estar deprimido
ⓑ VT **1** [+ *rubbish, waste etc*] verter, descargar **2** (•) (= *put down*) [+ *parcel*] dejar, soltar; [+ *passenger*] dejar, plantar•; [+ *sand, load*] descargar, verter **3** (•) (= *get rid of*) [+ *person*] deshacerse de, librarse de; [+ *girlfriend, boyfriend*] plantar•; [+ *thing*] tirar

4 (*Comput*) volcar

dumping ['dʌmpɪŋ] **ⓐ** N **1** [*of rubbish, waste*] vertido *m*; **"no dumping"** "prohibido verter basuras" **2** (*Comm*) dúmping *m* **ⓑ** CPD **➤ dumping ground** vertedero *m*

dumpling ['dʌmplɪŋ] N *bola de masa hervida para servir con guiso*

Dumpster® ['dʌmpstəʳ] N (*US*) contenedor *m* de escombros *or* deshechos

dumpy ['dʌmpɪ] ADJ (*compar* **dumpier**; *superl* **dumpiest**) regordete

dunce [dʌns] N zopenco/a *m/f*

dune [dju:n] N duna *f*

dung [dʌŋ] N (= *excrement*) excrementos *mpl*; (*as manure*) estiércol *m*

dungarees [ˌdʌŋgə'ri:z] NPL (*for work*) mono *m*sing, overol *m* (*LAm*); (= *casual wear*) pantalón *m*sing de peto

dungeon ['dʌndʒən] N calabozo *m*, mazmorra *f*

dunghill ['dʌŋhɪl] N estercolero *m*

dunk [dʌŋk] VT **1** [+ *biscuit, cake etc*] mojar **2** (*Basketball*) machacar

duo ['dju:əʊ] N (*Mus, Theat*) dúo *m*

duodenum [ˌdju:əʊ'di:nəm] N duodeno *m*

dupe [dju:p] **ⓐ** N inocentón/ona *m/f* **ⓑ** VT (= *trick*) engañar, embaucar; (= *swindle*) timar; **to ~ sb (into doing sth)** engañar *or* embaucar a algn (para que haga algo)

duplex ['dju:pleks] N (*US*) (*also ~* **house**) *casa compuesta por dos viviendas pareadas independientes*; (*also ~* **apartment**) dúplex *m inv*

duplicate ⓐ ['dju:plɪkeɪt] VT **1** (= *copy*) [+ *document*] duplicar; (*on machine*) copiar **2** (= *repeat*) [+ *action*] repetir **ⓑ** ['dju:plɪkɪt] N duplicado *m*, copia *f*; **in ~** por duplicado **ⓒ** ['dju:plɪkɪt] ADJ duplicado

duplicity [dju:'plɪsɪtɪ] N (*frm*) doblez *f*, duplicidad *f*

durability [ˌdjʊərə'bɪlɪtɪ] N durabilidad *f*, lo duradero

durable ['djʊərəbl] ADJ duradero; **~ goods** (*US*) bienes *mpl* (de consumo) duraderos *or* no perecederos

duration [djʊə'reɪʃən] N duración *f*; **for the ~ of the war** mientras dure la guerra

duress [djʊə'res] N **under ~** bajo presión

Durex® ['djʊəreks] N preservativo *m*

during ['djʊərɪŋ] PREP durante

dusk [dʌsk] N **1** (= *nightfall*) anochecer *m*, atardecer *m*; **at ~** al anochecer *or* atardecer **2** (= *darkness*) oscuridad *f*

dusky ['dʌskɪ] ADJ [*pink, blue*] oscuro; [*complexion*] moreno

dust [dʌst] **ⓐ** N **1** (*in house, on ground*) polvo *m*; **there was thick ~** había una gruesa capa de polvo; **✦** IDIOMS **not to see sb for ~•**: **if you ask for a volunteer, you won't see her for ~!** ¡en cuanto pides un voluntario pone los pies en polvorosa!; **when the ~ has settled** cuando haya pasado la tempestad **2** (= *act of dusting*) **to give sth a ~** quitar el polvo a algo **ⓑ** VT **1** [+ *furniture*] quitar el polvo a *or* de; [+ *room*] limpiar el polvo a *or* de; **✦** IDIOM **it's done and ~ed** (*Brit*) todo ha terminado; **the deal is done and ~ed** el trato está cerrado **2** (*with flour, icing sugar*) espolvorear **ⓒ** VI limpiar el polvo
ⓓ CPD **➤ dust bowl** (*Geog*) terreno erosionado por el viento **➤ dust cloth** (*US*) trapo *m* del polvo **➤ dust cover** [*of book*] sobrecubierta *f*; (*for furniture*) guardapolvo *m* **➤ dust jacket** sobrecubierta *f* **➤ dust sheet** (*Brit*) guardapolvo *m*, funda *f* **➤ dust storm** vendaval *m* de polvo, tormenta *f* de polvo **➤ dust down**, **dust off** VT + ADV quitar el polvo a *or* de, desempolvar; **✦** IDIOM **to ~ o.s. down** (*Brit*) sobreponerse

dustbag ['dʌstbæg] N bolsa *f* de aspiradora

dustbin ['dʌstbɪn] (*Brit*) N cubo *m* de la basura **➤ dustbin liner** bolsa *f* de basura **➤ dustbin man** (*Brit*) basurero *m*

dustcart ['dʌstkɑ:t] N (*Brit*) camión *m* de la basura

dustcloud ['dʌstklaʊd] N polvareda *f*

duster ['dʌstəʳ] N **1** (= *cloth*) trapo *m*; (*for blackboard*) borrador *m* **2** (*US*) (= *housecoat*) guardapolvo *m*

dusting ['dʌstɪŋ] N limpieza *f*

dustman ['dʌstmən] N (pl **dustmen**) (Brit) basurero m

dustpan ['dʌstpæn] N cogedor m

dust-up* ['dʌstʌp] N (Brit) pelea f, bronca f; **to have a ~ with** pelearse con, tener una bronca con

dusty ['dʌstɪ] ADJ (compar **dustier**; superl **dustiest**) 1 [furniture, book, car] cubierto de polvo; [ground, atmosphere] polvoriento; **to get ~** [table, book] cubrirse de polvo; [room, house] llenarse de polvo 2 (= greyish) grisáceo; **~ blue** azul m grisáceo; **~ pink** rosa m grisáceo

Dutch [dʌtʃ] **Ⓐ** ADJ holandés; **she's ~** es holandesa **Ⓑ** N 1 (Ling) neerlandés m, holandés m 2 **the ~** los holandeses **Ⓒ** ADV ✦ IDIOM **to go ~*** [two people] pagar a medias; [more than two] pagar a escote **Ⓓ** CPD ➤ **Dutch auction** subasta f a la baja ➤ **Dutch barn** granero abierto a los lados con el tejado curvo ➤ **Dutch cap*** diafragma m ➤ **Dutch courage** envalentonamiento del que ha bebido ➤ **Dutch elm disease** enfermedad f del olmo, grafiosis f

Dutchman ['dʌtʃmən] N (pl **Dutchmen**) holandés m; ✦ IDIOM **it's him or I'm a ~*** que me maten si no es él

Dutchwoman ['dʌtʃˌwʊmən] N (pl **Dutchwomen**) holandesa f

dutiful ['djuːtɪfʊl] ADJ [child] obediente; [husband] sumiso; [employee] cumplido

dutifully ['djuːtɪfəlɪ] ADV obedientemente, sumisamente

duty ['djuːtɪ] **Ⓐ** N 1 (moral, legal) deber m, obligación f; **it is my ~ to inform you that ...** es mi deber or obligación informarles de que ...; **I am ~ bound to say that ...** es mi deber decir que ...; **to do one's ~ (by sb)** cumplir con su deber (hacia algn, para con algn); **to make it one's ~ to do sth** encargarse de hacer algo; **out of a sense of ~** por sentido del deber 2 (= task, responsibility) función f, responsabilidad f; **my duties consist of ...** mis funciones or responsabilidades son ...; **to do ~ as** servir de; **to neglect one's duties** faltar a sus responsabilidades; **to be off ~** estar libre; **an off ~ policeman** un policía fuera de servicio; **to be on ~** [doctor, nurse, sentry] estar de guardia; [policeman] estar de servicio; (Admin, Scol) estar de turno; **to go on ~** entrar de servicio; **to take up one's duties** entrar en funciones 3 (= tax) derechos mpl; **to pay ~ on sth** pagar derechos por algo **Ⓑ** CPD ➤ **duty officer** (Mil) oficial mf de servicio; (Police) agente mf de servicio ➤ **duty roster, duty rota** lista f de turnos

duty-free ['djuːtɪ'friː] ADJ [goods, perfume] libre de impuestos, exento de derechos de aduana ➤ **duty-free shop** tienda f "duty free"

duvet ['duːveɪ] N (Brit) edredón m (nórdico) ➤ **duvet cover** funda f de edredón (nórdico)

DV ADV ABBR = **Deo volente** (= God willing) D. m.

DVD N ABBR (= **digital versatile** or **video disc**) DVD m, disco m de vídeo digital, disco digital polivalente ➤ **DVD player** lector m (de) DVD ➤ **DVD-Rom** DVD-Rom m

DVLA N ABBR (Brit) (= **Driver and Vehicle Licensing Agency**) organismo encargado de la expedición de permisos de conducir y matriculación de vehículos, ≈ DGT f (Sp)

DVM N ABBR (US Univ) = **Doctor of Veterinary Medicine**

dwarf [dwɔːf] **Ⓐ** N (pl **~s** or **dwarves** [dwɔːvz]) enano/a m/f **Ⓑ** ADJ enano **Ⓒ** VT [+ building, person] empequeñecer, hacer que parezca pequeño; [+ achievement] eclipsar

dwell [dwel] (pt, pp **dwelt**) VI (poet) morar, vivir ➤ **dwell (up)on** VI + PREP (= think about) dar vueltas a, pensar de forma obsesiva en; (= talk about) insistir en (hablar de); **don't let's ~ (up)on it** no hay que insistir

dweller ['dwelə'] N morador(a) m/f, habitante mf

dwelling ['dwelɪŋ] N morada f, vivienda f

dwelt [dwelt] PT, PP of **dwell**

dwindle ['dwɪndl] VI reducirse, menguar; **to ~ to** quedar reducido a; **to ~ away** [money, sound] disminuir, menguar

dwindling ['dwɪndlɪŋ] **Ⓐ** ADJ menguante **Ⓑ** N disminución f

dye [daɪ] N tinte m; **hair ~** tinte m para el pelo **Ⓑ** VT teñir; **to ~ sth red** teñir algo de rojo; **to ~ one's hair blond** teñirse el pelo de rubio

dyed-in-the-wool ['daɪdɪnðə'wʊl] ADJ testarudo

dying ['daɪɪŋ] **Ⓐ** PRESENT PARTICIPLE of **die¹** **Ⓑ** ADJ [man] moribundo, agonizante; [moments] final; [custom, race] en vías de extinción; **his ~ words were ...** sus últimas palabras fueron ...; **to my ~ day** hasta el fin de mis días, hasta el día de mi muerte **Ⓒ** NPL **the ~** los moribundos

dyke [daɪk] N 1 (= barrier) dique m; (= channel) canal m, acequia f; (= causeway) calzada f; (= embankment) terraplén m 2 (***) (= lesbian) tortillera*** f

dynamic [daɪ'næmɪk] **Ⓐ** ADJ dinámico **Ⓑ** N dinámica f

dynamically [daɪ'næmɪkəlɪ] ADV dinámicamente

dynamics [daɪ'næmɪks] NSING dinámica f

dynamism ['daɪnəmɪzəm] N dinamismo m

dynamite ['daɪnəmaɪt] N 1 (= explosive) dinamita f 2 (*) (fig) **he's ~!** ¡es estupendo!; **the story is ~** la noticia es una bomba or pura dinamita

dynamo ['daɪnəməʊ] N dínamo f or (LAm) m, dinamo f or (LAm) m

dynasty ['dɪnəstɪ] N dinastía f

dysentery ['dɪsntrɪ] N disentería f

dysfunction [dɪs'fʌŋkʃən] N disfunción f

dysfunctional [dɪs'fʌŋkʃənəl] ADJ disfuncional

dyslexia [dɪs'leksɪə] N dislexia f

dyslexic [dɪs'leksɪk] ADJ, N disléxico/a m/f

dysmenorrhoea, dysmenorrhea (US) [ˌdɪsmenə'rɪə] N dismenorrea f

dyspepsia [dɪs'pepsɪə] N dispepsia f

dystrophy ['dɪstrəfɪ] N distrofia f; **muscular ~** distrofia f muscular

Ee

E¹, e [iː] Ⓐ N **1** (= *letter*) E, e *f*; **E for Edward** E de Enrique **2** (*Mus*) **E** mi *m* Ⓑ CPD ➤ **E number** número *m* E

E² ABBR **1** (= **east**) E **2** (*Drugs**) = **ecstasy**

e- [iː] PREF electrónico

each [iːtʃ] Ⓐ ADJ cada; **~ day** cada día; **~ house has its own garden** todas las casas tienen jardín; **~ one of them** cada uno (de ellos)
Ⓑ PRON **1** cada uno; **~ of us** cada uno de nosotros, cada quien (*LAm*); **he gave ~ of us £10** nos dio diez libras a cada uno; **a little of ~** un poco de cada
2 ~ other: they love ~ other se quieren; **we write to ~ other** nos escribimos; **they looked at ~ other** se miraron; (*emphatic*) se miraron uno a otro; **they help ~ other** se ayudan mutuamente *or* entre ellos; **their houses are next to ~ other** sus casas están una al lado de la otra *or* (*LAm*) juntas
Ⓒ ADV **we gave them one apple ~** les dimos una manzana por persona; **they cost £5 ~** cuestan cinco libras cada uno

eager [ˈiːɡəʳ] ADJ [*person*] (= *enthusiastic*) entusiasta, entusiasmado; (= *hopeful*) ilusionado; (= *impatient*) impaciente, ansioso (**to do sth** por hacer algo); **to be ~ to please** desear complacer; **to be ~ to learn** tener muchas ganas *or* muchos deseos de aprender; **to be ~ for** [+ *affection, knowledge, power*] tener ansias de; **to be ~ for change** ansiar *or* desear mucho un cambio; ✦ IDIOM **to be an ~ beaver** ser muy diligente

eagerly [ˈiːɡəlɪ] ADV (= *enthusiastically*) con entusiasmo; (= *impatiently*) con impaciencia, ansiosamente; (= *hopefully*) con ilusión; (= *avidly*) con avidez

eagle [ˈiːɡl] N águila *f*

> Use **el/un** not **la/una** before feminine nouns beginning with stressed **a** or **ha** like **águila**.

with (an) ~ eye con ojos de lince

eagle-eyed [ˈiːɡlaɪd] ADJ **to be ~** tener ojos de lince

ear¹ [ɪəʳ] Ⓐ N **1** (*Anat*) (= *outer part*) oreja *f*; (= *rest of organ*) oído *m*; **he could not believe his ~s** no daba crédito a sus oídos; **he was grinning from ~ to ~** la sonrisa le llegaba de oreja a oreja; **inner/middle/outer ~** oído *m* interno/medio/externo; **he was looking for a sympathetic ~** buscaba a alguien que le escuchara; **a word in your ~** una palabra en confianza; ✦ IDIOMS **to be all ~s** ser todo oídos; **I bet his ~s were burning** apuesto a que le zumbaban *or* pitaban los oídos; **to close one's ~s to sth** hacer caso omiso de algo; **it goes in one ~ and out the other** por un oído le/me entra y por otro le/me sale; **to keep one's ~(s) to the ground** estar con la oreja pegada*, estar al tanto; **to be out on one's ~*** verse en la calle (sin trabajo)*; **to have money coming out of one's ~s** tener dinero para dar y tomar; **to be wet behind the ~s*** estar verde*
2 (= *sense of hearing*) oído *m*; **pleasing to the ~** agradable al oído; **to play sth by ~** [*musician*] tocar algo de oído; **we'll just have to play it by ~** (*fig*) tendremos que improvisar sobre la marcha
Ⓑ CPD ➤ **ear lobe** lóbulo *m* de la oreja ➤ **ear, nose and throat specialist** otorrinolaringólogo/a *m/f*

ear² [ɪəʳ] N (*of cereal*) espiga *f*

earache [ˈɪəreɪk] N dolor *m* de oídos; **to have ~** tener dolor de oídos

eardrum [ˈɪədrʌm] N tímpano *m*

earful* [ˈɪəfʊl] N (= *telling-off*) **to give sb an ~** echar una bronca a algn*, regañar a algn

earl [ɜːl] N conde *m*

early [ˈɜːlɪ] (*compar* **earlier**; *superl* **earliest**) Ⓐ ADJ **1** (= *before expected time*) [*death, menopause, frost*] prematuro, temprano; **you're ~!** ¡llegas temprano *or* pronto!; **you're five minutes ~** llegas con cinco minutos de adelanto; **I was half an hour ~ for the meeting** llegué a la reunión con media hora de adelanto; **Easter is ~ this year** la Semana Santa cae pronto este año; **to have an ~ lunch/night** comer/acostarse temprano; **~ retirement** jubilación *f* anticipada
2 (= *soon*) pronto; **it will happen in March at the earliest** ocurrirá en marzo como muy pronto; **at your earliest convenience** con la mayor brevedad posible
3 (*in morning*) **we need two seats on an ~ flight** necesitamos dos plazas en un vuelo que salga por la mañana temprano *or* un vuelo a primera hora de la mañana; **we arrived home in the ~ hours (of the morning)** llegamos a casa de madrugada; **we worked until the ~ hours of the morning** trabajamos hasta altas horas de la madrugada; **in the ~ morning** a primeras horas de la mañana; **to be an ~ riser** ser madrugador; **to get off to an ~ start** salir temprano
4 (*in period, process*) [*fruit, vegetable, crop*] temprano; **in the ~ 60s** a principios de los 60; **she's in her ~ forties** tiene poco más de cuarenta años; **there were two ~ goals** se marcaron dos goles al inicio del partido; **in ~ March** a principios de marzo; **it's still ~** (*in process*) es pronto todavía; **the ~ afternoon** a primera hora de la tarde; **at an ~ age** a una edad temprana; **from an ~ age** desde pequeño; **his ~ childhood** los primeros años de su infancia; **it was ~ evening** era media tarde; **we'll arrive in the ~ evening** llegaremos a media tarde; **the disease is hard to detect in its ~ stages** es difícil detectar la enfermedad en sus fases iniciales; **his ~ youth** su primera juventud; ✦ IDIOM **it's ~ days yet** (*esp Brit*): **we may have to modify the plans, but it's ~ days yet** quizás tengamos que modificar los planes, pero aún es pronto para saberlo
5 (= *first*) [*man, Church*] primitivo; [*settlers, pioneers, Christians*] primero/primer (*before m sing n*); **Shakespeare's ~ work** las primeras obras de Shakespeare
Ⓑ ADV **1** (= *ahead of time*) [*arrive, go to bed*] temprano, pronto; **I don't want to get there too ~** no quiero llegar demasiado pronto; **he arrived ten minutes ~** llegó diez minutos antes de la hora, llegó con diez minutos de anticipación; **to book ~** reservar con anticipación
2 (= *soon*) pronto; **the earliest I can do it is Tuesday** lo más pronto que lo podré hacer será el martes; **a month earlier** un mes antes; **as ~ as 1978** ya en 1978
3 (*in morning*) temprano; **you get up too ~** te levantas demasiado temprano, madrugas demasiado; **it was ~ in the morning** era muy de mañana, era muy temprano
4 (*in period, process*) **~ in the afternoon** a primera hora de la tarde; **~ in the book** en las primeras páginas del libro; **~ in the war/in 1915** a principios de la guerra/de 1915; **~ in the week/year** a principios de semana/año; **~ in his life** en su juventud; **~ last century/next year** a principios del siglo pasado/año que viene; **~ on in his career** en los primeros años de su carrera
Ⓒ CPD ➤ **early bird*** madrugador(a) *m/f*; ✦ PROV **it's the ~ bird that catches the worm** a quien madruga Dios le ayuda ➤ **early closing (day)** (*Brit*) día *m* en que muchas tiendas sólo abren por la mañana ➤ **early warning system** sistema *m* de alarma *or* alerta precoz

earmark [ˈɪəmɑːk] VT destinar (**for** a)

earmuff [ˈɪəmʌf] N orejera *f*

earn [ɜːn] VT [+ *money, wages etc*] ganar; [+ *interest*] devengar; **to ~ one's living** ganarse la vida

earner [ˈɜːnəʳ] N (= *person*) asalariado/a *m/f*; **the shop is a nice little ~** (*Brit**) la tienda es rentable *or* una buena fuente de ingresos

earnest [ˈɜːnɪst] Ⓐ ADJ [*person, character etc*] (= *serious*) serio, formal; (= *sincere*) sincero; [*wish, request*] vivo, ferviente Ⓑ N **in ~** en serio

earnestly [ˈɜːnɪstlɪ] ADV [*speak*] en serio; [*pray*] fervorosamente, fervientemente

earnings [ˈɜːnɪŋz] NPL (= *wages*) sueldo *msing*, salario *msing*; (= *income*) ingresos *mpl*

earphones [ˈɪəfəʊnz] NPL auriculares *mpl*

earpiece [ˈɪəpiːs] N (*Telec*) auricular *m*

earplugs [ˈɪəplʌgz] NPL tapones *mpl* para los oídos

earring ['ɪərɪŋ] N pendiente *m*, arete *m* (*LAm*)

earshot ['ɪəʃɒt] N **to be within** ~ estar al alcance del oído; **to be out of** ~ estar fuera del alcance del oído

ear-splitting ['ɪəˌsplɪtɪŋ] ADJ que rompe el tímpano, que taladra el oído, ensordecedor

earth [ɜ:θ] **Ⓐ** N **1** (**the**) **Earth** la Tierra; **here on** ~ en este mundo; **nothing on** ~ **would make me do it** no lo haría por nada del mundo; **what/where/who on** ~ **...?*** ¿qué/dónde/ quién demonios *or* diablos ...?; **✦** IDIOMS **to come down to** ~ volver a la realidad; **it must have cost the** ~**!** (*Brit**) ¡te habrá costado un ojo de la cara! **2** (= *ground*) tierra *f*, suelo *m*; (= *soil*) tierra *f* **3** [*of fox*] madriguera *f*, guarida *f*; **to go to** ~ [*fox*] meterse en su madriguera; [*person*] esconderse, refugiarse **4** (*Brit Elec*) toma *f* de tierra, tierra *f* **Ⓑ** VT (*Brit Elec*) [+ *apparatus*] conectar a tierra

earthenware ['ɜ:θənwɛəʳ] **Ⓐ** N loza *f* (de barro) **Ⓑ** CPD de barro

earthly ['ɜ:θlɪ] ADJ **1** (= *terrestrial*) terrenal; (= *worldly*) mundano **2** (*) (= *possible*) **there is no** ~ **reason to think ...** no existe razón alguna para pensar ...

earthquake ['ɜ:θkweɪk] N terremoto *m*

earthworm ['ɜ:θwɜ:m] N lombriz *f*

earthy ['ɜ:θɪ] ADJ **1** [*colour*] terroso; **an** ~ **taste** un sabor a tierra **2** [*character*] sencillo **3** [*humour*] grosero

earwig ['ɪəwɪg] N tijereta *f*

ease [i:z] **Ⓐ** N **1** (= *effortlessness*) facilidad *f*; **with** ~ con facilidad; **for** ~ **of reference** para facilitar la referencia **2** (= *relaxed state*) **his** ~ **with money** su soltura *or* ligereza con el dinero; **at** ~ **with** a gusto con, cómodo con; **I would feel more at** ~ **if I knew where she was** me sentiría más tranquilo si supiera dónde está; **to put sb's mind at** ~ tranquilizar a algn **3** (*Mil*) **stand at** ~**!** ¡descansen! **Ⓑ** VT **1** (= *relieve, lessen*) [+ *pain, suffering, pressure*] aliviar; [+ *burden*] aligerar; [+ *sanctions, restrictions*] relajar; **attempts to** ~ **traffic congestion** intentos de descongestionar el tráfico **2** (= *facilitate*) [+ *transition, task*] facilitar **3** (= *loosen*) aflojar **4** (= *move carefully*) **she ~d her foot off the clutch** soltó el pie del embrague con cuidado; **he ~d himself into the chair** se sentó con cuidado en la silla **Ⓒ** VI **1** [*pain, tension*] disminuir; [*wind, rain*] amainar **2** [*situation*] calmarse
➤ **ease off** **Ⓐ** VI + ADV = **ease C1** **Ⓑ** VT + ADV [+ *lid*] quitar (con cuidado); [+ *shoe*] quitarse (con cuidado)
➤ **ease up** VI + ADV **1** (= *take things more easily*) tomarse las cosas con más tranquilidad **2** (= *work less*) bajar el ritmo (de trabajo) **3** (= *relax*) relajarse **4** (= *slow down*) [*runner*] aflojar el paso, aminorar la marcha **5 to** ~ **up on** [+ *restrictions, sanctions*] relajar, aflojar; ~ **up on him, he's only a child** no seas tan estricto con él, es sólo un niño

easel ['i:zl] N caballete *m*

easily ['i:zɪlɪ] ADV **1** (= *without difficulty*) [*win, climb, cry*] fácilmente, con facilidad; **she's** ~ **pleased/upset** es fácil complacerla/disgustarla, se contenta/disgusta fácilmente; **that will cost you £50** ~ eso te costará fácilmente *or* por lo menos 50 libras **2** (= *very possibly*) perfectamente, fácilmente; **it could very** ~ **happen again** podría perfectamente *or* fácilmente ocurrir de nuevo **3** (= *by far*) con mucho; **he was** ~ **the best candidate** era con mucho el mejor candidato

east [i:st] **Ⓐ** N este *m*; **the East** (= *Orient*) el Oriente; (*Pol*) el Este; **in the** ~ en el este; **to the** ~ **of** al este de **Ⓑ** ADJ [*side, part*] este, del este; [*coast*] este, oriental; [*wind*] del este **Ⓒ** ADV (= *eastward*) hacia el este; **it's** ~ **of London** está al este de Londres **Ⓓ** CPD ➤ **East Africa** África *f* Oriental ➤ **the East End** *zona del Este de Londres* ➤ **East Germany** Alemania *f* Oriental ➤ **the East Indies** las Indias Orientales ➤ **East Timor** Timor *m* Oriental

eastbound ['i:stbaʊnd] ADJ en dirección este

Easter ['i:stəʳ] N Pascua *f* (de Resurrección), Semana *f* Santa; **at** ~ por Pascua, en Semana Santa ➤ **Easter Day** Domingo *m* de Resurrección ➤ **Easter egg** huevo *m* de Pascua ➤ **the Easter holidays** las vacaciones de Semana Santa ➤ **Easter Sunday** Domingo *m* de Resurrección ➤ **Easter week** Semana *f* Santa

easterly ['i:stəlɪ] ADJ [*wind*] del este; **in an** ~ **direction** hacia el este, en dirección este; **the most** ~ **point in Wales** el punto más oriental *or* más al este de Gales

eastern ['i:stən] ADJ [*side, part*] este, del este; [*coast, border*] este, del este, oriental; [*wind, front, town*] del este; **in** ~ **Spain** en el este de España; ~ **religions** religiones orientales ➤ **Eastern Europe** Europa *f* del Este, Europa *f* Oriental

East German [i:st'dʒɜ:mən] **Ⓐ** N (= *person*) alemán/ana *m/f* oriental **Ⓑ** ADJ germanooriental

eastward ['i:stwəd] **Ⓐ** ADJ [*movement, migration, journey*] hacia el este, en dirección este **Ⓑ** ADV (*also* ~**s**) hacia el este, en dirección este

easy ['i:zɪ] **Ⓐ** ADJ (*compar* **easier**; *superl* **easiest**) **1** (= *not difficult*) fácil; **it is** ~ **to see that ...** es fácil ver que ...; **fluorescent vests are** ~ **to see at night** las chalecos fluorescentes son fáciles de ver por la noche; **to be far from** ~ no ser nada fácil; **that's** ~ **for you to say** para ti es fácil decirlo; **to have it** ~ tenerlo fácil; **they made it very** ~ **for us** nos lo pusieron muy fácil; **"Russian made easy"** "ruso sin esfuerzo"; **it's an** ~ **mistake to make** es un error que se comete fácilmente; **to be** ~ **on the eye/ear** ser *or* resultar agradable a la vista/al oído; **to take the** ~ **option** optar por lo más fácil; **that's the** ~ **part** eso es lo fácil; ~ **pickings** botín *m* sing fácil; **to be within** ~ **reach of sth** estar muy cerca de algo; **that's easier said than done!** ¡eso se dice pronto!, es fácil decirlo, pero hacerlo ...; **to take the** ~ **way out** optar por el camino más fácil; **✦** IDIOM **it's as** ~ **as ABC** *or* **falling off a log** es facilísimo **2** (= *relaxed*) [*manners*] relajado, natural; [*pace*] lento, pausado; **I'm** ~ (*Brit**) me es igual *or* me da igual **Ⓑ** ADV **we can all breathe** ~ **now** ahora todos podemos respirar tranquilos; ~ **come,** ~ **go** tal y como viene se va; ~ **does it!** ¡despacio!, ¡cuidado!, ¡con calma!; **go** ~ **with the sugar** no te pases con el azúcar; **go** ~ **on him** no seas muy duro con él; **to take it** ~ (= *rest*) descansar; (= *go slowly*) tomárselo con calma **Ⓒ** CPD ➤ **easy chair** butaca *f*, sillón *m* (*Sp*) ➤ **easy listening** (**music**) música *f* fácil de escuchar

easy-care ['i:zɪkɛəʳ] ADJ (*Brit*) *que no necesita cuidados especiales*

easy-going ['i:zɪ'gəʊɪŋ] ADJ [*person*] acomodadizo; [*attitude*] de trato fácil, relajado

eat [i:t] (*pt* **ate**; *pp* ~**en**) **Ⓐ** VT comer; **would you like something to** ~? ¿quieres comer algo?; **to** ~ **one's lunch** comer, almorzar; **he won't** ~ **you*** no te va a morder; **what's** ~**ing you?*** ¿qué mosca te ha picado?; **✦** IDIOMS **he's** ~**ing us out of house and home*** come por ocho; **to** ~ **one's words** tragarse las palabras **Ⓑ** VI comer; **✦** IDIOMS **he** ~**s like a horse** come más que una lima (nueva), siempre tiene buen apetito; **I've got him** ~**ing out of my hand** lo tengo dominado
➤ **eat away** VT + ADV (= *wear away*) desgastar; (= *corrode*) corroer; [*mice etc*] roer
➤ **eat in** VI + ADV comer en casa
➤ **eat into** VI + PREP (= *wear away*) desgastar; [+ *metal*] corroer; [+ *savings*] mermar; [+ *leisure time*] reducir
➤ **eat out** VI + ADV comer fuera
➤ **eat up** **Ⓐ** VT + ADV [+ *meal, food*] comerse; **it** ~**s up electricity** consume mucha electricidad; **to be** ~**en up with envy** consumirse de envidia **Ⓑ** VI + ADV ~ **up!** ¡venga, come!, ¡apúrate! (*LAm*)

eaten ['i:tn] PP *of* **eat**

eater ['i:təʳ] N **to be a big** ~ tener siempre buen apetito, ser comilón; **I'm not a big** ~ yo como bastante poco

eatery* ['i:tərɪ] N (*US*) restaurante *m*

eating ['i:tɪŋ] CPD ➤ **eating apple** manzana *f* de mesa ➤ **eating disorder** desorden *m* alimenticio

eats* [i:ts] NPL comida *f* sing, comestibles *mpl*

eau de Cologne ['əʊdəkə'ləʊn] N (agua *f* de) colonia *f*

eaves [i:vz] NPL alero *m* sing

eavesdrop ['i:vzdrɒp] VI escuchar a escondidas; **to** ~ **on a conversation** escuchar una conversación a escondidas

ebb [eb] **Ⓐ** N [*of tide*] reflujo *m*; **the ~ and flow** [*of tide*] el flujo y reflujo; (*fig*) los altibajos; ✦ IDIOM **to be at a low ~** [*person*] estar decaído; [*business*] estar de capa caída **Ⓑ** VI bajar, menguar; **to ~ and flow** fluir y refluir

ebony ['ebənɪ] **Ⓐ** N ébano *m* **Ⓑ** CPD de ébano

e-book ['i:bʊk] N libro *m* electrónico

ebullient [ɪ'bʌlɪənt] ADJ entusiasta, animado

e-business ['i:ˌbɪznɪs] N **1** (= *company*) negocio *m* electrónico **2** (= *commerce*) comercio *m* electrónico

EC N ABBR (= **European Community**) CE *f*

ECB N (= **European Central Bank**) BCE *m*

eccentric [ɪk'sentrɪk] ADJ, N excéntrico/a *m/f*

eccentrically [ɪk'sentrɪkəlɪ] ADV de manera excéntrica

eccentricity [ˌeksən'trɪsɪtɪ] N excentricidad *f*

ecclesiastical [ɪˌkli:zɪ'æstɪkəl] ADJ eclesiástico

ECG N ABBR (= **electrocardiogram**) ECG *m*

echelon ['eʃəlɒn] N (= *level*) nivel *m*; (= *degree*) grado *m*; **the upper ~s of the corporation** los cuadros directivos de la compañía

echo ['ekəʊ] **Ⓐ** N (*pl* **-es**) eco *m* **Ⓑ** VT [+ *sound*] repetir; [+ *opinion etc*] hacerse eco de **Ⓒ** VI [*sound*] resonar, hacer eco; [*place*] resonar

éclair [ɪ'kleəʳ] N petisú *m*

eclectic [ɪ'klektɪk] ADJ, N ecléctico/a *m/f*

eclipse [ɪ'klɪps] **Ⓐ** N eclipse *m* **Ⓑ** VT eclipsar

eco-friendly ['i:kəʊ'frendlɪ] ADJ (*Brit*) amigo de la ecología, ecológicamente puro

E-coli [ˌi:'kəʊlaɪ] N (*Med*) E. coli *m*

ecological [ˌi:kəʊ'lɒdʒɪkəl] ADJ ecológico

ecologically [ˌi:kəʊ'lɒdʒɪkəlɪ] ADV ecológicamente; (*also ~ speaking*) desde el punto de vista ecológico

ecologist [ɪ'kɒlədʒɪst] N (= *scientist*) ecólogo/a *m/f*; (= *conservationist*) ecologista *mf*

ecology [ɪ'kɒlədʒɪ] N ecología *f*

e-commerce ['i:ˌkɒmɜ:s] N comercio *m* electrónico

economic [ˌi:kə'nɒmɪk] **Ⓐ** ADJ **1** (= *financial*) económico **2** (= *profitable*) rentable **Ⓑ** CPD ➤ **economic migrant** inmigrante *mf* (*por motivos económicos*)

economical [ˌi:kə'nɒmɪkəl] ADJ [*person, method, car*] económico; **my car is very ~ to run** mi coche me sale muy económico; **to be ~ with the truth** no decir toda la verdad, no ser muy pródigo con la verdad

economically [ˌi:kə'nɒmɪkəlɪ] ADV **1** (= *financially*) económicamente; (= *from an economic perspective*) desde el punto de vista económico **2** (= *cheaply*) [*use, live*] de manera económica; **to be ~ priced** tener un precio módico *or* muy económico

economics [ˌi:kə'nɒmɪks] **Ⓐ** NSING (= *science*) economía *f* **Ⓑ** NPL (= *financial aspects*) aspectos *mpl* económicos

economist [ɪ'kɒnəmɪst] N economista *mf*

economize [ɪ'kɒnəmaɪz] VI economizar (**on** en)

economy [ɪ'kɒnəmɪ] N economía *f*; (= *a saving*) ahorro *m*; **~ of scale** economía *f* de escala; **to make economies** economizar, ahorrar ➤ **economy class** clase *f* económica *or* turista ➤ **economy drive** **to have an ~ drive** economizar, ahorrar ➤ **economy pack** envase *m* familiar ➤ **economy size** tamaño *m* familiar

economy-class syndrome [ɪ'kɒnəmɪkla:s'sɪndrəʊm] N síndrome *m* de la clase turista

ecosystem ['i:kəʊˌsɪstɪm] N ecosistema *m*

eco-tourism [ˌi:kəʊ'tʊərɪzəm] N ecoturismo *m*, turismo *m* verde *or* ecológico

ecstasy ['ekstəsɪ] N éxtasis *m inv*; **to go into ecstasies over sth** extasiarse ante algo

ecstatic [eks'tætɪk] ADJ contentísimo, eufórico

ecstatically [eks'tætɪkəlɪ] ADV con gran euforia

ECT N ABBR = **electroconvulsive therapy**

ECU ['eɪkju:] N ABBR (= **European Currency Unit**) ECU *m*, UCE *f*

Ecuador [ˌekwə'dɔːʳ] N Ecuador *m*

Ecuadoran [ˌekwə'dɔːrən], **Ecuadorian** [ˌekwə'dɔːrɪən] ADJ, N ecuatoriano/a *m/f*

ecumenical [ˌi:kju'menɪkəl] ADJ ecuménico

eczema ['eksɪmə] N eczema *m*, eccema *m*

eddy ['edɪ] **Ⓐ** N remolino *m* **Ⓑ** VI [*water*] hacer remolinos, arremolinarse

edge [edʒ] **Ⓐ** N **1** [*of cliff, wood, bed, paper*] borde *m*; [*of town*] afueras *fpl*; [*of lake, river*] orilla *f*; [*of cube, brick*] arista *f*; [*of coin*] canto *m*; [*of blade*] filo *m*; **the trees at the ~ of the road** los árboles que bordean la carretera; ✦ IDIOMS **to be on ~** tener los nervios de punta; **to set sb's teeth on ~** [*sound, voice*] dar dentera a algn; [*person*] poner los pelos de punta a algn; **to drive/push sb over the ~** llevar a algn al límite; **to be on the ~ of one's seat** estar en suspense *or* vilo *or* ascuas; **talking to her took the ~ off my grief** hablar con ella mitigó mi dolor; **that took the ~ off my appetite** con eso maté el hambre *or* engañé el estómago **2** (= *advantage*) ventaja *f*; **their technology gave them the competitive ~** su tecnología les dio una posición de ventaja con respecto a la competencia; **to have the ~ over sb** llevar la delantera a algn, llevar ventaja a algn **Ⓑ** VT **1** (= *border*) [+ *garment*] ribetear; [+ *path*] bordear; **a top ~d with lace** un top ribeteado con encaje **2** (= *move*) **he ~d the car into the traffic** sacó el coche con cuidado y se unió al resto del tráfico; **she ~d her way through the crowd** se abrió paso poco a poco entre la multitud **Ⓒ** VI **she ~d away from him** poco a poco se alejó de él; **he ~d closer to the telephone** se acercó lentamente al teléfono; **to ~ forward** avanzar poco a poco; **Labour have ~d into the lead** el partido laborista ha conseguido tomar la delantera por muy poco; **to ~ past** pasar con dificultad

edgeways ['edʒweɪz], **edgewise** ['edʒwaɪz] ADV de lado, de canto; ✦ IDIOM **I couldn't get a word in ~*** no pude meter baza*

edging ['edʒɪŋ] N borde *m*; [*of ribbon, silk*] ribete *m*

edgy ['edʒɪ] ADJ (*compar* **edgier**; *superl* **edgiest**) crispado

edible ['edɪbl] ADJ comestible

edict ['i:dɪkt] N decreto *m*

edifice ['edɪfɪs] N (*frm*) edificio *m* (imponente)

edifying ['edɪfaɪɪŋ] ADJ edificante

Edinburgh ['edɪnbərə] N Edimburgo *m*

edit ['edɪt] VT **1** [+ *newspaper, magazine*] (= *be in charge of*) dirigir; (= *write*) redactar; (= *prepare for printing*) corregir, revisar; (= *cut*) cortar, reducir **2** (*Cine, TV*) montar; (*Rad, Comput*) editar

➤ **edit out** VT + ADV eliminar, suprimir

editing ['edɪtɪŋ] N **1** [*of newspaper, magazine*] (= *management*) dirección *f*; (= *writing*) redacción *f* **2** (= *preparation for printing*) [*of article, series of texts*] edición *f* **3** [*of film*] montaje *m*, edición *f*; [*of video*] edición *f* (*also Comput*)

edition [ɪ'dɪʃən] N edición *f*

editor ['edɪtəʳ] N [*of newspaper, magazine*] director(a) *m/f*; (= *publisher's editor*) redactor(a) *m/f*; (*Cine, TV*) montador(a) *m/f*, editor(a) *m/f*; (*Rad*) editor(a) *m/f*; **~'s note** nota *f* de la redacción; **the sports ~** el/la redactor(a) de la sección de deportes

editorial [ˌedɪ'tɔːrɪəl] **Ⓐ** ADJ [*decision, page, policy*] editorial; [*meeting, assistant*] de redacción; **~ staff** redacción *f* **Ⓑ** N editorial *m*, artículo *m* de fondo

editorialist [ˌedɪ'tɔːrɪəlɪst] N (*US*) editorialista *mf*

educate ['edjʊkeɪt] VT (= *teach*) enseñar; (= *train*) educar, formar; (= *provide instruction in*) instruir; **where were you ~d?** ¿dónde cursó sus estudios?

educated ['edjʊkeɪtɪd] ADJ [*person, voice*] culto; **an ~ guess** una suposición bien fundamentada

education [ˌedjʊ'keɪʃən] N [*of young people*] educación *f*; (= *teaching*) enseñanza *f*; (= *knowledge, culture*) cultura *f*; (= *studies*) estudios *mpl*; (= *training*) formación *f*; (*Univ*) (= *subject*) pedagogía *f*; **there should be more investment in ~** debería invertirse más dinero en educación; **they paid**

for his ~ le pagaron los estudios; **Department of Education** Ministerio *m or* (*LAm*) Secretaría *f* de Educación; **primary/secondary** ~ enseñanza *f* primaria/secundaria, primera/segunda enseñanza *f*; **higher** ~ educación *f* superior, enseñanza *f* superior ➤ **education authority** (*Brit*) ≈ delegación *f* de educación, ≈ consejería *f* de educación (*Sp*)

educational [ˌedjʊˈkeɪʃənl] ADJ (*gen*) educativo; [*role*] docente; [*establishment, institution*] docente, de enseñanza; [*theory*] pedagógico; **falling** ~ **standards** estándares *mpl* de educación cada vez más bajos ➤ **educational psychologist** psicopedagogo/a *m/f*

educationalist [ˌedjʊˈkeɪʃnəlɪst] N (*Brit*) pedagogo/a *m/f*

educationally [ˌedjʊˈkeɪʃnəlɪ] ADV desde el punto de vista educativo; ~ **sound principles** principios *mpl* con una base pedagógica sólida

educator [ˈedjʊkeɪtəʳ] N 1 (= *teacher*) educador(a) *m/f* 2 (*US*) (= *educationalist*) pedagogo/a *m/f*

edutainment [ˌedjʊˈteɪnmənt] N (*esp US*) juego de ordenador ameno y educativo al mismo tiempo

EEC N ABBR (= **European Economic Community**) CEE *f*

EEG N ABBR = **electroencephalogram**

eel [iːl] N anguila *f*

eerie [ˈɪərɪ] ADJ [*sound, experience*] sobrecogedor, espeluznante; [*silence*] sobrecogedor, estremecedor

eerily [ˈɪərɪlɪ] ADV [*similar, familiar*] sorprendentemente; **it was** ~ **quiet** había un silencio sobrecogedor *or* estremecedor

efface [ɪˈfeɪs] VT borrar

effect [ɪˈfekt] ❶ N 1 (*gen*) efecto *m*; (= *result*) resultado *m*, consecuencia *f*; **to have an** ~ **on sb** hacer efecto a algn; **to have an** ~ **on sth** afectar (a) algo; **it will have the** ~ **of preventing ...** tendrá como consecuencia impedir ...; **to have no** ~ no surtir efecto; **in** ~ (= *in fact*) en realidad; (= *practically*) de hecho; **to come into** ~ entrar en vigor; **to put into** ~ [+ *rule*] poner en vigor; [+ *plan*] poner en práctica; **to take** ~ [*drug*] surtir efecto; [*law*] entrar en vigor; **to no** ~ inútilmente, sin resultado; **with** ~ **from April** (*Brit*) a partir de abril; **an increase with immediate** ~ un aumento efectivo a partir de hoy 2 (= *sense*) **a circular to this** ~ **will be issued next week** la próxima semana se hará pública una circular en este sentido; **an announcement to the** ~ **that ...** un aviso informando de que ...; **or words to that** ~ o algo por el estilo 3 (= *impression*) efecto *m*, impresión *f*; **he said it for** ~ lo dijo sólo para impresionar; **special** ~**s** efectos *mpl* especiales 4 **effects** (= *property*) efectos *mpl* ❷ VT [+ *sale, payment, reduction*] efectuar; [+ *cure, improvement, transformation*] lograr

effective [ɪˈfektɪv] ADJ 1 (= *efficient, useful*) efectivo, eficaz; **to be** ~ **against sth** ser eficaz contra algo; **to be** ~ **in doing sth** ser eficaz para hacer algo 2 (= *striking*) [*display, outfit, decoration*] impresionante, logrado; [*combination*] logrado; **to look** ~ causar efecto 3 (= *operative*) **to become** ~ entrar en vigor, hacerse efectivo (**from, on** a partir de) 4 (= *actual*) [*aid, contribution, leader*] real; [*control, increase*] efectivo; [*income*] en efectivo 5 (*Econ, Fin*) [*demand, interest rate*] efectivo

effectively [ɪˈfektɪvlɪ] ADV 1 (= *efficiently*) [*treat, teach, work*] eficazmente, de manera eficaz; [*function*] de manera eficaz 2 (= *strikingly*) de manera impresionante, con mucho efecto 3 (= *in effect*) realmente, de hecho

effectiveness [ɪˈfektɪvnɪs] N eficacia *f*

effeminate [ɪˈfemɪnɪt] ADJ afeminado

effervescent [ˌefəˈvesnt] ADJ [*liquid, tablet*] efervescente

efficiency [ɪˈfɪʃənsɪ] N [*of person, manager*] eficiencia *f*; [*of method, remedy*] eficacia *f*

efficient [ɪˈfɪʃənt] ADJ [*person, service*] eficiente; [*method, remedy*] eficaz

efficiently [ɪˈfɪʃəntlɪ] ADV 1 (= *competently, well*) eficientemente, de manera eficiente 2 (= *effectively*) de manera eficaz

effigy [ˈefɪdʒɪ] N efigie *f*

effing** [ˈefɪŋ] ADJ (*Brit euph*) maldito

effluent [ˈefluənt] N aguas *fpl* residuales

effort [ˈefət] N 1 (= *hard work*) esfuerzo *m*; **put a bit of** ~ **into it!** ¡esfuérzate un poco!, ¡pon un poco más de esfuerzo!; **it's well worth the** ~ merece la pena 2 (= *try*) intento *m*; (= *endeavour*) esfuerzo *m*; **a good** ~ un feliz intento; **in an** ~ **to solve the problem/be polite** en un esfuerzo por resolver el problema/ser amable; **to make an** ~ **to do sth** esforzarse en hacer algo, hacer un esfuerzo por hacer algo; **please make every** ~ **to come** por favor, haz todo lo posible por venir; **it was a pretty poor** ~ fue un intento bastante flojo

effortless [ˈefətlɪs] ADJ [*success, victory*] fácil; [*charm, superiority, grace*] natural; **with** ~ **ease** sin ningún esfuerzo

effortlessly [ˈefətlɪslɪ] ADV [*win, succeed*] fácilmente; [*move, lift*] sin ningún esfuerzo

effrontery [ɪˈfrʌntərɪ] N descaro *m*

effusive [ɪˈfjuːsɪv] ADJ efusivo

effusively [ɪˈfjuːsɪvlɪ] ADV efusivamente, con efusión

E-fit [ˈiːfɪt] N fotorrobot *f* digital, retrato *m* robot digital

EFL N ABBR = **English as a Foreign Language**

EFT N ABBR = **electronic funds transfer**

e.g. ADV, ABBR (= **exempli gratia**) p.ej.

egalitarian [ɪˌɡælɪˈtɛərɪən] ADJ igualitario

egg [eɡ] ❹ N huevo *m*, blanquillo *m* (*Mex*); (= *cell*) óvulo *m*; ✦ IDIOMS **to have** ~ **on one's face*** quedar en ridículo; **as sure as** ~**s are** *or* **is** ~**s** como que dos y dos son cuatro, sin ningún género de dudas; ✦ PROV **don't put all your** ~**s in one basket** no te lo juegues todo a una carta ❸ CPD ➤ **egg beater** batidor *m* de huevos ➤ **egg cup** huevera *f* ➤ **egg custard** natillas *fpl* ➤ **egg roll** (= *sandwich*) bocadillo *m* con huevo duro ➤ **egg timer** reloj *m* de arena (*para cocer huevos*) ➤ **egg whisk** batidor *m* de huevos ➤ **egg white** clara *f* de huevo ➤ **egg yolk** yema *f* de huevo ➤ **egg on** VT + ADV incitar; **to** ~ **sb on to do sth** incitar a algn a hacer algo

egg-and-spoon race [ˈeɡənˌspuːnˌreɪs] N juego *m* del huevo con la cuchara

egghead* [ˈeɡhed] N (*pej*) lumbrera *f*, intelectual *mf*

eggplant [ˈeɡplɑːnt] N (*US*) berenjena *f*

egg-shaped [ˈeɡʃeɪpt] ADJ en forma de huevo

eggshell [ˈeɡʃel] N cáscara *f* de huevo

ego [ˈiːɡəʊ] N **the** ~ el ego, el yo ➤ **ego trip***: **to be on an** ~ **trip** creerse el centro del universo *or* el ombligo del mundo

egocentric [ˌeɡəʊˈsentrɪk] ADJ egocéntrico

egosurf [ˈeɡəʊˌsɜːf] VI buscarse en la Red

egotism [ˈeɡəʊtɪzəm] N egolatría *f*, egocentrismo *m*

egotist [ˈeɡəʊtɪst] Nególatra *mf*, egocéntrico(a) *m/f*

egotistic [ˌeɡəʊˈtɪstɪk], **egotistical** [ˌeɡəʊˈtɪstɪkəl] ADJ egotista

Egypt [ˈiːdʒɪpt] N Egipto *m*

Egyptian [ɪˈdʒɪpʃən] ADJ, N egipcio/a *m/f*

eh [eɪ] EXCL (= *what?*) ¿cómo?, ¿qué?; (*inviting assent*) ¿no?, ¿verdad?, ¿no es así?

eiderdown [ˈaɪdədaʊn] N edredón *m*

eight [eɪt] NUMBER ocho *m*; *see* **five**

eighteen [ˈeɪˈtiːn] NUMBER dieciocho *m*; *see* **five**

eighteenth [ˈeɪˈtiːnθ] ❹ ADJ decimoctavo ❸ PRON decimoctavo/a *m/f*; (= *fraction*) decimoctava parte *f*, dieciochoavo *m*; *see* **fifteenth**

eighth [eɪtθ] ❹ ADJ octavo ❸ PRON octavo/a *m/f*; (= *fraction*) octava parte *f*, octavo *m* ❸ CPD ➤ **eighth note** (*US*) corchea *f*; *see* **fifth**

eightieth [ˈeɪtɪɪθ] ❹ ADJ octogésimo ❸ PRON octogésimo/a *m/f*; (= *fraction*) octogésima parte *f*, octogésimo *m*; *see* **fiftieth**

eighty [ˈeɪtɪ] NUMBER ochenta *m*; *see* **fifty**

Eire ['ɛərə] N Eire m, República f de Irlanda

Eisteddfod [aɪs'teðvɒd] N *festival galés en el que se celebran concursos de música y poesía*

EISTEDDFOD

En Gales un **eisteddfod** es un concurso de poesía, canto, música y danza, en el que las canciones, los poemas y los relatos son mayormente en galés. Cada año tienen lugar muchos de estos **eisteddfodau** por todo Gales y el nivel de competición suele ser muy alto en los concursos más importantes. En Llangollen, al noreste de Gales, se celebra anualmente un concurso internacional en el que hay participantes de todo el mundo, pero el concurso principal, el **National Eisteddfod**, se celebra en un lugar diferente cada año. Ver tb www.eisteddfod.org.uk

---

either ['aɪðəʳ] Ⓐ ADJ 1 (= *one or other*) (*positive*) cualquiera de los dos; (*negative*) ninguno de los dos; **~ day would suit me** cualquiera de los dos días me viene bien; **I don't like ~ book** no me gusta ninguno de los dos libros; **you can do it ~ way** puedes hacerlo de este modo o del otro; **~ way I can't do anything about it** de cualquier forma yo no puedo hacer nada
2 (= *each*) cada; **on ~ side of the road** a ambos lados de la carretera
Ⓑ PRON (*positive*) cualquiera de los dos; (*negative*) ninguno de los dos; **give it to ~ of them** dáselo a cualquiera de los dos; **I don't want ~ of them** no quiero ninguno de los dos
Ⓒ CONJ **either ... or** o ... o; **~ come in or stay out** o entra o quédate fuera; **I have never been to ~ Paris or Rome** no he estado nunca ni en París ni en Roma
Ⓓ ADV tampoco; **he can't sing ~** tampoco sabe cantar; **no, I haven't ~** no, yo tampoco

ejaculate [ɪ'dʒækjʊleɪt] VT, VI (*Physiol*) eyacular

ejaculation [ɪˌdʒækjʊ'leɪʃən] N 1 (= *cry*) exclamación f 2 (*Physiol*) eyaculación f

eject [ɪ'dʒekt] Ⓐ VT expulsar Ⓑ VI [*pilot*] eyectarse

ejector seat [ɪ'dʒektəˌsi:t] N asiento m eyectable

eke [i:k] VT **to ~ out** [+ *food, supplies*] escatimar; [+ *money, income*] hacer que alcance; **to ~ out a living** ganarse la vida a duras penas

EKG N ABBR (*US*) = **ECG**

el* [el] N ABBR (*US*) = **elevated railroad**

elaborate [ɪ'læbərɪt] Ⓐ ADJ (*gen*) muy elaborado; (= *complicated*) complicado; [*excuse*] rebuscado; **an ~ hoax** un elaborado engaño Ⓑ [ɪ'læbəreɪt] VT 1 (= *develop*) [+ *plan, theory*] elaborar, desarrollar 2 (= *explain*) [+ *idea, point*] explicar en detalle, desarrollar Ⓒ [ɪ'læbəreɪt] VI **he refused to ~** se negó a dar más detalles; **he ~d on it** lo explicó con más detalles

elaborately [ɪ'læbərɪtlɪ] ADV 1 (= *ornately*) de forma muy elaborada 2 (= *carefully*) [*planned*] cuidadosamente, minuciosamente

elapse [ɪ'læps] VI pasar, transcurrir

elastic [ɪ'læstɪk] Ⓐ ADJ elástico Ⓑ N elástico m, jebe m (*SC*) Ⓒ CPD ➤ **elastic band** (*esp Brit*) gomita f, goma f elástica

elasticated [ɪ'læstɪkeɪtɪd] ADJ (*Brit*) con elástico

elasticity [i:læs'tɪsɪtɪ] N elasticidad f

elasticized [ɪ'læstɪsaɪzd] ADJ (*US*) con elástico

Elastoplast® [ɪ'læstəˌplɑ:st] N (*Brit*) esparadrapo m

elated [ɪ'leɪtɪd] ADJ (= *excited*) entusiasmado; (= *happy*) eufórico, alborozado

elation [ɪ'leɪʃən] N (= *excitement*) entusiasmo m; (= *happiness*) euforia f, alborozo m, júbilo m

elbow ['elbəʊ] Ⓐ N (*Anat*) codo m; **at one's ~** al alcance de la mano Ⓑ VT **to ~ sb aside** apartar a algn a codazos; **to ~ one's way through the crowd** abrirse paso a codazos por la muchedumbre Ⓒ CPD ➤ **elbow grease*** esfuerzo m; **it will take a bit of ~ grease to shift this** va a costar trabajo mover esto ➤ **elbow joint** articulación f del codo ➤ **elbow room** (= *space*) espacio m para moverse;

(= *leeway*) margen m de maniobra

elder¹ ['eldəʳ] Ⓐ ADJ [*brother etc*] mayor; **~ statesman** viejo estadista m; (*fig*) persona f respetada Ⓑ N (= *senior*) mayor m; [*of tribe*] anciano m; (*in certain Protestant churches*) *persona laica que ejerce funciones educativas, pastorales y/o administrativas*; **my ~s** mis mayores

elder² ['eldəʳ] N (= *tree*) saúco m

elderberry ['eldəˌberɪ] N baya f del saúco ➤ **elderberry wine** vino m de saúco

elderly ['eldəlɪ] Ⓐ ADJ mayor, de edad; **an ~ man** un anciano Ⓑ NPL **the ~** las personas mayores, los ancianos

eldest ['eldɪst] ADJ, N mayor mf; **my ~ sister** mi hermana mayor; **he ~** el es el mayor

elect [ɪ'lekt] Ⓐ VT 1 (*Pol etc*) elegir (**to** para); **he was ~ed chairman** fue elegido presidente 2 (= *choose*) elegir; **he ~ed to remain** eligió quedarse Ⓑ ADJ (*after noun*) electo; **the president ~** el/la presidente/a electo/a

election [ɪ'lekʃən] N elección f; **to call/hold an ~** convocar elecciones ➤ **election campaign** campaña f electoral

electioneer [ɪˌlekʃə'nɪəʳ] VI hacer campaña (electoral)

electioneering [ɪˌlekʃə'nɪərɪŋ] N campaña f electoral; (*pej*) electoralismo m

elective [ɪ'lektɪv] Ⓐ ADJ 1 [*course*] optativo 2 [*assembly*] electivo Ⓑ N (*US Scol*) (asignatura f) optativa f

elector [ɪ'lektəʳ] N elector(a) m/f

electoral [ɪ'lektərəl] ADJ electoral ➤ **electoral college** colegio m electoral ➤ **electoral register** (*Brit*), **electoral roll** (*Brit*) registro m electoral, censo m electoral (*Sp*)

electorate [ɪ'lektərɪt] N electorado m

electric [ɪ'lektrɪk] ADJ eléctrico ➤ **electric blue** azul m eléctrico ➤ **electric chair** silla f eléctrica ➤ **electric eye** célula f fotoeléctrica ➤ **electric fence** valla f electrificada, cercado m electrificado ➤ **electric kettle** hervidora f de agua eléctrica ➤ **electric shock** (*from wire, socket*) descarga f eléctrica; (*from static electricity*) calambre m; **I got an ~ shock from the heater** me dio calambre al tocar la estufa ➤ **electric window(s)** (PL) (*Aut*) elevalunas m inv eléctrico

electrical [ɪ'lektrɪkəl] ADJ eléctrico; **an ~ fault** una avería eléctrica; **household ~ goods** electrodomésticos mpl ➤ **electrical engineer** (= *electrician*) técnico/a m/f electricista; (*with university degree*) ingeniero/a m/f electrotécnico/a ➤ **electrical engineering** electrotecnia f; (*at university*) ingeniería f eléctrica ➤ **electrical failure** avería f eléctrica ➤ **electrical storm** tormenta f eléctrica

electrically [ɪ'lektrɪkəlɪ] ADV [*charged*] de electricidad; **to be ~ driven/powered** funcionar con electricidad

electrician [ɪlek'trɪʃən] N electricista mf

electricity [ɪlek'trɪsɪtɪ] N electricidad f; **to switch on/off the ~** encender/apagar la electricidad *or* la luz ➤ **electricity bill** (*Brit*) factura f *or* (*Sp*) recibo m de la electricidad ➤ **electricity board** (*Brit*) compañía f eléctrica, compañía f de luz (*LAm*)

electrification [ɪ'lektrɪfɪ'keɪʃən] N electrificación f

electrify [ɪ'lektrɪfaɪ] VT 1 (*with electricity*) electrificar; **electrified fence** valla f electrificada, cercado m eléctrico 2 [+ *audience*] electrizar

electrifying [ɪ'lektrɪfaɪɪŋ] ADJ [*performance*] electrizante

electrocardiogram [ɪˌlektrəʊ'kɑ:dɪəgræm] N electrocardiograma m

electrocute [ɪ'lektrəʊkju:t] VT electrocutar

electrocution [ɪˌlektrəʊ'kju:ʃən] N electrocución f

electrode [ɪ'lektrəʊd] N electrodo m

electrolysis [ɪlek'trɒlɪsɪs] N electrólisis f inv

electrolyte [ɪ'lektrəʊˌlaɪt] N electrolito m

electron [ɪ'lektrɒn] N electrón m

electronic [ɪlek'trɒnɪk] ADJ electrónico; **the ~ age** la edad de la electrónica ➤ **electronic banking** banca f informatizada ➤ **electronic engineer** ingeniero/a m/f electrónico/a ➤ **electronic engineering** ingeniería f electrónica ➤ **electronic tagging** (*Brit*) etiquetado m electrónico

electronically [ɪlek'trɒnɪklɪ] ADV electrónicamente

electronics [ɪlek'trɒnɪks] NSING electrónica *f* ➤ **electronics industry** industria *f* electrónica

elegance ['elɪɡəns] N elegancia *f*

elegant ['elɪɡənt] ADJ elegante

elegantly ['elɪɡəntlɪ] ADV con elegancia, elegantemente

elegiac [ˌelɪ'dʒaɪək] ADJ elegíaco

elegy ['elɪdʒɪ] N elegía *f*

element ['elɪmənt] N **1** (*gen, Chem*) elemento *m*; (= *factor*) factor *m*; (*Elec*) resistencia *f*; **an ~ of surprise** un elemento de sorpresa; **an ~ of truth** una parte de verdad; ✦ IDIOM **to be in one's ~** estar en su elemento, estar como pez en el agua **2** the **~s** la intemperie, los elementos; **to brave the ~s** salir a la intemperie

elemental [ˌelɪ'mentl] ADJ elemental

elementary [ˌelɪ'mentərɪ] ADJ elemental, básico ➤ **elementary school** (*US*) escuela *f* de (enseñanza) primaria ➤ **elementary teacher** (*US*) maestro/a *m/f* de (enseñanza) primaria

elephant ['elɪfənt] N elefante *m*

elevate ['elɪveɪt] VT (= *raise*) elevar; (*in rank*) ascender (**to** a)

elevated ['elɪveɪtɪd] ADJ elevado ➤ **elevated railway** (*US*), **elevated railroad** (*US*) ferrocarril *m* urbano elevado

elevation [ˌelɪ'veɪʃən] N **1** (= *raising*) elevación *f*; (*in rank*) ascenso *m* **2** (= *height*) (*esp above sea level*) altitud *f*

elevator ['elɪveɪtəʳ] Ⓐ N **1** (*US*) (= *lift*) ascensor *m*, elevador *m* (*Mex*) **2** (= *hoist for goods*) montacargas *m inv* **3** (*Agr*) elevador *m* de granos **4** (*US*) (*also* ~ **shoe**) zapato *m* de tacón alto Ⓑ CPD ➤ **elevator car** (*US*) caja *f* or cabina *f* de ascensor ➤ **elevator shaft** (*US*) hueco *m* del ascensor

eleven [ɪ'levn] NUMBER once *m*; *see* **five**

elevenses* [ɪ'levnzɪz] NPL (*Brit*) tentempié *msing* de las once, onces *fpl* (*LAm*); **to have ~** tomar un tentempié a las once, tomar las onces (*LAm*)

eleventh [ɪ'levnθ] Ⓐ ADJ undécimo; ✦ IDIOM **at the ~ hour** a última hora Ⓑ PRON undécimo/a *m/f*; (= *fraction*) undécima parte *f*, onceavo *m*; *see* **fifth**

elf [elf] N (*pl* **elves**) duende *m*, elfo *m*

elicit [ɪ'lɪsɪt] VT [+ *interest*] suscitar; [+ *reaction*] provocar; **to ~ sth (from sb)** [+ *reply, information*] obtener algo (de algn)

elide [ɪ'laɪd] Ⓐ VT elidir Ⓑ VI elidirse

eligibility [ˌelɪdʒə'bɪlɪtɪ] N elegibilidad *f*

eligible ['elɪdʒəbl] ADJ elegible; **to be ~ for** (= *suitable*) cumplir los requisitos para; (= *entitled*) tener derecho a; **an ~ young man** un buen partido

eliminate [ɪ'lɪmɪneɪt] VT (*gen*) eliminar; [+ *suspect, possibility*] descartar; [+ *mistakes, details*] suprimir, eliminar

elimination [ɪˌlɪmɪ'neɪʃən] N eliminación *f*; (= *suppression*) supresión *f*, eliminación *f*; **by process of ~** por eliminación ➤ **elimination round** eliminatoria *f*

eliminator [ɪ'lɪmɪneɪtəʳ] N (*Brit Boxing*) combate *m* eliminatorio

elision [ɪ'lɪʒən] N elisión *f*

elite, élite [eɪ'liːt] Ⓐ N élite *f* Ⓑ CPD [*group, unit, force*] de élite; [*school, university*] de élite, exclusivo

elitism [ɪ'liːtɪzəm] N elitismo *m*

elitist [ɪ'liːtɪst] ADJ, N elitista *mf*

elixir [ɪ'lɪksəʳ] N elixir *m*

Elizabethan [ɪˌlɪzə'biːθən] ADJ, N isabelino/a *m/f*

elk [elk] N (*Brit*) alce *m*

ellipse [ɪ'lɪps] N elipse *f*

elliptical [ɪ'lɪptɪkəl] ADJ elíptico

elm [elm] N (*also* ~ **tree**) olmo *m*

elocution [ˌelə'kjuːʃən] N elocución *f*

elongate ['iːlɒŋɡeɪt] VT alargar, extender

elope [ɪ'ləup] VI fugarse para casarse; **to ~ with sb** fugarse con algn

eloquence ['eləkwəns] N elocuencia *f*

eloquent ['eləkwənt] ADJ elocuente

eloquently ['eləkwəntlɪ] ADV con elocuencia, elocuentemente

El Salvador [el'sælvədɔːʳ] N El Salvador

else [els] ADV **all ~** todo lo demás; **anyone ~** cualquier otro; **anyone ~ would do it** cualquier otro lo haría; **I don't know anyone ~ here** aquí no conozco a nadie más; **anything ~ is impossible** cualquier otra cosa es imposible; **anything ~, sir?** (*in shop*) ¿algo más, señor?; **anywhere ~** en cualquier otro sitio; **everyone ~** todos los demás; **everything ~** todo lo demás; **how ~?** ¿de qué otra manera?; **there is little ~ to be done** poco se puede hacer aparte de eso; **no one ~** nadie más; **nothing ~** nada más; **nowhere ~** en ningún otro sitio; **do as I say, or ~!*** ¡haz lo que te digo o si no verás!; **keep quiet or ~ go away** cállate o vete; **someone ~** otra persona; **something ~** otra cosa; **(*)** (= *wonderful*) estupendo; **somewhere ~** ◇ **someplace ~** (*esp US*) en otro sitio, en otra parte; **what ~ ...?** ¿qué más ...?; **where ~ ...?** ¿en qué otro sitio ...?, ¿dónde más ...? (*LAm*); **who ~ ...?** ¿quién si no ...?, ¿quién más ...?

elsewhere ['els'weəʳ] ADV [*be*] en otra parte, en otro sitio; [*go, send*] a otra parte, a otro sitio; **~ in the country** en otros lugares *or* en otras partes del país

ELT N ABBR (*esp Brit*) = **English Language Teaching**

elucidate [ɪ'luːsɪdeɪt] VT aclarar, elucidar

elude [ɪ'luːd] VT [+ *pursuer*] burlar; [+ *capture, arrest*] eludir, escapar a; [+ *grasp, blow*] esquivar, zafarse de; [+ *question*] eludir; **success has ~d him** el éxito le ha eludido *or* le ha sido esquivo; **the answer has so far ~d us** hasta ahora no hemos dado con la respuesta

elusive [ɪ'luːsɪv] ADJ [*prey, enemy*] esquivo, escurridizo; [*success*] esquivo, difícil de conseguir; **he is very ~** no es fácil encontrarlo

elves [elvz] NPL *of* **elf**

emaciated [ɪ'meɪsɪeɪtɪd] ADJ demacrado

e-mail, email ['iːmeɪl] Ⓐ N e-mail *m*, correo *m* electrónico Ⓑ VT **to ~ sb** mandar un e-mail *or* un correo electrónico a algn; **to ~ sb sth** mandar algo a algn por Internet, mandar algo a algn en un e-mail *or* un correo electrónico Ⓒ CPD ➤ **e-mail account** cuenta *f* de correo ➤ **e-mail address** e-mail *m*, dirección *f* electrónica

emanate ['eməneɪt] VI **to ~ from** emanar de, proceder de

emancipate [ɪ'mænsɪpeɪt] VT emancipar

emancipated [ɪ'mænsɪpeɪtɪd] ADJ emancipado

emancipation [ɪˌmænsɪ'peɪʃən] N emancipación *f*

embalm [ɪm'bɑːm] VT embalsamar

embankment [ɪm'bæŋkmənt] N [*of path, railway*] terraplén *m*; [*of canal, river*] dique *m*

embargo [ɪm'bɑːɡəu] N (*pl* ~**es**) (*Comm, Naut*) embargo *m*; (= *prohibition*) prohibición *f* (**on** de); **there is an ~ on arms** está prohibido comerciar con armas, hay un embargo del comercio de armas; **to lift an ~** levantar un embargo/una prohibición; **to put an ~ on sth** establecer un embargo sobre algo, embargar algo

embark [ɪm'bɑːk] Ⓐ VT embarcar Ⓑ VI embarcarse (**for** con rumbo a; **on** en); **to ~ on** [+ *journey*] emprender; [+ *venture, explanation etc*] lanzarse a, embarcarse en

embarkation [ˌembɑː'keɪʃən] N embarque *m*

embarrass [ɪm'bærəs] VT avergonzar, apenar (*LAm*); **I was ~ed by the question** la pregunta me avergonzó *or* me hizo sentir incómodo, la pregunta hizo que me sintiera incómodo; **his decision could ~ the government** su decisión podría poner al gobierno en una situación embarazosa *or* comprometida

embarrassed [ɪm'bærəst] ADJ [*silence*] incómodo; [*laugh*] nervioso; **I was so ~!** ¡me dio tanta vergüenza *or* (*LAm*) pena! ; **many people are ~ about discussing their age** a mucha gente se le da vergüenza *or* (*LAm*) pena hablar de su edad; **it's nothing to be ~ about** no hay por qué avergonzarse *or* (*LAm*) apenarse

---

  ⚠ **embarrassed** ≠ *embarazada*

embarrassing [ɪmˈbærəsɪŋ] ADJ embarazoso; (*) [*performance*] penoso; **he finds it ~ to talk about himself** le da vergüenza *or* (*LAm*) pena hablar de sí mismo; **to put sb in an ~ position** poner a algn en una situación embarazosa *or* comprometida

embarrassingly [ɪmˈbærəsɪŋlɪ] ADV **there were ~ few people** era vergonzoso *or* (*LAm*) penoso la poca gente que había

embarrassment [ɪmˈbærəsmənt] N **1** (= *state*) vergüenza *f*, pena *f* (*LAm*) **2** (= *cause*) molestia *f*, vergüenza *f*

embassy [ˈembəsɪ] N embajada *f*

embed [ɪmˈbed] VT clavar, hincar (**in** en); **it is ~ded in my memory** lo tengo clavado en la memoria

embellish [ɪmˈbelɪʃ] VT (= *decorate*) embellecer (**with** con); [+ *story, truth*] adornar (**with** con)

ember [ˈembəʳ] N brasa *f*, ascua *f*

Use **el/un** not **la/una** before feminine nouns beginning with stressed **a** or **ha** like **ascua**.

---

the dying ~s el rescoldo

embezzle [ɪmˈbezl] VT malversar, desfalcar

embezzlement [ɪmˈbezlmənt] N malversación *f* (de fondos), desfalco *m*

embezzler [ɪmˈbezləʳ] N malversador(a) *m/f*, desfalcador(a) *m/f*

embittered [ɪmˈbɪtəd] ADJ resentido, amargado

emblazon [ɪmˈbleɪzən] VT engalanar *or* esmaltar con colores brillantes; (*fig*) escribir *or* adornar de modo llamativo

emblem [ˈembləm] N emblema *m*

emblematic [ˌemblɪˈmætɪk] ADJ emblemático

embodiment [ɪmˈbɒdɪmənt] N encarnación *f*; **to be the very ~ of virtue** ser la encarnación de la virtud, ser la virtud en persona

embody [ɪmˈbɒdɪ] VT [+ *spirit, quality*] encarnar; [+ *idea, thought, theory*] expresar, plasmar (**in** en)

embolism [ˈembəlɪzəm] N embolia *f*

embossed [ɪmˈbɒst] ADJ [*writing paper*] con membretes en relieve; [*wallpaper*] con relieve; [*metal, leather*] repujado, labrado

embrace [ɪmˈbreɪs] Ⓐ N abrazo *m* Ⓑ VT **1** [+ *person, religion, etc*] abrazar **2** (= *include*) abarcar Ⓒ VI abrazarse

embroider [ɪmˈbrɔɪdəʳ] Ⓐ VT **1** (= *sew*) bordar **2** (= *embellish*) [+ *truth, facts, story*] adornar Ⓑ VI bordar

embroidery [ɪmˈbrɔɪdərɪ] N bordado *m*; **I do ~ in the afternoon** bordo por las tardes

embroil [ɪmˈbrɔɪl] VT enredar; **to get ~ed in sth** enredarse en algo

embryo [ˈembrɪəʊ] N embrión *m*; **in ~** en embrión

embryonic [ˌembrɪˈɒnɪk] ADJ embrionario

emcee [ˈemˈsiː] (*US*) Ⓐ N presentador(a) *m/f* Ⓑ VT presentar

emend [ɪˈmend] VT enmendar

emerald [ˈemərəld] Ⓐ N (= *stone*) esmeralda *f*; (= *colour*) verde *m* esmeralda Ⓑ ADJ (*also* **~ green**) verde esmeralda *inv* Ⓒ CPD [*necklace, bracelet, ring*] de esmeraldas

emerge [ɪˈmɜːdʒ] VI salir (**from** de); [*truth*] saberse, resplandecer; [*facts, problems*] surgir, presentarse; [*theory, new nation*] surgir; **it ~s that** resulta que

emergence [ɪˈmɜːdʒəns] N aparición *f*

emergency [ɪˈmɜːdʒənsɪ] Ⓐ N **1** (= *crisis*) emergencia *f*; **in case of ~** en caso de emergencia; **a national ~** una crisis nacional; **to declare a state of ~** declarar el estado de excepción **2** (*Med*) urgencia *f* Ⓑ CPD [*meeting, measures*] de emergencia; [*operation*] de urgencia ➤ **emergency brake** (*US*) freno *m* de mano ➤ **emergency call** llamada *f* de urgencia ➤ **emergency exit** salida *f* de emergencia ➤ **emergency landing** (*Aer*) aterrizaje *m* forzoso ➤ **emergency lane** (*US*) arcén *m*

➤ **emergency powers** poderes *mpl* extraordinarios ➤ **emergency room** (*US Med*) sala *f* de urgencias ➤ **emergency services** servicios *mpl* de urgencia *or* emergencia ➤ **emergency stop** (*Aut*) parada *f* de emergencia ➤ **emergency supply** provisión *f* de reserva ➤ **emergency ward** sala *f* de urgencias

emerging [ɪˈmɜːdʒɪŋ] ADJ [*countries*] emergente

emery board [ˈemərɪbɔːd] N lima *f* de uñas

emetic [ɪˈmetɪk] N emético *m*

emigrant [ˈemɪgrənt] ADJ, N emigrante *mf*

emigrate [ˈemɪgreɪt] VI emigrar

emigration [ˌemɪˈgreɪʃən] N emigración *f*

eminence [ˈemɪnəns] N (= *fame*) prestigio *m*, renombre *m* (**as** como); **His/Your Eminence** Su/Vuestra Eminencia

eminent [ˈemɪnənt] ADJ [*doctor, scientist*] eminente, ilustre; **she is ~ in the field of avionics** es una eminencia en el campo de la aviónica

eminently [ˈemɪnəntlɪ] ADV sumamente

emirate [eˈmɪərɪt] N emirato *m*

emissary [ˈemɪsərɪ] N emisario/a *m/f*

emission [ɪˈmɪʃən] N emisión *f*; **emissions** emisiones *fpl* ➤ **emission controls** controles *mpl* de emisiones

emit [ɪˈmɪt] VT [+ *light, signal*] emitir; [+ *smoke, heat, smell*] despedir; [+ *sound*] producir

Emmy [ˈemɪ] N (*US TV*) Emmy *m*

e-money [ˈiːmʌnɪ] N dinero *m* electrónico

emotion [ɪˈməʊʃən] N **1** (= *passion*) emoción *f*; **her voice trembled with ~** su voz temblaba de emoción **2** (= *feeling*) sentimiento *m*; **to control one's ~s** controlar sus sentimientos

emotional [ɪˈməʊʃənl] Ⓐ ADJ **1** (= *psychological*) [*well-being, problem, development*] emocional; [*abuse, need*] afectivo **2** (= *moving, emotive*) [*experience, speech*] emotivo **3** (= *sentimental*) [*person, behaviour*] sentimental, emotivo; [*decision, outburst*] impulsivo; **to get ~** emocionarse; (*pej*) ponerse sentimental Ⓑ CPD ➤ **emotional blackmail** chantaje *m* emocional

emotionally [ɪˈməʊʃnəlɪ] ADV **1** (= *mentally*) [*mature, unstable*] emocionalmente; **to remain ~ detached** no involucrarse emocionalmente **2** (= *with emotion*) [*speak, appeal*] emotivamente, de forma conmovedora; **an ~ charged atmosphere** una atmósfera cargada de emotividad **3** (= *sentimentally*) **they became ~ involved** entablaron una relación sentimental

emotive [ɪˈməʊtɪv] ADJ emotivo

empathize [ˈempəθaɪz] VI identificarse (**with** con)

empathy [ˈempəθɪ] N identificación *f*, empatía *f*

emperor [ˈempərəʳ] N emperador *m*

emphasis [ˈemfəsɪs] N (*pl* **emphases** [ˈemfəsiːz]) **1** (*in word*) acento *m*; (*in sentence*) énfasis *m inv*; **the ~ is on the first syllable** el acento (re)cae en la primera sílaba **2** (*fig*) énfasis *m inv*; **he said it twice, for ~** lo dijo dos veces, para enfatizar *or* para recalcar; **the ~ is on sport** se da más énfasis al deporte; **to put ~ on sth** hacer hincapié en algo, poner énfasis en algo

emphasize [ˈemfəsaɪz] VT **1** [+ *word, syllable*] enfatizar; [+ *fact, point*] hacer hincapié en, enfatizar, subrayar, recalcar; **I must ~ that …** debo insistir en que … **2** (*Ling*) acentuar **3** [*garment*] hacer resaltar

emphatic [ɪmˈfætɪk] ADJ (= *forceful*) [*statement, denial, refusal*] categórico; [*tone, gesture*] enérgico, enfático; **they were quite ~ that they were not going** dijeron categóricamente que no iban; **she's ~ that business is improving** mantiene firmemente que el negocio está mejorando; **Pat was ~ about how valuable the course was** Pat hizo hincapié en lo valioso que era el curso; **an ~ no** un no rotundo; **an ~ yes** un sí contundente

emphatically [ɪmˈfætɪkəlɪ] ADV categóricamente

emphysema [ˌemfɪˈsiːmə] N enfisema *m*

empire [ˈempaɪəʳ] N imperio *m*

empirical [emˈpɪrɪkəl] ADJ empírico

employ [ɪmˈplɔɪ] VT [+ *person, object, method*] emplear; [+ *time*] ocupar; **thousands of people are ~ed in tourism** miles de personas trabajan en el sector del turismo

employable [ɪmˈplɔɪəbl] ADJ [*person*] con capacidad para trabajar; [*skill*] útil, utilizable

employee [ˌemplɔɪˈiː] N empleado/a *m/f*

employer [ɪmˈplɔɪəʳ] N (= *business person*) empresario/a *m/f*; (= *boss*) patrón/ona *m/f*; **my ~** mi jefe

employment [ɪmˈplɔɪmənt] N empleo *m*, trabajo *m*; **to be in ~** tener empleo *or* trabajo; **to give ~ to** emplear, dar trabajo a; **full ~** pleno empleo *m* ➤ **employment agency** agencia *f* de colocación

empower [ɪmˈpaʊəʳ] VT **1** (= *authorize*) **to ~ sb to do sth** autorizar a algn para hacer algo **2** [+ *women, workers, minorities*] atribuir poderes a

empowerment [ɪmˈpaʊəmənt] N [*of women, workers, minorities*] atribución *f* de poder

empress [ˈemprɪs] N emperatriz *f*

emptiness [ˈemptɪnɪs] N vacío *m*

empty [ˈemptɪ] Ⓐ ADJ (*compar* **emptier**; *superl* **emptiest**) **1** [*box, glass, street, room*] vacío; [*seat, chair*] (*in bus, restaurant*) libre, desocupado; (*in living room*) vacío; [*place*] desierto; **the flat next door is ~** el piso de al lado está desocupado; **she was staring into ~ space** miraba al infinito; **on an ~ stomach** en ayunas, con el estómago vacío

2 (= *meaningless*) [*threat, promise, dream*] vano; [*words, rhetoric*] hueco, vacío; **it's an ~ gesture** es un gesto vacío; **my life is ~ without you** mi vida no tiene sentido sin ti **3** (= *numb*) **when I heard the news I felt ~** cuando me enteré de la noticia me sentí vacío

Ⓑ N (= *empty bottle*) envase *m* (vacío), casco *m* (vacío); (= *empty glass*) vaso *m* (vacío); **the car was running on ~** el coche estaba con el depósito vacío

Ⓒ VT [+ *container, tank, glass, plate*] vaciar (**into** en); **to ~ out one's pockets** vaciarse los bolsillos

Ⓓ VI (= *become empty*) vaciarse

empty-handed [ˈemptɪˈhændɪd] ADJ con las manos vacías

empty-headed [ˈemptɪˈhedɪd] ADJ casquivano

EMS N ABBR (= **European Monetary System**) SME *m*

EMU N ABBR (= **economic and monetary union**) UME *f*, UEM *f*

emu [ˈiːmjuː] N emú *m*

emulate [ˈemjʊleɪt] VT emular

emulation [ˌemjʊˈleɪʃən] N emulación *f*

emulsion [ɪˈmʌlʃən] N (= *liquid*) emulsión *f*; (*also* **~ paint**) pintura *f* emulsión

enable [ɪˈneɪbl] VT **1** (= *make able*) **to ~ sb to do sth** permitir a algn hacer algo **2** (= *make possible*) posibilitar

enact [ɪˈnækt] VT **1** [+ *law*] promulgar **2** (= *perform*) [+ *play, scene, part*] representar

enamel [ɪˈnæməl] Ⓐ N esmalte *m* Ⓑ VT esmaltar Ⓒ CPD ➤ **enamel jewellery** alhajas *fpl* de esmalte ➤ **enamel paint** (pintura *f* al) esmalte *m* ➤ **enamel saucepan** cacerola *f* esmaltada

enamelled, enameled (US) [ɪˈnæməld] ADJ esmaltado

enamoured, enamored (US) [ɪˈnæməd] ADJ **to be ~ of** [+ *person*] estar enamorado de; [+ *thing*] estar entusiasmado con

enc. ABBR (= **enclosure(s), enclosed**) adj.

encampment [ɪnˈkæmpmənt] N campamento *m*

encapsulate [ɪnˈkæpsjʊleɪt] VT (= *include*) recoger; (= *summarize*) resumir

encase [ɪnˈkeɪs] VT encerrar; (*Tech*) revestir; **to be ~d in** estar revestido de

encephalogram [ɪnˈsefələgræm] N encefalograma *m*

enchant [ɪnˈtʃɑːnt] VT encantar; **we were ~ed with the place** el sitio nos encantó

enchanter [ɪnˈtʃɑːntəʳ] N hechicero/a *m/f*

enchanting [ɪnˈtʃɑːntɪŋ] ADJ encantador

enchantment [ɪnˈtʃɑːntmənt] N (= *delight*) encanto *m*; (= *charm, spell*) encantamiento *m*, hechizo *m*

enchantress [ɪnˈtʃɑːntrɪs] N hechicera *f*

encircle [ɪnˈsɜːkl] VT (= *surround*) rodear (**with** de); (*Mil*) sitiar; [+ *waist, shoulders*] ceñir

encl. ABBR (= **enclosure(s), enclosed**) adj.

enclave [ˈenkleɪv] N enclave *m*

enclose [ɪnˈkləʊz] VT **1** [+ *land, garden*] cercar, vallar **2** (*with letter*) remitir adjunto, adjuntar

enclosed [ɪnˈkləʊzd] ADJ **1** (*with letter*) adjunto; **please find ~ ...** le enviamos adjunto *or* anexo ...; **the ~ letter** la carta adjunta **2** [*garden, land*] cercado, vallado

enclosure [ɪnˈkləʊʒəʳ] N **1** (= *place*) recinto *m*; (*at racecourse*) reservado *m* **2** (*in letter*) anexo *m*

encode [ɪnˈkəʊd] VT (= *encrypt*) codificar, cifrar

encoder [ɪnˈkəʊdəʳ] N (*Comput*) codificador *m*

encompass [ɪnˈkʌmpəs] VT abarcar

encore [ɒŋˈkɔːʳ] Ⓐ EXCL ¡otra! Ⓑ N bis *m*; **to give an ~** hacer un bis, repetir a petición del público

encounter [ɪnˈkaʊntəʳ] Ⓐ N encuentro *m* Ⓑ VT [+ *person*] encontrar, encontrarse con; [+ *difficulty, enemy*] tropezar con

encourage [ɪnˈkʌrɪdʒ] VT animar, alentar; **to ~ sb to do sth** animar a algn a hacer algo

encouragement [ɪnˈkʌrɪdʒmənt] N ánimo(s) *m(pl)*, aliento *m*; **to give ~ to** dar ánimos a, animar

encouraging [ɪnˈkʌrɪdʒɪŋ] ADJ [*smile*] alentador; [*news, prospect*] alentador, halagüeño; [*words*] de aliento; **he was always very ~** siempre me daba ánimos

encroach [ɪnˈkrəʊtʃ] VI **to ~ (up)on** [+ *time*] quitar; [+ *rights*] usurpar

encrusted [ɪnˈkrʌstɪd] ADJ **~ with** incrustado de

encrypt [ɪnˈkrɪpt] VT codificar

encryption [ɪnˈkrɪpʃən] N codificación *f*

encumber [ɪnˈkʌmbəʳ] VT [+ *person, movement*] estorbar; [+ *place*] llenar (**with** de); **to be ~ed with debts** estar cargado de deudas

encumbrance [ɪnˈkʌmbrəns] N estorbo *m*

encyclopaedia, encyclopedia [enˌsaɪkləʊˈpiːdɪə] N enciclopedia *f*

encyclopaedic, encyclopedic [enˌsaɪkləʊˈpiːdɪk] ADJ enciclopédico

end [end] Ⓐ N **1** [*of street*] final *m*; [*of line, table*] extremo *m*; [*of rope, stick*] punta *f*; [*of town*] parte *f*, zona *f*; (*Sport*) lado *m*; **at the ~ of** [+ *street, corridor*] al final de; [+ *rope, cable*] en la punta de; **to change ~s** (*Sport*) cambiar de lado; **to go to the ~s of the earth** ir hasta el fin del mundo; **from one ~ to the other** de un extremo a otro; **the ~ of the line** (*fig*) el término, el acabóse; **to stand sth on ~** poner algo de punta; **his hair stood on ~** se le puso el pelo de punta; **the ~ of the road** (*fig*) el término, el acabóse; **to place ~ to ~** poner uno tras otro; **to start at the wrong ~** empezar por el fin; ✦ IDIOMS **to make ~s meet** hacer llegar *or* alcanzar el dinero; **to get hold of the wrong ~ of the stick** tomar el rábano por las hojas; **to be at the ~ of one's tether** no poder más, no aguantar más

2 [*of time, process, journey, resources*] fin *m*, final *m*; [*of story*] fin *m*, conclusión *f*; **at the ~ of the century** a fines del siglo; **at the ~ of three months** al cabo de tres meses; **to be at an ~** [*meeting, interview*] haber concluido; **we are almost at the ~ of our holidays** se nos están acabando las vacaciones; **to come to a bad ~** acabar mal; **to bring to an ~** [+ *work, speech, relationship*] dar por terminado; **to come to an ~** llegar a su fin, terminarse; **we'll never hear the ~ of it*** esto va a ser cuento de nunca acabar; **in the ~** al fin; **that's the ~ of the matter** asunto concluido; **there's no ~ to it*** esto no se acaba nunca; **no ~ of** (*esp Brit**) la mar de*; **I enjoyed it no ~*** me gustó muchísimo; **three days on ~** tres días seguidos; **for hours on ~** hora tras hora; **to put an ~ to** poner fin a, acabar con; **that was the ~ of that!** ¡y se acabó!; **that was the ~ of our car*** así se acabó el coche; **he's the ~!** (*Brit**) ¡es el colmo!; **towards the ~ of** [+ *book, film*] hacia el final de; [+ *century*] hacia fines de; [+ *month*] hacia fin de; **without ~** interminable; ✦ IDIOMS **at the ~ of the day** al fin

y al cabo, a fin de cuentas; **it's not the ~ of the world*** el mundo no se va a acabar por eso
3 (= *remnant*) [*of loaf, candle, meat*] resto *m*, cabo *m*
4 (= *aim*) fin *m*, propósito *m*; **an ~ in itself** un fin en sí; **to <u>achieve</u> one's ~** alcanzar su objetivo; **the ~ <u>justifies</u> the means** el fin justifica los medios; **<u>to</u> the ~ that ...** a fin de que ... + *subjun*; **to this ~** con este propósito; **<u>with</u> what ~?** ¿para qué?
B VT (= *finish*) terminar; [+ *abuse, speculation*] acabar con; **that was the meal to ~ <u>all</u> meals!*** ¡eso fue el no va más en comidas!; **to ~ one's <u>days</u>** vivir sus últimos días; **to ~ <u>it</u> all*** suicidarse
C VI (*gen*) terminar (**in** en; **with** con); [*road*] terminar(se); **to ~ <u>by</u> saying** terminar diciendo
D CPD ➤ **end product** (*Ind*) producto *m* final; (*fig*) consecuencia *f* ➤ **end result** resultado *m* ➤ **end user** usuario/a *m/f* final ➤ **end zone** (*US Sport*) zona *f* de anotación
➤ **end off** VT + ADV poner fin a
➤ **end up** VI + ADV terminar (**in** en); [*road, path*] llevar, conducir (**in** a)

endanger [ɪn'deɪndʒəʳ] VT poner en peligro; **an ~ed species** una especie en peligro de extinción

endear [ɪn'dɪəʳ] VT **to ~ sb to** ganar para algn la simpatía de

endearing [ɪn'dɪərɪŋ] ADJ [*person, smile, habit*] encantador, entrañable; [*characteristic, quality*] entrañable

endearingly [ɪn'dɪərɪŋlɪ] ADV [*say, smile*] de manera encantadora; **he is ~ shy/eccentric** es encantadoramente tímido/excéntrico

endearment [ɪn'dɪəmənt] N cariño *m*; **term of ~** palabra *f* de cariño

endeavour, endeavor (*US*) [ɪn'devəʳ] **A** N (= *attempt*) intento *m*, tentativa *f*; (= *effort*) esfuerzo *m*; **to make every ~ to do sth** procurar por todos los medios hacer algo **B** VI **to ~ to do sth** procurar hacer algo, esforzarse por hacer algo

endemic [en'demɪk] ADJ endémico

ending ['endɪŋ] N **1** (= *end*) fin *m*, final *m*; [*of book, story, play*] final *m*, desenlace *m*; **the tale has a happy ~** el cuento tiene un final *or* desenlace feliz **2** [*of word*] terminación *f*

endive ['endaɪv] N (*curly*) escarola *f*; (*US*) (*compact*) endibia *f*

endless ['endlɪs] ADJ **1** (= *interminable*) [*road, queue, summer, speech, list*] interminable; [*variety, patience, desert*] infinito; [*supply*] inacabable, inagotable; **an ~ round of meetings** una ronda interminable de reuniones
2 (= *continual*) continuo; **I'm tired of his ~ questions/ complaining** estoy cansado de sus continuas preguntas/ quejas; **the possibilities are ~** las posibilidades son infinitas

endlessly ['endlɪslɪ] ADV [*repeat*] una y otra vez, hasta la saciedad; [*discuss*] hasta la saciedad; [*argue*] continuamente; [*talk*] sin parar; [*recycle*] una y otra vez; **she talks ~ about her job** no para de hablar de su trabajo

endocrine ['endəʊkraɪn] ADJ endocrino

endorse [ɪn'dɔːs] VT **1** [+ *cheque, document*] endosar **2** (= *approve*) [+ *opinion, claim, plan*] aprobar; (= *support*) [+ *decision*] respaldar **3** (*Brit Aut*) **to ~ a licence** anotar los detalles de una sanción en el permiso de conducir

endorsement [ɪn'dɔːsmənt] N **1** (= *signature*) endoso *m* **2** (= *approval*) aprobación *f*; (= *support*) respaldo *m* **3** (*Brit Aut*) nota *f* de sanción

endow [ɪn'daʊ] VT (= *found*) [+ *prize, professorship*] fundar, crear; (= *donate*) dotar, hacer una donación a; **to be ~ed with** estar dotado de

endowment [ɪn'daʊmənt] **A** N **1** (= *act*) dotación *f*; (= *creation*) fundación *f*, creación *f*; (= *amount*) donación *f* **2** (*fig*) dote *f* **B** CPD ➤ **endowment mortgage** (*Brit*) hipoteca *f* avalada por una dote ➤ **endowment policy** (*Brit*) póliza *f* dotal

endurable [ɪn'djʊərəbl] ADJ aguantable, soportable

endurance [ɪn'djʊərəns] N resistencia *f*; **beyond ~** inaguantable, insoportable; **it tested his powers of ~** puso

a prueba su resistencia ➤ **endurance test** prueba *f* de resistencia

endure [ɪn'djʊəʳ] **A** VT (= *suffer*) [+ *pain, heat*] resistir, aguantar; (= *tolerate*) aguantar, soportar **B** VI (= *last*) durar

enduring [ɪn'djʊərɪŋ] ADJ duradero, perdurable

enema ['enɪmə] N enema *m*

enemy ['enɪmɪ] **A** N enemigo/a *m/f*; **to make an ~ of sb** enemistarse con algn; **✦** IDIOM **he is his own worst ~** su peor enemigo es él mismo **B** CPD [*territory, forces, aircraft*] enemigo

enemy-occupied [ˌenəmɪ'ɒkjʊpaɪd] ADJ ocupado por el enemigo

energetic [ˌenə'dʒetɪk] ADJ [*person, campaign*] activo; [*activity, sport*] enérgico, duro; [*performance*] lleno de energía; [*protest, efforts*] vigoroso; [*denial, refusal*] enérgico; **I've had a very ~ day** he tenido un día muy activo; **to feel ~** sentirse lleno de energía; **I'm not feeling very ~ today** hoy no me siento con muchas energías

energetically [ˌenə'dʒetɪkəlɪ] ADV [*play, run*] con energía; [*work, deny*] enérgicamente; [*campaign*] activamente, vigorosamente

energize ['enədʒaɪz] VT activar, dar energía a

energy ['enədʒɪ] N (*gen*) energía *f*; (= *strength*) vigor *m* ➤ **energy conservation** conservación *f* de la energía ➤ **energy crisis** crisis *f inv* energética

energy-efficient [ˌenədʒɪə'fɪʃənt] ADJ de bajo consumo energético

energy-saving ['enədʒɪˌseɪvɪŋ] ADJ [*device, system*] que ahorra energía; [*policy*] para ahorrar energía

enervating ['enəˌveɪtɪŋ] ADJ enervador

enfold [ɪn'fəʊld] VT envolver; **to ~ sb in one's arms** abrazar a algn, estrechar a algn entre los brazos

enforce [ɪn'fɔːs] VT [+ *law*] hacer cumplir; [+ *rights*] hacer respetar; [+ *sentence*] ejecutar; [+ *obedience, attendance*] imponer (**on** a)

enforced [ɪn'fɔːst] ADJ [*idleness, exile*] forzoso, forzado

enforcement [ɪn'fɔːsmənt] N [*of law*] aplicación *f*; [*of sentence*] ejecución *f*

enfranchise [ɪn'fræntʃaɪz] VT conceder el derecho de voto a

engage [ɪn'geɪdʒ] **A** VT **1** [+ *servant, lawyer, worker*] contratar **2** [+ *attention*] (= *attract*) llamar, captar; (= *occupy*) ocupar; **to ~ sb in conversation** entablar conversación con algn **B** VI **1** **to ~ in** [+ *discussion*] entablar; [+ *politics*] meterse en; [+ *sport*] tomar parte en **2** (*Mech*) engranar (**with** con)

engaged [ɪn'geɪdʒd] **A** ADJ **1** (= *busy*) **to be ~** [*person*] estar ocupado; (*Brit*) [*toilet*] estar ocupado; (*Brit*) [*telephone*] estar comunicando *or* (*LAm*) ocupado; **to be ~ in** estar ocupado en, dedicarse a **2** **to be ~** (**to be married**) estar prometido; **to get ~** prometerse (**to** con); **the ~ couple** los novios **B** CPD ➤ **engaged signal** *or* **tone** (*Brit*) señal *f* de comunicando *or* (*LAm*) ocupado

engagement [ɪn'geɪdʒmənt] **A** N **1** (= *betrothal*) compromiso *m*; (= *period of engagement*) noviazgo *m* **2** (= *appointment*) compromiso *m*, cita *f*; **I have a previous ~** ya tengo un compromiso **3** (*Mil*) (= *battle*) batalla *f*, combate *m* **4** (= *contract*) contrato *m* **B** CPD ➤ **engagement diary** dietario *m*; (*at work*) agenda *f* de trabajo ➤ **engagement party** fiesta *f* de compromiso ➤ **engagement ring** anillo *m* de compromiso

engaging [ɪn'geɪdʒɪŋ] ADJ atractivo

engine ['endʒɪn] **A** N **1** (*in car, ship, plane*) motor *m* **2** (*Rail*) locomotora *f*, máquina *f*; **with your back to the ~** de espaldas a la máquina **B** CPD ➤ **engine driver** (*Brit*) [*of train*] maquinista *mf* ➤ **engine failure** avería *f* del motor ➤ **engine room** (*Naut*) sala *f* de máquinas; (*fig*) motor *m*

engineer [ˌendʒɪ'nɪəʳ] **A** N ingeniero/a *m/f*; (*for repairs*) técnico/a *m/f*; (*US Rail*) maquinista *mf*; **electrical/TV ~** técnico/a *m/f* electricista/de televisión **B** VT [+ *plan*] maquinar; [+ *meeting*] organizar

engineering [ˌendʒɪ'nɪərɪŋ] N ingeniería *f* ➤ **engineering industry** industria *f* de ingeniería

England ['ɪŋglənd] N Inglaterra *f*

English ['ɪŋglɪʃ] **Ⓐ** ADJ inglés
Ⓑ N **1** (*Ling*) inglés *m*; **King's/Queen's ~** inglés *m* correcto; **in plain ~** (= *clearly*) claramente; (*hum*) ≈ en cristiano*; **~ as a Foreign Language** inglés para extranjeros; **~ as a Second Language** inglés como segunda lengua
2 the ~ los ingleses
Ⓒ CPD ➤ **English breakfast** desayuno *m* inglés *or* a la inglesa ➤ **the English Channel** el Canal de la Mancha ➤ **English Heritage** (*Brit*) ≈ Patrimonio *m* Histórico-Artístico ➤ **English Language Teaching** enseñanza *f* del inglés ➤ **English speaker** anglohablante *mf*

Englishman ['ɪŋglɪʃmən] N (*pl* **Englishmen**) inglés *m*

English-speaking ['ɪŋglɪʃ,spi:kɪŋ] ADJ de habla inglesa, anglohablante

Englishwoman ['ɪŋglɪʃ,wʊmən] N (*pl* **Englishwomen**) inglesa *f*

engrave [ɪn'greɪv] VT grabar; **it is ~d on my memory forever** lo tengo grabado para siempre en mi memoria

engraver [ɪn'greɪvəʳ] N grabador(a) *m/f*

engraving [ɪn'greɪvɪŋ] N grabado *m*

engross [ɪn'grəʊs] VT [+ *attention, person*] absorber; **to be ~ed in sth** estar absorto en algo

engrossing [ɪn'grəʊsɪŋ] ADJ absorbente

engulf [ɪn'gʌlf] VT (= *swallow up*) tragar; (= *immerse*) sumergir, hundir; **she felt ~ed by her grief** se sentía abrumada *or* hundida por el desconsuelo

enhance [ɪn'hɑ:ns] VT [+ *beauty, attraction*] realzar, dar realce a; [+ *position, reputation, chances*] mejorar; [+ *value, powers*] aumentar

enigma [ɪ'nɪgmə] N enigma *m*

enigmatic [,enɪg'mætɪk] ADJ enigmático

enjoin [ɪn'dʒɔɪn] VT (*frm*) **to ~ sb to do sth** exigir a algn hacer algo; **to ~ sb from doing sth** (*US*) prohibir a algn hacer algo

enjoy [ɪn'dʒɔɪ] VT **1** (= *take pleasure in*) [+ *meal, wine, occasion*] disfrutar (de); **to ~ life** disfrutar de la vida; **~ your meal!** ¡que aproveche!; **I ~ reading** me gusta leer; **did you ~ the game?** ¿te gustó el partido?; **I hope you ~ your holiday** que lo pases muy bien en las vacaciones; **to ~ o.s.** pasarlo bien, divertirse; **we really ~ed ourselves** lo pasamos en grande, nos divertimos mucho **2** (= *benefit from*) [+ *good health, income, respect*] disfrutar de, gozar de; [+ *advantage*] poseer

enjoyable [ɪn'dʒɔɪəbl] ADJ (= *pleasant*) agradable; (= *amusing*) divertido

enjoyment [ɪn'dʒɔɪmənt] N placer *m*; **to find ~ doing sth** disfrutar *or* gozar haciendo algo

enlarge [ɪn'lɑ:dʒ] **Ⓐ** VT (*Phot*) ampliar; [+ *house, business*] ampliar, extender **Ⓑ** VI **to ~ (up)on** (= *explain*) entrar en detalles sobre

enlarged [ɪn'lɑ:dʒd] ADJ [*edition*] aumentado; (*Med*) [*organ*] hipertrofiado; [*gland*] dilatado

enlargement [ɪn'lɑ:dʒmənt] N (= *act*) aumento *m*; (*Phot*) ampliación *f*

enlarger [ɪn'lɑ:dʒəʳ] N (*Phot*) ampliadora *f*

enlighten [ɪn'laɪtn] VT **can you ~ me?** ¿puedes explicármelo *or* aclarármelo?; **to ~ sb about sth** (= *inform*) poner a algn al corriente de algo; (= *clarify*) aclarar algo a algn

enlightened [ɪn'laɪtnd] ADJ progresista; **in these ~ times** (*esp iro*) en esta época de tantos adelantos *or* progresos

enlightening [ɪn'laɪtnɪŋ] ADJ instructivo

enlightenment [ɪn'laɪtnmənt] N **1** (= *clarification*) **we need some ~ on this point** necesitamos una aclaración sobre este punto **2** (= *tolerance*) progresismo *m*; **the (Age of) Enlightenment** el Siglo de las Luces

enlist [ɪn'lɪst] **Ⓐ** VT **1** (*Mil*) reclutar, alistar; **~ed man** (*US Mil*) soldado *m* raso **2** [+ *support etc*] conseguir **Ⓑ** VI (*Mil*) alistarse (**in** en)

enliven [ɪn'laɪvn] VT (= *stimulate*) animar; (= *make lively*) avivar, animar

en masse [ã:n'mæs] ADV en masa, masivamente

enmity ['enmɪtɪ] N enemistad *f*

enormity [ɪ'nɔ:mɪtɪ] N [*of task*] enormidad *f*; [*of crime, action*] gravedad *f*

enormous [ɪ'nɔ:məs] ADJ enorme

enormously [ɪ'nɔ:məslɪ] ADV [*improve, vary, help, enjoy*] muchísimo, enormemente; [*like*] muchísimo; [*difficult, relieved*] enormemente; **it's ~ important** es de gran importancia

enough [ɪ'nʌf] **Ⓐ** ADJ suficiente, bastante; **I've got ~ problems of my own** ya tengo suficientes *or* bastantes problemas con los míos; **did you get ~ sleep?** ¿has dormido bastante *or* lo suficiente?; **they didn't have ~ money to pay the rent** no tenían suficiente dinero (como) para pagar el alquiler; **more than ~ money/time** dinero/tiempo más que suficiente, dinero/tiempo de sobra
Ⓑ ADV **1** (*with vb*) [*suffer, help, talk*] bastante; **I can't thank you ~** no sabes cuánto te lo agradezco **2** (*with adj*) (lo) suficientemente, lo bastante; **he's old ~ to go alone** es (lo) suficientemente mayor *or* es lo bastante mayor (como) para ir solo; **I'm sorry, that's not good ~** lo siento, pero eso no basta; **she seems happy ~** parece bien contenta; **she was fool ~ to listen to him** fue tan estúpida que le hizo caso; **he was kind ~ to lend me the money** tuvo la bondad de prestarme el dinero; **it's hard ~ to cope with two children, let alone with five** ya es difícil defenderse con dos niños, cuanto peor con cinco
3 (*with adv*) **he can't do it fast ~** no lo puede hacer bastante *or* lo suficientemente rápido, no lo puede hacer con la suficiente rapidez; **curiously** *or* **oddly** *or* **strangely ~** por extraño *or* raro que parezca; **he writes well ~** no escribe mal
Ⓒ PRON bastante, suficiente; **there are ~ for everyone** hay bastantes *or* suficientes para todos; **will £15 be ~?** ¿habrá bastante *or* suficiente con 15 libras?, ¿bastarán 15 libras?, ¿serán suficientes 15 libras?; **that's ~, thanks** con eso basta *or* ya es suficiente, gracias; **that's ~!** ¡basta ya!, ¡ya está bien!; **as if that weren't ~** por si eso fuera poco; **have you had ~ to eat?** ¿has comido bastante *or* lo suficiente?; **it's ~ to drive you mad*** es (como) para volverse loco; **enough's enough!** ¡basta ya!, ¡ya está bien!; **we've got more than ~** tenemos más que suficiente(s) *or* más que de sobra; **I've had ~ of his silly behaviour** ya estoy harto de sus tonterías; **~ said!** ¡no hace falta que sigas!

enquire *etc* [ɪn'kwaɪəʳ] *see* **inquire** *etc*

enrage [ɪn'reɪdʒ] VT enfurecer, hacer rabiar

enrapture [ɪn'ræptʃəʳ] VT embelesar, extasiar

enrich [ɪn'rɪtʃ] VT enriquecer; [+ *soil*] fertilizar, abonar

enrol, enroll (*US*) [ɪn'rəʊl] **Ⓐ** VT [+ *member*] inscribir; [+ *student*] matricular **Ⓑ** VI (*in a club*) inscribirse, hacerse socio; (*on a course*) matricularse, inscribirse

enrolment, enrollment (*US*) [ɪn'rəʊlmənt] N **1** [*of member*] inscripción *f*; [*of student*] matrícula *f*, inscripción *f* **2** (= *numbers*) matrícula *f*

en route [ã:n'ru:t] ADV **to be ~ for** ir camino de; **to be ~ from** venir de camino de; **it was stolen ~** se lo robaron durante el viaje

ensconce [ɪn'skɒns] VT **to ~ o.s.** instalarse cómodamente, acomodarse; **to be ~d in** estar cómodamente instalado en

enshrine [ɪn'ʃraɪn] VT **to be ~d in law** ser consagrado por la ley

enslave [ɪn'sleɪv] VT esclavizar

ensue [ɪn'sju:] VI (= *follow*) seguir(se); (= *result*) resultar (**from** de)

ensuing [ɪn'sju:ɪŋ] ADJ (= *subsequent*) subsiguiente; (= *resulting*) consiguiente

en suite [ã:n'swi:t] ADJ (*Brit*) **with an ~ bathroom** con baño adjunto

ensure [ɪn'ʃʊəʳ] VT asegurar (**that** que)

ENT ABBR (*Med*) = **ear, nose and throat**

entail [ɪn'teɪl] VT (= *necessitate*) suponer, implicar; [+ *hardship, suffering*] acarrear, traer consigo; **it ~ed buying a new car** supuso comprar un coche nuevo; **what does the**

job ~? ¿en qué consiste el trabajo?

entangle [ɪnˈtæŋgl] VT **to become ~d in sth** verse envuelto en algo, enredarse en algo; **to get ~d with sb** liarse con algn*

entanglement [ɪnˈtæŋglmənt] N (= *love affair*) lío m amoroso*

enter [ˈentəʳ] Ⓐ VT **1** (= *go into, come into*) [+ *room, country, language*] entrar en; [+ *profession*] ingresar en, entrar en; [+ *market*] introducirse en; **the thought never ~ed my head** jamás se me ocurrió, jamás se me pasó por la cabeza **2** [+ *competition*] (= *enrol for*) inscribirse en; (= *take part in*) [*runner, competitor*] participar en, tomar parte en; [*contestant*] presentarse a; **to ~ an exam** presentarse a un examen
3 (= *enrol*) **to ~ sth for a competition** presentar algo a un concurso; **to ~ a horse for a race** inscribir a un caballo para una carrera
4 (= *write, submit*) [+ *name*] escribir, apuntar; [+ *claim, request*] presentar, formular; [+ *amount*] registrar, anotar; [+ *data*] introducir
Ⓑ VI **1** (= *come in, go in*) entrar; **~ Macbeth** entra en escena Macbeth
2 **to ~ for** [+ *competition*] (= *enrol for*) inscribirse en; (= *take part in*) [*runner, competitor*] participar en, tomar parte en; [*contestant*] presentarse a; **are you going to ~ for the exam?** ¿te vas a presentar al examen?
➤ **enter into** VI + PREP **1** [+ *agreement*] llegar a; [+ *contract*] firmar; [+ *relationship, argument*] iniciar; [+ *conversation, correspondence, negotiations*] entablar; **to ~ into the spirit of things** ambientarse **2** (= *affect*) [+ *plans, calculations*] influir en; **money doesn't ~ into it** el dinero no tiene nada que ver

enterprise [ˈentəpraɪz] N **1** (= *company, undertaking*) empresa f **2** (= *initiative*) iniciativa f

enterprising [ˈentəpraɪzɪŋ] ADJ [*person, spirit*] emprendedor; [*company, idea, scheme*] innovador; **that was ~ of her!** ¡qué emprendedora!

entertain [ˌentəˈteɪn] Ⓐ VT **1** (= *amuse*) [+ *audience*] divertir, entretener **2** (= *occupy*) distraer, entretener **3** (= *offer hospitality to*) [+ *guest*] recibir **4** (= *consider*) [+ *idea, hope*] abrigar; [+ *proposal*] tomar en consideración; [+ *doubts*] albergar; **I wouldn't ~ it for a moment** jamás se me ocurriría tal cosa Ⓑ VI **1** (= *amuse*) entretener **2** (= *have visitors*) recibir invitados; **they ~ a good deal** reciben muchos invitados

entertainer [ˌentəˈteɪnəʳ] N artista mf

entertaining [ˌentəˈteɪnɪŋ] Ⓐ ADJ [*person*] divertido; [*film, book, account, evening*] entretenido, ameno Ⓑ N **I like ~** me gusta tener invitados; **she does a lot of ~** invita a gente a menudo

entertainment [ˌentəˈteɪnmənt] Ⓐ N **1** (= *amusement*) diversión f; **for your ~** para divertiros **2** (= *show*) espectáculo m; **the world of ~** el mundo del espectáculo Ⓑ CPD ➤ **entertainment allowance** gastos mpl de representación

enthral, enthrall (US) [ɪnˈθrɔːl] VT cautivar, embelesar

enthralling [ɪnˈθrɔːlɪŋ] ADJ cautivador, embelesador

enthrone [ɪnˈθrəʊn] VT entronizar

enthuse [ɪnˈθuːz] VI **to ~ about sth/sb** entusiasmarse con algo/algn

enthusiasm [ɪnˈθuːzɪæzəm] N **1** (*gen*) entusiasmo m (**for** por); **the idea filled her with ~** la idea la entusiasmó **2** (= *interest, hobby*) interés m

enthusiast [ɪnˈθuːzɪæst] N entusiasta mf; **he is a jazz/ bridge ~** es un entusiasta del jazz/bridge

enthusiastic [ɪnˌθuːzɪˈæstɪk] ADJ [*skier, supporter, crowd, applause*] entusiasta; **to be ~ about** [+ *photography, chess, art*] ser un entusiasta de; [+ *idea, suggestion*] estar entusiasmado con; **to be ~ about doing sth** estar entusiasmado por hacer algo; **she was less than ~ about the idea** no le entusiasmaba nada la idea

enthusiastically [ɪnˌθuːzɪˈæstɪkəlɪ] ADV con entusiasmo; **he shouted ~** gritó entusiasmado

entice [ɪnˈtaɪs] VT (= *tempt*) atraer, tentar; (= *seduce*)

seducir; **to ~ sb away from sb** convencer a algn de que deje a algn; **to ~ sb into doing sth** engatusar a algn para que haga algo

enticement [ɪnˈtaɪsmənt] N (= *attraction*) tentación f, atracción f; (= *seduction*) seducción f; (= *bait*) atractivo m

enticing [ɪnˈtaɪsɪŋ] ADJ tentador, atractivo

entire [ɪnˈtaɪəʳ] ADJ **1** (= *whole*) entero; **the ~ world** el mundo entero, todo el mundo **2** (= *complete*) completo

entirely [ɪnˈtaɪəlɪ] ADV **1** (= *completely*) [*satisfied, convinced*] completamente, enteramente; [*different*] totalmente, completamente; [*possible*] totalmente; **that's another matter ~** eso es otra cosa, eso es una cosa completamente distinta; **I don't ~ agree** no estoy totalmente de acuerdo; **that is not ~ true** eso no es del todo or no es enteramente cierto **2** (= *exclusively*) enteramente, exclusivamente; **it was his fault ~** fue totalmente or enteramente culpa suya; **it's ~ up to you** tú verás

entirety [ɪnˈtaɪərətɪ] N **in its ~** en su totalidad, íntegramente

entitle [ɪnˈtaɪtl] VT **1** [+ *book etc*] titular **2 to ~ sb to sth/to do sth** dar derecho a algn a algo/a hacer algo; **to be ~d to sth/to do sth** tener derecho a algo/a hacer algo; **I think I am ~d to some respect** creo que se me debe cierto respeto

entitlement [ɪnˈtaɪtlmənt] N derecho m; **holiday ~** derecho m a vacaciones

entity [ˈentɪtɪ] N entidad f

entomologist [ˌentəˈmɒlədʒɪst] N entomólogo/a m/f

entomology [ˌentəˈmɒlədʒɪ] N entomología f

entrails [ˈentreɪlz] NPL entrañas fpl

entrance¹ [ˈentrəns] Ⓐ N **1** (= *way in*) entrada f; **front/ back ~** entrada f principal/trasera
2 (= *act*) entrada f (**into** en); (= *right to enter*) (derecho m de) entrada f; (*into profession etc*) ingreso m (**into** en); (*Theat*) entrada f en escena; **to gain ~ to** conseguir entrar en or acceder a; **to make one's ~** hacer su entrada Ⓑ CPD ➤ **entrance exam(ination)** (*to school*) examen m de ingreso ➤ **entrance fee** (*to a show*) (precio m de) entrada f; (*to a club, society etc*) cuota f de ingreso ➤ **entrance hall** vestíbulo m, antesala f ➤ **entrance ramp** (US *Aut*) rampa f de acceso ➤ **entrance requirements** requisitos mpl de ingreso

entrance² [ɪnˈtrɑːns] VT (= *bewitch*) encantar; **we listened ~d** escuchamos extasiados or embelesados

entrancing [ɪnˈtrɑːnsɪŋ] ADJ (= *captivating*) cautivador

entrant [ˈentrənt] N (*in race, competition*) participante mf, concurrente mf; (*in exam*) candidato/a m/f; (*to profession*) principiante mf

entrap [ɪnˈtræp] VT coger en una trampa; (*fig*) entrampar

entreat [ɪnˈtriːt] VT rogar, suplicar; **to ~ sb to do sth** suplicar a algn que haga algo

entreatingly [ɪnˈtriːtɪŋlɪ] ADV de modo suplicante

entreaty [ɪnˈtriːtɪ] N súplica f, ruego m

entrenched [ɪnˈtrentʃt] ADJ [*idea, belief, attitude*] arraigado; [*position, power*] afianzado; **deeply ~** [*idea, belief, attitude*] profundamente arraigado; [*position, power*] firmemente afianzado

entrepreneur [ˌɒntrəprəˈnɜːʳ] N empresario/a m/f

entrepreneurial [ˌɒntrəprəˈnɜːrɪəl] ADJ empresarial

entrepreneurship [ˌɒntrəprəˈnɜːʃɪp] N espíritu m empresarial or emprendedor

entrust [ɪnˈtrʌst] VT **to ~ sth to sb** ◇ **~ sb with sth** confiar algo a algn

entry [ˈentrɪ] Ⓐ N **1** (*into organization, building*) entrada f (**into** en); (*into profession*) ingreso m (**into** en); (= *access*) acceso m (**into** a); **"no entry"** "prohibida la entrada"; (*Aut*) "prohibido el paso"; **he gained ~ to the house by breaking a window** consiguió entrar en la casa rompiendo una ventana
2 (= *way in*) entrada f
3 (*in diary*) anotación f, apunte m; (*in account*) entrada f, partida f, rubro m (LAm); (*in record, reference book*) entrada f
4 (*in competition*) (= *total of competitors*) participantes mpl;

entries must be submitted by March 29 las cartas/los cuentos/los diseños *etc* deben llegar antes del 29 de marzo; **the winning ~ in a writing competition** la obra ganadora de un concurso de redacción

ⓑ CPD ➤ **entry fee** cuota *f* de inscripción ➤ **entry form** formulario *m* de inscripción, impreso *m* de inscripción ➤ **entry permit** permiso *m* de entrada ➤ **entry phone** portero *m* automático ➤ **entry requirements** requisitos *mpl* de entrada ➤ **entry word** (*US*) entrada *f*

entwine [ɪnˈtwaɪn] VT (= *plait*) entrelazar; (= *twist around*) enroscar

enumerate [ɪˈnjuːməreɪt] VT enumerar

enumeration [ɪˌnjuːməˈreɪʃən] N enumeración *f*

enunciate [ɪˈnʌnsɪeɪt] VT [+ *word, sound*] pronunciar, articular; [+ *theory, idea*] enunciar

enunciation [ɪˌnʌnsɪˈeɪʃən] N [*of word, sound*] pronunciación *f*, articulación *f*; [*of theory, idea*] enunciación *f*

envelop [ɪnˈveləp] VT envolver (**in** en)

envelope [ˈenvələʊp] N sobre *m*

enviable [ˈenvɪəbl] ADJ envidiable

envious [ˈenvɪəs] ADJ [*person*] envidioso; [*glance, look, tone*] de envidia; **to be ~ that** tener envidia de que + *subjun*, tener envidia porque; **it makes me ~** me da envidia; **to be ~ of sth/sb** tener envidia de algo/algn, envidiar algo/a algn

enviously [ˈenvɪəslɪ] ADV con envidia

environment [ɪnˈvaɪərənmənt] N entorno *m* (*also Comput*), ambiente *m*; **a safe working ~** un entorno *or* un ambiente de trabajo seguro; **the ~** el medio ambiente

environmental [ɪnˌvaɪərənˈmentl] ADJ [*pollution, policy, issues*] medioambiental; [*disaster, damage*] ecológico, medioambiental; [*group, movement*] ecologista; [*impact*] ambiental ➤ **environmental health** (*Brit*) salud *f* ambiental ➤ **environmental health officer** (*Brit*) funcionario/a *m/f* del Departamento de Sanidad y Medio Ambiente

environmentalist [ɪnˌvaɪərənˈmentəlɪst] ADJ, N ecologista *mf*

environmentally [ɪnˌvaɪərənˈmentlɪ] ADV **their policies are ~ sound** las medidas que adoptan son correctas desde el punto de vista medioambiental; **their products are ~ friendly** sus productos son ecológicos, sus productos no dañan el medio ambiente

environs [ɪnˈvaɪərənz] N alrededores *mpl*, inmediaciones *fpl*

envisage [ɪnˈvɪzɪdʒ] VT **1** (= *expect*) prever; **it is ~d that ...** se prevé que ... **2** (= *imagine*) imaginarse

envision [ɪnˈvɪʒən] VT (*US*) = **envisage**

envoy [ˈenvɔɪ] N (= *messenger*) mensajero/a *m/f*; (= *diplomat*) enviado/a *m/f*

envy [ˈenvɪ] **ⓐ** N envidia *f*; **✦** IDIOM **to be green with ~** morirse de envidia **ⓑ** VT envidiar, tener envidia de; **to ~ sb sth** envidiar algo a algn

enzyme [ˈenzaɪm] N enzima *f*

EPA N ABBR (*US*) = **Environmental Protection Agency**

epaulette [ˈepɔːlet] N charretera *f*

ephemeral [ɪˈfemərəl] ADJ efímero

epic [ˈepɪk] **ⓐ** ADJ épico **ⓑ** N epopeya *f*; (= *film*) película *f* épica

epicentre, epicenter (*US*) [ˈepɪsentəʳ] N epicentro *m*

epidemic [ˌepɪˈdemɪk] **ⓐ** ADJ epidémico **ⓑ** N epidemia *f*

epidermis [ˌepɪˈdɜːmɪs] N epidermis *f*

epidural [ˌepɪˈdjʊərəl] **ⓐ** ADJ epidural **ⓑ** N epidural *f*

epigram [ˈepɪgræm] N epigrama *m*

epilepsy [ˈepɪlepsɪ] N epilepsia *f*

epileptic [ˌepɪˈleptɪk] ADJ, N epiléptico/a *m/f* ➤ **epileptic fit** ataque *m* de epilepsia, acceso *m* epiléptico

epilogue, epilog (*US*) [ˈepɪlɒg] N epílogo *m*

Epiphany [ɪˈpɪfənɪ] N Epifanía *f*

episcopal [ɪˈpɪskəpəl] ADJ episcopal

Episcopalian [ɪˌpɪskəˈpeɪlɪən] ADJ, N episcopalista *mf*

episode [ˈepɪsəʊd] N (= *event*) acontecimiento *m*; (*TV, Rad*) capítulo *m*, episodio *m*; (*Press*) entrega *f*; (*Med*) ataque *m*

episodic [ˌepɪˈsɒdɪk] ADJ episódico

epitaph [ˈepɪtɑːf] N epitafio *m*

epithet [ˈepɪθet] N epíteto *m*

epitome [ɪˈpɪtəmɪ] N representación *f*, paradigma *m*; **to be the ~ of virtue** ser la virtud en persona *or* personificada

epitomize [ɪˈpɪtəmaɪz] VT personificar, resumir; **she ~s today's career woman** es el prototipo de la mujer de carrera moderna

epoch [ˈiːpɒk] N época *f*

eponymous [ɪˈpɒnɪməs] ADJ epónimo

Epsom salts [ˈepsɒmˌsɔːlts] NPL epsomita *fsing*

equable [ˈekwəbl] ADJ [*climate etc*] estable; [*person*] ecuánime; [*tone*] tranquilo, afable

equably [ˈekwəblɪ] ADV sosegadamente, con ecuanimidad

equal [ˈiːkwəl] **ⓐ** ADJ **1** [*number, amount*] igual; **to be of ~ importance/value** tener igual importancia/el mismo valor; **to come ~ first** (*in competition*) compartir el primer puesto; (*in race*) llegar ambos en primer lugar; **they are ~ in size** son del mismo tamaño, son iguales de tamaño; **they are ~ in value** tienen el mismo valor, tienen igual valor; **on ~ terms** de igual a igual; **all** *or* **other things being ~** si no intervienen otros factores; **an amount ~ to half your salary** una cantidad equivalente a la mitad de tu sueldo; **to be ~ to sth** (= *equivalent*) equivaler a algo

2 (= *capable*) **I'm confident that he is ~ to the task** tengo la seguridad de que está capacitado para desempeñar la tarea; **she did not feel ~ to going out** no se sentía con fuerzas *or* ánimo para salir

ⓑ N (= *person*) igual *mf*; **to treat sb as an ~** tratar a algn de igual a igual; **a talent without ~** un talento sin igual *or* sin par; **they are intellectual ~s** intelectualmente están a la par **ⓒ** VT **1** (*Math*) ser igual a; **let x ~ y** si x es igual a y, suponiendo que x sea igual a y; **two plus two ~s four** dos y dos son cuatro

2 [+ *record, rival, quality*] igualar

ⓓ CPD ➤ **equal opportunities** igualdad *fsing* de oportunidades ➤ **equal opportunity employer** empresa *f* con una política de no discriminación ➤ **equal pay** igual salario *m* ➤ **equal rights** igualdad *fsing* de derechos ➤ **equal sign, equals sign** (*Brit*) (*Math*) signo *m* de igual ➤ **equal time** (*US Rad, TV*) derecho *m* de respuesta

equality [ɪˈkwɒlɪtɪ] N igualdad *f*; **~ of opportunity** igualdad *f* de oportunidades

equalize [ˈiːkwəlaɪz] **ⓐ** VT igualar **ⓑ** VI (*Brit Sport*) empatar

equalizer [ˈiːkwəlaɪzəʳ] N **1** (*Brit Sport*) tanto *m* del empate **2** (*US***) (= *pistol*) pipa** *f*, pistola *f*

equally [ˈiːkwəlɪ] ADV **1** (= *evenly*) [*divide, share*] equitativamente, por igual; **the fence posts should be ~ spaced** el espacio entre los postes de la valla debería ser igual

2 (= *in the same way*) por igual; **this rule applies ~ to everyone** esta regla se aplica a todos por igual; **this applies ~ to men and to women** esto se aplica tanto a los hombres como a las mujeres

3 (= *just as*) [*important, difficult, responsible*] igualmente, igual de; [*well*] igual de; **his second novel was ~ successful** su segunda novela tuvo el mismo éxito

4 (= *by the same token*) al mismo tiempo

equanimity [ˌekwəˈnɪmɪtɪ] N ecuanimidad *f*

equate [ɪˈkweɪt] **ⓐ** VT **1** (= *compare*) equiparar (**to, with** con); (= *identify*) identificar (**to, with** con) **2** (*Math*) poner en ecuación **ⓑ** VI **to ~ to** equivaler a

equation [ɪˈkweɪʒən] N (*Math*) ecuación *f*; **✦** IDIOM **to enter (into) the ~** entrar en juego

equator [ɪˈkweɪtəʳ] N ecuador *m*

equatorial [ˌekwəˈtɔːrɪəl] ADJ ecuatorial

equestrian [ɪˈkwestrɪən] ADJ ecuestre

equidistant [ˈiːkwɪˈdɪstənt] ADJ equidistante

equilateral [ˈiːkwɪˈlætərəl] ADJ equilátero

equilibrium [ˌiːkwɪˈlɪbrɪəm] N equilibrio *m*

equinox ['iːkwɪnɒks] N equinoccio m

equip [ɪ'kwɪp] VT [+ office, workshop] equipar (**with** con); [+ person] proveer (**with** de); **to be ~ped with** [person] estar provisto de; [machine etc] estar equipado con, estar dotado de; **to be well ~ped to** (+ INFIN) estar bien preparado para + infin

equipment [ɪ'kwɪpmənt] N (gen) equipo m; (= tools, utensils etc) herramientas fpl

equitable ['ekwɪtəbl] ADJ equitativo

equitably ['ekwɪtəblɪ] ADV equitativamente, de forma equitativa

equity ['ekwɪtɪ] N (= fairness) equidad f; (also ~ **capital**) neto m patrimonial, patrimonio m neto; **equities** (St Ex) acciones fpl ordinarias

equivalence [ɪ'kwɪvələns] N equivalencia f

equivalent [ɪ'kwɪvələnt] **A** ADJ equivalente (**to** a; **in** en); **to be ~ to** equivaler a **B** N equivalente m (**in** en)

equivocal [ɪ'kwɪvəkəl] ADJ equívoco

equivocate [ɪ'kwɪvəkeɪt] VI ser evasivo

equivocation [ɪ,kwɪvə'keɪʃən] N evasivas fpl

ER ABBR **1** (= Elizabeth Regina) la reina Isabel **2** (US Med) = **emergency room**

era ['ɪərə] N era f

eradicate [ɪ'rædɪkeɪt] VT erradicar

eradication [ɪ,rædɪ'keɪʃən] N erradicación f

erase [ɪ'reɪz] VT **1** (gen, Comput) borrar **2** (US**) (= kill) liquidar*

eraser [ɪ'reɪzəʳ] N goma f de borrar

erect [ɪ'rekt] **A** ADJ [person, head, posture] erguido, derecho; [tail, ears] tieso, parado (LAm); [penis] erecto; **to hold o.s. ~** mantenerse derecho or erguido **B** ADV **to walk ~** caminar derecho or erguido **C** VT [+ monument, statue, temple] erigir; [+ mast, wall, building, barricade] levantar; [+ tent, scaffolding] montar

erection [ɪ'rekʃən] N **1** (= act) erección f, construcción f; (= assembly) montaje m **2** (= building) construcción f **3** [of penis] erección f

ergonomic [,ɜːgəʊ'nɒmɪk] ADJ ergonómico

ergonomically [,ɜːgəʊ'nɒmɪklɪ] ADV atendiendo a principios ergonómicos

ergonomics [,ɜːgəʊ'nɒmɪks] NSING ergonomía f

ERM N ABBR = **Exchange Rate Mechanism**

ermine ['ɜːmɪn] N armiño m

erode [ɪ'rəʊd] **A** VT **1** (Geol) erosionar; [acid] corroer **2** [+ confidence, power, authority, value] mermar; [+ support, rights] reducir **B** VI (Geol) erosionarse

erogenous [ɪ'rɒdʒənəs] ADJ erógeno

erosion [ɪ'rəʊʒən] N **1** (Geol) erosión f; [of metal] corrosión f **2** (fig) desgaste m

erotic [ɪ'rɒtɪk] ADJ erótico

erotica [ɪ'rɒtɪkə] NPL literatura fsing erótica

eroticism [ɪ'rɒtɪsɪzəm] N erotismo m

err [ɜːʳ] VI (= be mistaken) equivocarse; (= sin) pecar; **to ~ on the side of mercy/caution** etc pecar de piadoso/cauteloso etc; ✦ PROV **to ~ is human** errar es de humanos, quien tiene boca se equivoca

errand ['erənd] N recado m, mandado m (esp LAm); **to run ~s** hacer recados; **~ of mercy** tentativa f de salvamento ➤ **errand boy** recadero m, mandadero m (esp LAm)

erratic [ɪ'rætɪk] ADJ [person] (by temperament) imprevisible, voluble; (in performance) irregular; [behaviour, mood] imprevisible, variable; [movement, pulse, breathing] irregular; [progress, performance] desigual, poco uniforme

erratically [ɪ'rætɪkəlɪ] ADV [behave] de forma imprevisible; [work, drive, play] de modo irregular; [breathe] de forma irregular, irregularmente

erroneous [ɪ'rəʊnɪəs] ADJ erróneo

erroneously [ɪ'rəʊnɪəslɪ] ADV erróneamente

error ['erəʳ] N error m, equivocación f; **in ~** por error;

✦ IDIOM **to see the ~ of one's ways** reconocer su error ➤ **error message** (Comput) mensaje m de error

erudite ['erʊdaɪt] ADJ erudito

erudition [,erʊ'dɪʃən] N erudición f

erupt [ɪ'rʌpt] VI [volcano] (= start to erupt) entrar en erupción; (= go on erupting) estar en erupción; [spots] hacer erupción; [war, anger] estallar

eruption [ɪ'rʌpʃən] N [of volcano, spots] erupción f; [of war, anger] estallido m

escalate ['eskəleɪt] VI **1** [prices] subir vertiginosamente; **escalating costs** costes mpl que van en continuo aumento **2** [violence, tension, conflict] intensificarse; **the violence could ~ into a war** la violencia podría intensificarse hasta llegar a una guerra

escalation [,eskə'leɪʃən] N [of costs, prices] aumento m (vertiginoso), escalada f; [of tension, conflict] intensificación f; [of violence] intensificación f, escalada f

escalator ['eskəleɪtəʳ] N escalera f mecánica

escapade [,eskə'peɪd] N (= adventure) aventura f; (= misdeed) travesura f

escape [ɪs'keɪp] **A** N **1** (from detention) fuga f; (from country) huida f; **to make one's ~** escapar(se); **to have a lucky ~** salvarse por los pelos **2** (from real world) evasión f

B VT **1** (= avoid) [+ pursuer] escapar de, librarse de; [+ punishment, death] librarse de; [+ consequences] evitar; **they managed to ~ capture** consiguieron evitar que les capturaran; **they were lucky to ~ injury** tuvieron mucha suerte de salir ilesos; **there was no way I could ~ meeting him** no había manera de poder evitar verme con él; **he just ~d being run over** por poco lo atropellan

2 (= elude) **his name ~s me** no logro acordarme de su nombre; **nothing ~s her** no se le escapa nada; **it had ~d his notice** or **attention that ...** se le había escapado que ...

C VI **1** (= get away) (gen) escaparse; [prisoner] fugarse, escapar(se) (**from** de); **he ~d to a neutral country** huyó a un país neutral; **she ~d unhurt** salió ilesa; **he ~d with a few bruises** sólo sufrió algunas magulladuras

2 (= leak) [liquid, gas] salirse

D CPD ➤ **escape attempt** intento m de fuga ➤ **escape key** tecla f de escape ➤ **escape route** ruta f de escape

escapee [ɪsker'piː] N fugitivo/a m/f, prófugo/a m/f

escapism [ɪs'keɪpɪzəm] N escapismo m, evasión f

escapist [ɪs'keɪpɪst] ADJ, N escapista mf ➤ **escapist literature** literatura f de evasión

escarpment [ɪs'kɑːpmənt] N escarpa f

escort A ['eskɔːt] N **1** (Mil, Police) escolta f; **to travel under ~** viajar con escolta; **a police ~** una escolta policial **2** (= group) séquito m, acompañamiento m; (= lady's companion) acompañante m **3** (= girl from agency) señorita f de compañía **B** [ɪs'kɔːt] VT **1** (= accompany) acompañar; **to ~ sb home** acompañar a algn a su casa **2** (Mil, Police) escoltar **C** ['eskɔːt] CPD ➤ **escort agency** agencia m de servicios de compañía

Eskimo ['eskɪməʊ] ADJ, N esquimal mf

ESL N ABBR = **English as a Second Language**

esophagus [ɪ'sɒfəgəs] N (US) = **oesophagus**

esoteric [,esəʊ'terɪk] ADJ esotérico

ESP N ABBR **1** = **extrasensory perception 2** (Brit) = **English for Special Purposes**

esp. ABBR = **especially**

espadrille [,espə'drɪl] N alpargata f

especial [ɪs'peʃəl] ADJ especial, particular

especially [ɪs'peʃəlɪ] ADV especialmente; **not ~** no especialmente; **~ in summer/when it rains** especialmente or sobre todo en verano/cuando llueve; **why me, ~?** ¿por qué yo precisamente?

Esperanto [,espə'ræntəʊ] N esperanto m

espionage [,espɪə'nɑːʒ] N espionaje m

esplanade [,esplə'neɪd] N paseo m marítimo

espouse [ɪs'paʊz] VT [+ cause] adherirse a; [+ plan] adoptar

espresso [es'presəʊ] N café m exprés ➤ **espresso bar** café *m*, cafetería *f* (*donde se sirve café exprés*)

Esq. ABBR (*Brit frm*) (= **esquire**) Don, D.

esquire [ɪsˈkwaɪəʳ] N (*Brit*) (*on envelope*) Señor don; **Colin Smith Esquire** Sr. D. Colin Smith

essay [ˈeseɪ] N (*Literat*) ensayo *m*; (*Scol, Univ*) trabajo *m*

essence [ˈesəns] N **1** (= *extract*) esencia *f*, extracto *m* **2** (*fig*) (= *substance*) esencia *f*; **the ~ of the matter is ...** lo esencial del asunto es ...; **in ~** en lo esencial; **time is of the ~** el tiempo es primordial

essential [ɪˈsenʃəl] **Ⓐ** ADJ **1** (= *necessary*) esencial, imprescindible; **it is ~ that** es esencial que + *subjun*, es imprescindible que + *subjun*
2 (= *fundamental*) [*fact, difference*] fundamental, esencial
Ⓑ N (= *necessary thing*) **in my job a car is an ~** en mi trabajo, un coche es una necesidad; **we have all the ~s** tenemos todo lo necesario; **we picked up a few ~s for the trip** tomamos algunas cosas esenciales para el viaje; **accuracy is one of the ~s** la exactitud es uno de los elementos esenciales *or* fundamentales; **we can only take the bare ~s with us** sólo podemos llevarnos lo imprescindible
Ⓒ CPD ➤ **essential oil** aceite *m* esencial

essentially [ɪˈsenʃəlɪ] ADV **1** (= *basically*) básicamente; **she was ~ a generous person** era básicamente *or* en esencia una persona generosa **2** (= *on the whole*) en lo esencial, en lo fundamental; **~, we agree** estamos de acuerdo en lo esencial *or* fundamental

establish [ɪsˈtæblɪʃ] VT **1** (= *set up*) [+ *business, state, committee*] establecer, fundar; [+ *custom, rule, order*] establecer; [+ *relations*] establecer, entablar;
[+ *power, authority*] afirmar; [+ *reputation*] ganarse; **the book ~ed him as a writer** el libro lo consagró como escritor; **to ~ o.s.** establecerse, consolidarse **2** (= *prove*) [+ *fact, rights*] comprobar, demostrar; [+ *identity*] verificar; [+ *sb's innocence*] probar, demostrar **3** (= *find out, discover*) averiguar; [+ *date*] determinar

established [ɪsˈtæblɪʃt] ADJ [*person, business*] establecido, consolidado; [*custom*] establecido, arraigado; [*fact*] probado; [*church*] oficial, del Estado

establishment [ɪsˈtæblɪʃmənt] N **1** (= *business, house*) establecimiento *m*; **a teaching ~** un centro de enseñanza **2 the Establishment** la clase dirigente; **the literary/musical Establishment** las altas esferas del mundo literario/musical **3** (= *setting-up*) establecimiento *m*; (= *creation*) creación *f* **4** (= *proof*) [*of innocence, guilt*] determinación *f*

estate [ɪsˈteɪt] **Ⓐ** N **1** (= *land*) finca *f*, hacienda *f*; (= *country estate*) finca *f*, hacienda *f* (*LAm*), estancia *f* (*SC*); (*Brit*) (= *housing estate*) complejo *m* habitacional *or* residencial, urbanización *f* (*esp Sp*), fraccionamiento *m* (*Mex*) **2** (= *property*) propiedad *f*; (= *assets*) patrimonio *m*; [*of deceased*] herencia *f* **3** (*Pol*) estado *m* **4** (*Brit*) = **estate car**
Ⓑ CPD ➤ **estate agency** (*Brit*) agencia *f* inmobiliaria ➤ **estate agent** (*Brit*) agente *mf* inmobiliario/a ➤ **estate agent's** (*Brit*) agencia *f* inmobiliaria ➤ **estate car** (*Brit*) ranchera *f*, coche *m* familiar, rural *f* (*SC*), camioneta *f* (*LAm*)

esteem [ɪsˈtiːm] **Ⓐ** VT estimar **Ⓑ** N estima *f*, aprecio *m*; **to hold sb in high ~** tener a algn en gran estima; **he went down in my ~** bajó en mi estima; **he went up in my ~** ganó valor a mis ojos

esthete [ˈiːsθiːt] N (*US*) = **aesthete**

estimate **Ⓐ** [ˈestɪmɪt] N (= *judgment*) estimación *f*, cálculo *m*; (*for job, work*) presupuesto *m*; **rough ~** cálculo *m* aproximativo; **at a rough ~** aproximadamente **Ⓑ** [ˈestɪmeɪt] VT (= *calculate*) calcular aproximadamente; (= *assess*) juzgar, estimar; **to ~ that** calcular que; **to ~ the cost at ...** calcular el precio en ... **Ⓒ** [ˈestɪmeɪt] VI **to ~ for** [+ *building work etc*] hacer un presupuesto de

estimation [ˌestɪˈmeɪʃən] N **1** (= *judgment*) juicio *m*, opinión *f*; **in my ~** a mi juicio, en mi opinión **2** (= *esteem*) estima *f*, aprecio *m*

Estonia [eˈstəʊnɪə] N Estonia *f*

Estonian [eˈstəʊnɪən] ADJ, N estonio/a *m/f*

estranged [ɪsˈtreɪndʒd] ADJ separado; **his ~ wife** su mujer

que vive separada de él; **to become ~** separarse

estrangement [ɪsˈtreɪndʒmənt] N distanciamiento *m*

estrogen [ˈiːstrəʊdʒən] N (*US*) = **oestrogen**

estuary [ˈestjʊərɪ] N estuario *m*, ría *f*

e-tail [ˈiːteɪl] N venta *f* en línea ➤ **e-tail site** sitio *m* de venta en línea

e-tailer [ˈiːteɪləʳ] N vendedor *m* en línea

e-tailing [ˈiːteɪlɪŋ] N venta *f* en línea

etc ABBR (= **et cetera**) etc.

etch [etʃ] VT grabar al aguafuerte; (*fig*) grabar; **it is ~ed on my memory forever** lo tengo grabado para siempre en mi memoria

etching [ˈetʃɪŋ] N (= *process*) grabado *m* al aguafuerte; (= *print*) aguafuerte *m or f*

eternal [ɪˈtɜːnl] ADJ (= *everlasting*) eterno; (= *incessant*) constante

eternally [ɪˈtɜːnəlɪ] ADV eternamente

eternity [ɪˈtɜːnɪtɪ] N eternidad *f*; **it seemed like an ~** pareció una eternidad *or* un siglo

ether [ˈiːθəʳ] N (*Chem*) éter *m*

ethereal [ɪˈθɪərɪəl] ADJ etéreo

ethic [ˈeθɪk] N ética *f*

ethical [ˈeθɪkəl] ADJ ético

ethically [ˈeθɪklɪ] ADV [*behave*] éticamente, con ética; [*sound, unacceptable*] desde el punto de vista ético

ethics [ˈeθɪks] **Ⓐ** NSING (= *subject*) ética *f* **Ⓑ** NPL (= *honourableness*) moralidad *f* sing

Ethiopia [ˌiːθɪˈəʊpɪə] N Etiopía *f*

Ethiopian [ˌiːθɪˈəʊpɪən] ADJ, N etíope *mf*

ethnic [ˈeθnɪk] **Ⓐ** ADJ **1** (= *racial*) [*origin, community*] étnico; [*conflict, tension*] racial **2** (= *non-Western*) [*music*] étnico; [*food, jewellery*] exótico **Ⓑ** CPD ➤ **ethnic cleansing** limpieza *f* étnica ➤ **ethnic minority** minoría *f* étnica

ethnicity [eθˈnɪsɪtɪ] N etnicidad *f*

ethos [ˈiːθɒs] N espíritu *m*, escala *f* de valores

e-ticket [ˈiːˌtɪkɪt] N billete *m* electrónico (*Sp*), pasaje *m* electrónico (*LAm*)

etiquette [ˈetɪket] N etiqueta *f*, protocolo *m*

etymology [ˌetɪˈmɒlədʒɪ] N etimología *f*

EU N ABBR (= **European Union**) UE *f*

eucalyptus [juːkəˈlɪptəs] N (= *tree*) eucalipto *m*; (= *oil*) esencia *f* de eucalipto

eugenics [juːˈdʒenɪks] NSING eugenesia *f*

eulogize [ˈjuːlədʒaɪz] VT elogiar, encomiar

eulogy [ˈjuːlədʒɪ] N elogio *m*, encomio *m*

euphemism [ˈjuːfɪmɪzəm] N eufemismo *m* (**for** de)

euphemistic [juːfɪˈmɪstɪk] ADJ eufemístico

euphoria [juːˈfɔːrɪə] N euforia *f*

euphoric [juːˈfɒrɪk] ADJ eufórico

eureka [jʊˈriːkə] EXCL ¡eureka!

euro [ˈjʊərəʊ] N euro *m*

Eurocrat [ˈjʊərəʊkræt] N (*hum, pej*) eurócrata *mf* (*burócrata de la UE*)

Eurocurrency [ˈjʊərəʊˌkʌrənsɪ] N eurodivisa *f*

Eurodollar [ˈjʊərəʊˌdɒləʳ] N eurodólar *m*

Euroland [ˈjʊərəʊlænd] N eurozona *f*, zona *f* euro

Euro-MP [ˈjʊərəʊˌemˌpiː] N ABBR (= **Member of the European Parliament**) eurodiputado/a *m/f*

Europe [ˈjʊərəp] N Europa *f*

European [ˌjʊərəˈpiːən] ADJ, N europeo/a *m/f* ➤ **European Commission** Comisión *f* Europea ➤ **European Community** Comunidad *f* Europea ➤ **European Court of Justice** Tribunal *m* de Justicia Europeo ➤ **European Economic Community** Comunidad *f* Económica Europea ➤ **European Monetary System** Sistema *m* Monetario Europeo ➤ **European Parliament** Parlamento *m* Europeo ➤ **European plan** (*US*) habitación *f* (de hotel) con servicios (pero sin comidas) ➤ **European Union**Unión *f* Europea

europeanize[ˈjʊərəˈpɪənaɪz] VT europeizar

Europhile[ˈjʊərəʊfaɪl] ADJ, N europeísta *mf*

Europol[ˈjʊərəʊpɒl] N Europol *f*

Eurosceptic[ˈjʊərəʊskeptɪk] N euroescéptico/a *m/f*

Eurostar® [ˈjʊərəʊˌstɑːˈ] N Eurostar® *m*

Eurotunnel[ˈjʊərəʊˌtʌnl] N Eurotúnel *m*

Eurozone[ˈjʊərəʊˌzəʊn] N eurozona *f*, zona euro *f*

euthanasia[ˌjuːθəˈneɪzɪə] N eutanasia *f*

evacuate[ɪˈvækjʊeɪt] VT evacuar

evacuation[ɪˌvækjʊˈeɪʃən] N evacuación *f*

evacuee[ɪˌvækjʊˈiː] N evacuado/a *m/f*

evade[ɪˈveɪd] VT [+ *capture, pursuers*] eludir; [+ *punishment, blow*] evitar; [+ *question, responsibility*] eludir, evadir; [+ *military service*] librarse de; [+ *taxation, duty*] evadir

evaluate[ɪˈvæljʊeɪt] VT evaluar

evaluation[ɪˌvæljʊˈeɪʃən] N evaluación *f*

evangelical[iːvænˈdʒelɪkəl] ADJ, N evangélico/a *m/f*

evangelism[ɪˈvændʒəˌlɪzəm] N evangelismo *m*

evangelist[ɪˈvændʒəlɪst] N (= *preacher*) evangelizador(a) *m/f*

evaporate[ɪˈvæpəreɪt] VI [*liquid*] evaporarse; [*hopes, fears, anger*] desvanecerse

evaporated milk[ɪˌvæpəreɪtɪdˈmɪlk] N leche *f* evaporada

evaporation[ɪˌvæpəˈreɪʃən] N evaporación *f*

evasion[ɪˈveɪʒən] N evasión *f*; (= *evasive answer etc*) evasiva *f*

evasive[ɪˈveɪzɪv] ADJ evasivo; **to be ~ (about sth)** mostrarse evasivo (acerca de algo); **to take ~ action** (*Mil*) adoptar tácticas evasivas

eve[iːv] N víspera *f*; **on the ~ of** (*lit*) en la víspera de; (*fig*) en vísperas de

even[ˈiːvən] Ⓐ ADJ 1 (= *smooth, flat*) [*surface, ground*] plano; **to make sth ~** nivelar algo, allanar algo
2 (= *uniform*) [*speed, temperature, progress*] constante; [*breathing*] regular; [*distribution, colour, work*] uniforme
3 (= *equal*) [*quantities, distances*] igual; [*distribution*] equitativo; **to break ~** llegar a cubrir los gastos; **he has an ~ chance of winning the election** (*Brit*) tiene las mismas posibilidades de ganar las elecciones que de perderlas, tiene un cincuenta por ciento de posibilidades de ganar las elecciones; **to get ~ with sb** ajustar cuentas con algn; **I'll get ~ with you for that!** ¡me las pagarás por eso!*; **that makes us ~** (*regarding money*) así quedamos en paz *or* (*LAm*) a mano; **I'll give you ~ money that Arsenal will win** (*Brit*) para mí que Arsenal tiene las mismas posibilidades de ganar que de perder; **to be ~ with sb** (*in game*) estar igualado con algn; (*regarding money*) estar en paz *or* (*LAm*) a mano con algn; ✦ IDIOM **to give sb an ~ break** (*esp US*) dar a algn su *or* una oportunidad
4 (= *calm*) **he has an ~ temper** no se altera fácilmente; **to keep one's voice ~** no alterar la voz
5 (= *not odd*) [*number*] par

Ⓑ ADV 1 (= *including*) hasta, incluso; **~ on Sundays** hasta *or* incluso los domingos; **~ I know that!** ¡eso lo sé hasta yo!; **and he ~ sings** e incluso canta
2 (*with compar adj or adv*) aún, todavía; **~ faster** aún *or* todavía más rápido; **~ better** aún *or* todavía mejor; **~ less money** aún *or* todavía menos dinero
3 (*with negative*) **not ~ ...** ni siquiera ...; **he can't ~ read** ni siquiera sabe leer; **don't ~ think about it!** ¡ni lo pienses!; **without ~ reading it** sin leerlo siquiera
4 (*in phrases*) **~ as he spoke the door opened** en ese mismo momento se abrió la puerta; **~ as a child I used to drink cider** incluso de niño solía beber sidra; **~ if** aunque + *subjun*, incluso si + *subjun*; **~ if you tried** aunque lo intentaras, incluso si lo intentaras, así lo procuraras (*LAm*); **not (...) ~ if: I wouldn't do it ~ if you paid me a fortune** no lo haría aunque me pagaras una fortuna; **~ so** aun así; **and ~ then she wasn't happy** y aun así no estaba contenta; **~ though** aunque; **he didn't listen, ~ though he knew I was right** no me hizo caso, aunque sabía que tenía razón; **~ when** incluso cuando; **he never gets depressed, ~ when things go badly** nunca se deprime, incluso *or* ni siquiera cuando las cosas andan mal; **we were never in love, not ~**

when we got married nunca estuvimos enamorados, ni siquiera cuando nos casamos
Ⓒ **evens**NPL (*esp Brit*) **the bookmakers are offering ~s** los corredores de apuestas ofrecen el doble de la cantidad aportada
➤ **even out** Ⓐ VT + ADV 1 [+ *number, score*] igualar; **to ~ things out** nivelar la situación *or* las cosas 2 [+ *expenses, work, exports*] nivelar Ⓑ VI + ADV (= *become equal*) nivelarse, quedar compensado; **the work will ~ out** el trabajo irá siendo más regular
➤ **even up**VT + ADV igualar, poner parejos; **to ~ things up** nivelar la situación *or* las cosas

even-handed[ˈiːvənˈhændɪd] ADJ [*person, policy*] imparcial; [*distribution*] equitativo

evening[ˈiːvnɪŋ] N (*before dark*) tarde *f*; (*after dark*) noche *f*; **in the ~** por la tarde/noche; **this ~** esta tarde/noche; **tomorrow/yesterday ~** mañana/ayer por la tarde/noche; **on Sunday ~** el domingo por la tarde/noche; **good ~!** (*early*) ¡buenas tardes!; (*after sunset*) ¡buenas noches! ➤ **evening class**clase *f* nocturna ➤ **evening dress**(*woman's*) traje *m* de noche; (*man's*) traje *m* de etiqueta; **in ~ dress** [*man, woman*] vestido/a de etiqueta ➤ **evening paper**periódico *m* de la tarde, vespertino *m* ➤ **evening performance** (*Theat*) función *f* de noche

evenly[ˈiːvənlɪ] ADV 1 (= *uniformly*) [*breathe, flow*] con regularidad, regularmente; [*mix*] uniformemente; **the cake should rise ~** el pastel debe subir de manera uniforme *or* todo por igual 2 (= *equally*) [*distribute, share*] por igual, equitativamente; **to divide/split sth ~** dividir algo a partes iguales 3 (= *calmly*) [*say, reply, ask*] sin alterarse, serenamente

evensong[ˈiːvənsɒŋ] N vísperas *fpl*, misa *f* vespertina

event[ɪˈvent] N 1 (= *happening*) acontecimiento *m*; **this is quite an ~!** ¡esto es todo un acontecimiento!; **in** *or* **during the course of ~s** en el curso de los acontecimientos; **in the normal course of ~s** normalmente, por lo común; ✦ IDIOM **to be wise after the ~** mostrar sabiduría cuando ya no hay remedio
2 (= *case*) **in any ~** pase lo que pase, en todo caso; **in either ~** en cualquiera de los dos casos; **in the ~ ...** (*Brit*) resultó que ...; **in the ~ of ...** en caso de ...; **in the ~ of his dying** en caso de que muriese; **in the ~ that ...** en caso de que + *subjun*; **in that ~** en ese caso
3 (*in a programme*) número *m*; (= *ceremony*) acto *m*; **programme** of ~s (*civic*) programa *m* de actos; (= *shows*) programa *m* de atracciones
4 (*Sport*) prueba *f*

even-tempered[ˈiːvənˈtempəd] ADJ ecuánime, apacible

eventful[ɪˈventfʊl] ADJ [*journey, match*] lleno de incidentes; [*life*] azaroso

eventual[ɪˈventʃʊəl] ADJ final

⚠ **eventual** ≠ *eventual*

eventuality[ɪˌventʃʊˈælɪtɪ] N eventualidad *f*; **in the ~ of** ante la eventualidad de; **to be ready for any ~** estar preparado para cualquier eventualidad

eventually[ɪˈventʃʊəlɪ] ADV 1 (= *finally*) finalmente, al final 2 (= *at some future time*) con el tiempo

ever[ˈevəˈ] ADV 1 (= *always*) **they lived happily ~ after** vivieron felices; **as ~** como siempre; **for ~** para siempre; **for ~ and ~** por siempre jamás; **~ ready** siempre dispuesto; **~ since** (*as adv*) desde entonces; (*as conj*) desde que; **yours ~** (*Brit*) un abrazo ...
2 (= *at any time*) **all she ~ does is make jam** se pasa la vida haciendo mermelada; **if you ~ go there** si vas allí alguna vez; **have you ~ been there?** ¿has estado allí alguna vez?; **did you ~ meet him?** ¿llegaste a conocerlo?; **nothing ~ happens** nunca pasa nada; **we haven't ~ tried it** nunca lo hemos probado; **better than ~** mejor que nunca; **seldom, if ~** rara vez *or* nunca; **now, if ~, is the time** *or* **moment to ~** ahora o nunca es el momento de ...; **he's a liar if ~ there was one** él sí que es un mentiroso; **more beautiful than ~** más hermoso que nunca; ✦ IDIOM **did you ~?*** ¡habráse visto!
3 (*used as intensifier*) **is it ~ big!** (*US**) ¡qué grande es!, ¡si

vieras lo grande que es!; **as if I ~ would!** ¿me crees capaz de hacer algo semejante?; **never ~** (nunca) jamás; ~ **so** (*esp Brit**) (= *very*) muy; **it's ~ so cold** hace un frío terrible; ~ **many things** tantísimas cosas, la mar de cosas; ~ **so much** mucho, muchísimo; **why ~ did you do it?** ¿por qué demonios lo hiciste?; **why ~ not?** ¿y por qué no? **4** (*after superl*) **it's the best ~** jamás ha habido mejor; **the coldest night ~** la noche más fría que nunca hemos tenido

Everest ['evərɪst] N (*also* **Mount ~**) (monte *m*) Everest *m*

evergreen ['evəɡriːn] **Ⓐ** ADJ [*tree, shrub*] de hoja perenne **Ⓑ** N (= *tree*) árbol *m* de hoja perenne; (= *plant*) planta *f* de hoja perenne

everlasting [ˌevəˈlɑːstɪŋ] ADJ eterno

every ['evrɪ] ADJ **1** (= *each*) cada *inv*; (= *any*) todo; ~ **day** cada día; ~ **three days** ✧ ~ **third day** cada tres días; ~ **parent will have experienced this at one time or another** todo padre se habrá encontrado con esto en algún momento; ~ **bit as clever as ...*** tan *or* (*LAm*) igual de listo como ...; ~ **few days** cada dos o tres días; **I have to account for ~ last penny** tengo que dar cuentas de cada penique que gasto; **I enjoyed ~ minute of the party** disfruté cada minuto de la fiesta; **he was following my ~ move** me vigilaba constantemente; ~ **now and then** *or* **again** de vez en cuando; **not ~ child is as fortunate as you** no todos los niños son tan afortunados como tú; ~ **one of them passed the exam** todos ellos aprobaron el examen; **he criticized her at ~ opportunity** no dejaba escapar oportunidad alguna para criticarla; ~ **other** *or* **second month** un mes sí y otro no, cada dos meses; **he spends ~ penny he earns** gasta hasta el último centavo que gana; **he'd eaten ~ single chocolate** se había comido todos los bombones, se había comido hasta el último bombón; ~ **single time** cada vez sin excepción; ~ **so often** cada cierto tiempo, de vez en cuando; **he brings me a present ~ time he comes** cada vez que viene me trae un regalo; **this recipe gives you perfect results ~ time** esta receta siempre le dará resultados perfectos; **in ~ way** en todos los aspectos; ✦ IDIOM **(it's) ~ man for himself** ¡sálvese quien pueda!; ✦ PROV ~ **little helps** un grano no hace granero pero ayuda al compañero, todo es ayuda **2** (= *all possible*) **I gave you ~ assistance** te ayudé en todo lo que podía; **I have ~ confidence in him** tengo entera *or* plena confianza en él; ~ **effort is being made to trace him** se está haciendo todo lo posible para localizarlo; **I have ~ reason to think that ...** tengo razones sobradas para pensar que ...; **we wish you ~ success** te deseamos todo el éxito posible

everybody ['evrɪbɒdɪ] PRON todos/as, todo el mundo; ~ **else** todos los demás

everyday ['evrɪdeɪ] ADJ [*occurrence, experience*] cotidiano; [*expression*] corriente; [*use*] diario, cotidiano; [*shoes, clothes*] de uso diario; **for ~ use** de diario; **in ~ use** de uso corriente

everyone ['evrɪwʌn] PRON = **everybody**

everyplace ['evrɪpleɪs] ADV (*US*) = **everywhere**

everything ['evrɪθɪŋ] PRON todo; **he sold ~** lo vendió todo; ~ **you say is true** es verdad todo lo que dices; **time is ~** el tiempo lo es todo; **money isn't ~** el dinero no lo es todo; **he did ~ possible** hizo todo lo posible

everywhere ['evrɪweəʳ] ADV [*go*] a todas partes; [*be*] en todas partes; **I looked ~** busqué en todas partes; ~ **in Spain** en todas partes de España; ~ **you go** en todas partes

evict [ɪˈvɪkt] VT desahuciar, desalojar

eviction [ɪˈvɪkʃən] N desahucio *m*, desalojo *m* ➤ **eviction order** orden *f* de desalojo

evidence ['evɪdəns] N **1** (= *proof*) pruebas *fpl*; ~ **of/that ...** pruebas de/de que ...; **there is no ~ against him** no hay pruebas contra él **2** (= *testimony*) testimonio *m*; **to give ~** prestar declaración, deponer (*more frm*); **to call sb to give ~** llamar a algn como testigo; **to turn King's** *or* **Queen's** (*US*) **State's ~** delatar a un cómplice **3** (= *sign*) indicio *m*, señal *f*; **to show ~ of** dar muestras de; **to be in ~** (= *noticeable*) estar bien visible

evident ['evɪdənt] ADJ evidente, manifiesto; **it is ~ that ...** queda patente *or* manifiesto que ...; **it is ~ from his speech that ...** su discurso deja patente que ...

evidently ['evɪdəntlɪ] ADV **1** (= *clearly*) evidentemente; **the**

two men ~ knew each other era evidente que *or* evidentemente los dos hombres se conocían **2** (= *apparently*) aparentemente, por lo visto; ~ **not** por lo visto, no, parece que no

evil ['iːvl] **Ⓐ** ADJ (= *wicked*) [*person, deed*] malvado; [*spirit*] maligno, maléfico; [*influence*] maléfico, funesto; [*place, plan*] diabólico; (= *nasty*) [*smell, taste*] horrible; **to put the ~ eye on sb** echar el mal de ojo a algn; ~ **tongues may say that ...** las malas lenguas dirán que ... **Ⓑ** N mal *m*; **the lesser of two ~s** el menor de dos males

evil-smelling ['iːvlˈsmelɪŋ] ADJ fétido, maloliente, hediondo

evocation [ˌevəˈkeɪʃən] N evocación *f*

evocative [ɪˈvɒkətɪv] ADJ evocador (**of** de)

evoke [ɪˈvəʊk] VT [+ *memories*] evocar; [+ *admiration*] suscitar, provocar

evolution [ˌiːvəˈluːʃən] N evolución *f*

evolutionary [ˌiːvəˈluːʃnərɪ] ADJ evolutivo

evolve [ɪˈvɒlv] **Ⓐ** VT desarrollar **Ⓑ** VI [*species*] evolucionar; [*system, plan*] desarrollarse

ewe [juː] N oveja *f*

ex* [eks] N **my ex** (= *husband*) mi ex (marido); (= *wife*) mi ex (mujer); (= *boyfriend, girlfriend*) mi ex (novio/a)

ex- [eks] PREF (= *former*) ex; ~**president** ex-presidente/a *m/f*

exacerbate [eksˈæsəbeɪt] VT [+ *pain, disease*] exacerbar; [+ *relations, situation*] empeorar

exact [ɪɡˈzækt] **Ⓐ** ADJ **1** (= *precise*) [*number, translation, meaning, time, location*] exacto; [*cause, nature*] preciso; **his ~ words were ...** lo que dijo, exactamente, era ...; **to be ~,** **there were three of us** para ser exactos *or* en concreto, éramos tres; **can you be more ~?** precise, por favor; **the ~ same place/house** (*US*) exactamente el mismo sitio/la misma casa **2** (= *meticulous*) [*description, analysis, scientist, work, study*] preciso, meticuloso; [*instrument*] preciso **Ⓑ** VT [+ *money, payment, allegiance*] (= *demand*) exigir; (= *obtain*) obtener (**from** de); [+ *promise*] conseguir, arrancar; **to ~ revenge** vengarse

exacting [ɪɡˈzæktɪŋ] ADJ [*task, activity, profession*] duro; [*boss, person*] exigente; [*conditions*] severo, riguroso

exactly [ɪɡˈzæktlɪ] ADV [*resemble*] exactamente; [*calculate, measure, describe*] con precisión; **at ~ five o'clock** a las cinco en punto; **what ~ did you tell him?** ¿qué le dijiste exactamente?; **nobody knows who ~ will be in charge** nadie sabe con exactitud quién será el encargado; **I wanted to get everything ~ right** quería hacerlo todo a la perfección; **exactly!** ¡exacto!, ¡efectivamente!; **not ~** no exactamente; **he wasn't ~ pleased** (*iro*) no estaba precisamente contento, no estaba muy contento, que digamos

exaggerate [ɪɡˈzædʒəreɪt] VT, VI exagerar

exaggerated [ɪɡˈzædʒəreɪtɪd] ADJ exagerado

exaggeration [ɪɡˌzædʒəˈreɪʃən] N exageración *f*

exaltation [ˌeɡzɔːlˈteɪʃən] N exaltación *f*, elevación *f*

exalted [ɪɡˈzɔːltɪd] ADJ [*position*] elevado; [*person*] eminente

exam* [ɪɡˈzæm] N examen *m*; **our chemistry ~** nuestro examen de química; **to take an ~ (in)** presentarse a un examen (de), examinarse (de) (*Sp*); ➤ **exam paper** examen *m*

examination [ɪɡˌzæmɪˈneɪʃən] **Ⓐ** N **1** (*Scol, Univ*) examen *m* **2** [*of premises*] inspección *f*; [*of luggage*] registro *m*; [*of witness, suspect*] interrogatorio *m*; **on ~** al examinarlo/examinarlos *etc* **3** (*Med*) reconocimiento *m* **Ⓑ** CPD ➤ **examination board** (*Brit*) comisión *f* examinadora (*para alumnos preuniversitarios*)

examine [ɪɡˈzæmɪn] VT **1** [+ *student, patient, part of body*] examinar; [+ *premises*] inspeccionar; [+ *luggage*] registrar **2** (= *investigate*) estudiar, investigar

examiner [ɪɡˈzæmɪnəʳ] N examinador(a) *m/f*

example [ɪɡˈzɑːmpl] N ejemplo *m*; (= *copy, specimen*) ejemplar *m*; **for ~** por ejemplo; **to follow sb's ~** seguir el ejemplo de algn; **to set a good/bad ~** dar buen/mal ejemplo; **to make an ~ of sb** dar a algn un castigo ejemplar

exasperated [ɪgˈzɑːspəreɪtɪd] ADJ exasperado; **we were ~ with Joe/the situation** Joe/la situación nos tenía exasperados, estábamos exasperados con Joe/la situación; **to become** or **get** or **grow ~** exasperarse

exasperating [ɪgˈzɑːspəreɪtɪŋ] ADJ exasperante

exasperation [ɪgˌzɑːspəˈreɪʃən] N exasperación f; **"hurry!" he cried in ~** —¡date prisa! —gritó exasperado or con exasperación

excavate [ˈekskəveɪt] VT excavar

excavation [ˌekskəˈveɪʃən] N excavación f

excavator [ˈekskəveɪtəʳ] N (= machine) excavadora f

exceed [ɪkˈsiːd] VT [+ estimate] exceder (**by** en); [+ number, amount] pasar de, exceder de; [+ limit, bounds] sobrepasar, rebasar; [+ powers, instructions] excederse en; [+ expectations, fears] superar; **a fine not ~ing £50** una multa que no pase de 50 libras

exceedingly [ɪkˈsiːdɪŋlɪ] ADV sumamente, extremadamente

excel [ɪkˈsel] Ⓐ VI **to ~ at** or **in** sobresalir en, destacar en; **to ~ as** destacarse como Ⓑ VT **to ~ o.s.** (often iro) lucirse, pasarse (LAm)

excellence [ˈeksələns] N excelencia f

excellent [ˈeksələnt] ADJ excelente

excellently [ˈeksələntlɪ] ADV excelentemente, muy bien

except [ɪkˈsept] Ⓐ PREP **~ (for)** excepto, salvo, menos; **~ that/if/when** salvo que/si/cuando; **there is nothing we can do ~ wait** no nos queda otra (cosa) que esperar Ⓑ VT excluir, exceptuar (**from** de); **present company ~ed** con excepción de los presentes

excepting [ɪkˈseptɪŋ] PREP excepto, salvo; **always ~ the possibility that ...** excluyendo la posibilidad de que ...; **not ~ ...** incluso ..., inclusive ...

exception [ɪkˈsepʃən] N excepción f; **to make an ~** hacer una excepción; **with the ~ of** a excepción de; **without ~** sin excepción; **the ~ proves the rule** la excepción confirma la regla; **to take ~ to sth** ofenderse por algo

exceptional [ɪkˈsepʃənl] ADJ [courage, ability, circumstances] excepcional; [achievement, performance] extraordinario, excepcional ➤ **exceptional child** (US Scol) (= gifted) niño/a m/f superdotado/a; (= handicapped) niño/a m/f que requiere una atención diferenciada

exceptionally [ɪkˈsepʃənəlɪ] ADV [difficult, valuable, intelligent, high] excepcionalmente, extraordinariamente; [good, large, easy, rare] extraordinariamente

excerpt [ˈeksɜːpt] N extracto m

excess [ɪkˈses] Ⓐ N 1 (= surplus) exceso m; **a sum in ~ of £100,000** una cifra superior a las 100.000 libras; **I don't smoke or drink to ~** no fumo ni bebo en exceso; **to carry sth to ~** llevar algo al extremo 2 (= overindulgence) excesos mpl Ⓑ ADJ 1 (= surplus) **she burns off ~ energy by cycling** quema el exceso de energía montando en bicicleta 2 (= additional) [profit, charge] extraordinario Ⓒ CPD ➤ **excess baggage, excess luggage** exceso m de equipaje ➤ **excess weight** exceso m de peso

excessive [ɪkˈsesɪv] ADJ excesivo; **the accident was caused by the driver's ~ speed** el exceso de velocidad con que iba el conductor causó el accidente; **the dangers of ~ drinking** los peligros de beber en exceso; **£10? that's a bit ~** ¿diez libras? eso es pasarse* or eso es un poco exagerado

excessively [ɪkˈsesɪvlɪ] ADV [eat, smoke, worry etc] demasiado, en exceso; [ambitious, cautious etc] excesivamente

exchange [ɪksˈtʃeɪndʒ] Ⓐ N 1 (= act) [of prisoners, publications, stamps] intercambio m, canje m; [of ideas, information, contracts] intercambio m; **in ~ for** a cambio de; **~ of gunfire** tiroteo m 2 (Fin) [of currency] cambio m; **foreign ~** (= money) divisas fpl, moneda f extranjera 3 (telephone) **~** (public) central f telefónica; (private) centralita f, conmutador m (LAm) Ⓑ VT cambiar (**for** por); [+ prisoners, publications, stamps]

intercambiar, canjear (**for** por; **with** con); [+ greetings, shots] cambiar Ⓒ CPD ➤ **exchange rate** tipo m de cambio ➤ **Exchange Rate Mechanism** mecanismo m de paridades or de cambio del Sistema Monetario Europeo ➤ **exchange visit** visita f de intercambio

exchequer [ɪksˈtʃekəʳ] N **the Exchequer** (Brit Pol) (= budget) el erario público; (= treasury) el Ministerio de economía

excise [ˈeksaɪz] N (also ~ **duty**) impuestos mpl indirectos; **Customs and Excise** (Brit) la Aduana

excitable [ɪkˈsaɪtəbl] ADJ [person, creature] excitable; [mood, temperament] nervioso

excite [ɪkˈsaɪt] VT 1 (= make excited) entusiasmar 2 (= arouse) [+ curiosity, admiration, envy] provocar, suscitar; [+ enthusiasm, interest] despertar, suscitar

excited [ɪkˈsaɪtɪd] ADJ 1 (= exhilarated) [adult] entusiasmado; [child, voice, chatter] excitado; [cry, shout] de excitación; (= exhilarated) **I'm very ~ about the new house** estoy muy ilusionado or entusiasmado con la nueva casa; **to get ~ (about sth)** entusiasmarse (con algo) 2 (= agitated) [person, animal] agitado, nervioso; [crowd] alborotado; [state] de agitación, de nerviosismo; [voice] nervioso, excitado; **don't get ~!** ¡no te excites!, ¡no te pongas nervioso!; **it's nothing to get ~ about** no es para tanto

excitedly [ɪkˈsaɪtɪdlɪ] ADV [wave, shout] con excitación; **they were talking ~** hablaban muy excitados

excitement [ɪkˈsaɪtmənt] N (= exhilaration) emoción f, excitación f; **she's looking for a bit of ~ in her life** está buscando algo de emoción en su vida; **in her ~, she forgot to close the door** con la emoción, se olvidó de cerrar la puerta; **what's all the ~ about?** ¿a qué se debe tanta excitación?; **the book has caused great ~ in literary circles** el libro ha causado mucha conmoción en círculos literarios

exciting [ɪkˈsaɪtɪŋ] ADJ [experience, day, game, film] emocionante; [idea, discovery] apasionante

excl. ABBR = **exclusive (of)**

exclaim [ɪksˈkleɪm] VT exclamar

exclamation [ˌekskləˈmeɪʃən] N exclamación f ➤ **exclamation mark** (Brit), **exclamation point** (US) signo m de admiración

exclude [ɪksˈkluːd] VT 1 (= keep out) excluir; [+ pupil] expulsar 2 (= discount) [+ mistakes] exceptuar

excluding [ɪksˈkluːdɪŋ] PREP excepto, menos

exclusion [ɪksˈkluːʒən] N (gen) exclusión f; (Scol) expulsión f temporal (por mal comportamiento); **to the ~ of** con exclusión de

exclusive [ɪksˈkluːsɪv] Ⓐ ADJ 1 [information, use, pictures] exclusivo; **an ~ report/story** (Press) un reportaje en exclusiva; **to have (the) ~ rights to sth** tener la exclusiva or los derechos exclusivos para algo; **the designs are ~ to our store** son modelos exclusivos de nuestra tienda 2 [area, club, restaurant] selecto, exclusivo; **we attended an ~ gathering of theatre people** asistimos a una selecta reunión de gente del teatro 3 (= not inclusive) **from 1st to 15th ~** del 1 al 15 exclusive; **~ of postage and packing** sin incluir gastos de envío y empaquetado; **~ of taxes** impuestos mpl excluidos, excluyendo los impuestos Ⓑ N (= article) exclusiva f, reportaje m en exclusiva

exclusively [ɪksˈkluːsɪvlɪ] ADV exclusivamente; **available ~ from ...** de venta exclusiva en ...

excommunicate [ˌekskəˈmjuːnɪkeɪt] VT excomulgar

excommunication [ˈekskəˌmjuːnɪˈkeɪʃən] N excomunión f

ex-con* [ˌeksˈkɒn] N ex presidiario/a m/f

excrement [ˈekskrɪmənt] N excremento m

excrete [eksˈkriːt] VT excretar

excruciating [ɪksˈkruːʃieɪtɪŋ] ADJ 1 [pain, suffering] atroz, insoportable 2 (*) (= bad) [film, speech] horroroso

excruciatingly [ɪksˈkruːʃieɪtɪŋlɪ] ADV [hurt, suffer] terriblemente; **it was ~ painful** dolía terriblemente

excursion [ɪksˈkɜːʃən] N excursión f

excusable [ɪksˈkjuːzəbl] ADJ perdonable, disculpable

excuse Ⓐ [ɪksˈkjuːs] N excusa *f*, disculpa *f*; **he made his ~s and left** presentó sus excusas y se marchó; **he's only making ~s** está buscando pretextos; **it's only an ~** es un pretexto nada más; **there's no ~ for this** esto no admite disculpa
Ⓑ [ɪksˈkjuːz] VT 1 (= *forgive*) disculpar, perdonar; **to ~ sb sth** perdonar algo a algn; **~ me!** (*asking a favour, interrupting*) perdone; (*when passing*) perdón, con permiso; **~ me?** (*US*) (= *what?*) ¿perdone?, ¿mande? (*Mex*); **now, if you will ~ me ...** con permiso ...
2 (= *justify*) justificar; **that does not ~ his conduct** eso no justifica su conducta
3 (= *exempt*) **to ~ sb (from sth/from doing sth)** dispensar *or* eximir a algn (de algo/de hacer algo); **to ~ o.s. (from sth/from doing sth)** dispensarse (de algo/de hacer algo); **after ten minutes he ~d himself and left** después de diez minutos pidió permiso y se fue; **I must ask to be ~d this time** esta vez les ruego que me dispensen *or* disculpen
4 to ~ o.s. (for sth/for doing sth) (= *apologize*) pedir disculpas (por algo/por haber hecho algo)

ex-directory [ˌeksdɪˈrektərɪ] ADJ (*Brit*) **they are ~** su número no figura en la guía

exec* [ɪgˈzek] N ejecutivo/a *m/f*

execute [ˈeksɪkjuːt] VT 1 (= *put to death*) ejecutar; (*by firing squad*) fusilar **2** (= *carry out, perform*) [+ *plan*] llevar a cabo, ejecutar; (*Comput*) ejecutar

execution [ˌeksɪˈkjuːʃən] N 1 (= *killing*) ejecución *f*; (*by firing squad*) fusilamiento *m* **2** [*of plan*] ejecución *f*

executioner [ˌeksɪˈkjuːʃnəʳ] N verdugo *m*

executive [ɪgˈzekjʊtɪv] Ⓐ ADJ [*powers, role*] ejecutivo; [*position, duties, decision*] directivo, de nivel ejecutivo; [*pay, salaries*] de los ejecutivos; [*briefcase, chair, toy*] de ejecutivo
Ⓑ N 1 (= *person*) ejecutivo/a *m/f*; **a sales ~** un(a) ejecutivo/a de ventas
2 (= *management*) [*of company*] comité *m* ejecutivo; [*of trade union, party*] ejecutiva *f*; **to be on the ~** [*of company*] pertenecer al comité ejecutivo; [*of trade union, party*] pertenecer a la ejecutiva
3 (= *part of government*) poder *m* ejecutivo, ejecutivo *m*
Ⓒ CPD ➤ **executive privilege** (*US Pol*) inmunidad *f* del poder ejecutivo

exemplary [ɪgˈzemplərɪ] ADJ ejemplar

exemplify [ɪgˈzemplɪfaɪ] VT (= *illustrate*) ejemplificar, ilustrar; (= *be an example of*) demostrar

exempt [ɪgˈzempt] Ⓐ ADJ exento (**from** de); **to be ~ from paying** estar exento de pagar; **~ from tax** libre de impuestos
Ⓑ VT **to ~ sth/sb (from sth/from doing sth)** eximir algo/a algn (de algo/de hacer algo), dispensar algo/a algn (de algo/de hacer algo)

exemption [ɪgˈzempʃən] N exención *f* (**from** de); **tax ~** exención *f* de impuestos, exención *f* tributaria

exercise [ˈeksəsaɪz] Ⓐ N ejercicio *m*; **to take ~** hacer ejercicio; **to do (physical) ~s** hacer gimnasia Ⓑ VT
1 [+ *authority, right, influence*] ejercer **2** [+ *muscle, limb*] ejercitar; [+ *dog*] sacar a pasear Ⓒ VI ejercitarse Ⓓ CPD ➤ **exercise bicycle**, **exercise bike*** bicicleta *f* estática ➤ **exercise book** (*esp Brit*) cuaderno *m* de ejercicios

exert [ɪgˈzɜːt] VT [+ *strength, force*] emplear; [+ *influence, authority*] ejercer; **to ~ o.s.** esforzarse (**to do sth** por hacer algo); **don't ~ yourself!** (*iro*) ¡no te vayas a quebrar *or* herniar!

exertion [ɪgˈzɜːʃən] N esfuerzo *m*; (= *overdoing things*) esfuerzo *m* excesivo, trabajo *m* excesivo

exfoliate [eksˈfəʊlɪeɪt] Ⓐ VT exfoliar Ⓑ VI exfoliarse

ex gratia [ˌeksˈgreɪʃə] ADJ (*esp Brit*) [*payment*] ex-gratia, graciable

exhale [eksˈheɪl] Ⓐ VT despedir Ⓑ VI espirar

exhaust [ɪgˈzɔːst] Ⓐ N (= *fumes*) gases *mpl* de escape; (*Brit*) (*also* **~ pipe**) tubo *m* de escape Ⓑ VT agotar; **to ~ o.s.** agotarse Ⓒ CPD ➤ **exhaust fumes**, **exhaust gases** gases *mpl* de escape

exhausting [ɪgˈzɔːstɪŋ] ADJ agotador

exhaustion [ɪgˈzɔːstʃən] N agotamiento *m*

exhaustive [ɪgˈzɔːstɪv] ADJ exhaustivo

exhibit [ɪgˈzɪbɪt] Ⓐ N 1 (= *painting, object*) (*in museum, art gallery*) objeto *m* expuesto; (*US*) (= *exhibition*) [*of paintings, objects*] exposición *f* **2** (*Jur*) prueba *f* instrumental, documento *m* Ⓑ VT [+ *painting, object*] exponer; [+ *signs of emotion*] mostrar, manifestar; [+ *courage, skill*] demostrar Ⓒ VI [*painter, sculptor*] exponer (sus obras)

exhibition [ˌeksɪˈbɪʃən] N exposición *f*; **to be on ~** estar expuesto; **to make an ~ of o.s.** quedar en ridículo ➤ **exhibition game**, **exhibition match** partido *m* de exhibición

exhibitionist [ˌeksɪˈbɪʃənɪst] ADJ, N exhibicionista *mf*

exhibitor [ɪgˈzɪbɪtəʳ] N expositor(a) *m/f*

exhilarate [ɪgˈzɪləreɪt] VT alegrar, entusiasmar; **to feel ~d** sentirse muy entusiasmado *or* alegre

exhilarating [ɪgˈzɪləreɪtɪŋ] ADJ estimulante, vigorizador

exhilaration [ɪgˌzɪləˈreɪʃən] N (= *elation*) alegría *f*, regocijo *m*; (= *excitement*) excitación *f*

exhort [ɪgˈzɔːt] VT **to ~ sb (to sth/to do sth)** exhortar a algn (a algo/a hacer algo)

exhortation [ˌegzɔːˈteɪʃən] N exhortación *f*

exhume [eksˈhjuːm] VT exhumar, desenterrar

ex-husband [ˌeksˈhʌzbənd] N ex marido *m*

exile [ˈeksaɪl] Ⓐ N 1 (= *state*) exilio *m*, destierro *m*; **he spent many years in ~** vivió muchos años en el exilio *or* exiliado; **to send sb into ~** desterrar a algn, mandar a algn al exilio **2** (= *person*) exiliado/a *m/f*, desterrado/a *m/f* Ⓑ VT desterrar, exiliar

exiled [ˈeksaɪld] ADJ exiliado

exist [ɪgˈzɪst] VI 1 (= *live*) vivir; (= *survive*) subsistir; **to ~ on very little money** vivir *or* subsistir con muy poco dinero
2 (= *occur, be in existence*) existir

existence [ɪgˈzɪstəns] N existencia *f*; (= *way of life*) vida *f*; **to be in ~** existir; **to come into ~** nacer; **the only one in ~** el único existente

existential [ˌegzɪsˈtenʃəl] ADJ existencial

existentialism [ˌegzɪsˈtenʃəlɪzəm] N existencialismo *m*

existentialist [ˌegzɪsˈtenʃəlɪst] ADJ, N existencialista *mf*

existing [ɪgˈzɪstɪŋ] ADJ [*customers, products*] existente; [*law, arrangements, system*] actual, existente

exit [ˈeksɪt] Ⓐ N (= *place, act*) salida *f*; **"no exit"** "prohibida la salida"; **to make one's ~** salir, marcharse Ⓑ VI (*Theat*) hacer mutis; (*Comput*) salir; **~ Hamlet** vase Hamlet Ⓒ VT (*Comput*) salir de Ⓓ CPD ➤ **exit permit** permiso *m* de salida ➤ **exit poll** (*Pol*) encuesta de votantes a la salida del colegio electoral ➤ **exit ramp** (*US*) vía *f* de acceso ➤ **exit visa** visa *f or* visado *m* de salida

> ⚠ **exit** ≠ **éxito**

exodus [ˈeksədəs] N éxodo *m*

exonerate [ɪgˈzɒnəreɪt] VT exonerar (**from** de)

exorbitant [ɪgˈzɔːbɪtənt] ADJ exorbitante, abusivo

exorcise [ˈeksɔːsaɪz] VT exorcizar

exorcism [ˈeksɔːsɪzəm] N exorcismo *m*

exorcist [ˈeksɔːsɪst] N exorcista *mf*

exotic [ɪgˈzɒtɪk] ADJ exótico

expand [ɪksˈpænd] Ⓐ VT 1 [+ *market, operations, business, statement, notes*] ampliar; [+ *influence, knowledge*] aumentar, ampliar **2** (= *broaden*) [+ *mind*] ampliar, extender Ⓑ VI [*gas, metal, lungs*] dilatarse; [*market, operations, business*] ampliarse; **to ~ (up)on** [+ *notes, story*] ampliar, desarrollar

expanding [ɪksˈpændɪŋ] ADJ [*bracelet*] expandible; [*market, industry, profession*] en expansión; **a rapidly ~ industry** una industria en rápida expansión

expanse [ɪksˈpæns] N extensión *f*

expansion [ɪksˈpænʃən] N [*of metal*] dilatación *f*; [*of town, economy, territory*] desarrollo *m* (*also Math*); [*of subject, idea, trade, market*] ampliación *f*, desarrollo *m* ➤ **expansion card**

(*Comput*) tarjeta *f* de expansión

expansionism [ɪksˈpænʃənɪzəm] N expansionismo *m*

expansionist [ɪksˈpænʃənɪst] ADJ expansionista

expansive [ɪksˈpænsɪv] ADJ comunicativo, expansivo

expat [eksˈpæt] (*) N (*Brit*) = **expatriate**

expatriate [eksˈpætrɪɪt] ADJ, N expatriado/a *m/f*

expect [ɪksˈpekt] Ⓐ VT **1** (= *anticipate, wait for*) esperar; **I did not know what to ~** yo no sabía qué esperar; **you know what to ~** ya sabes a qué atenerte; **we'll ~ you for supper** te esperamos a cenar; **is he ~ing you?** ¿tiene usted cita con él?; **to ~ to do sth** esperar hacer algo; **I ~ him to arrive soon** creo que llegará pronto; **it is ~ed that ...** se espera que ... + *subjun*, se prevé que ...; **I ~ed as much** ya me lo imaginaba *or* figuraba; **that was (only) to be ~ed** eso era de esperar; **as was to be ~ed** como era de esperar; **when least ~ed** el día menos pensado; **~ me when you see me*** no cuentes conmigo
2 (= *imagine*) imaginarse; **I ~ it was Jo** me imagino que fue Jo; **I ~ she's there by now** me imagino que ya habrá llegado; **I ~ he'll be late** seguro que llega tarde; **I ~ so** supongo que sí, a lo mejor; **yes, I ~ it is** así tenía que ser
3 (= *require*) **to ~ sth (of/from sb)** esperar algo (de algn); **I think you're ~ing too much of me** creo que esperas demasiado de mí; **to ~ sb to do sth** esperar que algn haga algo; **I ~ you to be punctual** cuento con que serás puntual; **she can't be ~ed to know that** no se puede esperar *or* pretender que sepa eso; **what do you ~ me to do about it?** ¿qué pretendes que haga yo?
Ⓑ VI **she's ~ing** está encinta, está en estado

expectancy [ɪksˈpektənsɪ] N (= *hopefulness*) expectación *f*; (= *hope, chance*) expectativa *f* (**of** de); **life ~** esperanza *f* de vida

expectant [ɪksˈpektənt] ADJ [*person*] expectante; [*look*] de esperanza; **~ mother** mujer *f* encinta, futura madre *f*

expectantly [ɪksˈpektəntlɪ] ADV con expectación

expectation [ˌekspekˈteɪʃən] N **1** (= *hopefulness*) expectación *f* **2** (= *hope*) expectativa *f*, esperanza *f*; **against** *or* **contrary to all ~(s)** en contra de los pronósticos *or* todas las expectativas; **it didn't live up to our ~s** no estuvo a la altura de lo que esperábamos

expectorant [eksˈpektərənt] N expectorante *m*

expedience [ɪksˈpiːdɪəns], **expediency** [ɪksˈpiːdɪənsɪ] N conveniencia *f*, oportunidad *f*

expedient [ɪksˈpiːdɪənt] Ⓐ ADJ oportuno, conveniente Ⓑ N recurso *m*

expedite [ˈekspɪdaɪt] VT [+ *business, deal*] acelerar; [+ *official matter*] dar curso a; [+ *process*] facilitar

expedition [ˌekspɪˈdɪʃən] N expedición *f*; **to go on a fishing ~** ir de pesca, hacer una expedición de pesca; **to go on a shopping ~** ir de compras *or* de tiendas

expel [ɪksˈpel] VT [+ *person*] expulsar

expend [ɪksˈpend] VT [+ *money*] gastar; [+ *time, effort, energy*] dedicar (**on** a); [+ *resources*] consumir, agotar; [+ *ammunition*] usar

expendable [ɪksˈpendəbl] ADJ prescindible

expenditure [ɪksˈpendɪtʃəʳ] N (= *money spent*) gastos *mpl*

expense [ɪksˈpens] N gasto *m*, costo *m*; **expenses** gastos *mpl*; **travelling ~s** gastos *mpl* de viaje; **with all ~s paid** con todos los gastos pagados; **at great ~** gastándose muchísimo dinero; **at my ~** a cuenta mía; **they thought they would have a joke at my ~** querían reírse a costa mía; **you needn't go to the ~ of buying a new one** no es preciso que te gastes dinero en comprar uno nuevo; **they went to great ~ to send her to a private school** se metieron en muchos gastos para mandarla a un colegio privado; **he apologized for putting us to so much ~** se disculpó por habernos ocasionado tantos gastos ➤ **expense account** cuenta *f* de gastos de representación

expensive [ɪksˈpensɪv] ADJ caro; **he has ~ tastes** tiene gustos caros; **she has an ~ lifestyle** lleva un tren de vida caro; **it was an ~ mistake** el error nos ha salido caro

expensively [ɪksˈpensɪvlɪ] ADV [*furnished*] por todo lo alto; **she was ~ dressed** vestía con ropa cara

experience [ɪksˈpɪərɪəns] Ⓐ N experiencia *f*; **to learn by ~** aprender por la experiencia; **have you any previous ~?** ¿tiene usted experiencia previa?; **it was quite an ~** fue toda una experiencia Ⓑ VT [+ *emotion, sensation*] experimentar; [+ *defeat, loss, hardship*] sufrir; **he ~s some difficulty/pain in walking** tiene dificultades/dolor al andar

experienced [ɪksˈpɪərɪənst] ADJ [*teacher, nurse, etc*] con experiencia; **"experienced drivers required"** "se necesitan conductores con experiencia"; **she is not ~ enough** no tiene la suficiente experiencia; **to be ~ (in sth/in doing sth)** tener experiencia (en algo/en hacer algo); **to be sexually ~** tener experiencia sexual

experiment [ɪksˈperɪmənt] Ⓐ N experimento *m*; **to carry out an ~** realizar un experimento Ⓑ VI (*gen*) experimentar; (*scientifically*) experimentar, hacer experimentos (**on** con)

experimental [eksˌperɪˈmentl] ADJ [*science, method*] experimental; [*theatre, novel*] vanguardista

experimentally [eksˌperɪˈmentəlɪ] ADV [*study, test, introduce*] experimentalmente, de forma experimental; [*try out*] como experimento; **he lifted the cases ~ to see how heavy they were** hizo el experimento de levantar las maletas para ver lo que pesaban

experimentation [eksˌperɪmenˈteɪʃən] N experimentación *f*

expert [ˈekspɜːt] Ⓐ ADJ **we'll need an ~ opinion** necesitaremos la opinión de un experto *or* especialista; **with an ~ eye** con ojo experto; **to be ~ at (doing) sth** ser experto en (hacer) algo; **~ system** (*Comput*) sistema *m* experto Ⓑ N experto/a *m/f*; **to be an ~ at (doing) sth** ser un experto en (hacer) algo; **I'm no ~ on the subject** no soy un experto en la materia; **he's a computer ~** es especialista en ordenadores

expertise [ˌekspɜːˈtiːz] N (= *experience*) experiencia *f*; (= *knowledge*) conocimientos *mpl*; (= *skills*) pericia *f*

expertly [ˈekspɜːtlɪ] ADV con habilidad

expiate [ˈekspɪeɪt] VT expiar

expiration [ˌekspaɪəˈreɪʃən] N = **expiry**

expire [ɪksˈpaɪəʳ] VI **1** (= *end*) [*time, period*] terminar, finalizar; [*ticket, passport*] caducar, vencer; [*lease, contract*] vencer, expirar **2** (= *die*) expirar

expiry [ɪksˈpaɪərɪ] N [*of visa, passport*] vencimiento *m*, caducidad *f*; [*of lease, contract*] vencimiento *m*, expiración *f* ➤ **expiry date** [*of visa, contract*] fecha *f* de vencimiento; [*of medicine, food item*] fecha *f* de caducidad

explain [ɪksˈpleɪn] Ⓐ VT explicar; **I ~ed it to him** se lo expliqué; **that ~s it** eso lo explica, con eso queda todo aclarado; **to ~ o.s.** (*clearly*) explicarse; (*morally*) justificarse, defenderse; **kindly ~ yourself!** ¡explíquese Vd! Ⓑ VI **I tried to ~, but ...** intenté explicárselo, pero ...
➤ **explain away** VT + ADV (= *justify*) justificar; (= *excuse*) disculpar; **try and ~ that away!** ¡a ver cómo justificas eso!

explainable [ɪksˈpleɪnəbl] ADJ explicable

explanation [ˌekspləˈneɪʃən] N (*gen*) explicación *f*; (= *excuse*) disculpa *f*; **what is the ~ of this?** ¿cómo se explica esto?

explanatory [ɪksˈplænətərɪ] ADJ explicativo; [*note*] aclaratorio

expletive [eksˈpliːtɪv] N palabrota *f*, improperio *m*

explicit [ɪksˈplɪsɪt] ADJ [*instructions, reference, intention*] explícito, claro; [*description, picture*] gráfico; **to describe sth in ~ detail** describir algo gráficamente; **he was ~ about his intentions** fue explícito *or* claro acerca de sus intenciones; **sexually ~** con claro contenido sexual

explicitly [ɪksˈplɪsɪtlɪ] ADV [*mention, acknowledge*] explícitamente, de forma explícita; [*racist, political*] explícitamente, claramente

explode [ɪksˈpləʊd] Ⓐ VI (*lit*) estallar, explotar; **to ~ with laughter** estallar en carcajadas Ⓑ VT **1** (*lit*) hacer estallar, hacer explotar, explosionar **2** (= *refute*) [+ *myth, theory*] echar por tierra

exploit Ⓐ [ˈeksplɔɪt] N hazaña *f*, proeza *f* Ⓑ [ɪksˈplɔɪt] VT [+ *resources*] explotar, aprovechar; (*pej*) [+ *person, situation*] explotar

exploitation [ˌeksplɔɪˈteɪʃən] N explotación *f*

exploitative [eks'plɔɪtətɪv] ADJ explotador

exploration [,eksplɔː'reɪʃən] N exploración *f*

exploratory [eks'plɒrətərɪ] ADJ [*surgery, research, study*] exploratorio; [*discussions*] preliminares, de tanteo; [*drilling*] de sondeo

explore [ɪks'plɔː'] **Ⓐ** VT **1** [+ *country*] explorar **2** [+ *problem, subject*] investigar; **to ~ every possibility** considerar todas las posibilidades; **to ~ every avenue** estudiar todas las vías posibles **Ⓑ** VI explorar

explorer [ɪks'plɔːrə'] N explorador(a) *m/f*

explosion [ɪks'pləʊʒən] N **1** (*lit*) explosión *f* **2** (*fig*) [*of anger*] arranque *m*, arrebato *m*; [*of laughter*] estallido *m*; **population** ~ explosión *f* demográfica; **price** ~ aumento *m* general de precios

explosive [ɪks'pləʊzɪv] **Ⓐ** ADJ explosivo (*also fig*); **an ~ device** un artefacto explosivo **Ⓑ** N explosivo *m* **Ⓒ** CPD ➤ **explosives expert** artificiero/a *m/f*

exponent [eks'pəʊnənt] N [*of idea*] exponente *mf*; [*of cause*] partidario/a *m/f*; (= *interpreter*) intérprete *mf*

exponential [,ekspəʊ'nenʃəl] ADJ exponencial

export Ⓐ ['ekspɔːt] N (= *act*) exportación *f*; (= *commodity*) artículo *m* de exportación **Ⓑ** [eks'pɔːt] VT exportar **Ⓒ** ['ekspɔːt] CPD [*market, goods, permit, licence*] de exportación ➤ **export duty** derechos *mpl* de exportación

exportation [,ekspɔː'teɪʃən] N exportación *f*

exporter [eks'pɔːtə'] N exportador(a) *m/f*

expose [ɪks'pəʊz] VT (= *leave unprotected*) exponer (*also Phot*); (= *display*) exponer, presentar; (= *uncover*) dejar al descubierto; (= *reveal*) [+ *plot, crime*] poner al descubierto; [+ *criminal, imposter*] desenmascarar; [+ *weakness, one's ignorance*] revelar, poner en evidencia; **to be ~d to view** estar a la vista de todos; **to ~ o.s. to** [+ *risk, danger*] exponerse a; **to ~ o.s.** (*indecently*) hacer exhibicionismo

exposed [ɪks'pəʊzd] ADJ **1** (= *unsheltered, vulnerable*) desprotegido, expuesto; **~ to the wind** desprotegido del viento, expuesto al viento; **this leaves the party in an ~ position** esto deja al partido en una posición desprotegida *or* expuesta **2** (= *uncovered*) [*pipe, brickwork, skin*] al descubierto; [*nerve*] al descubierto, expuesto; [*wire*] al aire

exposition [,ekspə'zɪʃən] N exposición *f*

exposure [ɪks'pəʊʒə'] N **1** (*to weather, cold*) exposición *f*; **to die of ~** morir por exposición a las bajas temperaturas, morir por hipotermia **2** [*of plot*] denuncia *f*; [*of imposter, criminal*] desenmascaramiento *m*; **to threaten sb with ~** amenazar con desenmascarar *or* descubrir a algn **3** (= *publicity*) publicidad *f* **4** (*Phot*) (= *act*) exposición; (= *photo*) foto *f*, fotografía *f*

expound [ɪks'paʊnd] **Ⓐ** VT exponer, explicar **Ⓑ** VI **to ~ on sth** exponer algo en profundidad

express [ɪks'pres] **Ⓐ** VT **1** (*in words etc*) expresar; **they ~ed interest in ...** expresaron su interés en ...; **he ~ed his surprise at the result** expresó su sorpresa ante el resultado; **she had ~ed a wish to meet them** había manifestado su deseo de conocerlos; **to ~ o.s.** expresarse; **here it is ~ed as a percentage** aquí está expresado en forma de porcentaje **2** (*frm*) [+ *juice*] exprimir (**from** de); [+ *milk*] sacarse **Ⓑ** ADJ **1** [*purpose, intention, instructions*] expreso **2** (= *fast*) [*letter, delivery, mail*] urgente, exprés; [*laundry, photography service*] rápido **Ⓒ** ADV **to send sth ~** enviar algo por correo urgente *or* exprés **Ⓓ** N (*also* ~ **train**) expreso *m*, rápido *m*

expression [ɪks'preʃən] N (*gen*) expresión *f*; (*Ling*) frase *f*, expresión *f*; **as an ~ of gratitude** en señal de agradecimiento *or* gratitud

expressionism [ɪks'preʃənɪzəm] N expresionismo *m*

expressionist [ɪks'preʃənɪst] ADJ, N expresionista *mf*

expressionless [ɪks'preʃənlɪs] ADJ sin expresión, inexpresivo

expressive [ɪks'presɪv] ADJ [*person, face, language*] expresivo; [*ability*] de expresión

expressiveness [ɪks'presɪvnɪs] N expresividad *f*

expressly [ɪks'preslɪ] ADV [*state, inform, deny, forbid*] explícitamente, claramente; [*instruct*] expresamente

expresso [ɪk'spresəʊ] N = **espresso**

expressway [ɪks'preswei] N (*US*) autopista *f*

expropriate [eks'prəʊprɪeɪt] VT expropiar

expulsion [ɪks'pʌlʃən] N expulsión *f*; **in doing this she was risking ~** haciendo esto se arriesgaba a que la expulsaran ➤ **expulsion order** orden *f* de expulsión

expunge [ɪks'pʌndʒ] VT suprimir

expurgate ['ekspɜːgeɪt] VT expurgar

exquisite [eks'kwɪzɪt] ADJ [*craftmanship, food, manners, pleasure*] exquisito; [*object, ornament*] (= *beautiful*) de una belleza exquisita; (= *tasteful*) de un gusto exquisito; **he has ~ taste** tiene un gusto exquisito

exquisitely [eks'kwɪzɪtlɪ] ADV (= *tastefully*) con un gusto exquisito; (= *skilfully*) de forma exquisita; **~ beautiful/delicate** de una belleza/delicadeza exquisita

ex-serviceman ['eks'sɜːvɪsmən] N (*pl* **ex-servicemen**) (*Brit*) militar *m* retirado, ex militar *m*

extant [eks'tænt] ADJ existente

extemporize [ɪks'tempəraɪz] VI improvisar

extend [ɪks'tend] **Ⓐ** VT **1** [+ *hand, arm*] extender; (*to sb*) tender, alargar **2** (= *offer*) [+ *friendship, hospitality*] ofrecer; [+ *thanks, congratulations, condolences*] dar; [+ *invitation*] enviar; [+ *credit*] extender, otorgar **3** (= *prolong*) [+ *road, line, visit*] prolongar **4** (= *enlarge, increase*) [+ *building, knowledge, powers*] ampliar **Ⓑ** VI **1 to ~ to** or **as far as** [*land, wall*] extenderse a *or* hasta **2 to ~ to** or **into** [*meeting*] prolongarse hasta **3 to ~ to** (= *include*) abarcar, incluir

extendable [ɪk'stendɪbl] ADJ extensible

extended [ɪk'stendɪd] ADJ (= *stretched out*) extendido; (= *prolonged*) prolongado; **he has been granted ~ leave** se le ha concedido una prórroga del permiso ➤ **extended family** familia *f* extendida

extension [ɪks'tenʃən] N (= *act, part added*) extensión *f*; [*of powers, building*] ampliación *f*; [*of road, stay, visit*] prolongación *f*; [*of term, contract, credit*] prórroga *f*; (*Telec*) extensión, interno *m* (*RPl*), anexo *m* (*Chi, Peru*); **by ~** por extensión ➤ **extension ladder** escalera *f* extensible ➤ **extension lead** alargador *m*, alargadera *f* ➤ **extension number** (número *m* de) extensión *f* or (*RPl*) interno *m* or (*Chi, Peru*) anexo *m*

extensive [ɪks'tensɪv] ADJ **1** (= *large*) [*grounds, estate, area*] extenso; [*network, tour*] extenso, amplio; [*surgery*] de envergadura **2** (= *comprehensive*) [*collection, list*] extenso; [*range, reforms, interests, coverage*] amplio; [*inquiry, tests, research*] exhaustivo **3** (= *considerable*) [*damage, investments*] considerable, importante; [*experience, knowledge*] amplio, vasto; [*repairs*] de consideración; [*powers*] amplio; **to make ~ use of sth** usar *or* utilizar algo mucho

extensively [ɪks'tensɪvlɪ] ADV [*work, travel*] mucho; [*write, speak*] ampliamente, mucho; [*damage*] considerablemente; [*restore, modify*] considerablemente, en gran parte; [*discuss, write*] mucho; [*study, research, revise*] exhaustivamente, a fondo; **the story was covered ~ in the papers** la historia tuvo una amplia cobertura en la prensa

extent [ɪks'tent] N **1** (= *size*) extensión *f* **2** [*of knowledge, damage, activities*] alcance *m*; [*of power*] límite *m*; **the ~ of the problem** el alcance *or* la envergadura del problema **3** (= *degree*) [*of commitment, loss*] grado *m*; **to what ~?** ¿hasta qué punto?; **to a certain** or **to some ~** hasta cierto punto; **to a large ~** en gran parte *or* medida; **to a small ~** en menor grado; **to such an ~ that** hasta tal punto que

extenuating [eks'tenjueɪtɪŋ] ADJ **~ circumstances** circunstancias *fpl* atenuantes

exterior [eks'tɪərɪə'] **Ⓐ** ADJ [*wall, door, surface*] exterior **Ⓑ** N exterior *m*; (= *outward appearance*) apariencia *f*, aspecto *m* exterior; **on the ~** (*lit, fig*) por fuera

exterminate [eks'tɜːmɪneɪt] VT exterminar

extermination [eks,tɜːmɪ'neɪʃən] N [*of people*] exterminio *m*; [*of pests*] exterminación *f*

exterminator [eks'tɜːmɪneɪtə'] N (*US*) exterminador *m* de plagas

external [eks'tɜːnl] **Ⓐ** ADJ **1** [*wall, surface*] externo, exterior; [*appearance, injury, influences*] externo; **"for**

external use only" (*Med*) "de uso tópico *or* externo"
2 (= *foreign*) [*affairs, relations*] exterior Ⓑ CPD ➤ **external examiner** (*esp Brit*) examinador(a) *m/f* externo/a

externalize [ɪksˈtɜːnəlaɪz] VT [+ *ideas, feelings*] exteriorizar

externally [eksˈtɜːnəlɪ] ADV 1 (= *on the outside, outwardly*) por fuera, exteriormente 2 (*Med*) [*apply, use*] tópicamente, externamente; **"to be used externally"** "de uso tópico *or* externo"

extinct [ɪksˈtɪŋkt] ADJ [*volcano*] extinto, apagado; [*animal, race*] extinto, desaparecido; **to become ~** extinguirse, desaparecer

extinction [ɪksˈtɪŋkʃən] N extinción *f*

extinguish [ɪksˈtɪŋgwɪʃ] VT [+ *fire*] extinguir, apagar; [+ *light, cigarette*] apagar; [+ *hope, faith*] destruir

extinguisher [ɪksˈtɪŋgwɪʃəʳ] N extintor *m* (*Sp*), extinguidor *m* (*LAm*)

extn ABBR (*Telec*) (= **extension**) Ext.

extol, extoll (*US*) [ɪksˈtɒl] VT [+ *merits, virtues*] ensalzar, alabar; [+ *person*] alabar, elogiar

extort [ɪksˈtɔːt] VT [+ *promise, confession*] obtener por la fuerza, arrancar; **~ money from sb** extorsionar a algn

extortion [ɪksˈtɔːʃən] N extorsión *f*, exacción *f*; (*by public figure*) concusión *f*

extortionate [ɪksˈtɔːʃənɪt] ADJ [*price*] abusivo, exorbitante; [*demand*] excesivo, desmesurado

extra [ˈekstrə] Ⓐ ADJ 1 (= *reserve*) de más, de sobra; **take an ~ pair of shoes** lleva un par de zapatos de más *or* de sobra; **take some ~ money just to be on the safe side** coge dinero de más *or* de sobra para más seguridad
2 (= *additional*) más *inv*, adicional (*more frm*); **he gave me an ~ blanket** me dio una manta más; **they laid on some ~ trains** pusieron algunos trenes adicionales; **to earn an ~ £20 a week** ganar 20 libras más a la semana; **to go to ~ expense** gastar de más; **to work ~ hours** trabajar horas extra; **the ~ money will come in handy** el dinero extra vendrá bien; **~ pay** sobresueldo *m*
3 (= *special, added*) excepcional; **you must make an ~ effort** tienes que hacer un esfuerzo excepcional *or* extra; **for ~ safety** para mayor seguridad; **take ~ care!** ¡ten muchísimo cuidado!
4 (= *over, spare*) de más, de sobra; **these copies are ~** estas copias sobran
5 (= *not included in price*) **wine is ~** el vino es aparte *or* no está incluido; **~ charge** recargo *m*, suplemento *m*; **they delivered it at no ~ charge** lo enviaron sin recargo
Ⓑ ADV 1 (= *more*) más; **you have to pay ~ for a single room** hay que pagar más por una habitación individual, hay un recargo por habitación individual; **wine costs ~** el vino es aparte *or* no está incluido; **send 95p ~ for postage and packing** manda 95 peniques de más para los gastos de envío
2 (= *especially*) extraordinariamente, super*; **he did ~ well in the written exam** el examen escrito le salió super bien* *or* extraordinariamente bien; **he was ~ polite/nice to her** fue super educado/amable con ella*, fue re(te) educado/amable con ella (*esp LAm**); **to be ~ careful** tener un cuidado excepcional; **to work ~ hard** trabajar super duro*; **~ large** muy grande; **~ special** muy especial, super especial*
Ⓒ N 1 (= *add-on, charge*) extra *m*
2 (*Cine*) extra *mf*
3 (*US*) (= *gasoline*) súper *f*; (= *spare part*) repuesto *m*
Ⓓ CPD ➤ **extra time** (*Ftbl*) prórroga *f*

extract Ⓐ [ˈekstrækt] N (*gen*) extracto *m*; [*of book*] fragmento *m* Ⓑ [ɪksˈtrækt] VT 1 (= *take out*) [+ *cork, tooth*] sacar; [+ *bullet*] extraer; [+ *mineral*] extraer, obtener; [+ *juice*] exprimir 2 (= *obtain*) [+ *information, money*] obtener, sacar; [+ *confession*] sacar, arrancar 3 (*Math*) extraer

extraction [ɪksˈtrækʃən] N extracción *f*; **of Spanish ~** de extracción española

extractor [ɪksˈtræktəʳ] N extractor *m* ➤ **extractor fan** (*Brit*) extractor *m* de humos

extracurricular [ˌekstrəkəˈrɪkjʊləʳ] ADJ extraescolar

extradite [ˈekstrədaɪt] VT extraditar (**from/to** de/a)

extradition [ˌekstrəˈdɪʃən] N extradición *f*

extramarital [ˌekstreˈmærɪtəl] ADJ extramarital, fuera del matrimonio

extramural [ˈekstrəˈmjʊərəl] ADJ (*Brit*) [*course*] externo, de extensión; [*activities*] extracurricular

extraneous [eksˈtreɪnɪəs] ADJ [*influence*] extraño, externo; [*issue*] irrelevante, superfluo; **~ to** ajeno a

extraordinarily [ɪksˈtrɔːdnrɪlɪ] ADV extraordinariamente

extraordinary [ɪksˈtrɔːdnrɪ] ADJ 1 (= *exceptional*) [*courage, career, skill, person*] extraordinario 2 (= *strange*) [*tale, adventure, action*] increíble, insólito; **I find it ~ that he hasn't replied** me parece increíble que no haya contestado; **how ~!** (= *strange*) ¡qué raro!, ¡qué extraño!; (= *incredible*) ¡es increíble! 3 (*Brit frm*) (= *additional, special*) [*meeting, measure, powers*] extraordinario

extrapolate [ɪksˈtræpəleɪt] VT extrapolar; **to ~ sth from sth** extrapolar algo a partir de algo

extrapolation [ɪksˌtræpəˈleɪʃən] N extrapolación *f*

extrasensory [ˈekstrəˈsensərɪ] ADJ extrasensorial ➤ **extrasensory perception** percepción *f* extrasensorial

extraterrestrial [ˌekstrətəˈrestrɪəl] N, ADJ extraterrestre *mf*

extravagance [ɪksˈtrævəgəns] N 1 (= *wastefulness*) derroche *m*, despilfarro *m* 2 (= *indulgence*) extravagancia *f*

extravagant [ɪksˈtrævəgənt] ADJ 1 (= *wasteful, lavish*) [*person*] derrochador, despilfarrador; [*taste*] caro; [*lifestyle*] de muchos lujos; [*gift*] caro; [*price*] exorbitante, desorbitado; **it was very ~ of him to buy this ring** se ha pasado comprando este anillo; **to be ~ with electricity/ one's money** derrochar electricidad/el dinero
2 (= *exaggerated*) [*praise*] excesivo; [*claim, opinion*] extraordinario; [*behaviour, person, design*] extravagante; [*gesture*] exagerado

extravagantly [ɪksˈtrævəgəntlɪ] ADV (= *wastefully, lavishly*) [*spend*] profusamente, con gran despilfarro; [*live*] por todo lo alto, con todo lujo; **to use sth ~** derrochar algo; **the room was ~ furnished** la habitación estaba amueblada por todo lo alto *or* con mucho lujo

extravaganza [eksˌtrævəˈgænzə] N (= *show*) gran espectáculo *m*

extreme [ɪksˈtriːm] Ⓐ ADJ 1 (= *very great*) [*heat, danger, poverty, discomfort*] extremo; [*care, caution*] sumo, extremo; **a matter of ~ importance** una cuestión de suma importancia
2 (= *exceptional*) [*case, circumstances*] extremo
3 (= *radical*) [*views, opinion*] extremista; [*behaviour*] extremado; [*method, action, measure*] extremo; **the ~ left/ right** (*Pol*) la extrema izquierda/derecha; **to be ~ in one's opinions** tener opiniones extremistas
4 (= *furthest*) [*point,*] extremo
Ⓑ N extremo *m*; **to go to ~s** tomar medidas extremas; **to be driven to ~s** verse obligado a tomar medidas extremas; **to take** *or* **carry sth to ~s** llevar algo al extremo; **to go from one ~ to the other** pasar de un extremo al otro; **~s of temperature** las temperaturas extremas; **in the ~** en extremo, en sumo grado

extremely [ɪksˈtriːmlɪ] ADV sumamente, extremadamente; **it is ~ difficult** es dificilísimo, es sumamente *or* extremadamente difícil

extremism [ɪksˈtriːmɪzəm] N extremismo *m*

extremist [ɪksˈtriːmɪst] ADJ, N extremista *mf*

extremity [ɪksˈtremɪtɪ] N (= *end*) extremo *m*, punta *f*; **extremities** (*Anat*) extremidades *fpl*

extricate [ˈekstrɪkeɪt] VT (= *disentangle*) desenredar; (= *free*) [+ *victim*] rescatar, sacar; **to ~ o.s. from** [+ *difficulty, situation*] lograr salir de

extrovert [ˈekstrəʊvɜːt] Ⓐ ADJ (*esp Brit*) extrovertido Ⓑ N extrovertido/a *m/f*

extroverted [ˈekstrəvɜːtɪd] ADJ (*esp US*) extrovertido

exuberance [ɪgˈzuːbərəns] N (= *euphoria*) euforia *f*; (= *enthusiasm*) entusiasmo *m*; [*of style, painting*] exuberancia *f*

exuberant [ɪgˈzuːbərənt] ADJ (= *euphoric*) eufórico;

(= *enthusiastic*) entusiasta; [*style, colour, painting*] exuberante

exuberantly [ɪɡ'zu:bərəntlɪ] ADV eufóricamente

exude [ɪɡ'zju:d] VT **1** [+ *liquid*] rezumar, exudar; [+ *odour*] desprender **2** (*fig*) [+ *optimism, confidence*] rebosar

exult [ɪɡ'zʌlt] VI **to ~ in** *or* **at** *or* **over** regocijarse por

exultant [ɪɡ'zʌltənt] ADJ exultante, jubiloso

ex-wife [ˌeks'waɪf] N (*pl* **ex-wives**) ex mujer *f*

eye [aɪ] Ⓐ N **1** (*Anat*) ojo *m*; **I couldn't believe my (own) ~s** no daba crédito a lo que veían mis ojos; **to cry one's ~s out** llorar a moco tendido *or* a lágrima viva; **to have an ~ for a bargain** tener mucha vista *or* buen ojo para las gangas; **we need someone with an ~ for detail** nos hace falta alguien que sea meticuloso; **he's got his ~ on you** (= *monitoring*) no te quita ojo, no te pierde de vista; (= *attracted to*) te tiene echado el ojo; **I've got my ~ on that sofa in the sale** le tengo echado el ojo a ese sofá que vimos en las rebajas; **she had ~s only for me** sólo tenía ojos para mí, no tenía ojos más que para mí; **in the ~s of the law** a los ojos de la ley; **to keep an ~ on sth/sb** (= *watch*) vigilar algo/a algn, echar una mirada a algo/algn; (= *look after*) cuidar algo/a algn; **keep your ~s on the road!** ¡no quites los ojos de la carretera!; **to keep an ~ on things** estar al cuidado; **to look sb (straight) in the ~** mirar a algn (directamente) a los ojos; **he couldn't keep his ~s off the girl** se le fueron los ojos tras la chica; **I haven't seen any recently but I'll keep my ~s open** últimamente no he visto ninguno pero estaré al tanto; **I could hardly keep my ~s open** se me cerraban los ojos; **keep an ~ out for the postman** estáte atento *or* pendiente a ver si ves al cartero; **keep an ~ out for snakes** cuidado por si hay culebras; **I saw it with my own ~s** lo vi con mis propios ojos; **as far as the ~ can see** hasta donde alcanza la vista; **it's five years since I last set ~s on him** hace cinco años que no lo veo; **the sun is in my ~s** me da el sol en los ojos; **he didn't take his ~s off her for one second** no le quitó los ojos de encima ni por un segundo; **with an ~ to sth/to doing sth** con vistas *or* miras a algo/a hacer algo; **use your ~s!*** ¡abre los ojos!; **to look at sth with the ~ of an expert** ver algo con ojos de experto; ✦ IDIOMS **he was all ~s** era todo *or* (*LAm*) puros ojos; **to have ~s in the back of one's head** tener ojos en la nuca; **to give sb the (glad) ~*** tirar los tejos a algn con miraditas*; **to make ~s at sb*** lanzar miraditas insinuantes a algn, hacer ojitos a algn*; **there's more to this than meets the ~** esto tiene más enjundia de lo que parece, esto tiene su miga; **the decision was one in the ~ for the president*** la decisión supuso un auténtico varapalo para el presidente; **to open sb's ~s to sth** abrir los ojos de algn a algo; **to keep one's ~s peeled** estar alerta; **I don't see ~ to ~ with him** (= *agree with*) no estoy de acuerdo con él; **to shut one's ~s to** [+ *truth, evidence, dangers*] cerrar los ojos a; [+ *sb's shortcomings*] hacer la vista gorda a; **to be up to one's ~s in work/debt** (*Brit**) estar hasta aquí de deudas/agobiado de trabajo; ✦ PROV **an ~ for an ~ (and a tooth for a tooth)** ojo por ojo (y diente por diente)

2 [*of potato*] yema *f*
3 [*of storm*] ojo *m*
4 (*Sew*) [*of needle*] ojo *m*; [*of hook and eye*] hembra *f* de corchete
Ⓑ VT mirar (detenidamente), observar
Ⓒ CPD ➤ **eye contact** contacto *m* ocular ➤ **eye doctor** (*US*) oculista *mf* ➤ **eye drops** gotas *fpl* para los ojos ➤ **eye level at ~ level** a la altura de los ojos ➤ **eye patch** parche *m* ➤ **eye shadow** sombra *f* de ojos ➤ **eye socket** cuenca *f* del ojo ➤ **eye test** test *m* visual *or* de visión
➤ **eye up** VT + ADV (= *study*) estudiar detenidamente; **to ~ sb up** (*Brit**) (*sexually*) comerse a algn con los ojos

eyeball [ˈaɪbɔ:l] Ⓐ N globo *m* ocular; **to be ~ to ~*** (= *in confrontation*) enfrentarse cara a cara; **they've got him drugged up to the ~s*** lo tienen medicado hasta las cejas *or* (*Sp*) a tope* Ⓑ VT (*) clavar la mirada en

eyebath [ˈaɪbɑ:θ] N (= *bowl*) lavaojos *m inv*; (= *action*) baño *m* ocular *or* de ojos

eyebrow [ˈaɪbraʊ] N ceja *f*; **there were a lot of raised ~s when she was appointed** mucha gente se sorprendió cuando la nombraron a ella ➤ **eyebrow pencil** lápiz *m* de cejas

eye-catching [ˈaɪˌkætʃɪŋ] ADJ llamativo, vistoso

-eyed [aɪd] ADJ (*ending in compounds*) de ojos; **green-eyed** de ojos verdes; **one-eyed** tuerto

eyeful [ˈaɪfʊl] N **get an ~ of this!*** ¡echa un vistazo a esto!, ¡mira esto!

eyeglasses [ˈaɪglɑ:sɪz] NPL (*US*) gafas *fpl* (*Sp*), lentes *mpl or fpl* (*LAm*)

eyelash [ˈaɪlæʃ] N pestaña *f*

eyelid [ˈaɪlɪd] N párpado *m*

eyeliner [ˈaɪˌlaɪnəʳ] N lápiz *m* de ojos, delineador *m* de ojos

eye-opener* [ˈaɪˌəʊpnəʳ] N revelación *f*, sorpresa *f* grande

eyepiece [ˈaɪpi:s] N ocular *m*

eyeshade [ˈaɪʃeɪd] N visera *f*

eyesight [ˈaɪsaɪt] N vista *f*; **to have good/poor ~** tener buena/mala vista

eyesore [ˈaɪsɔ:ʳ] N monstruosidad *f*

eyestrain [ˈaɪstreɪn] N vista *f* cansada, fatiga *f* visual; **to cause ~** cansar la vista, producir fatiga visual

eyetooth [ˈaɪtu:θ] N (*pl* **eyeteeth**) colmillo *m*; ✦ IDIOM **I'd give my eyeteeth for a car like that/to see it*** daría cualquier cosa por un coche como ese/por verlo

eyewash [ˈaɪwɒʃ] N **it's a lot of ~!** ¡es puro cuento!

eyewitness [ˈaɪˌwɪtnɪs] N testigo *mf* presencial *or* ocular ➤ **eyewitness account** reportaje *m* en primera línea

eyrie [ˈaɪərɪ] N aguilera *f*

e-zine [ˈi:zi:n] N (*Comput*) revista *f* digital

Ff

F¹, f¹ [ef] **Ⓐ** N 1 (= *letter*) F, f *f*; **F for France** F de Francia 2 (*Mus*) F fa *m* **Ⓑ** ABBR = **female**

F² ABBR 1 = **Fahrenheit** 2 (*Rel*) (= **Father**) P., P.ᵉ

FA N ABBR (*Brit Sport*) (= **Football Association**) ≈ AFE *f*; **FA Cup** Copa *f* de la FA

FAA N ABBR (*US*) = **Federal Aviation Administration**

fable ['feɪbl] N fábula *f*

fabric ['fæbrɪk] **Ⓐ** N 1 (= *cloth*) tela *f*, tejido *m*; (= *textiles*) tejidos *mpl* 2 (*Archit*) estructura *f*; **the ~ of society** el tejido social, la estructura de la sociedad **Ⓑ** CPD ➤ **fabric conditioner, fabric softener** suavizante *m*

> ⚠️ **fabric ≠ fábrica**

fabricate ['fæbrɪkeɪt] VT [+ *goods etc*] fabricar; [+ *document, evidence*] falsificar

fabrication [ˌfæbrɪ'keɪʃən] N (= *manufacture*) fabricación *f*; [*of document, evidence*] falsificación *f*; **the whole thing is a ~** todo es pura invención *or* un cuento

fabulous* ['fæbjʊləs] ADJ (= *wonderful*) fabuloso, estupendo

façade [fə'sɑːd] N (*Archit*) fachada *f*; (*fig*) apariencia *f*

face [feɪs] **Ⓐ** N 1 (= *part of body*) cara *f*, rostro *m*; **the bomb blew up in his ~** la bomba estalló delante suyo; **it all blew up in his ~*** (*fig*) le salió el tiro por la culata*; **I could never look him in the ~ again** no tendría valor para mirarle a la cara de nuevo; **to say sth to sb's ~** decirle algo a la cara a algn; **to bring sb face to face with sb** confrontar algn con algn; **to come face to face with** [+ *person*] encontrarse cara a cara con; [+ *problem, danger*] enfrentarse con; ✦ IDIOMS **to put a brave** *or* (*US*) **good ~ on it** poner al mal tiempo buena cara; **to lose ~** quedar mal, desprestigiarse; **to put one's ~ on*** maquillarse, pintarse; **to save ~** salvar las apariencias, quedar bien; **to set one's ~ against sth** (*esp Brit*) oponerse resueltamente a algo; **to show one's ~** dejarse ver; **shut your ~!**** ¡cállate la boca!*, ¡calla la boca!*

2 (= *expression*) cara *f*, expresión *f*; **his ~ fell** puso cara larga; **a long ~** una cara larga; **to make** *or* (*Brit*) **pull ~s (at sb)** hacer muecas (a algn)

3 (= *person*) cara *f*; **there were plenty of familiar ~s at the party** había muchas caras conocidas en la fiesta; **we need some new** *or* **fresh ~s on the team** el equipo necesita sangre nueva

4 (= *surface*) superficie *f*; [*of dial, watch*] esfera *f*; [*of mountain, cliff, coin, playing card*] cara *f*; **~ down(ward)** (*person, card*) boca abajo; **~ up(ward)** boca arriba; ✦ IDIOM **it's vanished off the ~ of the earth** ha desaparecido de la faz de la tierra

5 (= *aspect*) **the unacceptable ~ of capitalism** los aspectos inadmisibles del capitalismo; **the changing ~ of modern politics** la cambiante fisonomía de la política actual

6 (= *effrontery*) descaro *m*, cara *f*, caradura *f*; **to have the ~ to do sth** tener el descaro de hacer algo

7 (*in set expressions*) **in the ~ of** [+ *enemy*] frente a; [+ *threats, danger*] ante; [+ *difficulty*] en vista de, ante; **on the ~ of it** a primera vista, a juzgar por las apariencias; ✦ IDIOM **to fly in the ~ of reason** oponerse abiertamente a la razón

Ⓑ VT 1 (= *be facing*) [+ *person, object*] estar de cara a; (= *be opposite*) estar enfrente de; **they sat facing each other** se sentaron uno frente al *or* enfrente del otro

2 [*room, building*] (= *overlook*) dar a, tener vista a; (= *be opposite to*) estar enfrente de

3 (= *confront*) [+ *enemy, danger, problem, situation*] enfrentarse a; [+ *consequences*] hacer frente a, afrontar; **many people are facing redundancy** muchas personas se ven enfrentadas al desempleo; **I can't ~ him** (*ashamed*) no podría mirarle a los ojos; **we are ~d with serious problems** se nos plantean graves problemas; **he ~s a fine of £200 if convicted** le espera una multa de £200 si lo declaran culpable; **~d with the prospect of living on his own, he ...** ante la perspectiva de vivir solo, ...; **to ~ facts** aceptar los

hechos *or* la realidad; **to ~ the fact that ...** reconocer que ...; **let's ~ it!** ¡seamos realistas!, ¡reconozcámoslo!; ✦ IDIOM **to ~ the music** afrontar las consecuencias

4 (= *bear, stand*) **I can't ~ breakfast this morning** hoy no podría desayunar nada; **I can't ~ this alone** no me veo capaz de enfrentar esto solo

Ⓒ VI **which way does the house ~?** ¿en qué dirección está orientada la casa?; **it ~s east/towards the east** da al este/mira hacia el este

Ⓓ CPD ➤ **face card** (*US*) figura *f* ➤ **face cloth** toallita *f* (*para la cara*) ➤ **face cream** crema *f* para la cara ➤ **face flannel** (*Brit*) toallita *f*; (= *glove*) manopla *f* (*para lavarse la cara*) ➤ **face mask** (*protective, cleansing*) mascarilla *f* ➤ **face pack** (*Brit*) mascarilla *f* ➤ **face powder** polvos *mpl* para la cara ➤ **face value** [*of coin, stamp*] valor *m* nominal; ✦ IDIOM **to take sb at ~ value** juzgar a algn por las apariencias; **I took his statement at (its) ~ value** tomé lo que dijo en sentido literal

➤ **face down** VT + ADV (*esp US*) amilanar

➤ **face on to** VI + PREP dar a, mirar hacia

➤ **face out** VT + ADV **to ~ it out** afrontar las consecuencias; **to ~ out a crisis** hacer frente a una crisis

➤ **face up to** VI + PREP [+ *difficulty*] afrontar, hacer frente a; **to ~ up to the fact that ...** reconocer *or* admitir (el hecho de) que ...

faceless ['feɪslɪs] ADJ sin rostro; (= *anonymous*) anónimo

facelift ['feɪslɪft] N 1 (*Med*) lifting *m*, estiramiento *m* (facial); **to have a ~** hacerse un lifting 2 (*fig*) reforma *f* (superficial), modernización *f* (ligera); **the building has had a ~** han remozado el edificio

face-saving ['feɪsˌseɪvɪŋ] ADJ para salvar las apariencias

facet ['fæsɪt] N faceta *f*, aspecto *m*

facetious [fə'siːʃəs] ADJ [*person*] ocurrente, ingenioso; [*remark*] jocoso, gracioso

face-to-face [ˌfeɪstə'feɪs] ADJ **a ~ argument** un enfrentamiento *or* una discusión cara a cara

facial ['feɪʃəl] **Ⓐ** ADJ de la cara, facial **Ⓑ** N tratamiento *m* facial

facile ['fæsaɪl] ADJ [*remark, expression*] superficial; [*writer*] vulgar; [*victory*] fácil

facilitate [fə'sɪlɪteɪt] VT (= *make easier*) facilitar; (= *assist progress of*) favorecer

facilitator [fə'sɪlɪteɪtəʳ] N facilitador(a) *m/f*

facility [fə'sɪlɪtɪ] N 1 **facilities** (= *equipment, place*) instalaciones *fpl*; (= *service*) servicio *m*sing; **the hotel's facilities are open to non-residents** las instalaciones del hotel están abiertas a los no residentes; **the flat has no cooking facilities** el piso no está equipado para cocinar; **recreational facilities** instalaciones *fpl* recreativas; **sports facilities** instalaciones *fpl* deportivas; **the company offers day-care facilities for children** la empresa ofrece un servicio de guardería para los niños; **toilet facilities** servicios *mpl*, aseos *mpl*

2 (*Fin*) **credit facilities** facilidades *fpl* (de pago), crédito *m*sing; **overdraft ~** crédito *m* al descubierto

3 (= *function*) función *f*; **the oven has an automatic timing ~** el horno dispone de una función de reloj automático

4 (= *centre*) centro *m*; **a medical ~** un centro médico, un punto de asistencia médica; **a nuclear ~** un complejo nuclear

5 (= *talent, ease*) facilidad *f*; **he writes with great ~** escribe con gran facilidad

6 (= *ability*) habilidad *f*, facultad *f*; (= *capacity*) capacidad *f*

facing ['feɪsɪŋ] **Ⓐ** PREP de cara a, frente a **Ⓑ** ADJ opuesto, de enfrente **Ⓒ** N (*Archit*) paramento *m*, revestimiento *m*; (*Sew*) guarnición *f*

facsimile [fæk'sɪmɪlɪ] **Ⓐ** N facsímile *m*, facsímil *m* **Ⓑ** ADJ facsímil

fact [fækt] **Ⓐ** N 1 (= *detail, circumstance*) hecho *m*; **the ~ that ...** el hecho de que ...; **the ~ that she knew is not the point** el hecho de que ella lo supiera no viene al caso; **he**

still loved her in spite of the ~ that she had left him aunque le había dejado él aún la quería; **their priority is to establish the ~s of the <u>case</u>** su prioridad es esclarecer los hechos *or* lo que ocurrió realmente; **to <u>stick</u> to the ~s** atenerse a los hechos

2 (= *piece of information*) dato *m*; **~s and <u>figures</u>** datos *mpl*; **the ~s of <u>life</u>** los detalles de la reproducción; **get your ~s <u>right</u> before you start accusing people** infórmate bien antes de empezar a acusar a la gente

3 (= *reality*) realidad *f*; **the ~ remains that ...** la realidad sigue siendo que ...; **the ~ (of the matter) is that ...** la verdad *or* el hecho es que ...; **it's a ~ that ...** es un hecho que ...; **I accept what he says as ~** acepto lo que dice como cierto; **a story founded on ~** una historia basada en hechos verídicos *or* reales; **it has no <u>basis</u> in ~** carece de base (real); **to <u>face</u> (the) ~s** enfrentarse a la realidad *or* los hechos; **he can't tell ~ from <u>fiction</u>** no es capaz de distinguir la realidad de la ficción; **to know <u>for</u> a ~ that ...** saber a ciencia cierta que ...; **<u>in</u> ~** de hecho; **it sounds simple, but in ~ it's very difficult** parece sencillo, pero de hecho *or* en realidad es muy difícil; **is <u>that</u> a ~!** (*iro*) ¡no me digas!; **he's a dull writer, and that's a ~** es un escritor aburrido, eso no hay quien lo discuta

Ⓑ CPD ➤ **fact sheet** hoja *f* informativa, informe *m*

fact-finding ['fækt,faɪndɪŋ] ADJ **on a ~ tour/mission** en viaje/misión de reconocimiento; **a ~ committee** una comisión de investigación

faction ['fækʃən] N facción *f*

factional ['fækʃənl] ADJ [*fighting, violence*] entre distintas facciones

factor ['fæktəʳ] N (*gen, Math*) factor *m*; **safety ~** factor *m* de seguridad; **highest common ~** máximo común divisor *m*; **to increase by a ~ of five** aumentar cinco veces, multiplicarse por cinco

factory ['fæktərɪ] N fábrica *f* ➤ **factory farming** (*esp Brit*) cría *f* intensiva ➤ **factory floor** fábrica *f*; **workers on the ~ floor** trabajadores *mpl* de fábrica ➤ **factory ship** buque *m* factoría ➤ **factory worker** obrero/a *m/f* industrial

factual ['fæktjʊəl] ADJ [*report, description*] objetivo, basado en datos objetivos; [*error*] de hecho

factually ['fæktjʊəlɪ] ADV objetivamente

faculty ['fækəltɪ] N **1** (*mental, physical*) facultad *f*; **to have or be in possession of all one's faculties** estar en pleno uso de sus facultades **2** (= *ability*) aptitud *f*, facilidad *f*; **to have a ~ for sth/doing sth** tener aptitud *or* facilidad para algo/hacer algo **3** (*Brit Univ*) facultad *f*; (*esp US*) (= *teaching staff*) profesorado *m* (de facultad *or* universidad)

fad [fæd] N (= *fashion*) moda *f*; **a passing ~** una moda pasajera; **it's just a ~** es la novedad nada más, es una moda pasajera; **he has his ~s** tiene sus caprichos

fade [feɪd] VI **1** [*fabric*] desteñirse, perder color; [*colour*] perder intensidad; **"guaranteed not to fade"** "no destiñe"; **my tan soon ~d** el moreno se me quitó pronto; **the light was fading rapidly** estaba oscureciendo rápidamente, la luz se iba rápidamente **2** [*sound*] desvanecerse; [*signal*] debilitarse; [*voice, music*] apagarse; (*Cine, TV*) [*image*] fundirse **3** (= *deteriorate, decline*) [*flower, beauty*] marchitarse; [*strength*] debilitarse; [*person*] consumirse **4** (= *begin to disappear*) [*hopes, memories, smile*] desvanecerse; [*appeal*] pasarse; [*scar*] borrarse; **he's the sort of person who always ~s into the background** es el tipo de persona que siempre se queda en un segundo plano; **to ~ from view** perderse de vista

➤ **fade in** (*Cine, TV*) Ⓐ VT + ADV [+ *image*] meter con un fundido; [+ *sound*] meter poco a poco Ⓑ VI + ADV [*image*] entrar en fundido (**to** con); [*sound*] entrar (**over** sobre)

➤ **fade out** Ⓐ VT + ADV (*Cine, TV*) [+ *image*] cerrar en fundido, fundir; [+ *sound*] apagar lentamente, bajar el volumen de Ⓑ VI + ADV (*Cine, TV*) [*image*] fundirse (**to** en); [*sound*] apagarse, dejar de oírse; **he ~d out of public life when he became ill** al enfermar desapareció de la vida pública

➤ **fade away** VI + ADV [*sound, music*] apagarse; [*emotion*] irse apagando; [*sick person*] consumirse

faded ['feɪdɪd] ADJ [*garment*] descolorido, desteñido; [*colour*] apagado, desvaído; [*photograph*] desvaído

faeces, feces (*US*) ['fiːsiːz] NPL (*frm*) excrementos *mpl*, heces *fpl* (*frm*)

faff* [fæf] VI (*Brit*): **to ~ about** *or* **around** perder el tiempo, ocuparse en bagatelas

fag [fæg] Ⓐ N **1** (*Brit**) (= *cigarette*) pitillo* *m*, cigarro *m* **2** (*US***) (= *homosexual*) marica* *m* Ⓑ CPD ➤ **fag end*** (= *remainder*) final *m*; (*Brit*) [*of cigarette*] colilla *f*

faggot¹, fagot (*US*) ['fægət] N **1** (*for fire*) haz *m* de leña **2** (*Brit Culin*) albóndiga *f*

faggot²** ['fægət] N (*esp US pej*) (= *homosexual*) marica* *m*

Fahrenheit ['færənhaɪt] N Fahrenheit *m*

fail [feɪl] Ⓐ VI **1** (= *not succeed*) [*candidate in examination*] suspender (*Sp*), reprobar (*LAm*); [*plan*] fracasar, no dar resultado; [*business*] quebrar; [*remedy*] fallar, no surtir efecto; **to ~ in one's duty** faltar a su deber, no cumplir con su obligación

2 [*light*], apagarse; [*crops*] perderse; [*health, sight, voice*] debilitarse; [*strength*] acabarse; [*engine, brakes, mechanism*] fallar, averiarse; [*power supply*] cortarse, fallar; **the light was ~ing** iba anocheciendo

Ⓑ VT **1** (+ *exam, subject, candidate*) suspender (*Sp*), reprobar (*LAm*); **a ~ed painter** un pintor fracasado

2 (= *let down*) [+ *person*] fallar (a); [*memory, strength*] fallar; **don't ~ me!** ¡no me falles!, ¡no faltes!; **his strength ~ed him** le fallaron las fuerzas; **his courage ~ed him** le faltó valor; **words ~ me!** ¡no encuentro palabras!

3 (= *not succeed*) **to ~ to be elected** no lograr ser elegido; **to ~ to win a prize** no obtener un premio

4 (= *omit, neglect*) **to ~ to do sth** no hacer algo, dejar de hacer algo

5 (= *be unable*) **I ~ to see why/what** *etc* no veo *or* alcanzo a ver por qué/qué *etc*

Ⓒ N **1 without ~** sin falta

2 (*Univ*) suspenso *m* (*Sp*), reprobado *m* (*LAm*), aplazo *m* (*Arg*) (**in** en)

failing ['feɪlɪŋ] Ⓐ PREP a falta de; **~ that, ...** de no ser posible, ... Ⓑ N (= *flaw*) falta *f*, defecto *m* Ⓒ ADJ **I had to stop work because of ~ eyesight** tuve que dejar de trabajar porque me fallaba la vista; **we reached the top in ~ light** anochecía cuando llegamos a la cumbre; **a ~ marriage** un matrimonio que anda mal

fail-safe ['feɪlseɪf] ADJ [*device*] de seguridad, a prueba de fallos; [*method*] infalible

failure ['feɪljəʳ] Ⓐ N **1** (= *lack of success*) fracaso *m*; (*in exam*) suspenso *m*; [*of crops*] pérdida *f*; [*of supplies*] corte *m*, interrupción *f*; [*of hopes*] frustración *f*, malogro *m*; **to end in ~** acabar mal, malograrse (*LAm*); **it was a complete ~** fue un fracaso total

2 (*Tech*) fallo *m*, avería *f*; (*Med*) crisis *f inv*, ataque *m*; (*Fin*) quiebra *f*

3 (= *person*) fracasado/a *m/f*

4 (= *neglect*) falta *f*; **~ to pay** incumplimiento *m* en el pago, impago *m*

Ⓑ CPD ➤ **failure rate** (*in exams*) porcentaje *m* de suspensos; [*of machine*] porcentaje *m* de averías

faint [feɪnt] Ⓐ ADJ (*compar* **~er**; *superl* **~est**) **1** (= *light, weak*) [*outline*] borroso, indistinto; [*trace, mark, line, light*] tenue; [*colour*] pálido; [*sound*] apagado, débil; [*smell*] tenue, casi imperceptible; [*taste, resemblance*] ligero; [*voice, breathing*] débil; [*hope*] remoto; [*smile*] leve; [*idea, memory*] vago; **I haven't the ~est idea*** no tengo ni la más remota idea

2 (*Med*) **to feel ~** marearse, tener vahídos; **she was ~ with hunger** estaba que se desmayaba de hambre

Ⓑ VI (*Med*) desmayarse, perder el conocimiento (**from** de)

fainthearted ['feɪntˈhɑːtɪd] ADJ pusilánime, apocado, medroso; **this film is not for the ~** es una película muy fuerte

fainting fit ['feɪntɪŋ,fɪt] N, **fainting spell** ['feɪntɪŋ,spel] N síncope *m*, desvanecimiento *m*

faintly ['feɪntlɪ] ADV **1** (= *slightly*) [*disappointed*] ligeramente **2** (= *weakly*) [*call, say*] débilmente; [*breathe, shine*] débilmente, ligeramente

fair¹ [feəʳ] **Ⓐ** ADJ (compar ~**er**; superl ~**est**) **1** (= just) [person, treatment, wage, exchange] justo; [decision, report] imparcial; [sample] representativo; [price] justo, razonable; [deal] justo, equitativo; [fight, election] limpio; [competition] leal; **it's not ~!** ¡no es justo!, ¡no hay derecho!; **be** ~ sé justo or razonable; **to be ~ ...** (= truth to tell) a decir verdad ..., en honor a la verdad ...; (= not to be unjust) para ser justo ...; **that's ~ comment** ésa es una observación razonable or válida; ~ **enough!** ¡muy bien!, ¡vale! (Sp); **fair's fair, it's my turn now** ya basta or (Sp) vale ya, ahora me toca a mí; ~ **game** (fig) blanco m legítimo; **it's not ~ on the old** es injusto or no es justo para (con) los ancianos; ~ **play** (in game) juego m limpio; **sense of ~ play** (fig) sentido m de la justicia; **it's ~ to say that ...** es cierto que ..., lo cierto es que ...; **she's had more than her ~ share of problems in life** ha pasado mucho or lo suyo en la vida; **they are not paying their ~ share** no están pagando la cantidad que les corresponde or que les toca; **to be ~ to him** para ser justo con él; ~ **trade** comercio m equitativo; ◆ IDIOM **by ~ means or foul** por las buenas o por las malas; ◆ PROV **all's ~ in love and war** todo vale en el amor y la guerra
2 (= reasonable, average) [work] pasable, regular; **she has a ~ chance** tiene bastantes posibilidades; **I have a ~ idea of what to expect** sé más o menos qué esperar; **he's been given ~ warning** no puede decir que no se le ha avisado
3 (= quite large) **a ~ amount of** bastante; **this happens in a ~ number of cases** esto sucede en bastantes casos; **we've still got a ~ way to go** aún nos queda un buen trecho que recorrer
4 (= light-coloured) [hair, person] rubio, güero (Mex*); [complexion, skin] blanco
5 (= good) [weather] bueno; **if it's ~ tomorrow** si hace buen tiempo mañana; **this ~ city of ours** esta bella ciudad nuestra; ~ **copy** copia f en limpio; **the ~ sex** el bello sexo **Ⓑ** ADV **to play** ~ jugar limpio; **to win ~ and square** ganar con todas las de la ley **Ⓒ** CPD ➤ **fair trade** comercio m justo

fair² [feəʳ] N **1** (= market) feria f; **antiques/craft** ~ feria f de antigüedades/artesanía; **book** ~ feria f del libro **2** (Brit) (= funfair) parque m de atracciones

fairground ['feəɡraʊnd] N parque m de atracciones

fair-haired ['feə'heəd] ADJ [person] rubio, güero (Mex)

fairly ['feəlɪ] ADV **1** (= justly) justamente, con justicia; (= impartially) con imparcialidad; (= equally) equitativamente **2** (= according to the rules) [play] limpiamente, limpio **3** (= quite) bastante; **I'm ~ sure** estoy bastante or casi seguro; ~ **good** bastante bueno

fair-minded ['feə'maɪndɪd] ADJ imparcial

fairness ['feənɪs] **Ⓐ** N **1** (= justice) justicia f; (= impartiality) imparcialidad f; **in all ~** (= truth to tell) a decir verdad, en honor a la verdad; (= not to be unjust) para ser justo; **in (all) ~ to him** para ser justo con él **2** [of hair, person] lo rubio, lo güero (Mex*); [of complexion, skin] blancura f **Ⓑ** CPD ➤ **fairness doctrine** (US) doctrina f de la imparcialidad

fair-sized ['feəsaɪzd] ADJ bastante grande

fair-skinned ['feə'skɪnd] ADJ de tez blanca

fairway ['feəweɪ] N (Golf) calle f

fair-weather friend [ˌfeəweðə'frend] N amigo/a m/f en la prosperidad or del buen viento

fairy ['feərɪ] **Ⓐ** N **1** (= creature) hada f

> Use **el/un** not **la/una** before feminine nouns beginning with stressed **a** or **ha** like **hada**.

2 (**) (= homosexual) maricón** m, marica* m
Ⓑ CPD ➤ **fairy godmother** hada f madrina; **a ~ godmother** un hada madrina ➤ **fairy lights** (Brit) bombillas fpl de colorines ➤ **fairy story**, **fairy tale** cuento m de hadas; (= lie) cuento m, patraña f

fairyland ['feərɪlænd] N país m de las hadas; ◆ IDIOM **he's living in ~*** vive en la luna

fairytale ['feərɪteɪl] ADJ [castle, world] fantástico, de ensueño ➤ **fairytale romance** (fig) amor m de cuento de hadas

fait accompli [ˌfeɪtə'kɒmplɪ] N hecho m consumado

faith [feɪθ] **Ⓐ** N **1** (Rel) fe f; (= doctrine) creencia f, doctrina f; (= sect, confession) religión f **2** (= trust) fe f, confianza f; **to have ~ in sth/sb** tener fe or confianza en algo/algn, fiarse de algo/algn; **to put one's ~ in sth/sb** confiar en algo/algn; **in (all) good ~** de buena fe; **in bad ~** de mala fe **Ⓑ** CPD ➤ **faith healer** curandero/a m/f

faithful ['feɪθfʊl] **Ⓐ** ADJ fiel (**to** a) **Ⓑ** NPL **the ~** (Rel) los fieles

faithfully ['feɪθfəlɪ] ADV [serve] fielmente, lealmente; [describe, translate] fielmente, con exactitud; **Yours ~** (Brit) le saluda atentamente

faithless ['feɪθlɪs] ADJ desleal, infiel

fake [feɪk] **Ⓐ** N (= thing, picture) falsificación f; (= person) impostor(a) m/f, embustero/a m/f; (as term of abuse) farsante mf **Ⓑ** ADJ falso **Ⓒ** VT **1** [+ accounts] falsificar; **to ~ an illness** fingirse enfermo **2** (US) (= improvise) improvisar **Ⓓ** VI fingir, simular

falcon ['fɔːlkən] N halcón m

Falkland Islands ['fɔːlkləndˌaɪləndz], **Falklands** ['fɔːlkləndz] NPL (Islas fpl) Malvinas fpl

fall [fɔːl] (vb: pt **fell**; pp ~**en**) **Ⓐ** N **1** (= tumble) caída f; [of rocks] desprendimiento m; **he had a bad** ~ sufrió una mala caída; **a ~ of snow** una nevada; ◆ IDIOM **to be heading** or **riding for a ~** presumir demasiado
2 (= decrease) (gen) disminución f; (in prices, temperature, demand) descenso m (**in** de); (St Ex, Fin) baja f, bajada f
3 (US) (= autumn) otoño m
4 falls (= waterfall) salto msing de agua, cascada fsing, catarata fsing; **Niagara Falls** las cataratas del Niágara
Ⓑ VI **1** (= fall down) [person, object] caerse; **to ~ into the river** caerse al río; **to ~ on one's feet** caer de pie; (fig) salir bien parado; **to ~ to one's knees** arrodillarse, caer de rodillas; ◆ IDIOM **to ~ flat** [joke] no hacer gracia; [party] fracasar
2 (= drop) [leaves, bomb, rain, snow, night] caer; [rocks] desprenderse; **he fell into bed exhausted** se desplomó en la cama, exhausto; **they left as darkness fell** partieron al caer la noche; **it all began to ~ into place** todo empezó a encajar; **to ~ short of sb's expectations** defraudar las esperanzas de algn; **to ~ short of perfection** no llegar a la perfección; **the arrow fell short of the target** la flecha no alcanzó la diana
3 (= decrease) disminuir; [price, level, temperature etc] bajar, descender; [wind] amainar; **at a time of ~ing interest rates** en un período cuando bajan los tipos de interés; **he fell in my estimation** perdió mucho a mis ojos
4 (= be defeated) [government] caer, ser derrotado; [city] rendirse, ser tomado
5 (liter) (= die) [soldier] caer, morir
6 (= become) **to ~ asleep** quedarse dormido, dormirse; **to ~ to bits** (Brit) hacerse pedazos; **to ~ ill** caer enfermo, enfermarse; **to ~ in love (with sth/sb)** enamorarse (de algo/algn); **to ~ to pieces** hacerse pedazos; **to ~ silent** callarse **Ⓒ** CPD ➤ **fall guy*** (= easy victim) víctima f (de un truco); (= scapegoat) cabeza f de turco
➤ **fall about*** VI + ADV (Brit) (also ~ **about laughing**) morirse or partirse de risa
➤ **fall apart** VI + ADV [object] caerse a pedazos, deshacerse; [empire] desmoronarse; [scheme, marriage] fracasar
➤ **fall back** VI + ADV (= retreat) retroceder; (Mil) replegarse; **to ~ back on sth** [+ remedy etc] recurrir a algo; **something to ~ back on** algo a lo que recurrir
➤ **fall behind** VI + ADV (in race etc) quedarse atrás, rezagarse; (with work, payments) retrasarse
➤ **fall down** **Ⓐ** VI + ADV **1** [person] caerse (al suelo); [building] hundirse, derrumbarse **2** (fig) (= fail) fracasar, fallar; **that is where you fell down** ahí es donde fallaste **Ⓑ** VI + PREP **to ~ down the stairs** caer rodando por la escalera
➤ **fall for*** VI + PREP **1** (= feel attracted to) [+ person] enamorarse de; [+ object, place] quedarse encantado con **2** (= be deceived by) [+ trick] dejarse engañar por, tragarse*; **he fell for it** picó*, se lo tragó*
➤ **fall in** VI + ADV **1** [person] caerse (dentro); [roof, walls] desplomarse **2** (Mil) formar filas; ~ **in!** ¡en filas!
➤ **fall into** VI + PREP **his poems ~ into three categories** sus poemas se dividen en tres categorías; **to ~ into error**

incurrir en error; **to ~ into bad habits** adquirir malos hábitos; **to ~ into conversation with sb** entablar conversación con algn
➤ **fall in with** VI + PREP **1** (= *meet*) [+ *person*] encontrarse *or* juntarse con **2** (= *agree to*) [+ *plan, proposal etc*] aceptar, quedar de acuerdo con; [+ *opinion*] adherirse a
➤ **fall off** Ⓐ VI + ADV **1** (*gen*) caerse; [*part*] desprenderse **2** (= *diminish*) (*in amount, numbers*) disminuir; [*interest*] decaer Ⓑ VI + PREP (*gen*) caerse de; [*part*] desprenderse de
➤ **fall on** VI + PREP **1** [*accent, stress*] recaer en **2** (*Mil*) caer sobre **3 to ~ on one's food** lanzarse sobre la comida, lanzarse a comer **4** [*birthday, Christmas etc*] caer en
➤ **fall out** VI + ADV **1** [*person, object*] caerse (*of* de) **2** (*Mil*) romper filas **3** (= *quarrel*) **to ~ out (with sb) (over sth)** enfadarse *or* (*LAm*) enojarse (con algn) (por algo)
➤ **fall over** Ⓐ VI + ADV [*person, object*] caer, caerse Ⓑ VI + PREP **1** [+ *object*] tropezar con **2** (*fig*) (*): **he was ~ing over himself to be polite** se desvivía en atenciones
➤ **fall through** VI + ADV [*plans etc*] fracasar
➤ **fall to** Ⓐ VI + ADV (= *begin working*) ponerse a trabajar; (= *begin eating*) empezar a comer; **~ to!** ¡a ello!, ¡vamos! Ⓑ VI + PREP **1** (= *begin*) **to ~ to doing sth** empezar *or* ponerse a hacer algo **2** (= *be one's duty*) corresponder a, tocar a; **it ~s to me to say ...** me corresponde a mí decir ...
➤ **fall upon** VI + PREP = **fall on**

fallacious [fəˈleɪʃəs] ADJ (*frm*) (= *incorrect*) erróneo; (= *misleading*) engañoso, falaz

fallacy [ˈfæləsɪ] N (= *false belief*) falacia *f*; (= *false reasoning*) sofisma *m*, argucia *f*

fallback [ˈfɔːlbæk] ADJ **~ position** segunda línea *f* de defensa; (*fig*) posición *f* de repliegue

fallen [ˈfɔːlən] Ⓐ PP of **fall** Ⓑ ADJ **1** (*lit*) caído **2** [*woman*] perdido; [*angel*] caído Ⓒ NPL **the ~** los caídos

fallible [ˈfæləbl] ADJ falible

falling [ˈfɔːlɪŋ] ADJ que cae; (*Comm*) en baja

falling-off [ˈfɔːlɪŋˈɒf] N (*in numbers etc*) disminución *f*; (*in standards*) empeoramiento *m*

falling-out* [ˈfɔːlɪŋˈaʊt] N altercado *m*, pelea *f*

Fallopian tube [fəˌləʊpɪənˈtjuːb] N trompa *f* de Falopio

fallout [ˈfɔːlaʊt] Ⓐ N **1** (*radioactive*) lluvia *f* radiactiva **2** (*fig*) consecuencias *fpl*, repercusiones *fpl* Ⓑ CPD ➤ **fallout shelter** refugio *m* atómico *or* nuclear

fallow [ˈfæləʊ] ADJ (*Agr*) en barbecho

false [fɔːls] Ⓐ ADJ **1** (= *untruthful*) [*statement, accusation*] falso; (= *mistaken*) [*idea, assumption, accusation*] equivocado; **to give a ~ impression** dar una impresión falsa; **~ move** movimiento *m* en falso; **a ~ sense of security** una falsa sensación de seguridad; **~ step** paso *m* en falso **2** (= *deceitful*) **under ~ pretences** *or* (*US*) **pretenses** con engaños, con insidias; **to bear ~ witness** (*esp Bible*) levantar falso testimonio **3** (= *inappropriate*) **that was ~ economy** fue un mal ahorro; **to give sb ~ hope(s)** dar falsas esperanzas a algn **4** (= *artificial*) [*hair, eyelashes*] postizo; [*name*] falso; **a suitcase with a ~ bottom** una maleta con doble fondo Ⓑ CPD ➤ **false alarm** falsa alarma *f* ➤ **false friend** (*Ling*) falso amigo *m* ➤ **false imprisonment** (*by police*) detención *f* ilegal; (*by criminal*) retención *f* ilegal ➤ **false memory syndrome** síndrome *m* de (la) falsa memoria ➤ **false start** (*Sport*) salida *f* nula; (*fig*) comienzo *m* fallido ➤ **false teeth** dentadura *fsing* postiza, dientes *mpl* postizos ➤ **false tooth** diente *m* postizo

falsehood [ˈfɔːlshʊd] N (= *falsity*) falsedad *f*; (= *lie*) mentira *f*

falsely [ˈfɔːlslɪ] ADV (= *untruthfully*) falsamente; (= *mistakenly*) equivocadamente; **she had been ~ diagnosed with cancer** se equivocaron cuando le diagnosticaron cáncer

falsetto [fɔːlˈsetəʊ] Ⓐ N falsete *m* Ⓑ ADJ [*voice*] con falsete

falsify [ˈfɔːlsɪfaɪ] VT [+ *document*] falsificar; [+ *evidence*] falsificar, falsear; [+ *accounts, figures*] falsear

falsity [ˈfɔːlsɪtɪ] N falsedad *f*

falter [ˈfɔːltəʳ] VI [*person*] vacilar, titubear; [*voice*] entrecortarse, quebrarse; [*steps*] vacilar; [*courage*] fallar, faltar; **without ~ing** sin vacilar

fame [feɪm] N fama *f*; **Margaret Mitchell, of "Gone with the Wind"** ~ Margaret Mitchell, famosa por su novela "Lo que el viento se llevó"

famed [feɪmd] ADJ famoso, afamado

familiar [fəˈmɪlɪəʳ] ADJ **1** (= *well-known*) [*face, person, place*] conocido, familiar; **his voice sounds ~** me suena (familiar) su voz
2 (= *common*) [*experience, complaint, event*] corriente, común
3 (= *well-acquainted*) **to be ~ with** estar familiarizado con, conocer; **to make o.s. ~ with** familiarizarse con
4 (= *intimate*) [*tone of voice etc*] íntimo, de confianza; [*language etc*] familiar; (= *over-intimate*) fresco, que se toma demasiadas confianzas; **to be on ~ terms with sb** tener confianza con algn; **he got too ~** se tomó demasiadas confianzas

familiarity [fəˌmɪlɪˈærɪtɪ] N **1** [*of sight, event etc*] familiaridad *f* **2** (= *knowledge*) conocimiento *m* (**with** de) **3** (= *intimacy*) [*of tone etc*] familiaridad *f*, confianza *f*; (*pej*) frescura *f*, exceso *m* de familiaridad

familiarize [fəˈmɪlɪəraɪz] VT familiarizar (**with** con); **to ~ o.s. with** familiarizarse con

family [ˈfæmɪlɪ] Ⓐ N familia *f* (*also Zool*); **she's one of the ~** es como de la familia; **do you have any ~?** (= *relatives*) ¿tiene usted parientes?; (= *children*) ¿tiene usted hijos?; **to run in the ~** ser cosa de familia Ⓑ CPD [*jewels*] de la familia; [*dinner, resemblance*] de familia ➤ **family allowance** (*Brit*) (*formerly*) ≈ ayuda *f* familiar ➤ **family business** negocio *m* familiar ➤ **family credit** (*Brit*) ≈ ayuda *f* familiar ➤ **family doctor** (*Brit*) médico/a *m/f* de cabecera ➤ **family friend** amigo/a *m/f* de la familia ➤ **family life** vida *f* doméstica ➤ **family man** (= *having family*) padre *m* de familia; (= *home-loving*) hombre *m* casero *or* de su casa ➤ **family name** apellido *m* ➤ **family pet** animal *m* doméstico ➤ **family planning** planificación *f* familiar ➤ **family planning clinic** centro *m* de planificación familiar ➤ **family practice** (*US Med*) (= *work*) medicina *f* general; (= *place*) consulta *f* ➤ **family room** (*in hotel*) habitación *f* familiar ➤ **family therapy** terapia *f* familiar ➤ **family tree** árbol *m* genealógico ➤ **family values** valores *m* (tradicionales) de la familia

family-size(d) [ˈfæmɪlɪsaɪz(d)] ADJ [*packet*] (tamaño) familiar

famine [ˈfæmɪn] N hambre *f*, hambruna *f*

Use **el/un** not **la/una** before feminine nouns beginning with stressed **a** or **ha** like **hambre**.

➤ **famine relief** ayuda *f* contra el hambre

famished* [ˈfæmɪʃt] ADJ famélico; (*fig*) muerto de hambre

famous [ˈfeɪməs] ADJ famoso, célebre (**for** por); (*hum*) dichoso

famously [ˈfeɪməslɪ] ADV **1** (= *notoriously*) **as Wilde ~ remarked** como bien señalara Wilde; **there have been hurricanes in England, most ~ in 1987** ha habido huracanes en Inglaterra, el más famoso ocurrido en 1987 **2** (†*) (= *very well*) **to get on ~** llevarse a las mil maravillas

fan¹ [fæn] Ⓐ N (*hand-held*) abanico *m*; (= *machine*) ventilador *m*; **electric ~** ventilador *m* eléctrico Ⓑ VT [+ *face, person*] abanicar; (*mechanically*) ventilar; (*fig*) avivar, excitar; **to ~ o.s.** abanicarse, darse aire Ⓒ CPD ➤ **fan belt** (*in motor*) correa *f* del ventilador ➤ **fan heater** (*Brit*) calentador *m* de aire, estufa *f* eléctrica (de aire caliente)
➤ **fan out** VI + ADV (*Mil etc*) desplegarse en abanico, avanzar en abanico

fan² [fæn] N (= *person*) (*gen*) aficionado/a *m/f*; (*Sport*) hincha *mf*, forofo/a *m/f* (*Sp*), adicto/a *m/f* (*LAm*); [*of pop star, etc*] fan *mf*, admirador(a) *m/f*; **the ~s** la afición; **I am not one of his ~s** no soy de sus admiradores, yo no soy de los que lo admiran ➤ **fan club** club *m* de admiradores; (*Mus*) club *m* de fans ➤ **fan mail** correspondencia *f* de los admiradores

fanatic [fəˈnætɪk] ADJ, N fanático/a *m/f*

fanatical [fəˈnætɪkəl] ADJ fanático

fanaticism [fəˈnætɪsɪzəm] N fanatismo *m*

fanciful ['fænsɪfʊl] ADJ [*idea, story, account*] descabalado, rocambolesco; [*person*] imaginativo, fantasioso; [*temperament*] caprichoso

fancy ['fænsɪ] Ⓐ N **1** (= *liking*) **to catch** *or* **take sb's ~** atraer a algn; **to take a ~ to** [+ *person*] (*amorously*) quedarse prendado de, prendarse de; [+ *thing*] encapricharse con **2** (= *whim*) capricho *m*, antojo *m*; **a passing ~** un capricho pasajero; **when the ~ takes him** cuando se le antoja **3** (= *imagination*) fantasía *f*, imaginación *f*
Ⓑ ADJ (*compar* **fancier**; *superl* **fanciest**) **1** (= *elaborate*) muy elaborado; **I like good, plain food, nothing ~** me gusta la buena comida, sencilla, nada muy elaborado *or* nada demasiado historiado **2** (= *elegant*) [*restaurant*] de lujo, muy chic; [*house, car*] lujoso; [*clothes*] elegante, chic
Ⓒ VT **1** (*esp Brit**) (= *like, want*) **what do you ~?** ¿qué quieres tomar?, ¿qué te apetece?; **do you ~ an Indian meal?** ¿te apetece *or* (*LAm*) se te antoja una comida india?; **what do you fancy doing?** ¿qué te apetece *or* (*LAm*) se te antoja hacer?; **he fancies himself*** es un creído *or* un presumido; **he fancies himself as a bit of an actor** se piensa que es un actor; **he fancies himself as a footballer** se las da de futbolista; **I could tell he fancied me** notaba que le gustaba mucho, notaba que se sentía atraído por mí **2** (= *imagine*) imaginarse, figurarse; **~ that!*** ¡fíjate!, ¡imagínate!; **~ meeting you here!** ¡qué casualidad encontrarte aquí!; **~ throwing that away!** ¡a quién se le ocurre tirar eso!; **he fancied he saw a glint of amusement in her face** le pareció ver una chispa de diversión en su rostro
Ⓓ CPD ➤ **fancy dress** disfraz *m*; **they were wearing ~ dress** iban disfrazados ➤ **fancy dress party** fiesta *f* de disfraces

fanfare ['fænfeə'] N fanfarria *f*

fang [fæŋ] N colmillo *m*

fanny ['fænɪ] Ⓐ N **1** (*Brit****) (= *vagina*) coño*** *m*, concha *f* (*LAm****) **2** (*US***) (= *buttocks*) culo** *m* Ⓑ CPD ➤ **fanny pack** (*US*) riñonera *f*

fantasize ['fæntəsaɪz] VI fantasear, hacerse ilusiones

fantastic [fæn'tæstɪk] ADJ **1** (*) (= *fabulous*) fantástico, estupendo, regio (*LAm**), macanudo (*SC**), chévere (*Col, Ven**); **you look ~!** (= *healthy*) ¡qué buen aspecto tienes!; (= *attractive*) ¡qué guapo estás! **2** (*) (= *huge*) [*amount, profit, speed*] increíble

fantastically [fæn'tæstɪkəlɪ] ADV (= *really*)] increíblemente

fantasy ['fæntəzɪ] N **1** (= *imagination*) fantasía *f*; **to live in a ~ world** *or* **in ~ land** vivir en un mundo de ensueño **2** (= *fanciful idea, wish*) fantasía *f*, sueño *m*

fanzine ['fænziːn] N fanzine *m*

FAO N ABBR (= **Food and Agriculture Organization**) OAA *f*, FAO *f*

FAQs NPL ABBR (= **frequently asked questions**) preguntas *f* frecuentes

far [fɑː'] (*compar* **~ther**, **further**; *superl* **~thest**, **furthest**)
Ⓐ ADV **1** (*distance*) (*lit, fig*) lejos; **is it ~ away?** ¿está lejos?; **is it ~ to London?** ¿hay mucho hasta Londres?; **it's not ~ (from here)** no está lejos (de aquí); **as ~ as** as hasta; **as ~ as the eye can see** hasta donde alcanza la vista; **to go as ~ as Milan** ir hasta Milán; **to come from as ~ away as Milan** venir de sitios tan lejanos como Milán; **as ~ back as I can remember** hasta donde me alcanza la memoria; **as ~ back as 1945** ya en 1945; **as ~ as possible** en lo posible; **the theory is good as ~ as it goes** la teoría es buena dentro de sus límites; **I will help you as ~ as I can** te ayudaré en lo que pueda; **as ~ as I know** que yo sepa; **as ~ as I am concerned** por lo que a mí se refiere *or* respecta; **~ away** lejos; **~ away in the distance** a lo lejos; **not ~ away** no muy lejos; **~ away from one's family** lejos de la familia; **~ from** [+ *place*] lejos de; **~ from approving it, I ...** lejos de aprobarlo, yo ...; **~ from it!** ¡todo lo contrario!, ¡ni mucho menos!; **he is ~ from well** no está nada bien; **~ be it from me to interfere, but ...** no quiero entrometerme, pero ...; **from easy** nada fácil; **to go ~:** **he'll go ~** (*fig*) llegará lejos; **it doesn't go ~ enough** (*fig*) no va bastante lejos, no tiene todo el alcance que quisiéramos; **he's gone too ~ this time** (*fig*) esta vez se ha pasado; **he's gone too ~ to back out now** (*fig*) ha ido demasiado lejos para echarse atrás *or* retirarse ahora; **it won't go ~** [*money, food*] no alcanzará mucho; **for**

a white wine you won't go ~ wrong with this si buscas un vino blanco éste ofrece bastante garantía; **how ~ is it to the river?** ¿qué distancia *or* cuánto hay de aquí al río?; **how ~ are you going?** ¿hasta dónde vas?; **how ~ have you got with your work/plans?** ¿hasta dónde has llegado en tu trabajo/tus planes?; ~ **into the night** hasta altas horas de la noche; ~ **off** lejos; ~ **off in the distance** a lo lejos; **not ~ off** no muy lejos; **Christmas is not ~ off** la Navidad no está lejos; **he's not ~ off 70** tiene casi 70 años, frisa en los 70 años; ~ **out at sea** en alta mar; **so ~ so good** por *or* hasta ahora, bien; **in so ~ as ...** en la medida en que ..., en cuanto ...; **so** *or* **thus ~ and no further** hasta aquí, pero ni un paso más; **I would go so ~ as to say that ...** me atrevería a decir que ...; **the plans are too ~ advanced** los proyectos están demasiado adelantados; ~ **and wide** por todas partes; **he wasn't ~ wrong** casi acertada, casi estaba en lo justo **2** (= *very much*) mucho; ~ **better** mucho mejor; **it is ~ better not to go** más vale que no vayamos/vayas *etc*, más vale no ir; **it's ~ and away the best** ◇ **it's by ~ the best** es con mucho el mejor; **she's the prettier by ~** es con mucho la más guapa; **this car is ~ faster (than)** este coche es mucho más rápido (que); ~ **superior to** muy superior a
Ⓑ ADJ **the ~ east** *etc* **of the country** el extremo este *etc* del país; **the ~ left/right** (*Pol*) la extrema izquierda/derecha; **at the ~ end of** en el otro extremo de, al fondo de; **on the ~ side of** en el lado opuesto de; ✦ IDIOM **it's a ~ cry from** tiene poco que ver con
Ⓒ CPD ➤ **the Far East** el Extremo *or* Lejano Oriente

faraway ['fɑːrəweɪ] ADJ remoto, lejano

farce [fɑːs] N **1** (*Theat*) farsa *f* **2** (*fig*) **this is a ~** esto es absurdo; **the trial was a ~** el proceso fue una farsa

farcical ['fɑːsɪkəl] ADJ absurdo, ridículo

fare [feə'] Ⓐ N **1** (= *cost*) precio *m*, tarifa *f*; (= *ticket*) billete *m* (*Sp*), boleto *m* (*LAm*); (*Naut*) pasaje *m*; **"fares please!"** "¡billetes por favor!" **2** (= *passenger in taxi*) pasajero/a *m/f* **3** (= *food*) comida *f* Ⓑ VI **they ~d badly/well** lo pasaron mal/bien, les fue mal/bien; **how did you ~?** ¿qué tal te fue?
Ⓒ CPD ➤ **fare dodger** (*Brit*) viajero/a *m/f* sin billete

farewell [feə'wel] Ⓐ N adiós *m*; **to bid ~ (to sb)** despedirse (de algn); **you can say ~ to your wallet** te puedes ir despidiendo de tu cartera Ⓑ EXCL (*liter*) ¡adiós! Ⓒ CPD ➤ **farewell dinner** cena *f* de despedida ➤ **farewell party** fiesta *f* de despedida

far-fetched ['fɑː'fetʃt] ADJ [*story, explanation*] inverosímil, poco probable; [*idea, scheme*] descabellado

far-flung ['fɑː'flʌŋ] ADJ (= *faraway*) remoto, lejano; (= *extensive*) extenso

farm [fɑːm] Ⓐ N granja *f*, chacra *f* (*LAm*); (*large*) hacienda *f*, finca *f*, estancia *f* (*LAm*), rancho *m* (*Mex*); [*of mink, oysters etc*] criadero *m* Ⓑ VT cultivar, labrar; **he ~s 300 acres** cultiva 300 acres Ⓒ VI (*as profession*) ser granjero; **he ~s in Devon** tiene una granja en Devon Ⓓ CPD agrícola ➤ **farm animal** animal *m* de granja ➤ **farm labourer, farm laborer** (*US*) jornalero/a *m/f* (del campo), obrero/a *m/f* agrícola ➤ **farm produce** productos *mpl* agrícolas
➤ **farm out*** VT + ADV [+ *work*] mandar hacer fuera (**to sb** a algn); (*hum*) [+ *children*] dejar (**on** a *or* con)

farmer ['fɑːmə'] N agricultor(a) *m/f*, granjero/a *m/f*, chacarero/a *m/f* (*LAm*); [*of large farm*] hacendado/a *m/f*, estanciero/a *m/f* (*LAm*), ranchero/a *m/f* (*Mex*)

farmhand ['fɑːmhænd] N obrero/a *m/f* agrícola, jornalero/a *m/f* (del campo)

farmhouse ['fɑːmhaus] N alquería *f*, casa *f* de labranza, caserío *m* (*Sp*), casa *f* grande (*LAm*), casa *f* de hacienda (*LAm*)

farming ['fɑːmɪŋ] Ⓐ N (*gen*) agricultura *f*; [*of land*] cultivo *m*; [*of animals*] cría *f* Ⓑ CPD agrícola ➤ **the farming community** los agricultores ➤ **farming methods** métodos *mpl* de cultivo

farmland ['fɑːmlænd] N tierras *fpl* de labranza *or* cultivo

farmyard ['fɑːmjɑːd] N corral *m*

Faroe Islands ['fεərəʊ,aɪləndz], **Faroes** ['fεərəʊz] NPL Islas *fpl* Feroe

far-off ['fɑːr'ɒf] ADJ lejano, remoto

far-out [,fɑː'raʊt] ADJ **1** (= *odd*) raro, extraño; (= *zany*) estrafalario **2** (= *superb*) fenomenal*, guay (*Sp**)

far-reaching ['fɑːˈriːtʃɪŋ] ADJ [*effect*] transcendental, de gran alcance

far-sighted ['fɑːˈsaɪtɪd] ADJ **1** (*US Med*) hipermétrope **2** (*fig*) [*person*] clarividente; [*plan, decision, measure*] con visión de futuro

fart** [fɑːt] **(A)** N **1** pedo** *m* **2 he's a boring old ~** es un pelmazo* **(B)** VI tirarse *or* echarse un pedo** ➤ **fart about***, **fart around*** VI + ADV perder el tiempo

farther ['fɑːðəʳ] **(A)** ADV = **further** **(B)** ADJ COMPAR *of* **far**; **she was sitting at the ~ end of the bar** estaba sentada al otro extremo de la barra; **on the ~ side of the lake** al otro lado del lago, en la otra orilla del lago

farthest ['fɑːðɪst] SUPERL *of* **far**; *see* **furthest**

fascia ['feɪʃə] N **1** (*Brit Aut*) salpicadero *m* **2** [*of mobile phone*] carcasa *f*

fascinate ['fæsɪneɪt] VT fascinar; **it ~s me how/why ...** me maravilla cómo/por qué ...

fascinated ['fæsɪneɪtɪd] ADJ fascinado; **to be ~ with sth** estar fascinado por algo

fascinating ['fæsɪneɪtɪŋ] ADJ fascinante

fascination [ˌfæsɪˈneɪʃən] N fascinación *f*; **his ~ with the cinema** su fascinación por el cine

fascism ['fæʃɪzəm] N fascismo *m*

fascist ['fæʃɪst] ADJ, N fascista *mf*

fashion ['fæʃən] **(A)** N **1** (= *manner*) manera *f*, modo *m*; **after a ~** así así, más o menos; **I play the ~** toco algo; **in his usual ~** a su manera *or* modo; **in the Greek ~** a la griega, al estilo griego
2 (= *latest clothes, ideas*) moda *f*; **it's all the ~ now** ahora está muy de moda; **it's no longer the ~** ya no está de moda; **to be in/out of ~** estar de moda/pasado de moda; **to come into/go out of ~** ponerse de/pasar de moda; **the latest ~** la última moda; **women's/men's ~s** moda para la mujer/el hombre **(B)** VT (= *shape*) formar; (= *make*) fabricar **(C)** CPD ➤ **fashion designer** modisto/a *m/f*, diseñador(a) *m/f* de modas ➤ **fashion editor** director(a) *m/f* de revista de modas ➤ **fashion house** casa *f* de modas ➤ **fashion magazine** revista *f* de modas ➤ **fashion model** modelo *mf* ➤ **fashion plate** figurín *m* de moda ➤ **fashion show** desfile *m or* pase *m* de modelos ➤ **fashion victim** esclavo/a *m/f* de la moda

fashionable ['fæʃnəbl] ADJ **1** [*dress etc*] de moda, moderno, a la moda; [*place, restaurant*] de moda; **~ people** gente *f* elegante, gente *f* guapa*; **in ~ society** en la buena sociedad; **it is ~ to do ...** está de moda hacer ...
2 (= *popular*) [*writer, subject for discussion*] de moda, popular

fashionably ['fæʃnəblɪ] ADV **to be ~ dressed** ir vestido a la moda

fashion-conscious ['fæʃənˌkɒnʃəs] ADJ pendiente de la moda

fast¹ [fɑːst] **(A)** ADJ (*compar* **-er**; *superl* **-est**) **1** (= *speedy*) rápido; **he's a ~ worker** trabaja muy rápido, trabaja a muy buen ritmo; ✦ IDIOM **to pull a ~ one on sb*** jugar una mala pasada a algn
2 [*clock*] adelantado; **my watch is five minutes ~** mi reloj está *or* va cinco minutos adelantado
3 [*colour, dye*] que no destiñe **(B)** ADV **1** (= *quickly*) rápidamente, deprisa; **as ~ as I can** lo más rápido posible; **he ran off as ~ as his legs would carry him** se fue corriendo a toda velocidad; **how ~ can you type?** ¿a qué velocidad escribes a máquina?; **don't speak so ~** habla más despacio; **~er!** ¡más (rápido)!; **not so ~!*** (*interrupting*) ¡un momento!
2 (= *firmly*) **~ asleep** profundamente dormido; **to stand ~** mantenerse firme; **to be stuck ~ in the mud** quedar atascado en el lodo **(C)** CPD ➤ **fast breeder reactor** autogenerador *m* ➤ **fast food** comida *f* rápida, platos *mpl* preparados ➤ **fast food restaurant** establecimiento *m or* restaurante *m* de comida rápida; (*selling hamburgers*) hamburguesería *f* ➤ **fast track** vía *f* rápida

fast² [fɑːst] VI ayunar

fasten ['fɑːsn] **(A)** VT (= *secure*) [+ *belt, dress, seat belt*] abrochar; [+ *door, box, window*] cerrar; (*with rope*) atar; (*with paste*) pegar; (*with bolt*) echar el cerrojo a; **to ~ two things**

together pegar/sujetar dos cosas **(B)** VI [*door, box*] cerrarse; [*dress*] abrocharse; **it ~s in front** se abrocha por delante ➤ **fasten up** **(A)** VT + ADV abrochar **(B)** VI + ADV abrocharse; **it ~s up in front** se abrocha por delante

fastener ['fɑːsnəʳ] N [*of necklace, bag, box*] cierre *m*; (*on dress*) corchete *m*; (= *zip fastener*) cremallera *f*

fast forward ['fɑːstˈfɔːwəd] **(A)** N (*also* ~ **button**) botón *m* de avance rápido **(B)** VT pasar para delante, adelantar **(C)** VI avanzar rápidamente

fastidious [fæsˈtɪdɪəs] ADJ [*person*] (*about cleanliness etc*) escrupuloso; (= *touchy*) quisquilloso; [*taste*] fino

fast-moving [ˌfɑːstˈmuːvɪŋ] ADJ rápido, veloz

fast-track ['fɑːstræk] ADJ rápido, por la vía rápida

fat [fæt] **(A)** ADJ (*compar* **~ter**; *superl* **~test**) **1** (= *plump*) [*person*] gordo; [*face, cheeks, limbs*] relleno, gordo; **to get ~** engordar; **he grew ~ on the proceeds** *or* **profits** (*fig*) se enriqueció con los beneficios
2 (= *fatty*) [*meat, pork*] graso
3 (= *thick*) [*book*] grueso
4 (= *substantial*) [*profit*] grande, pingüe; [*salary*] muy elevado, muy alto; **a ~ cheque** un cheque muy cuantioso
5 (*) (= *minimal*) **~ chance!** ¡ni soñarlo!; **a ~ lot he knows about it!** ¡qué sabrá él!; **a ~ lot of good that is!** ¡eso no sirve de nada!, y eso ¿de qué sirve? **(B)** N (*on person, in food*) grasa *f*; (*for cooking*) manteca *f*; **animal/vegetable ~s** grasas *fpl* animales/vegetales; ✦ IDIOM **to live off the ~ of the land** vivir a cuerpo de rey **(C)** CPD ➤ **fat cat*** pez *m* gordo*

fatal ['feɪtl] ADJ [*accident, injury*] mortal **2** (= *disastrous*) [*mistake*] fatal; [*consequences*] funesto (**to** para)

fatalism ['feɪtəlɪzəm] N fatalismo *m*

fatalist ['feɪtəlɪst] N fatalista *mf*

fatalistic [ˌfeɪtəˈlɪstɪk] ADJ fatalista

fatality [fəˈtælɪtɪ] N **1** (= *death*) muerte *f* **2** (= *victim*) muerto/a *m/f*, víctima *f*; **luckily there were no fatalities** por fortuna no hubo víctimas

fatally ['feɪtəlɪ] ADV mortalmente; **~ wounded** herido mortalmente *or* de muerte

fate [feɪt] N (= *destiny*) destino *m*; **to leave sb to his ~** abandonar a algn a su suerte

fated ['feɪtɪd] ADJ **to be ~ to do sth** estar predestinado a hacer algo; **it was ~ that ...** era inevitable que ...

fateful ['feɪtfʊl] ADJ [*day, event*] fatídico; [*words*] profético

fat-free ['fætfriː] ADJ [*diet, food*] sin grasa

fathead ['fæthed] N imbécil *mf*; **you ~!** ¡imbécil!

father ['fɑːðəʳ] **(A)** N **1** (*gen*) padre *m*; **my ~ and mother** mis padres; ✦ PROV **like ~, like son** de tal palo, tal astilla **2 Our Father** (*Rel*) Padre Nuestro **3 Father Brown** (*Rel*) (el) padre Brown **(B)** VT [+ *child*] engendrar **(C)** CPD ➤ **Father Christmas** (*Brit*) Papá *m* Noel ➤ **Father's Day** Día *m* del Padre

fatherhood ['fɑːðəhʊd] N paternidad *f*

father-in-law ['fɑːðərɪnlɔː] N (*pl* **fathers-in-law**) suegro *m*

fatherland ['fɑːðəlænd] N patria *f*

fatherless ['fɑːðəlɪs] ADJ huérfano de padre

fatherly ['fɑːðəlɪ] ADJ paternal

fathom ['fæðəm] **(A)** N braza *f* **(B)** VT (*fig*) (*also* ~ **out**) descifrar, llegar a entender; [+ *mystery*] desentrañar; **I can't ~ it out at all** no lo entiendo en absoluto

fatigue [fəˈtiːg] N (= *weariness*) cansancio *m*, fatiga *f*

fatness ['fætnɪs] N [*of person*] gordura *f*

fatten ['fætn] VT (*also* ~ **up**) cebar, engordar

fattening ['fætnɪŋ] ADJ [*food*] que hace engordar; **chocolate is ~** el chocolate engorda

fatty ['fætɪ] ADJ (*compar* **fattier**; *superl* **fattiest**) [*food*] graso; (*Anat*) [*tissue*] adiposo ➤ **fatty acid** ácido *m* graso

fatuous ['fætjʊəs] ADJ [*remark*] necio, fatuo; [*smile*] tonto

fatwa ['fætwə] N fatwa *f*

faucet ['fɔːsɪt] N (*US*) grifo *m* (*esp Sp*), llave *f* (*LAm*), canilla *f* (*esp RPl*)

fault [fɔːlt] **(A)** N **1** (= *defect*) (*in character*) defecto *m*; (*in*

manufacture) defecto *m*, falla *f* (*LAm*); (*in machine*) avería *f*; **with all his ~s** con todos sus defectos; **generous to a ~** excesivamente generoso; **to find ~ with sth/sb** criticar algo/a algn
2 (= *blame, responsibility*) culpa *f*; **it's all your ~** tú tienes toda la culpa; **it's not my ~** no es culpa mía; **your memory is at ~** no te acuerdas bien; **through no ~ of his own** sin falta alguna de su parte; **whose ~ is it (if ...)?** ¿quién tiene la culpa (si ...)?
3 (*Tennis, Geol*) falta *f*
B VT criticar; **it cannot be ~ed** es intachable; **you cannot ~ him on spelling** su ortografía es impecable

fault-finding [ˈfɔːltˌfaɪndɪŋ] N manía *f* de criticar

faultless [ˈfɔːltlɪs] ADJ [*person, behaviour*] intachable, impecable; [*appearance, clothing, logic*] impecable; [*work, performance*] perfecto; **Hans's English was ~** Hans hablaba un inglés perfecto

faulty [ˈfɔːltɪ] ADJ (*compar* **faultier**; *superl* **faultiest**)
1 [*machine etc*] defectuoso **2** (= *imperfect*) [*reasoning, argument etc*] imperfecto

faun [fɔːn] N fauno *m*

fauna [ˈfɔːnə] N fauna *f*

faux pas [ˈfəʊˈpɑː] N metedura *f* or (*LAm*) metida *f* de pata*

fava bean [ˈfɑːvəbiːn] N (*US*) haba *f*

> Use **el/un** not **la/una** before feminine nouns beginning with stressed **a** or **ha** like **haba**.

favour, favor (*US*) [ˈfeɪvər] **A** N **1** (= *kindness*) favor *m*; **I don't expect any ~s in return** no espero que me devuelvas/devuelvan *etc* el favor; **he did it as a ~ (to me)** (me) lo hizo como un favor; **to ask sb a ~** pedir un favor a algn; **to do sb a ~** hacer un favor a algn; **do me a ~!*** (*iro*) ¡haz el favor!; **do yourself a ~ and get a haircut** si te cortas el pelo te harás un favor
2 (= *approval*) **to find ~ with sb** [*person*] ganarse la aceptación de algn; [*suggestion*] tener buena acogida por parte de algn, ser bien acogido por algn; **to gain ~ with sb** ganarse la aceptación de algn; **to be in ~ of (doing) sth** estar a favor de (hacer) algo, ser partidario de (hacer) algo; **the result of the vote was 111 in ~ and 25 against** el resultado de la votación fue 111 votos a favor y 25 en contra; **the court found in their ~** el tribunal falló a *or* en su favor; **to fall out of ~** [*person*] caer en desgracia; [*product, style*] perder aceptación
3 favours (*euph*) (*sexual*) favores *mpl*
B VT **1** (= *support*) [+ *idea, scheme, view*] estar a favor de, ser partidario de
2 (= *be beneficial to*) favorecer
3 (= *prefer*) preferir
4 (= *honour*) **to ~ sb with sth** honrar a algn con algo; **he eventually ~ed us with a visit** (*hum*) por fin nos honró con su visita, por fin se dignó a visitarnos

favourable, favorable (*US*) [ˈfeɪvərəbl] ADJ [*report*] favorable (**to** para); [*conditions, weather*] propicio, favorable; **to show sb in a ~ light** dar una buena imagen de algn

favourably, favorably (*US*) [ˈfeɪvərəblɪ] ADV favorablemente

favourite, favorite (*US*) [ˈfeɪvərɪt] **A** ADJ favorito, preferido **B** N **1** (= *object*) favorito/a *m/f*; (= *person*) preferido/a *m/f*, favorito/a *m/f*; (*spoilt*) consentido/a *m/f*; (*at court*) valido *m*, privado *m*; (= *mistress*) querida *f*; **he sang some old ~s** cantó algunas de las viejas y conocidas canciones **2** (*in race, contest, election*) favorito/a *m/f*

favouritism, favoritism (*US*) [ˈfeɪvərɪtɪzəm] N favoritismo *m*

fawn[1] [fɔːn] **A** N (= *animal*) cervato *m* **B** ADJ de color pardo claro

fawn[2] [fɔːn] VI **to ~ (up)on sb** [*person*] adular *or* lisonjear a algn

fax [fæks] **A** N (= *document*) fax *m*; (= *machine*) fax *m*, telefax *m* **B** VT mandar por fax **C** CPD ➤ **fax machine** (máquina *f* or aparato *m* de) fax *m* ➤ **fax message** fax *m* ➤ **fax number** número *m* de (tele)fax

faze* [feɪz] VT perturbar, desconcertar

fazed* [feɪzd] ADJ pasmado, anonadado

FBI N ABBR (*US*) (= **Federal Bureau of Investigation**) ≈ BIC *f*

FC N ABBR (= **football club**) C. F. *m*

FCC N ABBR (*US*) (= **Federal Communications Commission**)

FCO N ABBR (*Brit*) (= **Foreign and Commonwealth Office**) ≈ Min. de AA.EE.

FD N ABBR (*US*) (= **Fire Department**)

FDA N ABBR (*US*) (= **Food and Drug Administration**) *organismo que fija niveles de calidad de los productos alimentarios y farmacéuticos*

FDD N ABBR (*Comput*) = **floppy disk drive**

FDIC N ABBR (*US*) = **Federal Deposit Insurance Corporation**

FE ABBR = **Further Education**

fear [fɪər] **A** N **1** (= *terror*) miedo *m*; **he has overcome his ~ of dogs** ha superado su miedo a los perros; **to be in ~ of or for one's life** temer por su propia vida; **she lives in ~ of being found out** vive atemorizada de que la descubran; **to have no ~** no tener ningún miedo; **~ of heights** miedo *m* a las alturas; **~ of flying** miedo *m* al avión; **she was trembling with ~** estaba temblando de miedo; **without ~ or favour** con imparcialidad, imparcialmente; ✦ IDIOM **to put the ~ of God into sb** meter el miedo en el cuerpo a algn
2 (= *worry*) temor *m*; **his worst ~s were confirmed** sus mayores temores se vieron confirmados; **there are ~s that ...** se teme que ... + *subjun*; **I didn't go in for ~ of disturbing them** no entré por temor *or* miedo a molestarlos; **she never goes out for ~ that it will happen again** nunca sale por temor *or* miedo a que suceda de nuevo; **have no ~!** (*freq hum*) (= *don't worry*) ¡no se preocupe!
3 (= *chance*) posibilidad *f*; (= *danger*) peligro *m*; **there's no ~ of that!** ¡no hay peligro de eso!; **no ~!** (*Brit**) ¡ni hablar!
B VT **1** (= *be afraid of*) temer, tener miedo a; **to ~ that** temer que + *subjun*; **two people are missing and ~ed dead** hay dos personas desaparecidas y se teme que hayan muerto; **to ~ the worst** temer(se) lo peor
2 (= *think regretfully*) temerse; **to ~ that** temerse que; **I ~ that he won't come** me temo que no vendrá; **I ~ that you are right** me temo que tiene razón; **I ~ you may be right** me temo que tenga razón; **I ~ so/not** me temo que sí/no
C VI temer; **to ~ for sth/sb** temer por algo/algn; **she ~ed for her life** temía por su vida; **never ~** no hay cuidado*

fearful [ˈfɪəfʊl] ADJ **1** (= *frightened*) temeroso (**of** de); **to be ~ that** tener miedo de que + *subjun* **2** (= *frightening*) espantoso **3** (†*) (= *awful*) horrible

fearless [ˈfɪəlɪs] ADJ (= *courageous*) valiente; (= *daring*) audaz; (= *adventurous*) intrépido; **she is completely ~** no le tiene miedo a nada

fearsome [ˈfɪəsəm] ADJ [*opponent, reputation*] temible

feasibility [ˌfiːzəˈbɪlɪtɪ] N viabilidad *f*; **to doubt the ~ of a scheme** poner en duda la viabilidad de un proyecto, dudar si un proyecto es factible ➤ **feasibility study** estudio *m* de viabilidad

feasible [ˈfiːzəbl] ADJ [*plan, suggestion*] factible, viable; **to make sth ~** posibilitar algo

feast [fiːst] **A** N **1** (= *meal*) banquete *m*; (*) (= *big meal*) comilona* *f*, tragadera *f* (*Mex**) **2** (*Rel*) fiesta *f* **B** VI darse un banquete; **to ~ on sth** darse un banquete con algo **C** CPD ➤ **feast day** fiesta *f*, día *m* festivo

feat [fiːt] N hazaña *f*, proeza *f*

feather ['feðəʳ] Ⓐ N pluma *f*; ✦ IDIOMS **that is a ~ in his cap** es un tanto que se apunta; **you could have knocked me down with a ~*** me quedé de piedra; **as light as a ~** (tan) ligero como una pluma Ⓑ VT ✦ IDIOM **to ~ one's nest** hacer su agosto Ⓒ CPD [*mattress, pillow*] de plumas ➤ **feather duster** plumero *m*

featherbrained ['feðəbreɪnd] ADJ [*idea*] disparatado, descabellado; **to be ~** [*person*] ser un/una cabeza de chorlito*

featherweight ['feðəweɪt] N (*Boxing*) peso *m* pluma ➤ **featherweight champion** campeón/ona *m/f* de peso pluma

feature ['fi:tʃəʳ] Ⓐ N **1** [*of face*] rasgo *m*; **~s** rasgos *mpl*, facciones *fpl*
2 (= *characteristic*) [*of countryside, building*] característica *f*; [*of product*] característica *f*, elemento *m*
3 (*Cine*) película *f*
4 (*Press*) artículo *m* de fondo; **a regular ~** una crónica regular
Ⓑ VT **1** [+ *actor, news*] presentar; (*in paper etc*) presentar; **a film featuring Garbo as ...** una película que presenta a la Garbo en el papel de ...
2 (= *be equipped with*) [*machine*] estar provisto de, ofrecer
Ⓒ VI **1** (*gen*) **it ~d prominently in ...** tuvo un papel destacado en ...
2 (*Cine*) figurar, aparecer (**in** en)
Ⓓ CPD ➤ **feature article** artículo *m* de fondo ➤ **feature film** (película *f* de) largometraje *m* ➤ **feature writer** articulista *mf*, cronista *mf*

featureless ['fi:tʃəlɪs] ADJ monótono, anodino

Feb. ABBR (= **February**) feb.

February ['februərɪ] N febrero *m*; *see* **July**

feces ['fi:si:z] NPL (*US*) = **faeces**

feckless ['feklɪs] ADJ (= *weak*) débil, incapaz; (= *irresponsible*) irresponsable

fecund ['fi:kənd] ADJ fecundo

Fed [fed] N ABBR (*US**) (= **federal officer**) federal* *mf*

fed [fed] PT, PP *of* **feed**

federal ['fedərəl] Ⓐ ADJ federal Ⓑ N (*US Hist*) federal *mf*
Ⓒ CPD ➤ **Federal Bureau** (*US*) Departamento *m* de Estado ➤ **Federal Bureau of Investigation** (*US*) FBI *m*, ≈ Brigada *f* de Investigación Criminal ➤ **federal holiday** (*US*) fiesta *f* nacional (*en EEUU*) ➤ **federal officer** (*US*) federal *mf* ➤ **Federal Republic of Germany** República *f* Federal de Alemania ➤ **Federal Reserve Bank** (*US*) banco *m* de la Reserva Federal

federalism ['fedərəlɪzəm] N federalismo *m*

federalist ['fedərəlɪst] ADJ, N federalista *mf*

federation [fedə'reɪʃən] N federación *f*

fed up* [fed'ʌp] ADJ harto; **to be ~ (with sth/sb)** estar harto (de algo/algn); **to be ~ with doing sth** estar harto de hacer algo

fee [fi:] N (= *professional*) honorarios *mpl*, emolumentos *mpl*; (*Comm*) pago *m*; (*for doctor's visit*) precio *m* de visita; **course/tuition/school ~s** matrícula *fsing*; **what's your ~?** ¿cuánto cobra Vd?; **for a small ~** por una pequeña *or* módica cantidad

feeble ['fi:bl] ADJ (*compar* **~r**; *superl* **~st**) **1** (= *weak*) [*person, cry*] débil; [*smile, laugh*] lánguido, débil **2** (= *poor*) [*effort, resistance*] débil; [*excuse, argument*] poco convincente, flojo; [*joke*] soso

feeble-minded ['fi:bl'maɪndɪd] ADJ bobo, zonzo (*LAm*)

feebly ['fi:blɪ] ADV [*struggle*] débilmente; [*laugh*] lánguidamente, débilmente; [*shine*] tenuemente

feed [fi:d] (*vb: pt, pp* **fed**) Ⓐ VT **1** (*with food*) [+ *person, animal*] dar de comer a; [+ *baby*] (= *bottle-feed*) dar el biberón a; (= *breastfeed*) dar de mamar a, dar el pecho a; [+ *plant*] alimentar; **"(please) do not feed the animals"** "prohibido dar de comer a los animales"; **you've made enough food to ~ an army** has hecho comida para un regimiento; **he has just started ~ing himself** acaba de empezar a comer solo; **now there was another mouth to ~** ahora había que dar de comer a una boca más, ahora había una boca más que alimentar; **to ~ sth to sb** dar algo (de comer) a algn; **they have been fed a diet of cartoons**

and computer games los han tenido a base de dibujos animados y juegos de ordenador
2 (= *supply*) suministrar; **he stole money to ~ his drug habit** robaba dinero para costear su drogadicción
3 (= *insert*) **to ~ data into a computer** meter *or* introducir datos en un ordenador
4 (= *fuel*) [+ *fire, emotion, feeling*] alimentar; **to ~ the flames** (*lit, fig*) echar leña al fuego
Ⓑ VI (= *take food*) comer; (*at breast*) mamar; **to ~ on sth** alimentarse de algo
Ⓒ N (= *food*) (*for animal*) forraje *m*, pienso *m*; **the six o'clock ~** (= *breast or bottle feed*) la toma de las seis; (= *baby food*) la papilla de las seis; **it's time for his ~** le toca comer ➤ **feed back** VT + ADV [+ *information, results*] proporcionar, facilitar ➤ **feed in** VT + ADV [+ *coins, paper*] meter, introducir; (*Comput*) [+ *data*] meter, introducir ➤ **feed up** VT + ADV [+ *person*] engordar; [+ *animal*] cebar, engordar

feedback ['fi:dbæk] N reacción *f*; **we're not getting much ~** no nos tienen demasiado informados de cómo vamos

feeder ['fi:dəʳ] N (*Mech*) alimentador *m*, tubo *m* de alimentación; (= *device*) (*for birds etc*) comedero *m* ➤ **feeder (primary) school** (*Brit*) escuela *primaria que envía alumnos a un determinado colegio de enseñanza secundaria*

feeding ['fi:dɪŋ] N (= *act*) alimentación *f*; (= *meals*) comida *f* ➤ **feeding bottle** (*esp Brit*) biberón *m* ➤ **feeding frenzy**: **she was caught in a media ~ frenzy** se vio convertida en el centro de una atención febril por parte de los medios de comunicación ➤ **feeding time** (*at zoo*) hora *f* de comer; (*baby's*) (= *time for breast feed*) hora *f* del pecho; (= *time for bottle feed*) hora *f* del biberón

feel [fi:l] (*vb: pt, pp* **felt**) Ⓐ VT **1** (= *touch*) tocar, palpar; [+ *pulse*] tomar; **I'm still ~ing my way** todavía me estoy familiarizando con la situación/el trabajo *etc*
2 (= *be aware of*) [+ *blow, pain, heat*] sentir; [+ *responsibility*] ser consciente de; **I felt something move** sentí que algo se movía; **I felt it getting hot** sentí que se iba calentando
3 (= *experience*) [+ *pity, anger, grief*] sentir; **the consequences will be felt next year** las consecuencias se harán sentir el año próximo; **they are beginning to ~ the effects of the trade sanctions** están empezando a sentir *or* notar los efectos de las sanciones económicas; **I felt myself blush** noté que me estaba sonrojando
4 (= *be affected by, suffer from*) ser sensible a; **he doesn't ~ the cold** no es sensible al frío
5 (= *think, believe*) **what do you ~ about it?** ¿qué te parece a ti?; **I ~ that you ought to do it** creo que deberías hacerlo; **I ~ strongly that we should accept their offer** me parece muy importante que aceptemos su oferta; **he felt it necessary to point out that ...** creyó *or* le pareció necesario señalar que ...
Ⓑ VI **1** (*physically*) sentirse, encontrarse; **how do you ~ now?** ¿qué tal *or* cómo te sientes *or* te encuentras ahora?; **to ~ cold/hungry/sleepy** tener frío/hambre/sueño; **I ~ much better** me siento *or* me encuentro mucho mejor; **she's not ~ing quite herself** no se encuentra del todo bien; **to ~ ill/old** sentirse mal/viejo; **do you ~ sick?** ¿estás mareado?; **I ~ quite tired** me siento bastante cansado; **I don't ~ up to a walk just now*** ahora mismo no me encuentro con fuerzas para dar un paseo
2 (*mentally*) **how does it ~ to go hungry?** ¿cómo se siente uno pasando hambre?; **how do you ~ about him/the idea?** ¿qué te parece él/la idea?; **he ~s bad about leaving his wife alone** siente haber dejado sola a su mujer; **I ~ for you!** ¡lo siento por ti!, ¡te compadezco!; **since you ~ so strongly about it ...** ya que te parece tan importante ...; **I ~ sure that ...** estoy seguro de que ...
3 to ~ like 3.1 it ~s like silk parece seda al tocarlo; **I felt like a new man/woman** me sentí como un hombre nuevo/una mujer nueva **3.2** (= *want*) **do you ~ like a walk?** ¿quieres dar un paseo?, ¿te apetece dar un paseo?; **I go out whenever I ~ like it** salgo cuando me apetece *or* cuando quiero; **I don't ~ like going out now** no tengo ganas de salir ahora
4 (= *give impression*) **it ~s colder out here** se siente más frío aquí fuera; **the house ~s damp** la casa parece húmeda; **to ~ hard/cold/damp** *etc* (*to the touch*) ser duro/frío/húmedo *etc* al tacto

5 (*also* ~ **around**) (= *grope*) tantear, ir a tientas; **to ~ around in the dark** ir a tientas *or* tantear en la oscuridad; **she felt in her pocket for her keys** rebuscó en el bolsillo para encontrar las llaves
◉ N **1** (= *sensation*) sensación *f*; **she liked the ~ of the breeze on her face** le gustaba sentir la brisa en la cara; **to know sth by the ~ of it** reconocer algo por el tacto
2 (= *sense of touch*) tacto *m*
3 (= *impression, atmosphere*) ambiente *m*, aspecto *m*; **the room has a cosy ~** la habitación tiene un ambiente acogedor; **to get the ~ of** [+ *new job, place*] ambientarse a, familiarizarse con; [+ *new car, machine*] familiarizarse con; **to have a ~ for languages/music** tener talento para los idiomas/la música
➤ **feel out*** VT + ADV (= *sound out*) tantear

feeler ['fi:lə'] N [*of insect, snail*] antena *f*; ◆ IDIOM **to put out ~s** hacer un sondeo

feelgood ['fi:lgʊd] ADJ **the ~ factor** la sensación de bienestar; **a ~ movie** una película que te hace sentir bien

feeling ['fi:lɪŋ] N **1** (*physical*) sensación *f*; **a cold ~** una sensación de frío; **to have no ~ in one's arm** no sentir un brazo
2 (= *emotion*) sentimiento *m*; **bad** *or* **ill ~** rencor *m*, hostilidad *f*; **to speak/sing with ~** hablar/cantar con sentimiento
3 **feelings** sentimientos *mpl*; **to appeal to sb's finer ~s** apelar a los sentimientos nobles de algn; **no hard ~s!** ¡todo olvidado!; **to hurt sb's ~s** herir los sentimientos de algn, ofender a algn; **you can imagine my ~s!** ¡ya te puedes imaginar cómo me sentía!; **~s ran high about it** causó mucha controversia; **to relieve one's ~s** desahogarse; **to spare sb's ~s** no herir los sentimientos de algn
4 (= *impression*) impresión *f*, sensación *f*; **I have a (funny) ~ that ...** tengo la (extraña) sensación de que ...; **I get the ~ that ...** me da la impresión de que ...
5 (= *opinion*) opinión *f*; **what are your ~s about the matter?** ¿qué opinas tú del asunto?; **my ~ is that ...** creo que ...
6 (= *sensitivity*) sensibilidad *f*

fee-paying ['fi:peɪɪŋ] ADJ [*pupil*] que paga pensión ➤ **fee-paying school** colegio *m* de pago

feet [fi:t] NPL *of* **foot**

feign [feɪn] VT [+ *surprise, indifference*] fingir; **to ~ madness/sleep/death** fingirse loco/dormido/muerto; **to ~ not to know** fingir no saber

feint [feɪnt] **◉** N (*Boxing, Fencing*) finta *f* **◉** VI fintar

feisty* ['faɪstɪ] ADJ (*compar* **feistier**; *superl* **feistiest**) (*esp US*) (= *lively*) animado; (= *quarrelsome*) pendenciero

felicitate [fɪ'lɪsɪteɪt] VT felicitar, congratular

feline ['fi:laɪn] **◉** ADJ felino **◉** N felino *m*

fell¹ [fel] PT *of* **fall**

fell² [fel] VT (*with a blow*) derribar; [+ *tree*] talar, cortar

fell³ [fel] N (*Brit*) (= *moorland*) páramo *m*, brezal *m*; (= *hill*) colina *f* rocosa

fellow ['feləʊ] **◉** N **1** (= *chap*) hombre *m*, tipo* *m*, tío *m* (*Sp**); **he's an odd ~** es un tipo raro; **my dear ~!** ¡hombre!; **nice ~** buen chico *m*, buena persona *f*; **old ~** viejo *m*; **poor ~!** ¡pobrecito!
2 (= *comrade*) compañero *m*
3 [*of association, society etc*] socio/a *m/f*
4 (*Brit Univ etc*) miembro *m* de la junta de gobierno de un colegio universitario
◉ CPD ➤ **fellow being** prójimo *m* ➤ **fellow citizen** conciudadano/a *m/f* ➤ **fellow countryman/-woman** compatriota *mf* ➤ **fellow creature** prójimo *m* ➤ **fellow feeling** compañerismo *m* ➤ **fellow member** consocio/a *m/f* ➤ **fellow men** prójimos *mpl*, semejantes *mpl* ➤ **fellow passenger** compañero/a *m/f* de viaje ➤ **fellow student** compañero/a *m/f* de clase *or* curso

fellowship ['feləʊʃɪp] N **1** (= *companionship*) compañerismo *m* **2** (= *society*) asociación *f* **3** (*Brit Univ*) (= *post*) puesto *m* de becario (de investigación); (*US Univ*) (= *grant*) beca *f* de investigación

felon ['felən] N (*Jur*) criminal *mf*, delincuente *mf* (de mayor cuantía)

felony ['felənɪ] N (*Jur*) crimen *m*, delito *m* grave

felt¹ [felt] PT, PP *of* **feel**

felt² [felt] N fieltro *m* ➤ **felt hat** sombrero *m* de fieltro

felt-tip ['felttɪp] N (*also* ~ **pen**) rotulador *m*

female ['fi:meɪl] **◉** ADJ **1** [*animal, plant*] hembra
2 [*population*] femenino; [*vote*] de las mujeres; [*subject*] del sexo femenino; **a ~ friend** una amiga; **the ~ sex** el sexo femenino; **a ~ student** una estudiante; **a ~ voice** una voz de mujer **◉** N (= *animal*) hembra *f*; (= *woman*) mujer *f*; (*hum*) fémina *f*

Femidom® ['femɪdɒm] N Femidón® *m*

feminine ['femɪnɪn] **◉** ADJ femenino **◉** N (*Gram*) femenino *m*; **in the ~** en femenino

femininity [femɪ'nɪnɪtɪ] N feminidad *f*

feminism ['femɪnɪzəm] N feminismo *m*

feminist ['femɪnɪst] ADJ, N feminista *mf*

femme fatale [ˌfæmfə'tɑːl] N mujer *f* fatal

femur ['fi:mə'] N fémur *m*

fence [fens] **◉** N **1** (*gen*) valla *f*, cerca *f*; (= *wire fence*) alambrada *f*; (*Racing*) valla *f*; ◆ IDIOM **to sit on the ~** no comprometerse, mirar los toros desde la barrera **2** (*) (= *receiver of stolen goods*) perista *mf* **◉** VI (*Sport*) practicar esgrima
➤ **fence in** VT + ADV [+ *animals, fig*] encerrar; [+ *land*] vallar, cercar
➤ **fence off** VT + ADV separar con una valla *or* cerca

fencing ['fensɪŋ] N (*Sport*) esgrima *f* ➤ **fencing master** maestro *m* de esgrima ➤ **fencing match** encuentro *m* de esgrima

fend [fend] VI **to ~ for o.s.** defenderse solo, arreglárselas por cuenta propia
➤ **fend off** VT + ADV [+ *attack*] repeler, rechazar; [+ *assailant*] repeler; [+ *blow*] desviar, esquivar; [+ *question*] soslayar, eludir

fender ['fendə'] N (*US Aut*) guardabarros *m inv*, guardafango *m* (*LAm*), salpicadera *f* (*Mex*), tapabarro *m* (*Per*)

fennel ['fenl] N hinojo *m*

ferment [fə'ment] VI fermentar

fermentation [fɜːmen'teɪʃən] N fermentación *f*

fern [fɜːn] N helecho *m*

ferocious [fə'rəʊʃəs] ADJ [*animal*] fiero, feroz; [*attack*] feroz

ferociously [fə'rəʊʃəslɪ] ADV [*bark, glare*] ferozmente, con ferocidad; [*fight, attack*] ferozmente

ferocity [fə'rɒsɪtɪ] N ferocidad *f*

ferret ['ferɪt] **◉** N hurón *m* **◉** VI cazar con hurones
➤ **ferret about*, ferret around*** VI + ADV (*Brit*) hurgar (**in** en)
➤ **ferret out** VT + ADV [+ *person*] dar con; [+ *secret, truth*] desentrañar

Ferris wheel ['ferɪswiːl] N (*US*) noria *f* (*Sp*), rueda *f* de la fortuna (*Mex*), rueda *f* gigante (*Chi*)

ferrous ['ferəs] ADJ ferroso

ferry ['ferɪ] **◉** N (*also* ~ **boat**) barca *f* (de pasaje); (*large*) (*for cars etc*) transbordador *m*, ferry *m* **◉** VT **to ~ sth/sb across** *or* **over** llevar algo/a algn a la otra orilla

ferryman ['ferɪmən] N (*pl* **ferrymen**) barquero *m*

fertile ['fɜːtaɪl] ADJ **1** [*land, soil, person, phase*] fértil; [*egg*] fértil, fecundo **2** (= *creative*) [*period*] fértil; [*imagination, mind*] fecundo, fértil; **a ~ breeding ground for racists** un caldo de cultivo propicio para el racismo, un buen caldo de cultivo para el racismo

fertility [fə'tɪlɪtɪ] N fertilidad *f* ➤ **fertility drug** medicamento *m* para el tratamiento de la infertilidad

fertilization [ˌfɜːtɪlaɪ'zeɪʃən] N fecundación *f*, fertilización *f*

fertilize ['fɜːtɪlaɪz] VT **1** [+ *egg*] fecundar **2** (*Agr*) [+ *land, soil*] abonar, fertilizar

fertilizer ['fɜːtɪlaɪzə'] N abono *m* (artificial), fertilizante *m*

fervent ['fɜːvənt] ADJ [*desire*] ardiente; [*belief*] firme; [*supporter*] acérrimo, ferviente; [*denial*] enfático; **it is my ~ hope that ...** espero fervientemente que ...

fervently ['fɜːvəntlɪ] ADV [*pray*] con fervor,

fervientemente; [*believe*] firmemente; [*hope, desire*] fervientemente, ardientemente; [*deny*] enfáticamente, con vehemencia; [*support*] con fervor, fervorosamente; **he was ~ opposed to the war** se oponía enérgicamente a la guerra

fervour, fervor (US) ['fɜːvəʳ] N fervor *m*

fester ['festəʳ] VI (*lit, fig*) enconarse

festival ['festɪvəl] N (*Rel etc*) fiesta *f*; (*Mus etc*) festival *m*

festive ['festɪv] ADJ (*gen*) festivo; (= *happy*) alegre; **the ~ season** las Navidades

festivity [fes'tɪvɪtɪ] N **1** (= *celebration*) fiesta *f*, festividad *f*; (= *joy*) regocijo *m* **2 festivities** festejos *mpl*, fiestas *fpl*

festoon [fes'tuːn] VT adornar, engalanar (**with** de); **to be ~ed with** estar adornado *or* engalanado de

feta ['fetə] N (*also* ~ **cheese**) feta *m*

fetal ['fiːtl] ADJ (US) = **foetal**

fetch [fetʃ] 🅐 VT **1** (= *go and get, bring*) [+ *object*] traer; [+ *person*] ir a buscar a; **can you ~ my coat?** ¿me trae el abrigo?; **I'll go and ~ it for you** yo te lo traigo; **they're ~ing the doctor** han ido (a) por el médico, han ido a buscar al médico; **please ~ the doctor** ¿puedes llamar *or* avisar al médico?; **to ~ sb back from Spain** hacer que algn vuelva de España
2 (= *sell for*) venderse por; **how much did it ~?** ¿por cuánto se vendió?
🅑 VI **to ~ and carry** ir de acá para allá, trajinar; **to ~ and carry for sb** ser el sirviente de algn
➤ **fetch up*** VI + ADV (= *end up*) ir a parar (**in** a)

fetching ['fetʃɪŋ] ADJ atractivo

fête [feɪt] N (*for charity*) feria *f* benéfica

fetid ['fetɪd] ADJ fétido

fetish ['fetɪʃ] N fetiche *m*; (= *obsession*) obsesión *f*

fetter ['fetəʳ] VT [+ *person*] encadenar, poner grilletes a; [+ *horse*] trabar; (*fig*) poner trabas a

fetters ['fetəz] NPL grilletes *mpl*; (*fig*) trabas *fpl*

fettle ['fetl] N **in fine ~** en buenas condiciones

fetus ['fiːtəs] N (US) = **foetus**

feud [fjuːd] 🅐 N enemistad *f* heredada; **a family ~** una disputa familiar 🅑 VI pelearse

feudal ['fjuːdl] ADJ feudal ➤ **feudal system** feudalismo *m*

fever ['fiːvəʳ] N (= *disease, high temperature*) fiebre *f*, calentura *f* (*LAm*); ~ **blister** (US) herpes *m inv* labial, pupa* *f* ➤ **fever pitch: it reached ~ pitch** se puso al rojo vivo

feverish ['fiːvərɪʃ] ADJ febril; **to be ~** tener fiebre

few [fjuː] ADJ, PRON (*compar* **~er**; *superl* **~est**) **1** (= *not many*) pocos/as; ~ **books** pocos libros; ~ **of them** pocos (de ellos); **only a ~** sólo unos pocos; **she is one of the ~ (people) who ...** ella es una de las pocos que ...; **every ~ weeks** cada dos o tres semanas; **they are ~ and far between** son contados; **the last ~ minutes** el poco tiempo que queda/quedaba; **the lucky ~** unos pocos *or* unos cuantos afortunados; **in** *or* **over the next ~ days** en *or* durante los próximos días, en estos días (*LAm*); **in** *or* **over the past ~ days** en *or* durante los últimos días
2 (= *some, several*) **a ~** algunos; **a good ~** (*esp Brit*) bastantes; **he'd had a ~ (drinks)*** llevaba ya una copa de más; **a ~ more** algunos más; **not a ~** (*Brit*) bastantes; **a ~ of them** algunos de ellos; **quite a ~** bastantes

fewer ['fjuːəʳ] ADJ, PRON, COMPAR *of* **few** menos; ~ **than ten** menos de diez; **no ~ than ...** no menos de ...; **they have ~ than I** tienen menos que yo; **the ~ the better** cuantos menos mejor

fewest ['fjuːɪst] ADJ, PRON, SUPERL *of* **few** los/las menos

fiancé [fɪ'ɑ̃ːnseɪ] N novio *m*, prometido *m*

fiancée [fɪ'ɑ̃ːnseɪ] N novia *f*, prometida *f*

fiasco [fɪ'æskəʊ] N fiasco *m*, desastre *m*

fib* [fɪb] N mentirijilla *f*

fibre, fiber (US) ['faɪbəʳ] 🅐 N **1** (= *thread*) fibra *f*, hilo *m*; (= *fabric*) fibra *f* **2** (*dietary*) fibra *f* 🅑 CPD ➤ **fibre optics, fiber optics** (US) SING transmisión *f* por fibra óptica

fibreglass, fiberglass (US) ['faɪbəglɑːs] N fibra *f* de vidrio

fibrositis [ˌfaɪbrə'saɪtɪs] N fibrositis *f inv*

fibrous ['faɪbrəs] ADJ fibroso

fickle ['fɪkl] ADJ inconstante, veleidoso, voluble

fiction ['fɪkʃən] N **1** (*Literat*) literatura *f* de ficción, narrativa *f*; **a work of ~** una obra de ficción **2** (= *untruth*) ficción *f*, invención *f*

fictional ['fɪkʃənl] ADJ ficticio

fictitious [fɪk'tɪʃəs] ADJ **1** (= *fictional*) ficticio **2** (= *false*) falso

fiddle ['fɪdl] 🅐 N **1** (= *violin*) violín *m*; ✦ IDIOMS **to play second ~** desempeñar un papel secundario; **to play second ~ to sb** estar a la sombra de algn **2** (*Brit**) (= *cheat*) trampa *f*, superchería *f*; **it's a ~** aquí hay trampa; **tax ~** evasión *f* fiscal; **to be on the ~** dedicarse a hacer chanchullos*
🅑 VI (= *fidget*) enredar; **to ~ (about** *or* **around) with sth** enredar *or* juguetear con algo
🅒 VT (*Brit**) [+ *accounts, results, expenses claim etc*] manipular; **to ~ one's income tax** defraudar impuestos

fiddler ['fɪdləʳ] N violinista *mf*

fiddling* ['fɪdlɪŋ] N (= *cheating*) chanchullos* *mpl*

fiddly ['fɪdlɪ] ADJ (*compar* **fiddlier**; *superl* **fiddliest**) (*Brit*) [*job*] complicado, difícil

fidelity [fɪ'delɪtɪ] N fidelidad *f*

fidget ['fɪdʒɪt] VI no parar de moverse; **don't ~!** ✧ **stop ~ing!** ¡estate quieto!

fidgety ['fɪdʒɪtɪ] ADJ nervioso, inquieto

fiduciary [fɪ'djuːʃɪərɪ] ADJ fiduciario

field [fiːld] 🅐 N **1** (*gen, Elec, Comput*) campo *m*; (*Geol*) yacimiento *m*; ~ **of vision** campo *m* visual; **to die in the ~** morir en combate
2 (*Sport*) campo *m*, terreno *m* de juego, cancha *f* (*LAm*); **to lead the ~** (*Sport, Comm*) llevar la delantera
3 (= *sphere of activity*) campo *m*, esfera *f*; ~ **of activity** esfera *f* de actividades, campo *m* de acción; **it's not my ~** no es mi campo *or* especialidad, no es lo mío; **what's your ~?** ¿qué especialidad tiene Vd?
🅑 VI (*Baseball, Cricket*) fildear
🅒 VT (*Sport*) [+ *team*] alinear; (*Baseball, Cricket*) [+ *ball*] recoger, fildear; (*fig*) [+ *question*] sortear
🅓 CPD ➤ **field day** ✦ IDIOM **to have a ~ day** sacar el máximo provecho ➤ **field event** concurso *m* (atlético) de salto/lanzamiento ➤ **field glasses** (= *binoculars*) gemelos *mpl* ➤ **field goal** (*Basketball*) canasta *f* de dos puntos; (US *Ftbl*) gol *m* de campo ➤ **field hockey** (US) hockey *m* (sobre hierba) ➤ **field hospital** hospital *m* de campaña ➤ **field marshal** (*Brit*) mariscal *m* de campo, ≈ capitán *m* general del ejército ➤ **field sports** *la caza y la pesca* ➤ **field study** estudio *m* de campo ➤ **field test, field trial** (*Comm*) prueba *f* de mercado ➤ **field trip** viaje *m* *or* excursión *f* de estudios ➤ **field work** (*Sociol etc*) trabajo *m* de campo ➤ **field worker** investigador/a *m/f* de campo

fieldmouse ['fiːldmaʊs] N (*pl* **fieldmice**) ratón *m* de campo

fiend [fiːnd] N **1** (= *devil*) demonio *m*, diablo *m* **2** (*) (= *fanatic*) **drugs ~** drogadicto/a *m/f*; **sex ~** maníaco *m* sexual

fiendish ['fiːndɪʃ] ADJ (= *clever and wicked*) diabólico

fiendishly ['fiːndɪʃlɪ] ADV terriblemente; ~ **difficult** terriblemente difícil; ~ **expensive** carísimo

fierce [fɪəs] ADJ (*compar* **~r**; *superl* **~st**) **1** (= *ferocious*) [*animal*] feroz, fiero; [*gesture, expression*] feroz; [*temper*] temible; **the prime minister came under ~ attack from the opposition** la oposición atacó ferozmente al primer ministro; **she gave me a ~ look** me lanzó una mirada furibunda
2 (= *intense*) [*competition, argument*] encarnizado; [*opposition, resistance*] violento; [*opponent*] empedernido, acérrimo; [*fire*] intenso; ~ **fighting broke out in the capital** se produjeron enfrentamientos encarnizados en la capital

fiercely ['fɪəslɪ] ADV **1** (= *ferociously*) [*look, scowl*] ferozmente, con ferocidad; [*attack*] ferozmente
2 (= *intensely*) [*independent, competitive, loyal*] tremendamente; [*oppose, resist*] ferozmente; [*fight, compete*] encarnizadamente; **it was a ~ contested match**

fue un partido extremadamente reñido

fiery ['faɪərɪ] ADJ (*compar* **fierier**; *superl* **fieriest**) [*sky, sunset, red*] encendido; [*temperament, speech*] acalorado

FIFA ['fiːfə] N ABBR (= **Fédération Internationale de Football Association**) FIFA *f*

fifteen [fɪf'tiːn] NUMBER quince *m*; (*Rugby*) quince *m*, equipo *m*; *see* **five**

fifteenth [fɪf'tiːnθ] Ⓐ ADJ decimoquinto; **on his ~ birthday** cuando cumpla/cumplió quince años, en su decimoquinto cumpleaños (*frm*); **in the ~ century** (*spoken form*) en el siglo quince; (*in writing*) en el siglo XV Ⓑ PRONOUN decimoquinto/a *m/f*; (= *fraction*) quinceava parte *f*, quinceavo *m*; **on the ~ of March ◇ on March (the) ~** el quince de marzo; **it's the ~ of July ◇ it's July (the) ~** estamos a quince de julio, es quince de julio; **I wrote to him on the ~** le escribí el día quince

fifth [fɪfθ] Ⓐ ADJ quinto; **on his ~ birthday** cuando cumpla/cumplió cinco años, en su quinto cumpleaños (*more frm*); **in the ~ century** (*spoken form*) en el siglo quinto *or* cinco; (*in writing*) en el siglo V; **~ form** (*Brit Scol*) quinto *m*, quinto curso Ⓑ PRONOUN **1** (*in series*) quinto/a *m/f*; **I was the ~ to arrive** yo fui el quinto en llegar; **on the ~ of July ◇ on July (the) ~** el cinco de julio; **it's the ~ of July ◇ it's July (the) ~** estamos a cinco de julio, es cinco de julio; **I wrote to him on the ~** le escribí el día cinco **2** (= *fraction*) quinta parte *f*, quinto *m* **3** (*in titles*) **Henry the Fifth** (*spoken form*) Enrique Quinto; (*in writing*) Enrique V **4** (*also* **~ gear**) quinta *f* (velocidad *f*) **5** (*Mus*) quinta *f* Ⓒ ADV (= *in fifth place*) en quinto lugar, en quinta posición; **he came ~ in the competition** ocupó el quinto lugar *or* terminó quinto en la competición Ⓓ CPD ➤ **fifth column** quinta columna *f* ➤ **fifth columnist** quintacolumnista *mf*

fiftieth ['fɪftɪɪθ] Ⓐ ADJ quincuagésimo; **the ~ anniversary** el cincuenta aniversario; **on his ~ birthday** cuando cumpla/cumplió cincuenta años Ⓑ PRON (*in series*) quincuagésimo/a *m/f*; (= *fraction*) quincuagésima parte *f*, quincuagésimo *m* Ⓒ ADV (*in fiftieth place*) en la posición número cincuenta, en quincuagésimo lugar

fifty ['fɪftɪ] NUMBER cincuenta *m*; **about ~ people/cars** alrededor de cincuenta personas/coches; **he's ~** tiene cincuenta años; **he'll be ~ (years old) this year** cumple *or* va a cumplir cincuenta años este año; **to be in one's fifties** tener más de cincuenta años, tener cincuenta y tantos años; **the temperature was in the fifties** hacía más de cincuenta (*Fahrenheit*) *or* diez (*Celsius*) grados; **to do ~ (miles per hour)** ir a cincuenta (millas por hora); **the fifties** (= *1950s*) los años cincuenta

fifty-fifty ['fɪftɪ'fɪftɪ] Ⓐ ADJ **we have a ~ chance of success** tenemos un cincuenta por ciento de posibilidades de éxito; **we'll do it on a ~ basis** lo haremos a medias Ⓑ ADV **to go ~ with sb** ir a medias con algn

fig [fɪg] Ⓐ N (*Bot*) higo *m*; (*early*) breva *f*; (*also* **~ tree**) higuera *f* Ⓑ CPD ➤ **fig leaf** hoja *f* de higuera; (*Art*) hoja *f* de parra (*also fig*)

fig. ABBR = **figure**

fight [faɪt] (*vb: pt, pp* **fought**) Ⓐ N **1** (*physical, verbal*) pelea *f* (**over** por); (*Boxing*) combate *m*, pelea *f*; (= *battle*) lucha *f*, contienda *f*; **to have a ~ with sb** pelearse con algn, tener una pelea con algn **2** (= *struggle, campaign*) lucha *f* (**for** por; **against** contra); **the ~ for justice/against inflation** la lucha por la justicia/contra la inflación; **he won't give up without a ~** no se rendirá sin luchar antes **3** (= *spirit*) ánimo *m* de lucha; **there was no ~ left in him** ya no le quedaba ánimo de lucha, ya no tenía ánimo para luchar **4** (= *resistance*) **police believe the victim put up a ~** la policía cree que la víctima opuso resistencia; **they beat us but we put up a good ~** nos vencieron pero nos defendimos bien Ⓑ VT **1** (*Mil*) [+ *enemy*] luchar contra, combatir contra; (*Boxing*) [+ *opponent*] pelear contra, luchar contra; **to ~ a**

battle (*Mil*) librar una batalla; (*fig*) luchar; **I'd like to ~ him for the title** me gustaría luchar *or* pelear contra él por el título; **to ~ one's way through a crowd** abrirse paso a la fuerza entre una multitud **2** (= *combat*) [+ *poverty, inflation, crime*] combatir, luchar contra; [+ *proposal*] oponerse a; **I had to ~ the urge to giggle** tuve que hacer un esfuerzo para no reír, tuve que contener las ganas de reír **3** (= *try to win*) [+ *campaign*] tomar parte en; [+ *election*] presentarse a Ⓒ VI **1** (= *do battle*) [*troops, countries*] luchar, combatir (**against** contra); [*person, animal*] pelear; (*Boxing*) luchar, pelear; **the dogs were ~ing over a bone** los perros estaban peleando por un hueso **2** (= *quarrel*) discutir, pelear(se) (**with** con); **they usually ~ about** *or* **over who pays the bills** suelen discutir *or* pelear(se) por quién paga las facturas **3** (= *struggle*) luchar (**for** por; **against** contra); **to ~ against disease/crime** luchar contra la enfermedad/el crimen; **to ~ for sth/sb** luchar por algo/algn; **he was ~ing for his life** estaba luchando por su vida
➤ **fight back** Ⓐ VI (= *resist*) (*in fight, argument*) defenderse; (*Sport*) contraatacar; **they fought back from 2-0 down to win 3-2** contraatacaron, pasando de perder por 2-0 a ganar por 3-2 Ⓑ VT + ADV [+ *tears*] contener; [+ *anger, feeling*] contener, reprimir; [+ *despair*] dominar
➤ **fight down** VT + ADV [+ *anger, feeling*] contener, reprimir
➤ **fight off** VT + ADV **1** (= *repel*) [+ *attack, attacker*] repeler, rechazar; **they successfully fought off a takeover bid** consiguieron defenderse contra una oferta de adquisición **2** (= *resist*) [+ *disease, infection*] combatir
➤ **fight on** VI + ADV seguir luchando
➤ **fight out** VT + ADV **1** (*with fists*) resolver a golpes **2** (= *resolve*) resolver **3** (= *compete*) **they'll be ~ing it out for the top prize** competirán por el primer premio

fightback ['faɪtbæk] N (*Brit*) contraataque *m*

fighter ['faɪtəʳ] Ⓐ N **1** (= *determined person*) luchador(a) *m/f*; (= *boxer*) boxeador(a) *m/f*, púgil *m*; (= *warrior*) guerrero/a *m/f*; (= *combatant*) combatiente *mf* **2** (= *plane*) avión *m* de combate, caza *m* Ⓑ CPD ➤ **fighter command** jefatura *f* de cazas ➤ **fighter pilot** piloto *mf* de caza

fighting ['faɪtɪŋ] Ⓐ N (*between troops, armies*) enfrentamientos *mpl*; (*between individuals*) (*lit, fig*) peleas *fpl* Ⓑ ADJ **we still have a ~ chance of beating them** aún tenemos una buena posibilidad de vencerles Ⓒ ADV **to be ~ fit** (*Brit**) estar en plena forma Ⓓ CPD ➤ **fighting force** fuerza *f* de combate ➤ **fighting man** guerrero *m*, soldado *m* ➤ **fighting spirit** espíritu *m* de lucha, combatividad *f*

figment ['fɪgmənt] N **a ~ of the imagination** un producto de la imaginación

figurative ['fɪgərətɪv] ADJ **1** [*meaning*] figurado; [*expression*] metafórico **2** (*Art*) figurativo

figuratively ['fɪgərətɪvlɪ] ADV figuradamente, en sentido figurado

figure ['fɪgəʳ] Ⓐ N **1** (= *shape, silhouette*) figura *f*; **a ~ in a blue dress** una figura vestida de azul **2** (= *bodily proportions*) tipo *m*, figura *f*; **she's got a nice ~** tiene buen tipo *or* una buena figura; **to watch one's ~** cuidar la línea *or* el tipo **3** (= *person*) figura *f*; **a key ~ in twentieth century music** una figura clave en la música del siglo veinte; **a ~ of authority** una figura de autoridad; **public ~** personaje *m* público; **these days he's become a ~ of fun** últimamente se ha convertido en el hazmerreír de todos **4** (= *numeral*) cifra *f*; **how did you arrive at these ~s?** ¿cómo has llegado a estas cifras?; **we want inflation brought down to single ~s** queremos que la inflación baje a menos del diez por cien **5 figures** (= *statistics*) estadísticas *fpl*, datos *mpl*; (= *calculations*) cálculos *mpl*; **he's always been good at ~s** siempre se le han dado bien los números, siempre se le ha dado bien la aritmética **6** (= *amount*) [*of money*] cifra *f*, suma *f*; (= *number*) [*of items*] cifra *f*, número *m*; **what sort of ~ did you have in mind?** ¿qué cifra *or* suma tenías en mente?; **I wouldn't like to put a ~ on it** no quisiera dar una cifra; **some estimates put the ~ as high as 20,000 dead** algunos cálculos dan una cifra *or*

un número de hasta 20.000 muertos
7 (= *diagram, picture*) figura *f* (*also Skating, Geom*)
Ⓑ VI **1** (= *appear*) figurar (**as** como; **among** entre)
2 (*esp US**) (= *make sense*) **it doesn't ~** no tiene sentido, no encaja; **that ~s!** ¡lógico!, ¡obvio!
Ⓒ VT (*esp US*) (= *think*) imaginarse, figurarse; (= *estimate*) calcular; **I ~ they'll come** me imagino *or* me figuro que vendrán; **I ~d there'd be about 20** calculé que habría unos 20
Ⓓ CPD ➤ **figure skating** patinaje *m* artístico
➤ **figure on*** VI + PREP (*esp US*) contar con; **he hadn't ~d on the problems that would arise** no había contado con los problemas que surgirían; **the meeting was longer than I'd ~d on** la reunión fue más larga de lo que yo esperaba; **I wasn't figuring on going** no contaba con ir
➤ **figure out*** VT + ADV **1** (= *understand*) [+ *person*] entender; [+ *writing*] entender, descifrar; **I just can't ~ it out!** ¡no me lo explico!, ¡no lo entiendo! **2** (= *work out*) [+ *sum*] calcular; [+ *problem*] resolver; **I couldn't ~ out the answer** no pude encontrar la respuesta *or* solución; **they had it all ~d out** lo tenían todo calculado
➤ **figure up** VT + ADV (*US*) calcular

-figure ['fɪɡə'] ADJ (*ending in compounds*) **a four-figure sum** una suma superior a mil (libras *etc*); **a seven-figure sum** un número de siete cifras

figurehead ['fɪɡəhed] N (*on ship*) mascarón *m* de proa; (*fig*) testaferro *m*

figure-hugging ['fɪɡə,hʌɡɪŋ] ADJ ajustado, ceñido al cuerpo

Fiji ['fi:dʒi:] N (*also* **the ~ Islands**) las Islas Fiji

filament ['fɪləmənt] N filamento *m*

filch* [fɪltʃ] VT birlar*, mangar*

file¹ [faɪl] **Ⓐ** N (= *tool*) lima *f*; (*for nails*) lima *f* (de uñas)
Ⓑ VT (*also* ~ **down**, ~ **away**) limar

file² [faɪl] **Ⓐ** N **1** (= *folder*) carpeta *f*; (= *dossier*) archivo *m*, carpeta *f*, expediente *m*; (*eg loose-leaf file*) archivador *m*, clasificador *m*; (= *filing system*) fichero *m*; **the ~s** los archivos; **police ~s** archivos policiales; **to close the ~ on sth** dar carpetazo a algo; **to have sth on ~** tener algo archivado; **to have a ~ on sb** tener fichado a algn
2 (*Comput*) fichero *m*, archivo *m*
Ⓑ VT **1** (*also* ~ **away**) [+ *notes, information, work*] archivar; (*under heading*) clasificar
2 (= *submit*) [+ *claim, application, complaint*] presentar; **to ~ a suit against sb** (*Jur*) entablar pleito *or* presentar una demanda contra algn
Ⓒ CPD ➤ **file cabinet** (*US*) fichero *m*, archivador *m* ➤ **file clerk** (*US*) archivero/a *m/f* ➤ **file name** (*Comput*) nombre *m* de fichero, nombre *m* de archivo
➤ **file for** VI + PREP (*Jur*) **to ~ for divorce** entablar pleito de divorcio; **to ~ for bankruptcy** presentar una declaración de quiebra

file³ [faɪl] **Ⓐ** N (= *row*) fila *f*, hilera *f*; **in single ~** en fila india **Ⓑ** VI **to ~ in/out** entrar/salir en fila; **to ~ past** desfilar; **they ~d past the general** desfilaron ante el general

filial ['fɪlɪəl] ADJ filial

filibuster ['fɪlɪbʌstə'] (*esp US*) **Ⓐ** N (= *act*) discurso *m* obstruccionista **Ⓑ** VI dar un discurso obstruccionista

filigree ['fɪlɪɡri:] **Ⓐ** N (*in metal*) filigrana *f* **Ⓑ** ADJ de filigrana

filing ['faɪlɪŋ] N [*of documents*] clasificación *f*; **to do the ~** archivar documentos ➤ **filing cabinet** fichero *m*, archivador *m* ➤ **filing clerk** (*esp Brit*) archivero/a *m/f*

filings ['faɪlɪŋz] NPL limaduras *fpl*

Filipino [ˌfɪlɪ'pi:nəʊ] **Ⓐ** ADJ filipino **Ⓑ** N **1** (= *person*) filipino/a *m/f* **2** (*Ling*) tagalo *m*

fill [fɪl] **Ⓐ** VT **1** (= *make full*) [+ *container, space*] llenar (**with** de); [+ *time*] ocupar; **I am ~ed with admiration for her achievements** sus logros me llenan de admiración; **he was ~ed with remorse** estaba lleno de remordimiento; **rooms ~ed with furniture** habitaciones *fpl* llenas de muebles; **shouts ~ed the air** resonaron unos gritos en el aire
2 (= *plug*) [+ *hole*] rellenar, tapar (**with** con), llenar (**with** de); [+ *tooth*] empastar, emplomar (*SC*) (**with** con); (*fig*) [+ *gap, vacuum*] llenar; **she ~ed a gap in his life** ella llenó

un hueco en su vida
3 (= *appoint sb to*) [+ *vacancy*] cubrir; [+ *post*] ocupar; **the position is already ~ed** la vacante ya está cubierta
Ⓑ VI llenarse (**with** de); **her eyes ~ed with tears** los ojos se le llenaron de lágrimas
Ⓒ N (= *sufficiency*) **to eat/drink one's ~ (of sth)** comer/beber (algo) hasta saciarse, hartarse de comer/beber (algo); **to have had one's ~ of sth** (*fig*) haberse hartado de algo, estar harto de algo
➤ **fill in Ⓐ** VT + ADV **1** [+ *hole, gap, outline*] rellenar
2 (= *occupy*) [+ *time*] ocupar, pasar; **I had an hour to ~ before my train** tenía que ocupar *or* pasar una hora de alguna forma hasta que llegase mi tren
3 (*esp Brit*) (= *complete*) [+ *form*] rellenar, llenar; [+ *details*] completar; [+ *name*] escribir, poner; **~ in the blanks in the following sentences** rellenar los espacios vacíos en las siguientes frases
4 (= *inform*) **to ~ sb in (on sth)** poner a algn al corriente (de algo)
Ⓑ VI + ADV **to ~ in for sb** suplir a algn, sustituir a algn
➤ **fill out** VT + ADV [+ *form, application*] rellenar, llenar; [+ *details*] completar; [+ *name*] escribir, poner
➤ **fill up Ⓐ** VI + ADV **1** [+ *room, hall*] llenarse **2** (*with petrol*) echar gasolina; (*with diesel*) echar diesel **Ⓑ** VT + ADV [+ *container, suitcase*] llenar (**with** de); ~ **it up!** (*Aut**) ¡llena el tanque!; **to ~ o.s. up with sth** llenarse (el estómago) de algo

filler ['fɪlə'] N **1** (*for cracks in wood, plaster*) masilla *f*
2 (*Press*) relleno *m* **3** (= *device*) [*of bottle, tank*] rellenador *m*

fillet ['fɪlɪt] **Ⓐ** N [*of meat, fish*] filete *m* **Ⓑ** VT [+ *fish*] cortar en filetes

fill-in ['fɪlɪn] N sustituto *m*, suplente *mf*

filling ['fɪlɪŋ] **Ⓐ** N **1** [*of tooth*] empaste *m*, emplomadura *f* (*SC*) **2** (*Culin*) relleno *m* **Ⓑ** ADJ [*food, dish*] que llena mucho; **this dish is very ~** este plato llena mucho **Ⓒ** CPD ➤ **filling station** (*esp Brit*) gasolinera *f*, estación *f* de servicio, bencinera *f* (*Chi*), surtidor *m* (*Bol*), grifo *m* (*Per*)

filly ['fɪlɪ] N potra *f*

film [fɪlm] **Ⓐ** N **1** (*esp Brit*) (= *movie*) película *f*, film *m*, filme *m*; **to make a ~ of** [+ *book*] llevar al cine, hacer una película de; [+ *event*] filmar
2 (*Phot*) (= *negatives*) película *f*; (= *roll of film*) carrete *m*, rollo *m*
3 (= *thin skin*) película *f*; [*of dust*] capa *f*; [*of smoke*] velo *m* **Ⓑ** VT [+ *book*] llevar al cine, hacer una película de; [+ *event*] filmar; [+ *scene*] rodar
Ⓒ VI rodar, filmar
Ⓓ CPD [*camera, festival*] cinematográfico, de cine ➤ **film buff** (*esp Brit*) cinéfilo/a *m/f* ➤ **film crew** (*esp Brit*) equipo *m* cinematográfico ➤ **film première** (*esp Brit*) estreno *m* oficial, premier *f* ➤ **film rights** (*esp Brit*) derechos *mpl* cinematográficos ➤ **film script** (*esp Brit*) guión *m* ➤ **film set** (*esp Brit*) plató *m* ➤ **film star** (*esp Brit*) estrella *f* de cine ➤ **film studio** (*esp Brit*) estudio *m* de cine ➤ **film test** (*esp Brit*) prueba *f* cinematográfica

filming ['fɪlmɪŋ] N rodaje *m*, filmación *f*

film-maker ['fɪlmmeɪkə'] N (*esp Brit*) cineasta *mf*

Filofax® ['faɪləʊfæks] N agenda *f* de anillas

filter ['fɪltə'] **Ⓐ** N filtro *m* **Ⓑ** VT filtrar **Ⓒ** VI [*liquid, light*] filtrarse; **to ~ to the left** (*Aut*) tomar el carril izquierdo
Ⓓ CPD ➤ **filter coffee** (= *grains*) café *m* para filtrar; (= *cup of coffee*) café *m* hecho con cafetera de filtro ➤ **filter lane** (*Brit*) carril *m* de giro ➤ **filter light** (*Brit*) semáforo *m* de flecha de desvío ➤ **filter paper** papel *m* de filtro
➤ **filter in** VI + ADV [*light*] filtrarse; [*news, rumour*] llegar; [*people*] entrar (poco a poco)
➤ **filter out** VT + ADV [+ *impurities*] quitar filtrando
➤ **filter through** VI + ADV = **filter in**

filter-tipped ['fɪltə,tɪpt] ADJ con filtro *or* boquilla

filth [fɪlθ] N (= *dirt*) suciedad *f*, mugre *f*; (= *bad language*) groserías *fpl*, obscenidades *fpl*

filthy ['fɪlθɪ] ADJ (*compar* **filthier**; *superl* **filthiest**) **1** (= *dirty*) [*hands, room, house*] asqueroso; [*bathtub*] mugriento, mugroso (*LAm*); [*clothes*] muy sucio **2** (= *indecent*) [*language*] grosero, obsceno; [*joke*] verde; [*sense of humour*] obsceno
3 (*) [*weather*] asqueroso*, de perros*; [*temper*] de perros*,

de mil diablos*

fin [fɪn] N (*all senses*) aleta *f*

fin. ABBR = **finance**

final ['faɪnl] **Ⓐ** ADJ **1** (= *last*) último; [*stage*] final, último; (*Univ*) [*exam*] de fin de carrera; **~ demand** último aviso *m* de pago **2** (= *conclusive*) [*approval*] definitivo; [*result*] final; **the judge's decision is ~** la decisión del juez es inapelable; **and that's ~!** ¡y punto!, ¡y no se hable más! **3** (= *ultimate*) [*destination*] final **Ⓑ** N **1** (*Sport*) final *f*; **she went on to reach the ~** siguió hasta llegar a la final **2** (*Univ*) **finals** exámenes *mpl* de fin de carrera

finale [fɪ'nɑːlɪ] N (*Mus*) final *m*; (*Theat*) escena *f* final; **the grand ~** el gran final, la gran escena final; (*fig*) el final apoteósico *or* triunfal

finalist ['faɪnəlɪst] N finalista *mf*

finality [faɪ'nælɪtɪ] N [*of death*] lo irreversible; [*of decision*] carácter *m* definitivo

finalize ['faɪnəlaɪz] VT [+ *preparations, arrangements*] concluir; [+ *agreement, plans, contract*] ultimar; [+ *report, text*] completar; [+ *date*] fijar, acordar

finally ['faɪnəlɪ] ADV **1** (= *lastly*) por último, finalmente **2** (= *eventually, at last*) por fin

finance ['faɪnæns] **Ⓐ** N **1** (*gen*) finanzas *fpl*, asuntos *mpl* financieros **2 finances** fondos *mpl*; **(the state of) the country's ~s** la situación económica del país; **Minister of Finance** Ministro/a *m/f* de Economía y Hacienda **Ⓑ** VT [+ *project*] financiar; **he stole to ~ his drug habit** robaba para costearse su adicción a las drogas **Ⓒ** CPD [*company, director*] financiero; [*page, section*] de economía, de negocios

financial [faɪ'nænʃəl] ADJ [*services, aid, affairs, security*] financiero; [*policy, resources, problems*] económico; [*page, section*] de economía, de negocios ➤ **financial adviser** asesor(a) *m/f* financiero/a ➤ **financial management** gestión *f* financiera ➤ **financial year** (*Brit*) [*of company*] ejercicio *m* (financiero); [*of government*] año *m* fiscal

financially [faɪ'nænʃəlɪ] ADV [*independent, sound*] económicamente; **~, he would be much better off** desde el punto de vista económico *or* económicamente, saldría ganando

financier [faɪ'nænsɪəʳ] N financiero/a *m/f*

finch [fɪntʃ] N pinzón *m*

find [faɪnd] (*vb: pt, pp* **found**) **Ⓐ** VT **1** encontrar; **I found some keys in the street** me he encontrado unas llaves en la calle; **can you ~ your (own) way to the station?** ¿sabes llegar a la estación sin ayuda?, ¿puedes encontrar la estación solo?; **the book is nowhere to be found** el libro no se encuentra por ninguna parte; **to ~ one's way around** (*in city, etc*) orientarse; (= *familiarize o.s.*) familiarizarse; **he found himself in a dark wood** se encontró en un bosque oscuro; **it has been found that ...** se ha comprobado que ... **2** (*in court*) declarar; **he was found guilty/innocent** fue declarado culpable/inocente **Ⓑ** VI **to ~ for/against sb** (*in court*) fallar a favor de/contra algn **Ⓒ** N hallazgo *m*; **your new assistant is a real ~** tu nueva ayudante es todo un hallazgo; **that was a lucky ~!** ¡qué buen hallazgo!

➤ **find out Ⓐ** VT + ADV **1** (= *check out*) averiguar; **she phoned to ~ out when the bus left** llamó por teléfono para averiguar cuándo *or* enterarse de cuándo salía el autobús **2** (= *discover*) descubrir; **I found out that she had been lying** descubrí *or* me enteré que había estado mintiendo; **~ out more by writing to ...** infórmese escribiendo a ... **3** (= *expose*) **to ~ sb out** descubrir a algn **4** (= *realize*) darse cuenta de, descubrir **Ⓑ** VI + ADV enterarse; **they'll soon ~ out** pronto se enterarán; **to ~ out about sth** (= *discover*) enterarse de algo, descubrir algo; (= *make inquiries*) informarse (acerca *or* de *or* sobre algo

findings ['faɪndɪŋz] NPL (= *conclusions*) conclusiones *fpl*; (= *results*) resultados *mpl*

fine¹ [faɪn] **Ⓐ** ADJ (*compar* **~r**; *superl* **~st**) **1** (= *delicate, thin*) [*thread, hair*] fino, delgado; [*rain, point, nib*] fino; [*line*] delgado, tenue; (= *small*) [*particle*] minúsculo

2 (= *good*) [*performance, example*] excelente; (= *imposing*) [*house, building*] magnífico; (= *beautiful*) [*object*] hermoso; **we use only the ~st ingredients** sólo usamos ingredientes de primerísima calidad; ✦ IDIOM **he's got it down to a ~ art** lo hace a la perfección **3** (= *subtle*) [*distinction*] sutil; **the ~r points of the argument** los puntos más sutiles del argumento; **there's a ~ line between love and hate** la línea que separa el amor del odio es muy tenue, del amor al odio sólo hay un paso; **not to put too ~ a point on it** hablando en plata **4** (= *refined*) [*taste, manners*] refinado **5** (= *acceptable*) bien; **"is this ok?" — "yes, it's ~"** —¿está bien así? *or* (*Sp*) ¿vale así? —si, está bien; **fine!** ¡de acuerdo!, ¡vale! (*Sp*), ¡cómo no! (*esp LAm*); **that's ~ by me** por mí bien, de acuerdo; **"would you like some more?" — "no, I'm ~, thanks"** —¿quieres un poco más? —no, gracias, con esto me basta; ✦ IDIOM **~ and dandy: everything may look ~ and dandy to you** puede que tú todo lo veas de color de rosa **6** (= *quite well*) muy bien; **he's ~, thanks** está muy bien, gracias **7** (*of weather*) bueno; **it's a ~ day today** hoy hace buen tiempo; **if it's ~** si hace buen tiempo **8** (*iro*) menudo; **a ~ friend you are!** ¡valiente amigo estás hecho! (*iro*), ¡menudo amigo eres tú! (*iro*); **you're a ~ one to talk!** ¡mira quién habla!; **a ~ thing!** ¡hasta dónde hemos llegado! **Ⓑ** ADV **1** (= *well*) bien; **"how did you get on at the dentist's?" — "fine"** —¿qué tal te ha ido en el dentista? —bien; **mother and baby are doing ~** la madre y el bebé están bien; **to feel ~** [*person*] encontrarse bien; **five o'clock suits me ~** a las cinco me viene bien **2** (= *finely*) **to chop sth up ~** picar algo en trozos menudos, picar algo muy fino; ✦ IDIOM **to cut it ~** (*of time*) ir con el tiempo justo; (*of money*) calcular muy justo; **we'll be cutting it pretty ~ if we leave at ten** vamos a ir con el tiempo muy justo si salimos a las diez **Ⓒ** CPD ➤ **fine art, the fine arts** las Bellas Artes ➤ **fine wines** vinos *mpl* selectos

fine² [faɪn] **Ⓐ** N multa *f*; **to get a ~ (for sth/doing sth)** ser multado (por algo/hacer algo); **I got a ~ for ...** me pusieron una multa por ... **Ⓑ** VT **to ~ sb (for sth/doing sth)** multar a algn (por algo/hacer algo)

finely ['faɪnlɪ] ADV **1** (= *splendidly, well*) [*dressed, written*] con elegancia **2** (= *delicately*) [*carved, woven*] delicadamente **3** (= *very small*) [*chopped*] en trozos muy menudos, muy fino; [*sliced*] en rodajas finas, en lonchas finas **4** (= *with precision*) [*tuned, judged*] con precisión

finery ['faɪnərɪ] N galas *fpl*

finesse [fɪ'nes] N (*in judgement*) finura *f*, delicadeza *f*; (*in action*) diplomacia *f*, sutileza *f*; (= *cunning*) astucia *f*

fine-tooth comb [,faɪn,tuː'θ'kəʊm] N ✦ IDIOM **to go over** *or* **through sth with a ~** revisar *or* examinar algo a fondo

fine-tune [faɪn'tjuːn] VT [+ *plans, strategy*] afinar, matizar; [+ *economy*] ajustar; [+ *text*] dar los últimos retoques a

fine-tuning [,faɪn'tjuːnɪŋ] N [*of plans, strategy*] matización *f*; [*of economy*] ajuste *m*; [*of text*] últimos retoques *mpl*

finger ['fɪŋgəʳ] **Ⓐ** N [*of hand, glove*] dedo *m*; **I can count on the ~s of one hand the number of times that ...** se pueden contar con los dedos de la mano las veces que ...; **I'll keep my ~s crossed for you** cruzo los dedos (por ti), ojalá tengas suerte; **~s crossed!** (*for someone*) ¡(que tengas) suerte!, ¡buena suerte!; (*for yourself*) ¡deséame suerte!; **index ~** (dedo *m*) índice *m*; **they never laid a ~ on her** no le pusieron la mano encima; **he didn't lift a ~ to help us** no movió un dedo para ayudarnos; **she never lifts a ~ around the house** nunca mueve un dedo para ayudar en la casa; **little ~** (dedo *m*) meñique *m*; **middle ~** (dedo *m*) corazón *m or* medio *m*; **ring ~** (dedo *m*) anular *m*; **to snap one's ~s** chasquear los dedos; **she only has to snap her ~s and he comes running** no tiene más que chasquear los dedos y él viene corriendo; ✦ IDIOMS **to burn one's ~s** ◇ **get one's ~s burned** pillarse los dedos; **to get** *or* **pull one's ~ out** (*Brit**) espabilarse; **to have a ~ in every pie** estar metido en todo; **to point the ~ at sb** acusar a algn, señalar a algn; **there's something wrong, but I can't put my ~ on it** hay algo que está mal, pero no sé exactamente qué; **there was nothing you could put your ~ on** no había nada concreto; **to slip**

through one's ~s escapársele de las manos; **to be all ~s and thumbs** ser un/una manazas, ser muy desmañado/a; **he's got her twisted round his little ~** hace con ella lo que quiere; **to give sb the two ~s*** ≈ hacer un corte de mangas a algn*; **to work one's ~s to the bone** dejarse la piel trabajando*
Ⓑ VT (= *touch*) toquetear
Ⓒ CPD ➤ **finger bowl** lavafrutas *m inv* ➤ **finger buffet** buffet *m* de canapés ➤ **finger food** (*for babies*) *comida que los bebés pueden agarrar y comer con las manos*; (*US*) canapés *mpl* ➤ **finger paint** pintura *f* para pintar con los dedos

fingermark ['fɪŋɡəmɑːk] N huella *f*

fingernail ['fɪŋɡəneɪl] N uña *f*

fingerprint ['fɪŋɡəprɪnt] **Ⓐ** N huella *f* digital *or* dactilar
Ⓑ VT [+ *person*] tomar las huellas digitales *or* dactilares a; (*Med*) identificar genéticamente

fingertip ['fɪŋɡətɪp] N punta *f or* yema *f* del dedo; **to have sth at one's ~s** tener algo a mano; (= *know sth*) saber(se) algo al dedillo

finicky ['fɪnɪki] ADJ **1** [*person*] melindroso (**about** con)
2 [*job*] complicado

finish ['fɪnɪʃ] **Ⓐ** N **1** (= *end*) final *m*; **from start to ~** de principio a fin; **a fight to the ~** una lucha a muerte
2 (*Sport*) [*of race*] final *m*; **it's going to be a close ~** va a ser un final reñido
3 (= *appearance*) acabado *m*; **a table with an oak ~** una mesa con un acabado en roble; **matt ~** acabado *m* mate
4 (= *refinement*) refinamiento *m*
Ⓑ VT (= *complete*) terminar, acabar; **I've nearly ~ed the ironing** casi he terminado *or* acabado de planchar; **what time do you ~ work?** ¿a qué hora terminas el trabajo?; **to ~ doing sth** terminar *or* acabar de hacer algo; **we ~ed the afternoon with tea at the Ritz** rematamos la tarde tomando té en el Ritz; **that last kilometre nearly ~ed me*** el kilómetro final casi acabó conmigo
Ⓒ VI (= *come to an end*) terminar, acabar; **have you quite ~ed?** ¿has acabado ya?; (= *can I speak now?*) ¿puedo hablar ya?; **she ~ed by saying that ...** terminó *or* acabó diciendo que ...; **she ~ed first/last** (*Sport*) terminó *or* acabó en primer lugar/en último lugar; **I've ~ed with the paper** he acabado el periódico, he terminado con el periódico; **come back, I haven't ~ed with you yet!** ¡vuelve, que todavía no he terminado *or* acabado contigo!; **she's ~ed with him** ha roto *or* terminado con él
Ⓓ CPD ➤ **finish line** (*US*) = **finishing line**
➤ **finish off** VT + ADV **1** (= *conclude*) terminar **2** (= *use up, consume*) terminar(se), acabar(se) **3** (= *kill*) [+ *victim*] acabar con, liquidar*; [+ *wounded person/animal*] rematar; (= *defeat*) [+ *opponent*] derrotar, vencer
➤ **finish up Ⓐ** VT + ADV [+ *food, leftovers*] terminarse, acabarse **Ⓑ** VI + ADV terminar, acabar

finished ['fɪnɪʃt] ADJ **1** (= *concluded*) terminado; **it's not ~ yet** aún no está terminado *or* acabado; **when will you be ~?** ¿(para) cuándo vas a terminar?; **he's ~ with politics** ha renunciado a la política; **I'm not ~ with you yet** aún no he terminado *or* acabado contigo
2 (= *completed*) acabado; **the ~ product** el producto acabado *or* final
3 (= *polished*) [*performance, production*] pulido
4 (*) (= *tired*) rendido, hecho polvo*; (= *destroyed*) acabado; **as a film star she's ~** como estrella está acabada
5 (= *surfaced*) **a building ~ in smoked glass** un edificio acabado con cristales ahumados

finishing ['fɪnɪʃɪŋ] CPD ➤ **finishing line** línea *f* de meta, meta *f* ➤ **finishing school** *escuela privada para señoritas donde se les enseña a comportarse en la alta sociedad*
➤ **finishing touch: to put the ~ touches to sth** dar los últimos toques a algo

finite ['faɪnaɪt] ADJ (= *limited*) finito; [*resources*] limitado
➤ **finite verb** verbo *m* conjugado

Finland ['fɪnlənd] N Finlandia *f*

Finn [fɪn] N finlandés/esa *m/f*

Finnish ['fɪnɪʃ] **Ⓐ** ADJ finlandés **Ⓑ** N (*Ling*) finlandés *m*

fir [fɜːʳ] N (*also ~ tree*) abeto *m* ➤ **fir cone** piña *f*

fire [faɪəʳ] **Ⓐ** N **1** (= *flames*) fuego *m*; **much of the town was**

destroyed by ~ el fuego causó la destrucción de gran parte de la ciudad; **to catch ~** [*curtains, furniture*] prender fuego; [*house*] incendiarse; [*engine, car*] empezar a arder; **to be on ~** estar ardiendo; **to set ~ to sth** ◇ **set sth on ~** prender fuego a algo; ✦ IDIOMS **to fight ~ with ~** pagar con la misma moneda; **to play with ~** jugar con fuego
2 (*in grate*) fuego *m*, lumbre *f*
3 (= *bonfire*) hoguera *f*, fogata *f*
4 (= *fireplace*) lumbre *f*, chimenea *f*
5 (*accidental*) incendio *m*; **87 people died in the ~** 87 personas murieron en el incendio; **forest ~** incendio *m* forestal
6 (*esp Brit*) (= *heater*) estufa *f*; **electric ~** estufa *f* eléctrica
7 (= *shots*) fuego *m*; **to draw sb's ~** distraer a algn (*disparando a algo que no es el objetivo real*); **to draw ~** (*fig*) provocar críticas; **to hold (one's) ~** (*lit*) no disparar; (*fig*) esperar; **hold your ~!** (*when already firing*) ¡alto al fuego!; **to open ~ (on sth/sb)** abrir fuego (sobre algo/algn); **to return (sb's) ~** responder a los disparos (de algn); [*troops*] responder al fuego enemigo; **to be/come under ~** (*lit*) estar/caer bajo fuego enemigo; (*fig*) ser atacado
Ⓑ VT **1** (= *shoot*) [+ *gun*] disparar; [+ *missile, arrow*] disparar, lanzar; [+ *rocket*] lanzar; [+ *shot*] efectuar; **to ~ a gun at sb** disparar contra algn; **he ~d a question at her** le lanzó una pregunta; **he continued to ~ (off) questions at her** continuó acosándola con preguntas
2 (= *operate*) **gas/oil ~d central heating** calefacción *f* central a *or* de gas/de petróleo
3 (= *set fire to*) [+ *property, building*] incendiar, prender fuego a
4 (*) (= *dismiss*) echar (a la calle), despedir; **you're ~d!** ¡queda usted despedido!
5 (*in kiln*) [+ *pottery*] cocer
6 (= *stimulate*) [+ *imagination*] estimular; **~d with enthusiasm/determination, the crowd ...** impulsados por el entusiasmo/por la determinación, la multitud ...
Ⓒ VI **1** (*Mil*) disparar (**at**, contra; **on** sobre); **ready, aim, ~!** ¡atención, apunten, fuego!
2 (*Aut*) [*engine*] encenderse, prender (*LAm*)
Ⓓ CPD ➤ **fire alarm** alarma *f* contra *or* de incendios ➤ **fire brigade** (*esp Brit*) cuerpo *m* de bomberos ➤ **fire chief** (*US*) jefe/a *m/f* de bomberos ➤ **fire department** (*US*) cuerpo *m* de bomberos ➤ **fire door** puerta *f* contra incendios ➤ **fire drill** simulacro *m* de incendio ➤ **fire engine** (*Brit*) coche *m* de bomberos ➤ **fire escape** escalera *f* de incendios ➤ **fire exit** salida *f* de incendios ➤ **fire extinguisher** extintor *m* (*Sp*), extinguidor *m* (*LAm*) ➤ **fire hazard: the spilt oil was a ~ hazard** el aceite derramado podía haber provocado un incendio ➤ **fire hydrant** boca *f* de incendios ➤ **fire insurance** seguro *m* contra incendios ➤ **fire prevention** prevención *f* de incendios ➤ **fire regulations** normas *fpl* para la prevención de incendios ➤ **fire retardant** ignifugante *m* ➤ **fire station** estación *f* or (*Sp*) parque *m* de bomberos ➤ **fire tender, fire truck** (*US*) coche *m* de bomberos ➤ **fire trap** *edificio muy peligroso en caso de incendio* ➤ **fire truck** (*US*) coche *m* de bomberos ➤ **fire warden** (*US*) *persona encargada de la lucha contra incendios*
➤ **fire up** VT + ADV (*fig*) enardecer; **to be/get ~d up about sth** estar enardecido/enardecerse por algo

firearm ['faɪərɑːm] N arma *f* de fuego

> Use **el/un** not **la/una** before feminine nouns beginning with stressed **a** or **ha** like **arma**.

firebomb ['faɪəbɒm] **Ⓐ** N bomba *f* incendiaria **Ⓑ** VT colocar una bomba incendiaria en; (*Aer*) bombardear con bombas incendiarias

firebrand ['faɪəbrænd] N agitador(a) *m/f*, revoltoso/a *m/f*

firecracker ['faɪəˌkrækəʳ] N petardo *m*

firefighter ['faɪəˌfaɪtəʳ] N bombero/a *m/f*

firefighting ['faɪəˌfaɪtɪŋ] N lucha *f* por apagar incendios
➤ **firefighting equipment** equipo *m* contra incendios

firefly ['faɪəflaɪ] N luciérnaga *f*

fireguard ['faɪəɡɑːd] N pantalla *f* de chimenea

firelight ['faɪəlaɪt] N luz *f* de la lumbre *or* del hogar; **by ~** a la luz de la lumbre *or* del hogar

firelighter ['faɪə,laɪtə'] N pastilla *f* de fuego, *barra de material inflamable que se utiliza para encender fuego en una chimenea*

fireman ['faɪəmən] N (*pl* **firemen**) bombero *m*

fireplace ['faɪəpleɪs] N chimenea *f*, hogar *m*

fireplug ['faɪəplʌg] N (*US*) boca *f* de incendios

firepower ['faɪə,paʊə'] N (*Mil*) potencia *f* de fuego

fireproof ['faɪəpruːf] ADJ [*material*] incombustible, ignífugo; [*suit, clothing*] ignífugo, a prueba de fuego; [*dish*] refractario

fire-raising ['faɪə,reɪzɪŋ] N (*Brit*) piromanía *f*

fire-resistant ['faɪərɪ,zɪstənt] ADJ ignífugo

fire-retardant ['faɪərɪ,tɑːdənt] ADJ resistente al fuego

fireside ['faɪəsaɪd] N **by the ~** junto a la chimenea, al amor de la lumbre

firewall ['faɪəwɔːl] N (*Internet*) firewall *m*

firewood ['faɪəwʊd] N leña *f*

firework ['faɪəwɜːk] N artilugio *m* pirotécnico (*frm*); **fireworks** fuegos *mpl* artificiales ➤ **firework display** fuegos *mpl* artificiales

firing ['faɪərɪŋ] N (= *bullets*) disparos *mpl*; (= *exchange of fire*) tiroteo *m* ➤ **firing line** línea *f* de fuego; ✦ IDIOM **to be in the ~ line** (*Mil, fig*) estar en la línea de fuego ➤ **firing squad** pelotón *m* (de fusilamiento)

firm¹ [fɜːm] **Ⓐ** ADJ (*compar* **~er**; *superl* **~est**) **1** (= *solid*) [*base*] firme, sólido; [*mattress, stomach, thighs*] duro; (= *secure*) [*hold*] firme, seguro; **beat the egg whites until ~** bata las claras a punto de nieve
2 (= *staunch*) [*belief, support*] firme; [*friends*] íntimo; [*friendship*] sólido; **she's a ~ believer in justice/discipline** cree firmemente en la justicia/la disciplina
3 (= *resolute, decisive*) [*decision, measures*] firme; [*voice*] seguro, firme; [*steps*] decidido, resuelto; **we are taking a ~ stand on this issue** mantenemos una postura firme con respecto a esta cuestión
4 (= *severe*) estricto, firme; **to be ~ with sb** ser estricto *or* firme con algn
5 (= *definite*) [*offer, order*] en firme; [*evidence*] concluyente, contundente
Ⓑ ADV **to stand ~** mantenerse firme
➤ **firm up** VT + ADV [+ *structure*] fortalecer, reforzar; [+ *thighs, muscles*] endurecer; [+ *proposal, deal*] concretar

firm² [fɜːm] N firma *f*, empresa *f*; **a ~ of accountants** una firma *or* empresa de contabilidad; **she joined a law ~** se incorporó a un bufete de abogados

firmly ['fɜːmlɪ] ADV [*fixed, entrenched*] firmemente; [*believe*] firmemente, con firmeza; [*speak, say*] con firmeza; **the crowd was ~ behind him** tenía todo el apoyo del público, el público le apoyaba firmemente; **they remain ~ opposed/ committed to the plan** se mantienen firmes en su oposición/entrega al proyecto

first [fɜːst] **Ⓐ** ADJ primero; (*before m sing noun*) primer; **I was ~!** ¡yo iba *or* estaba primero!; **he felt a bit lonely for the ~ few days** los primeros días se sentía un poco solo; **on his ~ birthday** en su primer cumpleaños, cuando cumpla/ cumplió un año; **in the ~ century** (*spoken form*) en el siglo primero *or* uno; (*in writing*) en el siglo I; **on the ~ floor** (*Brit*) en el primer piso; (*US*) en la planta baja; **at ~ hand** directamente; **in the ~ place** en primer lugar; **to win ~ place** (*in competition*) conseguir el primer puesto, ganar; **to win ~ prize** ganar el primer premio; **the ~ thing to do is ...** lo primero que hay que hacer es ...; **~ thing in the morning** a primera hora (de la mañana); **~ thing tomorrow** mañana a primera hora; **you don't know the ~ thing about it** no sabes nada en absoluto de esto; **the ~ time** la primera vez
Ⓑ ADV **1** (*in place, priority*) primero; **~ one, then another** primero uno, después otro; **we arrived ~** fuimos los primeros en llegar, llegamos los primeros; **~ of all** ante todo, antes que nada; **to come ~** (*in race*) ganar, llegar el primero *or* en primer lugar; (= *have priority*) estar primero, tener prioridad; **to get in ~** (*in conversation, process*) adelantarse; **~ and foremost** ante todo, antes que nada; **you go ~!** ¡tú primero!, ¡pasa tú!; **head ~** de cabeza; **you have to put your children's needs ~** primero están las

necesidades de tus hijos; **ladies ~** las señoras primero; ✦ IDIOM **~ come, ~ served** el que llega primero tiene prioridad
2 (= *before anything else*) primero, antes de nada; **~, I need a drink** primero *or* antes de nada *or* antes que nada, necesito una copa
3 (= *for the first time*) por primera vez; **the word was ~ used in 1835** la palabra se usó por primera vez en 1835; **I ~ met him in Paris** lo conocí en París
4 (= *rather*) primero, antes; **I'd die ~!** ¡antes me muero!
Ⓒ PRON **1** (*gen*) primero/a *m/f*; **to be the ~ to do sth** ser el primero en hacer algo; **the ~ of January** ◇ **January** (**the**) **~** el primero de enero, el uno de enero; **Charles the First** (*spoken form*) Carlos Primero; (*in writing*) Carlos I; **from the** (**very**) **~** desde el principio; **it's the ~ I've heard of it** ahora me entero, no lo sabía; **from ~ to last** de principio a fin
2 (= *first gear*) primera *f*; **in ~** en primera
3 (*Brit Univ*) ≈ sobresaliente *m*; **he got a ~ in French** ≈ se graduó en francés con sobresaliente
4 at ~ al principio
Ⓓ CPD ➤ **first aid** primeros auxilios *mpl* ➤ **first base** (*Baseball*) primera base *f*; ✦ IDIOM **not to get to ~ base** (*US**) quedar en agua de borrajas ➤ **first cousin** primo/a *m/f* hermano/a *or* carnal ➤ **first degree** licenciatura *f* ➤ **first edition** primera edición *f*; [*of early or rare book*] edición *f* príncipe ➤ **first form** *or* **year** (*Scol*) primer curso de secundaria; **~-year student** (*Univ*) estudiante *mf* de primer año (*de carrera universitaria*) ➤ **first gear** primera *f* ➤ **first lady** (*US*) primera dama *f* ➤ **first language** (= *mother tongue*) lengua *f* materna; [*of country*] lengua *f* principal ➤ **first lieutenant** (*US Aer*) teniente *mf*; (*Brit Naut*) teniente *mf* de navío ➤ **first light: at ~ light** al amanecer, al alba ➤ **first minister** presidente/a *m/f* ➤ **first name** nombre *m* (de pila); **to be on ~ name terms with sb** ≈ tutear a algn ➤ **first night** (*Theat*) estreno *m* ➤ **first officer** primer(a) oficial *m/f* ➤ **first performance** estreno *m* ➤ **first person** (*Gram*) primera persona *f*

first-aid [,fɜːst'eɪd] CPD ➤ **first-aid kit** botiquín *m* de urgencia ➤ **first-aid post, first-aid station** (*US*) puesto *m* de socorro

first-born ['fɜːstbɔːn] ADJ, N primogénito/a *m/f*

first-class ['fɜːstklɑːs] **Ⓐ** ADJ **1** [*passenger, accommodation*] de primera clase; [*travel, compartment, train*] de primera (clase); [*stamp*] *referido a un sello de correos, que asegura mayor rapidez en la entrega*
2 (= *very good*) [*education, performance*] de primera (calidad)
Ⓑ CPD ➤ **first-class honours degree** (*Univ*) licenciatura *f* con matrícula de honor ➤ **first-class mail, first-class post** *servicio de correos que asegura mayor rapidez en la entrega* ➤ **first-class ticket** (*Rail*) billete *m* (*Sp*) *or* boleto *m* (*LAm*) de primera clase
Ⓒ ADV **to travel ~** viajar en primera; **to send a letter ~** *enviar una carta por el sistema de correos que asegura una entrega rápida*

first-ever ['fɜːst,evə'] ADJ primerísimo

first-generation ['fɜːst,dʒenə'reɪʃən] ADJ de primera generación; **he's a ~ American** es americano de primera generación

first-hand ['fɜːst'hænd] **Ⓐ** ADJ [*information, account, experience, knowledge*] de primera mano **Ⓑ** ADV directamente

firstly ['fɜːstlɪ] ADV **1** (= *before anything else*) antes que nada, en primer lugar, **2** (= *on the first occasion*) primero **3** (= *in the first place*) en primer lugar; **~, it's too small and secondly it's too expensive** en primer lugar, es demasiado pequeño y en segundo lugar, es demasiado caro

first-rate ['fɜːst'reɪt] ADJ de primera categoría *or* clase

first-time ['fɜːst'taɪm] ADJ **~ buyer** *persona que compra su primera vivienda*

fiscal ['fɪskəl] ADJ fiscal ➤ **fiscal year** año *m* fiscal

fish [fɪʃ] **Ⓐ** N (*pl* **~** *or* **~es**) (*alive*) pez *m*; (*as food*) pescado *m*; ✦ IDIOMS **I've got other ~ to fry*** tengo cosas más importantes que hacer; **there are other ~ in the sea** hay otros peces en el mar; **to be like a ~ out of water** estar

como pez fuera del agua
Ⓑ VI pescar; [*trawler*] faenar; **I'm going ~ing** voy de pesca; **to go salmon ~ing** ir a pescar salmón; **to ~ for** [+ *trout, salmon etc*] pescar; [+ *compliments, information*] andar a la caza de
Ⓒ CPD ➤ **fish and chips** pescado *m* frito con patatas fritas ➤ **fish and chip shop** *tienda de comida rápida principalmente de pescado frito y patatas fritas* ➤ **fish cake** croqueta *f* de pescado ➤ **fish course** (plato *m* de) pescado *m* ➤ **fish factory** fábrica *f* de pescado ➤ **fish farm** piscifactoría *f*, criadero *m* de peces ➤ **fish farming** piscicultura *f*, cría *f* de peces ➤ **fish finger** (*Brit*) palito *m* de pescado empanado ➤ **fish glue** cola *f* de pescado ➤ **fish knife** cuchillo *m* de pescado ➤ **fish seller** (*US*) = **fishmonger** ➤ **fish shop** pescadería *f* ➤ **fish slice** (*Brit*) pala *f* para el pescado ➤ **fish soup** sopa *f* de pescado ➤ **fish stick** (*US*) palito *m* de pescado empanado ➤ **fish store** (*US*) pescadería *f* ➤ **fish tank** acuario *m*
➤ **fish out** VT + ADV sacar

fishbone ['fɪʃbəʊn] N espina *f*, raspa *f*

fishbowl ['fɪʃbəʊl] N pecera *f*

fisherman ['fɪʃəmən] N (*pl* **fishermen**) pescador *m*

fishery ['fɪʃərɪ] N (= *area*) caladero *m*, pesquería *f*; (= *industry*) pesca *f*, industria *f* pesquera

fishing ['fɪʃɪŋ] N pesca *f*; **to go on a ~ expedition** ir de pesca ➤ **fishing boat** barco *m* pesquero *or* de pesca ➤ **fishing fleet** flota *f* pesquera ➤ **fishing industry** industria *f* pesquera ➤ **fishing licence** licencia *f* de pesca ➤ **fishing line** sedal *m* ➤ **fishing net** red *f* de pesca ➤ **fishing permit** licencia *f* de pesca ➤ **fishing port** puerto *m* pesquero ➤ **fishing rod** caña *f* de pescar ➤ **fishing tackle** equipo *m* de pesca

fishmonger ['fɪʃmʌŋɡəʳ] N (*Brit*) pescadero/a *m/f*; **~'s (shop)** pescadería *f*

fishnet ['fɪʃnet] N (*US*) red *f* de pesca ➤ **fishnet stockings** medias *fpl* de red *or* malla

fishpaste ['fɪʃpeɪst] N pasta *f* de pescado

fishy ['fɪʃɪ] ADJ (*compar* **fishier**; *superl* **fishiest**) **1** [*smell, taste*] a pescado **2** (*) (= *suspect*) sospechoso; **there's something ~ going on here** aquí hay gato encerrado, me huele a chamusquina (*Sp**)

fission ['fɪʃən] N fisión *f*

fissure ['fɪʃəʳ] N hendidura *f*, grieta *f*; (*Anat, Geol, Metal*) fisura *f*

fist [fɪst] N puño *m*; **he banged his ~ on the table** dio un puñetazo en la mesa; **to shake one's ~ at sb** amenazar con el puño a algn ➤ **fist fight** pelea *f* a puñetazos

fistful ['fɪstfʊl] N puñado *m*

fit¹ [fɪt] ADJ (*compar* **~ter**; *superl* **~test**) **1** (= *suitable*) adecuado; **~ for sth**: **~ for human consumption/habitation** comestible/habitable; **he's not ~ for the job** no sirve para el puesto, no es apto para el puesto; **a meal ~ for a king** una comida digna de reyes; **~ for nothing** inútil; **to see/ think ~ to do sth**: **you must do as you think ~** debes hacer lo que estimes conveniente *or* lo que creas apropiado; **she didn't see ~ to mention it** no creyó apropiado mencionarlo; **to be ~ to do sth: he's not ~ to teach** no sirve para profesor; **you're not ~ to be seen** no estás presentable, no estás para que te vea la gente; **you're not ~ to drive** no estás en condiciones de conducir; **the meat was not ~ to eat** *or* **to be eaten** (= *unhealthy*) la carne no estaba en buenas condiciones; (= *bad-tasting*) la carne era incomible, la carne no se podía comer
2 (= *healthy*) (*Med*) sano; (*Sport*) en forma; **to be ~ for work** (*after illness*) estar en condiciones de trabajar; **to get ~** (*Med*) reponerse; (*Sport*) ponerse en forma; **to keep ~** mantenerse en forma; **she's not yet ~ to travel** todavía no está en condiciones de viajar; **✦** IDIOM **to be (as) ~ as a fiddle** estar rebosante de salud

fit² [fɪt] **Ⓐ** VT **1** (= *be right size*) [*clothes*] quedar bien a; [*key*] entrar en, encajar en; **it ~s me like a glove** me queda como un guante; **he can't find shirts to ~ him** no encuentra camisas que le queden *or* vengan bien
2 (= *match*) [+ *facts*] corresponderse con; [+ *description*] encajar con; [+ *need*] adecuarse a; **your story doesn't ~ the**

facts tu historia no se corresponde con los hechos; **she doesn't ~ the feminine stereotype** no encaja con el estereotipo femenino; **the punishment should ~ the crime** el castigo debe adecuarse al delito
3 (= *install*) [+ *windows*] instalar, poner; [+ *carpet*] poner; [+ *kitchen, bathroom, domestic appliance*] instalar; **they're having a new kitchen ~ted** les van a instalar una cocina nueva; **he ~ted the shelf to the wall** fijó el estante a la pared; **to ~ sth into place** hacer encajar algo; **I finally began to ~ the pieces together** (*fig*) finalmente empecé a encajar todas las piezas
4 (= *supply*) equipar de; **to be ~ted with sth** estar equipado con algo; **he has been ~ted with a new hearing aid** le han puesto un audífono nuevo
Ⓑ VI **1** (= *be the right size*) **the dress doesn't ~ very well** el vestido no me/le queda muy bien; **this key doesn't ~** esta llave no encaja *or* entra; **will the cupboard ~ into the corner?** ¿cabrá el armario en el rincón?; **it ~s in/on here** se encaja aquí; **the lid won't ~ on this saucepan** la tapa no encaja en esta cazuela
2 (= *match*) [*facts, description*] concordar, corresponderse; **it doesn't ~ with what he said to me** no concuerda *or* no se corresponde con lo que me dijo a mí; **it all ~s now!** ¡todo encaja ahora!
Ⓒ N **the lycra in the fabric ensures a good ~** la licra de la tela hace que se ajuste perfectamente; **it was a perfect ~** me/ le quedaba perfectamente; **it's rather a tight ~** me está un poco justo *or* apretado
➤ **fit in Ⓐ** VI + ADV **1** (= *correspond*) [*fact, statement*] concordar, cuadrar (**with** con); **that ~s in with what he told me** eso concuerda *or* cuadra *or* se corresponde con lo que me dijo él
2 (= *adapt*) **to ~ in with sb's plans** amoldarse *or* adaptarse a los planes de algn
3 (= *belong*) [*person*] **he left because he didn't ~ in** se marchó porque no congeniaba con los demás *or* no encajaba
4 (= *go in*) (*into cupboard, car, corner*) caber; (*into jigsaw puzzle*) encajar; **will we all ~ in?** ¿cabremos todos?
Ⓑ VT + ADV **1** (= *make room for*) **can you ~ another book/ passenger in?** ¿te cabe otro libro/pasajero más?; **you could ~ an illustration in here** aquí podrías poner *or* aquí tienes sitio para poner una ilustración
2 (= *make time for*) **I could ~ you in next Friday** podría hacerte un hueco el próximo viernes; **I managed to ~ in a trip to Ávila** logré incluir una excursión a Ávila
➤ **fit out** VT + ADV [+ *ship, expedition*] equipar; [+ *warship*] armar
➤ **fit up** VT + ADV **1** (= *install*) instalar **2** (*Brit*) (= *supply*) equipar; **to ~ sth/sb up with sth** proveer algo/a algn de algo, equipar algo/a algn con algo **3** (*) (= *frame*) **I've been ~ted up!** ¡han hecho que aparezca como el culpable!

fit³ [fɪt] N **1** (*Med*) ataque *m*; **epileptic ~** ataque *m* epiléptico; **she had a ~ last night** anoche tuvo un ataque **2** (= *outburst*) **a ~ of anger** un arranque *or* un arrebato *or* (*frm*) un acceso de cólera; **a ~ of coughing** un ataque *or* (*frm*) un acceso de tos; **I had a ~ of (the) giggles** me dio un ataque de risa; **he'd have a ~ if he knew** le daría un síncope si se enterara*, se pondría histérico si se enterara*; **to be in ~s*** partirse de risa*; **by** *or* **in ~s and starts** a tropezones, a trompicones*

fitful ['fɪtfʊl] ADJ intermitente; [*progress*] irregular; **she fell into a ~ sleep** se durmió pero no descansó bien

fitness ['fɪtnɪs] **Ⓐ** N **1** (= *suitability*) aptitud *f*, capacidad *f* (**for** para) **2** (= *state of health*) estado *m* físico; (= *good health*) buena forma *f* **Ⓑ** CPD ➤ **fitness fanatic** fanático/a *m/f* del mantenimiento físico ➤ **fitness test** prueba *f* de estado físico

fitted ['fɪtɪd] ADJ **1** (= *tailored*) [*jacket, shirt*] entallado; [*sheet*] de cuatro picos; **~ carpet** alfombra *f* de pared a pared, moqueta *f* (*Sp*) **2** (*Brit*) [*cupboards*] empotrado; **~ kitchen** cocina *f* con armarios empotrados, cocina *f* integral

fitter ['fɪtəʳ] N (*in garage*) mecánico/a *m/f*

fitting ['fɪtɪŋ] **Ⓐ** ADJ (= *appropriate*) adecuado, apropiado; (= *worthy*) digno; **it is ~ that ...** es apropiado que ...; **it seemed ~ to ...** (+ INFIN) parecía apropiado *or* oportuno ... + infin

❸ N **1** [of dress] prueba f **2 fittings** [of house] accesorios mpl; [of shop] mobiliario msing; **bathroom ~s** accesorios mpl de baño; **electrical/gas ~s** instalaciones fpl eléctricas/de gas **❹** CPD ➤ **fitting room** probador m

five [faɪv] NUMBER cinco m; **she is ~ (years old)** tiene cinco años (de edad); **it costs ~ pounds** cuesta or vale cinco libras; **it's ~ (o'clock)** son las cinco; **they live at number ~** viven en el número cinco; **~ and a quarter/half** cinco y cuarto/medio; **to divide sth into ~** dividir algo en cinco; **they are sold in ~s** se venden de cinco en cinco; **there are ~ of us** somos cinco; **all ~ of them came** vinieron los cinco

five-a-side ['faɪvə,saɪd] ADJ **~ football** (outdoors) futbito m; (indoors) fútbol m sala

five-day week [,faɪv,deɪ'wiːk] N semana f inglesa

five-o'clock shadow ['faɪvəklɒk'ʃædəʊ] N barba f crecida

fiver* ['faɪvə'] N (= banknote) (Brit) billete m de cinco libras; (US) billete m de cinco dólares; (= amount) (Brit) cinco libras fpl; (US) cinco dólares mpl

fix [fɪks] **❹** VT **1** (= position) fijar, asegurar; **to ~ sth in place** fijar or asegurar algo en su sitio
2 (= attach) (with nails) clavar; (with string) atar, amarrar; (with glue) pegar; **~ the mirror to the wall** fije el espejo a la pared; **the phone is ~ed to the wall** el teléfono está colgado de la pared; **the chairs and desks are ~ed to the floor** las sillas y mesas están sujetas or atornilladas al suelo; **they ~ed the two pieces of bone together with a metal plate** unieron los dos trozos de hueso con una placa de metal; **the image of her was now firmly ~ed in his mind** su imagen estaba ahora firmemente grabada en su mente
3 (= arrange, settle) [+ date, time] fijar; [+ meeting] fijar, convenir; **nothing's been ~ed yet** todavía no se ha decidido or acordado nada; **I've ~ed it for you to meet her** lo he arreglado para que la conozcas; **how are you ~ed for this evening?** ¿tienes planes para esta noche?; **how are we ~ed for money?** ¿qué tal andamos de dinero?
4 (= determine) [+ price, rate] fijar
5 (*) (= rig) [+ fight, race, election] amañar; [+ price] fijar; **they're in a dispute over price ~ing** tienen una disputa por la fijación de los precios
6 (= rivet) [+ eyes, gaze] fijar, clavar; [+ attention] fijar; **she ~ed her eyes on him** le clavó los ojos, fijó la mirada en él; **she had ~ed all her hopes on passing the exam** tenía todas sus esperanzas puestas en aprobar el examen
7 (= repair) [+ car, appliance] arreglar, reparar; **to get** or **have sth ~ed** arreglar or reparar algo; **I've got to get my car ~ed this week** tengo que arreglar or reparar el coche esta semana, tengo que llevar el coche a arreglar or reparar esta semana; **I should have my teeth ~ed** tendría que arreglarme los dientes
8 (*) (= deal with) encargarse de*
9 (= prepare) [+ meal, drink] preparar; **I ~ed myself a coffee** me preparé un café
10 (esp US) (= tidy up) [+ hair, makeup] arreglar; **to ~ one's hair** arreglarse el pelo
11 (= make permanent) [+ film, colour, dye] fijar
❸ VI (US) **1** (*) (= intend) tener intención de; **I'm ~ing to go to graduate school** tengo intención de or tengo pensado hacer estudios de postgraduado
2 (= arrange) **we had already ~ed to go to the theatre** ya habíamos quedado para ir al teatro
❹ N **1** (*) (= predicament) apuro m, aprieto m; **to be in/get into a ~** estar/meterse en un apuro or un aprieto
2 (*) [of drug] (gen) dosis f inv; (when injected) pinchazo* m, chute m (Sp**); **she needs her daily ~ of publicity** necesita su dosis diaria de publicidad
3 (Aer, Naut) posición f; **it's been hard to get a ~ on what's going on** (fig) ha sido difícil entender lo que pasa
4 (*) (= set-up) tongo* m; **the fight/result was a ~** hubo tongo en la pelea/el resultado*
5 (*) (= solution) arreglo m, apaño* m
➤ **fix up** VT + ADV **1** (= arrange) [+ date] fijar; [+ meeting] fijar, convenir; **to ~ sth up with sb** quedar con algn en algo, convenir algo con algn **2** (= repair, put in order) arreglar **3** (= set up, install) instalar, poner **4** (= provide) **I can ~ you up with a place to stay** puedo conseguirte un sitio donde alojarte **❸** VI + ADV **to ~ up with sb to** (+ INFIN) convenir con algn en + infin

fixation [fɪk'seɪʃən] N obsesión f, fijación f

fixative ['fɪksətɪv] N fijador m

fixed [fɪkst] **❹** ADJ **1** (= permanent) [amount, rate, interest] fijo; **of no ~ address** or (Brit) **abode** sin domicilio fijo
2 (= prearranged) establecido; **at a ~ time** a una hora establecida; **there's no ~ agenda** no hay un orden del día fijo **3** (= immovable) [smile] inamovible; [stare] fijo; **to keep one's eyes ~ on sth** mantener la mirada fija en algo
4 (= inflexible) [opinion] firme, rígido; [idea] fijo **❸** CPD ➤ **fixed assets** activo msing fijo ➤ **fixed penalty (fine)** sanción f fija ➤ **fixed price** precio m fijo

fixture ['fɪkstʃə'] **❹** N **1** [of house etc] **fixtures** instalaciones fpl fijas; **the house was sold with ~s and fittings** la casa se vendió totalmente equipada **2** (Brit Sport) encuentro m **3** (= permanent feature) elemento m fijo **❸** CPD ➤ **fixture list** (Brit) lista f de encuentros

fizz [fɪz] **❹** N **1** (= fizziness) efervescencia f, gas m; (= fizzing noise) silbido m, ruido m sibilante **2** (fig) chispa f; **the ~ had gone out of their relationship** a su relación no le quedaba chispa **❸** VI [drink] burbujear
➤ **fizzle out** VI + ADV [fire, firework] apagarse; [enthusiasm, interest] morirse

fizzy ['fɪzɪ] ADJ (compar **fizzier**; superl **fizziest**) (Brit) [drink] gaseoso, con gas

fjord [fjɔːd] N fiordo m

FL ABBR (US) = **Florida**

Fla. ABBR (US) = **Florida**

flab* [flæb] N gordura f

flabbergasted ['flæbəgɑːstɪd] ADJ pasmado, atónito

flabby ['flæbɪ] ADJ (compar **flabbier**; superl **flabbiest**) (= fat) gordo

flag¹ [flæg] **❹** N [of country] bandera f; (Naut) pabellón m; (small, as souvenir, also Sport) banderín m; **~ of convenience** pabellón m de conveniencia; ✦ IDIOMS **to keep the ~ flying** mantener alto el pabellón; **to show the ~** hacer acto de presencia; **to wrap o.s.** or **drape o.s. in the ~** (esp US) escudarse en el patriotismo
❸ VT (= mark) [+ path] señalar con banderitas; [+ item, reference] señalar, marcar; (also ~ **down**) [+ taxi] (hacer) parar **❹** CPD ➤ **flag day** (Brit) día m de colecta de una organización benéfica ➤ **Flag Day** (US) día m de la Bandera (14 junio) ➤ **flag stop** (US) parada f discrecional ➤ **flag down** VT + ADV [+ taxi] (hacer) parar; **to ~ sb down** hacer señales a algn para que se detenga

flag² [flæg] VI [strength, person] flaquear; [enthusiasm] enfriarse, decaer; [conversation] decaer; **he soon revived their ~ging spirits** les levantó el ánimo rápidamente

flag³ [flæg] N (also **~stone**) losa f

flagpole ['flægpəʊl] N asta f de bandera

> Use **el/un** not **la/una** before feminine nouns beginning with stressed **a** or **ha** like **asta**.

flagrant ['fleɪgrənt] ADJ flagrante

flagship ['flægʃɪp] N **1** (Naut) buque m insignia, buque m almirante **2** (fig) punta f de lanza

flagstaff ['flægstɑːf] N asta f de bandera

> Use **el/un** not **la/una** before feminine nouns beginning with stressed **a** or **ha** like **asta**.

flag-waving ['flæg,weɪvɪŋ] N (fig) patriotismo m de banderita

flail [fleɪl] VI **to ~ (about)** [arms, legs] agitarse; [person] revolverse

flair [fleə'] N (= gift) don m; (= instinct) instinto m; (= style) elegancia f, estilo m; **to have a ~ for languages** tener don de lenguas, tener facilidad para los idiomas

flak [flæk] **❹** N **1** fuego m antiaéreo **2** (*) (= criticism) críticas fpl; **to get a lot of ~** ser muy criticado **❸** CPD ➤ **flak jacket** chaleco m antibalas

flake [fleɪk] **❹** N [of paint] desconchón m; [of skin, soap]

escama *f*; [*of snow*] copo *m* **❸** VI (*also* ~ **off**, ~ **away**) [*paint*] descascarillarse, desconcharse; [*skin*] pelarse **❸** VT [+ *cooked fish*] desmenuzar
➤ **flake out*** VI + ADV (*Brit*) (= *faint*) desplomarse; (= *fall asleep*) caer rendido; **to be ~d out*** estar rendido

flaky ['fleɪkɪ] ADJ (*compar* **flakier**; *superl* **flakiest**) [*paintwork*] desconchado; [*skin*] escamoso ➤ **flaky pastry** (*Culin*) hojaldre *m*

flambé ['flɑ:mbeɪ] **❹** ADJ flam(b)eado **❸** VT flam(b)ear

flamboyant [flæm'bɔɪənt] ADJ [*person, behaviour, style*] extravagante; [*clothes, colour*] vistoso, llamativo

flame [fleɪm] **❹** N **1** [*of fire*] llama *f*; **to be in ~s** arder *or* estar en llamas; **to burst into ~s** [*car, plane*] estallar en llamas; **he watched the house go up in ~s** miraba cómo la casa era pasto de las llamas; **to fan the ~s** (*lit*) avivar el fuego; (*fig*) echar leña al fuego **2** (*) (= *lover*) **old ~*** antiguo amor *m* **❸** VI [*fire*] llamear; [*passion*] encenderse; [*eyes*] brillar **❸** VT (*Internet*) insultar a través de la Red, abuchear en la Red

flameproof ['fleɪmpru:f] ADJ ignífugo, a prueba de fuego

flamethrower ['fleɪm,θrəʊə'] N lanzallamas *m inv*

flaming ['fleɪmɪŋ] ADJ **1** [*torch*] llameante; [*vehicle*] en llamas **2** [*red, orange*] encendido; **she had ~ red hair** tenía el pelo de un rojo encendido **3 we had a ~ row** tuvimos una acalorada discusión **4** (*Brit***) (= *damn*) condenado*, maldito*

flamingo [flə'mɪŋgəʊ] N flamenco *m*

flammable ['flæməbl] ADJ inflamable

flan [flæn] N tarta *f*

⚠ **flan** ≠ *flan*

Flanders ['flɑ:ndəz] N Flandes *m*

flange [flændʒ] N (*on wheel*) pestaña *f*; (*on pipe*) reborde *m*

flank [flæŋk] **❹** N [*of person*] costado *m*; [*of animal*] ijar *m*, ijada *f*; (*Mil*) flanco *m* **❸** VT (= *stand at side of*) [+ *entrance, statue etc*] flanquear (*also Mil*); **he was ~ed by two policemen** iba escoltado por dos policías

flannel ['flænl] N **1** (= *fabric*) franela *f*; (*Brit*) (= *face flannel*) manopla *f* **2 flannels** (*Brit*) (= *trousers*) pantalones *mpl* de franela

flannelette [,flænə'let] N (*Brit*) franela *f* de algodón

flap [flæp] **❹** N **1** [*of pocket, envelope*] solapa *f*; [*of table*] hoja *f* (plegable); [*of counter*] trampa *f*; [*of skin*] colgajo *m*; (*Aer*) alerón *m* **2** (= *act*) [*of wing*] aletazo *m* **3** (*Brit**) (= *crisis*) crisis *f inv*; (= *row*) lío* *m*; **to get into a ~*** ponerse nervioso **❸** VT [+ *wings*] batir; [+ *arms*] agitar **❸** VI **1** [*wings*] aletear; [*sails*] agitarse; [*flag*] ondear, agitarse **2** (*) (= *panic*) ponerse nervioso; **don't ~!** ¡con calma!

flapjack ['flæpdʒæk] N (*US*) (= *pancake*) torta *f*, panqueque *m* (*LAm*); (*Brit*) *torta de avena*

flare [fleə'] **❹** N **1** (= *blaze*) llamarada *f*; (= *signal*) bengala *f* (*also Mil, for target*); (*on runway*) baliza *f*; **solar ~** erupción *f* solar **2** (*Sew*) vuelo *m* **3 flares** (= *trousers*) pantalones *mpl* de campana **❸** VI **1** [*match, torch*] llamear **2** [*nostrils*] ensancharse **3** [*tempers*] caldearse, calentarse
➤ **flare up** VI + ADV **1** [*fire*] llamear **2** (*fig*) [*person*] estallar, ponerse furioso (**at** con); [*riots*] estallar; [*epidemic*] declararse **3** [*wound*] resentirse, volver a dar problemas; [*illness, rash*] recrudecerse

flared [fleəd] ADJ [*trousers*] de campana; [*skirt*] de mucho vuelo, acampanado

flare-up ['fleər'ʌp] N [*of anger*] arranque *m*; (= *quarrel*) riña *f*; [*of violence*] estallido *m*; [*of illness, acne*] recrudecimiento *m*

flash [flæʃ] **❹** N **1** [*of light*] destello *m*; [*of gun*] fogonazo *m*; [*of jewel*] centelleo *m*, destellos *mpl*; **a ~ of lightning** un relámpago
2 (= *burst*) **a ~ of anger** un arranque *or* un arrebato de cólera; **a ~ of inspiration** una ráfaga *or* un momento de inspiración; ✦ IDIOM **a ~ in the pan** flor de un día
3 (= *instant*) instante *m*; **in a ~** en un abrir y cerrar de ojos, en un instante; **it all happened in a ~** todo sucedió en un

abrir y cerrar de ojos *or* en un instante; **it came to him in a ~** de repente lo vio todo claro; **quick as a ~** como un relámpago *or* un rayo
4 (*Phot*) flash *m*
5 (*US*) (= *torch*) linterna *f*
❸ VT **1** (= *direct*) [+ *look*] lanzar; [+ *smile*] dirigir
2 (= *shine*) **she ~ed the light in my eyes** me enfocó con la luz en los ojos; **to ~ one's (head)lights** (*Aut*) hacer señales con las luces
3 (= *send quickly*) [+ *news, information*] transmitir rápidamente; **the pictures were ~ed around the world** las imágenes circularon rápidamente por todo el mundo
4 (= *display briefly*) mostrar; **I ~ed my card at the security guard** le enseñé *or* mostré brevemente mi tarjeta al guardia de seguridad; **the screen ~es a message** aparece brevemente un mensaje en la pantalla, la pantalla muestra brevemente un mensaje
5 (= *flaunt*) hacer alarde de, fardar de (*Sp**)
❸ VI **1** (= *shine*) [*light*] brillar de forma intermitente *or* intermitentemente; [*eyes, teeth*] brillar; [*jewels*] brillar, lanzar destellos; **cameras ~ed as she stepped from the car** saltaron los flashes de las cámaras cuando ella salió del coche; **a police car raced past, lights ~ing** pasó un coche de policía a toda velocidad, con las luces lanzando destellos; **a ~ing neon sign** un anuncio de neón intermitente; **her eyes ~ed with anger** se le encendieron los ojos
2 (*Aut*) **I ~ed to let him out** le hice señales con las luces para que pasara
3 (= *move quickly*) **a thought ~ed through my mind** una idea me cruzó la mente como un relámpago; **his whole life ~ed before his eyes** volvió a revivir toda su vida en unos instantes; **a message ~ed up on the screen** apareció brevemente un mensaje en la pantalla; **to ~ by** *or* **past** [*vehicle, person*] pasar a toda velocidad, pasar como un rayo; [*time*] pasar volando
4 (*Cine*) **to ~ back to** retroceder a; **to ~ forward to** adelantarse hasta
5 (*) (= *expose o.s.*) exhibirse
❹ ADJ (*) (= *showy*) [*car, clothes*] llamativo, fardón (*Sp**); **a ~ restaurant** un restaurante ostentoso, un restaurante de esos impresionantes*
❺ CPD ➤ **flash bulb** bombilla *f* de flash ➤ **flash card** tarjeta *f* ➤ **flash flood** riada *f* ➤ **flash gun** (*Phot*) disparador *m* de flash

flashback ['flæʃbæk] N (*Cine*) escena *f* retrospectiva, flashback *m*

flashcube ['flæʃkju:b] N (*Phot*) cubo *m* de flash

flasher* ['flæʃə'] N (= *man*) exhibicionista *m*

flashlight ['flæʃlaɪt] N (*esp US*) (= *torch*) linterna *f*

flashy ['flæʃɪ] ADJ (*compar* **flashier**; *superl* **flashiest**) [*jewellery, clothes, car*] llamativo, ostentoso; [*colour*] chillón; [*person*] llamativo

flask [flɑ:sk] N (*for brandy*) petaca *f*; (= *vacuum flask*) termo *m*; (*Chem*) matraz *m*, redoma *f*

flat¹ [flæt] **❹** ADJ (*compar* **~ter**; *superl* **~test**) **1** (= *level*) [*surface, roof*] plano; [*countryside*] llano; **he was lying ~ on the floor** estaba tumbado en el suelo; **the sea was calm and ~** el mar estaba en calma y no había olas; **to fall ~ on one's face** (*lit*) caer(se) de bruces; **the government's campaign fell ~ on its face** la campaña del gobierno resultó un fracaso; ✦ IDIOM **~ as a pancake*** liso como la palma de la mano
2 (= *smooth, even*) [*road, surface*] liso, llano
3 (= *shallow*) [*dish*] llano; [*box*] plano
4 [*foot, shoe*] plano; [*nose*] chato; **to have ~ feet** tener los pies planos
5 (= *deflated*) [*tyre, ball*] pinchado, desinflado; **we got a ~ tyre** *or* (*US*) **tire** se nos pinchó una rueda, se nos ponchó una llanta (*Mex*)
6 (= *dull, lifeless*) [*voice, colour, atmosphere*] apagado; [*taste, style*] soso; [*light*] sin contraste; [*drink*] sin burbujas *or* gas; (*esp Brit*) [*battery*] descargado; **I've got a ~ battery** se me ha descargado la batería; **I'm feeling rather ~** estoy un poco deprimido; **she meant it as a joke, but it fell ~** lo dijo de broma, pero nadie le vio la gracia; **the champagne has gone ~** al champán se le ha ido la fuerza *or* se le han ido las burbujas

7 (= *inactive*) [*trade, business*] flojo
8 (= *outright*) [*refusal, denial*] rotundo, terminante; **his suggestion met with a ~ refusal** su sugerencia recibió una negativa rotunda *or* terminante
9 (*Mus*) **9.1** (*voice, instrument*) desafinado; **she/her singing was ~** desafinaba cantando **9.2** (*of key*) bemol; **E ~ major** mi bemol mayor
10 (= *fixed*) [*rate, fee, charge*] fijo
Ⓑ ADV **1** (= *absolutely*) **to be ~ broke*** estar pelado*, estar sin un duro (*Sp**), estar sin un peso (*LAm**)
2 (= *outright*) [*refuse*] rotundamente, terminantemente; **to turn sth down ~** rechazar algo rotundamente *or* de plano
3 (= *exactly*) **he did it in ten minutes ~** lo hizo en diez minutos justos *or* exactos
4 to go ~ out ir a toda máquina; **to go ~ out for sth** intentar conseguir algo por todos los medios
5 (*Mus*) **to play/sing ~** tocar/cantar demasiado bajo, desafinar
Ⓒ N **1** (*of hand*) palma *f*; (*of sword*) cara *f* de la hoja
2 (*Mus*) bemol *m*
3 (*Aut*) pinchazo *m*, ponchada *f* (*Mex*); **we got a ~** se nos pinchó una rueda, se nos ponchó una llanta (*Mex*)
Ⓓ CPD **➤ flat cap** (*esp Brit*) gorra de lana con visera **➤ flat pack it comes in a ~** viene en un paquete plano para su automontaje **➤ flat racing** carreras *fpl* de caballos sin obstáculos **➤ flat screen** (*TV, Comput*) pantalla *f* plana

flat² [flæt] N (*esp Brit*)(= *apartment*) apartamento *m*, piso *m* (*Sp*), departamento *m* (*LAm*)

flat-chested ['flæt'tʃestɪd] ADJ de pecho plano

flatly ['flætlɪ] ADV **1** (= *without emotion*) [*read, recite*] monótonamente; [*say, reply*] de manera inexpresiva
2 (= *categorically*) [*refuse, deny*] terminantemente, rotundamente; **we are ~ opposed to it** nos oponemos terminantemente *or* rotundamente a ello

flatmate ['flætmeɪt] N (*Brit*) compañero/a *m/f* de apartamento *or* (*Sp*) de piso *or* (*LAm*) de departamento

flatness ['flætnɪs] N **1** (*of land*) llanura *f*, lo llano; (*of surface*) lisura *f* **2** (*of atmosphere, relationship, voice*) monotonía *f*

flat-pack ['flætpæk] ADJ **~furniture** muebles *mpl* automontables (embalados en paquetes planos)

flatten ['flætn] VT **1** (= *compress, squash*) [+ *road, grass*] allanar, aplanar; [+ *hair, paper, map*] alisar; **I ~ed myself against the wall** me pegué a la pared **2** (= *level out*) [+ *surface*] nivelar **3** (= *knock down*) [+ *building, city*] arrasar; [+ *person*] tumbar **4** (= *defeat, subdue*) desanimar, desalentar

flatter ['flætə'] VT **1** (*sincerely*) halagar; (*insincerely*) adular, lisonjear; **to feel ~ed** sentirse halagado; **he only said it to ~ you** te lo dijo sólo para adularte; **to ~ o.s. on sth/that** enorgullecerse de algo/de que; **don't ~ yourself, I didn't come all this way just to see you** no te hagas ilusiones, no he venido hasta aquí sólo para verte a ti **2** (= *show to advantage*) favorecer; **that colour ~s you** ese color te favorece

flatterer ['flætərə'] N adulador(a) *m/f*

flattering ['flætərɪŋ] ADJ **1** (= *complimentary*) [*remark, words*] halagador; **it was ~ to be told how indispensable he was** te halagó que le dijeran lo indispensable que era **2** [*photo, clothes*] favorecedor; **that dress isn't ~ at all on you** ese vestido no te favorece nada

flattery ['flætərɪ] N halagos *mpl*, lisonjas *fpl*; **~ will get you nowhere!** ¡con halagos *or* lisonjas no vas a conseguir nada!

flatulence ['flætjʊləns] N flatulencia *f*

flatware ['flætweə'] N (*US*) cubertería *f*

flaunt [flɔːnt] VT (*pej*) [+ *wealth, knowledge*] alardear de, hacer alarde de; **to ~ o.s.** pavonearse

flautist ['flɔːtɪst] N (*esp Brit*) flautista *mf*

flavorsome ['fleɪvəsəm] ADJ (*US*) [*food, dish*] sabroso; [*wine*] con mucho sabor, sabroso

flavour, flavor (*US*) ['fleɪvə'] **Ⓐ** N (*gen*) sabor *m*, gusto *m* (**of** a); (= *flavouring*) condimento *m*; (*fig*) sabor *m*, aire *m*; **the decor has a Victorian ~** la decoración tiene un sabor *or* aire victoriano **Ⓑ** VT (*Culin*) condimentar, sazonar (**with**

con); **the pudding is ~ed with liqueur** el postre tiene licor

flavouring, flavoring (*US*) ['fleɪvərɪŋ] N condimento *m*; **artificial ~** aromatizante *m* artificial; **vanilla ~** esencia *f* de vainilla

flavourless, flavorless (*US*) ['fleɪvəlɪs] ADJ insípido, soso

flaw [flɔː] N (*in character, system*) defecto *m*; (*in material, diamond*) defecto *m*, tara *f*; (*in reasoning*) error *m*

flawed [flɔːd] ADJ [*system, goods*] defectuoso; [*theory*] erróneo; **the agreement is fatally ~** el acuerdo tiene defectos que lo condenan al fracaso

flawless ['flɔːlɪs] ADJ [*diamond, skin*] perfecto, sin defectos; [*beauty*] inmaculado; [*plan*] perfecto; [*conduct*] intachable, impecable; **she spoke in ~ English** habló en un inglés perfecto

flax [flæks] N lino *m* **➤ flax seed** linaza *f*

flaxen ['flæksən] ADJ [*hair*] muy rubio

flay [fleɪ] VT (= *skin*) desollar; **he'll ~ me alive if I'm late*** si llego tarde, me despelleja vivo

flea [fliː] N pulga *f*; **✦** IDIOM **to send sb away with a ~ in his ear*** despachar a algn con cajas destempladas **➤ flea collar** collar *m* antipulgas *or* antiparasitario **➤ flea market** mercadillo *m*, rastro *m* (*Sp*)

fleabag** ['fliːbæg] N (*US*) (= *hotel*) hotelucho *m* de mala muerte*

flea-bitten* ['fliːbɪtn] ADJ miserable

fleapit* ['fliːpɪt] N cine *m* de mala muerte

fleck [flek] **Ⓐ** N (*of mud, paint, dust*) mota *f*; (*of spit, foam*) salpicadura *f*; (*of colour*) mota *f* **Ⓑ** VT salpicar (**with** de); **black ~ed with white** negro moteado de blanco *or* con motas blancas

fled [fled] PT, PP *of* **flee**

fledg(e)ling ['fledʒlɪŋ] **Ⓐ** N (= *young bird*) pajarito *m*; (*fig*) novato/a *m/f* **Ⓑ** CPD [*democracy, writer*] en ciernes; [*company, industry*] joven

flee [fliː] (*pt, pp* **fled**) **Ⓐ** VT huir de; **to ~ the country** huir del país **Ⓑ** VI huir (**from** de), darse a la fuga; **they fled to the West/the mountains** huyeron hacia el oeste/las montañas

fleece [fliːs] **Ⓐ** N **1** (*on sheep*) lana *f*; (*shorn*) vellón *m* **2** (*jacket*) forro *m* polar **Ⓑ** VT (*) (= *rob*) desplumar*

fleecy ['fliːsɪ] ADJ (*compar* **fleecier**; *superl* **fleeciest**) (= *woolly*) lanoso, lanudo

fleet¹ [fliːt] N **1** (*Aer, Naut*) flota *f*; **the British ~** la armada británica **2** [*of cars, coaches etc*] parque *m* (móvil)

fleet² [fliːt] ADJ (*compar* **~er**; *superl* **~est**) (*also* **~- footed, ~ of foot**) veloz

fleeting ['fliːtɪŋ] ADJ (= *brief*) [*impression*] momentáneo; [*visit*] breve; [*moment*] breve, fugaz; **to have** *or* **catch a ~ glimpse of sth/sb** alcanzar a ver algo/a algn fugazmente; **a ~ glance** una breve mirada

Fleet Street ['fliːtˌstriːt] N (*Brit*) Fleet Street, *calle de Londres en la que muchos periódicos tenían sus oficinas*; (= *industry*) *prensa británica*

Flemish ['flemɪʃ] **Ⓐ** ADJ flamenco **Ⓑ** N (*Ling*) flamenco *m*

flesh [fleʃ] N (*gen*) carne *f*; (*of fruit*) pulpa *f*; **in the ~** en carne y hueso, en persona; **my own ~ and blood** mi propia sangre; **the sins of the ~** los pecados de la carne; **✦** IDIOM **to make sb's ~ crawl** *or* **creep** poner carne de gallina a algn **➤ flesh colour, flesh color** (*US*) (*gen, Art*) color *m* de la piel **➤ flesh wound** herida *f* superficial **➤ flesh out** VT + ADV desarrollar

flesh-coloured, flesh-colored (*US*) ['fleʃˌkʌləd] ADJ del color de la piel

fleshy ['fleʃɪ] ADJ (*compar* **fleshier**; *superl* **fleshiest**) (= *fat*) gordo; [*fruit*] carnoso

flew [fluː] PT *of* **fly²**

flex [fleks] **Ⓐ** N (*esp Brit*) [*of lamp, telephone*] cable *m*, cordón *m* **Ⓑ** VT [+ *arms, knees*] flexionar, doblar; **to ~ one's muscles** (*in exercises*) hacer ejercicios de calentamiento de músculos; (*to impress*) sacar los músculos

flexibility [ˌfleksɪˈbɪlɪtɪ] N flexibilidad *f*

flexible ['fleksəbl] ADJ flexible; **we have ~ (working) hours** tenemos un horario de trabajo flexible

flexitime ['fleksɪtaɪm] N (Brit) horario m flexible

flick [flɪk] **Ⓐ** N 1 [of tail] coletazo m; [of finger] capirotazo m, papirotazo m; [of duster] pasada f; **with a ~ of the wrist** con un movimiento rápido de la muñeca 2 (Brit*) película f, peli* f; **the ~s** el cine **Ⓑ** VT (with finger) dar un capirotazo a; **she ~ed her hair out of her eyes** se apartó el pelo de los ojos; **to ~ sth away** quitar algo con un movimiento rápido **Ⓒ** CPD ➤ **flick knife** (Brit) navaja f automática, navaja f de resorte (Mex)
➤ **flick off** VT + ADV [+ dust, ash] sacudir
➤ **flick through** VI + PREP [+ book, pages] hojear rápidamente

flicker ['flɪkə'] **Ⓐ** N 1 [of light, eyelid] parpadeo m; [of flame] destello m 2 [= hint] **a ~ of amusement crossed his face** por un momento se atisbó en su rostro una expresión divertida; **a ~ of surprise/dismay crossed his face** por un momento en su rostro pudo verse un atisbo de sorpresa/ consternación **Ⓑ** VI [light] parpadear; [flame] vacilar; **the candle ~ed and went out** la vela parpadeó y se apagó

flier ['flaɪə'] N 1 (= person) aviador(a) m/f 2 (= handbill) folleto m, volante m (LAm)

flight[1] [flaɪt] **Ⓐ** N 1 (plane, Aer) [of bird] vuelo m; [of bullet] trayectoria f; **in ~** en vuelo; **~s of fancy** ilusiones fpl 2 [of stairs] tramo m; **I walked up six ~s of stairs** subí seis tramos de escaleras; **he lives two ~s up** vive dos pisos más arriba
Ⓑ CPD ➤ **flight attendant** auxiliar mf de vuelo or de cabina, aeromozo/a m/f (LAm), sobrecargo mf (Mex), cabinero/a m/f (Col) ➤ **flight bag** bolso m de bandolera ➤ **flight crew** tripulación f ➤ **flight deck** (on aircraft carrier) cubierta f de aterrizaje/despegue; [of aeroplane] cubierta f de vuelo ➤ **flight engineer** mecánico/a m/f de vuelo ➤ **flight lieutenant** teniente mf de aviación ➤ **flight path** trayectoria f de vuelo ➤ **flight recorder** registrador m de vuelo ➤ **flight test** vuelo m de prueba

flight[2] [flaɪt] N (= act of fleeing) fuga f, huida f; **to take ~** fugarse, huir

flighty ['flaɪtɪ] ADJ (compar **flightier**; superl **flightiest**) [idea, remark] frívolo, poco serio; [girl] caprichoso, voluble

flimsy ['flɪmzɪ] ADJ (compar **flimsier**; superl **flimsiest**) 1 (= thin) [material] muy ligero, muy delgado; [paper] muy fino 2 (= weak) [structure] poco sólido, endeble; [excuse, pretext] pobre; [argument, evidence] poco sólido, inconsistente

flinch [flɪntʃ] VI (= shrink back) estremecerse; **without ~ing** sin inmutarse; **he did not ~ from his responsibilities** no se retrajo de sus obligaciones

fling [flɪŋ] (vb: pt, pp **flung**) **Ⓐ** N 1 (= period of fun) **to have a ~** echar una cana al aire 2 (*) (= affair) aventura f amorosa **Ⓑ** VT [+ stone] arrojar, lanzar; **she was flung to the ground by her horse** el caballo la lanzó or tiró or arrojó al suelo; **to ~ one's arms round sb** echar los brazos al cuello a algn; **the door was flung open** la puerta se abrió de golpe; **to ~ o.s. over a cliff** despeñarse por un precipicio; **to ~ o.s. into a chair** dejarse caer de golpe en una silla; **to ~ o.s. into a job** lanzarse a hacer un trabajo; **to ~ off/on one's clothes** quitarse/ponerse la ropa de prisa

flint [flɪnt] N (= material) sílex m; (= one piece) pedernal m; [of lighter] piedra f

flip[1] [flɪp] **Ⓐ** N [of coin] tirada f, echada f (esp LAm); [of tail] coletazo m **Ⓑ** VT (gen) tirar; **to ~ a coin** echar una moneda al aire, echar a cara o cruz; **he ~ped the book open** abrió el libro de golpe; **✦** IDIOM **to ~ one's lid*** perder los estribos **Ⓒ** VI (*) perder la chaveta* **Ⓓ** CPD ➤ **flip chart** flip chart m, bloc de papel de grandes dimensiones que se monta sobre un armazón f y sirve para ilustrar conferencias, charlas, demostraciones, etc ➤ **flip side** [of record] cara f B; (fig) otro lado m
➤ **flip through** VI + PREP [+ book] hojear; [+ records, index cards] repasar; **I ~ped through the pages/my notes** hojeé las páginas/mis notas

flip[2]* [flɪp] EXCL (Brit) ¡porras!*

flip[3]* [flɪp] ADJ = **flippant**

flip-flops ['flɪpflɒps] NPL (esp Brit) (= sandals) chancletas fpl

flippancy ['flɪpənsɪ] N ligereza f, frivolidad f, falta f de seriedad

flippant ['flɪpənt] ADJ [remark, reply] ligero, frívolo

flipper ['flɪpə'] N aleta f

flipping* ['flɪpɪŋ] ADJ (Brit) condenado*

flirt [flɜːt] **Ⓐ** N coqueto/a m/f; **he's/she's a great ~** es terriblemente coqueto/a, le gusta muchísimo flirtear **Ⓑ** VI coquetear, flirtear (**with** con)

flirtation [flɜːˈteɪʃən] N flirteo m, coqueteo m

flirty ['flɜːtɪ] ADJ coqueto

flit [flɪt] **Ⓐ** VI [bat, butterfly] revolotear; **to ~ in/out** [person] entrar/salir precipitadamente; **she ~s from one job to another** salta de un trabajo a otro **Ⓑ** N **✦** IDIOM **to do a (moonlight) ~** (Brit) marcharse de una casa a la francesa

float [fləʊt] **Ⓐ** N [of raft, seaplane] flotador m; (for fishing line) corcho m; (= swimming aid) flotador m; (in procession) carroza f; (Brit) (= sum of money) (gen) reserva f; (in shop) fondo m de caja, dinero en caja antes de empezar las ventas del día (para cambios etc)
Ⓑ VT 1 [+ boat, logs] hacer flotar
2 (= render seaworthy) poner a flote
3 (= launch) [+ company] fundar, constituir
4 (Fin) [+ currency] hacer fluctuar, hacer flotar; [+ shares] emitir, lanzar al mercado; [+ loan] emitir
5 **to ~ an idea** sugerir una idea
Ⓒ VI (gen) flotar; [bather] hacer la plancha; (= move in wind) flotar, ondear; **it ~ed to the surface** salió a la superficie; **to ~ downriver** ir río abajo
➤ **float around** VI + ADV [rumour] circular, correr
➤ **float away**, **float off** VI + ADV (in water) ir a la deriva; (in air) irse volando

floating ['fləʊtɪŋ] ADJ [object, assets, dock] flotante; (Brit) [voter] indeciso

flock [flɒk] **Ⓐ** N [of sheep, goats] rebaño m; [of birds] bandada f; [of people] tropel m, multitud f; (Rel) grey f, rebaño m **Ⓑ** VI (= move in numbers) ir en tropel; **they ~ed to the station** fueron en tropel hacia la estación; **to ~ around sb** apiñarse en torno a algn; **to ~ together** congregarse, reunirse

flog [flɒg] VT 1 (= whip) azotar; (= beat) dar una paliza a; **✦** IDIOM **to ~ a dead horse** (esp Brit*) predicar en el desierto, machacar en hierro frío 2 (Brit*) (= sell) vender

flogging ['flɒgɪŋ] N **to give sb a ~** azotar or flagelar a algn

flood [flʌd] **Ⓐ** N [of water] inundación f; (in river) avenida f; [of words, tears] torrente m; **the river is in ~** el río está crecido; **a ~ of letters** una avalancha de cartas; **she was in ~s of tears** lloraba a lágrima viva
Ⓑ VT (gen) inundar; **we have been ~ed with applications** nos han llovido las solicitudes, nos han inundado de solicitudes; **the room was ~ed with light** el cuarto se inundó de luz; **to ~ the engine** inundar el motor **Ⓒ** VI [river] desbordarse; **the people ~ed into the streets** la gente inundó la calle
➤ **flood in** VI + ADV [people] entrar a raudales
➤ **flood out** VT + ADV [+ house] inundar completamente; **they were ~ed out** tuvieron que abandonar su casa debido a la inundación

floodgate ['flʌdgeɪt] N compuerta f, esclusa f

flooding ['flʌdɪŋ] N inundación f

floodlight ['flʌdlaɪt] (vb: pt, pp **floodlit**) **Ⓐ** N foco m **Ⓑ** VT iluminar con focos

floor [flɔː'] **Ⓐ** N 1 (gen) suelo m; [of room] suelo m, piso m (LAm); [of sea] fondo m; (= dance floor) pista f; **✦** IDIOM **to wipe the ~ with sb*** dar un buen repaso a algn*, hacer picadillo a algn*
2 (= storey) 2.1 (Brit) piso m; **the first ~** el primer piso; **the ground ~** la planta baja; **the second ~** el segundo piso; **the top ~** el último piso 2.2 (US) piso m; **the first ~** la planta baja; **the second ~** el primer piso; **the top ~** el último piso **Ⓑ** VT 1 (*) (= knock down) [+ opponent] derribar
2 (*) (= baffle, silence) dejar sin respuesta
3 (US Aut) [+ accelerator] pisar

© CPD ➤ **floor area** superficie f total ➤ **floor cloth** bayeta f ➤ **floor covering** tapiz m para el suelo ➤ **floor lamp** (US) lámpara f de pie ➤ **floor manager** (in department store) jefe/a m/f de sección ➤ **floor plan** plano m, planta f ➤ **floor polish** cera f para suelos

floorboard ['flɔːbɔːd] N tabla f del suelo

flooring ['flɔːrɪŋ] N suelo m; (= material) solería f

floosie*, **floozie***, **floozy*** ['fluːzɪ] N putilla* f

flop [flɒp] **©** N (*) (= failure) fracaso m; **the film was a ~** la película fue un fracaso **®** VI **1** (= fall) [person] dejarse caer (**into, on** en) **2** (*) (= fail) [play, book] fracasar

flophouse* ['flɒphaʊs] N (US) pensión f de mala muerte*

floppy ['flɒpɪ] **©** ADJ (compar **floppier**; superl **floppiest**) [hat] flexible; **a dog with ~ ears** un perro con las orejas caídas **®** N (also ~ **disk**) (Comput) disquete m, disco m flexible

flora ['flɔːrə] N flora f

floral ['flɔːrəl] ADJ [display] de flores, floral; [fabric, dress] de flores, floreado; [fragrance, design, wallpaper, curtains] de flores ➤ **floral arrangement** arreglo m floral ➤ **floral tribute** ofrenda f floral; (at funeral) corona f de flores

Florence ['flɒrəns] N Florencia f

florid ['flɒrɪd] ADJ [complexion] colorado, rubicundo; [style] florido

Florida ['flɒrɪdə] N Florida f

florist ['flɒrɪst] N florista mf; ~'s **(shop)** floristería f, tienda f de flores

floss [flɒs] **©** N **1** (also ~ **silk**) cadarzo m **2** (for embroidery) seda f floja **3** (also **dental** ~) hilo m or seda f dental **®** VT (Dentistry) **to** ~ **one's teeth** limpiarse los dientes con hilo or seda dental **©** VI (Dentistry) limpiarse los dientes con hilo or seda dental

flotation [fləʊ'teɪʃən] N **1** (of boat etc) flotación f **2** (Fin) (of shares, loan etc) emisión f; (of company) lanzamiento m, salida f a bolsa

flotilla [flə'tɪlə] N flotilla f

flotsam ['flɒtsəm] N ~ **and jetsam** restos mpl (de naufragio); (Tech, frm) pecios mpl

flounce¹ [flaʊns] N (= frill) volante m

flounce² [flaʊns] VI **to** ~ **in/out** entrar/salir haciendo aspavientos

flounder¹ ['flaʊndəʳ] N (pl ~ or ~**s**) (= fish) platija f

flounder² ['flaʊndəʳ] VI **1** (also ~ **about**) (in water, mud etc) (= flap arms) debatirse; (= splash) revolcarse **2** (in speech etc) perder el hilo

flour ['flaʊəʳ] N harina f

flourish ['flʌrɪʃ] **©** N (= movement) floritura f, ademán m ostentoso; (under signature) rúbrica f; (Mus) floreo m; (= fanfare) toque m de trompeta **®** VT [+ weapon, stick etc] blandir **©** VI [plant etc] crecer; [person, business, civilization] florecer, prosperar

flourishing ['flʌrɪʃɪŋ] ADJ [plant] lozano; [person, business] floreciente, próspero

flout [flaʊt] VT (= ignore) no prestar atención a, ignorar; [+ law] incumplir

flow [fləʊ] **©** N (of river, tide, Elec) corriente f, flujo m; (= direction) curso m; (of blood) (from wound) flujo; (of words etc) torrente m; **the ~ of traffic** la circulación (del tráfico); **to maintain a steady ~** [of people, vehicles] mantener un movimiento constante; ✦ IDIOM **to go with the ~** dejarse llevar
® VI [river] fluir, discurrir; [tide] subir, crecer; [blood] (from wound) manar; (through body) circular; [tears] correr; [words] fluir; **tears ~ed down her cheeks** le corrían las lágrimas por las mejillas; **the river ~s into the sea** el río desemboca en el mar; **water was ~ing from the pipe** el agua brotaba de la tubería; **traffic is now ~ing normally** el tráfico ya circula or fluye or discurre con normalidad; **money ~ed in** el dinero entraba a raudales; **people are ~ing in** entra la gente a raudales; **to keep the conversation ~ing** mantener viva la conversación
© CPD ➤ **flow chart, flow diagram** organigrama m

flower ['flaʊəʳ] **©** N flor f; **in ~** en flor **®** VI florecer **©** CPD ➤ **flower arrangement** (on table) arreglo m floral ➤ **flower arranging** arte m floral ➤ **flower garden** jardín m (de flores) ➤ **flower seller** florista mf, vendedor(a) m/f de flores ➤ **flower shop** floristería f, tienda f de flores ➤ **flower show** exposición f de flores ➤ **flower stall** puesto m de flores

flowerbed ['flaʊəbed] N arriate m, parterre m, cantero m (SC)

flowerpot ['flaʊəpɒt] N maceta f, tiesto m

flowery ['flaʊərɪ] ADJ [meadow, field] florido; [fragrance, perfume] de flores; [fabric, dress, wallpaper] de flores, floreado; [language] florido

flowing ['fləʊɪŋ] ADJ [movement] fluido; [stream] corriente; [hair, clothing] suelto; [style] fluido

flown [fləʊn] PP of **fly²**

fl. oz. ABBR = **fluid ounce**

F/Lt ABBR = **Flight Lieutenant**

flu [fluː] N gripe f, gripa f (Col, Mex); **I've got ~** (esp Brit) or **the ~** (esp US) tengo gripe; **to get** or **catch ~** (esp Brit) or **the ~** (esp US) agarrar la gripe, agriparse (LAm)

fluctuate ['flʌktjʊeɪt] VI [cost] oscilar; [prices, temperature] fluctuar, oscilar; **to ~ between** [person] vacilar entre

fluctuation [ˌflʌktjʊ'eɪʃən] N (of prices, temperature) fluctuación f, oscilación f

flue [fluː] N humero m

fluency ['fluːənsɪ] N fluidez f, soltura f; **she speaks French with great ~** habla francés con mucha fluidez or soltura, domina bien el francés; **I was impressed by his ~ in English** me impresionó su dominio del inglés

fluent ['fluːənt] ADJ **1** (in foreign language) **he is a ~ Japanese speaker** or **speaker of Japanese** habla japonés con fluidez or soltura, domina bien el japonés; **to speak ~ French** ◇ **be ~ in French** hablar francés con fluidez or soltura, dominar bien el francés **2** (= not hesitant) [written style, speech, sentence] fluido; [speaker, debater, writer] desenvuelto; **a ~ reader** una persona que lee con fluidez or soltura

fluently ['fluːəntlɪ] ADV con fluidez, con soltura; **he speaks Russian ~** habla ruso con fluidez or soltura, domina bien el ruso

fluff [flʌf] **©** N (from blankets etc) pelusa f, lanilla f; (of chicks) plumón m; (of kittens) pelo m, pelusa f **®** VT **1 to ~ up the pillows** mullir las almohadas **2** (Theat*) [+ lines] hacerse un lío con

fluffy ['flʌfɪ] ADJ (compar **fluffier**; superl **fluffiest**) [material] mullido ➤ **fluffy toy** (muñeco m de) peluche m

fluid ['fluːɪd] **©** ADJ fluido **®** N fluido m; **drink plenty of ~s** tome mucho líquido, beba mucho **©** CPD ➤ **fluid ounce** onza f líquida

fluke¹ [fluːk] N (= stroke of luck) chiripa f, golpe m de suerte; **to win by a ~** ganar de or por chiripa

fluke² [fluːk] N (Zool) trematodo m; (Fishing) especie de platija

flummox ['flʌməks] VT (= disconcert) desconcertar, confundir; (= startle) asombrar; **I was completely ~ed** me quedé totalmente desconcertado

flung [flʌŋ] PT, PP of **fling**

flunk* [flʌŋk] VT, VI suspender (Sp), reprobar (LAm)

fluorescent [flʊə'resnt] ADJ fluorescente

fluoride ['flʊəraɪd] N fluoruro m ➤ **fluoride toothpaste** pasta f de dientes con flúor

flurry ['flʌrɪ] N (of wind, snow) racha f, ráfaga f; **a ~ of activity** un frenesí de actividad

flush¹ [flʌʃ] **©** N **1** (= blush) **there was a slight ~ on his cheeks** tenía las mejillas un poco coloradas **2** (= glow) [of beauty, health] resplandor m **3** (= surge) [of anger, excitement] arrebato m; **in the flush ~ of youth** en la flor de la juventud; **in the (first) ~ of victory** con la euforia del triunfo **4** (Med) **to have hot ~es** tener sofocos **®** VI [person, face] ponerse colorado, sonrojarse, ruborizarse (liter) (**with** de)

flush² [flʌʃ] **©** N (of toilet) (= device) cisterna f; (= sound) sonido m de la cisterna; (= action) descarga f de agua **®** VT (*also* ~ **out**) [+ *sink, yard*] limpiar con agua, baldear; **to ~ the toilet** *or* **lavatory** tirar de la cadena

flush³ [flʌʃ] ADJ **1** (= *level*) a ras (**with** de), al mismo nivel (**with** que) **2** (*) **to be ~ (with money)** estar forrado*, andar muy bien de dinero

flush⁴ [flʌʃ] VT (*also* ~ **out**) [+ *criminal*] sacar de su escondrijo a

flushed [flʌʃt] ADJ (= *red*) [*face, cheeks*] colorado, rojo; **be ~ with anger** estar rojo de ira; **to be ~ with success** estar eufórico por el éxito

fluster ['flʌstə'] **Ⓐ** N **to be in a ~** estar aturdido *or* confuso **Ⓑ** VT (= *confuse, upset*) aturdir, poner nervioso; **to get ~ed** ponerse nervioso, aturdirse

flute [fluːt] N flauta *f*

flutist ['fluːtɪst] N (*US*) flautista *mf*

flutter ['flʌtə'] **Ⓐ** VT [+ *wings*] batir; **to ~ one's eyelashes at sb** hacer ojitos a algn **Ⓑ** VI [*bird*] revolotear; [*butterfly*] mover las alas; [*flag*] ondear; [*heart*] palpitar

flux [flʌks] N **to be in a state of ~** estar inestable, estar cambiando continuamente

fly¹ [flaɪ] N (= *insect*) mosca *f*; ✦ IDIOMS **people were dropping like flies** la gente caía como moscas; **he wouldn't hurt a ~** sería incapaz de matar una mosca; **the ~ in the ointment** la única pega, el único inconveniente; **I wish I were a ~ on the wall** me gustaría estar allí para ver qué pasa ➤ **fly spray** (espray *m*) matamoscas *m inv*

fly² [flaɪ] (*pt* flew; *pp* flown) **Ⓐ** VI **1** [*plane, bird, insect*] volar; [*air passengers*] ir en avión; [*pilot*] pilotar un avión, volar; **"how did you get here?" — "I flew"** —¿cómo llegaste aquí? —en avión; **she's ~ing home tomorrow** sale en avión para casa mañana; **I'm ~ing back to New York tonight** esta noche tomo un vuelo de regreso a Nueva York; **we were ~ing at 5,000ft** volábamos a 5.000 pies de altura; **to ~ into London airport** llegar (en avión) al aeropuerto de Londres; **to learn to ~** aprender a pilotar un avión *or* a volar; **I had to ~ out to California to pick him up** tuve que ir en avión a California a recogerlo; **the plane flew over London** el avión sobrevoló Londres

2 (= *flutter, wave*) [*flag*] ondear

3 (= *rush*) ir volando, ir corriendo; **I must ~!** ¡me voy volando *or* corriendo!, ¡me tengo que ir volando *or* corriendo!; **to go ~ing:** the vase went ~ing el jarrón salió por los aires *or* salió volando; **my hat flew into the air** se me voló el sombrero, el sombrero salió volando; **to let ~ at sb** (*verbally*) empezar a despotricar contra algn, arremeter contra algn; **the door flew open** la puerta se abrió de golpe; **he/the ball came ~ing past me** él/la pelota pasó volando junto a mí; **to ~ into a rage** montar en cólera

4 (= *pass quickly*) [*time*] pasar *or* irse volando; **the years flew by** los años pasaron volando **Ⓑ** VT **1** [+ *aircraft*] pilotar, pilotear (*esp LAm*); [+ *passenger*] llevar en avión; [+ *goods*] transportar en avión; [+ *flag*] enarbolar; **which routes does the airline ~?** ¿qué rutas cubre la aerolínea?; **we ~ Iberia** volamos con Iberia; **to ~ a kite** hacer volar una cometa

2 (= *flee*) [+ *country*] abandonar, huir de **Ⓒ** N (*on trousers*) (*also Brit* **flies**) bragueta *f* **Ⓓ** CPD ➤ **fly button** botón *m* de la bragueta ➤ **fly away** VI + ADV [*bird*] salir volando, emprender el vuelo

fly³ [flaɪ] ADJ (*esp Brit*) avispado, espabilado

fly-by-night ['flaɪbaɪnaɪt] **Ⓐ** ADJ informal, poco fiable **Ⓑ** N casquivano/a *m/f*

fly-drive holiday [,flaɪdraɪv'hɒlɪdeɪ] N *paquete vacacional que incluye el alquiler de un vehículo*

fly-fishing ['flaɪ,fɪʃɪŋ] N pesca *f* a *or* con mosca

flying ['flaɪɪŋ] **Ⓐ** ADJ [*glass, debris*] que vuela por los aires; **he took a ~ leap at the man** dio un salto *or* saltó sobre el hombre; **to make a ~ visit** hacer una visita relámpago; ✦ IDIOMS **to come through (sth) with ~ colours** *or* (*US*) **colors** salir airoso (de algo); **he passed all his exams with ~ colours** aprobó todos sus exámenes con éxito; **to get off to a ~ start** empezar con muy buen pie **Ⓑ** N vuelo *m*; **I had done 60 hours of ~** había realizado 60 horas de vuelo; **I don't like ~** no me gusta ir en avión *or* volar; **to have a fear of ~** tener miedo al avión

Ⓒ CPD ➤ **flying doctor** médico/a *m/f* rural (que se traslada en avión) ➤ **flying saucer** platillo *m* volante ➤ **flying squad** (*Brit*) brigada *f* móvil ➤ **flying time** (= *length of journey*) duración *f* del vuelo; (= *hours flown*) horas *fpl* de vuelo

flyleaf ['flaɪliːf] N (*pl* **flyleaves**) guarda *f*

fly-on-the-wall documentary [,flaɪɒnðəwɔːl'dɒkjʊ'mentərɪ] N documental *m* en vivo

flyover ['flaɪ,əʊvə'] N (*Brit Aut*) paso *m* elevado, paso *m* a desnivel (*LAm*); (*US*) (= *flypast*) desfile *m* aéreo

flypaper ['flaɪ,peɪpə'] N papel *m* matamoscas

flypast ['flaɪpɑːst] N desfile *m* aéreo

fly-posting [,flaɪ'pəʊstɪŋ] N pegada *f* (ilegal) de carteles

fly-swat ['flaɪswɒt], **fly-swatter** ['flaɪswɒtə'] N matamoscas *m inv*

flyweight ['flaɪweɪt] N peso *m* mosca

flywheel ['flaɪwiːl] N (*Tech*) volante *m*

FM ABBR (= *frequency modulation*) FM *f*, M.F. *f*

FO N ABBR (*Brit Pol*) (= **Foreign Office**) Min. de AA.EE.

fo. ABBR (= **folio**) f.°, fol.

foal [fəʊl] **Ⓐ** N potro *m* **Ⓑ** VI [*mare*] parir

foam [fəʊm] **Ⓐ** N espuma *f* **Ⓑ** VI **to ~ at the mouth** echar espumarajos; (*fig*) subirse por las paredes **Ⓒ** CPD ➤ **foam bath** baño *m* de espuma ➤ **foam rubber** gomaespuma *f*

fob [fɒb] **Ⓐ** VT **to ~ sb off (with sth): I've asked her about it but she ~s me off** se lo he preguntado, pero me da largas; **she won't be ~bed off** no aceptará más evasivas; **don't be ~bed off with excuses** no te dejes engatusar con excusas **Ⓑ** CPD ➤ **fob watch** reloj *m* de cadena *or* de bolsillo

focal ['fəʊkəl] ADJ focal; **~ point** punto *m* focal; (*fig*) centro *m* de atención

focus ['fəʊkəs] **Ⓐ** N (*pl* **~es** *or* **foci** ['fəʊsaɪ]) (*gen*) foco *m*; [*of attention*] centro *m*, foco *m*; **to be in/out of ~** (*Phot*) estar enfocado/desenfocado **Ⓑ** VT [+ *camera, instrument*] enfocar (**on** a); [+ *attention*] centrar, concentrar (**on** en); **all eyes were ~ed on her** todos la miraban fijamente **Ⓒ** VI enfocar; **to ~ on sth** [*light*] concentrarse en algo; [*person*] (*with eyes*) fijarse en algo, concentrarse en algo; [*eyes*] detenerse en algo, concentrarse en algo; [*talk, investigation, report, speaker*] centrarse en algo; (*Phot*) enfocar algo **Ⓓ** CPD ➤ **focus group** grupo *m* formado por miembros del público escogidos para discutir sobre un tema o producto en particular

focus(s)ed ['fəʊkəst] ADJ (*fig*) centrado; [*sales, efforts, approach*] dirigido; **I wasn't ~** no estaba centrado

fodder ['fɒdə'] N pienso *m*, forraje *m*

foe [fəʊ] N (*poet*) enemigo *m*

foetal, fetal (*US*) ['fiːtl] ADJ fetal

foetus, fetus (*US*) ['fiːtəs] N feto *m*

fog [fɒg] **Ⓐ** N (*Met*) niebla *f* **Ⓑ** VI (*also* **to ~ up**) [*mirror, glasses*] empañarse **Ⓒ** CPD ➤ **fog lamp, fog light** faro *m* antiniebla

fogbound ['fɒgbaʊnd] ADJ inmovilizado por la niebla

fogey ['fəʊgɪ] N **old ~*** persona *f* chapada a la antigua, carroza *mf* (*Sp**)

foggy ['fɒgɪ] ADJ (*compar* **foggier**; *superl* **foggiest**) [*weather*] brumoso; [*day*] de niebla, brumoso; **it's ~** hay niebla; **I haven't the foggiest (idea)*** no tengo la más remota idea

foghorn ['fɒghɔːn] N sirena *f* de niebla

foible ['fɔɪbl] N manía *f*

foie gras [,fwɑː'grɑː] N foie-gras *m*

foil¹ [fɔɪl] N (*also* **tinfoil**) papel *m* de aluminio, papel *m* de plata

foil² [fɔɪl] N (*Fencing*) florete *m*

foil³ [fɔɪl] VT (= *thwart*) [+ *person*] desbaratar los planes de; [+ *attempt*] frustrar

foist [fɔɪst] VT **to ~ sth on sb** endosar algo a algn

fold¹ [fəʊld] N (= *enclosure*) redil *m*; **to return to the ~** (*Rel*) volver al redil

fold² [fəʊld] **Ⓐ** N (*in paper etc*) pliegue *m*, doblez *m* **Ⓑ** VT [+ *paper, map, blanket*] doblar; (*esp several times*) plegar; [+ *wings*] recoger; **to ~ sth in half** doblar algo por la mitad; **to ~ one's arms** cruzar los brazos **Ⓒ** VI (*esp Brit**) (= *fail*) [*business venture*] fracasar, quebrar; [*play*] fracasar
➤ **fold away** VI + ADV [*table, bed*] plegarse
➤ **fold up** VT + ADV [+ *paper, map, blanket*] doblar; [+ *chair*] plegar

-fold [fəʊld] ADJ, ADV (*ending in compounds*) **thirty-fold** (*as adj*) de treinta veces; (*as adv*) treinta veces

foldaway [ˈfəʊldəweɪ] ADJ plegable, plegadizo

folder [ˈfəʊldəʳ] N (= *file*) carpeta *f*; (= *binder*) carpeta *f* de anillas; (*Comput*) (= *directory*) carpeta *f*

folding [ˈfəʊldɪŋ] ADJ [*seat, table*] plegable

fold-up [ˈfəʊldʌp] ADJ plegable

foliage [ˈfəʊlɪɪdʒ] N follaje *m*, hojas *fpl*

folk [fəʊk] N (= *people*) gente *f*; **my ~s*** (= *parents*) mis viejos* *mpl*; (= *family*) mi familia ➤ **folk art** artesanía *f* popular *or* tradicional ➤ **folk dance** baile *m* popular ➤ **folk dancing** danza *f* folklórica ➤ **folk music** (*traditional*) música *f* tradicional *or* folklórica; (*contemporary*) música *f* folk ➤ **folk singer** cantante *mf* de música folk ➤ **folk song** canción *f* tradicional

folklore [ˈfəʊklɔːʳ] N folklore *m*

follow [ˈfɒləʊ] **Ⓐ** VT **1** (= *pursue*) seguir; **we're being ~ed** nos están *or* vienen siguiendo; **~ that car!** ¡siga a ese coche!; **she arrived first, ~ed by the ambassador** ella llegó primero, seguida del embajador; **the days ~ing her death** los días que siguieron a su muerte; **the dinner will be ~ed by a concert** después de la cena habrá un concierto; **~ing our meeting I spoke to the director** tras nuestra reunión hablé con el director; **to have sb ~ed** mandar seguir a algn; **he ~ed me into the room** entró en la habitación detrás de mí; **he ~ed his father into the business** siguió los pasos de su padre en el negocio; **to ~ a lead** seguir una pista
2 (= *observe*) [+ *instructions, advice, example, fashion*] seguir; [+ *rules*] obedecer, cumplir
3 (= *be interested in*) [+ *news*] seguir, mantenerse al corriente de; [+ *TV serial, progress*] seguir; **do you ~ football?** ¿eres aficionado al fútbol?; **which team do you ~?** ¿de qué equipo eres?
4 (= *understand*) [+ *person, argument*] seguir, entender; **do you ~ me?** ¿me sigue?, ¿me entiende?; **I don't quite ~ you** no te acabo de entender
Ⓑ VI **1** (= *go/come after*) **they led her in and I ~ed** la llevaron dentro y yo entré detrás; **to ~, there was roast lamb** de segundo había cordero asado; **what ~s is an eye-witness account** lo que viene a continuación es la versión de un testigo presencial; **the text reads as ~s** el texto dice lo siguiente, el texto dice así; **the winners are as ~s** los ganadores son los siguientes
2 (= *result, ensue*) deducirse; **that doesn't ~** eso no cuadra, de ahí no se puede deducir eso; **it ~s that ...** (de lo cual) se deduce que ..., se deduce pues que ...; **it doesn't ~ that ...** no significa que ...
3 (= *understand*) entender; **I don't quite ~** no lo sigo del todo, no lo acabo de entender
➤ **follow around, follow about** VT + ADV **to ~ sb around** seguir a algn a todas partes
➤ **follow on** VI + ADV **we'll ~ on behind** nosotros seguiremos, vendremos después; **it ~s on from what I said** es la consecuencia lógica de lo que dije
➤ **follow out** VT + ADV [+ *order*] ejecutar, cumplir; [+ *instructions*] seguir
➤ **follow through Ⓐ** VT + ADV **1** [+ *shot*] acompañar
2 (= *continue*) seguir con; **I was trained as an actress but I didn't ~ it through** estudié arte dramático pero luego no seguí con ello **Ⓑ** VI + ADV **1** (*Ftbl*) rematar; (*Golf, Tennis*) acompañar el golpe **2** (= *continue*) **to ~ through with sth** seguir con algo; **to ~ through on** (*US*) [+ *promise*] cumplir; [+ *threat*] cumplir, llevar a cabo
➤ **follow up Ⓐ** VT + ADV **1** (= *pursue*) [+ *offer*] reiterar; [+ *job application*] hacer un seguimiento de; [+ *suggestion*] investigar; **to ~ up a lead** seguir *or* investigar una pista

2 (= *reinforce*) [+ *visit, victory, advantage, success*] consolidar **Ⓑ** VI + ADV (*Ftbl*) rematar

follower [ˈfɒləʊəʳ] N (= *disciple*) discípulo/a *m/f*, seguidor(a) *m/f*; [*of team*] aficionado/a *m/f*; (*Pol etc*) partidario/a *m/f*; **the ~s of fashion** los que siguen la moda

following [ˈfɒləʊɪŋ] **Ⓐ** ADJ (= *next*) siguiente; **we saw him again the ~ day** lo volvimos a ver al día siguiente
Ⓑ N **1** (= *supporters*) [*of party, movement, person*] seguidores *mpl*, partidarios *mpl*; [*of product, company*] clientes *mpl*; [*of TV programme*] audiencia *f*, seguidores *mpl*; [*of sport*] afición *f*, aficionados *mpl*
2 (= *what follows*) **he said the ~** dijo lo siguiente; **do you use any of the ~?** ¿utiliza alguna de estas cosas?; **the ~ are all worth trying** se puede probar con cualquiera de las siguientes

follow-my-leader (*Brit*) [ˌfɒləʊməˈliːdəʳ], **follow-the-leader** (*US*) [ˌfɒləʊðəˈliːdəʳ] N *juego en el que los participantes hacen lo que alguien manda*; **to play ~** jugar a lo que haga el rey

follow-up [ˈfɒləʊʌp] N (= *further action*) seguimiento *m* (**to** de); (= *continuation*) continuación *f* (**to** de); **this is a ~ to the meeting held last Sunday** esto es la continuación de la reunión celebrada el domingo ➤ **follow-up call** (*Telec*) llamada *f* de reiteración ➤ **follow-up interview** entrevista *f* complementaria ➤ **follow-up visit** (= *inspection*) visita *f* de inspección *or* comprobación; (*Med*) revisión *f*

folly [ˈfɒlɪ] N locura *f*; **it would be ~ to do it** sería una locura hacerlo

foment [fəʊˈment] VT (*also Med*) fomentar; [+ *revolt, violence*] provocar, instigar a

fond [fɒnd] ADJ (*compar* ~**er**; *superl* ~**est**) **1 to be ~ of sb** tener cariño a algn, querer mucho a algn; **they were very ~ of each other** se tenían mucho cariño, se querían mucho; **I've become** *or* **grown ~ of him** me he encariñado con él, le he cogido cariño
2 to be ~ of sth: she is very ~ of marmalade/shopping le gusta mucho la mermelada/ir de compras; **she is very ~ of animals** le gustan mucho los animales; **he's very ~ of his old mini** le tiene mucho cariño a su viejo mini
3 (= *loving*) cariñoso, afectuoso; **to bid sb a ~ farewell** despedirse de algn cariñosamente
4 (= *pleasant*) **to have ~ memories of sth** tener muy buenos recuerdos de algo

fondant [ˈfɒndənt] N pasta *f* de azúcar, glaseado *m*

fondle [ˈfɒndl] VT acariciar

fondly [ˈfɒndlɪ] ADV **1** (= *affectionately*) [*say, smile*] cariñosamente, con cariño; [*remember*] con cariño
2 (= *foolishly*) [*imagine, believe, hope*] ingenuamente

fondness [ˈfɒndnɪs] N (*for person*) cariño *m* (**for** por); (*for thing*) afición *f* (**for** a)

font [fɒnt] N **1** (*Typ*) fundición *f*; (*Comput*) fuente *f*, tipo *m* de letra **2** (*in church*) pila *f*

food [fuːd] N comida *f*; (*for plants*) abono *m*; **I've no ~ left in the house** no me queda comida en casa; **the ~ at the hotel was terrible** la comida en el hotel era fatal; **the ~ is good here** aquí se come bien; **we need to buy some ~** hay que comprar cosas de comer; **she gave him ~** le dio de comer; **to be off one's ~*** estar desganado; **✚** IDIOM **to give ~ for thought** ser motivo de reflexión ➤ **food additive** aditivo *m* alimenticio ➤ **food chain** cadena *f* alimenticia ➤ **food colouring** colorante *m* alimentario ➤ **food mixer** batidora *f* ➤ **food parcel** paquete *m* de alimentos ➤ **food poisoning** intoxicación *f* alimenticia ➤ **food processing** preparación *f* de alimentos ➤ **food processor** robot *m* de cocina ➤ **food rationing** racionamiento *m* de víveres ➤ **food science** ciencia *f* de la alimentación ➤ **food shop**, **food store** tienda *f* de comestibles ➤ **food stamp** (*US*) *cupón para canjear por comida que reciben las personas de pocos recursos* ➤ **food supplies** víveres *mpl* ➤ **food supply** suministro *m* de alimentos; ▷ *FDA* ➤ **food technology** tecnología *f* de los alimentos

foodstuffs [ˈfuːdstʌfs] NPL comestibles *mpl*, productos *mpl* alimenticios

fool¹ [fuːl] **Ⓐ** N (= *idiot*) tonto/a *m/f*, zonzo/a *m/f* (*LAm*); **don't be a ~!** ¡no seas tonto!; **I was a ~ not to go!** ¡qué

tonto fui en no ir!; **to be ~ <u>enough</u> to do sth** ser lo bastante tonto como para hacer algo; **to <u>make</u> a ~ of sb** poner *or* dejar a algn en ridículo; **to make a ~ of o.s.** quedar en ridículo; **to <u>play</u> the ~** hacer el tonto; **you ~!** ¡idiota!, ¡imbécil!; ✦ IDIOM **to live in a ~'s paradise** vivir de ilusiones; ✦ PROVS **a ~ and his money are soon parted** a los tontos no les dura el dinero; **~s rush in where angels fear to tread** la ignorancia es osada
B VT (= *deceive*) engañar; **you <u>can't</u> ~ me** a mí no me engañas
C VI hacer el tonto; **<u>no</u> ~ing** en serio
➤ **fool around, fool about** (*Brit*) VI + ADV **1** (= *waste time*) perder el tiempo **2** (= *act the fool*) hacer el tonto; **to ~ around with sth** (= *play with*) jugar con algo; (*and damage*) estropear algo **3** (= *have an affair*) **to ~ around with sb** tontear con algn

fool² [fuːl] N (*Brit*) (= *dessert*) puré de frutas con nata o natillas

foolhardy [ˈfuːlˌhɑːdɪ] ADJ (= *rash*) temerario

foolish [ˈfuːlɪʃ] ADJ **1** (= *unwise, foolhardy*) [*person*] insensato; [*mistake*] estúpido, tonto; [*decision*] imprudente; **it would be ~ to believe him** sería de tontos creerle; **don't do anything ~** no hagas ninguna tontería *or* insensatez **2** (= *ridiculous*) ridículo; **to feel ~** sentirse ridículo, sentirse idiota; **to make sb look ~** dejar a algn en ridículo

foolishly [ˈfuːlɪʃlɪ] ADV tontamente, como un tonto; **to act ~** hacer el tonto

foolishness [ˈfuːlɪʃnɪs] N insensatez *f*, estupidez *f*

foolproof [ˈfuːlpruːf] ADJ [*mechanism, scheme etc*] infalible

foolscap [ˈfuːlskæp] N (*esp Brit*) papel *m* de tamaño folio

foot [fʊt] **A** N (*pl* **feet**) **1** (*Anat*) pie *m*; [*of animal, chair*] pata *f*; **my feet are <u>aching</u>** me duelen los pies; **to <u>get</u> to one's feet** ponerse de pie, levantarse, pararse (*LAm*); **lady, my ~!*** ¡dama, ni hablar!; **on ~** a pie, andando, caminando (*LAm*); **to be on one's feet** estar de pie, estar parado (*LAm*); **I've never <u>set</u> ~ there** nunca he estado allí; **to set ~ inside sb's door** poner los pies en la casa de algn, pasar el umbral de algn; **to trample sth <u>under</u> ~** pisotear algo; **the children are always under my feet** siempre tengo los niños pegados; ✦ IDIOMS **to get cold feet** entrarle miedo a algn; **to get one's ~ in the door** meter el pie en la puerta; **to put one's ~ down** (= *say no*) plantarse; (*Aut*) acelerar; **to drag one's feet** dar largas al asunto, hacerse el roncero; **to fall on one's feet** tener suerte, caer de pie; **to have one's feet on the ground** ser realista; **to put one's ~ in it*** meter la pata*; **to start off on the right ~** entrar con buen pie; **to stand on one's own two feet** volar con sus propias alas; **she never put a ~ wrong** no cometió ningún error; **to put one's feet up*** descansar
2 [*of mountain, page, stairs, bed*] pie *m*; **at the ~ of the hill** al pie de la colina
3 (= *measure*) pie *m*; **he's six ~ or feet tall** mide seis pies, mide un metro ochenta; ⊳ IMPERIAL SYSTEM
B VT ✦ IDIOM **to ~ the bill (for sth)** pagar (algo), correr con los gastos (de algo)
C CPD ➤ **foot brake** (*Aut*) freno *m* de pie ➤ **foot passenger** pasajero/a *m/f* de a pie ➤ **foot soldier** soldado *mf* de infantería

footage [ˈfʊtɪdʒ] N (= *pictures*) imágenes *fpl*, secuencias *fpl*

foot-and-mouth (disease) [ˈfʊtənˈmaʊθ(dɪˈziːz)] N fiebre *f* aftosa, glosopeda *f*

football [ˈfʊtbɔːl] **A** N **1** (*Brit*) (= *soccer*) fútbol *m*; **to play ~** jugar al fútbol **2** (*US*) (= *American football*) fútbol *m* americano **3** (= *ball*) balón *m* de fútbol **B** CPD ➤ **football ground** campo *m or* (*LAm*) cancha *f* de fútbol ➤ **football hooligan** (*Brit*) hooligan *m* ➤ **football league** liga *f* de fútbol ➤ **football match** partido *m* de fútbol ➤ **football player** jugador(a) *m/f* de fútbol, futbolista *mf* ➤ **football pools** (*Brit*) quinielas *fpl*

footballer [ˈfʊtbɔːlə^r] N (*Brit*) futbolista *mf*

footballing [ˈfʊtbɔːlɪŋ] ADJ (*Brit*) [*career, skills*] futbolístico

footbridge [ˈfʊtbrɪdʒ] N puente *m* peatonal

foothills [ˈfʊthɪlz] NPL estribaciones *fpl*

foothold [ˈfʊthəʊld] N asidero *m*, punto *m* de apoyo (*para el pie*); **to gain a ~** (*fig*) lograr establecerse

footie* [ˈfʊtɪ] N (*Brit*) = **football**

footing [ˈfʊtɪŋ] N **1** (= *foothold*) asidero *m*; **to lose one's ~** perder pie **2** (= *basis*) **on an equal ~** en pie de igualdad; **to be on a friendly ~ with sb** tener amistad con algn

footloose [ˈfʊtluːs] ADJ ✦ IDIOM **~ and fancy free** libre como el aire

footman [ˈfʊtmən] N (*pl* **footmen**) lacayo *m*

footmark [ˈfʊtmɑːk] N huella *f*, pisada *f*

footnote [ˈfʊtnəʊt] N nota *f* a pie de página

footpath [ˈfʊtpɑːθ] N (= *track*) sendero *m*, vereda *f*; (*Brit*) (= *pavement*) acera *f*, vereda *f* (*And, SC*), andén *m* (*CAm, Col*), banqueta *f* (*Mex*)

footprint [ˈfʊtprɪnt] N huella *f*, pisada *f*

footrest [ˈfʊtrest] N [*of wheelchair*] reposapiés *m inv*; [*of motorbike*] estribo *m*

footsie* [ˈfʊtsɪ] N ✦ IDIOM **to play ~ with** acariciar con el pie a

footstep [ˈfʊtstep] N paso *m*, pisada *f*; ✦ IDIOM **to follow in sb's ~s** seguir los pasos de algn

footstool [ˈfʊtstuːl] N escabel *m*

footwear [ˈfʊtweə^r] N calzado *m*

footwork [ˈfʊtwɜːk] N (*Sport*) juego *m* de piernas

for

*When **for** is part of a phrasal verb, eg **look for, stand for**, look up the verb. When it is part of a set combination, eg **as for, for sale, eager for**, look up the other word.*

for [fɔː^r] PREPOSITION **1** (= *going to*) para; **he left ~ Rome** salió para Roma; **the train ~ London** el tren para *or* de Londres
2 (= *intended for*) para; **a table ~ two** una mesa para dos; **there's a letter ~ you** hay una carta para ti; **is this ~ me?** ¿es para mí esto?; *BUT* **hats ~ women** sombreros de señora; **clothes ~ children** ropa infantil; **I decided that it was the job ~ me** decidí que era el puesto que me convenía; **she decided that hang-gliding was not ~ her*** decidió que el vuelo con ala delta no era lo suyo
3 (*to express purpose*) para; **he went there ~ a rest** fue allí para descansar; **a cloth ~ polishing silver** un paño para sacarle brillo a la plata; **<u>what</u> ~?** ¿para qué?; **what's it ~?** ¿para qué es *or* sirve?; **what do you want it ~?** ¿para qué lo quieres?; *BUT* **what did you do that ~?** ¿por qué hiciste eso?
4 (*employment*) para; **he works ~ the government** trabaja para el gobierno
5 (= *on behalf of*) **I'll ask him ~ you** se lo preguntaré de tu parte; **I'll go ~ you** iré yo en tu lugar; **"I can't iron this shirt" — "don't worry, I'll iron it ~ you"** —no puedo planchar esta camisa —no te preocupes, yo te la plancho; **"I still haven't booked the ticket" — "I'll do it ~ you"** —no he reservado el billete todavía —ya lo haré yo
6 (= *as in*); **G ~ George** G de Gerona
7 (= *in exchange for*) por; **I'll give you this book ~ that one** te cambio este libro por ése; **he'll do it ~ £25** lo hará por 25 libras; **~ every one who voted yes, 50 voted no** por cada persona que votó a favor, 50 votaron en contra; **to pay 50 pence ~ a ticket** pagar 50 peniques por una entrada; **I sold it ~ £5** lo vendí por *or* en cinco libras
8 (= *to the value of*) **a cheque ~ £500** un cheque *or* talón por valor de 500 libras
9 (*after adjective*) para; **he's tall/mature ~ his age** es alto/maduro para su edad *or* para la edad que tiene; **it's cold ~ July** para ser julio hace frío; **it was too difficult ~ her** era demasiado difícil para ella, le era demasiado difícil; **it was difficult ~ him to leave her** le resultó difícil dejarla
10 (= *in favour of*) a favor de; **I'm ~ helping him** yo estoy a favor de ayudarle; **anyone ~ a game of cards?** ¿alguien se apunta a una partida de cartas?; **are you ~ or <u>against</u> the idea?** ¿estás a favor o en contra de la idea?; **are you ~ or against us?** ¿estás con nosotros o en contra?
11 (= *as, by way of*) **what's ~ dinner?** ¿qué hay para cenar?
12 (= *because of*) por; **it's famous ~ its cathedral** es famosa

por su catedral; **if it weren't ~ you** si no fuera por ti; **he was sent to prison ~ fraud** lo mandaron a la cárcel por fraude; **we chose it ~ its climate** lo escogimos por el clima
13 (= *in spite of*) a pesar de; **~ all that** a pesar de todo
14 (*in expressions of time*)
14.1 (*future/past duration*)

> When translating **for** and a period of time, it is often unnecessary to translate **for**, as in the examples below where **durante** is optional:

she will be away ~ a month estará fuera (durante) un mes; **he worked in Spain ~ two years** trabajó (durante) dos años en España

> Alternatively, translate **for** using **durante**, or, especially when talking about very short periods, **por**. Use **por** also with the verb **ir**, although again it is often optional in this case:

they waited ~ over two hours estuvieron esperando durante más de dos horas; **~ a moment, he didn't know what to say** por un momento, no supo qué decir; **I'm going away ~ a few days** me voy (por) unos cuantos días; **we went to the seaside ~ the day** fuimos a pasar el día en la playa
14.2 (*with English perfect tenses*)

> Use **hace ... que** and the present to describe actions and states that started in the past and are still going on. Alternatively use the present and **desde hace**. Another option is sometimes **llevar** and the gerund. Don't use the present perfect in Spanish to translate phrases like these, unless they are in the negative.

I have known her ~ years hace años que la conozco, la conozco desde hace años; **he has been learning French ~ two years** hace dos años que estudia francés, estudia francés desde hace dos años, lleva dos años estudiando francés; **I haven't seen her ~ two years** hace dos años que no la veo, no la he visto desde hace dos años, no la veo desde hace dos años, llevo dos años sin verla

> Notice how the tenses change when talking about something that **had** happened or **had been** happening **for** a time:

he had been learning French ~ two years hacía dos años que estudiaba francés, estudiaba francés desde hacía dos años, llevaba dos años estudiando francés; **I hadn't seen her ~ two years** hacía dos años que no la veía, no la había visto desde hacía dos años, no la veía desde hacía dos años, llevaba dos años sin verla
15 (= *by, before*) para; **can you do it ~ tomorrow?** ¿lo puedes hacer para mañana?; **when does he want it ~?** ¿para cuándo lo quiere?
16 (= *on the occasion of*) para; **I'll be home ~ Christmas** estaré en casa para las Navidades; **what would you like ~ your birthday?** ¿qué quieres para tu cumpleaños?
17 (= *for a distance of*) **there were roadworks ~ five miles** había obras a lo largo de cinco millas; **we walked ~ two kilometres** caminamos dos kilómetros; **you can see ~ miles from here** desde aquí se puede ver hasta muy a lo lejos
18 (*with infinitive clauses*) **~ this to be possible ...** para que esto sea posible ...; **it's not ~ me to tell him what to do** yo no soy quien para decirle *or* no me corresponde a mí decirle lo que tiene que hacer; **he brought it ~ us to see** lo trajo para que lo viéramos; **there is still time ~ you to do it** todavía tienes tiempo para hacerlo
19 (*in other expressions*) **what's the German ~ "hill"?** ¿cómo se dice "colina" en alemán?; **✦ IDIOMS you're in ~ it!*** ♦ **you're ~ it!** (*Brit**) ¡las vas a pagar!*; **there's nothing ~ it but to jump** no hay más remedio que tirarse

fora ['fɔ:rə] NPL *of* **forum**

forage ['fɒrɪdʒ] Ⓐ N (*for cattle*) forraje *m* Ⓑ VI **to ~ for food** buscar algo para comer, buscar comida

foray ['fɒreɪ] N (*esp Mil*) incursión *f* (**into** en)
forbad(e) [fə'bæd] PT *of* **forbid**
forbearance [fɔ:'bɛərəns] N paciencia *f*
forbearing [fɔ:'bɛərɪŋ] ADJ paciente

forbid [fə'bɪd] (*pt* **forbad(e)**; *pp* **~den**) VT (= *not allow*) prohibir; **such actions are ~den by international law** el derecho internacional prohíbe este tipo de acciones; **to ~ sb to do sth** ♦ **~ sb from doing sth** prohibir a algn hacer algo, prohibir a algn que haga algo; **I ~ you to go** te prohíbo que vayas; **God** *or* **Heaven ~!*** ¡Dios nos libre!, ¡Dios no lo quiera!; **God** *or* **Heaven ~ that he should come here!** ¡quiera Dios *or* Dios quiera que no venga por aquí!

forbidden [fə'bɪdn] Ⓐ PT *of* **forbid** Ⓑ ADJ [*book, food, love*] prohibido; [*area, zone*] prohibido, vedado; [*word, feeling*] tabú; **to be ~** estar prohibido; **smoking is ~** está prohibido fumar

forbidding [fə'bɪdɪŋ] ADJ [*person, manner*] severo, intimidante; [*place, building*] imponente, intimidante

force [fɔ:s] Ⓐ N **1** (= *power*) fuerza *f*; **to do sth by ~** hacer algo por la fuerza; **by sheer ~ of personality** a fuerza de *or* a base de puro carácter; **from ~ of habit** por la fuerza de la costumbre; **the ~s of evil** las fuerzas del mal; **the ~ of gravity** la fuerza de la gravedad; **the police were out in ~** la policía había salido en masa, había un enorme despliegue policial; **to be in ~** [*law, tax*] estar vigente *or* en vigor; **to come into ~** entrar en vigor, hacerse vigente; **the ~s of nature** las fuerzas de la naturaleza; **he is a powerful ~ in the trade union movement** es una persona con mucho peso dentro del movimiento; **to resort to ~** recurrir a la fuerza; **to use ~** hacer uso de la fuerza
2 (= *body of people*) **allied ~s** fuerzas *fpl* aliadas, ejércitos *mpl* aliados; **sales ~** (*Comm*) personal *m* de ventas; **the ~s** (*Brit Mil*) las fuerzas armadas
Ⓑ VT **1** (= *compel*) [+ *person*] obligar, forzar; **to ~ sb to do sth** obligar *or* forzar a algn a hacer algo; **to ~ a smile** forzar una sonrisa, sonreír de manera forzada; **✦ IDIOM to ~ sb's hand** (*intentionally*) apretar las tuercas *or* las clavijas a algn; (*by circumstances*) no dejar a algn más remedio que actuar
2 (= *impose*) **to ~ sth on sb** imponer algo a algn
3 (= *push*) **they ~d their way into the flat** se metieron en el piso a *or* por la fuerza; **the lorry ~d the car off the road** el camión obligó *or* forzó al coche a salirse de la carretera, el camión hizo que el coche se saliera de la carretera; **she ~d her way through the crowd** se abrió paso entre la muchedumbre a *or* por la fuerza
4 (= *break open*) [+ *lock, door*] forzar; **to ~ sth open** forzar algo
5 (= *obtain by force*) conseguir a *or* por la fuerza; **to ~ a confession from** *or* **out of sb** obtener una confesión de algn a *or* por la fuerza
➤ **force back** VT + ADV **1** [+ *crowd, enemy*] obligar a retroceder, hacer retroceder (a la fuerza) **2** [+ *laughter, tears*] contener
➤ **force down** VT + ADV **1** [+ *food*] tragarse a la fuerza; **can you ~ a bit more down?** (*hum*) ¿te cabe un poco más? **2** [+ *prices*] hacer bajar, hacer que bajen

forced [fɔ:st] Ⓐ ADJ **1** (= *obligatory*) [*march*] forzado; [*repatriation*] forzoso; [*marriage*] forzado, por la fuerza
2 (= *from necessity*) [*landing*] forzoso **3** (= *contrived, strained*) [*smile*] forzado Ⓑ CPD ➤ **forced entry: there was no sign of ~ entry** no había señales de que hubieran forzado la entrada ➤ **forced labour, forced labor** (*US*) trabajos *mpl* forzados

force-feed ['fɔ:sfi:d] (*pt, pp* **force-fed**) VT alimentar a la fuerza

forceful ['fɔ:sfʊl] ADJ [*personality*] enérgico, fuerte; [*argument*] contundente, convincente

forcefully ['fɔ:sfəlɪ] ADV [*say, express*] enérgicamente; [*argue*] de forma convincente; [*push, shove*] violentamente

forceps ['fɔ:seps] NPL fórceps *m inv*

forcible ['fɔ:səbl] ADJ [*repatriation, deportation*] forzoso; **a ~ reminder of sth** un vivo recordatorio de algo

forcibly ['fɔ:səblɪ] ADV [*remove, restrain, separate*] a la fuerza, por la fuerza

ford [fɔ:d] Ⓐ N vado *m* Ⓑ VT vadear

fore [fɔːʳ] **Ⓐ** ADJ [*foot, limb*] anterior, delantero **Ⓑ** N **to come to the ~** empezar a destacar

forearm ['fɔːrɑːm] N (*Anat*) antebrazo *m*

forebears ['fɔːbɛəz] NPL antepasados *mpl*

foreboding [fɔː'bəʊdɪŋ] N presentimiento *m*; **to have a ~ that ...** presentir que ...

forecast ['fɔːkɑːst] (*vb: pt, pp* ~) **Ⓐ** N **1 the weather ~** el pronóstico meteorológico *or* del tiempo **2** (= *prediction*) previsión *f* **Ⓑ** VT (*gen*) pronosticar

forecaster ['fɔːkɑːstəʳ] N (*Met*) meteorólogo/a *m/f*; (*Econ, Pol, Sport*) pronosticador(a) *m/f*

foreclose [fɔː'kləʊz] **Ⓐ** VT [+ *mortgage*] extinguir el derecho de redimir **Ⓑ** VI extinguir el derecho de redimir una/la hipoteca; **to ~ on sth/sb** embargar algo/a algn

foreclosure [fɔː'kləʊʒəʳ] N apertura *f* de un juicio hipotecario

forecourt ['fɔːkɔːt] N (*esp Brit*) [*of hotel*] patio *m* (delantero), terraza *f*; [*of petrol station*] patio *m* (delantero)

forefathers ['fɔːfɑːðəz] NPL antepasados *mpl*

forefinger ['fɔːfɪŋgəʳ] N dedo *m* índice, índice *m*

forefront ['fɔːfrʌnt] N **to be in the ~ of** estar en la vanguardia de

forego [fɔː'gəʊ] (*pt* **forewent**; *pp* ~**ne**) VT (= *give up*) renunciar a; (= *do without*) pasar sin, privarse de

foregoing ['fɔːgəʊɪŋ] ADJ anterior, precedente

foregone ['fɔːgɒn] **Ⓐ** PP *of* **forego** **Ⓑ** ADJ **it was a ~ conclusion** era un resultado inevitable

foreground ['fɔːgraʊnd] N primer plano *m*, primer término *m*; **in the ~** (*fig*) en primer plano *or* término

forehand ['fɔːhænd] N (*Tennis*) drive *m*

forehead ['fɒrɪd] N frente *f*

foreign ['fɒrɪn] **Ⓐ** ADJ **1** (*gen*) [*person, country, language*] extranjero; [*import*] del extranjero; [*news*] internacional; **this was her first ~ holiday** éstas eran sus primeras vacaciones en el extranjero
2 [*minister, ministry*] de asuntos exteriores; [*policy, relations*] exterior
3 [*object, substance*] extraño
4 ~ to ajeno a; **it's an idea which is completely ~ to them** es una idea que les resulta totalmente ajena **Ⓑ** CPD ➤ **foreign affairs** asuntos *mpl* exteriores; **Secretary of State for Foreign Affairs** Secretario/a *m/f* de Estado para Asuntos Exteriores ➤ **foreign aid** (= *aid to other countries*) ayuda *f* al extranjero, ayuda *f* internacional; (= *aid from abroad*) ayuda *f* internacional ➤ **foreign body** (*frm*) cuerpo *m* extraño (*frm*) ➤ **foreign correspondent** corresponsal *mf* en el extranjero ➤ **foreign exchange** (= *currency*) divisas *fpl*; (= *reserves*) reservas *fpl* de divisas; (= *market*) mercado *m* de divisas ➤ **the Foreign Legion** la legión extranjera ➤ **foreign national** ciudadano/a *m/f* extranjero/a ➤ **the Foreign Office** (*Brit*) el Ministerio de Asuntos Exteriores ➤ **foreign policy** política *f* exterior ➤ **Foreign Secretary** (*Brit*) Ministro/a *m/f* de Asuntos Exteriores ➤ **the foreign service** (*US*) el servicio diplomático

foreigner ['fɒrɪnəʳ] N extranjero/a *m/f*

foreleg ['fɔːleg] N pata *f* delantera

foreman ['fɔːmən] N (*pl* **foremen**) [*of workers*] capataz *m*; (*Constr*) maestro *m* de obras; [*of jury*] presidente/a *m/f* del jurado

foremost ['fɔːməʊst] ADJ (= *outstanding*) más destacado; (= *main, first*) primero, principal

forename ['fɔːneɪm] N nombre *m*, nombre *m* de pila

forensic [fə'rensɪk] ADJ forense; [*medicine*] legal, forense ➤ **forensic evidence** prueba *f* legal

foreplay ['fɔːpleɪ] N caricias *fpl* estimulantes

forerunner ['fɔːrʌnəʳ] N precursor(a) *m/f*

foresee [fɔː'siː] (*pt* **foresaw**; *pp* ~**n**) VT prever

foreseeable [fɔː'siːəbl] ADJ [*opportunity*] previsible; **in the ~ future** en un futuro previsible

foreshadow [fɔː'ʃædəʊ] VT anunciar, presagiar

foreshore ['fɔːʃɔːʳ] N playa *f* (*entre pleamar y bajamar*)

foresight ['fɔːsaɪt] N previsión *f*; **he had the ~ to ...** tuvo la precaución de ...; **lack of ~** imprevisión *f*, falta *f* de previsión

foreskin ['fɔːskɪn] N (*Anat*) prepucio *m*

forest ['fɒrɪst] N (*temperate*) bosque *m*; (*tropical*) selva *f* ➤ **forest fire** incendio *m* forestal ➤ **forest ranger** guardabosques *mf inv*

forestall [fɔː'stɔːl] VT [+ *event, accident*] prevenir; [+ *rival, competitor*] adelantarse a

forestry ['fɒrɪstrɪ] N silvicultura *f*; (*Univ*) ingeniería *f* forestal

foretell [fɔː'tel] (*pt, pp* **foretold**) VT predecir, pronosticar

forethought ['fɔːθɔːt] N previsión *f*

forever [fər'evəʳ] ADV **1** (= *eternally*) para siempre; **he's gone ~** se ha ido para siempre **2** (***) (= *incessantly, repeatedly*) constantemente; **she's ~ complaining** se queja constantemente, siempre se está quejando

forewarn [fɔː'wɔːn] VT avisar, advertir; ✦ PROV ~**ed is forearmed** hombre prevenido *or* precavido vale por dos

forewent [fɔː'went] PT *of* **forego**

foreword ['fɔːwɜːd] N prefacio *m*, prólogo *m*

forfeit ['fɔːfɪt] **Ⓐ** N (*in game*) prenda *f*; (= *fine*) multa *f* **Ⓑ** VT [+ *one's rights etc*] perder

forgave [fə'geɪv] PT *of* **forgive**

forge [fɔːdʒ] **Ⓐ** N [*of blacksmith*] herrería *f* **Ⓑ** VT **1** (= *falsify*) [+ *document, painting, signature*] falsificar; ~**d money** moneda *f* falsa **2** (= *make*) fraguar, forjar **Ⓒ** VI **to ~ ahead** avanzar a grandes pasos

forger ['fɔːdʒəʳ] N falsificador(a) *m/f*

forgery ['fɔːdʒərɪ] N falsificación *f*; **it's a ~** es falso

forget [fə'get] (*pt* **forgot**; *pp* **forgotten**) **Ⓐ** VT olvidar, olvidarse de; **to ~ to do sth** olvidarse de hacer algo; **I forgot to close the window** me olvidé de *or* se me olvidó cerrar la ventana; **we shouldn't ~ that ...** no debemos olvidar que ...; **~ it!*** (= *don't worry*) ¡no te preocupes!, ¡no importa!; (= *you're welcome*) de nada, no hay de qué; **to ~ o.s.** (= *lose self-control*) pasarse, propasarse **Ⓑ** VI (*gen*) olvidar; (= *have a bad memory*) tener mala memoria; **I ~** no recuerdo, me he olvidado; **but I forgot** pero se me olvidó; **I forgot all about it** se me olvidó por completo

forgetful [fə'getfʊl] ADJ (= *lacking memory*) olvidadizo; (= *absent-minded*) despistado

forgetfulness [fə'getfʊlnɪs] N olvido *m*, falta *f* de memoria; (= *absentmindedness*) despiste *m*

forget-me-not [fə'getmɪnɒt] N nomeolvides *m inv*

forgive [fə'gɪv] (*pt* **forgave**; *pp* ~**n**) VT [+ *person, fault*] perdonar; **to ~ sb for doing sth** perdonar a algn por haber hecho algo; **~ me** (= *excuse me*) perdone

forgiveness [fə'gɪvnɪs] N (= *pardon*) perdón *m*; (= *willingness to forgive*) compasión *f*

forgiving [fə'gɪvɪŋ] ADJ compasivo

forgo [fɔː'gəʊ] (*pt* **forwent**; *pp* ~**ne**) VT (= *give up*) renunciar a; (= *do without*) pasar sin, privarse de

forgot [fə'gɒt] PT *of* **forget**

forgotten [fə'gɒtn] PP *of* **forget**

fork [fɔːk] **Ⓐ** N (*at table*) tenedor *m*; (*Agr*) horca *f*, horquilla *f*; (*in road*) bifurcación *f*; [*of tree*] horcadura *f* **Ⓑ** VI [*road*] bifurcarse ➤ **fork out*** **Ⓐ** VT + ADV [+ *money, cash*] aflojar* **Ⓑ** VI + ADV pagar

forked [fɔːkt] ADJ [*tail*] hendido; [*branch*] bifurcado; [*lightning*] en zigzag; [*tongue*] bífido

fork-lift truck ['fɔːklɪft,trʌk] N carretilla *f* elevadora

forlorn [fə'lɔːn] ADJ [*person*] triste, melancólico; (= *deserted*) [*cottage*] abandonado; (= *desperate*) [*attempt*] desesperado; **a ~ hope** una vana esperanza

form [fɔːm] **Ⓐ** N **1** (= *shape*) forma *f*; (= *figure, shadow*) bulto *m*, silueta *f*; (= *form and content*) forma *f* y contenido *m*; **in the ~ of** en forma de; **I'm against hunting in any ~** estoy en contra de cualquier forma de caza; **it took the ~ of a cash**

prize consistió en un premio en metálico; **what ~ will the ceremony take?** ¿en qué consistirá la ceremonia?
2 (= *kind, type*) clase *f*, tipo *m*
3 (= *way, means*) forma *f*; **~ of payment** modo *m* de pago
4 (*Sport, also fig*) forma *f*; **to be in good ~** (*Brit*) estar en buena forma; **he was in great ~ last night** (*Brit*) estaba en plena forma anoche
5 (= *document*) (*gen*) formulario *m*, impreso *m*; **application ~** solicitud *f*; **to fill in** *or* **out a ~** rellenar un formulario *or* un impreso
6 (*Brit Scol*) curso *m*, clase *f*; **she's in the first ~** está haciendo primer curso de secundaria *or* primero de secundaria
7 (*Brit Racing*) **to study ~** estudiar resultados anteriores
B VT (= *shape, make*) formar; [+ *company*] formar, fundar; [+ *plan*] elaborar, formular; [+ *sentence*] construir; [+ *queue*] hacer; [+ *opinion*] hacerse, formarse; **to ~ a government** formar gobierno; **to ~ part of sth** formar parte de algo
C VI tomar forma, formarse; **an idea ~ed in his mind** una idea tomó forma en su mente

formal ['fɔːməl] ADJ [*person*] (= *correct*) correcto; (= *reliable, stiff*) formal; (= *solemn*) [*greeting, language, occasion, announcement*] solemne; [*word, expression*] formal; [*dress*] de etiqueta; [*visit*] de cumplido; [*evidence*] documental; (*Pol*) [*visit*] oficial; **don't be so ~!** ¡no te andes con tantos cumplidos!; **there was no ~ agreement** no había un acuerdo en firme; **a ~ dinner** una cena de gala; **he has no ~ education** no tiene formación académica

formality [fɔː'mælɪtɪ] N formalidad *f*; **it's a mere ~** no es más que una formalidad

formalize ['fɔːməlaɪz] VT formalizar

formally ['fɔːməlɪ] ADV (*gen*) formalmente; (= *officially*) oficialmente; (= *ceremoniously*) con mucha ceremonia; [*dress etc*] de etiqueta; (= *stiffly*) con formalidad

format ['fɔːmæt] **A** N formato *m* **B** VT (*Comput*) formatear

formation [fɔː'meɪʃən] N formación *f* ➤ **formation flying** vuelo *m* en formación

formative ['fɔːmətɪv] ADJ [*influence*] formativo; [*years*] de formación

formatting ['fɔːmætɪŋ] N formateado *m*, formateo *m*

former ['fɔːmə'] **A** ADJ (= *earlier, previous*) antiguo; [*chairman, wife etc*] ex

In this sense, put **antiguo** before the noun:

a ~ pupil un antiguo alumno; **in ~ days** antiguamente; **the ~ president** el ex-presidente **B** PRON **night and day, the ~ dark, the latter light** la noche y el día, aquélla oscura y éste lleno de luz

formerly ['fɔːməlɪ] ADV antiguamente

Formica® [fɔː'maɪkə] N formica® *f*

formidable ['fɔːmɪdəbl] ADJ [*person*] formidable; [*opponent*] temible; [*task, challenge, obstacle*] tremendo, impresionante

formula ['fɔːmjʊlə] N (*pl* **~s** *or* **~e** ['fɔːmjʊliː]) **1** (*gen*) (*Maths*) fórmula *f*; **winning ~** fórmula *f* del éxito **2** (= *baby milk*) leche *f* en polvo (para bebés), leche *f* maternizada

formulate ['fɔːmjʊleɪt] VT [+ *theory, policy*] formular

formulation [ˌfɔːmjʊ'leɪʃən] N formulación *f*; (= *medicine*) fórmula *f*

fornicate ['fɔːnɪkeɪt] VI fornicar

forsake [fə'seɪk] (*pt* **forsook** [fə'sʊk]; *pp* **~n** [fə'seɪkən]) VT abandonar

fort [fɔːt] N (*Mil*) fortaleza *f*, fuerte *m*; ✦ IDIOM **to hold** *or* (*US*) **hold down the ~** quedarse a cargo; **hold the ~ till I get back** hazte cargo hasta que yo regrese

forte ['fɔːtɪ, (*US*) fɔːt] N fuerte *m*

forth [fɔːθ] ADV **1** (†) (= *onward*) adelante; **to go ~** marcharse; **from this day ~** de hoy en adelante **2 and so ~** etcétera, y así sucesivamente

forthcoming [fɔːθ'kʌmɪŋ] ADJ **1** (= *imminent*) [*event, election*] próximo; [*weeks, months*] venidero; [*book*] de próxima publicación **2** (= *available*) **no answer was ~** no

hubo respuesta; **no help was ~** no obtuvo ninguna ayuda; **if funds are ~** si nos facilitan fondos **3** (= *open*) [*person*] comunicativo

forthright ['fɔːθraɪt] ADJ franco, directo

forthwith ['fɔːθ'wɪθ] ADV en el acto, de inmediato

fortieth ['fɔːtɪɪθ] **A** ADJ cuadragésimo **B** N **1** (*in series*) cuadragésimo/a *m/f* **2** (= *fraction*) cuadragésima parte *f*, cuarenta y uno; *see* **fiftieth**

fortification [ˌfɔːtɪfɪ'keɪʃən] N fortificación *f*

fortify ['fɔːtɪfaɪ] VT (*Mil*) fortificar; (= *strengthen*) fortalecer; **fortified wine** vino *m* encabezado

fortitude ['fɔːtɪtjuːd] N fortaleza *f*, valor *m*

fortnight ['fɔːtnaɪt] N (*esp Brit*) quince días *mpl*, quincena *f*; **a ~ (from) today** de hoy en quince días

fortnightly ['fɔːtnaɪtlɪ] (*Brit*) **A** ADJ quincenal **B** ADV quincenalmente, cada quince días

fortress ['fɔːtrɪs] N fortaleza *f*, plaza *f* fuerte

fortuitous [fɔː'tjuːɪtəs] ADJ fortuito, casual

fortunate ['fɔːtʃənɪt] ADJ [*person, occurrence*] afortunado; [*coincidence*] feliz; **I was ~ enough to escape** yo tuve la suerte de poder escapar; **how ~!** ¡qué suerte!; **it was ~ that no one was injured** fue una suerte que nadie resultara herido

fortunately ['fɔːtʃənɪtlɪ] ADV afortunadamente, por suerte

fortune ['fɔːtʃən] **A** N **1** (= *luck*) fortuna *f*, suerte *f*; **by good ~** por fortuna; **we had the good ~ to find him** tuvimos la suerte de encontrarlo; **to tell sb's ~** decir a algn la buenaventura
2 (= *property, wealth*) fortuna *f*; **to come into a ~** heredar una fortuna
3 (= *huge amount of money*) dineral *m*, platal *m* (*LAm**); **to cost a ~** costar un ojo de la cara*, valer un dineral; **to make a ~** enriquecerse, ganar un dineral
B CPD ➤ **fortune cookie** (*esp US*) galleta china con un mensaje sobre la suerte ➤ **fortune hunter** cazafortunas *mf inv*

fortune-teller ['fɔːtʃən,telə'] N adivino/a *m/f*

fortune-telling ['fɔːtʃən,telɪŋ] N adivinación *f*

forty ['fɔːtɪ] NUMBER cuarenta *m*; ✦ IDIOM **to have ~ winks*** echar un sueñecito; *see* **fifty**

forum ['fɔːrəm] N (*pl* **~s** *or* **fora** ['fɔːrə]) foro *m*; (*fig*) tribunal *m*, foro *m*

forward ['fɔːwəd]

When **forward** is an element in a phrasal verb, eg **bring forward, come forward, step forward**, look up the verb.

A ADJ **1** (*in position*) delantero; (*in movement*) hacia adelante; (*in time*) adelantado, avanzado
2 (= *advanced*) [*child*] precoz; [*season, crop*] adelantado
3 (= *presumptuous*) [*person, remark*] atrevido
B ADV (*gen*) adelante, hacia adelante; **forward!** ¡adelante!; **~ march!** (*Mil*) de frente ¡mar!; **the lever is placed well ~** la palanca está colocada bastante hacia adelante; **from that day ~** desde ese día en adelante, a partir de entonces; **to come ~** hacerse conocer; **to go ~** ir hacia adelante, avanzar; (*fig*) progresar, hacer progresos
C N (*Sport*) delantero/a *m/f*
D VT (= *dispatch*) [+ *goods*] expedir, enviar; (= *send on*) [+ *letter*] remitir; **"please forward"** "remítase al destinatario"
E CPD ➤ **forward planning** planificación *f* por anticipado ➤ **forward slash** (*Typ*) barra *f* diagonal

forwarding address [ˌfɔːwədɪŋə'dres] N destinatario *m*; **she left no ~** no dejó dirección (a la que mandarle el correo)

forward-looking ['fɔːwəd,lʊkɪŋ] ADJ [*plan, policy*] con miras al futuro; [*person*] previsor; (*Pol*) progresista

forwards ['fɔːwədz] ADV (*esp Brit*) = **forward B**

forwent [fɔː'went] PT *of* **forgo**

fossil ['fɒsl] N fósil *m* ➤ **fossil fuel** hidrocarburo *m*

fossilized ['fɒsɪlaɪzd] ADJ fosilizado

foster ['fɒstə'] **A** VT **1** [+ *child*] acoger **2** (= *encourage*) fomentar, promover; (= *aid*) favorecer **③** CPD [*parent, child*] de acogida ➤ **foster brother** hermano *m* de leche ➤ **foster home** casa *f* de acogida ➤ **foster mother** madre *f* de acogida

fought [fɔːt] PT, PP *of* **fight**

foul [faʊl] **④** ADJ (*compar* **~er**; *superl* **~est**) **1** (= *disgusting*) [*place*] asqueroso; [*smell*] pestilente, fétido; [*taste*] repugnante, asqueroso
2 (*) (= *nasty*) [*weather*] de perros*, malísimo; **he was in a ~ mood** estaba de un humor de perros*; **she has a ~ temper** tiene muy malas pulgas*, tiene un genio de mil demonios*
3 (= *obscene*) ordinario, grosero; **to use ~ language** decir groserías; **✦** IDIOM **to have a ~ mouth*** ser mal hablado
4 (= *base, immoral*) [*lie, calumny, crime*] vil, terrible
5 (*Sport*) [*shot, ball*] nulo; [*blow, tackle*] sucio; [*kick*] antirreglamentaria
6 (*in phrases*) **someone is sure to cry ~** es seguro que alguien dice que no hemos jugado limpio; **to fall ~ of the law** (*esp Brit*) enfrentarse con la justicia, vérselas con la ley*
③ N (*Sport*) falta *f* (**on** contra)
④ VT **1** (= *pollute*) [+ *air*] viciar, contaminar; [+ *water*] contaminar; [*dog*] ensuciar
2 (*Sport*) [+ *opponent*] cometer una falta contra
3 (= *entangle*) [+ *fishing line, net, rope*] enredar; **something had ~ed the propellers** algo se había enredado en las hélices; **the boat had ~ed her anchor** el ancla del barco se había atascado
① CPD ➤ **foul play** (*Sport*) jugada *f* antirreglamentaria, juego *m* sucio; **the police suspect ~ play** (*Jur*) la policía sospecha que se trata de un crimen
➤ **foul up*** VT + ADV [+ *activity, event, plans*] dar al traste con, echar a perder; **he has ~ed up his exams** los exámenes le han ido mal, ha metido la pata en los exámenes*

foulmouthed [ˈfaʊlmaʊðd] ADJ malhablado

foul-smelling [ˈfaʊlsmelɪŋ] ADJ pestilente, fétido

foul-tempered [ˈfaʊlˈtempəd] ADJ **to be ~** (*habitually*) tener un genio de mil demonios*; (*on one occasion*) estar de mal humor, estar de un humor de perros*

found[1] [faʊnd] PT, PP *of* **find**

found[2] [faʊnd] VT [+ *town, school etc*] fundar; **a statement ~ed on fact** una declaración basada en los hechos

foundation [faʊnˈdeɪʃən] **④** N **1** (= *act*) fundación *f*, establecimiento *m* **2** (= *basis*) fundamento *m*, base *f*; **the story is without ~** la historia carece de fundamento
3 foundations (*Archit*) cimientos *mpl* **4** (= *organization*) fundación *f* **5** (= *make-up*) maquillaje *m* de fondo, base *f*
③ CPD ➤ **foundation course** (*Brit*) curso *m* preparatorio ➤ **foundation cream** crema *f* de base ➤ **foundation garment** corsé *m* ➤ **foundation stone** (*Brit*) primera piedra *f*; (*fig*) piedra *f* angular

founder[1] [ˈfaʊndəʳ] N (= *originator*) fundador(a) *m/f*
➤ **founder member** (*Brit*) miembro *mf* fundador(a)

founder[2] [ˈfaʊndəʳ] VI (*Naut*) hundirse, irse a pique; (*fig*) fracasar (**on** debido a)

foundry [ˈfaʊndrɪ] N fundición *f*, fundidora *f* (*LAm*)

fount [faʊnt] N **~ of knowledge/wisdom** fuente *f* de sabiduría

fountain [ˈfaʊntɪn] N (*natural, also fig*) fuente *f*, manantial *m*; (*artificial*) fuente *f*, surtidor *m*; **drinking ~** fuente *f* (de agua potable) ➤ **fountain pen** estilográfica *f*, plumafuente *f* (*LAm*)

four [fɔːʳ] NUMBER cuatro *m*; **to make up a ~ for bridge** completar los cuatro para jugar al bridge; **✦** IDIOM **on all ~s** a gatas; *see* **five**

four-door [ˈfɔːˈdɔːʳ] ADJ [*car*] de cuatro puertas

four-engined [ˈfɔːˈrendʒɪnd] ADJ cuatrimotor, tetramotor

four-eyes** [ˈfɔːraɪz] N cuatrojos* *mf inv*

four-legged [ˌfɔːˈlegɪd] ADJ cuadrúpedo

four-letter word [ˌfɔːletəˈwɜːd] N palabrota *f*, taco *m* (*Sp*)

four-poster [ˈfɔːˌpəʊstəʳ] N cama *f* de columnas

foursome [ˈfɔːsəm] N grupo *m* de cuatro

fourteen [ˈfɔːˈtiːn] NUMBER catorce *m*; *see* **five**

fourteenth [ˈfɔːˈtiːnθ] **④** ADJ decimocuarto **③** PRON **1** (*in series*) decimocuarto/a *m/f* **2** (= *fraction*) catorceava parte *f*, catorceavo *m*; *see* **fifteenth**

fourth [fɔːθ] **④** ADJ cuarto **③** PRON **1** (*in series*) cuarto/a *m/f*
2 (*US*) (= *fraction*) cuarta parte *f*, cuarto *m* **3** (*also* **~ gear**) cuarta *f* (velocidad *f*) **④** CPD **fourth dimension** cuarta dimensión *f* ➤ **the fourth estate** (*hum*) el cuarto poder, la prensa ➤ **fourth note** (*US*) cuarta *f*; *see* **fifth**

four-wheel drive [ˌfɔːwiːlˈdraɪv] N (= *system*) tracción *f* de cuatro por cuatro, tracción *f* a las cuatro ruedas; (= *car*) todoterreno *m inv*

fowl [faʊl] N ave *f*

> Use **el/un** not **la/una** before feminine nouns beginning with stressed **a** or **ha** like **ave**.

fox [fɒks] N zorro *m* ➤ **fox cub** cachorro *m* (de zorro)
➤ **fox terrier** foxterrier *m*

foxglove [ˈfɒksglʌv] N dedalera *f*

foxhound [ˈfɒkshaʊnd] N perro *m* raposero

foxhunting [ˈfɒksˌhʌntɪŋ] N caza *f* del zorro; **to go ~** ir a cazar zorros

foxtrot [ˈfɒkstrɒt] N fox *m inv*, foxtrot *m*

foxy [ˈfɒksɪ] ADJ **1** (= *crafty*) astuto **2** (*US**) [*woman*] sexy

foyer [ˈfɔɪeɪ] N vestíbulo *m*

Fr ABBR (*Rel*) (= *Father*) P., P.e

fracas [ˈfrækɑː] N gresca *f*, reyerta *f*

fraction [ˈfrækʃən] N **1** (*Math*) fracción *f*, quebrado *m*
2 (*fig*) pequeña porción *f*, parte *f* muy pequeña; **move it just a ~** muévelo una chispa; **for a ~ of a second** por un instante

fractionally [ˈfrækʃnəlɪ] ADV mínimamente

fractious [ˈfrækʃəs] ADJ (= *irritable*) irritable; (= *unruly*) díscolo

fracture [ˈfræktʃəʳ] **④** N fractura *f* **③** VT fracturar; **to ~ one's arm** fracturarse el brazo

fragile [ˈfrædʒaɪl] ADJ frágil; **"fragile, handle with care"** "cuidado, frágil"

fragment ④ [ˈfrægmənt] N fragmento *m* **③** [fræɡˈment] VI [*alliance, group*] fragmentarse

fragmentary [fræɡˈmentərɪ] ADJ fragmentario

fragmented [fræɡˈmentɪd] ADJ fragmentado

fragrance [ˈfreɪɡrəns] N (= *smell*) fragancia *f*; (= *perfume*) perfume *m*

fragrant [ˈfreɪɡrənt] ADJ fragante, oloroso

frail [freɪl] ADJ (*compar* **~er**; *superl* **~est**) [*person*] débil; [*health*] delicado, frágil

frailty [ˈfreɪltɪ] N [*of person*] debilidad *f*; [*of health*] lo delicado, fragilidad *f*

frame [freɪm] **④** N **1** (= *framework*) [*of ship, building etc*] armazón *m or f*, estructura *f*; [*of spectacles*] montura *f*; [*of bicycle*] cuadro *m*
2 (= *border*) [*of picture, window, door*] marco *m*
3 (*TV, Video*) cuadro *m*; (*Cine*) fotograma *m*
4 (= *body*) cuerpo *m*
5 (*fig*) **~ of mind** estado *m* de ánimo; **when you're in a better ~ of mind** cuando estés de mejor humor
③ VT **1** [+ *picture*] enmarcar, poner un marco a; **he appeared ~d in the doorway** apareció en el marco de la puerta
2 (*) [+ *innocent person*] **to ~ sb** tender una trampa a algn para incriminarlo; **I've been ~d!** ¡me han tendido una trampa!

frame-up* [ˈfreɪmʌp] N trampa *f*, montaje *m* (para incriminar a algn); **it's a ~** aquí hay trampa, esto es un montaje

framework [ˈfreɪmwɜːk] **④** N **1** (*lit*) armazón *m or f*, estructura *f* **2** (*fig*) [*of essay, society*] marco *m*; **within the ~ of the constitution** dentro del marco de la constitución
③ CPD ➤ **framework agreement** (*Ind, Pol*) acuerdo *m* marco

franc [fræŋk] N franco *m*

France [frɑːns] N Francia f

franchise ['fræntʃaɪz] **Ⓐ** N **1** (*Pol*) sufragio m **2** (*Comm*) concesión f, franquicia f **Ⓑ** VT (*Comm*) otorgar la concesión de, franquiciar **Ⓒ** CPD ➤ **franchise holder** franquiciado/a m/f, concesionario/a m/f

Franciscan [fræn'sɪskən] N franciscano/a m/f

Franco- ['fræŋkəʊ] PREF franco-; ~**British** franco-británico

frank¹ [fræŋk] ADJ (*compar* ~**er**; *superl* ~**est**) franco; **to be** ~ (**with you**) para serte franco, sinceramente

frank² [fræŋk] VT [+ *letter*] franquear

frankfurter ['fræŋk,fɜːtəʳ] N salchicha f de Frankfurt

frankincense ['fræŋkɪnsens] N incienso m

frankly ['fræŋklɪ] ADV francamente

frankness ['fræŋknɪs] N franqueza f, sinceridad f

frantic ['fræntɪk] ADJ [*activity, pace*] frenético; (= *desperate*) [*person*] desesperado; **she was** ~ **with worry** estaba loca de inquietud

frantically ['fræntɪkəlɪ] ADV frenéticamente, con frenesí

fraternal [frə'tɜːnl] ADJ fraterno

fraternity [frə'tɜːnɪtɪ] N **1** (= *comradeship*) fraternidad f **2** (*US Univ*) círculo m estudiantil **3** (= *world*) **the criminal** ~ el mundo del hampa; **the yachting** ~ los aficionados a la vela

fraternize ['frætənaɪz] VI confraternizar (**with** con)

fraud [frɔːd] **Ⓐ** N **1** (*Jur*) fraude m **2** (= *trickery*) estafa f; (= *trick, con*) engaño m, timo m **3** (= *person*) impostor(a) m/f, farsante mf **Ⓑ** CPD ➤ **Fraud Squad** brigada f de delitos económicos, brigada f anticorrupción

fraudulent ['frɔːdjʊlənt] ADJ fraudulento

fraught [frɔːt] ADJ **1** (= *tense*) tenso; **things got a bit** ~ la situación se puso difícil **2 to be** ~ **with** [+ *problems*] estar lleno de; **to be** ~ **with danger** ser peligrosísimo

fray¹ [freɪ] N (= *fight*) combate m, lucha f; **to be ready for the** ~ (*lit, fig*) estar dispuesto a pelear; **to enter the** ~ (*fig*) entrar en acción *or* en liza

fray² [freɪ] VI **1** [*cloth, garment, cuff*] deshilacharse; [*rope*] desgastarse **2** (*fig*) **tempers** ~**ed in the discussion that followed** los ánimos se caldearon en la discusión que siguió

frayed [freɪd] ADJ **1** [*cloth, garment, cuff,*] deshilachado, raído; [*rope*] desgastado **2** [*nerves*] crispado; **tempers were getting** ~ los ánimos se estaban caldeando, la gente estaba perdiendo la paciencia

frazzle* ['fræzl] **Ⓐ** N **it was burned to a** ~ (*Brit*) quedó carbonizado; **to beat sb to a** ~ (*Sport*) dar una soberana paliza a algn*; **to be worn to a** ~ estar hecho un trapo *or* migas* **Ⓑ** VT (*US*) agotar, rendir

freak [friːk] **Ⓐ** N **1** (= *person*) monstruo m, fenómeno m; (= *plant, animal*) monstruo m; (= *event*) anomalía f; **a** ~ **of nature** un fenómeno de la naturaleza; **the result was a** ~ el resultado fue totalmente anómalo **2** (*) (= *enthusiast*) fanático/a m/f, adicto/a m/f; **health** ~ maniático/a m/f en cuestión de salud **Ⓑ** ADJ [*storm, conditions*] anómalo, anormal; [*victory*] inesperado ➤ **freak out** **Ⓐ** VI + ADV alucinar (*Sp**), friquearse (*Mex**) **Ⓑ** VT + ADV alucinar (*Sp**), friquear (*Mex**)

freckle ['frekl] N peca f

free [friː] **Ⓐ** ADJ (*compar* ~**r**; *superl* ~**st**) **1** (= *at liberty*) libre; (= *untied*) libre, desatado; **to get** ~ escaparse; **to let sb go** ~ dejar a algn en libertad; **to pull sth/sb** ~ (*from wreckage*) sacar algo/a algn; (*from tangle*) sacar *or* desenredar algo/a algn; **to set** ~ [+ *prisoner*] liberar; [+ *animal*] soltar **2** (= *unrestricted*) libre; **she opened the door with her** ~ **hand** abrió la puerta con la mano que tenía libre; **to be** ~ **to do sth** ser libre de hacer algo, tener libertad para hacer algo; **"can I borrow your pen?" — "feel** ~**!"** —¿te puedo coger el bolígrafo? —¡por supuesto! *or* —¡claro que sí!; **feel** ~ **to help yourself** sírvete con toda libertad; ✦ IDIOMS **to give** ~ **rein to** dar rienda suelta a; **to give sb a** ~ **hand** dar a algn carta blanca; **to have a** ~ **hand to do sth** tener carta blanca para hacer algo **3** (= *clear, devoid*) ~ **from** *or* **of sth: a world** ~ **of nuclear weapons** un mundo sin armas nucleares; **to be** ~ **from pain**

no sufrir *or* padecer dolor; **we are** ~ **of him at last** por fin nos hemos librado de él **4** (*Pol*) (= *autonomous, independent*) [*country, state*] libre; ~ **elections** elecciones *fpl* libres; **it's a** ~ **country!*** ¡es una democracia! **5** (= *costing nothing*) [*ticket, delivery*] gratuito, gratis; [*sample, offer, transport, health care*] gratuito; **"admission free"** "entrada f libre"; ~ **of charge** gratis, gratuito; **to get sth for** ~* obtener algo gratis; ✦ IDIOMS **there's no such thing as a** ~ **lunch** no te regalan nada; **to get a** ~ **ride*** aprovecharse de la situación **6** (= *not occupied*) [*seat, room, person, moment*] libre; [*post*] vacante; [*premises*] desocupado; **is this seat** ~? ¿está libre este asiento?, ¿está ocupado (este asiento)?; **are you** ~ **tomorrow?** ¿estás libre mañana? **7** (= *generous*) generoso (**with** con); **to make** ~ **with sth** usar algo como si fuera cosa propia; **to be** ~ **with one's money** no reparar en gastos, ser manirroto*; **he's too** ~ **with his remarks** tiene una lengua muy suelta **Ⓑ** ADV **1** (= *without charge*) **I got in (for)** ~ entré gratis *or* sin pagar **2** (= *without restraint*) **animals run** ~ **in the park** los animales campan a sus anchas por el parque **Ⓒ** VT **1** (= *release*) [+ *prisoner, people*] liberar, poner en libertad; (*from wreckage etc*) rescatar; (= *untie*) desatar, soltar **2** (= *make available*) [+ *funds, resources*] hacer disponible, liberar; **this will** ~ **him to pursue other projects** esto lo dejará libre para *or* esto le permitirá dedicarse a otros proyectos **3** (= *rid, relieve*) **to** ~ **sb from sth** liberar a algn de algo; **to** ~ **sb from pain** quitar *or* aliviar a algn el dolor; **to** ~ **o.s. from sth** librarse de algo; **their aim is to** ~ **the country of disease** se han propuesto acabar con la enfermedad en el país **Ⓓ** CPD ➤ **free agent: he's a** ~ **agent** tiene libertad de acción, es libre de hacer lo que quiere ➤ **free enterprise** libre empresa f ➤ **free fall** caída f libre; **to go into** ~ **fall** empezar a caer en picado (*Sp*) *or* en picada (*LAm*) ➤ **free gift** obsequio m, regalo m ➤ **free house** (*Brit*) pub que es libre de vender cualquier marca de cerveza por no estar vinculado a ninguna cervecería en particular ➤ **free kick** (*Ftbl*) tiro m libre ➤ **free love** amor m libre ➤ **free market** (*Econ*) mercado m libre (**in** de); ~ **marketeer** partidario/a m/f del libre mercado ➤ **free pass** pase m gratuito ➤ **free period** (*Scol*) hora f libre ➤ **free speech** libertad f de expresión ➤ **free spirit** persona f libre de convencionalismos ➤ **free trade** libre cambio m ➤ **free trader** librecambista mf ➤ **free vote** (*Brit Parl*) voto m de confianza (independiente de la línea del partido) ➤ **free will** libre albedrío m; **he did it of his own** ~ **will** lo hizo por voluntad propia

freebie* ['friːbɪ] N (= *free gift*) obsequio m, regalo m; (= *free meal/drink*) comida f/bebida f gratuita; **it's a** ~ es gratis

freedom ['friːdəm] **Ⓐ** N **1** (*gen*) libertad f; ~ **of choice** libertad f de elección; ~ **of information** libertad f de información; ~ **of the press** libertad f de prensa; ~ **of speech** libertad f de expresión; **they want** ~ **from government control** no quieren estar sometidos al control del gobierno, quieren estar libres del control del gobierno; **she found her sudden** ~ **from responsibility exhilarating** viéndose de repente liberada de sus responsabilidades, se sentía eufórica **2** (= *liberation*) liberación f **Ⓑ** CPD ➤ **freedom fighter** guerrillero/a m/f ➤ **Freedom of Information Act** (*US*) ley f del derecho a la información

Freefone® ['friːfəʊn] N (*Brit Telec*) teléfono m gratuito

free-for-all* ['friːfə'rɔːl] N (= *brawl*) pelea f, bronca f; (= *argument*) discusión f general

freehold ['friːhəʊld] (*Brit*) **Ⓐ** ADJ [*property, land*] de pleno dominio **Ⓑ** N pleno dominio m, propiedad f absoluta

freelance ['friːlɑːns] ADJ freelance, por cuenta propia

freelancer ['friːlɑːnsəʳ] N trabajador(a) m/f por cuenta propia

freeloader* ['friːləʊdəʳ] N gorrón/ona m/f (*Sp, Mex**), gorrero/a m/f (*LAm**), bolsero/a m/f (*Chi**), garronero/a m/f (*RPl**)

freely ['fri:lɪ] ADV **1** (= *unrestrictedly*) libremente, con libertad; **to be ~ available** ser fácil de conseguir, conseguirse con facilidad **2** (= *openly*) [*speak*] con toda libertad, francamente **3** (= *willingly*) de buen grado; **I ~ admit I was wrong** soy el primero en admitir que estaba equivocado **4** (= *generously*) [*give*] generosamente, con liberalidad; [*flow*] copiosamente; [*spend money*] con liberalidad, a manos llenas; **the wine flowed ~** el vino fluía copiosamente **5** (= *loosely*) [*translate*] libremente

free-market economy [,fri:,mɑːkɪtɪ'kɒnəmɪ] N economía *f* de mercado libre

freemason ['fri:,meɪsn] N (franc)masón *m*

Freepost ['fri:,pəʊst] N (*Brit*) franqueo *m* pagado

free-range ['fri:reɪndʒ] ADJ (*Brit*) [*hen, eggs*] de corral

freesia ['fri:zɪə] N fresia *f*

freestyle ['fri:staɪl] N **100 metres ~**(*Swimming*) 100 metros libres

free-trade zone [,fri:'treɪdzəʊn] N zona *f* franca

freeware ['fri:wɜː] N (*Comput*) programas *mpl* de dominio público, software *m* gratuito

freeway ['fri:weɪ] N (*US*) autopista *f*

freewheel ['fri:'wi:l] VI (*on bicycle*) ir (en bicicleta) sin pedalear; (*in car*) ir en punto muerto

freeze [fri:z] (*pt* **froze**; *pp* **frozen**) Ⓐ VT [+ *water*] helar; [+ *food, prices, wages, assets*] congelar Ⓑ VI **1** (*gen*) helarse, congelarse; **it will ~ tonight** esta noche va a caer una helada; **to ~ to death** morirse de frío **2** (= *be motionless*) quedarse inmóvil; **freeze!** ¡no te muevas!; **the smile froze on his lips** se le heló la sonrisa en los labios Ⓒ N **1** (*Met*) helada *f* **2** [*of prices, wages etc*] congelación *f*
➤ **freeze out** VT + ADV marginar, excluir
➤ **freeze over** VI + ADV [*lake, river*] helarse; [*windows, windscreen*] cubrirse de escarcha; **the lake has frozen over** el lago está helado

freeze-dry [,fri:z'draɪ] VT liofilizar, deshidratar por congelación

freezer ['fri:zə] N congelador *m*

freezing ['fri:zɪŋ] Ⓐ ADJ glacial, helado; **I'm ~** estoy helado; **it's ~ in here** aquí se congela uno, aquí hace un frío que pela* Ⓑ ADV **it's ~ cold** hace un frío horrible *or* que pela* Ⓒ N **1** (*also* **~ point**) **five degrees below ~** cinco grados bajo cero **2** (= *deep freezing*) (ultra)congelación *f* **3** (*fig*) [*of prices, wages, assets*] congelación *f* Ⓓ CPD
➤ **freezing fog** niebla *f* helada ➤ **freezing point** punto *m* de congelación

freight [freɪt] Ⓐ N (= *goods transported*) flete *m*; (= *load*) carga *f*; (= *goods*) mercancías *fpl*; (= *charge*) flete *m*, gastos *mpl* *or* costos *mpl* de transporte; **to send sth (by) ~** enviar algo por flete; **~ paid** (*Comm*) porte *m* pagado Ⓑ CPD ➤ **freight car** (*esp US*) vagón *m* de mercancías
➤ **freight charges** gastos *mpl* *or* costos *mpl* de transporte
➤ **freight plane** avión *m* de transporte de mercancías
➤ **freight terminal** terminal *f* de mercancías; (*Aer*) terminal *f* de carga ➤ **freight train** (*US*) tren *m* de mercancías

freighter ['freɪtə] N (= *ship*) buque *m* de carga, nave *f* de mercancías; (= *person: carrier*) transportista *m*; (= *agent*) fletador *m*

French [frentʃ] Ⓐ ADJ francés; [*ambassador*] de Francia Ⓑ N **1** (*Ling*) francés *m* **2** **the ~** los franceses Ⓒ CPD
➤ **French bean** (*Brit*) judía *f* verde, ejote *m* (*Mex*), poroto *m* verde (*Chi*) ➤ **French doors** (*US*) puertaventana *fsing*
➤ **French dressing** vinagreta *f* ➤ **French fries** patatas *fpl* fritas, papas *fpl* fritas (*LAm*) ➤ **French horn** trompa *f* de llaves ➤ **French kiss** beso *m* en la boca (con la lengua)
➤ **French toast** (*Brit*) (= *toast*) tostada *f*; (= *fried bread in egg*) torrija *f* ➤ **French windows** puertaventana *fsing*

French-Canadian ['frentʃkə'neɪdɪən] N **1** (= *person*) francocanadiense *mf* **2** (*Ling*) francés *m* canadiense

Frenchman ['frentʃmən] N (*pl* **Frenchmen**) francés *m*

French-polish [,frentʃ'pɒlɪʃ] VT (*Brit*) lacar

French-speaking ['frentʃ,spi:kɪŋ] ADJ francófono, francoparlante, de habla francesa

Frenchwoman ['frentʃ,wʊmən] N (*pl* **Frenchwomen**)

francesa *f*

frenetic [frɪ'netɪk] ADJ frenético

frenzied ['frenzɪd] ADJ [*effort etc*] frenético; [*crowd etc*] enloquecido

frenzy ['frenzɪ] N frenesí *m*, delirio *m*

frequency ['fri:kwənsɪ] N (*gen, Elec*) frecuencia *f*
➤ **frequency band** banda *f* de frecuencia

frequent Ⓐ ['fri:kwənt] ADJ frecuente; **Fiona was a ~ visitor there** Fiona solía ir allí con frecuencia Ⓑ [frɪ'kwent] VT frecuentar

frequently ['fri:kwəntlɪ] ADV con frecuencia, frecuentemente; **all too ~** con demasiada frecuencia
➤ **frequently asked questions** preguntas *fpl* frecuentes

fresco ['freskəʊ] N (*pl* **~es** *or* **~s**) fresco *m*

fresh [freʃ] Ⓐ ADJ (*compar* **~er**; *superl* **~est**) **1** (= *not stale, not preserved*) [*fruit, vegetables, meat, milk*] fresco; [*bread*] recién hecho; [*smell, taste*] a fresco; **I need some ~ air** necesito un poco de aire fresco, necesito salir a respirar aire fresco; **to get some ~ air** tomar el fresco; ✦ IDIOM **as ~ as a daisy** fresco como una rosa
2 (= *not salt*) [*water*] dulce
3 (= *cool*) [*breeze*] fresco; [*wind*] fuerte
4 (= *healthy*) [*face, complexion*] lozano, saludable
5 (= *rested*) [*person*] descansado
6 (= *clean*) [*sheet of paper*] en blanco; [*shirt, sheets*] limpio; **to give sth a ~ coat of paint** dar otra mano de pintura a algo; **"fresh paint"** (*esp US*) "recién pintado"; **we need some ~ faces** necesitamos ver caras nuevas; **to make a ~ start** volver a empezar, empezar de nuevo
7 (= *further*) [*outbreak, supplies*] nuevo
8 (= *recent*) [*footprints, tracks*] reciente; **while it is still ~ in our minds** mientras lo tenemos fresco en la memoria; **I've just made a ~ pot of coffee** acabo de hacer una cafetera de café; **~ from the oven** recién salido del horno; **a teacher ~ from college** un profesor recién salido de la universidad; **milk ~ from the cow** leche recién ordeñada
9 (*) (= *cheeky*) [*person*] fresco, descarado; **to get ~ with sb** (= *be cheeky with*) ponerse impertinente con algn, ponerse chulo con algn*; (= *take liberties with*) propasarse con algn Ⓑ ADV **~ ground black pepper** pimienta *f* negra recién molida; **I picked the beans ~ this morning** acabo de recoger *or* coger las judías esta mañana

freshen ['freʃn] Ⓐ VT **1** [+ *air, breath*] refrescar **2 let me ~ your drink** déjame que te llene la copa Ⓑ VI [*wind*] arreciar
➤ **freshen up** VI + ADV (= *wash o.s.*) refrescarse, lavarse

fresher* ['freʃə] N (*Brit Univ*) = **freshman** ➤ **freshers' week** (*Brit*) *semana de bienvenida para nuevos alumnos*

freshly ['freʃlɪ] ADV recién; **~ squeezed orange juice** zumo *m* de naranja recién exprimido; **~ painted** recién pintado

freshman ['freʃmən] N (*pl* **freshmen**) (*Univ*) estudiante *mf* de primer año

freshness ['freʃnɪs] N [*of food, complexion*] frescura *f*; [*of air*] frescor *m*; [*of style*] originalidad *f*, frescura *f*

freshwater ['freʃ,wɔːtə] ADJ de agua dulce; **~ fish** pez *m* de agua dulce

fret¹ [fret] VI (= *worry*) preocuparse, apurarse; **don't ~** no te preocupes, no te apures

fret² [fret] N (*Mus*) traste *m*

fretful ['fretfʊl] ADJ [*child*] inquieto

fretsaw ['fretsɔː] N sierra *f* de calar *or* de marquetería

fretwork ['fretwɜːk] N calado *m*

Freudian ['frɔɪdɪən] ADJ freudiano; **~ slip** lapsus *m inv* linguae

Fri. ABBR = **Friday** vier.

friar ['fraɪə] N fraile *m*; (*before name*) fray *m*

friction ['frɪkʃən] N fricción *f* (*also fig*)

Friday ['fraɪdɪ] N viernes *m inv* ➤ **Friday 13th** ≈ martes y trece (*day traditionally associated with bad luck*); *see* **Tuesday**

fridge [frɪdʒ] N (*esp Brit*) N frigorífico *m*, nevera *f*, refrigerador *m*, refrigeradora *f* (*LAm*), heladera *f* (*SC*) ➤ **fridge freezer** frigorífico-congelador *m*, combi *m*

fried [fraɪd] ADJ (*Culin*) frito

friend [frend] N amigo/a m/f; (at school, work etc) compañero/a m/f; **a ~ of mine** un amigo mío; **let's be ~s** hagamos las paces; **to be ~s with sb** ser amigo de algn; **we're the best of ~s** somos muy amigos; **we're just good ~s with sb** somos sólo amigos, somos amigos nada más; **to make ~s with sb** hacerse amigo de algn, trabar amistad con algn

friendliness ['frendlɪnɪs] N **1** (= warmth) cordialidad f, simpatía f **2** (= friendship) cordialidad f, amistad f

friendly ['frendlɪ] **Ⓐ** ADJ (compar **friendlier**; superl **friendliest**) **1** [person, dog] simpático; [atmosphere, place] agradable; [smile, gesture] simpático, cordial; [relationship, greeting, tone] amistoso, cordial; **let me give you a piece of ~ advice** déjame que te dé un consejo de amigo; **it's nice to see a ~ face** es agradable ver una cara conocida; **to get ~ with sb** hacerse amigo de algn; **that wasn't a very ~ thing to do** eso no se hace con los amigos; **she wasn't very ~ to me** no estuvo demasiado amable conmigo, no se mostró muy amable conmigo; **Ian and Steve were ~ with one another** Ian y Steve eran amigos **2** (= not competitive) [match, rivalry, argument] amistoso **3** (= not enemy) [nation, forces] amigo **Ⓑ** N (Brit) (also ~ **match**) partido m amistoso **Ⓒ** CPD ➤ **friendly fire** (Mil) fuego m amigo ➤ **friendly society** (Brit) ≈ mutualidad f, ≈ mutua f, ≈ mutual f (LAm)

-friendly ['frendlɪ] ADJ (ending in compounds) **child-friendly hotel** hotel m con instalaciones para niños; **dolphin-friendly tuna** atún pescado sin causar daño a los delfines; see also **user-friendly**

friendship ['frendʃɪp] N amistad f

fries [fraɪz] NPL patatas fpl fritas, papas fpl fritas (LAm)

frieze [fri:z] N friso m

frigate ['frɪgɪt] N fragata f

frigging*** ['frɪgɪŋ] **Ⓐ** ADJ **do I need to do every ~ thing myself!** ¿por qué porras tengo que hacerlo yo todo?*; **it's a ~ nuisance!** ¡es un coñazo!** **Ⓑ** ADV **she's so ~ lazy!** ¡es una vaga de la hostia!**

fright [fraɪt] N **1** (= sudden fear) susto m, sobresalto m; (= state of alarm) miedo m; **to get a ~** asustarse; **what a ~ you gave me!** ¡qué susto me diste or has dado! **2** (*) (= person) espantajo m; **she looked a ~** iba hecha un espantajo

frighten ['fraɪtn] VT asustar; **to be ~ed** tener miedo (of a); **don't be ~ed!** ¡no te asustes!; **to ~ sb into doing sth** convencer a algn con amenazas de que haga algo; **I was ~ed out of my wits** or **to death** estaba aterrorizado ➤ **frighten away**, **frighten off** VT + ADV espantar, ahuyentar

frightening ['fraɪtnɪŋ] ADJ espantoso, aterrador

frightful†* ['fraɪtfʊl] ADJ (= terrible) [tragedy, experience, shame] horroroso; (= awful) [noise, weather] espantoso

frigid ['frɪdʒɪd] ADJ (sexually) frígido

frill [frɪl] N **1** (on dress etc) volante m **2** frills (fig) adornos mpl; **a package holiday without ~s** unas vacaciones organizadas de lo más sencillo or sin grandes lujos

frilly ['frɪlɪ] ADJ (compar **frillier**; superl **frilliest**) con volantes, con adornos

fringe [frɪndʒ] **Ⓐ** N **1** [of shawl, rug] (ribete m de) flecos mpl **2** (Brit) [of hair] flequillo m **3** (also ~s) [of forest] linde m or f, lindero m; [of city] periferia f; **to live on the ~ of society** vivir al margen de la sociedad **Ⓑ** CPD ➤ **fringe benefits** suplementos mpl, ventajas fpl adicionales ➤ **fringe group** grupo m marginal ➤ **fringe theatre** (Brit) teatro m experimental

Frisbee® ['frɪzbɪ] N disco m volador

frisk [frɪsk] VT (*) (= search) cachear, registrar

frisky ['frɪskɪ] ADJ (compar **friskier**; superl **friskiest**) [person, horse] juguetón

fritter¹ ['frɪtəʳ] N (Culin) buñuelo m

fritter² ['frɪtəʳ] VT (Brit) (also ~ **away**) malgastar, desperdiciar

frivolity [frɪ'vɒlɪtɪ] N frivolidad f

frivolous ['frɪvələs] ADJ frívolo

frizzy ['frɪzɪ] ADJ (compar **frizzier**; superl **frizziest**) **to go ~** ensortijarse, encresparse

fro [frəʊ] ADV **to and ~** de un lado para otro, de aquí para allá

frock [frɒk] N vestido m ➤ **frock coat** levita f

Frog* [frɒg] N (pej) gabacho/a m/f, franchute mf

frog [frɒg] N rana f; ✦ IDIOM **to have a ~ in one's throat** tener carraspera ➤ **frogs' legs** (Culin) ancas fpl de rana

frogman ['frɒgmən] N (pl **frogmen**) hombre rana m

frog-march ['frɒgmɑ:tʃ] VT (Brit): **to ~ sb in/out** meter/sacar a algn por la fuerza

frolic ['frɒlɪk] (pt, pp **~ked**) VI juguetear, brincar

from [frɒm] PREP **1** (indicating starting place) de, desde; **where are you ~?** ¿de dónde eres?; **he comes ~ Segovia** es de Segovia; **the train ~ Madrid** el tren de Madrid, el tren procedente de Madrid; **~ London to Glasgow** de Londres a Glasgow; **~ house to house** de casa en casa; **~ A to Z** de A a Z, desde A hasta Z **2** (indicating time) de, desde; **~ now on** de aquí en adelante; **~ that time** desde aquel momento; **~ one o'clock to** or **until two** desde la una hasta las dos; **(as) ~ Friday** a partir del viernes; **~ childhood** desde niño; **~ time to time** de vez en cuando **3** (indicating distance) de, desde; **the hotel is 1km ~ the beach** el hotel está a 1km de la playa; **a long way ~ home** muy lejos de casa **4** (indicating sender etc) de; **a letter ~ my sister** una carta de mi hermana; **a telephone call ~ Mr Smith** una llamada de parte del Sr. Smith; **a message ~ him** un mensaje de parte de él; **tell him ~ me** dile de mi parte **5** (indicating source) de; **to drink ~ the bottle** beber de la botella; **we learned it ~ him** lo aprendimos de él; **we learned it ~ a book** lo aprendimos en un libro; **a quotation ~ Shakespeare** una cita de Shakespeare; **to steal sth ~ sb** robar algo a algn; **I'll buy it ~ you** te lo compraré; **where did you get that ~?** ¿de dónde sacaste or has sacado eso?; **take the gun ~ him!** ¡quítale el revólver!; **one of the best performances we have seen ~ him** uno de los mejores papeles que le hayamos visto; **painted ~ life** pintado del natural **6** (indicating price, number etc) desde, a partir de; **we have shirts ~ £8 (upwards)** tenemos camisas desde or a partir de 8 libras; **prices range ~ £10 to £50** los precios varían entre 10 y 50 libras; **there were ~ 10 to 15 people there** había allí entre 10 y 15 personas **7** (indicating change) **things went ~ bad to worse** las cosas fueron de mal en peor; **the interest rate increased ~ 6% to 10%** la tasa de interés ha subido del 6 al 10 por ciento; **he went ~ office boy to director in five years** pasó de ser recadero a director en cinco años **8** (indicating difference) **to be different ~ sb** ser distinto de algn; **to know good ~ bad** saber distinguir entre el bien y el mal **9** (= because of) por; **~ sheer necessity** por pura necesidad; **~ what I can see** por lo que veo; **~ what he says** por lo que dice, según lo que dice; **~ experience** por experiencia **10** (= away from) **to escape ~ sth/sb** escapar de algo/algn; **to prevent sb ~ doing sth** impedir a algn hacer algo **11** (with prep, adv) desde; **~ above** desde arriba; **~ beneath** desde abajo

fromage frais [,frɒmɑ:ʒ'freɪ] N queso m fresco

frond [frɒnd] N fronda f

front [frʌnt] **Ⓐ** N **1** (= exterior) [of house, building] fachada f; [of shirt, dress] pechera f; [of book] portada f; **it fastens at the ~** se abrocha por delante; **to be a ~ for sth** (fig) servir de fachada or tapadera de algo; **he kept up a brave ~ to the world** delante de todos ponía buena cara **2** (= forepart) [of stage, desk, building] parte f de delante, parte f delantera; [of train, bus] parte f delantera; [of queue] principio m; **there's a dedication at the ~ of the book** hay una dedicatoria al principio del libro; **there are still some seats left at the ~** todavía quedan asientos delante; **he sat at the ~ of the train** se sentó en la parte delantera del tren; **he sat at the ~ of the class** se sentó en la primera fila de la clase; **he laid the baby on its ~** puso al bebé boca abajo; **the car's out ~** (US) el coche está delante or enfrente de la casa **3** **in ~** delante; **to send sb on in ~** enviar a algn por

829 **fuck-all**

delante; **the car in** ~ el coche de delante; **to be in** ~ (*gen*) ir primero, ir delante; (*in race*) ir a la cabeza, llevar la delantera; (*in scoring*) llevar (la) ventaja; **in ~ of** delante de; **don't argue in ~ of the children** no discutas delante de los niños
4 (*Met*) frente *m*; **cold/warm** ~ (*Met*) frente *m* frío/cálido
5 (*Mil, Pol*) frente *m*; **he fought at the ~ during the War** luchó en el frente durante la guerra; **we must present a united** ~ debemos parecer un frente unido
6 (*Brit*) (= *promenade*) paseo *m* marítimo; (= *beach*) playa *f*
7 (= *area of activity*) **is there any news on the wages ~?** ¿se sabe algo nuevo en materia de salarios?; **we have made progress on a variety of ~s** hemos avanzado en varios campos *or* varias esferas; **on all ~s** en todos los frentes
B ADJ (= *foremost*) [*wheel, leg*] delantero, de delante, de adelante (*LAm*); **he's in the ~ garden** está en el jardín de delante de la casa; **if we run, we can get a ~ seat** si corremos, podemos pillar un asiento en la parte delantera *or* la parte de delante *or* (*LAm*) la parte de adelante
C VT (*Brit*) [+ *organization*] estar al frente de, liderar
D CPD ➤ **front bench** (*Brit Pol*) en la *Cámara de Diputados británica, escaños de los ministros y sus equivalentes en la oposición* ➤ **front crawl** (*Swimming*) crol *m* ➤ **front desk** (*US*) recepción *f* (*de un hotel*) ➤ **front door** puerta *f* principal ➤ **front line** (*Mil*) primera línea *f* ➤ **front man** (*for activity*) testaferro *m*; [*of band, group*] líder *m*; (*TV*) presentador *m* ➤ **front page** (*Press*) primera plana *f* ➤ **front row** primera fila *f* ➤ **front runner** (*in race*) corredor(ora) *m/f* que va en cabeza; (*in election*) favorito/a *m/f* ➤ **front tooth** incisivo *m*, paleta* *f*

FRONT BENCH

El término genérico **front bench** se usa para referirse a los escaños situados en primera fila a ambos lados del Presidente (**Speaker**) de la Cámara de los Comunes del Parlamento británico. Dichos escaños son ocupados por los parlamentarios que son miembros del gobierno a un lado y por los del gobierno en la sombra (**shadow cabinet**) al otro y, por esta razón, se les conoce como **frontbenchers**. *Ver tb* www.parliament.uk

frontal ['frʌntl] ADJ [*attack*] de frente, frontal
frontbencher [ˌfrʌnt'bentʃəʳ] N (*Brit Parl*) (*in government*) *diputado con cargo oficial en el gobierno o la oposición*; (*in opposition*) *diputado con cargo oficial en la oposición*; ⊃ *FRONT BENCH*
frontier ['frʌntɪəʳ] **A** N (= *border, also fig*) frontera *f*; (= *dividing line*) línea *f* divisoria **B** CPD fronterizo ➤ **frontier dispute** conflicto *m* fronterizo ➤ **frontier post** puesto *m* fronterizo
frontispiece ['frʌntɪspiːs] N frontispicio *m*
front-line ['frʌntlaɪn] ADJ [*troops, news*] de primera línea; [*countries, areas*] fronterizo a una zona en guerra
front-loader [ˌfrʌnt'ləʊdəʳ] N (*also* **front-loading washing machine**) lavadora *f* de carga frontal
front-page news [ˌfrʌntpeɪdʒ'njuːz] N noticias *fpl* de primera plana
front-wheel drive [ˌfrʌntwiːl'draɪv] N tracción *f* delantera
frost [frɒst] **A** N (= *substance*) escarcha *f*; (= *weather*) helada *f* **B** VT (*US Culin*) escarchar **C** VI **to ~ over** *or* **up** cubrirse de escarcha, escarcharse
frostbelt ['frɒstbelt] N (*US*) *estados del norte de Estados Unidos caracterizados por su clima frío*; ⊃ *SUNBELT*
frostbite ['frɒstbaɪt] N congelación *f*
frostbitten ['frɒstˌbɪtn] ADJ congelado
frosted ['frɒstɪd] **A** ADJ (*US*) [*cake*] escarchado **B** CPD ➤ **frosted glass** vidrio *m or* cristal *m* esmerilado
frostily ['frɒstɪlɪ] ADV glacialmente
frosting ['frɒstɪŋ] N (*US*) (= *icing*) escarcha *f*
frosty ['frɒstɪ] ADJ (*compar* **frostier**; *superl* **frostiest**) **1** [*weather*] de helada; [*surface*] escarchado; **on a ~ morning** una mañana de helada; **it was ~ last night** anoche cayó una helada *or* heló **2** [*smile*] glacial

froth [frɒθ] **A** N (= *foam*) espuma *f* **B** VI hacer espuma; (*at the mouth*) echar espumarajos
frothy ['frɒθɪ] ADJ (*compar* **frothier**; *superl* **frothiest**) espumoso
frown [fraʊn] **A** N ceño *m*; **he said with a** ~ dijo frunciendo el ceño *or* entrecejo **B** VI fruncir el ceño, fruncir el entrecejo; **to ~ at** mirar con el ceño fruncido ➤ **frown (up)on** VI + PREP desaprobar
froze [frəʊz] PT *of* **freeze**
frozen ['frəʊzn] **A** PP *of* **freeze** **B** ADJ **1** [*food*] congelado **2 I'm ~ stiff** estoy helado, estoy muerto de frío **C** CPD ➤ **frozen assets** (*Fin*) activo *msing* congelado
fructose ['frʌktəʊz] N fructosa *f*
frugal ['fruːgəl] ADJ frugal
fruit [fruːt] **A** N **1** (*gen, Bot*) fruto *m*; (= *piece of fruit*) fruta *f*; **would you like some ~?** ¿quieres fruta?; **to bear ~** (*lit, fig*) dar fruto
2 *fruits* (*fig*) (= *benefits*) **the ~s of one's labour/success** los frutos del trabajo/éxito
B CPD ➤ **fruit basket** frutero *m*, canasto *m* de la fruta ➤ **fruit bowl** frutero *m* ➤ **fruit cocktail** macedonia *f* de frutas ➤ **fruit dish** frutero *m* ➤ **fruit farm** granja *f* frutícola *or* hortofrutícola ➤ **fruit farming** fruticultura *f* ➤ **fruit fly** mosca *f* de la fruta ➤ **fruit grower** fruticultor(a) *m/f*, granjero/a *m/f* frutícola *or* hortofrutícola ➤ **fruit juice** zumo *m or* jugo *m* de frutas ➤ **fruit machine** (*Brit*) máquina *f* tragaperras ➤ **fruit salad** macedonia *f* de frutas ➤ **fruit tree** árbol *m* frutal
fruitcake ['fruːtkeɪk] N tarta *f* de frutas
fruitful ['fruːtfʊl] ADJ productivo, provechoso
fruition [fruː'ɪʃən] N **to bring to ~** realizar; **to come to ~** [*hope*] cumplirse; [*plan*] realizarse, dar resultado
fruitless ['fruːtlɪs] ADJ infructuoso, inútil
fruity ['fruːtɪ] ADJ (*compar* **fruitier**; *superl* **fruitiest**) [*taste*] a fruta; [*wine*] afrutado
frump [frʌmp] N espantajo *m*, birria *f*
frumpish ['frʌmpɪʃ] ADJ desaliñado
frumpy ['frʌmpɪ] ADJ (*compar* **frumpier**; *superl* **frumpiest**) desaliñado
frustrate [frʌs'treɪt] VT [+ *plan, effort, person*] frustrar; [+ *hope*] defraudar; **to feel ~d** sentirse frustrado; **he's a ~d artist** es un artista frustrado
frustrating [frʌs'treɪtɪŋ] ADJ frustrante
frustration [frʌs'treɪʃən] N frustración *f*
fry [fraɪ] **A** VT (*Culin*) freír **B** VI freírse
frying pan ['fraɪɪŋˌpæn] N sartén *f or* (*LAm*) *m*; ✦ IDIOM **to jump out of the ~ into the fire** salir de Guatemala para entrar en Guatepeor
fry-up ['fraɪʌp] N (*Brit*) fritura *f*
FSA N ABBR (*Brit Fin*) (= **Financial Services Authority**) *organismo de control financiero en Reino Unido*
FT N ABBR (*Brit*) = **Financial Times**
F/T ABBR (*US*) = **full-time**
ft ABBR = **foot, feet**; ⊃ *IMPERIAL SYSTEM*
FTSE 100 Index [ˌfʊtsɪwʌnˌhʌndred'ɪndeks] N ABBR (*Brit St Ex*) = **Financial Times Stock Exchange 100 Index**
fuchsia ['fjuːʃə] N fucsia *f*
fuck*** [fʌk] **A** N **to have a ~** echar un polvo*** **B** VT joder***, tirarse***, follarse (*Sp****); **~ (it)!** ¡joder! (*Sp****), ¡carajo! (*LAm****), ¡chinga tu madre! (*Mex****); **~ you!** ¡que te den por culo!***, ¡jódete!***, ¡tu madre! (*LAm****); **~ this car!** ¡este jodido coche!***, ¡este coche del carajo! (*LAm****), ¡fregado coche! (*LAm****), ¡chingado coche! (*Mex****) **C** VI joder***, follar (*Sp****), coger (*LAm****) ➤ **fuck around*****, **fuck about***** VI + ADV joder***; **to ~ around with** joder***, manosear, estropear ➤ **fuck off***** VI + ADV irse a la mierda***; **~ off!** ¡vete a tomar por el culo!***, ¡vete al carajo! (*LAm****), ¡vete a la chingada! (*Mex****) ➤ **fuck up***** **A** VT + ADV joder*** **B** VI + ADV cagarla**
fuck-all*** [fʌk'ɔːl] (*Brit*) **A** ADJ **it's ~ use** no sirve para maldita la cosa* **B** N **I know ~ about it** no tengo ni puta

idea***; **he's done ~ today** hoy no ha hecho más que tocarse los huevos *or* cojones***, hoy no ha pegado ni golpe*

fucking*** [ˈfʌkɪŋ] **Ⓐ** ADJ de los cojones***, fregado (*LAm****), chingado (*Mex****); **~ hell!** ¡joder! (*Sp****), ¡coño!*** **Ⓑ** ADV **it was ~ awful** fue de puta pena***; **it's ~ cold!** ¡hace un frío del carajo!***; **I don't ~ know!** ¡no lo sé, coño!*** **Ⓝ** N joder*** *m*, jodienda*** *f*

fuddled [ˈfʌdld] ADJ confuso, aturdido

fuddy-duddy* [ˈfʌdɪˌdʌdɪ] N persona *f* chapada a la antigua, carroza *mf* (*Sp**)

fudge [fʌdʒ] **Ⓐ** N (*Culin*) dulce *m* de azúcar **Ⓑ** VT [+ *issue, problem*] esquivar, eludir **Ⓒ** VI eludir la cuestión

fuel [fjʊəl] **Ⓐ** N **1** (*gen*) combustible *m*; (*for engine*) carburante *m*; (*specifically coal*) carbón *m*; (*= wood*) leña *f* **2** (*fig*) pábulo *m*; ✦ IDIOM **to add ~ to the flames** echar leña al fuego **Ⓑ** VT [+ *furnace etc*] alimentar; [+ *aircraft, ship etc*] repostar; [+ *speculation etc*] estimular, provocar; [+ *dispute*] avivar, acalorar **Ⓒ** CPD ➤ **fuel crisis** crisis *f inv* energética ➤ **fuel injection** (**engine**) motor *m* de inyección ➤ **fuel oil** fuel oil *m*, mazut *m* ➤ **fuel pump** (*Aut*) surtidor *m* de gasolina ➤ **fuel tank** depósito *m* (de combustible)

fugitive [ˈfjuːdʒɪtɪv] N fugitivo/a *m/f*; (*= refugee*) refugiado/a *m/f*; **~ from justice** prófugo/a *m/f* (de la justicia)

fulfil, fulfill (*US*) [fʊlˈfɪl] VT **1** (*= carry out*) [+ *duty*] cumplir con; [+ *role*] desempeñar; [+ *order*] cumplir; [+ *plan, task*] llevar a cabo, realizar **2** (*= meet*) [+ *condition, requirement*] satisfacer, cumplir **3** (*= attain*) [+ *ambition*] realizar; [+ *potential*] alcanzar **4** (*= satisfy*) [+ *person*] satisfacer, llenar

fulfilling [fʊlˈfɪlɪŋ] ADJ **he has a ~ job** tiene un trabajo que le satisface *or* llena

fulfilment, fulfillment (*US*) [fʊlˈfɪlmənt] N **1** [*of duty, order*] cumplimiento *m* **2** [*of condition, requirement, need*] satisfacción *f* **3** [*of ambition, potential*] realización *f* **4** (*= satisfied feeling*) realización *f*, satisfacción *f*

full [fʊl] **Ⓐ** ADJ (*compar* ~**er**; *superl* ~**est**) **1** (*= filled*) [*room, hall, theatre*] lleno; [*vehicle*] completo; [*hotel*] lleno, completo; **"house full"** (*Theat*) "no hay localidades", "completo"; **I'm ~** no puedo más, estoy harto *or* ahíto; **~ to the brim** hasta el tope; **~ to bursting** lleno de bote en bote; **you'll work better on a ~ stomach** trabajarás mejor con el estómago lleno *or* después de haber comido; **we are ~ up for July** estamos completos para julio; **I'm ~ up*** no puedo más, estoy harto *or* ahíto **2 to be ~ of ...** estar lleno de ...; **to be ~ of o.s.** *or* **one's own importance** ser muy engreído *or* creído; **a look ~ of hate** una mirada cargada de odio; **~ of hope** lleno de esperanza, ilusionado; **he's ~ of good ideas** tiene muchísimas ideas buenas; **to be ~ of life** estar lleno de vida **3** (*= complete*) completo, entero; [*account*] detallado, extenso; [*meal*] completo; [*price, pay*] íntegro, sin descuento; [*speed, strength*] máximo; [*member*] de pleno derecho; **I waited a ~ hour** esperé una hora entera; **to take ~ advantage of the situation** aprovecharse al máximo de la situación; **to put one's headlights on ~ beam** poner las luces largas *or* de carretera; **to pay ~ fare** pagar la tarifa íntegra; **he's had a ~ life** ha llevado una vida muy completa; **he was suspended on ~ pay** se le suspendió sin reducción de sueldo; **to pay ~ price for sth** (*for goods, tickets*) pagar el precio íntegro de algo; **at ~ speed** a toda velocidad; **~ speed** *or* **steam ahead!** (*Naut*) ¡avance a toda

marcha!; **in ~ swing** en pleno apogeo; ✦ IDIOM **to go ~ steam ahead** ponerse en marcha a todo vapor **4** (*= ample*) [*face*] redondo; [*figure*] llenito; [*lips*] grueso; [*skirt, sleeves*] amplio; **clothes for the ~er figure** tallas *fpl* grandes **5** (*= busy*) [*day, timetable*] muy ocupado; **I've had a ~ day** he estado ocupado todo el día **Ⓑ** ADV **it hit him ~ in the face** le pegó en plena cara; **to turn the sound/volume up ~** subir el volumen al máximo; **to go ~ out to do sth** ir a por todas para hacer algo*; **~ well** muy bien, perfectamente **Ⓒ** N **name in ~** nombre *m* y apellidos; **text in ~** texto *m* íntegro; **to pay in ~** pagar la deuda entera; **to write sth in ~** escribir algo por extenso; **to the ~** al máximo **Ⓓ** CPD ➤ **full house** full *m* ➤ **full marks** (*Brit*) puntuación *fsing* máxima ➤ **full moon** luna *f* llena ➤ **full name** nombre *m* y apellidos ➤ **full stop** (*Brit Gram*) punto *m* (y seguido); **I'm not going, ~ stop!** ¡no voy, y punto *or* y se acabó! ➤ **full time** (*Brit Sport*) final *m* del partido

fullback [ˈfʊlbæk] N (*Ftbl*) defensa *mf*; (*Rugby*) zaguero *m*

full-beam [fʊlˈbiːm] ADJ (*Brit*): **~ headlights** luces *fpl* largas *or* de carretera

full-blown [fʊlˈbləʊn] ADJ [*attack, invasion etc*] a gran escala; **he has ~ AIDS** tiene el SIDA en su estado más avanzado

full-bodied [ˈfʊlˈbɒdɪd] ADJ [*cry*] fuerte; [*wine*] de mucho cuerpo

full-cream milk [ˌfʊlkriːmˈmɪlk] N leche *f* entera

full-face [ˌfʊlˈfeɪs] ADJ [*portrait*] de rostro entero

full-frontal [ˌfʊlˈfrʌntl] ADJ ➤ **full-frontal nude** desnudo *m* visto de frente ➤ **full-frontal nudity** desnudo *m* integral

full-grown [fʊlˈɡrəʊn] ADJ maduro

full-length [fʊlˈleŋθ] ADJ [*portrait, dress*] de cuerpo entero; [*swimming pool etc*] de tamaño normal

fullness [ˈfʊlnɪs] N **in the ~ of time** (*= eventually*) con el correr del tiempo; (*= at predestined time*) a su debido tiempo

full-page [fʊlˈpeɪdʒ] ADJ [*advert etc*] a toda plana

full-scale [fʊlˈskeɪl] ADJ [*plan, model*] de tamaño natural; [*search, retreat*] a gran escala

full-sized [fʊlˈsaɪzd] ADJ de tamaño normal

full-time [fʊlˈtaɪm] **Ⓐ** ADJ [*employment*] a tiempo completo; [*employee*] que trabaja una jornada completa, que trabaja a tiempo completo; **he's a ~ musician** es músico profesional; **a ~ job** un puesto de trabajo a tiempo completo; **a ~ course** un curso de dedicación plena **Ⓑ** ADV **to work** trabajar a tiempo completo

fully [ˈfʊlɪ] ADV **1** (*= completely*) **I was not ~ awake** no estaba completamente despierto, no estaba despierto del todo; **~ booked** todo reservado, completo; **I ~ expected to see you there** esperaba verte allí; **a ~ grown tiger** un tigre adulto; **she is a ~ qualified swimming instructor** es profesora titulada de natación; **when he has ~ recovered** cuando se haya recuperado completamente *or* del todo; **I don't ~ understand** no lo acabo de comprender, no lo entiendo del todo **2** (*= in full*) [*reimburse*] enteramente

fully-fledged [ˌfʊlɪˈfledʒd], **full-fledged** (*US*) [fʊlˈfledʒd] ADJ hecho y derecho

fulsome [ˈfʊlsəm] ADJ (*pej*) [*praise*] excesivo, exagerado

fumble [ˈfʌmbl] VI (*also* **~ about**) hurgar; **to ~ in one's pockets** hurgar en los bolsillos; **to ~ for sth** buscar algo con las manos; **to ~ with sth** manejar algo torpemente

fume [fjuːm] **Ⓐ** VI (*= be furious*) estar furioso, echar humo; **to be fuming at** *or* **with sb** echar pestes de algn **Ⓑ** **fumes** NPL (*gen*) humo *msing*, vapores *mpl*; (*= gas*) gases *mpl*

fumigate [ˈfjuːmɪɡeɪt] VT fumigar

fun [fʌn] **Ⓐ** N (*= enjoyment*) diversión *f*; (*= merriment*) alegría *f*; **it's great** ~ es muy divertido; **he's great** ~ es una persona muy divertida; **it's not much ~ for us** para nosotros no es nada divertido; **for ~** en broma; **to do sth for the ~ of it** hacer algo por divertirse; **~ and games** (*= lively behaviour*) travesuras *fpl*; (*= trouble*) jaleo *m*, bronca *f*; **to have** ~ divertirse; **have ~!** ¡que os divirtáis!, ¡que lo paséis bien!; **what ~ we had!** ¡qué bien lo pasamos!, ¡cómo

nos divertimos!; **in** ~ en broma; **to make** ~ **of sb** burlarse de algn, tomar el pelo a algn*
Ⓑ ADJ (*) divertido; **she's a ~ person** es una persona divertida
Ⓒ CPD ➤ **fun run** (*Brit*) maratón *m* corto (*de ciudad para los no atletas*)

function ['fʌŋkʃən] **Ⓐ** N **1** (= *purpose*) función *f*
2 (= *reception*) recepción *f*; (= *official ceremony*) acto *m* **Ⓑ** VI funcionar, marchar; **to** ~ **as** hacer (las veces) de **Ⓒ** CPD ➤ **function key** tecla *f* de función ➤ **function word** palabra *f* funcional

functional ['fʌŋkʃnəl] ADJ funcional

fund [fʌnd] **Ⓐ** N (*gen*) fondo *m*; (= *reserve*) reserva *f*; **funds** fondos *mpl*, recursos *mpl*; **to raise ~s** recaudar fondos **Ⓑ** VT [+ *project*] financiar

fundamental [,fʌndə'mentl] **Ⓐ** ADJ [*question, problem, principle, right, difference*] fundamental; **it is a ~ mistake to think that ...** es un error fundamental pensar que ...; **to be ~ to sth** ser fundamental *or* esencial para algo **Ⓑ** NPL **the ~s** los fundamentos, lo básico

fundamentalism [,fʌndə'mentəlɪzəm] N fundamentalismo *m*

fundamentalist [,fʌndə'mentəlɪst] ADJ, N fundamentalista *mf*, integrista *mf*

fundamentally [,fʌndə'mentəlɪ] ADV **1** (= *basically*) básicamente, en lo fundamental **2** (= *profoundly*) fundamentalmente; **there is something ~ wrong in what he says** hay un error fundamental en lo que dice; **it is ~ important that this project continues** es de vital importancia *or* es fundamental que el proyecto siga adelante **3** (= *intrinsically*) intrínsecamente

funding ['fʌndɪŋ] N (= *funds*) fondos *mpl*, finanzas *fpl*; (*act of funding*) financiación *f*

fund-raiser ['fʌnd,reɪzə'] N recaudador(a) *m/f* de fondos

fund-raising ['fʌnd,reɪzɪŋ] N recaudación *f* de fondos

funeral ['fjuːnərəl] N (= *burial*) funeral *m*, entierro *m*; (= *service*) exequias *fpl*; **state** ~ entierro *m or* funeral *m* con honores de estado ➤ **funeral cortège** cortejo *m* fúnebre ➤ **funeral director** director(a) *m/f* de funeraria ➤ **funeral home** (*US*) funeraria *f* ➤ **funeral march** marcha *f* fúnebre ➤ **funeral parlour** (*Brit*) funeraria *f* ➤ **funeral procession** cortejo *m* fúnebre ➤ **funeral service** exequias *fpl*

funfair ['fʌnfeə'] N (*Brit*) parque *m* de atracciones

fungi ['fʌngaɪ] NPL *of* **fungus**

fungicide ['fʌngɪsaɪd] N fungicida *m*

fungus ['fʌngəs] N (*pl* **fungi**) hongo *m*

funicular railway [fjuː,nɪkjʊlə'reɪlweɪ] N funicular *m*

funk [fʌŋk] **Ⓐ** N **1** (*) (= *fear*) **to be in a (blue)** ~ estar muerto de miedo **2** (*Mus*) funk *m* **Ⓑ** VT **to** ~ **it** rajarse

funky* ['fʌŋkɪ] ADJ (*compar* **funkier**; *superl* **funkiest**) [*music*] vibrante, marchoso

fun-loving ['fʌn,lʌvɪŋ] ADJ amigo de diversiones

funnel ['fʌnl] N (*for pouring*) embudo *m*; [*of ship, steam engine etc*] chimenea *f*

funnily ['fʌnɪlɪ] ADV **1** (= *amusingly*) con gracia **2** (= *oddly*) de forma extraña, de forma rara; **~ enough ...** aunque parezca extraño ...

funny ['fʌnɪ] **Ⓐ** ADJ (*compar* **funnier**; *superl* **funniest**)
1 (= *amusing*) [*person, joke, film, story*] gracioso; **that's not ~** eso no tiene gracia
2 (= *odd*) raro; **~! I thought he'd left** ¡qué raro! creía que ya se había marchado; **it's ~ that ...** me extraña que ... + *subjun*, me parece raro que ... + *subjun*; **(it's) ~ you should say that** qué curioso que digas eso; **there's something going on here** aquí hay gato encerrado; **he's ~ that way** tiene esa manía; **I feel ~** (= *ill*) no me encuentro muy bien; **I have the ~ feeling I'm going to regret this** tengo la extraña sensación de que me voy a arrepentir de esto; **children get some very ~ ideas sometimes!** ¡a los niños se les ocurre a veces cada idea!; **this smells/tastes ~** esto huele/sabe raro; **the ~ thing about it is that ...** lo curioso *or* extraño del caso es que ...
Ⓑ N **the funnies** (*US*) las tiras cómicas
Ⓒ CPD ➤ **funny bone** hueso *m* del codo ➤ **funny farm**

(*hum*) loquero* *m* ➤ **funny man** cómico *m* ➤ **funny money*** (= *large sum*) una millonada; (= *counterfeit money*) dinero *m* falso; (= *ill-gotten money*) dinero *m* mal habido

fur [fɜː'] **Ⓐ** N **1** [*of animal*] pelo *m*, pelaje *m*; (= *single skin*) piel *f*; (= *coat*) abrigo *m* de pieles **2** (*in kettle*) sarro *m* **Ⓑ** CPD ➤ **fur coat** abrigo *m* de pieles

furious ['fjʊərɪəs] ADJ **1** (= *angry*) [*person, reaction*] furioso; **to be ~ (with sb)** estar furioso (con algn); **to get ~** ponerse furioso **2** (= *violent*) [*argument, struggle*] violento; [*activity*] frenético; [*pace, speed*] vertiginoso

furiously ['fjʊərɪəslɪ] ADV **1** (= *angrily*) con furia, furiosamente **2** (= *energetically*) [*work, write*] frenéticamente

furlong ['fɜːlɒŋ] N estadio *m* (*octava parte de una milla*)

furlough ['fɜːləʊ] N (*US*) permiso *m*

furnace ['fɜːnɪs] N horno *m*; **the room was like a ~** la habitación era un horno

furnish ['fɜːnɪʃ] VT **1** [+ *room, house*] amueblar (**with** con); **~ed flat** (*esp Brit*) *or* **apartment** piso *m* amueblado, departamento *m* amoblado (*LAm*) **2** [+ *excuse, information*] proporcionar, facilitar; [+ *proof*] aducir; **to ~ sb with sth** [+ *supplies*] proveer a algn de algo; [+ *opportunity*] dar *or* proporcionar algo a algn

furnishings ['fɜːnɪʃɪŋz] NPL muebles *mpl*, mobiliario *msing*

furniture ['fɜːnɪtʃə'] N muebles *mpl*, mobiliario *m*; **a piece of ~** un mueble; **✦** IDIOM **part of the ~** parte *f* de la casa *or* del mobiliario ➤ **furniture mover** (*US*) compañía *f* de mudanzas ➤ **furniture polish** cera *f* para muebles ➤ **furniture remover** compañía *f* de mudanzas ➤ **furniture shop** tienda *f* de muebles ➤ **furniture van** (*Brit*) camión *m* de mudanzas

furore [fjʊə'rɔːrɪ], **furor** (*US*) ['fjʊərɔː'] N (= *protests*) ola *f* de protestas, escándalo *m*

furrier ['fʌrɪə'] N peletero/a *m/f*

furrow ['fʌrəʊ] **Ⓐ** N (*Agr*) surco *m*; (*on forehead*) arruga *f* **Ⓑ** VT [+ *forehead*] arrugar

furry ['fɜːrɪ] ADJ [*animal*] peludo; [*teddy bear*] de peluche ➤ **furry toy** (*muñeco m* de) peluche *m*

further ['fɜːðə'] **Ⓐ** ADV COMPAR *of* **far 1** (*in distance*) **how much ~ is it?** ¿cuánto camino nos queda?; **have you much ~ to go?** ¿le queda mucho camino por hacer?; **let's go ~ north/south** vayamos más al norte/sur; **his car was parked ~ along** su coche estaba aparcado un poco más arriba/abajo; **we were too tired to go any ~ that day** estábamos demasiado cansados para continuar ese día; **move it ~ away** apártalo un poco más; **~ back** más atrás; **I think it's ~ down the road** creo que está bajando un poco más la calle; **I don't think we want to go any ~ down that road** no creo que sea prudente seguir por ese camino (fig); **nothing was ~ from my thoughts** nada más lejos de mi intención; **the track ended a mile ~ on** el camino terminaba una milla más adelante; **the boat drifted ~ out to sea** la barca iba siendo arrastrada mar adentro; **~ to the south** más al sur; **we decided to go ~ up the track** decidimos seguir avanzando por el camino
2 (*in time*) **let's look a little ~ ahead** miremos un poco más adelante; **records go no ~ back than 1960** los archivos sólo se remontan a 1960
3 (= *in progress*) **you'll get ~ with her if you're polite** conseguirás más si se lo pides educadamente; **I got no ~ with him** (*in questioning*) no pude sacarle nada más; **to go ~**: **he went ~, claiming the man had attacked him** no se quedó ahí, sino que aseguró que el hombre lo había atacado; **this mustn't go any ~** [*confidential matter*] confidentia esto que no pase de aquí; **~ on in this chapter** más adelante en este capítulo; **I think we should take this matter ~** creo que deberíamos proseguir con este asunto
4 (= *more*) más; **they questioned us ~** nos hicieron más preguntas; **I heard nothing ~ from them** no supe más de ellos
5 (= *in addition*) además; **and I ~ believe that ...** y creo además que ...
6 (*in correspondence*) **~ to your letter of the 7th** (*Brit*) con *or* en relación a su carta del 7
Ⓑ ADJ (= *additional*) más; **after ~ consideration** tras considerarlo más detenidamente; **without ~ delay** sin más

demora; **we have no ~ need of your services** ya no necesitamos sus servicios; **until ~ notice** hasta nuevo aviso **C** VT (= *promote*) [+ *cause, aim, understanding, career*] promover, fomentar; **she was accused of ~ing her own interests** la acusaron de actuar en beneficio de sus propios intereses

D CPD ➤ **further education** (*esp Brit*) enseñanza *f* superior

furthermore ['fɜːðə:'mɔː'] ADV además

furthermost ['fɜːðəməʊst] ADJ más lejano

furthest ['fɜːðɪst] **A** ADV SUPERL *of* **far 1** (*in distance*) más lejos; **who has the ~ to go home?** ¿quién es el que vive más lejos? **2** (= *most*) más; **prices have fallen ~ in the south of England** donde más han bajado los precios ha sido en el sur de Inglaterra **B** ADJ más lejano; **the ~ point** el punto más lejano; **the seat ~ from the window** el asiento que está más lejos está de la ventana

furtive ['fɜːtɪv] ADJ [*glance, action*] furtivo; [*person*] sospechoso

furtively ['fɜːtɪvlɪ] ADV furtivamente

fury ['fjʊərɪ] N [*of person*] furia *f*, furor *m*; **to be in a ~** estar furioso; **like ~*** con encono

fuse [fjuːz] **A** N **1** (*Elec*) plomo *m*, fusible *m*; **to blow a ~** [*equipment*] fundirse un fusible; [*person*] salirse de sus casillas **2** [*of bomb*] (= *cord*) mecha *f*; (= *detonating device*) espoleta *f*; ✦ IDIOM **he has a very short ~*** tiene un genio muy vivo **B** VT **1** (*Brit*) [+ *lights, television etc*] fundir **2** [+ *metals*] fundir **C** VI **1** (*Brit Elec*) fundirse; **the lights have ~d** se han fundido los plomos **2** [*metals*] fundirse **D** CPD ➤ **fuse box** caja *f* de fusibles ➤ **fuse wire** hilo *m* fusible

fuselage ['fjuːzəlɑːʒ] N fuselaje *m*

fusillade [ˌfjuːzɪ'leɪd] N (*lit*) descarga *f* cerrada; (*fig*) lluvia *f*

fusion ['fjuːʒən] N fusión *f*

fuss [fʌs] **A** N **1** (= *complaints, arguments*) escándalo *m*, alboroto *m*; **to make a ~ about sth** armar un escándalo por algo, armar un lío *or* (*Sp*) un follón por algo*; **I think you were quite right to make a ~** creo que hiciste bien en protestar; **there's no need to make such a ~** no hay por qué ponerse así, no es para tanto **2** (= *agitation*) conmoción *f*, bulla *f*; **a lot of ~ about nothing** mucho ruido y pocas nueces; **such a ~ to get a passport!** ¡tanta lata para conseguir un pasaporte!*; **what's all the ~ about?** ¿a qué viene tanto jaleo? **3 to make a ~ of sb** (*Brit*) (= *spoil*) mimar *or* consentir a algn **B** VI preocuparse por pequeñeces

➤ **fuss over** VI + PREP [+ *person*] consentir a

fussily ['fʌsɪlɪ] ADV **1** (= *demandingly*) (*pej*) quisquillosamente; (= *scrupulously*) meticulosamente, escrupulosamente **2** (= *overelaborately*) [*designed, dressed*] de manera recargada

fusspot* ['fʌspɒt] N (*Brit*) quisquilloso/a *m/f*

fussy ['fʌsɪ] ADJ (*compar* **fussier**; *superl* **fussiest**) **1** (= *exacting*) [*person*] **1.1** (*pej*) quisquilloso; **they'll think you're ~ if you ring them** van a creer que eres quisquilloso *or* difícil si les llamas; **children are often ~ eaters** los niños son a menudo quisquillosos *or* especiales para la comida **1.2** (= *scrupulous*) **he's very ~ about detail** es muy escrupuloso *or* meticuloso con los detalles **1.3** (= *selective*) selectivo; **I'm not ~*** me da igual, me da lo mismo **2** (= *overelaborate*) [*design, clothes*] recargado, con muchos ringorrangos*

fusty ['fʌstɪ] ADJ (*compar* **fustier**; *superl* **fustiest**) rancio; [*air*] viciado; [*room*] que huele a cerrado

futile ['fjuːtaɪl] ADJ [*attempt*] vano; [*suggestion*] fútil

futility [fjuː'tɪlɪtɪ] N inutilidad *f*, lo inútil

futon ['fuːtɒn] N futón *m*

future ['fjuːtʃə'] **A** ADJ [*husband, generations*] futuro; [*plans*] para el futuro; **at some ~ date** *or* **time** en un futuro; **his ~ prospects are bleak** sus perspectivas de futuro no son nada halagüeñas; **in ~ years** en los años venideros **B** N **1** futuro *m*; **who knows what the ~ holds?** ¿quién sabe lo que nos depara el futuro?; **in ~** de ahora en adelante; **in the ~** en el futuro; **in the not too distant ~** en un futuro no muy lejano

2 (*Gram*) futuro *m*; **in the ~** en futuro

3 futures (*Fin*) futuros *mpl*

C CPD ➤ **the futures market** (*Fin*) el mercado de futuros

futuristic [ˌfjuːtʃə'rɪstɪk] ADJ futurista

fuzz [fʌz] N **1** (*on chin*) vello *m*; (= *fluff*) pelusa *f* **2 the ~** (*esp Brit†***) la poli*, la pasma (*Sp***), los tiras (*Chi***)

fuzzy ['fʌzɪ] **A** ADJ (*compar* **fuzzier**; *superl* **fuzziest**) **1** [*hair*] rizado; [*material*] velloso **2** (= *blurred*) [*photo, memory*] borroso; [*ideas, thinking*] confuso **B** CPD ➤ **fuzzy logic** (*Comput*) lógica *f* difusa, lógica *f* borrosa

fwd ABBR (*esp Comm*) = **forward**

FY ABBR = **fiscal year**

FYI ABBR = **for your information**

Gg

G¹, g¹ [dʒiː] N **1** (= *letter*) G, g *f*; **G for George** G de Gerona **2** (*Mus*) **G** sol *m*

G² ABBR (*US Cine*) (= **general audience**) todos los públicos

g² Ⓐ ABBR (= **gram(s), gramme(s)**) g, gr Ⓑ N ABBR (= **gravity**) g

GA ABBR (*US*) = **Georgia**

gab* [gæb] N *see* **gift**

gabble ['gæbl] (*Brit*) Ⓐ VT farfullar Ⓑ VI hablar atropelladamente; **they were gabbling away in French** parloteaban en francés

gable ['geɪbl] N aguilón *m*, gablete *m* ➤ **gable end** hastial *m*

Gabon [gə'bɒn] N Gabón *m*

gadget ['gædʒɪt] N (= *little thing*) artilugio *m*, chisme *m*; (= *device*) aparato *m*

gadgetry ['gædʒɪtrɪ] N chismes *mpl*, aparatos *mpl*

Gaelic ['geɪlɪk] Ⓐ ADJ gaélico Ⓑ N (*Ling*) gaélico *m*

gaff [gæf] N ✦ IDIOM **to blow the ~*** irse de la lengua, descubrir el pastel

gaffe [gæf] N plancha *f* (*Sp*), metedura *f* or (*LAm*) metida *f* de pata; **to make a ~** meter la pata, tirarse una plancha (*Sp*)

gaffer** ['gæfə'] N **1** (= *old man*) vejete* *m* **2** (*Brit*) (= *foreman*) capataz *m*; (= *boss*) jefe *m*

gag [gæg] Ⓐ N **1** (*over mouth*) mordaza *f*; **the new law will effectively put a ~ on the free press** en efecto la nueva ley va a poner una mordaza a la prensa libre **2** (*) (= *joke*) chiste *m* Ⓑ VT [+ *prisoner*] amordazar; (*fig*) amordazar, hacer callar Ⓒ VI (= *retch*) tener arcadas; **to ~ on** [+ *food*] atragantarse con

gaga* ['gaː'gaː] ADJ gagá, lelo, chocho; **to go ~** (= *senile*) chochear

gage [geɪdʒ] N, VT (*US*) = **gauge**

gaggle ['gægl] N [*of geese*] manada *f*

gaiety ['geɪtɪ] N [*of occasion, person*] alegría *f*; [*of dress, costumes*] colorido *m*, vistosidad *f*

gaily ['geɪlɪ] ADV **1** (= *brightly*) [*dressed, decorated*] vistosamente, alegremente; **~ coloured cushions** cojines de vistosos or alegres colores **2** (= *cheerfully*) [*chatter, sing*] alegremente

gain [geɪn] Ⓐ VT **1** (= *obtain, win*) [+ *respect*] ganarse; [+ *approval, support, supporters*] conseguir; [+ *experience*] adquirir, obtener; [+ *freedom*] obtener, conseguir; [+ *qualification*] obtener; **what do you hope to ~ by it?** ¿qué provecho esperas sacar con esto?, ¿qué esperas ganar or conseguir con esto?; **there is nothing to be ~ed by feeling bitter** no se gana or consigue nada guardando rencores; **to ~ an advantage over sb** sacar ventaja a algn; **to ~ control of sth** hacerse con el control de algo; **he has just ~ed a place at university** acaba de obtener una plaza en la universidad; **Jones ~ed possession of the ball** Jones se hizo con el balón

2 (= *increase*) **the shares have ~ed four points** las acciones han aumentado or subido cuatro enteros; **my watch has ~ed five minutes** mi reloj se ha adelantado cinco minutos; **to ~ speed** ganar or cobrar velocidad; **to ~ strength** (*physically*) cobrar fuerzas; (*mentally*) hacerse más fuerte; **to ~ weight** engordar, aumentar de peso

3 (= *arrive at*) llegar a

Ⓑ VI **1** (= *profit*) **to ~ by/from sth** beneficiarse de algo **2** (= *advance*) [*watch*] adelantar; [*runner*] ganar terreno **3** (= *increase, improve*) [*shares*] aumentar de valor, subir; **to ~ in popularity** adquirir mayor popularidad; **to ~ in prestige** ganar prestigio

Ⓒ N **1** (= *increase*) aumento *m*; **a ~ in weight** un aumento de peso; **a ~ of eight per cent** un aumento or una subida del ocho por ciento

2 (= *benefit, advantage*) beneficio *m*; **they are using the situation for personal/political ~** están utilizando la situación en beneficio propio/para ganar terreno político; ✦ IDIOM **their loss is our ~** ellos pierden y nosotros ganamos

3 (= *profit*) ganancia *f*, beneficio *m*; **the company reported pre-tax ~s of £759 million** la compañía anunció haber obtenido unos beneficios or unas ganancias brutas de 759 millones de libras

➤ **gain on** VI + PREP **to ~ on sb** (*in polls*) ganar terreno a algn; (*in race*) alcanzar a algn

gainful ['geɪnfəl] ADJ [*employment*] remunerado, retribuido

gainfully ['geɪnfəlɪ] ADV **to be ~ employed** tener un trabajo retribuido or remunerado

gait [geɪt] N paso *m*, modo *m* de andar

gal* [gæl] N = **girl**

gal. ABBR = **gallon(s)**

gala ['gaːlə] N (= *festive occasion*) gala *f*, fiesta *f*; (*Sport*) festival *m*; **swimming ~** festival *m* de natación ➤ **gala performance** función *f* de gala

Galapagos Islands [gə'læpəgəs,aɪləndz] NPL Islas *fpl* (de los) Galápagos

galaxy ['gæləksɪ] N (*Astron*) galaxia *f*; (*fig*) constelación *f*, pléyade *f*

gale [geɪl] N (= *strong wind*) vendaval *m*, viento *m* fuerte; (= *storm*) (*on land*) temporal *m*; (*at sea*) temporal *m*, tempestad *f* ➤ **gale warning** aviso *m* de temporal

gale-force ['geɪlfɔːs] ADJ **~ winds** vientos *mpl* huracanados

Galicia [gə'lɪʃə] N Galicia *f*

Galician [gə'lɪʃən] Ⓐ ADJ gallego Ⓑ N **1** (= *person*) gallego/a *m/f* **2** (*Ling*) gallego *m*

gall [gɔːl] Ⓐ N (= *bitterness*) hiel *f*; (= *cheek*) caradura *f*, descaro *m*; **she had the ~ to say that ...** tuvo la caradura or el descaro de decir que ... Ⓑ VT molestar, fastidiar Ⓒ CPD ➤ **gall bladder** vesícula *f* biliar

gall. ABBR = **gallon(s)**

gallant ['gælənt] ADJ (= *brave*) [*warrior, officer*] gallardo; [*effort*] valiente, noble

gallantry† ['gæləntrɪ] N **1** (= *bravery*) valor *m*, valentía *f* **2** (= *courtesy*) galantería *f*, cortesía *f*

galleon ['gælɪən] N galeón *m*

gallery ['gælərɪ] N (*gen*) galería *f* (*also Min, Theat*); (*for spectators*) tribuna *f*; (= *art gallery*) (*state owned*) museo *m* de arte; (*private*) galería *f* de arte

galley ['gælɪ] N (= *ship*) galera *f*; (= *ship's kitchen*) cocina *f*, fogón *m* ➤ **galley slave** galeote *m*

Gallic ['gælɪk] ADJ (= *of Gaul*) galo; (= *French*) francés

galling ['gɔːlɪŋ] ADJ mortificante

gallivant [gælɪ'vænt] VI callejear, salir de picos pardos*

gallon ['gælən] N galón *m* (*Brit* = 4.546 *litros*; *EEUU* = 3.785 *litros*); ⊃ *IMPERIAL SYSTEM*

gallop ['gæləp] Ⓐ N (= *pace*) galope *m*; (= *distance covered*) galopada *f*; **at a ~** al galope; **to break into a ~** ponerse a galopar Ⓑ VI [*horse*] galopar; **to ~ up/off** llegar/alejarse al galope; **he ~ed through his homework** terminó sus deberes a la carrera

galloping ['gæləpɪŋ] ADJ **~ inflation** inflación *f* galopante

gallows ['gæləʊz] NSING (*pl* ~) horca *f sing*

gallstone ['gɔːlstəʊn] N cálculo *m* biliar

Gallup poll ['gæləp,pəʊl] N sondeo *m* or encuesta *f* de Gallup

galore [gə'lɔː'] ADV en cantidad, a porrillo*; **bargains ~** gangas *fpl* a porrillo* or en cantidad

galosh [gə'lɒʃ] N chanclo *m* (de goma)

galvanize ['gælvənaɪz] VT [+ *metal*] galvanizar; **to ~ sb into action** mover a algn para que actúe

Gambia ['gæmbɪə] N **(the)** ~ Gambia *f*

gambit ['gæmbɪt] N (*Chess*) gambito *m*; (*fig*) táctica *f*

gamble ['gæmbl] Ⓐ N (= *risk*) riesgo *m*; (= *bet*) apuesta *f*;

the ~ came off la jugada salió bien; **to have a ~ on** [+ *horse*] jugar dinero a, apostar a; [+ *Stock Exchange*] jugar a; **to take a ~** arriesgarse

Ⓑ VT [+ *money*] jugar, apostar; [+ *one's life*] arriesgar; **to ~ everything/one's future (on sth)** jugarse todo/el porvenir (a algo)

Ⓒ VI (= *bet money*) jugar, apostar; (= *take a chance*) jugárselas; **to ~ on sth** confiar en algo, contar con algo; **to ~ on the Stock Exchange** jugar a la Bolsa; **to ~ with others' money** especular con el dinero ajeno

➤ **gamble away** VT + ADV perder en el juego

gambler ['gæmblə'] N jugador(a) *m/f*

gambling ['gæmblɪŋ] N juego *m* ➤ **gambling debts** deudas *fpl* de juego

gambol ['gæmbəl] VI [*lamb, child*] brincar, retozar

game [ɡeɪm] **Ⓐ** N **1** (*lit*) (= *form of entertainment*) juego *m*; (= *match*) [*of football, rugby, cricket, tennis*] partido *m*; (*within tennis set*) juego *m*; [*of cards, chess, snooker*] partida *f*; **games** (= *contest*) juegos *mpl*; (*Brit Scol*) deportes *mpl*; **it's only a ~** no es más que un juego; **this isn't a ~** esto no es ningún juego; **to have a ~ of football** jugar un partido de fútbol; **to have a ~ of chess** echar or jugar una partida de ajedrez; **they were (one) ~ all** (*Tennis*) iban iguales or empatados a un juego; **~, set and match** juego, set y partido; **~ to Johnston** juego para Johnston; ✦ IDIOMS **to beat sb at his/her own ~** ganar a algn con sus propias armas; **to give the ~ away** (*person*) descubrir el pastel*; **her nervousness gave the ~ away** los nervios la delataron or la pusieron en evidencia; **to play the ~** jugar limpio; **don't play ~s with me!** ¡no juegues conmigo!; **two can play at that ~** donde las dan las toman

2 (= *scheme*) juego *m*; **we know his little ~** sabemos de qué va*; **what's your ~?** ¿qué estás tramando?; ✦ IDIOM **the ~ is up** se acabó el juego*

3 (*) (= *business*) negocio *m*; **how long have you been in this ~?** ¿cuánto tiempo llevas metido en este negocio?, ¿cuánto tiempo hace que trabajas en esto?; ✦ IDIOM **to be ahead of the ~** llevar ventaja, llevar la delantera

4 (= *prostitution*) **to be on the ~*** hacer la calle*

5 (*Hunting*) (= *large animals*) caza *f* mayor; (= *birds, small animals*) caza *f* menor

Ⓑ ADJ (= *willing*) **are you ~?** ¿te animas?, ¿te apuntas?; **I'm ~ if you are** si tú te animas, yo también; **to be ~ to do sth** estar dispuesto a hacer algo; **to be ~ for anything** apuntarse a cualquier cosa or a todo

Ⓒ CPD ➤ **game bird** ave *f* de caza

> Use **el/un** not **la/una** before feminine nouns beginning with stressed **a** or **ha** like **ave**.

➤ **game park** parque *m* natural, reserva *f* natural ➤ **game plan** (*Sport*) plan *m* de juego; (*fig*) estrategia *f* ➤ **game reserve** coto *m* de caza ➤ **game show** programa *m* concurso ➤ **game warden** guarda *m* del coto or de caza

gamekeeper ['geɪm,kiːpə'] N guardabosques *mf inv*, guardabosque *mf*

gamely ['geɪmlɪ] ADV (= *bravely*) valientemente, con el mejor de los ánimos; (= *sportingly*) animosamente

gamesmanship ['geɪmzmənʃɪp] N astucia *f* en el juego

gaming ['geɪmɪŋ] N juego *m* ➤ **gaming laws** leyes *fpl* reguladoras del juego

gamma ['gæmə] N gamma *f* ➤ **gamma radiation** radiación *f* gamma ➤ **gamma ray** rayo *m* gamma

gammon ['gæmən] N (*Brit*) jamón *m*

gamut ['gæmət] N gama *f*; **to run the (whole) ~ of** recorrer toda la gama de

gander ['gændə'] N ganso *m* (macho)

gang [ɡæŋ] N [*of thieves*] banda *f*, pandilla *f*; [*of friends, youths*] grupo *m*; (*pej*) pandilla *f*; [*of workmen*] cuadrilla *f*, brigada *f* ➤ **gang rape** violación *f* en grupo

➤ **gang up** VI + ADV unirse (**with** a); **to ~ up on** or **against sb** unirse en contra de algn

Ganges ['gændʒiːz] N **the ~** el Ganges

gangland ['gæŋlænd] N mundo *m* del crimen ➤ **gangland boss** cabecilla *mf* del mundo del crimen ➤ **gangland**

murder asesinato *m* en el mundo del crimen, asesinato *m* por ajuste de cuentas entre criminales

gangling ['gæŋɡlɪŋ] ADJ [*youth*] larguirucho, desgarbado; [*legs*] larguirucho, desproporcionado

ganglion ['gæŋɡlɪən] N ganglio *m*

gangly ['gæŋɡlɪ] ADJ = **gangling**

gangplank ['gæŋplæŋk] N (*Naut*) plancha *f*

gangrene ['gæŋɡriːn] N gangrena *f*

gangster ['gæŋstə'] N gán(g)ster *m*

gangway ['gæŋweɪ] N **1** (*Brit*) (*in theatre, aircraft*) pasillo *m*, pasadizo *m* **2** (*Naut*) (*on ship*) escalerilla *f*, pasarela *f*; (*from ship to shore*) pasarela *f*; **gangway!** ¡abran paso!

gannet ['gænɪt] N alcatraz *m*

G&T N ABBR (= *gin and tonic*) gin-tonic *m*

gaol [dʒeɪl] N (*Brit*) = **jail**

gap [ɡæp] **Ⓐ** N (*gen, fig*) hueco *m*, vacío *m*; (*between teeth, floorboards*) hueco *m*; (*in traffic, vegetation*) claro *m*; (*in text*) espacio *m* (en blanco); (*in knowledge*) laguna *f*; (*in conversation*) silencio *m*; [*of time*] intervalo *m*; **to close the ~** cerrar la brecha; **we discerned a ~ in the market** vimos que había un hueco en el mercado; **leave a ~ for the name** deje un espacio para poner el nombre; **he left a ~ that will be hard to fill** dejó un hueco difícil de llenar **Ⓑ** CPD ➤ **gap year** (*Brit*) año *m* sabático (*antes de empezar a estudiar en la universidad*)

gape [ɡeɪp] VI **to ~ (at)** mirar boquiabierto (a); **he ~d at me in amazement** se me quedó mirando boquiabierto

gaping ['geɪpɪŋ] ADJ [*wound, mouth*] abierto; [*hole*] muy abierto, grande

garage ['gærɑːʒ] N [*of private house*] garaje *m*; (*for car repairs*) taller *m*; (*Brit*) (= *petrol station*) estación *f* de servicio, gasolinera *f*, grifo *m* (*Per*), bencinera *f* (*Chi*) ➤ **garage mechanic** mecánico/a *m/f* ➤ **garage proprietor** propietario/a *m/f* de un taller de reparaciones ➤ **garage sale** venta *f* de objetos usados (*en el garaje de una casa particular*)

garb [ɡɑːb] N atuendo *m*

garbage ['ɡɑːbɪdʒ] **Ⓐ** N **1** (*US*) (= *refuse*) basura *f*; (= *waste*) desperdicios *mpl*

2 (*) (*fig*) (= *goods, film etc*) birria *f*, porquería *f*; (*spoken, written*) bobadas *fpl*, tonterías *fpl*, disparates *mpl*; **he talks a lot of ~** dice muchas bobadas or tonterías; **~ in, ~ out** (*Comput*) basura entra, basura sale

Ⓑ CPD (*US*) ➤ **garbage bag** bolsa *f* de la basura ➤ **garbage can** cubo *m* de la basura ➤ **garbage collector** basurero/a *m/f* ➤ **garbage disposal unit** triturador *m* de basura ➤ **garbage dump** vertedero *m* ➤ **garbage man** basurero *m* ➤ **garbage truck** camión *m* de la basura

garbled ['ɡɑːbld] ADJ confuso, incoherente

garden ['ɡɑːdn] **Ⓐ** N jardín *m*; (= *vegetable garden*) huerto *m*; **the Garden of Eden** el Edén; (*public*) **~s** parque *m* sing, jardines *mpl*

Ⓑ VI trabajar en el jardín or el huerto

Ⓒ CPD ➤ **garden centre, garden center** (*US*) centro *m* de jardinería, vivero *m* ➤ **garden flat** (*Brit*), **garden apartment** (*US*) piso *m* con jardín en planta baja ➤ **garden furniture** muebles *mpl* de jardín ➤ **garden hose** manguera *f* de jardín ➤ **garden party** recepción *f* al aire libre ➤ **garden path** sendero *m*; ✦ IDIOM **to lead sb up** (*esp Brit*) or **down** (*esp US*) **the ~ path** embaucar a algn ➤ **garden shears** tijeras *fpl* de jardín ➤ **garden tools** útiles *mpl* de jardinería

gardener ['ɡɑːdnə'] N jardinero/a *m/f*

gardenia [ɡɑːˈdiːnɪə] N gardenia *f*

gardening ['ɡɑːdnɪŋ] N (*gen*) jardinería *f*; (= *market gardening*) horticultura *f*

garden-variety ['ɡɑːdnvəˌraɪətɪ] ADJ (*US*) común y corriente, normal y corriente

gargantuan [ɡɑːˈɡæntjʊən] ADJ colosal, gigantesco

gargle ['ɡɑːɡl] **Ⓐ** N gargarismo *m* **Ⓑ** VI hacer gárgaras, gargarear (*LAm*)

gargoyle ['ɡɑːɡɔɪl] N gárgola *f*

garish ['ɡɛərɪʃ] ADJ [*colour*] chillón, estridente; [*clothing*] chillón, llamativo, charro (*LAm*)

garland ['gɑːlənd] **A** N guirnalda f **B** VT engalanar (**with** con)

garlic ['gɑːlɪk] N ajo m ➤ **garlic mayonnaise** alioli m ➤ **garlic press** triturador m de ajo ➤ **garlic salt** sal f de ajo ➤ **garlic sausage** salchichón m al ajo

garlicky ['gɑːlɪkɪ] ADJ [taste] a ajo; [food] con ajo; [breath] con olor a ajo

garment ['gɑːmənt] N prenda f (de vestir); **garments** ropa fsing, indumentaria fsing

garnet ['gɑːnɪt] N granate m

garnish ['gɑːnɪʃ] **A** N (Culin) aderezo m, adorno m **B** VT aderezar, adornar (**with** con)

garret ['gærɪt] N (= attic room) desván m, altillo m (LAm)

garrison ['gærɪsən] **A** N guarnición f **B** VT guarnecer **C** CPD ➤ **garrison town** plaza f fuerte

garrotte [gə'rɒt] VT agarrotar

garrulous ['gærʊləs] ADJ gárrulo, parlanchín

garter ['gɑːtəʳ] N (for stocking, sock) liga f; (US) (= suspender) liguero m, portaligas m inv ➤ **garter belt** (US) liguero m, portaligas m inv

gas [gæs] **A** N (pl ~(s)es) **1** (gen) gas m; (as anaesthetic) gas m anestésico; (in mine) grisú m **2** (US) (= petrol) gasolina f, nafta f (SC), bencina f (Chi); **to step on the** ~* acelerar, pisar el acelerador **3** (esp US*) (= wind) gases mpl, flatulencia f **B** VT [+ person] asfixiar con gas; (Mil) gasear **C** CPD [industry, pipe] de gas ➤ **gas burner** mechero m de gas ➤ **gas can** (US) bidón m de gasolina ➤ **gas chamber** cámara f de gas ➤ **gas cooker** cocina f de or a gas ➤ **gas cylinder** bombona f de gas ➤ **gas fire** estufa f de gas ➤ **gas fitter** fontanero m (especializado en lo relacionado con el gas) ➤ **gas fittings** instalación fsing de gas ➤ **gas guzzler*** (US) chupagasolina* m inv, vehículo que consume mucha gasolina ➤ **gas jet** llama f de mechero de gas ➤ **gas leak** escape m de gas ➤ **gas lighter** encendedor m de gas ➤ **gas main** cañería f maestra de gas ➤ **gas mask** careta f or máscara f antigás ➤ **gas meter** contador m de gas, medidor m de gas (LAm) ➤ **gas oven** cocina f de gas ➤ **gas pedal** (esp US) acelerador m ➤ **gas pipe** tubo m de gas ➤ **gas pipeline** gasoducto m ➤ **gas pump** (US) (in car) bomba f de gasolina; (in gas station) surtidor m de gasolina ➤ **gas ring** (Brit) fuego m de gas ➤ **gas station** (US) gasolinera f, estación f de servicio, bencinera f (Chi), grifo m (Per) ➤ **gas stove** cocina f de or a gas ➤ **gas tank** (US Aut) tanque m or depósito m (de gasolina) ➤ **gas tap** llave f del gas

gaseous ['gæsɪəs] ADJ gaseoso

gas-fired [,gæs'faɪəd] ADJ de gas

gash [gæʃ] **A** N (in flesh) tajo m; (from knife) cuchillada f; (in material) raja f, hendidura f **B** VT [+ arm, head] hacer un tajo en; (with knife) acuchillar; [+ seat etc] rajar

gasket ['gæskɪt] N junta f

gaslight ['gæslaɪt] N luz f de gas, alumbrado m de gas

gasman ['gæsmæn] N (pl **gasmen**) (gen) empleado m del gas; (= gas fitter) fontanero m (especializado en lo relacionado con el gas)

gasoline ['gæsəliːn] N (US) gasolina f, nafta f (SC), bencina f (Chi)

gasp [gɑːsp] **A** N [of surprise] grito m ahogado; (for breath) boqueada f; **she gave a ~ of surprise** dio un grito ahogado de asombro **B** VI (for air) respirar con dificultad; (= pant) jadear; (in surprise) gritar; **he was ~ing for air or breath** le costaba respirar, le faltaba el aliento; **I was ~ing for a smoke** tenía unas ganas tremendas de fumar **C** VT (also ~ out) decir con voz entrecortada

gassy ['gæsɪ] ADJ (compar **gassier**; superl **gassiest**) gaseoso

gastric ['gæstrɪk] ADJ gástrico ➤ **gastric flu** gastroenteritis f inv

gastritis [gæs'traɪtɪs] N gastritis f inv

gastroenteritis [,gæstrəʊ,entə'raɪtɪs] N gastroenteritis f

gastronomy [gæs'trɒnəmɪ] N gastronomía f

gasworks ['gæswɜːks] NSING OR NPL fábrica fsing de gas

gate [geɪt] N **1** (wooden) puerta f (also of town, castle);

(metal) verja f; (= sluice) compuerta f; [of field, in station] barrera f; (Sport) entrada f; **please go to ~ seven** diríjanse a la puerta siete **2** (Sport) (= attendance) público m, concurrencia f; (= entrance money) taquilla f, recaudación f

gâteau ['gætəʊ] **A** N (pl ~x ['gætəʊz]) (esp Brit) torta f, pastel m, tarta f (Sp)

gatecrash* ['geɪtkræʃ] **A** VT [+ party] colarse en **B** VI colarse (de gorra)

gatecrasher* ['geɪt,kræʃəʳ] N colado/a m/f

gatehouse ['geɪthaʊs] N casa f del guarda or del portero

gatekeeper ['geɪt,kiːpəʳ] N portero/a m/f

gatepost ['geɪtpəʊst] N poste m (de una puerta)

gateway ['geɪtweɪ] N (gen) puerta f (de acceso); (Internet) portal m; **New York, the ~ to America** Nueva York, la puerta a América; **the ~ to success** la puerta al éxito

gather ['gæðəʳ] **A** VT **1** [+ flowers] coger, recoger (LAm); [+ information] reunir, recopilar **2** (also ~ **together**) [+ people, objects] reunir, juntar; **to ~ one's thoughts (together)** ordenar sus pensamientos; **she ~ed her coat around her** se envolvió en su abrigo **3** (also ~ **up**) [+ pins, sticks, etc] recoger; [+ hair] recoger **4** (also ~ **in**) [+ harvest, crop] recoger, recolectar; [+ taxes] recaudar **5** (Sew) fruncir **6** (= gain) **to ~ speed** ir ganando or adquiriendo velocidad; **to ~ strength** cobrar fuerzas; **to ~ dust** acumular polvo **7 to ~ that** (= understand) tener entendido que; (= discover) enterarse de que; **as you will have ~ed ...** se habrá dado cuenta de que ...; **as far as I could ~** hasta donde pude enterarme; **I ~ from him that ...** según lo que me dice ...; **what are we to ~ from this?** ¿qué consecuencia sacamos de esto? **B** VI [people] (also ~ **together**) reunirse, juntarse, congregarse; (= crowd together) amontonarse; [dust] acumularse; [clouds] acumularse, cerrarse; **they ~ed in the doorway** se apiñaron en la entrada **C** N (Sew) frunce m ➤ **gather round** VI + ADV, VI + PREP **to ~ round (sb)** agruparse alrededor (de algn); ~ **round!** ¡acercaos!

gathering ['gæðərɪŋ] **A** N (= assembly) reunión f; (= people present) concurrencia f **B** ADJ [force, speed] creciente, en aumento

GATT [gæt] N ABBR (= **General Agreement on Tariffs and Trade**) GATT m

gauche [gəʊʃ] ADJ [person, behaviour] torpe, desmañado; (socially) cohibido, falto de soltura

gaudy ['gɔːdɪ] ADJ (compar **gaudier**; superl **gaudiest**) [colour, clothes] chillón, llamativo

gauge, gage (US) [geɪdʒ] **A** N (= standard measure) [of wire, bullet, gun] calibre m; [of railway track] ancho m, entrevía f, trocha f (LAm); (= instrument) indicador m; (fig) indicación f, muestra f; **petrol** or (US) **gas ~** indicador m del nivel de gasolina **B** VT [+ temperature, pressure] medir; (fig) [+ sb's capabilities, character] estimar, juzgar; **he knows how to ~ the feeling of the crowd** sabe reconocer los deseos de la multitud; **to ~ the right moment** elegir el momento oportuno

Gaul [gɔːl] N **1** (= country) Galia f **2** (= person) galo/a m/f

gaunt [gɔːnt] ADJ [person] flaco y adusto; [face] (= drawn) chupado; (= unhealthy) demacrado

gauntlet ['gɔːntlɪt] N guante m; ✦ IDIOMS **to run the ~** (Mil, Hist) correr baquetas; **he had to run a ~ of abuse as he arrived for the meeting** tuvo que aguantar una sarta de improperios a su llegada a la reunión; **to throw down/take up the ~** arrojar/recoger el guante

gauze [gɔːz] N (gen) gasa f

gave [geɪv] PT of **give**

gavel ['gævl] N martillo m (de presidente de reunión o subastador)

gawk* [gɔːk] VI mirar boquiabierto (**at** a)

gawky* ['gɔːkɪ] ADJ (compar **gawkier**; superl **gawkiest**) desgarbado, torpe

gawp* [gɔːp] VI (Brit) = **gawk**

gay [geɪ] **Ⓐ** ADJ **1** (= *homosexual*) [*man, community, movement*] gay *inv*, homosexual; [*woman*] homosexual, lesbio; ~ **men and women** hombres y mujeres homosexuales, gays y lesbianas; ~ **sex** relaciones *fpl* homosexuales **2** (*compar* ~**er**; *superl* ~**est**) (†) (= *cheerful*) [*person, colour, costume*] alegre; [*atmosphere*] alegre, festivo **Ⓑ** N (= *man*) gay *m*, homosexual *m*; (= *woman*) lesbiana *f*, homosexual *f* **Ⓒ** CPD ➤ **gay rights** derechos *mpl* de los homosexuales

Gaza strip ['gɑːzə'strɪp] N franja *f* de Gaza

gaze [geɪz] **Ⓐ** N mirada *f* (fija); **his ~ met mine** se cruzaron nuestras miradas **Ⓑ** VI **to ~ at** mirar fijamente; **to ~ at o.s. in the mirror** mirarse (fijamente) en el espejo; **they ~d into each other's eyes** se miraron fijamente a los ojos; **to ~ into space** mirar distraídamente al vacío

gazelle [gə'zel] N gacela *f*

gazette [gə'zet] N (= *newspaper*) gaceta *f*; (= *official publication*) boletín *m* oficial

gazetteer [ˌgæzɪ'tɪəʳ] N diccionario *m* geográfico

gazump* [gə'zʌmp] VT (*Brit*) [*buyer*] ofrecer un precio más alto que; [*seller*] rehusar la venta de una propiedad a la persona con quien se había acordado aceptando una oferta más alta; **we were ~ed** ofrecieron más que nosotros

gazumping* [gə'zʌmpɪŋ] N (*Brit*) subida del precio de una casa tras haber sido apalabrado

GB N ABBR (= **Great Britain**) Gran Bretaña *f*

GBH N ABBR (*Brit Jur*) (= **grievous bodily harm**) graves daños *mpl* corporales

GCH N ABBR = **gas(-fired) central heating**

GCHQ N ABBR (*Brit*) (= **Government Communications Headquarters**) entidad gubernamental que recoge datos mediante escuchas electrónicas

GCSE N ABBR (*Brit*) = **General Certificate of Secondary Education**

GCSE

En Inglaterra, Gales e Irlanda del Norte, el **GCSE** o **General Certificate of Secondary Education** es el nombre del curso y del certificado académico que se obtiene una vez completada cada una de las asignaturas de la Educación Secundaria Obligatoria. Los exámenes tienen lugar a la edad de dieciséis años y las calificaciones van de la A a la G, (A es la máxima, G la mínima).

Gdns ABBR = **Gardens**

GDP N ABBR (= **gross domestic product**) PIB *m*, PGB *m* (*Chi*), PTB *m* (*And*)

gear [gɪəʳ] **Ⓐ** N **1** (*Mech*) engranaje *m*; (*Aut*) marcha *f*, velocidad *f*; **first/second** ~ primera *f*/segunda *f* (velocidad); **top** *or* (*US*) **high** ~ (= *fifth*) quinta velocidad *f*, superdirecta *f*; (= *fourth*) cuarta velocidad *f*, directa *f*; **to change** ~ (*Brit*) cambiar de marcha; **to put a car in** ~ meter una marcha; **he left the car in** ~ dejó el coche con una marcha metida; **out of** ~ desembragado; **to shift** ~ (*US*) cambiar de marcha **2** (*) (= *equipment*) equipo *m*; (= *tools*) herramientas *fpl*; (*for fishing*) aparejo *m*; (= *belongings*) cosas *fpl*, bártulos *mpl*; (= *clothing*) ropa *f*; (= *machinery*) mecanismo *m*, aparato *m* **Ⓑ** VT (*fig*) (= *adapt*) **the book is ~ed to adult students** el libro está dirigido a estudiantes adultos; **we both ~ed our lives to the children** los dos orientamos nuestras vidas hacia los niños; **the service is ~ed to meet the needs of the disabled** el servicio está pensado para satisfacer las necesidades de los minusválidos **Ⓒ** CPD ➤ **gear change** (= *act*) cambio *m* de marcha; (*US*) (= *control*) palanca *f* de cambios ➤ **gear lever** (*Brit*), **gear stick** (*Brit*) palanca *f* de cambios ➤ **gear up** **Ⓐ** VT + ADV (*fig*) **to ~ o.s. up to do sth** prepararse (psicológicamente) para hacer algo; **we're ~ed up to do it** estamos preparados para hacerlo **Ⓑ** VI + ADV prepararse, hacer preparativos

gearbox ['gɪəbɒks] N (*Aut*) caja *f* de cambios *or* velocidades; (*Mech*) caja *f* de engranajes

gearshift ['gɪəʃɪft] N (*US*) palanca *f* de cambios

GED N ABBR (*US Educ*) = **general equivalency diploma**

gee* [dʒiː] EXCL (*US*) ¡caramba!; ~ **whiz!** ¡córcholis! ➤ **gee up*** **Ⓐ** VI + ADV ~ **up!** ¡arre! **Ⓑ** VT + ADV (*fig*) dar ánimos a

geese [giːs] NPL *of* **goose**

Geiger counter ['gaɪgəˌkaʊntəʳ] N contador *m* Geiger

gel [dʒel] **Ⓐ** N gel *m*; **hair** ~ fijador *m* **Ⓑ** VI **1** (*lit*) gelificarse **2** (*fig*) [*ideas, plans*] encajar (**with** en)

gelatin(e) ['dʒelətiːn] N gelatina *f*

geld [geld] VT castrar, capar

gelding ['geldɪŋ] N caballo *m* castrado

gelignite ['dʒelɪgnaɪt] N gelignita *f*

gem [dʒem] N piedra *f* preciosa/semipreciosa, gema *f*; **my cleaner is a** ~ la señora que me hace la limpieza es una joya

Gemini ['dʒemɪniː] N **1** (= *sign, constellation*) Géminis *m* **2** (= *person*) géminis *mf inv*; **I'm (a)** ~ soy géminis

gemstone ['dʒemˌstəʊn] N piedra *f* preciosa/semipreciosa, gema *f*

Gen ABBR (*Mil*) (= **General**) Gen., Gral.

gender ['dʒendəʳ] N (*Ling*) género *m*; (= *sex*) sexo *m*

gene [dʒiːn] N gene *m*, gen *m* ➤ **gene mapping** cartografía *f* genética ➤ **gene therapy** terapia *f* génica, terapia *f* de genes

genealogy [ˌdʒiːnɪ'ælədʒɪ] N genealogía *f*

genera ['dʒenərə] NPL *of* **genus**

general ['dʒenərəl] **Ⓐ** ADJ general; **there was ~ agreement on this question** hubo un consenso general con respecto a esta cuestión; **we drove in the ~ direction of Aberdeen** íbamos conduciendo como en dirección a Aberdeen; **please direct any ~ enquiries to my secretary** le ruego solicite a mi secretaria cualquier información de carácter general; **I've got the ~ idea** tengo más o menos una idea; **the report was too ~** el informe era poco específico; **an introduction to psychology for the ~ reader** una introducción a la psicología para el lector no especializado; **as a ~ rule** por regla general; **secretary ~** secretario *m*/*f* general; **a ~ term** un término genérico; **in ~ terms** en líneas *or* términos generales; **for ~ use** para un uso general; **in ~ use** de uso general **Ⓑ** N **1 in** ~ en general **2** (*Mil*) general *mf* **Ⓒ** CPD ➤ **general anaesthetic, general anesthetic** (*US*) anestesia *f* general ➤ **general assembly** asamblea *f* general ➤ **General Certificate of Secondary Education** (*Brit Educ*) nombre del curso y del certificado que se obtiene al completar la enseñanza secundaria; ➙ GCSE ➤ **general delivery** (*US, Canada*) lista *f* de correos ➤ **general election** elecciones *fpl or* comicios *mpl* generales ➤ **general hospital** hospital *m* ➤ **general knowledge** cultura *f* general ➤ **general manager** director(a) *m*/*f* general ➤ **general medicine** medicina *f* general ➤ **general meeting** asamblea *f* general ➤ **general practice** (*Brit Med*) (= *medicine*) medicina *f* general; (= *group*) consultorio *m* médico; **to go into ~ practice** entrar a trabajar en medicina general ➤ **general practitioner** médico/a *m*/*f* de medicina general (*frm*), médico/a *m*/*f* de cabecera ➤ **the general public** el público en general, el gran público ➤ **general science** (*Scol*) Ciencias *fpl* ➤ **General Secretary** Secretario(a) *m*/*f* General ➤ **general store** tienda *f*, almacén *m* (*SC*)

generalization [ˌdʒenərəlaɪ'zeɪʃən] N generalización *f*

generalize ['dʒenərəlaɪz] VI generalizar (**about** sobre)

generally ['dʒenərəlɪ] ADV **1** (= *on the whole*) en general, en líneas generales; **~, the course is okay** en general *or* en líneas generales el curso está bien **2** (= *usually*) generalmente, por lo general; **we ~ meet on Tuesdays** generalmente *or* por lo general nos reunimos los martes **3** (= *widely*) generalmente; **it is ~ believed that ...** la mayoría de la gente cree que ..., generalmente, se cree que ...; **it's not yet ~ available** no está todavía a la venta *or* en el mercado **4** ~ **speaking** por lo general, en términos generales

general-purpose [ˌdʒenərəl'pɜːpəs] ADJ [tool, dictionary] de uso general

generate ['dʒenəreɪt] VT generar

generation [ˌdʒenə'reɪʃən] N generación f; **the younger ~** la nueva generación; **the older ~** los mayores; **first/second/ third ~** (Comput) de primera/segunda/tercera generación ➤ **the generation gap** la brecha entre las generaciones

generative ['dʒenərətɪv] ADJ generativo

generator ['dʒenəreɪtəʳ] N generador m

generic [dʒɪ'nerɪk] ADJ genérico

generosity [ˌdʒenə'rɒsɪtɪ] N generosidad f

generous ['dʒenərəs] ADJ 1 (= not mean) [person, mood, pay, offer] generoso; [gift] espléndido; [donation] cuantioso, generoso; **a ~ amount of sth** una buena cantidad de algo; **a ~ helping of sth** una ración generosa de algo, una buena ración de algo; **she was ~ in her praise of him** se deshizo en elogios (para) con él; **that's very ~ of you** eso es muy generoso de tu parte; **to be ~ with one's money** ser generoso or desprendido con el dinero; **he wasn't exactly ~ with the whisky** no fue muy espléndido que digamos con el whisky
2 (= kind) amable; **thank you for your ~ remarks** gracias por sus amables observaciones

generously ['dʒenərəslɪ] ADV generosamente

genesis ['dʒenɪsɪs] N (pl **geneses** ['dʒenɪsiːz]) génesis f inv; **Genesis** (Bible) Génesis m

genetic [dʒɪ'netɪk] ADJ genético ➤ **genetic engineering** ingeniería f genética ➤ **genetic fingerprinting** identificación f genética

genetically [dʒɪ'netɪkəlɪ] ADV genéticamente; **~ modified** transgénico, modificado genéticamente; **~-modified foods** alimentos mpl transgénicos; **~ modified organism** organismo m genéticamente modificado

geneticist [dʒɪ'netɪsɪst] N (Med) genetista mf

genetics [dʒɪ'netɪks] NSING genética f

Geneva [dʒɪ'niːvə] N Ginebra f

genial ['dʒiːnɪəl] ADJ [manner] cordial; [person] simpático, afable

genie ['dʒiːnɪ] N genio m

genital ['dʒenɪtl] Ⓐ ADJ genital Ⓑ N **genitals** (órganos mpl) genitales mpl

genitive ['dʒenɪtɪv] N genitivo m; **in the ~** en el genitivo

genius ['dʒiːnɪəs] N (pl **~es**) (= person) genio m; (= cleverness) genialidad f; (= talent) don m; **he's a ~** es un genio, es genial; **she's a mathematical ~** es un genio para las matemáticas; **a man of ~** un hombre genial; **to have a ~ for (doing) sth** tener un don especial para (hacer) algo

genocide ['dʒenəsaɪd] N genocidio m

genre [ʒɑ̃ːr] N género m

gent [dʒent] N ABBR 1 (= **gentleman**) caballero m 2 (Brit) **the ~s*** (= lavatory) el servicio (de caballeros), el baño (de señores) (LAm); **"gents"** "caballeros"

genteel [dʒen'tiːl] ADJ 1 (= middle-class) [person] elegante, refinado; [manners] refinado, fino; [atmosphere] elegante 2 (pej) (= affected) afectado

Gentile ['dʒentaɪl] N no judío/a m/f; (= pagan) gentil mf

gentle ['dʒentl] ADJ (compar **~r**; superl **~st**) 1 (= kind) [person] de carácter dulce; [manner, voice] dulce, delicado; [eyes, smile] dulce, tierno; [hint, reminder, rebuke] discreto; [animal] manso, dócil; **to be ~ with sb/sth** (= careful) tener cuidado con algn/algo; ✦ IDIOM **as ~ as a lamb** más bueno que el pan, más manso que un cordero
2 (= mild) [shampoo, soap, detergent] suave; **it is ~ on the skin** no irrita la piel
3 (= light) [touch, pressure, push, breeze] suave, ligero
4 (= moderate) [exercise] moderado; **cook for 30 minutes over a ~ heat** cocinar durante 30 minutos a fuego lento; **we jogged along at a ~ pace** hicimos footing a un ritmo suave
5 (= not steep) [slope] suave, poco pronunciado;

[curve] no muy cerrado

⚠ **gentle** ≠ **gentil**

gentleman ['dʒentlmən] N (pl **gentlemen**) (= man) señor m; (having gentlemanly qualities) caballero m; **there's a ~ waiting to see you** hay un señor esperando para verle; **"gentlemen"** (= lavatory) "caballeros"

gentlemanly ['dʒentlmənlɪ] ADJ caballeroso

gentleness ['dʒentlnɪs] N [of person, manner, voice] dulzura f; [of animal] mansedumbre f, docilidad f

gently ['dʒentlɪ] ADV 1 [say] dulcemente, suavemente; [hint, remind] con delicadeza 2 [handle] con cuidado; [shake, touch, push] ligeramente, suavemente; [simmer, cook] a fuego lento; [slope] suavemente; **~ does it!** ¡con cuidado!, ¡despacito!*

gentry† ['dʒentrɪ] N (Brit) alta burguesía f, pequeña aristocracia f; (pej) familias fpl bien, gente f bien; (= set of people) gente f

genuflect ['dʒenjʊflekt] VI hacer una genuflexión

genuine ['dʒenjʊɪn] ADJ 1 [picture, antique] auténtico; [claim, refugee] verdadero; **it is a ~ Renoir** es un Renoir auténtico; **a ~ leather sofa** un sofá de cuero legítimo or auténtico; **it's the ~ article** es genuino or auténtico 2 [interest, enthusiasm] verdadero, sincero; [commitment, difficulty] verdadero, auténtico; **it was a ~ mistake** fue realmente un error; **if this offer is ~ ...** si esta oferta va en serio or es seria ...; **she is very ~ and caring** es noble y bondadosa

genuinely ['dʒenjʊɪnlɪ] ADV 1 (= authentically) [funny] realmente, verdaderamente; **he claims, probably quite ~, to be ...** asegura, y probablemente sea cierto, ser ... 2 (= sincerely) [believe] sinceramente, realmente; [want] realmente, de verdad; [interested, worried, upset] verdaderamente, realmente

genus ['dʒenəs] N (pl **genera** or **~es**) género m

geographer [dʒɪ'ɒgrəfəʳ] N geógrafo/a m/f

geographic [dʒɪə'græfɪk] ADJ = **geographical**

geographical [dʒɪə'græfɪkəl] ADJ geográfico

geography [dʒɪ'ɒgrəfɪ] N geografía f

geological [dʒɪə'lɒdʒɪkəl] ADJ geológico

geologist [dʒɪ'ɒlədʒɪst] N geólogo/a m/f

geology [dʒɪ'ɒlədʒɪ] N geología f

geometric [dʒɪə'metrɪk] ADJ geométrico

geometrical [dʒɪə'metrɪkəl] ADJ = **geometric**

geometry [dʒɪ'ɒmɪtrɪ] N geometría f

geophysics [dʒɪəʊ'fɪzɪks] NSING geofísica f

geopolitics ['dʒiːəʊ'pɒlɪtɪks] NSING geopolítica f

Georgia ['dʒɔːdʒɪə] N (US and USSR) Georgia f

Georgian ['dʒɔːdʒɪən] ADJ (Brit) georgiano

geothermal [ˌdʒiːəʊ'θɜːməl] ADJ geotérmico

geranium [dʒɪ'reɪnɪəm] N geranio m

gerbil ['dʒɜːbɪl] N gerbo m, jerbo m

geriatric [ˌdʒerɪ'ætrɪk] Ⓐ ADJ geriátrico; **~ home** residencia f geriátrica, centro m geriátrico; **~ medicine** geriatría f Ⓑ N (Med) persona f mayor

geriatrician [ˌdʒerɪə'trɪʃən] N geriatra mf

geriatrics [ˌdʒerɪ'ætrɪks] NSING geriatría f

germ [dʒɜːm] N germen m; (Med) microbio m, germen m; **the ~ of an idea** el germen de una idea ➤ **germ warfare** guerra f bacteriológica

German ['dʒɜːmən] Ⓐ ADJ alemán Ⓑ N 1 (= person) alemán/ana m/f 2 (Ling) alemán m Ⓒ CPD ➤ **German Democratic Republic** (Hist) República f Democrática Alemana ➤ **German measles** rubeola f, rubéola f ➤ **German shepherd (dog)** pastor m alemán, perro m lobo

germane [dʒɜː'meɪn] ADJ **that's not ~ to the discussion** eso no atañe a la discusión; **the remark is not ~** el comentario no viene al caso

German-speaking ['dʒɜːmənˌspiːkɪŋ] ADJ de habla alemana

Germany ['dʒɜːmənɪ] N Alemania f; **East ~** Alemania f Oriental; **West ~** Alemania f Occidental

Germanic [dʒɜː'mænɪk] ADJ germánico

germ-free [,dʒɜːm'friː] ADJ estéril; (= sterilized) esterilizado

germicide ['dʒɜːmɪsaɪd] N germicida m

germinate ['dʒɜːmɪneɪt] VI germinar

germination [,dʒɜːmɪ'neɪʃən] N germinación f

gerontology [,dʒerɒn'tɒlədʒɪ] N gerontología f

gerrymandering ['dʒerɪmændərɪŋ] N manipulaciones fpl

gerund ['dʒerənd] N gerundio m

gestation [dʒes'teɪʃən] N gestación f

gesticulate [dʒes'tɪkjʊleɪt] VI gesticular

gesture ['dʒestʃəʳ] Ⓐ N 1 (lit) ademán m, gesto m 2 (fig) demostración f; (= small token) muestra f, detalle m; **what a nice ~!** ¡qué gesto or detalle más agradable!; **as a ~ of friendship** en señal de amistad; **as a ~ of support** para demostrar nuestro apoyo Ⓑ VI hacer gestos; **he ~d towards the door** señaló or apuntó hacia la puerta; **to ~ to sb to do sth** indicar a algn con la mano que haga algo

get

Ⓐ TRANSITIVE VERB	Ⓒ PHRASAL VERBS
Ⓑ INTRANSITIVE VERB	

*When **get** is part of a set combination, eg **get the sack**, **get hold of**, **get sth right**, look up the other word.*

get [get] (pt, pp **got**; US: pp **gotten**)
Ⓐ TRANSITIVE VERB
1 (= obtain) [+ information, money, visa, divorce] conseguir; **he got it for me** él me lo consiguió; **where did you ~ that idea from?** ¿de dónde sacaste esa idea?; **you won't ~ any money out of me** no vas a sacarme dinero; **a good coach knows how to ~ the best out of his players** un buen entrenador sabe cómo sacar lo mejor de sus jugadores
2 (= have) tener; **I go whenever I ~ the chance** voy siempre que tengo ocasión; **to ~ something to eat** comer algo
3 (= receive) [+ letter, phone call] recibir; [+ wage] ganar, cobrar; [+ TV station, radio station] coger, captar; [+ pension] cobrar; **how much did you ~ for it?** ¿cuánto te dieron por él?; **he ~s his red hair from his mother** el pelo rojizo lo ha heredado de su madre

*Some **get** + NOUN combinations are translated using a more specific Spanish verb. If in doubt, look up the noun.*

I never got an answer no me contestaron, no recibí nunca una respuesta; **this area doesn't ~ much rain** en este área no llueve mucho; **I got a shock/surprise** me llevé un susto/una sorpresa; **this room ~s a lot of sun** a esta habitación le da mucho el sol; **he got 15 years for murder** le condenaron a 15 años por asesinato
4 (= buy) comprar; **I got it cheap** me costó barato
5 (= fetch) [+ glasses, book] ir a buscar, traer; [+ person] ir a buscar, ir a por; (= pick up) [+ goods, person] recoger; **can you ~ my coat from the cleaner's?** ¿puedes recogerme el abrigo de la tintorería?; **quick, ~ help!** ¡rápido, ve a buscar ayuda!; **to ~ sth for sb** ◇ **~ sb sth** ir a buscar algo a algn, traer algo a algn; **can I ~ you a drink?** ¿te apetece beber or tomar algo?, ¿quieres beber or tomar algo?; **I'll go and ~ it for you** voy a buscártelo, voy a traértelo; **go and ~ Jane will you?** vete a buscar a Jane, ve a por Jane; **phone me when you arrive and I'll come and ~ you** cuando llegues llama por teléfono y te iré a buscar or recoger
6 (= call) [+ doctor, plumber] llamar
7 (= answer) [+ phone] contestar; **I'll ~ it!** (telephone) ¡yo contesto!; (door) ¡ya voy yo!
8 (= gain, win) [+ prize] ganar, llevarse, conseguir; [+ goal] marcar; [+ reputation] ganarse; **he's in it for what he can ~** lo único que quiere es sacarle provecho; **he got an A in French** sacó un sobresaliente en francés; **I have to ~ my**

degree first antes tengo que acabar la carrera or conseguir mi título
9 (= find) [+ job, flat] encontrar, conseguir
10 (= catch) [+ ball, disease, person] coger, agarrar (LAm); [+ thief] coger, atrapar (LAm); [+ bus] coger, tomar (LAm); **I'm ~ting the bus into town** voy a coger or tomar el autobús que va al centro; **got you!** ¡te pillé!*, ¡te cacé!*, ¡te agarré! (LAm); **I've been trying to ~ him alone** he estado intentando verle a solas; **to ~ sb by the throat/arm** agarrar or coger a algn de la garganta/del brazo; **I didn't ~ the details** no oí los detalles; **sorry, I didn't ~ your name** perdone, ¿cómo dice que se llama?, perdone, no me he enterado de su nombre; **did you ~ his (registration) number?** ¿viste el número de matrícula?; **you've got me there!*** ahí sí que me has pillado*; ✦ IDIOM **to ~ it from sb: he really got it from the teacher*** el profesor le echó una buena*
11 (= reach, put through to) **~ me Mr Jones, please** (Telec) póngame or (esp LAm) comuníqueme con el Sr. Jones, por favor; **you can ~ me on this number** puedes contactar conmigo en este número; **I've been trying to ~ you all week** he estado intentando hablar contigo toda la semana
12 (*) (= attack, take revenge on) **I feel like everyone is out to ~ me** siento que todo el mundo va contra mí; **I'll ~ you for that!** ¡esto me lo vas a pagar!; **they're out to ~ him** van a cargárselo*
13 (= hit) [+ target] dar en; **the bullet got him in the leg** la bala le dio en la pierna
14 (= finish) **the drink will ~ him in the end** la bebida acabará con él al final
15 (= take, bring) llevar, traer; **how can we ~ it home?** (speaker not at home) ¿cómo podemos llevarlo a casa?; (speaker at home) ¿cómo podemos traerlo a casa?; **I tried to ~ the blood off my shirt** intenté quitar la sangre de mi camisa; **~ the knife off him!** ¡quítale ese cuchillo!; **I couldn't ~ the stain out of the tablecloth** no podía limpiar la mancha del mantel; **to ~ sth past customs** conseguir pasar algo por la aduana; **we'll ~ you there somehow** le llevaremos de una u otra manera; **we can't ~ it through the door** no lo podemos pasar por la puerta; **to ~ sth to sb** hacer llegar algo a algn; **where will that ~ us?** ¿de qué nos sirve eso?; ✦ IDIOM **that won't ~ you/him anywhere** eso no te/le va a llevar a ningún sitio
16 (= prepare) [+ meal] preparar, hacer
17 (WITH ADJECTIVE)

get used with an adjective is often translated using a specific Spanish verb. Look up the relevant adjective.

he got his leg broken se rompió la pierna; **to ~ one's hands dirty** ensuciarse las manos; **to ~ sb drunk** emborrachar a algn; **to ~ one's feet wet** mojarse los pies; **you're ~ting me worried** estás haciendo que me preocupe
18 (WITH INFINITIVE/PRESENT PARTICIPLE) **to ~ sb to do sth** (= persuade) conseguir que algn haga algo, persuadir a algn a hacer algo; (= tell) decir a algn que haga algo; **I'll ~ him to ring you** le diré que te llame; **I can't ~ the door to open** no puedo abrir la puerta, no logro que se abra la puerta; **I couldn't ~ the car going** or **to go** no pude poner el coche en marcha, no pude arrancar el coche
19 ("get sth done" construction)
19.1 (= do oneself) **to ~ the washing done** lavar la ropa; **when do you think you'll ~ it finished?** ¿cuándo crees que lo vas a acabar?; **you'll ~ yourself killed driving like that** te vas a matar si conduces de esa forma
19.2 (= get someone to do) **to ~ one's hair cut** cortarse el pelo, hacerse cortar el pelo; **to ~ sth fixed** arreglar or reparar algo
20 (*) (= understand) entender; **I don't ~ you** no te entiendo; **(do you) ~ it?** ¿entiendes?; [+ joke] ¿lo coges?, ¿ya caes?*; **I've got it!** [+ joke] ¡ahora lo entiendo!; [+ solution] ¡ya lo tengo!
21 (*) (= annoy) molestar, fastidiar
22 **to have got sth** (Brit) (= have) tener algo; **I've got toothache** tengo dolor de muelas
Ⓑ INTRANSITIVE VERB
1 (= reach, go) llegar; **how do you ~ there?** ¿como se llega?; **how did you ~ here?** ¿cómo viniste or llegaste?; **to ~ from A to B** ir de A a B, trasladarse de A a B; **to ~ home** llegar a

casa; **how do you ~ to the cinema?** ¿cómo se llega al cine?; **where can he have got to?** ¿dónde se puede haber metido?; ✦ IDIOMS **you won't ~ anywhere with him** no conseguirás nada con él; **we're ~ting nowhere fast** no estamos llegando a ningún sitio; **now we're ~ting somewhere** ahora empezamos a hacer progresos; **"how's your thesis going?"** — **"I'm ~ting there"** —¿qué tal va tu tesis? —va avanzando; **don't let it ~ to you*** (= *affect*) no dejes que te afecte; (= *annoy*) no te molestes por eso **2** (= *become, be*) ponerse, volverse, hacerse; **it's ~ting late**

As expressions with **get** + ADJECTIVE, such as **get old**, **get drunk**, etc, are often translated by a specific verb, look up the adjective.

se está haciendo tarde; **how did it ~ like that?** ¿cómo se ha puesto así?; **this is ~ting ridiculous** esto roza los límites de lo ridículo; **how stupid can you ~?** ¿cómo se puede ser tan tonto?; **to ~ used to sth** acostumbrarse a algo
3 (WITH PAST PARTICIPLE)
3.1 (= *be*) **he often ~s asked for his autograph** a menudo le piden autógrafos; **we got beaten 3-2** perdimos 3 a 2; **several windows got broken** se rompieron varias ventanas; **to ~ killed** morir, matarse; **to ~ paid** cobrar
3.2 (*reflexive action*) **to ~ shaved** afeitarse; **to ~ washed** lavarse
4 (= *begin*) (WITH GERUND) empezar a + *infin*, ponerse a + *infin*; **to ~ going** (= *leave*) [*person*] ponerse en marcha; (= *liven up*) [*party*] empezar a animarse; **we got talking** empezamos a hablar *or* charlar
5 (*in set structures*)
✦ **to get to do sth** llegar a hacer algo; **when do we ~ to eat?** ¿cuándo comemos?; **to ~ to know sb** llegar a conocer a algn; **I never ~ to drive the car** nunca tengo oportunidad de conducir el coche; **to ~ to see sth/sb** lograr ver algo/a algn
✦ **to have got to do sth** tener que hacer algo
G PHRASAL VERBS
➤ **get about** VI + ADV **1** [*invalid*] (= *walk*) caminar; (= *move around*) moverse **2** (= *go out*) (*socially*) salir; (= *travel*) viajar **3** (*esp Brit*) (= *circulate*) [*rumour*] correr; [*story*] saberse, divulgarse; **it soon got about that ...** al poco tiempo corrió el rumor de que ...; **I don't want it to ~ about** no quiero que se sepa *or* divulgue
➤ **get above** VI + PREP **to ~ above o.s.** volverse un engreído
➤ **get across** **A** VI + PREP [+ *road*] cruzar; [+ *river, sea, desert*] cruzar, atravesar **B** VI + ADV **1** (= *cross road, river, etc*) cruzar **2** (= *be understood*) [*meaning*] ser comprendido; [*person*] hacerse entender; **the message seems to be ~ting across** parece que está empezando a captar el mensaje **G** VT + ADV **1** (= *communicate*) [+ *meaning, message*] comunicar, hacer entender **2** (= *transport across*) [+ *people, objects*] cruzar
➤ **get ahead** VI + ADV **1** (*in race*) tomar la delantera **2** (= *succeed*) (*by doing better than others*) ir por delante; (= *make progress*) progresar, avanzar; **to ~ ahead of sb** adelantar a algn **3** (*with work*) adelantar (**with** con)
➤ **get along** VI + ADV **1** (= *leave*) marcharse, irse; **it's time we were ~ting along** ya es hora de que nos marchemos *or* nos vayamos **2** (= *manage*) arreglárselas*, apañárselas*; **to ~ along without sth** arreglárselas sin algo*, apañárselas sin algo*; **we ~ along (somehow)** vamos tirando **3** (= *progress*) **how is he ~ting along?** ¿qué tal está?, ¿cómo le va? (*LAm*); **we we ~ting along fine until he arrived** la cosa iba perfectamente hasta que llegó él **4** (= *be on good terms*) llevarse bien (**with sb** con algn)
➤ **get around** **A** VI + PREP **1** [+ *corner*] dar la vuelta a; [+ *problem*] superar; [+ *regulation*] sortear
2 (= *persuade*) **to ~ around sb** engatusar a algn
B VI + ADV **1** (= *come*) venir; (= *go*) ir
2 (= *circulate*) [*rumour*] correr; [*story*] saberse, divulgarse; **it soon got around that ...** al poco tiempo corrió el rumor de que ...; **I don't want it to ~ around** no quiero que se sepa *or* divulgue
3 to ~ around to (doing) sth: I shan't ~ around to that before next week no lo podré hacer antes de la semana próxima; **we never got around to exchanging addresses** al final no llegamos a intercambiarnos las direcciones
G VT + ADV **1** (= *cause to come, go*) **we'll ~ a car around to**

you for nine le mandaremos un coche para las nueve **2** (= *persuade*) convencer; **we got him around to our way of thinking** logramos convencerlo de nuestra manera de pensar
➤ **get at** VI + PREP **1** (= *reach*) [+ *object*] alcanzar; [+ *place*] llegar a *or* hasta; [+ *facts, truth*] establecer **2** (*Brit**) (= *criticize*) meterse con*; **she's always ~ting at her brother** siempre se está metiendo con su hermano*; **I'm not ~ting at you, I just think that ...** no te estoy echando la bronca, simplemente creo que ...* **3** (*) (= *imply*) querer decir; (*negatively*) insinuar; **I couldn't see what he was ~ting at** no entendía qué quería decir **4** (*) (= *bribe*) sobornar; (= *pressurize*) presionar
➤ **get away** **A** VI + ADV **1** (= *leave*) salir (**from** de); (= *go away*) irse; **I didn't ~ away till seven** no conseguí marcharme hasta las siete; **I can't ~ away before the 15th** no puedo escaparme *or* irme antes del 15 **2** (= *move away*) apartarse (**from** de) **3** (= *escape*) escaparse (**from** de); **to ~ away from it all** escapar de todo **B** VT + ADV (= *remove*) **to ~ sth away from sb** (= *remove*) quitar algo a algn; **I can't ~ him away from that computer** no puedo despegarlo del ordenador
➤ **get away with** VI + PREP **1** (= *steal*) llevarse **2** (= *go unpunished*) **he got away with an official warning** sólo se llevó una amonestación; **we can ~ away with just repainting it** bastará con volver a pintarlo; **we mustn't let them ~ away with it** no debemos dejar que salgan impunes; **you won't ~ away with it!** (*with past action*) ¡esto no va a quedar así!; (*with possible action*) esto no te lo van a consentir; **he'll never ~ away with it** nunca se va a salir con la suya
➤ **get back** **A** VT + ADV **1** (= *recover*) [+ *possessions, money, spouse*] recuperar; [+ *strength*] recobrar
2 (= *return*) devolver; *see also* **own²** B
B VI + ADV **1** (= *return*) volver; **to ~ back (home)** volver a casa; **~ back into/bed/the car** vuelve a la cama/al coche; **things are ~ting back to normal** las cosas están volviendo a la normalidad; **to ~ back to work** volver al trabajo; **I'll ~ back to you on that** te daré una respuesta; **can you ~ back to Harry about the flat?** ¿puedes volver a llamar a Harry para lo del piso?
2 (= *move back*) **~ back!** ¡atrás!
➤ **get back at*** VI + PREP **to ~ back at sb (for sth)** vengarse de algn (por algo), desquitarse con algn (por algo)
➤ **get behind** **A** VI + ADV (*with work, payments*) retrasarse (**with** en) **B** VI + PREP **1** (= *move, sit behind*) ponerse detrás de; **to ~ behind the wheel** ponerse al volante **2** (= *support*) apoyar
➤ **get by** VI + ADV **1** (= *pass, be acceptable*) pasar **2** (*) (= *manage*) arreglárselas*, apañárselas*; (*in language*) defenderse; **we'll ~ by** nos las arreglaremos*, nos las apañaremos*; **she ~s by on what her son gives her** se las arregla *or* apaña para vivir con lo que le da su hijo*
➤ **get down** **A** VT + ADV **1** (*from shelf*) bajar (**from** de)
2 (= *swallow*) tragarse, tragar
3 (= *note down*) escribir; **to ~ sth down in writing** *or* **on paper** poner algo por escrito
4 (= *reduce*) **I need to ~ my weight down a bit** tengo que bajar de peso un poco
5 (*) (= *depress*) deprimir; **don't let it ~ you down** no dejes que eso te deprima
6 (*) (= *annoy*) molestar
B VI + ADV **1** (= *descend*) bajar (**from, off** de)
2 (= *crouch*) agacharse; **to ~ down on one's knees** ponerse de rodillas
3 (= *go*) bajar; **I'll try and ~ down this weekend** intentaré bajar este fin de semana
➤ **get down to** VI + PREP **to ~ down to doing sth** ponerse a hacer algo; **let's ~ down to business** (= *start work*) pongámonos manos a la obra; **to ~ down to work** ponerse a trabajar (en serio); **when you ~ down to it there's not much difference between them** cuando lo miras bien, no se diferencian mucho
➤ **get in** **A** VT + ADV **1** (= *bring in*) [+ *person, animal*] hacer entrar; [+ *harvest*] recoger; [+ *supplies*] traer; **I'll ~ some beer in** compraré cerveza
2 (= *hand over*) entregar; (= *post in*) mandar; **did you ~ your essay on time?** ¿entregaste tu trabajo a tiempo?
3 (= *plant*) [+ *bulbs etc*] plantar
4 (= *summon*) [+ *expert etc*] llamar a

5 (= *insert*) [+ *object, comment*] meter; **it was hard to ~ a word in** era muy difícil meter baza; **he managed to ~ in a game of golf** consiguió meter en un partido de golf; **I can't ~ any more in** no cabe nada más; **he got in a reference to his new book** logró mencionar su nuevo libro

6 (= *sneak in*) [+ *arms, drugs*] meter, pasar; [+ *visitor*] colar*; **I can ~ you in as a visitor** puedo colarte como visitante*

B VI + ADV **1** (= *enter*) entrar, meterse

2 (= *arrive*) [*train, bus, plane*] llegar; (= *reach home*) [*person*] llegar (a casa)

3 (*Pol*) (= *be elected*) ser elegido

➤ **get into** **A** VI + PREP **1** (= *enter*) [+ *house*] entrar en; [+ *vehicle*] subir a; [+ *bed, bath*] meterse en; **to ~ into politics** meterse en la política; ✦ IDIOM **what's got into him?** ¿qué mosca le ha picado?, ¿pero qué le pasa?

2 (= *reach*) [+ *office, school*] llegar a; **if this document ~s into the wrong hands ...** si este documento cae en en manos de quien no debe ...

3 (= *put on*) [+ *clothes*] ponerse

4 (= *become involved in*) meterse en; **I wish I'd never got into this** ojalá no me hubiera metido nunca en esto

5 (= *acquire*) **to ~ into the habit of doing sth** coger *or* (*LAm*) agarrar la costumbre de hacer algo

B VT + PREP meter en; **you got me into this** tú me has metido en esto

➤ **get in with** VI + PREP (= *gain favour with*) congraciarse con; **he got in with a bad crowd** empezó a andar con malas compañías

➤ **get off** **A** VT + ADV **1** (= *remove*) [+ *stain, lid*] quitar; **to ~ one's clothes off** quitarse la ropa

2 (= *send off*) [+ *letter*] mandar (**to** a); **to ~ sb off to school** despachar a algn al colegio; **she got the baby off to sleep** (*Brit*) logró dormir al niño

3 (= *save from punishment*) **his lawyer managed to ~ him off** su abogado logró que se librase del castigo

4 (= *have as leave*) [+ *day, time*] tener libre; **we ~ a day off** nos dan un día libre

B VT + PREP (= *remove*) **~ your dog off me!** ¡quítame al perro de encima!

C VI + PREP **1** [+ *bus, train, bike, horse*] bajarse de, apearse de (*frm*); ✦ IDIOM **I wish he would ~ off my back!*** ¡ojalá me dejara en paz!

2 (= *leave*) salir de; **what time do you ~ off work?** ¿a qué hora sales del trabajo?; **we've rather got off the subject** nos hemos alejado bastante del tema

3 (*) (= *escape*) [+ *chore etc*] librarse de, escaquearse de (*Sp**)

4 (= *get up from*) levantarse de

5 (= *give up*) [+ *drugs, alcohol, addiction*] dejar

D VI + ADV **1** (*from bus, train, bike, horse*) bajarse, apearse (*frm*); **~ off!** (= *let go*) ¡suelta!

2 (= *leave*) partir; **can you ~ off early tomorrow?** (*from work*) ¿puedes salir del trabajo temprano mañana?

3 (= *escape injury, punishment*) librarse; **he got off with a fine** se libró con una multa

4 **to ~ off (to sleep)** dormirse

➤ **get off with*** VI + PREP (*Brit*) liarse con*, enrollarse con (*Sp***)

➤ **get on** **A** VI + ADV **1** (= *mount*) subir

2 (= *proceed*) seguir; **we must be ~ting on** no podemos parar; **to ~ on with sth** seguir con algo; **now we can ~ on with our lives again** ahora podemos seguir con nuestras vidas; **~ on with it!** ¡venga!, ¡apúrese! (*LAm*); **~ on with your work, please** seguid trabajando, por favor; **this will do to be ~ting on with** esto basta por ahora

3 (= *manage*) **I was ~ting on fine till ...** me las iba apañando bien hasta que ...; **how did you ~ on?** (*in exam, interview*) ¿qué tal te fue?, ¿cómo te fue?; **she's ~ting on very well with Russian** está haciendo muchos progresos con el ruso

4 (*esp Brit*) (= *progress*) progresar; (= *succeed*) tener éxito; **if you want to ~ on in life, ...** si quieres tener éxito en la vida, ...

5 (*Brit*) **to be ~ting on: it's ~ting on for nine** son casi las nueve; **he's ~ting on for 70** está rondando los 70, anda cerca de los 70; **there were ~ting on for 50 people** había casi 50 personas; **her parents are ~ting on a bit** sus padres ya están un poco viejos; **time is ~ting on** se está haciendo tarde

6 (= *be on good terms*) llevarse bien; **to ~ on (well) with sb** llevarse bien con algn

B VI + PREP [+ *train, bus*] subir(se) a; [+ *horse, bicycle*] subir(se) a, montar a

C VT + ADV [+ *clothes*] ponerse; [+ *lid, dinner*] poner

➤ **get on to, get onto** **A** VI + PREP **1** [+ *bike, horse*] montarse en, subir(se) a; [+ *bus, train*] subir(se) a

2 (= *start talking of*) empezar a hablar de; (= *move on to*) pasar a; (= *reach*) llegar a; **we got on to the subject of money** empezamos a hablar de dinero

3 (*esp Brit*) (= *contact*) ponerse en contacto con; (= *phone*) llamar; (= *talk to*) hablar con; **I'll ~ on to him about it** (= *remind*) le insistiré, se lo recordaré

4 (= *deal with*) ocuparse de; **I'll ~ on to it right away** ahora mismo lo hago

5 (= *get wise to*) **how did they ~ on to us?** ¿cómo nos descubrieron?; **how did the press ~ on to this?** ¿cómo se ha enterado la prensa de esto?

B VT + PREP **1** (= *make deal with*) poner a trabajar en; **I'll ~ my men on to it right away** pondré a mis hombres a trabajar en esto enseguida; (= *send*) ahora mismo mando a mis hombres

2 (= *cause to talk about*) **we got him on to the subject of drugs** logramos que hablase de las drogas

➤ **get out** **A** VI + ADV **1** (*of room*) salir; (*of country*) marcharse; (*of vehicle*) bajarse, apearse (*frm*); (*of cage, prison*) escaparse (**of** de); **~ out!** ¡fuera de aquí!; **~ out of the way!** ¡apártate!, ¡hazte a un lado!; **to ~ out of bed/one's chair** levantarse de la cama/de la silla

2 (= *be released*) [*prisoner*] salir

3 (= *go out*) salir

4 [*secret*] llegarse a saber; [*news*] hacerse público

B VT + ADV **1** (= *remove, bring out*) [+ *object, person, library book, money from bank*] sacar; [+ *stain*] quitar; **I can't ~ it out of my mind** no me lo puedo quitar de la mente *or* de la cabeza; **it ~s me out of the house** me hace salir de casa

2 (= *send for*) [+ *doctor, plumber, electrician*] llamar

3 (= *pronounce*) **I couldn't ~ the words out** no me salían las palabras

➤ **get out of** VI + PREP [+ *duty, punishment*] librarse de; [+ *difficulty*] salir de; **how are you going to ~ out of this one?** ¿cómo vas a salir de ésta?; **to ~ out of doing sth** librarse de hacer algo; **to ~ out of the habit of doing sth** perder la costumbre de hacer algo; *see also* **get A1**

➤ **get over** **A** VI + PREP **1** (= *cross*) [+ *stream, road*] cruzar, atravesar; [+ *wall, fence*] (= *go over*) pasar por encima de; (= *jump over*) saltar por encima de

2 (= *overcome, recover from*) [+ *problem, serious illness, disappointment*] superar; [+ *cold, virus*] reponerse de; [+ *shock, fright, grief*] sobreponerse a; [+ *shyness*] vencer, dominar; **I can't ~ over how much he's changed** no puedo creer lo mucho que ha cambiado; **she never really got over him** nunca llegó realmente a olvidarlo

B VI + ADV (= *cross sth*) (*stream, road*) cruzar; (*wall, fence*) (= *go over*) pasar por encima; (*climb over*) saltar por encima

C VT + ADV **1** (= *transport across*) [+ *people, objects*] cruzar; (= *lift over*) hacer pasar por encima

2 (= *send*) **I'll ~ the documents over to you tomorrow** te haré llegar los documentos mañana

3 (= *have done with*) acabar de una vez; **let's ~ it over (with)** acabemos de una vez; **I just want to ~ this interview over (with)** lo único que quiero es sacarme de encima esta entrevista

4 (= *communicate*) [+ *idea, message*] transmitir

➤ **get round** VI + PREP, VI + ADV (*Brit*) = **get around**

➤ **get through** **A** VI + PREP **1** (= *pass through*) [+ *window, door, gap*] pasar por; [+ *crowd*] abrirse paso entre

2 (= *finish*) [+ *book, meal*] terminar; **we've got a lot of work to ~ through** tenemos mucho trabajo para hacer

3 (= *survive*) aguantar; **how are they going to ~ through the winter?** ¿cómo van a aguantar el invierno?

4 (*esp Brit*) (= *use up*) [+ *money*] gastar; [+ *food*] comer

5 (*esp Brit*) (= *pass*) [+ *exam*] aprobar, pasar; (*Sport*) [+ *qualifying round*] superar

B VT + ADV **we can't ~ it through the door** no lo podemos pasar por la puerta; **to ~ a bill through parliament** conseguir que una ley se apruebe en el parlamento

C VT + ADV **1** (= *succeed in sending*) [+ *supplies*] conseguir entregar

2 (= *cause to be understood*) **I can't ~ it through to him**

that ... no puedo hacerle entender que ...
D VI + ADV **1** (= *pass*) abrirse paso; (= *arrive*) [*news, supplies etc*] llegar (a su destino)
2 (*Telec*) (lograr) comunicar (**to** con); ✦ IDIOM **to ~ through to sb** hacerse entender por algn
3 (= *pass, succeed*) [*student*] aprobar; (*Sport*) [*team*] pasar
4 (*esp US*) (= *finish*) acabar
➤ **get together A** VT + ADV [+ *people, money, team*] reunir; [+ *objects*] reunir, juntar; [+ *show, concert*] preparar; [+ *thoughts, ideas*] poner en orden; **it won't take me long to ~ my stuff together** no tardaré mucho en recoger mis cosas **B** VI + ADV [*friends, group, club*] reunirse
➤ **get under A** VI + ADV (= *pass underneath*) pasar por debajo **B** VI + PREP **to ~ under a fence/rope** pasar por debajo de una cerca/cuerda **C** VT + ADV hacer pasar por debajo **D** VT + PREP hacer pasar por debajo de; **we couldn't ~ it under the bed** no podíamos meterlo debajo de la cama
➤ **get up A** VI + ADV **1** (= *stand*) levantarse, ponerse de pie; (*from bed*) levantarse; **~ up!** ¡levántate! **2** (= *climb up*) subir **3** [*wind*] (= *start to blow*) levantarse; (= *become fiercer*) empezar a soplar recio; [*sea*] embravecerse **B** VT + ADV **1** (= *raise*) [+ *person*] levantar **2** (= *gather*) [+ *courage*] reunir; **I want to ~ my strength up for this race** quiero ponerme en plena forma (física) para esta carrera, quiero cobrar fuerzas para esta carrera; **to ~ up speed** cobrar velocidad, ganar velocidad
➤ **get up to** VI + PREP **1** (= *reach*) llegar a **2** (*Brit*) (= *do*) hacer; **to ~ up to mischief** hacer travesuras; **what have you been ~ting up to lately?** ¿qué has estado haciendo últimamente?

getaway ['getəweɪ] N **to make one's ~** escaparse ➤ **getaway car the thieves' ~ car** el coche en el que huyeron los ladrones

get-rich-quick* [,get,rɪtʃ'kwɪk] ADJ **~ scheme** plan *m* para hacerse rico pronto, plan *m* para hacer una rápida fortuna

get-together* ['gettə,geðəʳ] N (= *meeting*) reunión *f*; (= *party*) fiesta *f*; **we're having a little ~ on Friday** vamos a reunirnos unos amigos el viernes; **a family ~** una reunión familiar

getup* ['getʌp] N atuendo *m*, traje *m*, atavío *m*

get-up-and-go* [,getʌpənd'gəʊ] N **he's got lots of ~** tiene mucho empuje

get-well card [,get'wel,kɑːd] N tarjeta para un enfermo *deseándole que se mejore*

geyser ['giːzəʳ, (*US*) 'gaɪzəʳ] N (*Geog*) géiser *m*; (= *water heater*) calentador *m* de agua

Ghana ['gɑːnə] N Ghana *f*

Ghanaian [gɑː'neɪən] ADJ, N ghanés/esa *m/f*

ghastly ['gɑːstlɪ] ADJ (*compar* **ghastlier**; *superl* **ghastliest**) **1** (*) (= *very bad*) [*person*] insoportable; [*dress, wallpaper*] horrible; [*situation, experience, mistake, accident*] espantoso, horroroso **2** (= *pale*) pálido, cadavérico

gherkin ['gɜːkɪn] N pepinillo *m*

ghetto ['getəʊ] N gueto *m*

ghetto-blaster ['getəʊ,blɑːstəʳ] N radiocasete *m* portátil (*muy grande*)

ghost [gəʊst] N fantasma *m*, espectro *m*; **he hasn't the ~ of a chance** no tiene la más remota posibilidad; **she managed the ~ of a smile** consiguió esbozar un amago de sonrisa; ✦ IDIOM **to give up the ~** (= *die*) entregar el alma; (*hum*) [*car, washing machine, etc*] pasar a mejor vida ➤ **ghost story** cuento *m* de fantasmas ➤ **ghost town** pueblo *m* fantasma ➤ **ghost train** (*Brit*) tren *m* fantasma

ghostly ['gəʊstlɪ] ADJ fantasmal, espectral

ghostwriter ['gəʊst,raɪtəʳ] N negro/a *m/f*

ghoul [guːl] N demonio *m* necrófago; (= *person*) morboso/a *m/f*

ghoulish ['guːlɪʃ] ADJ [*practice, activity*] macabro; [*person, curiosity*] morboso

GHQ N ABBR (= **General Headquarters**) cuartel *m* general

GI* N ABBR (*US*) (*also* **GI Joe**) soldado *m* (raso) americano

giant ['dʒaɪənt] **A** N **1** (*physically*) gigante/a *m/f* **2** (*fig*) (*in importance, power*) gigante *m*; **Sol, the computer ~** Sol,

líder en ordenadores **B** ADJ [*animal, plant*] gigante; [*portion*] gigantesco, enorme; [*packet*] gigante, familiar; [*strides*] de gigante

giant-killer ['dʒaɪənt,kɪləʳ] N (*esp Brit Sport*) matagigantes *m inv*, equipo que vence a otro muy superior

giant-size(d) ['dʒaɪəntsaɪz(d)] ADJ [*packet*] (de tamaño) gigante

gibber ['dʒɪbəʳ] VI farfullar, hablar atropelladamente; **I must have sounded like a ~ing idiot** debí de sonar como un tonto balbuceando

gibberish ['dʒɪbərɪʃ] N galimatías *m inv*, guirigay *m* (*Sp*)

gibbet ['dʒɪbɪt] N horca *f*

gibbon ['gɪbən] N gibón *m*

gibe [dʒaɪb] **A** N mofa *f*, burla *f* **B** VI mofarse, burlarse (**at** de)

giblets ['dʒɪblɪts] NPL menudillos *mpl*, menudencias *fpl* (*And, Chi*)

Gibraltar [dʒɪ'brɔːltəʳ] N Gibraltar *m*

Gibraltarian [,dʒɪbrɔː'teərɪən] ADJ, N gibraltareño/a *m/f*

giddiness ['gɪdɪnɪs] N vértigo *m*

giddy[1] ['gɪdɪ] ADJ (*compar* **giddier**; *superl* **giddiest**) (= *dizzy*) mareado; [*height, speed*] vertiginoso; **to feel ~** sentirse mareado; **it makes me ~** me marea, me da vértigo

giddy[2] ['gɪdɪ] EXCL **~ up!** (*to horse*) ¡arre!

gift [gɪft] **A** N **1** (= *present*) regalo *m*, obsequio *m* (*frm*); (*Jur*) donación *f*; (*Comm*) (*also* **free ~**) obsequio *m*; ✦ PROV **don't look a ~ horse in the mouth** a caballo regalado no le mires el dentado
2 (= *talent*) don *m*, talento *m*; **he has a ~ for administration** tiene talento para la administración; **to have a ~ for languages** tener mucha facilidad para los idiomas; ✦ IDIOM **to have the ~ of the gab** or (*US*) **~ of gab** tener mucha labia, tener un pico de oro
B CPD ➤ **gift certificate** (*US*) vale-obsequio *m* ➤ **gift coupon** cupón *m* de regalo ➤ **gift shop, gift store** (*US*) tienda *f* de regalos ➤ **gift token** (*Brit*), **gift voucher** (*Brit*) vale-obsequio *m*

gifted ['gɪftɪd] ADJ talentoso, de talento; **she is a very ~ writer** es una escritora de mucho talento; **the ~ child** el niño superdotado

giftwrap ['gɪft,ræp], **giftwrapping** ['gɪft,ræpɪŋ] N papel *m* de regalo

gift-wrap ['gɪft,ræp] VT envolver en papel de regalo

giftwrapped ['gɪft,ræpt] ADJ envuelto para regalo

gig [gɪg] N (*Mus**) actuación *f*, concierto *m*

gigabyte ['dʒɪgə,baɪt] N gigabyte *m*

gigantic [dʒaɪ'gæntɪk] ADJ gigantesco

giggle ['gɪgl] **A** N risita *f*; **she got the ~s** le dio la risa tonta; **they did it for a ~** (*Brit*) lo hicieron para reírse **B** VI reírse tontamente

giggly ['gɪglɪ] ADJ dado a la risa tonta

gigolo ['ʒɪgələʊ] N gigoló *m*

gild [gɪld] VT dorar

gilding ['gɪldɪŋ] N doradura *f*, dorado *m*

gill [gɪl] N [*of fish*] branquia *f*, agalla *f*; ✦ IDIOM **to look green about the ~s** tener mala cara

gilt [gɪlt] **A** N **1** (= *gold*) dorado *m* **2 gilts** (*Brit Fin*) papel *msing* del Estado, valores *mpl* de máxima confianza **B** ADJ dorado

gilt-edged ['gɪlt'edʒd] ADJ **1** (*Brit Fin*) **~ securities** papel *msing* del Estado **2** [*book*] con cantos dorados

gimlet ['gɪmlɪt] N barrena *f* de mano

gimme** ['gɪmɪ] = **give me**

gimmick ['gɪmɪk] N truco *m* publicitario; (= *gadget*) artilugio *m*; **it's just a sales ~** es un truco para vender más

gimmicky ['gɪmɪkɪ] ADJ efectista

gin [dʒɪn] N ginebra *f*; **~ and tonic** gin-tonic *m*

ginger ['dʒɪndʒəʳ] **A** N (= *spice*) jengibre *m* **B** ADJ [*hair*] rojo; [*cat*] de color melado; **to have ~ hair** ser pelirrojo **C** CPD ➤ **ginger ale, ginger beer** gaseosa *f* de jengibre

gingerbread [ˈdʒɪndʒəbred] N pan *m* de jengibre

gingerly [ˈdʒɪndʒəlɪ] ADV con cautela

gingham [ˈgɪŋəm] N guinga *f*

ginseng [ˈdʒɪnseŋ] N ginseng *m*

gipsy [ˈdʒɪpsɪ] ADJ, N = **gypsy**

giraffe [dʒɪˈrɑːf] N jirafa *f*

girder [ˈgɜːdəʳ] N viga *f*

girdle [ˈgɜːdl] N (= *corset*) faja *f*; (= *belt*) cinturón *m*

girl [gɜːl] N chica *f*, muchacha *f*; (= *small*) niña *f*; (= *young woman*) chica *f*, joven *f*; (*) (= *girlfriend*) novia *f*, polola *f* (*Chi*) ➤ **girl guide** (*Brit*), **girl scout** (*US*) exploradora *f*, guía *f*

girlfriend [ˈgɜːlfrend] N [*of girl*] amiga *f*; [*of boy*] novia *f*, compañera *f*, polola *f* (*Chi*)

girlie magazine* [ˈgɜːlɪˌmægəziːn] N revista *f* de desnudos

girlish [ˈgɜːlɪʃ] ADJ de niña; (*pej*) [*man, boy*] afeminado

giro [ˈdʒaɪrəʊ] (*Brit*) N giro *m*; **bank** ~ transferencia *f* bancaria ➤ **giro transfer by** ~ **transfer** mediante giro

girth [gɜːθ] N **1** (*for saddle*) cincha *f* **2** [*of tree*] circunferencia *f*; [*of waist*] contorno *m*

gist [dʒɪst] N [*of speech, conversation*] lo esencial; **to get the** ~ **of sth** captar lo esencial de algo

git** [gɪt] N (*Brit*) cretino/a* *m/f*

give

A TRANSITIVE VERB	**C** NOUN
B INTRANSITIVE VERB	**D** PHRASAL VERBS

When **give** *is part of a set combination, eg* **give evidence**, **give a lurch**, *look up the other word.*

give [gɪv] (*pt* **gave**; *pp* ~**n**)

A TRANSITIVE VERB

1 dar; (*as gift*) regalar, obsequiar (*frm*); [+ *title, award, prize*] dar, otorgar (*frm*); [+ *organ, blood*] dar, donar; (*Scol*) [+ *mark*] poner; **he gave her a dictionary for her birthday** le regaló un diccionario por su cumpleaños

2 (= *pass on*) [+ *message*] dar; [+ *goods, document*] dar, entregar (*more frm*); [+ *illness*] contagiar, pegar*; ~ **them my regards** *or* **best wishes** dales saludos de mi parte; **can you** ~ **Mary the keys when you see her?** ¿puedes darle las llaves a Mary cuando la veas?; **to** ~ **sb a cold** contagiar el resfriado a algn, pegar el resfriado a algn*

3 (= *offer*) [+ *party, dinner*] dar; **what can I** ~ **him to eat/for dinner?** ¿qué puedo hacerle para comer/cenar?

4 (= *provide*) [+ *money, information, idea*] dar; [+ *task*] dar, confiar; **can you** ~ **him something to do?** ¿puedes darle algo para hacer?; **they gave us a lot of help** nos ayudaron mucho; ✦ IDIOM ~ **or take: twelve o'clock,** ~ **or take a few minutes** más o menos las doce; **in A.D. 500** ~ **or take a few years** aproximadamente en el año 500 después de J.C.

5 (= *cause*) [+ *shock, surprise*] dar, causar; [+ *pain*] causar, provocar; **it** ~**s me great pleasure to welcome you all** es un gran placer para mí darles la bienvenida a todos; **I was** ~**n to believe that ...** me hicieron creer que ...; **to** ~ **sb to understand that ...** dar a entender a algn que ...

6 (= *grant, allow*) [+ *permission*] dar, conceder; [+ *chance*] dar; **I can** ~ **you ten minutes** le puedo conceder diez minutos; ~ **yourself an hour to get there** necesitas una hora para llegar; **he's honest, I'll** ~ **you that** es honrado, lo reconozco

7 (*) (*predicting future*) **how long would you** ~ **that marriage?** ¿cuánto tiempo crees que durará ese matrimonio?; **the doctors gave him two years to live** los médicos le dieron dos años de vida

8 (= *dedicate*) [+ *life, time*] dedicar; **he gave his life to helping the needy** dedicó su vida a ayudar a los necesitados; **he gave his life for his country** dio la vida por su país; **he gave it everything he'd got** dio lo mejor de sí

9 (= *pay*) dar; **what will you** ~ **me for it?** ¿qué me das por ello?; ✦ IDIOM **I'd** ~ **anything to know ...** daría cualquier cosa por saber ...

10 (= *put through to*) poner con; **could you** ~ **me Mr Smith/**

extension 3443? ¿me podría poner con el Sr. Smith/con la extensión 3443?

11 (= *punish with*) **the judge gave him five years** el juez le dio cinco años

12 (= *produce*) [+ *milk, fruit*] dar, producir; [+ *light, heat*] dar

13 (= *state*) [+ *name, age, address*] dar; (*on form*) poner

14 to ~ **way** (= *collapse*) [*bridge, floor, ceiling*] ceder, hundirse; [*cable, rope*] romperse; [*legs*] flaquear; **to** ~ **way (to sth)** (= *be replaced*) ser reemplazado (por algo); (*to demands*) ceder (a algo); (*to traffic*) ceder el paso (a algo); **to** ~ **way to an impulse** dejarse llevar por un impulso; **"give way"** (*Brit Aut*) "ceda el paso"; **to** ~ **way to the left** ceder el paso a la izquierda

15 (*in idiomatic expressions*) **I don't** ~ **a damn*** me importa un comino *or* un bledo*; **don't** ~ **me that!** ¡no me vengas con esas!*; **I'll** ~ **you something to cry about!*** ¡ya te daré yo razones para llorar!; **he wants £100? I'll** ~ **him £100!*** ¿que quiere cien libras? ¡ni cien libras ni nada!; **I'll** ~ **him what for!*** ¡se va a enterar!*; ~ **me a gas cooker every time!*** ¡prefiero mil veces una cocina de gas!; ✦ IDIOM **to** ~ **it to sb*** (= *beat*) dar una paliza a algn; (*verbally*) poner a algn como un trapo*

B INTRANSITIVE VERB

1 dar; **please** ~ **generously** por favor, sean generosos; **to** ~ **and take** hacer concesiones mutuas; ✦ IDIOM **to** ~ **as good as one gets** (*esp Brit*) pagar con la misma moneda, devolver golpe por golpe

2 (= *collapse, break*) [*bridge, floor*] ceder, hundirse; [*rope*] romperse; [*door*] ceder; [*knees*] flaquear; **the chair gave under his weight** la silla cedió bajo su peso, la silla no soportó su peso; ✦ IDIOM **something's got to** ~**!** ¡por algún lado tiene que salir!

3 (*US**) **what** ~**s?** ¿qué pasa?, ¿qué se cuece por ahí?*

C NOUN [*of material*] elasticidad *f*; **there's a lot of** ~ **in this rope** esta cuerda da mucho de sí

D PHRASAL VERBS

➤ **give away** VT + ADV **1** (*as gift*) [+ *money, goods*] regalar, obsequiar (*frm*); [+ *prizes*] entregar; [+ *bride*] llevar al altar; (*Sport, fig*) regalar **2** (= *reveal*) [+ *secret*] revelar; (= *betray*) [+ *person*] delatar; **his face gave nothing away** su rostro no delataba nada; **to** ~ **o.s. away** delatarse, descubrirse; ✦ IDIOM **to** ~ **the game away*** descubrir el pastel*

➤ **give back** VT + ADV (= *return*) devolver (**to** a)

➤ **give in A** VT + ADV (= *hand in*) [+ *form, essay*] entregar **B** VI + ADV (= *surrender*) rendirse; (= *yield*) ceder; (= *agree*) consentir; **I** ~ **in!** (*in guessing game*) ¡me rindo!, ¡me doy por vencido!; **to** ~ **in to** [+ *threats, pressure*] ceder *or* sucumbir ante; **she always** ~**s in to him** ella hace siempre lo que él quiere

➤ **give off** VT + ADV [+ *smell, smoke*] despedir; [+ *heat*] emitir

➤ **give out A** VT + ADV **1** (= *distribute*) repartir, distribuir **2** (= *make known*) [+ *news*] anunciar; (= *reveal*) revelar, divulgar **3** (= *emit*) [+ *smoke*] despedir; (*Rad*) [+ *signal*] emitir **B** VI + ADV [*supplies*] agotarse; [*strength, patience*] agotarse, acabarse; [*engine*] pararse; [*heart, legs*] fallar

➤ **give over** VI + ADV (*Brit**) (= *stop*) ~ **over!** ¡basta ya!

➤ **give up A** VT + ADV **1** (= *hand over*) [+ *seat, place*] ceder; [+ *authority*] ceder, traspasar; **to** ~ **o.s. up to the police** entregarse a la policía; **to** ~ **a child up for adoption** entregar a un hijo en adopción **2** (= *renounce*) [+ *habit*] dejar; [+ *job, post*] renunciar a, dejar; [+ *boyfriend*] dejar, romper con; [+ *beliefs, idea*] abandonar; **to** ~ **up smoking** dejar de fumar; **I gave it up as a bad job*** me di por vencido **3** (= *devote*) [+ *one's life, time*] dedicar (**to** a) **4** (= *sacrifice*) [+ *one's life*] entregar (**for** por); [+ *career*] renunciar a (**for** por) **5** (= *abandon hope for*) **we'd** ~ **n you up** creíamos que ya no venías; **they gave him up for dead** lo dieron por muerto **B** VI + ADV (= *stop trying*) rendirse; **I** ~ **up!** (*trying to guess*) ¡me rindo!, ¡me doy por vencido!

➤ **give up on** VI + PREP [+ *idea*] renunciar a; **I'd** ~ **n up on you** creía que ya no venías; **the car gave up on us** nos falló el coche

give-and-take* [ˈgɪvənˈteɪk] N toma y daca *m*, concesiones *fpl* mutuas

giveaway [ˈgɪvəweɪ] **A** N **1** (= *revelation*) revelación *f* involuntaria; **it's a dead** ~ (eso) lo dice todo **2** (= *gift*) regalo *m* **B** CPD ➤ **giveaway prices** precios *mpl* de regalo

given ['gɪvn] **A** PP *of* **give B** ADJ (= *fixed*) [*time, day, amount*] determinado; **on a ~ day** en un día determinado; **at any ~ time** en cualquier momento dado **C** CONJ **~ (that) ...** dado que ...; **~ the circumstances ...** dadas las circunstancias ...; **~ time, it would be possible** con el tiempo, sería posible **D** CPD ➤ **given name** (*esp US*) nombre *m* de pila

giver ['gɪvə'] N donante *mf*, donador(a) *m/f*

gizmo* ['gɪzməʊ] N artilugio *m*, chisme *m*, coso *m* (*LAm*)

glacé ['glæseɪ] ADJ [*fruit*] escarchado

glacial ['gleɪsɪəl] ADJ glacial

glacier ['glæsɪə'] N glaciar *m*

glad [glæd] ADJ (*compar* ~**der**; *superl* ~**dest**) (= *pleased*) **to be** ~ alegrarse; **"I had a great time" — "I'm (so) ~"** —me lo pasé fenomenal —me alegro (mucho); **I'm ~ that you could come** me alegro de que hayas podido venir; **I was ~ to see him** me alegré de verlo; **I am ~ to hear it** me alegra saberlo; **I'll be ~ to answer any questions** estaré encantado de responder a cualquier pregunta; **to be ~ about sth** alegrarse de algo; **I'd be very ~ of your advice** le agradeceré mucho que me aconseje

gladden ['glædn] (*liter*) VT alegrar, llenar de alegría; **to ~ sb's heart** llenar de alegría el corazón de algn, alegrar el corazón a algn

glade [gleɪd] N claro *m*

gladiator ['glædɪeɪtə'] N gladiador *m*

gladiolus [glædɪ'əʊləs] N (*pl* **gladioli** [glædɪ'əʊlaɪ]) gladiolo *m*

gladly ['glædlɪ] ADV con mucho gusto, de buena gana; **"will you help us?" — "gladly"** —¿nos ayudará? —con mucho gusto

glamor ['glæmə'] N (*US*) = **glamour**

glamorous ['glæmərəs] ADJ [*person, dress*] atractivo y sofisticado, glamo(u)roso; [*job*] con mucho glamour, rodeado de gloria *or* grandeza; [*life*] sofisticado; [*place, gathering*] elegante, sofisticado

glamour, glamor (*US*) ['glæmə'] N glamour *m*

glance [glɑːns] **A** VI (*at person*) mirada *f*; (*at object*) vistazo *m*, ojeada *f* (**at** a); **at a ~** de un vistazo; **we exchanged a ~** intercambiamos una mirada; **at first ~** a primera vista; **to take a ~ at sth/sb** echar un vistazo a algo/algn **B** VI (= *look*) mirar; **she ~d in my direction** miró hacia donde yo estaba; **to ~ at** [+ *person*] lanzar una mirada a; [+ *object*] echar un vistazo a, ojear; **to ~ over** *or* **through a report** hojear un informe

glancing ['glɑːnsɪŋ] ADJ [*blow*] oblicuo

gland [glænd] N glándula *f*

glandular ['glændjʊlə'] ADJ glandular ➤ **glandular fever** (*esp Brit*) mononucleosis *f* infecciosa

glare [glɛə'] **A** N 1 [*of light, sun*] luz *f* deslumbradora; (= *dazzle*) deslumbramiento *m*; **in the full ~ of publicity** bajo los focos de la publicidad 2 (= *look*) mirada *f* feroz **B** VI 1 [*light*] deslumbrar 2 (= *look*) **to ~ at sb** lanzar una mirada de odio a algn

glaring ['glɛərɪŋ] ADJ [*sun, light*] deslumbrante, resplandeciente; [*colour*] chillón; [*mistake*] patente, manifiesto

glaringly ['glɛərɪŋlɪ] ADV **to be ~ obvious** estar totalmente claro, saltar a la vista

glass [glɑːs] **A** N 1 (= *material*) vidrio *m*, cristal *m* (*Sp*); **under ~** [*exhibit*] en una vitrina, bajo vidrio; [*plant*] en invernadero
2 (= *tumbler, tumblerful*) vaso *m*; (*for wine, sherry, champagne*) copa *f*; (*for beer*) caña *f*; (*for liqueur, brandy*) copita *f*
3 (= *mirror*) espejo *m*
4 **glasses** (= *spectacles*) gafas *fpl*, lentes *mpl*, anteojos *mpl* (*esp LAm*); (= *binoculars*) gemelos *mpl*
B CPD [*bottle, ornament, eye*] de vidrio *or* (*Sp*) cristal ➤ **glass ceiling** tope *m or* barrera *f* invisible (*que impide ascender profesionalmente a las mujeres o miembros de minorías étnicas*) ➤ **glass door** puerta *f* vidriera *or* (*Sp*) de cristales

glassblower ['glɑːsˌbləʊə'] N soplador *m* de vidrio

glassblowing ['glɑːsˌbləʊɪŋ] N soplado *m* de vidrio

glasscutter ['glɑːsˌkʌtə'] N (= *tool*) cortavidrios *m inv*; (= *person*) cortador(a) *m/f* de vidrio

glassful ['glɑːsfʊl] N vaso *m*; [*of wine, sherry, champagne*] copa *f*

glasshouse ['glɑːshaʊs] N (*esp Brit*) invernadero *m*

glasspaper ['glɑːsˌpeɪpə'] N (*Brit*) papel *m* de vidrio

glassware ['glɑːswɛə'] N cristalería *f*

glassworks ['glɑːswɜːks] N fábrica *f* de vidrio

glassy ['glɑːsɪ] ADJ (*compar* **glassier**; *superl* **glassiest**) [*surface*] liso; [*water*] espejado; [*eye, look*] vidrioso

glaucoma [glɔː'kəʊmə] N glaucoma *m*

glaze [gleɪz] **A** N 1 (*on pottery*) vidriado *m* 2 (*on cake*) glaseado *m* **B** VT 1 [+ *window*] poner vidrios *or* cristales a 2 [+ *pottery*] vidriar 3 (*Culin*) glasear
➤ **glaze over** VI + ADV [*eyes*] ponerse vidrioso

glazed [gleɪzd] ADJ 1 (*Brit*) [*door, window etc*] con vidrio *or* (*Sp*) cristal 2 (*Culin*) glaseado

glazier ['gleɪzɪə'] N vidriero/a *m/f*

gleam [gliːm] **A** N 1 [*of light*] rayo *m*, destello *m*; [*of metal, water*] espejeo *m*; **with a ~ in one's eye** con ojos chispeantes 2 (*fig*) **a ~ of hope** un rayo de esperanza **B** VI [*light*] brillar, lanzar destellos; [*metal, water*] espejear, relucir; [*eyes*] brillar (**with** de)

gleaming ['gliːmɪŋ] ADJ reluciente

glean [gliːn] **A** VT (*Agr*) espigar; **from what I have been able to ~** por lo que yo he conseguido averiguar **B** VI espigar

glee [gliː] N (= *joy*) regocijo *m*, alegría *f*, júbilo *m*

gleeful ['gliːfəl] ADJ [*smile, laugh*] jubiloso, alegre

gleefully ['gliːfəlɪ] ADV con júbilo, con regocijo

glen [glen] N cañada *f*

glib [glɪb] ADJ [*person*] de mucha labia, poco sincero; [*explanation, excuse*] fácil; [*speech*] elocuente pero insincero

glide [glaɪd] VI 1 (= *move smoothly*) deslizarse; **she ~s to the door** se desliza hacia la puerta 2 (*Aer*) planear

glider ['glaɪdə'] N 1 (*Aer*) planeador *m*; (*towed*) avión *m* remolcado 2 (*US*) (= *swing*) columpio *m*

gliding ['glaɪdɪŋ] N (*Aer*) vuelo *m* sin motor, planeo *m*

glimmer ['glɪmə'] **A** N [*of light*] luz *f* trémula; [*of water*] espejeo *m*; **there is a ~ of hope** hay un rayo de esperanza **B** VI [*light*] brillar con luz trémula; [*water*] espejear

glimpse [glɪmps] **A** N vislumbre *f*, destello *m*; **to catch a ~ of** vislumbrar **B** VT vislumbrar

glint [glɪnt] **A** N [*of metal etc*] destello *m*, centelleo *m*; **he had a ~ in his eye** le chispeaban los ojos **B** VI lanzar destellos, centellear

glisten ['glɪsn] VI [*wet surface*] relucir; [*water*] espejear; [*eyes*] brillar; **her eyes ~ed with tears** le brillaban los ojos de las lágrimas

glitch* [glɪtʃ] N fallo *m* técnico (*Sp*), falla *f* técnica (*LAm*)

glitter ['glɪtə'] **A** N [*of gold etc*] brillo *m* **B** VI [*gold etc*] relucir, brillar; ✦ PROV **all that ~s is not gold** no es oro todo lo que reluce

glittering ['glɪtərɪŋ], **glittery** ['glɪtərɪ] ADJ reluciente, brillante (*also fig*)

glitz* [glɪts] N ostentación *f*

glitzy* ['glɪtsɪ] ADJ (*compar* **glitzier**; *superl* **glitziest**) ostentoso

gloat [gləʊt] VI relamerse; **to ~ over** [+ *money*] recrearse contemplando; [+ *victory, good news*] recrearse en; [+ *sb's misfortune*] saborear, regocijarse con

global ['gləʊbl] **A** ADJ 1 (= *worldwide*) mundial; **on a ~ scale** a escala mundial 2 (= *comprehensive*) global; **a ~ view** una visión global **B** CPD ➤ **the global village** la aldea global ➤ **global warming** calentamiento *m* global, calentamiento *m* del planeta

globalization [ˌgləʊbəlaɪˈzeɪʃən] N globalización *f*

globally ['gləʊbəlɪ] ADV (= *worldwide*) mundialmente

globe [gləʊb] N (= *sphere*) globo *m*, esfera *f*; (= *the world*) mundo *m*; (= *spherical map*) esfera *f* terrestre, globo *m* terráqueo

globe-trotter ['gləʊbˌtrɒtə'] N trotamundos *mf inv*

globe-trotting ['gləʊbˌtrɒtɪŋ] N viajar *m* por todo el mundo

globule ['glɒbjuːl] N [*of oil, water*] glóbulo *m*

gloom [gluːm] N **1** (= *darkness*) penumbra *f*, oscuridad *f* **2** (= *sadness*) melancolía *f*, tristeza *f*; **it's not all ~ and doom here** aquí no todo son pronósticos de desastre

gloomily ['gluːmɪlɪ] ADV [*say, look*] con tristeza; [*predict*] con pesimismo

gloomy ['gluːmɪ] ADJ (*compar* **gloomier**; *superl* **gloomiest**) **1** (= *dark*) [*place*] sombrío, lúgubre; [*day, weather*] triste, sombrío **2** (= *sad*) [*atmosphere*] triste, lúgubre; **he's a bit of a ~ character** es un tipo un poco sombrío; **to feel ~** estar bajo de moral, sentirse deprimido **3** (= *pessimistic*) [*person*] pesimista; [*forecast, assessment*] pesimista, nada prometedor; **to be ~ about sth** ser pesimista acerca de algo; **the outlook for next year is ~** las perspectivas para el próximo año no son nada prometedoras; **he paints a very ~ picture** pinta la cosa muy negra

glorify ['glɔːrɪfaɪ] VT (= *exalt*) [+ *God*] alabar; [+ *person*] glorificar; [+ *war, deeds*] embellecer; **it's just a glorified boarding house** es una simple pensión, aunque con pretensiones

glorious ['glɔːrɪəs] ADJ [*career, victory*] glorioso; [*weather, view*] magnífico

gloriously ['glɔːrɪəslɪ] ADV magníficamente; **it was ~ sunny** hacía un sol magnífico; **we were ~ happy** estábamos contentísimos

glory ['glɔːrɪ] Ⓐ N gloria *f* Ⓑ VI **to ~ in** [+ *one's success etc*] enorgullecerse *or* jactarse de; [+ *sb's misfortune*] disfrutar maliciosamente de

gloss¹ [glɒs] Ⓐ N (= *note*) glosa *f* Ⓑ VT glosar, comentar ➤ **gloss over** VI + PREP **1** (= *excuse*) disculpar **2** (= *play down*) paliar, restar importancia a **3** (= *cover up*) [+ *mistake etc*] encubrir

gloss² [glɒs] N **1** (= *shine*) brillo *m*, lustre *m* **2** (*also* ~ **paint**) pintura *f* de esmalte ➤ **gloss finish** (= *paint*) acabado *m* brillante; (*on photo*) brillo *m* satinado

glossary ['glɒsərɪ] N glosario *m*

glossy ['glɒsɪ] ADJ (*compar* **glossier**; *superl* **glossiest**) [*hair*] brillante; [*cloth, paper*] satinado; **~ magazine** revista *f* de moda

glove [glʌv] N guante *m*; ✦ IDIOM **to fit sb like a ~** sentar a algn como anillo al dedo ➤ **glove box**, **glove compartment** (*Aut*) guantera *f* ➤ **glove puppet** títere *m* (de guante)

glow [gləʊ] Ⓐ N [*of lamp, sunset, fire*] brillo *m*, resplandor *m*; [*of cheeks*] rubor *m*; (*in sky*) luz *f* difusa; (= *warm feeling*) sensación *f* de bienestar Ⓑ VI [*lamp, colour, sunset, fire*] brillar, resplandecer; **to ~ with pleasure** estar radiante de felicidad; **to ~ with health** rebosar salud Ⓒ CPD ➤ **glow worm** luciérnaga *f*

glower ['glaʊə'] VI mirar con el ceño fruncido (**at sb** a algn)

glowing ['gləʊɪŋ] ADJ [*light etc*] brillante; [*fire, colour*] vivo; [*complexion, cheeks*] encendido; [*report, description*] entusiasta

glucose ['gluːkəʊs] N glucosa *f*

glue [gluː] Ⓐ N cola *f*, pegamento *m*; (*as drug*) pegamento *m* Ⓑ VT pegar (**to** a); **her face was ~d to the window** tenía la cara pegada a la ventana; **she was ~d to the television** estaba pegada al televisor; **to be ~d to the spot** quedarse clavado Ⓒ CPD ➤ **glue sniffer** esnifador(a) *m/f* de pegamento, persona *f* que inhala *or* esnifa pegamento ➤ **glue sniffing** inhalación *f* de pegamento

glum [glʌm] ADJ (*compar* **~mer**; *superl* **~mest**) [*person*] melancólico; [*mood, expression*] triste; [*tone*] melancólico, sombrío

glut [glʌt] N superabundancia *f*, exceso *m*; **to be a ~ on the market** inundar el mercado

glutinous ['gluːtɪnəs] ADJ glutinoso

glutton ['glʌtn] N glotón/ona *m/f*, comilón/ona* *m/f*; **~ for work** trabajador(a) *m/f* incansable; **~ for punishment** masoquista *mf*

gluttonous ['glʌtənəs] ADJ glotón, goloso

gluttony ['glʌtənɪ] N glotonería *f*, gula *f*

glycerin(e) ['glɪsə'riːn] N glicerina *f*

GM ADJ ABBR (*esp Brit*) = **genetically-modified**; **GM foods** alimentos *mpl* transgénicos

GMO N ABBR (= **genetically modified organism**) OGM *m*, organismo *m* transgénico

GMT N ABBR (= **Greenwich Mean Time**) hora *f* media de Greenwich

gnarled [nɑːld] ADJ [*wood, hands*] nudoso

gnash [næʃ] VT **to ~ one's teeth** rechinar los dientes

gnat [næt] N mosquito *m*, jején *m* (*LAm*)

gnaw [nɔː] Ⓐ VT roer, carcomer; **~ed by doubts/hunger** atormentado por las dudas/el hambre Ⓑ VI roer; **to ~ through** roer; **to ~ at** (*lit, fig*) roer

gnawing ['nɔːɪŋ] ADJ [*remorse, anxiety etc*] corrosivo; [*hunger*] con retortijones; [*pain*] punzante

gnome [nəʊm] N gnomo *m*

GNP N ABBR (= **gross national product**) PNB *m*

GNVQ N ABBR (*Brit Scol*) (= **General National Vocational Qualification**) *diploma nacional de formación profesional*

go

Ⓐ INTRANSITIVE VERB	Ⓓ NOUN
Ⓑ TRANSITIVE VERB	Ⓔ PHRASAL VERBS
Ⓒ MODAL VERB	

When **go** *is part of a set combination such as* **go cheap**, **go far**, **go down the tube**, *look up the other word.*

go [gəʊ] (*vb*: *pt* **went**; *pp* **gone**)
Ⓐ INTRANSITIVE VERB
1 (= *move, travel*) ir; **she was going too fast** iba demasiado rápido; **I'll go and see** (*Brit*) ◇ **I'll go see** (*US*) voy a ver; **I'll go and fetch it for you** (*Brit*) ◇ **I'll go fetch it for you** (*US*) te lo voy a buscar; **now you've gone and done it!*** ¡ahora sí que la has hecho buena!; **to go at 30 mph** ir a 30 millas por hora; **to go by car/bicycle** ir en coche/bicicleta; **the train goes from London to Glasgow** el tren va de Londres a Glasgow; **to go home** irse a casa; **to go on a journey** ir de viaje; **to go to a party** ir a una fiesta; **to go to the doctor('s)** ir al médico; **to go to sb for advice** consultar a algn; **where do we go from here?** ¿qué hacemos ahora?
2 (= *depart*) [*person*] irse, marcharse; [*train, coach*] salir; **I'm going now** me voy ya, me marcho ya; **"food to go"** (*esp US*) "comida para llevar"
3 (*euph*) (= *die*) irse; **after I've gone** cuando yo me haya ido
4 (= *disappear*) [*object*] desaparecer; [*money*] gastarse; [*time*] pasar; **the cake is all gone** se ha acabado todo el pastel; **gone are the days when ...** ya pasaron los días cuando ...; **that sideboard will have to go** tendremos que deshacernos de ese aparador; **he'll have to go** [*employee*] habrá que despedirlo; **military service must go!** ¡fuera con el servicio militar!; **there goes my chance of promotion!** ¡adiós a mi ascenso!; **only two days to go** sólo faltan dos días; **eight down and two to go** ocho hechos y dos por hacer
5 (= *be sold*) venderse (**for** por, en); **it's going cheap** se vende barato; **going, going, gone!** (*at auction*) ¡a la una, a las dos, a las tres!
6 (= *extend*) extenderse, llegar; **the garden goes down to the lake** el jardín se extiende *or* llega hasta el lago; **money doesn't go far nowadays** hoy día el dinero apenas da para nada
7 (= *function*) [*machine*] funcionar; **I couldn't get the car to go at all** no podía arrancar el coche; **the washing machine was going** la lavadora estaba en marcha; **to make sth go** ◇ **get sth going** poner algo en marcha
8 (= *endure*) aguantar; **to go hungry/thirsty** pasar hambre/sed

9 (*with activities, hobbies*) **to go fishing/riding/swimming** ir a pescar/montar a caballo/nadar; **to go for a walk** dar un paseo; **to go for a swim** ir a nadar *or* a bañarse
10 (= *progress*) ir; **the meeting went well** la reunión fue bien; **how did the exam go?** ¿cómo te fue en el examen?; **how's it going?**** ◇ **what goes?** (*US**) ¿qué tal?*, ¿qué tal va?*, ¡qué hubo! (*Mex, Chi**); **we'll see how things go*** veremos cómo van las cosas; **the day went slowly** el día pasó lentamente
11 (= *match, combine with*) [*colours, clothes*] hacer juego, pegar* (**with** con); **mustard and lamb don't go** la mostaza no va bien con el cordero, la mostaza no le pega al cordero*; **cava goes well with anything** el cava va bien *or* combina con todo
12 (= *become*)

> For phrases with **go** and an adjective, such as **to go bad**, **go soft**, you should look under the adjective.

it's just gone seven (*Brit*) acaban de dar las siete; **to go red/green** ponerse rojo/verde; **don't go all sentimental/shy on me!** ¡no te me pongas sentimental/tímido!*, ¡no te hagas el sentimental/tímido conmigo!
13 (= *fit*) caber; **it won't go in the case** no cabe en la maleta; **four into three won't go** tres entre cuatro no cabe; **four into 12 goes three times** 12 (dividido) entre cuatro son tres
14 (= *be accepted*) valer; **anything goes*** todo vale; **that goes for me too** (= *applies to me*) por mí también va; (= *I agree*) yo también estoy de acuerdo
15 (= *fail*) [*material*] desgastarse; [*chair, branch*] romperse; [*elastic*] ceder; [*fuse, light bulb*] fundirse; [*strength*] fallar; **his hearing/mind is going** está perdiendo el oído/la cabeza; **my voice has gone** me he quedado afónico
16 (= *be kept*) ir; **where does this book go?** ¿dónde va este libro?
17 (= *be available*) **there are several jobs going** se ofrecen varios puestos; **is there any tea going?** (= *is there any left?*) ¿queda té?; (= *will you get me one?*) ¿me haces un té?; **I'll take whatever is going** acepto lo que sea
18 (= *get underway*) **whose turn is it to go?** (*in game*) ¿a quién le toca?, ¿quién va ahora?; **go!** (*Sport*) ¡ya!;
◆ IDIOMS **from the word go*** desde el principio; **there you go again!** ¡otra vez con lo mismo!*
19 (= *be destined*) [*inheritance*] pasar; [*fund*] destinarse; **all his money goes on drink** se le va todo el dinero en alcohol; **the prize went to Fiona Lilly** el premio fue para Fiona Lilly; **the qualities which go to make him a great writer** las cualidades que lo hacen un gran escritor; **the money will go towards the holiday** el dinero será para las vacaciones
20 (= *sound*) [*doorbell, phone*] sonar
21 (= *run*) **how does that song go?** (*tune*) ¿cómo es esa canción?; (*words*) ¿cómo es la letra de esa canción?; **the story does that ...** según dicen ...
22 (= *do*) hacer; **go like that (with your right hand)** haz así (con la mano derecha)
23 (*) (= *go to the toilet*) ir al baño
24 (*in set expressions*) **he's not bad, as estate agents go** no es un mal agente inmobiliario, dentro de lo que cabe; **let's get going!** (= *be on our way*) ¡vamos!, ¡vámonos!, ¡ándale! (*Mex*); (= *start sth*) ¡manos a la obra!, ¡adelante!; **to get going on** *or* **with sth** ponerse con algo; **once he gets going ...** una vez que se pone ..., una vez que empieza ...; **to keep going** (= *moving forward*) seguir; (= *enduring*) resistir, aguantar; (= *functioning*) seguir funcionando; **a cup of coffee is enough to keep him going all morning** una taza de café le basta para funcionar toda la mañana; **to let sb go** (= *release*) soltar a algn; (*euph*) (= *make redundant*) despedir a algn; **let (me) go!** ¡suéltame!; **we'll let it go at that** por esta vez pase; **you're wrong, but we'll let it go** no llevas razón, pero vamos a dejarlo así; **to let o.s. go** (*physically*) dejarse, descuidarse; (= *have fun*) soltarse el pelo*; **to let go of sth/sb** soltar algo/a algn
B TRANSITIVE VERB
1 (= *travel*) **which route does the number 29 go?** ¿qué itinerario hace el 29?; **which way are you going?** ¿por dónde vais a ir?, ¿qué camino vais a tomar?; **he went his way** siguió su camino; **we had only gone a few kilometres**

when ... sólo llevábamos unos kilómetros cuando ...
2 (= *make*) hacer; **the car went "bang!"** el coche hizo "bang"
3 (*) (= *say*) soltar*; **shut up! he goes** —¡cállate! —suelta
4 (*) ◆ IDIOMS **to go one better** ganar el remate; **to go it alone** obrar por su cuenta
C MODAL VERB ir; **I'm going/I was going to do it** voy/iba a hacerlo; **it's going to rain** va a llover; **there's going to be a storm** va a haber una tormenta
◆ **to go doing sth**: **don't go getting upset*** venga, no te enfades; **to go looking for sth/sb** ir a buscar algo/a algn
D NOUN (*pl* **goes**) **1** (= *turn*) **whose go is it?** ¿a quién le toca?; **it's your go** te toca a ti
2 (= *attempt*) intento *m*; **to have a go (at doing sth)** probar (a hacer algo); **shall I have a go?** ¿pruebo yo?, ¿lo intento yo?; **to have another go** probar otra vez, intentarlo otra vez; **at** *or* **in one go** de un (solo) golpe
3 (*) (= *success*) **to make a go of sth** tener éxito en algo
4 (*in expressions*) ◆ IDIOMS **it's all go** aquí no se para nunca; **to have a go at sb** (*esp Brit**) (*verbally*) tomarla con algn*; (*physically*) atacar a algn; **it's no go** es inútil; **he's always on the go** nunca para; **I've got two projects on the go** tengo dos proyectos en marcha
E PHRASAL VERBS
➤ **go about** **A** VI + PREP **1** (= *set to work on*) [+ *task*] emprender; [+ *problem*] abordar; **how does one go about joining?** ¿qué hay que hacer para hacerse socio?; **he knows how to go about it** sabe lo que hay que hacer, sabe cómo hacerlo **2** (= *busy o.s. with*) **to go about one's business** ocuparse de sus cosas **B** VI + ADV [*news, rumour*] correr, circular; [*virus*] rodar; **to go about barefoot** ir descalzo
➤ **go across** **A** VI + PREP [+ *river, road*] cruzar, atravesar **B** VI + ADV (= *cross*) cruzar
➤ **go after** VI + PREP (= *follow*) seguir; [+ *criminal*] perseguir; [+ *job, record*] andar tras
➤ **go against** VI + PREP **1** (= *be unfavourable to*) [*result, events, evidence*] ir en contra de; **the decision went against him** la decisión iba en contra de él **2** [+ *principles, conscience*] ser contrario a; [+ *sb's wishes*] actuar en contra de
➤ **go ahead** VI + ADV (= *carry on*) seguir adelante (**with** con); **the exhibition will go ahead as planned** la exposición seguirá adelante tal y como estaba planeado; **go (right) ahead!** ¡adelante!
➤ **go along** VI + ADV ir; **Ann's having a party, shall we go along?** Ann da una fiesta, ¿vamos?; **I'll tell you as we go along** te lo diré de camino; **check as you go along** ve corrigiendo sobre la marcha; **I'm learning as I go along** voy aprendiendo poco a poco; **things are going along nicely*** las cosas marchan bien; **to go along with** (= *accompany*) acompañar; (= *agree with*) estar de acuerdo con
➤ **go around** **A** VI + ADV **1** (= *revolve*) girar, dar vueltas; **the idea was going around in my head** la idea me daba vueltas en la cabeza; **my head is going around** la cabeza me da vueltas
2 (= *circulate*) **he goes around in a Rolls** se pasea por ahí en un Rolls; **to go around barefoot** andar descalzo; **people who go around spreading rumours** la gente que va por ahí esparciendo rumores; **there's a bug going around** hay un virus por ahí rondando; **there's a rumour going around that ...** corre *or* circula el rumor de que ...; **he often goes around with Jimmy** se le ve a menudo con Jimmy
3 (= *suffice*) alcanzar, bastar; **is there enough food to go around?** ¿hay comida suficiente para todos?
4 (= *visit*) **let's go around to John's place** vamos a casa de John
5 (= *make a detour*) dar la vuelta
B VI + PREP **1** (= *spin round*) girar alrededor de; **the Earth goes around the sun** la Tierra gira alrededor del sol
2 (= *visit*) [+ *museum*] visitar; **I love going around the shops** me encanta ir de tiendas; **to go around the world** dar la vuelta al mundo
3 (= *patrol*) [+ *grounds*] patrullar (por), recorrer
4 (= *make a detour around*) [+ *obstacle*] dar la vuelta a
➤ **go at*** VI + PREP (= *attack*) atacar, arremeter contra
➤ **go away** VI + ADV [*pain, problem*] desaparecer; [*person*] (= *depart*) irse, marcharse; (*on holiday*) irse de vacaciones; **go away!** ¡vete!, ¡lárgate!*; **we need to go away and think about this** ahora debemos pensárnoslo un poco
➤ **go back** VI + ADV **1** (= *return*) volver, regresar (**to** a); **to go**

back **home** volver or regresar a casa; **when do the schools go back?** ¿cuándo empieza el colegio?; **to go back to work** volver al trabajo; **he's gone back to his wife** ha vuelto con su mujer; **to go back to the beginning** volver al principio
2 (= retreat) volverse atrás; **there's no going back now** ya no podemos volvernos atrás
3 (= extend) extenderse; **the cave goes back 300 metres** la cueva tiene 300 metros de fondo, la cueva tiene una extensión de 300 metros
4 (= date back) remontarse; **we go back a long way** nos conocemos desde hace mucho; **my memories don't go back so far** mis recuerdos no se remontan tan lejos; **it goes back to Elizabeth I/1929** se remonta a Isabel I/1929
5 (= change) **the clocks go back on Sunday** los relojes se atrasan el domingo
➤ go back on VI + PREP [+ decision] volverse atrás en; [+ promise] incumplir; **to go back on one's word** faltar a su palabra
➤ go back to VI + PREP (= revert to) volver a; **go back to sleep!** ¡vuelve a dormir!
➤ go before Ⓐ VI + ADV (= precede) preceder; **all that has gone before** todo lo que ha pasado antes Ⓑ VI + PREP **the matter has gone before a grand jury** el asunto se ha sometido a un gran jurado
➤ go by Ⓐ VI + PREP 1 (= drop by) pasarse por 2 (= be guided by) [+ watch, compass] guiarse por; **to go by appearances** guiarse por las apariencias; **you can't go by what he says** no puedes fiarte de lo que dice Ⓑ VI + ADV [opportunity] pasar; [time] pasar, transcurrir; [person, car] pasar (cerca); **in days gone by** en tiempos pasados, antaño; **as time goes by** con el tiempo, con el transcurso del tiempo
➤ go down VI + ADV 1 (= descend) [sun] ponerse; [person] bajar; **to go down to the coast** bajar a la costa
2 (= fall) [person, horse] caerse; (= crash) [plane] estrellarse, caer; (= sink) [ship, person] hundirse
3 (= decrease, decline) [price, temperature] bajar, descender; [tide, flood, water level] bajar; **the house has gone down in value** la casa ha perdido valor or se ha devaluado
4 (= deflate) [balloon, airbed] desinflarse, deshincharse (Sp); **the swelling has gone down** me ha bajado la hinchazón
5 (= be defeated) perder
6 (Comput) (= break down) bloquearse, dejar de funcionar
7 (= be remembered) **to go down in history** pasar a la historia
8 (= be swallowed) **that omelette went down a treat*** esa tortilla estaba riquísima; **it went down the wrong way** se me atragantó
9 (= be accepted) **to go down well/badly** ser bien/mal recibido; **I wonder how that will go down with her parents** me pregunto cómo les sentará eso a sus padres
10 (Theat) [curtain] bajar; [lights] apagarse
➤ go down as VI + PREP (= be regarded as) considerarse; (= be remembered as) pasar a la historia como; **he will go down in history as ...** pasará a la historia como ...
➤ go down with* VI + PREP [+ illness, virus, food poisoning] pillar*, coger, agarrar (LAm)
➤ go for VI + PREP 1 (physically, verbally) atacar 2 (*) (= like) **I don't go for his films very much** no me gustan mucho sus películas 3 (= strive for) dedicarse a obtener; **go for it!*** ¡a por ello!, ¡adelante!; **I decided to go for it*** decidí intentarlo 4 (= choose) escoger, optar por; **I'll go for the cream caramel** para mí flan 5 ✦ IDIOM **to have a lot going for one: he has a lot going for him** tiene mucho a su favor; **the theory has a lot going for it** la teoría cuenta con muchas ventajas
➤ go forward VI + ADV 1 [person, vehicle] avanzar; **when do the clocks go forward?** ¿cuándo se adelantan los relojes?
2 (= proceed) seguir adelante (**with** con)
➤ go in VI + ADV 1 (= enter) entrar; **please do go in** pase, por favor 2 (= attack) atacar 3 (= fit) caber 4 (Brit) [sun] ocultarse
➤ go in for VI + PREP 1 (= enter for) [+ race, competition, examination] presentarse a 2 (= take as career) dedicarse a
3 (= be interested in) [+ hobby, sport] interesarse por 4 (= use) utilizar
➤ go into VI + PREP 1 (= enter) (lit) entrar en; **to go into politics** entrar en la política, dedicarse a la política; **he's had to go into hospital** ha tenido que ingresar en el hospital
2 (= embark on) [+ explanation, details] meterse en;

(= investigate, examine) examinar a fondo; **let's not go into all that now** dejemos todo eso por ahora
3 (= fall into) [+ trance, coma] entrar en
4 (= be spent on) dedicarse a; **a lot of money went into the research** se dedicó mucho dinero a la investigación
5 (Aut) **to go into first gear** meter primera velocidad or (la) primera; **they went into the back of a lorry** chocaron contra la parte trasera de un camión
➤ go off Ⓐ VI + ADV 1 (= leave) marcharse, irse; **he's gone off with my keys** se ha marchado or ido con mis llaves, se ha llevado mis llaves
2 (= stop) [TV, light, heating] apagarse; [pain] irse, pasarse
3 (= be activated) [bomb] estallar; [gun] dispararse; [alarm clock] sonar
4 (Brit) (= go bad) [food] echarse a perder; [milk] pasarse, echarse a perder
5 (= pass off) salir; **the party went off well** la fiesta salió bien Ⓑ VI + PREP (Brit) (= no longer like) [+ thing] perder el gusto por; [+ person] dejar de querer a; **I've gone off the idea** ya no me gusta la idea
➤ go on Ⓐ VI + PREP 1 (= be guided by) [+ evidence] basarse en; **there's nothing to go on** no hay nada en que basarse; **the police had no clues to go on** la policía no tenía pistas que le sirvieran de guía
2 (= continue) **to go on doing sth** seguir haciendo algo, continuar haciendo algo
3 (*) (= approach) **she's going on 50** anda cerca de la cincuentena, va para los cincuenta
4 (= be spent on) **most of their money goes on drink** la mayor parte del dinero se les va en bebida Ⓑ VI + ADV 1 (= fit) **the lid won't go on** la tapa no le va; **these shoes won't go on** no me entran estos zapatos
2 (= continue) [war, talks] seguir, continuar; [person] (on journey) seguir el camino; **everything is going on normally** todo sigue con normalidad; **"so," he went on ...** —así es que —continuó; **go on!** (= continue) sigue, continúa; (giving encouragement) ¡venga!; **go on with your work** sigue con tu trabajo; **that'll do to be going on with*** con eso basta por ahora; **I've got enough to be going on with** tengo suficiente por el momento; ✦ IDIOM **go on with you!*** (showing incredulity) ¡no digas bobadas!*, ¡anda ya!*, ¡venga ya!*
3 (= last) durar; **the concert went on until 11 o'clock at night** el concierto duró hasta las 11 de la noche
4 (= proceed) **to go on to do sth** pasar a hacer algo; **after having taught herself Italian, she went on to learn Arabic** después de haber aprendido italiano por su cuenta, empezó a estudiar árabe; **he went on to say that ...** añadió que ...
5 (*) (= talk) **he does go on so** habla más que siete*, no para de hablar; **to go on about sth** no parar de hablar de algo, dar la tabarra or la matraca con algo*; **he's always going on about the government** (= criticize) siempre está echando pestes contra el gobierno*
6 (Brit*) (= nag) **to go on at sb** dar la lata a algn* (about con)
7 (= happen) pasar, ocurrir; **there's something odd going on** aquí hay gato encerrado; **what's going on here?** ¿qué pasa or ocurre aquí?
8 (= pass, go by) [time, years] pasar, transcurrir
9 (= come on) [lights, machine] encenderse, prenderse (LAm)
10 (*) (= behave) **what a way to go on!** (pej) ¡qué manera de comportarse!
➤ go on for VI + PREP (with numbers) **he's going on for 60** anda por or cerca de los 60; **it's going on for two o'clock** son casi las dos, van a ser las dos; **it's going on for 50km to Vilafranca** Vilafranca está a unos 50km de aquí
➤ go out VI + ADV 1 (= be extinguished, switch off) [fire, light] apagarse; ✦ IDIOM **to go out like a light** dormirse enseguida, quedarse frito enseguida*
2 (= exit) salir; **to go out of a room** salir de un cuarto; **to go out shopping** salir de compras or de tiendas; **to go out for a meal** salir a comer/cenar (fuera); **she goes out to work** trabaja (fuera); **to go out of fashion** pasar de moda
3 (romantically) **how long have you been going out together?** ¿cuánto tiempo hace que salís juntos?; **to go out with sb** salir con algn
4 (= ebb) [tide] bajar, menguar
5 (Brit) (= travel) viajar (**to** a); (for long stay) marcharse (**to** a)

6 (= *be issued*) [*pamphlet, circular*] salir, publicarse; [*invitation*] mandarse; (= *be broadcast*) [*radio programme, TV programme*] emitirse; **an appeal has gone out for people to give blood** se ha hecho un llamamiento a la población para que done sangre
7 (*Sport*) (= *be eliminated*) quedar eliminado
8 (*commiserating*) **my heart** went out to him le compadecí mucho, sentí mucha pena por él; **all our sympathy goes out to you** te damos nuestro más sentido pésame, te acompañamos en el sentimiento
➤ **go over** Ⓐ VI + PREP **1** (= *examine, check*) [+ *report, figures*] examinar, revisar
2 (= *rehearse, review*) [+ *speech, lesson*] repasar, revisar; **to go over sth in one's mind** repasar algo mentalmente
3 (= *touch up*) retocar
4 (= *pass over*) [+ *wall*] pasar por encima de
Ⓑ VI + ADV **1 to go over to** (= *cross over to*) cruzar a; (*changing habit, sides etc*) pasarse a; (= *approach*) acercarse a, dirigirse a
2 (= *be received*) recibirse; **how did it go over?** ¿qué tal fue recibido *or* se recibió?; **his speech went over well** su discurso tuvo buena acogida
➤ **go past** VI + PREP, VI + ADV pasar
➤ **go round** VI + ADV, VI + PREP (*Brit*) = **go around**
➤ **go through** Ⓐ VI + PREP **1** (= *pass through*) pasar por; (= *cross*) atravesar
2 (= *suffer*) pasar por; (= *bear*) aguantar; **I know what you're going through** sé por lo que estás pasando
3 (= *examine*) [+ *list, book*] repasar; [+ *pile, possessions, pockets*] registrar
4 (= *use up*) [+ *money*] gastar; [+ *food*] comerse; [+ *drink*] beberse; (= *wear out*) [+ *garment*] gastar
5 (= *perform*) [+ *formalities*] cumplimentar; [+ *ceremony*] realizar
Ⓑ VI + ADV **1** (*lit*) pasar; **let's go through to the other room** vamos a pasar a la otra sala
2 [*proposal, bill, motion*] ser aprobado, aprobarse; [*deal*] concluirse, hacerse; **it all went through all right** todo se llevó a cabo sin problemas
➤ **go through with** VI + PREP [+ *plan, crime*] llevar a cabo; **I can't go through with it!** ¡no puedo seguir con esto!
➤ **go together** VI + ADV [*colours*] hacer juego; [*ideas*] complementarse; [*events, conditions*] ir de la mano
➤ **go under** VI + ADV **1** (= *sink*) [*ship, person*] hundirse
2 (= *fail*) [*business, firm*] quebrar
➤ **go up** VI + ADV **1** (= *rise*) [*temperature, price*] subir
2 (= *travel*) **to go up to London** ir a Londres **3** (= *approach*) **to go up to sb** acercarse a algn, abordar a algn **4** (= *go upstairs*) subir (*a la planta de arriba*) **5** (= *be built*) [*tower block, building*] levantarse **6** (= *explode*) estallar; **to go up in flames** arder en llamas, ser pasto de las llamas **7** (*Theat*) [*curtain*] subir, abrirse, levantarse
➤ **go with** VI + PREP (= *accompany*) ir con, acompañar a; **the house goes with the job** la casa va con el trabajo
➤ **go without** Ⓐ VI + PREP pasar sin, prescindir de Ⓑ VI + ADV **you'll have to go without** tendrás que arreglártelas *or* pasar sin ello
goad [gəʊd] VT (= *taunt*) provocar con insultos; **to ~ sb into doing sth/to do sth** incitar a algn a hacer algo
go-ahead ['gəʊəhed] Ⓐ ADJ (*esp Brit*) emprendedor Ⓑ N **to give sth/sb the** ~ autorizar algo/a algn
goal [gəʊl] Ⓐ N **1** (*Sport*) (= *score*) gol *m*; (= *net etc*) portería *f*, meta *f*, arco *m* (*LAm*); **to play in** ~ ser portero *or* (*LAm*) arquero; **to score a** ~ marcar un gol; **they won by two ~s to one** ganaron por dos goles a uno
2 (= *aim*) (*in life*) meta *f*, objetivo *m*; (*in journey*) fin *m*; **to reach one's** ~ llegar a la meta, realizar una ambición
Ⓑ CPD ➤ **goal area** área *f* de portería, área *f* de meta

Use **el/un** not **la/una** before feminine nouns beginning with stressed **a** or **ha** like **área**.

➤ **goal average** (*Brit*) promedio *m* de goles, golaverage *m*
➤ **goal kick** saque *m* de puerta ➤ **goal line** línea *f* de portería
goalie* ['gəʊlɪ] N = **goalkeeper**
goalkeeper ['gəʊl,ki:pə'] N portero/a *m/f*, guardameta *mf*,

arquero/a *m/f* (*LAm*)
goalless ['gəʊllɪs] ADJ sin goles, con empate a cero; **a ~ draw** un empate a cero (goles)
goalpost ['gəʊlpəʊst] N poste *m* (de la portería);
✦ IDIOM **to move the ~s** cambiar las reglas del juego
goalscorer ['gəʊl,skɔ:rə'] N goleador(a) *m/f*
goat [gəʊt] N (*gen*) cabra *f*; (*male*) chivo *m*, macho cabrío *m*; ✦ IDIOM **to get sb's ~*** fastidiar *or* molestar a algn ➤ **goat cheese, goat's cheese** queso *m* de cabra
goatee [gəʊ'ti:] N (*short*) perilla *f*; (*long*) barba *f* de chivo
goatherd ['gəʊthɜ:d] N cabrero *m*
gob** [gɒb] N (*Brit*) (= *mouth*) bocaza* *f*
gobbet* ['gɒbɪt] N [*of food etc*] trocito *m*, pequeña porción *f*; **~s of information** pequeños elementos *mpl* de información
gobble ['gɒbl] Ⓐ N gluglú *m* Ⓑ VT (*also ~ up*) engullir, tragar Ⓒ VI [*turkey*] gluglutear
gobbledegook*, **gobbledygook*** ['gɒbldɪgu:k] N jerigonza *f*, galimatías *m inv*
go-between ['gəʊbɪ,twi:n] N intermediario/a *m/f*
goblet ['gɒblɪt] N copa *f*
goblin ['gɒblɪn] N duende *m*, trasgo *m*
gobsmacked** ['gɒbsmækt] ADJ (*Brit*) **I was** ~ me quedé alucinado*
go-cart ['gəʊkɑ:t] N kart *m*
god [gɒd] N **1** dios *m*; **God** Dios *m*; **(my) God!** ✧ **good God!*** ¡Dios mío!, ¡santo Dios!; **God forbid!** ¡Dios me libre!; **he thinks he's God's gift to women*** se cree que lo creó Dios para ser la felicidad de las mujeres; **God help them if that's what they think** que Dios les ayude si piensan así; **I hope to** ~ **she'll be happy** Dios quiera que sea feliz; **God (only) knows** sólo Dios sabe, sabe Dios; **what in God's name is he doing?** ¿qué demonios está haciendo?; **for God's sake!** ¡por Dios!; **thank God!** ¡gracias a Dios!; **God willing** si Dios quiere, Dios mediante; ✦ PROV **God helps those who help themselves** a quien madruga Dios le ayuda
2 (*Brit*) **the ~s** (*Theat*) el gallinero, el paraíso
godchild ['gɒdtʃaɪld] N (*pl* **~ren**) ahijado/a *m/f*
goddam(n)** ['gɒd'dæm] (*US*) Ⓐ ADJ (*also* **goddamn(ed)**) maldito, puñetero (*Sp**) Ⓑ EXCL (*also* **goddammit**) ¡maldición!
goddaughter ['gɒd,dɔ:tə'] N ahijada *f*
goddess ['gɒdɪs] N diosa *f*
godfather ['gɒd,fɑ:ðə'] N padrino *m* (**to** de)
god-fearing ['gɒd,fɪərɪŋ] ADJ temeroso de Dios
godforsaken* ['gɒdfə,seɪkn] ADJ [*place*] olvidado de Dios; [*person*] dejado de la mano de Dios
godless ['gɒdlɪs] ADJ **1** (= *wicked*) [*life*] pecaminoso
2 (= *unbelieving*) ateo
godlike ['gɒdlaɪk] ADJ divino
godly ['gɒdlɪ] ADJ (*compar* **godlier**; *superl* **godliest**) devoto
godmother ['gɒd,mʌðə'] N madrina *f* (**to** de)
godparents ['gɒd,peərənts] NPL padrinos *mpl* (**to** de)
godsend ['gɒdsend] N don *m* del cielo; **it was a ~ to us** nos llegó en buena hora
godson ['gɒdsʌn] N ahijado *m*
goes [gəʊz] 3RD PERS PRESENT SING *of* **go**
gofer ['gəʊfə'] N recadero/a *m/f*
go-getter* ['gəʊgetə'] N ambicioso/a *m/f*
goggle ['gɒgl] VI **to ~ at** mirar con ojos desorbitados, mirar sin comprender
goggles ['gɒglz] NPL [*of diver*] gafas *fpl* de submarinismo; [*of driver*] anteojos *mpl*
go-go ['gəʊgəʊ] ADJ [*dancer, dancing*] gogó
going ['gəʊɪŋ] Ⓐ N **1** (= *departure*) salida *f*, partida *f*
2 (= *progress*) **it was slow ~** se avanzaba a paso lento; **the climb was hard** ~ la subida fue muy dura; **that was good** ~ eso fue muy rápido; **it's heavy** ~ **talking to her** es pesado hablar con ella; **we made money while the** ~ **was good**

cuando todo iba bien ganábamos dinero
3 (= *state of surface*) estado *m* del camino; (*Horse racing*) estado *m* de la pista
Ⓑ ADJ **1** (= *thriving*) [*business, concern*] establecido
2 (= *current*) [*price, rate*] corriente
3 (*) (= *available*) **the best one** = el mejor que hay
Ⓒ CPD ➤ **going concern** negocio *m* en marcha

going-over ['gəʊɪŋ'əʊvə'] N (*pl* **goings-over**) **1** (= *check*) inspección *f*; **we gave the car a thorough ~** revisamos el coche de arriba a abajo; **we gave the house a thorough ~** (= *search*) registramos la casa de arriba abajo; (= *clean*) le hicimos una limpieza profunda a la casa **2** (*Brit**) (*fig*) (= *beating*) paliza *f*; **they gave him a ~** le dieron una paliza

goings-on* ['gəʊɪŋz'ɒn] NPL tejemanejes *mpl*

goitre, goiter (*US*) ['gɔɪtə'] N bocio *m*

go-kart ['gəʊkɑːt] N (*Brit*) kart *m*

go-karting ['gəʊkɑːtɪŋ] N karting *m*

Golan Heights ['gəʊlæn'haɪts] NPL **the ~** los Altos del Golán

gold [gəʊld] **Ⓐ** N (= *metal, commodity, currency*) oro *m*; **autumnal browns and ~s** los marrones y dorados del otoño; **he won (the) ~ in Barcelona** ganó la medalla de oro en Barcelona
Ⓑ ADJ [*jewellery, coins, tooth*] de oro; [*paint, lettering, frame*] dorado; [*fabric, dress, shirt*] color oro *inv*, dorado; **a green and ~ flag** una bandera verde y oro
Ⓒ CPD ➤ **gold braid** galón *m* de oro ➤ **gold digger** (*lit*) buscador(a) *m/f* de oro; (*fig*) cazafortunas *mf inv* ➤ **gold disc** (*Mus*) disco *m* de oro ➤ **gold dust** ✦ IDIOM **biros are like ~ dust in this office** (*Brit*) (*fig*) en esta oficina no encuentras un bolígrafo ni por casualidad ➤ **gold filling** empaste *m* de oro ➤ **gold leaf** oro *m* en hojas, pan *m* de oro ➤ **gold medal** (*Sport*) medalla *f* de oro ➤ **gold mine** (*lit, fig*) mina *f* de oro ➤ **gold reserves** reservas *fpl* de oro ➤ **gold rush** fiebre *f* del oro ➤ **gold standard** patrón *m* oro

golden ['gəʊldən] ADJ (*in colour*) dorado; (= *made of gold*) de oro; **fry the chicken pieces until ~** dorar los trozos de pollo; **this is a ~ opportunity for peace** ésta es una oportunidad de oro *or* una excelente oportunidad para la paz ➤ **golden age** edad *f* de oro ➤ **the Golden Age** (*in Spanish Literature*) el Siglo de Oro ➤ **golden boy*** niño *m* bonito* ➤ **golden eagle** águila *f* real

> Use **el/un** not **la/una** before feminine nouns beginning with stressed **a** or **ha** like **águila**.

➤ **the Golden Gate** el Golden Gate ➤ **golden girl*** niña *f* bonita* ➤ **golden jubilee** cincuentenario *m*, cincuenta aniversario *m* ➤ **golden rule** regla *f* de oro ➤ **golden syrup** (*Brit*) miel *f* de caña, melaza *f* de caña ➤ **golden wedding** (**anniversary**) bodas *fpl* de oro

goldfinch ['gəʊldfɪntʃ] N jilguero *m*

goldfish ['gəʊldfɪʃ] N (*pl ~ or ~es*) pez *m* de colores ➤ **goldfish bowl** pecera *f*

gold-plated [gəʊld'pleɪtɪd] ADJ chapado en oro

gold-rimmed [gəʊld'rɪmd] ADJ [*spectacles*] con montura de oro

goldsmith ['gəʊldsmɪθ] N orfebre *mf*; **~'s (shop)** taller *m* de orfebrería

golf [gɒlf] **Ⓐ** N golf *m* **Ⓑ** VI jugar al golf **Ⓒ** CPD ➤ **golf ball** pelota *f* de golf ➤ **golf club** (= *society*) club *m* de golf; (= *stick*) palo *m* de golf ➤ **golf course** campo *m or* (*LAm*) cancha *f* de golf ➤ **golf links** campo *m* de golf (*junto al mar*)

golfer ['gɒlfə'] N golfista *mf*

golfing ['gɒlfɪŋ] **Ⓐ** N golf *m* **Ⓑ** ADJ [*equipment, trousers*] de golf; [*holiday*] golfístico

gondola ['gɒndələ] N góndola *f*

gone [gɒn] PP *of* **go**

goner** ['gɒnə'] N **he's a ~** está en las últimas, se nos va

gong [gɒŋ] N gong *m*

gonna* ['gɒnə] (*esp US*) = **going to**

gonorrhoea, gonorrhea (*US*) [gɒnə'rɪə] N gonorrea *f*

---

good

Ⓐ ADJECTIVE	**Ⓒ** NOUN
Ⓑ ADVERB	**Ⓓ** COMPOUNDS

> *When* **good** *is part of a set combination, eg* **in a good temper, a good deal of, good heavens,** *look up noun.*

good [gʊd]

> The commonest translation of **good** is **bueno**, which must be shortened to **buen** before a masculine singular noun. Note that **buen/buena** *etc* precede the noun in general comments where there is no attempt to compare or rank the person or thing involved.

Ⓐ ADJECTIVE (*compar* **better**; *superl* **best**)
1 (= *satisfactory*) bueno; **a ~ book** un buen libro; **it's a ~ investment** es una buena inversión

> **Bueno/buena** *etc* follow the noun when there is implied or explicit comparison:

we could make a list of ~ teachers podríamos hacer una lista de profesores buenos; **I'm not saying it's a ~ thing or a bad thing** no digo que sea una cosa buena, ni mala

> Use **ser** rather than **estar** with **bueno** when translating **to be good**, unless describing food:

it's ~ to be aware of the views of intelligent people es bueno conocer los puntos de vista de la gente inteligente; **the paella was very ~** la paella estaba muy buena

> Use **estar** with the adverb **bien** to give a general comment on a situation:

you've written a book, which is ~ has escrito un libro, lo que está bien; **his hearing is ~** del oído está bien
2 (= *pleasant*) [*holiday, day*] bueno, agradable; [*weather, news*] bueno; **have a ~ journey/trip!** ¡buen viaje!
3 (= *favourable*) [*moment, opportunity*] bueno; **it's a ~ chance to sort things out** es una buena oportunidad de *or* para arreglar las cosas; **it would be a ~ idea to ask him** no estaría mal *or* no sería mala idea preguntárselo
4 (= *useful*) **the only ~ chair** la única silla que está bien, la única silla servible *or* sana
5 (= *kind*) **that's very ~ of you** es usted muy amable, ¡qué amable (de su parte)!; **please would you be so ~ as to help me down with my case?** ¿me hace el favor de bajarme la maleta?, ¿tendría la bondad de bajarme la maleta? (*more frm*); **he was ~ to me** fue muy bueno *or* amable conmigo, se portó bien conmigo
6 (= *well-behaved*) [*child*] bueno; **be ~!** ¡pórtate bien!; ✦ IDIOM **to be as ~ as gold*** portarse como un ángel *or* santo
7 (= *upright, virtuous*) bueno; **he's a ~ man** es una buena persona, es un buen hombre; **she's too ~ for him** ella es más de lo que él se merece
8 (= *close*) bueno; **he's a ~ friend of mine** es un buen amigo mío
9 (= *considerable*) [*supply, number*] bueno; **a ~ three hours** tres horas largas; **a ~ 10km** 10kms largos; **a ~ £10** (por) lo menos diez libras; **a ~ many or few people** bastante gente
10 (= *thorough*) **to have a ~ cry** llorar a lágrima viva, llorar a moco tendido*; **to have a ~ laugh** reírse mucho; **to take a ~ look (at sth)** mirar bien (algo)
11 (*in greetings*) **~ afternoon/evening** buenas tardes; **~ morning** buenos días; **~ night** buenas noches; **with all ~ wishes** (*in letter*) saludos, un fuerte abrazo; **Robert sends (his) ~ wishes** Robert manda recuerdos
12 (*in exclamations*) **good!** ¡muy bien!; **(that's) ~!** ¡qué bien!, ¡qué bueno! (*LAm*); **~ for YOU!** ¡bien hecho!; (= *congratulations*) ¡enhorabuena!

13 (*in set structures*)
✦ **as good as**: **it's as ~ as new** está como nuevo; **it was as ~ as a holiday** aquello fue como unas vacaciones; **the job is as ~ as done** el trabajo puede darse por acabado; **as ~ as saying ...** tanto como decir ...; **she as ~ as told me so** poco menos que me lo dijo; **he as ~ as called me a liar** me llamó poco menos que mentiroso
✦ **good and ...**: **~ and hot*** bien calentito*; **I'll do it when I'm ~ and ready*** lo haré cuando a mí me parezca
✦ **good at**: **she's ~ at maths** se le dan bien las matemáticas, es buena en matemáticas; **she's ~ at singing** canta bien; **she's ~ at putting people at their ease** tiene la capacidad de hacer que la gente se sienta relajada
✦ **good enough**: **it's just not ~ enough!** ¡esto no se puede consentir!; **that's ~ enough for me** eso me basta
✦ **good for**: **it's ~ for burns** es bueno para las quemaduras; **it's ~ for you** *or* **your health** te hace bien, es bueno para tí *or* tu salud; **he eats more than is ~ for him** come más de lo que le conviene; **if you know what's ~ for you you'll say yes** por la cuenta que te tiene dirás que sí; **it'll be ~ for some years yet** durará todavía algunos años; **the ticket is ~ for three months** el billete (*Sp*) *or* boleto (*LAm*) es válido durante tres meses
✦ **to hold good** valer (**for** para)
✦ **it's a good job** (*Brit*): **it's a ~ job he came!*** ¡menos mal que ha venido!
✦ **to look good**: **you look ~ in that** eso te sienta *or* te va bien; **things are looking ~** las cosas van bien, la cosa tiene buena pinta*
✦ **good to do sth**: **it's ~ to see you** me alegro de verte, gusto en verte (*LAm*); **it's ~ to be here** da gusto estar aquí
✦ **good with**: **she's ~ with cats** entiende bien a los gatos, sabe manejarse bien con los gatos
✦ **it's [too] good to be true** no puede ser, es demasiado bueno para ser cierto
Ⓑ ADVERB
1 (*as intensifier*) bien; **a ~ strong stick** un palo bien fuerte; **a ~ long walk** un paseo bien largo, un buen paseo
2 (*esp US**) (= *well*) bien; **you did ~** hiciste bien; **"how are you?"** — **"thanks, I'm ~"** —¿cómo estás? —muy bien, gracias
Ⓒ NOUN
1 (= *virtuousness*) bien *m*; **to do ~** hacer (el) bien; **~ and evil** el bien y el mal; **there's some ~ in him** tiene algo bueno
2 (= *advantage, benefit*) bien *m*; **the common ~** el bien común; **a rest will do you some ~** un descanso te sentará bien; **a (fat) lot of ~ that will do you!*** (*iro*) ¡menudo provecho te va a traer!; **for your own ~** por tu propio bien; **that's all to the ~!** ¡menos mal!; **what ~ will that do you?** ¿y eso de qué te va a servir?; **what's the ~ of worrying?** ¿de qué sirve *or* para qué preocuparse?
3 (*in set expressions*)
✦ **any good**: **is he any ~?** [*worker, singer etc*] ¿qué tal lo hace?, ¿lo hace bien?; **is this any ~?** ¿sirve esto?; **if it's any ~ to you** si te sirve de algo; **is she any ~ at cooking?** ¿qué tal cocina?, ¿cocina bien?
✦ **for good (and all)** (= *for ever*) para siempre; **he's gone for ~** se ha ido para siempre *or* para no volver
✦ **no good**: **it's no ~** (= *no use*) no sirve; **it's no ~, I'll never get it finished in time** así no hay manera, nunca lo terminaré a tiempo; **it's no ~ worrying** de nada sirve *or* vale preocuparse, no saca nada preocupándose; **that's no ~** eso no vale *or* sirve; **I'm no ~ at maths** las matemáticas no se me dan nada bien; **that's no ~ to me** eso no me sirve para nada; **to come to no ~** acabar mal; **to be up to no ~*** estar tramando algo
Ⓓ COMPOUNDS ➤ **good faith** buena fe *f*; **in ~ faith** de buena fe ➤ **Good Friday** Viernes *m* Santo ➤ **good guy** (*Cine*) bueno *m*; **the ~ guys** los buenos

goodbye [ɡʊdˈbaɪ] **Ⓐ EXCL** ¡adiós!, ¡hasta luego! **Ⓑ N** despedida *f*; **to say ~ to sb** despedirse de algn; **you can say ~ to your wallet** ya puedes despedirte de tu cartera, ya no volverás a ver la cartera

good-for-nothing [ˈɡʊdfəˈnʌθɪŋ] **Ⓐ ADJ** inútil **Ⓑ N** inútil *mf*, gandul(a) *m/f*

good-humoured, good-humored (*US*) [ˈɡʊdˈhjuːməd] **ADJ** [*person*] amable, de buen humor; [*remark, joke*] jovial; [*discussion*] de tono amistoso

good-looking [ˈɡʊdˈlʊkɪŋ] **ADJ** guapo, bien parecido

good-natured [ˈɡʊdˈneɪtʃəd] **ADJ** [*person*] amable, simpático; [*discussion*] de tono amistoso

goodness [ˈɡʊdnɪs] **N** **1** (= *virtue*) bondad *f* **2** (= *kindness*) amabilidad *f*; **out of the ~ of his heart** de lo bondadoso que es **3** (= *quality*) calidad *f*; [*of food*] lo bueno; **to be full of natural ~** tener todo lo bueno de la naturaleza **4** (*) (*in phrases*) **thank ~!** ¡menos mal!; **for ~' sake!** ¡por Dios!; **I wish to ~ I'd never met him** ojalá nunca lo hubiera conocido

goods [ɡʊdz] **NPL** (= *possessions*) bienes *mpl*; (= *products*) productos *mpl*; (*Comm etc*) géneros *mpl*, mercancías *fpl*; (= *objects*) artículos *mpl*; **leather ~** géneros *mpl* de cuero; **consumer ~** bienes *mpl* de consumo; ✦ **IDIOM to deliver the ~** cumplir con lo prometido ➤ **goods train** (*Brit*) tren *m* de mercancías ➤ **goods vehicle** vehículo *m* de transporte, camión *m*

good-tempered [ˈɡʊdˈtempəd] **ADJ** [*person*] amable, de buen humor; [*discussion*] sereno, sin pasión

good-time girl* [ɡʊdˈtaɪmˈɡɜːl] **N** chica *f* alegre

goodwill [ˈɡʊdˈwɪl] **Ⓐ N** **1** (*gen*) buena voluntad *f*; **as a gesture of ~** como muestra de buena voluntad **2** (*Comm*) clientela *f* y renombre *m* comercial **Ⓑ CPD** ➤ **goodwill ambassador** embajador(a) *m/f* de buena voluntad ➤ **goodwill mission** misión *f* de buena voluntad

goody* [ˈɡʊdɪ] **Ⓐ EXCL** (*also* **~ ~**) ¡qué bien!, ¡qué estupendo!* **Ⓑ N** **1** (*Brit Cine**) bueno/a *m/f*; **the goodies** los buenos **2 goodies** (= *things*) cositas *fpl* buenas; (= *presents*) regalitos *mpl*; (= *nice food*) cositas *fpl* ricas **Ⓒ CPD** ➤ **goody bag*** bolsa *f* de regalos

goody-goody* (*pej*) [ˈɡʊdɪˈɡʊdɪ] **N** (*pl* **goody-goodies**) santito/a *m/f*

gooey* [ˈɡuːɪ] **ADJ** (*compar* **gooier**; *superl* **gooiest**) pegajoso, viscoso; (= *sweet*) empalagoso

goof* [ɡuːf] **Ⓐ N** (*US*) bobo/a *m/f* **Ⓑ VI 1** (= *err*) tirarse una plancha* **2** (*US*) (*also* **~ off**) gandulear ➤ **goof around*** VI + ADV (*US*) hacer el tonto

goofy* [ˈɡuːfɪ] **ADJ** (*compar* **goofier**; *superl* **goofiest**) (= *silly*) bobo

goolies*** [ˈɡuːlɪz] **N** pelotas*** *fpl*, cataplines *mpl* (*Sp****)

goose [ɡuːs] (*pl* **geese**) **Ⓐ N** (*domestic*) ganso/a *m/f*, oca *f*; (*wild*) ánsar *m*; ✦ **IDIOMS to cook sb's ~** hacer la santísima a algn; **to kill the ~ that lays the golden eggs** matar a la gallina de los huevos de oro **Ⓑ VT** (*) (= *prod*) meter mano a **Ⓒ CPD** ➤ **goose bumps, goose flesh, goose pimples** carne *fsing* de gallina

gooseberry [ˈɡʊzbərɪ] **N** (*Bot*) grosella *f* espinosa; (*Brit*) ✦ **IDIOM to play** ~ hacer de carabina ➤ **gooseberry bush** grosellero *m* espinoso

goose-step [ˈɡuːsstep] **Ⓐ N** paso *m* de ganso, paso *m* de la oca **Ⓑ VI** marchar a paso de ganso *or* de la oca

gopher [ˈɡəʊfəˈ] **N 1** (*Zool*) ardillón *m* **2** (*Comput*) gopher *m* **3** (*US for errands*) recadero/a *m/f*

gore¹ [ɡɔːˈ] **N** (= *blood*) sangre *f* derramada

gore² [ɡɔːˈ] **VT** (= *injure*) cornear

gorge [ɡɔːdʒ] **Ⓐ N** (*Geog*) cañón *m*, barranco *m* **Ⓑ VT** **to ~ o.s.** atracarse (**with, on** de) **Ⓒ VI** atracarse (**on** de)

gorgeous [ˈɡɔːdʒəs] **ADJ** (= *lovely*) [*object, scenery, colour, music*] precioso; [*food, wine*] delicioso, riquísimo; [*weather*] espléndido, magnífico; **the garden looks absolutely ~** el jardín está precioso; **it smells ~** huele delicioso; **this tastes ~** está riquísimo; **the weather was ~** hacía un tiempo espléndido *or* magnífico; **he/she's ~!** ¡es guapísimo/ guapísima!

gorilla [ɡəˈrɪlə] **N** gorila *m*

gormless* [ˈɡɔːmlɪs] **ADJ** (*Brit*) corto (de entendimiento)*

gorse [ɡɔːs] **N** aulaga *f*, tojo *m*

gory [ˈɡɔːrɪ] **ADJ** (*compar* **gorier**; *superl* **goriest**) sangriento; **he told me all the ~ details*** me contó todo con pelos y señales

gosh* [ɡɒʃ] **EXCL** ¡cielos!

gosling ['gɒzlɪŋ] N ansarino *m*

go-slow ['gəʊ'sləʊ] N (*Brit Ind*) huelga *f* de brazos caídos

gospel ['gɒspəl] N evangelio *m*; ✦ IDIOM **to take sth as ~*** aceptar algo como si estuviera escrito en el evangelio ➤ **gospel music** gospel *m* ➤ **gospel truth: as though it were ~ truth** como si estuviera escrito en el evangelio

gossamer ['gɒsəmə^r] N (= *web*) telaraña *f*; (= *fabric*) gasa *f*

gossip ['gɒsɪp] Ⓐ N **1** (= *rumours*) cotilleo *m*, chismorreo *m* **2** (= *chatter*) charla *f*; **we had a good old ~** charlamos un buen rato **3** (= *person*) cotilla *mf*, chismoso/a *m/f* Ⓑ VI **1** (*maliciously*) chismorrear, cotillear (*Sp**) **2** (= *chatter*) charlar Ⓒ CPD ➤ **gossip column** ecos *mpl* de sociedad ➤ **gossip columnist** cronista *mf* de sociedad

got [gɒt] PT, PP *of* **get**

Goth [gɒθ] N (*Hist*) godo/a *m/f*

Gothic ['gɒθɪk] Ⓐ ADJ [*race*] godo; [*novel etc*] gótico Ⓑ N (*Archit, Ling etc*) gótico *m*

gotta* ['gɒtə] (*esp US*) = **got to**

gotten ['gɒtn] (*US*) PP *of* **get**

gouge [gaʊdʒ] VT [+ *hole etc*] excavar ➤ **gouge out** VT + ADV [+ *hole etc*] excavar; **to ~ sb's eyes out** sacar los ojos a algn

goulash ['guːlæʃ] N *especie de guisado húngaro*

gourd [gʊəd] N calabaza *f*

gourmet ['gʊəmeɪ] Ⓐ N gastrónomo/a *m/f* Ⓑ ADJ [*food, dinner*] de gastronomía; **~ cooking** la gastronomía

gout [gaʊt] N gota *f*

gov** [gʌv] N ABBR (*Brit*) (= **governor**) jefe *m*, patrón *m*

Gov. ABBR = **Governor**

govern ['gʌvən] Ⓐ VT **1** (= *rule*) [+ *country*] gobernar **2** (= *choice, decision*) guiar; [+ *emotions*] dominar Ⓑ VI (*Pol*) gobernar

governess ['gʌvənɪs] N institutriz *f*, gobernanta *f*

governing ['gʌvnɪŋ] ADJ [*party*] gobernante, en el gobierno ➤ **governing body** consejo *m* de administración

government ['gʌvnmənt] N gobierno *m*; **the Labour Government** el gobierno *or* la administración laborista; [*intervention, support, loan*] estatal, del estado; [*responsibility, decision, policy*] gubernamental, del gobierno ➤ **government body** ente *m* gubernamental *or* oficial ➤ **government department** ministerio *m*, departamento *m* gubernamental, secretaría *f* (*Mex*) ➤ **government issue** propiedad *f* del Estado ➤ **government spending** el gasto público ➤ **government stock** reservas *fpl* del Estado

governmental [ˌgʌvən'mentl] ADJ gubernamental, gubernativo

governor ['gʌvənə^r] N **1** [*of colony, state etc*] gobernador(a) *m/f* **2** (*esp Brit*) [*of prison*] director(a) *m/f* **3** (*Brit*) [*of school*] miembro *mf* del consejo

Govt., govt. ABBR (= **government**) gob.^{no}

gown [gaʊn] N (= *dress*) vestido *m* largo; (*Jur, Univ*) toga *f*

GP N ABBR (= **general practitioner**) médico/a *m/f* de cabecera

GPA N ABBR (*US*) = **grade point average**

grab [græb] Ⓐ N (= *snatch*) **to make a ~ at** *or* **for sth** intentar agarrar algo; **it's all up for ~s*** está a disposición de cualquiera Ⓑ VT **1** (= *seize*) coger, agarrar (*LAm*); (*greedily*) echar mano a; **to ~ sth from sb** arrebatarle algo a algn; **to ~ hold of sth/ sb** agarrar algo/a algn **2** (*fig*) [+ *chance etc*] aprovechar; **we can ~ a sandwich on the way** comeremos un sándwich por el camino; **I managed to ~ him before he left** conseguí pillarlo antes de que se fuera; **how does that ~ you?*** ¿qué te parece? Ⓒ VI **to ~ at** (= *snatch*) tratar de coger *or* (*LAm*) agarrar; (*in falling*) tratar de asir Ⓓ CPD ➤ **grab bag*** (*US*) bolsa *f* de las sorpresas

grace [greɪs] Ⓐ N **1** [*of form, movement etc*] gracia *f*, elegancia *f* **2** (*Rel*) gracia *f*, gracia *f* divina; (= *prayer*) bendición *f* de la mesa; **by the ~ of God** por la gracia de Dios; **there but for the ~ of God go I** le podría ocurrir a cualquiera;

to say ~ bendecir la mesa **3** (= *graciousness*) cortesía *f*, gracia *f*; **he had the ~ to apologize** tuvo la cortesía de pedir perdón; **with (a) good ~** de buen talante; **with (a) bad ~** a regañadientes **4** (= *respite*) demora *f*; **three days' ~** un plazo de tres días **5** (*in titles*) **5.1** (= *duke*) **His Grace the Duke** su Excelencia el duque; **yes, Your Grace** sí, Excelencia **5.2** (*Rel*) **His Grace Archbishop Roberts** su Ilustrísima, Arzobispo Roberts; **yes, your Grace** sí, Ilustrísima Ⓑ VT (= *adorn*) adornar, embellecer; (= *honour*) [+ *occasion, event*] honrar; **he ~d the meeting with his presence** honró a los asistentes con su presencia Ⓒ CPD ➤ **grace note** (*Mus*) apoyadura *f* ➤ **grace period** (*Jur, Fin*) período *m* de gracia

graceful ['greɪsfəl] ADJ **1** (= *elegant*) [*person, animal, building*] elegante; [*movement*] elegante, airoso; [*lines*] grácil **2** (= *dignified*) digno

gracefully ['greɪsfəlɪ] ADV (= *elegantly*) elegantemente; (= *in a dignified manner*) con dignidad; **to grow old ~** envejecer con dignidad; **he never could lose ~** nunca supo perder con dignidad; **she apologized, none too ~** pidió perdón a regañadientes

gracious ['greɪʃəs] Ⓐ ADJ **1** (= *refined, courteous*) [*person, gesture, smile, letter*] gentil, cortés; **to be ~ to sb** ser gentil *or* cortés con algn; **by (the) ~ consent of** (*frm*) por la gracia de; **he was ~ in defeat/victory** era correcto a la hora de la derrota/del triunfo; **by ~ permission of** (*frm*) por la gracia de **2** (= *merciful*) [*God*] misericordioso **3** (= *elegant, comfortable*) [*place, building*] elegante, refinado; **~ living** la vida refinada Ⓑ EXCL **gracious!** ◇ **good ~ (me)!** ¡Santo cielo!, ¡Dios mío!; **"you know Jack, don't you?"** — **"good ~, yes!"** —conoces a Jack, ¿no? —¡por supuesto que sí!; **good ~, what does that matter?** ¡por amor de Dios! ¿qué importancia tiene eso?

graciously ['greɪʃəslɪ] ADV [*wave, smile*] gentilmente, cortésmente; [*accept*] gentilmente; [*live*] con refinamiento; **she has ~ consented to be my wife** (*frm*) ha tenido la gentileza de aceptar mi propuesta de matrimonio

grad* [græd] N (*esp US*) = **graduate** A

grade [greɪd] Ⓐ N **1** (= *level*) (*on scale*) clase *f*, categoría *f*; (*in job*) grado *m*, categoría *f*; (*US Mil*) graduación *f*, grado *m*; **to be promoted to a higher ~** ser ascendido a un grado *or* una categoría superior; ✦ IDIOM **to make the ~** llegar, alcanzar el nivel **2** (= *quality*) clase *f*, calidad *f* **3** (*Scol*) (= *mark*) nota *f*; **to get good/bad ~s** sacar buenas/ malas notas **4** (*US*) (= *school class*) **he's in fifth ~** está en quinto (curso); ⇨ **HIGH SCHOOL 5** (*US*) (= *gradient*) pendiente *f*, cuesta *f* **6** (*US*) (= *ground level*) **at ~** al nivel del suelo Ⓑ VT **1** [+ *goods, eggs*] clasificar, graduar; [+ *colours*] degradar **2** (*Scol*) (= *mark*) calificar Ⓒ CPD ➤ **grade crossing** (*US Rail*) paso *m* a nivel ➤ **grade point average** (*US*) nota *f* media ➤ **grade school** (*US*) escuela *f* primaria

graded ['greɪdɪd] ADJ graduado

gradient ['greɪdɪənt] N (*Brit*) pendiente *f*, cuesta *f*; **a ~ of one in seven** una pendiente del uno por siete

grading ['greɪdɪŋ] N (*gen*) graduación *f*; (*by size*) gradación *f*; (*Scol etc*) calificación *f*

gradual ['grædjʊəl] ADJ **1** [*change, improvement, decline*] gradual, paulatino **2** [*slope*] suave

gradually ['grædjʊəlɪ] ADV **1** (= *slowly*) gradualmente, paulatinamente **2** (= *not steeply*) suavemente

graduate Ⓐ ['grædjʊɪt] N (*Univ*) licenciado/a *m/f*, graduado/a *m/f*, egresado/a *m/f* (*LAm*) **2** (*US Scol*) bachiller *mf* Ⓑ ['grædjʊeɪt] VT **1** [+ *thermometer etc*] graduar **2** (*US Scol, Univ*) otorgar el título a Ⓒ ['grædjʊeɪt] VI **1** (*Univ*) graduarse *or* licenciarse (**from** en), recibirse (*LAm*) (**as** de) **2** (*US Scol*) acabar el bachillerato Ⓓ ['grædjʊɪt] CPD ➤ **graduate course** curso *m* para graduados ➤ **graduate school** (*US*) departamento *m* de graduados; ⇨ **COLLEGE** ➤ **graduate student** (*US*) estudiante *mf* de posgrado

graduation [ˌgrædjʊ'eɪʃən] N (= *ceremony*) (*Univ*) entrega *f* del título universitario; (US Scol) entrega f del título de bachillerato

graffiti [grə'fi:tɪ] NPL graffiti *msing or mpl*, pintadas *fpl* ➤ **graffiti artist** realizador(a) *m/f* de graffitis

graft¹ [grɑːft] (*Bot, Med*) Ⓐ N injerto *m* Ⓑ VT injertar (**in, into, on to** en)

graft² [grɑːft] Ⓐ N 1 (*esp US*) (= *corruption*) soborno *m*, coima *f* (*And, SC*), mordida *f* (*CAm, Mex*) 2 (*Brit**) **hard** ~ trabajo *m* muy duro Ⓑ VI 1 (*Brit**) (= *work*) currar (*Sp**), camellar (*Mex, Col**), laburar (*Cono Sur**) 2 (*esp US*) (= *swindle*) trampear

grain [greɪn] N 1 (= *cereals*) cereales *mpl*; (*US*) (= *corn*) trigo *m* 2 (= *single piece*) grano *m* 3 [*of sense, truth*] pizca *f*; **there's not a ~ of truth in it** en eso no hay ni pizca de verdad; ✦ IDIOM **with a ~ of salt** con reservas 4 [*of wood*] fibra *f*, hebra *f*; [*of stone*] veta *f*, vena *f*; [*of leather*] flor *f*; [*of cloth*] granilla *f*; (*Phot*) grano *m*; **against the ~** (*lit*) a contrapelo, ✦ IDIOM **it goes against the ~** (*Brit*) or **my ~** (*US*) no me pasa, no me entra

grainy ['greɪnɪ] ADJ (*compar* **grainier**; *superl* **grainiest**) (*Phot*) granulado, con grano; [*substance*] granulado

gram [græm] N gramo *m*

grammar ['græmə'] N gramática *f*; (*also* ~ **book**) libro *m* de gramática ➤ **grammar school** (*Brit*) instituto *m* de enseñanza secundaria (*al que se accede a través de un examen de ingreso*)

grammatical [grə'mætɪkəl] ADJ 1 [*rule, structure, error*] gramatical 2 (= *correct*) **in ~ English** en inglés correcto; **that's not ~** eso es gramaticalmente incorrecto

gramme [græm] N (*Brit*) gramo *m*

gramophone† ['græməfəʊn] N (*Brit*) gramófono *m*

gran* [græn] N (*Brit*) abuelita *f*

granary ['grænərɪ] N granero *m* ➤ **Granary loaf**® (*Brit*) pan *m* con granos enteros

grand [grænd] (*compar* **-er**; *superl* **-est**) Ⓐ ADJ 1 (= *impressive*) [*building, architecture*] imponente, grandioso; [*clothes*] elegante; [*person*] distinguido; **I went to a rather ~ dinner** fui a una cena bastante lujosa *or* solemne; **to make a ~ entrance** hacer una entrada solemne; **it was a very ~ occasion** fue una ocasión muy espléndida; **on a ~ scale** a gran escala; **to do sth in ~ style** hacer algo a lo grande *or* por todo lo alto 2 (= *ambitious*) [*scheme, plan, design*] ambicioso Ⓑ N (**) (= *thousand*) **ten ~** (*Brit*) diez mil libras; (*US*) diez mil dólares Ⓒ CPD ➤ **grand finale** broche *m* de oro; **for the ~ finale ...** como broche de oro ...; **the summit's ~ finale** la apoteosis de la conferencia cumbre ➤ **grand jury** (*esp US Jur*) jurado *m* de acusación (*que decide si hay suficiente causa para llevar a algn a juicio*) ➤ **grand larceny** (*US Jur*) hurto *m* de mayor cuantía ➤ **grand master** (*Chess*) gran maestro *m* (de ajedrez) ➤ **the Grand Old Party** (*US*) *mote que tiene el partido republicano de Estados Unidos desde 1880* ➤ **grand piano** piano *m* de cola ➤ **Grand Prix** [grɒn'priː] Grand Prix *m*, Gran Premio *m* ➤ **grand slam** (*Sport*) gran slam *m* ➤ **grand total** total *m*

grandad* ['grændæd] N abuelo *m*

grandchild ['græntʃaɪld] N (*pl* **~ren**) nieto/a *m/f*

granddad* ['grændæd] N abuelo *m*

granddaughter ['græn,dɔːtə'] N nieta *f*

grandeur ['grændjə'] N [*of occasion, house etc*] lo imponente

grandfather ['grænd,fɑːðə'] N abuelo *m* ➤ **grandfather clock** reloj *m* de pie, reloj *m* de caja

grandiose ['grændɪəʊz] ADJ 1 (= *imposing*) [*style, building etc*] imponente, grandioso 2 (*pej*) [*building etc*] ostentoso, hecho para impresionar; [*scheme, plan*] vasto, ambicioso; [*style*] exagerado, pomposo

grandma* ['grænmɑː] N abuela *f*

grandmother ['græn,mʌðə'] N abuela *f*

grandpa* ['grænpɑː] N abuelo *m*

grandparents ['græn,peərənts] NPL abuelos *mpl*

grandson ['grænsʌn] N nieto *m*

grandstand ['grændstænd] N (*Sport*) tribuna *f*

granite ['grænɪt] N granito *m*

granny*, grannie* ['grænɪ] N abuela *f* ➤ **granny flat*** (*Brit*) piso *m* or (*LAm*) departamento *m* para la abuela

grant [grɑːnt] Ⓐ N 1 (= *act*) otorgamiento *m*, concesión *f* 2 (*Brit*) (= *scholarship*) beca *f*; (= *subsidy*) subvención *f* Ⓑ VT 1 [+ *request, favour*] conceder; (*Jur*) ceder 2 (= *admit*) reconocer; **I ~ you that he is honest but ...** reconozco *or* no pongo en duda *or* no te discuto que sea honrado; **I ~ you that** eso no lo pongo en duda, eso no se lo discuto 3 **to take sth for ~ed** dar algo por supuesto *or* sentado; **he takes her for ~ed** no sabe valorarla

grant-aided [,grɑːnt'eɪdɪd] ADJ (*Brit*) subvencionado

grant-maintained [,grɑːntmeɪn'teɪnd] ADJ (*Brit*) [*school*] *que recibe dinero del gobierno central, y no de la administración local*

granulated sugar [,grænjʊleɪtɪd'ʃʊgə'] N azúcar *m or f* granulado *or* granulada

granule ['grænjuːl] N gránulo *m*

grape [greɪp] N uva *f* ➤ **grape harvest** vendimia *f* ➤ **grape juice** (*for making wine*) mosto *m*; (= *drink*) zumo *m* or (*LAm*) jugo *m* de uva

grapefruit ['greɪpfruːt] N (*pl* ~ *or* ~**s**) pomelo *m*, toronja *f* (*esp LAm*)

grapevine ['greɪpvaɪn] N vid *f*, parra *f*; ✦ IDIOM **I heard it on** *or* **through the ~*** me contó un pajarito, me enteré en radio macuto (*Sp**)

graph [grɑːf] N gráfica *f*, gráfico *m* ➤ **graph paper** papel *m* cuadriculado

graphic ['græfɪk] Ⓐ ADJ 1 [*description, picture*] muy gráfico; **to describe sth in ~ detail** describir algo con todo lujo de detalles 2 (*Art, Math*) gráfico Ⓑ CPD ➤ **graphic artist** grafista *mf* ➤ **graphic arts** artes *fpl* gráficas ➤ **graphic design** diseño *m* gráfico ➤ **graphic designer** grafista *mf*

graphics ['græfɪks] Ⓐ N 1 (= *art of drawing*) artes *fpl* gráficas 2 (= *graphs*) gráficas *fpl* 3 (*Comput*) gráficos *mpl* 4 (= *pictures*) dibujos *mpl* Ⓑ CPD ➤ **graphics pad** (*Comput*) tablero *m* de gráficos

graphite ['græfaɪt] N grafito *m*

grapple ['græpl] VI [*wrestlers etc*] luchar cuerpo a cuerpo (**with** con); **to ~ with a problem** confrontar un problema

grasp [grɑːsp] Ⓐ N (= *handclasp*) apretón *m*; **to be within sb's ~** estar al alcance de la mano de algn; **to lose one's ~ on sth** desasirse de algo; (= *understanding*) comprensión *f*; **it's within everyone's ~** está al alcance de todos; **it is beyond my ~** está fuera de mi alcance; **to have a good ~ of sth** dominar algo Ⓑ VT 1 (= *take hold of*) agarrar, asir; (= *hold firmly*) sujetar; [+ *hand*] estrechar, apretar; [+ *weapon etc*] empuñar 2 (*fig*) [+ *chance, opportunity*] aprovechar; [+ *power, territory*] apoderarse de 3 (= *understand*) comprender, entender ➤ **grasp at** VI + PREP 1 [+ *rope etc*] tratar de asir 2 (*fig*) [+ *hope*] aferrarse a; [+ *opportunity*] aprovechar

grasping ['grɑːspɪŋ] ADJ avaro, codicioso

grass [grɑːs] Ⓐ N 1 (*Bot*) hierba *f*, yerba *f*; (= *lawn*) césped *m*, pasto *m* (*LAm*), grama *f* (*LAm*); (= *pasture*) pasto *m*; "**keep off the grass**" "prohibido pisar la hierba"; ✦ IDIOM **not to let the ~ grow under one's feet** no dormirse (en los laureles); ✦ PROV **the ~ is always greener on the other side (of the fence)** nadie está contento con su suerte 2 (**) (= *marijuana*) marihuana *f*, mota *f* (*LAm**) 3 (*Brit***) (= *person*) soplón/ona *m/f* Ⓑ VI (*Brit***) soplar*, dar el chivatazo*; **to ~ on** delatar a Ⓒ CPD ➤ **grass court** (*Tennis*) pista *f* de hierba ➤ **grass roots** base *f* ➤ **grass snake** culebra *f* ➤ **grass widow** (*US*†) (*divorced, separated*) mujer *f* separada o divorciada; (*Brit hum*) mujer *f* cuyo marido está ausente ➤ **grass widower** (*US*†) (*divorced, separated*) hombre *m* separado o divorciado; (*Brit hum*) marido *m* cuya mujer está ausente

grasshopper ['grɑːs,hɒpə'] N saltamontes *m inv*, chapulín *m* (*Mex, CAm*)

grassland ['grɑːslænd] N pradera *f*, pampa *f* (*LAm*)

grassy ['grɑːsɪ] ADJ (compar **grassier**; superl **grassiest**) herboso, pastoso (LAm)

grate¹ [greɪt] N (= grid) parrilla f; (= fireplace) chimenea f

grate² [greɪt] Ⓐ VT [+ cheese etc] rallar Ⓑ VI **to ~ on the ear** hacer daño al oído; **it ~s on my nerves** me pone los nervios de punta, me destroza los nervios

grateful ['greɪtful] ADJ (= thankful) agradecido; [smile] de agradecimiento; **to be ~ for sth** agradecer algo; **I would be ~ if you would send me …** le agradecería que me enviara …; **with ~ thanks** con mi más sincero agradecimiento; **to be ~ to sb** estar agradecido a algn; **I am ~ to Dr Jones for the loan of the book** le estoy agradecido al Dr Jones por prestarme el libro, le agradezco al Dr Jones que me prestase el libro; **he was ~ that he was still alive** daba gracias por estar todavía vivo

gratefully ['greɪtfulɪ] ADV [accept, say, smile] con gratitud; **she shook my hand ~** me apretó la mano agradecida or con gratitud; **donations will be ~ received** agradecemos cualquier donativo

grater ['greɪtəʳ] N rallador m

gratification [grætɪfɪ'keɪʃən] N satisfacción f; **to my great ~** con gran satisfacción mía

gratified ['grætɪfaɪd] ADJ contento, satisfecho; **I was ~ to learn that …** me complació saber que …

gratify ['grætɪfaɪ] VT [+ person] complacer; [+ desire, whim] satisfacer

gratifying ['grætɪfaɪɪŋ] ADJ grato; **it is ~ to know that …** me es grato saber que …

grating¹ ['greɪtɪŋ] N reja f, enrejado m

grating² ['greɪtɪŋ] ADJ [tone etc] áspero

gratitude ['grætɪtjuːd] N gratitud f, agradecimiento m; **he felt a sense of ~ towards her** se sentía agradecido hacia ella; **there's or that's ~ for you!** (iro) ¡así me/te etc lo agradecen!

gratuitous [grə'tjuːɪtəs] ADJ gratuito

gratuitously [grə'tjuːɪtəslɪ] ADV gratuitamente, de manera gratuita

gratuity [grə'tjuːɪtɪ] N (= tip) propina f

grave¹ [greɪv] ADJ (compar **~r**; superl **~st**) [danger, problem, mistake] grave; [threat, suspicion] serio; [face, expression] grave, serio; [person] serio; **he expressed ~ concern about the matter** expresó su seria preocupación por el problema; **the situation is very ~** la situación es muy grave

grave² [greɪv] N tumba f, sepultura f; (with monument) sepulcro m, tumba f; **from beyond the ~** desde ultratumba

grave³ [grɑːv] ADJ (Ling) **~ accent** acento m grave

gravedigger ['greɪvdɪgəʳ] N sepulturero/a m/f

gravel ['grævəl] N grava f, gravilla f ➤ **gravel pit** gravera f

gravely ['greɪvlɪ] ADV **1** (= seriously) [ill, wounded, injured] gravemente; **we are ~ concerned about his decision** estamos muy or seriamente preocupados por su decisión **2** (= solemnly) [say, speak] con gravedad, con seriedad

gravestone ['greɪvstəun] N lápida f (sepulcral)

graveyard ['greɪvjɑːd] N cementerio m, camposanto m ➤ **graveyard shift** (esp US) turno m de noche, turno m nocturno

gravitate ['grævɪteɪt] VI gravitar; **to ~ toward(s)** (= move) dirigirse hacia; (fig) (= be drawn to) tender hacia

gravitation [grævɪ'teɪʃən] N (Phys) gravitación f

gravitational [grævɪ'teɪʃənl] ADJ gravitatorio, gravitacional

gravity ['grævɪtɪ] N gravedad f; **the law of ~** la ley de la gravedad; **a situation of the utmost ~** una situación de la mayor gravedad

gravy ['greɪvɪ] Ⓐ N **1** (Culin) salsa f de carne **2** (US******) (= easy money) dinero m fácil Ⓑ CPD ➤ **gravy boat** salsera f ➤ **gravy train*** (fig) dinero m fácil; ✦ IDIOM **to get on the ~ train** pillar un chollo**

gray etc [greɪ] (US) = **grey** etc

graze¹ [greɪz] VI (Agr) pacer, pastar

graze² [greɪz] Ⓐ N (= injury) rasguño m Ⓑ VT **1** (= touch

lightly) rozar **2** (= scrape) [+ skin] raspar; **to ~ one's knees** rasparse las rodillas

grazing ['greɪzɪŋ] N **1** (= land) pasto m **2** (= act) pastoreo m

grease [griːs] Ⓐ N (= oil, fat etc) grasa f; (= lubricant) lubricante m Ⓑ VT [+ baking tin] engrasar; (Aut etc) engrasar, lubricar; ✦ IDIOMS **like ~d lightning*** como un relámpago; **to ~ sb's palm** untar la mano a algn Ⓒ CPD ➤ **grease gun** pistola f engrasadora, engrasadora f a presión ➤ **grease monkey*** (US) mecánico/a m/f, maquinista mf

greasepaint ['griːspeɪnt] N maquillaje m

greaseproof paper [griːspruːf'peɪpəʳ] N (Brit) papel m encerado

greasy ['griːsɪ] ADJ (compar **greasier**; superl **greasiest**) **1** [substance, hands] grasiento, grasoso (esp LAm); [clothes] lleno de grasa, mugriento; [hair, skin] graso, grasoso (esp LAm); [food] grasiento; [road] resbaladizo **2** (*) (= ingratiating) adulón, zalamero

great [greɪt] Ⓐ ADJ (compar **~er**; superl **~est**)

> One of the commonest translations of **great** is **grande**, which must be shortened to **gran** before a singular noun.

1 (= huge) [effort, variety] grande; [shock, surprise] verdadero, enorme; **she lived to a ~ age** vivió hasta una edad muy avanzada; **he didn't say a ~ deal** no dijo mucho; **a ~ deal of time/money/effort** mucho tiempo/dinero/esfuerzo; **with ~ difficulty** con gran or mucha dificultad; **we had ~ difficulty convincing them** hemos tenido muchas dificultades para convencerlos; **to a ~ extent** en gran parte; **we had ~ fun** lo pasamos fenomenal; **to be a ~ help** ser de gran ayuda; **I'm not in any ~ hurry** no tengo mucha prisa; **a ~ many people** mucha gente; **with ~ pleasure** con gran placer; **the concert was a ~ success** el concierto fue un gran éxito

2 (= important) [achievement, occasion, event] grande; **the ~ cultural achievements of the past** los grandes logros culturales del pasado; **everyone said she was destined for ~ things** todos decían que llegaría lejos; **~ work** (= masterpiece) obra f maestra

3 (= outstanding) [person, nation, skill] grande; **one of the ~est engineers of this century** uno de los más grandes ingenieros de este siglo

4 (with names) **Frederick/Peter the Great** Federico/Pedro el Grande; **Alexander the Great** Alejandro Magno; **the ~ George Padmore** el gran George Padmore

5 (= real) (as intensifier) grande; **I am a ~ admirer of his work** soy un gran admirador de su obra; **they are ~ friends** son grandes amigos; **she is a ~ believer in hard work** es una gran partidaria del trabajo duro; **she's a ~ one for antique shops** le encantan las tiendas de antigüedades, es una fanática de las tiendas de antigüedades

6 (*) (= excellent) [person, thing, idea] estupendo, genial*; **you were ~!** ¡estuviste genial!*; **I think she's ~** creo que es genial*; **it's a ~ idea** es una idea estupenda, es una idea genial*; **(that's) ~!** ¡eso es estupendo!; **she was ~ about it** lo tomó muy bien; **he's ~ at football** juega estupendamente al fútbol; **she's ~ at maths** se le dan genial las matemáticas*; **to feel ~** sentirse fenómeno or fenomenal*; **you look ~!** (= attractive) ¡estás guapísimo!; (= healthy) ¡tienes un aspecto estupendo!; **the ~ thing is that you don't have to iron it** lo mejor de todo es que no tienes que plancharlo

Ⓑ EXCL **1** (*) (= excellent) **(oh) ~!** ¡fenómeno!*, ¡fenomenal!, ¡qué bien! **2** (iro) **(oh) ~! that's all I need!** ¡maravilloso! ¡eso es lo que me faltaba!

Ⓒ ADV ➤ **big*** grandísimo

Ⓓ CPD ➤ **the Great Bear** (Astron) la Osa Mayor ➤ **Great Britain** Gran Bretaña f ➤ **the Great Lakes** los Grandes Lagos ➤ **great tit** herrerillo m mayor ➤ **the Great Wall of China** la (Gran) Muralla China ➤ **the Great War** la Primera Guerra Mundial

great-aunt ['greɪt'ɑːnt] N tía f abuela

greatcoat ['greɪtkəut] N gabán m; (Mil etc) sobretodo m

greater ['greɪtə'] ADJ COMPAR of **great** mayor ➤ **Greater London** el gran Londres (incluyendo los barrios de la periferia)

greatest ['greɪtɪst] ADJ SUPERL of **great** el mayor, la mayor; **Ireland's ~ living poet** el mayor poeta vivo de Irlanda; **with the ~ difficulty** con suma dificultad; **he's the ~!*** ¡es el mejor!

great-grandchild ['greɪt'grænt∫aɪld] N (pl **~ren**) bisnieto/a m/f

great-granddaughter [ˌgreɪt'grænˌdɔːtə'] N bisnieta f

great-grandfather ['greɪt'grænˌfɑːðə'] N bisabuelo m

great-grandmother ['greɪt'grænˌmʌðə'] N bisabuela f

great-grandparents ['greɪt'grænˌpɛərənts] NPL bisabuelos mpl

great-grandson ['greɪt'grændsʌn] N bisnieto m

great-great-grandfather ['greɪt'greɪt'grænˌfɑːðə'] N tatarabuelo m

greatly ['greɪtlɪ] ADV **1** (with adj or pp used as adj) muy; **~ superior** muy superior; **he was ~ influenced by Debussy** estuvo muy or enormemente influenciado por Debussy **2** (with verb) [contribute, improve, vary, admire, regret] enormemente, mucho

greatness ['greɪtnɪs] N grandeza f

great-uncle ['greɪt,ʌŋkl] N tío m abuelo

Greece [griːs] N Grecia f

greed [griːd] N avaricia f, codicia f; (for food) gula f, glotonería f

greedily ['griːdɪlɪ] ADV (gen) con avidez; [eat] con voracidad

greedy ['griːdɪ] ADJ (compar **greedier**; superl **greediest**) codicioso (**for** de); (for food) goloso; **don't be so ~!** ¡no seas glotón!

Greek [griːk] Ⓐ ADJ griego Ⓑ N (= person) griego/a m/f; (Ling) griego m; ✦ IDIOM **it's all ~ to me*** me suena a chino, no entiendo ni papa* or palabra Ⓒ CPD ➤ **Greek Cypriot** grecochipriota mf

green [griːn] Ⓐ ADJ (compar **~er**; superl **~est**) **1** (in colour) verde; **dark ~** verde oscuro inv; **light ~** verde claro inv; ✦ IDIOMS **to be ~ with envy** morirse de envidia; **she's got ~ fingers** (Brit) ◇ **she's got a ~ thumb** (US) se le dan muy bien las plantas **2** (= unripe) [banana, tomato, wood] verde **3** (*) (= inexperienced) verde*; (= naive) inocente; **I'm not as ~ as I look!** ¡no soy tan inocente como parezco! **4** (= ecological) [movement, vote, person] verde, ecologista; [issues, policy, product] ecológico Ⓑ N (= colour) verde m **2** (= lawn) césped m; (also **village ~**) césped m comunal **3** (in Golf) green m; (for bowls) pista f **4 greens** (Culin) verdura f sing **5** (Pol) **the Greens** los verdes Ⓒ CPD ➤ **green bean** judía f verde, ejote m (Mex), poroto m verde (And, SC), chaucha f (Arg) ➤ **green belt** (Brit) zona f verde ➤ **green card** (in EC) (Aut) carta f verde; (in US) permiso de residencia y trabajo en los EE.UU. ➤ **the Green Cross Code** (Brit) código m de seguridad vial ➤ **green light** luz f verde; ✦ IDIOM **to give sb/sth the ~ light** dar luz verde a algn/algo ➤ **green onion** (US) cebolleta f, cebollino m ➤ **green paper** (Brit Pol) libro m verde ➤ **the Green Party** (Pol) el partido ecologista, los verdes* ➤ **green peas** guisantes mpl ➤ **green pepper** (= vegetable) pimiento m verde, pimentón m verde (LAm) ➤ **green salad** ensalada f (de lechuga, pepino, pimiento verde, etc)

greenback* ['griːnbæk] N (US) billete m (de banco)

greenery ['griːnərɪ] N follaje m

greenfield site [ˌgriːnfiːld'saɪt] N solar m or terreno m sin edificar

greenfly ['griːnflaɪ] N (pl **~ or greenflies**) pulgón m

greengage ['griːngeɪdʒ] N claudia f

greengrocer ['griːnˌgrəʊsə'] N (esp Brit) verdulero/a m/f; **~'s (shop)** verdulería f

greenhouse ['griːnhaʊs] N invernadero m ➤ **greenhouse effect** efecto m invernadero ➤ **greenhouse gas** gas m invernadero

greenish ['griːnɪ∫] ADJ verdoso

Greenland ['griːnlənd] N Groenlandia f

Greenwich mean time [ˌgrenɪt∫'miːntaɪm] N hora f media de Greenwich

greet [griːt] VT (gen) saludar; (= welcome) recibir; [sight, scene etc] presentarse a; **the statement was ~ed with laughter** la declaración fue recibida entre risas

greeting ['griːtɪŋ] N saludo m; (= welcome) bienvenida f, acogida f; **greetings** saludos mpl, recuerdos mpl; **greetings!** ¡bienvenido! ➤ **greeting card** (US), **greetings card** tarjeta f de felicitación

gregarious [grɪ'gɛərɪəs] ADJ [animal] gregario; [person] sociable

gremlin* ['gremlɪn] N duendecillo m, diablillo m

grenade [grɪ'neɪd] N (also **hand ~**) granada f ➤ **grenade launcher** lanzagranadas m inv

grenadier [ˌgrenə'dɪə'] N granadero m

grew [gruː] PT of **grow**

grey, gray (US) [greɪ] Ⓐ ADJ (compar **~er**; superl **~est**) **1** (in colour) gris; [face, complexion] ceniciento; [hair, beard] gris, canoso; [place, day] gris; **dark ~** gris oscuro inv; **light ~** gris claro adj inv; **to have ~ hair** tener el pelo gris or canoso; **to go ~** [hair] volverse gris or canoso; **she's going ~** le están saliendo canas; **to turn ~** [person, face] palidecer **2** (*) [pound, vote] de la tercera edad Ⓑ N (= colour) gris m; **dressed in ~** vestido de gris Ⓒ VI [hair] encanecer; **he was ~ing at the temples** se le estaban encaneciendo las sienes Ⓓ CPD ➤ **grey area** (= unclear area) área f poco definida, área f gris; (= intermediate area) área f intermedia

Use **el/un** not **la/una** before feminine nouns beginning with stressed **a** or **ha** like **área**:

it's rather a ~ area es un área poco definida or bastante gris ➤ **grey matter** (Anat, hum) materia f gris ➤ **grey squirrel** ardilla f gris

grey-haired, gray-haired (US) ['greɪ'hɛəd] ADJ canoso

Greyhound ['greɪhaʊnd] N (US) (also **~ bus**) autobús m de larga distancia

greyhound ['greɪhaʊnd] N galgo/a m/f ➤ **greyhound racing** carreras fpl de galgos ➤ **greyhound track** canódromo m

greying, graying (US) ['greɪɪŋ] ADJ [hair] grisáceo, canoso

grid [grɪd] Ⓐ N **1** (= grating) rejilla f **2** (Brit) **the (national) ~** la red nacional **3** (on map) cuadrícula f Ⓑ CPD ➤ **grid map** mapa m cuadriculado ➤ **grid reference** coordenadas fpl

griddle ['grɪdl] N plancha f

gridiron ['grɪd,aɪən] N **1** (= grill) parrilla f **2** (US Sport) campo m de fútbol (americano)

gridlock ['grɪdlɒk] N **1** (traffic) embotellamiento m **2** (in talks) punto m muerto

gridlocked ['grɪdlɒkt] ADJ **1** [traffic, road] paralizado **2** [negotiations] en (un) punto muerto

grief [griːf] N **1** (= sorrow) pena f, dolor m; ✦ IDIOM **to come to ~** fracasar, ir al traste **2** (= trouble) **to give sb ~** dar problemas a algn, dar la vara a algn* **3** (as exclamation) **good ~!** ¡qué demonio(s)!

grief-stricken ['griːf,strɪkən] ADJ apesadumbrado

grievance ['griːvəns] N (= complaint) queja f; (= cause for complaint) motivo m de queja; [of workers] reivindicación f; **to have a ~ against sb** tener queja de algn ➤ **grievance procedure** procedimiento m (de tramitación) de quejas

grieve [griːv] Ⓐ VT dar pena a, causar tristeza a, afligir; **it ~s me to see ...** me da pena or causa tristeza ver ... Ⓑ VI afligirse, acongojarse (**about, at** por); **to ~ for sb** llorar la pérdida de algn

grievous ['griːvəs] ADJ [loss etc] doloroso, penoso; [blow] severo; [pain] fuerte; [crime, offence, error] grave ➤ **grievous bodily harm** (Jur) daños mpl físicos graves, lesiones fpl corporales graves

grievously ['gri:vəslı] ADV [hurt, offend] gravemente; [err, be mistaken] lamentablemente; ~ **wounded** gravemente herido

grill [grɪl] **Ⓐ** N **1** (Brit) (= utensil, restaurant) parrilla f **2** (= food) parrillada f; **a mixed ~** una parrillada mixta **3** = **grille Ⓑ** VT **1** (Brit Culin) asar a la parrilla **2** (*) (= interrogate) interrogar

grille [grɪl] N rejilla f; [of window] reja f; (= screen) verja f

grilling* ['grɪlɪŋ] N (fig) interrogatorio m intenso; **to give sb a ~** interrogar a algn intensamente

grim [grɪm] (compar ~**mer**; superl ~**mest**) ADJ **1** (= gloomy) [news, situation, prospect] desalentador; [building, place, town] sombrío, lúgubre; **the situation looked ~** la situación se presentaba muy negra; **to paint a ~ picture of sth** pintar un cuadro muy negro de algo; **the ~ reality** la dura or cruda realidad
2 (= stern) [person] adusto; [face, expression] serio, adusto; [smile] forzado; **with ~ determination** con absoluta determinación
3 (= macabre) [humour, joke, story, discovery] macabro
4 (*) (= awful) [experience, effect] espantoso*, penoso*; **to feel ~** estar or encontrarse fatal*

grimace [grɪ'meɪs] **Ⓐ** N mueca f **Ⓑ** VI hacer muecas

grime [graɪm] N mugre f, suciedad f

grimly ['grɪmlɪ] ADV (= gravely) gravemente; (= determinedly) denodadamente; **"he's badly hurt," she said ~** —está muy malherido —dijo gravemente or en tono grave or con seriedad; **"this isn't good enough," he said ~** —esto no vale —dijo con seriedad

grimy ['graɪmɪ] ADJ (compar **grimier**; superl **grimiest**) mugriento, sucio

grin [grɪn] **Ⓐ** N sonrisa f **Ⓑ** VI sonreír abiertamente (**at** a); ♦ IDIOM **to ~ and bear it** poner al mal tiempo buena cara

grind [graɪnd] (pt, pp **ground**) **Ⓐ** VT **1** [+ coffee] moler; [+ corn, flour] moler, machacar; [+ stone] pulverizar; (US Culin) [+ meat] picar; **to ~ sth into** or **to a powder** reducir algo a polvo, pulverizar algo; **to ~ one's teeth** rechinar los dientes **2** (= sharpen) [+ knife] amolar, afilar **Ⓑ** VI [machine etc] funcionar con dificultad; **to ~ to a halt** pararse en seco **Ⓒ** N (*) (= dull hard work) trabajo m pesado; **the work was such a ~** el trabajo era tan pesado; **the daily ~** la rutina diaria ➤ **grind down** VT + ADV **1** (lit) pulverizar **2** (= wear away) desgastar **3** (= oppress) agobiar, oprimir; **to ~ down the opposition** destruir lentamente a la oposición ➤ **grind up** VT + ADV pulverizar

grinder ['graɪndəʳ] N **1** (for coffee) molinillo m; (US) (for meat) picadora f de carne **2** (for sharpening) afiladora f

grinding ['graɪndɪŋ] ADJ **to come to a ~ halt** [vehicle, traffic] detenerse en seco; [work, progress] llegar a un punto muerto, estancarse; **~ poverty** miseria f (absoluta)

grindstone ['graɪndstəʊn] N muela f; ♦ IDIOM **to keep one's nose to the ~** batir el yunque

grip [grɪp] **Ⓐ** N **1** (= handclasp) apretón m (de manos); **he lost his ~ on the branch** se le escapó la rama de las manos, la rama se le fue de las manos
2 (fig) **in the ~ of a strike** paralizado por una huelga; **to come to ~s with** luchar a brazo partido con; **to get to ~s with sth/sb** enfrentarse con algo/algn; **he's losing his ~** está perdiendo el control; **he lost his ~ of the situation** la situación se le fue de las manos; **to have a good ~ of a subject** entender algo a fondo; **get a ~ (on yourself)!*** ¡cálmate!, ¡contrólate!
3 (= handle) asidero m, asa f; [of weapon] empuñadura f

> Use **el/un** not **la/una** before feminine nouns beginning with stressed **a** or **ha** like **asa**.

4 (= bag) maletín m, bolsa f
Ⓑ VT **1** (= hold) agarrar, asir; [+ hands] apretar, estrechar; **the wheels ~ the road** las ruedas se agarran a la carretera **2** (fig) (= enthrall) fascinar; [fear] apoderarse de; **~ped by fear** presa del pánico
Ⓒ VI [wheel] agarrarse

gripe* [graɪp] **Ⓐ** N (= complaint) queja f **Ⓑ** VI (= complain) quejarse (**about** de)

gripping ['grɪpɪŋ] ADJ absorbente, muy emocionante

grisly ['grɪzlɪ] ADJ (compar **grislier**; superl **grisliest**) (= horrible) horroroso; (= horrifying) horripilante

grist [grɪst] N ♦ IDIOM **it's all ~ to the mill** de todo hay que sacar provecho

gristle ['grɪsl] N cartílago m, ternilla f

gristly ['grɪslɪ] ADJ cartilaginoso, ternilloso

grit [grɪt] **Ⓐ** N **1** (= gravel) grava f; (= dust) polvo m; (for birds, poultry) arenilla f silícea, arena f **2** (fig) (= courage) valor m, ánimo m; (= firmness of character) firmeza f; (= endurance) aguante m **3** **grits** (US Culin) sémola f sing **Ⓑ** VT **1** [+ road] echar grava a **2** **to ~ one's teeth** apretar los dientes

gritty ['grɪtɪ] ADJ (compar **grittier**; superl **grittiest**) **1** [soil, powder, texture] arenoso; [surface, floor] arenoso, granuloso **2** [person, display, performance] enérgico, resuelto; **~ determination** obstinada determinación **3** [drama, story, portrayal] crudo

grizzle ['grɪzl] VI (Brit) quejumbrar

grizzled ['grɪzld] ADJ [hair] entrecano

grizzly ['grɪzlɪ] N (also ~ **bear**) oso m pardo

groan [grəʊn] **Ⓐ** N [of pain, dismay] gemido m; (= grunt) gruñido m **Ⓑ** VI **1** (with pain, dismay) gemir; (= grunt) gruñir, refunfuñar **2** (= creak) [tree, gate etc] crujir **Ⓒ** VT gemir; **"yes," he ~ed** —sí —gimió

grocer ['grəʊsəʳ] N (esp Brit) tendero/a m/f, almacenero/a m/f (SC), abarrotero/a m/f (And, Mex, CAm), bodeguero/a m/f (And, Carib, CAm); **~'s (shop)** tienda f de comestibles, tienda f de abarrotes (And, Mex, CAm), almacén m (SC), bodega f (And, Carib, CAm)

grocery ['grəʊsərɪ] N **1** (US) (also ~ **store**) tienda f de comestibles, tienda de abarrotes (And, Mex, CAm), almacén m (SC), bodega f (And, Carib, CAm) **2** **groceries** comestibles mpl, abarrotes mpl (LAm)

groggy ['grɒgɪ] ADJ (compar **groggier**; superl **groggiest**) (from blow) atontado; (Boxing) groggy, grogui; (from alcohol) tambaleante; **I feel a bit ~** estoy un poco mareado

groin [grɔɪn] N ingle f

groom [gruːm] **Ⓐ** N **1** (in stable) mozo m de cuadra **2** (= bridegroom) novio m **Ⓑ** VT **1** [+ horse] almohazar, cuidar; **to ~ o.s.** acicalarse; **the cat was ~ing itself** el gato se lamía; **well ~ed** [person] muy acicalado **2** (= prepare) [+ person] **to ~ sb as/to be** preparar a algn para/para ser

groove [gruːv] **Ⓐ** N **1** (in wood, metal etc) ranura f, estría f; [of record] surco m **2** (Mus*) (= rhythm) ritmo m **Ⓑ** VI (*) (= dance) bailar

groovy* ['gruːvɪ] ADJ (compar **groovier**; superl **grooviest**) (= marvellous) estupendo*, total*, guay (Sp*)

grope [grəʊp] **Ⓐ** VI (also ~ **around**, ~ **about**) andar a tientas, tantear; **to ~ for sth** (lit, fig) buscar algo a tientas **Ⓑ** VT **1** **to ~ one's way (through/towards)** avanzar a tientas (por/hacia) **2** (*) **to ~ sb** (sexually) toquetear a algn **Ⓒ** N (*) (sexual) **they had a ~** se estuvieron toqueteando, se estuvieron metiendo mano*

gross [grəʊs] (compar ~**er**; superl ~**est**) **Ⓐ** ADJ **1** (= unacceptable) [injustice, inequality, mismanagement] flagrante; [exaggeration, simplification] burdo; **~ incompetence** incompetencia f absoluta; **that is a ~ understatement** eso es quedarse muy corto
2 (= revolting) [person, remark, joke] ordinario, basto; **he's totally ~*** es de lo más basto; **(how) ~!*** ¡qué asco!*
3 (*) (= tasteless) ordinario, de muy mal gusto
4 (= obese) gordísimo, cebón*
5 (= total) [income, profit, weight] bruto; **their ~ income is £205 a week** sus ingresos brutos son de 205 libras a la semana
Ⓑ ADV (= in total) [earn, pay, weigh] en bruto; **she earns £30,000 ~ per annum** gana 30.000 libras al año brutas or en bruto
Ⓒ VT (Comm) (gen) obtener unos ingresos brutos de; (from shares, bonds) obtener unos beneficios brutos de
Ⓓ CPD ➤ **gross domestic product** (Econ) producto m

interno bruto ➤ **gross indecency** (*Jur*) ultraje *m* contra la moral pública ➤ **gross misconduct** negligencia *f* grave ➤ **gross national product** (*Econ*) producto *m* nacional bruto ➤ **gross negligence** (*Jur*) culpa *f* grave

grossly [ˈɡrəʊslɪ] ADV (= *extremely*) [*unfair, inadequate*] sumamente; [*inaccurate, negligent, inefficient*] sumamente, extremadamente; [*misleading, incompetent, irresponsible, exaggerated*] sumamente, tremendamente; [*mislead*] de forma escandalosa; **he is ~ overweight** está obeso; **the police were ~ negligent** la policía incurrió en graves negligencias

grotesque [ɡrəʊˈtesk] ADJ [*appearance, idea, sight, spectacle*] grotesco (*also Art*); [*allegation, proposal*] absurdo

grotto [ˈɡrɒtəʊ] N (*pl* **-es** or **~s**) gruta *f*

grotty* [ˈɡrɒtɪ] ADJ (*compar* **grottier**; *superl* **grottiest**) (*Brit*) asqueroso; **I feel ~** me siento fatal*

grouch* [ɡraʊtʃ] **Ⓐ** VI refunfuñar, quejarse **Ⓑ** N
1 (= *person*) refunfuñón/ona *m/f*, cascarrabias *mf inv*
2 (= *complaint*) queja *f*

grouchy* [ˈɡraʊtʃɪ] ADJ (*compar* **grouchier**; *superl* **grouchiest**) malhumorado

ground¹ [ɡraʊnd] **Ⓐ** N **1** (= *soil*) tierra *f*, suelo *m*
2 (= *terrain*) terreno *m*; **high/hilly ~** terreno *m* alto/montañoso; **to break new ~** hacer algo nuevo; **common ~** terreno *m* común; **to cover a lot of ~** (*lit*) recorrer una gran distancia; **he covered a lot of ~ in his lecture** abarcó mucho en la clase; **to be on dangerous ~** entrar en territorio peligroso; **to be on firm ~** hablar con conocimiento de causa; **to gain ~** ganar terreno; **to lose ~** perder terreno; **to run sb to ~** localizar (por fin) a algn, averiguar el paradero de algn; **to stand one's ~** (*lit*) no ceder terreno; (*fig*) mantenerse firme; ✦ IDIOMS **to cut the ~ from under sb's feet** quitarle terreno a algn; **it suits me down to the ~** (*Brit**) me conviene perfectamente, me viene de perilla
3 (= *surface*) suelo *m*, tierra *f*; **above** ~ sobre la tierra; **below** ~ debajo de la tierra; **to get off the** ~ [*plans etc*] ponerse en marcha; **on the** ~ en el suelo
4 (= *pitch*) terreno *m*, campo *m*
5 grounds (= *gardens*) jardines *mpl*, parque *msing*
6 (*US Elec*) tierra *f*
7 (= *reason*) (*usu pl*) razón *f*, motivo *m*; (= *basis*) fundamento *m*; **~s for complaint** motivos *mpl* de queja; **what ~s do you have for saying so?** ¿en qué se basa para decir eso?; **on the ~s of ...** con motivo de ..., por causa de ..., debido a ...; **on the ~s that ...** a causa de que ..., por motivo de que ...; **on good ~s** con razón; **on medical ~s** por razones de salud
Ⓑ VT **1** [+ *ship*] varar, hacer encallar
2 [+ *plane, pilot*] obligar a permanecer en tierra; **he ordered the planes to be ~ed** ordenó que permaneciesen los aviones en tierra; **to be ~ed by bad weather** no poder despegar por el mal tiempo
3 [+ *teenager*] encerrar, no dejar salir
4 (*US Elec*) conectar con tierra
5 (*educationally*) **to be well ~ed in** tener un buen conocimiento de, estar versado en
Ⓒ CPD ➤ **ground attack** ataque *m* de tierra; (*Aer*) ataque *m* a superficie ➤ **ground control** control *m* desde tierra ➤ **ground crew** (*Aer*) personal *m* de tierra ➤ **ground floor** (*Brit*) planta *f* baja ➤ **ground forces** (*Mil*) fuerzas *fpl* de tierra ➤ **ground frost** escarcha *f* ➤ **ground level** nivel *m* del suelo ➤ **ground plan** plano *m*, planta *f* ➤ **ground rules** reglas *fpl* (básicas) ➤ **ground staff** personal *m* de tierra ➤ **ground wire** (*US*) cable *m* de toma de tierra ➤ **ground zero** zona *f* cero

ground² [ɡraʊnd] **Ⓐ** PT, PP *of* **grind** **Ⓑ** ADJ [*coffee etc*] molido; (*US*) [*meat*] picado (*Sp, RPl*), molido (*LAm*) **Ⓒ** N **grounds** [*of coffee*] poso *msing*, sedimento *msing* **Ⓓ** CPD ➤ **ground beef** (*US*) picadillo *m*

groundbreaking [ˈɡraʊndbreɪkɪŋ] ADJ [*research, work, book*] revolucionario

groundcloth [ˈɡraʊndklɒθ] N (*US*) (*in tent*) aislante *m* or suelo *m* (de tienda de campaña)

ground-floor flat [ˌɡraʊndˌflɔːˈflæt] N (*Brit*) piso *m* or (*LAm*) departamento *m* de planta baja

groundhog [ˈɡraʊndhɒɡ] N (*US*) marmota *f* de América

Groundhog Day (el día de la marmota) es una simpática tradición estadounidense según la cual se puede predecir supuestamente la duración del invierno. La marmota (en inglés **groundhog**, o **ground squirrel**, o **woodchuck**) despierta de su hibernación el dos de febrero (**Groundhog Day**). Si hace sol, el animal se asusta al ver su propia sombra y vuelve a su madriguera durante otras seis semanas, lo cual indica que el invierno será más largo. El acontecimiento tiene tal importancia que es televisado a todo el país desde la madriguera más famosa de Punxsutawney, en Pensilvania.

grounding [ˈɡraʊndɪŋ] N (*in education*) conocimientos *mpl* básicos; **to give sb a ~** enseñar a algn los rudimentos de

groundkeeper [ˈɡraʊndkiːpəʳ] (*US*) N encargado *m* (*del mantenimiento de una pista de deporte*)

groundless [ˈɡraʊndlɪs] ADJ sin fundamento

groundnut [ˈɡraʊndnʌt] N (*esp Brit*) cacahuete *m* (*Sp, Mex*), maní *m* (*LAm*) ➤ **groundnut oil** aceite *m* de cacahuete

groundsheet [ˈɡraʊndʃiːt] N (*Brit*) (*in tent*) aislante *m* or suelo *m* (de tienda de campaña)

groundskeeper [ˈɡraʊndzkiːpəʳ] (*US*) N = **groundkeeper**

groundsman [ˈɡraʊndzmən] N (*pl* **groundsmen**) (*Brit*) encargado *m* (*del mantenimiento de una pista de deporte*)

groundswell [ˈɡraʊndswel] N (*fig*) marejada *f*

groundwork [ˈɡraʊndwɜːk] N trabajo *m* preliminar or preparatorio; **to do the ~ for sth** poner las bases de algo

group [ɡruːp] **Ⓐ** N [*of people, objects, companies*] grupo *m*; (*for specific purpose*) agrupación *f*, asociación *f*; (*Mus*) conjunto *m*, grupo *m*; **they stood in a ~** estaban en grupo; **family ~** familia *f*, grupo *m* familiar; **a human rights ~** una agrupación or asociación pro derechos humanos **Ⓑ** VT (*also* **~ together**) agrupar **Ⓒ** VI agruparse; **the children ~ed around her** los niños se agruparon alrededor de ella **Ⓓ** CPD ➤ **group booking** reserva *f* hecha para un grupo ➤ **group captain** (*Brit Aer*) jefe *m* de escuadrilla ➤ **group photo** foto *f* de conjunto ➤ **group practice** (*Med*) consultorio *m* (de médicos) ➤ **group therapy** terapia *f* de grupo

groupie* [ˈɡruːpɪ] N grupi* *mf*, fan de un grupo pop

grouse [ɡraʊs] N (= *bird*) urogallo *m*

grout [ɡraʊt] **Ⓐ** N lechada *f* **Ⓑ** VT enlechar

grouting [ˈɡraʊtɪŋ] N lechada *f*

grove [ɡrəʊv] N arboleda *f*, bosquecillo *m*; **~ of pines** pineda *f*; **~ of poplars** alameda *f*

grovel [ˈɡrɒvl] VI (*lit, fig*) arrastrarse (**to** ante)

grow [ɡrəʊ] (*pt* **grew**; *pp* **~n**) **Ⓐ** VI **1** [*plant, hair, person, animal*] crecer; **how you've ~n!** ¡cómo has crecido!; **he has ~n five centimetres** ha crecido cinco centímetros; **she's letting her hair ~** se está dejando crecer el pelo, se está dejando el pelo largo; **these sharks can ~ to six metres** estos tiburones pueden llegar a medir hasta seis metros
2 (= *increase*) (*in number, amount*) aumentar; **the number of unemployed has ~n by more than 10,000** el número de parados ha aumentado en más de 10.000; **the economy continues to ~** la economía sigue en su fase de crecimiento; **opposition grew** la oposición cobró más fuerza; **to ~ in popularity** ganar popularidad
3 (= *develop*) [*friendship, love*] desarrollarse; [*person*] madurar
4 (*with adjective*) (*temporarily*) ponerse; (*changing character*) volverse; **he grew increasingly anxious/uncomfortable** empezó a ponerse cada vez más nervioso/incómodo, estaba cada vez más nervioso/incómodo; **he has ~n very impatient in the last few years** se ha vuelto muy

impaciente estos últimos años

---

grow + ADJECTIVE is often translated by a specific verb:

---

our eyes gradually grew accustomed to the light los ojos se nos fueron acostumbrando a la luz; **to ~ angry** enfadarse; **the light grew brighter** la luz se hizo más intensa; **to ~ dark** (gen) oscurecer; (at dusk) oscurecer, anochecer; **to ~ fat** engordar; **her eyes grew heavy** se le cerraban los ojos; **the noise grew louder** el ruido aumentó de volumen; **to ~ old** envejecer(se); **you will realize this as you ~ older** te darás cuenta de esto a medida que te hagas mayor; **he grew tired of waiting** se cansó de esperar

5 to ~ to like sb llegar a querer a algn, encariñarse con algn; **in time he grew to accept it** con el tiempo llegó a aceptarlo

Ⓑ VT **1** [+ plant, crop] cultivar; **I ~ my own vegetables** tengo mi propio huerto, cultivo mis verduras

2 [+ hair, beard, moustache, nails] dejarse crecer

➤ **grow apart** VI + ADV [friends, couple] distanciarse; **he and his wife grew apart** la relación entre él y su mujer se entibió or se debilitó

➤ **grow into** VI + PREP **1** [+ clothes] **the trousers are a bit big but he'll ~ into them** los pantalones son un poco grandes pero ya crecerá y le sentarán bien **2** (= get used to) acostumbrarse a **3** (= become) convertirse en

➤ **grow on** VI + PREP **the tune ~s on you after a while** la melodía te empieza a gustar con el tiempo

➤ **grow out of** VI + PREP **you've ~n out of your shoes again** se te han vuelto a quedar pequeños los zapatos; **to ~ out of the habit of doing sth** perder la costumbre de hacer algo; **most children who stammer ~ out of it** a casi todos los niños el tartamudeo se les quita con la edad

➤ **grow up** VI + ADV **1** (= become adult) hacerse mayor; **when I ~ up I'm going to be a doctor** cuando sea mayor voy a ser médico; **~ up!*** ¡no seas niño!; **we grew up together** crecimos juntos **2** (= develop) [friendship] desarrollarse; [hatred] crecer; [town, industry] desarrollarse, crecer; [custom] arraigar, imponerse

growbag ['grəʊbæg] N bolsa f de cultivo

grower ['grəʊəʳ] N cultivador(a) m/f

growing ['grəʊɪŋ] Ⓐ ADJ **1** [crop, plant] que está creciendo; [child] en edad de crecimiento **2** (= expanding, increasing) [business] en fase de desarrollo; [friendship, population, family] creciente; **a ~ number of** un número creciente or cada vez mayor de; **I felt a ~ sense of unease** me sentía cada vez más nervioso Ⓑ CPD ➤ **growing pains** (lit) dolores mpl de crecimiento; (fig) problemas mpl iniciales

growl [graʊl] Ⓐ N gruñido m Ⓑ VI [animal] gruñir; [person] refunfuñar Ⓒ VT **"yes,"** he **~ed** —sí —refunfuñó

grown [grəʊn] Ⓐ PP of **grow** Ⓑ ADJ (also **fully ~**) adulto, maduro

grown-up ['grəʊnʌp] Ⓐ ADJ adulto Ⓑ N adulto/a m/f, persona f mayor

growth [grəʊθ] Ⓐ N **1** [of person, animal, plant] crecimiento m; [of city] crecimiento m; (Econ) crecimiento m, desarrollo m

2 (= increase) (in productivity, profits, demand) aumento m; **population ~** crecimiento m demográfico

3 (Bot) (= vegetation) vegetación f; (= buds, leaves) brotes mpl

4 (Med) tumor m

Ⓑ CPD ➤ **growth area** (Econ) [of country] polo m de desarrollo; [of industry] sector m en crecimiento or expansión ➤ **growth industry** industria f en crecimiento or expansión ➤ **growth rate** (Econ) tasa f de crecimiento

grub [grʌb] N **1** (= larva) larva f, gusano m **2** (******) (= food) comida f; **~('s) up!** ¡la comida está servida!

grubby ['grʌbɪ] ADJ (compar **grubbier**; superl **grubbiest**) (= dirty) mugriento, sucio, mugroso (LAm)

grudge [grʌdʒ] Ⓐ N resentimiento m, rencor m (**against** a); **to bear sb a ~** ◇ **have a ~ against sb** guardar rencor a algn Ⓑ VT **1** (= resent) **to ~ doing sth** hacer algo de mala gana **2** (= envy) envidiar; **I don't ~ you your success** no te envidio el éxito; **he ~s us our pleasures** mira con malos ojos nuestros placeres

grudging ['grʌdʒɪŋ] ADJ [attitude, praise] reticente; **he earned the ~ admiration/respect of his rivals** se ganó, aunque con reticencias, la admiración/el respeto de sus rivales; **she gave us a ~ apology** se disculpó de mala gana or a regañadientes

grudgingly ['grʌdʒɪŋlɪ] ADV de mala gana, a regañadientes

gruelling, grueling (US) ['grʊəlɪŋ] ADJ [task] penoso, duro; [match, race] agotador

gruesome ['gruːsəm] ADJ espantoso, horrible

gruff [grʌf] ADJ (compar **~er**; superl **~est**) [voice] ronco; [manner] brusco

gruffly ['grʌflɪ] ADV bruscamente

grumble ['grʌmbl] Ⓐ N (= complaint) queja f Ⓑ VI (= complain) quejarse (**about** de)

grumbling ['grʌmblɪŋ] Ⓐ N **I couldn't stand his constant ~** no podía soportar que estuviera gruñendo todo el rato Ⓑ ADJ [person, tone] gruñón; **~ sound** gruñido m; **a ~ appendix** síntomas mpl de apendicitis

grumpy* ['grʌmpɪ] ADJ (compar **grumpier**; superl **grumpiest**) [person] malhumorado, gruñón; [voice] de gruñón

grungy* ['grʌndʒɪ] ADJ (compar **grungier**; superl **grungiest**) (= dirty) cutre (Sp), roñoso; (Mus) de grunge

grunt [grʌnt] Ⓐ N [of animal, person] gruñido m Ⓑ VI [animal, person] gruñir Ⓒ VT **"yes,"** he **~ed** —sí —gruñó

G-string ['dʒiːstrɪŋ] N (Mus) cuerda f de sol; (= clothing) tanga f, taparrabo m

Gt ABBR = **Great**

guacamole [ˌgwɑːkəˈməʊlɪ] N guacamole m

Guadeloupe [ˌgwɑːdəˈluːp] N Guadalupe f

guano ['gwɑːnəʊ] N guano m

guarantee [ˌgærənˈtiː] Ⓐ N garantía f; **it is under ~** está bajo garantía; **there is no ~ that** no hay seguridad de que + subjun; **I give you my ~** se lo aseguro Ⓑ VT (Comm) [+ goods] garantizar (**against** contra); [+ service, delivery] asegurar; [+ debt] ser fiador de; **~d for three months** garantizado durante tres meses; **I ~ that ...** les garantizo que ...; **he can't ~ that he'll come** no está seguro de poder venir

guarantor [ˌgærənˈtɔːʳ] N garante mf, fiador(a) m/f; **to act as ~ for sb** avalar a algn

guard [gɑːd] Ⓐ N **1** (= soldier) guardia mf; (= sentry) centinela mf; (= squad of soldiers) guardia f; (= escort) escolta f; **to change (the) ~** relevar la guardia

2 (Mil) (also **~ duty**) guardia f; (fig) (= watchfulness) vigilancia f; **to drop one's ~** bajar la guardia, descuidarse; **to keep ~** vigilar; **to keep ~ over sth/sb** (Mil, fig) vigilar algo/a algn; **to lower one's ~** bajar la guardia, descuidarse; **to be off one's ~** estar desprevenido; **to be on ~** estar en guardia; **to be on one's ~** (fig) estar en guardia (**against** contra); **to put sb on his ~** poner a algn en guardia, prevenir a algn (**against** contra); **to stand ~** montar guardia sobre algo; **to be under ~** estar vigilado; **to keep sb under ~** vigilar a algn

3 (= security guard) guardia mf de seguridad

4 (esp US) (= prison guard) carcelero/a m/f

5 (Brit Rail) jefe m de tren

6 (Fencing) guardia f; **on ~!** ¡en guardia!

7 (= safety device) (on machine) salvaguardia f, resguardo m; [of sword] guarda f, guarnición f; (also **fireguard**) guardafuego m; (= protection) protección f Ⓑ VT [+ prisoner, treasure] vigilar, custodiar; (while travelling) escoltar; [+ place] guardar, proteger (**against, from** de); [+ person] proteger (**against, from** de); **a closely ~ed secret** un secreto muy bien guardado Ⓒ CPD ➤ **guard dog** perro m guardián or de guarda ➤ **guard of honour** (Brit) guardia f de honor ➤ **guard's van** (Brit Rail) furgón m

➤ **guard against** VI + PREP [+ illness] guardarse de; [+ suspicion, accidents] evitar; **in order to ~ against this** para evitar esto; **to ~ against doing sth** evitar hacer algo

guarded ['gɑːdɪd] ADJ [person] cauto, comedido; [reply, tone] cauteloso; [optimism] comedido, moderado; **she was ~ about committing herself** fue cautelosa or cauta a la hora de comprometerse

guardedly ['gɑːdɪdlɪ] ADV [*say, reply*] cautelosamente, con cautela; [*optimistic*] comedidamente, moderadamente

guardhouse ['gɑːdhaʊs] N (*for guards*) cuartel *m* de la guardia; (*for prisoners*) cárcel *f* militar

guardian ['gɑːdɪən] N protector(a) *m/f*, guardián/ana *m/f*; (*Jur*) [*of child*] tutor(a) *m/f* ➤ **guardian angel** ángel *m* custodio, ángel *m* de la guarda

guardrail ['gɑːdreɪl] N pretil *m*, baranda *f*

guardroom ['gɑːdrʊm] N cuarto *m* de guardia

guardsman ['gɑːdzmən] N (*pl* **guardsmen**) (*Brit*) soldado *m* de la guardia real; (*US*) soldado *m* de la guardia (nacional)

Guatemala [ˌgwɑːtɪ'mɑːlə] N Guatemala *f*

Guatemalan [ˌgwɑːtɪ'mɑːlən] ADJ, N guatemalteco/a *m/f*

guava ['gwɑːvə] N guayaba *f*

Guayana [gaɪ'ɑːnə] N Guayana *f*

Guernsey ['gɜːnzɪ] N Guernesey *m*

guerrilla [gə'rɪlə] N guerrillero/a *m/f* ➤ **guerrilla warfare** guerra *f* de guerrillas

guess [ges] Ⓐ N (= *conjecture*) conjetura *f*, suposición *f*; (= *estimate*) estimación *f* aproximada; **to make/have a ~** adivinar; **I'll give you three ~es** a ver si lo adivinas; **at a (rough) ~** a ojo; **my ~ is that ...** yo creo que ...; **it's anybody's ~** ¿quién sabe?; **your ~ is as good as mine!** ¡vete a saber!

Ⓑ VT **1** (= *try to guess*) adivinar; (= *guess correctly*) acertar; **~ what!** ¡a que no lo adivinas!; **~ who!** ¡a ver si adivinas quién soy!; **I ~ed as much** me lo suponía; **you've ~ed it!** ¡has acertado!; **I never ~ed it was so big** nunca supuse que fuera tan grande; **I ~ed him to be about 20** le eché unos 20 años

2 (*) (= *think*) creer, suponer; **I ~ you're right** supongo que tienes razón; **I ~ we'll buy it** me imagino que lo compraremos

Ⓒ VI **1** (= *make a guess*) adivinar; (= *guess correctly*) acertar; **you'll never ~** no lo adivinarás nunca; **he's just ~ing** no hace más que especular; **to keep sb ~ing** mantener a algn a la expectativa; **to ~ at sth** intentar adivinar algo; **all that time we never ~ed** en todo ese tiempo no lo sospechábamos

2 (= *think*) suponer, creer; **I ~ so** creo que sí; **he's happy, I ~** supongo que está contento

guessing game ['gesɪŋˌgeɪm] N acertijo *m*, adivinanza *f*

guesstimate* ['gestɪmɪt] N estimación *f* aproximada

guesswork ['geswɜːk] N conjeturas *fpl*; **it's all ~** son meras conjeturas

guest [gest] Ⓐ N (*at home*) invitado/a *m/f*; (*at hotel, guesthouse*) huésped *mf*; **they had ~s that weekend** tenían invitados *or* visita(s) ese fin de semana; **~ of honour** invitado/a *m/f* de honor; **"do you mind if I sit here?" — "be my ~"*** —¿le importa si me siento aquí? —por supuesto que no

Ⓑ VI aparecer como invitado; **he's ~ing on tonight's show** aparecerá como invitado en el show de esta noche

Ⓒ CPD ➤ **guest book** libro *m* de los huéspedes ➤ **guest room** cuarto *m* de huéspedes ➤ **guest speaker** orador(a) *m/f* invitado/a ➤ **guest star** estrella *f* invitada

guesthouse ['gesthaʊs] N **1** (*Brit*) (= *hotel*) pensión *f*, casa *f* de huéspedes **2** (*US*) (*in grounds of large house*) casa *f* de invitados

guffaw [gʌ'fɔː] Ⓐ N carcajada *f* Ⓑ VI reírse a carcajadas

Guiana [gaɪ'ɑːnə] N Guayana *f*

guidance ['gaɪdəns] N **1** (= *counselling*) consejo *m*; (= *leadership*) dirección *f*; **marriage/vocational ~** orientación *f* matrimonial/profesional; **under the ~ of** bajo la dirección de **2** [*of missile*] dirección *f*

guide [gaɪd] Ⓐ N **1** (= *person*) guía *mf*; (= *girl guide*) exploradora *f*, guía *f*; (= *book*) guía *f* turística **2** (= *fig*) guía *f*; **let conscience be your ~** haz lo que te dicte tu conciencia Ⓑ VT (*round town, building*) guiar; (*in choice, decision*) orientar; **to be ~d by sth/sb** dejarse guiar por algo/algn Ⓒ CPD ➤ **guide dog** (*esp Brit*) perro *m* guía

guidebook ['gaɪdbʊk] N guía *f* turística

guided ['gaɪdɪd] ADJ [*missile, rocket*] teledirigido ➤ **guided**

tour visita *f* con guía; **I'll give you a ~ tour of the house** os enseñaré la casa

guideline ['gaɪdlaɪn] N (línea *f*) directriz *f*

guiding ['gaɪdɪŋ] ADJ **~ principle** principio *m* director; **~ star** estrella *f* de guía

guild [gɪld] N gremio *m*

guile [gaɪl] N astucia *f*

guileless ['gaɪllɪs] ADJ inocente, candoroso

guillotine ['gɪlə'tiːn] Ⓐ N guillotina *f* Ⓑ VT guillotinar

guilt [gɪlt] N (*gen*) culpa *f*, culpabilidad *f*; (*Jur*) culpabilidad *f*; **to admit one's ~** confesarse culpable; **she was racked with ~** la atormentaba el remordimiento

guiltily ['gɪltɪlɪ] ADV con aire de culpabilidad

guilty ['gɪltɪ] ADJ (*compar* **guiltier**; *superl* **guiltiest**) culpable; **to have a ~ conscience** tener remordimientos (de conciencia), sentirse culpable; **to feel ~ (about sth)** sentirse culpable (por algo); **to find sb ~/not ~** declarar a algn culpable/inocente; **he had a ~ look on his face** su rostro reflejaba culpabilidad; **she wondered why the children were looking so ~** se preguntaba por qué los niños tenían esa cara de culpa; **to be ~ of sth** ser culpable de algo; **the ~ party** el/la culpable; **"how do you plead?" — "~ or not ~?"** —¿cómo se declara? —¿culpable o inocente?; **a verdict of ~** una sentencia de culpabilidad; **a verdict of not ~** una declaración de inocencia

Guinea ['gɪnɪ] N Guinea *f* ➤ **guinea fowl** gallina *f* de Guinea, pintada *f* ➤ **guinea pig** cobayo *m*, cobaya *f*, conejillo *m* de Indias, cuy *m* (*And, SC*); (*fig*) conejillo *m* de Indias

guise [gaɪz] N **in that ~** de esa manera; **under the ~ of** con el pretexto de

guitar [gɪ'tɑːr] N guitarra *f*

guitarist [gɪ'tɑːrɪst] N guitarrista *mf*

gulf [gʌlf] N (= *bay*) golfo *m*; (= *chasm*) abismo *m* (also fig); **the (Persian) Gulf** el Golfo (Pérsico); **the Gulf of Mexico** el Golfo de Méjico *or* (*LAm*) México ➤ **the Gulf States** los países del Golfo ➤ **the Gulf Stream** la corriente del Golfo

gull [gʌl] N gaviota *f*

gullet ['gʌlɪt] N esófago *m*, garganta *f*

gullible ['gʌlɪbl] ADJ crédulo, simplón

gully ['gʌlɪ] N (= *ravine*) barranco *m*; (= *channel*) hondonada *f*

gulp [gʌlp] Ⓐ N trago *m*; **in** *or* **at one ~** de un trago; **"yes," he said with a ~** —sí —dijo tragando saliva Ⓑ VT (*also ~ down*) tragarse, engullir Ⓒ VI (*while drinking*) tragar; (= *swallow saliva*) tragar saliva

gum¹ [gʌm] N (*round teeth*) encía *f*

gum² [gʌm] Ⓐ N **1** (= *glue*) (*esp Brit*) goma *f*, pegamento *m*, cemento *m* (*LAm*) **2** (*also* **chewing ~**) chicle *m* Ⓑ VT (= *stick together*) pegar con goma; [+ *label, envelope*] pegar

gumboil ['gʌmbɔɪl] N flemón *m*

gumboots ['gʌmbuːts] NPL (*Brit†*) botas *fpl* altas de goma

gumdrop ['gʌmdrɒp] N pastilla *f* de goma

gummed [gʌmd] ADJ [*envelope, label*] engomado

gumption* ['gʌmpʃən] N (= *initiative*) iniciativa *f*; (*Brit*) (= *common sense*) seso *m*, sentido *m* común

gumshield ['gʌmʃiːld] N protector *m* de dientes

gumtree ['gʌmtriː] N ✦ IDIOM **to be up a ~** (*Brit**) estar en un aprieto

gun [gʌn] Ⓐ N **1** (= *pistol*) pistola *f*, revólver *m*; (= *rifle*) fusil *m*; (= *shotgun*) escopeta *f*; (= *cannon*) cañón *m*; **a 21-~ salute** una salva de 21 cañonazos; **to draw a ~ on sb** apuntar a algn con un arma; **to jump the ~** salir antes de tiempo; (*fig*) obrar con demasiada anticipación; ✦ IDIOMS **to be going great ~s** (*Brit**) hacer grandes progresos, ir a las mil maravillas; **to stick to one's ~s** mantenerse firme, mantenerse en sus trece

2 (*Brit*) (= *person*) pistolero/a *m/f*

Ⓑ VT disparar sobre

Ⓒ CPD ➤ **gun carriage** cureña *f*; (*at funeral*) armón *m* de artillería ➤ **gun crew** dotación *f* de un cañón ➤ **gun dog** perro *m* de caza ➤ **gun law** (*Jur*) ley *f* que rige la tenencia y uso de armas de fuego ➤ **gun licence, gun license** (*US*) licencia *f* de armas

➤ **gun down** VT + ADV abatir a tiros, abalear (*LAm*)

➤ **gun for** VI + PREP ir a por; **it's really the boss they're ~ning for** en realidad van a por el jefe

gunboat ['gʌnbəʊt] N cañonero *m* ➤ **gunboat diplomacy** diplomacia *f* cañonera

gunfight ['gʌnfaɪt] N tiroteo *m*

gunfire ['gʌnfaɪə^r] N disparos *mpl*; (*from artillery*) cañoneo *m*, fuego *m* de cañón

gunge* [gʌndʒ] N (*Brit*) mugre *f*

gung-ho ['gʌŋ'həʊ] ADJ **1** (= *over-enthusiastic*) (tontamente) optimista, (locamente) entusiasta **2** (= *jingoistic*) patriotero (en exceso), jingoísta

gunk* [gʌŋk] N mugre *f*

gunman ['gʌnmən] N (*pl* **gunmen**) pistolero *m*, gatillero *m* (*LAm*)

gunner ['gʌnə^r] N artillero/a *m/f*

gunpoint ['gʌnpɔɪnt] N **at ~** a punta de pistola; **to hold sb at ~** tener a algn a punta de pistola

gunpowder ['gʌn,paʊdə^r] N pólvora *f* ➤ **Gunpowder Plot** (*Brit*) Conspiración *f* de la Pólvora; ⊅ *GUY FAWKES NIGHT*

gunrunner ['gʌn,rʌnə^r] N contrabandista *mf or* traficante *mf* de armas

gunrunning ['gʌn,rʌnɪŋ] N contrabando *m or* tráfico *m* de armas

gunshot ['gʌnʃɒt] N (= *noise*) disparo *m* ➤ **gunshot wound** escopetazo *m*

gunsmith ['gʌnsmɪθ] N armero/a *m/f*

gurgle ['gɜːgl] Ⓐ N [*of liquid*] borboteo *m*, gluglú *m*; [*of baby*] gorjeo *m* Ⓑ VI [*liquid*] borbotear; [*baby*] gorjear

gurney ['gɜːnɪ] N (*US*) camilla *f*

guru ['gʊruː] N gurú *mf*

gush [gʌʃ] Ⓐ N **1** [*of liquid*] chorro *m*; [*of words*] torrente *m*; [*of feeling*] efusión *f* **2** (= *sentimentalism*) sentimentalismo *m* Ⓑ VI **1** (*also* ~ **out**) [*water, blood*] chorrear (**from** de) **2** (*) (= *enthuse*) hablar con entusiasmo (**about, over** de)

gushing ['gʌʃɪŋ] ADJ efusivo

gusset ['gʌsɪt] N escudete *m*

gust [gʌst] Ⓐ N [*of wind*] ráfaga *f*, racha *f* Ⓑ VI soplar racheado; **the wind ~ed up to 120km/h** el viento soplaba en rachas de hasta 120km/h

gusto ['gʌstəʊ] N **with ~** con entusiasmo

gusty ['gʌstɪ] ADJ (*compar* **gustier**; *superl* **gustiest**) [*weather*] borrascoso; [*wind*] racheado

gut [gʌt] Ⓐ N **1** (= *alimentary canal*) intestino *m*; (*for violin, racket*) cuerda *f* de tripa
2 guts* (= *innards*) tripas *fpl*; (= *courage*) agallas* *fpl*, coraje *m*; (= *staying power*) aguante *m*, resistencia *f*; (= *moral strength*) carácter *m*; (= *content*) meollo *m*, sustancia *f*; **to have ~s** tener agallas*; ✦ IDIOMS **I hate his ~s*** no lo puedo ver ni en pintura; **I'll have his ~s for garters!*** ¡le hago trizas!; **to work one's ~s out** echar los bofes, echar el hígado
Ⓑ VT **1** [+ *poultry, fish*] destripar
2 [+ *building*] no dejar más que las paredes de
Ⓒ CPD ➤ **gut feeling** instinto *m* visceral ➤ **gut reaction** reacción *f* instintiva

gutsy* ['gʌtsɪ] ADJ (*compar* **gutsier**; *superl* **gutsiest**) valiente, con agallas*

gutter ['gʌtə^r] N (*in street*) arroyo *m*, cuneta *f*, desagüe *m* (*CAm*); (*on roof*) canal *m*, canalón *m* ➤ **the gutter press** (*Brit pej*) la prensa amarilla; ⊅ *BROADSHEETS AND TABLOIDS*

guttering ['gʌtərɪŋ] N canales *mpl*, canalones *mpl*

guttural ['gʌtərəl] ADJ gutural

guv** [gʌv] N (= **governor**) jefe *m*; **thanks, ~!** ¡gracias, jefe!

guy¹* [gaɪ] N **1** (= *man*) tipo* *m*, tío *m* (*Sp**), cuate *m* (*Mex*); **he's a nice ~** es un buen tipo *or* (*Sp*) tío*; **hey, (you) ~s!** ¡eh, amigos!; **are you ~s ready to go?** ¿están todos listos para salir? **2** (*Brit*) (= *effigy*) efigie *f*

guy² [gaɪ] N (*also* ~ **rope**) (*for tent*) viento *m*, cuerda *f*

Guyana [gaɪˈænə] N Guayana *f*

Guy Fawkes [ˌgaɪˈfɔːks] CPD (*Brit*) ➤ **Guy Fawkes Day, Guy Fawkes Night** cinco de noviembre, aniversario de la Conspiración de la Pólvora

GUY FAWKES NIGHT

La noche del cinco de noviembre, **Guy Fawkes Night**, se celebra en el Reino Unido el fracaso de la conspiración de la pólvora, **Gunpowder Plot**, un intento fallido de volar el Parlamento de Jaime I en 1605. Esa noche se lanzan fuegos artificiales y se hacen hogueras en las que se queman unos muñecos de trapo que representan a **Guy Fawkes**, uno de los cabecillas de la revuelta. Días antes, los niños tienen por costumbre pedir a los transeúntes **a penny for the guy**, dinero que emplean en comprar cohetes.

guzzle ['gʌzl] VT **1** [+ *food*] engullirse, tragarse; [+ *drink*] soplarse, tragarse (*LAm*) **2** (*hum**) [+ *petrol*] tragar mucho

gym* [dʒɪm] N (= *gymnasium*) gimnasio *m*; (= *gymnastics*) gimnasia *f* ➤ **gym shoes** zapatillas *fpl* de deporte

gymkhana [dʒɪmˈkɑːnə] N gincana *f*

gymnasium [dʒɪmˈneɪzɪəm] N (*pl* **~s** *or* **gymnasia** [dʒɪmˈneɪzɪə]) gimnasio *m*

gymnast ['dʒɪmnæst] N gimnasta *mf*

gymnastic [dʒɪmˈnæstɪk] ADJ gimnástico

gymnastics [dʒɪmˈnæstɪks] N gimnasia *f*

gymslip ['dʒɪmslɪp] N (*Brit*) vestido *m* de peto

gynaecologist, gynecologist (*US*) [ˌgaɪnɪˈkɒlədʒɪst] N ginecólogo/a *m/f*

gynaecology, gynecology (*US*) [ˌgaɪnɪˈkɒlədʒɪ] N ginecología *f*

gyp¹** [dʒɪp] (*US*) Ⓐ N **1** (= *swindle*) estafa *f*, timo *m* **2** (= *swindler*) estafador(a) *m/f*, timador(a) *m/f* Ⓑ VT estafar, timar

gyp²* [dʒɪp] N (*Brit*) **it's giving me ~** me duele una barbaridad

gypsum ['dʒɪpsəm] N yeso *m*

gypsy ['dʒɪpsɪ] Ⓐ N gitano/a *m/f* Ⓑ CPD [*life, caravan, music*] gitano

gyrate [dʒaɪˈreɪt] VI (= *spin*) girar; (= *dance*) bailar enérgicamente

gyroscope ['dʒaɪrəskəʊp] N giroscopio *m*, giróscopo *m*

Hh

H, h [eɪtʃ] N H, h f; **H for Harry** H de Historia

habeas corpus [ˈheɪbɪəsˈkɔːpəs] N hábeas corpus m

haberdasher [ˈhæbədæʃəʳ] N (Brit) mercero/a m/f; (US) camisero/a m/f; **~'s (shop)** (Brit) mercería f; (US) camisería f

haberdashery [ˌhæbəˈdæʃərɪ] N **1** (= shop) (Brit) mercería f; (US) camisería f **2** (= goods) (Brit) mercería f; (US) artículos mpl de moda para caballeros

habit [ˈhæbɪt] N **1** costumbre f; **a bad** ~ un vicio, una mala costumbre; **to get into the ~ of doing sth** acostumbrarse a hacer algo; **to get out of the ~ of doing sth** perder la costumbre de hacer algo; **to have a ~*** [drug user] drogarse habitualmente; **to be in the ~ of doing sth** tener la costumbre de hacer algo, acostumbrar or soler hacer algo; **we mustn't make a ~ of arriving late** no debemos acostumbrarnos a llegar tarde; **out of ~** por costumbre **2** (monk's) hábito m

habitable [ˈhæbɪtəbl] ADJ habitable

habitat [ˈhæbɪtæt] N hábitat m

habitation [ˌhæbɪˈteɪʃən] N **to be fit/unfit for (human) ~** estar/no estar en condiciones de habitabilidad; **there was no sign of (human) ~** no había señales de que estuviera habitado

habit-forming [ˈhæbɪtˌfɔːmɪŋ] ADJ que crea hábito

habitual [həˈbɪtjʊəl] ADJ habitual, acostumbrado; [drunkard, liar etc] inveterado, empedernido

habitually [həˈbɪtjʊəlɪ] ADV (= usually) por costumbre; (= constantly) constantemente

habituate [həˈbɪtjʊeɪt] VT acostumbrar, habituar (**to** a)

hack¹ [hæk] **Ⓐ** VT **1** (= cut) cortar; **to ~ sth to pieces** hacer algo pedazos (a hachazos) **2 I can't ~ it*** no puedo hacerlo **Ⓑ** VI **1** (= cut) dar tajos (**at** a) **2** (Comput) **to ~ into a system** piratear un sistema, conseguir entrar en un sistema

hack² [hæk] **Ⓐ** N **1** (= writer) escritorzuelo/a m/f, plumífero/a m/f; (= journalist) gacetillero/a m/f **2** (US*) (= taxi) taxi m **Ⓑ** CPD ➤ **hack reporter** reportero/a m/f de poca monta

hacker [ˈhækəʳ] N (Comput) pirata mf informático/a

hacking¹ [ˈhækɪŋ] ADJ [cough] seco

hacking² [ˈhækɪŋ] N (Comput) piratería f informática

hackneyed [ˈhæknɪd] ADJ [saying] trillado, gastado

hacksaw [ˈhæksɔː] N sierra f para metales

had [hæd] PT, PP of **have**

haddock [ˈhædək] N (pl ~) eglefino m

hadn't [ˈhædnt] = **had not**; see **have**

haematologist, hematologist (US) [ˌhiːməˈtɒlədʒɪst] N hematólogo/a m/f

haematology, hematology (US) [ˌhiːməˈtɒlədʒɪ] N hematología f

haemoglobin, hemoglobin (US) [ˌhiːməʊˈgləʊbɪn] N hemoglobina f

haemophilia, hemophilia (US) [ˌhiːməʊˈfɪlɪə] N hemofilia f

haemophiliac, hemophiliac (US) [ˌhiːməʊˈfɪlɪæk] ADJ, N hemofílico/a m/f

haemorrhage, hemorrhage (US) [ˈhemərɪdʒ] **Ⓐ** N hemorragia f **Ⓑ** VI sangrar profusamente

haemorrhoids, hemorrhoids (US) [ˈhemərɔɪdz] NPL hemorroides fpl

hag [hæg] N vieja f fea, bruja f

haggard [ˈhægəd] ADJ (from tiredness) ojeroso; (= unwell, unhealthy) demacrado, macilento

haggis [ˈhægɪs] N (Scot Culin) asaduras de cordero, avena y especias, cocidas en las tripas del animal

haggle [ˈhægl] VI regatear; **to ~ over the price** regatear, regatear el precio

haggling [ˈhæglɪŋ] N (over price) regateo m

Hague [heɪg] N **The ~** La Haya

hail¹ [heɪl] **Ⓐ** N **1** (Met) granizo m, pedrisco m **2** (fig) [of bullets] lluvia f; [of abuse, insults] sarta f, torrente m **Ⓑ** VI granizar

hail² [heɪl] VT **1** (= acclaim) aclamar (**as** como) **2** (= call to) llamar, gritar a; [+ taxi] llamar, hacer señas a

hailstone [ˈheɪlstəʊn] N granizo m, piedra f (de granizo)

hailstorm [ˈheɪlstɔːm] N granizada f

hair [hɛəʳ] N **1** pelo m, cabello m; (on legs etc) vello m; [of animal] pelo m, piel f; (= fluff) pelusa f; **to do one's ~/have one's ~ done** arreglarse el pelo; **she's got long ~** tiene el pelo largo; **to wash one's ~** lavarse la cabeza or el pelo; ✦ IDIOMS **keep your ~ on!** (Brit*) ¡cálmate!; **to let one's ~ down*** soltarse la melena*, relajarse (esp LAm); **to make sb's ~ stand on end** poner los pelos de punta a algn **2** (= single hair) pelo m; **to be within a ~'s breadth of** estar a dos dedos de **Ⓑ** CPD [follicle, transplant] capilar; [lacquer] para el pelo ➤ **hair appointment: to have/make a ~ appointment** tener/pedir hora en la peluquería ➤ **hair clip** horquilla f, clipe m ➤ **hair conditioner** suavizante m or (LAm) enjuague m para el cabello ➤ **hair curler** rulo m, bigudí m ➤ **hair gel** fijador m ➤ **hair grip** (Brit) horquilla f, clipe m ➤ **hair oil** brillantina f ➤ **hair remover** depilatorio m ➤ **hair restorer** loción f capilar ➤ **hair slide** (Brit) pasador m, hebilla f (SC) ➤ **hair style** peinado m ➤ **hair stylist** peluquero/a m/f estilista

hairband [ˈhɛəbænd] N cinta f

hairbrush [ˈhɛəbrʌʃ] N cepillo m (para el pelo)

haircut [ˈhɛəkʌt] N corte m de pelo, corte m; **to have** or **get a ~** cortarse el pelo

hairdo* [ˈhɛəduː] N peinado m

hairdresser [ˈhɛəˌdresəʳ] N peluquero/a m/f; **~'s** peluquería f

hairdressing [ˈhɛədresɪŋ] N peluquería f ➤ **hairdressing salon** salón m de peluquería

hairdryer, hairdrier [ˈhɛədraɪəʳ] N secador m de pelo

hairless [ˈhɛəlɪs] ADJ sin pelo, calvo; (= beardless) lampiño

hairline [ˈhɛəlaɪn] N (on head) nacimiento m del pelo ➤ **hairline crack** grieta f fina ➤ **hairline fracture** fractura f fina

hairnet [ˈhɛənet] N redecilla f

hairpiece [ˈhɛəpiːs] N postizo m, tupé m; (= false plait) trenza f postiza

hairpin [ˈhɛəpɪn] N horquilla f ➤ **hairpin bend, hairpin curve** (US) revuelta f, curva f muy cerrada

hair-raising [ˈhɛəˌreɪzɪŋ] ADJ espeluznante

hair-splitting [ˈhɛəˌsplɪtɪŋ] N nimiedades fpl, sutilezas fpl

hairspray [ˈhɛəspreɪ] N laca f (para el pelo)

hairy [ˈhɛərɪ] ADJ (compar **hairier**; superl **hairiest**) **1** [chest, legs, arms] peludo, velludo **2** (*) (= frightening) espeluznante

Haiti [ˈheɪtɪ] N Haití m

Haitian [ˈheɪʃən] ADJ, N haitiano/a m/f

hake [heɪk] N (pl ~) merluza f

halcyon [ˈhælsɪən] ADJ **~ days** días mpl felices

hale [heɪl] ADJ **~ and hearty** robusto, sano y fuerte

half [hɑːf] N (pl **halves**) **Ⓐ** N **1** (gen) mitad f; **give me ~** dame la mitad; **~ of my friends** la mitad de mis amigos; **~ a cup** media taza f; **~ a day** medio día m; **a pound and a ~** ◇ **one and a ~ pounds** libra f y media; **three and a ~ hours** tres horas y media; **we have a problem and a ~*** tenemos un problema mayúsculo, vaya problemazo que tenemos; **one's better ~*** (hum) su media naranja*; **he's too clever by ~*** se pasa de listo; **he doesn't do things by halves** no hace las cosas a medias; **~ a dozen** media docena f; **to go halves (with sb) (on sth)** ir a medias (con algn) (en algo); **~ an**

hour media hora *f*; **to cut/break sth <u>in</u>** ~ cortar/partir algo por la mitad; **one's <u>other</u> ~*** (*hum*) su media naranja*; ~ **a <u>second</u>!*** ¡un momento!; **they don't know <u>the</u> ~ of it*** no saben de la misa la media; **she's asleep ~ the <u>time</u>** (*iro*) se pasa la mitad del tiempo dormida
2 (*Sport*) (= *player*) medio *m*; **first/second** ~ primer/segundo tiempo *m*
3 (*Brit*) [*of beer*] media pinta *f*
4 (= *child's ticket*) billete *m* (*Sp*) *or* boleto *m* (*LAm*) de niño
5 (*time*) ~ **past four** ◇ ~ **four** (*Brit**) las cuatro y media
Ⓑ ADJ [*bottle, quantity*] medio; **I have a ~ <u>share</u> in the flat** la mitad del piso es mío *or* de mi propiedad
Ⓒ ADV **1** (*gen*) medio, a medias; ~ **laughing,** ~ **crying** medio riendo, medio llorando; **I was ~ <u>afraid</u> that ...** medio temía que ...; ~ **<u>as much</u>** la mitad; ~ **as big** la mitad de grande; **they paid ~ as much again** pagaron la mitad más; **there were only ~ as many people as before** había solamente la mitad de los que había antes; **it wasn't ~ as bad as I had thought*** no lo pasé ni con mucho *or* ni de lejos tan mal como había imaginado; ~ **<u>asleep</u>** medio dormido; ~ **<u>closed</u>** entreabierto; ~ **<u>done</u>** a medio hacer; ~ **<u>naked</u>** semidesnudo; **I only ~ <u>read</u> it** lo leí sólo a medias; **I was only ~ <u>serious</u> when I said that** aquello sólo lo dije medio en broma
2 (*with neg*) (*Brit**): **not ~!** ¡y cómo!, ¡ya lo creo!; **he didn't ~ run** corrió muchísimo, corrió como un bólido
Ⓓ CPD ► **half board** (*Brit*) (*in hotel*) media pensión *f* ► **half brother** medio hermano *m*, hermanastro *m* ► **half day** medio día *m*, media jornada *f* ► **half dozen** media docena *f* ► **half fare** medio pasaje *m*; **to travel ~ fare** viajar pagando medio pasaje ► **half hour** media hora *f*; **the clock struck the ~ hour** el reloj dio y media *or* dio la media ► **half life** (*Phys*) media vida *f* ► **half measures** paños *mpl* calientes, medias tintas *fpl*; **we don't want any ~ measures** no queremos andarnos con medias tintas *or* paños calientes ► **half moon** media luna *f* ► **half note** (*US Mus*) blanca *f* ► **half pay** media paga *f*; **to retire on ~ pay** jubilarse con media paga ► **half pint** media pinta *f* ► **half sister** media hermana *f*, hermanastra *f* ► **half term** (*Brit*) vacaciones *fpl* de mediados del trimestre ► **half time** (*Sport*) descanso *m*; **at ~ time** en el descanso ► **half-time score** marcador *m* en el descanso

half-and-half [ˌhɑːfənd'hɑːf] ADV (= *in equal parts*) (*gen*) a partes iguales, mitad y mitad; (*Culin*) a partes iguales, en cantidades iguales; **to split sth ~** dividir algo en dos mitades (a partes iguales)

halfback ['hɑːfbæk] N medio/a *m/f*

half-baked ['hɑːf'beɪkt] ADJ mal concebido, sin perfilar

half-cock ['hɑːf'kɒk] N ✦ IDIOM **to go off at ~** [*person*] hacer las cosas antes de tiempo; [*plan*] irse al garete (por falta de preparación)*

half-dead ['hɑːf'ded] ADJ medio muerto, más muerto que vivo

half-empty ['hɑːf'emptɪ] ADJ [*bottle, box, room, train*] medio vacío; [*hall*] semidesierto

half-hearted ['hɑːf'hɑːtɪd] ADJ [*effort*] tibio; [*applause*] tímido, poco entusiasta

half-heartedly ['hɑːf'hɑːtɪdlɪ] ADV con poco entusiasmo

half-mast ['hɑːf'mɑːst] N **at ~** a media asta

halfpenny ['heɪpnɪ] N (*pl* **halfpennies** *or* **halfpence** ['heɪpəns]) (*Brit Hist*) medio penique *m*

half-price ['hɑːf'praɪs] ADJ, ADV a mitad de precio

half-timbered [ˌhɑːf'tɪmbəd] ADJ con entramado de madera

halfway ['hɑːf'weɪ] **Ⓐ** ADV **1** (*lit*) a mitad de camino, a medio camino; **Reading is ~ between Oxford and London** Reading está a mitad de camino *or* a medio camino entre Oxford y Londres; **we're ~ there** (*lit, fig*) estamos a mitad de camino *or* a medio camino; ~ **up/down the hill** a media cuesta; **her hair reaches ~ down her back** el pelo le llega hasta la mitad de la espalda; **they've travelled ~ around the world** han recorrido medio mundo; ~ **through the film** hacia la mitad de la película, a (la) mitad de la película; **the decision only goes ~ toward giving the strikers what they want** la decisión sólo satisface a medias las demandas de los huelguistas; ✦ IDIOM **to meet sb ~** llegar a un

compromiso con algn
2 (*) (= *at all*) **anything ~ decent will be incredibly expensive** cualquier cosa mínimamente decente va a ser carísima
Ⓑ ADJ [*stage*] intermedio; **the ~ mark** (*lit*) (la) mitad del camino; **we're at the ~ mark** (*fig*) estamos a mitad de camino
Ⓒ CPD ► **halfway house** (*for rehabilitation*) centro *m* de reinserción; (*fig*) punto *m* medio, término *m* medio

halfwit ['hɑːfwɪt] N imbécil *mf*, tonto/a *m/f*

half-yearly ['hɑːf'jɪəlɪ] (*Brit*) **Ⓐ** ADV semestralmente **Ⓑ** ADJ semestral

halibut ['hælɪbət] N (*pl* ~) halibut *m*, hipogloso *m*

hall [hɔːl] **Ⓐ** N **1** (*Brit*) (= *entrance hall*) hall *m*, entrada *f* **2** (*esp US*) (= *passage*) pasillo *m* **3** (= *large room, building*) sala *f* **4** (= *mansion*) casa *f* solariega **5** (*Brit*) (*also* ~ **of residence**) residencia *f*, colegio *m* mayor **Ⓑ** CPD ► **hall porter** (*Brit*) portero/a *m/f*, conserje *mf*

hallelujah [ˌhælɪ'luːjə] N, EXCL aleluya *f*

hallmark ['hɔːlmɑːk] N (*lit*) contraste *m*; (*fig*) sello *m*

hallo [hʌ'ləʊ] EXCL = **hello**

hallowed ['hæləʊd] ADJ sagrado, santificado

Hallowe'en ['hæləʊ'iːn] N víspera *f* de Todos los Santos

HALLOWE'EN

En la noche del 31 de octubre se celebra en el Reino Unido y en EE.UU. la festividad de **Hallowe'en**. Aunque antes estaba asociada a la creencia de que las almas de los difuntos regresaban a sus hogares en esa fecha, actualmente **Hallowe'en** no es más que una excusa para celebrar fiestas de disfraces y el tradicional **trick or treat**, una costumbre en la que los niños, disfrazados de fantasmas o brujas, llevan una calabaza hueca con una vela de casa en casa y amenazan al vecino con gastarle una broma si no les dan dinero o golosinas.

---

hallucinate [hə'luːsɪneɪt] VI alucinar, tener alucinaciones

hallucination [həˌluːsɪ'neɪʃən] N alucinación *f*

hallucinatory [hə'luːsɪnətərɪ] ADJ alucinante

hallucinogenic [həˌluːsɪnəʊ'dʒenɪk] ADJ alucinógeno

hallway ['hɔːlweɪ] N (= *passage*) pasillo *m*; (*Brit*) (= *entrance hall*) hall *m*, entrada *f*

halo ['heɪləʊ] N (*pl* ~**es** *or* ~**s**) halo *m*, aureola *f*

halogen ['heɪləʊdʒɪn] N halógeno *m*

halt [hɔːlt] **Ⓐ** N (= *stop*) alto *m*, parada *f*; **to come to a ~** [*car*] pararse, detenerse; [*train*] hacer alto, detenerse; [*negotiations*] interrumpirse; **to call a ~ (to sth)** poner fin (a algo) **Ⓑ** VT [+ *vehicle, production*] parar, detener **Ⓒ** VI (*gen*) pararse, detenerse; [*train*] hacer alto, detenerse; **halt!** (*Mil*) ¡alto! **Ⓓ** CPD ► **halt sign** señal *f* de stop

halter ['hɔːltə'] N (*for horse*) cabestro *m*, ronzal *m*

halter-neck ['hɔːltənek] ADJ [*dress, top*] atado a la nuca

halting ['hɔːltɪŋ] ADJ titubeante, vacilante

halve [hɑːv] **Ⓐ** VT (= *divide*) partir por la mitad, partir en dos; (= *reduce by half*) reducir a la mitad **Ⓑ** VI reducirse a la mitad

halves [hɑːvz] NPL *of* **half**

ham [hæm] N **1** (*Culin*) jamón *m* **2** (*Theat*) (*also* ~ **actor**) comicastro *m*, actor *m* histriónico; (*also* ~ **actress**) actriz *f* histriónica **3** (= *radio ham*) radioaficionado/a *m/f*
► **ham up*** VT + ADV **to ~ it up*** actuar de manera exagerada *or* melodramática

hamburger ['hæmˌbɜːgə'] N hamburguesa *f*; (*US*) (*also* ~ **meat**) carne *f* picada

ham-fisted [ˌhæm'fɪstɪd], **ham-handed** [ˌhæm'hændɪd] ADJ torpe, desmañado

hamlet ['hæmlɪt] N aldea *f*, caserío *m*

hammer ['hæmə'] **Ⓐ** N martillo *m*; **to come under the ~** ser subastado; ✦ IDIOM **to go at it ~ and tongs*** (= *argue*) discutir acaloradamente; (= *fight*) luchar a brazo partido

ⓑ VT **1** [+ *nail*] clavar; [+ *metal*] martillar, batir; **to ~ a post into the ground** hincar un poste en el suelo a martillazos; **to ~ sth into sb** (*fig*) meter algo en la cabeza de algn **2** (*Brit**) (= *defeat*) dar una paliza a*, machacar* **ⓒ** VI **to ~ at a door** dar golpes en *or* golpear una puerta
➤ **hammer in** VT + ADV meter a martillazos
➤ **hammer out** VT + ADV [+ *agreement*] negociar no sin esfuerzo

hammering ['hæmərɪŋ] N (*) (= *defeat*) paliza* *f*; **to give sb a ~** dar una paliza a algn*

hammock ['hæmək] N hamaca *f*; (*Naut*) coy *m*

hamper¹ ['hæmpə*ʳ*] N cesto *m*, canasta *f*

hamper² ['hæmpə*ʳ*] VT [+ *efforts, work*] dificultar, entorpecer; [+ *movement*] obstaculizar, impedir

hamster ['hæmstə*ʳ*] N hámster *m*

hamstring ['hæmstrɪŋ] N [*of person*] tendón *m* de la corva
➤ **hamstring injury** lesión *f* del tendón de la corva

hand [hænd] **ⓐ** N **1** (= *part of body*) mano *f*; **to have sth in one's ~** tener algo en la mano; **to be good with one's ~s** ser hábil con las manos, ser un manitas; **to hold ~s** [*children*] ir cogidos de la mano, ir tomados de la mano (*LAm*); [*lovers*] hacer manitas; **on (one's) ~s and knees** a gatas; **~s off!*** ¡fuera las manos!, ¡no se toca!; **~s off those chocolates!** ¡los bombones ni tocarlos!; **~s up!** (*to criminal*) ¡arriba las manos!; (*to pupils*) ¡que levanten la mano!; ✦ IDIOMS **to be making money ~ over fist** ganar dinero a espuertas; **to be losing money ~ over fist** hacerle agua el dinero; **to be ~ in glove with sb** (= *very close*) ser uña y carne con algn; (= *in cahoots*) estar conchabado con algn; **to live from ~ to mouth** vivir al día; **my ~s are tied** tengo las manos atadas, no puedo hacer nada; **I could do it with one ~ tied behind my back** lo podría hacer con una mano atada a la espalda; **he never does a ~'s turn** no da golpe; ✦ PROV **many ~s make light work** muchas manos facilitan el trabajo
2 (= *needle*) [*of instrument*] aguja *f*; [*of clock*] manecilla *f*, aguja *f*; **the big ~*** la manecilla grande, el minutero; **the little ~*** la manecilla pequeña, el horario
3 (= *agency, influence*) mano *f*, influencia *f*; **to have a ~ in** tomar parte en, intervenir en; **he had no ~ in it** no tuvo arte ni parte en ello
4 (= *worker*) (*in factory*) obrero *a m/f*; (= *farm hand*) peón *m*; (= *deck hand*) marinero *m* (de cubierta); **all ~s on deck!** (*Naut*) ¡todos a cubierta!; **to be lost with all ~s** hundirse con toda la tripulación; ✦ IDIOM **to be an old ~ (at sth)** ser perro viejo (en algo)
5 (= *help*) mano *f*; **to give** *or* **lend sb a ~** echar una mano a algn
6 (= *handwriting*) letra *f*, escritura *f*; **in one's own ~** de su (propio) puño y letra
7 (*Cards*) (= *round*) mano *f*, partida *f*; (= *cards held*) mano *f*
8 (*) (= *round of applause*) **they gave him a big ~** le aplaudieron calurosamente; **let's have a big ~ for ...!** ¡muchos aplausos para ...!
9 (*phrases with verb*) **to ask for sb's ~** (**in marriage**) pedir la mano de algn; **to change ~s** cambiar de mano *or* de dueño; **just wait till I get my ~s on him!** ¡espera (a) que le ponga la mano encima!; **to raise one's ~ to sb** poner a algn la mano encima; **to take a ~ in sth** tomar parte *or* participar en algo; **to try one's ~ at sth** probar algo; ✦ IDIOMS **to give with one ~ and take away with the other** quitar con una mano lo que se da con la otra; **to keep one's ~ in** conservar *or* no perder la práctica (**at** de); **to sit on one's ~s** (*US**) [*audience*] aplaudir con desgana; [*committee etc*] no hacer nada; **to turn one's ~ to sth** dedicarse a algo; **to wait on sb ~ and foot** desvivirse por algn, ponérselo todo en bandeja a algn
10 (*phrases with adjective*) **to rule with a firm ~** gobernar con firmeza; **to give sb a free ~** dar carta blanca a algn; **to have one's ~s full** estar muy ocupado; **don't worry, she's in good ~s** no te preocupes, está en buenas manos; **with a heavy ~** con mano dura; **to have the upper ~** tener *or* llevar la ventaja; **if this should get into the wrong ~ ...** si esto cayera en manos de quien no debiera ...
11 (= *after preposition*) **don't worry, help is at ~** no te preocupes, disponemos de *or* contamos con ayuda; **we're close at ~ in case she needs help** nos tiene a mano *or* muy cerca si necesita ayuda; **at first ~** de primera mano; **I heard**

it only at second ~ lo supe sólo de modo indirecto; **at the ~s of** a manos de; **made by ~** hecho a mano; **delivered by ~** entregado en mano; **to take sb by the ~** coger *or* tomar a algn de la mano; **to fall into the ~s of the enemy** caer en manos del enemigo; **they were going along ~ in ~** iban cogidos de la mano; **it goes ~ in ~ with** está estrechamente relacionado con; **to be in sb's ~s** estar en manos de algn; **it's in his ~s now** depende de él ahora; **I put myself in your ~s** me pongo en tus manos; **to have £50 in ~** (*Brit*) tener 50 libras en el haber; **the situation is in ~** tenemos la situación controlada *or* bajo control; **let's concentrate on the job in ~** centrémonos en el trabajo que tenemos entre manos; **to take sth in ~** tomar algo a cuestas; **to take sb in ~** (= *take charge of*) hacerse cargo de algn; (= *discipline*) imponer disciplina a algn; **on the right/left ~** a (mano) derecha/izquierda; **on the one ~ ... on the other ~** por una parte ... por otra parte, por un lado ... por otro lado; **on the other ~, she did agree to do it** pero el caso es que ella (sí) había accedido a hacerlo; **there are experts on ~ to give you advice** hay expertos a su disposición para ofrecerle asesoramiento; **I've got him on my ~s all day** está conmigo todo el día; **we've got a difficult job on our ~s** tenemos entre manos una difícil tarea; **he's got time on his ~s** tiene todo el tiempo del mundo; **to dismiss sth out of ~** descartar algo sin más; **the situation was getting out of ~** la situación se estaba escapando de las manos; **to play into sb's ~s** hacer el juego a algn; **to take justice into one's own ~s** tomar la justicia por su propia mano; **to have sth to ~** tener algo a mano
ⓑ VT (= *pass*) **to ~ sb sth** ✧ **~ sth to sb** pasar algo a algn; ✦ IDIOM **you've got to ~ it to him*** hay que reconocérselo
ⓒ CPD [*lotion, cream*] para las manos ➤ **hand baggage** (*US*) equipaje *m* de mano ➤ **hand controls** controles *mpl* manuales ➤ **hand drier, hand dryer** secamanos *m inv* automático ➤ **hand grenade** granada *f* (de mano) ➤ **hand luggage** equipaje *m* de mano ➤ **hand towel** toalla *f* de manos
➤ **hand around** VT + ADV [+ *information, bottle*] pasar (de mano en mano); [+ *biscuits*] ofrecer; [+ *copies*] repartir
➤ **hand back** VT + ADV devolver
➤ **hand down** VT + ADV [+ *suitcase etc*] bajar, pasar; [+ *heirloom*] pasar, dejar en herencia; [+ *tradition*] transmitir
➤ **hand in** VT + ADV [+ *form, homework*] entregar; [+ *resignation*] presentar
➤ **hand on** VT + ADV [+ *tradition*] transmitir; [+ *news*] comunicar; [+ *object*] pasar
➤ **hand out** VT + ADV [+ *leaflets*] repartir, distribuir; [+ *advice*] dar
➤ **hand over ⓐ** VT + ADV **1** (= *pass over*) pasar **2** (= *give in*) [+ *driving licence, passport*] entregar; (= *surrender*) [+ *property, business*] traspasar, ceder; [+ *power, government*] ceder **ⓑ** VI + ADV (*to successor*) ceder su puesto a; **I'm now ~ing over to the studio** (*Rad, TV*) ahora devolvemos la conexión al estudio
➤ **hand round** VT + ADV (*Brit*) = **hand around**

handbag ['hændbæg] N bolso *m* (de mano), bolsa *f* (de mano), cartera *f* (*LAm*)

handball ['hændbɔ:l] N **1** (= *game*) balonmano *m* **2** (*Brit*) (= *offence in football*) mano *f*

handbasin ['hændˌbeɪsn] N lavabo *m*

handbill ['hændbɪl] N folleto *m*, octavilla *f*

handbook ['hændbʊk] N manual *m*

handbrake ['hændbreɪk] N (*Brit*) freno *m* de mano

handcream ['hændkri:m] N crema *f* para las manos

handcuff ['hændkʌf] **ⓐ** VT poner las esposas a, esposar **ⓑ** N **handcuffs** esposas *fpl*

handful ['hændfʊl] N (*measuring out*) manojo *m*, puñado *m*; (= *small number*) puñado *m*; **a ~ of people** un puñado de gente; **that child's a real ~*** ese niño es muy travieso

handgun ['hændgʌn] N (*esp US*) revólver *m*, pistola *f*

hand-held ['hændheld] ADJ de mano; (= *portable*) portátil

handicap ['hændɪkæp] **ⓐ** N **1** (= *disadvantage*) desventaja *f*; (= *impediment*) obstáculo *m*, estorbo *m* **2** (*Sport*) hándicap *m* **3** (*Med*) discapacidad *f*, minusvalía *f* **ⓑ** VT perjudicar; (*Sport*) establecer un hándicap para

handicapped ['hændɪkæpt] Ⓐ ADJ discapacitado; **mentally** ~ mentalmente discapacitado, psíquicamente disminuido; **physically** ~ (físicamente) discapacitado, minusválido; **to be mentally/physically** ~ tener una discapacidad mental/física, ser (un) discapacitado mental/físico Ⓑ N **the** ~ (gen) los discapacitados; (physically) los discapacitados, los minusválidos; **the mentally** ~ los discapacitados mentales, los disminuidos psíquicos

handicraft ['hændɪkrɑːft] N artesanía f

handiwork ['hændɪwɜːk] N obra f; **this looks like his** ~ (pej) parece que es obra de él

handkerchief ['hæŋkətʃɪf] N pañuelo m

hand-knitted [ˌhændˈnɪtɪd] ADJ tricotado a mano, tejido a mano (LAm)

handle ['hændl] Ⓐ N [of knife, brush, spade, saucepan] mango m; [of broom] palo m; [of basket, bucket, jug] asa f; [of drawer] tirador m, manija f; [of door] (= round knob) pomo m; (= lever) picaporte m, manilla f (LAm); [of pump] palanca f

> Use **el/un** not **la/una** before feminine nouns beginning with stressed **a** or **ha** like **asa**.

✦ IDIOMS **to fly off the** ~ perder los estribos, salirse de sus casillas; **to have a** ~ **on sth*** tener algo controlado
Ⓑ VT **1** (with hands) (= touch) tocar; (= move) manipular; (= use) [+ gun, machine] manejar; **"please do not handle the fruit"** "se ruega no tocar la fruta"; **to** ~ **the ball** (Ftbl) tocar la pelota con la mano; **"handle with care"** "manéjese or trátese con cuidado"
2 (= use) [+ gun, machine] manejar; [+ car] conducir, manejar (LAm)
3 (= tackle) [+ situation] manejar; [+ people] tratar; **he** ~**d the situation very well** manejó or llevó muy bien la situación
4 (= manage effectively) [+ people] manejar bien; [+ emotions] controlar; **she can't** ~ **pressure** no puede con la presión
5 (= be responsible for) [+ case, investigation] llevar, encargarse de; **the treasurer** ~**s large sums of money** el tesorero maneja grandes cantidades de dinero; **I'll** ~ **this** yo me encargo (de esto)
6 (= deal in) [+ goods] comerciar con; **to** ~ **stolen goods** comerciar con objetos robados; **we don't** ~ **that type of business** no hacemos ese tipo de trabajos
7 (= process) **a computer can store and** ~ **large amounts of information** un ordenador puede almacenar y trabajar con or procesar muchísima información; **there is an extra fee for handling and packing your order** hay un recargo por tramitación y embalaje de su pedido; **we** ~ **ten per cent of their total sales** movemos or trabajamos un diez por ciento del total de sus ventas; **we** ~ **2,000 travellers a day** (gen) por aquí pasan 2.000 viajeros cada día; [airport spokesperson] hacemos el handling para 2,000 pasajeros cada día
Ⓒ VI [car, plane, horse] comportarse; **this car** ~**s like a dream** este coche va or se comporta de maravilla

handlebars ['hændlbɑːz] NPL manillar msing, manubrio msing

handler ['hændlə'] N (also **dog** ~) adiestrador(a) m/f

handling ['hændlɪŋ] Ⓐ N **1** (lit) (= treatment) trato m; (= manipulation) manejo m; (= touching) manoseo m
2 (= management) [of situation, animal, money] manejo m; [of person] trato m; **the minister was criticized for his** ~ **of the economy** el ministro fue criticado por su forma de manejar or llevar la economía Ⓑ CPD ➤ **handling charges** gastos mpl de tramitación

handmade ['hændmeɪd] ADJ hecho a mano

hand-me-down* ['hændmɪdaʊn] N prenda f usada

handout ['hændaʊt] N **1** (= leaflet) octavilla f, panfleto m; (= pamphlet) folleto m; (= press handout) nota f de prensa; (at lecture) hoja f **2** (*) (= money) limosna f

handover ['hændəʊvə'] N (Pol) entrega f, transferencia f

hand-picked ['hændˈpɪkt] ADJ [people, staff] cuidadosamente seleccionado, muy escogido; [fruit] cosechado or (LAm) recogido a mano

handrail ['hændreɪl] N (on staircase etc) pasamanos m inv, barandilla f; (on ship) barandilla f

handset ['hændset] N (Telec) aparato m, auricular m

hands-free ['hændzfriː] ADJ [telephone etc] manos libres

handshake ['hændʃeɪk] N apretón m de manos; (Comput) coloquio m; (as data signal) "acuse de recibo"; **she had a firm** ~ estrechaba la mano con fuerza

hands-off [hændzˈɒf] ADJ [policy, approach] de no intervención

handsome ['hænsəm] ADJ (compar ~**r**; superl ~**st**) **1** [man] guapo, bien parecido; [house, furniture] bello, espléndido **2** [fortune, profit] cuantioso; [salary, sum] generoso, espléndido; [increase] importante; [win, victory] amplio, holgado

handsomely ['hænsəmlɪ] ADV **1** [illustrated] espléndidamente **2** [pay, reward] generosamente, espléndidamente **3** [win] fácilmente, por un amplio margen; **this strategy has paid off** ~ esta estrategia bien ha merecido la pena

hands-on [hændzˈɒn] ADJ [experience] práctico

handstand ['hændstænd] N **to do a** ~ hacer el pino

hand-to-hand ['hændtəˈhænd] ADV, ADJ cuerpo a cuerpo

hand-to-mouth ['hændtəˈmaʊθ] ADJ [existence] precario

hand-wash ['hændwɒʃ] VT lavar a mano

hand-woven [hændˈwəʊvən] ADJ tejido a mano

handwriting ['hændˌraɪtɪŋ] N letra f, escritura f

handwritten ['hændˈrɪtn] ADJ escrito a mano

handy ['hændɪ] ADJ (compar **handier**; superl **handiest**)
1 (= at hand) [scissors, book] a mano; (= conveniently close) [shops, station] cerca, a mano; **have you got a pen** ~? ¿tienes un bolígrafo a mano?; **our house is** ~ **for the shops** nuestra casa está or queda cerca de las tiendas; **to keep sth** ~ tener algo a mano
2 (= useful) [tool, gadget, hint] práctico, útil; **credit cards can be** ~ las tarjetas de crédito pueden resultar muy prácticas or útiles; **the cheque came in very** ~ el cheque nos vino muy bien
3 (= skilful) [carpenter, mechanic] hábil, diestro; **he's** ~ **around the home** es un manitas en la casa; **she's** ~ **with a paintbrush/needle** es muy mañosa para la pintura/costura, se le da muy bien la pintura/costura

handyman ['hændɪmən] N (pl **handymen**) manitas mf (Sp, Mex) (hombre que tiene dotes prácticas para hacer trabajos de carpintería etc en casa)

hang

Ⓐ TRANSITIVE VERB	Ⓒ NOUN
Ⓑ INTRANSITIVE VERB	Ⓓ PHRASAL VERBS

hang [hæŋ] (pt, pp **hung**)
Ⓐ TRANSITIVE VERB
1 (= suspend) [+ coat, curtains] colgar; [+ picture] (on wall) colgar; (as exhibit) exponer; [+ washing] tender; [+ door] colocar; **are you any good at** ~**ing wallpaper?** ¿se te da bien empapelar?; ✦ IDIOM **to** ~ **one's head** bajar or agachar la cabeza
2 (= decorate) adornar; **the walls were hung with tapestries** las paredes estaban adornadas con tapices
3 (pt, pp ~**ed**) (= execute) ahorcar; **to** ~ **o.s.** ahorcarse
Ⓑ INTRANSITIVE VERB
1 (= be suspended) colgar; **a light-bulb was** ~**ing from the ceiling** una bombilla colgaba del techo; **his portrait** ~**s in the National Gallery** su retrato está expuesto en la National Gallery
2 (= be positioned) **to** ~ **open:** **the door hung open** (= not closed) la puerta estaba abierta; (= partly off hinges) la puerta estaba encajada; **to** ~ **out of the window** [person] asomarse por la ventana; [thing] colgar de la ventana
3 (= flow) [rope, garment, hair] caer; **her hair** ~**s down her back** el pelo le cae por la espalda
4 (pt, pp ~**ed**) (= be hanged) [criminal] morir en la horca; **he'll** ~ **for it** lo ahorcarán por esto
5 (= hover) [fog] flotar; **the threat** ~**ing over us** la amenaza que se cierne sobre nosotros; **a question mark** ~**s over many of their futures** se cierne un or una interrogante sobre el porvenir de muchos de ellos

ⒸNOUN
1 [*of garment*] caída *f*
2 ✦ IDIOM **to get the ~ of sth*** coger el tranquillo a algo*,
agarrarle la onda a algo (*esp Mex*)
ⒹPHRASAL VERBS
➤ **hang around, hang about** (*Brit*) Ⓐ VI + ADV **1** (= *spend
time*) **they always ~ around together** siempre van *or* andan
juntos; **to ~ around with sb** juntarse *or* andar con algn
2 (= *loiter*) holgazanear **3** (= *wait*) quedarse a esperar; **to
keep sb ~ing around** hacer esperar a algn, tener a algn
esperando Ⓑ VI + PREP **the crowd who hung around the café**
el grupo que frecuentaba el café; **schoolboys who ~ around
the streets after school** colegiales que rondan por las
calles después de clase
➤ **hang back** VI + ADV **1** (= *hesitate*) no decidirse **2** (= *stay
behind*) quedarse atrás
➤ **hang down** VI + ADV colgar, pender
➤ **hang in*** VI + ADV **~ in there!** ¡aguanta!
➤ **hang on** Ⓐ VI + PREP **1 she hung on his arm** iba agarrada
de su brazo; ✦ IDIOM **to ~ on sb's every word** estar
pendiente de todo lo que dice algn, no perder detalle de
lo que dice algn
2 (= *depend on*) depender de; **everything ~s on his decision**
todo depende de su decisión
Ⓑ VI + ADV **1** (= *grip, hold*) **to ~ on (to sth)** agarrarse (a *or* de
algo); **~ on tight** agárrate fuerte
2 (*) (= *wait*) esperar; **~ on a minute!** ¡espera (un
momento)!; **could you ~ on, please?** (*Telec*) no cuelgue,
por favor
3 (= *hold out*) aguantar; **he managed to ~ on till help came**
consiguió aguantar hasta que llegó ayuda; **~ on in there!***
¡aguanta!
➤ **hang out** Ⓐ VT + ADV [+ *washing*] tender; [+ *flags, banner*]
poner, colgar
Ⓑ VI + ADV **1** (= *hang loose*) colgar; **your shirt is ~ing out**
llevas la camisa colgando, tienes la camisa fuera **2** (*)
(= *spend time*) pasar el rato; (= *live*) vivir; **on Saturdays we ~
out in the park** los sábados pasamos el rato en el parque;
she ~s out with some strange people anda *or* se junta con
gente rara **3** (*) (= *hold out*) **they're ~ing out for more
money** siguen exigiendo más dinero, insisten en pedir más
dinero
➤ **hang round** VI + ADV, VI + PREP = **hang around**
➤ **hang together** VI + ADV (*logically*) (= *back one another up*)
sostenerse; (= *follow internal logic*) tener coherencia; **his
arguments just don't ~ together** sus argumentos no se
sostienen; **it all ~s together** todo tiene coherencia
➤ **hang up** Ⓐ VT + ADV **1** [+ *coat*] colgar **2** (*): **to be hung up
on sth** estar obsesionado por algo **3** (*Telec*) [+ *receiver*]
colgar Ⓑ VI + ADV **1** (= *be suspended*) estar colgado **2** (*Telec*)
colgar; **don't ~ up!** ¡no cuelgues!; **to ~ up on sb** colgar a
algn

hangar ['hæŋəʳ] N hangar *m*

hangdog ['hæŋdɒg] ADJ [*look, expression*] (= *guilty*)
avergonzado; (= *depressed*) abatido

hanger ['hæŋəʳ] N (*for clothes*) percha *f*, gancho *m* (*LAm*)

hanger-on* ['hæŋəʳˈɒn] N (*pl* **hangers-on**) parásito/a *m/f*,
pegote *mf* (*Sp**)

hang-glider ['hæŋˌglaɪdəʳ] N ala *f* delta

hang-gliding ['hæŋˌglaɪdɪŋ] N vuelo *m* con ala delta

hanging ['hæŋɪŋ] Ⓐ N **1** (= *death penalty*) (ejecución *f* en)
la horca, ahorcamiento *m*; **the last ~ in Britain** la última
ejecución en la horca en Gran Bretaña; **~s were
commonplace then** entonces los ahorcamientos eran
moneda corriente **2** (= *curtain*) colgadura *f*; **wall ~** tapiz *m*
Ⓑ ADJ [*bridge, plant, garden*] colgante Ⓒ CPD ➤ **hanging
basket** macetero *m* colgante

hangman ['hæŋmən] N (*pl* **hangmen**) verdugo *m*

hangover ['hæŋˌəʊvəʳ] N **1** (*after drinking*) resaca *f*, cruda *f*
(*LAm*) **2** (= *sth left over*) vestigio *m*, reliquia *f*

hang-up* ['hæŋʌp] N (= *complex*) complejo *m* (**about** con)

hanker ['hæŋkəʳ] VI **to ~ after sth** añorar *or* anhelar algo

hankering ['hæŋkərɪŋ] N añoranza *f* (**for** de), anhelo *m*
(**for** por); **to have a ~ for sth** añorar *or* anhelar algo

hankie*, **hanky*** ['hæŋkɪ] N pañuelo *m*

hanky-panky* ['hæŋkɪˈpæŋkɪ] N **1** (*US*) (= *trickery*) **there's
some ~ going on here** aquí hay trampa, esto huele a
camelo* **2** (*sexual*) relaciones *fpl* sospechosas; **we want no ~
with the girls** nada de meterse mano con las chicas*

Hanukkah ['hɑːnəkə] N celebración judía dedicada al
Templo de Jerusalén

haphazard ['hæpˈhæzəd] ADJ [*selection*] al azar; [*manner,
method*] poco sistemático; **the town has developed in a ~
way** la ciudad ha crecido sin planificación alguna *or* muy
desordenadamente

hapless ['hæplɪs] ADJ desventurado

happen ['hæpən] VI **1** (= *occur*) pasar, ocurrir, suceder; **what's
~ing?** ¿qué pasa *or* ocurre *or* sucede?; **these things ~** estas
cosas pasan, son cosas que pasan; **whatever ~s** pase lo que
pase; **don't let it ~ again** que no vuelva a ocurrir; **as if
nothing had ~ed** como si nada, como si tal cosa; **what has
~ed to him?** (= *befall*) ¿qué le ha pasado?; (= *become of*) ¿qué
ha sido de él?
2 (= *chance*) **if you ~ to see John, ...** si acaso vieras a John, ...,
si da la casualidad de que ves a John, ...; **I ~ to know that ...**
da la casualidad de que sé que ...; **if anyone should ~ to see
you** si acaso alguien te viera; **would you ~ to have a pen?** ¿no
tendrá un bolígrafo por casualidad?; **it ~s to be true** da la
casualidad de que es verdad; **as it ~s ...,** ✧ **it (just) so ~s
that ...** da la casualidad de que ...; **I do know him, as it ~s**
pues da la casualidad de que sí le conozco
➤ **happen (up)on** VI + PREP [+ *thing*] dar con, encontrar

happening ['hæpnɪŋ] N suceso *m*, acontecimiento *m*

happily ['hæpɪlɪ] ADV **1** (= *contentedly*) [*smile, say, play*]
alegremente, felizmente; **it all ended ~** todo acabó
felizmente, todo tuvo un final feliz; **he said he would ~
lend us the money** dijo que nos dejaría el dinero con
mucho gusto, dijo que gustosamente nos dejaría el
dinero; **and they all lived ~ ever after** y vivieron felices y
comieron perdices
2 (= *without difficulty*) sin ningún problema; **she'll ~ spend
£1,000 on a dress** se puede gastar 1.000 libras en un
vestido tan tranquilamente
3 (= *fortunately*) afortunadamente, por fortuna

happiness ['hæpɪnɪs] N (= *contentment*) felicidad *f*;
(= *cheerfulness*) alegría *f*

happy ['hæpɪ] Ⓐ ADJ (*compar* **happier**; *superl* **happiest**)
1 (= *contented*) feliz; (= *cheerful*) alegre; **we've been very ~
here** aquí hemos sido muy felices; **she has always been a ~
little girl** siempre ha sido una niña muy alegre; ✦ IDIOM **to
be as ~ as Larry** *or* **a lark** *or* **a sandboy** estar como unas
pascuas
2 (= *satisfied, pleased*) contento; (= *at ease, unworried*)
tranquilo; **to be ~ to do sth: I'm just ~ to be back running**
sólo estoy contento de poder volver a correr; **I am ~ to tell
you that ...** tengo el gusto de comunicarle que ...; **we'll be
~ to help** estaremos encantados de ayudar; **I'm quite ~ to
wait** no me importa esperar; **yes, I'd be ~ to** sí, con mucho
gusto; **we're very ~ for you** nos alegramos mucho por ti; **to
keep sb ~** tener a algn contento; **she wasn't ~ with his work**
no estaba contenta con su trabajo
3 (= *pleasant, joyful*) [*childhood, life, marriage, home*] feliz;
[*place, atmosphere*] alegre; **it was the happiest day of my life**
fue el día más feliz de mi vida; **we spent many ~ hours
playing on the beach** pasamos muchas horas maravillosas
jugando en la playa; **~ birthday!** ¡feliz cumpleaños!; **~
Christmas!** ¡feliz Navidad!, ¡felices Navidades!; **a ~ ending**
un final feliz; **a ~ event** un feliz acontecimiento; **~ New
Year!** ¡feliz Año Nuevo!
4 (= *felicitous*) [*position, chance*] afortunado; [*coincidence*]
feliz
5 (*) (= *tipsy*) contentillo*, alegre*
Ⓑ CPD ➤ **happy families** SING (*Cards*) juego *m* de las
familias ➤ **happy hour** hora *f* feliz, *hora durante la cual se
paga menos por la bebida en los bares* ➤ **a happy medium** un
término medio; **to strike a ~ medium** encontrar un
término medio

happy-go-lucky ['hæpɪgəʊ'lʌkɪ] ADJ despreocupado

harangue [hə'ræŋ] VT arengar

harass ['hærəs] VT acosar, hostigar

harassed ['hærəst] ADJ (= *exhausted*) agobiado; (= *under* *pressure*) presionado

harassment ['hærəsmənt] N acoso *m*; **sexual** ~ acoso *m* sexual

harbinger ['hɑːbɪndʒəʳ] N (= *person*) heraldo *m*, precursor *m*; (= *sign*) presagio *m*, precursor *m*; ~ **of doom** presagio *m* del desastre

harbour, harbor (*US*) ['hɑːbəʳ] Ⓐ N puerto *m* Ⓑ VT [+ *fear, hope*] abrigar; [+ *criminal, spy*] dar abrigo *or* refugio a; (= *conceal*) esconder; **to** ~ **a grudge** guardar rencor Ⓒ CPD ➤ **harbour dues** derechos *mpl* portuarios ➤ **harbour master** capitán *m* de puerto

hard [hɑːd] Ⓐ ADJ (*compar* ~**er**; *superl* ~**est**) 1 (= *not soft*) [*object, substance, cheese, skin*] duro; [*ground, snow*] duro, compacto; **baked** ~ endurecido (*al sol o en el horno*); **to become** *or* **go** ~ ponerse duro, endurecerse; **the water is very** ~ **here** aquí el agua es muy dura *or* tiene mucha cal; ✦ IDIOM **to be as** ~ **as nails** [*person*] (*physically*) ser duro como una roca; (*in temperament*) ser muy duro, tener el corazón muy duro
2 (= *harsh*) [*climate, winter, person*] duro, severo; [*life, times, drugs*] duro; [*words, tone*] duro, áspero; [*expression, eyes, voice*] serio, duro; [*drink, liquor*] fuerte; **a** ~ **blow** (*fig*) un duro golpe; **no** ~ **feelings!** ¡todo olvidado!; **it's a** ~ **life!** ¡qué vida más dura!; **to take a** ~ **line against/over sth** adoptar una postura intransigente contra algo/respecto a algo; **to take a long** ~ **look at sth** examinar algo detenidamente; **to be** ~ **on sb** ser muy duro con algn, darle duro a algn (*LAm*); **to have a** ~ **time** pasarlo mal; **to have a** ~ **time doing sth** tener problemas para hacer algo; **to give sb a** ~ **time** hacérselo pasar mal a algn; **her family had fallen on** ~ **times** su familia estaba pasando por dificultades económicas
3 (= *strenuous*) [*work, day*] duro; [*fight, match*] muy reñido; **to be a** ~ **worker** ser muy trabajador(a)
4 (= *difficult*) [*exam, decision, choice*] difícil; **he found it** ~ **to make friends** le resultaba difícil hacer amigos; **I find it** ~ **to believe that ...** me cuesta (trabajo) creer que ...; **bloodstains are** ~ **to remove** las manchas de sangre son difíciles de quitar; **to be** ~ **to please** ser muy exigente *or* quisquilloso; **to be** ~ **of hearing** ser duro de oído
5 (= *forceful*) [*push, tug, kick*] fuerte
6 (= *concrete*) [*fact*] concreto; [*evidence*] irrefutable
7 (*Phon, Ling*) [*sound*] fuerte; [*consonant*] oclusivo
Ⓑ ADV (*compar* ~**er**; *superl* ~**est**) 1 (= *with a lot of effort*) [*work*] duro, mucho; [*study*] mucho; **she always tries** ~ siempre se esfuerza mucho; **I can't do it, no matter how** ~ **I try** no puedo hacerlo, por mucho que lo intente; **to try one's** ~**est to do sth** esforzarse al máximo por hacer algo; ✦ IDIOM **to be** ~ **at it*: Bill was** ~ **at it in the garden*** Bill se estaba empleando a fondo en el jardín, Bill se estaba metiendo buena caña al jardín**
2 (= *with force*) [*hit*] fuerte, duro; [*pull, push, blow*] con fuerza; [*snow, rain*] fuerte, mucho; **she was feeling** ~ **done by** (*Brit*) pensaba que la habían tratado injustamente; ~ **hit** seriamente afectado; **I would be** ~ **put to think of another plan** me resultaría difícil pensar en otro plan; **to take sth** ~ tomarse algo muy mal*; **to be** ~ **up*** estar pelado*, no tener un duro (*Sp**)
3 (= *solid*) **to freeze** ~ quedarse congelado; **to set** ~ [*cement etc*] fraguar, endurecerse
4 (= *intently*) [*listen*] atentamente; [*concentrate*] al máximo; **think** ~ **before you make a decision** piénsalo muy bien antes de tomar una decisión
5 (= *sharply*) **to turn** ~ **left/right** girar todo a la izquierda/derecha
6 (= *closely*) **behind** sth justo detrás de algo; ~ **upon sth** (= *just after*) justo después de algo
Ⓒ CPD ➤ **hard cash** dinero *m* contante y sonante, (dinero *m* en) efectivo *m* ➤ **hard cider** (*US*) sidra *f* ➤ **hard copy** (*Comput*) copia *f* impresa ➤ **the hard core** (= *intransigents*) los incondicionales, el núcleo duro ➤ **hard court** (*Tennis*) cancha *f* (de tenis) de cemento, pista *f* (de tenis) de cemento ➤ **hard currency** moneda *f* fuerte, divisa *f* fuerte ➤ **hard disk** (*Comput*) disco *m* duro ➤ **hard goods** productos *mpl* no perecederos ➤ **hard hat** (= *riding hat*) gorra *f* de montar; [*of construction worker*] casco *m*; (*US*) (= *construction worker*) albañil *mf* ➤ **hard labour, hard labor** (*US*) trabajos *mpl* forzados ➤ **the hard left** (*esp Brit*) la extrema izquierda, la izquierda radical ➤ **hard porn***

porno *m* duro ➤ **the hard right** (*esp Brit*) la extrema derecha, la derecha radical ➤ **hard rock** (*Mus*) rock *m* duro ➤ **hard sell** venta *f* agresiva ➤ **hard shoulder** (*Brit*) arcén *m*, hombrillo *m* ➤ **hard stuff*** (= *alcohol*) alcohol *m* duro, bebidas *fpl* fuertes; (= *drugs*) droga *f* dura ➤ **hard water** agua *f* dura, agua *f* con mucha cal

> Use **el/un** not **la/una** before feminine nouns beginning with stressed **a** or **ha** like **agua**.

hard-and-fast ['hɑːdən'fɑːst] ADJ [*rule*] rígido; [*decision*] definitivo, irrevocable

hardback ['hɑːdbæk] N libro *m* encuadernado, libro *m* de tapa dura

hardboard ['hɑːdbɔːd] N aglomerado *m* (*de madera*)

hard-boiled ['hɑːd'bɔɪld] ADJ [*egg*] duro

hard-core ['hɑːdkɔːʳ] ADJ [*pornography*] duro; [*conservative, communist*] acérrimo, empedernido

hardcover ['hɑːdkʌvəʳ] N (*US*) libro *m* encuadernado, libro *m* de tapa dura

hard-drinking ['hɑːd'drɪŋkɪŋ] ADJ bebedor

hard-earned ['hɑːd'ɜːnd] ADJ ganado con el sudor de la frente

harden ['hɑːdn] Ⓐ VT endurecer; **these experiences ~ed her resolve** estas experiencias la afianzaron en su propósito; ✦ IDIOM **to** ~ **one's heart: she ~ed her heart and refused to have him back** hizo de tripas corazón *or* se hizo fuerte y se negó a aceptarlo de nuevo Ⓑ VI 1 [*clay, arteries, icing*] endurecerse; [*cement*] fraguar 2 [*tone, person*] endurecerse 3 (*Fin*) [*prices, economy*] estabilizarse, consolidarse

hardened ['hɑːdnd] ADJ [*drinker*] empedernido; [*criminal*] reincidente; **we are becoming** ~ **to violence** nos hemos ido acostumbrando a la violencia

hardening ['hɑːdnɪŋ] N endurecimiento *m*

hard-fought ['hɑːd'fɔːt] ADJ muy reñido

hard-headed ['hɑːd'hedɪd] ADJ realista, práctico

hard-hearted ['hɑːd'hɑːtɪd] ADJ duro de corazón; **to be** ~ tener un corazón de piedra

hard-hitting ['hɑːd,hɪtɪŋ] ADJ [*speech etc*] contundente

hard-line ['hɑːd'laɪn] ADJ [*communist, conservative*] de línea dura, extremista; [*approach, policy*] radical

hard-liner [,hɑːd'laɪnəʳ] N duro/a *m/f*; (*Pol*) (= *supporter*) partidario/a *m/f* de línea dura; (= *politician*) político/a *m/f* de línea dura; **the ~s of the party** el ala dura del partido

hardly ['hɑːdlɪ] ADV apenas; **I** ~ **know him** apenas lo conozco, casi no lo conozco; **I could** ~ **understand a word** no entendí casi nada, apenas entendí una palabra; **she had** ~ **any money** apenas tenía dinero, no tenía casi dinero; ~ **a day goes by when we don't argue** apenas pasa un día sin que discutamos; **we could** ~ **refuse** ¿cómo podíamos negarnos?; **he's** ~ **what you'd call a cordon bleu chef** no es precisamente *or* no es lo que se dice un cocinero de primera; **that is** ~ **likely** eso es poco probable; **"do you think he'll pass?" — "hardly!"** —¿crees que aprobará? —¡qué va! *or* ¡ni hablar!; ~ **anyone** casi nadie; ~ **anything** casi nada; ~ **ever** casi nunca

hardness ['hɑːdnɪs] N dureza *f*

hard-nosed [,hɑːd'nəʊzd] ADJ (*fig*) duro

hard-on* ['hɑːdɒn] N **he had a** ~ se le puso dura, se empalmó (*Sp***), se le empinó (*Sp***)

hard-pressed ['hɑːdprest] ADJ **our** ~ **economy** nuestra agobiada economía; **you'd be** ~ **to find a better deal than that** le va a ser difícil encontrar una oferta mejor

hardship ['hɑːdʃɪp] N (= *deprivation*) privación *f*; (*financial*) apuro *m*; (= *condition of life*) miseria *f*; **it's no** ~ **to him (to give up the car)** no le cuesta nada (dejar de usar el coche)

hardware ['hɑːdweəʳ] N (*for domestic use*) ferretería *f*, quincalla *f*; (*Mil*) armas *fpl*, armamento *m*; (*Comput*) hardware *m* ➤ **hardware dealer** ferretero/a *m/f* ➤ **hardware**

shop, hardware store ferretería *f*

hard-wearing ['hɑː'dwɛərɪŋ] ADJ (*esp Brit*) resistente, duradero

hardwood ['hɑːdwʊd] N madera *f* noble *or* dura

hard-working ['hɑːd'wɜːkɪŋ] ADJ trabajador

hardy ['hɑːdɪ] ADJ (*compar* **hardier**; *superl* **hardiest**) fuerte, robusto; (*Bot*) resistente

hare [hɛəʳ] **Ⓐ** N liebre *f* **Ⓑ** VI **to ~ off** (*Brit**) irse a todo correr *or* a toda pastilla*, salir disparado*

harebrained ['hɛəbreɪnd] ADJ [*idea, scheme*] disparatado, descabellado; [*person*] casquivano

harelip ['hɛə'lɪp] N labio *m* leporino

harem [hɑː'riːm] N harén *m*

haricot ['hærɪkəʊ] N (*Brit*) (*also* **~ bean**) frijol *m*, judía *f* blanca (*Sp*)

hark [hɑːk] VI **hark!** (*poet*) ¡escucha!; **~ at him!*** ¡qué cosas dice!, ¡quién fue a hablar!
➤ hark back VI + ADV (= *return to*) volver (**to** a); (= *recall*) recordar (**to** a)

Harley Street ['hɑːlɪstriːt] N (*Brit*) *calle de Londres donde tienen su consulta muchos médicos especialistas prestigiosos*

harm [hɑːm] **Ⓐ** N daño *m*, mal *m*, perjuicio *m*; **to <u>do</u> sb ~** hacer daño a algn; (*fig*) perjudicar a algn; **it does more ~ than good** es peor el remedio que la enfermedad; **the ~ is done now** el daño *or* mal ya está hecho; **don't worry, <u>no</u> ~ done** no te preocupes, no ha sido nada; **there's no ~ in trying** nada se pierde con probar; **I see no ~ in that** no veo nada en contra de eso; **he means no ~** no tiene malas intenciones; **out of ~'s <u>way</u>** a salvo, fuera de peligro; **to keep out of ~'s way** evitar el peligro
Ⓑ VT [+ *person*] hacer daño a, hacer mal a; [+ *health, reputation, interests*] perjudicar

harmful ['hɑːmfʊl] ADJ [*substance, chemical*] dañino, nocivo; [*effects, consequences*] perjudicial, pernicioso; (*to reputation*) perjudicial (**to** para); **tobacco is ~ to the health** el tabaco perjudica seriamente la salud

harmless ['hɑːmlɪs] ADJ [*person, animal*] inofensivo; [*substance, chemical*] inocuo; (= *innocent*) inocente

harmonica [hɑː'mɒnɪkə] N armónica *f*

harmonious [hɑː'məʊnɪəs] ADJ armonioso; [*atmosphere*] de armonía

harmonize ['hɑːmənaɪz] VT, VI armonizar (**with** con)

harmony ['hɑːmənɪ] N armonía *f*; **in ~ with** en armonía con

harness ['hɑːnɪs] **Ⓐ** N (*for horse*) arreos *mpl*, jaeces *mpl*; (*for mountaineer, dog etc*) arnés *m* **Ⓑ** VT **1** [+ *horse*] enjaezar, poner los arreos a; **to ~ a horse to sth** enganchar un caballo a algo **2** [+ *resources, energy*] utilizar, aprovechar

harp [hɑːp] N arpa *f*

Use **el/un** not **la/una** before feminine nouns beginning with stressed **a** or **ha** like **arpa**.

➤ harp on* VI + ADV **to ~ on (about)** estar siempre con la misma historia (de), machacar (sobre)*

harpist ['hɑːpɪst] N arpista *mf*

harpoon [hɑː'puːn] **Ⓐ** N arpón *m* **Ⓑ** VT arponear

harpsichord ['hɑːpsɪkɔːd] N clavicémbalo *m*, clavecín *m*

harpy ['hɑːpɪ] N arpía *f*

harrow ['hærəʊ] N (*Agr*) grada *f*, rastra *f*

harrowing ['hærəʊɪŋ] ADJ (= *distressing*) angustioso; (= *awful*) espeluznante, terrible; (= *moving*) conmovedor

harsh [hɑːʃ] ADJ (*compar* **~er**; *superl* **~est**) **1** (= *severe*) [*winter, punishment*] duro, riguroso; [*remark, criticism, conditions*] duro; [*person, sentence*] duro, severo **2** [*light*] fuerte; [*colour*] chillón, estridente **3** [*material, sound*] áspero

harshly ['hɑːʃlɪ] ADV [*treat, judge, speak*] con dureza; [*criticize*] duramente; [*say*] con voz áspera

harshness ['hɑːʃnɪs] N [*of climate*] rigor *m*, dureza *f*; [*of conditions, words*] dureza *f*; [*of punishment*] dureza *f*,

---

severidad *f*; [*of light*] crudeza *f*; [*of colour*] estridencia *f*; [*of sound, fabric*] aspereza *f*

harvest ['hɑːvɪst] **Ⓐ** N (= *picking, cutting*) [*of cereals*] siega *f*; [*of fruit, vegetables*] cosecha *f*, recolección *f*; [*of grapes*] vendimia *f* **2** (= *fruit, vegetables, grain etc*) cosecha *f* (*also fig*) **Ⓑ** VT [+ *cereals*] cosechar; [+ *fruit, vegetables*] cosechar, recolectar; [+ *grapes*] vendimiar; (*fig*) cosechar **Ⓒ** VI cosechar, segar **Ⓓ** CPD **➤ harvest festival** (*esp Brit*) fiesta *f* de la cosecha **➤ harvest moon** luna *f* llena **➤ harvest time** cosecha *f*, siega *f*

harvester ['hɑːvɪstəʳ] N **1** (= *person*) [*of cereals*] segador(a) *m/f*; [*of fruit, vegetables*] recolector(a) *m/f*; [*of grapes*] vendimiador(a) *m/f* **2** (= *machine*) cosechadora *f*; (= *combine harvester*) segadora-trilladora *f*

has [hæz] 3RD PERS SING PRESENT OF **have**

has-been* ['hæzbiːn] N vieja gloria *f*

hash¹ [hæʃ] **Ⓐ** N **1** (*Culin*) picadillo *m* **2** (*) (= *mess*) lío* *m*, embrollo *m*; **to make a ~ of sth** hacer algo muy mal; **he made a complete ~ of the interview** la entrevista le fue fatal **Ⓑ** CPD **➤ hash browns** croquetas de patata hervida y cebolla

hash²* [hæʃ] N (= *hashish*) hachís *m*, chocolate *m* (*Sp***), mota *f* (*CAm**)

hash³ [hæʃ] N (= *sign*) almohadilla *f*

hashish ['hæʃɪʃ] N hachís *m*

hasn't ['hæznt] = **has not**; *see* **have**

hassle ['hæsl] **Ⓐ** N (*) lío *m*, problema *m*; **it's not worth the ~** no vale la pena **Ⓑ** VT molestar, fastidiar

hassock ['hæsək] N (*esp Brit*) cojín *m*

haste [heɪst] N prisa *f*, apuro *m* (*LAm*); **to do sth in ~** hacer algo precipitadamente *or* de prisa; **to make ~** darse prisa, apurarse (*LAm*); **✦ PROV more ~ less speed** vísteme despacio que tengo prisa

hasten ['heɪsn] VT [+ *process*] acelerar; [+ *sb's end, downfall*] precipitar; **to ~ sb's departure** acelerar la partida *or* marcha de algn **Ⓑ** VI apresurarse, darse prisa; **to ~ to do sth** apresurarse a hacer algo

hastily ['heɪstɪlɪ] ADV **1** (= *hurriedly*) de prisa, apresuradamente; **I ~ suggested that ...** me apresuré a sugerir que ... **2** (= *rashly*) [*speak*] precipitadamente

hasty ['heɪstɪ] ADJ (*compar* **hastier**; *superl* **hastiest**) **1** (= *hurried*) apresurado, precipitado **2** (= *rash*) precipitado; **don't be so ~** no te precipites

hat [hæt] N sombrero *m*; **to raise one's ~** (*in greeting*) descubrirse; **to take off one's ~** quitarse el sombrero; **✦ IDIOMS I'll eat my ~ if ...** que me maten si ...; **to pass the ~ round** (*Brit*) ◇ **pass the ~** (*US*) pasar el platillo; **I take my ~ off to him** me descubro ante él; **to talk through one's ~*** decir disparates *or* tonterías; **to keep sth under one's ~** no decir palabra sobre algo; **keep it under your ~** de esto no digas ni pío*; **to wear two ~s** ejercer un doble papel **➤ hat trick** (= *three goals etc*) tres tantos *mpl or* goles *mpl* en un partido; (= *three consecutive wins*) serie *f* de tres victorias, tres triunfos *mpl* seguidos; **to get a ~ trick** marcar tres tantos *or* goles en un partido

hatch¹ [hætʃ] N **1** (*on boat*) escotilla *f* **2** (*Brit*) (= *serving hatch*) ventanilla *f*

hatch² [hætʃ] **Ⓐ** VT **1** (*lit*) [+ *chick*] empollar; [+ *egg*] incubar **2** (*fig*) (= *scheme*) idear; [+ *plot*] tramar **Ⓑ** VI [*chick*] salir del huevo; [*insect, larva*] eclosionar (*frm*)

hatchback ['hætʃbæk] N **1** (= *car*) **a** = un tres/cinco puertas, un coche con puerta trasera **2** (= *door*) puerta *f* trasera, portón *m*

hat-check girl ['hættʃek,gɜːl] N (*US*) encargada *f* del guardarropa

hatchery ['hætʃərɪ] N criadero *m*, vivero *m*

hatchet ['hætʃɪt] N hacha *f* (pequeña)

Use **el/un** not **la/una** before feminine nouns beginning with stressed **a** or **ha** like **hacha**.

➤ hatchet job* crítica *f* vitriólica; **to do a ~ job on sb** poner por los suelos a algn, poner a algn a caer de un burro *or* a parir* ➤ **hatchet man*** *ejecutor de faenas desagradables por cuenta de otro*; (= *assassin*) sicario *m*, asesino *m* a sueldo

hate [heɪt] **A** N odio *m* **B** VT odiar; **he ~s to be** *or* **he ~s being corrected** no soporta que se le corrija *or* que le corrijan; **I ~ to see him unhappy** me duele mucho *or* no soporto verlo triste; **I ~ to say it, but ...** lamento tener que decirlo, pero ...; **I ~ to trouble you, but ...** siento muchísimo molestarle, pero ...; ✦ IDIOM **to ~ sb like poison** odiar a algn a muerte **C** CPD ➤ **hate campaign** campaña *f or* operación *f* de acoso (y derribo) ➤ **hate crime** delito *m* de odio ➤ **hate mail** cartas *fpl* amenazantes

hateful [ˈheɪtfʊl] ADJ odioso

hatpin [ˈhætpɪn] N alfiler *m* de sombrero

hatred [ˈheɪtrɪd] N odio *m* (**for** a)

haughty [ˈhɔːtɪ] ADJ (*compar* **haughtier**; *superl* **haughtiest**) altanero, altivo

haul [hɔːl] **A** N **1** (= *distance*) recorrido *m*, trayecto *m*; **it's a long ~** hay mucho trecho, hay una buena tirada*; **revitalizing the economy will be a long ~** hay por delante un largo trecho hasta conseguir revitalizar la economía

2 [*of fish*] redada *f*; (*financial*) ganancia *f*; (*from robbery etc*) botín *m*; (= *arms haul, drugs haul*) alijo *m*

B VT (= *drag*) [+ *heavy object*] arrastrar, jalar (*LAm*); **they ~ed me out of bed at five o'clock in the morning** me sacaron de la cama a las cinco de la mañana; **he was ~ed before the manager** tuvo que presentarse al gerente

➤ **haul down** VT + ADV [+ *flag, sail*] arriar

➤ **haul in** VT + ADV [+ *fishing net*] ir recogiendo

➤ **haul up** VT + ADV [+ *object*] ir levantando; **he was ~ed up in court** fue llevado ante el tribunal

haulage [ˈhɔːlɪdʒ] N (*esp Brit*) (= *road transport*) transporte *m*, acarreo *m*; (= *cost*) gastos *mpl* de transporte ➤ **haulage company** compañía *f* de transportes (por carretera) ➤ **haulage contractor** transportista *mf*

haulier [ˈhɔːlɪəʳ], **hauler** (*US*) [ˈhɔːləʳ] N transportista *mf*

haunch [hɔːntʃ] N [*of animal*] anca *f*; [*of person*] cadera *f*; **to sit on one's ~es** sentarse en cuclillas

> Use **el/un** not **la/una** before feminine nouns beginning with stressed **a** or **ha** like **anca**.

haunt [hɔːnt] **A** N [*of criminals*] guarida *f*; [*of person*] lugar *m* predilecto; **I know his usual/favourite ~s** sé dónde suele ir/cuáles son sus lugares predilectos **B** VT [+ *place*] [*ghost*] aparecerse en, rondar; [*person*] (= *frequent*) frecuentar, rondar; **the house is ~ed** en la casa hay fantasmas, la casa está encantada *or* embrujada; **he is ~ed by the thought that ...** le obsesiona el pensamiento de que ...; **he is ~ed by memories** le persiguen los recuerdos

haunted [ˈhɔːntɪd] ADJ [*look*] de angustia, obsesionado; ~ **house** casa encantada *or* embrujada

haunting [ˈhɔːntɪŋ] ADJ [*sight, music*] evocador; [*melody*] inolvidable

Havana [həˈvænə] N La Habana

> ## have
>
> | | |
> |---|---|
> | **A** TRANSITIVE VERB | **C** MODAL VERB |
> | **B** AUXILIARY VERB | **D** PHRASAL VERBS |

> *When* **have** *is part of a set combination, eg* **have a look**, **have a good time**, **have breakfast**, **had better**, *look up the other word. For* **have** + *adverb/preposition combinations, see also the phrasal verb section of this entry.*

have [hæv] (*3rd pers sing present* **has**; *pt, pp* **had**)
A TRANSITIVE VERB

1 (= *possess*) tener; **he's got** (*esp Brit*) *or* **he has blue eyes** tiene los ojos azules; **you got** (*esp Brit*) *or* **do you ~ any brothers or sisters?** ¿tienes hermanos?; **he hasn't got** (*esp Brit*) *or* **he doesn't ~ any friends** no tiene amigos; **she had**

her eyes closed tenía los ojos cerrados

> Don't translate the **a** in sentences like **has he got a girlfriend?**, **I haven't got a washing-machine** if the number of such items is not significant since people normally only have one at a time:

has he got (*esp Brit*) *or* **does he ~ a girlfriend?** ¿tiene novia?; **I ~n't got** (*esp Brit*) *or* **I don't ~ a washing-machine** no tengo lavadora

> Do translate the **a** if the person or thing is qualified:

he has got (*esp Brit*) *or* **he has a Spanish girlfriend** tiene una novia española; **can I ~ a pencil please?** ¿me puedes dar un lápiz, por favor?; **to ~ something to do** tener algo que hacer; **I've got** (*esp Brit*) *or* **I ~ some letters to write** tengo algunas cartas que escribir; **I've got** (*esp Brit*) *or* **I ~ nothing to do** no tengo nada que hacer

2 (= *eat, drink*) tomar; **what are we having for lunch?** ¿que vamos a comer?; **we had ice-cream for dessert** tomamos helado de postre; **to ~ something to eat/drink** comer/beber algo, tomar algo; **what will you ~?** ¿qué quieres tomar?, ¿qué vas a tomar?; **will you ~ some more?** ¿te sirvo más?

3 (= *receive*) recibir; **thank you for having me** gracias por su hospitalidad; **you can ~ my ticket** puedes quedarte con mi entrada; **we had some help from the government** recibimos ayuda del gobierno; **I had a letter from John** tuve carta de John, recibí una carta de John; **they had a lot of presents** recibieron *or* les hicieron muchos regalos

4 (= *obtain*) **they can be had for as little as £10 each** pueden conseguirse por tan sólo diez libras; **there was no bread to be had** no quedaba pan en ningún sitio, no podía conseguirse pan en ningún sitio

5 (= *take*) **I'll ~ a dozen eggs, please** ¿me pones una docena de huevos, por favor?; **which one will you ~?** ¿cuál quiere?; **can I ~ your name please?** ¿me da su nombre, por favor?; **you can ~ it** *or* **I'll let you ~ it for £10** te lo dejo en diez libras, te lo puedes llevar por diez libras

6 (= *give birth to*) [+ *baby, kittens*] tener

7 (= *hold, catch*) tener; **I ~ him in my power** lo tengo en mi poder; **he had him by the throat** lo tenía agarrado por la garganta; **I ~ it on good authority that ...** me consta que ..., sé a ciencia cierta que ..., sé de buena tinta que ...*; **I've got it!** ¡ya!; **you ~ me there** ahí sí que me has pillado*

8 (= *allow*) consentir, tolerar; **we can't ~ that** eso no se puede consentir; **I won't ~ it!** ¡no lo voy a consentir! *or* tolerar!

9 (= *spend*) pasar; **to ~ a pleasant afternoon/evening** pasar una tarde agradable; ~ **a nice day!** ¡que pases un buen día!; **I had a horrible day at school today** he tenido un día horrible en el colegio

10 (*on telephone*) **can I ~ Personnel please?** ¿me puede poner con Personal, por favor?

11 (= *make*) **I'll soon ~ it nice and shiny** enseguida lo dejo bien brillante; **he had us confused** nos tenía confundidos

12 (*in set structures*)

✦ **to have sb do sth** mandar a algn hacer algo; **he had me do it again** me hizo hacerlo otra vez, me hizo que lo hiciese otra vez; **I'll ~ you know that ...** quiero que sepas que ...

✦ **to have sb doing sth**: **she soon had them all reading and writing** (= *organized them*) enseguida los puso a leer y a escribir; (= *taught them*) enseguida les habían enseñado a leer y a escribir

✦ **to have sth done**: **we had our luggage brought up** mandamos subir el equipaje, hicimos *or* mandamos que nos subieran el equipaje; **I've had the brakes checked** he mandado revisar los frenos; **to ~ one's hair cut** cortarse el pelo; **they had him killed** lo mataron

✦ **to have sth happen**: **she had her bag stolen** le robaron el bolso

13 (*in set expressions*)

✦ **to have sth against sb/sth** tener algo en contra de algn/algo

✦ **to have had it***: **you've had it now!*** ¡ahora sí que te la has cargado!; **this sofa has had it*** este sofá ya no da para

más*; **I've had it up to here with his nonsense*** estoy hasta la coronilla *or* hasta el moño de sus tonterías*
✦ **to be had: you've been had!*** ¡te han engañado!
✦ **to have to do with** tener que ver con; **that's got** *or* **that has nothing to do with it!** ¡eso no tiene nada que ver!; **you'd better not ~ anything to do with him** más te vale no tener tratos con él
✦ **to let sb have sth** (= *give*) dar algo a algn; (= *lend*) dejar algo a algn, prestar algo a algn; **let me ~ your address** dame tus señas; **let me ~ your pen for a moment** déjame el boli un momento; **let him ~ it!*** ¡dale!
✦ **what have you: ... and what ~ you** ... y qué sé yo qué más
Ⓑ AUXILIARY VERB
1 haber; **he's been very kind** ha sido muy amable; **has he gone?** ¿se ha ido?; **hasn't he told you?** ¿no te lo ha dicho?; **she said she had spoken to them** dijo que había hablado con ellos; **had you phoned me** (*frm*) *or* **if you had phoned me I would ~ come round** si me hubieras llamado habría venido; **having finished** *or* **when he had finished, he left** cuando terminó *or* cuando hubo terminado, se fue
2 (*in tag responses*) **"he's already eaten" — "so ~ I"** —él ya ha comido —yo también; **"we ~n't had any news yet" — "neither ~ we"** —no hemos tenido noticias todavía —nosotros tampoco; **"you've made a mistake" — "no I ~n't"** —has cometido un error —no es verdad *or* cierto; **"we ~n't paid" — "yes we ~!"** —no hemos pagado —¡qué sí!; **"he's got a new job" — "oh has he?"** —tiene un trabajo nuevo —¿ah, sí?; **"you've written it twice" — "so I ~"** —lo has escrito dos veces —es verdad *or* cierto; **"~ you read the book?" — "yes, I ~/no, I ~n't"** —¿has leído el libro? —sí/no
3 (*in question tags*) **he hasn't done it, has he?** no lo ha hecho, ¿verdad?; **you've done it, ~n't you?** lo has hecho, ¿verdad? *or* ¿no?
4 (*avoiding repetition of verb*) **you've got more than I ~** tienes más que yo; **you've all been there before, but I ~n't** ustedes han estado allí antes, pero yo no; **he has never met her, but I ~ it's had to know a conocer, pero yo sí; ~ you ever been there? if you ~ ...** ¿has estado alguna vez allí? si es así ...; ~ **you tried it? if you ~n't ...** ¿lo has probado? (porque) si no ...
Ⓒ MODAL VERB (= *be obliged*) **to ~ to do sth** ◇ → **got to do sth** (*Brit*) tener que hacer algo; **I ~ to** *or* (*Brit*) **I've got to finish this work** tengo que terminar este trabajo; **I don't ~ to** *or* (*Brit*) **I ~n't got to wear glasses** no necesito (usar) gafas; **he had to pay all the money back** tuvo que devolver todo el dinero; **you didn't ~ to tell her!** ¡no tenías por qué decírselo!; **does it ~ to be ironed?** ¿hay que plancharlo?
Ⓓ PHRASAL VERBS
➤ **have around** VT + ADV **1** (= *have near*) tener cerca; **Sarah was a joy to ~ around** era una delicia tener a Sarah cerca; **a useful person to ~ around** una persona que conviene tener a tu lado *or* tener cerca; **the sort of player I'd like to ~ around** el tipo de jugador con el que me gustaría contar **2** (= *invite*) **we're having Mary around tomorrow** hemos invitado a Mary para que venga mañana; **we're having some people around** tenemos invitados
➤ **have in** VT + ADV **1** [+ *doctor, plumber*] llamar; **let's ~ the next one in** que pase el siguiente; **2** ✦ IDIOM **to ~ it in for sb*** tenerla tomada con algn*
➤ **have off** VT + ADV **1** (= *have as holiday*) **I'm having a fortnight off in July** me voy a tomar dos semanas de vacaciones *or* permiso en julio; **the children ~ (got) a week off for half term** los niños tienen una semana de vacaciones a mitad del trimestre **2** (*Brit*): **to ~ it off**** echar un polvo***; **to ~ it off with sb**** tirarse a algn***
➤ **have on** VT + ADV **1** (= *wear*) [+ *dress, hat*] llevar; **she had on a beautiful black evening dress** llevaba (puesto) un precioso vestido de noche negro **2** (= *be busy with*) **I've got a lot on this week** tengo mucho que hacer esta semana; ~ **you anything on tomorrow?** ¿tienes algo que hacer mañana?, ¿tienes compromiso para mañana? **3** (*Brit**) (= *tease*) **to ~ sb on** tomar el pelo a algn*
➤ **have out** VT + ADV **to ~ a tooth out** sacarse una muela; **to ~ one's tonsils out** operarse de las amígdalas; **we'll ~ the piano out in a trice** enseguida sacamos el piano; ✦ IDIOM **to ~ it out with sb** ajustar cuentas con algn
➤ **have round** VT + ADV = **have around**
➤ **have up** VT + ADV (*Brit**): **to be had up** (= *be prosecuted*) ser

---

llevado a juicio; **he was had up for assault** le llevaron a juicio por asalto
haven ['heɪvn] N refugio *m*; (= *port*) puerto *m*
haven't ['hævnt] = **have not**
haversack ['hævəsæk] N (*esp Brit*) mochila *f*, macuto *m* (*LAm*)
haves* [hævz] NPL **the ~ and the have-nots** los ricos y los pobres
havoc ['hævək] N estragos *mpl*; **to cause** *or* **create ~** hacer estragos; **the weather played ~ with sporting fixtures this weekend** el mal tiempo arruinó los acontecimientos deportivos del fin de semana
Hawaii [hə'waɪiː] N (Islas *fpl*) Hawai *m*
Hawaiian [hə'waɪjən] ADJ, N hawaiano/a *m/f*
hawk¹ [hɔːk] N (*Orn, Pol*) halcón *m*; **he was watching me like a ~** me vigilaba estrechamente, no me quitaba ojo
hawk² [hɔːk] VT [+ *goods for sale*] pregonar
hawker ['hɔːkəʳ] N vendedor(a) *m/f* ambulante
hawthorn ['hɔːθɔːn] N espino *m*
hay [heɪ] N heno *m*; ✦ IDIOMS **that ain't ~** (*US**) eso no es moco de pavo*; **to hit the ~*** acostarse; **to make ~ while the sun shines** aprovechar la ocasión ➤ **hay fever** fiebre *f* del heno, alergia *f* al polen
haystack ['heɪstæk] N almiar *m*; ✦ IDIOM **it's like looking for a needle in a ~** es como buscar una aguja en un pajar
haywire* ['heɪwaɪəʳ] ADJ ✦ IDIOM **to go ~** [*person*] volverse loco, perder la chaveta*; [*machine*] averiarse, malograrse (*LAm*)
hazard ['hæzəd] Ⓐ N peligro *m*; (*less serious*) riesgo *m*; **this heater is a fire ~** esta estufa puede provocar un incendio Ⓑ VT [+ *answer, remark*] aventurar; **would you like to ~ a guess?** ¿quieres intentar adivinarlo? Ⓒ CPD ➤ **hazard (warning) lights** luces *fpl* de emergencia
hazardous ['hæzədəs] ADJ [*waste, chemicals, weather conditions*] peligroso; [*occupation, journey, enterprise*] arriesgado, peligroso; **~ to health** peligroso para la salud ➤ **hazardous pay** (*US*) prima *f or* plus *m* de peligrosidad
haze¹ [heɪz] N (= *mist*) bruma *f*, neblina *f*; (*in hot weather*) calina *f*, calima *f*
haze² [heɪz] VT (*US*) gastar novatadas a
hazel ['heɪzl] Ⓐ N (= *tree*) avellano *m* Ⓑ ADJ [*eyes*] color de avellana *inv*
hazelnut ['heɪzlnʌt] N avellana *f*
hazy ['heɪzɪ] ADJ (*compar* **hazier**; *superl* **haziest**) **1** [*sunshine, morning*] (*due to mist*) brumoso, neblinoso; (*due to heat*) calinoso; **it's a bit ~ today** (*due to mist*) hoy hay un poco de neblina *or* bruma; (*due to heat*) hoy hay un poco de calima **2** [*notion, details*] confuso; [*memory*] vago, confuso; [*idea*] poco claro, confuso; **I'm ~ about what happened** tengo solamente una vaga idea de lo que ocurrió, no recuerdo muy bien lo que ocurrió **3** [*outline, vision*] borroso; [*photograph*] nublado
H-bomb ['eɪtʃbɒm] N bomba *f* H
HDD N ABBR (*Comput*) = **hard disk drive**
HDTV N ABBR = **high definition television**
he [hiː] Ⓐ PERS PRON **1** (*emphatic, to avoid ambiguity*) él; **we went to the cinema but he didn't** nosotros fuimos al cine pero él no; **it is he who ...** es él quien ...; **you've got more money than he has** tienes más dinero que él

> Don't translate the subject pronoun when not emphasizing or clarifying:

he's very tall es muy alto; **there he is** allí está **2** (*frm*) **he who wishes to ...** el que desee ..., quien desee ...
Ⓑ N **it's a he*** (= *animal*) es macho; (= *baby*) es un niño, es un varón (*LAm*)
Ⓒ CPD macho ➤ **he-goat** cabra *f* macho
head [hed] Ⓐ N **1** (= *part of body*) cabeza *f*; **my ~ aches** me duele la cabeza; **he went ~ first into the ditch** se cayó de cabeza en la zanja; **from ~ to foot** de pies a cabeza; **wine goes to my ~** el vino se me sube a la cabeza; **success has**

gone to his ~ el éxito se le ha subido a la cabeza; ~ **of hair** cabellera *f*; **to go** ~ **over heels** caer de cabeza; **to fall** ~ **over heels in love with sb** enamorarse perdidamente de algn; **to keep one's** ~ **down** (*lit*) no levantar la cabeza; (= *work hard*) trabajar de lo lindo; (= *avoid being noticed*) intentar pasar desapercibido; **he stands** ~ **and shoulders above the rest** (*lit*) les saca más de una cabeza a los demás; (*fig*) los demás no le llegan a la suela del zapato; **to stand on one's** ~ hacer el pino; **I could do it standing on my** ~* lo podría hacer con los ojos cerrados; **from** ~ **to toe** de pies a cabeza; **I'm going to knock your ~s together** os voy a dar un coscorrón a los dos*; ✦ IDIOMS **I can't get my** ~ **around that*** no consigo entenderlo, para mí eso es un misterio; **to bite sb's** ~ **off** poner a algn de vuelta y media; **to give sb his/her** ~ dar rienda suelta a algn; **to go over sb's** ~: **they went over my** ~ **to the manager** pasaron por encima de mí y fueron directamente al gerente; **to hold one's** ~ **up (high)** ir con la frente bien alta *or* erguida; **to stand** *or* **turn sth on its** ~ dar la vuelta a algo; **on your own** ~ **be it!** ¡allá tú!, tú sabrás lo que haces; **~s will roll** van a rodar cabezas; **to scream/shout one's** ~ **off** desgañitarse; **I can't make** ~ **nor tail of it** no le encuentro ni pies ni cabeza; **I can't make** ~ **nor tail of what he's saying** no entiendo nada de lo que dice; **to keep one's** ~ **above water** ir tirando
2 (= *intellect, mind*) cabeza *f*; **use your** ~! ¡usa la cabeza!; **it's gone right out of my** ~ se me ha ido de la cabeza, se me ha olvidado; **it was the first thing that came into my** ~ fue lo primero que me vino a la cabeza; **it never entered my** ~ ni se me pasó por la cabeza siquiera; **you need your** ~ **examining** *or* **examined*** tú estás mal de la cabeza; **to have a** ~ **for business/figures** ser bueno para los negocios/con los números; **I have no** ~ **for heights** tengo vértigo; **to do a sum in one's** ~ hacer un cálculo mental; **he added it all up in his** ~ lo sumó todo mentalmente; **he has got it into his** ~ **that ...** se le ha metido en la cabeza que ...; **don't put ideas into his** ~ no le metas ideas en la cabeza; **I can't get that tune out of my** ~ no puedo quitarme esa música de la cabeza; **it went over their** ~**s** no lo entendían; **I'm sure if we put our ~s together** we can work something out estoy seguro de que si intercambiamos ideas encontraremos una solución; **to take it into one's** ~ **to do sth**: **he took it into his** ~ **to go to Australia** se le metió en la cabeza ir a Australia; ✦ IDIOMS **to keep one's** ~ mantener la calma; **to lose one's** ~ perder la cabeza *or* los estribos; **to be off one's** ~ (*esp Brit**) estar como una cabra, estar majara (*Sp**); **to go off one's** ~ (*esp Brit**) volverse loco *or* (*Sp*) majara*; **he's got his** ~ **screwed on (the right way)** tiene la cabeza sobre los hombros; ✦ PROV **two ~s are better than one** cuatro ojos ven más que dos
3 (= *leader*) [*of school, firm*] director(a) *m/f*; ~ **of department** (*in school, firm*) jefe/a *m/f* de departamento; ~ **of state** (*Pol*) jefe/a *m/f* de Estado
4 (= *part*) [*of pin, spot*] cabeza *f*; [*of bed*] cabecera *f*; [*of flower*] cabeza *f*, flor *f*; (*on tape-recorder*) cabezal *m*, cabeza *f* magnética; (*Comput*) cabeza *f*; (*on beer*) espuma *f*; **at the** ~ **of** [+ *organization*] a la cabeza de; **to be at the** ~ **of the queue** ser el primero en la cola; **to sit at the** ~ **of the table** sentarse en la cabecera de la mesa, presidir la mesa; **a** ~ **of garlic** una cabeza de ajo; **a** ~ **of lettuce** una lechuga *f*
5 (= *culmination*) punto *m* crítico; **this will bring matters to a** ~ esto llevará las cosas a un punto crítico; **to come to a** ~ alcanzar un punto crítico
6 heads (*on coin*) cara *f*; **it came down ~s** salió cara; **~s or tails?** ¿cara o cruz?, ¿águila o sol? (*Mex*)
7 (*no pl*) (= *unit*) **20** ~ **of cattle** 20 cabezas de ganado (vacuno); **£15 a** *or* **per** ~ 15 libras por cabeza *or* persona
Ⓑ VT **1** [+ *procession, league, poll*] encabezar, ir a la cabeza de; [+ *list, chapter*] encabezar
2 [+ *organization*] dirigir; (*Sport*) [+ *team*] capitanear
3 [+ *goal*] cabecear; **to** ~ **the ball** cabecear (el balón)
Ⓒ VI **where are you ~ing** *or* **~ed?** ¿hacia dónde vas?, ¿para dónde vas?; **he ~ed up the hill** se dirigió hacia la cima de la colina; **they were ~ing home/back to town** volvían a casa/a la ciudad; **he's ~ing for trouble** se está buscando problemas
Ⓓ CPD ➤ **head boy** (*Brit*) ≈ delegado *m* de la escuela (*alumno*) ➤ **head buyer** jefe/a *m/f* de compras ➤ **head cheese** (*US*) queso *m* de cerdo, cabeza *f* de jabalí (*Sp*), queso *m* de cabeza (*Chi*), queso *m* de puerco (*Mex*), queso *m* de

chancho (*River Plate*) ➤ **head cold** resfriado *m* (de cabeza) ➤ **head count** recuento *m* de personas ➤ **head gardener** jefe/a *m/f* de jardineros ➤ **head girl** (*Brit Scol*) ≈ delegada *f* de la escuela (*alumna*) ➤ **head nurse** enfermero/a *m/f* jefe ➤ **head office** sede *f* central ➤ **head prefect** (*Brit Scol*) ≈ delegado/a *m/f* de la escuela (*alumno/alumna*) ➤ **head start** ventaja *f*; **a good education gives your child a** ~ **start in life** una buena educación sitúa a su hijo en una posición aventajada en la vida ➤ **head teacher** (*Brit*) director(a) *m/f* ➤ **head waiter** maître *m*
➤ **head for** VI + PREP **where are you ~ing for?** ¿hacia *or* para dónde vas?; **the car was ~ing straight for us** el coche venía derecho hacia nosotros; **you're ~ing for trouble** vas por mal camino; **he's ~ing for a fall** va camino del fracaso
➤ **head off Ⓐ** VI + ADV marcharse (**for** para, hacia; **toward(s)** hacia) **Ⓑ** VT + ADV atajar
➤ **head up** VT + ADV [+ *group, team*] estar a la cabeza de, dirigir

headache ['hedeɪk] N dolor *m* de cabeza; **that's his ~*** allá él

headband ['hedbænd] N cinta *f* (para la cabeza), vincha *f* (*And, SC*), huincha *f* (*And, SC*)

headboard ['hedbɔːd] N cabecera *f*

headcount ['hedkaʊnt] N (= *workforce*) personal *m*, plantilla *f* (*Sp*); (= *count*) recuento *m* de personas; **to take a** ~ hacer un recuento de personas

headdress ['heddres] N tocado *m*

headed ['hedɪd] ADJ [*notepaper*] membretado, con membrete

header ['hedə'] N (*Ftbl*) cabezazo *m*, remate *m* de cabeza

headgear ['hedɡɪə'] N (*gen*) tocado *m*; (= *hat*) sombrero *m*; (= *cap*) gorra *f*; (= *helmet*) casco *m*

headhunt ['hedhʌnt] **Ⓐ** VI buscar talentos **Ⓑ** VT **he was ~ed by a bank** un banco contactó con él para ofrecerle trabajo

headhunter ['hedhʌntə'] N (*fig*) cazatalentos *mf inv*

heading ['hedɪŋ] N (= *title*) encabezamiento *m*, título *m*; **under various ~s** en varios apartados; **to come under the** ~ **of** estar incluido en

headlamp ['hedlæmp] N (*Brit*) faro *m*

headland ['hedlənd] N cabo *m*, punta *f*

headlight ['hedlaɪt] N faro *m*

headline ['hedlaɪn] N (*in newspaper*) titular *m*, cabecera *f*; **the (news) ~s** (*TV, Rad*) el resumen de las noticias; **to hit** *or* **make the ~s** salir en primera plana ➤ **headline news: to be** ~ **news** ser noticia de cabecera

headlong ['hedlɒŋ] **Ⓐ** ADJ [*fall*] de cabeza; **he made a** ~ **dive for the ball** se lanzó en plancha a por la pelota **Ⓑ** ADV **1** (= *head first*) de cabeza; **the lorry ploughed** ~ **into a wall** el camión se estrelló de frente contra una pared **2** (= *swiftly*) precipitadamente

headmaster ['hedmɑːstə'] N (*esp Brit*) director *m* (de colegio)

headmistress ['hedmɪstrɪs] N (*esp Brit*) directora *f* (de colegio)

head-on ['hedɒn] **Ⓐ** ADJ [*collision*] de frente, frontal **Ⓑ** ADV [*collide*] de frente, frontalmente; [*meet*] cara a cara; ✦ IDIOM **to tackle sth** ~ enfrentarse de lleno con algo

headphones ['hedfəʊnz] NPL auriculares *mpl*, audífono(s) *m(pl)*

headquarters ['hedkwɔːtəz] NPL (*Mil*) cuartel *msing* general; (*Police etc*) jefatura *fsing* de policía; [*of party, organization*] sede *fsing*; (*Comm*) oficina *fsing* central, central *fsing*

headrest ['hedrest] N (*in car*) reposacabezas *m inv*; (*on chair*) cabezal *m*

headroom ['hedrʊm] N espacio *m* para estar (derecho) de pie; (*under bridge etc*) altura *f* libre; **"2m headroom"** "2m de altura libre"

headscarf ['hedskɑːf] N (*pl* **headscarves**) pañuelo *m*

headset ['hedset] N auriculares *mpl*, audífono(s) *m(pl)*

headstand ['hedstænd] N **to do a** ~ hacer el pino

headstone ['hedstəʊn] N lápida f (mortuoria)

headstrong ['hedstrɒŋ] ADJ testarudo

headway ['hedweɪ] N **to make** ~ hacer progresos; **I didn't make much** ~ **with him** no conseguí hacer carrera con él

headwind ['hedwɪnd] N viento m contrario

heady ['hedɪ] ADJ (*compar* **headier**; *superl* **headiest**)
1 (= *intoxicating*) [*wine*] que se sube a la cabeza, cabezón*; [*scent*] embriagador; **a** ~ **brew** una mezcla embriagadora **2** (= *exhilarating*) [*days, experience*] excitante, emocionante; [*atmosphere*] excitante, embriagador; **the** ~ **heights of sth** las vertiginosas alturas de algo

heal [hi:l] ⒶVT [+ *wound*] curar; [+ *person*] sanar, curar; (*fig*) [+ *differences*] reconciliar ⒷVI (*also* ~ **up**) cicatrizar

healer ['hi:lə'] N curandero(a) m/f

healing ['hi:lɪŋ] ⒶADJ curativo, sanativo ⒷN curación f

health [helθ] N salud f; **to be in good/bad** ~ estar bien/ mal de salud; **good ~!** ¡(a tu) salud!; **to drink (to) sb's** ~ beber a la salud de algn, brindar por algn; **Department of Health** Ministerio m de Sanidad ➤ **health authority** administración f sanitaria ➤ **health benefit** (*US*) subsidio m de enfermedad ➤ **health care** asistencia f sanitaria, atención f sanitaria ➤ **health centre, health center** (*US*) centro m de salud, centro m médico ➤ **health club** gimnasio m ➤ **health education** educación f sanitaria ➤ **health farm** (*esp Brit*) centro m de adelgazamiento ➤ **health food(s)** alimentos mpl dietéticos, alimentos mpl naturales ➤ **health food shop, health food store** (*US*) tienda f de alimentos dietéticos, herbolario m ➤ **health hazard** peligro m para la salud, riesgo m para la salud ➤ **health insurance** seguro m de enfermedad, seguro m médico ➤ **Health Service** (*Brit*) Servicio m de Sanidad, Servicio m de Salud Pública ➤ **health spa** balneario m ➤ **health visitor** (*Brit*) auxiliar mf sanitario/a (*en asistencia domiciliaria*) ➤ **health warning** (*on cigarette packets, adverts*) texto m de advertencia

healthful ['helθfʊl], **health-giving** ['helθ,gɪvɪŋ] ADJ sano, saludable

healthily ['helθɪlɪ] ADV de forma sana, sanamente

healthy ['helθɪ] ADJ (*compar* **healthier**; *superl* **healthiest**)
1 [*person, plant, mind*] sano; [*skin, hair*] sano, saludable, que goza de buena salud; **to be** ~ [*person*] tener buena salud, estar sano; **to have a** ~ **appetite** tener buen apetito **2** [*diet, lifestyle, air, place*] sano, saludable **3** [*economy, company*] próspero; [*profit*] pingüe; [*bank account*] sustancioso **4** [*attitude, scepticism*] razonable

heap [hi:p] ⒶN **1** (= *pile*) montón m, pila f; **her clothes lay in a** ~ **on the floor** su ropa estaba amontonada en el suelo; **a whole** ~ **of trouble*** un montón de disgustos* **2** (= *lots of*) montones de, un montón de; **you've had ~s of opportunities** has tenido montones *or* un montón de oportunidades; **we have ~s of time** tenemos tiempo de sobra; **~s of times** muchísimas veces ⒷVT (*also* ~ **up**) amontonar; **to** ~ **praise on sb** colmar a algn de elogios; **~ed tablespoonful** cucharada f colmada

hear [hɪə'] (*pt, pp* **~d**) ⒶVT **1** oír; **did you** ~ **what he said?** ¿has oído lo que ha dicho?; **can you** ~ **me?** ¿me oyes?; **I can't** ~ **you** no te oigo; **I can't** ~ **a thing** no oigo nada; **I ~d someone come in** he oído entrar a alguien; **I ~d you talking to her** te oí hablar con ella; **have you ~d the news?** ¿has oído la noticia?, ¿te has enterado de la noticia?; **what's this I ~ about you getting married?** ¿qué es eso que he oído de que te vas a casar?; **from what I** ~ ... por lo que he oído parece que ...; **I've ~d it all before** ya conozco la historia; **have you ~d anything from him since he left?** ¿has sabido algo *or* has tenido noticias de él desde que se fue?; **the first I ~d of it was when ...** lo primero que supe al respecto fue cuando ...; **that's the first I've ~d of it** no tenía ni idea, es la primera noticia que tengo; **I'm glad to** ~ **it** me alegro; **you haven't ~d the last of this!** ¡aquí no se acaba esto!; **let's** ~ **it for ...** un aplauso para ...; **I could hardly make myself ~d** apenas puede lograr que se me oyera; **I have ~d it said that ...** he oído decir que ...; **I'm sorry to** ~ **it** lo siento; **to** ~ **that ...** enterarse de que ...; **I can't** ~ **myself think** el ruido no me deja pensar *or* concentrarme; **where did you** ~ **that?** ¿quién te ha dicho eso?; **I haven't ~d yet whether I've passed** aún no sé si he aprobado

2 (= *listen to*) [+ *radio programme, story*] escuchar, oír; [+ *lecture*] escuchar **3** (*Jur*) [+ *case*] ver **4** (*Rel*) **to** ~ **mass** oír misa
ⒷVI oír; **I can't** ~ no oigo; **I'll call the police, (do) you ~?** llamaré a la policía, ¿me oyes? *or* ¿me entiendes?; **I ~d about it from Maria** me enteré por María, lo supe a través de María; **did you** ~ **about Liz?** ¿te enteraste de lo de Liz?; **to** ~ **from sb** saber de algn, tener noticias de algn; **hoping to** ~ **from you** (*in letter*) esperando recibir noticias tuyas; **to** ~ **of sth** (= *come across*) oír hablar de algo; (= *become aware of*) saber de algo; **I've never ~d of such a thing!** ¡en mi vida he oído cosa igual!; **I won't** ~ **of it!** (= *allow*) ¡ni hablar!; **I always wanted to be an actor but Dad wouldn't** ~ **of it** siempre quise ser actor pero papá no me dejó; **to** ~ **of sb** (= *come across*) oír hablar de algn; (= *have news of*) saber de algn, tener noticias de algn; **he was never ~d of again** nunca se supo más de él
ⒸEXCL **hear! hear!** (*Brit*) ¡sí señor!, ¡eso, eso!
➤ **hear out** VT + ADV [+ *story*] escuchar; **let's** ~ **him out** vamos a dejarle que termine de hablar

heard [hɜ:d] PT, PP *of* **hear**

hearing ['hɪərɪŋ] ⒶN **1** (= *sense of hearing*) oído m; **to have good/poor** ~ oír bien/poco; **in my** ~ estando yo delante, en mi presencia; **within/out of** ~ al alcance/fuera del alcance del oído **2** (= *chance to speak*) oportunidad f de hablar; (*Jur*) vista f, audiencia f; **he never got a fair** ~ en ningún momento se le permitió explicar su punto de vista; (*Jur*) no tuvo un juicio justo ⒷCPD ➤ **hearing aid** audífono m ➤ **hearing problem** problema m de oído

hearsay ['hɪəseɪ] N rumores mpl; **it's just** ~ son rumores nada más

hearse [hɜ:s] N coche m *or* (*LAm*) carro m fúnebre

heart [hɑ:t] ⒶN **1** (= *organ, symbol of love*) corazón m; **to have a weak** ~ padecer *or* sufrir del corazón
2 (= *seat of emotions*) corazón m; **with all one's** ~ de todo corazón, con toda su alma; **at** ~ en el fondo; **to have sb's interests at** ~ tener presente el corazón de algn; **this is an issue which is close to his** ~ este es un asunto que le toca muy de cerca; **to one's ~'s content** a gusto; **he knew in his** ~ **that it was a waste of time** él en el fondo sabía que era una pérdida de tiempo; ✦ IDIOMS **he's a man after my own** ~ es un hombre de los que me gustan; **from the bottom of one's** ~ con toda sinceridad, de corazón; **to break sb's** ~ (*in love*) partir el corazón a algn; (*by behaviour etc*) matar a algn a disgustos; **to break one's** ~ **over** partirse el corazón por; **to die of a broken** ~ morir de pena; **he has a** ~ **of gold** tiene un corazón de oro; **have a ~!*** ¡ten un poco de compasión *or* corazón!; **with a heavy** ~ con el corazón encogido, compungido; **his** ~ **was not in it** lo hacía sin ganas, no tenía fe en lo que estaba haciendo; **in his** ~ **of ~s** en lo más íntimo de su corazón; **to cry one's** ~ **out** llorar a lágrima viva; **to sing one's** ~ **out** cantar a voz en grito; **his** ~ **is in the right place** tiene buen corazón; **to let one's** ~ **rule one's head** dejar que el corazón guíe a la cabeza; **to set one's** ~ **on sth: I've set my** ~ **on that coat I saw yesterday** quiero a toda costa (comprarme) ese abrigo que vi ayer; **she's set her** ~ **on winning the championship** ha puesto todo su empeño en ganar el campeonato; **she is the** ~ **and soul of the organization** ella es el alma de la organización; **to throw o.s. into sth** ~ **and soul** entregarse en cuerpo y alma a algo, meterse de lleno en algo; **to take sth to** ~ tomarse algo a pecho; **to wear one's** ~ **on one's sleeve** llevar el corazón en la mano; **to win sb's ~: she won the ~s of the people** se ganó el corazón *or* el afecto de la gente
3 (= *courage*) **I did not have the** ~ **to tell her** no tuve valor para decírselo; ✦ IDIOMS **to be in good** ~ [*person*] estar de buen ánimo; **to lose** ~ descorazonarse; **to have one's** ~ **in one's mouth** tener el alma en un hilo, tener el corazón en un puño; **my** ~ **sank** me descorazoné, se me cayó el alma a los pies; **to take** ~ cobrar ánimos, animarse
4 (= *centre*) [*of lettuce, celery*] cogollo m; [*of place, earth etc*] corazón m, seno m, centro m; **in the** ~ **of the country** en pleno campo; **the** ~ **of the matter** lo esencial *or* el meollo *or* el quid del asunto
5 (= *memory*) **to learn/know/recite sth by** ~ aprender/saber/recitar algo de memoria
6 hearts (*Cards*) corazones mpl

heart Ⓑ CPD ➤ **heart attack** ataque *m* al corazón, infarto *m* (de miocardio) ➤ **heart condition** condición *f* cardíaca ➤ **heart disease** enfermedad *f* cardíaca ➤ **heart failure** (= *attack*) paro *m* cardíaco, fallo *m* del corazón (*Sp*); (*chronic*) insuficiencia *f* cardíaca ➤ **heart murmur** soplo *m* en el corazón ➤ **heart rate** ritmo *m* del corazón ➤ **heart surgery** cirugía *f* cardíaca ➤ **heart transplant** trasplante *m* del corazón ➤ **heart trouble** problemas *mpl* de corazón, afecciones *fpl* cardíacas; **to have ~ trouble** padecer *or* sufrir del corazón

heartache ['hɑːteɪk] N pena *f*, dolor *m*

heartbeat ['hɑːtbiːt] N (*gen*) latido *m* del corazón

heartbreak ['hɑːtbreɪk] N congoja *f*, sufrimiento *m*

heartbreaking ['hɑːtˌbreɪkɪŋ] ADJ desgarrador, que parte el corazón

heartbroken ['hɑːtˌbrəʊkən] ADJ acongojado, desconsolado; **she was ~ about it** estaba desconsolada

heartburn ['hɑːtbɜːn] N acidez *f*, ardor *m*

hearten ['hɑːtn] VT alentar, animar

heartening ['hɑːtnɪŋ] ADJ alentador

heartfelt ['hɑːtfelt] ADJ [*sympathy*] sentido; [*thanks, apology*] sincero

hearth [hɑːθ] N (= *fireplace*) chimenea *f*; (*fig*) hogar *m* ➤ **hearth rug** alfombrilla *f*, tapete *m*

heartily ['hɑːtɪlɪ] ADV [*laugh*] a carcajadas, de buena gana; [*eat*] con ganas, con apetito; [*say*] efusivamente; [*recommend*] encarecidamente; [*agree*] completamente, totalmente; **to be ~ sick of sth** estar completamente *or* realmente harto de algo

heartland ['hɑːtlænd] N **1** (*Geog*) zona *f* central, zona *f* interior **2** (*fig*) **the conservative ~ in southeast England** el feudo conservador del sudeste de Inglaterra

heartless ['hɑːtlɪs] ADJ despiadado, cruel

heartlessness ['hɑːtlɪsnɪs] N crueldad *f*, inhumanidad *f*

heartrending ['hɑːtˌrendɪŋ] ADJ desgarrador, que parte el corazón; **it was ~ to see them** se me partía el corazón de verlos

heart-searching ['hɑːtˌsɜːtʃɪŋ] N examen *m* de conciencia

heart-shaped ['hɑːtʃeɪpt] ADJ en forma de corazón

heartstrings ['hɑːtstrɪŋz] NPL ✦ IDIOM **to pull at** *or* **touch sb's ~** tocar la fibra sensible de algn

heartthrob* ['hɑːtθrɒb] N **he's the ~ of the teenagers** es el ídolo de las quinceañeras

heart-to-heart ['hɑːttəˈhɑːt] Ⓐ ADJ íntimo, franco Ⓑ N conversación *f* íntima

heart-warming ['hɑːtˌwɔːmɪŋ] ADJ (= *pleasing*) grato, reconfortante; (= *moving*) conmovedor, emocionante

hearty ['hɑːtɪ] (*compar* **heartier**; *superl* **heartiest**) ADJ **1** [*voice, welcome, thanks*] cordial, caluroso; [*laugh*] efusivo, campechano; [*person*] campechano, sanote **2** [*slap*] fuerte **3** [*meal*] copioso; [*appetite*] bueno

heat [hiːt] Ⓐ N **1** (= *warmth*) calor *m*; **in the ~ of the day** en las horas de más calor; **on a low ~** (*Culin*) a fuego lento **2** (= *excitement*) calor *m*; (= *vehemence*) vehemencia *f*; (= *pressure*) presión *f*; **in the ~ of the moment/battle** en el calor del momento/de la batalla; ✦ IDIOMS **to turn on the ~** empezar a ejercer presión; **the ~ is on** ha llegado la hora de la verdad; **when the ~ is on** cuando hay presión; **it'll take the ~ off us** esto nos dará un respiro; **to take the ~ out of a situation** reducir la tensión de una situación **3** (*US*) (= *heating*) calefacción *f* **4** (*Sport*) prueba *f* (eliminatoria); **dead ~** empate *m* **5** (*Zool*) **to be in** *or* (*Brit*) **on ~** estar en celo **6** **the ~** (*US***) (= *police*) la poli*, la pasma (*Sp***), la cana (*SC***) **7** (*US*) (= *criticism*) **he took a lot of ~ for that mistake** se llevó muchos palos por ese error Ⓑ VT calentar; **they ~ their house with coal** su casa tiene calefacción de carbón Ⓒ VI calentarse Ⓓ CPD ➤ **heat exhaustion** agotamiento *m* por el calor ➤ **heat haze** calina *f*, calima *f* ➤ **heat loss** pérdida *f* de calor ➤ **heat treatment** tratamiento *m* de calor

➤ **heat up** Ⓐ VI + ADV (*lit*) calentarse; (*fig*) [*discussion, debate*] acalorarse Ⓑ VT + ADV (*gen*) calentar; [+ *food*] calentar, recalentar

heated ['hiːtɪd] ADJ [*swimming pool*] climatizado; [*rollers*] caliente; [*discussion*] acalorado; **to grow** *or* **become ~** [*discussion, debate*] acalorarse

heater ['hiːtəʳ] N calentador *m*, estufa *f*

heath [hiːθ] N (*Brit*) brezal *m*, páramo *m* (*esp LAm*)

heathen ['hiːðən] Ⓐ ADJ (= *pagan*) pagano; (= *uncivilized*) bárbaro, salvaje Ⓑ N pagano/a *m/f*; (*fig*) bárbaro/a *m/f*, salvaje *mf*

heather ['heðəʳ] N brezo *m*

heating ['hiːtɪŋ] N calefacción *f*

heatproof ['hiːtpruːf], **heat-resistant** ['hiːtrɪˌzɪstənt] ADJ termorresistente, a prueba de calor; [*ovenware*] refractario

heatstroke ['hiːtstrəʊk] N insolación *f*

heatwave ['hiːtweɪv] N ola *f* de calor

heave [hiːv] Ⓐ N (= *lift*) gran esfuerzo *m* (para levantar *etc*); (= *pull*) tirón *m*, jalón *m* (*LAm*) (**on** de); (= *push*) empujón *m*; (= *throw*) echada *f*, tirada *f* Ⓑ VT (= *pull*) tirar, jalar (*LAm*); (= *drag*) arrastrar; (= *carry*) llevar; (= *lift*) levantar (con dificultad); (= *push*) empujar; (= *throw*) lanzar, tirar; **he ~d himself to a sitting position** se incorporó con gran esfuerzo; **to ~ a sigh** dar *or* echar un suspiro, suspirar; **to ~ a sigh of relief** suspirar aliviado Ⓒ VI **1** [*chest, bosom*] palpitar **2** (= *pull*) tirar, jalar (*LAm*) (**at, on** de) **3** (= *retch*) hacer arcadas; **her stomach was heaving** le daban arcadas, se le revolvía el estómago **4** (*Naut*) (*pt, pp* **hove**) (= *move*) virar; (= *pitch*) cabecear; (= *roll*) balancearse; **to ~ in(to) sight** aparecer

heaven ['hevn] N **1** (*Rel, gen*) cielo *m*; **to go to ~** ir al cielo; **(good) ~s!** ¡cielos!; **~ forbid!** ¡no lo quiera Dios!; **~ forbid that ...!** ¡ojalá no ...! + *subjun*, ¡quiera Dios que no ...! + *subjun*; **~ help them if they do** que Dios les ayude si lo hacen; **~ knows why** Dios sabe por qué; **what in ~'s name ...?** ¿qué demonios ...?; **the ~s opened** se abrieron los cielos, las nubes descargaron con fuerza; **for ~'s sake!** ¡por Dios!; **thank ~!** ¡gracias a Dios!, ¡menos mal!; ✦ IDIOMS **to move ~ and earth to do sth** remover cielo y tierra *or* Roma con Santiago para hacer algo; **to stink to high ~** heder a perro muerto **2** (*fig*) paraíso *m*; **this place is ~** este lugar es el paraíso; **the trip was ~** el viaje fue una maravilla

heavenly ['hevnlɪ] ADJ (*Rel*) celestial; (*) (= *lovely*) divino

heaven-sent ['hevn'sent] ADJ milagroso, (como) llovido del cielo

heavily ['hevɪlɪ] ADV **1** (= *very much*) [*rain, bleed*] mucho; [*drink, smoke*] mucho, en exceso; [*depend, rely*] en gran medida; [*biased, laden, influenced*] muy; [*populated*] densamente; **he had to borrow ~** tuvo que pedir grandes cantidades de *or* mucho dinero prestado; **to be ~ in debt** tener muchísimas deudas, estar muy endeudado; **he's ~ into jazz/football*** le ha dado fuerte por el jazz/el fútbol; **he's ~ into drugs*** está muy metido en las drogas; **he invested ~ in commodities** invirtió grandes cantidades de dinero *or* invirtió mucho en materias primas; **to be ~ involved in** *or* **with sth** estar muy metido en algo*; **to lose ~** (*gambling*) perder grandes cantidades de dinero, perder muchísimo dinero; (*in vote, match*) sufrir una derrota aplastante; **she was ~ made up** llevaba muchísimo maquillaje; **she was ~ pregnant** le quedaba poco para dar a luz, se encontraba en avanzado estado de gestación (*frm*) **2** (= *well, strongly*) [*armed*] fuertemente; [*guarded, fortified*] muy bien **3** (= *deeply*) [*sleep*] profundamente; **to breathe ~** (= *pant*) resoplar, jadear; **he sighed ~** exhaló un profundo suspiro **4** (= *weightily*) [*tread*] con paso pesado; [*move, walk*] pesadamente; **~ built** corpulento, fornido; **it weighs ~ on him** (*fig*) le pesa mucho

heavy ['hevɪ] Ⓐ ADJ (*compar* **heavier**; *superl* **heaviest**) **1** (= *weighty*) pesado; **to be ~** pesar mucho; **how ~ are you?** ¿cuánto pesas?; **with ~ (with sleep)** los párpados le pesaban de sueño; **my arms felt so ~** me pesaban tanto los brazos; **the mayor's ~ mob*** los gorilas del alcalde

2 (= *considerable*) [*traffic*] denso; [*rain, shower*] fuerte; [*loss*] considerable, cuantioso; [*fine*] fuerte; [*defeat*] aplastante; [*irony, symbolism*] enorme; [*fighting, fire*] intenso; **to be a ~ drinker** beber mucho; **the car is ~ on petrol** (*Brit*) or **gas** (*US*) el coche consume mucha gasolina; **to be a ~ smoker** fumar mucho
3 (= *thick, solid*) [*cloth, coat, line*] grueso; [*features*] tosco; [*meal, food*] fuerte, pesado
4 (= *oppressive, gloomy*) [*atmosphere*] cargado; [*sky*] encapotado; [*burden, responsibility*] pesado; **with a ~ heart** con el corazón encogido, compungido
5 (= *deep*) [*sigh, sleep, silence*] profundo; **to be a ~ sleeper** tener el sueño profundo
6 (= *arduous*) [*task, work*] pesado; [*schedule*] apretado; **I've had a ~ day** he tenido un día muy liado or ajetreado; ✦ IDIOM **to make ~ weather of sth** (*Brit**) complicar algo, hacer algo más difícil de lo que es
7 (= *boring, laboured*) [*book, film, humour*] denso, pesado; **to be ~ going** [*book, film*] ser muy denso; **the conversation was ~ going** era difícil encontrar temas de conversación; **his new album/book is pretty ~ stuff** su nuevo álbum es bastante fuerte
8 (= *bad*) **to have a ~ cold** estar muy resfriado or acatarrado; **things got a bit ~** (= *nasty*) la cosa se puso fea
9 (= *rough*) [*sea*] grueso
Ⓑ N (*) (= *thug*) matón* m, gorila* m; (= *eminent person*) peso m pesado
Ⓒ ADV **time hung ~ (on our hands)** las horas/los días se nos hacían interminables
Ⓓ CPD ➤ **heavy cream** (*US*) nata f (para montar) (*Sp*), crema f doble (*LAm*), doble crema f (*Mex*) ➤ **heavy goods vehicle** vehículo m pesado ➤ **heavy metal** (*Mus*) heavy m (metal)

heavy-duty [ˌhevɪˈdjuːtɪ] ADJ fuerte, resistente
heavy-handed [ˌhevɪˈhændɪd] ADJ **1** (= *clumsy, tactless*) torpe, patoso **2** (= *harsh*) severo
heavyweight [ˈhevɪweɪt] N (*Boxing, fig*) peso m pesado
Hebrew [ˈhiːbruː] **Ⓐ** ADJ hebreo **Ⓑ** N **1** (= *person*) hebreo/a m/f **2** (*Ling*) hebreo m
Hebrides [ˈhebrɪdiːz] NPL Hébridas fpl
heck* [hek] **Ⓐ** EXCL ¡jo! (*Sp**), ¡la pucha! (*LAm**) **Ⓑ** N **a ~ of a lot (of)** un montón (de)*; **I'm in one ~ of a mess** estoy metido en un lío de narices*; **what the ~ is he doing?** ¿qué narices está haciendo?*; **what the ~!** ¡qué narices!*
heckle [ˈhekl] VI interrumpir, molestar con preguntas
heckler [ˈheklər] N persona que interrumpe or molesta a un orador
heckling [ˈheklɪŋ] N interrupciones fpl, protestas fpl
hectare [ˈhektɑːr] N hectárea f
hectic [ˈhektɪk] ADJ [*life, pace*] agitado; [*activity*] frenético; **things are pretty ~ here** vamos como locos
hector [ˈhektər] **Ⓐ** VT intimidar con bravatas **Ⓑ** VI echar bravatas
he'd [hiːd] = **he had, he would**
hedge [hedʒ] **Ⓐ** N (*Hort, Agr*) seto m (vivo); **as a ~ against inflation** como protección contra la inflación **Ⓑ** VT ✦ IDIOM **to ~ one's bets** jugar a dos bandas **Ⓒ** VI (= *be evasive*) contestar con evasivas **Ⓓ** CPD ➤ **hedge clippers** tijeras fpl de podar
hedgehog [ˈhedʒhɒg] N erizo m
hedgerow [ˈhedʒrəʊ] N seto m vivo
hedonism [ˈhiːdənɪzəm] N hedonismo m
heed [hiːd] **Ⓐ** N **to pay (no) ~ to sb** (no) hacer caso a algn; **to take (no) ~ of sth** (no) tener en cuenta algo **Ⓑ** VT [+ *person*] hacer caso a; [+ *warning*] tomar en cuenta
heedless [ˈhiːdlɪs] ADJ **to be ~ of** [+ *consequences*] no hacer caso de ..., no prestar atención a ...; **she ran outside, ~ of whether the others were following her** salió a la calle corriendo, sin fijarse en si los demás la seguían
heel [hiːl] **Ⓐ** N **1** (*Anat*) talón m; ✦ IDIOMS **to bring sb to ~** sobreponerse a algn, meter a algn en cintura; **to follow hard on the ~s of sth** venir a renglón seguido de algo; **to be hot on sb's ~s** pisar los talones a algn; **to take to one's ~s*** echar a correr, poner pies en polvorosa* **2** [of sock] talón m; [of shoe] tacón m; ✦ IDIOM **to be down at ~** ir

desharrapado **Ⓑ** VT [+ *shoe*] poner tapas a **Ⓒ** VI **heel!** ¡ven aquí! **Ⓓ** CPD ➤ **heel bar** rápido m, tienda f de reparación de calzado en el acto
hefty* [ˈheftɪ] ADJ (*compar* **heftier**; *superl* **heftiest**) [*person*] corpulento, fornido; [*object*] enorme, imponente*; [*increase*] considerable; [*profit, payment*] cuantioso; [*price, salary, fees*] alto; [*bill, debt*] enorme; **a ~ fine** una multa muy cuantiosa, una buena multa*
heifer [ˈhefər] N novilla f, vaquilla f
height [haɪt] N **1** (= *measurement*) [of object] altura f; [of person] estatura f; **to be 20 metres in ~** medir or tener 20 metros de alto, tener una altura de 20 metros; **he was of average ~ and build** era de estatura y constitución media; **he drew himself up to his full ~** se irguió todo lo alto que era; **she's about my ~** tiene mi altura or es de mi estatura más o menos
2 (= *altitude*) altura f; **~ above sea level** altura f or altitud f sobre el nivel del mar; **at a ~ of 2,000 m** a una altura or altitud de 2.000 m; **to gain/lose ~** ganar/perder altura
3 (= *high place*) cumbre f; **to be afraid of ~s** tener miedo a las alturas, tener vértigo
4 (= *peak, zenith*) cumbre f, cima f; **at the ~ of her career** en la cumbre o la cima de su carrera; **at its ~, the movement had millions of supporters** en su punto más álgido, el movimiento tenía millones de seguidores; **the ~ of fashion** la última moda; **at the ~ of summer** en pleno verano
5 (= *utmost degree*) colmo m; **it is the ~ of arrogance/ stupidity** es el colmo de la arrogancia/la estupidez
heighten [ˈhaɪtn] **Ⓐ** VT (= *increase*) aumentar, acrecentar; (= *enhance*) realzar, hacer destacar **Ⓑ** VI aumentarse
heinous [ˈheɪnəs] ADJ atroz, nefasto
heir [ɛər] N heredero/a m/f; **~ apparent** heredero/a m/f forzoso/a; **~ to the throne** heredero/a m/f al trono
heiress [ˈɛəres] N (= *wealthy woman*) soltera f adinerada; (= *heir*) heredera f
heirloom [ˈɛəluːm] N reliquia f de familia
heist* [haɪst] N atraco m a mano armada
held [held] PT, PP of **hold**
helicopter [ˈhelɪkɒptər] N helicóptero m
heliport [ˈhelɪpɔːt] N helipuerto m
helium [ˈhiːlɪəm] N helio m
hell [hel] **Ⓐ** N **1** (= *underworld, also fig*) infierno m; **life became ~** la vida se convirtió en un infierno; ✦ IDIOMS **to be ~ on earth** ser un infierno; **to give sb ~: she gave me ~ when she found out** (= *scolded*) me puso de vuelta y media cuando se enteró, me puso como un trapo cuando se enteró*; **my back's giving me ~** esta espalda me está haciendo la vida imposible; **to go through ~** pasar las de Caín; **I've been going through ~, wondering where you were** he estado preocupadísimo, preguntándome dónde estarías; **come ~ or high water** pase lo que pase; **~ for leather** como un(os) endemoniado(s); **all ~ broke loose** se armó un lío padre; **to raise ~ (about sth)*** (= *protest*) armarla (por algo)*, liar un taco (por algo)*; **I'll see you/ him in ~ first** antes prefiero morir; ✦ PROV **the road to ~ is paved with good intentions** el camino del infierno está lleno de buenas intenciones
2 (*) (*as intensifier*) **it was (as) hot as ~** hacía un calor infernal; **I'm mad as ~** estoy como una cabra* or una chota*; **they did it just for the ~ of it** lo hicieron por puro capricho or porque sí; **"I'll go myself" — "like ~ you will!"** —iré yo mismo —¡ni lo sueñes! or ¡ni hablar!; **to run like ~** correr como un demonio or un diablo; **it hurts like ~** duele una barbaridad; **there were a ~ of a lot of people there** había un montañazo de gente; **that's one ~ of a lot of money** eso sí que es un verdadero dineral; **a ~ of a noise** un ruido de todos los demonios, un ruido tremendo; **we had a ~ of a time** (= *bad*) lo pasamos fatal; (= *good*) lo pasamos en grande or (*LAm*) regio; **to beat the ~ out of sb** dar una paliza de padre y muy señor mío a algn*; **to scare the ~ out of sb** dar un susto de muerte a algn; **I hope to ~ you're right** Dios quiera que tengas razón; **I wish to ~ he'd go** ojalá se fuera de una vez por todas; **what the ~!** I've got nothing to lose ¡qué narices! or ¡qué más da! no tengo nada que perder; **what the ~ do you want?** ¿qué demonios

or diablos quieres?; **who the ~ are you?** ¿quién demonios *or* diablos eres tú?
3 (**) (*as interjection*) **(oh) ~!** ¡caray!*, ¡mierda!***; **get the ~ out of here!** ¡vete al diablo!**; **let's get the ~ out of here!** ¡larguémonos de aquí!*; **go to ~!** ¡vete al diablo!**; **to ~ with it!** ¡a hacer puñetas!**; **to ~ with him!** ¡que se vaya a hacer puñetas!**
Ⓑ CPD ➤ **hell's angel** ángel *m* del infierno

he'll [hi:l] = **he will, he shall**

hellbent ['hel'bent] ADJ **to be ~ on doing sth** *or* (*US*) **to do sth** estar totalmente resuelto a hacer algo

hellish* ['helɪʃ] ADJ infernal, de muerte

hellishly* ['helɪʃlɪ] ADV muy, terriblemente

hello [hʌ'ləʊ] EXCL **1** (= *greeting*) ¡hola!, ¿qué tal?, ¿qué hubo? (*Mex, Chi*); (*Telec: answering*) ¡diga!, ¡hola!, ¡bueno! (*Mex*), ¡aló! (*SC*); (*calling*) ¡oiga!, ¡escuche! **2** (*in surprise*) ¡vaya!, ¡ándale! (*LAm*); **~, what's all this?** ¡vaya *or* hombre!, ¿qué tenemos aquí? **3** (*attracting attention*) ¡oiga!, ¡escuche!

helm [helm] N timón *m*; **to be at the ~** estar al timón

helmet ['helmɪt] N (*gen*) casco *m*; (*Hist*) yelmo *m*

help [help] **Ⓐ** N **1** (= *assistance*) ayuda *f*; **thanks for your ~** gracias por ayudarme, gracias por tu ayuda; **the books were not much ~** los libros no me sirvieron de mucho; **to ask (sb) for ~** pedir ayuda (a algn); **to call for ~** (= *ask for help*) pedir ayuda *or* auxilio; (= *shout for help*) pedir ayuda *or* auxilio a gritos; **he rushed off to get ~** salió corriendo en busca de ayuda; **you'll get no ~ from me** yo no te pienso ayudar; **you've been a great ~ to me** me has ayudado muchísimo; **you're a great ~!** (*iro*) ¡valiente ayuda!; **it's no ~ (to say that)** no sirve de nada (decir eso); **to be of ~ to sb** ayudar a algn; **I was glad to be of ~** me alegré de poder ayudar; **you should seek professional ~** deberías consultar a un profesional, deberías pedir asesoramiento; **with his son's ~** con la ayuda de su hijo; **with the ~ of a knife** con un cuchillo, ayudándose con un cuchillo
2 (= *helpers*) **we're short of ~ in the shop** nos falta personal en la tienda; **she has no ~ in the house** no tiene a nadie que le ayude en la casa
3 (= *cleaner*) asistenta *f*
Ⓑ VT **1** (= *aid, assist*) ayudar; **that won't ~ you** eso no te va a servir de nada, eso no te va a ayudar; **can I ~ you?** (*in shop*) ¿qué deseaba?, ¿en qué le puedo servir?; **to ~ (to) do sth** ayudar a hacer algo; **to ~ sb (to) do sth** ayudar a algn a hacer algo; **to ~ each other/one another** ayudarse el uno al otro; **to ~ sb across the road** ayudar a algn a cruzar la calle; **to ~ sb on/off with his coat** ayudar a algn a ponerse/quitarse el abrigo; **so ~ me, I'll kill him!*** ¡te lo juro que lo mato!*; **let me ~ you with that suitcase** deja que te ayude *or* que te eche una mano con esa maleta
2 (*at table*) **to ~ sb to soup/vegetables** servir sopa/verdura a algn
3 (= *avoid*) evitar; **"why are you laughing?" — "I can't ~ it"** —¿por qué te ríes? —no lo puedo evitar; **I can't ~ it, I just don't like him** es superior a mí, me cae mal; **I can't ~ that** (= *it's not my fault*) no es mi culpa; **it can't be ~ed** no hay más remedio, ¿qué se le va a hacer?; **he won't if I can ~ it** si de mí depende, no lo hará; **don't spend more than you can ~** no gastes más de lo necesario; **you can't ~ feeling sorry for him** no puede uno (por) menos de sentir lástima por él
4 to ~ o.s. (= *assist o.s.*) ayudarse a sí mismo; (= *serve o.s.*) servirse; **~ yourself!** ¡sírvete!; **she ~ed herself to vegetables** se sirvió verdura; **"can I borrow your pen?" — "~ yourself"** —¿me prestas el bolígrafo? —cógelo; **he's ~ed himself to my pencil*** me ha mangado el lápiz*
Ⓒ VI ayudar; **that doesn't ~ much** eso no sirve de mucho
Ⓓ EXCL **help!** ¡socorro!, ¡auxilio!
Ⓔ CPD ➤ **help menu** (*Comput*) menú *m* de ayuda
➤ **help along** VT + ADV **she has done much to ~ these negotiations along** ha contribuido considerablemente a que las negociaciones sigan adelante
➤ **help out Ⓐ** VI + ADV ayudar, echar una mano **Ⓑ** VT + ADV **to ~ sb out** ayudar a algn, echar una mano a algn

helper ['helpə'] N (*gen*) ayudante *mf*; (= *co-worker*) colaborador(a) *m/f*

helpful ['helpfʊl] ADJ [*person*] atento, servicial; [*suggestion, book, explanation*] útil; [*attitude, remark*] positivo; **it would be ~ if you could come** sería de gran ayuda que vinieses; **you have been most ~** ha sido muy amable; **to be ~ to sb** ayudar a algn

helpfully ['helpfəlɪ] ADV [*say, suggest, offer*] amablemente; **"it might be here," she said ~** —puede que esté aquí —dijo para ayudar

helping ['helpɪŋ] **Ⓐ** ADJ **to give** *or* **lend sb a ~ hand** echar una mano a algn **Ⓑ** N porción *f*, ración *f*; **he came back for second ~s** vino a servirse más

helpless ['helplɪs] ADJ (= *powerless*) [*victim, baby*] indefenso; [*feeling*] impotente; [*gesture*] de impotencia; (= *incapacitated*) incapacitado; **he lay ~ on the ground** yacía indefenso *or* inerme en el suelo; **to feel ~** sentirse impotente; **we were ~ to prevent it** no pudimos hacer nada para impedirlo; **to be ~ with laughter** estar muerto de (la) risa

helplessly ['helplɪslɪ] ADV [*watch, stand by*] sin poder hacer nada; [*shrug*] en un gesto de impotencia; [*laugh*] sin poder contenerse

helpline ['helplaɪn] N (*esp Brit*) línea *f* de socorro

Helsinki ['helsɪŋkɪ] N Helsinki *m*

helter-skelter ['heltə'skeltə'] **Ⓐ** ADV atropelladamente **Ⓑ** N (*Brit*) (*at fair*) tobogán *m*

hem [hem] **Ⓐ** N dobladillo *m*, bastilla *f* **Ⓑ** VT (*Sew*) hacer el dobladillo de, coser el dobladillo de
➤ **hem in** VT + ADV (*lit*) (= *surround*) cercar; (= *corner*) arrinconar; **I feel ~med in** me siento constreñido *or* limitado

he-man ['hi:mæn] N (*pl* **he-men**) macho *m*

hematology *etc* [,hi:mə'tɒlədʒɪ] (*US*) = **haematology** *etc*

hemiplegic [,hemɪ'pli:dʒɪk] ADJ, N hemiplégico/a *m/f*

hemisphere ['hemɪsfɪə'] N hemisferio *m*

hemline ['hemlaɪn] N bajo *m* (del vestido)

hemlock ['hemlɒk] N cicuta *f*

hemp [hemp] N **1** (= *plant, fibre*) cáñamo *m* **2** (= *drug*) hachís *m*

hen [hen] N (= *fowl*) gallina *f*; (= *female bird*) hembra *f*
➤ **hen coop** gallinero *m* ➤ **hen night*, hen party*** (*Brit*) (= *girls' night*) reunión *f* de mujeres; (*before marriage*) despedida *f* de soltera

hence [hens] ADV **1** (= *therefore*) por lo tanto, de ahí, ~ **my letter** de allí que le escribiera; ~ **the fact that ...** de ahí que ... **2** (= *from now*) **five years ~** de aquí a cinco años

henceforth ['hens'fɔ:θ] ADV (= *from now on*) de hoy en adelante, a partir de hoy; (= *from then on*) en lo sucesivo

henchman ['hentʃmən] N (*pl* **henchmen**) (*esp Pol*) (= *follower*) secuaz *m*; (= *guard*) guardaespaldas *m inv*

henhouse ['henhaʊs] N gallinero *m*

henna ['henə] N alheña *f*

henpecked ['henpekt] ADJ dominado por su mujer; **a ~ husband*** un marido dominado por su mujer, un calzonazos (*Sp*)

hepatitis [,hepə'taɪtɪs] N hepatitis *f*

her [hɜ:'] **Ⓐ** PRON **1** (= *direct object*) la; **I can see ~** la veo; **look at ~!** ¡mírala!; **I have never seen HER** a ella no la he visto nunca
2 (= *indirect object*) le; (*combined with direct object pronoun*) se; **you must tell ~ the truth** tienes que decirle la verdad; **yes of course I gave ~ the book** sí, claro que le di el libro; **yes of course I gave them to ~** sí, claro que se los di; **I'm speaking to HER not you** le estoy hablando a ella, no a ti; **give it to ~ when you go to Liverpool** dáselo cuando vayas a Liverpool; **I gave it to HER not Peter** se lo di a ella, no a Peter
3 (*after prep, in comparisons, with verb "to be"*) ella; **I'm going with ~** voy con ella; **she was carrying it on ~** lo llevaba encima *or* consigo; **younger than ~** más joven *or* menor que ella; **it's ~** es ella
Ⓑ POSS ADJ (*with singular noun*) su; (*with plural noun*) sus;

~ **book/table** su libro/mesa; ~ **friends** sus amigos

---

her is usually translated by the definite article **el/los** or **la/las** when it's clear from the sentence who the possessor is or when referring to clothing or parts of the body:

---

they stole ~ **car** le robaron el coche; **she took off** ~ **coat** se quitó el abrigo; **she's washing** ~ **hair** se está lavando la cabeza

herald ['herəld] **A** N (= *messenger*) heraldo *m*; (*fig*) precursor(a) *m/f* **B** VT (*fig*) anunciar

heraldry ['herəldrɪ] N heráldica *f*

herb [hɜːb, (*US*) ɜːb] N hierba *f* ➤ **herb garden** jardín *m* de hierbas finas ➤ **herb tea** infusión *f* de hierbas

herbaceous [hɜː'beɪʃəs] ADJ herbáceo

herbal ['hɜːbəl] ADJ de hierbas, herbario ➤ **herbal tea** infusión *f* de hierbas

herbalist ['hɜːbəlɪst] N herbolario/a *m/f*

herbicide ['hɜːbɪsaɪd] N herbicida *m*

herbivore ['hɜːbɪˌvɔː] N herbívoro *m*

herd [hɜːd] **A** N [*of cattle*] rebaño *m*, manada *f*; [*of elephants*] manada *f*; [*of people*] multitud *f*, tropel *m* **B** VT [+ *animals*] llevar en manada; [+ *people*] reunir ➤ **herd together** **A** VI + ADV apiñarse, agruparse **B** VT + ADV agrupar, reunir

herdsman ['hɜːdzmən] N (*pl* **herdsmen**) [*of cattle*] vaquero *m*; [*of sheep*] pastor *m*

here [hɪəʳ] **A** ADV **1** (= *in this place*) aquí; (= *to this place*) aquí, acá (*esp LAm*); **I live** ~ vivo aquí; **she's not** ~ **at the moment** no está (aquí) en este momento; **here!** (*at roll call*) ¡presente!; **winter is** ~ ha llegado el invierno, ya está aquí el invierno; **my friend** ~ **will do it** este amigo mío lo hará; ~ **I should remind you that ...** ahora os debería recordar que ...; **it's my job that's at risk** ~ lo que me estoy jugando es el trabajo; **he's well known** <u>around</u> ~ es muy conocido por aquí; **come** ~! ¡ven aquí *or* (*esp LAm*) acá!; **in** ~, **please** aquí (dentro), por favor

2 (*offering or showing sth*) ~ **are the books** aquí están los libros; ~ **he comes** ya viene; ~ **'s what I think** esto es lo que pienso; ~ **it is, under the cushion** aquí está, debajo del cojín; ~ **you are, I've fixed it** toma *or* aquí lo tienes, lo he arreglado

3 (*in phrases*) ~ **we** <u>go</u> **again!** ¡ya estamos otra vez!; ~ **goes!** ¡ahí va!; ~ <u>lies</u> **...** aquí yacen los restos de ...; **whether or not he realized was** <u>neither</u> ~ **nor there** el que se hubiera dado cuenta o no no venía al caso; ~ **and** <u>now</u> aquí y ahora mismo; **he could only understand a word** ~ **and** <u>there</u> sólo entendía palabras sueltas; ~**'s** <u>to</u> **the happy couple!** ¡a la salud de los novios!; ~**'s to your new job!** ¡por tu nuevo trabajo!

B EXCL ~ **, you try and open it!** ¡toma, intenta abrirlo tú!; ~**, that's my dinner you're eating!** ¡oye tú, que ésa es mi cena!

C N **the** ~ **and now** el presente

hereabouts ['hɪərəbaʊts] ADV por aquí (cerca)

hereafter [hɪər'ɑːftəʳ] **A** ADV (*frm*) a continuación; (= *from now on*) de aquí en adelante, a partir de ahora **B** N **the** ~ el más allá

hereby ['hɪəbaɪ] ADV (*frm*) por este medio; (*in letter, document*) por la presente

hereditary [hɪ'redɪtərɪ] ADJ hereditario

heredity [hɪ'redɪtɪ] N herencia *f*

heresy ['herəsɪ] N herejía *f*

heretic ['herətɪk] N hereje *mf*

heretical [hɪ'retɪkəl] ADJ herético

hereupon ['hɪərə'pɒn] ADV (*frm*) en ese momento, en esto

herewith ['hɪə'wɪð] ADV (*frm*) **I enclose** ~ **a letter** le adjunto (con la presente) una carta

heritage ['herɪtɪdʒ] N herencia *f*; (*fig*) patrimonio *m* (nacional) ➤ **heritage centre** (*Brit*) museo *m* (*local, de artesanía etc*)

hermaphrodite [hɜː'mæfrədaɪt] ADJ, N hermafrodita *mf*

hermetic [hɜː'metɪk] ADJ hermético

hermetically [hɜː'metɪkəlɪ] ADV herméticamente; ~ **sealed** cerrado herméticamente

hermit ['hɜːmɪt] N ermitaño/a *m/f*

hernia ['hɜːnɪə] N (*Med*) hernia *f*

hero ['hɪərəʊ] N (*pl* ~**es**) héroe *m*; [*of film, book*] protagonista *mf*, personaje *m* principal ➤ **hero worship** adulación *f*

heroic [hɪ'rəʊɪk] ADJ heroico

heroics [hɪ'rəʊɪks] NPL acciones *fpl* heroicas, actos *mpl* de heroicidad

heroin ['herəʊɪn] N heroína *f* (*droga*) ➤ **heroin addict** heroinómano/a *m/f* ➤ **heroin addiction** adicción *f* a la heroína, dependencia *f* de la heroína, heroinomanía *f* ➤ **heroin user** heroinómano/a *m/f*

heroine ['herəʊɪn] N heroína *f*; [*of film, book*] protagonista *f*, personaje *m* principal

heroism ['herəʊɪzəm] N heroísmo *m*

heron ['herən] N garza *f* real

herpes ['hɜːpiːz] N herpes *m*

herring ['herɪŋ] N (*pl* ~**s** *or* ~) arenque *m*; **red** ~ (*fig*) pista *f* falsa, despiste *m*

herringbone pattern [ˌherɪŋbəʊn'pætən] ADJ (*on material*) diseño *m* en espiga

hers [hɜːz] POSS PRON (*referring to singular possession*) (el/la) suyo/a; (*referring to plural possession*) (los/las) suyos/as

---

Only use the article with **suyo/suyos** etc when you mean "the one(s) belonging to her".

---

this car is ~ este coche es suyo *or* de ella; **is that car** ~**?** ¿es suyo *or* de ella ese coche?; **"whose is this?" — "it's** ~**"** —¿de quién es esto? —es de ella; **a friend of** ~ un amigo suyo; **my car is much bigger than** ~ mi coche es mucho más grande que el suyo *or* el de ella; **my parents and** ~ mis padres y los suyos *or* los de ella

herself [hɜː'self] PRON **1** (*reflexive*) se; **she washed** ~ se lavó **2** (*emphatic*) ella misma; **she did it** ~ lo hizo ella misma; **she went** ~ fue ella misma, fue en persona **3** (*after prep*) sí misma, ella misma; **she talked mainly about** ~ habló principalmente de sí misma *or* ella misma; **she said to** ~ dijo entre *or* para sí, se dijo a sí misma **4** (*phrases*) **by** ~: **she came by** ~ vino sola; **she did it by** ~ lo hizo ella sola; **she's not** ~ no se encuentra nada bien, parece otra

he's [hiːz] = **he is, he has**

hesitant ['hezɪtənt] ADJ (*gen*) vacilante; (*in character*) indeciso; **to be** ~ **about doing sth** no decidirse a hacer algo

hesitantly ['hezɪtəntlɪ] ADV indecisamente; [*speak, suggest*] con vacilación

hesitate ['hezɪteɪt] VI (*gen*) vacilar; (*in speech*) vacilar, titubear; **to** ~ **to do sth** dudar *or* vacilar en hacer algo

hesitation [ˌhezɪ'teɪʃən] N vacilación *f*, indecisión *f*; **I have no** ~ **in saying ...** no vacilo en decir ...; **without the slightest** ~ sin vacilar siquiera, sin pensarlo dos veces

hessian ['hesɪən] (*esp Brit*) **A** N arpillera *f* **B** ADJ de arpillera

heterogeneous ['hetərəʊ'dʒiːnɪəs] ADJ heterogéneo

heterosexual ['hetərəʊ'seksjʊəl] ADJ, N heterosexual *mf*

heterosexuality ['hetərəʊˌseksjʊ'ælɪtɪ] N heterosexualidad *f*

het up★ [ˌhet'ʌp] ADJ **to get** ~ acalorarse, emocionarse (**about, over** por)

heuristic [hjʊə'rɪstɪk] ADJ heurístico

hew [hjuː] (*pt* ~**ed**; *pp* ~**ed**, ~**n** [hjuːn]) VT (= *cut*) cortar; [+ *trees*] talar; (= *shape, work*) labrar, tallar

hex★ [heks] (*US*) **A** N maleficio *m*, mal *m* de ojo **B** VT embrujar

hexagon ['heksəgən] N hexágono *m*

hexagonal [hek'sægənəl] ADJ hexagonal

hey [heɪ] EXCL ¡oye!, ¡oiga!

heyday ['heɪdeɪ] N auge *m*; **in the** ~ **of the theatre** cuando el teatro estaba en su apogeo; **in his** ~ en sus buenos tiempos

HGV N ABBR (= **heavy goods vehicle**) vehículo *m* pesado

HI ABBR (*US*) = **Hawaii**

hi [haɪ] EXCL ¡oye!; (*greeting*) ¡hola!, ¡qué hubo! (*Mex, Chi*)

hiatus [haɪˈeɪtəs] N (*Gram*) hiato *m*; (*fig*) vacío *m*, interrupción *f*

hibernate [ˈhaɪbəneɪt] VI hibernar, invernar

hibernation [ˌhaɪbəˈneɪʃən] N hibernación *f*, invernación *f*

hiccup [ˈhɪkʌp] Ⓐ N hipo *m*; **it gives me ~s** me da hipo, me hace hipar; **to have ~s** tener hipo; **a slight ~ in the proceedings** una pequeña dificultad *or* interrupción en los actos Ⓑ VI hipar

hick* [hɪk] (*US pej*) Ⓐ ADJ rústico, de aldea Ⓑ N pueblerino/a *m/f*, paleto/a *m/f* (*Sp**)

hickey* [ˈhɪkɪ] N (*US*) (= *pimple*) grano *m*; (= *love-bite*) mordisco *m* amoroso, chupón* *m*

hide¹ [haɪd] (*pt* **hid** [hɪd]; *pp* **hidden** [ˈhɪdn]) Ⓐ VT (*gen*) esconder (**from** de); [+ *grief*] ocultar, disimular; **to ~ one's face in one's hands** taparse la cara con las manos; **I have nothing to ~** no tengo nada que ocultar Ⓑ VI esconderse, ocultarse (**from** de); **he's hiding behind his illness** se ampara en su enfermedad; **he's hiding behind his boss** está buscando la protección de su jefe
➤ **hide away** Ⓐ VI + ADV esconderse Ⓑ VT + ADV esconder, ocultar
➤ **hide out, hide up** VI + ADV esconderse

hide² [haɪd] N (= *skin*) piel *f*, pellejo *m*; (*tanned*) cuero *m*; ✦ IDIOMS **to save one's ~** salvar el pellejo; **I haven't seen ~ nor hair of him** no le he visto el pelo*

hide³ [haɪd] N (*Brit Hunting*) paranza *f*, trepa *f*; (*Orn*) observatorio *m*

hide-and-seek [ˌhaɪdənˈsiːk], **hide-and-go-seek** (*US*) [ˌhaɪdəngəʊˈsiːk] N escondite *m*; **to play ~** jugar al escondite

hideaway [ˈhaɪdəweɪ] N escondite *m*, escondrijo *m*

hideous [ˈhɪdɪəs] ADJ (*gen*) espantoso, horroroso; (= *repugnant*) repugnante, asqueroso

hideously [ˈhɪdɪəslɪ] ADV horriblemente; **~ ugly** feísimo

hideout [ˈhaɪdaʊt] N guarida *f*, escondrijo *m*

hiding¹ [ˈhaɪdɪŋ] N **to be in ~** estar escondido; **to go into ~** esconderse; (*Pol*) pasar a la clandestinidad ➤ **hiding place** escondite *m*, escondrijo *m*

hiding² [ˈhaɪdɪŋ] N (= *beating*) paliza *f*; **to give sb a ~** dar una paliza a algn

hierarchy [ˈhaɪərɑːkɪ] N jerarquía *f*

hieroglyphics [ˌhaɪərəˈglɪfɪks] NPL jeroglíficos *mpl*; (*fig*) (*) garabatos *mpl*

hi-fi [ˈhaɪfaɪ] ABBR *of* **high fidelity** Ⓐ N estéreo *m* Ⓑ ADJ de alta fidelidad Ⓒ CPD ➤ **hi-fi equipment** equipo *m* de alta fidelidad ➤ **hi-fi system** sistema *m* de alta fidelidad

higgledy-piggledy* [ˈhɪgldɪˈpɪgldɪ] ADJ revuelto, desordenado, en desorden

high [haɪ] Ⓐ ADJ (*compar* **~er**; *superl* **~est**) **1** [*building, mountain*] alto; [*plateau*] elevado; [*altitude*] grande; **it's 20 metres ~** tiene 20 metros de alto *or* de altura; **~ cheekbones** pómulos *mpl* salientes; **how ~ is Ben Nevis/ that tree?** ¿qué altura tiene el Ben Nevis/ese árbol?; **economic reform is ~ on the agenda** la reforma económica figura entre los asuntos más importantes a tratar; **I've known her since she was so ~*** la conozco desde que era así (de pequeña); ✦ IDIOM **to leave sb ~ and dry** dejar a algn en la estacada
2 (= *considerable*) [*level, risk, rent, salary, principles*] alto; [*price, tax, number*] alto, elevado; [*speed*] alto, gran; [*quality*] alto, bueno; [*wind*] fuerte; **temperatures were in the ~ 30s** las temperaturas llegaron casi a *or* rondaron los 40 grados; **to have ~ blood pressure** tener la tensión alta, ser hipertenso; **I had ~ hopes of being elected** tenía muchas esperanzas de que me eligieran; **parsley is ~ in calcium** el perejil es rico en calcio; **to have a ~ opinion of sb** (= *think highly of*) tener muy buena opinión *or* concepto de algn; (= *be fond of*) tener a algn en alta estima; **to pay a ~ price for sth** (*lit*) pagar mucho dinero por algo; (*fig*) pagar algo muy caro; **to have a ~**

temperature tener mucha fiebre, tener una fiebre muy alta; ✦ IDIOM **it's ~ time you were in bed*** ya deberías estar acostado desde hace un buen rato
3 (= *important, superior*) [*rank, position, office*] alto; **she's too ~ and mighty** es demasiado engreída; ✦ IDIOMS **to get (up) on one's ~ horse** subirse a la parra; **to get off one's ~ horse** bajar los humos; **to have friends in ~ places** tener amigos importantes *or* con influencias
4 (= *high-pitched*) [*sound, note*] alto; [*voice*] agudo; ✦ IDIOM **he ended his career on a ~ note** terminó su carrera con un gran éxito
5 (*) (= *intoxicated*) **to be ~ (on)** [+ *drink, drugs*] estar puesto (de)*; **to get ~ (on)** [+ *drink, drugs*] ponerse (de)*; **she was ~ on her latest success** estaba encantada *or* entusiasmada con su último éxito; ✦ IDIOM **to be (as) ~ as a kite** (*on drugs, drink*) estar volado*; (= *confident*) estar que no se cabe en sí
Ⓑ ADV (*compar* **~er**; *superl* **~est**) **1** (*in height*) [*fly, rise*] a gran altura; **an eagle circled ~ above** un águila circulaba en las alturas; **~ above my head** muy por encima de mi cabeza; **feelings were running ~** los ánimos estaban exaltados; ✦ IDIOMS **to hold one's head (up) ~** mantener la cabeza bien alta; **to live ~ on the hog** (*US**) vivir como un rajá; **to hunt ~ and low (for sth/sb)** remover el cielo y la tierra (en busca de algo/algn)
2 (*in degree, number*) **the bidding went as ~ as £500** las ofertas llegaron hasta 500 libras
Ⓒ N **1 on ~** (= *in heaven*) en el cielo, en las alturas; **there's been a new directive from on ~** (*iro*) ha habido una nueva directriz de arriba
2 (= *peak*) **sales have reached an all-time ~** las ventas han alcanzado cifras récord; ✦ IDIOM **to be on a ~*** estar a las mil maravillas
3 (*Fin*) máximo *m*; **the Dow Jones index reached a ~ of 2,503** el índice de Dow Jones alcanzó un máximo de 2.503
4 (*Met*) zona *f* de altas presiones; (*esp US*) temperatura *f* máxima
5 (*US Aut*) (= *top gear*) directa *f*; **to be in ~** ir en directa
Ⓓ CPD ➤ **high beam** (*US Aut*) **he had his lights on ~ beam** llevaba las luces largas *or* de cruce ➤ **high chair** silla *f* alta (para niño), trona *f* (*Sp*) ➤ **high command** alto mando *m* ➤ **High Court** (*Brit*) Tribunal *m* Supremo; **a ~ court judge** un juez del Tribunal Supremo ➤ **high definition** alta definición *f* ➤ **high explosive** explosivo *m* de gran potencia ➤ **high fidelity** alta fidelidad *f* ➤ **high finance** altas finanzas *fpl* ➤ **high flier, high flyer: he's a ~ flier** es ambicioso, tiene talento y promete ➤ **high ground: they believe they have** *or* **occupy the moral ~ ground in this conflict** creen que tienen moralmente la razón de su parte en este conflicto ➤ **high heels** (= *heels*) tacones *mpl* altos; (= *shoes*) zapatos *mpl* de tacón ➤ **high jump** (*Sport*) salto *m* de altura ➤ **high jumper** (*Sport*) saltador(a) *m/f* de altura ➤ **high living** la buena vida ➤ **high point** [*of show, evening*] punto *m* culminante, clímax *m inv*; [*of visit, holiday*] lo más destacado; [*of career*] punto *m* culminante, cenit *m* ➤ **high priest** sumo sacerdote *m* ➤ **high road** (*Brit*) carretera *f* ➤ **high roller** (*US*) (*gen*) derrochón/ona *m/f*; (*gambling*) jugador/ora *m/f* empedernido ➤ **high school** (*US, Brit*) instituto *m* de enseñanza secundaria, ≈ liceo *m* (*LAm*); **junior ~ (school)** (*US*) instituto donde se imparten los dos primeros años de bachillerato ➤ **high school diploma** (*US*) ≈ bachillerato *m* ➤ **the high seas** alta mar *fsing*; **on the ~ seas** en alta mar ➤ **high season** (*Brit*) temporada *f* alta ➤ **high society** la alta sociedad ➤ **high spirits: to be in ~ spirits** estar animadísimo, estar muy alegre ➤ **high spot** [*of show, evening*] punto *m* culminante, clímax *m inv*; [*of visit, holiday*] lo más destacado; [*of career*] punto *m* culminante, cenit *m* ➤ **high stakes: to play for ~ stakes** (*lit*) apostar fuerte; (*fig*) tener mucho en juego ➤ **high street** (*esp Brit*) calle *f* mayor, calle *f* principal; ~ **banks** bancos *mpl* principales; ~ **street shops** tiendas *fpl* de la calle principal ➤ **high table** (*gen*) mesa *f* principal, mesa *f* presidencial; (*Univ, Scol*) mesa *f* de los profesores ➤ **high tide** pleamar *f*, marea *f* alta; **at ~ tide** en la pleamar, en marea alta ➤ **high water** pleamar *f*, marea *f* alta ➤ **high wire** cuerda *f* floja ➤ **high wire act** número *m*

en la cuerda floja, número *m* de funambulismo

HIGH SCHOOL

En EE.UU. las **high schools** son los institutos donde los alumnos de 15 a 18 años estudian los tres cursos (del noveno al duodécimo **grades**) correspondientes al bachillerato; al final del último curso se edita un anuario con fotos de los alumnos y profesores (**Yearbook**) y se entrega el diploma de **high school** en la ceremonia de graduación, que precede al baile de fin de curso, conocido como **Senior Prom**.

highball ['haɪbɔːl] N (*US*) jaibol *m*, whisky *m* con soda

highboy ['haɪbɔɪ] N (*US*) cómoda *f* alta

highbrow ['haɪbraʊ] Ⓐ N intelectual *mf*, persona *f* culta; (*pej*) intelectualoide *mf* Ⓑ ADJ [*book, play, film*] para intelectuales

high-class [,haɪ'klɑːs] ADJ de (alta) categoría

high-definition [,haɪdefɪ'nɪʃən] ADJ de alta definición

high-density [,haɪ'densɪtɪ] ADJ ~ **housing** alta densidad *f* de inquilinos

higher ['haɪə'] Ⓐ ADJ COMPAR *of* **high** más alto; [*form of life, court*] superior; [*price*] más elevado; [*number, speed*] mayor; **any number ~ than six** cualquier número superior a *or* mayor de seis; **~ interest rates are a possibility** existe la posibilidad de una subida de los tipos de interés Ⓑ ADV COMPAR *of* **high 1** (*lit*) más alto; **~ and ~** más y más (alto); **try hanging the picture a bit ~ up** prueba a poner el cuadro un poquito más alto *or* más arriba; **to fly ~ than the clouds** volar encima de las nubes; **to fly ~ still** volar a mayor altura todavía **2** (*fig*) **the dollar closed ~ today** la cotización del dólar ha cerrado más alta hoy; **unemployment is expected to rise even ~** se espera que el desempleo aumente aún más Ⓒ N (*Scot Scol*) = **Higher Grade** Ⓓ CPD ► **higher education** educación *f* superior, enseñanza *f* superior ► **Higher Grade** (*Scot*) *examen de estado que se realiza a la edad de 16 años* ► **Higher National Certificate** (*Brit*) Certificado *m* Nacional de Estudios Superiores ► **Higher National Diploma** (*Brit*) Diploma *m* Nacional de Estudios Superiores

higher-up ['haɪər∧p] N = **high-up**

highfalutin(g) [,haɪfə'luːtɪn] ADJ presuntuoso, pomposo

high-fibre, high-fiber (*US*) ['haɪ'faɪbə'] ADJ **a ~ diet** una dieta rica en fibra

high-flown ['haɪfləʊn] ADJ exagerado, altisonante

high-flying [,haɪ'flaɪɪŋ] ADJ **1** [*aircraft*] de gran altura **2** (*fig*) (= *promising*) prometedor; (= *in high-calibre job*) bien situado, de prestigio

high-frequency [,haɪ'friːkwənsɪ] ADJ de alta frecuencia

high-grade ['haɪ'greɪd] ADJ de calidad superior

high-handed ['haɪ'hændɪd] ADJ arbitrario, despótico

high-heeled ['haɪhiːld] ADJ de tacón (alto)

highjack *etc* ['haɪdʒæk] = **hijack** *etc*

highlander ['haɪləndə'] N montañés/esa *m/f*; **Highlander** (*Brit*) *habitante de las tierras altas de Escocia*

highlands ['haɪləndz] NPL tierras *fpl* altas, sierra *fsing* (*LAm*); **the Highlands** (*Brit*) las Tierras Altas de Escocia

high-level ['haɪ'levl] ADJ de alto nivel (*also Comput*)

highlight ['haɪlaɪt] Ⓐ N **1** (*Art*) toque *m* de luz **2** (*fig*) punto *m* culminante; **the ~ of the evening** el punto culminante de la velada; **they showed the ~s of the game on television** mostraron los momentos más interesantes del partido por televisión; (*Ftbl*) mostraron las jugadas más interesantes del partido por televisión **3 highlights** (*in hair*) reflejos *mpl* Ⓑ VT (*gen*) poner de relieve, destacar; [+ *hair*] poner reflejos en; (*Comput*) marcar

highlighter ['haɪlaɪtə'] N rotulador *m* (*Sp*), marcador *m* (*LAm*)

highly ['haɪlɪ] ADV **1** (*with adj, pp used as adj*) [*effective, sensitive, controversial*] muy, sumamente; [*qualified,*

developed, sophisticated] sumamente, altamente; [*significant*] sumamente, tremendamente; **~ acclaimed** sumamente elogiado; **~ intelligent** sumamente inteligente, inteligentísimo; **it is ~ likely that ...** es muy *or* sumamente probable que + *subjun*; **~ paid** muy bien pagado; **~ qualified** muy preparado, muy cualificado; **~ strung** muy nervioso, muy excitable; **a ~ successful businessman** un hombre de negocios de muchísimo éxito; **it is ~ unlikely that ...** es muy poco probable que + *subjun* **2** (*with verb*) **to praise sb ~** alabar *or* elogiar mucho a algn; **I can't praise him ~ enough** todo elogio que haga de él es poco; **I don't rate him very ~** no tengo muy buena opinión de él; **he is ~ regarded by all his staff** está muy bien considerado por todo su personal; **to speak ~ of sb/sth** hablar muy bien de algn/algo; **to think ~ of sb/sth** tener muy buena opinión de algn/algo

high-minded ['haɪ'maɪndɪd] ADJ [*person*] de nobles pensamientos, magnánimo; [*act*] noble, altruista

high-necked [,haɪ'nekt] ADJ de cuello alto

highness ['haɪnɪs] N altura *f*; **Highness** (*as title*) Alteza *f*; **His/Her/Your Royal Highness** Su Alteza Real

high-performance [,haɪpə'fɔːməns] ADJ de gran rendimiento

high-pitched ['haɪ'pɪtʃt] ADJ [*sound, voice*] agudo; [*instrument*] de tono agudo, de tono alto

high-powered ['haɪ'paʊəd] ADJ [*engine*] de gran potencia; [*person*] (= *dynamic*) enérgico, dinámico; (= *important*) importante

high-pressure ['haɪ'preʃə'] ADJ de alta presión; (*fig*) enérgico, dinámico; **~ selling** venta *f* agresiva

high-profile [,haɪ'prəʊfaɪl] ADJ **~ activity** actividad *f* prominente

high-ranking [,haɪ'ræŋkɪŋ] ADJ [*official*] de alto rango, de alto grado; (*Mil*) de alta graduación

high-resolution [,haɪrezə'luːʃən] ADJ de alta resolución

high-rise ['haɪraɪz] Ⓐ ADJ **~ block** (*residential*) torre *f* de pisos; **~ office block** edificio *m* de oficinas (de muchas plantas) Ⓑ N torre *f* de pisos

high-risk [,haɪ'rɪsk] ADJ [*investment, policy*] de alto riesgo

high-speed [,haɪ'spiːd] ADJ [*vehicle, tram*] de alta velocidad

high-spirited [,haɪ'spɪrɪtɪd] ADJ [*person*] animado; [*horse*] fogoso

high-strung [,haɪ'strʌŋ] ADJ (*US*) muy nervioso, muy excitable

hightail* ['haɪteɪl] VT **to ~ it** (*esp US*) darse el piro**, salir pitando*

high-tech* [,haɪ'tek] ADJ al-tec*, de alta tecnología

high-up* ['haɪ∧p], **higher-up** ['haɪər∧p] N pez *m* gordo*, mandamás* *mf inv*

highway ['haɪweɪ] N (*esp US*) (= *main road*) carretera *f*; (= *motorway*) autopista *f*; **~s department** administración *f* de carreteras ► **Highway Code** (*Brit*) Código *m* de la Circulación ► **highway robbery** salteamiento *m*, atraco *m* (en el camino); ♦ IDIOM **it's ~ robbery!** ¡es un robo *or* una estafa!, ¡es un atraco a mano armada!

highwayman ['haɪweɪmən] N (*pl* **highwaymen**) salteador *m* de caminos

hijack ['haɪdʒæk] Ⓐ VT secuestrar; (*fig*) apropiarse de Ⓑ N secuestro *m*; (*fig*) apropiación *f*

hijacker ['haɪdʒækə'] N secuestrador(a) *m/f*

hijacking ['haɪdʒækɪŋ] N secuestro *m*; (*fig*) apropiación *f*

hike¹ [haɪk] Ⓐ VI ir de excursión a pie, dar una caminata Ⓑ N excursión *f* a pie, caminata *f*; **to go on a ~** hacer una excursión (a pie), dar una caminata

hike²* [haɪk] N (= *increase*) aumento *m*

hiker ['haɪkə'] N excursionista *mf*

hiking ['haɪkɪŋ] N excursionismo *m* (a pie); **to go ~** ir de excursión a pie

hilarious [hɪ'lɛərɪəs] ADJ divertidísimo, graciosísimo

hilarity [hɪ'lærɪtɪ] N hilaridad *f*

hill [hɪl] N (*gen*) colina *f*, cerro *m*, loma *f* (*esp LAm*); (*high*) montaña *f*; (= *slope*) cuesta *f*; **a house at the top of a** ~ una casa en lo alto de una colina; **I climbed the** ~ **up to the office** subí la cuesta hasta la oficina; **the hills** la montaña *fsing*, la sierra *fsing*; ✦ IDIOMS **to be over the** ~* ir cuesta abajo; **as old as the** ~**s** más viejo que Matusalén ➤ **hill farmer** agricultor(a) *m/f* de montaña ➤ **hill farming** agricultura *f* de montaña ➤ **hill walker** montañero/a *m/f*, senderista *mf* ➤ **hill walking** montañismo *m*, senderismo *m*; **to go** ~ **walking** hacer montañismo, hacer senderismo

hillbilly* ['hɪl,bɪlɪ] N (*US*) rústico/a *m/f* montañés/esa; (*pej*) palurdo/a *m/f*

hillock ['hɪlək] N montículo *m*, altozano *m*

hillside ['hɪlsaɪd] N ladera *f*, falda *f*

hilltop ['hɪltɒp] N cumbre *f*

hilly ['hɪlɪ] ADJ (*compar* **hillier**; *superl* **hilliest**) [*terrain*] montañoso, accidentado; [*road*] con fuertes pendientes

hilt [hɪlt] N puño *m*, empuñadura *f*; **to back sb up to the** ~ apoyar a algn incondicionalmente

him [hɪm] PRON **1** (= *direct object*) lo, le (*Sp*); **I saw** ~ lo vi; **look at** ~! ¡míralo!; **I have never seen HIM** a él no lo *or* (*also Sp*) le he visto nunca
2 (= *indirect object*) le; (*combined with direct object pron*) se; **you must tell** ~ **the truth** tienes que decirle la verdad; **yes of course I gave** ~ **the book** sí, claro que le di el libro; **yes of course I gave them to** ~ sí, claro que se los di; **I gave the book to HIM not his sister** le di el libro a él no a su hermana; **I'm speaking to HIM not you** le estoy hablando a él, no a ti; **give it to** ~ **when you go to Liverpool** dáselo cuando vayas a Liverpool; **I gave it to HIM not Charlotte** se lo di a él no a Charlotte
3 (*after prep, in comparisons, with verb "to be"*) él; **without** ~ sin él; **I'm going with** ~ voy con él; **he was carrying it on** ~ lo llevaba encima *or* consigo; **if I were** ~ yo de él, yo que él, si yo fuera él; **younger than** ~ más joven *or* menor que él; **it's** ~ es él

Himalayas [,hɪmə'leɪəz] NPL **the** ~ los montes Himalaya, el Himalaya

himself [hɪm'self] PRON **1** (*reflexive*) se; **he washed** ~ se lavó
2 (*emphatic*) él mismo; **he did it** ~ lo hizo él mismo; **he went** ~ fue él mismo, fue en persona **3** (*after prep*) sí mismo, él mismo; **he talked mainly about** ~ habló principalmente de sí mismo *or* él mismo; **he said to** ~ dijo entre *or* para sí, se dijo a sí mismo **4** (*phrases*) **by** ~**: he came by** ~ vino solo; **he did it by** ~ lo hizo él solo; **he's not** ~ no se encuentra nada bien, parece otro

hind¹ [haɪnd] ADJ [*leg, foot*] trasero, posterior; ✦ IDIOM **he could talk the** ~ **leg(s) off a donkey** (*Brit**) habla hasta por los codos*

hind² [haɪnd] N (*pl* ~**s** *or* ~) cierva *f*

hinder ['hɪndə] VT (= *disturb, make difficult*) estorbar, dificultar; (= *prevent*) impedir; (= *obstruct*) obstaculizar, poner dificultades a; (= *slow down*) entorpecer; **to** ~ **sb from doing sth** impedir a algn hacer algo

Hindi ['hɪndiː] N hindi *m*

hindquarters ['haɪnd,kwɔːtəz] NPL cuartos *mpl* traseros

hindrance ['hɪndrəns] N (= *obstacle*) obstáculo *m* (**to** para); (= *disturbance*) estorbo *m*; (= *problem*) impedimento *m*; **to be a** ~ **to sb/sth** ser un estorbo para algn/algo

hindsight ['haɪndsaɪt] N **with the benefit of** ~ en retrospectiva

Hindu ['hɪn'duː] ADJ, N hindú *mf*

Hinduism ['hɪnduːɪzəm] N (*Rel*) hinduismo *m*

hinge [hɪndʒ] Ⓐ N [*of door, window*] bisagra *f*, gozne *m*; (*fig*) eje *m* Ⓑ VI **to** ~ **on** (*fig*) depender de

hinged [hɪndʒd] ADJ de bisagra, con goznes

hint [hɪnt] Ⓐ N **1** (= *suggestion*) indirecta *f*, insinuación *f*; (= *tip*) consejo *m*; ~**s for purchasers** consejos *mpl* a los compradores; **broad** ~ indicación *f* inconfundible; **to drop a** ~ soltar *or* tirar una indirecta; **give me a** ~ dame una idea; **to take the** ~ (*unspoken*) tomar algo a corazón; (*spoken*) darse por aludido
2 (= *trace*) señal *f*, indicio *m*; **without the least** ~ **of** sin la menor señal de; **with just a** ~ **of garlic** con un ligerísimo

sabor a ajo; **with a** ~ **of irony** con un dejo de ironía Ⓑ VT dar a entender, insinuar Ⓒ VI soltar indirectas
➤ **hint at** VI + PREP referirse indirectamente a, hacer alusión a; **what are you** ~**ing at?** ¿qué estás insinuando?

hip¹ [hɪp] N (*Anat*) cadera *f* ➤ **hip joint** articulación *f* de la cadera ➤ **hip pocket** bolsillo *m* de atrás, bolsillo *m* trasero ➤ **hip replacement (operation)** operación *f* de trasplante de cadera ➤ **hip size** talla *f* de cadera

hip² [hɪp] EXCL **hip hip hurray!** ¡viva!

hip³* [hɪp] ADJ **to be** ~ (= *up-to-date*) estar al día; (= *well-informed*) estar al tanto (de lo que pasa), estar enterado

hippie* ['hɪpɪ] = **hippy**

hippo* ['hɪpəʊ] N hipopótamo/a *m/f*

hippopotamus [,hɪpə'pɒtəməs] N hipopótamo/a *m/f*

hippy* ['hɪpɪ] ADJ, N hippy* *mf*, hippie* *mf*

hire ['haɪə] Ⓐ VT [+ *employee, lawyer*] contratar; (*esp Brit*) [+ *car, house*] alquilar, arrendar (*LAm*); ~**d hand** jornalero/a *m/f*, enganchado/a *m/f*; ~**d assassin** *or* **killer** asesino/a *m/f* a sueldo; ~**d car** (*esp Brit*) coche *m* de alquiler
Ⓑ VI **she's in charge of hiring and firing at the company** es la encargada de contratar y despedir al personal en la empresa
Ⓒ N (*esp Brit*) [*of car*] alquiler *m*, arriendo *m* (*LAm*); **"for hire"** se alquila *or* (*LAm*) arrienda; (*on taxi*) libre; **we've got it on** ~ **for a week** lo tenemos alquilado por una semana
Ⓓ CPD ➤ **hire car** (*Brit*) coche *m* de alquiler ➤ **hire purchase** (*Brit*) compra *f* a plazos; **to buy sth on** ~ **purchase** comprar algo a plazos ➤ **hire purchase agreement** acuerdo *m* de compra a plazos
➤ **hire out** VT + ADV (*Brit*) alquilar, arrendar (*LAm*)

his [hɪz] Ⓐ POSS ADJ (*with singular noun*) su; (*with plural noun*) sus; ~ **book/table** su libro/mesa; ~ **friends** sus amigos

---

his is usually translated by the definite article **el/los** or **la/las** when it's clear from the sentence who the possessor is or when referring to clothing or parts of the body:

he took off ~ **coat** se quitó el abrigo; **he's washing** ~ **face** se está lavando la cara; **he had** ~ **car stolen** le robaron el coche
Ⓑ POSS PRON (*referring to singular possession*) (el/la) suyo/a; (*referring to plural possession*) (los/las) suyos/as

---

Only use the article with **suyo/suyos** etc when you mean "the one(s) belonging to him".

---

this book is ~ este libro es suyo *or* de él; **is that car** ~**?** ¿es suyo *or* de él ese coche?; **"whose is this?" — "it's** ~**"** —¿de quién es esto? —es de él; **a friend of** ~ un amigo suyo; **my car is much bigger than** ~ mi coche es mucho más grande que el suyo *or* el de él; **my parents and** ~ mis padres y los suyos

Hispanic [hɪs'pænɪk] Ⓐ ADJ hispánico; (*within US*) hispano Ⓑ N (*within US*) hispano/a *m/f*

hispanicism [hɪs'pænɪsɪzəm] N hispanismo *m*

hispanist ['hɪspənɪst] N hispanista *mf*

hiss [hɪs] Ⓐ N siseo *m*, silbido *m*; [*of protest*] silbido *m*, chiflido *m*; (*Elec*) silbido *m* Ⓑ VI sisear; (*in protest*) silbar, chiflar Ⓒ VT **to** ~ **an actor off the stage** abuchear a un actor (hasta que abandone la escena)

histogram ['hɪstəgræm] N histograma *m*

historian [hɪs'tɔːrɪən] N historiador(a) *m/f*

historic [hɪs'tɒrɪk] ADJ histórico

historical [hɪs'tɒrɪkəl] ADJ histórico

history ['hɪstərɪ] N historia *f*; **to go down in** ~ pasar a la historia (**as** como); **to make** ~ hacer época, marcar un hito; **he has a** ~ **of psychiatric disorder** tiene antecedentes de problemas psiquiátricos; **a piece of** ~ un trozo *or* fragmento de la historia; ✦ IDIOMS **that's ancient** ~ ésa es cosa vieja; **the rest is** ~ el resto ya lo sabéis, el resto ya es historia

histrionic [ˌhɪstrɪ'ɒnɪk] ADJ histriónico

hit [hɪt] (*vb: pt, pp ~*) **Ⓐ** N 1 (= *blow*) golpe *m*; (*Sport*) (= *shot*) tiro *m*; (*on target*) tiro *m* certero, acierto *m*; (*Baseball*) jit *m*; [*of bomb*] impacto *m* directo; (= *good guess*) acierto *m*
2 (*Mus, Theat*) éxito *m*; **to be a ~** tener éxito, ser un éxito; **the film was a massive ~** la película fue un éxito enorme; **to make a ~ with sb** caerle bien a algn
3 (*Internet*) (= *match when searching Web*) correspondencia *f*; (= *visit to website*) visitante *mf*
Ⓑ VT 1 (= *strike*) [+ *person*] pegar, golpear; (= *come into contact with*) dar con, dar contra; (*violently*) chocar con, chocar contra; [+ *ball*] pegar; [+ *target*] dar en; **to ~ sb a blow** dar un golpe a algn; **to ~ one's head against a wall** dar con la cabeza contra una pared; **the president was ~ by three bullets** el presidente fue alcanzado por tres balas; **the house was ~ by a bomb** la casa sufrió un directo; **I realized my plane had been ~** me di cuenta de que mi avión había sido tocado; **he was ~ by a stone** le alcanzó una piedra; **the car ~ a road sign** el coche chocó con una señal de tráfico; **he was ~ by a car** le pilló un coche; **✦** IDIOMS **to ~ sb when he's down** rematar a algn; **then it ~ me*** (*realization*) entonces caí en la cuenta; **to ~ one's head against a wall** dar golpes al viento; **to ~ home: a lot of what he said ~ home** gran parte de lo que dijo dio en el blanco *or* hizo mella; **to ~ the mark** dar en el blanco, acertar
2 (= *damage*) dañar; [+ *person*] afectar, golpear; **the news ~ him hard** la noticia le afectó mucho; **the company has been hard ~** la empresa se ha visto muy afectada
3 (= *find, reach*) [+ *speed*] alcanzar; [+ *difficulty*] tropezar con; **we ~ London at nightfall*** llegamos a Londres al anochecer; **✦** IDIOMS **to ~ the bottle*** beber mucho; **to ~ the jackpot** sacar el premio gordo; **to ~ the sack*** tumbarse; **to ~ the road** *or* **the trail*** ponerse en camino *or* en marcha
4 (*Press*) **✦** IDIOMS **to ~ the front page** *or* **the headlines*** salir en primera plana; **to ~ the papers*** salir en el periódico
Ⓒ VI golpear; (= *collide*) chocar; **to ~ against** chocar con, dar contra; **to ~ at** asestar un golpe a
Ⓓ CPD **➤ hit list** (= *death list*) lista *f* de personas a las que se planea eliminar; (= *target list*) lista *f* negra **➤ hit parade** lista *f* de éxitos **➤ hit song** canción *f* éxito **➤ hit squad** escuadrón *m* de la muerte
➤ hit back Ⓐ VI + ADV (*lit, fig*) devolver el golpe **Ⓑ** VT + ADV devolver el golpe a
➤ hit off VT + ADV **to ~ it off with sb** hacer buenas migas con algn; **they don't ~ it off** no se llevan bien
➤ hit on VI + PREP 1 (= *stumble on*) dar con; **I ~ on the idea of ...** se me ocurrió la idea de ... 2 (*esp US***) (= *make advances to*) intentar ligar con
➤ hit out VI + ADV 1 (*Brit*) (*physically*) asestar un golpe; (*wildly*) repartir golpes (**at** a) 2 **to ~ out at sb** (= *criticize*) atacar a algn
➤ hit upon = hit on 1

hit-and-miss [ˌhɪtən'mɪs] ADJ **it's all rather ~** es todo un poco a la buena de Dios; **to have a ~ way of doing things** hacer las cosas al azar *or* sin ton ni son

hit-and-run [ˈhɪtən'rʌn] ADJ **➤ hit-and-run accident** *accidente de carretera en el que el conductor se da a la fuga* **➤ hit-and-run driver** *conductor(a) que atropella a alguien y huye*

hitch [hɪtʃ] **Ⓐ** N (= *impediment, obstacle*) obstáculo *m*, impedimento *m*; **without a ~** sin ningún problema; **there's been a slight ~** ha habido un pequeño contratiempo
Ⓑ VT 1 **to ~ a lift** hacer autostop, hacer dedo*, pedir aventón (*Mex*); **they ~ed a lift to Rome** llegaron a Roma haciendo autostop 2 (= *fasten*) atar, amarrar (**to** a); **to ~ a horse to a wagon** enganchar un caballo a un carro 3 **to get ~ed*** casarse
Ⓒ VI (* *also* **~hike**) hacer autostop, ir a dedo, hacer dedo*, pedir aventón (*Mex*)
➤ hitch up VT + ADV [+ *trousers, sleeves*] remangarse, subirse

hitchhike [ˈhɪtʃhaɪk] VI hacer autostop, hacer dedo*, pedir aventón (*Mex*)

hitchhiker [ˈhɪtʃhaɪkəʳ] N autostopista *mf*

hitchhiking [ˈhɪtʃhaɪkɪŋ] N autostop *m*

hi-tech* [ˈhaɪtek] ADJ al-tec*, de alta tecnología

hither [ˈhɪðəʳ] ADV **~ and thither** acá y acullá

hitherto [ˈhɪðə'tuː] ADV hasta ahora

hitman [ˈhɪtmæn] N (*pl* **hitmen**) sicario *m*, asesino *m* a sueldo

hit-or-miss [ˈhɪtɔː'mɪs] ADJ = **hit-and-miss**

HIV N ABBR (= **human immunodeficiency virus**) VIH *m*; **~ positive/negative** VIH positivo/negativo

hive [haɪv] N colmena *f*; **a ~ of activity** un hervidero de actividad
➤ hive off* VT + ADV (*esp Brit*) (= *sell off*) vender (por separado); (= *privatize*) privatizar

HM ABBR (= **Her/His Majesty**) S.M.

hm ABBR (= **hectometre(s)**) hm

HMO N ABBR (*US*) (= **health maintenance organization**) *seguro médico global*

HMS N ABBR (*Brit*) (= **Her/His Majesty's Ship**) *buque de guerra*

HNC N ABBR (*Brit*) = **Higher National Certificate**

HND N ABBR (*Brit*) = **Higher National Diploma**

hoard [hɔːd] **Ⓐ** N (= *stockpile*) provisión *f*; (= *treasure*) tesoro *m* **Ⓑ** VT (= *accumulate*) amontonar, acumular; [+ *money*] atesorar

hoarding [ˈhɔːdɪŋ] N (*Brit*) valla *f* publicitaria

hoarse [hɔːs] ADJ (*compar* **~r**; *superl* **~st**) ronco

hoary [ˈhɔːrɪ] ADJ (*compar* **hoarier**; *superl* **hoariest**) 1 (= *grey-haired*) cano 2 (= *old*) [*joke*] muy viejo

hoax [həʊks] N engaño *m* **➤ hoax call** *llamada efectuada a la policía, los bomberos, etc. para dar un falso aviso de bomba, incendio, etc*

hob [hɒb] N (*Brit*) quemador *m*

hobble [ˈhɒbl] **Ⓐ** VT [+ *horse*] manear **Ⓑ** VI (*also* **to ~ along**) cojear, andar cojeando

hobby [ˈhɒbɪ] N hobby *m*, pasatiempo *m* favorito; **he began to paint as a ~** empezó a pintar como hobby

hobbyhorse [ˈhɒbɪhɔːs] N 1 (= *toy*) caballito *m* (de niño) 2 (*fig*) (= *preoccupation*) caballo *m* de batalla, tema *m* preferido; **he's on his ~ again** ya está otra vez con lo mismo

hobnailed [ˈhɒbneɪld] ADJ con clavos

hobnob* [ˈhɒbnɒb] VI **to ~ with** codearse con, alternar con

hobo [ˈhəʊbəʊ] N (*pl* **~es** *or* **~s**) (*US*) vagabundo/a *m/f*

Hobson's choice [ˈhɒbsənz'tʃɔɪs] N (*Brit*) **it's ~** o lo tomas o lo dejas

hock¹ [hɒk] N [*of animal*] corvejón *m*

hock² [hɒk] N (= *wine*) vino *m* blanco del Rin

hockey [ˈhɒkɪ] **Ⓐ** N 1 (*Brit*) (*on grass*) hockey *m* (sobre hierba) 2 (*US*) (= *ice hockey*) hockey *m* sobre hielo **Ⓑ** CPD **➤ hockey stick** palo *m* de hockey

hocus-pocus [ˈhəʊkəs'pəʊkəs] **Ⓐ** N (= *trickery*) juego *m* de manos; (= *words*) jerigonza *f* **Ⓑ** EXCL abracadabra

hodgepodge [ˈhɒdʒpɒdʒ] N (*esp US*) mezcolanza *f*

hoe [həʊ] **Ⓐ** N azada *f*, azadón *m* **Ⓑ** VT [+ *earth*] azadonar, trabajar con la azada; [+ *crop*] sachar

hog [hɒg] **Ⓐ** N (*esp US*) (= *pig*) cerdo *m*, puerco *m*, chancho *m* (*LAm*) **Ⓑ** VT (*) acaparar; **to ~ the limelight** acaparar toda la atención

Hogmanay [ˈhɒgməneɪ] N (*Scot*) Nochevieja *f*

hogwash [ˈhɒgwɒʃ] N tonterías *fpl*

hoi polloi [ˌhɔɪpə'lɔɪ] N **the ~** (*hum, iro*) la plebe, el vulgo

hoist [hɔɪst] **Ⓐ** VT (*also* **to ~ up**) levantar, alzar; [+ *flag, sail*] izar **Ⓑ** N (= *lift*) montacargas *m inv*; (= *crane*) grúa *f*; **to give sb a ~ (up)** ayudar a algn a subir

hoity-toity* [ˈhɔɪtɪ'tɔɪtɪ] ADJ presumido, engreído

hokum* [ˈhəʊkəm] N (*esp US*) tonterías *fpl*

hold [həʊld] (*vb: pt, pp* **held**) **Ⓐ** N 1 (= *grasp*) agarro *m*, asimiento *m*; **to catch ~ of** coger, agarrar (*LAm*); **to get ~ of** coger, agarrar (*LAm*); (= *take over*) adquirir, apoderarse de; (= *obtain*) procurarse, conseguir; **where did you get ~ of that idea?** ¿de dónde te salió esa idea?; **to get ~ of sb**

(= *find, contact*) localizar a algn; **to get (a) ~ of o.s.** dominarse; **to keep ~ of** seguir agarrado a; (*fig*) guardar para sí; **to be on ~** (*Telec*) estar en espera; **to put sb on ~** (*Telec*) poner a algn en espera; **to put a plan on ~** suspender temporalmente la ejecución de un plan; **to seize ~ of** apoderarse de; **to take ~ of** coger, agarrar (*LAm*) **2** (*Mountaineering*) asidero *m* **3** (*Wrestling*) presa *f*, llave *f*; **with no ~s barred** (*fig*) sin restricción, permitiéndose todo **4** (= *influence*) influencia *f*, dominio *m* (**on, over** sobre); **her powerful ~ on her son** su poderosa influencia sobre su hijo; **this broke the dictator's ~** esto acabó con el dominio del dictador; **to have a ~ on** or **over sb** dominar a algn, tener dominado a algn; **drink has a ~ on him** la bebida está muy arraigada en él, está atrapado por la bebida **5** (*on ship, plane*) bodega *f*, compartimento *m* de carga **Ⓑ** VT **1** (= *grasp*) tener; (= *grasp firmly*) sujetar; (= *take hold of*) coger, agarrar (*LAm*); (= *embrace*) abrazar; (= *bear weight of*) soportar; **he was ~ing a little mouse in his hand** tenía un ratoncillo en la mano; **she came in ~ing a baby/bunch of flowers** entró con un niño en brazos/con un ramo de flores en las manos; **he held my arm** me tuvo por el brazo; **~ the ladder** sujeta la escalera; **~ this for a moment** coge esto un momento; **~ him or he'll fall** sostenle que va a caer; **to ~ sth tight** agarrar algo fuertemente; **to ~ sb tight** abrazar a algn estrechamente **2** (= *maintain, keep*) [+ *attention, interest*] mantener; [+ *belief, opinion*] tener, sostener; [+ *note*] (*Mus*) sostener; **to ~ the line** (*Telec*) no colgar; **to ~ one's own** defenderse; **to ~ sb to his promise** hacer que algn cumpla su promesa; **he held us spellbound** nos tuvo embelesados **3** (= *keep back*) retener, guardar; **"hold for arrival"** (*US*) (*on letters*) "no reexpedir", "reténgase"; **we are ~ing it pending inquiries** lo guardamos mientras se hagan indagaciones **4** (= *restrain*) [+ *enemy, breath*] contener; **~ it!** ¡para!, ¡espera!; **the police held him for three days** lo detuvo la policía durante tres días; **there was no ~ing him** no había manera de detenerle; **to ~ sb prisoner** tener preso a algn; **to ~ one's tongue** morderse la lengua, callarse la boca **5** (= *possess*) [+ *post, town, lands*] ocupar; [+ *passport, ticket, shares, title*] tener; (*Fin*) [+ *reserves*] tener en reserva, tener guardado; [+ *record*] ostentar; (*Mil*) [+ *position*] mantenerse en; **to ~ office** (*Pol*) ocupar un cargo **6** (= *contain*) contener, tener capacidad or cabida para; **this bag won't ~ them all** en este saco no caben todos; **what does the future ~?** ¿qué nos reserva el futuro? **7** (= *carry out*) [+ *conversation*] mantener; [+ *interview, meeting, election*] celebrar; [+ *event*] realizar; (*formally*) celebrar; **the maths exam is being held today** hoy tiene lugar el examen de matemáticas; **the meeting will be held on Monday** se celebrará la reunión el lunes, la reunión tendrá lugar el lunes **8** (= *consider, believe*) creer, sostener; **to ~ that** creer que, sostener que; **to ~ sth dear** apreciar mucho algo; **to ~ sb in high esteem** tener a algn en gran or alta estima; **to ~ sb responsible for sth** echar la culpa a algn de algo, hacer a algn responsable de algo **Ⓒ** VI **1** (= *stick*) pegarse; (= *not give way*) mantenerse firme, resistir; [*weather*] continuar, seguir bueno; **to ~ firm** or **fast** mantenerse firme **2** (= *be valid*) valer, ser valedero **3** (*Telec*) **please ~** no cuelge, por favor
➤ **hold against** VT + PREP tener contra; **you won't ~ this against me, will you?** ¿verdad que no vas a pensar mal de mí por esto?
➤ **hold back Ⓐ** VT + ADV (= *keep*) guardar, retener; (= *stop*) [+ *river, flood*] retener; [+ *progress*] refrenar; [+ *information*] ocultar, no revelar; [+ *names*] no comunicar; [+ *emotion, tears*] reprimir, contener; **are you ~ing sth back from me?** ¿me estás ocultando algo? **Ⓑ** VI + ADV refrenarse; (*in doubt*) vacilar; **to ~ back from** refrenarse de; **to ~ back from doing sth** refrenarse de hacer algo
➤ **hold down** VT + ADV **1** [+ *object*] sujetar **2** [+ *prices*] mantener bajo **3 to ~ down a job** (= *retain*) mantenerse en su puesto; (= *be equal to*) estar a la altura de su cargo; **he can't ~ down a job** pierde todos los trabajos
➤ **hold forth** VI + ADV hablar largo y tendido (**about, on** de), perorar
➤ **hold in** VT + ADV [+ *stomach, emotion*] contener

➤ **hold off Ⓐ** VT + ADV **1** (= *resist*) [+ *attack, enemy*] rechazar; [+ *person*] defenderse contra; [+ *visitor*] hacer esperar **2** (= *postpone*) aplazar **Ⓑ** VI + ADV **if the rain ~s off** si no llueve
➤ **hold on Ⓐ** VI + ADV **1** (= *grip, cling*) agarrarse **2** (= *persevere*) aguantar, resistir; **~ on!** ¡ánimo! **3** (= *wait*) esperar, seguir esperando; **~ on!** ¡espera!; (*Telec*) ¡no cuelgue!; **~ on, I'm coming!** ¡espera que ya voy! **Ⓑ** VT + ADV sujetar
➤ **hold on to** VT + PREP **1** (= *grasp*) agarrarse a, agarrarse de **2** (= *keep*) guardar, quedarse con; [+ *post, job*] retener
➤ **hold out Ⓐ** VT + ADV [+ *object*] ofrecer, alargar; [+ *hand*] tender, alargar; [+ *arm*] extender; [+ *possibility*] ofrecer; [+ *hope*] dar; **to ~ out sth to sb** ofrecer algo a algn **Ⓑ** VI + ADV **1** (= *resist*) resistir (**against** a), aguantar; **to ~ out for sth** insistir hasta conseguir algo; **he held out for £10** insistió en diez libras **2** (= *last*) [*supplies*] durar; [*weather*] seguir bueno
➤ **hold out on*** VI + PREP **you've been ~ing out on me!** ¡no me habías dicho nada!
➤ **hold over** VT + ADV [+ *meeting*] aplazar, posponer
➤ **hold to** VI + PREP atenerse a
➤ **hold together Ⓐ** VT + ADV [+ *people*] mantener unidos; [+ *company, group*] mantener la unidad de **Ⓑ** VI + ADV **1** [*people*] mantenerse unidos **2** [*argument*] ser sólido, ser lógico; [*deal*] mantenerse
➤ **hold up Ⓐ** VT + ADV **1** (= *support*) sujetar, sostener **2** (= *raise*) [+ *hand*] levantar, alzar; [+ *head*] mantener erguido; **to ~ sth up to the light** poner algo a contraluz **3** (= *display*) mostrar, enseñar; **to ~ sth up as a model** presentar algo como modelo **4** (= *delay*) [+ *person, traffic*] retrasar; (= *stop*) detener, parar; [+ *work*] interrumpir; [+ *delivery, payment*] suspender; **we were held up by the traffic** nos retrasamos por culpa del tráfico; **I was held up at the office** me entretuvieron en la oficina; **we were held up for three hours** no nos pudimos mover durante tres horas; **the train was held up** el tren sufrió un retraso; **the train was held up by fog** el tren venía con retraso debido a la niebla **5** (= *rob*) atracar, asaltar; **to ~ up a bank** atracar un banco **Ⓑ** VI + ADV **1** [*weather*] seguir bueno **2** (= *survive*) resistir; **to ~ up under the strain** soportar bien la presión **3** (= *remain strong*) mantenerse bien

holdall ['həʊldɔːl] N (*esp Brit*) bolsa *f* de viaje

holder ['həʊldə'] N [*of bonds*] tenedor(a) *m/f*; [*of title, office*] titular *mf*; [*of record*] poseedor(a) *m/f*

holding ['həʊldɪŋ] N (= *land*) pequeña propiedad *f*, parcela *f*, chacra *f* (*SC*); **holdings** terrenos *mpl* ➤ **holding company** (*Comm*) holding *m*

holdup ['həʊldʌp] N **1** (= *robbery*) atraco *m* (a mano armada), asalto *m* (a mano armada) **2** (= *stoppage, delay*) demora *f*, retraso *m* **3** (= *traffic jam*) embotellamiento *m*, atasco *m*

hole [həʊl] **Ⓐ** N **1** (*gen*) agujero *m*, hoyo *m*; (*in road*) bache *m*; (= *gap, opening*) boquete *m*; (*in wall, defences, dam*) brecha *f*; (= *burrow*) madriguera *f*; (*Golf*) hoyo *m*; **to dig a ~** cavar un hoyo; **these socks are full of ~s** estos calcetines están llenos de agujeros; **his argument is full of ~s** sus argumentos están llenos de fallas; **~ in the heart** soplo *m* cardíaco; **buying the car made a ~ in his savings** la compra del coche le costó una buena parte de sus ahorros; **to wear a ~ in sth** agujerear algo; ✦ IDIOM **to pick ~s in sth** encontrar defectos en algo **2** (***) (= *difficulty*) aprieto *m*, apuro *m* **3** (***) (= *dwelling, room*) cuchitril *m*, tugurio *m* (*esp LAm*); (= *town*) poblacho *m*, pueblo *m* de mala muerte* **Ⓑ** VT [+ *ship*] abrir una brecha en
➤ **hole up** VI + ADV esconderse

hole-in-the-wall* ['həʊlɪnðə'wɔːl] N (*Brit*) cajero *m* automático

holiday ['hɒlədɪ] N (= *public*) fiesta *f*; (= *day*) día *m* de fiesta, día *m* feriado, feriado *m* (*LAm*); (*esp Brit*) (= *vacation*) vacaciones *fpl*; **tomorrow is a ~** mañana es fiesta; **to be/go on ~** (*esp Brit*) estar/ir de vacaciones; **to take a ~** (*esp Brit*) tomarse unas vacaciones; **the school ~s** (*esp Brit*) las vacaciones escolares ➤ **holiday camp** (*at beach*) colonia *f* de veraneo, colonia f de vacaciones ➤ **holiday home** (*esp Brit*) casa f or piso m etc para ocupar durante las vacaciones ➤ **holiday job** (*Brit*) trabajo m para las vacaciones ➤ **holiday pay** (*esp Brit*) paga f de las vacaciones ➤ **holiday resort** (*esp Brit*) lugar m de veraneo ➤ **holiday season** (*Brit*) época f de vacaciones; (*US*) Navidades *fpl* ➤ **holiday traffic** (*esp Brit*) tráfico m de las vacaciones

holiday-maker ['hɒlədɪˌmeɪkəʳ] N (*Brit*) turista *mf*; (*in summer*) veraneante *mf*

holier-than-thou ['hɒʊlɪəðənˈðaʊ] ADJ [*attitude, tone of voice*] de superioridad moral

holiness ['hɒʊlɪnɪs] N [*of place, person*] santidad f; [*of day*] lo sagrado; **His Holiness (the Pope)** Su Santidad (el Papa)

holistic [həʊˈlɪstɪk] ADJ holístico

Holland ['hɒlənd] N Holanda f

hollandaise [ˌhɒlənˈdeɪz] ADJ ~ **sauce** salsa f holandesa

holler• ['hɒləʳ] VT, VI (*esp US*) gritar

hollow ['hɒləʊ] **Ⓐ** ADJ 1 [*tree, object*] hueco; [*cheeks, eyes*] hundido; **it's ~ (inside)** está hueco (por dentro); **she had a ~ feeling in her stomach** tenía una sensación de vacío en el estómago; **he felt ~ inside** se sentía vacío por dentro 2 [*gesture, laugh*] falso; [*threat*] vano, falso; [*words*] hueco, vacío; [*person, victory, success*] vacío; **to ring ~** sonar (a) falso **Ⓑ** N (= *hole*) hueco m; (= *depression*) hoyo m **Ⓒ** ADV **to beat sb ~**• dar una paliza a algn• ➤ **hollow out** VT + ADV ahuecar

holly ['hɒlɪ] N acebo m

hollyhock ['hɒlɪhɒk] N malva f loca

Hollywood ['hɒlɪˌwʊd] N Hollywood m

holocaust ['hɒləkɔːst] N holocausto m

hologram ['hɒləgræm] N holograma m

hols• [hɒlz] NPL (*Brit*) (= **holidays**) vacaciones *fpl*

holster ['hɒʊlstəʳ] N funda f de pistola

holy ['hɒʊlɪ] (*compar* **holier**; *superl* **holiest**) ADJ [*place, book*] sagrado, santo; [*church, shrine*] sagrado; [*person, war*] santo; [*day*] de precepto ➤ **the Holy Bible** la Santa Biblia ➤ **Holy Communion** Sagrada Comunión f ➤ **the Holy Father** el Santo Padre ➤ **the Holy Ghost** el Espíritu Santo ➤ **the Holy Grail** el Santo Grial ➤ **the Holy Land** la Tierra Santa ➤ **holy man** santón m ➤ **holy matrimony** santo matrimonio m ➤ **holy orders: to be in ~ orders** ser sacerdote; **to take ~ orders** ordenarse sacerdote ➤ **the Holy See** la Santa Sede ➤ **the Holy Spirit** el Espíritu Santo ➤ **the Holy Trinity** la Santísima Trinidad ➤ **holy water** agua f bendita

> Use **el/un** not **la/una** before feminine nouns beginning with stressed **a** or **ha** like **agua**.

➤ **Holy Week** Semana f Santa

homage ['hɒmɪdʒ] N homenaje m; **to pay ~ to** rendir homenaje a

home [həʊm] **Ⓐ** N 1 (= *house*) casa f; (= *residence*) domicilio m; **there's no place like ~** como su casa no hay dos; **at ~** en casa; **to feel at ~** sentirse como en casa; **make yourself at ~** estás en tu casa; **is Mr Lyons at ~?** ¿está el señor Lyons?; **he is at ~ with the topic** domina bien la materia; **~ from ~** (*Brit*) ◇ **~ away from ~** (*US*) segunda casa; **for us this is a ~ from ~** aquí estamos como en casa, ésta es como una segunda casa para nosotros; **to give sb/sth a ~** dar casa a algn/algo; (= *position, niche*) encontrar sitio para algn/algo 2 (= *refuge*) hogar m; (= *hospital, hostel*) asilo m; **children's ~** centro m de acogida de menores; **old people's ~** residencia f de ancianos, asilo m de ancianos 3 (= *country*) patria f; (= *town*) ciudad f natal; (= *origin*) cuna f; **Scotland is the ~ of the haggis** Escocia es la patria del haggis; **at ~ and abroad** dentro y fuera del país 4 (*Bio*) hábitat m 5 (*Sport*) (= *target area*) meta f; **to play at ~** jugar en casa; **Villasanta are at ~ to Castroforte** Villasanta recibe en casa a Castroforte; **they lost nine games at ~** perdieron nueve partidos en casa 6 (*Internet*) **"home"** "inicio"

Ⓑ ADV 1 (*lit*) (= *at home*) en casa; (= *to home*) a casa; **I'll be ~ at five o'clock** (*upon return*) estaré en casa a las cinco; **as we say** **back** ~ como decimos en mi tierra; **to come** ~ volver a casa; **to get** ~ llegar a casa; **to go** ~ volver a casa; **he leaves** ~ **at eight** sale de casa a las ocho; **she left** ~ **at the age of 17** se marchó de casa cuando tenía 17 años; **to see sb** ~ acompañar a algn a su casa; **to stay** ~ quedarse en casa; ✦ IDIOMS **to be ~ and dry** (*Brit*) ◇ **be ~ free** (*US*) respirar tranquilo/a; **it's nothing to write ~ about*** no tiene nada de particular 2 (*fig*) **to bring sth ~ to sb** hacer ver algo a algn; **it came ~ to me** me di cuenta de ello

Ⓒ CPD ➤ **home address** (*on form*) domicilio m; **my ~ address** mi dirección particular, las señas de mi casa ➤ **home banking** banco m en casa ➤ **home brew** (= *beer*) cerveza f casera; (= *wine*) vino m casero ➤ **home comforts** comodidades *fpl* domésticas ➤ **home computer** ordenador m doméstico (*Sp*), computadora f doméstica (*LAm*), computador m doméstico (*LAm*) ➤ **home cooking** cocina f casera ➤ **the Home Counties** (*Brit*) los condados alrededor de Londres ➤ **home country** patria f, país m de origen ➤ **home economics** SING ciencia f del hogar ➤ **home field** (*US*): **to play on one's ~ field** jugar en casa ➤ **home fries** (*US*) carne picada frita con patatas y col ➤ **home front** frente m interno ➤ **home ground** (*Brit*): **to play on one's ~ ground** jugar en casa; ✦ IDIOM **to be on ~ ground** estar en su terreno or lugar ➤ **home help** (= *act*) atención f domiciliaria, ayuda f a domicilio; (*esp Brit*) (= *person*) asistente/a *m/f* (*especialmente los que, a cargo de la seguridad social, ayudan en las tareas domésticas a personas necesitadas*) ➤ **home helper** (*US*) asistente/a *m/f* ➤ **home improvements** reformas *fpl* en casa ➤ **home leave** permiso m para irse a casa ➤ **home life** vida f de familia, vida f doméstica ➤ **home loan** préstamo m para la vivienda ➤ **home match** (*Sport*) partido m en casa ➤ **home movie** película f hecha por un aficionado ➤ **Home Office** (*Brit*) Ministerio m del Interior, Gobernación f (*Mex*) ➤ **home owner** propietario/a *m/f* de una casa; **~ owners** propietarios *mpl* de viviendas ➤ **home page** página f de inicio ➤ **home rule** autonomía f ➤ **home run** (*Baseball*) jonrón m; (= *return journey*) [*of ship, truck*] viaje m de vuelta ➤ **Home Secretary** (*Brit*) Ministro m del Interior ➤ **home shopping** venta f por correo; (*TV, Telec*) televenta f ➤ **the home side** (*Sport*) el equipo de casa, el equipo local ➤ **home straight** recta f final; ✦ IDIOM **to be on the ~ straight** estar en la última recta ➤ **the home team** el equipo de casa, el equipo local ➤ **home town** ciudad f natal ➤ **home truths: to tell sb a few ~ truths** decir cuatro verdades a algn ➤ **home visit** visita f a domicilio ➤ **home win** (*Sport*) victoria f en casa

➤ **home in on, home on to** VI + PREP 1 [*missiles*] dirigirse hacia; **to ~ in on the target** buscar el blanco 2 (*fig*) concentrarse en

homebody ['həʊmbɒdɪ] N (*pl* **homebodies**) (*US*) persona f hogareña, persona f casera

homeboy• ['həʊmbɔɪ] N (*US*) chico m del barrio

home-brewed ['həʊmˈbruːd] ADJ hecho en casa, casero

homecoming ['həʊmkʌmɪŋ] N regreso m al hogar ➤ **Homecoming Queen** (*US*) reina de la fiesta de antiguos alumnos

homegirl• ['həʊmgɜːl] N (*US*) chica f del barrio

home-grown ['həʊmˈgrəʊn] ADJ de cosecha propia; (= *not imported*) del país

homeland ['həʊmlænd] N patria f, tierra f natal

homeless ['həʊmlɪs] **Ⓐ** ADJ sin hogar, sin vivienda; **to be made ~** quedarse sin hogar; **to make ~** (*gen*) dejar sin hogar; [+ *tenant*] desahuciar **Ⓑ** NPL **the ~** las personas sin hogar

homelessness ['həʊmlɪsnɪs] N el estar sin hogar; **the increase in ~** el aumento de la cifra de los que no tienen hogar

home-loving ['həʊmˌlʌvɪŋ] ADJ hogareño, casero

homely ['həʊmlɪ] ADJ (*compar* **homelier**; *superl* **homeliest**) 1 (= *like home*) (*esp Brit*) [*food*] casero; [*atmosphere*] familiar; **it's very ~ here** aquí se está como en casa 2 (*Brit*) [*woman*] sencillo 3 (*US*) (= *unattractive*) poco atractivo

home-made ['həʊm'meɪd] ADJ hecho en casa
home-maker ['həʊm,meɪkə'] N (US) ama f de casa

> Use **el/un** not **la/una** before feminine nouns beginning with stressed **a** or **ha** like **ama**.

homeopath ['həʊmɪəʊpæθ] N homeópata mf
homeopathic [,həʊmɪəʊ'pæθɪk] ADJ homeopático
homeopathy ['həʊmɪ'ɒpəθɪ] N homeopatía f
homepage ['həʊmpeɪdʒ] N página f de inicio
homesick ['həʊmsɪk] ADJ **to be** ~ echar de menos la tierra, tener morriña (Sp); **I feel** ~ echo de menos mi tierra or mi casa
homesickness ['həʊmsɪknɪs] N nostalgia f, morriña f (Sp)
homespun ['həʊmspʌn] ADJ tejido en casa, hecho en casa; (fig) llano
homestead ['həʊmsted] N (US) casa f, caserío m; (= farm) granja f
homeward ['həʊmwəd] **(A)** ADJ de regreso **(B)** ADV (also esp Brit ~s) hacia casa; ~ **bound** camino a la casa
homework ['həʊmwɜːk] N deberes mpl, tarea f; **my geography** ~ mis deberes de geografía, mi tarea de geografía; **to do one's** ~ (= schoolwork) hacer los deberes or la tarea; (fig) documentarse, hacer el trabajo preparatorio
homey* ['həʊmɪ] ADJ (compar **homier**; superl **homiest**) (US) íntimo, cómodo
homicidal [,hɒmɪ'saɪdl] ADJ homicida; ~ **maniac** maniaco/a m/f con tendencias homicidas
homicide ['hɒmɪsaɪd] N (esp US) (= act) homicidio m
homing ['həʊmɪŋ] ADJ [missile] buscador, cazador
> **homing device** dispositivo m buscador de blancos
> **homing instinct** instinto m de volver al hogar > **homing pigeon** paloma f mensajera
hominy ['hɒmɪnɪ] N (US) maíz m molido
homoeopath etc ['həʊmɪəʊpæθ] (Brit) = **homeopath** etc
homogeneous [,hɒmə'dʒiːnɪəs] ADJ homogéneo
homogenize [hə'mɒdʒənaɪz] VT homogeneizar
homograph ['hɒməʊɡrɑːf] N homógrafo m
homonym ['hɒmənɪm] N homónimo m
homophobia ['hɒməʊ'fəʊbɪə] N homofobia f
homophobic ['hɒməʊ'fəʊbɪk] ADJ homofóbico
homophone ['hɒməfəʊn] N homófono m
homosexual ['hɒməʊ'seksjʊəl] ADJ, N homosexual mf
homosexuality ['hɒməʊseksjʊ'ælɪtɪ] N homosexualidad f
Hon. ABBR (in titles) = **Honorary; Honourable**
hon* [hʌn] N (US) (= **honey**) cariño m; **hi, ~!** ¡hola, cariño!
Honduras [hɒn'djʊərəs] N Honduras f
hone [həʊn] VT (= sharpen) afilar; [+ skills] poner a punto
honest ['ɒnɪst] **(A)** ADJ **1** (= frank) sincero; **to be (perfectly)** ~ ... para ser (totalmente) sincero or franco ...; **to be ~ about sth** ser sincero or franco con respecto a algo; **to be ~ with you** para serle sincero or franco, si quiere que le diga la verdad; **that's the ~ truth** eso es la pura verdad **2** (= trustworthy, law-abiding) [person] honrado, honesto; **to make an ~ living** ganarse la vida honradamente; **by ~ means** de forma honrada; **it was an ~ mistake** no fue un error deliberado; **he hasn't done an ~ day's work in his life** no ha trabajado honradamente en su vida
(B) ADV (*) de verdad; **I didn't know about it,** ~ no lo sabía, de verdad, de verdad que no lo sabía; ~ **to God** or **goodness** palabra (de honor), te lo juro
honestly ['ɒnɪstlɪ] ADV **1** (= truly) sinceramente, francamente; **I can ~ say that it doesn't bother me** puedo decir con toda sinceridad or franqueza que no me importa; **no, ~, I'm fine** no, de verdad or de veras or en serio, estoy bien; **I didn't do it,** ~ de verdad que no lo hice; **do you ~ expect me to believe that?** ¿de verdad or de veras esperas que me lo crea? **2** (= truthfully) [speak, answer] sinceramente, con sinceridad **3** (= legally) honradamente

4 (showing exasperation) vamos, por favor; **"honestly," said Barbara, "that woman ..."** —vamos or por favor —dijo Barbara —esa mujer ...; **oh, ~!** ¡por favor!, ¡anda, anda!
honesty ['ɒnɪstɪ] N **1** (= sincerity) sinceridad f; **I admire his** ~ admiro su sinceridad; **in all** ~ ... para ser sincero or franco ... **2** (= trustworthiness) honradez f, honestidad f
honey ['hʌnɪ] N **1** (from bees) miel f **2** (esp US*) (= form of address) cariño m
honeybee ['hʌnɪbiː] N abeja f
honeycomb ['hʌnɪkəʊm] N panal m; (fig) laberinto m
honeymoon ['hʌnɪmuːn] **(A)** N luna f de miel; **to go on** ~ irse de luna de miel **(B)** VI pasar la luna de miel **(C)** CPD
> **the honeymoon couple** la pareja de recién casados
> **honeymoon period** (Pol) período m de gracia, cien días mpl > **honeymoon suite** suite f nupcial
honeysuckle ['hʌnɪsʌkl] N madreselva f
Hong Kong [,hɒŋ'kɒŋ] N Hong Kong m
honk [hɒŋk] VI [driver] tocar la bocina, tocar el claxon (LAm); [goose] graznar
Honolulu [,hɒnə'luːluː] N Honolulú m
honor ['ɒnə'] N (US) = **honour**
honorable ['ɒnərəbl] ADJ (US) = **honourable**
honorably ['ɒnərəblɪ] ADV (US) = **honourably**
honorary ['ɒnərərɪ] ADJ [member, president] de honor, honorario; [title] honorífico; [secretary] no remunerado; **an ~ degree** un doctorado "honoris causa"
honour, honor (US) ['ɒnə'] **(A)** N **1** honor m; **I had the ~ of meeting him** tuve el honor de conocerlo; **to be ~ bound to do sth** estar moralmente obligado a hacer algo; **would you do me the ~ of having lunch with me?** ¿me haría el honor de almorzar conmigo?; **in ~ of sth/sb** en honor a algo/algn; **it's a matter of ~** es una cuestión de honor; **on my ~!** ¡palabra de honor!; **you are on your ~ to report any irregularities** es su deber moral informar de cualquier irregularidad; **to be an ~ to one's profession** ser un orgullo para su profesión;
✦ IDIOM **to do the ~s** (introducing people, serving drinks or food) hacer los honores
2 (= award) (by the state) condecoración f; (in contest) galardón m
3 (as title) **His Honour Judge Brodrick** el señor Juez Brodrick; **Your Honour** (to judge) su Señoría, señor Juez; (US) (to mayor) Excelentísimo Señor, su Señoría
4 (†) (= chastity) honra f
5 honours (Brit Univ) **she got first/second class ~s in French** ≈ terminó la carrera de francés con matrícula de honor/con notable; **to graduate with ~s** ≈ licenciarse (con nota)
(B) VT **1** honrar; **I am deeply ~ed to be asked** me siento muy honrado de que me lo pidan; **I should be ~ed if ...** sería un honor para mí si ...; **~ed guest** invitado/a m/f de honor
2 (= decorate) [the state, authorities] condecorar; (in contest) galardonar
3 [+ agreement, promise] cumplir, cumplir con
4 [+ cheque] aceptar, pagar
(C) CPD > **honor guard** (US) guardia f de honor > **honor roll** (US) cuadro m de honor > **honours degree** (Brit Univ) ≈ licenciatura f; **she has ~s degree in French** es licenciada en filología francesa; ver tb www.education.org.uk
> **Honours List** (Brit) lista f de condecoraciones; **New Year Honours List** lista de condecoraciones que otorga el monarca el día de Año Nuevo
honourable, honorable (US) ['ɒnərəbl] ADJ (= upright) honrado; (in title) honorable; **the ~ member for Woodford** (Brit Parl) ≈ el señor diputado de Woodford
honourably, honorably (US) ['ɒnərəblɪ] ADV honradamente
Hons. ABBR (Brit) = **Honours**
hooch* [huːtʃ] N licor m (esp ilícito)
hood [hʊd] N **1** [of cloak, raincoat] capucha f; (Univ) muceta f **2** (US Aut) capó m **3** (on cooker) tapa f **4** (esp US*) (= hoodlum) matón/ona m/f, gorila* m
hooded ['hʊdɪd] ADJ encapuchado
hoodlum* ['huːdləm] N matón/ona m/f, gorila* m
hoodwink ['hʊdwɪŋk] VT engañar
hoof [huːf] N (pl ~s or **hooves**) [of horse] casco m; [of other

animals] pezuña f

hoo-ha* ['huː;haː] N lío* *m*, marimorena* *f*, follón *m* (*Sp**); **there was a great ~ about it** se armó la marimorena*

hook [hʊk] **Ⓐ** N **1** (*gen*) gancho *m*; (*for hanging painting*) alcayata *f*; (= *meat hook*) garfio *m*; (*Fishing*) anzuelo *m* ✦ IDIOMS **by ~ or by crook** por las buenas o por las malas, a como dé lugar (*LAm*); **he fell for it ~, line and sinker** se tragó el anzuelo; **to get sb off the ~** sacar a algn de un apuro; **to let sb off the ~** dejar escapar a algn **2** (*Telec*) **to take the phone off the ~** descolgar el teléfono; **to leave the phone off the ~** dejar el teléfono descolgado; ✦ IDIOM **the phone was ringing off the ~** (*esp US**) el teléfono echaba humo, el teléfono no paraba de sonar **3** (= *hanger*) percha *f*, colgadero *m* **4** (*Sew*) **~s and eyes** corchetes *mpl*, macho y hembra *msing* **5** (*Boxing*) gancho *m*, crochet *m* **Ⓑ** VT **1** (= *fasten*) enganchar; (*Fishing*) pescar **2** (*) (= *catch*) **she finally ~ed him** por fin lo enganchó **Ⓒ** VI **1** (= *fasten*) [*dress*] abrocharse **2** (*US***) trabajar como prostituta, hacer la calle* ➤ **hook on Ⓐ** VI + ADV engancharse (**to** a) **Ⓑ** VT + ADV enganchar (**to** a) ➤ **hook up Ⓐ** VI + ADV [*dress*] abrocharse **Ⓑ** VT + ADV [+ *dress*] abrochar

hooked [hʊkt] ADJ **1** (= *having a hook*) ganchudo **2** (*) (= *addicted*) **to be ~ on sth** estar enganchado a algo*, ser adicto a algo; **to get ~ on sth** volverse adicto a algo

hooker ['hʊkəʳ] N (*esp US**) puta *f*

hook-up ['hʊkʌp] N (*Rad, TV*) transmisión *f* en cadena; (*Elec*) acoplamiento *m*; **a ~ with Eurovision** una conexión con Eurovisión

hooky*, hookey* ['hʊkɪ] N (*esp US*) **to play ~** hacer rabona*, hacer novillos

hooligan ['huːlɪgən] N vándalo/a *m/f*, gamberro/a *m/f* (*Sp*), patotero/a *m/f* (*SC*)

hooliganism ['huːlɪgənɪzəm] N vandalismo *m*, gamberrismo *m* (*Sp*), patoterismo *m* (*SC*)

hoop [huːp] N aro *m*, argolla *f*

hooray [hʊ'reɪ] EXCL ¡hurra! ➤ **Hooray Henry** (*Brit pej*) señorito *m*

hoot [huːt] **Ⓐ** N [*of owl*] ululato *m*; (*esp Brit*) [*of car*] bocinazo *m*; [*of train*] silbato *m*; [*of siren*] toque *m* de sirena; **I don't care a ~*** (no) me importa un comino* **Ⓑ** VT (*esp Brit*) [+ *horn*] tocar **Ⓒ** VI [*owl*] ulular; [*ship, train*] silbar; (*esp Brit*) [*driver*] tocar la bocina, tocar el claxon (*esp LAm*); **to ~ with laughter** carcajear

hooter ['huːtəʳ] N (*Brit*) [*of ship, factory*] sirena *f*; (*Aut*) bocina *f*, claxon *m* (*esp LAm*)

Hoover®, hoover ['huːvəʳ] (*Brit*) **Ⓐ** N aspiradora *f* **Ⓑ** VT pasar la aspiradora por **Ⓒ** VI pasar la aspiradora

hooves [huːvz] NPL *of* **hoof**

hop¹ [hɒp] **Ⓐ** N (= *jump*) salto *m*, brinco *m*; ✦ IDIOM **to catch sb on the ~** (*Brit**) pillar *or* (*LAm*) agarrar a algn desprevenido **Ⓑ** VI [*person, bird, animal*] dar saltos, brincar (*LAm*); ✦ IDIOM **to be ~ping mad*** echar chispas* **Ⓒ** VT (*Brit**): **to ~ it** largarse*; **~ it!** ¡lárgate!* ➤ **hop along** VI + ADV avanzar a saltos ➤ **hop on Ⓐ** VI + PREP subir a **Ⓑ** VI + ADV subir

hop² [hɒp] N (= *plant*) **hops** lúpulo *msing* ➤ **hop picking** recolección *f* del lúpulo

hope [həʊp] **Ⓐ** N **1** (= *expectation*) esperanza *f*; **where there's life there's ~** mientras hay vida, hay esperanza; **to build** *or* **get one's ~s up (over sth)** hacerse ilusiones (con algo); **don't get your ~s up** no te hagas ilusiones; **to give up ~ (of doing sth)** perder las esperanzas (de hacer algo); **he set out with high ~s** empezó lleno de esperanzas *or* ilusión, empezó con muchas esperanzas; **I ignored him in the ~ that he would go away** no le hice caso con la esperanza de que se fuera; **you are my last/only ~** tú eres mi última/única esperanza; **to raise sb's ~s** dar esperanzas a algn; **don't raise your ~s** no te hagas ilusiones **2** (= *chance*) posibilidad *f*; **he hasn't much ~ of winning** no tiene muchas posibilidades de ganar; **you haven't got a ~ in hell*** no tienes la más remota posibilidad; **not a ~!*** ¡ni

en sueños!; **your only ~ is to ...** tu única esperanza es ...; **"have you got the day off tomorrow?" — "some ~(s)!"*** —¿libras mañana? —¡qué va! *or* ¡ya quisiera yo! **Ⓑ** VT esperar; **your mother is well, I ~?** espero que su madre esté bien; **to ~ that ...** esperar que ... + *subjun*; **I ~ he comes soon** espero que venga pronto, ojalá venga pronto; **I ~ you don't think I'm going to do it!** ¡no pensarás que lo voy a hacer yo!; **I ~ to goodness she remembers*** quiera el cielo que se acuerde; **to ~ to do sth** esperar hacer algo; **hoping to hear from you** en espera *or* a la espera de recibir noticias tuyas; **I ~ not/so** espero que no/sí **Ⓒ** VI esperar; **to ~ against ~** esperar en vano; **to ~ for sth** esperar algo; **I always knew it was too much to ~ for** siempre supe que era mucho pedir; **we'll just have to ~ for the best** esperemos que todo salga bien **Ⓓ** CPD ➤ **hope chest** (*US*) ajuar *m* (de novia)

hopeful ['həʊpfʊl] **Ⓐ** ADJ **1** (= *optimistic*) [*person*] esperanzado, optimista; [*face*] esperanzado, lleno de esperanza; **to feel ~** sentirse optimista; **I'll ask her, but I'm not too ~** le preguntaré, pero no me hago demasiadas ilusiones *or* no tengo muchas esperanzas; **to be ~ that** tener esperanzas de que, esperar que + *subjun*; **to be ~ of doing sth** tener esperanzas de hacer algo, esperar poder hacer algo **2** (= *promising*) [*sign, news*] esperanzador(a), prometedor(a) **Ⓑ** N aspirante *mf*; **presidential ~s** aspirantes *mpl* a la presidencia

hopefully ['həʊpfəlɪ] ADV **1** (= *with feeling of hope*) ... **I asked ~** ... pregunté esperanzado **2** (= *with luck*) **~ we'll be able to sort something out** con un poco de suerte podremos arreglar algo; **the new legislation will ~ lead to some improvements** es de esperar que la nueva legislación traiga consigo algunas mejoras; **~, it won't rain** esperemos que no llueva

hopeless ['həʊplɪs] ADJ **1** (= *impossible*) [*task*] imposible; [*attempt*] vano; [*cause*] perdido; [*situation, position*] desesperado; [*love*] imposible; **it's ~!** ¡es inútil!; **he's a ~ case** es un caso perdido, no tiene remedio; **the doctor says it is a ~ case** el médico dice que no tiene salvación, el médico lo ha desahuciado; **a ~ drunk** un borracho empedernido **2** (*) (= *useless*) **he's completely ~** es un inútil*; **she's a ~ manager** como jefa es una nulidad *or* es penosa*; **the buses round here are ~** los autobuses de por aquí son un desastre; **he's ~ at football** es un desastre jugando al fútbol, es una nulidad para el fútbol*; **I'm ~ at maths/ cooking** soy un negado para las matemáticas/la cocina

hopelessly ['həʊplɪslɪ] ADV [*inadequate, confused, lost*] totalmente, completamente; **he is ~ in debt** está totalmente *or* completamente endeudado; **to be ~ in love** estar perdidamente enamorado

hopelessness ['həʊplɪsnɪs] N **1** [*of situation*] lo desesperado **2** (= *despair*) desesperanza *f* **3** (= *incompetence*) inutilidad *f*

hopper ['hɒpəʳ] N (= *chute*) tolva *f*

hopscotch ['hɒpskɒtʃ] N tejo *m*, rayuela *f* (*River Plate*)

horde [hɔːd] N multitud *f*

horizon [hə'raɪzn] N horizonte *m*; **there are new schemes on the ~** hay nuevos planes en perspectiva

horizontal [ˌhɒrɪ'zɒntl] **Ⓐ** ADJ horizontal **Ⓑ** N horizontal *f*

horizontally [ˌhɒrɪ'zɒntəlɪ] ADV horizontalmente

hormone ['hɔːməʊn] N hormona *f* ➤ **hormone replacement therapy** terapia *f* hormonal sustitutiva

horn [hɔːn] N **1** [*of bull*] cuerno *m*, cacho *m* (*LAm*); [*of deer*] asta *f*, cacho *m* (*LAm*)

Use **el/un** not **la/una** before feminine nouns beginning with stressed **a** or **ha** like **asta**.

---

2 (*Mus*) trompa *f*, cuerno *m* **3** (*in car*) bocina *f*, claxon *m* (*esp LAm*); **to sound one's ~** tocar la bocina *or* (*esp LAm*) el claxon **4** (*US***) teléfono *m*; **to get on the ~ to sb** llamar a algn (por teléfono)

hornet ['hɔːnɪt] N avispón *m*; ✦ IDIOM **to stir up a ~'s nest**

armar mucho revuelo

horn-rimmed ['hɔːnrɪmd] ADJ de concha, de carey

horny** ['hɔːnɪ] ADJ (compar **hornier**; superl **horniest**) (= randy) caliente*, cachondo (Sp*), arrecho (LAm***)

horoscope ['hɒrəskəup] N horóscopo m

horrendous [hɒ'rendəs] ADJ [injury, attack, accident] horrible, horrendo; [weather, traffic] horroroso*, espantoso*

horrible ['hɒrɪbl] ADJ [crime, accident] horrible, espantoso; [food, smell, thought] horroroso*, horrible*; **you're ~!** ¡qué malo eres!; **I've got a ~ feeling that ...** tengo la horrible sensación de que ...; **to be ~ to sb** tratar fatal a algn*; **don't be ~ to your brother** no seas malo con tu hermano

horribly ['hɒrɪblɪ] ADV **1** (*) (= terribly) [difficult, rich, expensive] terriblemente, tremendamente; **it's all gone ~ wrong** todo ha salido terriblemente mal **2** (= horrifically) [die, injure, scream] de una forma horrible; [mutilated, disfigured] horriblemente, espantosamente

horrid ['hɒrɪd] ADJ (= disagreeable) horrible; (= unkind) antipático; **to be ~ to sb** tratar a algn muy mal, portarse muy mal con algn; **don't be ~!** ¡no seas antipático!

horrific [hɒ'rɪfɪk] ADJ horrible, horrendo

horrify ['hɒrɪfaɪ] VT **1** (= fill with horror) horrorizar; **I was horrified to discover that ...** me horrorizó descubrir que ... **2** (= shock) escandalizar; **they were all horrified** se escandalizaron todos

horrifying ['hɒrɪfaɪɪŋ] ADJ horroroso, horripilante

horror ['hɒrə'] N (= terror) horror m, pavor m; (= hatred) horror m; **to have a ~ of** tener horror a; **to my ~ I discovered that ...** descubrí con horror que ...; **then, to my ~, it moved!** luego ¡qué susto!, se movió!; **that child is a little ~*** ese niño es un diablillo; **you ~!*** ¡bestia! ➤ **horror film** (esp Brit), **horror movie** (esp US) película f de terror

horror-stricken ['hɒrəstrɪkən], **horror-struck** ['hɒrəstrʌk] ADJ horrorizado

hors d'oeuvres [ɔː'dɜːvr] NPL entremeses mpl

horse [hɔːs] **A** N **1** (= animal) caballo m; ✦ IDIOMS **to eat like a ~** comer como una vaca*; **hold your ~s!** ¡para el carro!, ¡despacito!; **to be straight from the ~'s mouth** ser de buena tinta **2** (in gymnastics) potro m **3** (carpenter's) caballete m **B** CPD ➤ **horse chestnut** (= tree) castaño m de Indias; (= fruit) castaña f de Indias ➤ **Horse Guards** (Brit) Guardia fsing Montada ➤ **horse opera** (US) película f del Oeste ➤ **horse race** carrera f de caballos ➤ **horse racing** (gen) carreras fpl de caballos; (as sport) hípica f ➤ **horse riding** (Brit) equitación f ➤ **horse sense** sentido m común ➤ **horse show** concurso m hípico ➤ **horse trading** (Pol) toma y daca m, chalaneo m ➤ **horse trials** concurso msing hípico ➤ **horse around***, **horse about*** VI + ADV hacer el tonto

horseback ['hɔːsbæk] N **on ~** a caballo ➤ **horseback riding** (US) equitación f

horsebox ['hɔːsbɒks] N (Brit) remolque m para caballerías; (Rail) vagón m para caballerías

horse-drawn ['hɔːsdrɔːn] ADJ de tracción animal, tirado por caballos

horsefly ['hɔːsflaɪ] N (pl **horseflies**) tábano m

horsehair ['hɔːsheə'] N crin f

horseman ['hɔːsmən] N (pl **horsemen**) (= rider) jinete m; (skilful) caballista m, charro m (Mex)

horsemanship ['hɔːsmənʃɪp] N (= activity) equitación f; (= skill) manejo m del caballo

horseplay ['hɔːspleɪ] N payasadas fpl

horsepower ['hɔːsˌpauə'] N caballo m de vapor; **a 20 ~ engine** un motor de 20 caballos

horseradish ['hɔːsˌrædɪʃ] N (= plant) rábano m picante; (also **~ sauce**) salsa f de rábano

horseshoe ['hɔːsʃuː] N herradura f

horsewhip ['hɔːswɪp] **A** VT azotar **B** N fusta f

horsewoman ['hɔːsˌwumən] N (pl **horsewomen**) amazona f, charra f (Mex)

horsey*, **horsy*** ['hɔːsɪ] ADJ (compar **horsier**; superl **horsiest**) [person] aficionado a los caballos; [appearance] caballuno

horticultural [ˌhɔːtɪ'kʌltʃərəl] ADJ hortícola; **~ show** exposición f de horticultura

horticulture ['hɔːtɪkʌltʃə'] N horticultura f

horticulturist [ˌhɔːtɪ'kʌltʃərɪst] N horticultor(a) m/f

hose [həuz] N **1** (also **~pipe**) manga f, manguera f **2** (= stockings) medias fpl ➤ **hose down** VT + ADV regar con manguera ➤ **hose out** VT + ADV regar con manguera

hosepipe ['həuzpaɪp] N (esp US) manga f, manguera f

hosiery ['həuʒɪərɪ] N calcetería f

hospice ['hɒspɪs] N hospicio m

hospitable [hɒs'pɪtəbl] ADJ acogedor, hospitalario

hospital ['hɒspɪtl] N hospital m; **to go into ~** or (US) **the ~** ingresar en el hospital ➤ **hospital case** caso m clínico ➤ **hospital doctor** interno/a m/f ➤ **hospital facilities** instalaciones fpl hospitalarias

hospitality [ˌhɒspɪ'tælɪtɪ] N hospitalidad f; **corporate ~** hospitalidad f corporativa ➤ **hospitality tent** carpa f de recepción para invitados importantes

hospitalize ['hɒspɪtəlaɪz] VT hospitalizar

host¹ [həust] **A** N **1** [to guest] anfitrión(ona) m/f; [of programme] presentador(a) m/f; [of inn] hostelero m, mesonero m **2** (Bot, Zool) huésped m **B** VT [+ TV programme, games] presentar; [+ conference] ser anfitrión de; [+ festival, games etc] acoger **C** CPD ➤ **host country** país m anfitrión

host² [həust] N (= crowd) multitud f; **for a whole ~ of reasons** por un sinfín de razones; **I have a ~ of problems** tengo un sinfín or un montón de problemas

host³ [həust] N (Rel) hostia f

hostage ['hɒstɪdʒ] N rehén mf; **to take sb ~** tomar or (LAm) agarrar a algn como rehén

hostel ['hɒstəl] N (esp Brit) residencia f; (= youth hostel) albergue m juvenil; (Univ) residencia f de estudiantes

hostess ['həustes] N huéspeda f, anfitriona f; (in night club) azafata f; (Aer) azafata f

hostile ['hɒstaɪl, (US) 'hɒstəl] ADJ **1** [person, question, atmosphere, reception] hostil (also Mil, Fin); **to be ~ to** or **towards sth/sb** ser hostil a algo/con algn; **~ (takeover) bid** OPA f hostil **2** [conditions, weather, environment] adverso, desfavorable

hostility [hɒs'tɪlɪtɪ] N hostilidad f; **to cease/resume hostilities** cesar/reanudar las hostilidades

hot [hɒt] **A** ADJ (compar **~ter**; superl **~test**) **1** (gen) caliente; [climate] cálido; [day, summer] caluroso, de calor; **it was a very ~ day** fue un día de mucho calor; **a nice ~ bath** un buen baño caliente; **to be ~** [thing] estar caliente; [weather] hacer calor; [person] tener calor; **this room is ~** hace calor en esta habitación; **I'm too ~** tengo demasiado calor; **it made me go ~ and cold** me dio escalofríos; **to get ~** [thing] calentarse; [weather] empezar a hacer calor; **I'm getting ~** me está entrando calor; **to get (all) ~ and bothered** sofocarse **2** (= spicy, peppery) [taste, food] picante **3** (fig) **~ favourite** or (US) **favorite** gran favorito m; **to make it ~ for sb** hacerle la vida imposible a algn; **~ money** dinero m caliente; **~ news** noticias fpl de última hora; **he's a pretty ~ player** es un jugador experto; **he has a ~ temper** tiene mal genio or carácter; **a ~ tip** información f de buenas tintas or de fuente fidedigna; ✦ IDIOMS **to be in/get into ~ water** estar/meterse en problemas; **to be ~ under the collar*** estar acalorado; **to get ~ under the collar*** acalorarse; **that's a ~ button** or **~-button issue** (US) ése es un asunto polémico, ése es un tema candente **B** ADV **to be ~ on sb's trail** or **heels** pisar los talones a algn; **news ~ from the press** una noticia que acaba de publicarse en la prensa; ✦ IDIOM **to blow ~ and cold** ser veleta, mudar a todos los vientos **C** N **he's got the ~s for her*** ella le pone cachondo **D** CPD ➤ **hot air** (fig) palabras fpl al aire ➤ **hot cross bun** bollo a base de especias y pasas marcado con una cruz y que se

come en Viernes Santo ➤ **hot dog** perrito *m* caliente, hot dog *m*, pancho *m* (*SC*) ➤ **hot flash** (*US*), **hot flush** (*Brit*) sofoco *m* de calor ➤ **hot goods** artículos *mpl* robados ➤ **hot line** teléfono *m* rojo ➤ **hot potato*** cuestión *f* muy discutida ➤ **hot seat***: **to be in the ~ seat** estar expuesto ➤ **hot spot*** (*Pol*) lugar *m* de peligro; (*for amusement*) lugar *m* de diversión; (= *night club*) sala *f* de fiestas ➤ **hot springs** aguas *fpl* termales ➤ **hot stuff: he's pretty ~ stuff at maths*** es un hacha *or* un as para las matemáticas ➤ **hot tub** jacuzzi® *m*
➤ **hot up*** VI + ADV (*esp Brit*) [*party, competition, battle*] animarse, empezar a animarse; [*dispute*] acalorarse

hot-air balloon [ˌhɒtˈɛəbəˈluːn] N globo *m* de aire caliente

hotbed [ˈhɒtbed] N semillero *m*

hot-blooded [ˈhɒtˈblʌdɪd] ADJ apasionado

hotchpotch [ˈhɒtʃpɒtʃ] N (*Brit*) mezcolanza *f*

hot-desking [ˌhɒtˈdeskɪŋ] N práctica consistente en la asignación variable de mesas en una oficina, de tal forma que nadie ocupa permanentemente la misma

hotel [həʊˈtel] N hotel *m* ➤ **the hotel industry** el sector hotelero ➤ **hotel staff** personal *m* de hotel ➤ **hotel workers** trabajadores/oras *mpl/fpl* de hostelería

hotelier [həʊˈtelɪə^r] N hotelero/a *m/f*

hotfoot [ˈhɒtˈfʊt] **Ⓐ** ADV a toda prisa **Ⓑ** VT **to ~ it*** ir volando

hothead [ˈhɒthed] N exaltado/a *m/f*

hot-headed [ˈhɒtˈhedɪd] ADJ impulsivo, impetuoso

hothouse [ˈhɒthaʊs] N invernadero *m*

hotly [ˈhɒtlɪ] ADV con pasión, con vehemencia; **he was ~ pursued by the policeman** el policía le seguía muy de cerca

hotplate [ˈhɒtpleɪt] N (*for keeping food warm*) calientaplatos *m inv*; (*esp Brit*) (*on stove*) hornillo *m*

hotpot [ˈhɒtpɒt] N (*Brit Culin*) estofado *m*

hotrod* [ˈhɒtrɒd] N (*US Aut*) bólido *m*

hotshot* [ˈhɒtʃɒt] **Ⓐ** ADJ de primera, de aúpa* **Ⓑ** N personaje *m*, pez *m* gordo*

hot-tempered [ˌhɒtˈtempəd] ADJ de mal genio, de mal carácter

hot-water bottle [hɒtˈwɔːtəˌbɒtl] N bolsa *f* de agua caliente

hound [haʊnd] **Ⓐ** N perro *m* de caza; **the ~s** la jauría **Ⓑ** VT perseguir, acosar

hour [aʊə^r] N hora *f*; **after ~s** fuera de horario; **at all ~s (of the day and night)** a cualquier hora; **she's out till all ~s** no regresa hasta muy tarde, vuelve a casa a las tantas; **at 30 miles an ~** a 30 millas por hora; **~s and ~s** horas y horas, horas enteras; **to pay sb by the ~** pagar a algn por horas; **in the early ~s** en la *or* de madrugada; **at the eleventh ~** a última hora; **I've been waiting for ~s** llevo horas esperando; **half an ~** media hora; **two and a half ~s** dos horas y media; **to work long ~s** trabajar muchas horas; **on the ~** a la hora en punto; **out of ~s** (*esp Brit*) fuera de horario; **a quarter of an ~** un cuarto de hora; **to keep regular ~s** llevar una vida ordenada; **in the small ~s** en la *or* de madrugada; **to strike the ~** dar la hora ➤ **hour hand** horario *m*

hourglass [ˈaʊəglɑːs] N reloj *m* de arena

hourly [ˈaʊəlɪ] **Ⓐ** ADJ [*rate, pay, earnings*] por hora; [*news*] de cada hora; **they come at ~ intervals** llegan cada hora; **there are ~ buses** hay autobuses cada hora; **~ rate** *or* **wage** paga *f* por hora **Ⓑ** ADV **1** (= *every hour*) cada hora **2** (= *by the hour*) **she's paid ~** le pagan por horas

house Ⓐ [haʊs] N (*pl* **~s** [ˈhaʊzɪz]) **1** casa *f*; **the party's at my/John's ~** la fiesta es en mi casa/en casa de John; **to keep ~ (for sb)** llevar la casa (a algn); **to move ~** mudarse (de casa); **to keep open ~** tener la puerta siempre abierta, recibir a todo el mundo; **to set up ~** poner casa; **the noise woke the whole ~** el ruido despertó a toda la casa;
✦ IDIOMS **to get on like a ~ on fire** llevarse de maravilla*; **to put one's ~ in order** poner sus asuntos en orden
2 (*Pol*) cámara *f*; **the upper/lower ~** la cámara alta/baja; **the House** (*Brit*) la Cámara de los Comunes; (*US*) la Cámara de Representantes

3 (*in debate*) asamblea *f*; **this ~ believes that …** esta asamblea cree que …
4 (*Brit Scol*) subdivisión de alumnos que se crea en algunos colegios para promover la competición entre ellos
5 (*Theat*) (= *auditorium*) sala *f*; (= *audience*) público *m*; **full ~** (teatro *m*) lleno *m*; **they played to packed ~s** llenaban las salas; **✦** IDIOM **to bring the ~ down** [*act, scene*] hacer que se venga abajo la sala *or* el teatro; [*joke*] hacer morirse de risa a todos
6 (*Comm*) casa *f*; **fashion ~** casa *f* de modas; **we do our printing in ~** hacemos nuestra propia impresión, hacemos la impresión en la empresa; **it's on the ~** invita la casa; **TV programmes made out of ~** programas de televisión realizados por productoras externas
7 (= *family, line*) casa *f*, familia *f*; **the House of Windsor** la casa de los Windsor
Ⓑ [haʊz] VT **1** (= *give housing to*) [+ *person, family*] alojar, dar alojamiento a
2 (= *have space for, contain*) albergar; **the building will not ~ them all** el edificio no podrá albergarlos a todos, no cabrán todos en el edificio
Ⓒ [haʊs] CPD ➤ **house agent** (*Brit*) agente *mf* inmobiliario/a ➤ **house arrest** arresto *m* domiciliario; **to be under ~ arrest** estar bajo arresto domiciliario ➤ **house call** consulta *f* a domicilio ➤ **house guest** invitado/a *m/f* ➤ **house martin** avión *m* común ➤ **the House of Commons/Lords** (*Brit*) la Cámara de los Comunes/Lores ➤ **the House of Representatives** (*US*) la Cámara de Representantes ➤ **house owner** propietario/a *m/f* de una casa ➤ **house party** (= *event*) fiesta de varios días en una casa de campo; (= *people*) grupo *m* de invitados (*que pasan varios días en una casa de campo*) ➤ **house plant** planta *f* de interior ➤ **house prices** el precio de la vivienda ➤ **the Houses of Parliament** (*Brit*) el Parlamento ➤ **house wine** vino *m* de la casa

houseboat [ˈhaʊsbəʊt] N casa *f* flotante

housebound [ˈhaʊsbaʊnd] ADJ confinado en casa

housebreaker [ˈhaʊsˌbreɪkə^r] N ladrón/ona *m/f*

housebroken [ˈhaʊsˌbrəʊkən] ADJ (*US*) enseñado

housecleaning [ˈhaʊsˈkliːnɪŋ] N limpieza *f* de la casa

housecoat [ˈhaʊskəʊt] N bata *f*

housefly [ˈhaʊsflaɪ] N (*pl* **houseflies**) mosca *f*

household [ˈhaʊshəʊld] N (= *home*) casa *f*; (= *family*) familia *f* ➤ **household chores** quehaceres *mpl* domésticos, tareas *fpl* de la casa ➤ **household goods** enseres *mpl* domésticos ➤ **household name: he's a ~ name** es una persona conocidísima ➤ **household word: it's a ~ word** es el pan de cada día

householder [ˈhaʊsˌhəʊldə^r] N (= *owner*) propietario/a *m/f*; (= *tenant*) inquilino/a *m/f*; (= *head of house*) cabeza *f* de familia

house-hunt [ˈhaʊshʌnt] VI (*Brit*) buscar casa

house-hunting [ˈhaʊsˌhʌntɪŋ] N **to go ~** ir buscando casa

house-husband [ˈhaʊsˌhʌzbənd] N marido que se ocupa de las tareas de la casa

housekeeper [ˈhaʊsˌkiːpə^r] N ama *f* de llaves; (*in hotel*) gobernanta *f*

> Use **el/un** not **la/una** before feminine nouns beginning with stressed **a** or **ha** like *ama*.

housekeeping [ˈhaʊsˌkiːpɪŋ] N (= *administration*) gobierno *m* de la casa; (= *housework*) quehaceres *mpl* domésticos, tareas *fpl* de la casa; (*Comput*) gestión *f* interna; (*esp Brit*) (= *money*) dinero *m* para gastos domésticos

housemaid [ˈhaʊsmeɪd] N criada *f*

houseman [ˈhaʊsmən] N (*pl* **housemen**) (*Brit*) (*in hospital*) interno/a *m/f*

housemaster [ˈhaʊsˌmɑːstə^r] N (*Brit Scol*) profesor a cargo de la subdivisión de un colegio de internado

housemistress [ˈhaʊsˌmɪstrɪs] N (*Brit Scol*) profesora a cargo de la subdivisión de un colegio de internado

house-proud [ˈhaʊspraʊd] ADJ (*esp Brit*): **she's very ~** le gusta tener la casa impecable

houseroom ['haʊsrʊm] N **to give sth ~** guardar algo en su casa; **I wouldn't give it ~*** no lo tendría en casa

house-sit ['haʊssɪt] VI (*pt, pp* **house-sat**) **I'm ~ting for the Sinclairs** vivo en la casa de los Sinclair para vigilarla en ausencia de los dueños

house-to-house ['haʊstə'haʊs] ADJ de casa en casa

house-trained ['haʊstreɪnd] ADJ (*Brit*) enseñado

house-warming ['haʊs,wɔːmɪŋ] N (*also* **~ party**) fiesta *f* de estreno de una casa

housewife ['haʊswaɪf] N (*pl* **housewives**) ama *f* de casa

> Use **el/un** not **la/una** before feminine nouns beginning with stressed **a** or **ha** like **ama**.

housework ['haʊswɜːk] N quehaceres *mpl* domésticos, tareas *fpl* de la casa

housing ['haʊzɪŋ] N (= *houses*) casas *fpl*, viviendas *fpl*; **the ~ problem** el problema de la vivienda ➤ **housing association** asociación *f* de la vivienda ➤ **housing development** (*US*) complejo *m* habitacional *or* residencial, urbanización *f* (*esp Sp*), fraccionamiento *m* (*Mex*) ➤ **housing estate** (*Brit*) (*privately owned*) complejo *m* habitacional *or* residencial, urbanización *f* (*esp Sp*), fraccionamiento *m* (*Mex*); (= *council estate*) barrio *m* de viviendas protegidas ➤ **housing market** mercado *m* de la vivienda ➤ **housing project** (*US*) barrio *m* de viviendas protegidas

hove [həʊv] PT, PP *of* **heave C4**

hovel ['hɒvəl] N casucha *f*, cuchitril *m*, tugurio *m* (*esp LAm*)

hover ['hɒvəʳ] VI **1** (*bird*) planear, cernerse **2** (*fig*) (*person*) rondar; **a couple of waiters were ~ing near our table** un par de camareros rondaban cerca de nuestra mesa

hovercraft ['hɒvəkrɑːft] N aerodeslizador *m*

hoverport ['hɒvə,pɔːt] N puerto *m* de aerodeslizadores

how

how [haʊ] ADVERB
1 (*in direct and indirect questions, reported speech*)
1.1 (WITH VERB)

> You can usually use **cómo** (with an accent) to translate **how** in questions as well as after report verbs and verbs of (un)certainty and doubt (eg **no sé**):

cómo; **~ did you do it?** ¿cómo lo hiciste?; **~ are you?** ¿cómo estás?, ¿cómo *or* qué tal te va? (*LAm**), ¿qué tal (estás)? (*Sp**); **~ was the film?** ¿qué tal la película?; **please tell me ~ to do it** por favor, dígame cómo hacerlo; **I know ~ you did it** ya sé cómo lo hiciste; **to know ~ to do sth** saber hacer algo; **to learn ~ to do sth** aprender a hacer algo, aprender cómo se hace algo; **~ do you like your steak?** ¿cómo le gusta el filete?; **I can't understand ~ it happened** no entiendo cómo ocurrió
1.2 (WITH ADJECTIVE/ADVERB)

>> **how** + ADJECTIVE in questions can often be translated using **cómo es/era de** + ADJECTIVE (agreeing with the noun), but other constructions might be more usual depending on the context:

~ big is it? ¿cómo es de grande?; **~ difficult was the exam?** ¿cómo fue de difícil el examen?; *BUT* **~ old are you?** ¿cuántos años tienes?; **~ wide is this bed?** ¿qué anchura tiene esta cama?, ¿cuánto mide de ancho esta cama?

>> With adverbs, various translations are possible depending on the context. A very common construction is PREPOSITION + **qué** + NOUN:

~ far away is it? ¿a qué distancia queda?, ¿qué tan lejos queda? (*LAm*); **~ far is it (from here) to Edinburgh?** ¿qué distancia hay de aquí a Edimburgo?; **~ fast can it go?** ¿a qué velocidad puede ir?; **~ soon can you come?** ¿cuándo

puedes venir?

> To translate **how** + ADJECTIVE/ADVERB in reported speech, **lo** + ADJECTIVE/ADVERB is used. Note that the adjective agrees with the noun.

you don't know ~ difficult it is no sabes lo difícil que es; **I didn't know ~ expensive the tickets were** no sabía lo caras que eran las entradas; **they've been telling me ~ well you did in your exams** ya me han hablado de lo bien que hiciste los exámenes
✦ how about: ~ about tomorrow? ¿qué te parece mañana?; **~ about a cup of tea?** ¿te apetece una taza de té?; **I like it, but ~ about you?** a mí me gusta, pero ¿y a ti?; **~ about going to the cinema?** ¿qué tal si vamos al cine?, ¿y si vamos al cine?
✦ how long: ~ long is this bed? ¿qué longitud tiene esta cama?, ¿cuánto mide de largo esta cama?; **~ long will you be?** ¿cuánto vas a tardar?; **~ long have you been here?** ¿cuánto tiempo llevas aquí?
✦ how many: ~ many are there? ¿cuántos hay?
✦ how much: ~ much sugar do you want? ¿cuánto azúcar quieres?; **~ much is it?** ¿cuánto vale?, ¿cuánto es?
✦ how often: ~ often do you go? ¿con qué frecuencia vas?
2 (*in other statements*)

> Translate **how** with verbs other than report ones or verbs of (un)certainty and doubt using **como** without an accent:

como; **this is ~ you do it** así es como se hace
3 (*in exclamations*)

> You can often translate **how** + ADJECTIVE/ADVERB using **qué** + ADJECTIVE/ADVERB:

qué; **~ beautiful!** ¡qué bonito!; **~ strange!** ¡qué raro!; *BUT* **~ glad I am to see you!** ¡cuánto me alegro de verte!; **~ they talk!** ¡cuánto hablan!

howdy* ['haʊdɪ] EXCL (*US*) ¡hola!

however [haʊ'evəʳ] **Ⓐ** ADV **1** (= *nevertheless*) sin embargo, no obstante

> Don't put **sin embargo** or **no obstante** at the end of the sentence; put them at the beginning or between the clauses:

he has one problem, ~ sin embargo, tiene un problema
2 (= *no matter how*) **~ cold it is, we still manage to have fun** por mucho frío que haga, nos las arreglamos para pasarlo bien; **he'll never catch us ~ fast he runs** por muy rápido que vaya *or* por mucho que corra no nos alcanzará; **~ hard she tried, she couldn't remember his name** por mucho *or* más que lo intentara, no lograba acordarse de su nombre; **the 5,000 spectators, or ~ many were there** los 5.000 espectadores, o los que fuesen; **take about a metre of fabric, or ~ much you need** toma un metro de tela o lo que necesites
3 (*in questions*) cómo
Ⓑ CONJ **~ we add it up, it doesn't come to 83** lo sumemos como lo sumemos, no da 83, hagamos la suma como la hagamos, no da 83; **you can do it ~ you want** puedes hacerlo como quieras

howl [haʊl] **Ⓐ** N (*of animal*) aullido *m*; (*of wind*) rugido *m*; (*of protest*) clamor *m*, grito *m*; **a ~ of pain/rage** un alarido de dolor/furia; **~s of laughter** carcajadas *fpl* **Ⓑ** VI (*animal*) aullar; (*person*) dar alaridos; (*wind*) rugir, bramar; (*child*) (= *weep*) berrear; **he ~ed with pain** aullaba de dolor, daba alaridos de dolor; **to ~ with laughter** reír a carcajadas **Ⓒ** VT (= *shout*) gritar

howler* ['haʊləʳ] N (*esp Brit*) falta *f* garrafal

howling ['haʊlɪŋ] ADJ (*success*) clamoroso

h.p. N ABBR (= **horsepower**) C.V. *mpl*

HQ N ABBR (= **headquarters**) E.M.

HR N ABBR **1** = **Human Resources 2** (*US*) = **House of Representatives**

hr ABBR (= **hour**) h

HRH N ABBR (= **Her/His Royal Highness**) S.A.R.

HRT N ABBR = **hormone replacement therapy**

HSS N ABBR (*US*) = **Health and Social Services**

HST N ABBR (*US*) = **Hawaiian Standard Time**

ht. ABBR (= **height**) alt.

HTML N ABBR (= **hypertext markup language**) HTML *m*

http ABBR (*Comput*) (= **hypertext transfer protocol**) http *m*

hub [hʌb] N cubo *m*; (*fig*) eje *m*

hubbub ['hʌbʌb] N algarabía *f*, barahúnda *f*; **a ~ of voices** un barullo de voces

hubby* ['hʌbɪ] N marido *m*, maridito* *m*

hubcap ['hʌbkæp] N (*Aut*) tapacubos *m inv*

HUD N ABBR (*US*) = **Department of Housing and Urban Development**

huddle ['hʌdl] **Ⓐ** N [*of people*] tropel *m*; [*of things*] montón *m* **Ⓑ** VI acurrucarse; **we ~d round the fire** nos arrimamos al fuego
➤ **huddle together** VI + ADV apiñarse; **they were huddling together for warmth** estaban apiñados *or* acurrucados para darse calor

hue[1] [hjuː] N (= *colour*) color *m*; (= *shade*) matiz *m* (*also fig*)

hue[2] [hjuː] N **~ and cry** [*of protest*] griterío *m*, clamor *m*; **to raise a ~ and cry** levantar protestas

huff* [hʌf] **Ⓐ** N **to be in a ~** estar de morros (*Sp**), estar enojado (*esp LAm*); **to go off in a ~** irse ofendido, picarse; **to take the ~** ofenderse **Ⓑ** VI **to ~ and puff** (*out of breath*) jadear, resollar

huffy ['hʌfɪ] ADJ (*compar* **huffier**; *superl* **huffiest**) (*of character*) enojadizo; (*in mood*) malhumorado, ofendido; **he was a bit ~ about it** se ofendió un tanto por ello

hug [hʌg] **Ⓐ** N abrazo *m*; **to give sb a ~** dar un abrazo a algn **Ⓑ** VT **1** (*lovingly*) abrazar; **they ~ged each other** se abrazaron **2** (= *keep close to*) arrimarse a

huge [hjuːdʒ] (*compar* **~r**; *superl* **~st**) ADJ enorme; **to be a ~ success** tener un éxito enorme, ser todo un éxito; **~ numbers of** gran número de; **the result was human suffering on a ~ scale** el resultado fue sufrimiento humano en proporciones gigantescas

hugely ['hjuːdʒlɪ] ADV **1** [*expensive, popular, entertaining, important*] tremendamente, enormemente; **a ~ enjoyable book** un libro que se disfruta muchísimo; **a ~ successful film** una película de enorme éxito **2** [*vary, increase*] enormemente

hulk [hʌlk] N **a great ~ of a man*** un gigantón

hulking* ['hʌlkɪŋ] ADJ pesado; **a ~ great brute** un hombracho

hull [hʌl] N [*of ship*] casco *m*

hullabaloo* [ˌhʌləbə'luː] N (= *noise*) algarabía *f*; (= *fuss*) jaleo *m*, revuelo *m*; **that ~ about the money** ese jaleo *or* revuelo que se armó por el dinero*

hullo [hʌ'ləʊ] EXCL (*Brit*) = **hello**

hum [hʌm] **Ⓐ** N (*gen, Elec*) zumbido *m*; [*of voices*] murmullo *m* **Ⓑ** VT [+ *tune*] canturrear, tararear **Ⓒ** VI [*insect, wire*] zumbar; [*person*] canturrear, tararear una canción; **to ~ and haw** vacilar

human ['hjuːmən] **Ⓐ** ADJ humano; ✦ IDIOM **I'm/he's etc only ~** todos somos humanos **Ⓑ** N ser *m* humano **Ⓒ** CPD ➤ **human being** ser *m* humano ➤ **human chain: to form a ~ chain** formar una cadena humana ➤ **human consumption: to be fit for ~ consumption** ser apto para el consumo humano ➤ **human nature** naturaleza *f* humana; **it's ~ nature to do that** hacer eso es humano ➤ **the human race** la raza humana, el género humano ➤ **human resources** recursos *mpl* humanos ➤ **human rights** derechos *mpl* humanos ➤ **human rights organization** organización *f* pro derechos humanos ➤ **human shield: to use sb as a ~ shield** usar a algn como escudo (humano)

humane [hjuː'meɪn] ADJ humano, humanitario

humanely [hjuː'meɪnlɪ] ADV humanamente

humanism ['hjuːmənɪzəm] N humanismo *m*

humanitarian [hjuːˌmænɪ'tɛərɪən] ADJ, N humanitario/a *m/f*

humanity [hjuː'mænɪtɪ] N humanidad *f*; **the humanities** las humanidades

humankind ['hjuːmən'kaɪnd] N el género humano

humanly ['hjuːmənlɪ] ADV humanamente; **to do everything ~ possible** hacer todo lo humanamente posible

humble ['hʌmbl] **Ⓐ** ADJ (*compar* **~r**; *superl* **~st**) humilde; **in my ~ opinion** en mi humilde *or* modesta opinión **Ⓑ** VT dar una lección de humildad a; **it was a humbling experience** fue una lección de humildad **Ⓒ** CPD ➤ **humble pie** ✦ IDIOM **to eat ~ pie** morder el polvo

humbly ['hʌmblɪ] ADV humildemente

humbug* ['hʌmbʌg] N **1** (= *person*) charlatán/ana *m/f*; **he's an old ~** es un farsante **2** (= *nonsense*) tonterías *fpl*; **humbug!** ¡bobadas!* **3** (*Brit*) (= *sweet*) caramelo *m* de menta

humdrum ['hʌmdrʌm] ADJ monótono, rutinario

humid ['hjuːmɪd] ADJ húmedo

humidifier [hjuː'mɪdɪfaɪəʳ] N humedecedor *m*

humidity [hjuː'mɪdɪtɪ] N humedad *f*

humiliate [hjuː'mɪlɪeɪt] VT humillar

humiliating [hjuː'mɪlɪeɪtɪŋ] ADJ humillante, vergonzoso

humiliation [hjuːmɪlɪ'eɪʃən] N humillación *f*

humility [hjuː'mɪlɪtɪ] N humildad *f*

hummingbird ['hʌmɪŋbɜːd] N colibrí *m*, picaflor *m*

hummus ['hʊməs] N *paté de garbanzos originario del Oriente Medio*

humongous* [hjuː'mɒŋgəs] ADJ **she is such a ~ star** es una superestrella; **we had a ~ row** tuvimos una pelea de órdago*

humor ['hjuːməʳ] N, VT (*US*) = **humour**

humorist ['hjuːmərɪst] N humorista *mf*

humorless ['hjuːməlɪs] ADJ (*US*) = **humourless**

humorous ['hjuːmərəs] ADJ [*person*] gracioso, divertido; [*book, story*] divertido; [*situation, idea, tone*] cómico, gracioso

humorously ['hjuːmərəslɪ] ADV con gracia

humour, humor (*US*) ['hjuːməʳ] **Ⓐ** N (*gen*) humor *m*; [*of book, situation*] gracia *f*; **sense of ~** sentido *m* del humor **Ⓑ** VT complacer, consentir

humourless, humorless (*US*) ['hjuːmələs] ADJ [*person*] arisco; [*joke*] sin gracia

hump [hʌmp] N (*Anat*) joroba *f*; [*of camel*] giba *f*; (*in ground*) montecillo *m*

humpbacked ['hʌmpbækt] ADJ [*person*] jorobado; **~ bridge** (*Brit*) puente *m* encorvado

humungous* [hjuː'mʌŋgəs] ADJ = **humongous**

humus ['hjuːməs] N humus *m*

hunch [hʌntʃ] **Ⓐ** N (*) corazonada *f*, presentimiento *m*; **it's only a ~** no es más que una corazonada *or* un presentimiento que tengo **Ⓑ** VT (*also* ~ **up**) encorvar; **to ~ one's back** encorvarse; **to be ~ed up** ser jorobado **Ⓒ** VI encorvarse

hunchback ['hʌntʃbæk] N jorobado/a *m/f*

hunchbacked ['hʌntʃbækt] ADJ jorobado

hundred ['hʌndrɪd] NUMBER ciento *m*; (*before noun*) cien; **a or one ~ people** cien personas; **a or one ~ and ten** ciento diez; **I've got a ~ and one things to do** tengo la mar de cosas que hacer; **a or one ~ thousand** cien mil; **two ~** doscientos; **three ~** trescientos; **five ~ people** quinientas personas; **five ~ and one** quinientos uno; **to live to be a ~** llegar a los cien años; **in ~s** ◇ **by the ~** a centenares; **~s of people** centenares de personas; **I've told you ~s of times** te lo he dicho cientos *or* centenares de veces

hundredth ['hʌndrɪdθ] **Ⓐ** ADJ centésimo **Ⓑ** PRON centésima parte *f*, centésimo *m*

hundredweight ['hʌndrɪdweɪt] N (*Brit*) = *112 libras*,

= 50,8 kilogramos; (approx) quintal m; (US) = 100 libras, = 45,4 kilogramos

hung [hʌŋ] **Ⓐ** PT, PP of **hang** **Ⓑ** CPD ➤ **hung jury** jurado cuyos miembros no se pueden poner de acuerdo ➤ **hung parliament** (Brit) parlamento en el que ningún partido alcanza mayoría absoluta

Hungarian [hʌŋˈgɛərɪən] **Ⓐ** ADJ húngaro **Ⓑ** N 1 (= person) húngaro/a m/f 2 (Ling) húngaro m

Hungary [ˈhʌŋgərɪ] N Hungría f

hunger [ˈhʌŋgəʳ] **Ⓐ** N 1 (for food) hambre f 2 (fig) hambre f, sed f; **to have a ~ for** [+ adventure, knowledge] tener hambre or sed de, estar hambriento or sediento de **Ⓑ** CPD ➤ **hunger strike** huelga f de hambre; **to be on ~ strike** estar haciendo huelga de hambre

> Use **el/un** not **la/una** before feminine nouns beginning with stressed **a** or **ha** like **hambre**.

➤ **hunger after** VI + PREP [+ adventure, knowledge] tener hambre or sed de, estar hambriento or sediento de

hung over* [hʌŋˈəʊvəʳ] ADJ **to be ~** tener resaca

hungrily [ˈhʌŋgrɪlɪ] ADV 1 [eat] ávidamente, con ansia; [look] con anhelo 2 (fig) (= eagerly) ansiosamente

hungry [ˈhʌŋgrɪ] ADJ (compar **hungrier**; superl **hungriest**) 1 (gen) [person, animal] hambriento; **to be ~** tener hambre; **to go ~** pasar hambre; **all this work is making me ~** todo este trabajo me está dando hambre 2 (fig) (= eager) **to be ~ for** [+ adventure, knowledge] tener hambre or sed de, estar hambriento or sediento de

hunk [hʌŋk] N 1 [of bread, cheese, cake] (buen) trozo m, pedazo m (grande) 2 (*) (= man) monumento* m, cachas m inv (Sp*)

hunky* [ˈhʌŋkɪ] ADJ (compar **hunkier**; superl **hunkiest**) (= strong) fuerte, macizo; (= attractive) bueno*

hunt [hʌnt] **Ⓐ** N 1 (for animals) caza f, cacería f (**for** de); (= huntsmen) partida f de caza, (grupo m de) cazadores mpl 2 (= search) busca f, búsqueda f (**for** de); (= pursuit) persecución f; **we joined in the ~ for the missing key** ayudamos a buscar la llave perdida

Ⓑ VT 1 [+ animal] cazar

2 (= search for) buscar; (= pursue) perseguir

Ⓒ VI 1 (Sport) cazar, ir de caza or cacería; **to go ~ing** ir de caza or cacería

2 (= search) buscar por todas partes; **to ~ for** buscar

Ⓓ CPD ➤ **hunt ball** baile organizado tras una cacería

➤ **hunt down** VT + ADV [+ person] dar caza a; [+ thing] buscar (hasta encontrar)

➤ **hunt out** VT + ADV buscar (hasta encontrar)

hunter [ˈhʌntəʳ] **Ⓐ** N 1 (= person) cazador(a) m/f 2 (Brit) (= horse) caballo m de caza **Ⓑ** CPD ➤ **hunter gatherer** cazador-recolector m

hunting [ˈhʌntɪŋ] N caza f, cacería f ➤ **hunting lodge** pabellón m de caza ➤ **hunting season** época f de caza

huntsman [ˈhʌntsmən] N (pl **huntsmen**) cazador m

hurdle [ˈhɜːdl] N (Sport) valla f; (fig) obstáculo m, barrera f; **the 100m ~s** (= race) los 100 metros vallas; **✦** IDIOM **to fall at the first** = fracasar a las primeras de cambio, no superar el primer escollo ➤ **hurdle race** carrera f de vallas

hurdler [ˈhɜːdləʳ] N vallista mf, corredor(a) m/f de vallas

hurl [hɜːl] VT (= throw) arrojar; **to ~ abuse** or **insults at sb** lanzar or soltar una sarta de insultos a algn; **to ~ o.s. at sth/sb** abalanzarse sobre algo/algn

hurly-burly [ˈhɜːlɪˈbɜːlɪ] N alboroto m, tumulto m; **the ~ of politics** la vida tumultuosa de la política

hurrah [hʊˈrɑː], **hurray** [hʊˈreɪ] EXCL ¡hurra!; **~ for Mr Brown!** ¡viva el señor Brown!

hurricane [ˈhʌrɪkən] N huracán m ➤ **hurricane lamp** lámpara f a prueba de viento

hurried [ˈhʌrɪd] ADJ [footsteps] apresurado; [visit, meeting] rápido, cortísimo; [phone call, conversation] rápido

hurriedly [ˈhʌrɪdlɪ] ADV [go, dress] apresuradamente, a toda prisa; [study, look at, read] por encima, rápidamente; [write] apresuradamente, a vuela pluma; **Tim ~ made his**

excuses and left Tim se excusó atropelladamente y se marchó; **he rose and ~ left** se levantó y se marchó precipitadamente; **"it doesn't matter," he said ~** —no importa —se apresuró a decir

hurry [ˈhʌrɪ] **Ⓐ** N prisa f, apuro m (LAm); **to be in a ~ (to do sth)** tener prisa or (LAm) apuro (por hacer algo); **I'm not in any ~** no tengo prisa; **they were in no ~ to pay us** no se dieron prisa por pagarnos; **in our ~ to leave ...** con las prisas de or con nuestro empeño por marcharnos ...; **to do sth in a ~** hacer algo de prisa; **he won't do that again in a ~*** eso no lo vuelve a hacer; **there's no** (great) ~ no hay or corre prisa; **what's the ~?** ¿a qué viene tanta prisa?

Ⓑ VT [+ person] meter prisa a, apresurar, apurar (LAm); [+ work, job] hacer apresuradamente, hacer deprisa y corriendo; **they hurried him to a doctor** lo llevaron a toda prisa a un médico

Ⓒ VI darse prisa, apurarse (LAm); **hurry!** ¡date prisa!, ¡apúrate! (LAm); **to ~ to do sth** darse prisa or (LAm) apurarse en hacer algo, apresurarse a hacer algo; **to ~ after sb** correr detrás de algn; **to ~ back** volver de prisa; **she hurried home** se dio prisa para llegar a casa; **I must ~** tengo que correr or darme prisa

➤ **hurry along** **Ⓐ** VI + ADV apresurarse, correr; **~ along now!** ¡vamos, rápido! **Ⓑ** VT + ADV [+ person] meter prisa a, apresurar, apurar (LAm); [+ work, job] acelerar

➤ **hurry away, hurry off** **Ⓐ** VI + ADV irse corriendo **Ⓑ** VT + ADV [+ object] llevar a la carrera; **to ~ sb away** llevarse a algn apresuradamente or a la carrera

➤ **hurry on** **Ⓐ** VI + ADV (= move) pasar rápidamente; (= speak) continuar apresuradamente **Ⓑ** VT + ADV = **hurry along** B

➤ **hurry up** **Ⓐ** VI + ADV darse prisa, apurarse (LAm); **~ up!** ¡date prisa!, ¡apúrate! (LAm) **Ⓑ** VT + ADV [+ person] meter prisa a, apresurar, apurar (LAm); [+ job] apurar, acelerar

hurt [hɜːt] (pt, pp ~) **Ⓐ** VT 1 (= cause pain to, injure) hacer daño a, lastimar (LAm); **did I ~ you?** ¿te he hecho daño?, ¿te he lastimado? (LAm); **stop it! you're ~ing me!** ¡para! ¡me estás haciendo daño!, ¡para! ¡me estás lastimando! (LAm); **how did you ~ your finger/leg?** ¿cómo te has hecho daño en el dedo/la pierna?, ¿cómo te has lastimado el dedo/la pierna? (LAm); **ten people were ~ in the accident** diez personas resultaron heridas en el accidente; **did you ~ yourself?** ¿te has hecho daño?, ¿te has lastimado? (LAm); **he's not badly ~** no está herido de gravedad; **to get ~** resultar herido; **✦** IDIOM **he wouldn't ~ a fly** sería incapaz de matar una mosca

2 (= harm) [+ prospects, chances, reputation] perjudicar; **it wouldn't ~ her to try and save some money** no le vendría mal intentar ahorrar algo de dinero; **one little glass of wine won't ~ him** un vasito de vino no le va a hacer daño; **a little hard work never ~ anyone** nadie se ha muerto nunca por trabajar un poco duro, trabajar duro nunca le ha hecho daño a nadie

3 (= upset) hacer daño a; **I was deeply ~ by his attitude** su actitud me hizo mucho daño; **to be easily ~** ser muy susceptible; **you've ~ her feelings** la has ofendido; **she was bound to get ~** estaba claro que iba a terminar sufriendo

Ⓑ VI (physically, emotionally) doler; **it doesn't ~ much** no duele mucho; **does it ~?** ¿te duele?; **where does it ~?** ¿dónde te duele?; **my feet ~** me duelen los pies; **it ~s to admit it but ...** duele or cuesta admitirlo pero ...; **my shoes are ~ing** me hacen daño los zapatos

2 (= harm) **it doesn't ~ to ask** por preguntar no se pierde nada; **it wouldn't ~ to let your mum know you'll be late** no te costaría nada avisarle a tu madre que vas a llegar tarde

3 (esp US*) (= feel pain) sufrir

Ⓒ ADJ 1 (= injured) [part of body] lastimado; **are you ~?** ¿te has hecho daño?, ¿te has lastimado? (esp LAm)

2 (= upset) dolido; **he gave me a slightly ~ look** me miró un poco dolido; **to be/feel ~** estar/sentirse dolido

Ⓓ N (= emotional pain) dolor m, pena f

hurtful [ˈhɜːtfʊl] ADJ [remark] hiriente; [act, behaviour] ofensivo; [experience] doloroso

hurtle [ˈhɜːtl] VI precipitarse; **to ~ along** ir como un rayo or a toda velocidad

husband [ˈhʌzbənd] **Ⓐ** N marido m, esposo m **Ⓑ** VT [+ resources] administrar bien, gestionar bien

husbandry ['hʌzbəndrɪ] N 1 (Agr) agricultura f; **animal ~** cría f de animales 2 (= administration) (also **good ~**) buena administración f, buena gestión f

hush [hʌʃ] 🅐 N silencio m; **a ~ fell** se hizo un silencio 🅑 VI callarse; **hush!** ¡cállate!, ¡chitón!; **~ now, don't cry** shh, no llores 🅒 CPD ➤ **hush money*** soborno m, coima f (And, SC), mordida f (Mex)
➤ **hush up** 🅐 VT + ADV [+ affair] encubrir, echar tierra a; [+ person] tapar la boca a 🅑 VI + ADV (US) callarse

hushed [hʌʃt] ADJ [silence] profundo; [tone] callado, muy bajo

hush-hush* ['hʌʃ'hʌʃ] ADJ muy secreto

husk [hʌsk] 🅐 N (gen) cascarilla f, cáscara f, cascabillo m (Agr) 🅑 VT quitar la cascarilla a, descascarillar

husky¹ ['hʌskɪ] ADJ (compar **huskier**; superl **huskiest**) ronco

husky² ['hʌskɪ] N (= dog) perro m esquimal

hussy ['hʌsɪ] N fresca* f; **she's a little ~** es una fresca

hustings ['hʌstɪŋz] NPL (esp Brit) campaña f sing electoral

hustle ['hʌsl] 🅐 N 1 (= activity) bullicio m; **~ and bustle** ajetreo m, vaivén m
2 (US*) timo m, chanchullo* m
🅑 VT 1 (= jostle) empujar, codear; (= hurry up) [+ person] dar prisa a; **they ~d him in/out** le hicieron entrar/salir a empujones or sin ceremonia; **he was ~d into a car** lo metieron en un coche a empujones or sin ceremonia
2 (fig) **to ~ sb into making a decision** meter prisa a algn para que tome una decisión; **I won't be ~d into anything** no voy a dejar que me empujen a nada
3 (US*) **they were paid to ~ drinks out of the customers** les pagaban para sacarles bebidas a los clientes; **they were hustling him for payment of the debt** le apretaban las clavijas para que saldara la deuda

hustler* ['hʌslər] N 1 (= go-getter) persona f dinámica 2 (= swindler) estafador(a) m/f, timador(a) m/f 3 (= prostitute) puto/a m/f

hut [hʌt] N (= shed) cobertizo m; (= small house) cabaña f; (= hovel) barraca f, choza f; (Mil) barracón m, barraca f; **mountain ~** albergue m de montaña

hutch [hʌtʃ] N conejera f

hyacinth ['haɪəsɪnθ] N jacinto m

hybrid ['haɪbrɪd] 🅐 N híbrido m 🅑 ADJ híbrido

hydrangea [haɪ'dreɪndʒə] N hortensia f

hydrant ['haɪdrənt] N **fire ~** boca f de incendios

hydraulic [haɪ'drɒlɪk] ADJ hidráulico

hydraulics [haɪ'drɒlɪks] N SING hidráulica f

hydrochloric [ˌhaɪdrə'klɒrɪk] ADJ **~ acid** ácido m clorhídrico

hydroelectric [ˌhaɪdrəʊ'lektrɪk] ADJ [power] hidroeléctrico; **~ power station** central f hidroeléctrica

hydrofoil ['haɪdrəʊfɔɪl] N hidroala m, aliscafo m

hydrogen ['haɪdrɪdʒən] N hidrógeno m ➤ **hydrogen bomb** bomba f de hidrógeno ➤ **hydrogen chloride** cloruro m de hidrógeno ➤ **hydrogen peroxide** agua f oxigenada

> Use **el/un** not **la/una** before feminine nouns beginning with stressed **a** or **ha** like **agua**.

➤ **hydrogen sulphide** ácido m sulfhídrico

hydroplane ['haɪdrəʊpleɪn] N hidroavión m

hyena [haɪ'iːnə] N hiena f; **to laugh like a ~** reírse como una hiena

hygiene ['haɪdʒiːn] N higiene f

hygienic [haɪ'dʒiːnɪk] ADJ higiénico

hygienist [haɪ'dʒiːnɪst] N higienista mf

hymen ['haɪmen] N himen m

hymn [hɪm] N himno m ➤ **hymn book** himnario m

hymnal ['hɪmnəl] N himnario m

hype* [haɪp] 🅐 N exageraciones fpl; (Comm) bombo m publicitario*; **it's just media ~** no es más que una campaña orquestada por los medios de comunicación 🅑 VT (Comm) (= publicize) hacer una gran campaña publicitaria a*; (= plug) dar bombo publicitario a*
➤ **hype up**** VT + ADV [+ product] dar bombo a*; [+ claim] exagerar

hyper* ['haɪpər] ADJ hiperactivo

hyperactive [ˌhaɪpər'æktɪv] ADJ hiperactivo

hyperbole [haɪ'pɜːbəlɪ] N hipérbole f

hyperlink ['haɪpəlɪŋk] N (Comput) hipervínculo m

hypermarket ['haɪpəˌmɑːkɪt] N (esp Brit) hipermercado m

hypersensitive ['haɪpə'sensɪtɪv] ADJ hipersensible

hypertext ['haɪpəˌtekst] N hipertexto m

hyphen ['haɪfən] N guión m

hyphenate ['haɪfəneɪt] VT escribir con guión, unir con guión

hypnosis [hɪp'nəʊsɪs] N (pl **hypnoses** [hɪp'nəʊsiːz]) hipnosis f; **she revealed under ~ that ...** bajo los efectos de la hipnosis reveló que ...

hypnotherapy [ˌhɪpnəʊ'θerəpɪ] N hipnoterapia f

hypnotic [hɪp'nɒtɪk] ADJ [state] hipnótico; [rhythm, sound] hipnótico, hipnotizador

hypnotism ['hɪpnətɪzəm] N hipnotismo m

hypnotist ['hɪpnətɪst] N hipnotista mf

hypnotize ['hɪpnətaɪz] VT hipnotizar

hypoallergenic [ˌhaɪpəʊˌælə'dʒenɪk] ADJ hipoalergénico

hypochondria [ˌhaɪpəʊ'kɒndrɪə] N hipocondría f

hypochondriac [ˌhaɪpəʊ'kɒndrɪæk] ADJ, N hipocondríaco/a m/f

hypocrisy [hɪ'pɒkrɪsɪ] N hipocresía f

hypocrite ['hɪpəkrɪt] N hipócrita mf

hypocritical [ˌhɪpə'krɪtɪkəl] ADJ hipócrita

hypodermic [ˌhaɪpə'dɜːmɪk] 🅐 ADJ hipodérmico 🅑 N (also ~ **needle**) aguja f hipodérmica

hypotenuse [haɪ'pɒtɪnjuːz] N hipotenusa f

hypothermia [ˌhaɪpəʊ'θɜːmɪə] N hipotermia f

hypothesis [haɪ'pɒθɪsɪs] N (pl **hypotheses** [haɪ'pɒθɪsiːz]) hipótesis f inv

hypothesize [haɪ'pɒθɪsaɪz] 🅐 VI realizar hipótesis, hacer hipótesis (**about** sobre) 🅑 VT plantear la hipótesis de; **to ~ that** plantear la hipótesis de que

hypothetic [ˌhaɪpəʊ'θetɪk] ADJ = **hypothetical**

hypothetical [ˌhaɪpəʊ'θetɪkəl] ADJ hipotético

hypothetically [ˌhaɪpəʊ'θetɪkəlɪ] ADV hipotéticamente

hysterectomy [ˌhɪstə'rektəmɪ] N histerectomía f; **she had to have a ~** le tuvieron que hacer una histerectomía

hysteria [hɪs'tɪərɪə] N histeria f, histerismo m; **mass ~** histeria f colectiva

hysterical [hɪs'terɪkəl] ADJ 1 (Psych) histérico; **to get ~** ponerse histérico 2 (*) (= funny) [situation] para morirse de (la) risa; [person] graciosísimo, desternillante

hysterically [hɪs'terɪkəlɪ] ADV histéricamente; **it was funny*** fue para morirse de (la) risa, fue graciosísimo

hysterics [hɪs'terɪks] NPL 1 (= tears, shouts) histeria f, histerismo m; **she was in ~** tenía un ataque de histeria, estaba histérica; **to have ~** ponerse histérico 2 (*) (= laughter) ataque m de risa; **we were in ~ about it** estábamos muertos de risa

I, i¹ [aɪ] N (= *letter*) I, i *f*; **I for Isabel** I de Isabel; ✦ IDIOM **to dot the i's and cross the t's** poner los puntos sobre las íes

I² [aɪ] PERS PRON (*emphatic, to avoid ambiguity*) yo; **I'm not one to exaggerate** yo no soy de los que exageran; **it is I who ...** soy yo quien ...; **he was frightened but I wasn't** él estaba asustado pero yo no; **if I were you** yo de ti, yo que tú, si yo fuera tú, yo en tu lugar; **Ann and I** Ann y yo; **he is taller than I am** es más alto que yo

> Don't translate the subject pronoun when not emphasizing or clarifying:

I've got an idea tengo una idea; **I'll go and see** voy a ver

I. ABBR (*Geog*) (= **Island, Isle**) isla *f*

IA, Ia. ABBR (*US*) = **Iowa**

IAEA N ABBR (= **International Atomic Energy Agency**) OIEA *f or m*

IBA N ABBR (*Brit*) (= **Independent Broadcasting Authority**) entidad que controla los medios privados de televisión y radio

Iberia [aɪˈbɪərɪə] N Iberia *f*

Iberian [aɪˈbɪərɪən] Ⓐ ADJ ibero, ibérico Ⓑ N ibero/a *m/f* Ⓒ CPD ➤ **the Iberian Peninsula** la Península Ibérica

ice [aɪs] Ⓐ N 1 (= *frozen water*) hielo *m*; **we put the champagne on** = pusimos el champán a enfriar; ✦ IDIOMS **to break the ~** romper el hielo; **arguments like that cut no ~ with him** ese tipo de argumentos lo dejan frío 2 (*esp Brit*) (= *ice cream*) helado *m* Ⓑ VT [+ *cake*] glasear, escarchar Ⓒ CPD ➤ **the Ice Age** la edad de hielo, el periodo glacial ➤ **ice axe, ice ax** (*US*) piqueta *f* (de alpinista), piolet *m* ➤ **ice bucket** cubo *m* del hielo, hielera *f* (*LAm*) ➤ **ice cream** helado *m* ➤ **ice-cream cone** cucurucho *m* (de helado) ➤ **ice-cream parlour, ice-cream parlor** (*US*) heladería *f* ➤ **ice-cream soda** soda *f* mezclada con helado ➤ **ice cube** cubito *m* de hielo ➤ **ice floe** témpano *m* de hielo ➤ **ice hockey** (*esp Brit*) hockey *m* sobre hielo ➤ **ice lolly** (*Brit*) polo *m* (*Sp*), paleta *f* (*LAm*) ➤ **ice pack** compresa *f* de hielo ➤ **ice pick** (*Culin*) punzón *m* para el hielo ➤ **ice rink** pista *f* de patinaje sobre hielo, pista *f* de hielo ➤ **ice skate** patín *m* de hielo, patín *m* de cuchilla ➤ **ice skater** patinador(a) *m/f* (artístico/a), patinador(a) *m/f* sobre hielo ➤ **ice skating** patinaje *m* sobre hielo; **to go ~ skating** ir a patinar sobre hielo ➤ **ice water** (*US*) agua *f* helada, agua *f* fría (*de la nevera*)

> Use **el/un** not **la/una** before feminine nouns beginning with stressed **a** or **ha** like **agua**.

➤ **ice over, ice up** VI + ADV helarse, congelarse

iceberg [ˈaɪsbɜːg] N iceberg *m*; ✦ IDIOM **that's just the tip of the ~!** no es más que la punta del iceberg ➤ **iceberg lettuce** lechuga *f* repollo

icebox [ˈaɪsbɒks] N (*Brit*) (= *part of refrigerator*) congelador *m*; (*US†*) = **refrigerator**

icebreaker [ˈaɪsˌbreɪkəʳ] N rompehielos *m inv*; **we used the video as an** ~ el vídeo nos sirvió para romper el hielo

icecap [ˈaɪskæp] N casquete *m* glaciar, casquete *m* de hielo

ice-cold [ˈaɪsˈkəʊld] ADJ [*hands, drink*] helado

iced [aɪst] ADJ [*water*] helado, frío (*de la nevera*); [*drink*] con hielo; [*cake*] glaseado, escarchado

Iceland [ˈaɪslənd] N Islandia *f*

Icelander [ˈaɪsləndəʳ] N islandés/esa *m/f*

Icelandic [aɪsˈlændɪk] Ⓐ ADJ islandés Ⓑ N (*Ling*) islandés *m*

ice-skate [ˈaɪsskeɪt] VI patinar sobre hielo

icicle [ˈaɪsɪkl] N carámbano *m*

icily [ˈaɪsɪlɪ] ADV glacialmente

icing [ˈaɪsɪŋ] N (*on plane, car, road, railway*) formación *f* de hielo; (*on cake*) glaseado *m*; ✦ IDIOM **this is the ~ on the cake** esto es la guinda que corona la torta ➤ **icing sugar** (*Brit*) azúcar *m* glasé, azúcar *m* en polvo, azúcar *m* flor (*SC*)

icon [ˈaɪkɒn] N icono *m*

iconoclast [aɪˈkɒnəklæst] N iconoclasta *mf*

ICT N ABBR (= **Information and Communications Technology**) informática *f*, TI *f*, tecnología *f* de la información

ICU N ABBR (= **intensive care unit**) UCI *f*, UMI *f*, UVI *f* (*Sp*)

icy [ˈaɪsɪ] ADJ (*compar* **icier**; *superl* **iciest**) 1 (= *covered with ice*) [*road, ground*] helado, cubierto de hielo; **the ~ conditions caused accidents** las heladas provocaron accidentes; **I don't like driving when it's** ~ no me gusta conducir cuando hiela 2 (= *freezing*) [*air, wind, weather*] glacial; [*hand, water*] helado; **the water was ~ cold** el agua estaba helada 3 (= *unfriendly*) [*stare, silence, tone, reception*] glacial

ID Ⓐ ABBR (*US*) = **Idaho** Ⓑ N ABBR = **identification, identity** Ⓒ CPD [*bracelet, tag, number*] de identidad ➤ **ID card** carnet *m* de identidad, ≈ DNI *m* (*Sp*), ≈ cédula *f* (de identidad) (*LAm*), C.I. *f* (*LAm*)

id [ɪd] N (*Psych*) id *m*

I'd [aɪd] = **I would, I had**

Ida. ABBR (*US*) = **Idaho**

idea [aɪˈdɪə] N 1 (*gen*) idea *f*; **it wasn't my ~** no fue idea mía; **that's the ~** así es; **have you <u>any</u> ~ how ridiculous you look?** ¿tienes idea de lo ridículo que estás?; **it wouldn't be a <u>bad</u> ~ to paint it** no le vendría mal pintarlo; **it might not be a bad ~ to wait a few days** puede que no sea mala idea esperar unos cuantos días; **I haven't the <u>foggiest</u>** ~ no tengo ni la menor *or* más remota *or* más mínima idea; **what(ever) <u>gave</u> you that ~?** ¿de dónde has sacado esa idea?, ¿qué te ha dado esa idea?; **you're <u>getting</u> the ~** (= *understanding*) estás empezando a comprender; (= *getting the knack*) estás cogiendo el tino *or* truco; **don't go getting ~s** (= *build up one's hopes*) no te hagas ilusiones; (= *be presumptuous*) no se te ocurra; **once she gets an ~ into her head there's no stopping her** como se le meta una idea en la cabeza no hay quien se la quite; **to <u>get</u> used to the ~ of sth** hacerse a la idea de algo; **to <u>give</u> sb ~s** meter ideas en la cabeza a algn; **he <u>hit</u> on the ~ of painting it red** se le ocurrió pintarlo de rojo; **it wasn't <u>my</u> ~ of a holiday** no era la idea que yo tengo de unas vacaciones; **I've <u>no</u> ~!** ¡ni idea!; **it was awful, you've <u>no</u>** ~ no te puedes hacer una idea de lo horrible que fue; **I had no ~ that ...** no tenía ni idea *or* la menor idea de que ...; **to <u>put</u> ~s into sb's head** meter ideas en la cabeza a algn; **can you give me a <u>rough</u> ~ of how many you want?** ¿puede darme una idea aproximada de cuántos quiere?; **<u>what</u> an ~!** ¡qué ocurrencias!; **let's forget the <u>whole</u> ~** olvidémonos de todo el asunto; **if that's <u>your</u> ~ of fun** si eso es lo que tú entiendes por diversión 2 (= *vague idea*) impresión *f*; **to <u>have</u> an~ that ...** tener la impresión de que ...; **I have an ~ that she was going to Paris** tengo la impresión de que se iba a París 3 (= *purpose*) intención *f*, idea *f*; **we went with the ~ of meeting new people** fuimos con la intención *or* idea de conocer a gente nueva; **what's the <u>big</u>~?*** ¿a qué viene eso?*

ideal [aɪˈdɪəl] ADJ, N ideal *m*

idealism [aɪˈdɪəlɪzəm] N idealismo *m*

idealist [aɪˈdɪəlɪst] N idealista *mf*

idealistic [aɪˌdɪəˈlɪstɪk] ADJ idealista

idealize [aɪˈdɪəlaɪz] VT idealizar

ideally [aɪˈdɪəlɪ] ADV **they're ~ suited** hacen una pareja ideal; **the hotel is ~ situated** el hotel tiene una situación ideal; **~, I'd like a garden** de ser posible, me gustaría tener jardín; **~, all the children should live together** lo ideal *or* lo mejor sería que todos los hijos vivieran juntos

identical [aɪˈdentɪkəl] ADJ idéntico (**to** a); ➤ **identical twins** gemelos *mpl* idénticos

identification [aɪˌdentɪfɪ'keɪʃən] N identificación f; **we have a positive ~ of the victim** disponemos ya de la identidad de la víctima ➤ **identification papers** documentos mpl de identidad, documentación fsing ➤ **identification parade** (Brit) rueda f de reconocimiento, rueda f de identificación

identify [aɪ'dentɪfaɪ] **Ⓐ** VT identificar; **to ~ o.s.** identificarse **Ⓑ** VI **to ~ with** identificarse con

Identikit ® [aɪ'dentɪkɪt] N (esp Brit) retrato-robot m (Sp), retrato m hablado (LAm)

identity [aɪ'dentɪtɪ] N identidad f; **a case of mistaken ~** un caso de identificación errónea ➤ **identity bracelet** pulsera f identificativa, brazalete m identificativo ➤ **identity card** carnet m de identidad, cédula f (de identidad) (LAm) ➤ **identity disc** (Brit) chapa f de identidad ➤ **identity papers** documentos mpl de identidad, documentación fsing ➤ **identity parade** (Brit) rueda f de reconocimiento, rueda f de identificación

ideological [ˌaɪdɪə'lɒdʒɪkəl] ADJ ideológico

ideologically [ˌaɪdɪə'lɒdʒɪkəlɪ] ADV ideológicamente

ideology [ˌaɪdɪ'ɒlədʒɪ] N ideología f

idiocy [ˈɪdɪəsɪ] N idiotez f, imbecilidad f

idiom [ˈɪdɪəm] N **1** (= phrase) modismo m, giro m **2** (= style of expression) lenguaje m

> ⚠ **idiom** ≠ **idioma**

idiomatic [ˌɪdɪə'mætɪk] ADJ idiomático

idiosyncrasy [ˌɪdɪə'sɪŋkrəsɪ] N peculiaridad f; **Spanish ~** la idiosincrasia española

idiosyncratic [ˌɪdɪəsɪŋ'krætɪk] ADJ idiosincrásico

idiot [ˈɪdɪət] N (= fool) tonto/a m/f; (= imbecile) idiota mf, imbécil mf

idiotic [ˌɪdɪ'ɒtɪk] ADJ [person] idiota, imbécil; [behaviour, laughter, idea] estúpido, idiota; **that was an ~ thing to do!** ¡eso que hiciste fue una idiotez or estupidez!

idiot-proof* [ˈɪdɪətpruːf] ADJ para torpes*, de fácil manejo

idle [ˈaɪdl] ADJ (compar ~r; superl ~st) **1** (= lazy) perezoso, holgazán, flojo (LAm); (= without work) parado, desocupado; (= inactive) [machine, factory] parado; [moment] de ocio, libre; **to stand ~** [factory, machine] estar parado **2** (= futile) [speculation] infundado; [threat] vano; **out of ~ curiosity** por pura curiosidad; **it's just ~ gossip** no es más que cotilleo
➤ **idle away** VT + ADV [+ time] (= fritter) desperdiciar, echar a perder; (= spend) pasar; **he ~s away his days in the garden** se pasa las horas muertas en el jardín

idleness [ˈaɪdlnɪs] N (= leisure) ocio m, ociosidad f; (= having nothing to do) inactividad f, desocupación f; (= laziness) holgazanería f, pereza f, flojera f (LAm)

idler [ˈaɪdlə'] N ocioso/a m/f, holgazán/ana m/f, vago/a m/f

idly [ˈaɪdlɪ] ADV (= in a leisurely way) ociosamente; (= without doing anything) sin hacer nada; (= absentmindedly) distraídamente; (= to pass the time) [chat] para pasar el rato; (= uselessly) vanamente, inútilmente; **to stand or sit ~ by** estarse de brazos cruzados

idol [ˈaɪdl] N ídolo m

idolatry [aɪ'dɒlətrɪ] N idolatría f

idolize [ˈaɪdəlaɪz] VT idolatrar

idyll [ˈɪdɪl] N idilio m

idyllic [ɪ'dɪlɪk] ADJ idílico

i.e. ABBR = **id est** (= that is) esto es, es decir, i.e.

if [ɪf] **Ⓐ** CONJ **1** (conditional) si; **I'll go if you come with me** yo iré si tú me acompañas; **if you studied harder you would pass your exams** si estudiaras más aprobarías los exámenes; **if they are to be believed** si hacemos caso de lo que dicen; **if you had come earlier, you would have seen him** si hubieras venido antes, le habrías visto; **if I had known I would have told you** de haberlo sabido te lo habría dicho, si lo sé te lo digo*; **if it hadn't been for you we would have all died** de no ser or de no haber sido por ti hubiéramos muerto todos; **you can go if you like** puedes ir si quieres; **if necessary** si es necesario, si hace falta; **if I were you I would go to Spain** yo que tú iría a España, yo en tu lugar iría a España; **if it weren't for him, we wouldn't be in this mess!** ¡si estamos metidos en este lío, es por él!*, ¡no estaríamos metidos en este lío de no ser por él!*
2 (= whenever) si, cuando; **if she wants any help she asks me** si or cuando necesita ayuda me la pide; **if it was fine we went out for a walk** si or cuando hacía buen tiempo dábamos un paseo
3 (= although) aunque, si bien; **it's a nice film if rather long** es una buena película, aunque or si bien algo larga; **I'll finish it even if it takes me all day** lo terminaré aunque me lleve todo el día; **even if he tells me himself I won't believe it** ni aunque me lo diga él mismo me lo creo; **I couldn't eat it if I tried** aunque me lo propusiera no lo podría comer
4 (= whether) si; **I don't know if he's here** no sé si está aquí; **I wonder if it's true** me pregunto si es or será verdad
5 (in phrases) **if anything this one is better** hasta creo que éste es mejor, éste es mejor si cabe; **it's no bigger than our last house, if anything, it's even smaller** no es más grande que nuestra última casa, en todo acaso, es incluso más pequeña; **as if** como si; **she acts as if she were the boss** se comporta como si fuera la jefa; **as if by chance** como por casualidad; **it isn't as if we were rich** no es que seamos precisamente ricos, no es que seamos ricos que digamos; **if it isn't old Garfield!** ¡pero si es el bueno de Garfield!, ¡hombre, Garfield, tú por aquí!; **if not** si no; **if only I had known!** ¡de haberlo sabido!; **if only we had a car!** ¡ojalá tuviéramos coche!, ¡quién tuviera coche!; **I'll come, if only to see him** voy, aunque sólo sea para verlo; **if so** si es así, de ser así
Ⓑ N **there are a lot of ifs and buts** hay muchas dudas sin resolver

iffy* [ˈɪfɪ] ADJ dudoso, incierto

igloo [ˈɪgluː] N iglú m

ignite [ɪg'naɪt] **Ⓐ** VT encender, prender fuego a (LAm) **Ⓑ** VI encenderse, prender (LAm)

ignition [ɪg'nɪʃən] N (Aut) encendido m, arranque m; **to switch on/off the ~** arrancar/apagar el motor, dar al/quitar el contacto; **I left the key in the ~** (intentionally) dejé la llave de contacto puesta; (unintentionally) me dejé la llave de contacto puesta ➤ **ignition key** llave f de contacto

ignoble [ɪg'nəʊbl] ADJ innoble, vil

ignominious [ˌɪgnə'mɪnɪəs] ADJ [act, behaviour] ignominioso, oprobioso; [defeat] vergonzoso

ignominy [ˈɪgnəmɪnɪ] N ignominia f, oprobio m, vergüenza f

ignoramus [ˌɪgnə'reɪməs] N ignorante mf, inculto/a m/f

ignorance [ˈɪgnərəns] N ignorancia f (of de); **to be in ~ of** ignorar, desconocer; **to keep sb in ~ of sth** ocultar algo a algn

ignorant [ˈɪgnərənt] ADJ ignorante; **to be ~ of** ignorar, desconocer; **they are surprisingly ~ about their own culture** es sorprendente lo poco que saben de or conocen su propia cultura

ignore [ɪg'nɔː'] VT [+ person] (= disregard) no hacer caso a; (= spurn) ignorar; [+ remark, danger] hacer caso omiso de, no hacer caso de; [+ behaviour, rudeness] pasar por alto; [+ awkward fact] cerrar los ojos ante

IL ABBR (US) = **Illinois**

ilk [ɪlk] N índole f, clase f; **and others of that ~** y otros así or de esa clase, y otros de ese jaez

I'll [aɪl] = **I will, I shall**

ill [ɪl] **Ⓐ** ADJ (compar **worse**; superl **worst**) **1** (Med) enfermo; **to be ~** estar enfermo; **to feel ~** encontrarse mal, sentirse mal; **to look ~** tener mal aspecto or mala cara; **to make sb ~** [food, wine] sentar mal a algn; [lifestyle, diet] afectar a la salud de algn; **to make o.s. ~** ponerse enfermo, ponerse malo*; **to be taken ~** caer or ponerse enfermo, enfermarse (LAm)
2 (= bad) [fortune, luck] malo; **~ effects** efectos mpl adversos; **~ feeling** (= hostility) hostilidad f; (= spite) rencor m; **there are no ~ feelings** no quedan rencores; **~ health** mala salud f; **~ humour** or (US) **humor** mal humor m; **~ will** (= hostility) hostilidad f; (= spite) rencor m; **I bear you no ~**

will for that no le guardo rencor por eso
B ADV mal; **to speak/think ~ of sb** hablar/pensar mal de algn
C N **ills** males *mpl*

Ill. ABBR (*US*) = **Illinois**

ill-advised ['ɪləd'vaɪzd] ADJ [*remark*] inoportuno; [*plan*] desacertado; [*attempt*] imprudente; **you would be ~ to go** harías mejor en no ir, sería poco aconsejable que fueras

ill-at-ease ['ɪlət'iːz] ADJ (= *awkward*) molesto, incómodo; (= *uneasy*) inquieto, intranquilo

ill-bred ['ɪl'bred] ADJ mal educado, malcriado

ill-considered ['ɪlkən'sɪdəd] ADJ [*plan, remark*] poco pensado, poco meditado; [*act, decision*] apresurado, irreflexivo

ill-disposed [,ɪldɪs'pəʊzd] ADJ **to be ~ toward sb** estar predispuesto en contra de algn

illegal [ɪ'liːgəl] ADJ ilegal ➤ **illegal immigrant** inmigrante *mf* ilegal ➤ **illegal substance** sustancia *f* ilegal

illegality [,ɪliː'gælɪtɪ] N ilegalidad *f*

illegally [ɪ'liːgəlɪ] ADV [*act, occupy, fish*] ilegalmente

illegible [ɪ'ledʒəbl] ADJ ilegible

illegitimate [,ɪlɪ'dʒɪtɪmɪt] ADJ ilegítimo

ill-equipped ['ɪl'kwɪpt] ADJ [*expedition etc*] mal equipado; **he was ~ for the task** no estaba preparado para esa tarea

ill-fated ['ɪl'feɪtɪd] ADJ [*day*] funesto, nefasto; [*expedition, journey, attempt*] desafortunado

ill-founded ['ɪl'faʊndɪd] ADJ [*claim, fear*] infundado, sin fundamento

ill-gotten ['ɪl'gɒtn] ADJ **~ gains** (*liter or hum*) ganancias *fpl* ilícitas

ill-humoured, ill-humored (*US*) ['ɪl'hjuːməd] ADJ malhumorado

illicit [ɪ'lɪsɪt] ADJ ilícito

ill-informed ['ɪlɪn'fɔːmd] ADJ [*judgment, criticism*] desinformado, inexacto; [*person*] mal informado

illiteracy [ɪ'lɪtərəsɪ] N analfabetismo *m*

illiterate [ɪ'lɪtərɪt] ADJ analfabeto

ill-kempt ['ɪl'kempt] ADJ desaliñado, desaseado

ill-mannered ['ɪl'mænəd] ADJ mal educado, sin educación

illness ['ɪlnɪs] N enfermedad *f*

illogical [ɪ'lɒdʒɪkəl] ADJ ilógico, falto de lógica

ill-prepared [,ɪlprɪ'peəd] ADJ mal preparado

ill-suited ['ɪl'suːtɪd] ADJ **as a couple they are ~** como pareja no son compatibles, no hacen buena pareja; **he is ~ to the job** no es la persona indicada para el trabajo

ill-tempered ['ɪl'tempəd] ADJ [*person*] de mal genio; [*remark, tone etc*] malhumorado

ill-timed ['ɪl'taɪmd] ADJ inoportuno, intempestivo

ill-treat ['ɪl'triːt] VT [+ *person, animal*] maltratar, tratar mal

ill-treatment ['ɪl'triːtmənt] N maltrato *m*, malos tratos *mpl*

illuminate [ɪ'luːmɪneɪt] VT **1** [+ *room, building, street*] iluminar; **~d sign** letrero *m* luminoso **2** (= *clarify*) [+ *problem, question*] aclarar, echar luz sobre **3** (= *enlighten*) [+ *person*] iluminar

illuminating [ɪ'luːmɪneɪtɪŋ] ADJ [*remark, observation*] esclarecedor; [*lecture, experience*] instructivo

illumination [ɪ,luːmɪ'neɪʃən] N (*gen*) iluminación *f*; (*Art*) iluminación *f*; (*fig*) aclaración *f*; **illuminations** (*esp Brit*) (= *decorative lights*) luces *fpl*, iluminación *f*

illusion [ɪ'luːʒən] N ilusión *f*; **optical ~** ilusión *f* óptica; **it gives an ~ of space** crea una ilusión *or* impresión de espacio; **to be under an ~** hacerse falsas ilusiones, estar en un error; **I am under no ~s on that score** sobre ese punto no me hago (falsas) ilusiones; **to be under the ~ that ...** creerse que ...

illusive [ɪ'luːsɪv], **illusory** [ɪ'luːsərɪ] ADJ ilusorio

illustrate ['ɪləstreɪt] VT **1** [+ *book*] ilustrar **2** (= *exemplify*) [+ *subject*] ilustrar; [+ *point*] demostrar; **this can best be ~d**

as follows esto puede ilustrarse del modo siguiente

illustration [,ɪləs'treɪʃən] N (*in book, paper*) ilustración *f*; (= *example*) ejemplo *m*, ilustración *f*; **by way of ~** a modo de ejemplo, a título ilustrativo

illustrative ['ɪləstrətɪv] ADJ ilustrativo; **to be ~ of sth** ejemplificar *or* demostrar algo

illustrator ['ɪləstreɪtə'] N ilustrador(a) *m/f*

illustrious [ɪ'lʌstrɪəs] ADJ ilustre

I'm [aɪm] = **I am**

image ['ɪmɪdʒ] N **1** (*gen*) imagen *f*; **we must improve our ~** tenemos que mejorar nuestra imagen; ✦ IDIOM **to be the spitting ~ of sb** ser el vivo retrato *or* la viva imagen de algn **2** (= *reflection*) reflejo *m*; **mirror ~** reflejo *m* exacto

imagery ['ɪmɪdʒərɪ] N imágenes *fpl*, imaginería *f*

imaginable [ɪ'mædʒɪnəbl] ADJ imaginable; **the biggest party ~** la fiesta más grande que se pueda imaginar

imaginary [ɪ'mædʒɪnərɪ] ADJ imaginario

imagination [ɪ,mædʒɪ'neɪʃən] N imaginación *f*; **it's all in your ~** te lo estás imaginando, son imaginaciones tuyas; **was it my ~ or did I see you there?** ¿me lo he imaginado o te vi allí de verdad?; **she let her ~ run away with her** se dejó llevar por la imaginación; **her story caught the popular ~** su historia atrapó el interés popular

imaginative [ɪ'mædʒɪnətɪv] ADJ [*person*] imaginativo, lleno de imaginación; [*drawing, story*] imaginativo

imaginatively [ɪ'mædʒɪnətɪvlɪ] ADV con imaginación

imagine [ɪ'mædʒɪn] VT **1** (= *visualize*) imaginarse, figurarse; **~ my surprise** imagínate *or* figúrate mi sorpresa; **you can ~ how I felt!** ¡imagínate *or* figúrate cómo me sentí!; **(just) ~!** ¡imagínate!, ¡figúrate!; **you can't begin to ~ what it was like** no puedes hacerte (ni) idea de lo que fue aquello; **~ yourself on a Caribbean island** imagínate (que estás) en una isla del Caribe **2** (= *falsely believe*) **you're just imagining things** te lo estás imaginando, son imaginaciones tuyas; **he ~d himself to be the Messiah** se creía *or* se imaginaba que era el Mesías **3** (= *suppose, think*) suponer, creer; **don't ~ that you're going to get it free** no te vayas a pensar *or* no te creas que te va a salir gratis

imbalance [ɪm'bæləns] N desequilibrio *m*, falta *f* de equilibrio

imbecile ['ɪmbəsiːl] N imbécil *mf*; **you ~!** ¡imbécil!

imbibe [ɪm'baɪb] **A** VT (*frm or hum*) (= *drink*) beber; (*fig*) [+ *information*] imbuirse de (*frm*), empaparse de **B** VI (*frm or hum*) beber

imbue [ɪm'bjuː] VT **to ~ sb with sth** [+ *quality, virtue*] infundir *or* conferir algo a algn, imbuir a algn de algo (*frm*)

IMF N ABBR (= **International Monetary Fund**) FMI *m*

imitate ['ɪmɪteɪt] VT [+ *person, action, accent*] imitar

imitation [,ɪmɪ'teɪʃən] **A** N (= *act*) imitación *f*; (= *copy*) reproducción *f*, copia *f*; **in ~ of** a imitación de; **beware of ~s** desconfíe de las imitaciones **B** CPD de imitación ➤ **imitation fur** piel *f* sintética ➤ **imitation gold** oro *m* de imitación ➤ **imitation leather** imitación *f* a piel

immaculate [ɪ'mækjʊlɪt] ADJ impecable; **a hotel where the service is ~** un hotel donde el servicio es impecable; **to be in ~ condition** estar en perfectas condiciones; **the Immaculate Conception** la Inmaculada Concepción

immaculately [ɪ'mækjʊlɪtlɪ] ADV impecablemente; **~ clean** impecablemente limpio, de un limpio inmaculado

immaterial [,ɪmə'tɪərɪəl] ADJ irrelevante; **that is quite ~** eso no tiene ninguna importancia, eso es irrelevante; **the difference between them is ~ to me** la diferencia entre ellos me es indiferente; **it is ~ whether ...** no importa si ...

immature [,ɪmə'tjʊə'] ADJ **1** (= *childish*) [*person, attitude*] inmaduro **2** (= *half-grown*) [*tree, plant*] joven; [*fruit*] verde, inmaduro

immaturity [,ɪmə'tjʊərɪtɪ] N inmadurez *f*, falta *f* de madurez; [*of tree, plant*] inmadurez *f*

immeasurable [ɪ'meʒərəbl] ADJ (= *not measurable*) inconmensurable, imposible de medir; (= *enormous*) [*benefit, value*] inconmensurable, incalculable

immediacy [ɪ'miːdɪəsɪ] N inmediatez *f*

immediate [ɪ'miːdɪət] ADJ **1** (= *instant*) [*decision, answer, reaction*] inmediato; **to take ~ action** actuar inmediatamente *or* de inmediato; **these changes will take place with ~ effect** estos cambios tendrán lugar con un efecto inmediato
2 (= *urgent*) [*needs, problem*] urgente, apremiante; [*danger, threat, task*] inmediato; **my ~ concern was for Max** Max era mi primera preocupación; **what are your ~ plans?** ¿cuáles son tus planes más inmediatos?
3 (= *future, cause*) inmediato; **my ~ family** mi familia más cercana

immediately [ɪ'miːdɪətlɪ] **Ⓐ** ADV **1** (= *at once*) [*reply, come, agree*] inmediatamente, de inmediato; **the cause of the accident was not ~ apparent** la causa del accidente no se apreciaba a simple vista
2 (= *directly*) [*affect, concern*] directamente; **~ above/below sth** justo *or* justamente encima de/debajo de algo; **~ after/before sth** inmediatamente después de/antes de algo
Ⓑ CONJ (*Brit*) **~ he put the phone down, he remembered** nada más colgar el teléfono se acordó, en cuanto *or* (*LAm*) no más colgó el teléfono se acordó; **let me know ~ he arrives** avíseme en cuanto llegue, avíseme en el momento en que llegue

immemorial [ˌɪmɪ'mɔːrɪəl] ADJ inmemorial; **from time ~** desde tiempo(s) inmemorial(es)

immense [ɪ'mens] ADJ [*distance, difficulty, effort*] inmenso, enorme; **to his ~ relief/satisfaction** para gran alivio suyo/ satisfacción suya; **it has been of ~ benefit to her** le ha resultado enormemente beneficioso

immensely [ɪ'menslɪ] ADV [*like, enjoy*] muchísimo; [*differ*] enormemente; [*powerful*] inmensamente, enormemente; **I was ~ grateful/relieved** me sentía enormemente agradecido/aliviado

immensity [ɪ'mensɪtɪ] N inmensidad *f*

immerse [ɪ'mɜːs] VT **to ~ sth in water** sumergir algo en el agua; **he was totally ~d in his work** estaba metido de lleno *or* inmerso en su trabajo; **to ~ o.s. in sth** (*fig*) sumergirse en algo

immersion [ɪ'mɜːʃən] N (*in liquid*) inmersión *f*, sumersión *f*; (*in work, thoughts*) absorción *f* ➤ **immersion heater** (*Brit*) calentador *m* de inmersión

immigrant ['ɪmɪɡrənt] ADJ, N inmigrante *mf*

immigrate ['ɪmɪɡreɪt] VI inmigrar

immigration [ˌɪmɪ'ɡreɪʃən] N inmigración *f* ➤ **immigration control** control *m* de inmigración

imminent ['ɪmɪnənt] ADJ inminente

immobile [ɪ'məʊbaɪl] ADJ inmóvil

immobility [ˌɪməʊ'bɪlɪtɪ] N inmovilidad *f*

immobilize [ɪ'məʊbɪlaɪz] VT inmovilizar

immoderate [ɪ'mɒdərɪt] ADJ [*opinion, reaction*] desmesurado; [*demand*] excesivo, inmoderado; [*person*] extremista, radical; **with ~ haste** (*frm*) con excesiva *or* desmesurada celeridad (*frm*)

immodest [ɪ'mɒdɪst] ADJ [*behaviour*] indecoroso, impúdico; [*dress*] poco recatado; [*claim, statement*] poco modesto, presuntuoso

immodesty [ɪ'mɒdɪstɪ] N (= *indecency*) falta *f* de decoro, impudicia *f*; (= *boastfulness*) falta *f* de modestia, presunción *f*

immoral [ɪ'mɒrəl] ADJ inmoral

immorality [ˌɪmə'rælɪtɪ] N inmoralidad *f*

immortal [ɪ'mɔːtl] ADJ, N inmortal *mf*

immortality [ˌɪmɔː'tælɪtɪ] N inmortalidad *f*

immortalize [ɪ'mɔːtəlaɪz] VT inmortalizar

immovable [ɪ'muːvəbl] ADJ [*object*] imposible de mover, inamovible; [*feast, post*] inamovible

immune [ɪ'mjuːn] ADJ (*to disease*) inmune (**to** a); (*from tax, regulations*) exento (**from** de); **they seemed ~ to the cold** parecían inmunes al frío ➤ **immune deficiency** inmunodeficiencia *f* ➤ **immune system** sistema *m* inmunológico

immunity [ɪ'mjuːnɪtɪ] N (*Med, fig*) inmunidad *f* (**to** contra); (*from tax, regulations*) exención *f* (**from** de)

immunization [ˌɪmjʊnaɪ'zeɪʃən] N inmunización *f*

immunize ['ɪmjʊnaɪz] VT inmunizar

immunodeficiency [ˌɪmjuːnəʊdɪ'fɪʃənsɪ] N inmunodeficiencia *f*

immutable [ɪ'mjuːtəbl] ADJ inmutable

imp [ɪmp] N diablillo *m*; (*fig*) diablillo *m*, pillín/ina *m/f*

impact ['ɪmpækt] N impacto *m*; **to explode on ~** explotar con el impacto; **the book had a great ~ on me** el libro me impactó mucho *or* me causó gran impacto; **the measure would have considerable ~ on consumers** la medida afectaría considerablemente a los consumidores; **the speech made no ~** el discurso no hizo mella

impacted [ɪm'pæktɪd] ADJ [*tooth*] incrustado

impair [ɪm'peər] VT [+ *health, relations*] perjudicar, afectar; [+ *sight, hearing*] afectar, dañar; [+ *ability*] mermar; [+ *visibility*] reducir; **~ed hearing** problemas *mpl* de audición

impale [ɪm'peɪl] VT (*as punishment*) empalar; (*on sword, spike*) ensartar, atravesar; **to ~ o.s. on** atravesarse con

impalpable [ɪm'pælpəbl] ADJ impalpable

impart [ɪm'pɑːt] VT [+ *knowledge*] impartir, transmitir; [+ *information, ideas, values*] transmitir

impartial [ɪm'pɑːʃəl] ADJ imparcial

impartiality [ˌɪmˌpɑːʃɪ'ælɪtɪ] N imparcialidad *f*

impassable [ɪm'pɑːsəbl] ADJ [*road*] intransitable; [*barrier, river*] infranqueable

impasse ['ɪmpɑːs] N punto *m* muerto, impasse *m or f*; **to reach an ~** llegar a un punto muerto *or* impasse

impassioned [ɪm'pæʃnd] ADJ apasionado

impassive [ɪm'pæsɪv] ADJ impasible, imperturbable

impassively [ɪm'pæsɪvlɪ] ADV impasiblemente, sin inmutarse; **he listened ~** escuchó impasible *or* sin inmutarse

impatience [ɪm'peɪʃəns] N impaciencia *f*

impatient [ɪm'peɪʃənt] ADJ **1** (= *irascible*) [*person*] impaciente, sin paciencia; [*gesture*] de impaciencia
2 (= *eager*) impaciente; **to be ~ to do sth** estar impaciente por hacer algo

impatiently [ɪm'peɪʃəntlɪ] ADV con impaciencia, impacientemente

impeach [ɪm'piːtʃ] VT [+ *public official*] (= *accuse*) acusar de prevaricación; (= *try*) procesar por prevaricación; (*US*) [+ *president*] someter a un proceso de destitución

impeachment [ɪm'piːtʃmənt] N (= *accusation*) acusación *f* de prevaricación; (= *trial*) proceso *m* por prevaricación; (*US*) [*of president*] proceso *m* de destitución

impeccable [ɪm'pekəbl] ADJ impecable; **she speaks ~ English** habla un inglés impecable

impeccably [ɪm'pekəblɪ] ADV impecablemente

impede [ɪm'piːd] VT dificultar, obstaculizar

impediment [ɪm'pedɪmənt] N **1** (= *obstacle*) obstáculo *m*, impedimento *m* (**to** para) **2** (*Med*) defecto *m*; **speech ~** defecto *m* del habla

impel [ɪm'pel] VT obligar; **I feel ~led to say ...** me veo obligado a decir ...; **hunger ~led him to do it** el hambre lo impulsó a hacerlo

impending [ɪm'pendɪŋ] ADJ inminente

impenetrable [ɪm'penɪtrəbl] ADJ [*jungle, barrier, fortress*] impenetrable; [*writing, idea, accent*] incomprensible; [*mystery*] insondable, inescrutable; [*expression*] inescrutable

impenitent [ɪm'penɪtənt] ADJ impenitente

imperative [ɪm'perətɪv] **Ⓐ** ADJ imprescindible, fundamental; **it is ~ that he comes** es imprescindible *or* fundamental que venga; **it was ~ to destroy the bridge** era fundamental destruir el puente **Ⓑ** N imperativo *m*

imperceptible [ˌɪmpə'septəbl] ADJ imperceptible

imperceptibly [ˌɪmpə'septəblɪ] ADV imperceptiblemente

imperfect [ɪm'pɜːfɪkt] **Ⓐ** ADJ **1** [*machine, product*] defectuoso; [*hearing, vision*] deficiente; [*understanding, world, method*] imperfecto; [*knowledge*] incompleto, limitado **2** [*tense*] imperfecto **Ⓑ** N imperfecto *m*; **a verb in the ~** un verbo en imperfecto

imperfection [ˌɪmpəˈfekʃən] N **1** (= *state of being imperfect*) imperfección *f* **2** (= *fault*) defecto *m*

imperial [ɪmˈpɪərɪəl] ADJ imperial ➤ **imperial system** sistema *m* británico de pesos y medidas

imperialism [ɪmˈpɪərɪəlɪzəm] N imperialismo *m*

imperialist [ɪmˈpɪərɪəlɪst] ADJ, N imperialista *mf*

IMPERIAL SYSTEM

Aunque el sistema métrico decimal se implantó oficialmente en el Reino Unido en 1971 y es el que se enseña en los colegios, en el lenguaje cotidiano aún se sigue usando en muchos casos el llamado **imperial system**. Por ejemplo, en muchas tiendas se sigue pesando en libras (**pounds**) y la gente suele decir su peso en **stones** y **pounds**. La cerveza se mide en pintas (**pints**), las distancias en millas (**miles**) y la longitud, la altura o la profundidad en pies (**feet**) y pulgadas (**inches**).

En Estados Unidos el sistema imperial también se usa para todas las medidas y pesos, aunque la capacidad de la onza (**ounce**), del galón (**gallon**) y de la pinta (**pint**) es ligeramente inferior a la del Reino Unido. Por otro lado, en EE.UU. la gente mide su peso sólo en libras (**pounds**) y no en **stones**.

imperil [ɪmˈperɪl] VT (*frm*) arriesgar, poner en peligro

imperious [ɪmˈpɪərɪəs] ADJ imperioso

impermeable [ɪmˈpɜːmɪəbl] ADJ impermeable (**to** a)

impersonal [ɪmˈpɜːsnl] ADJ impersonal

impersonate [ɪmˈpɜːsəneɪt] VT hacerse pasar por; (*Theat*) imitar

impersonation [ɪmˌpɜːsəˈneɪʃən] N (*to commit crime*) suplantación *f*; (*Theat*) imitación *f*

impersonator [ɪmˈpɜːsəneɪtəʳ] N imitador(a) *m/f*

impertinence [ɪmˈpɜːtɪnəns] N impertinencia *f*, insolencia *f*

impertinent [ɪmˈpɜːtɪnənt] ADJ impertinente, insolente (**to sb** con algn)

impertinently [ɪmˈpɜːtɪnəntlɪ] ADV impertinentemente

imperturbable [ˌɪmpəˈtɜːbəbl] ADJ imperturbable, impasible

impervious [ɪmˈpɜːvɪəs] ADJ **1** (*to water*) impermeable (**to** a) **2** (*to remarks, threats*) inmune, insensible (**to** a); **he is ~ to criticism** es inmune *or* insensible a las críticas, no le afectan las críticas

impetuosity [ɪmˌpetjʊˈɒsɪtɪ] N impulsividad *f*

impetuous [ɪmˈpetjʊəs] ADJ [*person*] impetuoso, impulsivo; [*behaviour*] precipitado, impulsivo

impetuously [ɪmˈpetjʊəslɪ] ADV [*say*] impetuosamente, de forma impetuosa, impulsivamente; [*behave*] precipitadamente, impulsivamente

impetus [ˈɪmpɪtəs] N (= *force*) ímpetu *m*; (*fig*) impulso *m*; **to give an ~ to sales** impulsar *or* incentivar las ventas

impiety [ɪmˈpaɪətɪ] N impiedad *f*

impinge [ɪmˈpɪndʒ] VI **to ~ on sth/sb** incidir en algo/algn, afectar a algo/algn; **to ~ on sb's freedom/rights** vulnerar la libertad/los derechos de algn

impish [ˈɪmpɪʃ] ADJ [*expression, smile*] pícaro, travieso

implacable [ɪmˈplækəbl] ADJ [*enemy, hatred*] implacable

implant **Ⓐ** [ˈɪmplɑːnt] N implante *m* **Ⓑ** [ɪmˈplɑːnt] VT [+ *organ, tissue*] injertar, implantar; [+ *idea, principle*] inculcar

implausible [ɪmˈplɔːzəbl] ADJ inverosímil, poco convincente

implement **Ⓐ** [ˈɪmplɪmənt] N herramienta *f*, instrumento *m* **Ⓑ** [ˈɪmplɪment] VT [+ *plan, decision, idea*] llevar a cabo,

poner en práctica; [+ *measure*] aplicar, poner en práctica; [+ *law*] aplicar

implementation [ˌɪmplɪmenˈteɪʃən] N [*of plan, decision*] ejecución *f*, puesta *f* en práctica; [*of idea*] puesta *f* en práctica; [*of law, measure*] aplicación *f*

implicate [ˈɪmplɪkeɪt] VT implicar; **to ~ sb in sth** implicar *or* involucrar a algn en algo

implication [ˌɪmplɪˈkeɪʃən] N **1** (= *consequence*) implicación *f*, consecuencia *f*; **the proposal has major ~s for schools** la propuesta tiene importantes implicaciones *or* acarrea importantes consecuencias para los colegios; **we shall have to study all the ~s** tendremos que estudiar las posibles consecuencias *or* repercusiones **2** (= *inference*) **the ~ of this is that ...** esto significa que ...; **he did not realize the full ~s of his words** no se dio cuenta de la trascendencia de sus palabras; **by ~ then ...** de ahí (se deduce) que ...

implicit [ɪmˈplɪsɪt] ADJ **1** (= *implied*) implícito **2** (= *unquestioning*) incondicional, absoluto

implicitly [ɪmˈplɪsɪtlɪ] ADV **1** (= *by implication*) implícitamente **2** (= *unquestioningly*) [*trust*] sin reservas, incondicionalmente

implied [ɪmˈplaɪd] ADJ implícito, tácito; **it is ~** se sobreentiende

implode [ɪmˈpləʊd] VT, VI implosionar

implore [ɪmˈplɔːʳ] VT suplicar; **to ~ sb to do sth** suplicar a algn que haga algo; **I ~ you!** ¡se lo suplico!

imploring [ɪmˈplɔːrɪŋ] ADJ suplicante, de súplica

imploringly [ɪmˈplɔːrɪŋlɪ] ADV de modo suplicante

imply [ɪmˈplaɪ] VT (= *hint, suggest*) insinuar; (= *involve*) suponer, implicar; **what are you ~ing?** ¿qué insinúas?; **are you ~ing that ...?** ¿quieres decir que ...?, ¿insinúas que ...?; **he implied he would do it** dio a entender que lo haría; **it implies a lot of work** supone *or* implica mucho trabajo

impolite [ˌɪmpəˈlaɪt] ADJ [*person*] mal educado, descortés; [*behaviour*] descortés

impolitely [ˌɪmpəˈlaɪtlɪ] ADV con descortesía

imponderable [ɪmˈpɒndərəbl] ADJ imponderable

import **Ⓐ** [ˈɪmpɔːt] N **1** (*Comm*) (= *article*) artículo *m* importado, artículo *m* de importación; (= *importing*) importación *f* **2** (*frm*) (= *importance*) trascendencia *f*, importancia *f* **Ⓑ** [ɪmˈpɔːt] VT importar (**from** de; **into** en) **Ⓒ** [ˈɪmpɔːt] CPD [*licence, quota*] de importación ➤ **import duty** derechos *mpl* de importación

importance [ɪmˈpɔːtəns] N importancia *f*; **to be of great/ little ~** ser de gran/escasa importancia, tener mucha/poca importancia; **to be of no ~** carecer de importancia, no tener importancia; **to be full of one's own ~** darse ínfulas, creerse muy importante

important [ɪmˈpɔːtənt] ADJ importante; **he told Henry to touch nothing, and more ~, to say nothing** le dijo a Henry que no tocase nada y, lo que era más importante, que no dijese nada; **to become ~** cobrar importancia; **it is ~ for everyone to be here on time** es importante que todo el mundo esté aquí a la hora

importantly [ɪmˈpɔːtəntlɪ] ADV **I was hungry, and, more ~, my children were hungry** yo tenía hambre y, lo que era aún más importante, mis hijos tenían hambre

importation [ˌɪmpɔːˈteɪʃən] N importación *f*

importer [ɪmˈpɔːtəʳ] N (*Comm*) importador(a) *m/f*

impose [ɪmˈpəʊz] **Ⓐ** VT [+ *condition, fine, tax, sentence*] imponer (**on** a); **to ~ o.s. on sb** abusar de la amabilidad de algn **Ⓑ** VI **to ~ (up)on** [+ *kindness, hospitality*] abusar de; **I don't wish to ~ (upon you)** no quiero abusar, no quiero molestar(le)

imposing [ɪmˈpəʊzɪŋ] ADJ imponente, impresionante

imposition [ˌɪmpəˈzɪʃən] N [*of fine*] imposición *f*; [*of tax*] aplicación *f*; **it's a bit of an ~** me parece un abuso; **I'm afraid it's rather an ~ for you** me temo que le vaya a resultar molesto

impossibility [ɪmˌpɒsəˈbɪlɪtɪ] N imposibilidad *f*; **the ~ of doing sth** la imposibilidad de hacer algo

impossible [ɪmˈpɒsəbl] **Ⓐ ADJ 1** (= *not possible*) imposible; **it's almost ~ to read her writing** leer su letra es casi imposible, es casi imposible leer su letra; **this cooker is ~ to clean!** ¡esta cocina es imposible de limpiar!, ¡limpiar esta cocina es imposible!; **the fog made it ~ to see very far** la niebla impedía ver a mucha distancia; **it is ~ for me to leave now** me es imposible salir ahora; **it's not ... that ...** existe la posibilidad de que ...; **to be physically ~** ser físicamente imposible
2 (= *intolerable*) [*person*] insufrible, insoportable; [*situation*] insostenible
Ⓑ N the ~ lo imposible; **to ask for/do the ~** pedir/hacer lo imposible

impossibly [ɪmˈpɒsəblɪ] ADV [*late, expensive, small*] increíblemente, tremendamente

imposter, **impostor** [ɪmˈpɒstəʳ] N impostor(a) *m/f*

impotence [ˈɪmpətəns] N impotencia *f*

impotent [ˈɪmpətənt] ADJ impotente

impound [ɪmˈpaʊnd] VT [+ *vehicle*] retener, retirar de la vía pública; [+ *goods*] confiscar, incautar

impoverished [ɪmˈpɒvərɪʃt] ADJ [*person*] empobrecido

impracticable [ɪmˈpræktɪkəbl] ADJ impracticable, no factible

impractical [ɪmˈpræktɪkəl] ADJ [*person*] poco práctico, falto de sentido práctico; [*plan*] poco factible

imprecise [ˌɪmprɪˈsaɪs] ADJ impreciso

imprecision [ˌɪmprɪˈsɪʒən] N imprecisión *f*

impregnable [ɪmˈpregnəbl] ADJ [*castle*] inexpugnable; (*lit, fig*) [*position*] invulnerable

impregnate [ˈɪmpregneɪt] VT (= *permeate*) impregnar, empapar (**with** de); (= *fertilize*) fecundar

impresario [ˌɪmpreˈsɑːrɪəʊ] N empresario/a *m/f*

impress [ɪmˈpres] **Ⓐ VT 1** (= *make good impression on*) impresionar; **he is not easily ~ed** no se deja impresionar fácilmente; **I'm very ~ed!** ¡estoy admirado!; **I was not ~ed** no me causó buena impresión **2 to ~ sth (up)on sb** convencer a algn de la importancia de algo; **I must ~ upon you that ...** tengo que subrayar que ... **Ⓑ VI** causar buena impresión

impression [ɪmˈpreʃən] N **1** (= *effect*) impresión *f*; **to make an ~ (on sb)** impresionar (a algn); **to make a good/bad ~ (on sb)** causar buena/mala impresión (a algn); **to make no ~ (on sth)** no tener el menor efecto (sobre algo) **2** (= *vague idea, illusion*) impresión *f*; **to be under the ~ that ...** tener la impresión de que ...; **I don't want you to get the wrong ~** no quiero que te lleves una falsa impresión **3** (*Theat*) imitación *f*; **to do ~s** hacer imitaciones

impressionable [ɪmˈpreʃnəbl] ADJ impresionable, influenciable

impressionism [ɪmˈpreʃənɪzəm] N impresionismo *m*

impressionist [ɪmˈpreʃənɪst] **Ⓐ** ADJ impresionista **Ⓑ N 1** (*Art*) impresionista *mf* **2** (*Theat*) imitador(a) *m/f*

impressive [ɪmˈpresɪv] ADJ impresionante

impressively [ɪmˈpresɪvlɪ] ADV [*play, perform*] admirablemente, extraordinariamente; **she was ~ brave** tuvo un valor admirable *or* extraordinario

imprint Ⓐ [ɪmˈprɪnt] VT **1** (= *print*) imprimir **2** (*fig*) grabar; **it was ~ed on his mind** lo tenía grabado en la mente **Ⓑ** [ˈɪmprɪnt] N (= *mark, trace*) impresión *f*, huella *f*; **under the HarperCollins ~** publicado por HarperCollins

imprison [ɪmˈprɪzn] VT encarcelar, meter en la cárcel

imprisonment [ɪmˈprɪznmənt] N (= *act*) encarcelamiento *m*; (= *term of imprisonment*) cárcel *f*, prisión *f*; **he was sentenced to ten years' ~** fue condenado a diez años de prisión; **life ~** cadena *f* perpetua

improbability [ɪmˌprɒbəˈbɪlɪtɪ] N (= *unlikelihood*) improbabilidad *f*; (= *implausibility*) inverosimilitud *f*

improbable [ɪmˈprɒbəbl] ADJ [*event*] improbable; [*excuse, story*] inverosímil; **it is ~ that it will happen** es improbable *or* poco probable que ocurra

impromptu [ɪmˈprɒmptjuː] ADJ [*performance, speech*] improvisado; [*remark*] espontáneo, impremeditado

improper [ɪmˈprɒpəʳ] ADJ **1** (= *unseemly*) [*behaviour*] indecoroso, impropio **2** (= *indecent*) [*suggestion*] deshonesto **3** (= *incorrect*) [*use*] indebido **4** (= *illicit*) [*dealings*] deshonesto

improperly [ɪmˈprɒpəlɪ] ADV (= *in unseemly way*) incorrectamente, indecorosamente, impropiamente; (= *indecently*) indecentemente; (= *incorrectly*) [*use*] indebidamente; (= *illicitly*) deshonestamente

impropriety [ˌɪmprəˈpraɪətɪ] N [*of person, behaviour*] (= *unseemliness*) incorrección *f*, falta *f* de decoro; (= *indecency*) indecencia *f*; [*of language*] impropiedad *f*; (= *illicit nature*) deshonestidad *f*

improve [ɪmˈpruːv] **Ⓐ VT 1** (= *make better*) [+ *work*] mejorar; [+ *property*] hacer mejoras en; **to ~ one's mind** cultivarse, instruirse; **to ~ one's Spanish** perfeccionar sus conocimientos del español **2** (= *increase*) [+ *production, yield*] aumentar **Ⓑ VI** [*person*] (*in skill etc*) hacer progresos; (*after illness*) mejorar(se); [*health, weather, work, quality*] mejorar; [*production, yield*] aumentar; [*business*] mejorar, prosperar; **to ~ with age** mejorar con el tiempo
➤ **improve (up)on** VI + PREP (*gen*) mejorar; **it cannot be ~d (up)on** es inmejorable; **to ~ (up)on sb's offer** ofrecer más que algn, mejorar la oferta de algn

improvement [ɪmˈpruːvmənt] N (*in quality*) mejora *f* (**in** de); (= *increase*) aumento *m* (**in** de); (= *progress*) progresos *mpl* (**in** en); **there is room for ~** podría mejorarse; **there has been some ~ in the patient's condition** el paciente ha mejorado algo; **to make ~s to** (*gen*) mejorar; [+ *property*] hacer mejoras en

improvident [ɪmˈprɒvɪdənt] ADJ [*person*] imprevisor; [*action*] carente de previsión

improvisation [ˌɪmprəvaɪˈzeɪʃən] N improvisación *f*

improvise [ˈɪmprəvaɪz] VI, VT improvisar

imprudent [ɪmˈpruːdənt] ADJ imprudente

impudence [ˈɪmpjʊdəns] N insolencia *f*, descaro *m*; **he had the ~ to say that ...** tuvo la insolencia *or* el descaro de decir que ...; **what ~!** ¡qué insolencia *or* descaro!

impudent [ˈɪmpjʊdənt] ADJ insolente

impugn [ɪmˈpjuːn] VT [+ *integrity, honesty, motives*] poner en duda; [+ *testimony*] impugnar

impulse [ˈɪmpʌls] N impulso *m*; **on ~** llevado por un impulso, impulsivamente ➤ **impulse buy** compra *f* impulsiva

impulsion [ɪmˈpʌlʃən] N impulsión *f*

impulsive [ɪmˈpʌlsɪv] ADJ [*person, temperament*] impulsivo; [*act, remark*] irreflexivo

impunity [ɪmˈpjuːnɪtɪ] N impunidad *f*; **with ~** con impunidad, impunemente

impure [ɪmˈpjʊəʳ] ADJ impuro

impurity [ɪmˈpjʊərɪtɪ] N impureza *f*

impute [ɪmˈpjuːt] VT **to ~ sth to sb** imputar *or* atribuir algo a algn

IN ABBR (*US*) = **Indiana**

in	
Ⓐ PREPOSITION	**Ⓒ** ADJECTIVE
Ⓑ ADVERB	**Ⓓ** NOUN

When **in** *is the second element in a phrasal verb, eg* **ask in**, **fill in**, **look in**, *etc, look up the verb. When it is part of a set combination, eg* **in the country**, **in danger**, **dressed in**, *look up the other word.*

in [ɪn] **Ⓐ** PREPOSITION
1 (*in expressions of place*) en; (= *inside*) dentro de; **it's in London/Scotland/Galicia** está en Londres/Escocia/Galicia; **in the garden** en el jardín; **in the house** en casa; (= *inside*) dentro de la casa; **our bags were stolen, and our passports were in them** nos robaron los bolsos, y nuestros

pasaportes iban dentro

When phrases like **in Madrid**, **in Germany** are used to identify a particular group, **de** is the usual translation:

---

our colleagues in Madrid nuestros colegas de Madrid; **in here/there** aquí/allí dentro
2 (*in expressions of time*)
2.1 (= *during*) en; **in 1986** en 1986; **in May/spring** en mayo/primavera; **in the eighties/the 20th century** en los años ochenta/el siglo 20; **in the morning(s)/evening(s)** por la mañana/la tarde; **at four o'clock in the morning/afternoon** a las cuatro de la mañana/la tarde
2.2 (= *for*) **she hasn't been here in years** hace años que no viene
2.3 (= *in the space of*) en; **I did it in three hours/days** lo hice en tres horas/días
2.4 (= *within*) dentro de; **I'll see you in three weeks' time** *or* **in three weeks** te veré dentro de tres semanas
3 (*indicating manner, medium*) en; **in a loud/soft voice** en voz alta/baja; **in Spanish/English** en español/inglés; **to pay in dollars** pagar en dólares
4 (= *clothed in*) **she opened the door in her dressing gown** abrió la puerta en bata; **they were all in shorts** todos iban en *or* llevaban pantalón corto; **you look nice in that dress** ese vestido te sienta bien

---

When phrases like **in the blue dress**, **in the glasses** are used to identify a particular person, **de** is the usual translation:

---

the man in the hat el hombre del sombrero; **the boy in the checked trousers** el chico de los pantalones de cuadros; *BUT* **the girl in green** la chica vestida de verde
5 (*giving ratio, number*) **one person in ten** una persona de cada diez; **he had only a one in fifty chance of survival** sólo tenía una posibilidad entre cincuenta de sobrevivir; **20 pence in the pound** 20 peniques por (cada) libra; **once in a hundred years** una vez cada cien años; **in twos** de dos en dos; **these jugs are produced in their millions** estas jarras se fabrican por millones, se fabrican millones de estas jarras; **people came in their hundreds** acudieron cientos de personas, la gente acudió a centenares
6 (= *among*) entre; **this is common in children/cats** es cosa común entre los niños/los gatos
7 (*talking about people*) **she has it in her to succeed** tiene la capacidad de triunfar; **it's not in him to do that** no es capaz de hacer eso; **it's something I admire in her** es algo que admiro de *or* en ella
8 (*in profession etc*) **to be in teaching** dedicarse a la enseñanza; **to be in publishing** trabajar en el mundo editorial
9 (*after superlative*) de; **the biggest/smallest in Europe** el más grande/pequeño de Europa
10 (*with verb*) **in saying this** al decir esto
11 (*in set expressions*)
✦ **in all** en total
✦ **in itself** de por sí
✦ **in that** (= *since*) puesto que, ya que
✦ **what's in it for me: I want to know what's in it for me** quiero saber qué gano yo con eso
B ADVERB
1 ✦ **to be in** (= *be at home*) estar (en casa); (= *be at work*) estar; (= *be at destination*) [*train, ship, plane*] haber llegado; (*Sport*) [*ball, shuttlecock*] entrar; **he wasn't in** no estaba (en casa); **there's nobody in** no hay nadie; **is Mr Eccles in?** ¿está el Sr. Eccles?; **the boss isn't in yet** el jefe no ha llegado aún; **he's in for tests** (*in hospital*) está ingresado para unas pruebas; **he's in for larceny** (*in prison*) está encerrado por ladrón; **what's he in for?** ¿de qué delito se le acusa?; **when the Tories were in*** (*in power*) cuando los conservadores estaban en el poder; **the essays have to be in by Friday** hay que entregar los trabajos para el viernes
✦ **to be in for sth*: he's in for a surprise** le espera una sorpresa; **you don't know what you're in for!** ¡no sabes lo que te espera!; **we're in for a hard time** vamos a pasar un mal rato; **he's in for it** lo va a pagar

✦ **to be in on sth*** (= *be aware*) **to be in on the plan/ secret** estar al tanto del plan/del secreto
✦ **to be well in with sb*** (= *be friendly*) llevarse muy bien con algn
2 (*with other verbs*) **she opened the door and they all rushed in** abrió la puerta y todos entraron *or* se metieron corriendo; **she opened her bag and put the ticket in** abrió el bolso y metió el billete
3 (*with time words*) **day in, day out** día tras día; **week in, week out** semana tras semana
4 (*Sport*) **in!** ¡entró!
C ADJECTIVE
(*) (= *fashionable*) de moda; **to be in** estar de moda, llevarse; **it's the in place to eat** es el restaurante que está de moda
D NOUN
the ins and outs of: the ins and outs of the problem los pormenores del problema; **the ins and outs of high finance** los entresijos de las altas finanzas

in. ABBR = **inch**; ⇨ *IMPERIAL SYSTEM*

inability [ˌɪnəˈbɪlɪtɪ] N incapacidad *f*; **~ to do sth** incapacidad para hacer algo

inaccessibility [ˈɪnækˌsesəˈbɪlɪtɪ] N inaccesibilidad *f*

inaccessible [ˌɪnækˈsesəbl] ADJ inaccesible; **to be ~ to sb** ser inaccesible para algn; **to be ~ to cars** resultar inaccesible en coche

inaccuracy [ɪnˈækjʊrəsɪ] N **1** (= *imprecision*) [*of figures, information*] inexactitud *f*; [*of aim, instrument, method*] falta *f* de precisión, imprecisión *f* **2** (= *mistake*) error *m*

inaccurate [ɪnˈækjʊrɪt] ADJ [*figures, information*] inexacto, erróneo; [*aim, instrument, method*] impreciso, poco preciso

inaccurately [ɪnˈækjʊrɪtlɪ] ADV **he described the event ~** su descripción del suceso fue inexacta

inaction [ɪnˈækʃən] N inacción *f*, inactividad *f*

inactive [ɪnˈæktɪv] ADJ inactivo

inactivity [ˌɪnækˈtɪvɪtɪ] N inactividad *f*

inadequacy [ɪnˈædɪkwəsɪ] N [*of resources, measures*] insuficiencia *f*; [*of person*] incompetencia *f*, ineptitud *f*; [*of system*] deficiencia *f*

inadequate [ɪnˈædɪkwɪt] ADJ [*supply, measures*] insuficiente; [*housing, diet*] inadecuado; [*person*] incompetente, inepto

inadequately [ɪnˈædɪkwɪtlɪ] ADV **the police were ~ trained** la policía no estaba lo suficientemente entrenada, la policía no había recibido el entrenamiento adecuado

inadmissible [ˌɪnədˈmɪsəbl] ADJ inadmisible

inadvertent [ˌɪnədˈvɜːtənt] ADJ [*error, oversight*] involuntario

inadvertently [ˌɪnədˈvɜːtəntlɪ] ADV sin darse cuenta, sin querer

inadvisable [ˌɪnədˈvaɪzəbl] ADJ poco aconsejable, desaconsejable

inane [ɪˈneɪn] ADJ [*remark*] necio, fatuo, sonso (*LAm*); [*laugh, task, activity*] tonto; [*expression*] (*on face*) estúpido

inanimate [ɪnˈænɪmɪt] ADJ [*object*] inanimado

inanity [ɪˈnænɪtɪ] N (= *quality*) necedad *f*

inapplicable [ɪnˈæplɪkəbl] ADJ inaplicable

inappropriate [ˌɪnəˈprəʊprɪɪt] ADJ [*action, treatment*] inadecuado, poco apropiado; [*expression*] inoportuno; [*behaviour*] impropio

inappropriately [ˌɪnəˈprəʊprɪɪtlɪ] ADV [*act*] de manera impropia; [*dressed*] de manera poco adecuada *or* apropiada

inarticulate [ˌɪnɑːˈtɪkjʊlət] ADJ [*person*] con dificultad para expresarse; [*speech*] mal pronunciado

inasmuch [ˌɪnəzˈmʌtʃ] ADV **~ as** (= *seeing that*) puesto que, ya que, en vista de que; (= *insofar as*) en la medida en que

inattention [ˌɪnəˈtenʃən] N (= *inattentiveness*) falta *f* de atención; (= *neglect*) falta *f* de interés, desinterés *m*

inattentive [ˌɪnəˈtentɪv] ADJ (= *distracted*) desatento, distraído; (= *neglectful*) poco atento

inaudible [ɪnˈɔːdəbl] ADJ inaudible; **he was almost ~** apenas se le podía oír

inaugural [ɪˈnɔːgjʊrəl] ADJ [*lecture, debate*] inaugural; [*speech*] de apertura

inaugurate [ɪˈnɔːgjʊreɪt] VT [+ *policy, new era, building*] inaugurar; (= *swear in*) [+ *president, official*] investir

inauguration [ɪˌnɔːgjʊˈreɪʃən] N (= *start*) inauguración *f*; (= *opening*) ceremonia *f* de apertura; [*of president*] investidura *f*, toma *f* de posesión ➤ **inauguration ceremony** [*of building*] ceremonia *f* de inauguración; [*of president*] ceremonia *f* de investidura *or* de toma de posesión ➤ **inauguration speech** [*of president*] discurso *m* de investidura *or* de toma de posesión

inauspicious [ˌɪnɔːsˈpɪʃəs] ADJ [*occasion*] poco propicio; [*circumstances*] desfavorable

inboard [ˈɪnbɔːd] ADJ [*engine*] interior

inborn [ˈɪnbɔːn] ADJ [*ability, talent*] innato

inbound [ˈɪnbaʊnd] ADJ [*flight*] de llegada

inbred [ˈɪnbred] ADJ (= *innate*) innato

inbreeding [ˈɪnˌbriːdɪŋ] N endogamia *f*

inbuilt [ˈɪnbɪlt] ADJ (*esp Brit*) **1** (= *innate*) [*feeling*] innato; [*prejudice*] inherente **2** (= *integral*) incorporado

Inc. ABBR (*US Comm*) (= **Incorporated**) S.A.

inc. ABBR (= **included, including, inclusive (of)**) inc.

Inca [ˈɪŋkə] Ⓐ ADJ incaico, incásico Ⓑ N (*pl* ~ *or* ~**s**) inca *mf*

incalculable [ɪnˈkælkjʊləbl] ADJ incalculable

incandescent [ˌɪnkænˈdesnt] ADJ incandescente

incantation [ˌɪnkænˈteɪʃən] N conjuro *m*

incapable [ɪnˈkeɪpəbl] ADJ **1** (= *unable*) **to be ~ of doing sth** ser incapaz de hacer algo **2** (= *incompetent*) incompetente **3** (= *helpless*) inútil

incapacitate [ˌɪnkəˈpæsɪteɪt] VT [+ *person*] incapacitar

incapacity [ˌɪnkəˈpæsɪtɪ] N incapacidad *f*

incarcerate [ɪnˈkɑːsəreɪt] VT encarcelar

incarceration [ɪnˌkɑːsəˈreɪʃən] N encarcelamiento *m*, encarcelación *f*

incarnate Ⓐ [ɪnˈkɑːnɪt] ADJ encarnado Ⓑ [ˈɪnkɑːneɪt] VT encarnar

incarnation [ˌɪnkɑːˈneɪʃən] N encarnación *f*

incendiary [ɪnˈsendɪərɪ] Ⓐ ADJ incendiario Ⓑ N (= *bomb*) bomba *f* incendiaria

incense¹ [ˈɪnsens] N incienso *m* ➤ **incense burner** incensario *m*

incense² [ɪnˈsens] VT indignar, encolerizar

incensed [ɪnˈsenst] ADJ [*person*] furioso, furibundo

incentive [ɪnˈsentɪv] N incentivo *m*, estímulo *m* ➤ **incentive bonus** prima *f* de incentivación ➤ **incentive scheme** plan *m* de incentivos

inception [ɪnˈsepʃən] N comienzo *m*, principio *m*; **from its ~** desde el comienzo *or* principio, desde los comienzos

incessant [ɪnˈsesnt] ADJ incesante, constante

incessantly [ɪnˈsesntlɪ] ADV sin cesar, incesantemente

incest [ˈɪnsest] N incesto *m*

incestuous [ɪnˈsestjʊəs] ADJ incestuoso

inch [ɪntʃ] N pulgada *f* (= *2,54 cm*); **not an ~ of territory** ni un palmo de territorio; **the car missed me by ~es** faltó poco para que me atropellara el coche; **~ by ~** palmo a palmo; **we searched every ~ of the room** registramos todos los rincones del cuarto; **every ~ of it was used** se aprovechó hasta el último centímetro; **he's every ~ a soldier** es todo un soldado; **to be within an ~ of death/disaster** estar a dos dedos de la muerte/del desastre; ✦ IDIOM **give him an ~ and he'll take a mile** dale un dedo y se toma hasta el codo; ◇ *IMPERIAL SYSTEM* ➤ **inch forward** VI + ADV avanzar muy lentamente

incidence [ˈɪnsɪdəns] N incidencia *f*

incident [ˈɪnsɪdənt] N (= *event*) incidente *m*, suceso *m*; (*in book, play etc*) episodio *m*, incidente *m*; (= *confrontation*) incidente *m*; **without ~** sin incidentes ➤ **incident room** (*Brit*) centro *m* de coordinación

incidental [ˌɪnsɪˈdentl] Ⓐ ADJ **1** (= *related*) [*benefit*] adicional; [*effect*] secundario; **~ music** música *f* de acompañamiento **2** (= *secondary, minor*) [*details*] incidental, secundario Ⓑ **incidentals** NPL (= *expenses*) (gastos *mpl*) imprevistos *mpl*

incidentally [ˌɪnsɪˈdentəlɪ] ADV a propósito, por cierto; **he spoke no English, ~** por cierto *or* a propósito, no hablaba inglés

incinerate [ɪnˈsɪnəreɪt] VT incinerar

incineration [ɪnˌsɪnəˈreɪʃən] N incineración *f*

incinerator [ɪnˈsɪnəreɪtəʳ] N incinerador *m*

incipient [ɪnˈsɪpɪənt] ADJ incipiente

incision [ɪnˈsɪʒən] N incisión *f*

incisive [ɪnˈsaɪsɪv] ADJ [*mind*] penetrante; [*remark, criticism, wit*] incisivo, mordaz

incisor [ɪnˈsaɪzəʳ] N incisivo *m*

incite [ɪnˈsaɪt] VT [+ *violence, riots, hatred*] incitar; **to ~ sb to do sth** incitar a algn a hacer algo; **to ~ sb to violence** incitar a algn a la violencia

incitement [ɪnˈsaɪtmənt] N incitación *f* (**to** a)

incivility [ˌɪnsɪˈvɪlɪtɪ] N descortesía *f*

incl. ABBR (= **included, including, inclusive (of)**) inc.

inclement [ɪnˈklemənt] ADJ inclemente

inclination [ˌɪnklɪˈneɪʃən] N **1** (= *tendency*) tendencia *f*, inclinación *f*; **his natural ~s** su tendencia *or* inclinación natural **2** (= *desire*) **I have neither the time nor the ~ to get involved** no tengo ni tiempo ni ganas de meterme en el asunto; **I decided to follow my own ~ and stay at home** decidí hacer lo que más me apetecía y quedarme en casa **3** (= *slope, bow*) inclinación *f*

incline Ⓐ [ˈɪnklaɪn] N pendiente *f*, cuesta *f* Ⓑ [ɪnˈklaɪn] VT **1** [+ *head*] bajar, inclinar **2** (= *slope*) inclinar **3** (= *dispose*) **to ~ sb to do sth** predisponer a algn a hacer algo Ⓒ [ɪnˈklaɪn] VI **1** (= *slope*) inclinarse **2** (= *tend*) **I ~ towards the opinion that ...** me inclino a pensar que ...

inclined [ɪnˈklaɪnd] ADJ **1** (= *tilted*) inclinado **2** (= *apt*) **he was ~ to be moody** tenía tendencia *or* tendía a sufrir cambios de humor, era propenso a los cambios de humor **3** (= *disposed*) **I'm ~ to believe you** estoy dispuesto a creerte; **to ~ to agree** yo me inclino a pensar lo mismo; **to be academically/artistically ~** estar dotado para los estudios/tener inclinaciones artísticas; **I didn't feel at all ~ to go out** no me apetecía nada salir, no tenía ninguna gana de salir; **if you feel so ~** si te apetece; (*more formal*) si así lo deseas

include [ɪnˈkluːd] VT incluir; (*with letter*) adjuntar, incluir; **your name is not ~d in the list** su nombre no figura en la lista; **he sold everything, books ~d** vendió todo, incluso los libros; **service is/is not ~d** el servicio está/no está *or* va/no va incluido; **myself ~d** incluido yo ➤ **include out*** VT + ADV (*hum*) excluir, dejar fuera; **~ me out!** ¡no contéis conmigo!

including [ɪnˈkluːdɪŋ] PREP **not ~ service** servicio no incluido; **$20, ~ post and packing** 20 dólares incluidos gastos de envío; **seven ~ this one** siete con éste; **everyone, ~ the President** todos, incluido el Presidente; **up to and ~ chapter seven** hasta el capítulo siete inclusive

inclusion [ɪnˈkluːʒən] N inclusión *f*

inclusive [ɪnˈkluːsɪv] Ⓐ ADJ [*sum, price*] global; **£5,000 fully ~** 5.000 libras con todo incluido; **~ of postage and packing** incluidos los gastos de envío; **to be ~ of sth** incluir algo Ⓑ ADV **from the 10th to the 15th ~** del 10 al 15, ambos inclusive *or* ambos incluidos

incognito [ɪnˈkɒgnɪtəʊ] Ⓐ ADV [*travel*] de incógnito Ⓑ ADJ **to remain ~** permanecer en el anonimato

incoherence [ˌɪnkəʊˈhɪərəns] N incoherencia *f*, falta *f* de coherencia

incoherent [ˌɪnkəʊˈhɪərənt] ADJ incoherente; **he was ~ with rage** estaba tan furioso que casi no podía hablar, balbuceaba de rabia

incoherently [ˌɪnkəʊˈhɪərəntlɪ] ADV [*mumble, ramble, argue, write*] de forma incoherente; [*speak*] con incoherencia, incoherentemente

income ['ɪnkʌm] N (gen) ingresos mpl; (from property) renta f; **private ~** rentas fpl ➤ **income bracket, income group** categoría f económica ➤ **incomes policy** política f salarial or de salarios ➤ **income support** (Brit) ≈ ayuda f compensatoria ➤ **income tax** impuesto m sobre la renta ➤ **income tax return** declaración f de impuestos or de la renta

incoming ['ɪn,kʌmɪŋ] ADJ [passenger, flight] que llega/ llegaba; [president] entrante; **all ~ calls are monitored** todas las llamadas que se reciben están sujetas a control

incommunicado [,ɪnkəmjʊnɪ'kɑːdəʊ] ADJ incomunicado

incomparable [ɪn'kɒmpərəbl] ADJ [beauty, skill] incomparable, sin par; [achievement] inigualable, sin par

incomparably [ɪn'kɒmpərəblɪ] ADV incomparablemente

incompatibility ['ɪnkəm,pætə'bɪlɪtɪ] N incompatibilidad f

incompatible [,ɪnkəm'pætəbl] ADJ incompatible (**with** con)

incompetence [ɪn'kɒmpɪtəns] N incompetencia f

incompetent [ɪn'kɒmpɪtənt] ADJ incompetente

incomplete [,ɪnkəm'pliːt] ADJ incompleto

incomprehensible [ɪn,kɒmprɪ'hensəbl] ADJ incomprensible; **it is ~ to me** me resulta incomprensible

incomprehension [,ɪnkɒmprɪ'henʃən] N incomprensión f

inconceivable [,ɪnkən'siːvəbl] ADJ inconcebible

inconclusive [,ɪnkən'kluːsɪv] ADJ [result, evidence] no concluyente; (= not convincing) [argument] no convincente

incongruity [,ɪnkɒŋ'gruːɪtɪ] N incongruencia f

incongruous [ɪn'kɒŋgrʊəs] ADJ incongruente; **it seems ~ that ...** parece extraño que ...

inconsequential [ɪn,kɒnsɪ'kwenʃəl] ADJ [conversation] sin trascendencia

inconsiderable [,ɪnkən'sɪdərəbl] ADJ **a not ~ sum** una cifra nada desdeñable or despreciable, una suma considerable

inconsiderate [,ɪnkən'sɪdərɪt] ADJ [behaviour, person] desconsiderado; **to be ~ to sb** no tener consideración con algn

inconsistency [,ɪnkən'sɪstənsɪ] N [of behaviour] carácter m contradictorio or incongruente; [of statement, account, evidence, policy] falta f de coherencia

inconsistent [,ɪnkən'sɪstənt] ADJ 1 [person] inconsecuente, voluble; [quality, work] irregular, desigual 2 (= contradictory) [statement, account, evidence] contradictorio; **to be ~ with sth** (= contradict) contradecir algo, no concordar con algo; (= not correspond with) no encajar con algo, no concordar con algo

inconsolable [,ɪnkən'səʊləbl] ADJ inconsolable

inconspicuous [,ɪnkən'spɪkjʊəs] ADJ [person] que no llama la atención; **she tried to make herself ~** trató de no llamar la atención or de pasar desapercibida

inconspicuously [,ɪnkən'spɪkjʊəslɪ] ADV discretamente

incontinence [ɪn'kɒntɪnəns] N incontinencia f

incontinent [ɪn'kɒntɪnənt] ADJ incontinente

incontrovertible [ɪn,kɒntrə'vɜːtəbl] ADJ incontrovertible

inconvenience [,ɪnkən'viːnɪəns] Ⓐ N 1 [of time, location] inconveniencia f; [of arrangements, house] incomodidad f 2 (= drawback) inconveniente m 3 (= trouble) molestias fpl, inconvenientes mpl; **to put sb to great ~** causar muchas molestias or muchos inconvenientes a algn Ⓑ VT (= cause problems to) causar molestias a; (= disturb) molestar; **I'm sorry to ~ you, but ...** perdone que lo moleste, pero ...

inconvenient [,ɪnkən'viːnɪənt] ADJ [time, appointment] inoportuno; [location, design] poco práctico, incómodo; **to be ~ for sb** venir mal a algn; (more formal) resultar inconveniente a algn

incorporate [ɪn'kɔːpəreɪt] VT (= include) incluir, comprender; (= integrate) incorporar (**in, into** a)

incorporated [ɪn'kɔːpəreɪtɪd] ADJ (US Comm) **Jones & Lloyd Incorporated** Jones y Lloyd Sociedad Anónima

incorrect [,ɪnkə'rekt] ADJ 1 (= wrong) [answer, spelling]

incorrecto; [information, statement, assumption] erróneo 2 (= bad) [diet] incorrecto, inadecuado

incorrectly [,ɪnkə'rektlɪ] ADV [spell, answer] mal, incorrectamente; [inform] mal, erróneamente; [behave] incorrectamente

incorrigible [ɪn'kɒrɪdʒəbl] ADJ incorregible, sin remedio

increase Ⓐ [ɪn'kriːs] VI aumentar; **to ~ in weight/value** aumentar de peso/valor Ⓑ [ɪn'kriːs] VT aumentar; **to ~ one's efforts** redoblar sus esfuerzos; **there has been an ~d interest in his work** ha aumentado el interés por su trabajo Ⓒ ['ɪnkriːs] N aumento m; **an ~ in size/volume** un aumento de tamaño/volumen; **to be on the ~** estar or ir en aumento

increasing [ɪn'kriːsɪŋ] ADJ [number, amount] creciente, cada vez mayor; **the president is under ~ pressure to resign** el presidente recibe cada vez más presiones para presentar la dimisión

increasingly [ɪn'kriːsɪŋlɪ] ADV cada vez más; **Spanish food is becoming ~ popular** la comida española se está volviendo cada vez más popular or está alcanzando una popularidad cada vez mayor

incredible [ɪn'kredəbl] ADJ increíble; **they found it ~ that I was still alive** les pareció increíble que todavía estuviera viva; **~ though it may seem** por increíble que parezca, aunque parezca mentira

incredibly [ɪn'kredəblɪ] ADV [ugly, rich, intelligent] increíblemente; **it all happened ~ fast** todo sucedió con una rapidez increíble

incredulity [,ɪnkrɪ'djuːlɪtɪ] N incredulidad f

incredulous [ɪn'kredjʊləs] ADJ [expression] de incredulidad; **I was ~** no lo creí

incredulously [ɪn'kredjʊləslɪ] ADV con incredulidad

increment ['ɪnkrɪmənt] N aumento m, incremento m (**in** de)

incremental [ɪnkrɪ'mentəl] ADJ [change, process] gradual; [costs] incremental

incriminate [ɪn'krɪmɪneɪt] VT incriminar

incriminating [ɪn'krɪmɪneɪtɪŋ] ADJ incriminatorio

incrimination [ɪn,krɪmɪ'neɪʃən] N incriminación f

in-crowd* ['ɪn,kraʊd] N grupo m exclusivista or excluyente, camarilla f; **to be in with the ~** ser amigo de los que cortan el bacalao*

incubate ['ɪnkjʊbeɪt] Ⓐ VT incubar Ⓑ VI incubarse

incubation [,ɪnkjʊ'beɪʃən] N incubación f ➤ **incubation period** período m de incubación

incubator ['ɪnkjʊbeɪtə'] N incubadora f

inculcate ['ɪnkʌlkeɪt] VT **to ~ sth in sb** inculcar algo a algn

incumbent [ɪn'kʌmbənt] Ⓐ ADJ **to be ~ on sb to do sth** incumbir a algn hacer algo Ⓑ N titular mf, poseedor(a) m/f (de un cargo o dignidad)

incur [ɪn'kɜː'] VT [+ debt, obligation] contraer; [+ expense, charges] incurrir en; [+ loss] sufrir; [+ anger] provocar

incurable [ɪn'kjʊərəbl] Ⓐ ADJ 1 (Med) incurable 2 [optimist, romantic] incorregible Ⓑ N incurable mf

incurably [ɪn'kjʊərəblɪ] ADV **to be ~ ill** tener una enfermedad incurable; **to be ~ romantic/optimistic** ser un romántico/optimista incurable or incorregible

incursion [ɪn'kɜːʃən] N incursión f

Ind. ABBR (US) = **Indiana**

indebted [ɪn'detɪd] ADJ 1 (= owing money) endeudado 2 (= grateful) **I am ~ to you for your help** estoy muy agradecido por su ayuda

indebtedness [ɪn'detɪdnɪs] N 1 (Fin) endeudamiento m, deuda f (**to** con) 2 (fig) deuda f (**to** con)

indecency [ɪn'diːsnsɪ] N indecencia f

indecent [ɪn'diːsnt] ADJ indecente; **to make an ~ suggestion** sugerir algo indecente ➤ **indecent assault** (Jur) abusos mpl deshonestos ➤ **indecent exposure** exhibicionismo m

indecently [ɪn'diːsntlɪ] ADV indecentemente, de una forma indecente; **to ~ assault sb** realizar abusos deshonestos de algn; **to ~ expose o.s.** cometer un acto de exhibicionismo

indecipherable [ˌɪndɪˈsaɪfərəbl] ADJ indescifrable

indecision [ˌɪndɪˈsɪʒən] N indecisión *f*, falta *f* de decisión, irresolución *f (frm)*

indecisive [ˌɪndɪˈsaɪsɪv] ADJ **1** (= *hesitant*) indeciso **2** (= *inconclusive*) no concluyente, no decisivo

indecisively [ˌɪndɪˈsaɪsɪvlɪ] ADV (= *hesitantly*) con indecisión

indeed [ɪnˈdiːd] ADV **1** (= *in fact*) de hecho; **if ~ he is wrong** si es que realmente se equivoca, si efectivamente se equivoca; **the document was ~ missing** efectivamente el documento había desaparecido; **it is ~ true that …** es en efecto verdad que …
2 (*as intensifier*) **that is praise ~** eso es todo un elogio, eso sí es una alabanza; **to be very good ~** ser verdaderamente *or* realmente bueno; **you're doing very well ~** vas realmente bien; **we are taking the matter very seriously ~** nos estamos tomando la cuestión sumamente en serio *or* pero que muy en serio; **thank you very much ~** muchísimas gracias
3 (*in answer to a question*) **"isn't it a beautiful day?" — "yes, ~!"** —¿a que es un día precioso? —¡desde luego! *or* —¡y que lo digas! *or* —¡ya lo creo!; **"did you know him?" — "I did ~"** —¿lo conocías? —sí que lo conocía *or* —claro que sí; **"are you Professor Ratburn?" — "I am ~"** —¿es usted el profesor Ratburn? —sí, señor *or* —el mismo
4 (*expressing interest*) **indeed?** ◇ **did you ~?** ¿de veras?, ¿de verdad?, ¿ah, sí?
5 (*expressing disbelief, surprise, scorn*) **"he said he would do it" — "did he ~?"** —dijo que lo haría —¿eso dijo? *or* —¡no me digas?

indefatigable [ˌɪndɪˈfætɪgəbl] ADJ incansable, infatigable

indefensible [ˌɪndɪˈfensəbl] ADJ [*conduct, action*] injustificable, inexcusable; [*idea, policy, town*] indefendible

indefinable [ˌɪndɪˈfaɪnəbl] ADJ indefinible

indefinite [ɪnˈdefɪnɪt] ❶ ADJ **1** (= *vague*) [*answer*] impreciso; **our plans are somewhat ~ as yet** nuestros planes están todavía por concretar **2** (= *not fixed*) [*time*] indefinido, indeterminado **3** (*Gram*) indefinido ❷ CPD ➤ **indefinite article** artículo *m* indefinido ➤ **indefinite pronoun** pronombre *m* indefinido

indefinitely [ɪnˈdefɪnɪtlɪ] ADV por tiempo indefinido

indelible [ɪnˈdeləbl] ADJ indeleble

indelicate [ɪnˈdelɪkɪt] ADJ (= *tactless*) indiscreto, falto de tacto; (= *crude*) indelicado

indemnify [ɪnˈdemnɪfaɪ] VT **1** (= *compensate*) **to ~ sb for sth** indemnizar a algn por algo **2** (= *safeguard*) **to ~ sb against sth** asegurar a algn contra algo

indemnity [ɪnˈdemnɪtɪ] N (= *compensation*) indemnización *f*, reparación *f*; (= *insurance*) indemnidad *f*

indent [ɪnˈdent] VT [+ *word, line*] sangrar

indentation [ˌɪndenˈteɪʃən] N (= *dent*) (*in wood, metal*) hendidura *f*; (*Typ*) sangría *f*

independence [ˌɪndɪˈpendəns] N independencia *f*
➤ **Independence Day** Día *m* de la Independencia

INDEPENDENCE DAY

El cuatro de julio, Día de la Independencia (**Independence Day**), es la fiesta nacional más importante de Estados Unidos y se celebra para conmemorar el aniversario de la Declaración de Independencia en 1776. Como una auténtica fiesta de cumpleaños del país, las celebraciones presentan un marcado carácter patriótico y la bandera nacional ondea en las casas de muchos norteamericanos, a la vez que tienen lugar acontecimientos públicos por todo el país, con fuegos artificiales, desfiles y comidas en el campo.

---

independent [ˌɪndɪˈpendənt] ADJ [*person, country, inquiry*] independiente; [*income*] propio; [*sector, radio*] privado; **you are advised to seek an ~ opinion** le aconsejamos que se haga asesorar por un tercero ➤ **independent school** (*Brit*) escuela *f* privada, colegio *m* privado

independently [ˌɪndɪˈpendəntlɪ] ADV **1** (= *self-reliantly*) [*live*] independientemente; [*act*] por su cuenta; **each child will work ~** cada niño trabajará de forma independiente *or* por su cuenta *or* sólo; **he behaves very ~** es muy independiente; **~ of sth/sb** independientemente de algo/algn **2** (= *separately*) por separado

in-depth [ˈɪnˌdepθ] ADJ [*study*] a fondo, exhaustivo

indescribable [ˌɪndɪsˈkraɪbəbl] ADJ indescriptible

indescribably [ˌɪndɪsˈkraɪbəblɪ] ADV indescriptiblemente; **~ bad** indescriptiblemente malo

indestructible [ˌɪndɪsˈtrʌktəbl] ADJ indestructible

indeterminable [ˌɪndɪˈtɜːmɪnəbl] ADJ indeterminable

indeterminate [ˌɪndɪˈtɜːmɪnɪt] ADJ indeterminado

index [ˈɪndeks] ❶ N (*pl* ~**es**) (*in book*) índice *m* **2** (*pl* ~**es** *or* **indices**) (*Econ*) índice *m*; **cost of living ~** índice *m* del costo de la vida ❷ VT (= *put index in*) [+ *book*] poner índice a ❸ CPD ➤ **index card** ficha *f* ➤ **index finger** dedo *m* índice

index-linked [ˌɪndeksˈlɪŋkt] ADJ (*esp Brit*) indexado, indiciado

India [ˈɪndɪə] N India *f*; *ver tb* **http://goidirectory.nic.in** ➤ **India rubber** caucho *m*

Indian [ˈɪndɪən] ❶ ADJ (= *from India*) indio, hindú; (= *American Indian*) indígena, indio ❷ N (*from India*) indio/a *m/f*, hindú *mf*; (= *American Indian*) indígena *mf*, indio/a *m/f* ❸ CPD ➤ **Indian elephant** elefante *m* asiático ➤ **Indian ink** tinta *f* china ➤ **the Indian Ocean** el Océano Índico ➤ **Indian summer** (*in northern hemisphere*) veranillo *m* de San Martín; (*in southern hemisphere*) veranillo *m* de San Juan

indicate [ˈɪndɪkeɪt] ❶ VT **1** (= *point out*) [+ *place*] indicar, señalar; [+ *temperature, speed*] marcar **2** (= *show, suggest*) [+ *change*] ser indicio de **3** (= *gesture*) indicar; **he ~d that I was to sit down** me indicó que me sentara **4** (= *recommend, require*) **in this particular case, surgery is not ~d** en este caso en particular no es aconsejable operar ❷ VI (*esp Brit*) indicar, señalizar; **to ~ left/right** indicar *or* señalizar a la izquierda/derecha

indication [ˌɪndɪˈkeɪʃən] N **1** (= *sign*) indicio *m*; **there is every ~ that …** todo hace suponer que …; **there is no ~ that …** no hay indicios de que …; **this is some ~ of …** esto da una idea de … **2** (*Med*) indicación *f*

indicative [ɪnˈdɪkətɪv] ❶ ADJ **1 to be ~ of sth** ser indicio de algo **2** (*Gram*) indicativo ❷ N (*Gram*) indicativo *m*

indicator [ˈɪndɪkeɪtər] N (*gen*) indicador *m*; **indicators** (*esp Brit Aut*) intermitentes *mpl*, direccionales *mpl* (*LAm*)

indices [ˈɪndɪsiːz] NPL *of* **index**

indict [ɪnˈdaɪt] VT (*US Jur*) (= *charge*) acusar

indictable [ɪnˈdaɪtəbl] ADJ **~ offence** delito *m* procesable

indictment [ɪnˈdaɪtmənt] N (= *charge, document*) acusación *f*; (= *act*) procesamiento *m*; **to bring an ~ against sb** formular cargos contra algn; **the report is an ~ of our system** el informe critica durante nuestro sistema

indie* [ˈɪndɪ] ADJ (*Brit Mus*) [*music, band*] independiente

Indies [ˈɪndɪz] NPL *see* **East D, West D**

indifference [ɪnˈdɪfrəns] N indiferencia *f* (**to** ante)

indifferent [ɪnˈdɪfrənt] ADJ **1** (= *uninterested, unmoved*) indiferente; **he seemed ~ to what was happening** parecía que lo que ocurría le resultaba indiferente **2** (= *mediocre*) mediocre, regular **3** (= *unimportant*) **it is ~ to me** me es igual *or* indiferente

indifferently [ɪnˈdɪfrəntlɪ] ADV **1** (= *uninterestedly, unsympathetically*) con indiferencia **2** (= *in a mediocre way*) regularmente

indigenous [ɪnˈdɪdʒɪnəs] ADJ indígena, autóctono; **the elephant is ~ to India** el elefante es autóctono de India

indigestible [ˌɪndɪˈdʒestəbl] ADJ **1** (= *difficult to digest*) indigesto **2** (*information, style, wording*) difícil de digerir

indigestion [ˌɪndɪˈdʒestʃən] N indigestión *f*; **lentils give me ~** las lentejas me resultan indigestas

indignant [ɪnˈdɪgnənt] ADJ [*person, mood, tone*] indignado; **to be ~ at/about sth** estar indignado ante/por algo; **to become ~** indignarse

indignantly [ɪnˈdɪgnəntlɪ] ADV con indignación; **"that's not true," she said ~** —eso no es verdad —dijo indignada *or* con indignación

indignation [ˌɪndɪgˈneɪʃən] N indignación *f*

indignity [ɪnˈdɪgnɪtɪ] N indignidad *f*, humillación *f*

indigo [ˈɪndɪgəʊ] **Ⓐ** N (= *colour*) añil *m*, índigo *m* **Ⓑ** ADJ añil *inv*, índigo *inv* **Ⓒ** CPD ➤ **indigo blue** azul *m* añil *or* índigo

indirect [ˌɪndɪˈrekt] ADJ indirecto; **in an ~ way** de una forma indirecta ➤ **indirect discourse** (*US*) estilo *m* indirecto ➤ **indirect lighting** iluminación *f* indirecta ➤ **indirect object** objeto *m* or complemento *m* indirecto ➤ **indirect question** (*esp Brit*) oración *f* interrogativa indirecta ➤ **indirect speech** (*esp Brit*) estilo *m* indirecto

indirectly [ˌɪndɪˈrektlɪ] ADV indirectamente

indiscernible [ˌɪndɪˈsɜːnəbl] ADJ imperceptible

indiscreet [ˌɪndɪsˈkriːt] ADJ indiscreto

indiscreetly [ˌɪndɪsˈkriːtlɪ] ADV indiscretamente

indiscretion [ˌɪndɪsˈkreʃən] N indiscreción *f*

indiscriminate [ˌɪndɪsˈkrɪmɪnɪt] ADJ [*killing, violence, use*] indiscriminado; [*person*] falto de discernimiento

indiscriminately [ˌɪndɪsˈkrɪmɪnɪtlɪ] ADV [*kill*] indiscriminadamente; [*use, view, read*] sin discernimiento, de forma indiscriminada

indispensable [ˌɪndɪsˈpensəbl] ADJ imprescindible, indispensable; **to be ~ to sth/sb** ser indispensable para algo/algn

indisposed [ˌɪndɪsˈpəʊzd] ADJ (= *ill*) indispuesto; (= *disinclined*) poco dispuesto (**to do sth** a hacer algo)

indisputable [ˌɪndɪsˈpjuːtəbl] ADJ [*evidence*] irrefutable; [*fact*] incuestionable; [*winner*] indiscutible

indisputably [ˌɪndɪsˈpjuːtəblɪ] ADV indiscutiblemente

indissoluble [ˌɪndɪˈsɒljʊbl] ADJ indisoluble

indistinct [ˌɪndɪsˈtɪŋkt] ADJ [*voice, noise*] indistinto; (= *blurred*) [*figure, shape, outline*] poco definido, borroso

indistinctly [ˌɪndɪsˈtɪŋktlɪ] ADV [*hear*] con poca claridad; [*see*] con poca claridad, borrosamente

indistinguishable [ˌɪndɪsˈtɪŋgwɪʃəbl] ADJ indistinguible (**from** de)

individual [ˌɪndɪˈvɪdjʊəl] **Ⓐ** ADJ **1** (= *separate*) individual **2** (= *personal*) [*tastes*] personal; **the constitution respects ~ rights** la constitución respeta los derechos del individuo; **the programme is tailored to your ~ needs** el programa se adapta a sus necesidades particulares **3** (= *distinctive*) personal; **he has a very ~ style** tiene un estilo muy personal *or* original **Ⓑ** N individuo *m*

individualist [ˌɪndɪˈvɪdjʊəlɪst] N individualista *mf*

individualistic [ˈɪndɪˌvɪdjʊəˈlɪstɪk] ADJ individualista

individuality [ˌɪndɪˌvɪdjʊˈælɪtɪ] N individualidad *f*

individually [ˌɪndɪˈvɪdjʊəlɪ] ADV **1** (= *separately*) por separado **2** (= *for each individual*) **an ~ designed exercise programme** un programa de ejercicios diseñado según las necesidades de cada individuo

indivisible [ˌɪndɪˈvɪzəbl] ADJ indivisible

Indo-China [ˈɪndəʊˈtʃaɪnə] N Indochina *f*

indoctrinate [ɪnˈdɒktrɪneɪt] VT adoctrinar (**with, in** en)

indoctrination [ɪnˌdɒktrɪˈneɪʃən] N adoctrinamiento *m*

Indo-European [ˈɪndəʊˌjʊərəˈpiːən] ADJ, N indoeuropeo/a *m/f*

indolence [ˈɪndələns] N indolencia *f*

indolent [ˈɪndələnt] ADJ indolente

indomitable [ɪnˈdɒmɪtəbl] ADJ indómito, indomable

Indonesia [ˌɪndəʊˈniːzɪə] N Indonesia *f*

Indonesian [ˌɪndəʊˈniːzɪən] ADJ, N indonesio/a *m/f*

indoor [ˈɪndɔːʳ] ADJ [*shoes*] para estar por casa; [*plant*] de interior; [*stadium, pool*] cubierto; [*photography*] de interiores ➤ **indoor aerial** antena *f* interior ➤ **indoor games** deportes *mpl* de interior

indoors [ɪnˈdɔːz] ADV dentro; **what's it like ~?** ¿cómo es por dentro?; **to go ~** entrar (en la casa)

indubitable [ɪnˈdjuːbɪtəbl] ADJ indudable

indubitably [ɪnˈdjuːbɪtəblɪ] ADV indudablemente, sin duda

induce [ɪnˈdjuːs] VT **1** (= *persuade*) inducir, persuadir; **to ~ sb to do sth** inducir *or* persuadir a algn a hacer algo **2** (= *cause*) [+ *sleep*] producir, inducir **3** (*Med*) [+ *birth*] inducir; **I was ~d** me tuvieron que provocar el parto

inducement [ɪnˈdjuːsmənt] N incentivo *m*, aliciente *m*

induct [ɪnˈdʌkt] VT (*Rel*) instalar; [+ *new member*] iniciar (**into** en); (*US Mil*) reclutar

induction [ɪnˈdʌkʃən] N (*Rel*) instalación *f*; [*of new member, worker*] iniciación *f* (**into** en); (*US Mil*) reclutamiento *m*; (*Med, Philos*) inducción *f* ➤ **induction course** curso *m* or cursillo *m* introductorio

inductive [ɪnˈdʌktɪv] ADJ [*reasoning*] inductivo

indulge [ɪnˈdʌldʒ] **Ⓐ** VT (= *give in to*) [+ *desire, appetite*] satisfacer; [+ *person*] complacer; (= *spoil*) [+ *child*] mimar, consentir; **to ~ o.s.** darse un gusto; **go on, ~ yourself!** venga, ¡date ese gustazo *or* capricho!* **Ⓑ** VI **to ~ in** permitirse

indulgence [ɪnˈdʌldʒəns] N **1** [*of desire, appetite*] satisfacción *f* **2** (= *spoiling*) complacencia *f* **3** (= *tolerance*) indulgencia *f*; **she was treated with great ~ as a child** cuando era niña la trataban con mucha indulgencia *or* estaba muy consentida **4** (= *luxury item*) lujo *m*

indulgent [ɪnˈdʌldʒənt] ADJ indulgente; **to be ~ to sb** consentir a algn, ser indulgente con algn

industrial [ɪnˈdʌstrɪəl] ADJ industrial ➤ **industrial accident** accidente *m* laboral *or* de trabajo ➤ **industrial action** (*esp Brit*) medidas *fpl* de presión *or* protesta laboral; **to take ~ action** tomar medidas de presión *or* protesta laboral ➤ **industrial dispute** (*Brit*) conflicto *m* laboral ➤ **industrial engineering** ingeniería *f* industrial ➤ **industrial estate** (*Brit*), **industrial park** (*US*) zona *f* or (*Sp*) polígono *m* industrial ➤ **industrial relations** relaciones *fpl* laborales ➤ **Industrial Revolution** Revolución *f* Industrial ➤ **industrial tribunal** magistratura *f* de trabajo, tribunal *m* laboral ➤ **industrial unrest** agitación *f* obrera, conflictos *mpl* laborales

industrialist [ɪnˈdʌstrɪəlɪst] N industrial *mf*

industrialization [ɪnˌdʌstrɪəlaɪˈzeɪʃən] N industrialización *f*

industrialize [ɪnˈdʌstrɪəlaɪz] VT [+ *area, region*] industrializar

industrious [ɪnˈdʌstrɪəs] ADJ (= *hardworking*) trabajador, laborioso; (= *studious*) aplicado, diligente

industriously [ɪnˈdʌstrɪəslɪ] ADV [*work*] laboriosamente; [*study*] con aplicación

industry [ˈɪndəstrɪ] N industria *f*; **the steel/coal/textile ~** la industria siderúrgica/minera/textil; **the banking/insurance/ hotel ~** el sector bancario/de seguros/hotelero; **the tourist ~** el turismo; **a career in ~** una carrera en el sector empresarial

inebriated [ɪˈniːbrɪeɪtɪd] ADJ ebrio

inedible [ɪnˈedɪbl] ADJ (= *unpleasant*) incomible; (= *poisonous*) no comestible

ineffective [ˌɪnɪˈfektɪv] ADJ [*measure, policy, drug*] ineficaz; [*person, committee*] incompetente, ineficaz; [*effort, attempt*] infructuoso; **to be ~ in doing sth** [*law, measure, drug*] ser ineficaz a la hora de hacer algo; [*person, committee*] ser incompetente *or* carecer de eficacia a la hora de hacer algo

ineffectual [ˌɪnɪˈfektjʊəl] ADJ inútil

inefficacy [ɪnˈefɪkəsɪ] N ineficacia *f*

inefficiency [ˌɪnɪˈfɪʃənsɪ] N [*of method*] ineficiencia *f*; [*of person*] incompetencia *f*

inefficient [ˌɪnɪˈfɪʃənt] ADJ [*method*] ineficiente; [*person*] incompetente; [*factory, mine, industry*] poco productivo

inefficiently [ˌɪnɪˈfɪʃəntlɪ] ADV de forma ineficaz

inelegant [ɪnˈelɪgənt] ADJ poco elegante, inelegante

ineligible [ɪnˈelɪdʒəbl] ADJ inelegible; **to be ~ for sth** (*for candidacy, competition*) ser inelegible para algo; **I was ~ for unemployment benefit** no tenía derecho a cobrar el desempleo; **to be ~ to vote** no tener derecho al voto

inept [ɪ'nept] ADJ [*person*] inepto, incapaz; [*performance*] malo

ineptitude [ɪ'neptɪtjuːd], **ineptness** [ɪ'neptnɪs] N [*of person*] ineptitud *f*, incapacidad *f*

inequality [ˌɪnɪ'kwɒlɪtɪ] N desigualdad *f*; ~ **of wealth/ between nations** la desigualdad en el reparto de la riqueza/ entre naciones

inequitable [ɪn'ekwɪtəbl] ADJ no equitativo

inert [ɪ'nɜːt] ADJ inerte

inertia [ɪ'nɜːʃə] N inercia *f*

inescapable [ˌɪnɪs'keɪpəbl] ADJ [*duty*] ineludible; [*result, conclusion*] inevitable; [*fact*] que no se puede ignorar

inestimable [ɪn'estɪməbl] ADJ [*value, benefit*] inapreciable, inestimable; [*harm*] incalculable

inevitability [ɪnˌevɪtə'bɪlɪtɪ] N inevitabilidad *f*

inevitable [ɪn'evɪtəbl] Ⓐ ADJ inevitable; **it was ~ that he would refuse** era inevitable que se negara Ⓑ N **the ~** lo inevitable

inevitably [ɪn'evɪtəblɪ] ADV inevitablemente, forzosamente

inexact [ˌɪnɪg'zækt] ADJ inexacto

inexcusable [ˌɪnɪks'kjuːzəbl] ADJ imperdonable, inexcusable

inexcusably [ˌɪnɪks'kjuːzəblɪ] ADV [*behave*] de modo inexcusable, de modo imperdonable

inexhaustible [ˌɪnɪg'zɔːstəbl] ADJ inagotable

inexorable [ɪn'eksərəbl] ADJ inexorable, implacable

inexorably [ɪn'eksərəblɪ] ADV inexorablemente, implacablemente

inexpensive [ˌɪnɪks'pensɪv] ADJ económico

inexperience [ˌɪnɪks'pɪərɪəns] N inexperiencia *f*, falta *f* de experiencia

inexperienced [ˌɪnɪks'pɪərɪənst] ADJ [*player, team, pilot, driver*] inexperto, falto de experiencia; [*staff*] sin experiencia; **to be ~ in sth/doing sth** no tener experiencia en algo/hacer algo

inexplicable [ˌɪnɪks'plɪkəbl] ADJ inexplicable

inexplicably [ˌɪnɪks'plɪkəblɪ] ADV inexplicablemente

inexpressible [ˌɪnɪks'presəbl] ADJ [*feelings, thoughts*] inexpresable; [*joy, beauty, sorrow*] inefable, indescriptible

inexpressive [ˌɪnɪks'presɪv] ADJ inexpresivo

inextricable [ˌɪnɪks'trɪkəbl] ADJ inextricable, inseparable

inextricably [ˌɪnɪks'trɪkəblɪ] ADV inextricablemente

infallibility [ɪnˌfælə'bɪlɪtɪ] N infalibilidad *f*; **Papal ~** la infalibilidad del Papa

infallible [ɪn'fæləbl] ADJ infalible

infamous ['ɪnfəməs] ADJ infame; **to be ~ for sth** ser infame por algo

infamy ['ɪnfəmɪ] N infamia *f*

infancy ['ɪnfənsɪ] N infancia *f*, niñez *f*; **from ~** desde niño, desde muy pequeño; **the project is still in its ~** el proyecto está todavía en mantillas

infant ['ɪnfənt] N niño/a *m/f* ➤ **infant class** (*Brit*) clase *f* de párvulos ➤ **infant mortality** mortandad *f or* mortalidad *f* infantil ➤ **infant school** (*Brit*) *centro de educación primaria (primer ciclo)*

infanticide [ɪn'fæntɪsaɪd] N (= *act*) infanticidio *m*

infantile ['ɪnfəntaɪl] ADJ infantil

infantry ['ɪnfəntrɪ] N infantería *f*

infantryman ['ɪnfəntrɪmən] N (*pl* **infantrymen**) soldado *m* de infantería

infatuated [ɪn'fætjʊeɪtɪd] ADJ **to be ~ with sb** estar encaprichado con algn; **to become ~ with sb/sth** encapricharse con algn/algo

infatuation [ɪnˌfætjʊ'eɪʃən] N encaprichamiento *m*

infect [ɪn'fekt] VT [+ *wound, foot*] infectar; [+ *person*] contagiar; [+ *food*] contaminar; **to ~ sb with sth** contagiar algo a algn (*also fig*); **to become** *or* **get ~ed** [*wound, eye*] infectarse

infection [ɪn'fekʃən] N 1 (= *illness*) infección *f* 2 (= *process*) contagio *m*; **the risk of ~** el riesgo de contagio

infectious [ɪn'fekʃəs] ADJ 1 [*disease*] infeccioso, contagioso; **he is no longer ~** ya le ha pasado el periodo de contagio 2 (*fig*) [*person, laugh, enthusiasm, rhythm*] contagioso

infer [ɪn'fɜːʳ] VT 1 (= *deduce*) inferir, deducir (**from** de) 2 (*) (= *imply*) insinuar; **what are you ~ring?** ¿qué estás insinuando?

inference ['ɪnfərəns] N deducción *f*, inferencia *f*; **by ~** por deducción; **to draw ~s** sacar conclusiones

inferior [ɪn'fɪərɪəʳ] Ⓐ ADJ (*gen*) inferior; [*product, work, service*] de calidad inferior; **to be ~ to sth/sb** ser inferior a algo/algn Ⓑ N inferior *mf*

inferiority [ɪnˌfɪərɪ'ɒrɪtɪ] N inferioridad *f* (**to sth/sb** frente a *or* con respecto a algo/algn); ➤ **inferiority complex** complejo *m* de inferioridad

infernal [ɪn'fɜːnl] ADJ infernal

inferno [ɪn'fɜːnəʊ] N (= *hell*) infierno *m*; **a blazing ~** una hoguera; **it's like an ~ in there** allí dentro hace un calor insoportable

infertile [ɪn'fɜːtaɪl] ADJ [*land, soil*] yermo, infecundo; [*person, animal*] estéril

infertility [ˌɪnfɜː'tɪlɪtɪ] N [*of land, soil*] infecundidad *f*; [*of person, animal*] esterilidad *f*

infest [ɪn'fest] VT infestar; **to be ~ed with sth** estar infestado *or* plagado de algo

infidelity [ˌɪnfɪ'delɪtɪ] N infidelidad *f* (**to** a)

infighting* ['ɪnfaɪtɪŋ] N (*in organization*) lucha *f* interna; **political ~** peleas *fpl* políticas

infiltrate ['ɪnfɪltreɪt] Ⓐ VT [+ *organization*] infiltrarse en, infiltrar; **to ~ sb into sth** infiltrar a algn en algo Ⓑ VI infiltrarse

infiltration [ˌɪnfɪl'treɪʃən] N infiltración *f*

infiltrator ['ɪnfɪltreɪtəʳ] N infiltrado/a *m/f*

infinite ['ɪnfɪnɪt] Ⓐ ADJ infinito; **he took ~ pains over it** lo hizo con el mayor esmero; **an ~ amount of time/money** una infinidad de tiempo/dinero; **in their ~ wisdom** en su infinita sabiduría Ⓑ N **the ~** el infinito

infinitely ['ɪnfɪnɪtlɪ] ADV infinitamente; **this is ~ harder** esto es muchísimo más difícil, esto es mil veces más difícil

infinitesimal [ˌɪnfɪnɪ'tesɪməl] ADJ infinitesimal

infinitive [ɪn'fɪnɪtɪv] N infinitivo *m*

infinity [ɪn'fɪnɪtɪ] N (*gen*) infinidad *f*; (*Math*) infinito *m*

infirm [ɪn'fɜːm] ADJ (= *weak*) débil, endeble; (= *ill*) enfermo; **the old and ~** los ancianos y enfermos; **~ of purpose** irresoluto

infirmary [ɪn'fɜːmərɪ] N (= *hospital*) hospital *m*, clínica *f*; (*in school*) enfermería *f*

infirmity [ɪn'fɜːmɪtɪ] N (= *weakness*) debilidad *f*; (= *illness*) enfermedad *f*; **the infirmities of (old) age** los achaques de la vejez

inflame [ɪn'fleɪm] VT 1 (*Med*) [+ *wound*] inflamar; **to become ~d** inflamarse 2 (*fig*) [+ *person, feelings*] encender, inflamar; [+ *situation*] exacerbar; **to be ~d with passion/ anger/jealousy** estar encendido de pasión/ira/celos

inflammable [ɪn'flæməbl] ADJ 1 [*liquid, substance, fabric*] inflamable 2 [*situation*] explosivo

inflammation [ˌɪnflə'meɪʃən] N inflamación *f*

inflammatory [ɪn'flæmətərɪ] ADJ (*Med*) inflamatorio; [*speech*] incendiario

inflatable [ɪn'fleɪtəbl] ADJ [*boat*] inflable, hinchable (*Sp*)

inflate [ɪn'fleɪt] Ⓐ VT 1 [+ *tyre, balloon*] inflar, hinchar (*Sp*) (**with** de) 2 [+ *prices*] inflar; [+ *currency*] provocar la inflación de Ⓑ VI inflarse, hincharse (*Sp*)

inflated [ɪn'fleɪtɪd] ADJ 1 [*tyre, balloon*] inflado, hinchado (*Sp*) 2 [*price, salary*] inflado; **he has an ~ ego** se cree muy importante

inflation [ɪn'fleɪʃən] N inflación *f*

inflationary [ɪn'fleɪʃnərɪ] ADJ inflacionario, inflacionista

inflationist [ɪnˈfleɪʃənɪst] N partidario/a m/f de la inflación

inflation-proof [ɪnˈfleɪʃən,pruːf] ADJ resistente a la inflación

inflect [ɪnˈflekt] ⓐ VI [verb] conjugarse; [noun, ending] cambiar de forma, declinarse ⓑ VT 1 [+ voice] modular 2 (Gram) [+ noun] declinar; [+ verb] conjugar

inflection [ɪnˈflekʃən] N inflexión f

inflexibility [ɪn,fleksɪˈbɪlɪtɪ] N inflexibilidad f

inflexible [ɪnˈfleksəbl] ADJ inflexible

inflexion [ɪnˈflekʃən] N inflexión f

inflict [ɪnˈflɪkt] VT **to ~ (on)** [+ wound] causar (a), inferir (a); [+ penalty, tax, punishment] imponer (a); [+ pain, suffering, damage] causar (a), infligir (a)

in-flight [ˈɪnflaɪt] ADJ ~ **entertainment/meal/movie** amenidades fpl ofrecidas/comida f servida/película f proyectada durante el vuelo

inflow [ˈɪnfləʊ] N [of capital] afluencia f; [of water] entrada f

influence [ˈɪnfluəns] ⓐ N influencia f (**on** sobre); **a man of** ~ un hombre influyente; **to have an ~ on sth/sb** tener influencia sobre algo/algn; **to be a good/bad ~ on sb** ejercer buena/mala influencia sobre algn; **to bring every ~ to bear on sb** ejercer todas las presiones posibles sobre algn; **to be under the ~** (hum) borracho ⓑ VT [+ person] influenciar, influir en; [+ action, decision] influir en or sobre; **don't let him ~ you** no te dejes influenciar por él; **to be easily ~d** ser muy influenciable

influential [,ɪnfluˈenʃəl] ADJ [person, ideas] influyente; [organization] prestigioso; **he was ~ in securing the loan** influyó para que se consiguiera el préstamo; **he was ~ in government circles** tenía influencia en círculos gubernamentales

influenza [,ɪnfluˈenzə] N gripe f

influx [ˈɪnflʌks] N [of people] afluencia f; [of objects, ideas] flujo m

info* [ˈɪnfəʊ] N = **information**

inform [ɪnˈfɔːm] ⓐ VT (= give information) informar, avisar; (= bring up to date) poner al corriente or al día; **to ~ sb about** or **of sth** informar a algn sobre or de algo; **I am pleased to ~ you that ...** tengo el gusto de comunicarle que ...; **keep me ~ed** téngame or manténgame al corriente ⓑ VI **to ~ on sb** delatar or denunciar a algn

informal [ɪnˈfɔːməl] ADJ 1 (= relaxed, unceremonious) informal; [expression] coloquial, familiar; **dress is ~** vista ropa informal, no es necesaria etiqueta 2 (= unofficial) [meeting, visit] informal

informality [,ɪnfɔːˈmælɪtɪ] N informalidad f, falta f de ceremonia

informally [ɪnˈfɔːməlɪ] ADV 1 [speak, greet, welcome, dress] de manera informal; [write] con un lenguaje informal, con un estilo familiar 2 (= unofficially) [meet, discuss, agree] informalmente; **I have been ~ told that ...** me han dicho de manera informal or extraoficial que ...

informant [ɪnˈfɔːmənt] N informante mf; **my ~** el que me lo dijo; **who was your ~?** ¿quién se lo dijo?

information [,ɪnfəˈmeɪʃən] N (gen) información f; (= knowledge) conocimientos mpl; (US Telec) información f (telefónica); **"information"** "información"; **to ask for ~** pedir información; **to gather ~ about sth** reunir información sobre algo, informarse sobre algo; **for your ~** para su información; **for your ~, I asked him to come!** para que te enteres, ¡le pedí que viniera!; **a piece of ~** un dato ➤ **information bureau** oficina f de información ➤ **information desk** información f ➤ **information pack** material m informativo ➤ **information retrieval** recuperación f de la información ➤ **information service** servicio m de información ➤ **information superhighway** superautopista f de la información ➤ **information technology** informática f

informative [ɪnˈfɔːmətɪv] ADJ informativo

informed [ɪnˈfɔːmd] ADJ [person] bien informado; [debate] llevado a cabo con conocimiento de causa; **an ~ guess** una

conjetura bien fundamentada; ~ **opinion is that ...** la opinión de los que saben del tema es que ...

informer [ɪnˈfɔːməʳ] N informante mf; (pej) delator(a) m/f; soplón/ona* m/f; **police ~** informante mf de la policía; **to turn ~** convertirse en delator

infraction [ɪnˈfrækʃən] N infracción f, contravención f

infrared [ˈɪnfrəˈred] ADJ [rays, light] infrarrojo

infrastructure [ˈɪnfrə,strʌtʃəʳ] N infraestructura f

infrequent [ɪnˈfriːkwənt] ADJ poco frecuente, infrecuente

infrequently [ɪnˈfriːkwəntlɪ] ADV rara vez, pocas veces; **not ~** no raramente, no pocas veces

infringe [ɪnˈfrɪndʒ] ⓐ VT [+ law, rights] infringir, violar ⓑ VI **to ~ (up)on** [+ sb's rights, privacy] violar

infringement [ɪnˈfrɪndʒmənt] N [of law, rule] infracción f, violación f; [of rights] violación f; (Sport) falta f

infuriate [ɪnˈfjʊərɪeɪt] VT enfurecer, poner furioso; **to be/ get ~d** estar/ponerse furioso

infuriating [ɪnˈfjʊərɪeɪtɪŋ] ADJ exasperante

infuriatingly [ɪnˈfjʊərɪeɪtɪŋlɪ] ADV ~, **I was cut off** se cortó la línea, vamos, como para volverse loco; **his answer was ~ vague** su respuesta fue de una vaguedad exasperante

infuse [ɪnˈfjuːz] ⓐ VT 1 [+ courage, enthusiasm] infundir (**into** a); **they were ~d with a new hope** se les infundió nuevas esperanzas 2 [+ herbs, tea] hacer una infusión de ⓑ VI **to let sth ~** dejar algo en infusión

infusion [ɪnˈfjuːʒən] N [of new talent, capital] inyección f; (= tea etc) infusión f

ingenious [ɪnˈdʒiːnɪəs] ADJ ingenioso

ingeniously [ɪnˈdʒiːnɪəslɪ] ADV ingeniosamente, con inventiva

ingenuity [,ɪndʒɪˈnjuːɪtɪ] N [of person] ingenio m, inventiva f; [of idea, scheme] lo ingenioso

ingenuous [ɪnˈdʒenjʊəs] ADJ (= naive) ingenuo; (= candid) cándido

ingest [ɪnˈdʒest] VT ingerir

ingot [ˈɪŋgət] N lingote m

ingrained [ˈɪnˈgreɪnd] ADJ 1 [dirt, blood, stain] incrustado 2 (= deep-seated) [attitude, ideas, tradition] arraigado

ingratiate [ɪnˈgreɪʃɪeɪt] VT **to ~ o.s. with sb** congraciarse con algn

ingratiating [ɪnˈgreɪʃɪeɪtɪŋ] ADJ [smile, speech] obsequioso; [person] halagador, congraciador, zalamero

ingratitude [ɪnˈgrætɪtjuːd] N ingratitud f

ingredient [ɪnˈgriːdɪənt] N (Culin) ingrediente m; [of beauty product, medicine] componente m; (fig) elemento m, factor m

ingrowing (Brit) [ˈɪn,grəʊɪŋ], **ingrown** (US) [ˈɪn,grəʊn] ADJ ~ **(toe)nail** uña f encarnada

inhabit [ɪnˈhæbɪt] VT [+ house] ocupar; [+ town, country] vivir en, habitar (frm); [animal] habitar

inhabitable [ɪnˈhæbɪtəbl] ADJ habitable

inhabitant [ɪnˈhæbɪtənt] N habitante mf

inhabited [ɪnˈhæbɪtɪd] ADJ habitado

inhale [ɪnˈheɪl] ⓐ VT [+ gas] inhalar, aspirar; [+ smoke, vomit] tragar ⓑ VI [smoker] tragar el humo; (Med) aspirar

inhaler [ɪnˈheɪləʳ] N inhalador m

inherent [ɪnˈhɪərənt] ADJ inherente, intrínseco (**in** a); **with all the ~ difficulties** con todas las dificultades que conlleva

inherently [ɪnˈhɪərəntlɪ] ADV intrínsecamente

inherit [ɪnˈherɪt] VT (gen) heredar (**from** de)

inheritance [ɪnˈherɪtəns] N herencia f ➤ **inheritance tax** (Brit) impuesto m sobre sucesiones

inhibit [ɪnˈhɪbɪt] VT (= check) inhibir, reprimir; (= prevent) impedir

inhibited [ɪnˈhɪbɪtɪd] ADJ cohibido, inhibido

inhibition [,ɪnhɪˈbɪʃən] N inhibición f

inhospitable [,ɪnhɒsˈpɪtəbl] ADJ [person] inhospitalario, poco hospitalario; [place, country, climate] inhóspito

in-house [ˈɪnˈhaʊs] ⓐ ADV dentro de la empresa ⓑ ADJ

[*staff*] interno ➤ **in-house training** formación *f* en la empresa

inhuman [ɪnˈhjuːmən] ADJ inhumano

inhumane [ˌɪnhjuːˈmeɪn] ADJ [*behaviour, treatment*] inhumano; [*person*] cruel

inhumanity [ˌɪnhjuːˈmænɪtɪ] N inhumanidad *f*, crueldad *f*

inimical [ɪˈnɪmɪkəl] ADJ [*attitude*] hostil; [*influence*] adverso; **to be ~ to sth** ser adverso a algo

inimitable [ɪˈnɪmɪtəbl] ADJ inimitable

iniquitous [ɪˈnɪkwɪtəs] ADJ inicuo, injusto

initial [ɪˈnɪʃəl] **Ⓐ** ADJ [*shock, success, cost, report*] inicial; **in the ~ stages** al principio, en la etapa inicial, en la primera etapa **Ⓑ** N (*also* ~ **letter**) inicial *f* **Ⓒ** VT [+ *letter, document*] firmar con las iniciales

initialize [ɪˈnɪʃəlaɪz] VT (*Comput*) inicializar

initially [ɪˈnɪʃəlɪ] ADV al principio, en un principio

initiate Ⓐ VT [ɪˈnɪʃɪeɪt] **1** (= *begin*) iniciar, dar comienzo a; [+ *talks*] entablar; [+ *reform*] poner en marcha; [+ *fashion*] introducir; **to ~ proceedings against sb** (*Jur*) entablar una demanda contra algn **2 to ~ sb into a society** admitir a algn en una asociación; **to ~ sb into a secret** iniciar a algn en un secreto **Ⓑ** [ɪˈnɪʃɪɪt] N iniciado/a *m/f*

initiation [ɪˌnɪʃɪˈeɪʃən] N (= *beginning*) inicio *m*, comienzo *m*; (= *admission*) admisión *f* (**into** en); ➤ **initiation ceremony** ceremonia *f* de iniciación

initiative [ɪˈnɪʃɪɪtɪv] N iniciativa *f*; **to use one's ~** obrar por propia iniciativa; **on one's own ~** por iniciativa propia, motu propio; **to take the ~** tomar la iniciativa

initiator [ɪˈnɪʃɪeɪtəʳ] N iniciador(a) *m/f*

inject [ɪnˈdʒekt] VT **1** [+ *medicine*] inyectar (**into** en); **to ~ sb with sth** inyectar algo a algn **2** [+ *enthusiasm*] infundir (**into** a); [+ *money, capital*] inyectar (**into** en); **they've ~ed new life into the club** han infundido un espíritu nuevo al club

injection [ɪnˈdʒekʃən] N inyección *f*; **to give sb an ~** poner *or* dar una inyección a algn

injudicious [ˌɪndʒuˈdɪʃəs] ADJ imprudente, indiscreto

injunction [ɪnˈdʒʌŋkʃən] N (*Jur*) mandamiento *m* judicial; **to seek an ~ (against sth/sb) (to do sth)** obtener un mandamiento judicial (contra algo/algn) (para hacer algo)

injure [ˈɪndʒəʳ] VT **1** (*physically*) herir; (*esp Sport*) lesionar; **he ~d his arm** resultó herido en el brazo; (*Sport*) se lesionó el brazo; **to ~ o.s.** (*in an accident*) resultar herido; (*in a match, race etc*) lesionarse **2** (*fig*) [+ *feelings, pride*] herir; [+ *reputation*] dañar; [+ *trade, chances*] perjudicar

injured [ˈɪndʒəd] **Ⓐ** ADJ **1** [*person, animal, limb*] herido, lesionado; [*player*] lesionado **2** [*tone, look*] dolido; [*feelings*] herido; ~ **pride** orgullo *m* herido **3** (*Jur*) **the ~ party** la parte perjudicada **Ⓑ** NPL **the ~** los heridos

injurious [ɪnˈdʒʊərɪəs] ADJ perjudicial (**to** para)

injury [ˈɪndʒərɪ] **Ⓐ** N **1** (*physical*) herida *f*; (*esp Sport*) lesión *f*; **to do o.s. an ~** hacerse daño; **to do sb an ~** hacer daño a algn **2** (*fig*) (*to reputation*) daño *m*, perjuicio *m*; (*to feelings*) agravio *m* **Ⓑ** CPD ➤ **injury time** (*esp Brit*) tiempo *m* de descuento

⚠ **injury ≠ injuria**

injustice [ɪnˈdʒʌstɪs] N injusticia *f*; **you do me an ~** está siendo injusto conmigo

ink [ɪŋk] **Ⓐ** N tinta *f*; (= *printing ink*) tinta *f* de imprenta; **in ~** con tinta **Ⓑ** VT (*Typ*) entintar **Ⓒ** CPD ➤ **ink blot** borrón *m* de tinta ➤ **ink pad** almohadilla *f*, tampón *m* (de entintar)

ink-jet printer [ˈɪŋkdʒetˈprɪntəʳ] N impresora *f* de chorro de tinta

inkling [ˈɪŋklɪŋ] N idea *f*; **I had no ~ that ...** no tenía ni la menor idea de que ...; **we had some ~ of it** teníamos una vaga idea

inky [ˈɪŋkɪ] ADJ (*lit*) [*page, fingers*] manchado de tinta; (*fig*) [*darkness*] profundo

inlaid [ˈɪnˈleɪd] **Ⓐ** PP *of* **inlay Ⓑ** ADJ (*with wood, tiles*) taraceado (**with** de); (*with jewels*) incrustado (**with** de); [*table, box*] de marquetería

inland Ⓐ [ˈɪnlənd] ADJ [*town*] del interior; [*trade*] interior **Ⓑ** [ɪnˈlænd] ADV (*in*) tierra adentro; (*towards*) hacia el interior **Ⓒ** [ˈɪnlənd] CPD ➤ **Inland Revenue** (*Brit*) ≈ Hacienda *f* ➤ **inland sea** mar *m* interior

in-laws* [ˈɪnlɔːz] NPL (= *partner's family*) parientes *mpl* políticos; (= *partner's parents*) suegros *mpl*

inlay Ⓐ [ˈɪnleɪ] N [*of wood, tiles*] taracea *f*; [*of jewels*] incrustación *f* **Ⓑ** [ˈɪnleɪ] VT (*pt, pp* **inlaid**) (*with wood*) taracear, embutir; (*with jewels*) incrustar

inlet [ˈɪnlet] N (*Geog*) ensenada *f*, entrante *m*; (*Tech*) admisión *f*, entrada *f*

inmate [ˈɪnmeɪt] N [*of hospital*] enfermo/a *m/f*; [*of prison*] preso/a *m/f*, presidiario/a *m/f*; [*of asylum*] internado/a *m/f*

inmost [ˈɪnməʊst] ADJ [*place, chamber*] más recóndito; [*thoughts, feelings*] más íntimo, más secreto

inn [ɪn] N (= *pub*) taberna *f*; (= *hotel*) hostería *f*; (= *tavern*) posada *f*, mesón *m*

innards* [ˈɪnədz] NPL tripas* *fpl*

innate [ɪˈneɪt] ADJ innato

innately [ɪˈneɪtlɪ] ADV de manera innata; **it is not ~ evil** no es malo de por sí

inner [ˈɪnəʳ] **Ⓐ** ADJ **1** [*room, wall, door, part*] interior **2** [*thoughts, emotions*] íntimo; [*voice, calm, conflict, life*] interior; **the ~ man** (= *soul*) el alma; **one's ~ self** el fuero interno de uno **Ⓑ** CPD ➤ **the inner city** *barrios céntricos pobres de la ciudad que presentan problemas sociales* ➤ **inner ear** oído *m* interno ➤ **Inner London** el centro de Londres ➤ **inner tube** (*in tyre*) cámara *f*, llanta *f* (*LAm*)

inner-city [ˈɪnəˈsɪtɪ] ADJ [*schools, problems*] de las zonas céntricas pobres, de los barrios céntricos pobres; **an ~ area** un área pobre del centro

innermost [ˈɪnəməʊst] ADJ [*thoughts, feelings*] más íntimo, más secreto; [*place, chamber*] más recóndito

inning [ˈɪnɪŋ] N (*US Baseball*) inning *m*, entrada *f*; innings (*Cricket*) turno *m*sing, entrada *f*sing; ✦ IDIOM **he's had a good ~s** ha disfrutado de una larga vida, ha vivido sus buenos años

innkeeper [ˈɪnkiːpəʳ] N [*of pub*] tabernero/a *m/f*

innocence [ˈɪnəsns] N inocencia *f*; **in all ~** con toda inocencia, de la forma más inocente

innocent [ˈɪnəsnt] **Ⓐ** ADJ **1** (= *not guilty*) inocente; (= *naive*) inocente, ingenuo; **to be ~ of a crime** ser inocente de un crimen; **he was found ~ of murder** lo declararon inocente de asesinato **2** [*question, remark*] inocente, sin malicia; [*mistake*] inocente **Ⓑ** N inocente *mf*

innocently [ˈɪnəsntlɪ] ADV [*ask, smile*] inocentemente, con inocencia

innocuous [ɪˈnɒkjʊəs] ADJ [*substance*] inocuo; [*person, remark*] inofensivo

innovate [ˈɪnəʊveɪt] VI innovar

innovation [ˌɪnəʊˈveɪʃən] N innovación *f*

innovative [ˈɪnəʊveɪtɪv] ADJ innovador

innovator [ˈɪnəʊveɪtəʳ] N innovador(a) *m/f*

innuendo [ˌɪnjʊˈendəʊ] N (*pl* **~es** *or* **~s**) indirecta *f*, insinuación *f*; **sexual ~** alusiones *fpl or* connotaciones *fpl* sexuales

innumerable [ɪˈnjuːmərəbl] ADJ innumerable

innumerate [ɪˈnjuːmərɪt] ADJ incompetente en el cálculo aritmético

inoculate [ɪˈnɒkjʊleɪt] VT vacunar (**against** contra)

inoculation [ɪˌnɒkjʊˈleɪʃən] N inoculación *f*

inoffensive [ˌɪnəˈfensɪv] ADJ inofensivo

inoperable [ɪnˈɒpərəbl] ADJ inoperable

inoperative [ɪnˈɒpərətɪv] ADJ inoperante

inopportune [ɪnˈɒpətjuːn] ADJ inoportuno

inordinate [ɪˈnɔːdɪnɪt] ADJ (= *excessive*) excesivo; (= *unrestrained*) desmesurado, desmedido

inordinately [ɪˈnɔːdɪnɪtlɪ] ADV desmesuradamente, excesivamente

inorganic [ˌɪnɔːˈgænɪk] ADJ inorgánico

inpatient [ˈɪnˌpeɪʃənt] N paciente *mf* hospitalizado/a

input [ˈɪnpʊt] **Ⓐ** N (*Elec*) entrada *f*; (*Comput*) entrada *f*, input *m*; (= *contribution*) contribución *f*, aportación *f*, aporte *m*; (= *effort, time*) inversión *f*; (*Fin*) dinero *m* invertido, inversión *f* **Ⓑ** VT [+ *data*] entrar

inquest [ˈɪnkwest] N investigación *f* (*llevada a cabo para averiguar las causas de una muerte violenta o sospechosa*)

inquire [ɪnˈkwaɪəʳ] (*esp Brit*) **Ⓐ** VT preguntar; **to ~ when/whether ...** preguntar cuándo/si ... **Ⓑ** VI preguntar; **to ~ about sth** preguntar por algo or acerca de algo; **to ~ after sb** preguntar por algn; **to ~ into sth** investigar or indagar algo

inquiring [ɪnˈkwaɪərɪŋ] ADJ (*esp Brit*) [*mind*] inquieto, inquisitivo; [*look*] inquisitivo

inquiringly [ɪnˈkwaɪərɪŋlɪ] ADV (*esp Brit*) inquisitivamente

inquiry [ɪnˈkwaɪərɪ] (*esp Brit*) **Ⓐ** N **1** (= *question*) interrogante *m or f*, pregunta *f*; **"all inquiries to reception"** "para cualquier información diríjanse a recepción"; **to make inquiries (about sth)** pedir información or informarse (sobre algo)
2 (= *investigation*) investigación *f*, pesquisa *f*; (= *commission*) comisión *f* investigadora, comisión *f* de investigación; **to hold an ~ into sth** llevar a cabo una investigación sobre algo, investigar algo; **they set up an ~ into the disaster** nombraron a una comisión para investigar el desastre; **the police are making inquiries** la policía está investigando el caso **Ⓑ** CPD ➤ **inquiry desk** mesa *f* de información ➤ **inquiry office** oficina *f* de información

inquisition [ˌɪnkwɪˈzɪʃən] N inquisición *f*, investigación *f*; **the Spanish Inquisition** la Inquisición, el Santo Oficio

inquisitive [ɪnˈkwɪzɪtɪv] ADJ curioso; [*mind*] inquisitivo

inquisitively [ɪnˈkwɪzɪtɪvlɪ] ADV con curiosidad

inquisitiveness [ɪnˈkwɪzɪtɪvnɪs] N curiosidad *f*

inroads [ˈɪnrəʊdz] NPL **to make ~ into** [+ *savings*] recurrir a, echar mano de; [+ *market*] adentrar en

INS N ABBR (*US*) = **Immigration and Naturalization Service**

insalubrious [ˌɪnsəˈluːbrɪəs] ADJ [*conditions*] insalubre, malsano; [*part of town*] deprimido

insane [ɪnˈseɪn] **Ⓐ** ADJ (= *mentally ill*) loco (*also fig*), demente; (***) [*suggestion, idea*] descabellado; **to drive sb ~** (*lit*) enloquecer or volver loco a algn; (*fig*) sacar a algn de quicio; **to go ~** volverse loco; **it would be ~ to let him go by himself** sería una locura dejarle ir solo **Ⓑ** NPL **the ~** los enfermos mentales **Ⓒ** CPD ➤ **insane asylum** (*US*) manicomio *m*, psiquiátrico *m*

insanely [ɪnˈseɪnlɪ] ADV **to laugh ~** reírse como un loco; **to be ~ jealous** (*by nature*) ser terriblemente celoso; (*at particular moment*) estar loco de celos

insanitary [ɪnˈsænɪtərɪ] ADJ insalubre, malsano

insanity [ɪnˈsænɪtɪ] N (= *illness*) demencia *f*; (= *foolishness*) locura *f*, insensatez *f*; **it was sheer ~** fue una verdadera locura or insensatez

insatiable [ɪnˈseɪʃəbl] ADJ insaciable

insatiably [ɪnˈseɪʃəblɪ] ADV **to be ~ hungry/curious** tener un hambre/una curiosidad insaciable

inscribe [ɪnˈskraɪb] VT (= *engrave*) grabar; (= *write*) inscribir; (= *dedicate*) [+ *book*] dedicar

inscription [ɪnˈskrɪpʃən] N (*on stone*) inscripción *f*; (*in book*) dedicatoria *f*

inscrutable [ɪnˈskruːtəbl] ADJ inescrutable

insect [ˈɪnsekt] N insecto *m* ➤ **insect bite** picadura *f* de insecto ➤ **insect repellent** repelente *m* contra insectos ➤ **insect spray** insecticida *m* en aerosol or spray

insecticide [ɪnˈsektɪsaɪd] N insecticida *m*

insecure [ˌɪnsɪˈkjʊəʳ] ADJ **1** (= *not confident*) inseguro **2** (= *not secure, not safe*) [*job, country, ladder*] poco seguro; [*situation*] inestable; **an ~ future** un futuro incierto or poco seguro

insecurity [ˌɪnsɪˈkjʊərɪtɪ] N inseguridad *f*

inseminate [ɪnˈsemɪneɪt] VT inseminar

insemination [ɪnˌsemɪˈneɪʃən] N inseminación *f*

insensibility [ɪnˌsensəˈbɪlɪtɪ] N insensibilidad *f* (**to** a)

insensible [ɪnˈsensəbl] ADJ (*frm*) **1** (= *unconscious*) inconsciente, sin conocimiento; **he drank himself ~** bebió hasta perder el conocimiento **2** (= *insensitive*) **to be ~ to sth** ser insensible a algo **3** (= *unaware*) **to be ~ of sth** no ser consciente de algo

insensibly [ɪnˈsensəblɪ] ADV imperceptiblemente, insensiblemente

insensitive [ɪnˈsensɪtɪv] ADJ [*person*] insensible; [*behaviour, remark*] falto de sensibilidad; **to be ~** [*person*] no tener sensibilidad; **to be ~ to sth** ser insensible a algo

insensitivity [ɪnˌsensɪˈtɪvɪtɪ] N (*physical*) insensibilidad *f* (**to** a); (*emotional*) falta *f* de sensibilidad (**to** ante)

inseparable [ɪnˈsepərəbl] ADJ inseparable (**from** de)

inseparably [ɪnˈsepərəblɪ] ADV inseparablemente, indisolublemente

insert **Ⓐ** [ˈɪnsɜːt] N encarte *m* **Ⓑ** [ɪnˈsɜːt] VT [+ *coin, finger*] introducir, meter; [+ *word*] intercalar, insertar; [+ *advertisement*] insertar, poner; (*Comput*) insertar

insertion [ɪnˈsɜːʃən] N inserción *f*, introducción *f*

in-service [ˈɪnˈsɜːvɪs] ADJ **~ course/training** cursillo *m*/ formación *f* en la empresa

inset [ˈɪnset] **Ⓐ** N (*Typ*) recuadro *m*; (= *page(s)*) encarte *m* **Ⓑ** VT (*pt, pp ~*) [+ *diagram, map*] insertar, imprimir como recuadro; [+ *page(s)*] imprimir como encarte; (= *indent*) sangrar

inshore [ˈɪnˈʃɔːʳ] **Ⓐ** ADV [*be, fish*] cerca de la costa; [*sail, blow*] hacia la costa **Ⓑ** ADJ costero ➤ **inshore fishing** pesca *f* de bajura

inside [ˈɪnˈsaɪd] **Ⓐ** N **1** (= *inner part*) interior *m*, parte *f* de dentro; **the doors were locked from the ~** las puertas estaban cerradas (con llave) por dentro; **crisp on the outside and soft on the ~** crujiente por fuera y tierno por dentro; **your sweater's ~ out** llevas el jersey al or del revés; **she turned the sock ~ out** le dio la vuelta al calcetín, volvió el calcetín del revés; **to know a subject ~ out** conocer un tema de cabo a rabo; **he knows the district ~ out** se conoce el distrito como la palma de la mano
2 (= *lining*) parte *f* de dentro
3 **to overtake** or **pass (sb) on the ~** (*Brit/other countries*) adelantar (a algn) por la izquierda/derecha
4 **insides** [*of person, animal, fruit*] tripas *fpl* **Ⓑ** ADV **1** (= *indoors, in*) dentro, adentro (*LAm*); **wait for me ~** espérame dentro or (*LAm*) adentro; **please step ~** pase (usted); **to come/go ~** entrar; **it gives me a lovely warm feeling ~** me produce una sensación muy agradable por dentro
2 (= *towards the inside*) adentro, dentro; **he opened the car door and shoved her ~** abrió la puerta del coche y la empujó adentro or dentro
3 (***) (= *in prison*) **to be ~** estar en chirona*, estar a la sombra* **Ⓒ** PREP (*also US* ~ **of**) **1** dentro de, en el interior de (*frm*); **the envelope** dentro del sobre, en el interior del sobre (*frm*); **he went ~ the house** entró en la casa
2 (*of time*) en menos de; **~ four hours** en menos de cuatro horas; **her time was five seconds ~ the record** superó el récord por cinco segundos **Ⓓ** ADJ (= *internal*) interior; **it must be an ~ job*** tiene que haber sido alguien de dentro; **the KGB: the ~ story** la KGB: la historia secreta **Ⓔ** CPD ➤ **inside information** información *f* confidencial ➤ **the inside lane** (*Aut*) (*Brit/other countries*) el carril de la izquierda/derecha; (*Athletics*) la calle interior ➤ **inside leg** medida *f* de la entrepierna ➤ **inside pocket** bolsillo *m* interior

insider [ɪnˈsaɪdəʳ] N [*of firm*] empleado/a *m/f* de la empresa ➤ **insider dealing, insider trading** abuso *m* de información privilegiada

insidious [ɪnˈsɪdɪəs] ADJ insidioso

insight [ˈɪnsaɪt] N **1** (= *understanding*) perspicacia *f* **2** (= *new* *perception)* **to get an ~ into sth** comprender algo mejor, adquirir una nueva percepción de algo

insightful [ˈɪnˌsaɪtfʊl] ADJ (*US*) penetrante, perspicaz

insignia [ɪnˈsɪɡnɪə] N (*pl* ~) insignia *f*

insignificance [ˌɪnsɪɡˈnɪfɪkəns] N insignificancia *f*

insignificant [ˌɪnsɪɡˈnɪfɪkənt] ADJ insignificante

insincere [ˌɪnsɪnˈsɪəʳ] ADJ insincero, poco sincero

insincerity [ˌɪnsɪnˈserɪtɪ] N falta *f* de sinceridad, insinceridad *f*

insinuate [ɪnˈsɪnjʊeɪt] VT (= *hint*) insinuar; **what are you insinuating?** ¿qué insinúas?

insinuating [ɪnˈsɪnjʊeɪtɪŋ] ADJ [*remark*] malintencionado, con una segunda intención, con segundas*

insinuation [ɪnˌsɪnjʊˈeɪʃən] N (= *hint*) insinuación *f*

insipid [ɪnˈsɪpɪd] ADJ insípido, soso

insist [ɪnˈsɪst] **Ⓐ** VI insistir; **if you** ~ si insistes; **to ~ on** (= *repeat*) insistir en; (= *demand*) exigir; (= *emphasize*) hacer hincapié en; **she always ~s on the best** siempre exige lo mejor; **to ~ on doing sth** insistir en hacer algo **Ⓑ** VT **to ~ that** insistir en que; **he ~ed that it was so** insistió en que era así

insistence [ɪnˈsɪstəns] N insistencia *f*; **his ~ that we should have a drink/he had switched the light off** su insistencia *or* su empeño en que tomásemos una copa/en que había apagado la luz; **at his/her ~** ante su insistencia; **~ on sth** insistencia en algo

insistent [ɪnˈsɪstənt] ADJ insistente; **to be ~ on/about sth** insistir en algo; **to be ~ that** insistir en que; **he was ~ that we should have a drink** insistió en que tomásemos una copa; **he was ~ that he had switched the light off** insistía en que había apagado la luz

insistently [ɪnˈsɪstəntlɪ] ADV insistentemente, con insistencia

in situ [ɪnˈsɪtjuː] ADV in situ

insofar [ɪnsəˈfɑːʳ] ADV ~ **as ...** en la medida en que ...

insole [ˈɪnsəʊl] N plantilla *f*

insolence [ˈɪnsələns] N insolencia *f*

insolent [ˈɪnsələnt] ADJ insolente

insoluble [ɪnˈsɒljʊbl] ADJ insoluble

insolvency [ɪnˈsɒlvənsɪ] N insolvencia *f*

insolvent [ɪnˈsɒlvənt] ADJ insolvente

insomnia [ɪnˈsɒmnɪə] N insomnio *m*

insomniac [ɪnˈsɒmnɪæk] ADJ, N insomne *mf*

insomuch [ˌɪnsəʊˈmʌtʃ] CONJ ~ **as** puesto que, ya que, por cuanto que; ~ **that** hasta tal punto que

Insp., insp. ABBR = **inspector**

inspect [ɪnˈspekt] VT **1** [+ *goods, luggage*] inspeccionar, examinar; (*officially*) [+ *premises, school, machinery*] inspeccionar; [+ *ticket, document*] revisar **2** [+ *troops*] pasar revista a

inspection [ɪnˈspekʃən] N **1** [*of goods, premises, school*] inspección *f*; [*of ticket, document*] revisión *f*; **on closer ~** tras un examen más minucioso **2** [*of troops*] revista *f*

inspector [ɪnˈspektəʳ] N (= *official*) inspector(a) *m/f* (*also Police, Educ*); (*on bus, train*) revisor(a) *m/f*, controlador(a) *m/f* (*LAm*); ~ **of taxes** ≈ Inspector(a) *m/f* de Hacienda

inspiration [ˌɪnspəˈreɪʃən] N **1** (= *motivation*) inspiración *f*; (= *source of inspiration*) fuente *f* de inspiración; **to find ~ in** inspirarse en; **she has been an ~ to us all** ha sido un gran estímulo para todos nosotros **2** (= *inspired idea*) idea *f* genial

inspirational [ˌɪnspɪˈreɪʃənl] ADJ inspirador

inspire [ɪnˈspaɪəʳ] VT inspirar; **to ~ sb to do sth** mover a algn a hacer algo; **this painting was ~d by Greek mythology** este cuadro está inspirado en la mitología griega; **to ~ confidence in sb** infundir *or* inspirar confianza a algn

inspired [ɪnˈspaɪəd] ADJ [*musician, poet, artist*] genial; [*performance*] inspirado; [*idea*] genial, excelente; **it was an ~ choice** fue todo un acierto; **to feel ~** sentirse inspirado; **to make an ~ guess** tener una inspiración

inspiring [ɪnˈspaɪərɪŋ] ADJ **it is ~ to work with people like them** es estimulante trabajar con gente como ellos; **he was a brilliant and ~ speaker** fue un magnífico orador que conseguía inspirar a la gente

instability [ˌɪnstəˈbɪlɪtɪ] N inestabilidad *f*

instal, install (*US*) [ɪnˈstɔːl] VT instalar

installation [ˌɪnstəˈleɪʃən] N instalación *f*

instalment, installment (*US*) [ɪnˈstɔːlmənt] **Ⓐ** N **1** (*Comm*) (= *part payment*) plazo *m*, cuota *f* (*LAm*); **to pay in ~s** pagar a plazos; **monthly ~** plazo *m* mensual, cuota *f* mensual (*LAm*) **2** [*of serial, in magazine*] fascículo *m*; (*on radio, TV*) episodio *m* **Ⓑ** CPD ➤ **installment plan** (*US*) plan *m* de financiación; **to buy sth/pay for sth on an installment plan** comprar/pagar algo a plazos

instance [ˈɪnstəns] N **1** (= *example*) ejemplo *m*; **for ~** por ejemplo **2** (= *case*) caso *m*; **in many ~s** en muchos casos; **in the first ~** en primer lugar

instant [ˈɪnstənt] **Ⓐ** ADJ **1** (= *immediate*) instantáneo, inmediato; **he took an ~ dislike to Derek** Derek le cayó mal desde el primer momento **2** [*coffee, soup*] instantáneo **Ⓑ** N instante *m*, momento *m*; **the ~ I heard it** en el instante *or* momento en que lo supe; **Tom hesitated for an ~** Tom dudó un instante *or* un momento; **in an ~** en un instante *or* momento; **put it down this ~!** ¡deja eso ahora mismo! **Ⓒ** CPD ➤ **instant access account** cuenta *f* de acceso instantáneo *or* inmediato ➤ **instant replay** (*US Sport*) repetición *f* de la jugada

instantaneous [ˌɪnstənˈteɪnɪəs] ADJ instantáneo

instantaneously [ˌɪnstənˈteɪnɪəslɪ] ADV instantáneamente

instantly [ˈɪnstəntlɪ] ADV [*recognize, know*] inmediatamente, al instante; [*die*] en el acto, instantáneamente

instead [ɪnˈsted] ADV **1** **he was busy, so I went ~** él estaba ocupado, así es que fui yo en su lugar; **I was tempted to spend the money, but I put it in the bank ~** tuve la tentación de gastar el dinero, pero en lugar de ello *or* en vez de eso, lo metí en el banco; **we had expected to make £2,000, ~ we barely made £200** esperábamos sacar unas 2.000 libras y en cambio sacamos 200 **2** ~ **of** en vez de, en lugar de; **he went ~ of me** fue en mi lugar

instep [ˈɪnstep] N empeine *m*

instigate [ˈɪnstɪɡeɪt] VT [+ *rebellion, strike, crime*] instigar a; [+ *new ideas*] fomentar; [+ *change*] promover

instigation [ˌɪnstɪˈɡeɪʃən] N instigación *f*; **at Brown's ~** a instancias de Brown

instigator [ˈɪnstɪɡeɪtəʳ] N instigador(a) *m/f*

instil, instill (*US*) [ɪnˈstɪl] VT **to ~ sth into sb** [+ *fear, confidence*] inspirar *or* infundir algo a algn; [+ *awareness, responsibility*] inculcar algo a algn

instinct [ˈɪnstɪŋkt] N instinto *m*; **the ~ for self-preservation** el instinto de conservación *or* supervivencia; **by ~** por instinto

instinctive [ɪnˈstɪŋktɪv] ADJ instintivo

instinctively [ɪnˈstɪŋktɪvlɪ] ADV instintivamente, por instinto

institute [ˈɪnstɪtjuːt] **Ⓐ** N (= *research centre*) instituto *m*; (= *professional body*) colegio *m*, asociación *f*; (*for professional training*) escuela *f*; (*US*) (= *course*) curso *m*, cursillo *m* **Ⓑ** VT (= *begin*) [+ *inquiry*] iniciar, empezar; (= *found*) fundar, instituir; (*Jur*) [+ *proceedings*] entablar

institution [ˌɪnstɪˈtjuːʃən] N **1** (= *founding*) fundación *f*, institución *f*; (= *initiation*) iniciación *f*; [*of proceedings*] entablación *f* **2** (= *organization*) institución *f* **3** (= *custom*) institución *f*

institutional [ˌɪnstɪˈtjuːʃənl] ADJ institucional

institutionalize [ˌɪnstɪˈtjuːʃənəˌlaɪz] VT **1** [+ *patient*] internar en una institución **2** [+ *practices, values*] institucionalizar

institutionalized [ˌɪnstɪˈtjuːʃənəˌlaɪzd] ADJ **1** (= *living in an institution*) ~ **elderly people** personas *fpl* mayores internadas en residencias; ~ **mental patients** enfermos *mpl* mentales ingresados en una institución

2 (= *affected by institution*) **to become** ~ habituarse al régimen de vida de un hospital, una cárcel u otra institución de forma que se convierte en un modo de vida
3 (= *established*) [*custom, practice, value*] institucionalizado; **to become** ~ institucionalizarse

in-store ['ɪnstɔːʳ] ADJ en el establecimiento

instruct [ɪn'strʌkt] VT **1** (= *teach*) **to** ~ **sb in sth** enseñar algo a algn, instruir a algn en algo **2** (= *order*) **to** ~ **sb to do sth** mandar *or* ordenar a algn que haga algo **3** (*Brit*) [+ *solicitor, barrister*] dar instrucciones a, instruir

instruction [ɪn'strʌkʃən] **Ⓐ** N **1** (= *teaching*) instrucción *f*, enseñanza *f*; **to give sb** ~ **in mathematics** dar clases de *or* enseñar matemáticas a algn **2** (= *order*) orden *f*; **to give sb** ~**s to do sth** dar órdenes *or* instrucciones a algn de que haga algo; ~**s for use** modo *m* sing de empleo; **on the** ~**s of** por orden de **Ⓑ** CPD ➤ **instruction book**, **instruction manual** manual *m* de instrucciones

instructive [ɪn'strʌktɪv] ADJ [*experience*] instructivo

instructor [ɪn'strʌktəʳ] N instructor(a) *m/f*; (*US Univ*) profesor(a) *m/f* auxiliar; **dance** ~ profesor(a) *m/f* de baile; **flying** ~ monitor(a) *m/f* de vuelo; **ski** ~ instructor(a) *m/f* de esquí, monitor(a) *m/f* de esquí

instrument ['ɪnstrəmənt] **Ⓐ** N **1** (*gen, Mus*) instrumento *m*; **surgical** ~**s** instrumental *m* quirúrgico; **set of** ~**s** instrumental *m* **2** (*Jur*) instrumento *m* **Ⓑ** CPD ➤ **instrument panel** (*Aer*) tablero *m* de instrumentos, cuadro *m* de instrumentos; (*US Aut*) tablero *m* de mandos, salpicadero *m* (*Sp*)

instrumental [ˌɪnstrʊ'mentl] ADJ **1 to be** ~ **in** contribuir decisivamente a **2** [*music, piece*] instrumental

instrumentalist [ˌɪnstrʊ'mentəlɪst] N instrumentista *mf*

instrumentation [ˌɪnstrʊmen'teɪʃən] N instrumentación *f*

insubordinate [ˌɪnsə'bɔːdənɪt] ADJ insubordinado

insubordination ['ɪnsəˌbɔːdɪ'neɪʃən] N insubordinación *f*

insubstantial [ˌɪnsəb'stænʃəl] ADJ (*gen*) insustancial; [*meal*] poco sustancioso

insufferable [ɪn'sʌfərəbl] ADJ insufrible, insoportable

insufficient [ˌɪnsə'fɪʃənt] ADJ insuficiente

insufficiently [ˌɪnsə'fɪʃəntlɪ] ADV insuficientemente

insular ['ɪnsjələʳ] ADJ [*person, attitude*] estrecho de miras

insularity [ˌɪnsjʊ'lærɪtɪ] N estrechez *f* de miras

insulate ['ɪnsjʊleɪt] VT aislar (**from** de)

insulating tape ['ɪnsjʊleɪtɪŋˌteɪp] N cinta *f* aislante

insulation [ˌɪnsjʊ'leɪʃən] N aislamiento *m* ➤ **insulation material** material *m* aislante

insulin ['ɪnsjʊlɪn] N insulina *f*

insult Ⓐ ['ɪnsʌlt] N insulto *m*; ✦ IDIOM **and to add** ~ **to injury** y para colmo de males, y por si esto fuera poco **Ⓑ** [ɪn'sʌlt] VT insultar, ofender

insulting [ɪn'sʌltɪŋ] ADJ insultante, ofensivo

insultingly [ɪn'sʌltɪŋlɪ] ADV [*behave, talk*] ofensivamente, de modo insultante

insuperable [ɪn'suːpərəbl] ADJ insuperable

insurance [ɪn'ʃʊərəns] N seguro *m*; ~ **against theft/fire/ damage** seguro *m* contra robo/incendio/daños; **to take out** ~ hacerse un seguro ➤ **insurance adjuster** (*US*) ajustador(a) *m/f* de pérdidas, tasador(a) *m/f* de pérdidas ➤ **insurance agent** agente *mf* de seguros ➤ **insurance broker** corredor(a) *m/f* de seguros, agente *mf* de seguros ➤ **insurance certificate** certificado *m* de seguro ➤ **insurance claim** demanda *f* de seguro ➤ **insurance company** compañía *f* de seguros ➤ **insurance policy** póliza *f* de seguros ➤ **insurance premium** prima *f* del seguro

insure [ɪn'ʃʊəʳ] VT [+ *house, property*] asegurar; **to** ~ **o.s.** *or* **one's life** hacerse un seguro de vida; **to** ~ **sth against fire/ theft** asegurar algo contra incendios/robo; **to** ~ **one's life for £500,000** hacerse un seguro de vida por valor de 500.000 libras; **I'm** ~**d to drive any car** tengo un seguro que me permite conducir cualquier coche

insured [ɪn'ʃʊəd] **Ⓐ** ADJ [*person, building, vehicle*] asegurado; **are you** ~? ¿estás asegurado?, ¿tienes seguro?; **to be** ~ **against fire/theft** estar asegurado contra incendios/

robo; **it's** ~ **for £5,000** está asegurado en 5.000 libras **Ⓑ** N **the** ~ el/la asegurado/a

insurer [ɪn'ʃʊərəʳ] N asegurador(a) *m/f*

insurgency [ɪn'sɜːdʒənsɪ] N insurrección *f*

insurgent [ɪn'sɜːdʒənt] ADJ, N insurgente *mf*, insurrecto/a *m/f*

insurmountable [ˌɪnsə'maʊntəbl] ADJ insuperable

insurrection [ˌɪnsə'rekʃən] N insurrección *f*

intact [ɪn'tækt] ADJ intacto

intake ['ɪnteɪk] N [*of food*] consumo *m*; **what is your student** ~? ¿cuántos alumnos se matriculan (cada año)?

intangible [ɪn'tændʒəbl] ADJ intangible

integer ['ɪntɪdʒəʳ] N entero *m*, número *m* entero

integral ['ɪntɪgrəl] ADJ [*part*] integrante, esencial; **it is an** ~ **part of the plan** es parte integrante *or* esencial del proyecto

integrate ['ɪntɪgreɪt] **Ⓐ** VT integrar **Ⓑ** VI integrarse

integrated ['ɪntɪgreɪtɪd] ADJ integrado

integration [ˌɪntɪ'greɪʃən] N integración *f* (**in, into** en)

integrity [ɪn'tegrɪtɪ] N integridad *f*

intellect ['ɪntɪlekt] N intelecto *m*, inteligencia *f*

intellectual [ˌɪntɪ'lektjʊəl] ADJ, N intelectual *mf*

intellectualize [ˌɪntɪ'lektjʊəlaɪz] **Ⓐ** VT intelectualizar, racionalizar **Ⓑ** VI dar razones

intellectually [ˌɪntɪ'lektjʊəlɪ] ADV intelectualmente

intelligence [ɪn'telɪdʒəns] **Ⓐ** N **1** (= *cleverness*) inteligencia *f* **2** (= *information*) información *f*, inteligencia *f* **Ⓑ** CPD ➤ **intelligence agent** agente *mf* de inteligencia, agente *mf* secreto ➤ **intelligence officer** oficial *mf* de informaciones ➤ **intelligence quotient (IQ)** cociente *m* intelectual *or* de inteligencia ➤ **intelligence service** servicio *m* de información *or* inteligencia ➤ **intelligence test** test *m* de inteligencia

intelligent [ɪn'telɪdʒənt] ADJ inteligente

intelligently [ɪn'telɪdʒəntlɪ] ADV inteligentemente

intelligentsia [ɪnˌtelɪ'dʒentsɪə] N intelectualidad *f*

intelligible [ɪn'telɪdʒəbl] ADJ inteligible, comprensible

intemperate [ɪn'tempərɪt] ADJ [*person*] (= *immoderate*) desmedido, destemplado; (= *drunken*) dado a la bebida, que bebe en exceso; [*climate*] inclemente

intend [ɪn'tend] VT **1** (*with noun*) **it's** ~**ed for John** está destinado a John, es para John; **no offence was** ~**ed** no tenía intención de ofender a nadie, no fue su intención ofender a nadie; **that remark was** ~**ed for you** esa observación iba dirigida a ti; **it was** ~**ed as a compliment** se dijo como un cumplido; **is that what you** ~**ed?** ¿fue eso lo que se proponía?
2 (*with verb*) **to** ~ **to do sth** ✧ ~ **doing sth** pensar hacer algo; **what do you** ~ **to do about it?** ¿qué piensas hacer al respecto?; **this scheme is** ~**ed to help** este proyecto tiene la finalidad de ayudar; **I fully** ~ **to punish him** tengo la firme intención de castigarlo

intended [ɪn'tendɪd] ADJ [*effect*] deseado

intense [ɪn'tens] ADJ **1** (= *extreme*) [*heat, pain, emotion, light, colour*] intenso; [*enthusiasm, happiness*] enorme **2** (= *impassioned*) [*person, face, expression*] apasionado, vehemente; [*relationship*] intenso; [*gaze*] intenso, penetrante

intensely [ɪn'tenslɪ] ADV **1** (= *extremely*) sumamente **2** (= *concentratedly*) [*work, fight, concentrate*] intensamente **3** (= *with passion*) [*look, love*] intensamente; [*discuss*] apasionadamente; [*say*] con pasión; **I dislike it** ~ me desagrada profundamente

intensification [ɪnˌtensɪfɪ'keɪʃən] N intensificación *f*

intensifier [ɪn'tensɪˌfaɪəʳ] N intensificador *m*

intensify [ɪn'tensɪfaɪ] **Ⓐ** VI [*desire, frustration, dislike*] intensificarse; [*pain*] agudizarse; [*odour*] hacerse más intenso; [*fighting*] recrudecerse, intensificarse **Ⓑ** VT [+ *attack*] recrudecer, intensificar

intensity [ɪn'tensɪtɪ] N intensidad *f*

intensive [ɪn'tensɪv] ADJ intensivo ➤ **intensive care**

cuidados mpl intensivos ➤ **intensive care unit** unidad f de cuidados intensivos

intensively [ɪn'tensɪvlɪ] ADV intensivamente

intent [ɪn'tent] **Ⓐ** ADJ 1 (= *determined*) **to be ~ on doing sth** estar resuelto *or* decidido a hacer algo 2 (= *absorbed*) **to be ~ on sth** estar absorto en algo **Ⓑ** N propósito *m*, intención *f*; **with ~ to** (+ INFIN) con el propósito de + *infin*; **with ~ to kill** con intentos homicidas; **to all ~s and purposes** prácticamente, en efecto

intention [ɪn'tenʃən] N intención *f*, propósito *m*; **I have no ~ of going** no tengo la menor intención de ir; **I have every ~ of going** tengo plena intención de ir; **with the best of ~s** con la mejor intención; **what are your ~s?** ¿qué piensas hacer?

intentional [ɪn'tenʃənl] ADJ deliberado; **if I offended you it wasn't ~** si te ofendí fue sin querer *or* no fue a propósito

intentionally [ɪn'tenʃnəlɪ] ADV [*do, hurt, discriminate*] a propósito, adrede; [*mislead*] intencionadamente; **the figures are ~ misleading** las cifras están presentadas de manera equívoca a propósito

intently [ɪn'tentlɪ] ADV atentamente, fijamente

interact [ˌɪntər'ækt] VI influirse mutuamente, interactuar; **to ~ with sb** relacionarse con algn

interaction [ˌɪntər'ækʃən] N interacción *f*, interrelación *f*

interactive [ˌɪntər'æktɪv] ADJ interactivo

interbreed ['ɪntə'briːd] (*pt, pp* **interbred**) VI cruzarse

intercede [ˌɪntə'siːd] VI interceder (**for** por; **with** con)

intercept [ˌɪntə'sept] VT [+ *message, missile*] interceptar; (= *stop*) detener; (= *cut off*) atajar, cortar; (*Sport*) [+ *pass*] cortar, interceptar

interception [ˌɪntə'sepʃən] N [*of message, missile*] intercepción *f*; (*Sport*) corte *m*, intercepción *f*

interchange Ⓐ [ˌɪntə'tʃeɪndʒ] VT 1 [+ *views, ideas*] intercambiar, cambiar; [+ *prisoners*] canjear 2 (= *alternate*) alternar **Ⓑ** ['ɪntətʃeɪndʒ] N 1 [*of views, ideas*] intercambio *m*, cambio *m*; [*of prisoners*] canje *m* 2 (*on motorway*) nudo *m* de carreteras, paso *m* elevado, paso *m* a desnivel (*LAm*)

interchangeable [ˌɪntə'tʃeɪndʒəbl] ADJ intercambiable

intercity ['ɪntə'sɪtɪ] **Ⓐ** N (*Brit Rail*) (*also* ~ **train**) tren *m* de largo recorrido, tren *m* intercity (*Sp*) **Ⓑ** ADJ interurbano, intercity (*Sp*)

intercollegiate ['ɪntəkə'liːdʒɪɪt] ADJ (*US*) interuniversitario

intercom* ['ɪntəkɒm] N intercomunicador *m*, interfono *m*

interconnect [ˌɪntəkə'nekt] **Ⓐ** VT (*Elec, Comput*) interconectar; **all these problems are ~ed** todos estos problemas están interrelacionados **Ⓑ** VI [*concepts*] interrelacionarse

intercourse ['ɪntəkɔːs] N 1 (*frm*) relaciones *fpl*, trato *m* 2 (*also* **sexual ~**) acto *m* sexual, coito *m*; **to have ~ with sb** tener relaciones sexuales con algn

interdepartmental ['ɪntəˌdiːpɑː't'mentl] ADJ interdepartamental

interdependence [ˌɪntədɪ'pendəns] N interdependencia *f*

interdependent [ˌɪntədɪ'pendənt] ADJ interdependiente

interdisciplinary [ˌɪntə'dɪsɪplɪnərɪ] ADJ interdisciplinario

interest ['ɪntrɪst] **Ⓐ** N 1 (= *curiosity*) interés *m*; **to have an ~ in sth** estar interesado en algo; **to lose ~ (in sth)** perder el interés (por *or* en algo); **it is of no ~ to us** no nos interesa; **is this of any ~ to you?** ¿te interesa esto?; **I'm doing it just out of ~, how much did it cost?** por simple curiosidad, ¿cuánto costó?; **to take an ~ in sth/sb** interesarse por *or* en algo/por algn

2 (= *hobby*) interés *m*; **what are your ~s?** ¿qué cosas te interesan?

3 (= *profit, advantage*) interés *m*; **a conflict of ~s** un conflicto de intereses; **it is not in his ~ to sell the house** no le conviene vender la casa; **in the ~s of hygiene** por razones de higiene; **in the ~s of national unity** con el fin de preservar la unidad nacional

4 (= *share, stake*) (*gen*) interés *m*; (*in company*) participación *f*; **he has sold his ~ in the company** ha vendido su participación en la empresa; **the West has an ~ in promoting democracy there** Occidente tiene interés *or* está interesado en promover allí la democracia

5 (*on loan, shares, savings*) interés *m*; **to bear ~** devengar *or* dar intereses; **to earn ~** cobrar intereses; **the ~ on an investment** los intereses de una inversión

Ⓑ VT interesar; **can I ~ you in a new car?** ¿estaría interesado en comprar un coche nuevo?

Ⓒ CPD ➤ **interest rate** tipo *m or* tasa *f* de interés

interested ['ɪntrɪstɪd] ADJ interesado; **I've got some books to sell, are you ~?** tengo unos libros que quiero vender, ¿te interesan?; **he's ~ in buying a car** está interesado en comprar un coche; **I'm not ~ in football** no me interesa el fútbol; **to get ~ in sth/sb** interesarse por algn/algo; **to get sb ~ in sth** hacer que algn se interese por algo; **the ~ party** la parte interesada; **I'd be ~ to know the outcome** me interesaría saber el resultado

interest-free [ˌɪntrɪst'friː] ADJ sin interés

interesting ['ɪntrɪstɪŋ] ADJ interesante; **it is ~ that** es interesante el hecho de que; **it will be ~ to see what happens** será interesante ver lo que ocurre

interestingly ['ɪntrɪstɪŋlɪ] ADV [*speak, write*] de manera interesante; **~ enough** curiosamente

interface ['ɪntəfeɪs] N (*Comput*) interfaz *m or f*, interface *m or f*

interfere [ˌɪntə'fɪə'] VI 1 (= *pry, intrude*) entrometerse, meterse (**in** en); **stop interfering!** ¡deja de entrometerte!; **he's always interfering** se mete en todo 2 (= *meddle*) **to ~ with sth** manosear *or* tocar algo 3 (= *hinder*) **to ~ with sth** afectar a algo; **it mustn't ~ with my work** no debe afectar a mi trabajo; **I don't want to ~ with your plans** no quiero interferir con tus planes

interference [ˌɪntə'fɪərəns] N 1 (= *intrusion*) intromisión *f* 2 (*Rad, TV*) interferencia *f*

interfering [ˌɪntə'fɪərɪŋ] ADJ [*neighbour*] entrometido, metomentodo*

intergovernmental [ˌɪntəˌɡʌvn'mentl] ADJ intergubernamental

interim ['ɪntərɪm] **Ⓐ** N **in the ~** en el ínterin *or* interín **Ⓑ** ADJ [*president*] interino, provisional; [*measure, government, report, result*] provisional **Ⓒ** CPD ➤ **interim payment** pago *m* a cuenta ➤ **the interim period** el ínterin *or* interín

interior [ɪn'tɪərɪə'] **Ⓐ** ADJ interior **Ⓑ** N interior *m*; **Minister of the Interior** Ministro/a *m/f* del Interior; **Ministry of the Interior** Ministerio *m* del Interior, Secretaría *f* de Gobernación (*Mex*) **Ⓒ** CPD ➤ **interior decoration** interiorismo *m* ➤ **interior decorator** interiorista *mf* ➤ **interior design** interiorismo *m*, decoración *f* de interiores ➤ **interior designer** interiorista *mf*

interject [ˌɪntə'dʒekt] VT interponer; **"that's not true," he ~ed** —eso no es cierto —interpuso él

interjection [ˌɪntə'dʒekʃən] N (= *exclamation*) exclamación *f*; (*Ling*) interjección *f*; (= *insertion*) interposición *f*

interlink [ˌɪntə'lɪŋk] **Ⓐ** VT [+ *issues, interests*] interrelacionar, vincular; **the two issues are ~ed** las dos cuestiones están interrelacionadas, las dos cuestiones están vinculadas (entre sí) **Ⓑ** VI interrelacionarse

interlock [ˌɪntə'lɒk] **Ⓐ** VT trabar, entrelazar; [+ *wheels*] endentar, engranar **Ⓑ** VI trabarse, entrelazarse; [*wheels*] endentarse, engranar

interloper ['ɪntələʊpə'] N intruso/a *m/f*

interlude ['ɪntəluːd] N intervalo *m*, intermedio *m*; (*esp Brit*) (*in theatre*) intermedio *m*; (= *musical interlude*) interludio *m*

intermarriage [ˌɪntə'mærɪdʒ] N (*between races*) matrimonio *m* mixto; (*between relatives*) matrimonio *m* entre parientes

intermarry ['ɪntə'mærɪ] VI (*gen*) casarse entre sí; (*within family*) casarse entre parientes

intermediary [ˌɪntə'miːdɪərɪ] ADJ, N intermediario/a *m/f*

intermediate [ˌɪntə'miːdɪət] ADJ intermedio; **beginner, ~ and advanced** elemental, medio *or* intermedio y avanzado

interminable [ɪn'tɜːmɪnəbl] ADJ interminable

interminably [ɪnˈtɜːmɪnəblɪ] ADV interminablemente

intermingle [ˌɪntəˈmɪŋgl] **A** VT entremezclar **B** VI entremezclarse

intermission [ˌɪntəˈmɪʃən] N (= *pause*) interrupción *f*, intermisión *f*; (*between events*) intervalo *m*; (*Theat*) intermedio *m*

intermittent [ˌɪntəˈmɪtənt] ADJ intermitente

intermittently [ˌɪntəˈmɪtəntlɪ] ADV a ratos, a intervalos

intern [ɪnˈtɜːn] VT internar, recluir **B** [ˈɪntɜːn] N (*US*) (= *doctor*) interno/a *m/f*

internal [ɪnˈtɜːnl] ADJ (*gen*) interno; [*wall*] interior ➤ **internal audit** auditoría *f* interna ➤ **Internal Revenue Service** (*US*) ≈ Hacienda *f*

internalize [ɪnˈtɜːnəlaɪz] VT interiorizar

internally [ɪnˈtɜːnəlɪ] ADV internamente; **"not to be taken internally"** "sólo para uso externo *or* tópico"

international [ˌɪntəˈnæʃnəl] **A** ADJ internacional **B** N (*Brit*) (= *match*) partido *m* internacional; (= *player*) internacional *mf* **C** CPD ➤ **International Court of Justice** Corte *f* Internacional de Justicia ➤ **international date line** línea *f* de cambio de fecha ➤ **International Monetary Fund** Fondo *m* Monetario Internacional ➤ **international reply coupon** cupón *m* de respuesta internacional

internationally [ˌɪntəˈnæʃnəlɪ] ADV [*function, compete*] internacionalmente; [*known, recognized*] mundialmente

internee [ˌɪntɜːˈniː] N prisionero/a *m/f* de guerra (*civil*)

Internet [ˈɪntənet] N **the ~** Internet *m or f* ➤ **Internet café** cibercafé *m* ➤ **Internet Service Provider** proveedor *m* de servicios de Internet ➤ **Internet user** internauta *mf*

internment [ɪnˈtɜːnmənt] N internamiento *m*

interpersonal [ˌɪntəˈpɜːsənl] ADJ interpersonal

interplay [ˈɪntəpleɪ] N interacción *f*

Interpol [ˈɪntəpɒl] N ABBR (= **International Criminal Police Organization**) Interpol *f*

interpose [ˌɪntəˈpəʊz] VT interponer

interpret [ɪnˈtɜːprɪt] **A** VT (= *translate, understand*) interpretar; **that is not how I ~ it** yo no lo entiendo así, yo lo entiendo de otro modo **B** VI (= *translate*) hacer de intérprete, traducir; (= *work as interpreter*) trabajar de intérprete

interpretation [ɪnˌtɜːprɪˈteɪʃən] N interpretación *f*; **what ~ am I to place on your conduct?** ¿cómo he de interpretar tu conducta?

interpreter [ɪnˈtɜːprɪtəʳ] N intérprete *mf*

interpreting [ɪnˈtɜːprɪtɪŋ] N interpretación *f*

interrelate [ˌɪntərɪˈleɪt] **A** VT interrelacionar **B** VI interrelacionarse

interrelated [ˌɪntərɪˈleɪtɪd] ADJ interrelacionado

interrogate [ɪnˈterəgeɪt] VT interrogar, someter a un interrogatorio

interrogation [ɪnˌterəˈgeɪʃən] N interrogatorio *m* ➤ **interrogation mark, interrogation point** (*US*) signo *m* de interrogación, punto *m* de interrogación

interrogative [ˌɪntəˈrɒgətɪv] **A** ADJ [*look, tone*] interrogador; (*Gram*) interrogativo **B** N interrogativo *m*; **in the ~** en (forma) interrogativa

interrogator [ɪnˈterəgeɪtəʳ] N interrogador(a) *m/f*

interrupt [ˌɪntəˈrʌpt] VT, VI interrumpir

interruption [ˌɪntəˈrʌpʃən] N interrupción *f*

intersect [ˌɪntəˈsekt] VI (*Math*) cortarse, intersecarse; [*roads*] cruzarse

intersection [ˌɪntəˈsekʃən] N (= *crossing*) intersección *f*, cruce *m*; (*Math*) intersección *f*

intersperse [ˌɪntəˈspɜːs] VT **begonias ~d with geraniums** begonias entremezcladas *or* intercaladas con geranios; **a speech ~d with jokes** un discurso salpicado de chistes; **sunny periods ~d with showers** periodos *mpl* de sol con intervalos de chubascos irregulares

interstate [ˌɪntəˈsteɪt] **A** ADJ interestatal **B** N (*US*) autopista *f* interestatal

intertwine [ˌɪntəˈtwaɪn] **A** VI [*fingers, plants*] entrelazarse; [*fates, destinies*] cruzarse, entrecruzarse **B** VT [+ *fingers, plants*] entrelazar; [+ *fates, destinies*] cruzar, entrecruzar

interval [ˈɪntəvəl] N (*in time, space, also Mus*) intervalo *m*; (*Sport*) (= *half time*) descanso *m*; (*esp Brit Theat*) intermedio *m*, entreacto *m* (*more frm*); **at ~s** a intervalos; **at 15-minute ~s** cada 15 minutos; **sunny ~s** claros *mpl*

intervene [ˌɪntəˈviːn] VI (= *take part*) intervenir (**in** en); (= *step in*) interponerse; **we were to marry but the war ~d** íbamos a casarnos pero se interpuso la guerra; **to ~ (with sb) on sb's behalf** interceder por algn (ante algn); **if nothing ~s to prevent it** si no surge nada que lo impida

intervening [ˌɪntəˈviːnɪŋ] ADJ intermedio; **in the ~ period** en el ínterin *or* interín; **in the ~ years** en el transcurso de esos años

intervention [ˌɪntəˈvenʃən] N intervención *f*

interventionist [ˌɪntəˈvenʃənɪst] ADJ, N intervencionista *mf*

interview [ˈɪntəvjuː] **A** N entrevista *f*; (*for press, TV*) entrevista *f*, interviú *f or m*; **to have an ~ with sb** entrevistarse con algn **B** VT (*for press, TV*) hacer una entrevista *or* interviú a **C** VI **they are ~ing for this post tomorrow** mañana realizarán las entrevistas para este puesto

interviewee [ˈɪntəvjuːˈiː] N entrevistado/a *m/f*

interviewer [ˈɪntəvjuːəʳ] N entrevistador(a) *m/f*

inter-war [ˌɪntəˈwɔːʳ] ADJ **the ~ years** el período de entreguerras

interweave [ˌɪntəˈwiːv] (*pt* **interwove**; *pp* **interwoven**) VT entretejer

intestate [ɪnˈtestɪt] ADJ **to die ~** morir intestado

intestinal [ˌɪntesˈtaɪnl] ADJ [*tract, complaint*] intestinal

intestine [ɪnˈtestɪn] N intestino *m*; **small/large ~** intestino *m* delgado/grueso

intimacy [ˈɪntɪməsɪ] N **1** (= *closeness*) intimidad *f*; **there had never been any sexual ~ between them** nunca habían mantenido relaciones íntimas **2 intimacies** (*spoken*) intimidades *fpl*; (*sexual*) intimidad *fsing* (física), proximidad *fsing* (física)

intimate **A** ADJ [ˈɪntɪmɪt] íntimo; **to have an ~ knowledge of a subject** tener un profundo conocimiento de una materia, conocer una materia a fondo; **he had an ~ knowledge of the city** conocía muy bien la ciudad; **to be on ~ terms with sb** ser íntimo de algn **B** [ˈɪntɪmeɪt] VT insinuar, dar a entender; **she ~d that she was ready for a change** insinuó *or* dio a entender que estaba lista para un cambio **C** [ˈɪntɪmɪt] N amigo/a *m/f* de confianza

intimately [ˈɪntɪmɪtlɪ] ADV íntimamente; **to know sb ~** (*as friends*) conocer a algn íntimamente; (*sexually*) tener relaciones íntimas con algn; **musicians whose work she knew ~** músicos cuyo trabajo conocía a fondo *or* en profundidad

intimation [ˌɪntɪˈmeɪʃən] N **1** (= *suggestion*) indicación *f*; **did you have any ~ that this would happen?** ¿hubo algo que te hiciera pensar que esto sucedería? **2** (= *hint*) insinuación *f*

intimidate [ɪnˈtɪmɪdeɪt] VT intimidar

intimidating [ɪnˈtɪmɪdeɪtɪŋ] ADJ amedrentador, intimidante

intimidation [ɪnˌtɪmɪˈdeɪʃən] N intimidación *f*

into [ˈɪntʊ] PREP

When **into** is an element in a phrasal verb, eg **break into, enter into, look into, walk into**, look up the verb.

---

1 (*of place*) en, dentro de; **put it ~ the box** mételo en *or* dentro de la caja; **to get ~ bed** meterse a la cama; **to get ~ a car** subir(se) a un coche; **to go ~ the country** ir al campo; **I poured the milk ~ a cup** vertí la leche en una taza; **it fell ~ the lake** se cayó al lago; **they got ~ the plane** subieron al avión; **to come/go ~ a room** entrar en una habitación; **to go ~ town** ir al centro de la ciudad; **to go ~ the wood** adentrarse *or* penetrar en el bosque

2 (*of time*) **we talked far ~ the night** charlamos hasta bien entrada la noche; **he's well ~ his fifties** tiene cincuenta y tantos largos

3 (*change in condition etc*) **to <u>change</u> ~ a monster** volverse un *or* convertirse en un monstruo; **to change pounds ~ dollars** cambiar libras por dólares; **the rain changed ~ snow** la lluvia se convirtió en nieve

4 (*Math*) **to <u>divide</u> three ~ 12** dividir doce entre tres; **two ~ six <u>goes</u> three** seis entre dos son tres

5 to be ~ sth*: he is really ~ jazz es un gran aficionado al *or* del jazz; **to be ~ drugs** meterse drogas, andar metido en drogas; **she's ~ health food** le va mucho lo de la comida sana; **the children/puppies are ~ everything!** ¡los críos/ perritos andan revolviéndolo todo!

intolerable [ɪnˈtɒlərəbl] ADJ intolerable; **it is ~ that** es intolerable que + *subjun*, no se puede consentir que + *subjun*

intolerably [ɪnˈtɒlərəblɪ] ADJ [*ache*] insoportablemente; **it was ~ hot** hacía un calor insoportable

intolerance [ɪnˈtɒlərəns] N (*gen*) intolerancia *f*; (= *bigotry*) intransigencia *f*

intolerant [ɪnˈtɒlərənt] ADJ (*gen*) intolerante (**of** con *or* para con); (= *bigoted*) intransigente (**of** con); **to be ~ of sth** (*gen*) no tolerar algo

intonation [ˌɪntəʊˈneɪʃən] N entonación *f*

intone [ɪnˈtəʊn] VT entonar

intoxicate [ɪnˈtɒksɪkeɪt] VT embriagar

intoxicated [ɪnˈtɒksɪkeɪtɪd] ADJ (= *drunk*) ebrio, en estado de embriaguez; **to become ~** alcanzar un estado de embriaguez; **to be ~ with sth** (*fig*) estar embriagado *or* ebrio de algo

intoxicating [ɪnˈtɒksɪkeɪtɪŋ] ADJ **1** [*substance*] narcótico, estupefaciente; **an ~ mixture of gin, vodka and coke** una mezcla de ginebra, vodka y Coca Cola con un efecto narcótico **2** [*success, perfume, atmosphere*] embriagador

intoxication [ɪnˌtɒksɪˈkeɪʃən] N embriaguez *f*

intractable [ɪnˈtræktəbl] ADJ [*person*] intratable; (= *unruly*) indisciplinado; [*problem*] insoluble, espinoso; [*illness*] incurable

intramural [ˌɪntrəˈmjʊərəl] ADJ (*US Univ*) dentro de la universidad; (= *within organization, country*) interno

intramuscular [ˌɪntrəˈmʌskjʊləʳ] ADJ intramuscular

intranet [ˈɪntrənet] N intranet *f*

intransigence [ɪnˈtrænsɪdʒəns] N intransigencia *f*

intransigent [ɪnˈtrænsɪdʒənt] ADJ intransigente

intransitive [ɪnˈtrænsɪtɪv] ADJ intransitivo

intrauterine [ˌɪntrəˈjuːtəraɪn] ADJ intrauterino ➤ **intrauterine device** dispositivo *m* intrauterino

intravenous [ˌɪntrəˈviːnəs] ADJ intravenoso; **~ drug users** drogadictos *mpl* que se inyectan por vía intravenosa ➤ **intravenous drip** gota a gota *m*

intravenously [ˌɪntrəˈviːnəslɪ] ADV por vía intravenosa

in-tray [ˈɪnˌtreɪ] N bandeja *f* de entrada

intrepid [ɪnˈtrepɪd] ADJ intrépido

intricacy [ˈɪntrɪkəsɪ] N [*of pattern, design*] lo intrincado, complejidad *f*; [*of plot, problem*] complejidad *f*

intricate [ˈɪntrɪkɪt] ADJ [*pattern, design*] intrincado; [*plot, problem*] complejo

intricately [ˈɪntrɪkɪtlɪ] ADV intrincadamente, de modo intrincado

intrigue [ɪnˈtriːɡ] 🄐 N (= *plot*) intriga *f*; (*amorous*) aventura *f* (sentimental), amorío *m* 🄑 VT fascinar; **I am ~d to know whether ...** me intriga saber si ..., estoy intrigado por saber si ...; **we were ~d by a sign outside a shop** nos llamó la atención el letrero de una tienda 🄒 VI intrigar (**against** contra)

intriguing [ɪnˈtriːɡɪŋ] ADJ [*question, problem*] intrigante; [*prospect, possibility*] fascinante

intrinsic [ɪnˈtrɪnsɪk] ADJ intrínseco

intrinsically [ɪnˈtrɪnsɪklɪ] ADV intrínsecamente

intro* [ˈɪntrəʊ] N (= *introduction*) (*between people*) presentación *f*; (*Mus*) entrada *f*

introduce [ˌɪntrəˈdjuːs] VT **1** (= *make acquainted*) presentar;

to ~ sb to sb presentar a algn a algn; **may I ~ ...?** permítame presentarle a ..., le presento a ...; **I don't think we've been ~d** creo que no nos han presentado; **to ~ sb to sth** hacer conocer algo a algn, iniciar a algn en algo; **I was ~d to chess at eight** empecé a jugar al ajedrez a los ocho años

2 (= *bring in*) [+ *reform, idea*] introducir; (*Pol*) [+ *bill*] presentar; [+ *programme*] presentar; [+ *product, new fashion*] lanzar; **be careful how you ~ the subject** ten cuidado a la hora de abordar el tema

3 (= *insert*) introducir

introduction [ˌɪntrəˈdʌkʃən] N **1** [*of person*] presentación *f*; **a letter of ~** una carta de recomendación; **will you do the ~s?** ¿quieres hacer las presentaciones? **2** (= *initiation*) introducción *f*; **a good ~ to his teachings** una buena introducción a sus enseñanzas; **my ~ to maths** mi iniciación en las matemáticas **3** (*in book*) prólogo *m*, introducción *f* **4** [*of legislation*] introducción *f*; [*of bill*] presentación *f* **5** (= *insertion*) introducción *f*, inserción *f*

introductory [ˌɪntrəˈdʌktərɪ] ADJ [*remarks*] preliminar; [*lecture, talk*] introductorio, de introducción; [*course*] introductorio, de iniciación ➤ **introductory offer** oferta *f* de lanzamiento

introspection [ˌɪntrəʊˈspekʃən] N introspección *f*

introspective [ˌɪntrəʊˈspektɪv] ADJ introspectivo

introvert [ˈɪntrəʊvɜːt] ADJ, N introvertido/a *m/f*

introverted [ˌɪntrəʊˈvɜːtɪd] ADJ introvertido

intrude [ɪnˈtruːd] VI (= *disturb*) molestar; (= *intervene*) entrometerse, inmiscuirse (**on, upon** en); **am I intruding?** ¿les molesto?; **to ~ on sb** molestar a algn; **we mustn't ~ on their grief** debemos respetar la intimidad de su dolor

intruder [ɪnˈtruːdəʳ] N intruso/a *m/f*

intrusion [ɪnˈtruːʒən] N intrusión *f*; (*on sb's privacy*) intromisión *f*, invasión *f*; **pardon the ~** siento tener que importunarla

intrusive [ɪnˈtruːsɪv] ADJ [*reporter*] entrometido, indiscreto; [*question*] indiscreto; [*noise, presence*] molesto

intuit [ɪnˈtjʊɪt] VT intuir

intuition [ˌɪntjuːˈɪʃən] N intuición *f*

intuitive [ɪnˈtjuːɪtɪv] ADJ [*knowledge*] intuitivo; [*powers*] de intuición; **she had an ~ grasp of what was needed** intuía qué era lo que hacía falta

intuitively [ɪnˈtjuːɪtɪvlɪ] ADV intuitivamente, por intuición

Inuit [ˈɪnjuɪt] (*pl ~ or ~s*) ADJ, N Inuit *mf inv*

inundate [ˈɪnʌndeɪt] VT inundar; **we have been ~d with replies** nos hemos visto inundados *or* desbordados por las respuestas

inure [ɪnˈjʊəʳ] VT (= *accustom*) acostumbrar, habituar (**to** a); **to become ~d to sth** acostumbrarse *or* habituarse a algo

invade [ɪnˈveɪd] VT invadir

invader [ɪnˈveɪdəʳ] N invasor(a) *m/f*

invading [ɪnˈveɪdɪŋ] ADJ invasor

invalid¹ [ˈɪnvəlɪd] ADJ, N inválido/a *m/f* ➤ **invalid car**, **invalid carriage** coche *m* de inválido

invalid² [ɪnˈvælɪd] ADJ [*ticket, contract*] inválido; [*theory, results*] sin validez; **to become ~** caducar

invalidate [ɪnˈvælɪdeɪt] VT [+ *document, argument, theory*] invalidar; [+ *contract*] anular, invalidar

invalidity [ˌɪnvəˈlɪdɪtɪ] N invalidez *f* ➤ **invalidity benefit** (*Brit*) prestación *f* por invalidez

invaluable [ɪnˈvæljʊəbl] ADJ inapreciable, inestimable

invariable [ɪnˈvɛərɪəbl] ADJ invariable

invariably [ɪnˈvɛərɪəblɪ] ADV invariablemente, siempre; **he is ~ late** siempre llega tarde, llega tarde invariablemente

invasion [ɪnˈveɪʒən] N invasión *f*; **it would be an ~ of privacy to ...** sería una invasión de la intimidad ...

invasive [ɪnˈveɪsɪv] ADJ [*surgery, cancer*] invasivo

invective [ɪnˈvektɪv] N (= *accusation*) invectiva *f*; (= *abuse*) improperios *mpl*, palabras *fpl* fuertes

inveigh [ɪnˈveɪ] VI **to ~ against** vituperar, lanzar invectivas contra

inveigle [ɪn'viːɡl] VT inducir; **he let himself be ~d into it** se dejó inducir a ello; **to ~ sb into doing sth** inducir a algn mediante engaño a que haga algo

invent [ɪn'vent] VT inventar

invention [ɪn'venʃən] N **1** (= *act*) invención *f*; (= *machine*) invento *m*, invención *f* **2** (= *falsehood*) mentira *f*, invención *f*; **it's pure ~** es pura invención

inventive [ɪn'ventɪv] ADJ ingenioso, lleno de inventiva

inventiveness [ɪn'ventɪvnɪs] N inventiva *f*, ingenio *m*

inventor [ɪn'ventə'] N inventor(a) *m/f*

inventory ['ɪnvəntrɪ] ⒶN inventario *m*; **to draw up an ~ of sth** hacer un inventario de algo ⒷVT inventariar

inverse ['ɪn'vɜːs] ⒶADJ inverso ⒷN **the ~** lo inverso, lo contrario

inversely [ɪn'vɜːslɪ] ADV a la inversa; **A is ~ proportional to B** A es inversamente proporcional a B

inversion [ɪn'vɜːʃən] N inversión *f*

invert [ɪn'vɜːt] VT invertir, poner al revés

invertebrate [ɪn'vɜːtɪbrɪt] ADJ, N invertebrado/a *m/f*

inverted [ɪn'vɜːtɪd] ADJ ➤ **inverted commas** (*Brit*) comillas *fpl*; **in ~ commas** entre comillas ➤ **inverted snobbery** esnobismo *m* regresivo

invest [ɪn'vest] ⒶVT **1** [+ *money, funds*] invertir (**in** en); [+ *time, effort*] dedicar (**in** a) **2** [+ *person*] (*in office*) investir; **to ~ sb with sth** investir a algn de *or* con algo; **to ~ sth with sth** revestir algo de algo ⒷVI **to ~ in** [+ *company, project*] invertir dinero en; (= *buy*) comprarse

investigate [ɪn'vestɪɡeɪt] ⒶVT [+ *crime, case*] investigar; [+ *person*] hacer indagaciones sobre; [+ *claim, possibility*] examinar, estudiar; [+ *complaint*] estudiar ⒷVI investigar

investigation [ɪn,vestɪ'ɡeɪʃən] N (*by police, authorities, scientist*) investigación *f*; **the ~ into the causes of the accident** la investigación sobre las causas del accidente; **these allegations need further ~** estas acusaciones se tienen que investigar más a fondo

investigative [ɪn'vestɪɡətɪv] ADJ investigador ➤ **investigative journalism** periodismo *m* de investigación

investigator [ɪn'vestɪɡeɪtə'] N investigador(a) *m/f*

investiture [ɪn'vestɪtʃə'] N investidura *f*

investment [ɪn'vestmənt] N (*Comm*) inversión *f* ➤ **investment bank** banco *m* de inversión ➤ **investment company** compañía *f* de inversiones ➤ **investment portfolio** cartera *f* de valores

investor [ɪn'vestə'] N inversionista *mf*

inveterate [ɪn'vetərɪt] ADJ [*gambler*] empedernido; [*laziness, selfishness*] inveterado

invidious [ɪn'vɪdɪəs] ADJ [*job, task*] odioso, ingrato; [*comparison*] injusto; **I find myself in an ~ position** me encuentro en una situación ingrata; **it would be ~ to mention names** sería inapropiado mencionar nombres

invigilate [ɪn'vɪdʒɪleɪt] VT, VI (*Brit*) vigilar (*durante los exámenes*)

invigilator [ɪn'vɪdʒɪleɪtə'] N (*Brit*) vigilante *m* (*en un examen*)

invigorate [ɪn'vɪɡəreɪt] VT [+ *person*] vigorizar; [+ *campaign*] dar nuevo ímpetu a; [+ *economy*] estimular; **I felt refreshed, ~d and ready to tackle anything** me sentía descansado, lleno de energía y dispuesto a abordar cualquier tarea

invigorating [ɪn'vɪɡəreɪtɪŋ] ADJ [*walk, shower, air*] vigorizante, tonificante; **how ~ she was to talk to!** ¡qué estimulante resultaba su conversación!

invincible [ɪn'vɪnsəbl] ADJ [*army, team*] invencible; [*faith, belief*] inquebrantable

inviolable [ɪn'vaɪələbl] ADJ inviolable

invisible [ɪn'vɪzəbl] ADJ invisible ➤ **invisible earnings** ingresos *mpl* invisibles ➤ **invisible exports** exportaciones *fpl* invisibles ➤ **invisible ink** tinta *f* simpática *or* invisible

invisibly [ɪn'vɪzɪblɪ] ADV de manera invisible

invitation [,ɪnvɪ'teɪʃən] N invitación *f*; **an ~ to dinner** una

invitación para cenar; **at the ~ of** por invitación de ➤ **invitation card** tarjeta *f* de invitación

invite Ⓐ[ɪn'vaɪt] VT **1** [+ *person*] invitar; (*esp to important celebration*) convidar; **to ~ sb to do sth** invitar a algn a hacer algo; **to ~ sb to dinner/lunch** invitar a algn a cenar/almorzar; **to ~ sb in/up** invitar a algn a pasar/subir; **they ~d me out to dinner** me invitaron a cenar (a un restaurante) **2** (= *request*) [+ *opinions*] pedir, solicitar (*more frm*) **3** (= *provoke*) [+ *discussion, ridicule*] provocar; **to ~ trouble** buscarse problemas Ⓑ['ɪnvaɪt] N (*) invitación *f*

inviting [ɪn'vaɪtɪŋ] ADJ [*atmosphere, place, room*] acogedor; [*prospect*] atractivo; [*food*] apetitoso, apetecible; [*smell*] apetitoso; **the water looked warm and ~** el agua aparecía cálida y tentadora

in vitro [ɪn'viːtrəʊ] ADJ, ADV in vitro

invoice ['ɪnvɔɪs] ⒶN factura *f*; **as per ~** según factura; **to send an ~** pasar *or* presentar factura ⒷVT [+ *goods*] facturar; **to ~ sb for sth** pasar a algn factura por algo

invoicing ['ɪnvɔɪsɪŋ] N facturación *f*

invoke [ɪn'vəʊk] VT [+ *law, principle*] recurrir a, invocar; [+ *protection, spirit*] invocar

involuntarily [ɪn'vɒləntərɪlɪ] ADV involuntariamente

involuntary [ɪn'vɒləntərɪ] ADJ involuntario

involve [ɪn'vɒlv] VT **1** (= *implicate, associate*) implicar, involucrar; **a dispute involving a friend of mine** una disputa en la que estaba implicado *or* involucrado un amigo mío; **a crash involving three vehicles** una colisión en la que se vieron envueltos *or* involucrados tres vehículos; **he was ~d in a fight** se vio envuelto en una pelea; **we would prefer not to ~ the children** preferiríamos no meter *or* involucrar a los niños; **try to ~ him in your leisure activities** intenta hacer que participe contigo en tus actividades de tiempo libre; **the persons ~d** (*gen*) los implicados; (= *culprits*) los implicados; **to become ~d (in sth): the police became ~d** la policía tomó cartas en el asunto; **I don't want to get ~d** no quiero meterme; **she got ~d with some really weird people** se mezcló con una gente muy rara; **she likes him but she doesn't want to get ~d** él le gusta, pero no quiere comprometerse

2 (= *entail*) suponer; **it ~d a lot of expense** supuso *or* acarreó muchos gastos; **the job ~s moving to London** el trabajo requiere que se traslade a Londres; **what does your job ~?** ¿en qué consiste su trabajo?

involved [ɪn'vɒlvd] ADJ complicado, enrevesado

involvement [ɪn'vɒlvmənt] N **1** (= *intervention*) intervención *f*; (= *participation*) participación *f*; **we don't know the extent of his ~** no sabemos hasta qué punto está implicado; **I knew of his past ~ with drugs** sabía que en el pasado había estado metido en drogas **2** (= *relationship*) relación *f*

invulnerable [ɪn'vʌlnərəbl] ADJ invulnerable (**to** a)

inward ['ɪnwəd] ⒶADJ **1** [*peace, happiness*] interior **2** [*movement*] hacia el interior ⒷADV hacia dentro; **the door swung ~** la puerta se abrió hacia dentro ⒸCPD ➤ **inward investment** inversiones *fpl* extranjeras ➤ **inward investor** inversor(a) *m/f* extranjero/a

inward-looking ['ɪnwəd,lʊkɪŋ] ADJ [*person*] introvertido; **the country is too ~** el país está muy encerrado en sí mismo

inwardly ['ɪnwədlɪ] ADV [*sigh, groan, smile*] para sus adentros; [*know, struggle*] en su interior; [*feel*] por dentro; **she was ~ furious** por dentro estaba furiosa

inwards ['ɪnwədz] ADV (*Brit*) = **inward B**

IOC N ABBR (= **International Olympic Committee**) COI *m*

iodine ['aɪədiːn] N yodo *m*

IOM ABBR (*Brit*) = **Isle of Man**

ion ['aɪən] N ion *m*

Ionian [aɪ'əʊnɪən] ADJ jonio, jónico ➤ **Ionian Sea** Mar *m* Jónico

ionize ['aɪənaɪz] VT ionizar

iota [aɪ'əʊtə] N (= *letter*) iota *f*; (*fig*) pizca *f*, ápice *m*; **there's not one ~ of truth in it** eso no tiene ni pizca de verdad; **if he had an ~ of sense** si tuviera un pizca de inteligencia

IOU N ABBR (= **I owe you**) pagaré *m*, vale *m* (*LAm*)

IOW ABBR (*Brit*) = **Isle of Wight**

IPA N ABBR = **International Phonetic Alphabet**

IP address [aɪ'piːəˌdres] N (*Comput*) (= **Internet Protocol address**) dirección *f* IP

IQ N ABBR (= **intelligence quotient**) C.I. *m*

IRA N ABBR (= **Irish Republican Army**) IRA *m*

Iran [ɪ'rɑːn] N Irán *m*

Iranian [ɪ'reɪnɪən] ADJ, N iraní *mf*

Iraq [ɪ'rɑːk] N Irak *m*, Iraq *m*

Iraqi [ɪ'rɑːkɪ] ADJ, N iraquí *mf*

irascible [ɪ'ræsɪbl] ADJ irascible, colérico

irate [aɪ'reɪt] ADJ indignado, furioso; **he got very ~** se indignó mucho, se puso furioso

IRC N ABBR (*Comput*) (= **Internet Relay Chat**) IRC *m*

ire [aɪəʳ] N (*liter*) ira *f*, cólera *f*; **to rouse sb's ~** provocar la ira de algn

Ireland ['aɪələnd] N Irlanda *f*; **Northern ~** Irlanda *f* del Norte; **Republic of ~** República *f* de Irlanda

iridescent [ɪrɪ'desnt] ADJ iridiscente, irisado, tornasolado

iris ['aɪrɪs] N (*pl* **-es**) **1** (*Anat*) iris *m inv* **2** (*Bot*) lirio *m*

Irish ['aɪərɪʃ] **Ⓐ** ADJ irlandés **Ⓑ** N **1 the ~** los irlandeses **2** (*Ling*) irlandés *m* **Ⓒ** CPD ➤ **Irish coffee** café *m* irlandés ➤ **the Irish Sea** el Mar de Irlanda ➤ **Irish stew** estofado *m* irlandés

Irishman ['aɪərɪʃmən] N (*pl* **Irishmen**) irlandés *m*

Irishwoman ['aɪərɪʃˌwʊmən] N (*pl* **Irishwomen**) irlandesa *f*

irk [ɜːk] VT fastidiar, molestar

irksome ['ɜːksəm] ADJ [*child, chore*] fastidioso, pesado

iron ['aɪən] **Ⓐ** N **1** (= *metal*) hierro *m*, fierro *m* (*LAm*); **✦ IDIOM to strike while the ~ is hot** a hierro candente batir de repente **2 irons** (= *fetters*) grilletes *mpl*, grillos *mpl* **3** (*Golf*) hierro *m* **4** (*for ironing clothes*) plancha *f*; **✦ IDIOM to have too many ~s in the fire** tener demasiados asuntos entre manos **Ⓑ** VT [+ *clothes*] planchar **Ⓒ** VI [*person*] planchar **Ⓓ** CPD [*bridge, bar, tool*] de hierro, de fierro (*LAm*); (*fig*) [*will, determination*] férreo ➤ **the Iron Age** la Edad de hierro ➤ **Iron Cross** cruz *f* de hierro ➤ **the Iron Curtain** (*Hist, Pol*) el telón de acero, la cortina de hierro (*LAm*) ➤ **iron foundry** fundición *f*, fundidora *f* (*LAm*) ➤ **iron ore** mineral *m* de hierro ➤ **iron rations** ración *fsing* or víveres *mpl* de reserva ➤ **iron out** VT + ADV [+ *unevenness*] allanar; [+ *crease*] quitar, planchar; [+ *difficulties*] allanar, suprimir; [+ *problems, differences*] resolver

ironic [aɪ'rɒnɪk], **ironical** [aɪ'rɒnɪkəl] ADJ irónico

ironically [aɪ'rɒnɪkəlɪ] ADV irónicamente; (*say etc*) con ironía; **~ enough** paradójicamente, como quiso la suerte

ironing ['aɪənɪŋ] N (= *act*) planchado *m*; (= *clothes*) (*for ironing*) ropa *f* por planchar; (*ironed*) ropa *f* planchada; **to do the ~** planchar ➤ **ironing board** tabla *f* de planchar

ironmonger ['aɪənˌmʌŋgəʳ] N (*Brit*) ferretero/a *m/f*, quincallero/a *m/f*; **~'s (shop)** ferretería *f*, quincallería *f*

irony ['aɪərənɪ] N ironía *f*; **the ~ of it is that ...** lo irónico es que ...

irradiate [ɪ'reɪdɪeɪt] VT irradiar

irrational [ɪ'ræʃənl] ADJ irracional

irrationally [ɪ'ræʃnəlɪ] ADV irracionalmente

irreconcilable [ɪˌrekən'saɪləbl] ADJ [*enemies*] irreconciliable; [*ideas*] incompatible

irredeemable [ɪrɪ'diːməbl] ADJ irredimible; (*Fin*) perpetuo, no amortizable

irrefutable [ɪrɪ'fjuːtəbl] ADJ irrefutable

irregular [ɪ'regjʊləʳ] **Ⓐ** ADJ **1** [*shape, surface, pattern, attendance, pulse, verb, noun*] irregular **2** (= *unorthodox*) [*practice*] poco ortodoxo, irregular; [*treatment*] poco ortodoxo; [*action*] poco ortodoxo, contrario a la práctica; [*payment*] irregular; **all this is very ~** todo esto es muy poco

ortodoxo **Ⓑ** N soldado *mf* irregular

irregularity [ɪˌregjʊ'lærɪtɪ] N irregularidad *f*

irrelevance [ɪ'reləvəns] N irrelevancia *f*, intrascendencia *f*; **it highlighted the ~ of the project to the local community** puso de relieve lo intrascendente del proyecto para la comunidad local; **they dismiss religion as an ~** rechazan la religión como algo irrelevante *or* intrascendente

irrelevant [ɪ'reləvənt] ADJ [*details, information*] irrelevante, intrascendente; **those remarks are ~ to the present discussion** esas observaciones no tienen relación con lo que se está discutiendo

irreligious [ɪrɪ'lɪdʒəs] ADJ irreligioso

irreparable [ɪ'repərəbl] ADJ irreparable

irreparably [ɪ'repərəblɪ] ADV irreparablemente

irreplaceable [ɪrɪ'pleɪsəbl] ADJ irre(e)mplazable, insustituible

irrepressible [ɪrɪ'presəbl] ADJ [*person*] irrefrenable

irreproachable [ɪrɪ'prəʊtʃəbl] ADJ irreprochable, intachable

irresistible [ɪrɪ'zɪstəbl] ADJ irresistible

irresistibly [ɪrɪ'zɪstəblɪ] ADV irresistiblemente; **he found her ~ beautiful** la encontraba de una belleza irresistible

irresolute [ɪ'rezəluːt] ADJ indeciso, irresoluto

irrespective [ɪrɪ'spektɪv] ADJ **~ of** sin tomar en consideración *or* en cuenta; **the same treatment for all, ~ of age or gender** el mismo trato para todos, sin distinción de edad o sexo

irresponsibility ['ɪrɪsˌpɒnsə'bɪlɪtɪ] N irresponsabilidad *f*, falta *f* de responsabilidad

irresponsible [ɪrɪs'pɒnsəbl] ADJ irresponsable

irresponsibly [ɪrɪs'pɒnsəblɪ] ADV irresponsablemente, de modo irresponsable

irretrievable [ɪrɪ'triːvəbl] ADJ [*object*] irrecuperable; [*loss, damage, error*] irreparable

irretrievably [ɪrɪ'triːvəblɪ] ADV irreparablemente

irreverence [ɪ'revərəns] N irreverencia *f*, falta *f* de respeto

irreverent [ɪ'revərənt] ADJ irreverente, irrespetuoso

irreversible [ɪrɪ'vɜːsəbl] ADJ [*process*] irreversible; [*decision*] irrevocable

irrevocable [ɪ'revəkəbl] ADJ [*decision*] irrevocable

irrigate [ɪrɪgeɪt] VT [+ *land*] regar; (*Med*) irrigar

irrigation [ɪrɪ'geɪʃən] N (*Agr*) irrigación *f*, riego *m*; (*Med*) irrigación *f* ➤ **irrigation channel** acequia *f*, canal *m* de riego

irritability [ɪrɪtə'bɪlɪtɪ] N irritabilidad *f*

irritable ['ɪrɪtəbl] ADJ irritable; **to get ~** irritarse; **to be in an ~ mood** estar irritable

irritably ['ɪrɪtəblɪ] ADV **he said ~** dijo malhumorado

irritant ['ɪrɪtənt] N (*Med*) agente *m* irritante; (*fig*) molestia *f*

irritate ['ɪrɪteɪt] VT **1** (= *annoy*) irritar, fastidiar; **to get ~d** irritarse, enfadarse **2** (*Med*) irritar

irritating ['ɪrɪteɪtɪŋ] ADJ **1** (= *annoying*) irritante; **it's really most ~** es de lo más irritante **2** (*to skin, eyes*) irritante

irritation [ɪrɪ'teɪʃən] N **1** (= *annoyance*) irritación *f*, enfado *m* **2** (= *irritant*) molestia *f* **3** (*Med*) irritación *f*

irruption [ɪ'rʌpʃən] N irrupción *f*

IRS N ABBR (*US*) = **Internal Revenue Service**

is [ɪz] *see* **be**

Is. ABBR = **Isle(s), Island(s)**

ISA ['aɪsə] N ABBR (*Brit Fin*) (= **Individual Savings Account**) *plan de ahorro personal para pequeños inversores con fiscalidad cero*

ISBN N ABBR (= **International Standard Book Number**) ISBN *f*

ISDN N ABBR (= **Integrated Services Digital Network**) RDSI *f*

Islam ['ɪzlɑːm] N Islam *m*

Islamic [ɪz'læmɪk] ADJ islámico

island ['aɪlənd] N isla *f*; (*in street*) refugio *m*, isla *f* (peatonal)

islander ['aɪləndəʳ] N isleño/a *m/f*

isle [aɪl] N isla *f*

isn't ['ɪznt] = **is not**

isobar ['aɪsəʊbɑːʳ] N isobara *f*

isolate ['aɪsəʊleɪt] VT **1** (= *cut off*) aislar (**from** de) **2** (= *pinpoint*) [+ *cause, source*] identificar; [+ *problem, virus, gene*] aislar

isolated ['aɪsəʊleɪtɪd] ADJ aislado

isolation [ˌaɪsəʊ'leɪʃən] N aislamiento *m*; **we cannot discuss this in ~** no podemos discutir esto aisladamente; **things like this don't happen in ~** estas cosas no ocurren aisladas; **she's being kept in ~** la mantienen aislada
  ➤ **isolation ward** pabellón *m* de infecciosos

isolationism [ˌaɪsəʊ'leɪʃənɪzəm] N aislacionismo *m*

isolationist [aɪsəʊ'leɪʃənɪst] ADJ, N aislacionista *mf*

isometric [ˌaɪsə'metrɪk] ADJ isométrico

isotope ['aɪsəʊtəʊp] N isótopo *m*

ISP N ABBR (= **Internet Service Provider**) proveedor *m* de servicios de Internet

Israel ['ɪzreɪl] N Israel *m*

Israeli [ɪz'reɪlɪ] ADJ, N israelí *mf*

Israelite ['ɪzrɪəlaɪt] ADJ, N israelita *mf*

issue ['ɪʃuː] **Ⓐ** N **1** (= *matter, question*) asunto *m*, cuestión *f*; **the point at ~** el punto en cuestión; **his integrity is not at ~** no se está cuestionando su integridad; **I think we should make an ~ of this** creo que deberíamos insistir en este punto; **do you want to make an ~ of it?** ¿quieres hacer un problema de esto?; **he makes an ~ of every tiny detail** a todo le da mucha más importancia de la que tiene; **it's not a political ~** no es una cuestión política; **the real ~ is ...** lo fundamental es ...; **to take ~ with sth/sb** discrepar de algo/de *or* con algn **2** [*of shares, stamps, banknotes*] emisión *f*; [*of library book*] préstamo *m*; [*of document*] expedición *f*; [*of rations*] distribución *f*, reparto *m* **3** (= *copy*) [*of magazine*] ejemplar *m*, número *m*; **the March ~** el ejemplar *or* número de marzo **4** (*frm*) (= *outcome*) resultado *m*, consecuencia *f* **5** (= *offspring*) descendencia *f*; **to die without ~** morir sin (dejar) descendencia
  Ⓑ VT [+ *library book*] prestar; [+ *tickets*] emitir; [+ *shares, stamps*] poner en circulación, emitir; [+ *rations*] distribuir, repartir; [+ *order*] dar; [+ *statement, proclamation*] hacer público; [+ *decree*] promulgar; [+ *passport, certificate*] expedir; [+ *licence*] facilitar; [+ *writ, summons*] extender; **a warrant has been ~d for his arrest** se ha ordenado su detención; **we were ~d with ten rounds each** nos dieron diez cartuchos a cada uno
  Ⓒ VI **to ~ from sth** [*blood, water*] brotar *or* salir de algo; [*sound*] salir de algo

Istanbul ['ɪstæn'buːl] N Estambul *m*

isthmus ['ɪsməs] N istmo *m*

IT N ABBR (*Comput*) (= **information technology**) informática *f*

it [ɪt] PRON **1** (*specific*)

It as subject or following a preposition is often not translated.

(= *direct object*) lo *m*, la *f*; (= *indirect object*) le; (*after prep*) (*if translated*) él *m*, ella *f*; (*neuter*) ello; **it's on the table** está en la mesa; **where is it?** ¿dónde está?; **"here's the book"** — **"give it to me"** —aquí está el libro —dámelo; **if you have the list, give it to him** si tienes la lista, dásela; **it's a good film, have you seen it?** es una buena película, ¿la has visto?; **give it a kick** dale una patada; **I doubt it** lo dudo; **there's a wall in front of/behind it** hay una pared delante/detrás (de ello); **she put a plate on top of it** le puso un plato encima, lo tapó con un plato; **it's a she** [*dog, cat etc*] es hembra; **it's a boy** [*baby*] es un niño **2** (*indefinite*)

The indefinite subject is not translated.
---

it's raining está lloviendo; **it's Friday tomorrow** mañana es viernes; **it's the tenth of October** es diez de octubre; **it's six o'clock** son las seis; **how far is it?** ¿a qué distancia está?, ¿está muy lejos?; **it's ten miles to London** hay diez millas de aquí a Londres; **it's easy to talk** hablar no cuesta nada; **hello, it's Peter here** hola, soy Peter; **it's me** soy yo; **it's no use worrying** no vale la pena inquietarse; **it is said that ...** se dice que ...; **it was Peter who phoned** fue Peter quien llamó; **what is it?** (= *what's the matter?*) ¿qué pasa?; **who is it?** ¿quién es? **3** (*special uses with "to be"*) **that's it for today** eso es todo por hoy; **that's it! just there is fine** ¡eso es! ahí mismo está bien; **that's it! I've had enough of this waiting!** ¡ya está bien! ¡estoy harto de esperar!; **that's it then! we leave on Sunday** ¡muy bien! *or* ¡solucionado! salimos el domingo; **that's just it!** ¡ahí está el problema!; **this is it** (= *it's time*) ya llegó la hora; (= *train, bus etc*) ahí viene **4** (*referring to situation*) **I spoke to him about it** lo hablé con él; **I'm against it** estoy en contra; **I'm (all) for it*** estoy (muy) a favor; **he won't agree to it** no lo aceptará **5** (*in games*) **you're it!** ¡te tocó! **6** (*) (= *sexual attraction*) **you've either got it or you haven't** ese algo, o se tiene o no **7** (*) (= *something special*) **she thinks she's just it!*** no sé de qué se las da*

Italian [ɪ'tæljən] **Ⓐ** ADJ italiano **Ⓑ** N **1** (= *person*) italiano/a *m/f* **2** (*Ling*) italiano *m*

italic [ɪ'tælɪk] ADJ (*Typ*) en cursiva *or* bastardilla

italics [ɪ'tælɪks] NPL cursiva *fsing*, (letra *fsing*) bastardilla *fsing*

Italy ['ɪtəlɪ] N Italia *f*

itch [ɪtʃ] **Ⓐ** N picor *m*; **I've got an ~ here** me pica aquí, tengo un picor aquí **Ⓑ** VI (= *be itchy*) **my leg ~es** me pica la pierna; **I was ~ing all over** me picaba todo; **to be ~ing for sth*** estar deseando algo; **to be ~ing to do sth*** rabiar por hacer algo

itchiness ['ɪtʃɪnɪs] N picor *m*

itching ['ɪtʃɪŋ] N picor *m*

itchy ['ɪtʃɪ] ADJ (*compar* **itchier**; *superl* **itchiest**) (= *irritated*) [*eyes, skin, scalp*] irritado; [*rash*] que produce picor; **I've got an ~ nose** me pica la nariz

it'd ['ɪtd] = **it would, it had**

item ['aɪtəm] N (*in list, bill, catalogue*) artículo *m*; (*on agenda*) asunto *m* (a tratar), punto *m* (a tratar); (*in programme*) número *m*; (*in newspaper*) artículo *m*; (*TV, Rad*) noticia *f*; **~ of clothing** prenda *f* (de vestir); **basic/luxury food ~s** productos *mpl* alimenticios básicos/suntuarios; **a news ~** una noticia; **they're something of an ~*** son pareja

itemize ['aɪtəmaɪz] VT detallar; **~d bill** factura *f* detallada

itinerant [ɪ'tɪnərənt] ADJ [*preacher, lecturer, worker*] itinerante; [*salesperson*] ambulante

itinerary [aɪ'tɪnərərɪ] N (= *route*) itinerario *m*; (= *map*) ruta *f*

it'll ['ɪtl] = **it will, it shall**

ITN N ABBR (*Brit*) (= **Independent Television News**) *servicio de noticias en las cadenas privadas de televisión*

it's [ɪts] = **it is, it has**

its [ɪts] POSS ADJ (*with singular noun*) su; (*with plural noun*) sus; **everything in ~ place** cada cosa en su sitio; **it has ~ advantages** tiene sus ventajas

---
Its is usually translated by the definite article **el/los** or **la/las** when its clear from the sentence who the possessor is or when referring to clothing or parts of the body:
---

the bird was in ~ cage el pájaro estaba en la jaula; **the dog was wagging ~ tail** el perro iba moviendo la cola

itself [ɪt'self] PRON **1** (*reflexive*) se; (*after preposition*) sí; **the dog was scratching ~** el perro se estaba rascando; **their record speaks for ~** su historial habla por sí mismo **2** (*emphatic*) **Christmas ~ was an anticlimax** lo que es la

Navidad en sí fue muy decepcionante; **he is always politeness** ~ siempre es la cortesía personificada; **the door closed by** ~ la puerta se cerró sola; **I loved him more than life** ~ lo quería más que a mi propia vida; **that was an achievement in** ~ eso fue un triunfo de por sí

ITV N ABBR (*Brit*) (= **Independent Television**) *cadena privada de televisión*

IUD N ABBR (= **intrauterine device**) DIU *m*

IV ABBR (= **intravenous(ly)**) ➤ IV drip gota a gota *m*

I've [aɪv] = **I have**

IVF N ABBR (= **in vitro fertilization**) FIV *f*

ivory ['aɪvərɪ] **A** N marfil *m* **B** ADJ [*cane, box*] de marfil; [*skin*] de color marfil **C** CPD ➤ Ivory Coast Costa *f* de Marfil ➤ ivory tower torre *f* de marfil

ivy ['aɪvɪ] N (*Bot*) hiedra *f*, yedra *f* ➤ the Ivy League (*US*) *grupo de ocho universidades privadas muy prestigiosas de Nueva Inglaterra*

IVY LEAGUE

En el noreste de los Estados Unidos, la **Ivy League** está formada por ocho universidades de gran prestigio, tanto académico como social. El término procede de la época en la que estas ocho universidades, **Harvard, Yale, Pennsylvania, Princeton, Columbia, Brown, Dartmouth** y **Cornell** formaron una liga para impulsar las competiciones deportivas entre ellas y tiene su origen en la hiedra (**ivy**) que cubre los muros de las facultades y colegios universitarios. A los estudiantes de estas universidades se les denomina **Ivy Leaguers**.

Jj

J, j [dʒeɪ] N (= letter) J, j f; **J for Jack** J de José

jab [dʒæb] Ⓐ N **1** (= poke) pinchazo m; (with elbow) codazo m **2** (Brit Med*) inyección f Ⓑ VT **to ~ sb with one's elbow** dar un codazo a algn; **to ~ a finger at sth** señalar algo con el dedo; **I ~bed the knife in my arm** me pinché el brazo con el cuchillo Ⓒ VI **to ~ at** [+ fire] atizar; **he ~bed at the map with a finger** dio con el dedo en el mapa

jabber ['dʒæbəʳ] Ⓐ N (= fast talk) chapurreo m, farfulla f; (= chatter) cotorreo m Ⓑ VI (= talk fast) farfullar; (= chatter) charlotear, parlotear

jack [dʒæk] Ⓐ N **1** (Aut, Tech) gato m; (Elec) toma f de corriente, enchufe m hembra **3** (Cards) jota f; (in Spanish pack) sota f Ⓑ CPD ➤ **jack plug** enchufe m de clavija
➤ **jack in*** VT + ADV (Brit) dejar, abandonar
➤ **jack up** VT + ADV **1** (Tech) levantar con el gato
2 (= increase) [+ price, production] aumentar

jackal ['dʒækɔːl] N chacal m

jackass ['dʒækæs] N burro m

jackboot ['dʒækbuːt] N bota f militar; ✦ IDIOM **under the Nazi ~** bajo el dominio nazi

jackdaw ['dʒækdɔː] N grajilla f

jacket ['dʒækɪt] Ⓐ N **1** (= garment) chaqueta f, americana f (Sp), saco m (LAm) **2** [of book] sobrecubierta f; (US) [of record] funda f Ⓑ CPD ➤ **jacket potatoes** (Brit) patatas fpl asadas con piel, papas fpl asadas con cáscara (LAm)

jack-in-the-box ['dʒækɪnðəbɒks] N caja f sorpresa, caja f de resorte

jackknife ['dʒæknaɪf] Ⓐ N (pl **jackknives**) navaja f, chaveta f (LAm) Ⓑ VI [lorry] colear

jack-of-all-trades ['dʒækəvɔːl'treɪdz] N (pl **jacks-of-all-trades**) **he's a ~** (multiskilled) le mete mano a todo; **he's a ~ (and master of none)** es aprendiz de mucho y maestro de nada

jackpot ['dʒækpɒt] N premio m gordo; **to hit the ~** (= be successful) ser todo un éxito or un exitazo

Jacobean [,dʒækə'biːən] ADJ de la época de Jacobo I (de Inglaterra)

Jacobite ['dʒækəbaɪt] ADJ, N jacobita mf

Jacuzzi ® [dʒə'kuːzɪ] N jacuzzi® m, baño m de burbujas

jade [dʒeɪd] Ⓐ N jade m Ⓑ ADJ verde jade inv

jaded ['dʒeɪdɪd] ADJ hastiado, harto

jade-green ['dʒeɪd'griːn] ADJ verde jade inv

jagged ['dʒægɪd] ADJ dentado

jaguar ['dʒægjʊəʳ] N jaguar m, tigre m (LAm)

jail [dʒeɪl] Ⓐ N cárcel f, prisión f; **to go to ~** ir a la cárcel Ⓑ VT encarcelar (**for doing sth** por haber hecho algo); **to ~ sb for two months** condenar a algn a dos meses de cárcel Ⓒ CPD ➤ **jail sentence** pena f de cárcel

jailbird ['dʒeɪlbɜːd] N presidiario/a m/f reincidente, preso/a m/f reincidente

jailbreak ['dʒeɪlbreɪk] N fuga f, evasión f (de la cárcel)

jailer ['dʒeɪləʳ] N carcelero/a m/f

jailhouse ['dʒeɪlhaʊs] N cárcel f, prisión f

Jakarta [dʒə'kɑːtə] N Yakarta f

jam¹ [dʒæm] (Brit) Ⓐ N (= food) mermelada f; **strawberry ~** mermelada f de fresas ➤ **jam jar** (Brit) tarro m de mermelada ➤ **jam tart** tarta f de mermelada

jam² [dʒæm] Ⓐ N **1** [of people] aglomeración f **2** (= traffic jam) embotellamiento m, atasco m **3** (*) (= difficulty) apuro m, aprieto m; **to be in/get into a ~** estar/meterse en un aprieto, estar/meterse en apuros Ⓑ VT **1** [+ mechanism, drawer, pipe] atascar; [+ road] cerrar, obstruir; **it's got ~med** se ha atascado, no se puede mover/quitar/retirar etc
2 [+ passage] atestar, abarrotar; [+ container] atestar, llenar; **people ~med the exits** la gente se agolpaba en las salidas;

the room was ~med with people el cuarto estaba atestado de gente; **streets ~med with cars** calles atascadas por el tráfico
Ⓒ VI [mechanism] atascarse, atorarse (LAm); [part, wheel] atascarse, atrancarse; [gun] encasquillarse; **the drawer had ~med (shut/open)** el cajón no se podía abrir/cerrar
Ⓓ CPD ➤ **jam session** jam session f (actuación improvisada de jazz, rock etc)

Jamaica [dʒə'meɪkə] N Jamaica f

Jamaican [dʒə'meɪkən] ADJ, N jamaicano/a m/f

jamb [dʒæm] N jamba f

jamboree [,dʒæmbə'riː] N **1** [of Scouts] congreso m de exploradores **2** (*) francachela f, juerga f

jammy* ['dʒæmɪ] ADJ (Brit) (compar **jammier**; superl **jammiest**) (= lucky) suertudo*, potrudo*

jam-packed ['dʒæm'pækt] ADJ (with people) abarrotado, atestado; (with things) atestado, repleto

Jan. ABBR (= January) ene., en.

jangle ['dʒæŋgl] Ⓐ N tintineo m Ⓑ VT [+ coins, bracelets] hacer tintinear Ⓒ VI tintinear

janitor ['dʒænɪtəʳ] N (= doorkeeper) portero/a m/f; (= caretaker) conserje mf

January ['dʒænjʊərɪ] N enero m; see **July**

Jap**** [dʒæp] ADJ, N (offensive) = **Japanese**

Japan [dʒə'pæn] N el Japón

Japanese [,dʒæpə'niːz] Ⓐ ADJ japonés Ⓑ N (pl ~) **1** (= person) japonés/esa m/f; **the ~** los japoneses **2** (Ling) japonés m

jar¹ [dʒɑːʳ] N (= container) tarro m, bote m; (= jug) jarra f; (large) tinaja f; **to have a ~** (Brit*) tomar un trago or una copa

jar² [dʒɑːʳ] Ⓐ N **1** (= jolt) sacudida f, choque m **2** (= shock) **it gave me a ~** me dejó de piedra Ⓑ VT (= jog) tocar; (= shake) sacudir, hacer vibrar; **I've ~red my back** me he lastimado la espalda Ⓒ VI [colours, sounds] desentonar; **to ~ on sb's nerves** poner a algn los nervios de punta

jargon ['dʒɑːgən] N jerga f

jarring ['dʒɑːrɪŋ] ADJ [sound] discordante, desafinado; [colour] discordante, que desentona

jasmine ['dʒæzmɪn] N jazmín m

jaundice ['dʒɔːndɪs] N ictericia f

jaundiced ['dʒɔːndɪst] ADJ (= embittered) amargado, resentido; (= disillusioned) desilusionado

jaunt [dʒɔːnt] N excursión f

jauntily ['dʒɔːntɪlɪ] ADV [walk] garbosamente, airosamente; [dress] de manera alegre or desenfadada

jaunty ['dʒɔːntɪ] ADJ (compar **jauntier**; superl **jauntiest**) [air, tone] desenvuelto, desenfadado; [hat] alegre; [step] garboso, airoso

Java ® ['dʒɑːvə] N (Comput) Java m

javelin ['dʒævlɪn] N jabalina f; **she won a gold medal in the ~** ganó la medalla de oro en lanzamiento de jabalina
➤ **javelin thrower** lanzador(a) m/f de jabalina

jaw [dʒɔː] N **1** [of person] mandíbula f; [of animal] quijada f **2** jaws [of animal] fauces fpl

jawbone ['dʒɔːbəʊn] N [of person] mandíbula f; [of animal] quijada f

jawline ['dʒɔːlaɪn] N mandíbula f

jay [dʒeɪ] N arrendajo m

jaywalk ['dʒeɪwɔːk] VI cruzar la calle imprudentemente

jaywalker ['dʒeɪwɔːkəʳ] N peatón/ona m/f imprudente

jazz [dʒæz] N (Mus) jazz m; **and all that ~*** y otras cosas por el estilo ➤ **jazz band** orquesta f de jazz
➤ **jazz up** VT + ADV [+ party] animar; [+ room] alegrar

jazzy* ['dʒæzɪ] ADJ (compar **jazzier**; superl **jazziest**) [dress etc] de colores llamativos, de colores chillones

JCB® N ABBR *excavadora para la construcción con pala hidráulica*

jealous ['dʒeləs] ADJ **1** [*husband, wife, lover*] celoso; **to be ~ of sb** tener celos de algn; **to make sb ~** dar celos a algn **2** (= *envious*) envidioso

jealously ['dʒeləslɪ] ADV **1** (= *protectively*) celosamente **2** (= *enviously*) con envidia

jealousy ['dʒeləsɪ] N [*of husband, wife, lover*] celos *mpl*

jeans [dʒiːnz] NPL vaqueros *mpl*, bluejeans *m* (*esp LAm*)

Jeep®, jeep [dʒiːp] N jeep® *m*, yip *m*

jeer [dʒɪəʳ] **Ⓐ** N (*from crowd*) abucheo *m* **Ⓑ** VI (= *mock*) burlarse (**at** de); (= *boo*) abuchear (**at** a)

jeering ['dʒɪərɪŋ] **Ⓐ** ADJ [*remark, laughter*] burlón, sarcástico **Ⓑ** N (= *mockery*) burlas *fpl*; (= *booing*) abucheo *m*

Jehovah [dʒɪˈhəʊvə] N Jehová *m* ➤ **Jehovah's Witness** Testigo *mf* de Jehová

jell [dʒel] VI (*esp US*) = **gel B**

Jell-O® ['dʒeləʊ] N (*US*) jalea *f*, gelatina *f*

jelly ['dʒelɪ] **Ⓐ** N **1** (*Brit*) (= *dessert*) jalea *f*, gelatina *f* **2** (*US*) (= *jam*) mermelada *f* **Ⓑ** CPD ➤ **jelly baby** caramelo *m* de goma (*en forma de niño*) ➤ **jelly jar** (*US*) tarro *m* de mermelada ➤ **jelly roll** (*US*) brazo *m* de gitano

jellybean ['dʒelɪbiːn] N caramelo *m* de goma (*en forma de judía*), gominola *f* (*Sp*)

jellyfish ['dʒelɪfɪʃ] N (*pl ~ or ~es*) medusa *f*, aguamala *f* (*Mex*), aguaviva *f* (*SC*)

jemmy ['dʒemɪ] N (*Brit*) palanqueta *f*

jeopardize ['dʒepədaɪz] VT (= *endanger*) arriesgar, poner en peligro; (= *compromise*) comprometer

jeopardy ['dʒepədɪ] N riesgo *m*, peligro *m*; **to be in ~** estar en peligro

jerk [dʒɜːk] **Ⓐ** N **1** (= *shake*) sacudida *f*; (= *pull*) tirón *m*, jalón *m* (*LAm*) **2** (*US**) imbécil *mf* **Ⓑ** VT (= *pull*) dar un tirón a, tirar bruscamente de, jalar bruscamente de (*LAm*) **Ⓒ** VI **to ~ along** moverse a sacudidas; **the bus ~ed to a halt** el autobús dio unas sacudidas y se paró

jerkin ['dʒɜːkɪn] N chaleco *m*

jerky ['dʒɜːkɪ] ADJ (*compar* **jerkier**; *superl* **jerkiest**) [*movement, motion*] brusco; [*speech*] entrecortado, vacilante

jerry-built ['dʒerɪbɪlt] ADJ mal construido, hecho con malos materiales

jerry can ['dʒerɪkæn] N bidón *m*

Jersey ['dʒɜːzɪ] N Isla *f* de Jersey, Jersey *m* ➤ **Jersey cow** vaca *f* de Jersey

jersey ['dʒɜːzɪ] N (= *garment*) jersey *m*, suéter *m*

Jerusalem [dʒəˈruːsələm] N Jerusalén *f* ➤ **Jerusalem artichoke** aguaturma *f*, pataca *f*

jest [dʒest] **Ⓐ** N guasa *f*, broma *f*; **in ~** en broma, de guasa **Ⓑ** VI bromear, estar de guasa

jester ['dʒestəʳ] N bufón *m*

Jesuit ['dʒezjʊɪt] **Ⓐ** ADJ jesuita **Ⓑ** N jesuita *m*

Jesus ['dʒiːzəs] N Jesús *m*; **~ Christ** Jesucristo *m*

jet¹ [dʒet] N (= *stone*) azabache *m* ➤ **jet black** negro *m* azabache

jet² [dʒet] **Ⓐ** N **1** [*of liquid, steam*] chorro *m* **2** (= *plane*) avión *m* a reacción, reactor *m* **Ⓑ** CPD [*fighter, plane*] a reacción ➤ **jet engine** [*of plane*] motor *m* a reacción, reactor *m* ➤ **jet lag** jet lag *m* (*desfase debido a un largo viaje en avión*); **to be suffering from ~ lag** tener jet lag ➤ **jet propulsion** propulsión *f* a reacción, propulsión *f* a chorro ➤ **the jet set** la jet set (*Sp*), el jet set (*LAm*) ➤ **jet stream** corriente *f* en chorro

jet-black ['dʒet'blæk] ADJ negro azabache *inv*

jetlagged ['dʒetˌlægd] ADJ **to be ~** tener jet lag, estar desfasado por el viaje en avión

jet-propelled ['dʒetprəˈpeld] ADJ a reacción, a chorro

jetsam ['dʒetsəm] N echazón *f*, cosas *fpl* desechadas

jet-ski ['dʒetskiː] VI practicar el motociclismo acuático; **they were ~ing** iban en moto acuática

jettison ['dʒetɪsn] VT (*Naut*) echar al mar, echar por la borda; (*Aer*) vaciar

jetty ['dʒetɪ] N (= *breakwater*) malecón *m*; (= *pier*) muelle *m*, embarcadero *m*

Jew [dʒuː] N judío/a *m/f*

jewel ['dʒuːəl] N (= *precious stone*) piedra *f* preciosa; (= *ornament*) joya *f*, alhaja *f* ➤ **jewel case** joyero *m*

jewelled, jeweled (*US*) ['dʒuːəld] ADJ adornado con piedras preciosas; [*watch*] con rubíes

jeweller, jeweler (*US*) ['dʒuːələʳ] N joyero/a *m/f*; **~'s (shop)** joyería *f*

jewellery, jewelry (*US*) ['dʒuːəlrɪ] N joyas *fpl*, alhajas *fpl*; **a piece of ~** una joya ➤ **jewellery box** joyero *m* ➤ **jewelry store** (*US*) joyería *f*

Jewish ['dʒuːɪʃ] ADJ judío

jib [dʒɪb] N (*Naut*) foque *m*; [*of crane*] aguilón *m*, brazo *m*

jibe [dʒaɪb] N, VI = **gibe**

jiffy ['dʒɪfɪ] N momento *m*, segundo *m*; **in a ~** en un santiamén, en un momento, en un segundito (*LAm*) ➤ **Jiffy bag®** sobre *m* acolchado

jig [dʒɪg] **Ⓐ** N **1** (= *dance, tune*) giga *f* **2** (*Mech*) plantilla *f* **Ⓑ** VI (= *dance*) bailar dando brincos

jigger* ['dʒɪgəʳ] N (*esp US*) (= *measure*) medida *f* (de whisky etc)

jiggery-pokery* ['dʒɪgərɪ'pəʊkərɪ] N (*Brit*) trampas *fpl*, embustes *mpl*; **there's some ~ going on** hay gato encerrado

jigsaw ['dʒɪgsɔː] N **1** (*also ~ puzzle*) rompecabezas *m inv*, puzzle *m* **2** (= *tool*) sierra *f* de vaivén

jilt [dʒɪlt] VT [+ *fiancé*] dejar plantado a

jingle ['dʒɪŋgl] **Ⓐ** N **1** (= *sound*) tintineo *m*, retintín *m* **2** (= *advertising jingle*) cancioncilla *f*, musiquilla *f* (de anuncio) **Ⓑ** VT hacer tintinear **Ⓒ** VI tintinear

jingoism ['dʒɪŋgəʊɪzəm] N (*pej*) patriotería *f*

jingoistic [ˌdʒɪŋgəʊ'ɪstɪk] ADJ (*pej*) patriotero

jinx [dʒɪŋks] **Ⓐ** N **there's a ~ on it** está gafado, tiene la negra; **to put a ~ on sth** echar mal de ojo a algo **Ⓑ** VT traer mala suerte a, gafar (*Sp**); **to be ~ed** traer mala suerte, tener gafe (*Sp**)

jitters* ['dʒɪtəz] NPL **to have the ~** tener tembleque*

jittery* ['dʒɪtərɪ] ADJ muy inquieto, nervioso

jiujitsu [dʒuː'dʒɪtsuː] N = **jujitsu**

jive [dʒaɪv] **Ⓐ** N (= *music, dancing*) swing *m* **Ⓑ** VI bailar el swing

Jnr ABBR (*Brit*) (= **junior**) jr.

job [dʒɒb] **Ⓐ** N **1** (= *employment*) trabajo *m*, empleo *m*; **what's her ~?** ¿de qué trabaja?; **he got a ~ as a clerk** consiguió un trabajo *or* empleo de oficinista; **he's the best man for the ~** es el más apropiado para el puesto; **to look for a ~** buscar (un) trabajo *or* empleo; **to lose one's ~** (= *gen*) perder el trabajo *or* empleo; (= *be sacked*) ser despedido; **to be out of a ~** estar sin trabajo *or* empleo
2 (= *piece of work*) trabajo *m* (*also Comput*); **I have a ~ for you** tengo un trabajo para ti; **I've got a few ~s to do** tengo algunas cosillas que hacer; **can you do a ~ for me?** ¿te puedo hacer un encargo?, ¿te puedo encargar algo?; **we could make a better ~ of it than they have** podríamos hacerlo mejor que ellos; **it's not ideal but it'll do the ~** no es lo ideal pero valdrá; **he really knows his ~** es un experto en lo suyo; **you've made a good ~ of painting the doors** (*Brit*) has pintado muy bien las puertas; **he's out on a ~** ha salido a hacer un trabajo; **he fell asleep on the ~** se quedó dormido trabajando
3 (= *duty, responsibility*) **my ~ is to sell them** yo estoy encargado de venderlos; **that's not my ~** eso no me incumbe *or* toca a mí; **I had the ~ of telling him** a mí me tocó decírselo
4 (*) (= *difficulty*) **we had quite a ~ getting here!** ¡vaya que nos costó (trabajo) llegar!; **we'll have a (hard) ~ to finish it in time** nos va a costar mucho trabajo terminarlo a tiempo
5 (*) (= *state of affairs*) **it's a good ~ he didn't see us** menos mal que no nos vio; ✦ IDIOMS **to make the best of a bad ~** poner al mal tiempo buena cara; **to give sth up as a bad ~**

dejar algo por imposible
6 (*) (= *crime*) golpe* *m*; **he was planning a bank ~** planeaba un golpe en un banco*
7 (*Brit**) (= *thing*) **this machine is just the ~** esta máquina nos viene que ni pintada *or* nos viene al pelo*
Ⓑ CPD ➤ **job application** solicitud *f* de trabajo *or* empleo ➤ **Job Centre** (*Brit*) oficina *f* de empleo ➤ **job creation scheme** plan *m* de creación de puestos de trabajo, plan *m* de creación de nuevos empleos ➤ **job description** descripción *f* del trabajo ➤ **job hunting** búsqueda *f* de trabajo, búsqueda *f* de empleo; **to go ~ hunting** salir a buscar trabajo *or* empleo ➤ **job interview** entrevista *f* de trabajo ➤ **job lot** lote *m* ➤ **job number** número *m* del trabajo ➤ **job opportunity** oportunidad *f* de trabajo ➤ **job queue** (*Comput*) cola *f* de trabajos ➤ **job satisfaction** satisfacción *f* en el trabajo, satisfacción *f* profesional ➤ **job security** seguridad *f* en el trabajo ➤ **job seeker** demandante *mf* de empleo, persona *f* que busca trabajo ➤ **job seeker's allowance** (*Brit*) prestación *f* por desempleo ➤ **job sharing**: **I'm interested in the possibility of ~ sharing** me interesaría poder compartir el empleo con otra persona ➤ **job title** (nombre *m* del) puesto *m* ➤ **job vacancy** puesto *m* vacante

jobbing ['dʒɒbɪŋ] ADJ (*Brit*) [*gardener, carpenter*] que trabaja a destajo

Jobcentre ['dʒɒbsentə'] N (*Brit*) oficina *f* de empleo

jobless ['dʒɒblɪs] **Ⓐ** ADJ sin trabajo, desempleado, parado (*Sp*), cesante (*Chi*) **Ⓑ** NPL **the ~** los desempleados, los parados (*Sp*), los cesantes (*Chi*)

job-share ['dʒɒbʃeə'] ADJ **we operate a ~ scheme** tenemos en marcha un plan de empleo compartido

jock [dʒɒk] N (*US*) deportista *m*

jockey ['dʒɒkɪ] **Ⓐ** N jockey *m* **Ⓑ** VI **to ~ for position** (*fig*) maniobrar para conseguir una posición **Ⓒ** CPD ➤ **Jockey Shorts®** calzoncillos *mpl* de jockey

jockstrap ['dʒɒkstræp] N suspensorio *m*

jocular ['dʒɒkjʊlə'] ADJ [*person*] gracioso; (= *merry*) alegre; [*manner*] bromista, chistoso; [*reply*] jocoso, divertido

jodhpurs ['dʒɒdpɜːz] NPL pantalones *mpl* de montar

jog [dʒɒg] **Ⓐ** N **1** (= *push*) empujoncito *m* **2** (= *pace*) trote *m* corto **3** (= *run*) **to go for a ~** ir a hacer footing *or* jogging **Ⓑ** VT empujar (ligeramente); **he ~ged my arm** me dio ligeramente con el codo; **to ~ sb's memory** refrescar la memoria a algn **Ⓒ** VI andar a trote corto; (*Sport*) (*also* **to go ~ging**) hacer footing, hacer jogging **Ⓓ** CPD ➤ **jog trot**: **at a ~ trot** a trote corto
➤ **jog along** VI + ADV **we keep ~ging along** vamos tirando; **the work is ~ging along nicely** el trabajo marcha bien

jogger ['dʒɒgə'] N corredor(a) *m/f* (de footing)

jogging ['dʒɒgɪŋ] N footing *m*, jogging *m* ➤ **jogging suit** chandal *m* (*Sp*), pants *mpl* (*Mex*), buzo *m* (*SC*), jogging *m* (*Argentina*)

john** [dʒɒn] N (*esp US*) (= *lavatory*) **the ~** el váter*, el retrete, el baño (*LAm*)

John [dʒɒn] N Juan ➤ **John Doe** (*US*) fulano *m* ➤ **John Q Public*** (*US*) el hombre de la calle

joie de vivre ['ʒwɑːdə'viːvr] N alegría *f* de vivir

join [dʒɔɪn] **Ⓐ** VT **1** (= *link*) [+ *ends, pieces, parts*] unir, juntar; [+ *tables*] juntar; **the island is ~ed to the mainland by a bridge** un puente une *or* conecta la isla a tierra firme; **to ~ hands** cogerse *or* (*LAm*) tomarse de la mano **2** (= *merge with*) [+ *river*] desembocar en, confluir con; [+ *sea*] desembocar en; [+ *road*] empalmar con **3** (= *become part of*) [+ *university, firm, religious order*] ingresar en, entrar en; [+ *club*] hacerse socio de; [+ *political party*] afiliarse a, hacerse miembro de; [+ *army, navy*] alistarse en, ingresar en; [+ *queue*] meterse en; [+ *procession, strike*] sumarse a, unirse a; **~ the club!*** ¡bienvenido al club!; **to ~ forces (with sb to do sth)** juntarse (con algn para hacer algo); (*Mil*) aliarse (con algn para hacer algo); **we ~ed the motorway at junction 15** nos metimos en la autopista por la entrada 15 **4** (= *accompany*) [+ *person*] acompañar a; **may I ~ you?** ¿les importa que les acompañe?; **I'll ~ you later if I can** yo iré luego si puedo

Ⓑ VI **1** [*ends, pieces*] unirse, juntarse; [*roads*] empalmar, juntarse; [*rivers*] confluir, juntarse; **to ~ together (to do sth)** (= *meet*) reunirse (para hacer algo); (= *unite*) unirse (para hacer algo); (= *pool resources*) asociarse (para hacer algo); **Moscow and Washington have ~ed in condemning these actions** Moscú y Washington se han unido para protestar por estas acciones **2** (= *become a member*) hacerse socio **Ⓒ** N (*in wood*) juntura *f*, unión *f*; (*Tech*) junta *f*
➤ **join in** VI + PREP [+ *game, celebration, conversation*] tomar parte en, participar en **Ⓑ** VI + ADV (*in game, celebration, conversation*) participar; **she started singing, and the audience ~ed in** empezó a cantar, y el público se unió a ella; **~ in everyone!** (*in chorus*) ¡todo el mundo!, ¡todos!
➤ **join up Ⓐ** VI + ADV **1** (*Mil*) alistarse **2** (= *meet*) [*people*] reunirse, juntarse **3** (= *team up*) unirse, asociarse **Ⓑ** VT + ADV [+ *ends, pieces*] unir, juntar; **~ed up writing** escritura *f* cursiva, escritura *f* corrida

joiner ['dʒɔɪnə'] N (*esp Brit*) (= *carpenter*) carpintero/a *m/f*

joinery ['dʒɔɪnərɪ] N (*esp Brit*) carpintería *f*

joint [dʒɔɪnt] **Ⓐ** ADJ [*agreement*] mutuo; [*decision*] de común acuerdo; [*responsibility*] compartido **Ⓑ** N (*in wood*) ensambladura *f*; (= *hinge*) bisagra *f* **2** (*Brit*) [*of meat*] cuarto *m* **3** (*Anat*) articulación *f*, coyuntura *f*; **to be out of ~** [*bone*] estar descoyuntado, estar dislocado; ✦ IDIOM **to put sb's nose out of ~*** bajar los humos a algn **4** (*) (= *place*) garito *m* **5** (*) (= *cigarette containing cannabis*) porro *m* (*Sp**), toque *m* (*Mex***), cacho *m* (*Carib**), pito *m* (*Chi**) **Ⓒ** VT (*Brit*) [+ *chicken*] despiezar, cortar en trozos **Ⓓ** CPD ➤ **joint account** cuenta *f* conjunta ➤ **joint heir** coheredero/a *m/f* ➤ **joint ownership** copropiedad *f* ➤ **joint stock bank** banco *m* comercial ➤ **joint venture** empresa *f* conjunta

jointly ['dʒɔɪntlɪ] ADV en común, conjuntamente

joist [dʒɔɪst] N viga *f*, vigueta *f*

joke [dʒəʊk] **Ⓐ** N (= *witticism, story*) chiste *m*; (= *practical joke, hoax*) broma *f*; **to treat sth as a ~** tomar algo a broma; **it's (gone) beyond a ~** (*Brit*) esto no tiene nada de gracioso; **for a ~** en broma; **is that your idea of a ~?** ¿es que eso tiene gracia?; **to make a ~** hacer un chiste (**about sth** sobre algo); **it's no ~ having to go out in this weather** no tiene nada de divertido salir con este tiempo; **to play a ~ on sb** gastar una broma a algn; **I don't see the ~** no le veo la gracia; **he can't take a ~** no le gusta que le tomen el pelo; **to tell a ~** contar un chiste (**about sth** sobre algo); **what a ~!** (*iro*) ¡qué gracia!
Ⓑ VI (= *make jokes*) contar chistes, hacer chistes; (= *be frivolous*) bromear; **I was only joking** lo dije en broma, no iba en serio; **I'm not joking** hablo en serio; **you're joking!** ✧ **you must be joking!** ¡no lo dices en serio!

joker ['dʒəʊkə'] N **1** (= *wit*) chistoso/a *m/f*, guasón/ona *m/f*; (= *practical joker*) bromista *mf* **2** (*) (= *idiot*) payaso/a *m/f*; (*stronger*) idiota *mf* **3** (*Cards*) comodín *m*

joking ['dʒəʊkɪŋ] **Ⓐ** ADJ [*tone*] burlón; [*reference*] humorístico **Ⓑ** N (= *jokes*) (*practical*) bromas *fpl*; (*verbal*) chistes *mpl*, cuentos *mpl* (*LAm*)

jokingly ['dʒəʊkɪŋlɪ] ADV en broma

jollity ['dʒɒlɪtɪ] N alegría *f*, regocijo *m*

jolly ['dʒɒlɪ] **Ⓐ** ADJ (*compar* **jollier**; *superl* **jolliest**) (= *cheerful*) alegre; (= *amusing*) divertido; [*laugh*] gracioso **Ⓑ** ADV (*Brit**) muy, la mar de*, bastante; **we were ~ glad** estábamos la mar de contentos*, nos alegramos muchísimo; **you've ~ well got to** no tienes otro remedio, no te queda otra (*LAm*); **~ good!** ¡estupendo!, ¡macanudo! (*Per, SC*)

jolt [dʒəʊlt] **Ⓐ** N (= *jerk*) sacudida *f*; (= *sudden bump*) choque *m*; **to give sb a ~** (*fig*) dar un susto a algn **Ⓑ** VT [*vehicle*] sacudir; [+ *person, elbow*] empujar (ligeramente), sacudir (levemente); **to ~ sb out of his complacency** hacer que algn se dé cuenta de la necesidad de hacer algo **Ⓒ** VI [*vehicle*] traquetear, dar tumbos

Jordan ['dʒɔːdn] N **1** (= *country*) Jordania *f* **2** (= *river*) Jordán *m*

Jordanian [dʒɔːˈdeɪnɪən] ADJ, N jordano/a *m/f*

joss stick [ˈdʒɒsstɪk] N pebete *m*

jostle [ˈdʒɒsl] ❶ VT empujar ❷ VI empujar, dar empujones; **to ~ for a place** abrirse paso a empujones

jot [dʒɒt] ❶ N pizca *f*; **there's not a ~ of truth in it** no tiene ni pizca de verdad ❷ VT **to ~ down** apuntar, anotar

jotter [ˈdʒɒtəʳ] N (*Brit*) (= *notebook, pad*) bloc *m* (de notas)

jottings [ˈdʒɒtɪŋz] NPL apuntes *mpl*, anotaciones *fpl*

journal [ˈdʒɜːnl] N **1** (= *diary*) diario *m* **2** (= *periodical*) periódico *m*; (= *magazine*) revista *f*

journalese [ˌdʒɜːnəˈliːz] N (*pej*) jerga *f* periodística

journalism [ˈdʒɜːnəlɪzəm] N periodismo *m*

journalist [ˈdʒɜːnəlɪst] N periodista *mf*, reportero/a *m/f* (*LAm*)

journey [ˈdʒɜːnɪ] N (= *trip*) viaje *m*; (= *distance*) trayecto *m*, tramo *m* (*LAm*); (= *expedition*) expedición *f*; (= *trajectory*) trayecto *m*; **to go on a ~** hacer un viaje; **pleasant ~!** ¡buen viaje!

jovial [ˈdʒəʊvɪəl] ADJ jovial

jowls [dʒaʊlz] N **a man with heavy ~** un hombre mofletudo

joy [dʒɔɪ] N (= *happiness*) alegría *f*; (= *delight*) júbilo *m*, regocijo *m*; **to jump for ~** saltar de alegría; **it's a ~ to hear him** es un gusto oírlo, da gusto oírlo; **the ~s of camping** los placeres del camping; **did you have any ~ in finding it?** ¿tuviste éxito en encontrarlo?; **no ~!** (*Brit**) ¡sin resultado!, ¡sin éxito!

joyful [ˈdʒɔɪfʊl] ADJ [*person*] feliz; [*event, occasion*] festivo

joyfully [ˈdʒɔɪfəlɪ] ADV [*sing, play*] alegremente; [*greet, announce*] con júbilo

joyous [ˈdʒɔɪəs] ADJ (*liter*) = **joyful**

joyride* [ˈdʒɔɪraɪd] VI dar una vuelta en un coche robado

joyrider [ˈdʒɔɪraɪdəʳ] N *persona que se da una vuelta en un coche robado*

joyriding [ˈdʒɔɪraɪdɪŋ] N *delito de robar un coche para dar una vuelta en él*

joystick [ˈdʒɔɪstɪk] N (*Aer*) palanca *f* de mando; (*Comput*) palanca *f* de control, joystick *m*

JP N ABBR (*Brit*) = **Justice of the Peace**

Jr ABBR (*US*) (= *junior*) jr.

jubilant [ˈdʒuːbɪlənt] ADJ [*crowd*] jubiloso, exultante; [*cry, shout*] de júbilo, alborozado

jubilation [ˌdʒuːbɪˈleɪʃən] N júbilo *m*

jubilee [ˈdʒuːbɪliː] N (= *celebration*) jubileo *m*; (= *anniversary*) aniversario *m*

Judaism [ˈdʒuːdeɪɪzəm] N judaísmo *m*

Judas [ˈdʒuːdəs] N (= *name*) Judas; (= *traitor*) judas *m*

judder [ˈdʒʌdəʳ] (*Brit*) ❶ N vibración *f* ❷ VI vibrar

judge [dʒʌdʒ] ❶ N (*Jur*) juez *mf*, juez(a) *m/f*; [*of contest*] juez *mf*, miembro *mf* del jurado; (*Sport*) árbitro *m*; (*in races*) juez *mf*; **to be a good ~ of character** ser buen psicólogo, tener psicología para conocer a la gente; **I'm no ~ of wines** no entiendo de vinos; **I'll be the ~ of that** yo decidiré eso, lo juzgaré yo mismo ❷ VT [+ *person, case, contest*] juzgar; [+ *weight, size, distance*] calcular; (*Sport*) arbitrar; ✦ PROV **you can't ~ a book by its cover** no hay que fiarse de las apariencias, las apariencias engañan ❸ VI juzgar, ser juez; **judging from his expression** a juzgar por su expresión; **to ~ for o.s.** juzgar por sí mismo

judg(e)ment [ˈdʒʌdʒmənt] ❶ N **1** (*Jur*) (= *decision*) sentencia *f*, fallo *m*; (= *act*) juicio *m*; **to pass ~ (on sb/sth)** (*Jur*) pronunciar or dictar sentencia (sobre algn/en algo), emitir un fallo (sobre algn/algo); **Last Judg(e)ment** Juicio *m* Final **2** (= *opinion*) opinión *f*, parecer *m* **3** (= *understanding*) juicio *m*, criterio *m*; **in my ~** a mi juicio; **against my better ~** a pesar mío; **to have good** or **sound ~** tener buen juicio or criterio ❷ CPD ➤ **Judg(e)ment Day** Día *m* del Juicio Final

judg(e)mental [dʒʌdʒˈmentl] ADJ crítico

judicial [dʒuːˈdɪʃəl] ADJ [*decision, proceedings*] judicial;

[*separation*] legal ➤ **judicial inquiry** investigación *f* judicial

judiciary [dʒuːˈdɪʃɪərɪ] ❶ ADJ judicial ❷ N (= *judges*) judicatura *f*; (= *court system*) poder *m* judicial

judicious [dʒuːˈdɪʃəs] ADJ sensato, juicioso

judiciously [dʒuːˈdɪʃəslɪ] ADV juiciosamente

judo [ˈdʒuːdəʊ] N judo *m*, yudo *m*

jug [dʒʌɡ] N jarro *m*, jarra *f*

juggernaut [ˈdʒʌɡənɔːt] N (*Brit*) camión *m* de gran tonelaje

juggle [ˈdʒʌɡl] ❶ VI hacer juegos malabares (**with** con) ❷ VT [+ *balls, plates*] hacer juegos malabares con; [+ *figures*] hacer malabarismos con; **to ~ a career and a family** compaginar las responsabilidades profesionales con las familiares

juggler [ˈdʒʌɡləʳ] N malabarista *mf*

juggling [ˈdʒʌɡlɪŋ] N juegos *mpl* malabares, malabarismo *m*

jugular [ˈdʒʌɡjʊləʳ] ADJ ~ **vein** yugular *f*, vena *f* yugular

juice [dʒuːs] N [*of fruit*] jugo *m*, zumo *m* (*Sp*); [*of meat*] jugo *m*; **digestive ~s** jugos digestivos or gástricos

juicy [ˈdʒuːsɪ] ADJ (*compar* **juicier**; *superl* **juiciest**) [*fruit*] jugoso; [*story*] sabroso, picante

jujitsu [dʒuːˈdʒɪtsuː] N jiu-jitsu *m*

jukebox [ˈdʒuːkbɒks] N máquina *f* de discos, gramola® *f*, rocanola *f* (*LAm*)

Jul. ABBR (= *July*) jul.

July [dʒuːˈlaɪ] N julio *m*; **at the beginning/end of ~** a principios/finales de julio; **every ~** todos los meses de julio; **in (the month of) ~** en (el mes de) julio; **there are 31 days in ~** julio tiene treinta y un días; **on the first/eleventh of ~** ✧ **on ~ (the) first/eleventh** el primero/once de julio; **it's the third of ~** ✧ **it's ~ (the) third** estamos a tres de julio, es tres de julio

jumble [ˈdʒʌmbl] ❶ N [*of objects*] revoltijo *m*, batiburrillo *m*; **a ~ of sounds** unos ruidos confusos ❷ VT (*also* ~ **together**, ~ **up**) mezclar, amontonar ❸ CPD ➤ **jumble sale** (*Brit*) mercadillo *m* benéfico (*venta de objetos usados con fines benéficos*)

JUMBLE SALE/RUMMAGE SALE

Se conoce como **jumble sale** en el Reino Unido o como **rummage sale** en Estados Unidos al mercadillo que se organiza con fines benéficos en los locales de un colegio, iglesia, ayuntamiento u otro centro público. En él se venden artículos baratos de segunda mano como por ejemplo libros, juguetes, joyas o ropa y también se suelen colocar puestos de té o café.

---

jumbo [ˈdʒʌmbəʊ] ADJ (*) gigante, de tamaño extra ➤ **jumbo jet** jumbo *m*

jump [dʒʌmp] ❶ N **1** (*Sport, Parachuting*) salto *m*; (= *leap*) salto *m*, brinco *m*

2 (= *start*) **she gave an involuntary ~** se sobresaltó sin querer **3** (= *fence, obstacle*) obstáculo *m*

4 (= *step*) salto *m*; **in one ~ he went from novice to master** de un salto or golpe pasó de novicio a maestro; ✦ IDIOMS **to be one ~ ahead (of sb)** llevar ventaja or la delantera (a algn); **to get a** or **the ~ on sb** (*esp US**) adelantarse a algn

5 (= *increase*) aumento *m*, subida *f*

❷ VI **1** (= *leap*) saltar; (*from aeroplane*) lanzarse, tirarse; **to ~ across a stream** cruzar un arroyo de un salto, saltar por encima de un arroyo; **she ~ed into the river** se tiró al río; **to ~ off/on a bus** bajar de/subir a un autobús de un salto; **he ~ed over the fence** saltó (por encima de) la valla; **he ~ed to his feet** se puso de pie de un salto; **to ~ up** ponerse de pie de un salto; **I ~ed up and down to keep warm** me puse a dar saltos para que no me entrara frío

2 (= *start*) sobresaltarse; **to make sb ~** dar un susto a algn, sobresaltar a algn

3 (*fig*) **to ~ at sth** no dejar escapar algo; **to ~ from one subject to another** saltar de un tema a otro; **he ~s on everything I say** le pone faltas a todo lo que digo

4 (= *increase*) [*sales, profits*] subir, aumentar; [*shares*] subir

© VT [+ *ditch, fence*] saltar (por encima de); **one of them ~ed him from behind*** uno de ellos se le echó encima por detrás; **to ~ bail** (*Jur*) fugarse estando bajo fianza; **to ~ the lights** (*Aut*) saltarse el semáforo (en rojo); **you've ~ed a page** te has saltado una página; **to ~ the queue** (*Brit*) colarse; **to ~ the rails** [*train*] descarrilar, salirse de la vía; **✦** IDIOM **to ~ the gun*** precipitarse
© CPD **➤ jump jet** avión *m* de despegue vertical **➤ jump leads** (*Brit Aut*) cables *mpl* de arranque (de batería) **➤ jump rope** (*US*) cuerda *f* de saltar, comba *f* (*Sp*)
➤ jump around, jump about VI + ADV dar saltos; **the story ~s around a bit** la historia da muchos saltos
➤ jump in VI + ADV **1** (*into water*) tirarse; **~ in!** (*into car*) ¡sube!, ¡vamos! **2** (*in situation, conversation*) intervenir
➤ jump out VI + ADV (*from vehicle*) bajar de un salto; **he ~ed out from behind a tree** salió de un salto de detrás de un árbol; **it ~s out at you** salta a la vista

jumped-up* [ˈdʒʌmptˈʌp] ADJ (*Brit pej*) presumido

jumper [ˈdʒʌmpəʳ] **Ⓐ** N **1** (*Sport*) saltador(a) *m/f* **2** (*Brit*) (= *sweater*) jersey *m*, suéter *m* **3** (*US*) (= *pinafore dress*) pichi *m* (*Sp*), jumper *m* (*Mex, SC*), falda *f* tipo mono **Ⓑ** CPD **➤ jumper cables** (*US*) cables *mpl* de arranque (de batería)

jumping [ˈdʒʌmpɪŋ] N (*Sport*) pruebas *fpl* de salto
➤ jumping rope (*US*) cuerda *f* de saltar, comba *f* (*Sp*)

jumping-off point [ˌdʒʌmpɪŋˈɒfˌpɔɪnt] N punto *m* de partida

jump-start [ˈdʒʌmpstɑːt] **Ⓐ** N **he gave me a ~** (*pushing*) me ayudó a arrancar el coche empujándolo; (*using jump leads*) me ayudó a arrancar el coche haciendo un puente **Ⓑ** VT [+ *car*] (*by pushing*) arrancar empujando; (*using jump leads*) arrancar haciendo un puente

jumpsuit [ˈdʒʌmpsuːt] N (*US*) mono *m*

jumpy [ˈdʒʌmpɪ] ADJ (*compar* **jumpier**; *superl* **jumpiest**) nervioso; (= *easily startled*) asustadizo

Jun. ABBR **1** (= **June**) jun. **2** (= **junior**) jr.

junction [ˈdʒʌŋkʃən] N (*esp Brit*) (= *meeting place*) [*of roads*] cruce *m*, crucero *m* (*LAm*); [*of railway lines*] empalme *m*; [*of rivers*] confluencia *f* **➤ junction box** caja *f* de empalmes

juncture [ˈdʒʌŋktʃəʳ] N **at this ~** en este momento, a estas alturas

June [dʒuːn] N junio *m*; *see* **July**

jungle [ˈdʒʌŋgl] N selva *f*, jungla *f*; (*fig*) maraña *f*, selva *f*

junior [ˈdʒuːnɪəʳ] **Ⓐ** ADJ (*in age*) más joven; (*in length of service*) de menor antigüedad; (*in position, rank*) subalterno, auxiliar; [*partner*] segundo; [*section*] (*in competition*) juvenil; **Roy Smith, Junior** Roy Smith, hijo **Ⓑ** N **1** (= *younger person*) menor *mf*, joven *mf*; **he is three years my ~** tiene tres años menos que yo, le llevo tres años **2** (*Brit Scol*) alumno/a *m/f* (*de 7 a 11 años*); (*US Univ*) estudiante *mf* de penúltimo año **Ⓒ** CPD **➤ junior college** (*US*) *centro universitario donde se imparten cursos de dos años* **➤ junior high school** (*US*) ≈ *centro de enseñanza secundaria* **➤ junior school** (*Brit*) escuela *f* primaria

juniper [ˈdʒuːnɪpəʳ] N enebro *m* **➤ juniper berries** bayas *fpl* de enebro

junk [dʒʌŋk] **Ⓐ** N **1** (= *worthless things*) trastos *mpl* viejos, cacharros* *mpl*; (= *bric-à-brac*) cachivaches *mpl*; (= *cheap goods*) baratijas *fpl*; (= *things thrown away*) desperdicios *mpl*, desechos *mpl*; (= *iron*) chatarra *f* **2** (*) (= *rubbish*) porquería *f*; **he eats nothing but ~** no come más que porquerías **Ⓑ** VT (*) [+ *object*] tirar, tirar a la basura **Ⓒ** CPD **➤ junk bond** bono *m* basura **➤ junk food** comida *f* basura **➤ junk heap: to end up on the ~ heap** terminar en el cubo de la basura **➤ junk mail** propaganda *f* por correo **➤ junk shop** tienda *f* de objetos usados

junket [ˈdʒʌŋkɪt] N **1** (= *sweet*) dulce *m* de leche cuajada, cajeta *f* (*LAm*) **2** (*) (= *party*) fiesta *f* **3** (*US*) (= *excursion at public expense*) viaje de placer realizado por un funcionario público o miembro de un comité a expensas del contribuyente

junkie* [ˈdʒʌŋkɪ] N (= *drug addict*) yonqui* *mf*; (= *esp of heroin*) heroinómano/a *m/f*

junkyard [ˈdʒʌŋkjɑːd] N depósito *m* de chatarra, chatarrería *f*

junta [ˈdʒʌntə] N junta *f* militar

Jupiter [ˈdʒuːpɪtəʳ] N Júpiter *m*

jurisdiction [ˌdʒʊərɪsˈdɪkʃən] N jurisdicción *f*

juror [ˈdʒʊərəʳ] N (*Jur*) jurado *m*; (*for contest*) juez *m*

jury [ˈdʒʊərɪ] N jurado *m*; **to be on a ~** ser miembro de un jurado **➤ jury box** tribuna *f* del jurado **➤ jury duty: to do ~ duty** actuar como jurado

just¹ [dʒʌst] ADJ [*person, system*] justo; [*reward*] merecido; [*punishment*] apropiado, justo; [*complaint, criticism*] justificado; [*account, assessment*] correcto

just²

just² [dʒʌst] ADVERB
1 (= *at this or that moment*) ahora mismo; **we're ~ off** nos vamos ahora mismo; **I'm ~ coming!** ¡ya voy!; **he was ~ leaving when ...** estaba justo saliendo cuando ...; **~ as I arrived** justo cuando yo llegaba
2 (= *recently, a moment ago*) precisamente *or* ahora mismo estábamos hablando de eso; **to have ~ done sth** acabar de hacer algo; **he has ~ left** acaba de irse; **~ cooked** recién hecho
3 (= *slightly*) **~ after I arrived** poco después de mi llegada; **it's ~ after nine o'clock** son las nueve un poco pasadas; **it's ~ gone** *or* **past ten o'clock** acaban de dar las diez; **~ over two kilos** un poco más de dos kilos; **it's ~ over two kilos** pasa de los dos kilos
4 (= *barely*) por poco; **we (only) ~ missed it** lo perdimos por muy poco; **we had ~ enough money** teníamos el dinero justo; **he passed, but only ~** aprobó pero por los pelos; **we arrived ~ in time** por poco no llegamos, llegamos justo a tiempo
5 (= *exactly*) justo, exactamente; **it's ~ my size** es justo *or* exactamente mi talla; **~ here/there** aquí/ahí mismo; **~ behind/next to** *etc* justo detrás de/al lado de *etc*; **it's ~ (on) ten (o'clock)** son las diez en punto; **that's ~ it!** ¡ahí está!*, ¡ésa es la cuestión!; **he's ~ like his father** (*physically, or behaviour*) es idéntico a su padre; **I can't find £1,000 ~ like that** no puedo conseguir mil libras así sin más; **that's ~ the point!** ¡ahí está!*, ¡ésa es la cuestión!; **he likes everything ~ so*** le gusta que todo esté perfecto; **it's ~ what I wanted** es justo *or* precisamente lo que quería; **~ what are you implying?** ¿qué es exactamente lo que estás insinuando?
6 (= *only*) sólo, nomás (*LAm*); **he's ~ a lad** no es más que un chaval, es sólo un chaval; **it's ~ a mouse** es sólo un ratón; **she's ~ jealous** lo que le pasa es que está celosa; **~ a little** sólo un poco, un poco nada más; **~ this morning** esta misma mañana; **it's ~ a suggestion** es sólo una sugerencia; **he's ~ teasing** sólo está bromeando, está bromeando, nada más; **~ yesterday** ayer mismo
7 (= *simply*) sencillamente; **I ~ told him to go away** le dije sencillamente que se fuera; **let's ~ wait and see** es mejor esperar a ver (qué pasa); **you should ~ send it back** deberías devolverlo sin más; **he ~ couldn't wait to see them** tenía unas ganas enormes de verlos; **it's ~ one of those things*** son cosas que pasan; **it's ~ that I don't like it** lo que pasa es que no me gusta
8 (= *specially*) sólo; **I did it ~ for you** lo hice sólo por ti; **we went ~ to see the museum** fuimos sólo para ver el museo
9 (= *conceivably*) **it may ~ be possible** puede que sea posible
10 (*in comparisons*) **it's ~ as good as yours** es tan bueno como el tuyo; **the new one is ~ as big** el nuevo es igual de grande
11 (*in imperatives*) **~ you dare!*** ¡inténtalo si te atreves!; **~ look at this mess!** ¡fíjate qué desorden!; **~ (you) wait until I tell your father** ya verás cuando se lo cuente a tu padre, espera (nomás (*LAm*)) a que se lo cuente a tu padre
12 (*emphatic*) **she's ~ amazing!** ¡es una mujer increíble!; **"that dress is awful" — "isn't it ~?"** (*Brit*) —ese vestido es francamente horrible —¡y tanto!; **it's ~ perfect!** ¡es absolutamente perfecto!
13 (*imagining something*) **I can ~ imagine her reaction** me imagino muy bien *or* perfectamente su reacción
14 (*in set expressions*) **~ about: it's ~ about finished** está casi terminado; **it was ~ about here that I saw him** yo estaba más o menos aquí cuando lo vi; **to be ~ about to do sth** estar a punto de hacer algo; **come ~ as you are** ven tal

como estás; ~ **as I thought!** ¡ya me lo figuraba *or* imaginaba!, ¡lo que yo me figuraba *or* imaginaba!; ~ **in case** por si acaso; ~ **in case it rains** por si acaso llueve, por si llueve; ~ **a minute!** (= *coming*) ¡un momento, por favor!, ¡voy!; ~ **a minute, I don't know if I agree with that ...** un momento, no sé si estoy de acuerdo con eso ...; ~ **the same, I'd rather ...** de todas formas, prefiero ...; **that's** ~ **too bad!** (*iro*) ¡qué lástima!, ¡qué mala pata!*; **it's** ~ **as well** menos mal; **it's** ~ **as well it's insured** menos mal que está asegurado

justice ['dʒʌstɪs] **Ⓐ** N **1** (*Jur*) justicia *f*; **to bring sb to** ~ llevar a algn ante los tribunales **2** (= *fairness*) justicia *f*; **to do sb** ~ hacer justicia a algn; **this doesn't do him** ~ [*photo etc*] no le favorece **3** (= *judge*) juez *mf* **Ⓑ** CPD ➤ **Justice Department** Ministerio *m* de Justicia ➤ **Justice of the Peace** (*Brit*) juez *mf* de paz

justifiable ['dʒʌstɪfaɪəbl] ADJ [*anger, pride, concern*] justificado; **that sort of behaviour is not** ~ ese tipo de comportamiento no puede justificarse

justifiably ['dʒʌstɪfaɪəblɪ] ADV justificadamente, con razón; **he was** ~ **angry** estaba enfadado y con razón, su enfado era justificado

justification [ˌdʒʌstɪfɪ'keɪʃən] N justificación *f*; **there's no** ~ **for it** esto no tiene justificación posible

justify ['dʒʌstɪfaɪ] VT **1** [+ *decision, action*] justificar **2** [+ *text*] alinear, justificar

justly ['dʒʌstlɪ] ADV (= *fairly*) justamente, con justicia; (= *rightly*) con razón

justness ['dʒʌstnɪs] N justicia *f*

jut [dʒʌt] VI (*also* ~ **out**) sobresalir

juvenile ['dʒuːvənaɪl] **Ⓐ** ADJ [*books, sports etc*] juvenil; (*pej*) infantil; (*Jur*) [*court*] de menores **Ⓑ** N joven *mf*, menor *mf* **Ⓒ** CPD ➤ **juvenile delinquency** delincuencia *f* juvenil ➤ **juvenile delinquent** delincuente *mf* juvenil

juxtapose ['dʒʌkstəpəʊz] VT yuxtaponer

juxtaposition [ˌdʒʌkstəpə'zɪʃən] N yuxtaposición *f*

Kk

K¹, k [keɪ] N (= *letter*) K, k *f*; **K for Kilo** K de Kilo

K² ABBR **1** (= **kilobyte**) K *m* **2** (*) (= *thousand*) **he earns 30K** gana 30.000 libras

kaftan ['kæftæn] N caftán *m*

kale [keɪl] N col *f* rizada

kaleidoscope [kə'laɪdəskəʊp] N calidoscopio *m*, caleidoscopio *m*

kamikaze [ˌkæmɪ'kɑːzɪ] N kamikaze *m*

Kampuchea [ˌkæmpʊ'tʃɪə] N Kampuchea *f*

Kan. ABBR (*US*) = **Kansas**

kangaroo [ˌkæŋgə'ruː] N canguro/a *m/f* ➤ **kangaroo court** tribunal *m* desautorizado

Kans. ABBR (*US*) = **Kansas**

kaolin ['keɪəlɪn] N caolín *m*

kaput* [kə'pʊt] ADJ kaput

karaoke [kɑːrə'əʊkɪ] N karaoke *m* ➤ **karaoke machine** máquina *f* de karaoke

karat ['kærət] N (*US*) = **carat**

karate [kə'rɑːtɪ] N karate *m*

karma ['kɑːmə] N karma *m*

karting ['kɑːtɪŋ] N (*Sport*) kárting *m*

Kashmir [kæʃ'mɪər] N Cachemira *f*

kayak ['kaɪæk] N kayac *m*, kayak *m*

Kazakhstan [ˌkæzəks'tɑːn] N Kazajstán *m*

KB ABBR (= **kilobyte**) K *m*

kebab [kə'bæb] N kebab *m*, pincho *m* moruno, anticucho *m* (*Per, Bol, Chi*)

kedgeree [ˌkedʒə'riː] N (*Brit*) *plato de pescado desmenuzado, huevos y arroz*

keel [kiːl] N (*Naut*) quilla *f*; **on an even ~** en equilibrio, estable; ✦ IDIOM **to keep sth on an even ~** mantener algo estable ➤ **keel over** VI + ADV [*person*] desplomarse

keen [kiːn] ADJ (*compar* **~er**; *superl* **~est**) **1** (= *enthusiastic*) [*supporter*] entusiasta; [*student*] aplicado; **she's a photographer** es muy aficionada a la fotografía; **I was ~ to get started** tenía muchas ganas de empezar; **to be ~ on sth** (*Brit*): **I'm not all that ~ on grapes** no me gustan mucho las uvas; **he's ~ on fishing** es muy aficionado a la pesca, le gusta mucho la pesca; **I'm not ~ on the idea** no me entusiasma *or* no me hace mucha gracia la idea; **I'm not ~ on going** no me apetece mucho ir
2 (= *intense*) [*desire*] fuerte, vivo; [*interest*] vivo, grande; [*competition, match, struggle*] reñido
3 (= *sharp*) [*edge, blade*] afilado; [*wind*] cortante; [*mind, intelligence*] agudo, penetrante; [*intellect, sense of humour*] agudo; [*eyesight*] agudo, muy bueno; [*hearing*] fino; **to have a ~ eye for detail** tener buen ojo para los detalles; **to have a ~ sense of smell** tener buen olfato

keenly ['kiːnlɪ] ADV **1** (= *intensely*) [*discuss, debate*] vivamente, intensamente; [*feel*] profundamente; [*look*] fijamente; [*listen*] con interés **2** (= *enthusiastically*) con entusiasmo

keenness ['kiːnnɪs] N **1** (= *sharpness*) [*of mind, sense of humour, eyesight*] agudeza *f*; [*of blade*] lo afilado
2 (= *intensity*) intensidad *f* **3** (= *enthusiasm*) entusiasmo *m*

---

keep

A TRANSITIVE VERB	**C** NOUN
B INTRANSITIVE VERB	**D** PHRASAL VERBS

When **keep** *is part of a set combination, eg* **to keep an appointment**, **to keep a promise***, look up the noun.*

---

keep [kiːp] (*vb: pt, pp* **kept**)
A TRANSITIVE VERB
1 (= *retain*) [+ *change, copy*] quedarse con; [+ *receipt*]

guardar; [+ *customer, colour*] conservar; **to ~ sth for o.s.** quedarse con algo; ✦ IDIOM **if this is fashion, you can ~ it!*** ¡si esto es moda no la quiero ni regalada!
2 (= *save, put aside*) guardar, reservar; **I was ~ing it for you** lo guardaba para ti
3 (= *have ready*) **I always ~ a torch in the car** siempre tengo una linterna en el coche
4 (= *store, put*) guardar; (*in museum*) conservar; **where do you ~ the sugar?** ¿dónde guardas el azúcar?; **~ it somewhere safe** guárdalo en un sitio seguro
5 (= *house*) **the tarantulas were kept in cages** las tarántulas estaban metidas en jaulas; **the prisoners were kept in a dark room** los prisioneros estaban encerrados en una habitación oscura
6 (= *detain*) tener; **~ him in bed for a couple of days** tenlo en cama un par de días; **to ~ sb in prison** tener a algn preso; **he was kept in hospital overnight** lo tuvieron una noche en el hospital
7 (= *delay*) entretener; **don't let me ~ you** no le entretengo más; **what kept you?** ¿por qué te has retrasado?
8 (= *have*) [+ *shop, hotel, house*] tener; [+ *pigs, bees*] criar
9 (= *stock*) tener; **we don't ~ that model any more** ya no tenemos ese modelo
10 (= *support*) [+ *family*] mantener; **to ~ o.s.** mantenerse
11 (= *fulfil, observe*) [+ *promise, agreement, obligation*] cumplir; [+ *law, rule*] observar; [+ *appointment*] acudir a, ir a; [+ *feast day, Sabbath*] observar
12 (= *not divulge*) **to ~ sth from sb** ocultar algo a algn; **~ it quiet** de esto no digas ni una palabra; **~ it to yourself*** no se lo digas a nadie
13 [+ *accounts*] llevar; [+ *diary*] escribir; **to ~ a record of sth** llevar nota de algo
14 (= *maintain*)
14.1 (WITH ADJECTIVE) mantener, tener (*less frm*); **to ~ sth clean** conservar *or* mantener algo limpio, tener algo limpio (*less frm*); **exercise ~s you fit** haciendo ejercicio te mantienes en forma; **to ~ sth safe** guardar algo bien *or* en un lugar seguro; **try to ~ your head still** intenta no mover la cabeza; **to ~ sth warm** mantener algo caliente
14.2 (+ *-ING*) **he kept them working all night** los tuvo trabajando toda la noche; **to ~ the engine running** dejar el motor en marcha; **to ~ sb talking** entretener a algn hablando; **to ~ sb waiting** hacer esperar a algn
15 (= *hold*) **I'll ~ you to your promise** haré que cumplas tu promesa
16 (= *prevent*) **to ~ sb from doing sth** impedir que algn haga algo; **what can we do to ~ it from happening again?** ¿qué podemos hacer para evitar que se repita?
17 **to ~ o.s. to o.s.** guardar las distancias
B INTRANSITIVE VERB
1 (= *remain*) **try to ~ calm** intenta mantener la calma; **to ~ fit** mantenerse en forma; **you must ~ still** tienes que estarte *or* quedarte muy quieto
2 **to ~ doing sth** (= *continue*) seguir haciendo algo; (= *do repeatedly*) no hacer más que hacer algo; **he kept walking** siguió caminando; **he ~s mentioning his uncle** no hace más que mencionar a su tío; **he kept interrupting us** no paraba de interrumpirnos; **I ~ forgetting to pay the gas bill** siempre se me olvida pagar la factura del gas
3 (*in directions*) (= *continue*) seguir; **to ~ straight on** seguir todo recto *or* derecho; **"keep left"** "circule por la izquierda"
4 (= *not go off*) [*food*] conservarse fresco, conservarse bien
5 (*) (= *wait*) esperar; **the news will ~ till I see you** la noticia puede esperar hasta que nos veamos
6 (*) (*talking about health*) **how are you ~ing?** ¿qué tal (estás)? (*Sp**), ¿como *or* qué tal te va?*, ¿cómo sigues? (*LAm**), ¿qué hubo? (*Mex, Chi**); **he's not ~ing very well** no está muy bien de salud
7 (= *avoid*) **to ~ from doing sth** evitar hacer algo
C NOUN
1 (= *livelihood, food*) **I pay £50 a week for my ~** la pensión me cuesta 50 libras a la semana; **to earn one's ~** ganarse el sustento

2 (*of castle*) torreón *m*, torre *f* del homenaje
3 for ~s* (= *permanently*) para siempre
Ⓓ PHRASAL VERBS
➤ **keep at** VI + PREP **1** (= *persevere with*) **to ~ at sth***
perseverar en algo; **~ at it!*** ¡ánimo!, ¡no te aflojes! (*LAm*)
2 (= *pester*) **she kept at him until she got an interview*** no
paró hasta que le concedió una entrevista
➤ **keep away** Ⓐ VT + ADV mantener alejado, mantener a
distancia; **the police kept the crowds away** la policía
mantuvo a la multitud alejada *or* a distancia; **~ medicines
away from children** mantener los medicamentos fuera del
alcance de los niños Ⓑ VI + ADV no acercarse; **~ away from
the fire** no te acerques al fuego
➤ **keep back** Ⓐ VT + ADV **1** (= *restrain*) [+ *crowds*] contener;
[+ *enemy*] no dejar avanzar, tener a raya **2** [+ *tears*]
contener, reprimir **3** (= *conceal*) [+ *information*] no
comunicar; **I'm sure he's ~ing sth back** estoy segura de que
oculta algo Ⓑ VI + ADV **~ back, please!** ¡no se acerquen, por
favor!; **I kept well back** me mantuve bien alejado
➤ **keep down** Ⓐ VT + ADV **1** (= *not raise*) **~ your head down**
no levantes la cabeza
2 (= *control*) [+ *anger, rebellion*] contener, reprimir; [+ *prices,
temperature*] mantener bajo; [+ *costs, inflation*] mantener al
mismo nivel; **could you ~ the noise down?** ¿puedes hacer
menos ruido?; **you must try to ~ your weight down** tienes
que intentar no subir de peso
3 (= *hold back*) oprimir; **it's just a way to ~ women down** es
sólo una forma de oprimir a las mujeres
4 (= *retain*) [+ *food*] **he can't ~ anything down** lo devuelve *or*
vomita todo
Ⓑ VI + ADV seguir agachado, no levantar la cabeza
➤ **keep in** Ⓐ VT + ADV **1** (= *prevent from going out*) impedir
que salga, no dejar salir **2** (= *hold in*) [+ *stomach*] meter;
[+ *anger*] contener Ⓑ VI + ADV **to ~ in with sb** (*esp Brit**)
mantener buenas relaciones con algn
➤ **keep off** Ⓐ VT + ADV (= *keep distant, repel*) **put a cloth
over it to ~ the flies off** pon un trapo encima para que no
se posen las moscas; **~ your hands off!*** ¡no toques!
Ⓑ VT + PREP **they want to ~ young people off the streets**
quieren evitar que los jóvenes pierdan el tiempo
vagabundeando por las calles; **he couldn't ~ his eyes off
her*** no podía apartar los ojos de ella; **try to ~ him off the
subject of budgets** intenta que no toque el tema de los
presupuestos
Ⓒ VI + PREP **~ off my land!** ¡fuera de mi propiedad!; **"keep
off the grass"** "prohibido pisar el césped"
Ⓓ VI + ADV **if the rain ~s off** si no llueve
➤ **keep on** Ⓐ VT + ADV [+ *hat, coat*] no quitarse; **they kept
him on for years** siguieron empleándole durante muchos
años
Ⓑ VI + ADV **1** (= *continue*) seguir, continuar; **~ on along this
road until ...** siga por esta carretera hasta ...; **~ on doing
sth** (*ceaselessly*) seguir *or* continuar haciendo algo;
(*repeatedly*) no dejar de hacer algo
2 (*Brit**) (= *talk*) **she ~s on about how much money they've
got** no hace más que hablar *or* siempre está hablando de
todo el dinero que tienen
3 (*Brit**) (= *nag*) **she does ~ on** es muy machacona*; **she ~s
on at him to look for a job** le está siempre insistiendo que
busque un trabajo
➤ **keep out** Ⓐ VT + ADV (= *exclude*) [+ *person, dog*] no dejar
entrar; **this coat should ~ out the cold** este abrigo tiene
que proteger del frío Ⓑ VI + ADV (= *not enter*) no entrar,
quedarse fuera; **"keep out"** "prohibida la entrada"; **to ~
out of trouble** no meterse en líos; **to ~ out of sb's way**
(= *avoid*) evitar encontrarse con algn; (= *try not to annoy*)
procurar no molestar a algn; **you ~ out of this!** ¡no te
metas en esto!
➤ **keep to** VI + PREP [+ *promise*] cumplir con; [+ *subject,
schedule, text*] ceñirse a; **to ~ to the left** circular *or*
mantenerse por la izquierda; **to ~ to the main roads** no
salir de las carreteras principales; **they ~ to themselves**
guardan las distancias
➤ **keep up** Ⓐ VT + ADV **1** (= *hold up*) [+ *shelf*] sostener,
sujetar; [+ *trousers*] sujetar
2 (= *continue*) [+ *tradition, correspondence, standards,
pressure*] mantener; [+ *payments*] no retrasarse en; **~ up the
good work!** ¡bien hecho!, ¡sigue así!, ¡síguele dando! (*LAm*)
3 (= *keep out of bed*) **I don't want to ~ you up** no quiero

entretenerte más
Ⓑ VI + ADV **1** [*weather*] seguir, mantenerse
2 (*in race etc*) mantener el ritmo, no quedarse atrás; (*in
comprehension*) seguir (el hilo); **to ~ up with sb** (*in race*)
seguir el ritmo a algn; (*in comprehension*) seguir el hilo a
algn; **to ~ up with the times** ir con los tiempos,
mantenerse al día; **to ~ up with the news** estar al día de las
noticias; ✦ IDIOM **to ~ up with the Joneses** no ser menos
que el vecino

keeper ['kiːpəʳ] N (*in park, zoo etc*) guarda *mf*,
guardián/ana *m/f*; (= *gamekeeper*) guardabosque *mf*,
guardabosques *mf inv*; (*in museum, art gallery*)
conservador(a) *m/f*; (*Brit*) (= *goalkeeper*) portero/a *m/f*,
arquero/a *m/f* (*LAm*)

keep-fit [ˌkiːpˈfɪt] (*esp Brit*) N gimnasia *f* (para mantenerse
en forma) ➤ **keep-fit classes** clases *fpl* de gimnasia (para
mantenerse en forma)

keeping ['kiːpɪŋ] N **1** (= *harmony*) **to be in ~ with** estar de
acuerdo con, estar en armonía con; **to be out of ~ with**
estar en desacuerdo con **2** (= *care, custody*) **to give sth to sb
for safe ~** poner algo al cuidado de algn

keepsake ['kiːpseɪk] N recuerdo *m*

keg [keg] N (*Brit*) barrilete *m*

Ken. ABBR (*US*) = **Kentucky**

kennel ['kenl] N **1** (*esp Brit*) (= *doghouse*) caseta *f* de perro
2 kennels (*sing and pl*) (= *dogs' home*) residencia *f* canina;
(*for breeding*) criadero *m* de perros

Kenya ['kenjə] N Kenia *f*

Kenyan ['kenjən] ADJ, N keniano/a *m/f*

kept [kept] PT, PP *of* **keep**

kerb, curb (*US*) [kɜːb] N bordillo *m*, cordón *m* (*SC*), cuneta
f (*Chi*) ➤ **kerb crawler** (*Brit*) *conductor que busca prostitutas
desde su coche*

kerfuffle* [kəˈfʌfl] N (*Brit*) jaleo* *m*, follón *m* (*Sp**)

kernel ['kɜːnl] N [*of nut*] almendra *f*; [*of fruit*] pepita *f*, pepa
f (*LAm*); [*of grain*] grano *m*

kerosene ['kerəsiːn] N keroseno *m*, queroseno *m*,
querosén *m* (*LAm*)

kestrel ['kestrəl] N cernícalo *m* (vulgar)

ketchup ['ketʃəp] N salsa *f* de tomate, catsup *m*

kettle ['ketl] N hervidor *m*, caldera *f* (*Bol, Uru*), pava *f* (*SC*);
I'll put the ~ on voy a poner a hervir el agua (*para hacer
café/té*); ✦ IDIOM **that's a different ~ of fish** (*Brit**) eso es
harina de otro costal

kettledrum ['ketldrʌm] N timbal *m*

key [kiː] Ⓐ N **1** (*to door, car etc*) llave *f*
2 [*of typewriter, piano*] tecla *f*
3 (*to code*) clave *f*; **the ~ to success** (*fig*) la clave del éxito
4 (*to map, diagram*) explicación *f* de los signos
convencionales
5 (*Mus*) clave *f*; **what ~ is it in?** ¿en qué clave está?; **to
change ~** cambiar de tonalidad; **to sing off ~** cantar
desafinado; **major/minor ~** tono *m* mayor/menor
Ⓑ ADJ (= *crucial*) [*issue, job, role, witness*] clave *inv*
Ⓒ VT (*Comput, Typ*) (*also ~ in, ~ up*) teclear
Ⓓ CPD ➤ **key card** (*at hotel etc*) tarjeta-llave *f* ➤ **key money**
entrada *f* ➤ **key ring** llavero *m*
➤ **key in** VT + ADV teclear
➤ **key up** VT + ADV **1 to be all ~ed up** (= *tense*) estar
nervioso; (= *excited*) estar entusiasmado **2** (*Comput, Typ*)
teclear

keyboard ['kiːbɔːd] Ⓐ N teclado *m* Ⓑ VT [+ *text*] teclear
Ⓒ CPD ➤ **keyboard player** teclista *mf*

keyboarder ['kiːbɔːdəʳ] N teclista *mf*

keyhole ['kiːhəʊl] N ojo *m* de la cerradura ➤ **keyhole
surgery** cirugía *f* laparoscópica

keynote ['kiːnəʊt] N (*Mus*) tónica *f*; (*fig*) (= *main emphasis*)
tónica *f*, piedra *f* clave ➤ **keynote speech** discurso *m* de
apertura, *discurso en que se sientan las bases de una política o
programa*

keypad ['kiːpæd] N teclado *m* numérico

keystroke ['kiːstrəʊk] N pulsación *f* (*de la tecla*)

Kg, kg ABBR (= **kilogram(s), kilogramme(s)**) kg

khaki ['kɑːkɪ] ⒶN (= *cloth, colour*) caqui *m*; **khakis** (= *military uniform*) uniforme *m* caqui ⒷADJ caqui *inv*

kibbutz [kɪ'bʊts] N (*pl* ~**im** [kɪ'bʊtsɪm]) kibutz *m*

kibosh ['kaɪbɒʃ] N ✦ IDIOM **to put the ~ on sth*** dar al traste con algo*

kick [kɪk] ⒶN **1** (*with foot*) patada *f*, puntapié *m*; (*Sport*) puntapié *m*, tiro *m*; (*by animal*) coz *f*; **to give sth/sb a ~** dar una patada a algo/algn; **it was a ~ in the teeth for him*** (*fig*) le sentó como una patada (en la barriga)*
2 (*) (= *zest*) **a drink with a ~ to it*** una bebida que pega fuerte*
3 (*) (= *thrill*) **he gets a ~ out of teasing her** se refocila tomándole el pelo; **to do something for ~s** hacer algo sólo para divertirse *or* por pura diversión
ⒷVT **1** [+ *ball etc*] dar una patada a *or* un puntapié a; [+ *person*] dar una patada a; [*animal*] dar una coz a; **to ~ sth out of the way** quitar algo de en medio de una patada; **she ~ed the door shut** cerró la puerta de una patada; **I could have ~ed myself*** ¡me hubiera dado de tortas!*; ✦ IDIOMS **to ~ the bucket*** estirar la pata*; **to ~ a man when he's down** dar a moro muerto gran lanzada
2 (= *give up*) **to ~ a habit** dejar un hábito
ⒸVI **1** [*person*] dar patadas *or* puntapiés; [*baby*] patalear; [*animal*] dar coces, cocear
2 (*gun*) dar un culetazo, recular
ⒹCPD ➤ **kick boxing** kick boxing *m*
➤ **kick around, kick about** ⒶVT + ADV dar patadas a; [+ *idea*] darle vueltas a; **to ~ a ball around** divertirse dándole puntapiés a un balón de un lado para otro; **to ~ sb around** (*fig*) tratar a algn a patadas* ⒷVI + ADV (*) **it's ~ing around here somewhere** anda por aquí en algún sitio
➤ **kick down** VT + ADV derribar *or* echar abajo a patadas
➤ **kick in** ⒶVT + ADV **1** [+ *door*] derribar *or* echar abajo a patadas; (= *break*) romper a patadas; **to ~ sb's teeth in*** romper la cara a algn* **2** (*US**) (= *contribute*) contribuir, apoquinar (*Sp**) ⒷVI + ADV (*US**) **1** (= *take effect*) surtir efecto **2** (= *contribute*) contribuir, apoquinar (*Sp**)
➤ **kick off** VI + ADV (*Ftbl*) hacer el saque inicial; (*fig**) [*meeting etc*] empezar
➤ **kick out*** VT + ADV echar a patadas*; (*from job, home*) echar, poner de patitas en la calle*
➤ **kick up*** VT + ADV **to ~ up a fuss** *or* (*esp US*) **a storm about sth** armar un escándalo por algo

kickoff ['kɪkɒf] N (*Ftbl*) saque *m* (inicial)

kick-start ['kɪk'stɑːt] ⒶN (*also* ~**er**) pedal *m* de arranque ⒷVT [+ *engine*] arrancar con el pedal; [+ *economy*] activar

kid [kɪd] ⒶN **1** (*Zool*) (= *goat*) cabrito *m*, chivo *m*
2 (*) (= *child*) chiquillo/a *m/f*, crío/a *m/f*, chaval/a *m/f* (*Sp*), cabro/a *m/f* (*Chi*), chamaco/a *m/f* (*CAm, Mex*), escuincle/a *m/f* (*Mex**), pibe/a *m/f* (*SC**); **that's ~'s stuff** (= *childish*) eso es de *or* para niños; (= *easy*) eso es un juego de niños
ⒷVT (*) **1** (= *deceive*) engañar; **don't ~ yourself** no te engañes
2 (= *tease*) **to ~ sb about sth** tomar el pelo a algn por algo
ⒸVI (*) bromear; **I'm only ~ding** lo digo en broma; **really! no ~ding!** ¡en serio!, ¡de verdad!
ⒹCPD ➤ **kid brother*** hermano *m* menor *or* pequeño *m* (*LAm*) chico ➤ **kid gloves** ✦ IDIOM **to handle sth/sb with ~ gloves** tratar algo/a algn con guante blanco ➤ **kid sister*** hermana *f* menor *or* pequeña *or* (*LAm*) chica
➤ **kid on*** VT + ADV **he's ~ding you on** te está tomando el pelo*

kidnap ['kɪdnæp] VT secuestrar, raptar, plagiar (*Mex*)

kidnapper, kidnaper (*US*) ['kɪdnæpə'] N secuestrador(a) *m/f*, raptor(a) *m/f*, plagiador(a) *m/f* (*Mex*)

kidnapping, kidnaping (*US*) ['kɪdnæpɪŋ] N secuestro *m*, rapto *m*, plagio *m* (*Mex*)

kidney ['kɪdnɪ] ⒶN (*Anat, Culin*) riñón *m* ⒷCPD (*disease*) renal ➤ **kidney bean** (*red*) frijol *m*, alubia *f* (*Sp*), judía *f* (*Sp*), poroto *m* (*SC*); (*US*) (*green*) habichuela *f*, judía *f* verde (*Sp*), ejote *m* (*Mex*), poroto *m* verde (*Chi*) ➤ **kidney donor** donante *mf* de riñón ➤ **kidney failure** insuficiencia *f* renal ➤ **kidney machine** riñón *m* artificial ➤ **kidney stone** cálculo *m* renal ➤ **kidney transplant** trasplante *m* renal *or* de riñón

kill [kɪl] ⒶVT **1** (*gen*) matar, dar muerte a (*frm*); (= *murder*) asesinar, matar; [+ *animal*] matar, sacrificar; **he was ~ed in the explosion** murió en la explosión; **I'll do it if it ~s me*** lo haré aunque me vaya en ello la vida; **my feet are ~ing me*** los pies me están matando*; **to ~ o.s.** matarse; (= *commit suicide*) suicidarse; **he was ~ing himself laughing*** se moría de (la) risa; ✦ IDIOM **to ~ two birds with one stone** matar dos pájaros de un tiro
2 [+ *rumour*] acabar con; [+ *proposal*] echar abajo; [+ *hope*] destruir; [+ *pain*] calmar; [+ *engine*] parar, apagar; [+ *lights*] apagar; **to ~ time** matar el rato
ⒷN (*Hunting*) muerte *f*; (= *animal killed*) pieza *f*; **to be in at the ~** (*lit*) asistir a la matanza
➤ **kill off** VT + ADV acabar con

killer ['kɪlə'] ⒶN **1** (= *murderer*) asesino/a *m/f* **2** (*) (*fig*) **it's a ~** (*task, journey*) es agotador ⒷCPD [*bee, shark*] asesino ➤ **killer disease** enfermedad *f* mortal ➤ **killer instinct** (*also fig*) instinto *m* asesino ➤ **killer whale** orca *f*

killing ['kɪlɪŋ] ⒶADJ (*) (= *exhausting*) [*work, journey*] agotador, durísimo ⒷN (= *murder*) asesinato *m*; (*large scale, also of animals*) matanza *f*; ✦ IDIOM **to make a ~*** hacer su agosto ⒸCPD ➤ **killing fields** campo *msing* de exterminio

killjoy ['kɪldʒɔɪ] N aguafiestas *mf inv*

kiln [kɪln] N horno *m*

kilo ['kiːləʊ] N kilo *m*

kilobyte ['kɪləʊˌbaɪt] N kilobyte *m*, kilocteto *m*

kilogram(me) ['kɪləʊgræm] N kilo(gramo) *m*

kilohertz ['kɪləʊˌhɜːts] N kilohercio *m*

kilometre, kilometer (*US*) ['kɪləʊmiːtə'] N kilómetro *m*

kilowatt ['kɪləʊwɒt] N kilovatio *m*

kilt [kɪlt] N falda *f* escocesa

kilter ['kɪltə'] N **to be out of ~** [*mechanism*] estar descentrado; **business is bad and everything's out of ~** el negocio va mal y todo anda desbaratado

kimono [kɪ'məʊnəʊ] N (*pl* ~**s**) kimono *m*, quimono *m*

kin [kɪn] N familiares *mpl*, parientes *mpl*; **next of ~** familiar(es) *m(pl)* *or* pariente(s) *m(pl)* más cercano(s)

kind [kaɪnd] ⒶADJ (*compar* ~**er**; *superl* ~**est**) [*person*] amable, atento; [*act, word, offer*] amable; [*voice*] tierno, cariñoso; **he was ~ enough to help** tuvo la amabilidad de ayudar; **to have a ~ heart** tener buen corazón; **that's very ~ of you** es usted muy amable; (*more frm*) es muy amable de su parte; **it was very ~ of you to pick us up** fuiste muy amable viniéndonos a recoger; (*more frm*) fue muy amable de su parte el venir a recogernos; **would you be so ~ as to close the door?** (*frm*) ¿haría el favor de cerrar la puerta, por favor?, ¿tendría la bondad de cerrar la puerta, por favor? (*frm*); **she was very ~ to me** fue muy amable conmigo, se portó muy bien conmigo
ⒷN **1** (= *type*) clase *f*, tipo *m*; **I prefer the ~ with handles** prefiero los que tienen asas; **all ~s of things** toda clase de cosas; **you know the ~ of thing I mean** ya sabes a lo que me refiero; **she's the ~ (of person) that ...** ella es de las que ...; **it's not his ~ of film** no es el tipo de película que a él le gusta; **payment in ~** pago *m* en especie; **it was tea of a ~** (*pej*) se supone que era té (*pej*); **they're two of a ~** son tal para cual; **it's the only one of its ~** es único (en su género); **something of the ~** algo por el estilo; **she never said anything of the ~** nunca dijo nada parecido
2 ~ of* (= *rather*) algo; **we're ~ of busy right now** ahora mismo estamos algo ocupados

kindergarten ['kɪndəˌgɑːtn] N jardín *m* de infancia, kindergarten *m*, kinder *m* (*LAm**)

kind-hearted ['kaɪnd'hɑːtɪd] ADJ bondadoso, de buen corazón; **to be ~** ser bondadoso, tener buen corazón

kindle ['kɪndl] ⒶVT [+ *wood*] prender fuego a; [+ *fire*] encender; [+ *emotion, interest*] despertar, suscitar ⒷVI [*wood, fire*] prender, encenderse

kindling ['kɪndlɪŋ] N leña *f* (menuda), astillas *fpl*

kindly ['kaɪndlɪ] ⒶADJ (*compar* **kindlier**; *superl* **kindliest**) [*person*] bondadoso; [*face, smile*] afable, dulce ⒷADV **1** (= *thoughtfully*) amablemente; **he very ~ helped** tuvo la amabilidad de ayudar

2 (= *favourably*) **he didn't take very ~ to her suggestion** no acogió muy bien su sugerencia; **he doesn't take ~ to being kept waiting** no le hace ninguna gracia que le hagan esperar; **to think ~ of sb** tener un buen concepto de algn **3** (= *please*) (*frm*) **~ wait a moment** haga el favor de esperar un momento, tenga la amabilidad de esperar un momento

kindness ['kaɪndnɪs] N amabilidad *f*; **out of the ~ of her heart** por pura amabilidad

kindred ['kɪndrɪd] ADJ emparentado; (*fig*) afín, semejante ➤ **kindred spirits** almas *fpl* gemelas

kinetic [kɪ'netɪk] ADJ cinético

king [kɪŋ] N rey *m*; (*Draughts*) dama *f*; **the ~ and queen** los reyes; ✦ IDIOM **to live like a ~** vivir a cuerpo de rey ➤ **King's Counsel** (*Brit*) abogado *mf* (*de categoría superior*); ⊃ QC/KC

kingdom ['kɪŋdəm] N reino *m*; **animal/plant ~** reino *m* animal/vegetal

kingfisher ['kɪŋfɪʃəʳ] N martín *m* pescador

kingpin ['kɪŋpɪn] N (*fig*) piedra *f* angular

king-size(d) ['kɪŋsaɪz(d)] ADJ tamaño gigante *or* familiar ➤ **king-size(d) bed** cama *f* de matrimonio extragrande

kink [kɪŋk] N (*in rope etc*) retorcedura *f*, vuelta *f*; (*in hair*) onda *f*; (*in paper*) arruga *f*, pliegue *m*

kinky ['kɪŋkɪ] ADJ (*compar* **kinkier**; *superl* **kinkiest**) **1** (*) (*sexually*) pervertido **2** (= *curly*) [*hair*] ondulado

kinship ['kɪnʃɪp] N (*of family*) parentesco *m*; (*fig*) afinidad *f*

kinsman ['kɪnzmən] N (*pl* **kinsmen**) familiar *m*, pariente *m*

kinswoman ['kɪnz,wʊmən] N (*pl* **kinswomen**) familiar *f*

kiosk ['kiːɒsk] N quiosco *m*; **telephone ~** (*Brit*) cabina *f* telefónica

kip* [kɪp] (*Brit*) Ⓐ N (= *sleep*) siestecita* *f*, sueño* *m*; **to have a ~** echar un sueño* Ⓑ VI dormir

kipper ['kɪpəʳ] N arenque *m* ahumado

kirk [kɜːk] N (*Scot*) iglesia *f*; **the Kirk** la Iglesia (Presbiteriana) de Escocia

kiss [kɪs] Ⓐ N beso *m*; (= *light touch*) roce *m*; **to give sb a ~** dar un beso a algn; **the ~ of life** (*Brit*) (= *artificial respiration*) respiración *f* boca a boca Ⓑ VT besar; **to ~ sb's cheek/hand** besar a algn en la mejilla/besar la mano a algn; **to ~ sb goodbye** dar un beso de despedida a algn Ⓒ VI besarse

kissagram ['kɪsə,græm] N besograma *m*

kit [kɪt] N **1** (= *equipment, gear*) avíos *mpl*; (= *instruments, tools*) útiles *mpl*, herramientas *fpl*; (*Mil*) pertrechos *mpl*, petate *m* **2** (*esp Brit**) (= *clothes*) ropa *f*; (*for sports*) equipo *m*, indumentaria *f* **3** (= *set of items*) equipo *m*, kit *m*; **first-aid ~** botiquín *m* **4** (= *parts for assembly*) (= *toy, model*) maqueta *f*; (= *assembly kit*) kit *m*, juego *m* por piezas para armar ➤ **kit out, kit up** VT + ADV (*Brit*) equipar (**with** de); **to be ~ted out in** [+ *clothing*] llevar puesto

kitbag ['kɪtbæg] N (*esp Brit*) mochila *f*

kitchen ['kɪtʃɪn] Ⓐ N cocina *f* Ⓑ CPD [*cupboard, knife*] de cocina; [*window*] de la cocina ➤ **kitchen foil** papel *m* de aluminio ➤ **kitchen paper, kitchen roll** rollo *m* de cocina ➤ **kitchen sink** fregadero *m*, pila *f*; ✦ IDIOM **they took everything but the ~ sink*** (*hum*) se llevaron la casa a cuestas* ➤ **kitchen unit** mueble *m* de cocina

kitchenette [,kɪtʃɪ'net] N cocina *f* pequeña

kitchenware ['kɪtʃɪnwɛəʳ] N artículos *mpl* de cocina

kite [kaɪt] N **1** (= *toy*) cometa *f* **2** (= *bird*) milano *m* real

kith [kɪθ] N **~ and kin** parientes *mpl* y amigos

kitten ['kɪtn] N gatito/a *m/f*; ✦ IDIOM **to have ~s*: I nearly had ~s when I saw it** casi me da un ataque (de nervios) cuando lo vi

kitty ['kɪtɪ] N (= *funds*) fondo *m* común; (*Cards*) bote *m*, puesta *f*

kiwi ['kiːwiː] Ⓐ N **1** (= *bird*) kiwi *m* **2** (*Brit, Australian**) (= *New Zealander*) neozelandés/esa *m/f* Ⓑ CPD ➤ **kiwi fruit** kiwi *m*

KKK N ABBR (*US*) = **Ku Klux Klan**

kleptomania [,kleptəʊ'meɪnɪə] N cleptomanía *f*

kleptomaniac [,kleptəʊ'meɪnɪæk] N cleptómano/a *m/f*

km ABBR (= **kilometre(s)**) km

kmh, km/h ABBR (= **kilometre(s) per hour**) km/h, k.p.h.

knack [næk] N **it's just a ~** es un truco que se aprende; **to get the ~ of (doing) sth** coger el tranquillo a (hacer) algo (*Sp**), agarrarle la onda a algo (*esp Mex**); **she has the ~ of making people feel at home** tiene el don de hacer que la gente se sienta cómoda a su alrededor

knacker ['nækəʳ] (*Brit*) Ⓐ N (*for horses*) matarife *mf* de caballos Ⓑ VT (*) agotar, reventar*; **I'm ~ed** estoy reventado *or* hecho polvo* Ⓒ CPD ➤ **knacker's yard** (*for horses*) matadero *m*

knapsack ['næpsæk] N (= *small rucksack*) mochila *f*

knave [neɪv] N **1** (††) (= *rascal*) bellaco *m*, bribón *m* **2** (*esp Brit Cards*) valet *m*; (*in Spanish pack*) sota *f*

knead [niːd] VT [+ *dough*] amasar, sobar

knee [niː] N rodilla *f*; **on one's ~s** de rodillas; **the embargo has brought the country to its ~s** el embargo ha llevado al país al borde del desastre; **to go down on one's ~s (to sb)** arrodillarse (ante algn)

kneecap ['niːkæp] N rótula *f*

knee-deep ['niː'diːp] ADJ **the water was ~** el agua cubría hasta las rodillas; **to be ~ in** estar metido hasta las rodillas en; (*fig*) estar metido hasta el cuello en

knee-high ['niː'haɪ] ADJ [*grass*] hasta las rodillas; [*boots*] de caña alta; ✦ IDIOM **he's been riding since he was ~ to a grasshopper*** lleva montando a caballo desde que era un renacuajo*

knee-jerk ['niːdʒɜːk] ADJ [*reaction*] instintivo, automático

kneel [niːl] [*pt, pp* **knelt** *or* **~ed**] VI (*also* **~ down**) arrodillarse, ponerse de rodillas; (= *be kneeling*) estar de rodillas

knee-length ['niːlenθ] ADJ [*boots*] de caña alta; [*socks*] largo; [*coat, skirt*] hasta la rodilla

kneepad ['niːpæd] N (*for sport, work*) rodillera *f*

knell [nel] N toque *m* de difuntos, doble *m*

knelt [nelt] PT, PP *of* **kneel**

knew [njuː] PT *of* **know**

knickerbocker glory [,nɪkəbɒkə'glɔːrɪ] N (*Brit*) especial *m* de helado (*servido en copa alta*)

knickerbockers ['nɪkəbɒkəz] NPL pantalones *mpl* cortos

knickers ['nɪkəz] NPL (*Brit*) bragas *fpl*, calzones *mpl* (*LAm*); ✦ IDIOM **to get one's ~ in a twist*** ponerse nervioso

knick-knack ['nɪknæk] N chuchería *f*, chisme *m*

knife [naɪf] Ⓐ N (*pl* **knives**) (= *table knife*) cuchillo *m*; (= *pocket knife*) navaja *f*, cortaplumas *m inv*; (= *dagger*) puñal *m*; (= *flick knife*) navaja *f*, chaveta *f* (*LAm*); (= *blade*) cuchilla *f*; **I'll get the knives and forks out** voy a sacar los cubiertos; ✦ IDIOMS **to turn the ~ in the wound** hurgar en la herida; **to put *or* stick the ~ in** ensañarse, tirar con bala Ⓑ VT (= *stab*) acuchillar, apuñalar Ⓒ CPD ➤ **knife edge** filo *m* (de cuchillo); ✦ IDIOM **to be (balanced) on a ~ edge** [*person*] estar con el alma pendiente de un hilo; [*result*] estar pendiente de un hilo

knife-point ['naɪfpɔɪnt] N **at ~** a punta de navaja

knight [naɪt] Ⓐ N (*Hist*) caballero *m*; (*Chess*) caballo *m*; (*modern*) (*Brit*) Sir *m*, caballero de una orden; **~ in shining armour** príncipe *m* azul Ⓑ VT (*Brit*) otorgar el título de Sir a

knighthood ['naɪthʊd] N (*Brit*) título *m* de Sir; **he was given a ~** le otorgaron el título de Sir

knit [nɪt] Ⓐ VT [+ *garment*] tejer, hacer (*Sp*); **to ~ one's brows** fruncir el ceño Ⓑ VI tejer, hacer punto (*Sp*); [*bones*] (*also* **~ together**) soldarse

knitting ['nɪtɪŋ] N (= *activity*) labor *f* de punto; (= *product*) prenda *f* de punto; (= *piece being worked on*) labor *f*; **I think I'll do some ~** creo que voy a ponerme a tejer *or* (*Sp*) a hacer punto ➤ **knitting machine** máquina *f* de tejer, tricotosa *f* (*Sp*) ➤ **knitting needle** aguja *f* de tejer *or* (*Sp*) de hacer punto

knitwear ['nɪtwɛəʳ] N géneros *mpl* de punto

knives [naɪvz] NPL *of* **knife**

knob [nɒb] N **1** (= *control*) [*of radio etc*] botón *m*, mando *m* **2** (= *handle*) [*of door*] pomo *m*, tirador *m*; [*of drawer*] tirador *m* **3** (= *piece*) **a ~ of butter** (*esp Brit*) un pedazo de mantequilla

knobbly ['nɒblɪ] ADJ (*compar* **knobblier**; *superl* **knobbliest**) [*stick*] nudoso; [*knees*] huesudo

knock [nɒk] **Ⓐ** N golpe *m*; (*in collision*) choque *m*; (*on door*) llamada *f*; **there was a ~ at the door** llamaron a la puerta; **his pride took a ~** su orgullo sufrió un golpe **Ⓑ** VT **1** (= *strike*) golpear; **to ~ one's head on sth** (*by accident*) dar con la cabeza contra algo; **to ~ sb to the ground** tirar *or* echar a algn al suelo; **to ~ sb unconscious** dejar a algn sin sentido; **to ~ sth to the floor** dar con algo en el suelo; ✦ IDIOMS **to ~ sth on the head** (*Brit*) [*+ idea*] echar algo por tierra; **to ~ some sense into sb*** hacer entrar en razón a algn; **to ~ sb sideways*** dejar de piedra *or* patidifuso a algn*; **to ~ spots off sb*** dar mil vueltas a algn* **2** (*) (= *criticize*) criticar, hablar mal de **Ⓒ** VI **1** (= *strike*) golpear; (*at door*) llamar a la puerta; **he ~ed on the table** golpeó con un golpe en la mesa **2** (= *bump*) **to ~ into sth/sb** chocar *or* tropezar con algo/algn; **to ~ against sth** chocar *or* dar con *or* contra algo
➤ **knock around*, knock about*** (*Brit*) **Ⓐ** VT + ADV [*+ person*] pegar, maltratar; [*+ object*] golpear; **to ~ an idea around** dar vueltas a una idea **Ⓑ** VI + ADV **he's ~ing around somewhere** anda por algún lado; **she ~s around with a bad crowd** anda con malas compañías
➤ **knock back*** VT + ADV **1** [*+ drink*] beberse (de un trago) **2** (= *cost*) **it ~ed me back £10** me costó diez libras **3** (*esp Brit*) (= *reject*) [*+ offer, person*] echar para atrás
➤ **knock down** VT + ADV **1** [*+ building*] derribar, demoler; [*+ person*] tirar al suelo; [*+ pedestrian*] atropellar; [*+ tree, door etc*] derribar, echar abajo; [*+ price*] rebajar, reducir; **I ~ed him down to £20** conseguí que me rebajara el precio a 20 libras
➤ **knock off Ⓐ** VT + ADV **1** (= *make fall*) hacer caer; (*intentionally*) echar abajo **2** (= *deduct*) **he ~ed £5 off** (*from price*) rebajó el precio en cinco libras, hizo un descuento de cinco libras; **to ~ three seconds off the record** mejorar el récord en tres segundos **3** (*Brit**) (= *steal*) birlar* **4** (*) (= *do quickly*) [*+ meal*] preparar enseguida; [*+ garment*] hacer enseguida; [*+ novel*] escribir rápidamente **5** (*) (= *stop*) **it off!** ¡déjalo ya! **6** (*) (= *kill*) liquidar* **Ⓑ** VI + ADV (*) **he ~s off at five** sale del trabajo a las cinco
➤ **knock out** VT + ADV **1** (= *stun*) dejar sin sentido, hacer perder el conocimiento; (*Boxing*) poner fuera de combate, dejar K.O. **2** (*in competition*) eliminar
➤ **knock over** VT + ADV [*+ object*] tirar, voltear (*LAm*); [*+ pedestrian*] atropellar
➤ **knock together** VT + ADV [*+ two objects*] golpear (uno contra otro); **I ought to ~ your heads together!** ¡os debería dar una buena paliza!
➤ **knock up Ⓐ** VT + ADV **1** (*Brit*) (= *waken*) despertar, llamar **2** (= *make hastily*) hacer; [*+ meal*] preparar en seguida **3** (**) (= *make pregnant*) dejar embarazada **Ⓑ** VI + ADV (*Tennis*) pelotear

knockabout ['nɒkəbaʊt] N (*Sport*) **to have a ~** pelotear

knockback* ['nɒkbæk] N (= *setback*) revés *m*, duro golpe *m*

knockdown ['nɒkdaʊn] ADJ [*price*] de ganga, regalado

knocker ['nɒkəʳ] N (*on door*) aldaba *f*

knocking ['nɒkɪŋ] N (= *sound*) golpes *mpl*, golpeteo *m*; (*at door*) golpes *mpl*, llamada *f*

knock-kneed ['nɒk'niːd] ADJ patizambo

knock-on effect [,nɒkɒnə'fekt] N (*Brit*) repercusiones *fpl*; **the rise in interest rates will have a ~ on the housing market** la subida en los tipos de interés repercutirá en el mercado inmobiliario

knockout ['nɒkaʊt] **Ⓐ** N **1** (*Boxing*) knock-out *m*, K.O. *m*, nocaut *m* **2** (= *competition*) concurso *m* eliminatorio, eliminatoria *f* **3** (*) (= *stunner*) maravilla *f* **Ⓑ** CPD
➤ **knockout competition** concurso *m* eliminatorio, eliminatoria *f* ➤ **knockout punch** golpe *m* aplastante

knot [nɒt] **Ⓐ** N **1** (*gen*) nudo *m*; **to tie a ~** hacer un nudo; **her hair was all in ~s** tenía el pelo enredado; ✦ IDIOMS **to tie sb up in ~s** enredar a algn; **to get tied up** *or* **tie o.s. up in ~s** armarse un lío*; **to tie the ~** casarse **2** (= *unit of speed*) nudo *m* **3** (*in wood*) nudo *m* **Ⓑ** VT anudar, atar

knotty ['nɒtɪ] ADJ (*compar* **knottier**; *superl* **knottiest**) [*wood*] nudoso; [*problem*] espinoso

know

Ⓐ TRANSITIVE VERB	**Ⓒ** NOUN
Ⓑ INTRANSITIVE VERB	✦ IDIOMS

Look up set combinations such as **know the ropes**, **know one's stuff**, **know sth backward** *at the other word.*

know [nəʊ] (*pt* **knew**; *pp* **~n**)
Ⓐ TRANSITIVE VERB
1 (= *be aware of*) [*+ facts, dates*] saber; **to ~ that** saber que; **you ~ as well as I do that ...** sabes tan bien como yo que ...; **I knew it!** ¡lo sabía!; **I don't ~ much about history** no sé mucho de historia; **I don't ~ anything about it** no sé nada de eso; **what does he ~ about dictionaries!** ¡qué sabrá él de diccionarios!; **to ~ the difference between ...** saber la diferencia entre ...; **to ~ how to do sth** saber hacer algo; **how was I to ~ that ...?** ¿cómo iba yo a saber que ...?; **let me ~ if you can't come** avísame si no puedes venir; **let me ~ how you get on** ya me contarás cómo te fue; **I should have ~n you'd mess things up** debería haberme figurado *or* imaginado que ibas a estropear las cosas; **I ~ what I said** ya sé qué *or* lo que dije; **he doesn't ~ what to do** no sabe qué hacer; **do you ~ what, I think she did it!** ¿sabes una cosa? creo que lo hizo ella; **I ~ what! let's drop in on Daphne!** ¡ya sé! ¡vamos a pasarnos por casa de Daphne!; ✦ IDIOM **to ~ what's what** saber cuántas son cinco
2 (= *be acquainted with*) [*+ person, place*] conocer; [*+ subject, language*] saber; **civilization as we ~ it** la civilización tal y como la conocemos; **don't you ~ me better than that?** ¿no es que no me conoces?, ¡como si no me conocieras!; **to ~ sb by sight/name** conocer a algn de vista/de nombre; **they ~ each other from university** se conocen de la universidad; **to get to ~ sb** (llegar a) conocer a algn; **if I ~ him, he'll say no** me apuesto a que dice que no; **she ~s her own mind** sabe lo que quiere; ✦ PROV **it's not what you ~, it's who you ~** lo importante no es lo que sabes sino a quién conoces
3 (*with infinitive*) **he is ~n to have been there** se sabe que ha estado allí; **I've never ~n her to be wrong** que yo sepa nunca se ha equivocado; **it has never been ~n to happen** no se tienen noticias de que haya pasado nunca
4 (= *understand*) **you ~ what I mean** ya me entiendes, ya sabes lo que quiero decir
5 (= *recognize*) reconocer; **he knew me at once** me reconoció en seguida; **to ~ right from wrong** saber distinguir el bien del mal; ✦ IDIOM **she ~s a good thing when she sees it*** sabe reconocer algo bueno cuando lo ve
6 (= *be certain*) **I don't ~ if it's a very good idea** no sé si es una buena idea, no estoy seguro de que sea una buena idea
Ⓑ INTRANSITIVE VERB
1 saber; **I don't ~** no (lo) sé; **yes, I ~** si, ya lo sé; **I ~, let's ...** ya sé, vamos a ...; **it's not easy, you ~** no es fácil, sabes; **you ~, I think I'm beginning to like Richard** ¿sabes? creo que me está empezando a gustar Richard; **mummy ~s best** mamá sabe lo que te conviene; **he doesn't ~ any better** no sabe lo que hace; **you ought to ~ better than to ...** ya deberías saber que no se puede ...; **how should I ~?** ¿cómo iba yo a saberlo?; **you never ~** nunca se sabe; **there's no way of ~ing** no hay manera de saberlo; **who ~s?** ¿quién sabe?
2 (*in set expressions*)
✦ **to know about**: **did you ~ about Paul?** ¿te has enterado de *or* sabes lo de Paul?; **I didn't ~ about the accident** no me había enterado de lo del accidente, no sabía nada de lo del accidente; **I'd ~n about his illness for some time** sabía lo de su enfermedad hacía tiempo; **"you must be delighted!" — "I don't ~ about that"** ¡debes estar encantado! —no sé qué decirte; **I don't ~ about you, but I think it's terrible** a ti no sé, pero a mí me parece terrible
✦ **to get to know about sth** enterarse de algo

◆ **to know of: I ~ of a nice little café** conozco un pequeño café muy agradable; **I don't ~ him but I ~ OF him** no lo conozco pero he oído hablar de él; **I ~ of no reason why he should have committed suicide** que yo sepa no tenía razones para suicidarse; **that was the first I knew of it** esa fue la primera noticia que tuve del asunto; **not that I ~ of** que yo sepa, no

◆ **to let sb know: we'll let you ~** ya te diremos lo que sea, ya te avisaremos; **why didn't you let me ~?** ¿por qué no me lo dijiste?

Ⓒ NOUN **to be in the know*** (= *well-informed*) estar enterado; (= *privy to sth*) estar al tanto *or* al corriente

know-all ['nəʊɔːl] N (*Brit pej*) sabelotodo *mf inv*, sabihondo/a *m/f*

know-how ['nəʊhaʊ] N (= *knowledge*) conocimientos *mpl*; (= *experience*) experiencia *f*; (= *expertise*) pericia *f*

knowing ['nəʊɪŋ] **Ⓐ** ADJ [*look, smile*] de complicidad **Ⓑ** N **there's no ~** no hay modo de saberlo; **there's no ~ what he'll do** es imposible adivinar lo que hará

knowingly ['nəʊɪŋlɪ] ADV **1** (= *intentionally*) a sabiendas, adrede **2** (= *archly*) [*smile, look, nod*] con complicidad

know-it-all ['nəʊɪtɔːl] N (*US pej*) sabelotodo *mf inv*, sabihondo/a *m/f*

knowledge ['nɒlɪdʒ] N **1** (= *awareness, understanding*) conocimiento *m*; **to bring sth to sb's ~** poner a algn al tanto de algo; **it has come to my ~ that ...** me he enterado de que ...; **it is common ~ that ...** todo el mundo sabe que ..., es del dominio público que ...; **to have no ~ of sth** no tener conocimiento de algo; **not to my ~** que yo sepa, no; **without my ~** sin saberlo yo **2** (= *person's range of information*) conocimientos *mpl*; **my ~ of Spanish** mis conocimientos del español; **he has some ~ of computers** sabe algo de informática **3** (= *learning*) saber *m*; **the pursuit of ~** la búsqueda del saber

knowledgeable ['nɒlɪdʒəbl] ADJ [*person*] informado; (*in specific subject*) entendido; **she's very ~ about antiques** es muy entendida en *or* sabe mucho de antigüedades

known [nəʊn] **Ⓐ** PP *of* **know** **Ⓑ** ADJ [+ *person, fact*] conocido; **a ~ expert** un experto reconocido como tal; **she wishes to be ~ as Jane Beattie** quiere que se la conozca como Jane Beattie; **it soon became ~ that ...** tardó poco en saberse que ...; **he is best ~ for his fiction** se le conoce sobre todo por sus obras de ficción; **he let it be ~ that ...** dio a entender que ...; **they made it ~ that ...** dieron a saber que ...; **to make one's wishes ~** hacer que se sepa lo que uno desea; **he is ~ to be unreliable** tiene fama de no ser una persona en la que se pueda confiar; **the most dangerous snake ~ to man** la serpiente más peligrosa de todas las conocidas por el hombre; **it's well ~ that ...** es bien sabido que ..., es de todos conocido que ...

knuckle ['nʌkl] N (*Anat*) nudillo *m*; [*of ham*] jarrete *m*
➤ **knuckle down*** VI + ADV ponerse a trabajar en serio
➤ **knuckle under** VI + ADV someterse, bajar la cerviz

knuckleduster ['nʌkl,dʌstəʳ] N (*esp Brit*) puño *m* de hierro

KO* (= *knockout*) **Ⓐ** N ABBR K.O. *m*, nocaut *m* **Ⓑ** VT dejar K.O.

koala [kəʊ'ɑːlə] N (*also* ~ **bear**) koala *m*

kookie*, kooky* ['kuːkɪ] ADJ (*compar* ~**r**; *superl* ~**st**) (*US*) [*person*] chiflado*, majareta (*Sp**); [*idea*] descabellado, disparatado

Koran [kɒ'rɑːn] N Corán *m*, Alcorán *m*

Korea [kə'rɪə] N Corea *f*; **North/South ~** Corea *f* del Norte/Sur

Korean [kə'rɪən] ADJ, N coreano/a *m/f*

kosher ['kəʊʃəʳ] ADJ **1** (*Rel*) autorizado por la ley judía, kosher **2** (*) (= *genuine*) legal*

kowtow ['kaʊ'taʊ] VI saludar humildemente; **to ~ to sb** (*fig*) bajar la cabeza *or* doblegarse ante algn

kph ABBR (= *kilometres per hour*) km/h, kph

Kremlin ['kremlɪn] N **the ~** el Kremlin

KS ABBR (*US*) = **Kansas**

kudos ['kjuːdɒs] N prestigio *m*

kumquat ['kʌmkwɒt] N naranja *f* china

Kurd [kɜːd] N kurdo/a *m/f*

Kurdish ['kɜːdɪʃ] **Ⓐ** ADJ kurdo **Ⓑ** N (*Ling*) kurdo *m*

Kurdistan [,kɜːdɪ'stæn] N Kurdistán *m*

Kuwait [kʊ'weɪt] N Kuwait *m*

Kuwaiti [kʊ'weɪtɪ] ADJ, N kuwaití *mf*

kW, kw ABBR (= *kilowatt(s)*) kw

KY ABBR (*US*) = **Kentucky**

Kyrgyzstan [,kɜːgɪs'tɑːn] N Kirguizistán *m*

Ll

L¹, l¹ [el] **Ⓐ** N (= *letter*) L, l *f*; **L for Lucy** L de Lorenzo **Ⓑ** ABBR (= **left**) izq., izq.°

L² ABBR **1** (= **large**) G **2** (*Brit Aut*) = **learner**

l² ABBR (= **litre(s)** *or* (*US*) **liter(s)**) l

LA Ⓐ N ABBR = **Los Angeles Ⓑ** ABBR = **Louisiana**

La. ABBR **1** = **Louisiana 2** = **Lane**

Lab. ABBR = **Labrador**

lab* [læb] N ABBR (= **laboratory**) laboratorio *m* ➤ **lab coat** bata *f* de laboratorio ➤ **lab technician** técnico/a *m/f* de laboratorio

label ['leɪbl] **Ⓐ** N **1** (*on merchandise, luggage, also fig*) etiqueta *f* **2** (= *brand*) marca *f* **3** (*also* **record ~**) sello *m* discográfico **Ⓑ** VT etiquetar, poner etiqueta a; **the jar was not ~led** *or* (*US*) **~ed** el bote no llevaba etiqueta *or* no estaba etiquetado; **the bottle was ~led** *or* (*US*) **~ed "poison"** la botella llevaba una etiqueta que decía "veneno"; **to ~ sb as sth** calificar a algn de algo, tachar a algn de algo (*pej*)

labelling, labeling (*US*) ['leɪbəlɪŋ] N etiquetado *m*, etiquetaje *m*

labor ['leɪbəʳ] (*US*) **Ⓐ** N, VT, VI = **labour Ⓑ** CPD ➤ **labor union** sindicato *m*; *see also* **labour**

laboratory [ləˈbɒrətərɪ, (*US*) ˈlæbrəˌtɔːrɪ] N laboratorio *m* ➤ **laboratory assistant** ayudante *mf* de laboratorio ➤ **laboratory technician** técnico/a *m/f* de laboratorio

laborer ['leɪbərəʳ] N (*US*) = **labourer**

laborious [ləˈbɔːrɪəs] ADJ laborioso

labour, labor (*US*) ['leɪbəʳ] **Ⓐ** N **1** (= *work, toil*) trabajo *m*; **the division of ~** la división del trabajo; **a ~ of love** un trabajo realizado con amor, una tarea realizada con amor **2** (= *workers*) obreros *mpl*; (= *workforce*) mano *f* de obra; **women were used as a source of cheap ~** se utilizaba a las mujeres como mano de obra barata **3 Labour** (*Brit Pol*) el Partido Laborista, los laboristas **4** (= *birth*) parto *m*; **to be in ~** estar de parto; **to go into ~** ponerse de parto **Ⓑ** VT [+ *point*] insistir en **Ⓒ** VI **1** (= *work*) trabajar (**at** en); **to ~ to do sth** esforzarse *or* afanarse por hacer algo **2** (= *struggle*) [*engine*] sonar forzado; **to ~ up a hill** [*person, vehicle*] subir una cuesta con esfuerzo *or* dificultad; **✦** IDIOM **to ~ under the illusion that** engañarse pensando que, creerse que **Ⓓ** CPD ➤ **labour camp** campamento *m* de trabajos forzados ➤ **labour costs** costo *msing* de la mano de obra ➤ **Labour Day** Día *m* del Trabajo, Día *m* de los Trabajadores ➤ **labour force** mano *f* de obra ➤ **labour market** mercado *m* laboral, mercado *m* del trabajo ➤ **labour pains** dolores *mpl* de parto ➤ **Labour party** Partido *m* Laborista ➤ **labour relations** relaciones *fpl* laborales ➤ **labour ward** sala *f* de partos

laboured, labored (*US*) ['leɪbəd] ADJ [*breathing*] pesado; [*style*] forzado; [*text*] farragoso, recargado

labourer, laborer (*US*) ['leɪbərəʳ] N (*on roads, building site*) peón *m*; (= *farm labourer*) trabajador(a) *m/f* del campo, peón *m*

labour-intensive, labor-intensive (*US*) ['leɪbərɪn'tensɪv] ADJ que emplea mucha mano de obra

labour-saving, labor-saving (*US*) ['leɪbəˌseɪvɪŋ] ADJ que ahorra trabajo

labrador ['læbrədɔːʳ] N labrador *m*

labyrinth ['læbərɪnθ] N laberinto *m*

lace [leɪs] **Ⓐ** N **1** (= *fabric*) encaje *m*; (*as trimming*) puntilla *f* **2** [*of shoe, corset*] cordón *m*, agujeta *f* (*Mex*) **Ⓑ** ADJ de encaje **Ⓒ** VT **1** [+ *shoes*] atar (los cordones de) **2** (*with spirits*) echar licor a; **a drink ~d with brandy** una bebida con un chorrito de coñac; **a drink ~d with cyanide** una bebida envenenada con cianuro *or* con dosis de cianuro

lacerate ['læsəreɪt] VT lacerar

laceration [ˌlæsəˈreɪʃən] N laceración *f*

lace-up ['leɪsʌp] ADJ (*Brit*) de cordones, con cordones

lack [læk] **Ⓐ** N falta *f*, carencia *f* (*frm*); **the charges were dropped for ~ of evidence** retiraron la acusación por falta de pruebas; **there was no ~ of applicants for the job** no faltaban candidatos al puesto **Ⓑ** VT **he ~s confidence** le falta confianza en sí mismo, carece de confianza en sí mismo (*frm*) **Ⓒ** VI **to be ~ing** faltar; **he is ~ing in confidence** le falta confianza en sí mismo, carece de confianza en sí mismo (*frm*)

lackadaisical [ˌlækəˈdeɪzɪkəl] ADJ (= *careless*) descuidado, informal; (= *lazy*) perezoso, flojo (*LAm*); (= *dreamy*) distraído

lackey ['lækɪ] N lacayo *m*

lacklustre, lackluster (*US*) ['læk,lʌstəʳ] ADJ [*performance, style, campaign*] mediocre, deslucido

laconic [ləˈkɒnɪk] ADJ lacónico

lacquer ['lækəʳ] **Ⓐ** N laca *f* **Ⓑ** VT [+ *wood*] lacar, barnizar con laca; **to ~ one's hair** (*Brit*) ponerse *or* echarse laca en el pelo

lacrosse [ləˈkrɒs] N lacrosse *m*

lactate ['lækteɪt] VI lactar

lacy ['leɪsɪ] ADJ (*compar* **lacier**; *superl* **laciest**) (= *of lace*) de encaje; (= *like lace*) como de encaje

lad [læd] N muchacho *m*, chico *m*, chaval *m* (*Sp**), pibe *m* (*SC**), cabro *m* (*Chi**), chavo *m* (*Mex**); **come on, ~s!** ¡vamos, muchachos!; **when I was a ~** cuando yo era un muchacho, cuando yo era joven; **he's gone for a drink with the ~s** (*Brit**) ha salido a tomar algo con los amiguetes; **he's a bit of a ~** (*Brit**) es un golfillo, está hecho una buena pieza*

ladder ['lædəʳ] **Ⓐ** N **1** (= *steps*) escalera *f* de mano; **it's a first step up the ~ of success** es el primer paso hacia el éxito; **to be at the top of the ~** estar en la cumbre de su profesión *etc* **2** (*Brit*) (*in stockings*) carrera *f* **Ⓑ** VT (*Brit*) hacer una carrera en **Ⓒ** VI (*Brit*) hacerse una carrera

ladderproof ['lædəpruːf] ADJ (*Brit*) indesmallable

laden ['leɪdn] ADJ **~ with** cargado de

la-di-da* ['lɑːdɪ'dɑː] ADJ afectado, cursi*, repipi (*Sp**)

ladle ['leɪdl] N cazo *m*, cucharón *m* ➤ **ladle out** VT + ADV [+ *soup etc*] servir con cucharón; [+ *money, advice*] repartir generosamente

lady ['leɪdɪ] **Ⓐ** N **1** (= *woman*) señora *f*, dama *f* (*frm*); **ladies' clothing** ropa *f* de señora; **ladies' hairdresser's** peluquería *f* de señoras; **ladies and gentlemen!** ¡señoras y señores!, ¡damas y caballeros!; **he's a ladies' man** es un donjuán **2** (*educated*) dama *f*; **she's a real ~** es toda una dama **3** (*in titles*) **Lady Jane Grey** Lady Jane Grey **4** (*US**) (*as form of address*) señora *f* **5** (*Rel*) **Our Lady** Nuestra Señora **6** (*Brit**) **the ladies** (= *lavatory*) el servicio (de señoras), el baño (de señoras) (*LAm*); **"Ladies"** "Señoras", "Damas" **Ⓑ** CPD ➤ **ladies' room** servicio *m* de señoras, baño *m* de señoras (*LAm*) ➤ **lady doctor** doctora *f*, médico *f* ➤ **lady friend**† (*Brit*) amiga *f*

ladybird (*Brit*) ['leɪdɪbɜːd] , **ladybug** (*US*) ['leɪdɪbʌg] N mariquita *f*, vaca *f* de San Antón†

lady-in-waiting ['leɪdɪɪn'weɪtɪŋ] N (*pl* **ladies-in-waiting**) dama *f* de honor

ladylike ['leɪdɪlaɪk] ADJ elegante, fino

ladyship ['leɪdɪʃɪp] N **Her/Your Ladyship** su señoría *f*

lag [læg] VT (*esp Brit*) [+ *boiler, pipes*] revestir (**with** de) ➤ **lag behind** VI + ADV quedarse atrás, rezagarse **Ⓑ** VI + PREP **to ~ behind sb** quedarse atrás con respecto a algn, ir a la zaga de algn

lager ['lɑːgəʳ] N (*Brit*) cerveza *f* rubia ➤ **lager lout*** vándalo *m or* (*Sp*) gamberro *m* borracho

lagging ['lægɪŋ] N (*esp Brit*) revestimiento *m* calorífugo

lagoon [ləˈguːn] N laguna *f*

laid [leɪd] PT, PP *of* **lay¹**

laid-back* [ˌleɪd'bæk] ADJ (= easy-going) relajado; (= casual) despreocupado

lain [leɪn] PP of **lie²**

lair [lɛəʳ] N guarida f, cubil m

laity ['leɪtɪ] N **the ~** los seglares, los legos

lake [leɪk] N lago m; **Lake Michigan** el Lago Michigan ➤ **the Lake District** el País de los Lagos (región de lagos en el noroeste de Inglaterra)

lama ['lɑːmə] N lama m

lamb [læm] Ⓐ N (= animal) cordero m; (older) borrego m; (= meat) (carne f de) cordero m; **my poor ~!** ¡pobrecito! Ⓑ VI parir Ⓒ CPD ➤ **lamb chop** chuleta f de cordero

lambast(e) [læm'beɪst] VT fustigar, despellejar

lambing ['læmɪŋ] N parición f de las ovejas, época f del parto de las ovejas

lambswool ['læmzwʊl] N lambswool m, lana f de oveja

lame [leɪm] Ⓐ ADJ (compar ~r; superl ~st) 1 [person] cojo; **to be ~** (permanently) ser cojo, cojear; (temporarily) estar cojo, cojear; **to go ~** (permanently) quedar cojo; (temporarily) empezar a cojear 2 (= weak) [excuse] débil, pobre; [attempt] patético; [joke] malo; [argument, performance] flojo, pobre Ⓑ CPD ➤ **lame duck** (= person) caso m perdido; **the project was a ~ duck** el proyecto estaba condenado al fracaso

lamé ['lɑːmeɪ] N lamé m

lamely ['leɪmlɪ] ADV [say] de forma poco convincente

lament [lə'ment] Ⓐ N lamento m; (= poem) elegía f, endecha f **(for** por); (= song) canción f elegíaca, endecha f Ⓑ VT [+ absence, lack, loss] llorar, lamentar; **it is much to be ~ed that ...** es de lamentar que ... + subjun

lamentable ['læməntəbl] ADJ lamentable

lamentably ['læməntəblɪ] ADV lamentablemente; **there are still ~ few women surgeons** es de lamentar or es lamentable que todavía existan muy pocas cirujanas

laminated ['læmɪneɪtɪd] ADJ [metal] laminado; [glass] inastillable; [wood] contrachapado; [document] plastificado

lamp [læmp] N (= table lamp, floor lamp) lámpara f; (hand-held) linterna f; (in street) farol m, farola f; (Aut) faro m; (= bulb) bombilla f, bombillo m (LAm), foco m (LAm)

lamplight ['læmplaɪt] N luz f de (la) lámpara; (from street lamp) luz f de(l) farol

lampoon [læm'puːn] Ⓐ N sátira f Ⓑ VT satirizar

lamppost ['læmppəʊst] N (esp Brit) farol m, farola f

lampshade ['læmpʃeɪd] N pantalla f (de lámpara)

lance [lɑːns] Ⓐ N (= weapon) lanza f; (Med) lanceta f Ⓑ VT (Med) abrir con lanceta Ⓒ CPD ➤ **lance corporal** (Brit) soldado mf de primera

lancet ['lɑːnsɪt] N lanceta f

land [lænd] Ⓐ N 1 (= ground) tierra f; **agricultural ~** tierra(s) f(pl) agrícola(s), terreno m agrícola; **to go/travel by ~** ir/viajar por tierra; **dry ~** tierra f firme; **a piece/plot of ~** un terreno, una parcela; **to live off the ~** vivir de la tierra; ✦ IDIOM **to see how the ~ lies** tantear el terreno 2 (= property) tierras fpl; **get off my ~!** ¡fuera de mis tierras! 3 (= region) **desert/equatorial/temperate ~s** tierras fpl desérticas/ecuatoriales/templadas 4 (= nation, country) país m; **a ~ of opportunity** un país de oportunidades; ✦ IDIOM **to be in the ~ of the living** (hum) estar en el mundo de los vivos, estar vivito y coleando Ⓑ VI 1 [plane] aterrizar; (on water) amerizar, amarizar; (on moon) alunizar; **to ~ on sth** [bird, insect] posarse en algo 2 (from boat) [passenger] desembarcar 3 (after fall, jump, throw) caer; **I ~ed awkwardly** caí en una mala postura; **to ~ on one's back** caer de espaldas; ✦ IDIOM **to ~ on one's feet** caer de pie 4 (*) (in prison, hospital) ir a parar* (**in** a), acabar (**in** en) Ⓒ VT [+ passengers] desembarcar; [+ cargo] descargar 2 [+ plane] hacer aterrizar 3 [+ fish] pescar, conseguir pescar; [+ job, contract] conseguir; [+ prize] obtener 4 (*) (in set expressions) **to ~ sb in sth: his comments ~ed him in court** sus comentarios hicieron que fuera a parar a los tribunales or que acabara en los tribunales*; **to ~ sb in**

it fastidiar or jorobar a algn pero bien*; **to ~ sb in trouble** causar problemas a algn; **to ~ o.s. in trouble** meterse en problemas; **they ~ed the children on me** me endilgaron or endosaron a los niños*; **I got ~ed with the job** (Brit) me endilgaron or endosaron el trabajo*; **getting overdrawn could ~ you with big bank charges** girar al descubierto te puede ocasionar enormes intereses bancarios ➤ **land up*** (esp Brit) Ⓐ VI + ADV ir a parar*, acabar; **eventually we ~ed up in Rome** al final fuimos a parar a Roma*, al final aterrizamos en Roma* Ⓑ VT + ADV **this sort of behaviour could ~ you up in prison** este tipo de comportamiento puede llevarte a la cárcel

landed ['lændɪd] ADJ ➤ **the landed gentry** los terratenientes, la aristocracia rural

landfill ['lændfɪl] N entierro m de basuras ➤ **landfill site** vertedero m de basuras

landing ['lændɪŋ] Ⓐ N 1 [of aircraft, spacecraft] (on land) aterrizaje m; (on sea) amerizaje m; (on moon) alunizaje m 2 [of troops] desembarco m 3 (in house) descansillo m, rellano m Ⓑ CPD ➤ **landing card** tarjeta f de desembarque ➤ **landing craft** lancha f de desembarco ➤ **landing gear** tren m de aterrizaje ➤ **landing stage** (Brit) desembarcadero m ➤ **landing strip** pista f de aterrizaje

landlady ['lænd,leɪdɪ] N [of flat] casera f, dueña f; (Brit) [of pub] (= owner) dueña f, patrona f; (= manager) encargada f, jefa f; (esp US) [of boarding house] patrona f

landlocked ['lændlɒkt] ADJ sin acceso al mar

landlord ['lændlɔːd] N [of property, land] propietario m, dueño m; [of flat] casero m, dueño m; (Brit) [of pub] (= owner) dueño m, patrón m; (= manager) encargado m, jefe m; (esp US) [of boarding house] patrón m

landmark ['lændmɑːk] N punto m de referencia; **to be a ~ in history** marcar un hito en la historia, ser un hito histórico

landmine ['lændmaɪn] N mina f terrestre

landowner ['lænd,əʊnəʳ] N terrateniente mf, hacendado/a m/f

landscape ['lænskeɪp] Ⓐ N (= scenery, painting) paisaje m; **the political ~** el panorama político Ⓑ VT [+ terrain, grounds] ajardinar; [+ park, garden] diseñar Ⓒ CPD ➤ **landscape format** formato m apaisado ➤ **landscape gardener** jardinero/a m/f paisajista ➤ **landscape gardening** jardinería f paisajista ➤ **landscape painter** paisajista mf

landslide ['lændslaɪd] N 1 (lit) corrimiento m or desprendimiento m de tierras 2 (also ~ **victory**) victoria f arrolladora or aplastante

lane [leɪn] Ⓐ N 1 (in country) camino m; (in town) callejuela f, callejón m 2 (= carriageway) carril m, vía f (LAm); **bus/cycle ~** carril m de autobuses/bicicletas; **the fast ~** (Brit) el carril de la derecha; (most other countries) el carril de la izquierda; **"get in lane"** "incorpórese al carril"; **"keep in lane"** "manténgase en su carril" 3 (for ships) ruta f; **sea/shipping ~** ruta f marítima/de navegación 4 (also **air ~**) corredor m aéreo, ruta f aérea 5 (Sport) calle f; **inside/outside ~** calle f de dentro/fuera Ⓑ CPD ➤ **lane closure** corte m de carril; **there will be ~ closures on the M1** habrá carriles cortados en la M1

language ['læŋgwɪdʒ] Ⓐ N 1 (= faculty, style of speech) lenguaje m 2 (= national tongue) lengua f, idioma m; **the Spanish ~** la lengua española, el idioma español; **he studies ~s** estudia idiomas or lenguas; **first ~** lengua f materna; ✦ IDIOM **we don't talk the same ~** no hablamos el mismo idioma 3 (= style, jargon) lenguaje m; **in plain ~** en lenguaje sencillo; **legal/technical ~** lenguaje m jurídico/técnico 4 (Comput) lenguaje m 5 (= swear words) **watch your ~** no digas palabrotas; **bad ~** palabrotas fpl, lenguaje m grosero Ⓑ CPD ➤ **language barrier** barrera f del idioma ➤ **language laboratory** laboratorio m de idiomas ➤ **language school** academia f de idiomas

languid ['læŋgwɪd] ADJ lánguido

languish ['læŋgwɪʃ] VI (= pine) languidecer, consumirse; (in prison) pudrirse

lank [læŋk] ADJ [hair] lacio

lanky ['læŋkɪ] ADJ (compar **lankier**; superl **lankiest**) larguirucho*

lanolin(e) ['lænəlɪn] N lanolina f

lantern ['læntən] N farol m, linterna f

Laos [laʊs] N Laos m

lap¹ [læp] N (= knee) regazo m; **to sit on sb's ~** sentarse en el regazo or las rodillas de algn; ✦ IDIOMS **to fall into sb's ~**: **he expects the money to fall into his ~** espera que el dinero le caiga como llovido del cielo; **the outcome is in the ~ of the gods now** del resultado Dios dirá, la suerte está echada y ya veremos qué pasa; **to live in the ~ of luxury** vivir or nadar en la abundancia

lap² [læp] Ⓐ N 1 (Sport) vuelta f; **~ of honour** (esp Brit) vuelta f de honor 2 (= stage) etapa f, fase f; **we're on the last ~ now** (fig) ya estamos en la recta final Ⓑ VT **to ~ sb** doblar a algn Ⓒ CPD ➤ **lap record** récord m del circuito

lap³ [læp] Ⓐ VT 1 (= drink) [+ water, milk] beber a lengüetazos 2 (= wash against) [+ shore, cliff] lamer, besar Ⓑ VI [waves] chapalear; **to ~ against sth** lamer or besar algo ➤ **lap up** VT + ADV [+ milk, water] beber a lengüetazos; [+ compliments, attention] disfrutar con

lapdog ['læpdɒg] N perro m faldero

lapel [lə'pel] N solapa f

Lapland ['læplænd] N Laponia f

Lapp [læp] ADJ, N lapón/ona m/f

lapse [læps] Ⓐ N 1 (= error) lapsus m inv, fallo m (Sp), falla f (LAm); **she has the occasional ~ of memory** de vez en cuando tiene lapsus or (Sp) fallos or (LAm) fallas de memoria; **it was a ~ of judgement on his part** fue un error de cálculo por su parte; **a momentary ~ of concentration** un despiste momentáneo 2 [of time] lapso m, intervalo m, período m Ⓑ VI 1 (= slip) **to ~ into one's old ways** volver a las andadas; **he ~d into silence** se calló, se quedó callado 2 (= expire) [season ticket] caducar, vencer 3 (= decline) [standards] entrar en declive

lapsed [læpst] ADJ (Rel) que ya no practica

laptop ['læptɒp] N (also **~ computer**) ordenador m portátil, computador(a) m/f portátil (LAm)

larceny ['lɑːsənɪ] N hurto m, robo m; **grand ~** (US) hurto m mayor; **petty ~** hurto m menor

larch [lɑːtʃ] N (also **~ tree**) alerce m

lard [lɑːd] Ⓐ N manteca f de cerdo Ⓑ VT (esp Brit) lardear, mechar; **to ~ sth with** (fig) salpicar algo de, adornar algo con

larder ['lɑːdər] N (esp Brit) despensa f

large [lɑːdʒ] Ⓐ ADJ (compar **~r**; superl **~st**)

The commonest translation of **large** is **grande**, which must be shortened to **gran** before a singular noun.

---

1 (in size) [house, object, organization] grande; [person] corpulento; [area] grande, extenso; **as ~ as life** en carne y hueso, en persona; **in ~ part** en gran parte 2 (in number) [family, group, army] numeroso, grande; [sum, amount] grande, importante; **~ numbers of people came** vinieron muchísimas personas, vinieron gran número de personas; **a ~ quantity of** una gran cantidad de 3 (Comm) de tamaño grande; **a dozen ~ envelopes** una docena de sobres de tamaño grande; **"large"** (on clothing label) "grande"; (on food packet, washing powder) "tamaño familiar" Ⓑ N **at ~: the country/society at ~** el país/la sociedad en general; **to be at ~** andar suelto Ⓒ ADV **by and ~** en general Ⓓ CPD ➤ **the large intestine** el intestino grueso

---

⚠ **large ≠ largo**

---

largely ['lɑːdʒlɪ] ADV en gran parte, en gran medida; **this is ~ due to …** esto se debe en gran parte or medida a …; **it is a ~ working-class area** es en su mayor parte una zona de clase obrera

large-scale ['lɑːdʒ'skeɪl] ADJ a or en gran escala

lark¹ [lɑːk] N (= bird) alondra f; ✦ IDIOM **to get up with the ~** levantarse con las gallinas, madrugar mucho

lark² [lɑːk] N (esp Brit) 1 (= joke) broma f; **what a ~!** ¡qué risa!, ¡qué divertido!; **to do sth for a ~** hacer algo por diversión or para divertirse 2 (= business, affair) **that ice-cream ~** ese tinglado* or asunto de los helados; **this dinner-jacket ~** esto de ponerse esmoquin ➤ **lark around***, **lark about*** VI + ADV (Brit) hacer el tonto, hacer tonterías; **to ~ around with sth** divertirse con algo, jugar con algo

larva ['lɑːvə] N (pl **~e** ['lɑːviː]) larva f

laryngitis [ˌlærɪn'dʒaɪtɪs] N laringitis f inv

larynx ['lærɪŋks] N laringe f

lasagna, lasagne [lə'zænjə] N lasaña f

lascivious [lə'sɪvɪəs] ADJ lascivo

laser ['leɪzər] N láser m ➤ **laser beam** rayo m láser ➤ **laser printer** impresora f láser

lash [læʃ] Ⓐ N 1 (= eyelash) pestaña f 2 (= blow from whip) latigazo m, azote m Ⓑ VT 1 (= beat) azotar 2 (= tie) atar 3 (= move) **it ~ed its tail** dio coletazos Ⓒ VI **the rain was ~ing against the windows** la lluvia azotaba las ventanas ➤ **lash down** Ⓐ VT + ADV sujetar con cuerdas Ⓑ VI + ADV [rain] caer con fuerza; **it was ~ing down** llovía con fuerza ➤ **lash out** VI + ADV (with fists) repartir golpes a diestro y siniestro; (with feet) soltar patadas, tirar coces; **to ~ out at** or **against sb** arremeter contra algn

lashing ['læʃɪŋ] N 1 (= beating) azotes mpl; **to give sb a ~** azotar a algn 2 **~s of** (esp Brit*) montones de*

lass [læs] N (esp Scot) muchacha f, chica f, chavala f (Sp*), cabra f (Chi*), piba f (SC*), chamaca f (CAm, Mex*)

lasso [læ'suː] Ⓐ N (pl **~s** or **~es**) lazo m Ⓑ VT lazar, coger con el lazo

last¹ [lɑːst] Ⓐ ADJ 1 (= most recent) último; **over the ~ few months** durante los últimos meses 2 (= past, previous) [Christmas, Easter, month, year] pasado; [time, meeting, birthday] último; **~ Friday** el viernes pasado; **this time ~ year** el año pasado por estas fechas; **this time ~ week** la semana pasada a estas horas 3 (= final) último; **the ~ Friday of the month** el último viernes del mes; **the ~ door on the right** la última puerta a la derecha; **the ~ three pages of the book** las tres últimas paginas del libro; **~ but one** penúltimo; **I'm down to my ~ pound** sólo me queda una libra; **down to the ~ detail** hasta el más mínimo or el último detalle; **I was the ~ person to arrive/to see him alive** fui la última en llegar/la última persona que lo vió vivo; **~ thing at night** antes de acostarse; **I'll finish it if it's the ~ thing I do!** ¡lo terminaré aunque sea la última cosa que haga en esta vida!; **that was the ~ time I saw him** ésa fue la última vez que lo vi; ✦ IDIOM **to be on one's ~ legs*** estar en las últimas 4 (= least likely) **you're the ~ person I'd trust with it** lo confiaría a cualquiera menos a ti, eres la última persona a la que se lo confiaría; **that was the ~ thing I expected** eso era lo que menos me esperaba; **retirement is the ~ thing on his mind** jubilarse es lo último en lo que piensa Ⓑ PRON 1 (in series) último/a m/f; **he was the ~ of the Tudors** fue el último de los Tudores; **the ~ but one** el/la penúltimo/a; **if we don't go we shall never hear the ~ of it** si no vamos no dejarán de recordárnoslo; **the ~ we heard of him he was in Rio** según las últimas noticias estaba en Río; **you haven't heard the ~ of this!** ¡esto no se acaba aquí!, ¡esto no se va a quedar así!; **we're always the ~ to know** siempre somos los últimos en enterarnos; **to leave sth till ~** dejar algo para lo último or el final; **that was the ~ I saw of him** después de aquello no volví a verlo más; **to the ~** hasta el final 2 (= previous one) **each one is better than the ~** son cada vez mejores; **the night before ~** anteanoche; **the week before ~** la semana anterior a la pasada, la semana pasada no, la anterior 3 (= all that remains) **this is the ~ of the bread/wine** esto es lo que queda de pan/vino 4 **at ~** por fin Ⓒ ADV 1 (= finally) **~ of all, take out the screws** por último, saca los tornillos; **~ but not least** por último, pero no por ello menos importante

2 (= *in last place, at the end*) **he came ~ in the 100 metres** terminó en último lugar *or* en última posición en los 100 metros; **to arrive ~** llegar el *or* (*LAm*) al último

3 (= *most recently*) **when I ~ saw them** la última vez que los vi; **I ~ saw her in 1997** la vi por última vez en 1997
ⓓ CPD ➤ **the last rites** la extremaunción

last² [lɑ:st] **ⓐ** VI durar; **it ~s (for) two hours** dura dos horas; **it can't ~** esto no puede durar; **he wouldn't have ~ed ten minutes in those conditions** no hubiera durado *or* aguantado ni diez minutos en esas condiciones; **"only available while stocks last"** "sólo hasta que se agoten las existencias" **ⓑ** VT durar; **it will ~ you a lifetime** te durará toda la vida; **I've had enough publicity to ~ me a lifetime!** ¡me han dado publicidad suficiente para toda una vida!
➤ **last out** VI + ADV **1** [*money, resources*] alcanzar; **my money doesn't ~ out the month** el dinero no me alcanza para todo el mes **2** [*person*] (= *go on*) aguantar; (= *survive*) sobrevivir

last-ditch [ˈlɑ:stˈdɪtʃ] ADJ último, desesperado

lasting [ˈlɑ:stɪŋ] ADJ (*gen*) duradero, perdurable; [*shame*] eterno

lastly [ˈlɑ:stlɪ] ADV por último, finalmente

last-minute [ˈlɑ:stˈmɪnɪt] ADJ de última hora

lat. ABBR = **latitude**

latch [lætʃ] N pestillo *m*; **the door is on the ~** la puerta no tiene echado el pestillo
➤ **latch on*** VI + ADV comprender, darse cuenta
➤ **latch onto** VI + PREP [+ *person, group*] pegarse a; [+ *idea*] agarrarse a; **the media were quick to ~ onto the story** la prensa no tardó en recoger la noticia

latchkey [ˈlætʃki:] N llave *f* ➤ **latchkey child** niño/a *m/f* cuya madre trabaja

late [leɪt] (*compar* **~r**; *superl* **~st**) **ⓐ** ADV **1** (= *after usual time*) tarde; **the chemist is open ~ on Thursdays** la farmacia cierra tarde los jueves; **to stay up ~** irse a la cama tarde, trasnochar; **to work ~** trabajar hasta tarde
2 (= *after scheduled time*) [*arrive*] tarde, con retraso; **he arrived ten minutes ~** llegó con diez minutos de retraso, llegó diez minutos tarde; **we're running ~ this morning** llevamos retraso esta mañana; **we're running about 40 minutes ~** llevamos unos 40 minutos de retraso, llevamos un retraso de unos 40 minutos; **◆** PROV **better ~ than never** más vale tarde que nunca
3 (*in period*) **he had arrived ~ the previous evening** había llegado tarde la noche anterior; **~ at night** muy de noche, ya entrada la noche; **~ in the morning** a última hora de la mañana; **~ in 1992/May** a finales del año 1992/de mayo; **they scored ~ in the second half** metieron un gol ya bien entrado el segundo tiempo; **~ into the night** hasta bien entrada la noche; **~ that night I got a phone call** ya entrada la noche recibí una llamada de teléfono; **too ~** demasiado tarde; **◆** IDIOM **it's a bit ~ in the day to be changing your mind** es un poco tarde para cambiar de opinión
4 (= *recently*) **as ~ as 1950** aún en 1950; **of ~** últimamente, recientemente
ⓑ ADJ **1** (*in period*) **it was very ~ and I was tired** era muy tarde y estaba cansado; **by ~ morning we had finished** a última hora de la mañana habíamos acabado; **in the ~ afternoon** a media tarde; **in ~ September/spring** a finales de septiembre/de la primavera; **in the ~ 1960s** a finales de los años sesenta; **in the ~ 18th century** a fines del siglo XVIII; **to be in one's ~ thirties** rondar los cuarenta, tener cerca de cuarenta años; **it's getting ~** se está haciendo tarde; **~ goal** gol *m* de última hora; **even at this ~ stage** incluso a estas alturas
2 (= *after arranged or scheduled time*) **sorry I'm ~!** ¡siento llegar tarde *or* con retraso!; **you're ~!** ¡llegas tarde!; **we apologize for the ~ arrival/departure of this train** les rogamos disculpen el retraso en la llegada/salida de este tren; **our train was ~ again** nuestro tren se retrasó *or* llegó con retraso otra vez; **the train is 20 minutes ~** el tren llega con 20 minutos de retraso, el tren lleva un retraso de 20 minutos; **he was ~ (in) finishing his essay** terminó la redacción con retraso; **I'm ~ for my train** voy a perder el

tren; **I'm ~ for work** voy a llegar tarde al trabajo; **a fault on the plane made us two hours ~** una avería en el avión nos retrasó dos horas; **you're going to make me ~ for my appointment** vas a hacer que llegue tarde a la cita; **we got off to a ~ start** empezamos tarde *or* con retraso; **I was ~ with the payments** me había retrasado en los pagos
3 (= *after usual or normal time*) [*reservation, booking*] de última hora; [*crop, flowers*] tardío; **we had a ~ breakfast** desayunamos tarde; **to have a ~ night** acostarse muy tarde; **you've had too many ~ nights** llevas muchos días acostándote muy tarde; **"late opening till ten pm on Fridays"** "los viernes cerramos a las diez"; **my period is ~** se me está retrasando la regla; **spring is ~ this year** la primavera llega tarde este año
4 **too ~** demasiado tarde; **it's too ~ to change your mind** es demasiado tarde para cambiar de opinión; **it's not too ~ (for you) to change your mind** aún estás a tiempo para cambiar de opinión
5 (*Hist, Art*) **the ~ Middle Ages** la baja edad media; **a ~ Georgian house** una casa de finales del periodo Georgiano
6 (= *dead*) difunto; **the ~ Joe Tay** el difunto Joe Tay
ⓒ CPD ➤ **late developer: I was a ~ developer** maduré tarde
➤ **late edition** edición *f* de última hora

latecomer [ˈleɪtkʌmər] N rezagado/a *m/f*, el/la que llega tarde; **~s will not be admitted** no se permitirá la entrada una vez comenzado el acto/espectáculo

lately [ˈleɪtlɪ] ADV últimamente, recientemente; **until ~** hasta hace poco; **it's only ~ that ...** hace poco que ...

lateness [ˈleɪtnɪs] N [*of person, vehicle*] retraso *m*, tardanza *f*, atraso *m* (*LAm*); [*of hour*] lo avanzado

late-night [ˈleɪtˈnaɪt] ADJ **~ film** (*Cine*) película *f* de sesión de noche; (*TV*) película *f* de medianoche; **~ opening** *or* **shopping is on Thursdays** se abre hasta tarde los jueves

latent [ˈleɪtənt] ADJ [*heat*] latente; [*tendency*] implícito

later [ˈleɪtər] **ⓐ** ADV **1** más tarde; **ten years/minutes ~** diez años/minutos después *or* más tarde; **I'll do it ~** lo haré luego *or* más tarde; **~, when all the guests had left** luego *or* más tarde, cuando todos los invitados se habían marchado; **all essays should be handed in no ~ than Monday** todos los trabajos deben entregarse el lunes a más tardar; **~ that day** más tarde *or* posteriormente ese día
2 **~ on** más tarde, más adelante; **~ on that night** aquella noche más tarde; **~ on in the film** más adelante en la película; **~ on in the morning/afternoon/evening** más entrada la mañana/tarde/noche
ⓑ ADJ [*chapter, version, work*] posterior; **I took a ~ flight** tomé un avión que salía más tarde; **in ~ life** más adelante

lateral [ˈlætərəl] ADJ lateral ➤ **lateral thinking** pensamiento *m* lateral

latest [ˈleɪtɪst] **ⓐ** SUPERL *of* **late** ADJ **1** (= *most recent*) [*figures, boyfriend, book*] último, más reciente; **the ~ fashion** la última moda; **it's the ~ model** es el último modelo
2 (= *last*) [*flight, train, bus*] último; **the ~ (possible) date** la fecha límite; **the ~ possible moment** el último momento; **the ~ (possible) time** lo más tarde
ⓑ N **the ~ 1** (= *news*) **have you heard the ~?** ¿te has enterado de la última noticia?; **for the ~ on where to go and what to do ...** para la información más actualizada acerca de dónde ir y qué hacer ...
2 (= *most modern type*) **it's the ~ in food processors** es lo último en robots de cocina
3 (= *last possible time*) lo más tarde; **it has to be here by Friday at the (very) ~** tiene que estar aquí el viernes como muy tarde

latex [ˈleɪteks] N látex *m*

lathe [leɪð] N torno *m*

lather [ˈlæðər] **ⓐ** N espuma *f*; **the horse was in a ~** el caballo estaba empapado en sudor; **◆** IDIOM **to be in/get into a ~ (about sth)** estar/ponerse frenético (por algo) **ⓑ** VT [+ *one's face*] enjabonarse **ⓒ** VI hacer espuma

Latin [ˈlætɪn] **ⓐ** ADJ latino **ⓑ** N **1** (= *person*) latino/a *m/f*; **the ~s** los latinos **2** (*Ling*) latín *m* **ⓒ** CPD ➤ **Latin America** América *f* Latina, Latinoamérica *f*, Hispanoamérica *f*
➤ **Latin quarter** barrio *m* latino

Latin American [ˈlætɪnəˈmerɪkən] ADJ, N latinoamericano/a *m/f*

latitude [ˈlætɪtjuːd] N latitud f

latrine [ləˈtriːn] N letrina f

latter [ˈlætəʳ] **Ⓐ** ADJ **1** (= last) último; **the ~ part of the story** la última parte del relato; **in the ~ part of the century** hacia fines or finales del siglo **2** (of two) segundo **Ⓑ** N **the ~** éste/ésta; (pl) éstos/éstas; **the former ... the ~ ...** aquél ... éste ...

latterly [ˈlætəlɪ] ADV últimamente, recientemente

lattice [ˈlætɪs] N enrejado m; (on window) reja f, celosía f ➤ **lattice window** ventana f de celosía

Latvia [ˈlætvɪə] N Letonia f, Latvia f

Latvian [ˈlætvɪən] ADJ, N letón/ona m/f, latvio/a m/f

laudable [ˈlɔːdəbl] ADJ loable, laudable

laugh [lɑːf] **Ⓐ** N **1** (lit) risa f; (loud) carcajada f, risotada f; **she gave a little ~** soltó una risita; **to get a ~** (esp Brit) hacer reír (a la gente); **to have a (good) ~ about sth** reírse (mucho) de algo; **that sounds like a ~ a minute** (iro*) suena como para mondarse de risa*; **to raise a ~** hacer reír (a la gente); **... he said with a ~ ...** dijo riéndose; **✦** IDIOM **to have the last ~** ser el que ríe el último

2 (*) (= fun) **he's a ~** es un tipo gracioso or divertido*, es muy cachondo (Sp*); **it'll be a ~** será divertido; **to do sth for a ~** hacer algo por divertirse; **he's always good for a ~** siempre te ríes or te diviertes con él; **if you want a ~, read on** si te quieres reír, sigue leyendo

3 (*) (= joke) **that's a ~!** (iro) ¡no me hagas reír!

Ⓑ VI reírse, reír; **I didn't know whether to ~ or cry** no sabía si reír(me) o llorar; **you may ~, but ...** tú te ríes, pero ...; **once we get this contract signed we're ~ing*** una vez que nos firmen este contrato, lo demás es coser y cantar; **to ~ about sth** reírse de algo; **there's nothing to ~ about** no es cosa de risa or (LAm) reírse; **to ~ at sb/sth** reírse de algn/algo; **you have (got) to ~** hay que reírse; **to make sb ~** hacer reír a algn; **I ~ed till the tears ran down my cheeks** me reí a más no poder, me tronché de (la) risa; **I ~ed to myself** me reí para mis adentros; **✦** IDIOMS **they'll be ~ing all the way to the bank** estarán contentísimos contando el dinero; **he'll soon be ~ing on the other side of his face** (Brit) or **mouth** (US) pronto se le quitarán las ganas de reír **Ⓒ** VT **"don't be silly," he ~ed** —no seas bobo —dijo riéndose; **his idea was ~ed out of court** se rieron de su idea; **✦** IDIOM **to ~ one's head off*** partirse or desternillarse or troncharse de risa

➤ **laugh off** VT + ADV tomarse a risa

laughable [ˈlɑːfəbl] ADJ [sum, amount] irrisorio; [suggestion] ridículo; **it's really quite ~ that ...** es realmente un poco ridículo or irrisorio que ...

laughing [ˈlɑːfɪŋ] ADJ risueño, alegre; **it's no ~ matter** no tiene ninguna gracia, no es cosa de risa ➤ **laughing gas** gas m hilarante ➤ **laughing stock** hazmerreír m

laughter [ˈlɑːftəʳ] N risa f, risas fpl; **their ~ could be heard in the next room** se oían sus risas or se les oía reír desde la habitación de al lado; **there was loud ~ at this remark** el comentario provocó carcajadas or grandes risas

launch [lɔːntʃ] **Ⓐ** N **1** (= boat) lancha f; **motor ~** lancha f motora

2 (of ship) botadura f; (of lifeboat, rocket, campaign, product) lanzamiento m; (of film, play) estreno m; (of company) creación f, fundación f; (of shares) emisión f

Ⓑ VT [+ ship] botar; [+ lifeboat] echar al mar; [+ rocket, missile, campaign, product, attack] lanzar; [+ film, play] estrenar; [+ company] crear, fundar; [+ shares] emitir; **it was this novel that really ~ed him as a writer** fue esta novela la que lo lanzó a la fama como escritor; **to ~ sb on his/her way** iniciar a algn en su carrera

Ⓒ VI **she ~ed into a long speech about patriotism** se puso a soltar or empezó un largo discurso sobre el patriotismo; **he ~ed into an attack on the president** emprendió un ataque contra el presidente, se puso a despotricar contra el presidente

Ⓓ CPD ➤ **launch pad** rampa f or plataforma f de lanzamiento ➤ **launch party** fiesta f de lanzamiento ➤ **launch site** lugar m del lanzamiento

➤ **launch out** VI + ADV lanzarse; **the company needs to ~ out into new markets** la compañía necesita lanzarse a nuevos mercados; **now we can afford to ~ out a bit** ahora nos podemos permitir algunos lujos

launching [ˈlɔːntʃɪŋ] N (of ship) botadura f; (of missile, rocket, lifeboat, company, product) lanzamiento m ➤ **launching pad** rampa f or plataforma f de lanzamiento

launder [ˈlɔːndəʳ] VT (lit) lavar y planchar; [+ money] blanquear, lavar (LAm)

Launderette® [ˌlɔːndəˈret] N (Brit) lavandería f automática

Laundromat® [ˈlɔːndrəˌmæt] N (US) lavandería f automática

laundry [ˈlɔːndrɪ] **Ⓐ** N **1** (= clothes) (= dirty) ropa f sucia, ropa f para lavar; (= clean) ropa f lavada, colada f (Sp); **to do the ~** lavar la ropa **2** (= establishment) lavandería f; (domestic) lavadero m **Ⓑ** CPD ➤ **laundry basket** cesto m de la ropa sucia ➤ **laundry detergent** (US) jabón m en polvo, detergente m

laureate [ˈlɔːrɪɪt] N laureado m; **the Poet Laureate** (Brit) el Poeta Laureado

laurel [ˈlɔrəl] N laurel m; **✦** IDIOM **to rest on one's ~s** dormirse en los laureles

lava [ˈlɑːvə] N lava f ➤ **lava flow** torrente m or río m de lava

lavatory [ˈlævətrɪ] (esp Brit) **Ⓐ** N **1** (= room) (in house) wáter m (Sp), baño m (LAm); (in public place) aseos mpl, servicio(s) m(pl) (Sp), baño(s) m(pl) (LAm) **2** (= appliance) inodoro m, wáter m (Sp), taza f (LAm) **Ⓑ** CPD ➤ **lavatory paper** papel m higiénico

lavender [ˈlævɪndəʳ] N espliego m, lavanda f ➤ **lavender water** lavanda f

lavish [ˈlævɪʃ] **Ⓐ** ADJ [apartment, meal, production, costume] suntuoso; [gift, hospitality] espléndido, generoso; [amount] abundante, generoso; **to be ~ in one's praise** ser pródigo en elogios, no escatimar elogios **Ⓑ** VT **to ~ sth on sb** colmar a algn de algo

lavishly [ˈlævɪʃlɪ] ADV [decorated, furnished] suntuosamente; [entertain, pay] espléndidamente, generosamente; [praise] profusamente

law [lɔː] **Ⓐ** N **1** (= legislation) ley f; **it's the ~** es la ley; **to be above the ~** estar por encima de la ley; **there's no ~ against it** no hay ley que lo prohíba; **the bill became ~ on 6th August** el proyecto de ley se hizo ley el seis de agosto; **by ~** por ley, de acuerdo con la ley; **civil/criminal ~** derecho m civil/penal; **the ~ of the land** la ley vigente; **the ~ on abortion** la legislación sobre el aborto; **to have the ~ on one's side** tener la justicia de su lado; **to keep within the ~** obrar legalmente; **his word is ~** su palabra es ley; **✦** IDIOMS **to lay down the ~*** imponer su criterio, obrar autoritariamente; **to take the ~ into one's own hands** tomarse la justicia por su mano; **to be a ~ unto o.s.** dictar sus propias leyes

2 (= field of study) derecho m; **to study ~** estudiar derecho

3 (= profession) abogacía f; **to practise ~** ejercer de abogado, ejercer la abogacía

4 (= legal proceedings) **court of ~** tribunal m de justicia; **to go to ~** recurrir a la justicia or a los tribunales

5 (= standard) norma f; **there seemed to be one ~ for the rich and another for the poor** parecía haber unas normas para los ricos y otras para los pobres

6 (Sci, Math) ley f; **the ~s of physics** las leyes de la física; **by the ~ of averages** por la estadística, estadísticamente; **the ~ of gravity** la ley de la gravedad

Ⓑ CPD ➤ **law and order** el orden público ➤ **law court** tribunal m de justicia ➤ **Law Faculty** facultad f de Derecho ➤ **the Law Lords** (Brit) jueces que son miembros de la Cámara de los Lores y constituyen el Tribunal Supremo ➤ **law school** (US) facultad f de derecho ➤ **law student** estudiante mf de derecho

law-abiding [ˈlɔːəˌbaɪdɪŋ] ADJ (lit) cumplidor de la ley; (fig) decente

lawful [ˈlɔːfʊl] ADJ [owner, government, action] legítimo; [contract] legal, válido

lawfully [ˈlɔːfəlɪ] ADV legalmente

lawless [ˈlɔːlɪs] ADJ [person] rebelde, que rechaza la ley; [country] ingobernable, anárquico

lawn¹ [lɔːn] N césped m, pasto m (LAm) ➤ **lawn bowling** (US) bochas fpl ➤ **lawn tennis** tenis m sobre hierba

lawn² [lɔ:n] N (= *cloth*) linón *m*

lawnmower ['lɔ:n,məʊəʳ] N cortacésped *m* (*Sp*), segadora *f* (*LAm*)

lawsuit ['lɔ:su:t] N pleito *m*, juicio *m*; **to bring a ~ against sb** entablar demanda judicial contra algn

lawyer ['lɔ:jəʳ] N abogado/a *m/f*

lax [læks] ADJ (*compar* **~er**; *superl* **~est**) [*person, discipline*] poco estricto, poco riguroso; [*standards*] laxo, relajado; **to be ~ about punctuality** ser negligente en la puntualidad

laxative ['læksətɪv] N laxante *m*

laxity ['læksɪtɪ], **laxness** ['læksnɪs] N falta *f* de rigor

lay¹ [leɪ] **Ⓐ** VT (*pt, pp* **laid**) **1** (= *place, put*) (*gen*) poner, colocar; [+ *carpet, lino*] poner, extender; [+ *bricks*] poner, colocar; [+ *pipes*] (*in building*) instalar; [+ *cable, mains, track, trap*] tender; [+ *foundations*] echar; [+ *mines*] sembrar; **I haven't laid eyes on him for years** hace años que no lo veo; **I didn't ~ a finger on it!** ¡no lo toqué!; **I don't know where to ~ my hands on ...** no sé dónde echar mano a *or* conseguir ... **2** (= *prepare*) [+ *fire*] preparar; [+ *plans*] hacer; **to ~ the table** (*esp Brit*) poner la mesa **3** (= *present*) [+ *plan, proposal, facts*] presentar (**before** a); [+ *accusation, charge*] hacer **4** (= *attribute*) [+ *responsibility*] atribuir (**on** a); **to ~ the blame (for sth) on sb** echar la culpa (de algo) a algn **5** (= *cause to be*) **he has been laid low with flu** la gripe lo ha tenido en cama; **to ~ o.s. open to attack** exponerse al ataque; **to be laid to rest** ser enterrado **6** [+ *bet*] hacer; [+ *money*] apostar (**on** a); **I'll ~ you a fiver on it!** ¡te apuesto cinco libras a que es así!; **they're ~ing bets on who is going to leave next** hacen apuestas sobre quién será el próximo en marcharse **7** [+ *egg*] poner **8** (******) (= *have sex with*) tirarse a***, follarse a (*Sp****) **Ⓑ** VI [*hen*] poner (huevos) **Ⓒ** N **1** [*of countryside, district etc*] disposición *f*, situación *f*; **the ~ of the land** (*US*) la configuración del terreno; (*fig*) la situación, el estado de las cosas **2 she's an easy ~**** es una tía fácil*

➤ **lay aside** VT + ADV **1** [+ *food, provisions*] guardar; [+ *money*] ahorrar **2** [+ *prejudices, differences*] dejar de lado

➤ **lay down** VT + ADV **1** (= *put down*) [+ *book, pen*] dejar, poner a un lado; [+ *burden*] posar, depositar en tierra **2** (= *give up*) [+ *arms*] deponer, rendir; **to ~ down one's life for sth/sb** dar su vida por algo/algn **3** (= *establish*) [+ *condition*] establecer; [+ *precedent*] sentar, establecer; **to ~ it down that ...** asentar que ..., dictaminar que ... **4** (= *impose*) [+ *condition*] imponer

➤ **lay in** VT + ADV [+ *food, fuel, water*] proveerse de, abastecerse de; (= *buy*) comprar; **to ~ in supplies of sth** proveerse *or* abastecerse de algo

➤ **lay into*** VI + PREP [+ *person*] arremeter contra

➤ **lay off Ⓐ** VT + ADV [+ *workers*] (= *sack*) despedir; (*temporarily*) despedir *or* suspender (temporalmente por falta de trabajo) **Ⓑ** VI + ADV **~ off, will you?*** ¡déjalo!, ¡por Dios!

➤ **lay on** VT + ADV (*esp Brit*) [+ *food, drink*] proporcionar; **you rent the hall and we'll ~ the refreshments** usted alquila la sala y nosotros nos hacemos cargo de *or* ponemos los refrigerios; **everything's laid on** todo está dispuesto; **they laid on a car for me** pusieron un coche a mi disposición; **✦ IDIOM to ~ it on thick** *or* **with a trowel*** recargar las tintas*

➤ **lay out** VT + ADV **1** [+ *cloth, rug*] tender, extender;

[+ *objects*] disponer, arreglar; [+ *goods for sale*] exponer; [+ *garden, town*] trazar, hacer el trazado de; [+ *page, letter*] presentar, diseñar; [+ *clothes*] preparar; [+ *ideas*] exponer, explicar; **the house is well laid out** la casa está bien distribuida; **the town is well laid out** la ciudad tiene un trazado elegante **2** [+ *corpse*] amortajar **3** [+ *money*] (= *spend*) gastar; (= *invest*) invertir, emplear (**on** en) **4** (*) (= *knock out*) derribar; (*Boxing*) dejar K.O.

➤ **lay up** VT + ADV **1** (= *store*) guardar, almacenar; (= *amass*) acumular **2** (*Med*) **to be laid up (with sth)** estar en cama (con algo); **she was laid up for weeks** tuvo que guardar cama durante varias semanas

lay² [leɪ] PT *of* **lie²**

lay³ [leɪ] ADJ (*Rel*) laico, lego, seglar

layabout* ['leɪəbaʊt] N (*esp Brit*) holgazán/ana *m/f*, vago/a *m/f*

lay-by ['leɪbaɪ] N (*Brit*) área *f* de descanso, área *f* de estacionamiento

layer ['leəʳ] **Ⓐ** N (*gen*) capa *f*; (*Geol*) estrato *m* **Ⓑ** VT [+ *vegetables, pasta, pancakes*] poner en capas

layman ['leɪmən] N (*pl* **laymen**) **1** (*Rel*) seglar *mf*, lego/a *m/f* **2** (= *not specialist*) profano(a) *m/f*, lego(a) *m/f*; **in ~'s terms** para entendernos, para los profanos en la materia

lay-off ['leɪɒf] N despido *m*

layout ['leɪaʊt] N [*of building*] plan *m*, distribución *f*; [*of town*] trazado *m*; (*Typ*) composición *f*

layover ['leɪəʊvəʳ] N (*US*) parada *f* intermedia; (*Aer*) escala *f*

laze [leɪz] VI (*also* **~ about, ~ around**) no hacer nada, descansar; (*pej*) holgazanear, gandulear; **we ~d in the sun for a week** pasamos una semana tirados al sol

lazily ['leɪzɪlɪ] ADV perezosamente

laziness ['leɪzɪnɪs] N pereza *f*, flojera *f* (*esp LAm**)

lazy ['leɪzɪ] (*compar* **lazier**; *superl* **laziest**) ADJ **1** (= *idle*) perezoso, vago; **to feel ~** tener pereza, tener flojera (*esp LAm**) **2** (= *relaxed*) [*smile, gesture*] perezoso; [*meal, day*] relajado; [*holiday*] descansado; **we spent a ~ Sunday on the river** pasamos un domingo de lo más relajado en el río

lazybones ['leɪzɪ,bəʊnz] NSING gandul(a) *m/f*, vago/a *m/f*, flojo/a *m/f* (*LAm*)

LB ABBR (*Canada*) = **Labrador**

lb ABBR (= *pound*) libra *f*

LCD, lcd N ABBR **1** = **liquid crystal display 2** = **lowest common denominator**

lead¹ [led] N (= *metal*) plomo *m*; (*in pencil*) mina *f*; **they filled him full of ~*** lo acribillaron a balazos ➤ **lead balloon ✦ IDIOM that went down like a ~ balloon*** eso cayó muy mal, eso cayó fatal* ➤ **lead pencil** lápiz *m* ➤ **lead poisoning** saturnismo *m*, plumbismo *m*, intoxicación *f* por plomo ➤ **lead replacement petrol** gasolina *m* aditivada

lead² [li:d] (*vb: pt, pp* **led**) **Ⓐ** N **1** (*Sport*) (= *leading position*) delantera *f*, cabeza *f*; (= *distance, time, points ahead*) ventaja *f*; **to be in the ~** (*gen*) ir a la *or* en cabeza; (*Sport*) llevar la delantera; (*in league*) ocupar el primer puesto; **to have two minutes' ~ over sb** llevar a algn una ventaja de dos minutos; **to have a ~ of half a length** tener medio cuerpo de ventaja; **to take the ~** (*Sport*) tomar la delantera **2** (= *example*) ejemplo *m*; **to follow sb's ~** seguir el ejemplo de algn; **to give sb a ~** guiar a algn, dar el ejemplo a algn, mostrar el camino a algn **3** (= *clue*) pista *f*; **to follow up a ~** seguir *or* investigar una pista; **the police have a ~** la policía tiene una pista **4** (*Theat*) (= *part*) papel *m* principal; (= *person*) primer actor *m*, primera actriz *f*; **to play the ~** tener el papel principal; **to sing the ~** llevar la voz cantante **5** (*esp Brit*) (= *leash*) cuerda *f*, traílla *f*, correa *f* (*LAm*); **dogs must be kept on a ~** los perros deben llevarse con traílla **6** (*Elec*) cable *m* **7** (*Press*) (= *main story*) reportaje *m* principal; (= *opening paragraph*) primer párrafo *m*, entrada *f* **Ⓑ** VT **1** (= *conduct*) llevar, conducir; **to ~ sb to a table**

conducir a algn a una mesa; **this ~s me to an important point** esto me lleva a un punto importante
2 (= *be the leader of*) [+ *government*] dirigir, encabezar; [+ *party*] encabezar, ser jefe de; [+ *expedition, regiment*] mandar; [+ *discussion*] conducir
3 (= *be first in*) [+ *procession*] ir a la or en cabeza de, encabezar; **to ~ the field** (*Sport*) ir a la cabeza, llevar la delantera; **they ~ the field in this area of research** son los líderes en este campo de la investigación
4 (= *be in front of*) [+ *opponent*] aventajar; **they led us by 30 seconds** nos llevaban una ventaja de 30 segundos; **to ~ the way** (*lit*) ir primero; (*fig*) mostrar el camino, dar el ejemplo
5 [+ *life, existence*] llevar; **to ~ a busy life** llevar una vida muy ajetreada
6 (= *influence*) **to ~ sb to do sth** llevar or inducir or mover a algn a hacer algo; **we were led to believe that ...** nos hicieron creer que ...; **what led you to this conclusion?** ¿qué te hizo llegar a esta conclusión?
🄲 VI **1** (= *go in front*) ir primero
2 (*in match, race*) llevar la delantera; **he is ~ing by an hour/ten metres** lleva una hora/diez metros de ventaja
3 (*Cards*) ser mano, salir; **you ~** sales tú, tú eres mano
4 (= *be in control*) estar al mando
5 **to ~ to** [*street*] salir a, acabar en, desembocar en; [*corridor*] llevar a, llegar hasta; [*door*] dar a
6 (= *result in*) **to ~** to llevar a; **it led to his arrest** llevó a su detención; **it led to war** condujo a la guerra; **it led to a change** produjo un cambio; **one thing led to another ...** una cosa nos/los *etc* llevó a otra ...
🄳 CPD ► **lead singer** cantante *mf* ► **lead story** reportaje *m* principal
► **lead away** VT + ADV llevar; **he was led away by the police** se lo llevó la policía
► **lead off** 🄐 VT + ADV **1** (= *take away*) llevar **2** (= *begin*) empezar (**with** con) 🄑 VI + PREP [*street*] salir de; [*room*] comunicar con
► **lead on** 🄐 VT + ADV **1** (= *tease*) engañar, engatusar; (*amorously*) ir dando esperanzas a **2** (= *incite*) **to ~ sb on** (**to do sth**) incitar a algn (a hacer algo) 🄑 VI + ADV ir primero, ir a la cabeza; **you ~ on** tú primero; **~ on!** ¡vamos!, ¡adelante!
► **lead up to** VI + PREP llevar a, conducir a; **what's all this ~ing up to?** ¿a dónde lleva or a qué conduce todo esto?, ¿a qué vas con todo esto?; **the years that led up to the war** los años que precedieron a la guerra; **the events that led up to the war** los sucesos que condujeron a la guerra

leaded petrol ['ledɪd,petrəl] N gasolina *f* con plomo

leaden ['ledn] ADJ (*in colour*) plomizo

leader ['liːdəʳ] 🄐 N **1** [*of group, party*] líder *mf*, jefe/a *m/f*; (= *guide*) guía *mf*, conductor(a) *m/f*; [*of rebels*] cabecilla *mf*; **he's a born ~** ha nacido para mandar **2** (*in race, field etc*) primero/a *m/f*; (*in league*) líder *m*; (= *horse*) caballo *m* que va primero **3** (*in newspaper*) (*Brit*) (= *editorial*) editorial *m*; (*US*) (= *main story*) reportaje *m* principal 🄑 CPD ► **Leader of the House** (*of Commons*) Presidente/a *m/f* de la Cámara de los Comunes; (*of Lords*) Presidente/a *m/f* de la Cámara de los Lores

leadership ['liːdəʃɪp] N **1** (= *position*) dirección *f*, liderazgo *m*; **under the ~ of ...** bajo la dirección or liderazgo de ...; **take over the ~ (of sth)** asumir la dirección (de algo) **2** (= *leaders*) dirección *f*, jefatura *f*

lead-free [,led'friː] ADJ sin plomo

lead-in ['liːd'ɪn] N introducción *f* (**to** a)

leading ['liːdɪŋ] 🄐 ADJ **1** (= *foremost*) [*expert, politician, writer, producer*] principal; [*company, product, brand*] líder; (*Theat, Cine*) [*part, role*] principal, de protagonista **2** (= *prominent*) [*expert, politician, writer*] destacado; **a ~ industrial nation** uno de los países más industrializados; **to play a ~ role** or **part in sth** jugar un papel importante or destacado en algo **3** (*in race*) [*athlete, horse, driver*] en cabeza, que va a la cabeza; (*in procession, convoy*) que va a la cabeza 🄑 CPD ► **leading article** (*Brit*) (= *editorial*) editorial *m*, artículo *m* de fondo; (*US*) (= *main story*) reportaje *m* principal ► **leading edge** (= *forefront*) vanguardia *f* ► **leading lady** (*Theat*) primera actriz *f*; (*Cine*) protagonista *f*

► **leading light** figura *f* principal ► **leading man** (*Theat*) primer actor *m*; (*Cine*) protagonista *m* ► **leading question** pregunta *f* capciosa

leaf [liːf] N (*pl* **leaves**) **1** [*of plant*] hoja *f* **2** [*of book*] página *f*; ✦ IDIOMS **to turn over a new ~** pasar página, hacer borrón y cuenta nueva; **to take a ~ out of sb's book** seguir el ejemplo de algn
► **leaf through** VI + PREP hojear

leaflet ['liːflɪt] N (*containing several pages*) folleto *m*; (= *single piece of paper*) octavilla *f*

leafy ['liːfɪ] ADJ (*compar* **leafier**; *superl* **leafiest**) frondoso, con muchas hojas; **the ~ suburbs of the city** los barrios residenciales de la ciudad

league¹ [liːg] N (= *measure*) legua *f*

league² [liːg] N (= *group*) liga *f*; ✦ IDIOMS **they're not in the same ~** no hay comparación; **to be in ~ with sb** estar de manga con algn, haberse confabulado con algn ► **league champion(s)** campeón *msing* de liga ► **league table** (*esp Brit*) clasificación *f*

leak [liːk] 🄐 N **1** (*in roof*) gotera *f*; (*in pipe, radiator, tank*) rotura *f*; (*in boat*) vía *f* de agua
2 [*of gas, water, chemical*] escape *m*, fuga *f*
3 [*of information, document*] filtración *f*
🄑 VI [*roof*] tener goteras; [*pipe, radiator, tank*] gotear, tener una fuga; [*boat*] hacer agua; [*pen*] perder tinta; **the window is ~ing a bit** entra un poco de agua por la ventana; **radioactive gas was ~ing from a reactor** había un escape or fuga de gas radiactivo en un reactor
🄒 VT **1** (= *discharge*) perder; (= *pour out*) derramar; **it is feared that these weapons could ~ plutonium** se teme que se produzca un escape de plutonio de estas armas
2 [+ *information, document*] filtrar (**to** a); **his letter was ~ed to the press** su carta se filtró a la prensa
► **leak out** VI + ADV [*gas, liquid*] salirse; [*secret, news, information*] filtrarse

leakage ['liːkɪdʒ] N **1** [*of gas, liquid*] escape *m*, fuga *f* **2** (*fig*) filtración *f*

leakproof ['liːkpruːf] ADJ [*container*] hermético; [*nappy, pants*] impermeable

leaky ['liːkɪ] ADJ (*compar* **leakier**; *superl* **leakiest**) [*roof*] con goteras; [*pipe, container*] que gotea, con fugas; [*boat*] que hace agua; [*pen*] que pierde tinta

lean¹ [liːn] ADJ (*compar* **~er**; *superl* **~est**) **1** (= *slim*) [*person, body*] delgado, enjuto; [*animal*] flaco **2** (= *not prosperous*) [*times*] difícil; [*harvest*] pobre; **to have a ~ time of it** pasar por una mala racha; **~ years** años *mpl* de vacas flacas **3** (= *not fatty*) [*meat*] magro, sin grasa

lean² [liːn] (*pt, pp* **~ed** or **~t**) 🄐 VI **1** (= *slope*) inclinarse, ladearse; **to ~ to/towards the left/right** (*lit*) estar inclinado hacia la izquierda/derecha; (*Pol*) inclinarse hacia la izquierda/derecha **2** (*for support*) apoyarse; **to ~ on/against sth** apoyarse en/contra algo; **to ~ on sb** (*lit*) apoyarse en algn; (*fig*) presionar a algn 🄑 VT apoyar (**against** contra)
► **lean back** VI + ADV reclinarse, recostarse
► **lean forward** VI + ADV inclinarse hacia delante
► **lean out** VI + ADV asomarse; **to ~ out of the window** asomarse a or por la ventana
► **lean over** VI + ADV inclinarse; ✦ IDIOM **to ~ over backwards to help sb** volcarse or desvivirse por ayudar a algn

leaning ['liːnɪŋ] N inclinación *f* (**to, towards** hacia), tendencia *f* (**to, towards** a)

leanness ['liːnnɪs] N [*of animal*] flacura *f*, flaqueza *f*; [*of meat*] lo magro

leant [lent] PT, PP *of* **lean²**

lean-to ['liːntuː] N (*pl* **~s**) cobertizo *m*

leap [liːp] (*vb: pp, pt* **~ed** or **~t**) 🄐 N **1** (= *jump*) salto *m*; **by ~s and bounds** a pasos agigantados; **a ~ in the dark** un salto al vacío; **his heart gave a ~** le dio un vuelco el corazón; **to make** or **take a huge ~ forward** (*fig*) dar un gran salto or paso hacia adelante; **to make** or **take a ~ of faith** hacer un gran esfuerzo de fe, hacer profesión de fe **2** (= *increase*) subida *f*
🄑 VI **1** (= *jump*) saltar; **the dog ~t at the man** el perro saltó or se arrojó sobre el hombre; **she ~t at the chance to play**

the part no dejó escapar la oportunidad de representar el papel; **to ~ at an offer** aceptar una oferta al vuelo; **he ~t down from his horse** se bajó del caballo de un salto; **my heart ~t** me dio un vuelco el corazón; **he ~t into the river** saltó *or* se tiró al río; **he ~t off/onto the bus** bajó del/subió al autobús de un salto; **the headline ~t out at her** el titular le saltó a la vista; **she ~t out of bed** se levantó de la cama de un salto, saltó de la cama; **to ~ over** [+ *obstacle*] saltar por encima de; [+ *stream*] cruzar de un salto; **to ~ to one's feet** levantarse de un salto; **he ~t to his brother's defence** enseguida saltó a defender a su hermano **2** (= *increase*) **sales ~t by one third** las ventas se incrementaron repentinamente en un tercio **⊙** VT [+ *fence, ditch*] saltar por encima de; [+ *stream, river*] cruzar de un salto **⊙** CPD **➤ leap year** año *m* bisiesto **➤ leap up** VI + ADV **1** [*person*] levantarse de un salto; [*flame*] subir; **the dog ~t up at him** el perro le saltó *or* se le echó encima **2** [*profits, unemployment*] subir de repente

leapfrog ['liːpfrɒg] **Ⓐ** N pídola *f* **Ⓑ** VI **to ~ over sth/sb** saltar por encima de algo/algn

leapt [lept] PT, PP *of* **leap**

learn [lɜːn] (*pt, pp* **-ed** *or* **~t**) **Ⓐ** VT **1** (*by study, practice*) [+ *language, words, skill*] aprender; [+ *instrument*] aprender a tocar; **to ~ (how) to do sth** aprender a hacer algo; **✦** IDIOMS **to ~ sth by heart** aprender(se) algo de memoria; **to ~ one's lesson** aprender la lección, escarmentar **2** (= *find out*) enterarse de; **to ~ that** enterarse de que **Ⓑ** VI **1** (*by study, practice*) aprender; **he'll ~!** ¡un día aprenderá!, ¡ya aprenderá!; **we are ~ing about the Romans** estamos estudiando los romanos; **to ~ from experience** aprender por experiencia; **to ~ from one's mistakes** aprender de los errores (cometidos) **2** (= *find out*) **to ~ of** *or* **about sth** enterarse de algo

learned ['lɜːnɪd] ADJ [*person*] docto, erudito; [*remark, speech, book*] erudito; [*profession*] liberal

learner ['lɜːnəʳ] N (= *novice*) principiante *mf*; (= *student*) estudiante *mf*; (*Brit*) (*also* **~ driver**) conductor(a) *m/f* en prácticas, aprendiz(a) *m/f* de conductor(a); **to be a fast ~** aprender con mucha rapidez

learning ['lɜːnɪŋ] **Ⓐ** N **1** (= *act*) aprendizaje *m* **2** (= *knowledge*) conocimientos *mpl*, saber *m*; (= *erudition*) saber *m*, erudición *f*; **man of ~** sabio *m*, erudito *m* **Ⓑ** CPD **➤ learning curve** curva *f* de aprendizaje, proceso *m* de aprendizaje; **it's going to be a steep ~ curve** va a ser un proceso de aprendizaje rápido pero difícil, resultará una curva de aprendizaje muy marcada (*more tech*) **➤ learning difficulties** dificultades *fpl* de aprendizaje

learnt [lɜːnt] PT, PP *of* **learn**

lease [liːs] **Ⓐ** N contrato *m* de arrendamiento; **✦** IDIOMS **to give sb a new ~ of life** hacer revivir a algn; **to take on a new ~ of life** [*person*] recobrar su vigor; [*thing*] renovarse **Ⓑ** VT (= *take*) arrendar (**from** de), tomar en arriendo; (*also* **~ out**) arrendar, alquilar, dar en arriendo **➤ lease back** VT + ADV subarrendar

leasehold ['liːshəʊld] (*esp Brit*) **Ⓐ** N (= *contract*) derechos *mpl* de arrendamiento; (= *property*) inmueble *m* arrendado **Ⓑ** ADJ [*property, house, flat*] arrendado **Ⓒ** ADV [*buy*] en arriendo, en arrendamiento

leaseholder ['liːshəʊldəʳ] N (*esp Brit*) arrendatario/a *m/f*

leash [liːʃ] N correa *f*, traílla *f*

least [liːst] SUPERL *of* **little²** **Ⓐ** ADJ **1** (= *minimum, smallest amount of*) menor; **with the ~ possible delay** con el menor retraso posible; **choose yoghurts which contain the ~ fat** elija los yogures que contengan la menor cantidad de grasa **2** (= *smallest, slightest*) [*hint, complaint*] más mínimo; **she wasn't the ~ bit jealous** no estaba celosa en lo más mínimo; **we haven't the ~ idea where he is** no tenemos la más mínima *or* la menor idea de dónde está; **the ~ thing upsets her** se ofende a la mínima *or* por lo más mínimo **3** (*in comparisons*) menos; **he has the ~ money** es el que menos dinero tiene **Ⓑ** PRON **1** (= *the very minimum*) (*gen*) lo menos; (= *amount*) lo mínimo; **it was the ~ I could do** era lo menos que podía hacer; **what's the ~ you are willing to accept?** ¿qué es lo

mínimo que estás dispuesto a aceptar?; **accommodation was basic to say the ~** el alojamiento era muy sencillo, por no decir otra cosa; **✦** PROV **~ said, soonest mended** cuanto menos se diga, antes se arregla **2** (*in comparisons*) **the country that spends the ~ on education** el país que menos (se) gasta en materia de enseñanza; **that's the ~ of my worries** eso es lo que menos me preocupa **3 in the ~: I don't mind in the ~** no me importa lo más mínimo; **Pete wasn't in the ~ in love with me** Pete no estaba ni mucho menos enamorado de mí; **"don't you mind?" — "not in the ~"** —¿no te importa? —en absoluto *or* —para nada **4 at ~ 4.1** (*with quantity, comparison*) por lo menos, como mínimo, al menos; **I must have slept for at ~ 12 hours** debo de haber dormido por lo menos *or* como mínimo *or* al menos 12 horas; **he earns at ~ as much as you do** gana por lo menos *or* al menos tanto como tú **4.2** (*other uses*) al menos, por lo menos; **it's rather laborious but at ~ it is not dangerous** requiere bastante trabajo pero al menos *or* por lo menos no es peligroso; **Lucy appeared to be asleep, at ~ her eyes were shut** Lucy parecía estar dormida, al menos *or* por lo menos tenía los ojos cerrados; **at the very ~** como mínimo, como poco **Ⓒ** ADV menos; **the ~ expensive car** el coche menos caro; **when ~ expected** cuando menos se espera; **~ of all me** y yo menos, yo menos que nadie; **for a variety of reasons, not ~ because it is cheap** por toda una serie de razones, entre ellas que es barato

leather ['leðəʳ] **Ⓐ** N **1** (= *hide*) cuero *m*, piel *f* **2** (*esp Brit*) **leathers** (*for motorcyclist*) ropa *fsing* de cuero **Ⓑ** CPD de cuero, de piel **➤ leather goods** artículos *mpl* de cuero

leathery ['leðərɪ] ADJ [*meat*] correoso; [*skin*] curtido

leave [liːv] (*vb: pt, pp* **left**) **Ⓐ** N **1** (= *time off*) (*gen*) permiso *m*; (*Mil*) (*brief*) permiso *m*; (*lengthy, compassionate*) licencia *f*; **~ of absence** permiso *m* para ausentarse; **to be on ~** estar de permiso **2** (= *departure*) **to take (one's) ~ (of sb)** despedirse (de algn); **have you taken ~ of your senses?** ¿te has vuelto loco? **3** (= *permission*) permiso *m*; **to ask ~ to do sth** pedir permiso para hacer algo **Ⓑ** VT **1** (= *go away from*) dejar, marcharse de; [+ *room*] salir de, abandonar; [+ *hospital*] salir de; [+ *person*] abandonar, dejar; **I'll ~ you at the station** te dejo en la estación; **I must ~ you** tengo que despedirme *or* marcharme; **she ~s home at 8am** sale de casa a las ocho; **he left home when he was 18** se fue de casa a los 18 años; **to ~ school** (= *finish studies*) terminar el colegio **2** (= *forget*) dejar, olvidar **3** (= *bequeath*) dejar, legar **4** (= *allow to remain*) dejar; **it's best to ~ him alone** es mejor dejarlo solo; **let's ~ it at that** dejémoslo así, ¡ya está bien (así)!; **it ~s much to be desired** deja mucho que desear; **take it or ~ it** lo tomas o lo dejas; **~ it to me!** ¡yo me encargo!, ¡tú, déjamelo a mí!; **I'll ~ it up to you** lo dejo a tu criterio; **he ~s a wife and a child** le sobreviven su viuda y un hijo, deja mujer y un hijo; **~ it with me** yo me encargaré del asunto **5 to be left** (= *remain*) quedar; **how many are (there) left?** ¿cuántos quedan?; **we were left with four** quedamos con cuatro, nos quedaron cuatro; **all the money I have left** todo el dinero que me queda; **there are three left over** sobran tres; **she saved whatever was left over of her wages** ahorraba lo que le sobraba del sueldo; **there is some wine left over from the party** queda un poco de vino de la fiesta **6** (*Math*) **three from ten ~s seven** diez menos tres son siete, de tres a diez van siete **Ⓒ** VI (= *go out*) salir; (= *go away*) [*person*] irse, marcharse, partir; [*train, bus*] salir **➤ leave around, leave about** VT + ADV dejar tirado **➤ leave aside** VT + ADV dejar de lado **➤ leave behind** VT + ADV **1** (= *not take*) dejar, no llevar consigo; **we had to ~ the furniture behind** no pudimos llevarnos los muebles; **we have left all that behind us** todo eso ha quedado atrás *or* ya es historia **2** (= *forget*) olvidarse **3** (= *outdistance*) dejar atrás **➤ leave in** VT + ADV [+ *passage, words*] dejar tal como está/

leaves

932

estaba, conservar; [+ *plug*] dejar puesto
➤ **leave off** Ⓐ VT + ADV **1** [+ *lid*] no poner, dejar sin poner; [+ *clothes*] no ponerse **2** [+ *gas*] no poner, no encender; [+ *light*] dejar apagado **3** (*) (= *stop*) **to ~ off doing sth** dejar de hacer algo Ⓑ VI + ADV (*) (= *stop*) parar; **when the rain ~s off** cuando deje de llover; **~ off, will you!** ¡déjalo!; **we'll carry on where we left off last time** continuaremos por donde quedamos la última vez
➤ **leave on** VT + ADV [+ *clothes*] dejar puesto, no quitarse; [+ *light, TV*] dejar encendido *or* (*LAm*) prendido
➤ **leave out** VT + ADV **1** (= *omit*) [+ *word, passage*] (*on purpose*) omitir; (*accidentally*) omitir, saltarse; [+ *person*] dejar fuera, excluir; **he feels left out** se siente excluido; ✦ IDIOM **~ it out!** (*Brit***) ¡venga ya!*, ¡no me vengas con esas!*, ¡tírate de la moto! (*Sp***) **2** (= *not put back*) no devolver a su lugar, no guardar; (= *leave outside*) dejar fuera; **it got left out in the rain** quedó fuera bajo la lluvia **3** (= *leave ready*) [+ *food, meal*] dejar preparado

leaves [liːvz] NPL *of* **leaf**

leaving ['liːvɪŋ] N (= *departure*) salida *f*; [*ceremony, present*] de despedida

Lebanese [ˌlebə'niːz] ADJ, N libanés/esa *m/f*

Lebanon ['lebənən] N Líbano *m*

lecherous ['letʃərəs] ADJ lascivo, lujurioso

lectern ['lektən] N atril *m*; (*Rel*) facistol *m*

lecture ['lektʃəʳ] Ⓐ N **1** (*Univ*) clase *f*; (*by visitor*) conferencia *f*; (*less formal*) charla *f* **2** (*fig*) sermón *m*; **I gave him a ~ on good manners** le eché un sermón sobre buenos modales Ⓑ VI **to ~ (in** *or* **on sth)** dar clases (de algo); **he ~s at Princeton** es profesor en Princeton Ⓒ VT (= *scold*) sermonear Ⓓ CPD ➤ **lecture theatre** (*Brit*), **lecture theater** (*US*) (*gen*) sala *f* de conferencias; (*Univ*) aula *f*

> Use **el/un** not **la/una** before feminine nouns beginning with stressed **a** or **ha** like **aula**.

lecturer ['lektʃərəʳ] N (= *visitor*) conferenciante *mf*; (*Brit Univ*) profesor(a) *m/f*

LED N ABBR = **light-emitting diode**

led [led] PT, PP *of* **lead²**

ledge [ledʒ] N (*on wall, of window*) alféizar *m*; (= *shelf*) repisa *f*, anaquel *m*; (*on mountain*) saliente *m*, cornisa *f*

ledger ['ledʒəʳ] N libro *m* mayor

leech [liːtʃ] N sanguijuela *f* (*also fig*); ✦ IDIOM **to stick to sb like a ~** pegarse a algn como una lapa*

leek [liːk] N puerro *m*

leer [lɪəʳ] VI **to ~ at sb** lanzar una mirada lasciva a algn

leeway ['liːweɪ] N (= *scope*) libertad *f* de acción; **that doesn't give me much ~** (= *scope*) eso no me deja mucha libertad de acción; (= *time to spare*) eso no me deja mucho margen de tiempo

left¹ [left] PT, PP *of* **leave**

left² [left] Ⓐ ADJ **1** izquierdo; ✦ IDIOM **to have two ~ feet*** ser un patoso* **2** (*Pol*) de izquierda, de izquierdas (*Sp*) Ⓑ ADV [*turn, look*] a la izquierda; ✦ IDIOM **~, right and centre** ◇ **~ and right** (*US*) a diestra y siniestra, a diestro y siniestro (*Sp*) Ⓒ N **1** (= *left side*) izquierda *f*; **pictured from ~ to right are ...** de izquierda a derecha vemos a ...; **the third from the ~** el tercero empezando por la izquierda; **on** *or* **to my/your ~** a mi/tu izquierda; **on the ~** a la izquierda; **it's the second door on the ~** es la segunda puerta a la izquierda; **to drive on the ~** conducir *or* (*LAm*) manejar por la izquierda; **"keep left"** "manténgase a la izquierda" **2** (= *turning*) **take the next ~** toma la próxima a la izquierda **3 the ~** (*Pol*) la izquierda; **the parties of the ~** los partidos de izquierda *or* (*Sp*) izquierdas Ⓓ CPD ➤ **left back** (= *player*) lateral *mf* izquierdo/a; (= *position*) lateral *m* izquierdo ➤ **left half** (= *player*) lateral *mf* izquierdo/a; (= *position*) lateral *m* izquierdo ➤ **left wing**

(*Sport*) banda *f* izquierda; (*Pol*) ala *f* izquierda

> Use **el/un** not **la/una** before feminine nouns beginning with stressed **a** or **ha** like **ala**.

left-hand ['lefthænd] ADJ [*page*] izquierdo; **a ~ drive car** un coche con el volante a la izquierda; **is it a ~ drive?** ¿tiene el volante a la izquierda?; **the house is on the ~ side** la casa está a la izquierda; **~ turn** vuelta *f* a la izquierda

left-handed ['left'hændɪd] ADJ [*person*] zurdo

left-hander [ˌleft'hændəʳ] N (= *person*) zurdo/a *m/f*

leftie* ['leftɪ] N (*Brit*) izquierdista *mf*

leftist ['leftɪst] ADJ, N izquierdista *mf*

left-click ['leftklɪk] Ⓐ VI clicar con el botón izquierdo del ratón Ⓑ VT **to ~ an icon** clicar en un icono con el botón izquierdo del ratón

left-luggage ['left'lʌgɪdʒ] N (*Brit*) (*also* **~ office**) consigna *f* ➤ **left-luggage locker** (*Brit*) consigna *f* automática

leftover ['leftəʊvəʳ] Ⓐ ADJ sobrante, restante; **we used up the ~ turkey** usamos el pavo que había sobrado Ⓑ N **1** (= *relic*) reliquia *f*; **a ~ from another age** una reliquia de otra edad **2 leftovers** sobras *fpl*, restos *mpl*

left-wing ['left,wɪŋ] ADJ de izquierda, izquierdista, de izquierdas (*Sp*)

left-winger ['left'wɪŋəʳ] N izquierdista *mf*

lefty* ['leftɪ] N (*Brit*) izquierdista *mf*

leg [leg] Ⓐ N **1** [*of person*] pierna *f*; [*of animal, bird, insect*] pata *f*; [*of furniture*] (= *one of set*) pata *f*; (= *central support*) pie *m*; [*of trousers*] pernera *f*; **to give sb a ~ up** (*Brit**) (*lit*) aupar a algn; (*fig*) dar un empujoncito a algn*, echar un cable a algn*; ✦ IDIOMS **to get one's ~ over** (*Brit***) darse un revolcón*; **to pull sb's ~** tomar el pelo a algn; **he hasn't got a ~ to stand on** no tiene donde agarrarse* **2** (*Culin*) [*of lamb, mutton, pork*] pierna *f*; [*of chicken, turkey*] muslo *m*, pata *f*; **frogs' ~s** ancas *fpl* de rana **3** (= *stage*) [*of journey*] tramo *m*, etapa *f* Ⓑ VT **to ~ it*** (= *run*) echarse una carrera*; (= *run away*) salir por piernas *or* patas* Ⓒ CPD ➤ **leg room** sitio *m* para las piernas

legacy ['legəsɪ] N legado *m*

legal ['liːgəl] Ⓐ ADJ **1** (= *judicial*) [*error*] judicial; [*document*] legal; [*firm*] de abogados; [*question, matter*] legal, jurídico; **to take ~ action** poner una denuncia; **to take ~ action against sb** poner una denuncia a algn, presentar una demanda (judicial) contra algn; **to take ~ advice** consultar a un abogado; **~ adviser** asesor(a) *m/f* jurídico/a; **~ costs** *or* **fees** costas *fpl*, gastos *mpl* judiciales; **~ department**] departamento *m* jurídico; **~ proceedings** procedimiento *msing* jurídico, pleito *msing*; **to start ~ proceedings against sb** entablar un pleito contra algn; **the ~ profession** la abogacía; **to go into the ~ profession** hacerse abogado **2** (= *lawful*) [*activity, action*] legal, legítimo; [*owner*] legítimo; (= *under the law*) [*right, protection*] legal; **to make sth ~** legalizar algo Ⓑ CPD ➤ **legal aid** asistencia *f* de un abogado de oficio ➤ **legal holiday** (*US*) fiesta *f* oficial, día *m* festivo oficial, (día *m*) feriado *m* (*LAm*) ➤ **legal system** sistema *m* jurídico ➤ **legal tender** moneda *f* de curso legal

legality [lɪ'gælɪtɪ] N legalidad *f*

legalization [ˌliːgəlaɪ'zeɪʃən] N [*of party*] legalización *f*; [*of drugs, euthanasia, abortion*] legalización *f*, despenalización *f*

legalize ['liːgəlaɪz] VT [+ *party*] legalizar; [+ *drugs, euthanasia, abortion*] legalizar, despenalizar

legally ['liːgəlɪ] ADV **1** (= *from a legal point of view*) [*obliged, required*] por ley; [*entitled*] legalmente, según la ley; **~ ...** desde el punto de vista legal ...; **this contract is ~ binding** el contrato vincula jurídicamente, el contrato implica obligatoriedad jurídica **2** (= *lawfully*) legalmente

legend ['ledʒənd] N leyenda *f*

legendary ['ledʒəndərɪ] ADJ legendario

leggings ['legɪŋz] NPL mallas *fpl*, leotardos *mpl*; (*baby's*) pantalones *mpl* polainas

legible ['ledʒəbl] ADJ legible

legibly ['ledʒəblɪ] ADV legiblemente

legion ['liːdʒən] N legión f

legionnaire [ˌliːdʒə'nɛəʳ] N legionario m ➤ **legionnaire's disease** enfermedad f del legionario, legionella f

legislate ['ledʒɪsleɪt] VI legislar

legislation [ˌledʒɪs'leɪʃən] N (= law) ley f; (= body of laws) legislación f

legislative ['ledʒɪslətɪv] ADJ legislativo ➤ **legislative body** cuerpo m legislativo

legislator ['ledʒɪsleɪtəʳ] N legislador(a) m/f

legislature ['ledʒɪslətʃəʳ] N asamblea f legislativa, legislatura f (LAm)

legitimacy [lɪ'dʒɪtɪməsɪ] N [of government, action, birth] legitimidad f; [of argument] validez f

legitimate [lɪ'dʒɪtɪmɪt] ADJ [government, right, interest, son, daughter] legítimo; [complaint, conclusion] justificado

legitimize [lɪ'dʒɪtɪmaɪz] VT (gen) legitimar; [+ child, birth] legalizar

legless* ['leglɪs] ADJ (Brit) (= drunk) como una cuba*

legwork ['legwɜːk] N trabajo m de campo, preparativos mpl; **to do the ~** hacer los preparativos

leisure ['leʒəʳ, (US) 'liːʒəʳ] N ocio m; **a life of ~** una vida ociosa or de ocio; **do it at your ~** hazlo cuando tengas tiempo or te convenga ➤ **leisure activities** pasatiempos mpl ➤ **leisure centre** (Brit) polideportivo m ➤ **leisure industry** sector m del ocio ➤ **leisure time** tiempo m libre; **in one's ~ time** en sus ratos libres, en los momentos de ocio ➤ **leisure wear** (Brit) ropa f de sport

leisurely ['leʒəlɪ] 🅐 ADJ [stroll, swim, meal] relajado, sin prisas; **at a ~ pace** sin prisas 🅑 ADV despacio, con calma

leitmotiv ['laɪtməʊˌtiːf] N leitmotiv m

lemming ['lemɪŋ] N lem(m)ing m

lemon ['lemən] 🅐 N (= fruit) limón m; (= tree) limonero m; (= drink) limonada f; ✦ IDIOM **I felt a bit of a ~*** me sentí como un auténtico imbécil 🅑 ADJ [colour] amarillo limón inv 🅒 CPD ➤ **lemon cheese, lemon curd** (Brit) crema f de limón ➤ **lemon juice** zumo m or (LAm) jugo m de limón ➤ **lemon sole** (Brit) platija f ➤ **lemon squash** limonada f (sin burbujas) ➤ **lemon squeezer** exprimelimones m inv, exprimidor m ➤ **lemon tea** té m con limón ➤ **lemon tree** limonero m ➤ **lemon yellow** amarillo m limón

lemonade [ˌlemə'neɪd] N limonada f, gaseosa f (Sp)

lend [lend] (pt, pp **lent**) VT **1** (as favour) prestar, dejar; **to ~ sb sth** ⋄ **~ sth to sb** prestar algo a algn, dejar algo a algn **2** [bank] prestar **3** (= give) **~ credibility to sth** conceder credibilidad a algo **4** (reflexive) **the system does not ~ itself to rapid reform** el sistema no se presta a una reforma rápida
➤ **lend out** VT + ADV prestar

lender ['lendəʳ] N (= bank, building society) entidad f crediticia or de crédito; (= person) prestamista mf

lending ['lendɪŋ] CPD ➤ **lending library** biblioteca f de préstamo ➤ **lending rate** tipo m de interés sobre los préstamos

length [leŋkθ] N **1** (= size) largo m, longitud f; **what ~ is it?** ¿cuánto tiene or mide de largo?; **it was two metres in ~** tenía or medía dos metros de largo
2 (= extent) **2.1** [of street, river, house] **the room runs the ~ of the house** la habitación tiene el largo de la casa; **I walked the entire ~ of the street** recorrí la calle de una punta a la otra; **I have travelled the ~ and breadth of the country** he viajado a lo largo y ancho del país, he viajado por todo el país **2.2** [of book, letter, essay] extensión f; **an essay 4,000 words in ~** un ensayo de 4.000 palabras (de extensión)
2.3 ✦ IDIOMS **to go to great ~s to do sth** esforzarse mucho para hacer algo; **I'd go to any ~(s) to protect her** haría cualquier cosa por protegerla
3 (= duration) duración f; **you couldn't keep that effort up for any ~ of time** un esfuerzo así no se puede mantener (durante) mucho tiempo
4 at ~ (= finally) finalmente, por fin; (= in detail) [discuss] detenidamente; [explain] con mucho detalle; (= for a long time) largo y tendido

5 (= piece) trozo m, pedazo m
6 (in horse races) cuerpo m; (in rowing, swimming) largo m

lengthen ['leŋθən] 🅐 VT [+ dress, trousers] alargar; [+ term, period, life, jail sentence] prolongar, alargar 🅑 VI [shadows, queue, days, nights] alargarse

lengthways ['leŋkθˌweɪz], **lengthwise** ['leŋkθˌwaɪz] ADV longitudinalmente, a lo largo; **to measure sth ~** medir el largo de algo

lengthy ['leŋkθɪ] ADJ (compar **lengthier**; superl **lengthiest**) largo

lenience ['liːnɪəns], **leniency** ['liːnɪənsɪ] N indulgencia f, benevolencia f; **to show leniency to or towards sb** ser or mostrarse indulgente con or hacia algn

lenient ['liːnɪənt] ADJ [sentence, treatment] benévolo, poco severo; [person, attitude] indulgente, poco severo

leniently ['liːnɪəntlɪ] ADV con indulgencia, con benevolencia

lens [lenz] N [of spectacles] lente f; [of camera] objetivo m; (Anat) cristalino m; (= contact lens) lente f de contacto, lentilla f ➤ **lens cap** tapa f de objetivo

Lent [lent] N Cuaresma f

lent [lent] PT, PP of **lend**

lentil ['lentl] N lenteja f

Leo ['liːəʊ] N **1** (= sign, constellation) Leo m **2** (= person) leo mf inv; **she's (a) ~** es leo

leopard ['lepəd] N leopardo m

leopardskin ['lepədskɪn] N piel f de leopardo

leotard ['liːətɑːd] N malla f

leper ['lepəʳ] N leproso/a m/f

leprosy ['leprəsɪ] N lepra f

lesbian ['lezbɪən] 🅐 ADJ lesbiano, lésbico 🅑 N lesbiana f

lesion ['liːʒən] N lesión f

less [les] COMPAR of **little²** 🅐 ADJ menos; **she has ~ spare time now** ahora tiene menos tiempo libre; **he has ~ money than his sister** tiene menos dinero que su hermana; **no ~ a person than the bishop** no otro que el obispo, el mismísimo obispo
🅑 PRON menos; **it's ~ than you think** es menos de lo que piensas; **can't you let me have it for ~?** ¿no me lo puedes dar en menos?; **~ than £1/three metres** menos de una libra/tres metros; **at a price of ~ than £1** a un precio inferior or menor a una libra; **a tip of £10, no ~!** ¡una propina de diez libras, nada menos!; **that was told me by the minister no ~** eso me lo dijo el mismo ministro; **nothing ~ than** nada menos que; **it's nothing ~ than a disaster** es un verdadero or auténtico desastre; **the ~ he works the ~ he earns** cuanto menos trabaja menos gana; **the ~ said about it the better** cuanto menos se hable de eso mejor
🅒 ADV menos; **to go out ~ (often)** salir menos; **you work ~ than I do** trabajas menos que yo; **in ~ than an hour** en menos de una hora; **it's ~ expensive than the other one** cuesta menos que el otro; **~ and ~** cada vez menos; **that doesn't make her any ~ guilty** no por eso es menos culpable; **still ~** todavía menos, menos aún
🅓 PREP menos; **the price ~ 10%** el precio menos 10 por ciento; **the price ~ VAT** el precio excluyendo el IVA

lessee [le'siː] N [of house] inquilino/a m/f; [of land] arrendatario/a m/f

lessen ['lesn] 🅐 VT [+ risk, danger] reducir; [+ pain] aliviar; [+ cost, stature] rebajar; **it will ~ your chances of getting the job** disminuirá las posibilidades que tienes de conseguir el puesto 🅑 VI [noise, anger, love] disminuir; [pain] aliviarse

lesser ['lesəʳ] ADJ menor; **to a ~ extent or degree** en menor grado; **the ~ of two evils** el menor de dos males

lesson ['lesn] N (= class) clase f; (in textbook, also fig) lección f; (Rel) lectura f; **to give swimming/piano ~s** dar clases de natación/piano; **let that be a ~ to you!** ¡que te sirva de lección!, ¡para que aprendas!; **his courage is a ~ to us all** su valor debe servirnos a todos de lección; **if there is a single ~ to be drawn from this, it is that ...** si hay algo que podemos aprender de esto, es que ...

let¹ [let] 🅐 VT (pt, pp **~**) **1** (= allow to) dejar; **to ~ sb do sth**

dejar que algn haga algo, dejar a algn hacer algo; **my parents wouldn't ~ me go out with boys** mis padres no dejaban que saliera con chicos, mis padres no me dejaban salir con chicos; **she wanted to help but her mother wouldn't ~ her** quería ayudar, pero su madre no la dejaba; **when can you ~ me have it?** ¿cuándo me lo puedes dejar?; **he really ~ her have it about being late*** le echó una buena bronca por llegar tarde*; **they won't ~ you into the country** no te dejarán entrar en el país; **he ~ himself into the flat** entró en el piso; **you must ~ me be the judge of that** eso seré yo quien lo decida; **to ~ it be known that** hacer saber que; **he wouldn't ~ me past** no me dejaba pasar
2 (*in imperative constructions*) **2.1 ~ me: don't ~ me catch you cheating again!** ¡no quiero volver a pillarte haciendo trampa!, ¡que no vuelva a pillarte haciendo trampa!; **don't ~ me forget to post the letters** recuérdame que eche las cartas al correo; **~ me help you** déjame ayudarle *or* que le ayude; **don't ~ me keep you** no quiero entretenerle; **now ~ me see** ¿a ver?, déjame que vea; **~ me take your coat** permítame que tome su abrigo; **~ me think** déjame pensar, a ver que piense; **it's hard work, ~ me tell you** es mucho trabajo, te lo aseguro **2.2 ~'s: her then boyfriend — ~'s call him Dave ...** el entonces novio suyo — llamémoslo *or* vamos a llamarlo Dave ...; **~'s go!** ¡vámonos!; **~'s go for a walk** vamos a dar un paseo; **~'s not** *or* **don't ~'s jump to conclusions** no nos precipitemos a sacar conclusiones; **if you weigh, ~'s say, 175 pounds ...** si pesas, digamos, 175 libras ...; **~'s see, what was I saying?** a ver *or* déjame ver, ¿qué decía yo?; **"shall we eat now?" — "yes, ~'s"** —¿comemos ahora? —sí, vamos *or* (*Sp*) venga; **"shall we go home now?" — "yes, ~'s!"** —¿nos vamos a casa ahora? —¡sí, vamos! *or* —¡sí, vámonos! **2.3** (*forming 3rd-person imperative*) **"people may complain" — "~ them"** —puede que la gente se queje —pues que lo hagan; **~ X equal six** supongamos que X equivale a seis; **never ~ it be said that ...** que nunca se diga que ...; **~ people say what they will ...** que la gente diga lo que quiera ...; **~ them wait** que esperen **2.4** (*in prayers, wishes*) **don't ~ him die, she prayed** no dejes que se muera, le pidió a Dios; **please don't ~ it rain** por favor, que no llueva
3 (*esp Brit*) (= *rent out*) alquilar, arrendar (**to** a); **"to let"** "se alquila"
Ⓑ N **long/short ~** alquiler *m* a corto/largo plazo
➤ **let down** VT + ADV **1** (= *lower*) bajar; [+ *hair*] soltar, dejar suelto; ✦ IDIOM **to ~ one's hair down*** relajarse (*esp LAm*) **2** (= *lengthen*) [+ *dress, hem*] alargar **3** (*esp Brit*) (= *deflate*) [+ *tyre*] desinflar **4** (= *disappoint*) defraudar; (= *fail*) fallar; **we all felt ~ down** todos nos sentimos defraudados; **I trusted you and you ~ me down** confié en ti y me fallaste; **to ~ o.s. down** quedar mal; ✦ IDIOM **to ~ the side down: she would never ~ the side down** jamás nos haría quedar mal, jamás nos fallaría
➤ **let in** VT + ADV **1 to ~ sb in** (= *allow to enter*) dejar entrar a algn; (= *usher in*) hacer pasar a algn; (= *open door to*) abrir la puerta a algn
2 (= *allow through*) [+ *light*] dejar entrar; **shoes which ~ the water in** zapatos que dejan calar el agua
3 to ~ sb in on sth: to ~ sb in on a secret contar un secreto a algn; **to ~ sb in on a deal** dejar que algn participe en un negocio
4 to ~ o.s. in for sth: you don't know what you're ~ting yourself in for no sabes bien a lo que te estás exponiendo, no sabes bien en lo que te estás metiendo
➤ **let off Ⓐ** VT + ADV **1** [+ *bomb*] hacer explotar; [+ *firework*] tirar; [+ *firearm*] disparar
2 (= *release*) **to ~ off steam** (*lit*) soltar vapor; (*) (= *release anger*) desahogarse; (= *unwind*) relajarse
3 (= *allow to leave*) dejar salir
4 (= *exempt, not punish*) perdonar; **the headmaster ~ him off with a warning** el director le dejó escapar con sólo una advertencia
Ⓑ VT + PREP **to ~ sb off sth** perdonar algo a algn; **I'll ~ you off the £5 you owe me** te perdono las cinco libras que me debes; **the authorities ~ him off National Service** las autoridades le permitieron librarse del servicio militar
➤ **let on* Ⓐ** VI + ADV **he's not ~ting on** no dice nada; **don't ~ on!** ¡no digas nada!, ¡no te vayas de la lengua!*; **don't ~ on to her about what they did** no le digas lo que hicieron
Ⓑ VT + ADV (= *reveal*) **to ~ on that** decir que

➤ **let out** VT + ADV **1** (= *allow to leave*) [+ *visitor*] acompañar a la puerta; [+ *prisoner*] poner en libertad; [+ *penned animal*] dejar salir; **~ me out!** ¡déjenme salir!; **he ~ himself out quietly** salió sin hacer ruido; **can you ~ yourself out?** ¿hace falta que te acompañe a la puerta?; **they are ~ out of school at four** salen de la escuela a las cuatro; **to ~ the air out of a tyre** desinflar *or* deshinchar un neumático; **to ~ the water out of the bath** dejar salir el agua de la bañera; ✦ IDIOM **to ~ the cat out of the bag** descubrir el pastel
2 (= *reveal*) [+ *secret, news*] contar, revelar
3 [+ *dress, skirt*] ensanchar; **to ~ out a seam** soltar una costura
4 (*esp Brit*) (= *rent out*) alquilar
5 (= *utter*) **to ~ out a cry/sigh** dar un grito/un suspiro
6 [+ *clutch*] soltar
➤ **let past** VI + ADV dejar pasar
➤ **let through** VT + ADV dejar pasar
➤ **let up** VI + ADV [*bad weather*] mejorar; [*storm, wind*] amainar; **when the rain ~s up** cuando deje de llover tanto; **he never ~s up** (*talking*) no deja de hablar, habla sin parar; (*working*) trabaja sin descanso; **in spite of his health, he did not ~ up** a pesar de su salud, no aflojó el ritmo (*del trabajo, de las actividades etc*)

let² [let] N (*Tennis*) dejada *f*, let *m*

letdown ['letdaʊn] N decepción *f*, desilusión *f*

lethal ['liːθəl] ADJ [*weapon*] mortífero, letal; [*dose, injection, effects*] mortal, letal; [*force*] letal; **the roads are ~ in these conditions** las carreteras son nefastas en estas condiciones; **this schnapps is ~** (*hum*) este aguardiente es mortal

lethargic [leˈθɑːdʒɪk] ADJ letárgico, aletargado

lethargy ['leθədʒɪ] N letargo *m*

letter ['letə^r] **Ⓐ** N **1** (*of alphabet*) letra *f*; **the ~ G** la letra G; **capital ~** (letra *f*) mayúscula *f*; **small ~** (letra *f*) minúscula *f*; **to the ~** al pie de la letra **2** (= *communication*) carta *f*; **by ~** por carta, por escrito **3** (*letters*) (= *learning*) letras *fpl*; **man of ~s** hombre *m* de letras, literato *m* **Ⓑ** CPD ➤ **letter bomb** carta *f* bomba ➤ **letter card** (*Brit*) carta-tarjeta *f* ➤ **letter carrier** (*US*) cartero/a *m/f* ➤ **letter opener** abrecartas *m inv*

letterbox ['letəbɒks] N (*esp Brit*) buzón *m*

letterhead ['letəhed] N membrete *m*

lettering ['letərɪŋ] N letras *fpl*

letting ['letɪŋ] N arrendamiento *m*, alquiler *m* ➤ **letting agency** (agencia) *f* inmobiliaria *f* (*especializada en alquilar propiedades*)

lettuce ['letɪs] N lechuga *f*

let-up* ['letʌp] N (= *rest*) descanso *m*; (= *reduction*) reducción *f*, disminución *f* (**in** de); **if there is a ~ in the rain** si deja un momento de llover; **there has been no ~ in the fighting** se ha luchado sin descanso *or* sin tregua

leukaemia, leukemia (*US*) [luːˈkiːmɪə] N leucemia *f*

level ['levl] **Ⓐ** ADJ **1** (*lit*) (= *not sloping*) nivelado; (= *not uneven*) plano, llano; **a ~ spoonful** una cucharada rasa; ✦ IDIOMS **to compete on a ~ playing field** competir en igualdad de condiciones; **to do one's ~ best to do sth** (*Brit**) hacer todo lo posible para hacer algo
2 to be ~ (with sb) (*in race*) estar *or* ir igualado (con algn); (*in league, competition*) estar *or* ir empatado (con algn); **to be ~ (with sth)** (= *at same height*) estar a la misma altura (que algo); **to be ~ with the ground** estar a ras del suelo; **to draw ~ with sth/sb** (*esp Brit*) (*gen*) alcanzar algo/a algn; (*in league, competition*) empatar con algo/algn
3 [*voice, tone*] sereno; [*gaze*] penetrante; ✦ IDIOM **to keep a ~ head** no perder la cabeza
Ⓑ N **1** nivel *m*; **at advanced/elementary ~** a nivel avanzado/elemental; **at eye ~** a la altura de los ojos; **to be on a ~ with** (*lit*) estar al nivel *or* a la altura de algo; **bankruptcies have reached record ~s** el número de bancarrotas ha alcanzado cifras récord; **~ of unemployment** índice *m* de desempleo *or* (*Sp*) paro
2 (= *floor*) [*of building*] piso *m*
3 (= *flat place*) llano *m*; **on the ~** en superficie plana *or* llana; ✦ IDIOM **to be on the ~*** [*person*] ser de fiar, ser un tipo cabal*; **it's on the ~** es un negocio serio *or* limpio
4 (*also* **spirit ~**) nivel *m* de burbuja
Ⓒ VT **1** (= *make level*) [+ *ground, site*] nivelar, allanar;

[+ *match, game*] igualar; **to ~ the score(s)** igualar el marcador
2 (= *raze*) [+ *building, city*] arrasar
3 (= *direct*) **he has denied the charges ~led** *or* (*US*) **~ed against him** ha negado las acusaciones que se han hecho en su contra; **he has not responded to the criticism ~led** *or* (*US*) **~ed at him** no ha reaccionado ante las críticas que se le han dirigido; **to ~ a gun at sb** apuntar a *or* contra algn con una pistola
D VI (*) **I'll ~ with you** te voy a hablar con franqueza, te voy a ser franco
E CPD ➤ **level crossing** (*Brit*) paso *m* a nivel
➤ **level off A** VI + ADV [*ground, road*] nivelarse; [*prices, rate of growth*] estabilizarse **B** VT + ADV nivelar, allanar
➤ **level out A** VI + ADV [*road, ground*] nivelarse; [*prices, rate of growth*] estabilizarse **B** VT + ADV nivelar, allanar
level-headed ['levl'hedɪd] ADJ sensato, equilibrado
levelling, leveling (*US*) ['levlɪŋ] N nivelación *f*
levelling-off [ˌlevəlɪŋ'ɒf] N nivelación *f*
level-pegging [ˌlevl'pegɪŋ] ADJ (*Brit*) **it's ~ now** van muy iguales, están empatados
lever ['liːvəʳ, (*US*) 'levəʳ] **A** N (*gen, fig*) palanca *f* **B** VT **to ~ sth up/off** levantar/quitar algo con palanca
leverage ['liːvərɪdʒ, (*US*) 'levərɪdʒ] N apalancamiento *m*; (= *influence*) influencia *f*, palanca *f*
levy ['levɪ] **A** N impuesto *m* **B** VT (= *impose*) [+ *tax, fine*] imponer (**on** a); (= *collect*) [+ *contribution*] recaudar
lewd [luːd] ADJ (*compar* **~er**; *superl* **~est**) [*person*] lascivo; [*song, story*] verde, colorado (*LAm*)
lexicographer [ˌleksɪ'kɒɡrəfəʳ] N lexicógrafo/a *m/f*
lexicography [ˌleksɪ'kɒɡrəfɪ] N lexicografía *f*
lexicon ['leksɪkən] N léxico *m*
LI ABBR (*US*) = **Long Island**
liability [ˌlaɪə'bɪlɪtɪ] N **1** (= *responsibility*) responsabilidad *f*; **to admit/deny ~ (for sth)** admitir/negar ser responsable (de algo) **2** (= *debts*) pasivo *msing*; **tax ~** carga *f* fiscal **3** (= *burden*) **this car's a bit of a ~** este coche da muchos problemas
liable ['laɪəbl] ADJ **1** (= *likely*) **he's ~ to do something stupid** puede fácilmente hacer alguna tontería, es muy posible que haga una tontería; **he's ~ to have an accident** es probable que tenga un accidente; **it's ~ to rain at any moment** puede empezar a llover en cualquier momento **2** (= *prone*) **we are all ~ to make mistakes** todos podemos cometer errores; **some people are more ~ to depression than others** algunas personas son más propensas a la depresión *or* tienen más tendencia a la depresión que otras **3** (= *responsible*) responsable (**for** de) **4** (= *subject*) **to be ~ to duty** estar sujeto a derechos de aduana; **to be ~ to prosecution** poder ser procesado; **to be ~ to** *or* **for tax** [*person*] deber pagar impuestos; [*thing*] estar sujeto a impuestos, ser gravable
liaise [lɪ'eɪz] VI **to ~ with** (*Brit*) (= *work with*) trabajar en colaboración con; **the agency will ~ between youth groups and the government** la agencia servirá de puente *or* enlace entre los grupos juveniles y el gobierno
liaison [lɪ'eɪzɒn] N (= *coordination*) enlace *m*, coordinación *f*; (= *relationship*) relación *f*
liar ['laɪəʳ] N mentiroso/a *m/f*, embustero/a *m/f*; **liar!** ¡mentira!
libel ['laɪbl] **A** N difamación *f*, calumnia *f*, escrito *m* difamatorio **B** VT difamar, calumniar **C** CPD ➤ **libel action** pleito *m* por difamación
libellous, libelous (*US*) ['laɪbələs] ADJ difamatorio, calumnioso
liberal ['lɪbərəl] **A** ADJ **1** (= *tolerant*) liberal **2** (= *generous*) [*quantity, amount*] abundante, generoso; [*portion*] generoso; **he is very ~ with his money** es muy generoso con el dinero; **she was rather ~ with the mayonnaise** puso mucha mayonesa **3** **Liberal** (*Brit Pol*) (*formerly*) [*MP*] del partido liberal; [*government, policy*] liberal **4** (= *free*) [*interpretation, translation*] libre

B N **Liberal** (*Brit Pol*) (*formerly*) liberal *mf*
C CPD ➤ **the liberal arts** (*US*) las humanidades, las artes liberales ➤ **Liberal Democrat** (*Brit*) demócrata *mf* liberal
liberalize ['lɪbərəlaɪz] VT liberalizar
liberally ['lɪbərəlɪ] ADV **1** (= *generously*) [*give*] generosamente **2** (= *tolerantly*) con tolerancia **3** (= *freely*) [*interpret*] libremente
liberate ['lɪbəreɪt] VT liberar, libertar (**from** de); [+ *prisoner, slave*] poner en libertad
liberated ['lɪbəreɪtɪd] ADJ liberado
liberation [ˌlɪbə'reɪʃən] N liberación *f*
Liberia [laɪ'bɪərɪə] N Liberia *f*
liberty ['lɪbətɪ] N **1** (= *freedom*) libertad *f*; **to be at ~ to do sth** tener libertad para hacer algo, ser libre de hacer algo; **I'm not at ~ to say who it was** no puedo decir quién fue **2** (= *impertinence*) atrevimiento *m*; **what a ~!** ¡qué atrevimiento *or* descaro!; **to take liberties with sb** (= *be cheeky*) tomarse libertades *or* demasiadas confianzas con algn; (*sexually*) propasarse con algn; **to take the ~ of doing sth** tomarse la libertad de hacer algo
libido [lɪ'biːdəʊ] N libido *f*
Libra ['liːbrə] N **1** (= *sign, constellation*) Libra *f* **2** (= *person*) libra *mf inv*; **he's (a) ~** es libra
librarian [laɪ'brɛərɪən] N bibliotecario/a *m/f*; (*professionally qualified*) bibliotecólogo/a *m/f*
library ['laɪbrərɪ] N biblioteca *f* ➤ **library book** libro *m* de biblioteca ➤ **library pictures** (*TV*) imágenes *fpl* de archivo ➤ **library ticket** carnet *m* de biblioteca

⚠ **library** ≠ *librería*

Libya ['lɪbɪə] N Libia *f*
lice [laɪs] NPL **of louse**
licence, license[1] (*US*) ['laɪsəns] **A** N **1** (= *permit*) permiso *m*, licencia *f*; (*Aut*) permiso *m* de conducir, carnet *m* (de conducir); **export ~** permiso *m* *or* licencia *f* de exportación; **to manufacture sth under ~** fabricar algo bajo licencia **2** (= *freedom*) licencia *f* **B** CPD ➤ **licence fee** (*Brit*) cuota que debe pagarse para el uso de un televisor ➤ **licence number, licence plate** matrícula *f*, placa *f*, patente *f* (*SC*)
license[2] ['laɪsəns] **A** VT [+ *drug, medicine*] autorizar la comercialización de; [+ *company, operator*] registrar; [+ *vehicle*] [*authority*] conceder el permiso de circulación a; [*owner*] (*initially*) obtener el permiso de circulación de; (*thereafter*) renovar el permiso de circulación de; [+ *sale, use*] autorizar; **to be ~d to do sth** tener licencia para hacer algo, estar autorizado para hacer algo **B** N, CPD (*US*) = **licence**
licensed ['laɪsənst] ADJ [*dealer*] autorizado; (*Brit*) [*restaurant, premises*] autorizado para la venta de bebidas alcohólicas
licensee [ˌlaɪsən'siː] N concesionario/a *m/f*; (*Brit*) [*of bar*] patrón/ona *m/f*
licensing ['laɪsənsɪŋ] CPD ➤ **licensing hours** (*Brit*) horas *fpl* durante las cuales se permite la venta y consumo de alcohol (*en un bar etc*) ➤ **licensing laws** (*Brit*) leyes *fpl* reguladoras de la venta y consumo de alcohol
lichee [ˌlaɪ'tʃiː] N lichi *m*
lichen ['laɪkən] N liquen *m*
lick [lɪk] **A** VT **1** lamer; ✦ IDIOMS **to ~ sb's boots*** hacer la pelota *or* dar coba a algn*; **to ~ sth into shape*** poner algo a punto **2** (*) (= *defeat*) dar una paliza a* (*with tongue*) lametazo *m*, lengüetada *f*; **a ~ of paint** una mano de pintura **2** (*Brit**) (= *speed*) **to go at a fair old ~** ir a buen tren*
➤ **lick up** VT + ADV beber a lengüetazos
licorice ['lɪkərɪs] N regaliz *m*, orozuz *m*
lid [lɪd] N **1** tapa *f* **2** (= *eyelid*) párpado *m*
lie[1] [laɪ] **A** N (= *untruth*) mentira *f*; **it's a ~!** ¡(es) mentira!; **to tell ~s** mentir **B** VI mentir
lie[2] [laɪ] (*pt* **lay**; *pp* **lain**) **A** VI **1** [*person, animal*] (= *lie down*) echarse, acostarse, tumbarse; (= *be lying down*) estar echado *or* acostado *or* tendido *or* tumbado; **to ~ in bed**

cama; **here** ~s ... aquí yace ...; **to let things** ~ dejar estar las cosas como están; **to** ~ **still** quedarse inmóvil; ✦ IDIOM **to** ~ **low** mantenerse a escondidas
2 (= be situated) [object] estar; [town, house] estar situado, encontrarse, ubicarse (LAm); (= remain) quedarse; **the book lay on the table** el libro estaba sobre la mesa; **where does the difficulty** ~? ¿en qué consiste or radica la dificultad?; **how does the land** ~? ¿cuál es el estado actual de las cosas?; **the problem** ~s **in his refusal** el problema estriba en su negativa; **the snow lay half a metre deep** había medio metro de nieve; **the book lay unopened** el libro quedaba sin abrir; **the fault** ~s **with you** la culpa es tuya, tú eres el culpable
🅑 N **the** ~ **of the land** (Geog) la configuración del terreno; (fig) el estado de las cosas
➤ **lie around, lie about** (Brit) VI + ADV [objects] estar por ahí tirado; [person] pasar el tiempo sin hacer nada; **it must be lying around somewhere** estará por aquí, debe de andar por aquí
➤ **lie back** VI + ADV recostarse (**against, on** sobre)
➤ **lie behind** VI + PREP **I wonder what** ~s **behind all this** me pregunto qué hay detrás de todo esto
➤ **lie down** VI + ADV echarse, acostarse, tumbarse; ~ **down!** (to dog) ¡échate!; ✦ IDIOM **to take sth lying down** aguantar or soportar algo sin rechistar; **he's not one to take things lying down** no es de los que se callan, no es de los que tragan con todo*; **we're not going to take this lying down** no nos vamos a callar con este tema, no vamos a permitir que esto se quede así
➤ **lie in** VI + ADV quedarse en la cama hasta tarde
Liechtenstein ['lɪktənstaɪn] N Liechtenstein m
lie-down* [ˌlaɪ'daʊn] N (Brit) descanso m; **I must have a** ~ necesito echarme un rato
lie-in* [ˌlaɪ'ɪn] N (Brit) **to have a** ~ quedarse en la cama hasta tarde
lieu [luː] N (esp LAm) **in** ~ **of** en lugar de, en vez de
Lieut. ABBR (= Lieutenant) Tte.
lieutenant [lef'tenənt, (US) luː'tenənt] N teniente mf
life [laɪf] 🅐 N (pl **lives**) **1** (gen) vida f; **to breathe new** ~ **into sth/sb** infundir nueva vida a algo/algn; **to bring sb back to** ~ resucitar or reanimar a algn; **to come to** ~ animarse; **country/city** ~ la vida de la ciudad/del campo; **it's a matter of** ~ **and death** es cosa f de vida o muerte; **in early/later** ~ en los años juveniles/maduras; **friends for** ~ amigos mpl para siempre; **a job for** ~ un trabajo para toda la vida; **I can't for the** ~ **of me remember*** por más que lo intento no puedo recordar; **she was fighting for her** ~ se debatía entre la vida y la muerte; **run for your** ~! ¡sálvese quien pueda!; **get a** ~!* ¡espabílate y haz algo!; ~ **must go on** la vida sigue; **I've had a good** ~ la vida me ha tratado bien; **it's a hard** ~ la vida es muy dura; **how's** ~?* ¿cómo te va (la vida)?, ¿qué hubo? (Mex, Chi); **there is not much insect** ~ **here** aquí hay pocos insectos; **never in my** ~ en mi vida; **to make a new** ~ **for o.s.** comenzar una vida nueva; **in the next** ~ en el más allá, en la otra vida; **not on your** ~!* ¡ni hablar!; ~ **on earth** la vida en la tierra; **to have a** ~ **of its own** [object, machine] tener vida propia; **plant** ~ vida f vegetal, las plantas; **to lead a quiet** ~ llevar una vida tranquila; **in real** ~ en la vida real; **the** ~ **and soul of the party** el alma de la fiesta; **to take one's own** ~ quitarse la vida, suicidarse; **you'll be taking your** ~ **in your hands if you climb up there** subir allí es jugarse la vida; **that's** ~! ¡así es la vida!; **this is the** ~! ¡esto sí que es vida!, ¡esto es jauja!; **what a** ~! ¡qué vida ésta!; **it was her** ~**'s work** fue el trabajo de toda su vida; **his** ~ **won't be worth living** más le valdría morirse; **it's more than my** ~**'s worth** sería jugarme la vida
2 (*) (= life imprisonment) **to do** ~ cumplir una condena de cadena or reclusión perpetua; **to be sentenced to** ~ ser condenado a cadena or reclusión perpetua
3 (Art) **to paint from** ~ pintar del natural; **true to** ~ fiel a la realidad
4 (US**) **she's in the** ~ hace la calle*
🅑 CPD ➤ **life assurance** (Brit) seguro m de vida ➤ **life coach** profesional encargado de mejorar la situación laboral y personal de sus clientes ➤ **life cycle** ciclo m vital ➤ **life expectancy** esperanza f de vida ➤ **life force** fuerza f vital ➤ **life form** forma f de vida ➤ **life history** (historia f de la) vida f ➤ **life imprisonment** cadena f perpetua ➤ **life**

insurance seguro m de vida ➤ **life jacket** chaleco m salvavidas ➤ **life membership: to take out a** ~ **membership** inscribirse como miembro vitalicio or de por vida ➤ **life peer** (Brit) miembro de la Cámara de los Lores de carácter no hereditario ➤ **life preserver** (US) chaleco m salvavidas ➤ **life raft** balsa f salvavidas ➤ **life sentence** condena f a perpetuidad ➤ **life span** [of person] vida f; [of product] vida f útil ➤ **life story** biografía f ➤ **life vest** (US) chaleco m salvavidas
lifebelt ['laɪfbelt] N salvavidas m inv, flotador m
lifeblood ['laɪfblʌd] N sangre f vital; (fig) alma f, sustento m

---

Use **el/un** not **la/una** before feminine nouns beginning with stressed **a** or **ha** like **alma**.

---

lifeboat ['laɪfbəʊt] N (from shore) lancha f de socorro; (from ship) bote m salvavidas
lifebuoy ['laɪfbɔɪ] N boya f salvavidas, guindola f
lifeguard ['laɪfgɑːd] N salvavidas mf inv, socorrista mf
lifeless ['laɪflɪs] ADJ [body] sin vida, exánime; [face, voice, eyes] apagado, sin vida; [hair] sin cuerpo, lacio
lifelike ['laɪflaɪk] ADJ (= seemingly real) que parece vivo; **her photo is so** ~ la foto es el vivo retrato de ella
lifeline ['laɪflaɪn] N cuerda f de salvamento; (fig) cordón m umbilical, sustento m
lifelong ['laɪflɒŋ] ADJ de toda la vida
life-saver ['laɪfˌseɪvəʳ] N salvador(a) m/f; (= lifeguard) salvavidas mf inv, socorrista mf
life-saving ['laɪfseɪvɪŋ] 🅐 N salvamento m; (= training for life-saving) socorrismo m 🅑 ADJ [equipment] de salvamento, salvavidas; **she was rushed to hospital for a** ~ **operation** la ingresaron de urgencia en el hospital para operarla a vida o muerte
life-size(d) ['laɪf'saɪz(d)] ADJ de tamaño natural
lifestyle ['laɪfstaɪl] N estilo m de vida
life-support ['laɪfsəˌpɔːt] ADJ ➤ **life-support machine** (esp Brit) máquina f corazón-pulmón; **he's been on a** ~ **machine for six weeks** ha estado con respiración artificial durante seis semanas ➤ **life-support system** sistema m de respiración artificial (pulmón artificial etc)
lifetime ['laɪftaɪm] N **1** (= lifespan) vida f; **in my** ~ ◇ **within my** ~ durante mi vida, en el curso de mi vida; **once in a** ~ una vez en la vida **2** (= eternity) eternidad f
lift [lɪft] 🅐 N **1** (Brit) (= elevator) ascensor m; (for goods) montacargas m inv
2 (esp Brit) (in car) **never accept** ~s **from strangers** nunca te montes en un coche con extraños; **can I give you a** ~? ¿quiere que le lleve (en coche)?, ¿quiere que le dé (Mex) aventón or (Col) un aventón?; **she gave me a** ~ **home** me llevó a casa en coche, me acompañó con su coche a casa
3 (= boost) **to give sb a** ~ levantar el ánimo a algn
🅑 VT **1** (= raise, pick up) [+ cover, box, head] levantar; [+ phone, receiver] descolgar, coger (Sp); [+ child] tomar en brazos, coger en brazos (Sp), alzar; [+ invalid] mover; **he** ~**ed the lid off the pan** levantó la tapadera de la olla, destapó la olla; **he** ~**ed the child onto his knee** alzó or (Sp) cogió al niño y lo sentó en su rodilla; **he** ~**ed his case onto the table** levantó la maleta y la puso encima de la mesa; **to** ~ **sb's spirits** levantar el ánimo a algn; **to** ~ **weights** (Sport) hacer or levantar pesas; ✦ IDIOMS **she never** ~s **a finger to help** no mueve un dedo para ayudar; **to** ~ **the lid on sth** destapar algo
2 (= remove) [+ restrictions, sanctions, siege] levantar
3 (*) (= steal) [+ goods, money] mangar*, birlar*; [+ idea, quotation] copiar, plagiar
🅒 VI **1** (= rise) levantarse, alzarse (LAm)
2 [fog] disiparse
🅓 CPD ➤ **lift attendant** (Brit) ascensorista mf ➤ **lift shaft** (Brit) caja f or hueco m del ascensor
➤ **lift down** VT + ADV bajar
➤ **lift off** 🅐 VT + ADV [+ lid, cover] quitar, levantar 🅑 VI + ADV **1** (= gen) levantarse; **the top** ~s **off** la parte de arriba se levanta **2** [spacecraft] despegar
➤ **lift out** VT + ADV sacar

> lift up Ⓐ VT + ADV levantar Ⓑ VI + ADV levantarse

lift-off ['lɪftɒf] N despegue *m*

ligament ['lɪgəmənt] N ligamento *m*

light¹ [laɪt] (*vb: pt, pp* **lit** *or* **~ed**) Ⓐ N **1** (= *not darkness*) luz *f*; **the ~ was beginning to fade** estaba empezando a oscurecer; **against the ~** al trasluz; **by the ~ of the moon/a candle** a la luz de la luna/de una vela; **at first ~** al rayar el día; **you're in my ~** me quitas la luz, me haces sombra; **~ and shade** luz y sombra; (*Art*) claroscuro *m*; **to hold sth up to the ~** acercar algo a la luz, mirar algo al trasluz; ✦ IDIOMS **in the cold ~ of day** pensándolo con calma; **to come to ~** salir a la luz (pública); **(the) ~ dawned on him/her** se dio cuenta, comprendió; **to see (a) ~ at the end of the tunnel** ver la salida del túnel, ver una solución al problema; **to bring sth to ~** sacar algo a la luz; **to see the ~** ver la luz; **to throw ~ on sth** arrojar luz sobre algo **2** (= *lamp*) luz *f*; **to turn the ~ on/off** encender/apagar la luz; ✦ IDIOM **to go out like a ~*** dormirse al instante **3** (= *electricity*) luz *f*; **electric ~** luz *f* eléctrica **4** (*on vehicle*) luz *f*; **rear** *or* **tail ~s** pilotos *mpl*, luces *fpl* traseras, calaveras *fpl* (*Mex*) **5** (= *traffic signal*) semáforo *m*; **to go through a red ~** saltarse un semáforo en rojo; **the ~s** el semáforo; **the ~s were at** *or* **on red** el semáforo estaba en rojo **6** (= *viewpoint*) **to see things in a different** *or* **new ~** ver las cosas con una perspectiva distinta *or* desde otro punto de vista; **to show sth/sb in a good/bad ~** dar una buena/mala imagen de algo/algn; **in the ~ of what you have said ...** en vista de *or* a la luz de lo que has dicho ... **7** (= *glint, twinkle*) brillo *m* **8** (= *flame*) **have you got a ~?** ¿tienes fuego?; **to set ~ to sth** (*Brit*) prender fuego a algo

Ⓑ ADJ (*compar* **~er**; *superl* **~est**) **1** (= *bright*) [*evening, room, house*] claro; **while it's still ~** mientras es de día *or* hay luz; **to get ~** hacerse de día **2** (= *pale*) [*colour*] claro; [*hair*] rubio, güero (*CAm, Mex*); [*skin*] blanco

Ⓒ VT **1** [+ *match, candle, fire, cigarette*] encender **2** (= *illuminate*) iluminar

Ⓓ VI (= *ignite*) encenderse, prender

Ⓔ CPD **> light bulb** bombilla *f*, foco *m* (*And*), bombillo *m* (*Col, Ven*) **> light fitting** *instalación eléctrica donde se colocan bombillas, tubos fluorescentes, etc* **> light meter** fotómetro *m* **> light pen** lápiz *m* óptico **> light show** espectáculo *m* de luces **> lights out** hora *f* de apagar las luces **> light switch** interruptor *m* **> light year** año *m* luz

> light up Ⓐ VI + ADV **1** (*gen*) iluminarse; **her face lit up** se le iluminó la cara **2** (*light cigarette*) encender un cigarrillo Ⓑ VT + ADV iluminar

light² [laɪt] Ⓐ ADJ (*compar* **~er**; *superl* **~est**) **1** (= *not heavy*) ligero, liviano (*LAm*); [*breeze, sound, sentence*] leve; **she can only manage ~ work** sólo puede realizar tareas ligeras; **traffic was ~** había poco tráfico; **I want to be ten pounds ~er** quiero adelgazar diez libras; **to make ~ of sth** quitar importancia a algo; **on a ~er note** hablando de cosas menos serias; **to be a ~ sleeper** tener el sueño ligero; ✦ IDIOMS **as ~ as a feather** ligero como una pluma; **to make ~ work of sth** hacer algo con facilidad **2** (= *low-alcohol*) de bajo contenido alcohólico, de bajo contenido en alcohol; (= *low-calorie*) light, bajo en calorías; (= *low-tar*) light, de bajo contenido en alquitrán

Ⓑ ADV **to travel ~** viajar con poco equipaje

Ⓒ CPD **> light aircraft** avión *m* ligero **> light cream** (*US*) crema *f* de leche líquida, nata *f* líquida (*Sp*) **> light entertainment** (*TV*) programas *mpl* de variedades **> light industry** industria *f* ligera **> light opera** (= *show*) opereta *f*; (= *genre*) género *m* lírico

lighten¹ ['laɪtn] Ⓐ VT [+ *sky*] iluminar; [+ *color*] hacer más claro Ⓑ VI [*sky*] clarear

lighten² ['laɪtn] **1** [+ *load*] aligerar, hacer menos pesado; [+ *atmosphere*] relajar; [+ *heart*] alegrar

lighter ['laɪtəʳ] N (*also* **cigarette ~**) encendedor *m*, mechero *m* **> lighter fuel** gas *m* de encendedor

light-footed ['laɪt'fʊtɪd] ADJ ligero (de pies)

light-haired ['laɪt'hɛəd] ADJ rubio, güero (*CAm, Mex*)

light-headed ['laɪt'hɛdɪd] ADJ mareado

light-hearted ['laɪt'hɑːtɪd] ADJ desenfadado, alegre; [*remark*] poco serio, dicho en tono festivo

lighthouse ['laɪthaʊs] N faro *m* **> lighthouse keeper** farero/a *m/f*, torrero/a *m/f*

lighting ['laɪtɪŋ] N (= *system*) alumbrado *m*; (*at pop show*) equipo *m* de luces, iluminación *f*; (*Theat*) iluminación *f* **> lighting effects** efectos *mpl* luminosos **> lighting engineer** luminotécnico/a *m/f*

lighting-up time [ˌlaɪtɪŋ'ʌptaɪm] N hora *f* de encender los faros

lightly ['laɪtlɪ] ADV **1** (= *gently, softly*) [*touch, knock*] suavemente; [*tread, walk*] con paso ligero **2** (= *slightly*) levemente, ligeramente; **a ~ boiled egg** un huevo pasado por agua **3** (= *frivolously*) a la ligera; **to get off ~** librarse de una buena

lightness¹ ['laɪtnɪs] N [*of room*] luminosidad *f*; [*of colour*] claridad *f*

lightness² ['laɪtnɪs] N (*gen*) ligereza *f*, liviandad *f* (*LAm*); [*of tone, voice*] suavidad *f*; [*of sentence*] levedad *f*

lightning ['laɪtnɪŋ] N (= *flash*) relámpago *m*; (= *stroke*) rayo *m*; **a flash of ~** un relámpago; ✦ IDIOM **like (greased) ~*** como un rayo; ✦ PROV **~ never strikes twice in the same place** desgracias así no suelen repetirse **> lightning conductor** (*Brit*), **lightning rod** (*US*) pararrayos *m inv* **> lightning visit** visita *f* relámpago

lightweight ['laɪtweɪt] ADJ (*gen*) ligero, de poco peso, liviano (*esp LAm*); (*Boxing*) de peso ligero

likable ['laɪkəbl] ADJ = **likeable**

like¹ [laɪk] Ⓐ ADJ (*frm*) (= *similar*) parecido, semejante; ✦ IDIOM **they are as ~ as two peas (in a pod)** se parecen como dos gotas de agua

Ⓑ PREP **1** (= *similar to*) como; **a house ~ mine** una casa como la mía, una casa parecida a la mía; **I found one ~ it** encontré uno parecido *or* igual; **I never saw anything ~ it** nunca he visto cosa igual *or* semejante; **to be ~ sth/sb** parecerse a algo/algn, ser parecido a algo/algn; **it was more ~ a prison than a house** se parecía más a una cárcel que a una casa; **the figure is more ~ 300** la cifra se acerca más bien a 300; **that's more ~ it!*** ¡así está mejor!, ¡así me gusta!; **something ~ that** algo así, algo por el estilo; **they earn something ~ £50,000 a year** ganan alrededor de 50.000 libras al año; **people ~ that can't be trusted** esa clase *or* ese tipo de gente no es de fiar; **what's he ~?** ¿cómo es (él)?; **what's Spain ~?** ¿cómo es España?; **what's the weather ~?** ¿qué tiempo hace?; **what's he ~ as a teacher?** ¿qué tal es como profesor?; **you know what she's ~** ya la conoces, ya sabes cómo es **2** (= *typical of*) **it's not ~ him to do that** no es propio de él hacer eso; **isn't it just ~ him!** ¡no cambia!, ¡eso es típico de él! **3** (= *similarly to*) como; **he thinks ~ us** piensa como nosotros; **~ me, he is fond of Brahms** le gusta Brahms, igual que a mí; **she behaved ~ an idiot** se comportó como una idiota; **just ~ anybody else** igual que cualquier otro; **~ this/that** así; **I'm sorry to intrude on you ~ this** siento importunarte de este modo; ✦ PROV **~ father ~ son** de tal palo tal astilla **4** (= *such as*) como; **large cities ~ New York** las grandes urbes como Nueva York

Ⓒ ADV **on company advice, well, orders, more ~** siguiendo los consejos de la empresa, bueno, más bien sus órdenes; **£500 will be nothing ~ enough** 500 libras no serán suficientes, ni mucho menos

Ⓓ CONJ (*) **1** (= *as*) como; **do it ~ I do** hazlo como yo; **it's just ~ I say** es como yo digo*; ✦ IDIOM **to tell it ~ it is** decir las cosas como son **2** (= *as if*) como si; **you look ~ you've seen a ghost** parece que acabas de ver un fantasma

Ⓔ N **we shall not see his ~ again** (*frm, liter*) no volveremos a ver otro igual; **did you ever see the ~ (of it)?** ¿has visto cosa igual?; **I've no time for the ~s of him*** no soporto a la gente como él; **sparrows, starlings and the ~** gorriones, estorninos y otras aves por el estilo; **to compare ~ with ~** comparar dos cosas semejantes

like² [laɪk] Ⓐ VT **1** (= *find pleasant*) **I ~ dancing/football** me gusta bailar/el fútbol; **I ~ bright colours** me gustan los colores vivos; **your father won't ~ it** esto no le va a gustar a tu padre; **we ~ it here** nos gusta este sitio; **I ~ him** me cae bien *or* simpático; **I don't ~ him at all** me resulta antipático, no me cae nada bien; **you know he ~s you very much** sabes que te tiene mucho cariño *or* que te quiere mucho; **which do you ~ best?** ¿cuál es el que más te gusta?; **I don't think they ~ each other** creo que no se caen bien; **I don't ~ the look of him** no me gusta su aspecto, no me gusta la pinta que tiene*; **well, I ~ that!*** *(iro)* ¡será posible!, ¡habráse visto!; **she is well ~d here** aquí se la quiere mucho

2 (= *feel about*) **how do you ~ it here?** ¿qué te parece este sitio?; **how would you ~ to go to the cinema?** ¿te apetece *or* (*LAm*) se te antoja ir al cine?; **how would you ~ it if somebody did the same to you?** ¿cómo te sentirías si alguien te hiciera lo mismo?; **how do you ~ that!** ¡qué te parece!

3 (= *have a preference for*) **I ~ my whisky neat** me gusta el whisky solo; **I ~ to know the facts before I form opinions** me gusta conocer los hechos antes de formarme una opinión

4 (= *want*) **I didn't ~ to say no** no quise decir que no; *(because embarrassed)* me dio vergüenza decir que no; **take as much as you** ~ toma *or* coge todo lo que quieras; **whenever you** ~ cuando quieras

5 would/should ~ **5.1** *(specific request, offer, desire)* **would you ~ a drink?** ¿quieres tomar algo?; **would you ~ me to wait?** ¿quiere que espere?; **I'd ~ to take this opportunity to thank you all** quisiera aprovechar esta oportunidad para darles las gracias a todos; **I'd ~ the roast chicken, please** querría el pollo asado; **I'd ~ three kilos of tomatoes, please** ¿me da tres kilos de tomates? **5.2** *(wishes, preferences)* **I'd ~ a bigger flat** me gustaría tener un piso más grande; **I should ~ to have been there** me hubiera gustado estar allí

Ⓑ VI querer; **as you** ~ como quieras; **"shall we go now?"** — **"if you ~"** —¿nos vamos ya? —si quieres

Ⓒ N **likes** gustos *mpl*

likeable ['laɪkəbl] ADJ simpático, agradable

likelihood ['laɪklɪhʊd] N probabilidad *f*; **what is the ~ of a successful outcome?** ¿qué probabilidad hay de que el resultado sea favorable?; **there is little/every ~ that he'll come** es poco/muy probable que venga; **in all ~ the explosion was caused by a bomb** lo más probable es que una bomba causase la explosión

likely ['laɪklɪ] **Ⓐ** ADJ *(compar* **likelier**; *superl* **likeliest**)

1 (= *probable*) probable; **it is ~ that** es probable que + *subjun*; **they are not ~ to come** no es probable que vengan; **the ~ outcome** el resultado más probable; **he's the man most ~ to win** es el que más probabilidades tiene de ganar; **a ~ story!** *(iro)* ¡menudo cuento!, ¡y yo que me lo creo!

2 (= *suitable*) apropiado

3 (= *promising*) prometedor

Ⓑ ADV (= *probably*) **she will very** *or* **most ~ arrive late** lo más probable es que llegue tarde; **some prisoners will ~ be released soon** (*US*) es probable que pronto se deje en libertad a algunos prisioneros; **(as) ~ as not he'll arrive early** lo más probable es que llegue pronto, seguramente llegará pronto; **not ~!*** ¡ni hablar!*

like-minded ['laɪk'maɪndɪd] ADJ con ideas afines, de igual parecer

liken ['laɪkən] VT comparar (**to** con)

likeness ['laɪknɪs] N **1** (= *resemblance*) semejanza *f*, parecido *m*; **family ~** aire *m* de familia **2** (= *portrait*) retrato *m*; **it's a good ~** se parece mucho

likewise ['laɪkwaɪz] ADV (= *similarly*) asimismo, igualmente, también; (= *the same*) lo mismo, igualmente; **~ it is true that ...** asimismo es verdad que ...; lo mismo se puede decir; **do ~** hacer lo mismo

liking ['laɪkɪŋ] N *(for thing)* gusto *m* **(for** por), afición *f* **(for** a); *(for person)* simpatía *f*, aprecio *m* (*LAm*); **to have a ~ for sth** ser aficionado *or* tener afición a algo; **to be to sb's ~** ser del gusto de algn; **to take a ~ to sb** tomar *or* coger simpatía a algn; **it's too strong for my ~** para mí es demasiado fuerte, es demasiado fuerte para mi gusto

lilac ['laɪlək] **Ⓐ** N *(Bot)* lila *f*; (= *colour*) lila *m*, color *m* lila **Ⓑ** ADJ de color lila

Lilo® ['laɪləʊ] N colchoneta *f* inflable

lilt [lɪlt] N *(in voice)* tono *m* cantarín; *(in song)* ritmo *m* alegre; **a song with a ~ to it** una canción de ritmo alegre

lilting ['lɪltɪŋ] ADJ *[voice]* cantarín

lily ['lɪlɪ] N lirio *m*, azucena *f* ➤ **lily of the valley** muguete *m*, lirio *m* de los valles

Lima ['liːmə] N Lima *f*

limb [lɪm] N (= *arm, leg*) miembro *m*, extremidad *f*; *[of tree]* rama *f*; ✦ IDIOMS **to be/go out on a ~** *(in danger)* estar/quedar en peligro; (= *be isolated*) estar/quedarse aislado; (= *take risk*) correr el riesgo; **to tear sb ~ from ~** despedazar a algn

➤ **limber up** VI + ADV *(Sport)* entrar en calor, hacer ejercicios preparatorios; *(fig)* entrenarse, prepararse

limbo ['lɪmbəʊ] N limbo *m*; ✦ IDIOM **to be in ~** quedarse nadando entre dos aguas

lime¹ [laɪm] N *(Geol)* cal *f*; *(birdlime)* liga *f*

lime² [laɪm] N (= *linden*) tilo *m*

lime³ [laɪm] N (= *citrus fruit*) lima *f*; (= *tree*) limero *m*; *(also* **~ green**) verde *m* lima ➤ **lime juice** zumo *m or* (*LAm*) jugo *m* de lima

limelight ['laɪmlaɪt] N luz *f* de calcio; ✦ IDIOM **to be in the ~** ser el centro de atención, estar en el candelero

limerick ['lɪmərɪk] N *especie de quintilla jocosa*

limestone ['laɪmstəʊn] N *(piedra f)* caliza *f*

limit ['lɪmɪt] **Ⓐ** N límite *m*; **there is a ~ to my patience** mi paciencia tiene un límite; **there's a ~ to what doctors can do in such cases** lo que pueden hacer los médicos en estos casos es limitado; **one glass of wine's my ~** con un vaso de vino me basta y me sobra; **these establishments are off ~s to ordinary citizens** los ciudadanos de a pie tienen prohibido el acceso a estos establecimientos; **he was three times over the ~** (*Brit*) había ingerido tres veces más de la cantidad de alcohol permitida (para conducir); **it's the ~!*** ¡es el colmo!, ¡es demasiado!; **she tried my patience to the ~** puso mi paciencia a prueba

Ⓑ VT *(gen)* limitar; *[+ spending]* restringir; **he ~ed himself to a few remarks** se limitó a hacer algunas observaciones; **I ~ myself to ten cigarettes a day** me permito sólo diez cigarrillos al día

limitation [,lɪmɪ'teɪʃən] N limitación *f*, restricción *f*

limited ['lɪmɪtɪd] **Ⓐ** ADJ **1** *[number, space]* limitado; *[resources]* limitado, escaso; *[range, scope]* limitado, reducido; **to a ~ extent** hasta cierto punto; **"for a limited period only"** "sólo por un periodo limitado"; **the choice is ~** hay poca elección

2 *(Brit)* *(in company names)* **Hourmont Travel Limited** ≈ Hourmont Travel, Sociedad Anónima

Ⓑ CPD ➤ **limited company** *(esp Brit)* ≈ sociedad *f* anónima, ≈ sociedad *f* limitada ➤ **limited edition** *[of book]* edición *f* limitada; *[of picture, record]* tirada *f* limitada; *[of car]* serie *f* limitada

limitless ['lɪmɪtlɪs] ADJ ilimitado, sin límites

limo* ['lɪməʊ] N limusina *f*

limousine ['lɪməziːn] N limusina *f*

limp¹ [lɪmp] **Ⓐ** N cojera *f*; **to walk with a ~** cojear **Ⓑ** VI cojear, renguear (*LAm*); **he ~ed to the door** fue cojeando a la puerta; **the ship managed to ~ to port** el buque llegó con dificultad al puerto

limp² [lɪmp] ADJ *(compar* **~er**; *superl* **~est**) *[person, body]* sin fuerzas; *[handshake]* flojo; *[lettuce]* mustio; **his body went ~**

se le fueron las fuerzas del cuerpo

limpet ['lɪmpɪt] N lapa f; **like a** ~ como una lapa

limpid ['lɪmpɪd] ADJ [*water*] límpido, cristalino; [*eyes*] claro

linchpin ['lɪntʃpɪn] N (*lit*) pezonera f; (*fig*) eje m

linden ['lɪndən] N tilo m

line[1] [laɪn] **Ⓐ** N **1** (*gen*) línea f, raya f; **to draw a** ~ trazar una línea *or* raya; **there's a <u>fine</u> ~ between genius and madness** la línea que separa la genialidad de la locura es muy sutil; **to <u>put</u> a ~ through sth** tachar *or* (*LAm*) rayar algo; **✦ IDIOMS to draw the ~ at sth** no tolerar *or* aceptar algo; **one must draw the ~ somewhere** hay que fijar ciertos límites; **to draw a ~ under** [+ *episode, event*] poner punto final a; **to put one's reputation on the ~** arriesgar su reputación
2 (= *rope*) cuerda f; (= *fishing line*) sedal m; (= *washing line*) cuerda f para tender la ropa
3 (= *wrinkle*) (*on face etc*) arruga f
4 [*of print, verse*] renglón m, línea f; **"new ~"** (*in dictation*) "otra línea"; **lines** (*as school punishment*) copias; **<u>drop</u> me a ~*** escríbeme; **to <u>learn</u> one's ~s** (*Theat*) aprenderse el papel; **✦ IDIOM to read between the ~s** leer entre líneas
5 (= *row*) hilera f, fila f, línea f; **a ~ of winning numbers** (*in bingo, lottery*) una línea ganadora; **to be in ~ with** estar de acuerdo con, ser conforme a; **to be in ~ for promotion** estar bajo consideración para un ascenso; **to keep people in ~** mantener a la gente a raya; **to bring sth <u>into</u> ~ with sth** poner algo de acuerdo con algo; **to get into ~** (= *formation*) meterse en fila; **to be <u>out of</u> ~ with** no ser conforme con; **he was completely out of ~ to suggest that ...*** estaba totalmente fuera de lugar que propusiera que ...;
✦ IDIOM all along the ~ desde principio a fin; **somewhere along the ~ we went wrong** en algún punto nos hemos equivocado
6 (*US*) (= *queue*) cola f; **to <u>form</u> a ~** hacer una cola; **to <u>get into</u> ~** ponerse en la cola *or* a la cola; **to <u>stand</u> in ~** hacer cola
7 (= *series*) serie f; **the latest in a <u>long</u> ~ of tragedies** la última de una larga serie *or* lista de tragedias
8 (= *lineage*) linaje m; **he comes from a <u>long</u> ~ of artists** proviene de un extenso linaje de artistas
9 (= *hierarchy*) ~ **of <u>command</u>** cadena f de mando
10 (*Mil*) línea f; **behind <u>enemy</u> ~s** tras las líneas enemigas
11 (= *direction*) línea f; **something <u>along</u>** *or* **<u>on</u> the ~s of** algo por el estilo de; **something along those** *or* **the same ~s** algo por el estilo; **along** *or* **on political ~s** según criterios políticos; **on the right ~s** por buen camino; ~ **of <u>argument</u>** argumento m; ~ **of <u>attack</u>** (*Mil*) modo m de ataque; (*fig*) planteamiento m; **in the ~ of <u>duty</u>** en cumplimiento de sus deberes; **it's all in the ~ of duty** es una parte normal del deber; **in the ~ of <u>fire</u>** (*Mil*) en la línea de fuego; ~ **of <u>inquiry</u>** línea f de investigación; ~ **of <u>vision</u>** visual f
12 (*Comput*) **to be/come <u>on</u> ~** estar/entrar en (pleno) funcionamiento
13 (*Telec*) línea f; **it's a very <u>bad</u> ~** se oye muy mal; ~**s of communication** líneas fpl de comunicación; **the ~'s gone <u>dead</u>** se ha cortado la línea; **the ~s are <u>down</u>** no hay línea; **the ~ is <u>engaged</u>** *or* (*US*) **<u>busy</u>** está comunicando; **hold the ~ please** no cuelgue, por favor; **Mr Smith is <u>on</u> the ~ (for you)** el Sr. Smith está al teléfono (y quiere hablar con usted); **the ~s are <u>open</u> from six o'clock onwards** las líneas están abiertas de seis en adelante
14 (= *shape*) **the rounded ~s of this car** la línea redondeada *or* el contorno redondeado de este coche
15 (= *field, area*) **what ~ (of business) are you in?** ¿a qué se dedica?; **we're in the same ~ (of business)** nos dedicamos a lo mismo, trabajamos en el mismo campo; ~ **of research** campo m de investigación; **it's not my ~** (= *speciality*) no es de mi especialidad; **fishing's more (in) my ~** me interesa más la pesca, de pesca sí sé algo
16 (= *stance, attitude*) actitud f; **to <u>take</u> a firm ~ on sth** adoptar una actitud firme sobre algo; **what ~ is the government taking?** ¿cuál es la actitud del gobierno?; **to take the ~ that ...** ser de la opinión que ...
17 (= *product*) línea f
18 (= *track*) vía f; **the ~ to Palencia** el ferrocarril de Palencia, la línea de Palencia
19 (*also* **shipping** ~) (= *company*) naviera f; (= *route*) línea f marítima, ruta f marítima

20 (= *spiel*) **✦ IDIOM to feed sb a ~ (about sth)*** soltar un rollo *or* contar un cuento chino a algn (sobre algo)*
21 (= *assembly line*) línea f
22 [*of cocaine*] raya f
Ⓑ VT [+ *face*] arrugar
Ⓒ CPD ➤ **line dancing** *danza folclórica en que los que bailan forman líneas y filas* ➤ **line drawing** dibujo m lineal ➤ **line judge** (*Tennis*) juez mf de fondo ➤ **line manager** (*Brit*) jefe/a m/f de línea
➤ **line up Ⓐ** VT + ADV **1** (= *stand in line*) poner en fila
2 (= *arrange*) **I wonder what he's got ~d up for us** me pregunto qué nos tendrá preparado; **have you got something ~d up for this evening?** ¿tienes algún plan para esta noche?; **have you got someone ~d up for the job?** ¿tienes pensado *or* tienes en mente a alguien para el puesto? **Ⓑ** VI + ADV (*in queue*) hacer cola; (*behind one another*) formar fila; (*in row*) ponerse en fila

line[2] [laɪn] VT **1** (= *put lining in*) [+ *garment*] forrar (**with** de); (*Tech*) revestir (**with** de); **eat something to ~ your stomach** come algo para no tener el estómago vacío **2** (= *border*) **streets ~d with trees** calles fpl bordeadas de árboles; **to ~ the route** alinearse a lo largo de la ruta

lineage ['lɪnɪɪdʒ] N linaje m

linear ['lɪnɪəʳ] ADJ [*design*] lineal; [*measure*] de longitud

lined[1] [laɪnd] ADJ [*paper*] de rayas, pautado; [*face*] arrugado

lined[2] [laɪnd] ADJ [*garment*] forrado; (*Tech*) revestido

linen ['lɪnɪn] **Ⓐ** N **1** (= *cloth*) lino m **2** (= *household linen*) ropa f blanca; (= *bed linen*) ropa f de cama; **dirty ~** ropa f sucia *or* para lavar **Ⓑ** CPD de lino ➤ **linen basket** canasta f *or* cesto m de la ropa ➤ **linen closet** (*US*), **linen cupboard** (*Brit*) armario m para la ropa blanca

liner ['laɪnəʳ] N (= *ship*) transatlántico m

linesman ['laɪnzmən] N (*pl* **linesmen**) juez m de línea, linier m

line-up ['laɪnʌp] N (*Sport*) formación f, alineación f; (*Theat, Cine*) [*of actors*] reparto m, elenco m; (*US*) (= *suspects*) rueda f de reconocimiento; (*US*) (= *queue*) cola f

linger ['lɪŋgəʳ] VI **1** [*person*] (= *not go*) rezagarse, tardar en marcharse; **to ~ over doing sth** tardar *or* no darse prisa en hacer algo; **to ~ over a meal** comer despacio **2** (*also* ~ **on**) [*pain*] persistir, durar; [*doubts*] persistir, quedar; [*tradition*] sobrevivir; [*memory*] pervivir, seguir vivo

lingerie ['lænʒəriː] N lencería f, ropa f interior femenina

lingering ['lɪŋgərɪŋ] ADJ [*smell, doubt*] persistente; [*death*] lento

lingo* ['lɪŋgəʊ] N (*pl* **-es**) (= *language*) lengua f, idioma m; (= *specialist jargon*) jerga f

linguist ['lɪŋgwɪst] N (= *specialist*) lingüista mf; **I'm no ~** se me dan mal los idiomas, no puedo con los idiomas; **the company needs more ~s** la compañía necesita más gente que sepa idiomas

linguistic [lɪŋˈgwɪstɪk] ADJ lingüístico

linguistics [lɪŋˈgwɪstɪks] NSING lingüística f

liniment ['lɪnɪmənt] N linimento m

lining ['laɪnɪŋ] N [*of garment*] forro m; (*Tech*) revestimiento m; [*of brake*] guarnición f

link [lɪŋk] **Ⓐ** N **1** [*of chain*] eslabón m; **weak ~** (*fig*) punto m débil
2 (= *relation*) relación f, conexión f; **the ~ between smoking and lung cancer** la relación *or* conexión entre el tabaco y el cáncer de pulmón
3 (= *tie, association*) vínculo m, lazo m; **cultural ~s** vínculos mpl *or* lazos mpl culturales
4 (*Travel*) enlace m, conexión f; **rail/air/road ~s** enlaces mpl ferroviarios/aéreos/por carretera, conexiones fpl ferroviarias/aéreas/por carretera
5 (*Telec, TV, Rad*) **radio/telephone/satellite ~** conexión f radiofónica/telefónica/vía satélite
6 (*Internet*) enlace m
Ⓑ VT **1** (= *join, connect*) [+ *parts, units*] unir (**to** a), conectar (**to** con); [+ *computers*] conectar (**to** con); [+ *towns, buildings, countries*] comunicar, conectar; **to ~ arms** tomarse del brazo, cogerse del brazo (*Sp*)

2 (= *relate*) relacionar; **the evidence ~ing smoking with early death** las pruebas que relacionan *or* que establecen una relación entre el tabaco y las muertes prematuras; **there is evidence ~ing the group to a series of terrorist attacks** hay pruebas que implican al grupo en una serie de atentados terroristas
ⓒ VI **1 to ~ together** [*parts, components*] encajar
2 (*Internet*) **to ~ (in) to** tener un enlace con
➤ **link up ⓐ** VI + ADV [*people*] unirse; [*companies*] unir fuerzas; [*spacecraft*] acoplarse; [*railway lines, roads*] empalmar **ⓑ** VT + ADV conectar (**to** a)

linkage ['lɪŋkɪdʒ] N conexión *f*, enlace *m*

links [lɪŋks] NPL (= *golf links*) campo *msing or* (*LAm*) cancha *fsing* de golf

linkup ['lɪŋkʌp] N conexión *f*, vinculación *f*; (*Rad, TV*) conexión *f*, enlace *m*

lino ['laɪnəʊ], **linoleum** [lɪ'nəʊlɪəm] N (*Brit*) linóleo *m*

linseed ['lɪnsiːd] N linaza *f* ➤ **linseed oil** aceite *m* de linaza

lint [lɪnt] N **1** (*Med*) hilas *fpl* **2** (*US*) (*on sweaters*) bolas *fpl*

lintel ['lɪntl] N dintel *m*

lion ['laɪən] N león *m*; ✦ IDIOM **the ~'s share** la parte del león, la mejor parte ➤ **lion cub** cachorro *m* de león ➤ **lion tamer** domador(a) *m/f* de leones

lioness ['laɪənɪs] N leona *f*

lip [lɪp] **ⓐ** N **1** (*Anat*) labio *m*; [*of cup, crater*] borde *m*; [*of jug*] pico *m*; **my ~s are sealed** (= *I won't tell*) soy una tumba; (= *I can't tell*) no puedo contar nada **2** (*) (= *insolence*) impertinencia *f*, insolencia *f*; **none of your ~!** ¡cállate la boca!*
ⓑ CPD ➤ **lip balm** = **lip salve** ➤ **lip gloss** brillo *m* de labios ➤ **lip salve** (*Brit*) vaselina *f*, cacao *m*, protector *m* labial
➤ **lip service** ✦ IDIOM **to pay ~ service to an ideal** defender un ideal de boquilla; **he's just paying ~ service** todo lo que dice es boquilla

liposuction ['lɪpəʊˌsʌkʃən] N liposucción *f*

lip-read ['lɪpriːd] **ⓐ** VT leer los labios a **ⓑ** VI leer los labios

lip-reading ['lɪpˌriːdɪŋ] N lectura *f* de labios

lipstick ['lɪpstɪk] N lápiz *m* de labios, barra *f* de labios; **to put (one's) ~ on** pintarse los labios

liquefy ['lɪkwɪfaɪ] **ⓐ** VT licuar **ⓑ** VI licuarse

liqueur [lɪ'kjʊəʳ] N licor *m* ➤ **liqueur chocolate** bombón *m* de licor ➤ **liqueur glass** copa *f* de licor

liquid ['lɪkwɪd] **ⓐ** ADJ líquido **ⓑ** N líquido *m* **ⓒ** CPD ➤ **liquid assets** activo *msing* líquido ➤ **liquid crystal display** pantalla *f* de cristal líquido

liquidate ['lɪkwɪdeɪt] VT liquidar

liquidation [ˌlɪkwɪ'deɪʃən] N liquidación *f*; **to go into ~** entrar en liquidación

liquidator ['lɪkwɪdeɪtəʳ] N liquidador(a) *m/f*

liquidity [lɪ'kwɪdɪtɪ] N liquidez *f*

liquidize ['lɪkwɪdaɪz] **ⓐ** VT licuar **ⓑ** VI licuarse

liquidizer ['lɪkwɪdaɪzəʳ] N (*esp Brit*) licuadora *f*

liquor ['lɪkəʳ] N (*Brit frm*) licores *mpl*; (*US*) alcohol *m*; **hard ~** licores *mpl* espiritosos, bebidas *fpl* fuertes ➤ **liquor store** (*US*) bodega *f*, tienda *f* de bebidas alcohólicas, licorería *f* (*LAm*)

liquorice ['lɪkərɪs] N regaliz *m*, orozuz *m*

Lisbon ['lɪzbən] N Lisboa *f*

lisp [lɪsp] **ⓐ** N ceceo *m*; **to speak with a ~** cecear **ⓑ** VI cecear **ⓒ** VT decir ceceando

list¹ [lɪst] **ⓐ** N (*gen*) lista *f*; (= *catalogue*) catálogo *m*; **that job is at the top of my ~** para mí ese trabajo es lo primero *or* lo más importante **ⓑ** VT (= *include in list*) poner en una/la lista; (= *make a list of*) hacer una lista de; (*verbally*) enumerar; (*Fin*) cotizar (**at** a); (*Comput*) listar; **it is not ~ed** no aparece en la lista **ⓒ** CPD ➤ **list price** precio *m* de catálogo

list² [lɪst] VI (*Naut*) escorar; **to ~ badly** escorar de modo peligroso

listed ['lɪstɪd] ADJ ➤ **listed building** (*Brit*) edificio *m* protegido ➤ **listed company** empresa *f* con cotización

listen ['lɪsn] VI escuchar; **he wouldn't ~** no quiso escuchar; **~, I finish at one, why don't we have lunch together?** mira, yo termino a la una, ¿por qué no almorzamos juntos?; **to ~ to sth/sb** escuchar algo/a algn; **you never ~ to a word I say!** ¡nunca escuchas nada de lo que te digo!, ¡nunca me haces caso!; **we ~ed for footsteps approaching** estuvimos atentos por si oíamos venir a alguien
➤ **listen in** VI + ADV (= *eavesdrop*) escuchar; **to ~ in on** *or* **to a conversation** escuchar una conversación a hurtadillas

listener ['lɪsnəʳ] N (*gen*) oyente *mf*; (*Rad*) radioyente *mf*; **to be a good ~** saber escuchar

listeria [lɪs'tɪərɪə] N listeria *f*

listing ['lɪstɪŋ] N **1** (*gen, Comput*) listado *m* **2** (*Comm*) **they have a ~ on the Stock Exchange** cotizan en Bolsa **3** listings (= *publication*) cartelera *fsing*, guía *fsing* del ocio

listless ['lɪstlɪs] ADJ lánguido

lit [lɪt] PT, PP *of* **light¹**; **to be ~ up*** estar achispado*

Lit., lit.¹* [lɪt] N ABBR = **literature**

lit.² ABBR = **literal(ly)**

litany ['lɪtənɪ] N letanía *f*

liter ['liːtəʳ] N (*US*) litro *m*

literacy ['lɪtərəsɪ] N alfabetismo *m*, capacidad *f* de leer y escribir

literal ['lɪtərəl] **ⓐ** ADJ [*sense, translation*] literal **ⓑ** N (*Typ*) errata *f*

literally ['lɪtərəlɪ] ADV **1** (= *actually*) literalmente; **he's crazy, I mean ~** está loco, y lo digo en el verdadero sentido de la palabra **2** (= *word for word*) [*translate, mean*] literalmente, palabra por palabra; **to take sth ~** tomarse algo al pie de la letra

literary ['lɪtərərɪ] ADJ [*prize, award, work*] de literatura, literario; **~ circles** círculos *mpl* literarios

literate ['lɪtərɪt] ADJ que sabe leer y escribir; **highly ~** culto; **not very ~** poco culto, que tiene poca cultura

literature ['lɪtərɪtʃəʳ] N **1** (= *writings*) literatura *f* **2** (= *promotional material*) información *f*, publicidad *f*

lithe [laɪð] ADJ ágil

lithium ['lɪθɪəm] N litio *m*

lithograph ['lɪθəʊɡrɑːf] N litografía *f*

Lithuania [ˌlɪθjʊ'eɪnɪə] N Lituania *f*

Lithuanian [ˌlɪθjʊ'eɪnɪən] ADJ, N lituano/a *m/f*

litigation [ˌlɪtɪ'ɡeɪʃən] N litigio *m*, pleito *m*

litigious [lɪ'tɪdʒəs] ADJ litigioso

litmus test ['lɪtməsˌtest] N (*lit*) prueba *f* de tornasol; (*fig*) prueba *f* de fuego

litre, liter (*US*) ['liːtəʳ] N litro *m*

litter ['lɪtəʳ] **ⓐ** N **1** (= *rubbish*) basura *f*; (= *papers*) papeles *mpl* (tirados); **"no litter"** "prohibido arrojar basura" **2** (= *number of young*) camada *f*
3 cat ~ arena *f* higiénica (para gatos)
ⓑ VT **a pavement ~ed with papers** una acera sembrada de papeles; **a room ~ed with books** un cuarto con libros por todas partes
ⓒ CPD ➤ **litter bin** (*Brit*) papelera *f* ➤ **litter box** (*US*) = **litter tray** ➤ **litter lout*** persona que tira papeles o basura a la vía pública ➤ **litter tray** (*Brit*) lecho *m* de arena higiénica para animales domésticos

litterbug ['lɪtəbʌɡ] N (*US*) = **litter lout**

little¹ ['lɪtl] **ⓐ** ADJ **1** (= *small*) pequeño, chico (*LAm*); **when I was ~** cuando era pequeño, de pequeño; **the ~ ones** (= *children*) los pequeños; **she had a ~ girl yesterday** ayer tuvo una niñita; **a ~ book/boat/piece** un librito/barquito/trocito **2** (= *short*) corto; **a ~ walk** un paseo corto
3 (= *younger*) **her ~ brother** su hermano menor, su hermanito **ⓑ** CPD ➤ **little finger** dedo *m* meñique, meñique *m* ➤ **little toe** dedo *m* pequeño del pie

little² ['lɪtl] (*compar* **less**; *superl* **least**) **ⓐ** PRON **1** (= *not much*) poco; **that has ~ to do with it!** ¡eso tiene poco que ver!; **there was ~ we could do** apenas había nada que hacer; **as ~ as £5** cinco libras, nada más; **there's very ~ left**

queda muy poco; **to make ~ of sth** (= *play down*) quitar importancia a algo; (= *fail to exploit*) desaprovechar algo; **they made ~ of loading the huge boxes** cargaron las enormes cajas como si nada; **~ or nothing** poco o nada 2 (= *some*) **give me a ~** dame un poco; **a ~ of everything** un poco de todo; **~ by ~** poco a poco; **the ~ I have seen is excellent** lo poco que he visto me ha parecido excelente; **I did what ~ I could** hice lo poco que pude 3 (= *short time*) **they'll have to wait a ~** tendrán que esperar un poco; **for a ~** (durante) un rato

B ADJ 1 (= *not much*) poco; **there is ~ hope of finding them alive** hay pocas esperanzas de encontrarlos con vida; **so much to do, so ~ time** tanto que hacer y en tan poco tiempo; **I have very ~ money** tengo muy poco dinero 2 (= *some*) **a ~ wine** un poco de vino; **I speak a ~ Spanish** hablo un poco de español; **a ~ bit (of)** un poquito (de); **for a ~ time** *or* **while** un ratito

C ADV 1 (= *not much*) poco; **he reads ~** lee poco; **they spoke very ~** hablaron muy poco; **try to move as ~ as possible** intenta moverte lo menos posible; **(as) ~ as I like him, I must admit that ...** aunque me gusta muy poco, debo admitir que ...; **a ~ known fact** un hecho poco conocido; **~ more than** poco más que; **it's ~ short of a miracle** es casi un milagro 2 (= *somewhat*) algo; **we were a ~ surprised/happier** nos quedamos algo sorprendidos/más contentos; **a ~ better** un poco mejor, algo mejor; **a ~ less/more than ...** un poco menos/más que ...; **a ~ less/more milk** un poco menos/más de leche; **a ~ more slowly** un poco más despacio 3 (= *not at all*) **~ does he know that ...** no tiene la menor idea de que ... 4 (= *rarely*) poco; **I watch television very ~ nowadays** ahora veo la televisión muy poco

liturgy ['lɪtədʒɪ] N liturgia *f*

livable ['lɪvəbl] ADJ [*house*] habitable; [*life*] llevadero

live¹ [lɪv] **A** VI 1 vivir; **where do you ~?** ¿dónde vives?; **to ~ in a flat/in London** vivir en un piso/en Londres; **the times we ~ in** los tiempos en que vivimos, los tiempos que corremos; **she has only six months to ~** sólo le quedan seis meses de vida; **she ~d for her work** vivía por y para su trabajo; **I've got nothing left to ~ for** no tengo nada por lo que vivir; **to ~ for the moment** vivir al día; **to ~ with sb** vivir con algn; **I'd never be able to ~ with myself if ...** jamás podría vivir tranquilo *or* vivir con mi conciencia si ...; **✦ IDIOM to ~ and let ~** vivir y dejar vivir; **✦ PROV you ~ and learn** nunca te acostarás sin saber una cosa más 2 (= *survive*) sobrevivir; **you'll ~!** (*hum*) ¡de ésta no te mueres!; **he ~d to a ripe old age/to be 103** llegó a viejo/a cumplir 103 años 3 (*Brit**) (= *go, belong*) ir, guardarse; **where does the teapot ~?** ¿dónde va *or* se guarda la tetera? 4 (= *enjoy life*) **let's ~ a little!*** ¡vivamos la vida un poquito!*; **if you've never been to an opera, you haven't ~d*** si no has ido nunca a la ópera no sabes lo qué es vivir **B** VT [+ *life*] (*gen*) vivir; (*in particular way*) llevar; **to ~ life to the full** vivir la vida al máximo; **to ~ a life of luxury/crime** llevar una vida de lujos/de delincuencia; **how you ~ your life is your business** tu vida es cosa tuya ➤ **live down** VT + ADV **I thought I'd never ~ it down** pensé que no se iba a olvidar nunca ➤ **live in** VI + ADV [*servant, nanny*] vivir en la casa ➤ **live off** VI + PREP [+ *person*] vivir a costa de; [+ *income*] vivir de; [+ *food*] alimentarse de ➤ **live on A** VI + PREP 1 (= *subsist on*) **what does he ~ on?** ¿de qué vive?; **he ~s on £50 a week** vive con 50 libras por semana; **we have just enough to ~ on** tenemos lo justo para vivir 2 (= *feed on*) alimentarse de **B** VI + ADV [*person, memory, tradition*] seguir vivo ➤ **live through** VI + PREP 1 (= *experience*) vivir; **she has ~d through two world wars** ha vivido dos guerras mundiales 2 (= *survive*) sobrevivir ➤ **live together** VI + ADV (*in amity*) convivir; (*as lovers*) vivir juntos ➤ **live up** VT + ADV **✦ IDIOM to ~ it up*** (= *have fun*) pasárselo en grande*; (= *live in luxury*) darse la gran vida* ➤ **live up to** VI + PREP 1 (= *be true to*) vivir de acuerdo con; [+ *promises*] cumplir 2 (= *be equal to*) [+ *reputation, expectations*] estar a la altura de

live² [laɪv] **A** ADJ 1 (= *living*) [*animal, person*] vivo; **a real ~ duke** un duque de carne y hueso 2 (*Rad, TV*) [*broadcast, coverage*] en vivo, en directo; [*performance, show, recording*] en vivo; **performed before a ~ audience** interpretado delante del público 3 [*shell, ammunition*] cargado; [*bomb*] sin explotar 4 (*Elec*) [*cable, wire, appliance*] conectado, con corriente **B** ADV en vivo, en directo; **the match is brought to you ~ from Madrid** le ofrecemos el partido en vivo *or* en directo desde Madrid; **we'll be going ~ to Montreal later on** conectaremos con Montreal en directo más adelante **C** CPD ➤ **live wire** (*Elec*) alambre *m* conectado, alambre *m* con corriente; **I IDIOM he's a real ~ wire!** ¡es un torbellino!*, ¡tiene mucha marcha!* ➤ **live yoghurt** yogur *m* Bio®

lived-in ['lɪvd,ɪn] ADJ **the cushions give the room a ~ look** los cojines le dan un aspecto acogedor a la habitación

live-in ['lɪv,ɪn] ADJ [*servant*] interno ➤ **live-in lover** compañero/a *m/f*

livelihood ['laɪvlɪhʊd] N sustento *m*; **to earn a** *or* **one's ~** ganarse la vida *or* el sustento

lively ['laɪvlɪ] ADJ (*compar* **livelier**; *superl* **liveliest**) 1 [*person, personality*] vivaz, alegre; [*atmosphere, conversation, party, town, debate*] animado; [*dog*] juguetón; [*performance*] enérgico; [*description, style*] vivo, vívido; **things were getting quite ~** (= *heated*) el ambiente se estaba caldeando; **look ~!** ¡espabila! 2 (= *keen*) [*mind*] vivaz, inquieto; [*imagination*] vivo; **she took a ~ interest in everything** ponía un gran interés en todo

liver ['lɪvə'] **A** N hígado *m* **B** CPD [*disease*] hepático, del hígado ➤ **liver pâté** foie gras *m*, paté *m* de hígado ➤ **liver sausage** salchicha *f* de hígado ➤ **liver spots** manchas *fpl* de la vejez

livery ['lɪvərɪ] N (= *uniform*) librea *f*; (*on vans etc*) colores *mpl*

lives [laɪvz] NPL *of* **life**

livestock ['laɪvstɒk] N ganado *m*

livid ['lɪvɪd] ADJ 1 (*) (= *furious*) furioso, furibundo* (**about** por) 2 (*in colour*) (= *pale*) lívido; [*bruise, scar*] amoratado

living ['lɪvɪŋ] **A** ADJ vivo; **Ireland's greatest ~ playwright** el mejor dramaturgo irlandés vivo *or* aún con vida; **the worst drought in** *or* **within ~ memory** la peor sequía que se recuerda **B** N 1 (= *livelihood*) **to earn a ~** ganarse la vida; **what do you do for a ~?** ¿cómo te ganas la vida?, ¿en qué trabajas?; **now he has to work for a ~** ahora tiene que trabajar para ganarse la vida 2 (= *way of life*) vida *f*; **clean ~** vida *f* ordenada **C** NPL **the ~** los vivos **D** CPD ➤ **living area** zona *f* destinada a la vivienda ➤ **living conditions** condiciones *fpl* de vida ➤ **living expenses** gastos *mpl* de mantenimiento ➤ **living quarters** (*for students*) residencia *f*; (*for soldiers, servants, staff*) dependencias *fpl* ➤ **living room** sala *f* de estar, living *m* ➤ **living standards** nivel *msing* de vida ➤ **living wage** salario *m* de subsistencia; **£20 a week isn't a ~ wage** con 20 libras a la semana no se puede vivir

lizard ['lɪzəd] N (*large*) lagarto *m*; (*small*) lagartija *f*

llama ['lɑːmə] N llama *f*

LLB N ABBR (= **Bachelor of Laws**) Ldo./Lda. *m/f* en Dcho.

load [ləʊd] **A** N 1 (= *cargo*) carga *f*; (= *weight*) peso *m*; **"maximum load: 17 tons"** "carga máxima: 17 toneladas"; **the lorry had a full ~ of** el camión iba lleno; **they were forced to carry heavy ~s** les obligaron a cargar con pesos pesados; **I put another ~ in the washing machine** puse otra vez la lavadora 2 (= *burden*) carga *f*; **he finds his new responsibilities a heavy ~** sus nuevas responsabilidades le resultan una gran carga; **that's (taken) a ~ off my mind!** ¡eso me quita un peso de encima! 3 **loads*** cantidad* *fsing*, un montón*; **we've got ~s of time** tenemos cantidad *or* un montón de tiempo*; **I've got ~s (of them) at home** tengo cantidad *or* un montón en casa* 4 **a ~ of*: the book is a ~ of rubbish** el libro es una basura*, el libro no vale nada; **he talks a ~ of rubbish** no dice más

que tonterías; **get a ~ of this!**** (= *look*) ¡échale un vistazo a esto!*, ¡mírame esto!; (= *listen*) ¡escucha esto! **Ⓑ** VT cargar; **the branch was ~ed with fruit** la rama estaba cargada de fruta; **we're ~ed with debts** estamos cargados *or* agobiados de deudas
➤ **load down** VT + ADV cargar (**with** de)
➤ **load up** **Ⓐ** VT + ADV cargar (**with** de) **Ⓑ** VI + ADV [*vehicle*] cargarse; [*person*] cargar

load-bearing ['ləʊd,beərɪŋ] ADJ [*beam*] maestro; [*wall*] de carga

loaded ['ləʊdɪd] ADJ **1** (= *full*) cargado **2** [*remark, question*] lleno de implicaciones, cargado de implicaciones **3** [*dice*] cargado; **✦ IDIOM the dice are ~ against him** todo está en su contra **4** (*) (= *rich*) **✦ IDIOM to be ~** estar forrado de dinero*, estar podrido de dinero* **5 ✦ IDIOM to be ~ for bear** (*US*) estar preparado para el ataque

loaf¹ [ləʊf] N (*pl* **loaves**) [*of bread*] pan *m* de molde; (= *French bread*) barra *f*; **✦ IDIOM use your ~!** (*Brit**) ¡espabílate!; ⇨ *RHYMING SLANG*

loaf² [ləʊf] VI (*also* **~ about, ~ around**) holgazanear, flojear (*LAm*)

loafer ['ləʊfə'] N (*esp US*) (= *shoe*) mocasín *m*

loan [ləʊn] **Ⓐ** N (*between individuals*) préstamo *m*; (*from bank*) crédito *m*, préstamo *m*; **it's on ~** está prestado; **I had it on ~ from the company** me lo prestó la empresa; **she is on ~ to another department** presta temporalmente sus servicios en otra sección; **I asked for the ~ of the book** le pedí prestado el libro **Ⓑ** VT prestar **Ⓒ** CPD ➤ **loan shark** prestamista *mf* usurero/a, tiburón *m* ➤ **loan word** préstamo *m*

loath [ləʊθ] ADJ **to be ~ to do sth** estar poco dispuesto a hacer algo, ser reacio a hacer algo

loathe [ləʊð] VT detestar, odiar; **I ~ doing it** detesto *or* odio hacerlo; **he ~s being corrected** detesta que se le corrija

loathing ['ləʊðɪŋ] N odio *m*; **it fills me with ~** me repugna

loathsome ['ləʊðsəm] ADJ [*thing, person*] detestable, odioso; [*smell, disease*] repugnante

loaves [ləʊvz] NPL *of* **loaf¹**

lob [lɒb] **Ⓐ** VT [+ *ball*] volear por alto; **to ~ sth over to sb** tirar *or* echar algo a algn **Ⓑ** N lob *m*, globo *m* **Ⓒ** VI lanzar un globo

lobby ['lɒbɪ] **Ⓐ** N **1** (= *entrance hall*) vestíbulo *m*; (= *corridor*) pasillo *m*; (= *anteroom*) antecámara *f* **2** (= *pressure group*) grupo *m* de presión; **the environmental ~** el grupo de presión ecologista **Ⓑ** VT **to ~ one's member of parliament** ejercer presiones sobre su diputado **Ⓒ** VI ejercer presiones, presionar; **to ~ for a reform** presionar para conseguir una reforma

lobbyist ['lɒbɪɪst] N cabildero/a *m/f*

lobe [ləʊb] N lóbulo *m*

lobster ['lɒbstə'] N langosta *f* ➤ **lobster pot** nasa *f*, langostera *f*

local ['ləʊkəl] **Ⓐ** ADJ **1** (= *of the area*) [*custom, newspaper, radio*] local; [*school, shop, doctor*] del barrio; [*bus, train*] urbano; [*news, weather forecast*] regional; **the ~ community** el vecindario, el barrio; (*wider*) la zona, el área; **to be of ~ interest** ser de interés local; **he's a ~ man** es de aquí; **~ residents** los residentes del barrio *or* de la zona **2** (= *municipal*) [*administration, taxes, elections*] municipal **3** (*Med*) [*pain*] localizado **Ⓑ** N **1** (*) (= *local resident*) **the ~s** los vecinos; (*wider*) la gente de la zona; **he's a ~** es de aquí **2** (*Brit**) (= *pub*) bar *m* de la zona donde alguien vive **3** (*) (*also* **~ anaesthetic**) anestesia *f* local **4** (*US*) (= *train, bus etc*) tren, autobús etc que hace parada en todas las estaciones **Ⓒ** CPD ➤ **local anaesthetic, local anesthetic** (*US*) anestesia *f* local ➤ **local authority** (*Brit, New Zealand*) gobierno *m* local; [*of city, town*] ayuntamiento *m* ➤ **local education authority** secretaría *f* municipal de educación ➤ **local government** (*Brit*) administración *f* municipal; (*US*) gobierno *m* local; [*of city, town*] ayuntamiento *m* ➤ **local government elections** elecciones *fpl* municipales

locality [ləʊˈkælɪtɪ] N localidad *f*

localize ['ləʊkəlaɪz] VT localizar

locally ['ləʊkəlɪ] ADV (= *nearby*) en las cercanías; (= *in the region*) en la región; (= *in the area*) en la zona; (= *in the locality*) en la localidad; (= *in local shops*) en las tiendas del barrio/de la zona *etc*; (*on a local level*) a nivel local; **she's very well known ~** es muy conocida en el barrio *or* la zona *or* la localidad *etc*; **to be known ~ as** conocerse localmente como

locate [ləʊˈkeɪt] **Ⓐ** VT **1** (= *situate*) situar, ubicar (*esp LAm*); **to be ~d at** estar situado en, estar ubicado en (*esp LAm*) **2** (= *find*) localizar; **we ~d it eventually** por fin lo encontramos **Ⓑ** VI (*esp US*) establecerse

location [ləʊˈkeɪʃən] N **1** (= *place*) lugar *m*; **the house is set in a beautiful ~** la casa está situada en un lugar precioso **2** (= *positioning*) [*of building*] situación *f*, ubicación *f*; **"central location near the sea"** (*in brochure*) "situación *f or* ubicación *f* céntrica próxima al mar" **3** (= *exact position*) [*of missing person, suspect*] paradero *m*; [*of airplane, ship*] posición *f* **4** (= *finding*) localización *f* **5** (*Cine*) **to be on ~ in Mexico** estar rodando exteriores en México; **to film on ~** filmar en exteriores

loch [lɒx] N (*Scot*) lago *m*; (= *sea loch*) ría *f*, brazo *m* de mar

lock¹ [lɒk] N [*of hair*] mecha *f*, mechón *m*; (= *ringlet*) bucle *m*; **locks** (*poet*) cabellos *mpl*

lock² [lɒk] **Ⓐ** N **1** (*on door, box, safe*) cerradura *f*, chapa *f* (*LAm*); (*on steering wheel*) tope *m*, retén *m*; **to put sth under ~ and key** guardar algo bajo llave; **✦ IDIOM ~, stock, and barrel** con todo incluido **2** (*on canal*) esclusa *f* **Ⓑ** VT **1** (*with key*) cerrar con llave; **to ~ sth/sb in a place** encerrar algo/a algn en un lugar; **she ~ed herself in her bedroom** se encerró en su habitación; **he got ~ed in the toilet** se quedó encerrado en el baño **2** (= *immobilize*) [+ *steering wheel*] (*to prevent theft*) bloquear, inmovilizar; (= *jam*) bloquear; (*Comput*) [+ *screen*] desactivar **3** (= *entwine*) (*usu pass*) **they were ~ed in each other's arms** estaban unidos en un abrazo; **the armies were ~ed in combat** los ejércitos luchaban encarnizadamente; **✦ IDIOM to ~ horns with sb** enzarzarse en una disputa *or* pelea con algn **Ⓒ** VI **1** [*door, box, safe*] cerrarse con llave **2** (*Mech*) trabarse; **the front wheels of the car ~ed** las ruedas delanteras se trabaron **Ⓓ** CPD ➤ **lock gate** puerta *f* de esclusa ➤ **lock keeper** esclusero/a *m/f*
➤ **lock away** VT + ADV (*gen*) guardar bajo llave; [+ *criminal, mental patient*] encerrar
➤ **lock in** VT + ADV dejar encerrado dentro; **to ~ o.s. in** encerrarse
➤ **lock out** VT + ADV cerrar la puerta a, dejar fuera con la puerta cerrada; **to find o.s. ~ed out** estar fuera sin llave para abrir la puerta; **the workers were ~ed out** los obreros se quedaron sin trabajo por cierre patronal
➤ **lock up** VT + ADV [+ *object*] guardar bajo llave; [+ *house*] cerrar con llave; [+ *criminal*] encarcelar; [+ *funds*] inmovilizar; **you ought to be ~ed up!** ¡irás a parar a la cárcel! **Ⓑ** VI + ADV echar la llave

locker ['lɒkə'] N cajón *m* con llave; (*for left luggage*) casillero *m* (de consigna), consigna *f* automática; (*US*) cámara *f* de frío; (*of gymnasium*) taquilla *f* ➤ **locker room** vestuario *m*

locket ['lɒkɪt] N relicario *m*, guardapelo *m*

lockjaw ['lɒkdʒɔ:] N trismo *m*

lockout ['lɒkaʊt] N cierre *m* patronal

locksmith ['lɒksmɪθ] N cerrajero/a *m/f*

lock-up ['lɒkʌp] N **1** (*US**) (= *prison*) cárcel *f* **2** (*Brit*) (*also* **~ garage**) garaje *m*, cochera *f* (*LAm*)

locomotive [,ləʊkəˈməʊtɪv] N locomotora *f*, máquina *f*

locum ['ləʊkəm] N (*also* **~ tenens**) (*Brit*) interino/a *m/f*

locust ['ləʊkəst] N langosta *f*

lodge [lɒdʒ] **Ⓐ** N (*at gate of park*) casa *f* del guarda; [*of* *porter*] portería f; (*Freemasonry*) logia f **B** VT [+ *person*] alojar, hospedar; [+ *complaint*] presentar; [+ *appeal*] interponer; **the bullet is ~d in the lung** la bala se ha alojado en el pulmón **C** VI (= *reside*) alojarse, hospedarse (**with** con, en casa de); (= *get stuck*) alojarse, meterse

lodger ['lɒdʒəʳ] N inquilino/a m/f (*de habitación en una casa particular*), huésped(a) m/f; **she takes ~s** alquila habitaciones en su casa

lodging ['lɒdʒɪŋ] N alojamiento m, hospedaje m; **lodgings** alojamiento msing

loft [lɒft] N **1** (= *attic*) desván m **2** (= *apartment*) loft m

lofty ['lɒftɪ] ADJ (*compar* **loftier**; *superl* **loftiest**) **1** [*ceiling, building, tower*] alto, elevado; **he rose to a ~ position in the organization** ascendió a una posición elevada dentro de la organización **2** [*aim, ideal*] elevado, noble **3** (= *haughty*) ~ **air/manner** aire m de superioridad, altivez f

log¹ [lɒg] **A** N **1** (*of wood*) tronco m, leño m **2** = **logbook B** VT (*Naut, Aer*) anotar, apuntar **C** VI cortar (y transportar) troncos **D** CPD ► **log cabin** cabaña f de troncos *or* de madera ► **log fire** fuego m de leña ► **log in A** VI + ADV acceder al sistema, entrar en el sistema **B** VT + ADV meter en el sistema ► **log off** VI + ADV, VT + ADV = **log out** ► **log on** VI + ADV, VT + ADV = **log in** ► **log out A** VI + ADV salir del sistema, terminar de operar **B** VT + ADV sacar del sistema

log² [lɒg] **A** N ABBR (= **logarithm**) logaritmo m **B** CPD ► **log tables** tablas *fpl* de logaritmos

logarithm ['lɒgərɪθəm] N logaritmo m

logbook ['lɒgbʊk] N (*ship's*) cuaderno m de bitácora, diario m de navegación; (*Brit*) (*for car*) documentación f

logger ['lɒgəʳ] N **1** (= *dealer*) maderero/a m/f, negociante mf en maderas **2** (*US*) (= *lumberjack*) leñador(a) m/f

loggerheads ['lɒgəhedz] NPL (*esp Brit*): **to be at ~ with sb** estar a matar con algn, estar picado con algn

logic ['lɒdʒɪk] N lógica f; **I can't see the ~ of it** no le veo la lógica

logical ['lɒdʒɪkəl] ADJ lógico

logically ['lɒdʒɪkəlɪ] ADV (= *by a logical process*) lógicamente; [*think, speak, act*] de manera lógica, de forma lógica; [*designed, laid out*] con lógica; **~ enough** como es lógico

login ['lɒgɪn] N login m

logistics [lɒ'dʒɪstɪks] NSING logística f

logo ['ləʊgəʊ] N logo m, logotipo m

loin [lɔɪn] N [*of meat*] lomo m ► **loin chop** chuleta f de lomo

loincloth ['lɔɪnklɒθ] N taparrabo m, taparrabos m inv

loiter ['lɔɪtəʳ] VI (= *idle*) merodear; (= *lag behind*) rezagarse; (= *dally*) entretenerse; **to ~ (with intent)** (*Jur*) merodear con fines sospechosos *or* delictivos

loll [lɒl] VI [*head*] colgar, caer; **to ~ against** recostarse en ► **loll about, loll around** VI + ADV repantigarse

lollipop ['lɒlɪpɒp] N pirulí m, chupete m (*LAm*) ► **lollipop man/lady** (*Brit**) *persona encargada de ayudar a los niños a cruzar la calle*

LOLLIPOP MAN/LADY

Se llama **lollipop man** o **lollipop lady** a la persona encargada de parar el tráfico en las calles cercanas a los colegios en el Reino Unido, para que los niños las crucen sin peligro. Suelen ser personas ya jubiladas, que van vestidas con una gabardina fosforescente y que llevan una señal de stop en un poste portátil, lo que recuerda por su forma a una piruleta, y de ahí su nombre.

---

lolly ['lɒlɪ] N **1** (*esp Brit*) = **lollipop**; *see also* **ice 2** (*Brit**) (= *money*) pasta* f, lana f (*LAm**)

London ['lʌndən] **A** N Londres m **B** CPD londinense

Londoner ['lʌndənəʳ] N londinense mf

lone [ləʊn] ADJ (= *solitary*) solitario ► **lone parent** (*esp Brit*)

(= *woman*) madre f sin pareja; (= *man*) padre m sin pareja

loneliness ['ləʊnlɪnɪs] N soledad f

lonely ['ləʊnlɪ] ADJ (*compar* **lonelier**; *superl* **loneliest**) [*person*] solo; [*life, place, time*] solitario; (= *remote*) [*village, house*] solitario, aislado; **to feel ~** sentirse solo ► **lonely hearts (column)** sección f de corazones solitarios

loner ['ləʊnəʳ] N solitario/a m/f

lonesome ['ləʊnsəm] ADJ (*esp US*) [*person*] solo; **to be/feel ~** sentirse solo

long¹ [lɒŋ] (*compar* **~er**; *superl* **~est**) **A** ADJ **1** (*in size*) [*dress, hair*] largo; **it's six metres ~** tiene seis metros de largo; **to pull a ~ face** poner cara larga; **to get ~er** [*queue*] hacerse más largo; [*hair*] crecer (más); **how ~ is it?** [*table, hallway, piece of material, stick*] ¿cuánto mide de largo?; ✦ IDIOMS **a list as ~ as your arm*** una lista larguísima; **not by a ~ chalk** ni con mucho; **he's a bit ~ in the tooth*** es bastante viejo ya

2 (*in distance*) [*journey*] largo; **it's a ~ way** está lejos; **it's a ~ way to the shops** las tiendas están lejos

3 (*in time*) [*film, holiday*] largo; [*visit*] prolongado; [*wait*] largo, prolongado; **there will be ~ delays** habrá grandes retrasos, habrá retrasos considerables; **the days are getting ~er** los días se están alargando; **how ~ is the film?** ¿cuánto (tiempo) dura la película?; **the reply was not ~ in coming** la respuesta no tardó en llegar; **it will be a ~ job** será un trabajo que llevará mucho tiempo; **at ~ last** por fin; **he's not ~ for this world*** no le queda mucho de vida; **in the ~ run** a la larga; **a ~ time ago** hace mucho tiempo; **it takes a ~ time** lleva mucho tiempo

B ADV **1** (= *a long time*) **don't be ~!** ¡vuelve pronto!; **I shan't be ~** (*in finishing*) termino pronto, no tardo; (*in returning*) vuelvo pronto, no tardo; **will you be ~?** ¿vas a tardar mucho?; **we didn't stay ~** nos quedamos poco tiempo; **have you been waiting ~?** ¿hace mucho que esperas?; **I have ~ believed that ...** creo desde hace tiempo que ..., hace tiempo que creo que ...; **he died ~ after his wife** murió mucho tiempo después que su mujer; **how ~ ago was it?** ¿cuánto tiempo hace de eso?; **not ~ ago** no hace mucho (tiempo); **all day ~** todo el (santo) día; **~ before** mucho antes; **~ before you came** mucho antes de que llegaras; **~ before now** hace mucho tiempo; **not ~ before** poco antes; **not ~ before the war** poco antes de la guerra; **not ~ before his wife died** poco antes de que muriera su mujer; **they left ~ before ~** se marcharon muy pronto; **we won't stay for ~** nos quedaremos un rato nada más; **are you going away for ~?** ¿te vas para mucho tiempo?; **he hesitated, but not for ~** dudó, pero sólo por un instante; **how ~ will you be?** (*in finishing*) ¿cuánto (tiempo) tardarás?; (*in returning*) ¿cuánto tiempo te quedarás?; **how ~ have you been here?** ¿cuánto tiempo llevas aquí?; **how ~ have you been learning Spanish?** ¿desde cuándo llevas aprendiendo español?; **how ~ is it since you saw her?** ¿cuánto tiempo hace que no la ves?; **he hasn't ~ to live** no le queda mucho de vida; **~ live the King!** ¡viva el rey!; **it's not ~ since he died** no hace mucho que murió, murió hace poco; **so ~!** (*esp US**) ¡hasta luego!; **it won't take ~** no tardará mucho; **it didn't take him ~ to realize that ...** no tardó en darse cuenta de que ...

2 ~er más tiempo; **we stayed ~er than you** quedamos más tiempo que vosotros; **wait a little ~er** espera un poco más; **how much ~er do we have to wait?** ¿hasta cuándo tenemos que esperar?; **I can't stand it any ~er** ya no lo aguanto más; **no ~er** ya no; **he no ~er comes** ya no viene

3 ~est: six months at the ~est seis meses, como máximo *or* como mucho

4 **as** *or* **so ~ as** (= *while*) mientras; (= *provided that*) siempre que; **as ~ as I live** mientras viva; **stay (for) as ~ as you like** quédate hasta cuando quieras; **as ~ as (is) necessary** el tiempo que haga falta, lo que haga falta

C N **the ~ and the short of it is that ...** en resumidas cuentas, es que ..., concretamente, es que ...

D CPD ► **long division** división f larga ► **long johns** calzoncillos *mpl* largos ► **long jump** salto m de longitud ► **long jumper** saltador(a) m/f de longitud ► **long shot*: it's a ~ shot** dudo que resulte; ✦ IDIOM **not by a ~ shot** ni con mucho ► **the long term: in** *or* **over the ~ term** a largo plazo ► **long trousers** (*as opposed to shorts*) pantalones *mpl* largos ► **the long vac***, **the long vacation** (*Brit Univ*) las vacaciones de verano ► **long wave** onda f larga; (*used as* *adj*) de onda larga

long² [lɒŋ] VI **to ~ for sth** anhelar algo, desear algo; **to ~ to do sth** tener muchas ganas de hacer algo, estar deseando hacer algo; **to ~ for sb to do sth** desear que algn haga algo

long-distance ['lɒŋ'dɪstəns] Ⓐ ADJ [*flight*] largo, de larga distancia; [*race, runner*] de fondo Ⓑ ADV **to call sb ~** hacer una llamada de larga distancia, poner una conferencia a algn (*Sp*) Ⓒ CPD ➤ **long-distance call** llamada *f* de larga distancia, conferencia *f* (*Sp*)

long-drawn-out ['lɒŋdrɔːn'aʊt] ADJ interminable

longevity [lɒn'dʒevɪtɪ] N longevidad *f*

long-grain ['lɒŋɡreɪn] ADJ [*rice*] de grano largo

long-haired ['lɒŋ'heəd] ADJ de pelo largo

longhand ['lɒŋhænd] Ⓐ N **in ~** escrito a mano Ⓑ ADV a mano

long-haul ['lɒŋ,hɔːl] ADJ [*flight*] de larga distancia

longing ['lɒŋɪŋ] Ⓐ N (*for place*) nostalgia *f*, añoranza *f*; (*for past time*) añoranza *f*; (*for person, thing*) anhelo *m*; **he felt a ~ for his homeland** sentía nostalgia por su país, añoraba su país; **people have a ~ for normality** la gente anhela la normalidad Ⓑ ADJ [*look*] anhelante

longingly ['lɒŋɪŋlɪ] ADV (= *yearningly*) con anhelo, con ansia; (= *nostalgically*) con nostalgia, con añoranza

longitude ['lɒŋɡɪtjuːd] N longitud *f*

long-lasting ['lɒŋ'lɑːstɪŋ] ADJ duradero

long-legged ['lɒŋ'legɪd] ADJ [*person*] de piernas largas; [*animal*] de patas largas; [*bird*] zancudo

long-life ['lɒŋ'laɪf] ADJ de larga duración

long-lost ['lɒŋ'lɒst] ADJ perdido hace mucho tiempo

long-range ['lɒŋ'reɪndʒ] ADJ [*gun, missile*] de largo alcance; [*forecast, plan*] a largo plazo

long-running ['lɒŋ'rʌnɪŋ] ADJ [*dispute*] largo; [*play*] taquillero, que se mantiene mucho tiempo en la cartelera; [*programme*] que lleva mucho tiempo en antena

longshoreman ['lɒŋʃɔːmən] N (*pl* **longshoremen**) (*US*) estibador *m*

long-sighted ['lɒŋ'saɪtɪd] ADJ (*Brit Med*) hipermétrope, présbita; (*fig*) previsor

long-sleeved ['lɒŋsliːvd] ADJ de manga larga

long-standing ['lɒŋ'stændɪŋ] ADJ antiguo

long-stay ['lɒŋsteɪ] ADJ (*Brit*) [*car park*] para aparcamiento *or* (*LAm*) estacionamiento prolongado; [*hospital*] para enfermos de larga duración; [*patient*] de larga duración

long-suffering ['lɒŋ'sʌfərɪŋ] ADJ sufrido

long-term ['lɒŋ'tɜːm] ADJ [*effect, investment, care, solution*] a largo plazo; **they're in a ~ relationship** llevan tiempo juntos; **the ~ unemployed** *las personas que llevan mucho tiempo sin trabajo*

long-wearing ['lɒŋ'weərɪŋ] ADJ (*US*) resistente, duradero

long-winded ['lɒŋ'wɪndɪd] ADJ [*person*] prolijo; [*speech, explanation*] prolijo, interminable

loo* [luː] N (*Brit*) retrete *m*, wáter *m* (*Sp*), baño *m* (*LAm*)

loofah ['luːfə] N esponja *f* de lufa

look [lʊk] Ⓐ N **1** (= *glance*) vistazo *m*; **to have** *or* **take a ~ at sth** echar un vistazo a algo; **take a ~ at this!** ¡mira esto!, ¡échale un vistazo a esto!; **let me have a ~** déjame ver; **shall we have a ~ round the town?** ¿damos una vuelta por la ciudad?; **to take a good ~ at sth** mirar algo detenidamente; **to take a long hard ~ at o.s.** examinarse a sí mismo detenidamente

2 (= *expression*) mirada *f*; **he gave me a furious ~** me miró furioso, me lanzó una mirada furiosa; **we got some very odd ~s** la gente nos miró extrañada; **a ~ of despair** una cara de desesperación; **if ~s could kill ...*** si las miradas mataran ...

3 (= *search*) **to have a ~ for sth** buscar algo; **have another ~!** ¡vuelve a buscar!

4 (= *air, appearance*) aire *m*, aspecto *m*, pinta* *f*; **he had a sad ~** tenía un aspecto *or* aire triste; **he had the ~ of a sailor** tenía aire de marinero; **by the ~(s) of it*** a juzgar por las apariencias; **by the ~(s) of him ...*** viéndole, se diría que ...; **I don't like the ~ of him*** me cae mal, no me fío de él; **I don't like the ~ of it*** no me gusta nada

5 looks (= *attractiveness*) **~s aren't everything** la belleza no lo es todo; **she has kept her ~s** sigue tan guapa como siempre

6 (= *fashion*) moda *f*, estilo *m*; **I need a new ~** quiero cambiar de imagen

Ⓑ VI **1** (= *see, glance*) mirar; **look!** ¡mira!; **~ here!** ¡oye!; **just ~!** ¡mira!, ¡fíjate!; **I'll ~ and see** voy a ver; **to ~ into sb's eyes** mirar a los ojos a algn; **to ~ the other way** (= *avert one's eyes*) apartar la vista; (*fig*) hacer como que no se da cuenta; ✦ IDIOMS **to ~ down one's nose at sth/sb** menospreciar algo/a algn; **to be ~ing over sb's shoulder** estar siempre vigilando a algn; ✦ PROV **~ before you leap** mira bien lo que haces

2 (= *search*) buscar; **~ again!** ¡vuelve a buscar!

3 (= *seem, appear*) parecer, verse (*LAm*); **he ~s happy/tired** parece contento/cansado; **he ~s about 60 (years old)** aparenta tener alrededor de los 60 años; **to ~ one's age** aparentar *or* representar su edad; **it ~s all right to me** me parece que está bien; **it will ~ bad** (*fig*) quedará mal; **he just does it to ~ big*** lo hace sólo para impresionar; **they made me ~ a fool** me hicieron quedar como un idiota; **he ~s good in a uniform** está muy guapo en uniforme; **Manchester United are ~ing good for the championship** el Manchester United tiene muchas posibilidades de ganar el campeonato; **it ~s good on you** te sienta bien; **she wasn't ~ing herself** parecía otra, no parecía la misma; **how does it ~ to you?** ¿qué te parece?; **how do I ~?** ¿cómo estoy?; **she's 70 but doesn't ~ it** tiene 70 años pero no los aparenta *or* representa; **~ lively!*** ¡muévete!*; **that cake ~s nice** ese pastel tiene buena pinta*; **that hairstyle makes her ~ old** ese peinado la hace parece mayor; **to ~ the part** (*fig*) parecerlo; **how pretty you ~!** ¡qué guapa estás!; **it ~s promising** parece prometedor; **to make sb ~ small** (*fig*) rebajar a algn; **to ~ well** tener buena cara

4 to ~ like sb (= *resemble*) parecerse a algn; **this photo doesn't ~ like him** la foto no se le parece, en esta foto no parece él **4.2** (= *seem, appear*) **what does she ~ like?** ¿cómo es físicamente?; **it ~s like cheese to me** a mí me parece (que es) queso; **the festival ~s like being lively** la fiesta se anuncia animada; **it ~s like rain** parece que va a llover; **it certainly ~s like it** parece que sí

5 it ~s as if *or* **as though the train will be late** parece que el tren va a llegar tarde; **try to ~ as if** *or* **as though you're glad to see me** haz como que te alegras de verme

6 (= *face*) **it ~s onto the garden** da al jardín; **it ~s south** [*house*] mira hacia el sur, está orientada hacia el sur

Ⓒ VT **1** (= *look at*) **to ~ sb (straight) in the eye** mirar directamente a los ojos de algn; **I would never be able to ~ her in the face again** no podría resistir su mirada, siempre me avergonzaría al verla; **to ~ sb up and down** mirar a algn de arriba abajo

2 (= *pay attention to*) **~ how she does it** fíjate cómo lo hace; **~ what you've done now!** ¡mira lo que has hecho!; **~ where you're going!** ¡fíjate por donde vas!; **~ who's here!** ¡mira quién está aquí!

➤ **look after** VI + PREP **1** (= *take care of*) [+ *invalid, animal, plant*] cuidar, cuidar de; [+ *one's possessions*] velar por; **he can ~ after himself** sabe cuidar de *or* valerse por sí mismo **2** (= *mind*) [+ *child*] vigilar, cuidar; [+ *shop, business*] encargarse de; **to ~ after sth for sb** (= *watch over*) vigilar algo a algn; (= *keep temporarily*) guardar algo a algn

➤ **look ahead** VI + ADV (*in front*) mirar hacia delante; (*to future*) hacer proyectos para el futuro

➤ **look around** Ⓐ VI + ADV **1** (= *look about one*) mirar a su alrededor **2** (= *turn*) volver la cabeza, volverse **3** (*in shop*) mirar; **we're just ~ing around** estamos mirando solamente; **do you mind if we ~ around?** ¿le importa que echemos un vistazo? **4** (= *search*) **to ~ around for** buscar Ⓑ VI + PREP [+ *town, factory*] visitar, recorrer

➤ **look at** VI + PREP **1** (= *observe*) mirar; **just ~ at this mess!** ¡mira qué desorden!; **to ~ at him you would never think that ...** por la apariencia nunca pensarías que ...; **it isn't much to ~ at** no es muy bonito; **~ at how she does it** fíjate cómo lo hace

2 (= *consider*) [+ *alternatives*] considerar, examinar; [+ *problem*] estudiar; **it depends (on) how you ~ at it**

depende de cómo se enfoca la cuestión, depende del punto de vista de uno; **whichever way you ~ at it** se mire por donde se mire; **I wouldn't even ~ at the job** no aceptaría el puesto por nada del mundo
3 (= check) [+ patient, wound, heart] examinar; [+ engine, spelling] revisar
4 (*) (= have in prospect) **you're ~ing at a minimum of £200** calcula 200 libras como mínimo
➤ **look away** VI + ADV apartar la mirada (**from** de)
➤ **look back** VI + ADV **1** (= look behind) mirar hacia atrás **2** (= remember) pensar en el pasado; **~ing back, I'm surprised ...** pensándolo ahora, me sorprende que ...; **to ~ back on** or **at** [+ event, period] recordar, rememorar; **after that he never ~ed back** (esp Brit) desde entonces todo le ha ido sobre ruedas
➤ **look down** VI + ADV (= lower eyes) bajar la mirada; (= look downward) mirar hacia abajo
➤ **look down on** VI + PREP **1** (= despise) despreciar **2** (= overlook) dominar; **the castle ~s down on the town** el castillo domina la ciudad
➤ **look for** VI + PREP **1** (= seek) buscar; **to be ~ing for trouble*** andar buscando camorra* **2** (= expect) [+ praise, reward] esperar
➤ **look forward to** VI + PREP [+ event] esperar con ansia, esperar con impaciencia; **we're ~ing forward to the journey** tenemos muchas ganas de hacer el viaje, estamos deseando hacer el viaje; **to ~ forward to doing sth** tener muchas ganas de or estar deseando hacer algo; **~ing forward to hearing from you ...** a la espera de sus noticias ...
➤ **look in** VI + ADV **1** (= see in) mirar por dentro **2** (= visit) pasar or caer por casa; **to ~ in on sb** pasar a ver a algn
➤ **look into** VI + PREP [+ matter, possibility] estudiar, investigar
➤ **look on** Ⓐ VI + ADV mirar (como espectador) Ⓑ VI + PREP considerar; **I ~ on him as a friend** lo considero un amigo
➤ **look out** Ⓐ VI + ADV **1** (= look outside) mirar fuera; **to ~ out of the window** mirar por la ventana; **it ~s out on to the garden** da al jardín **2** (= take care) tener cuidado; **~ out!** ¡cuidado!, ¡aguas! (Mex) Ⓑ VT + ADV (Brit) (= search for) buscar; (= find) encontrar
➤ **look out for** VI + PREP **1** (= watch for) **to ~ out for sth/sb** esperar algo/a algn, estar atento a algo/algn; **do ~ out for pickpockets** ten mucho ojo con los carteristas **2** (*) (= look after) [+ person] cuidar; **to ~ out for o.s.** cuidar de sí mismo, cuidarse; **we ~ out for each other** nos cuidamos el uno al otro, cuidamos el uno del otro
➤ **look over** VT + ADV (gen) echar un vistazo a; (= examine) examinar
➤ **look round** VI + ADV, VI + PREP (Brit) = **look around**
➤ **look through** VI + PREP **1** [+ window] mirar por; **he ~ed right through me** me miró sin verme, me miró como si no existiera **2** (= search) registrar; (= leaf through) hojear; (= re-read) revisar
➤ **look to** VI + PREP **1** (= turn to) contar con, recurrir a; **it's no good ~ing to me for help** es inútil recurrir a mí en busca de ayuda; **to ~ to sb to do sth** esperar que algn haga algo, contar con algn para hacer algo **2** (= think of) **we must ~ to the future** tenemos que pensar en el futuro or mirar hacia adelante **3** (= attend to) ocuparse de, mirar por
➤ **look up** Ⓐ VI + ADV **1** (= glance up) levantar or alzar la vista **2** (= improve) mejorar; **things are ~ing up** las cosas van mejor Ⓑ VT + ADV **1** [+ information] buscar **2** [+ person] ir a visitar
➤ **look upon** VI + PREP = **look on** B
➤ **look up to** VI + PREP respetar, admirar

lookalike ['lʊkəˌlaɪk] N doble mf

look-in* ['lʊkɪn] N (Brit) **to get a ~** tener una oportunidad, tener chance (LAm); **we never got** or **had a ~** [losers] nunca tuvimos posibilidades de ganar

looking-glass† ['lʊkɪŋglɑːs] N espejo m

lookout ['lʊkaʊt] N **1** (= act) **to keep a ~ for sth** estar atento a or al acecho de algo; **keep a ~ for the postman** estáte atento por si viene el cartero **2** (= watchperson) centinela mf **3** (= prospect) perspectiva f; **that's his ~!** ¡eso es asunto suyo!, ¡allá él!

loom¹ [luːm] N (for weaving) telar m

loom² [luːm] VI **1** (= appear) surgir, aparecer **2** (= threaten)

amenazar; **dangers ~ ahead** se vislumbran los peligros que hay por delante

loony* ['luːnɪ] N loco/a m/f ➤ **loony bin** manicomio m
➤ **the loony left** (Brit pej) la izquierda radical

loop [luːp] Ⓐ N **1** (in string, ribbon) lazo m, lazada f **2** (Comput) bucle m **3** (Elec) circuito m cerrado **4** (= informed group) **to be in the ~** estar en el grupo de informados **to be out of the ~** estar fuera del grupo de informados Ⓑ VT **to ~ a rope round a post** pasar una cuerda alrededor de un poste; **to ~ the ~** hacer el rizo, rizar el rizo

loophole ['luːphəʊl] N escapatoria f; (in law) laguna f, resquicio m legal

loopy* ['luːpɪ] ADJ (compar **loopier**; superl **loopiest**) chiflado*

loose [luːs] Ⓐ ADJ (compar **~r**; superl **~st**) **1** (= not firmly attached) [thread, wire, screw, brick, page] suelto; [handle, knob] desatornillado; [tooth] flojo, que se mueve; **this button is ~** este botón está a punto de caerse; **to come** or **work ~** [thread, wire, brick] soltarse; [screw] aflojarse; [knob, handle] aflojarse, desatornillarse
2 [hair] suelto; **to wear one's hair ~** llevar el pelo suelto
3 [clothes] holgado, amplio; **these trousers are too ~ round the waist** estos pantalones son muy anchos de cintura
4 [skin] flácido, colgón*
5 (= not dense) [mixture, soil, powder] suelto
6 (= not tied up) [animal] suelto; **to let sth/sb ~** soltar algo/a algn; **inexperienced doctors were let ~ on seriously ill patients** se dejó que médicos sin experiencia trataran a pacientes gravemente enfermos
7 (= not strict) [alliance, coalition] libre; [arrangement] flexible; [interpretation] libre; [translation] aproximado
8 (= not packaged) [carrots, potatoes] suelto, a granel
Ⓑ VT [+ animal] soltar; [+ prisoner] poner en libertad, soltar; [+ arrow, missile] lanzar
Ⓒ N **to be on the ~** andar suelto
Ⓓ CPD ➤ **loose box** establo m móvil ➤ **loose cannon** (fig) bomba f de relojería ➤ **loose change** dinero m suelto ➤ **loose chippings** (on roadway) gravilla fsing suelta ➤ **loose connection** (Elec) mala conexión f ➤ **loose end: to tie up ~ ends** atar los cabos sueltos; **to be at a ~ end*** no saber qué hacer

loose-fitting ['luːsˈfɪtɪŋ] ADJ [clothes] holgado

loose-leaf ['luːsˈliːf] ADJ [book] de hojas sueltas ➤ **loose-leaf binder** carpeta f de anillas

loosely ['luːslɪ] ADV **1** (= not tightly) [fasten, tie] con un nudo flojo, ligeramente **2** (= not precisely) [translated] libremente; **~ speaking** hablando en términos generales **3** (= informally) [organized, structured] sin mucha rigidez, con bastante flexibilidad; **groups ~ connected to the Hezbollah movement** grupos mpl que tienen cierta conexión con el movimiento Hezbolá

loosen ['luːsn] VT (= slacken) aflojar (also fig); (= untie) desatar; **to ~ one's grip on** [+ handle, sb's arm] dejar de apretar con tanta fuerza
➤ **loosen up** Ⓐ VI + ADV (gen) desentumecerse; (*) (= relax) soltarse, relajarse Ⓑ VT + ADV [+ muscles] desentumecer

loot [luːt] Ⓐ N botín m, presa f; (*) (= money) pasta* f, plata f (LAm*) Ⓑ VT saquear Ⓒ VI entregarse al saqueo

looter ['luːtər] N saqueador(a) m/f

looting ['luːtɪŋ] N saqueo m

lop [lɒp] VT [+ tree] mochar, desmochar; (also ~ **away**, ~ **off**) [+ branches] podar; (fig) cortar

lopsided ['lɒpˈsaɪdɪd] ADJ (lit) torcido, ladeado, chueco (LAm); (fig) [view] desequilibrado

lord [lɔːd] Ⓐ N **1** (= master, ruler) señor m; (= British title) lord m; **~ of the manor** señor m feudal; **~ and master** dueño y señor; **Lord (John) Smith** (Brit) Lord (John) Smith; **the (House of) Lords** (Brit) la Cámara de los Lores; **my Lord** (to bishop) Ilustrísima; (to noble) señor; (to judge) señoría, señor juez
2 (Rel) **the Lord** el Señor; **Our Lord** Nuestro Señor; **good Lord!** ¡Dios mío!; **Lord knows where ...!*** ¡Dios sabe dónde ...!
Ⓑ CPD ➤ **Lord Chancellor** jefe de la administración de la justicia en Inglaterra y Gales, y presidente de la Cámara de

los Lores ➤ **Lord Mayor** (Brit) alcalde m ➤ **the Lord's Prayer** el padrenuestro

lordship ['lɔːdʃɪp] N señoría f; **your Lordship** Señoría

lorry ['lɒrɪ] (Brit) N camión m; **it fell off the back of a ~*** (euph) es de trapicheo* ➤ **lorry driver** camionero/a m/f ➤ **lorry load** carga f

lose [luːz] (pt, pp **lost**) Ⓐ VT **1** perder; **I've lost my pen** he perdido el bolígrafo; **he's lost his licence** le han retirado el carnet; **to ~ one's life** perder la vida; **there was not a moment to ~** no había ni un momento que perder; **you've got nothing to ~** no tienes nada que perder; **you've nothing to ~ by helping him** no vas a perder nada ayudándole; **to be lost at sea** desaparecer en el mar; **I wouldn't ~ any sleep over it!** ¡no pierdas el sueño por ello!, ¡no te preocupes por ello!; **she lost no time in making up her mind** se decidió enseguida, no le costó nada decidirse; **to ~ one's way** (lit) perderse; (fig) perder el rumbo; ✦ IDIOM **to ~ it*** perder los papeles, perder el control
2 (*) (= get rid of) [+ unwanted companion] deshacerse de; [+ pursuers] zafarse de; **to ~ weight** perder peso, adelgazar; **I lost two kilos** perdí or adelgacé dos kilos
3 (= fall behind) [watch, clock] atrasarse; **this watch ~s five minutes every day** este reloj se atrasa cinco minutos cada día
4 (= cause loss of) **it lost him the job/the match** le costó el puesto/el partido, le hizo perder el puesto/el partido
5 (*) (= confuse) confundir; **you've lost me there** ahora sí que me has confundido, ahora sí que no te entiendo
Ⓑ VI **1** [player, team] perder (**to sb** contra algn); **they lost (by) three goals to two** perdieron (por) tres goles a dos; **you can't ~** no tienes pérdida, tienes que forzosamente salir ganando; **he lost on the deal** salió perdiendo en el negocio
2 [watch, clock] atrasarse
➤ **lose out** VI + ADV salir perdiendo

loser ['luːzəʳ] N perdedor(a) m/f; **to be a good/bad ~** saber/ no saber perder, tener buen/mal perder

losing ['luːzɪŋ] ADJ perdedor; **the ~ team** el equipo perdedor; **to fight a ~ battle** luchar por una causa perdida; **to be on the ~ side** estar en el lado de los perdedores or vencidos; **to be on a ~ streak** estar pasando por una racha de mala suerte

loss [lɒs] N pérdida f; **it's your ~** el que sales perdiendo eres tú; **to operate at a ~** funcionar con pérdida de capital; **to sell sth at a ~** vender algo con pérdida; **he's no great ~** no vamos a perder nada con su marcha; **the army suffered heavy ~es** el ejército sufrió pérdidas cuantiosas; **we want to prevent further ~ of life** queremos evitar que se produzcan más muertes or que se pierdan más vidas; **the company made a ~ in 1999** la empresa tuvo un balance adverso en 1999; **the company made a ~ of £2 million** la empresa sufrió pérdidas de dos millones de libras; **the ~ of a loved one** la pérdida or muerte de un ser querido; ✦ IDIOMS **to be at a ~: they are at a ~ to explain how such a mistake could have been made** no se explican cómo se pudo haber cometido semejante error; **to be at a ~ for words** no encontrar palabras con qué expresarse; **he's never at a ~ for words** tiene mucha facilidad de palabra; **to cut one's ~es** cortar por lo sano ➤ **loss adjuster** (Brit) ajustador(a) m/f de pérdidas, tasador(a) m/f de pérdidas ➤ **loss leader** artículo m de lanzamiento

lossmaking ['lɒs,meɪkɪŋ] ADJ [enterprise] deficitario

lost [lɒst] Ⓐ PT, PP of **lose**
Ⓑ ADJ **1** [person, thing] perdido; **I'm ~** (lit) me he perdido, estoy perdido; (= confused) estoy perdido; **he was looking for a ~ contact lens** buscaba una lente de contacto que se le había perdido; **all is not ~!** ¡no se ha perdido todo!; **to get ~** [person, thing] perderse; [issue, fact] olvidarse; **get ~!*** ¡vete al cuerno!**, ¡vete a la porra!**; **to give sb up for ~** dar a algn por desaparecido; **to give sth up for ~** dar algo por perdido; **to be ~ in sth** estar absorto en algo; **the meaning of that was ~ on me** no entendí or no capté el significado de eso; **an irony/a fact which was not ~ on me** una ironía/un hecho que no se me escapaba; **to make up for ~ time** recuperar el tiempo perdido; ✦ IDIOM **to be ~ for words** no tener palabras, no saber qué decir
2 (= vanished) [civilization] desaparecido; [skill, art] desaparecido, perdido; **he pined for his ~ youth** suspiraba por su juventud perdida

Ⓒ CPD ➤ **lost and found** (US) oficina f de objetos perdidos ➤ **lost property** (= belongings) objetos mpl perdidos; (= office) oficina f de objetos perdidos ➤ **lost property office** oficina f de objetos perdidos

lot [lɒt] N **1 a ~ 1.1** (used as adv) mucho; **I read a ~** leo mucho; **we don't go out a ~** no salimos mucho; **he drinks an awful ~** bebe una barbaridad; **"do you like football?" — "not a ~"** —¿te gusta el fútbol? —no mucho; **thanks a ~!** ¡muchísimas gracias!, ¡muy agradecido! **1.2** (= large quantity) **a ~ of money** mucho dinero; **a ~ of people** mucha gente; **an awful ~ of things to do** la mar de cosas que hacer; **I'd give a ~ to know** me gustaría muchísimo saberlo; **quite/such a ~ of books** bastantes/tantos libros; **quite/such a ~ of noise** bastante/tanto ruido; **there wasn't a ~ we could do** apenas había nada que pudiéramos hacer
2 ~s : take as much as you want, I've got ~s llévate cuanto quieras, tengo un montón or (LAm) harto(s)*; **~s of people** mucha gente, cantidad de gente*; **she has ~s of friends** tiene muchos amigos, tiene un montón de or (LAm) hartos amigos*; **he feels ~s better** se encuentra mucho mejor
3 (esp Brit*) (= group) grupo m; **a fine ~ of students** un buen grupo de estudiantes; **Melissa's friends? I don't like that ~** ¿los amigos de Melissa? no me cae bien ese grupo
4 the ~* (= all, everything) todo; **that's the ~** eso es todo; **the (whole) ~ of them** todos
5 (= destiny) suerte f, destino m; **to throw in one's ~ with sb** unirse a la suerte de algn
6 (= random selection) **by ~** por sorteo; **to draw ~s (for sth)** echar suertes (para algo)
7 (at auction) lote m; ✦ IDIOM **he's a bad ~** (esp Brit) es un mal sujeto
8 (esp US) (= plot) terreno m, solar m
9 (= share) porción f, parte f

loth [ləʊθ] ADJ = **loath**

lotion ['ləʊʃən] N loción f

lottery ['lɒtərɪ] N lotería f

lotus ['ləʊtəs] N loto m ➤ **lotus position** postura f del loto

loud [laʊd] (compar **~er**; superl **~est**) Ⓐ ADJ **1** (= noisy) [music] alto, fuerte; [applause, noise, explosion, scream] fuerte; **she has a ~ voice** tiene una voz muy fuerte; **in a ~ voice** en voz alta
2 (= garish) [colour] chillón, llamativo; [pattern, clothes] llamativo
Ⓑ ADV [speak] alto; [laugh, shout] fuerte; [play] a todo volumen; **you'll have to speak ~er** tendrás que hablar más fuerte or alto; **I am reading or receiving you ~ and clear** te recibo perfectamente; **out ~** [think, read, laugh] en voz alta

loudhailer ['laʊd'heɪləʳ] N (Brit) megáfono m

loudly ['laʊdlɪ] ADV **1** (= not quietly) [say] en voz alta; [talk, speak] alto, en voz alta; [sing, shout, scream] fuerte; [laugh, knock, applaud] con fuerza; [complain, proclaim] enérgicamente **2** (= garishly) [dress] llamativamente

loudmouth* ['laʊdmaʊθ] N gritón/ona m/f, bocazas mf inv (Sp*)

loudmouthed ['laʊd'maʊðd] ADJ gritón, bocazas inv (Sp*)

loudspeaker ['laʊd'spiːkəʳ] N altavoz m, altoparlante m (LAm)

Louisiana [luˌiːzɪˈænə] N Luisiana f

lounge [laʊndʒ] Ⓐ N (at airport) sala f; (on liner) salón m; (Brit) (in house) salón m, sala f de estar, living m (LAm) Ⓑ VI (= be idle) gandulear, pasar el rato sin hacer nada Ⓒ CPD ➤ **lounge bar** salón-bar m ➤ **lounge suit** traje m de calle, terno m de calle (LAm)
➤ **lounge around, lounge about** (Brit) VI + ADV gandulear, holgazanear

louse [laʊs] N (pl **lice**) **1** (= insect) piojo m **2** (pej*) (= person) canalla* mf, sinvergüenza mf
➤ **louse up*** VT + ADV fastidiar, echar a perder

lousy* ['laʊzɪ] ADJ (compar **lousier**; superl **lousiest**) [climate, food] asqueroso*; [secretary, driver] malísimo, pésimo; **I'm a ~ player** juego fatal*; **all for a few ~ quid** todo por unas cochinas libras*; **we had a ~ time** lo pasamos fatal*; **I feel ~** me siento fatal*

lout [laʊt] N bruto m, gamberro m (Sp)

loutish ['laʊtɪʃ] ADJ grosero, maleducado

louvre, louver (US) ['luːvəʳ] N (Archit) lumbrera f; (= blind) persiana f

lovable ['lʌvəbl] ADJ adorable

love [lʌv] **Ⓐ** N **1** (between people) amor m; **it was ~ at first sight** fue amor a primera vista, fue un flechazo; **her ~ for her children** su amor m por sus hijos; **for ~ of her son** por amor a su hijo, por el amor que le tiene/tenía a su hijo; **for the ~ of God** or **Mike!** ¡por el amor de Dios!; **to be/fall in ~ (with sb)** estar enamorado/enamorarse (de algn); **to make ~** hacer el amor; ✦ IDIOM **I wouldn't do it for ~ nor money** no lo haría por nada del mundo; **it wasn't to be had for ~ nor money** era imposible conseguirlo

2 (= liking) [of activity, food, place] afición f, pasión f

3 (in greetings, letters) **(with) ~ (from)** Jim con cariño (de) Jim, besos (de) Jim; **give him my ~** dale or mándale recuerdos míos; **lots of ~, Jim** muchos besos, Jim; **he sends (you) his ~** te da or manda recuerdos

4 (= person loved) amor m; (= thing loved) pasión f; **she was my first ~** fue mi primer amor; **football was his first ~** el fútbol era su principal pasión; **he was the ~ of her life** fue el amor de su vida

5 (Brit*) (as term of address) (= darling) cariño m; **yes, ~** sí, cariño; **thanks, ~** (to woman) gracias, guapa or (Sp) maja; (to man) gracias, guapo or (Sp) majo; (to child) gracias, cielo or cariño; **my ~** amor mío, mi vida

6 (Tennis) **~ all** cero cero; **15 ~** 15 a cero

Ⓑ VT **1** (= feel affection for) querer, amar (frm); **I ~ you** te quiero; **you don't ~ me any more** ya no me quieres; **she ~s her children/her cat/that car** quiere mucho a or siente mucho cariño por sus hijos/su gato/ese coche

2 (= like very much) **I ~ Madrid** me encanta Madrid, me gusta muchísimo Madrid; **I ~ strawberries** me encantan las fresas; **"would you like a drink?" — "I'd ~ one!"** —¿quieres tomar algo? —¡sí, por favor!; **I'd ~ a beer** daría cualquier cosa por una cerveza; **he ~s swimming** le encanta nadar, le gusta muchísimo nadar; **I'd ~ to come** me encantaría ir, me gustaría muchísimo ir; **I'd ~ to!** ¡con mucho gusto!, ¡yo, encantado!

Ⓒ CPD ➤ **love affair** aventura f (sentimental), amorío m; (fig) pasión f ➤ **love child** hijo/a m/f natural ➤ **love handles**✺✺ agarraderas✺✺ fpl ➤ **love letter** carta f de amor ➤ **love life** (emotional) vida f sentimental; (sexual) vida f sexual ➤ **love nest** nido m de amor ➤ **love song** canción f de amor ➤ **love story** historia f de amor

lovebirds ['lʌvbɜːdz] NPL (hum) palomitos mpl, tórtolos mpl

lovebite ['lʌvˌbaɪt] N mordisco m amoroso

lovely ['lʌvlɪ] ADJ (compar **lovelier**; superl **loveliest**) ADJ (esp Brit) **1** (= beautiful) [face, figure, thing, day] precioso; [food, meal] delicioso, riquísimo; **you look ~, María** estás preciosa, María; **look at these ~ flowers!** ¡mira qué flores más bonitas!; **what ~ weather!** ¡hace un tiempo estupendo or buenísimo!

2 (= pleasant) [person, family, character] encantador, amoroso (LAm); **you do say some ~ things** dices unas cosas preciosas; **it's ~ to see you again** que alegría volver a verte; **what a ~ surprise!** ¡qué sorpresa más agradable!

3 (as intensifier) **it's ~ and hot/cold** [drink, water] está calentito/fresquito; [air] hace calorcito/fresquito

lovemaking ['lʌvˌmeɪkɪŋ] N relaciones fpl sexuales

lover ['lʌvəʳ] N **1** (sexually) amante mf; (romantically) enamorado/a m/f; **he became her ~** se hizo su amante

2 (= fan) aficionado/a m/f; **music ~** ✧ ~ **of music** aficionado/a m/f a la música, amante mf de la música

lovesick ['lʌvsɪk] ADJ enfermo de amor

loving ['lʌvɪŋ] ADJ cariñoso, tierno; **with ~ care** con amoroso cuidado; **~ kindness** bondad f

lovingly ['lʌvɪŋlɪ] ADV **1** (= affectionately) [look, speak] cariñosamente, tiernamente; (stronger) amorosamente

2 (= carefully) [cook, prepare, inscribe] con cariño; **~ restored** cuidadosamente restaurado

low [ləʊ] **Ⓐ** ADJ (compar **~er**; superl **~est**) **1** (in height) [wall, shelf, seat, level] bajo; [bow] profundo; **on ~ ground** a nivel del mar, en tierras bajas; **a dress with a ~ neckline** un vestido escotado

2 (= quiet) [voice, TV, radio] bajo

3 (= low-pitched) [voice, musical note] grave, bajo

4 [number] bajo; [price, income] reducido, bajo; [stock, supplies] escaso; **the battery is ~** la batería se está acabando; **stocks are running ~** las existencias empiezan a escasear

5 (in intensity) [light, rate, speed, temperature] bajo; **the temperature is in the ~ 40s** la temperatura es de 40 grados y algo más; **to cook on a ~ heat** cocer a fuego lento

6 (= inferior) [standard, quality] inferior

7 (= humble) [rank] humilde; [card] pequeño

8 (Aut) **in a ~ gear** en primera or segunda

9 (= depressed) deprimido; **to be in ~ spirits** sentirse deprimido, estar bajo de moral

10 [character, behaviour, opinion] malo; [joke, song] verde; [trick] sucio, malo

Ⓑ ADV (compar **~er**; superl **~est**) **1** [aim, fly, sing] bajo; **to bow ~** hacer una reverencia profunda; **to be laid ~ with flu** (Brit) ser postrado por la gripe; **to lie ~** (= hide) mantenerse escondido; (= be silent) mantenerse quieto

2 [quietly] [say, sing] bajo, en voz baja

3 **to turn the lights/the volume down ~** bajar las luces/el volumen

Ⓒ N **1** (Meteo) área f de baja presión

> Use **el/un** not **la/una** before feminine nouns beginning with stressed **a** or **ha** like **área**.

2 (= low point) punto m más bajo; **to reach a new** or **an all-time ~** estar más bajo que nunca

Ⓓ CPD ➤ **low beam headlights** (US) luces fpl de cruce ➤ **the Low Countries** los Países Bajos ➤ **low point** punto m (más) bajo ➤ **low season** (Brit) temporada f baja ➤ **low tide** marea f baja ➤ **low water** bajamar f ➤ **low water mark** línea f de bajamar

lowbrow ['ləʊbraʊ] ADJ poco culto

low-budget [ˌləʊ'bʌdʒɪt] ADJ de bajo presupuesto; **~ film** película f de presupuesto modesto

low-calorie [ˌləʊ'kælərɪ] ADJ [diet, menu, food] bajo en calorías, con pocas calorías; [beer, cola] light inv

low-cost ['ləʊ'kɒst] ADJ económico

low-cut ['ləʊ'kʌt] ADJ [dress] escotado

low-down ['ləʊdaʊn] **Ⓐ** N (*) **he gave me the ~ on it** me contó todo sobre el tema; **come on, give us the ~** venga, cuéntanos todo lo que sabes **Ⓑ** ADJ rastrero, bajo

lower ['ləʊəʳ] **Ⓐ** ADJ COMPAR of **low 1** (= bottom) [part, section, floors, windows] de abajo, inferior; [slopes] inferior, bajo; **the ~ bunk** la litera de abajo; **the ~ left corner** la esquina inferior izquierda; **the ~ half of** la mitad inferior de, la mitad de abajo de

2 (= less important) [level, rank, caste] inferior

3 (Anat) inferior; **the ~ back** la parte inferior de la espalda **Ⓑ** VT (gen) bajar; [+ boat] echar al agua; [+ flag, sail] arriar; [+ price] bajar, rebajar; **to ~ o.s. to do sth** rebajarse a hacer algo; **to ~ one's headlights** (US) poner las luces de cruce; **to ~ one's voice** bajar la voz

Ⓒ CPD ➤ **lower case** minúsculas fpl; **in ~ case** en minúsculas ➤ **lower class the ~ class** or **classes** la clase baja ➤ **lower deck** [of bus] piso m de abajo; [of ship] cubierta f inferior ➤ **the Lower House** (Parl) la Cámara Baja

lower-class ['ləʊəˌklɑːs] ADJ de (la) clase baja

lowest ['ləʊɪst] **Ⓐ** ADJ SUPERL of **low Ⓑ** CPD ➤ **lowest common denominator** (Math) mínimo común denominador m; **to appeal to the ~ common denominator** dirigirse al estrato social más bajo ➤ **lowest common multiple** mínimo común múltiplo m

low-fat ['ləʊ'fæt] ADJ [margarine, cheese] bajo en grasas; [milk, yoghurt] desnatado

low-flying ['ləʊ,flaɪɪŋ] ADJ que vuela bajo

low-grade ['ləʊ,greɪd] ADJ de baja calidad

low-key* [ˌləʊ'kiː] ADJ discreto

lowland ['ləʊlənd] ADJ de tierra baja

low-level ['ləʊ'levl] ADJ de bajo nivel

lowly ['ləʊlɪ] ADJ (compar **lowlier**; superl **lowliest**) humilde

low-lying [ˈləʊˌlaɪɪŋ] ADJ bajo

low-paid [ˌləʊˈpeɪd] ADJ [work] mal pagado, de baja remuneración (more frm); [worker] mal pagado, mal remunerado (more frm)

low-pitched [ˈləʊpɪtʃt] ADJ bajo

low-powered [ˈləʊpaʊəd] ADJ de baja potencia

low-pressure [ˈləʊˈpreʃəʳ] ADJ de baja presión

low-profile [ˈləʊˈprəʊfaɪl] ADJ [activity] discreto

low-rent [ˈləʊrent] ADJ de renta baja, de alquiler bajo

low-rise [ˈləʊraɪz] ADJ de baja altura

low-risk [ˌləʊˈrɪsk] ADJ de bajo riesgo

low-slung [ˈləʊslʌŋ] ADJ [chair] con el asiento bajo; [sports car] con el suelo bajo

low-tar [ləʊˈtɑːʳ] ADJ ~ **cigarettes** cigarrillos mpl de bajo contenido en alquitrán

loyal [ˈlɔɪəl] ADJ [friend, subject, employee, wife] leal, fiel; [customer, reader] fiel; **to remain ~ to** [+ leader, government] permanecer leal a; [+ beliefs, principles] permanecer fiel a

loyalist [ˈlɔɪəlɪst] N (gen) partidario/a m/f del régimen; (in Spain, 1936) republicano/a m/f; (N Irl Pol) unionista mf

loyally [ˈlɔɪəlɪ] ADV lealmente, fielmente

loyalty [ˈlɔɪəltɪ] N (to leader, government) lealtad f (to a); (to beliefs, principles) fidelidad f (to a); **he has divided loyalties** tiene un conflicto de lealtades ➤ **loyalty card** (Brit) tarjeta que reparten los hipermercados a sus clientes, mediante la que se acumulan puntos u otras ventajas

lozenge [ˈlɒzɪndʒ] N (Med) pastilla f; (Math) rombo m

L-plate [ˈelpleɪt] N (Brit) (placa f de) la L

LRP N ABBR (= **lead replacement petrol**) gasolina f aditivada

LSD N ABBR (= **lysergic acid diethylamide**) LSD m

LSE N ABBR (Brit) = **London School of Economics**

Lt ABBR (= **lieutenant**) Tte.

Ltd ABBR (Brit) (= **limited**) ≈ S.A.

lubricant [ˈluːbrɪkənt] N lubricante m

lubricate [ˈluːbrɪkeɪt] VT lubricar, engrasar

lubricating [ˈluːbrɪkeɪtɪŋ] ADJ lubricante ➤ **lubricating oil** aceite m lubricante

lubrication [ˌluːbrɪˈkeɪʃən] N lubricación f

lucid [ˈluːsɪd] ADJ lúcido; ~ **interval** intervalo m de lucidez

lucidity [luːˈsɪdɪtɪ] N lucidez f

luck [lʌk] N suerte f; **I couldn't believe my ~** no me podía creer la suerte que tenía; **good/bad ~** buena/mala suerte f; **good ~!** ¡(buena) suerte!; **bad ~!** ¡(qué) mala suerte!, ¡qué pena!; **to bring sb (good) ~** traer buena suerte a algn; **to have the good ~/bad ~ to do sth** tener la buena/mala suerte de hacer algo; **it's good/bad ~ to see a black cat** cruzarse con un gato negro trae buena/mala suerte; **any ~?** ¿hubo suerte?; **best of ~!** ¡muchísima suerte!, ¡que tengas suerte!; **better ~ next time!** ¡otra vez será!; **that was a bit of ~!** ¡eso fue un golpe de suerte!; **once more for ~!** ¡una vez más por si trae suerte!; **I'll take one more photo for ~** sacaré una foto más por si acaso; **his ~ held** siguió con su racha de buena suerte; **to be in ~** estar de or con suerte; **it would be just my ~ to meet the boss!** mira que toparme con el jefe; ¡sólo me pasan a mí estas cosas!; **knowing my ~** con la suerte que tengo; **no such ~!** ¡ojalá!; **if it's money you want you're out of ~** si lo que quieres es dinero, me temo que no estás de suerte; **to push one's ~** tentar a la suerte; **to have ~ on one's side** tener la suerte de su parte; **wish me ~!** ¡deséame suerte!; **with (any) ~** con (un poco de) suerte; **worse ~** desgraciadamente; **as ~ would have it ...** quiso la suerte que ...; ✦ IDIOMS **it's the ~ of the draw** es cuestión de suerte; **to be down on one's ~** estar de mala racha ➤ **luck out*** VI + ADV (US) tener un golpe de suerte

luckily [ˈlʌkɪlɪ] ADV afortunadamente, por suerte

lucky [ˈlʌkɪ] (compar **luckier**; superl **luckiest**) Ⓐ ADJ
1 (= fortunate) [person, coincidence, shot] afortunado; **to be ~** [person] tener suerte; **I'm ~ to have an excellent teacher** tengo la suerte de tener un profesor excelente; **he is ~ to be alive** tiene suerte de seguir vivo; **he will be ~ to get £5 for it**

con mucha suerte conseguirá cinco libras por ello; **he was ~ that I didn't kill him** tuvo suerte de que no lo matara; **it's ~ that it didn't rain** es una suerte or menos mal que no haya llovido; **a ~ break** un golpe de suerte; **it's your ~ day** es tu día de suerte; **~ devil!*** ¡qué suertudo!*; **he was ~ enough to get a seat** tuvo la suerte de conseguir un sitio; **to have a ~ escape** salvarse de milagro; **to get ~*** tener suerte; **it was just a ~ guess** acerté de casualidad; **to be ~ in love** tener suerte or ser afortunado en el amor; **who's the ~ man/woman?*** ¿quién es el afortunado/la afortunada?; **you should be so ~!*** ¡ya quisieras!*, ¡ojalá!*; **~ winner** afortunado/a ganador(a) m/f; **~ (old) you!*** ¡qué suerte!, ¡vaya or menuda suerte la tuya!*; **you'll be ~!*** ¡sería un milagro!*
2 (= bringing luck) [number, shirt] de la suerte
Ⓑ CPD ➤ **lucky charm** amuleto m ➤ **lucky dip** (Brit) caja f de las sorpresas; (fig) lotería f

lucrative [ˈluːkrətɪv] ADJ lucrativo

ludicrous [ˈluːdɪkrəs] ADJ ridículo, absurdo

ludo [ˈluːdəʊ] N (Brit) ludo m

lug* [lʌg] VT (= drag) arrastrar, jalar (LAm); (= carry) cargar (con trabajo); **I've been ~ging this camera around with me all day** llevo cargando con esta cámara todo el día; **he ~ged the cases upstairs** llevó a rastras las maletas al piso de arriba

luggage [ˈlʌgɪdʒ] N equipaje m ➤ **luggage car** (US) furgón m de equipaje ➤ **luggage checkroom** (US) consigna f ➤ **luggage label** etiqueta f de equipaje ➤ **luggage locker** consigna f automática ➤ **luggage rack** (on train, bus etc) rejilla f, redecilla f; (US Aut) baca f, portaequipajes m inv ➤ **luggage van** (Brit) furgón m de equipajes

lugubrious [luːˈguːbrɪəs] ADJ lúgubre

lukewarm [ˈluːkwɔːm] ADJ [water, food, coffee] tibio; [reception, applause, support] tibio, poco entusiasta; **he was ~ about the idea** no le entusiasmaba la idea

lull [lʌl] Ⓐ N (in storm, wind) pausa f, momento m de calma; (in fighting, bombardment) tregua f; (in activity) respiro m, pausa f Ⓑ VT [+ fears] calmar, sosegar; **to ~ sb to sleep** arrullar a algn, adormecer a algn; ✦ IDIOM **he was ~ed into a false sense of security** se le inspiró un falso sentimiento de seguridad

lullaby [ˈlʌləbaɪ] N canción f de cuna, nana f

lumbago [lʌmˈbeɪgəʊ] N lumbago m

lumber[1] [ˈlʌmbəʳ] Ⓐ N **1** (esp US) (= wood) maderas mpl **2** (esp Brit*) (= junk) trastos mpl viejos Ⓑ VT (Brit*) **to ~ sb with sth** hacer que algn cargue con algo, endilgar algo a algn; **I got ~ed with the girl for the afternoon** tuve que cargar toda la tarde con la chica, me endilgaron a la chica toda la tarde Ⓒ CPD ➤ **lumber jacket** chaqueta f de leñador ➤ **lumber room** trastero m ➤ **lumber yard** (US) almacén m de madera

lumber[2] [ˈlʌmbəʳ] VI (also ~ **about**) moverse pesadamente; (also ~ **along**) avanzar pesadamente

lumberjack [ˈlʌmbədʒæk] N leñador(a) m/f

luminous [ˈluːmɪnəs] ADJ luminoso

lump [lʌmp] Ⓐ N **1** (= piece) [of sugar] terrón m; [of cheese, earth, clay, ice] trozo m, pedazo m **2** (= swelling) bulto m; **she found a ~ in her breast** se encontró un bulto en el pecho; **he had a nasty ~ on his head** tenía un buen chichón en la cabeza; **with a ~ in one's throat** con un nudo en la garganta **3** (pej*) (= person) zoquete* mf
Ⓑ VT **if he doesn't like it he can ~ it*** si no le gusta que se aguante
Ⓒ CPD ➤ **lump sugar** azúcar m en terrones ➤ **lump sum** cantidad f global, suma f global
➤ **lump together** VT + ADV [+ things] amontonar; [+ people] agrupar; **these problems can't be ~ed together under any one heading** estos problemas no pueden agruparse or englobarse bajo el mismo encabezamiento

lumpy [ˈlʌmpɪ] ADJ (compar **lumpier**; superl **lumpiest**) [sauce] grumoso, lleno de grumos; [bed] desigual

lunacy [ˈluːnəsɪ] N locura f; **it's ~!** ¡es una locura!

lunar [ˈluːnəʳ] ADJ lunar ➤ **lunar landing** alunizaje m, aterrizaje m lunar

lunatic [ˈluːnətɪk] Ⓐ N loco/a m/f Ⓑ ADJ [person] loco; [plan, scheme] descabellado Ⓒ CPD ➤ **lunatic asylum**

manicomio *m* ➤ **the lunatic fringe** el sector más fanático *or* radical

lunch [lʌntʃ] N comida *f*, almuerzo *m*, lonche *m* (*Mex*); **to have ~** comer, almorzar; ✦ IDIOM **to be out to ~*** (*hum*) estar como una regadera *or* cabra* ➤ **lunch break** hora *f* de la comida *or* del almuerzo *or* (*Mex*) del lonche ➤ **lunch counter** (*US*) (= *café*) *cafetería donde se sirven comidas*; (= *counter*) *mostrador o barra donde se come* ➤ **lunch hour** hora *f* de la comida *or* del almuerzo *or* (*Mex*) del lonche

lunchbox ['lʌntʃbɒks] N fiambrera *f*, tartera *f*

luncheon ['lʌntʃən] N (*esp Brit*) comida *f*, almuerzo *m* ➤ **luncheon voucher** (*Brit*) vale *m or* (*LAm*) tíquet *m* de comida

lunchpail ['lʌntʃpeɪl] N (*US*) fiambrera *f*, tartera *f*

lunchtime ['lʌntʃtaɪm] N hora *f* de comer *or* de la comida, hora *f* del almuerzo *or* (*Mex*) lonche

lung [lʌŋ] N pulmón *m* ➤ **lung cancer** cáncer *m* de pulmón ➤ **lung disease** enfermedad *f* pulmonar

lunge [lʌndʒ] VI (*also* **~ forward**) arremeter, embestir; **to ~ at sth/sb (with sth)** arremeter contra algo/algn (con algo), lanzarse *or* abalanzarse sobre algo/algn (con algo)

lurch¹ [lɜːtʃ] Ⓐ N sacudida *f*, tumbo *m*; (*Naut*) bandazo *m*; **to give a ~** dar una sacudida *or* un tumbo Ⓑ VI [*person*] tambalearse; [*vehicle*] (*continually*) dar sacudidas, dar tumbos; (*once*) dar una sacudida, dar un tumbo; (*Naut*) dar un bandazo; **he ~ed in/out** entró/salió tambaleándose; **the bus ~ed forward** el autobús avanzó dando tumbos/dando un tumbo

lurch² [lɜːtʃ] N ✦ IDIOM **to leave sb in the ~** dejar a algn en la estacada

lure [ljʊəʳ] Ⓐ N (= *decoy*) señuelo *m*; (= *bait*) cebo *m*; (*fig*) atractivo *m*, aliciente *m*, encanto *m* Ⓑ VT [+ *person*] atraer; [+ *animal*] atraer (con un señuelo); **to ~ sb into a trap** hacer que algn caiga en una trampa; **they ~d him into the house** consiguieron con artimañas que entrara en la casa; **he was ~d away from the company by a more lucrative offer** dejó la empresa atraído por una oferta más lucrativa

lurid ['ljʊərɪd] ADJ **1** (= *sordid, prurient*) [*description, novel, photo, crime*] morboso, escabroso; [*imagination, headline*] morboso; **in ~ detail** sin omitir los detalles más escabrosos **2** (= *garish*) [*colour, tie , shirt*] chillón

lurk [lɜːk] VI **1** [*person*] (= *lie in wait*) estar al acecho, merodear; (= *hide*) estar escondido; **I saw him ~ing around the building** lo vi merodeando *or* al acecho por el edificio **2** [*danger*] acechar; [*doubt*] persistir

luscious ['lʌʃəs] ADJ [*fruit*] suculento; [*girl*] deliciosa, atractiva

lush [lʌʃ] ADJ (*compar* **~er**; *superl* **~est**) **1** (= *luxuriant*) [*vegetation*] exuberante, lozano; [*pastures*] rico **2** (= *opulent*) opulento, lujoso

lust [lʌst] N (= *greed*) codicia *f*; (*sexual*) lujuria *f*; **~ for money** codicia *f*; **~ for power** ansia *f or* sed *f* de poder

---

Use **el/un** not **la/una** before feminine nouns beginning with stressed **a** or **ha** like **ansia**.

➤ **lust after** VI + PREP [+ *person*] desear; [+ *thing*] codiciar

luster ['lʌstəʳ] N (*US*) = **lustre**

lustful ['lʌstfʊl] ADJ lujurioso, libidinoso

lustre, luster (*US*) ['lʌstəʳ] N lustre *m*, brillo *m*

lusty ['lʌstɪ] ADJ (*compar* **lustier**; *superl* **lustiest**) [*person*] vigoroso, lozano; [*cry, cheer*] fuerte

lute [luːt] N laúd *m*

Luxembourg ['lʌksəmbɜːg] N Luxemburgo *m*

Luxembourger ['lʌksəmbɜːgəʳ] N luxemburgués/esa *m/f*

luxuriant [lʌgˈzjʊərɪənt] ADJ exuberante, lozano

luxuriate [lʌgˈzjʊərɪeɪt] VI **to ~ in** disfrutar (de), deleitarse con, entregarse al lujo de

luxurious [lʌgˈzjʊərɪəs] ADJ [*house, furnishings*] lujoso, de lujo; [*life*] de lujo

luxury ['lʌkʃərɪ] Ⓐ N (*gen*) lujo *m*; (= *article*) artículo *m* de lujo; **to live in ~** vivir con mucho lujo; **a holiday is a ~ we can't afford** unas vacaciones son un lujo que no nos podemos permitir Ⓑ ADJ de lujo

LW N ABBR (= **long wave**) OL *f*

lychee [ˌlaɪˈtʃiː] N lichi *m*

Lycra® ['laɪkrə] N licra® *f*

lying ['laɪɪŋ] Ⓐ ADJ [*statement, story*] falso; [*person*] mentiroso Ⓑ N mentiras *fpl*

lymph [lɪmf] N linfa *f* ➤ **lymph gland** ganglio *m* linfático

lynch [lɪntʃ] Ⓐ VT linchar Ⓑ CPD ➤ **lynch mob** *muchedumbre dispuesta a linchar a alguien*

lynching ['lɪntʃɪŋ] N linchamiento *m*

lynchpin ['lɪntʃpɪn] N (*lit*) pezonera *f*; (*fig*) eje *m*

lynx [lɪŋks] N lince *m*

lyre ['laɪəʳ] N lira *f*

lyric ['lɪrɪk] Ⓐ ADJ lírico Ⓑ N **lyrics** letra *fsing*

lyrical ['lɪrɪkəl] ADJ lírico; **to wax ~ about sth** deshacerse en elogios a algo

M¹, m¹ [em] **Ⓐ** N (= *letter*) M, m *f*; **M for Mary** M de Madrid **Ⓑ** ABBR = **male**

M² ABBR **1** = **million(s) 2** (= **medium**) M **3** (*Brit*) = **motorway**; **the M8** ≈ la A8

m² ABBR **1** (= **metre(s)** *or* (*US*) **meter(s)**) m **2** = **mile(s)**

MA Ⓐ N ABBR (*Univ*) = **Master of Arts Ⓑ** ABBR (*US*) = **Massachusetts**

ma* [mɑː] N mamá *f*

ma'am [mæm] N (*esp US*) = **madam**

mac* [mæk] N (*Brit*) (= *mackintosh*) impermeable *m*; (= *cagoule*) chubasquero *m*

macabre [məˈkɑːbr] ADJ macabro

macaroni [ˌmækəˈrəʊnɪ] N macarrones *mpl* ➤ **macaroni cheese** macarrones *mpl* gratinados (con queso)

macaroon [ˌmækəˈruːn] N macarrón *m*, mostachón *m*

mace¹ [meɪs] N (= *ceremonial staff*) maza *f*

mace² [meɪs] N (= *spice*) macis *f*

Macedonia [ˌmæsɪˈdəʊnɪə] N Macedonia *f*

machete [məˈtʃeɪtɪ] N machete *m*

Machiavellian [ˌmækɪəˈvelɪən] ADJ maquiavélico

machinations [ˌmækɪˈneɪʃənz] NPL maquinaciones *fpl*, intrigas *fpl*, manipulaciones *fpl*

machine [məˈʃiːn] **Ⓐ** N **1** máquina *f*, aparato *m*; (= *machinery*) maquinaria *f* **2** (*Pol*) organización *f*, aparato *m*

Ⓑ VT (*Tech*) elaborar a máquina; (*Sew*) coser a máquina

Ⓒ CPD ➤ **machine code** (*Comput*) lenguaje *m* (de) máquina ➤ **machine error** error *m* de la máquina ➤ **machine gun** ametralladora *f* ➤ **machine intelligence** inteligencia *f* artificial ➤ **machine language** lenguaje *m* (de) máquina ➤ **machine operator** operario/a *m/f*, maquinista *mf* ➤ **machine tool** máquina *f* herramienta ➤ **machine translation** traducción *f* automática

machine-gun [məˈʃiːnˌɡʌn] VT ametrallar

machine-readable [məˈʃiːnˈriːdəbl] ADJ legible por máquina; **in ~ form** en forma legible por máquina

machinery [məˈʃiːnərɪ] N **1** (= *machines*) maquinaria *f*; (= *mechanism*) mecanismo *m* **2** (*fig*) maquinaria *f*, aparato *m*

machine-stitch [məˈʃiːnˌstɪtʃ] VT coser a máquina

machine-washable [məˈʃiːnˈwɒʃəbl] ADJ lavable en la lavadora

machinist [məˈʃiːnɪst] N (*Tech*) operario/a *m/f*; (*Sew*) costurero/a *m/f* a máquina

machismo [məˈtʃɪzməʊ] N machismo *m*

macho [ˈmætʃəʊ] ADJ muy de macho, muy masculino

mackerel [ˈmækrəl] N (*pl* ~ *or* ~**s**) caballa *f*

mackintosh [ˈmækɪntɒʃ] N (*esp Brit*) impermeable *m*; (= *cagoule*) chubasquero *m*

macro [ˈmækrəʊ] N (*Comput*) macro *m*

macro... [ˈmækrəʊ] PREF macro...

macrobiotic [ˌmækrəʊbaɪˈɒtɪk] ADJ macrobiótico

macrocosm [ˈmækrəʊkɒzəm] N macrocosmo *m*

macroeconomics [ˌmækrəʊˌiːkəˈnɒmɪks] NSING macroeconomía *f*

mad [mæd] **Ⓐ** ADJ (*compar* ~**der**; *superl* ~**dest**) **1** (= *mentally ill*) loco; **to drive sb ~** volver loco a algn; **to go ~** volverse loco

2 (*) (= *crazy*) [*person*] loco; [*plan, idea, scheme*] descabellado, de locos; **are you ~?** ¿estás loco?; **you must be ~!** ¡tú estás loco *or* mal de la cabeza!; **she drove me ~ with her constant questions** me volvió loco con sus constantes preguntas; **don't go ~! we've only got £100** ¡no te pases! sólo tenemos 100 libras; **after the news came through the phones went ~** tras saberse la noticia los teléfonos sonaban como locos; **I worked/ran/pedalled like**

~ trabajé/corrí/pedaleé como (un) loco

3 (*) (= *angry*) furioso; **I was really ~ when I found out** me puse furiosísimo *or* (*Sp*) me enfadé muchísimo *or* (*esp LAm*) me enojé muchísimo cuando me enteré; **to be ~ at** *or* **with sb** estar furioso con algn, estar muy enfadado con algn (*Sp*), estar muy enojado con algn (*esp LAm*); **to go ~** ponerse furioso; **it makes her ~ when you do that** cuando haces eso la sacas de quicio

4 (*esp Brit**) (= *keen*) **to be ~ about sb** estar loco por algn; **he's ~ about football** el fútbol le vuelve loco, es un fanático del fútbol; **I can't say I'm ~ about the idea** no es precisamente que la idea me vuelva loco

5 (= *frantic*) [*race*] desenfrenado; **the daily ~ dash to work** la desenfrenada carrera diaria por llegar al trabajo; **there was a ~ rush for the exit** todo el mundo corrió *or* se lanzó desenfrenado hacia la salida, todo el mundo corrió como loco hacia la salida; **the audience went ~** el público se puso como loco

Ⓑ ADV (= *very*) **she's ~ keen to go** tiene unas ganas locas de ir

Ⓒ CPD ➤ **mad cow disease** (*esp Brit**) enfermedad *f* de las vacas locas*, encefalopatía *f* espongiforme bovina

-mad [mæd] ADJ (*ending in compounds*) **he's football-mad** el fútbol le vuelve loco, es un fanático del fútbol

Madagascar [ˌmædəˈɡæskər] N Madagascar *m*

madam [ˈmædəm] N señora *f*; **yes, ~** sí, señora; **she's a little ~** (*Brit**) es una niña muy enteradilla

madcap [ˈmædkæp] **Ⓐ** ADJ alocado, disparatado **Ⓑ** N locuelo/a *m/f*, tarambana *mf*

madden [ˈmædn] VT (= *infuriate*) enfurecer, sacar de quicio; (= *make demented*) enloquecer

maddening [ˈmædnɪŋ] ADJ [*delay, habit*] exasperante; **he can be absolutely ~ at times** a veces puede sacarte de quicio

made [meɪd] PT, PP *of* **make**

Madeira [məˈdɪərə] N Madeira *f*; (= *wine*) (vino *m* de) madeira *m*

made-to-measure [ˌmeɪdtəˈmeʒər] ADJ (*Brit*) hecho a (la) medida

made-up [ˈmeɪdʌp] ADJ **1** (= *wearing make-up*) [*face*] maquillado; [*eyes*] pintado, maquillado **2** (= *invented*) [*story, character*] inventado, ficticio; [*word*] inventado

madhouse* [ˈmædhaʊs] N manicomio *m*, casa *f* de locos

madly [ˈmædlɪ] ADV [*scream, laugh, wave, rush*] (*one person*) como (un) loco/(una) loca; (*more than one person*) como locos; **they were ~ in love** estaban locamente *or* perdidamente enamorados

madman [ˈmædmən] N (*pl* **madmen**) loco *m*

madness [ˈmædnɪs] N **1** (= *mental illness*) locura *f*, demencia *f* **2** (= *foolishness*) locura *f*; **it would be sheer ~ to continue** sería una auténtica locura seguir

Madrid [məˈdrɪd] **Ⓐ** N Madrid *m* **Ⓑ** ADJ madrileño

madwoman [ˈmædwʊmən] N (*pl* **madwomen**) loca *f*

maelstrom [ˈmeɪlstrəum] N torbellino *m*, remolino *m*

maestro [ˈmaɪstrəʊ] N (*pl* ~**s** *or* **maestri** [ˈmaɪstrɪ]) maestro *m*

MAFF [mæf] N ABBR (*Brit*) (= **Ministry of Agriculture, Fisheries and Food**) ≈ MAPA *m*

mafia [ˈmæfɪə] N mafia *f*

mag* [mæɡ] N ABBR (= **magazine**) revista *f*

magazine [ˌmæɡəˈziːn] N **1** (= *journal*) revista *f* **2** (*in rifle*) recámara *f*

magenta [məˈdʒentə] **Ⓐ** N magenta *m* **Ⓑ** ADJ magenta *inv*

maggot [ˈmæɡət] N cresa *f*, gusano *m*

Magi [ˈmeɪdʒaɪ] NPL **the ~** los Reyes Magos

magic [ˈmædʒɪk] **Ⓐ** N magia *f*; **as if by ~** como por arte de magia, como por encanto **Ⓑ** ADJ **1** (= *supernatural*) mágico;

to say the ~ word decir la palabra mágica **2** (*esp Brit**) (= *super*) fabuloso, estupendo **⊙** CPD ➤ **magic carpet** alfombra *f* mágica ➤ **magic mushrooms*** setas *fpl* alucinógenas, hongos *mpl* alucinógenos ➤ **magic spell** hechizo *m*, encanto *m* ➤ **magic wand** varita *f* mágica

magical ['mædʒɪkəl] ADJ mágico

magician [mədʒɪʃən] N **1** (= *sorcerer*) mago/a *m/f* **2** (= *conjuror*) prestidigitador(a) *m/f*

magistrate ['mædʒɪstreɪt] N magistrado/a *m/f*, juez *mf* ➤ **magistrates' court** juzgado *m* de primera instancia

magnanimity [,mægnə'nɪmɪtɪ] N magnanimidad *f*

magnanimous [mæg'nænɪməs] ADJ magnánimo (*frm*), generoso; **to be ~ to sb** mostrarse magnánimo (*frm*) *or* generoso con algn

magnate ['mægneɪt] N magnate *mf*, potentado/a *m/f*

magnesium [mæg'niːzɪəm] N magnesio *m*

magnet ['mægnɪt] N imán *m*

magnetic [mæg'netɪk] ADJ magnético; (*fig*) carismático ➤ **magnetic disk** disco *m* magnético ➤ **magnetic field** campo *m* magnético ➤ **magnetic strip** banda *f* magnética ➤ **magnetic tape** cinta *f* magnética

magnetism ['mægnɪtɪzəm] N magnetismo *m*; (*fig*) magnetismo *m*, atractivo *m*

magnetize ['mægnɪtaɪz] VT magnetizar, imantar

magnification [,mægnɪfɪ'keɪʃən] N (*Opt*) aumento *m*, ampliación *f*

magnificence [mæg'nɪfɪsəns] N magnificencia *f*

magnificent [mæg'nɪfɪsənt] ADJ [*display, performance, achievement, animal, view*] magnífico, espléndido; [*building*] espléndido; **the princess looked ~** la princesa estaba esplendorosa

magnify ['mægnɪfaɪ] VT (*Opt*) aumentar, ampliar

magnifying glass ['mægnɪfaɪɪŋ,glɑːs] N lupa *f*

magnitude ['mægnɪtjuːd] N magnitud *f*

magnolia [mæg'nəʊlɪə] N magnolia *f*

magnum ['mægnəm] N (= *bottle*) botella *f* doble

magpie ['mægpaɪ] N urraca *f*, marica *f*

mahogany [mə'hɒgənɪ] N caoba *f*

maid [meɪd] N (= *servant*) criada *f*, muchacha *f* (*SC*), mucama *f* (*SC*), recamarera *f* (*Mex*); (*in hotel*) camarera *f* ➤ **maid of honor** (*US*) dama *f* de honor

maiden ['meɪdn] **Ⓐ** N (*poet†*) doncella *f* **Ⓑ** ADJ [*flight, speech*] inaugural, de inauguración **⊙** CPD ➤ **maiden aunt** tía *f* solterona ➤ **maiden name** apellido *m* de soltera

mail [meɪl] **Ⓐ** N **1** (= *postal system*) correo *m*; **by** *or* **through the ~** por correo **2** (= *letters*) cartas *fpl*, correspondencia *f*; **is there any ~ for me?** ¿hay alguna carta para mí? **3** = **e-mail** **Ⓑ** VT **1** (*esp US*) (= *post*) echar al correo; (= *send by mail*) enviar por correo **2** = **e-mail** **⊙** CPD ➤ **mail coach** (*Rail*) furgón *m* postal, vagón *m* correo ➤ **mail merge** combinación *f* de correspondencia ➤ **mail order** (= *system*) venta *f* por correo; (= *order*) pedido *m* por correo ➤ **mail room** (*esp US*) sala *f* de correo, departamento *m* de registro (de entradas y salidas) ➤ **mail van** (*Brit Aut*) camioneta *f* de correos; (*Rail*) furgón *m* postal, vagón *m* correo

mailbag ['meɪlbæg] N saca *f* de correos

mailbox ['meɪlbɒks] N **1** (*US*) (*in street*) buzón *m* **2** (*esp US*) (*in office etc*) casilla *f* **3** (*Comput*) buzón *m*

mailing ['meɪlɪŋ] N envío *m* ➤ **mailing list** lista *f* de direcciones

mailman ['meɪlmæn] N (*pl* **mailmen**) (*US*) cartero *m*

mail-order ['meɪl,ɔːdə*r*] CPD ➤ **mail-order catalogue, mail-order catalog** (*US*) catálogo *m* de venta por correo

mailshot ['meɪlʃɒt] N (*Brit*) mailing *m*

maim [meɪm] VT mutilar, lisiar; **to be ~ed for life** quedar lisiado de por vida

main [meɪn] **Ⓐ** ADJ [*reason, problem, aim, concern*] principal, fundamental; [*gate, entrance*] principal; **the ~ thing is that no one was hurt** lo principal es que nadie resultó herido **Ⓑ** N **1** (= *pipe*) cañería *f* principal, conducto *m* principal; (= *cable*) cable *m* principal; **the ~s** (*esp Brit Gas, Water*) la red de suministro; (*esp Brit Elec*) la red, la red de suministro; **to turn the gas/water off at the ~s** cerrar la llave principal del gas/agua; **to turn the electricity off at the ~s** apagar la electricidad **2 in the ~** (= *generally speaking*) por lo general, por regla general, en general; (= *in the majority*) por lo general, en su mayoría, en su mayor parte **⊙** CPD ➤ **main course** plato *m* principal ➤ **main line** (*Rail*) línea *f* principal ➤ **main office** sede *f*, oficina *f* central ➤ **main road** carretera *f* principal ➤ **Main Street** (*US*) **1** calle *f* principal **2** (*fig*) *gente que vive en poblaciones pequeñas* ➤ **the mains supply** el suministro de la red

mainframe ['meɪnfreɪm] N (*also* **~ computer**) ordenador *m* central, computadora *f* central

mainland ['meɪnlənd] N tierra *f* firme, continente *m*; **they want to move to the ~** [*islanders*] quieren trasladarse a Inglaterra/Francia *etc*

mainline ['meɪn'laɪn] ADJ **1** (*Rail*) [*service, station*] principal, interurbano **2** (= *mainstream*) tradicional, al uso

mainly ['meɪnlɪ] ADV **1** (= *fundamentally*) principalmente, fundamentalmente; (= *for the greater part*) mayormente, principalmente; **they have stayed together ~ because of their children** han seguido juntos principalmente *or* fundamentalmente por sus hijos; **it was ~ his idea** fue mayormente *or* principalmente idea suya **2** (= *in the majority*) en su mayoría, en su mayor parte; **her customers are ~ women** sus clientes son en su mayoría *or* en su mayor parte mujeres

mainsail ['meɪnsl] N vela *f* mayor

mainspring ['meɪnsprɪŋ] N [*of watch*] muelle *m* real

mainstay ['meɪnsteɪ] N (*Naut*) estay *m* mayor; (*fig*) sostén *m* principal, pilar *m*

mainstream ['meɪnstriːm] **Ⓐ** N [*of ideology, philosophy, literature*] corriente *f* principal; **they remain outside the political ~** permanecen fuera de la escena política mayoritaria **Ⓑ** ADJ [*political party*] mayoritario; [*press, media, culture*] dominante; [*fashion*] de masas; [*education*] convencional; **the rise of the right in ~ politics** el ascenso de la derecha dentro de la corriente política dominante

maintain [meɪn'teɪn] VT **1** (= *keep up*) mantener; [+ *silence*] guardar **2** (= *support*) [+ *family, dependants*] mantener **3** (= *keep in good condition*) [+ *road, building, car*] mantener en buen estado **4** (= *claim*) [+ *one's innocence*] mantener, sostener; **he ~ed that the earth was round** mantenía *or* sostenía que la tierra era redonda

maintenance ['meɪntɪnəns] **Ⓐ** N **1** [*of car*] mantenimiento *m*; [*of building*] manutención *f*, cuidado *m* **2** (*after divorce*) pensión *f* alimenticia **Ⓑ** CPD ➤ **maintenance costs** gastos *mpl* de mantenimiento ➤ **maintenance grant** (*Univ*) beca *f* ➤ **maintenance order** *orden judicial que obliga al pago de una pensión alimenticia*

maisonette [,meɪzə'net] N (*esp Brit*) dúplex *m inv*

maize [meɪz] N (*esp Brit*) maíz *m* ➤ **maize field** maizal *m*

Maj. ABBR = **Major**

majestic [mə'dʒestɪk] ADJ majestuoso

majesty ['mædʒɪstɪ] N majestad *f*; **His/Her Majesty** Su Majestad; **Your Majesty** (Vuestra) Majestad

major ['meɪdʒə*r*] **Ⓐ** ADJ **1** (= *large, important*) [*city, company*] muy importante; [*change, role*] fundamental, muy importante; [*factor*] clave, muy importante, fundamental; [*problem*] serio, grave; [*worry*] enorme; [*breakthrough*] de enorme importancia; **of ~ importance** de la mayor importancia; **a hysterectomy is a ~ operation** la histerectomía es una operación seria *or* grave; **getting him off to school is a ~ operation** (*hum*) llevarlo al colegio es una operación a gran escala (*hum*) **2** (= *principal*) [*cities, political parties*] más importante **3** (*Mus*) [*chord, key*] mayor; **C ~** do mayor **Ⓑ** N **1** (*Mil*) comandante *m*, mayor *m* (*LAm*)

2 (*US Univ*) (= *subject*) asignatura *f* principal; **he's a Spanish ~** estudia español como asignatura principal
Ⓒ VI **to ~ in sth** (*US Univ*) especializarse en algo
Ⓓ CPD ➤ **major league** (*US*) liga *f* principal

Majorca [məˈjɔːkə] N Mallorca *f*

Majorcan [məˈjɔːkən] ADJ, N mallorquín/ina *m/f*

majorette [ˌmeɪdʒəˈret] N majorette *f*, batonista *f*

majority [məˈdʒɒrɪtɪ] Ⓐ N **1** mayoría *f*; **they won by a ~** ganaron por mayoría; **in the ~ of cases** en la mayoría *or* la mayor parte de los casos; **the vast ~** la inmensa mayoría
2 (*Jur*) **to attain one's ~** llegar a la mayoría de edad Ⓑ CPD ➤ **majority decision: by a ~ decision** por decisión mayoritaria *or* de la mayoría ➤ **majority rule** gobierno *m* mayoritario, gobierno *m* en mayoría ➤ **majority verdict: by a ~ verdict** por fallo *or* veredicto mayoritario

make

Ⓐ TRANSITIVE VERB	Ⓒ NOUN
Ⓑ INTRANSITIVE VERB	Ⓓ PHRASAL VERBS

When **make** *is part of a set combination, eg* **make an attempt, make a bow, make a case, make sure,** *look up the other word.*

make [meɪk] (*pt, pp* **made**)
Ⓐ TRANSITIVE VERB
1 (= *create, prepare*) [+ *fire, bed, tea, cake, will, remark, plan, suggestion*] hacer; [+ *dress*] hacer, confeccionar; [+ *meal*] hacer, preparar; [+ *record*] grabar; [+ *film*] rodar; (= *manufacture*) [+ *tool, machine*] fabricar, hacer; **I ~ my bed every morning** me hago la cama cada mañana; **he made it himself** lo hizo él mismo; **"made in Spain"** [*machine*] "fabricado en España"; [*dress*] "confeccionado en España"; [*chocolate*] "elaborado en España"; **this car isn't made to carry eight people** este coche no está pensado para ocho personas; **they were made for each other** estaban hechos el uno para el otro; **her shoes weren't made for walking** llevaba unos zapatos poco adecuados para caminar; **we had the curtains made to measure** nos hicieron las cortinas a medida; **it's made of gold** es de oro, está hecho de oro
2 (= *carry out*) [+ *journey, effort, phone call*] hacer; [+ *speech*] pronunciar; [+ *payment*] efectuar; [+ *error*] cometer
3 (= *earn*) ganar; **he ~s £350 a week** gana 350 libras a la semana; **the film made millions** la película recaudó millones
4 (= *reach, achieve*) [+ *place*] llegar a; **will we ~ Paris before lunch?** ¿llegaremos a París antes de la hora de comer?; **we made it just in time** llegamos justo a tiempo; **sorry, I can't ~ it** lo siento, no puedo *or* no me va bien; **he made (it into) the first team** consiguió entrar en el primer equipo;
✦ IDIOM **he's got it made*** tiene el éxito asegurado
5 (= *say, agree*) **let's ~ it nine o'clock** pongamos las nueve; **another beer, please, no, ~ that two** otra cerveza por favor, no, que sean dos
6 (= *cause to succeed*) **this film made her** esta película la consagró; **he was made for life** se aseguró un porvenir brillante; ✦ IDIOM **this deal will ~ or break him** con este negocio o fracasa o se asegura el éxito
7 (= *constitute*) **he'll ~ somebody a good husband** va a ser *or* hará un buen marido para algn; **they ~ a lovely couple** hacen muy buena pareja; **he'll ~ a good footballer** será buen futbolista
8 (= *equal*) **two and two ~ four** dos y dos son cuatro; **this one ~s 20** con éste son *or* hacen 20; **how much does that ~ (altogether)?** ¿a cuánto sube (en total)?
9 (= *calculate*) calcular; **how many do you ~ it?** ¿cuántos calculas que hay?; **what time do you ~ it?** ¿qué hora tienes?; **I ~ it six o'clock** yo tengo las seis
10 (*set structures and expressions*)
✦ **to make sb sth** (= *cause to be*) **to ~ sb king** hacer rey a algn; **he made his wife** la hizo su esposa; **he made her a star** hizo de ella una estrella
✦ **to make sb/sth** (+ ADJECTIVE/PAST PARTICIPLE) **to ~ sb happy** hacer feliz a algn; **to ~ sb angry** poner furioso a algn; **to ~ o.s. heard** hacerse oír; **the noise made it difficult to concentrate** con ese ruido era difícil concentrarse

✦ **to make sth/sb into sth** convertir algo/a algn en algo; **we made the guest room into a study** convertimos la habitación de los invitados en estudio
✦ **to make sb do sth** hacer a algn hacer algo; **to ~ sb laugh/cry** hacer reír/llorar a algn; **now look what you've made me do!** ¡mira lo que me has hecho hacer!; **what made you say that?** ¿cómo se te ocurrió decir eso?, ¿por qué dijiste eso?; **it ~s you think, doesn't it?** da que pensar ¿no?; **you can't ~ me (do it)** no puedes obligarme (a hacerlo)
✦ **to make o.s. sth** obligarse a hacer algo
✦ **to make sth do, make do with sth** arreglárselas *or* apañárselas con algo
✦ **to make believe that** fingir que, hacer que
✦ **to make good** [+ *promise*] cumplir; [+ *claim*] justificar; [+ *loss*] compensar; [+ *damage*] reparar; (= *pay*) pagar
✦ **to make of** (= *understand*) **I don't know what to ~ of it** no sé qué pensar; **what do you ~ of Anna?** ¿qué piensas de Anna?, ¿qué te parece Anna?; **what do you ~ of this?** ¿qué te parece esto?; (= *give importance to*) **I think you're making too much of what I said** creo que le estás dando demasiada importancia a lo que dije
✦ **to make something of o.s./one's life** ser alguien (en la vida)
Ⓑ INTRANSITIVE VERB (*in set expressions*) **to ~ after sb** perseguir a algn, correr tras algn; **he made as if to** (+ INFIN) hizo como si + *subjun*, hizo además de + *infin*; **he made as if to strike me** hizo como si me fuera a pegar, hizo además de pegarme; **to ~ good** [*ex-criminal*] rehabilitar, reformar
Ⓒ NOUN (= *brand*) marca *f*; **what ~ of car was it?** ¿qué marca de coche era?; **they are our own ~** son de nuestra propia marca; ✦ IDIOM **to be on the ~*** (*for money*) estar intentando sacar tajada*; (*for power*) ser muy ambicioso
Ⓓ PHRASAL VERBS
➤ **make for** VI + PREP **1** (= *go towards*) [+ *place*] dirigirse hacia *or* a; **he made for the door** se dirigió hacia la puerta
2 (= *attack*) **to ~ for sb** atacar a algn, abalanzarse sobre algn **3** (= *contribute to*) contribuir a; (= *lead to*) conducir a; **it ~s for an easy life** contribuye a hacer la vida más fácil; **it doesn't ~ for good customer relations** no conduce a una buena relación con los clientes
➤ **make off** VI + ADV irse rápidamente, largarse*; **to ~ off with sth** llevarse algo, escaparse *or** largarse con algo
➤ **make out** Ⓐ VT + ADV **1** (= *write out*) [+ *cheque*] hacer, extender; [+ *receipt, list*] hacer; [+ *document*] redactar; (= *fill in*) [+ *form*] llenar; **the cheque should be made out to Pérez** el cheque debe extenderse a nombre de Pérez
2 (= *see*) [+ *distant object*] distinguir, divisar
3 (= *decipher*) [+ *writing*] descifrar
4 (= *understand*) entender, comprender; **I can't ~ her out at all** no la entiendo *or* comprendo en absoluto
5 (= *claim, imply*) **he's not as rich as people ~ out** no es tan rico como dice la gente; **the situation is not so bad as you ~ it out to be** la situación no es tan grave como la pintas; **to ~ out that** dar a entender que; **she made out it was a wrong number** hizo como que se había equivocado de número
Ⓑ VI + ADV (*) (= *get on*) (*with person*) llevarse; **how did you ~ out at the audition?** ¿qué tal te fue en la audición?; **to ~ out with sb** (*esp US**) (*sexually*) hacérselo con algn*
➤ **make over** VT + ADV **1** (= *assign*) ceder, traspasar (**to** a); **he had made over the farm to his son** le había cedido *or* traspasado la granja a su hijo **2** (= *revamp*) [+ *organization*] modernizar, poner al día
➤ **make up** Ⓐ VT + ADV **1** (= *invent*) inventar(se); **you're making it up!** ¡te lo estás inventando!
2 (= *prepare*) [+ *list*] hacer, preparar; [+ *parcel, bed*] hacer; [+ *medicine*] preparar; [+ *sweater, dress*] montar y coser
3 (= *settle*) [+ *differences*] resolver; **to ~ it up with sb** hacer las paces con algn, reconciliarse con algn
4 (= *complete*) completar; **I paid £200 and my parents made up the difference** pagué 200 libras y mis padres pusieron la diferencia; **we need someone to ~ up the numbers** necesitamos a alguien para completar el grupo
5 (= *decide*) **to ~ up one's mind** decidirse
6 (= *compensate for, replace*) [+ *loss*] compensar; [+ *deficit*] cubrir; **if I take time off I have to ~ up the hours later** si me tomo tiempo libre después tengo que recuperar las horas; **I'd like to ~ it up to him for spoiling his birthday** me gustaría compensarle por haberle estropeado el

cumpleaños; **he tried to ~ it up to her by buying her a bunch of flowers** intentó hacerse perdonar comprándole un ramo de flores; **to ~ up (lost) time** recuperar el tiempo perdido
7 (= *constitute*) componer; **women ~ up 13% of the police force** las mujeres componen el 13% del cuerpo de policía; **blood is made up of red and white cells** la sangre se compone de glóbulos rojos y glóbulos blancos
8 (*with cosmetics*) maquillar; **to ~ o.s. up** maquillarse, pintarse
Ⓑ VI + ADV **1** (*after quarrel*) hacer las paces, reconciliarse **2** (= *apply cosmetics*) maquillarse, pintarse
➤ **make up for** VI + PREP (= *compensate for*) compensar; **her willingness to learn more than made up for her lack of experience** sus ganas de aprender compensaban con creces su falta de experiencia; **to ~ up for lost time** recuperar el tiempo perdido

make-believe ['meɪkbɪ‚liːv] **Ⓐ** ADJ (= *pretend*) fingido, simulado; (= *fantasy*) de ensueño, de fantasía **Ⓑ** N **don't worry, it's just ~** no te preocupes, no es de verdad; **a land or world of ~** un mundo de ensueño *or* fantasía

makeover ['meɪkəʊvəʳ] N **1** (*by beautician*) sesión *f* de maquillaje y peluquería **2** (= *change of image*) lavado *m* de cara

maker ['meɪkəʳ] N **1** (= *manufacturer*) fabricante *mf* **2** (*Rel*) **Maker** Creador *m*, Hacedor *m*; **prepare to meet your Maker** prepárate a morir

makeshift ['meɪkʃɪft] **Ⓐ** ADJ (= *improvised*) improvisado; (= *provisional*) provisional **Ⓑ** N arreglo *m* provisional

make-up ['meɪkʌp] **Ⓐ** N **1** (= *cosmetics*) maquillaje *m*, pintura *f*; **to put on one's ~** maquillarse, pintarse **2** (= *composition*) composición *f*; (= *structure*) estructura *f*; (= *character*) carácter *m*, modo *m* de ser **Ⓑ** CPD ➤ **make-up artist** maquillador(a) *m/f* ➤ **make-up bag** neceser *m* del maquillaje ➤ **make-up remover** desmaquillador *m*, desmaquillante *m*

making ['meɪkɪŋ] N **1** (= *production*) fabricación *f*; (= *preparation*) preparación *f*; (= *shooting*) [*of film*] rodaje *m*; **it's history in the ~** esto pasará a la historia; **she was caught in a trap of her own ~** había caído en su propia trampa **2 makings: a chain of events that had all the ~s of a Hollywood epic** una cadena de acontecimientos que tenía todos los elementos *or* ingredientes de una epopeya de Hollywood; **he has the ~s of an actor** tiene madera de actor

maladjusted [‚mælə'dʒʌstɪd] ADJ (*Psych*) inadaptado

malady ['mælədɪ] N mal *m*, enfermedad *f*

malaise [mæ'leɪz] N malestar *m*

malapropism ['mæləprɒpɪzəm] N lapsus *m inv* linguae, equivocación *f* de palabras

malaria [mə'lɛərɪə] N malaria *f*, paludismo *m*

Malawi [mə'lɑːwɪ] N Malawi *m*, Malaui *m*

Malay [mə'leɪ] ADJ, N malayo/a *m/f*

Malaysia [mə'leɪzɪə] N Malaisia *f*

Malaysian [mə'leɪzɪən] ADJ, N malaisio/a *m/f*

Maldives ['mɔːldaɪvz], **Maldive Islands** [‚mɔːldaɪv'aɪləndz] NPL (islas *fpl*) Maldivas *fpl*

male [meɪl] **Ⓐ** N (= *animal*) macho *m*; (= *person*) varón *m* **Ⓑ** ADJ [*rat, plant*] macho; [*baby, child*] varón; [*friend, colleague*] del sexo masculino; [*population, hormone, sex, behaviour*] masculino; [*voice*] de hombre, masculino **Ⓒ** CPD ➤ **male chauvinism** machismo *m* ➤ **male chauvinist** machista *m* ➤ **male menopause** menopausia *f* masculina, andropausia *f* ➤ **male model** modelo *m* del sexo masculino ➤ **male nurse** enfermero *m* ➤ **male voice choir** coro *m* masculino *or* de hombres

malevolence [mə'levələns] N malevolencia *f*

malevolent [mə'levələnt] ADJ malévolo

malformation ['mælfɔː'meɪʃən] N malformación *f*, deformidad *f*

malformed [‚mæl'fɔːmd] ADJ malformado, deforme

malfunction [mæl'fʌŋkʃən] **Ⓐ** N [*of machine*] fallo *m* (*Sp*), falla *f* (*LAm*) **Ⓑ** VI funcionar mal

malice ['mælɪs] N (= *grudge*) rencor *m*; (= *badness*) malicia *f*; **I bear him no ~** no le guardo rencor

malicious [mə'lɪʃəs] ADJ [*person, remark*] malicioso

malign [mə'laɪn] **Ⓐ** ADJ maligno, malévolo **Ⓑ** VT [+ *person, reputation*] calumniar, difamar

malignancy [mə'lɪgnənsɪ] N malignidad *f*

malignant [mə'lɪgnənt] ADJ (= *evil*) malvado; (*Med*) maligno

malingerer [mə'lɪŋgərəʳ] N enfermo/a *m/f* fingido/a

mall [mɔːl, mæl] N **1** (= *avenue*) alameda *f*, paseo *m* **2** (*US*) (= *pedestrian street*) calle *f* peatonal **3** (*also* **shopping ~**) centro *m* comercial

mallard ['mælɑːd] N ánade *m* real

malleable ['mælɪəbl] ADJ maleable, dúctil

mallet ['mælɪt] N mazo *m*

malnourished [‚mæl'nʌrɪʃt] ADJ desnutrido

malnutrition ['mælnjʊ'trɪʃən] N desnutrición *f*

malpractice ['mæl'præktɪs] N (= *negligence*) negligencia *f* profesional; (= *wrongdoing*) práctica *f* abusiva
➤ **malpractice suit** (*US*) juicio *m* por negligencia profesional

malt [mɔːlt] N malta *f* ➤ **malt whisky** (*Brit*) whisky *m* de malta

Malta ['mɔːltə] N Malta *f*

Maltese ['mɔːl'tiːz] **Ⓐ** ADJ maltés **Ⓑ** N (*pl* ~) **1** (= *person*) maltés/esa *m/f* **2** (*Ling*) maltés *m*

maltreat [mæl'triːt] VT maltratar, tratar mal

mama†* [mə'mɑː] N (*Brit*) mamá *f*

mamma* [mə'mɑː] N (*esp US*) mamá *f*

mammal ['mæməl] N mamífero *m*

mammary ['mæmərɪ] ADJ mamario ➤ **mammary gland** mama *f*, glándula *f* mamaria

mammogram ['mæməgræm] N mamografía *f*

mammoth ['mæməθ] **Ⓐ** N (= *animal*) mamut *m* **Ⓑ** ADJ descomunal, gigante

mammy ['mæmɪ] N **1** (*) mami *f*, mamaíta *f*, mamacita *f* (*LAm*) **2** (*US†*) (= *black nurse*) nodriza *f* negra

man [mæn] **Ⓐ** N (*pl* **men**) **1** (= *not woman*) hombre *m*; (= *husband*) marido *m*; (= *boyfriend*) novio *m*; (= *servant*) criado *m*; (= *workman*) obrero *m*; (= *ordinary soldier*) soldado *m*; (= *ordinary sailor*) marinero *m*; **he's been a different ~ since he got married** es otro hombre desde que se casó; **the ~ who does the garden** el señor que hace el jardín; **he's not the ~ for the job** no es el más indicado para esa tarea; **good ~!** ¡bravo!, ¡muy bien!; **the army will make a ~ out of him** el ejército le hará un hombre; **to feel (like) a new ~** sentirse como nuevo; **my old ~*** (= *father*) el viejo*; (= *husband*) mi marido; **the ~ in the street** el hombre de la calle; **~ to ~** de hombre a hombre; **he's a ~ about town** (*Brit*) es un gran vividor; **~ and wife** marido y mujer; **to live as ~ and wife** vivir como casados *or* en matrimonio; **a ~ of the world** un hombre de mundo; **a young ~** un joven; **her young ~** su novio; ✦ IDIOMS **this will separate or sort the men from the boys** con esto se verá quiénes son hombres y quiénes no; **to be ~ enough to do sth** ser lo bastante hombre *or* tener valor suficiente como para hacer algo **2** (= *humanity in general*) (*also* **Man**) el hombre **3** (= *individual, person*) persona *f*; **no ~** ninguno, nadie; **as one ~** como un solo hombre; **they're communists to a ~** todos sin excepción son comunistas; **then I'm your ~** entonces soy la persona que estás buscando **4** (= *type*) **I'm not a drinking ~** yo no bebo; **he's a family ~** (= *with family*) es padre de familia; (= *home-loving*) es muy casero; **I'm not a football ~** no soy aficionado al fútbol, no me gusta mucho el fútbol; **he's a man's ~** es un hombre estimado entre otros hombres; **I'm a whisky ~ myself** yo prefiero el whisky **5** (*Chess*) pieza *f*; (*Draughts*) ficha *f* **Ⓑ** VT [+ *ship*] tripular; [+ *fortress*] guarnecer; [+ *pumps*] acudir a, hacer funcionar; **the gun is ~ned by four soldiers** cuatro soldados manejan el cañón; **the telephone is ~ned all day** el teléfono está atendido todo el día **Ⓒ** CPD ➤ **man hour** (*Comm, Ind*) hora-hombre *f* ➤ **men's**

doubles (*Tennis*) dobles *mpl* masculinos ➤ **men's room** (*esp US*) lavabo *m* de caballeros

manacle ['mænəkl] **Ⓐ** NPL **manacles** esposas *fpl*, grillos *mpl* **Ⓑ** VT esposar, poner esposas a

manage ['mænɪdʒ] **Ⓐ** VT **1** (= *direct*) [+ *firm, shop*] dirigir, administrar; [+ *employees*] dirigir; [+ *time, money*] administrar; [+ *household*] llevar; (*Comput*) [+ *system, network*] gestionar

2 (= *handle, control*) [+ *situation, person*] manejar; [+ *suitcases, packages*] poder con; [+ *animal*] dominar; [+ *children*] manejar, controlar

3 (= *achieve*) **I can't ~ Friday** el viernes no puedo; **£20 is all I can ~** 20 libras es todo lo que puedo dar *or* pagar; **I couldn't ~ another mouthful** no podría comer ni un bocado más; **to ~ to do sth** lograr *or* conseguir hacer algo; **how did you ~ not to spill it?** ¿cómo lograste *or* conseguiste no derramarlo?; **he ~d to annoy everybody** consiguió irritar a todo el mundo

Ⓑ VI arreglárselas; (*financially*) arreglarse, arreglárselas; **can you ~?** (= *deal with situation*) ¿puedes arreglártelas?; (= *carry sth*) ¿puedes con eso?; **thanks, I can ~** gracias, yo puedo; **she ~s on £60 a week** se (las) arregla con 60 libras a la semana; **"do you need the car?" — "I can ~ without it"** —¿necesitas el coche? —me (las) puedo arreglar *or* apañar sin él; **I don't know how we'd have ~d without her** no sé cómo nos (las) hubiéramos arreglado *or* apañado sin ella

manageable ['mænɪdʒəbl] ADJ **1** (= *controllable*) [*size, number, level, rate*] razonable; [*situation*] controlable; [*problem*] que se puede solucionar; [*vehicle*] manejable, fácil de maniobrar; [*hair*] dócil **2** (= *achievable*) [*task*] que se puede realizar **3** (= *docile*) [*person, child, animal*] dócil

management ['mænɪdʒmənt] **Ⓐ** N **1** (= *managing*) [*of firm*] dirección *f*, administración *f*, gestión *f* **2** (= *people in charge*) directivos *mpl*; (= *managing body*) [*of firm*] dirección *f*, gerencia *f*; **"under new management"** "bajo nueva dirección"; **~ and workers** empresarios y trabajadores **3** (= *handling*) [*of situation*] manejo *m* **Ⓑ** CPD ➤ **management accounting** contabilidad *f* de gestión ➤ **management consultant** consultor(a) *m/f* en gestión de empresas

manager ['mænɪdʒəʳ] N [*of firm, bank*] director(a) *m/f*, gerente *mf*; [*of estate*] administrador(a) *m/f*; [*of football team*] director(a) *m/f* técnico/a; [*of restaurant, shop*] encargado/a *m/f*; [*of actor, singer*] representante *mf*, mánager *mf*; [*of boxer*] mánager *mf*; **she's a good ~** es buena administradora

manageress [,mænɪdʒə'res] N [*of restaurant, shop*] encargada *f*

managerial [,mænə'dʒɪərɪəl] ADJ directivo, de gestión; **at ~ level** a nivel directivo; **~ staff** personal *m* directivo *or* de gerencia

managing ['mænɪdʒɪŋ] CPD ➤ **managing director** (*esp Brit*) director(a) *m/f* gerente

Mandarin ['mændərɪn] N (*Ling*) mandarín *m*

mandarin ['mændərɪn] N **1** (= *person*) mandarín *m* **2** (*also* **~ orange**) mandarina *f*

mandate ['mændeɪt] **Ⓐ** N (= *authority*) mandato *m*; **they have no ~ to intervene in the fighting** no tienen mandato para intervenir en el conflicto; **he does not have a ~ to rule this country** carece de autoridad para gobernar este país **Ⓑ** VT (= *authorize*) [+ *person*] encomendar, encargar

mandatory ['mændətərɪ] ADJ (= *compulsory*) obligatorio; (*Jur*) [*sentence, penalty, fine*] preceptivo, obligatorio

mandolin(e) ['mændəlɪn] N mandolina *f*, bandolina *f* (*LAm*)

mane [meɪn] N [*of lion, person*] melena *f*; [*of horse*] crin *f*, crines *fpl*

man-eater ['mæn,iːtəʳ] N **1** (= *animal*) fiera *f* devoradora de hombres **2** (*) (= *woman*) devoradora *f* de hombres

maneuver [mə'nuːvəʳ] (*US*) = **manoeuvre**

manfully ['mænfəlɪ] ADV valientemente, resueltamente

manganese [,mæŋgə'niːz] N (*Chem*) manganeso *m*

mange [meɪndʒ] N sarna *f*

manger ['meɪndʒəʳ] N pesebre *m*

mangle¹ ['mæŋgl] N escurridor *m*

mangle² ['mæŋgl] VT (= *crush*) aplastar; [+ *text etc*] mutilar, estropear

mango ['mæŋgəʊ] N (*pl* **~es**) mango *m*

mangrove ['mæŋgrəʊv] N mangle *m*

mangy ['meɪndʒɪ] ADJ (*compar* **mangier**; *superl* **mangiest**) roñoso, sarnoso

manhandle ['mæn,hændl] VT **1** (*esp Brit*) (= *move by hand*) mover a base de brazos **2** (= *treat roughly*) maltratar

manhole ['mænhəʊl] N boca *f* de alcantarilla, registro *m* de alcantarilla

manhood ['mænhʊd] N **1** (= *age of majority*) mayoría *f* de edad, madurez *f*; **to reach ~** alcanzar la mayoría de edad, llegar a la madurez **2** (= *manliness*) hombría *f*, virilidad *f*

manhunt ['mænhʌnt] N búsqueda *f* (*de delincuente, desaparecido*)

mania ['meɪnɪə] N manía *f*

maniac ['meɪnɪæk] **Ⓐ** ADJ maníaco **Ⓑ** N maníaco/a *m/f*; **he drives like a ~*** conduce como un loco

manic ['mænɪk] **Ⓐ** ADJ **1** (= *insane*) [*person, behaviour*] maníaco; [*laughter, stare*] de maníaco **2** (= *frenetic*) [*activity, energy*] frenético **Ⓑ** CPD ➤ **manic depression** maniacodepresión *f* ➤ **manic depressive** maniacodepresivo/a *m/f*

manicure ['mænɪkjʊəʳ] **Ⓐ** N manicura *f* **Ⓑ** VT [+ *person*] hacer la manicura a; [+ *nails*] limpiar, arreglar **Ⓒ** CPD ➤ **manicure set** estuche *m* de manicura

manifest ['mænɪfest] **Ⓐ** ADJ manifiesto, patente; **to make sth ~** poner algo de manifiesto **Ⓑ** VT manifestar

manifestation [,mænɪfes'teɪʃən] N manifestación *f*

manifesto [,mænɪ'festəʊ] N (*pl* **~es** *or* **~s**) manifiesto *m*

manifold ['mænɪfəʊld] ADJ (= *numerous*) múltiple; (= *varied*) diverso

Manila [mə'nɪlə] N Manila *f*

manil(l)a [mə'nɪlə] ADJ [*envelope, paper*] manila *inv*

manipulate [mə'nɪpjʊleɪt] VT [+ *tool, vehicle*] manipular, manejar; [+ *facts, figures, person*] manipular

manipulation [mə,nɪpjʊ'leɪʃən] N [*of tool, vehicle*] manipulación *f*, manejo *m*; [*of facts, figures, person*] manipulación *f*

manipulative [mə'nɪpjʊlətɪv] ADJ manipulador

mankind [mæn'kaɪnd] N humanidad *f*, género *m* humano

manliness ['mænlɪnɪs] N masculinidad *f*, virilidad *f*

manly ['mænlɪ] ADJ (**manlier, manliest**) [*person, physique*] varonil, viril; [*quality, pursuit*] masculino, varonil

man-made ['mæn'meɪd] ADJ [*material*] sintético, artificial; [*lake, island, environment*] artificial; [*gas, chemical*] producido por el hombre; **~ fibres** fibras *fpl* sintéticas

manna ['mænə] N maná *m*; ✦ IDIOM **~ from heaven** maná *m* caído del cielo

mannequin ['mænɪkɪn] N **1** (= *dressmaker's dummy*) maniquí *m* **2** (= *fashion model*) modelo *f*, maniquí *f*

manner ['mænəʳ] N **1** (= *mode, way*) manera *f*, modo *m*; **in a ~ of speaking** (= *so to speak*) por así decirlo, como si dijéramos; (= *up to a point*) hasta cierto punto, en cierto modo; **in such a ~ that ...** de tal manera que ... **2** (= *behaviour etc*) forma *f* de ser, comportamiento *m*; **I don't like his ~** no me gusta su forma de ser **3** (= *class, type*) clase *f*; **all ~ of** toda clase *or* suerte de **4 manners** [*of person*] modales *mpl*, educación *fsing*; **to have bad ~s** ser maleducado; **it's bad ~s to yawn** es de mala educación bostezar; **good ~s** educación *f*, buenos modales *mpl*; **it's good ~s to say "please"** se dice "por favor"; **he's got no ~s** es un maleducado

mannerism ['mænərɪzəm] N (= *gesture etc*) gesto *m*

manoeuvre, maneuver (*US*) [mə'nuːvəʳ] **Ⓐ** N maniobra *f*; **to be on ~s** estar de maniobras; **this leaves us little room for ~** esto apenas nos deja margen de maniobra **Ⓑ** VT maniobrar; **he ~d the car through the gate** cruzó la puerta haciendo maniobras; **to ~ sb into doing sth** manipular a algn para que haga algo

manor ['mænə^r] N (*modern*) finca *f*; (*Brit*) (*feudal*) señorío *m* ➤ **manor house** (*Brit*) casa *f* solariega, casa *f* señorial

manpower ['mænpaʊə^r] N (= *workers*) mano *f* de obra

mansion ['mænʃən] N mansión *f*; (*of ancient family*) casa *f* solariega

manslaughter ['mæn,slɔːtə^r] N homicidio *m* involuntario

mantelpiece ['mæntlpiːs] N repisa *f* (de chimenea)

mantle ['mæntl] N **1** (= *layer*) capa *f*; **a ~ of snow** una capa de nieve **2** (††) (= *cloak*) manto *m* **3** (*fig*) **he accepted the ~ of leader** asumió el liderazgo, aceptó el cargo de líder

man-to-man ['mæntə'mæn] ADJ de hombre a hombre

manual ['mænjʊəl] **Ⓐ** ADJ manual; **~ labour** *or* (*US*) **labor** trabajo *m* manual **Ⓑ** N (= *book*) manual *m*

manufacture [,mænjʊ'fæktʃə^r] **Ⓐ** N fabricación *f* **Ⓑ** VT fabricar; **~d goods** productos *mpl* manufacturados

manufacturer [,mænjʊ'fæktʃərə^r] N fabricante *mf*

manufacturing [,mænjʊ'fæktʃərɪŋ] **Ⓐ** N fabricación *f* **Ⓑ** ADJ [*town, city, sector*] industrial, manufacturero/a **Ⓒ** CPD ➤ **manufacturing costs** costes *mpl* de fabricación

manure [mə'njʊə^r] N estiércol *m*, abono *m* ➤ **manure heap** estercolero *m*

manuscript ['mænjʊskrɪpt] N, ADJ manuscrito *m*

Manx [mæŋks] ADJ de la Isla de Man

many ['menɪ] **Ⓐ** ADJ muchos/as; **~ people** mucha gente, muchas personas; **a good** *or* **a great ~ houses** muchas *or* (*LAm*) bastantes casas; **however ~ books you have** por muchos libros que tengas; **not ~ people** poca gente; **so ~ tantos/as**; **~'s the time I've seen him act** muchas veces lo he visto actuar; **too ~** demasiados/as **Ⓑ** PRON muchos/as; **he has as ~ as I have** tiene tantos como yo; **he has three times as ~ as I have** tiene tres veces más que yo; **there were as ~ as a hundred at the meeting** asistieron a la reunión hasta cien personas; **as ~ again** otros tantos; **how ~ are there?** ¿cuántos hay?; **however ~ you have** por muchos que tengas; **not ~** pocos; **~ of them came** muchos (de ellos) vinieron

Maori ['maʊrɪ] ADJ, N maorí *mf*

map [mæp] **Ⓐ** N (*of town*) plano *m*; (*of world, country*) mapa *m*; ✦ IDIOM **this will put us on the ~** esto nos dará a conocer **Ⓑ** VT [+ *area*] levantar un mapa de ➤ **map out** VT + ADV [+ *strategy, future*] planificar, planear; [+ *plan*] trazar

maple ['meɪpl] N arce *m* ➤ **maple syrup** jarabe *m* de arce

mapmaking ['mæp,meɪkɪŋ], **mapping** ['mæpɪŋ] N cartografía *f*

mar [mɑː^r] VT estropear, echar a perder; **to ~ sb's enjoyment** aguar la fiesta a algn

Mar. ABBR (= **March**) mar.

marathon ['mærəθən] **Ⓐ** N (*Sport*) maratón *m* **Ⓑ** ADJ (= *very long*) maratoniano **Ⓒ** CPD ➤ **marathon runner** corredor(a) *m/f* de maratón

marauder [mə'rɔːdə^r] N merodeador(a) *m/f*, intruso/a *m/f*

marauding [mə'rɔːdɪŋ] ADJ merodeador, intruso

marble ['mɑːbl] **Ⓐ** N **1** (= *material*) mármol *m* **2** (= *work in marble*) obra *f* en mármol **3** (= *glass ball*) canica *f*, bolita *f* (*And, SC*), metra *f* (*Ven*); **to play ~s** jugar a las canicas; ✦ IDIOM **to lose one's ~s*** perder la chaveta* **Ⓑ** CPD marmóreo, de mármol ➤ **marble staircase** escalera *f* de mármol

March [mɑːtʃ] N marzo *m*; *see* **July**

march [mɑːtʃ] **Ⓐ** N marcha *f*; **an army on the ~** un ejército en marcha **Ⓑ** VT **I was ~ed into an office** me llevaron a un despacho, me hicieron entrar en un despacho **Ⓒ** VI **1** (*Mil*) marchar; **forward ~!** de frente ¡ar!; **quick ~!** al trote ¡ar!; **to ~ past sb** desfilar ante algn **2** (= *demonstrate*) manifestarse, hacer una manifestación **3** (*fig*) **to ~ into a room** entrar resueltamente en un cuarto; **to ~ up to sb** abordar a algn

marcher ['mɑːtʃə^r] N (*on demonstration*) marchista *mf*, manifestante *mf*

marching orders ['mɑːtʃɪŋ,ɔːdəz] NPL (*Brit*) ✦ IDIOMS **to get one's ~*** ser despedido; **to give sb his ~*** despedir a algn, poner a algn en la calle*

---

mare [mɛə^r] N yegua *f*

margarine [,mɑːdʒə'riːn] N margarina *f*

marge* [mɑːdʒ] N (*Brit*) = **margarine**

margin ['mɑːdʒɪn] N margen *m*; **to write sth in the ~** escribir algo al margen; **~ of error/safety** margen *m* de error/seguridad; **to win by a wide/narrow ~** vencer por un amplio/estrecho margen; **profit ~** margen *m* de beneficios

marginal ['mɑːdʒɪnl] **Ⓐ** ADJ **1** (= *very small*) [*improvement, difference, increase*] mínimo, insignificante **2** (= *peripheral*) [*issue*] menor; [*character, public figure*] marginal, al margen **3** (*Brit Parl*) [*seat*] obtenido con escasa mayoría **Ⓑ** N (*Brit Parl*) (*also* **~ seat**) escaño *m* obtenido por escasa mayoría

marginalize ['mɑːdʒɪnəlaɪz] VT marginar

marginally ['mɑːdʒɪnəlɪ] ADV ligeramente

marigold ['mærɪɡəʊld] N maravilla *f*

marijuana, marihuana [,mærɪ'hwɑːnə] N marihuana *f*, mariguana *f*

marina [mə'riːnə] N puerto *m* deportivo

marinade [,mærɪ'neɪd] **Ⓐ** N adobo *m* **Ⓑ** VT adobar

marinate ['mærɪneɪt] VT adobar

marine [mə'riːn] **Ⓐ** N (= *person*) infante *m* de marina; (= *fleet*) marina *f*; **the Marines** (*Brit*) la infantería de marina; (*US*) los marines; ✦ IDIOM **tell that to the ~s!** (*Brit*†*) ¡a otro perro con ese hueso!* **Ⓑ** ADJ marino **Ⓒ** CPD ➤ **marine biology** biología *f* marina ➤ **marine life** vida *f* marina, flora y fauna *f* marina

mariner ['mærɪnə^r] N (*liter*) marinero *m*, marino *m*

marital ['mærɪtl] ADJ [*home, bliss*] conyugal; [*problems*] matrimonial, conyugal ➤ **marital rape** violación *f* dentro del matrimonio ➤ **marital status** estado *m* civil

maritime ['mærɪtaɪm] ADJ marítimo

marjoram ['mɑːdʒərəm] N mejorana *f*

mark¹ [mɑːk] N (= *currency*) marco *m*

mark² [mɑːk] **Ⓐ** N **1** (= *stain, spot*) mancha *f*; **he left the ring without a ~ on his body** salió del cuadrilátero sin llevar señal alguna en el cuerpo

2 (= *written symbol on paper etc*) señal *f*, marca *f*; (= *imprint, trace*) huella *f*; ✦ IDIOM **to make one's ~** dejar huella, distinguirse; **he has made his ~ on British politics** ha dejado huella en la política británica

3 (= *indication*) señal *f*; **as a ~ of our gratitude** en señal de nuestro agradecimiento; **it bears the ~ of genius** lleva la marca de un genio

4 (*in exam*) nota *f*, calificación *f*; **to get high ~s in French** sacar buena nota en francés

5 (= *target*) blanco *m*; ✦ IDIOMS **to hit the ~** dar en el clavo; **he's on the ~** ha dado en el blanco, está en lo cierto; **he's way off the ~** no acierta ni con mucho; **to be wide of the ~** estar lejos de la verdad

6 (*Sport*) **on your ~s** *or* (*US*) **~, get set, go!** ¡preparados, listos, ya!; ✦ IDIOM **to be quick/slow off the ~** ser muy vivo/ parado

7 (= *level, standard*) **to hit the £1,000 ~** alcanzar el total de 1.000 libras; **gas ~ one** (*Brit Culin*) número uno del gas; ✦ IDIOM **to be up to the ~** [*person*] estar a la altura de las circunstancias; [*work*] alcanzar el nivel necesario

8 (= *brand name*) marca *f*

Ⓑ VT **1** (= *make a mark on*) (*gen*) marcar; [+ *furniture, paintwork*] (= *scratch*) dejar una marca en; (= *stain*) dejar una mancha en; **~ it with an asterisk** ponga un asterisco allí

2 (= *price*) **the chair is ~ed at £12** la silla tiene un precio de 12 libras

3 (= *indicate*) señalar, indicar; **stones ~ the path** unas piedras señalan el camino; **~s a change of policy** indica un cambio de política; **it's not ~ed on the map** no está indicado en el mapa; **we must do something special to ~ the occasion** tenemos que hacer algo especial para celebrarlo

4 (= *heed*) **~ my words!** ¡fíjese *or* acuérdese bien de lo que le digo!, ¡te lo advierto!; **~ you** ahora (bien)

5 [+ *exam*] calificar; **to ~ sth right** aprobar algo; **to ~ sth wrong** rechazar *or* (*LAm*) reprobar algo

6 (*esp Brit Ftbl*) marcar, doblar

7 ✦ IDIOM to ~ time estancarse
ⓒ VI mancharse
➤ **mark down** VT + ADV **1** (= *note down*) apuntar, anotar
2 [+ *prices, goods*] rebajar **3** [+ *student*] bajar la nota a
➤ **mark off** VT + ADV **1** (= *separate*) separar, dividir **2** [+ *items on list etc*] (= *tick off*) marcar, poner una señal contra; (= *cross out*) tachar
➤ **mark out** VT + ADV **1** [+ *road etc*] marcar, jalonar
2 (= *single out*) señalar; (= *distinguish*) distinguir, señalar; **he's ~ed out for promotion** se le ha señalado para un ascenso
➤ **mark up** VT + ADV **1** (= *write up*) (*on board, paper etc*) apuntar **2** [+ *price*] subir; [+ *goods*] subir el precio de **3** [+ *student*] subir la nota a

markdown ['mɑːkdaʊn] N (*Comm*) rebaja *f*, reducción *f*

marked [mɑːkt] ADJ **1** (= *noticeable*) [*improvement, increase, deterioration*] marcado, notable; [*difference, change*] acusado, marcado; [*contrast*] acusado, fuerte; [*accent*] marcado, fuerte; [*effect*] acusado, notable; **the difference has become more ~** la diferencia se ha vuelto más acusada *or* marcada, la diferencia se acusa cada vez más
2 (= *targeted*) **to be a ~ man** ser un hombre marcado

markedly ['mɑːkɪdlɪ] ADV [*better, worse*] visiblemente, notablemente; (*with verb*) notablemente

marker ['mɑːkəʳ] N **1** (= *indicator*) marcador *m*; (*in field*) jalón *m* **2** (*also* ~ **pen**) rotulador *m* **3** (= *bookmark*) marca *f*, señal *f* **4** (*Ftbl*) (= *person*) marcador(a) *m/f*, secante *mf*

market ['mɑːkɪt] **ⓐ** N mercado *m*; **overseas/domestic ~** mercado exterior/nacional; **to corner the ~ in maize** acaparar el mercado del maíz; **to flood the ~ with sth** inundar el mercado de algo; **there's no ~ for pink socks** los calcetines de color rosa no encuentran salida; **to be on the ~** estar en venta *or* a la venta; **to play the ~** jugar a la bolsa **ⓑ** VT (= *sell*) comercializar, poner en venta; (= *promote*) publicitar
ⓒ CPD ➤ **market analysis** análisis *m inv* de mercado(s)
➤ **market economy** economía *f* de mercado ➤ **market forces** fuerzas *fpl* del mercado, tendencias *fpl* del mercado
➤ **market garden** (*esp Brit*) (*small*) huerto *m*; (*large*) huerta *f* ➤ **market leader** líder *m* del mercado ➤ **market place** plaza *f* (del mercado); (= *world of trade*) mercado *m* ➤ **market price** precio *m* de mercado ➤ **market research** estudios *mpl* de mercados ➤ **market share** cuota *f* de mercado ➤ **market value** valor *m* de mercado

marketability [ˌmɑːkɪtə'bɪlɪtɪ] N comerciabilidad *f*, vendibilidad *f*

marketable ['mɑːkɪtəbl] ADJ [*commodity, product*] vendible, comercializable; [*skill*] con mucha salida; **the more specialized your skill, the more ~ you are** cuanto más especializado estés, mayores posibilidades tendrás en el mercado laboral

market-driven [ˌmɑːkɪt'drɪvn] ADJ impulsado por el mercado

marketing ['mɑːkɪtɪŋ] **ⓐ** N márketing *m*, mercadotecnia *f* **ⓑ** CPD [*plan, strategy, agreement*] de comercialización ➤ **marketing department** departamento *f* de márketing ➤ **marketing manager** director(a) *m/f* de márketing ➤ **marketing strategy** estrategia *f* de comercialización

market-led [ˌmɑːkɪt'led] ADJ dirigido por el mercado

marking ['mɑːkɪŋ] N **1** (= *mark*) señal *f*, marca *f*; (*on animal*) pinta *f*; (= *coloration*) coloración *f* **2** (*esp Brit Ftbl*) marcaje *m*

marksman ['mɑːksmən] N (*pl* **marksmen**) tirador *m*

marksmanship ['mɑːksmənʃɪp] N puntería *f*

mark-up ['mɑːkʌp] N (= *profit*) margen *m* (de beneficio); (= *price increase*) aumento *m* de precio

marmalade ['mɑːməleɪd] N mermelada *f* (de naranja amarga)

maroon¹ [mə'ruːn] **ⓐ** ADJ granate *inv* **ⓑ** N granate *m*

maroon² [mə'ruːn] VT [+ *castaway*] abandonar (en una isla desierta); (*fig*) aislar, dejar aislado; **we were ~ed by floods** quedamos aislados debido a las inundaciones

marquee [mɑː'kiː] N (= *tent*) carpa *f*; (*open-sided*) entoldado *m*

marquess, marquis ['mɑːkwɪs] N marqués *m*

marriage ['mærɪdʒ] **ⓐ** N **1** (= *state of being married*) matrimonio *m*; **to be related by ~** estar emparentados **2** (= *wedding*) boda *f*, casamiento *m*; (*fig*) unión *f* **ⓑ** CPD ➤ **marriage ceremony** ceremonia *f* nupcial, matrimonio *m* ➤ **marriage certificate** partida *f* matrimonial *or* de matrimonio ➤ **marriage counseling** (*US*) orientación *f* matrimonial ➤ **marriage counselor** (*US*) consejero/a *m/f* matrimonial ➤ **marriage guidance** (*Brit*) orientación *f* matrimonial ➤ **marriage guidance counsellor** (*Brit*) consejero/a *m/f* matrimonial ➤ **marriage of convenience** matrimonio *m* de conveniencia ➤ **marriage vows** votos *mpl* matrimoniales

married ['mærɪd] ADJ casado; **~ man** (hombre *m*) casado *m*; **~ woman** (mujer *f*) casada *f*; **~ couple** matrimonio *m*; **~ life** vida *f* matrimonial; **"just married"** "recién casados"; **he's ~ to his job** vive por y para el trabajo, vive para trabajar *or* para el trabajo ➤ **married name** nombre *m* de casada

marrow ['mærəʊ] N **1** (*in bone*) médula *f*, tuétano *m*; ✦ IDIOM **to be frozen to the ~** estar helado hasta los huesos **2** (*Brit*) (*also* **vegetable ~**) calabacín *m*

marrowbone ['mærəʊbəʊn] N hueso *m* con tuétano

marry ['mærɪ] **ⓐ** VT **1** (= *take in marriage*) casarse con; **to be married to sb** estar casado con algn; **we have been married for 14 years** llevamos 14 años (de) casados **2** (= *give or join in marriage*) casar **ⓑ** VI (*also* **to get married**) casarse

Mars [mɑːz] N Marte *m* ➤ **~ landing, landing on ~** amartizaje *m*

marsh [mɑːʃ] N pantano *m*, ciénaga *f*

marshal ['mɑːʃəl] **ⓐ** N **1** (*Mil*) mariscal *m* **2** (*at demonstration, meeting*) oficial *m* **3** (*US*) alguacil *m*, oficial *m* de justicia **ⓑ** VT **1** [+ *soldiers, procession*] formar **2** [+ *facts etc*] ordenar; [+ *evidence*] presentar

marshmallow ['mɑːʃ'mæləʊ] N (= *flower*) malvavisco *m*; (= *sweet*) esponja *f*, dulce *m* de merengue blando

marshy ['mɑːʃɪ] ADJ (*compar* **marshier**; *superl* **marshiest**) pantanoso

marsupial [mɑː'suːpɪəl] ADJ, N marsupial *m*

martial ['mɑːʃəl] ADJ marcial ➤ **martial arts** artes *fpl* marciales ➤ **martial law** ley *f* marcial

Martian ['mɑːʃən] ADJ, N marciano/a *m/f*

martinet [ˌmɑːtɪ'net] N ordenancista *mf*, rigorista *mf*

Martinique [ˌmɑːtɪ'niːk] N Martinica *f*

martyr ['mɑːtəʳ] **ⓐ** N mártir *mf*; **to be a ~ to arthritis** ser víctima de la artritis **ⓑ** VT martirizar

martyrdom ['mɑːtədəm] N martirio *m*

marvel ['mɑːvəl] **ⓐ** N maravilla *f*; **it's a ~ to me how she does it** no llego a entender cómo lo hace; **if he gets there it will be a ~** si llega será un milagro **ⓑ** VI maravillarse, asombrarse (**at** de)

marvellous, marvelous (*US*) ['mɑːvələs] ADJ maravilloso, estupendo

Marxism ['mɑːksɪzəm] N marxismo *m*

Marxist ['mɑːksɪst] ADJ, N marxista *mf*

marzipan ['mɑːzɪpæn] N mazapán *m*

mascara [mæs'kɑːrə] N rímel® *m*

mascot ['mæskət] N mascota *f*

masculine ['mæskjʊlɪn] ADJ, N masculino *m*

masculinity [ˌmæskjʊ'lɪnɪtɪ] N masculinidad *f*

mash [mæʃ] **ⓐ** N (*Brit**) (= *mashed potatoes*) puré *m* de patata(s) (*Sp*) *or* papas (*LAm*) **ⓑ** VT **1** (= *crush*) triturar, machacar **2** [+ *potatoes*] hacer puré de

mask [mɑːsk] N máscara *f*; (*just covering eyes and nose*) antifaz *m*; (*protective, cosmetic*) mascarilla *f*; (*surgeon's*) mascarilla *f*, barbijo *m*; (*in baseball, fencing, ice hockey*) careta *f*; **the man in the ~ produced a gun** el hombre enmascarado *or* que llevaba la máscara sacó una pistola

masked [mɑːskt] ADJ enmascarado; [*terrorist, attacker*] encapuchado ➤ **masked ball** baile *m* de máscaras

masking tape ['mɑːskɪŋˌteɪp] N cinta *f* adhesiva protectora (*del margen del área a pintar*)

masochism ['mæsəkɪzəm] N masoquismo *m*

masochist ['mæsəkɪst] N masoquista *mf*

mason ['meɪsn] N **1** (= *builder*) albañil *mf*; (= *stonework specialist*) mampostero/a *m/f*
2 (= *freemason*) masón *m*, francmasón *m*

masonic [mə'sɒnɪk] ADJ (*also* **Masonic**) masónico

masonry ['meɪsnrɪ] N **1** (= *building trade*) albañilería *f*
2 (= *stonework*) mampostería *f* **3** (= *rubble*) escombros *mpl*
4 (= *freemasonry*) masonería *f*, francmasonería *f*

masquerade [ˌmæskə'reɪd] **Ⓐ** N **1** (= *pretence*) farsa *f*, mascarada *f* **2** (= *fancy-dress ball*) baile *m* de máscaras, mascarada *f* **Ⓑ** VI to ~ **as** hacerse pasar por

Mass [mæs] N (*Rel*) misa *f*; **to go to** ~ ir a misa, oír misa

mass [mæs] **Ⓐ** N **1** (= *concentration*) masa *f*; **the garden was a ~ of colour** el jardín era una masa de color; **a ~ of auburn hair** una mata de pelo castaño rojizo; **he's a ~ of bruises** está cubierto de cardenales; **the (great) ~ of the population** la (gran) masa de la población
2 masses* (= *great quantity*) montones* *mpl*, cantidad* *fsing*; **~es of work** montones *or* cantidad de trabajo*; **~es of people** una masa de gente
3 the ~es (= *ordinary people*) las masas
4 (*Phys*) masa *f*
Ⓑ VI [*crowds, troops*] concentrarse; [*clouds*] agruparse
Ⓒ CPD [*movement*] de masas; [*protest, unemployment, support*] masivo; [*hysteria, suicide*] colectivo ➤ **mass grave** fosa *f* común ➤ **mass media** medios *mpl* de comunicación (de masas) ➤ **mass murder** matanza *f*, masacre *f* ➤ **mass murderer** autor(a) *m/f* de una matanza *or* masacre ➤ **mass production** fabricación *f* en serie ➤ **mass transit** (*US*) transporte *m* público

Mass. ABBR (*US*) = **Massachusetts**

massacre ['mæsəkə'] **Ⓐ** N **1** (= *killing*) masacre *f*, carnicería *f*
2 (*) (= *defeat*) derrota *f* aplastante, paliza* *f* **Ⓑ** VT **1** (= *kill*) masacrar, aniquilar **2** (*) (= *defeat*) aplastar, dar una paliza a*

massage ['mæsɑːʒ] **Ⓐ** N masaje *m* **Ⓑ** VT **1** [+ *person*] dar un masaje a; [+ *body*] masajear **2** (*) [+ *figures*] maquillar*

masseur [mæ'sɜː'] N masajista *mf*

masseuse [mæ'sɜːz] N masajista *f*

massive ['mæsɪv] ADJ [*boulder, increase, dose, person, body, explosion*] enorme; [*wall*] macizo, sólido; [*job losses*] cuantioso; ~ **heart attack** infarto *m* masivo; **on a ~ scale** a gran escala

massively ['mæsɪvlɪ] ADV [*overweight, popular*] tremendamente; [*increase*] enormemente

mass-produce ['mæsprə'djuːs] VT fabricar en serie, producir en serie

mast [mɑːst] N [*of ship*] mástil *m*, palo *m*

mastectomy [mæ'stektəmɪ] N mastectomía *f*

master ['mɑːstə'] **Ⓐ** N **1** [*of the house*] señor *m*, amo *m*; [*of dog, servant*] amo *m*; **to be one's own** ~ ser dueño de sí mismo; **to be ~ of the situation** dominar la situación
2 (= *musician, painter*) maestro *m*
3 (*Brit†*) (= *teacher*) (*primary*) maestro *m*; (*secondary*) profesor *m*

4 (*Univ*) **Master of Arts/Science** (= *qualification*) master *m* en letras/ciencias; (= *person*) persona que posee un master en letras/ciencias; **she's working for her Master's (degree)** está estudiando para sacarse el máster
Ⓑ VT [+ *subject, situation, technique*] dominar
Ⓒ CPD ➤ **master bedroom** dormitorio *m* principal ➤ **master builder** maestro *m* de obras ➤ **master class** clase *f* magistral ➤ **master copy** original *m* ➤ **master disk** disco *m* maestro ➤ **master key** llave *f* maestra ➤ **master of ceremonies** maestro *m* de ceremonias; [*of show*] presentador *m*, animador *m* ➤ **master plan** plan *m* maestro, plan *m* rector ➤ **master switch** interruptor *m* general

masterful ['mɑːstəful] ADJ [*performance*] magistral; [*leadership*] capaz; [*person*] imperioso, autoritario

masterly ['mɑːstəlɪ] ADJ magistral, genial

mastermind ['mɑːstəmaɪnd] **Ⓐ** N (= *genius*) genio *m*; (*in crime etc*) cerebro *m* **Ⓑ** VT dirigir, planear

masterpiece ['mɑːstəpiːs] N obra *f* maestra

masterstroke ['mɑːstəˌstrəʊk] N golpe *m* maestro

mastery ['mɑːstərɪ] N **1** [*of subject, technique*] dominio *m*
2 (= *skill*) maestría *f* **3** (= *control*) (*over competitors etc*) dominio *m*, superioridad *f*

mastiff ['mæstɪf] N mastín *m*, alano *m*

mastitis [mæs'taɪtɪs] N mastitis *f inv*

masturbate ['mæstəbeɪt] VI masturbarse

masturbation [ˌmæstə'beɪʃən] N masturbación *f*

mat [mæt] N **1** (*on floor*) estera *f*, esterilla *f*; (= *doormat*) felpudo *m* **2** (= *tablemat*) (mantel *m*) individual *m*; (*in centre of table*) salvamanteles *m inv*

match¹ [mætʃ] N (*for lighting*) fósforo *m*, cerilla *f*, cerillo *m* (*Mex*)

match² [mætʃ] **Ⓐ** N **1** (*esp Brit*) (*Tennis, Cricket*) partido *m*; (*Ftbl*) partido *m*, encuentro *m*; (*Boxing*) combate *m*
2 (= *complement*) **the two of them are a good** ~ hacen una buena pareja
3 (= *equal*) **to be no** ~ **for sb** no estar a la altura de algn; **he was more than a ~ for Paul** venció fácilmente a Paul; **to meet one's** ~ **(in sb)** encontrar la horma de su zapato (en algn)
4 (= *marriage*) casamiento *m*, matrimonio *m*; (= *potential partner*) partido *m*; **he's a good** ~ es un buen partido
Ⓑ VT **1** (= *pair*) emparejar; **they're well ~ed** [*couple*] hacen buena pareja; **the teams were well ~ed** los equipos estaban muy igualados *or* (*esp LAm*) eran muy parejos; **the children were asked to ~ the pictures with the words** se pidió a los niños que emparejaran las imágenes con las palabras
2 (= *equal*) igualar; **her performance would be hard to** ~ su actuación sería difícil de igualar; **I can ~ any offer** puedo igualar cualquier oferta
3 (= *correspond to*) ajustarse a, corresponder a; **a man ~ing the police description** un hombre que se ajustaba a *or* que correspondía a la descripción de la policía
4 (= *put in opposition to*) enfrentar; **she ~ed her wits against his strength** enfrentó *or* midió su ingenio con la fuerza de él
5 [+ *clothes, colours*] combinar con, hacer juego con
Ⓒ VI **1** (= *go together*) [*colours*] combinar bien; [*clothes*] hacer juego; **with a skirt to** ~ con una falda a tono *or* que hace juego
2 (= *be the same*) corresponderse, coincidir
Ⓓ CPD ➤ **match point** (*Tennis*) bola *f* de partido, match point *m*

matchbox ['mætʃbɒks] N caja *f* de fósforos *or* cerillas

matching ['mætʃɪŋ] ADJ haciendo juego, a juego (*Sp*); **a blue silk dress with ~ shoes** un vestido de seda azul con zapatos haciendo juego *or* (*Sp*) a juego

matchmaker ['mætʃˌmeɪkə'] N casamentero/a *m/f*, alcahuete/a *m/f*

matchstick ['mætʃstɪk] N fósforo *m*

mate¹ [meɪt] (*Chess*) **Ⓐ** N mate *m* **Ⓑ** VT dar jaque mate a, matar

mate² [meɪt] **Ⓐ** N **1** (*Zool*) (*male*) macho *m*; (*female*) hembra *f* **2** (*Brit Naut*) primer(a) oficial *mf*; (*US*) segundo/a

m/f de a bordo **3** (*at work*) compañero/a *m/f*, colega *mf*
4 (*Brit**) (= *friend*) amigo/a *m/f*, compinche* *mf*, colega* *mf*,
cuate/a *m/f* (*Mex*); **look here,** ~* mire, amigo
B VT (*Zool*) aparear **C** VI (*Zool*) aparearse

material [məˈtɪərɪəl] **A** ADJ **1** (= *physical*) [*goods, needs,
comforts, benefits, damage*] material; ~ **possessions** bienes
mpl materiales; **the ~ world** el mundo físico
2 (*Jur*) (= *relevant*) [*fact*] pertinente; [*witness*] primordial,
principal; ~ **evidence** pruebas *fpl* palpables
B N **1** (= *cloth*) tela *f*, tejido *m*
2 (= *substance*) materia *f*, material *m*; **raw ~s** materias *fpl*
primas
3 materials (= *equipment, components*) material(es) *m(pl)*;
building ~s material(es) *m(pl)* de construcción; **teaching ~s**
material(es) *m(pl)* didácticos; **writing ~s** artículos *mpl* de
escritorio
4 (= *information for book, article*) datos *mpl*, información *f*
5 (= *potential*) **he is university ~** tiene madera de
universitario

materialism [məˈtɪərɪəlɪzəm] N materialismo *m*

materialistic [məˌtɪərɪəˈlɪstɪk] ADJ materialista

materialize [məˈtɪərɪəlaɪz] VI **1** (= *come into being*) [*idea,
hope etc*] realizarse **2** (= *appear*) aparecer; **the funds haven't
~d so far** hasta ahora no han aparecido los fondos

maternal [məˈtɜːnl] ADJ **1** (= *motherly*) [*woman, behaviour,
instinct*] maternal; [*feelings, love*] maternal, de madre
2 (= *on the mother's side*) materno (*por parte de madre*)

maternity [məˈtɜːnɪtɪ] N maternidad *f* ➤ **maternity dress**
vestido *m* de futura mamá, vestido *m* de premamá (*Sp*)
➤ **maternity hospital** maternidad *f* ➤ **maternity leave** baja
f por maternidad ➤ **maternity ward** sala *f* de maternidad

matey* [ˈmeɪtɪ] ADJ (*Brit*) **she's quite ~ with my wife** es
bastante amiga con mi mujer

math* [mæθ] N ABBR (*US*) (= **mathematics**) mates* *fpl*

mathematical [ˌmæθəˈmætɪkəl] ADJ matemático; **I'm not
very ~** no se me dan bien las matemáticas; **he's a ~ genius**
es un genio para las matemáticas

mathematician [ˌmæθəməˈtɪʃən] N matemático/a *m/f*

mathematics [ˌmæθəˈmætɪks] NSING matemáticas *fpl*

maths* [mæθs] N ABBR (*Brit*) (= **mathematics**) mates* *fpl*

matinée [ˈmætɪneɪ] N función *f* de tarde, matiné(e) *f* (*SC*)

mating [ˈmeɪtɪŋ] N apareamiento *m* ➤ **mating call** aullido
m/rugido *m* de la época de celo ➤ **mating season** época *f*
de celo

matriarchal [ˌmeɪtrɪˈɑːkl] ADJ matriarcal

matrices [ˈmeɪtrɪsiːz] NPL *of* **matrix**

matriculation [məˌtrɪkjʊˈleɪʃən] N matriculación *f*

matrimonial [ˌmætrɪˈməʊnɪəl] ADJ [*problems*] matrimonial;
[*vow, bed*] de matrimonio; [*life*] conyugal

matrimony [ˈmætrɪmənɪ] N matrimonio *m*

matrix [ˈmeɪtrɪks] N (*pl* **matrices**) matriz *f*

matron [ˈmeɪtrən] **A** N **1** (*Brit*) (*in nursing home*) supervisora
f **2** (*Brit*†) (*in hospital*) enfermera *f* jefe **3** (*Brit*) (*in school*)
enfermera *f* **4** (= *married woman*) matrona *f* **B** CPD
➤ **matron of honour** dama *f* de honor (*casada*)

matronly [ˈmeɪtrənlɪ] ADJ matronal, de matrona; [*figure*]
maduro y algo corpulento

matt [mæt] ADJ mate

matted [ˈmætɪd] ADJ enmarañado y apelmazado

matter [ˈmætəʳ] **A** N **1** (= *substance*) materia *f*, sustancia *f*
2 (*Typ, Publishing*) material *m*; **printed ~** impresos *mpl*
3 (= *question, affair*) asunto *m*, cuestión *f*; **that's another ~
altogether** ésa es otra cuestión, eso es totalmente distinto;
the ~ is closed el asunto está concluido; **as a ~ of course**
automáticamente; **that's a very different ~** ésa es otra
cuestión, eso es totalmente distinto; **it's an easy ~ to
phone him** es cosa fácil llamarle; **as a ~ of fact ...: as a ~ of
fact I know her very well** de hecho *or* en realidad la
conozco muy bien; **"don't tell me you like it?" — "as a ~ of
fact I do"** —no me digas que te gusta —pues sí, la verdad
es que sí; **for that ~** en realidad; **the ~ in hand** la cuestión
del momento; **there's the ~ of my wages** queda el asunto

de mi sueldo; **a ~ of minutes** cosa de minutos; **it's a ~ of
great concern to us** es motivo de gran preocupación para
nosotros; **it's a ~ of taste** es cuestión de gusto; **it's a serious
~** es cosa seria; **to make ~s worse** para colmo de males
4 (= *importance*) **no ~!** ¡no importa!, ¡no le hace! (*LAm*) **no ~
how you do it** no importa cómo lo hagas; **no ~ how big it is**
por grande que sea; **no ~ how hot it is** por mucho calor
que haga; **no ~ what he says** diga lo que diga; **no ~ when**
no importa cuándo; **no ~ who goes** quienquiera que vaya
5 (= *difficulty, problem etc*) **what's the ~?** ¿qué pasa?, ¿qué
hay?; **what's the ~ with you?** ¿qué te pasa?, ¿qué tienes?;
something's the ~ with the lights algo les pasa a las luces,
algo pasa con las luces; **what's the ~ with my hat?** ¿qué pasa
con mi sombrero?; **what's the ~ with singing?** ¿por qué no
se puede cantar?, ¿es que está prohibido cantar?; **nothing's
the ~** no pasa nada
B VI importar; **does it ~ to you if I go?** ¿te importa que yo
vaya?; **why should it ~ to me?** ¿a mí qué me importa *or* qué
más me da?; **it doesn't ~** (*unimportant*) no importa; (*no
preference*) (me) da igual *or* lo mismo; **what does it ~?** ¿qué
más da?, ¿y qué?; **some things ~ more than others** algunas
cosas son más importantes que otras

matter-of-fact [ˈmætərəvˈfækt] ADJ [*style*] prosaico; [*person*]
(*practical*) práctico

matting [ˈmætɪŋ] N estera *f*

mattress [ˈmætrɪs] N colchón *m*

mature [məˈtjʊəʳ] **A** ADJ (*compar* **~r**; *superl* **~st**) [*person*]
maduro; [*animal, plant*] adulto; [*wine, whisky*] añejo;
[*cheese*] curado; [*policy, investment*] vencido **B** VI [*person*]
(*emotionally*) madurar; [*child, young animal*] (*physically*)
desarrollarse; [*wine, whisky*] añejarse; [*cheese*] curarse; (*Fin*)
[*insurance policy, investment*] vencer **C** CPD ➤ **mature
student** (*Brit*) estudiante *mf* mayor

maturity [məˈtjʊərɪtɪ] N madurez *f*

maudlin [ˈmɔːdlɪn] ADJ (= *weepy*) llorón; (= *sentimental*)
sensiblero

maul [mɔːl] VT [*tiger, bear*] atacar y malherir

Maundy Thursday [ˌmɔːndɪˈθɜːzdɪ] N Jueves *m* Santo

Mauritius [məˈrɪʃəs] N Isla *f* Mauricio *m*

mausoleum [ˌmɔːsəˈliːəm] N mausoleo *m*

mauve [məʊv] **A** ADJ malva *inv* **B** N malva *m*

maverick [ˈmævərɪk] N (= *nonconformist*) inconformista *mf*;
(*Pol etc*) disidente *mf*

mawkish [ˈmɔːkɪʃ] ADJ empalagoso, sensiblero, insulso

max [mæks] **A** ABBR (= **maximum**) máx.; **a couple of weeks,
~** dos semanas como máximo **B** N **to do sth to the ~***
hacer algo al máximo, hacer algo a tope (*Sp**)

maxim [ˈmæksɪm] N máxima *f*

maximization [ˌmæksɪmaɪˈzeɪʃən] N maximización *f*

maximize [ˈmæksɪmaɪz] VT maximizar

maximum [ˈmæksɪməm] **A** ADJ [*amount, temperature, speed,
load, efficiency*] máximo; **for ~ effect** para conseguir el
máximo efecto; **a ~ security prison** una prisión de máxima
seguridad **B** N máximo *m*; **at the ~** como máximo, a lo
sumo; **up to a ~ of £20** hasta 20 libras como máximo; **to
the ~** al máximo **C** ADV como máximo

May [meɪ] N mayo *m* ➤ **May Day** el primero de mayo; *see*
July

may[1] [meɪ] MODAL AUX VB **1** (*possibility*) **it ~ rain** puede *or* es
posible que llueva; **he ~ not be hungry** a lo mejor no tiene
hambre; **it ~ be that he has had to go out** puede (ser) que
haya tenido que salir; **that's as ~ be** eso puede ser; **be that
as it ~** sea como sea; **we ~ as well go** vámonos ya *or* de una
vez; **they ~ have gone out** puede que hayan salido, a lo
mejor han salido; **they ~ well be related** puede que sean
parientes
2 (*permission*) poder; **~ I go now?** ¿puedo irme ya?; **~ I
come in?** ¿se puede?, con permiso; **~ I help you?** (*in shop*)
¿qué desea?; **yes, you ~** sí, puedes; **you ~ smoke** se permite
fumar; **you ~ not smoke** se prohíbe fumar
3 (*wishes*) **~ you have a happy life together!** ¡que seáis
felices!; **~ God bless you!** ¡Dios te bendiga!

may[2] [meɪ] N (= *blossom*) flor *f* del espino; (= *tree*) espino *m*

Maya ['maɪjə], **Mayan** ['maɪjən] ADJ, N maya *mf*

maybe ['meɪbiː] ADV a lo mejor, quizá(s), tal vez; **~ he'll come tomorrow** a lo mejor viene mañana, puede que *or* quizá(s) *or* tal vez venga mañana; **~ I should grow a moustache** a lo mejor debería dejarme bigote; **maybe, maybe not** puede que sí, puede que no, a lo mejor sí, a lo mejor no

Mayday ['meɪdeɪ] N (= *distress call*) socorro *m*, SOS *m*

mayfly ['meɪflaɪ] N cachipolla *f*, efímera *f*

mayhem ['meɪhem] N alboroto *m*, caos *m*

mayo* ['meɪəʊ] N (*US*) = **mayonnaise**

mayonnaise [meɪə'neɪz] N mayonesa *f*

mayor [mɛəʳ] N alcalde *m*, alcaldesa *f*, intendente *mf* (*SC, Mex*), regente *mf* (*Mex*); **Mr Mayor** Señor Alcalde; **Madam Mayor** Señora Alcaldesa

mayoress ['mɛəres] (*Brit*) N alcaldesa *f*, intendente *f* (*SC, Mex*), regente *f* (*Mex*)

maypole ['meɪpəʊl] N mayo *m*

maze [meɪz] N laberinto *m*

MB Ⓐ N ABBR (*Brit Univ*) = **Bachelor of Medicine** Ⓑ ABBR (*Canada*) = **Manitoba**

Mb N ABBR (*Comput*) (= *megabyte*) Mb

MBA N ABBR (*Univ*) = **Master of Business Administration**

MBE N ABBR (= *Member of the Order of the British Empire*) *título ceremonial británico*

MC N ABBR 1 = **Master of Ceremonies** 2 (*US*) = **Member of Congress** 3 (*Brit Mil*) = **Military Cross**

MD Ⓐ N ABBR 1 = **Doctor of Medicine** 2 (*esp Brit*) = **managing director** 3 (= *MiniDisc®*) MiniDisc®, minidisc *m* Ⓑ CPD ➤ **MD® player** MiniDisc®, minidisc *m*

Md. ABBR (*US*) = **Maryland**

me¹ [miː] PRON 1 (*direct/indirect object*) me; (*after prep*) mí; **he loves me** me quiere; **look at me!** ¡mírame!; **without me** sin mí; **come with me** ven conmigo; **like me** como yo 2 (*emphatic, in comparisons, after verb "to be"*) yo; **who, me?** ¿quién, yo?; **he's taller than me** es más alto que yo; **it's me** soy yo; **it's me, Paul** soy Paul

me² [miː] N (*Mus*) mi *m*

ME Ⓐ N ABBR 1 = **myalgic encephalomyelitis** 2 (*US*) = **medical examiner** Ⓑ ABBR (*US*) = **Maine**

Me. ABBR (*US*) = **Maine**

mead [miːd] N aguamiel *f*, hidromiel *m*

meadow ['medəʊ] N prado *m*, pradera *f*

meagre, meager (*US*) ['miːgəʳ] ADJ [*amount, salary, rations*] escaso, exiguo

meal¹ [miːl] N comida *f*; **to go for a ~** ir a comer fuera; **to have a (good) ~** comer (bien); **I don't eat between ~s** no como entre horas; ✦ IDIOM **to make a ~ of sth** (*Brit**) (= *take time over*) tardar lo suyo en hacer algo ➤ **meals on wheels** (*Brit*) servicio *m* de comidas a domicilio (*para ancianos*) ➤ **meal ticket** ✦ IDIOM **she's just looking for a ~ ticket** sólo busca a alguien que la mantenga

meal² [miːl] N (= *flour*) harina *f*

mealtime ['miːltaɪm] N hora *f* de comer

mealy ['miːlɪ] ADJ harinoso

mealy-mouthed ['miːlɪ'maʊðd] ADJ modoso, evasivo

mean¹ [miːn] ADJ (*compar ~er*; *superl ~est*) 1 (*esp Brit*) (= *stingy*) tacaño, agarrado*, amarrete (*And, SC**) 2 (= *nasty*) malo; **don't be ~!** ¡no seas malo!; **a ~ trick** una jugarreta, una mala pasada; **that was pretty ~ of them** se han portado bastante mal 3 (= *vicious*) [*dog*] malo 4 (= *inferior*) **she's no ~ cook** es una cocinera excelente; **it was no ~ feat** fue toda una hazaña 5 (*US*) formidable, de primera; **he plays a ~ game** juega estupendamente

mean² [miːn] Ⓐ N (= *middle term*) término *m* medio; (= *average*) promedio *m*; (*Math*) media *f* Ⓑ ADJ medio

mean³ [miːn] (*pt, pp ~t*) VT 1 [*word*] (= *signify*) significar, querer decir; [*person*] (= *imply*) querer decir; **what does this word ~?** ¿qué significa *or* quiere decir esta palabra?; **what do you ~?** ¿qué quieres decir?; **18, I ~ 19** 18, digo 19; **don't**

I ~ anything to you? ¿no significo yo nada para ti?; **what do you ~ by that?** ¿qué quieres decir con eso?; **your friendship ~s a lot to me** tu amistad es muy importante *or* significa mucho para mí; **it ~s a lot of expense for us** supone un gasto muy fuerte para nosotros; **the name ~s nothing to me** el nombre no me suena
2 (= *refer to*) referirse a; **do you ~ me?** ¿te refieres a mí?
3 (= *intend*) **I meant to come yesterday** quería venir ayer; **what do you ~ to do?** ¿qué piensas hacer?; **he didn't ~ to do it** lo hizo sin querer; **I ~ to have you sacked** voy a encargarme de que te despidan; **I ~ it** va en serio; **I meant it as a joke** lo dije en broma; **was the remark meant for me?** ¿el comentario iba por mí?; **I meant no harm by what I said** no lo dije con mala intención; **he meant no offence** no tenía intención de ofender a nadie; **he ~s well** tiene buenas intenciones
4 (= *suppose*) suponer; **to be meant to do sth: it's meant to be a good car** este coche se supone que es bueno; **parents are meant to love their children** se supone que los padres quieren a sus hijos; **we were meant to arrive at eight** se suponía que llegaríamos a las ocho; **this portrait is meant to be Anne** este retrato es de Anne, aunque no lo parezca; **you're not meant to drink it!** ¡no es para beber!

meander [mɪ'ændəʳ] Ⓐ VI 1 [*river*] serpentear 2 [*person*] (= *roam*) deambular, vagar; (*in speech*) divagar Ⓑ N meandro *m*

meandering [mɪ'ændərɪŋ] ADJ 1 [*river*] con meandros; [*road*] serpenteante 2 [*account, speech etc*] lleno de digresiones

meaning ['miːnɪŋ] N 1 (= *sense*) [*of word*] significado *m*, acepción *f*; [*of phrase*] significado *m*; [*of life, work*] sentido *m*; **life has no ~ for her now** ahora para ella la vida no tiene sentido; **double ~** doble sentido; **he doesn't know the ~ of the word** (*fig*) ni sabe lo que eso significa; **what's the ~ of this?** (*as reprimand*) ¿se puede saber qué significa esto? 2 (= *intention*) intención *f*, propósito *m*

meaningful ['miːnɪŋfʊl] ADJ 1 (= *worthwhile*) [*discussion*] valioso, positivo; [*experience*] valioso, significativo; [*relationship*] serio, significativo; [*question, explanation, comment, analogy*] que tiene sentido 2 (= *eloquent*) [*smile, look*] significativo, elocuente

meaningless ['miːnɪŋlɪs] ADJ sin sentido; **it is ~** no tiene sentido

meanness ['miːnnɪs] N 1 (*esp Brit*) (= *stinginess*) tacañería *f*, mezquindad *f* 2 (= *nastiness*) maldad *f*, vileza *f*

means [miːnz] Ⓐ N 1 (*with sing vb*) (= *way*) manera *f*, modo *m*; (= *method*) medio *m*; **by any ~** de cualquier manera, del modo que sea; **not by any ~** de ninguna manera *or* ningún modo; **by any ~ possible** como sea/ fuera posible, a como dé/diera lugar (*CAm, Mex*); **there is no ~ of doing it** no hay manera *or* modo de hacerlo; **a ~ to an end** un medio para conseguir algo *or* un fin; **by ~ of** por medio de; **~ of transport** medio *m* de transporte
2 (*in phrases*) **by all ~!** ¡claro que sí!, ¡por supuesto!; **by all ~ take one** por favor toma uno; **"is she a friend of yours?" — "by no means"** —¿es amiga suya? —de ninguna manera *or* ningún modo; **they're by no ~ rich** no son ricos, ni mucho menos; **it is by no ~ difficult** no es nada difícil
3 (*with pl vb*) (*Fin*) recursos *mpl*, medios *mpl*; **we haven't the ~ to do it** no contamos con los recursos *or* los medios para hacerlo; **to live beyond one's ~** vivir por encima de sus posibilidades, gastar más de lo que se gana; **a man of ~** un hombre acaudalado; **to live within one's ~** vivir de acuerdo con sus posibilidades Ⓑ CPD ➤ **means test** prueba *f* de haberes (*para determinar si una persona tiene derecho a determinada prestación*)

means-test ['miːnztest] VT **this benefit is ~ed** este subsidio se otorga después de averiguar los recursos económicos del solicitante

meant [ment] PT, PP *of* **mean³**

meantime ['miːntaɪm] Ⓐ ADV entretanto, mientras tanto Ⓑ N **for the ~** (*referring to now*) por ahora, de momento; (*referring to past*) entretanto; **in the ~** (*referring to now*) mientras tanto; (*referring to past*) en el ínterin

meanwhile ['miːn'waɪl] Ⓐ ADV entretanto, mientras tanto Ⓑ N **in the ~** entretanto, mientras tanto

measles ['mi:zlz] NSING sarampión *m*

measly* ['mi:zlɪ] ADJ (*compar* **measlier**; *superl* **measliest**) miserable, mezquino

measurable ['meʒərəbl] ADJ **1** (*lit*) mensurable, que se puede medir **2** (= *perceptible*) apreciable, perceptible

measure ['meʒə^r] Ⓐ N **1** (= *system*) medida *f*; **a suit made to** ~ un traje hecho a (la) medida **2** (= *rule*) metro *m* **3** (= *indication*) indicativo *m*; **it is a ~ of how serious the situation is** es un indicativo de lo grave de la situación **4** (= *amount measured*) cantidad *f*; (*sold in pub*) medida *f*; **I poured two equal ~s into the glasses** eché dos cantidades iguales en los vasos; **to give (sb) short ~** dar una medida escasa (a algn); ✦ IDIOM **for good ~: he gave me a few extra for good** ~ me dio unos pocos más por añadidura; **I repeated my question for good** ~ repetí la pregunta por si acaso **5** (= *step*) medida *f*; **to take ~s against sb/to do sth** tomar medidas contra algn/para hacer algo **6** (= *extent*) **we had some ~ of success** tuvimos cierto éxito Ⓑ VT [+ *object, speed, length*] medir; [+ *person*] (*for height*) medir; (*for clothes*) tomar las medidas a; **I have to be ~d for my costume** me tienen que tomar las medidas para el traje; **how can you ~ success?** ¿cómo puedes medir el éxito?; **I don't like being ~d against other people** no me gusta que se me compare con otra gente Ⓒ VI medir; **what does it ~?** ¿cuánto mide?; **the room ~s four metres across** la habitación mide cuatro metros de ancho
➤ **measure out** VT + ADV [+ *solid ingredients*] pesar; [+ *liquid, piece of ground, length*] medir
➤ **measure up** Ⓐ VT + ADV **1** [+ *wood, material*] medir **2** (= *evaluate*) [+ *sb's intentions*] averiguar; [+ *situation*] evaluar Ⓑ VI + ADV (= *fulfil expectations*) dar la talla, estar a la altura; **to ~ up to sth** estar a la altura de algo

measured ['meʒəd] ADJ [*tread, pace*] acompasado; [*tone, statement*] mesurado, comedido

measurement ['meʒəmənt] N (= *size*) medida *f*; **bust/hip** ~ contorno *m* de pecho/de caderas; **to take sb's ~s** tomar las medidas a algn

measuring ['meʒərɪŋ] N medición *f* ➤ **measuring jug** jarra *f* medidora *or* graduada ➤ **measuring tape** cinta *f* métrica, metro *m*

meat [mi:t] N carne *f*; (= *cold meat*) fiambre *m*; **a book with some ~ in it** un libro con enjundia *or* sustancia ➤ **meat eater** (= *person*) persona *f* que come carne; (= *animal*) carnívoro/a *m/f*; **we're not ~ eaters** no comemos carne ➤ **meat grinder** (*US*) máquina *f* de picar carne ➤ **meat hook** gancho *m* carnicero ➤ **meat loaf** rollo *m* de carne picada sazonado, cocido y servido como fiambre ➤ **meat pie** pastel *m* de carne; (*individual*) empanada *f*

meatball ['mi:tbɔ:l] N albóndiga *f*

meaty ['mi:tɪ] ADJ (*compar* **meatier**; *superl* **meatiest**) **1** [*soup, filling*] con carne; [*flavour*] a carne **2** (= *substantial*) [*book*] sustancioso, enjundioso; [*part, role*] importante, de peso

Mecca ['mekə] N La Meca; **a ~ for tourists** una de las mecas del turismo

mechanic [mɪ'kænɪk] N mecánico/a *m/f*

mechanical [mɪ'kænɪkəl] Ⓐ ADJ **1** [*toy, problem, failure, device*] mecánico **2** (= *unthinking*) [*behaviour, reply*] mecánico, maquinal Ⓑ CPD ➤ **mechanical engineer** ingeniero/a *m/f* mecánico/a ➤ **mechanical engineering** ingeniería *f* mecánica

mechanics [mɪ'kænɪks] Ⓐ NSING (= *science*) mecánica *f* Ⓑ NPL (= *machinery*) mecanismo *msing*; (*fig*) mecánica *fsing*

mechanism ['mekənɪzəm] N mecanismo *m*

mechanization [,mekənaɪ'zeɪʃən] N mecanización *f*

mechanize ['mekənaɪz] VT [+ *process, task*] mecanizar; [+ *factory*] automatizar

MEd [em'ed] N ABBR (*Univ*) = **Master of Education**

Med* [med] N **the** ~ el Mediterráneo

medal ['medl] N medalla *f*

medallion [mɪ'dælɪən] N medallón *m*

medallist, medalist (*US*) ['medəlɪst] N medallista *mf*; **bronze/silver/gold** ~ medalla *mf* de bronce/plata/oro

meddle ['medl] VI **1** (= *interfere*) (entro)meterse (**in** en) **2 to ~ with sth** (= *touch*) toquetear algo, manosear algo

meddlesome ['medlsəm], **meddling**[1] ['medlɪŋ] ADJ entrometido

meddling[2] ['medlɪŋ] N intromisión *f*

media ['mi:dɪə] NPL *of* **medium**; **the** ~ los medios de comunicación (de masas) ➤ **media coverage** cobertura *f* informativa ➤ **media research** investigación *f* de los medios de comunicación ➤ **media studies** (*Univ*) ciencias *fpl* de la información (*frm*), periodismo* *msing*

mediaeval [,medɪ'i:vəl] ADJ = **medieval**

median ['mi:dɪən] Ⓐ ADJ mediano Ⓑ N (*US*) (*also* ~ **strip**) mediana *f*, franja *f* central

mediate ['mi:dɪeɪt] Ⓐ VI mediar (**between** entre; **in** en) Ⓑ VT [+ *talks*] mediar en, actuar de mediador en; [+ *dispute*] mediar en, arbitrar; [+ *agreement*] conseguir mediante mediación

mediation [,mi:dɪ'eɪʃən] N mediación *f*

mediator ['mi:dɪeɪtə^r] N mediador(a) *m/f*

medic* ['medɪk] N **1** (= *doctor*) médico/a *m/f* **2** (= *student*) estudiante *mf* de medicina

Medicaid ['medɪ,keɪd] N (*US*) seguro médico estatal para personas de bajos ingresos

medical ['medɪkəl] Ⓐ ADJ [*care, facilities, staff, treatment*] médico; [*records*] médico, clínico; [*student*] de medicina; [*problems*] de salud; **to seek ~ advice** consultar a un médico; **he is in urgent need of ~ attention** necesita atención médica urgente; **on ~ grounds** por razones de salud; **the ~ history of a patient** el historial médico *or* clínico de un paciente, la historia clínica de un paciente; **the ~ profession** la profesión médica Ⓑ N reconocimiento *m* médico, revisión *f* médica, examen *m* médico Ⓒ CPD ➤ **medical board** (*Mil*) consejo *m* de médicos ➤ **medical certificate** certificado *m* médico ➤ **medical examination** reconocimiento *m* médico, revisión *f* médica, examen *m* médico ➤ **medical examiner** (*US*) médico/a *m/f* forense ➤ **medical insurance** seguro *m* médico ➤ **medical officer** médico/a *m/f*; (*Mil*) oficial *mf* médico/a ➤ **medical practitioner** (*frm*) médico/a *m/f* ➤ **medical school** facultad *f* de medicina ➤ **medical science** medicina *f*, ciencia *f* médica

Medicare ['medɪkeə^r] N (*US*) seguro médico estatal para ancianos y minusválidos

medicated ['medɪkeɪtɪd] ADJ [*soap, shampoo*] medicinal

medication [,medɪ'keɪʃən] N (= *drugs*) medicación *f*

medicinal [me'dɪsɪnl] ADJ medicinal

medicine ['medsən] Ⓐ N **1** (= *drug*) medicina *f*, medicamento *m*; ✦ IDIOM **to give sb a taste of his own** ~ pagar a algn con la misma moneda **2** (= *science*) medicina *f* Ⓑ CPD ➤ **medicine cabinet** botiquín *m* ➤ **medicine man** hechicero *m*

medieval [,medɪ'i:vəl] ADJ medieval

mediocre [,mi:dɪ'əʊkə^r] ADJ mediocre

mediocrity [,mi:dɪ'ɒkrɪtɪ] N mediocridad *f*

meditate ['medɪteɪt] Ⓐ VI (= *think*) reflexionar, meditar (**on** sobre); (*Rel, Health*) meditar Ⓑ VT meditar

meditation [,medɪ'teɪʃən] N (= *thought*) meditación *f*, reflexión *f*; (*Rel, Health*) meditación

Mediterranean [,medɪtə'reɪnɪən] Ⓐ ADJ mediterráneo; **the ~ Sea** el Mar Mediterráneo Ⓑ N (= *sea*) **the** ~ el Mediterráneo; (= *person*) mediterráneo/a *m/f*

medium ['mi:dɪəm] Ⓐ ADJ **1** (= *not small or large*) [*object*] mediano; [*length, size, build*] mediano, medio; **available in small, ~ and large** disponible en talla pequeña, mediana y grande; **of ~ height** de estatura regular; **in the ~ term** a medio plazo **2** (*Culin*) **a ~ steak** un filete no muy hecho Ⓑ N **1** (*pl* **media** *or* ~**s**) (= *gen*) medio *m* (*also Art*); **the advertising media** los medios publicitarios *or* de publicidad; **through the ~ of television** por medio de *or* a

través de la televisión; **happy** ~ término *m* medio
2 (*pl* **~s**) (= *spiritualist*) médium *mf*
Ⓒ CPD ➤ **medium wave** (*esp Brit Rad*) onda *f* media

medium-dry [ˌmiːdɪəmˈdraɪ] ADJ [*wine*] semi seco

medium-range [ˌmiːdɪəmˈreɪndʒ] ADJ [*missile*] de alcance
medio; [*weather forecast*] a medio plazo

medium-rare [ˌmiːdɪəmˈrɛəʳ] ADV [*steak*] medio hecho,
sonrosado

medium-size(d) [ˌmiːdɪəmˈsaɪz(d)] ADJ de tamaño
mediano *or* medio

medium-sweet [ˌmiːdɪəmˈswiːt] ADJ [*wine*] semidulce

medley [ˈmedlɪ] N [*of music*] popurrí *m*

meek [miːk] ADJ (*compar* **~er**; *superl* **~est**) [*person*] sumiso,
dócil, manso (*liter*); ✦ IDIOM **~ and mild** como una malva

meet [miːt] (*pt, pp* **met**) Ⓐ VT **1** (*by arrangement*) quedar
con, verse con; (*by chance*) encontrarse con, tropezar
con; **I'm ~ing them for lunch tomorrow** he quedado para
almorzar con ellos mañana; **I had arranged to ~ her in town**
había quedado con ella en el centro, había acordado en
verla en el centro; **I'll ~ you outside the cinema** te veré en
la entrada del cine
2 (= *go/come to get*) ir/venir a buscar; (= *welcome*) recibir;
I'm being met at the airport me vendrán a buscar al
aeropuerto; **she ran out to ~ us** salió corriendo a
recibirnos; **to ~ sb off the train** ir a esperar a algn a la
estación
3 (= *make acquaintance of*) conocer; **I met my wife in 1994**
conocí a mi mujer en 1994; **pleased to ~ you!** ¡mucho
gusto!, ¡encantado de conocerlo!
4 (= *come together with*) **where the sea ~s the horizon**
donde el mar se junta con el horizonte; **the sound which
met his ears** el sonido que llegó a sus oídos; **I could not ~
his eye** no podía mirarle a los ojos; **her eyes met her
sister's across the table** tropezó con la mirada de su
hermana al otro lado de la mesa
5 (= *come across*) [+ *problem*] encontrarse con
6 (= *confront*) [+ *opponent*] enfrentarse con; (*in duel*) batirse
con; [+ *problem*] hacer frente a; **he met his death in 1800**
halló *or* encontró la muerte en 1800; **to ~ sth head-on**
enfrentarse de lleno con algo, hacer frente *or* plantar cara
directamente a algo; **this suggestion was met with angry
protests** la gente reaccionó con protestas de indignación
ante la sugerencia
7 (= *satisfy*) [+ *need*] satisfacer, cubrir; [+ *demand*] atender
a, satisfacer; [+ *wish*] satisfacer; [+ *requirement*] cumplir
con; [+ *expense, cost*] correr con, hacer frente a;
[+ *obligation*] atender a, cumplir con; [+ *target, goal*]
alcanzar; [+ *challenge*] hacer frente a; [+ *expectations*] estar
a la altura de; **it did not ~ our expectations** no estuvo a la
altura de nuestras expectativas
Ⓑ VI **1** (= *encounter each other*) (*by arrangement*) quedar,
verse; (*by chance*) encontrarse; (= *hold meeting*) reunirse; **we
could ~ for a drink after work** podríamos vernos *or* quedar
para tomar una copa después del trabajo; **what time shall
we ~?** ¿a qué hora quieres que quedemos *or* nos veamos?;
let's ~ at eight quedemos para las ocho; **the two ministers
met to discuss the treaty** los dos ministros se entrevistaron
or se reunieron para discutir el tratado; **to ~ again** volver a
verse
2 (= *convene*) [*Parliament, club, committee*] reunirse
3 (= *become acquainted*) conocerse; **we have met before** nos
conocemos ya; **have we met?** ¿nos conocemos de antes?
4 (= *come together*) [*rivers*] confluir; [*roads*] empalmar;
our eyes met cruzamos una mirada
Ⓒ N (*Brit Hunting*) cacería *f*; (*esp US Sport*) encuentro *m*
➤ **meet up** VI + ADV **to ~ up (with sb)** (*by arrangement*)
quedar (con algn), verse (con algn); (*by chance*)
encontrarse (con algn), tropezar (con algn)
➤ **meet with** VI + PREP **1** (= *experience*) [+ *hostility*]
experimentar; [+ *difficulties*] encontrarse con, tropezar con;
[+ *accident*] tener, sufrir; [+ *success*] tener; **we hope the idea
~s with your approval** esperamos que la idea reciba su
aprobación **2** (*esp US*) [+ *person*] (*by arrangement*) quedarse
con, verse con; (*by chance*) encontrarse con, tropezar con;
(*formally*) reunirse con

meeting [ˈmiːtɪŋ] Ⓐ N **1** [*of manager, members, staff etc*]
reunión *f*; [*of legislative body*] sesión *f*; **to call a ~** convocar

una reunión; **I have a ~ at ten** tengo una reunión a las
diez; **to hold a ~** celebrar una reunión; **John's in a ~** John
está en una reunión *or* (*Sp*) está reunido
2 (*between two people*) (*arranged*) cita *f*, compromiso *m*;
(*accidental*) encuentro *m*; (*with politician, person in authority*)
entrevista *f*, encuentro *m*; **I liked him from our first ~** me
gustó desde el día que le conocí *or* desde nuestro primer
encuentro; **I had a ~ with the headmistress today** hoy he
tenido una entrevista *or* reunión con la directora
3 (*Athletics*) competición *f* (*Sp*), competencia *f* (*LAm*); (*Horse
racing*) jornada *f*
4 [*of rivers*] confluencia *f*
Ⓑ CPD ➤ **meeting place** [*of two people*] lugar *m* de cita; [*of
many*] lugar *m* de reunión *or* encuentro; **this bar was their
usual ~ place** solían citarse en este bar, acostumbraban
reunirse en este bar

mega* [ˈmegə] ADJ súper*

megabucks* [ˈmegəˌbʌks] N **now he's making ~** ahora está
ganando un dineral*, ahora se está forrando*; **we're
talking ~** hablamos de un montón *or* (*Sp*) un porrón de
dinero*

megabyte [ˈmegəˌbaɪt] N megabyte *m*, mega *m*

megalithic [ˌmegəˈlɪθɪk] ADJ megalítico

megalomania [ˈmegələʊˈmeɪnɪə] N megalomanía *f*

megaphone [ˈmegəfəʊn] N megáfono *m*

megawatt [ˈmegəwɒt] N megavatio *m*

melancholy [ˈmelənkəlɪ] Ⓐ ADJ [*person, mood*]
melancólico; [*sight*] triste Ⓑ N melancolía *f*

melanin [ˈmelənɪn] N melanina *f*

melanoma [ˌmeləˈnəʊmə] N melanoma *m*

melée [ˈmeleɪ] N **1** (= *confusion*) tumulto *m* **2** (= *fight*) pelea
f confusa, refriega *f*

mellow [ˈmeləʊ] Ⓐ ADJ (*compar* **~er**; *superl* **~est**)
1 (= *smooth*) [*wine*] suave, añejo; [*fruit*] maduro, dulce;
[*colour, light*] suave y dorado, tenue y dorado; [*voice, tone*]
dulce, meloso
2 (= *calm-tempered*) apacible, sosegado; (= *relaxed*) relajado;
he has grown more ~ over the years los años le han
suavizado el carácter, se ha vuelto más afable con los
años; **to be in a ~ mood** sentirse relajado
Ⓑ VI **1** (= *relax*) relajarse; **he has ~ed with age** los años le
han suavizado el carácter, con los años se ha vuelto más
afable
2 [*wine*] añejarse; [*fruit*] madurar; [*voice, character*]
suavizarse
Ⓒ VT [+ *wine*] añejar; **old age has ~ed him** la vejez le ha
suavizado el carácter *or* lo ha hecho más afable

melodic [mɪˈlɒdɪk] ADJ melódico

melodious [mɪˈləʊdɪəs] ADJ melodioso

melodrama [ˈmeləˌdrɑːmə] N melodrama *m*

melodramatic [ˌmelədrəˈmætɪk] ADJ melodramático

melody [ˈmelədɪ] N melodía *f*

melon [ˈmelən] N melón *m*

melt [melt] Ⓐ VT [+ *snow, chocolate, butter*] derretir, fundir;
[+ *metal*] fundir Ⓑ VI [*snow, chocolate, butter*] derretirse,
fundirse; [*metal*] fundirse; **it ~s in the mouth** se deshace en
la boca; **he ~ed into the crowd** desapareció entre la
multitud; ✦ IDIOM **her heart ~ed with pity** se le ablandó el
corazón de lástima
➤ **melt away** VI [*snow*] derretirse; [*confidence*]
desvanecerse; [*crowd*] dispersarse
➤ **melt down** VT + ADV fundir

meltdown [ˈmeltdaʊn] N **1** (*in nuclear reactor*) fusión *f* de
un reactor, fundido *m* **2** (*fig*) catástrofe *f*

melting [ˈmeltɪŋ] CPD ➤ **melting point** punto *m* de fusión
➤ **melting pot** crisol *m*; ✦ IDIOM **to be in the ~ pot** (*esp Brit*)
estar sobre el tapete

member [ˈmembəʳ] N [*of organization, committee*] miembro
mf; [*of society, club*] miembro *mf*, socio/a *m/f*; [*of political
party, trade union*] miembro *mf*, afiliado/a *m/f*; **"members
only"** "sólo para socios", "reservado para los socios"; **if any
~ of the audience ...** si cualquiera de los espectadores ..., si
cualquier miembro del público ...; **a ~ of the family** un

miembro de la familia ➤ **Member of Congress** (US) miembro *mf* del Congreso ➤ **Member of Parliament** (Brit) diputado/a *m/f*, parlamentario/a *m/f*; ⊃ BY-ELECTION, CONSTITUENCY ➤ **member of staff** [of firm] empleado/a *m/f*; [of school] miembro *mf* del profesorado ➤ **Member of the European Parliament** diputado/a *m/f* del Parlamento Europeo, eurodiputado/a *m/f* ➤ **member of the public** ciudadano/a *m/f*; **the library is open to ~s of the public** la biblioteca está abierta al público ➤ **member state** estado *m* miembro

membership ['membəʃɪp] **Ⓐ** N **1** (= members) [of club, society] socios *mpl*, miembros *mpl*; [of political party, trade union] miembros *mpl*, afiliados *mpl*

2 (= position) ~ **of the union is compulsory** es obligatorio afiliarse a or hacerse miembro del sindicato; **to apply for ~** solicitar el ingreso como socio or miembro; **Spain's ~ of** or (US) **in the Common Market** la pertenencia de España al Mercado Común

3 (= numbers) número *m* de miembros or socios *etc*, membresía *f* (Mex); **a ~ of more than 800** más de 800 socios or miembros

Ⓑ CPD ➤ **membership card** tarjeta *f* or carné *m* de socio ➤ **membership fee** cuota *f* de socio

membrane ['membreɪn] N membrana *f*

memento [mɪ'mentəʊ] N recuerdo *m*

memo* ['meməʊ] N ABBR (= **memorandum**) memo *m* ➤ **memo pad** bloc *m* de notas

memoirs ['memwɑːz] NPL memorias *fpl*, autobiografía *fsing*

memorabilia [,memərə'bɪlɪə] N recuerdos *mpl*

memorable ['memərəbl] ADJ memorable

memorandum [,memə'rændəm] N (pl **~s** or **memoranda** [,memə'rændə]) memorándum *m*

memorial [mɪ'mɔːrɪəl] **Ⓐ** ADJ conmemorativo **Ⓑ** N (= monument) monumento *m* conmemorativo **Ⓒ** CPD ➤ **memorial park** (US) cementerio *m* ➤ **memorial service** servicio religioso en memoria del difunto

memorize ['meməraɪz] VT memorizar, aprender de memoria

memory ['memərɪ] **Ⓐ** N **1** (= faculty) memoria *f* (also Comput); **to commit sth to ~** aprender algo de memoria; **to lose one's ~** perder la memoria; **I have a bad ~ for faces** se me olvida la cara de la gente; **he recited the poem from ~** recitó el poema de memoria; **to the best of my ~** que yo recuerde; ✦ IDIOM **to have a ~ like a sieve** tener malísima memoria

2 (= recollection) recuerdo *m*; **to have happy memories of sth** tener or guardar buenos recuerdos de algo; **to keep sb's ~ alive** guardar el recuerdo de algn, mantener vivo el recuerdo de algn; **in ~ of** en memoria de

Ⓑ CPD ➤ **memory bank** banco *m* de memoria ➤ **memory chip** chip *m* de memoria ➤ **memory lane** ✦ IDIOM **to take a trip down ~ lane** adentrarse en el mundo de los recuerdos

men [men] NPL of **man**

menace ['menɪs] **Ⓐ** N **1** (= threat) amenaza *f*; **a voice full of ~** una voz amenazadora **2** (= danger) peligro *m*, amenaza *f*; **he's a ~ to the public*** es un peligro público **Ⓑ** VT amenazar

menacing ['menɪsɪŋ] ADJ amenazador

ménage à trois [me,nɑ:ʒɑ:'trwɑ:] N trío *m*, ménage à trois *m*

menagerie [mɪ'nædʒərɪ] N casa *f* or colección *f* de fieras

mend [mend] **Ⓐ** N ✦ IDIOM **to be on the ~** ir mejorando **Ⓑ** VT [+ watch, toy] arreglar, reparar; [+ shoes] arreglar; ✦ IDIOM **to ~ one's ways** enmendarse **Ⓒ** VI (= improve) mejorar

mending ['mendɪŋ] N reparación *f*, arreglo *m*

menfolk ['menfəʊk] NPL hombres *mpl*

menial ['miːnɪəl] ADJ (= lowly) servil; (= domestic) doméstico, de la casa; **~ work** trabajo *m* de baja categoría

meningitis [,menɪn'dʒaɪtɪs] N meningitis *f inv*

menopause ['menəʊpɔːz] N menopausia *f*

menstrual ['menstrʊəl] ADJ menstrual ➤ **menstrual cycle**

ciclo *m* menstrual

menstruate ['menstrʊeɪt] VI menstruar, tener la menstruación

menstruation [,menstrʊ'eɪʃən] N menstruación *f*

menswear ['menzweəʳ] N ropa *f* de caballero

mental ['mentl] **Ⓐ** ADJ **1** (= not physical) mental; **to make a ~ note of sth** tomar nota mentalmente de algo **2** (Brit*) (= crazy) chiflado* **Ⓑ** CPD ➤ **mental arithmetic** cálculos *mpl* mentales ➤ **mental block** bloqueo *m* mental ➤ **mental handicap** retraso *m* mental ➤ **mental home, mental hospital** hospital *m* psiquiátrico, manicomio *m* ➤ **mental illness** enfermedad *f* mental ➤ **mental patient** paciente *mf* psiquiátrico/a

mentality [men'tælɪtɪ] N mentalidad *f*

mentally ['mentəlɪ] ADV mentalmente; **to be ~ disturbed** estar trastornado; **to be ~ handicapped** ser un disminuido psíquico; **to be ~ ill** tener una enfermedad mental, ser un enfermo mental

menthol ['menθɒl] **Ⓐ** N mentol *m* **Ⓑ** CPD [cigarette, sweet] mentolado

mention ['menʃən] **Ⓐ** N mención *f*; **at the ~ of food, she looked up** al oír que se mencionaba comida, levantó la vista; **it got a ~ in the news** lo mencionaron en las noticias; **there was no ~ of any surcharge** no se hizo mención de or no se mencionó ningún recargo adicional **Ⓑ** VT mencionar; **I will ~ it to him** se lo mencionaré, se lo diré; **don't ~ it to anyone** no se lo digas a nadie; **don't ~ it!** ¡de nada!, ¡no hay de qué!; **he didn't ~ any names** no dijo or dio los nombres; **they make so much mess, not to ~ the noise** lo dejan todo patas arriba, y no digamos ya el ruido que arman; **to ~ sb in one's will** dejar algo a algn en el testamento, legar algo a algn; **it's worth ~ing that ...** merece la pena mencionar que ...

mentor ['mentɔːʳ] N mentor *m*

menu ['menjuː] N **1** (in restaurant) carta *f*; (= set meal) menú *m* **2** (Comput) menú *m*

MEP N ABBR (Brit) (= **Member of the European Parliament**) eurodiputado/a *m/f*

mercantile ['mɜːkəntaɪl] ADJ mercantil

mercenary ['mɜːsnərɪ] ADJ, N mercenario/a *m/f*

merchandise ['mɜːtʃəndaɪz] N mercancías *fpl*

merchandising ['mɜːtʃəndaɪzɪŋ] N (US) comercialización *f*

merchant ['mɜːtʃənt] N (= trader, dealer) comerciante *mf*; (US) (= retailer) minorista *mf*, detallista *mf* ➤ **merchant bank** (esp Brit) banco *m* mercantil or comercial ➤ **merchant banker** (esp Brit) ejecutivo/a *m/f* de un banco mercantil or comercial ➤ **merchant marine** (US), **merchant navy** (Brit) marina *f* mercante ➤ **merchant seaman** marino *m* mercante

merciful ['mɜːsɪfʊl] ADJ **1** (= compassionate) [God] misericordioso, clemente, compasivo; [person] clemente, compasivo; **to be ~ to** or **towards sb** ser clemente con algn, mostrarse compasivo con algn **2** (= welcome) **death came as a ~ release** la muerte fue como una bendición

mercifully ['mɜːsɪfəlɪ] ADV **1** (= kindly) con clemencia, con compasión **2** (= fortunately) afortunadamente, gracias a Dios

merciless ['mɜːsɪlɪs] ADJ [person, attack] despiadado, cruel; [killing, beating] cruel; [sun, heat] implacable

mercurial [mɜː'kjʊərɪəl] ADJ (= lively) vivo; (= changeable) veleidoso, voluble

Mercury ['mɜːkjʊrɪ] N Mercurio *m*

mercury ['mɜːkjʊrɪ] N mercurio *m*, azogue *m*

mercy ['mɜːsɪ] **Ⓐ** N **1** (= compassion) misericordia *f*; (= clemency) clemencia *f*, piedad *f*; **to beg for ~** pedir clemencia; **to have ~ on sb** tener misericordia or piedad de algn, tener clemencia para con algn; **have ~!** ¡por piedad!; **to show sb no ~** no mostrarse misericordioso or clemente con algn

2 (= discretion) **to be at the ~ of sth/sb** estar a merced de algo/algn; **to be left to the tender mercies of sb** (esp hum) quedar a merced de algn

3 (= blessing) **it's a ~ that no-one was hurt*** es un milagro que nadie resultara herido, menos mal que nadie resultó herido; **we should be grateful for small mercies** y demos gracias, porque podría haber sido peor ⓑ CPD ➤ **mercy killing** eutanasia f

mere [mɪəʳ] ADJ (*superl* ~**st**) mero, simple; **it was sold for a ~ £45** lo vendieron por apenas 45 libras; **I was a ~ child when I married him** no era más que una niña *or* era solamente una niña cuando me casé con él; **a ~ formality** una mera *or* pura *or* simple formalidad; **the merest hint of a smile** apenas un atisbo de sonrisa; **it's way beyond the abilities of ~ mortals like us** está más allá de la capacidad del común de los mortales como nosotros; **a ~ nothing** casi nada; **the ~ sight of blood is enough to make her faint** sólo con ver la sangre *or* con sólo ver la sangre se desmaya

merely ['mɪəlɪ] ADV simplemente, solamente; **I ~ said that ...** sólo dije que ..., lo único que dije era que ...; **she ~ smiled** sonrió nada más, se limitó a sonreír

merge [mɜːdʒ] ⓐ VT **1** [+ *company*] fusionar, unir **2** (*Comput*) [+ *text, files*] fusionar ⓑ VI **1** [*colours, sounds*] fundirse; [*roads*] empalmar; **to ~ into the background** confundirse con el fondo **2** [*companies, organizations*] fusionarse (**with** con) ⓒ N (*Comput*) fusión f

merger ['mɜːdʒəʳ] N fusión f

meridian [məˈrɪdɪən] N meridiano m

meringue [məˈræŋ] N merengue m

merit ['merɪt] ⓐ N mérito m; **it has the ~ of being clear** tiene el mérito de ser claro; **to treat a case on its ~s** juzgar un caso según sus propios méritos ⓑ VT merecer

meritocracy [ˌmerɪˈtɒkrəsɪ] N meritocracia f

mermaid ['mɜːmeɪd] N sirena f

merrily ['merɪlɪ] ADV **1** (= *cheerfully*) alegremente **2** (= *blithely*) **she quite ~ wrote out a cheque for £3,000** extendió tranquilamente *or* tan tranquila un cheque por 3.000 libras

merriment ['merɪmənt] N alegría f, regocijo m; (= *laughter*) risas fpl

merry ['merɪ] ADJ (*compar* **merrier**; *superl* **merriest**) **1** (= *cheerful*) alegre; **Merry Christmas!** ¡Feliz Navidad! **2** (*Brit**) (= *tipsy*) achispado, alegre

merry-go-round ['merɪɡəʊˌraʊnd] N caballitos mpl, carrusel m (*esp LAm*), calesita(s) f(pl) (*And, SC*)

merrymaking ['merɪˌmeɪkɪŋ] N (= *enjoyment*) diversión f; (= *happiness*) alegría f, regocijo m; (= *parties*) fiestas fpl

mesh [meʃ] ⓐ N **1** [*of net*] malla f **2** (= *netting*) **wire ~** tela f metálica, malla f metálica **3** (= *network, net, also fig*) red f ⓑ VI (*Tech*) engranar (**with** con)

mesmerize ['mezməraɪz] VT hipnotizar; (*fig*) fascinar

mess [mes] ⓐ N **1** (*untidy*) desorden m; (*dirty*) porquería f; (= *shambles*) desastre m, desbarajuste m; (= *predicament*) lío* m, follón m (*Sp**); (= *bad job*) chapuza* f, desastre m; **excuse the ~** perdone el desorden; **this place is a ~** esta casa es un desastre; **her hair is a ~** tiene el pelo hecho un desastre; **to be in a ~: the house was in a ~** la casa estaba hecha un desastre; **the toys were in a ~** había un desorden de juguetes; **to leave things in a ~** dejarlo todo desordenado *or* hecho un desastre; **her life is in a ~** su vida es un desastre *or* un desbarajuste; **we're in a ~** estamos metidos en un lío *or* (*Sp*) un follón*; **to get (o.s.) into a ~** (*fig*) meterse en un lío *or* (*Sp*) un follón*; **you look a ~** vas hecho un desastre; **to make a ~: look what a ~ you've made!** ¡mira cómo lo has puesto todo!; **he made a ~ of his audition** la audición le fue fatal*; **I've made such a ~ of my life** he arruinado *or* echado a perder mi vida **2** (*euph*) (= *excrement*) caca f **3** (*Mil*) comedor m; **officers' ~** comedor m de oficiales ⓑ VT **to ~ one's pants/trousers** hacerse caca encima*

➤ **mess around***, **mess about*** (*Brit*) ⓐ VT + ADV **to ~ sb around** fastidiar a algn; **they kept ~ing me around over the dates** ya me estaban fastidiando con tanto cambio de fechas ⓑ VI + ADV (= *play the fool*) hacer tonterías; (= *do nothing in particular*) pasar el rato, gandulear; (= *waste time*) perder el tiempo; **he enjoys ~ing around in boats** le gusta entretenerse con las barcas; **she's not one to ~ around, she**

gets on with the job no es de las que pierde el tiempo, saca el trabajo adelante; **stop ~ing around!** ¡déjate de tonterías!; **to ~ around with sb/sth: he isn't the kind of guy you ~ around with** no es de los que se deja enredar *or* tomar el pelo; **she'd been ~ing around with other men** había estado liada con otros hombres*; **he was ~ing around with his watchstrap** estaba juguetando con la correa del reloj; **who's been ~ing around with the video?** ¿quién ha estado manoseando *or* toqueteando el vídeo?

➤ **mess up** ⓐ VT + ADV **1** (= *disarrange*) [+ *books, papers*] descolocar; [+ *hair*] desarreglar; [+ *room*] desordenar, desarreglar **2** (= *dirty*) ensuciar **3** (= *ruin*) [+ *plans, arrangements*] estropear, echar por tierra ⓑ VI + ADV (*) meter la pata*

➤ **mess with*** VI + PREP **1** (= *challenge, confront*) meterse con* **2** (= *interfere with*) interferir con **3** (= *get involved with*) **I used to ~ with drugs** estaba metido en drogas*

message ['mesɪdʒ] N recado m; (*frm, fig, Comput*) mensaje m; **to leave a ~** dejar un recado; **a secret ~** un mensaje secreto; **the ~ of the film** el mensaje de la película. ✦ IDIOM **to get the ~*: do you think he got the ~?*** ¿crees que lo comprendió *or* entendió? ➤ **message switching** (*Comput*) conmutación f de mensajes

messenger ['mesɪndʒəʳ] N mensajero/a m/f ➤ **messenger boy** recadero m

Messiah [mɪˈsaɪə] N Mesías m

Messrs ['mesəz] NPL ABBR (*Brit*) (= **Messieurs**) Srs., Sres.

mess-up* ['mesʌp] N (*Brit*) lío* m, follón m (*Sp**)

messy ['mesɪ] ADJ (*compar* **messier**; *superl* **messiest**) **1** (= *creating mess*) [*person*] desordenado; [*animal, activity, job*] sucio; **he's such a ~ eater** lo deja todo perdido *or* lo ensucia todo cuando come **2** (= *dirty, untidy*) [*place, room*] desordenado; [*clothes*] desarreglado, desordenado; [*hair*] despeinado **3** (= *confused and awkward*) [*divorce, relationship*] turbio, turbulento; [*process, dispute*] enrevesado, complicado

met [met] PT, PP *of* **meet**

Met. [met] ⓐ ADJ ABBR (*Brit*) = **meteorological**; **the ~ Office** el instituto meteorológico británico ⓑ N ABBR **1** (*Brit*) (= **Metropolitan Police**) *la policía de Londres* **2** (*US*) = **Metropolitan Opera**

metabolic [ˌmetəˈbɒlɪk] ADJ metabólico; **~ rate** ciclo m metabólico

metabolism [meˈtæbəlɪzəm] N metabolismo m

metal ['metl] ⓐ N metal m ⓑ ADJ metálico, de metal ⓒ CPD ➤ **metal detector** detector m de metales ➤ **metal fatigue** fatiga f del metal

metallic [mɪˈtælɪk] ADJ metálico

metallurgy [meˈtælədʒɪ] N metalurgia f

metalwork ['metlwɜːk] N (= *craft*) metalistería f

metamorphose [ˌmetəˈmɔːfəʊz] VI metamorfosearse (**into** en)

metamorphosis [ˌmetəˈmɔːfəsɪs] N (*pl* **metamorphoses** [ˌmetəˈmɔːfəsiːz]) metamorfosis f inv

metaphor ['metəfɔːʳ] N metáfora f

metaphorical [ˌmetəˈfɒrɪkəl] ADJ metafórico

metaphorically [ˌmetəˈfɒrɪkəlɪ] ADV metafóricamente

metaphysical [ˌmetəˈfɪzɪkəl] ADJ metafísico

metaphysics [ˌmetəˈfɪzɪks] NSING metafísica f

metatarsal [ˌmetəˈtɑːsl] N metatarsiano m

meteor ['miːtɪəʳ] N meteoro m

meteoric [ˌmiːtɪˈɒrɪk] ADJ **1** (*lit*) meteórico **2** (*fig*) [*rise*] rápido, meteórico

meteorite ['miːtɪəraɪt] N meteorito m

meteorological [ˌmiːtɪərəˈlɒdʒɪkəl] ADJ meteorológico

meteorologist [ˌmiːtɪəˈrɒlədʒɪst] N meteorólogo/a m/f

meteorology [ˌmiːtɪəˈrɒlədʒɪ] N meteorología f

mete out [ˌmiːtˈaʊt] VT [+ *punishment, justice*] imponer; [+ *challenge*] asignar

meter[1] ['miːtəʳ] N contador m, medidor m (*LAm*); (*in taxi*) taxímetro m; **gas/electricity ~** contador de gas/de electricidad; **parking** ~ parquímetro *m*

meter² ['mi:tə'] N (*US*) = **metre**

methane ['mi:θeɪn] N metano *m*

method ['meθəd] N (= *manner, way*) método *m*; (= *procedure*) procedimiento *m*; (= *technique*) técnica *f*; ~ **of payment** forma *f* de pago; ✦ IDIOM **there's ~ in his madness** no está tan loco como parece ➤ **method acting** método *m* (de) Stanislavski ➤ **method actor** actor/actriz *m/f* de(l) método, seguidor(a) *m/f* del método (de) Stanislavski

methodical [mɪ'θɒdɪkəl] ADJ metódico

Methodist ['meθədɪst] ADJ, N metodista *mf*

methodology [,meθə'dɒlədʒɪ] N metodología *f*

meths* [meθs] N ABBR (*Brit*) = **methylated spirit(s)**

methylated spirit(s) ['meθɪleɪtɪd'spɪrɪt(s)] NSING (*Brit*) alcohol *m* desnaturalizado

meticulous [mɪ'tɪkjʊləs] ADJ meticuloso

métier ['meɪtɪeɪ] N (= *trade*) oficio *m*; (= *strong point*) fuerte *m*; (= *speciality*) especialidad *f*; **it's not my** ~ no es mi especialidad

metre, meter (*US*) ['mi:tə'] N metro *m*

metric ['metrɪk] ADJ métrico; **to go** ~ pasar al sistema métrico ➤ **metric system** sistema *m* métrico

metrication [,metrɪ'keɪʃən] N conversión *f* al sistema métrico

metrics ['metrɪks] NSING métrica *f*

metro ['metrəʊ] N metro *m*

metronome ['metrənəʊm] N metrónomo *m*

metropolis [mɪ'trɒpəlɪs] N metrópoli *f*

metropolitan [,metrə'pɒlɪtən] ADJ metropolitano ➤ **the Metropolitan Police** la policía de Londres

mettle ['metl] N ánimo *m*, valor *m*; **to be on one's** ~ estar dispuesto a demostrar su valía; **to show one's** ~ mostrar lo que uno vale

mew [mju:] Ⓐ N maullido *m* Ⓑ VI maullar, hacer miau

mews [mju:z] (*Brit*) NSING callejuela *f* ➤ **mews cottage** *casa acondicionada en antiguos establos o cocheras*

Mexican ['meksɪkən] Ⓐ ADJ mejicano, mexicano (*LAm*) Ⓑ N mejicano/a *m/f*, mexicano/a *m/f* (*LAm*) Ⓒ CPD ➤ **Mexican wave** (*Brit*) ola *f* (mejicana *or* (*LAm*) mexicana)

Mexico ['meksɪkəʊ] N México *m* ➤ **Mexico City** (Ciudad *f* de) México *m*

mezzanine ['mezəni:n] N (*in shop*) entresuelo *m*; (*US*) (*in theatre*) = **dress circle**

mezzo-soprano ['metsəʊsə'prɑː:nəʊ] N (= *singer*) mezzosoprano *f*

mg ABBR (= **milligram(s)**) mg

Mgr ABBR (*Rel*) (= **Monseigneur** *or* **Monsignor**) Mons.

MHR N ABBR (*US*) = **Member of the House of Representatives**

MI ABBR (*US*) = **Michigan**

mi [mi:] N (*Mus*) mi *m*

MI5 [,emaɪ'faɪv] N ABBR (*Brit*) (= **Military Intelligence five**) *servicio de inteligencia contraespionaje*

MI6 [,emaɪ'sɪks] N ABBR (*Brit*) (= **Military Intelligence six**) *servicio de inteligencia*

miaow [mi:'aʊ] Ⓐ N maullido *m* Ⓑ VI maullar, hacer miau

mice [maɪs] NPL *of* **mouse**

Mich. ABBR (*US*) = **Michigan**

mickey* ['mɪkɪ] N ✦ IDIOM **to take the** ~ **(out of sb)** (*Brit*) tomar el pelo (a algn)

micro ['maɪkrəʊ] N microcomputador *m*, microcomputadora *f*, microordenador *m* (*Sp*)

micro... ['maɪkrəʊ] PREF micro...

microbe ['maɪkrəʊb] N microbio *m*

microbiology [,maɪkrəʊbaɪ'ɒlədʒɪ] N microbiología *f*

microchip ['maɪkrəʊtʃɪp] N microchip *m*

microcomputer [,maɪkrəʊkəm'pjuːtə'] N microcomputador *m*, microcomputadora *f*, microordenador *m* (*Sp*)

microcosm ['maɪkrəʊkɒzəm] N microcosmo *m*

microeconomics ['maɪkrəʊ,i:kə'nɒmɪks] NSING microeconomía *f*

microelectronics ['maɪkrəʊ,i:lek'trɒnɪks] NSING microelectrónica *f*

microfiche ['maɪkrəʊfiːʃ] N microficha *f*

microfilm ['maɪkrəʊfɪlm] N microfilme *m* ➤ **microfilm reader** lector *m* de microfilmes

microlight ['maɪkrəʊlaɪt] N (avión *m*) ultraligero *m*

microorganism ['maɪkrəʊ'ɔːgənɪzəm] N microorganismo *m*

microphone ['maɪkrəfəʊn] N micrófono *m*

microprocessor ['maɪkrəʊ'prəʊsəsə'] N microprocesador *m*

micro-scooter ['maɪkrəʊ,skuː:tə'] N patinete *m*

microscope ['maɪkrəskəʊp] N microscopio *m*

microscopic [,maɪkrə'skɒpɪk] ADJ microscópico

microsurgery [,maɪkrəʊ'sɜ:dʒərɪ] N microcirugía *f*

microwavable, microwaveable ['maɪkrə,weɪvəbl] ADJ apto para microondas

microwave ['maɪkrə,weɪv] N 1 (*Phys*) microonda *f* 2 (= *oven*) (horno *m*) microondas *m inv*

mid [mɪd] ADJ **in** ~ **June** a mediados de junio; **he's in his** ~ **twenties** tiene unos veinticinco años, tiene veinte y tantos años; **in** ~ **afternoon/morning** a media tarde/mañana

mid-air ['mɪdeə'] Ⓐ N **to catch sth in** ~ agarrar *or* atrapar algo al vuelo; **to refuel in** ~ repostar combustible en pleno vuelo; ✦ IDIOM **to leave sth in** ~ dejar algo a medio hacer Ⓑ ADJ ~ **collision** colisión *f* en el aire

midday ['mɪd'deɪ] Ⓐ N mediodía *m*; **at** ~ a(l) mediodía Ⓑ CPD ➤ **the midday sun** el sol de(l) mediodía

middle ['mɪdl] Ⓐ N 1 (*of object, area*) centro *m*, medio *m*; **in the** ~ **of the table** en medio *or* en el centro de la mesa; **he was in the** ~ **of the road** estaba en medio *or* en (la) mitad de la carretera; **the potatoes were raw in the** ~ las patatas estaban crudas por el centro; **in the** ~ **of nowhere** quién sabe dónde, en el quinto pino (*Sp**); **right in the** ~ en el mismo centro

2 (*of period*) **in the** ~ **of the night** en mitad de la noche; **in the** ~ **of summer** en pleno verano; **in the** ~ **of May** a mediados de mayo; **in the** ~ **of the morning** a media mañana; **he was in his** ~ **thirties** tenía unos treinta y cinco años, tenía treinta y tantos años

3 (*of activity*) **to be in the** ~ **of sth** estar en mitad de algo; **I'm in the** ~ **of reading it** lo estoy leyendo

4 (*) (= *waist*) cintura *f*

Ⓑ ADJ **the** ~ **shelf of the oven** la bandeja del medio del horno; **my ~ daughter** mi hija de en medio; ✦ IDIOM **to steer a** ~ **course** tomar por la calle de en medio

Ⓒ CPD ➤ **middle age** madurez *f* ➤ **the Middle Ages** la Edad Media ➤ **Middle America** (= *Central America*) Mesoamérica *f*, Centroamérica *f*; (*US Geog*) el centro de los Estados Unidos; (= *middle class*) la clase media norteamericana ➤ **the middle class(es)** (*pl*) la clase media ➤ **middle distance: in the** ~ **distance** a una distancia intermedia; (*Art*) en segundo plano ➤ **middle ear** oído *m* medio ➤ **the Middle East** el Oriente Medio ➤ **middle finger** dedo *m* corazón ➤ **middle ground** terreno *m* neutral ➤ **middle management** mandos *mpl* medios ➤ **middle manager** mando *mf* medio ➤ **middle name** segundo nombre *m* de pila; ✦ IDIOM **"discretion" is my** ~ **name** soy la discreción en persona ➤ **middle school** (*Brit*) *colegio para niños de ocho o nueve a doce o trece años*; (*US*) *colegio para niños de diez a trece o catorce años* ➤ **the Middle West** (*US*) *la región central de los Estados Unidos*

middle-aged ['mɪdl'eɪdʒd] ADJ de mediana edad

middlebrow ['mɪdlbraʊ] ADJ de *or* para gusto medianamente culto, de gusto entre intelectual y plebeyo

middle-class [mɪdl'klɑ:s] ADJ de (la) clase media

middle-distance [,mɪdl'dɪstəns] CPD ➤ **middle-distance race** carrera *f* de medio fondo ➤ **middle-distance runner** mediofondista *mf*

middleman ['mɪdlmæn] N (*pl* **middlemen**) intermediario/a *m/f*

middle-of-the-road ['mɪdləvðə'rəʊd] ADJ moderado

middle-sized ['mɪdl,saɪzd] ADJ mediano

middleweight ['mɪdlweɪt] N peso *m* medio

middling ['mɪdlɪŋ] ADJ mediano; (*pej*) regular

midfield ['mɪdfi:ld] N centro *m* del campo

midge [mɪdʒ] N (*Brit*) mosquito *m* pequeño

midget ['mɪdʒɪt] Ⓐ N enano/a *m/f* Ⓑ ADJ en miniatura, en pequeña escala; [*submarine*] de bolsillo

Midlands ['mɪdləndz] NPL the ~ *la región central de Inglaterra*

midlife crisis ['mɪd,laɪf'kraɪsɪs] N crisis *f inv* de los cuarenta

midnight ['mɪdnaɪt] N medianoche *f*; **at** ~ a medianoche; ✦ IDIOM **to burn the** ~ **oil** quemarse las pestañas

midriff ['mɪdrɪf] N estómago *m*

midst [mɪdst] N **in the** ~ **of** [+ *place*] en medio de, a mitad de (*LAm*); **in our** ~ entre nosotros; **we are in the** ~ **of an economic crisis** estamos inmersos en una crisis económica, estamos en plena crisis económica

midstream ['mɪd'stri:m] N **in** ~ en el medio de la corriente/del río; (*fig*) antes de terminar, a mitad de camino; **he stopped talking in** ~ dejó de hablar a mitad de la frase

midsummer ['mɪd'sʌmə'] N pleno verano *m*; **in** ~ en pleno verano ➤ **Midsummer('s) Day** Día *m* de San Juan (*24 junio*)

midterm ['mɪd'tɜːm] CPD ➤ **midterm elections** (*US*) elecciones *fpl* a mitad del mandato (presidencial) ➤ **midterm exam** examen *m* de mitad del trimestre

midway ['mɪd'weɪ] ADV a mitad de camino, a medio camino; ~ **between Edinburgh and Glasgow** a mitad de camino *or* a medio camino entre Edimburgo y Glasgow; ~ **through the interview** a mitad de la entrevista

midweek ['mɪd'wi:k] Ⓐ ADV entre semana Ⓑ ADJ de entre semana

Midwest ['mɪd'west] N (*US*) mediooeste *m* (*llanura central de EEUU*)

Midwestern ['mɪd,westən] ADJ (*US*) del mediooeste (*de EEUU*)

midwife ['mɪdwaɪf] N (*pl* **midwives**) comadrona *f*, partera *f*

midwifery ['mɪd,wɪfərɪ] N partería *f*

midwinter ['mɪd'wɪntə'] N pleno invierno *m*; **in** ~ en pleno invierno

midwives ['mɪdwaɪvz] NPL *of* **midwife**

miffed* [mɪft] ADJ **he was pretty** ~ **about it** se ofendió bastante por eso

might[1] [maɪt] MODAL AUX VB 1 (*possibility*) **it** ~ **snow** puede *or* es posible que nieve; **he** ~ **not be hungry** a lo mejor no tiene hambre; **we** ~ **as well** go vámonos ya *or* de una vez; **as you** ~ **expect** como era de esperar; **they** ~ **have gone out** puede que hayan salido, a lo mejor han salido; **they** ~ **well be related** puede que sean parientes 2 (= *should*) **I** ~ **have known!** ¡debería haberlo sabido! 3 (*making suggestions*) **you** ~ **try Smith's** podrías probar en la tienda de Smith; ~ **I suggest that ...?** me permito sugerir que ...; ~**n't it be better to ...?** (+ INFIN) ¿no sería mejor ...? + *infin* 4 (*criticizing*) **you** ~ **shut the door!** ¡podrías *or* podías cerrar la puerta!; **he** ~ **have offered to help** podría haberse prestado a ayudar; **you** ~ **have told me!** ¡habérmelo dicho! 5 (*emphatic*) **who** ~ **you be?** ¿quién es usted?; **how old** ~ **you be?** ¿cuántos años tendrás?; **run as he** ~ por mucho que corriese

might[2] [maɪt] N poder *m*, fuerza *f*; **with all one's** ~ con todas sus fuerzas

mighty ['maɪtɪ] Ⓐ ADJ (*compar* **mightier**; *superl* **mightiest**) (*liter*) 1 (= *powerful*) [*blow*] tremendo*; [*effort*] grandísimo; [*nation*] poderoso 2 (= *large*) [*river, fortress, wall*] enorme, inmenso Ⓑ ADV (*esp US**) (= *very*) muy; **it's a** ~ **long way** está tremendamente lejos *or* está lejísimos

migraine ['mi:greɪn] N jaqueca *f*, migraña *f*; **I've got a** ~ tengo jaqueca *or* migraña

migrant ['maɪgrənt] Ⓐ ADJ migratorio Ⓑ N emigrante *mf*;

(= *bird*) ave *f* migratoria *or* de paso

> Use **el/un** not **la/una** before feminine nouns beginning with stressed **a** or **ha** like **ave**.

migrate [maɪ'greɪt] VI emigrar

migration [maɪ'greɪʃən] N migración *f*

migratory [maɪ'greɪtərɪ] ADJ migratorio

mike* [maɪk] N ABBR (= **microphone**) micro *m*

mild [maɪld] ADJ (*compar* **-er**; *superl* **-est**) 1 (= *not severe*) [*winter*] moderado, poco frío; [*weather, climate, evening*] templado; **it's very** ~ no hace mucho frío 2 (= *not strong*) [*cheese, cigar, detergent, shampoo, sedative*] suave; [*curry*] suave, no muy picante; [*protest*] moderado; [*criticism*] suave, moderado 3 (= *slight*) [*infection*] pequeño; [*symptoms*] leve; [*pain*] leve, ligero; **he had a** ~ **stroke** tuvo un derrame cerebral de poca seriedad; **they listened with** ~ **interest** escuchaban con cierto interés; **he turned to Mona with a look of** ~ **surprise** se volvió hacia Mona y la miró ligeramente sorprendido

mildew ['mɪldju:] N (*on plants*) añublo *m*; (*on food, leather etc*) moho *m*

mildly ['maɪldlɪ] ADV 1 (= *gently*) [*say, reply, rebuke*] suavemente, con suavidad; [*protest*] débilmente; **he's a low-down thief, and that's putting it** ~ es un cochino ladrón por no decir algo peor 2 (= *slightly*) [*amusing, surprised, interested, irritated*] ligeramente

mildness ['maɪldnɪs] N 1 [*of weather, climate*] lo templado 2 [*of cigar, detergent, criticism*] suavidad *f*; [*of symptoms*] levedad *f* 3 [*of person, disposition*] afabilidad *f*, placidez *f*

mile [maɪl] N 1 milla *f* (= *1609,33m*); **30** ~ **s a** *or* **to the gallon** 30 millas por galón; **50** ~ **s per hour** 50 millas por hora; **we walked** ~**s!** ¡anduvimos millas y millas!; **people came from** ~**s around** la gente vino de millas a la redonda; **they live** ~**s away** viven lejísimos de aquí; **you could see for** ~**s** se veía hasta lejísimos; ✦ IDIOMS **sorry, I was** ~**s away** lo siento, estaba pensando en otra cosa; **the shot missed by a** ~ el disparo falló por mucho; **not a million** ~**s from here** (*hum*) no muy lejos de aquí; **you can smell it a** ~ **off** eso se huele a la legua; **as soon as he sees me coming, he runs a** ~ en cuanto me ve venir sale pitando*; ⊳ *IMPERIAL SYSTEM* **2 miles*** (= *very much*) **she's** ~**s better than I am at maths** las matemáticas se le dan cien mil veces mejor que a mí; **the sleeves are** ~**s too long** las mangas no me van largas, me van larguísimas

mileage ['maɪlɪdʒ] Ⓐ N 1 (= *distance covered*) distancia *f* en millas; (*on mileometer*) ≈ kilometraje *m*; **what** ~ **has this car done?** ≈ ¿qué kilometraje tiene este coche?, ¿cuántas millas/cuántos kilómetros tiene este coche? 2 (*fig*) **he got a lot of** ~ **out of it** le sacó mucho partido Ⓑ CPD ➤ **mileage allowance** dietas *fpl* por desplazamiento en vehículo propio, ≈ dietas *fpl* por kilometraje ➤ **mileage indicator** ≈ cuentakilómetros *m inv*

mileometer [maɪ'lɒmɪtə'] N (*Brit*) ≈ cuentakilómetros *m inv*

milestone ['maɪlstəʊn] N 1 (*on road*) mojón *m* 2 (*in life, career*) hito *m*

milieu ['mi:ljɜː] (*pl* ~**s** *or* ~**x** ['mi:ljɜː]) N medio *m*, entorno *m*

militant ['mɪlɪtənt] Ⓐ ADJ [*group*] militante, combativo; [*person, attitude*] combativo Ⓑ N militante *mf*

militarism ['mɪlɪtərɪzəm] N militarismo *m*

militaristic [,mɪlɪtə'rɪstɪk] ADJ militarista

military ['mɪlɪtərɪ] Ⓐ ADJ militar Ⓑ NPL **the** ~ los militares Ⓒ CPD ➤ **military academy** academia *f* militar ➤ **military police** policía *f* militar ➤ **military service** servicio *m* militar; **to do (one's)** ~ **sevice** hacer *or* prestar el servicio militar, hacer la mili*

militate ['mɪlɪteɪt] VI **to** ~ **against** militar en contra de

militia [mɪ'lɪʃə] N milicia(s) *f(pl)*

milk [mɪlk] Ⓐ N leche *f*; **powdered** ~ leche *f* en polvo; ✦ PROV **it's no good crying over spilt** ~ a lo hecho pecho Ⓑ VT [+ *cow*] ordeñar; [+ *applause*] arrancar del público, sacar todo el partido a; **they're ~ing the company for all they can get** chupan todo lo que pueden de la compañía Ⓒ CPD ➤ **milk chocolate** chocolate *m* con leche ➤ **milk float** (*Brit*) carro *m* de la leche ➤ **milk jug** jarrita *f* para la leche ➤ **milk products** productos *mpl* lácteos ➤ **milk round** (*Brit*) (*lit*) recorrido *m* del lechero; (*Univ*) recorrido anual de las principales empresas por las universidades para entrevistar a estudiantes del último curso con vistas a una posible contratación ➤ **milk run** (*Aer*) vuelo *m* rutinario ➤ **milk saucepan** cazo *m* or cacerola *f* para la leche ➤ **milk shake** batido *m*, malteada *f* (*LAm*) ➤ **milk tooth** diente *m* de leche

milking ['mɪlkɪŋ] N ordeño *m* ➤ **milking machine** ordeñadora *f* mecánica

milkman ['mɪlkmən] N (*pl* **milkmen**) lechero *m*, repartidor *m* de leche

milky ['mɪlkɪ] (*compar* **milkier**; *superl* **milkiest**) Ⓐ ADJ **1** (= *pale white*) lechoso **2** (*containing a lot of milk*) [*tea, coffee*] con mucha leche; **a ~ drink** una bebida hecha con leche Ⓑ CPD ➤ **the Milky Way** (*Astron*) la Vía Láctea

mill [mɪl] Ⓐ N **1** (= *textile factory*) fábrica *f* (de tejidos); (= *sugar mill*) ingenio *m* de azúcar; (= *spinning mill*) hilandería *f*; (= *steel mill*) acería *f* **2** (= *machine*) molino *m*; (*for coffee, pepper*) molinillo *m*; (*Tech*) fresadora *f* Ⓑ VT moler
➤ **mill around, mill about** (*Brit*) VI + ADV arremolinarse

millennium [mɪ'lenɪəm] N (*pl* **~s** *or* **millennia** [mɪ'lenɪə]) milenio *m*; **the ~** el milenio ➤ **the millennium bug** el (problema del) efecto 2000

miller ['mɪlər] N molinero/a *m/f*

millet ['mɪlɪt] N mijo *m*

milligram(me) ['mɪlɪgræm] N miligramo *m*

millilitre, milliliter (*US*) ['mɪlɪˌliːtər] N mililitro *m*

millimetre, millimeter (*US*) ['mɪlɪˌmiːtər] N milímetro *m*

milliner ['mɪlɪnər] N sombrerero/a *m/f*; **~'s (shop)** sombrerería *f*

million ['mɪljən] NUMBER millón *m*; **four ~ dogs** cuatro millones de perros; **I've got ~s of letters to write*** tengo miles de cartas que escribir; **I've told you ~s of times*** te lo he dicho infinidad de veces

millionaire [ˌmɪljə'neər] N millonario/a *m/f*

millionairess [ˌmɪljə'neəres] N millonaria *f*

millionth ['mɪljənθ] Ⓐ ADJ millonésimo Ⓑ PRON millonésimo *m*

millipede ['mɪlɪpiːd] N milpiés *m inv*

millisecond ['mɪlɪˌsekənd] N milésima *f* de segundo, milisegundo *m*

millstone ['mɪlstəun] N piedra *f* de molino, muela *f*; **it's a ~ round his neck** es una cruz que lleva a cuestas

millwheel ['mɪlwiːl] N rueda *f* de molino

milometer [maɪ'lɒmɪtər] N = **mileometer**

mime [maɪm] Ⓐ N (= *acting*) mimo *m*, mímica *f*; (= *actor*) mimo *mf* Ⓑ VI (= *act*) hacer mímica; **to ~ to a song** cantar una canción haciendo playback Ⓒ CPD ➤ **mime artist** mimo *mf*

mimic ['mɪmɪk] Ⓐ N mímico/a *m/f* Ⓑ VT imitar, remedar

mimicry ['mɪmɪkrɪ] N mímica *f*; (*Bio*) mimetismo *m*

Min. ABBR (*Brit*) (= **Ministry**) Min.

min. ABBR **1** (= **minute(s)**) m. **2** (= **minimum**) mín.

minaret [mɪnə'ret] N alminar *m*, minarete *m*

mince [mɪns] Ⓐ N (*esp Brit*) (= *minced meat*) carne *f* picada Ⓑ VT **1** (*esp Brit*) [+ *meat*] picar **2** ✦ IDIOM **not to ~ one's words** no tener pelos en la lengua Ⓒ CPD ➤ **mince pie** pastel *m* de picadillo de fruta

mincemeat ['mɪnsmiːt] N **1** (= *dried fruit*) conserva *f* de picadillo de fruta **2** (*Brit*) (= *minced meat*) carne *f* picada **3** ✦ IDIOM **to make ~ of sb*** hacer picadillo or pedazos a algn

mincer ['mɪnsər] N (*Brit*) (= *machine*) máquina *f* de picar carne

---

<table>
<tr><td colspan="2" style="text-align:center">mind</td></tr>
<tr><td>Ⓐ NOUN</td><td>Ⓓ COMPOUNDS</td></tr>
<tr><td>Ⓑ TRANSITIVE VERB</td><td>Ⓔ PHRASAL VERBS</td></tr>
<tr><td>Ⓒ INTRANSITIVE VERB</td><td></td></tr>
</table>

mind [maɪnd] Ⓐ NOUN
1 = (*brain, head*) mente *f*; **he has the ~ of a five-year-old** tiene la edad mental de un niño de cinco años; **it's all in the ~** es pura sugestión; **at the back of my ~ I had the feeling that ...** tenía la remota sensación de que ...; **it came to my ~** *or* **crossed my ~ that ...** se me ocurrió que ...; **my ~ was elsewhere** tenía la cabeza en otro sitio; **it never entered my ~** jamás se me pasó por la cabeza; **I can't get it out of my ~** no me lo puedo quitar de la cabeza; **to go over sth in one's ~** repasar algo mentalmente; **it's a question of ~ over matter** es cuestión de voluntad; **to have sth on one's ~** estar preocupado por algo; **if you put** *or* **set your ~ to it** si te concentras en ello; **knowing that he had arrived safely set my ~ at ease** *or* **rest** el saber que había llegado sano y salvo me tranquilizó; **that will take your ~ off it** eso te distraerá; **he let his ~ wander** dejó que los pensamientos se le fueran a otras cosas; ✦ IDIOMS **in my ~'s eye I could still see her sitting there** mentalmente todavía la veía allí sentada; **that's a load** *or* **weight off my ~!** ¡eso me quita un peso de encima!; ✦ PROV **great ~s think alike** (*hum*) los sabios siempre pensamos igual
2 (= *memory*) **to bear sth/sb in ~** tener en cuenta algo/a algn; **he puts me in ~ of his father** me recuerda a su padre; **it went right out of my ~** se me fue por completo de la cabeza; **to bring** *or* **call sth to ~** recordar algo, traer algo a la memoria
3 (= *intention*) **you can do it if you have a ~ to** puedes lograrlo si de verdad estás empeñado en ello; **I have a good ~ to do it** ganas de hacerlo no me faltan; **I have half a ~ to do it** estoy tentado *or* me dan ganas de hacerlo; **nothing was further from my ~** nada más lejos de mi intención; **to have sth in ~** tener pensado algo; **who do you have in ~ for the job?** ¿a quién piensas darle el puesto *or* tienes en mente para el puesto?
4 (= *opinion*) opinión *f*, parecer *m*; **to change one's ~** cambiar de opinión o idea *or* parecer; **to know one's own ~** saber lo que uno quiere; **to make up one's ~** decidirse; **I can't make up my ~ about him** todavía tengo ciertas dudas con respecto a él; **he has made up his ~ to leave home** ha decidido irse de casa, está decidido a irse de casa; **to my ~** a mi juicio; **to have an open ~** tener una mente *or* mentalidad abierta; **to have a ~ of one's own** [*person*] pensar por sí mismo, (*hum*) [*machine etc*] tener voluntad propia, hacer lo que quiere; **to be in** *or* (*esp US*) **of two ~s** dudar, estar indeciso
5 (= *mental balance*) juicio *m*; **to lose one's ~** perder el juicio; **we were bored out of our ~s** estábamos muertos de aburrimiento; **to go out of one's ~ (with worry)** volverse loco (de preocupación); **nobody in his right ~ would do it** nadie que esté en su sano juicio lo haría
Ⓑ TRANSITIVE VERB
1 (*Brit*) (= *be careful of*) tener cuidado con; **~ you don't fall** ten cuidado, no te vayas a caer; **~ your head!** ¡cuidado con la cabeza!; **~ how you go!*** (*as farewell*) ¡cuídate!; **~ your language!** ¡qué manera de hablar es ésa!; **~ the step!** ¡cuidado con el escalón!; **~ what you're doing!** ¡cuidado con lo que haces!; **~ where you're going!** ¡mira por dónde vas!
2 (= *pay attention to*) hacer caso de; **~ your own business!** ¡no te metas donde no te llaman!; **don't ~ me** por mí no se preocupe; (*iro*) ¡y a mí que me parta un rayo!*; **never ~ that now** olvídate de eso ahora; **never ~ him** no le hagas caso
3 (*Brit*) (= *oversee*) [+ *child, belongings*] cuidar
4 (= *dislike, object to*) **I don't ~ the cold** a mí no me molesta el frío; **I don't ~ waiting** no me importa esperar; **if you don't ~ my** *or* **me saying so ...** perdona que te diga pero ..., permíteme que te diga que ...; **I don't ~ telling you, I was shocked** estaba horrorizado, lo confieso; **I wouldn't ~ a cup of tea** no me vendría mal un té
5 (*in requests*) **would you ~ opening the door?** ¿me hace el favor de abrir la puerta?, ¿le importa(ría) abrir la puerta?

ⓒ INTRANSITIVE VERB
1 (*Brit*) (= *be careful*) **mind!** ¡cuidado!, ¡ojo!, ¡abusado! (*Mex*)
2 (= *object*) **do you ~ if I open the window?** ¿te molesta que abra *or* si abro la ventana?; **"do you ~ if I take this book?" — "I don't ~ at all"** —¿te importa si me llevo *or* que me lleve este libro? —en absoluto; **"cigarette?" — "I don't ~ if I do"** —¿un cigarrillo? —pues muchas gracias *or* bueno *or* no digo que no; **I don't ~** (= *it's the same to me*) me da igual; **never ~** (= *don't worry*) no te preocupes; (= *it makes no odds*) es igual, da lo mismo; (= *it's not important*) no importa; **I can't walk, never ~ run** no puedo andar, ni mucho menos correr
✦ **mind you:** ~ **you, it was raining at the time** claro que *or* te advierto que en ese momento llovía; **it was a big one, ~ you** era grande, eso sí
3 (*Brit*) (= *make sure*) ~ **you get there first** procura llegar primero
ⓓ COMPOUNDS ➤ **mind game** juego *m* psicológico ➤ **mind reader** adivinador(a) *m/f* de pensamientos; **I'm not a ~ reader you know!*** ¿tú te crees que yo soy adivino?*
➤ **mind set** actitud *f*, disposición *f*
ⓔ PHRASAL VERBS
➤ **mind out** VI + ADV (*Brit*) tener cuidado; ~ **out!** ¡cuidado!, ¡ojo!, ¡abusado! (*Mex*)

mind-bending* [ˈmaɪndˌbendɪŋ], **mind-blowing*** [ˈmaɪndˌbləʊɪŋ], **mind-boggling*** [ˈmaɪndˌbɒglɪŋ] ADJ increíble, alucinante (*Sp**)

minded [ˈmaɪndɪd] ADJ **if you are so ~** si estás dispuesto a hacerlo, si quieres hacerlo

-minded [ˈmaɪndɪd] ADJ (*ending in compounds*) **fair-minded** imparcial; **scientifically-minded** con aptitudes científicas

minder* [ˈmaɪndəʳ] N **1** (*esp Brit*) (= *bodyguard*) guardaespaldas *mf inv*, acompañante *mf*, escolta *mf* **2** (*Brit*) = **childminder**

mindful [ˈmaɪndfʊl] ADJ **to be ~ of** tener presente *or* en cuenta

mindless [ˈmaɪndlɪs] ADJ **1** (*Brit*) [*violence*] sin sentido **2** [*work, task, repetition*] mecánico; [*entertainment*] sin sentido, absurdo **3** [*person*] tonto

mine¹ [maɪn] POSS PRON (*referring to singular possession*) (el/la) mío/a; (*referring to plural possession*) (los/las) míos/as

> Only use the article with **mío/míos** etc when you mean "the one(s) belonging to me".

that car is ~ ese coche es mío; **which is ~?** ¿cuál es el mío?; **is this glass ~?** ¿es éste mi vaso?; **a friend of ~** un amigo mío; **I think that brother of ~ is responsible*** creo que mi hermano es el responsable

mine² [maɪn] **ⓐ** N **1** (*for minerals, coal*) mina *f*; **a coal ~** una mina de carbón; ✦ IDIOM **the book is a ~ of information** este libro es una mina de información **2** (*Mil, Naut etc*) mina *f* **ⓑ** VT **1** [+ *minerals, coal*] extraer **2** [+ *area, beach*] minar, poner minas en **ⓒ** VI extraer mineral; **to ~ for sth** abrir una mina para extraer algo **ⓓ** CPD ➤ **mine detector** detector *m* de minas

minefield [ˈmaɪnfiːld] N campo *m* de minas; (*fig*) avispero *m*, campo *m* minado

miner [ˈmaɪnəʳ] N minero/a *m/f*

mineral [ˈmɪnərəl] N mineral *m* ➤ **mineral deposit** yacimiento *m* minero ➤ **mineral water** agua *f* mineral

> Use **el/un** not **la/una** before feminine nouns beginning with stressed **a** or **ha** like **agua**.

mineshaft [ˈmaɪnʃɑːft] N pozo *m* de mina

minestrone [ˌmɪnɪˈstrəʊnɪ] N minestrone *f* ➤ **minestrone soup** sopa *f* minestrone

minesweeper [ˈmaɪnswiːpəʳ] N dragaminas *m inv*

mingle [ˈmɪŋgl] **ⓐ** VT mezclar **ⓑ** VI **1** (= *mix*) mezclarse **2** (= *become indistinguishable*) [*sounds*] confundirse (**in, with** con); **to ~ with the crowd** perderse entre la multitud **3** (*at party*) **she ~d for a while** alternó con los invitados durante un rato

mingy* [ˈmɪndʒɪ] ADJ (*compar* **mingier**; *superl* **mingiest**) (*Brit*) [*person*] tacaño; [*amount, portion*] mísero, miserable

miniature [ˈmɪnɪtʃəʳ] **ⓐ** N miniatura *f*; **in ~** en miniatura **ⓑ** ADJ (= *not full-sized*) (en) miniatura; (= *tiny*) diminuto **ⓒ** CPD ➤ **miniature golf** minigolf *m*

minibar [ˈmɪnɪbɑːʳ] N minibar *m*

minibus [ˈmɪnɪbʌs] N microbús *m*, micro *m*

minicab [ˈmɪnɪkæb] N (*Brit*) radiotaxi *m*

minicam [ˈmɪnɪkæm] N minicámara *f*

minicomputer [ˌmɪnɪkəmˈpjuːtəʳ] N minicomputadora *f*, miniordenador *m* (*Sp*)

MiniDisc®, **minidisc** [ˈmɪnɪdɪsk] **ⓐ** N MiniDisc® *m*, minidisc *m* **ⓑ** CPD ➤ **MiniDisc® player** MiniDisc® *m*, minidisc *m*

minim [ˈmɪnɪm] N (*Brit Mus*) blanca *f*

minimal [ˈmɪnɪml] ADJ mínimo

minimalist [ˈmɪnɪməlɪst] ADJ, N minimalista *mf*

minimarket [ˈmɪnɪˌmɑːkɪt], **minimart** [ˈmɪnɪˌmɑːt] N autoservicio *m*

minimize [ˈmɪnɪmaɪz] VT **1** (= *reduce*) reducir al mínimo, minimizar **2** (= *play down*) menospreciar

minimum [ˈmɪnɪməm] **ⓐ** N mínimo *m*; **to reduce sth to a ~** reducir algo al mínimo; **he always does the bare ~** siempre sigue la ley del mínimo esfuerzo; **with a ~ of effort** con un mínimo de esfuerzo **ⓒ** CPD ➤ **minimum wage** salario *m* mínimo

mining [ˈmaɪnɪŋ] N [*of coal*] minería *f*, explotación *f* de minas ➤ **mining engineer** ingeniero/a *m/f* de minas ➤ **mining industry** industria *f* minera

minion [ˈmɪnjən] N (= *follower*) secuaz *mf*; (= *servant*) paniaguado *m*

miniseries [ˈmɪnɪˌsɪərɪz] N (*pl* ~) (*TV*) miniserie *f*

miniskirt [ˈmɪnɪskɜːt] N minifalda *f*

minister [ˈmɪnɪstəʳ] **ⓐ** N **1** (*Pol*) ministro/a *m/f*, secretario/a *m/f* (*Mex*); **the Minister for Education** el/la Ministro/a de Educación **2** (*Rel*) pastor(a) *m/f*, clérigo/a *m/f* **ⓑ** VI **to ~ to sb** atender a algn; **to ~ to sb's needs** atender *or* satisfacer las necesidades de algn

ministerial [ˌmɪnɪsˈtɪərɪəl] ADJ (*Pol*) [*meeting*] del gabinete; [*post, career, duties*] ministerial; **at ~ level** a nivel ministerial

ministry [ˈmɪnɪstrɪ] N **1** (*Pol*) ministerio *m*, secretaría *f* (*Mex*); **Ministry of Transport** Ministerio *m* de Transporte **2** (*Rel*) sacerdocio *m*; **to enter the ~** hacerse sacerdote; (*Protestant*) hacerse pastor

mink [mɪŋk] N (*pl* ~ *or* ~**s**) (= *animal*) visón *m*; (= *fur*) piel *f* de visón ➤ **mink coat** abrigo *m* de visón

Minn. ABBR (*US*) = **Minnesota**

minnow [ˈmɪnəʊ] N pececillo *m* (*de agua dulce*)

minor [ˈmaɪnəʳ] **ⓐ** ADJ **1** [*problem, operation*] de poca importancia; [*adjustment, detail*] menor, de poca importancia; [*change, damage, poet, work*] menor; [*role*] (*in film, play*) secundario; (*in negotiations*) de poca importancia; [*road*] secundario; [*injury*] leve; [*illness*] poco grave; **of ~ importance** de poca importancia **2** (*Mus*) [*chord, key*] menor; **in F ~** en fa menor **ⓑ** N **1** (*Jur*) menor *mf* (de edad) **2** (*US Univ*) asignatura *f* secundaria **ⓒ** VI (*US Univ*) **to ~ in sth** estudiar algo como asignatura secundaria **ⓓ** CPD ➤ **minor league** (*US*) liga *f* menor ➤ **minor offence** (*Brit*), **minor offense** (*US*) delito *m* de menor cuantía

Minorca [mɪˈnɔːkə] N Menorca *f*

minority [maɪˈnɒrɪtɪ] **ⓐ** N **1** (= *small number*) minoría *f*; **a small ~ of children** una pequeña minoría de niños; **to be in a** *or* **the ~** ser minoría, estar en minoría; **ethnic ~** minoría *f* étnica **2** (= *age*) minoría *f* de edad **ⓑ** ADJ minoritario

minster [ˈmɪnstəʳ] N (= *cathedral*) catedral *f*; (= *church*) iglesia *f* de un monasterio

minstrel [ˈmɪnstrəl] N juglar *m*

mint¹ [mɪnt] **ⓐ** N casa *f* de la moneda **ⓑ** ADJ **in ~ condition** como nuevo, en perfecto estado

Ⓒ VT [+ *coin*] acuñar

mint² [mɪnt] **Ⓐ** N **1** (= *plant*) hierbabuena *f*, menta *f* **2** (= *sweet*) pastilla *f* de menta **Ⓑ** CPD ➤ **mint sauce** salsa *f* de menta ➤ **mint tea** té *m* de menta

minuet [ˌmɪnjʊ'et] N minué *m*

minus ['maɪnəs] **Ⓐ** PREP **1** (*Math*) menos; **nine ~ six** nueve menos seis **2** (= *without*) sin; **he appeared ~ his trousers** apareció sin pantalón **Ⓑ** ADJ [*number*] negativo; **it's ~ 20 outside** fuera hace una temperatura de 20 bajo cero; **I got a B ~ for my French** me pusieron un notable bajo en francés **Ⓒ** N (= *sign*) signo *m* menos; (= *amount*) cantidad *f* negativa **Ⓓ** CPD ➤ **minus sign** signo *m* menos

minuscule ['mɪnəskjuːl] ADJ minúsculo

minute¹ ['mɪnɪt] **Ⓐ** N **1** (= *60 secs*) minuto *m*; **it is twenty-three ~s past two** son las dos y veintitrés (minutos); **a ten-~ break** un descanso de diez minutos; **it won't take five ~s** es cosa de pocos minutos; **it's a few ~s' walk from the station** está a unos minutos de la estación andando; **they were on the scene within ~s** llegaron al lugar de los hechos a los pocos minutos **2** (= *short time*) momento *m*; **I won't be a ~** (*on going out*) vuelvo enseguida; (*when busy*) termino enseguida; **every ~ counts** no hay tiempo que perder; **have you got a ~?** ¿tienes un momento?; **I'll come in a ~** ahora voy, vengo dentro de un momento; **wait a ~!** ¡espera un momento!, ¡un momento!, ¡momentito! (*LAm*) **3** (= *instant*) instante *m*; **I haven't had a ~ to myself all day** no he tenido ni un instante *or* momento para mí en todo el día; **we expect him any ~** le esperamos de un momento a otro; **any ~ now he's going to fall off there** se va caer en cualquier momento; **I bet you loved every ~ of it!** ¡seguro que te lo pasaste en grande!; **at the last ~** a última hora, en el último momento; **to leave things until the last ~** dejar las cosas hasta última hora *or* hasta el último momento; **one ~ she was there, the next she was gone** estaba allí, y al momento se había ido; **we caught the train without a ~ to spare** cogimos el tren justo a tiempo; **tell me the ~ he arrives** avísame en cuanto llegue; **sit down this ~!** ¡siéntate ya!; **I've just this ~ heard** me acabo de enterar; **this very ~** ahora mismo; ✦ IDIOM **I don't believe him for a** *or* **one ~** no le creo para nada *or* en absoluto **4 minutes** [*of meeting*] acta *f*

Use **el/un** not **la/una** before feminine nouns beginning with stressed **a** or **ha** like **acta**.

---

to take the ~s (of a meeting) levantar (el) acta (de una reunión) **Ⓑ** CPD ➤ **minute hand** minutero *m* ➤ **minute steak** biftec *m* pequeño (que se hace rápidamente)

minute² [maɪ'njuːt] ADJ **1** (= *very small*) [*amount, change*] mínimo; [*particles*] diminuto **2** (= *detailed*) [*examination, scrutiny*] minucioso; **in ~ detail** hasta el mínimo detalle

minutely [maɪ'njuːtlɪ] ADV **1** (= *in detail*) [*describe*] detalladamente, minuciosamente; [*examine*] minuciosamente **2** (= *slightly*) mínimamente

minutiae [mɪ'njuːʃiː] NPL detalles *mpl* minuciosos

minx [mɪŋks] N picaruela *f*, mujer *f* descarada

miracle ['mɪrəkl] N milagro *m*; **it's a ~ that you weren't hurt!** ¡fue un milagro que salieras ileso!; **by some ~ he passed his exam** milagrosamente aprobó el examen ➤ **miracle cure** remedio *m* milagroso ➤ **miracle drug** medicamento *m* milagro ➤ **miracle worker: I'm not a ~ worker!*** yo no puedo hacer milagros

miraculous [mɪ'rækjʊləs] ADJ milagroso; **he made a ~ recovery** tuvo una recuperación milagrosa, se recuperó de forma milagrosa; **it was nothing short of ~** fue un verdadero *or* auténtico milagro

mirage ['mɪrɑːʒ] N espejismo *m*

mire [maɪə'] N fango *m*, lodo *m*

mirror ['mɪrə'] **Ⓐ** N espejo *m*; (*in car*) (espejo *m*) retrovisor *m*; **to look at o.s. in the ~** mirarse en el *or* al espejo **Ⓑ** VT reflejar **Ⓒ** CPD ➤ **mirror image** reflejo *m* exacto

mirth [mɜːθ] N (= *good humour*) alegría *f*, júbilo *m*;

(= *laughter*) risas *fpl*

mirthless ['mɜːθlɪs] ADJ triste, sin alegría

misadventure [ˌmɪsəd'ventʃə'] N desgracia *f*, contratiempo *m*; **death by ~** muerte *f* accidental

misanthrope ['mɪzənθrəʊp] N misántropo/a *m/f*

misanthropic [ˌmɪzən'θrɒpɪk] ADJ misantrópico

misapprehension [ˌmɪsæprɪ'henʃən] N malentendido *m*; **to be under a ~** estar equivocado

misappropriate [ˌmɪsə'prəʊprɪeɪt] VT malversar, desfalcar

misappropriation [ˌmɪsəprəʊprɪ'eɪʃən] N malversación *f*, desfalco *m*

misbehave [ˌmɪsbɪ'heɪv] VI portarse mal, comportarse mal

misbehaviour, misbehavior (*US*) [ˌmɪsbɪ'heɪvjə'] N mala conducta *f*, mal comportamiento *m*

misc. ABBR = **miscellaneous**

miscalculate [ˌmɪs'kælkjʊleɪt] VT, VI calcular mal

miscalculation [ˌmɪskælkjʊ'leɪʃən] N error *m* de cálculo

miscarriage ['mɪskærɪdʒ] N **1** (*during pregnancy*) aborto *m* (natural); **to have a ~** tener un aborto, abortar **2 ~ of justice** error *m* judicial

miscarry [mɪs'kærɪ] VI **1** (*Med*) abortar **2** (= *fail*) [*plans*] fracasar, malograrse (*Per*)

miscast [ˌmɪs'kɑːst] VT (*pt, pp ~*) **he was ~ as Othello** no fue muy acertado darle el papel de Otelo

miscellaneous [ˌmɪsə'leɪnɪəs] ADJ [*objects*] variado, de todo tipo; [*writings, collection*] variado; **~ expenses** gastos *mpl* diversos

miscellany [mɪ'selənɪ] N [*of objects*] miscelánea *f*

mischance [mɪs'tʃɑːns] N desgracia *f*, mala suerte *f*; **by some ~** por desgracia

mischief ['mɪstʃɪf] N travesura *f*, diablura *f*; **he's up to some ~** está haciendo alguna travesura; **he's always getting into ~** siempre anda haciendo travesuras; **to keep sb out of ~** evitar que algn haga travesuras; **to do o.s. a ~*** hacerse daño

mischievous ['mɪstʃɪvəs] ADJ [*person, smile*] pícaro; [*child, kitten*] travieso

misconceived [ˌmɪskən'siːvd] ADJ **a ~ plan** un proyecto descabellado

misconception [ˌmɪskən'sepʃən] N malentendido *m*, concepto *m* erróneo; **but this is a ~** pero esta idea es errónea

misconduct [mɪs'kɒndʌkt] N mala conducta *f*; (*professional*) falta *f* de ética profesional, mala conducta *f* profesional

misconstrue [ˌmɪskən'struː] VT interpretar mal, malinterpretar

miscount Ⓐ [ˌmɪs'kaʊnt] VT, VI contar mal **Ⓑ** ['mɪskaʊnt] N **there was a ~** hubo un error en el recuento

misdeed [ˌmɪs'diːd] N fechoría *f*

misdemeanour, misdemeanor (*US*) [ˌmɪsdɪ'miːnə'] N fechoría *f*; (*Jur*) delito *m* menor, falta *f*

misdirect [ˌmɪsdɪ'rekt] VT [+ *operation*] manejar mal; [+ *person*] informar mal

miser ['maɪzə'] N avaro/a *m/f*

miserable ['mɪzərəbl] ADJ **1** (= *unhappy*) [*person*] abatido, con el ánimo por los suelos; [*face*] triste; **to feel ~** tener el ánimo por los suelos, sentirse abatido *or* deprimido; **my job was making me really ~** mi trabajo me estaba deprimiendo **2** (= *depressing*) [*place, life, weather*] deprimente; [*childhood*] desdichado, infeliz; **to make sb's life ~** amargar la vida a algn; **to have a ~ time** pasarlo mal, pasarlo fatal* **3** (= *wretched*) [*hovel, beggar*] mísero **4** (= *paltry*) [*pay*] miserable; [*meal*] triste, mísero; **a ~ two pounds** dos miserables libras

miserably ['mɪzərəblɪ] ADV **1** (= *unhappily*) tristemente, con desconsuelo **2** (= *depressingly*) [*furnished*] miserablemente, míseramente; **to fail ~** fracasar rotundamente

miserly ['maɪzəlɪ] ADJ **1** (= *mean*) [*person*] mezquino, ruin, tacaño 2 (= *paltry*) [*sum*] mísero

misery ['mɪzərɪ] N 1 (= *sadness*) tristeza *f*, pena *f*
2 (= *poverty*) miseria *f*, pobreza *f* 3 (= *misfortune*) desgracia
f; **a life of** ~ una vida desgraciada 4 (= *suffering*)
sufrimiento *m*, dolor *m*; **to put an animal out of its** ~
rematar a un animal (para que no sufra); **to put sb out of
his/her** ~ (*fig*) sacar a algn de la incertidumbre; **to make
sb's life a** ~ amargar la vida a algn 5 (*esp Brit**) (= *person*)
aguafiestas *mf inv*

misfire [ˌmɪs'faɪəʳ] VI [*plan, engine*] fallar; [*gun*]
encasquillarse

misfit ['mɪsfɪt] N (= *person*) inadaptado/a *m/f*; **he's always
been a** ~ **here** no se ha adaptado nunca a las condiciones
de aquí

misfortune [mɪs'fɔːtʃən] N desgracia *f*; **I had the** ~ **to meet
him** tuve la desgracia de conocerlo

misgiving [mɪs'gɪvɪŋ] N recelo *m*, duda *f*; **I had** ~**s about
the scheme** tuve mis dudas sobre el proyecto

misguided [ˌmɪs'gaɪdɪd] ADJ [*attempt*] torpe; [*belief, view*]
equivocado; [*person*] descaminado, desacertado; **in the** ~
belief that ... creyendo, equivocadamente *or*
erróneamente, que ...

mishandle [ˌmɪs'hændl] VT [*+ situation*] llevar mal, manejar
mal; [*+ problem*] no saber tratar

mishap ['mɪshæp] N contratiempo *m*; **we had a slight** ~
tuvimos un pequeño contratiempo

mishear [ˌmɪs'hɪəʳ] (*pt, pp* ~**d**) VT, VI oír mal

mishit Ⓐ ['mɪshɪt] N golpe *m* defectuoso Ⓑ [ˌmɪs'hɪt] VT
golpear mal

mishmash ['mɪʃmæʃ] N revoltijo *m*, batiburrillo* *m*

misinform [ˌmɪsɪn'fɔːm] VT informar mal

misinformation [ˌmɪsɪnfəˈmeɪʃən] N (= *wrong information*)
mala información *f*, información *f* errónea; (= *deliberate
act*) desinformación *f*

misinterpret [ˌmɪsɪn'tɜːprɪt] VT interpretar mal,
malinterpretar; (*deliberately*) tergiversar

misinterpretation [ˌmɪsɪntɜːprɪˈteɪʃən] N mala
interpretación *f*; (*deliberate*) tergiversación *f*; **to be open to**
~ prestarse a malas interpretaciones

misjudge [ˌmɪs'dʒʌdʒ] VT 1 (= *miscalculate*) [*+ distance,
time*] calcular mal 2 (= *judge wrongly*) [*+ person*] juzgar mal

mislay [mɪs'leɪ] (*pt, pp* **mislaid**) VT extraviar, perder

mislead [mɪs'liːd] (*pt, pp* **misled**) VT (*deliberately*) engañar; **I
wouldn't like to** ~ **you** no quisiera inducirle a error, no me
gustaría que se hiciera una idea equivocada

misleading [mɪs'liːdɪŋ] ADJ engañoso

misled [mɪs'led] PT, PP *of* **mislead**

mismanage [ˌmɪs'mænɪdʒ] VT [*+ business, shop*] administrar
mal; [*+ situation*] llevar mal, manejar mal

mismanagement [ˌmɪs'mænɪdʒmənt] N [*of business*] mala
administración *f*; [*of situation*] manejo *m* inadecuado

mismatch [ˌmɪs'mætʃ] N **a** ~ **of styles/colours** una falta de
armonía en los estilos/colores

misnomer [mɪs'nəuməʳ] N nombre *m* equivocado *or*
inapropiado; **that is a** ~ ese nombre es impropio

misogynist [mɪ'sɒdʒɪnɪst] ADJ, N misógino/a *m/f*

misplace [ˌmɪs'pleɪs] VT perder

misplaced [ˌmɪs'pleɪst] ADJ [*confidence, trust*] inmerecido;
[*enthusiasm*] que no viene a cuento; [*humour*] fuera de
lugar, inoportuno

misprint ['mɪsprɪnt] N error *m* de imprenta, errata *f*

mispronounce [ˌmɪsprə'naʊns] VT pronunciar mal

mispronunciation [ˌmɪsprənʌnsɪ'eɪʃən] N mala
pronunciación *f*

misquote [ˌmɪs'kwəʊt] VT citar incorrectamente; **he was
~d in the press** la prensa no reprodujo con exactitud sus
palabras

misread [ˌmɪs'riːd] (*pt, pp* ~ [ˌmɪs'red]) VT (= *read wrongly*)
leer mal; (= *misinterpret*) interpretar mal, malinterpretar

misrepresent [ˌmɪsreprɪ'zent] VT [*+ person*] dar una

imagen falsa de; [*+ views, situation*] tergiversar; **he was ~ed
in the papers** los periódicos tergiversaron sus palabras

miss[1] [mɪs] Ⓐ N [*of shot*] tiro *m* errado, fallo *m* (*Sp*);
✦ IDIOM **to give sth a** ~ (*Brit**): **you could give rehearsals a** ~
for once* por una vez podrías faltar a los ensayos; **I'll give
the wine a** ~ **this evening*** esta noche no tomaré vino
Ⓑ VT 1 [*+ target*] no dar en; **the shot just ~ed me** la bala
me pasó rozando; **the plane just ~ed the tower** faltó poco
para que el avión chocara con la torre; **he narrowly ~ed
being run over** por poco lo atropellan, faltó poco para que
lo atropellaran

2 [*+ bus, train, plane, flight*] perder; [*+ opportunity, chance*]
dejar pasar, perder; [*+ meeting, class, appointment*] faltar a,
no asistir a; [*+ film, match*] perderse; **don't** ~ **this film** no te
pierdas *or* no dejes de ver esta película; **we ~ed our lunch**
nos quedamos sin comer; **you haven't ~ed much!** ¡no te
has perdido mucho!; **I ~ed you at the station** no te vi en la
estación; **I ~ed you by five minutes** si hubiera llegado cinco
minutos antes te hubiera visto *or* (*Sp**) cogido; **to** ~ **one's
vocation** equivocarse de vocación; **to** ~ **one's way**
equivocarse de camino

3 (= *skip*) [*+ meal, page*] saltarse; **my heart ~ed a beat** me
dio un vuelco el corazón

4 (= *overlook*) **you've ~ed that bit in the corner** se te ha
pasado por alto ese trozo en la esquina

5 (= *fail to understand*) no entender, no coger (*Sp*); **she's ~ed
the joke** no ha entendido *or* cogido el chiste; **you're ~ing
the point** no lo entiendes

6 (= *fail to hear, see*) **I ~ed what you said** no he oído lo que
has dicho; **you don't** ~ **much, do you?** no se te escapa nada
¿verdad?; **you can't** ~ **the house** la casa no tiene pérdida;
he ~ed the turning se pasó de cruce

7 (= *long for*) echar de menos, extrañar (*esp LAm*); **they're
~ing one another** se echan de menos *or* se extrañan; **he
won't be ~ed** no se le echará de menos *or* no se le echará
en falta que digamos; **I** ~ **having a garden** echo de menos
tener un jardín

8 (= *notice absence of*) echar en falta; **we're ~ing eight
dollars** nos faltan ocho dólares

Ⓒ VI [*shot*] errar el blanco; [*person*] fallar, errar el tiro

➤ **miss out** Ⓐ VT + ADV (*esp Brit*) [*+ word, line, page*] saltarse;
tell me if I ~ **anybody out** decidme si me salto a algn Ⓑ VI
+ ADV **I'm glad you can come, I wouldn't want you to** ~ **out**
me alegro de que puedas venir, no quisiera que te lo
perdieras

➤ **miss out on** VI + PREP [*+ opportunity*] dejar pasar, perder;
did you think you were ~ing out on something? ¿creías que
te estabas perdiendo algo?

miss[2] [mɪs] N señorita *f*; (*in address*) Srta.; **Miss Peters
wants to see you** la señorita Peters quiere verte

Miss. ABBR (*US*) = **Mississippi**

missal ['mɪsəl] N misal *m*

misshapen [ˌmɪs'ʃeɪpən] ADJ deforme

missile ['mɪsaɪl] N (*Mil*) misil *m* ➤ **missile launcher**
lanzamisiles *m inv*

missing ['mɪsɪŋ] Ⓐ ADJ 1 (= *lost*) [*object*] perdido; [*child,
cat*] desaparecido, extraviado; [*explorer*] desaparecido; **an
important document was found to be** ~ se descubrió que
faltaba un importante documento; **to go** ~ desaparecer
2 [*soldier, plane*] desaparecido; **reported** ~ declarado como
desaparecido 3 (= *lacking*) [*piece, button, tooth, word*] que
falta; **to be** ~ faltar; **your shirt has a button** ~ te falta un
botón en la camisa Ⓑ CPD ➤ **missing person**
desaparecido/a *m/f*

mission ['mɪʃən] N misión *f*; **to send sb on a secret** ~
enviar a algn en misión secreta ➤ **mission control** centro
m de control ➤ **mission statement** (*Comm, Ind*) principio
m básico

missionary ['mɪʃənrɪ] N misionero/a *m/f* ➤ **missionary
zeal** fervor *m* apostólico

missis* ['mɪsɪz] N (*Brit*) **my** ~ ~ ⬦ **the** ~ mi mujer, la parienta
(*Sp**), la patrona (*SC**); **John and his** ~ John y su mujer

missive ['mɪsɪv] N misiva *f*

misspell [ˌmɪs'spel] (*pt, pp* ~**ed**, **misspelt**) VT escribir mal

misspent [ˌmɪs'spent] ADJ **a** ~ **youth** una juventud
malgastada *or* desperdiciada

missus* ['mɪsɪz] N (*Brit*) = **missis**

mist [mɪst] **Ⓐ** N neblina *f*; (= *rain*) llovizna *f*, garúa *f* (*LAm*); (*at sea*) bruma *f*; (*on glass*) vaho *m*; **morning ~** bruma *f* del alba; **lost in the ~s of time** (*liter*) perdido en la noche de los tiempos **Ⓑ** VI (*also ~ over, ~ up*) [*scene, landscape*] nublarse; [*mirror, window*] empañarse

mistake [mɪs'teɪk] (*vb: pt* **mistook**; *pp* **~n**) **Ⓐ** N error *m*; (*in piece of work*) error *m*, fallo *m* (*Sp*); **there must be some ~** debe de haber algún error; **by ~** por error *or* equivocación; **to make a ~** (*gen*) cometer un error; (= *be mistaken*) equivocarse; **they made the ~ of asking too much** cometieron el error de pedir demasiado; **you're making a big ~** estás cometiendo un grave error; **make no ~ about it** y que no quepa la menor duda; **my ~!** ¡la culpa es mía!, es culpa mía; **spelling ~** falta *f* de ortografía
Ⓑ VT [+ *meaning, remark*] malinterpretar; **he is often ~n for Peter** se le confunde muchas veces con Peter; **she could easily be ~n for a boy** se la podría confundir fácilmente con un chico; **there's no mistaking her voice** su voz es inconfundible; **there was no mistaking his intention** su intención estaba clarísima

mistaken [mɪs'teɪkən] **Ⓐ** PP *of* **mistake** **Ⓑ** ADJ [*belief, idea*] equivocado, falso; **in the ~ belief that ...** creyendo, equivocadamente *or* erróneamente, que ...; **to be ~** equivocarse, estar equivocado; **unless I'm very much ~, that's him** si no me equivoco, ése es él, o mucho me equivoco o es él; **that's just where you're ~!** ¡ahí es donde te equivocas!; **~ identity** identificación *f* errónea

mistakenly [mɪs'teɪkənlɪ] ADV **1** (= *wrongly*) [*believe, assume*] equivocadamente, erróneamente **2** (= *accidentally*) por equivocación, por error

mister ['mɪstəʳ] N (*gen abbr* Mr) señor *m* (*gen abbr* Sr.)

mistime ['mɪs'taɪm] VT **to ~ sth** hacer algo a destiempo

mistletoe ['mɪsltəʊ] N muérdago *m*

mistook [mɪs'tʊk] PT *of* **mistake**

mistranslation [ˌmɪstræns'leɪʃən] N mala traducción *f*

mistreat [mɪs'triːt] VT maltratar

mistreatment [mɪs'triːtmənt] N maltrato *m*, malos tratos *mpl*

mistress ['mɪstrɪs] N **1** [*of household, servant*] señora *f*, ama *f*

> Use **el/un** not **la/una** before feminine nouns beginning with stressed **a** or **ha** like **ama**.

2 (= *lover*) amante *f*, querida *f*, amasia *f* (*Mex*) **3** (*Brit†*) (= *teacher*) (*in primary school*) maestra *f*; (*in secondary school*) profesora *f*

mistrial [ˌmɪs'traɪəl] N (*invalidated*) juicio *m* viciado de nulidad; (*US*) (*inconclusive*) juicio *m* nulo por desacuerdo del jurado

mistrust [ˌmɪs'trʌst] **Ⓐ** N desconfianza *f* **Ⓑ** VT desconfiar de

mistrustful [ˌmɪs'trʌstfʊl] ADJ desconfiado, receloso; **to be ~ of sth/sb** desconfiar de algo/algn

misty ['mɪstɪ] ADJ (*compar* **mistier**; *superl* **mistiest**) [*day, morning*] neblinoso; [*valley, shore*] cubierto de neblina; [*mirror, window*] empañado; [*eyes*] empañado, lloroso; **it is ~** hay neblina; (*US*) está lloviznando

misty-eyed ['mɪstɪˌaɪd] ADJ sentimental

misunderstand [ˌmɪsʌndə'stænd] (*pt, pp* **misunderstood**) VT entender mal; **don't ~ me** entiéndeme, no me malinterpretes

misunderstanding [ˌmɪsʌndə'stændɪŋ] N (= *confusion*) malentendido *m*; (= *mistake*) equivocación *f*; (= *disagreement*) desacuerdo *m*

misunderstood [ˌmɪsʌndə'stʊd] **Ⓐ** PT, PP *of* **misunderstand** **Ⓑ** ADJ incomprendido

misuse Ⓐ [ˌmɪs'juːs] N [*of power, drug*] abuso *m*; [*of machine*] mal uso *m*, mal manejo *m*; [*of funds*] malversación *f* **Ⓑ** [ˌmɪs'juːz] VT [+ *power, drug*] abusar de; [+ *machine*] usar mal, manejar mal; [+ *funds*] malversar

MIT N ABBR (*US*) = **Massachusetts Institute of Technology**

mite¹ [maɪt] N (= *insect*) ácaro *m*, acárido *m*

mite² [maɪt] N **1** (= *small quantity*) pizca *f*; **we were a ~ surprised** nos quedamos un tanto sorprendidos **2** (*esp Brit**) (= *child*) chiquillo/a *m/f*, criatura *f*; **poor little ~!** ¡pobrecito!

miter ['maɪtəʳ] N (*US*) = **mitre**

mitigate ['mɪtɪgeɪt] VT aliviar, mitigar; **mitigating circumstances** circunstancias *fpl* atenuantes

mitigation [ˌmɪtɪ'geɪʃən] N mitigación *f*, alivio *m*

mitre, miter (*US*) ['maɪtəʳ] N **1** (*of bishop*) mitra *f* **2** (*also ~ joint*) inglete *m*, ensambladura *f* de inglete

mitt [mɪt] N **1** (= *glove*) mitón *m* **2** (= *baseball glove*) guante *m* de béisbol **3** (*) (= *hand*) zarpa* *f*; **get your ~s off my dictionary!** ¡quita tus zarpas de mi diccionario!*

mitten ['mɪtn] N **1** (= *glove*) mitón *m*, manopla *f* **2** (*Boxing*) guante *mpl* de boxeo

mix [mɪks] **Ⓐ** VT [+ *ingredients, colours, liquids*] mezclar; [+ *concrete, cocktail*] preparar; **~ all the ingredients together** mezcle todos los ingredientes; **never ~ your drinks!** ¡no mezcle nunca bebidas!; **to ~ business and *or* with pleasure** mezclar los negocios con el placer
Ⓑ VI **1** (= *combine*) mezclarse; **oil and water don't ~** el aceite y el agua no se mezclan; **politics and sport don't ~** la política y el deporte no hacen buena combinación
2 (= *socialize*) **she ~es with all kinds of people** se mezcla con toda clase de gente
Ⓒ N **1** (= *combination*) mezcla *f*; **there was a good ~ of people at the party** había una mezcla variada *or* una buena variedad de gente en la fiesta
2 (= *for cooking*) preparado *m*; **a cake ~** un preparado para pasteles
> **mix in** VT + ADV [+ *ingredients*] añadir
> **mix up** VT + ADV **1** (= *prepare*) [+ *paint, paste*] preparar **2** (= *combine*) [+ *ingredients*] mezclar
3 (= *jumble up*) mezclar; **the letter got ~ed up with my things** la carta se mezcló con mis cosas
4 (= *confuse*) [+ *person*] confundir; **you've got me all ~ed up** me has confundido, me has hecho un lío*
5 (= *mistake*) [+ *names, dates, person*] confundir; **we got the dates ~ed up** confundimos las fechas; **I'm ~ing you up with somebody else** te estoy confundiendo con otra persona
6 (= *involve*) **to be/get ~ed up in sth** estar metido/meterse en algo; **he's got ~ed up with a bad crowd** se ha mezclado con mala gente, anda con malas compañías; **to ~ sb up in sth** meter *or* mezclar a algn en algo
7 ♦ IDIOM **to ~ it up (with sb)** (*US**) (= *cause trouble*) buscar camorra (con algn)*

mixed [mɪkst] **Ⓐ** ADJ **1** (= *varied*) [*selection*] variado; (= *assorted*) [*biscuits, sweets, vegetables*] surtido, variado; **a ~ crowd ◇ a ~ bunch*** un grupo muy variopinto, un grupo con gente de todo tipo; **♦** IDIOM **a ~ bag*** (= *some good, some bad*) un poco de todo, una mezcla de todo; (= *with good variety*) una gran variedad
2 (= *both good and bad*) [*reviews, reactions*] diverso; [*results*] desigual, diverso; [*weather*] variable; **to have a ~ blessing** tener su lado bueno y su lado malo; **to have ~ feelings about sth** no tener muy claro algo, tener sus dudas acerca de algo; **the government's proposals have had a ~ reception** las propuestas del gobierno han sido recibidas con reservas *or* han tenido una acogida desigual
3 (= *of different races*) [*parentage, marriage*] mixto; **of ~ race** mestizo
4 (= *for both sexes*) [*school, education, bathing*] mixto; **in ~ company** con personas de ambos sexos
Ⓑ CPD **► mixed ability class** (*Brit*) clase *f* con niveles de aptitud distintos **► mixed doubles** (*Sport*) (dobles *mpl*) mixtos *mpl* **► mixed economy** economía *f* mixta **► mixed fruit** frutas *fpl* surtidas **► mixed grill** (*Brit*) parrillada *f* mixta **► mixed herbs** surtido *m* de hierbas **► mixed marriage** matrimonio *m* mixto (*de esposos de religión o raza distintas*) **► mixed metaphor** metáfora *f* disparada **► mixed salad** ensalada *f* mixta **► mixed spice** mezcla *f* de especias

mixed-up ['mɪkst'ʌp] ADJ [*person, idea*] confuso; [*things*] revuelto; **he's very ~** (= *disturbed*) es una persona con problemas (psicológicos); (= *confused*) está muy confuso

mixer ['mɪksə^r] N **1** (*for cooking*) batidora *f* **2** (= *cement mixer*) hormigonera *f* **3** (= *sound mixer*) mezclador(a) *m/f* **4** (= *sociable person*) **he's a good ~** tiene don de gentes **5** (= *drink*) refresco *m* (*para mezclar con licores*)

mixing bowl ['mɪksɪŋˌbəʊl] N cuenco *m* grande

mixture ['mɪkstʃə^r] N mezcla *f*; (*Med*) preparado *m*, compuesto *m*

mix-up ['mɪksˌʌp] N lío *m*, confusión *f*; **there was a ~ over the tickets** hubo un lío *or* una confusión con las entradas

ml ABBR (= **millilitre(s)**) ml

MLA ABBR (*Pol*) (= **Member of the Legislative Assembly**) *miembro de la asamblea legislativa*

mm ABBR (= **millimetre(s)**) mm

MMR vaccine [ˌemem'ɑːˌvæksiːn] N (*against measles, mumps, rubella*) vacuna *f* triple vírica

MN ABBR (*US*) = **Minnesota**

mnemonic [nɪ'mɒnɪk] N *figura o frase etc mnemotécnica*

MO Ⓐ N ABBR = **medical officer** Ⓑ ABBR (*US*) = **Missouri**

mo* [məʊ] N ABBR (*Brit*) = **moment**

Mo. ABBR (*US*) = **Missouri**

moan [məʊn] Ⓐ N **1** (= *groan*) gemido *m* **2** (= *complaint*) queja *f* Ⓑ VI **1** (= *groan*) gemir **2** (= *complain*) quejarse

moaner* ['məʊnə^r] N protestón/ona* *m/f*

moat [məʊt] N foso *m*

mob [mɒb] Ⓐ N **1** (= *crowd*) multitud *f*, muchedumbre *f*, bola *f* (*Mex*); (= *rabble*) populacho *m*, turba *f* (*esp LAm*); **the ~** (*pej*) (= *the masses*) el populacho **2** (*) (= *criminal gang*) pandilla *f*; **the Mob** la Mafia Ⓑ VT **1** (= *attack*) asaltar **2** (= *surround*) **the minister was ~bed by journalists** los periodistas se apiñaban en torno al ministro Ⓒ CPD ➤ **mob rule** ley *f* de la calle

mobile ['məʊbaɪl] Ⓐ ADJ [*shop*] ambulante; [*society*] con movilidad; [*features*] expresivo; **I'm still very ~** todavía me muevo bastante; **now that we're ~*** ahora que tenemos coche, ahora que estamos motorizados* Ⓑ N **1** (= *decoration*) móvil *m* **2** (*Brit**) (= *mobile phone*) móvil* *m*, teléfono *m* celular (*LAm*) Ⓒ CPD ➤ **mobile home** caravana *f*, casa *f* rodante (*SC, Ven*) ➤ **mobile library** biblioteca *f* ambulante, bibliobús *m* ➤ **mobile phone** (*Brit*) teléfono *m* móvil, teléfono *m* celular (*LAm*)

mobility [məʊ'bɪlɪtɪ] N movilidad *f*

mobilize ['məʊbɪlaɪz] Ⓐ VT movilizar Ⓑ VI movilizarse

moccasin ['mɒkəsɪn] N mocasín *m*

mocha ['mɒkə] N moca *m*

mock [mɒk] Ⓐ VT mofarse de, burlarse de Ⓑ VI mofarse, burlarse (**at** de) Ⓒ ADJ [*solemnity, terror*] fingido, simulado; [*leather, fur*] de imitación; **in ~ horror** fingiendo estar horrorizado Ⓓ NPL **mocks** (*Brit Scol**) exámenes *mpl* de prueba Ⓔ CPD ➤ **mock exam** examen *m* de prueba ➤ **mock trial** juicio *m* de prueba

mockery ['mɒkərɪ] N **1** (= *derision*) burla *f*, mofa *f* **2** (= *farce*) **this is a ~ of justice** esto es una negación de la justicia; **it was a ~ of a trial** fue un simulacro de juicio; **to make a ~ of sth** poner algo en ridículo

mocking ['mɒkɪŋ] Ⓐ ADJ burlón, socarrón Ⓑ N burlas *fpl*

mockingbird ['mɒkɪŋbɜːd] N sinsonte *m*, zenzontle *m* (*LAm*)

mock-up ['mɒkʌp] N maqueta *f*, modelo *m* a escala

MOD N ABBR (*Brit*) (= **Ministry of Defence**) ≈ Min. de D.

mod cons* [ˌmɒd'kɒnz] NPL (*Brit*) **"all mod cons"** "todo confort"

mode [məʊd] N **1** (= *way, manner*) manera *f*, modo *m* **2** (= *fashion*) moda *f* **3** (*Comput*) función *f*, modalidad *f*

model ['mɒdl] Ⓐ N **1** (= *small-scale representation*) modelo *m* a escala, maqueta *f* **2** (= *example*) modelo *m*; **he is a ~ of patience** es un modelo de paciencia **3** (= *person*) (*Art*) modelo *mf*; (*Fashion*) modelo *mf*, maniquí *mf* **4** (= *design*) modelo *m* Ⓑ ADJ **1** (= *miniature*) [*railway, village*] en miniatura, a escala; **~ aeroplane** aeromodelo *m*

2 (= *perfect*) [*husband, wife*] modelo *inv* Ⓒ VT **1 to ~ sth on sth: their new socialist state is ~led** *or* (*US*) **~ed on that of China** su nuevo estado socialista toma como modelo el de China; **to ~ o.s. on sb** tomar a algn como modelo **2** (*Art*) modelar **3** (*Fashion*) **she ~s children's clothes** es modelo de ropa de niños Ⓓ VI **1** (*Art*) (= *make models*) modelar **2** (*Phot, Art*) posar; (*Fashion*) ser modelo, trabajar de modelo

modelling, modeling (*US*) ['mɒdlɪŋ] N (*Fashion*) **she does ~** es modelo

modem ['məʊdem] N módem *m*

moderate Ⓐ ['mɒdərɪt] ADJ [*amount, speed, wind, heat, success, policy*] moderado; [*price*] módico; [*improvement, achievement*] regular; **bake the fish in a ~ oven** hacer el pescado al horno a una temperatura moderada Ⓑ ['mɒdərɪt] N (*Pol*) moderado/a *m/f* Ⓒ ['mɒdəreɪt] VT moderar

moderately ['mɒdərɪtlɪ] ADV [*good, wealthy*] medianamente; [*drink, eat*] con moderación; **she did ~ well in her exams** los exámenes le salieron medianamente bien; **~ priced** de precio módico

moderation [ˌmɒdə'reɪʃən] N moderación *f*; **in ~** con moderación

moderator ['mɒdəreɪtə^r] N **1** (*Brit*) (= *examiner*) árbitro *mf*, asesor(a) *m/f* **2** (*in assembly, discussion*) moderador(a) *m/f*

modern ['mɒdən] ADJ moderno; [*features*] **"all modern conveniences"** "todo confort" ➤ **modern art** arte *m* moderno ➤ **modern history** historia *f* contemporánea ➤ **modern languages** lenguas *fpl* modernas

modernity [mɒ'dɜːnɪtɪ] N modernidad *f*

modernization [ˌmɒdənaɪ'zeɪʃən] N modernización *f*

modernize ['mɒdənaɪz] VT modernizar

modest ['mɒdɪst] ADJ **1** (= *humble*) modesto; **to be ~ about sth** ser modesto con algo **2** (= *small*) [*garden, income*] modesto, pequeño; [*amount, sum*] módico, modesto; [*increase, improvement*] moderado **3** (= *chaste, proper*) [*person, clothes*] púdico, recatado

modestly ['mɒdɪstlɪ] ADV **1** (= *humbly*) modestamente **2** (= *moderately*) con moderación **3** (= *chastely*) pudorosamente, con pudor

modesty ['mɒdɪstɪ] N **1** (= *humbleness*) modestia *f* **2** (= *propriety*) pudor *m*, recato *m*

modicum ['mɒdɪkəm] N **a ~ of** un mínimo de

modification [ˌmɒdɪfɪ'keɪʃən] N modificación *f* (**to** de)

modifier ['mɒdɪfaɪə^r] N modificante *m*

modify ['mɒdɪfaɪ] VT **1** (= *change*) modificar **2** (= *moderate*) moderar

modish ['məʊdɪʃ] ADJ muy de moda

Mods* [mɒdz] N ABBR (*at Oxford university*) (= (**Honour**) **Moderations**) *examen de la licenciatura de la universidad de Oxford*

modular ['mɒdjʊlə^r] ADJ modular

modulate ['mɒdjʊleɪt] VT modular

modulation [ˌmɒdjʊ'leɪʃən] N modulación *f*

module ['mɒdjuːl] N módulo *m*

modus operandi ['məʊdəsˌɒpə'rændiː] N modo *m* de proceder, modus operandi *m inv*

Mogadishu [ˌmɒgə'dɪʃuː] N Mogadiscio *m*

mogul ['məʊgəl] N magnate *m*; **film ~** magnate *m* de la cinematografía

mohair ['məʊheə^r] N mohair *m*

Mohammed [məʊ'hæmed] N Mahoma *m*

moist [mɔɪst] ADJ (*compar* **~er**; *superl* **~est**) [*soil, cloth*] húmedo; [*cake*] esponjoso

moisten ['mɔɪsn] VT humedecer, mojar

moisture ['mɔɪstʃə^r] N (*on glass*) vaho *m*

moisturize ['mɔɪstʃəraɪz] VT [+ *skin, face, hands*] hidratar

moisturizer ['mɔɪstʃəraɪzə^r] N crema *f* hidratante

molar ['məʊləʳ] N muela *f*

molasses [mə'læsɪz] NSING melaza *f*

mold *etc* [məʊld] *(US)* = **mould** *etc*

Moldavia [mɒl'deɪvɪə] N *(formerly)* Moldavia *f*

Moldova [mɒl'dəʊvə] N Moldova *f*

mole¹ [məʊl] N *(on skin)* lunar *m*

mole² [məʊl] N (= *animal, spy*) topo *m*

molecular [mə'lekjʊləʳ] ADJ molecular

molecule ['mɒlɪkjuːl] N molécula *f*

molehill ['məʊlhɪl] N topera *f*

molest [mə'lest] VT *(sexually)* (= *attack*) agredir sexualmente; (= *abuse*) abusar de

⚠ **molest** ≠ *molestar*

molester [mə'lestəʳ] N *(also* **child ~**) *persona que abusa sexualmente de niños*

mollify ['mɒlɪfaɪ] VT aplacar, apaciguar

mollusc, mollusk *(US)* ['mɒləsk] N molusco *m*

mollycoddle ['mɒlɪkɒdl] VT *(esp Brit)* mimar, sobreproteger

Molotov cocktail [,mɒlətɒf'kɒkteɪl] N cóctel *m* Molotov

molt [məʊlt] VI, VT, N *(US)* = **moult**

molten ['məʊltən] ADJ fundido, derretido; *[lava]* líquido

mom* [mɒm] *(US)* N mamá* *f*

moment ['məʊmənt] N momento *m*; **a ~ ago** hace un momento; **they should be arriving any ~ (now)** deberían llegar ahorita *(LAm)* or de un momento a otro; **at the ~** en este momento; **at that ~** en ese momento *or* instante; **at this ~ in time** en este mismo momento; **for the ~** por el momento, por lo pronto; **he didn't hesitate for a ~** no vaciló ni un momento *or* instante; **from the ~ I saw him** desde el momento en que lo vi; **from that ~ on** desde entonces, desde ese *or* aquel momento; **the play has its ~s** la obra tiene sus momentos; **I'll come in a ~** vengo en seguida, vengo dentro de un momento; **just a ~!** ¡un momento!; **at the last ~** a última hora, en el último momento; **a ~ later** un momento después; **I was waiting for the right ~ to tell him** estaba esperando el momento adecuado *or* oportuno para decírselo; **tell me the ~ he arrives** avísame en cuanto llegue; **the ~ of truth** la hora de la verdad

momentarily ['məʊməntərɪlɪ] ADV **1** (= *for a moment*) por un momento, momentáneamente **2** *(US)* (= *at any moment*) de un momento a otro, en seguida, ahorita *(LAm)*

momentary ['məʊməntərɪ] ADJ momentáneo

momentous [məʊ'mentəs] ADJ trascendental, de gran trascendencia

momentum [məʊ'mentəm] N *(Phys)* momento *m*; *(fig)* ímpetu *m*, impulso *m*; **to gather** *or* **gain ~** *(lit)* cobrar velocidad; *(fig)* ganar fuerza

mommy* ['mɒmɪ] *(US)* N mamá* *f*

Mon. ABBR (= **Monday**) lun.

Monaco ['mɒnəkəʊ] N Mónaco *m*

monarch ['mɒnək] N monarca *mf*

monarchist ['mɒnəkɪst] ADJ, N monárquico/a *m/f*

monarchy ['mɒnəkɪ] N monarquía *f*

monastery ['mɒnəstrɪ] N monasterio *m*

monastic [mə'næstɪk] ADJ monástico

Monday ['mʌndɪ] N lunes *m inv*; *see* **Tuesday**

monetarism ['mʌnɪtərɪzəm] N monetarismo *m*

monetarist ['mʌnɪtərɪst] ADJ, N monetarista *mf*

monetary ['mʌnɪtərɪ] ADJ monetario

money ['mʌnɪ] Ⓐ N dinero *m*; **there's ~ in second-hand cars** los coches de segunda mano son (un) buen negocio; **I want my ~ back** quiero que me devuelvan mi dinero; **to come into** ~ heredar dinero; **to earn good** ~ ganar un buen sueldo, ganar su buen dinero *or* dinerito*; **I paid good ~ for it** pagué un buen dinero por ello; **to make** ~ [*person*]

ganar dinero; *[business]* rendir, dar dinero; **to put ~ into sth** invertir dinero en algo; **it was ~ well spent** fue dinero bien empleado; ✦ IDIOMS **~ doesn't grow on trees** el dinero no cae del cielo *or* de los árboles; **to have ~ to burn** estar cargado *or* podrido de dinero*; **~ isn't everything** el dinero no lo es todo; **to be in the ~*** estar bien de dinero; **to be made of ~** ser millonario, tener un banco; **to put one's ~ where one's mouth is** predicar con el ejemplo; **to spend ~ like water** tener un agujero en el bolsillo, ser un/una manirroto/a; **to throw one's ~ around** tirar *or* derrochar el dinero; **to throw ~ at a problem** intentar solucionar un problema a base de dinero; **to get one's ~'s worth** sacar partido a su dinero; ✦ PROVS **(the love of) ~ is the root of all evil** el dinero es la raíz de todos los males; **~ talks** poderoso caballero es don Dinero

Ⓑ CPD *[worries, problems]* de dinero, económico ➤ **money back guarantee** garantía *f* de devolución (del dinero) ➤ **money belt** riñonera *f* ➤ **money laundering** blanqueo *m* de dinero, lavado *m* de dinero *(LAm)* ➤ **money market** bolsa *f* or mercado *m* de valores, mercado *m* monetario ➤ **money matters** asuntos *mpl* financieros ➤ **money order** *(US)* giro *m* postal ➤ **money spinner** *(Brit)* fuente *f* de ganancias ➤ **the money supply** la oferta *or* masa monetaria, el volumen de moneda

moneybags* ['mʌnɪbægz] NSING **he's a ~** está forrado*

moneybox ['mʌnɪbɒks] N *(esp Brit)* hucha *f (Sp)*, alcancía *f (LAm)*

moneyed ['mʌnɪd] ADJ adinerado

money-grubbing* ['mʌnɪˌgrʌbɪŋ] ADJ *(Brit)* avaro

moneylender ['mʌnɪˌlendəʳ] N prestamista *mf*

moneymaker ['mʌnɪˌmeɪkəʳ] N fuente *f* de ganancias

money-making ['mʌnɪˌmeɪkɪŋ] Ⓐ ADJ *[business etc]* rentable Ⓑ N ganancia *f*, lucro *m*

money-spinner ['mʌnɪˌspɪnəʳ] N *(Brit)* = **moneymaker**

Mongol ['mɒŋgəl] N mongol(a) *m/f*

Mongolia [mɒŋ'gəʊlɪə] N Mongolia *f*

mongoose ['mɒŋguːs] N *(pl* **-s**) mangosta *f*

mongrel ['mʌŋgrəl] N perro *m* mestizo, perro *m* cruzado

monitor ['mɒnɪtəʳ] Ⓐ N **1** *(TV, Comput, Med)* monitor *m* **2** (= *person*) supervisor(a) *m/f* Ⓑ VT *[+ progress, process]* seguir (la marcha de), controlar; **we are ~ing the situation closely** estamos observando *or* controlando la situación de cerca

monk [mʌŋk] N monje *m*

monkey ['mʌŋkɪ] N *(Zool)* mono *m*; *(fig)* (= *child*) diablillo *m*; ✦ IDIOMS **I don't give a ~'s*** me importa un rábano*; **to make a ~ out of sb** poner a algn en ridículo ➤ **monkey bars** *(US)* estructura metálica en la cual los niños juegan trepando ➤ **monkey business*** *(dishonest)* trapisondas *fpl*, tejemanejes *mpl*; *(mischievous)* travesuras *fpl*, diabluras *fpl* ➤ **monkey nut** *(Brit)* cacahuete *m*, maní *m (LAm)*, cacahuate *m (Mex)* ➤ **monkey puzzle** (= *tree*) araucaria *f* ➤ **monkey wrench** llave *f* inglesa
➤ **monkey around, monkey about** *(Brit)* VI + ADV hacer tonterías; **to ~ around with sth** juguetear con algo, toquetear algo

monkfish ['mʌŋkfɪʃ] N *(pl ~)* rape *m*

mono ['mɒnəʊ] ADJ ABBR (= **monophonic**) mono *inv*, monoaural, monofónico

monochrome ['mɒnəkrəʊm] ADJ, N monocromo *m*

monocle ['mɒnəkl] N monóculo *m*

monogamous [mɒ'nɒgəməs] ADJ monógamo

monogamy [mɒ'nɒgəmɪ] N monogamia *f*

monogram ['mɒnəgræm] N monograma *m*, iniciales *fpl*

monograph ['mɒnəgræf] N monografía *f*

monolingual [,mɒnəʊ'lɪŋgwəl] ADJ monolingüe

monolith ['mɒnəlɪθ] N monolito *m*

monolithic [,mɒnə'lɪθɪk] ADJ monolítico

monologue, monolog *(US)* ['mɒnəlɒg] N monólogo *m*

mononucleosis [,mɒnəʊˌnjuːklɪ'əʊsɪs] N *(US)* mononucleosis *f* infecciosa

monopolistic [mə,nɒpə'lɪstɪk] ADJ monopolístico

monopolize [məˈnɒpəlaɪz] VT monopolizar

monopoly [məˈnɒpəlɪ] N monopolio *m*

monorail [ˈmɒnəʊreɪl] N monocarril *m*, monorraíl *m*

monosodium glutamate [ˈmɒnəʊˌsəʊdɪəmˈgluːtəmeɪt] N glutamato *m* monosódico

monosyllable [ˈmɒnəˌsɪləbl] N monosílabo *m*

monotone [ˈmɒnətəʊn] N monotonía *f*; **to speak in a ~** hablar en un solo tono

monotonous [məˈnɒtənəs] ADJ monótono

monotony [məˈnɒtənɪ] N monotonía *f*

monsignor [mɒnˈsiːnjəʳ] N monseñor *m*

monsoon [mɒnˈsuːn] N monzón *m*

monster [ˈmɒnstəʳ] Ⓐ ADJ (*) enorme, gigantesco Ⓑ N monstruo *m*

monstrosity [mɒnsˈtrɒsɪtɪ] N monstruosidad *f*

monstrous [ˈmɒnstrəs] ADJ **1** (= *huge*) enorme, gigantesco **2** (= *dreadful*) monstruoso

Mont. ABBR (*US*) = **Montana**

montage [mɒnˈtɑːʒ] N montaje *m*

Mont Blanc [mɔ̃ˈblɑ̃] N el Mont Blanc

Montenegro [ˌmɒntəˈniːgrəʊ] N Montenegro *m*

month [mʌnθ] N mes *m*; **in the ~ of May** en el mes de mayo; **a ~'s unlimited rail travel** uso ilimitado del tren por el periodo de un mes; **what** or **which day of the ~ is it?** ¿a cuántos estamos?; **at the end of the ~** a fin or finales de mes; **every** ~ todos los meses; **it went on for ~s** duró meses y meses; **six ~s pregnant** embarazada de seis meses; ✦ IDIOM **not in a ~ of Sundays** ni de casualidad

monthly [ˈmʌnθlɪ] Ⓐ ADJ [*publication, salary, rainfall*] mensual; **on a ~ basis** mensualmente, todos los meses; **~ payment** or **instalment** or (*US*) **installment** mensualidad *f*, cuota *f* mensual Ⓑ ADV [*publish*] mensualmente, todos los meses; [*pay*] mensualmente, por meses Ⓒ N (= *journal*) publicación *f* mensual

monty [ˈmɒntɪ] N **the full ~** todo completo, el paquete or lote completo*

monument [ˈmɒnjʊmənt] N monumento *m* (**to** a)

monumental [ˌmɒnjʊˈmentl] ADJ [*building, arch*] monumental; [*task, success, effort*] monumental, colosal; [*blunder, error*] garrafal; **on a ~ scale** a una escala gigantesca

moo [muː] Ⓐ N mugido *m* Ⓑ VI mugir Ⓒ EXCL ¡mu!

mooch [muːtʃ] VI **to ~ about** (*Brit*) or **around the shops** pasear por las tiendas; **to ~ about** (*Brit*) or **around the house** dar vueltas por la casa

mood [muːd] N humor *m*; **he's in a bit of a ~** está de mal humor; **to be in a bad/good ~** estar de mal/buen humor; **I'm in no ~ to argue** no tengo ganas de discutir, no estoy (de humor) para discutir; **she's in one of her ~s** está de malas, está con un humor de perros; **to be in the ~ for sth/ to do sth** tener ganas de algo/de hacer algo, estar de humor para algo/para hacer algo; **he plays well when he's in the ~** toca bien cuando está en vena or por la labor; **I'm not in the ~** no tengo ganas, no me apetece

moodily [ˈmuːdɪlɪ] ADV de mal humor

moodiness [ˈmuːdɪnɪs] N (= *variability*) humor *m* variable; (= *bad mood*) mal humor *m*

moody [ˈmuːdɪ] ADJ (*compar* **moodier**; *superl* **moodiest**) (= *variable*) de humor cambiante, de humor variable; (= *bad-tempered*) de mal humor, malhumorado; **he's very ~** (= *variable*) tiene un humor muy cambiante; (= *bad-tempered*) siempre está de mal humor

moon [muːn] Ⓐ N luna *f*; **there's a full ~ tonight** esta noche hay luna llena; **by the light of the ~** a la luz de la luna; ✦ IDIOMS **once in a blue ~** de Pascuas a Ramos; **to be over the ~** (*Brit**) estar loco de contento, estar en el séptimo cielo Ⓑ VI (*) enseñar el culo* Ⓒ CPD ➤ **moon landing** alunizaje *m*
➤ **moon around, moon about** (*Brit*) VI + ADV mirar a las musarañas
➤ **moon over** VI + PREP **she was ~ing over the photo** miraba amorosamente la foto, contemplaba extasiada la foto

moonbeam [ˈmuːnbiːm] N rayo *m* de luna

moonlight [ˈmuːnlaɪt] Ⓐ N luz *f* de la luna; **by ~** a la luz de la luna Ⓑ VI (*) practicar el pluriempleo

moonlighting [ˈmuːnˌlaɪtɪŋ] N pluriempleo *m*

moonlit [ˈmuːnlɪt] ADJ [*object*] iluminado por la luna; [*night*] de luna

moonshine [ˈmuːnʃaɪn] N **1** (*) (= *nonsense*) pamplinas *fpl* **2** (*esp US*) (= *illegal spirits*) licor *m* destilado ilegalmente

Moor [mʊəʳ] N moro/a *m/f*

moor[1] [mʊəʳ] N (*esp Brit*) páramo *m*, brezal *m*

moor[2] [mʊəʳ] Ⓐ VT amarrar Ⓑ VI echar las amarras

mooring [ˈmʊərɪŋ] N **1** (= *place*) amarradero *m* **2 moorings** (= *ropes, fixtures*) amarras *fpl*

Moorish [ˈmʊərɪʃ] ADJ [*person*] moro; [*culture, influence, invasion*] árabe; [*architecture*] morisco

moorland [ˈmʊələnd] N páramo *m*, brezal *m*

moose [muːs] N (*pl ~*) alce *m*

moot [muːt] Ⓐ ADJ **it's a ~ point** or **question** es un punto discutible Ⓑ VT **it has been ~ed that ...** se ha sugerido que ...

mop [mɒp] Ⓐ N **1** (*for floor*) fregona *f*, trapeador *m* (*LAm*) **2 ~ of hair** pelambrera *f*, melena *f* Ⓑ VT [+ *floor*] fregar, trapear (*LAm*); [+ *brow*] enjugar
➤ **mop up** VT + ADV [+ *spilt water*] secar; [+ *floor, surface*] limpiar

mope [məʊp] VI quedar abatido
➤ **mope around, mope about** (*Brit*) VI + ADV andar con cara mustia

moped [ˈməʊped] N (*esp Brit*) ciclomotor *m*

moral [ˈmɒrəl] Ⓐ ADJ moral; **a fall in ~ standards** una decadencia moral; **~ fibre** fibra *f* moral Ⓑ N **1** (= *lesson*) moraleja *f* **2 morals** moralidad *f*; **he has no ~s** no tiene moralidad Ⓒ CPD ➤ **moral support** apoyo *m* moral

morale [mɒˈrɑːl] N moral *f*; **~ was at an all-time low** la moral estaba más baja que nunca

morality [məˈrælɪtɪ] N moralidad *f*, moral *f*

moralize [ˈmɒrəlaɪz] VI moralizar

morally [ˈmɒrəlɪ] ADV [*superior, responsible*] moralmente; [*right, wrong*] desde el punto de vista moral

morass [məˈræs] N cenagal *m*, pantano *m*; **a ~ of problems** un laberinto de problemas

moratorium [ˌmɒrəˈtɔːrɪəm] N (*pl ~s* or **moratoria** [ˌmɒrəˈtɔːrɪə]) moratoria *f*

morbid [ˈmɔːbɪd] ADJ morboso, malsano; **don't be so ~!** ¡no seas morboso!; **~ curiosity** curiosidad *f* malsana

morbidly [ˈmɔːbɪdlɪ] ADV morbosamente

mordant [ˈmɔːdənt] ADJ mordaz

more [mɔːʳ] Ⓐ ADJ más; **there's ~ tea in the cupboard** hay más té en el aparador; **is there any ~ wine in the bottle?** ¿queda vino en la botella?; **it'll take a few ~ days** llevará unos cuantos días más; **many ~ people** muchas más personas; **much ~ butter** mucha más mantequilla; **I have no ~ money** no me queda más dinero; **do you want some ~ tea?** ¿quieres más té?; **you have ~ money than I** tienes más dinero que yo
Ⓑ N, PRON más; **four ~** cuatro más; **we can't afford ~** no podemos pagar más; **is there any ~?** ¿hay más?; **there isn't any ~** ya no hay más; **a bit ~?** ¿un poco más?; **a few ~** algunos más; **a little ~** un poco más; **many ~** muchos más; **much ~** mucho más; **there's no ~ left** no queda (nada); **some ~** ya he's got ~ than me! ¡él tiene más que yo!; **~ than ever** más que nunca; **~ than half** más de la mitad; **~ than fifteen** más de quince; **not ~ than fifteen** no más de quince; **all the ~ so because ...** tanto más cuanto que ...; **the ~ you give him the ~ he wants** cuanto más se le da, (tanto) más quiere; **and what's ~ ...** y además ...; ✦ IDIOM **the ~ the merrier** cuantos más mejor
Ⓒ ADV más; **~ difficult** más difícil; **~ easily** con mayor facilidad; **more and more** cada vez más; **if he says that any ~** si vuelve a decir eso, si dice eso otra vez; **he doesn't live here any ~** ya no vive aquí; **~ or less** más o menos; **once ~** otra vez, una vez más; **he's ~ intelligent than me** es más inteligente que yo; **I had ~ than carried out my obligation**

había cumplido con creces mi obligación; **it's ~ a short story than a novel** más que novela es un cuento

moreover [mɔːˈrəʊvəʳ] ADV además

mores [ˈmɔːreɪz] NPL costumbres *fpl*

morgue [mɔːg] N depósito *m* de cadáveres, morgue *f* (*esp LAm*)

MORI [ˈmɔːrɪ] N ABBR = **Market & Opinion Research Institute** (*Brit*) empresa británica que realiza sondeos de opinión y estudios de mercado

moribund [ˈmɒrɪbʌnd] ADJ moribundo

Mormon [ˈmɔːmən] ADJ, N mormón/ona *m/f*

morning [ˈmɔːnɪŋ] Ⓐ N mañana *f*; (*before dawn*) madrugada *f*; **the ~ after** (*hum*) la mañana después de la juerga; **good ~!** ¡buenos días!; **in the ~** (= *during the morning*) por la mañana, en la mañana (*LAm*); (*tomorrow*) mañana por la mañana; **early in the ~** a primera hora de la mañana, muy de mañana; **at seven o'clock in the ~** a las siete de la mañana; **at three in the ~** a las tres de la madrugada; **the next ~** la mañana siguiente; **on Saturday ~** el sábado por la mañana; **tomorrow ~** mañana por la mañana; **yesterday ~** ayer por la mañana
Ⓑ CPD ➤ **morning dress** chaqué *m*, traje *m* de etiqueta ➤ **morning sickness** (*Med*) náuseas *fpl* del embarazo ➤ **morning star** lucero *m* del alba

morning-after [ˈmɔːnɪŋˈɑːftəʳ] CPD ➤ **the morning-after pill** la píldora (anticonceptiva) del día después

Moroccan [məˈrɒkən] ADJ, N marroquí *mf*

Morocco [məˈrɒkəʊ] N Marruecos *m*

moron* [ˈmɔːrɒn] N imbécil *mf*

moronic [məˈrɒnɪk] ADJ imbécil

morose [məˈrəʊs] ADJ malhumorado

morphia [ˈmɔːfɪə], **morphine** [ˈmɔːfiːn] N morfina *f*

morphology [mɔːˈfɒlədʒɪ] N morfología *f*

morris dance [ˈmɒrɪsdɑːns] N baile tradicional inglés de hombres en el que éstos llevan cascabeles en la ropa

Morse code [ˌmɔːsˈkəʊd] N alfabeto *m* Morse

morsel [ˈmɔːsl] N [*of food*] bocado *m*; (*fig*) pedazo *m*

mortal [ˈmɔːtl] Ⓐ ADJ mortal; **to be in ~ danger** estar en peligro de muerte Ⓑ N mortal *mf* Ⓒ CPD ➤ **mortal sin** pecado *m* mortal

mortality [mɔːˈtælɪtɪ] N mortalidad *f* ➤ **mortality rate** tasa *f* de mortalidad

mortally [ˈmɔːtəlɪ] ADV 1 (= *fatally*) **to be ~ wounded** estar herido de muerte, estar mortalmente herido
2 (= *extremely*) **~ offended** profundamente ofendido

mortar [ˈmɔːtəʳ] N 1 (= *cannon*) mortero *m* 2 (= *cement*) argamasa *f*, mortero *m* 3 (= *bowl*) mortero *m*

mortgage [ˈmɔːgɪdʒ] Ⓐ N hipoteca *f*; **to take out a ~** obtener una hipoteca (**on** sobre) Ⓑ VT hipotecar Ⓒ CPD ➤ **mortgage lender** sociedad *f* hipotecaria ➤ **mortgage payment** pago *m* de la hipoteca, plazo *m* de la hipoteca ➤ **mortgage rate** tipo *m* de interés hipotecario

mortician [mɔːˈtɪʃən] N (*US*) director/a *m/f* de pompas fúnebres

mortify [ˈmɔːtɪfaɪ] VT avergonzar; **I was mortified (to find that ...)** me moría de vergüenza (al descubrir que ...)

mortifying [ˈmɔːtɪfaɪɪŋ] ADJ humillante

mortise lock [ˈmɔːtɪsˌlɒk] N cerradura *f* de muesca

mortuary [ˈmɔːtjʊərɪ] N depósito *m* de cadáveres

mosaic [məʊˈzeɪɪk] N mosaico *m*

Moscow [ˈmɒskəʊ] N Moscú *m*

mosey [ˈməʊzɪ] VI **to ~ along*** pasearse

Moslem [ˈmɒzlem] ADJ, N musulmán/ana *m/f*

mosque [mɒsk] N mezquita *f*

mosquito [mɒsˈkiːtəʊ] N (*pl* ~**es**) mosquito *m*, zancudo *m* (*LAm*) ➤ **mosquito bite** picadura *f* de mosquito ➤ **mosquito net** mosquitero *m*, mosquitera *f*

moss [mɒs] N musgo *m*

mossy [ˈmɒsɪ] ADJ musgoso, cubierto de musgo

most [məʊst] Ⓐ ADJ SUPERL 1 (*making comparisons*) más;

who has (the) ~ money? ¿quién tiene más dinero?; **for the ~ part** por lo general
2 (= *the majority of*) la mayoría de, la mayor parte de; **~ men** la mayoría de *or* la mayor parte de los hombres
Ⓑ N, PRON **~ of it** la mayor parte; **~ of them** la mayoría de ellos, la mayor parte de ellos; **~ of the time** la mayor parte del tiempo, gran parte del tiempo; **do the ~ you can** haz lo que puedas; **at the very ~** como máximo, a lo sumo; **20 minutes at the ~** 20 minutos como máximo *or* a lo sumo; **to make the ~ of sth** (= *make good use of*) aprovechar algo al máximo, sacar el máximo partido a algo; (= *enjoy*) disfrutar algo al máximo
Ⓒ ADV 1 (*superl*) más; **he spent ~** él gastó más; **the ~ difficult question** la pregunta más difícil
2 (= *extremely*) sumamente, muy; **a ~ interesting book** un libro interesantísimo *or* sumamente interesante; **you have been ~ kind** ha sido usted muy amable; **~ likely** lo más probable

mostly [ˈməʊstlɪ] ADV (= *mainly*) en su mayoría, en su mayor parte; **they are ~ women** en su mayoría *or* en su mayor parte son mujeres, la mayoría *or* casi todas son mujeres; **owls hunt ~ at night** el búho caza principalmente *or* sobre todo de noche; **it's ~ finished** está casi terminado

MOT (*Brit*) Ⓐ N ABBR 1 (= **Ministry of Transport**) ≈ Ministerio *m* de Transportes 2 (*also* ~ **test**) ≈ ITV *f* (*Sp*), ≈ Inspección *f* Técnica de Vehículos (*Sp*), Revisión *f* Técnica de Vehículos (*LAm*); **to pass the ~** ≈ pasar la ITV (*Sp*), ≈ pasar la revisión técnica (*LAm*) Ⓑ VT **I got my car ~'d last month** ≈ el coche pasó la ITV (*Sp*) *or* la revisión técnica (*LAm*) el mes pasado Ⓒ CPD ➤ **MOT certificate** ≈ certificado *m* de la ITV (*Sp*), certificado *m* de la revisión técnica (*LAm*)

motel [məʊˈtel] N motel *m*

moth [mɒθ] N mariposa *f* nocturna; (= *clothes moth*) polilla *f*

mothball [ˈmɒθbɔːl] Ⓐ N bola *f* de naftalina; **to put sth in ~s** [+ *project*] aparcar algo, dejar algo aparcado Ⓑ VT [+ *ship*] poner en la reserva; [+ *project*] aparcar, dejar aparcado

moth-eaten [ˈmɒθiːtn] ADJ apolillado

mother [ˈmʌðəʳ] Ⓐ N madre *f*; **to be like a ~ to sb** ser como una madre para algn Ⓑ VT (= *care for*) cuidar como una madre; (= *spoil*) mimar, consentir Ⓒ CPD ➤ **mother country** patria *f*; (*more sentimentally*) madre patria *f* ➤ **mother figure** figura *f* materna, figura *f* de la madre ➤ **Mother Nature** la madre *f* Naturaleza ➤ **Mother's Day** Día *m* de la Madre ➤ **Mother Superior** madre *f* superiora ➤ **mother tongue** lengua *f* materna

motherfucker*** [ˈmʌðəˌfʌkəʳ] N (*US*) hijoputa*** *m*, hijaputa*** *f*

motherhood [ˈmʌðəhʊd] N maternidad *f*

mother-in-law [ˈmʌðərɪnlɔː] N (*pl* **mothers-in-law**) suegra *f*

motherland [ˈmʌðəlænd] N patria *f*

motherly [ˈmʌðəlɪ] ADJ maternal

mother-of-pearl [ˈmʌðərəvˈpɜːl] Ⓐ N madreperla *f*, nácar *m* Ⓑ ADJ nacarado

mother-to-be [ˈmʌðətəˈbiː] N (*pl* **mothers-to-be**) futura madre *f*

mothproof [ˈmɒθpruːf] ADJ a prueba de polillas

motif [məʊˈtiːf] N (*Art, Mus*) motivo *m*; [*of speech*] tema *m*

motion [ˈməʊʃən] Ⓐ N 1 (= *movement*) movimiento *m*; **to be in ~** (*lit*) estar en movimiento; **plans are already in ~ for ...** ya hay planes en marcha para ...; **to set in ~** [+ *mechanism*] poner en marcha; [+ *chain of events*] desencadenar; ✦ IDIOM **to set the wheels in ~ (to do sth)** poner las cosas en marcha (para hacer algo)
2 (= *gesture*) gesto *m*, ademán *m*; **they went through the ~s of consulting members** siguieron la formalidad de consultar a los miembros
3 (= *proposal*) moción *f*
4 (*US Jur*) petición *f*
Ⓑ VI **he ~ed for the doors to be opened** hizo un gesto *or* hizo señas para que se abrieran las puertas; **to ~ to sb to do sth** indicar a algn con un gesto que haga algo, hacer señas a algn para que haga algo

⊙ CPD ➤ **motion picture** *(esp US)* película *f* ➤ **motion sickness** mareo *m*

motionless ['məʊʃənlɪs] ADJ inmóvil

motivate ['məʊtɪveɪt] VT motivar; **to be ~d to do sth** tener motivación *or* estar motivado para hacer algo; **he is highly ~d** tiene una fuerte motivación, está muy motivado

motivation [,məʊtɪ'veɪʃən] N motivación *f*

motive ['məʊtɪv] N motivo *m*; *(for crime)* móvil *m*

motley ['mɒtlɪ] ADJ *[collection, bunch]* variopinto; **they were a ~ crew** era una pandilla de lo más variopinto

motocross ['məʊtəkrɒs] N motocross *m*

motor ['məʊtə'] **⒜** N **1** *(= engine)* motor *m* **2** *(esp Brit*)* *(= car)* coche *m*, automóvil *m*, carro *m* *(LAm)*, auto *m* *(esp LAm)* **⒝** ADJ *[nerve, muscle]* motor *(fem: motora/motriz)* **⒞** CPD *(esp Brit)* ➤ **motor insurance** *(esp Brit)* seguro *m* de automóvil ➤ **motor mechanic** *(esp Brit)* mecánico/a *m/f* de automóviles ➤ **motor racing** *(esp Brit Sport)* carreras *fpl* de coches, automovilismo *m* ➤ **motor show** *(esp Brit)* feria *f* de automóviles

motorail ['məʊtəreɪl] N motorraíl *m*

motorbike ['məʊtəbaɪk] N *(Brit)* motocicleta *f*, moto *f*

motorboat ['məʊtəbəʊt] N lancha *f* motora, motora *f*

motorcade ['məʊtəkeɪd] N desfile *m* de automóviles

motorcar ['məʊtəkɑ:'] N *(frm)* coche *m*, automóvil *m*

motorcycle ['məʊtə,saɪkl] N motocicleta *f*, moto *f*

motorcyclist ['məʊtə,saɪklɪst] N motociclista *mf*, motorista *mf*

motoring ['məʊtərɪŋ] *(esp Brit)* **⒜** ADJ *[accident]* de tráfico, de circulación; **~ holiday** vacaciones *fpl* en coche **⒝** N automovilismo *m*; **school of ~** autoescuela *f*, escuela *f* de manejo *(LAm)*

motorist ['məʊtərɪst] N *(esp Brit)* conductor(a) *m/f*, automovilista *mf*

motormouth** ['məʊtəməʊθ] N cotorra* *f*

motorway ['məʊtəweɪ] N *(Brit)* autopista *f*

mottled ['mɒtld] ADJ *[egg]* moteado; *[leaf, colour]* jaspeado; *[complexion, skin]* con manchas

motto ['mɒtəʊ] N *(pl ~es or ~s)* *[of family, person]* lema *m*; *(= watchword)* consigna *f*

mould¹, **mold** *(US)* [məʊld] N *(= fungus)* moho *m*

mould², **mold** *(US)* [məʊld] **⒜** N *(= container)* molde *m*; **✦** IDIOM **they broke the ~ when they made him** rompieron el molde después de hacerlo a él **⒝** VT **1** *(= fashion)* moldear; *(= cast)* vaciar **2** *[+ sb's character]* moldear, formar

moulder, molder *(US)* ['məʊldə'] VI *(also ~ away)* desmoronarse

mouldy, moldy *(US)* ['məʊldɪ] ADJ *(compar* **mouldier;** *superl* **mouldiest)* **1** *[cheese, bread]* mohoso, enmohecido; *[mattress, clothing]* enmohecido, lleno de moho; **to go ~** enmohecerse, criar moho; **to smell ~** oler a moho *or* a humedad **2** *(Brit*)* *(= lousy)* cochino*

moult, molt *(US)* [məʊlt] VI *[bird]* mudar las plumas; *[mammal]* mudar el pelo

mound [maʊnd] N **1** *(= pile)* montón *m* **2** *(= hillock)* montículo *m*; *(= burial mound)* túmulo *m*

mount¹ [maʊnt] N *(= mountain)* monte *m*; **Mount Everest** el Everest

mount² [maʊnt] **⒜** N **1** *(= horse)* montura *f*, caballería *f* *(frm)* **2** *[of machine]* soporte *m*, base *f*; *[of jewel]* engaste *m*, montura *f*; *(for transparency)* marco *m*; *[of specimen, exhibit]* soporte *m* **⒝** VT **1** *[+ horse]* montar; *[+ bicycle]* montar en; *[+ platform, stage]* subir a; **the vehicle ~ed the pavement** el vehículo se subió a la acera **2** *[+ jewel]* engastar; *[+ exhibit, specimen]* fijar; *[+ picture]* poner un fondo a **3** *[+ exhibition, campaign, event]* montar, organizar; *[+ attack, offensive]* preparar **⒞** VI **1** *(= get on horse)* montar **2** *[prices, temperature]* subir, aumentar; *[excitement, tension]* crecer, aumentar

3 *(also ~ up)* *[bills, debts, problems]* amontonarse

mountain ['maʊntɪn] N montaña *f*; *[of work etc]* montón *m*; **in the ~s** en la montaña; **✦** IDIOM **to make a ~ out of a molehill** hacer una montaña de un grano de arena ➤ **mountain bike** bicicleta *f* de montaña ➤ **mountain climber** alpinista *mf*, andinista *mf* *(LAm)* ➤ **mountain lion** *(esp US)* puma *m* ➤ **mountain pass** puerto *m* de montaña, paso *m* de montaña ➤ **mountain range** *(large)* cordillera *f*; *(smaller)* sierra *f* ➤ **mountain rescue** servicio *m* de rescate de montaña

mountaineer [,maʊntɪ'nɪə'] N alpinista *mf*, andinista *mf* *(LAm)*

mountaineering [,maʊntɪ'nɪərɪŋ] N alpinismo *m*, andinismo *m* *(LAm)*

mountainous ['maʊntɪnəs] ADJ **1** *(= hilly)* montañoso **2** *(= immense)* gigantesco

mountainside ['maʊntɪn,saɪd] N ladera *f* de montaña, falda *f* de montaña

mountaintop ['maʊntɪntɒp] N cima *f* de la montaña, cumbre *f* de la montaña

mounted ['maʊntɪd] ADJ montado ➤ **the mounted police** la policía montada

mourn [mɔ:n] **⒜** VT *[+ person]* *(= grieve for)* llorar (la muerte de); *(= be in mourning for)* estar de luto *or* duelo por; *[+ death, loss]* lamentar, sentir **⒝** VI *(= be in mourning)* estar de luto *or* duelo; **to ~ for sb** llorar a algn, llorar la muerte de algn

mourner ['mɔ:nə'] N doliente *mf*; *(hired)* plañidero/a *m/f*

mournful ['mɔ:nfʊl] ADJ *[person]* afligido; *[tone, sound]* triste, lúgubre; *[occasion]* triste, luctuoso

mourning ['mɔ:nɪŋ] N luto *m*, duelo *m*; *(= dress)* luto *m*; **to be in ~ (for sb)** estar de luto *or* duelo (por algn); **to come out of ~** dejar el luto

mouse [maʊs] N *(pl* **mice)** ratón *m* *(also Comput)* ➤ **mouse mat, mouse pad** alfombrilla *f*, almohadilla *f*

mousetrap ['maʊstræp] N ratonera *f*

moussaka [mʊ'sɑ:kə] N musaca *f*

mousse [mu:s] N **1** *(= dessert)* mousse *m or f*; **chocolate ~** mousse *m or f* de chocolate **2** *(for hair)* espuma *f*

moustache, mustache *(US)* [məs'tɑ:ʃ] N bigote *m*; **he's got a ~** tiene bigote

mousy ['maʊsɪ] ADJ *(compar* **mousier;** *superl* **mousiest)* *[person]* tímido; *[colour, hair]* pardusco

mouth **⒜** [maʊθ] N *(pl ~s* [maʊðz]) *[of person, animal, bottle]* boca *f*; *[of cave]* entrada *f*; *[of river]* desembocadura *f*; **to open one's ~** abrir la boca; **✦** IDIOMS **to be down in the ~** estar deprimido; **to shoot one's ~ off*** hablar más de la cuenta; **to keep one's ~ shut*** callarse, no decir ni esta boca es mía; **shut your ~!**** ¡cállate ya!; **to put words into sb's ~** poner palabras en boca de algn **⒝** [maʊð] VT *(insincerely)* soltar; **"go away!" she ~ed** *(silently)* —¡vete de aquí! —dijo moviendo mudamente los labios **⒞** [maʊθ] CPD ➤ **mouth organ** *(esp Brit)* armónica *f*

mouthful ['maʊθfʊl] N *[of food]* bocado *m*; *[of drink]* trago *m*; *[of smoke, air]* bocanada *f*; **the name is a bit of a ~** es un nombre kilométrico

mouthpiece ['maʊθpi:s] N **1** *[of musical instrument]* boquilla *f* **2** *[of telephone]* micrófono *m* **3** *(= person)* portavoz *m*

mouth-to-mouth resuscitation [,maʊθtə'maʊθ rɪ,sʌsɪ'teɪʃən] N (respiración *f*) boca a boca *m*

mouthwash ['maʊθwɒʃ] N elixir *m* bucal

mouthwatering ['maʊθ'wɔ:tərɪŋ] ADJ muy apetitoso, que hace la boca agua

movable ['mu:vəbl] **⒜** ADJ movible, móvil **⒝** NPL **~s** muebles *mpl*, mobiliario *msing*; *(Jur)* bienes *mpl* muebles

move [mu:v] **⒜** N **1** *(= movement)* movimiento *m*; **to watch sb's <u>every</u> ~** observar a algn sin perder detalle, acechar a algn cada movimiento; **to <u>get</u> a ~ on (with sth)*** darse prisa *or* *(LAm)* apurarse (con algo); **get a ~ on!*** ¡date prisa!, ¡apúrate! *(LAm)*; **to <u>make</u> a ~** *(= start to leave, go)* ponerse en marcha; **it's time we made a ~** es hora de irnos; **to be <u>on</u> the ~** (= *travelling*) estar de viaje; [*troops, army*] estar avanzando; **to be always on the ~** [*nomads, circus, busy person*] andar siempre de aquí para allá; [*animal, child*] no saber estar quieto

2 (*in game*) jugada *f*; **whose ~ is it?** ¿a quién le toca jugar?; **it's my ~** es mi turno, me toca a mí

3 (= *step, action*) **what's the next ~?** ¿qué hacemos ahora?, y ahora ¿qué?; **that was a bad ~** fue una mala decisión; **to <u>make</u> a ~** dar un paso; **it's up to him to make the first ~** le toca a él dar el primer paso

4 (*to new home*) mudanza *f*; (*to new job*) traslado *m*

⑧ VT **1** (= *change place of*) cambiar de lugar, cambiar de sitio; [+ *part of body*] mover; [+ *chess piece etc*] jugar, mover; (= *transport*) transportar, trasladar; **you've ~d all my things!** ¡has cambiado de sitio todas mis cosas!; **can you ~ your fingers?** ¿puedes mover los dedos?; **the breeze ~d the leaves gently** la brisa movía *or* agitaba dulcemente las hojas; **to ~ <u>house</u>** mudarse; **~ your chair <u>nearer</u> the fire** acerca *or* arrima la silla al fuego; **he asked to be ~d to a new department** pidió el traslado a otro departamento

2 [+ *event, date*] **to ~ sth forward/back** adelantar/aplazar algo

3 (= *motivate*) **to ~ sb to do sth** mover *or* inducir a algn a hacer algo

4 (*emotionally*) conmover, emocionar; **to be ~d** estar conmovido; **to be easily ~d** ser impresionable, ser sensible; **to ~ sb to tears/anger** hacer llorar/enfadar a algn

5 (*frm*) (= *propose*) **to ~ that ...** proponer que ...

⓪ VI **1** (*gen*) moverse; **don't ~!** ¡no te muevas!; **I saw something moving in the bushes** vi moverse algo entre los arbustos; **let's ~ <u>into</u> the garden** vamos al jardín; **keep moving!** ¡no te pares!; (*order from traffic policeman*) ¡circulen!; **it's <u>time</u> we were moving** es hora de irnos; **she ~d <u>to</u> the next room** pasó a la habitación de al lado; **he ~d slowly <u>towards</u> the door** avanzó *or* se acercó lentamente hacia la puerta

2 (= *move house*) mudarse, trasladarse; **to ~ to the country** mudarse *or* trasladarse al campo

3 (= *travel*) ir; (= *be in motion*) estar en movimiento; **the bus was moving at 50kph** el autobús iba a 50kph; **the car was not moving** el coche no estaba en movimiento; **do not get out while the bus is moving** no se baje mientras el autobús esté en marcha

4 (= *progress*) **things are moving at last** por fin se empiezan a mover las cosas; **he certainly knows how to get things moving** ése sí que sabe poner las cosas en marcha

5 (*in games*) jugar, hacer una jugada

6 (= *take steps*) dar un paso, tomar medidas; **the council ~d to stop the abuse** el consejo tomó medidas para corregir el abuso; **we'll have to ~ quickly if we want to get that contract** tendremos que actuar inmediatamente si queremos hacernos con ese contrato

➤ **move about** (*Brit*) = **move around**

➤ **move along ⓐ** VT + ADV [+ *crowd*] hacer circular **⑧** VI + ADV **1** [*crowd*] circular; **~ along there!** ¡circulen! **2** (= *move forward*) avanzar, adelantarse **3** (*on bench etc*) correrse, hacerse a un lado

➤ **move around ⓐ** VT + ADV **1** (= *place in different position*) cambiar de sitio **2** (= *employee*) trasladar de un sitio a otro **⑧** VI + ADV **1** (= *fidget*) moverse **2** (= *walk about*) andar **3** (= *travel*) viajar de un sitio a otro

➤ **move away ⓐ** VT + ADV apartar, alejar; (= *to another place*) mover **⑧** VI + ADV **1** (= *move aside*) apartarse **2** (= *leave*) irse, marcharse **3** (= *move house*) mudarse

➤ **move back ⓐ** VT + ADV [+ *crowd*] hacer retroceder **2** (*to former place*) volver, regresar **3** (= *postpone*) aplazar, posponer **⑧** VI + ADV **1** (= *withdraw*) retroceder, retirarse **2** (*to former place*) volver, regresar **3** (= *move house*) **they ~d back to Burgos** volvieron a mudarse a Burgos

➤ **move forward ⓐ** VT + ADV **1** avanzar **2** (= *bring forward*) [+ *date, meeting*] adelantar; **to ~ the clocks forward** adelantar los relojes **⑧** VI + ADV adelantarse

➤ **move in ⓐ** VT + ADV (= *take inside*) meter, llevar hacia dentro **⑧** VI + ADV **1** (*into accommodation*) instalarse; **to ~ in with sb** irse a vivir con algn **2** (= *start operations*) ponerse manos a la obra, intervenir **3** (= *come closer*) acercarse (**on** a); [*army*] avanzar (**on** sobre)

➤ **move off ⓐ** VT + ADV sacar **⑧** VI + ADV **1** (= *go away*) irse,

marcharse **2** (= *start moving*) ponerse en marcha

➤ **move on ⓐ** VT + ADV [+ *crowd etc*] hacer circular **⑧** VI + ADV **1** [*person, vehicle*] circular **2** (*to new job*) **this training will prove useful when you want to ~ on** esta formación te resultará útil cuando quieras cambiar de trabajo **3** (*in discussion*) **let's ~ on (to the next point)** pasemos al punto siguiente **4** (= *change*) cambiar; **things have ~d on since your visit** las cosas han cambiado desde tu visita

➤ **move out ⓐ** VT + ADV [+ *person, object*] sacar; [+ *troops*] retirar **⑧** VI + ADV **1** (= *leave accommodation*) mudarse; **to ~ out of an area** marcharse de un barrio; **to ~ out of a flat** mudarse de un piso *or* (*LAm*) departamento **2** (= *withdraw*) [*troops*] retirarse

➤ **move over ⓐ** VT + ADV hacer a un lado, correr **⑧** VI + ADV correrse, hacerse a un lado; **~ over!** ¡córrete!

➤ **move up ⓐ** VT + ADV **1** [+ *object, person*] subir **2** (= *promote*) ascender **⑧** VI + ADV **1** (= *make room*) correrse **2** (= *be promoted*) ascender, ser ascendido; **to ~ up a class** pasar de curso, pasar al curso inmediatamente superior

moveable ['mu:vəbl] = **movable**

movement ['mu:vmənt] N **1** (= *motion*) movimiento *m*; [*of traffic*] circulación *f*; **there was a ~ towards the door** algunos se dirigieron hacia la puerta; **the police questioned him about his ~s** la policía le pidió informes sobre sus actividades **2** (*political, artistic*) movimiento *m* **3** (*Mus*) tiempo *m*, movimiento *m* **4** (*also* **bowel ~**) evacuación *f*

mover ['mu:və'] N **1** [*of motion*] promotor(a) *m/f* **2** (*esp US*) agente *m* de mudanzas

movie ['mu:vɪ] N (*esp US*) película *f*, film(e) *m*; **the ~s** el cine; **to go to the ~s** ir al cine ➤ **movie camera** cámara *f* cinematográfica ➤ **movie house** (*US*) cine *m* ➤ **the movie industry** (*US*) la industria cinematográfica ➤ **movie star** (*esp US*) estrella *f* de cine ➤ **movie theater** (*US*) cine *m*

moviegoer ['mu:vɪgəʊə'] N (*US*) aficionado/a *m/f* al cine

moving ['mu:vɪŋ] **ⓐ** ADJ **1** (= *not fixed*) móvil; **~ part** pieza *f* móvil **2** (= *not stationary*) [*vehicle*] en marcha, en movimiento; [*target*] móvil, en movimiento **3** (= *touching*) [*book, film, sight*] conmovedor, emotivo **4** (= *instigating*) **the ~ force behind sth** la fuerza motora *or* motriz *or* impulsora de algo **⑧** CPD ➤ **moving van** (*US*) camión *m* de mudanzas ➤ **moving walkway** cinta *f* móvil

mow [məʊ] (*pt* **~ed**; *pp* **~n**, **~ed**) VT **to ~ the lawn** cortar el césped; **to ~ sb down** acabar con algn, segar la vida de algn

mower ['məʊə'] N (*also* **lawn ~**) cortacésped *m*

mown [məʊn] PP *of* **mow**

Mozambique [,məʊzəm'bi:k] N Mozambique *m*

mozzarella [,mɒtsə'relə] N mozzarella *f*

MP [em'pi:] N ABBR **1** (*Brit*) (= **Member of Parliament**) Dip., diputado/a *m/f*, parlamentario/a *m/f* **2** (= **Military Police**) PM *f*

MP3 [empi:'θri:] N MP3 *m* ➤ **MP3 player** reproductor *m* (de) MP3

mpg N ABBR (= **miles per gallon**) ≈ k.p.l.

mph N ABBR (= **miles per hour**) ≈ km/h, ≈ k.p.h.

Mr ['mɪstə'] N ABBR (*pl* **Messrs**) (= **Mister**) Sr., señor; **Mr Jones wants to see you** el señor Jones quiere verte; **yes, Mr Brown** sí, señor Brown

MRI [emɑ:'raɪ] N ABBR = **magnetic resonance imaging**

Mrs ['mɪsɪz] N ABBR (*pl inv*) (= **Mistress**) Sra., señora; **~ Pitt wants to see you** la señora (de) Pitt quiere verte; **yes, ~ Brown** sí, señora Brown

MS ⓐ N ABBR **1** = **multiple sclerosis 2** (*US*) = **Master of Science ⑧** ABBR **1** (*US*) = **Mississippi 2** (*also* **ms**) = **manuscript**

Ms [mɪz, məz] N ABBR (= **Miss** *or* **Mrs**) *prefijo de nombre de*

mujer que evita expresar su estado civil

Ms

La fórmula de tratamiento **Ms** es el equivalente femenino de **Mr** y se utiliza frecuentemente en la actualidad para evitar la distinción que los términos tradicionales establecen entre mujer casada (**Mrs**) y soltera (**Miss**). Las formas **Ms** y **Miss** nunca llevan punto, pero **Mr** y **Mrs** a veces sí.

MSc N ABBR (*Brit*) = **Master of Science**

MSP N ABBR (*Brit*) = **Member of the Scottish Parliament**

MST N ABBR (*US*) = **Mountain Standard Time**

MT ABBR (*US*) = **Montana**

Mt ABBR (*Geog*) (= **Mount, Mountain**) M.

mth ABBR (= **month**) mes *m*

MTV N ABBR = **music television**

much [mʌtʃ] **Ⓐ** ADJ mucho; **there isn't ~ time** no tenemos mucho tiempo, tenemos poco tiempo; **I haven't got** <u>as</u> ~ **energy as you** no tengo tanta energía como tú; <u>how</u> ~ **sugar do you want?** ¿cuánto azúcar quieres?; **she's got so** ~ **energy** tiene tanta energía; **too** ~ **jam** demasiada mermelada *f*; <u>very</u> ~ mucho **Ⓑ** ADV mucho; (*before pp*) muy; **she doesn't go out** ~ no sale mucho; **it won't finish** ~ **before midnight** no terminará mucho antes de la media noche; ~ **better** mucho mejor; **he's** ~ **richer than I am** *or* **than me** es mucho más rico que yo; ~ <u>as</u> **I would like to go** a pesar de que me gustaría mucho ir, aunque me gustaría mucho ir; <u>however</u> ~ **he tries** por mucho que se esfuerce; **I hardly know her,** ~ <u>less</u> **her mother** apenas la conozco, y mucho menos a su madre; **a** ~ <u>needed</u> **holiday** unas vacaciones que me/le *etc* hacían mucha falta; <u>not</u> ~ no mucho; **I would** ~ <u>rather</u> **stay** prefiero mucho más quedarme; **they're** ~ **the** <u>same</u> **size** tienen más o menos el mismo tamaño; **thank you (ever)** <u>so</u> ~ muchísimas gracias, muy agradecido; ~ <u>to my</u> **astonishment** para gran sorpresa mía; **he talks** <u>too</u> ~ habla demasiado; <u>very</u> ~ mucho **Ⓒ** PRON mucho; **there isn't** ~ **to do** no hay mucho que hacer; **you've got** <u>as</u> ~ **as she has** tienes tanto como ella; **it didn't cost as** ~ **as I had expected** no costó tanto como yo me esperaba; **it can cost as** ~ **as $2,000** puede llegar a costar 2.000 dólares; **that's a** <u>bit</u> ~!* ¡eso es demasiado!; <u>how</u> ~ **is it a kilo?** ¿cuánto vale el kilo?; **how** ~ **does it cost?** ¿cuánto cuesta?; **there isn't** ~ <u>in it</u> (*between alternatives*) no hay mucha diferencia, no va mucho de uno a otro; **she won but there wasn't** ~ **in it** ganó, pero no por mucho; ~ <u>of</u> **this is true** gran parte de esto es verdad; **we don't see** ~ **of each other** no nos vemos mucho; **we haven't heard** ~ **of him lately** últimamente apenas sabemos nada de él; **I'm not** ~ **of a cook** no cocino muy bien; **that wasn't** ~ **of a dinner** eso apenas se podía llamar cena; **we spent** <u>so</u> ~ gastamos tanto; **I've got so** ~ **to do** tengo tantísimo que hacer; **that's** <u>too</u> ~ eso es demasiado; **it's not** <u>up to</u> ~ (*esp Brit**) no vale gran cosa

muchness [ˈmʌtʃnɪs] N **they're much of a** ~ son poco más o menos lo mismo

muck [mʌk] **Ⓐ** N **1** (= *dirt*) suciedad *f*, mugre *f*; (= *manure*) estiércol *m* **2** (*fig*) porquería *f* **Ⓑ** CPD ➤ **muck heap** estercolero *m*
➤ **muck around***, **muck about*** (*esp Brit*) **Ⓐ** VT + ADV **to** ~ **sb around** fastidiar *or* (*LAm**) fregar a algn **Ⓑ** VI + ADV **1** (= *lark about*) hacer tonterías; (= *do nothing in particular*) gandulear; **he enjoys** ~**ing around in boats** le gusta hacer el gandul navegando; **stop** ~**ing around!** ¡déjate de tonterías! **2** (= *tinker*) manosear
➤ **muck in*** VI + ADV (*esp Brit*) compartir el trabajo, arrimar el hombro
➤ **muck out** VT + ADV (*Brit*) limpiar
➤ **muck up*** VT + ADV **1** (= *dirty*) ensuciar **2** (*esp Brit*) (= *spoil*) echar a perder, fastidiar

muckraking* [ˈmʌkˌreɪkɪŋ] N revelación *f* de trapos sucios; (*in journalism*) amarillismo *m*, sensacionalismo *m*

muck-up* [ˈmʌkʌp] N (*esp Brit*) lío *m* grande

mucky [ˈmʌkɪ] ADJ (*compar* **muckier**; *superl* **muckiest**) (= *muddy*) lleno de barro, embarrado; (= *filthy*) sucio, asqueroso, mugroso (*LAm*); **to get** ~ (= *muddy*) llenarse de barro, embarrarse; (= *filthy*) ponerse hecho un asco*, ensuciarse

mucus [ˈmjuːkəs] N moco *m*

mud [mʌd] N barro *m*, lodo *m*; ✦ IDIOMS **to drag sb's name through the** ~ ensuciar el nombre de algn; **to throw** ~ **at sb** vilipendiar *or* insultar a algn, poner a algn como un trapo *or* por los suelos ➤ **mud flap** cortina *f* ➤ **mud flats** marisma *f* ➤ **mud hut** choza *f* de barro ➤ **mud pack** mascarilla *f* de barro

muddle [ˈmʌdl] **Ⓐ** N (*untidy*) desorden *m*, lío* *m*; (= *tricky situation*) lío* *m*, follón *m* (*Sp**); (= *mix-up*) confusión *f*; **to be in a** ~ [*room, books*] estar en desorden, estar revuelto, estar hecho un desbarajuste*; [*person*] estar confuso, estar hecho un lío*; **to get into a** ~ [*things*] desordenarse, revolverse; [*person*] hacerse un lío* **Ⓑ** VT = **muddle up**
➤ **muddle along** VI + ADV arreglárselas de alguna manera, ir tirando*
➤ **muddle through** VI + ADV arreglárselas de alguna manera, ir tirando*; **I expect we shall** ~ **through** espero que lo logremos de algún modo u otro
➤ **muddle up** VT + ADV **1** (= *jumble*) [+ *photos, papers*] revolver, desordenar; **to get** ~**d up** [*things*] desordenarse, revolverse
2 (= *mix up*) **I kept getting my words** ~**d up** no hacía más que confundirme al hablar; **the copies had got** ~**d up with the original documents** las copias se habían mezclado *or* confundido con los documentos originales; **you're getting me** ~**d up with the other Julie** me estás confundiendo con la otra Julie
3 (= *confuse*) [+ *person*] confundir; **to get** ~**d up** [*person*] confundirse, hacerse un lío*, liarse*

muddleheaded [ˈmʌdlˌhedɪd] ADJ [*person*] despistado, atolondrado; [*ideas*] confuso

muddy [ˈmʌdɪ] **Ⓐ** ADJ (*compar* **muddier**; *superl* **muddiest**) [*clothes, hands, floor, field*] lleno de barro, embarrado; [*water, stream*] turbio; [*ideas, thinking*] confuso, poco claro **Ⓑ** VT [+ *floor, carpet*] llenar de barro; ✦ IDIOM **to** ~ **the waters** confundir el tema *or* la cuestión, enredar las cosas

mudguard [ˈmʌdɡɑːd] N (*esp Brit*) guardabarros *m inv*

mudslide [ˈmʌdslaɪd] N alud *m* de lodo

mudslinging [ˈmʌdˌslɪŋɪŋ] N injurias *fpl*

muesli [ˈmjuːzlɪ] N muesli *m*

muff¹ [mʌf] N (*for hands*) manguito *m*

muff² [mʌf] VT [+ *shot, catch etc*] fallar; **to** ~ **it** fastidiarla, hacerlo fatal

muffin [ˈmʌfɪn] N **1** (= *cake*) magdalena *f* (generalmente con sabor a chocolate o con trocitos de fruta) **2** (*eaten with butter*) (*Brit*) ≈ mollete *m*; (*US*) especie de pan dulce, ≈ bollo *m*

muffle [ˈmʌfl] VT [+ *sound*] amortiguar

muffled [ˈmʌfld] ADJ **1** (= *deadened*) [*sound, shot, cry, sob*] sordo, apagado; [*voice*] apagado **2** (= *warmly wrapped*) envuelto, abrigado; **children** ~ **up in scarves and woolly hats** niños envueltos *or* abrigados con bufandas y gorros de lana

muffler [ˈmʌflər] N **1** (= *scarf*) bufanda *f* **2** (*US Aut*) silenciador *m*, mofle *m* (*LAm*)

mufti [ˈmʌftɪ] N **in** ~ (*vestido*) de paisano

mug [mʌɡ] **Ⓐ** N **1** (= *cup*) tazón *m* (*más alto que ancho*) **2** (*Brit**) (= *dupe*) bobo/a *m/f*, primo/a *m/f*; **smoking is a** ~**'s game** fumar es cosa de bobos **3** (**) (= *face*) jeta* *f*, careto *m* (*Sp***) **Ⓑ** VT (= *attack and rob*) atracar, asaltar **Ⓒ** CPD
➤ **mug shot*** fotografía *f* para las fichas
➤ **mug up*** VT + ADV (*Brit*) (*also* ~ **up on**) empollar

mugger [ˈmʌɡər] N atracador(a) *m/f*, asaltante *mf*

mugging [ˈmʌɡɪŋ] N atraco *m* (callejero)

muggins* [ˈmʌɡɪnz] N (*Brit*) ~ **will do it** lo haré yo, como un tonto

muggy [ˈmʌɡɪ] ADJ (*compar* **muggier**; *superl* **muggiest**) [*weather*] bochornoso; **it's** ~ **today** hoy hace bochorno

Muhammad [mʊˈhæməd] N = **Mohammed**

mujahedin, mujaheddin, mujahideen [mʊdʒəhəˈdiːn] NPL mujahedines *mpl*

mulatto [mjuːˈlætəʊ] ADJ, N mulato/a *m/f*

mulberry [ˈmʌlbərɪ] N (= *fruit*) mora *f*; (= *tree*) morera *f*, moral *m*

mule¹ [mjuːl] N (= *animal*) mulo/a *m/f*; (= *person*) testarudo/a *m/f*; ✦ IDIOM **(as) stubborn as a ~** terco como una mula

mule² [mjuːl] N (= *slipper*) babucha *f*

mulish [ˈmjuːlɪʃ] ADJ terco, testarudo

mull [mʌl] VT (*US*) reflexionar sobre, meditar
➤ **mull over** VT + ADV reflexionar sobre, meditar

mullah [ˈmʌlə] N mullah *m*

mulled [mʌld] ADJ ➤ **mulled wine** ponche *m*

mullet [ˈmʌlɪt] N **grey ~** mújol *m*; **red ~** salmonete *m*

multi... [ˈmʌltɪ] PREF multi...

multi-access [ˌmʌltɪˈækses] ADJ multiacceso *inv*, de acceso múltiple

multicoloured, multicolored (*US*) [ˈmʌltɪˈkʌləd] ADJ multicolor

multicultural [ˌmʌltɪˈkʌltʃərəl] ADJ multicultural

multidisciplinary [ˌmʌltɪˈdɪsɪplɪnərɪ] ADJ multidisciplinar

multifaceted [ˌmʌltɪˈfæsɪtɪd] ADJ [*personality*] multifacético; [*job*] con múltiples aspectos

multifarious [ˌmʌltɪˈfɛərɪəs] ADJ múltiple, vario

multigym [ˈmʌltɪdʒɪm] N estación *f* de musculación

multilateral [ˈmʌltɪˈlætərəl] ADJ (*Pol*) multilateral

multilingual [ˌmʌltɪˈlɪŋgwəl] ADJ plurilingüe

multimedia [ˈmʌltɪˈmiːdɪə] ADJ multimedia

multimillion [ˈmʌltɪˈmɪljən] ADJ multimillonario

multimillionaire [ˈmʌltɪmɪljəˈnɛəʳ] N multimillonario/a *m/f*

multinational [ˌmʌltɪˈnæʃənl] ⒶN compañía *f* multinacional, multinacional *f* ⒷADJ multinacional

multi-party [ˌmʌltɪˈpɑːtɪ] ADJ (*Pol*) [*system, democracy*] multipartidista

multiple [ˈmʌltɪpl] ⒶADJ múltiple ⒷN (*Math*) múltiplo *m* ⒸCPD ➤ **multiple choice test** examen *m* de elección múltiple, examen *m* tipo test ➤ **multiple personality (disorder)** (*Psych*) personalidad *f* múltiple ➤ **multiple sclerosis** esclerosis *f* múltiple

multiplex [ˈmʌltɪˌpleks] N (*also* ~ **cinema**) multicines *mpl*

multiplication [ˌmʌltɪplɪˈkeɪʃən] N multiplicación *f* ➤ **multiplication table** tabla *f* de multiplicar

multiplicity [ˌmʌltɪˈplɪsɪtɪ] N multiplicidad *f*

multiply [ˈmʌltɪplaɪ] ⒶVT (*Math*) multiplicar; **to ~ eight by seven** multiplicar ocho por siete ⒷVI **1** (*Math*) multiplicar **2** (= *reproduce o.s.*) multiplicarse

multipurpose [ˌmʌltɪˈpɜːpəs] ADJ multiuso

multiracial [ˈmʌltɪˈreɪʃəl] ADJ multirracial

multistorey [ˌmʌltɪˈstɔːrɪ], **multistoreyed, multistoried** (*US*) [ˌmʌltɪˈstɔːrɪd], **multistory** (*US*) [ˌmʌltɪˈstɔːrɪ] ADJ de varias plantas, de varios pisos ➤ **multistorey car park** (*Brit*) aparcamiento *m* de varias plantas

multitasking [ˈmʌltɪˈtɑːskɪŋ] N multitarea *f*

multitude [ˈmʌltɪtjuːd] N (= *crowd*) multitud *f*, muchedumbre *f*; **a ~ of problems** una infinidad de problemas, multitud de problemas; **for a ~ of reasons** por múltiples razones

mum¹* [mʌm] N (*esp Brit*) (= *mother*) mamá* *f*; **I'll ask Mum** le preguntaré a mamá

mum²* [mʌm] ADJ **to keep ~ (about sth)** guardar silencio (sobre algo)

mumble [ˈmʌmbl] VI, VT mascullar

mumbo jumbo [ˈmʌmbəʊˈdʒʌmbəʊ] N (= *nonsense*) galimatías *m inv*

mummify [ˈmʌmɪfaɪ] ⒶVT momificar ⒷVI momificarse

mummy¹ [ˈmʌmɪ] N (= *preserved corpse*) momia *f*

mummy²* [ˈmʌmɪ] N (*Brit*) mamá* *f*

mumps [mʌmps] NSING paperas *fpl*

munch [mʌntʃ] VT, VI mascar, masticar

munchies* [ˈmʌntʃɪz] NPL (*US*) **1** (= *snacks*) algo para picar **2 to have the ~** tener hambre

mundane [mʌnˈdeɪn] ADJ [*task*] rutinario; [*matter, problem*] trivial; [*existence*] prosaico

municipal [mjuːˈnɪsɪpəl] ADJ municipal

municipality [mjuːˌnɪsɪˈpælɪtɪ] N municipio *m*

munitions [mjuːˈnɪʃənz] NPL municiones *fpl* ➤ **munitions dump** polvorín *m*, depósito *m* de municiones ➤ **munitions factory** fábrica *f* de municiones

mural [ˈmjʊərəl] ⒶADJ mural *m* ⒷN mural *m*, pintura *f* mural

murder [ˈmɜːdəʳ] ⒶN **1** asesinato *m*; (*Jur*) homicidio *m*; **to commit ~** cometer un asesinato *or* un crimen **2** (*) **the heat in here is ~** el calor que hace aquí es insoportable; ✦ IDIOMS **to scream blue ~** poner el grito en el cielo; **she lets the children get away with ~** a los niños les consiente todo, a los niños les deja hacer lo que les da la gana* ⒷVT **1** [+ *person*] asesinar, matar, ultimar (*LAm*); ✦ IDIOM **I could ~ a cup of tea*** daría cualquier cosa por una taza de té **2** (*) [+ *song, play*] destrozar, cargarse (*Sp**); [+ *opponent*] aniquilar* ⒸCPD ➤ **murder case** caso *m* de asesinato *or* homicidio ➤ **murder trial** juicio *m* por asesinato ➤ **the murder weapon** el arma homicida

murderer [ˈmɜːdərəʳ] N asesino/a *m/f*; (*as legal term*) homicida *mf*

murderess [ˈmɜːdərɪs] N asesina *f*; (*as legal term*) homicida *f*

murderous [ˈmɜːdərəs] ADJ (= *homicidal*) homicida; [*look*] asesino, homicida; **this heat is ~*** este calor es cruel

murk [mɜːk] N oscuridad *f*, tinieblas *fpl*

murkiness [ˈmɜːkɪnɪs] N (= *darkness*) oscuridad *f*; (*fig*) lo turbio, tenebrosidad *f*; [*of water, river*] lo turbio

murky [ˈmɜːkɪ] ADJ (*compar* **murkier**; *superl* **murkiest**) [*night, evening*] tenebroso, oscuro; [*water*] turbio; (*Brit*) [*past*] turbio

murmur [ˈmɜːməʳ] ⒶN murmullo *m*; **there were ~s of disagreement** hubo un murmullo de desaprobación; **without a ~** sin una queja ⒷVI murmurar; **to ~ about sth** (= *complain*) quejarse *or* murmurar de algo ⒸVT murmurar, decir en voz baja

Murphy's law* [ˈmɜːfɪzlɔː] N *ley de la indefectible mala voluntad de los objetos inanimados*

muscle [ˈmʌsl] N músculo *m*; **he didn't move a ~** ni se inmutó; **political ~** poder *m* político ➤ **muscle in*** VI + ADV **to ~ in (on sth)** meterse por la fuerza (en algo)

musclebound [ˈmʌslbaʊnd] ADJ exageradamente musculoso

Muscovite [ˈmʌskəvaɪt] ADJ, N moscovita *mf*

muscular [ˈmʌskjʊləʳ] ⒶADJ **1** [*tissue, pain, control*] muscular **2** (= *brawny*) [*person, body*] musculoso ⒷCPD ➤ **muscular dystrophy** distrofia *f* muscular

Muse [mjuːz] N musa *f*; **the ~s** las Musas

muse [mjuːz] ⒶVI **to ~ on** *or* **about sth** reflexionar sobre algo, meditar algo ⒷVT **"should we?" he ~d** —¿debemos hacerlo? —dijo pensativo

museum [mjuːˈzɪəm] N museo *m*

mush [mʌʃ] N **1** (= *food*) gachas *fpl* **2** (*sentimental*) sensiblería *f*, sentimentalismo *m*

mushroom [ˈmʌʃrʊm] ⒶN (*round-topped*) champiñón *m*; (*flat-topped*) seta *f*; (*Bot*) seta *f*, hongo *m*, callampa *f* (*Chi*); **a great ~ of smoke** un enorme hongo de humo ⒷVI [*town* *etc*] crecer vertiginosamente Ⓖ CPD ➤ **mushroom cloud** hongo *m* nuclear

mushy ['mʌʃi] ADJ (*compar* **mushier**; *superl* **mushiest**) **1** (*in texture*) pulposo, mollar; ~ **peas** (*Brit*) puré *m* de guisantes *or* (*LAm*) arvejas, chícharos *mpl* aguados (*Mex*) **2** (= *sentimental*) sensiblero, sentimentaloide

music ['mjuːzɪk] N música *f*; ✦ IDIOMS **it was ~ to my ears** daba gusto escucharlo, me sonaba a música celestial; **to face the ~** afrontar las consecuencias ➤ **music box** caja *f* de música ➤ **music centre**, **music center** (*US*) equipo *m* estereofónico ➤ **music festival** festival *m* de música ➤ **music hall** (*esp Brit*) teatro *m* de variedades ➤ **music lover** aficionado/a *m/f* a la música, amante *mf* de la música ➤ **music stand** atril *m*

musical ['mjuːzɪkəl] ⒶADJ **1** (= *relating to music*) [*career, style, accompaniment*] musical; [*talent*] musical, para la música
2 (= *musically talented*) dotado para la música, con aptitudes musicales; **he came from a ~ family** venía de una familia de músicos *or* dotada para la música
3 (= *melodious*) [*laugh, voice*] musical
ⒷN (*Cine, Theat*) musical *m*
ⒸCPD ➤ **musical box** (*Brit*) caja *f* de música ➤ **musical chairs**: **to play ~ chairs** jugar a las sillas, jugar al stop ➤ **musical director** (*esp US*) director(a) *m/f* musical ➤ **musical instrument** instrumento *m* musical

musician [mjuːˈzɪʃən] N músico/a *m/f*

musicianship [mjuːˈzɪʃənʃɪp] N maestría *f* musical

musicology [ˌmjuːzɪˈkɒlədʒɪ] N musicología *f*

musk [mʌsk] N (= *scent*) perfume *m* de almizcle

musket ['mʌskɪt] N mosquete *m*

musketeer [ˌmʌskɪˈtɪəʳ] N mosquetero *m*

muskrat ['mʌskræt] N ratón *m* almizclero

musky ['mʌskɪ] ADJ almizcleño, almizclado; [*smell*] a almizcle

Muslim ['muslɪm] ADJ, N musulmán/ana *m/f*

muslin ['mʌzlɪn] ⒶN muselina *f* Ⓑ ADJ de muselina

mussel ['mʌsl] N mejillón *m*

must [mʌst] ⒶMODAL AUX VB **1** (*obligation*) deber, tener que; **I ~ do it** debo hacerlo, tengo que hacerlo; **you ~ come again next year** tienes que volver el año que viene; **you ~n't forget to send her a card** no te vayas a olvidar de mandarle una tarjeta; **I'll do it if I ~** si me obligan, lo haré, lo haré si es necesario; **if you ~ know, I'm Portuguese** para que lo sepa, soy portugués; **I ~ say, he's very irritating** tengo que decir que es muy irritante; **why ~ you always be so rude?** ¿por qué tienes que ser siempre tan maleducado?
2 (*probability*) deber de; **you ~ be tired** debes de estar cansado; **it ~ be eight o'clock by now** ya deben de ser las ocho; **but you ~ have seen her!** ¡pero debes de haberla visto!; **there ~ be a reason** debe de haber *or* tiene que haber una razón
ⒷN **this programme is a ~*** no hay que perderse este programa, este programa hay que verlo

mustache ['mʌstæʃ] N (*US*) = **moustache**

mustang ['mʌstæŋ] N potro *m*, mesteño mustang(o) *m*

mustard ['mʌstəd] ⒶN mostaza *f* Ⓑ ADJ **a ~ (yellow) dress** un vestido color mostaza Ⓒ CPD ➤ **mustard gas** (*Chem, Mil*) gas *m* mostaza

muster ['mʌstəʳ] ⒶN ✦ IDIOM **to pass ~** ser aceptable Ⓑ VT [+ *helpers*] reunir; (*also ~ up*) [+ *courage*] armarse de; [+ *strength*] cobrar

mustiness ['mʌstɪnɪs] N [*of room*] olor *m* a cerrado, olor *m* a humedad

mustn't ['mʌsnt] = **must not**

musty ['mʌstɪ] ADJ (*compar* **mustier**; *superl* **mustiest**) [*room etc*] que huele a humedad, que huele a cerrado

mutant ['mjuːtənt] ADJ, N mutante *mf*

mutate [mjuːˈteɪt] VI (*Bio*) mutarse, sufrir mutación; (= *change*) transformarse

mutation [mjuːˈteɪʃən] N mutación *f*

mute [mjuːt] ⒶADJ mudo Ⓑ N (= *person*) mudo/a *m/f* **2** (*Mus*) sordina *f*

muted ['mjuːtɪd] ADJ [*noise*] sordo; [*criticism*] callado, silencioso; [*colour*] apagado

mutilate ['mjuːtɪleɪt] VT mutilar

mutilation [ˌmjuːtɪˈleɪʃən] N mutilación *f*

mutinous ['mjuːtɪnəs] ADJ [*crew, soldiers*] amotinado; [*child, attitude*] rebelde

mutiny ['mjuːtɪnɪ] ⒶN motín *m* Ⓑ VI amotinarse

mutt* [mʌt] N **1** (= *fool*) bobo *m* **2** (= *dog*) chucho *m*

mutter ['mʌtəʳ] ⒶN murmullo *m* Ⓑ VT murmurar, decir entre dientes Ⓒ VI murmurar; (= *complain*) quejarse

mutton ['mʌtn] N cordero *m*; ✦ IDIOM ~ **dressed as lamb** (*Brit***) vejestorio *m* emperifollado

mutual ['mjuːtjʊəl] ⒶADJ **1** (= *reciprocal*) [*affection, help, understanding*] mutuo; **the feeling is ~** el sentimiento es mutuo **2** (= *common*) [*friend, cousin*] común; **they had a ~ interest in rugby** tenían un interés común *or* compartían su interés por el rugby; **by ~ consent** de mutuo *or* común acuerdo Ⓑ CPD ➤ **mutual fund** (*US*) fondo *m* de inversión mobiliaria

mutually ['mjuːtjʊəlɪ] ADV **1** (= *reciprocally*) mutuamente; **these views are ~ exclusive** estas opiniones se excluyen mutuamente **2** (= *for/by both parties involved*) **we arranged to meet at a ~ convenient time** acordamos vernos a una hora que nos viniera bien a los dos

Muzak ® ['mjuːzæk] N hilo *m* musical

muzzle ['mʌzl] ⒶN **1** (= *snout*) hocico *m* **2** [*of gun*] boca *f* **3** (= *restraint for dog*) bozal *m* Ⓑ VT **1** [+ *dog*] poner bozal a **2** (*fig*) [+ *person*] amordazar

muzzy* ['mʌzɪ] ADJ (*compar* **muzzier**; *superl* **muzziest**) (*esp Brit*) [*outline, ideas*] borroso; [*person*] atontado, confuso

MW N ABBR (*Rad*) = **medium wave** OM *f*

my [maɪ] POSS ADJ (*with singular noun*) mi; (*with plural noun*) mis; **my friend** mi amigo; **my books** mis libros; **my own car** mi propio coche

---

My is usually translated by the definite article **el/los** or **la/las** when it's clear from the sentence who the possessor is or when referring to clothing or parts of the body:

---

they stole my car me robaron el coche; **I'm washing my hair** me estoy lavando la cabeza; **I took off my coat** me quité el abrigo

myalgic encephalomyelitis [maɪˈældʒɪk enˌsefələʊmaɪəˈlaɪtɪs] N encefalomielitis *f inv* miálgica

Myanmar ['maɪænmɑːʳ] N Myanmar *f*

myopia [maɪˈəʊpɪə] N (*frm*) miopía *f*

myopic [maɪˈɒpɪk] ADJ (*frm*) miope

myriad ['mɪrɪəd] (*frm*) ⒶADJ **a ~ flies** un sinnúmero *or* una miríada de moscas Ⓑ N miríada *f*

myrrh [mɜːʳ] N mirra *f*

myself [maɪˈself] PRON **1** (*reflexive*) me; **I've hurt ~** me he hecho daño; **I couldn't see ~ in the mirror** no pude verme en el espejo
2 (*emphatic*) yo mismo/a; **I made it ~** lo hice yo mismo; **I went ~** fui en persona
3 (*after prep*) mí, mí mismo/a; **I talked mainly about ~** hablé principalmente de mí (mismo)
4 (*phrases*) **by ~** solo/a; **I did it all by ~** lo hice yo solo; **I don't like travelling by ~** no me gusta viajar solo; **don't leave me all by ~!** ¡no me dejes aquí solo!; **a beginner like ~** un principiante como yo; **I'm not ~** no me encuentro nada bien; **I was talking to ~** hablaba a *or* para mí mismo

mysterious [mɪsˈtɪərɪəs] ADJ misterioso; **there is nothing ~ about it** no tiene nada de misterioso, no tiene ningún misterio; **why are you being so ~?** ¿por qué andas con tanto misterio?, ¿a qué viene tanto misterio?

mysteriously [mɪsˈtɪərɪəslɪ] ADV misteriosamente

mystery ['mɪstərɪ] N misterio *m*; **there's no ~ about it** no tiene ningún misterio; **it's a ~ to me where it can have**

gone no entiendo dónde puede haberse metido ➤ **mystery story** novela *f* de misterio ➤ **mystery tour** viaje *m* sorpresa

mystic ['mɪstɪk] ADJ, N místico/a *m/f*

mystical ['mɪstɪkəl] ADJ místico

mysticism ['mɪstɪsɪzəm] N misticismo *m*

mystify ['mɪstɪfaɪ] VT dejar perplejo, desconcertar; **I was mystified** me quedé perplejo *or* desconcertado

mystifying ['mɪstɪfaɪɪŋ] ADJ desconcertante

mystique [mɪs'tiːk] N mística *f*

myth [mɪθ] N (= *story*) mito *m*; (= *imaginary person, thing*) mito *m*, ilusión *f*; **a Greek ~** un mito griego; **that's a ~** eso es un mito

mythical ['mɪθɪkəl] ADJ [*beast, creature*] mítico; (= *imaginary*) imaginario

mythological [ˌmɪθəˈlɒdʒɪkəl] ADJ mitológico

mythology [mɪˈθɒlədʒɪ] N mitología *f*

myxomatosis [ˌmɪksəməˈtəʊsɪs] N mixomatosis *f inv*

N¹, n [en] N (= *letter*) N f, n f; **N for Nellie** N de Navarra

N² ABBR (= **north**) N

'n'** [ən] CONJ = **and**

n/a ABBR (= **not applicable**) no interesa

NAACP N ABBR (*US*) = **National Association for the Advancement of Colored People**

naan bread ['nɑːnbred] N *pan indio sin apenas levadura*

nab* [næb] VT pescar*, coger, agarrar (*LAm*)

naff* [næf] ADJ (*Brit*) de mal gusto, hortera (*Sp**), naco (*Mex**)

NAFTA ['næftə] N ABBR (= **North American Free Trade Agreement**) Zona f de Libre Comercio del Atlántico Norte

nag¹ [næg] 🅐 VT fastidiar, dar la lata a*; **to ~ sb about sth** dar la lata a algn con algo*; **to ~ sb to do sth** fastidiar a algn *or* dar la lata a algn para que haga algo* 🅑 VI fastidiar, dar la lata* 🅒 N (= *person*) gruñón/ona m/f

nag² [næg] N (= *horse*) rocín m, jaco m

nagging ['nægɪŋ] 🅐 ADJ persistente 🅑 N quejas fpl, críticas fpl

NAHT N ABBR (*Brit*) = **National Association of Head Teachers**

nail [neɪl] 🅐 N **1** (*on finger, toe*) uña f
2 (*metal*) clavo m; ✦ IDIOMS **it was another ~ in his coffin** representó otro paso hacia su destrucción; **to hit the ~ on the head** dar en el clavo; **to pay (cash) on the ~** (*Brit*) pagar en el acto, pagar a tocateja (*Sp**)
🅑 VT **1** (= *fix with nails*) clavar; **to ~ two things together** clavar dos cosas
2 (*) (= *catch*) agarrar, pillar*
🅒 CPD ➤ **nail bomb** bomba f de metralla ➤ **nail clippers** cortauñas m inv ➤ **nail file** lima f (para las uñas) ➤ **nail polish** esmalte m de uñas ➤ **nail polish remover** quitaesmalte m ➤ **nail scissors** tijeras fpl para las uñas ➤ **nail varnish** (*Brit*) esmalte m de uñas ➤ **nail varnish remover** (*Brit*) quitaesmalte m
➤ **nail down** VT + ADV **1** (= *with nails*) clavar, sujetar con clavos **2** (= *identify*) identificar **3** (= *commit*) **to ~ sb down** hacer que algn se comprometa; **we ~ed him down to a date** le obligamos a fijar una fecha **4** (= *force to be specific*) obligar a concretar; **you can't ~ him down** es imposible hacerle concretar
➤ **nail up** VT + ADV (*on wall*) clavar

nail-biting ['neɪl,baɪtɪŋ] ADJ [*tension*] angustioso; [*contest, finish*] emocionantísimo

nailbrush ['neɪlbrʌʃ] N cepillo m de uñas

naïve, naive [naɪ'iːv] ADJ (*gen*) ingenuo; (*Art*) naïf

naïvely, naively [naɪ'iːvlɪ] ADV ingenuamente

naïveté, naivety [naɪ'iːvtɪ] N ingenuidad f

naked ['neɪkɪd] ADJ **1** (= *unclothed*) desnudo; **visible/invisible to the ~ eye** visible/invisible a simple vista
2 (= *exposed*) [*light bulb*] sin pantalla; **~ flame** llama f
3 (= *undisguised*) [*hatred*] manifiesto; [*ambition*] patente

nakedness ['neɪkɪdnɪs] N desnudez f

NAM N ABBR (*US*) = **National Association of Manufacturers**

namby-pamby ['næmbɪ'pæmbɪ] ADJ (*esp Brit**) soso, ñoño*

name [neɪm] 🅐 N **1** [*of person, firm*] nombre m; (= *surname*) apellido m; [*of book, film*] título m; **what's your ~?** ¿cómo te llamas?; **my ~ is Peter** me llamo Peter; **what ~ shall I say?** (*Telec*) ¿de parte de quién?; **I know him by ~ only** lo conozco solamente de nombre; **a man by the ~ of Ian Kelly** un hombre llamado Ian Kelly; **a man by the ~ of Kelly** un hombre apellidado *or* que se apellidaba Kelly; **she's the boss in all but ~** para jefa sólo le falta el nombre; **open up, in the ~ of the law!** ¡abran en nombre de la ley!; **to put one's ~ down for** [+ *new car etc*] apuntarse para; [+ *school, course*] inscribirse en; **to write under the ~ of** escribir bajo el nombre de; ✦ IDIOM **that's the ~ of the game*** (= *how it is*) así son las cosas; (= *what's important*) eso es lo importante
2 (*insulting*) **to call sb ~s** insultar a algn

3 (= *reputation*) reputación f, fama f; **to get (o.s.) a bad ~** crearse mala reputación *or* fama; **to make a ~ for o.s.** hacerse famoso; **to make one's ~** llegar a ser famoso
4 (= *person*) **big ~*** (gran) figura f
🅑 VT **1** (= *call*) llamar; **a man ~d Joe** un hombre llamado Joe; **they ~d the child Zoë** a la niña le pusieron Zoë; **they ~d him Winston after** *or* (*US*) **for Winston Churchill** le pusieron Winston por Winston Churchill
2 (= *mention*) mencionar; **you were not ~d in the speech** no se te nombró *or* mencionó en el discurso; **he is not ~d in this list** no figura en esta lista; **~ 20 British birds** nómbra(me) 20 pájaros británicos; **you ~ it, we've got it** cualquier cosa que pidas, la tenemos; **to name names** dar *or* mencionar nombres
3 (= *fix*) fijar; **have they ~d the day yet?** ¿han fijado ya la fecha de la boda?; **they're so keen to buy it you can ~ your price** tienen tanto afán por comprarlo que puedes pedirles el precio que quieras
4 (= *nominate*) nombrar
🅒 CPD ➤ **name day** día m del santo, santo m, fiesta f onomástica ➤ **name tape** etiqueta f con el nombre

name-dropper ['neɪm,drɒpər] N **he's a ~** siempre está mencionando a la gente importante que conoce

nameless ['neɪmlɪs] ADJ anónimo, sin nombre; **someone, who shall remain ~ ...** cierta persona, cuyo nombre me callo ...

namely ['neɪmlɪ] ADV a saber, concretamente

nameplate ['neɪmpleɪt] N (*on door*) placa f (con el nombre); (*on goods*) placa f del fabricante

namesake ['neɪmseɪk] N tocayo/a m/f, homónimo/a m/f

name-tag ['neɪmtæg] N placa f de identificación

Namibia [nɑː'mɪbɪə] N Namibia f

nan* [næn], **nana*** ['nænə] N (*Brit*) abuelita* f, yaya* f

nanny ['nænɪ] N (*esp Brit*) niñera f ➤ **nanny goat** cabra f ➤ **nanny state** (*esp Brit*) papá-estado m

nanosecond ['nænəʊ,sekənd] N nanosegundo m

nanotechnology [,nænəʊtek'nɒlədʒɪ] N nanotecnología f

nap [næp] 🅐 N (= *sleep*) sueñecito m; (*in afternoon*) siesta f; **to have a ~** echar un sueñecito/una siesta 🅑 VI dormitar; ✦ IDIOM **to catch sb ~ping** pillar a algn desprevenido

napalm ['neɪpɑːm] N napalm m

nape [neɪp] N (*also ~ of the neck*) nuca f, cogote m

naphthalene ['næfθəliːn] N naftalina f

napkin ['næpkɪn] N (*also table ~*) servilleta f; (*US*) (= *sanitary towel*) compresa f higiénica, paño m higiénico ➤ **napkin ring** servilletero m

nappy ['næpɪ] N (*Brit*) pañal m ➤ **nappy liner** gasa f ➤ **nappy rash** irritación f; **to have ~ rash** estar escaldado *or* escocido

narcissistic [,nɑː'sɪsɪstɪk] ADJ narcisista

narcissus [nɑː'sɪsəs] N (*pl* **narcissi** [nɑː'sɪsaɪ]) narciso m

narcotic [nɑː'kɒtɪk] 🅐 N **1** (*Med*) narcótico m **2** (*esp US*) **narcotics** (= *illegal drugs*) estupefacientes mpl, narcóticos mpl 🅑 CPD ➤ **narcotics agent** (*US*) agente mf de narcóticos ➤ **narcotics trafficking** (*US*) narcotráfico m, tráfico m de estupefacientes *or* drogas

narked* [nɑːkt] ADJ (*Brit*) **to be ~** estar cabreado *or* mosqueado*; **to get ~** cabrearse*, mosquearse*

narrate [nə'reɪt] VT narrar

narration [nə'reɪʃən] N narración f

narrative ['nærətɪv] 🅐 ADJ narrativo 🅑 N narración f

narrator [nə'reɪtər] N narrador(a) m/f

narrow ['nærəʊ] 🅐 ADJ (*compar* **~er**; *superl* **~est**) **1** (*in width*) estrecho, angosto (*esp LAm*); **to get ~(er)** estrecharse **2** (= *limited*) [*range*] reducido, limitado; [*definition*] restringido; **in a ~ sense** en sentido estricto **3** (= *small*) [*margin, majority*] escaso; [*victory, defeat*] por un

escaso margen; **to have a ~ escape** salvarse por los pelos*
4 (= *closed*) [*person*] estrecho de miras; [*view*] cerrado
Ⓑ VI [*road, path, river*] estrecharse, angostarse (*esp LAm*);
[*eyes*] entrecerrarse; [*gap, majority*] reducirse
Ⓒ VT [+ *gap*] reducir
Ⓓ CPD ➤ **narrow boat** (*Brit*) barcaza *f*
➤ **narrow down Ⓐ** VT + ADV [+ *search, investigation,
possibilities*] restringir, limitar; [+ *list*] reducir **Ⓑ** VI + ADV
[*search, investigation*] restringirse; [*list*] reducirse

narrowly ['nærəʊlɪ] ADV **1** [*escape, avoid, miss*] por poco; **to
be ~ defeated** (*in election*) ser derrotado por un escaso
margen; (*Sport*) perder por poco **2** [*define*] de forma
restringida

narrow-minded ['nærəʊ'maɪndɪd] ADJ estrecho de miras

narrow-mindedness ['nærəʊ'maɪndɪdnɪs] N estrechez *f* de
miras

narrowness ['nærəʊnɪs] N estrechez *f*

NAS N ABBR (*US*) = **National Academy of Sciences**

NASA ['næsə] N ABBR (*US*) (= **National Aeronautics and
Space Administration**) NASA *f*

nasal ['neɪzəl] ADJ (*Anat, Phon*) nasal; (= *twanging*) gangoso

nastily ['nɑːstɪlɪ] ADV [*speak, behave*] con mala idea

nastiness ['nɑːstɪnɪs] N (= *spitefulness*) maldad *f*

nasturtium [nəs'tɜːʃəm] N capuchina *f*

nasty ['nɑːstɪ] ADJ (*compar* **nastier**; *superl* **nastiest**)
1 (= *unpleasant*) desagradable; **I've got a ~ feeling that ...**
tengo la horrible sensación de que ...; **history has a ~ habit
of repeating itself** la historia tiene la mala costumbre de
repetirse; **he had a ~ shock** se llevó un susto terrible
2 (= *serious*) [*accident*] serio, grave; [*cut, wound*] feo;
[*infection*] fuerte; **a ~ case of** un caso grave de
3 (= *dangerous*) [*bend, junction*] peligroso
4 (= *difficult*) [*question*] difícil; [*problem*] complicado
5 (= *spiteful*) [*person, remark*] cruel, desagradable; [*joke*] de
mal gusto, grosero; **he's a ~ piece of work** es un canalla*;
don't be ~ to your little brother no seas malo con tu
hermanito; **a ~ trick** una mala jugada; **he turned ~** se puso
agresivo

NAS/UWT N ABBR (*Brit*) = **National Association of
Schoolmasters/Union of Women Teachers**

NATFHE N ABBR (*Brit*) = **National Association of Teachers in
Further and Higher Education**

nation ['neɪʃən] N nación *f* ➤ **nation state** estado-nación
m

national ['næʃənl] **Ⓐ** ADJ nacional
Ⓑ N **1** (= *person*) ciudadano/a *m/f*
2 (= *newspaper*) periódico *m* nacional
Ⓒ CPD ➤ **national anthem** himno *m* nacional ➤ **national
bank** (*state-owned*) banco *m* nacional, banco *m* estatal; (*US*)
(*commercial*) banco que forma parte del Sistema de Reservas
Federal ➤ **national costume** traje *m* típico nacional
➤ **National Curriculum** (*Brit*) plan de estudios oficial que se
sigue en las escuelas de enseñanza pública de Inglaterra y
Gales ➤ **national debt** deuda *f* pública ➤ **national dress**
traje *m* típico nacional ➤ **the National Front** (*Brit*) el Frente
Nacional (británico) (*partido político de extrema derecha e
ideología racista*) ➤ **national grid** red *f* eléctrica nacional
➤ **the National Guard** (*US*) la Guardia Nacional ➤ **the
National Health (Service)** (*Brit*) servicio Nacional de Salud; **to
have an operation done on the National Health** ≈ operarse
por la Seguridad Social *or* el Seguro ➤ **national holiday** (*esp
US*) fiesta *f*, día *m* festivo, (día *m*) feriado *m* (*LAm*)
➤ **National Insurance** (*Brit*) ≈ Seguridad *f* Social ➤ **National
Insurance contributions** cotizaciones *fpl* a la Seguridad
Social, aportes *mpl* a la Seguridad Social (*SC*) ➤ **National
Insurance number** número *m* de la Seguridad Social ➤ **the
National Lottery** (*Brit*) ≈ la lotería primitiva ➤ **National
Savings (Bank)** (*Brit*) ≈ caja *f* postal de ahorros ➤ **National
Savings Certificate** (*Brit*) ≈ bono *m* del Estado ➤ **the
National Security Council** (*US*) el Consejo para la
Seguridad Nacional ➤ **national service** (*esp Brit*) servicio *m*
militar ➤ **National Socialism** nacionalsocialismo *m* ➤ **the
National Trust** (*Brit*) ≈ la Dirección General del Patrimonio
Nacional; *ver tb* www.nationaltrust.org.uk

nationalism ['næʃnəlɪzəm] N nacionalismo *m*

nationalist ['næʃnəlɪst] ADJ, N nacionalista *mf*

nationalistic [,næʃnə'lɪstɪk] ADJ nacionalista

nationality [,næʃə'nælɪtɪ] N nacionalidad *f*

nationalization [,næʃnəlaɪ'zeɪʃən] N nacionalización *f*

nationalize ['næʃnəlaɪz] VT nacionalizar

nationally ['næʃnəlɪ] ADV [*distribute*] por todo el país;
[*recognize*] a nivel nacional, en todo el país; [*available*] en
todo el país; **this is the case locally, but not ~** eso es cierto
a nivel local, pero no a nivel nacional

nationwide ['neɪʃənwaɪd] **Ⓐ** ADJ [*survey, campaign*] a nivel
nacional; [*interest, support*] en todo el país; [*network,
referendum*] nacional; [*tour, hunt*] por todo el país **Ⓑ** ADV
[*deliver*] en todo el territorio nacional, por todo el país; **we
now have over 300 branches** ~ ya tenemos más de 300
sucursales por todo el país; **the film will be released ~ on
the 28th** la película se estrena en todo el país el día 28

native ['neɪtɪv] **Ⓐ** ADJ **1** [*town, country, soil*] natal;
[*inhabitant, culture, population*] indígena; [*plant, animal,
species*] autóctono; **the ~ peoples of the Amazon** los
pueblos indígenas del Amazonas; ~ **Britons** los nacidos en
Gran Bretaña; **to be ~ to** [*plant, animal*] ser originario de
2 (= *innate*) [*ability, talent*] natural, innato
Ⓑ N (= *local*) nativo/a *m/f*; (†*pej*) indígena *mf*
Ⓒ CPD ➤ **native land** patria *f* ➤ **native language** lengua *f*
materna ➤ **native speaker** hablante *mf* nativo/a; **a Spanish
~ speaker** un hablante nativo de español

Native American [,neɪtɪvə'merɪkən] ADJ, N americano/a
m/f nativo/a

Nativity [nə'tɪvɪtɪ] N **the** ~ la Natividad ➤ **Nativity play** auto
m de Navidad ➤ **Nativity scene** belén *m*, nacimiento *m*

NATO ['neɪtəʊ] N ABBR (= **North Atlantic Treaty
Organization**) OTAN *f*

natter* ['nætə'] (*Brit*) **Ⓐ** N charla *f*, plática *f* (*Mex*); **to have
a ~** charlar, platicar (*Mex*) (**with** con) **Ⓑ** VI charlar, platicar
(*Mex*)

natural ['nætʃrəl] **Ⓐ** ADJ **1** [*substance, disaster, remedy,
manner*] natural; **he died of ~ causes** murió de muerte
natural; **the rest of his ~ life** el resto de sus días
2 (= *understandable*) [*reaction, feeling*] natural, normal;
[*mistake*] comprensible; **it's only ~ that she should be upset**
es normal *or* natural que esté disgustada
3 (= *inborn*) [*ability, talent*] innato; [*reaction, fear*] instintivo;
he's a ~ leader es un líder innato
4 (= *biological*) [*father, mother, child*] biológico
Ⓑ N **1** (= *person*) **she's a ~ with computers** tiene un don
innato para los ordenadores
2 (*Mus*) (= *note*) nota *f* natural; (= *sign*) becuadro *m*
Ⓒ CPD ➤ **natural childbirth** parto *m* natural ➤ **natural gas**
gas *m* natural ➤ **natural history** historia *f* natural ➤ **natural
science** ciencia *f* de la naturaleza ➤ **natural selection**
selección *f* natural ➤ **natural wastage** (*Brit Ind*) bajas
voluntarias de los empleados de una empresa, y cuyos puestos
quedan sin cubrir; **the jobs will be lost through ~ wastage**
los puestos irán desapareciendo a medida que se
produzcan bajas voluntarias

naturalist ['nætʃrəlɪst] N naturalista *mf*

naturalization [,nætʃrələ'zeɪʃən] N naturalización *f*

naturalize ['nætʃrəlaɪz] VT **to become ~d** [*person*]
naturalizarse; [*plant, animal*] aclimatarse, establecerse

naturally ['nætʃrəlɪ] ADV **1** (= *by a natural process*) [*happen,
develop*] de forma natural
2 (= *by nature*) [*cheerful, cautious*] por naturaleza; **her hair is
~ curly** tiene el pelo rizado natural; **winning seems to come
~ to him** se diría que ganar no le supone ningún esfuerzo
3 (= *unaffectedly*) [*behave, speak*] con naturalidad
4 (= *as a result*) [*follow, lead*] como consecuencia natural
5 (= *obviously*) naturalmente, por supuesto; **naturally!** ¡por
supuesto!, ¡naturalmente!; ~ **enough** como es natural,
lógicamente

naturalness ['nætʃrəlnɪs] N naturalidad *f*

nature ['neɪtʃə'] **Ⓐ** N **1** (*of things*) naturaleza *f*; **situations
of an unusual ~** situaciones de naturaleza poco común;
evidence of this ~ pruebas de esta naturaleza; **by its very ~**
por su propia naturaleza; **documents of a technical ~**

documentos de carácter técnico; **the project is experimental in** ~ el proyecto es de carácter experimental; **we were unaware of the serious** ~ **of his illness** ignorábamos que su enfermedad fuera tan grave; **something of that** ~ algo por el estilo
2 [*of person*] carácter *m*; **to appeal to sb's better** ~ apelar al buen corazón de algn; **by** ~ por naturaleza; **to take advantage of sb's good** ~ abusar de la amabilidad de algn; **it is not in his** ~ **to lie** mentir no es propio de él
3 (= *natural life, environment*) naturaleza *f*; **to paint from** ~ pintar del natural; **it's ~'s way of fighting infection** es el mecanismo natural para combatir la infección
Ⓑ CPD ➤ **nature lover** amante *mf* de la naturaleza ➤ **nature reserve** reserva *f* natural ➤ **nature study** estudio *m* de la historia natural, historia *f* natural ➤ **nature trail** ruta *f* para el estudio de la naturaleza

-natured ['neɪtʃəd] ADJ (*ending in compounds*) de carácter ...; **good-natured** de carácter bondadoso

naturism ['neɪtʃərɪzəm] N (*esp Brit*) naturismo *m*

naturist ['neɪtʃərɪst] N (*esp Brit*) naturista *mf*

naturopath ['neɪtʃərəˌpæθ] N naturópata *mf*

naught [nɔːt] N **1** (*esp US Math*) = **nought 2** (†*poet*) (= *nothing*) nada *f*

naughtiness ['nɔːtɪnɪs] N (= *mischief*) travesuras *fpl*; (= *bad behaviour*) mala conducta *f*

naughty ['nɔːtɪ] ADJ (*compar* **naughtier**; *superl* **naughtiest**)
1 [*child*] travieso, malo; **you** ~ **boy!** (*angrily*) ¡mira que eres travieso or malo!; (*indulgently*) ¡anda, pillín or picaruelo!*; **you've been very** ~ has sido muy malo; **that was very** ~ **of you** eso ha estado muy feo; **I'm going to be** ~ **and have two cakes** voy a portarme mal y a comerme dos pasteles; **it was very** ~ **of you to leave without telling anyone** no estuvo nada bien que te marcharas sin decir nada
2 (= *risqué*) [*joke, song*] verde, colorado (*LAm*)

nausea ['nɔːsɪə] N náusea *f*

nauseate ['nɔːsɪeɪt] VT (*lit*) dar náuseas de; (*fig*) repugnar, asquear, dar asco de

nauseating ['nɔːsɪeɪtɪŋ] ADJ [*smell*] nauseabundo; [*crime, violence, hypocrisy*] repugnante, asqueroso

nauseatingly ['nɔːsɪeɪtɪŋlɪ] ADV **the film is** ~ **violent** la película es de una violencia repugnante; **he is** ~ **virtuous** es tan perfecto que da asco

nauseous ['nɔːsɪəs] ADJ **to feel** ~ sentir náuseas; **to make sb (feel)** ~ dar náuseas a algn

nautical ['nɔːtɪkəl] ADJ [*terms, matters, charts*] náutico, marítimo ➤ **nautical mile** milla *f* marina

naval ['neɪvəl] ADJ [*warfare, base, tradition*] naval; [*affairs, forces*] de la marina; [*officer*] de marina; [*power*] marítimo ➤ **naval academy** escuela *f* naval

nave [neɪv] N nave *f*

navel ['neɪvəl] N ombligo *m* ➤ **navel orange** naranja *f* návell

navigable ['nævɪɡəbl] ADJ [*river*] navegable

navigate ['nævɪɡeɪt] Ⓐ VT [+ *ship, plane*] conducir; [+ *sea, river*] navegar por Ⓑ VI (*at sea*) navegar; (*in car*) hacer de copiloto

navigation [ˌnævɪˈɡeɪʃən] N **1** (= *act*) navegación *f*
2 (= *science*) náutica *f*, navegación *f*

navigational [ˌnævɪˈɡeɪʃənl] ADJ [*instruments, system*] de navegación; ~ **aids** ayudas *fpl* a la navegación

navigator ['nævɪɡeɪtəʳ] N (*on ship*) oficial *mf* de derrota, oficial *mf* de navegación; (*Aer*) navegante *mf*

navvy†* ['nævɪ] N (*Brit*) peón *m* caminero

navy ['neɪvɪ] Ⓐ N **1** (= *ships*) armada *f*, flota *f*
2 (= *organization*) marina *f* de guerra **3** (= *colour*) (*also* ~ **blue**) azul *m* marino Ⓑ ADJ (*also* ~**-blue**) azul marino Ⓒ CPD ➤ **Navy Department** (*US*) Ministerio *m* de Marina

Nazareth ['næzərəθ] N Nazaret *m*

Nazi ['nɑːtsɪ] Ⓐ ADJ nazi, nazista Ⓑ N nazi *mf*

Nazism ['nɑːtsɪzəm] N nazismo *m*

NB ABBR **1** (= *nota bene*) NB **2** (*Canada*) = **New Brunswick**

NBA N ABBR (*US*) **1** = **National Basketball Association**

2 = **National Boxing Association**

NBC N ABBR (*US*) = **National Broadcasting Company**

NC ABBR (*US*) = **North Carolina**

NCO N ABBR (*Mil*) (= **non-commissioned officer**) suboficial *m*

ND, N.Dak. ABBR (*US*) = **North Dakota**

NDP N ABBR (= **Net Domestic Product**) PIN *m*

NE ABBR **1** (= **northeast**) NE **2** (*US*) = **Nebraska 3** (*US*) = **New England**

NEA N ABBR (*US*) = **National Educational Association**

Neanderthal [nɪˈændətɑːl] ADJ Neandertal, de Neandertal ➤ **Neanderthal man** hombre *m* de Neandertal

near [nɪəʳ] Ⓐ ADV **1** (*in place*) cerca; **he lives quite** ~ vive bastante cerca; **don't come any ~er!** ¡no te acerques más!
2 (*in time*) **the agreement brings peace a little ~er** este acuerdo nos acerca un poco más a la paz; **winter is drawing** ~ el invierno se acerca; **to be** ~ **at hand** [*object*] estar al alcance de la mano; [*event, season*] estar a la vuelta de la esquina
3 (*in level, degree*) **the ~est I ever got to winning** lo más cerca que estuve de ganar; **that's** ~ **enough*** [*numbers*] no merece la pena precisar más; [*amount*] con eso vale; **it isn't anywhere** ~ **enough*** con eso no basta ni mucho menos; **"have you finished it yet?" — "nowhere** ~**"*** —¿has terminado ya? —qué va, me falta muchísimo
4 (= *almost*) casi; **I came** ~ **to telling her everything** llegué casi a decírselo todo; ~ **on 3,000 people** casi 3.000 personas; **it's in** ~ **perfect condition** está casi en perfectas condiciones
Ⓑ PREP (*also* ~ **to**) **1** (*of place*) cerca de; **we weren't anywhere** ~ **the station** estábamos bastante or muy lejos de la estación; **if you come** ~ **me I'll kill you** como te me acerques, te mato; **nobody comes anywhere** ~ **him at swimming** (*fig*) en natación no le llega nadie ni a la suela del zapato; **the passage is** ~ **the end of the book** el trozo viene hacia el final del libro; **don't go** ~ **the edge** no te acerques al borde; **is there a bank** ~ **here?** ¿hay algún banco por aquí cerca?; **the schools** ~ **where I live** los colegios de mi barrio
2 (*in time*) **her birthday is** ~ **mine** su cumpleaños cae cerca del mío
3 (= *almost*) **she was** ~ **death** estaba al borde de la muerte; ~ **to tears** a punto de llorar
Ⓒ ADJ **1** (*in place*) cercano; **where's the ~est service station?** ¿dónde está la gasolinera más cercana?; **my house is** ~ **enough to walk** mi casa está muy cerca, se puede ir andando; **he had a** ~ **miss** (*Aut*) por poco chocó
2 (*in time*) próximo; **in the** ~ **future** en un futuro próximo; **the time is** ~ **when ...** falta poco para ...
3 (*in level, degree*) **£250 or ~est offer** 250 libras o precio a discutir; **he calculated the price to the ~est pound** redondeó el precio a la libra entera; **he won, but it was a** ~ **thing** ganó, pero por los pelos
4 [*relative*] cercano; **your ~est and dearest** tus seres más allegados y queridos
Ⓓ VT **1** (*in space*) acercarse a
2 (*in time*) **it was ~ing lunchtime** faltaba poco para la hora de comer; **I'm ~ing the end of my contract** falta poco para que venza mi contrato; **he is ~ing 50** frisa en los 50, tiene casi 50 años
3 (*in level, degree*) **the building is ~ing completion** el edificio está casi terminado
Ⓔ CPD ➤ **the Near East** el Cercano Oriente

nearby ['nɪəˈbaɪ] Ⓐ ADV cerca Ⓑ ADJ cercano; **we had a drink in a** ~ **pub** tomamos una copa en un bar cercano or que había cerca

nearly ['nɪəlɪ] ADV **1** (= *almost*) casi; **it's** ~ **three o'clock** son casi las tres; **I've** ~ **finished** casi he terminado; **we are** ~ **there** casi hemos llegado; **I (very)** ~ **lost it** casi lo pierdo, por poco lo pierdo; **he (very)** ~ **succeeded** estuvo a punto de conseguirlo **2** (*with negative*) **not** ~ ni con mucho, ni mucho menos; **that's not** ~ **enough** eso no es ni mucho menos suficiente; **it's not** ~ **ready** falta mucho para que esté listo

nearness ['nɪənɪs] N (*in place*) proximidad *f*, cercanía *f*; (*in time*) proximidad *f*, inminencia *f*

nearside ['nɪəsaɪd] (Brit Aut) **A** N (in Brit) lado m izquierdo; (most other countries) lado m derecho **B** ADJ [door, lane] (in Brit) de la izquierda; (most other countries) de la derecha

near-sighted ['nɪə'saɪtɪd] ADJ miope, corto de vista

near-sightedness ['nɪə'saɪtɪdnɪs] N miopía f

neat [niːt] ADJ (compar ~er; superl ~est) **1** (= tidy-looking) [room, desk, pile] ordenado; [garden] bien cuidado; [appearance] cuidado, pulcro, prolijo (SC); [clothes] muy cuidado; [work] bien presentado; **everything looks ~ and tidy** todo parece muy ordenado; **she always looks very ~** siempre va muy arreglada; **he has very ~ writing** tiene muy buena letra
2 (= organized) [person] ordenado, pulcro, prolijo (SC)
3 (= compact) [figure] bien proporcionado; [waist] delgado
4 (= clever) [solution] ingenioso, bueno; [explanation] claro
5 (US*) (= wonderful) **that's a ~ idea** ésa es una idea genial*; **those new apartments are really ~** esos nuevos apartamentos son muy chulos*
6 (Brit) (= undiluted) **I take it ~** [+ whisky, brandy] lo tomo solo; **half a litre of ~ whisky** medio litro de whisky puro

neatly ['niːtlɪ] ADV **1** (= tidily) [arrange, put] con cuidado, cuidadosamente; [write] claramente; **she is always very ~ dressed** siempre va muy arreglada **2** (= cleverly) [summarize, explain] con claridad, bien; [avoid] ingeniosamente, con habilidad **3** (= conveniently) [fit] perfectamente; [divide] claramente, fácilmente; **they do not fit ~ into categories** no se los puede encasillar tan fácilmente; **everything worked out very ~** todo se resolvió muy bien

neatness ['niːtnɪs] N **1** (= tidiness) [of room, garden, things] orden m; [of handwriting] claridad f; [of person's appearance] pulcritud f, prolijidad f (SC) **2** (= cleverness) habilidad f, destreza f **3** (= clarity) [of explanation] claridad f

Nebr. ABBR (US) = **Nebraska**

nebulizer ['nebjʊˌlaɪzə'] N nebulizador m

nebulous ['nebjʊləs] ADJ vago, nebuloso

NEC N ABBR = **National Executive Committee**

necessarily ['nesɪsərɪlɪ] ADV necesariamente, forzosamente; **not ~** no necesariamente; **it doesn't ~ follow that ...** no implica necesariamente or por fuerza que ...; **this is not ~ the case** esto no tiene por qué ser así

necessary ['nesɪsərɪ] **A** ADJ **1** (= required) necesario; **to be ~ to do sth** ser necesario or preciso hacer algo; **is it ~ for us to go?** ¿es necesario or preciso que vayamos?; **if ~** si es necesario or preciso; **don't do more than is ~** no hagas más de lo necesario; **do whatever (is) ~ to find him** haz todo lo posible para encontrarlo; **when/where ~** cuando/donde sea necesario or preciso
2 (= inevitable) [consequence, conclusion] inevitable
B N **I'll do the ~** haré lo que haga falta, haré lo que sea necesario

necessitate [nɪ'sesɪteɪt] VT requerir, exigir

necessity [nɪ'sesɪtɪ] N necesidad f; **there is no ~ for you to do it** no es necesario que lo hagas; **a regrettable ~** un mal necesario; **of ~** necesariamente, forzosamente, por fuerza; **♦ PROV ~ is the mother of invention** la necesidad agudiza el ingenio

neck [nek] **A** N **1** [of person] cuello m; [of animal] pescuezo m, cuello m; **the rain ran down my ~** la lluvia me corría por el cuello; **to be ~ and ~** ir parejos; **to break one's ~** desnucarse; **♦ IDIOMS to get it in the ~*** (= be punished) cargársela*; (= be told off) llevarse una buena bronca or (Sp) un buen rapapolvo*; **to risk one's ~** jugarse el pellejo or el tipo*; **to save one's ~** salvar el pellejo or el tipo*; **to stick one's ~ out** arriesgarse; **to be in sth up to one's ~*** (in trouble, plot) estar metido hasta el cuello en algo*; **to be up to one's ~ (in work)*** estar hasta arriba de trabajo*
2 [of dress, T-shirt etc] cuello m, escote m; [of bottle] cuello m, gollete m; [of womb] cuello m; **♦ IDIOM in your ~ of the woods*** por tu zona
3 (Brit*) = **nerve A4**
B VI (*) [couple] besuquearse*

neckerchief ['nekətʃiːf] N pañuelo m

necklace ['neklɪs] N collar m

neckline ['neklaɪn] N escote m; **with a low ~** escotado

necktie ['nektaɪ] N (US) corbata f

necropolis [ne'krɒpəlɪs] N necrópolis f inv

nectar ['nektə'] N néctar m

nectarine ['nektərɪːn] N nectarina f

née [neɪ] ADJ **Mary Green, ~ Smith** Mary Green, Smith de (apellido de) soltera

need [niːd] **A** N (= necessity) necesidad f (for, of de); **the ~s of industry** las necesidades de la industria; **my ~s are few** es poco lo que necesito; **to be in ~ of ♦ have ~ of** necesitar; **there's no ~ to worry** no hay por qué preocuparse; **there's no ~ for you to go** no hace falta or no es preciso que vayas; **there's no ~ for that sort of language!** ¡no hay ninguna necesidad de usar ese vocabulario!, ¡no hace falta usar ese vocabulario!; **in times of ~** en momentos de apuro or necesidad
B VT **1** [person] necesitar; **I ~ a bigger car** necesito or me hace falta un coche más grande; **I ~ two more to make up the series** me faltan dos para completar la serie; **he ~s watching** hay que vigilarlo; **that's all I ~!** (iro) ¡sólo me faltaba eso!, ¡lo que me faltaba!; **it's just what I ~ed** es precisamente lo que necesitaba; **a much ~ed holiday** unas vacaciones muy necesarias; **he ~ed no asking** no se hizo de rogar; **you only ~ed to ask** no tenía más que pedírmelo; **I ~ to get some petrol** tengo que echar gasolina; **they don't ~ to be told all the details** no es preciso or no hace falta contarles todos los detalles; **who ~s more motorways?** ¿para qué queremos más autopistas?
2 (= require) [+ concentration, skill, care] requerir; **this room ~s painting** este cuarto hay que or hace falta pintarlo; **I gave it a much ~ed wash** le di un buen lavado, que era lo que necesitaba
3 (impersonal) **it doesn't ~ to be done now** no hace falta hacerlo ahora; **it doesn't ~ me to tell him** no hace falta que yo se lo diga; **it ~ed a war to alter that** fue necesaria una guerra para cambiar eso
C AUX VB **~ I go?** ¿es necesario que vaya?, ¿tengo que ir?; **I ~ hardly remind you that ...** no hace falta que les recuerde que ...; **it ~ not follow that ...** lo que no significa necesariamente que ...; **she ~n't have worried** no tenía de qué preocuparse; **I ~n't have bothered** fue trabajo perdido

needle ['niːdl] **A** N aguja f; **♦ IDIOMS to give sb the ~** (US*) pinchar a algn, meterse con algn; **it's like looking for a ~ in a haystack** es como buscar una aguja en un pajar **B** VT **1** (*) (= nag) pinchar*, fastidiar **2** (US**) [+ drink] añadir alcohol a **C** CPD **► needle exchange** (centro m de) intercambio m de jeringuillas

needlepoint ['niːdlpɔɪnt] N bordado m sobre cañamazo, cañamazo m

needless ['niːdlɪs] ADJ innecesario, superfluo; **~ to say ...** huelga decir que ..., ni qué decir tiene que ...; **he was, ~ to say, drunk** ni qué decir tiene que estaba borracho

needlessly ['niːdlɪslɪ] ADV innecesariamente; **you worry quite ~** te inquietas sin motivo alguno

needlework ['niːdlwɜːk] N (= sewing) labor f de aguja; (= embroidery) bordado m; **to do ~** hacer labores de aguja

needn't ['niːdnt] = **need not**

needy ['niːdɪ] **A** ADJ (compar **needier**; superl **neediest**) necesitado **B** NPL **the ~** los necesitados

negate [nɪ'geɪt] VT anular, invalidar

negative ['negətɪv] **A** ADJ negativo; **a ~ answer** una negativa, una respuesta negativa; **the test proved ~** el análisis dio negativo **B** N **1** (= negative answer) negativa f; **he answered in the ~** contestó negativamente, contestó que no **2** (Gram) negación f; **in the ~** en negativo **3** (Phot) negativo m **4** (Elec) polo m negativo **C** CPD **► negative equity** (Brit) cantidad hipotecada que sobrepasa el valor de la vivienda

negativity [ˌnegə'tɪvɪtɪ] N negatividad f

neglect [nɪ'glekt] **A** N (= state) abandono m; [of rules, duty] incumplimiento m; [of friends, family] desatención f; **the garden was in a state of ~** el jardín estaba muy descuidado or abandonado; **the plants had died of ~** las plantas se habían muerto de no cuidarlas
B VT **1** [+ obligations] descuidar, desatender; [+ duty] no cumplir con, faltar a; [+ friends, family] desatender;

[+ *opportunity*] desperdiciar, desaprovechar; [+ *work, garden*] descuidar
2 (= *omit*) **to ~ to do sth** omitir hacer algo; **they ~ed to mention this fact** omitieron mencionar este hecho, no mencionaron este hecho

neglected [nɪˈglektɪd] ADJ [*child*] desatendido; [*house, garden*] descuidado, abandonado; **he is a much ~ composer** es un compositor insuficientemente reconocido

neglectful [nɪˈglektfʊl] ADJ negligente; **to be ~ of** [+ *family, children*] desatender a; [+ *work*] descuidar; [+ *duty*] no cumplir con

negligee [ˈneglɪʒeɪ] N (= *nightdress*) salto *m* de cama, negligé *m*; (= *housecoat*) bata *f*, negligé *m*

negligence [ˈneglɪdʒəns] N negligencia *f*; **through ~** por negligencia

negligent [ˈneglɪdʒənt] ADJ negligente; **to be ~ in doing sth** pecar de negligencia al hacer algo

negligently [ˈneglɪdʒəntlɪ] ADV con negligencia

negligible [ˈneglɪdʒəbl] ADJ [*amount*] insignificante; [*damage, difference*] insignificante, sin importancia

negotiable [nɪˈgəʊʃɪəbl] ADJ **1** (*Comm*) negociable; **"salary negotiable"** "salario o sueldo a convenir" **2** [*road etc*] transitable; [*river*] salvable

negotiate [nɪˈgəʊʃɪeɪt] Ⓐ VT **1** (= *arrange*) [+ *treaty*] negociar; [+ *loan, deal*] negociar, gestionar **2** (= *pass*) [+ *bend*] tomar; [+ *hill*] subir; [+ *obstacle*] salvar, franquear; [+ *river, stream*] pasar, cruzar Ⓑ VI negociar (**with** con); **to ~ for** negociar para obtener

negotiating table [nɪˈgəʊʃɪeɪtɪŋˌteɪbl] N mesa *f* de negociaciones

negotiation [nɪˌgəʊʃɪˈeɪʃən] N **1** (= *negotiating*) negociación *f*; **the treaty is under ~** el tratado está siendo negociado; **that will be a matter for ~** eso tendrá que ser negociado, eso tendrá que someterse a negociación **2** negotiations negociaciones *fpl*, tratativas *fpl* (*SC*); **to be in/enter into ~s with sb** estar/entrar en negociaciones con algn

negotiator [nɪˈgəʊʃɪeɪtəʳ] N negociador(a) *m/f*

Negro [ˈniːgrəʊ] Ⓐ ADJ († *or* ***) negro Ⓑ N (*pl* **~es**) († *or* ***) negro *m* Ⓒ CPD ➤ **Negro spiritual** espiritual *m*

neigh [neɪ] Ⓐ N relincho *m* Ⓑ VI relinchar

neighbour, neighbor (*US*) [ˈneɪbəʳ] N (*lit*) vecino/a *m/f*; (= *fellow being*) prójimo/a *mf*, semejante *m*

neighbourhood, neighborhood (*US*) [ˈneɪbəhʊd] Ⓐ N **1** (= *area*) barrio *m*, vecindario *m* **2** (= *surrounding area*) alrededores *mpl*, cercanías *fpl* **3** (*fig*) **in the ~ of** alrededor de; **somewhere in the ~** por allí Ⓑ CPD [*supermarket, chemist, policeman*] de barrio ➤ **neighbourhood watch scheme** grupo *m* de vigilancia de los (propios) vecinos

neighbouring, neighboring (*US*) [ˈneɪbərɪŋ] ADJ [*towns, villages*] cercano, vecino; [*houses, streets, fields*] cercano, de las proximidades; [*state, country*] vecino; **the people at the ~ table** la gente de la mesa de al lado

neighbourly, neighborly (*US*) [ˈneɪbəlɪ] ADJ [*person*] amable; [*attitude*] de buen vecino, amable

neither [ˈnaɪðəʳ] Ⓐ ADV **~ ... nor** ni ... ni; **~ he nor I can go** ni él ni yo podemos ir; **he ~ smokes nor drinks** ni fuma ni bebe; **that's ~ here nor there** eso no viene al caso Ⓑ CONJ tampoco; **if you aren't going, ~ am I** si tú no vas, yo tampoco; **"I don't like it" — "~ do I"** —a mí no me gusta —a mí tampoco; **~ will he agree to sell it** ni consiente en venderlo tampoco Ⓒ PRON **~ of them has any money** ninguno de los dos tiene dinero, ni el uno ni el otro tiene dinero Ⓓ ADJ ninguno de los dos; **~ car is for sale** ninguno de los dos coches está a la venta

neofascism [ˈniːəʊˈfæʃɪzəm] N neofascismo *m*

neofascist [ˈniːəʊˈfæʃɪst] ADJ, N neofascista *mf*

neolithic [ˌniːəʊˈlɪθɪk] ADJ neolítico

neologism [nɪˈɒlədʒɪzəm] N neologismo *m*

neon [ˈniːɒn] CPD ➤ **neon light** luz *f* de neón ➤ **neon sign** anuncio *m* de neón

neonatal [ˈniːəʊˌneɪtl] ADJ neonatal

neonazi [ˈniːəʊˈnɑːtsɪ] Ⓐ ADJ neonazi, neonazista Ⓑ N neonazi *mf*

Nepal [nɪˈpɔːl] N Nepal *m*

Nepalese [ˌnepɔːˈliːz] ADJ, N nepalés/esa *m/f*

nephew [ˈnevjuː] N sobrino *m*

nephritis [neˈfraɪtɪs] N nefritis *f*

nepotism [ˈnepətɪzəm] N nepotismo *m*

Neptune [ˈneptjuːn] N Neptuno *m*

nerd** [nɜːd] N pazguato/a *m/f*

nerdy** [ˈnɜːdɪ] ADJ pazguato, timorato

nerve [nɜːv] Ⓐ N **1** nervio *m*; **my ~s are on edge** tengo los nervios de punta; **it/he gets on my ~s*** me pone los nervios de punta, me saca de quicio; **to be living on one's ~s** (*Brit*) vivir en estado de tensión constante; ✦ IDIOM **to have ~s of steel** tener nervios de acero
2 nerves (= *nervousness*) nerviosismo *msing*, nervios *mpl*; **she suffers from ~s** padece de los nervios, sufre trastornos nerviosos; **to be in a state of ~s** estar muy nervioso, estar hipertenso
3 (= *courage*) valor *m*; **I wouldn't have the ~ to do that!** ¡yo no me atrevería a *or* yo no tendría el valor de hacer eso!; **to keep one's ~** mantenerse firme, no amilanarse; **to lose one's ~** perder el valor, rajarse*
4 (*) (= *cheek*) caradura* *f*, cara* *f*; **of all the ~!** ◇ **what a ~!** ¡qué caradura!*, ¡qué frescura!*; **you've got a ~!** ¡qué cara tienes!*, ¡eres un caradura!*; **he had the ~ to ask for money** tuvo la cara de pedir dinero*
Ⓑ CPD ➤ **nerve cell** neurona *f*, célula *f* nerviosa ➤ **nerve centre, nerve center** (*US*) centro *m* nervioso; (*fig*) punto *m* neurálgico ➤ **nerve gas** gas *m* nervioso

nerve-racking [ˈnɜːvˌrækɪŋ] ADJ [*wait, experience*] angustioso; [*drive, journey, interview*] estresante

nervous [ˈnɜːvəs] ADJ (= *anxious*) nervioso; **to be/feel ~** estar nervioso; (= *frightened*) tener miedo; **I was ~ about the meeting** estaba nervioso pensando en la reunión, la reunión me tenía nervioso; **I was ~ about speaking in public** me asustaba hablar en público; **to get ~** ponerse nervioso; **to make sb ~** (*gen*) poner nervioso a algn; (= *frighten*) dar miedo a algn; **to be a ~ wreck*** (*temporarily*) ser un manojo de nervios; (*more permanently*) estar hecho polvo de los nervios* ➤ **nervous breakdown** crisis *f inv* nerviosa ➤ **nervous exhaustion** agotamiento *m* nervioso ➤ **nervous system** sistema *m* nervioso

nervously [ˈnɜːvəslɪ] ADV nerviosamente; **he laughed ~** soltó una risa nerviosa, rió nerviosamente; **I waited ~ in the hall** esperé nervioso en el hall

nervy* [ˈnɜːvɪ] ADJ (*compar* **nervier**; *superl* **nerviest**) **1** (*Brit*) (= *tense*) nervioso **2** (*US*) (= *cheeky*) descarado, caradura*

nest [nest] Ⓐ N [*of bird*] nido *m*; [*of hen*] nidal *m*; [*of rat*] madriguera *f*; [*of mouse*] ratonera *f*; [*of wasps, hornets*] avispero *m*; [*of ants*] hormiguero *m* Ⓑ VI anidar, hacer su nido Ⓒ CPD ➤ **nest egg** ahorros *mpl*

nestle [ˈnesl] VI **to ~ up to sb** arrimarse *or* acurrucarse junto a algn; **to ~ down in bed** acurrucarse en la cama; **a village nestling among the hills** un pueblo abrigado por las colinas

NET N ABBR (*US*) = **National Educational Television**

net¹ [net] Ⓐ N **1** (*for fish, butterflies, also Sport*) red *f*; (*for hair*) redecilla *f*; (= *fabric*) tul *m*; ✦ IDIOMS **to fall into the ~** caer en la trampa; **to slip through the ~** escapar de la red
2 (= *network*) red *f*; **the Net** (= *Internet*) la Red, Internet *m or f* Ⓑ VT [+ *fish*] pescar (con red); [+ *criminal*] atrapar Ⓒ CPD ➤ **net curtain** (*Brit*) visillo *m*

net², **nett** (*Brit*) [net] Ⓐ VT (= *earn*) ganar en limpio; (= *produce*) producir en limpio; **the new tax will ~ the government £50m** el nuevo impuesto le supondrá al gobierno unos ingresos netos de 50 millones de libras; **the deal ~ted him £50,000** se embolsó 50.000 libras en el negocio Ⓑ ADJ **1** (*Fin etc*) neto; **~ of tax** deducidos los impuestos; **at a ~ profit of 5%** con un beneficio neto del 5% **2** [*result, effect*] final, global Ⓒ CPD ➤ **net assets** activo *msing* neto ➤ **net income** renta *f* neta ➤ **net loss** pérdida *f* neta ➤ **net payment** importe *m* neto ➤ **net weight** peso *m* neto

netball ['netbɔːl] N (*Brit*) *especie de baloncesto jugado especialmente por mujeres*

Netherlands ['neðələndz] NPL **the** ~ los Países Bajos

netiquette ['netiket] N netiqueta *f*, *normas de conducta oficiosas para navegar por Internet*

netsurfer ['net,sɜːfəʳ] N internauta *m/f*

nett [net] (*Brit*) = **net²**

netting ['netɪŋ] N (= *mesh*) malla *f*; (= *nets*) redes *fpl*

nettle ['netl] ➊ N ortiga *f*; ✦ IDIOM **to grasp the** ~ (*Brit*) agarrar el toro por los cuernos ➌ VT (*) picar*, molestar; **somewhat ~d by this** algo molesto por esto ➍ CPD ➤ **nettle rash** urticaria *f*

network ['netwɜːk] ➊ N (*gen, Comput*) red *f*; (*Rad, TV*) red *f*, cadena *f*; **the national railway** ~ la red nacional de ferrocarriles ➌ VT (*Rad, TV*) difundir por la red de emisoras, emitir en cadena; (*Comput*) conectar a la red ➍ VI hacer contactos (*en el mundo de los negocios*)

networking ['netwɜːkɪŋ] N establecimiento *m* de contactos

neuralgia [njʊəˈrældʒə] N neuralgia *f*

neurological [,njʊərəˈlɒdʒɪkəl] ADJ neurológico

neurologist [njʊəˈrɒlədʒɪst] N neurólogo/a *m/f*

neurology [njʊəˈrɒlədʒɪ] N neurología *f*

neuron ['njʊərɒn] N neurona *f*

neurosis [njʊəˈrəʊsɪs] N (*pl* **neuroses** [njʊəˈrəʊsiːz]) neurosis *f inv*

neurosurgeon [,njʊərəʊˈsɜːdʒən] N neurocirujano/a *m/f*

neurotic [njʊˈrɒtɪk] ADJ, N neurótico/a *m/f*

neurotransmitter [,njʊərəʊtrænzˈmɪtəʳ] N neurotransmisor *m*

neuter ['njuːtəʳ] ➊ ADJ (*Ling*) neutro ➌ N (*Ling*) neutro *m*; **in the** ~ en género neutro ➍ VT [+ *male animal*] castrar, capar; [+ *female animal*] esterilizar

neutral ['njuːtrəl] ➊ ADJ (*gen*) neutro; (= *impartial*) neutral; **~ shoe cream** betún *m* incoloro ➌ N **1** (*Pol*) (= *person*) persona *f* neutral; (= *country*) país *m* neutral **2** (*Aut*) **in** ~ en punto muerto

neutrality [njuːˈtrælɪtɪ] N neutralidad *f*

neutralize ['njuːtrəlaɪz] VT neutralizar

neutron ['njuːtrɒn] N neutrón *m* ➤ **neutron bomb** bomba *f* de neutrones

Nev. ABBR (*US*) = **Nevada**

never ['nevəʳ] ADV **1** (= *not ever*) nunca; **you** ~ **saw anything like it** nunca se ha visto nada parecido; ~ **leave valuables in your car** no dejen nunca objetos de valor en el coche; **never!** ¡jamás!; ~ **again!** ¡nunca más!; **I** ~ **expected to see him again** no contaba con volverlo a ver; **scenes** ~ **before shown on TV** imágenes *fpl* nunca vistas con anterioridad en televisión; **it had** ~ **been tried before** no se había intentado antes; ~**, ever do that again!** ¡no vuelvas a hacer eso nunca jamás!; ~ **in all my life have I been so embarrassed** en mi vida *or* jamás en la vida he pasado tanta vergüenza; **I've** ~ **yet known him to fail** no lo he visto nunca fracasar **2** (*in expressions*) **never!*** ¿en serio?, ¡no puede ser!; ~ **mind** no importa, no te preocupes; **well I** ~**!*** ¡no me digas!, ¡no me lo puedo creer!; ✦ IDIOM **never say never** nunca digas nunca jamás

never-ending ['nevəˈrendɪŋ] ADJ interminable, inacabable

nevertheless [,nevəðəˈles] ADV sin embargo, no obstante; **it is** ~ **true that ...** sin embargo *or* no obstante es verdad que ...

new [njuː] ➊ ADJ (*compar* ~**er**; *superl* ~**est**) **1** nuevo

> Put **nuevo** after the noun when **new** means brand-new but before the noun when it means another or latest:

the sales of ~ **cars** las ventas de automóviles nuevos; **I've bought a** ~ **coat** me he comprado un abrigo nuevo; **the** ~ **prime minister** el nuevo primer ministro; **the** ~ **people at number five** los nuevos vecinos del número cinco; **the** ~ **model** el nuevo modelo; ~ **boy/girl** (*Scol*) alumno/a *f*

nuevo/a; ~ **face** cara *f* nueva; **it's as good as** ~ está como nuevo; **I feel like a** ~ **man** me siento como nuevo; **he's been a** ~ **man since he got divorced** desde que se ha divorciado parece otro; **that's a** ~ **one on me!** ¡la primera vez que lo oigo!; **I'm** ~ **to the area** hace poco que vivo aquí; **hi, what's** ~**?*** hola, ¿que hay de nuevo?; **so what's** ~**?*** (*iro*) ¡qué *or* vaya novedad! **2** (= *recent*) [*bread*] recién hecho; [*wine*] joven; [*crop*] nuevo ➌ CPD ➤ **new age** new age *f*; (*as adj*) [*music, philosophy*] new age *inv* ➤ **New Brunswick** Nuevo Brunswick *m* ➤ **New Caledonia** Nueva Caledonia *f* ➤ **New England** Nueva Inglaterra *f* ➤ **New Englander** habitante *o* nativo de Nueva Inglaterra ➤ **New Guinea** Nueva Guinea *f* ➤ **New Hampshire** Nuevo Hampshire *m*, Nueva Hampshire *f* ➤ **the New Hebrides** las Nuevas Hébridas ➤ **New Jersey** Nueva Jersey *f* ➤ **new man** (*esp Brit*) hombre de ideas modernas que se ocupa de tareas tradicionalmente femeninas como el cuidado de la casa y de los niños ➤ **New Mexico** Nuevo México *m* ➤ **new moon** luna *f* nueva ➤ **New Orleans** Nueva Orleáns *f* ➤ **new potatoes** patatas *f* nuevas ➤ **New South Wales** Nueva Gales *f* del Sur ➤ **the New Testament** el Nuevo Testamento ➤ **new town** (*Brit*) ciudad recién creada de la nada ➤ **the New World** el Nuevo Mundo ➤ **New Year** Año *m* Nuevo; **to bring** *o* **see in the New Year** celebrar el Año Nuevo; **happy New Year!** ¡feliz Año Nuevo! ➤ **New Year resolutions** buenos propósitos *mpl* del año nuevo ➤ **New Year's** (*US**) = **New Year's Day, New Year's Eve** ➤ **New Year's Day** el día de Año Nuevo ➤ **New Year's Eve** Nochevieja *f* ➤ **New York** Nueva York *f*; (*before noun*) neoyorquino ➤ **New Yorker** neoyorquino/a *m/f* ➤ **New Zealand** Nueva Zelanda *f*, Nueva Zelandia *f* (*LAm*); *ver tb* www.govt.nz/en/aboutnz; (*before noun*) neocelandés, neozelandés ➤ **New Zealander** neocelandés/esa *m/f*, neozelandés/esa *m/f*

newbie* ['njuːbɪ] N novato/a *m/f*, principiante *mf*

newborn ['njuːbɔːn] ADJ [*baby*] recién nacido

newcomer ['njuːˌkʌməʳ] N recién llegado/a *m/f*; **they were ~s to the area** eran nuevos en la zona, en la zona eran unos recién llegados

new-fangled ['njuːˌfæŋɡld] ADJ (*pej*) moderno, tan de moda

new-found ['njuːfaʊnd] ADJ [*talent*] recién descubierto; [*wealth, freedom*] recién adquirido; [*friend*] nuevo; **his ~ enthusiasm** su recién estrenado entusiasmo

Newfoundland ['njuːfəndlənd] N **1** (*Geog*) Terranova *f* **2** (*also* ~ **dog**) perro *m* de Terranova

new-laid ['njuːˈleɪd] ADJ [*egg*] fresco, recién puesto

new-look [,njuːˈlʊk] ADJ nuevo, renovado; **the ~ Labour Party** el nuevo *or* renovado Partido Laborista; **this is the ~ me** esta es mi nueva imagen

newly ['njuːlɪ] ADV recién; ~ **made/arrived** recién hecho/llegado

newlyweds ['njuːlɪwedz] NPL recién casados *mpl*

new-mown ['njuːˈməʊn] ADJ recién segado, recién cortado

newness ['njuːnɪs] N [*of car, clothes*] lo nuevo; [*of idea, fashion*] novedad *f*

news [njuːz] ➊ NSING **1** (*also* **piece of** ~) noticia *f*; **that's wonderful ~!** ¡qué buena noticia!; **some sad** ~ ◇ **a sad piece of** ~ una triste noticia; **is there any ~ about Bob?** ¿hay noticias de Bob?; **so you think you're going out tonight? well, I've got** ~ **for you!** (*iro*) si crees que vas a salir esta noche, te vas a llevar una sorpresa; **to be bad ~*** [*person*] ser un ave de mal agüero; [*thing*] ser mal asunto*; **when the** ~ **broke** al saberse la noticia; **that's good** ~ es una buena noticia; **they're in the** ~ son de actualidad; **it was** ~ **to me** me pilló de nuevas*; ✦ PROV **no** ~ **is good** ~ la falta de noticias es una buena señal **2** **the** ~ (*Rad*) las noticias, el noticiario; (*TV*) las noticias, el telediario (*Sp*), el noticiero (*LAm*), el noticioso (*And*) ➌ CPD ➤ **news agency** agencia *f* de noticias ➤ **news broadcast, news bulletin** boletín *m* informativo ➤ **news conference** rueda *f* de prensa ➤ **news dealer** (*US*) vendedor/a *m/f* de periódicos ➤ **news desk** redacción *f* ➤ **the news headlines** el resumen de las noticias ➤ **news item** noticia *f* ➤ **news magazine** revista *f* de información general ➤ **news release** (*US*) comunicado *m* de prensa

newsagent ['njuːzˌeɪdʒənt] N (*Brit*) vendedor(a) *m/f* de periódicos; **~'s tienda** *f or* quiosco *m* de periódicos

newscast ['nju:zka:st] N (*esp US*) noticiario *m*, noticiero *m* (*LAm*), noticioso *m* (*And*)

newscaster ['nju:z'ka:stə'] N locutor(a) *m/f*

newsdealer ['nju:z'di:lə'] N (*US*) vendedor(a) *m/f* de periódicos

newsflash ['nju:zflæʃ] N flash *m*, noticia *f* de última hora

newsgroup ['nju:zgru:p] N (*Internet*) grupo *m* de noticias

newsletter ['nju:z,letə'] N boletín *m* informativo

newsman ['nju:zmæn] N (*pl* **newsmen**) (*Press*) periodista *m*, reportero *m*; (*TV, Rad*) locutor *m*

newspaper ['nju:s,peɪpə'] N (*gen*) periódico *m*; (= *daily*) diario *m*; (= *material*) papel *m* de periódico ➤ **newspaper cutting** recorte *m* de periódico ➤ **newspaper report** reportaje *m*

newspaperman ['nju:z,peɪpəmæn] N (*pl* **newspapermen**) periodista *m*, reportero *m*

newsprint ['nju:zprɪnt] N papel *m* prensa, papel *m* continuo; **acres of ~ have been devoted to the subject** han corrido ríos de tinta sobre el asunto

newsreader ['nju:z,ri:də'] N (*Brit*) locutor(a) *m/f*

newsreel ['nju:zri:l] N noticiario *m*, documental *m* de actualidades, ≈ Nodo *m* (*Sp*)

newsroom ['nju:zrʊm] N sala *f* de redacción

newsstand ['nju:zstænd] N quiosco *m* de periódicos y revistas

newsworthy ['nju:z,wɜ:ðɪ] ADJ de interés periodístico; **it's not ~** no es noticia, no tiene interés periodístico

newsy* ['nju:zɪ] ADJ lleno de noticias

newt [nju:t] N tritón *m*

next [nekst] Ⓐ ADJ **1** (*time*) (*in future*) próximo; (*in past*) siguiente; **~ month/year** (*in future*) el mes/año que viene, el mes/año próximo, el mes/año entrante (*esp LAm*); **the ~ month/year** (*in past*) el mes/año siguiente; **(the) ~ day/ morning** al día/a la mañana siguiente; **she'll have been gone six months ~ Friday** el viernes que viene *or* el viernes próximo hará seis meses que se marchó; **the week after ~** la semana que viene *or* la semana próxima no, la siguiente *or* la otra; **this time ~ week** la semana que viene a estas horas; **this time ~ year** el año que viene por estas fechas; **(the) ~ time you see him** la próxima vez que lo veas; **from one moment/day to the ~** de un momento/día para otro **2** (*in order*) próximo, siguiente; **~ please!** ¡el siguiente por favor!; **I'm/you're ~** me/te toca (a mí/ti); **she was ~ to arrive** ella fue la próxima *or* siguiente en llegar; **he's ~ after me** es el primero después de mí; **it's the ~ road but one** es la segunda calle después de ésta; **on the ~ page** en la siguiente página; **the ~ size up/down** (*in clothes*) una talla más grande/más pequeña; (*in shoes*) un número más grande/más pequeño; **I get out at the ~ stop** me bajo en la próxima *or* siguiente parada; **the ~ thing I knew he was gone** cuando me quise dar cuenta se había ido; **who's ~?** ¿a quién le toca ahora?, ¿quién sigue? **3** (= *adjacent*) **the ~ house/room** la casa/el cuarto de al lado; **she lives in the ~ street to me** vive en la calle contigua a la mía; **~ door** (= *in adjacent house*) (en la casa de) al lado; **I went ~ door to the bathroom** fui al baño que estaba (en el cuarto de) al lado; **~ door to** al lado de; **I live ~ door to her** vivo en la casa del lado de la suya *or* contigua a la suya; **the girl/boy ~ door** la hija/el hijo del vecino; **I'm as much against violence as the ~ person, but ...** estoy tan en contra de la violencia como cualquiera, pero ...

Ⓑ ADV **1** (*in past*) después, luego; **what did he do ~?** ¿qué hizo después *or* luego?; **when I ~ saw him** cuando lo volví a ver; **I ~ saw him in Rome** la siguiente vez que lo vi fue en Roma

2 (*in future*) **what do we do ~?** ¿y ahora qué hacemos?; **~ we put the salt in** a continuación *or* ahora añadimos la sal; **when ~ you see him** cuando lo vuelvas a ver, la próxima vez que lo veas; **whatever ~!** ¡lo que faltaba!

3 (*of place, order*) **who's the ~ tallest boy?** ¿quién le sigue en altura?; **it's the ~ best thing to having your own swimming pool** si no puedes tener tu propia piscina, esto es lo mejor; **what comes ~?** ¿qué viene ahora?, ¿qué sigue?

4 ~ to (= *beside, compared to*) al lado de; (= *after*) después de; (= *almost*) casi; **his room is ~ to mine** su habitación está al lado de la mía; **I was sitting ~ to her** estaba sentado a su lado; **to wear silk ~ to one's skin** llevar seda en contacto directo con la piel; **~ to her I felt totally inept** al lado de ella, me sentía totalmente inútil; **~ to Spain, what country do you like best?** ¿después de España, cuál es tu país preferido?; **the ~ to last row** la penúltima fila; **I know ~ to nothing about computers** no sé casi nada de ordenadores, sé poquísimo de ordenadores; **we got it for ~ to nothing** lo conseguimos por poquísimo dinero

Ⓒ CPD ➤ **next of kin** familiar(es) *m(pl)* más cercano(s), pariente(s) *m(pl)* más cercano(s)

next-door ['neks'dɔ:'] ADJ **~ flat** piso *m* de al lado; **~ neighbour** vecino/a *m/f* de al lado

NF ABBR (*Canada*) = **Newfoundland**

NFL N ABBR (*US*) = **National Football League**

Nfld. ABBR (*Canada*) = **Newfoundland**

NFU N ABBR (*Brit*) = **National Farmers' Union**

NG ABBR (*US*) = **National Guard**

NGO N ABBR (= *non-governmental organization*) ONG *f*

NH ABBR (*US*) = **New Hampshire**

NHL N ABBR (*US*) = **National Hockey League**

NHS N ABBR (*Brit*) (= *National Health Service*) Sistema *m* Nacional de Salud

NI ABBR = **National Insurance**

Niagara [naɪˈægrə] N Niágara *m* ➤ **Niagara Falls** Cataratas *fpl* del Niágara

nib [nɪb] N plumilla *f*, plumín *m*

nibble ['nɪbl] Ⓐ N **1** (= *bite*) mordisquito *m* **2** (= *food*) bocado *m*; **I feel like a ~** me apetece comer algo, no me vendría mal un bocado; **nibbles** (*Brit*) (*at party etc*) comida *f* sing para picar Ⓑ VT [*person*] mordisquear, mordiscar; [*fish*] picar; [*rat, mouse*] roer Ⓒ VI **to ~ (at)** picar

NIC N ABBR (*Brit*) = **National Insurance Contribution**

NICAM ['naɪkæm] N ABBR = **near-instantaneous companding audio multiplex**

Nicaragua [,nɪkəˈrægjʊə] N Nicaragua *f*

Nicaraguan [,nɪkəˈrægjʊən] ADJ, N nicaragüense *mf*

nice [naɪs] ADJ (*compar* **~r**; *superl* **~st**) **1** (= *pleasant*) [*book, holiday, evening*] bueno, agradable, lindo (*LAm*); [*weather*] bueno; [*food, aroma*] rico

---

Use **buen** not **bueno** before a masculine singular noun:

~ weather buen tiempo; **it's very ~ here** se está muy bien aquí; **it would be ~ to speak a foreign language** estaría bien poder hablar otro idioma; **it was ~ to see you** me ha alegrado mucho verte; **did you have a ~ day?** (*on trip*) ¿lo pasaste bien?; **it would be ~ if you came too** me gustaría que tú también vinieses; **it smells ~** huele bien **2** (= *likeable*) simpático, buena gente*, majo (*Sp**) **3** (= *kind*) amable; **he was very ~ about it** se mostró *or* (*LAm*) se portó muy amable al respecto; **it was ~ of you to help us** fuiste muy amable ayudándonos; **to say ~ things about sb** hablar bien de algn; **to be ~ to sb** ser amable con algn, tratar bien a algn **4** (= *attractive*) [*person*] guapo, lindo (*LAm*); [*thing, place, house*] bonito, lindo (*LAm*); **you look ~!** ¡qué guapa estás!, ¡qué bien te ves! (*LAm*) **5** (= *polite*) fino, educado; **that's not ~** eso no está bien, eso no se hace; **he has ~ manners** es muy educado **6** (*emphatic*) bien; **a ~ cold drink** una bebida bien fría; **a ~ little house** una casita muy mona*; **~ and early** bien temprano; **just take it ~ and easy** tú tómatelo con calma; **it's ~ and warm here** aquí hace un calorcito muy agradable **7** (*iro*) (= *not nice*) **~ friends you've got!** ¡vaya amigos que tienes!, ¡menudos amigos tienes!; **here's a ~ state of affairs!** ¡dónde hemos ido a parar!

nice-looking ['naɪs'lʊkɪŋ] ADJ atractivo, guapo

nicely ['naɪslɪ] ADV bien; **she is coming along ~ at school** en el colegio le va bien; **that will do ~** así está perfecto *or* bien; **your driver's licence will do ~** su carnet de conducir sirve;

he's doing very ~ (for himself) le van muy bien las cosas

niceties ['naɪsɪtɪz] NPL detalles *mpl*, sutilezas *fpl*; **legal ~** pormenores *mpl* legales; **she went through the social ~** realizó las formalidades *or* los cumplidos de rigor

niche [niːʃ] N (*Archit*) nicho *m*, hornacina *f*; (*fig*) hueco *m*; **to find a ~ for o.s.** hacerse con una buena posición *or* un huequecito*

nick [nɪk] Ⓐ N **1** (= *cut*) (*on person*) corte *m*; (*on wood*) muesca *f*; (*on metal*) mella *f*; (= *crack*) hendedura *f* **2** (*Brit**) (= *prison*) chirona* *f*, trullo *m* (*Sp***); (= *police station*) comisaría *f* **3** ✦ IDIOMS **in good ~*** en buen estado; **in the ~ of time** justo a tiempo
Ⓑ VT **1** (= *cut*) [+ *wood*] hacer una muesca en; [+ *metal*] mellar; **he ~ed his chin shaving** se hizo un corte en la barbilla afeitándose; **to ~ o.s.** cortarse **2** (*Brit**) (= *steal*) robar, afanar*; (= *arrest*) agarrar*, trincar (*Sp**), apañar (*Mex**); **you're ~ed!** ¡estás detenido!

nickel ['nɪkl] N **1** (= *metal*) níquel *m* **2** (= *US coin*) moneda *f* de cinco centavos

nickname ['nɪkneɪm] Ⓐ N apodo *m*, mote *m*; (*Internet*) nick *m* Ⓑ VT apodar, dar el apodo de

nicotine ['nɪkətiːn] N nicotina *f* ➤ **nicotine patch** parche *m* de nicotina

niece [niːs] N sobrina *f*

nifty* ['nɪftɪ] ADJ (*compar* **niftier**; *superl* **niftiest**)
1 (= *excellent*) [*person*] sensacional*, chachi (*Sp**); [*place*] chulo*; [*gadget, idea*] ingenioso, chulo* **2** (= *skilful*) diestro, hábil **3** (= *quick*) **you'd better be ~ about it!** ¡ya puedes ir ligerito!, ¡más vale que te des prisa! **4** (= *stylish*) elegante, chulo*

Niger ['naɪdʒəʳ] N Níger *m*

Nigeria [naɪ'dʒɪərɪə] N Nigeria *f*; *ver tb* www.nigeria.gov.ng

Nigerian [naɪ'dʒɪərɪən] ADJ, N nigeriano/a *m/f*

niggardly ['nɪgədlɪ] ADJ [*person*] tacaño; [*allowance*] miserable

nigger******* ['nɪgəʳ] N negro/a *m/f*

niggle ['nɪgl] Ⓐ (*esp Brit*) VI quejarse Ⓑ VT preocupar; **it's something that has always ~d me** es algo que siempre me ha inquietado Ⓒ N (= *complaint*) queja *f*; (= *worry*) preocupación *f*

niggling ['nɪglɪŋ] ADJ [*detail*] engorroso; [*doubt, suspicion*] persistente, constante; [*ache*] molesto, molestoso (*LAm*)

night [naɪt] Ⓐ N **1** (= *time of day*) noche *f*; **it's ~** es de noche; **Monday ~** el lunes por la noche; **all ~ (long)** toda la noche; **at ~** por la noche, de noche; **11 o'clock at ~** las 11 de la noche; **to stay up late at ~** trasnochar; **to have a bad ~** dormir mal, pasar una mala noche; **the ~ before the ceremony** la víspera de la ceremonia; **by ~** de noche, por la noche; **~ and day** noche y día; **good ~!** ¡buenas noches!; **in the ~** durante la noche; **last ~** (= *late*) anoche; (= *in the evening*) ayer por la tarde; **the ~ before last** anteanoche; **we decided to make a ~ of it and go to a club** decidimos continuar la marcha y nos fuimos a una discoteca*; **night, night!*** ¡buenas noches!; **to have a ~ out** salir por la noche; **I can't sleep ~s** no puedo dormir la noche; **tomorrow ~** mañana por la noche; **to work ~s** trabajar de noche **2** (*Theat*) **first ~** estreno *m*; **last ~** última representación *f* Ⓑ CPD ➤ **night light** lamparilla *f*, mariposa *f* ➤ **night owl*** (*fig*) ave *f* nocturna

> Use **el/un** not **la/una** before feminine nouns beginning with stressed **a** or **ha** like **ave**.

➤ **night porter** (*esp Brit*) guarda *m* nocturno ➤ **night safe** caja *f* de seguridad nocturna ➤ **night school** escuela *f* nocturna ➤ **night shift** turno *m* nocturno, turno *m* de noche ➤ **night stand** (*US*), **night table** mesita *f* de noche ➤ **night watchman** vigilante *m* nocturno

nightcap ['naɪtkæp] N **1** (= *hat*) gorro *m* de dormir **2** (= *drink*) bebida que se toma antes de acostarse

nightclothes ['naɪtkləʊðz] N ropa *fsing* de dormir

nightclub ['naɪtklʌb] N club *m* nocturno

nightclubber ['naɪtklʌbəʳ] N discotequero/a *m/f*

nightclubbing ['naɪtklʌbɪŋ] N **to go ~** ir de discotecas

nightdress ['naɪtdres] N (*Brit*) camisón *m* de noche

nightfall ['naɪtfɔːl] N anochecer *m*; **at ~** al anochecer

nightgown ['naɪtgaʊn] N (*US*) camisón *m* de noche

nightie* ['naɪtɪ] N camisón *m* de noche

nightingale ['naɪtɪŋgeɪl] N ruiseñor *m*

nightlife ['naɪtlaɪf] N vida *f* nocturna

nightly ['naɪtlɪ] Ⓐ ADV todas las noches Ⓑ ADJ de todas las noches

nightmare ['naɪtmeəʳ] N pesadilla *f*

nightshade ['naɪtʃeɪd] N **deadly ~** belladona *f*

nightshirt ['naɪtʃɜːt] N camisa *f* de dormir

nightspot ['naɪtspɒt] N local *m* nocturno

nightstick ['naɪtstɪk] N (*US*) porra *f* (de policía)

night-time ['naɪttaɪm] Ⓐ N noche *f* Ⓑ ADJ nocturno

Nikkei average [nɪˌkeɪ'ævərɪdʒ] N índice *m* Nikkei

nil [nɪl] N (= *nothing*) nada *f*; (*Brit Sport*) cero *m*; **Granada beat Murcia two-~** el Granada venció al Murcia dos-cero *or* por dos a cero

Nile [naɪl] N Nilo *m*

nimble ['nɪmbl] ADJ (*compar* **~r**; *superl* **~st**) [*person, mind*] ágil; [*feet*] ligero; [*fingers*] hábil, diestro; **~-fingered** de dedos hábiles; **~-footed** de pies ligeros

nimbly ['nɪmblɪ] ADV ágilmente

NIMBY ['nɪmbɪ] N ABBR (= **not in my backyard**) "no en el patio de mi casa" (*campaña contra la colocación de vertederos o servicios comunitarios no deseados en la vecindad*)

nine [naɪn] NUMBER nueve *m*; ✦ IDIOMS **a ~ days' wonder** una maravilla de un día; **to be dressed up to the ~s** (*Brit**) ir de punta en blanco; **~ times out of ten** casi siempre, en el noventa por ciento de los casos; *see* **five**

9-11, Nine-Eleven [ˌnaɪn'levn] N 11-S *m*

nineteen ['naɪn'tiːn] NUMBER diecinueve *m*; ✦ IDIOM **to talk ~ to the dozen** (*Brit**) hablar por los codos*; *see* **five**

nineteenth ['naɪn'tiːnθ] Ⓐ ADJ decimonoveno, decimonono Ⓑ PRON (*in series*) decimonoveno/a *m/f*, decimonono *m/f*; (= *fraction*) decimonovena parte *f*, decimonoveno *m*; *see* **fifteenth**

ninetieth ['naɪntɪɪθ] Ⓐ ADJ nonagésimo; **the ~ anniversary** el noventa aniversario Ⓑ PRON (*in series*) nonagésimo/a *m/f*; (= *fraction*) nonagésima parte *f*, nonagésimo *m*; *see* **fiftieth**

nine-to-five ['naɪntə'faɪv] ADJ **~ job** trabajo *m* de nueve a cinco

ninety ['naɪntɪ] NUMBER noventa *m*; **temperatures were in the nineties** ≈ las temperaturas superaban los treinta grados centígrados; *see* **fifty**

ninth [naɪnθ] Ⓐ ADJ noveno, nono Ⓑ PRON (*in series*) noveno/a *m/f*; (= *fraction*) novena parte *f*, noveno *m*; *see* **fifth**

nip [nɪp] Ⓐ N **1** (= *pinch*) pellizco *m*; (= *bite*) mordisco *m*; **there's a ~ in the air** hace bastante frío **2** [*of drink*] trago *m*, traguito* *m* **3** (*US*) ✦ IDIOM **~ and tuck: it was ~ and tuck throughout the match** el encuentro estuvo muy reñido *or* igualado
Ⓑ VT (= *pinch*) pellizcar, pinchar; (= *bite*) mordiscar, mordisquear; ✦ IDIOM **to ~ sth in the bud** cortar algo de raíz
Ⓒ VI (*Brit**) **to ~ out/down** salir/bajar un momento; **I ~ped round to the shop** fui un momento a la tienda; **we were ~ping along at 100kph** íbamos a 100kph

nipple ['nɪpl] N (*on female*) pezón *m*; (*on male*) tetilla *f*; (*US*) (*on baby's bottle*) tetina *f*

nippy* ['nɪpɪ] ADJ (*compar* **nippier**; *superl* **nippiest**) **1** (*Brit*) (= *quick*) [*person*] ágil, rápido!; [*car*] rápido; **we shall have to be ~** tendremos que darnos prisa, tendremos que apurarnos *or* movernos (*LAm*) **2** (= *cold*) [*weather*] fresquito

NIREX ['naɪreks] N ABBR (*Brit*) = **Nuclear Industry Radioactive Waste Executive**

nit [nɪt] N **1** (= *parasite*) liendre *f* **2** (*Brit**) (= *idiot*) imbécil *mf*, bobo/a *m/f*, zonzo/a *m/f* (*LAm*); **you ~!** ¡imbécil!

nite* [naɪt] N (= *night*) noche *f*

nitpick* ['nɪt,pɪk] VI sacar faltas a todo, buscar tres pies al gato*

nit-picker* ['nɪt,pɪkəʳ] N criticón/ona *m/f*, quisquilloso/a *m/f*

nit-picking* ['nɪt,pɪkɪŋ] **Ⓐ** ADJ [*question, criticism*] quisquilloso **Ⓑ** N quisquillosidad *f*

nitrate ['naɪtreɪt] N nitrato *m*

nitric ['naɪtrɪk] ADJ nítrico ➤ **nitric acid** ácido *m* nítrico

nitrogen ['naɪtrədʒən] N nitrógeno *m* ➤ **nitrogen dioxide** dióxido *m* de nitrógeno

nitroglycerin(e) ['naɪtrəʊˈglɪsəriːn] N nitroglicerina *f*

nitty-gritty* [,nɪtɪˈgrɪtɪ] N ✦ IDIOM **to get down to the ~** ir al grano

nitwit* ['nɪtwɪt] N imbécil *mf*, bobo/a *mf*, zonzo/a *m/f* (*LAm*)

nix** [nɪks] (*US*) **Ⓐ** N nada **Ⓑ** EXCL ¡ni hablar!

NJ ABBR (*US*) = **New Jersey**

NLF N ABBR = **National Liberation Front**

NLRB N ABBR (*US*) = **National Labor Relations Board**

NM, N. Mex. ABBR (*US*) = **New Mexico**

no [nəʊ] **Ⓐ** ADV (*as answer*) no; **I am no taller than you** yo no soy más alto que tú; **it's no good** es inútil **Ⓑ** ADJ

For set expressions such as **no parking, no smoking, it's no use**, look up the other word.

Put the Spanish verb in the negative when translating **no** + UNCOUNT NOUN:

I have no money/furniture no tengo dinero/muebles

Also put the Spanish verb in the negative when translating **no** + PLURAL NOUN. For extra emphasis use **ningún/ninguna** + singular noun:

---

there are no trains after midnight no hay trenes después de medianoche; **they've got no friends in London** no tienen ningún conocido en Londres; **there's no <u>denying</u> it** es imposible negarlo; **he's no <u>fool</u>** no es tonto, ni mucho menos, no es ningún tonto; **he's no <u>friend</u> of mine** no es precisamente amigo mío; **there's no <u>getting</u> out of it** no hay posibilidad de evitarlo; **there is no coffee <u>left</u>** no queda café; **no <u>place</u>** (*esp US**) = **nowhere**; **there's no <u>pleasing</u> him** es imposible tenerlo contento; **we'll be there in no <u>time</u>** llegamos en un dos por tres, no tardamos nada; **no <u>two</u> of them are alike** no hay dos iguales **Ⓒ** N (*pl* **noes**) **1** (= *refusal*) no *m*; **I won't take no for an answer** no acepto un no por respuesta **2** (*Pol*) voto *m* en contra **Ⓓ** CPD ➤ **no one** nadie; **no one spoke** nadie habló, no habló nadie ➤ **no throw** lanzamiento *m* nulo

No., no. ABBR (= **number**) núm., nº

Noah ['nəʊə] N Noé ➤ **Noah's ark** arca *f* de Noé

Use **el/un** not **la/una** before feminine nouns beginning with stressed **a** or **ha** like **arca**.

---

nobble* ['nɒbl] (*Brit*) VT **1** (= *bribe*) sobornar, comprar **2** (= *arrest*) pescar*, coger, agarrar (*LAm*); (= *waylay*) pescar* **3** (= *drug*) [+ *horse*] drogar

Nobel [nəʊˈbel] CPD ➤ **Nobel prize** premio *m* Nobel ➤ **Nobel prizewinner** ganador(a) *m/f* del premio Nobel

nobility [nəʊˈbɪlɪtɪ] N nobleza *f*

noble ['nəʊbl] **Ⓐ** ADJ (*compar* **~r**; *superl* **~st**) (*by birth*) noble; (= *worthy*) magnánimo, generoso **Ⓑ** N noble *mf*, aristócrata *mf*; (*Spanish Hist*) hidalgo *m*

nobleman ['nəʊblmən] N (*pl* **noblemen**) noble *m*, aristócrata *m*; (*Spanish Hist*) hidalgo *m*

noblewoman ['nəʊblwʊmən] N (*pl* **noblewomen**) noble *f*, aristócrata *f*

nobly ['nəʊblɪ] ADV con generosidad

nobody ['nəʊbədɪ] **Ⓐ** PRON nadie; **~ spoke** nadie habló, no habló nadie **Ⓑ** N **he's a mere ~** es un don nadie; **I knew him when he was a ~** lo conocí cuando no era nadie

no-claim(s) bonus [,nəʊˈkleɪm(z)bəʊnəs], **no-claim(s) discount** [,nəʊˈkleɪm(z)dɪskaʊnt] N prima *f* de no reclamación

nocturnal [nɒkˈtɜːnl] ADJ nocturno

nocturne ['nɒktɜːn] N (*Mus*) nocturno *m*

nod [nɒd] **Ⓐ** N **give me a ~ when you want me to start** hazme una señal con la cabeza cuando quieras que empiece; **she greeted me with a ~** me saludó con (un gesto de) la cabeza; **he answered me with a ~** (*saying yes*) asintió con la cabeza; ✦ IDIOM **the Land of Nod** el país de los sueños **Ⓑ** VT **to ~ (one's) agreement** asentir con la cabeza; **to ~ (one's) approval** hacer un gesto *or* una señal de aprobación con la cabeza; **he answered yes** (*saying yes*) asintió con la cabeza; **she ~ded her head** (*saying yes*) asintió con la cabeza; **she ~ded her head in greeting** nos saludó con un gesto de cabeza **Ⓒ** VI (= *bow*) inclinar la cabeza; (*in agreement*) asentir con la cabeza; **she ~ded to him** (*in greeting*) lo saludó con la cabeza
➤ **nod off** VI + ADV dormirse, quedarse dormido

node [nəʊd] N nodo *m*

nodule ['nɒdjuːl] N nódulo *m*

no-fault ['nəʊfɔːlt] ADJ **~ divorce** divorcio *m* en el que no se culpa a ninguno de los esposos

no-fly zone [,nəʊˈflaɪzəʊn] N zona *f* de exclusión aérea

no-frills ['nəʊˌfrɪlz] ADJ sencillo

no-go [,nəʊˈgəʊ] ADJ **~ area** (*Brit*) (*prohibited*) zona *f* prohibida; (*fig*) zona *f* en la que no se puede entrar

no-good* ['nəʊgʊd] ADJ (*US*) inútil

no-holds-barred [,nəʊhəʊldzˈbaːd] ADJ [*battle, contest*] sin cuartel; [*account, book*] sin prejuicios; [*interview*] sin barreras

no-hoper* ['nəʊ,həʊpəʳ] N nulidad *f*

noise [nɔɪz] N ruido *m*; **tell them not to make any ~** diles que no hagan ruido ➤ **noise pollution** contaminación *f* acústica

noiseless ['nɔɪzlɪs] ADJ silencioso

noisily ['nɔɪzɪlɪ] ADV ruidosamente

noisy ['nɔɪzɪ] ADJ (*compar* **noisier**; *superl* **noisiest**) ruidoso; **it's very ~ here** hay mucho ruido aquí; **don't be too ~** no hagáis mucho ruido

nomad ['nəʊmæd] N nómada *mf*

nomadic [nəʊˈmædɪk] ADJ nómada

no-man's land ['nəʊmænzlænd] N tierra *f* de nadie

nom de plume ['nɒmdəˈpluːm] N (*pl* **noms de plume**) seudónimo *m*, nombre *m* artístico

nominal ['nɒmɪnl] ADJ [*Christian, Catholic*] solamente de nombre, nominal; [*sum, charge*] simbólico; [*partner, value, wage*] nominal

nominally ['nɒmɪnəlɪ] ADV nominalmente, sólo de nombre

nominate ['nɒmɪneɪt] VT (= *propose*) proponer; (= *appoint*) nombrar; **to ~ sb as** *or* **for chairman** proponer a algn como candidato a la presidencia; **she was ~d for an Oscar** la nominaron para un Oscar

nomination [,nɒmɪˈneɪʃən] N (= *proposal*) propuesta *f*; (= *appointment*) nombramiento *m*

nominative ['nɒmɪnətɪv] N nominativo *m*

nominee [,nɒmɪˈniː] N (= *person proposed*) candidato/a *m/f*; (= *person appointed*) persona *f* nombrada; **the Democratic ~** el candidato propuesto por los demócratas

non- [nɒn] PREF no ...

non-addictive [,nɒnəˈdɪktɪv] ADJ que no crea dependencia

non-aggression ['nɒnə'greʃən] N no agresión *f*
➤ **non-aggression pact** pacto *m* de no agresión
non-alcoholic ['nɒnælkə'hɒlɪk] ADJ no alcohólico
non-aligned ['nɒnə'laɪnd] ADJ [*country*] no alineado
non-attendance ['nɒnə'tendəns] ausencia *f*, no asistencia *f*
non-believer ['nɒnbɪ'liːvə'] N no creyente *mf*
non-belligerent ['nɒnbɪ'lɪdʒərənt] ADJ, N no beligerante *mf*
non-biological ['nɒnbaɪəʊ'lɒdʒɪkl] ADJ no biológico
non-Catholic ['nɒn'kæθlɪk] ADJ, N no católico/a *m/f*
nonchalant ['nɒnʃələnt] ADJ despreocupado; **I tried to look ~** intenté adoptar un aire despreocupado
non-Christian [,nɒn'krɪstɪən] ADJ, N no cristiano/a *m/f*
non-combatant ['nɒn'kɒmbətənt] ADJ, N no combatiente *mf*
non-combustible ['nɒnkəm'bʌstɪbl] ADJ incombustible
non-commissioned ['nɒnkə'mɪʃənd] ADJ **~ officer** suboficial *mf*
non-committal ['nɒnkə'mɪtl] ADJ [*person*] poco comprometido; [*answer*] evasivo
non-committally [,nɒnkə'mɪtəlɪ] ADV sin comprometerse
non-compliance ['nɒnkəm'plaɪəns] N incumplimiento *m* (**with** de)
nonconformist ['nɒnkən'fɔːmɪst] ADJ, N inconformista *mf*; **Nonconformist** (*Brit Rel*) no conformista *mf*
non-contagious ['nɒnkən'teɪdʒəs] ADJ no contagioso
non-contributory [,nɒnkən'trɪbjʊtərɪ] ADJ **~ pension scheme** plan *m* de jubilación no contributivo (*costeado por la empresa*)
non-cooperation ['nɒnkəʊˌɒpə'reɪʃən] N no cooperación *f*
non-custodial sentence ['nɒnkʌs'təʊdɪəl'sentəns] N *sentencia que no implica privación de libertad*
non-denominational ['nɒndɪnɒmɪ'neɪʃənl] ADJ aconfesional
nondescript ['nɒndɪskrɪpt] ADJ [*building, furniture*] corriente; [*colour*] indefinido; [*person, clothes, face*] (= *unremarkable*) anodino; (= *uninteresting*) insulso, soso*
non-drinker ['nɒn'drɪŋkə'] N no bebedor(a) *m/f*
non-drip ['nɒn'drɪp] ADJ que no gotea
none [nʌn] **(A)** PRON (= *not one*) ninguno; (= *not a little*) nada; **~ of them** ninguno de ellos; **we have ~ of your books** no tenemos ninguno de tus libros *or* ningún libro tuyo; **there are ~ left** no queda ninguno; **~ of this is true** nada de esto es verdad; **"any news?" — "none!"** —¿alguna noticia? —¡nada! *or* ¡ninguna!, —¿se sabe algo? —¡nada!; **we'll have ~ of that!** ¡basta ya!, ¡vale ya! (*Sp*); **he would have ~ of it** no hubo forma de convencerlo; **everyone wanted her to win, ~ more so than I** todos querían que ganara, y yo más que nadie; **it was ~ other than the bishop** fue el obispo mismo **(B)** ADV **I was ~ too comfortable** no me sentía nada cómodo; **he did ~ too well in his exams** los exámenes no le fueron nada bien; **it was ~ too soon** ya era hora; **it's ~ the worse for that** no es peor por eso
nonentity [nɒ'nentɪtɪ] N nulidad *f*, cero *m* a la izquierda
non-essential ['nɒnɪ'senʃəl] **(A)** ADJ no esencial **(B)** N cosa *f* secundaria
nonetheless [,nʌnðə'les] ADV sin embargo, aún así
non-EU [,nɒnɪ'juː] ADJ [*citizens, passports*] no comunitario; [*imports*] de fuera de la Unión Europea
non-event [,nɒnɪ'vent] N fracaso *m*, fiasco *m*; **it was a ~** fue un fiasco
non-executive [,nɒnɪg'zekjʊtɪv] ADJ **~ director** vocal *mf*, consejero/a *m/f* (*no ejecutivo*)
non-existence ['nɒnɪg'zɪstəns] N inexistencia *f*, no existencia *f*
non-existent ['nɒnɪg'zɪstənt] ADJ inexistente
non-fattening [,nɒn'fætnɪŋ] ADJ que no engorda
non-fiction ['nɒn'fɪkʃən] N literatura *f* no novelesca

non-flammable ['nɒn'flæməbl] ADJ ininflamable
non-fulfilment ['nɒnfʊl'fɪlmənt] N incumplimiento *m*
non-governmental ['nɒnˌgʌvn'mentl] ADJ no gubernamental
non-intervention ['nɒnˌɪntə'venʃən] N no intervención *f*
non-iron ['nɒn'aɪən] ADJ que no necesita plancha
non-malignant ['nɒnmə'lɪgnənt] ADJ no maligno
non-member ['nɒnˌmembə'] N no miembro *mf*
non-negotiable [,nɒnnɪ'gəʊʃɪəbl] ADJ innegociable
non-nuclear ['nɒn'njuːklɪə'] ADJ [*defence, policy*] no nuclear; [*area*] desnuclearizado
no-no* ['nəʊnəʊ] N **that's a ~** (= *undesirable*) eso no se hace; (= *not an option*) no existe tal posibilidad
no-nonsense [,nəʊ'nɒnsəns] ADJ sensato
non-participating ['nɒnpa:'tɪsɪpeɪtɪŋ] ADJ no participante
nonpartisan ['nɒnˌpa:tɪ'zæn] ADJ imparcial
non-party ['nɒn'pa:tɪ] ADJ (*Pol*) independiente
non-paying ['nɒn'peɪɪŋ] ADJ [*member*] que no paga
non-payment ['nɒn'peɪmənt] N falta *f* de pago, impago *m*; **sued for ~ of debts** demandado por no pagar sus deudas
nonplussed ['nɒn'plʌst] ADJ perplejo, desconcertado
non-polluting ['nɒnpə'lu:tɪŋ] ADJ no contaminante
non-practising ['nɒn'præktɪsɪŋ] ADJ no practicante
non-productive [,nɒnprə'dʌktɪv] ADJ improductivo
non-professional ['nɒnprə'feʃnəl] ADJ no profesional, aficionado
non-profit-making (*esp Brit*) ['nɒn'prɒfɪtmeɪkɪŋ], **non-profit** (*US*) [,nɒn'prɒfɪt] ADJ no lucrativo
non-proliferation treaty [nɒnprəlɪfə'reɪʃn,tri:tɪ] N tratado *m* de no proliferación
non-resident ['nɒn'rezɪdənt] **(A)** ADJ [*citizen, population*] no residente, transeúnte; [*staff, workers*] no fijo **(B)** N [*of hotel*] no residente *mf*; [*of country*] no residente *mf*, transeúnte *mf*
non-residential ['nɒnˌrezɪ'denʃl] ADJ no residencial
non-returnable [,nɒnrɪ'tɜːnəbl] ADJ [*deposit*] no reembolsable; **~ bottle** envase *m* no retornable
non-scheduled ['nɒn'ʃedju:ld] ADJ [*flight*] no regular
nonsense ['nɒnsəns] N tonterías *fpl*; **(what) ~!** ¡tonterías!, ¡qué tontería!; **but that's ~!** ¡eso es absurdo *or* ridículo!; **it is ~ to say that ...** es absurdo *or* ridículo decir que ...; **I've never heard such ~!** ¡vaya (una) tontería!, ¡jamás oí (una) tontería igual!; **to make (a) ~ of** [+ *claim, system, law*] quitar sentido a; **a piece of ~** una tontería; **I'll stand no ~ from you!** ¡no voy a tolerar tus tonterías!; **to talk ~** decir tonterías *or* disparates; **stop this ~!** ¡ya vale de tonterías!
nonsensical [nɒn'sensɪkəl] ADJ absurdo
non sequitur [,nɒn'sekwɪtə'] N incongruencia *f*, falta *f* de lógica; **it's a ~** es una incongruencia
non-shrink ['nɒn'ʃrɪŋk] ADJ que no encoge
non-skilled ['nɒn'skɪld] ADJ [*worker*] no cualificado; [*work*] no especializado
non-slip ['nɒn'slɪp] ADJ antideslizante, antirresbaladizo
non-smoker ['nɒn'sməʊkə'] N no fumador(a) *m/f*
non-smoking ['nɒn'sməʊkɪŋ] ADJ [*person*] no fumador; [*compartment, area*] de no fumadores
non-specialist ['nɒn'speʃəlɪst] N no especialista *mf*
non-standard [,nɒn'stændəd] ADJ (*Ling*) no estándar
non-starter [,nɒn'sta:tə'] N **that idea is a ~** esa idea es imposible
non-stick [,nɒn'stɪk] ADJ antiadherente, que no se pega
non-stop ['nɒn'stɒp] **(A)** ADV (= *without a pause*) sin cesar, sin parar; (*Rail*) sin hacer paradas; (*Aer*) sin hacer escalas; **he talks ~** no para de hablar **(B)** ADJ (= *without a pause*) continuo; [*flight*] directo; [*music*] ininterrumpido
non-taxable ['nɒn'tæksəbl] ADJ no sujeto a impuestos, exento de impuestos

non-toxic [ˌnɒnˈtɒksɪk] ADJ no tóxico

non-transferable [ˈnɒntrænsˈfɜːrəbl] ADJ intransferible

non-verbal [ˈnɒnˈvɜːbl] ADJ sin palabras

non-violent [ˈnɒnˈvaɪələnt] ADJ no violento, pacífico

non-white [ˌnɒnˈwaɪt] **Ⓐ** ADJ de color **Ⓑ** N persona *f* de color

noodle [ˈnuːdl] N noodles fideos *mpl*, tallarines *mpl* ➤ **noodle soup** sopa *f* de fideos

nook [nʊk] N rincón *m*; **we looked in every ~ and cranny** buscamos hasta el último rincón

noon [nuːn] N mediodía *m*; **at ~** a mediodía

no-one [ˈnəʊwʌn] PRON = **nobody**

noose [nuːs] N (= *loop*) nudo *m* corredizo; (*for animal, as trap*) lazo *m*; [*of hangman*] soga *f*; ✦ IDIOM **to put one's head in the ~** echarse la soga al cuello

nope** [nəʊp] EXCL no

nor [nɔː[r]] CONJ 1 (*following "neither"*) ni; **neither Pat ~ Zoë is coming to the party** no vienen ni Pat ni Zoë a la fiesta, ni Pat ni Zoë vienen a la fiesta; **she neither eats ~ drinks** ni come ni bebe; **he was neither fat ~ thin** no estaba ni gordo ni delgado 2 (= *neither*) **"I don't work here" — "~ do I"** —yo no trabajo aquí —ni yo (tampoco) *or* —yo tampoco; **"I didn't like the film" — "~ did I"** —no me gustó la película —a mí tampoco *or* —ni a mí; **~ does it seem likely** ni tampoco parece probable

norm [nɔːm] N **the ~** (= *standard*) la norma; (= *average*) lo normal; **social ~s** las normas sociales; **larger than the ~** más grande de lo normal

normal [ˈnɔːml] **Ⓐ** ADJ normal; **it's perfectly ~ to feel that way** es muy normal sentirse así, no hay nada raro en sentirse así; **"normal service will be resumed as soon as possible"** (*TV*) "se reanudará la emisión lo antes posible"; **I woke at the ~ time** me desperté a la hora de siempre **Ⓑ** N **above/below ~** por encima/debajo de lo normal; **to carry on as ~** seguir haciendo todo como de costumbre; **to get back to ~** [*situation*] normalizarse, volver a la normalidad

normality [nɔːˈmælɪtɪ] N normalidad *f*

normalize [ˈnɔːməlaɪz] VT normalizar

normally [ˈnɔːməlɪ] ADV normalmente; **he ~ arrives at seven o'clock** normalmente llega *or* suele llegar a las siete; **the trains are running ~** los trenes están funcionando con normalidad

Norman [ˈnɔːmən] ADJ normando; **the ~ Conquest** la conquista de los normandos; **~ architecture** arquitectura *f* románica

Norse [nɔːs] ADJ nórdico

north [nɔːθ] **Ⓐ** N norte *m*; **in the ~** en el norte; **to the ~ of** al norte de **Ⓑ** ADJ [*side, part*] norte, del norte; [*coast*] norte, del norte, septentrional; [*wind*] del norte **Ⓒ** ADV (= *northward*) hacia el norte; **~ of the border** al norte de la frontera; **it's ~ of London** está al norte de Londres **Ⓓ** CPD ➤ **North Africa** África *f* del Norte ➤ **North America** Norteamérica *f*, América *f* del Norte ➤ **the North Atlantic Treaty Organization** la Organización del Tratado del Atlántico Norte ➤ **North Korea** Corea *f* del Norte ➤ **the North Pole** el Polo Norte ➤ **the North Sea** el Mar del Norte ➤ **the north star** la estrella polar, la estrella del norte

North African [ˈnɔːθˈæfrɪkən] ADJ, N norteafricano/a *m/f*

North American [ˈnɔːθəˈmerɪkən] ADJ, N norteamericano/a *m/f*

northbound [ˈnɔːθbaʊnd] ADJ en dirección norte

northeast [ˈnɔːθˈiːst] **Ⓐ** N nor(d)este *m* **Ⓑ** ADJ [*side, part*] nor(d)este, del nor(d)este; [*coast*] nor(d)este, del nor(d)este, nororiental; [*wind*] del nor(d)este **Ⓒ** ADV (= *northeastward*) hacia el nor(d)este; **it's ~ of London** está al nor(d)este de Londres

northeasterly [ˈnɔːθˈiːstəlɪ] ADJ [*wind*] del nor(d)este; **in a ~ direction** hacia el nor(d)este, en dirección nor(d)este

northeastern [ˈnɔːθˈiːstən] ADJ [*side, part*] nor(d)este, del nor(d)este; [*coast, border*] nor(d)este, del nor(d)este, nororiental; [*wind, front, town*] del nor(d)este; **in ~ Spain** al *or* en el nor(d)este de España

northerly [ˈnɔːðəlɪ] ADJ [*wind*] del norte; **in a ~ direction** hacia el norte, en dirección norte; **the most ~ point in Europe** el punto más al norte *or* más septentrional de Europa

northern [ˈnɔːðən] ADJ [*side, part*] norte, del norte; [*coast, border*] norte, del norte, septentrional; [*wind, front, town*] del norte; [*person*] norteño; **in ~ Spain** al norte *or* en el norte de España, en la España septentrional ➤ **the northern hemisphere** el hemisferio norte, el hemisferio boreal ➤ **Northern Ireland** Irlanda *f* del Norte ➤ **the northern lights** la aurora boreal

northerner [ˈnɔːðənə[r]] N persona *f* del norte, habitante *mf* del norte, norteño/a *m/f*; **he's a ~** es del norte

Northern Irish [ˌnɔːðənˈaɪrɪʃ] **Ⓐ** ADJ norirlandés **Ⓑ** NPL **the ~** los norirlandeses

northernmost [ˈnɔːðənməʊst] ADJ más septentrional, más al norte

north-facing [ˈnɔːθˌfeɪsɪŋ] ADJ con cara al norte, orientado hacia el norte; **~ slope** vertiente *f* norte

North Korean [ˈnɔːθkəˈrɪən] ADJ, N norcoreano/a *m/f*

North Vietnamese [ˈnɔːθvɪetnəˈmiːz] ADJ, N norvietnamita *mf*

northward [ˈnɔːθwəd] **Ⓐ** ADJ [*movement, migration, journey*] hacia el norte, en dirección norte **Ⓑ** ADV (*also* ~s) hacia el norte, en dirección norte

northwest [ˈnɔːθˈwest] **Ⓐ** N noroeste *m* **Ⓑ** ADJ [*side, part*] noroeste, del noroeste; [*coast*] noroeste, del noroeste, noroccidental; [*wind*] del noroeste **Ⓒ** ADV (= *toward northwest*) hacia el noroeste; **it's ~ of London** está al noroeste de Londres

northwesterly [ˈnɔːθˈwestəlɪ] ADJ [*wind*] del noroeste; **in a ~ direction** hacia el noroeste, en dirección noroeste

northwestern [ˈnɔːθˈwestən] ADJ [*side, part*] noroeste, del noroeste; [*coast, border*] noroeste, del noroeste, noroccidental; [*wind, front, town*] del noroeste; **in ~ Spain** al noroeste *or* en el noroeste de España, en la España noroccidental

Norway [ˈnɔːweɪ] N Noruega *f* ➤ **Norway lobster** cigala *f*

Norwegian [nɔːˈwiːdʒən] **Ⓐ** ADJ noruego **Ⓑ** N 1 (= *person*) noruego/a *m/f* 2 (*Ling*) noruego *m*

Nos., nos. ABBR (= *numbers*) núms.

no-score draw [ˌnəʊskɔːˈdrɔː] N partido *m* sin goles

nose [nəʊz] **Ⓐ** N 1 [*of person*] nariz *f*; [*of animal*] hocico *m*; **his ~ was bleeding** le sangraba la nariz, le salía sangre de la nariz; **to have one's ~ in a book** estar enfrascado en un libro; ✦ IDIOMS **to keep one's ~ clean*** no meterse en problemas *or* líos*; **to cut off one's ~ to spite one's face** tirar piedras a su tejado; **he gets up my ~** (*Brit**) me revienta*; **to have a (good) ~ for sth** tener (buen) olfato para algo; **to keep one's ~ out (of sth)** no entrometerse (en algo); **that's it! you've hit it on the ~!** ¡eso es! ¡has dado en el clavo!; **to poke one's ~ into sth*** meter las narices en algo*, meterse en algo; **to put sb's ~ out of joint** molestar a algn; **to see no further than the end of one's ~** no ver más allá de sus narices; **to turn up one's ~ at sth** hacer ascos a algo; **it's right under your ~** lo tienes delante de las narices* 2 (*esp US*) (= *distance*) to win by a ~ [*horse*] ganar por una nariz; (*fig*) ganar por los pelos 3 (= *front*) [*of aeroplane*] morro *m*, parte *f* delantera; **the traffic was ~ to tail** (*esp Brit*) los coches iban pegados unos a otros **Ⓑ** CPD ➤ **nose cone** [*of missile*] ojiva *f* ➤ **nose drops** gotas *fpl* para la nariz ➤ **nose job: to have a ~ job** operarse la nariz ➤ **nose ring** [*of animal*] argolla *f* (en el hocico); [*of person*] pendiente *m* en la nariz ➤ **nose around, nose about** (*Brit*) **Ⓐ** VI + ADV curiosear, fisgonear **Ⓑ** VI + PREP curiosear por, fisgonear por ➤ **nose out** VT + ADV 1 (= *smell*) olfatear 2 (= *discover*) [+ *secret, truth*] averiguar, lograr descubrir; [+ *fugitive*] encontrar

nosebag ['nəʊzbæg] N morral *m*

nosebleed ['nəʊzbliːd] N hemorragia *f* nasal (*Med*); **to have a ~** sangrar *or* echar sangre por la nariz, tener una hemorragia nasal (*Med*)

nose-dive ['nəʊzdaɪv] Ⓐ N (*Aer*) picado *m* (*Sp*) *or* picada *f* (*LAm*) vertical; (*fig*) caída *f* súbita; **to take a ~** [*profits, shares, reputation*] caer en picado (*Sp*) *or* en picada (*LAm*) Ⓑ VI (*Aer*) descender en picado (*Sp*) *or* en picada (*LAm*); [*profits, shares, reputation*] caer en picado (*Sp*) *or* en picada (*LAm*)

nosey*, **nosy*** ['nəʊzɪ] ADJ (*compar* **nosier**; *superl* **nosiest**) entrometido; **don't be so ~!** ¡no seas tan entrometido!

nosey-parker* ['nəʊzɪ'pɑːkəʳ] N (*Brit*) metomentodo/a* *m/f*

nosh* [nɒʃ] N (*Brit*) comida *f*, papeo** *m*, manduca *f* (*Sp**)

no-show ['nəʊ'ʃəʊ] N ausente *mf* (*persona que no ocupa una plaza reservada previamente*)

nosh-up** ['nɒʃʌp] N (*Brit*) comilona* *f*, tragadera *f* (*LAm**)

nosily ['nəʊzɪlɪ] ADV de forma entrometida

nosiness ['nəʊzɪnɪs] N entrometimiento *m*

no-smoking ['nəʊˌsməʊkɪŋ] ADJ [*area, carriage*] de no fumadores; [*policy*] de prohibición del tabaco

nostalgia [nɒs'tældʒɪə] N nostalgia *f*, añoranza *f*

nostalgic [nɒs'tældʒɪk] ADJ nostálgico

nostril ['nɒstrəl] N (*gen*) ventana *f* de la nariz, orificio *m* nasal (*frm*); [*of horse*] ollar *m*

nosy* ['nəʊzɪ] ADJ = **nosey**

nosy-parker* ['nəʊzɪ'pɑːkəʳ] N = **nosey-parker**

not [nɒt] ADV **1** (*with vb*)

Often contracted to **n't** on the end of modals, auxiliaries and parts of the verb **to be** in everyday language.

---

no; **I'm ~ sure** no estoy seguro; **he's ~ here** ◇ **he isn't here** no está aquí; **it's too late, isn't it?** es demasiado tarde, ¿no?; **you owe me money, don't you?** me debes dinero, ¿verdad? *or* (*esp LAm*) ¿no es cierto?; **he asked me ~ to do it** me pidió que no lo hiciera; **I hope/suppose ~** espero/supongo que no; **to tell sb ~ to do sth** decir a algn que no haga algo; **~ thinking that ...** sin pensar que ...
2 (*with pronoun etc*) **~ one** ni uno; **~ me/you** *etc* yo/tú *etc* no; **~ everybody can do it** no lo puede hacer cualquiera, no todos pueden hacerlo; **~ any more** ya no
3 (*in expressions*) **~ at all** (*after verb*) no ... en absoluto; (*responding to thanks*) ¡de nada!, ¡no hay de qué!; **I don't mind at all** no me importa en absoluto; **"are you cold?" — "~ at all!"** —¿tienes frío? —¡en absoluto! *or* —¡qué va!; **he's ~ at all selfish** no es nada egoísta; **~ for anything (in the world)** por nada (del mundo); **~ guilty** no culpable; **are you coming or ~?** ¿vienes o no?; **big, ~ to say enormous** grande, por no decir enorme; **~ that I don't like him** no es que no me guste; **~ that I know of** no que yo sepa

notable ['nəʊtəbl] ADJ [*person*] destacado; **to be ~ for** distinguirse por; **it is ~ that ...** es de notar que ...

notably ['nəʊtəblɪ] ADV particularmente, en particular

notary ['nəʊtərɪ] N (*also* **~ public**) notario/a *m/f*

notation [nəʊ'teɪʃən] N notación *f*

notch [nɒtʃ] N **1** (= *cut*) corte *m*, muesca *f* **2** (*US*) (= *mountain pass*) desfiladero *m*
➤ **notch up** VT + ADV apuntarse

note [nəʊt] Ⓐ N **1** (= *record, letter*) nota *f*; (*on text*) anotación *f*, nota *f*; (*more detailed*) comentario *m*; **just a quick ~ to tell you that ...** sólo una nota para decirte que ...; **see ➤ 16 on page 223** véase nota número 16 en la página 223; **keep a ~ of all your expenses** apunta *or* anota todos tus gastos; **to make a ~ of sth** apuntar *or* anotar algo **2 notes** apuntes *mpl*, notas *fpl*; **to speak from/without ~s** hablar con/sin la ayuda de apuntes *or* notas; **to make ~s** hacer anotaciones; **to take ~s** tomar apuntes; **✦ IDIOM to compare ~s (about sth)** intercambiar impresiones (acerca de algo)
3 (= *tone*) (*gen*) nota *f*; (*in voice*) dejo *m*, deje *m*; **on a more positive ~** mirando el lado positivo ...; **to sound a ~ of**

---

caution llamar a la prudencia
4 (*Mus*) (= *sound*) nota *f*; (= *key*) tecla *f*
5 (*Brit*) (= *bank note*) billete *m*; **a five-pound ~** un billete de cinco libras
6 (= *importance*) **a writer/an artist of ~** un escritor/un artista destacado *or* de renombre; **nothing of ~** nada digno de mención
7 (= *notice*) **the government should take ~ of this survey** el gobierno debería tomar nota del resultado de esta encuesta; **they will take ~ of what you say** tendrán en cuenta lo que digas; **worthy of ~** digno de mención
Ⓑ VT **1** (= *observe*) **~ the statue by Rodin** tomen nota de *or* fíjense en la estatua de Rodin; **she ~d that his hands were dirty** notó que tenía las manos sucias, se dio cuenta de que tenía las manos sucias; **please ~ that there are a limited number of tickets** les informamos que el número de entradas es limitado
2 (= *point out*) señalar, indicar; **the report ~s that this trend is on the increase** el informe señala *or* indica que esta tendencia se está extendiendo
3 (= *record officially*) tomar nota de
4 (*also* **~ down**) anotar, apuntar

notebook ['nəʊtbʊk] N **1** (= *notepad, jotter*) libreta *f*, bloc *m*; (= *exercise book*) cuaderno *m* **2** (*also* **~ computer**) ordenador *m* portátil, computador *m* portátil (*LAm*), computadora *f* portátil (*LAm*)

noted ['nəʊtɪd] ADJ [*historian, writer*] destacado, renombrado; **to be ~ for sth** ser conocido *or* famoso por algo

notepad ['nəʊtpæd] N bloc *m*, libreta *f* para notas

notepaper ['nəʊtˌpeɪpəʳ] N papel *m* de carta

noteworthy ['nəʊtˌwɜːðɪ] ADJ notable, digno de atención; **it is ~ that ...** es notable que ..., es de notar que ...

nothing ['nʌθɪŋ] Ⓐ PRON nada *f*; (= *nought*) cero *m*; **~ but** solamente; **to come to ~** parar en nada, quedarse en aguas de borraja; **~ else** nada más; **there's ~ to fear** no hay de qué tener miedo; **for ~** (= *free*) gratis; (= *unpaid*) sin sueldo; (= *in vain*) en vano, en balde; **it is not for ~ that ...** no es sin motivo que ..., por algo será que ...; **there was ~ for it but to pay** (*Brit*) no había más remedio *or* (*LAm*) no nos quedaba otra que pagar; **I have ~ to give you** no tengo nada que darte; **to have ~ to do with** no tener nada que ver con; **he is ~ if not careful** es de lo más cauteloso; **there is ~ in the rumours** los rumores no tienen nada de verdad; **there's ~ in it** (*in race*) van muy iguales; **~ much** poco, no mucho; **to have ~ on** (= *naked*) estar desnudo; (= *not busy*) estar libre; **to say ~ of ...** sin mencionar ...; **to get something for ~** obtener algo gratis; **there's ~ special about it** no tiene nada de particular; **think ~ of it!** ¡no hay de qué!, ¡no tiene cuidado! (*LAm*); **there's ~ to it!** ¡es facilísimo!; **✦ IDIOM he has ~ on her** (*comparing*) no le llega ni a la suela del zapato*
Ⓑ ADV **it's ~ like him** no se le parece en nada; **it was ~ like as expensive as we thought** era mucho menos caro de lo que nos imaginábamos
Ⓒ N **a mere ~** una friolera, una bagatela; **to her he was a ~** para ella él no tenía ningún valor

notice ['nəʊtɪs] Ⓐ N **1** (= *intimation, warning*) aviso *m*; **we require 28 days' ~ for delivery** se requieren 28 días para la entrega; **until further ~** hasta nuevo aviso; **to give sb ~ to do sth** avisar a algn que haga algo; **at a moment's ~** en seguida, inmediatamente, luego (*Mex*), al tiro (*Chi*); **to quit** (*Brit*) *or* **vacate** (*US*) aviso *or* notificación de desalojo; **at short ~** con poca antelación; **a week's ~** una semana de antelación; **without prior ~** sin previo aviso
2 (= *order to leave job etc*) **to get one's ~** ser despedido; **to give sb ~** despedir a algn; **to give sb a week's ~** despedir a algn con una semana de preaviso *or* plazo; **to give in** *or* **hand in one's ~** dimitir, renunciar
3 (= *sign*) letrero *m*; (= *poster*) cartel *m*; (= *announcement*) anuncio *m*, nota *f*; **the ~ says "keep out"** el letrero dice "prohibida la entrada"; **birth/marriage ~** anuncio *m* de nacimiento/matrimonio; **death ~** nota *f* necrológica, esquela *f* (*Sp*)
4 (= *review*) [*of play, opera etc*] reseña *f*, crítica *f*
5 (= *attention*) atención *f*; **to bring a matter to sb's ~** llamar la atención de algn sobre un asunto; **it has come to my ~ that ...** ha llegado a mi conocimiento que ...; **to**

escape ~ pasar inadvertido; **to take (no)** ~ **of sb/sth** (no) hacer caso a algn/de algo; **take no** ~ **!** ¡no hagas caso! **B** VT (*with eyes*) fijarse en; (= *perceive*) notar; **did you** ~ **the picture?** ¿te fijaste en el cuadro?; **I don't** ~ **such things** no me fijo en tales cosas; **I didn't** ~ **anything odd** no noté nada raro; **have you ever** ~**d how slowly time passes?** ¿te has fijado en *or* te has dado cuenta de lo lento que pasa el tiempo?; **I** ~ **you've removed the bookcase** veo que has quitado la estantería **C** VI fijarse, darse cuenta; **I never** ~**d** no me había fijado; **yes, so I've** ~**d!** (*iro*) ¡sí, ya me he dado cuenta *or* ya lo he notado! **D** CPD ➤ **notice board** (*Brit*) tablón *m* de anuncios

⚠ **notice ≠ noticia**

noticeable ['nəʊtɪsəbl] ADJ [*difference, change, increase*] sensible, perceptible; **it is** ~ **that ...** se nota que ..., es evidente que ..., está claro que ...; **it isn't** ~ [*mark, stain*] no se nota; **a** ~ **lack of enthusiasm** una evidente falta de entusiasmo

noticeably ['nəʊtɪsəblɪ] ADV [*different, changed, improved*] sensiblemente, perceptiblemente; **the next day it was** ~ **warmer** al día siguiente se notaba que hacía más calor

notifiable ['nəʊtɪfaɪəbl] ADJ de declaración obligatoria

notification [ˌnəʊtɪfɪˈkeɪʃən] N (= *warning, prior notice*) notificación *f*, aviso *m*; (= *announcement*) anuncio *m*

notify ['nəʊtɪfaɪ] VT avisar; **to** ~ **sb of sth** comunicar *or* notificar algo a algn

notion ['nəʊʃən] N **1** (= *idea*) idea *f*; (= *view*) opinión *f*, noción *f*; (= *whim*) capricho *m*; **I have a** ~ **that ...** tengo la idea de que ...; **I had no** ~ **that he was planning to leave** no tenía ni idea de que tuviera pensado marcharse **2 notions** (*Sew*) artículos *mpl* de mercería, mercería *f*

notional ['nəʊʃənl] ADJ hipotético, teórico

notoriety [ˌnəʊtəˈraɪətɪ] N mala fama *f*, mala reputación *f*

notorious [nəʊˈtɔːrɪəs] ADJ [*criminal*] muy conocido, celebérrimo; [*area, prison*] de mala fama, de mala reputación; [*case, crime*] muy sonado; **a** ~ **womanizer** un hombre con fama de donjuán; **to be** ~ **for sth** ser conocido por algo, tener fama de algo

notoriously [nəʊˈtɔːrɪəslɪ] ADJ **anorexia nervosa is** ~ **difficult to treat** tratar la anorexia nerviosa es de notoria dificultad, es bien sabido que tratar la anorexia nerviosa entraña gran dificultad; **he is** ~ **unreliable** tiene fama de informal

Notts [nɒts] N ABBR (*Brit*) = **Nottinghamshire**

notwithstanding ['nɒtwɪðˈstændɪŋ] **A** PREP a pesar de, no obstante **B** ADV sin embargo, no obstante **C** CONJ (*also* ~ **that**) a pesar de que, por más que + *subjun*

nougat ['nuːgɑː] N turrón *m*

nought [nɔːt] N (*esp Brit*) cero *m* ➤ **noughts and crosses** (*Brit*) tres *m* en raya

noun [naʊn] N nombre *m*, sustantivo *m*

nourish ['nʌrɪʃ] VT alimentar, nutrir

nourishing ['nʌrɪʃɪŋ] ADJ nutritivo, alimenticio

nourishment ['nʌrɪʃmənt] N (= *food*) alimento *m*; (= *nutrition*) nutrición *f*

nouveau riche [ˌnuːvəʊˈriːʃ] N (*pl* **nouveaux riches**) nuevo/a rico/a *m/f*

nouvelle cuisine ['nuːvelkwiːˈziːn] N nueva cocina *f*, nouvelle cuisine *f*

Nov. ABBR (= **November**) nov., N.

Nova Scotia ['nəʊvəˈskəʊʃə] N Nueva Escocia *f*

Nova Scotian ['nəʊvəˈskəʊʃən] **A** ADJ de Nueva Escocia **B** N habitante *mf* de Nueva Escocia

novel ['nɒvəl] **A** ADJ [*idea, suggestion, method*] original, novedoso; **it was a** ~ **experience for him** era una experiencia nueva para él **B** N novela *f*

novelist ['nɒvəlɪst] N novelista *mf*

novelty ['nɒvəltɪ] N (= *quality, thing*) novedad *f*; **once the** ~ **has worn off** cuando pase la novedad

November [nəʊˈvembəʳ] N noviembre *m*; *see* **July**

novice ['nɒvɪs] N principiante *mf*, novato/a *m/f*; (*Rel*) novicio/a *m/f*

NOW [naʊ] N ABBR (*US*) = **National Organization for Women**

now [naʊ] **A** ADV **1** (= *at this time, immediately*) ahora; (= *these days*) hoy (en) día, ahora; (= *at last, already*) ya; **what shall we do** ~? ¿qué hacemos ahora?; **nobody would think of doing that** ~ hoy (en) día *or* ahora a nadie se le ocurriría hacer eso; **it's too late** ~ ya es demasiado tarde; **can I go** ~? ¿ya me puedo ir?

2 (= *up to present*) **they've been married** ~ **for 30 years** ya llevan 30 años casados, hace 30 años que se casaron; **it's some days** ~ **since I heard anything** hace varios días que no sé nada

3 (*in time expressions*) **(every)** ~ **and again** de vez en cuando; **any moment** ~ de un momento a otro; **any day** ~ cualquier día de estos; **as of** ~ a partir de ahora; **before** ~ (= *already*) ya, antes; **you should have done that before** ~ ya tendrías que haber hecho eso, tendrías que haber hecho eso antes; **she should have arrived long before** ~ hace tiempo que tenía que haber llegado; **between** ~ **and next Tuesday** entre hoy y el martes que viene; **they must be there by** ~ ya deben de haber llegado; **by** ~ **everybody was tired** para entonces ya estaban todos cansados; **by** ~ **it was clear that ...** en ese momento ya estaba claro que ...; **that will do for** ~ por ahora *or* por el momento basta con eso; **(in) three weeks/one hundred years from** ~ dentro de tres semanas/cien años; **just** ~ (= *at this moment*) ahora mismo, en este momento; (= *a moment ago*) hace un momento; **they won't be long** ~ no tardarán en venir, al rato vienen (*Mex*); **it's** ~ **or never** es ahora o nunca; **from** ~ **on** (*with present, future tense*) a partir de ahora, de ahora en adelante; (*with past tense*) a partir de entonces; **(every)** ~ **and then** de vez en cuando; **until** ~ ◇ **up to** ~ (= *till this moment*) hasta ahora; (= *till that moment*) hasta entonces

4 (= *in these circumstances*) ya; ~ **we won't be able to go** ya no podemos ir; **how can I believe you** ~? ¿cómo puedo seguir confiando en ti?; ~ **what (do we do)?** ¿y ahora, qué (hacemos)?; ~ **you've gone and done it!**[*] ¡ahora sí que la has hecho buena!*; ~ **look what you've done!** ¡mira lo que has hecho!

5 (= *well*) bien, bueno; ~**, as you all know ...** bien *or* bueno, como todos sabéis ...; ~ **there's a coincidence!** ¡eso sí que es una coincidencia!; ~ **there's a thought** pues no es mala idea

6 (= *come on*) ~ **Fred, you don't really mean that** vamos Fred, no lo dices en serio; **now, now, don't get so upset!** ¡vamos *or* (*Sp*) venga, no te pongas así!; **now, now, we'll have none of that!** ¡basta *or* (*Sp*) vale ya, nada de tonterías!; **come** ~**, you must be hungry** venga ya, no me digas que no tienes hambre; ~ **then, what's the trouble?** ¡entonces a ver! ¿cuál es el problema?

B PRON ~ **is your chance to talk to him** está es tu oportunidad de hablar con él; ~ **is the best time to go to Scotland** ésta es la mejor época para ir a Escocia

C CONJ ~ **(that)** ahora que; ~ **(that) you mention it** ahora que lo dices

nowadays ['naʊədeɪz] ADV hoy (en) día, en la actualidad

nowhere ['nəʊwɛəʳ] ADV **1** (*lit*) [*be*] en ninguna parte; [*go*] a ninguna parte; **you're going** ~ no vas a ninguna parte; **they have** ~ **to go** no tienen dónde ir; **there was** ~ **to hide** no había dónde esconderse; **there is** ~ **more romantic than Paris** no hay lugar más romántico que París; **it's** ~ **you'll ever find it** está en un sitio donde no lo encontrarás nunca; **she had** ~ **else to go** no tenía otro lugar a donde ir; ~ **in Europe** en ninguna parte de Europa; **she was** ~ **to be seen** no se la veía por ninguna parte

2 (*fig*) **without me he would be** ~ sin mí no habría llegado a ninguna parte; **the party came from** ~ **to win the election** el partido surgió de la nada y ganó las elecciones; **we're getting** ~ no estamos consiguiendo nada; **five pounds goes** ~ **these days** cinco libras no se hace nada hoy en día; **it's** ~ **near as big/good** no es tan grande/bueno ni con mucho; **£10 is** ~ **near enough** diez libras no bastan, ni mucho menos

no-win ['nəʊˈwɪn] ADJ **a** ~ **situation** una situación imposible *or* sin salida

noxious ['nɒkʃəs] ADJ nocivo

nozzle ['nɒzl] N [of hose, vacuum cleaner] boquilla f; [of spray] pulverizador m; (Mech) tobera f, inyector m

nr ABBR (Brit) = **near**

NRA N ABBR (US) = **National Rifle Association of America**

NS ABBR (Canada) = **Nova Scotia**

NSC N ABBR (US) = **National Security Council**

NSPCC N ABBR (Brit) = **National Society for the Prevention of Cruelty to Children**

NSW ABBR = **New South Wales**

nth [enθ] ADJ enésimo; **to the ~ power** a la enésima potencia; **for the ~ time*** por enésima vez

nuance ['njuːɑ̃ːns] N matiz m

nubile ['njuːbaɪl] ADJ [girl, woman] núbil; (hum) joven y guapa

nuclear ['njuːklɪəʳ] ADJ (Phys, Mil) nuclear ➤ **nuclear deterrent** fuerza f disuasiva nuclear ➤ **Nuclear Non-Proliferation Treaty** Tratado m de No Proliferación Nuclear ➤ **nuclear physicist** físico/a m/f nuclear ➤ **nuclear power** energía f nuclear ➤ **nuclear power station** central f nuclear ➤ **nuclear waste** desechos mpl nucleares

nuclear-free ['njuːklɪəˌfriː] ADJ desnuclearizado, no nuclear ➤ **nuclear-free zone** zona f desnuclearizada

nuclear-powered [,njuːklɪəˈpaʊəd] ADJ nuclear

nucleus ['njuːklɪəs] N (pl **nuclei** ['njuːklɪaɪ]) núcleo m

nude [njuːd] Ⓐ ADJ desnudo Ⓑ N 1 (Art) desnudo m 2 **in the ~** desnudo/a

nudge [nʌdʒ] Ⓐ N codazo m; **to give sb a ~** dar un codazo a algn; **he said she's his secretary, ~ ~** dijo que era su secretaria, tú ya me entiendes Ⓑ VT dar un codazo a

nudist ['njuːdɪst] N (des)nudista mf ➤ **nudist camp** colonia f nudista

nudity ['njuːdɪtɪ] N desnudez f

nugget ['nʌɡɪt] N (Min) pepita f; **gold ~** pepita de oro

nuisance ['njuːsns] Ⓐ N 1 (= situation, thing) fastidio m, lata* f; **what a ~!** ¡qué lata!*; **it's a ~ having to shave!** ¡qué lata tener que afeitarse!* 2 (= person) pesado/a m/f, latoso/a* m/f; **what a ~ you are!** ¡eres un pesado!, ¡eres un latoso!*; **to make a ~ of o.s.** dar la lata*, ponerse pesado Ⓑ CPD ➤ **nuisance call** llamada f anónima ➤ **nuisance caller** llamante mf anónimo/a ➤ **nuisance value:** **he's only of ~ value** no hace más que fastidiar, sólo vale para crear problemas

NUJ N ABBR (Brit) = **National Union of Journalists**

nuke* [njuːk] VT atacar con arma nuclear

null [nʌl] ADJ **~ and void** nulo

nullify ['nʌlɪfaɪ] VT anular, invalidar

NUM N ABBR (Brit) = **National Union of Mineworkers**

numb [nʌm] Ⓐ ADJ 1 (with cold) entumecido; **my feet were ~ with cold** tenía los pies entumecidos de frío; **my fingers have gone ~** (with cold) se me han entumecido los dedos; (from posture) se me han dormido los dedos 2 (with fear, shock) paralizado; **when I heard about the accident I just felt ~** cuando me enteré del accidente me quedé atontado or sin poder reaccionar Ⓑ VT (= deaden) (with injection) adormecer; **alcohol was the only thing that ~ed the pain** el alcohol era la única cosa que aplacaba el dolor

number ['nʌmbəʳ] Ⓐ N 1 número m; (also **registration ~**) matrícula f; **an even/odd ~** un número par/impar; **we live at ~ 15** vivimos en el número 15; **my ~ is 414 3925** mi (número de) teléfono es el 414 3925; **it's (at) ~ three in the charts** está tercero or es el número tres en la lista de éxitos; **she's the world ~ one** es la campeona mundial; **the ~ one Spanish player** el mejor jugador español, el número uno de los jugadores españoles; **it's my ~ one priority** es lo más importante para mí; ✦ IDIOMS **I've got his ~ now*** ya lo tengo calado*; **he only thinks of ~ one** sólo piensa en sí mismo; **his ~ is up*** le ha llegado la hora 2 (= quantity, amount) número m; **equal ~s of women and men** el mismo número de mujeres y hombres; **a ~ of** (= several) varios; **in a large ~ of cases** en muchos casos, en

un gran número de casos; **in a small ~ of cases** en contados or unos pocos casos; **I've had an enormous ~ of letters** he recibido muchísimas cartas; **there must be any ~ of people in my position** debe de haber gran cantidad de personas en mi situación; **any ~ can play** puede jugar cualquier número de personas, pueden jugar cuantos quieran; **they were eight/few in ~** eran ocho/pocos 3 (= group) **one of their ~** uno de ellos 4 (= edition) número m 5 (= song, act) número m; **and for my next ~ I shall sing …** ahora voy a cantar …; ✦ IDIOM **to do a ~ on sb** (US*) hacer una jugada a algn* 6 (Bible) **(the Book of) Numbers** (el libro de) Números Ⓑ VT 1 (= assign number to) numerar; **they are ~ed from one to ten** están numerados del uno al diez 2 (= include) contar; **to ~ sb among one's friends** contar a algn entre sus amigos; **to be ~ed among** figurar entre 3 (= limit) ✦ IDIOM **his days are ~ed** tiene los días contados Ⓒ CPD ➤ **number plate** (Brit) matrícula f, placa f (esp LAm), chapa f (de matrícula) (SC) ➤ **numbers game, numbers racket** (US) (= lottery) lotería f; (illegal) lotería clandestina ➤ **Number Ten** (Brit) la casa del Primer Ministro británico

numbly ['nʌmlɪ] ADV **she watched ~ …** se quedó mirando atontada

numbness ['nʌmnɪs] N 1 (lit) **I had a feeling of ~ in my legs** (from position) se me habían dormido las piernas; (from cold) tenía las piernas entumecidas 2 (from grief, fear, shock) atontamiento m

numeracy ['njuːmərəsɪ] N conocimientos mpl básicos de aritmética

numeral ['njuːmərəl] Ⓐ N número m Ⓑ ADJ numeral

numerate ['njuːmərɪt] ADJ **to be ~** tener conocimientos básicos de aritmética

numeric [njuːˈmerɪk] ADJ numérico ➤ **numeric keypad** teclado m numérico

numerical [njuːˈmerɪkəl] ADJ numérico; **in ~ order** por orden numérico

numerous ['njuːmərəs] ADJ numeroso; **in ~ cases** en numerosos casos; **~ people believe that …** mucha gente cree que …

nun [nʌn] N monja f, religiosa f; **to become a ~** hacerse monja, meterse (a) monja*

nuptial ['nʌpʃəl] ADJ nupcial

nuptials ['nʌpʃəlz] NPL (hum) nupcias fpl

nurse [nɜːs] Ⓐ N 1 (in hospital, clinic) enfermero/a m/f; **male ~** enfermero m; **student ~** estudiante mf de enfermería 2 (children's) niñera f Ⓑ VT 1 [+ patient] cuidar, atender; **she ~d him back to health** lo cuidó hasta que se repuso 2 [+ baby] (= suckle) amamantar; (= cradle) mecer 3 [+ anger, grudge] alimentar; [+ hope] abrigar

nursemaid ['nɜːsmeɪd] N (esp US) niñera f, aya f

> Use **el/un** not **la/una** before feminine nouns beginning with stressed **a** or **ha** like **aya**.

✦ IDIOM **to play ~ to sb** hacer de niñera de algn

nursery ['nɜːsrɪ] Ⓐ N 1 (= crèche) guardería f, jardín m de infancia; (= school) parvulario m, escuela f de párvulos, escuela f infantil (Sp), kínder m (LAm); (= room at home) cuarto m del bebé, habitación f del bebé 2 (Agr, Hort) vivero m Ⓑ CPD ➤ **nursery education** educación f preescolar ➤ **nursery nurse** (Brit) puericultor(a) m/f ➤ **nursery rhyme** canción f infantil ➤ **nursery school** parvulario m, escuela f de párvulos, escuela f infantil (Sp), kínder m (LAm) ➤ **nursery slopes** (Brit Ski) pistas fpl para principiantes ➤ **nursery teacher** maestro/a m/f de parvulario, maestro/a m/f de preescolar

nursing ['nɜːsɪŋ] Ⓐ N 1 (= career, course, profession) enfermería f; **to go in for ~** hacerse enfermero/a, dedicarse a la enfermería 2 (= care) [of patient] asistencia f, cuidado m 3 (= suckling) lactancia f Ⓑ CPD ➤ **nursing bottle** (US) biberón m ➤ **nursing home** (for elderly) hogar m de ancianos; (for convalescents) clínica f (particular) ➤ **nursing**

mother madre *f* que amamanta ➤ **nursing staff** personal *m* de enfermería

nurture ['nɜːtʃəʳ] **Ⓐ** VT **1** (= *bring up*) criar, educar **2** (= *nourish*) nutrir, alimentar **Ⓑ** N educación *f*, crianza *f*; **nature or** ~ naturaleza o educación

NUS N ABBR (*Brit*) = **National Union of Students**

NUT N ABBR (*Brit*) = **National Union of Teachers**

nut [nʌt] N **1** (*Tech*) tuerca *f*; ✦ IDIOM **the ~s and bolts of a scheme** los aspectos prácticos de un proyecto **2** (*Bot*) nuez *f*; ✦ IDIOMS **it's a tough ~ to crack** es un hueso duro de roer; **he's a tough ~** es un tipo duro; **~s!*** ¡narices!* **3** (*) (= *head*) coco* *m*; ✦ IDIOMS **to do one's ~** (*Brit*) salirse de sus casillas*; **to be off one's ~** estar chiflado *or* chalado* **4** (*) (= *crazy person*) chiflado/a* *m/f*, chalado/a* *m/f* **5** **nuts***** (= *testicles*) cojones*** *mpl*, huevos*** *mpl*

nutcase* ['nʌtkeɪs] N chiflado/a* *m/f*, chalado/a* *m/f*

nutcrackers ['nʌtˌkrækəz] NPL cascanueces *m inv*

nutmeg ['nʌtmeg] N nuez *f* moscada

nutrient ['njuːtrɪənt] N nutriente *m*

nutrition [njuːˈtrɪʃən] N nutrición *f*, alimentación *f*

nutritional [njuːˈtrɪʃənl] ADJ nutritivo, nutricional

nutritionist [njuːˈtrɪʃənɪst] N nutricionista *mf*

nutritious [njuːˈtrɪʃəs] ADJ nutritivo, alimenticio

nuts* [nʌts] ADJ chiflado*, chalado*; **to be ~ about sth/sb** estar chiflado por algo/algn*; **to drive sb ~** volver loco a

algn; **to go** ~ volverse loco

nutshell ['nʌtʃel] N cáscara *f* de nuez; ✦ IDIOMS **in a ~** en pocas palabras; **to put it in a ~** para decirlo en pocas palabras

nutter** ['nʌtəʳ] N (*Brit*) chiflado/a* *m/f*, chalado/a* *m/f*

nutty ['nʌtɪ] ADJ (*compar* **nuttier**; *superl* **nuttiest**) **1** [*cake*] con nueces; [*taste*] a nuez **2** (*) (= *crazy*) chiflado*; **to be ~ about sth/sb** estar chiflado por algo/algn*

nuzzle ['nʌzl] **Ⓐ** VT acariciar con el hocico **Ⓑ** VI arrimarse

NV ABBR (*US*) = **Nevada**

NVQ N ABBR (*Brit*) = **National Vocational Qualification**

NW ABBR (= *northwest*) NO

NWT ABBR (*Canada*) = **Northwest Territories**

NY ABBR (*US*) = **New York**

NYC ABBR (*US*) = **New York City**

nylon ['naɪlɒn] **Ⓐ** N **1** (= *fabric*) nilón *m*, nailon *m* **2** **nylons**† medias *fpl* de nilón *or* nailon **Ⓑ** ADJ de nilón, de nailon

nymph [nɪmf] N ninfa *f*

nymphomaniac [ˌnɪmfəˈmeɪnɪæk] **Ⓐ** N ninfómana *f* **Ⓑ** ADJ ninfómano

NYSE N ABBR (*US*) = **New York Stock Exchange**

NZ, N. Zeal ABBR = **New Zealand**

Oo

O, o [əʊ] N **1** (= *letter*) O, o *f*; **O for Oliver** O de Oviedo **2** (= *number*) (*Telec etc*) cero *m*

oaf [əʊf] N zoquete* *mf*

oak [əʊk] **Ⓐ** N (= *wood, tree*) roble *m*; (= *holm oak*) encina *f* **Ⓑ** ADJ [*table, furniture*] de roble

OAP N ABBR (*Brit*) = **old age pensioner**

OAPEC [əʊˈeɪpek] N ABBR (= **Organization of Arab Petroleum-Exporting Countries**) OPAEP *f*

oar [ɔːʳ] N remo *m*

oarsman [ˈɔːzmən] N (*pl* **oarsmen**) remero *m*

oarswoman [ˈɔːzwʊmən] N (*pl* **oarswomen**) remera *f*

OAS N ABBR (= **Organization of American States**) OEA *f*

oasis [əʊˈeɪsɪs] N (*pl* **oases** [əʊˈeɪsiːz]) oasis *m inv*

oat bran [ˈəʊtbræn] N salvado *m* de avena

oatcake [ˈəʊtkeɪk] N torta *f* de avena

oath [əʊθ] N (*pl* **~s** [əʊðz]) **1** (*sworn*) juramento *m*; **under ~** bajo juramento; **to take the ~** prestar juramento; **to take an ~ of allegiance** (*Mil*) jurar la bandera **2** (= *swear word*) palabrota *f*, grosería *f* (*esp LAm*), lisura *f* (*And, SC*); (= *curse*) blasfemia *f*, maldición *f*

oatmeal [ˈəʊtmiːl] N (*for cooking*) harina *f* de avena; (*US*) (= *porridge*) avena *f* (cocida), atole *m* (*Mex*)

oats [əʊts] NPL avena *fsing*

obdurate [ˈɒbdjʊrɪt] ADJ (= *stubborn*) obstinado, terco; (= *unyielding*) inflexible, firme

OBE N ABBR (*Brit*) (= **Officer of the Order of the British Empire**) *título ceremonial*

obedience [əˈbiːdɪəns] N obediencia *f*; **to show ~ to sb/sth** obedecer a algn/algo

obedient [əˈbiːdɪənt] ADJ obediente; **to be ~ to sth/sb** obedecer a algo/algn

obediently [əˈbiːdɪəntlɪ] ADV obedientemente

obelisk [ˈɒbɪlɪsk] N obelisco *m*

obese [əʊˈbiːs] ADJ obeso

obesity [əʊˈbiːsɪtɪ] N obesidad *f*

obey [əˈbeɪ] **Ⓐ** VT [+ *person*] obedecer; [+ *law*] observar, acatar; [+ *order*] cumplir; **I like to be ~ed** exijo obediencia **Ⓑ** VI obedecer

obituary [əˈbɪtjʊərɪ] N necrología *f*, obituario *m* ➤ **obituary column** sección *f* necrológica

object[1] [ˈɒbdʒɪkt] **Ⓐ** N **1** (= *item*) objeto *m* **2** (= *focus*) objeto *m*; **the ~ of her hatred/love** el objeto de su odio/su amor; **he became an ~ of ridicule** quedó en ridículo **3** (= *aim*) objetivo *m*; **the ~ of the exercise is to raise money for charity** lo que se persigue con esto es recaudar dinero con fines benéficos; **that's the whole ~ of the exercise** de eso precisamente se trata **4** (= *obstacle*) **I want the best, money is no ~** quiero lo mejor, no importa cuánto cueste **5** (*Gram*) complemento *m* **Ⓑ** CPD ➤ **object lesson** (*fig*) **it was an ~ lesson in how not to drive a car** fue un perfecto ejemplo de cómo no conducir un coche ➤ **object pronoun** (*Gram*) pronombre *m* que funciona como objeto

object[2] [əbˈdʒekt] **Ⓐ** VT objetar **Ⓑ** VI **1** (= *disapprove*) oponerse (**to** a); **if you don't ~** si no tiene inconveniente; **I wouldn't ~ to a bite to eat** no diría que no a algo que comer; **I would ~ to Paul as chairman** me opondría a que Paul fuera presidente; **do you ~ to my smoking?** ¿le molesta que fume? **2** (= *protest*) oponerse, poner objeciones; **I ~!** (*frm*) ¡protesto!

objection [əbˈdʒekʃən] N **1** (= *aversion*) **do you have any ~ to my smoking?** ¿le molesta que fume?; **I have no ~ to people having a celebration, but ...** no tengo nada en contra de que la gente celebre cosas, pero ... **2** (= *opposing view*) objeción *f*; **are there any ~s?** ¿alguna

objeción?, ¿alguien en contra?; **we have no ~ to the plan** no tenemos ninguna objeción al plan; **I have no ~** no tengo inconveniente; **do you have any ~ to my going?** ¿tienes algún inconveniente en que vaya (yo)? **3** (*Jur*) **objection!** ¡protesto!; **~ overruled** no ha lugar a la protesta

objectionable [əbˈdʒekʃnəbl] ADJ [*person*] grosero, desagradable; [*behaviour, attitude, remark*] inaceptable; [*language*] (= *indecent*) grosero, soez; (= *offensive*) ofensivo; [*smell*] desagradable, molesto

objective [əbˈdʒektɪv] **Ⓐ** ADJ **1** (= *impartial*) objetivo; **to take an ~ look at sth** mirar algo desde un punto de vista objetivo **2** (= *real*) [*evidence, facts*] objetivo **Ⓑ** N (= *aim*) objetivo *m*, propósito *m*

objectively [əbˈdʒektɪvlɪ] ADV **1** (= *impartially*) objetivamente, de manera objetiva; **~, such criticism is hardly fair** objetivamente or desde un punto de vista objetivo, críticas semejantes no son lo que se dice justas **2** (= *actually*) realmente

objectivity [ˌɒbdʒɪkˈtɪvɪtɪ] N objetividad *f*

objector [əbˈdʒektəʳ] N opositor(a) *m/f*

obligate [ˈɒblɪgeɪt] VT (*frm*) **to ~ sb to do sth** obligar a algn a hacer algo; **to be ~d to do sth** estar obligado a hacer algo

obligation [ˌɒblɪˈgeɪʃən] N obligación *f*; **"no obligation to buy"** "sin compromiso a comprar"; **you have an ~ to see that ...** le cumple a usted comprobar que ... + *subjun*; **to be under an ~ to sb/to do sth** estar comprometido con algn/a hacer algo

obligatory [ɒˈblɪgətərɪ] ADJ obligatorio; **to make it ~ for sb to do sth** hacer obligatorio que algn haga algo

oblige [əˈblaɪdʒ] VT **1** (= *compel*) obligar, forzar; **to ~ sb to do sth** obligar a algn a hacer algo; **you are not ~d to do it** no estás obligado a hacerlo **2** (= *gratify*) complacer, hacer un favor a; **he did it to ~ us** lo hizo como favor or para complacernos; **anything to ~!** ¡cualquier cosa!, ¡con mucho gusto!; **much ~d!** ¡muchísimas gracias!, ¡muy agradecido!; **I should be much ~d if ...** agradecería que ... + *subjun*; **I am ~d to you for your help** le agradezco mucho su ayuda

obliging [əˈblaɪdʒɪŋ] ADJ amable, atento; **it was very ~ of them** fue muy amable de su parte

obligingly [əˈblaɪdʒɪŋlɪ] ADV amablemente, atentamente

oblique [əˈbliːk] **Ⓐ** ADJ **1** [*angle*] oblicuo **2** (*fig*) [*reference*] indirecto, tangencial; [*reply*] evasivo **Ⓑ** N (*Typ*) oblicua *f*

obliquely [əˈbliːklɪ] ADV indirectamente

obliterate [əˈblɪtəreɪt] VT **1** (= *destroy*) arrasar con, destruir **2** (= *blot out*) borrar; (= *hide*) ocultar

obliteration [əˌblɪtəˈreɪʃən] N (= *destruction*) arrasamiento *m*, destrucción *f*

oblivion [əˈblɪvɪən] N olvido *m*

oblivious [əˈblɪvɪəs] ADJ **~ to** inconsciente de

oblong [ˈɒblɒŋ] **Ⓐ** ADJ rectangular, oblongo **Ⓑ** N rectángulo *m*

obnoxious [əbˈnɒkʃəs] ADJ odioso, aborrecible

oboe [ˈəʊbəʊ] N oboe *m*

oboist [ˈəʊbəʊɪst] N oboe *mf*

obscene [əbˈsiːn] ADJ **1** (= *indecent*) [*gesture, language, remark*] obsceno, soez; [*phone call, act*] obsceno, indecente **2** (= *shocking*) [*profit, salary*] escandaloso

obscenely [əbˈsiːnlɪ] ADV **1** (= *indecently*) [*gesture, remark*] obscenamente **2** (= *shockingly*) [*fat*] repugnantemente; [*rich, expensive*] escandalosamente

obscenity [əbˈsenɪtɪ] N (= *indecency*) obscenidad *f*, indecencia *f*; (= *word*) palabrota *f*, grosería *f* (*esp LAm*), lisura *f* (*And, SC*)

obscure [əbˈskjʊəʳ] **Ⓐ** ADJ **1** (= *not well-known*) [*book, artist, poet*] poco conocido, oscuro **2** (= *not obvious*) **the meaning**

is ~ el significado es oscuro *or* poco claro; **for some ~ reason** por alguna extraña razón **3** (= *indistinct*) [*shape, figure*] borroso **Ⓑ** VT (= *hide*) [+ *object, face, truth*] ocultar; **this news should not be allowed to ~ the fact that ...** no se debería permitir que esta noticia impida ver claramente que *or* que esta noticia vele el hecho de que ...

obscurity [əbˈskjʊərɪtɪ] N oscuridad *f*

obsequious [əbˈsiːkwɪəs] ADJ servil, sumiso

observable [əbˈzɜːvəbl] ADJ [*benefit, consequence, effect*] visible; [*phenomenon*] observable, perceptible; [*rise, fall, improvement, increase*] apreciable, perceptible

observance [əbˈzɜːvəns] N [*of rule etc*] observancia *f* (**of** de), cumplimiento *m* (**of** de); [*of customs, rites etc*] práctica *f*

observant [əbˈzɜːvənt] ADJ observador

observation [ˌɒbzəˈveɪʃən] **Ⓐ** N **1** (= *perception*) observación *f*; **he is under ~ in hospital** lo tienen en observación en el hospital; **the police are keeping him under ~** la policía lo tiene vigilado; **powers of ~** capacidad *fsing* de observación **2** (= *remark*) observación *f*, comentario *m* **Ⓑ** CPD ➤ **observation post** (*Mil*) puesto *m* de observación ➤ **observation tower** torre *f* de vigilancia

observatory [əbˈzɜːvətrɪ] N observatorio *m*

observe [əbˈzɜːv] VT **1** (= *see, notice*) observar, ver **2** (= *watch carefully, study*) observar, mirar; [+ *suspect*] vigilar **3** (= *remark*) observar, comentar **4** (= *obey*) [+ *rule, custom*] observar; [+ *Sabbath, silence*] guardar; [+ *anniversary*] celebrar

observer [əbˈzɜːvəʳ] N observador(a) *m/f*

obsess [əbˈses] VT obsesionar

obsessed [əbˈsest] ADJ obsesionado; **he's ~ with the idea** está obsesionado con la idea, le obsesiona la idea

obsession [əbˈseʃən] N obsesión *f*; **to have an ~ about sth** estar obsesionado con algo; **football is an ~ with him** está obsesionado con el fútbol, el fútbol es una obsesión para él

obsessional [əbˈseʃənəl] ADJ [*behaviour, love, hatred, thought*] obsesivo; **to be ~ about sth** estar obsesionado con algo

obsessive [əbˈsesɪv] ADJ [*behaviour, jealousy, interest, need*] obsesivo; **his ~ tidiness was driving her crazy** su obsesión *or* manía con *or* por la limpieza la estaba sacando de quicio; **to be ~ about sth** estar obsesionado con algo

obsessively [əbˈsesɪvlɪ] ADV [*work*] de (una) forma obsesiva; [*love, hate*] de (una) forma obsesiva *or* enfermiza; **she is ~ tidy** tiene obsesión *or* manía con *or* por la limpieza

obsolescence [ˌɒbsəˈlesns] N obsolescencia *f*

obsolescent [ˌɒbsəˈlesnt] ADJ que está cayendo en desuso

obsolete [ˈɒbsəliːt] ADJ [*weapon, equipment, machine*] obsoleto; [*attitude, idea, system*] obsoleto, anticuado; [*process, practice, word, law*] obsoleto, en desuso; [*ticket*] caduco

obstacle [ˈɒbstəkl] N obstáculo *m*; **that is no ~ to our doing it** eso no impide que lo hagamos ➤ **obstacle course** pista *f* de obstáculos ➤ **obstacle race** (*Sport*) carrera *f* de obstáculos

obstetric [ɒbˈstetrɪk] ADJ obstétrico

obstetrical [ɒbˈstetrɪkəl] ADJ obstétrico

obstetrician [ˌɒbstəˈtrɪʃən] N tocólogo/a *m/f*, obstetra *mf*

obstetrics [ɒbˈstetrɪks] NSING obstetricia *f*, tocología *f*

obstinacy [ˈɒbstɪnəsɪ] N obstinación *f*, terquedad *f*

obstinate [ˈɒbstɪnɪt] ADJ (= *stubborn*) obstinado, terco; **to be ~ about sth** obstinarse en algo, ser obstinado con algo

obstinately [ˈɒbstɪnɪtlɪ] ADV obstinadamente, tercamente

obstreperous [əbˈstrepərəs] ADJ [*person, behaviour*] escandaloso; **he became ~** empezó a demandarse

obstruct [əbˈstrʌkt] VT **1** (= *block*) obstruir; [+ *pipe*] atascar; [+ *road*] cerrar, bloquear; [+ *view*] tapar **2** (= *hinder*) [+ *person*] estorbar, impedir; [+ *plan, progress etc*] dificultar, obstaculizar; (*Parl, Sport*) obstruir, bloquear

obstruction [əbˈstrʌkʃən] N **1** (= *blockage*) obstrucción *f*; (*in pipe, road*) atasco *m*; (*Med*) oclusión *f*; **to cause an ~** estorbar; (*Aut*) obstruir el tráfico **2** (= *obstacle*) (*to progress*)

dificultad *f*, obstáculo *m* **3** (*Ftbl*) obstrucción *f*, bloqueo *m*

obstructionism [əbˈstrʌkʃənɪzəm] N obstruccionismo *m*

obstructive [əbˈstrʌktɪv] ADJ obstruccionista; **he's just being ~** está poniendo dificultades nada más

obtain [əbˈteɪn] VT obtener, conseguir; (= *acquire*) adquirir

obtainable [əbˈteɪnəbl] ADJ (= *on sale*) a la venta; (= *available*) disponible

obtrude [əbˈtruːd] (*frm*) **Ⓐ** VT [+ *tongue etc*] sacar **Ⓑ** VI [*person*] entrometerse

obtrusive [əbˈtruːsɪv] ADJ [*presence, person*] molesto; [*smell*] penetrante; [*colours*] llamativo; [*building*] demasiado prominente

obtuse [əbˈtjuːs] ADJ **1** (*Math*) obtuso **2** [*person*] obtuso, torpe

obtuseness [əbˈtjuːsnɪs] N (*fig*) torpeza *f*, obtusidad *f*

obverse [ˈɒbvɜːs] N anverso *m*; (*fig*) complemento *m*

obviate [ˈɒbvɪeɪt] VT obviar, evitar; **to ~ the need for sth** evitar *or* ahorrar la necesidad de algo

obvious [ˈɒbvɪəs] **Ⓐ** ADJ (= *clear, perceptible*) [*disadvantage, solution*] obvio, claro; [*danger*] evidente; [*question*] obvio; **it's ~ that he's unhappy/we can't win** está claro *or* es evidente que es infeliz/no podemos ganar; **he isn't going to resign, that much is ~** no va a dimitir, eso está claro *or* es evidente; **she made it very ~ that she didn't like him** dejó muy claro que no le gustaba, hizo patente que no le gustaba; **he's the ~ man for the job** es la persona obvia para el puesto; **it's the ~ thing to do** está claro que es eso lo que hay que hacer; **it was ~ to everyone that it had been a mistake** todo el mundo se daba cuenta de que había sido un error
Ⓑ N **to state the ~** afirmar lo obvio

obviously [ˈɒbvɪəslɪ] ADV **1** (= *clearly*) obviamente; **he was ~ very angry/tired** se notaba que estaba muy enfadado/cansado, estaba claro *or* era evidente *or* era obvio que estaba muy enfadado/cansado; **he was ~ not drunk** estaba claro *or* era evidente *or* era obvio que no estaba borracho; **he was not ~ drunk** no se le notaba que estaba borracho; **~, I am delighted** lógicamente *or* por supuesto, estoy encantado; **obviously!** ¡por supuesto!, ¡lógico!, ¡obvio!; **"aren't they coming?" — "~ not!"** —¿no vienen? —¡evidentemente no *or* obviamente no! **2** (= *unsubtly*) **she asked him rather too ~ where he had been** le preguntó sin mucha delicadeza (que) dónde había estado

ocarina [ˌɒkəˈriːnə] N ocarina *f*

OCAS N ABBR (= *Organization of Central American States*) ODECA *f*

occasion [əˈkeɪʒən] **Ⓐ** N **1** (= *particular time*) ocasión *f*; **(on) the first ~ that it happened** la primera vez que ocurrió; **on ~** de vez en cuando; **on one ~** una vez; **on that ~** esa vez, en aquella ocasión; **on the ~ of his retirement** con motivo de su jubilación; **to take (the) ~ to do sth** aprovechar la oportunidad para hacer algo **2** (= *event*) acontecimiento *m*; **it was quite an ~** fue todo un acontecimiento; **what's the ~?** ¿qué se celebra?; **I wasn't dressed for the ~** no estaba vestida de forma adecuada para la ocasión; **to rise or be equal to the ~** ponerse a la altura de las circunstancias **3** (= *reason*) razón *f*, motivo *m*; **should the ~ arise ◇ if the ~ arises** si se da el caso; **to have ~ to do sth** (= *opportunity*) tener ocasión de hacer algo; (= *reason*) tener motivo para hacer algo; **you had no ~ to say that** no había necesidad de que dijeras eso, no había motivo para decir eso **Ⓑ** VT (*frm*) ocasionar (*frm*), causar

occasional [əˈkeɪʒənl] ADJ (= *infrequent*) [*lapse, meeting*] esporádico; [*rain, showers*] ocasional, aislado; **she made ~ visits to England** hacía alguna que otra visita a Inglaterra, hacía visitas esporádicas a Inglaterra; **I have the or an ~ drink** tomo una copa de vez en cuando; **he smokes only the or a very ~ cigar** sólo muy de vez en cuando *or* muy de tarde en tarde se fuma un puro ➤ **occasional table** mesa *f* auxiliar

occasionally [əˈkeɪʒnəlɪ] ADV de vez en cuando, a veces; ocasionalmente (*frm*), cada cuando (*LAm*); **we see each**

other (only) **very ~** nos vemos (sólo) muy de vez en cuando *or* muy de tarde en tarde

occult [ɒˈkʌlt] Ⓐ ADJ oculto Ⓑ N **the ~** lo oculto

occupancy [ˈɒkjʊpənsɪ] N ocupación *f*; (= *tenancy*) inquilinato *m*; [*of post*] tenencia *f*

occupant [ˈɒkjʊpənt] N 1 (= *tenant*) inquilino/a *m/f* 2 [*of boat, car etc*] ocupante *mf* 3 [*of job, post*] titular *mf*

occupation [ˌɒkjʊˈpeɪʃən] N 1 (= *employment*) empleo *m*, profesión *f*; **what is his ~?** ¿cuál es su profesión?; **by ~** de profesión 2 (= *pastime*) pasatiempo *m* 3 (*Mil etc*) ocupación *f*; **under (military) ~** ocupado por el ejército 4 [*of house etc*] tenencia *f*; **the house is ready for ~** la casa está lista para habitar 5 [*of post, office*] tenencia *f*

occupational [ˌɒkjʊˈpeɪʃənl] ADJ (*gen*) profesional ➤ **occupational accident** accidente *m* laboral ➤ **occupational disease** enfermedad *f* profesional ➤ **occupational hazard** [*of job*] riesgo *m* laboral; (*hum*) gaje *m* del oficio ➤ **occupational pension scheme** plan *m* de jubilación ➤ **occupational therapist** terapeuta *mf* ocupacional ➤ **occupational therapy** terapia *f* ocupacional ➤ **occupational training** formación *f* profesional, formación *f* ocupacional

occupier [ˈɒkjʊpaɪəʳ] N [*of house, land*] inquilino/a *m/f*; [*of post*] titular *mf*

occupy [ˈɒkjʊpaɪ] VT 1 [+ *house*] habitar, vivir en; [+ *office, seat*] ocupar 2 (*Mil etc*) ocupar 3 [+ *post, position*] ocupar 4 (= *take up, fill*) [+ *space, time*] ocupar; **this job occupies all my time** este trabajo me ocupa *or* absorbe todo el tiempo 5 (= *keep busy*) ocupar; **he is very occupied at the moment** está muy ocupado en este momento; **she occupies herself by knitting** se entretiene haciendo punto 6 (*US Telec*) **to be occupied** estar comunicando

occur [əˈkɜːʳ] VI 1 (= *happen*) ocurrir, suceder; **don't let it (ever) ~ again** que no se vuelva a repetir (nunca) 2 (= *be found*) darse, encontrarse; **the plant ~s all over Spain** la planta se da en todas partes en España 3 (= *come to mind*) **to ~ to sb** ocurrírsele a algn; **it ~s to me that ...** se me ocurre que ...; **such an idea would never have ~red to her** semejante idea jamás se le hubiera ocurrido *or* pasado por la mente

occurrence [əˈkʌrəns] N (= *happening*) suceso *m*, hecho *m*; **it's an everyday ~** es cosa de todos los días, es un hecho cotidiano; **that is a common ~** eso sucede a menudo

ocean [ˈəʊʃən] Ⓐ N océano *m*; **~s of*** (*fig*) la mar de* Ⓑ CPD [*climate, region*] oceánico ➤ **ocean bed** fondo *m* del océano ➤ **ocean cruise** crucero *m* ➤ **ocean liner** transatlántico *m*

ocean-going [ˈəʊʃənˌgəʊɪŋ] ADJ [*ship*] transatlántico

Oceania [ˌəʊʃɪˈeɪnɪə] N Oceanía *f*

oceanography [ˌəʊʃəˈnɒgrəfɪ] N oceanografía *f*

ochre, ocher (*US*) [ˈəʊkəʳ] N ocre *m*

o'clock [əˈklɒk] ADV (*time*) **it is seven ~** son las siete; **it is one ~** es la una; **at nine ~ (exactly)** a las nueve (en punto); **it is just after two ~** son las dos pasadas, son un poco más de las dos; **it is nearly eight ~** son casi las ocho; **the six ~ (train/bus)** el (tren/autobús) de las seis

OCR N ABBR (*Comput*) 1 (= **optical character reader**) LOC *m* 2 (= **optical character recognition**) ROC *m*

Oct. ABBR (= **October**) oct.

octagon [ˈɒktəgən] N octágono *m*

octagonal [ɒkˈtægənl] ADJ octagonal

octane [ˈɒkteɪn] N octano *m*

octave [ˈɒktɪv] N octava *f*

octet, octette [ɒkˈtet] N octeto *m*

October [ɒkˈtəʊbəʳ] N octubre *m*; *see* **July**

octogenarian [ˌɒktəʊdʒɪˈnɛərɪən] ADJ, N octogenario/a *m/f*

octopus [ˈɒktəpəs] N (*pl* **~es**) pulpo *m*

ocular [ˈɒkjʊləʳ] ADJ ocular

oculist [ˈɒkjʊlɪst] N oculista *mf*

OD¹, O/D ABBR 1 = **on demand** 2 = **overdraft** 3 = **overdrawn**

OD²∗∗ [əʊˈdiː] ABBR = **overdose** Ⓐ N sobredosis *f* Ⓑ VI tomar una sobredosis

odd [ɒd] Ⓐ ADJ (*compar* **~er**; *superl* **~est**) 1 (= *strange*) raro, extraño; **how ~!** ¡qué raro!, ¡qué curioso!, ¡qué extraño!; **the ~ thing about it is ...** lo raro *or* lo extraño que tiene es que ...
2 (= *occasional*) algún que otro; **he enjoys the ~ glass of champagne** le gusta tomar una copa de champán de vez en cuando, le gusta tomar alguna que otra copa de champán
3 (*Math*) [*number*] impar; **~ or even** par o impar
4 (= *unpaired*) [*shoe, sock*] desparejado, sin pareja
5 (= *extra, left over*) **to be the ~ one out** (= *be over*) ser el que sobra, estar de más; (= *different*) ser distinto; (= *be the exception*) ser la excepción; **£5 and some ~ pennies** cinco libras y algunos peniques; **an ~ scrap of paper** un trozo de papel
6 (*) (*with approximate numbers*) **thirty ~** treinta y pico, treinta y tantos; **she must be forty ~** debe tener cuarenta y tantos *or* y pico años; **£20 ~** unas 20 libras
Ⓑ ADV **he acted a bit ~ when I told him** reaccionó de manera extraña *or* se puso algo raro cuando se lo dije
Ⓒ CPD ➤ **odd jobs** trabajillos *mpl* ➤ **odd lot** (*St Ex*) cantidad *f* irregular (y normalmente pequeña) de acciones *or* valores

oddball∗ [ˈɒdbɔːl] N bicho *m* raro*, excéntrico/a *m/f*

oddity [ˈɒdɪtɪ] N (= *odd thing*) cosa *f* rara; (= *odd trait*) manía *f*

odd-job man [ɒdˈdʒɒbˌmæn] N (*pl* **odd-job men**) *hombre que se dedica a hacer pequeños trabajos u arreglos*, manitas *m inv* (*Sp, Mex**)

odd-looking [ˈɒdˌlʊkɪŋ] ADJ de aspecto singular

oddly [ˈɒdlɪ] ADV [*behave, act*] de (una) manera rara, de (una) manera extraña, en forma extraña; **~ attractive/calm** extrañamente atractivo/tranquilo; **an ~ shaped room** una habitación con una forma rara *or* extraña; **~ enough** por extraño que parezca

oddments [ˈɒdmənts] NPL (*Comm*) restos *mpl*; [*of fabric*] retazos *mpl*, retales *mpl*

oddness [ˈɒdnɪs] N rareza *f*

odds [ɒdz] Ⓐ NPL 1 (*in betting*) puntos *mpl* de ventaja; **to give ~ of three to one** ofrecer tres puntos de ventaja a uno; **the ~ on the horse are five to one** las apuestas al caballo están a cinco contra uno; **short/long ~** pocas/muchas probabilidades; ✦ IDIOM **to pay over the ~** (*Brit*) pagar en demasía
2 (= *chances for or against*) probabilidades *fpl*; **the ~ are in his favour** lo tiene todo a su favor; **to fight against overwhelming ~** luchar con todo en contra; **to succeed against all the ~** tener éxito en contra de todas las predicciones; **the ~ are that ...** lo más probable es que ...
3 (*) (= *difference*) **it makes no ~** da lo mismo, da igual; **it makes no ~ to me** me da igual
4 (= *variance, strife*) **to be at ~ with sb over sth** estar reñido *or* en desacuerdo con algn por algo
Ⓑ CPD ➤ **odds and ends** (= *bits and pieces*) trozos *mpl*, pedacitos *mpl*; [*of food*] restos *mpl*, sobras *fpl*

odds-on [ˈɒdzˈɒn] CPD ➤ **odds-on favourite** (= *horse*) caballo *m* favorito, caballo *m* con puntos de ventaja; **he's ~ favourite for the job** él tiene las mejores posibilidades de ganar el puesto

odd-sounding [ˈɒdˌsaʊndɪŋ] ADJ [*name*] raro; **~ words** palabras que suenan raras

ode [əʊd] N oda *f*

odious [ˈəʊdɪəs] ADJ [*person, task*] odioso, detestable; [*behaviour, crime*] detestable; [*comparison*] odioso

odium [ˈəʊdɪəm] N (*frm*) odio *m*

odometer [ɒˈdɒmɪtəʳ] N (*US*) cuentakilómetros *m inv*

odontologist [ˌɒdɒnˈtɒlədʒɪst] N odontólogo/a *m/f*

odontology [ˌɒdɒnˈtɒlədʒɪ] N odontología *f*

odour, odor (*US*) [ˈəʊdəʳ] N olor *m* (**of** a); ✦ IDIOM **to be in bad ~ with sb** estar mal con algn

odourless, odorless (*US*) [ˈəʊdəlɪs] ADJ inodoro

odyssey [ˈɒdɪsɪ] N odisea *f*

OECD N ABBR (= **Organization for Economic Cooperation and Development**) OCDE *f*

oecumenical [ˌiːkjuːˈmenɪkəl] ADJ ecuménico

oedema [ɪˈdiːmə] N (*pl* **~ta** [ɪˈdiːmətə]) edema *m*

Oedipus [ˈiːdɪpəs] N Edipo ➤ **Oedipus complex** (*Psych*) complejo *m* de Edipo

oenologist, enologist (*US*) [iːˈnɒlədʒɪst] N enólogo/a *m/f*

oenology, enology (*US*) [iːˈnɒlədʒɪ] N enología *f*

oesophagus, esophagus (*US*) [iːˈsɒfəgəs] N esófago *m*

oestrogen, estrogen (*US*) [ˈiːstrəʊdʒən] N estrógeno *m*

oeuvre [ˈɜːvrə] N obra *f*

of [ɒv, əv] PREP **1** (*indicating possession*) de; **the house of my uncle** la casa de mi tío; **a friend of mine** un amigo mío
2 (*objective genitive*) a, hacia; **hatred of injustice** odio a la injusticia; **love of country** el amor a la patria
3 (*partitive etc*) de; **a pound of flour** una libra de harina; **there were four of them** eran cuatro; **all of them** todos ellos; **you of all people ought to know** debieras saberlo más que nadie; **most of all** sobre todo, más que nada; **we're the best of friends** somos muy (buenos) amigos
4 (*indicating cause*) por, de; **out of fear** por temor, **out of anger** de rabia; **of necessity** por necesidad; **to die of pneumonia** morir de pulmonía
5 (*agent*) **it was rude of him to say that** fue de mala educación que dijese eso; **it was nice of him to offer** fue muy amable ofreciéndose; **that was very kind of you** fue muy amable de su parte
6 (*indicating material*) de; **made of steel/paper** hecho de acero/papel
7 (*descriptive*) de; **a boy of eight** un niño de ocho años; **a man of great ability** un hombre de gran talento; **that idiot of a minister** ese idiota de ministro
8 (*concerning*) **what do you think of him?** ¿qué piensas de él?; **what of it?** ¿y a ti qué (te) importa?, ¿y qué?
9 (*indicating deprivation, riddance*) **loss of faith** pérdida de fe; **lack of water** falta de agua
10 (*indicating separation in space or time*) de; **south of Glasgow** al sur de Glasgow; **it's a quarter of six** (*US*) son las seis menos cuarto, falta un cuarto para las seis (*LAm*)
11 (*in time phrases*) **I go to the pub of an evening*** al pub suelo ir por las noches

---

off

A ADVERB	**D** NOUN
B ADJECTIVE	**E** COMPOUNDS
C PREPOSITION	

When **off** *is the second element in a phrasal verb, eg* **get off**, **keep off**, **take off***, look up the verb. When it is part of a set combination, eg* **off duty/work**, **far off***, look up the other word.*

---

off [ɒf] **A** ADVERB
1 (= *distant*) **a place two miles ~** un lugar a dos millas (de distancia); **it's some way ~** está algo lejos
2 (*in time*) **the game is three days ~** faltan tres días para el partido
3 (= *removed*) **the lid is ~** la tapa está quitada; **he had his coat ~** no llevaba el abrigo puesto; **with his shoes ~** descalzo, sin zapatos; **hands ~!** ¡fuera las manos!, ¡sin tocar!; **~ with those wet socks!** ¡quítate esos calcetines mojados!
4 (= *departing*) **to be ~** irse, marcharse; **I'm ~** me voy, me marcho; **they're ~!** (*race*) ¡ya salen!; **he's ~ fishing** ha ido a pescar; **~ with you!** (= *go away*) ¡fuera de aquí!, ¡lárgate!; (*affectionately*) ¡vete ya!; **~ we go!** ¡vamos!
5 (= *not at work*) **to be ~** (= *away*) estar fuera, no estar; **Ana is ~ sick today** (= *indisposed*) Ana no ha venido a trabajar hoy porque está enferma; (= *with doctor's note*) Ana está de baja hoy; **she's ~ on Tuesdays** los martes no viene (a trabajar); **to have** *or* **take a day ~** tomarse un día de descanso; **he gets two days ~ each week** tiene dos días libres a la semana
6 (*Elec, Mech, etc*) **to be ~** [*radio, TV, light*] estar apagado; [*tap*] estar cerrado; [*water etc*] estar cortado; [*brake*] no

estar puesto, estar quitado; [*machinery*] estar parado
7 (*Comm*) **"10% off"** "10% de descuento"; **I'll give you 5% ~** te hago el 5 por ciento de descuento, te hago un descuento del 5 por ciento
8 (*in phrases*) **~ and on** de vez en cuando, a ratos; **right ~** ◇ **straight ~** inmediatamente, enseguida
B ADJECTIVE
1 (*Brit*) (= *bad*) **to be ~** [*fish, yoghurt, meat*] estar malo *or* pasado; [*milk*] estar cortado
2 (= *cancelled*) **the game is ~** se ha cancelado el partido; **sorry, but the party's ~** lo siento, pero no hay fiesta; **their engagement is ~** han roto el noviazgo; **salmon is ~** (*on menu*) ya no hay salmón, se acabó el salmón
3 (*) (= *not right*) **it's a bit ~, isn't it?** eso no está muy bien ¿no?; **she's feeling rather ~** se siente bastante mal
4 (*for money, supplies, time*) **how are you ~ for money/bread?** ¿qué tal andas de dinero/pan?; **how are we ~ for time?** ¿qué tal vamos de tiempo?
5 (*Sport*) = **offside** A1
6 (*Elec, Mech etc*) **in the ~ position** en posición de apagado
C PREPOSITION
1 (= *from*) de; **to fall ~ a table** caer de una mesa; **to eat ~ a dish** comer en un plato
2 (= *near*) **a street ~ the square** una calle que sale de la plaza; **a flat just ~ the high street** un piso junto a la calle mayor
3 (= *away from*) **a house ~ the main road** una casa algo apartada de la carretera; **height ~ the ground** altura del suelo, altura sobre el suelo
4 (= *missing from*) **there are two buttons ~ my coat** a mi chaqueta le faltan dos botones
5 (= *absent from*) **he was ~ work for three weeks** estuvo sin poder ir a trabajar tres semanas; **to take three days ~ work** tomarse tres días libres
6 (*Comm*) **to take 5% ~ the price** rebajar el precio en un cinco por ciento
7 (= *not taking*) **he's been ~ drugs for a year** hace un año que no prueba las drogas, dejó las drogas hace un año; **I'm ~ coffee** (= *not taking*) he dejado de tomar café; (= *disliking*) tengo aborrecido el café, no puedo ver el café; **to be ~ one's food** no tener apetito
D NOUN (*) (= *start*) comienzo *m*; (*Sport*) salida *f*; **at the ~** en la salida; **ready for the ~** (*Sport*) listos para salir
E COMPOUNDS ➤ **off day**: **to have an ~ day** tener un día malo ➤ **off season** temporada *f* baja; **in the ~ season** fuera de temporada

offal [ˈɒfəl] N asaduras *fpl*, menudillos *mpl*

offbeat [ˈɒfˌbiːt] ADJ excéntrico, original

Off-Broadway [ˌɒfˈbrɔːdweɪ] ADJ *que no pertenece a las superproducciones de Broadway*

off-centre, off-center (*US*) [ˌɒfˈsentər] ADJ descentrado

off-chance [ˈɒftʃɑːns] N (**let's go) on the ~** (vamos) por si acaso; **he bought it on the ~ that it would come in useful** lo compró pensando que tal vez resultaría útil

off-colour [ˌɒfˈkʌlər] ADJ (*Brit*) (= *ill*) indispuesto, pachucho (*Sp**)

offcut [ˈɒfkʌt] N **1** (= *piece left over*) trozo *m* **2** offcuts restos *mpl*, sobras *fpl*

offence, offense (*US*) [əˈfens] N **1** (= *crime*) delito *m*; (*Sport*) falta *f*; **first ~** primer delito *m*; **second ~** reincidencia *f*; **it is an ~ to ...** está prohibido ..., se prohíbe ... **2** (= *insult*) ofensa *f*, agravio *m*; **no ~ was intended** ◇ **he intended no ~** no tenía intención de ofender a nadie; **to give** *or* **cause ~ (to sb)** ofender (a algn); **to take ~ (at sth)** ofenderse *or* sentirse ofendido (por algo)

offend [əˈfend] **A** VT ofender; **to be ~ed** ofenderse; **don't be ~ed** no te vayas a ofender; **to be ~ed at or by sth** ofenderse por algo **B** VI **1** (= *cause offence*) ofender; **scenes that may ~** escenas que pueden ofender; **to ~ against** [+ *good taste*] atentar contra; [+ *law*] infringir; **to ~ against God** pecar contra Dios **2** (*criminally*) (= *commit an offence*) cometer una infracción; (= *commit offences*) cometer infracciones; **to ~ again** reincidir

offender [əˈfendər] N **1** (= *lawbreaker*) delincuente *mf*; (*against traffic regulations etc*) infractor(a) *m/f*; **first ~**

delincuente *mf* sin antecedentes penales **2** (*moral*) transgresor(a) *m/f*, pecador(a) *m/f*; **regarding air pollution, industry is the worst** = en lo que se refiere a la contaminación atmosférica, la industria es la mayor culpable

offending [əˈfendɪŋ] ADJ (*esp hum*) **the dentist proceeded to fill the ~ tooth** el dentista procedió a empastar el diente culpable; **he put the ~ object out of sight** guardó el objeto causante del conflicto

offense [əˈfens] N (*US*) = **offence**

offensive [əˈfensɪv] **Ⓐ** ADJ **1** (= *causing offence*) [*behaviour, book, joke*] ofensivo; [*remark, language*] insultante; [*smell*] muy desagradable; **to find sth/sb ~** encontrar algo/a algn ofensivo; **he doesn't mean to be ~** no pretende ofender; **to be ~ to sb** ofender a algn **2** (*Mil*) [*operation, action, capability*] ofensivo **3** (*esp US Sport*) [*player, play*] de ataque
Ⓑ N (*Comm, Mil, Sport*) ofensiva *f*; **an advertising ~** una ofensiva publicitaria; **to go on the ~** pasar a la ofensiva, pasar al ataque
Ⓒ CPD ➤ **offensive weapon** (*Jur*) arma *f* ofensiva; (*Mil*) arma *f* de ataque

> Use **el/un** not **la/una** before feminine nouns beginning with stressed **a** or **ha** like **arma**.

offer [ˈɒfəʳ] **Ⓐ** N (*gen, Comm*) oferta *f*; **"offers over £25"** "ofertas a partir de 25 libras"; **"£50 or nearest offer"** "50 libras, negociable"; **I accepted his ~ of a lift** acepté cuando se ofreció a llevarme en coche; **to make (sb) an ~ (for sth)** hacer una oferta (a algn) (por algo); **they made me an ~ I couldn't refuse** me hicieron una oferta que no pude rechazar; **~ of marriage** propuesta *f* de matrimonio; **to be on ~** (*Comm*) estar de oferta; **the house is under ~** tenemos una oferta para la casa pendiente de formalizar el contrato
Ⓑ VT **1** (= *invite to*) **can I ~ you sth to drink?** ¿quieres tomar algo?; **"can I get you a drink?" she ~ed** —¿te sirvo algo?— preguntó ofreciéndose
2 (= *make available*) [+ *help, services, money*] ofrecer; [+ *information, advice*] dar, ofrecer; **to ~ sb sth ◇ ~ sth to sb** ofrecer algo a algn; **to ~ to do sth** ofrecerse a hacer algo; **to ~ one's hand** (*to shake*) tender la mano
3 (= *express, make*) [+ *opinion*] expresar; [+ *comment, remark, suggestion*] hacer; **he ~ed no explanation** no dio ninguna explicación
4 (= *afford*) [+ *opportunity, prospect, solution*] ofrecer
5 (= *show*) **he ~ed no resistance** no opuso resistencia
6 (*Rel*) (*also ~ up*) [+ *sacrifice*] ofrecer; [+ *prayer*] ofrecer, rezar
Ⓒ VI (= *volunteer*) ofrecerse
Ⓓ CPD ➤ **offer price** (*St Ex*) precio *m* de oferta

offering [ˈɒfərɪŋ] N (*gen*) ofrenda *f*; (= *gift*) regalo *m*; (*Rel*) exvoto *m*

offertory [ˈɒfətərɪ] N (*Rel*) (= *part of service*) ofertorio *m*; (= *collection*) colecta *f*

offhand [ɒfˈhænd] **Ⓐ** ADJ **1** (= *casual*) **he was very ~ about his achievements** no daba importancia a sus logros; **"it was nothing," he said in an ~ manner** —no fue nada —dijo como quitándole importancia; **his attitude to work/punctuality is very ~** se toma el trabajo/la puntualidad muy a la ligera
2 (= *cavalier*) displicente; **the next day he was very ~ with her** al día siguiente estuvo muy displicente con ella
Ⓑ ADV (= *without some thought*) sin pensarlo; **I can't tell you ~** no te lo puedo decir así de pronto or sin pensarlo un poco or (*LAm*) así nomás; **~, I'd say that there were around 40** así, a ojo, diría que eran unos cuarenta; **do you know ~ where the copies are kept?** ¿sabes por casualidad dónde se guardan las copias?

offhandedly [ɒfˈhændɪdlɪ] ADV (= *casually*) a la ligera

office [ˈɒfɪs] **Ⓐ** N **1** (= *workplace*) oficina *f*; (= *room*) despacho *m*; [*of lawyer*] bufete *m*; (*US*) [*of doctor*] consultorio *m*
2 (= *part of organization*) sección *f*, departamento *m*; (= *ministry*) ministerio *m*; (= *branch*) sucursal *f*
3 (= *public position*) cargo *m*; (= *duty, function*) función *f*; **to**

be in/hold ~ [*person*] desempeñar or ocupar un cargo; [*political party*] ocupar el poder; **to come into** or **take ~** [*person*] tomar posesión del cargo (**as** de); [*political party*] acceder al poder; **to leave ~** [*person*] dejar el cargo; [*government*] salir del poder
4 offices (*frm*) **through his good ~s** mediante sus buenos oficios; **through the ~s of** por mediación or medio de
5 (*Rel*) oficio *m*
Ⓑ CPD de oficina ➤ **office block** (*Brit*) bloque *m* de oficinas ➤ **office boy** recadero *m*, mandadero *m* (*LAm*) ➤ **office equipment** mobiliario *m* de oficina ➤ **office furniture** mobiliario *m* de oficina ➤ **office hours** (*gen*) horas *fpl* de oficina; (*US Med*) horas *fpl* de consulta ➤ **office job** trabajo *m* de oficina ➤ **Office of Management and Budget** (*US*) *servicio que asesora al presidente en materia presupuestaria* ➤ **office party** fiesta *f* de la oficina ➤ **office politics** relaciones *fpl* de poder en la oficina ➤ **office staff** personal *m* de oficina ➤ **office supplies** material *m* de oficina ➤ **office worker** (*gen*) oficinista *mf*; (= *civil servant etc*) funcionario/a *m/f*

officer [ˈɒfɪsəʳ] **Ⓐ** N **1** (*Mil, Naut, Aer*) oficial *mf* **2** (= *official*) funcionario/a *m/f*; [*of company*] directivo/a *m/f* **3** (= *police officer*) policía *mf*, agente *mf* de policía; **excuse me, ~** perdone agente **Ⓑ** CPD ➤ **officer of the watch** (*Naut*) oficial *mf* de guardia ➤ **officers' mess** comedor *m* de oficiales

official [əˈfɪʃəl] **Ⓐ** ADJ oficial; **is that ~?** ¿es oficial?, ¿se ha confirmado eso oficialmente?; **~ channels** conductos *mpl* or vías *fpl* oficiales; **"for official use only"** "sólo para uso oficial" **Ⓑ** N (*in civil service*) funcionario/a *m/f*; (*elsewhere*) oficial *mf*; **trade union ~** representante *mf* sindical **Ⓒ** CPD ➤ **official receiver** síndico *m* ➤ **Official Secrets Act** (*Brit*) *ley relativa a los secretos de Estado*

officialdom [əˈfɪʃəldəm] N (*pej*) burocracia *f*

officially [əˈfɪʃəlɪ] ADV oficialmente

officiate [əˈfɪʃɪeɪt] VI oficiar; **to ~ as Mayor** ejercer las funciones de alcalde; **to ~ at a marriage** oficiar un enlace or una boda

officious [əˈfɪʃəs] ADJ oficioso

officiously [əˈfɪʃəslɪ] ADV oficiosamente

offing [ˈɒfɪŋ] N **in the ~** a la vista; **a recession may be in the ~** puede que estemos a las puertas de una recesión

off-key [ɒfˈkiː] **Ⓐ** ADJ desafinado **Ⓑ** ADV desentonadamente, fuera de tono

off-licence [ˈɒfˌlaɪsəns] N (*Brit*) bodega *f*, tienda *f* de licores (*LAm*)

off-limits [ɒfˈlɪmɪts] ADJ **1** (*US Mil*) prohibido, de acceso prohibido **2** (*fig*) [*activity, substance*] prohibido

off-line, offline [ɒfˈlaɪn] **Ⓐ** ADJ (= *not connected to system*) fuera de línea; (= *switched off*) desconectado; **to be ~** [*Internet user*] no estar conectado (*a Internet*) **Ⓑ** ADV fuera de línea; **to read one's email ~** leer el email offline or sin estar conectado

offload [ˈɒfləʊd] VT (*esp Brit*) **1** [+ *goods*] descargar; [+ *passengers*] desembarcar, hacer bajar **2** (= *get rid of*) librarse de

off-message [ˈɒfˌmesɪdʒ] ADJ **to be ~** [*politician*] salirse de la línea del partido

off-peak [ɒfˈpiːk] **Ⓐ** ADJ (*gen*) fuera de las horas punta (*Sp*) or peak (*Chi*) or pico (*LAm*); [*holiday*] de temporada baja; [*times*] de tarifa reducida, valle *inv*; [*rate*] reducido, valle *inv* **Ⓑ** ADV (*gen*) fuera de las horas punta (*Sp*) or peak (*Chi*) or pico (*LAm*), en horario de tarifa reducida; [*travel, have holiday*] en temporada baja; [*telephone, consume electricity*] en horas de menor consumo, en horario de tarifa reducida

off-piste [ɒfˈpiːst] ADJ, ADV fuera de pista

off-putting [ˈɒfˌpʊtɪŋ] ADJ (*esp Brit*) (= *dispiriting*) desalentador; (= *unpleasant*) [*taste, smell etc*] desagradable; [*behaviour*] desagradable, chocante; (= *unfriendly*) [*person*] difícil, poco amable

off-road [ˈɒfrəʊd] ADJ [*driving, racing*] todoterreno

off-roader* [ˈɒfrəʊdəʳ] N todoterreno *m*

off-sales [ˈɒfseɪlz] NSING (*Scot*) (= *shop*) bodega *f*, tienda *f* de licores (*LAm*)

off-screen [ˈɒfskriːn] (*Cine, TV*) **Ⓐ** ADJ real, en la vida privada **Ⓑ** ADV fuera de la pantalla, en la vida privada

off-season ['ɒf,si:zn] **Ⓐ** N temporada *f* baja; **in the ~** en temporada baja **Ⓑ** ADJ [*rates, prices*] de temporada baja **Ⓒ** ADV [*travel, have holiday*] en temporada baja

offset ['ɒfset] (*vb: pt, pp ~*) **Ⓐ** N **1** (= *counterbalancing factor*) compensación *f* **2** (*Typ*) offset *m* **Ⓑ** VT **1** (= *compensate for*) compensar **2** (= *counteract*) contrarrestar, contrapesar; **to ~ A against B** contrapesar A y B **Ⓒ** CPD ➤ **offset printing** impresión *f* con offset

offshoot ['ɒfʃu:t] N (*Bot*) vástago *m*; (*Comm*) rama *f*; (*fig*) ramificación *f*

offshore [,ɒf'ʃɔːʳ] **Ⓐ** ADJ **1** (= *near the shore*) [*island*] cercano a la costa, del litoral; [*waters*] de la costa, del litoral; **~ fishing** pesca *f* de bajura **2** (= *out at sea*) [*rig, platform, drilling*] off-shore *inv*, costa afuera; [*well*] submarino **3** (*Fin*) [*account, fund*] en un paraíso fiscal/en paraísos fiscales, offshore *inv* (*Tech*); **~ investments** inversiones *fpl* en paraísos fiscales **Ⓑ** ADV **1** (= *near the coast*) [*lie, anchor, fish*] cerca de la costa **2** (= *out at sea*) [*drill*] off-shore, costa afuera; **they were rescued 20 miles ~** los rescataron a 20 millas de la costa **3** (*Fin*) [*invest*] en un paraíso fiscal/en paraísos fiscales

offside [,ɒf'saɪd] **Ⓐ** ADJ **1** (*Sport*) [*player, goal*] en fuera de juego **2** (*Brit Aut*) [*door, verge, lane*] del lado del conductor **Ⓑ** ADV (*Sport*) en fuera de juego **Ⓒ** N **1** (*Ftbl*) fuera de juego *m*, orsay *m*, offside *m* **2** (*Aut*) lado *m* del conductor **Ⓓ** EXCL ¡fuera de juego!, ¡orsay!, ¡offside!

offspring ['ɒfsprɪŋ] N (*pl inv*) descendencia *f*, prole* *f*

offstage [,ɒf'steɪdʒ] **Ⓐ** ADJ de entre bastidores **Ⓑ** ADV entre bastidores, fuera del escenario

off-the-cuff [,ɒfðə'kʌf] **Ⓐ** ADJ [*remark*] espontáneo, dicho sin pensar; [*speech*] improvisado **Ⓑ** ADV de improviso

off-the-job training [,ɒfðədʒɒb'treɪnɪŋ] N formación *f* fuera del trabajo

off-the-peg (*Brit*) [,ɒfðə'peg] , **off-the-rack** (*US*) ['ɒfðə'ræk] ADJ confeccionado, de percha

off-the-record [,ɒfðə'rekəd] ADJ no oficial, extraoficial

off-the-wall* [,ɒfðə'wɔːl] ADJ [*idea etc*] disparatado

off-white [,ɒf'waɪt] ADJ de color hueso *inv*, blanquecino

Ofgas ['ɒfgæs] N ABBR (*Brit*) (= **Office of Gas Supply**) *organismo que controla a las empresas del gas en Gran Bretaña*

Oflot ['ɒflɒt] N ABBR (*Brit*) (= **Office of the National Lottery**) *organismo regulador de la lotería nacional en Gran Bretaña,* ≈ Organismo Nacional de Loterías y Apuestas del Estado, ≈ ONLAE *m* (*Sp*)

Ofsted ['ɒfsted] N ABBR (*Brit*) (= **Office for Standards in Education**) *organismo regulador de los centros escolares*

OFT N ABBR (*Brit*) = **Office of Fair Trading**

Oftel ['ɒftel] N ABBR (*Brit*) (= **Office of Telecommunications**) *organismo que controla a las telecomunicaciones británicas*

often ['ɒfən] ADV a menudo, con frecuencia, seguido (*LAm*); **I've ~ wondered why you turned the job down** me he preguntado muchas veces *or* a menudo *or* con frecuencia por qué no aceptaste el trabajo; **it's not ~ that I ask you to help me** no es frecuente que te pida ayuda; **we ~ meet here** solemos reunirnos aquí; **do you ~ argue?** ¿discutís mucho?, ¿discutís muy a menudo?; **we visit her as ~ as possible** la visitamos tanto como nos es posible; **every so ~** de vez en cuando; **how ~ do you see him?** ¿cada cuánto lo ves?, ¿con qué *or* cuánta frecuencia lo ves?; **how ~ she had asked herself that very question!** ¡cuántas veces se había hecho esa misma pregunta!; **he's read it so ~ he knows it off by heart** lo ha leído tantas veces que se lo sabe de memoria; **(all) too ~** con demasiada frecuencia, demasiado a menudo, demasiadas veces; **very ~** muchísimas veces, muy a menudo

oftentimes ['ɒfəntaɪmz] ADV (*US*) muchas veces, seguido (*LAm*)

Ofwat ['ɒfwɒt] N ABBR (*Brit*) (= **Office of Water Services**) *organismo que controla a las empresas suministradores de agua en Inglaterra y Gales*

ogle ['əʊgl] VT comerse con los ojos

ogre ['əʊgəʳ] N ogro *m*

OH ABBR (*US*) = **Ohio**

oh [əʊ] EXCL (*gen*) ¡ah!; **oh is he?** ¿en serio?; **oh dear, I've spilt the milk!** ¡ay, se me ha caído la leche!; **oh good!** ¡qué bien!; **oh really?** ¿no me digas?, ¿de veras?; **oh really!** ¡no puede ser!; **oh yes?** ¿ah sí?

ohm [əʊm] N ohmio *m*, ohm *m*

OHMS ABBR (*Brit*) = **On Her/His Majesty's Service**

OHP N ABBR (= **overhead projector**) retroproyector *m*

oil [ɔɪl] **Ⓐ** N **1** (*gen, also Aut*) aceite *m*; (= *holy oil*) crisma *f*, santo óleo *m*; ✦ IDIOMS **to pour ~ on troubled waters** calmar los ánimos; **to pour ~ on the flames** echar más leña al fuego **2** (*Geol*) (*as mineral*) petróleo *m* **3** (*Art*) óleo *m*; **to paint in ~s** pintar al óleo **Ⓑ** VT lubricar, engrasar **Ⓒ** CPD ➤ **oil change** (*Aut*) cambio *m* de aceite ➤ **oil drum** bidón *m* de aceite ➤ **oil field** yacimiento *m* petrolífero ➤ **oil filter** (*Aut*) filtro *m* de aceite ➤ **oil gauge** (*Aut*) indicador *m* de(l) aceite ➤ **oil industry** industria *f* del petróleo ➤ **oil lamp** lámpara *f* de aceite, quinqué *m* ➤ **oil level** nivel *m* del aceite ➤ **oil paint** (*Art*) óleo *m*, pintura *f* al óleo ➤ **oil painting** (*Art*) pintura *f* al óleo ➤ **oil pan** (*US*) cárter *m* ➤ **oil pipeline** oleoducto *m* ➤ **oil platform** plataforma *f* petrolífera ➤ **oil pressure** (*Aut*) presión *f* del aceite ➤ **oil refinery** refinería *f* de petróleo ➤ **oil rig** torre *f* de perforación; (*Naut*) plataforma *f* de perforación submarina ➤ **oil slick** (*large*) marea *f* negra; (*small*) mancha *f* de petróleo, capa *f* de petróleo (en el agua) ➤ **oil spill** (= *act*) fuga *f* de petróleo; (= *substance*) = **oil slick** ➤ **oil stove** (*for cooking*) cocina *f* de petróleo; (*for heating*) estufa *f* de petróleo ➤ **oil tanker** petrolero *m* ➤ **oil terminal** terminal *f* petrolífera ➤ **oil well** pozo *m* de petróleo

oil-based ['ɔɪlbeɪst] ADJ [*product*] derivado del petróleo

oilcan ['ɔɪlkæn] N aceitera *f*

oilcloth ['ɔɪlklɒθ] N hule *m*, encerado *m*

oil-fired ['ɔɪlfaɪəd] ADJ [*central heating*] al petróleo

oilskin ['ɔɪlskɪn] N **1** (= *oilcloth*) hule *m*, encerado *m* **2 oilskins** (*Brit*) (= *clothes*) chubasquero *msing*, impermeable *msing*

oily ['ɔɪlɪ] **Ⓐ** ADJ (*compar* **oilier**; *superl* **oiliest**) **1** (= *greasy*) [*food*] aceitoso, grasiento, grasoso (*LAm*); [*hands, rag*] grasiento, lleno de aceite; [*skin, hair*] graso, grasoso (*LAm*); [*substance, liquid*] oleaginoso **2** (= *smarmy*) zalamero, empalagoso **Ⓑ** CPD ➤ **oily fish** (*Culin*) pescado *m* azul

ointment ['ɔɪntmənt] N ungüento *m*, pomada *f*

OK¹* ['əʊ'keɪ] **Ⓐ** EXCL (= *all right*) ¡vale! (*Sp*), ¡okey! (*LAm*); (= *yes*) ¡sí!; (= *understood*) ¡comprendo!; (= *enough*) ¡basta ya!, ¡ya estuvo bueno! (*LAm*); **OK, OK!** ¡ya, ya!, ¡vale, vale! (*Sp*); **OK, the next item on the agenda is ...** bueno, el siguiente punto en el orden del día es ... **Ⓑ** ADJ **1** (= *undamaged, in good health*) bien; **is the car OK?** ¿anda bien el coche? **2** (= *agreed*) **it's OK with** *or* **by me** yo estoy de acuerdo, por mí vale (*Sp*); **is it OK with you if ...?** ¿te importa si ...?, ¿te molesta que ...?; **OK it's difficult, but ...** estoy de acuerdo que es difícil pero ...; **I'm coming too, OK?** yo también voy, ¿vale (*Sp*) *or* okey (*LAm*)? **3** (= *acceptable*) **that may have been OK last year** eso puede haber estado bien el año pasado **4** (= *well provided for*) **are you OK for money/time?** ¿andas *or* (*esp LAm*) vas bien de dinero/tiempo?; **"do you want another drink?" — "I'm OK, thanks"** —¿te apetece otro trago? —no quiero más, gracias **5** (= *likeable*) **he's OK** ✧ **he's an OK guy** es un buen tipo*, es un tío majo (*Sp**) **Ⓒ** ADV **he's doing OK** las cosas le van bien **Ⓓ** N visto *m* bueno; **to give sth the OK** dar el visto bueno a algo, aprobar algo **Ⓔ** VT dar el visto bueno a, aprobar

OK² ABBR (*US*) = **Oklahoma**

okay* [əʊ'keɪ] = **OK¹**

Okla. ABBR (*US*) = **Oklahoma**

okra ['əʊkrə] N kimbombó *m*

old [əʊld] **Ⓐ** ADJ (compar ~**er**; superl ~**est**) **1** (= not young) viejo; (more respectful) mayor, anciano; [civilization] antiguo; **an ~ man/woman** un(a) viejo/a, un(a) anciano/a; **a little ~ lady** una viejecita, una ancianita; **~ people** ◊ **~ folks*** los viejos; (more respectful) los ancianos, las personas mayores; **to be ~ before one's time** hacerse mayor antes de tiempo; **he's ~ for his age** [child] es muy maduro para su edad; **that dress is too ~ for you** ese vestido es para alguien mayor que tú or no es apropiado para tu edad; **to get** or **grow ~(er)** envejecer; **as we get ~er ...** según envejecemos ...; **he's getting ~** se está haciendo viejo; **to get ~er** envejecer; **to look ~** parecer viejo, estar avejentado; ✦ IDIOM **to have an ~ head on young shoulders** ser maduro/a para su edad

2 (relating to ages) **how ~ are you?** ¿cuántos años tienes?, ¿qué edad tienes?; **Laura is six weeks/years ~** Laura tiene seis semanas/años; **he'll be six weeks ~ tomorrow** cumplirá seis semanas mañana; **a five-year-~ (child)** un niño de cinco años; **the building is 300 years ~** el edificio tiene 300 años; **she is two years ~er than you** tiene dos años más que tú; **you'll understand when you are ~er** cuando seas mayor lo entenderás; **their ~est child** su hijo mayor; **she is the ~est** es la mayor; **she is the ~est teacher in the school** es la profesora de más edad del colegio; **to be ~ enough for sth/ to do sth** tener edad para algo/para hacer algo; **he's ~ enough to know better** (to have more sense) a su edad debería tener más sentido común, ya es mayorcito para saber lo que está bien y lo que está mal; **she's ~ enough to be your mother** con la edad que tiene, podría ser tu madre

3 (= not new) **3.1** (= antique) [painting, book, building] antiguo; **the ~ part of Glasgow** el casco viejo or antiguo de Glasgow; ✦ IDIOM **to be as ~ as the hills** ◊ **be as ~ as Adam** ser de tiempos de Maricastaña, ser más viejo que el mundo **3.2** [clothes, furniture] (= tatty) viejo; (= worn) usado, gastado ✦ IDIOM **that's ~ hat** eso no es nada nuevo

4 (= long-standing) viejo; **he's an ~ friend of mine** es un viejo amigo mío

5 (= former) antiguo; **my ~ flat was very small** mi antiguo piso era muy pequeño; **in the ~ days** antaño, en los viejos tiempos; **the good ~ days** los viejos tiempos; **it's not as good as our ~ one** no es tan bueno como el anterior; **my ~ school** mi antiguo or viejo colegio

6 (*) (expressing affection) **~ Peter** el bueno de Peter; **good ~ Mike!** ¡este Mike!; **my ~ lady** (= mother) mi or la vieja**; (= wife) la parienta*; **my ~ man** (= father) mi or el viejo**; (= husband) mi marido

7 (*) (as intensifier) **any ~:: any ~ thing will do** cualquier cosa sirve; **he leaves his things any ~ how** deja sus cosas de cualquier manera

Ⓑ N **1 the ~** los viejos mpl, los ancianos mpl
2 (liter) **to know sb of ~** conocer a algn desde hace tiempo
Ⓒ CPD ➤ **old age** vejez f ➤ **old age pension** (Brit) subsidio m de la tercera edad, pensión f ➤ **old age pensioner** (Brit) pensionista mf, jubilado/a m/f ➤ **the Old Bill**** (Brit) la poli*, la pasma (Sp**) ➤ **old boy** (Brit) (= former pupil) ex-alumno m, antiguo alumno m ➤ **Old English** inglés m antiguo; ⇨ ANGLO-SAXON ➤ **old folks' home** residencia f de ancianos ➤ **old girl** (Brit) (= former pupil) ex-alumna f, antigua alumna f ➤ **Old Glory** (US) bandera de los Estados Unidos ➤ **old hand** veterano/a m/f ➤ **old maid** (pej) solterona f ➤ **old master** (= work) obra f maestra de la pintura clásica; (= painter) gran maestro m de la pintura clásica ➤ **old people's home** (esp Brit) residencia f de ancianos ➤ **old school tie** (Brit) (lit) corbata con los colores representativos de la escuela a la que alguien ha asistido; **the ~ school tie** (fig) el amiguismo ➤ **Old Testament** Antiguo Testamento m ➤ **old wives' tale** cuento m de viejas, patraña f ➤ **the Old World** el Viejo Mundo, el Viejo Continente

old-boy network [əʊld'bɔɪˌnetwɜːk] N (Brit) amiguismo m

olden ['əʊldən] ADJ **in ~ times** or **days** antaño (liter), antiguamente

olde-worlde ['əʊldɪ'wɜːldɪ] ADJ (hum) viejísimo, antiquísimo; **a very ~ interior** un interior pintoresco de antaño

old-fashioned ['əʊld'fæʃnd] ADJ (= outmoded) [thing] pasado de moda; [person, attitude] anticuado, chapado a la antigua; **good ~ honesty** la honestidad de toda la vida

oldster ['əʊldstəʳ] N (US) viejo/a m/f, anciano/a m/f

old-style ['əʊld'staɪl] ADJ antiguo, al estilo antiguo, a la antigua

old-time ['əʊldtaɪm] ADJ de antaño ➤ **old-time dancing** baile m antiguo, baile m de antaño

old-timer [əʊld'taɪməʳ] N veterano/a m/f; (US*) (= old person) viejo/a m/f, anciano/a m/f

old-world ['əʊld'wɜːld] ADJ (= traditional) antiguo

oleander [əʊlɪ'ændəʳ] N adelfa f

O-level ['əʊˌlevl] N (Brit Scol) (formerly) (= Ordinary level) ≈ BUP m

olfactory [ɒl'fæktərɪ] ADJ olfativo, olfatorio

oligarchy ['ɒlɪgɑːkɪ] N oligarquía f

olive ['ɒlɪv] **Ⓐ** N (= fruit) aceituna f, oliva f; (also ~ **tree**) olivo m **Ⓑ** ADJ [complexion, skin] aceitunado; (also **~-green**) [shirt, paint] verde oliva inv **Ⓒ** CPD ➤ **olive branch** rama f de olivo; ✦ IDIOM **to hold out an ~ branch** hacer un gesto de paz ➤ **olive green** verde m oliva ➤ **olive grove** olivar m ➤ **olive grower** oleicultor(a) m/f ➤ **olive growing** oleicultura f ➤ **olive oil** aceite m de oliva ➤ **olive tree** olivo m

olive-green ['ɒlɪv'griːn] ADJ verde oliva inv

olive-growing ['ɒlɪv,grəʊɪŋ] ADJ **~ region** región f olivera

Olympiad [ə'lɪmpɪæd] N olimpíada f

Olympic [ə'lɪmpɪk] **Ⓐ** ADJ olímpico **Ⓑ** N **the ~s** las Olimpiadas **Ⓒ** CPD ➤ **the Olympic Games** las Olimpiadas

Oman [əʊ'mɑːn] N Omán m

Omani [əʊ'mɑːnɪ] ADJ, N omaní mf

OMB N ABBR (US) (= Office of Management and Budget) servicio que asesora al presidente en materia presupuestaria

ombudsman ['ɒmbʊdzmən] N (pl **ombudsmen**) ≈ defensor m del pueblo

omega ['əʊmɪgə] N omega f

omelette, omelet (US) ['ɒmlɪt] N tortilla f francesa, torta f de huevos (Mex)

omen ['əʊmən] N augurio m, presagio m

ominous ['ɒmɪnəs] ADJ [development, event] de mal agüero; [sound] siniestro; **it was an ~ sign** era una señal de mal agüero; **to look/sound ~** no augurar or presagiar nada bueno

ominously ['ɒmɪnəslɪ] ADV **"we have a problem," she said ~** —tenemos un problema —dijo en un tono que resultaba inquietante; **"I would not do that if I were you," he said ~** —yo que tú no haría eso —dijo con un tono inquietante or en tono amenazador

omission [əʊ'mɪʃən] N omisión f

omit [əʊ'mɪt] VT (on purpose) suprimir; (by accident) olvidarse de; **to ~ to do sth** (on purpose) omitir hacer algo, decidir no hacer algo; (by accident) olvidarse de hacer algo

omnibus ['ɒmnɪbəs] N **1** (also ~ **edition**) (= book) antología f de obras escogidas; (Brit TV, Rad) programa m especial (que incluye varios episodios) **2** (†) (= bus) ómnibus m, autobús m, camión m (Mex)

omnipotence [ɒm'nɪpətəns] N omnipotencia f

omnipotent [ɒm'nɪpətənt] ADJ omnipotente

omnipresent ['ɒmnɪ'prezənt] ADJ omnipresente

omniscient [ɒm'nɪsɪənt] ADJ omnisciente

omnivorous [ɒm'nɪvərəs] ADJ omnívoro

ON ABBR (Canada) = Ontario

on [ɒn] **Ⓐ** PREP **1** (indicating place, position) en, sobre; **on**

> When **on** is the second element in a phrasal verb, eg **have on**, **get on**, **go on**, look up the verb. When it is part of a set combination, such as **further on**, look up the other word.

the table en or sobre la mesa; **on the ceiling** sobre el techo; **on page two** en la página dos; **on the right** a la derecha; **hanging on the wall** colgado en la pared
2 (indicating time) **on Friday** el viernes; **on Fridays** los viernes; **on May 14th** el 14 de mayo; **on the evening of July**

2nd el dos de julio por la tarde
3 (= *at the time of*) **on seeing him** al verlo; **on my arrival** al llegar, a mi llegada
4 (= *about, concerning*) sobre, acerca de; **a book on physics** un libro de *or* sobre física; **he gave a lecture on Keats** dio una conferencia sobre Keats; **while we're on the subject** como hablamos de esto
5 (= *towards, against*) **the march on Rome** la marcha sobre Roma; **an attack on the government** un ataque contra el gobierno
6 (= *earning, receiving*) **he's on £6,000 a year** gana seis mil libras al año; **a student on a grant** un estudiante con beca; **many live on less than that** muchos viven con menos
7 (= *taking, consuming*) **I'm on a milk diet** sigo un régimen lácteo; **he's on heroin** está enganchado a la heroína; **I'm on three pills a day** tomo tres píldoras al día
8 (= *engaged in*) **I'm on a new project** trabajo sobre un nuevo proyecto; **we're on irregular verbs** estamos con los verbos irregulares; **he's away on business** está en viaje de negocios; **to be on holiday** estar de vacaciones
9 (*indicating membership*) **he's on the committee** es miembro del comité; **he's on the permanent staff** forma parte del personal fijo, está en plantilla (*Sp*)
10 (= *playing*) **with Louis Armstrong on trumpet** con Louis Armstrong a la trompeta; **he played it on the violin** lo tocó al violín
11 (*TV, Rad*) **on the radio** en *or* por la radio; **on television** en *or* por (la) televisión; **there's a good film on TV tonight** esta noche dan una buena película en la tele
12 (= *about one's person*) **I haven't any money on me** no llevo dinero encima
13 (= *compared to*) **prices are up on last year('s)** los precios han subido frente a los del año pasado
14 (= *at the expense of*) **this round's on me** esta ronda la pago yo, invito yo
Ⓑ ADV **1** (= *in place*) [*lid etc*] puesto; **the lid is on** la tapa está puesta; **it's not on properly** no está bien puesto
2 (*with clothes*) **what's she got on?** ¿qué lleva puesto?, ¿cómo va vestida?; **to have one's coat on** tener el abrigo puesto; **she had not got much on** iba muy ligera de ropa
3 (*indicating time*) **from that day on** a partir de aquel día, de aquel día en adelante; **on and off** de vez en cuando, a intervalos; **well on in June** bien entrado junio; **they talked well on into the night** hablaron hasta bien entrada la noche
4 (*indicating continuation*) **to go/walk on** seguir adelante; **to read on** seguir leyendo; **on with the show!** ¡que empiece/continúe el espectáculo!
5 (*in phrases*) **what are you on about?*** ¿de qué (me) hablas?; **he's always on at me about it*** me está majando continuamente con eso*
Ⓒ ADJ **1** (= *functioning, in operation*) **to be on** [*engine*] estar encendido, estar en marcha; [*machine*] estar encendido *or* funcionando; [*light, TV*] estar encendido, estar prendido (*LAm*); [*tap*] estar abierto; [*brake etc*] estar puesto, estar echado
2 (= *being performed, shown*) **the programme is on in a minute** el programa empieza dentro de un minuto; **there's a good film on tonight** hay una película buena esta noche; **the show was on for only two weeks** el show estuvo solamente 15 días en cartelera; **what's on at the cinema?** ¿qué ponen en el cine?; **what's on at the theatre?** ¿qué dan en el teatro?
3 (= *taking place*) **is the meeting still on tonight?** ¿sigue en pie la reunión de esta noche?, ¿se lleva a cabo siempre la reunión de esta noche? (*LAm*)
4 (= *arranged*) **have you got anything on this evening?** ¿tienes compromiso para esta noche?
5 (= *working*) **are you on tomorrow?** ¿trabajas mañana?, ¿estás de turno mañana?; **to have one day on and the next off** trabajar un día y el otro no
6 (*) (*indicating agreement, acceptance*) **you're on!** ¡te tomo la palabra!; **that's not on** (*Brit*) eso no se hace, no hay derecho
Ⓓ EXCL ¡adelante!

ONC N ABBR (*Brit Scol*) = **Ordinary National Certificate**

once [wʌns] **Ⓐ** ADV **1** (= *on one occasion*) una vez; **~ a week** una vez a la *or* por semana; **~ again** otra vez, una vez

más; **~ and for all** de una vez (por todas); **~ every two days** una vez cada dos días; **for ~** por una vez; **~ more** otra vez, una vez más; **not** ~ ni una sola vez; **~ or twice** un par de veces, una o dos veces; **(every) ~ in a while** de vez en cuando, de cuando en cuando, cada cuando (*LAm*)
2 (= *formerly*) antes; **a ~ powerful nation** un país que antes *or* en su día había sido poderoso; **~ when we were young** hace tiempo cuando éramos jóvenes; **Texas was ~ ruled by Mexico** Tejas estuvo en su tiempo gobernada por Méjico; **~ upon a time there was** (*as start of story*) érase una vez, había una vez
3 **at ~** (= *immediately*) inmediatamente; (= *now*) ahora mismo; (= *simultaneously*) a la vez, al mismo tiempo; **all at ~** (= *suddenly*) de repente, de pronto; (= *simultaneously*) a la vez, al mismo tiempo
Ⓑ CONJ una vez que; **~ they finish, we can start** una vez que *or* en cuanto ellos terminen podemos empezar nosotros
Ⓒ N **just this** ~ esta vez sólo, esta vez nada más

once-over* ['wʌnsˌəʊvəʳ] N **to give sth/sb the ~** echar un vistazo a algo/algn

oncologist [ɒŋ'kɒlədʒɪst] N oncólogo/a *m/f*

oncology [ɒŋ'kɒlədʒɪ] N oncología *f*

oncoming ['ɒn,kʌmɪŋ] ADJ [*car, traffic*] que viene en el sentido opuesto

OND N ABBR (*Brit Scol*) = **Ordinary National Diploma**

one [wʌn] **Ⓐ** ADJ **1** (= *number*) un (*before masc noun*), una (*before fem noun*); **~ man** un hombre; **~ man out of two** uno de cada dos hombres; **the baby is ~ (year old)** el bebé tiene un año; **it's ~ (o'clock)** es la una; **for ~ reason or another** por diferentes razones; **~ or two people** algunas personas
2 (*indefinite*) un (*before masc noun*), una (*before fem noun*), cierto; **~ day** un día, cierto día; **~ hot July evening** una tarde de julio de mucho calor; **~ Pérez** un tal Pérez
3 (= *sole*) único; **his ~ worry** su única preocupación; **no ~ man could do it** ningún hombre podría hacerlo por sí solo
4 (= *same*) mismo; **it is ~ and the same thing** es la misma cosa
Ⓑ N uno *m*; **✦** IDIOM **to be at ~ (with sb)** estar completamente de acuerdo (con algn)
Ⓒ PRON **1** (*indefinite*) **have you got ~?** ¿tienes uno?; **~ after the other** uno tras otro; **it's all ~** (= *the same*) es lo mismo; **it's all ~ to me** me da igual, me da lo mismo; **~ by ~** uno tras otro, uno a uno; **I for ~ am not going** yo, por mi parte, no voy; **she's cook and housekeeper in ~** es a la vez cocinera y ama de llaves; **it's made all in ~** está hecho en una sola pieza; **you've got it in ~!*** ¡y que lo digas!*; **not ~** ni uno; **~ of them** uno de ellos; **any ~ of us** cualquiera de nosotros; **he's ~ of the family now** ya es de la familia; **two for the price of ~** dos por el precio de uno; **~ or two** unos pocos; **in ~s and twos** en pequeños grupos; **to be ~ up** (*Sport etc*) llevar un punto/gol *etc* de ventaja; **to be ~ up on sb** llevar ventaja a algn
2 (*specific*) **this ~** éste *m*, ésta *f*; **that ~** ése *m*, ésa *f*, aquél *m*, aquélla *f*; **which ~ do you want?** ¿cuál quieres?; **the white dress and the grey** ~ el vestido blanco y el gris
3 (*relative*) **the ~ who** *or* **that** el/la que; **the ~s who** *or* **that** los/las que; **they were the ~s who told us** ellos fueron quienes nos lo dijeron
4 (= *person*) **he's a clever ~** es un taimado; **he's the troublesome ~** él es el revoltoso; **he's a great ~ for arguing** es de los que les encanta discutir; **the little ~s** los pequeños, los chiquillos; **he is not ~ to protest** no es de los que protestan
5 **~ another: they kissed ~ another** se besaron (el uno al otro); **do you see ~ another much?** ¿se ven mucho?
6 (*generalizing*) **~** uno/a *m/f*; **~ has ~'s pride** uno tiene cierto amor propio; **~ never knows** nunca se sabe; **~ must eat** hay que comer; **to cut ~'s finger** cortarse el dedo

one-armed ['wʌn'ɑːmd] ADJ manco **➤ one-armed bandit*** máquina *f* tragamonedas, máquina *f* tragaperras (*Sp*)

one-eyed ['wʌn'aɪd] ADJ tuerto

one-handed ['wʌn'hændɪd] **Ⓐ** ADV **to catch the ball ~** recoger la pelota con una sola mano **Ⓑ** ADJ manco

one-horse ['wʌn'hɔːs] ADJ **1** (*) insignificante, de poca monta; **~ town** pueblucho* *m* **2 a ~ race** (*fig*) una contienda en la que no hay color, un paseo triunfal

one-legged [ˈwʌnˈlegɪd] ADJ con una sola pierna

one-liner [ˌwʌnˈlaɪnəʳ] N chiste m breve

one-man [ˈwʌnˈmæn] ADJ (= *individual*) individual; [*job*] para una sola persona; [*business*] llevado por una sola persona ➤ **one-man band** (*Mus*) hombre m orquesta; **it's a ~ band*** (*fig*) lo hace todo uno solo ➤ **one-man exhibition**, **one-man show** exposición f individual

one-night stand [ˌwʌnnaɪtˈstænd] N conquista m or (*Sp*) ligue m de una noche

one-off* [ˈwʌnɒf] (*Brit*) 🅐 N **it's a ~** es un caso único 🅑 ADJ [*appearance, exhibition, show*] aislado; [*payment*] único

one-on-one [wʌnɒnˈwʌn] ADJ, ADV (*US*) = **one-to-one**

one-parent family [ˌwʌnpεərəntˈfæmɪlɪ] N familia f monoparental

one-party [ˌwʌnˈpɑːtɪ] ADJ [*state etc*] de partido único

one-piece [ˌwʌnˈpiːs] ADJ de una pieza; **~ swimsuit** bañador m de una pieza

onerous [ˈɒnərəs] ADJ [*debt*] oneroso; [*task, duty*] pesado

oneself [wʌnˈself] PRON **1** (*reflexive*) se; **to wash ~** lavarse **2** (*for emphasis*) uno/a mismo/a; (*after prep*) sí mismo/a; **it's quicker to do it ~** es más rápido si lo hace uno mismo **3** (*phrases*) **to be ~** (= *behave naturally*) conducirse con naturalidad; **to be by ~** estar solo or a solas; **to do sth by ~** hacer algo solo or por sí solo; **it's nice to have the museum to ~** es agradable tener el museo para uno mismo; **to say to ~** decir para sí, decirse a uno mismo; **to talk to ~** hablar solo

one-shot* [ˈwʌnʃɒt] N, ADJ (*US*) = **one-off**

one-sided [ˌwʌnˈsaɪdɪd] ADJ [*view etc*] parcial; [*decision*] unilateral; [*contest*] desigual

one-time [ˈwʌntaɪm] ADJ antiguo

one-to-one [ˈwʌntəˈwʌn], **one-on-one** (*US*) [wʌnɒnˈwʌn] 🅐 ADJ [*conversation*] de uno a uno; [*meeting*] entre dos 🅑 ADJ (*also* **on a ~ basis**) [*discuss, talk*] de uno a uno; [*teach*] individualmente

one-track [ˈwʌntræk] ADJ **to have a ~ mind** no tener más que una idea en la cabeza

one-upmanship [wʌnˈʌpmənʃɪp] N arte m de aventajar a los demás, arte m de llevar siempre la delantera

one-way [ˈwʌnweɪ] ADJ [*street*] de dirección única, de sentido único (*esp LAm*); (*esp US*) [*ticket*] de ida, sencillo (*Mex*)

ongoing [ˈɒnˌgəʊɪŋ] ADJ (= *in progress*) en curso; (= *continuing*) en desarrollo

onion [ˈʌnjən] 🅐 N cebolla f 🅑 CPD de cebolla ➤ **onion dome** (*Archit*) cúpula f bulbosa ➤ **onion rings** aros mpl de cebolla rebozados ➤ **onion soup** sopa f de cebolla

on-line, **online** [ˈɒnlaɪn] 🅐 ADJ [*business, service, purchase*] online, en línea; **to be ~** [*Internet user*] estar conectado (a Internet); [*printer*] estar conectado 🅑 ADV online, en línea; **to go ~** [*company*] saltar a la Red; [*Internet user*] conectarse a Internet; **to shop ~** comprar por Internet, comprar online 🅒 CPD ➤ **on-line banking** banca f online

onlooker [ˈɒnˌlʊkəʳ] N espectador(a) m/f

only [ˈəʊnlɪ] 🅐 ADJ único; **your ~ hope is to hide** la única posibilidad que te queda es esconderte; **it's the ~ one left** es el único que queda; **you're not the ~ one** no eres el único; **the ~ thing I don't like about it is ...** lo único que no me gusta de esto es ... 🅑 ADV **1** (= *just*) sólo, solamente; **he's ~ ten** sólo or solamente tiene diez años; **I'm ~ the porter** no soy más que el portero; **I'm ~ a porter** soy un simple portero; **you ~ have to ask** ◇ **you have ~ to ask** no tienes más que pedirlo, sólo tienes que pedirlo; **he raced onto the platform ~ to find the train pulling out** llegó corriendo al andén para encontrarse con que el tren estaba saliendo; **I ~ wish he were here now** ojalá estuviese ahora aquí **2** (= *exclusively*) sólo; **a ticket for one person ~** una entrada para una persona sólo; **"members only"** "sólo socios"; **I saw her ~ yesterday** ayer mismo la vi, la vi ayer nomás (*LAm*), recién ayer la vi (*LAm*) **3** (*in phrases*) **I've ~ just arrived** acabo de llegar ahora mismo, no he hecho más que llegar; **it fits him, but ~ just** le cabe pero le queda muy justo; **not ~ ... but also:** **not ~**

was he late but he also forgot the tickets no sólo llegó tarde sino que además olvidó las entradas; **a machine that is not ~ efficient but looks good as well** una máquina que no sólo es eficaz sino también atractiva; **I've ~ recently met him** hace poco que lo conocí; **~ too:** **I'd be ~ too pleased to help** estaría encantado de or me encantaría poder ayudar(les); **it is ~ too true** por desgracia es verdad or cierto 🅒 CONJ sólo que, pero; **it's a bit like my house, ~ nicer** es un poco como mi casa, sólo que or pero más bonita 🅓 CPD ➤ **only child** hijo/a m/f único/a

on-message [ˈɒnmesɪdʒ] ADJ **to be ~** [*politician*] seguir la línea del partido

o.n.o. ABBR (*Brit*) (= **or nearest offer**) abierto ofertas

on-off switch [ˌɒnɒfˈswɪtʃ] N botón m de conexión

onomatopoeia [ˌɒnəʊmætəˈpiːə] N onomatopeya f

onrush [ˈɒnrʌʃ] N [*of water*] oleada f; (*fig*) oleada f, avalancha f

on-screen [ˌɒnˈskriːn] ADJ **1** (*Comput etc*) en pantalla **2** (*Cine, TV*) [*romance, kiss*] cinematográfico

onset [ˈɒnset] N principio m, comienzo m; [*of disease*] aparición f; **the ~ of winter** el comienzo del invierno

onshore [ˈɒnʃɔːʳ] ADJ [*breeze*] que sopla del mar hacia la tierra

onside [ˈɒnsaɪd] ADJ (*Ftbl etc*) **to be ~** estar en posición correcta

on-site [ˈɒnˌsaɪt] ADJ in situ

onslaught [ˈɒnslɔːt] N (*gen*) ataque m, arremetida f

Ont. ABBR (*Canada*) = **Ontario**

on-the-job training [ˌɒnðədʒɒbˈtreɪnɪŋ] N formación f en el trabajo, formación f sobre la práctica

on-the-spot [ˈɒnðəˈspɒt] ADJ [*fine*] en el acto; [*investigation*] sobre el terreno; [*decision*] instantáneo; [*report*] inmediato

onto [ˈɒntʊ] PREP **1** (= *on top of*) **he got ~ the table** se subió a la mesa **2** (= *on track of*) **to be ~ sth** haber encontrado algo; **he knows he's ~ a good thing** sabe que ha encontrado algo que vale la pena; **the police are ~ the villain** la policía tiene una pista que le conducirá al criminal; **we're ~ them** les conocemos el juego; **they were ~ him at once** le calaron en seguida, le identificaron en el acto

ontological [ˌɒntəˈlɒdʒɪkəl] ADJ ontológico

ontology [ɒnˈtɒlədʒɪ] N ontología f

onus [ˈəʊnəs] N (*pl* **-es**) responsabilidad f; **the ~ is upon him to prove it** es suya la responsabilidad de demostrarlo, le incumbe a él demostrarlo

onward [ˈɒnwəd] 🅐 ADJ [*flight, journey*] de conexión 🅑 ADV (*also* **~s**) adelante, hacia adelante; **from that time ~** desde entonces; **from the 12th century ~** desde el siglo doce en adelante, a partir del siglo doce

onwards [ˈɒnwədz] ADV (*esp Brit*) = **onward B**

onyx [ˈɒnɪks] N ónice m, ónix m

oodles* [ˈuːdlz] NPL **we have ~ (of)** tenemos cantidad or montones (de)*

oomph** [ʊmf] N brío m, marcha* f

oops* [ʊps] EXCL ¡ay!

ooze [uːz] 🅐 VI [*liquid*] rezumar(se); [*blood*] salir; (= *leak*) gotear 🅑 VT (*fig*) rebosar; **he simply ~s confidence** rebosa confianza

op[1]* [ɒp] N ABBR (*Med, Mil*) = **operation**

op[2] ABBR (*Mus*) = **opus**

opal [ˈəʊpəl] N ópalo m

opaque [əʊˈpeɪk] ADJ opaco

OPEC [ˈəʊpek] N ABBR (= **Organization of Petroleum-Exporting Countries**) OPEP f

open [ˈəʊpən] 🅐 ADJ **1** (= *not closed*) abierto; [*bottle, tin*] destapado; **the book was ~ at page seven** el libro estaba abierto por la página siete; **to fling** or **throw a door ~** abrir una puerta de golpe or de par en par; **wide ~** [*door etc*] abierto de par en par; ✦ IDIOM **to welcome sb with ~ arms** dar la bienvenida or recibir a algn con los brazos abiertos **2** (= *unfolded*) desplegado; (= *unfastened*) desabrochado;

with his shirt ~ con la camisa desabotonada
3 (= *not enclosed*) [*countryside, view, fire, sewer*] abierto; [*carriage*] descubierto; [*car*] descapotable; **in the ~ air** al aire libre; **~ sea** mar *m* abierto
4 (= *not blocked*) [*border, tunnel*] abierto; [*road*] sin obstáculos; **the speed permitted on the ~ road** la velocidad permitida circulando en carretera; **road ~ to traffic** carretera abierta al tráfico, vía libre
5 (= *unrestricted*) [*championship, race, scholarship, ticket*] abierto; **~ to the public on Mondays** abierto al público los lunes; **the competition is ~ to all** todos pueden participar en el certamen, el certamen se abre a todos
6 (= *available, permissible*) **what choices are ~ to me?** ¿qué posibilidades *or* opciones me quedan?
7 (= *not biased*) abierto; **I am ~ to offers** estoy dispuesto a recibir ofertas; **I am ~ to persuasion** se me puede convencer
8 (= *frank*) [*person, admiration*] franco
9 (= *undecided*) por resolver, por decidir; [*race, contest*] muy abierto, muy igualado; **to leave the matter ~** dejar el asunto pendiente
10 (= *exposed, not protected*) abierto, descubierto; **to lay o.s. ~ to criticism/attack** exponerse a ser criticado/atacado; **it is ~ to doubt whether ...** queda la duda sobre si ...; **it is ~ to question whether ...** es cuestionable que ...; **it's an ~ secret that ...** es un secreto a voces que ...
Ⓑ N 1 **(out) in the ~** (= *out of doors*) al aire libre; (= *in the country*) en campo raso *or* abierto; **to bring a dispute (out) into the ~** hacer que una disputa llegue a ser del dominio público
2 (*Golf, Tennis*) **the Open** el (Torneo) Abierto, el Open
Ⓒ VT 1 (*gen*) abrir; [+ *bottle etc*] destapar; **I didn't ~ my mouth** ni abrí la boca, no dije ni pío
2 (= *unfold*) [+ *map, newspaper*] desplegar
3 (= *begin*) [+ *conversation, debate, negotiations*] entablar, iniciar; **to ~ fire** (*Mil*) romper *or* abrir el fuego
4 (= *declare open, inaugurate*) inaugurar
Ⓓ VI 1 [*door, flower*] abrirse; **a door that ~s onto the garden** una puerta que da al jardín; **✦** IDIOM **the heavens ~ed** se abrieron las cataratas del cielo
2 (*for business*) [*shop, bank*] abrir
3 (= *begin*) dar comienzo, iniciarse; [*play*] estrenarse; **when we ~ed in Bradford** (*Theat*) cuando dimos la primera representación en Bradford; **the book ~s with a long description** el libro empieza con una larga descripción
Ⓔ CPD ➤ **open cheque** (*Brit*) cheque *m* sin cruzar ➤ **open day** (*Brit*), **open house** (*US*) día *m* abierto a todos ➤ **open letter** carta *f* abierta ➤ **open market** (*Econ*) mercado *m* libre, mercado *m* abierto ➤ **open pit** (*US*) mina *f* a cielo abierto ➤ **open policy** (*Insurance*) póliza *f* abierta ➤ **open prison** (*Brit*) cárcel *f* abierta ➤ **open sandwich** sandwich *m* sin tapa, sandwich *m* abierto (*esp LAm*) ➤ **Open University** (*Brit*) ≈ Universidad *f* Nacional de Enseñanza a Distancia; *ver tb* www.open.ac.uk ➤ **open verdict** (*Jur*) juicio *m* en el que se determina el crimen sin designar el culpable
➤ **open out** VI + ADV [*passage, tunnel, street*] ensancharse; [*view, panorama*] extenderse
➤ **open up Ⓐ** VT + ADV [+ *new business*] abrir, poner; [+ *possibility*] crear; **to ~ up a market** abrirse un mercado, conquistar un mercado; **to ~ up a country for trade** incorporar un país al comercio **Ⓑ** VI + ADV 1 [*flower*] abrirse; [*new shop, business*] abrir, inaugurarse; **~ up!** ¡abran!; (*police order*) ¡abran a la autoridad! **2** (*Brit*) (*emotionally*) abrirse, confiarse

open-air [ˌəʊpənˈɛəˈ] ADJ al aire libre

open-and-shut case [ˌəʊpənənˈʃʌtˈkeɪs] N caso *m* claro, caso *m* evidente

opencast [ˈəʊpənkɑːst] ADJ (*Brit*) **~ mine** mina *f* a cielo abierto; **~ mining** minería *f* a cielo abierto

open-ended [ˌəʊpənˈendɪd] ADJ (*fig*) [*contract, offer etc*] indefinido, sin plazo definido; [*discussion*] sin desarrollo preestablecido

opener [ˈəʊpənəˈ] N (= *bottle opener*) sacacorchos *m inv*; (= *can opener*) abrelatas *m inv*; **for ~s** (*US**) de entrada

open-handed [ˌəʊpənˈhændɪd] ADJ (= *generous*) generoso

open-heart surgery [ˌəʊpənhɑːˈtˈsɜːdʒərɪ] N cirugía *f* a corazón abierto

opening [ˈəʊpnɪŋ] **Ⓐ** ADJ [*ceremony, speech*] de apertura, inaugural; [*price*] inicial
Ⓑ N 1 (= *gap*) abertura *f*; (*in wall*) brecha *f*, agujero *m*; (*in clouds, trees*) claro *m* 2 (*Theat*) estreno *m*; [*of exhibition*] inauguración *f*; [*of parliament*] apertura *f*
3 (= *chance*) oportunidad *f*; (= *post*) puesto *m* vacante, vacante *f*
Ⓒ CPD ➤ **opening hours** horas *fpl* de abrir ➤ **opening night** (*Theat*) noche *f* de estreno; [*of club etc*] inauguración *f* ➤ **opening price** cotización *f* de apertura ➤ **opening time** hora *f* de apertura

openly [ˈəʊpənlɪ] ADV (= *frankly*) abiertamente, francamente; (= *publicly*) públicamente

open-minded [ˌəʊpənˈmaɪndɪd] ADJ libre de prejuicios, de miras amplias; **I'm still ~ about it** no me he decidido todavía

open-mouthed [ˈəʊpənˈmaʊðd] ADJ boquiabierto

open-necked [ˈəʊpənˈnekt] ADJ sin corbata

openness [ˈəʊpənnɪs] N franqueza *f*

open-plan [ˈəʊpənˌplæn] ADJ sin tabiques, de planta abierta

opera [ˈɒpərə] **Ⓐ** N ópera *f* ➤ **opera glasses** gemelos *mpl* de teatro ➤ **opera house** teatro *m* de la ópera ➤ **opera singer** cantante *mf* de ópera **Ⓑ** *of* **opus**

operable [ˈɒpərəbl] ADJ (*Med*) operable

opera-goer [ˈɒpərəˌɡəʊəˈ] N aficionado/a *m/f* a la ópera

operate [ˈɒpəreɪt] **Ⓐ** VT 1 (= *work*) [+ *machine, vehicle, switchboard*] manejar; [+ *switch, lever*] accionar; **this switch ~s a fan** este interruptor activa un ventilador
2 (= *run, manage*) [+ *company*] dirigir; [+ *service*] ofrecer; [+ *system*] aplicar; [+ *mine, oil well, quarry*] explotar; **they ~ a system of flexible working hours** aplican un horario flexible de trabajo
Ⓑ VI 1 (= *function*) [*machine, system, principle, mind*] funcionar; [*person*] actuar, obrar
2 (= *act, influence*) [*drug, propaganda*] actuar (**on** sobre); [*factors*] intervenir
3 (= *carry on one's business*) [*person*] trabajar; [*company, factory, criminal, service*] operar; [*airport*] funcionar
4 (*Med*) operar; **to ~ on sb (for sth)** operar a algn (de algo); **to ~ on sb's back/eyes** operar a algn de la espalda/de la vista

operatic [ˌɒpəˈrætɪk] ADJ operístico

operating [ˈɒpəreɪtɪŋ] **Ⓐ** ADJ 1 (*Comm*) [*budget, profit, costs, loss*] de explotación 2 (*Comput*) **~ system** sistema *m* operativo 3 (*Tech*) **~ conditions** condiciones *fpl* de funcionamiento **Ⓑ** CPD ➤ **operating room** (*US*) quirófano *m*, sala *f* de operaciones ➤ **operating table** mesa *f* de operaciones ➤ **operating theatre** (*Brit*) quirófano *m*, sala *f* de operaciones

operation [ˌɒpəˈreɪʃən] **Ⓐ** N 1 (= *functioning*) funcionamiento *m*; **to be in ~** [*machine, system, business*] estar en funcionamiento *or* en marcha, estar funcionando; [*law*] ser vigente, estar en vigor; **to come into ~** [*machine, system*] entrar en funcionamiento; [*law*] entrar en vigor; **to put sth into ~** [+ *plan, factory*] poner algo en funcionamiento *or* en marcha
2 (= *use*) [*of controls, machine*] manejo *m*; [*of system*] uso *m*
3 (= *activity*) operación *f* (*also Med, Comm, Mil, Fin*); **United Nations peacekeeping ~s** las operaciones de paz de las Naciones Unidas; **will I need an ~?** ¿hará falta que me operen?; **to have an ~ for appendicitis** operarse de apendicitis; **to perform an ~ on sb** operar a algn
Ⓑ CPD ➤ **operations room** (*Police*) centro *m* de coordinación; (*Mil*) centro *m* de operaciones

operational [ˌɒpəˈreɪʃənl] ADJ 1 (= *relating to operations*) [*control, plan*] operativo, de operaciones; [*problems, cost, expenses*] de funcionamiento; [*staff*] de servicio; **for ~ reasons** por necesidades operativas 2 (= *ready for service*) [*aircraft, service, airport*] en funcionamiento; [*bus, train*] en servicio; [*troops*] operacional; **the bridge could be ~ in three years' time** el puente podría entrar en funcionamiento dentro de tres años; **to be fully ~** estar en pleno funcionamiento

operative [ˈɒpərətɪv] **Ⓐ** ADJ 1 (*gen*) operativo 2 (*Jur*) **to be ~** estar en vigor; **to become ~ from the 9th** entrar en vigor a partir del nueve 3 (*Med*) operatorio **Ⓑ** N (= *worker*) obrero/a *m/f*; (*with a special skill*) operario/a *m/f*, obrero/a *m/f* especializado/a; (*in intelligence*) agente *mf*

operator ['ɒpəreɪtəʳ] N **1** [*of equipment*] operador(a) *m/f*; (*Ind*) (= *machinist*) maquinista *mf*; (*Telec*) telefonista *mf* **2** (*) (*fig*) **a smooth ~** (*in business*) un tipo hábil; (*in love*) un engatusador **3** (= *company*) (*Telec*) operadora *f*; **Britain's biggest bus/train ~** la mayor compañía de autobuses/ trenes del Reino Unido

operetta [ˌɒpəˈretə] N zarzuela *f*, opereta *f*

ophthalmic [ɒfˈθælmɪk] ADJ oftálmico

ophthalmologist [ˌɒfθælˈmɒlədʒɪst] N oftalmólogo/a *m/f*

ophthalmology [ˌɒfθælˈmɒlədʒɪ] N oftalmología *f*

opiate ['əʊpɪɪt] N opiata *f*

opinion [əˈpɪnjən] N (= *belief, view*) opinión *f*; **what's your ~ of him?** ¿qué opinas de él?, ¿qué opinión te merece?; **there are differences of ~ as to what happened** hay discordancia *or* discrepancia de opiniones respecto a lo que pasó; **to have a high** *or* **good ~ of sth/sb** tener un alto concepto de algo/algn, tener muy buena opinión de algo/ algn; **to have a poor** *or* **low ~ of sth/sb** tener un bajo concepto de algo/algn, tener muy mala opinión de algo/ algn; **in my ~** en mi opinión, a mi juicio; <u>medical</u> **~ was divided over the case** la opinión médica estaba dividida con respecto al caso; **could you give us your <u>professional</u> ~?** ¿nos puede dar su opinión (como) profesional? ➤ **opinion poll** sondeo *m* (de opinión)

opinionated [əˈpɪnjəneɪtɪd] ADJ testarudo

opium ['əʊpɪəm] N opio *m* ➤ **opium addiction** opiomanía *f* ➤ **opium den** fumadero *m* de opio

opossum [əˈpɒsəm] N zarigüeya *f*

opponent [əˈpəʊnənt] N adversario/a *m/f*, contrincante *mf*; (*in debate, discussion*) oponente *mf*, adversario/a *m/f*

opportune ['ɒpətjuːn] ADJ oportuno; **at an ~ moment** en un momento oportuno

opportunism [ˌɒpəˈtjuːnɪzəm] N oportunismo *m*

opportunist [ˌɒpəˈtjuːnɪst] ADJ, N oportunista *mf*

opportunity [ˌɒpəˈtjuːnɪtɪ] N oportunidad *f*, ocasión *f*; **at the <u>earliest</u> ~** en la primera oportunidad, cuanto antes; <u>equality</u> **of ~** igualdad *f* de oportunidades; **opportunities for promotion** oportunidades de promoción; **when I <u>get</u> the ~** cuando se me presente la oportunidad *or* la ocasión, cuando tenga ocasión; **to <u>have</u> the ~ to do sth** tener la oportunidad de hacer algo; **to <u>miss</u> one's ~** perder la oportunidad; **he never missed an ~ to criticize her** aprovechaba cualquier oportunidad para criticarla; **to <u>take</u> the ~ to do sth** aprovechar la oportunidad *or* la ocasión para hacer algo

oppose [əˈpəʊz] VT **1** (= *disagree with*) oponerse a, estar en contra de; **they ~d the motion** se opusieron a la moción **2** (= *combat*) luchar contra, combatir

opposed [əˈpəʊzd] ADJ **1** (= *in disagreement*) **to be ~ to sth** oponerse a algo, estar en contra de algo; **they have diametrically ~ views on abortion** tienen opiniones diametralmente opuestas sobre el aborto **2 as ~ to** (= *rather than*) en vez de; (= *compared to*) a diferencia de

opposing [əˈpəʊzɪŋ] ADJ [*views, ideas*] opuesto, contrario; [*team*] contrario; [*army*] enemigo

opposite ['ɒpəzɪt] **A** ADV enfrente; **I looked at the director, sitting ~** miré al director que estaba sentado enfrente (de mí) **B** PREP (*also* **~ to**) **1** (= *across from*) frente a, enfrente de; **~ the library** frente a *or* enfrente de la biblioteca; **they sat ~ one another** se sentaron uno frente a(l) otro, se sentaron frente a frente **2** (= *next to*) junto a, al lado de; **to play ~ sb** (*Theat*) aparecer junto a algn **C** ADJ **1** (*in position*) de enfrente; **the house ~** la casa de enfrente; **on the ~ page** en la página opuesta *or* de al lado **2** (= *far*) [*end, corner*] opuesto; **we sat at ~ ends of the sofa** nos sentamos cada uno a un extremo del sofá, nos sentamos en extremos opuestos del sofá **3** (= *contrary*) contrario, opuesto; **in the ~ direction** en dirección contraria *or* opuesta, en sentido contrario *or* opuesto; **~ number** homólogo/a *m/f*; **the ~ sex** el otro sexo,

el sexo opuesto; **we take the ~ view** nosotros pensamos lo contrario **D** N **the ~** lo contrario; **quite the ~!** ¡todo lo contrario!; **the ~ is true** la verdad es todo lo contrario

opposition [ˌɒpəˈzɪʃən] **A** N **1** (= *resistance*) resistencia *f*, oposición *f*; (= *people opposing*) oposición *f*; (*Sport*) (= *team*) equipo *m* contrario; **he made his ~ known** indicó su disconformidad; **in ~ to** (= *against*) en contra de; (= *unlike*) a diferencia de **2** (*Brit Pol*) **the Opposition** los partidos de la oposición, la oposición **B** CPD [*member, party*] de la oposición ➤ **the Opposition benches** los escaños de la Oposición, la Oposición

oppress [əˈpres] VT **1** (*Mil, Pol etc*) oprimir; **the ~ed** los oprimidos **2** [*heat, anxiety etc*] agobiar

oppression [əˈpreʃən] N opresión *f*

oppressive [əˈpresɪv] ADJ **1** (= *unjust*) [*regime, law, system*] opresivo; [*tax*] gravoso **2** (= *stifling*) [*heat, air, atmosphere*] sofocante, agobiante; [*mood, feeling, silence*] opresivo, agobiante

oppressively [əˈpresɪvlɪ] ADV **1** (= *unjustly*) [*rule, govern*] de manera opresiva, de modo opresivo **2** (= *stiflingly*) **the room was ~ hot** en la habitación hacía un calor sofocante *or* agobiante

oppressor [əˈpresəʳ] N opresor(a) *m/f*

opprobrium [əˈprəʊbrɪəm] N (*frm*) oprobio *m*

opt [ɒpt] VI **to ~ for sth** optar por algo; **to ~ to do sth** optar por hacer algo ➤ **opt out** VI + ADV **1** (= *decide against*) **to ~ out of doing sth** optar por no hacer algo **2** (= *withdraw*) retractarse

optic ['ɒptɪk] ADJ óptico ➤ **optic nerve** nervio *m* óptico

optical ['ɒptɪkəl] ADJ óptico ➤ **optical illusion** ilusión *f* óptica

optician [ɒpˈtɪʃən] N óptico/a *m/f*; **~'s** óptica *f*

optics ['ɒptɪks] NSING óptica *fsing*

optimal ['ɒptɪml] ADJ óptimo

optimism ['ɒptɪmɪzəm] N optimismo *m*

optimist ['ɒptɪmɪst] N optimista *mf*

optimistic [ˌɒptɪˈmɪstɪk] ADJ optimista; **to be ~ that** ser optimista respecto a que; **to be ~ about sth** ser optimista acerca de *or* con respecto a algo; **to remain ~** mantener el optimismo

optimistically [ˌɒptɪˈmɪstɪklɪ] ADV con optimismo

optimize ['ɒptɪmaɪz] VT optimizar

optimum ['ɒptɪməm] ADJ [*level, number*] óptimo

option ['ɒpʃən] N **1** (= *choice*) opción *f*; **what are my ~s?** ¿qué opciones tengo?; **she had no ~ but to leave** no tuvo más remedio que irse; **to have the ~ of doing sth** tener la posibilidad de hacer algo; **to keep one's ~s open** no descartar ninguna posibilidad **2** (*Comm*) opción *f*; **stock ~** (*Fin*) compra *f* opcional de acciones; **with the ~ to buy** con opción de compra **3** (*Scol, Univ*) asignatura *f* optativa

optional ['ɒpʃənl] ADJ [*course, subject*] optativo, facultativo; [*part, accessory*] opcional; **~ extra** (*Aut*) accesorio *m* opcional, extra *m*; **"dress optional"** "no se requiere (ir de) etiqueta"

optometrist [ɒpˈtɒmətrɪst] N optometrista *mf*

opt-out ['ɒptaʊt] **A** ADJ (*esp Brit*) **~ clause** cláusula *f* de exclusión voluntaria, cláusula *f* de no participación **B** N (*from agreement, treaty*) opción *f* de exclusión voluntaria, opción *f* de no participación

opulence ['ɒpjʊləns] N opulencia *f*

opulent ['ɒpjʊlənt] ADJ opulento

opus ['əʊpəs] N (*pl* **~es** *or* **opera**) (*Mus*) opus *m*

OR ABBR (*US*) = **Oregon**

or [ɔːʳ] CONJ **1** (*giving alternative*) o; (*before o-, ho-*) u; (*between numerals*) ó; **would you like tea or coffee?** ¿quieres té o café?; **seven or eight** siete u ocho; **men or women** mujeres u hombres; **15 or 16** 15 ó 16; **hurry up or you'll miss the bus** date prisa, que vas a perder el autobús; <u>not</u> ... **or ...** no ... ni ...; **I don't eat meat or fish** no como carne ni pescado; **she can't dance or sing** no sabe bailar ni cantar; **20 or <u>so</u>** unos veinte, veinte más o menos; **an hour or so**

una hora más o menos; **without relatives or friends** sin parientes ni amigos
2 (= *that is*) es decir; **botany, or the science of plants** botánica, es decir la ciencia que estudia las plantas; **or rather ...** o mejor dicho ..., o más bien ...

oracle ['ɒrəkl] N oráculo *m*

oral ['ɔːrəl] Ⓐ ADJ **1** (= *spoken*) oral **2** (*Med, Anat*) [*contraceptive, vaccine*] oral; [*hygiene*] bucal Ⓑ N examen *m* oral

orally ['ɔːrəlɪ] ADV **1** (= *verbally*) verbalmente, oralmente **2** (*Med*) por vía oral

orange ['ɒrɪndʒ] Ⓐ N (= *fruit*) naranja *f*; (= *tree*) naranjo *m*; (= *colour*) naranja *m*; (= *orange squash*) naranjada *f* Ⓑ ADJ **1** (*in colour*) naranja *inv*, (de) color naranja *inv* **2** [*flavour*] a naranja Ⓒ CPD ➤ **orange blossom** azahar *m*, flor *f* de naranjo ➤ **orange box, orange crate** (*US*) caja *f* de fruta ➤ **orange drink** refresco *m* de naranja ➤ **orange grove** naranjal *m* ➤ **orange juice** jugo *m* de naranja, zumo *m* de naranja (*Sp*) ➤ **orange peel** cáscara *f* de naranja ➤ **orange squash** naranjada *f* (*sin burbujas*) ➤ **orange stick** palito *m* de naranjo ➤ **orange tree** naranjo *m*

orangeade ['ɒrɪndʒ'eɪd] N (*natural*) naranjada *f*; (*fizzy*) refresco *m* de naranja

orange-coloured, **orange-colored** (*US*) ['ɒrɪndʒ,kʌləd] ADJ naranja *inv*, (de) color naranja *inv*

Orangeman ['ɒrɪndʒmən] N (*pl* **Orangemen**) *miembro de las logias protestantes de la Orden de Orange*

orang-outang [ɔː,ræŋuː'tæŋ], **orang-utan** [ɔː,ræŋuː'tæn] N orangután *m*

oration [ɔː'reɪʃən] N discurso *m*

orator ['ɒrətər] N orador(a) *m/f*

oratorio [,ɒrə'tɔːrɪəʊ] N (*pl* **~s**) (*Mus*) oratorio *m*

oratory ['ɒrətərɪ] N (= *art of speaking*) oratoria *f*

orb [ɔːb] N (= *sphere*) esfera *f*, globo *m*

orbit ['ɔːbɪt] Ⓐ N órbita *f*; **to be in/go into ~ (round the earth/moon)** estar en/entrar en órbita (alrededor de la tierra/luna) Ⓑ VI [*satellite*] orbitar, girar; [*astronaut*] estar en órbita Ⓒ VT [+ *earth, moon*] girar alrededor de

orchard ['ɔːtʃəd] N huerto *m*; **apple ~** manzanar *m*, manzanal *m*

orchestra ['ɔːkɪstrə] Ⓐ N **1** (*Mus*) orquesta *f* **2** (*US Theat*) patio *m* de butacas, platea *f* Ⓑ CPD ➤ **orchestra pit** foso *m* de orquesta

orchestral [ɔː'kestrəl] ADJ orquestal

orchestrate ['ɔːkɪstreɪt] VT **1** (*Mus*) orquestar **2** (*fig*) [+ *rebellion*] tramar; [+ *campaign*] organizar

orchestration [,ɔːkɪs'treɪʃən] N orquestación *f*

orchid ['ɔːkɪd] N orquídea *f*

ordain [ɔː'deɪn] Ⓐ VT **1** (= *order*) (*gen*) ordenar, disponer; (*by law*) decretar; [*God*] mandar, disponer; **it was ~ed that ...** se dispuso *or* ordenó *or* decretó que ... **2** (*Rel*) ordenar; **to be ~ed** ordenarse Ⓑ VI mandar, disponer; **as God ~s** según manda Dios, como Dios manda

ordeal [ɔː'diːl] N **1** (= *bad experience*) terrible experiencia *f*; **exams are an ~ for me** para mí los exámenes son un suplicio **2** ➤ **by fire** ordalías *fpl* del fuego

order ['ɔːdər] Ⓐ N **1** (= *sequence*) orden *m*; **in ~** en orden, por orden; **what ~ should these documents be in?** ¿en qué orden deben estar estos documentos?; **in alphabetical ~** por *or* en orden alfabético; **"cast in order of appearance"** (*Theat, Cine*) "por orden de aparición"; **in chronological ~** por *or* en orden cronológico; **they are out of ~** están mal ordenados; **in ~ of seniority** por *or* en orden de antigüedad; **word ~** orden *m* de las palabras; **they are in the wrong ~** están mal ordenados
2 (= *system*) orden *m*; **a new political/social ~** un nuevo orden político/social; **the old ~ is changing** el viejo orden está cambiando; **it is in the ~ of things** es ley de vida; **a new world ~** un nuevo orden mundial
3 (= *good order*) buen estado *m*, orden *m*; **in ~** (*legally*) en regla; [*room*] en orden, ordenado; **his papers are in ~** tiene los papeles en regla; **everything is in ~** todo está en regla;

to put one's affairs in ~ poner sus asuntos en orden; **in good ~** en buen estado, en buenas condiciones; **to be out of ~** [*machine*] estar estropeado *or* (*LAm*) descompuesto; **the line is out of ~** (*Telec*) no hay línea, la línea no funciona; **"out of order"** "no funciona"
4 (= *peace, control*) orden *m*; **the forces of ~** las fuerzas del orden; **to keep ~** mantener el orden
5 (= *command*) orden *f*; [*of court etc*] sentencia *f*, fallo *m*; **~s are ~s** las órdenes no se discuten; **bankruptcy ~** orden *f* de quiebra; **by ~ of** por orden de; **to give ~s** dar órdenes; **he gave the ~ for it to be done** ordenó que se hiciera; **on the ~s of** a las órdenes de; **to take ~s from sb** recibir órdenes de algn; **I don't take ~s from anyone** a mí no me da órdenes nadie; **under ~s** bajo órdenes; **we are under ~s not to allow it** tenemos orden de no permitirlo
6 (*at meeting, Parliament etc*) orden *m*; **order (order)!** ¡orden!; **to call sb to ~** llamar a algn al orden; **strikes are the ~ of the day** las huelgas están a la orden del día; **a beer would be in ~** sería indicado tomarse una cerveza; **it seems congratulations are in ~!** ¡enhorabuena!; **to be out of ~*** [*remark*] estar fuera de lugar; [*person*] comportarse mal; **a point of ~** una cuestión de procedimiento
7 (*Comm*) pedido *m*, encargo *m*; **we have it on ~ for you** está pedido para usted; **we will put it on ~ for you** se lo pediremos para usted al fabricante; **to place an ~ for sth with sb** encargar *or* hacer un pedido de algo a algn; **made to ~** hecho a medida
8 (*in restaurant*) **the waiter took our ~** el camarero tomó nota de lo que íbamos a comer; **an ~ of French fries** una ración de patatas fritas
9 **in ~ to do sth** para *or* a fin de hacer algo; **in ~ that he may stay** para que pueda quedarse
10 [*of society etc*] clase *f*, categoría *f*; (*Bio*) orden *m*; **the present crisis is of a different ~** la crisis actual es de un orden distinto; **talents of the first ~** talentos *mpl* de primer orden; **holy ~s** órdenes *fpl* sagradas; **to be in/take (holy) ~s** ser/ordenarse sacerdote; **of the ~ of 500** del orden de los quinientos; **something in ~ of** (*or US*) **on the ~ of £3,000** unas 3.000 libras, alrededor de 3.000 libras; **of ~ of magnitude** magnitud *f*
11 (*Fin*) libranza *f*; (*postal*) giro *m*; **pay to the ~ of** páguese a la orden de
12 in short ~ (*US*) rápidamente
13 (*Mil*) **in battle ~** en orden de batalla; **in marching ~** en orden de marchar
Ⓑ VT **1** (= *command*) mandar, ordenar; **to ~ sb to do sth** mandar *or* ordenar a algn hacer algo; **he was ~ed to be quiet** le ordenaron que se callara; **the referee ~ed the player off the field** el árbitro expulsó al jugador del campo
2 (= *put in order*) ordenar, poner en orden; **they are ~ed by date/size** están ordenados por fecha/tamaño
3 (= *organize*) organizar, arreglar; **to ~ one's life properly** organizar bien su vida, vivir de acuerdo a cierto método
4 [+ *goods, meal, taxi*] pedir, encargar; **we ~ed steak and chips** pedimos un filete con patatas fritas
Ⓒ VI (*in restaurant*) pedir; **are you ready to ~?** ¿han decidido qué van a pedir?
Ⓓ CPD ➤ **order book** (*esp Brit Comm*) libro *m* de pedidos, cartera *f* de pedidos ➤ **order form** (*Comm*) hoja *f* de pedido ➤ **order number** (*Comm*) número *m* de pedido

➤ **order around, order about** (*Brit*) VT + ADV dar órdenes a, mandonear*; **she was fed up with being ~ed around** estaba harta de que le dieran órdenes

orderly ['ɔːdəlɪ] Ⓐ ADJ (= *tidy*) ordenado; (= *methodical*) ordenado, metódico; (= *disciplined*) obediente, disciplinado; [*crowd*] pacífico; **in an ~ fashion** *or* **way** *or* **manner** de forma *or* manera ordenada Ⓑ N (*Mil*) ordenanza *mf*; (*Med*) celador(a) *m/f*

ordinal ['ɔːdɪnl] ADJ ordinal

ordinarily [ˈɔːdnˈeərɪlɪ] ADV por lo común, generalmente

ordinary ['ɔːdnrɪ] Ⓐ ADJ **1** (= *usual, normal*) [*milk, coffee*] normal, corriente; **my ~ doctor** el médico al que voy normalmente; **in the ~ way** normalmente
2 (= *unexceptional*) normal y corriente; **he's a normal, ~ guy** es un tipo normal y corriente; **it's not what you'd call an ~ present** no es lo que se dice un regalo de todos los días; **an ~ citizen** un simple ciudadano, un ciudadano de a pie; **it was no ~ bar** no era un bar corriente; **the meal was very ~**

(pej) la comida fue bastante mediocre, la comida no fue nada del otro mundo *or* del otro jueves
Ⓑ N **a man above the ~** un hombre fuera de serie, un hombre excepcional; **out of the ~** fuera de lo común, extraordinario
Ⓒ CPD ➤ **ordinary degree** *(Brit Univ)* diploma *m*, título universitario de categoría inferior al Honours degree ➤ **Ordinary National Certificate** *(Brit)* ≈ diploma *m* de técnico especialista ➤ **Ordinary National Diploma** *(Brit)* diploma profesional, ≈ diploma *m* de técnico especialista ➤ **ordinary seaman** *(Brit Navy)* marinero *m*

ordination [ˌɔːdɪˈneɪʃən] N ordenación *f*

ordnance [ˈɔːdnəns] *(Mil)* N (= *guns*) artillería *f*; (= *supplies*) pertrechos *mpl* de guerra, material *m* de guerra ➤ **ordnance factory** fábrica *f* de artillería ➤ **Ordnance Survey map** *(Brit)* mapa *m* del servicio estatal de cartografía

ore [ɔː'] N mineral *m*, mena *f*

Ore., Oreg. ABBR *(US)* = **Oregon**

oregano [ˌɒrɪˈɡɑːnəʊ, *(US)* əˈreɡənəʊ] N orégano *m*

organ [ˈɔːɡən] **Ⓐ** N **1** *(Mus, Anat)* órgano *m* **2** (= *mouthpiece*) *[of opinion]* órgano *m*, portavoz *mf* **Ⓑ** CPD ➤ **organ donor** donante *mf* de órganos ➤ **organ transplant** transplante *m* de órganos

organdie, organdy *(US)* [ˈɔːɡəndɪ] N organdí *m*

organ-grinder [ˈɔːɡənˌɡraɪndə'] N organillero/a *m/f*

organic [ɔːˈɡænɪk] ADJ **1** (= *living*) *[matter, waste]* orgánico; *[fertilizer]* orgánico, natural **2** (= *not chemical*) *[farmer, farm, methods, meat]* ecológico; *[vegetables, produce]* de cultivo biológico, biológico; *[flour]* integral; *[wine, beer]* sin sustancias artificiales; **~ food** alimentos *mpl* biológicos, alimentos *mpl* de cultivo biológico; **~ farming** agricultura *f* ecológica *or* biológica; **~ restaurant** restaurante *m* de cocina natural **3** *(Chem)* orgánico; **~ chemistry** química *f* orgánica

organically [ɔːˈɡænɪkəlɪ] ADV *(Agr)* *[grow, produce, farm]* biológicamente, sin utilizar pesticidas ni fertilizantes artificiales

organism [ˈɔːɡənɪzəm] N organismo *m*

organist [ˈɔːɡənɪst] N organista *mf*

organization [ˌɔːɡənaɪˈzeɪʃən] N **1** (= *act*) organización *f* **2** (= *body*) organización *f*, organismo *m*

organizational [ˌɔːɡənaɪˈzeɪʃənl] ADJ organizativo

organize [ˈɔːɡənaɪz] VT (= *arrange*) organizar; **I will ~ transport** yo me encargaré del transporte; **she tried to ~ her thoughts** intentó ordenar *or* poner en orden sus pensamientos; **to get ~d** organizarse

organized [ˈɔːɡənaɪzd] ADJ organizado; **it was ~ chaos** era un caos organizado *or* ordenado ➤ **organized labour** *(Ind)* trabajadores *mpl* *or* obreros *mpl* sindicados

organizer [ˈɔːɡənaɪzə'] N organizador(a) *m/f*

organophosphate [ɔːˌɡænəʊˈfɒsfeɪt] N organofosfato *m*

orgasm [ˈɔːɡæzəm] **Ⓐ** N orgasmo *m* **Ⓑ** VI tener un orgasmo, llegar al orgasmo

orgy [ˈɔːdʒɪ] N orgía *f*

Orient [ˈɔːrɪənt] N Oriente *m*

orient [ˈɔːrɪənt] VT = **orientate**

oriental [ˌɔːrɪˈentəl] ADJ oriental, de Oriente

orientate [ˈɔːrɪenteɪt] VT orientar; *(fig)* encaminar; **to ~ o.s.** orientarse

-orientated [ˈɔːrɪenteɪtɪd] ADJ *(ending in compounds)* **career-orientated** orientado hacia una carrera

orientation [ˌɔːrɪenˈteɪʃən] N orientación *f*

-oriented [ˈɔːrɪentɪd] ADJ *(ending in compounds)* = **-orientated**

orienteering [ˌɔːrɪənˈtɪərɪŋ] N carrera *f* con mapa y brújula

orifice [ˈɒrɪfɪs] N orificio *m*

origami [ˌɒrɪˈɡɑːmɪ] N papiroflexia *f*

origin [ˈɒrɪdʒɪn] N origen *m*; **country of ~** país *m* de origen *or* de procedencia

original [əˈrɪdʒɪnl] **Ⓐ** ADJ *(gen)* original; **one of the ~ members** uno de los primeros miembros **Ⓑ** N original *m*; **he reads Homer in the ~** lee a Homero en versión original **Ⓒ** CPD ➤ **original sin** pecado *m* original

originality [əˌrɪdʒɪˈnælɪtɪ] N originalidad *f*

originally [əˈrɪdʒənəlɪ] ADV **1** (= *at first*) originariamente, en un principio; **he's ~ from Armenia** es originario de Armenia **2** (= *in an original way*) con originalidad, de manera original

originate [əˈrɪdʒɪneɪt] VI **to ~ (from** *or* **in)** originarse (en), tener su origen (en); **these oranges ~ from Israel** estas naranjas son de Israel; **where do you ~ from?** ¿de dónde eres?; **with whom did the idea ~?** ¿quién tuvo la idea primero?

originator [əˈrɪdʒɪneɪtə'] N inventor(a) *m/f*, creador(a) *m/f*

Orkneys [ˈɔːknɪz], **Orkney Islands** [ˈɔːknɪˌaɪləndz] NPL **the ~** las (Islas) Órcadas

ornament [ˈɔːnəmənt] N *(gen)* adorno *m*, ornamento *m*; (= *vase etc*) objeto *m* de adorno, adorno *m*

ornamental [ˌɔːnəˈmentl] ADJ decorativo, de adorno

ornamentation [ˌɔːnəmenˈteɪʃən] N (= *act*) ornamentación *f*, decoración *f*; (= *ornaments*) adornos *mpl*

ornate [ɔːˈneɪt] ADJ *[decor]* ornamentado; *[building, ceiling, vase, architectural style]* ornamentado, ricamente decorado; *[written style, language]* florido, recargado *(pej)*

ornithologist [ˌɔːnɪˈθɒlədʒɪst] N ornitólogo/a *m/f*

ornithology [ˌɔːnɪˈθɒlədʒɪ] N ornitología *f*

orphan [ˈɔːfən] **Ⓐ** N huérfano/a *m/f* **Ⓑ** VT **to be ~ed** quedarse huérfano

orphanage [ˈɔːfənɪdʒ] N orfanato *m*, orfanatorio *m* *(Mex)*

orthodontics [ˌɔːθəˈdɒntɪks] NSING ortodoncia *f*

orthodontist [ˌɔːθəˈdɒntɪst] N ortodoncista *mf*

orthodox [ˈɔːθədɒks] ADJ ortodoxo

orthodoxy [ˈɔːθədɒksɪ] N ortodoxia *f*

orthopaedic, orthopedic *(US)* [ˌɔːθəˈpiːdɪk] ADJ ortopédico; **~ surgeon** ortopedista *mf*, traumatólogo/a *m/f*

orthopaedics, orthopedics *(US)* [ˌɔːθəˈpiːdɪks] NSING ortopedia *f*

o/s ABBR *(Comm)* (= *outsize*) de tamaño extraordinario

oscillate [ˈɒsɪleɪt] VI oscilar

Oslo [ˈɒzləʊ] N Oslo *m*

osmosis [ɒzˈməʊsɪs] N ósmosis *f inv*, osmosis *f inv*

osprey [ˈɒspreɪ] N pigargo *m*, quebrantahuesos *m inv*

ossify [ˈɒsɪfaɪ] VI osificarse

Ostend [ɒsˈtend] N Ostende *m*

ostensible [ɒsˈtensəbl] ADJ aparente

ostensibly [ɒsˈtensəblɪ] ADV aparentemente, en apariencia

ostensive [ɒˈstensɪv] ADJ ostensivo

ostentation [ˌɒstenˈteɪʃən] N ostentación *f*, boato *m*

ostentatious [ˌɒstenˈteɪʃəs] ADJ *[behaviour, car, clothes]* ostentoso; *[surroundings, style of living]* suntuoso, fastuoso

ostentatiously [ˌɒstenˈteɪʃəslɪ] ADV ostentosamente, con ostentación

osteoarthritis [ˌɒstɪəʊɑːˈθraɪtɪs] N osteoartritis *f*

osteopath [ˈɒstɪəpæθ] N osteópata *mf*

osteopathy [ˌɒstɪˈɒpəθɪ] N osteopatía *f*

osteoporosis [ˌɒstɪəʊpɔːˈrəʊsɪs] N osteoporosis *f inv*

ostracism [ˈɒstrəsɪzəm] N ostracismo *m*

ostracize [ˈɒstrəsaɪz] VT condenar al ostracismo

ostrich [ˈɒstrɪtʃ] N avestruz *m*

OTC N ABBR *(Brit)* = **Officer Training Corps**

other [ˈʌðə'] **Ⓐ** ADJ otro; **all the ~ books have been sold** todos los otros *or* los demás libros se han vendido; **the ~ five** los otros cinco; **the ~ day** el otro día; **every ~ day** cada dos días; **if there are no ~ questions ...** si no hay más preguntas ...; **the ~ one** el otro/la otra; **some actor or ~** un actor cualquiera; **~ people** los otros, los demás; **~ people's**

property la propiedad ajena; **some ~ time** en otro momento, en otra ocasión
B PRON **the** ~ el otro/la otra; **the ~s** los otros/las otras, los/las demás; **some do, ~s don't** algunos sí, otros no; **and these five ~s** y estos otros cinco; **we must respect the rights of ~s** hay que respetar los derechos ajenos; **one after the ~** uno tras otro; **among ~s** entre otros; **are there any ~s?** (*gen*) ¿hay algún otro?; (= *any unaccounted for*) ¿falta alguno?; (= *anybody unaccounted for*) ¿falta alguien?; **one or ~ of them will come** uno de ellos vendrá; **somebody or ~** alguien, alguno; **he had no clothes ~ than** those he stood up in no tenía más ropa que la que llevaba puesta; **none ~ than** el mismísimo/la mismísima
C ADV **somewhere or ~** en alguna parte, en algún lado; **~ than him** aparte de él; **he could not have acted ~ than he did** no le quedaba otro recurso que hacer lo que hizo; **I wouldn't wish him ~ than he is** no quisiera que fuera distinto de como es

otherwise [ˈʌðəwaɪz] **A** CONJ (= *if not*) si no, de lo contrario; **let's go with them, ~ we shall have to walk** vámonos con ellos, si no *or* de lo contrario tendremos que ir a pie; **of course I'm interested, I wouldn't be here ~** claro que me interesa, si no *or* de lo contrario no estaría aquí
B ADV **1** (= *another way, differently*) de otra manera; **unless your doctor advises ~** a menos que el médico le recomiende otra cosa; **it's true, and nothing you can say will convince me ~** es verdad, y nada que puedas decir me convencerá de lo contrario; **she was ~ engaged** tenía otro compromiso; **Miller, ~ known as Dusty** Miller, también conocido como Dusty; **until proven** *or* **proved ~** hasta que se demuestre lo contrario; **unless ~ stated** (*frm*) salvo indicación de lo contrario (*frm*), a no ser que se indique lo contrario; **we had no reason to think ~** no teníamos motivo para creer otra cosa
2 (= *in other respects*) aparte de esto, por lo demás
3 (= *in other circumstances*) en otras circunstancias
4 (= *of another sort*) **he would do it by any means, legal or ~** lo haría por todos los medios, legales o no; **it may not be transmitted by any means, electronic or ~** está prohibida su transmisión por cualquier medio, ya sea electrónico o de otra clase

other-worldly [ˈʌðəˈwɜːldlɪ] ADJ [*person*] muy espiritual; [*experience*] (como) de otro mundo

OTT* ADJ ABBR (*Brit*) (= **over the top**) excesivo

Ottawa [ˈɒtəwə] N Ottawa *f*

otter [ˈɒtəʳ] N nutria *f*

Ottoman [ˈɒtəmən] ADJ, N otomano/a *m/f*

OU N ABBR (*Brit*) (= **Open University**) ≈ UNED *f*

ouch [aʊtʃ] EXCL ¡ay!

ought [ɔːt] MODAL AUX VB **1** (*moral obligation*) deber; **I ~ to do it** debería hacerlo, debiera hacerlo; **you ~ to have warned me** me deberías haber avisado; **he ~ to have known** debía saberlo; **I thought I ~ to tell you** me creí en el deber de decírselo; **to behave as one ~** comportarse como se debe
2 (*vague desirability*) **you ~ to go and see it** vale la pena ir a verlo; **you ~ to have seen him!** ¡tenías que haberle visto!
3 (*probability*) deber; **he ~ to win** debería ganar; **that ~ to be enough** con eso debería ser suficiente; **he ~ to have arrived by now** debería de haber llegado ya

Ouija®, ouija [ˈwiːdʒə] N (*also* ~ **board**) tabla *f* de espiritismo

ounce [aʊns] N onza *f*; **if you had an ~ of common sense** si tuvieras una gota de sentido común; ⊳ *IMPERIAL SYSTEM*

our [aʊəʳ] POSS ADJ (*with singular noun*) nuestro/a; (*with plural noun*) nuestros/as; **~ house** nuestra casa; **~ neighbours are very nice** nuestros vecinos son muy simpáticos

---

Our is usually translated by the definite article **el/los** or **la/las** when it's clear from the sentence who the possessor is or when referring to clothing or parts of the body:

---

we took off ~ coats nos quitamos los abrigos; **they stole ~ car** nos robaron el coche

ours [aʊəz] POSS PRON (*referring to singular possession*) (el/la) nuestro/a; (*referring to plural possession*) (los/las) nuestros/as

---

Only use the article with **nuestro/nuestros** etc when you mean "the one(s) belonging to us".

---

this house is ~ esta casa es nuestra; **a friend of ~** un amigo nuestro; **your car is much bigger than ~** tu coche es mucho más grande que el nuestro

ourselves [ˌaʊəˈselvz] PERS PRON **1** (*reflexive*) nos; **we really enjoyed ~** nos divertimos mucho
2 (*emphatic, also after prep*) nosotros/as (mismos/as); **we built our garage ~** construimos el garaje nosotros mismos; **we went ~** fuimos en persona; **let's not talk about ~ any more** no hablemos más de nosotros (mismos); **we said to ~** nos dijimos
3 (*phrases*) **we were talking among ~** hablábamos entre nosotros; **by ~: we prefer to be by ~** preferimos estar solos; **we did it (all) by ~** lo hicimos nosotros solos

oust [aʊst] VT (*gen*) expulsar, echar; (*from house*) desahuciar, desalojar; **to ~ sb from a post** hacer que algn renuncie a un puesto

out [aʊt] **A** ADV

When **out** is the second element in a phrasal verb, eg **go out, put out, walk out**, look up the verb.

---

1 (= *not in*) fuera, afuera; **they're ~ in the garden** están fuera *or* afuera en el jardín; **to be ~** (= *not at home*) no estar (en casa); **Mr Green is ~** el señor Green no está *or* (*LAm*) no se encuentra; **"way out"** "salida"; **to be ~ and about again** estar bien otra vez (*después de una enfermedad*); **it's cold ~ here** hace frío aquí fuera; **the journey ~** el viaje de ida; **to have a night ~** salir por la noche (*a divertirse*); (*drinking*) salir de juerga *or* (*LAm*) de parranda; **to run ~** salir corriendo; **the tide is ~** la marea está baja; **~ with him!** ¡fuera con él!, ¡que le echen fuera!
2 (= *on strike*) **the railwaymen are ~** los ferroviarios están en huelga
3 (*indicating distance*) **she's ~ in Kuwait** se fue a Kuwait, está en Kuwait; **the boat was ten km ~** el barco estaba a diez kilómetros de la costa; **it carried us ~ to sea** nos llevó mar adentro
4 **to be ~:** **when the sun is ~** cuando brilla el sol; **the dahlias are ~** las dalias están en flor; **when the sun comes ~** cuando sale el sol; **the roses are coming ~** los rosales están floreciendo
5 (= *in existence*) **it's the biggest swindle ~*** es la mayor estafa que se ha conocido jamás; **the book is ~** se ha publicado el libro, ha salido el libro; **the film is now ~ on video** la película ya ha salido en vídeo
6 (= *in the open*) **your secret's ~** tu secreto se ha descubierto *or* ha salido a la luz; **~ with it!** ¡desembucha!, ¡suéltalo ya!, ¡suelta la lengua! (*LAm*)
7 (= *to or at an end*) **before the week was ~** antes de que terminara la semana
8 [*lamp, fire, gas*] apagado/a; **all the lights are ~** todas las luces están apagadas; **"lights out at ten pm"** "se apagan las luces a las diez"
9 (= *not in fashion*) pasado/a de moda
10 (= *not in power*) **now that the Liberals are ~** ahora que los liberales están fuera del poder
11 (*Sport*) [*player*] fuera de juego; [*boxer*] fuera de combate; [*loser*] eliminado/a; **that's it, Liverpool are ~** ya está, el Liverpool queda eliminado *or* fuera de la eliminatoria; **you're ~** (*in games*) quedas eliminado; **the ball is ~** el balón está fuera del terreno; **out!** ¡fuera!
12 (*indicating error*) equivocado/a; **he was ~ in his reckoning** calculó mal; **I was not far ~** por poco acierto; **your watch is five minutes ~** su reloj lleva cinco minutos de atraso/de adelanto; **I'm two dollars ~** ◇ **I'm ~ two dollars** (*US*) he perdido dos dólares en el cálculo
13 (*indicating loudness, clearness*) en voz alta, en alto; **speak ~ (loud)!** ¡habla en voz alta *or* fuerte!

14 (*indicating purpose*) **he's ~ to make money** lo que busca es hacerse rico; **to be ~ for sth** buscar algo; **they're ~ to make trouble** quieren armar un escándalo
15 to be ~ (= *unconscious*) estar inconsciente; (= *drunk*) estar completamente borracho; (= *asleep*) estar durmiendo como un tronco; **he was ~ cold** estuvo completamente sin conocimiento; **I was ~ for some minutes** estuve inconsciente durante varios minutos, estuve varios minutos sin conocimiento
16 ~ and away con mucho
Ⓑ **~ of** PREP

> When **out of** is part of a set combination, eg **out of danger**, **out of proportion**, **out of sight**, look up the other word.

1 (= *outside, beyond*) fuera de; **~ of town** fuera de la ciudad; **three kilometres ~ of town** a tres kilómetros de la ciudad; **to go ~ of the house** salir de la casa; **to look ~ of the window** mirar por la ventana; **we're well ~ of it*** de buena nos hemos librado; ✦ IDIOM **to feel ~ of it*** sentirse aislado or fuera de contacto
2 (*cause, motive*) por; **~ of curiosity** por curiosidad; **~ of respect for you** por el respeto que te tengo
3 (*origin*) de; **to copy sth ~ of a book** copiar algo de un libro; **to take sth ~ of a drawer** sacar algo de un cajón; **a box made ~ of wood** una caja (hecha) de madera
4 (= *from among*) de cada; **one ~ of every three smokers** uno de cada tres fumadores
5 (= *without*) sin; **we're ~ of paper** nos hemos quedado sin papel; **we're ~ of milk** se nos ha acabado la leche; **it's ~ of stock** (*Comm*) está agotado
Ⓒ VT revelar la homosexualidad de
Ⓓ VI **the truth will ~** se descubrirá la verdad

outage ['aʊtɪdʒ] N (*US*) (*also* **power ~**) corte *m* de luz or de corriente, apagón *m*, corte *m* del suministro eléctrico

out-and-out ['aʊtən'aʊt] ADJ **1** (= *absolute*) [*liar, villain*] redomado, empedernido; [*defeat, lie*] absoluto
2 (= *dedicated*) acérrimo

outback ['aʊtbæk] N (*in Australia*) despoblado *m*, campo *m*

outbid [aʊt'bɪd] (*pt, pp* ~) VT pujar más alto que

outboard ['aʊtbɔːd] N (*also* ~ **motor**) motor *m* fuera borda or bordo

outbound ['aʊtbaʊnd] ADJ [*flight*] (= *departing*) de salida; (= *as opposed to return*) de ida; **all ~ flights from Heathrow have been cancelled** todas las salidas (de vuelo) de Heathrow han sido canceladas

outbreak ['aʊtbreɪk] N [*of war*] declaración *f*; [*of hostilities*] comienzo *m*; [*of disease*] brote *m*; [*of violence*] arranque *m*; **at the ~ of war** al estallar la guerra

outbuilding ['aʊtbɪldɪŋ] N dependencia *f*

outburst ['aʊtbɜːst] N (*gen*) estallido *m*, explosión *f*; [*of anger*] arrebato *m*, arranque *m*; [*of applause*] salva *f*; **forgive my ~ last week** perdona que perdiera los estribos la semana pasada

outcast ['aʊtkɑːst] N (= *rejected person*) paria *mf*; (*in exile*) desterrado/a *m/f*; **he's a social ~** vive marginado por la sociedad

outclass [aʊt'klɑːs] VT aventajar a, superar

outcome ['aʊtkʌm] N (= *result*) resultado *m*; (= *consequences*) consecuencias *fpl*

outcrop ['aʊtkrɒp] N afloramiento *m*

outcry ['aʊtkraɪ] N (= *protest*) protesta *f*, clamor *m*; **there was a great ~** hubo fuertes protestas

outdated [aʊt'deɪtɪd] ADJ anticuado, pasado de moda

outdistance [aʊt'dɪstəns] VT dejar atrás

outdo [aʊt'duː] (*pt* **outdid**; *pp* **outdone**) VT **to ~ sb (in sth)** superar a algn (en algo); **he was not to be outdone** no quiso quedarse atrás; **not to be outdone, he added ...** ni corto ni perezoso, añadió que ...

outdoor ['aʊtdɔːʳ] ADJ [*sports, work, market*] al aire libre; [*swimming pool, tennis court*] descubierto, al aire libre;

[*clothes, shoes*] de calle; [*plant*] de exterior

outdoors ['aʊt'dɔːz] Ⓐ ADV **1** (= *outside*) fuera, afuera; **to go ~** salir fuera or afuera; **~, there are three heated swimming pools** fuera or afuera, hay tres piscinas climatizadas **2** (= *in the open air*) [*exercise, bathe*] al aire libre; [*sleep*] al raso Ⓑ N campo *m* abierto; **the great ~** (*hum*) la naturaleza

outer ['aʊtəʳ] ADJ [*layer, surface*] exterior; [*wall, door*] exterior, de fuera; [*garment*] externo; **the ~ reaches of the solar system** los extremos del sistema solar ➤ **outer space** espacio *m* exterior, espacio *m* sideral

outermost ['aʊtəmaʊst] ADJ [*place*] más extremo, más remoto; [*cover, layer*] más externo, más exterior

outfit ['aʊtfɪt] N **1** (= *suit*) traje *m*; (= *ensemble*) conjunto *m*; **a cowboy ~** un traje de vaquero **2** (= *equipment*) equipo *m*; (= *tools*) juego *m* de herramientas **3** (*) (= *organization*) grupo *m*, organización *f*; (*Mil*) unidad *f*, cuerpo *m*

outfitter ['aʊtfɪtəʳ] N (*esp Brit*) **gentlemen's ~'s** tienda *f* de ropa para caballero

outflow ['aʊtfləʊ] N (= *pipe*) tubo *m* de salida; [*of capital etc*] fuga *f*, salida *f*

outgo ['aʊtgəʊ] N (*US*) gastos *mpl*

outgoing ['aʊtgəʊɪŋ] ADJ **1** [*president*] saliente; [*government*] cesante; [*boat, train, mail*] de salida; [*flight*] (= *departing*) de salida; (*as opposed to return*) de ida; [*tide*] que baja **2** [*character*] extrovertido, sociable

outgoings ['aʊtgəʊɪŋz] NPL (*Brit*) gastos *mpl*

outgrow [aʊt'grəʊ] (*pt* **outgrew**; *pp* ~**n**) VT [+ *habit etc*] perder con la edad; [+ *defect, illness*] curarse de ... con la edad; **she has ~n her gloves** se le han quedado pequeños los guantes; **we've ~n all that** todo eso ha quedado ya atrás

outhouse ['aʊthaʊs] N **1** (*Brit*) = **outbuilding 2** (*US*) (= *toilet*) retrete *m* fuera de la casa

outing ['aʊtɪŋ] N (= *trip*) excursión *f*, paseo *m* (*LAm*); **everyone went on an ~ to Toledo** todos fueron de excursión a Toledo

outlandish [aʊt'lændɪʃ] ADJ [*appearance, clothes*] estrafalario, extravagante; [*behaviour, ideas*] extraño, disparatado

outlast [aʊt'lɑːst] VT durar más tiempo que; [+ *person*] sobrevivir a

outlaw ['aʊtlɔː] Ⓐ N (= *fugitive*) prófugo/a *m/f*, fugitivo/a *m/f*; (= *bandit*) bandido/a *m/f*, matrero/a *m/f* (*And, SC*); (*in Westerns*) forajido/a *m/f* Ⓑ VT [+ *person, slavery*] proscribir; [+ *drug*] ilegalizar; [+ *practice*] declarar ilegal

outlay ['aʊtleɪ] N desembolso *m*, gastos *mpl*

outlet ['aʊtlet] N **1** (*for water etc*) salida *f*; (= *drain*) desagüe *m*, distribuidora *f* **2** (*Comm*) (= *shop*) tienda *f*; (= *agency*) sucursal *f*; **to find an ~ for a product** encontrar una salida or un mercado para un producto **3** (*US Elec*) toma *f* **4** (*for emotion, talents etc*) desahogo *m*; **it provides an ~ for his energies** ofrece una válvula de escape para su energía

outline ['aʊtlaɪn] Ⓐ N **1** (= *shape*) contorno *m*, perfil *m* **2** (= *draft*) [*of book, film, plan, theory*] esbozo *m*, boceto *m*; (= *summary*) resumen *m*; **I'll give you the broad** or **general ~ of what we mean to do** te voy a explicar a grandes rasgos lo que pensamos hacer, te voy a resumir lo que pensamos hacer; **in ~, the story goes like this** en resumen, la historia es así Ⓑ VT **1** (= *sketch*) esbozar, bosquejar; (= *silhouette*) perfilar; **the mountain was ~d against the sky** la montaña se perfilaba or recortaba contra el cielo **2** (= *summarize*) resumir, explicar a grandes rasgos Ⓒ CPD ➤ **outline drawing** esbozo *m*, bosquejo *m*

outlive [aʊt'lɪv] VT sobrevivir a; **she dropped men as soon as they ~d their usefulness** abandonaba a los hombres tan pronto como dejaban de resultarle útiles

outlook ['aʊtlʊk] N **1** (= *view*) vista *f*, perspectiva *f* **2** (= *prospects*) perspectivas *fpl*, panorama *m*; **the ~ for the economy is good** las perspectivas económicas son favorables **3** (= *attitude*) actitud *f* **4** (*Met*) **the ~ for next Saturday is sunny** la previsión para el próximo sábado es que hará sol

outlying [ˈaʊtˌlaɪɪŋ] ADJ (= *distant*) [*towns, villages*] remoto, lejano; (= *surrounding*) [*areas*] periférico; [*suburb*] periférico, circundante

outmanoeuvre, outmaneuver (*US*) [ˌaʊtməˈnuːvəʳ] VT [+ *opposition, competition*] superar a

outmatch [aʊtˈmætʃ] VT superar, aventajar

outmoded [aʊtˈməʊdɪd] ADJ anticuado, pasado de moda

outnumber [aʊtˈnʌmbəʳ] VT exceder en número, ser más numeroso que; **the actors ~ed the audience** había más actores que público; **we were ~ed ten to one** ellos eran diez veces más que nosotros

out-of-bounds [ˌaʊtəvˈbaʊndz] *see* **bound** A

out-of-court [aʊtəvˈkɔːt] ADJ **an ~ settlement** un arreglo sin acudir a los tribunales

out-of-date [ˈaʊtəvˈdeɪt] ADJ [*ideas*] anticuado; [*clothes*] pasado de moda, [*passport, ticket*] caducado, vencido

out-of-doors [ˈaʊtəvˈdɔːz] ADV = **outdoors** A

out-of-pocket [ˈaʊtəvˈpɒkɪt] ADJ **~ expenses** gastos *mpl* varios

out-of-school [ˌaʊtəvˈskuːl] ADJ **~ activities** actividades *fpl* extraescolares

out-of-the-way [ˈaʊtəvðəˈweɪ] ADJ (= *remote*) remoto, apartado; (= *inaccessible*) inaccesible

out-of-town [ˌaʊtəvˈtaʊn] ADJ [*shopping centre etc*] en las afueras

out-of-towner [ˌaʊtəvˈtaʊnəʳ] N (*US*) forastero/a *m/f*

outpace [aʊtˈpeɪs] VT dejar atrás

outpatient [ˈaʊtˌpeɪʃənt] N paciente *mf* externo/a

outperform [ˈaʊtpəˈfɔːm] VT hacer mejor que, superar a; [+ *shares, investment fund*] dar mayores beneficios que

outpost [ˈaʊtpəʊst] N **1** (*Mil*) avanzada *f*, puesto *m* avanzado **2** (*fig*) avanzada *f*

outpouring [ˈaʊtˌpɔːrɪŋ] N [*of emotion*] efusión *f*

output [ˈaʊtpʊt] **A** N [*of factory*] producción *f*; [*of person, machine*] rendimiento *m*; (*Comput*) salida *f*; (*Elec*) potencia *f* de salida **B** VT (*Comput*) imprimir

outrage [aʊtˈreɪdʒ] **A** N **1** (= *atrocity*) atrocidad *f*; **bomb ~** atentado *m* (con bomba) **2** (*scandalous*) escándalo *m*; **a public ~** un escándalo público; **it's an ~!** ¡es un escándalo!, ¡qué barbaridad! **B** VT [+ *person*] ultrajar; [+ *standards, decency*] atentar contra; **to be ~d by sth** indignarse ante algo

outrageous [aʊtˈreɪdʒəs] ADJ **1** (= *intolerable*) [*conduct, decision, accusation*] escandaloso; [*price, demands*] exorbitante, escandaloso; [*act, crime*] atroz, monstruoso; **it is ~ that taxpayers will have to foot the bill** es escandaloso que sean los contribuyentes los que tengan que pagar **2** (= *extravagant*) [*clothes, fashion*] extravagante, estrafalario; [*idea, story*] estrambótico

outrageously [aʊtˈreɪdʒəslɪ] ADV **1** (= *shockingly*) [*behave*] de manera escandalosa; **she flirted with him ~** era escandaloso cómo flirteaba con él, flirteaba de manera escandalosa con él **2** (= *extravagantly*) [*dress*] de forma extravagante, de forma estrafalaria **3** (= *extremely*) [*unfair, racist*] terriblemente; [*expensive*] escandalosamente

outran [aʊtˈræn] PT *of* **outrun**

outrank [aʊtˈræŋk] VT ser de rango superior a

outrider [ˈaʊtˌraɪdəʳ] N motociclista *mf* de escolta

outright [aʊtˈraɪt] **A** ADJ **1** (= *complete*) [*failure*] completo, total; [*winner, victory*] absoluto; [*lie*] descarado; [*owner*] absoluto (*sin hipotecas*); [*refusal, rejection*] rotundo, absoluto **2** (= *open, forthright*) franco; [*rudeness, hostility*] abierto, franco **B** ADV **1** (= *completely*) [*own, buy*] en su totalidad; [*win*] de manera absoluta; [*refuse, reject*] rotundamente, de pleno; **to reject an offer ~** rechazar una oferta de pleno; **they won the cup ~** ganaron la copa indiscutiblemente; **he was killed ~** murió en el acto **2** (= *openly, forthrightly*) abiertamente, francamente; **to laugh ~ at sth** reírse abiertamente de algo

outrun [aʊtˈrʌn] (*pt* **outran**; *pp* ~) VT dejar atrás

outsell [ˌaʊtˈsel] (*pt, pp* **outsold**) VT venderse más que; **this product ~s all the competition** este producto se vende más que todos los competidores

outset [ˈaʊtset] N principio *m*, comienzo *m*; **at the ~** al principio *or* comienzo; **from the ~** desde el principio *or* comienzo

outshine [aʊtˈʃaɪn] (*pt, pp* **outshone** [aʊtˈʃɒn]) VT eclipsar

outside [ˈaʊtˈsaɪd] **A** ADV fuera, afuera (*esp LAm*); **to be/go ~** estar/salir fuera
B PREP (*also ~ of*) **1** (*lit*) fuera de, afuera de (*LAm*); (= *beyond*) más allá de; **~ the city** fuera de la ciudad, en las afueras de la ciudad; **the car ~ the house** el coche que está frente a la casa
2 (*fig*) fuera de; **it's ~ my experience** no tengo experiencia en eso
C ADJ **1** (= *exterior*) [*wall*] exterior; [*door*] que da a la calle; (= *outdoors*) [*patio, swimming pool*] descubierto, al aire libre; (= *alien*) [*influence*] externo; **~ broadcast** (*Brit Rad, TV*) retransmisión *f* desde exteriores; **the ~ lane** (*Brit Aut*) el carril de la derecha; (*most other countries*) el carril de la izquierda; **~ line** (*Telec*) línea *f* exterior; **an ~ seat** un asiento al lado del pasillo; **the ~ world** el mundo exterior **2** (= *unlikely*) **an ~ chance** una posibilidad remota **3** (= *from another organization, person*) **to get an ~ opinion** pedir una opinión independiente
D N **1** (= *outer part*) exterior *m*, parte *f* exterior; **to open a window from the ~** abrir una ventana desde fuera; **on the ~** por fuera; **judging from the ~** a juzgar por las apariencias; **to overtake on the ~** (*Brit Aut*) adelantar *or* (*Mex*) rebasar por la derecha; (*most other countries*) adelantar *or* (*Mex*) rebasar por la izquierda
2 (= *maximum*) **at the (very) ~** a lo sumo, como máximo
E CPD ➤ **the outside lane** (*Brit*) el carril de la derecha; (*most countries*) el carril de la izquierda

outside-forward [ˈaʊtsaɪdˈfɔːwəd] N delantero/a *m/f* extremo/a

outside-left [ˈaʊtsaɪdˈleft] N extremo/a *m/f* izquierdo/a

outsider [ˈaʊtˈsaɪdəʳ] N **1** (= *stranger*) forastero/a *m/f*, desconocido/a *m/f* **2** (= *independent*) persona *f* independiente, persona *f* ajena al asunto **3** (*in horse race*) caballo *m* que no figura entre los favoritos; (*in election*) candidato *m* poco conocido; (*pej*) segundón *m*

outside-right [ˈaʊtsaɪdˈraɪt] N extremo/a *m/f* derecho/a

outsize [ˈaʊtsaɪz] ADJ (*Brit*) [*clothes*] de talla muy grande

outskirts [ˈaʊtskɜːts] NPL [*of town*] afueras *fpl*, alrededores *mpl*; **on the ~ of the town** en las afueras de la ciudad

outsmart [aʊtˈsmɑːt] VT **to ~ sb** engañar a algn

outsold [ˌaʊtˈsəʊld] PT, PP *of* **outsell**

outsourcing [ˈaʊtsɔːsɪŋ] N [*of labour*] *contratación de mano de obra que no pertenece a la empresa*; **the ~ of components** la adquisición de componentes de fuentes externas

outspoken [aʊtˈspəʊkən] ADJ [*criticism*] franco, abierto; [*opponent, critic*] declarado; **to be ~** ser muy franco, no tener pelos en la lengua*

outspread [ˈaʊtˈspred] ADJ [*wings*] extendido, desplegado; [*legs, feet*] extendido; **with ~ arms** con los brazos abiertos

outstanding [aʊtˈstændɪŋ] ADJ **1** (= *exceptional*) [*person, achievement, feature*] destacado; [*beauty, performance, service*] excepcional, extraordinario; [*example*] sobresaliente **2** (= *not settled*) [*issue, problem*] pendiente, por resolver; [*bill*] por cobrar; [*debt, balance, account*] pendiente

outstandingly [aʊtˈstændɪŋlɪ] ADV [*beautiful, effective, well-written*] excepcionalmente, extraordinariamente; **an ~ gifted musician** un músico de excepcional *or* extraordinario talento

outstay [aʊtˈsteɪ] VT quedarse más tiempo que; **I don't want to ~ my welcome** no quiero quedarme más de lo debido, no quiero abusar de su hospitalidad

outstretched [ˈaʊtstretʃt] ADJ extendido

outstrip [aʊtˈstrɪp] VT [+ *business rival*] dejar atrás, aventajar; (*Sport*) aventajar, adelantarse a

out-tray [ˈaʊtˌtreɪ] N bandeja *f* de salida

outturn ['aʊtɜ:n] N (US) rendimiento *m*, producción *f*

outvote [aʊt'vəʊt] VT [+ *proposal*] rechazar (por mayoría de votos); [+ *party, person*] vencer (en la votación); **but I was ~d** pero en la votación perdí

outward ['aʊtwəd] Ⓐ ADJ 1 [*flight*] (= *departing*) de salida; (*as opposed to return*) de ida; [*movement*] hacia fuera; **on the ~ journey** en el viaje de ida 2 (= *exterior*) [*appearance etc*] exterior, externo Ⓑ ADV hacia fuera; **~ bound (from/for)** saliendo (de/con rumbo a)

outwardly ['aʊtwədlɪ] ADV por fuera, aparentemente

outwards ['aʊtwədz] ADV (*esp Brit*) = **outward** B

outweigh [aʊt'weɪ] VT pesar más que; **the advantages ~ the disadvantages** las ventajas pesan más que *or* superan a las desventajas

outwit [aʊt'wɪt] VT ser más listo que

outworker ['aʊtwɜ:kə'] N *persona que trabaja en su propio domicilio*

ova ['əʊvə] NPL *of* **ovum**

oval ['əʊvəl] Ⓐ ADJ oval, ovalado Ⓑ N óvalo *m*

ovarian [əʊ'veərɪən] ADJ ovárico

ovary ['əʊvərɪ] N ovario *m*

ovation [əʊ'veɪʃən] N ovación *f*; **to give sb an ~** ovacionar a algn; **to give sb a standing ~** ponerse en pie *or* levantarse para ovacionar a algn

oven ['ʌvn] N horno *m*; **it's like an ~ in there** aquello es un horno ➤ **oven glove** guante *m* para el horno, manopla *f* para el horno

ovenproof ['ʌvnpru:f] ADJ [*dish*] refractario, (a prueba) de horno

oven-ready [ˌʌvn'redɪ] ADJ listo para el horno

ovenware ['ʌvnweə'] N vajilla *f* refractaria

---

over

Ⓐ ADVERB	Ⓒ ADJECTIVE
Ⓑ PREPOSITION	Ⓓ NOUN

When **over** *is the second element in a phrasal verb, eg* **come over, go over, start over, turn over,** *look up the verb.*

---

over ['əʊvə'] Ⓐ ADVERB
1 (= *across*) por encima, por arriba (*LAm*); **this one goes under and that one goes ~** éste pasa por debajo y ése por encima; **the (whole) world ~** en *or* por todo el mundo, en el mundo entero
2 (= *here, there*) **I'll be ~ at seven o'clock** estaré ahí a las siete; **they're ~ for the day** han venido a pasar el día; **when you're next ~ this way** la próxima vez que pases por aquí

With prepositions and adverbs **over** is usually not translated:

---

they're ~ from Canada for the summer han venido desde Canadá a pasar el verano; **~ here** aquí; **he's ~ in the States** está en Estados Unidos; **~ there** allí; **~ to you!** (*to speak*) ¡te paso la palabra!; **now ~ to our Paris correspondent** ahora damos paso a nuestro corresponsal en París
3 (*indicating repetition*) **it happened all ~ again** (*Brit*) volvió a ocurrir, ocurrió otra vez; **to start (all) ~ again** volver a empezar; **~ and ~ (again)** repetidas veces, una y otra vez; **several times ~** varias veces seguidas
4 (*US*) (= *again*) otra vez; **to do sth ~** volver a hacer algo, hacer algo otra vez
5 (= *remaining*) **there are three (left) ~** sobran *or* quedan tres; **is there any cake left ~?** ¿queda *or* sobra (algo de) pastel?; **four into 29 goes seven and one ~** 29 dividido entre cuatro son siete y me llevo uno
6 (= *more*) **sums of £50,000 and ~** cantidades iguales *or* superiores a 50.000 libras; **persons of 21 and ~** las personas de 21 años para arriba
7 (*Telec*) **over!** ¡cambio!; **~ and out!** ¡cambio y corto!
Ⓑ PREPOSITION
1 (*indicating position*) (= *situated above*) encima de, arriba de

(*LAm*); (= *across*) por encima de, por arriba de (*LAm*); **a washbasin with a mirror ~ it** un lavabo con un espejo encima; **the water came ~ his knees** el agua le llegaba por encima de las rodillas; **the ball went ~ the wall** la pelota pasó por encima del muro; **to jump ~ sth** saltar por encima de algo; **I put a blanket ~ her** le eché una manta por encima; **she put an apron on ~ her dress** se puso un delantal encima del vestido; *BUT* **the bridge ~ the river** el puente sobre el río
2 (= *superior to*) **he's ~ me (in the company)** está por encima mío (en la empresa)
3 (= *on the other side of*) **the bar ~ the road** el bar de enfrente; **it's ~ the river** está en la otra orilla del río; **the noise came from ~ the wall** el ruido venía del otro lado de la pared; **~ the page** en la página siguiente
4 (= *more than*) más de; **~ two hundred** más de doscientos; **well ~ 200 people** bastante más de 200 personas; **(the) ~~18s** los mayores de 18 años; **spending has gone up by 7% ~ and above inflation** el gasto ha aumentado un 7% por encima de la inflación; **this was ~ and above his normal duties** eso iba más allá de sus deberes habituales
5 (= *during*) durante; **~ Christmas** durante las Navidades; **~ the winter** durante *or* en el invierno; **why don't we discuss it ~ dinner?** ¿por qué no vamos a cenar y lo hablamos?; **they talked ~ a cup of coffee** hablaron mientras se tomaban un café
6 (= *because of*) por; **they fell out ~ money** se pelearon por una cuestión de dinero
7 (= *about*) sobre; **they disagreed ~ how much should be spent** discrepaban sobre cuánto debería gastarse
8 (= *recovered from*) **he's not ~ that yet** (*illness*) todavía no se ha repuesto de aquello; (*shock*) todavía no se ha repuesto *or* sobrepuesto a aquello; **I hope you'll soon be ~ your cold** espero que se te pase pronto el resfriado, espero que te repongas pronto del resfriado; **she's still not ~ her last boyfriend** aún no ha olvidado a su último novio; **we're ~ the worst now** ya pasó lo peor
9 (*indicating means of communication*) por; **~ the telephone** por teléfono
10 (= *contrasted with*) **the issue of quality ~ economy** la cuestión de la calidad en contraposición a la rentabilidad
Ⓒ ADJECTIVE (= *finished*) **when** *or* **after the war is ~, we'll go ...** cuando (se) acabe la guerra, nos iremos ...; **our troubles are ~** (se) han acabado nuestros problemas; **the danger was soon ~** el peligro pasó pronto; **it's all ~** se acabó; **it's all ~ between us** lo nuestro se acabó; **I'll be glad when it's all ~ and done** estaré contento cuando todo (se) haya acabado *or* terminado; **to get sth ~ and done with: if we've got to tell her, best get it ~ and done with** si tenemos que decírselo, cuanto antes (lo hagamos) mejor
Ⓓ NOUN (*Cricket*) serie *f* de seis lanzamientos

overact [ˌəʊvər'ækt] VI sobreactuar, exagerar (el papel)

overactive [ˌəʊvər'æktɪv] ADJ [*thyroid*] hiperactivo; [*imagination*] muy activo

overage ['əʊvərɪdʒ] N (*US Comm*) excedente *m* de mercancías

over-age [ˌəʊvər'eɪdʒ] ADJ demasiado mayor, mayor de la edad permitida

overall[1] Ⓐ ['əʊvərɔ:l] ADJ [*view*] de conjunto, global; [*width, length, cost*] total; **what was your ~ impression?** ¿cuál fue tu impresión general? Ⓑ [ˌəʊvər'ɔ:l] ADV en conjunto, en su totalidad; **~, we are well pleased** en términos generales estamos muy contentos

overall[2] ['əʊvərɔ:l] N 1 (*Brit*) (= *protective coat*) guardapolvo *m*, bata *f* 2 **overalls** (*Brit*) (= *boiler suit*) mono *msing* (*Sp*), overol *msing* (*LAm*); (*US*) (= *dungarees*) peto *msing* (*Sp*), overol *msing* (*LAm*), mameluco *m* (*SC*)

overambitious [ˌəʊvəræm'bɪʃəs] ADJ demasiado ambicioso

overanxious [ˌəʊvər'æŋkʃəs] ADJ 1 (= *worried*) demasiado preocupado 2 (= *eager*) **I'm not ~ to go** tengo pocas ganas de ir

overarching [ˌəʊvər'ɑ:tʃɪŋ] ADJ [*question*] global; [*desire*] general

overarm ['əʊvərɑ:m] ADV [*throw, bowl*] por encima de la cabeza

overate [ˌəʊvə'reɪt] PT *of* **overeat**

overawe [ˌəʊvər'ɔ:] VT intimidar

overbalance [ˌəʊvə'bæləns] VI perder el equilibrio

overbearing [ˌəʊvə'bɛərɪŋ] ADJ (= *imperious*) imperioso, autoritario; (= *despotic*) despótico

overbill [ˌəʊvə'bɪl] VT (*US*) = **overcharge A**

overblown [ˌəʊvə'bləʊn] ADJ 1 [*flower*] marchito, pasado 2 [*style*] pomposo, pretencioso

overboard ['əʊvəbɔ:d] ADV (*Naut*) por la borda; **to fall ~** caer al agua *or* por la borda; **man ~!** ¡hombre al agua!; ✦ IDIOM **let's not go ~** no hay que exagerar, no nos pasemos*

overbook [ˌəʊvə'bʊk] VI tener overbooking, aceptar más reservas que plazas

overbooking [ˌəʊvə'bʊkɪŋ] N overbooking *m* (*reserva de habitaciones en un hotel, plazas en un vuelo etc, que sobrepasa al número real de las mismas*)

overburden [ˌəʊvə'bɜ:dn] VT sobrecargar; (*with work*) abrumar, agobiar; **~ed with worries** abrumado *or* agobiado por las preocupaciones

overcame [ˌəʊvə'keɪm] PT *of* **overcome**

over-capacity [ˌəʊvəkə'pæsɪtɪ] N sobrecapacidad *f*

overcapitalize [ˌəʊvə'kæpɪtəlaɪz] VI sobrecapitalizar

overcast ['əʊvəka:st] ADJ [*sky*] encapotado, cubierto; [*day*] nublado; **to grow ~** nublarse

overcautious [ˌəʊvə'kɔ:ʃəs] ADJ demasiado cauteloso

overcharge [ˌəʊvə'tʃɑ:dʒ] Ⓐ VT **to ~ sb for sth** cobrar a algn de más por algo Ⓑ VI cobrar más de la cuenta

overcoat ['əʊvəkəʊt] N abrigo *m*, sobretodo *m*

overcome [ˌəʊvə'kʌm] (*pt* **overcame**; *pp* ~) Ⓐ VT 1 (= *conquer*) [+ *enemy, opposition*] vencer; [+ *problem, temptation, inhibitions, disease*] superar, vencer; [+ *rage, fear, disgust*] superar, dominar 2 (= *overwhelm*) [*feeling*] adueñarse de; [*sleep, fatigue*] vencer; **he was ~ by the smoke** el humo le impidió respirar; **she was quite ~ by the occasion** la ocasión la conmovió mucho; **she was ~ with remorse** le abrumaba el remordimiento; **she was so ~ with emotion she couldn't answer** estaba tan conmovida que no podía responder Ⓑ VI vencer, triunfar; **we shall ~!** ¡venceremos!

overcompensate [ˌəʊvə'kɒmpen,seɪt] VI **to ~ for sth** compensar algo en exceso

overconfidence [ˌəʊvə'kɒnfɪdəns] N confianza *f* excesiva, exceso *m* de confianza

overconfident [ˌəʊvə'kɒnfɪdənt] ADJ demasiado confiado (**of** en); (= *conceited*) presumido

overcook [ˌəʊvə'kʊk] VT cocer demasiado, recocer

overcrowded [ˌəʊvə'kraʊdɪd] ADJ [*room, bus, train*] atestado de gente; [*road, suburb*] congestionado; [*city, country*] superpoblado

overcrowding [ˌəʊvə'kraʊdɪŋ] N [*of housing, prison*] hacinamiento *m*; [*of bus, train*] abarrotamiento *m*; [*of town*] superpoblación *f*

overdependence [ˌəʊvədɪ'pendəns] N dependencia *f* excesiva

overdependent [ˌəʊvədɪ'pendənt] ADJ excesivamente dependiente (**on** de)

overdeveloped [ˌəʊvədɪ'veləpt] ADJ (*gen*) excesivamente desarrollado; (*Phot*) sobreprocesado, sobrerrevelado

overdo [ˌəʊvə'du:] (*pt* **overdid**; *pp* ~**ne**) VT 1 (= *exaggerate*) exagerar; (= *use to excess*) pasarse con*; **to ~ it** (= *work too hard*) trabajar demasiado; (= *exaggerate*) exagerar 2 (= *cook too long*) cocer demasiado, recocer

overdone [ˌəʊvə'dʌn] Ⓐ PP *of* **overdo** Ⓑ ADJ (= *exaggerated*) exagerado; (= *overcooked*) recocido, muy hecho

overdose ['əʊvədəʊs] N Ⓐ N sobredosis *f inv* Ⓑ VI tomar una sobredosis (**on** de); **she ~d on the chocolate** comió demasiado chocolate

overdraft ['əʊvədrɑ:ft] N sobregiro *m*, giro *m* en descubierto; **to have an ~** tener la cuenta en descubierto ➤ **overdraft facility** crédito *m* al descubierto ➤ **overdraft**

limit límite *m* del descubierto

overdraw [ˌəʊvə'drɔ:] (*pt* **overdrew**; *pp* ~**n**) VT girar en descubierto; **your account is ~n (by £50)** su cuenta tiene un saldo deudor (de 50 libras); **I'm ~n** tengo un descubierto

overdressed [ˌəʊvə'drest] ADJ demasiado arreglado

overdrive ['əʊvədraɪv] N **to go into ~** ponerse *or* empezar a funcionar a toda marcha

overdue [ˌəʊvə'dju:] ADJ [*salary, wages*] atrasado; [*bill*] vencido y no pagado; [*train, plane*] retrasado, con retraso; **the train is 30 minutes ~** el tren tiene *or* lleva 30 minutos de retraso; **the baby is two weeks ~** el niño tenía que haber nacido hace quince días; **her period was ~** se le había atrasado la regla; **that change was long ~** ese cambio tenía que haberse hecho hace tiempo

overeat [ˌəʊvə'i:t] (*pt* **overate**; *pp* ~**en**) VI comer en exceso

overemphasis [ˌəʊvər'emfəsɪs] N énfasis *m* excesivo

overemphasize [ˌəʊvər'emfəsaɪz] VT poner demasiado énfasis en

overenthusiastic [ˌəʊvərɪnθju:zɪ'æstɪk] ADJ demasiado entusiasta

overestimate Ⓐ [ˌəʊvər'estɪmɪt] N sobre(e)stimación *f*, estimación *f* excesiva; (*Fin*) presupuesto *m* excesivo Ⓑ [ˌəʊvər'estɪmeɪt] VT [+ *importance, value, cost, person*] sobre(e)stimar

overexcite [ˌəʊvərɪk'saɪt] VT sobreexcitar

overexert [ˌəʊvərɪg'zɜ:t] VT **to ~ o.s.** hacer un esfuerzo excesivo

overexpose [ˌəʊvərɪks'pəʊz] VT (*Phot*) sobreexponer

overfamiliar [ˌəʊvəfə'mɪlɪə'] ADJ **to be ~ with sb** tomarse demasiadas libertades *or* confianzas con algn

overfeed [ˌəʊvə'fi:d] (*pt, pp* **overfed**) VT sobrealimentar, dar demasiado de comer a

overflow Ⓐ ['əʊvəfləʊ] N 1 (= *outlet, hole*) rebosadero *m* 2 (= *excess*) exceso *m* Ⓑ [ˌəʊvə'fləʊ] VI [*liquid*] rebosar, derramarse; [*container, room, hall*] rebosar; [*river*] desbordarse; **the crowd filled the stadium to ~ing** el estadio estaba a rebosar de público Ⓒ ['əʊvəfləʊ] CPD ➤ **overflow pipe** desagüe *m*, tubo *m* de desagüe

overfly [ˌəʊvə'flaɪ] (*pt* **overflew**; *pp* **overflown**) VT sobrevolar

overfull [ˌəʊvə'fʊl] ADJ demasiado lleno, rebosante (**of** de)

overgenerous [ˌəʊvə'dʒenərəs] ADJ [*person*] demasiado generoso; [*helping, portion*] excesivamente grande

overgrown [ˌəʊvə'grəʊn] ADJ [*garden*] descuidado, cubierto de malas hierbas; **he's just an ~ schoolboy** es como un niño grande

overhang (*vb: pt, pp* **overhung**) Ⓐ ['əʊvəhæŋ] N proyección *f*; [*of roof*] alero *m*; (*in rock climbing*) saliente *m*, extraplomo *m* Ⓑ [ˌəʊvə'hæŋ] VT sobresalir por encima de; **the mists that overhung the valley** la neblina que flotaba sobre el valle

overhanging [ˌəʊvə'hæŋɪŋ] ADJ [*cliff, rock*] saliente; [*branches, trees, balcony*] que sobresale

overhaul Ⓐ ['əʊvəhɔ:l] N repaso *m* general, revisión *f* Ⓑ [ˌəʊvə'hɔ:l] VT (= *check*) [+ *machine*] revisar, repasar, dar un repaso general a; [+ *plans etc*] volver a pensar, rehacer, replantear

overhead Ⓐ [ˌəʊvə'hed] ADV por lo alto, en alto, por encima de la cabeza Ⓑ ['əʊvəhed] N (*US*) = **overheads** Ⓒ ['əʊvəhed] **overheads** NPL (*Brit*) gastos *mpl* generales Ⓓ ['əʊvəhed] CPD ➤ **overhead cable** línea *f* eléctrica aérea ➤ **overhead light** luz *f* de techo ➤ **overhead projector** retroproyector *m*

overhear [ˌəʊvə'hɪə'] (*pt, pp* ~**d**) Ⓐ VT oír (por casualidad) Ⓑ VI **be careful, someone might ~** ten cuidado, alguien podría oírnos

overheat [ˌəʊvə'hi:t] Ⓐ VT (*lit*) recalentar, sobrecalentar Ⓑ VI recalentarse

overheating [ˌəʊvə'hi:tɪŋ] N recalentamiento *m*

overhung [ˌəʊvə'hʌŋ] PT, PP *of* **overhang**

overindulge [ˌəʊvərɪn'dʌldʒ] Ⓐ VT [+ *child*] mimar, consentir; [+ *passion*] dar rienda suelta a, dejarse llevar por Ⓑ VI excederse

overindulgence [ˌəʊvərɪnˈdʌldʒəns] N **1** (= *excess*) abuso *m* (**in** de) **2** (*with children*) exceso *m* de tolerancia (**towards** con)

overjoyed [ˌəʊvəˈdʒɔɪd] ADJ lleno de alegría (**at** por), contentísimo; **he was ~ at the news** no cabía en sí de contento con la noticia; **she will be ~ to see you** estará encantada de verte

overkill [ˈəʊvəkɪl] N (*Mil*) capacidad *f* excesiva de destrucción

overland Ⓐ [ˈəʊvəˈlænd] ADV por tierra, por vía terrestre Ⓑ [ˈəʊvəlænd] ADJ terrestre

overlap Ⓐ [ˈəʊvəlæp] N **1** (*lit*) superposición *f* (parcial) **2** (*fig*) coincidencia *f* (parcial) Ⓑ [ˌəʊvəˈlæp] VI **1** (*lit*) superponerse (parcialmente) **2** (*fig*) coincidir (en parte) Ⓒ [ˌəʊvəˈlæp] VT colocar parcialmente unos sobre otros

overlay (*pt, pp* **overlaid**) Ⓐ [ˌəʊvəˈleɪ] VT cubrir (**with** con), revestir (**with** de) Ⓑ [ˈəʊvəleɪ] N capa *f* sobrepuesta, revestimiento *m*; (= *applied decoration*) incrustación *f*; (*on map etc*) transparencia *f* superpuesta

overleaf [ˌəʊvəˈliːf] ADV al dorso; **"see overleaf"** "véase al dorso"

overload Ⓐ [ˈəʊvələʊd] N sobrecarga *f* Ⓑ [ˌəʊvəˈləʊd] VT sobrecargar (**with** de); **to be ~ed with** estar sobrecargado de; (*with work*) estar agobiado de

overlong [ˌəʊvəˈlɒŋ] ADJ demasiado largo

overlook [ˌəʊvəˈlʊk] VT **1** [*building*] tener vista a, dar a **2** (= *leave out*) pasar por alto; (= *not notice*) pasar por alto, no darse cuenta de; (= *tolerate*) pasar por alto, dejar pasar; (= *turn a blind eye to*) hacer la vista gorda a; **we'll ~ it this time** por esta vez lo pasaremos por alto *or* lo dejaremos pasar

overlord [ˈəʊvəlɔːd] N (*feudal*) señor *m*; (= *leader*) jefe *m* supremo

overly [ˈəʊvəlɪ] ADV (*esp US*) demasiado

overmanning [ˌəʊvəˈmænɪŋ] N exceso *m* de mano de obra

overmuch [ˌəʊvəˈmʌtʃ] Ⓐ ADV demasiado, en demasía Ⓑ ADJ demasiado

overnight [ˌəʊvəˈnaɪt] Ⓐ ADV **1** (= *through the night*) **we drove ~** condujimos durante la noche; **we'd like to keep him in ~ for observation** nos gustaría que se quedase la noche en observación; **we stayed ~ in Pisa** pasamos la noche *or* hicimos noche en Pisa; **we stayed ~ at John's place** nos quedamos a dormir en casa de John, pasamos la noche en casa de John **2** (= *quickly*) [*disappear, spring up*] de la noche a la mañana Ⓑ ADJ **1** (= *night-time*) [*journey*] de noche; **accommodation is included** el precio de la estancia por la noche está incluido; **the operation requires an ~ stay in hospital** esta operación requiere que se quede una noche *or* que haga noche en el hospital; **we arrived in Rio after an ~ stop in Madrid** llegamos a Río tras hacer noche en Madrid **2** (= *quick*) [*change, transformation*] repentino; **he became an ~ success in America** de la noche a la mañana, se convirtió en una estrella en América Ⓒ CPD ➤ **overnight bag** bolso *m* de viaje

overoptimistic [ˌəʊvərɒptɪˈmɪstɪk] ADJ optimista

overparticular [ˌəʊvəpəˈtɪkjʊləʳ] ADJ **he's not ~ about hygiene** no es muy escrupuloso en cuestiones de higiene

overpass [ˈəʊvəpɑːs] N (*US*) paso *m* elevado *or* (*LAm*) a desnivel

overpay [ˌəʊvəˈpeɪ] (*pt, pp* **overpaid**) VT [+ *person*] pagar demasiado a

overpayment [ˌəʊvəˈpeɪmənt] N pago *m* excesivo

overplay [ˌəʊvəˈpleɪ] VT **to ~ one's hand** pasarse, ir demasiado lejos

overpopulated [ˌəʊvəˈpɒpjʊleɪtɪd] ADJ superpoblado

overpopulation [ˌəʊvəpɒpjʊˈleɪʃən] N superpoblación *f*

overpower [ˌəʊvəˈpaʊəʳ] VT (= *subdue physically*) dominar; (= *defeat*) [+ *enemy, opponent*] derrotar, vencer

overpowering [ˌəʊvəˈpaʊərɪŋ] ADJ [*smell*] penetrante, intensísimo; [*perfume*] embriagado; [*heat*] asfixiante, sofocante; [*flavour*] fortísimo; [*desire*] irresistible; [*need*] acuciante; [*person, manner*] apabullante, abrumador

overprice [ˌəʊvəˈpraɪs] VT cargar demasiado sobre el precio de; **these goods are ~d** el precio de estas mercancías es excesivo, estas mercancías son demasiado caras para lo que son

overproduction [ˌəʊvəprəˈdʌkʃən] N superproducción *f*, exceso *m* de producción

overprotect [ˌəʊvəprəˈtekt] VT proteger demasiado

overprotective [ˌəʊvəprəˈtektɪv] ADJ excesivamente protector

overqualified [ˌəʊvəˈkwɒlɪfaɪd] ADJ **he's ~ for the job** tiene más titulación de la que se pide para el trabajo

overran [ˌəʊvəˈræn] PT *of* **overrun**

overrate [ˌəʊvəˈreɪt] VT sobrevalorar, sobre(e)stimar

overreach [ˌəʊvəˈriːtʃ] VT **to ~ o.s.** ir más allá de las propias posibilidades

overreact [ˌəʊvərɪˈækt] VI reaccionar de manera exagerada

overreliance [ˌəʊvərɪˈlaɪəns] N dependencia *f* excesiva (**on** de)

override [ˌəʊvəˈraɪd] (*pt* **overrode**; *pp* **overridden**) VT (= *ignore*) hacer caso omiso de, ignorar; (= *cancel*) anular, invalidar

overriding [ˌəʊvəˈraɪdɪŋ] ADJ [*need, importance, reason*] primordial; [*principle*] fundamental

overripe [ˌəʊvəˈraɪp] ADJ demasiado maduro, pasado

overrode [ˌəʊvəˈrəʊd] PT *of* **override**

overrule [ˌəʊvəˈruːl] VT [+ *judgment, decision*] anular, invalidar; [+ *request, suggestion*] denegar, rechazar; [+ *objection*] ignorar; **"objection overruled"** (*Jur*) "objeción desestimada"

overrun [ˌəʊvəˈrʌn] (*pt* **overran**; *pp* ~) Ⓐ VT invadir; **the town is ~ with tourists** el pueblo está inundado de turistas Ⓑ VI exceder el tiempo previsto; **his speech overran by 15 minutes** su discurso se pasó 15 minutos del tiempo que tenía, su discurso se excedió al tiempo que tenía en 15 minutos

overseas [ˌəʊvəˈsiːz] Ⓐ ADV [*be, live*] en el extranjero; **to go ~** ir al extranjero Ⓑ ADJ [*student*] extranjero; [*duty, trade, market*] exterior

oversee [ˌəʊvəˈsiː] (*pt* **oversaw**; *pp* ~**n**) VT supervisar

overseer [ˈəʊvəsɪəʳ] N (= *foreman*) capataz *mf*; (= *supervisor*) supervisor(a) *m/f*

oversensitive [ˌəʊvəˈsensɪtɪv] ADJ hipersensible, demasiado susceptible

oversexed [ˌəʊvəˈsekst] ADJ de deseo sexual excesivo; (*hum or pej*) sexualmente obsesionado

overshadow [ˌəʊvəˈʃædəʊ] VT (= *eclipse*) eclipsar; **it was ~ed by greater events** fue eclipsado por sucesos de mayor trascendencia; **the event was ~ed by his death** su muerte ensombreció el acontecimiento

overshoot [ˌəʊvəˈʃuːt] (*pt, pp* **overshot**) VT [+ *destination*] ir más allá de; [+ *turning*] pasarse de; **to ~ the runway** salirse de la pista de aterrizaje; ✦ IDIOM **to ~ the mark** pasarse de la raya, excederse

oversight [ˈəʊvəsaɪt] N descuido *m*; **it was an ~** fue un descuido; **by an ~** por descuido

oversimplification [ˌəʊvəsɪmplɪfɪˈkeɪʃən] N simplificación *f* excesiva

oversimplify [ˌəʊvəˈsɪmplɪfaɪ] VT simplificar demasiado

oversize(d) [ˌəʊvəˈsaɪz(d)] ADJ demasiado grande, descomunal; (*US*) [*clothes*] de talla muy grande

oversleep [ˌəʊvəˈsliːp] (*pt, pp* **overslept**) VI quedarse dormido, no despertar(se) a tiempo; **I overslept** me quedé dormido, no (me) desperté a tiempo

overspend [ˌəʊvəˈspend] (*pt, pp* **overspent**) Ⓐ VT **to ~ one's allowance** gastar más de lo que permite su asignación Ⓑ VI gastar demasiado *or* más de la cuenta; **we have overspent by 50 dollars** hemos gastado 50 dólares de más *or* más de lo que debíamos

overspending [ˌəʊvəˈspendɪŋ] N gasto *m* excesivo

overspill ['əʊvəspɪl] N (*Brit*) **the ~ from the cities** la gente que no cabe en las ciudades

overstaffed [,əʊvə'stɑːft] ADJ con exceso de personal, con exceso de plantilla (*Sp*)

overstaffing [,əʊvə'stɑːfɪŋ] N exceso *m* de personal, exceso *m* de plantilla (*Sp*)

overstate [,əʊvə'steɪt] VT exagerar

overstatement [,əʊvə'steɪtmənt] N exageración *f*

overstay [,əʊvə'steɪ] VT **to ~ one's leave** quedarse más tiempo de lo que la licencia permite; **I don't want to ~ my welcome** no quiero ser un pesado, no quiero abusar de su hospitalidad

overstep [,əʊvə'step] VT (*fig*) [+ *boundary*] traspasar; [+ *authority*] excederse en el ejercicio de; ✦ IDIOM **to ~ the mark** pasarse de la raya, excederse

overstock [,əʊvə'stɒk] VT abarrotar; **to be ~ed with** tener existencias excesivas de

overstretch [,əʊvə'stretʃ] VT [+ *resources, budget, finances*] estirar; **to ~ o.s.** exigirse demasiado; (*financially*) ponerse en una situación (económica) comprometida

oversubscribed [,əʊvəsəb'skraɪbd] ADJ **the course is heavily ~** existe un exceso enorme de solicitudes para el curso

overt [əʊ'vɜːt] ADJ [*racism, discrimination, hostility*] manifiesto, patente; [*criticism*] abierto, manifiesto

overtake [,əʊvə'teɪk] (*pt* **overtook**; *pp* **~n**) Ⓐ VT **1** (*esp Brit*) (= *pass*) [+ *car*] adelantar, rebasar (*Mex*); [+ *runner*] adelantar, dejar atrás; [+ *competition, rival*] tomar la delantera a; **he doesn't want to be ~n** no quiere dejarse adelantar **2** (*fig*) pillar desprevenido; **we have been ~n by events** los sucesos nos pillaron desprevenidos *or* de sorpresa Ⓑ VI (*esp Brit Aut*) adelantar, rebasar (*Mex*); **"no overtaking"** "prohibido adelantar", "prohibido rebasar" (*Mex*)

overtax [,əʊvə'tæks] VT **1** (*Fin*) gravar en exceso **2** (*fig*) [+ *strength, patience*] agotar, abusar de; **to ~ o.s.** exigirse demasiado a sí mismo

over-the-counter ['əʊvəθə'kaʊntə'] ADJ **~ drugs** medicamentos *mpl* sin receta

overthrow [,əʊvə'θrəʊ] (*vb*: *pt* **overthrew**; *pp* **~n**) Ⓐ N [*of president, dictator, government*] derrocamiento *m* Ⓑ VT [+ *president, dictator, government*] derrocar

overtime ['əʊvətaɪm] Ⓐ N **1** (*Ind*) horas *fpl* extra(s); **to do/ work ~** hacer/trabajar horas extra(s); **your imagination has been working ~!** ¡tienes una imaginación demasiado activa! **2** (*US Sport*) prórroga *f*, tiempo *m* suplementario Ⓑ CPD ➤ **overtime ban** prohibición *f* de horas extra(s) ➤ **overtime pay** pago *m* de horas extra(s)

overtired [,əʊvə'taɪəd] ADJ agotado

overtly [əʊ'vɜːtlɪ] ADV abiertamente

overtone ['əʊvətəʊn] N (= *connotation*) connotación *f*; (= *insinuation*) insinuación *f*; **a speech with a hostile ~** un discurso con cierto tono hostil; **the strike has political ~s** la huelga tiene un trasfondo político

overtook [,əʊvə'tʊk] PT *of* **overtake**

overture ['əʊvətjʊə'] N **1** (*Mus*) obertura *f* **2** (*fig*) **to make ~s to sb** (*Pol, Comm*) hacer una propuesta a algn; (*sexual*) hacer insinuaciones a algn

overturn [,əʊvə'tɜːn] Ⓐ VT [+ *car, boat, saucepan*] volcar; [+ *government*] derrocar, derribar; [+ *decision, ruling*] anular Ⓑ VI [*car*] volcar, dar una vuelta de campana; [*boat*] zozobrar

overuse [,əʊvə'juːz] VT usar demasiado

overvalue [,əʊvə'væljuː] VT sobrevalorar

overview ['əʊvəvjuː] N visión *f* de conjunto

overweight [,əʊvə'weɪt] ADJ **to be ~** [*person*] estar demasiado gordo; **he is 8 kilos ~** pesa 8 kilos de más; **the suitcase is a kilo ~** la maleta tiene un exceso de peso de un kilo

overwhelm [,əʊvə'welm] VT **1** (= *overcome*) [*difficulties, fear, loneliness*] abrumar; **sorrow ~ed him** estaba abrumado por el dolor **2** (= *inundate, overload*) (*with work*) abrumar, agobiar; (*with questions, requests, information*) atosigar

overwhelming [,əʊvə'welmɪŋ] ADJ [*defeat, victory*]

arrollador, aplastante; [*success*] arrollador; [*majority*] abrumador, aplastante; [*heat*] agobiante; [*pressure, urge*] irresistible; [*desire*] irresistible, imperioso; [*emotion*] incontenible

overwhelmingly [,əʊvə'welmɪŋlɪ] ADV **they voted ~ for Blake** Blake obtuvo una mayoría aplastante *or* abrumadora, la inmensa mayoría votó por Blake; **the legal profession is ~ male** en la abogacía la inmensa mayoría son hombres

overwork [,əʊvə'wɜːk] Ⓐ N agotamiento *m* por trabajo excesivo Ⓑ VT [+ *person*] hacer trabajar demasiado Ⓒ VI trabajar demasiado

overworked [,əʊvə'wɜːkt] ADJ **we're ~** tenemos demasiado trabajo, nos hacen trabajar demasiado

overwrite [,əʊvə'raɪt] (*pt* **overwrote**; *pp* **overwritten**) VT (*Comput*) sobreescribir

overwrought [,əʊvə'rɔːt] ADJ **to be ~** estar crispado

overzealous [,əʊvə'zeləs] ADJ demasiado entusiasta

ovulate ['ɒvjʊleɪt] VI ovular

ovulation [,ɒvjʊ'leɪʃən] N ovulación *f*

ovule ['əʊvjuːl] N óvulo *m*

ovum ['əʊvəm] N (*pl* **ova** ['əʊvə]) óvulo *m*

ow [aʊ] EXCL ¡ay!

owe [əʊ] VT (*gen*) deber; **to ~ sb £2** deber dos libras a algn; **I'll ~ it to you** te lo quedo a deber; **he claims he is still ~d for the work** asegura que todavía se le debe dinero por el trabajo; **to what do I ~ the honour of your visit?** ¿a qué debo el honor de su visita?; **you ~ it to yourself to come** venir es un deber que tienes contigo mismo; **I ~ it to her to confess** mi deber con ella me obliga a confesarlo; **I think I ~ you an explanation** creo que es necesaria una explicación

owing ['əʊɪŋ] Ⓐ ADJ **how much is ~ to you now?** ¿cuánto se le debe ahora? Ⓑ PREP **~ to** (= *due to*) debido a, a causa de; **~ to the bad weather** debido al mal tiempo

owl [aʊl] N (= *barn owl*) lechuza *f*; (= *little owl*) mochuelo *m*; (= *long-eared owl*) búho *m*; (= *tawny owl*) cárabo *m*

own¹ [əʊn] VT (= *possess*) [+ *object, goods*] tener, poseer; [+ *land, house, company*] ser dueño de, poseer; **who ~s the newspaper?** ¿quién es el propietario *or* dueño del periódico?; **who ~s this pen?** ¿de quién es esta pluma?
➤ **own up** VI + ADV confesar (**to sth** algo); **~ up!** ¡confiésalo!; **they ~ed up to having stolen the apples** confesaron haber robado las manzanas

own² [əʊn] Ⓐ ADJ propio; **the house has its ~ garage** la casa tiene garaje propio; **in her ~ house** en su propia casa; **it's all my ~ money** todo el dinero es mío
Ⓑ PRON **the house is her ~** la casa es de su propiedad *or* le pertenece; **my time is my ~** dispongo de mi tiempo como quiero; **we all look after our ~** todos cuidamos lo nuestro; **he has a style all his ~** tiene un estilo muy suyo *or* propio; **without a chair to call my ~** sin una silla que pueda decir que es mía; **can I have it for my ~?** ¿puedo quedarme con él?; **he made the theory his ~** hizo suya la teoría, adoptó la teoría; **she has money of her ~** tiene su propio dinero; **a place of one's ~** (= *una*) casa propia; **I'll give you a copy of your ~** te daré una copia para ti; **to be on one's ~** estar solo; **if I can get him on his ~** si puedo hablar con él a solas; **to do sth on one's ~** (= *unaccompanied*) hacer algo por su cuenta; (= *unaided*) hacer algo solo *or* sin ayuda (de nadie); **you'll have a room of your very ~** tendrás una habitación para ti solo; ✦ IDIOMS **to get one's ~ back (on sb)** (*esp Brit*) vengarse (de algn); **to come into one's ~:** **women came into their ~ during the war** las mujeres mostraron su valía durante la guerra; **to hold one's ~** defenderse; **I can hold my ~ in German** me defiendo en alemán; ✦ PROV **each to his ~** cada uno a lo suyo, cada cual a lo suyo
Ⓒ CPD ➤ **own brand**, **own label** (*Comm*) marca *f* propia (*de un supermercado etc*) ➤ **own goal** (*Brit Sport*) autogol *m*

own-brand ['əʊn,brænd] ADJ **~ products** productos *mpl* de marca propia (*de un supermercado etc*)

owner ['əʊnə'] N [*of goods*] dueño/a *m/f*; [*of land, property, company*] dueño/a *m/f*, propietario/a *m/f* ➤ **owner occupier** (*Brit*) ocupante *mf* propietario/a

owner-occupied [ˌəʊnəˈɒkjʊpaɪd] ADJ (*Brit*) [*property, house*] ocupado por el dueño, ocupado por el propietario

ownership [ˈəʊnəʃɪp] N propiedad *f*; **the ~ of the land is in dispute** está en disputa la propiedad de la tierra; **"under new ownership"** "nuevo propietario", "nuevo dueño"

ox [ɒks] N (*pl* **oxen**) buey *m*

oxalic [ɒkˈsælɪk] ADJ ~ **acid** ácido *m* oxálico

Oxbridge [ˈɒksbrɪdʒ] N (*Brit*) *universidades de Oxford y Cambridge*

OXBRIDGE

Oxbridge es el término que se usa en el Reino Unido para hacer referencia a las universidades de **Oxford** y **Cambridge**, sobre todo cuando se quiere destacar el ambiente de privilegio con el que se las asocia, por ser las dos universidades más antiguas y prestigiosas del Reino Unido y por el hecho de que muchos licenciados de **Oxbridge** suelen acabar en puestos muy influyentes del ámbito empresarial, político o diplomático. Un buen número de estudiantes de estas universidades todavía proviene de colegios privados, aunque ambas instituciones tratan de aumentar el número de alumnos procedentes de centros estatales.
Ver tb www.ox.ac.uk, www.cam.ac.uk

oxen [ˈɒksən] NPL *of* **ox**

Oxfam [ˈɒksfæm] N ABBR = **Oxford Committee for Famine Relief**

oxidation [ˌɒksɪˈdeɪʃən] N oxidación *f*

oxide [ˈɒksaɪd] N óxido *m*

oxidize [ˈɒksɪdaɪz] **Ⓐ** VT oxidar **Ⓑ** VI oxidarse

oxtail [ˈɒksteɪl] N ➤ **oxtail soup** sopa *f* de rabo de buey

oxyacetylene [ˈɒksɪəˈsetɪliːn] ADJ oxiacetilénico ➤ **oxyacetylene torch** soplete *m* oxiacetilénico

oxygen [ˈɒksɪdʒən] N oxígeno *m* ➤ **oxygen mask** máscara *f* de oxígeno, mascarilla *f* de oxígeno ➤ **oxygen tent** cámara *f* de oxígeno

oxygenate [ɒkˈsɪdʒəneɪt] VT oxigenar

oxygenation [ˌɒksɪdʒəˈneɪʃən] N oxigenación *f*

oxymoron [ˌɒksɪˈmɔːrɒn] N (*pl* **oxymora** [ˌɒksɪˈmɔːrə]) oxímoron *m*

oyster [ˈɔɪstəʳ] N ostra *f* ➤ **oyster farm** criadero *m* de ostras

oysterbed [ˈɔɪstəbed] N criadero *m* de ostras, vivero *m* de ostras

Oz ** [ɒz] N ABBR = **Australia**

OZ ABBR = **ounce(s)**

ozone [ˈəʊzəʊn] N ozono *m* ➤ **ozone hole** agujero *m* de ozono ➤ **ozone layer** capa *f* de ozono

ozone-friendly [ˈəʊzəʊnˈfrendlɪ] ADJ que no daña la capa de ozono

ozonosphere [əʊˈzəʊnəˌsfɪəʳ] N ozonosfera *f*

Pp

P¹, p¹ [piː] N (= *letter*) P, p *f*; **P for Peter** P de Pedro; ✦ IDIOM **to mind** *or* **watch one's Ps and Qs*** cuidarse *or* tener mucho cuidado de no meter la pata*

P² ABBR = **parking**

p² ABBR (= *penny*) penique *m*; (= *pence*) peniques *mpl*

PA Ⓐ N ABBR **1** (= *personal assistant*) ayudante *mf* personal **2** (= *public address system*) (sistema *m* de) megafonía *f* Ⓑ ABBR (*US*) = **Pennsylvania**

pa* [pɑː] N papá* *m*

p.a. ABBR (= *per annum*) por año, al año

pace ['peɪs] Ⓐ N **1** (= *step*) paso *m*; **I took a couple of ~s forward/back** di un par de pasos hacia delante/atrás; **to put sb through his/her ~s** poner a algn a prueba **2** (= *speed*) (*when walking, running*) paso *m*, ritmo *m*; (*fig*) ritmo *m*; **to do sth at one's own ~** hacer algo a su (propio) ritmo; **the ~ of change/life** el ritmo de cambio/vida; **salaries are not keeping ~ with inflation** los sueldos no avanzan al mismo ritmo *or* paso que la inflación, los sueldos no siguen el ritmo de la inflación; **to set the ~** (*Sport*) marcar el paso *or* el ritmo; (*fig*) marcar la pauta; **he can't stand the ~** las cosas se desarrollan demasiado rápidamente para él Ⓑ VT **1** (*anxiously*) **to ~ the floor** ir *or* andar de un lado para otro **2** (= *set pace of*) **to ~ o.s.: it was a tough race and I had to ~ myself** era una carrera difícil y tuve que tener cuidado de no gastar toda mi energía al principio; **you should ~ yourself and not attempt too much at once** tienes que tomártelo poco a poco y no intentar hacer demasiado de una vez Ⓒ VI **to ~ up and down** ir *or* pasearse de un lado para otro

pacemaker ['peɪsˌmeɪkə'] N **1** (*Med*) marcapasos *m inv* **2** (*Sport*) liebre *f*

pacesetter ['peɪsˌsetə'] N **1** (*in market, business*) persona *f* que marca la pauta **2** (*Sport*) liebre *f*

Pacific [pə'sɪfɪk] N **the ~ (Ocean)** el (Océano) Pacífico ➤ **the Pacific Rim** los países de la Costa del Pacífico

pacifier ['pæsɪfaɪə'] N (*US*) (= *dummy*) chupete *m*

pacifist ['pæsɪfɪst] ADJ, N pacifista *mf*

pacify ['pæsɪfaɪ] VT [+ *person*] apaciguar, calmar

pack [pæk] Ⓐ N **1** (= *packet*) paquete *m*; (*esp US*) [*of cigarettes*] paquete *m*, cajetilla *f*; (= *packaging*) envase *m*; **for sell-by date see back of ~** para la fecha de caducidad ver el reverso del envase **2** (*also* **backpack**) mochila *f*; (*on animal*) fardo *m* **3** (*esp Brit*) [*of cards*] baraja *f*; **he told me a ~ of lies** me contó una sarta *or* (*LAm*) bola de mentiras **4** [*of hounds, dogs*] jauría *f*; [*of wolves*] manada *f* **5** (= *group*) [*of tourists, reporters*] manada *f*; [*of idiots, fools*] hatajo *m*; [*of brownies, cubs*] patrulla *f*; [*of runners, cyclists*] pelotón *m*; **they're like a ~ of kids** son (como) un hatajo de críos* **6** (*Rugby*) **the ~** (= *forwards*) los delanteros; (= *scrum*) el pack Ⓑ VT **1** (= *put in container*) **1.1** (*in case, bag etc*) **I decided to ~ a few things** decidí meter algunas cosas en la maleta; **~ your things and get out!** ¡coge tus cosas y lárgate de aquí!* **1.2** [+ *goods for transport*] (*in package*) empaquetar; (*in crate, container*) embalar, empacar (*esp LAm*) **1.3** (*Comm*) (*in individual packaging*) envasar; **she spent the summer ~ing apricots** se pasó el verano envasando albaricoques **2** (= *fill*) [+ *box, crate*] llenar; **a crate ~ed with books** una caja llena de libros; **to ~ one's bags** (*lit*) hacer las maletas; **to ~ one's bags (and go** *or* **leave)** (*fig*) coger sus cosas e irse, coger sus cosas y largarse*; **to ~ one's/a (suit)case** hacer la maleta **3** (= *fill tightly*) [+ *hall, stadium*] llenar a rebosar **4** (*US**) (= *carry*) **he ~s a gun** lleva un revólver **5 he ~s a powerful punch** (*lit*) pega duro; **this play ~s a powerful punch** esta es una obra con mucho impacto emocional

Ⓒ VI **1** (= *do one's packing*) hacer la(s) maleta(s); ✦ IDIOM **to send sb ~ing*** [+ *visitor, caller*] echar a algn con cajas destempladas; (*from job*) despedir a algn sin contemplaciones **2** (= *cram*) **to ~ into a room/theatre** apiñarse *or* apretujarse en una habitación/un teatro Ⓓ CPD ➤ **pack animal** bestia *f or* animal *m* de carga ➤ **pack ice** banco *m* de hielo, masa *f* flotante de hielo

➤ **pack in*** VT + ADV **1** (= *cram*) **airlines make money by ~ing people in** las compañías aéreas hacen dinero metiendo a un montón de gente en los aviones; **they were ~ed in like sardines** estaban como sardinas en lata; **the show's ~ing them in** el espectáculo llena la sala al completo *or* a rebosar **2** (*esp Brit*) (= *stop doing*) [+ *job, activity*] dejar; ➤ **it in!** ¡déjalo ya!

➤ **pack off** VT + ADV largar*; **I ~ed him off in a taxi** lo despaché en un taxi, lo largué en un taxi*; **to ~ a child off to bed/school** mandar a un niño a la cama/al colegio

➤ **pack up** Ⓐ VI + ADV **1** (*Brit**) (= *cease to function*) [*washing-machine, car*] estropearse, descomponerse (*esp Mex*); [*battery*] agotarse; [*engine*] averiarse, estropearse **2** (*) (= *stop activity*) **let's ~ up now** vamos a dejarlo *or* terminar ya **3** (*) (= *collect things together*) recoger (sus cosas) Ⓑ VT + ADV **1** (= *put away*) [+ *belongings*] recoger **2** (*) (= *give up*) dejar

package ['pækɪdʒ] Ⓐ N **1** (= *parcel, container, packet*) paquete *m* **2** (*fig*) **2.1** (= *deal*) oferta *f*; **a generous remuneration ~** una generosa oferta de remuneración **2.2** [*of measures, aid*] paquete *m*; **an economic aid ~** un paquete de ayuda económica **2.3** (= *holiday*) viaje *m* organizado, vacaciones *fpl* organizadas **3** (*Comput*) paquete *m* Ⓑ VT **1** (*US Comm*) (*in paper, packet*) empaquetar, embalar, empacar (*LAm*); (*in bottle, jar*) envasar **2** (*fig*) presentar Ⓒ CPD ➤ **package deal** (= *holiday*) viaje *m* organizado, vacaciones *fpl* organizadas; (= *deal*) oferta *f*; (= *agreement*) acuerdo *m* global ➤ **package holiday** (*Brit*), **package vacation** (*US*) viaje *m* organizado, vacaciones *fpl* organizadas ➤ **package store** (*US*) tienda con licencia para vender bebidas alcohólicas ➤ **package tour** viaje *m* organizado

packaging ['pækɪdʒɪŋ] N **1** (= *packet, box, etc*) embalaje *m*; (= *wrapping*) envoltorio *m* **2** (= *presentation*) presentación *f*

packed [pækt] Ⓐ ADJ **1** (= *crowded*) (*with people, vehicles*) lleno, repleto, a rebosar (**with** *o*) **2** (= *filled*) lleno, repleto **3** (= *with luggage ready*) **she was ~ and ready to leave** ya había hecho la(s) maleta(s) y estaba lista para irse **4** (= *compressed*) **the snow was ~ hard** la nieve se había convertido en una masa compacta Ⓑ CPD ➤ **packed lunch** (*Brit*) bolsa *f* de bocadillos, bocadillos *o* comida preparada para llevar al colegio, a la oficina, a una excursión, etc

packer ['pækə'] N empaquetador(a) *m/f*

packet ['pækɪt] N **1** (*esp Brit*) (= *carton*) cajita *f*; [*of cigarettes*] paquete *m*, cajetilla *f*; [*of seeds, needles*] sobre *m*; [*of crisps etc*] bolsa *f*; (= *small parcel*) paquete *m* **2** (*Brit**) (= *sum*) dineral *m*; **to make a ~** ganar un dineral; **that must have cost a ~** eso habrá costado un dineral

packhorse ['pækhɔːs] N caballo *m* de carga

packing ['pækɪŋ] N **1** (= *product wrapping, act of packing*) embalaje *m* **2** [*of suitcase*] **to do one's ~** hacer la(s) maleta(s) ➤ **packing case** (*esp Brit*), **packing box** (*US*) cajón *m* or caja *f* de embalaje

pact [pækt] N pacto *m*; **to make a ~ (with sb)** hacer un pacto (con algn); **to make a ~ (not) to do sth** acordar (no) hacer algo, pactar (no) hacer algo

pad¹ [pæd] Ⓐ N **1** (*to prevent friction etc*) almohadilla *f*, cojinete *m* **2** (= *knee pad*) rodillera *f*; (= *elbow pad*) codera *f*; (= *shin pad*) espinillera *f* **3** (= *note pad, writing pad*) bloc(k) *m*, cuaderno *m* **4** (*for helicopter*) plataforma *f*; (= *launch pad*) plataforma *f* de lanzamiento **5** [*of animal's foot*] almohadilla *f* Ⓑ VT **1** [+ *shoulders etc*] acolchonar, poner

hombreras a **2** [+ *book, speech etc*] meter paja en
© VI **to ~ about** andar *or* (*esp LAm*) caminar sin hacer ruido
➤ **pad out** VT + ADV [+ *speech, essay*] meter paja en

pad²* [pæd] N (= *home*) casa *f*; (= *flat*) piso *m*,
departamento *m* (*LAm*); (= *room*) agujero** *m*, habitación *f*

padded ['pædɪd] ADJ [*bra*] reforzado; [*cell*] acolchonado;
[*envelope*] acolchado ➤ **padded shoulders** hombreras *fpl*

padding ['pædɪŋ] N (= *material*) relleno *m*, almohadilla *f*;
(*in speech etc*) paja *f*, borra *f*

paddle ['pædl] **Ⓐ** N **1** (= *oar*) zagual *m*, pala *f*, remo *m*
(*LAm*) **2** (*US*) (= *bat*) raqueta *f* **3** (*in water*) **to have a ~** ir a
chapotear, ir a mojarse los pies **Ⓑ** VT [+ *boat*] remar con
pala **©** VI **1** (*in boat*) remar con pala **2** (= *walk in water*)
mojarse los pies **Ⓓ** CPD ➤ **paddle boat, paddle steamer**
vapor *m* de ruedas *or* paletas

paddling pool ['pædlɪŋpu:l] N (*Brit*) piscina *f* para
niños

paddock ['pædək] N (= *field*) prado *m*; potrero *m*; [*of
racecourse*] paddock *m*

paddy field ['pædɪˌfi:ld] N arrozal *m*

padlock ['pædlɒk] **Ⓐ** N candado *m* **Ⓑ** VT cerrar con
candado

paediatric, pediatric (*US*) [ˌpiːdɪˈætrɪk] ADJ de pediatría,
pediátrico

paediatrician, pediatrician (*US*) [ˌpiːdɪəˈtrɪʃən] N
pediatra *mf*

paediatrics, pediatrics (*US*) [ˌpiːdɪˈætrɪks] NSING
pediatría *f*

paedophile, pedophile (*US*) ['piːdəʊfaɪl] N pederasta
mf, pedófilo/a *m/f* ➤ **paedophile ring** red *f* de
pederastas

pagan ['peɪɡən] ADJ, N pagano/a *m/f*

page¹ [peɪdʒ] N página *f*; **see ~ 20** véase en la página 20;
on ~ 14 en la página 14 ➤ **page break** salto *m* de página

page² [peɪdʒ] **Ⓐ** N **1** (*at court, wedding*) paje *m* **2** (*US*) (*in
Congress*) mensajero *m* **Ⓑ** VT **to ~ sb** (*over public address*)
llamar a algn por megafonía; (*with pager*) llamar a algn al
busca*

pageant ['pædʒənt] N (= *show*) espectáculo *m*;
(= *procession*) desfile *m*

pageantry ['pædʒəntrɪ] N pompa *f*, boato *m*

pageboy ['peɪdʒbɔɪ] N **1** (*in hotel*) botones *m inv*; (*Brit*) (*at
wedding*) paje *m* **2** (*also ~ **hairstyle***) estilo *m* paje

pager ['peɪdʒəʳ] N (*esp Brit*) buscapersonas *m inv*, busca *m
inv* (*Sp**), bipper *m* (*LAm**)

pagination [ˌpædʒɪˈneɪʃən] N paginación *f*

pagoda [pəˈɡəʊdə] N pagoda *f*

paid [peɪd] **Ⓐ** PT, PP *of* **pay** **Ⓑ** ADJ [*official*] asalariado, que
recibe un sueldo; [*work*] remunerado, rentado (*SC*); [*bill,
holiday etc*] pagado; **to put ~ to sth** (*esp Brit*) acabar con *or*
poner fin a algo

paid-up ['peɪdʌp] ADJ [*member*] con sus cuotas pagadas *or*
al día

pail [peɪl] N balde *m*, cubo *m*; (*child's*) cubito *m*

pain [peɪn] N **1** (*in body*) dolor *m*; **where is the ~?** ¿dónde
le duele? **back/chest** – dolor *m* de espalda/pecho; **I have a
~ in my leg** me duele la pierna; **to be in ~** sufrir dolor(es),
tener dolor(es)
2 (*) (= *nuisance*) **to be a ~** [*person*] ser un pesado*;
[*situation*] ser una lata*
3 pains (= *efforts*) **to be at ~s to do sth** esforzarse al

máximo por hacer algo, intentar por todos los medios
hacer algo; **for my ~s** después de todos mis esfuerzos; **to
take ~s to do sth** poner especial cuidado en hacer algo
4 on ~ of sth bajo pena de algo, so pena de algo

pained [peɪnd] ADJ [*expression*] dolorido, de dolor

painful ['peɪnfəl] ADJ [*injury, swelling, death, memory*]
doloroso; [*foot, arm*] dolorido; [*decision, duty, task*] penoso;
is it ~? ¿te duele?

painfully ['peɪnfəlɪ] ADV **his tooth throbbed ~** la muela le
producía un dolor punzante; **to die slowly and ~** tener una
muerte lenta y dolorosa; **to be ~ aware that ...** ser
plenamente consciente de que ...; **it was ~ clear that ...**
estaba totalmente claro que ...; **she was ~ shy** era tan
tímida que daba pena; **he was ~ thin** estaba tan delgado
que daba pena

painkiller ['peɪnkɪləʳ] N analgésico *m*

painless ['peɪnlɪs] ADJ (= *without pain*) indoloro, sin dolor;
(= *easy*) sin mayor(es) dificultad(es)

painstaking ['peɪnzˌteɪkɪŋ] ADJ meticuloso

paint [peɪnt] **Ⓐ** N pintura *f*; **"wet paint"** "(ojo,) recién
pintado"; **a box of ~s** una caja de pinturas
Ⓑ VT **1** [+ *picture, subject, wall*] pintar; [+ *slogan,
message*] escribir con pintura; **to ~ sth blue** pintar algo
de azul; ✦ IDIOM **to ~ the town red** irse de juerga *or*
parranda*
2 [+ *nails, lips*] pintarse
3 (= *portray*) describir, pintar; **to ~ a gloomy picture of sth**
dar una imagen deprimente de algo
© VI pintar; **to ~ in oils** pintar al óleo; **to ~ in
watercolours** pintar con acuarelas
Ⓓ CPD ➤ **paint roller** rodillo *m* (pintor) ➤ **paint scraper**
raspador *m* de paredes ➤ **paint stripper** quitapintura *f*

paintbox ['peɪntbɒks] N caja *f* de pinturas

paintbrush ['peɪntbrʌʃ] N (*Art*) pincel *m*; (*for decorating*)
brocha *f*

painter ['peɪntəʳ] N (*Art*) pintor(a) *m/f*; (= *decorator*)
pintor(a) *m/f* de brocha gorda

painting ['peɪntɪŋ] N (= *picture*) cuadro *m*, pintura *f*;
(= *activity*) pintura *f*; **~ and decorating** pintura *f* y
decoración

paintwork ['peɪntwɜːk] N pintura *f*

pair [pɛəʳ] **Ⓐ** N **1** (= *set*) [*of gloves, shoes, socks, etc*] par *m*;
these socks are not a ~ estos calcetines no son del mismo
par; **a ~ of glasses** *or* **spectacles** unas gafas, unos
anteojos; **I've only got one ~ of hands** sólo tengo dos
manos; **a ~ of pyjamas** un pijama; **a ~ of scissors** unas
tijeras, un par de tijeras; **six ~s of scissors** seis tijeras; **a ~
of trousers** un pantalón, unos pantalones, un par de
pantalones
2 (= *group of two things*) pareja *f*; **to arrange in ~s** [+ *glasses,
chairs*] colocar de dos en dos; [+ *related words, pictures*]
colocar en parejas
3 [*of people*] (= *group of two*) par *m*; (= *couple*) pareja *f*; **to do
sth in ~s** hacer algo en parejas *or* de dos en dos
4 [*of animals, birds*] pareja *f*
Ⓑ VT (= *put together*) [+ *socks, gloves*] emparejar; **trainees
will be ~ed with experienced managers** a los aprendices se
les pondrá formando pareja con gerentes con
experiencia
➤ **pair off** VI + ADV (*as a couple, team*) formar pareja(s)

paisley ['peɪzlɪ] N (= *fabric, design*) cachemira *f*

pajamas [pəˈdʒɑːməz] NPL (*US*) = **pyjamas**

Paki*** ['pækɪ] N ABBR (*Brit offensive*) = **Pakistani**

Pakistan [ˌpɑːkɪsˈtɑːn] N Pakistán *m*, Paquistán *m*

Pakistani [ˌpɑːkɪsˈtɑːnɪ] ADJ, N pakistaní *mf*, paquistaní *mf*

pal* [pæl] N amigo/a *m/f*, compinche* *mf*, cuate/a *m/f*
(*Mex**), pata *mf* (*Per**); **be a ~!** ¡venga, pórtate como un
amigo!; **they're great ~s** son muy amigos

palace ['pælɪs] N palacio *m*

palatable ['pælətəbl] ADJ (= *tasty*) sabroso, apetitoso;
(= *just passable*) comible; (*fig*) aceptable (**to** a)

palate ['pælɪt] N paladar *m*

palatial [pəˈleɪʃəl] ADJ suntuoso, espléndido

palaver* [pə'lɑːvəˠ] N (= *fuss*) jaleo *m*, desmadre* *m*; **what a ~!** ¡qué jaleo!

pale¹ [peɪl] **Ⓐ** ADJ (*compar* **~r**; *superl* **~st**) **1** [*person, face*] (*naturally*) blanco; (*from illness, shock*) pálido; **you look very ~** estás muy pálido; **to turn ~** [*person*] palidecer, ponerse pálido **2** (= *not bright*) [*light, daylight*] tenue, pálido; [*moon*] pálido **3** [*colour*] claro; **a ~ blue dress** un vestido azul claro **Ⓑ** VI [*person*] palidecer, ponerse pálido/blanco; **it ~s into insignificance beside ...** se vuelve insignificante en comparación con *or* al compararse con ... **Ⓒ** CPD ➤ **pale ale** (*Brit*) cerveza *f* rubia suave

pale² [peɪl] N ✦ IDIOM **to be beyond the ~** ser inaceptable

paleness ['peɪlnɪs] N palidez *f*; [*of skin*] blancura *f*

Palestine ['pælɪstaɪn] N Palestina *f*

Palestinian [pæləs'tɪnɪən] ADJ, N palestino/a *m/f*

palette ['pælɪt] N paleta *f* ➤ **palette knife** espátula *f*

palimony* ['pælɪmənɪ] N alimentos *mpl* pagados a una ex compañera

pall¹ [pɔːl] N (*on coffin*) paño *m* mortuorio; **a ~ of smoke** una cortina de humo; **to cast a ~ over sth** empañar algo

pall² [pɔːl] VI perder el interés (**on** para), dejar de gustar (**on a**)

pallbearer ['pɔːlˌbeərəˠ] N portador(a) *m/f* del féretro

pallet ['pælɪt] N (*for goods*) paleta *f*

palliative ['pælɪətɪv] **Ⓐ** ADJ paliativo, lenitivo **Ⓑ** N paliativo *m*, lenitivo *m*

pallid ['pælɪd] ADJ pálido

pallor ['pæləˠ] N palidez *f*

pally* ['pælɪ] ADJ (*compar* **pallier**; *superl* **palliest**) **to be ~ with sb** ser muy amigo de algn

palm¹ [pɑːm] N (*also* **~ tree**) palma *f*, palmera *f*; (*as carried at Easter*) ramo *m* ➤ **palm oil** aceite *m* de palma ➤ **Palm Sunday** Domingo *m* de Ramos

palm² [pɑːm] N [*of hand*] palma *f*; **to read sb's ~** leer la mano a algn; ✦ IDIOM **to have sb in the ~ of one's hand** tener a algn en la palma de la mano ➤ **palm off*** VT + ADV (*esp Brit*) **to ~ sth off on sb** encajar algo a algn*; **I managed to ~ the visitor off on John** le encajé la visita a John*; **I ~ed him off with the excuse that ...** me lo saqué de encima con la excusa de que ...

palmistry ['pɑːmɪstrɪ] N quiromancia *f*

palmtop ['pɑːmtɒp] N (*also* **~ computer**) ordenador *m* de bolsillo, computador *m or* computadora *f* de bolsillo (*LAm*), palmtop *m*

palpable ['pælpəbl] ADJ palpable

palpitate ['pælpɪteɪt] VI [*heart*] palpitar

palpitation [pælpɪ'teɪʃən] N palpitación *f*

paltry ['pɔːltrɪ] (*compar* **paltrier**; *superl* **paltriest**) ADJ ínfimo, miserable; **for a few ~ euros** por unos miserables euros, por unos pocos euros

pampas ['pæmpəs] NPL pampa *fsing*

pamper ['pæmpəˠ] VT mimar, consentir

pamphlet ['pæmflɪt] N folleto *m*

pan¹ [pæn] **Ⓐ** N **1** (= *saucepan*) cazuela *f*, cacerola *f*, olla *f* (*LAm*); (= *frying pan*) sartén *f or* (*LAm*) *m*; (*US*) (= *baking tin*) molde *m* para el horno **2** [*of scales*] platillo *m*; [*of lavatory*] taza *f*; ✦ IDIOM **to go down the ~**** irse al traste* **Ⓑ** VT (*) (= *criticize*) [+ *play etc*] dejar por los suelos* **Ⓒ** VI **to ~ for gold** cribar oro **Ⓓ** CPD ➤ **pan scrub** estropajo *m* (*para sartenes*) ➤ **pan out** VI + ADV resultar, salir (bien *etc*); **if it ~s out as we hope** si sale como (nosotros) lo esperamos

pan² [pæn] (*Cine*) VI tomar panorámicas *or* vistas pan

panacea [pænə'sɪə] N panacea *f*

panache [pə'næʃ] N garbo *m*, gracia *f*; **with ~** con garbo

Panama ['pænəmɑː] N Panamá *m* ➤ **Panama Canal** Canal *m* de Panamá ➤ **Panama hat** (sombrero *m* de) jipijapa *f*, panamá *m*

Panamanian [pænə'meɪnɪən] ADJ, N panameño/a *m/f*

pancake ['pænkeɪk] N tortita *f*, panqueque *m* (*LAm*) ➤ **Pancake Day** (*Brit*) martes *m inv* de carnaval

pancreas ['pæŋkrɪəs] N páncreas *m*

panda ['pændə] N panda *m* ➤ **panda car** (*Brit*) coche *m* patrulla

pandemonium [pændɪ'məʊnɪəm] N (= *chaos*) jaleo *m*, desmadre* *m*; **at this there was ~** en esto se armó un tremendo jaleo, en esto se armó las de Caín

pander ['pændəˠ] VI **to ~ to sb** consentir a algn; **to ~ to sb's desire for sth** complacer el deseo de algn por algo

p & h ABBR (*US*) (= **postage and handling**) gastos *mpl* de envío

Pandora's box [pæn,dɔːrəz'bɒks] N caja *f* de Pandora

p & p N ABBR (*Brit*) (= **postage and packing**) gastos *mpl* de envío

pane [peɪn] N cristal *m*, vidrio *m*

panel ['pænl] **Ⓐ** N **1** [*of wall*] panel *m*; [*of door*] entrepaño *m* **2** [*of instruments, switches*] tablero *m* **3** (*Sew*) paño *m*; (*Art*) tabla *f* **4** [*of judges, in a competition*] jurado *m*; (*TV, Rad*) panel *m* **Ⓑ** CPD ➤ **panel beater** (*Brit*) carrocero/a *m/f* ➤ **panel game** programa *m* concurso para equipos

panelled, paneled (*US*) ['pænld] ADJ con paneles

panelling, paneling (*US*) ['pænlɪŋ] N paneles *mpl*

panellist, panelist (*US*) ['pænəlɪst] N miembro *mf* del jurado/de la mesa redonda

pang [pæŋ] N (= *pain*) punzada *f*; **hunger ~s** retortijones *mpl* de hambre; **to feel a ~ of remorse** sentir (un) remordimiento

panhandle ['pænhændl] (*US*) **Ⓐ** N (*Geog*) faja angosta de territorio de un estado que entra en el de otro **Ⓑ** VI (*) mendigar, pedir limosna

panhandler* ['pænhændləˠ] N (*US*) pordiosero/a *m/f*

panic ['pænɪk] (*vb*: *pt*, *pp* **~ked**) **Ⓐ** N pánico *m*; **to be in a ~** ser presa del pánico; **I get into a ~ about all sorts of things** me entra el pánico por cualquier cosa **Ⓑ** VI dejarse llevar por el pánico; **don't ~!** ¡calma!, ¡cálmate! **Ⓒ** VT [+ *crowd, population*] provocar el pánico entre; [+ *person*] provocar *or* infundir el pánico en, causar pánico a **Ⓓ** CPD ➤ **panic attack** ataque *m* de pánico ➤ **panic button** botón *m* de alarma ➤ **panic buying** **buying has caused shortages of some foodstuffs** las compras masivas originadas por el pánico han provocado la escasez de algunos alimentos ➤ **panic stations** ✦ IDIOM **it was ~ stations*** reinaba el pánico

panicky ['pænɪkɪ] ADJ [*person, behaviour*] nervioso

panic-stricken ['pænɪkˌstrɪkən] ADJ **to be ~** ser presa del pánico, estar aterrorizado

pannier ['pænɪəˠ] N (*also* **~ bag**) cartera *f*, bolsa *f*

panoply ['pænəplɪ] N (= *array*) despliegue *m*

panorama [pænə'rɑːmə] N panorama *m*

panoramic [pænə'ræmɪk] ADJ panorámico

panpipes ['pænpaɪps] NPL zampoña *fsing*

pansy ['pænzɪ] N (= *flower*) pensamiento *m*

pant [pænt] **Ⓐ** N (= *gasp*) jadeo *m*, resuello *m* **Ⓑ** VI jadear, resollar **Ⓒ** VT (*also* **~ out**) decir jadeando, decir de manera entrecortada

pantechnicon [pæn'teknɪkən] N (*Brit*) camión *m* de mudanzas

panther ['pænθəˠ] N pantera *f*, jaguar *m* (*LAm*)

panties ['pæntɪz] NPL bragas *fpl* (*Sp*), calzones *mpl* (*LAm*); **a pair of ~** unas bragas (*Sp*), unos calzones (*LAm*)

pantihose ['pæntɪhəʊz] NPL = **pantyhose**

panto* ['pæntəʊ] N ABBR (*Brit*) = **pantomime**

pantomime ['pæntəmaɪm] N (*Brit*) (*at Christmas*) revista *f* musical navideña; **what a ~!** (fig) ¡qué farsa!

PANTOMIME

Una **pantomime**, abreviado en inglés como **panto**, es una obra teatral que se representa normalmente en Navidad. Suele estar basada en un cuento de hadas u otra historia conocida y en ella nunca faltan personajes como la vieja dama (**dame**), papel que siempre interpreta un actor, el protagonista joven (**principal boy**), normalmente interpretado por una actriz, y el malvado (**villain**). Aunque es un espectáculo familiar dirigido fundamentalmente a los niños, en él se alienta la participación de todo el público y posee una gran dosis de humor para adultos.

---

pantry ['pæntrɪ] N despensa f

pants [pænts] NPL (Brit) (= underwear) (man's) calzoncillos mpl; (woman's) bragas fpl (Sp), calzones mpl (LAm); (US) (= slacks) pantalones mpl; **a pair of ~** (Brit) (= underwear) (man's) unos calzoncillos, (woman's) unas bragas, unos calzones (LAm); (US) (= slacks) un pantalón, unos pantalones; ◆ IDIOMS **to bore the ~ off sb*** aburrir terriblemente a algn; **to catch sb with his ~ down*** pillar a algn desprevenido; **she wears the ~** (US*) ella es la que manda or lleva los pantalones ➤ **pants press** (US) prensa f para pantalones ➤ **pants suit** (US) = **pantsuit**

pantsuit ['pæntsuːt] N (US) traje-pantalón m, traje m de chaqueta y pantalón

pantyhose ['pæntɪhəʊz] NPL (US) pantys mpl, pantimedias fpl

panty liner ['pæntɪˌlaɪnəʳ] N protege-slip m, salva-slip m

papa [pəˈpɑː] N papá m

papacy ['peɪpəsɪ] N papado m, pontificado m

papal ['peɪpəl] ADJ papal, pontificio

papaya [pəˈpaɪə] N (= fruit) papaya f; (= tree) árbol m de papaya

paper ['peɪpəʳ] Ⓐ N 1 (= material) papel m; (= wallpaper) papel m pintado; **a piece of ~** un papel, una hoja (de papel); **to put sth down on ~** poner algo por escrito; **on ~** (fig) en teoría, sobre el papel
2 (= newspaper) periódico m, diario m; **the ~s** los periódicos, la prensa
3 **papers** (= writings, documents) papeles mpl; (= identity papers) documentación fsing, papeles mpl
4 (Univ) (= essay) ejercicio m, ensayo m; (= exam) examen m
5 (= scholarly article) (written) artículo m; (spoken) ponencia f, comunicación f
Ⓑ VT [+ wall, room] empapelar, tapizar (Mex)
Ⓒ CPD de papel ➤ **paper bag** bolsa f de papel ➤ **paper clip** clip m, sujetapapeles m inv ➤ **paper cup** vaso m de cartón ➤ **paper handkerchief, paper hankie** pañuelo m de papel ➤ **paper industry** industria f papelera ➤ **paper knife** abrecartas m inv ➤ **paper lantern** farolillo m (de papel) ➤ **paper mill** fábrica f de papel, papelera f ➤ **paper money** papel m moneda ➤ **paper qualifications** títulos mpl ➤ **paper round** (Brit), **paper route** (US) reparto m de periódicos; **to do a ~ round** (Brit) or **route** (US) repartir periódicos ➤ **paper shop** (Brit) tienda f de periódicos, ≈ quiosco m ➤ **paper tiger** tigre m de papel ➤ **paper towel** toallita f de papel
➤ **paper over** VI + PREP (lit) empapelar; ◆ IDIOM **to ~ over the cracks** (Brit) guardar las apariencias

paperback ['peɪpəbæk] N libro m en rústica; **in ~** en rústica

paperboy ['peɪpəbɔɪ] N repartidor m de periódicos

papergirl ['peɪpəgɜːl] N repartidora f de periódicos

paper-thin ['peɪpəˌθɪn] ADJ muy fino

paperweight ['peɪpəweɪt] N pisapapeles m inv

paperwork ['peɪpəwɜːk] N trabajo m administrativo

papier-mâché ['pæpɪeɪˈmæʃeɪ] N cartón m piedra, papel maché m

papist ['peɪpɪst] ADJ, N (pej) papista mf

---

paprika ['pæprɪkə] N paprika f, pimentón m picante

Pap smear (US) ['pæpˌsmɪəʳ], **Pap test** (US) ['pæpˌtest] N frotis m (cervical)

Papua New Guinea ['pæpjʊənjuːˈgɪnɪ] N Papúa f Nueva Guinea, Nueva Guinea f Papúa

par [pɑːʳ] N 1 (Fin) par f 2 (Golf) par m; **two over/under ~** dos sobre/bajo par 3 (fig) **to be on a ~ with sth/sb** estar en pie de igualdad con algo/algn; **to be under** or **below ~** (= ill) sentirse mal, estar indispuesto; ◆ IDIOM **that's ~ for the course** eso es lo más normal

para ABBR (= paragraph) párr.

parable ['pærəbl] N parábola f

parabola [pəˈræbələ] N parábola f

parabolic [ˌpærəˈbɒlɪk] ADJ parabólico ➤ **parabolic aerial** antena f parabólica

paracetamol [ˌpærəˈsiːtəmɒl] N (Brit) paracetamol m

parachute ['pærəʃuːt] Ⓐ N paracaídas m inv Ⓑ VT lanzar en paracaídas Ⓒ VI (also ~ **down**) lanzarse or saltar en paracaídas Ⓓ CPD ➤ **parachute jump** salto m en paracaídas

parachutist ['pærəʃuːtɪst] N paracaidista mf

parade [pəˈreɪd] Ⓐ N (= procession) desfile m; (Mil) desfile m, parada f; (= series) **a ~ of** una serie de Ⓑ VT hacer alarde de, lucir Ⓒ VI desfilar Ⓓ CPD ➤ **parade ground** (Mil) plaza f de armas
➤ **parade around***, **parade about*** VI + ADV pavonearse

paradigm ['pærədaɪm] N paradigma m

paradise ['pærədaɪs] N paraíso m

paradox ['pærədɒks] N paradoja f

paradoxical [ˌpærəˈdɒksɪkəl] ADJ paradójico

paradoxically [ˌpærəˈdɒksɪkəlɪ] ADV paradójicamente

paraffin ['pærəfɪn] N (Brit) (= oil) petróleo m lampante, queroseno m, parafina f; (US) (= paraffin wax) ➤ **paraffin heater** (Brit) estufa f de parafina or queroseno ➤ **paraffin lamp** (Brit) quinqué m ➤ **paraffin wax** parafina f

paragliding ['pærəglaɪdɪŋ] N parapente m

paragon ['pærəgən] N modelo m, dechado m

paragraph ['pærəgrɑːf] N párrafo m, (punto) acápite m (LAm); **"new ~"** "(punto y) aparte"

Paraguay ['pærəgwaɪ] N Paraguay m

Paraguayan [ˌpærəˈgwaɪən] ADJ, N paraguayo/a m/f

parakeet ['pærəkiːt] N perico m, periquito m

parallel ['pærəlel] Ⓐ ADJ 1 (Geom) paralelo (**to** a); (Comput, Elec) en paralelo
2 (= similar) análogo (**to** a); **this is a ~ case to the last one** este caso es análogo al anterior
Ⓑ N 1 (Geom) paralela f
2 (Geog) paralelo m; **the 49th ~** el paralelo 49
3 (fig) paralelo m; **to draw a ~ between X and Y** establecer un paralelo entre X e Y; **these things occur in ~** estas cosas corren parejas (**with** con), estas cosas ocurren paralelamente (**with** con); **a case without ~** un caso inaudito or insólito
Ⓒ CPD ➤ **parallel bars** paralelas fpl ➤ **parallel processing** (Comput) procesamiento m en paralelo

parallelogram [ˌpærəˈleləgræm] N paralelogramo m

Paralympic Games [ˌpærəˌlɪmpɪkˈgeɪmz] NPL juegos mpl paralímpicos

paralyse, paralyze (US) ['pærəlaɪz] VT (lit, fig) paralizar; **to be ~d with fright** estar paralizado de(l) miedo; **the factory was ~d by the strike** la fábrica quedó paralizada por la huelga

paralysis [pəˈræləsɪs] N parálisis f inv

paralytic [ˌpærəˈlɪtɪk] ADJ 1 (Med) paralítico 2 (Brit**) (= drunk) como una cuba*

paralyze ['pærəlaɪz] VT (US) = **paralyse**

paramedic [ˌpærəˈmedɪk] N paramédico/a m/f

parameter [pəˈræmɪtəʳ] N parámetro m

paramilitary [ˌpærəˈmɪlɪtərɪ] ADJ, N paramilitar mf

paramount ['pærəmaʊnt] ADJ primordial; **solvency must be ~** la solvencia es primordial or lo más importante; **of ~ importance** de suma importancia

paranoia [ˌpærəˈnɔɪə] N paranoia f

paranoid [ˈpærənɔɪd] **Ⓐ** ADJ paranoide **Ⓑ** N paranoico/a m/f

paranormal [ˌpærəˈnɔːməl] **Ⓐ** ADJ paranormal **Ⓑ** N **the ~** lo paranormal

parapet [ˈpærəpɪt] N [*of balcony, roof*] pretil m, antepecho m; [*of fortification*] parapeto m; ✦ IDIOMS **to put one's head above the ~** (*Brit*) arriesgar el cuello; **to keep one's head below the ~** (*Brit*) mantenerse al margen

paraphernalia [ˈpærəfəˈneɪlɪə] N parafernalia f

paraphrase [ˈpærəfreɪz] **Ⓐ** N paráfrasis f inv **Ⓑ** VT parafrasear

paraplegic [ˌpærəˈpliːdʒɪk] ADJ, N parapléjico/a m/f

parascending [ˈpærəsendɪŋ] N parascending m; **to go ~** hacer parascending

parasite [ˈpærəsaɪt] N parásito/a m/f (**on** de)

parasitic [ˌpærəˈsɪtɪk] ADJ parásito, parasitario

parasitical [ˌpærəˈsɪtɪkəl] ADJ parásito, parasitario

parasol [ˈpærəsɒl] N sombrilla f, parasol m

paratrooper [ˈpærətruːpəʳ] N paracaidista mf

parboil [ˈpɑːbɔɪl] VT sancochar, cocer a medias

parcel [ˈpɑːsl] N (*esp Brit*) paquete m ➤ **parcel bomb** (*Brit*) paquete-bomba m ➤ **parcel post** servicio m de paquetes postales ➤ **parcel out** VT + ADV repartir; [+ *land*] parcelar ➤ **parcel up** VT + ADV empaquetar; (*large size*) embalar

parched [pɑːtʃt] ADJ [*land*] abrasado, reseco; **I'm ~*** me muero de sed

parchment [ˈpɑːtʃmənt] N pergamino m

pardon [ˈpɑːdn] **Ⓐ** N **1** perdón m; **pardon?** (= *what?*) ¿perdón?, ¿cómo?, ¿mande? (*Mex*) **2** (*Jur*) indulto m; **free ~** indulto m absoluto **Ⓑ** VT **1** (= *forgive*) perdonar, disculpar (*esp LAm*); **to ~ sb sth** perdonar algo a algn; **~ me, but could you ...?** perdone or (*esp LAm*) disculpe la molestia, pero ¿podría usted ...?; **~ me!** ¡perdone!, ¡ay, perdone!; **~ me?** (*US*) ¿perdón?, ¿cómo?, ¿mande? (*Mex*); **~ my mentioning it** siento tener que decirlo, perdone que se lo diga **2** [+ *criminal*] indultar

pardonable [ˈpɑːdnəbl] ADJ perdonable, disculpable

pare [peəʳ] VT [+ *nails*] cortar; [+ *fruit etc*] pelar; (*also ~ down*) reducir

parent [ˈpeərənt] N (= *father*) padre m; (= *mother*) madre f; **parents** padres mpl ➤ **parent company** casa f matriz ➤ **parents' evening** reunión f de padres de alumnos ➤ **parent teacher association** asociación f de padres de alumnos y profesores

> ⚠ **parent ≠ pariente**

parentage [ˈpeərəntɪdʒ] N familia f; **of humble ~** de origen or nacimiento humilde; **of unknown ~** de padres desconocidos

parental [pəˈrentl] ADJ [*care etc*] de los padres ➤ **parental leave** permiso m por maternidad/paternidad

parenthesis [pəˈrenθɪsɪs] N (*pl* **parentheses** [pəˈrenθɪsiːz]) paréntesis m inv; **in ~** entre paréntesis

parenthood [ˈpeərənthʊd] N paternidad f

parenting [ˈpeərəntɪŋ] N el ser padres; **~ is a full-time occupation** el cuidar de los hijos es una labor de plena dedicación

par excellence [ˌpɑːˈreksəlɑːns] ADV por excelencia

Paris [ˈpærɪs] **Ⓐ** N París m **Ⓑ** ADJ parisiense, parisino

parish [ˈpærɪʃ] N parroquia f ➤ **parish church** iglesia f parroquial ➤ **parish council** concejo m parroquial ➤ **parish priest** párroco m ➤ **parish register** libro m parroquial

parishioner [pəˈrɪʃənəʳ] N feligrés/esa m/f

parity [ˈpærɪtɪ] N (*Fin etc*) paridad f; [*of wages, conditions*] igualdad f

park [pɑːk] **Ⓐ** N parque m **Ⓑ** VT **1** (*Aut*) aparcar (*Sp*), estacionar (*esp LAm*) **2** (*)** (= *put*) poner, dejar; **she ~ed**

herself on the sofa se apalancó or apoltronó en el sofá **Ⓒ** VI aparcar (*Sp*), estacionarse (*esp LAm*) **Ⓓ** CPD ➤ **park keeper** guardián/ana m/f (de parque), guardabosque(s) mf

parka [ˈpɑːkə] N chaquetón m acolchado con capucha, parka f, anorak m

park-and-ride [ˌpɑːkəndˈraɪd] N *aparcamiento en estaciones periféricas que conectan con el transporte público urbano*

parking [ˈpɑːkɪŋ] N aparcamiento m (*Sp*), parking m, estacionamiento m (*esp LAm*); **"no parking"** "prohibido aparcar", "prohibido estacionarse" (*esp LAm*) ➤ **parking attendant** guardacoches mf inv ➤ **parking brake** (*US*) freno m de mano ➤ **parking garage** (*US*) aparcamiento m, parking m, (playa f de) estacionamiento m (*LAm*) ➤ **parking lights** luces fpl de estacionamiento ➤ **parking lot** (*US*) aparcamiento m (*Sp*), (playa f de) estacionamiento m (*esp LAm*) ➤ **parking meter** parquímetro m ➤ **parking offence** (*Brit*) infracción f por aparcamiento or (*esp LAm*) estacionamiento indebido ➤ **parking place, parking space** aparcamiento m (*Sp*), parking m, estacionamiento m (*esp LAm*) ➤ **parking ticket** multa f por aparcamiento or (*esp LAm*) estacionamiento indebido ➤ **parking violation** (*US*) = **parking offence**

Parkinson's disease [ˈpɑːkɪnsənzdɪˌziːz] N enfermedad f de(l) Parkinson

parkway [ˈpɑːkweɪ] N (*US*) alameda f

parlance [ˈpɑːləns] N lenguaje m; **in common ~** en lenguaje corriente; **in technical ~** en lenguaje técnico

parliament [ˈpɑːləmənt] N parlamento m; **to enter ~** ser elegido diputado or senador; *ver tb* www.parliament.uk

parliamentarian [ˌpɑːləmənˈteərɪən] ADJ, N parlamentario/a m/f

parliamentary [ˌpɑːləˈmentərɪ] ADJ parlamentario

parlour, parlor (*US*) [ˈpɑːləʳ] N sala f, salón m ➤ **parlour game, parlor game** (*US*) juego m de salón or sala

parlourmaid, parlormaid (*US*) [ˈpɑːləmeɪd] N camarera f

parlous [ˈpɑːləs] ADJ [*state*] lamentable, crítico, pésimo

Parmesan [ˌpɑːmɪˈzæn] N parmesano m

parochial [pəˈrəʊkɪəl] ADJ (*Rel*) parroquial; (*pej*) (= *provincial*) provinciano; (= *narrow-minded*) de miras estrechas

parody [ˈpærədɪ] **Ⓐ** N parodia f **Ⓑ** VT parodiar

parole [pəˈrəʊl] **Ⓐ** N libertad f condicional; **to be on ~** estar en libertad condicional; **to break one's ~** quebrantar las condiciones impuestas por la libertad condicional **Ⓑ** VT dejar en libertad condicional

paroxysm [ˈpærəksɪzəm] N paroxismo m; **it sent him into ~s of rage** le produjo un ataque de ira

parquet [ˈpɑːkeɪ] N parquet m, parqué m

parrot [ˈpærət] N loro m, papagayo m

parrot-fashion [ˈpærətˌfæʃən] ADV (*Brit*) como un loro

parry [ˈpærɪ] VT [+ *blow*] parar, desviar; [+ *question*] esquivar, eludir

parse [pɑːz] VT analizar (sintácticamente)

parsimonious [ˌpɑːsɪˈməʊnɪəs] ADJ parco, excesivamente frugal

parsley [ˈpɑːslɪ] N perejil m

parsnip [ˈpɑːsnɪp] N chirivía f, pastinaca f

parson [ˈpɑːsn] N pastor m

parsonage [ˈpɑːsnɪdʒ] N casa f del párroco, parroquia f

part [pɑːt] **Ⓐ** N **1** (= *portion, proportion*) parte f; **it was all ~ of the job** todo formaba parte del trabajo; **it went on for the best ~ of an hour** continuó durante casi una hora; **you haven't heard the best ~ yet** todavía no has oído lo mejor; **in the early ~ of this century** a principios de este siglo; **the funny ~ of it is that ...** lo gracioso es que ...; **in ~** en parte; **the book is good in ~s** hay partes del libro que son buenas, el libro es bueno en partes; **a large ~ of sth** gran parte de algo; **in large ~** en gran parte; ✦ IDIOM **to be ~ and parcel of sth** ser parte integrante de algo **2** (= *measure*) parte f; **one ~ alcohol to two ~s water** una parte de alcohol por cada dos partes de agua **3** (= *share, role*) **to do one's ~** poner de su parte; **work plays**

an important ~ **in her life** el trabajo juega un papel importante en su vida; **to take ~ (in sth)** tomar parte (en algo), participar (en algo); **I want no ~ of this** no quiero tener nada que ver con esto
4 (*Theat, Cine*) papel *m*; **to look the ~** vestir el cargo; **to play the ~ of Hamlet** hacer el papel de Hamlet
5 (= *region*) [*of city*] parte *f*, zona *f*; [*of country, world*] región *f*; **in this/that ~ of the world** en esta/esa región; **in** *or* **round these ~s** por aquí, por estos pagos
6 (= *side*) **for my ~, ...** en lo que a mí se refiere *or* por mi parte, ...; **it was bad organization on their ~** fue mala organización por su parte
7 (*Mech*) pieza *f*
8 (*Mus*) parte *f*
9 (= *instalment*) [*of journal*] número *m*; [*of serialized publication*] fascículo *m*; (*TV, Rad*) (= *episode*) parte *f*
10 (*US*) (*in hair*) raya *f*; **side/center ~** raya *f* al lado/al medio
B ADV (= *partly*) en parte; **it is ~ fiction and ~ fact** es en parte ficción y en parte realidad, contiene partes ficticias y partes reales; **she is ~ French** tiene algo de sangre francesa
C VT **1** (= *separate*) separar
2 (= *open*) [+ *curtains*] abrir, correr; [+ *legs, lips*] abrir
3 (= *divide*) **to ~ one's hair on the left/right** peinarse con raya a la izquierda/derecha
D VI **1** (= *separate*) [*people*] separarse
2 (= *move to one side*) [*crowd, clouds*] apartarse
3 (= *open*) [*lips, curtains*] abrirse
E CPD ➤ **part exchange** (*Brit*): **they take your old car in ~ exchange** aceptan tu coche viejo como parte del pago; **they offer ~ exchange on older vehicles** aceptan vehículos más antiguos como parte del pago de uno nuevo ➤ **part of speech** parte *f* de la oración, categoría *f* gramatical; **what ~ of speech is "of"?** ¿qué parte de la oración es "de"?, ¿a qué categoría gramatical pertenece "de"? ➤ **part payment** pago *m* parcial; **to accept sth as ~ payment for sth** aceptar algo como parte del pago *or* como pago parcial de algo

partake [pɑːˈteɪk] (*pt* **partook**; *pp* **~n**) VI (*frm*) **to ~ of** [+ *food*] comer; [+ *drink*] beber; **to ~ in an activity** tomar parte *or* participar en una actividad

partial [ˈpɑːʃəl] ADJ **1** (= *not complete*) parcial **2** (= *biased*) parcial (**towards** hacia) **3 to be ~ to sth** tener debilidad por algo

partiality [ˌpɑːʃɪˈælɪtɪ] N **1** (= *bias*) parcialidad *f* (**towards** hacia) **2** (= *liking*) debilidad *f*, gusto *m* (**for, to** por)

partially [ˈpɑːʃəlɪ] ADV **1** (= *partly*) parcialmente, en parte **2** (= *with bias*) con parcialidad

participant [pɑːˈtɪsɪpənt] N (*in debate, fight, argument*) participante *mf*; (*in competition*) concursante *mf*

participate [pɑːˈtɪsɪpeɪt] VI participar, tomar parte (**in** en)

participation [pɑːˌtɪsɪˈpeɪʃən] N participación *f* (**in** en)

participle [ˈpɑːtɪsɪpl] N participio *m*

particle [ˈpɑːtɪkl] N (*gen, Physics, Gram*) partícula *f*; [*of dust*] partícula *f*, grano *m* ➤ **particle physics** física *f* de partículas

particular [pəˈtɪkjʊləʳ] **A** ADJ **1** (= *special*) especial; **is there anything ~ you want?** ¿quieres algo en particular *or* en concreto?; **nothing ~ happened** no pasó nada en especial **2** (= *specific*) **in this ~ case** en este caso concreto; **is there any ~ food you don't like?** ¿hay algún alimento en particular *or* en especial *or* en concreto que no te guste?; **for no ~ reason** por ninguna razón especial *or* en particular *or* en concreto **3** (= *fussy*) exigente; **he's very ~ about his food** es muy exigente con *or* especial para la comida; **I'm rather ~ about my friends** escojo mis amigos con cierto cuidado; **they weren't too ~ about where the money came from** no les importaba *or* preocupaba mucho de dónde viniera el dinero **4** (= *insistent*) **he was most ~ that I shouldn't go to any trouble** insistió mucho en que no me tomara ninguna molestia
B N **1** (*frm*) (= *detail*) detalle *m*; **her account was accurate in every ~** su versión fue exacta en todos los detalles; **full ~s** todos los detalles; **for further ~s apply to ...** para más información diríjase a ...; **the nurse took her ~s** la enfermera le tomó sus datos personales

2 in ~ en particular

particularly [pəˈtɪkjʊləlɪ] ADV (= *especially*) especialmente; **in many countries, ~ France** en muchos países, especialmente *or* particularmente en Francia; **he ~ dislikes quiz shows** siente especial aversión por los concursos televisivos; **he was not ~ pleased** no se puso loco de contento que digamos; **not ~** no especialmente

parting [ˈpɑːtɪŋ] **A** ADJ de despedida; **his ~ words** sus palabras de despedida; **~ shot** golpe *m* de gracia **B** N **1** (= *separation*) separación *f*, despedida *f*; **the ~ of the ways** la encrucijada, el momento de la separación **2** (*Brit*) (*in hair*) raya *f*; **side/centre ~** raya *f* al lado/al medio

partisan [ˌpɑːtɪˈzæn] N partidario/a *m/f* (**of** de); (*Mil*) partisano/a *m/f*, guerrillero/a *m/f*

partition [pɑːˈtɪʃən] **A** N **1** (= *wall*) tabique *m* **2** (*Pol*) partición *f*, división *f* **B** VT (= *divide*) [+ *country*] partir, dividir; [+ *room, area*] tabicar, dividir con tabiques ➤ **partition off** VT + ADV separar con tabiques

partitive [ˈpɑːtɪtɪv] ADJ partitivo

partly [ˈpɑːtlɪ] ADV en parte

partner [ˈpɑːtnəʳ] **A** N **1** (*in activity*) compañero/a *m/f*; **work with a ~ for this exercise** realizar este ejercicio con un compañero *or* en/por parejas; **~(s) in crime** cómplice(s) *m(pl)* **2** (*in dance, tennis, cards*) pareja *f* **3** (*in business*) socio/a *m/f* **4** (*in relationship*) pareja *f*, compañero/a *m/f* **B** VT **to ~ sb in a waltz** bailar un vals con algn; **he ~ed her at bridge** jugó al bridge en pareja con ella, fue su pareja al bridge

partnership [ˈpɑːtnəʃɪp] N **1** (= *relationship*) asociación *f*; (= *couple*) relación *f* de pareja; **the ~ between government and industry** la alianza entre el gobierno y la industria **2** (= *company*) sociedad *f* colectiva; **in ~ with** asociado con; **to go** *or* **enter into ~ (with sb)** asociarse (con algn); **we work in ~ with our clients** trabajamos conjuntamente con nuestros clientes; **they've offered me a ~** me han ofrecido hacerme socio

partook [pɑːˈtʊk] PT *of* **partake**

partridge [ˈpɑːtrɪdʒ] N perdiz *f*

part-time [ˈpɑːtˈtaɪm] **A** ADV a tiempo parcial (*Sp*), medio tiempo (*LAm*) **B** ADJ [*worker, job*] de media jornada, a tiempo parcial (*Sp*), de medio tiempo (*LAm*)

part-timer [ˌpɑːtˈtaɪməʳ] N trabajador(a) *m/f* a tiempo parcial (*Sp*), trabajador(a) *m/f* a medio tiempo (*LAm*)

partway [ˈpɑːtˈweɪ] ADV (= *partially*) parcialmente; **~ through the week** a mitad de la semana; **it goes ~ toward explaining his strange behaviour** explica en parte su extraño comportamiento; **we're only ~ through the work** hemos hecho sólo una parte del trabajo

party [ˈpɑːtɪ] **A** N **1** (= *celebration*) fiesta *f*; **to have a ~** dar una fiesta; **✦** IDIOM **the ~'s over** se acabó la fiesta **2** (*Pol*) partido *m* **3** (= *group*) grupo *m* **4** (*in dispute, contract*) parte *f*; **the parties concerned** los interesados, las partes interesadas; **to be (a) ~ to a crime** ser cómplice en un delito
B VI (*) (= *go to parties*) ir a fiestas; (= *have a good time*) irse de juerga*, irse de marcha (*Sp*); **let's ~!** ¡vámonos de juerga!*, ¡vámonos de marcha! (*Sp*)
C CPD ➤ **party animal** fiestero/a *m/f*, juerguista *mf* ➤ **party dress** vestido *m* de fiesta ➤ **the party line** (*Pol*) la línea del partido ➤ **party piece** numerito *m* (de fiesta)*; **to do one's ~ piece** hacer su numerito* ➤ **party political broadcast** (*Brit*) emisión *f* de propaganda política, ≈ espacio *m* electoral ➤ **party politics** (*gen*) política *f* sing de partido; (*pej*) partidismo *msing*, politiqueo *msing* ➤ **party pooper** aguafiestas *mf inv* ➤ **party wall** pared *f* medianera

party-goer [ˈpɑːtɪˌɡəʊəʳ] N (*gen*) asiduo/a *m/f* a fiestas; (*on specific occasion*) invitado/a *m/f*; **one of London's most dedicated ~s** uno de los asistentes más asiduos a fiestas de Londres; **I'm not much of a ~** yo voy a pocas fiestas

party political [ˌpɑːtɪpəˈlɪtɪkəl] ADJ [*advantage, issue*] de(l) partido ➤ **party political broadcast** emisión *f* de propaganda política, ≈ espacio *m* electoral

pass [pɑːs] **A** N **1** (= *permit*) (*gen*) pase *m*; (*Mil*) permiso *m*, pase *m*; **bus ~** abono *m* *or* pase *m* de autobús

2 (*Sport*) pase *m*
3 (*Brit*) (*in exam*) aprobado *m*; **to get a ~ (in sth)** aprobar (algo)
4 (= *state*) **things have come to a pretty ~!** ¡hasta dónde hemos llegado!; **things had reached such a ~ that …** las cosas habían llegado a tal extremo que …
5 (= *sexual advance*) **to make a ~ at sb*** tirar a algn los tejos*, intentar ligar con algn*
6 (*Geog*) puerto *m*, paso *m*
Ⓑ VT **1** (= *go past*) pasar; (*go in front of*) pasar por delante de; (*while looking*) pasar por (delante de); (= *cross paths with*) cruzarse con; (= *overtake*) adelantar, pasar, rebasar (*Mex*); **have we ~ed the Plaza de España yet?** ¿ya hemos pasado la Plaza de España?; **the road ~es a church** la carretera pasa por delante de una iglesia; **we'll shortly be ~ing Buckingham Palace** pronto pasaremos por (delante de) Buckingham Palace
2 (= *surpass*) superar; **total membership has ~ed the six million mark** el número total de miembros supera los seis millones
3 (= *cross*) [+ *barrier, frontier*] cruzar; **not a word has ~ed my lips** de mí no ha salido una palabra, no he dicho ni una palabra
4 (= *convey, hand over*) (*gen, also Sport*) pasar; **the gas is then ~ed along a pipe** el gas se pasa luego por una tubería; **to ~ sb sth ◇ ~ sth to sb** pasar algo a algn; **~ me the salt, please** ¿me pasas *or* alcanzas la sal, por favor?
5 (= *spend*) [+ *time*] pasar; **it ~es the time** ayuda a pasar el rato
6 (= *not fail*) [+ *exam, essay, candidate, law, motion*] aprobar; [+ *inspection*] pasar
7 (= *express*) [+ *remark, comment*] hacer; **to ~ sentence** fallar, dictar sentencia; **to ~ sentence on sb** sentenciar *or* condenar a algn
8 (*Physiol*) [+ *blood*] echar; **to ~ water** orinar; **to ~ wind** ventosear
9 [+ *counterfeit money, stolen goods*] pasar
Ⓒ VI **1** (= *go past*) pasar; (*Aut*) (= *overtake*) pasar, adelantar, rebasar (*Mex*); **to let sb ~** dejar pasar a algn; **we ~ed in the corridor** nos cruzamos en el pasillo
2 (= *go, be transferred*) pasar; **the estate ~ed to my brother** la herencia pasó a mi hermano; **the bullet ~ed through her shoulder** la bala le atravesó el hombro
3 (*Sport*) hacer un pase
4 (= *happen*) **all that ~ed between them** todo lo que hubo entre ellos
5 (= *go by*) [*time, deadline*] pasar; **as the years ~ed** a medida que pasaban los años, con el paso de los años; **how time ~es!** ¡como pasa el tiempo!
6 (= *disappear*) [*storm, pain, danger*] pasar
7 (*in exam*) aprobar
8 (= *be accepted*) pasar; **"will this do?" — "oh, it'll ~"** —¿esto servirá? —bueno, pasará; **what ~es in New York may not be good enough here** lo que es aceptable en Nueva York puede no serlo aquí; **she could easily ~ for 20** podría pasar fácilmente por una chica de 20 años; **we can't let that ~!** ¡eso no lo podemos consentir *or* pasar por alto!
9 (*at cards, in quiz*) (**I**) **~!** ¡paso!; **I'm afraid I don't know, I'll have to ~ on that one** me temo que no lo sé, no puedo contestar esa pregunta; **I think I'll ~ on the hiking next time*** creo que la próxima vez voy a pasar de la excursión*
Ⓓ CPD **➤ pass key** llave *f* maestra **➤ pass mark** aprobado *m*, nota *f* de aprobado **➤ pass rate** índice *m* de aprobados
➤ pass around VT + ADV [+ *object*] pasar de uno a otro; **a bottle of whisky was ~ed around** se pasaron una botella de whisky de mano en mano *or* de uno a otro; **you ~ around the biscuits** pasa las galletas entre todos; **to ~ around the hat** pasar la gorra
➤ pass away VI + ADV fallecer
➤ pass by Ⓐ VI + ADV pasar **Ⓑ** VT + ADV **life has ~ed her by** la vida se le ha pasado sin enterarse, no ha disfrutado de la vida; **don't let this opportunity ~ you by** no dejes pasar (por alto) esta oportunidad **Ⓒ** VI + PREP pasar por; **I'll ~ by your place to pick you up** pasaré por tu casa a recogerte
➤ pass down Ⓐ VT + ADV [+ *custom, disease, trait*] pasar, transmitir; [+ *inheritance*] pasar; **my clothes were always ~ed down from my elder sister** yo siempre heredaba la ropa de mi hermana mayor **Ⓑ** VI + ADV [*custom*] pasar, transmitirse; **the farm ~ed down to me** yo heredé la granja
➤ pass off Ⓐ VI + ADV **1** (= *happen*) transcurrir; **it all ~ed off**

without incident todo transcurrió sin percances **2** (= *wear off*) pasarse; **her headache ~ed off after an hour** el dolor de cabeza se le pasó una hora después **Ⓑ** VT + ADV **to ~ sth/sb off as sth** hacer pasar algo/algn por algo; **to ~ o.s. off as sth/sb** hacerse pasar por algo/algn
➤ pass on Ⓐ VT + ADV **1** (= *transfer*) [+ *information*] pasar, comunicar, dar; [+ *object*] pasar; [+ *disease*] contagiar; **they ~ the increase on to the consumer** hacen que el consumidor cargue con el incremento; **we ~ our savings on to the customer** los ahorros redundan en favor de nuestros clientes; **Sheila's having a party, ~ it on!*** Sheila va a dar una fiesta, ¡corre la voz!
2 (= *put in contact*) **to ~ sb on to sb** poner a algn en contacto con algn; (*on telephone*) poner a algn con algn; **I'll ~ you on to my supervisor** le pongo con mi supervisor
Ⓑ VI + ADV **1** (= *proceed*) pasar (**to** a)
2 (= *die*) fallecer
➤ pass out VI + ADV **1** (= *faint*) perder el conocimiento, desmayarse **2** (*Brit Mil*) graduarse
➤ pass over Ⓐ VI + ADV (= *die*) fallecer **Ⓑ** VT + ADV (= *omit*) pasar por alto, omitir; **he was ~ed over for promotion** a la hora de los ascensos lo dejaron de lado
➤ pass round VT + ADV (*Brit*) = **pass around**
➤ pass through VI + ADV **1** (= *not stay*) estar de paso; **I'm just ~ing through** estoy de paso nada más **2** (= *go through*) pasar; **he wouldn't let me ~ through without identification** no me dejaba pasar sin documentación
➤ pass up VT + ADV (= *forgo*) echar a perder, desperdiciar

passable ['pɑːsəbl] ADJ **1** (= *tolerable*) pasable **2** [*road*] transitable

passage ['pæsɪdʒ] N **1** (= *corridor*) pasillo *m*; (*between buildings*) pasaje *m*; (*secret, underground*) pasadizo *m*; (= *alley*) callejón *m* **2** (= *voyage*) travesía *f*, viaje *m*; (= *fare*) pasaje *m* **3** (= *access, progress*) paso *m*; **free ~** paso *m* libre; **safe ~** salvoconducto *m*; **the ~ of time** el paso del tiempo; **one's ~ into womanhood/manhood** el paso de uno a la edad adulta **4** [*of book, music*] pasaje *m*

passageway ['pæsɪdʒweɪ] N (*in house*) pasillo *m*, corredor *m*; (*between buildings etc*) pasaje *m*

passbook ['pɑːsbʊk] N (*Brit*) libreta *f or* cartilla *f* de ahorros

passé ['pæseɪ] ADJ pasado de moda

passenger ['pæsndʒəʳ] **Ⓐ** N **1** (= *traveller*) pasajero/a *m/f* **2** (= *parasite*) parásito *m* **Ⓑ** CPD [*jet, ship, train*] de pasajeros **➤ passenger door** puerta *f* del pasajero **➤ passenger list** lista *f* de pasajeros **➤ passenger miles** millas por pasajero *fpl* **➤ passenger seat** asiento *m* de(l) pasajero

passer-by ['pɑːsəˈbaɪ] N (*pl* **passers-by**) transeúnte *mf*

passing ['pɑːsɪŋ] **Ⓐ** ADJ [*fad*] pasajero; [*glance*] rápido, superficial; [*remark*] hecho de paso; **a ~ car** un coche que pasaba; **with each ~ day it gets more difficult** cada día (que pasa) se hace más difícil; **the story aroused no more than ~ interest** la noticia no despertó más que un interés pasajero; **the speech made only a ~ reference to the Middle East** el discurso hizo sólo una breve alusión a Oriente Medio
Ⓑ N **1** (= *disappearance*) desaparición *f*; (= *death*) fallecimiento *m*; **with the ~ of the years** con el paso de los años, conforme pasan *or* van pasando los años; **to mention sth in ~** mencionar algo de paso *or* pasada
2 (*US Aut*) adelantamiento *m*
Ⓒ CPD **➤ passing lane** (*US*) carril *m* de adelantamiento **➤ passing place** (*Brit*) apartadero *m*

passing-out [ˌpɑːsɪŋ'aʊt] N graduación *f* **➤ passing-out parade** desfile *m* de promoción

passion ['pæʃən] N (= *love, emotion*) pasión *f*; **his ~ for accuracy** su pasión por la exactitud; **I have a ~ for shellfish** el marisco me apasiona **➤ passion fruit** granadilla *f*, maracuyá *m*

passionate ['pæʃənɪt] ADJ [*affair, love, kiss*] apasionado; [*believer, supporter*] ardiente, ferviente; [*speech*] apasionado, vehemente; **we're both ~ gardeners** a los dos nos apasiona *or* entusiasma la jardinería

passionately ['pæʃənɪtlɪ] ADV [*love, embrace, kiss*] apasionadamente, con pasión; [*believe, desire*] ardientemente, fervientemente; **she argued ~ in his**

defence abogó con vehemencia en su favor, lo defendió con vehemencia; **I was ~ in love with him** estaba locamente enamorada de él, lo amaba apasionadamente or con pasión

passive ['pæsɪv] **Ⓐ** ADJ pasivo **Ⓑ** N voz f pasiva **Ⓒ** CPD ➤ **passive resistance** resistencia f pasiva ➤ **passive smoking** fumar m pasivamente

Passover ['pɑːsəʊvəʳ] N Pascua f (judía)

passport ['pɑːspɔːt] N pasaporte m ➤ **passport control** control m de pasaportes ➤ **passport holder: British ~ holder** titular mf de pasaporte británico

password ['pɑːswɜːd] N contraseña f

past [pɑːst] **Ⓐ** ADV 1 (in place) **she walked slowly ~** pasó despacio; **the days flew ~** los días pasaron volando 2 (in time) **it's ten ~** son y diez; **I've been waiting since half ~** llevo esperando desde y media **Ⓑ** PREP 1 (= in front of) por delante de; (= beyond) más allá de; **we went ~ your house** pasamos por delante de tu casa; **we drove ~ a flock of sheep** pasamos al lado de un rebaño de ovejas con el coche; **just ~ the town hall** un poco más allá del Ayuntamiento; **it's the first house ~ the park** es la primera casa después del parque 2 (in time) **at quarter/twenty ~ four** a las cuatro y cuarto/ veinte; **it's ~ twelve** son las doce pasadas; **it's long ~ the time he normally gets back** él normalmente hubiese llegado hace tiempo; **it's ~ your bedtime** ya tenías que estar durmiendo 3 (= beyond the limits of) **he's ~ 40** tiene más de 40 años; **I'm ~ caring** ya me trae sin cuidado; ✦ IDIOMS **to be ~ it*** [person] estar para el arrastre*; **those jeans are a bit ~ it** esos vaqueros ya están como para jubilarlos*; **I wouldn't put it ~ him*** no me extrañaría en él, lo creo capaz hasta de eso **Ⓒ** ADJ 1 (= previous) [occasion] anterior; **experience tells me not to trust him** sé por experiencia que no debo fiarme de él; **in ~ years** en años anteriores 2 (= former) antiguo 3 (= most recent, last) último; **the ~ few weeks** las últimas semanas; **what has happened over the ~ week?** ¿qué ha pasado en la última semana? 4 (= over) **all that is ~ now** todo eso ya ha pasado, todo eso ya ha quedado atrás; **what's ~ is** lo pasado, pasado (está); **in times ~** antiguamente **Ⓓ** N 1 (= past times) **the ~** el pasado; **in the ~ ...** (= in former times) antes or antiguamente ...; **I've always done it like this in the ~** yo siempre lo he hecho así; **you're living in the ~** estás viviendo en el pasado; **it's a thing of the ~** pertenece a la historia 2 [of person] pasado m; [of place] historia f 3 (= tense) pasado m, pretérito m **Ⓔ** CPD ➤ **past participle** (Ling) participio m (de) pasado or (de) pretérito or pasivo ➤ **past perfect** (Ling) (pretérito m) pluscuamperfecto m ➤ **past tense** (Ling) (tiempo m) pasado m

pasta ['pæstə] N pasta(s) f(pl)

paste [peɪst] **Ⓐ** N 1 (= substance, consistency) pasta f; (= glue) engrudo m, cola f; **anchovy ~** pasta f de anchoas; **fish ~** paté m de pescado; **tomato ~** concentrado m de tomate **Ⓑ** VT 1 (= put paste on) engomar, encolar; (= stick) pegar; **to ~ sth onto sth** pegar algo a algo 2 (Comput) pegar **Ⓒ** CPD [jewellery] (lit) de estrás; (costume) de fantasía

pastel ['pæstəl] **Ⓐ** N 1 (= crayon, colour) pastel m; (= drawing) pintura f al pastel **2 pastels** (= colours) colores mpl pastel **Ⓑ** ADJ [colour, shade, blue] pastel inv; [drawing] al pastel

pasteurization [,pæstəraɪˈzeɪʃən] N paste(u)rización f

pasteurize ['pæstəraɪz] VT paste(u)rizar

pastiche [pæsˈtiːʃ] N pastiche m, imitación f

pastille ['pæstɪl] N pastilla f

pastime ['pɑːstaɪm] N pasatiempo m

pasting* ['peɪstɪŋ] N paliza f; **to give sb a ~** dar una paliza a algn; **the city took a ~ during the war** la ciudad fue muy castigada durante la guerra; **he got a ~ from the critics** los críticos fueron muy duros con él

pastor ['pɑːstəʳ] N pastor(a) m/f

pastoral ['pɑːstərəl] ADJ [care, economy] pastoral; (Literat) pastoril

pastry ['peɪstrɪ] N (= dough) masa f; (baked) pasta f; (= cake) pastel m ➤ **pastry brush** cepillo m de repostería ➤ **pastry case** cobertura f de pasta ➤ **pastry cook** pastelero/a m/f, repostero/a m/f

pasture ['pɑːstʃəʳ] N (= field) pasto m, prado m; (= pastureland) tierra(s) f(pl) de pastoreo; **they're putting me out to ~** (hum) me echan al pasto (como a caballo viejo); ✦ IDIOM **to seek ~s new** buscar nuevos horizontes

pastureland ['pɑːstʃələænd] N pradera f, tierra(s) f(pl) de pastoreo

pasty¹ ['pæstɪ] N (Brit) (= pie) pastel m (de carne), empanada f

pasty² ['peɪstɪ] ADJ (compar **pastier**; superl **pastiest**) [substance] pastoso; [complexion] pálido

pat¹ [pæt] **Ⓐ** N 1 (= light blow) palmadita f, golpecito m; (= caress) caricia f; **to give sb a ~ on the back** (fig) felicitar a algn 2 [of butter] porción f **Ⓑ** VT (= touch) [+ hair, face etc] tocar, pasar la mano por; (= tap) dar una palmadita en; [+ child's head, dog] acariciar

pat² [pæt] **Ⓐ** ADV **he knows it (off) ~** lo sabe al dedillo or de memoria; **he always has an excuse just ~** siempre tiene su excusa lista; ✦ IDIOM **to stand ~** (US) mantenerse firme or en sus trece **Ⓑ** ADJ [answer] fácil

Patagonia [,pætəˈɡəʊnɪə] N Patagonia f

patch [pætʃ] **Ⓐ** N 1 (= mend) (on clothing) remiendo m, parche m; (on tyre, wound, over eye) parche m; **nicotine ~** parche m de nicotina; ✦ IDIOM **this book's not a ~ on the other one** (Brit*) este libro no tiene ni punto de comparación con el otro 2 (= stain) mancha f; (= bit) pedazo m; **a ~ of blue flowers** un área de flores azules; **the team is going through a bad ~** (esp Brit) el equipo está pasando por una mala racha; **then we hit a bad ~ of road** dimos luego con un tramo de carretera bastante malo 3 (= piece of land) parcela f, terreno m; **the cabbage ~** la parcela or el terreno or el bancal de las coles 4 (*) (= territory) territorio m; **they must get off our ~** tienen que largarse de nuestro territorio* 5 (Comput) ajuste m **Ⓑ** VT [+ garment, hole] remendar, poner remiendos a ➤ **patch up** VT + ADV [+ clothes] remendar provisionalmente; [+ marriage, relationship] salvar; **the doctor soon ~ed him up** el doctor enseguida le curó las heridas; **to ~ things up (with sb)** hacer las paces (con algn); **they ~ed up their differences** resolvieron sus diferencias

patchwork ['pætʃwɜːk] N labor f de retazos, arpillería f (LAm); **a ~ of fields** un mosaico de campos ➤ **patchwork quilt** edredón m de retazos multicolores or patchwork

patchy ['pætʃɪ] ADJ (compar **patchier**; superl **patchiest**) [performance] desigual, poco uniforme; [knowledge] incompleto; [fog] discontinuo

pâté ['pæteɪ] N paté m

patent ['peɪtənt] **Ⓐ** ADJ (= obvious) patente, evidente **Ⓑ** N patente f **Ⓒ** VT patentar **Ⓓ** CPD ➤ **patent law** derecho m de patentes ➤ **patent leather** charol m ➤ **Patent Office** (Brit) registro m de la propiedad industrial

patently ['peɪtəntlɪ] ADV evidentemente; **to be ~ obvious** saltar a la vista, ser evidente

paternal [pəˈtɜːnl] ADJ [love, feelings, authority] paterno; [pride] de padre; [grandparent] por parte de padre, paterno

paternalistic [pə,tɜːnəˈlɪstɪk] ADJ paternalista

paternity [pəˈtɜːnɪtɪ] N paternidad f ➤ **paternity leave** permiso m por paternidad, licencia f por paternidad ➤ **paternity suit** litigio m por paternidad

path [pɑːθ] **Ⓐ** N (pl **~s** [pɑːðz]) 1 (surfaced) camino m; (unsurfaced) camino m, sendero m 2 (= course) [of person, vehicle] camino m; [of missile, earth, storm] trayectoria f; **the hurricane destroyed everything in its ~** el huracán destruyó todo a su paso; **he stepped into the ~ of an oncoming car** se cruzó en el camino de un coche que se acercaba 3 (= way) paso m; **a group of reporters blocked his ~** un

grupo de periodistas le cerraba el paso
4 (*fig*) camino *m*; **our ~s first crossed in Milan** nuestros caminos se cruzaron por primera vez en Milán, la primera vez que coincidimos fue en Milán; **the ~ to independence** el camino hacia la independencia
Ⓑ CPD ➤ **path name** (*Comput*) dirección *f* de fichero

pathetic [pəˈθetɪk] ADJ **1** (= *piteous*) [*sight*] patético, lastimoso; [*smile*] conmovedor **2** (*) (= *useless*) [*excuse, attempt*] pobre; [*performance*] penoso, patético; **~, isn't it?** da pena ¿no?

pathetically [pəˈθetɪklɪ] ADV **1** (= *piteously*) [*whimper, moan*] lastimeramente; **~ thin/weak** tan delgado/débil que da/daba pena; **she was ~ grateful** su gratitud resultaba penosa **2** (= *uselessly*) [*play, perform*] que da/daba pena; **a ~ inadequate answer** una respuesta penosa *or* patética

pathogen [ˈpæθədʒen] N patógeno *m*

pathological [ˌpæθəˈlɒdʒɪkəl] ADJ (*lit, fig*) patológico

pathologist [pəˈθɒlədʒɪst] N patólogo/a *m/f*

pathology [pəˈθɒlədʒɪ] N patología *f*

pathos [ˈpeɪθɒs] N patetismo *m*

patience [ˈpeɪʃəns] N **1** paciencia *f*; **to lose one's ~ (with sth/sb)** perder la paciencia (con algn/algo); **to try sb's ~** poner a prueba la paciencia de algn; **I have no ~ with you** no tengo paciencia contigo **2** (*Brit Cards*) solitario *m*; **to play ~** hacer un solitario

patient¹ [ˈpeɪʃənt] ADJ paciente; **to be ~** tener paciencia (**with sb** con algn)

patient² [ˈpeɪʃənt] N (*on doctor's list*) paciente *mf*; (*having medical treatment*) enfermo/a *m/f*

patiently [ˈpeɪʃəntlɪ] ADV con paciencia, pacientemente

patio [ˈpætɪəʊ] N patio *m* ➤ **patio doors** puertas *fpl* que dan al patio

patois [ˈpætwɑː] N (*pl* ~ [ˈpætwɑːz]) dialecto *m*, jerga *f*

patriarchal [ˌpeɪtrɪˈɑːkəl] ADJ patriarcal

patrimony [ˈpætrɪmənɪ] N patrimonio *m*

patriot [ˈpeɪtrɪət] N patriota *mf*

patriotic [ˌpætrɪˈɒtɪk] ADJ patriótico

patriotism [ˈpætrɪətɪzəm] N patriotismo *m*

patrol [pəˈtrəʊl] **Ⓐ** N patrulla *f*; **to be on ~** estar de patrulla **Ⓑ** VT [+ *streets*] patrullar por; [+ *frontier*] patrullar **Ⓒ** VI patrullar **Ⓓ** CPD ➤ **patrol boat** patrullero *m*, (lancha *f*) patrullera *f* ➤ **patrol car** (*Brit*) coche *m* patrulla ➤ **patrol wagon** (*US*) coche *m* celular

patrolman [pəˈtrəʊlmən] N (*pl* **patrolmen**) **1** (*US*) guardia *m*, policía *m* **2** (*Brit Aut*) mecánico del servicio de ayuda en carretera

patrolwoman [pəˈtrəʊlˌwʊmən] N (*pl* **patrolwomen**) **1** (*US*) mujer *f* policía **2** (*Brit Aut*) mecánica del servicio de ayuda en carretera

patron [ˈpeɪtrən] N [*of charity, society*] patrocinador(a) *m/f*; (*Comm*) [*of shop, hotel*] cliente/a *m/f*; **a ~ of the arts** un mecenas ➤ **patron saint** patrono/a *m/f*

patronage [ˈpætrənɪdʒ] N (= *support*) patrocinio *m*; [*of the arts*] mecenazgo *m*; (*political*) apoyo *m*

patronize [ˈpætrənaɪz] VT **1** (= *treat condescendingly*) tratar con condescendencia **2** (= *be customer of*) [+ *shop*] ser cliente de, comprar en; [+ *hotel, cinema*] frecuentar

patronizing [ˈpætrənaɪzɪŋ] ADJ [*person, attitude*] condescendiente; **a few ~ remarks** unas cuantas observaciones dichas en tono condescendiente

patsy* [ˈpætsɪ] N (*US*) bobo/a *m/f*, primo* *m*

patter¹* [ˈpætə*] N (= *talk*) labia *f*; [*of salesman*] rollo* *m*, discursito* *m*

patter² [ˈpætə*] **Ⓐ** N [*of feet*] golpeteo *m*; [*of rain*] tamborileo *m* **Ⓑ** VI [*feet*] golpetear; (*rain*) golpetear, tamborilear

pattern [ˈpætən] **Ⓐ** N **1** (= *design*) dibujo *m*; **a fabric in** *or* **with a floral ~** una tela con un dibujo *or* diseño floral **2** (*Sew, Knitting*) patrón *m*, molde *m* (*SC*) **3** (= *model, style*) modelo *m*; **behaviour ~** modelo *m* de comportamiento; **a clear ~ began to emerge** empezaron a surgir unas pautas

definidas; **a healthy eating ~** unos hábitos alimenticios sanos; **to follow a ~** seguir unas pautas **Ⓑ** CPD ➤ **pattern book** muestrario *m*

patterned [ˈpætənd] ADJ estampado

patty [ˈpætɪ] N (*esp US*) empanada *f*

paucity [ˈpɔːsɪtɪ] N escasez *f*, insuficiencia *f*

paunch [pɔːntʃ] N panza* *f*, barriga* *f*

pauper [ˈpɔːpə*] N pobre *mf*, indigente *mf*; **~'s grave** fosa *f* común

pause [pɔːz] **Ⓐ** N **1** (= *interruption*) pausa *f* (*also Mus*); (= *silence*) silencio *m*; (= *rest*) descanso *m*; **to give sb ~ for thought** dar que pensar a algn **2** (*on cassette-player*) botón *m* de pausa **Ⓑ** VI (*in activity*) hacer un descanso; (*when speaking*) callarse (momentáneamente), detenerse; (*when moving*) detenerse; **to ~ for breath** detenerse para tomar aliento **Ⓒ** CPD ➤ **pause button** botón *m* de pausa

pave [peɪv] VT (*gen*) pavimentar; (*with flagstones*) enlosar; (*with stones*) adoquinar, empedrar; **✦** IDIOM **to ~ the way for sth/sb** preparar el terreno para algo/algn

pavement [ˈpeɪvmənt] **Ⓐ** N **1** (*Brit*) (*for walking on*) acera *f*, vereda *f* (*LAm*), andén *m* (*CAm, Col*), banqueta *f* (*Mex*) **2** (*US*) (= *road surface*) calzada *f*, pavimento *m* **Ⓑ** CPD ➤ **pavement artist** (*Brit*) pintor(a) *m/f* callejero/a ➤ **pavement café** (*Brit*) café *m* con terraza, café *m* al aire libre

pavilion [pəˈvɪlɪən] N (*for band*) quiosco *m*; (*Brit Sport*) caseta *f*, vestuario *m*; (*at trade fair*) pabellón *m*

paving [ˈpeɪvɪŋ] N (*concrete*) pavimento *m*; (= *flagstones*) enlosado *m*; (= *stones*) adoquinado *m*, empedrado *m* ➤ **paving stone** adoquín *m*, baldosa *f* (*LAm*); (*esp Brit*) (= *flagstone*) losa *f*

paw [pɔː] **Ⓐ** N [*of animal*] pata *f*; [*of cat*] garra *f*; [*of lion*] zarpa *f*, garra *f* **Ⓑ** VT **1 to ~ the ground** [*horse*] piafar **2** (*pej*) [+ *person*] manosear, tocar

pawn¹ [pɔːn] N (*Chess*) peón *m*; (*fig*) instrumento *m*; **he was just a ~ in their game** era sólo un títere en sus manos

pawn² [pɔːn] VT empeñar

pawnbroker [ˈpɔːnˌbrəʊkə*] N prestamista *mf*

pawnshop [ˈpɔːnʃɒp] N monte *m* de piedad, casa *f* de empeños

pawpaw [ˈpɔːpɔː] N **1** (*Brit*) = **papaya 2** (*US*) (= *custard apple*) asimina *f*, chirimoya *f*

pay [peɪ] (*vb*: *pt, pp* **paid**) **Ⓐ** N (= *wages*) [*of professional person*] sueldo *m*; [*of worker*] salario *m*, sueldo *m*; **the ~'s not very good** no pagan muy bien
Ⓑ VT **1** [+ *bill, duty, fee*] pagar; [+ *account*] liquidar; [+ *debt*] saldar, liquidar; [+ *employee, worker*] pagar a; **to ~ sb £10** pagar diez libras a algn; **to ~ sb to do a job** pagar a algn para que haga un trabajo; **to ~ cash (down)** pagar al contado; **I paid £5 for that record** pagué cinco libras por ese disco; **how much did you ~ for it?** ¿cuánto pagaste por él?, ¿cuánto te costó?; **that's what you're paid for** para eso te pagan; **to get paid on Fridays** cobrar los viernes; **does your current account ~ interest?** ¿le rinde intereses su cuenta corriente?; **to ~ money into an account** depositar *or* (*Sp*) ingresar dinero en una cuenta
2 (= *be profitable to*) **it wouldn't ~ him to do it** (*lit*) no le compensaría hacerlo; (*fig*) no le valdría la pena hacerlo **3** [+ *attention*] prestar (**to** a); [+ *homage*] rendir (**to** a); [+ *respects*] ofrecer, presentar; **to ~ sb a visit** ir a ver a algn **Ⓒ** VI **1** pagar; **I'll ~** lo pago yo; **can I ~ by cheque?** ¿puedo pagar con cheque?; **to ~ for sth** pagar algo; **they paid for her to go** pagaron para que fuera; **she paid for it with her life** le costó la vida; **they made him ~ dearly for it** le hicieron pagarlo muy caro; **you'll ~ for this!** ¡me las pagarás!; **to ~ in instalments** pagar a plazos
2 (= *be profitable*) [*business*] rendir, ser rentable; **his job ~s well** tiene un buen sueldo, le pagan bien en el trabajo ; **it ~s to advertise** compensa hacer publicidad; **it ~s to be courteous/tell the truth** vale la pena ser cortés/decir la verdad
Ⓓ CPD ➤ **pay as you earn** (*Brit*) retención *f* fiscal (hecha por la empresa) ➤ **pay award** adjudicación *f* de aumento de salarios ➤ **pay bed** habitación *f* privada en un hospital público ➤ **pay check** (*US*), **pay cheque** (*Brit*) cheque *m* de la

paga; (= *salary*) sueldo *m* ➤ **pay day** día *m* de paga ➤ **pay desk** caja *f* ➤ **pay dirt** (*US*) grava *f* provechosa ➤ **pay envelope** (*US*) sobre *m* de la paga ➤ **pay increase** incremento *m or* aumento *m* salarial ➤ **pay negotiations** negociaciones *fpl* salariales ➤ **pay packet** (*Brit*) sobre *m* de la paga ➤ **pay phone** (*Brit*) teléfono *m* público ➤ **pay raise** (*US*), **pay rise** (*Brit*) incremento *m or* aumento *m* salarial ➤ **pay scale** escala *f* salarial ➤ **pay slip** (*Brit*) nómina *f*, hoja *f* salarial *or* de sueldo ➤ **pay station** (*US*) teléfono *m* público ➤ **pay structure** estructura *f* salarial ➤ **pay TV** televisión *f* de pago ➤ **pay back** VT + ADV **1** [+ *money*] devolver; [+ *loan*] pagar **2 I'll ~ you back for the meal tomorrow** te devuelvo el dinero de la comida mañana; **I'll never be able to ~ you back for all you've done** nunca podré corresponderte por todo lo que has hecho; **I'll ~ you back for this!** ¡me las vas a pagar!
➤ **pay down** VT + ADV [+ *cash*] pagar al contado; [+ *deposit*] pagar como desembolso inicial
➤ **pay in** VT + ADV [+ *money*] ingresar, depositar; [+ *cheque*] ingresar, abonar
➤ **pay off Ⓐ** VT + ADV **1** [+ *debt*] liquidar, saldar; [+ *mortgage*] amortizar; **to ~ sth off in instalments** pagar algo a plazos **2** (= *discharge*) [+ *workers, crew*] pagar y despedir **Ⓑ** VI + ADV merecer *or* valer la pena
➤ **pay out Ⓐ** VT + ADV (*for purchase*) gastar, desembolsar; (*to shareholder, prizewinner*) pagar **Ⓑ** VI + ADV **to ~ out on a policy** pagar una póliza
➤ **pay up** VI + ADV pagar (lo que se debe); **~ up!** ¡a pagar!

payable ['peɪəbl] ADJ pagadero; **~ on demand** pagadero a presentación *or* a vista; **to make a cheque ~ to sb** extender un cheque a favor de algn

pay-and-display [,peɪəndɪs'pleɪ] ADJ (*Brit*) [*car park*] de pago (*colocando el ticket en el interior del parabrisas*)

pay-as-you-go [,peɪəzjə'gəʊ] (*US*) = **pay as you earn**; *see* **pay D**

payback ['peɪbæk] N (*esp US*) restitución *f*

PAYE N ABBR (*Brit*) retención *f* fiscal (hecha por la empresa)

payee [peɪ'iː] N portador(a) *m/f*, tenedor(a) *m/f*; [*of cheque*] beneficiario/a *m/f*

paying guest [,peɪɪŋ'gest] N huésped *mf*, inquilino/a *m/f* (*de habitación en una casa particular*)

paying-in slip [,peɪɪŋ'ɪn,slɪp], **pay-in slip** [,peɪ'ɪn,slɪp] N hoja *f or* resguardo *m* de ingreso

payload ['peɪləʊd] N carga *f* útil

paymaster ['peɪmɑːstə'] **Ⓐ** N **1** (oficial *m*) pagador *m* **2** (*pej*) **the ~s of terrorism** los mecenas del terrorismo **Ⓑ** CPD ➤ **Paymaster General** (*Brit*) *encargado del departamento del ministerio de Hacienda a través del que se paga a los funcionarios públicos*

payment ['peɪmənt] **Ⓐ** N **1** [*of salary, debt, invoice*] pago *m*; (*for services*) remuneración *f*; **~ of this invoice is now due** ya hay que hacer efectivo el pago de esta factura; **in ~ for** en pago por/de; **to make a ~** efectuar un pago; **on ~ of £5** mediante pago de cinco libras, pagando cinco libras **2** (= *instalment*) plazo *m*; **ten monthly ~s of £50** diez plazos mensuales *or* diez mensualidades de 50 libras **Ⓑ** CPD ➤ **payment card** tarjeta *f* de pago

payoff* ['peɪɒf] N **1** (= *payment*) pago *m* **2** (= *reward*) recompensa *f*, beneficios *mpl* **3** (= *bribe*) soborno *m*, coima *f* (*And, SC*), mordida *f* (*CAm, Mex*)

payout ['peɪaʊt] N pago *m*; (= *share-out*) reparto *m*; (*in competition*) premio *m* en metálico; (*from insurance*) indemnización *f*

pay-per-click [,peɪpə'klɪk] N pago *m* por clic

payroll ['peɪrəʊl] N nómina *f or* plantilla *f* (de sueldos); **he has 1,000 people on his ~** tiene una nómina de 1.000 empleados

PC Ⓐ N ABBR **1** (= **personal computer**) PC *m*, OP *m* (*Sp*), CP *m or f* (*LAm*) **2** (*Brit*) (= **police constable**) policía *mf* **Ⓑ** ADJ ABBR (*) = **politically correct**

pc N ABBR = **postcard**

PCB N ABBR **1** (= **printed circuit board**) TCI *f* **2** (= **polychlorinated biphenyl**) PCB *m*

pcm ADV ABBR (*Brit*) (= **per calendar month**) p/mes

PD N ABBR (*US*) = **police department**

pd ABBR (= **paid**) pgdo.

PDA N ABBR (= **personal digital assistant**) PDA *m*

PDF N ABBR (*Comput*) (= **Portable Document Format**) PDF *m*

PDSA N ABBR (*Brit*) = **People's Dispensary for Sick Animals**

PE Ⓐ N ABBR (= **physical education**) gimnasia *f*, educación *f* física, ed. física **Ⓑ** ABBR (*Canada*) = **Prince Edward Island**

pea [piː] N guisante *m* (*Sp*), chícharo *m* (*CAm, Mex*), arveja *f* (*LAm*), alverja *f* (*LAm*) ➤ **pea soup** sopa *f* de guisantes *etc*

peace [piːs] **Ⓐ** N paz *f*; **to be at ~** (= *dead*) descansar en paz; **at ~ with** en paz con; **he gave her no ~ until she agreed** no la dejó tranquila *or* en paz hasta que accedió; **to leave sb in ~** dejar a algn tranquilo *or* en paz; **to live in ~ (with sb)** vivir en paz (con algn); **to make ~ (with sb)** hacer las paces (con algn); **~ of mind** tranquilidad *f* (de espíritu); **anything for the sake of ~ and quiet** lo que sea por un poco de tranquilidad **Ⓑ** CPD [*agreement, plan, settlement*] de paz; [*campaign, conference*] por la paz ➤ **peace campaigner** *persona que participa en una campaña por la paz* ➤ **peace conference** conferencia *f* de paz ➤ **Peace Corps** (*US*) Cuerpo *m* de la Paz ➤ **peace dividend** beneficios *mpl* reportados por la paz ➤ **peace initiative** iniciativa *f* de paz ➤ **peace movement** movimiento *m* pacifista ➤ **peace offering** prenda *f* de paz ➤ **the peace process** el proceso de paz ➤ **peace settlement** acuerdo *m* de paz ➤ **peace studies** (*Univ*) estudios *mpl* de la paz ➤ **peace talks** negociaciones *fpl* por la paz *or* de paz ➤ **peace treaty** tratado *m* de paz

peaceable ['piːsəbl] ADJ pacífico

peaceably ['piːsəblɪ] ADV [*live, settle*] pacíficamente

peaceful ['piːsfʊl] ADJ **1** (= *non-violent*) [*person, tribe, nation*] pacífico; [*demonstration, protest*] pacífico, no violento; **by ~ means** por medios pacíficos; **for ~ purposes** para fines pacíficos **2** (= *calm*) [*place, life, day*] tranquilo

peacefully ['piːsfʊlɪ] ADV (= *non-violently*) pacíficamente; (= *calmly*) tranquilamente; **to die ~** morir sin sufrir

peacekeeper ['piːs,kiːpə'] N **UN ~s** tropas *fpl* de las Naciones Unidas encargadas de mantener la paz

peace-keeping ['piːs,kiːpɪŋ] N mantenimiento *m* de la paz ➤ **peace-keeping force(s)** fuerzas *fpl* encargadas de mantener la paz

peacemaker ['piːs,meɪkə'] N (= *pacifier*) pacificador(a) *m/f*; (= *conciliator*) conciliador(a) *m/f*

peacetime ['piːstaɪm] N tiempos *mpl* de paz

peach [piːtʃ] **Ⓐ** N **1** (= *fruit*) melocotón *m* (*Sp*), durazno *m* (*LAm*); (*also* ~ **tree**) melocotonero *m* (*Sp*), duraznero *m* (*LAm*) **2** (*) **she's a ~** es un bombón *or* una monada*, es una belleza (*LAm*); **it's a ~ of a job** es un trabajo muy cómodo, es un chollo (*Sp**) **Ⓑ** ADJ de color melocotón *or* (*LAm*) durazno

peacock ['piːkɒk] N pavo *m* real ➤ **peacock blue** azul *m* (de) pavo real

pea-green ['piː'griːn] ADJ verde claro

peak [piːk] **Ⓐ** N **1** [*of mountain*] cumbre *f*, cima *f*; (= *mountain itself*) pico *m* **2** [*of cap*] visera *f* **3** (= *high point*) [*of career, fame, popularity*] cumbre *f*, cúspide *f*; **at the ~ of the morning rush hour** en el momento de mayor intensidad de la hora punta matinal; **~s and troughs** auges *mpl* y depresiones *fpl* **Ⓑ** VI [*temperatures*] alcanzar su punto más alto; [*inflation, sales*] alcanzar su nivel máximo; [*crisis*] alcanzar su momento crítico; [*career*] alcanzar la cumbre *or* la cúspide; [*sportsperson*] alcanzar su mejor momento **Ⓒ** ADJ (*before noun*) **in ~ condition** [*athlete*] en óptimas condiciones, en plena forma; [*animal*] en óptimas condiciones; **~ hours** [*of traffic*] horas *fpl* punta; (*Elec*) horas *fpl* de mayor consumo; **~ rate** (*Telec*) tarifa *f* alta; **~ season** temporada *f* alta; **~ time** (*Brit TV*) horas *fpl* de máxima audiencia; (*Telec, Elec*) horas *fpl* de máxima demanda; (= *rush hour*) horas *fpl* punta

peaked [piːkt] ADJ **~ cap** gorra *f* de visera

peaky* ['piːkɪ] ADJ (*compar* **peakier**; *superl* **peakiest**) (*Brit*) paliducho*; **to look ~** estar paliducho*

peal [piːl] **Ⓐ** N (= *sound of bells*) repique *m*; **a ~ of thunder** un trueno; **~s of laughter** carcajadas *fpl* **Ⓑ** VI [*bell*] repicar, tocar a vuelo

peanut ['piːnʌt] N cacahuete *m* (*Sp*), maní *m* (*LAm*), cacahuate *m* (*Mex*); **he gets paid ~s*** le pagan una miseria ➤ **peanut butter** mantequilla *f or* crema *f* de cacahuete (*Sp*), mantequilla *f* de maní (*LAm*), mantequilla *f* de cacahuate (*Mex*) ➤ **peanut oil** aceite *m* de cacahuete *etc*

peapod ['piːpɒd] N vaina *f* de guisante (*Sp*), vaina *f* de arveja (*LAm*), vaina *f* de chícharo (*CAm*)

pear [pɛəʳ] N (= *fruit*) pera *f*; (*also* ~ **tree**) peral *m*

pearl [pɜːl] **Ⓐ** N perla *f*; **~ of wisdom** joya *f* de sabiduría **Ⓑ** CPD [*earring, button*] de perla(s); (*in colour*) color perla ➤ **pearl barley** cebada *f* perlada ➤ **pearl necklace** collar *m* de perlas

pearl-grey ['pɜːl'greɪ] ADJ gris perla

pearly ['pɜːlɪ] ADJ (*compar* **pearlier**; *superl* **pearliest**) [*teeth*] de perla; [*colour*] perlado, nacarado; **~ white/pink** blanco/rosa perla ➤ **the Pearly Gates** (*hum*) las puertas del cielo

pear-shaped ['pɛəʃeɪpt] ADJ en forma de pera; ✦ IDIOM **things started to go ~** (*Brit**) las cosas empezaron a ir mal

peasant ['pɛzənt] N campesino/a *m/f* ➤ **peasant farmer** campesino *m*

peashooter ['piːʃuːtəʳ] N cerbatana *f*

peat [piːt] N turba *f* ➤ **peat bog** turbera *f*, turbal *m*

pebble ['pɛbl] N guijarro *m*; ✦ IDIOM **you're not the only ~ on the beach*** no eres el único

pebbledash [,pɛbl'dæʃ] **Ⓐ** N enguijarrado *m* **Ⓑ** VT enguijarrar

pecan ['piːkæn] N pacana *f*

peck [pɛk] **Ⓐ** N picotazo *m*; (= *kiss*) besito *m*, beso *m* rápido **Ⓑ** VT picotear; (= *kiss*) dar un besito a, dar un beso rápido a **Ⓒ** VI picotear; **to ~ at** [*bird*] picar; **he ~ed at his food** picaba la comida (con desgana)

pecking order ['pɛkɪŋ'ɔːdəʳ] N jerarquía *f*

peckish* ['pɛkɪʃ] ADJ (*Brit*) **to feel ~** tener ganas de comer algo

pecs* [pɛks] NPL pectorales *mpl*

pectoral ['pɛktərəl] **Ⓐ** ADJ pectoral **Ⓑ** **pectorals** NPL (músculos *mpl*) pectorales *mpl*

peculiar [pɪ'kjuːlɪəʳ] ADJ 1 (= *strange*) extraño, raro; **I'm feeling a bit ~** me siento algo raro, no me siento del todo bien 2 (= *exclusive, special*) **the style of dress ~ to that period in history** la forma de vestir peculiar *or* característica *or* propia de esa época de la historia; **a species ~ to Africa** una especie que existe únicamente en África

peculiarity [pɪ,kjuːlɪ'ærɪtɪ] N 1 (= *strangeness*) rareza *f* 2 (= *specific quality*) peculiaridad *f*; **he has his peculiarities** tiene sus rarezas *or* manías 3 (= *distinctive feature*) rasgo *m* singular

peculiarly [pɪ'kjuːlɪəlɪ] ADV 1 (= *strangely*) de forma rara 2 (= *specifically*) típicamente, peculiarmente 3 (= *unusually, exceptionally*) particularmente, especialmente

pecuniary [pɪ'kjuːnɪərɪ] ADJ pecuniario

pedagogical [,pɛdə'gɒdʒɪkəl] ADJ pedagógico

pedal ['pɛdl] **Ⓐ** N pedal *m* **Ⓑ** VI pedalear **Ⓒ** VT [+ *bicycle*] darle a los pedales de **Ⓓ** CPD ➤ **pedal bin** (*Brit*) cubo *m* de la basura con pedal ➤ **pedal boat** patín *m* a pedal ➤ **pedal car** cochecito *m* con pedales ➤ **pedal cycle** bicicleta *f* a pedales

pedalo ['pɛdələu] N patín *m* a pedal

pedant ['pɛdənt] N pedante *mf*

pedantic [pɪ'dæntɪk] ADJ pedante

pedantry ['pɛdəntrɪ] N pedantería *f*

peddle ['pɛdl] VT (= *sell*) ir vendiendo (de puerta en puerta); [+ *drugs*] pasar*; [+ *ideas*] difundir

peddler ['pɛdləʳ] N (*esp US*) vendedor(a) *m/f* ambulante

pedestal ['pɛdɪstl] N pedestal *m*, basa *f*; ✦ IDIOM **to knock sb off his ~** bajar los humos *or* el copete a algn*

pedestrian [pɪ'dɛstrɪən] **Ⓐ** N peatón/ona *m/f* **Ⓑ** ADJ [*style, speech*] prosaico, pedestre **Ⓒ** CPD ➤ **pedestrian crossing** (*Brit*) paso *m* de peatones ➤ **pedestrian mall** (*US*), **pedestrian precinct** (*Brit*), **pedestrian zone** (*US*) zona *f* peatonal

pedestrianize [pɪ'dɛstrɪənaɪz] VT peatonalizar, hacer peatonal (una calle)

pediatric *etc* [,piːdɪ'ætrɪk] (*US*) = **paediatric** *etc*

pedicure ['pɛdɪkjuəʳ] N pedicura *f*

pedigree ['pɛdɪgriː] **Ⓐ** N (= *lineage*) linaje *m*, genealogía *f*; [*of animal*] pedigrí *m*; (= *family tree*) árbol *m* genealógico; (= *record*) historial *m* **Ⓑ** CPD de raza, de casta

pedlar ['pɛdləʳ] N vendedor(a) *m/f* ambulante

pedophile ['piːdəufaɪl] N (*US*) = **paedophile**

pee* [piː] **Ⓐ** N pipí *m*; **to go for a ~** ir a hacer pipí*; **to have a ~** hacer pipí* **Ⓑ** VI hacer pipí*

peek [piːk] **Ⓐ** N ojeada *f*, miradita *f*; **to have a ~ at** echar una ojeada *or* miradita a; (*furtively*) mirar furtivamente *or* a hurtadillas **Ⓑ** VI (= *glance*) echar una ojeada *or* miradita; (*furtively*) mirar (a hurtadillas); **no ~ing!** ¡sin mirar!

peel [piːl] **Ⓐ** N [*of apple, potato*] piel *f*; [*of citrus fruit*] cáscara *f*; (= *peelings*) [*of apple, potato*] peladuras *fpl*, mondas *fpl*; [*of citrus fruit*] cáscaras *fpl* **Ⓑ** VT [+ *fruit, vegetable*] pelar; [+ *layer of paper*] quitar; ✦ IDIOM **to keep one's eyes ~ed** estar alerta **Ⓒ** VI [*wallpaper*] despegarse, desprenderse; [*paint*] desconcharse; [*skin, person*] pelarse; **I'm ~ing** me estoy pelando

➤ **peel off Ⓐ** VT + ADV [+ *layer, paper*] quitar, despegar; [+ *clothes*] quitarse rápidamente **Ⓑ** VI + ADV 1 (= *separate*) separarse (**from** de); (= *leave formation*) [*vehicle, plane*] despegarse; **he ~ed off to the east** se desvió hacia el este 2 (*) (= *undress*) desnudarse rápidamente

peeler ['piːləʳ] N (*also* **potato ~**) pelapatatas *m inv* (*Sp*), pelapapas *m inv* (*LAm*)

peelings ['piːlɪŋz] NPL [*of apple, potato*] peladuras *fpl*, mondas *fpl*; [*of citrus fruit*] cáscaras *fpl*

peep¹ [piːp] **Ⓐ** N ojeada *f*, miradita *f*; **to have a ~ (at sth)** echar una ojeada *or* miradita (a algo) **Ⓑ** VI (= *look*) mirar rápidamente; (*furtively*) mirar furtivamente *or* a hurtadillas; **to ~ at** echar una ojeada *or* miradita a ➤ **peep out** VI + ADV asomar(se); **the sun ~ed out from behind the clouds** el sol se asomó tras las nubes

peep² [piːp] N [*of bird*] pío *m*; [*of whistle*] silbido *m*; **there hasn't been a ~ out of them** no han dicho ni pío*; **I don't want to hear ~ out of you!** ¡tú ni chistar!, ¡tú ni pío!*

peephole ['piːphəul] N mirilla *f*, atisbadero *m*

Peeping Tom [,piːpɪŋ'tɒm] N mirón *m*

peer¹ [pɪəʳ] **Ⓐ** N 1 (= *noble*) par *m*, lord *m* 2 (= *equal*) (*in status*) par *mf*, igual *mf*; (*in age*) coetáneo/a *m/f* **Ⓑ** CPD ➤ **peer group** grupo *m* paritario ➤ **peer pressure** presión *f* ejercida por los iguales *or* (*frm*) por el grupo paritario ➤ **peer review** evaluación *f* por los iguales

peer² [pɪəʳ] VI **to ~ at sth/sb** (*short-sightedly*) mirar algo/a algn con ojos de miope; (*closely*) escudriñar algo/a algn

peerage ['pɪərɪdʒ] N (= *nobility*) nobleza *f*; **he was given a ~** le otorgaron un título de nobleza; **to marry into the ~** casarse con un título

peerless ['pɪəlɪs] ADJ sin par, incomparable

peeved* [piːvd] ADJ picado*, molesto

peevish ['piːvɪʃ] ADJ [*look, glance*] malhumorado; [*tone*] de irritación

peg [pɛg] **Ⓐ** N 1 (*in ground, tent peg*) estaca *f*; (*Brit*) (= *clothes peg*) pinza *f*, broche *m* (*LAm*); (*in board game*) ficha *f*; ✦ IDIOM **to take sb down a ~ (or two)*** bajar los humos *or* el copete a algn*

2 (*for coat, hat*) gancho *m*, colgador *m*; **he always buys clothes off the ~** (*Brit*) siempre compra ropa confeccionada *or* de confección

Ⓑ VT 1 (= *secure*) (*gen*) fijar; [+ *clothes*] (*on line*) tender; [+ *tent*] fijar con estacas, sujetar con estacas

2 (*fig*) 2.1 (= *fix*) [+ *prices, wages, rates*] fijar, estabilizar (**at,**

to en) 2.2 (= *link*) vincular (**to** a)
➤ **peg out*** VI + ADV (*Brit*) (= *die*) estirar la pata*; (= *collapse*) caerse redondo*

PEI ABBR (*Canada*) = **Prince Edward Island**

pejorative [prˈdʒɒrətɪv] ADJ peyorativo, despectivo

Pekin [piːˈkɪn], **Peking** [piːˈkɪŋ] N Pekín *m*

pekinese [ˌpiːkɪˈniːz], **pekingese** [ˌpiːkɪŋˈiːz] N pequinés/esa *m/f*

pelican [ˈpelɪkən] N pelícano *m* ➤ **pelican crossing** (*Brit*) semáforo *m* sonoro

pellet [ˈpelɪt] N (= *little ball*) bolita *f*; (*for gun*) perdigón *m*; (= *granule*) gránulo *m*

pell-mell [ˈpelˈmel] ADV en tropel, atropelladamente

pelmet [ˈpelmɪt] N (*Brit*) galería *f* (para cubrir la barra de las cortinas)

pelt¹ [pelt] Ⓐ VT **to ~ sb with eggs** arrojar *or* tirar huevos a algn; **to ~ sb with stones** apedrear a algn Ⓑ VI **the rain is ~ing down*** está lloviendo a cántaros, está diluviando Ⓒ N **to go full ~** ir a todo correr, ir a toda pastilla*

pelt² [pelt] N (= *fur*) piel *f*; (= *skin*) pellejo *m*

pelvic [ˈpelvɪk] ADJ pélvico

pelvis [ˈpelvɪs] N pelvis *f*

pen¹ [pen] Ⓐ N (= *fountain pen*) (pluma *f*) estilográfica *f*, pluma *f*, pluma *f* fuente (*LAm*); (= *ballpoint*) bolígrafo *m*, boli* *m*; (= *felt tip*) rotulador *m*; **to put ~ to paper** ponerse a escribir Ⓑ VT escribir Ⓒ CPD ➤ **pen friend** amigo/a *m/f* por correspondencia ➤ **pen name** seudónimo *m*, nombre *m* de guerra ➤ **pen pal*** amigo/a *m/f* por correspondencia

pen² [pen] Ⓐ N 1 (= *enclosure*) (*for cattle*) corral *m*; (*for sheep*) redil *m*, aprisco *m*; (*for bulls*) toril *m* 2 (*US**) (= *prison*) cárcel *f*, chirona *f* (*Sp**) Ⓑ VT (*also* – **up**) [+ *animal*] encerrar, acorralar

pen³ [pen] N (= *swan*) cisne *m* hembra

penal [ˈpiːnl] ADJ penal ➤ **penal code** código *m* penal

penalize [ˈpiːnəlaɪz] VT (= *punish*) castigar; (*by law*) penar; (*accidentally, unfairly*) perjudicar; (*Sport*) sancionar, penalizar

penalty [ˈpenltɪ] Ⓐ N 1 (*Jur*) (= *punishment*) pena *f*, castigo *m*; (= *fine*) multa *f*; (*Comm*) recargo *m*; (= *disadvantage*) desventaja *f*; **there is a ~ for paying the loan off early** se cobra un recargo si se paga el préstamo antes de que venza; **the ~ for this is death** esto se castiga con la muerte; **to pay the ~ (for** *or* **of sth/for doing sth)** pagar las consecuencias (de algo/de haber hecho algo) 2 (*Ftbl*) penalti *m*, penalty *m*; (*Golf*) penalización *f*; (*Bridge*) multa *f*, castigo *m*; **there is a seven-second ~ for each error** se descuentan siete segundos por cada error; **to give sb a ~** (*Ftbl*) conceder un penalti *or* penalty a algn; **to take a ~** lanzar penalti *or* penalty Ⓑ CPD ➤ **penalty area, penalty box** (*esp Brit Ftbl*) área *f* de castigo *or* de penalti *or* de penalty

> Use **el/un** not **la/una** before feminine nouns beginning with stressed **a** or **ha** like **área**.

➤ **penalty clause** cláusula *f* penal ➤ **penalty kick** penalti *m*, penalty *m* ➤ **penalty point** (*on driving licence, in showjumping*) punto *m* de castigo ➤ **penalty shoot-out** (*esp Brit*) desempate *m* a penaltis

penance [ˈpenəns] N penitencia *f*; **to do ~ for** hacer penitencia por

pence [pens] NPL *of* **penny**

penchant [ˈpɑːʃɑː] N predilección *f* (**for** por), inclinación *f* (**for** hacia, por); **to have a ~ for** tener predilección por

pencil [ˈpensl] Ⓐ N lápiz *m*; **to write in ~** escribir a lápiz Ⓑ VT escribir a lápiz Ⓒ CPD ➤ **pencil case** estuche *m* (para lápices), plumier *m* (*Sp*) ➤ **pencil drawing** dibujo *m* a lápiz ➤ **pencil pusher** (*US pej*) chupatintas* *m inv* ➤ **pencil sharpener** sacapuntas *m inv*

➤ **pencil in** VT + ADV [+ *appointment*] apuntar con carácter provisional; **I'll ~ you in for Thursday** de momento te apunto para el jueves

pendant [ˈpendənt] N colgante *m*

pending [ˈpendɪŋ] Ⓐ ADJ pendiente; **to be ~** estar pendiente *or* en trámite Ⓑ PREP ~ **the arrival of ...** hasta que llegue ...; **he has been suspended ~ further investigation** ha sido suspendido en espera de que continúe la investigación

pendulum [ˈpendjʊləm] N péndulo *m*

penetrate [ˈpenɪtreɪt] VT 1 (= *go right through*) [+ *skin, armour*] penetrar (por), traspasar 2 (*Mil*) [+ *defences*] infiltrar, penetrar; [+ *territory*] penetrar en 3 (= *enter, infiltrate*) [+ *organization*] infiltrarse en; (*Comm*) [+ *market*] introducirse en, entrar en

penetrating [ˈpenɪtreɪtɪŋ] ADJ [*eyes, sound*] penetrante; [*mind*] perspicaz

penetration [ˌpenɪˈtreɪʃən] N penetración *f*

penguin [ˈpeŋgwɪn] N pingüino *m*

penicillin [ˌpenɪˈsɪlɪn] N penicilina *f*

peninsula [prˈnɪnsjʊlə] N península *f*

penis [ˈpiːnɪs] N pene *m*

penitence [ˈpenɪtəns] N penitencia *f*

penitent [ˈpenɪtənt] ADJ arrepentido; (*Rel*) penitente

penitentiary [ˌpenɪˈtenʃərɪ] N (*US*) penitenciaría *f*

penknife [ˈpennaɪf] N (*pl* **penknives**) navaja *f*, cortaplumas *m inv*

Penn., Penna. ABBR (*US†*) = **Pennsylvania**

pennant [ˈpenənt] N banderín *m*; (*Naut*) gallardete *m*

pennies [ˈpenɪz] NPL *of* **penny**

penniless [ˈpenɪlɪs] ADJ sin dinero; **to be ~** no tener un céntimo *or* un centavo

Pennsylvania [ˌpensɪlˈveɪnɪə] N Pensilvania *f*

penny [ˈpenɪ] Ⓐ N 1 (*pl* **pence**) (= *value*) penique *m*; (*US*) (= *cent*) centavo *m*; **it costs five pence** cuesta cinco peniques; **I don't owe you a ~** no te debo nada; **it cost £500 but it was worth every ~** costó 500 libras, pero mereció la pena pagarlas; ✦ IDIOMS **he hasn't a ~ to his name** no tiene dónde caerse muerto; **he thinks jobs are two a ~** (*esp Brit**) cree que hay trabajos a montones; ✦ PROV **in for a ~, in for a pound** de perdidos, al río 2 (*pl* **pennies**) (= *coin*) (*Brit*) penique *m*; (*US*) centavo *m*; **I have five pennies** tengo cinco peniques *or* centavos; ✦ IDIOMS **to count the pennies** mirar el euro (*Sp*), mirar el dinero; **then the ~ dropped** (*Brit**) por fin cayó en la cuenta; **a ~ for your thoughts*** ¿en qué estás pensando? Ⓑ CPD ➤ **penny arcade** (*US*) sala *f* de juegos *or* máquinas tragaperras, salón *m* recreativo ➤ **penny loafer** (*US*) mocasín *m* ➤ **penny whistle** flautín *m*

penny-pinching [ˈpenɪˌpɪntʃɪŋ] Ⓐ N tacañería *f* Ⓑ ADJ [*person*] tacaño, avaro

penpusher [ˈpenˌpʊʃəʳ] N (*Brit pej*) chupatintas* *m inv*

pension [ˈpenʃən] N pensión *f*; **to retire on full ~** retirarse con toda la jubilación; **disability/invalidity ~** pensión *f* de invalidez; **personal** *or* **private ~** plan *m* de pensiones personal; **retirement ~** retiro *m*, (pensión *f* de) jubilación *f*; **state ~** pensión *f* estatal ➤ **pension book** (*Brit*) libreta *f* de pensión ➤ **pension contributions** aportaciones *mpl* a la pensión ➤ **pension fund** fondo *m* de pensiones ➤ **pension plan, pension scheme** plan *m* de pensiones ➤ **pension off** VT + ADV (*Brit*) jubilar

pensionable [ˈpenʃənəbl] ADJ [*age*] de jubilación

pensioner [ˈpenʃənəʳ] N (= *old age pensioner*) jubilado/a *m/f*

pensive [ˈpensɪv] ADJ pensativo, meditabundo

pentagon [ˈpentəgən] N pentágono *m*; **the Pentagon** el Pentágono

pentathlon [penˈtæθlən] N pentatlón *m*

Pentecost [ˈpentɪkɒst] N Pentecostés *m*

penthouse [ˈpenthaʊs] N ático *m*

pent-up [ˈpentʌp] ADJ [*rage*] contenido, reprimido; [*emotion, frustration, energy*] contenido

penultimate [prˈnʌltɪmɪt] ADJ penúltimo

penury ['penjʊrɪ] N miseria *f*, penuria *f*

peony ['pɪənɪ] N peonía *f*

people ['piːpl] **Ⓐ** N **1** (*with pl vb*) **1.1** (*seen as a mass*) gente *f*; **what will ~ think?** ¿qué va a pensar la gente?; **the place was full of ~** el local estaba lleno de gente; **English ~** los ingleses; **here ~ quarrel a lot** aquí se riñe mucho; **what a lot of ~!** ¡cuánta gente!; **old ~** los ancianos, la gente mayor; **~ say that ...** dicen que ..., la gente dice que ...; **young ~** los jóvenes, la gente joven **1.2** (= *persons, individuals*) personas *fpl*; **20 ~** 20 personas; **~ are more important than animals** las personas son más importantes que los animales; **how many ~ are there in your family?** ¿cuántos sois en tu familia?; **the gas ~ are coming tomorrow** los del gas vienen mañana; **many ~ think that ...** mucha gente cree que ..., muchos creen que ...; **they're strange ~** son gente rara **1.3** (= *inhabitants*) habitantes *mpl* **1.4** (= *citizens, public*) pueblo *m*; **the ~** el pueblo; **the will of the ~** la voluntad popular *or* del pueblo; **a man of the ~** un hombre del pueblo **1.5** (= *family*) familia *f*; **my ~** mi familia **1.6** (= *colleagues*) **I asked one of our ~ in Boston to handle it** pedí a uno de nuestro equipo de Boston que se encargara de ello
2 (*countable noun*) (= *ethnic group*) pueblo *m*; **an oppressed ~** un pueblo oprimido
Ⓑ VT poblar; **~d with** poblado de

PEP [pep] N ABBR (*Brit Fin*) = **personal equity plan**

pep* [pep] N energía *f*, dinamismo *m* ➤ **pep pill** estimulante *m* ➤ **pep rally** (*US*) encuentro de motivación ➤ **pep talk** palabras *fpl* que motivan, palabras *fpl* para levantar la moral
➤ **pep up** VT + ADV (= *encourage*) animar, estimular; (= *revive*) dar un nuevo impulso a

pepper ['pepə'] **Ⓐ** N **1** (= *spice*) pimienta *f*; **black/white ~** pimienta *f* negra/blanca
2 (= *vegetable*) pimiento *m*, pimentón *m* (*LAm*); **green/red ~** pimiento *m* verde/rojo, pimentón *m* verde/rojo (*LAm*)
Ⓑ VT **1** (*lit*) echar *or* poner pimienta a, sazonar con pimienta
2 (= *bombard*) acribillar; (= *sprinkle*) salpicar; **to ~ sth/sb with bullets** acribillar algo/a algn a balazos; **to ~ a work with quotations** salpicar una obra de citas
Ⓒ CPD ➤ **pepper mill** molinillo *m* de pimienta ➤ **pepper pot** (*esp Brit*), **pepper shaker** (*US*) pimentero *m*

peppercorn ['pepəkɔːn] N grano *m* de pimienta

peppermint ['pepəmɪnt] N (= *herb*) menta *f*; (= *sweet*) caramelo *m* de menta; (= *lozenge*) pastilla *f* de menta; **~ flavour ice cream** helado *m* con sabor a menta *or* de menta

pepperoni [pepə'rəʊnɪ] N salchichón *m*, pepperoni *m*

peppery ['pepərɪ] ADJ (= *hot, sharp*) picante; (= *tasting of pepper*) con sabor a pimienta

peptic ['peptɪk] ADJ péptico ➤ **peptic ulcer** úlcera *f* péptica

per [pɜː'] PREP por; **~ annum** al año; **as ~ invoice** de acuerdo con *or* según la factura; **£10 ~ dozen** diez libras la docena; **30 miles ~ gallon** 30 millas por cada galón; **~ head** por cabeza; **60 miles ~ hour** 60 millas por hora; **~ person** por persona; **~ se** por sí; *see also* **per cent**

perceive [pə'siːv] VT **1** (= *see, hear*) percibir; (= *realize*) darse cuenta de, notar; **now I ~ that ...** ahora veo que ...; **do you ~ anything strange?** ¿notas algo raro?; **~d need/interest** necesidad *f*/interés *m* que se ha detectado **2** (= *understand*) comprender **3** (= *consider*) considerar; **their action may be ~d as a threat** su actuación puede considerarse *or* puede verse como una amenaza; **the things children ~ as being important** las cosas que los niños consideran importantes

per cent [pə'sent] N por ciento; **20 ~** el 20 por ciento; **there's a ten ~ discount** hay un descuento del diez por cien(to), hay un diez por ciento de descuento; **the population is 90 ~ Catholic** el 90 por ciento de la población es católica; **100 ~** cien por cien

percentage [pə'sentɪdʒ] N porcentaje *m*; **a high ~ are girls** un alto *or* elevado porcentaje son chicas; **to get a ~ on all sales** recibir un tanto por cien sobre todas las ventas; **on a ~ basis** a porcentaje ➤ **percentage increase** aumento *m* porcentual ➤ **percentage point** punto *m* porcentual

perceptible [pə'septəbl] ADJ (= *appreciable*) sensible; (= *discernible*) perceptible

perceptibly [pə'septəblɪ] ADV (= *appreciably*) sensiblemente; (= *discernibly*) perceptiblemente; **it has improved ~** ha mejorado sensiblemente

perception [pə'sepʃən] N **1** (= *act*) percepción *f*; **it changes one's ~ of time** cambia la percepción que uno tiene del tiempo **2** (= *impression*) impresión *f*; **the public ~ is that ...** la gente tiene la impresión de que ... **3** (= *insight*) perspicacia *f*, agudeza *f*

perceptive [pə'septɪv] ADJ perspicaz

perch¹ [pɜːtʃ] **Ⓐ** N [*of bird*] percha *f* **Ⓑ** VT encaramar; **the village is ~ed on a hilltop** el pueblo está levantado en lo alto de una colina **Ⓒ** VI [*bird*] posarse (**on** en); [*person*] sentarse (**on** en)

perch² [pɜːtʃ] N (= *fish*) perca *f*

percolate ['pɜːkəleɪt] **Ⓐ** VT filtrar; **~d coffee** café *m* (de) filtro **Ⓑ** VI **1** (= *filter*) filtrarse; **to ~ down to** filtrarse hasta **2** [*coffee*] hacerse (*en una cafetera de filtro*)

percolator ['pɜːkəleɪtə'] N cafetera *f* de filtro

percussion [pə'kʌʃən] N percusión *f*; **to play ~** ser percusionista ➤ **percussion instrument** instrumento *m* de percusión

peregrine falcon [ˌperɪɡrɪn'fɔːlkən] N halcón *m* peregrino

peremptory [pə'remptərɪ] ADJ [*tone*] perentorio, imperioso; [*person*] imperioso, autoritario

perennial [pə'renɪəl] **Ⓐ** ADJ (*Bot*) perenne; [*problem*] perenne, eterno; **it's a ~ complaint** es una queja constante **Ⓑ** N planta *f* perenne, planta *f* vivaz

perfect Ⓐ ['pɜːfɪkt] ADJ **1** (= *faultless*) perfecto (*also Gram, Mus*); **nobody is ~** nadie es perfecto; **in ~ condition** en perfectas condiciones; **he spoke ~ English** hablaba un inglés perfecto; **his Spanish is far from ~** su español dista mucho de ser perfecto
2 (= *ideal*) [*moment, solution, place*] ideal, perfecto **3** (= *absolute, utter*) **a ~ fool/stranger** un perfecto idiota/desconocido; **I have a ~ right to be here** estoy en mi perfecto derecho de estar aquí, tengo todo el derecho del mundo a estar aquí; **it makes ~ sense to me** me parece completamente *or* totalmente lógico
Ⓑ ['pɜːfɪkt] **the ~** el tiempo perfecto
Ⓒ [pə'fekt] VT perfeccionar
Ⓓ ['pɜːfɪkt] CPD ➤ **perfect pitch** (*Mus*) oído *m* perfecto ➤ **perfect tense** tiempo *m* perfecto

perfection [pə'fekʃən] N perfección *f*

perfectionist [pə'fekʃənɪst] N perfeccionista *mf*

perfectly ['pɜːfɪktlɪ] ADV **1** (= *very well*) perfectamente; **the plan worked ~** el plan salió perfectamente *or* a la perfección **2** (= *absolutely, entirely*) [*frank, normal, innocent*] totalmente; **I'm ~ all right** estoy perfectamente; **you know ~ well what my answer will be** bien sabes *or* sabes muy bien qué respuesta te voy a dar

perfidious [pɜː'fɪdɪəs] ADJ (*liter*) pérfido

perforate ['pɜːfəreɪt] VT perforar

perforation [ˌpɜːfə'reɪʃən] N perforación *f*; [*of stamp*] perforado *m*

perform [pə'fɔːm] **Ⓐ** VT **1** (*Theat, Mus*) [+ *play*] representar; [+ *part, piece, song, dance*] interpretar
2 (= *carry out*) [+ *task, experiment, feat*] realizar, llevar a cabo; [+ *function, role*] desempeñar, cumplir
Ⓑ VI **1** (*Theat, Mus*) [*entertainer, actor*] actuar; [*musician*] tocar; [*orchestra, pop group*] actuar, tocar; [*singer*] cantar; [*dancer*] bailar; **he ~ed brilliantly as Hamlet** interpretó brillantemente el papel de Hamlet, se lució en el papel de Hamlet
2 (= *respond, behave*) [*vehicle, machine, team*] responder; [*investment, shares*] rendir; **our economy has been ~ing well recently** nuestra economía ha estado generando buenos resultados últimamente

performance [pə'fɔːməns] **Ⓐ** N **1** (*Theat, Mus etc*) **1.1** (= *session*) (*Theat*) función *f*; (*Cine*) sesión *f*; **two ~s nightly** (*Theat*) dos funciones *or* representaciones por noche; (*Cine*) dos sesiones por noche **1.2** (= *presentation*) [*of play, opera, ballet*] representación *f*; [*of piece of music*]

interpretación f; **it has not had a ~ since 1950** (*Theat*) no se ha representado desde 1950; (*Mus*) no se ha interpretado desde 1950 **1.3** (*by actor, singer*) actuación f, interpretación f; (*by pianist, orchestra*) interpretación f; (*by comedian*) actuación f; **his ~ as Don Juan was excellent** su actuación en el papel *or* su interpretación del papel de Don Juan fue excelente
2 (= *effectiveness*) [*of investment, worker*] rendimiento m; [*of team, athlete*] actuación f; [*of company, exam candidate*] resultados mpl; [*of vehicle*] rendimiento m, performance f (*LAm*); [*of machine*] (= *productivity*) rendimiento m; (= *working*) funcionamiento m; **the ~ of the pound against the mark** el comportamiento de la libra con respecto al marco
3 (= *execution*) [*of task*] realización f, ejecución f; [*of duty*] cumplimiento m; [*of function*] ejercicio m; [*of rite, ritual*] práctica f, celebración f
4 (*) (= *bother, rigmarole*) jaleo* m, follón m (*Sp**); **it's such a ~ getting here** llegar aquí supone tal jaleo *or* (*Sp*) follón* **Ⓑ** CPD ➤ **performance art** performance art m, arte m de interpretar

performer [pəˈfɔːməʳ] N (*Theat*) actor/actriz m/f, artista mf; (*Mus*) intérprete mf

performing [pəˈfɔːmɪŋ] ADJ [*animal*] amaestrado ➤ **performing arts** artes fpl de la interpretación *or* interpretativas

perfume Ⓐ [ˈpɜːfjuːm] N perfume m **Ⓑ** [pəˈfjuːm] VT perfumar

perfunctory [pəˈfʌŋktərɪ] ADJ [*inspection, glance*] superficial, somero; [*kiss*] indiferente, mecánico

perhaps [pəˈhæps] ADV quizá(s), tal vez; ~ **he'll come** quizá *or* tal vez venga, a lo mejor viene; **"will you be seeing her later?" — "perhaps"** —¿la vas a ver después? —a lo mejor *or* —tal vez *or* —puede que sí; ~ **not** puede que no; ~ **so** puede que sí, puede que así sea, quizá sea así

peril [ˈperɪl] N riesgo m, peligro m; **to be in ~** estar en *or* correr peligro; **do it at your ~** hágalo por su cuenta y riesgo

perilous [ˈperɪləs] ADJ peligroso, arriesgado

perilously [ˈperɪləslɪ] ADV peligrosamente; **he came ~ close to being caught** estuvieron a punto de cogerlo, por poco lo agarran*

perimeter [pəˈrɪmɪtəʳ] N perímetro m ➤ **perimeter fence** valla f que rodea el recinto

period [ˈpɪərɪəd] **Ⓐ** N **1** (= *length of time*) período m; (= *time limit*) plazo m; (= *era*) época f; (= *stage*) (*in career, development etc*) etapa f; **for a ~ of three weeks** durante (un período de) tres semanas; **within a three month ~** en tres meses, dentro de (un plazo de) tres meses; **the postwar ~** la posguerra; **the Victorian ~** la época victoriana; **a painting from his early ~** un cuadro de su primera época
2 (= *lesson*) clase f, hora f; **we have two French ~s** tenemos dos clases *or* horas de francés
3 (*US*) (= *full stop*) punto m; **I said no, ~** he dicho que no, y punto
4 (= *menstruation*) período m, regla f; **I've got my ~** estoy con *or* tengo la regla
Ⓑ CPD [*furniture*] de época ➤ **period costume, period dress** traje(s) mpl de época ➤ **period pain** dolores fpl menstruales ➤ **period piece** (= *film*) película f de época; (= *novel*) novela f de época *or* histórica

periodic [ˌpɪərɪˈɒdɪk] ADJ periódico ➤ **periodic table** tabla f periódica

periodical [ˌpɪərɪˈɒdɪkəl] **Ⓐ** ADJ periódico **Ⓑ** N revista f, publicación f periódica

periodically [ˌpɪərɪˈɒdɪkəlɪ] ADV (= *at regular intervals*) periódicamente; (= *from time to time*) cada cierto tiempo, de vez en cuando

peripatetic [ˌperɪpəˈtetɪk] ADJ [*teacher*] que trabaja en varios centros

peripheral [pəˈrɪfərəl] ADJ [*vision, area*] periférico; [*role, concern*] secundario

periphery [pəˈrɪfərɪ] N periferia f

periscope [ˈperɪskəʊp] N periscopio m

perish [ˈperɪʃ] VI **1** [*person*] perecer, fallecer; **he ~ed at sea**

murió en el mar; ~ **the thought!** ¡Dios me libre! **2** [*food, material*] deteriorarse, estropearse

perishable [ˈperɪʃəbl] **Ⓐ** ADJ perecedero **Ⓑ** N **perishables** productos mpl perecederos

perishing* [ˈperɪʃɪŋ] ADJ (*Brit*) (*also* ~ **cold**) **it's ~** hace un frío de muerte*, hace un frío que pela*

peritonitis [ˌperɪtəˈnaɪtɪs] N peritonitis f

periwinkle [ˈperɪwɪŋkl] N (= *flower*) vincapervinca f; (= *animal*) caracol m de mar, bígaro m

perjure [ˈpɜːdʒəʳ] VT **to ~ o.s.** jurar en falso, perjurar

perjury [ˈpɜːdʒərɪ] N perjurio m; **to commit ~** cometer perjurio

perk* [pɜːk] N (= *money*) beneficio m adicional; **it's one of the ~s of the job** es uno de los incentivos *or* las ventajas del puesto
➤ **perk up Ⓐ** VT + ADV [+ *person*] animar **Ⓑ** VI + ADV [*person*] animarse, reanimarse; (*in health*) sentirse mejor; **business is ~ing up** el negocio va mejorando

perky [ˈpɜːkɪ] ADJ (*compar* **perkier**; *superl* **perkiest**) alegre, animado

perm* [pɜːm] (*Brit*) **Ⓐ** N permanente f; **to have a ~** hacerse una permanente **Ⓑ** VT **to ~ sb's hair** hacer una permanente a algn; **to have one's hair ~ed** hacerse una permanente

permanence [ˈpɜːmənəns] N permanencia f

permanent [ˈpɜːmənənt] **Ⓐ** ADJ permanente; [*damage*] irreparable; [*job*] estable, fijo; [*relationship*] estable; **on a ~ basis** de forma permanente; **I lived in a ~ state of fear** vivía en un estado de miedo continuo *or* permanente **Ⓑ** N (*US*) = **perm A Ⓒ** CPD ➤ **permanent address** domicilio m permanente ➤ **permanent staff** personal m fijo *or* (*Sp*) de plantilla

permanently [ˈpɜːmənəntlɪ] ADV [*live, go away, come back*] permanentemente; [*damage*] irreparablemente, de forma permanente; [*stain, disqualify, ban*] para siempre

permeable [ˈpɜːmɪəbl] ADJ permeable

permeate [ˈpɜːmɪeɪt] **Ⓐ** VT **1** [*liquid*] penetrar, impregnar; [*smell*] impregnar; [*substance, chemical*] penetrar; **to be ~d with** estar impregnado de **2** [*ideology, corruption*] estar presente en **Ⓑ** VI **1 to ~ through sth** [*liquid, substance, chemical*] penetrar a través de algo **2** [*ideology, corruption*] extenderse, propagarse (**through** por)

permissible [pəˈmɪsəbl] ADJ permisible, lícito; **it is not ~ to do that** no se permite *or* está permitido hacer eso

permission [pəˈmɪʃən] N permiso m; **to ask (sb's) ~ to do sth** pedir permiso (a algn) para hacer algo; **by ~ of** con permiso *or* autorización de; **to get ~ from sb (to do sth)** obtener permiso de algn (para hacer algo); **to give ~ (for sth)** dar *or* conceder permiso (para algo); **to give sb ~ (to do sth)** dar permiso a algn (para hacer algo); **with your ~** con su permiso; **without ~** sin permiso

permissive [pəˈmɪsɪv] ADJ permisivo; **the ~ society** la sociedad permisiva

permit Ⓐ [ˈpɜːmɪt] N (= *licence*) permiso m, licencia f; (= *pass*) pase m; (= *permission*) permiso m; **building ~** permiso m de de obras
Ⓑ [pəˈmɪt] VT permitir; **"smoking is not permitted on the car deck"** "está prohibido fumar *or* no se permite fumar en la cubierta de automóviles"; **to ~ sb to do sth** permitir a algn hacer algo, permitir que algn haga algo
Ⓒ [pəˈmɪt] VI **if time ~s** si hay tiempo (suficiente); **weather ~ting** si el tiempo lo permite
Ⓓ [ˈpɜːmɪt] CPD ➤ **permit holder** titular mf de un permiso

permutation [ˌpɜːmjʊˈteɪʃən] N **1** (*Math*) permutación f **2** (= *variety, combination*) combinación f

pernicious [pɜːˈnɪʃəs] ADJ pernicioso

pernickety* [pəˈnɪkɪtɪ] ADJ [*person*] quisquilloso, chinche*, remilgado; **she's ~ about food** es exigente para la comida; **he's terribly ~ about punctuality** tiene la manía de la puntualidad

peroxide [pəˈrɒksaɪd] N peróxido m ➤ **peroxide blonde** rubia f teñida, rubia f de bote (*Sp*)

perpendicular [ˌpɜːpənˈdɪkjʊləʳ] **Ⓐ** ADJ perpendicular **Ⓑ** N perpendicular f

perpetrate [ˈpɜːpɪtreɪt] VT cometer; (Jur) perpetrar

perpetrator [ˈpɜːpɪtreɪtəʳ] N autor(a) m/f, responsable mf

perpetual [pəˈpetjʊəl] ADJ [youth] eterno; [state, smile, snow] perpetuo; [complaints] continuo, constante

perpetually [pəˈpetjʊəlɪ] ADV (= eternally) permanentemente; (= continually) constantemente, continuamente; **we were ~ hungry** teníamos siempre hambre

perpetuate [pəˈpetjʊeɪt] VT perpetuar

perpetuity [ˌpɜːpɪˈtjuːɪtɪ] N perpetuidad f; **in ~ a** perpetuidad

perplex [pəˈpleks] VT (= puzzle) dejar perplejo; (= confuse) desconcertar, confundir

perplexed [pəˈplekst] ADJ perplejo, confuso

perplexing [pəˈpleksɪŋ] ADJ [issue, question, problem] complicado

persecute [ˈpɜːsɪkjuːt] VT perseguir; (= harass) acosar; **they were ~d under the Nazis** sufrieron persecución bajo los nazis

persecution [ˌpɜːsɪˈkjuːʃən] N persecución f
➤ **persecution complex** complejo m persecutorio

perseverance [ˌpɜːsɪˈvɪərəns] N perseverancia f

persevere [ˌpɜːsɪˈvɪəʳ] VI perseverar, persistir (**in** en); **to ~ with** perseverar con, continuar con

persevering [ˌpɜːsɪˈvɪərɪŋ] ADJ perseverante, tenaz

Persia [ˈpɜːʃə] N Persia f

Persian [ˈpɜːʃən] **Ⓐ** ADJ persa **Ⓑ** N 1 (= person) persa mf 2 (Ling) persa m **Ⓒ** CPD ➤ **Persian carpet** alfombra f persa ➤ **Persian cat** gato m persa ➤ **Persian Gulf** Golfo m Pérsico

persist [pəˈsɪst] VI 1 [belief, rumour, symptoms] persistir 2 (= insist) **we shall ~ in our efforts to do it** seguiremos esforzándonos por hacerlo; **he ~s in calling me at all hours of the day** se empeña or insiste en llamarme a todas horas del día

persistence [pəˈsɪstəns] N 1 (= tenacity) perseverancia f 2 (of symptoms, disease) persistencia f

persistent [pəˈsɪstənt] **Ⓐ** ADJ 1 (= tenacious) [person] insistente 2 (= constant) [rumours, rain, headache] persistente; [problem] continuo, que persiste; [questions, refusal, denial] continuo, constante **Ⓑ** CPD ➤ **persistent offender** multirreincidente mf, delincuente mf habitual ➤ **persistent vegetative state** estado m vegetativo persistente

persistently [pəˈsɪstəntlɪ] ADV 1 (= tenaciously) persistentemente, con persistencia 2 (= continually) constantemente

persnickety* [pəˈsnɪkɪtɪ] ADJ (US) = **pernickety**

person [ˈpɜːsn] N (pl **people** or (frm)~**s**) (= individual) persona f; **Jane was the last ~ to see him** Jane fue la última (persona) que lo vio; **I don't know of any such ~** no conozco a tal persona; **to have a weapon concealed about one's ~** llevar encima una arma oculta; **Steve is a cat ~** Steve es muy amante de los gatos; **I'm not much of a city ~ myself** no soy de los que les gusta la ciudad*; **in ~** en persona; **in the first/third ~** en primera/tercera persona

persona [pɜːˈsəʊnə] N (pl **-e** [pɜːˈsəʊniː]) personaje m

personable [ˈpɜːsnəbl] ADJ bien parecido

personage [ˈpɜːsnɪdʒ] N personaje m

personal [ˈpɜːsnl] **Ⓐ** ADJ 1 (= individual) personal; **I will give it my ~ attention** me encargaré personalmente; **I know from ~ experience that ...** sé por experiencia personal que ...; **he was a ~ friend** era un amigo íntimo or personal; **to have/take a ~ interest in sth** tener un interés personal en or por algo, interesarse personalmente en or por algo; **my ~ opinion is that ...** en mi opinión personal ... 2 (= private) personal; **"personal"** (on letter) "confidencial"; **~ belongings** efectos mpl or cosas fpl personales; **they don't allow ~ calls on the office phone** no permiten que se hagan llamadas particulares en el teléfono de la oficina; **his ~ life** su vida personal or privada; **a ~ matter** un asunto personal; **for ~ reasons** por razones personales

3 [visit, interview] en persona; **to make a ~ appearance** hacer acto de presencia 4 [abuse, insult, remark] de carácter personal; **there's no need to get ~** no hace falta llevar las cosas al terreno personal; **I have nothing ~ against him** no tengo nada personal en contra suya; **to ask ~ questions** hacer preguntas personales or de carácter personal 5 (= physical) personal; **~ appearance** aspecto m (físico) **Ⓑ** N (US) (= advert) anuncio m en la sección de citas; **personals = personal column Ⓒ** CPD ➤ **personal assistant** ayudante mf personal (**to** de); ➤ **personal best** (Sport) marca f personal ➤ **personal column** (Brit) (for births, deaths and marriages) (páginas fpl) sociales fpl (y necrológicas); (for lonely hearts) (sección f de) anuncios mpl personales ➤ **personal computer** ordenador (Sp) m or (LAm) computadora f personal ➤ **personal effects** efectos mpl personales ➤ **personal identification number** número m de identificación personal ➤ **personal loan** préstamo m personal ➤ **personal organizer** (paper) agenda f personal; (electronic) agenda f personal electrónica ➤ **personal pronoun** pronombre m personal ➤ **personal secretary** secretario/a m/f personal ➤ **personal stereo** Walkman® m, equipo m de música personal ➤ **personal trainer** preparador(a) m/f

personality [ˌpɜːsəˈnælɪtɪ] **Ⓐ** N 1 (= nature, charisma) personalidad f; **a woman of great ~** una mujer de gran personalidad 2 (= celebrity) figura f, personaje m; **a well-known TV ~** una conocida figura de la TV **Ⓑ** CPD ➤ **personality clash** incompatibilidad f de caracteres ➤ **personality cult** culto m a la personalidad ➤ **personality disorder** trastornos mpl de personalidad

personalize [ˈpɜːsənəlaɪz] VT [+ argument, issue] llevar al terreno de lo personal

personalized [ˈpɜːsənəlaɪzd] ADJ [stationery] con membrete; [service] personalizado, individualizado ➤ **personalized number plate** matrícula personalizada, que contiene, por ejemplo, las iniciales del propietario

personally [ˈpɜːsnəlɪ] ADV personalmente; **~ I think that ...** personalmente creo que ...; **I didn't mean it ~** no pretendía ofenderte; **don't take it too ~** no te lo tomes a mal

personification [pɜːˌsɒnɪfɪˈkeɪʃən] N personificación f

personify [pɜːˈsɒnɪfaɪ] VT personificar; **he is greed personified** es la codicia personificada or en persona, es la personificación de la codicia

personnel [ˌpɜːsəˈnel] N (= staff) personal m; (= department) departamento m de personal, sección f de personal ➤ **personnel carrier** vehículo m militar para transporte de tropas ➤ **personnel department** departamento m de personal, sección f de personal ➤ **personnel management** administración f de personal, gestión f de personal ➤ **personnel manager** jefe/a m/f de personal ➤ **personnel officer** jefe/a m/f de personal (subordinado al "personnel manager" si lo hay)

person-to-person [ˌpɜːsntəˈpɜːsn] ADJ ➤ **person-to-person call** llamada f (de) persona a persona

perspective [pəˈspektɪv] N 1 (Art) perspectiva f; **to be in/out of ~** estar/no estar en perspectiva 2 (fig) perspectiva f; **it has given him a new ~ on life** le ha dado una nueva perspectiva or visión de la vida; **from our ~** desde nuestro punto de vista; **let's get things in ~** pongamos las cosas en su sitio; **to keep sth in ~** guardar algo en su justa medida; **it helped me put things into ~** me ayudó a ver las cosas con cierta perspectiva or en su justa medida

Perspex® [ˈpɜːspeks] N (Brit) plexiglás® m

perspicacious [ˌpɜːspɪˈkeɪʃəs] ADJ perspicaz

perspicacity [ˌpɜːspɪˈkæsɪtɪ] N perspicacia f

perspiration [ˌpɜːspəˈreɪʃən] N transpiración f (frm), sudor m; **to be bathed in ~** estar bañado en sudor, estar todo sudoroso

perspire [pəsˈpaɪəʳ] VI transpirar (frm), sudar

persuadable [pəˈsweɪdəbl] ADJ influenciable, persuasible

persuade [pəˈsweɪd] VT convencer, persuadir (frm); **she is easily ~d** se deja convencer or persuadir fácilmente; **she didn't need any persuading** no hizo falta insistirle, no hizo falta que la persuadieran or convencieran; **he is not ~d of**

the need for electoral reform la necesidad de una reforma electoral no lo convence; **to ~ sb to do sth** convencer a algn de que *or* para que haga algo, persuadir a algn para que haga algo; **to ~ sb that** convencer a algn de que

persuasion [pə'sweɪʒən] N **1** (= *act*) persuasión *f*; **I wouldn't need much ~ to stop working nights** costaría poco convencerme de *or* para que dejara de trabajar por la noche **2** (= *belief*) (*Rel*) creencia *f*; (*Pol*) ideología *f*

persuasive [pə'sweɪsɪv] ADJ [*person, voice, tone*] persuasivo; [*argument, evidence*] convincente

persuasively [pə'sweɪsɪvlɪ] ADV de modo persuasivo

persuasiveness [pə'sweɪsɪvnɪs] N persuasiva *f*

pert [pɜːt] ADJ **1** (= *coquettish*) [*young woman, hat*] coqueto **2** [*nose*] respingón; [*breasts*] levantado

pertain [pɜː'teɪn] VI **to ~ to** (= *concern*) concernir a, estar relacionado con

pertinence ['pɜːtɪnəns] N pertinencia *f*

pertinent ['pɜːtɪnənt] ADJ pertinente (**to** a)

perturb [pə'tɜːb] VT **1** (= *distress*) inquietar, preocupar; **he didn't seem in the least ~ed** no parecía estar inquieto *or* preocupado en lo más mínimo **2** (= *disturb*) [+ *calm, harmony*] perturbar

Peru [pə'ruː] N Perú *m*

perusal [pə'ruːzəl] N examen *m*; **a copy is enclosed for your ~** adjunta se ha enviado una copia para que la examine

peruse [pə'ruːz] VT [+ *book, menu*] leer detenidamente, examinar con detenimiento

Peruvian [pə'ruːvɪən] ADJ, N peruano/a *m/f*

pervade [pɜː'veɪd] VT [*smell*] extenderse por; [*light*] difundirse por; [*feeling, atmosphere*] impregnar; [*influence, ideas*] extenderse por; **this prejudice ~s our society** este prejuicio está extendido en nuestra sociedad

pervasive [pɜː'veɪsɪv] ADJ [*smell*] penetrante; [*feeling, influence*] dominante; [*superstition, belief, presence*] generalizado

perverse [pə'vɜːs] ADJ (= *contrary*) retorcido; (= *obstinate*) terco, contumaz; (= *wicked*) perverso

perversely [pə'vɜːslɪ] ADV (= *irrationally*) sin ninguna lógica; (= *obstinately*) tercamente; (= *wickedly*) con perversidad

perversion [pə'vɜːʃən] N (*Med, Psych*) perversión *f*; [*of justice*] deformación *f*; [*of truth, facts*] tergiversación *f*

perversity [pə'vɜːsɪtɪ] N (= *contrariness*) contrariedad *f*; (= *obstinacy*) terquedad *f*, contumacia *f*

pervert **Ⓐ** [pə'vɜːt] VT **1** (= *corrupt*) pervertir **2** (= *twist*) [+ *facts, truth*] distorsionar, tergiversar; **to ~ the course of justice** torcer el curso de la justicia **Ⓑ** ['pɜːvɜːt] N pervertido/a *m/f*

perverted [pə'vɜːtɪd] ADJ pervertido

peseta [pə'setə] N peseta *f*

pesky* ['peskɪ] ADJ (*compar* **peskier**; *superl* **peskiest**) molesto

pessary ['pesərɪ] N pesario *m*

pessimism ['pesɪmɪzəm] N pesimismo *m*

pessimist ['pesɪmɪst] N pesimista *mf*

pessimistic [ˌpesɪ'mɪstɪk] ADJ pesimista

pest [pest] **Ⓐ** N **1** (*Zool*) plaga *f*; (= *insect*) insecto *m* nocivo; (= *animal*) animal *m* dañino, animal *m* nocivo **2** (*fig*) (= *person*) pelma *mf* (*Sp***), pelmazo/a *m/f* (*Sp***), fregón/ona *m/f* (*LAm***) **Ⓑ** CPD ➤ **pest control** lucha *f* contra las plagas de insectos y ratas

pester ['pestə'] VT molestar, fregar (*LAm*); **he's always ~ing me** siempre me está dando la lata*; **she ~ed me for the book** estuvo dando la lata para que le prestara el libro*; **he ~s me with his questions** me fastidia con sus preguntas; **to ~ sb to do sth** dar la lata a algn para que haga algo*

pesticide ['pestɪsaɪd] N pesticida *m*

pestilence ['pestɪləns] N pestilencia *f*, peste *f*

pestle ['pesl] N mano *f* (de mortero)

pet [pet] **Ⓐ** N **1** (= *animal*) animal *m* doméstico, mascota *f* **2** (*) (= *favourite*) preferido/a *m/f*; **she's teacher's ~** es la preferida de la profesora, es la enchufada de la profesora* **3** (*Brit***) (*term of affection*) cielo *m*; **come here, (my) ~** ven aquí mi cielo *or* amor; **be a ~ and fetch me my glasses** sé un cielo y alcánzame las gafas **Ⓑ** ADJ **1** (= *domesticated*) **he had a ~ monkey** tenía un mono domesticado; **he lives alone with his ~ dog** vive solo con su perro **2** [*theory, project*] preferido, favorito; **~ hate** pesadilla *f* **Ⓒ** VT (= *fondle*) acariciar **Ⓓ** VI (*sexually*) sobarse*, acariciarse **Ⓔ** CPD ➤ **pet door** (*US*) gatera *f* ➤ **pet food** comida *f* para animales ➤ **pet name** diminutivo *m* cariñoso ➤ **pet owner** dueño/a *m/f* de animal ➤ **pet shop**, **pet store** (*US*) tienda *f* de animales

petal ['petl] N pétalo *m*

Pete [piːt] N ♦ IDIOM **for ~'s sake!*** ¡por (el amor de) Dios!

peter out [ˌpiːtər'aʊt] VI [*conversation*] irse acabando; [*road, stream*] perderse, desaparecer; [*interest, excitement*] desvanecerse, decaer; [*plan*] quedar en nada; [*song, noise, voice*] apagarse; **the road ~ed out into a track** la carretera dio paso a un camino, la carretera se transformó en camino

petit bourgeois [ˌpetɪ'bʊəʒwaː] ADJ, N pequeñoburgués/ esa *m/f*

petite [pə'tiːt] ADJ chiquita

petition [pə'tɪʃən] N (= *list of names*) petición *f*; **to get up a ~** organizar una recogida de firmas

petitioner [pə'tɪʃnə'] N (*gen*) peticionario/a *m/f*; (*Jur*) demandante *mf*

petrify ['petrɪfaɪ] VT (= *terrify*) aterrorizar, horrorizar

petrochemical [ˌpetrəʊ'kemɪkəl] **Ⓐ** ADJ petroquímico **Ⓑ** N petrochemicals productos *mpl* petroquímicos

petrodollar ['petrəʊˌdɒlə'] N petrodólar *m*

petrol ['petrəl] (*Brit*) N gasolina *f*, nafta *f* (*Arg*), bencina *f* (*Chi*); (*for lighter*) bencina *f*; **to run out of ~** quedarse sin gasolina ➤ **petrol bomb** bomba *f* de gasolina ➤ **petrol can** bidón *m* de gasolina ➤ **petrol cap** tapón *m* del depósito ➤ **petrol engine** motor *m* de gasolina ➤ **petrol gauge** indicador *m* de nivel de gasolina ➤ **petrol pump** surtidor *m* de gasolina ➤ **petrol station** gasolinera *f*, estación *f* de servicio, bencinera *f* (*Chi*), surtidor *m* (*Bol*), grifo *m* (*Per*) ➤ **petrol tank** depósito *m* de gasolina ➤ **petrol tanker** camión *m* cisterna

petroleum [pɪ'trəʊlɪəm] N petróleo *m* ➤ **petroleum jelly** vaselina *f*

petticoat ['petɪkəʊt] N (= *underskirt*) enagua(s) *f(pl)*; (= *slip*) combinación *f*

pettifogging ['petɪfɒgɪŋ] ADJ [*detail*] insignificante, nimio; [*lawyer*] pedante; [*suggestion*] hecho para entenebrecer el asunto

pettiness ['petɪnɪs] N mezquindad *f*, estrechez *f* de miras

petting* ['petɪŋ] N caricias *fpl*, manoseo *m*

petty ['petɪ] **Ⓐ** ADJ (*compar* **pettier**; *superl* **pettiest**) **1** (= *trivial*) [*detail*] insignificante, nimio; [*squabble, rivalry, concerns*] pequeño, trivial **2** (= *small-minded*) mezquino **Ⓑ** CPD ➤ **petty cash** dinero *m* para gastos menores, caja *f* chica* ➤ **petty crime** delito *m* menor ➤ **petty officer** suboficial *mf* de marina ➤ **petty thief** ladrón/ona *m/f* de poca monta

petulance ['petjʊləns] N mal humor *m*, irritabilidad *f*

petulant ['petjʊlənt] ADJ [*person, voice*] malhumorado, irritable; [*gesture*] malhumorado, de irritación

pew [pjuː] N banco *m* (de iglesia); **take a ~!*** (*hum*) ¡siéntate!

pewter ['pjuːtə'] **Ⓐ** N peltre *m* **Ⓑ** CPD de peltre

PG ABBR (*Brit*) (= **Parental Guidance**) ≈ menores acompañados

PG 13 [ˌpiːdʒiː'θɜːtiːn] ABBR (*US*) (= **Parental Guidance 13**) no apto para menores de 13 años

PGCE N ABBR (*Brit*) (= **Postgraduate Certificate in Education**) ≈ C.A.P. *m*

PH ABBR (*US Mil*) (= **Purple Heart**) *decoración otorgada a los heridos de guerra*

pH ABBR (= **potential of hydrogen**) pH *m*

phallic ['fælɪk] ADJ fálico

phallus ['fæləs] N (*pl* **phalli** ['fælaɪ]) falo *m*

phantom ['fæntəm] N fantasma *m* ➤ **phantom pregnancy** embarazo *m* psicológico

Pharaoh ['feərəʊ] N Faraón *m*

pharmaceutical [ˌfɑːmə'sjuːtɪkəl] ❹ ADJ farmacéutico ❸ pharmaceuticals NPL productos *mpl* farmacéuticos

pharmacist ['fɑːməsɪst] N farmacéutico/a *m/f*; **the ~'s** (*esp Brit*) la farmacia

pharmacology [ˌfɑːmə'kɒlədʒɪ] N farmacología *f*

pharmacy ['fɑːməsɪ] N farmacia *f*

phase [feɪz] ❹ N **1** (= *stage*) etapa *f*, fase *f*; **she'll get over it, it's just a ~** (**she's going through**) se le pasará, es algo pasajero; **a passing ~** una etapa pasajera **2** (*Astron*) fase *f*; **the ~s of the moon** las fases de la luna ❸ VT (= *introduce gradually*) escalonar, llevar a cabo de forma escalonada; **~d withdrawal** retirada *f* progresiva
➤ **phase in** VT + ADV introducir progresivamente
➤ **phase out** VT + ADV [+ *machinery, product*] retirar progresivamente; [+ *job*] eliminar por etapas; [+ *subsidy*] eliminar progresivamente; [+ *production*] parar progresivamente

PhD N ABBR = **Doctor of Philosophy** (= *qualification*) doctorado *m*; (= *person*) doctor(a) *m/f* en filosofía

pheasant ['feznt] N faisán *m*

phenomena [fɪ'nɒmɪnə] NPL *of* **phenomenon**

phenomenal [fɪ'nɒmɪnl] ADJ [*memory, success, strength*] extraordinario; [*speed*] espectacular

phenomenally [fɪ'nɒmɪnəlɪ] ADV extraordinariamente; **to be ~ successful** tener un éxito extraordinario

phenomenon [fɪ'nɒmɪnən] N (*pl* **phenomena**) fenómeno *m*

pheromone ['ferəməʊn] N feromona *f*

phew [fjuː] EXCL ¡uf!, ¡puf!

phial ['faɪəl] N ampolla *f*, redoma *f*

Phi Beta Kappa [ˌfaɪbeɪtə'kæpə] N (*US Univ*) *asociación de antiguos alumnos sobresalientes*

Phil. [fɪl] ABBR = **Philadelphia**

Philadelphia [ˌfɪlə'delfɪə] N Filadelfia *f*

philanderer [fɪ'lændərər] N Don Juan *m*, tenorio *m*

philanthropic [ˌfɪlən'θrɒpɪk] ADJ filantrópico

philanthropist [fɪ'lænθrəpɪst] N filántropo/a *m/f*

philanthropy [fɪ'lænθrəpɪ] N filantropía *f*

philatelist [fɪ'lætəlɪst] N filatelista *mf*

philately [fɪ'lætəlɪ] N filatelia *f*

Philippines ['fɪlɪpiːnz] NPL **the ~** (las) Filipinas *fpl*

Philistine ['fɪlɪstaɪn] N (= *ignorant person*) inculto/a *m/f*

Phillips screwdriver® [ˌfɪlɪps'skruːdraɪvər] N destornillador *m* de estrella

philologist [fɪ'lɒlədʒɪst] N filólogo/a *m/f*

philology [fɪ'lɒlədʒɪ] N filología *f*

philosopher [fɪ'lɒsəfər] N filósofo/a *m/f*

philosophical [ˌfɪlə'sɒfɪkəl] ADJ filosófico; **she was ~ about the delay** se tomó el retraso con filosofía

philosophically [ˌfɪlə'sɒfɪkəlɪ] ADV (= *with resignation*) con filosofía

philosophize [fɪ'lɒsəfaɪz] VI filosofar

philosophy [fɪ'lɒsəfɪ] N filosofía *f*; **his ~ of life** su filosofía de la vida

phlegm [flem] N flema *f*

phlegmatic [fleg'mætɪk] ADJ flemático

phobia ['fəʊbɪə] N fobia *f*

phoenix ['fiːnɪks] N fénix *m*

phone [fəʊn] ❹ N teléfono *m*; **to be on the ~** (*Brit*) (= *have a telephone*) tener teléfono; (= *be in conversation*) estar hablando por teléfono; **there's someone on the ~ for you**

te llama alguien por teléfono, hay alguien al teléfono que quiere hablar contigo; **I spent an hour on the ~** me pasé una hora al teléfono; **I can't talk about it <u>over</u> the ~** no puedo hablar de ello por teléfono; **to <u>put down</u> the ~** colgar el teléfono
❸ VT [+ *person*] llamar (por teléfono); [+ *number*] llamar a ❺ VI llamar (*por teléfono*); **shall I ~ for a taxi?** ¿llamo a un taxi?, ¿quieres que llame a *or* pida un taxi?
❹ CPD ➤ **phone bill** cuenta *f* del teléfono, factura *f* del teléfono ➤ **phone book** guía *f* (telefónica) ➤ **phone book** (*US*), **phone box** (*Brit*) cabina *f* (telefónica) ➤ **phone call** llamada *f* (telefónica) ➤ **phone company** compañía *f* telefónica ➤ **phone line** línea *f* de teléfono ➤ **phone number** número *m* de teléfono ➤ **phone tapping** intervención *f* telefónica, pinchazo *m* de teléfono*
➤ **phone back** VT + ADV, VI + ADV (= *return call*) llamar; (= *call again*) volver a llamar
➤ **phone in** ❹ VI + ADV llamar; **you could always ~ in sick** siempre podrías llamar diciendo que estás enfermo
❸ VT + ADV **our reporter ~d in this account of what had happened** nuestro reportero nos mandó por teléfono esta versión de lo ocurrido; **you can ~ in your order on 0898 060606** puede hacer su pedido llamando al 0898 060606

phonecard ['fəʊnkɑːd] N tarjeta *f* telefónica *or* de teléfonos

phone-in ['fəʊnɪn] N (*also* **~ programme**) (*esp Brit*) *programa de radio o televisión con participación telefónica del público*

phoneme ['fəʊniːm] N fonema *m*

phonetic [fə'netɪk] ADJ fonético

phonetics [fə'netɪks] N fonética *f*

phoney*, **phony** (*US**) ['fəʊnɪ] ❹ ADJ [*name, document, smile*] falso; [*accent*] fingido; **there's something ~ about it** esto huele a camelo*; **the ~ war** (*Brit*) (*1939*) la guerra ilusoria ❸ N (= *person*) farsante* *mf*

phonograph ['fəʊnəgrɑːf] N (*US*) fonógrafo *m*, tocadiscos *m inv*

phonology [fə'nɒlədʒɪ] N fonología *f*

phony ['fəʊnɪ] (*US*) = **phoney**

phosphate ['fɒsfeɪt] N fosfato *m*

phosphorescent [ˌfɒsfə'resnt] ADJ fosforescente

phosphorus ['fɒsfərəs] N fósforo *m*

photo ['fəʊtəʊ] N (*pl* **~s**) foto *f*; **to take a ~** hacer *or* (*esp LAm*) sacar una foto; **I took a ~ of the bride and groom** les hice una foto a los novios ➤ **photo album** álbum *m* de fotos ➤ **photo booth** cabina *f* de fotos, fotomatón *m* (*Sp*) ➤ **photo finish** resultado *m* comprobado por fotocontrol; (*fig*) final *m* muy reñido ➤ **photo opportunity**, **photo session** sesión *f* de fotos

photocall ['fəʊtəʊkɔːl] N sesión *f* de fotos

photocopier ['fəʊtəʊˌkɒpɪər] N fotocopiadora *f*

photocopy ['fəʊtəʊˌkɒpɪ] ❹ N fotocopia *f* ❸ VT fotocopiar

Photofit® ['fəʊtəʊfɪt] N (*Brit*) retrato *m* robot

photogenic [ˌfəʊtəʊ'dʒenɪk] ADJ fotogénico

photograph ['fəʊtəgrɑːf] ❹ N fotografía *f*, foto *f*; **to take a ~ (of sth/sb)** hacer *or* (*esp LAm*) sacar una foto (a algo/algn) ❸ VT fotografiar, hacer *or* (*esp LAm*) sacar una foto(grafía) a ❺ CPD ➤ **photograph album** álbum *m* de fotos

photographer [fə'tɒgrəfər] N fotógrafo/a *m/f*; **he's a keen ~** es muy aficionado a la fotografía; **a ~'s** (= *shop*) una tienda de fotografía

photographic [ˌfəʊtə'græfɪk] ADJ fotográfico

photography [fə'tɒgrəfɪ] N fotografía *f*

photojournalism [ˌfəʊtəʊ'dʒɜːnəlɪzəm] N fotoperiodismo *m*

photomontage [ˌfəʊtəʊmɒn'tɑːʒ] N fotomontaje *m*

photon ['fəʊtɒn] N fotón *m*

photosensitive [ˌfəʊtəʊ'sensɪtɪv] ADJ fotosensible

photostat† ['fəʊtəʊstæt] ❹ N fotocopia *f* ❸ VT fotocopiar

photosynthesis [ˌfəʊtəʊ'sɪnθəsɪs] N fotosíntesis *f*

phrasal verb [ˌfreɪzəl'vɜːb] N verbo *m* con preposición *or* adverbio

phrase [freɪz] **A** N frase f; **noun/verb** ~ frase f nominal/verbal; **she had picked up some useful ~s** había aprendido algunas frases útiles **B** VT 1 (*orally*) expresar, formular; (*in writing*) redactar, expresar 2 (*Mus*) frasear **C** CPD ➤ **phrase book** libro m de frases

phraseology [ˌfreɪzɪ'ɒlədʒɪ] N fraseología f

phrasing ['freɪzɪŋ] N (= *act*) redacción f; [*of question*] formulación f; (= *style*) estilo m, términos mpl; (*Mus*) fraseo m; **the ~ is rather unfortunate** la forma en que está expresado es bastante desafortunada

phylloxera [ˌfɪlɒk'sɪərə] N filoxera f

physical ['fɪzɪkəl] **A** ADJ (*gen*) físico; [*punishment*] corporal; [*world*] material; **he's a very ~ man** es un hombre que recurre mucho al contacto físico; ~ **evidence** pruebas fpl materiales; **it's a ~ impossibility** es materialmente imposible **B** N (*also* ~ **examination**) reconocimiento m físico **C** CPD ➤ **physical education** educación f física ➤ **physical examination** reconocimiento m físico ➤ **physical exercise** ejercicio m (físico) ➤ **physical fitness** (buena) forma f física ➤ **physical therapist** (*US*) fisioterapeuta mf ➤ **physical therapy** (*US*) fisioterapia f ➤ **physical training** entrenamiento m, ejercicio m (físico)

physically ['fɪzɪkəlɪ] ADV físicamente; **it's very ~ demanding work** es un trabajo que requiere mucho esfuerzo físico; **to be ~ fit** estar en buena forma (física); **it's ~ impossible** es materialmente imposible; **he had to be ~ removed from the premises** lo tuvieron que sacar del local por la fuerza; **the thought of food made me ~ sick** sólo pensar en comer me daba náuseas

physician [fɪ'zɪʃən] N médico/a m/f

physicist ['fɪzɪsɪst] N físico/a m/f

physics ['fɪzɪks] NSING física f

physio* ['fɪzɪəʊ] N ABBR 1 (*esp Brit Sport*) = **physiotherapist** 2 (*Brit*) = **physiotherapy**

physio... ['fɪzɪəʊ] PREF fisio...

physiognomy [ˌfɪzɪ'ɒnəmɪ] N fisonomía f

physiological [ˌfɪzɪə'lɒdʒɪkəl] ADJ fisiológico

physiology [ˌfɪzɪ'ɒlədʒɪ] N fisiología f

physiotherapist [ˌfɪzɪə'θerəpɪst] N fisioterapeuta mf

physiotherapy [ˌfɪzɪə'θerəpɪ] N fisioterapia f

physique [fɪ'ziːk] N físico m

pi [paɪ] N (*pl* **pis**) (*Math*) pi f

pianist ['pɪənɪst] N pianista mf

piano ['pjɑːnəʊ] N (*pl* **~s**) piano m ➤ **piano accordion** acordeón-piano m ➤ **piano concerto** concierto m para piano ➤ **piano lesson** lección f de piano ➤ **piano stool** taburete m de piano ➤ **piano teacher** profesor(a) m/f de piano ➤ **piano tuner** afinador(a) m/f de pianos

picayune* [ˌpɪkə'juːn] (*US*) ADJ insignificante, de poca monta

piccolo ['pɪkələʊ] N (*pl* **~s**) flautín m, píccolo m

pick [pɪk] **A** N 1 (= *choice*) **to have one's ~ of sth** escoger *or* elegir lo que uno quiere de algo; **take your ~!** ¡escoja *or* elija lo que quiera!; **take your ~ of** *or* **from ten luxury hotels** escoja *or* elija el que quiera de entre diez hoteles de lujo 2 (= *best*) **the ~ of sth** lo mejor de algo, la flor y nata de algo; **the ~ of the bunch** *or* **the crop** (*fig*) lo mejor del grupo 3 (*also* ~**axe**) pico m, piqueta f 4 (*US*) (= *plectrum*) púa f **B** VT 1 (= *choose*) (*gen*) escoger, elegir; [+ *team, candidate*] seleccionar; **to ~ a fight (with sb)** (*lit*) buscar pelea *or* pleito (con algn); (*fig*) (= *argument*) discutir (con algn); **to ~ one's way through/across sth** abrirse camino cuidadosamente a través de algo 2 (= *gather*) [+ *flowers, fruit, tea, cotton*] coger, recoger (*LAm*) 3 (= *lift, remove*) **to ~ sth off the ground** recoger algo del suelo; **let me ~ that bit of fluff off your collar** deja que te quite esa pelusa del cuello; **to ~ o.s. off the floor** levantarse del suelo; **to ~ names out of a hat** sacar nombres de un sombrero 4 (= *make*) [+ *hole*] hacer 5 [+ *scab, spot*] toquetear; [+ *lock*] forzar *or* abrir con

ganzúa; [+ *guitar, banjo*] puntear; **their bones had been ~ed clean by the birds** los pájaros habían dejado limpios los huesos; **to ~ one's nose** hurgarse la nariz; **to ~ sb's pocket** robar algo a algn del bolsillo; ✦ IDIOM **to ~ sb's brains** exprimir el coco a algn* **C** VI 1 (= *choose*) escoger, elegir; **you can't ~ and choose** no puedes ponerte a escoger *or* elegir, no puedes ser muy exigente 2 (= *examine*) **dogs ~ through the garbage on the streets** los perros hurgan en *or* por la basura de las calles

➤ **pick at** VI + PREP 1 (= *toy with*) **to ~ at one's food** comer con poca gana, picar (la comida) 2 (*US**) (= *nag*) meterse con

➤ **pick off** VT + ADV 1 (= *remove*) [+ *leaves, fluff, paint*] quitar; [+ *scab*] arrancar 2 (= *shoot*) liquidar*, cargarse (*Sp***); (= *eliminate*) [+ *opponents*] acabar uno a uno con

➤ **pick on** VI + PREP 1 (*esp Brit*) (= *choose, single out*) escoger, elegir 2 (*) (= *harass*) meterse con*; ~ **on someone your own size!** ¡métete con alguien de tu tamaño!*

➤ **pick out** VT + ADV 1 (= *choose*) elegir, escoger 2 (= *draw out*) sacar 3 (= *discern*) distinguir; **I could just ~ out the letters ALG** sólo podía distinguir, y con dificultad, las letras ALG 4 (= *identify*) reconocer; **can you ~ me out in this photo?** ¿sabes quién soy yo en esta foto?, ¿eres capaz de reconocerme en esta foto? 5 (= *highlight*) resaltar; **the name is ~ed out in gold letters** el nombre está resaltado en letras doradas 6 (= *play*) [+ *tune*] tocar de oído

➤ **pick over** VT + ADV ~ **over the raspberries** escoge las frambuesas que estén mejor; **she was ~ing over the shirts in the sale** estaba seleccionando las camisas en las rebajas

➤ **pick up** **A** VT + ADV 1 (= *lift*) [+ *box, suitcase, cat*] levantar; [+ *dropped object*] recoger, coger; (= *take hold of*) tomar, coger, agarrar (*LAm*); **I saw her fall and ran to ~ her up** la vi caerse y fui corriendo a levantarla; **that child is always wanting to be ~ed up** ese niño siempre quiere que lo cojan *or* (*LAm*) levanten; **to ~ up the bill** *or* **tab (for sth)*** pagar la cuenta (de algo); **to ~ o.s. up** (*lit*) levantarse, ponerse de pie; (*fig*) recuperarse, reponerse 2 (= *collect*) [+ *person*] recoger, ir a buscar (*esp LAm*); (= *give lift to*) [+ *hitch-hiker, passenger*] recoger, coger; **did you ~ up my laundry?** ¿recogiste la ropa? 3 (= *learn*) [+ *language, skill*] aprender; [+ *accent, habit*] coger, agarrar (*LAm*) 4 (= *buy*) comprar; (= *find*) encontrar; (= *catch*) [+ *disease*] coger, agarrar (*LAm*), pillar* 5 (*) (= *earn, gain*) ganar; **it ~ed up the best musical award** ganó *or* se llevó el premio al mejor musical; **to ~ up speed** acelerar, coger velocidad, tomar velocidad (*LAm*) 6 (*) (*sexually*) ligarse a* 7 (*Rad, TV*) [+ *station, channel*] captar, coger; (*Tech*) [+ *signal*] captar, registrar 8 (= *notice, detect*) **he ~ed up ten misprints** encontró diez erratas; **she ~ed up every mistake** no se le escapó ni un error 9 (= *resume*) [+ *conversation, narrative*] continuar; [+ *relationship*] reanudar 10 (= *focus on*) **I'd like to ~ up the point David made** quisiera volver al punto que planteó David; **the papers ~ed up the story** los periódicos publicaron la historia 11 (= *reprimand*) reñir, reprender (**for** por) 12 (*esp Brit*) (= *correct*) **he ~ed me up on my grammar** me señaló diversas faltas de gramática; **if I may ~ you up on that point** si me permites corregirte en ese punto 13 (= *arrest*) detener 14 (*US**) (= *tidy*) [+ *room, house*] recoger **B** VI + ADV 1 (= *improve*) [*conditions, weather, sales*] mejorar; [*market, economy*] reponerse; [*business, trade*] ir mejor; [*prices*] volver a subir 2 (= *increase*) [*wind*] levantarse 3 (= *continue*) **to ~ up where one left off** continuar donde se había dejado 4 (= *notice, react to*) **I was getting nervous and he ~ed up on that** me estaba poniendo nervioso y él lo captó *or* se dió cuenta; **the press did not ~ up on it** la prensa no reaccionó ante la noticia 5 (*) (= *become involved with*) **to ~ up with sb** juntarse con algn 6 (= *tidy up*) **to ~ up after sb** ir recogiendo detrás de algn

pickaxe, pickax (*US*) ['pɪkæks] N pico m, piqueta f

picket ['pɪkɪt] **Ⓐ** N (= *strikers*) piquete *m* **Ⓑ** VT [+ *factory*] poner piquetes a la puerta de, piquetear (*LAm*) **Ⓒ** VI formar piquetes, piquetear (*LAm*) **Ⓓ** CPD ➤ **picket duty to be on - duty** estar de guardia ➤ **picket fence** estacada *f*, cerca *f* ➤ **picket line** piquete *m*; **to cross a - line** no hacer caso de un piquete

picketing ['pɪkɪtɪŋ] N formación *f* de piquetes

pickings ['pɪkɪŋz] NPL (= *profits*) ganancias *fpl*; **there are rich - for bargain hunters at these sales** en esta liquidación hay pingües beneficios para los que van a la caza de gangas

pickle ['pɪkl] **Ⓐ** N (= *relish*) salsa *f* macerada; **pickles** encurtidos *mpl*; ✦ IDIOM **to be in a -*** estar en un apuro *or* aprieto **Ⓑ** VT encurtir, escabechar

pickled ['pɪkld] ADJ encurtido, escabechado, en conserva ➤ **pickled herrings** arenques *mpl* en escabeche ➤ **pickled onions** cebollas *fpl* en vinagre

pick-me-up ['pɪkmiːʌp] N estimulante *m*; (= *drink*) bebida *f* tonificante; (*Med*) tónico *m*, reconstituyente *m*

pickpocket ['pɪk,pɒkɪt] N carterista *mf*, bolsista *mf* (*Mex*)

pick-up ['pɪkʌp] **Ⓐ** N **1** (*also* ~ **truck**) furgoneta *f*, camioneta *f* **2** (*in economy, trade, sales*) mejora *f*; (*in prices*) subida *f* **Ⓑ** CPD ➤ **pick-up point** (*for people*) parada *f*

picky* ['pɪkɪ] ADJ (*US*) (*compar* **pickier**; *superl* **pickiest**) **1** (= *critical*) criticón **2** (= *choosy*) melindroso, quisquilloso

picnic ['pɪknɪk] (*vb: pt, pp* **~ked**) **Ⓐ** N picnic *m*, comida *f* al aire libre; **it was no -*** (= *unpleasant*) fue muy desagradable; (= *difficult*) no fue nada fácil **Ⓑ** VI ir de picnic, comer al aire libre; **we ~ked by the river** comimos a la orilla del río **Ⓒ** CPD ➤ **picnic basket** cesta *f or* (*LAm*) canasta *f* de la merienda *or* comida *etc* ➤ **picnic site** lugar *m* destinado para picnics

picnicker ['pɪknɪkəʳ] N excursionista *mf*

pictorial [pɪk'tɔːrɪəl] ADJ [*record, history*] gráfico

picture ['pɪktʃəʳ] **Ⓐ** N **1** (*Art*) (= *print, engraving*) cuadro *m*; (= *drawing*) dibujo *m*; (= *painting*) cuadro *m*, pintura *f*; (= *portrait*) retrato *m*; **to draw a - (of sth/sb)** hacer un dibujo (de algo/algn); **to paint a - (of sth/sb)** pintar un cuadro (de algo/algn); **he painted a black - of the future** nos pintó un cuadro muy negro del porvenir **2** (= *photo*) foto *f*, fotografía *f*; **to take a - of sth/sb** hacer *or* (*esp LAm*) sacar una foto a algo/algn **3** (= *illustration*) ilustración *f* **4** (= *personification*) **he looked the - of health** era la salud personificada **5** (= *wonderful sight*) **the garden is a - in June** el jardín es una preciosidad en junio; **his face was a -*** ¡vaya cara que puso!, ¡vieras *or* hubieras visto su cara! (*LAm*) **6** (= *situation*) panorama *m*; **the overall - is encouraging** el panorama general es alentador; **I get the -*** ya comprendo; **these figures give the general -** estas cifras ofrecen una idea general *or* una visión de conjunto **7** (*Cine*) película *f*; **the -s** (*Brit*) el cine **Ⓑ** VT **1** (= *imagine*) imaginarse; **I never ~d you as a family man** nunca te imaginé *or* te vi como hombre de familia; **~ the scene** figuraos la escena; **~ yourself lying on the beach** imagínate que estás tumbado en la playa **2** (*in painting, film, novel*) representar **Ⓒ** CPD ➤ **picture book** libro *m* ilustrado ➤ **picture frame** marco *m* ➤ **picture messaging** (envío *m* de) mensajes *mpl* con imágenes ➤ **picture postcard** (tarjeta *f*) postal *f* ➤ **picture rail** (*esp Brit*) moldura para colgar cuadros ➤ **picture window** ventanal *m*

picturesque [pɪktʃə'resk] ADJ (= *quaint*) [*village*] pintoresco; [*name, title*] pintoresco, peculiar; (= *vivid*) [*language*] expresivo, vívido

piddling* ['pɪdlɪŋ] ADJ [*sum, amount*] ridículo, irrisorio

pidgin ['pɪdʒɪn] N pidgin *m*

pie [paɪ] N [*of fruit*] tarta *f*, pay *m* (*LAm*); [*of meat, fish*] (= *large*) pastel *m*; (= *small*) empanada *f*; ✦ IDIOM **it's all - in the sky** son castillos en el aire, es pura ilusión ➤ **pie chart** (*Math, Comput*) gráfico *m* de sectores, gráfico *m* circular

piebald ['paɪbɔːld] **Ⓐ** ADJ pío, picazo **Ⓑ** N caballo *m* pío, picazo *m*

piece [piːs] N **1** (= *fragment*) trozo *m*, pedazo *m*; **to come to ~s** (= *fall apart*) hacerse pedazos, romperse; **to fall to ~s** caerse a pedazos, romperse; **a - of bread/cake/cheese** un trozo de pan/queso/tarta; **a - of paper** un trozo *or* una hoja de papel, un papel; **a - of string** un trozo de cuerda, un cabo; **a - of toast** una tostada; **the vase is still in one -** el jarrón sigue intacto; **we got back all in one -** llegamos sanos y salvos; **I smashed the vase to ~s** rompí el jarrón en mil pedazos, hice el jarrón añicos; **the boat was smashed to ~s on the rocks** el barco se estrelló contra las rocas y se hizo añicos; ✦ IDIOMS **to go to ~s** (*emotionally*) quedar deshecho, quedar hecho pedazos; **it's a - of cake*** es pan comido*; **to give sb a - of one's mind** decir cuatro verdades a algn, cantar las cuarenta a algn* **2** (= *part, member of a set*) pieza *f*; **it comes to ~s** se desmonta, es desmontable; **to take sth to ~s** desmontar *or* desarmar algo; **a fifteen-~ tea set** un juego de té de quince piezas **3** (= *item*) **a - of advice** un consejo; **to sell sth by the -** vender algo suelto; **a - of evidence** una prueba; **a - of furniture** un mueble; **a - of information** un dato; **what a - of luck** you called round qué suerte que te hayas pasado por aquí; **you are allowed two ~s of luggage** se le permite llevar dos bultos **4** (= *composition*) (*Press*) artículo *m*; (*Mus, Art, Theat*) pieza *f*; **a piano -** una pieza para piano **5** (*in chess*) pieza *f*; (*in draughts, backgammon*) ficha *f* **6** (= *coin*) moneda *f*; **a 10-pence -** una moneda de 10 peniques; **a - of eight** un real de a ocho **7** (*US**) (= *distance*) **his place is down the road a -** su casa está un poco más allá bajando la calle ➤ **piece together** VT + ADV [+ *jigsaw puzzle, events*] reconstruir; [+ *plan, strategy*] concebir; **we eventually ~d together what had happened** por fin logramos atar todos los cabos de lo que había pasado

piecemeal ['piːsmiːl] **Ⓐ** ADV (= *gradually*) poco a poco, por partes; (= *unsystematically*) de manera poco sistemática **Ⓑ** ADJ [*approach, reform*] poco sistemático; **a - solution** una solución de compromiso

piecework ['piːswɜːk] N trabajo *m* a destajo

pied-à-terre [pjeɪdɑː'teəʳ] N (*pl* **pieds-à-terre** [pjeɪdɑː'teəʳ]) segunda vivienda *f* (*en una ciudad*)

pier [pɪəʳ] N (= *amusement centre*) paseo marítimo situado *como zona de ocio sobre un muelle o malecón*; (= *landing-stage*) embarcadero *m*, muelle *m*

pierce [pɪəs] VT **1** (= *puncture*) perforar; (= *go right through*) atravesar, traspasar; (= *make hole in*) agujerear; **to have one's ears ~d** hacerse los agujeros de las orejas **2** [*sound*] desgarrar, penetrar

piercing ['pɪəsɪŋ] ADJ penetrante, agudo; [*eyes, gaze, cold*] penetrante; [*cry*] desgarrador; [*wind*] cortante; [*pain*] punzante

piety ['paɪətɪ] N piedad *f*, devoción *f*

piffling* ['pɪflɪŋ] ADJ [*dispute, task*] de poca monta, insignificante; [*sum, amount*] ridículo, irrisorio

pig [pɪg] N **1** (= *animal*) cerdo *m*, chancho *m* (*LAm*); ✦ IDIOMS **he made a right ~'s ear of it** (*Brit**) le salió muy mal, le salió un verdadero churro (*Sp**), le salió una auténtica cagada**; **in a ~'s eye!** (*US**) ¡ni hablar!; **yes, and ~s might fly!** cuando las ranas críen pelo; **to be - in the middle** (= *powerless to act, etc*) estar entre dos fuegos; **to buy a - in a poke** comprar algo a ciegas; **to sell sb a - in a poke** dar gato por liebre a algn **2** (*) (= *person*) (*dirty, nasty*) cerdo/a** *m/f*, puerco/a* *m/f*, chancho/a* *m/f* (*LAm*); (*greedy*) comilón/ona* *m/f*, tragón/ona* *m/f*; **you ~!** (*hum*) ¡bandido!; ✦ IDIOM **to make a - o.s.** darse un atracón*, ponerse las botas* **3** (**) (= *policeman*) poli* *m*; **the ~s** la poli*, la pasma (*Sp***), la cana (*SC***) ➤ **pig out*** VI + ADV **to - out (on sth)** darse un atracón *or* ponerse las botas (de algo)*

pig-breeding ['pɪg,briːdɪŋ] N cría *f* de cerdos

pigeon ['pɪdʒən] N (*gen*) paloma *f*; (*as food*) pichón *m* ➤ **pigeon fancier** colombófilo/a *m/f* ➤ **pigeon fancying**

colombofilia *f* ➤ **pigeon loft** palomar *m* ➤ **pigeon post by ~ post** por paloma mensajera

pigeonhole ['pɪdʒənhəʊl] **Ⓐ** N casilla *f* **Ⓑ** VT (= *classify*) encasillar, clasificar

pigeon-toed ['pɪdʒən'təʊd] ADJ **to be ~** tener los pies torcidos hacia dentro

piggy ['pɪgɪ] N cerdito *m*, chanchito *m* (*LAm*); **to play ~ in the middle** jugar al balón prisionero; ✦ IDIOM **to be ~ in the middle** (= *powerless to act, influence*) estar entre dos fuegos

piggyback ['pɪgɪbæk] **Ⓐ** N **to give sb a ~** llevar a algn a cuestas *or* a caballo **Ⓑ** ADV **to carry sb ~** llevar a algn a cuestas

piggybank ['pɪgɪˌbæŋk] N hucha *f* (*Sp*) (en forma de cerdito), alcancía *f* (*LAm*)

pigheaded ['pɪg'hedɪd] ADJ [*person*] terco, testarudo; [*attitude*] obstinado

piglet ['pɪglɪt] N cerdito *m*, lechón *m*, chanchito *m* (*LAm*)

pigment ['pɪgmənt] N pigmento *m*

pigmentation [ˌpɪgmən'teɪʃən] N pigmentación *f*

pigmy ['pɪgmɪ] ADJ, N = **pygmy**

pigpen ['pɪgpen] N (*US*) pocilga *f*, porqueriza *f*

pigskin ['pɪgskɪn] N piel *f* de cerdo, cuero *m* de chancho (*LAm*)

pigsty ['pɪgstaɪ] N (*esp Brit*) pocilga *f*, porqueriza *f*

pigtail ['pɪgteɪl] N (= *plait*) trenza *f*; (*of Chinese*) coleta *f*

pike[1] [paɪk] N (*Mil*) pica *f*

pike[2] [paɪk] (*pl ~ or ~s*) N (= *fish*) lucio *m*

pilchard ['pɪltʃəd] N sardina *f*

pile[1] [paɪl] **Ⓐ** N **1** (= *heap*) [*of books, clothes*] montón *m*; **to put things in a ~** amontonar cosas, juntar cosas en un montón
2 (*) (= *large amount*) montón* *m*; **I've got ~s of work to do** tengo un montón *or* tengo montones de trabajo que hacer*
3 (*) (= *fortune*) dineral* *m*, fortuna *f*; **he made his ~ in oil** hizo su fortuna con el petróleo
4 (*hum**) (= *building*) mole *f* (*hum*); **some stately ~ in the country** una mole de casa *or* un caserón en el campo
Ⓑ VT amontonar, apilar; **he ~d the plates onto the tray** amontonó *or* apiló los platos en la bandeja; **the tables were ~d high with food** en las mesas había montones *or* montañas de comida
Ⓒ VI (*) (= *squeeze*) **we all ~d into the car** nos metimos todos apretujados en el coche; **we ~d off the bus** salimos en avalancha *or* en tropel del autobús
➤ **pile on*** **Ⓐ** VI + ADV (= *crowd on*) meterse a empujones, meterse apretujados **Ⓑ** VT + ADV **they really ~ the work on, don't they?** te dan muchísimo trabajo, ¿verdad?; **to ~ on the pressure** apretar las clavijas; **they were piling it on** estaban exagerando
➤ **pile up** **Ⓐ** VI + ADV (= *accumulate*) [*work*] amontonarse, acumularse **Ⓑ** VT + ADV **1** (= *put in heap*) [+ *books, clothes*] apilar, amontonar **2** (= *accumulate*) [+ *possessions*] acumular; [+ *debts*] acumular, llenarse de

pile[2] [paɪl] N (*Constr*) pilote *m*, pilar *m*

pile[3] [paɪl] N [*of carpet, cloth*] pelo *m*

piles [paɪlz] NPL (= *haemorrhoids*) almorranas *fpl*, hemorroides *fpl*

pile-up* ['paɪlʌp] N (*Aut*) accidente *m* múltiple, choque *m* en cadena; **there was a ~ on the motorway** chocaron varios coches en cadena en la autopista, hubo un accidente múltiple en la autopista

pilfer ['pɪlfə'] **Ⓐ** VT ratear*, hurtar, robar **Ⓑ** VI ratear*, robar cosas

pilfering ['pɪlfərɪŋ] N ratería* *f*, hurto *m*, robo *m*

pilgrim ['pɪlgrɪm] N peregrino/a *m/f*, romero/a *m/f*
➤ **the Pilgrim Fathers** *los primeros colonos de Nueva Inglaterra*

pilgrimage ['pɪlgrɪmɪdʒ] N peregrinación *f*; **to go on a ~**

(to) ir de peregrinación (a)

pill [pɪl] N píldora *f*, pastilla *f*; **the ~** (= *contraceptive*) la píldora (anticonceptiva); **to be on/take the ~** tomar la píldora (anticonceptiva)

pillage ['pɪlɪdʒ] **Ⓐ** N pillaje *m*, saqueo *m* **Ⓑ** VT, VI saquear

pillar ['pɪlə'] N pilar *m*, columna *f*; **a ~ of the church** un pilar de la iglesia; ✦ IDIOM **to go from ~ to post** (*Brit*) ir de la Ceca a la Meca ➤ **pillar box** (*Brit*) buzón *m*

pillion ['pɪljən] **Ⓐ** N (*also ~ seat*) asiento *m* trasero **Ⓑ** ADV **to ride ~** ir en el asiento trasero ➤ **pillion passenger** pasajero/a *m/f* de atrás

pillory ['pɪlərɪ] **Ⓐ** N picota *f* **Ⓑ** VT poner en ridículo

pillow ['pɪləʊ] N almohada *f*

pillowcase ['pɪləʊkeɪs], **pillowslip** ['pɪləʊslɪp] N funda *f* de almohada

pilot ['paɪlət] **Ⓐ** N **1** (*Aer*) piloto *mf* **2** (*Naut*) práctico *mf*, piloto *mf* **Ⓑ** VT pilotar, pilotear (*esp LAm*) **Ⓒ** CPD [*project, scheme*] piloto *inv*, experimental ➤ **pilot light** piloto *m* ➤ **pilot programme** (*TV*) programa *m* piloto ➤ **pilot's licence** (*Brit*), **pilot's license** (*US*) licencia *f* de piloto ➤ **pilot study** estudio *m* piloto

pimento [pɪ'mentəʊ] N pimiento *m*, pimentón *m* morrón (*SC*)

pimp [pɪmp] N proxeneta *m* (*frm*), chulo *m* (de putas) (*Sp**), cafiche *m* (*SC**)

pimple ['pɪmpl] N (*gen*) grano *m*; (*on face*) espinilla *f*

pimply ['pɪmplɪ] ADJ (*compar* **pimplier**; *superl* **pimpliest**) lleno de granos, cubierto de granos

PIN [pɪn] N ABBR = **personal identification number**; **~ (number)** NPI *m*

pin [pɪn] **Ⓐ** N **1** (*Sew*) alfiler *m*; **~s and needles** hormigueo *msing*; ✦ IDIOMS **to be on ~s and needles** (*US*) estar hecho un manojo de nervios, estar en *or* sobre ascuas; **you could have heard a ~ drop** se oía el vuelo de una mosca; **like a new ~** (= *clean*) como una patena, limpio como un espejo; (= *tidy*) pulcro y muy ordenado; **for two ~s I'd hand in my resignation*** un poco más y presento la dimisión
2 (*Elec*) [*of plug*] polo *m*; **three-~ plug** clavija *f* de tres polos, clavija *f* tripolar
3 (*Med*) (*in limb*) clavo *m*
4 (*on grenade*) anilla *f*
5 (*Bowls*) bolo *m*; (*Golf*) banderín *m*
6 (*US*) = **brooch**
Ⓑ VT **1** [+ *fabric, seam, hem*] prender *or* sujetar con alfileres; **there was a note on *or* to the door** había una nota clavada en la puerta; **to ~ a medal to sb's uniform** prender una medalla al uniforme de algn
2 (*fig*) **to ~ one's hopes on sth/sb** cifrar *or* depositar sus esperanzas en algo/algn; **you can't ~ the blame on me** no podéis cargarme con la culpa; **there was nothing they could ~ on him** no podían acusarlo *or* culparlo de nada
3 (= *immobilize*) **they ~ned me against the wall/to the floor** me sujetaron contra la pared/en el suelo
Ⓒ CPD ➤ **pin money** dinero *m* para gastos menores
➤ **pin down** VT + ADV **1** (= *fasten or hold down*) sujetar; (= *trap*) atrapar
2 (*fig*) **2.1** (= *oblige to be specific*) **to ~ sb down** hacer que algn concrete; **the minister refused to be ~ned down on the timing of the reforms** el ministro no quiso comprometerse a dar fechas específicas para las reformas; **you can't ~ him down to a date** es imposible lograr que nos

dé una fecha concreta **2.2** (= *identify*) [+ *problem*] identificar; [+ *concept*] precisar, definir; [+ *reason*] dar con; [+ *date*] precisar; **there's something wrong but I can't ~ it down** algo va mal pero no sé exactamente qué

pinafore ['pɪnəfɔːʳ] N (= *overall, apron*) delantal *m*, mandil *m* ➤ **pinafore dress** (*Brit*) jumper *m*, pichi *m* (*Sp*)

pinball ['pɪnbɔːl] N (*also* ~ **machine**) millón *m*, flíper *m*; **to play** ~ jugar al millón *or* al flíper

pincer ['pɪnsəʳ] Ⓐ N **1** [*of crab, etc*] pinza *f* **2** (*Tech*) pincers tenazas *fpl*, pinzas *fpl*; **a pair of ~s** unas tenazas Ⓑ CPD ➤ **pincer movement** movimiento *m* de pinza *or* tenaza

pinch [pɪntʃ] Ⓐ N **1** (*with fingers*) pellizco *m*; **to give sb a ~ on the arm** dar a algn un pellizco en el brazo, pellizcar el brazo a algn

2 (= *small quantity*) pizca *f*; ✦ IDIOM **to take sth with a ~ of salt** tomarse algo con reservas, no creerse algo a pies juntillas

3 (*fig*) apuro *m*; **at** *or* (*US*) **in a** ~ en caso de apuro *or* necesidad; **if it comes to the** ~ en un caso extremo; ✦ IDIOM **to feel the** ~ (empezar a) pasar apuros *or* estrecheces Ⓑ VT **1** (*with fingers*) pellizcar; [*shoe*] apretar

2 (*Brit**) (= *steal*) robar, birlar*, guindar (*Sp**) Ⓒ VI [*shoe*] apretar

pinched ['pɪntʃt] ADJ (= *drawn*) **to look** ~ tener un aspecto demacrado; **to be ~ with cold** estar aterido de frío

pincushion ['pɪn,kʊʃən] N acerico *m*, almohadilla *f*

pine¹ [paɪn] N pino *m* ➤ **pine cone** piña *f* ➤ **pine kernel** piñón *m* ➤ **pine needle** aguja *f* de pino ➤ **pine nut** piñón *m* ➤ **pine tree** pino *m*

pine² [paɪn] VI (*also* **to** ~ **away**) consumirse, languidecer; **to** ~ **for sth/sb** suspirar por algo/algn

pineapple ['paɪn,æpl] N piña *f*, ananá(s) *m* (*LAm*)

ping [pɪŋ] Ⓐ N (*on striking*) sonido *m* metálico; [*of bell*] tilín *m*, tintín *m*; [*of timer*] tin *m* Ⓑ VI (*on striking*) producir un sonido metálico; [*bell*] tintinear, hacer tintín

ping-pong® ['pɪŋpɒŋ] N ping-pong® *m*, tenis *m* de mesa ➤ **ping-pong ball** pelota *f* de ping-pong

pinion ['pɪnjən] VT [+ *person*] atar los brazos a; **he was ~ed against the wall** lo tenían inmovilizado contra la pared

pink¹ [pɪŋk] Ⓐ N (= *colour*) rosa *m*, rosado *m* (*LAm*); ✦ IDIOMS **to be in the** ~ (= *healthy*) rebosar salud; (= *happy*) estar feliz y contento; **to be in the** ~ **of condition** estar en perfecto estado Ⓑ ADJ (*compar* ~**er**; *superl* ~**est**) **1** (= *colour*) (*gen*) (color de) rosa, rosado (*LAm*); [*cheeks, face*] sonrosado; **to go** ~ (*with embarrassment*) ponerse colorado, sonrojarse **2** (*) (= *gay*) [*pound, vote*] homosexual, gay *inv* Ⓒ CPD ➤ **pink gin** ginebra *f* con angostura ➤ **pink slip** (*US*) notificación *f* de despido

pink² [pɪŋk] VI (*Brit Aut*) [*engine*] picar

pinkie* ['pɪŋkɪ] N (*Scot, US*) (dedo *m*) meñique *m*

pinking shears ['pɪŋkɪŋ,ʃɪəz] NPL tijeras *fpl* dentadas

pinnacle ['pɪnəkl] N [*of fame, success*] cumbre *f*, cúspide *f*

pinpoint ['pɪnpɔɪnt] VT [+ *location, source, problem*] identificar, determinar; [+ *cause*] precisar, señalar con precisión

pinprick ['pɪnprɪk] N (*lit*) pinchazo *m*; (*fig*) pequeña molestia *f*

pinstripe ['pɪnstraɪp] ADJ de raya diplomática ➤ **pinstripe suit** traje *m* de raya diplomática

pint [paɪnt] N **1** (= *measure*) pinta *f* (*Brit* = 0,57 *litros*; *US* = 0,47 *litros*); ⊘ IMPERIAL SYSTEM **2** (*Brit**) [*of beer*] **a** ~ una cerveza; **to go for a** ~ salir a tomar una cerveza

pint-size(d)* ['paɪntsaɪz(d)] ADJ diminuto, pequeñito*

pin-up ['pɪnʌp] N foto *o* póster de un famoso, de una chica atractiva, *etc* ➤ **pin-up girl** chica *f* de revista (*modelo*)

pioneer [,paɪə'nɪəʳ] Ⓐ N pionero/a *m/f*; **he was a ~ in the study of bats** fue uno de los primeros en estudiar los murciélagos Ⓑ VT [+ *technique*] ser el/la primero/a en utilizar Ⓒ CPD ➤ **pioneer work** trabajo *m* pionero

pioneering [,paɪə'nɪərɪŋ] ADJ pionero, innovador

pious ['paɪəs] ADJ piadoso, pío; (*pej*) beato

pip¹ [pɪp] N **1** [*of fruit*] pepita *f*, pepa *f* (*esp LAm*) **2** (= *sound*) bip *m*, pitido *m*; **the ~s** (*Telec*) la señal

pip² [pɪp] VT ✦ IDIOM **to be ~ped at** *or* **to the post** (*Brit**) perder por un pelo*

pipe [paɪp] Ⓐ N **1** (= *tube*) tubo *m*, caño *m*; (*larger*) tubería *f*, cañería *f*; **a length of copper** ~ una tubería de cobre

2 (*Mus*) [*of organ*] cañón *m*, tubo *m*; (= *wind instrument*) flauta *f*, caramillo *m*; **pipes** (*also* **bagpipes**) gaita *f* **3** (*smoker's*) pipa *f*, cachimba *f* (*esp LAm*) Ⓑ VT (= *convey*) [+ *water*] canalizar por tuberías; [+ *gas*] llevar por gasoducto; [+ *oil*] llevar por oleoducto; **~d music** música *f* ambiental, hilo *m* musical (*Sp*) Ⓒ CPD ➤ **pipe band** banda *f* de gaiteros ➤ **pipe dream** sueño *m* imposible ➤ **pipe smoker** fumador(a) *m/f* de pipa

➤ **pipe down*** VI + ADV callarse, cerrar el pico*; **~down, will you!** ¡cerrad ya el pico!*

➤ **pipe up*** VI + ADV meter baza*; **then somebody ~d up with another question** y entonces alguien metió baza con otra pregunta* Ⓑ VT + ADV soltar de sopetón*

pipeline ['paɪplaɪn] N (*for water*) tubería *f*, cañería *f*; (*for oil*) oleoducto *m*; (*for gas*) gasoducto *m*; ✦ IDIOM **it's in the** ~ está en proyecto, se está tramitando; **a sequel to the series is in the** ~ ya hay planes para una segunda parte de la serie

piper ['paɪpəʳ] N (*on bagpipes*) gaitero/a *m/f*

piping ['paɪpɪŋ] Ⓐ N **1** (*in house, building*) tubería *f*, cañería *f* **2** [*of bagpipes*] música *f* de gaita **3** (*Sew*) ribete *m*, cordoncillo *m* Ⓑ ADJ [*voice*] agudo Ⓒ ADV ~ **hot** bien caliente

piquant ['piːkənt] ADJ [*taste*] fuerte; [*humour*] corrosivo, ácido

pique [piːk] Ⓐ N resentimiento *or*; **to do sth in a fit of** ~ hacer algo por resentimiento *or* por despecho Ⓑ VT (= *offend*) **I was ~d at his refusal to acknowledge me** me ofendió que se negara a saludarme

piracy ['paɪərəsɪ] N (*lit*) piratería *f*; [*of book*] publicación *f* pirata; [*of tape, video, software*] reproducción *f* pirata

piranha [pɪ'rɑːnə] N piraña *f*

pirate ['paɪərɪt] Ⓐ N pirata *mf* (*also in publishing*) Ⓑ VT [+ *book, tape, video, software*] piratear Ⓒ CPD pirata *inv* ➤ **pirate radio station** (*Brit*) emisora *f* pirata

pirouette [,pɪru'et] Ⓐ N pirueta *f* Ⓑ VI piruetear, hacer piruetas

Pisces ['paɪsiːz] N **1** (= *sign, constellation*) Piscis *m* **2** (= *person*) piscis *mf inv*; **he's (a)** ~ es piscis

piss*** [pɪs] Ⓐ N (= *urine*) meados*** *mpl*; (= *act*) meada*** *f*; **to have a** ~ mear***, echar una meada***; ✦ IDIOM **to take the ~ out of sb** (*Brit*) tomar el pelo a algn, cachondearse de algn (*Sp**); **it's a piece of** ~ (*Brit*) está tirado*, está chupado* (*Sp**) Ⓑ VI mear***; **it's ~ing down** (*Brit*) están cayendo chuzos de punta* Ⓒ VT **to ~ o.s. mearse** (encima)***; **to ~ o.s. (laughing)** (*Brit*) mearse de (la) risa***

➤ **piss off***** Ⓐ VT + ADV reventar*, cabrear**, joder***; **to be ~ed off (with sth/sb)** estar hasta las narices (de algo/algn)*, estar hasta los cojones (de algo/algn)***, estar cabreado (por algo/con algn)** Ⓑ VI + ADV largarse*; ~ **off!** ¡vete a la mierda!***, ¡vete al cuerno!*

pissed** [pɪst] ADJ **1** (*Brit*) **to be** ~ (= *drunk*) estar mamado** **2** (*US*) **to be** ~ **(at sth/sb)** (= *angry*) estar cabreado (por algo/con algn)**, estar de mala leche (por algo/con algn) (*Sp***)

piss-up*** ['pɪsʌp] N (*Brit*) juerga *f* de borrachera

pistachio [pɪs'tɑːʃɪəʊ] N pistacho *m*; (= *tree*) pistachero *m*

piste [piːst] N pista *f*

pistol ['pɪstl] N pistola *f*, revólver *m*

piston ['pɪstən] N pistón *m*, émbolo *m* ➤ **piston engine** motor *m* a pistón

pit¹ [pɪt] Ⓐ N **1** (= *hole in ground*) hoyo *m*, foso *m*; (*as grave*) fosa *f*; (*as trap*) trampa *f*; (*fig*) abismo *m*; **the ~ of one's stomach** la boca del estómago

2 (*Brit*) (= *mine*) mina *f* (de carbón); (= *quarry*) cantera *f*

3 (also **inspection** ~) foso *m* de reparación
4 **the** ~**s** 4.1 (*Motor racing*) los boxes 4.2 (*US**) **to be in the**
~**s** [*person, economy*] estar por los suelos* 4.3 (*Brit**) **this**
town really is the ~**s** este pueblo es para echarse a llorar;
he's the ~**s** es insoportable
5 (*Brit Theat*) **the** ~ el patio de butacas, la platea
6 (*US St Ex*) parquet *m* de la Bolsa; **the cotton** ~ la bolsa del
algodón
7 (= *small depression*) (*in metal, glass*) muesca *f*, marca *f*; (*on*
face) marca *f*, picadura *f*
B VT (= *mark*) [+ *surface*] picar, marcar; **the tarmac was**
~**ted with craters** la calzada estaba llena de hoyos
C CPD ➤ **pit bull (terrier)** pit bull terrier *m*, bull terrier *m*
de pelea ➤ **pit stop** entrada *f* en boxes

pit² [pɪt] (*US*) **A** N (*in fruit*) pepita *f*, hueso *m*, pepa *f* (*esp LAm*)
B VT deshuesar, quitar el hueso a

pita (bread) ['piːtə(ˌbred)] N (*US*) pan *m* árabe

pitapat ['pɪtə'pæt] ADV **to go** ~ [*feet, rain*] golpetear; **my**
heart went ~ el corazón me latía con fuerza

pitch¹ [pɪtʃ] **A** N 1 (*Brit Sport*) (= *ground*) campo *m*, cancha
f (*LAm*)
2 (*Baseball*) (= *throw*) lanzamiento *m*, tiro *m*
3 [*of note, voice, instrument*] tono *m*
4 (*Brit*) [*of trader*] puesto *m*
5 (= *height, degree*) extremo *m*, punto *m*; **matters reached**
such a ~ **that ...** las cosas llegaron a tal extremo *or* a tal
punto que ...
6 (*) (= *sales talk*) rollo* *m*
7 [*of roof*] pendiente *f*
B VT 1 (= *throw*) [+ *ball*] lanzar; [+ *person*] arrojar
2 (*Mus*) [+ *note*] dar; [+ *instrument*] graduar el tono de
3 (= *present*) **it must be** ~**ed at the right level for the**
audience el tono ha de ajustarse al público
4 (= *set up*) [+ *tent*] armar, montar; **to** ~ **camp** acampar,
montar el campamento
C VI 1 **to** ~ **forward: the passengers** ~**ed forward as the**
coach stopped los pasajeros salieron despedidos hacia
adelante cuando se paró el autocar
2 [*ship*] cabecear
3 (*Baseball*) lanzar; ✦ IDIOM **to be in there** ~**ing** (*esp US**)
seguir en la brecha*, seguir al pie del cañón*
D CPD ➤ **pitch pipe** (*Mus*) diapasón *m*
➤ **pitch in*** VI + ADV 1 (= *start work*) **we all** ~**ed in together**
todos nos pusimos manos a la obra, todos nos pusimos a
trabajar juntos 2 (= *cooperate*) echar una mano, arrimar el
hombro; **we all** ~**ed in to help** todos echamos una mano,
todos arrimamos el hombro

pitch² [pɪtʃ] N (= *tar*) brea *f*, pez *f*; **it was** ~ **black** *or* **dark**
outside afuera estaba oscuro como (la) boca de(l) lobo

pitch-and-putt [ˌpɪtʃən'pʌt] N minigolf *m*

pitch-black ['pɪtʃ'blæk] ADJ [*night*] oscuro como (la) boca
de(l) lobo; [*water, sea*] muy oscuro

pitch-dark ['pɪtʃ'dɑːk] ADJ oscuro como (la) boca de(l)
lobo

pitched [pɪtʃt] ADJ ~ **battle** (*Mil, fig*) batalla *f* campal; **a** ~
roof un tejado a dos aguas

pitcher¹ ['pɪtʃəʳ] N (*esp US*) (= *jar*) cántaro *m*, jarro *m*

pitcher² ['pɪtʃəʳ] N (*Baseball*) pítcher *mf*, lanzador(a) *m/f*

pitchfork ['pɪtʃfɔːk] N horca *f*

piteous ['pɪtɪəs] ADJ [*cry*] lastimero; [*expression, story*]
lastimoso; **it was a** ~ **sight** daba lástima verlo

pitfall ['pɪtfɔːl] N (= *danger*) peligro *m*; (= *problem*)
dificultad *f*, escollo *m*; (= *trap*) trampa *f*

pith [pɪθ] N [*of orange etc*] blanco *m* de la cáscara; (*fig*)
meollo *m*

pithead ['pɪthed] N bocamina *f*

pithy ['pɪθɪ] ADJ (*compar* **pithier**; *superl* **pithiest**) [*statement,*
comment, style] sucinto, conciso

pitiable ['pɪtɪəbl] ADJ [*condition*] lastimoso; [*attempt*]
penoso

pitiful ['pɪtɪfəl] ADJ 1 (= *moving to pity*) [*sight*] lastimoso,
penoso; [*cry*] lastimero 2 (= *contemptible*) [*efforts*]
lamentable; [*sum, amount*] irrisorio; **it was a** ~ **performance**
fue una actuación pésima *or* lamentable

pitifully ['pɪtɪfəlɪ] ADV 1 (= *pathetically*) lastimosamente;
she was ~ **thin** estaba tan delgada que daba lástima
2 (= *contemptibly*) lamentablemente; ~ **inadequate supplies**
equipamiento *m* de una pobreza lamentable

pitiless ['pɪtɪlɪs] ADJ [*enemy*] despiadado; [*sun, storm*]
implacable

pitta (bread) ['pɪtə(ˌbred)] N pan *m* árabe

pittance ['pɪtəns] N miseria *f*

pitted ['pɪtɪd] ADJ 1 [*surface*] picado 2 (*US*) [*fruit*]
deshuesado, sin hueso

pituitary gland [pɪ'tjuːɪtərɪˌglænd] N glándula *f* pituitaria

pity ['pɪtɪ] **A** N 1 (= *compassion*) piedad *f*, compasión *f*;
have ~ **on us** ten piedad de nosotros; **to take** ~ **on sb**
compadecerse *or* apiadarse de algn; **out of** ~ por
compasión; **for** ~**'s sake!** ¡por piedad!; (*less seriously*) ¡por el
amor de Dios!
2 (= *cause of regret*) lástima *f*, pena *f*; **what a** ~**!** ¡qué
lástima!, ¡qué pena!; **it is a** ~ **that ...** es una lástima *or* pena
que ... + *subjun*; **what a** ~ **he didn't see it!** ¡qué pena que no
lo viera!; **more's the** ~ desgraciadamente, pero ¿qué le
vamos a hacer?
B VT compadecer(se de), tener lástima a/de

pitying ['pɪtɪɪŋ] ADJ [*look, smile*] (= *compassionate*) lleno de
compasión, compasivo; (= *contemptuous*) de desprecio

pivot ['pɪvət] **A** N (*Tech*) pivote *m*; (*fig*) eje *m* (central)
B VT (= *turn*) hacer girar **C** VI girar (**on** sobre); **to** ~ **on sth**
(*fig*) girar alrededor de algo, depender de algo

pivotal ['pɪvətl] ADJ central, fundamental

pixel ['pɪksel] N pixel *m*, punto *m*

pixie ['pɪksɪ] N duendecillo *m* ➤ **pixie hat, pixie hood**
caperucita *f*, caperuza *f*

pizza ['piːtsə] N pizza *f*

piz(z)azz* [pə'zæz] N energía *f*, dinamismo *m*

pizzeria [ˌpiːtsə'rɪə] N pizzería *f*

Pl. ABBR (= *Place*) Plaza *f*

placard ['plækɑːd] N (*on wall*) cartel *m*; (= *sign,*
announcement) letrero *m*; (*carried in demonstration*)
pancarta *f*

placate [plə'keɪt] VT aplacar, apaciguar

place [pleɪs] **A** N 1 (*gen*) lugar *m*, sitio *m*; **this is the** ~ éste
es el lugar, aquí es; **the furniture was** <u>all over</u> **the** ~ los
muebles estaban todos manga por hombro; **it all began to**
fall into ~ todo empezó a tener sentido; **when the new law**
is in ~ cuando la nueva ley entre en vigor; **the snow was a**
metre deep in ~**s** había tramos *or* trozos en que la nieve
cubría un metro; **this is** <u>no</u> ~ **for you** éste no es sitio para ti;
there was no ~ **to hide** no había donde esconderse; **to** <u>run</u>
in ~ (*US*) correr en parada
2 (= *town, area*) lugar *m*, sitio *m*; **it's a small** ~ es un pueblo
pequeño; **to** <u>go</u> ~**s** (*US*) (= *travel*) viajar, conocer mundo;
he's going ~**s*** (*fig*) llegará lejos
3 (= *house*) casa *f*; (= *building*) sitio *m*; **we were at Peter's** ~
estuvimos en casa de Pedro, estuvimos donde Pedro*; **my**
~ **or yours?** ¿en mi casa o en la tuya?; **there's a new pizza** ~
in town han abierto un sitio de pizzas en el centro
4 (*in street names*) plaza *f*
5 (= *proper or natural place*) sitio *m*, lugar *m*; **does this have**
a ~**?** ¿tiene esto un sitio determinado?; **to put sth back in**
its ~ devolver algo a su sitio; **this isn't the** ~ **to discuss**
politics no es el lugar más indicado para hablar de
política; **to be** <u>out of</u> ~ estar fuera de lugar; **to laugh in the**
<u>right</u> ~ reírse en el momento oportuno
6 (*in book*) **to** <u>find/lose</u> **one's** ~ encontrar/perder la página
7 (= *seat*) asiento *m*; (*in cinema, theatre*) localidad *f*; (*at*
table) cubierto *m*; (*in queue*) turno *m*; (*in school, university,*
on trip) plaza *f*; (*in team*) puesto *m*; **is this** ~ **taken?** ¿está
ocupado este asiento?; **a university** ~ una plaza en la
universidad; **to** <u>change</u> ~**s with sb** cambiar de sitio con
algn; **to** <u>lay</u> **an extra** ~ **for sb** poner otro cubierto para algn;
to <u>lose</u> **one's** ~ (*in queue*) perder su turno
8 (= *job, vacancy*) puesto *m*
9 (= *position*) lugar *m*; **it is not my** ~ **to do it** no me
corresponde a mí hacerlo; **put yourself in my** ~ ponte en
mi lugar; **if I were in your** ~ yo en tu lugar, yo que tú; **I**

wouldn't mind changing ~s with her! ¡no me importaría estar en su lugar!; **friends in high ~s** amigos *mpl* bien situados; **to know one's ~** saber cuál es su lugar; **racism has no ~ here** aquí no hay sitio para el racismo; **to take the ~ of sth/sb** sustituir *or* suplir algo/a algn

10 (*in series, rank*) posición *f*, lugar *m*; **to work sth out to three ~s of decimals** calcular algo hasta las milésimas *or* hasta con tres decimales; **Madrid won, with Bilbao in second** ~ ganó Madrid, con Bilbao en segunda posición *or* segundo lugar; ✦ IDIOM **to put sb in his ~** poner a algn en su lugar, bajar los humos a algn*

11 (*other phrases*) **in the first/second ~** en primer/segundo lugar; **in ~ of** en lugar de, en vez de; **to take ~** tener lugar ⑧ VT **1** (= *put*) poner; (*more precisely*) colocar; **she ~d the dish on the table** puso el plato en la mesa; **~ the mask over your nose and mouth** colóquese la mascarilla sobre la nariz y la boca

2 (= *give, attribute*) [+ *blame*] echar (**on** a); [+ *responsibility*] achacar (**on** a); [+ *importance*] dar, otorgar (*more frm*) (**on** a); **they ~ too much emphasis on paper qualifications** le dan demasiada importancia a los títulos

3 (= *situate*) situar, ubicar; **we are better ~d than a month ago** estamos en mejor situación que hace un mes; **he is well ~d to see it all** está en una buena posición para observarlo todo; **how are you ~d for money?** ¿qué tal andas de dinero?

4 (*Comm*) [+ *order*] hacer; [+ *goods*] colocar; (*Fin*) [+ *money, funds*] colocar, invertir; **goods that are difficult to ~** mercancías *fpl* que no encuentran salida; **to ~ an advert in a paper** poner un anuncio en un periódico

5 (= *find employment for*) [*agency*] encontrar un puesto a, colocar; [*employer*] ofrecer empleo a, colocar; (= *find home for*) colocar

6 (*of series, rank*) colocar, clasificar; **to be ~d** (*in horse race*) llegar colocado; **they are currently ~d second in the league** actualmente ocupan el segundo lugar de la clasificación

7 (= *recall*) recordar; (= *recognize*) reconocer; (= *identify*) identificar, ubicar (*LAm*); **I can't ~ her** no recuerdo de dónde la conozco, no la ubico (*LAm*) ⑥ CPD ➤ **place mat** bajoplatos *m inv*, salvamanteles *m inv* individual ➤ **place name** topónimo *m*; **place names** (*as study, in general*) toponimia *f* ➤ **place of birth** lugar *m* de nacimiento ➤ **place of business** [*of employment*] lugar *m* de trabajo; (= *office*) oficina *f*, despacho *m*; (= *shop*) comercio *m* ➤ **place setting** cubierto *m*

placebo [pləˈsiːbəʊ] N placebo *m* ➤ **placebo effect** efecto *m* placebo

placement [ˈpleɪsmənt] N (= *positioning*) colocación *f*; (*Comm*) emplazamiento *m*

placenta [pləˈsentə] N placenta *f*

placid [ˈplæsɪd] ADJ apacible, plácido

plagiarism [ˈpleɪdʒɪərɪzəm] N plagio *m*

plagiarize [ˈpleɪdʒɪəraɪz] VT plagiar

plague [pleɪɡ] ⓐ N (= *disease*) peste *f*; (*fig*) plaga *f*, fastidio *m*; ✦ IDIOM **to avoid sth/sb like the ~** huir de algo/algn como de la peste, evitar algo/a algn a toda costa ⑧ VT plagar; **the project has been ~d with problems from the beginning** el proyecto se ha visto plagado de problemas desde el comienzo; **a country ~d by recession** un país asolado por la recesión; **the thought has been plaguing me** la idea me viene atormentando

plaice [pleɪs] N (*pl ~*) platija *f*

plaid [plæd] ⓐ N (= *cloth*) tela *f* escocesa *or* a/de cuadros ⑧ CPD [*skirt, trousers, shirt*] escocés

plain [pleɪn] ⓐ ADJ (*compar ~er*; *superl ~est*) **1** (= *clear, obvious*) claro, evidente; **it is ~ that** es evidente *or* obvio que, está claro que; **to make sth ~ (to sb)** poner algo de manifiesto (a algn), dejar algo claro (a algn)

2 (= *frank*) franco; **~ dealing** negocios *mpl* limpios

3 (= *unadorned*) [*answer*] franco; [*living*] sencillo, sin lujo; [*food, cooking*] sencillo, corriente; [*language, style*] sencillo, llano; [*envelope*] en blanco; [*paper*] liso; [*fabric*] de un solo color, liso; **she used to be ~ Miss Jones** antes se llamaba la Srta. Jones sin más; **it's just ~ common sense** es de sentido común; **in ~ clothes** [*policeman*] (vestido) de civil *or* paisano; **in ~ language** (= *understandably*) en lenguaje claro

or sencillo; (= *frankly*) (hablando) sin rodeos; ✦ IDIOM **it's ~ sailing from now on*** a partir de ahora es pan comido*

4 (= *not pretty*) poco atractivo; **she's terribly ~** no es nada atractiva

⑧ ADV **1** (*) (= *completely*) **he's ~ wrong** no tiene razón, y punto; **it's just ~ stupid** es una ridiculez absoluta *or* total

2 (= *simply*) **I can't put it ~er than that** más claramente no lo puedo decir, no lo puedo decir con más claridad

ⓒ N **1** (*Geog*) llanura *f*, llano *m*; **the Great Plains** (*US*) las Grandes Llanuras

2 (*Knitting*) punto *m* sencillo

ⓓ CPD ➤ **plain chocolate** (*Brit*) chocolate *m* amargo *or* sin leche ➤ **plain flour** (*Brit*) harina *f* sin levadura

plain-clothes [ˈpleɪnˈkləʊðz] ADJ **~ policeman** policía *m* de civil *or* de paisano

plainly [ˈpleɪnlɪ] ADV **1** (= *clearly*) **~ I was not welcome** estaba claro *or* era evidente *or* era obvio que no era bienvenido; **I can remember it all quite ~** lo recuerdo con todo detalle *or* perfectamente **2** (= *frankly*) **to put it ~, he's not wanted** hablando claro *or* sin rodeos, él sobra; **to speak ~ to sb** hablar claro a algn, hablar a algn sin rodeos

3 (= *simply*) con sencillez, sencillamente

plainness [ˈpleɪnnɪs] N **1** (= *clarity*) claridad *f*; (= *frankness*) franqueza *f*; (= *simplicity*) sencillez *f* **2** (= *unattractiveness*) falta *f* de atractivo

plaintiff [ˈpleɪntɪf] N demandante *mf*, querellante *mf*

plaintive [ˈpleɪntɪv] ADJ lastimero, quejumbroso

plait [plæt] (*esp Brit*) ⓐ N trenza *f*; **she wears her hair in ~s** lleva trenzas ⑧ VT trenzar

plan [plæn] ⓐ N **1** (= *scheme*) proyecto *m*, plan *m*; **~ of action** plan *m* de acción; **to make ~s for the future** hacer planes *or* planear para el futuro

2 (= *idea, intention*) plan *m*; **do you have any ~s for the weekend?** ¿tienes planes para el fin de semana?; **if everything goes according to ~** si todo sale como está previsto *or* planeado; **to change one's ~s** cambiar de planes

3 (= *diagram, map*) plano *m* (*also* Archit, Tech)

4 (= *outline*) [*of story, essay*] esquema *m*

⑧ VT **1** (= *organize*) [+ *schedule, event, crime*] planear; [+ *party, surprise*] preparar; [+ *route*] planificar, planear; [+ *essay*] hacer un esquema de, planear; [+ *family*] planificar; **as ~ned** según lo previsto, como estaba planeado

2 (= *intend*) **I had been ~ning a trip to New York** había estado pensando en *or* planeando un viaje a Nueva York; **how long do you ~ to stay?** ¿cuánto tiempo piensas quedarte?

3 (= *design*) diseñar

ⓒ VI hacer planes; **to ~ ahead** planear con antelación; **to ~ for the future** hacer planes *or* planear para el futuro

➤ **plan on** VI + PREP **1** (= *intend*) **to ~ on doing sth** tener pensado hacer algo **2** (= *expect*) contar con; **I hadn't ~ned on the bad weather** no había contado con el mal tiempo

plane [pleɪn] ⓐ N **1** (= *aeroplane, airplane*) avión *m*; **to go by ~** ir en avión; **to send goods by ~** enviar mercancías por avión

2 (*Art, Math, Constr*) plano *m*

3 (*fig*) nivel *m*; **he seems to exist on another ~** parece vivir en otro nivel *or* en una esfera distinta

4 (= *tool*) (= *small*) cepillo *m* (de carpintero); (= *large*) garlopa *f*

5 (*Bot*) (*also* **~ tree**) plátano *m*

⑧ VT cepillar; **to ~ sth down** cepillar *or* desbastar algo ⓒ CPD ➤ **plane crash** accidente *m* de avión ➤ **plane journey** viaje *m* en avión ➤ **plane ticket** billete *m* (*Sp*) *or* pasaje *m* (*LAm*) de avión

planet [ˈplænɪt] N planeta *m*

planetarium [ˌplænɪˈtɛərɪəm] N planetario *m*

planetary [ˈplænɪtərɪ] ADJ planetario

plank [plæŋk] N **1** [*of wood*] tabla *f*, tablón *m* **2** (*fig*) [*of policy*] punto *m*

plankton [ˈplæŋktən] N plancton *m*

planned [plænd] ADJ [*economy*] dirigido; [*development, redundancy*] programado; [*crime, murder*] premeditado; [*pregnancy*] deseado

planner ['plænəʳ] N planificador(a) *m/f*

planning ['plænɪŋ] **Ⓐ** N planificación *f*; **the trip needs careful ~** hay que planear bien el viaje; **we're still at the ~ stage** estamos todavía en la etapa de la planificación **Ⓑ** CPD [*committee, department, process*] de planificación ➤ **planning permission** (*Brit*) permiso *m* de obra ➤ **planning regulations** normas *fpl* urbanísticas

plant [plɑːnt] **Ⓐ** N **1** (*Bot*) planta *f* **2** (*no pl*) (= *machinery*) maquinaria *f*; (*fixed*) instalaciones *fpl*; **heavy ~** maquinaria *f* pesada **3** (= *factory*) fábrica *f*, planta *f* **4** (***) (= *infiltrator*) infiltrado/a *m/f*, espía *mf* **Ⓑ** VT **1** [+ *tree, flower, crop*] plantar; [+ *seed, garden, field*] sembrar; **to ~ sth with sth** sembrar algo de algo **2** (= *put*) **he ~ed himself right in her path** se le plantó en el camino*, se plantó en mitad de su camino*; **to ~ an idea in sb's mind** meter a algn una idea en la cabeza; **to ~ a kiss on sb's cheek** plantar un beso en la mejilla a algn* **3** (*furtively*) [+ *bomb, evidence*] colocar, poner; [+ *informer, spy*] poner, infiltrar; **he accused the police of ~ing the drug on him** acusó a la policía de colocarle *or* meterle droga en la ropa **Ⓒ** CPD ➤ **plant life** vida *f* vegetal, las plantas ➤ **plant pot** (*esp Brit*) maceta *f*, tiesto *m* ➤ **plant out** VT + ADV [+ *seedlings*] trasplantar

plantain ['plæntɪn] N llantén *m*, plátano *m* (*LAm*)

plantation [plæn'teɪʃən] N [*of tea, sugar etc*] plantación *f*; (= *large estate*) hacienda *f*; [*of trees*] arboleda *f*; [*of young trees*] plantel *m*

planter ['plɑːntəʳ] N (= *plantpot*) tiesto *m*, maceta *f*

plaque [plæk] N (= *plate*) placa *f*; (*on teeth*) sarro *m*, placa *f* (dental)

plasma ['plæzmə] N plasma *m*

plaster ['plɑːstəʳ] **Ⓐ** N **1** (*Constr*) yeso *m*; (= *layer on wall*) enlucido *m* **2** (*Brit*) (*for broken limb*) escayola *f* (*Sp*), yeso *m* (*LAm*); **with his leg in ~** con la pierna escayolada (*Sp*) *or* enyesada (*LAm*) **3** (*Brit*) (= *sticking plaster*) tirita *f* (*Sp*), curita *f* (*LAm*) **Ⓑ** VT **1** (*Constr*) enyesar; [+ *wall*] enyesar, enlucir **2** (= *cover*) cubrir, llenar; **the children came back ~ed with mud** los niños volvieron cubiertos de lodo; **the story was ~ed all over the front page** el reportaje llenaba toda la primera plana **Ⓒ** CPD [*model, statue*] de yeso ➤ **plaster cast** (*Med*) escayola *f* (*Sp*), enyesado *m* (*LAm*); (= *model, statue*) vaciado *m* de yeso ➤ **plaster of Paris** yeso *m* mate

plasterboard ['plɑːstəbɔːd] N cartón *m* de yeso, pladur® *m* (*Sp*)

plastered* ['plɑːstəd] ADJ **to be ~** estar como una cuba*, estar tomado (*LAm**); **to get ~** ponerse como una cuba*

plasterer ['plɑːstərəʳ] N yesero/a *m/f*, enlucidor(a) *m/f*

plastic ['plæstɪk] **Ⓐ** N **1** plástico *m*; **plastics** (*materiales mpl*) plásticos *mpl* **2** (= *credit cards*) plástico *m* **Ⓑ** ADJ **1** (= *made of plastic*) de plástico **2** (= *flexible*) plástico **Ⓒ** CPD ➤ **plastic bag** bolsa *f* de plástico ➤ **plastic bullet** bala *f* de goma ➤ **plastic explosive** goma *f* dos ➤ **plastic mac** (*Brit*) impermeable *m* ➤ **plastic surgeon** cirujano/a *m/f* plástico/a ➤ **plastic surgery** cirugía *f* plástica *or* estética ➤ **plastic wrap** (*US*) film *m* adherente (para envolver alimentos)

Plasticine® ['plæstɪsiːn] N Plastilina® *f*, arcilla *f* de modelar

Plate [pleɪt] N **the River ~** el Río de la Plata

plate [pleɪt] **Ⓐ** N **1** (= *flat dish*) plato *m*; [*of metal etc*] lámina *f*, plancha *f*; **✦** IDIOMS **to hand sth to sb on a ~** (*esp Brit**) ofrecer algo a algn en bandeja (de plata); **to have a lot on one's ~*** estar muy atareado **2** (*on cooker*) quemador *m*, fuego *m* **3** (= *silverware etc*) vajilla *f* **4** (= *plaque*) placa *f* **5** [*of microscope*] placa *f* **6** (= *number plate*) matrícula *f*, placa *f* **7** (= *dental plate*) dentadura *f* (postiza) **8** (= *book illustration*) lámina *f*, grabado *m* **9** (*Geol*) placa *f* **Ⓑ** VT (*with gold*) dorar; (*with silver*) platear

Ⓒ CPD ➤ **plate glass** vidrio *m* cilindrado, cristal *m* cilindrado (*Sp*) ➤ **plate rack** (*Brit*) escurreplatos *m inv*

plateau ['plætəu] N (*pl* **~s** *or* **~x** ['plætəuz]) **1** (*Geog*) meseta *f* **2** (*fig*) estancamiento *m*, punto *m* muerto

plateful ['pleɪtfəl] N plato *m*

platform ['plætfɔːm] **Ⓐ** N **1** (= *structure*) plataforma *f* (*also fig*); [*of oil rig*] plataforma *f* base; (*for band etc*) estrado *m*; (*at meeting*) plataforma *f*, tribuna *f* **2** (*Rail*) andén *m*, vía *f*; **on ~ eight** en/por la vía (número) ocho **3** (*Pol*) programa *m* **Ⓑ** CPD ➤ **platform shoes** zapatos *mpl* de plataforma ➤ **platform ticket** (*Brit Rail*) billete *m* (*Sp*) *or* boleto *m* (*LAm*) de andén

platinum ['plætɪnəm] N platino *m* ➤ **platinum blonde** rubio/a *m/f* platino

platitude ['plætɪtjuːd] N tópico *m*, lugar *m* común

platonic [plə'tɒnɪk] ADJ platónico

platoon [plə'tuːn] N (*Mil*) pelotón *m*, sección *f*

platter ['plætəʳ] N **1** (= *dish*) fuente *f* **2** (= *meal, course*) plato *m*; **a cheese ~** una tabla de quesos

platypus ['plætɪpəs] N ornitorrinco *m*

plaudits ['plɔːdɪts] NPL aplausos *mpl*

plausibility [ˌplɔːzə'bɪlɪtɪ] N [*of argument*] verosimilitud *f*; [*of person*] credibilidad *f*

plausible ['plɔːzəbl] ADJ [*argument*] verosímil, plausible; [*person*] convincente

play [pleɪ] **Ⓐ** N **1** (*Sport*) juego *m*; (= *move, manoeuvre*) jugada *f*, movida *f*; **neat ~** una bonita jugada; **~ began at three o'clock** el partido empezó a las tres **2** (*Theat*) obra *f* (de teatro), pieza *f*; **the ~s of Lope** las obras de teatro de Lope, el teatro de Lope; **radio/television ~** obra *f* para radio/televisión **3** (*fig*) (= *interaction*) **the ~ of light on the water** el rielar de la luz sobre el agua; **the ~ of light and dark in this picture** el efecto de luz y sombra en este cuadro **4** (*fig phrases*) **to bring** *or* **call into ~** poner en juego; **to come into ~** entrar en juego; **to make a ~ for sth/sb** intentar conseguir algo/conquistar a algn; **to make (a) great ~ of sth** insistir en algo, hacer hincapié en algo **Ⓑ** VT **1** [+ *football, chess*] jugar a; [+ *game, match*] jugar, disputar; **to ~ football/chess** jugar al fútbol/al ajedrez; **what position does he ~?** ¿de qué juega?; **to ~ a game of tennis** jugar un partido de tenis; **to ~ a game of cards (with sb)** echar una partida de cartas (con algn); **the children were ~ing a game in the garden** los niños estaban jugando (a un juego) en el jardín; **don't ~ games with me!** ¡no me vengas con jueguecitos!, ¡no trates de engañarme!; **✦** IDIOMS **to ~ the field*** (= *have many girlfriends, boyfriends*) dedicarse a ligar*; **to ~ the game** (= *play fair*) acatar las normas **2** [+ *team, opponent*] jugar contra; **to ~ sb at chess** jugar contra algn al ajedrez **3** [+ *card*] jugar; [+ *chess piece etc*] mover; **✦** IDIOMS **to ~ one's cards right** *or* **well** jugar bien sus cartas; **to ~ ball (with sb)** (= *cooperate*) colaborar (con algn) **4** (= *perform*) [+ *role, part*] hacer, interpretar; [+ *work*] representar; **what part did you ~?** ¿qué papel tuviste?; **when we ~ed "Hamlet"** cuando representamos "Hamlet"; **when I ~ed Hamlet** cuando hice el papel de Hamlet; **✦** IDIOMS **to ~ it cool*** mantener el tipo, actuar como si nada; **to ~ (it) safe** obrar con cautela, ser prudente **5** [+ *instrument, note*] tocar; [+ *tune, concerto*] tocar, interpretar (*more frm*); [+ *tape, CD*] poner, tocar **6** (= *direct*) [+ *light, hose*] dirigir **Ⓒ** VI **1** (= *amuse o.s.*) [*child*] jugar; [*puppy, kitten etc*] jugar, juguetear; **to ~ (about) with a stick** juguetear con un palo; **to ~ with an idea** dar vueltas a una idea, barajar una idea; **to ~ with fire** jugar con fuego; **how much time/money do we have to ~ with?** ¿con cuánto tiempo/dinero contamos?, ¿de cuánto tiempo/dinero disponemos? **2** (*Sport, Gambling, Games*) jugar; **I've not ~ed for a long time** hace mucho tiempo que no juego; **England are ~ing against Scotland in the final** Inglaterra jugará contra *or* se enfrentará a Escocia en la final; **they're ~ing at soldiers** están jugando a (los) soldados; **what are you ~ing at?*** pero ¿qué haces?, ¿qué te pasa?; **to ~ by the rules** (*fig*) acatar las normas; **to ~ dead** hacerse el muerto; **to ~ fair** jugar

limpio; **he ~s for Liverpool** juega en el Liverpool; **to ~ for money** jugar por dinero; ✦ IDIOMS **to ~ for time** tratar de ganar tiempo; **to ~ into sb's hands** hacer el juego a algn **3** (*Mus*) [*person*] tocar; [*instrument, record etc*] sonar; **a record was ~ing in the background** de fondo sonaba un disco; **will you ~ for us?** ¿nos tocas algo?
Ⓓ CPD ► **play on words** juego *m* de palabras
► **play along** VI + ADV **to ~ along (with sb)** (*fig*) seguir el juego (a algn)
► **play around** VI + ADV **to ~ around with sth** (= *fiddle with*) juguetear con algo; (= *tamper with*) toquetear algo; **to ~ around with an idea** dar vueltas a una idea, barajar una idea
► **play back** VT + ADV [+ *tape*] poner
► **play down** VT + ADV minimizar, quitar importancia a
► **play off** VT + ADV **to ~ one person off against another** enfrentar a una persona con otra
► **play on** Ⓐ VI + PREP (= *take advantage of*) aprovecharse de, explotar; **to ~ on sb's emotions** jugar con las emociones de algn; **to ~ on words** jugar con las palabras Ⓑ VI + ADV (*Mus*) seguir tocando; (*Sport*) seguir jugando; **~ on!** ¡adelante!
► **play out** VT + ADV (= *enact*) llevar a cabo; [+ *fantasy*] realizar
► **play up** Ⓐ VI + ADV (*Brit****) (= *cause trouble*) [*child*] dar guerra*; **the car is ~ing up** el coche no anda bien; **my stomach is ~ing up again** el estómago me está dando problemas otra vez, mi estómago vuelve a darme problemas Ⓑ VT + ADV **1** (*Brit****) (= *cause trouble to*) **his rheumatism is ~ing him up** el reúma le está fastidiando **2** (= *exaggerate*) exagerar, encarecer

play-act ['pleɪækt] VI (*lit*) hacer teatro, actuar; (*fig*) (= *pretend*) hacer teatro

playback ['pleɪbæk] N repetición *f*, reproducción *f*; (*TV etc*) playback *m*

playboy ['pleɪbɔɪ] N playboy *m*

Play-Doh® ['pleɪdəʊ] N ≈ Plastilina® *f*

player ['pleɪəʳ] N **1** (*Sport*) jugador(a) *m/f*; **football ~** jugador(a) *m/f* de fútbol, futbolista *mf* **2** (*Theat*) actor *m*, actriz *f* **3** (*Mus*) músico/a *m/f*; **piano ~** pianista *mf*

playful ['pleɪfəl] ADJ [*person*] juguetón; [*mood*] alegre; [*remark*] dicho en broma, festivo

playgoer ['pleɪˌɡəʊəʳ] N aficionado/a *m/f* al teatro

playground ['pleɪɡraʊnd] N (*in school*) patio *m* de recreo

playgroup ['pleɪˌɡruːp] N jardín *m* de infancia, guardería *f*, kinder *m* (*LAm*)

playhouse ['pleɪhaʊs] N (= *theatre*) teatro *m*

playing ['pleɪɪŋ] Ⓐ N **1** (*Sport*) juego *m*; **~ in the wet is tricky** es difícil jugar cuando llueve **2** (*Mus*) interpretación *f* Ⓑ CPD ► **playing card** naipe *m* ► **playing field** campo *m* or (*LAm*) cancha *f* de deportes

playmate ['pleɪmeɪt] N compañero/a *m/f* de juego

play-off ['pleɪɒf] N (*in case of draw*) (partido *m* de) desempate *m*; (*US*) (*to select competing teams*) eliminatoria *f*

playpen ['pleɪpen] N parque *m*, corral *m*

playroom ['pleɪrʊm] N cuarto *m* de juego

playschool ['pleɪˌskuːl] N (*esp Brit*) = **playgroup**

plaything ['pleɪθɪŋ] N juguete *m*

playtime ['pleɪtaɪm] N (*Scol*) (hora *f* de) recreo *m*

playwright ['pleɪraɪt] N dramaturgo/a *m/f*

plaza ['plɑːzə] N **1** (= *public square*) plaza *f* **2** (*US*) (= *motorway complex*) zona *f* de servicios; (= *toll*) peaje *m*; (= *shopping complex*) centro *m* comercial

PLC, plc N ABBR (*Brit*) (= **public limited company**) S.A.

plea [pliː] Ⓐ N **1** (= *entreaty*) súplica *f*, petición *f*; **he made a ~ for mercy** pidió clemencia **2** (*Jur*) alegato *m*, defensa *f*; **a ~ of insanity** un alegato por desequilibrio mental; **a ~ of guilty/not guilty** una declaración de culpabilidad/ inocencia; **to enter a ~ of innocent** declararse inocente Ⓑ CPD ► **plea bargaining** (*Jur*) *acuerdo táctico entre fiscal y defensor para agilizar los trámites judiciales*

plead [pliːd] (*pt, pp* **~ed, pled** (*esp US*)) Ⓐ VT **1** (= *argue*) **to ~ sb's cause** hablar por algn, interceder por algn; **to ~ sb's**

case (*Jur*) defender a algn en juicio **2** (*as excuse*) aducir, pretextar; **to ~ ignorance** aducir *or* pretextar desconocimiento Ⓑ VI **1** (= *beg*) **I ~ed and ~ed but it was no use** le supliqué mil veces pero de nada sirvió; **to ~ with sb (to do sth)** suplicar a algn (que haga algo); **to ~ with sb for sth** rogar a algn que conceda algo **2** (*Jur*) (*as defendant*) presentar declaración; (*as barrister*) abogar; **how do you ~?** ¿cómo se declara el acusado?; **to ~ guilty/not guilty** declararse culpable/inocente

pleading ['pliːdɪŋ] Ⓐ N (= *entreaties*) súplicas *fpl* Ⓑ ADJ suplicante

pleasant ['plezənt] ADJ **1** (= *agreeable*) agradable; **it's very ~ here** aquí se está muy bien **2** (= *friendly*) agradable, simpático

pleasantly ['plezəntlɪ] ADV [*say*] amablemente, en tono agradable; **the evening passed ~ enough** la velada fue bastante agradable; **it was ~ warm** hacía un calor agradable; **we were ~ surprised** fue una grata *or* agradable sorpresa para nosotros

pleasantry ['plezəntrɪ] N **to exchange pleasantries** intercambiar los cumplidos de rigor

please [pliːz] Ⓐ EXCL **please!** ¡por favor!; (*as protest*) ¡por Dios!; **(yes,) ~** sí, gracias; **~ don't interfere, Boris** haz el favor de no meterte, Boris, no te metas, Boris, por favor

---

> **por favor** is not as common as **please** and can be omitted in many cases. Spanish speakers may show their politeness by their intonation, or by using **usted**.

~ be seated siéntese; **~ accept this book** le ruego acepte este libro; **"may I?"** — **"~ do!"** —¿puedo? —¡por supuesto! *or* —¡cómo no!; **"please do not smoke"** "se ruega no fumar"
Ⓑ VI **1** (= *like, prefer*) querer; **he does whatever he ~s** hace lo que quiere *or* lo que le place; **do as you ~** haz lo que quieras, haz lo que te dé la gana*
2 (= *cause satisfaction*) **we aim to ~** nuestro objetivo es complacer; **to be anxious to ~** tener muchas ansias de quedar bien; **a gift that is sure to ~** un regalo que siempre gusta, un regalo que de seguro gustará
Ⓒ VT (= *give pleasure to*) agradar, complacer; (= *satisfy*) complacer; **he is hard to ~** es difícil de contentar *or* complacer; **~ yourself!** ¡haz lo que quieras!, ¡haz lo que te dé la gana!*

pleased [pliːzd] ADJ **to be ~** (= *happy*) estar contento; (= *satisfied*) estar satisfecho; **I am ~ to hear it** me alegra saberlo; **~ to meet you** mucho gusto (en conocerlo), encantado (de conocerlo); **we are ~ to inform you that ...** nos complace *or* nos es grato comunicarle que ...; **to be ~ about/at sth** **I am ~ at the decision** me alegro de la decisión; **we were ~ at the news** la noticia nos alegró; **I'm not very ~ about it** no me hace mucha gracia; **to be ~ with sb/sth** estar contento con algn/algo; **he is/looks very ~ with himself** está/parece estar muy satisfecho de sí mismo *or* consigo mismo

pleasing ['pliːzɪŋ] ADJ [*manner*] agradable; [*news*] grato; [*result*] satisfactorio

pleasurable ['pleʒərəbl] ADJ agradable, grato

pleasure ['pleʒəʳ] Ⓐ N **1** (= *satisfaction*) placer *m*, gusto *m*; (= *happiness*) alegría *f*; **my ~!** (*returning thanks*) ¡de nada!, ¡no hay de qué! (*esp LAm*); **to do sth for ~** hacer algo por gusto *or* placer; **is this trip for business or ~?** ¿este viaje es de negocios o de placer?; **to get ~ from sth** disfrutar con algo; **I have much ~ in informing you that ...** tengo el gran placer de comunicarles que ...; **I take great ~ in watching them grow** disfruto muchísimo viéndolos crecer **2** (= *source of pleasure*) placer *m*, gusto *m*; **it's a real ~** es un verdadero placer; **it's a ~ to see her** da gusto verla Ⓑ CPD ► **pleasure boat** barco *m* de recreo

pleat [pliːt] Ⓐ N pliegue *m*, doblez *m*; [*of skirt*] tabla *f* Ⓑ VT plisar, plegar

pleb* [pleb] (*Brit*) N plebeyo/a *m/f*; **the ~s** la plebe

plebeian [plɪ'biːən] ADJ plebeyo; (*pej*) ordinario

plebiscite ['plebɪsɪt] N plebiscito *m*

plectrum ['plektrəm] N púa f, plectro m

pled [pled] (esp US) PT, PP of **plead**

pledge [pledʒ] **Ⓐ** N (= promise, assurance) (gen) compromiso m, promesa f; [of money] promesa f de donación; **the Pledge of Allegiance** (US) ≈ la jura de (la) bandera; **he sent his brother as a ~ of his sincerity** envió a su hermano en señal or como muestra de su sinceridad; **to break a ~** romper una promesa; **to give (sb) a ~ to do sth** prometer (a algn) hacer algo; **to honour** or **keep a ~** cumplir una promesa; **to make (sb) a ~ to do sth** prometer (a algn) hacer algo; ✦ IDIOM **to take the ~** (hum) jurar renunciar al alcohol

Ⓑ VT 1 (= promise) [+ money, donation] prometer; **to ~ to do sth** prometer hacer algo; **to ~ (one's) support (for sth/sb)** comprometerse a prestar apoyo (a algo/algn) 2 (= pawn) empeñar, dejar en prenda

plenary ['pliːnərɪ] ADJ plenario; **in ~ session** en sesión plenaria

plentiful ['plentɪfəl] ADJ [wildlife, game, hair] abundante; **a ~ supply of ...** un suministro abundante de ...

plenty ['plentɪ] **Ⓐ** N abundancia f

Ⓑ PRON 1 (= lots) **that's ~, thanks** ¡así basta, gracias!; **she's got ~ to do** tiene muchas cosas que hacer, tiene un montón que hacer*; **there are ~ like me** hay mucha gente or hay muchos como yo

2 **~ of** (= much) mucho/a; (= many) muchos/as; **they have ~ of money** tienen mucho dinero; **we've got ~ of time to get there** tenemos tiempo de sobra para llegar; **drink ~ of fluids** beba muchos líquidos; **we see ~ of Mum and Dad** vemos a mis padres con frecuencia, vemos mucho a mis padres

Ⓒ ADV (esp US*) **it's ~ big enough** es bastante grande

plethora ['pleθərə] N plétora f

pleurisy ['plʊərɪsɪ] N pleuresía f, pleuritis f

pliable ['plaɪəbl] ADJ flexible

pliant ['plaɪənt] ADJ dócil, flexible

pliers ['plaɪəz] NPL alicates mpl; **a pair of ~** unos alicates

plight [plaɪt] N situación f grave; **the country's economic ~** la grave situación económica del país; **to be in a sorry ~** estar en un estado lamentable

plimsoll ['plɪmsəl] N (Brit) zapatilla f de tenis, playera f

Plimsoll line ['plɪmsəl,laɪn] N línea f de máxima carga

plinth [plɪnθ] N plinto m

PLO N ABBR (= **Palestine Liberation Organization**) OLP f

plod [plɒd] VI 1 (lit) andar con paso pesado; **to ~ along** or **on** ir andando con paso lento 2 (fig) **to ~ away at a task** seguir dándole a un trabajo; **we must ~ on** tenemos que seguir trabajando

plodder ['plɒdə⁺] N trabajador diligente pero lento

plonk¹* [plɒŋk] (Brit) VT (also ~ **down**) dejar caer; **to ~ o.s. down** dejarse caer

plonk² [plɒŋk] N (Brit*) (= wine) vino m peleón*

plop [plɒp] **Ⓐ** N plaf m **Ⓑ** VI hacer plaf **Ⓒ** EXCL plaf

plot¹ [plɒt] N (Agr) parcela f, terreno m; [of vegetables, flowers etc] cuadro m; **a ~ of grass** un cuadro de césped; **a ~ of land** (gen) un terreno; (for building) un solar, un lote (esp LAm); **a vegetable ~** un cuadro de hortalizas

plot² [plɒt] **Ⓐ** N 1 (= conspiracy) complot m, conjura f 2 (Literat, Theat) trama f, argumento m; ✦ IDIOMS **to lose the ~*** perderse, perder el hilo; **the ~ thickens** la cosa se complica **Ⓑ** VT 1 (on graph etc) [+ progress, course, position] trazar 2 [+ downfall, ruin etc] urdir, fraguar **Ⓒ** VI maquinar, conspirar; **to ~ to do sth** conspirar para hacer algo

plotter ['plɒtə⁺] N (= conspirator) conspirador(a) m/f

plough, plow (US) [plaʊ] **Ⓐ** N (Agr) arado m; **the Plough** (Astron) el Carro, la Osa Mayor **Ⓑ** VT (Agr) arar; **to ~ money into a project** invertir (grandes cantidades de) dinero en un proyecto; **to ~ one's way through a book** leer un libro con dificultad **Ⓒ** VI (Agr) arar; **the car ~ed into the wall** el coche dio fuerte(mente) contra la pared; **the lorry ~ed into the crowd** el camión se metió en la multitud

➤ **plough back** VT + ADV [+ profits] reinvertir

➤ **plough up** VT + ADV [+ field] arar, roturar

ploughman, plowman (US) ['plaʊmən] N (pl ploughmen) arador m, labrador m ➤ **ploughman's lunch** (Brit) pan m con queso y cebolla

plow etc [plaʊ] (US) = **plough** etc

ploy [plɔɪ] N truco m, estratagema f

pls* ABBR (= **please**) porfa*

pluck [plʌk] **Ⓐ** N (= courage) valor m, ánimo m; (= guts) agallas fpl; **it takes ~ to do that** hace falta mucho valor para hacer eso; **he's got plenty of ~** tiene muchas agallas **Ⓑ** VT [+ fruit, flower] arrancar; [+ bird] desplumar; [+ guitar] pulsar, puntear; **to ~ one's eyebrows** depilarse las cejas

➤ **pluck up** VT + ADV **to ~ up (one's) courage** armarse de valor; **to ~ up the courage to do sth** armarse de valor para hacer algo

plucky ['plʌkɪ] ADJ (compar **pluckier**; superl **pluckiest**) valiente, valeroso

plug [plʌg] **Ⓐ** N 1 (in bath, basin, barrel, for leak) tapón m; ✦ IDIOM **to pull the ~ on sth***: **the bank pulled the ~ on my overdraft** el banco me canceló el descubierto or (Sp) me cerró el grifo del descubierto

2 (Elec) (on flex, apparatus) enchufe m, clavija f; (= socket) toma f de corriente; (Telec) clavija f; (Aut) (= spark plug) bujía f; **two-/three-pin ~** clavija f bipolar/tripolar, clavija f de dos/tres polos

3 (*) (= piece of publicity) publicidad f; **to give sth/sb a ~** dar publicidad a algo/algn **Ⓑ** VT 1 (also ~ **up**) [+ hole] llenar, tapar; [+ leak] cubrir

2 (= insert) introducir; **to ~ sth into a socket** enchufar algo a una toma

3 (*) (= publicize) dar publicidad a

4 (*) (= advocate, put forward) insistir or hacer hincapié en; **he's been ~ging that line for years** hace años que viene diciendo lo mismo

➤ **plug away*** VI + ADV **to ~ away (at sth)** perseverar (en algo), darle (a algo)*

➤ **plug in Ⓐ** VT + ADV (Elec) enchufar **Ⓑ** VI + ADV (Elec) enchufarse, ir enchufado

plug-and-play [plʌgən'pleɪ] ADJ (Comput) fácil de conectar

plughole ['plʌghəʊl] N (Brit) desagüe m, desaguadero m; ✦ IDIOM **to go down the ~*** irse al traste

plum [plʌm] **Ⓐ** N 1 (= fruit) ciruela f; (also ~ **tree**) ciruelo m 2 (= colour) color m ciruela or (LAm) guinda 3 (*) (fig) **it's a real ~ (of a) job** es un trabajo fantástico, es un chollo (Sp*) **Ⓑ** CPD ➤ **plum pudding** pudín m or budín m de pasas ➤ **plum tomato** tomate m pera

plumage ['pluːmɪdʒ] N plumaje m

plumb [plʌm] **Ⓐ** N plomo m **Ⓑ** ADJ vertical, a plomo **Ⓒ** ADV 1 (= vertically) verticalmente, a plomo 2 (US*) (= wholly) totalmente, completamente; ~ **crazy** completamente loco; **he's ~ stupid** es un tonto perdido; ~ **in the middle** en el mismo or (Mex) mero centro **Ⓓ** VT sondear; **to ~ the depths of the human mind** penetrar en las profundidades de la mente humana; **to ~ the depths of despair** conocer la mayor desesperación **Ⓔ** CPD ➤ **plumb line** plomada f

➤ **plumb in** VT + ADV (Brit) conectar (con el suministro de agua)

plumber ['plʌmə⁺] N fontanero/a m/f, plomero/a m/f (LAm), gasfitero/a m/f (Chi)

plumbing ['plʌmɪŋ] N 1 (= craft) fontanería f, plomería f (LAm), gasfitería f (Chi) 2 (= piping) tuberías fpl, cañerías fpl

plumbline ['plʌmlaɪn] N plomada f

plume [pluːm] N (= feather) pluma f; (on helmet) penacho m; (fig) [of smoke etc] columna f, hilo m

plummet ['plʌmɪt] VI [bird, plane etc] caer en picado (Sp) or en picada (LAm); [temperature, price, sales] bajar de golpe; [spirits, morale] caer a plomo

plump [plʌmp] **Ⓐ** ADJ (compar ~**er**; superl ~**est**) [person] relleno, rollizo; [face] llenito, rollizo; [baby] rechoncho; [animal] gordo; [fruit, vegetable] gordo, orondo **Ⓑ** VT (also ~ **up**) [+ pillow] mullir

➤ **plump for*** VI + PREP (esp Brit) (= choose) decidirse por, optar por; (= vote for) votar por

plunder ['plʌndəʳ] **A** N (= *act*) pillaje *m*, saqueo *m*; (= *loot*) botín *m* **B** VT pillar, saquear

plunge [plʌndʒ] **A** N 1 (= *dive*) (*from bank etc*) salto *m*; (*under water*) zambullida *f*
2 [*of currency etc*] caída *f* repentina, desplome *m*;
✦ IDIOM **to take the ~** aventurarse, dar el paso decisivo; (*hum*) (= *get married*) decidir casarse **B** VT 1 (= *immerse*) sumergir, hundir (**into** en); **he ~d his hand into his pocket** metió la mano bien dentro del bolsillo; **to ~ a dagger into sb's chest** clavar un puñal en el pecho de algn
2 (*fig*) **to ~ a room into darkness** sumir un cuarto en la oscuridad; **we were ~d into gloom by the news** la noticia nos hundió *or* sumió en la tristeza **C** VI 1 (= *dive*) arrojarse, tirarse; (*into water*) lanzarse, zambullirse
2 (= *fall*) caer, hundirse; [*road, cliff*] precipitarse; **he ~d to his death** tuvo una caída mortal; **the aircraft ~d into the sea** el avión cayó al *or* se precipitó en el mar
3 [*share prices, currency etc*] desplomarse

plunger ['plʌndʒəʳ] N (*for clearing drain*) desatascador *m*

plunging ['plʌndʒɪŋ] ADJ **~ neckline** escote *m* muy bajo

plunk* [plʌŋk] VT (*US*) dejar caer

pluperfect ['pluː'pɜːfɪkt] N (*Ling*) pluscuamperfecto *m*

plural ['plʊərəl] **A** ADJ plural; **the ~ form of the noun** la forma del sustantivo en plural **B** N plural *m*; **in the ~** en (el) plural

pluralism ['plʊərəlɪzəm] N pluralismo *m*

plus [plʌs] **A** PREP (*Math*) más; **three ~ four** tres más cuatro; **~ what I have to do already** además de lo que ya tengo que hacer
B ADJ **a ~ factor** un factor a favor; **twenty ~** veinte y pico, veintitantos; **two pounds ~** dos libras y algo más, más de dos libras; **on earnings of £40,000 ~** de un sueldo de 40.000 libras en adelante
C N 1 (= *plus sign*) signo *m* (de) más, signo *m* de sumar
2 (= *advantage*) punto *m* a favor; **that is a ~ for him** es un punto a su favor **D** CPD ➤ **plus sign** signo *m* (de) más, signo *m* de sumar

plush [plʌʃ] ADJ afelpado; (*fig*) de mucho lujo

Pluto ['pluːtəʊ] N (*Astron, Myth*) Plutón *m*

plutocrat ['pluːtəʊkræt] N plutócrata *mf*

plutonium [pluː'təʊnɪəm] N plutonio *m*

ply [plaɪ] **A** VT 1 [+ *needle, tool*] manejar, emplear; [+ *oars*] emplear; [+ *river, route*] navegar por; **to ~ one's trade** ejercer su profesión 2 **to ~ sb with questions** acosar a algn con preguntas; **to ~ sb with drink** no parar de ofrecer de beber a algn **B** VI **to ~ between** ir y venir de

-ply [plaɪ] ADJ (*ending in compounds*) **three-ply wood** madera *f* de tres capas; **three-ply wool** lana *f* de tres cabos

plywood ['plaɪwʊd] N madera *f* contrachapada

PM N ABBR 1 (*Brit*) = **Prime Minister** 2 (*Jur, Med*) = **post mortem**

pm [piː'em] ADV ABBR = **post meridiem** (*before dark*) de la tarde; (*after dark*) de la noche

PMS N ABBR (= **premenstrual syndrome**) SPM *m*

PMT N ABBR (*Brit*) (= **premenstrual tension**) SPM *m*

pneumatic [njuː'mætɪk] ADJ neumático ➤ **pneumatic drill** taladradora *f* neumática

pneumonia [njuː'məʊnɪə] N pulmonía *f*, neumonía *f*

PO N ABBR (= **Post Office**) oficina *f* de correos; **PO Box** apdo. de correos, aptdo., CP (*LAm*)

poach¹ [pəʊtʃ] VT [+ *egg*] escalfar; [+ *fish*] hervir

poach² [pəʊtʃ] **A** VT 1 (= *hunt*) cazar en vedado; (= *fish*) pescar en vedado 2 (*) (= *steal*) birlar*, quitar **B** VI (= *hunt*) cazar furtivamente; (= *fish*) pescar furtivamente

poacher ['pəʊtʃəʳ] N (= *person*) cazador(a) *m/f* furtivo/a

poaching ['pəʊtʃɪŋ] N caza *f*/pesca *f* furtiva

pocket ['pɒkɪt] **A** N 1 (*in trousers etc*) bolsillo *m*, bolsa *f* (*Mex*); **with his hands in his ~s** con las manos (metidas) en los bolsillos; ✦ IDIOMS **to have sth/sb in one's ~** tener algo/ a algn en el bolsillo; **to line one's ~s** forrarse; **to put one's**

hand in one's ~ echar mano al bolsillo
2 (= *finances, budget*) **to be in ~** salir ganando; **to be £5 in ~** haber ganado cinco libras; **to be out of ~** salir perdiendo; **to be £5 out of ~** haber perdido cinco libras
3 (*Billiards*) tronera *f*
4 (= *restricted area, space*) **~ of resistance** foco *m* de resistencia; **~ of warm air** bolsa *f* de aire caliente **B** VT 1 (*lit*) meter *or* guardar en el bolsillo
2 (*Billiards*) entronerar
3 (= *gain, steal*) embolsar **C** CPD de bolsillo ➤ **pocket billiards** (*US*) billar *msing* americano ➤ **pocket calculator** calculadora *f* de bolsillo ➤ **pocket handkerchief** pañuelo *m* (de bolsillo) ➤ **pocket money** (*Brit*) dinero *m* para gastos (personales); (*children's*) dinero *m* de bolsillo

pocketbook ['pɒkɪtbʊk] N 1 (= *notebook*) cuaderno *m*
2 (*US*) (= *handbag*) bolso *m*, cartera *f* (*LAm*); (= *wallet*) cartera *f*, billetero *m*; (= *purse*) monedero *m*

pocketknife ['pɒkɪtnaɪf] N (*pl* **pocketknives**) navaja *f*

pocket-size(d) ['pɒkɪtsaɪz(d)] ADJ de bolsillo

pockmarked ['pɒkmɑːkt] ADJ [*face*] picado de viruelas; [*surface*] marcado de hoyos

pod [pɒd] N vaina *f*

podgy* ['pɒdʒɪ] ADJ (*compar* **podgier**; *superl* **podgiest**) (*Brit*) gordinflón*; [*face*] mofletudo*

podiatrist [pɒ'diːətrɪst] N (*US*) pedicuro/a *m/f*

podiatry [pɒ'diːətrɪ] N (*US*) pedicura *f*

podium ['pəʊdɪəm] N podio *m*

poem ['pəʊɪm] N (*short*) poesía *f*; (*long, narrative*) poema *m*

poet ['pəʊɪt] N poeta *mf*

poetic [pəʊ'etɪk] ADJ poético ➤ **poetic justice** justicia *f* divina

poetry ['pəʊɪtrɪ] N poesía *f* ➤ **poetry reading** recital *m or* lectura *f* de poesías

pogrom ['pɒgrəm] N pogrom *m*

poignancy ['pɔɪnjənsɪ] N patetismo *m*

poignant ['pɔɪnjənt] ADJ conmovedor, patético

poinsettia [pɔɪn'setɪə] N flor *f* de pascua

point [pɔɪnt] **A** N 1 (*Geom*) (= *dot*) punto *m*; (= *decimal point*) punto *m* decimal, coma *f*; **two ~ six (2.6)** dos coma seis (2,6)
2 (*on scale, thermometer*) punto *m*; **the shares went down two ~s** las acciones bajaron dos enteros
3 (*on compass*) cuarta *f*, grado *m*
4 [*of needle, pencil, knife, star etc*] punta *f*; [*of pen*] puntilla *f*; **with a sharp ~** puntiagudo; ✦ IDIOM **not to put too fine a ~ on it** hablando sin rodeos
5 (= *place*) punto *m*; **he had reached the ~ of resigning** había llegado al punto de la dimisión; **this was the low/ high ~ of his career** este fue el momento más bajo/el momento cumbre de su carrera; **at this ~** (*in space*) aquí, allí; (*in time*) en este *or* aquel momento; **when it comes to the ~** en el momento de la verdad; **there was no ~ of contact between them** no existía ningún nexo de unión entre ellos; **~ of departure** (*lit, fig*) punto *m* de partida; **~ of entry** (*into a country*) punto *m* de entrada, paso *m* fronterizo; **from that ~ on …** de allí en adelante …; **to reach the ~ of no return** (*lit, fig*) llegar al/a un punto sin retorno; **to be on the ~ of doing sth** estar a punto de hacer algo; **up to a ~** (= *in part*) hasta cierto punto, en cierta medida
6 (= *mark*) punto *m*; **to win on ~s** ganar por puntos; **to give sth/sb ~s out of ten** dar a algo/algn un número de puntos sobre diez; **to score ten ~s** marcar diez puntos
7 (= *most important thing*) **the ~ is that …** el caso es que …;

that's just the ~! ¡eso es!, ¡ahí está!; the ~ of the joke/story la gracia del chiste/cuento; to be beside the ~ no venir al caso; do you get the ~? ¿entiendes por dónde voy or lo que quiero decir?; to miss the ~ no comprender; that's not the ~ esto no viene al caso, no es eso; to get off the ~ salirse del tema; his remarks were to the ~ sus observaciones venían al caso; to come or get to the ~ ir al grano; to get back to the ~ volver al tema; to keep to the ~ no salirse del tema

8 (= purpose, use) [of action, visit] finalidad f, propósito m; there's little ~ in telling him no merece la pena or no tiene mucho sentido decírselo; there's no ~ in staying no tiene sentido quedarse; a long story that seemed to have no ~ at all una larga historia que no parecía venir al caso en absoluto; to see the ~ of sth encontrar or ver sentido a algo, entender el porqué de algo; what's the ~? ¿para qué?, ¿a cuento de qué?; what's the ~ of or in trying? ¿de qué sirve intentar?

9 (= detail, argument) punto m; five-~ plan proyecto m de cinco puntos; in ~ of fact en realidad, el caso es que; you've got or you have a ~ there! ¡tienes razón!, ¡es cierto! (LAm); the ~ at issue el asunto, el tema en cuestión; you've made your ~ nos etc has convencido; he made the following ~s dijo lo siguiente; to make the ~ that ... hacer ver or comprender que ...; to make a ~ of doing sth poner empeño en hacer algo; on this ~ sobre este punto; on that ~ en cuanto a eso; I take your ~ acepto lo que dices; ~ taken! ¡de acuerdo!

10 (= matter) cuestión f
11 (= characteristic) cualidad f; bad ~s cualidades fpl malas; good ~s cualidades fpl buenas
12 points (Brit Rail) agujas fpl; (Aut) platinos mpl
13 (Brit Elec) (also power ~) toma f de corriente, tomacorriente m (SC)
14 (Geog) punta f, promontorio m, cabo m
15 (Ballet) (usu pl) punta f; to dance on ~s bailar sobre las puntas

B VT 1 (= aim, direct) apuntar (at a); to ~ a gun at sb apuntar a algn con un fusil; to ~ one's finger at sth/sb señalar con el dedo algo/a algn; to ~ one's toes hacer puntas

2 (= indicate, show) señalar, indicar; would you ~ me in the direction of the town hall? ¿me quiere decir dónde está el ayuntamiento?; we ~ed him in the right direction le indicamos el camino; to ~ the way (lit, fig) señalar el camino

3 (Constr) [+ wall] rejuntar

C VI 1 (lit) señalar; to ~ at or towards sth/sb (with finger) señalar algo/a algn con el dedo; the car isn't ~ing in the right direction el coche no va en la dirección correcta; the hands ~ed to midnight las agujas marcaban las 12 de la noche; it ~s (to the) north apunta hacia el norte

2 (= indicate) indicar; everything ~s that way todo parece indicar eso; the evidence ~s to her las pruebas indican que ella es la culpable; everything ~s to his success todo anuncia su éxito

3 to ~ to sth (= call attention to) señalar algo

D CPD ➤ point duty (Brit Police) control m de la circulación; to be on ~ duty dirigir la circulación or el tráfico ➤ point of detail detalle m ➤ point of honour cuestión f or punto m de honor ➤ a point of principle una cuestión de principios ➤ point of reference punto m de referencia ➤ point of sale punto m de venta ➤ point of view punto m de vista ➤ points failure (Brit Rail) fallo m (Sp) or falla f (LAm) en el sistema de agujas ➤ points system sistema m de puntos ➤ points victory, points win victoria f a los puntos ➤ point out VT + ADV señalar; to ~ out sth to sb señalar algo a algn; to ~ out sb's mistakes señalar los errores de algn; to ~ out that señalar que; may I ~ out that ... permítaseme observar que ... ➤ point up VT + ADV subrayar, destacar

point-blank ['pɔɪnt'blæŋk] **A** ADJ 1 [shot] (hecho) a quemarropa, a bocajarro; at ~ range a quemarropa, a bocajarro 2 [question] directo; [refusal] rotundo, categórico **B** ADV [shoot] a quemarropa, a bocajarro; [demand] tajantemente, categóricamente; [refuse] rotundamente, categóricamente; to ask sb sth ~ preguntar algo a algn a quemarropa

point-by-point ['pɔɪntbaɪ'pɔɪnt] ADJ punto por punto

pointed ['pɔɪntɪd] ADJ 1 (lit) [chin, nose, shoes] puntiagudo; [stick] de punta afilada; [hat] de pico; [arch, window, roof] apuntado, ojival 2 (fig) [remark] mal intencionado; [criticism] mordaz; [question] directo; [look] penetrante

pointedly ['pɔɪntɪdlɪ] ADV [say] intencionadamente; [ask] sin rodeos, directamente

pointer ['pɔɪntəʳ] N 1 (= indicator) indicador m, aguja f; [of balance] fiel m 2 (= stick) puntero m 3 (= dog) perro m de muestra 4 (esp Brit) (= clue, indication) indicación f, pista f; (= piece of advice) consejo m; it is a ~ to a possible solution es una indicación or pista para una posible solución

pointing ['pɔɪntɪŋ] N (Constr) (= action) rejuntado m; (= mortar) juntas fpl

pointless ['pɔɪntlɪs] ADJ 1 (= useless) inútil; it is ~ to complain es inútil quejarse, de nada sirve quejarse 2 (= motiveless) sin motivo, inmotivado 3 (= meaningless) sin sentido

pointlessness ['pɔɪntlɪsnɪs] N falta f de sentido, inutilidad f; the ~ of war la insensatez de la guerra

point-to-point ['pɔɪnttə'pɔɪnt] N carrera de caballos a campo traviesa

poise [pɔɪz] N 1 (= balance) equilibrio m 2 (= carriage of head, body) porte m 3 (= composure) elegancia f, aplomo m

poised [pɔɪzd] ADJ 1 (= self-possessed) sereno, ecuánime 2 to be ~ (fig) (= ready, all set) estar listo; they are ~ to attack or for the attack están listos para atacar

poison ['pɔɪzn] **A** N (lit, fig) veneno m **B** VT envenenar; (chemically) intoxicar; (fig) envenenar, emponzoñar; to ~ sb's mind (against sth/sb) envenenar la mente de algn (contra algo/algn); a ~ed chalice (esp Brit) un arma de doble filo **C** CPD ➤ poison gas gas m tóxico ➤ poison ivy (= plant) hiedra f venenosa; (= rash) urticaria f ➤ poison pen letter anónimo m ofensivo

poisoner ['pɔɪznəʳ] N envenenador(a) m/f

poisoning ['pɔɪznɪŋ] N (lit, fig) envenenamiento m, intoxicación f

poisonous ['pɔɪznəs] ADJ 1 [snake etc] venenoso; [substance, plant, fumes etc] tóxico 2 (fig) (= damaging) pernicioso

poke [pəʊk] **A** N (= jab) empujón m, empellón m; (with elbow) codazo m; he gave me a ~ in the ribs (with elbow) me dio un codazo en las costillas; to give the fire a ~ atizar la lumbre, remover la lumbre

B VT 1 (= jab with stick, finger etc) pinchar, clavar; [+ fire] hurgar, atizar, remover; to ~ sb in the ribs dar a algn un codazo en las costillas; to ~ sb with a stick dar a algn un empujón con un palo; you nearly ~d me in the eye with that! ¡casi me saltas un ojo con eso!

2 (= thrust) introducir; to ~ a stick into a crack meter un palo en una grieta; to ~ one's head out (of a window) sacar or asomar la cabeza (por una ventana)

3 to ~ a hole in sth hacer un agujero en algo
4 to ~ fun at sb reírse de algn
5 (US*) (= punch) pegar un puñetazo a

C VI to ~ at sth with a stick hurgar algo con un bastón ➤ poke around*, poke about (Brit*) VI + ADV (in drawers, attic etc) fisgonear, hurgar; (round shops) curiosear; (pej) fisgar, hacer indagaciones a hurtadillas; and now you come poking around! ¡y ahora te metes a husmear!* ➤ poke out **A** VI + ADV (= stick out) salir **B** VT + ADV you almost ~d my eye out casi me saltas el ojo

poker¹ ['pəʊkəʳ] N (for fire) atizador m, hurgón m

poker² ['pəʊkəʳ] N (Cards) póker m, póquer m

poker-faced ['pəʊkə'feɪst] ADJ de cara impasible, con cara de póquer; they looked on ~ miraron impasibles

poky ['pəʊkɪ] ADJ (compar pokier; superl pokiest) (pej) 1 (= cramped) a ~ room un cuartucho*; a ~ town un pueblucho* 2 (US*) parado

Poland ['pəʊlənd] N Polonia f

polar ['pəʊləʳ] ADJ (Elec, Geog) polar ➤ polar bear oso m polar ➤ polar (ice) cap casquete m polar

polarity [pəʊ'lærɪtɪ] N polaridad f

polarization [ˌpəʊləraɪ'zeɪʃən] N polarización f
polarize ['pəʊləraɪz] **A** VT polarizar **B** VI polarizarse
Pole [pəʊl] N (= *Polish person*) polaco/a *m/f*
pole¹ [pəʊl] N (= *rod*) palo *m*; (= *flag pole*) asta *f*; (= *telegraph pole*) poste *m*; (= *tentpole*) mástil *m*; (*for gymnastics*) percha *f*; (*for vaulting, punting*) pértiga *f*, garrocha *f* (*LAm*)

> Use **el/un** not **la/una** before feminine nouns beginning with stressed **a** or **ha** like **asta**, the translation of (**flag**) **pole**

✦ IDIOMS **I wouldn't touch it with a ten-foot ~** (*US**) yo no lo querría ni regalado; **to be up the ~** (*Brit**) estar chiflado* ➤ **pole bean** (*US*) judía *f* trepadora ➤ **pole position** (*Motor racing*) posición *f* de cabeza en la parrilla de salida, pole *f*; (*fig*) posición *f* de ventaja ➤ **pole vault** salto *m* de pértiga *or* (*LAm*) garrocha ➤ **pole vaulter** saltador(a) *m/f* de pértiga *or* (*LAm*) garrocha, pertiguista *mf*, garrochista *mf* (*LAm*) ➤ **pole vaulting** salto *m* de pértiga *or* (*LAm*) garrocha

pole² [pəʊl] N (*Elec, Geog, Astron*) polo *m*; **North/South Pole** Polo *m* Norte/Sur; ✦ IDIOM **to be ~s apart** ser polos opuestos ➤ **the Pole Star** la Estrella Polar
poleaxe, poleax (*US*) ['pəʊlæks] VT desnucar; (*fig**) **to be poleaxed** quedarse pasmado
polecat ['pəʊlkæt] N (*Brit*) (= *weasel-like animal*) turón *m*; (*US*) (= *skunk*) mofeta *f*
polemic [pɒ'lemɪk] **A** ADJ polémico **B** N polémica *f*
polemical [pɒ'lemɪkəl] ADJ polémico
pole-vault ['pəʊlvɔːlt] VI saltar con pértiga *or* (*LAm*) garrocha
police [pə'liːs] **A** NPL (= *organization*) policía *fsing*; **to join the ~** hacerse policía; **a hundred ~** cien policías **B** VT [+ *frontier*] vigilar, patrullar por; [+ *area*] mantener el orden público en; [+ *process*] vigilar, controlar **C** CPD de policía ➤ **police brutality** violencia *f* policial ➤ **police captain** (*US*) subjefe *mf* ➤ **police car** coche *m* de policía ➤ **police constable** (*Brit*) guardia *mf*, policía *mf* ➤ **police custody**: **in ~ custody** bajo custodia policial ➤ **police department** (*US*) policía *f* ➤ **police dog** perro *m* policía ➤ **police force** cuerpo *m* de policía ➤ **police inspector** inspector(a) *m/f* de policía ➤ **police officer** guardia *mf*, policía *mf* ➤ **police protection** protección *f* policial ➤ **police record** antecedentes *mpl* penales ➤ **police state** estado *m* policía ➤ **police station** comisaría *f*
policeman [pə'liːsmən] N (*pl* **policemen**) guardia *m*, policía *m*
policewoman [pə'liːsˌwʊmən] N (*pl* **policewomen**) mujer *f* policía
policing [pə'liːsɪŋ] N mantenimiento *m* del orden público
policy¹ ['pɒlɪsɪ] N (*gen, principles*) política *f*; [*of party, at election*] programa *m*; [*of newspaper*] normas *fpl* de conducta; **it's a matter of ~** es cuestión de política; **it's company ~ not to comment on such matters** no entra en la política de la empresa tratar esos asuntos; **that's not my ~** ése no es mi sistema; **to change one's ~** cambiar de táctica; **it is a good/bad ~** es buena/mala táctica ➤ **policy decision** decisión *f* de principio ➤ **policy maker** diseñador(a) *m/f* de políticas ➤ **policy statement** declaración *f* de política
policy² ['pɒlɪsɪ] N (*also* **insurance ~**) póliza *f*; **to take out a ~** sacar una póliza, hacerse un seguro ➤ **policy holder** asegurado/a *m/f*
policy-making ['pɒlɪsɪˌmeɪkɪŋ] **A** N elaboración *f* de la política a seguir **B** ADJ [*body, process, role*] normativo
polio ['pəʊlɪəʊ] N poliomielitis *f*, polio *f*
Polish ['pəʊlɪʃ] **A** ADJ polaco **B** N **1** (*Ling*) polaco *m* **2 the ~** los polacos
polish ['pɒlɪʃ] **A** N **1** (= *shoe polish*) betún *m*, bola *f* (*Mex*); (= *furniture polish, floor polish*) cera *f*; (= *metal polish*) limpiametales *m*; (= *nail polish*) esmalte *m or* laca *f* (de uñas)
2 (= *clean*) **my shoes need a ~** mis zapatos necesitan una limpieza; **to give sth a ~** dar brillo a algo
3 (= *shine*) lustre *m*, brillo *m*

4 (= *refinement*) refinamiento *m*; **he lacks ~** le falta refinamiento
B VT **1** (*gen*) pulir; [+ *shoes*] limpiar, lustrar (*esp LAm*), bolear (*Mex*), embolar (*Chi*); [+ *floor, furniture*] encerar; (*mechanically, industrially*) pulimentar
2 (*also* **~ up**) (= *improve*) perfeccionar; [+ *one's Spanish etc*] pulir, perfeccionar
➤ **polish off*** VT + ADV [+ *work, food, drink*] despacharse
polished ['pɒlɪʃt] ADJ **1** (*lit*) [*metal, wood*] pulido **2** [*style etc*] pulido, elegante; [*person*] culto, refinado
polite [pə'laɪt] ADJ [*person*] cortés, educado; [*smile*] cortés, amable; [*request*] cortés; **I was too ~ to ask** no pregunté por educación; **it's ~ to ask permission** es de buena educación pedir permiso; **it's not ~ to stare** es una falta de educación *or* es de mala educación quedarse mirando a la gente; **to make ~ conversation** dar conversación; **in ~ society** en la buena sociedad
politely [pə'laɪtlɪ] ADV **1** (= *courteously*) [*ask, listen, refuse*] cortésmente; [*smile*] cortésmente, amablemente **2** (= *out of politeness*) por educación
politeness [pə'laɪtnɪs] N cortesía *f*, educación *f*; **to do sth out of ~** hacer algo por cortesía *or* por educación
politic ['pɒlɪtɪk] ADJ prudente
political [pə'lɪtɪkəl] **A** ADJ **1** (*gen*) político; **the play is very ~** esta obra tiene mucho contenido político **2** (= *expedient, tactical*) estratégico **B** CPD ➤ **political asylum** asilo *m* político ➤ **political correctness** corrección *f* política ➤ **political correspondent** corresponsal *mf* político/a ➤ **political prisoner** preso/a *m/f* político/a ➤ **political science** ciencias *fpl* políticas
politically [pə'lɪtɪkəlɪ] ADV políticamente; **~ correct** [*person, attitude, terminology*] políticamente correcto; **~ incorrect** políticamente incorrecto

---

POLITICALLY CORRECT

Una persona o su comportamiento es **politically correct** o **PC** cuando sus actitudes o palabras no reflejan ningún signo de discriminación hacia las minorías o las personas con alguna minusvalía física, psíquica o social. Los que propugnan el uso de este tipo de lenguaje y actitudes se enfrentan así a los valores que la sociedad occidental ha tratado de imponer a lo largo de la historia. Sin embargo, el término **politically correct** se emplea también de forma irónica por quienes consideran excesivo este tipo de actitudes. Algunos ejemplos de expresiones políticamente correctas son: **Native American** en vez de **Red Indian** (indio americano), **visually impaired** en vez de **blind** (ciego) y **vertically challenged** en vez de **short** (bajo). Ésta última suele usarse en tono de humor.

---

politician [ˌpɒlɪ'tɪʃən] N político/a *m/f*
politicize [pə'lɪtɪsaɪz] VT politizar
politics ['pɒlɪtɪks] **A** NSING (= *subject, career*) política *f*; **to talk ~** hablar de política **B** NPL **1** (= *views*) postura *fsing* política **2** (= *political aspects*) **the ~ of health care** la política *or* los aspectos políticos de la asistencia médica
polka ['pɒlkə] N (= *dance*) polca *f* ➤ **polka dot** dibujo *m* de puntos
poll [pəʊl] **A** N **1** (= *voting*) votación *f*; (= *election*) elecciones *fpl*; **to take a ~ on sth** someter algo a votación
2 (= *total votes*) votos *mpl*, votación *f*; **there was a ~ of 84%** el 84% del electorado acudió a las urnas
3 to go to the ~s acudir a las urnas
4 (= *opinion poll*) encuesta *f*, sondeo *m*; **to take a ~** hacer una encuesta
B VT **1** [+ *votes*] obtener
2 (*in opinion poll*) [+ *people*] encuestar
C VI **he ~ed badly** obtuvo pocos votos, tuvo escaso apoyo; **we expect to ~ well** esperamos obtener muchos votos
D CPD ➤ **poll tax** impuesto *m* de capitación
pollen ['pɒlən] N polen *m* ➤ **pollen count** recuento *m* polínico

pollinate ['pɒlɪneɪt] VT polinizar

polling ['pəʊlɪŋ] N elecciones *fpl*; **~ will be on Thursday** las elecciones se celebrarán el jueves, se votará el jueves ➤ **polling booth** cabina *f* electoral ➤ **polling day** (*esp Brit*) día *m* de las elecciones ➤ **polling place** (*US*), **polling station** (*Brit*) centro *m* electoral

pollster ['pəʊlstəʳ] N encuestador(a) *m/f*

pollutant [pə'luːtənt] N contaminante *m*, agente *m* contaminador

pollute [pə'luːt] VT **1** (= *contaminate*) contaminar, polucionar; **to become ~d** contaminarse (**with** de) **2** (*fig*) corromper

polluter [pə'luːtəʳ] N contaminador(a) *m/f*

pollution [pə'luːʃən] N **1** contaminación *f*, polución *f* **2** (*fig*) corrupción *f*

polo ['pəʊləʊ] N (*Sport*) polo *m* ➤ **polo neck (sweater)** (*esp Brit*) (jersey *m* de) cuello *m* vuelto *or* cisne ➤ **polo shirt** polo *m*

poltergeist ['pɒltəgaɪst] N duende *m*, poltergeist *m*

poly* ['pɒlɪ] N (*Brit*) = **polytechnic**

polycotton [,pɒlɪ'kɒtən] N polycotton *m*, *mezcla de algodón y poliéster*

polyester [,pɒlɪ'estəʳ] Ⓐ N poliéster *m* Ⓑ ADJ de poliéster

polyethylene [,pɒlɪ'eθəliːn] N (*esp US*) polietileno *m*

polygamist [pɒ'lɪgəmɪst] N polígamo *m*

polygamous [pɒ'lɪgəməs] ADJ polígamo

polygamy [pɒ'lɪgəmɪ] N poligamia *f*

polyglot ['pɒlɪglɒt] ADJ, N políglota/a *m/f*

polygon ['pɒlɪgən] N polígono *m*

polygraph ['pɒlɪgrɑːf] N (*US*) polígrafo *m*, detector *m* de mentiras

polymath ['pɒlɪmæθ] N polímata *mf*, erudito/a *m/f*

polymer ['pɒlɪməʳ] N polímero *m*

Polynesia [,pɒlɪ'niːzɪə] N Polinesia *f*

polyp ['pɒlɪp] N pólipo *m*

polypropylene [,pɒlɪ'prɒpɪliːn] N polipropileno *m*

polystyrene [,pɒlɪ'staɪriːn] Ⓐ N poliestireno *m* Ⓑ ADJ de poliestireno

polytechnic [,pɒlɪ'teknɪk] N (*Brit*) (*formerly*) escuela *f* politécnica, politécnico *m*

polythene ['pɒlɪθiːn] N (*esp Brit*) polietileno *m* ➤ **polythene bag** bolsa *f* de plástico *or* polietileno

polyunsaturated [,pɒlɪʌn'sætʃəreɪtɪd] ADJ poliinsaturado

polyurethane [,pɒlɪ'jʊərɪθeɪn] N poliuretano *m*

pomegranate ['pɒməgrænɪt] N (= *fruit*) granada *f*; (= *tree*) granado *m*

pomelo ['pɒmɪ,ləʊ] N (*pl* **~s**) pomelo *m*

pommel ['pʌml] N pomo *m*

pommy* ['pɒmɪ] (*Australia pej*) ADJ, N inglés/esa *m/f*

pomp [pɒmp] N pompa *f*

Pompeii [pɒm'peɪiː] N Pompeya *f*

pompom ['pɒmpɒm], **pompon** ['pɒmpɒn] N borla *f*, pompón *m*

pomposity [pɒm'pɒsɪtɪ] N pomposidad *f*

pompous ['pɒmpəs] ADJ [*person*] pretencioso; [*occasion*] ostentoso; [*language*] ampuloso, inflado

poncho ['pɒntʃəʊ] N (*pl* **~s**) poncho *m*, manta *f*, ruana *f* (*Col, Ven*), sarape *m* (*Mex*), jorongo *m* (*Mex*)

pond [pɒnd] N (= *natural*) charca *f*; (*artificial*) estanque *m*

ponder ['pɒndəʳ] Ⓐ VT considerar, sopesar Ⓑ VI reflexionar *or* meditar (**on, over** sobre)

ponderous ['pɒndərəs] ADJ pesado

pong* [pɒŋ] (*Brit*) Ⓐ N peste *f* Ⓑ VI apestar

pontiff ['pɒntɪf] N pontífice *m*

pontificate [pɒn'tɪfɪkeɪt] VI pontificar

pontoon¹ [pɒn'tuːn] N pontón *m* ➤ **pontoon bridge** puente *m* de pontones

pontoon² [pɒn'tuːn] N (*Brit Cards*) veintiuna *f*

pony ['pəʊnɪ] Ⓐ N **1** (= *animal*) pony *m*, poney *m* (*Sp*) **2** (*US Scol**) chuleta* *f* Ⓑ CPD ➤ **pony trekking** excursión *f* en pony

ponytail ['pəʊnɪteɪl] N cola *f* de caballo, coleta *f*

poo** [puː] (*Brit baby talk*) N caca**; **to do a ~** hacer caca**

poodle ['puːdl] N caniche *mf*

poof** [pʊf] N (*Brit pej*) maricón*** *m*

pooh [puː] EXCL (*in response to smell*) ¡puaf!; (*expressing scorn*) ¡bah!

pooh-pooh [puː'puː] VT despreciar; [+ *proposal etc*] rechazar con desdén

pool¹ [puːl] N **1** (*natural*) charca *f*; (*artificial*) estanque *m*; (= *swimming pool*) piscina *f*, alberca *f* (*Mex*), pileta *f* (de natación) (*SC*) **2** [*of spilt liquid*] charco *m*; (*fig*) [*of light*] foco *m*

pool² [puːl] Ⓐ N **1** (= *common fund*) fondo *m* (común); (*Cards*) polla *f* **2** (= *supply, source*) reserva *f*; [*of genes etc*] fondo *m*, reserva *f*; **an untapped ~ of ability** una reserva de inteligencia no utilizada **3 the ~s** (*Brit*) (= *football pools*) las quinielas (*Sp*) **4** (= *form of snooker*) billar *m* americano; **to shoot ~** (*US*) jugar al billar americano Ⓑ VT juntar, poner en común Ⓒ CPD ➤ **pool room** sala *f* de billar ➤ **pool table** mesa *f* de billar

poop¹** [puːp] N (= *excrement*) caca** *f*

poop²** [puːp] N (*US*) (= *information*) onda* *f*, información *f*

pooped** [puːpt] ADJ (*US*) **to be ~** (= *tired*) estar hecho polvo*

pooper-scooper* ['puːpə,skuːpəʳ], **poop-scoop*** ['puːpskuːp] N caca-can* *m*

poor [pʊəʳ] Ⓐ ADJ (*compar* **~er**; *superl* **~est**)

> A common translation of **poor** is **pobre**. Note that **pobre** generally follows any noun it modifies when **poor** means not rich and precedes it when **poor** means unfortunate.

1 (= *not rich*) [*person, family, country*] pobre; **a ~ family** una familia pobre; **a ~ man** un pobre
2 (= *inferior, bad*) [*goods, service*] malo, de mala calidad; **he's a ~ actor** es un mal actor; **Britain's ~ economic performance** el bajo rendimiento económico obtenido por Gran Bretaña; **to have a ~ opinion of sb** tener un concepto poco favorable de algn; **his family comes a ~ second to his career** su familia queda relegada a segundo lugar tras su carrera
3 (= *deficient*) [*memory*] malo; [*soil*] pobre, estéril; [*harvest*] pobre, escaso; **I had a ~ education** la educación que recibí no fue muy buena; **a ~ diet** una dieta pobre; **"poor"** (*Scol*) (*as mark*) "deficiente"
4 (= *untalented*) **he was a ~ actor** era un actor flojo; **she was a ~ swimmer** no era buena nadadora; **to be ~ at maths** no ser muy bueno en matemáticas
5 (= *unfortunate*) pobre; **~ little thing!** ¡pobrecito!, ¡pobre criaturita!; **~ Mary** la pobre María
Ⓑ NPL **the ~** los pobres

poorly ['pʊəlɪ] Ⓐ ADV **1** (= *badly*) [*designed, equipped*] mal; **she did ~ in history** sacó mala nota en historia; **she did ~ at school** sacaba malas notas en el colegio; **~ lit** mal iluminado; **the job was ~ paid** el trabajo estaba mal pagado; **he was ~ paid** le pagaban poco **2** (= *meagrely, shabbily*) pobremente Ⓑ ADJ (*esp Brit*) (= *ill*) enfermo; **to be/feel ~** estar/encontrarse mal; **to look ~** tener mal aspecto

pop¹ [pɒp] Ⓐ N **1** (= *sound*) pequeño estallido *m*; [*of cork*] taponazo *m*; (= *imitative sound*) ¡pum!
2 (*esp Brit**) (= *drink*) refresco *m*, gaseosa *f* (*Sp*)
3 to have *or* **take a ~ at*** (= *criticize*) criticar
4 the drinks go for $3.50 a ~ (*esp US**) las bebidas son a 3.50 dólares cada una
Ⓑ ADV **to go ~** [*balloon*] reventar, hacer ¡pum!; [*cork*] salir disparado, hacer ¡pum!
Ⓒ VT **1** [+ *balloon*] hacer reventar; [+ *cork*] hacer saltar;
✦ IDIOM **to ~ one's clogs** (*Brit hum**) estirar la pata*
2 (*Brit**) (= *put*) poner (rápidamente); **to ~ sth into a drawer**

meter algo (rápidamente) en un cajón; **to ~ pills** drogarse (con pastillas); ✦ IDIOM **to ~ the question** declararse
Ⓓ VI **1** [*balloon*] reventar; [*cork*] saltar, salir disparado; **his eyes nearly ~ped out of his head** se le saltaban los ojos; **my ears ~ped** se me taponaron los oídos
2 (*Brit**) (= *go*) **we ~ped over to see them** fuimos a hacerles una breve visita; **let's ~ round to Joe's** vamos a pasarnos por casa de Joe
➤ **pop in*** VI + ADV entrar un momento; **to ~ in to see sb** pasar a ver a algn; **I just ~ped in to say hello** sólo quería saludarte
➤ **pop off*** VI + ADV **1** (*Brit*) (= *die*) estirar la pata* **2** (= *leave*) irse, marcharse
➤ **pop out* Ⓐ** VT + ADV **she ~ped her head out** asomó de repente la cabeza **Ⓑ** VI + ADV salir un momento
➤ **pop up*** VI + ADV aparecer inesperadamente

pop²* [pɒp] **Ⓐ** N (música *f*) pop *m* **Ⓑ** CPD [*music, song, singer, concert, group*] pop *inv* ➤ **pop art** pop-art *m* ➤ **pop star** estrella *f* de la música pop *or* del pop

pop³* [pɒp] N (*esp US*) (= *dad*) papá* *m*

pop. ABBR (= **population**) h.

popcorn [ˈpɒpkɔːn] N palomitas *fpl* de maíz, alborotos *mpl* (*SC, Per*), cabritas *fpl* (*SC, Per*)

pope [pəʊp] N papa *m*; **Pope John XXIII** el Papa Juan XXIII

pop-eyed [ˈpɒpˈaɪd] ADJ **they looked at me ~** me miraron con los ojos desorbitados

popgun [ˈpɒpɡʌn] N pistola *f* de juguete (de aire comprimido)

poplar [ˈpɒpləʳ] N (*black*) chopo *m*, álamo *m*; (*white*) álamo *m* blanco

poppa* [ˈpɒpə] N (*US*) papá* *m*

poppadom [ˈpɒpədəm] N torta *f* india

popper [ˈpɒpəʳ] N **1** (*Brit**) (= *press-stud*) corchete *m* **2** (*Drugs***) cápsula de nitrito amílico

poppet* [ˈpɒpɪt] N (*Brit*) encanto *m*, cielo *m*; **she's a ~** es un cielo; **yes, my ~** (*to little girl*) sí, hija, sí, querida

poppy [ˈpɒpɪ] N amapola *f* ➤ **Poppy Day** (*Brit*) día en el que se recuerda a los caídos en las dos guerras mundiales ➤ **poppy seed** semilla *f* de amapola

---

POPPY DAY

Poppy Day es la expresión coloquial para referirse al **Remembrance Day** o **Remembrance Sunday**, día en que se recuerda a los caídos en las dos grandes guerras mundiales del siglo XX. La celebración se hace el segundo domingo de noviembre y en los días que preceden a esta fecha se venden amapolas de papel con el fin de recaudar fondos destinados a las instituciones de caridad que prestan ayuda a los veteranos de guerra y a sus familias. Las amapolas representan las que florecieron en los campos franceses, donde tantos soldados perecieron durante la Primera Guerra Mundial. Ver tb www.britishlegion.org.uk

---

Popsicle® [ˈpɒpsɪkl] N (*US*) polo *m* (*Sp*), paleta *f* (helada) (*LAm*)

populace [ˈpɒpjʊlɪs] N (*gen*) pueblo *m*; (= *mob*) populacho *m*, turba *f*

popular [ˈpɒpjʊləʳ] **Ⓐ** ADJ **1** (= *well-liked*) **to be ~** [*show*] gozar de mucho éxito, gozar de mucha popularidad; [*person, boss*] gozar de mucha simpatía; **this is one of our most ~ lines** esta es una de nuestras líneas más vendidas; **he's ~ with the girls** tiene éxito con las chicas; **I'm not very ~ with her at the moment** en este momento no soy santo de su devoción; **she's very ~ with her colleagues** goza de mucha simpatía entre sus colegas; **the area is ~ with tourists** es una zona muy frecuentada por los turistas
2 (= *fashionable*) de moda
3 (= *widespread*) [*image, belief*] generalizado; **contrary to ~ belief** en contra de *or* contrario a lo que comúnmente se cree; **by ~ demand** a petición del público, respondiendo a la demanda general
4 (= *of the people*) [*unrest, support, culture, music*] popular;

[*uprising*] popular, del pueblo; **~ opinion** la opinión general **Ⓑ** CPD ➤ **the popular press** la prensa popular

popularity [ˌpɒpjʊˈlærɪtɪ] N popularidad *f*; **to gain** *or* **grow in ~** gozar de una popularidad cada vez mayor

popularize [ˈpɒpjʊləraɪz] VT **1** (= *make well-liked*) popularizar **2** (= *make available*) divulgar

popularly [ˈpɒpjʊləlɪ] ADV **it is ~ thought that ...** comúnmente se cree que ...; **Albert, ~ known as Bertie** Albert, corrientemente conocido como Bertie

populate [ˈpɒpjʊleɪt] VT poblar

population [ˌpɒpjʊˈleɪʃən] N población *f*; **75% of the male ~** el 75% de la población masculina ➤ **population density** densidad *f* de población ➤ **population explosion** explosión *f* demográfica ➤ **population growth** crecimiento *m* demográfico

populous [ˈpɒpjʊləs] ADJ populoso; **the most ~ city in the world** la ciudad más populosa del mundo

pop-up [ˈpɒpʌp] ADJ ➤ **pop-up advertisement** anuncio *m* emergente ➤ **pop-up book** libro *m* con historietas o escenas plegables ➤ **pop-up menu** menú *m* emergente ➤ **pop-up toaster** tostador *m* automático

porcelain [ˈpɔːslɪn] N porcelana *f*

porch [pɔːtʃ] N [*of church*] pórtico *m*; [*of house*] porche *m*, portal *m*; (*US*) (= *veranda*) porche *m*, terraza *f*

porcupine [ˈpɔːkjʊpaɪn] N puerco *m* espín

pore¹ [pɔːʳ] N (*Anat, Zool*) poro *m*

pore² [pɔːʳ] VI **to ~ over sth** estudiar algo

pork [pɔːk] N carne *f* de cerdo *or* puerco *or* (*LAm*) chancho ➤ **pork chop** chuleta *f* de cerdo *or* puerco ➤ **pork pie** (*Brit Culin*) empanada *f* de carne de cerdo ➤ **pork sausage** salchicha *f* de cerdo *or* puerco

porn* [pɔːn] **Ⓐ** N pornografía *f*, porno* *m*; **hard/soft ~** pornografía *f* dura/blanda **Ⓑ** CPD [*magazine, video, actor*] porno* *inv* ➤ **porn shop** tienda *f* de pornografía

pornographic [ˌpɔːnəˈɡræfɪk] ADJ pornográfico

pornography [pɔːˈnɒɡrəfɪ] N pornografía *f*

porous [ˈpɔːrəs] ADJ poroso

porpoise [ˈpɔːpəs] N marsopa *f*, puerco *m* de mar

porridge [ˈpɒrɪdʒ] N (*esp Brit Culin*) avena *f* (cocida), ≈ atole *m* (*Mex*) ➤ **porridge oats** copos *mpl* de avena

port¹ [pɔːt] **Ⓐ** N (= *harbour, town*) puerto *m*; **to put into ~** tomar puerto; **~ of call** puerto *m* de escala; **his next ~ of call was the chemist's** (*fig*) luego fue a la farmacia; ✦ IDIOM **any ~ in a storm** la necesidad carece de ley **Ⓑ** CPD portuario ➤ **port authority** autoridad *f* portuaria

port² [pɔːt] N (*Naut, Aer*) (*also ~ side*) babor *m*; **land to ~!** ¡tierra a babor!

port³ [pɔːt] N (*Comput*) puerta *f*, puerto *m*, port *m*

port⁴ [pɔːt] N (= *wine*) oporto *m*

portability [ˌpɔːtəˈbɪlɪtɪ] N (*esp Comput*) portabilidad *f*; [*of software*] transferibilidad *f*

portable [ˈpɔːtəbl] **Ⓐ** ADJ portátil **Ⓑ** N máquina *f*/ televisor *m* etc portátil

Portakabin® [ˈpɔːtəˌkæbɪn] N (*gen*) caseta *f* prefabricada

portal [ˌpɔːtl] N (*gen, Comput*) portal *m*

portcullis [pɔːtˈkʌlɪs] N rastrillo *m*

portend [pɔːˈtend] VT (*liter*) augurar, presagiar; **what does this ~?** ¿qué significa esto?

portent [ˈpɔːtent] N augurio *m*, presagio *m*; **a ~ of doom** un presagio de la catástrofe

porter [ˈpɔːtəʳ] **Ⓐ** N **1** (*Rail, Aer*) maletero *m*, mozo *m* de cuerda *or* de estación, changador *m* (*SC*); (*US Rail*) mozo *m* de los coches-cama, camarero *m* (*LAm*); (*touting for custom*) mozo *m* de cuerda **2** (*Brit*) [*of hotel, office etc*] portero/a *m/f* **3** (= *Sherpa*) porteador *m* **4** (*esp Brit*) (*in hospital*) camillero/a *m/f* **Ⓑ** CPD ➤ **porter's lodge** portería *f*, conserjería *f*

portfolio [pɔːtˈfəʊlɪəʊ] N (*pl ~s*) [*of artist, designer*] carpeta *f*, porfolio *m*; [*of politician*] cartera *f*; **~ of shares** cartera *f* de acciones

porthole [ˈpɔːthəʊl] N portilla *f*

portico ['pɔːtɪkəʊ] N (pl ~**es** or ~**s**) pórtico m

portion ['pɔːʃən] Ⓐ N 1 (= part, piece) porción f, parte f; [of food] ración f; [of cake] porción f, trozo m 2 (= quantity, in relation to a whole) porción f, porcentaje m Ⓑ VT (also ~ **out**) repartir, dividir

portly ['pɔːtlɪ] ADJ grueso, corpulento

portrait ['pɔːtrɪt] N retrato m; **to have one's ~ painted** ◇ **sit for one's ~** hacerse un retrato ➤ **portrait format** (Comput, Publishing) formato m vertical ➤ **portrait painter** retratista mf

portray [pɔː'treɪ] VT representar, pintar

portrayal [pɔː'treɪəl] N 1 (Art) retrato m 2 (= description) descripción f, representación f

Portugal ['pɔːtjʊgəl] N Portugal m

Portuguese [,pɔːtjʊ'giːz] Ⓐ ADJ portugués Ⓑ N (pl ~) 1 (= person) portugués/esa m/f 2 (Ling) portugués m

pose [pəʊz] Ⓐ N 1 (of body) postura f, actitud f 2 (fig) afectación f, pose f; **it's only a ~** es pura pose Ⓑ VT [+ problem, question, difficulty] plantear; [+ threat] representar, encerrar Ⓒ VI 1 (for artist etc) posar; **she once ~d for Picasso** una vez posó para Picasso 2 (affectedly) presumir, hacer pose 3 **to ~ as** (= pretend to be) hacerse pasar por; (= disguise o.s. as) disfrazarse de

poser* ['pəʊzəʳ] N 1 (= problem) problema m or pregunta f difícil 2 (= person) persona f afectada

poseur [pəʊ'zɜːʳ] N persona f afectada

posh* [pɒʃ] Ⓐ ADJ (compar ~**er**; superl ~**est**) (= high-class) elegante, pijo (Sp*); (= affected) afectado; [wedding etc] de mucho rumbo; [school] de buen tono; **a ~ car/hotel** un coche/un hotel de lujo; ~ **people** gente f bien; **it's a very ~ neighbourhood** es un barrio de lo más elegante Ⓑ ADV **to talk ~** hablar con acento afectado

position [pə'zɪʃən] Ⓐ N 1 (= location) [of object, person] posición f; [of house, town] situación f, ubicación f (LAm); **to be in ~** estar en su sitio; **to get into ~** ponerse en posición 2 (= posture) (gen) posición f, postura f; **to change (one's) ~** cambiar de posición or postura; **he had raised himself to a sitting ~** se había incorporado 3 (Sport) **what ~ do you play (in)?** ¿de qué juegas? 4 (Mil) [of troops] posición f 5 (in race, competition) puesto m, posición f, lugar m; (in class, league) puesto m; **he finished in third ~** terminó en tercer puesto or lugar, terminó en tercera posición 6 (in society) posición f 7 (= post) (gen) puesto m; (high-ranking) cargo m; **a high ~ in government** un alto cargo en el gobierno; **a ~ of trust** un puesto de confianza 8 (= situation, circumstance) situación f; **this is the ~** la situación es ésta; **put yourself in my ~** ponte en mi lugar; **(if I were) in his ~, I'd say nothing** yo que él or yo en su lugar no diría nada; **we are in a strong negotiating ~** estamos en una buena posición para negociar; **they were in a ~ to help** su situación les permitía ayudar; **he's in no ~ to criticize** no es quién para criticar, él no está en condiciones de criticar 9 (= opinion) postura f (**on** con respecto a); **what is our ~ on Greece?** ¿cuál es nuestra nuestra política or postura con respecto a Grecia? Ⓑ VT [+ furniture, object, ball] colocar; [+ police, troops] apostar; **to ~ o.s.** colocarse, situarse; **the house was strategically ~ed** la casa estaba situada or ubicada de forma estratégica; **he is well ~ed to act as intermediary** está en una buena posición para hacer de intermediario

positive ['pɒzɪtɪv] Ⓐ ADJ 1 (= sure, certain) seguro (**about** de); **"are you sure?" — "yes, ~"** —¿estás seguro? —segurísimo; **we have ~ proof that ...** tenemos pruebas concluyentes de que ... 2 (= affirmative, constructive) [attitude, view, influence] positivo; [criticism] constructivo; [person] que tiene una actitud positiva; ~ **discrimination** (Brit) discriminación f positiva; **on the ~ side** en el lado positivo 3 (Elec, Phot, Math, Med, Ling) positivo Ⓑ N **the ~s outweigh the negatives** los aspectos positivos tienen más peso que or superan a los negativos Ⓒ ADV **to test ~** dar positivo; **you have to think ~** hay que ser positivo

positively ['pɒzɪtɪvlɪ] ADV 1 (= with certainty) [guarantee] con seguridad; (= categorically) [refuse] tajantemente; **the body has been ~ identified** se ha hecho una identificación definitiva del cadáver 2 (= affirmatively) [respond, act] de manera positiva; **most employees view the new system ~** la mayoría de los empleados han reaccionado favorablemente al nuevo sistema, la mayoría de los empleados ve el nuevo sistema con buenos ojos; **you must think and act ~** debes tener una actitud positiva 3 (*) (= really, absolutely) [amazed, delighted] realmente, verdaderamente; **this is ~ the last time I'm going to tell you** está sí que es la última vez que te lo digo 4 (Elec) **a ~ charged ion** un ión con carga positiva

poss* [pɒs] ADJ ABBR = **possible**; **as soon as ~** cuanto antes, lo más pronto posible

posse ['pɒsɪ] N (US) pelotón m

possess [pə'zes] VT 1 (= have) tener, poseer 2 (= control, take over) **to be ~ed by an idea** estar poseído por una idea; **whatever can have ~ed you?** ¿cómo se te ocurrió?

possession [pə'zeʃən] N 1 (gen) posesión f; ~ **of arms** tenencia f de armas; **to come into the ~ of** pasar a manos de; **to get ~ of** [+ building, property] ganar derecho de entrada a; **to get/have ~ of the ball** (Sport) hacerse con/tener el balón; **to have sth in one's ~** tener algo (en su posesión or sus manos); **to be in ~ of sth** estar en posesión de algo; **to be in full ~ of one's faculties** estar en pleno uso de sus facultades mentales; **to take ~ of sth** (Jur) tomar posesión de algo; (by force) apoderarse de algo 2 **possessions** posesiones fpl, bienes mpl; **Spain's overseas ~s** las posesiones de España en ultramar

possessive [pə'zesɪv] Ⓐ ADJ posesivo; **to be ~ about sth/towards sb** ser posesivo con algo/algn Ⓑ N (Ling) posesivo m Ⓒ CPD ➤ **possessive pronoun** pronombre m posesivo

possessor [pə'zesəʳ] N poseedor/a m/f, dueño/a m/f

possibility [,pɒsə'bɪlɪtɪ] N 1 (= chance, likelihood) posibilidad f; **is there any ~ (that) they could help?** ¿hay alguna posibilidad de que nos ayuden?; **there is a strong ~ I'll be late** es muy posible que me retrase, hay muchas posibilidades de que me retrase; **it is within the bounds of ~** está dentro de lo posible; **it is not beyond the bounds of ~ that he'll succeed** cabe dentro de lo posible or no es imposible que lo consiga; **there is no ~ of his agreeing to it** no existe ninguna posibilidad de que lo consienta 2 (usu pl) (= potential) **the scheme has real possibilities** es un plan que promete, es un plan de gran potencial; **it's a job with great possibilities** es un trabajo con mucho futuro or porvenir

possible ['pɒsəbl] Ⓐ ADJ posible; **it is ~ that he'll come** es posible que venga, puede (ser) que venga; **will it be ~ for me to leave early?** ¿hay algún inconveniente en que me vaya antes de la hora?; **try to make the lesson as interesting as ~** trata de que la lección sea lo más interesante posible; **you must practise as much as ~** debes practicar todo lo que puedas or todo lo posible; **as soon as ~** cuanto antes, lo antes posible; **we provide the best ~ accommodation for our students** nuestros estudiantes disponen del mejor de los alojamientos; **if (at all) ~** si es posible, a ser posible; **it's just ~ he may still be there** existe una pequeña posibilidad de que siga allí; **to make sth ~**: **improvements made ~ by new technology** mejoras fpl que la nueva tecnología ha hecho posible; **the new legislation would make it ~ for alcohol to be sold on Sundays** la nueva legislación posibilitaría la venta de alcohol los domingos; **there is no ~ excuse for his behaviour** su comportamiento no tiene excusa que valga; **what ~ motive could she have?** ¿qué motivo puede tener?; **where ~** donde sea posible; **they have joined the job market at the worst ~ time** se han incorporado al mercado de trabajo en el peor momento posible or en el peor de los momentos Ⓑ N 1 (*) (= suitable person) (for job) candidato/a m/f; **he's a ~ for Saturday's match** es posible que juegue en el partido del sábado 2 **the ~** lo posible

possibly ['pɒsəblɪ] ADV 1 (= feasibly, conceivably) **if I ~ can** si me es posible, si puedo; **I go as often as I ~ can** voy siempre que puedo, voy lo más a menudo posible; **could**

you ~ **come another day?** ¿le sería posible venir otro día?, ¿podría venir otro día?; **I can't ~ eat all this** me es totalmente imposible comer todo esto; **it can't ~ be true!** ¡no puede ser verdad!; **she will do everything she ~ can to help you** hará todo lo que esté en su mano *or* todo lo que pueda para ayudarte **2** (= *perhaps*) **"will you be able to come?" — "possibly"** —¿podrás venir? —es posible *or* —puede que sí; ~ **not** puede que no; **of the 200 who apply, ~ five may be accepted** de los 200 solicitantes, tal vez se elija a cinco

possum ['pɒsəm] N (US) zarigüeya *f*

post¹ [pəʊst] **Ⓐ** N **1** [*of wood, metal*] poste *m*; (*also* **goalpost**) poste *m* (de la portería); (*for fencing, marking*) estaca *f* **2** (*Sport*) **the starting/finishing ~** el poste de salida/llegada **Ⓑ** VT **1** (*also* ~ **up**) [+ *bill, notice*] poner; **"post no bills"** "prohibido fijar carteles" **2** (= *announce*) [+ *exam results*] hacer público, sacar; **to ~ sth/sb (as) missing** dar algo/a algn por desaparecido **3** (= *inform*) **to keep sb ~ed (on** *or* **about sth)** tener *or* mantener a algn al corriente *or* al tanto *or* informado (de algo) **4** (US *Sport*) [+ *time, score*] registrar, obtener

post² [pəʊst] **Ⓐ** N **1** (*esp Brit*) (= *mail service*) correo *m*; **by ~** por correo; **your cheque is in the ~** su cheque está en el correo; **to drop** *or* **put sth in the ~** echar algo al correo *or* al buzón; **to drop** *or* **put sth in the ~ to sb** enviar *or* mandar algo a algn **2** (*esp Brit*) (= *letters*) correo *m*; **is there any ~ for me?** ¿hay correo para mí? **3** (*esp Brit*) (= *collection*) recogida *f*; (= *delivery*) entrega *f*; **to catch the ~** echar el correo antes de la recogida **Ⓑ** VT (*esp Brit*) (= *send by post*) mandar *or* enviar por correo; (*Brit*) (= *put in mailbox*) echar al correo *or* al buzón **Ⓒ** CPD ➤ **post and packing** gastos *mpl* de envío ➤ **post office** oficina *f* de correos, correos *m*, correo *m* (*LAm*); **I'm going to the ~ office** voy a correos, voy al correo (*LAm*) ➤ **the Post Office** ≈ la Dirección General de Correos ➤ **post office box** apartado *m* de correos, casilla *f* (postal *or* de correo(s)) (*LAm*)

post³ [pəʊst] **Ⓐ** N **1** (= *job*) (*gen*) puesto *m*; (*high-ranking*) cargo *m* **2** (*Mil*) (= *place of duty, stronghold*) puesto *m* **Ⓑ** VT **1** (*Brit*) (= *send*) [+ *diplomat, soldier*] destinar; **to ~ sb abroad** destinar a algn al extranjero **2** (US *Jur*) [+ *collateral*] pagar; **to ~ bail** pagar la fianza

post... [pəʊst] PREF post..., pos...

postage ['pəʊstɪdʒ] N franqueo *m*, porte *m*; ~ **due** a pagar; ~ **paid** porte *m* pagado ➤ **postage and handling** (*US*), **postage and packing** (*Brit*) gastos *mpl* de envío ➤ **postage meter** (*US*) franqueadora *f* ➤ **postage rates** tarifa *fsing* de correo ➤ **postage stamp** sello *m* (de correos), estampilla *f* (*LAm*), timbre *m* (*Mex*)

postal ['pəʊstəl] ADJ postal ➤ **postal code** (*Brit*) = **postcode** ➤ **postal order** (*Brit*) giro *m* postal ➤ **postal rates** tarifa *fsing* de correo ➤ **postal service** servicio *m* postal ➤ **postal vote** voto *m* postal

postbag ['pəʊstbæg] N (*Brit*) (= *sack*) saco *m* postal; (= *letters*) correspondencia *f*, cartas *fpl*

postbox ['pəʊstbɒks] N (*Brit*) buzón *m*

postcard ['pəʊstkɑːd] N (tarjeta *f*) postal *f*

postcode ['pəʊstkəʊd] N (*Brit*) código *m* postal

postdate ['pəʊst'deɪt] VT poner una fecha posterior a

postdated ['pəʊst'deɪtɪd] ADJ [*cheque*] con fecha posterior

post-doctoral ['pəʊst'dɒktərəl] ADJ posdoctoral

poster ['pəʊstə'] N cartel *m*, póster *m*, afiche *m* (*LAm*) ➤ **poster paint** témpera *f*

poste restante ['pəʊst'restɑːnt] N (*esp Brit*) lista *f* de correos, poste *f* restante (*LAm*)

posterior [pɒs'tɪərɪə'] ADJ (*frm*) posterior

posterity [pɒs'terɪtɪ] N posteridad *f*

postgraduate ['pəʊst'grædjʊɪt] (*Brit*) N posgraduado/a *m/f* ➤ **postgraduate course** curso *m* para posgraduados

posthumous ['pɒstjʊməs] ADJ póstumo

posthumously ['pɒstjʊməslɪ] ADV póstumamente, con carácter póstumo

post-impressionist ['pəʊstɪm'preʃənɪst] ADJ, N posimpresionista *mf*

posting ['pəʊstɪŋ] N (*esp Brit Mil etc*) destino *m*

postman ['pəʊstmən] N (*pl* **postmen**) (*Brit*) cartero *m*

postmark ['pəʊstmɑːk] **Ⓐ** N matasellos *m inv* **Ⓑ** VT matasellar; **it is ~ed "León"** lleva el matasellos de León

postmaster ['pəʊst,mɑːstə'] N administrador *m* de correos

postmistress ['pəʊst,mɪstrɪs] N administradora *f* de correos

postmodern ['pəʊst'mɒdən] ADJ posmoderno

post-mortem ['pəʊst'mɔːtəm] N autopsia *f*; **to carry out a ~** practicar una autopsia

post-natal ['pəʊst'neɪtl] ADJ postnatal, pos(t)parto ➤ **post-natal depression** depresión *f* pos(t)parto

post-operative [,pəʊst'ɒpərətɪv] ADJ posoperatorio

post-paid ['pəʊst'peɪd] ADV porte pagado, franco de porte

postpone [pəʊst'pəʊn] VT aplazar, postergar (*LAm*); **to ~ sth for a month** aplazar algo por un mes

postponement [pəʊst'pəʊnmənt] N aplazamiento *m*

postscript ['pəʊsskrɪpt] N (*to letter*) posdata *f*; (*fig*) epílogo *m*

post-traumatic ['pəʊstrɔː,mætɪk] ADJ postraumático ➤ **post-traumatic stress** estrés *m* postraumático

postulate **Ⓐ** ['pɒstjʊlɪt] N postulado *m* **Ⓑ** ['pɒstjʊleɪt] VT postular

posture ['pɒstʃə'] **Ⓐ** N postura *f*, actitud *f* **Ⓑ** VI (*pej*) adoptar una postura afectada

postwar ['pəʊst'wɔː'] ADJ de la posguerra; **the ~ period** la pos(t)guerra

postwoman ['pəʊst,wʊmən] N (*pl* **postwomen**) (*Brit*) cartera *f*

posy ['pəʊzɪ] N ramillete *m*

pot¹ [pɒt] **Ⓐ** N **1** (*for cooking*) cazuela *f*, olla *f* (*LAm*); (*for jam*) tarro *m*, pote *m* (*SC*); (*for flowers*) tiesto *m*, maceta *f*; (= *teapot*) tetera *f*; (= *coffee pot*) cafetera *f*; (= *piece of pottery*) cacharro *m*; ~**s and pans** batería *fsing* de cocina, cacharros *mpl* **2** (= *potful*) cazuela *f*; **a ~ of coffee for two** café *m* para dos; **to make a ~ of tea** hacer el té **3** (*Cards*) pozo *m*; (*esp US*) (= *kitty*) bote *m*; **to have ~s of money*** estar forrado de dinero* **Ⓑ** VT **1** [+ *jam, meat, etc*] conservar en tarros **2** [+ *plant*] poner en tiesto *or* maceta; [+ *seedling*] enmacetar **3** (*Snooker, Billiards*) meter en la tronera **Ⓒ** CPD ➤ **pot belly** (*from overeating*) panza* *f*; (*from malnutrition*) barriga *f* hinchada ➤ **pot cheese** (*US*) ≈ requesón *m* ➤ **pot herb** hierba *f* aromática ➤ **pot luck to take ~ luck** conformarse con lo que haya ➤ **pot plant** (*esp Brit*) planta *f* de interior ➤ **pot roast** carne *f* asada a la cazuela ➤ **pot shot*** tiro *m* al azar; **to take a ~ shot at sth** disparar contra algo al azar

pot²** [pɒt] N (= *marijuana*) maría *f* (*Sp**), mota *f* (*LAm**)

potash ['pɒtæʃ] N potasa *f*

potassium [pə'tæsɪəm] N potasio *m* ➤ **potassium cyanide** cianuro *m* de potasio ➤ **potassium sulphate** sulfato *m* potásico

potato [pə'teɪtəʊ] N (*pl* ~**es**) patata *f* (*Sp*), papa *f* (*LAm*); **baked ~** patata *f* (*Sp*) *or* papa *f* (*LAm*) al horno ➤ **potato chip** (*US*), **potato crisp** (*Brit*) patata *f* frita (*Sp*), papa *f* frita (*LAm*) ➤ **potato masher** utensilio *m* para aplastar las patatas/papas al hacer puré ➤ **potato peeler** pelapatatas *m inv* (*Sp*), pelapapas *m inv* (*LAm*)

pot-bellied ['pɒt,belɪd] ADJ (*from overeating*) barrigón*; (*from malnutrition*) de vientre hinchado

potency ['pəʊtənsɪ] N potencia *f*; [*of drink*] fuerza *f*; [*of remedy*] eficacia *f*

potent ['pəʊtənt] ADJ potente, poderoso; [*drink*] fuerte; [*remedy*] eficaz

potentate ['pəʊtənteɪt] N potentado *m*

potential [pə'tenʃəl] **Ⓐ** ADJ en potencia; ~ **earnings**

ganancias *fpl* potenciales; **a ~ prime minister** un primer ministro en ciernes; **a ~ threat** una posible amenaza **Ⓑ** N potencial *m*; **he hasn't yet realized his full ~** todavía no ha desarrollado plenamente su potencial; **to have the ~ to do sth** [*person*] tener aptitudes *or* capacidad para hacer algo; **our ~ for increasing production** nuestras posibilidades de incrementar la producción

potentially [pə'tenʃəlɪ] ADV en potencia, potencialmente

pothole ['pɒthəʊl] N **1** (*in road*) bache *m* **2** (*Geol*) marmita *f* de gigante, gruta *f*; (*loosely*) cueva *f*, caverna *f*, profunda gruta *f*

potholer ['pɒthəʊlə'] N (*Brit*) espeleólogo/a *m/f*

potholing ['pɒthəʊlɪŋ] N (*Brit*) espeleología *f*; **to go ~** hacer espeleología; (*on specific occasion*) ir de espeleología

potion ['pəʊʃən] N poción *f*, pócima *f*

potpourri [pəʊ'pʊərɪ] N (*pl* ~**s**) **1** (= *flowers*) flores *fpl* secas aromáticas, popurrí *m* **2** (*of music, writing*) popurrí *m*

pot-roast ['pɒtrəʊst] VT asar

potted ['pɒtɪd] ADJ **1** [*food*] conservado en tarros; [*plant*] en tiesto, en maceta **2** (*Brit*) (= *shortened*) [*history, version*] resumido

potter¹ ['pɒtə'] N alfarero/a *m/f*; (*artistic*) ceramista *mf* ➤ **potter's wheel** torno *m* de alfarero

potter² ['pɒtə'] VI (*Brit*) entretenerse haciendo un poco de todo; **I ~ed round the house all day** estuve todo el día en casa haciendo un poco de todo; **we ~ed round the shops** nos paseamos por las tiendas

pottery ['pɒtərɪ] N **1** (= *craft*) alfarería *f*; (= *art*) cerámica *f* **2** (= *pots*) cerámica *f*; (*of fine quality*) loza *f*

potting compost ['pɒtɪŋˌkɒmpɒst] N (*Brit*) compost *m* para macetas

potty¹* ['pɒtɪ] N orinal *m* de niño, bacinica *f* (*LAm*)

potty²* ['pɒtɪ] ADJ (*compar* **pottier**; *superl* **pottiest**) (*Brit*) (= *mad*) chiflado*; **she's ~ about him** anda loca por él*, se chifla por él*; **you must be ~!** ¡tú estás loco!; **to drive sb ~** volver loco a algn

potty-trained ['pɒtɪˌtreɪnd] ADJ (*Brit*) que ya no necesita pañales

potty-training ['pɒtɪˌtreɪnɪŋ] N (*Brit*) *adiestramiento de los niños pequeños en el uso del orinal para hacer sus necesidades*

pouch [paʊtʃ] N (*for tobacco*) petaca *f*; (*for ammunition*) cartuchera *f*; (*Zool, Anat*) bolsa *f*

pouf(fe) [puːf] N **1** (= *seat*) puf(f) *m* **2** (*Brit***) = poof**

poultice ['pəʊltɪs] N cataplasma *f*, emplasto *m*

poultry ['pəʊltrɪ] N (*alive*) aves *fpl* de corral; (*as food*) aves *fpl* ➤ **poultry farm** granja *f* avícola ➤ **poultry farmer** avicultor(a) *m/f* ➤ **poultry farming** avicultura *f* ➤ **poultry shop** (*US*) pollería *f*

pounce [paʊns] **Ⓐ** N salto *m*, ataque *m* **Ⓑ** VI abalanzarse (**on** sobre); **to ~ on sth/sb** (*lit*) abalanzarse sobre algo/algn, echarse encima de algo/algn; **to ~ on sb's mistake** saltar sobre el error de algn

pound¹ [paʊnd] **Ⓐ** N **1** (= *weight*) libra *f* (= 453,6*gr*); **they sell it by the ~** lo venden por libras; ⟳ *IMPERIAL SYSTEM* **2** (= *money*) libra *f*; **the ~** la libra esterlina **Ⓑ** CPD ➤ **pound coin** moneda *f* de una libra

pound² [paʊnd] **Ⓐ** VT **1** (*strike*) (*with fists*) [+ *door, table*] aporrear, golpear; (*with hammer*) martillear; (*with other instrument*) golpear; [*sea, waves*] azotar, batir contra; **he ~ed the table with his fist** aporreó *or* golpeó la mesa con el puño; **the waves ~ed the boat to pieces** las olas batieron contra el bote hasta destrozarlo; **day after day long-range artillery ~ed the city** día tras día fuego de artillería de largo alcance cayó sobre la ciudad causando estragos; **the bombs ~ed the city to rubble** las bombas redujeron la ciudad a escombros

2 (*Culin*) [+ *herbs, spices*] machacar; [+ *garlic, mixture*] machacar, majar; [+ *meat*] golpear; [+ *dough*] trabajar **3** (= *thump*) [+ *piano, typewriter*] aporrear

Ⓑ VI **1** (= *throb, pulsate*) [*head*] estar a punto de estallar; [*heart*] palpitar; [*music*] retumbar

2 (= *strike*) **the sea ~ed against the rocks** el mar azotaba las rocas *or* batía contra las rocas; **somebody began ~ing at the**

door alguien empezó a aporrear la puerta; **we listened to the rain ~ing on the roof** oíamos la lluvia cayendo con fuerza sobre el tejado

3 (= *move heavily*) **to ~ up/down the stairs** subir/bajar las escaleras con paso pesado *or* pesadamente

pound³ [paʊnd] N (*for dogs*) perrera *f*; (*for cars*) depósito *m* de coches

pounding ['paʊndɪŋ] N **1** [*of feet, hooves*] pisadas *fpl*; [*of guns*] martilleo *m*; [*of sea, waves*] embate *m*; [*of heart*] palpitaciones *fpl*, latidos *mpl* violentos **2** (*from shells, bombs*) bombardeo *m*; **the city took a ~ last night** la ciudad fue muy castigada en el bombardeo de anoche

3 Barcelona gave us a real ~* el Barcelona nos dio una paliza de las buenas*

pour [pɔː'] **Ⓐ** VT **1** (= *serve*) servir; **to ~ sb a drink** servir una copa a algn

2 (= *tip*) [+ *liquid*] verter, echar; [+ *salt, powder*] echar; **I ~ed the milk down the sink** vertí *or* eché la leche por el fregadero; **he ~ed some wine into a glass** vertió *or* echó un poco de vino en un vaso; **~ the sauce over the meat** vierta *or* eche la salsa sobre la carne

3 (= *invest*) invertir (**into** en); **we can't go on ~ing money into this project** no podemos seguir invirtiendo ese caudal en este proyecto

Ⓑ VI **1** (= *serve*) servir; **shall I ~?** ¿sirvo?

2 (= *flow*) **water was ~ing down the walls** el agua caía a raudales por las paredes; **tears ~ed down his face** las lágrimas le resbalaban por la cara; **blood ~ed from the wound** la sangre salía a borbotones de la herida; **water came ~ing into the room** el agua entraba a raudales en el cuarto; **the sweat was ~ing off him** sudaba a chorros

3 (*Met*) **it's ~ing (with rain)** está lloviendo a cántaros, está diluviando

4 (*fig*) **refugees ~ed into the country** entraban grandes cantidades de refugiados en el país; **sunshine ~ed into the room** el sol entraba a raudales en la habitación; **cars ~ed off the ferry** muchísimos coches salían del transbordador

➤ **pour away** VT + ADV tirar; **he had to ~ the wine away** tuvo que tirar el vino

➤ **pour in Ⓐ** VI + ADV **1** [*water*] entrar; **sunshine ~ed in from the courtyard** desde el patio el sol entraba a raudales en la habitación

2 (*fig*) [*people*] (*to country, area*) llegar a raudales; (*to shop, office*) entrar a raudales; **letters ~ed in from their fans** les llovían cartas de sus admiradores, llegaban avalanchas de cartas de sus admiradores

Ⓑ VT + ADV **1** (*lit*) [+ *liquid*] (*into mixture*) añadir; (*into container*) echar

2 (*fig*) **we can't keep ~ing in capital** no podemos seguir invirtiendo tanto capital *or* ese caudal

➤ **pour out Ⓐ** VT + ADV **1** (= *serve*) [+ *tea, milk, cornflakes*] servir **2** (= *emit*) [+ *smoke, fumes*] arrojar **3** (*fig*) [+ *anger, emotion*] desahogar; [+ *words, abuse*] soltar; **to ~ out one's feelings (to sb)** desahogarse (con algn) **Ⓑ** VI + ADV **1** [*water, liquid*] salir a raudales; [*blood*] salir a borbotones **2** (= *come out in large numbers*) [*people, crowds*] salir en tropel

pouring ['pɔːrɪŋ] ADJ **1** [*custard, cream etc*] líquido **2** [*rain*] torrencial; **in the ~ rain** bajo la lluvia torrencial

pout [paʊt] **Ⓐ** N puchero *m*, mohín *m* **Ⓑ** VI hacer pucheros, hacer un mohín

poverty ['pɒvətɪ] N pobreza *f*; **to live in ~** vivir en la pobreza; **~ of ideas** pobreza *f* de ideas ➤ **poverty line**, **poverty level** (*US*) umbral *m* de pobreza; **to live above/ below the ~ line** vivir por encima de/por debajo del umbral de pobreza

poverty-stricken ['pɒvətɪˌstrɪkn] ADJ [*person*] muy pobre, indigente; [*area*] muy pobre; **to be ~** estar en la miseria

POW N ABBR = **prisoner of war**

powder ['paʊdə'] **Ⓐ** N polvo *m*; (= *face powder, talcum powder*) polvos *mpl*; (= *gun powder*) pólvora *f* **Ⓑ** VT **1** (= *reduce to powder*) pulverizar, reducir a polvo **2** (*with face powder, talcum powder*) empolvar; (*with flour, icing sugar*) espolvorear (**with** de); **to ~ one's nose** (*lit*) empolvarse la nariz; (*euph*) ir al baño **Ⓒ** CPD ➤ **powder blue** azul *m* pálido ➤ **powder compact** polvera *f* ➤ **powder keg: the country is a ~ keg** el país es un polvorín ➤ **powder puff** borla *f* ➤ **powder room**

tocador *m*, aseos *mpl* (de señora)

powder-blue [ˈpaʊdəˈbluː] ADJ azul pálido

powdered [ˈpaʊdəd] ADJ en polvo ➤ **powdered milk** leche *f* en polvo ➤ **powdered sugar** (*US*) azúcar *m* glasé, azúcar *m* en polvo, azúcar *m* flor (*SC*)

powdery [ˈpaʊdərɪ] ADJ [*substance*] pulverulento; [*snow*] en polvo

power [paʊəʳ] Ⓐ N **1** (= *control*) poder *m*; (*physical strength*) fuerza *f*; **to have sb in one's ~** tener a algn en su poder; **to have the ~ of life and death over sb** tener poder para decidir sobre la vida de algn
2 (*Pol*) poder *m*, poderío *m*; **to be in ~** estar en el poder; **to come to ~** subir al poder
3 (*Mil*) **a nation's air/sea ~** la potencia aérea/naval de un país, el poderío aéreo/naval de un país
4 (= *authority*) poder *m*, autoridad *f*; **they have no ~ in economic matters** carecen de autoridad en asuntos económicos; **it was seen as an abuse of his ~** se percibió como un abuso de poder por su parte; **that is beyond or outside my ~(s)** eso no es de mi competencia; **to exceed one's ~s** excederse en el ejercicio de sus atribuciones *or* facultades
5 (= *ability*) **it is beyond his ~ to save her** no está dentro de sus posibilidades salvarla, no puede hacer nada para salvarla; **~s of concentration** capacidad *f* de concentración; **to be at the height of one's ~s** estar en plenitud de facultades; **to do everything in one's ~ to help sb** hacer todo lo posible por ayudar a algn; **~s of persuasion** poder *msing* de persuasión *or* convicción
6 (= *nation*) potencia *f*
7 (= *person in authority*) **they are the real ~ in the government** son los que ostentan el auténtico poder en el gobierno; **the ~s that be** las autoridades, los que mandan; **the ~s of darkness** *or* **evil** las fuerzas del mal; ✦ IDIOM **the ~ behind the throne** la eminencia gris
8 (= *forcefulness*) [*of argument*] fuerza *f*; **the ~ of love/ thought** el poder del amor/del intelecto
9 [*of engine, machine*] potencia *f*, fuerza *f*; [*of telescope*] aumento *m*; (= *output*) rendimiento *m*; **microwave on full ~ for one minute** póngalo con el microondas a plena potencia durante un minuto; **the ship returned to port under her own ~** el buque volvió al puerto impulsado por sus propios motores
10 (= *source of energy*) energía *f*; (= *electric power*) electricidad *f*; **they cut off the ~** cortaron la corriente; **nuclear ~** energía *f* nuclear
11 (*Math*) potencia *f*; **seven to the ~ (of) three** siete elevado a la tercera potencia, siete elevado al cubo; **to the nth ~** a la enésima potencia
12 (*) (= *a lot of*) **that holiday did me a ~ of good** esas vacaciones me hicieron mucho bien
Ⓑ VT **a plane ~ed by four jets** un avión propulsado por cuatro motores a reacción; **a racing car ~ed by a 4.2 litre engine** un coche de carreras impulsado por un motor de 4,2 litros
Ⓒ CPD ➤ **power base** base *f* de poder ➤ **power cable** cable *m* de energía eléctrica ➤ **power cut** (*esp Brit*) corte *m* de luz *or* de corriente, apagón *m* ➤ **power dressing** moda *f* de ejecutivo ➤ **power drill** taladro *m*, taladradora *f* eléctrica ➤ **power failure** corte *m* del suministro eléctrico ➤ **power line** línea *f* de conducción eléctrica, cable *m* de alta tensión ➤ **power of attorney** (*Jur*) poder *m*, procuración *f* ➤ **power outage** (*US*) = **power cut** ➤ **power pack** transformador *m* ➤ **power plant** (= *generator*) grupo *m* electrógeno; (*US*) central *f* eléctrica, usina *f* eléctrica (*SC*) ➤ **power point** (*Brit Elec*) enchufe *m*, toma *f* de corriente ➤ **power station** central *f* eléctrica, usina *f* eléctrica (*SC*) ➤ **power steering** (*Aut*) dirección *f* asistida ➤ **power struggle** lucha *f* por el poder ➤ **power supply** suministro *m* eléctrico ➤ **power tool** herramienta *f* eléctrica
➤ **power down** VT + ADV [+ *computer*] apagar; [+ *engine*] parar
➤ **power up** VT + ADV [+ *computer*] encender; [+ *engine*] poner en marcha

power-assisted [ˈpaʊərəˌsɪstɪd] ADJ **~ brakes** servofrenos *mpl*; **~ steering** dirección *f* asistida

powerboat [ˈpaʊəˌbəʊt] N lancha *f* a motor, motora *f*

powerful [ˈpaʊəfəl] ADJ **1** (= *influential*) [*person, government, force, influence*] poderoso **2** (= *strong*) [*person, physique, muscles, smell, explosion*] fuerte; [*engine, magnet, computer, explosive, drug*] potente; [*swimmer*] resistente; [*emotion*] intenso, profundo; [*argument*] poderoso, convincente; [*performance, film, novel*] impactante, que deja huella; [*speech*] conmovedor

powerfully [ˈpaʊəfəlɪ] ADV [*affect*] profundamente; [*speak, argue, express*] de forma convincente; [*hit, strike*] con fuerza

powerhouse [ˈpaʊəhaʊs] N **the town is the industrial ~ of Germany** el pueblo es el centro neurálgico de la industria alemana; **he's a ~ of ideas** es una fuente inagotable de ideas

powerless [ˈpaʊəlɪs] ADJ impotente; **I felt ~ to resist** no tuve fuerzas para resistir, no pude resistir; **they are ~ in the matter** no tienen autoridad para intervenir en el asunto

powerlessness [ˈpaʊəlɪsnɪs] N impotencia *f*

power-sharing [ˈpaʊəˌʃeərɪŋ] N reparto *m* del poder

powwow* [ˈpaʊwaʊ] N asamblea *f*, reunión *f*

pp ABBR (= **per procurationem**) p.p.

pp. ABBR (= **pages**) págs.

PPV ABBR (= **pay-per-view**) PPV *m*

PQ ABBR (*Canada*) = **Province of Quebec**

PR Ⓐ N ABBR **1** (*Pol*) = **proportional representation**
2 (= **public relations**) relaciones *fpl* públicas, RR.PP. *fpl*, RRPP *fpl* Ⓑ ABBR (*US*) = **Puerto Rico**

Pr. ABBR (= **prince**) P.

practicability [ˌpræktɪkəˈbɪlɪtɪ] N viabilidad *f*, factibilidad *f*

practicable [ˈpræktɪkəbl] ADJ practicable, viable, factible

practical [ˈpræktɪkəl] Ⓐ ADJ **1** (= *not theoretical*) práctico; **for all ~ purposes** a efectos prácticos
2 (= *sensible*) práctico; **let's be ~ (about this)** seamos prácticos (con respecto a esto)
3 (= *feasible*) factible; **what's the most ~ way of doing this?** ¿cuál es la forma más factible de hacer esto?
4 (= *functional*) [*clothing, suggestion, guide*] práctico
5 (= *virtual*) **it's a ~ certainty** es casi seguro Ⓑ N (*esp Brit Scol, Univ*) (= *exam*) examen *m* práctico; (= *lesson*) práctica *f*
Ⓒ CPD ➤ **practical joke** broma *f* ➤ **practical nurse** (*US*) enfermero/a *m/f* de prácticas *or* sin título

practicality [ˌpræktɪˈkælɪtɪ] N [*of design, model*] utilidad *f*; [*of scheme, project*] lo factible; [*of person*] sentido *m* práctico; **practicalities** detalles *mpl* prácticos

practically [ˈpræktɪklɪ] ADV **1** (= *almost*) casi, prácticamente; **you've eaten ~ nothing** apenas has comido, casi no has comido; **it ~ killed me** por poco me mata, casi me mata **2** (= *sensibly*) con sentido práctico **3** (= *in practice*) en la práctica

practice [ˈpræktɪs] Ⓐ N **1** (= *custom, tradition*) costumbre *f*, práctica *f*; (= *procedure*) práctica *f*; **it is not our ~ to do that** no tenemos por norma hacer eso; **unfair trade ~s** prácticas *fpl* de comercio desleales; **it is bad ~** no es una práctica recomendable; **it is common ~ among modern companies to hire all their office equipment** entre las empresas modernas es una práctica muy extendida alquilar todo su material y mobiliario de oficina; **it is good ~ to interview several candidates before choosing one** es una práctica recomendable entrevistar a varios aspirantes antes de decidirse por uno; **to make a ~ of doing sth** acostumbrar a hacer algo
2 (= *experience, drilling*) práctica *f*; **I need more ~** (= *practical experience*) necesito más práctica; (= *to practise more*) necesito practicar más; **I haven't got a job yet but the interviews are good ~** aún no tengo trabajo pero las entrevistas me sirven de práctica; **to be out of ~** (*at sport*) no estar en forma; **it gets easier with ~** resulta más fácil con la práctica
3 (*Sport*) (= *training session*) sesión *f* de entrenamiento, entrenamiento *m*
4 (= *rehearsal*) ensayo *m*; **choir ~** ensayo *m* de coro
5 (*as opposed to theory*) práctica *f*; **in ~** en la práctica; **to put sth into ~** poner algo en práctica
6 (= *exercise*) [*of profession*] ejercicio *m*; [*of religion*] práctica

f; **the ~ of medicine** el ejercicio de la medicina; **to be in ~ (as a doctor/lawyer)** ejercer (de médico/abogado); **to go into ~** (*Med*) empezar a ejercer de médico; **to set up in ~** (*Med*) poner consulta; (*Jur*) poner bufete
7 (= *premises, firm*) (*Jur*) bufete *m*; (*Med*) consultorio *m*, consulta *f*; (*veterinary, dental*) clínica *f*
🅑 VT, VI (*US*) = **practise**
🅒 CPD [*match, run*] de entrenamiento ➤ **practice flight** vuelo *m* de entrenamiento ➤ **practice session** (*Sport*) sesión *f* de entrenamiento ➤ (*Scol, Mus*) ensayo *m*

practiced ['præktɪst] ADJ (*US*) = **practised**

practicing ['præktɪsɪŋ] ADJ (*US*) = **practising**

practise, practice (*US*) ['præktɪs] 🅐 VI **1** (*to improve skill*) (*Sport*) entrenar; (*Theat*) ensayar; (*Mus*) practicar **2** (= *work professionally*) [*lawyer, doctor*] ejercer; **to ~ as a doctor/lawyer** ejercer de *or* como médico/abogado 🅑 VT **1** (= *put into practice*) [+ *medicine*] practicar; [+ *law*] ejercer; [+ *self-denial, one's religion, method*] practicar; ✦ IDIOM **to ~ what one preaches** predicar con el ejemplo **2** (= *work on*) [+ *piano, language, technique*] practicar; [+ *song, speech*] ensayar

practised, practiced (*US*) ['præktɪst] ADJ [*politician, surgeon, climber*] experto; **with a ~ eye** con ojo experto

practising, practicing (*US*) ['præktɪsɪŋ] ADJ [*lawyer, physician, teacher*] que ejerce como tal; [*Catholic, Muslim*] practicante; **he's a ~ homosexual** mantiene relaciones homosexuales

practitioner [præk'tɪʃənəʳ] N **1** [*of an art, a science*] practicante *mf* **2** (*Med*) médico/a *m/f*

pragmatic [præg'mætɪk] ADJ pragmático

pragmatism ['prægmətɪzəm] N pragmatismo *m*

Prague [prɑ:g] N Praga *f*

prairie ['prɛərɪ] N pradera *f*, llanura *f*, pampa *f* (*LAm*); **the Prairies** (*US*) las Grandes Llanuras ➤ **prairie dog** perro *m* de las praderas

praise [preɪz] 🅐 N **1** (= *approval, acclaim*) elogios *mpl*, alabanzas *fpl*; **I have nothing but ~ for her** merece todos mis elogios *or* alabanzas; **he is full of ~ for the medical staff** se deshace en elogios para con el personal médico **2** (*Rel*) alabanza *f*; **a hymn of ~** un himno de alabanza 🅑 VT **1** (= *applaud*) alabar, elogiar **2** (*Rel*) alabar

praiseworthy ['preɪz,wɜ:ðɪ] ADJ loable, digno de elogio

pram [præm] N (*Brit*) cochecito *m* (*de niño*)

prance [prɑ:ns] VI [*horse*] hacer cabriolas; [*person*] (*proudly*) pavonearse; (*gaily*) brincar, saltar

prank [præŋk] N broma *f*

prat** [præt] (*Brit*) N (= *ineffectual person*) inútil* *mf*; (= *fool*) imbécil *mf*; **you ~!** ¡imbécil!

pratfall** ['prætfɔ:l] N (*US*) (= *blunder*) metedura *f* de pata*

prattle ['prætl] 🅐 VI parlotear, cotorrear; [*child*] balbucear 🅑 N parloteo *m*, cotorreo *m*; (*child's*) balbuceo *m*

prawn [prɔ:n] N (*Brit*) (*medium*) gamba *f*, camarón *m* (*esp LAm*); (*small*) camarón *m*, quisquilla *f* (*Sp*); (= *Dublin Bay prawn, large prawn*) langostino *m* ➤ **prawn cocktail** (*Brit*) cóctel *m* de gambas

pray [preɪ] 🅐 VI (= *say prayers*) rezar, orar; **let us ~** oremos; **to ~ for sth/sb** rezar *or* rogar por algo/algn; **to ~ for sb's soul** rezar por el alma de algn; **we ~ed for rain** rezamos para que lloviera 🅑 VT **we ~ that it won't happen** rezamos para que no ocurra; **I was ~ing that he wouldn't notice** le pedía a Dios que no lo notara

prayer [prɛəʳ] N (*Rel*) oración *f*, rezo *m*; (= *entreaty*) oración *f*, plegaria *f*; **a ~ for peace** una oración por la paz; **Lord, hear our ~** Señor, escucha nuestras plegarias *or* súplicas; **to say one's ~s** orar, rezar; **say a ~ for me** reza por mí ➤ **prayer book** devocionario *m*, misal *m* ➤ **prayer mat** alfombra *f* de rezo ➤ **prayer meeting** reunión *f* de oraciones

pre... [pri:] PREF **1** (= *before*) **~-Columbian** precolombino; **I had a ~-breakfast swim** me di un baño antes del desayuno **2** (= *beforehand*) **a ~-recorded interview** una entrevista pregrabada

preach [pri:tʃ] 🅐 VT **1** (*Rel*) predicar; **to ~ the gospel** predicar el Evangelio; **to ~ a sermon** dar un sermón

2 [+ *virtues*] predicar; [+ *patience*] aconsejar 🅑 VI predicar; **to ~ at sb** sermonear a algn, dar un sermón a algn; ✦ IDIOM **to ~ to the converted** querer convertir a los que ya lo están

preacher ['pri:tʃəʳ] N [*of sermon*] predicador(a) *m/f*; (*US*) (= *minister*) pastor(a) *m/f*

preamble [pri:'æmbl] N preámbulo *m*

prearrange [,pri:ə'reɪndʒ] VT arreglar de antemano

prearranged [,pri:ə'reɪndʒd] ADJ [*time, location, signal*] convenido; [*meeting*] fijado

precarious [prɪ'kɛərɪəs] ADJ precario

precaution [prɪ'kɔ:ʃən] N precaución *f*; **as a ~** como precaución, para mayor seguridad; **to take ~s** tomar precauciones; **to take the ~ of doing sth** tomar la precaución de hacer algo

precautionary [prɪ'kɔ:ʃənərɪ] ADJ preventivo, de precaución; **as a ~ measure** como medida preventiva *or* de precaución

precede [prɪ'si:d] VT preceder, anteceder; **the concert was ~d by a talk** el concierto vino precedido de una charla

precedence ['presɪdəns] N (*in rank*) precedencia *f*; (*in importance*) prioridad *f*; **in order of ~** (= *rank*) por orden de precedencia; (= *importance*) por orden de prioridad; **to take ~ over** tener prioridad/precedencia sobre

precedent ['presɪdənt] N precedente *m* (*also Jur*); **without ~** sin precedentes; **to set a ~ (for sth)** sentar un precedente (para algo)

preceding [prɪ'si:dɪŋ] ADJ [*day, week, month, year*] anterior; [*chapter, paragraph, sentence*] precedente, anterior

precept ['pri:sept] N precepto *m*

precinct ['pri:sɪŋkt] N **1** (= *area*) recinto *m*; (*US Pol*) distrito *m* electoral, circunscripción *f*; (*US*) [*of police*] distrito *m* policial; **shopping ~** (*Brit*) centro *m* comercial; **pedestrian ~** (*Brit*) zona *f* peatonal **2 precincts** (= *grounds, premises*) límites *mpl*; (= *environs*) alrededores *mpl*; [*of cathedral etc*] recinto *msing*

precious ['preʃəs] 🅐 ADJ **1** (= *costly*) [*jewel, stone*] precioso; [*commodity, resource*] preciado; [*possession*] muy valioso; **we're wasting ~ time** estamos desperdiciando un tiempo precioso
2 (= *treasured*) preciado; **her friendship is very ~ to me** aprecio *or* valoro mucho su amistad; **the book is very ~ to me** para mí el libro tiene gran valor
3 I couldn't care less about your ~ golf clubs (*iro*) me traen sin cuidado tus queridos palos de golf
🅑 ADV **~ little/few*** bien poco/pocos; **~ little has been gained** se ha logrado muy poco
🅒 CPD ➤ **precious metal** metal *m* precioso ➤ **precious stone** piedra *f* preciosa

precipice ['presɪpɪs] N precipicio *m*, despeñadero *m*

precipitate 🅐 [prɪ'sɪpɪtɪt] ADJ precipitado, apresurado 🅑 [prɪ'sɪpɪteɪt] VT (= *bring on*) precipitar, provocar

precipitation [prɪ,sɪpɪ'teɪʃən] N precipitación *f*

precipitous [prɪ'sɪpɪtəs] ADJ **1** (= *steep*) escarpado, cortado a pico **2** (= *hasty*) precipitado, apresurado

précis ['preɪsi:] 🅐 N (*pl* ~ ['preɪsi:z]) resumen *m* 🅑 VT hacer un resumen de, resumir

precise [prɪ'saɪs] ADJ **1** (= *exact*) [*description, figure, measurements*] exacto; [*instructions*] preciso; [*details, information*] concreto; **the timing had to be very ~** había que calcular el tiempo con mucha precisión; **there were five, to be ~** para ser exacto *or* preciso, fueron cinco; **can you be more ~?** ¿puedes ser más concreto?; **at that ~ moment** en ese preciso instante **2** (= *meticulous*) meticuloso

precisely [prɪ'saɪslɪ] ADV **1** (= *exactly*) exactamente; **at four o'clock ~** a las cuatro en punto; **precisely!** ¡exactamente!, ¡efectivamente!; **~ what was it that you wanted?** ¿qué era lo que quería usted exactamente? **2** (= *with precision*) [*calculate, measure*] con precisión **3** (= *meticulously*) meticulosamente

precision [prɪ'sɪʒən] N (*gen*) precisión *f*; [*of calculations*] exactitud *f* ➤ **precision instrument** instrumento *m* de precisión

preclude [prɪ'kluːd] VT (= *prevent*) impedir; [+ *possibility*] excluir; **so as to ~ all doubt** para disipar cualquier duda; **we are ~d from doing that** nos vemos imposibilitados para hacer eso

precocious [prɪ'kəʊʃəs] ADJ precoz

preconceived ['priːkən'siːvd] ADJ preconcebido

preconception ['priːkən'sepʃən] N preconcepción *f*, idea *f* preconcebida

precondition ['priːkən'dɪʃən] N condición *f* previa

precursor [prɪ'kɜːsəʳ] N precursor(a) *m/f*

predate ['priː'deɪt] VT (= *put earlier date on*) poner fecha anterior a, antedatar; (= *precede*) preceder, ser anterior a

predator ['predətəʳ] N (= *animal*) depredador *m*; (= *bird*) ave *f* de presa, ave *f* rapaz

> Use **el/un** not **la/una** before feminine nouns beginning with stressed **a** or **ha** like **ave**.

predatory ['predətərɪ] ADJ [*animal*] depredador; [*bird*] de presa, rapaz; [*person*] rapaz; [*look*] devorador

predecessor ['priːdɪsesəʳ] N predecesor(a) *m/f*, antecesor(a) *m/f*

predestination [priːˌdestɪ'neɪʃən] N predestinación *f*

predestine [priː'destɪn] VT predestinar

predetermine ['priːdɪ'tɜːmɪn] VT (*Philos*, *Rel*) predeterminar; (= *arrange beforehand*) determinar de antemano

predicament [prɪ'dɪkəmənt] N apuro *m*, aprieto *m*; **to be in a ~** (= *in a fix*) estar en un apuro *or* un aprieto

predicate Ⓐ ['predɪkɪt] N (*Ling*) predicado *m* Ⓑ ['predɪkeɪt] VT **to be ~d (up)on** estar basado en, partir de

predict [prɪ'dɪkt] VT predecir, pronosticar; **to ~ that** predecir que, pronosticar que; **"it'll end in disaster," he ~ed** —será un desastre, —predijo *or* —pronosticó; **the motion was passed, as ~ed** la moción se aprobó como se había previsto *or* pronosticado; **I can't ~ the future** no puedo predecir *or* prever el futuro

predictable [prɪ'dɪktəbl] ADJ [*result, outcome*] previsible; **his reaction was ~** su reacción era de esperar; **people were so ~** era tan fácil prever las reacciones de la gente; **you're so ~!** (= *always saying the same*) ¡siempre sales con las mismas!*; (= *always behaving the same*) ¡siempre estás igual!

predictably [prɪ'dɪktəblɪ] ADV como era de esperar

prediction [prɪ'dɪkʃən] N (*by expert, layman*) predicción *f*; (*by clairvoyant, oracle*) vaticinio *m*, profecía *f*; **to make a ~ about sth** pronosticar *or* predecir algo

predilection [ˌpriːdɪ'lekʃən] N predilección *f*; **to have a ~ for** tener predilección por

predispose ['priːdɪs'pəʊz] VT predisponer

predisposition ['priːˌdɪspə'zɪʃən] N predisposición *f*

predominance [prɪ'dɒmɪnəns] N predominio *m*

predominant [prɪ'dɒmɪnənt] ADJ predominante

predominantly [prɪ'dɒmɪnəntlɪ] ADV (= *mainly*) predominantemente; (= *in the majority*) en su mayoría; **a population of ~ Italian residents** una población en su mayoría de residentes italianos

predominate [prɪ'dɒmɪneɪt] VI predominar (**over** sobre)

pre-eminence [priː'emɪnəns] N preeminencia *f*

pre-eminent [priː'emɪnənt] ADJ preeminente

pre-empt [priː'empt] VT [+ *person, attack, opposition*] adelantarse a, anticiparse a; **we found they had ~ed us in buying it** encontramos que se nos habían adelantado a comprarlo; **I did it to ~ any family arguments** lo hice para evitar discusiones familiares

pre-emptive [priː'emptɪv] ADJ [*measure*] preventivo ➤ **pre-emptive strike** ataque *m* preventivo

preen [priːn] VT [+ *feathers*] arreglarse las plumas con el pico; **to ~ o.s.** [*person*] pavonearse, atildarse

pre-established ['priːɪs'tæblɪʃt] ADJ establecido de antemano

pre-existent ['priːɪg'zɪstənt] ADJ preexistente

prefab* ['priːfæb] N (*esp Brit*) casa *f* prefabricada

prefabricated ['priː'fæbrɪkeɪtɪd] ADJ prefabricado

preface ['prefɪs] Ⓐ N prólogo *m*, prefacio *m* Ⓑ VT **he ~d this by saying that ...** a modo de prólogo a esto dijo que ..., introdujo este tema diciendo que ...

prefect ['priːfekt] N 1 (*Brit Scol*) monitor(a) *m/f* 2 (*Admin*) (*esp in France*) prefecto *m*

prefer [prɪ'fɜːʳ] Ⓐ VT 1 (= *like better*) preferir (**to** a); **which do you ~?** ¿cuál prefieres?, ¿cuál te gusta más?; **I ~red it the way it was** lo prefería tal como estaba; **to ~ doing sth** preferir hacer algo; **I ~ walking to going by car** prefiero ir andando *or* (*LAm*) caminando a ir en coche; **I'd ~ it if you didn't come with me** preferiría que no vinieras conmigo; **I much ~ Scotland** Escocia me gusta mucho más; **we'd ~ that this visit be kept confidential** preferimos que esta visita se mantenga en secreto; **to ~ to do sth** preferir hacer algo; **"will you do it?" — "I'd ~ not to"** —¿lo harás? —preferiría no hacerlo; **to ~ sb to do sth** preferir que algn haga algo; **would you ~ me to drive?** ¿preferirías que condujera yo? 2 (*Jur*) **to ~ charges (against sb)** presentar cargos (contra algn) Ⓑ VI preferir; **if you ~ ...** si usted quiere *or* lo prefiere ...

preferable ['prefərəbl] ADJ preferible (**to** a)

preferably ['prefərəblɪ] ADV de preferencia, preferentemente

preference ['prefərəns] N 1 (= *liking*) preferencia *f*; **she has a ~ for older men** prefiere a *or* tiene preferencia por los hombres maduros; **for ~** de preferencia; **in ~ to sth** antes que algo, más que algo; **I have no ~** no tengo preferencia 2 (= *priority*) **to give ~ to sth/sb** dar prioridad a algo/algn

preferential [ˌprefə'renʃəl] ADJ preferente, preferencial; **on ~ terms** con condiciones preferenciales

prefix ['priːfɪks] N [*of word, phone number*] prefijo *m*

pregnancy ['pregnənsɪ] N [*of woman*] embarazo *m*; [*of animal*] preñez *f* ➤ **pregnancy test** prueba *f* del embarazo

pregnant ['pregnənt] ADJ [*woman*] embarazada; [*animal*] preñado; **to be six months ~** estar embarazada de seis meses; **Tina was ~ with their first son** Tina estaba embarazada de su primer hijo

preheat ['priː'hiːt] VT precalentar

prehensile [prɪ'hensaɪl] ADJ prensil

prehistoric ['priːhɪs'tɒrɪk] ADJ prehistórico

prehistory ['priː'hɪstərɪ] N prehistoria *f*

prejudge ['priː'dʒʌdʒ] VT prejuzgar

prejudice ['predʒʊdɪs] Ⓐ N 1 (= *bias*) prejuicio *m*; **there's a lot of racial ~** hay muchos prejuicios raciales; **to have a ~ against/in favour of sth/sb** estar predispuesto en contra de/a favor de algo/algn 2 (*Jur*) (= *injury, detriment*) perjuicio *m*; **without ~** (*Jur*) sin detrimento de sus propios derechos Ⓑ VT 1 (= *bias*) predisponer, prevenir (**against** contra) 2 (= *damage*) perjudicar; **to ~ one's chances** perjudicar sus posibilidades

prejudiced ['predʒʊdɪst] ADJ [*view*] parcial, interesado; **he's very ~** tiene muchos prejuicios; **to be ~ against sth/sb** estar predispuesto en contra de algo/algn

prejudicial [ˌpredʒʊ'dɪʃəl] ADJ perjudicial (**to** para); **it would be ~ to her career** sería perjudicial para *or* perjudicaría a su carrera

prelate ['prelɪt] N prelado *m*

preliminary [prɪ'lɪmɪnərɪ] Ⓐ ADJ preliminar Ⓑ N (= *preface*) prolegómeno *m*; (*Sport*) fase *f* previa

prelude ['preljuːd] N preludio *m* (**to** de)

premarital ['priː'mærɪtl] ADJ prematrimonial

premature ['premətʃʊəʳ] ADJ [*baby, ageing*] prematuro; **it would be ~ to conclude that ...** sería prematuro deducir que ...; **you're being a little ~** te estás adelantando a los acontecimientos

prematurely ['premətʃʊəlɪ] ADV prematuramente, antes de tiempo; **to be born ~** nacer prematuramente

pre-med ['priː'med] Ⓐ N (*Brit*) (= **premedication**) premedicación *f* Ⓑ ADJ (*US*) = **premedical**; **~ course** curso *m* preparatorio para ingresar en la Facultad de Medicina

premeditate [priˈmedɪteɪt] VT premeditar

premeditation [ˌpriːmedɪˈteɪʃən] N premeditación f

premenstrual [ˌpriːˈmenstrʊəl] ADJ premenstrual ➤ **premenstrual syndrome** (esp Brit) síndrome m premenstrual

premier [ˈpremɪəʳ] Ⓐ ADJ primero, principal Ⓑ N (= prime minister) primer(a) ministro/a m/f; (= president) presidente/a m/f Ⓒ CPD ➤ **Premier League** (Brit Ftbl) primera división f, división f de honor

première [ˈpremɪeəʳ] Ⓐ N estreno m; **world** ~ estreno m mundial; **the film had its** ~ se estrenó la película Ⓑ VT estrenar

premiership [ˈpremɪəʃɪp] N cargo m del primer ministro, puesto m de primer ministro; (= period in office) mandato m

premise [ˈpremɪs] N 1 (= hypothesis) premisa f 2 **premises** (gen) local msing; (= shop, restaurant, hotel) establecimiento m; (= building) edificio m; **they're moving to new** ~s se trasladan de local

premium [ˈpriːmɪəm] Ⓐ N 1 (Insurance) prima f 2 (= surcharge) recargo m 3 (= bonus) prima f 4 (US) (= gasoline) súper f 5 (in phrases) **to be at a** ~ (Comm) estar por encima de la par; (= be scarce) estar muy solicitado; **space is at a** ~ **in our house** en casa no nos sobra espacio; **to put a** ~ **on sth** (= value) valorar mucho algo; (= make valuable) hacer que suba el valor de algo; (= make important) hacer que se dé más importancia a algo Ⓑ ADJ [brand, product] de calidad superior, de primera calidad Ⓒ CPD ➤ **premium bond** (Brit) bono del estado que permite participar en la lotería nacional ➤ **premium price** precio m con prima, precio m más elevado ➤ **premium rate** tarifa f de primas

premonition [ˌpreməˈnɪʃən] N presentimiento m, premonición f; **to have a** ~ **that ...** presentir que ...

prenatal [ˈpriːˈneɪtl] ADJ prenatal

preoccupation [priːˌɒkjʊˈpeɪʃən] N preocupación f; **keeping warm was his main** ~ su principal preocupación or lo que más le preocupaba era no pasar frío

preoccupied [priːˈɒkjʊpaɪd] ADJ (= worried) preocupado; (= absorbed, distracted) ensimismado, absorto; **you're too** ~ **with winning** estás demasiado obsesionado por ganar

preoccupy [priːˈɒkjʊpaɪ] VT preocupar

preordained [ˈpriːɔːˈdeɪnd] ADJ predestinado

prep [prep] Ⓐ N (Brit Scol) (= work) tareas fpl, deberes mpl; (= period) tiempo m de estudio, hora f de los deberes Ⓑ VI (US*) **to** ~ **for** (gen) prepararse para; (Educ) hacer el curso de preparación para (los estudios universitarios) Ⓒ VT (US*) preparar; **to** ~ **o.s.** prepararse Ⓓ CPD ➤ **prep school** (Brit) escuela privada para niños de 6 a 13 años; (US) colegio m privado

prepacked [ˌpriːˈpækt], **prepackaged** [ˌpriːˈpækɪdʒd] ADJ (pre)empaquetado

prepaid [ˌpriːˈpeɪd] ADJ pagado con antelación

preparation [ˌprepəˈreɪʃən] N (= activity) preparación f; **her latest novel has been four years in** ~ lleva cuatro años preparando su última novela; **preparations** preparativos mpl (**for** para, de); **to make** ~s (**for sth/to do sth**) hacer preparativos (para algo/para hacer algo)

preparatory [prɪˈpærətərɪ] ADJ preparatorio, preliminar; ~ **to** como preparación para, antes de ➤ **preparatory school** (Brit) escuela privada para niños de 6 a 13 años; (US) colegio m privado

prepare [prɪˈpeəʳ] Ⓐ VT [+ meal, lesson, defence] preparar; [+ report] redactar, preparar; [+ plan, strategy] idear, preparar; **to** ~ **sb for sth** preparar a algn para algo; **to** ~ **sth for sb** preparar algo a algn; **they had** ~**d a room for him** le habían preparado una habitación Ⓑ VI prepararse; **to** ~ **for sth** prepararse para algo; **to** ~ **to do sth** prepararse para hacer algo

prepared [prɪˈpeəd] ADJ 1 (= ready) preparado; **I am** ~ **for**

anything estoy preparado para cualquier eventualidad; **we were** ~ **for it** íbamos preparados; **we were not** ~ **for this** esto no lo esperábamos, no contábamos con esto 2 (= willing) **to be** ~ **to do sth** estar dispuesto a hacer algo

prepayment [ˈpriːˈpeɪmənt] N pago m por adelantado, pago m anticipado

preponderance [prɪˈpɒndərəns] N preponderancia f, predominio m

preposition [ˌprepəˈzɪʃən] N preposición f

prepossessing [ˌpriːpəˈzesɪŋ] ADJ agradable, atractivo; **not very** ~ no muy atractivo

preposterous [prɪˈpɒstərəs] ADJ absurdo, ridículo

preppie*, **preppy*** [ˈprepɪ] Ⓐ ADJ de muy buen tono Ⓑ N 1 (= prep school student) alumno de colegio privado de secundaria 2 (= rich kid) niño/a m/f bien, niño/a m/f pijo (Sp*)

preprogrammed, preprogramed (US) [ˌpriːˈprəʊɡræmd] ADJ preprogramado

prerecord [ˈpriːrɪˈkɔːd] VT grabar de antemano, pregrabar

prerequisite [ˈpriːˈrekwɪzɪt] N requisito m indispensable, condición f previa; **a maths degree is a** ~ **for the job** la titulación en matemáticas es requisito indispensable para el puesto

prerogative [prɪˈrɒɡətɪv] N prerrogativa f

Pres. ABBR (= President) Presidente/a m/f

presage [ˈpresɪdʒ] (liter) Ⓐ N presagio m Ⓑ VT presagiar

Presbyterian [ˌprezbɪˈtɪərɪən] ADJ, N presbiteriano/a m/f

presbytery [ˈprezbɪtərɪ] N casa f parroquial; (Archit) presbiterio m

pre-school [ˈpriːˈskuːl] Ⓐ ADJ preescolar Ⓑ N (US) parvulario m, escuela f de párvulos, escuela f infantil (Sp), kínder m (LAm)

prescribe [prɪˈskraɪb] VT 1 (= lay down, order) prescribir, ordenar 2 [+ medicine] recetar; **to** ~ **sth for sb** ◊ ~ **sb sth** recetar algo a algn; **the** ~**d dose** la dosis prescrita

prescription [prɪˈskrɪpʃən] N (Med) receta f; **to make up** or (US) **fill a** ~ preparar una receta; **"only available on prescription"** "de venta únicamente bajo receta médica" ➤ **prescription charges** (Brit) precio msing de las recetas ➤ **prescription lenses** (US) lentillas fpl graduadas

prescriptive [prɪˈskrɪptɪv] ADJ (gen) prescriptivo; (Gram) normativo

presence [ˈprezns] N presencia f; **in sb's** ~ en presencia de algn, delante de algn; **to make one's** ~ **felt** hacerse notar or sentir; **military** ~ presencia f militar; **there was a massive police** ~ **at the match** hubo una importante presencia policial en el partido ➤ **presence of mind** presencia f de ánimo

present¹ [ˈpreznt] Ⓐ ADJ 1 [person] **to be** ~ (in place) estar presente; (at function) asistir, estar presente; **nobody else was** ~ no había nadie más, nadie más estuvo presente; **present!** ¡presente!; **ssh! there are ladies** ~ ¡sss! hay señoras delante; **to be** ~ **at** [+ function] asistir a, estar presente en; [+ scene, accident] presenciar; ~ **company excepted** exceptuando a los presentes; **those** ~ los presentes 2 [thing, substance] **to be** ~ encontrarse 3 (= current) actual; **how long have you been in your** ~ **job?** ¿cuánto tiempo llevas en tu puesto actual?; **the** ~ **government** el actual gobierno; **from Roman times to the** ~ **day** desde los tiempos romanos hasta nuestros días; **a solution to the problems of the** ~ **day** una solución a los problemas actuales or de nuestros días; **at the** ~ **time** (= at this instant) en este momento; (= currently) actualmente, hoy día 4 (Gram) presente Ⓑ N 1 (= present time) **the** ~ el presente; **for the** ~ de momento, por lo pronto; **up to the** ~ hasta ahora; ✦ IDIOM **to live for the** ~ vivir el momento; ✦ PROV **(there's) no time like the** ~ no dejes para mañana lo que puedas hacer hoy 2 **at** ~ (= at this instant) en este momento; (= currently) ahora, actualmente; **I don't want to get married at** ~ de momento no me quiero casar 3 (Gram) (tiempo m) presente m

© CPD ➤ **the present continuous** el presente continuo ➤ **present participle** participio *m* activo, participio *m* (de) presente ➤ **the present perfect** el pretérito perfecto ➤ **the present simple** el presente simple ➤ **the present tense** el (tiempo) presente

present² ['preznt] N (= *gift*) regalo *m*, obsequio *m* (*frm*); **she gave me the book as a** ~ me regaló el libro; **to give sb a** ~ hacer un regalo a algn

present³ [prɪ'zent] VT **1** (= *give*) **1.1** [+ *prize, award*] entregar, hacer entrega de; **to** ~ **sth to sb** entregar algo a algn, hacer entrega de algo a algn; **they have** ~**ed a petition to Parliament** han hecho entrega de *or* han presentado una petición al parlamento **1.2** [+ *gift*] **to** ~ **sb with sth** ◇ ~ **sth to sb** regalar algo a algn, obsequiar a algn con algo (*more frm*), obsequiar algo a algn (*LAm*) **2** (= *introduce*) presentar **3** (= *offer formally*) presentar; **to** ~ **one's apologies (to sb)** presentar sus excusas (ante algn); **to** ~ **one's compliments (to sb)** presentar *or* ofrecer sus saludos (a algn) **4** (= *show*) [+ *documents, tickets*] presentar, mostrar **5** (= *put forward, communicate*) [+ *report, proposal, evidence, bill*] presentar; [+ *case, argument, plan*] exponer **6** (= *pose*) [+ *challenge*] representar; [+ *opportunity*] presentar, ofrecer; [+ *sight*] ofrecer; **the patrol** ~**ed an easy target** la patrulla era un blanco fácil **7** (= *provide, confront*) **the author** ~**s us with a vivid chronicle of contemporary America** el autor nos brinda *or* ofrece una vívida crónica de la América contemporánea; **she bought a new car and** ~**ed me with the bill** se compró un coche nuevo y me pasó la factura **8** (= *represent, portray*) presentar; **the report** ~**s her in a favourable light** el informe presenta una imagen favorable de ella **9** (*Comm*) (= *tender, submit*) [+ *bill*] presentar, pasar; [+ *cheque*] presentar; **the cheque was** ~**ed for payment on the 24th** el cheque se presentó para el cobro el día 24 **10** (*esp Brit Rad, TV*) [+ *programme*] presentar; ~**ing Garbo as Mimi** con Garbo en el papel de Mimi **11** (*Mil*) **to** ~ **arms** presentar las armas; ~ **arms!** ¡presenten armas! **12 to** ~ **o.s.** [*person*] presentarse; **she's thinking of** ~**ing herself as a candidate** está pensando en presentarse como candidata; **to** ~ **o.s. for (an) interview** presentarse a una entrevista; **a problem has** ~**ed itself** ha surgido *or* se ha presentado un problema

presentable [prɪ'zentəbl] ADJ presentable; **I must go and make myself** ~ voy a arreglarme un poco

presentation [,prezən'teɪʃən] N **1** (= *act of presenting*) presentación *f*; **on** ~ **of the voucher** al presentar el vale **2** (= *ceremony*) ceremonia *f* de entrega; **to make the** ~ hacer la presentación; **to make sb a** ~ **on their retirement** hacer un obsequio a algn con ocasión de su jubilación **3** (= *talk*) presentación *f*

present-day ['preznt'deɪ] ADJ actual, de hoy (en día)

presenter [prɪ'zentəʳ] N (*esp Brit Rad*) locutor(a) *m/f*; (*TV*) presentador/a *m/f*

presentiment [prɪ'zentɪmənt] N presentimiento *m*

presently ['prezntlɪ] ADV **1** (= *shortly*) dentro de poco, al rato; **you'll feel better** ~ enseguida te sentirás mejor **2** (= *a little later*) poco después **3** (*US*) (= *now*) en este momento, actualmente

preservation [,prezə'veɪʃən] N [*of antiquities, food*] conservación *f*; [*of wildlife, land, buildings*] conservación *f*, preservación *f*; [*of order, democracy*] mantenimiento *m*

preservative [prɪ'zɜːvətɪv] N conservante *m*

preserve [prɪ'zɜːv] **©** VT **1** (= *keep in existence*) [+ *endangered species, jobs, language*] proteger, preservar; [+ *customs, silence, reputation*] conservar, mantener; [+ *sense of humour, memory*] conservar; [+ *peace*] mantener **2** (= *keep from decay*) [+ *object, environment, meat*] conservar; **perfectly** ~**d medieval houses** casas *fpl* medievales en perfecto estado; **the body was** ~**d in ice** el cuerpo se conservaba en hielo **3** (*esp Brit Culin*) (= *bottle, pickle, etc*) [+ *fruit*] hacer conservas de; [+ *meat, fish*] conservar **4** (= *protect*) proteger; **to** ~ **sth from sth** proteger algo de algo

© N **1** (*Culin*) (= *jam*) mermelada *f*, confitura *f*; (= *bottled fruit, chutney*) conserva *f*; **preserves** conservas *fpl* **2** (*Hunting*) coto *m*, vedado *m*; (*for wildlife*) reserva *f* **3** (*fig*) dominio *m*; **banking has remained almost exclusively a male** ~ la banca sigue siendo casi exclusivamente del dominio masculino

preset ['priː'set] (*pt, pp* ~) VT programar

preshrunk ['priː'ʃrʌŋk] ADJ ya lavado

preside [prɪ'zaɪd] VI presidir; **to** ~ **at** *or* **over a meeting** presidir una reunión

presidency ['prezɪdənsɪ] N presidencia *f*

president ['prezɪdənt] N [*of country, company, organization*] presidente/a *m/f*; (*US Univ*) rector(a) *m/f* ➤ **Presidents' Day** (*US*) *fiesta celebrada el tercer lunes de febrero, en memoria de los presidentes Lincoln y Washington*

presidential [,prezɪ'denʃəl] ADJ presidencial; ~ **election(s)** elecciones *fpl* presidenciales

press	
Ⓐ NOUN	**Ⓓ** COMPOUNDS
Ⓑ TRANSITIVE VERB	**Ⓔ** PHRASAL VERBS
Ⓒ INTRANSITIVE VERB	

press [pres] **Ⓐ** NOUN **1** (= *newspapers collectively*) prensa *f*; **to get a good/bad** ~ (*lit, fig*) tener buena/mala prensa; **the** ~ (= *newspapers, journalists*) la prensa; **the national** ~ la prensa nacional **2** (*also* **printing** ~) imprenta *f*; **correct at the time of going to** ~ correcto en el momento de impresión; **hot off the** ~**(es)** recién salido de la imprenta **3** (= *publishing firm*) editorial *f* **4** (= *touch*) (*with hand*) apretón *m*; **at the** ~ **of a button** con sólo apretar *or* pulsar un botón **5** (*with iron*) **to give sth a** ~ planchar algo **6** (= *apparatus*) (*for wine, olives, moulding*) prensa *f* **Ⓑ** TRANSITIVE VERB **1** (= *push*) [+ *button, switch, doorbell*] pulsar, apretar; [+ *hand, trigger*] apretar; [+ *accelerator*] pisar; **select the option required, then** – **"enter"** escoja la opción que desee, y luego pulse *or* apriete "intro"; **he** ~**ed his face against the window** apretó la cara contra la ventana; **she** ~**ed a note into his hand** le metió un billete en la mano; **✦** IDIOM **to** ~ **the flesh** (*US**) ir estrechando manos a diestro y siniestro **2** (= *crush*) apretujar **3** (*using press*) [+ *grapes, olives, flowers*] prensar **4** (= *iron*) [+ *clothes*] planchar **5** (= *pressurize*) presionar; **he didn't need much** ~**ing** no hubo que presionarle mucho; **don't** ~ **me on this point** no me insistas sobre este punto; **to** ~ **sb for an answer** exigir una respuesta de algn; **to** ~ **sb for payment** insistir en que algn pague, exigir a algn el pago de lo que se debe; **to** ~ **sb into doing sth** obligar a algn a hacer algo; **to** ~ **sb to do sth** (= *urge*) insistir en que algn haga algo; (= *pressurize*) presionar a algn para que haga algo **6** (= *force*) **to** ~ **sth on sb** insistir en que algn acepte algo; **food and cigarettes were** ~**ed on him** le estuvieron ofreciendo insistentemente comida y cigarros **7 to be** ~**ed into service: we were all** ~**ed into service** todos tuvimos que ponernos a trabajar; **the town hall has been** ~**ed into service as a school** se han visto obligados a usar el ayuntamiento como escuela **8** (= *pursue*) [+ *claim*] insistir en; [+ *demand*] exigir; **to** ~ **charges (against sb)** presentar cargos (contra algn); **the champion failed to** ~ **home** his advantage el campeón no supo aprovechar su ventaja; **I shan't** ~ **the point** no insistiré más sobre eso **Ⓒ** INTRANSITIVE VERB **1** (= *exert pressure*) apretar; **does it hurt when I** – **here?** ¿le duele cuando le aprieto aquí? **2** (= *move, push*) **he** ~**ed against her** se apretó contra ella; **the crowd** ~**ed round him** la muchedumbre se apiñó en torno a él **3** (= *urge, agitate*) **to** ~ **for sth** exigir algo, insistir en algo **Ⓓ** COMPOUNDS ➤ **press agency** agencia *f* de prensa ➤ **press agent** encargado/a *m/f* de prensa ➤ **press**

conference rueda *f* de prensa, conferencia *f* de prensa ➤ **press corps** prensa *f* acreditada ➤ **press cutting** (*esp Brit*) recorte *m* (de periódico) ➤ **press office** oficina *f* de prensa ➤ **press officer** agente *mf* de prensa ➤ **press photographer** fotógrafo/a *m/f* de prensa ➤ **press release** comunicado *m* de prensa ➤ **press report** nota *f* de prensa, reportaje *m* de prensa ➤ **press room** sala *f* de prensa ➤ **press run** (*US*) tirada *f* ➤ **press secretary** secretario/a *m/f* de prensa ➤ **press stud** (*Brit*) automático *m*, broche *m* de presión
Ⓔ PHRASAL VERBS
➤ **press ahead** VI + ADV seguir adelante (**with** con)
➤ **press on** VI + ADV (*with work, journey*) seguir adelante, continuar (**with** con)

pressed [prest] ADJ **to be ~ for money/time** andar muy escaso de dinero/tiempo

press-gang ['presgæŋ] VT (*esp Brit*) **to ~ sb into doing sth** forzar a algn a hacer algo

pressie* ['prezɪ] N (*Brit*) = **prezzie**

pressing ['presɪŋ] ADJ [*matter, problem*] urgente; [*request, invitation*] insistente

press-up ['presʌp] N (*Brit*) flexión *f*

pressure ['preʃəʳ] Ⓐ N presión *f*; oil/water ~ presión *f* del aceite/del agua; **he felt the ~ of her hand on his shoulder** notó la presión de su mano en el hombro; **the ~s of modern life** las presiones de la vida moderna; **high/low ~** alta/baja presión *f*; **to put ~ on sb (to do sth)** presionar a algn (para que haga algo); **it will put intense ~ on our already overstretched resources** supondrá una gran carga sobre nuestros recursos, ya apurados al máximo; **could you check the tyre ~?** ¿me puede mirar la presión de los neumáticos?; **to act/work under ~** obrar/trabajar bajo presión; **he is under ~ to sign the agreement** le están presionando para que firme el acuerdo; **he's under a lot of ~** está bajo mucha presión, está sometido a mucha presión; **I was unable to go due to ~ of work** no pude ir por razones de trabajo
Ⓑ VT (= *pressurize*) presionar; **to ~ sb to do sth** presionar a algn para que haga algo; **to ~ sb into doing sth** obligar a algn a hacer algo
Ⓒ CPD ➤ **pressure cooker** olla *f* a presión, olla *f* exprés ➤ **pressure gauge** manómetro *m* ➤ **pressure group** grupo *m* de presión ➤ **pressure pan** (*US*) = **pressure cooker** ➤ **pressure point** (*Anat*) punto *m* de presión

pressurize ['preʃəraɪz] VT 1 (*Phys, Tech*) presurizar 2 (*fig*) presionar; **to ~ sb to do sth** presionar a algn para que haga algo; **to ~ sb into doing sth** obligar a algn a hacer algo

pressurized ['preʃəraɪzd] ADJ [*cabin, aircraft*] presurizado; [*chamber, container*] cerrado a presión

pressy* ['prezɪ] N (*Brit*) = **prezzie**

Prestel® ['prestel] N videotex *m*

prestige [pres'tiːʒ] N prestigio *m*

prestigious [pres'tɪdʒəs] ADJ prestigioso

presto ['prestəʊ] ADV **hey ~!** ¡abracadabra!

presumably [prɪ'zjuːməblɪ] ADV ~ supongo *or* me imagino que nos avisará; **"will they be coming later?" — "presumably"** —¿vendrán más tarde? — es de suponer

presume [prɪ'zjuːm] VT 1 (= *suppose*) suponer; **to ~ that ...** suponer que ...; **it may be ~d that ...** es de suponer que ...; **to ~ sb to be innocent** suponer que algn es inocente 2 (= *venture*) **to ~ to do sth** atreverse a hacer algo

presumption [prɪ'zʌmpʃən] N 1 (= *arrogance*) presunción *f*; (= *liberty-taking*) atrevimiento *m* 2 (= *thing presumed*) suposición *f*, presunción *f*; **the ~ is that ...** se supone que ..., es de suponer que ...

presumptive [prɪ'zʌmptɪv] ADJ presunto

presumptuous [prɪ'zʌmptjʊəs] ADJ atrevido

presuppose [ˌpriːsə'pəʊz] VT presuponer

presupposition [ˌpriːsʌpə'zɪʃən] N presuposición *f*

pre-tax [ˌpriː'tæks] ADJ bruto; ~ **profits** beneficios *mpl* brutos *or* antes de impuestos

pretence, pretense (*US*) [prɪ'tens] N 1 (= *make-believe*) fingimiento *m*, simulación *f*; **to make a ~ of doing sth** fingir hacer algo; **it's all a ~*** todo es fingido 2 (= *claim*) pretensión *f*; **to make no ~ to learning** no pretender ser erudito 3 (= *pretext*) pretexto *m*; **under the ~ of doing sth** so pretexto de hacer algo

pretend [prɪ'tend] Ⓐ VT 1 (= *feign*) fingir, simular; **to ~ that ...** (querer) hacer creer que ...; **he's ~ing that he can't hear** finge no oír; **to ~ to do sth** fingir hacer algo; **to ~ to be asleep** hacerse el dormido, fingir estar dormido; **to ~ to be mad** fingirse loco; **to ~ not to understand** hacerse el desentendido
2 (= *claim*) pretender; **I don't ~ to know the answer** no pretendo saber la respuesta
Ⓑ VI fingir; **she's only ~ing** es de mentira
Ⓒ ADJ (*) de mentira, fingido; ~ **money*** dinero *m* de juego

pretense [prɪ'tens] N (*US*) = **pretence**

pretension [prɪ'tenʃən] N 1 (= *claim*) pretensión *f* 2 (= *pretentiousness*) presunción *f*, pretenciosidad *f*

pretentious [prɪ'tenʃəs] ADJ pretencioso

preterite ['pretərɪt] N (*Gram*) pretérito *m*

pretext ['priːtekst] N pretexto *m*, excusa *f*; **on the ~ of doing sth** so pretexto *or* con la excusa de hacer algo

pretty ['prɪtɪ] Ⓐ ADJ (*compar* **prettier**; *superl* **prettiest**) (= *attractive*) [*dress, object, baby*] bonito, mono*, lindo (*LAm*); [*girl*] bonito, guapo, lindo (*LAm*); **it'll cost you a ~ penny*** te va a costar un ojo de la cara *or* un dineral; **it was not a ~ sight** no era nada agradable de ver; ✚ IDIOM **as ~ as a picture** precioso
Ⓑ ADV bastante; **she got ~ good marks** sacó unas notas bastante buenas; **he got ~ cross** se enfadó bastante; ~ **damn** *or* **damned quick*** bien pronto; **it's ~ much the same** es mas o menos igual, es prácticamente lo mismo; **I'm ~ well finished** ya casi he terminado; **that's ~ well everything** eso es todo más o menos

pretzel ['pretsl] N galleta *f* salada

prevail [prɪ'veɪl] VI 1 (= *gain mastery*) prevalecer; **finally good sense ~ed** por fin se impuso el buen sentido; **eventually peace ~ed** al final se restableció la paz 2 (= *be current*) [*views, opinions*] predominar; (= *be in fashion*) estar de moda, estar en boga; **the conditions that now ~** las condiciones que ahora imperan 3 (= *persuade*) **to ~ (up)on sb to do sth** convencer a algn para que haga algo

prevailing [prɪ'veɪlɪŋ] ADJ [*opinion, wind*] predominante; [*price*] imperante; **under ~ conditions** bajo las condiciones actuales

prevalence ['prevələns] N 1 (= *dominance*) predominio *m* 2 (= *frequency*) frecuencia *f*

prevalent ['prevələnt] ADJ 1 (= *dominant*) dominante 2 (= *widespread*) extendido 3 (= *fashionable*) de moda; (= *current*) actual

prevaricate [prɪ'værɪkeɪt] VI andar con rodeos

prevarication [prɪˌværɪ'keɪʃən] N evasivas *fpl*

prevent [prɪ'vent] VT 1 (= *avert*) (*by taking precautions*) [+ *accident, disaster, death, war, pregnancy*] prevenir, evitar; [+ *illness*] prevenir 2 (= *impede, put a stop to*) [+ *crime, corruption*] impedir; [+ *attempt*] prevenir, impedir; **to ~ the spread of nuclear weapons** impedir la proliferación de las armas nucleares; **to ~ sb (from) doing sth** impedir que algn haga algo; **don't let this ~ you from going** no dejes que esto te impida ir

preventable [prɪ'ventəbl] ADJ evitable

preventative [prɪ'ventətɪv] ADJ = **preventive**

prevention [prɪ'venʃən] N prevención *f*; ✚ PROV ~ **is better than cure** más vale prevenir que curar

preventive [prɪ'ventɪv] ADJ preventivo

preview ['priːvjuː] N [*of film*] preestreno *m*; [*of exhibition*] inauguración *f* (*para la prensa, socios, personalidades etc*); **to give sb a ~ of sth** (*fig*) permitir a algn ver algo de antemano; **to have a ~ of sth** (*fig*) ver algo con anticipación, lograr ver algo antes que otros

previous ['priːvɪəs] ADJ (= *former, earlier*) [*night, day, year, page, life*] anterior; [*experience*] previo; **I have a ~ engagement** tengo un compromiso previo; **on ~ occasions** en ocasiones anteriores; **the car has had two ~ owners** el coche ha pasado por dos manos; **in the five years ~ to 1992** durante los cinco años anteriores a 1992; **~ to that ...** antes de eso ...

previously ['priːvɪəslɪ] ADV (= *earlier, formerly*) antes, anteriormente; (= *in advance*) con antelación, previamente

prewar ['priːˈwɔːʳ] ADJ de antes de la guerra; **the ~ period** la preguerra

prewash ['priːwɒʃ] N prelavado *m*

prey [preɪ] Ⓐ N (*lit, fig*) presa *f*, víctima *f*; **bird of ~** ave *f* de rapiña

> Use **el/un** not **la/una** before feminine nouns beginning with stressed **a** or **ha** like **ave**.

to be (a) ~ to ser víctima de; **she is ~ to irrational fears** (*fig*) es presa de temores irracionales
Ⓑ VI **to ~ on** [+ *animals*] (= *attack*) cazar; (= *feed on*) alimentarse de; [+ *person*] aprovecharse de; **rabbits are ~ed on by foxes** los conejos son presa de los zorros; **to ~ on sb's mind** traer preocupado *or* obsesionar a algn

prezzie*, prezzy* ['prezɪ] N (*Brit*) regalito

price [praɪs] Ⓐ N 1 (*Comm*) precio *m*; **we pay top ~s for gold** pagamos los mejores precios por el oro; **that's my ~, take it or leave it** eso es lo que pido, o lo tomas o lo dejas; **you can get it at a ~** se puede conseguir, pero pagando; **it's not for sale at any ~** no está a la venta a ningún precio; **their loyalty cannot be bought at any ~** su lealtad no tiene precio; **he'll do it for a ~** él lo hará, pero será caro, lo hará si le pagan; **you can get anything you want for a ~** puedes conseguir todo lo que quieras pagando; **two for the ~ of one** dos al *or* por el precio de uno; **he got a good ~ for it** sacó una buena suma por ello; **everyone has their ~** todos tenemos un precio; **there's a ~ on his head** se ha puesto precio a su cabeza; **to come down/go up in ~** bajar/subir de precio; **you can't put a ~ on friendship** la amistad no tiene precio; **he is prepared to make a comeback if the ~ is right** está dispuesto a volver si se le paga bien; **as long as the ~ is right, property will sell** si está a un buen precio, la propiedad se vende
2 (*Fin, St Ex*) (= *quotation*) cotización *f*
3 (*Gambling*) (= *odds*) puntos *mpl* de ventaja; ✦ IDIOM **what ~ ...?*** (= *what's the betting*) ¿qué apuestas ...?; **what ~ she'll change her mind?** ¿qué apuestas a que cambia de opinión?
4 (= *sacrifice*) precio *m*; **that's the ~ of progress** es el precio que tenemos que pagar por el progreso; **at any ~** (*with affirmative*) a toda costa; **they want peace at any ~** quieren la paz a toda costa; **a concert I wasn't going to miss at any ~** un concierto que no me iba a perder por nada del mundo; **to pay a high ~ for sth** pagar algo muy caro; **that's a small ~ to pay for independence** eso es poco sacrificio a cambio de la independencia
Ⓑ VT 1 (= *fix price of*) poner precio a; **tickets, ~d £20, are now available** las entradas ya están a la venta a un precio de 20 libras; **it was ~d too high/low** su precio era demasiado alto/bajo; ✦ IDIOM **to ~ sb out of the market** hacer que algn pierda competitividad (*rebajando uno sus precios artificialmente*)
2 (= *label with price*) **the tins of salmon weren't clearly ~d** el precio de la latas de salmón no estaba claro *or* claramente indicado; **it was ~d at £15** estaba marcado a un precio de 15 libras
3 (= *estimate value of*) calcular el valor de; **it was ~d at £1,000** estaba valorado en mil libras
4 (= *find out price of*) comprobar el precio de
Ⓒ CPD ➤ **price bracket he's looking for a property in the £70,000 ~ bracket** está buscando una vivienda que cueste alrededor de las setenta mil libras; **a traditional restaurant in the middle ~ bracket** un restaurante tradicional con precios de un nivel medio (dentro de la escala) ➤ **price cut** rebaja *f* ➤ **price cutting** reducción *f* de precios ➤ **price**

fixing fijación *f* de precios ➤ **price freeze** congelación *f* de precios ➤ **price list** lista *f* de precios ➤ **price range: there are lots of good products in all ~ ranges** hay gran cantidad de productos de buena calidad en una amplia gama de precios; **in the medium** *or* **middle ~ range** dentro de un nivel medio de la escala de precios; **in/out of one's ~ range** dentro de/fuera de las posibilidades de uno ➤ **prices and incomes policy** política *f* de precios y salarios, política *f* de precios y rentas ➤ **price tag** (*lit*) etiqueta *f* (del precio); (*fig*) precio *m* ➤ **price war** guerra *f* de precios

priceless ['praɪslɪs] ADJ 1 [*picture, jewel*] inestimable 2 (*) (= *amusing*) divertidísimo

pricey* ['praɪsɪ] ADJ (*compar* **pricier**; *superl* **priciest**) (*Brit*) carito*, caro

pricing ['praɪsɪŋ] N fijación *f* de precios ➤ **pricing policy** política *f* tarifaria

prick [prɪk] Ⓐ N 1 (*with pin, needle*) pinchazo *m*
2 (***) (= *penis*) polla *f* (*Sp****), picha *f* (*Sp****), pinga *f* (*And, Mex****), pico *m* (*Chi****), pija *f* (*River Plate****)
3 (***) (= *person*) gilipollas *mf inv* (*Sp****), cojonudo/a *m/f* (*And****), boludo/a *m/f* (*SC***), huevón/ona *m/f* (*Chi****)
Ⓑ VT pinchar; **to ~ one's finger (with** *or* **on sth)** pincharse el dedo (con algo); **it ~ed his conscience** le remordía la conciencia
➤ **prick up** VT + ADV **to ~ up one's ears** (*lit, fig*) aguzar el oído, parar la oreja (*LAm*)

prickle ['prɪkl] Ⓐ N 1 (*on plant, animal*) espina *f*
2 (= *sensation*) picor *m*, comezón *f* Ⓑ VT picar
Ⓒ VI picar, hormiguear; **my eyes are prickling** me pican los ojos; **I could feel my skin prickling** me escocía la piel

prickly ['prɪklɪ] Ⓐ ADJ (*compar* **pricklier**; *superl* **prickliest**)
1 (= *spiky*) espinoso 2 [*person*] enojadizo; **he's rather ~ about that** sobre ese tema es algo quisquilloso
Ⓑ CPD ➤ **prickly heat** (*Med*) sarpullido *m* (causado por exceso de calor) ➤ **prickly pear** (= *plant*) chumbera *f*, nopal *m* (*LAm*); (= *fruit*) higo *m* chumbo, tuna *f* (*LAm*)

pride [praɪd] Ⓐ N 1 (= *satisfaction*) orgullo *m*; **to take (a) ~ in sth/in doing sth** enorgullecerse de algo/de hacer algo, estar orgulloso de algo/de hacer algo; **his roses are his ~ and joy** sus rosas son su orgullo; ✦ IDIOM **to have ~ of place** ocupar el lugar de honor
2 (= *conceit*) orgullo *m*, soberbia *f*, arrogancia *f*;
✦ PROV **~ comes** *or* **goes before a fall** más dura será la caída
3 (= *self-respect*) orgullo *m*, amor *m* propio; **I wouldn't ask him any favours, I have my ~** no le pediría ningún favor, tengo mi orgullo *or* amor propio
4 [*of lions*] manada *f*
Ⓑ VT **to ~ o.s. on sth: she ~s herself on not owning a TV** está orgullosa de no tener televisor; **he ~s himself on his punctuality** se precia de ser puntual

priest [priːst] N (*gen, pagan*) sacerdote *m*; (*Christian*) sacerdote *m*, cura *m*; **woman ~** diaconisa *f*

priestess ['priːstɪs] N sacerdotisa *f*

priesthood ['priːsthʊd] N (= *function*) sacerdocio *m*; (= *priests collectively*) clero *m*; **to enter the ~** ordenarse sacerdote

prig [prɪg] N gazmoño/a *m/f*, mojigato/a *m/f*

prim [prɪm] ADJ (*compar* **~mer**; *superl* **~mest**) (= *formal*) formal, estirado; (= *demure*) remilgado, cursi; (= *prudish*) mojigato, gazmoño

primacy ['praɪməsɪ] N primacía *f*

prima donna ['priːməˈdɒnə] N primadonna *f*, diva *f*

primaeval [praɪˈmiːvl] ADJ (*Brit*) = **primeval**

prima facie ['praɪməˈfeɪʃɪ] ADJ suficiente a primera vista; **~ evidence** prueba *f* semiplena; **to have a ~ case** (*Jur*) tener razón a primera vista

primal ['praɪməl] ADJ (= *first in time*) original; (= *first in* *importance*) principal; ~ **scream** grito *m* primal

PRIMARIES

Las elecciones primarias (**primaries**) sirven para preseleccionar a los candidatos de los partidos demócrata (**Democratic**) y republicano (**Republican**) durante la campaña que precede a las elecciones a la presidencia de Estados Unidos. Se inician en New Hampshire y tienen lugar en 35 estados entre los meses de febrero y junio. El número de votos obtenidos por cada candidato determina el número de delegados que votarán en el congreso general (**National Convention**) de julio y agosto, en el que se decide el candidato definitivo de cada partido.

primarily ['praɪmərɪlɪ] ADV ante todo, principalmente

primary ['praɪmərɪ] **A** ADJ 1 (= *chief, main*) [*reason, purpose, source*] principal
2 (= *fundamental*) primordial
3 (= *first*) primario
4 (*esp Brit Scol*) (= *elementary*) primario
B N 1 (*US*) (*also* ~ **election**) (elección *f*) primaria *f*
2 (= *colour*) color *m* primario
3 = **primary school**
C CPD ➤ **primary colour, primary color** (*US*) color *m* primario ➤ **primary education** (*Brit*) enseñanza *f* primaria, educación *f* primaria ➤ **primary election** (*US*) (elección *f*) primaria *f* ➤ **primary school** (*Brit*) escuela *f* primaria; (*US*) escuela *f* primaria (de primer ciclo) (6-9 años) ➤ **primary school teacher** (*Brit*) profesor(a) *m/f* de enseñanza primaria, maestro/a *m/f*

primate ['praɪmeɪt] N 1 (*Zool*) primate *m* 2 (*Rel*) primado *m*

prime [praɪm] **A** ADJ 1 (= *major, main*) [*cause, objective, target*] principal; **our ~ concern is public safety** nuestra mayor *or* principal preocupación es la seguridad ciudadana; **to be of ~ importance** ser de primordial *or* fundamental importancia; **he's the ~ suspect** es el principal sospechoso
2 (= *top-quality, excellent*) [*real estate, property*] de primera; [*ingredient, cut*] de primera (calidad); **a ~ site** un lugar privilegiado
3 (*Math*) [*number*] primo
B N (= *best years*) **when trade unionism was in its ~** cuando el sindicalismo estaba en su apogeo; **to be in the ~ of life** *or* **in one's ~** estar en la flor de la vida; **to be cut down in one's ~** morir en la flor de la vida; **he's past his ~** ya ha dejado atrás los mejores años de su vida
C VT 1 (= *prior to painting*) imprimar, preparar; (*with primer*) aplicar una capa de imprimación a; (*with anticorrosive*) aplicar una capa de pintura anticorrosiva a
2 (*prior to use*) [+ *gun, pump, bomb*] cebar
3 (= *prepare*) [+ *student, politician, soldier*] preparar
4 (*with drink*) **he arrived well ~d** llegó ya bien bebido
D CPD ➤ **prime minister** primer(a) ministro/a *m/f* ➤ **prime mover** (= *person*) promotor(a) *m/f* ➤ **prime number** (*Math*) número *m* primo ➤ **prime rate** tipo *m* de interés preferencial; ~ **lending rate** tipo *m* de interés preferencial sobre los préstamos ➤ **prime time** (*TV*) horas *fpl* de máxima *or* mayor audiencia

primer ['praɪmə'] N 1 (= *textbook*) manual *m* básico
2 (= *paint*) pintura *f* base, imprimación *f*

prime-time ['praɪmtaɪm] ADJ en horario de máxima audiencia, en horario de mayor audiencia; **the documentary will be broadcast on ~ television** el documental se emitirá por televisión durante las horas de máxima *or* mayor audiencia

primeval [praɪ'miːvəl] ADJ primitivo

primitive ['prɪmɪtɪv] ADJ (*gen, also Art*) primitivo; (= *basic*) rudimentario, básico

primordial [praɪ'mɔːdɪəl] ADJ primordial

primrose ['prɪmrəʊz] **A** N (= *flower*) primavera *f* **B** ADJ (*also* ~ **yellow**) amarillo pálido

primula ['prɪmjʊlə] N (*Bot*) prímula *f*

Primus (stove)® ['praɪməs(ˌstəʊv)] N (*Brit*) cocina *f* de camping, camping-gas® *m*

prince [prɪns] N príncipe *m*; **Prince Charles** el príncipe Carlos; **Prince Charming** el Príncipe Azul, el Príncipe Encantador

princely ['prɪnslɪ] ADJ (*lit*) principesco; (*fig*) magnífico, espléndido; **the ~ sum of five dollars** (*iro*) la bonita suma de cinco dólares

princess [prɪn'ses] N (= *royal*) princesa *f*; **Princess Victoria** la Princesa Victoria

principal ['prɪnsɪpəl] **A** ADJ [*reason, cause, source*] principal; **our ~ concern** nuestra mayor *or* principal preocupación **B** N 1 [*of school, college*] director(a) *m/f*; (*Univ*) rector(a) *m/f* 2 (*Fin*) capital *m*, principal *m* **C** CPD ➤ **principal boy** (*Brit Theat*) joven héroe *m* (*papel de actriz en la "pantomime" navideña*); ▷ *PANTOMIME*

principality [ˌprɪnsɪ'pælɪtɪ] N principado *m*

principally ['prɪnsɪpəlɪ] ADV principalmente

principle ['prɪnsəpl] N (*gen, Sci*) principio *m*; **it goes against my ~s** va (en) contra (de) mis principios; **to have high ~s** tener principios nobles; **in ~** en principio; **I make it a ~ never to lend money** tengo por norma no prestar nunca dinero, yo, por principio, nunca presto dinero; **as a matter of ~** por principio; **it's a matter of ~** ◆ **it's the ~ of the thing** es cuestión de principios

print [prɪnt] **A** N 1 (*Typ*) (= *letters*) letra *f*; (= *printed matter*) texto *m* impreso; **in bold** ~ en negrita; **the fine** ~ la letra pequeña *or* menuda; **to be in** ~ (= *be published*) estar publicado; (= *be available*) estar a la venta; **to appear in** ~ [*work*] publicarse; **the first time the term appeared in** ~ **was in 1530** la primera vez que apareció el término en una publicación fue en 1530; **in large** ~ con letra grande; **to be out of** ~ estar agotado; **to go out of** ~ agotarse; **in small** ~ con letra pequeña *or* menuda; **read the small** ~ **before you sign** lea la letra pequeña *or* menuda antes de firmar
2 (= *mark, imprint*) [*of foot, finger, tyre*] huella *f*, marca *f*; (= *fingerprint*) huella *f* digital, huella *f* dactilar
3 (= *fabric*) estampado *m*
4 (*Art*) (= *etching, woodcut, lithograph*) grabado *m*; (= *reproduction*) reproducción *f*
5 (*Phot, Cine*) copia *f*
B VT 1 (= *set in print*) [+ *letters, text*] imprimir; [+ *money*] emitir; **they ~ed 300 copies** hicieron una tirada de 300 ejemplares; **~ed in England** impreso en Inglaterra; **to ~ sth on sth** estampar algo en algo
2 (= *write in block letters*) escribir con *or* en letra de imprenta, escribir con *or* en letra de molde; **~ it in block capitals** escríbalo con *or* en mayúsculas
3 (*Phot*) [+ *negative*] imprimir; [+ *photo*] sacar una copia de; [+ *copy*] sacar
4 (*fig*) grabar; **her face was ~ed in my mind** su cara se me había quedado grabada en la mente
C VI [*person*] escribir con *or* en letra de imprenta, escribir con *or* en letra de molde; [*machine*] imprimir
D CPD ➤ **print dress** vestido *m* estampado ➤ **print out** VT + ADV (*Comput*) imprimir

printable ['prɪntəbl] ADJ imprimible

printer ['prɪntə'] N 1 (= *person*) impresor(a) *m/f* 2 (*Comput*) (= *machine*) impresora *f*

printing ['prɪntɪŋ] **A** N 1 (= *process*) impresión *f* 2 (= *block writing*) letras *fpl* de molde; (= *characters, print*) letra *f* **B** CPD ➤ **printing press** prensa *f*

printout ['prɪntaʊt] N copia *f* impresa, listado *m*

prior[1] ['praɪə'] **A** ADJ (= *previous*) previo; **I have a ~ engagement** tengo un compromiso previo; **to have a ~ claim to** *or* **on sth/sb: there are others who have a ~ claim on my time** hay otros que tienen prioridad (sobre mi tiempo); **she felt that her past connection with him gave her a ~ claim to him** le parecía que su pasada relación con él le daba ciertos derechos
B ADV (*frm*) 1 ~ **to sth** anterior *or* previo a algo; **in the years** ~ **to his death** en los años anteriores *or* previos a su muerte; ~ **to that day we had not met** antes de ese día no nos conocíamos, hasta ese día no nos conocíamos; ~ **to this/that** antes de esto/eso; ~ **to doing sth** antes de hacer algo
2 (*US*) antes; **it happened two days** ~ ocurrió dos días antes

prior² ['praɪə'] N (*Rel*) prior *m*
prioritize [praɪ'ɒrɪtaɪz] VT (*esp US*) priorizar
priority [praɪ'ɒrɪtɪ] N **1** (= *precedence*) prioridad *f;* **to give ~ to sth/sb** dar prioridad a algo/algn; **to give sth (a) high/low ~** dar mucha/poca importancia a algo; **to give sth top ~** dar máxima prioridad a algo; **to have ~ (over sth/sb)** tener prioridad (sobre algo/algn)
2 (= *concern, aim*) prioridad *f;* **try to decide what your priorities are** intenta establecer tu orden de prioridades; **our first ~ is to cut costs** nuestra máxima prioridad es reducir los gastos; **to be high/low on sb's list of priorities** ocupar un lugar alto/bajo en el orden de prioridades de algn; **my number one** *or* **top ~** lo más importante para mí
3 (*on highway*) preferencia *f* de paso; **to have ~** tener preferencia de paso
priory ['praɪərɪ] N priorato *m*
prise, prize (*US*) [praɪz] VT **to ~ the lid off** levantar la tapa haciendo palanca; **to ~ sth open** abrir algo haciendo palanca; **we had to ~ the secret out of him** tuvimos que sacarle el secreto a la fuerza
prism ['prɪzəm] N (*Geom, Tech*) prisma *m*
prison ['prɪzn] N cárcel *f*, prisión *f;* **to be in ~** estar en la cárcel, estar en prisión; **to be in ~ for five years** pasar cinco años en la cárcel *or* en prisión; **to send sb to ~** (= *imprison*) encarcelar a algn; **to send sb to ~ for two years** (= *sentence*) condenar a algn a dos años de prisión ➤ **prison camp** campamento *m* para prisioneros ➤ **prison cell** celda *f* de la cárcel *or* prisión ➤ **prison officer** carcelero/a *m/f* ➤ **prison sentence** (*Brit*), **prison term** (*US*) condena *f*
prisoner ['prɪznə'] ❹ N **1** (*under arrest*) detenido/a *m/f;* (*in court*) acusado/a *m/f;* (*convicted*) preso/a *m/f*, reo/a *m/f;* (*Mil*) prisionero/a *m/f;* **to hold sb ~** detener a algn; **to take sb ~** tomar preso a algn, hacer prisionero a algn
2 (*fig*) preso/a *m/f*, prisionero/a *m/f* ❺ CPD ➤ **prisoner of conscience** preso/a *m/f* de conciencia ➤ **prisoner of war** prisionero/a *m/f* de guerra, preso/a *m/f* de guerra
prisoner-of-war camp [ˌprɪznərəv'wɔːˌkæmp] N campamento *m* para prisioneros de guerra
prissy* ['prɪsɪ] ADJ (*compar* **prissier;** *superl* **prissiest**) remilgado
pristine ['prɪstaɪn] ADJ prístino
privacy ['prɪvəsɪ] N intimidad *f;* **in ~** en la intimidad; **lack of ~** falta *f* de intimidad
private ['praɪvɪt] ❹ ADJ **1** (= *not public*) [*conversation, visit, land, matter*] privado; [*letter, reason, opinion*] personal; [*language*] secreto; [*thoughts, grief, fantasy*] íntimo; **"private"** (*on door*) "privado"; (*on envelope*) "confidencial"; **"private and confidential"** "confidencial"; **"private fishing"** "coto *m* de pesca"; **"private parking"** "aparcamiento *m* or (*LAm*) estacionamiento *m* privado"; **it's a ~ joke of ours** es un chiste que sólo nosotros entendemos; **I've always tried to keep my ~ life** [*famous person*] siempre he intentado mantener mi vida privada alejada de la mirada del público; [*ordinary person*] siempre he intentado mantener mi vida privada fuera del alcance de los demás; **he's a very ~ person** es una persona muy reservada
2 (= *own, individual*) [*car, house, lesson, room*] particular; [*bank account*] personal
3 (= *independent*) [*medicine, education, finance*] privado; [*school*] privado, particular; [*patient, tutor, teacher*] particular; **a ~ hospital** una clínica (privada), un hospital privado *or* particular
4 (= *secluded*) [*place*] retirado; **is there somewhere we can be ~?** ¿hay algún sitio donde podamos hablar en privado? ❺ N **1** (*Mil*) soldado *mf* raso; **Private Jones** el soldado Jones; **Private Jones!** ¡Jones!
2 could I talk to you in ~? ¿te puedo hablar en privado?; **what people do in ~ is up to them** lo que cada uno haga en su vida privada es asunto suyo
3 privates* (*euph, hum*) partes *fpl* pudendas
❻ CPD ➤ **private detective** detective *mf* privado/a ➤ **private enterprise** (= *industry*) el sector privado; (= *initiative*) la iniciativa privada ➤ **private eye** (*US**) detective *mf* privado/a ➤ **private health care** servicio *m* médico privado ➤ **private health insurance** seguro *m* médico privado ➤ **private investigator** investigador(a) *m/f*

private life vida *f* privada ➤ **private means** rentas *fpl* ➤ **private member, Private Member** (*Brit Parl*) diputado/a *m/f* sin responsabilidades de gobierno ➤ **private parts** (*euph, hum*) partes *fpl* pudendas ➤ **private patient** paciente *mf* privado/a ➤ **private practice** (*Brit Med*) consulta *f* privada; **to be in ~ practice** (*Med*) ejercer la medicina de forma privada; **he decided to set up in ~ practice** (*Med*) decidió establecerse como médico privado ➤ **private property** propiedad *f* privada ➤ **private prosecution** (*Jur*) demanda *f* civil; **to bring a ~ prosecution against sb** presentar una demanda civil contra algn ➤ **private school** escuela *f* privada, escuela *f* particular ➤ **the private sector** el sector privado ➤ **private soldier** soldado *mf* raso
privately ['praɪvɪtlɪ] ADV **1** (= *not publicly*) en privado; **senior officials from the two sides met ~** altos funcionarios de ambas partes se reunieron en privado *or* a puerta(s) cerrada(s); **~ I was very angry with her** por dentro estaba muy enfadado con ella; **the Foreign Office was ~ appalled** extraoficialmente, el Ministerio de Exterior estaba horrorizado
2 (= *independently*) **one in every four of these operations is done ~** una de cada cuatro operaciones de este tipo se hace en clínicas privadas; **he is being ~ educated** va a un colegio privado *or* particular; **~ financed projects** proyectos *mpl* de financiación privada; **~ owned land** tierras *fpl* que son propiedad privada
privation [praɪ'veɪʃən] N privación *f*
privatization [ˌpraɪvətaɪ'zeɪʃən] N privatización *f*
privatize ['praɪvətaɪz] VT privatizar
privet ['prɪvɪt] N alheña *f* ➤ **privet hedge** seto *m* de alheña, seto *m* vivo
privilege ['prɪvɪlɪdʒ] ❹ N privilegio *m;* **I had the ~ of meeting her** tuve el privilegio *or* el honor de conocerla; **that's your ~** estás en tu derecho ❺ VT (= *favour*) privilegiar
privileged ['prɪvɪlɪdʒd] ADJ privilegiado; **for a ~ few** unos pocos privilegiados *or* afortunados; **to be ~ to do sth** tener el privilegio *or* el honor de hacer algo
privy ['prɪvɪ] ADJ **to be ~ to sth** estar al tanto *or* enterado de algo ➤ **Privy Council** (*Brit*) consejo *m* privado (del monarca), ≈ Consejo *m* de Estado

---

PRIVY COUNCIL

El consejo de asesores de la Corona, conocido como **Privy Council,** se creó en la época de los normandos y fue adquiriendo mayor importancia hasta ser substituido en 1688 por el actual Consejo de Ministros **Cabinet.** Hoy día sigue existiendo con un carácter fundamentalmente honorífico y los ministros y otras personalidades políticas, eclesiásticas y jurídicas se convierten en miembros de forma automática.

---

prize¹ [praɪz] ❹ N **1** (*in competition, lottery*) premio *m;* **he won first ~** (*in race, competition*) se llevó el primer premio
2 (*Sport*) (= *trophy*) trofeo *m;* (= *money*) premio *m*
3 (*fig*) premio *m*, galardón *m* (*frm*)
❺ ADJ **1** (= *outstanding*) de primera, de primera clase; **a ~ idiot*** un tonto de remate*
2 (= *prizewinning*) [*entry, rose*] galardonado, premiado; (*fig*) digno de premio
❻ VT apreciar mucho, estimar mucho; **to ~ sth highly** estimar algo en mucho; **a ~d possession** un bien preciado
❼ CPD ➤ **prize day** (*Scol*) día *m* de reparto de premios ➤ **prize draw** sorteo *m* con premio, tómbola *f* ➤ **prize fight** (*Boxing*) partido *m* (de boxeo) profesional ➤ **prize fighter** boxeador *m* profesional ➤ **prize money** (= *cash*) premio *m* en metálico; (*Boxing*) bolsa *f*
prize² [praɪz] VT (*US*) = **prise**
prize-giving ['praɪzˌgɪvɪŋ] N (*Brit*) reparto *m* de premios
prizewinner ['praɪzˌwɪnə'] N premiado/a *m/f*
prizewinning ['praɪzˌwɪnɪŋ] ADJ premiado
pro¹ [prəʊ] N **the ~s and cons** los pros y los contras
pro²* [prəʊ] N profesional *mf*

pro... [prəʊ] PREF (*esp Brit*) (= *in favour of*) pro, en pro de; **~-Soviet** pro-soviético; **~-European** europeísta; **they were terribly ~-Franco** eran unos franquistas furibundos, eran partidarios acérrimos de Franco

proactive [ˌprəʊˈæktɪv] ADJ proactivo

probability [ˌprɒbəˈbɪlɪtɪ] N (*gen, also Math*) probabilidad *f*; **the ~ is that ...** es probable que ... + *subjun*; **in all ~ he won't turn up** lo más probable es que no aparezca; **there is little ~ of anyone finding out** es muy poco probable que alguien se entere

probable [əbl] ADJ 1 (= *likely*) probable; **it is ~ that ...** es probable que ... + *subjun* 2 (= *credible*) verosímil; **her story didn't sound very ~ to me** su historia no me pareció muy verosímil

probably ['prɒbəblɪ] ADV probablemente; **she ~ forgot** se habrá olvidado, seguramente se ha olvidado, probablemente se haya olvidado; **he will ~ come** es probable que venga; **~ not** puede que no, quizá no; **very ~, but ...** es muy posible *or* bien puede ser, pero ...

probate ['prəʊbɪt] N validación *f* de un testamento, validación *f* testamentaria

probation [prəˈbeɪʃən] N libertad *f* condicional; **to be on ~** (*Jur*) estar en libertad condicional; (*in employment*) estar a prueba ➤ **probation officer** funcionario que vigila a las personas que están en libertad condicional

probationary [prəˈbeɪʃnərɪ] ADJ de prueba ➤ **probationary period** período *m* de prueba

probationer [prəˈbeɪʃnəʳ] N (= *worker*) persona *f* a prueba; (= *criminal*) persona *f* en libertad condicional

probe [prəʊb] Ⓐ N 1 (*Med*) sonda *f*
2 (*also* space ~) sonda *f* espacial
3 (= *inquiry*) investigación *f* (**into** de)
Ⓑ VT 1 [+ *hole, crack*] (*with instrument, probe*) sondear; (*with hands*) palpar, tantear
2 (*Med*) sondar
3 (= *explore*) explorar
4 (= *investigate*) investigar; **the policeman kept probing me** el policía siguió sondeándome; **to ~ a mystery** investigar un misterio
Ⓒ VI investigar; **to ~ into sb's past** investigar el pasado de algn; **you should have ~d more deeply** deberías haber llevado a cabo una investigación más a fondo

probing ['prəʊbɪŋ] N (= *investigation*) investigación *f*

probity ['prəʊbɪtɪ] N probidad *f*

problem ['prɒbləm] N (*gen, also Math*) problema *m*; **what's the ~?** ¿cuál es el problema?; **that's your ~** eso es problema tuyo; **it's not my ~** no es problema mío; **the ~ is that she can't cook** el problema es que no sabe cocinar; **he has a drink ~** tiene problemas con la bebida, bebe demasiado; **he shouldn't have any ~ finding a job** no le será difícil encontrar trabajo; **phone me if you have any ~s** llámame si tienes cualquier problema; **I had no ~ getting a mortgage** no tuve problemas para conseguir una hipoteca; **do you have a ~ with that?*** ¿te molesta?; **I have no ~ with the ordination of women** no tengo nada en contra de la ordenación de las mujeres; **health ~s** problemas *mpl* de salud; **no ~!*** (= *of course*) ¡claro!, ¡cómo no!; (= *it doesn't matter*) ¡no importa!, ¡no hay problema!; **the ~ with men is that ...** lo malo de los hombres es que ... ➤ **problem case** (*Med, Sociol*) caso *m* difícil ➤ **problem child** niño/a *m/f* problemático/a ➤ **problem drinker: he's a ~ drinker** tiene problemas con la bebida ➤ **problem page** consultorio *m* sentimental ➤ **problem solving** resolución *f* de problemas

problematic [ˌprɒblɪˈmætɪk] ADJ problemático

problem-free [ˌprɒbləmˈfriː] ADJ sin problema

procedural [prəˈsiːdjʊrəl] ADJ relativo al procedimiento; (*Jur*) procesal; **a ~ question** una cuestión de procedimiento

procedure [prəˈsiːdʒəʳ] N 1 (*gen*) procedimiento *m*; **what is the ~ for emergencies?** ¿cuál es el procedimiento a seguir *or* cómo se procede en caso de emergencia?; **the usual ~ is to write a letter** lo que se hace por lo general es escribir una carta 2 (*Admin*) trámites *mpl*; **what's the ~ for obtaining a visa?** ¿qué trámites *or* gestiones hay que hacer para conseguir un visado?

proceed [prəˈsiːd] Ⓐ VI 1 (= *go forward*) [*person, vehicle*] avanzar; [*plan, project*] desarrollarse; [*events*] transcurrir; **he was ~ing along the road** avanzaba por la calle; **things are ~ing according to plan** las cosas se están desarrollando conforme estaban previstas
2 (= *go on, continue*) seguir, continuar; **before we ~ any further** antes de seguir adelante; **to ~ to sth: let us ~ to the next item** pasemos al siguiente punto; **we ~ed to the bar** nos dirigimos al bar; **to ~ to do sth** pasar a hacer algo; **he ~ed to drink the lot** acto seguido comenzó a bebérselo todo; **to ~ with sth** seguir adelante con algo
3 (= *act*) proceder, obrar
Ⓑ VT (= *say*) proseguir; **"well," she ~ed** —bueno — prosiguió

proceedings [prəˈsiːdɪŋz] NPL 1 (= *event*) acto *msing*; (= *record*) [*of learned society*] actas *fpl*; **the ~ began at seven o'clock** el acto comenzó a las siete; **hecklers attempted to disrupt the ~** hubo gente que intentó perturbar el desarrollo del acto *or* de la reunión 2 (*esp Jur*) (= *measures*) medidas *fpl*; **legal ~** proceso *msing*; **to start (legal) ~ (against sb)** (*Jur*) entablar pleito *or* una demanda (contra algn)

proceeds ['prəʊsiːdz] NPL [*of sale, transaction*] ganancias *fpl*; **all ~ will go to charity** toda la recaudación se destinará a obras benéficas

process¹ ['prəʊses] Ⓐ N 1 (*gen*) proceso *m*; **the production ~** el proceso de producción; **I got what I wanted but made a lot of enemies in the ~** conseguí lo que quería pero a costa de crearme muchos enemigos; **it is in (the) ~ of construction** está en (vías de) construcción; **we are in the ~ of moving house** estamos en medio de una mudanza 2 (= *specific method*) proceso *m*, procedimiento *m*; **the Bessemer ~** el proceso de Bessemer
Ⓑ VT 1 (= *treat*) [+ *raw materials*] procesar; [+ *food*] (*industrially*) procesar, tratar; (*with food processor*) pasar por el robot de cocina
2 (= *deal with*) [+ *application, claim, order*] tramitar; [+ *applicants*] atender
3 (*Comput*) procesar
4 (*Phot*) revelar

process² [prəˈses] VI (*Brit frm*) (= *go in procession*) desfilar; (*Rel*) ir en procesión

processed ['prəʊsest], **process** (*US*) ['prɑːses] ADJ [*food*] procesado ➤ **process(ed) cheese** queso *m* fundido

processing ['prəʊsesɪŋ] N [*of raw materials*] procesamiento *m*, tratamiento *m*; [*of food*] procesamiento *m*; [*of application, claim, order*] tramitación *f*; (*Comput*) procesamiento *m*; (*Phot*) revelado *m* ➤ **processing plant** planta *f* de procesamiento

procession [prəˈseʃən] N [*of people, cars etc*] desfile *m*; (*ceremonial, funeral*) cortejo *m*; (*Rel*) procesión *f*; **to go or walk in ~** desfilar; (*Rel*) ir en procesión

pro-choice [ˌprəʊˈtʃɔɪs] ADJ en favor de la libertad de elección

proclaim [prəˈkleɪm] VT 1 (= *announce*) [+ *independence*] proclamar, declarar; **to ~ sb king** proclamar a algn rey; **to ~ one's innocence** declararse inocente 2 (= *reveal*) revelar, anunciar

proclamation [ˌprɒkləˈmeɪʃən] N (= *act*) proclamación *f*; (= *document*) proclama *f*

proclivity [prəˈklɪvɪtɪ] N propensión *f*, proclividad *f* (**for, towards** a)

procrastinate [prəʊˈkræstɪneɪt] VI dejar las cosas para más tarde, aplazar las cosas; **to ~ over a decision** aplazar una decisión, buscar pretextos para no tomar una decisión; **stop procrastinating!** ¡hazlo ya!, ¡deja de buscar pretextos para no hacerlo!

procrastination [prəʊˌkræstɪˈneɪʃən] N indecisión *f*, falta *f* de resolución

procreate ['prəʊkrieɪt] VI procrear

procreation [ˌprəʊkrɪˈeɪʃən] N procreación *f*

procure [prəˈkjʊəʳ] VT obtener, conseguir; **to ~ sth for sb** conseguir *or* procurar algo para algn; **to ~ sb's release** lograr *or* gestionar la liberación de algn

procurement [prəˈkjʊəmənt] N obtención f
➤ **procurement agency** agencia f de aprovisionamiento
➤ **procurement price** precio m al productor

prod [prɒd] **ⓐ** N **1** (= *push*) empujón m; (*with elbow*)
codazo m; (= *jab*) pinchazo m; **to give sb a ~** dar un
pinchazo a algn; **he needs an occasional ~** hay que darle
un empujón de vez en cuando **2** (*also* **cattle ~**) aguijada
f, picana f (LAm) **ⓑ** VT (= *push*) empujar; (*with elbow*)
codear, dar un codazo a; (= *jab*) pinchar, punzar; (*with
goad*) aguijar; **to ~ sb into doing sth** instar a algn a hacer
algo **ⓒ** VI **he ~ded at the fire with a stick** atizó el fuego
con un palo

prodigal [ˈprɒdɪgəl] ADJ pródigo

prodigious [prəˈdɪdʒəs] ADJ [*amount, quantity*] enorme,
ingente; [*appetite*] enorme; [*memory, energy*] prodigioso

prodigy [ˈprɒdɪdʒɪ] N prodigio m; **child ~** niño/a m/f
prodigio

produce ⓐ [prəˈdjuːs] VT **1** (= *yield*) [+ *coal, crop, electricity,
sound*] producir; [+ *profit, benefits*] producir, reportar; **oil-
producing countries** países mpl productores de petróleo
2 (= *manufacture*) [+ *cars, weapons*] fabricar, producir
3 (= *create*) [+ *novel*] escribir; [+ *magazine*] publicar;
[+ *musical work*] componer
4 (= *give birth to*) [*animal*] parir; [*woman*] tener, dar a luz a;
[*parents*] tener
5 (= *bring out, supply*) [+ *gift, handkerchief, gun*] sacar;
[+ *ticket, documents, evidence, proof*] presentar; [+ *argument*]
dar, presentar; [+ *witness*] nombrar; [+ *meal*] preparar
6 (*Cine, Theat*) [+ *film, play, show*] producir; (*TV, Rad*)
realizar, producir; (*Publishing*) [+ *magazine*] publicar
7 (= *cause*) [+ *symptoms*] producir, causar; [+ *response*]
provocar, producir
8 (*Geom*) [+ *line, plane*] prolongar
ⓑ [prəˈdjuːs] VI producir
ⓒ [ˈprɒdjuːs] N (*Agr*) productos mpl agrícolas, productos
mpl del campo; **"produce of Turkey"** "producto m de
Turquía"

producer [prəˈdjuːsəʳ] N **1** [*of oil, coal, ore, crop*]
productor(a) m/f; [*of product*] fabricante mf **2** (*Theat*)
director(a) m/f de escena; (*Cine*) productor(a) m/f; (*TV*)
realizador(a) m/f, productor(a) m/f

product [ˈprɒdʌkt] N producto m; **food ~s** productos mpl
alimenticios; **it is a ~ of his imagination** es producto de su
imaginación ➤ **product line** línea f de productos

production [prəˈdʌkʃən] **ⓐ** N **1** (= *making*) producción f;
(= *manufacture*) producción f, fabricación f; **the car is due
to go into ~** este año está previsto que el coche
empiece a fabricarse este año; **to put sth into ~** lanzar algo
a la producción; **to take sth out of ~** dejar de fabricar algo
2 (= *output*) (*Ind, Agr*) producción f; **industrial/oil ~**
producción f industrial/de aceite
3 (= *act of showing*) presentación f; **on ~ of this card** al
presentar esta tarjeta
4 (= *act of producing*) (*Theat*) producción f, puesta f en
escena; (*Cine, TV, Rad*) realización f; **the series goes into ~
in March** la serie empezará a realizarse en marzo
5 (= *work produced*) (*Theat*) representación f, montaje m;
(*Cine, TV*) producción f
ⓑ CPD [*process, department, costs, quota*] de producción
➤ **production company** (*TV*) (compañía f) productora f
➤ **production line** cadena f de fabricación *or* montaje
➤ **production manager** jefe/a m/f de producción

productive [prəˈdʌktɪv] ADJ [*worker, land, industry*]
productivo; [*meeting, discussion*] fructífero

productivity [ˌprɒdʌkˈtɪvɪtɪ] N productividad f
➤ **productivity bonus** prima f de productividad *or*
rendimiento

prof* [prɒf] N profe* mf

Prof. [prɒf] N ABBR (= **professor**) Prof.

profane [prəˈfeɪn] **ⓐ** ADJ **1** (= *secular*) profano
2 (= *irreverent*) [*person, language*] blasfemo **ⓑ** VT profanar

profanity [prəˈfænɪtɪ] N (= *blasphemy, oath*) blasfemia f; **to
utter a string of profanities** soltar una sarta de blasfemias

profess [prəˈfes] VT **1** (*Rel*) [+ *faith, religion*] profesar
2 (= *state*) [+ *innocence*] declarar; [+ *regret, surprise*]

manifestar; [+ *ignorance*] confesar **3** (= *claim*) pretender; **I
do not ~ to be an expert** no pretendo ser experto; **he ~es
to know all about it** afirma estar enterado de ello; **to ~ o.s.
satisfied** declararse satisfecho

professed [prəˈfest] ADJ declarado

profession [prəˈfeʃən] N **1** (= *calling*) profesión f, oficio m;
by ~ de profesión **2** (= *body of people*) profesión f, cuerpo m
profesional; **to enter a ~** entrar a formar parte de una
profesión *or* un cuerpo profesional; **the legal ~** el cuerpo
de abogados; **the medical ~** la profesión médica, el cuerpo
médico; **the teaching ~** el cuerpo docente **3** (= *declaration*)
declaración f, manifestación f; **~ of faith** profesión f de fe

professional [prəˈfeʃənl] **ⓐ** ADJ **1** (= *non-amateur*) [*sport,
sportsperson, musician*] profesional; [*soldier*] de carrera; **he
plays ~ football** se dedica al fútbol profesional; **to take ~
advice** consultar a un profesional; (*from lawyer*) consultar a
un abogado; **to turn ~** hacerse profesional,
profesionalizarse
2 (= *employed in a profession*) **the flat is ideal for the ~ single
person** el piso es idóneo para el profesional soltero
3 (= *relating to a profession*) profesional; **his ~ life/conduct**
su vida/conducta profesional
4 (= *appropriate to a professional*) **that wasn't a very ~ thing
to do** eso no fue propio de un profesional, eso fue una
falta de profesionalidad
5 (= *competent, skilled*) **it was a very ~ performance** fue una
representación hecha con mucha profesionalidad; **a ~ job**
obra f de un profesional *or* experto; **you've done a really ~
job of the decorating** has pintado la casa como un
verdadero profesional *or* experto
ⓑ N profesional mf
ⓒ CPD ➤ **professional foul** falta f profesional
➤ **professional school** (*US*) escuela f profesional superior

professionalism [prəˈfeʃnəlɪzəm] N profesionalismo m

professionally [prəˈfeʃnəlɪ] ADV **1** (*Sport, Mus*) [*play,
sing*] profesionalmente **2** (= *in a professional capacity*)
profesionalmente; **I only knew her ~** sólo la traté
profesionalmente **3** (= *expertly*) con profesionalidad,
profesionalmente **4** (= *by an expert*) [*made, built*] por
un profesional *or* un experto **5** (= *as befits a professional*)
con profesionalidad

professor [prəˈfesəʳ] N **1** (*Brit, US Univ*) catedrático/a m/f (*de
universidad*); **he is a ~ of economics** es catedrático de
economía; **Professor Cameron** el profesor Cameron **2** (*US*)
(= *teacher*) profesor(a) m/f (universitario/a)

professorship [prəˈfesəʃɪp] N cátedra f

proffer [ˈprɒfəʳ] VT [+ *gift*] ofrecer; [+ *advice, help*] brindar,
ofrecer; [+ *congratulations*] dar

proficiency [prəˈfɪʃənsɪ] N habilidad f, competencia f
➤ **proficiency test** prueba f de aptitud

proficient [prəˈfɪʃənt] ADJ competente (**at, in** en); **she was
already ~ in German** tenía ya un gran dominio del alemán,
dominaba ya el alemán

profile [ˈprəʊfaɪl] **ⓐ** N **1** (= *side view*) perfil m; **in ~** de perfil
2 (= *description, portrait*) reseña f, perfil m; (*TV programme*)
perfil m **3** (= *public image*) **to keep a low ~** tratar de pasar
desapercibido; **to raise the ~ of sth/sb** realzar la imagen de
algo/algn **ⓑ** VT [+ *person's life*] hacer un perfil de

profit [ˈprɒfɪt] **ⓐ** N **1** (*Comm*) ganancias fpl, beneficios
mpl, utilidades fpl (LAm); **to operate at a ~** ser rentable; **to
sell (sth) at a ~** vender (algo) obteniendo una ganancia; **to
make a ~** obtener ganancias *or* beneficios **2** (*fig*) utilidad f,
beneficio m **ⓑ** VI **1** (*financially*) obtener ganancia, obtener
beneficio **2** (*fig*) **to ~ from sth** aprovecharse de algo **ⓒ** CPD
➤ **profit and loss account** cuenta f de pérdidas y
ganancias ➤ **profit margin** margen m de beneficios

profitability [ˌprɒfɪtəˈbɪlɪtɪ] N rentabilidad f

profitable [ˈprɒfɪtəbl] ADJ (*Comm*) lucrativo; (= *economic to
run*) rentable; (= *beneficial*) provechoso

profitably [ˈprɒfɪtəblɪ] ADV (*Comm*) [*run*] de forma
rentable, obteniendo beneficios; [*sell*] con ganancia; (*fig*)
(= *beneficially*) provechosamente

profiteer [ˌprɒfɪˈtɪəʳ] **ⓐ** N especulador(a) m/f **ⓑ** VI
especular, obtener ganancias excesivas

profiteering [ˌprɒfɪ'tɪərɪŋ] N especulación f

profit-making ['prɒfɪtˌmeɪkɪŋ] ADJ (= profitable) rentable; (= aiming to make profit) [organization] con fines lucrativos

profit-related ['prɒfɪtrə'leɪtɪd] ADJ [pay, bonus] proporcional a los beneficios

profit-sharing ['prɒfɪtˌʃeərɪŋ] N reparto m de los beneficios

profligate ['prɒflɪgɪt] ADJ (= extravagant) despilfarrador, derrochador

pro forma [ˌprəʊ'fɔːmə] ADJ ➤ **pro forma invoice** factura f detallada que precede a la entrega ➤ **pro forma letter** carta f estándar

profound [prə'faʊnd] ADJ profundo

profoundly [prə'faʊndlɪ] ADV profundamente; **to be ~ deaf** ser totalmente sordo

profundity [prə'fʌndɪtɪ] N profundidad f

profuse [prə'fjuːs] ADJ [vegetation] profuso, abundante; [sweating] copioso; [bleeding] intenso

profusely [prə'fjuːslɪ] ADV [grow] con profusión, en abundancia; [sweat, bleed] profusamente, copiosamente; **he apologized ~** se deshizo en disculpas; **she thanked me ~** me dio las gracias efusivamente

profusion [prə'fjuːʒən] N profusión f, abundancia f

progeny ['prɒdʒɪnɪ] N progenie f

progesterone [prəʊ'dʒestərəʊn] N progesterona f

prognosis [prɒg'nəʊsɪs] N (pl **prognoses** [prɒg'nəʊsiːz]) pronóstico m

program ['prəʊgræm] Ⓐ N (Comput) programa m; (US Univ) (= syllabus) plan m de estudios, programa m; (= course) curso m; see also **programme** Ⓑ VT (Comput) programar; **to ~ sth to do sth** programar algo para que haga algo; see also **programme** Ⓒ VI (Comput) programar; see also **programme**

programmable [prəʊ'græməbl] ADJ programable

programme, program (esp US) ['prəʊgræm] Ⓐ N 1 (= plan, schedule) programa m; **what's (on) the ~ for today?** ¿qué planes or programa tenemos para hoy? 2 (TV, Rad) programa m; **television ~** programa m de televisión 3 (= performance details) programa m; **can I have a look at the ~?** ¿puedo echarle un vistazo al programa? 4 (Comput) = **program** 5 (on washing machine) programa m Ⓑ VT 1 (gen) programar 2 (Comput) = **program** Ⓒ VI (Comput) = **program**

programmer, programer (US) ['prəʊgræməʳ] N programador(a) m/f

programming, programing (US) ['prəʊgræmɪŋ] N programación f ➤ **programming language** lenguaje m de programación

progress Ⓐ ['prəʊgres] N 1 (= forward movement) avance m; **we are making good ~** estamos avanzando rápidamente 2 (= development) [of activity, student] progresos mpl; [of events, talks] marcha f, desarrollo m; [of patient] evolución f; [of disease] curso m, evolución f; **he came in to check on my ~** vino para ver cómo iba progresando; **to make ~** (gen) hacer progresos, progresar; [patient] mejorar; **the two sides have made little ~ towards agreement** las dos partes apenas han avanzado hacia un acuerdo 3 (= innovation) progreso m; **it was all done in the name of ~** todo se hizo con la excusa del progreso 4 (= course) **the game was already in ~** había comenzado ya el partido; **negotiations are still in ~** aún se están manteniendo las negociaciones; **I went to see the work in ~** fui a ver cómo marchaba el trabajo Ⓑ [prə'gres] VI 1 (= go forward) [work] avanzar; [events] desarrollarse; [disease] evolucionar; **as the evening ~ed** a medida que avanzaba la noche; **he started sketching, then ~ed to painting** empezó haciendo bosquejos para luego pasar a pintar 2 (= improve) [student] hacer progresos; [patient] mejorar Ⓒ [prə'gres] VT seguir adelante con Ⓓ ['prəʊgres] CPD ➤ **progress report** (Admin) informe m sobre la marcha del trabajo; (Med) informe m médico; (Scol) informe m sobre el progreso del alumno

progression [prə'greʃən] N [of disease, career] evolución f;

arithmetical/geometric ~ progresión f aritmética/geométrica

progressive [prə'gresɪv] Ⓐ ADJ 1 (= increasing) progresivo 2 (Pol) progresista Ⓑ N progresista mf

progressively [prə'gresɪvlɪ] ADV progresivamente, poco a poco; **it's getting ~ better** va mejorando poco a poco

prohibit [prə'hɪbɪt] VT 1 (= forbid) prohibir; **to ~ sb from doing sth** prohibir a algn hacer algo; **"feeding the animals is prohibited"** "se prohíbe dar de comer a los animales"; **"smoking prohibited"** "se prohíbe or está prohibido fumar" 2 (= prevent) **to ~ sb from doing sth** impedir a algn hacer algo

prohibition [ˌprəʊɪ'bɪʃən] N prohibición f

prohibitive [prə'hɪbɪtɪv] ADJ prohibitivo

project Ⓐ ['prɒdʒekt] N 1 (= scheme, plan) proyecto m 2 (Scol, Univ) trabajo m 3 (also **housing ~**) (US) barrio m de viviendas protegidas Ⓑ [prə'dʒekt] VT 1 (= estimate) [+ costs, expenditure] hacer una proyección de 2 (= forecast) prever; **a ~ed deficit of two million dollars** un déficit previsto de dos millones de dólares 3 (= send forward) [+ object] lanzar 4 [+ slide, image, light, voice, image, personality] proyectar (also Math) Ⓒ [prə'dʒekt] VI (= jut out) sobresalir Ⓓ ['prɒdʒekt] CPD ➤ **project management** administración f de proyectos ➤ **project manager** director(a) m/f de proyecto

projectile [prə'dʒektaɪl] N proyectil m

projection [prə'dʒekʃən] Ⓐ N 1 [of image, voice] proyección f (also Psych, Cartography) 2 (= overhang) saliente m, resalto m; (= knob) protuberancia f 3 (= forecast) (Fin) pronóstico m Ⓑ CPD ➤ **projection room** (Cine) cabina f de proyección

projectionist [prə'dʒekʃnɪst] N (Cine) operador(a) m/f (de proyector), proyeccionista mf

projector [prə'dʒektəʳ] N (Cine) proyector m

prolapse ['prəʊlæps] N prolapso m

proletarian [ˌprəʊlə'tɛərɪən] ADJ, N proletario/a m/f

proletariat [ˌprəʊlə'tɛərɪət] N proletariado m

pro-life [ˌprəʊ'laɪf] ADJ pro-vida

proliferate [prə'lɪfəreɪt] VI proliferar

proliferation [prəˌlɪfə'reɪʃən] N proliferación f

prolific [prə'lɪfɪk] ADJ prolífico

prologue, prolog (US) ['prəʊlɒg] N prólogo m (**to** de)

prolong [prə'lɒŋ] VT prolongar, alargar

prolonged [prə'lɒŋd] ADJ prolongado

prom [prɒm] N 1 (Brit*) (= promenade) paseo m marítimo 2 (Brit*) = **promenade concert** 3 (US) baile de gala bajo los auspicios de los alumnos de un colegio

promenade [ˌprɒmɪ'nɑːd] Ⓐ N 1 (= act) paseo m 2 (= avenue) paseo m, avenida f 3 (esp Brit) (at seaside) paseo *m* marítimo **Ⓑ** CPD ➤ **promenade concert** *concierto en el que una parte del público permanece de pie*; ⟳ **PROM**

prominence ['prɒmɪnəns] N **1** (= *importance*) importancia *f*; **to bring sth/sb to ~** hacer que algo/algn destaque *or* resalte; **to come (in)to** *or* **rise to ~** [*idea, subject*] adquirir importancia; [*person*] empezar a ser conocido; **to give ~ to sth** hacer que algo destaque *or* resalte **2** (= *conspicuousness*) prominencia *f*

prominent ['prɒmɪnənt] ADJ **1** (= *projecting*) [*nose*] prominente; [*cheekbones*] marcado, prominente; [*teeth*] salido, hacia fuera; [*eyes*] saltón **2** (= *conspicuous*) destacado, prominente **3** (= *important*) [*person*] destacado, prominente; [*position, role*] prominente, importante, destacado

prominently ['prɒmɪnəntlɪ] ADV **to display sth ~** exponer algo muy a la vista; **the newspapers had carried the story ~** los periódicos habían publicado la historia en grandes titulares; **he figured ~ in the case** desempeñó un papel prominente *or* importante *or* destacado en el juicio

promiscuity [ˌprɒmɪs'kjuːɪtɪ] N promiscuidad *f*

promiscuous [prə'mɪskjʊəs] ADJ promiscuo

promise ['prɒmɪs] **Ⓐ** N **1** (= *pledge*) promesa *f*; **a ~ is a ~** lo prometido es deuda; **~s, ~s!** (*iro*) ¡mucho prometer y poco hacer!; **is that a ~?** ¿me lo prometes?; **to keep one's ~** cumplir su promesa; **to make (sb) a ~** hacer una promesa (a algn); **I made him a ~ that I'd come and visit him** le hice la promesa de que *or* le prometí que vendría a visitarlo **2** (= *hope, prospect*) **full of ~** muy prometedor; **she showed considerable ~ as a pianist** prometía mucho como pianista **Ⓑ** VT **1** (= *pledge*) prometer; **to ~ do sth** prometer hacer algo; **to ~ (sb) that** prometer (a algn) que; **~ me you won't tell her** prométeme que no se lo dirás; **you must ~ me to do as I say** tienes que prometerme que harás lo que yo te diga; **he ~d faithfully to return it** dio su palabra de que lo devolvería

2 (= *forecast, augur*) augurar; **their policies ~ little for the future** su política no augura un futuro muy prometedor; **the debate ~s to be lively** el debate se presenta animado **3** (= *assure*) prometer, jurar; **there's no-one here, I ~ you** no hay nadie aquí, te lo prometo *or* juro **Ⓒ** VI **1** (= *pledge*) prometer; **"(do you) ~?"** — **"all right, I ~"** —¿lo prometes? —bueno, lo prometo; **I can't ~ but I'll try** no te prometo nada, pero haré lo que pueda

2 (= *augur*) **such a good beginning ~s well for the future** un principio tan bueno resulta muy prometedor *or* augura un buen futuro

promising ['prɒmɪsɪŋ] ADJ [*student*] prometedor; [*future, prospect*] esperanzador, halagüeño; **two ~ candidates** dos candidatos buenos; **it doesn't look very ~** no promete mucho, no parece muy prometedor

promissory note ['prɒmɪsərɪ,nəʊt] N (*esp US*) pagaré *m*

promontory ['prɒməntrɪ] N promontorio *m*

promote [prə'məʊt] VT **1** (*in rank*) [*+ employee, soldier*] ascender; **he was ~d (to) colonel** *or* **to the rank of colonel** lo ascendieron a coronel; **Tarifa was ~d to the first division** el Tarifa subió *or* ascendió a primera división

2 (*US Scol*) **I failed to get ~d and had to redo my year** no conseguí aprobar y tuve que repetir el curso **3** (= *encourage*) [*+ trade, cooperation, peace*] promover, fomentar; [*+ growth*] estimular; [*+ sales, campaign, project, cause*] promover **4** (= *advertise*) [*+ product*] promocionar, dar publicidad a

promoter [prə'məʊtəʳ] N (*gen*) promotor(a) *m/f*; (= *backer*) patrocinador(a) *m/f*; (*Boxing*) empresario/a *m/f*

promotion [prə'məʊʃən] **Ⓐ** N **1** (*in rank*) [*of employee*] ascenso *m*, promoción *f*; (*Sport*) ascenso *m*; **to get ~** ser ascendido (**to** a); **they narrowly missed ~** [*team*] por muy poco no han ascendido a otra división

2 (*US Scol*) ascenso *m* **3** (= *encouragement*) [*of trade, peace*] fomento *m*, promoción *f*; [*of campaign, project*] apoyo *m* **4** (= *organization*) [*of concert, event*] organización *f* **5** (= *publicity, advertising*) promoción *f*; (= *advertising campaign*) campaña *f* (de promoción); **special ~** oferta *f* de promoción **Ⓑ** CPD ➤ **promotion prospects** perspectivas *fpl* de ascenso

promotional [prə'məʊʃənl] ADJ promocional, de promoción

prompt [prɒmpt] **Ⓐ** ADJ **1** (= *speedy*) [*delivery, reply, service*] rápido; **it is not too late, but ~ action is needed** no es demasiado tarde pero hay que actuar inmediatamente *or* es necesario tomar medidas inmediatas

2 (= *punctual*) puntual; **there is a discount for ~ payment** se hace un descuento por prontitud en el pago **Ⓑ** ADV puntualmente; **at two o'clock ~** a las dos en punto **Ⓒ** VT **1** (= *motivate*) mover, impulsar; **I was ~ed by a desire to see justice done** me movía *or* impulsaba el deseo de que se hiciera justicia; **to ~ sb to do sth** mover *or* incitar a algn a hacer algo

2 (= *give rise to*) [*+ thought, question*] dar lugar a; [*+ reply, reaction, speculation*] provocar, dar lugar a **3** (= *help with speech*) apuntar (*also Theat*) **Ⓓ** VI (*Theat*) apuntar **Ⓔ** N **1** (= *reminder*) apunte *m*, palabra *f* clave (*que ayuda a recordar*); **to give sb a ~** apuntar a algn **2** (*Comput*) aviso *m*

prompter ['prɒmptəʳ] N (*Theat*) apuntador(a) *m/f*

prompting ['prɒmptɪŋ] N **without ~** (= *on one's own initiative*) por iniciativa propia, motu propio

promptly ['prɒmptlɪ] ADV (= *immediately*) inmediatamente; (= *fast*) [*pay, deliver, reply*] rápidamente, con prontitud; (= *punctually*) [*start, arrive*] en punto, puntualmente; **they left ~ at six** partieron a las seis en punto

promulgate ['prɒməlgeɪt] VT promulgar

prone [prəʊn] ADJ **1** (= *liable*) **to be ~ to do sth** ser propenso *or* tener tendencia a hacer algo; **to be ~ to sth** ser propenso a algo **2** (= *face down*) **to be ~** estar postrado (boca abajo)

prong [prɒŋ] N [*of fork*] punta *f*, diente *m*

pronoun ['prəʊnaʊn] N (*Gram*) pronombre *m*

pronounce [prə'naʊns] **Ⓐ** VT **1** [*+ letter, word*] pronunciar; **how do you ~ it?** ¿cómo se pronuncia? **2** (= *declare*) declarar; **"I now ~ you man and wife"** —yo os declaro marido y mujer; **he was ~d dead** se dictaminó que estaba muerto **Ⓑ** VI **to ~ in favour of/against sth** pronunciarse a favor de/en contra de algo; **to ~ on sth** pronunciarse sobre algo

pronounced [prə'naʊnst] ADJ [*tendency, influence*] marcado; [*limp*] fuerte, pronunciado

pronouncement [prə'naʊnsmənt] N declaración *f*

pronto* ['prɒntəʊ] ADV en seguida

pronunciation [prəˌnʌnsɪ'eɪʃən] N pronunciación *f*

proof [pruːf] **Ⓐ** N **1** (= *evidence*) prueba(s) *f(pl)*; **do you have any ~ of this?** ¿tienes pruebas de esto?; **it is ~ that he is innocent** eso prueba su inocencia; **as (a) ~ of** como *or* en prueba de; **by way of ~** a modo de prueba; **you will need ~ of identity** necesitará algo que acredite su identidad; **to be living ~ of sth** ser prueba viviente de algo; ✦ PROV **the ~ of the pudding (is in the eating)** para saber si algo es bueno hay que probarlo

2 (*Typ, Phot*) prueba *f*; **to read the ~s** corregir las pruebas **3** [*of alcohol*] graduación *f* (alcohólica); **it is 70 degrees ~** tiene una graduación del 40%; (*US*) tiene una graduación del 35% **4** (*Math, Geom*) prueba *f* **Ⓑ** ADJ **to be ~ against sth** estar a prueba de algo **Ⓒ** VT [*+ fabric, tent*] impermeabilizar **Ⓓ** CPD ➤ **proof of identity** prueba *f* de identidad ➤ **proof of purchase** comprobante *m* de compra; **to obtain a refund you must produce ~ of purchase** para cualquier devolución necesitará el comprobante de compra

-proof [pruːf] ADJ (*ending in compounds*) **bomb-proof** a prueba de bombas; **bullet-proof** a prueba de balas

proofread ['pruːfriːd] (*pt, pp* ~ ['pruːfred]) VT corregir las pruebas de

proofreader ['pruːfˌriːdəʳ] N corrector(a) *m/f* de pruebas

prop [prɒp] **Ⓐ** N **1** (*lit*) (*Archit, Min*) puntal *m*; (*for clothesline*) palo *m*; (*Theat*) accesorio *m*; **props** accesorios *mpl*, at(t)rezzo *m*sing **2** (*fig*) sostén *m*, apoyo *m* **Ⓑ** VT (= *support*) apuntalar; (= *rest, lean*) apoyar, (*fig*) sostener, apoyar; **to ~ a ladder against a wall** apoyar una escalera contra una pared; **the door was ~ped open with a bucket** habían puesto un cubo para que no se cerrara la puerta ➤ **prop up** VT + ADV **1** (*lit*) [+ *roof, structure*] apuntalar; **she ~ped herself up on one elbow** se enderezó apoyándose en el codo **2** [+ *economy, currency, regime*] respaldar

propaganda [ˌprɒpəˈgændə] Ⓐ N propaganda *f* Ⓑ ADJ [*leaflet, campaign*] de propaganda

propagate [ˈprɒpəgeɪt] Ⓐ VT propagar Ⓑ VI propagarse

propagation [ˌprɒpəˈgeɪʃən] N propagación *f*

propane [ˈprəʊpeɪn] N propano *m*

propel [prəˈpel] VT [+ *vehicle, rocket*] impulsar, propulsar; **to ~ sth/sb along** impulsar algo/a algn; **they ~led him into the room** (*violently*) lo metieron en la habitación de un empujón

propeller [prəˈpelə'] N hélice *f* ➤ **propeller shaft** (*Aer*) árbol *m* de la hélice; (*Aut*) árbol *m* or eje *m* de transmisión; (*Naut*) eje *m* portahélices

propelling pencil [prəˈpelɪŋˈpensl] N (*Brit*) lapicero *m*, portaminas *m inv*

propensity [prəˈpensɪtɪ] N propensión *f* (**to** a)

proper [ˈprɒpə'] Ⓐ ADJ **1** (= *right, suitable*) [*equipment, tools*] apropiado, adecuado; **at the ~ time** en el momento oportuno; **that's not the ~ way to do it** así no se hace; **you'll have to apply for a permit in the ~ way** tendrás que solicitar el permiso por las vías establecidas
2 (= *correct*) **do as you think** ~ haz lo que te parezca bien; **I thought it ~ to inform you** pensé que debía informarte
3 (= *actual, real*) propiamente dicho; **in the city ~** en la ciudad propiamente dicha, en la ciudad en sí; **he's never had a ~ job** nunca ha tenido un trabajo serio; **in the ~ sense of the word** en el sentido estricto de la palabra
4 (*) (= *complete, downright*) verdadero; **I felt a ~ idiot** me sentí como un perfecto or verdadero idiota
5 (= *seemly*) [*person, behaviour*] correcto
6 (= *prim and proper*) correcto y formal
Ⓑ ADV (*Brit**) **he was ~ upset about it** estaba verdaderamente or realmente disgustado por ello
Ⓒ CPD ➤ **proper name, proper noun** nombre *m* propio

properly [ˈprɒpəlɪ] ADV **1** (= *suitably, adequately*) adecuadamente, apropiadamente; **not ~ dressed** (*for occasion*) no vestido de la manera adecuada; (*for activity*) no vestido de la manera apropiada; **I had not eaten ~ for the past few days** hacía unos días que no comía como es debido
2 (= *correctly*) [*function, work*] bien; **to do sth ~** hacer algo bien or como es debido; **sit up ~!** (*to child*) ¡siéntate como es debido!; **if you don't sit up ~ you can damage your back** si no te sientas correctamente, puedes fastidiarte la espalda; **~ speaking** hablando con propiedad, propiamente dicho
3 (= *in seemly fashion*) correctamente

property [ˈprɒpətɪ] Ⓐ N **1** (= *possession*) propiedad *f*; **whose ~ is this?** ¿de quién es (propiedad) esto?, ¿a quién pertenece esto?; **she left her ~ to her daughter** dejó sus propiedades or bienes a su hija
2 (= *land*) propiedad *f*, terreno *m*; (= *real estate*) propiedades *fpl*; **get off my ~** salga de mi propiedad; **"private property"** "propiedad *f* privada"; **he owns ~ in Ireland** tiene propiedades en Irlanda
3 (= *building*) propiedad *f*, inmueble *m*
4 (*Theat*) accesorio *m*; **properties** accesorios *mpl*, at(t)rezzo *msing*
5 (= *quality*) propiedad *f*; **this plant has healing properties** esta planta tiene propiedades curativas
Ⓑ CPD ➤ **property developer** promotor(a) *m/f* inmobiliario/a ➤ **property market** mercado *m* inmobiliario ➤ **property owner** (*rural*) terrateniente *mf*; (*urban*) dueño/a *m/f* de propiedades

prophecy [ˈprɒfɪsɪ] N profecía *f*

prophesy [ˈprɒfɪsaɪ] VT (= *foretell*) profetizar; (= *predict*) predecir, vaticinar

prophet [ˈprɒfɪt] N profeta *m*

prophetic [prəˈfetɪk] ADJ profético

prophylactic [ˌprɒfɪˈlæktɪk] Ⓐ ADJ profiláctico Ⓑ N (= *contraceptive*) profiláctico *m*

propitious [prəˈpɪʃəs] ADJ propicio, favorable

proponent [prəˈpəʊnənt] N defensor(a) *m/f*

proportion [prəˈpɔːʃən] Ⓐ N **1** (= *ratio*) proporción *f*; **the ~ of women to men** la proporción entre mujeres y hombres; **in/out of ~** proporcionado/desproporcionado; **to be in/out of ~ (to** or **with sth)** estar en/no guardar proporción (con algo); **in ~ as** a medida que; **to see sth in ~** ver algo en su justa medida; **it has been magnified out of all ~** se ha exagerado mucho; **sense of ~** sentido *m* de la medida
2 (= *part, amount*) parte *f*; **in equal ~s** por partes iguales; **what ~ is in private hands?** ¿qué porción queda en manos de particulares?
3 proportions (= *size*) dimensiones *fpl*
Ⓑ VT **to ~ sth to sth** [+ *charge, cost*] adecuar algo a algo; **well-proportioned** [*room*] de buenas proporciones; [*woman's figure*] bien proporcionado; [*man's figure*] bien armado

proportional [prəˈpɔːʃənl] ADJ proporcional (**to** a), en proporción (**to** con); ➤ **proportional representation** (*Pol*) representación *f* proporcional

proportionally [prəˈpɔːʃnəlɪ] ADV proporcionalmente

proportionate [prəˈpɔːʃnɪt] ADJ proporcionado (**to** a)

proposal [prəˈpəʊzl] N **1** (= *offer, suggestion*) (*gen*) propuesta *f*, proposición *f*; (= *written submission*) propuesta *f*; **the latest peace ~** la última propuesta de paz; **let me make a ~** permítame hacer una propuesta or proposición; **I made the ~ that we should adjourn the meeting** propuse que levantásemos la sesión **2** (*also* ~ **of marriage**) proposición *f* de matrimonio, propuesta *f* de matrimonio

propose [prəˈpəʊz] Ⓐ VT **1** (= *suggest*) proponer; [+ *motion*] presentar; **the idea was first ~d in 1789** la idea se propuso por primera vez en 1789; **what do you ~?** ¿qué propones?; **to ~ sth to sb** proponer algo a algn; **to ~ doing sth: I ~ writing her a letter** (= *I suggest I write*) me propongo escribirle una carta; (= *I suggest that someone writes*) yo propongo que se le escriba una carta; **to ~ sb's health** beber a la salud de algn, brindar por algn; **to ~ marriage to sb** proponer a algn en matrimonio, hacer una proposición or propuesta de matrimonio a algn; **to ~ that** proponer que + *subjun*
2 (= *nominate*) proponer; **he ~d Smith as** or **for chairman** propuso a Smith como presidente
3 (= *intend*) **to ~ to do sth** ◊ ~ **doing sth** pensar hacer algo
Ⓑ VI (= *offer marriage*) **to ~ to sb** proponer a algn en matrimonio, hacer una proposición de matrimonio a algn; **have you ~d yet?** ¿le has propuesto en matrimonio ya?, ¿le has hecho una proposición de matrimonio ya?

proposer [prəˈpəʊzə'] N [*of motion*] proponente *mf*

proposition [ˌprɒpəˈzɪʃən] Ⓐ N proposición *f*; **to make sb a ~** proponer algo a algn; **an attractive ~** una proposición atractiva; **she had received a number of unwanted sexual ~s** había sido objeto de varias proposiciones sexuales no deseadas Ⓑ VT hacer proposiciones deshonestas a

propound [prəˈpaʊnd] VT (*frm*) [+ *ideas etc*] exponer, plantear

proprietary [prəˈpraɪətərɪ] ADJ (*Comm*) patentado ➤ **proprietary brand** marca *f* comercial ➤ **proprietary goods** artículos *mpl* de marca ➤ **proprietary interest** interés *m* patrimonial

proprietor [prəˈpraɪətə'] N [*of shop, hotel etc*] dueño/a *m/f*

propriety [prəˈpraɪətɪ] N decoro *m*, decencia *f*; **the proprieties** los cánones sociales

propulsion [prəˈpʌlʃən] N propulsión *f*

pro rata [ˌprəʊˈrɑːtə] ADV, ADJ a prorrateo

prosaic [prəʊˈzeɪɪk] ADJ (= *dull*) prosaico

proscribe [prəʊˈskraɪb] VT proscribir

prose [prəʊz] Ⓐ N **1** (*Literat*) prosa *f* **2** (*also* ~ **translation**) texto *m* para traducir Ⓑ CPD ➤ **prose poem** poema *m* en prosa ➤ **prose writer** prosista *mf*

prosecute [ˈprɒsɪkjuːt] Ⓐ VT (*Jur*) (= *try*) procesar, enjuiciar; **to ~ sb for theft** procesar a algn por robo; **"trespassers will be prosecuted"** "se procederá contra los intrusos" Ⓑ VI (*Jur*) interponer una acción judicial;

prosecuting attorney (*US*)**, prosecuting counsel** (*Brit*) fiscal *mf*

prosecution [ˌprɒsɪˈkjuːʃən] N (= *act, proceedings*) proceso *m*, juicio *m*; (= *case, side*) acusación *f*; **counsel for the ~** fiscal *mf*; **witness for the ~** testigo *mf* de cargo; **to bring** *or* **start a ~ against sb** entablar juicio *or* una acción judicial contra algn

prosecutor [ˈprɒsɪkjuːtəʳ] N (= *lawyer*) abogado/a *m/f* de la acusación; (*also* **public ~**) fiscal *mf*

prospect ❶ [ˈprɒspekt] N **1** (= *outlook*) perspectiva *f*; **the ~s look grim** las perspectivas son desalentadoras; **she was excited at the ~ of going to China** estaba entusiasmada con la perspectiva de irse a China; **in ~** en perspectiva; **to have sth in ~** tener algo en perspectiva
2 (= *possibility*) posibilidad *f*; **the job held out the ~ of rapid promotion** el trabajo ofrecía la posibilidad de ascender con rapidez; **he has little ~ of success/of succeeding** tiene pocas posibilidades de tener éxito; **I see no ~ of that (happening)** eso no lo creo probable
3 prospects (= *future possibilities*) porvenir *m*, futuro *m*; **a job with no ~s** un trabajo sin porvenir, un trabajo sin (perspectivas de) futuro; **what are his ~s?** ¿qué perspectivas de futuro tiene?; **job/promotion ~s** perspectivas *fpl* de trabajo/ascenso; **future ~s** perspectivas *fpl* de futuro; **she has good ~s** tiene buen porvenir *or* un buen futuro
4 (= *prospective candidate, champion, etc*) **the company is not an attractive ~ for shareholders** la empresa no representa una opción *or* posibilidad atractiva para los accionistas; **the man who is Britain's best ~ for a gold medal** el hombre que tiene mayores posibilidades de (conseguir una) medalla de oro para Gran Bretaña
❷ [prəˈspekt] VI hacer prospecciones, prospectar; **to ~ for gold** buscar oro

prospecting [prəˈspektɪŋ] N (*Min*) prospección *f*

prospective [prəˈspektɪv] ADJ **1** (= *likely, possible*) [*customer, candidate*] posible **2** (= *future*) [*son-in-law, home*] futuro

prospector [prəˈspektəʳ] N buscador(a) *m/f*, cateador(a) *m/f* (*LAm*); **gold ~** buscador(a) *m/f* de oro; **oil ~s** prospectores *mpl* petroleros

prospectus [prəˈspektəs] N prospecto *m*

prosper [ˈprɒspəʳ] VI prosperar, medrar

prosperity [prɒˈsperɪtɪ] N prosperidad *f*

prosperous [ˈprɒspərəs] ADJ próspero

prostate [ˈprɒsteɪt] N (*also* **~ gland**) próstata *f*

prostitute [ˈprɒstɪtjuːt] ❶ N prostituto/a *m/f* ❷ VT prostituir; **to ~ o.s.** prostituirse

prostitution [ˌprɒstɪˈtjuːʃən] N prostitución *f*

prostrate ❶ [ˈprɒstreɪt] ADJ **1** (*lit*) boca abajo, postrado **2** (*fig*) [*nation, country etc*] abatido; (= *exhausted*) postrado, abatido (**with** por) ❷ [prɒˈstreɪt] VT (*lit*) postrar; (*fig*) postrar, abatir; **to ~ o.s.** (*lit, fig*) postrarse

protagonist [prəʊˈtægənɪst] N protagonista *mf*

protect [prəˈtekt] VT proteger (**against** contra; **from** de)

protection [prəˈtekʃən] N protección *f*; **to be under sb's ~** estar bajo la protección de algn, estar amparado por algn; **the policy offers ~ against ...** la póliza protege contra ...
➤ **protection factor** [*of sun cream*] factor *m* de protección
➤ **protection money he pays 200 dollars a week ~ money** paga 200 dólares de protección a la semana ➤ **protection racket** chantaje *m*

protectionism [prəˈtekʃənɪzəm] N proteccionismo *m*

protectionist [prəˈtekʃənɪst] ADJ, N proteccionista *mf*

protective [prəˈtektɪv] ADJ [*layer, covering, cream, attitude*] protector; [*clothing*] de protección; [*tariffs*] proteccionista; **to be ~ of sth** proteger algo; **he's very ~ towards his little sister** tiene una actitud muy protectora hacia su hermanita, protege mucho a su hermanita ➤ **protective custody** detención *f* preventiva

protectively [prəˈtektɪvlɪ] ADV en actitud protectora, en actitud de protección

protector [prəˈtektəʳ] N **1** (= *defender*) protector(a) *m/f* **2** (= *device*) protector *m*

protégé [ˈprɒteʒeɪ] N protegido *m*, ahijado *m*

protégée [ˈprɒteʒeɪ] N protegida *f*, ahijada *f*

protein [ˈprəʊtiːn] N proteína *f* ➤ **protein content** contenido *m* proteínico

pro tem [ˈprəʊˈtem] ❶ ADV provisionalmente ❷ ADJ interino; **the ~ chairman** el presidente interino; **on a ~ basis** de manera provisional

protest ❶ [ˈprəʊtest] N (*gen*) protesta *f*; (= *demonstration*) manifestación *f* (de protesta); **under ~** bajo protesta; **to make a ~** hacer una protesta ❷ [prəˈtest] VT **1** (= *complain*) protestar; **to ~ that** protestar diciendo que **2** (*US*) (= *complain about*) protestar de **3** (= *declare*) declarar, afirmar ❸ [prəˈtest] VI protestar; **to ~ at** *or* **against** protestar de ❹ [ˈprəʊtest] CPD de protesta ➤ **protest demonstration** manifestación *f* (de protesta) ➤ **protest march** marcha *f* (de protesta)

Protestant [ˈprɒtɪstənt] ADJ, N protestante *mf*

Protestantism [ˈprɒtɪstəntɪzəm] N protestantismo *m*

protestation [ˌprɒteˈsteɪʃən] N **1** (= *affirmation*) [*of love, loyalty etc*] afirmación *f*, declaración *f* **2** (= *protest*) protesta *f*

protester, protestor [prəˈtestəʳ] N protestador(a) *m/f*; (*on march, in demonstration etc*) manifestante *mf*

protocol [ˈprəʊtəkɒl] N protocolo *m*

proton [ˈprəʊtɒn] N protón *m*

prototype [ˈprəʊtəʊtaɪp] N prototipo *m*

protracted [prəˈtræktɪd] ADJ prolongado, (excesivamente) largo

protractor [prəˈtræktəʳ] N transportador *m*

protrude [prəˈtruːd] VI salir, sobresalir

protruding [prəˈtruːdɪŋ] ADJ saliente, sobresaliente; [*eye, tooth*] saltón

protuberance [prəˈtjuːbərəns] N protuberancia *f*, saliente *m*

proud [praʊd] ADJ (*compar* **~er**; *superl* **~est**) **1** (= *satisfied*) [*person*] orgulloso; [*expression, smile*] de orgullo; **I'm ~ that I did it on my own** estoy *or* me siento orgulloso de haberlo hecho solo; **I'm ~ to call her my friend** me enorgullece que sea mi amiga; **we are ~ to present ...** tenemos el honor de presentarles ...; **to be ~ of sth/sb** estar orgulloso de algo/algn; **that's nothing to be ~ of!** ¡esto no es motivo de orgullo!; ✦ IDIOM **to do sb/o.s. ~*: the team have done their country ~** el equipo ha sido motivo de orgullo para su país; **his honesty did him ~** su honradez decía mucho en su favor; **the hotel did them ~** el hotel los trató a cuerpo de rey; **she did herself ~ in the piano competition** se lució en el concurso de piano
2 (= *self-respecting*) [*people, nation*] digno
3 (= *arrogant*) orgulloso, soberbio
4 (= *causing pride*) [*day, moment*] glorioso, de orgullo
5 (*Brit*) (= *protruding*) **to be/stand ~ (of sth)** sobresalir (de algo)

proudly [ˈpraʊdlɪ] ADV (= *with satisfaction*) con orgullo; (= *arrogantly*) arrogantemente, con arrogancia; **he ~ showed me his drawing** orgulloso, me enseñó su dibujo, me enseñó con orgullo su dibujo

prove [pruːv] (*pt* **~d**; *pp* **~d** *or* **~n**) ❶ VT **1** (= *give proof of*) [+ *theory, statement*] demostrar, probar; [+ *one's love, loyalty, strength*] demostrar; **can you ~ it?** ¿lo puede demostrar *or* probar?; **you can't ~ anything against me** usted no tiene ninguna prueba en mi contra, usted no puede demostrar *or* probar nada en mi contra; **it just ~s how stupid he is** simplemente demuestra *or* prueba lo tonto que es; **to ~ sb innocent** demostrar *or* probar la inocencia de algn; **she took him to court just to ~ a point** lo llevó a los tribunales simplemente para demostrar *or* probar que estaba en lo cierto *or* que ella tenía razón; **he was ~d right in the end** al fin se demostró que tenía razón; **to ~ that** demostrar que, probar que
2 (= *verify*) comprobar; **you can ~ how effective this method is by trying it out yourself** puede comprobar la eficacia de este método probándolo usted mismo
❷ VI **1** (= *turn out*) resultar; **it ~d (to be) useful** resultó (ser) útil; **it may ~ difficult to secure funding** puede que resulte difícil conseguir fondos; **the news ~d false** resultó que la noticia era falsa
2 (*Culin*) [*dough*] leudarse

proven Ⓐ ['pru:vən] PP *of* **prove** Ⓑ ['pru:vən] ADJ **1** (*gen*) [*formula, method*] de eficacia probada; [*abilities*] probado **2** ['prəʊvən] (*Scot Jur*) **the case was found not** ~ el acusado fue absuelto por falta de pruebas

proverb ['prɒvɜ:b] N refrán *m*, proverbio *m*

proverbial [prə'vɜ:bɪəl] ADJ proverbial

provide [prə'vaɪd] VT **1** (= *supply*) **1.1** [+ *materials, food*] proporcionar, suministrar; [+ *money, information, evidence*] proporcionar, facilitar; [+ *service*] prestar; **the meeting ~d an opportunity to talk** la reunión les brindó *or* ofreció la oportunidad de hablar; **candidates must ~ their own pencils** los candidatos deben traer sus propios lápices; **to ~ sth for sb/sth: I will ~ food for everyone** proveeré a todo el mundo de comida, proporcionaré *or* daré comida a todo el mundo; **it ~s accommodation for five families** provee a cinco familias de alojamiento, da *or* proporciona alojamiento a cinco familias; **to ~ funding/money for sth** proporcionar *or* facilitar fondos/dinero para algo **1.2 to ~ sb with sth** [+ *materials, food*] proveer a algn de algo, suministrar algo a algn; [+ *money, information, details*] proporcionar *or* facilitar algo a algn; [+ *service*] proporcionar algo a algn; [+ *means*] facilitar algo a algn; [+ *opportunity*] brindar algo a algn **1.3 to ~ o.s. with sth** proveerse de algo
2 (= *have available*) estar provisto de
➤ **provide for** VI + PREP **1** (*financially*) [+ *person, family*] mantener; **he wanted to see that the children were well ~d for** quería asegurarse de que las necesidades de los niños estaban bien cubiertas; **they are well ~d for** tienen medios de sobra **2** (= *take care of*) prever; **it's impossible to ~ for all eventualities** es imposible prever todas las eventualidades *or* tomar precauciones contra toda eventualidad

provided [prə'vaɪdɪd] CONJ ~ **(that)** con tal (de) que, a condición de que

providence ['prɒvɪdəns] N providencia *f*; **Providence** la Divina Providencia

providential [ˌprɒvɪ'denʃəl] ADJ providencial; (= *fortunate*) afortunado, milagroso

providentially [ˌprɒvɪ'denʃəlɪ] ADV providencialmente, afortunadamente, milagrosamente

providing [prə'vaɪdɪŋ] CONJ = **provided**

province ['prɒvɪns] N **1** (*Geog*) provincia *f*; **they live in the ~s** viven en provincias **2** (= *area of knowledge, activity*) esfera *f*, campo *m*; (= *jurisdiction*) competencia *f*; **it's not within my ~** no es de mi competencia

provincial [prə'vɪnʃəl] Ⓐ ADJ provincial, de provincia; (*pej*) pueblerino, provinciano Ⓑ N (*usu pej*) provinciano/a *m/f*

proving ground ['pru:vɪŋˌɡraʊnd] N terreno *m* de prueba

provision [prə'vɪʒən] Ⓐ N **1** [*of funds, accommodation, jobs*] provisión *f*; [*of food, water*] suministro *m*; [*of service, care*] prestación *f*; **there is inadequate housing ~ for the poor** la provisión de viviendas para los pobres es insuficiente
2 (= *arrangements*) **2.1** (*gen*) previsiones *fpl*; **to make ~ for sth/sb** hacer previsiones para algo/algn **2.2** (= *financial*) provisiones *fpl*; **you must make ~ for your old age** debes hacer provisiones para la vejez; **to make ~ for one's family** asegurar el porvenir de su familia
3 provisions (= *food*) provisiones *fpl*, víveres *mpl*
4 (= *stipulation*) estipulación *f*, disposición *f*; **under** *or* **according to the ~s of the treaty** en virtud de las estipulaciones *or* disposiciones del tratado; **the rules make no ~ for this** las reglas no disponen en previsión de esto **5** (= *condition, proviso*) condición *f*; **with the ~ that** con la condición de que
Ⓑ VT aprovisionar, abastecer; **to be ~ed with sth** (*frm*) estar provisto de algo

provisional [prə'vɪʒənl] Ⓐ ADJ provisional, provisorio (*LAm*) Ⓑ N **the Provisionals** el IRA provisional Ⓒ CPD ➤ **provisional driving licence** (*Brit*) permiso *m* de conducción provisional (*Sp*), licencia *f* provisional (*esp LAm*) ➤ **the Provisional IRA** el IRA provisional

provisionally [prə'vɪʒnəlɪ] ADV provisionalmente

proviso [prə'vaɪzəʊ] N salvedad *f*; **with the ~ that ...** a condición de que ...

provocation [ˌprɒvə'keɪʃən] N provocación *f*

provocative [prə'vɒkətɪv] ADJ **1** (= *inflammatory*) provocador **2** (= *thought-provoking*) sugestivo, que hace reflexionar **3** (= *seductive*) [*person*] seductor; [*clothing, look, smile*] provocativo

provoke [prə'vəʊk] VT **1** (= *cause*) [+ *reaction, response*] provocar; [+ *violence*] provocar, causar; [+ *crisis*] causar **2** (= *rouse, move*) incitar (**to** a); **to ~ sb into doing sth** incitar a algn a hacer algo **3** (= *anger*) provocar, irritar; **he is easily ~d** se irrita por cualquier cosa, se le provoca fácilmente

provost ['prɒvəst] N **1** (*Univ*) (*Brit*) (= *principal*) rector(a) *m/f*; (*US*) (*in charge of admin*) secretario/a *m/f* de facultad **2** (*Scot*) alcalde/esa *m/f*

prow [praʊ] N proa *f*

prowess ['praʊɪs] N **1** (= *skill*) habilidad *f*, capacidad *f* **2** (= *courage*) valor *m*

prowl [praʊl] Ⓐ N **to be on the ~** merodear, rondar Ⓑ VI (*also* ~ **about** *or* **around**) merodear, rondar Ⓒ CPD ➤ **prowl car** (*US Police*) coche-patrulla *m*

prowler ['praʊləʳ] N merodeador(a) *m/f*

proximity [prɒk'sɪmɪtɪ] N proximidad *f*; **in ~ to** cerca *or* en las cercanías de

proxy ['prɒksɪ] N (= *person*) apoderado/a *m/f*; **by ~** por poderes ➤ **proxy vote** voto *m* por poderes

Prozac® ['prəʊzæk] N Prozac® *m*

PRP N ABBR (*Brit*) (= **performance-related pay**) *sistema salarial que incluye un plus de productividad*

prude [pru:d] N gazmoño/a *m/f*, mojigato/a *m/f*

prudence ['pru:dəns] N prudencia *f*

prudent ['pru:dənt] ADJ cauteloso, prudente

prudently ['pru:dəntlɪ] ADV prudentemente, con prudencia

prudish ['pru:dɪʃ] ADJ gazmoño, remilgado

prune¹ [pru:n] N (= *fruit*) ciruela *f* pasa

prune² [pru:n] VT [+ *tree, branches*] podar; (*fig*) reducir, recortar

pruning shears ['pru:nɪŋˌʃɪəz] NPL podadera *f*

prurient ['prʊərɪənt] ADJ salaz, lascivo

Prussia ['prʌʃə] N Prusia *f*

pry¹ [praɪ] VI (= *snoop*) fisgonear, curiosear; (= *spy*) atisbar; **to ~ into sb's affairs** (entro)meterse en los asuntos de algn

pry² [praɪ] VT (*US*) = **prise**

prying ['praɪɪŋ] ADJ fisgón

PS N ABBR (= **postscript**) P.D.

psalm [sɑ:m] N salmo *m*

PSAT N ABBR (*US*) = **Preliminary Scholastic Aptitude Test**

PSBR N ABBR (*Econ*) (= **public sector borrowing requirement**) *necesidades de endeudamiento del sector público*

pseud* [sju:d] N (*Brit*) farsante *mf*

pseudo... ['sju:dəʊ] PREF seudo...; **a ~-artist** un seudo artista

pseudonym ['sju:dənɪm] N seudónimo *m*

psoriasis [sə'raɪəsɪs] N soriasis *f*

psyche ['saɪkɪ] N (*Psych*) psique *f*, psiquis *f*

psychedelic [ˌsaɪkə'delɪk] ADJ psicodélico

psychiatric [ˌsaɪkɪ'ætrɪk] ADJ psiquiátrico

psychiatrist [saɪ'kaɪətrɪst] N psiquiatra *mf*

psychiatry [saɪ'kaɪətrɪ] N psiquiatría *f*

psychic ['saɪkɪk] Ⓐ ADJ **1** (= *supernatural*) psíquico **2** (= *telepathic*) telepático; **I'm not ~!** ¡no soy adivino!* Ⓑ N vidente *mf*

psycho* ['saɪkəʊ] N psicópata *mf*

psychoanalyse, psychoanalyze (*US*) [ˌsaɪkəʊ'ænəlaɪz] VT psicoanalizar

psychoanalysis [ˌsaɪkəʊə'nælɪsɪs] N psicoanálisis *m*

psychoanalyst [ˌsaɪkəʊ'ænəlɪst] N psicoanalista *mf*

psychoanalytic [ˌsaɪkəʊænəˈlɪtɪk] ADJ psicoanalítico
psychoanalyze [ˌsaɪkəʊˈænəlaɪz] VT (US) = **psychoanalyse**
psychological [ˌsaɪkəˈlɒdʒɪkəl] ADJ psicológico
psychologically [ˌsaɪkəˈlɒdʒɪkəlɪ] ADV psicológicamente
psychologist [saɪˈkɒlədʒɪst] N psicólogo/a m/f
psychology [saɪˈkɒlədʒɪ] N psicología f
psychopath [ˈsaɪkəʊpæθ] N psicópata mf
psychopathic [ˌsaɪkəʊˈpæθɪk] ADJ psicopático
psychosis [saɪˈkəʊsɪs] N (pl **psychoses** [saɪˈkəʊsiːz]) psicosis f inv
psychosomatic [ˈsaɪkəʊsəʊˈmætɪk] ADJ psicosomático
psychotherapist [ˌsaɪkəʊˈθerəpɪst] N psicoterapeuta mf
psychotherapy [ˌsaɪkəʊˈθerəpɪ] N psicoterapia f
psychotic [saɪˈkɒtɪk] ADJ, N psicótico/a m/f
psych out* [ˌsaɪkˈaʊt] VT + ADV **1** (= make uneasy) poner nervioso **2** (US) (= analyse, work out) [+ person] calar*; **I psyched it all out for myself** me di cuenta de por dónde iban los tiros*
psych up* [ˌsaɪkˈʌp] VT + ADV **to get o.s. psyched up for sth** mentalizarse para algo; **he was all psyched up to start, when ...** ya estaba mentalizado para empezar, cuando ...
PT† N ABBR (= **physical training**) gimnasia f, educación f física, ed. física
pt ABBR = **pint(s)**
P/T ABBR = **part-time**
PTA N ABBR (= **Parent-Teacher Association**) ≈ APA f
Pte ABBR (Mil) = **Private**
PTO ABBR (= **please turn over**) sigue
pub [pʌb] (Brit) N pub m, bar m ➤ **pub crawl to go on a ~ crawl*** ir de chateo or de parranda (de bar en bar)*
puberty [ˈpjuːbətɪ] N pubertad f
pubic [ˈpjuːbɪk] ADJ púbico ➤ **pubic hair** vello m púbico
public [ˈpʌblɪk] Ⓐ ADJ público; **to be in the ~ domain** (= not secret) ser de dominio público; **to be in the ~ eye** ser objeto del interés público; **he has kept his family out of the ~ eye** ha mantenido a su familia alejada de la atención pública; **to go ~** (Comm) empezar a cotizar en bolsa; **they decided to go ~ about their relationship*** decidieron revelar su relación a la prensa or al público; **it is ~ knowledge** ya es de dominio público; **can we talk somewhere less ~?** ¿podemos hablar en algún sitio más privado or menos expuesto al público?; **to make** sth ~ hacer público algo, publicar algo; **to run for ~ office** presentarse como candidato a un cargo público; **in a bid to gain ~ support** en un intento de hacerse con el apoyo de la gente; **it's too ~ here** aquí estamos demasiado expuestos al público, aquí no tenemos intimidad
Ⓑ N **the ~** el público; **the general ~** el gran público; **in ~** en público; **a member of the ~** un ciudadano
Ⓒ CPD ➤ **public access television** (US) televisión abierta al público ➤ **public address system** (sistema m de) megafonía f, altavoces mpl, altoparlantes mpl (LAm) ➤ **public assistance** (US) asistencia f pública ➤ **public bar bar** m ➤ **public convenience** (Brit frm) servicios mpl, aseos mpl públicos ➤ **public defender** (US) defensor(a) m/f de oficio ➤ **public health** salud f pública, sanidad f pública ➤ **public health inspector** inspector/a m/f de salud or sanidad pública ➤ **Public Health Service** (US) servicio público de asistencia sanitaria ➤ **public holiday** fiesta f nacional, fiesta f oficial, (día m) feriado m (LAm) ➤ **public house** (Brit frm) bar m ➤ **public inquiry** investigación f oficial ➤ **public law** (= discipline, body of legislation) derecho m público; (US) (= piece of legislation) ley f pública ➤ **public library** biblioteca f pública ➤ **public limited company** ≈ sociedad f anónima ➤ **public opinion** opinión f pública ➤ **public opinion poll** sondeo m (de la opinión pública) ➤ **public property** (= land, buildings) dominio m público; (fig) ➤ **public prosecutor** fiscal m/f; **the Public Prosecutor's Office** la fiscalía ➤ **Public Record Office** (Brit) archivo m nacional ➤ **public relations** relaciones fpl públicas; **it's just a ~ relations exercise** es sólo una operación publicitaria or de relaciones públicas ➤ **public school** (Brit) colegio m privado; (US) escuela f pública ➤ **the public sector** el

sector público ➤ **public speaker** orador(a) m/f; **she is a good ~ speaker** habla muy bien en público, es una buena oradora ➤ **public speaking** oratoria f ➤ **public spending** gasto m (del sector) público ➤ **public television** (US) cadenas fpl públicas (de televisión) ➤ **public transport**, **public transportation** (US) transporte(s) m(pl) público(s); **to ban smoking on ~ transport** prohibir fumar en los medios de transporte público ➤ **public utility** empresa f del servicio público
publican [ˈpʌblɪkən] N (Brit) dueño/a m/f or encargado/a m/f de un pub or bar
publication [ˌpʌblɪˈkeɪʃən] N publicación f
publicist [ˈpʌblɪsɪst] N publicista mf
publicity [pʌbˈlɪsɪtɪ] Ⓐ N publicidad f Ⓑ CPD [agent, manager] de publicidad ➤ **publicity campaign** campaña f publicitaria ➤ **publicity stunt** truco m publicitario
publicize [ˈpʌblɪsaɪz] VT **1** (= make public) publicar, divulgar **2** (= advertise) anunciar, hacer propaganda de
publicly [ˈpʌblɪklɪ] ADV [acknowledge, criticize, accuse] públicamente, en público; [announce, state, humiliate] públicamente; [funded] con fondos públicos; **land and buildings that are ~ owned** tierras fpl y edificios mpl que son propiedad pública or del Estado
public-spirited [ˈpʌblɪkˈspɪrɪtɪd] ADJ [act] de espíritu cívico, solidario; [person] lleno de civismo, consciente del bien público
publish [ˈpʌblɪʃ] VT **1** [+ book etc] publicar; [+ author] publicar las obras de **2** (= make public) [+ list, information] divulgar, hacer público
publisher [ˈpʌblɪʃəʳ] N (= person) editor(a) m/f; (= firm) editorial f
publishing [ˈpʌblɪʃɪŋ] N (= trade) industria f editorial; **he's in ~** publica libros, está con una casa editorial ➤ **publishing company, publishing house** (casa f) editorial f
puce [pjuːs] ADJ de color castaño rojizo; (with shame etc) colorado
puck [pʌk] N (Sport) puck m, disco m
pucker [ˈpʌkəʳ] Ⓐ VT (also ~ up) arrugar; [+ brow, material] fruncir Ⓑ VI (also ~ up) arrugarse, formar buches
pud* [pʊd] N (Brit) = **pudding**
pudding [ˈpʊdɪŋ] N (= steamed pudding) pudín m, budín m; (Brit) (= dessert) postre m ➤ **pudding basin** (Brit) cuenco m ➤ **pudding rice** arroz m con leche
puddle [ˈpʌdl] N charco m
pudgy* [ˈpʌdʒɪ] ADJ (compar pudgier; superl pudgiest) (US) = **podgy**
puerile [ˈpjʊəraɪl] ADJ pueril
Puerto Rican [ˈpwɜːtəʊˈriːkən] ADJ, N puertorriqueño/a m/f
Puerto Rico [ˈpwɜːtəʊˈriːkəʊ] N Puerto Rico m
puff [pʌf] Ⓐ N **1** [of air] soplo m; [of wind] racha f, ráfaga f; [of smoke] bocanada f; (on cigarette) calada f; (on pipe) chupada f; **in one ~** de un soplo; **I'm out of ~** (Brit*) estoy sin aliento
2 (= powder puff) borla f
3 (Culin) **cream ~** petisú m, pastel m de crema
Ⓑ VT (= blow) soplar; [+ pipe etc] chupar; **to ~ smoke** echar bocanadas de humo; **to ~ smoke in sb's face** echar humo a la cara de algn
Ⓒ VI **1** (= breathe heavily) jadear, resoplar; **to ~ (away) at** or **on one's pipe** chupar la pipa
2 the train ~ed into/out of the station el tren entró en/ salió de la estación echando humo
Ⓓ CPD ➤ **puff paste** (US), **puff pastry** (Brit) hojaldre m ➤ **puff sleeves** mangas fpl filipinas
➤ **puff out** VT + ADV **1** [+ smoke etc] echar, arrojar, despedir **2** [+ cheeks, chest, sails] hinchar (Sp), inflar (LAm)
➤ **puff up** VT + ADV **1** (= inflate) [+ tyre etc] hinchar (Sp), inflar (LAm) **2** = **puff out 2 3** (*) (= exaggerate) dar bombo a
puffed [pʌft] ADJ **I'm ~ (out)*** me he quedado sin aliento
puffer* [ˈpʌfəʳ] N (= train) locomotora f; (= inhaler) inhalador m
puffin [ˈpʌfɪn] N frailecillo m

puffy ['pʌfɪ] ADJ (*compar* **puffier**; *superl* **puffiest**) hinchado

pug [pʌg] N doguillo *m*

pugnacious [pʌg'neɪʃəs] ADJ pugnaz, agresivo

puke** [pjuːk] ⒶN vómito *m* ⒷVI (*also* ~ **up**) devolver; **it makes me (want to)** ~ me da asco

pukka* ['pʌkə] ADJ (*Brit*) (= *real*) auténtico, genuino; (= *posh*) esnob, elegante, lujoso

pull [pʊl] ⒶN 1 (= *tug*) tirón *m*, jalón *m* (*LAm*); **to give sth a** ~ tirar de algo, jalar algo (*LAm*); **suddenly it gave a** ~ de repente dio un tirón
2 [*of moon, magnet, sea etc*] (fuerza *f* de) atracción *f*; [*of current*] fuerza *f*, ímpetu *m*; (= *attraction*) atracción *f*; **the** ~ **of the south** la atracción del Sur, lo atractivo del Sur
3 (*) (= *influence*) enchufe* *m*, palanca *f* (*LAm**)
4 (*at pipe, cigarette*) chupada *f*; (*at drink*) trago *m*; **he took a** ~ **at his pipe** le dio una chupada a la pipa; **he took a** ~ **from the bottle** tomó un trago de la botella, dio un tiento a la botella (*Sp*)
5 (= *journey, drive etc*) **we had a long** ~ **up the hill** nos costó mucho trabajo subir la cuesta
6 (= *handle of drawer etc*) tirador *m*; [*of bell*] cuerda *f*
Ⓑ VT 1 (= *draw, drag*) tirar de, jalar (*LAm*); (= *drag along*) arrastrar; **to** ~ **a door shut/open** cerrar/abrir una puerta de un tirón *or* (*LAm*) jalón; ~ **your chair over** acerca la silla
2 (= *tug*) tirar de, jalar (*LAm*); [+ *trigger*] apretar; [+ *oar*] tirar de; [+ *tooth*] sacar; **to** ~ **sb's hair** tirar del pelo a algn, jalar del pelo a algn (*LAm*), jalar el pelo a algn (*LAm**); ♦ IDIOM ~ **the other one!** (*Brit**) ¡cuéntaselo a tu abuela!*
3 (= *extract, draw out*) sacar, arrancar; [+ *beer*] servir; **to** ~ **a gun on sb** amenazar a algn con una pistola
4 (= *injure*) **to** ~ **a muscle** sufrir un tirón en un músculo
5 (*) (= *cancel*) [+ *TV programme*] suspender
6 (*) **to** ~ **a fast one on sb** jugar una mala pasada a algn
7 (*) (= *attract*) **this will really** ~ **the punters** esto seguramente atraerá clientela; **he knows how to** ~ **the birds** (*Brit*) sabe ligar con las chicas*
Ⓒ VI 1 tirar, jalar (*LAm*); **to** ~ **at** *or* **on a rope** tirar *or* (*LAm*) jalar de una cuerda
2 **to** ~ **at one's pipe** dar chupadas a la pipa; **to** ~ **at a bottle** tomar un trago de una botella
3 (= *move*) [*vehicle*] ir; **he** ~**ed sharply to one side to avoid the lorry** torció bruscamente a un lado para no chocar con el camión; **the train** ~**ed into the station** el tren entró en la estación; **the car is** ~**ing to the right** el coche tira hacia la derecha; **the car isn't** ~**ing very well** el coche no tira
Ⓓ CPD ➤ **pull ring, pull tab** anilla *f*
➤ **pull about** VT + ADV (= *handle roughly*) maltratar, manosear
➤ **pull apart** VT + ADV 1 (= *separate*) separar; (= *take apart*) desmontar 2 (*fig**) (= *search thoroughly*) registrar de arriba abajo, revolver 3 (*fig**) (= *criticize*) deshacer, hacer pedazos
➤ **pull away** ⒶVT + ADV (= *move off*) salir, arrancar; **he soon** ~**ed away from the others** (*in race*) pronto dejó atrás a los demás
2 (= *draw back*) **to** ~ **away from sb** apartarse bruscamente de algn
➤ **pull back** ⒶVT + ADV [+ *lever etc*] tirar hacia sí; [+ *curtains*] descorrer Ⓑ VI + ADV 1 (= *refrain*) contenerse 2 (*Mil*) (= *withdraw*) retirarse
➤ **pull down** VT + ADV 1 (= *lower*) [+ *blinds etc*] bajar; **he** ~**ed his hat down** se caló el sombrero, se encasquetó el sombrero* 2 (= *demolish*) derribar, demoler; (*fig*) [+ *government*] derribar 3 (= *weaken*) debilitar; **the mark in chemistry** ~**s her down** la nota de química es la que la perjudica *or* la que le baja la media 4 (*US**) (= *earn*) ganar
➤ **pull in** ⒶVT + ADV 1 [+ *net*] recoger; [+ *rope*] cobrar 2 (*) (= *attract*) [+ *crowds*] atraer; **the film is** ~**ing them in** la película atrae un público numeroso, la película es muy popular; **this will** ~ **them in** esto les hará venir en masa 3 (*) (= *take into custody*) detener Ⓑ VI + ADV (= *enter*) (*into station, harbour*) llegar; (*into driveway*) entrar; (= *stop, park*) parar
➤ **pull off** ⒶVT + ADV 1 (= *remove*) quitar, arrancar; [+ *clothes*] quitarse (de prisa) 2 (*) (= *cause to succeed*) [+ *plan etc*] llevar a cabo, conseguir; [+ *deal*] cerrar, concluir con éxito (algo inesperadamente); **to** ~ **it off** lograrlo Ⓑ VI + ADV **we** ~**ed off into a lay-by** (*Aut*) salimos de la carretera y paramos en un apartadero Ⓒ VI + PREP **we**

~**ed off the road into a lay-by** salimos de la carretera y paramos en un apartadero
➤ **pull on** VT + ADV [+ *gloves etc*] ponerse (de prisa)
➤ **pull out** ⒶVT + ADV 1 (= *take out*) (*from pocket, drawer*) sacar; (*from ground*) arrancar; [+ *tooth*] sacar, extraer 2 (= *withdraw*) retirar Ⓑ VI + ADV 1 (*Aut, Rail*) (= *come out*) salir; **the red car** ~**ed out from behind that black one** el coche rojo salió de detrás de aquel negro 2 (*Mil*) (= *withdraw*) retirarse (**from** de) 3 (= *leave*) salir, partir
➤ **pull over** ⒶVT + ADV 1 (= *bring closer*) [+ *chair*] acercar 2 (= *topple*) volcar 3 (*Police*) [+ *car, driver*] parar Ⓑ VI + ADV (*Aut*) hacerse a un lado
➤ **pull through** VI + ADV (*from illness*) reponerse, recobrar la salud; (*from difficulties etc*) reponerse
➤ **pull together** ⒶVT + ADV **to** ~ **o.s. together** calmarse, tranquilizarse; ~ **yourself together!** ¡cálmate! Ⓑ VI + ADV (= *cooperate*) ir todos a una
➤ **pull up** ⒶVT + ADV 1 (= *raise by pulling*) levantar, subir; [+ *socks etc*] subir 2 (= *bring closer*) [+ *chair*] acercar 3 (= *uproot*) sacar, arrancar 4 (= *stop*) parar 5 (*Brit*) (= *scold*) regañar 6 (= *strengthen*) **his mark in French has** ~**ed him up** la nota de francés le ha subido la media Ⓑ VI + ADV (= *stop*) detenerse, parar; (*Aut*) parar(se)

pulley ['pʊlɪ] N polea *f*

pull-in ['pʊl,ɪn] N (*Brit Aut*) (= *lay-by*) apartadero *m*; (*for food*) café *m* de carretera, restaurante *m* de carretera

Pullman® ['pʊlmən] N (*pl* ~**s**) 1 (*Brit*) (*also* ~ **carriage**) vagón *m* de primera clase 2 (*US*) (*also* ~ **car**) coche *m* cama

pull-off ['pʊlɒf] N (*US Aut*) área *f* de descanso, área *f* de estacionamiento

---

Use **el/un** not **la/una** before feminine nouns beginning with stressed **a** or **ha** like **área**.

---

pull-out ['pʊlaʊt] ⒶN 1 (*in magazine*) suplemento *m* separable 2 (*Mil etc*) retirada *f* Ⓑ CPD [*magazine section*] separable; [*table leaf etc*] extensible

pullover ['pʊləʊvə'] N (*esp Brit*) jersey *m*, suéter *m*, chompa *f* (*Per, Bol*)

pull-up ['pʊlʌp] N 1 (*Brit*) = **pull-in** 2 (*US*) = **press-up**

pulmonary ['pʌlmənərɪ] ADJ pulmonar

pulp [pʌlp] ⒶN 1 (= *paper pulp, wood pulp*) pasta *f*, pulpa *f*; (*for paper*) pulpa *f* de madera; **a leg crushed to** ~ una pierna hecha trizas; **to beat sb to a** ~* dar a algn una tremenda paliza, hacer a algn papilla* 2 [*of fruit, vegetable*] pulpa *f* Ⓑ VT reducir a pulpa

pulpit ['pʊlpɪt] N púlpito *m*

pulsate [pʌl'seɪt] VI vibrar, palpitar

pulse[1] [pʌls] ⒶN (*Anat*) pulso *m*; (*Phys*) pulsación *f*; [*of drums, music*] ritmo *m*, compás *m*; **to take sb's** ~ tomar el pulso a algn; ♦ IDIOM **he keeps his finger on the company's** ~ está tomando constantemente el pulso a la compañía, se mantiene al tanto de lo que pasa en la compañía Ⓑ VI pulsar, latir Ⓒ CPD ➤ **pulse rate** frecuencia *f* del pulso

pulse[2] [pʌls] N (*Bot, Culin*) legumbre *f*

pulverize ['pʌlvəraɪz] VT pulverizar; (*fig*) hacer polvo

puma ['pjuːmə] N (*esp Brit*) puma *m*

pumice ['pʌmɪs], **pumice stone** ['pʌmɪs,stəʊn] N piedra *f* pómez

pummel ['pʌml] VT aporrear, apalear

pump[1] [pʌmp] ⒶN 1 (*for liquid, gas, air*) bomba *f*; **foot/hand** ~ bomba *f* de pie/de mano
2 (*also* **petrol** ~) surtidor *m* de gasolina
Ⓑ VT 1 (*with a pump*) bombear; **to** ~ **gas** (*US*) echar *or* meter gasolina; **a respirator** ~**ed oxygen into her lungs** un respirador le bombeaba oxígeno a los pulmones; **to** ~ **air into a tyre** inflar un neumático; **the heart** ~**s the blood round the body** el corazón hace circular la sangre por el cuerpo; **to** ~ **sb's stomach** hacer un lavado de estómago a algn; ♦ IDIOM **to** ~ **sb dry** dejar a algn seco
2 (*fig*) **we can't go on** ~**ing money into this project** no podemos seguir metiendo tanto dinero en *or* inyectándole tanto dinero a este proyecto; **he** ~**ed five bullets into her head** le metió cinco balas en la cabeza; **to** ~ **sb full of drugs**

atiborrar a algn de drogas
3 (= *move up and down*) [+ *pedal*] pisar repetidamente; [+ *handle*] darle repetidamente a; **he ~ed the accelerator** pisó repetidamente el pedal del acelerador, se puso a darle al pedal del acelerador; ✦ IDIOM **to ~ iron*** hacer pesas
4 (*) (= *question*) **I ~ed him discreetly about his past** le sonsaqué discretamente todo lo que pude acerca de su pasado, le tiré de la lengua discretamente acerca de su pasado*; **to ~ sb <u>for</u> information** sonsacar información a algn
Ⓒ VI **1** [*person*] (*at pump*) **here's a bucket, get ~ing!** aquí tienes un balde, ¡a trabajar la bomba!
2 [*pump, machine*] **the machine is ~ing (away) all the time** la máquina de bombeo está en funcionamiento constantemente; **the piston was ~ing up and down** el émbolo subía y bajaba
3 [*heart*] (= *circulate blood*) bombear la sangre; (= *beat*) latir; **blood ~ed <u>from</u> the severed artery** la sangre salía a borbotones de la arteria cortada
Ⓓ CPD ➤ **pump attendant** encargado/a *m/f* de la gasolinera ➤ **pump price** [*of petrol*] precio *m* de la gasolina
➤ **pump in** VT + ADV **1** (*with pump*) bombear, meter *or* introducir con una bomba **2** (*fig*) [+ *money*] inyectar
➤ **pump out** VT + ADV **1** (= *extract, remove*) [+ *oil, water*] bombear, extraer *or* sacar con una bomba **2** (= *empty*) [+ *boat*] achicar el agua de; [+ *flooded cellar, building*] sacar el agua de; **it's no fun having your stomach ~ed out** un lavado de estómago no es nada divertido **3** (= *emit*) despedir; **cars which ~ out deadly exhaust fumes** los coches que despiden gases letales **4** (= *produce*) producir; **this station ~s out music 24 hours a day** esta cadena emite música las veinticuatro horas del día
➤ **pump up** VT + ADV (= *inflate*) [+ *tyre*] hinchar (*Sp*), inflar (*LAm*)

pump² [pʌmp] N (*esp Brit*) (= *sports shoe*) zapatilla *f*; (= *dancing shoe*) bailarina *f*; (= *slip-on shoe*) zapato *m* de salón; (*US*) (= *court shoe*) escarpín *m*

pumpkin ['pʌmpkɪn] N (= *vegetable*) calabaza *f*, zapallo *m* (*And, SC*); (= *plant*) calabacera *f*

pun [pʌn] Ⓐ N juego *m* de palabras (**on** sobre), retruécano *m*, albur *m* (*Mex*) Ⓑ VI hacer un juego de palabras (**on** sobre), alburear (*Mex*)

Punch [pʌntʃ] N (*Theat*) Polichinela *m*; ✦ IDIOM **to be as pleased as ~** estar como unas pascuas ➤ **Punch and Judy show** teatro *de títeres cuyos personajes principales se llaman Punch y Judy*

punch¹ [pʌntʃ] Ⓐ N **1** (*for making holes*) (*in paper*) perforadora *f*; (*in ticket*) máquina *f* de picar
2 (= *blow*) puñetazo *m*; **he floored him with one ~** lo derribó de un solo puñetazo; **a ~ on the nose** un puñetazo en la nariz; ✦ IDIOM **he didn't pull any ~es** no se mordió la lengua
3 (*fig*) (= *vigour*) empuje *m*, garra *f*; **think of a phrase that's got some ~ to it** piensa una frase que tenga garra
Ⓑ VT **1** (= *perforate*) [+ *paper, card, metal*] perforar; [+ *ticket*] picar; **to ~ a hole in sth** hacer un agujero a algo
2 (= *hit*) (*with fist*) dar un puñetazo a; **to ~ sb in the stomach/on the nose** dar un puñetazo a algn en el estómago/la nariz; **to ~ sb in the face** ◇ **~ sb's face** dar un puñetazo a algn en la cara; **I ~ed the ball into the net** metí el balón en la red de un manotazo; **he ~ed the wall angrily** golpeó la pared furioso
3 (= *press*) [+ *button, key*] presionar
Ⓒ VI pegar (puñetazos)
Ⓓ CPD ➤ **punch bag** (*Brit*) saco *m* de arena ➤ **punch card** tarjeta *f* perforada ➤ **punch line** remate *m*
➤ **punch in** VT + ADV [+ *code, number*] teclear
➤ **punch out** VT + ADV **1** [+ *hole*] perforar **2** [+ *number, code*] teclear

punch² [pʌntʃ] N (= *drink*) ponche *m* ➤ **punch bowl** ponchera *f*

punch-drunk ['pʌntʃ'drʌŋk] ADJ (*fig*) aturdido; **to be ~** estar grogui*

punching bag ['pʌntʃɪŋbæg] N (*US*) = **punch bag**

punch-up* ['pʌntʃʌp] N (*Brit*) pelea *f*, refriega *f*

punctilious [pʌŋk'tɪlɪəs] ADJ puntilloso, quisquilloso

punctual ['pʌŋktjʊəl] ADJ puntual; **"please be punctual"** "se ruega la mayor puntualidad"

punctuality [ˌpʌŋktjʊ'ælɪtɪ] N puntualidad *f*

punctually ['pʌŋktjʊəlɪ] ADV puntualmente, en punto; **the bus arrived ~** el autobús llegó puntualmente *or* a la hora; **~ at six o'clock** a las seis en punto

punctuate ['pʌŋktjʊeɪt] VT (*with punctuation*) puntuar; **his speech was ~d by applause** los aplausos interrumpieron repetidamente su discurso

punctuation [ˌpʌŋktjʊ'eɪʃən] N puntuación *f*

puncture ['pʌŋktʃəʳ] Ⓐ N (*in tyre, balloon*) pinchazo *m*, ponchadura *f* (*Mex*); **I have a ~** se me ha pinchado *or* (*Mex*) ponchado un neumático *or* (*esp LAm*) una llanta; **I had a ~ on the motorway** tuve un pinchazo *or* (*Mex*) una ponchadura en la autopista Ⓑ VT [+ *tyre*] pinchar, ponchar (*Mex*)

pundit ['pʌndɪt] N experto/a *m/f*

pungent ['pʌndʒənt] ADJ [*smell, flavour*] acre; [*remark, style*] mordaz

punish ['pʌnɪʃ] VT castigar; **to ~ sb for sth/for doing sth** castigar a algn por algo/por hacer algo

punishable ['pʌnɪʃəbl] ADJ punible; **a ~ offence** una infracción penada *or* sancionada por la ley; **a crime ~ by death** un delito castigado con la pena de muerte

punishing ['pʌnɪʃɪŋ] Ⓐ ADJ [*race, schedule*] duro, agotador Ⓑ N castigo *m*

punishment ['pʌnɪʃmənt] N castigo *m*; **to make the ~ fit the crime** determinar un castigo acorde con la gravedad del crimen

punitive ['pjuːnɪtɪv] ADJ (*gen*) punitivo; [*damages*] punitorio

Punjabi [pʌn'dʒɑːbɪ] ADJ, N (= *person*) punjabí *mf*

punk [pʌŋk] Ⓐ N **1** (= *person*) punki *mf*, punk *mf*; (= *music*) música *f* punk, punk *m* **2** (*US**) (= *hoodlum*) rufián *m*, matón *m* (*LAm*) Ⓑ CPD ➤ **punk rock** música *f* punk, punk *m*

punnet ['pʌnɪt] N (*Brit*) canastilla *f*

punt¹ [pʌnt] (*esp Brit*) Ⓐ N (= *boat*) batea *f* Ⓑ VT [+ *boat*] impulsar (con percha) Ⓒ VI **to go ~ing** ir a pasear en batea

punt² [pʊnt] N (= *currency*) libra *f* (irlandesa)

punter ['pʌntəʳ] N **1** (*Brit Racing*) (= *gambler*) jugador(a) *m/f*, apostador(a) *m/f* **2** (*) (= *customer*) cliente *mf*; **the ~(s)** (*Brit*) el público

puny ['pjuːnɪ] ADJ (*compar* **punier**; *superl* **puniest**) enclenque, endeble

pup [pʌp] N [*of dog*] cachorro/a *m/f*; [*of other animal*] cría *f*; **seal ~** cría *f* de foca

pupil¹ ['pjuːpl] N (= *student*) alumno/a *m/f*

pupil² ['pjuːpl] N (*Anat*) pupila *f*

puppet ['pʌpɪt] N (*lit*) títere *m*, marioneta *f*; (*fig*) títere *m* ➤ **puppet government, puppet régime** gobierno *m* títere ➤ **puppet show** teatro *m* de títeres *or* marionetas

puppy ['pʌpɪ] N cachorro/a *m/f*, perrito/a *m/f* ➤ **puppy fat** gordura *f* infantil ➤ **puppy love** amor *m* juvenil

purchase ['pɜːtʃɪs] Ⓐ N **1** (= *buy*) compra *f*, adquisición *f*; **to make a ~** hacer una compra **2** (= *grip*) agarre *m*, asidero *m*; (= *leverage*) palanca *f*; **I got a ~ on the rope and pulled** me agarré de la cuerda y tiré Ⓑ VT comprar, adquirir; **to ~ sth from sb** comprar algo a algn Ⓒ CPD ➤ **purchase price** precio *m* de compra

purchaser ['pɜːtʃɪsəʳ] N comprador(a) *m/f*

purchasing power ['pɜːtʃəsɪŋˌpaʊəʳ] N [*of person, currency*] poder *m* adquisitivo

pure [pjʊəʳ] ADJ (*compar* **~r**; *superl* **~st**) (*gen*) puro; [*silk*] natural; **the whole story was ~ invention** todo fue puro cuento

---

Put **pure** after the noun when **pure** means literally "uncontaminated" or "unadulterated" and before the noun when it means "sheer" or "plain":

~ olive oil aceite puro de oliva; **by ~ chance** por pura casualidad; **it's blackmail, ~ and simple** esto es chantaje, lisa y llanamente; ✦ IDIOM **as ~ as the driven snow** puro como la nieve

purebred ['pjʊəˈbred] ADJ [*horse*] de pura sangre; [*dog*] de raza

purée ['pjʊəreɪ] N puré *m*; **tomato ~** puré *m* de tomate, concentrado *m* de tomate

purely ['pjʊəlɪ] ADV puramente; **~ and simply** lisa y llanamente

purgatory ['pɜːgətərɪ] N purgatorio *m*; **it was ~!** ¡fue un purgatorio!

purge [pɜːdʒ] Ⓐ N purga *f*, depuración *f* Ⓑ VT purgar, depurar

purification [ˌpjʊərɪfɪˈkeɪʃən] N [*of air*] purificación *f*; [*of water*] depuración *f*

purify ['pjʊərɪfaɪ] VT [+ *air*] purificar; [+ *water*] depurar

purist ['pjʊərɪst] N purista *mf*

puritan ['pjʊərɪtən] ADJ, N puritano/a *m/f*

puritanical [ˌpjʊərɪˈtænɪkəl] ADJ puritano

purity ['pjʊərɪtɪ] N pureza *f*

purl [pɜːl] Ⓐ N punto *m* del revés Ⓑ VT hacer punto del revés; **"~ two"** "dos del revés"

purloin [pɜːˈlɔɪn] VT robar

purple ['pɜːpl] Ⓐ ADJ morado; **to go ~ (in the face)** enrojecer; **~ prose** prosa *f* de estilo inflado Ⓑ N (= *colour*) púrpura *f*, morado *m* Ⓒ CPD ➤ **Purple Heart** (*US Mil*) *decoración otorgada a los heridos de guerra*

purport [pɜːˈpɔːt] VT **to ~ to be** pretender ser

purportedly [pɜːˈpɔːtɪdlɪ] ADV supuestamente

purpose ['pɜːpəs] N **1** (= *intention*) propósito *m*, objetivo *m*; **she has a ~ in life** tiene un objetivo *or* una meta *or* un norte en la vida; **"purpose of visit"** "motivo *m* del viaje"; **I put that there for a ~** he puesto eso ahí a propósito *or* por una razón; **this is good enough for our ~s** esto sirve para nuestros fines; **for all practical ~s** en la práctica; **for the ~s of this meeting** para los fines de esta reunión; **for the ~ of doing sth** con el fin de hacer algo; **on ~** a propósito, adrede; **with the ~ of** con el fin de **2** (= *use*) uso *m*, utilidad *f*; **what is the ~ of this tool?** ¿qué uso *or* utilidad tiene esta herramienta?; **it wasn't designed for this** – no se diseñó para este fin *or* uso; **it was all to no useful ~** todo fue inútil *or* en vano; **it serves no ~** no tiene uso práctico, no tiene utilidad práctica **3** (= *direction*) **to have a sense of ~** tener un rumbo en la vida; **he has no sense of ~** no tiene rumbo en la vida; **she has great strength of ~** tiene muchísima resolución *or* determinación, es muy resuelta

purpose-built [ˌpɜːpəsˈbɪlt] ADJ (*esp Brit*) construido especialmente

purposeful ['pɜːpəsfəl] ADJ [*look, expression*] de determinación; [*manner*] resuelto, decidido

purposely ['pɜːpəslɪ] ADV a propósito, adrede, expresamente; **a ~ vague statement** una declaración realizada en términos vagos a propósito *or* adrede

purr [pɜːʳ] Ⓐ N ronroneo *m* Ⓑ VI [*cat, engine*] ronronear

purse [pɜːs] Ⓐ N **1** (*Brit*) (*for money*) monedero *m* **2** (*US*) (= *handbag*) bolso *m*, cartera *f* (*LAm*) **3** (= *sum of money as prize*) premio *m* en metálico Ⓑ VT **to ~ one's lips** fruncir los labios Ⓒ CPD ➤ **purse snatcher** (*US*) carterista *mf* ➤ **purse strings** ✦ IDIOM **to hold the ~ strings** (*Brit*) administrar el dinero

purser ['pɜːsəʳ] N comisario/a *m/f*

pursue [pəˈsjuː] VT **1** (= *chase*) perseguir, seguir **2** (= *engage in*) [+ *interests, career*] dedicarse a; [+ *studies, war, talks*] proseguir; [+ *profession*] ejercer, dedicarse a **3** (= *continue with*) [+ *course of action*] seguir; [+ *policy, reform*] aplicar; **he had been pursuing his own inquiries** había estado haciendo sus propias averiguaciones; **we have decided not to ~ the matter further** hemos decidido no seguir adelante con el asunto

pursuer [pəˈsjuːəʳ] N perseguidor(a) *m/f*

pursuit [pəˈsjuːt] N **1** (= *chase*) caza *f*, persecución *f*; [*of pleasure, happiness, knowledge*] busca *f*, búsqueda *f*; **the ~ of wealth** el afán de riqueza; **in (the) ~ of sth/sb** en busca de algo/algn; **with two policemen in hot ~** con dos policías pisándole los talones **2** (= *occupation*) **outdoor ~s** actividades *fpl* al aire libre; **literary ~s** intereses *mpl* literarios, actividades *fpl* literarias; **leisure ~s** pasatiempos *mpl*

purveyor [pɜːˈveɪəʳ] N proveedor(a) *m/f*, abastecedor(a) *m/f*

pus [pʌs] N pus *m*

push [pʊʃ] Ⓐ N **1** (= *shove*) empujón *m*; **the car needs a ~** hay que empujar el coche; **at the ~ of a button** con sólo apretar *or* pulsar un botón; **to give sth/sb a ~** dar a algo/algn un empujón **2** (*Brit**) (= *dismissal*) **to get the ~: he got the ~** [*worker*] lo pusieron de patitas en la calle*, lo echaron; [*lover*] ella lo plantó*, ella lo dejó; **to give sb the ~** [+ *worker*] poner a algn de patitas en la calle*, echar a algn; [+ *lover*] plantar a algn*, dejar a algn **3** (= *effort*) esfuerzo *m*; **in its ~ for economic growth ...** en su esfuerzo por desarrollar la economía ... **4** (= *encouragement*) empujoncito* *m*; **we need a ~ to take the first step** necesitamos un empujoncito para dar el primer paso* **5** (*Mil*) (= *offensive*) ofensiva *f* **6** (*) **at a ~** a duras penas; **if** *or* **when it comes to the ~** en último caso, en el peor de los casos Ⓑ VT **1** (= *shove, move by pushing*) empujar; **she ~ed him down the stairs** lo empujó escaleras abajo; **to ~ sb into a room** hacer entrar a algn en una habitación de un empujón; **to ~ a car into the garage** empujar un coche dentro del garaje; **they ~ed the car off the cliff** empujaron el coche por el acantilado; **to ~ a door open/shut** abrir/cerrar una puerta empujándola *or* de un empujón; **he ~ed the thought to the back of his mind** intentó quitárselo de la cabeza; **to ~ one's way through the crowd** abrirse paso a empujones por la multitud; **he ~ed the box under the table** empujó *or* metió la caja debajo de la mesa **2** (= *press*) [+ *button etc*] apretar, pulsar **3** (= *press, advance*) [+ *product*] promover; **to ~ home one's advantage** aprovechar la ventaja; **don't ~ your luck!*** ¡no te pases!*, ¡no desafíes a la suerte! **4** (= *put pressure on*) **when we ~ed her, she explained it all** cuando la presionamos, nos lo explicó todo; **don't ~ her too far** no te pases con ella*; **to ~ sb into doing sth** obligar a algn a hacer algo; **to ~ o.s.** esforzarse; **to be ~ed for time/money** (*Brit**) andar justo de tiempo/escaso de dinero; **to ~ sb to do sth** presionar a algn para que haga algo **5** (*) [+ *drugs*] pasar* **6** (*) **he's ~ing 50** raya en los 50 Ⓒ VI **1** (= *press*) empujar; (*on bell*) pulsar; **he ~ed past me** pasó por mi lado dándome un empujón; **she ~ed through the crowd** se abrió paso entre la multitud a empujones **2** (= *campaign*) **they're ~ing for better conditions** hacen campaña para mejorar sus condiciones (de trabajo) Ⓓ CPD ➤ **push bike**† (*Brit*) bicicleta *f*, bici* *f*
➤ **push about*** VT + ADV = **push around**
➤ **push ahead** VI + ADV (= *make progress*) seguir adelante; **to ~ ahead with a plan** seguir adelante con un proyecto
➤ **push around*** VT + ADV (= *bully*) intimidar; **he's not one to be ~ed around** no se deja intimidar, no se deja mandonear*; **he likes ~ing people around** le gusta mandonear*, le gusta dar órdenes a la gente
➤ **push aside** VT + ADV [+ *person, chair*] apartar, hacer a un lado; [+ *objection, suggestion*] hacer caso omiso de
➤ **push away** VT + ADV [+ *plate*] apartar; [+ *person*] apartar a un lado; (*more violently*) apartar de un empujón
➤ **push back** VT + ADV [+ *hair etc*] echar hacia atrás; [+ *enemy, crowd*] hacer retroceder
➤ **push down** VT + ADV [+ *prices, value*] hacer bajar
➤ **push forward** Ⓐ VI + ADV (*Mil*) avanzar Ⓑ VT + ADV [+ *person, object*] empujar hacia adelante; [+ *plan, work*] llevar adelante
➤ **push in** Ⓐ VT + ADV **1** [+ *screw etc*] introducir (a la fuerza) **2** (= *break*) [+ *window, door*] romper **3** [+ *person*] (*in lake etc*) empujar al agua Ⓑ VI + ADV **1** (*in queue*) colarse **2** (*fig*) (= *interfere*) entrometerse

➤ **push off** VI + ADV (*Brit**) (= *leave*) marcharse; ~ **off!** ¡lárgate!*
➤ **push on** VI + ADV (= *carry on*) continuar; (*on journey*) seguir adelante; **to** ~ **on with sth** continuar con algo
➤ **push over** VT + ADV **1** (= *cause to fall*) hacer caer, derribar **2** (= *knock over*) [+ *chair, table*] volcar
➤ **push through** VT + ADV **1** (*through door, hole*) introducir, meter; **I** ~**ed my way through** me abrí paso a empujones **2** (= *get done quickly*) [+ *deal*] expeditar, apresurar; (*Parl*) [+ *bill*] hacer aprobar
➤ **push up** VT + ADV **1** [+ *lever, window*] levantar, subir **2** (= *raise, increase*) [+ *price, value*] hacer subir

push-button ['pʊʃ,bʌtn] ADJ de mando de botón; **with ~ control** con mando de botón ➤ **push-button warfare** guerra *f* a control remoto

pushcart ['pʊʃkɑːt] N carretilla *f* de mano

pushchair ['pʊʃtʃɛəʳ] N (*Brit*) sillita *f* de paseo

pusher* ['pʊʃəʳ] N (*of drugs*) camello* *mf*, traficante *mf*

pushover* ['pʊʃ,əʊvəʳ] N **it's a ~** está tirado*; **he was a ~** era fácil de convencer

push-up ['pʊʃʌp] N (*US*) = **press-up**

pushy* ['pʊʃɪ] ADJ (*compar* **pushier**; *superl* **pushiest**) (*pej*) agresivo, avasallador, prepotente (*esp LAm*)

puss* [pʊs] N (= *cat*) minino* *m*, gatito *m*

pussy ['pʊsɪ] Ⓐ N **1** = **pussycat 2** (***) (= *genitals*) coño*** *m* Ⓑ CPD ➤ **pussy willow** sauce *m*

pussycat* ['pʊsɪkæt] N minino* *m*, gatito *m*

pussyfoot* ['pʊsɪfʊt] VI (*also* ~ **around**) andarse con demasiado tiento

---

put

Ⓐ TRANSITIVE VERB	Ⓒ PHRASAL VERBS
Ⓑ INTRANSITIVE VERB	

For set combinations consisting of **put** + *noun, eg* **put a price on, put at risk, put out of business** *look up the noun. For* **put** + *adverb/preposition combinations, see also phrasal verbs.*

put [pʊt] (*pt, pp* ~) Ⓐ TRANSITIVE VERB
1 (= *place, thrust*)
1.1 (*physically*) poner; (*with precision*) colocar; (= *insert*) meter, introducir (*more frm*); (= *leave*) dejar; **I** ~ **a serviette by each plate** puse *or* coloqué una servilleta junto a cada plato; ~ **it in the drawer** ponlo en el cajón; **shall I** ~ **milk in your coffee?** ¿te pongo leche en el café?; **to** ~ **an ad in the paper** poner un anuncio en el periódico; **he** ~ **the letter in his pocket** se metió la carta en el bolsillo; **he** ~ **his keys on the table** puso *or* dejó las llaves en la mesa; **my brother** ~ **me on the train** mi hermano me dejó en el tren; **she** ~ **her head out of the window** asomó la cabeza por la ventana; **he** ~ **his hand over his mouth** se tapó la boca con la mano, se puso la mano en la boca; **he** ~ **his head round the door** asomó la cabeza por la puerta; **I** ~ **my fist through the window** rompí la ventana con el puño; ✦ IDIOMS ~ **yourself in my place** ponte en mi lugar; **I didn't know where to** ~ **myself*** creí que me moría de vergüenza, no sabía dónde meterme
1.2 (*with abstract nouns*)

Some **put** + noun combinations require a more specific Spanish verb. For very set combinations look up the noun.

the syllabus ~**s a lot of emphasis on languages** el programa (de estudios) hace *or* pone mucho énfasis en los idiomas; **you can** ~ **that idea out of your head** ya te puedes quitar esa idea de la cabeza
2 (= *cause to be*) poner; **to** ~ **sb in a good/bad mood** poner a algn de buen/mal humor; **to** ~ **sb on a diet** poner a algn a dieta *or* a régimen; **the doctor has** ~ **me on antibiotics** el médico me ha recetado (un tratamiento de) antibióticos *or* me ha puesto un tratamiento de antibióticos

3 (= *cause to undertake*) **to** ~ **sb to sth: it** ~ **us to a lot of extra expense** nos supuso muchos gastos adicionales; **I don't want to** ~ **you to any trouble** no quiero causarte ninguna molestia; **she** ~ **him to work immediately** lo puso a trabajar en seguida
4 (= *express*) decir; **I don't quite know how to** ~ **this** la verdad, no sé cómo decir esto; **as Shakespeare** ~**s it** como dice Shakespeare; **to** ~ **it bluntly** para decirlo claramente, hablando en plata*; **I find it hard to** ~ **into words** me resulta difícil expresarlo con palabras; **how shall I** ~ **it?** ¿cómo lo diría?; **let me** ~ **it this way ...** digámoslo de esta manera ..., por decirlo de alguna manera ...
5 (= *write*) poner, escribir; **what do you want me to** ~**?** ¿qué quieres que ponga *or* escriba?; **to** ~ **sth in writing** poner algo por escrito; ~ **it on my account** cárguelo a mi cuenta
6 (= *invest*) invertir; **he** ~ **all his savings into the project** invirtió todos sus ahorros en el proyecto; **I've** ~ **a lot of time and effort into this** he invertido un montón de tiempo y esfuerzo en esto, le he dedicado a esto mucho tiempo y esfuerzo; **she has** ~ **a lot into the relationship** se ha esforzado mucho en su relación
7 (= *contribute*) **to** ~ **sth towards sth** contribuir (con) algo hacia algo; **I'll pay for the bike but you'll have to** ~ **something towards it** yo pagaré la bici pero tú tienes que contribuir con algo; **I'm going to** ~ **the money towards a holiday** voy a poner *or* guardar el dinero para unas vacaciones
8 (= *submit*) [+ *views*] expresar, exponer; **he** ~**s the case for a change in the law** plantea *or* expone argumentos a favor de un cambio en la ley; **the proposal was** ~ **before Parliament** la propuesta se presentó ante el parlamento; **to** ~ **sth to sb: how will you** ~ **it to him?** ¿cómo se lo vas a decir *or* comunicar?; **I** ~ **it to you that ...** les sugiero que ...; **we shall have to** ~ **it to our members** tendremos que someterlo a la votación de nuestros miembros
9 (= *estimate*) **they** ~ **the loss at around £50,000** calcularon *or* valoraron las pérdidas en unas 50.000 libras; **the number of dead was** ~ **at 6,000** se calculó *or* estimó el número de muertos en 6.000
10 (= *rank*) **I wouldn't** ~ **him among the greatest poets** yo no le pondría entre los más grandes poetas; **we should never** ~ **money before happiness** no deberíamos nunca anteponer el dinero a la felicidad; **I** ~ **the needs of my children before anything else** para mí las necesidades de mis hijos van por delante de todo lo demás *or* son más importantes que todo lo demás; **she has always** ~ **her career first** para ella su carrera siempre ha sido lo primero
Ⓑ INTRANSITIVE VERB Naut **to** ~ **into port** entrar a puerto; **the ship** ~ **into Southampton** el barco entró a *or* en Southampton; **to** ~ **to sea** hacerse a la mar
Ⓒ PHRASAL VERBS
➤ **put about** Ⓐ VT + ADV **1** (*esp Brit*) [+ *rumour*] hacer correr; **to** ~ **it about that ...** hacer correr el rumor de que ... **2 he's** ~**ting it about a bit*** (*sexually*) se está ofreciendo a todo quisque*; **to** ~ **o.s. about** (= *make o.s. noticed*) hacerse notar Ⓑ VI + ADV (*Naut*) cambiar de rumbo, virar
➤ **put across** VT + ADV (= *communicate*) [+ *idea*] comunicar; [+ *meaning*] hacer entender; **the play** ~**s the message across very well** la obra transmite el mensaje muy bien; **to** ~ **o.s. across** (= *present o.s.*) presentarse
➤ **put aside** VT + ADV **1** (= *lay down*) dejar a un lado, poner a un lado **2** (= *save*) [+ *money*] ahorrar, guardar; [+ *time*] reservar; [+ *food*] apartar; **to have money** ~ **aside** tener ahorros **3** (*in shop*) [+ *goods*] guardar, reservar, apartar **4** (= *ignore*) [+ *differences, feelings*] dejar de lado
➤ **put away** VT + ADV **1** (*in proper place*) [+ *clothes, toys, books*] guardar, poner en su sitio; [+ *shopping*] guardar, colocar **2** (*) (*in prison*) meter en la cárcel, encerrar; (*in asylum*) encerrar en un manicomio **3** (= *save*) [+ *money*] ahorrar, guardar **4** (*) (= *consume*) [+ *food, drink*] tragarse*, zamparse* **5** (= *reject*) [+ *thought*] desechar, descartar **6** (*Sport*) [+ *ball*] meter, marcar
➤ **put back** Ⓐ VT + ADV **1** (= *replace*) poner otra vez en su sitio; (*in pocket, drawer etc*) volver a guardar; ~ **that back!** ¡deja eso en su sitio *or* donde estaba!
2 (*esp Brit*) (= *postpone*) aplazar, posponer (**till, to** hasta)
3 (= *delay*) [+ *development, progress*] retrasar, atrasar; **this will** ~ **us back ten years** esto nos retrasará diez años; **he has**

been ~ **back a class** *or* **year** (*Scol*) tiene que repetir el curso
4 (= *change*) [+ *clock, watch*] atrasar, retrasar
5 (= *reinvest*) [+ *money, profits*] reinvertir (**into** en)
6 (*) (= *drink*) beber, beberse
B VI + ADV (*Naut*) volver, regresar; **to ~ back to port** volver *or* regresar a puerto
➤ **put by** VT + ADV **1** (*Brit*) (= *save*) ahorrar; **to have money ~ by** tener ahorros **2** (*in shop*) guardar, reservar, apartar
➤ **put down (A)** VT + ADV **1** [+ *object*] (= *leave*) dejar; (= *let go of*) soltar; [+ *telephone*] colgar; [+ *passenger*] dejar (bajar), dejar (apearse); **she ~ her glass down and stood up** dejó el vaso y se levantó; ~ **it down!** ¡déjalo!, ¡suéltalo!; **once I started the book I couldn't ~ it down** una vez que empecé el libro no podía dejarlo *or* dejar de leerlo
2 (= *lay*) [+ *carpets, poison, trap*] poner, colocar
3 (= *lower*) [+ *blinds, hand*] bajar
4 (= *close*) [+ *umbrella, parasol*] cerrar
5 (= *write down*) [+ *ideas*] anotar, apuntar; [+ *name on list*] poner, inscribir; **I've ~ you down as unemployed** lo he inscrito *or* apuntado como desempleado; ~ **me down for £15** apúntame 15 libras; **I've ~ myself down for the computer course** me he inscrito para el curso de informática; **to ~ sth down in writing** poner algo por escrito
6 (= *suppress*) [+ *revolt*] reprimir, sofocar
7 (*) (= *criticize, snub*) hacer de menos, rebajar; **you must stop ~ting yourself down** debes dejar de rebajarte *or* quitarte importancia
8 (= *pay*) **to ~ down a deposit** dejar un depósito; **she ~ down £500 on the car** dejó una señal *or* un anticipo de 500 libras para el coche
9 (*esp Brit euph*) **to have an animal ~ down** sacrificar a un animal
B VI + ADV (*Aer*) aterrizar
➤ **put down as** VT + PREP **to ~ sb down as sth** catalogar a algn como algo; **I had ~ him down as a complete fool** lo tenía catalogado como un tonto perdido
➤ **put down to** VT + PREP **to ~ sth down to sth** atribuir algo a algo
➤ **put forward** VT + ADV **1** (= *propose*) [+ *theory, idea, argument*] presentar; [+ *plan, proposal*] presentar, proponer; [+ *suggestion*] hacer; [+ *name, candidate*] proponer; **to ~ o.s. forward for a job** presentarse como candidato para un puesto **2** (= *make earlier*) [+ *clock, meeting, starting time*] adelantar
➤ **put in (A)** VT + ADV **1** (*inside box, drawer, room*) meter; **I'll ~ some more sugar in** voy a poner más azúcar; **I've ~ the car in for repairs** he llevado el coche a que lo reparen
2 (= *install*) instalar, poner
3 (= *include*) [+ *word, paragraph, joke*] meter
4 (= *interject*) interponer
5 (= *submit*) [+ *request, claim*] presentar; **to ~ sb in for an award** proponer a algn para un premio; **to ~ one's name in for sth** inscribirse para algo; **to ~ in a plea of not guilty** declararse inocente
6 (*Pol*) [+ *party, government, candidate*] elegir, votar a
7 (= *devote, expend*) [+ *time*] dedicar
8 (= *work*) trabajar; **can you ~ in a few hours at the weekend?** ¿puede trabajar unas horas el fin de semana?
B VI + ADV (*Naut*) hacer escala (**at** en)
➤ **put in for** VI + PREP [+ *promotion, transfer, pay rise, divorce*] solicitar; **I've ~ in for a new job** he solicitado otro empleo
➤ **put off (A)** VT + ADV **1** (= *postpone, delay*) [+ *departure, appointment, meeting, decision*] aplazar, posponer; **he ~ off writing the letter** pospuso *or* aplazó el escribir la carta; **I keep ~ting it off** no hago más que aplazarlo
2 (= *discourage*) **her brusque manner ~s some people off** desanima a la gente con sus maneras tan bruscas; **he's not easily ~ off** no es de los que se desaniman fácilmente
3 (= *distract*) distraer
4 (= *dissuade*) disuadir
5 (= *fob off*) dar largas a; **to ~ sb off with an excuse** dar largas a algn con excusas
6 (= *switch off*) apagar
B VT + PREP **1** (= *cause not to like, want*) **it ~ me off opera for good** me quitó las ganas de ir más a la ópera; **you've ~ me off my meal** me has quitado las ganas de comer; **it ~ me off going to Greece** me quitó las ganas de ir a Grecia
2 (= *dissuade from*) **we tried to ~ him off the idea**

intentamos quitarle la idea de la cabeza, intentamos disuadirlo; **I tried to ~ her off going by herself** intenté convencerla de que no fuera sola
C VI + ADV (*Naut*) hacerse a la mar, salir (**from** de)
➤ **put on (A)** VT + ADV **1** [+ *one's coat, socks, hat*] ponerse; [+ *ointment, cream*] ponerse, aplicarse (*more frm*); **to ~ on one's make-up** ponerse maquillaje, maquillarse
2 (= *add, increase*) **he's ~ on 3 kilos** ha engordado 3 kilos; **to ~ on weight** engordar
3 [+ *concert*] presentar; [+ *exhibition*] montar; [+ *play*] representar, poner en escena; [+ *extra bus, train*] poner
4 (= *assume*) [+ *expression, air*] adoptar; **to ~ on a French accent** fingir (tener) un acento francés; **she's not ill, she's just ~ting it on** no está enferma, es puro teatro *or* está fingiendo; **she ~ on a show of enthusiasm** fingió entusiasmo
5 (= *switch on, start*) [+ *light, radio*] encender, prender (*LAm*); [+ *CD, tape, music*] poner; [+ *vegetables*] (= *begin to cook*) poner (a cocer); (= *begin to heat*) poner (a calentar); **to ~ the kettle on** poner agua a hervir
6 [+ *clock*] adelantar
7 (*esp US**) (= *deceive*) engañar; **you're ~ting me on, aren't you?** me estás tomando el pelo, ¿verdad?
B VT + PREP **1** (= *add to*) **the proposal would ~ 5p on (to) a litre of petrol** la propuesta aumentaría en cinco peniques el litro de gasolina; **they ~ £2 on (to) the price** añadieron dos libras al precio
2 (= *bet on*) **to ~ money on a horse** apostar dinero a un caballo, jugarse dinero en un caballo
➤ **put onto, put on to** VT + PREP **1** (= *inform about*) **who ~ the police onto him?** ¿quién lo denunció a la policía?
2 (= *put in touch with*) **can you ~ me onto a good dentist?** ¿me puede recomendar un buen dentista?; **Sue ~ us onto you** Sue nos dio su nombre
➤ **put out (A)** VT + ADV **1** (= *place outside*) [+ *rubbish*] sacar; [+ *cat*] sacar fuera, dejar afuera; **to ~ the clothes out to dry** sacar la ropa a secar
2 (= *stretch out*) [+ *hand*] alargar, tender; [+ *tongue, claws, horns*] sacar; [+ *leaves, shoots*] echar; **to ~ one's head out of a window** asomar la cabeza por una ventana
3 (= *lay out in order*) [+ *cards, chessmen, chairs*] disponer, colocar; [+ *clothes, best china*] sacar, poner
4 (= *publish*) [+ *appeal, statement, propaganda*] hacer; [+ *warning*] dar; (= *broadcast*) [+ *programme*] transmitir; **they have ~ out a press release denying the allegations** han desmentido las alegaciones en un comunicado de prensa, han emitido un comunicado de prensa negando las alegaciones
5 (= *extinguish*) [+ *light, cigarette, fire*] apagar
6 (= *annoy, upset*) enfadar (*Sp*), enojar (*esp LAm*); **he was very ~ out at finding her there** se enfadó (*Sp*) *or* se enojó (*esp LAm*) mucho al encontrarla allí; **he's a bit ~ out that nobody came** le sentó mal que no viniera nadie
7 (= *inconvenience*) molestar; **to ~ o.s. out: she really ~ herself out for us** se tomó muchas molestias por nosotros; **I don't want to ~ you out** no quiero molestarle
8 [+ *calculations*] desbaratar, echar por tierra
9 (*Sport*) [+ *team, contestant*] eliminar (**of** de)
10 (= *dislocate*) [+ *shoulder, knee*] dislocar
11 (= *give anaesthetic to*) anestesiar, dormir
12 to ~ sth out to tender sacar algo a concurso *or* a licitación; **to ~ work out to contract** sacar una obra a contrata
B VI + ADV (*Naut*) salir, zarpar (**from** de); **to ~ out to sea** hacerse a la mar
➤ **put over** VT + ADV **1** = **put across 2 to ~ one over on sb*** engañar a algn, dar a algn gato por liebre*
➤ **put through (A)** VT + ADV **1** [+ *plan, reform, change*] llevar a cabo; [+ *deal*] cerrar
2 (*Telec*) (= *connect*) [+ *call, caller*] pasar; **who? Martha? all right, ~ her through** ¿quién? ¿Marta? bueno, ponme con ella; **can you ~ me through to Miss Blair, please** por favor, póngame *or* (*esp LAm*) me comunica con la Srta. Blair
B VT + PREP **1** (*by providing finance*) **she ~ two sons through university** mandó a dos hijos a la universidad
2 (= *make suffer*) **she didn't want to ~ him through another ordeal like that** no quiso hacerle pasar por otra prueba tan dura como esa; **they really ~ him through it at the interview** se las hicieron pasar mal en la entrevista, se las hicieron

pasar canutas en la entrevista*; ✦ IDIOM **to ~ sb through hell*** hacérselas pasar canutas a algn*
➤ **put together** VT + ADV **1** (= *place together*) poner juntos, juntar; ✦ IDIOM **she's worth more than all the others ~ together** vale más que todos los demás juntos **2** (= *assemble*) [+ *model kit, piece of furniture*] armar, montar; [+ *meal*] preparar; [+ *collection*] juntar, reunir; [+ *team*] reunir, formar **3** (= *formulate*) [+ *plan, scheme*] formular, preparar
➤ **put up** VT + ADV **1** (= *raise, lift up*) [+ *window, blinds*] subir; [+ *hand*] levantar; [+ *flag, sail*] izar
2 (= *hang*) [+ *picture, decorations*] colgar; [+ *notice*] poner **3** (= *erect*) [+ *building, wall*] construir, levantar; [+ *statue, monument*] erigir, levantar; [+ *fence, barrier*] poner; [+ *tent*] montar; [+ *umbrella*] abrir; [+ *ladder*] montar, poner
4 (= *increase*) [+ *price, tax, sb's temperature, blood pressure*] aumentar, subir; **that ~s the total up to over 1,000** con eso el total asciende a más de 1.000
5 (= *offer*) [+ *reward, prize, prayer*] ofrecer; [+ *resistance*] oponer; **he didn't ~ up much of a fight** *or* **struggle** no se resistió mucho, no opuso mucha resistencia; **to ~ sth up for sale** poner algo a la venta; **to ~ a child up for adoption** ofrecer un niño en adopción
6 (= *provide*) [+ *money*] poner, dar
7 (= *give accommodation to*) alojar, hospedar
8 (= *present, put forward*) [+ *plan, petition*] presentar; [+ *proposal, suggestion*] hacer; [+ *argument, case, defence*] presentar; [+ *candidate*] proponer (**for** para)
➤ **put upon** VI + PREP **to ~ upon sb** (= *inconvenience*) molestar a algn, incomodar a algn; (= *impose on*) abusar de la amabilidad de algn
➤ **put up to** VT + PREP (= *incite*) **they said that she had ~ him up to the murder** dijeron que ella le había incitado *or* instigado al asesinato; **somebody must have ~ him up to it** alguien ha debido sugerírselo
➤ **put up with** VI + PREP aguantar; **you'll just have to ~ up with it** tendrás que aguantarte

putative ['pjuːtətɪv] ADJ supuesto

put-down* ['pʊt,daʊn] N (= *act*) humillación *f*; (= *words*) frase *f* despectiva

put-on* ['pʊt,ɒn] Ⓐ ADJ (= *feigned*) fingido Ⓑ N (= *pretence*) teatro* *m*; (= *hoax*) broma *f* (de mal gusto)

putrid ['pjuːtrɪd] ADJ (= *rotten*) putrefacto, podrido

putsch [pʊtʃ] N golpe *m* de estado

putt [pʌt] Ⓐ N putt *m* Ⓑ VT golpear Ⓒ VI golpear la bola

putter¹ ['pʌtəʳ] N putter *m*

putter² ['pʌtəʳ] VI (*US*) = **potter²**

putting ['pʌtɪŋ] N minigolf *m* ➤ **putting green** (= *miniature golf*) campo *m* de minigolf; (*on golf course*) green *m*

putty ['pʌtɪ] N masilla *f*

put-up ['pʊtʌp] ADJ ➤ **put-up job** (*Brit**) chanchullo* *m*

put-upon ['pʊtə,pɒn] ADJ **she's feeling very ~** cree que los demás la están explotando

puzzle ['pʌzl] Ⓐ N **1** (= *game, jigsaw*) rompecabezas *m inv*; (= *crossword*) crucigrama *m* **2** (= *mystery*) misterio *m*, enigma *m*; (= *riddle*) acertijo *m*, adivinanza *f*; **it's a real ~** es un verdadero misterio *or* enigma Ⓑ VT dejar perplejo, desconcertar; **that properly ~d him** eso lo dejó totalmente perplejo Ⓒ VI **to ~ over** dar vueltas (en la cabeza) a Ⓓ CPD ➤ **puzzle book** libro *m* de pasatiempos
➤ **puzzle out** VT + ADV **we're still trying to ~ out why he did it** seguimos tratando de comprender por qué lo hizo

puzzled ['pʌzld] ADJ perplejo; **to be ~ about sth** no entender algo

puzzlement ['pʌzlmənt] N perplejidad *f*

puzzling ['pʌzlɪŋ] ADJ curioso

PVC N ABBR (= **polyvinyl chloride**) PVC *m*

Pvt. ABBR (*US Mil*) = **Private**

PW N ABBR (*US*) = **prisoner of war**

p.w. ABBR (= **per week**) por semana, a la semana

PX N ABBR (*US Mil*) (= **Post Exchange**) economato militar

pygmy ['pɪgmɪ] Ⓐ N pigmeo/a *m/f*; (*fig*) enano/a *m/f* Ⓑ ADJ pigmeo; (*fig*) miniatura, minúsculo

pyjamas [pɪ'dʒɑːməz] NPL pijama *msing*, piyama *msing* (*LAm*); **a pair of ~** un pijama

pylon ['paɪlən] N (*Elec*) torre *f* de conducción eléctrica

pyramid ['pɪrəmɪd] N pirámide *f* ➤ **pyramid selling** venta *f* piramidal

pyre ['paɪəʳ] N pira *f*

Pyrenean [,pɪrə'niːən] ADJ pirenaico, pirineo

Pyrenees [,pɪrə'niːz] NPL **the ~** el Pirineo, los Pirineos

Pyrex® ['paɪreks] Ⓐ N pyrex® *m*, pirex® *m* Ⓑ CPD [*bowl, dish*] de pyrex® *or* pirex®

pyromaniac [,paɪərəʊ'meɪnɪæk] N pirómano/a *m/f*

pyrotechnics [,paɪərəʊ'teknɪks] NSING pirotecnia *f*

Pyrrhic ['pɪrɪk] ADJ **~ victory** victoria *f* pírrica

python ['paɪθən] N pitón *f*

pzazz* [pə'zæz] N energía *f*, dinamismo *m*

Qq

Q¹, q [kjuː] N (= *letter*) Q, q *f*; **Q for Queen** Q de queso
Q² ABBR (= **question**) P
Q and A [ˌkjuːənˈeɪ] N ABBR (= **question and answer**) ~
session sesión *f* de preguntas y respuestas
Qatar [kæˈtɑːʳ] N Qatar *m*, Katar *m*
QC N ABBR (*Brit*) = **Queen's Counsel**

QC/KC

QC o **KC**, abreviaturas de **Queen's** o **King's Counsel**, es el título que se les da a los abogados de más alto rango en el Reino Unido. Los letrados denominados **barristers** (o **advocates** en Escocia) que hayan practicado la abogacía durante al menos diez años pueden solicitar este título al **Lord Chancellor**, quien a su vez los recomienda a la Corona para su designación. Pasar a ser un **QC** o **KC** se conoce como **taking silk** (recibir la seda), haciendo referencia al material de la túnica que llevan estos letrados.

QED ABBR (= **quod erat demonstrandum**) QED
qty ABBR (= **quantity**) cant.
quack¹ [kwæk] **Ⓐ** N [*of duck*] graznido *m* **Ⓑ** VI graznar
quack²* [kwæk] N charlatán/ana *m/f*; (= *doctor*) curandero/a *m/f*; (*pej*) matasanos* *mf inv*
quad* [kwɒd] ABBR 1 = **quadrangle** 2 = **quadruplet**
quadrangle [ˈkwɒdræŋgl] N 1 (*Geom*) cuadrilátero *m*, cuadrángulo *m* 2 (= *courtyard*) patio *m*
quadrant [ˈkwɒdrənt] N cuadrante *m*
quadratic [kwɒˈdrætɪk] ADJ [*equation*] cuadrático, de segundo grado
quadruped [ˈkwɒdruped] N cuadrúpedo *m*
quadruple **Ⓐ** [ˈkwɒdrupl] ADJ cuádruple, cuádruplo **Ⓑ** [ˈkwɒdrupl] N cuádruple *m*, cuádruplo *m* **Ⓒ** [kwɒˈdruːpl] VT cuadruplicar **Ⓓ** [kwɒˈdruːpl] VI cuadruplicarse
quadruplet [kwɒˈdruːplɪt] N cuatrillizo/a *m/f*
quagmire [ˈkwægmaɪəʳ] N cenagal *m*
quail¹ [kweɪl] N (*pl ~ or ~s*) (= *bird*) codorniz *f*
quail² [kweɪl] VI (= *cower*) temblar (**at** ante)
quaint [kweɪnt] ADJ (*compar* **-er**; *superl* **-est**) 1 (= *picturesque*) [*building, street, village*] pintoresco 2 (= *odd*) [*custom, notion*] curioso; [*person*] peculiar, poco corriente
quake [kweɪk] **Ⓐ** VI [*person*] (= *shake*) temblar; (*inwardly*) estremecerse; **to ~ with fright** temblar de miedo **Ⓑ** N (*) (= *earthquake*) terremoto *m*, temblor *m*
Quaker [ˈkweɪkəʳ] ADJ, N cuáquero/a *m/f*
qualification [ˌkwɒlɪfɪˈkeɪʃən] N 1 (= *diploma*) título *m*; **he left school without any ~s** dejó la escuela sin sacarse ningún título; **what are his ~s?** ¿qué títulos tiene?; **a teaching ~** un título de profesor 2 (= *requirement*) requisito *m*; **the ~s for membership** lo que se requiere para ser socio 3 (= *reservation*) reserva *f*; (= *modification*) salvedad *f*; **without ~** sin reserva; **this is true, with the ~ that ...** esto es verdad, con la salvedad de que ...
qualified [ˈkwɒlɪfaɪd] ADJ 1 (= *trained*) [*instructor*] diplomado, titulado; [*doctor, teacher*] (= *having completed training*) titulado; (= *skilled*) cualificado (*Sp*), calificado (*LAm*); **to be ~ to do sth** (*having passed exams*) estar titulado para hacer algo; (*having right expertise*) estar cualificado (*Sp*) *or* calificado (*LAm*) para hacer algo; (*being capable*) estar capacitado para hacer algo; (*being eligible*) reunir los requisitos necesarios para algo; **I don't feel ~ to judge that** no me siento capacitado para juzgar eso; **highly ~ young people** jóvenes altamente cualificados (*Sp*) *or* calificados (*LAm*); **suitably ~ staff** personal adecuadamente cualificado (*Sp*) *or* calificados (*LAm*) 2 (= *limited*) **he gave it his ~ approval** lo aprobó con

reservas; **it was a ~ success** fue un éxito relativo
qualify [ˈkwɒlɪfaɪ] **Ⓐ** VI 1 (= *gain qualification*) (*degree*) terminar la carrera, sacar el título, recibirse (*LAm*); (*professional exams*) obtener la licencia para ejercer (como profesional); **to ~ as an engineer** sacar el título de ingeniero
2 (= *meet criteria*) **it may ~ as a medical expense** puede que cuente como gastos médicos; **to ~ as disabled, he must ...** para ser declarado minusválido, tiene que ...; **she doesn't ~ for a grant** no tiene derecho a una beca, no puede optar a una beca
3 (*Sport*) clasificarse (**for** para)
Ⓑ VT 1 (= *give qualifications, knowledge to*) **to ~ sb to do sth/ for sth** capacitar a algn para hacer algo/para algo; **the basic course does not ~ you to practise as a therapist** el curso básico no le capacita para ejercer de terapeuta
2 (= *make eligible*) **your age may ~ you for a special discount** puede que tu edad te dé derecho a un descuento especial; **that doesn't ~ him to speak on this** eso no le da derecho a hablar sobre esto
3 (= *modify*) [+ *statement, remark*] matizar; (= *limit*) [+ *support, conclusion*] condicionar
4 (= *describe*) calificar (**as** de); **some of her statements could be qualified as racist** algunos de sus comentarios se podrían calificar de racistas
qualifying [ˈkwɒlɪfaɪɪŋ] ADJ [*exam, round, game*] eliminatorio; [*team, contestant*] clasificado; **~ heat** prueba *f* clasificatoria
qualitative [ˈkwɒlɪtətɪv] ADJ cualitativo
quality [ˈkwɒlɪti] **Ⓐ** N 1 (= *standard*) calidad *f*; **of good/ high ~** de buena/alta calidad; **of poor/low ~** de mala/baja calidad; **the ~ of life** la calidad de vida
2 (= *personal attribute*) cualidad *f*; **one of his good qualities** una de sus buenas cualidades
3 (= *physical property*) propiedad *f*
Ⓑ CPD [*product, work*] de calidad; (*Brit*) [*newspaper*] serio ➤ **quality control** control *m* de calidad ➤ **the quality press** la prensa seria; ⇨ *BROADSHEETS AND TABLOIDS* ➤ **quality time: I need to spend some ~ time with my children** necesito pasar tiempo disfrutando con mis hijos; **to spend ~ time studying** pasar tiempo estudiando en serio
qualm [kwɑːm] N 1 (= *scruple*) escrúpulo *m*; **he had no ~s about throwing them out on the street** no tuvo ningún escrúpulo para echarlos a la calle 2 (= *misgiving*) duda *f*; **she signed it without a ~** no tuvo ninguna duda al firmarlo
quandary [ˈkwɒndərɪ] N dilema *m*; **to be in a ~** estar en un dilema; **he was in a ~ about whether to accept** estaba en un dilema sobre si aceptar o no
quango [ˈkwæŋgəʊ] N (*Brit*) (= **quasi-autonomous non-governmental organization**) ONG *f*, *organización no gubernamental cuasi autónoma*

QUANGO

El término **quango**, que corresponde a las siglas de **quasi-autonomous non-governmental organization**, se empezó a usar en el Reino Unido para referirse a organizaciones tales como la **Equal Opportunities Commission** o la **Race Relations Board**, que fueron establecidas por el gobierno pero que no dependen de ningún ministerio. Algunos **quangos** poseen funciones ejecutivas, mientras que otros son meramente consultivos. La práctica de poner demasiadas responsabilidades en manos de **quangos** ha sido criticada debido al hecho de que sus miembros son a menudo nombrados a dedo por el gobierno y no tienen la obligación de responder de sus actividades ante el electorado.

---

quanta [ˈkwɒntə] NPL *of* **quantum**
quantifiable [ˈkwɒntɪfaɪəbl] ADJ cuantificable

quantify ['kwɒntɪfaɪ] VT cuantificar

quantitative ['kwɒntɪtətɪv] ADJ cuantitativo

quantity ['kwɒntɪtɪ] N cantidad *f*; **in large quantities** en grandes cantidades; **unknown** ~ incógnita *f* ➤ **quantity surveyor** (*Brit*) aparejador(a) *m/f*

quantum ['kwɒntəm] Ⓐ N (*pl* **quanta**) cuanto *m*, quantum *m* Ⓑ CPD [*physics, theory, number*] cuántico ➤ **quantum leap** salto *m* espectacular

quarantine ['kwɒrəntiːn] Ⓐ N cuarentena *f*; **to be in** ~ estar en cuarentena Ⓑ VT poner en cuarentena

quarrel ['kwɒrəl] Ⓐ N (= *argument*) riña *f*, pelea *f*, disputa *f*; **to have a** ~ **with sb** reñir *or* pelearse con algn; **I have no** ~ **with you** no tengo nada en contra de usted, no tengo queja de usted Ⓑ VI reñir, pelearse; **they** ~**led** *or* (*US*) ~**ed over money** riñeron por cuestión de dinero; **I can't** ~ **with that** eso no lo discuto

quarrelling, quarreling (*US*) ['kwɒrəlɪŋ] N riñas *fpl*, disputas *fpl*, peleas *fpl*

quarrelsome ['kwɒrəlsəm] ADJ provocador, peleón*

quarry[1] ['kwɒrɪ] N (= *victim*) presa *f*

quarry[2] ['kwɒrɪ] Ⓐ N (= *mine*) cantera *f* Ⓑ VT sacar, extraer

quart [kwɔːt] N (*gen*) cuarto *m* de galón (*Brit= 1,136 litros; US= 0,946 litros*)

quarter ['kwɔːtəʳ] Ⓐ N **1** (= *fourth part*) [*of kilo, kilometre, second, moon*] cuarto *m*; [*of price, population*] cuarta parte *f*; **a** ~ **of a mile** un cuarto de milla; **a** ~ **(of a pound) of tea** un cuarto de libra de té; **for a** ~ **of the price** por la cuarta parte del precio; **to divide sth into** ~**s** dividir algo en cuartos *or* en cuatro
2 (*in time*) cuarto *m*; **a** ~ **of an hour/century** un cuarto de hora/siglo; **an hour and a** ~ una hora y cuarto; **it's a** ~ **past** *or* (*US*) **after seven** son las siete y cuarto; **it's a** ~ **to** *or* (*US*) **of seven** son las siete menos cuarto, es un cuarto para las siete (*LAm*)
3 (*US*) (= *25 cents*) (moneda *f* de) cuarto *m* de dólar
4 [*of year*] trimestre *m*; **to pay by the** ~ pagar trimestralmente *or* al trimestre *or* cada tres meses
5 (= *part of town*) barrio *m*; **the business** ~ el barrio comercial; **the old** ~ el casco viejo *or* antiguo
6 (= *direction, area*) **protest is growing in some** ~**s** las protestas aumentan en algunos círculos; **from all** ~**s** de todas partes; **at close** ~**s** de cerca
7 (*frm*) (= *mercy*) clemencia *f*
8 quarters (= *accommodation*) **8.1** (*for staff*) (= *building, section*) dependencias *fpl*; (= *rooms*) cuartos *mpl*, habitaciones *fpl*; **the servants'** ~**s** las dependencias del servicio **8.2** (= *barracks*) cuartel *msing*; (*also* **sleeping** ~**s**) barracones *mpl*
Ⓑ ADJ cuarto; **he has a** ~ **share** tiene una cuarta parte; **a** ~ **pound/century** un cuarto de libra/siglo
Ⓒ VT cortar en cuatro (trozos)
Ⓓ CPD ➤ **quarter note** (*US Mus*) negra *f* ➤ **quarter turn** cuarto *m* de vuelta

quarterback ['kwɔːtəbæk] N (*US Ftbl*) mariscal *mf* de campo

quarterdeck ['kwɔːtədek] N alcázar *m*

quarter-final [ˌkwɔːtəˈfaɪnl] N cuarto *m* de final

quarter-finalist [ˌkwɔːtəˈfaɪnəlɪst] N cuartofinalista *mf*

quarter-hour [ˌkwɔːtəˈaʊəʳ] N cuarto *m* de hora

quarterly ['kwɔːtəlɪ] Ⓐ ADV trimestralmente, cada tres meses Ⓑ ADJ trimestral Ⓒ N publicación *f* trimestral

quartermaster ['kwɔːtəˌmɑːstəʳ] N intendente *m*

quartet, quartette [kwɔːˈtet] N cuarteto *m*

quartz ['kwɔːts] N cuarzo *m* ➤ **quartz watch** reloj *m* de cuarzo

quash ['kwɒʃ] VT [+ *rebellion*] sofocar; [+ *proposal*] rechazar; [+ *verdict*] anular, invalidar

quasi- ['kweɪzaɪ, 'kwɑːzɪ] PREF cuasi-; ~**religious** cuasi-religioso; ~**revolutionary** cuasi-revolucionario

quaver ['kweɪvəʳ] Ⓐ N **1** (*when speaking*) temblor *m*; **with a** ~ **in her voice** con voz trémula **2** (*Brit*) (= *musical note*) corchea *f* Ⓑ VI temblar

quay [kiː] N muelle *m*; **on the** ~ en el muelle

quayside ['kiːsaɪd] N muelle *m*

queasy ['kwiːzɪ] ADJ (*compar* **queasier**; *superl* **queasiest**) [*stomach*] revuelto; **to be** *or* **feel** ~ tener náuseas; **the food made her (feel)** ~ la comida le revolvió el estómago; **the slight rocking made her feel** ~ el ligero balanceo la mareó

Quebec [kwɪˈbek] N Quebec *m*

queen [kwiːn] N reina *f*; (*Cards*) dama *f* ➤ **queen bee** abeja *f* reina ➤ **queen mother** reina *f* madre ➤ **Queen's Counsel** (*Brit*) abogado/a *m/f* (*de categoría superior*); ⊕ QC/KC

QUEEN'S/KING'S SPEECH

En el Reino Unido, el **Queen's** o **King's Speech** es el discurso que el monarca dirige cada año a las dos cámaras del Estado en la apertura del nuevo curso parlamentario. El discurso se retransmite por radio y televisión y es preparado por el gobierno, ya que en él se indican las directrices del programa de gobierno para el curso que comienza, así como la nueva legislación que se introducirá ese año. Para seguir con la tradición, en este discurso el monarca sigue refiriéndose al gobierno como **my government**.

---

queer [kwɪəʳ] Ⓐ ADJ (*compar* ~**er**; *superl* ~**est**) **1** (= *odd*) raro, extraño **2** (*Brit*[†]) (= *ill*) **to feel** ~ no sentirse bien, encontrarse mal **3** (*pej***) (= *homosexual*) maricón***, marica** Ⓑ N (*pej***) (= *homosexual*) maricón*** *m*, marica** *m*, mariquita** *m*

queerly ['kwɪəlɪ] ADV de modo raro *or* extraño, de forma rara *or* extraña

quell [kwel] VT [+ *uprising*] sofocar; [+ *opposition*] sobreponerse a, dominar; [+ *fears*] desechar

quench [kwentʃ] VT [+ *flames, thirst*] apagar

querulous ['kwerʊləs] ADJ quejumbroso

query ['kwɪərɪ] Ⓐ N **1** (= *question*) pregunta *f*; (= *doubt*) duda *f*, interrogante *m or f*; **if you have any queries, please do not hesitate to call** si tiene alguna pregunta, no dude en llamar **2** (= *question mark*) signo *m* de interrogación Ⓑ VT (= *ask*) preguntar; (= *doubt*) dudar de, expresar dudas acerca de; (= *disagree with, dispute*) cuestionar, poner en duda; (*Comput*) interrogar; **I would** ~ **that** dudo si eso es cierto, tengo mis dudas acerca de eso; **they queried the bill** pidieron explicaciones sobre la factura

quest [kwest] N búsqueda *f* (**for** de); **to go in** ~ **of** ir en busca de

question ['kwestʃən] Ⓐ N **1** (= *query*) (*also in exam*) pregunta *f*; **(are there) any** ~**s?** ¿(hay) alguna pregunta?; **to ask (sb) a** ~ hacer una pregunta (a algn); **ask yourself this** ~ hágase esta pregunta; **to obey orders without** ~ obedecer órdenes sin rechistar
2 (= *matter, issue*) cuestión *f*; **that is not the** ~ no se trata de eso, no es cuestión de eso; **at the time in** ~ a la hora en cuestión; **it is a** ~ **of money** es una cuestión de dinero; **this raises the** ~ **of her suitability** esto plantea la cuestión de si es la persona adecuada
3 (= *possibility*) posibilidad *f*; **there is no** ~ **of outside help** no hay posibilidad de ayuda externa; **it's out of the** ~! ¡imposible!, ¡ni hablar!
4 (= *doubt*) duda *f*; **there is no** ~ **about it** no cabe la menor duda de esto; **to bring** *or* **call sth into** ~ poner algo en duda; **to be in** ~ estar en duda; **this disaster raises** ~**s about air safety** con el desastre se ha puesto en duda la seguridad aérea; **there is some** ~ **as to whether he will sign** hay *or* existen ciertas dudas sobre si firmará; **without** ~ sin duda, indudablemente
Ⓑ VT **1** (= *interrogate*) [+ *exam candidate, interviewee*] hacer preguntas a; [+ *suspect*] interrogar; **a suspect is being** ~**ed by police** la policía está interrogando a un sospechoso; **they** ~**ed him about his past** le hicieron preguntas *or* le preguntaron acerca de su pasado
2 (= *doubt*) [+ *honesty, loyalty, motives*] dudar de, poner en duda; [+ *decision, beliefs*] poner en duda, cuestionar
Ⓒ CPD ➤ **question mark** signo *m* de interrogación; **a big** ~ **mark hangs over his future** se plantea un enorme interrogante sobre su futuro

questionable ['kwestʃənəbl] ADJ [*assumption, significance, value*] discutible, cuestionable; [*behaviour, method, practice*] cuestionable; **it is ~ whether ...** es discutible si ...; **in ~ taste** de dudoso gusto

questioner ['kwestʃənəʳ] N interrogador(a) *m/f*; (*at meeting*) interpelante *mf*

questioning ['kwestʃənɪŋ] Ⓐ ADJ [*tone, mind*] inquisitivo, inquisidor; **she gave him a ~ look** le lanzó una mirada inquisitiva *or* inquisidora Ⓑ N interrogatorio *m*; **he is wanted for ~ by police** la policía requiere su presencia para someterlo a un interrogatorio

questionnaire [,kwestʃə'neəʳ] N cuestionario *m*

queue [kjuː] (*esp Brit*) Ⓐ N cola *f*; **to stand in a ~** hacer cola Ⓑ VI (*also ~ up*) hacer cola; **to ~ for three hours** pasar tres horas haciendo cola

queue-jump ['kjuːˌdʒʌmp] VI (*Brit*) colarse*

queue-jumper ['kjuːˌdʒʌmpəʳ] N (*Brit*) colón/ona* *m/f*

queue-jumping ['kjuːˌdʒʌmpɪŋ] N (*Brit*) colarse *m*

quibble ['kwɪbl] Ⓐ N objeción *f* de poca monta Ⓑ VI hacer objeciones de poca monta; **to ~ over** *or* **about sth** discutir por algo sin importancia

quiche [kiːʃ] N quiche *m*

quick [kwɪk] Ⓐ ADJ (*compar ~er; superl ~est*) **1** (= *fast*) rápido; **this is the ~est way to do it** ésta es la forma más rápida de hacerlo; **it's ~er by train** es más rápido ir en tren; **be ~!** ¡rápido!, ¡date prisa!, ¡apúrate! (*LAm*); **he was ~ to point out that ...** señaló rápidamente que ...; **to be ~ to act** obrar con prontitud; **to be ~ to anger** enfadarse (*Sp*) *or* enojarse (*esp LAm*) con facilidad; **to be ~ to take offence** ofenderse por nada; **and be ~ about it!** ¡y date prisa!, ¡y apúrate! (*LAm*); **he gave me a ~ kiss on the cheek** me dio un besito en la mejilla; **he made a ~ recovery** se recuperó rápidamente; **to have a ~ temper** tener un genio vivo; **can I have a ~ word (with you)?** ¿puedo hablar un segundo contigo?, ¿podemos hablar un segundo?; **he's a ~ worker** trabaja rápido, es un trabajador rápido **2** (= *sharp*) [*person*] listo; [*wit*] agudo; [*mind, reflexes*] ágil, rápido; **he is very ~ at maths** es muy rápido para las matemáticas Ⓑ N **the ~: her nails were bitten down to the ~** se había mordido las uñas hasta dejárselas como muñones; ✦ IDIOM **to cut sb to the ~** herir a algn en lo vivo Ⓒ ADV deprisa, rápido; **I left as ~ as I could** me fui lo más rápido *or* deprisa que pude; **come as ~ as you can** ven cuanto antes; ✦ IDIOM **as ~ as a flash** como un rayo *or* relámpago

quick-drying ['kwɪk'draɪɪŋ] ADJ de secado rápido

quicken ['kwɪkən] Ⓐ VT (= *speed up*) acelerar, apresurar; **to ~ one's pace** apretar *or* acelerar el paso Ⓑ VI [*breathing, pulse*] acelerarse; [*interest*] acrecentarse, avivarse

quick-fire ['kwɪkfaɪəʳ] ADJ [*question*] rápido, hecho a quemarropa

quickie* ['kwɪkɪ] N **to have a ~** (= *drink*) tomarse una copita*; (= *sex*) echar un polvo rápido**

quicklime ['kwɪklaɪm] N cal *f* viva

quickly ['kwɪklɪ] ADV **1** (= *fast*) [*move, work*] deprisa, rápidamente; **I'm working as ~ as I can** estoy trabajando lo más rápido *or* lo más rápidamente que puedo, no puedo trabajar más deprisa **2** (= *with minimal delay*) [*arrive, answer, react*] en seguida, con prontitud (*more frm*); **the police were ~ on the scene** la policía llegó en seguida; **come as ~ as you can** ven cuanto antes **3** (= *not lengthily*) [*embrace, smile*] rápidamente; **he glanced ~ at the note** echó un vistazo rápido a la nota

quickness ['kwɪknɪs] N **1** (= *speed*) rapidez *f*, velocidad *f* **2** (= *lack of delay*) prontitud *f*

quicksand ['kwɪksænd] N arenas *fpl* movedizas

quick-setting ['kwɪkˌsetɪŋ] ADJ **~ glue** pegamento *m* rápido

quicksilver ['kwɪkˌsɪlvəʳ] N azogue *m*, mercurio *m*

quick-tempered ['kwɪk'tempəd] ADJ de genio vivo, irascible

quick-witted ['kwɪk'wɪtɪd] ADJ agudo, perspicaz

quid* [kwɪd] N (*pl ~*) (*Brit*) libra *f* (esterlina); **15 ~** 15 libras

quid pro quo ['kwɪdprəʊ'kwəʊ] N (*pl ~s*) compensación *f* (**for** por)

quiet ['kwaɪət] Ⓐ ADJ (*compar ~er; superl ~est*) **1** (= *not loud*) [*engine*] silencioso; [*music*] tranquilo, suave; [*laughter*] suave; **in a ~ voice** en (un) tono bajo **2** (= *silent*) [*person*] callado; **you're very ~ today** hoy estás muy callado; **be ~!** ¡cállate!, ¡silencio!; **to go ~** callarse; **to keep** *or* **stay ~** (= *say nothing*) quedarse callado; (= *not make a noise*) no hacer ruido; **to keep ~ about sth** no decir nada acerca de algo; **that book should keep him ~ for a while** ese libro le tendrá entretenido durante un rato; **he managed to keep the whole thing ~** consiguió que nadie se enterara del asunto **3** [*place, street*] silencioso; **isn't it ~!** ¡qué silencio!; ✦ IDIOM **it was ~ as the grave** había un silencio sepulcral **4** (= *peaceful, not busy*) [*life, night, village, area*] tranquilo; **this town is too ~ for me** esta ciudad es demasiado tranquila para mí; **he'll do anything for a ~ life** hará lo que sea para que lo dejen en paz; **business is ~ at this time of year** hay poco movimiento en esta época **5** (= *calm, placid*) [*person*] callado; [*temperament*] tranquilo, sosegado; [*dog, horse*] manso **6** (= *discreet*) [*manner, decor, humour*] discreto; [*clothes, dress*] discreto, no llamativo; [*colour*] suave, apagado; [*despair*] callado; [*optimism*] comedido; [*ceremony*] íntimo; **we had a ~ supper** cenamos en la intimidad; **we had a ~ laugh over it** nos reímos en privado; **it was a ~ wedding** la boda se celebró en la intimidad; **I'll have a ~ word with him** hablaré discretamente con él Ⓑ N **1** (= *silence*) silencio *m*; **let's have complete ~ for a few minutes** vamos a tener unos minutos de completo silencio; **on the ~** a escondidas **2** (= *peacefulness*) tranquilidad *f*; **there was a period of ~ after the fighting** hubo un periodo de tranquilidad tras los enfrentamientos Ⓒ VT (*esp US*) = **quieten**

⚠ **quiet ≠ quieto**

quieten ['kwaɪətn] (*esp Brit*) (*also ~ down*) Ⓐ VT (= *calm*) calmar, tranquilizar Ⓑ VI (= *calm down*) calmarse, tranquilizarse; (= *fall silent*) callarse; (*after unruly youth etc*) calmarse, sentar cabeza

quietly ['kwaɪətlɪ] ADV **1** (= *not loudly*) [*say*] en voz baja; [*sing*] en voz baja, suavemente; [*drink, leave, walk*] silenciosamente, sin hacer ruido **2** (= *silently*) en silencio; **she said nothing, but listened ~** no dijo nada, sino que escuchó en silencio **3** (= *peacefully, calmly*) [*play, read*] tranquilamente; **I was ~ drinking a cup of coffee** estaba tomando café tranquilamente; **are you coming ~ or are you going to make trouble?** ¿nos acompaña usted pacíficamente o va a causar problemas?; **I'm ~ confident about the future** aunque no lo exteriorice, soy optimista respecto al futuro **4** (= *discreetly*) discretamente; **the plan had been ~ shelved** el plan se había dejado de lado discretamente; **to be ~ dressed** vestirse con discreción; **he slipped off ~** se marchó sin que nadie lo notara

quietness ['kwaɪətnɪs] N **1** (= *softness*) [*of voice, music*] suavidad *f* **2** (= *silence*) silencio *m* **3** (= *calm*) tranquilidad *f*

quilt [kwɪlt] Ⓐ N edredón *m* Ⓑ VT acolchar

quilted ['kwɪltɪd] ADJ acolchado

quin* [kwɪn] N (*Brit*) = **quintuplet**

quintessential [,kwɪntɪ'senʃəl] ADJ quintaesencial

quince [kwɪns] N membrillo *m* ➤ **quince jelly** (dulce *m* de) membrillo *m*

quinine [kwɪ'niːn] N quinina *f*

quintessence [kwɪn'tesns] N quintaesencia *f*

quintet, quintette [kwɪn'tet] N quinteto *m*

quintuplet [kwɪn'tjuːplɪt] N quintillizo/a *m/f*

quip [kwɪp] VT **"you'll have to go on a diet!" he ~ped** —¡tendrás que ponerte a dieta! —dijo bromeando

quirk [kwɜːk] N rareza *f*; **it's just one of his little ~s** es una de sus rarezas; **by some ~ of nature** por algún capricho de la naturaleza

quirky ['kwɜːkɪ] ADJ (*compar* **quirkier**; *superl* **quirkiest**) raro, estrafalario

quit [kwɪt] (*pt, pp ~, ~ted*) **A** VT **1** (= *cease*) **to ~ doing sth** (*esp US*) dejar de hacer algo; **to ~ work** (*during job*) suspender el trabajo, dejar de trabajar; (*at end of day*) salir del trabajo; **~ stalling!** (*esp US**) ¡déjate de evasivas! **2** (= *leave*) [+ *place*] abandonar, salir de; [+ *premises*] desocupar; (*Comput*) [+ *application*] abandonar; **to ~ one's job** dejar el trabajo, renunciar a su puesto **B** VI (*esp US*) (= *go away*) irse, marcharse; (= *resign*) dimitir, renunciar; (= *stop work*) suspender el trabajo, dejar de trabajar; (= *give up*) abandonar; (*Comput*) salir; **I ~!** ¡lo dejo!; (*from job*) ¡renuncio!

quite [kwaɪt] ADV **1** (= *completely*) totalmente, completamente; **that's not ~ right** eso no es totalmente cierto; **I'm not ~ sure** no estoy del todo seguro; **it's ~ clear that ...** está clarísimo que ...; **that's ~ enough for me** eso me basta a mí; **I ~ understand** comprendo perfectamente; **I don't ~ understand it** no acabo de entenderlo; **~ frankly ...** para ser totalmente sincero ...; **he has not ~ recovered yet** no se ha repuesto todavía del todo **2** (= *exactly*) exactamente; **it's not ~ what we wanted** no es exactamente lo que queríamos; **not ~ as many as last time** no tantos como la última vez **3** (= *rather*) bastante; **it's ~ good/important** es bastante bueno/importante; **it was ~ a surprise** me sorprendió bastante; **it was ~ a shock** fue bastante chocante; **~ a lot** bastante; **there were ~ a few people there** había bastante gente allí **4** (*emphatic use*) **that's ~ a car!** ¡vaya coche!; **~ a hero** todo un héroe

quits [kwɪts] ADJ **to be ~ with sb** estar en paz con algn; **let's call it ~** (*in argument*) hagamos las paces; (*when settling bill*) digamos que quedamos en paz

quiver[1] ['kwɪvəʳ] N [*of arrows*] carcaj *m*, aljaba *f*

quiver[2] ['kwɪvəʳ] VI [*person*,] temblar, estremecerse (**with** de); [*voice*] temblar

Quixote ['kwɪksət] N Quijote; **Don ~** don Quijote

quiz [kwɪz] **A** N (*pl ~zes*) (*TV, Rad*) concurso *m*; (*in magazine*) encuesta *f*; (*US*) test *m*, prueba *f* **B** VT (= *interrogate*) interrogar (**about** sobre) **C** CPD ➤ **quiz programme**, **quiz show** programa *m* concurso

quizzical ['kwɪzɪkəl] ADJ [*glance*] burlón, socarrón

quoit [kwɔɪt] N aro *m*, tejo *m*; **quoits** juego *msing* de los aros; **to play ~s** jugar a los aros

Quorn® [kwɔːn] N *alimento a base de proteínas vegetales*

quorum ['kwɔːrəm] N quórum *m*

quota ['kwəʊtə] N (*gen*) cuota *f*; (*Comm*) cupo *m*, contingente *m*; **I've done my ~ of chores** he hecho mi parte de las tareas ➤ **quota system** sistema *m* de cuotas

quotation [kwəʊ'teɪʃən] **A** N **1** (= *words quoted*) cita *f* **2** (*Comm*) (= *estimate*) presupuesto *m* **B** CPD ➤ **quotation marks** comillas *fpl*; **in ~ marks** (*lit, fig*) entre comillas

quote [kwəʊt] **A** VT **1** (= *cite*) [+ *writer, line, passage, source*] citar; **to ~ my aunt ...** para citar a mi tía ..., como decía mi tía ...; **you can ~ me** puedes decir que te lo he dicho yo; **don't ~ me on that** no te lo puedo decir a ciencia cierta; **he is ~d as saying that ...** se le atribuye haber dicho que ... **2** (= *mention*) [+ *example*] dar, citar; [+ *reference number*] indicar; **to ~ sth/sb as an example (of sth)** poner algo/a algn como ejemplo (de algo) **3** (*Comm*) (= *estimate*) **he ~d/I was ~d a good price** me dio un presupuesto *or* precio muy razonable **4** (*Fin*) [+ *shares, company, currency*] cotizar (**at** a); **last night, Hunt shares were ~d at 346 pence** anoche las acciones Hunt cotizaron a 346 peniques; **it is not ~d on the Stock Exchange** no se cotiza en (la) Bolsa; **~d company** empresa *f* que cotiza en Bolsa **B** VI **1** (= *recite, repeat*) citar; **to ~ from the Bible** citar (palabras) de la Biblia; **he said, and I ~, ...** dijo, y cito sus propias palabras, ... **2** (*Comm*) **to ~ for sth** hacer un presupuesto de algo, presupuestar algo; **I got several firms to ~ for the building work** pedí a varias empresas que me hicieran un presupuesto *or* me presupuestaran la obra **C** N (*) **1** (= *line, passage*) cita *f* **2** (*Comm*) (= *estimate*) presupuesto *m* **3** (*St Ex*) cotización *f* **4 quotes** (= *inverted commas*) comillas *fpl*; **in ~s** entre comillas **D** EXCL **she said, ~, "he was as drunk as a lord", unquote** sus palabras textuales fueron: —estaba como una cuba; **she died in a, ~, "accident", unquote** murió en un accidente, entre comillas *or* por así decirlo; **"quote"** (*in dictation*) "comienza la cita"

quotient ['kwəʊʃənt] N cociente *m*

Rr

R¹, r [ɑːʳ] **Ⓐ** N (= *letter*) R, r *f*; **R for Robert** R de Ramón; **the three Rs** lectura, escritura y aritmética; ⇨ *THREE RS* **Ⓑ** ABBR **1** (= **river**) R. **2** (= **right**) dcha., der., der.ᵒ

R² ADJ ABBR (*US Cine*) (= **restricted**) ≈ sólo mayores

rabbi ['ræbaɪ] N rabino/a *m/f*; (*before name*) rabí *mf*

rabbit ['ræbɪt] N conejo *m* ➤ **rabbit hole** madriguera *f* ➤ **rabbit hutch** conejera *f* ➤ **rabbit on*** VI + ADV (*Brit*) cotorrear*, enrollarse (*Sp**)

rabble ['ræbl] N gentío *m*, muchedumbre *f*

rabid ['ræbɪd] ADJ [*animal*] rabioso

rabies ['reɪbiːz] NSING rabia *f*

RAC N ABBR (*Brit*) (= **Royal Automobile Club**) *servicio de asistencia para averías en carretera*, ≈ RACE *m* (*Sp*)

raccoon [rə'kuːn] N mapache *m*

race¹ [reɪs] **Ⓐ** N carrera *f*; **the ~ for the White House** la carrera hacia la Casa Blanca; **a ~ against time/the clock** una carrera contra el tiempo/contra reloj; **cycle ~** carrera *f* ciclista; **the ~s** las carreras (de caballos)
Ⓑ VT **1** (= *enter in race*) [+ *horse*] presentar
2 (= *run against*) echar una carrera a; **(I'll) ~ you home!** ¡te echo una carrera hasta casa!
Ⓒ VI **1** (= *compete*) correr, competir; **to ~ against sb** competir con algn (en una carrera)
2 (= *go fast*) correr, ir a toda velocidad; **we ~d to get back home for eight o'clock** nos dimos prisa para estar en casa para las ocho; **to ~ against time/the clock (to do sth)** trabajar contra reloj (para hacer algo); **he ~d down the street** bajó la calle corriendo *or* a toda velocidad; **he ~d past us** nos pasó a toda velocidad *or* a toda carrera; **he ~d through the paperwork as quickly as he could** hizo el papeleo todo lo rápido que pudo
3 [*pulse, heart*] acelerarse; **my mind was racing** los pensamientos me invadían la mente
Ⓓ CPD ➤ **race car** (*US*) coche *m* de carreras ➤ **race (car) driver** (*US*) piloto *mf* de carreras, corredor(a) *m/f* de coches

race² [reɪs] N (= *racial origin*) raza *f*; **the human ~** la raza humana, el género humano ➤ **race relations** relaciones *fpl* interraciales ➤ **race riot** disturbio *m* racial

racecourse ['reɪskɔːs] N hipódromo *m*

racegoer ['reɪsɡəʊəʳ] N (*esp Brit*) aficionado/a *m/f* a las carreras

racehorse ['reɪshɔːs] N caballo *m* de carreras

racetrack ['reɪstræk] N (*for runners*) pista *f*; (*for horses*) hipódromo *m*; (*for cars*) circuito *m* de carreras; (*for cycles*) velódromo *m*

racial ['reɪʃəl] ADJ racial

racially ['reɪʃəlɪ] ADV racialmente; **a ~ motivated attack** un ataque racista, un ataque por motivos racistas *or* raciales

racing ['reɪsɪŋ] N carreras *fpl*; **greyhound/horse ~** carreras *fpl* de galgos/caballos ➤ **racing bike** bicicleta *f* de carreras ➤ **racing car** coche *m* de carreras ➤ **racing driver** piloto *mf* de carreras, corredor(a) *m/f* de carreras de coches ➤ **racing pigeon** paloma *f* de carreras

racism ['reɪsɪzəm] N racismo *m*

racist ['reɪsɪst] ADJ, N racista *mf*

rack [ræk] **Ⓐ** N (= *dish rack*) escurridor *m*, escurreplatos *m inv*; (= *luggage rack*) (*Rail*) portaequipajes *m inv*, rejilla *f*; (= *roof rack*) baca *f*, portaequipajes *m inv*, parrilla *f* (*And*); **to buy clothes off the ~** (*US*) comprar ropa de confección
Ⓑ VT [*pain*] atormentar; [*cough*] sacudir; **to be ~ed by remorse** estar atormentado por el remordimiento;
✦ IDIOM **to ~ one's brains** devanarse los sesos

racket¹, racquet ['rækɪt] N (*Sport*) raqueta *f*

racket² ['rækɪt] N **1** (= *din*) [*of machine, engine*] estruendo *m*; (= *loud voices*) bulla *f*, jaleo *m*; **to make a ~** armar bulla* *or* jaleo **2** (= *fraudulent*) estafa *f*; **the drug ~** el tráfico de drogas

racketeer [rækɪ'tɪəʳ] N estafador(a) *m/f*

racketeering [rækɪ'tɪərɪŋ] N chantaje *m* sistematizado, crimen *m* organizado

raconteur [rækɒn'tɜːʳ] N anecdotista *mf*

racquet ['rækɪt] N = **racket¹**

racy ['reɪsɪ] ADJ (*compar* **racier**; *superl* **raciest**) picante

RADA ['rɑːdə] N ABBR (*Brit*) = **Royal Academy of Dramatic Art**

radar ['reɪdɑːʳ] N radar *m* ➤ **radar screen** pantalla *f* de radar ➤ **radar trap** trampa *f* de radar

radial ['reɪdɪəl] ADJ radial ➤ **radial tyre** neumático *m* radial

radiance ['reɪdɪəns] N [*of face, beauty*] lo radiante

radiant ['reɪdɪənt] ADJ **1** [*smile, person*] radiante; **to look ~** estar radiante; **~ with joy** radiante *or* rebosante de alegría **2** [*sunshine*] resplandeciente **3** (*Phys*) [*heat, light*] radiante

radiantly ['reɪdɪəntlɪ] ADV **he smiled ~** sonrió radiante; **she looked ~ happy** estaba radiante *or* rebosante de felicidad

radiate ['reɪdɪeɪt] **Ⓐ** VT (*lit, fig*) irradiar **Ⓑ** VI **to ~ from** [*lines, streets*] partir de; **hostility ~d from him** irradiaba hostilidad

radiation [reɪdɪ'eɪʃən] N radiación *f* ➤ **radiation sickness** enfermedad *f* por radiación, radiotoxemia *f* ➤ **radiation treatment** tratamiento *m* con radiaciones, radioterapia *f*

radiator ['reɪdɪeɪtəʳ] N radiador *m*

radical ['rædɪkəl] ADJ, N radical *mf*

radically ['rædɪkəlɪ] ADV [*differ, improve, reduce*] radicalmente, de forma radical; [*different, new*] radicalmente

radii ['reɪdɪaɪ] NPL *of* **radius**

radio ['reɪdɪəʊ] **Ⓐ** N radio *f*; **by ~** por radio; **over the ~** por radio; **on the ~** en *or* por la radio
Ⓑ VI **to ~ to sb** enviar un mensaje a algn por radio; **to ~ for help** pedir socorro por radio
Ⓒ VT [+ *information, news*] radiar, transmitir por radio
Ⓓ CPD ➤ **radio alarm clock** radio-reloj *m* despertador ➤ **radio announcer** locutor(a) *m/f* de radio ➤ **radio broadcast** emisión *f* de radio ➤ **radio cassette (player)** (*Brit*) radiocasete *m* ➤ **radio frequency** frecuencia *f* de radio ➤ **radio ham** radioaficionado/a *m/f* ➤ **radio operator** radiotelegrafista *mf* ➤ **radio programme, radio program** (*US*) programa *m* de radio ➤ **radio station** emisora *f* (de radio) ➤ **radio taxi** radiotaxi *m* ➤ **radio telescope** radiotelescopio *m* ➤ **radio transmitter** radiotransmisor *m* ➤ **radio wave** onda *f* de radio

radioactive ['reɪdɪəʊ'æktɪv] ADJ radiactivo, radioactivo ➤ **radioactive waste** residuos *mpl* radiactivos

radioactivity ['reɪdɪəʊæk'tɪvɪtɪ] N radiactividad *f*, radioactividad *f*

radio-controlled ['reɪdɪəʊkən'trəʊld] ADJ [*car*] teledirigido

radiographer [reɪdɪ'ɒɡrəfəʳ] N (*Brit*) radiógrafo/a *m/f*

radiologist [reɪdɪ'ɒlədʒɪst] N radiólogo/a *m/f*

radiology [reɪdɪ'ɒlədʒɪ] N radiología *f*

radiotherapy [reɪdɪəʊ'θerəpɪ] N radioterapia *f*

radish ['rædɪʃ] N rábano *m*

radium ['reɪdɪəm] N radio *m*

radius ['reɪdɪəs] N (*pl* **radii**) radio *m*; **within a ~ of 50 miles** en un radio de 50 millas

RAF N ABBR = **Royal Air Force**

raffia ['ræfɪə] N rafia *f*

raffle ['ræfl] **Ⓐ** N rifa *f*, sorteo *m* **Ⓑ** VT [+ *object*] rifar, sortear; **ten bottles will be ~d for charity** se rifarán *or* se sortearán diez botellas con fines benéficos **Ⓒ** CPD ➤ **raffle ticket** papeleta *f* de rifa

raft [rɑːft] N balsa *f*

rafter ['rɑːftəʳ] N viga *f*, cabrio *m*; **the ~s** (*loosely*) el techo

rag¹ [ræɡ] **Ⓐ** N **1** (= *piece of cloth*) trapo *m*; **rags** (= *old clothes*) harapos *mpl*, trapos *mpl* viejos; **dressed in ~s** cubierto de *or* vestido con harapos; ✦ IDIOMS **to chew the ~** (*US**) (= *chat*) charlar, pasar el rato; (= *argue*) discutir; **to lose**

one's ~ (*Brit**) perder los estribos; **from ~s to riches** de pobre a rico **2** (*) (= *newspaper*) periodicucho* *m*, periódico *m* de mala muerte* **C** CPD ➤ **rag doll** muñeca *f* de trapo ➤ **the rag trade*** la industria de la confección

rag² [ræg] (*Brit*) **A** N (= *joke*) broma *f* pesada **B** VT (*) tomar el pelo a* **C** CPD ➤ **rag week** semana *f* de funciones benéficas (estudiantiles)

RAG WEEK

Los universitarios británicos suelen organizar cada año lo que llaman **rag week**. Es costumbre que, durante esa semana, los estudiantes se disfracen y salgan así vestidos a la calle, pidiendo dinero a los transeúntes con el fin de recaudar fondos para fines benéficos.

---

ragamuffin ['rægə,mʌfɪn] N granuja *mf*

rag-and-bone man [,rægən'bəʊnmæn] N (*pl* **rag-and-bone men**) (*Brit*) trapero *m*

ragbag ['rægbæg] N mezcolanza *f*, batiburrillo *m*

rage [reɪdʒ] **A** N **1** (= *anger*) furia *f*, cólera *f*, ira *f* (**at** *or* **over sth** ante algo); **in a fit of ~** en un ataque de furia *or* cólera *or* ira; **to fly into a ~** montar en cólera, ponerse hecho una furia; **to be in a ~** estar furioso **2** (= *fashion*) **to be all the ~** hacer furor **B** VI [*person*] estar furioso (**at sth** ante algo); [*fire*] propagarse con furia; [*epidemic*] propagarse causando estragos; [*battle*] proseguir con furia; [*wind, storm*] bramar; [*sea*] enfurecerse, embravecerse; **to ~ against sth/sb** protestar furiosamente contra algo/algn, estar furioso con algo/algn; **controversy is raging over her new economic policy** hay una encendida polémica en torno a su nueva política económica

ragged ['rægɪd] ADJ **1** (= *in tatters*) [*clothes*] andrajoso, hecho jirones; [*person*] andrajoso, harapiento; ♦ IDIOM **they ran themselves ~*** sudaron tinta *or* la gota gorda **2** (= *untidy*) [*beard*] descuidado, desgreñado; [*animal's coat*] desgreñado; [*edge*] mellado, irregular; [*hole, line*] irregular; [*coastline*] accidentado, recortado

raging ['reɪdʒɪŋ] ADJ [*debate*] acalorado; [*nationalist, feminist*] acérrimo, a ultranza; [*storm*] violento, rugiente; [*temperature*] altísimo; [*thirst*] horroroso; **he was in a ~ temper*** estaba muy furioso

raid [reɪd] **A** N **1** (*into territory, across border*) incursión *f* (**into** en); (*on specific target*) asalto *m* (**on** a) **2** (*by air*) ataque *m* (aéreo) (**on** contra), bombardeo *m* (**on** de) **3** (*by police*) redada *f*; **a police ~** una redada policial **4** (*Brit*) (*by criminals*) asalto *m* (**on** a); **a bank ~** un asalto a un banco **B** VT **1** [+ *village, bank*] asaltar; [+ *territory*] invadir, hacer una incursión en **2** [*police*] llevar a cabo una redada en

raider ['reɪdəʳ] N (*across frontier*) invasor(a) *m/f*; (*Brit*) (*in bank etc*) asaltante *mf*

rail [reɪl] **A** N **1** (= *handrail*) (*on stairs, bridge, balcony*) baranda *f*, barandilla *f*, pasamanos *m inv*; (*on ship*) barandilla *f*; (*for curtains*) riel *m* **2** (*for train*) carril *m*, riel *m*; **rails** vía *f* sing; **to leave the ~s** descarrilar; **to travel by ~** viajar por ferrocarril *or* en tren; ♦ IDIOM **to go off the ~s** (*Brit**) [*person*] descarrilarse **B** CPD ➤ **rail journey** viaje *m* por ferrocarril *or* en tren ➤ **rail strike** huelga *f* de ferroviarios *or* de trenes ➤ **rail travel** viajes *mpl* por ferrocarril *or* en tren

railcard ['reɪlkɑːd] N (*Brit*) carnet *m* para obtener descuento en los ferrocarriles; **family/student's ~** carnet *m* de familia/ estudiante (*para viajes en tren*)

railing ['reɪlɪŋ] N baranda *f*, barandilla *f*, pasamanos *m inv*; **~s** verja *f* sing, enrejado *m* sing

railroad ['reɪlrəʊd] **A** N (*US*) = **railway B** VT **to ~ sb into doing sth** obligar a algn a hacer algo precipitadamente; **to ~ a bill through Parliament** hacer que se apruebe un decreto de ley sin discutirse **C** CPD ➤ **railroad crossing** paso *m* a nivel

railway ['reɪlweɪ] (*esp Brit*) N (= *system*) ferrocarril *m*, ferrocarriles *mpl*; (= *track*) vía *f*, vía *f* férrea ➤ **railway bridge** puente *m* de ferrocarril ➤ **railway carriage** (*Brit*) vagón *m*, coche *m* (de ferrocarril) ➤ **railway engine**

máquina *f*, locomotora *f* ➤ **railway line** (= *route*) línea *f* ferroviaria *or* de ferrocarril; (= *track*) vía *f* (férrea) ➤ **railway network** red *f* ferroviaria ➤ **railway station** estación *f* (de ferrocarril) ➤ **railway timetable** horario *m* de trenes

railwayman ['reɪlweɪmən] N (*pl* **railwaymen**) (*Brit*) ferroviario *m*, ferrocarrilero *m* (*Mex*)

rain [reɪn] **A** N lluvia *f*; **in the ~** bajo la lluvia; **it looks like ~** parece que va a llover; **come in out of the ~!** ¡entra, que te vas a mojar! **B** VI (*Met*) llover; **it's ~ing** está lloviendo; ♦ IDIOM **to ~ on sb's parade** (*US*) aguar la fiesta a algn; ♦ PROVS **it never ~s but it pours** (*Brit*) ◇ **when it ~s it pours** (*US*) las desgracias nunca vienen solas, siempre llueve sobre mojado **C** VT llover; ♦ IDIOM **it's ~ing cats and dogs** está lloviendo a cántaros **D** CPD ➤ **rain barrel** (*US*) tina *f* para recoger el agua de la lluvia ➤ **rain check** (*US Sport*) contraseña para usar otro día *en caso de cancelación por lluvia*; **I'll take a ~ check*** (*fig*) de momento, paso ➤ **rain cloud** nube *f* de lluvia, nubarrón *m* ➤ (*tropical*) **rain forest** pluviselva *f*, selva *f* tropical ➤ **rain off** (*Brit*), **rain out** (*US*) VT + ADV **the match was ~ed off** el partido se canceló por la lluvia

rainbow ['reɪnbəʊ] N arco *m* iris ➤ **rainbow trout** trucha *f* arco iris

raincoat ['reɪnkəʊt] N gabardina *f*, impermeable *m*

raindrop ['reɪndrɒp] N gota *f* de lluvia

rainfall ['reɪnfɔːl] N (= *showers*) precipitaciones *fpl*; (= *recorded amount*) cantidad *f* de lluvia *or* agua caída *or* registrada

rainproof ['reɪnpruːf] ADJ impermeable

rainstorm ['reɪnstɔːm] N aguacero *m*, chaparrón *m*

rainwater ['reɪnwɔːtəʳ] N agua *f* de lluvia

Use **el/un** not **la/una** before feminine nouns beginning with stressed **a** or **ha** like **agua**.

---

rainy ['reɪnɪ] ADJ (*compar* **rainier**; *superl* **rainiest**) [*climate*] lluvioso; [*day*] de lluvia, lluvioso; ♦ IDIOM **to save sth for a ~ day** [+ *money*] ahorrar algo para cuando lleguen tiempos peores ➤ **rainy season** época *f* de las lluvias

raise [reɪz] **A** VT **1** (= *lift*) [+ *fallen object, weight, hand*] levantar, alzar; [+ *hat*] levantarse; [+ *blinds, window*] subir; [+ *flag*] izar; [+ *eyebrows*] arquear; **to ~ one's glass to sth/sb** brindar por algo/algn **2** (= *increase*) [+ *prices, salaries, taxes*] aumentar, subir; [+ *temperature*] subir, aumentar, elevar; [+ *standard, level*] subir; [+ *age limit*] extender; [+ *awareness, consciousness*] aumentar; **we want to ~ the profile of rugby** queremos realzar la imagen del rugby; **don't you ~ your voice to me!** ¡no me levantes or alces la voz! **3** (= *erect*) [+ *building, statue*] erigir, levantar **4** (= *bring up*) [+ *child, livestock*] criar; **the house where she was ~d** la casa donde se crió **5** (= *produce*) [+ *laugh*] provocar; [+ *doubts, fears*] suscitar; [+ *suspicion*] levantar, despertar; **his speech ~d a cheer from the crowd** su discurso suscitó una ovación del público; **she could barely ~ a smile** apenas pudo sonreír **6** (= *present, put forward*) [+ *question, possibility*] plantear; [+ *subject*] sacar; **I'll ~ the point with them** se lo mencionaré; **you'll have to ~ that with the director** tendrás que plantearle *or* comentarle eso al director; **to ~ objections to sth** poner objeciones *or* peros a algo **7** (= *get together*) [+ *funds, money*] recaudar; [+ *capital*] movilizar; [+ *loan*] conseguir, obtener; [+ *army*] reclutar; **to ~ money for charity** recaudar dinero con fines benéficos **8** (*Cards*) **I'll ~ you!** ¡subo la apuesta!; **I'll ~ you £10** te subo diez libras más **B** N (*esp US*) (*in salary*) aumento *m*, subida *f*; (*in taxes*) subida *f*

raised [reɪzd] ADJ [*platform*] elevado; [*temperature, blood pressure, level*] alto, elevado; [*voice*] exaltado

raisin ['reɪzən] N pasa *f*, uva *f* pasa

raison d'être ['reɪzɔːn'dɛːtr] N razón *f* de ser

rake¹ [reɪk] **A** N (= *tool*) rastrillo *m* **B** VT **1** [+ *leaves, soil*] rastrillar; [+ *fire*] hurgar **2** (= *strafe*) [+ *ship, men*] barrer

➤ **rake in** (*) VT + ADV **to ~ it in** acuñar dinero
➤ **rake up** VT + ADV [+ *subject*] sacar a relucir; [+ *memories, the past*] remover; **why did you have to ~ that up?** ¿para qué has vuelto a mencionar eso?

rake² [reɪk] N (= *man*) calavera *m*; **old ~** viejo *m* verde

rake-off* ['reɪkɒf] N comisión *f*, tajada* *f*

rakish ['reɪkɪʃ] ADJ **1** [*person*] libertino, disoluto **2 at a ~ angle** ladeado

rally ['rælɪ] **Ⓐ** N **1** (= *mass meeting*) (*gen*) concentración *f*; (*with speeches*) mitin *m* **2** (*Aut*) rally *m* **3** (*Tennis*) intercambio *m* de golpes **4** (= *revival*) recuperación *f* **Ⓑ** VT (*Pol*) concentrar; (*Mil*) reunir; (= *revitalize*) levantar el ánimo de, fortalecer el espíritu de **Ⓒ** VI **1 to ~ behind sb** ◇ **~ to sb's side** solidarizarse con algn **2** (= *recover*) recuperarse; (= *improve*) mejorar **Ⓓ** CPD ➤ **rally car** coche *m* de rally ➤ **rally driver** piloto *mf* de rally
➤ **rally around, rally round** (*Brit*) VI + ADV **everyone must ~ around** todos tenemos que cooperar; **we all rallied around to help** todos nos juntamos para ayudar

rallying ['rælɪɪŋ] CPD ➤ **rallying call, rallying cry** llamamiento *m* (*para reanimar la resistencia etc*) ➤ **rallying point** punto *m* de reunión

RAM [ræm] N ABBR (= **random access memory**) RAM *f*

ram [ræm] **Ⓐ** N carnero *m*
Ⓑ VT **1** (= *force*) **to ~ clothes into a case** meter la ropa a la fuerza en una maleta; **to ~ a hat down on one's head** incrustarse el sombrero; **to ~ a nail into a wall** incrustar un clavo en una pared; **they ~ their ideas down your throat** te hacen tragar sus ideas a la fuerza
2 (= *collide with*) (*deliberately*) embestir contra; (*accidentally*) chocar con *or* contra
Ⓒ CPD ➤ **ram raid*** robo *m* (*rompiendo el escaparate etc con un coche*) ➤ **ram raider*** ladrón/ona *m/f* (*que entra en el establecimiento rompiendo el escaparate etc con un coche*)

Ramadan [ˌræmə'dæn] N ramadán *m*

ramble ['ræmbl] **Ⓐ** N (*esp Brit*) (= *walk*) vuelta *f* pl; (*longer*) excursión *f*; **to go for a ~** ir a andar un rato
Ⓑ VI **1** (*esp Brit*) (= *walk*) pasear; **we spent a week rambling in the hills** pasamos una semana de excursión en la montaña *or* la sierra **2** (*in speech*) divagar, perder el hilo; **he just ~d on and on** siguió divagando

rambler ['ræmblə'] N (*Brit*) excursionista *mf* (a pie)

rambling ['ræmblɪŋ] **Ⓐ** ADJ [*speech, book*] farragoso, inconexo **Ⓑ** N (*esp Brit*) excursionismo *m* (a pie)

ramification [ˌræmɪfɪ'keɪʃən] N ramificación *f*; **in all its ~s** en toda su complejidad

ramp [ræmp] N rampa *f*

rampage [ræm'peɪdʒ] N **to go on the ~** desbocarse, desmandarse

rampant ['ræmpənt] ADJ [*inflation*] galopante; **anarchism is ~ here** aquí el anarquismo está muy extendido

rampart ['ræmpɑːt] N muralla *f*

ramrod ['ræmrɒd] N baqueta *f*

ramshackle ['ræmˌʃækl] ADJ [*house*] destartalado

ran [ræn] PT of **run**

ranch [rɑːntʃ] N rancho *m*, hacienda *f* (de ganado) (*LAm*), estancia *f* (*SC*) ➤ **ranch hand** peón *m*

rancher ['rɑːntʃə'] N ganadero/a *m/f*, ranchero/a *m/f*

rancid ['rænsɪd] ADJ rancio

rancour, rancor (*US*) ['ræŋkə'] N rencor *m*

R & D [ˌɑːrən'diː] N ABBR (= **research and development**) I + D, I & D

random ['rændəm] **Ⓐ** ADJ (= *haphazard*) [*selection, arrangement*] hecho al azar; [*sample, distribution*] aleatorio **Ⓑ** N **at ~** al azar; **we picked the number at ~** elegimos el número al azar; **to hit out at ~** repartir golpes por todos lados **Ⓒ** CPD ➤ **random access memory** memoria *f* de acceso aleatorio ➤ **random number** número *m* al azar

R & R [ˌɑːrən'ɑː'] N ABBR (*US*) (= **rest and recreation**) descanso *m*

randy* ['rændɪ] ADJ (*compar* **randier**; *superl* **randiest**) (*Brit*) (= *aroused*) caliente**, cachondo (*Sp****), arrecho (*LAm**)

rang [ræŋ] PT of **ring²**

range [reɪndʒ] **Ⓐ** N **1** [*of hills*] cadena *f*; **a ~ of mountains** una cadena montañosa *or* de montañas, una cordillera **2** (= *extent*) **your weight is within the normal ~** su peso está dentro de lo normal **3** (*Mus*) [*of instrument, voice*] registro *m* **4** (= *selection, variety*) **4.1** (*gen*) variedad *f*; **there was a wide ~ of opinions** había gran variedad de opiniones, las opiniones variaban mucho; **she has a wide ~ of interests** tiene muchos y diversos intereses **4.2** (*Comm*) (= *product line*) línea *f*; (= *selection*) gama *f*, selección *f*; **they come in a ~ of sizes** vienen en varios *or* diversos tamaños **5** [*of gun, missile*] alcance *m*; [*of plane, ship*] autonomía *f*, radio *m* de acción; [*of transmitter*] radio *m* de acción; **within ~ (of sth/sb)** (*Mil, also fig*) a tiro (de algo/algn); **to come within ~ (of sth/sb)** (*Mil, also fig*) ponerse a tiro (de algo/algn); **out of ~ (of sth/sb)** (*Mil, also fig*) fuera del alcance (de algo/algn) **6** (= *distance from target*) distancia *f*; **at close ~** de cerca, a corta distancia; **at long ~** de lejos, a larga distancia **7** (*US Agr*) pradera *f*, pampa *f* (*SC*), llano *m* (*esp Ven*) **8** (*also* **shooting ~**) campo *m* de tiro **9** (*Brit*) (*also* **kitchen ~**) fogón *m* **10** (*US*) cocina *f*, estufa *f* (*LAm*) **Ⓑ** VT (= *line up*) alinear; **chairs were ~d against one wall** las sillas estaban alineadas frente a una pared **Ⓒ** VI **1** (= *extend*) extenderse; **the search ~d over the whole country** se llevó a cabo la búsqueda por todo el país; **the conversation ~d over many issues** la conversación abarcó muchos temas **2** (= *vary*) **prices ~ from £3 to £9** los precios varían de tres a nueve libras, los precios oscilan entre las tres y las nueve libras; **the women ~d in age from 14 to 40** la edad de las mujeres iba de los 14 a los 40 años *or* oscilaba entre los 14 y los 40 años

ranger ['reɪndʒə'] N (= *forest ranger*) guardabosques *mf inv*

rank¹ [ræŋk] **Ⓐ** N **1** (= *status*) rango *m*, categoría *f*; (*Mil*) grado *m*, rango *m*; **to attain the ~ of major** ser ascendido a comandante, llegar a(l grado de) comandante; **✦ IDIOM to pull ~*** aprovecharse de tener un rango superior **2** (= *row*) fila *f*, hilera *f*, línea *f*; **to break ~(s)** romper filas; **to close ~s** (*Mil, also fig*) cerrar filas; **the ~ and file** (*Mil*) los soldados rasos; (*Pol*) la base; **the ~s** (*Mil*) la tropa; **to rise from the ~s** ascender desde soldado raso **3** (*esp Brit*) (*also* **taxi ~**) parada *f* de taxis **Ⓑ** VT clasificar; **he's ~ed third** está clasificado tercero; **I ~ her among ...** yo la pongo entre ...; **she was ~ed as (being) ...** se la consideraba ... **Ⓒ** VI **to ~ fourth** ocupar el cuarto lugar; **to ~ second to sb** tener el segundo lugar después de algn; **to ~ above sb** ser superior a *or* sobrepasar a algn; **to ~ among ...** figurar entre ...; **to ~ high** ocupar una posición privilegiada; **to ~ with** ser igual a

rank² [ræŋk] ADJ **1** (= *smelly*) maloliente, apestoso; **to smell ~** oler mal **2** (= *utter*) [*hypocrisy, injustice*] manifiesto, absoluto; [*beginner, outsider*] completo, puro

ranking ['ræŋkɪŋ] N **1** ránking *m*; (*Mil*) graduación *f* **2 rankings** (*Sport*) clasificación *fsing*, ránking *msing*

rankle ['ræŋkl] VI doler; **the fact that he won still ~s with me** todavía me duele *or* me molesta el hecho de que él haya ganado

ransack ['rænsæk] VT **1** (= *search*) registrar de arriba abajo; **they ~ed the house for arms** registraron la casa de arriba abajo buscando armas **2** (= *pillage*) saquear; [+ *house, shop*] desvalijar; **the place had been ~ed** el lugar había sido saqueado

ransom ['rænsəm] N rescate *m*; **to hold sb (to) ~** (*Brit*) ◇ **hold sb for ~** (*US*) pedir un rescate por algn; (*fig*) poner a algn entre la espada y la pared ➤ **ransom demand** petición *f* de rescate

rant [rænt] **Ⓐ** VI despotricar; **to ~ at sb** (= *be angry*) ponerse hecho una furia con algn, ponerse hecho un(a) energúmeno/a con algn; **to ~ on about sb** (*angrily*) echar pestes de algn; **to ~ and rave** despotricar (**about** contra) **Ⓑ** N diatriba *f*

rap [ræp] **Ⓐ** N **1** golpecito *m*, golpe *m* seco; **there was a ~**

at the door llamaron (suavemente) a la puerta; **to give sb a ~ on the knuckles** leer la cartilla a algn
2 (= *blame*) **to take the ~*** pagar los platos rotos*; **to take the ~ for sth** cargar con la culpa de algo
3 (*esp US**) (= *charge*) acusación *f*; **murder ~** acusación *f* de homicidio
4 (*Mus*) rap *m*
Ⓑ VT **to ~ sb on the knuckles** (*lit*) dar a algn en los nudillos; (*fig*) leer la cartilla a algn
Ⓒ VI **1** (= *knock*) **to ~ at the door** llamar a la puerta
2 (*Mus*) hacer rap

rapacious [rə'peɪʃəs] ADJ rapaz

rape¹ [reɪp] **Ⓐ** N (= *crime*) violación *f*; **attempted ~** intento *m* de violación **Ⓑ** VT violar

rape² [reɪp] N (= *crop*) colza *f*

rapeseed ['reɪpsiːd] N semilla *f* de colza **➤ rapeseed oil** aceite *m* de colza

rapid ['ræpɪd] ADJ rápido **➤ rapid reaction force** fuerza *f* de reacción rápida

rapid-fire ['ræpɪd,faɪə] ADJ [*gun*] de fuego racheado; (*fig*) trepidante; **a ~ succession of questions** una sucesión trepidante de preguntas

rapidity [rə'pɪdɪtɪ] N rapidez *f*

rapidly ['ræpɪdlɪ] ADV rápidamente, rápido

rapids ['ræpɪdz] NPL rápidos *mpl*

rapier ['reɪpɪə] N estoque *m*

rapist ['reɪpɪst] N violador(a) *m/f*

rappel [ræ'pel] VI (*US*) hacer rappel, descender en rappel; **he ~led down the rock** hizo rappel roca abajo

rapper ['ræpə] N músico *mf* de rap

rapport [ræ'pɔː] N relación *f*; **I have a good ~ with him** tengo muy buena relación con él, me entiendo muy bien con él

rapprochement [ræ'prɒʃmɑ̃] N acercamiento *m*

rapt [ræpt] ADJ **they were sitting with ~ attention** estaban sentados prestando mucha atención

rapture ['ræptʃə] N éxtasis *m inv*; **to be in ~s** (*esp Brit*) estar extasiado, extasiarse; **to go into ~s over sth** (*esp Brit*) extasiarse con algo

rapturous ['ræptʃərəs] ADJ entusiasta

rare [rɛə] ADJ (*compar* **~r**; *superl* **~st**) **1** [*item, book*] raro; [*plant, animal*] poco común; [*ability, opportunity*] excepcional; [*case, occurrence*] poco frecuente; **it is ~ to find that ...** es raro encontrarse con que ...; **on the ~ occasions when he spoke** en las poquísimas ocasiones en las que hablaba **2** [*steak, meat*] vuelta y vuelta, poco hecho (*Sp*)

rarefied ['rɛərɪfaɪd] ADJ enrarecido

rarely ['rɛəlɪ] ADV casi nunca, rara vez, raramente

raring ['rɛərɪŋ] ADJ **to be ~ to do sth** tener muchas ganas de hacer algo; **to be ~ to go** tener muchas ganas de empezar

rarity ['rɛərɪtɪ] N **1** (= *scarcity*) rareza *f* **2** (= *rare thing*) rareza *f*, cosa *f* rara

rascal ['rɑːskəl] N granuja *mf*

rash¹ [ræʃ] N **1** (*Med*) sarpullido *m*, erupción *f* (cutánea); **I've got a ~ on my chest** tengo un sarpullido *or* una erupción en el pecho; **she came out in a ~** le salieron ronchas en la piel **2** (= *spate*) racha *f*, avalancha *f*

rash² [ræʃ] ADJ [*act, statement*] temerario, precipitado; [*person*] temerario, imprudente

rasher ['ræʃə] N (*Brit*) **a ~ of bacon** una loncha de beicon

rashly ['ræʃlɪ] ADV temerariamente

rasp [rɑːsp] **Ⓐ** N (= *tool*) escofina *f*, raspador *m*; (= *sound*) chirrido *m*. **Ⓑ** VT (*gen*) decir con voz áspera; [+ *order*] espetar

raspberry ['rɑːzbərɪ] N **1** (= *fruit*) frambuesa *f* **2 to blow a ~** (*Brit**) hacer una pedorreta*

rasping ['rɑːspɪŋ] ADJ [*voice*] áspero; [*noise*] chirriante

Rasta* ['ræstə], **Rastafarian** [,ræstə'fɛərɪən] ADJ, N rastafario/a *m/f*

---

rat [ræt] **Ⓐ** N **1** (= *animal*) rata *f*; **✦** IDIOMS **I smell a ~** aquí hay gato encerrado, aquí se está tramando algo; **he could smell a ~** se olió algo (sospechoso), le olió a gato encerrado
2 (= *person*) **you dirty ~!*** ¡canalla!*
Ⓑ VI (*) **to ~ on sb** (= *inform on*) chivarse de algn; **to ~ on a deal** rajarse de un negocio
Ⓒ CPD **➤ rat pack** (*Brit*) paparazzi *mpl* **➤ rat poison** matarratas *m inv* **➤ the rat race** la lucha por la supervivencia, la competencia; **it's a ~ race** es un mundo muy competitivo **➤ rat trap** trampa *f* para ratas, ratonera *f*

rat-a-tat [,rætə'tæt], **rat-a-tat-tat** [,rætə,tæt'tæt] N (*at door*) golpecitos *mpl*; [*of machine-gun*] martilleo *m*

ratatouille [,rætə'twiː] N ≈ pisto *m*

ratcatcher ['rætˌkætʃə] N cazarratas *mf inv*, cazador(a) *m/f* de ratas

ratchet ['rætʃɪt] N trinquete *m*

rate [reɪt] **Ⓐ** N **1** (= *proportion, ratio*) **birth ~** índice *m or* tasa *f* de natalidad, natalidad *f*; **death ~** índice *m or* tasa *f* de mortalidad, mortalidad *f*; **the failure/success ~ for this exam is high** el índice de suspensos/aprobados en este examen es alto; **at a ~ of** a razón de
2 (= *speed*) (*gen*) velocidad *f*; [*of work*] ritmo *m*; **at an alarming ~** a una velocidad alarmante; **at a ~ of knots*** a toda pastilla*; **at this ~** a este paso; **at the ~ you're going, you'll be dead before long** al paso que vas no vas a durar mucho
3 (= *price*) (*for tickets*) precio *m*; [*of hotel, telephone service*] tarifa *f*; **there is a reduced ~ for children under 12** a los niños menores de 12 años se les hace un descuento, hay una tarifa reducida para niños menores de 12 años; **they were paid a ~ of £5 an hour** les pagaban a razón de cinco libras la hora; **the ~ for the job** el sueldo que corresponde al trabajo; **~s of pay** sueldos *mpl*
4 (*Fin*) [*of stocks*] cotización *f*; **bank ~** tipo *m* de interés bancario; **~ of exchange** (tipo *m* de) cambio *m*; **~ of inflation** tasa *f* de inflación; **~ of interest** tipo *m or* tasa *f* de interés
5 rates (*Brit*) (*formerly*) contribución *fsing* municipal, impuesto *msing* municipal
6 at any ~ (= *at least*) al menos, por lo menos; (= *anyway*) en todo caso
Ⓑ VT **1** (= *consider*) considerar; **how do you ~ her?** ¿qué opinas de ella?; **she is ~d fifth in the world** ocupa el quinto lugar en la clasificación mundial; **I ~ the book highly** tengo muy buena opinión del libro; **I ~ him highly** lo tengo en muy alta estima
2 (*esp Brit**) (= *regard as good*) **I don't ~ your chances** creo que tienes pocas posibilidades; **I don't ~ him (as a composer)** no le valoro (como compositor)
Ⓒ VI **to ~ as**: **it must ~ as one of the most boring films around** debe de estar considerada una de las películas más aburridas del momento

rate-capping ['reɪtˌkæpɪŋ] N (*Brit*) (*formerly*) *limitación de la contribución municipal impuesta por el Estado*

ratepayer ['reɪtpeɪə] N (*Brit*) (*formerly*) contribuyente *mf*

rather ['rɑːðə] ADV **1** (*preference*) **we decided to camp, ~ than stay at a hotel** decidimos acampar, en lugar de quedarnos en un hotel; **anything ~ than that!** (*hum*) ¡cualquier cosa menos eso!; **~ you than me!** ¡allá tú!; **"would you like a sweet?" — "I'd ~ have an apple"** —¿quieres un caramelo? —preferiría una manzana; **I'd ~ stay in tonight** preferiría no salir esta noche; **I'd ~ he didn't come to the party** preferiría que no viniera a la fiesta; **I'd ~ not say** prefiero no decirlo
2 (= *somewhat*) algo, un poco; **he looks ~ like his mother** se parece un poco a su madre; **I feel ~ more happy today** hoy me siento algo más contento
3 (= *quite*) bastante; **it's ~ a difficult task** es una tarea bastante difícil; **he did ~ well in the exam** le fue bastante *or* muy bien en el examen; **"isn't she pretty?" — "yes, she is ~"** —¿es guapa, eh? —sí, bastante *or* mucho; **there's ~ a lot** hay un poco más de la cuenta; **£20! that's ~ a lot, isn't it?** ¡20 libras! es mucho *or* demasiado, ¿no?
4 (= *more accurately*) **or ~** o mejor dicho, es decir

ratification [,rætɪfɪ'keɪʃən] N ratificación *f*

ratify ['rætɪfaɪ] VT ratificar

rating ['reɪtɪŋ] N 1 (= *ranking*) **each wine was given a ~ out of ten** cada vino recibió una puntuación del uno al diez; **Labour's ~s in the polls are high** las encuestas demuestran que el partido laborista goza de un alto nivel de popularidad 2 (*TV, Rad*) **ratings** índice *msing* de audiencia 3 (*Brit*) (= *sailor*) marinero *m*

ratio ['reɪʃɪəʊ] N razón *f*; **in the ~ of two to one** a razón de dos a uno; **in direct ~ to** en proporción *or* razón directa con; **the ~ of wages to raw materials** la relación entre los sueldos y las materias primas

ration ['ræʃən] Ⓐ N (= *portion*) ración *f*, porción *f*; **rations** (*Mil etc*) víveres *mpl*, suministro *msing* Ⓑ VT (*also ~ out*) racionar; **they are ~ed to one kilo a day** están racionados a un kilo por día Ⓒ CPD ➤ **ration book, ration card** cartilla *f* de racionamiento

rational ['ræʃənl] ADJ [*explanation*] racional, lógico; [*person*] (= *reasonable*) razonable; (= *sane*) sensato, cuerdo; **the ~ thing to do would be to ...** lo lógico *or* racional sería ...

rationale [ræʃə'nɑːl] N base *f*, fundamento *m*; **the ~ of or behind sth** la razón fundamental de algo

rationalization [ˌræʃnəlaɪ'zeɪʃən] N 1 [*of ideas*] racionalización *f* 2 (= *reorganization*) reconversión *f*, reorganización *f*

rationalize ['ræʃnəlaɪz] VT 1 [+ *ideas*] racionalizar 2 [+ *industry*] reconvertir, reorganizar

rationally ['ræʃnəlɪ] ADV racionalmente

rationing ['ræʃnɪŋ] N racionamiento *m*

rattle ['rætl] Ⓐ N 1 (= *sound*) [*of cart, train, gunfire*] traqueteo *m*; [*of window, chains, stone in tin*] ruido *m* 2 (= *toy*) (*child's*) sonajero *m*, sonajas *fpl* (*Mex*); (*football fan's*) carraca *f*, matraca *f* Ⓑ VT 1 (= *shake*) **the wind ~d the window** el viento hizo vibrar la ventana; **he banged on the table, rattling the cups** golpeó la mesa, haciendo que las tazas tintinearan; **he ~d the tin** agitó la lata (*haciendo sonar lo que tenía dentro*); **she ~d the door handle** sacudió el picaporte de la puerta 2 (= *disconcert*) [+ *person*] desconcertar; **to get ~d** ponerse nervioso, perder la calma Ⓒ VI [*cart, train*] traquetear; [*window, chains, stone in tin*] sonar, hacer ruido
➤ **rattle off** VT + ADV recitar de un tirón *or* una tirada
➤ **rattle on*** VI + ADV parlotear (sin parar)

rattlesnake ['rætlsneɪk] N serpiente *f* de cascabel, yarará *f* (*And*)

rattling ['rætlɪŋ] ADJ **at a ~ pace** muy rápidamente, a gran velocidad

ratty* ['rætɪ] ADJ (*compar* **rattier**; *superl* **rattiest**) 1 (*Brit*) (= *bad-tempered*) **to be/get ~** estar/ponerse de malas 2 (*US*) (= *shabby*) andrajoso

raucous ['rɔːkəs] ADJ chillón, estridente

raunchy* ['rɔːntʃɪ] ADJ (*compar* **raunchier**; *superl* **raunchiest**) [*story, film, song*] picante, atrevido; [*person*] sexy, provocativo; [*clothing*] atrevido, provocativo

ravage ['rævɪdʒ] Ⓐ N **ravages** estragos *mpl*; **the ~s of time** los estragos del tiempo Ⓑ VT hacer estragos en; **the region was ~d by floods** las inundaciones hicieron estragos en la región, la región fue asolada por las inundaciones

rave [reɪv] Ⓐ VI 1 (= *be delirious*) delirar, desvariar 2 (= *talk furiously*) despotricar 3 (= *talk enthusiastically*) **to ~ about sth** entusiasmarse por algo; **to ~ about sb** pirrarse por algn* Ⓑ N (*Brit**) fiesta *f* acid* Ⓒ CPD ➤ **rave review** reseña *f* entusiasta; **the play got ~ reviews** los críticos pusieron la obra por las nubes

raven ['reɪvn] N cuervo *m*

ravenous ['rævənəs] ADJ 1 (= *starving*) hambriento; **I'm ~!** ¡me comería un toro! 2 (= *voracious*) voraz

raver* ['reɪvəʳ] N (*Brit*) juerguista* *mf*, marchoso/a** *m/f*

ravine [rə'viːn] N barranco *m*, quebrada *f* (*esp LAm*)

raving ['reɪvɪŋ] Ⓐ ADJ **he's a ~ lunatic** está loco de remate Ⓑ ADV **you must be ~ mad!** ¡tú estás loco de atar!

ravings ['reɪvɪŋz] NPL delirio *msing*, desvarío *msing*

ravioli [ˌrævɪ'əʊlɪ] N ravioles *mpl*, ravioli *mpl*

ravishing ['rævɪʃɪŋ] ADJ [*smile*] encantador; [*woman*]
bellísimo; **you look ~** estás deslumbrante

raw [rɔː] Ⓐ ADJ 1 (= *uncooked*) crudo 2 (= *unprocessed*) [*sugar*] sin refinar; [*spirit*] puro; [*silk*] crudo, salvaje; [*cotton*] en rama, sin refinar; [*sewage*] sin tratar 3 (= *sore*) **to be red and ~** estar en carne viva; **his wife's words touched a ~ nerve** las palabras de su mujer le dieron donde más le dolía *or* le dieron en lo más sensible 4 (= *basic*) [*anger, hate, ambition*] puro; [*talent*] en bruto 5 (= *inexperienced*) [*person, troops*] novato, inexperto 6 (*) (= *unfair*) **he got a ~ deal** lo trataron injustamente; **he's got a ~ deal from life** la vida lo ha tratado mal Ⓑ CPD ➤ **raw materials** materias *fpl* primas

rawhide ['rɔːhaɪd] N (*US*) cuero *m* crudo *or* sin curtir

ray¹ [reɪ] N [*of light, heat, sun, hope*] rayo *m*

ray² [reɪ] N (= *fish*) raya *f*

rayon ['reɪɒn] N rayón *m*

raze [reɪz] VT (*also ~ to the ground*) arrasar, asolar

razor ['reɪzəʳ] N (*open*) navaja *f*, chaveta *f* (*Per*); (*safety*) maquinilla *f* de afeitar; **electric ~** máquina *f* de afeitar ➤ **razor blade** hoja *f* or cuchilla *f* de afeitar

razor-sharp ['reɪzə'ʃɑːp] ADJ [*edge*] muy afilado; [*mind*] agudo, perspicaz

razzle* ['ræzl] N **to be/go on the ~** estar/ir de juerga*

razzmatazz* [ˌræzmə'tæz] N bombo *m* publicitario

RC ABBR = **Roman Catholic**

Rd ABBR = (**road**) C/, ctra.

RE N ABBR (*Brit*) (= **religious education**) religión *f*, educación *f* religiosa, ed. religiosa

re [riː] PREP (= *concerning*) relativo a, respecto a; **re my previous account** con referencia a mi cuenta anterior

reach [riːtʃ] Ⓐ VT 1 [+ *place, person, stage, age, compromise*] llegar a; [+ *speed, level*] alcanzar, llegar a; [+ *goal, target*] lograr; [+ *decision*] tomar; **by the time I ~ed her she was dead** cuando llegué a donde estaba, la encontré muerta; **the cancer had already ~ed her liver** el cáncer ya le había llegado al hígado; **we hope to ~ a wider <u>audience</u>** esperamos llegar a un público más variado; **to ~ <u>home</u>** llegar a casa; **she ~ed the <u>semi-finals</u>** llegó hasta las semifinales 2 (= *stretch to*) alcanzar; **he is tall enough to ~ the top shelf** es lo suficientemente alto como para alcanzar el estante de arriba del todo 3 (= *contact*) [+ *person*] ponerse en contacto con, contactar 4 (*US Jur*) [+ *witness*] sobornar Ⓑ VI 1 (= *stretch out hand*) alargar la mano (**for sth** para tomar *or* coger algo); **~ for the sky!** (*US**) ¡arriba las manos!; **she ~ed <u>into</u> her bag** metió la mano en el bolso; **she ~ed <u>up</u> and put the book on the shelf** alargó la mano y puso el libro en el estante; ✦ IDIOM **to ~ for the stars** apuntar muy alto 2 (= *extend*) [*land*] extenderse (**to, as far as** hasta); [*clothes, curtains, water level*] llegar (**to, up to** a) 3 (= *stretch far enough*) [*person*] alcanzar; [*cable, hose*] llegar; **can you ~?** ¿alcanzas?; **it <u>won't</u> ~** no va a llegar Ⓒ N 1 alcance *m*; **the price is <u>beyond</u> the ~ of ordinary people** el precio está fuera del alcance de la gente corriente; **<u>out of</u> ~** fuera del alcance; **the gun was just out of ~** la pistola estaba justo fuera de su alcance; **<u>within</u> sb's ~** (*lit*) al alcance (de la mano) de algn; **cars are within everyone's ~ nowadays** ahora los coches están al alcance (del bolsillo) de cualquiera; **the shops are within easy ~** las tiendas están cerca *or* a mano 2 **the upper/lower ~es of the Amazon** la cuenca alta/baja del Amazonas; **the outer ~es of the solar system** los límites exteriores del sistema solar

react [riː'ækt] VI reaccionar

reaction [riː'ækʃən] N reacción *f*; **to have quick/slow ~s** reaccionar rápidamente/lentamente; **his ~s were slow because he'd been drinking** tardaba en reaccionar porque había estado bebiendo

reactionary [riː'ækʃənrɪ] ADJ, N reaccionario/a *m/f*

reactor [riː'æktəʳ] N reactor *m*

read [riːd] (*pt, pp ~* [red]) Ⓐ VT 1 [+ *book, poem, story,* music, sign] leer; **can you ~ Russian?** ¿sabes leer en ruso?; **I can't ~ your writing** no entiendo tu letra, no puedo leer tu letra; **to ~ sb sth** leer algo a algn; **to ~ sb's lips** leer los labios a algn; ✦ IDIOM **to take sth as ~** dar algo por sentado **2** (*esp Brit*) (= *study*) estudiar, cursar estudios de; **to ~ chemistry** estudiar química, cursar estudios de química **3** (= *interpret*) [+ *map, meter, thermometer*] leer; [+ *information, remarks, expression, situation*] interpretar; [+ *person*] entender; **to ~ sth as sth** interpretar algo como algo; **to ~ the future** leer *or* adivinar el porvenir; **to ~ sb's hand** *or* **palm** leer la mano a algn; **you're ~ing too much into it** le estás dando demasiada importancia; **to ~ sb's mind** leer el pensamiento a algn, adivinar el pensamiento a algn **4** (*Telec*) **do you ~ me?** ¿me oye?; **I ~ you loud and clear** le oigo perfectamente **5** (= *show*) [*thermometer, instrument*] indicar, marcar **6** (*Comput*) leer **Ⓑ** VI **1** [*person*] leer; **I ~ about it in the papers** lo leí en los periódicos; **I've ~ about him** he leído sobre *or* acerca de él; **to ~ aloud** leer en voz alta; **to ~ to o.s.** leer para sí; ✦ IDIOM **to ~ between the lines** leer entre líneas **2** (= *give impression*) **the book ~s well** el libro está bien escrito; **his article ~s like an official report** su artículo está escrito como un informe oficial **Ⓒ** N lectura *f*; **it's a good ~** es un libro ameno; **I was having a quiet ~** leía tranquilamente ➤ **read back Ⓐ** VT + ADV volver a leer; **can you ~ it back to me?** ¿puedes volvérmelo a leer? **Ⓑ** VI + ADV **I was ~ing back over my notes** estaba releyendo *or* repasando mis apuntes ➤ **read on** VI + ADV seguir leyendo ➤ **read out** VT + ADV leer (en voz alta) ➤ **read over** VT + ADV repasar, volver a leer ➤ **read through** VT + ADV leer (entero) ➤ **read up Ⓐ** VT + ADV [+ *subject*] estudiar; [+ *notes*] repasar **Ⓑ** VI + ADV **to ~ up for an exam** estudiar *or* repasar para un examen; **to ~ up on sth** leer sobre algo, ponerse al tanto de algo

readable ['riːdəbl] ADJ (= *legible*) legible; (= *interesting*) entretenido, que puede leerse

reader ['riːdəʳ] N lector(a) *m/f*; **he's a great ~** lee mucho, es muy aficionado a la lectura

readership ['riːdəʃɪp] N número *m* de lectores

readily ['redɪlɪ] ADV **1** (= *willingly*) [*accept, admit*] de buena gana **2** (= *easily*) [*accessible*] fácilmente; **they are ~ available** se pueden adquirir fácilmente

readiness ['redɪnɪs] N **1** (= *willingness*) buena disposición *f*; **his ~ to help us** su buena disposición para ayudarnos **2** (= *preparedness*) **equipment that is kept in ~ for an emergency** material que se mantiene listo *or* preparado para una emergencia

reading ['riːdɪŋ] **Ⓐ** N **1** (= *activity*) lectura *f*; **the book makes interesting ~** el libro es *or* resulta interesante; **to give a bill a second ~** leer un proyecto de ley por segunda vez **2** (= *interpretation*) interpretación *f* **3** (on *thermometer, instrument*) lectura *f*; **to take a ~ of sth** hacer una lectura de algo, leer algo **4** (= *recital*) recital *m* **Ⓑ** CPD ➤ **reading age** nivel *m* de lectura; **he has a ~ age of eight** tiene el nivel de lectura de un niño de ocho años ➤ **reading book** libro *m* de lectura ➤ **reading glasses** gafas *fpl* para leer ➤ **reading lamp** lámpara *f* para leer, lámpara *f* portátil ➤ **reading list** lista *f* de lecturas ➤ **reading matter** material *m* de lectura ➤ **reading room** sala *f* de lectura

readjust ['riːə'dʒʌst] **Ⓐ** VT reajustar **Ⓑ** VI reajustarse

readjustment ['riːə'dʒʌstmənt] N reajuste *m*

read-only memory [ˌriːdəʊnlɪ'meməri] N memoria *f* ROM, memoria *f* de sola lectura *or* acceso aleatorio

ready ['redɪ] **Ⓐ** ADJ (*compar* **readier**; *superl* **readiest**) **1** (*physically*) [*person, thing*] listo; **to be ~ to do sth** estar listo para hacer algo; **to be ~ for sth** estar listo para algo; **~ for use** listo para usar; **the doctor's ~ for you now** el doctor ya puede verlo; **to get (o.s.) ~** prepararse, arreglarse; **to get ~ for school/bed** prepararse para ir al colegio/a la cama; **to get sth ~** preparar algo; **he was getting the children ~ to go out** estaba arreglando a los niños para salir; **I'll have everything ~** lo tendré todo listo; **I**

had my camera ~ tenía la cámara preparada; **~, steady, go!** (*Brit*) ¡preparados, listos, ya!; **~ and waiting** a punto; **~ when you are!** ¡cuando quieras! **2** (*mentally, emotionally*) preparado; **are you ~ to order?** (*in restaurant*) ¿desean pedir ya?; **to be ~ for anything** estar preparado para lo que sea, estar dispuesto a lo que sea **3** (= *willing*) dispuesto (**to do sth** a hacer algo) **4** (= *quick*) [*solution, explanation, smile*] fácil; [*wit*] agudo, vivo; [*market*] muy receptivo; **to have a ~ answer (for sth)** tener una respuesta a punto (para algo); **don't be so ~ to criticize** no seas tan dado a criticar **5** (= *on the point of*) **we were ~ to give up there and then** estábamos a punto de abandonar sin más **Ⓑ** N **at the ~** listo, preparado; **with rifles at the ~** con los fusiles listos *or* preparados para disparar **Ⓒ** CPD ➤ **ready cash**, **ready money** dinero *m* en efectivo ➤ **ready meal** plato *m* precocinado *or* preparado ➤ **ready reckoner** tabla *f* de equivalencias

ready-cooked ['redɪˈkʊkt] ADJ precocinado, preparado

ready-made ['redɪˈmeɪd] ADJ [*clothes, curtains*] confeccionado, ya hecho; [*excuses, ideas*] preparado

ready-mixed [ˌredɪˈmɪkst] ADJ [*concrete*] mezclado de antemano, ya preparado; [*cake*] de sobre

ready-to-wear [ˌredɪtəˈweəʳ] ADJ confeccionado, listo para llevar

reaffirm ['riːəˈfɜːm] VT reafirmar, reiterar

reafforestation ['riːəˌfɒrɪsˈteɪʃən] N (*esp Brit*) repoblación *f* forestal

real [rɪəl] **Ⓐ** ADJ **1** (= *true*) [*reason, surprise, talent, achievement, progress*] verdadero; [*power*] efectivo, verdadero; [*cost, income*] real; **the only ~ car accident that I've ever had** el único accidente de coche de verdad que he tenido jamás; **I was never in any ~ danger** nunca estuve realmente en peligro; **there was no ~ evidence that ...** no había pruebas contundentes de que ...; **get ~!*** ¡baja de las nubes!; **in ~ life** en la vida real, en la realidad; **in ~ terms** en términos reales; **the ~ world** el mundo real **2** (= *not fake*) [*gold*] de ley, auténtico; [*leather, diamond*] auténtico; [*flowers*] de verdad; **~ coffee** café de cafetera, café de verdad; **this isn't the ~ thing, it's just a copy** esto no es auténtico *or* genuino, es sólo una copia; **this was definitely love, the ~ thing** esto era amor de verdad **3** (= *great*) verdadero; **it's a ~ shame** es una verdadera lástima **Ⓑ** ADV (*US**) muy; **he wrote some ~ good stories** escribió unos relatos muy buenos *or* buenísimos; **we had a ~ good time** lo pasamos realmente bien **Ⓒ** N **for ~*** de veras, de verdad; **is this guy for ~?** (*esp US**) ¿de qué va este tío?* **Ⓓ** CPD ➤ **real ale** (*esp Brit*) cerveza *f* de barril tradicional ➤ **real assets** propiedad *fsing* inmueble, bienes *mpl* raíces ➤ **real estate** (*US*) bienes *mpl* raíces, bienes *mpl* inmuebles ➤ **real estate agency** (*US*) agencia *f* inmobiliaria ➤ **real estate agent** (*US*) agente *mf* inmobiliario/a ➤ **real time** tiempo *m* real

real-estate ['rɪəlɪsˌteɪt] ADJ ➤ **real-estate agent** agente *mf* inmobiliario/a ➤ **real-estate office** (*US*) (agencia *f*) inmobiliaria *f*

realign [riːəˈlaɪn] VT realinear

realism ['rɪəlɪzəm] N realismo *m*

realist ['rɪəlɪst] N realista *mf*

realistic [rɪəˈlɪstɪk] ADJ realista; **we had no ~ chance of winning** no teníamos posibilidades reales de ganar

realistically [rɪəˈlɪstɪkəlɪ] ADV [*think, describe*] de manera realista; **they are ~ priced** tienen un precio razonable; **~, he had little chance of winning** siendo realistas, tenía pocas posibilidades de ganar

reality [riːˈælɪtɪ] N realidad *f*; **in ~** en realidad

reality TV [riːˈælɪtɪˌviː] N telerrealidad *f*

realization [ˌrɪəlaɪˈzeɪʃən] N **1** (= *comprehension*) comprensión *f*, entendimiento *m* **2** (= *completion*) realización *f*

realize ['rɪəlaɪz] VT **1** (= *understand*) darse cuenta de; **he ~d his mistake and went back** se dio cuenta de su error y

volvió; **without realizing it** sin darse cuenta; **to ~ that** darse cuenta de que, comprender que; **I ~ it's difficult, but ...** (ya) sé que es difícil, pero ..., comprendo or entiendo que es difícil, pero ...
2 (= carry out) [+ plan] llevar a cabo; **my worst fears were ~d** mis mayores temores se hicieron realidad; **to ~ one's ambitions** hacer realidad sus ambiciones; **to ~ one's potential** desarrollar al máximo su potencial
3 [+ assets] realizar; **the sale of the house ~d £250,000** la venta de la casa generó 250.000 libras

reallocate [riːˈæləˌkeɪt] VT redistribuir

really [ˈrɪəlɪ] **Ⓐ** ADV **1** (as intensifier) **it's ~ ugly** es feísimo, es feo de verdad; **a ~ good film** una película buenísima or verdaderamente buena; **I ~ ought to go** de verdad que me tengo que ir; **I ~ don't know** de verdad que no lo sé; **you ~ must see it** no puedes perdértelo
2 (= actually) **what ~ happened?** ¿qué fue lo que pasó en realidad or realmente?; **has he ~ gone?** ¿de verdad que or es cierto que se ha ido?; **"would you like to go?" — "not ~"** —¿te gustaría ir? —la verdad es que no mucho
Ⓑ EXCL **really?** (expressing doubt) ¿de verdad?, ¿de veras?; (expressing interest) ¿ah sí?; **really!** (esp Brit) (in surprise, disbelief) ¡no me digas!; **(well) ~!** (Brit) (in disapproval) ¡de verdad!

realm [relm] N (= kingdom) reino m; (= field) esfera f, campo m; **in the ~s of fantasy** en el reino de la fantasía

realtor [ˈrɪəltɔːʳ] N (US) corredor(a) m/f de bienes raíces, agente mf inmobiliario/a

ream [riːm] N [of paper] resma f; **reams*** (= lots) montones mpl

reap [riːp] VT (= cut) segar; (= harvest) cosechar, recoger; **who ~s the reward?** ¿quién se lleva los beneficios?;
◆ IDIOM **to ~ what one has sown** recoger lo que uno ha sembrado

reaper [ˈriːpəʳ] N (= person) segador(a) m/f; (= machine) segadora f, agavilladora f, cosechadora f; **the Grim Reaper** la Parca, la muerte

reappear [ˌriːəˈpɪəʳ] VI reaparecer, volver a aparecer

reappearance [ˌriːəˈpɪərəns] N reaparición f

reapply [ˈriːəˈplaɪ] VI hacer una nueva solicitud, presentar una nueva solicitud; **he reapplied for a transfer** volvió a solicitar traslado, hizo or presentó una nueva solicitud de traslado

reappoint [ˈriːəˈpɔɪnt] VT volver a nombrar

reappraisal [ˈriːəˈpreɪzəl] N reevaluación f

reappraise [ˈriːəˈpreɪz] VT reevaluar

rear¹ [rɪəʳ] **Ⓐ** N **1** (= back part) (gen) parte f de atrás, parte f trasera, parte f posterior; [of procession] cola f, final m; [of battle formation] retaguardia f; **there were empty seats at the ~** había asientos libres al final; **we sat in the ~ of the car** nos sentamos en la parte de atrás or en la parte trasera or en el asiento de atrás del coche; **my bedroom is at the ~ of the house** mi habitación da a la parte de atrás or trasera de la casa; **there is a garden at** or (US) **in the ~ of the house** detrás de la casa hay un jardín; **to bring up the ~** cerrar la marcha; **from the ~ he looked just like everybody else** por detrás parecía como todo el mundo; **to attack the enemy from the ~** atacar al enemigo por la retaguardia; **to the ~** (gen) detrás, en la parte trasera or de atrás; **to the ~ of** detrás de
2 (= buttocks) trasero* m
Ⓑ ADJ (gen) de atrás, trasero
Ⓒ CPD ➤ **rear door** puerta f trasera or de atrás ➤ **rear end** [of vehicle] parte f trasera or posterior; (hum*) (= buttocks) trasero* m ➤ **rear light** piloto m, luz f trasera, calavera f (Mex) ➤ **rear wheel** rueda f trasera or de atrás ➤ **rear window** [of building] ventana f de atrás; [of vehicle] luneta f trasera, cristal m de atrás

rear² [rɪəʳ] **Ⓐ** VT **1** [+ children, animals] criar **2** (= show) **to ~ its head** levantar la cabeza; **fascism/jealousy ~s its ugly head again** el fascismo/la envidia vuelve a levantar la cabeza **Ⓑ** VI (also ~ **up**) [horse] (gen) empinarse; (in fright) encabritarse

rearguard [ˈrɪəɡɑːd] N (Mil) retaguardia f ➤ **rearguard action** combate m para cubrir una retirada; **to fight a ~**

action (fig) resistir en lo posible

rearm [ˈriːˈɑːm] **Ⓐ** VT rearmar **Ⓑ** VI rearmarse

rearmament [ˈriːˈɑːməmənt] N rearme m

rearrange [ˈriːəˈreɪndʒ] VT [+ meeting, appointment] cambiar de fecha/hora; [+ furniture] cambiar de sitio

rear-view mirror [ˌrɪəvjuːˈmɪrəʳ] N (espejo m) retrovisor m

rear-wheel drive [ˌrɪəwiːlˈdraɪv] N tracción f trasera

reason [ˈriːzn] **Ⓐ** N **1** (= motive) razón f, motivo m; **the only ~ (that) I went was because ...** la única razón por la que or el único motivo por el que fui fue porque ...; **we have ~ to believe that ...** tenemos motivos para creer que ...; **he had every ~ to be upset** estaba disgustado y con razón; **the ~ for my going** la razón por la que or el motivo por el que me marcho; **for ~s best known to himself** por razones or motivos que sólo él sabe; **for no ~** sin motivo, sin razón; **for personal ~s** por razones or motivos personales; **for some ~** por la razón or el motivo que sea; **for this ~** por esta razón, por eso; **all the more ~ why you should not sell it** razón de más para que no lo vendas; **with good ~** con razón
2 (= faculty) razón f
3 (= good sense) sentido m común, sensatez f; **the Age of Reason** la Edad de la Razón; **to listen to ~** atender a razones; **to see ~** entrar en razón; **he tried to make her see ~** intentó hacerla entrar en razón; **the voice of ~** la voz de la razón; **within ~** dentro de lo razonable
Ⓑ VT, VI razonar

reasonable [ˈriːznəbl] ADJ **1** [person, explanation, request] razonable; [behaviour] sensato; **it is ~ to suppose that ...** es razonable suponer que ...; **beyond ~ doubt** sin que quede lugar a dudas; **~ grounds** motivos mpl fundados; **within a ~ time** dentro de un plazo de tiempo razonable
2 (= acceptable) [amount, distance, price, offer] razonable; [standard, results] aceptable; **there was a ~ chance of finding a peaceful solution** existían bastantes posibilidades de encontrar una solución pacífica

reasonably [ˈriːznəblɪ] ADV **1** (= sensibly) [discuss, expect, suppose] razonablemente; [behave] de manera razonable; **he argued, quite ~, that ...** argumentó, con toda la razón, que ... **2** (= fairly) [good, happy, sure, safe] bastante

reasoned [ˈriːznd] ADJ [argument] razonado

reasoning [ˈriːznɪŋ] N razonamiento m, lógica f

reassemble [ˈriːəˈsembl] **Ⓐ** VT **1** (Tech) montar de nuevo, volver a armar **2** [+ people] volver a reunir **Ⓑ** VI [people] volver a reunirse, juntarse de nuevo

reassert [ˈriːəˈsɜːt] VT [+ authority, influence] reafirmar

reassess [ˈriːəˈses] VT [+ situation] estudiar de nuevo, reestudiar; [+ tax] calcular de nuevo

reassurance [ˈriːəˈʃʊərəns] N consuelo m, confianza f

reassure [ˈriːəˈʃʊəʳ] VT tranquilizar; **we ~d her that everything was OK** le aseguramos que todo iba bien

reassuring [ˈriːəˈʃʊərɪŋ] ADJ (= calming) tranquilizador; (= encouraging) alentador

reawakening [ˈriːəˈweɪknɪŋ] N despertar m

rebate [ˈriːbeɪt] N (= discount) rebaja f, descuento m; (= money back) reembolso m, devolución f

rebel Ⓐ [ˈrebl] ADJ, N rebelde mf **Ⓑ** [rɪˈbel] VI rebelarse **Ⓒ** [ˈrebl] CPD ➤ **rebel leader** cabecilla mf

rebellion [rɪˈbeljən] N rebelión f, sublevación f

rebellious [rɪˈbeljəs] ADJ rebelde

rebirth [ˈriːˈbɜːθ] N (gen) renacimiento m; (= re-emergence) resurgimiento m

reboot [ˌriːˈbuːt] VT, VI reinicializar, reiniciar

rebound Ⓐ [ˈriːbaʊnd] N **on the ~** (Sport) de rebote; **she married him on the ~** se casó con él por despecho **Ⓑ** [rɪˈbaʊnd] VI rebotar
➤ **rebound on** VI + PREP estallar en la cara de

rebuff [rɪˈbʌf] **Ⓐ** N desaire m, rechazo m; **to meet with a ~** sufrir un desaire or rechazo **Ⓑ** VT desairar, rechazar

rebuild [ˈriːˈbɪld] (pt, pp **rebuilt**) VT reconstruir

rebuke [rɪˈbjuːk] **Ⓐ** N reprimenda f, reproche m **Ⓑ** VT reprender, reprochar; **to ~ sb for having done sth**

reprender a algn por haber hecho algo

rebut [rɪ'bʌt] VT rebatir, impugnar

rebuttal [rɪ'bʌtl] N refutación f, impugnación f

recalcitrant [rɪ'kælsɪtrənt] ADJ recalcitrante, contumaz (*frm*)

recall [rɪ'kɔ:l] **Ⓐ** N **1** (= *calling back*) [*of Parliament*] convocatoria f extraordinaria; [*of troops*] nueva convocatoria f
2 (= *withdrawal*) [*of ambassador*] retirada f; [*of defective product*] retirada f (del mercado); (*US*) [*of elected official*] destitución f
Ⓑ VT **1** (= *call back*) [+ *Parliament*] convocar en sesión extraordinaria; [+ *ambassador*] retirar; [+ *player*] volver a llamar; [+ *library book*] reclamar; [+ *defective product*] retirar (*del mercado*); (*US Pol*) (= *dismiss*) destituir
2 (= *remember*) recordar; **I don't ~ saying that** no recuerdo haber dicho eso

recant [rɪ'kænt] **Ⓐ** VT retractar, desdecir **Ⓑ** VI retractarse, desdecirse

recap* ['ri:kæp] VI recapitular, resumir; **well, to ~, ...** resumiendo ..., en resumen ...

recapitulate [ˌri:kə'pɪtjʊleɪt] VI recapitular, resumir

recapture ['ri:'kæptʃəʳ] **Ⓐ** VT [+ *prisoner*] volver a detener; [+ *town*] reocupar, reconquistar (*Hist*); [+ *memory, scene*] hacer revivir, recordar **Ⓑ** N [*of prisoner*] detención f; [*of town*] reocupación f, reconquista f (*Hist*)

recast ['ri:'ka:st] (*pt, pp* ~) VT [+ *play*] hacer un nuevo reparto para

recd., rec'd ABBR (= **received**) rbdo.

recede [rɪ'si:d] VI [*tide, flood*] bajar; [*view*] alejarse; [*danger*] disminuir; [*chin*] retroceder; **his hair is receding** tiene entradas

receding [rɪ'si:dɪŋ] ADJ [*forehead*] huidizo, achatado ➤ **receding hairline** entradas *fpl*

receipt [rɪ'si:t] N **1** (= *document*) recibo m **2** (= *act*) recepción f, recibo m; **to acknowledge ~ of** acusar recibo de; **on ~ of** al recibo de, al recibir; **payment on ~** pago m contra entrega *or* al recibo

receive [rɪ'si:v] **Ⓐ** VT **1** (= *get*) recibir; (*esp Brit*) [+ *stolen goods*] comerciar con; **"received with thanks"** "recibí"
2 (= *greet*) [+ *visitors*] recibir; **to be well ~d** [*book, idea*] tener buena acogida **3** (*Rad, TV*) recibir; **are you receiving me?** ¿me recibe? **Ⓑ** VI **1** (= *get*) recibir **2** (= *handle stolen goods*) comerciar con artículos robados

received [rɪ'si:vd] ADJ [*opinion*] aceptado; [*pronunciation*] estándar; **the ~ wisdom is that ...** la creencia popular es que ...

receiver [rɪ'si:vəʳ] N **1** [*of gift, letter*] destinatario/a *m/f*; [*of stolen goods*] comerciante *mf* (*de artículos robados*) **2** (*Telec*) auricular m; **to pick up the ~** coger *or* levantar el auricular; **to put down** *or* **replace the ~** colgar el auricular **3** (*Rad, TV*) receptor m **4** (*also* **official ~**) síndico/a *m/f*; **to call in the ~(s)** entrar en liquidación **5** (*US Ftbl*) receptor(a) *m/f*

receivership [rɪ'si:vəʃɪp] N **to go into ~** entrar en liquidación

receiving [rɪ'si:vɪŋ] **Ⓐ** N [*of stolen goods*] receptación f, encubrimiento m **Ⓑ** ADJ ✦ IDIOM **to be on the ~ end (of sth)*** ser el blanco *or* la víctima (de algo)

recent ['ri:snt] ADJ reciente; **a ~ arrival** (= *person*) un recién llegado; **in the ~ past** en los últimos tiempos, en un pasado reciente; **in ~ years** en los últimos años

recently ['ri:sntlɪ] ADV **1** (= *not long ago*) recientemente, hace poco, recién (*LAm*); **until ~** hasta hace poco; **as ~ as March he was living in London** hace muy poco, en marzo, estaba viviendo en Londres **2** (= *lately*) últimamente, recientemente **3** (*before pp*) recién; **~ arrived** recién llegado

receptacle [rɪ'septəkl] N receptáculo m, recipiente m

reception [rɪ'sepʃən] **Ⓐ** N **1** (= *party, desk, also Rad*) recepción f **2** (= *welcome*) acogida f; **to get a warm ~** tener buena acogida, ser bien recibido **3** (*Brit Scol*) clase f de primer año **Ⓑ** CPD ➤ **reception class** (*Brit*) clase f de primer año ➤ **reception desk** (*esp Brit*) mostrador m de recepción, recepción f ➤ **reception room** (*Brit*) sala f de visitas

receptionist [rɪ'sepʃənɪst] N recepcionista *mf*

receptive [rɪ'septɪv] ADJ receptivo

receptor [rɪ'septəʳ] N receptor m

recess [rɪ'ses] N **1** (*Jur, Pol*) (= *cessation of business*) clausura f; (*US Jur*) (= *short break*) descanso m; (*US Scol*) recreo m; **parliament is in ~** la sesión del parlamento está suspendida **2** (*in wall*) hueco m, nicho m

recession [rɪ'seʃən] N recesión f; **to be in ~** estar en recesión *or* retroceso

recharge ['ri:'tʃɑ:dʒ] VT [+ *battery*] recargar, volver a cargar

rechargeable [rɪ'tʃɑ:dʒəbl] ADJ recargable

recidivist [rɪ'sɪdɪvɪst] N reincidente *mf*

recipe ['resɪpɪ] N receta f (de cocina); **it's a ~ for disaster** es una forma segura de buscarse problemas ➤ **recipe book** libro m de cocina, recetario m

recipient [rɪ'sɪpɪənt] N [*of letter, gift*] destinatario/a *m/f*

reciprocal [rɪ'sɪprəkəl] ADJ recíproco, mutuo

reciprocate [rɪ'sɪprəkeɪt] **Ⓐ** VT [+ *good wishes*] intercambiar, devolver; **her kindness was not ~d** su amabilidad no fue correspondida **Ⓑ** VI corresponder

recital [rɪ'saɪtl] N recital m

recitation [ˌresɪ'teɪʃən] N [*of poetry*] recitación f; [*of facts*] relación f

recite [rɪ'saɪt] VT [+ *poetry*] recitar; [+ *story*] relatar; [+ *list*] enumerar

reckless ['reklɪs] ADJ **1** [*person*] (= *rash*) temerario; (= *wild*) descabellado; (= *thoughtless*) imprudente **2** [*speed*] peligroso; [*statement*] inconsiderado; **~ driving** conducción f temeraria; **he's a ~ driver** conduce temerariamente

recklessly ['reklɪslɪ] ADV (= *rashly*) temerariamente; (= *thoughtlessly*) imprudentemente

reckon ['rekən] **Ⓐ** VT **1** (= *calculate*) calcular
2 (= *consider*) considerar; **she is ~ed to be the best Spanish tennis player** se la considera la mejor tenista española
3 (*) (= *think*) creer; **I ~ she'll come** creo *or* me parece que vendrá, se me hace que vendrá (*Mex*); **you ~?** ¿tú crees?, ¿te parece a ti?; **I ~ so** eso creo, creo *or* me parece que sí; **I ~ he must be about 40** calculo que debe de estar rondando los 40
4 (= *plan, expect*) **to ~ to do sth** contar con poder hacer algo, esperar poder hacer algo
Ⓑ VI (= *count*) contar

reckoning ['rekənɪŋ] N **1** (= *calculation*) cálculo m; **according to my ~** según mis cálculos; **by any ~** a todas luces **2** **day of ~** ajuste m de cuentas

reclaim [rɪ'kleɪm] VT **1** [+ *throne, title*] reclamar; [+ *inheritance, rights*] reclamar, reivindicar; [+ *language, culture*] recuperar; [+ *baggage*] recoger, reclamar; **you may be eligible to ~ income tax** puede que tenga derecho a que le devuelvan parte de lo que ha pagado del impuesto sobre la renta; **he intended to ~ the money as expenses** tenía intención de que le pagaran los gastos como dietas *or* de que le reembolsaran los gastos
2 (= *salvage*) [+ *land*] (*gen*) aprovechar; (*from sea*) ganar al mar; [+ *materials*] recuperar, reciclar

recline [rɪ'klaɪn] **Ⓐ** VI recostarse, reclinarse **Ⓑ** VT [+ *head*] recostar, reclinar

reclining [rɪ'klaɪnɪŋ] ADJ [*seat*] reclinable; [*figure*] yacente ➤ **reclining chair** sillón m reclinable

recluse [rɪ'klu:s] N solitario/a *m/f*

recognition [ˌrekəg'nɪʃən] N reconocimiento m; **in ~ of** en reconocimiento de; **she has changed beyond ~** ha cambiado tanto que está irreconocible

recognizable [ˈrekəgnaɪzəbl] ADJ reconocible; **it is ~ as ...** se le reconoce *or* identifica como ...

recognize ['rekəgnaɪz] VT reconocer

recoil [rɪ'kɔɪl] VI [*person*] echarse atrás, retroceder; [*gun*] dar un culatazo; **to ~ from sth** retroceder *or* dar marcha atrás ante algo; **to ~ in fear** retroceder espantado

recollect [ˌrekə'lekt] **Ⓐ** VT recordar, acordarse de **Ⓑ** VI recordar, acordarse

recollection [ˌrekə'lekʃən] N recuerdo m; **to the best of**

my ~ que yo recuerde

recommend [ˌrekəˈmend] **Ⓐ** VT (= *speak well of*) recomendar; (= *advise*) recomendar, aconsejar; **to** ~ **sb for a job** recomendar a algn para un trabajo; **the town has much/little to** ~ **it** el pueblo tiene mucho/poco atractivo; **the** ~**ed daily intake** el consumo diario recomendado *or* aconsejado; **this method is not to be** ~**ed** este método no es nada recomendable *or* aconsejable; **to** ~ **doing sth** recomendar *or* aconsejar hacer algo; ~**ed retail price** precio *m* de venta al público recomendado **Ⓑ** VI **they** ~**ed against using mobiles during takeoff** recomendaron no utilizar los teléfonos móviles durante el aterrizaje

recommendation [ˌrekəmenˈdeɪʃən] N recomendación *f*; **to do sth on the** ~ **of sb** hacer algo por recomendación *or* consejo de algn, hacer algo siguiendo la recomendación *or* consejo de algn

recompense [ˈrekəmpens] **Ⓐ** N (*gen*) recompensa *f*; (*financial*) indemnización *f* **Ⓑ** VT (*gen*) recompensar; (*financially*) indemnizar

reconcilable [ˈrekənsaɪləbl] ADJ conciliable, reconciliable

reconcile [ˈrekənsaɪl] VT [+ *people*] reconciliar; [+ *theories*] conciliar; **to be** ~**d (with)** estar reconciliado (con); **you must try and** ~ **your differences** tenéis que intentar resolver vuestras diferencias; **to** ~ **o.s. to sth** resignarse a algo

reconciliation [ˌrekənsɪlɪˈeɪʃən] N reconciliación *f*

recondition [ˈriːkənˈdɪʃən] VT reacondicionar

reconnaissance [rɪˈkɒnɪsəns] N reconocimiento *m* ➤ **reconnaissance flight** vuelo *m* de reconocimiento

reconnoitre, reconnoiter (*US*) [ˌrekəˈnɔɪtəʳ] VT reconocer, explorar

reconquest [ˈriːˈkɒŋkwest] N reconquista *f*

reconsider [ˈriːkənˈsɪdəʳ] VT, VI reconsiderar

reconstitute [ˈriːˈkɒnstɪtjuːt] VT reconstituir

reconstruct [ˈriːkənˈstrʌkt] VT reconstruir

reconstruction [ˈriːkənˈstrʌkʃən] N reconstrucción *f*

reconvene [ˌriːkənˈviːn] **Ⓐ** VT reconvocar **Ⓑ** VI [*committee, jury etc*] reunirse

record Ⓐ [ˈrekɔːd] N **1** (= *document*) documento *m*; (= *note*) nota *f*, apunte *m*; [*of attendance*] registro *m*; [*of meeting*] acta *f*

Use **el/un** not **la/una** before feminine nouns beginning with stressed **a** or **ha** like **acta**.

---

there is no ~ **of it** no hay constancia de ello, no consta en ningún sitio; **for the** ~**, I disagree** no estoy de acuerdo, que conste; **to keep a** ~ **of sth** apuntar algo, tomar nota de algo; **it is a matter of (public)** ~ **that ...** hay constancia de que ...; **off the** ~ [*statement, comment*] extraoficial; [*speak, say*] extraoficialmente; **there is no similar example on** ~ no existe constancia de nada semejante; **the police had kept his name on** ~ la policía lo había fichado; **to be on** ~ **as saying that ...** haber declarado públicamente que ...; **to put sth on** ~ hacer constar algo, dejar constancia de algo; **the highest temperatures since** ~**s began** las temperaturas más altas que se han registrado hasta la fecha; **just to set the** ~ **straight, let me point out that ...** simplemente para que quede claro, permítanme señalar que ...
2 (*Comput*) registro *m*
3 records (= *files*) archivos *mpl*; **according to our** ~**s ...** según nuestros datos ...; **public** ~**s** archivos *mpl* públicos
4 (= *case history*) **4.1** (*in work*) historial *m*; **his past** ~ **is against him** su historial obra en perjuicio suyo; **the airline has a good safety** ~ la compañía aérea tiene un buen historial en materia de seguridad **4.2** (*Med*) historial *m* **4.3** (*also* **criminal** ~) antecedentes *mpl* (penales); **he's got a clean** ~ no tiene antecedentes (penales) **4.4** (*Mil*) hoja *f* de servicios
5 (*Sport etc*) récord *m*; **the long jump** ~ el récord del salto de longitud
6 (*for record player*) disco *m*; **to make a** ~ grabar un disco **Ⓑ** [ˈrekɔːd] ADJ récord, sin precedentes **Ⓒ** [rɪˈkɔːd] VT **1** (= *set down*) [+ *facts*] registrar; [+ *events*] (*in*

journal, diary) tomar nota de; **it is not** ~**ed anywhere** no consta en ninguna parte; **her letters** ~ **the details of diplomatic life in China** sus cartas dejan constancia de *or* recogen los detalles de la vida diplomática en China **2** (= *show*) [*instrument*] registrar, marcar **3** [+ *sound, images, data*] grabar **Ⓓ** [ˈrekɔːd] CPD ➤ **record breaker** (= *man*) recordman *m*, plusmarquista *m*; (= *woman*) plusmarquista *f* ➤ **record company** casa *f* discográfica ➤ **record holder** (= *man*) recordman *m*, plusmarquista *m*; (= *woman*) plusmarquista *f*; **she is the world 800 metre** ~ **holder** tiene *or* ostenta el récord mundial de los 800 metros, es la plusmarquista mundial de los 800 metros ➤ **record player** tocadiscos *m inv* ➤ **record producer** productor(a) *m/f* discográfico/a ➤ **record token** vale *m* para discos

---

⚠ **record** ≠ *recordar*

---

record-breaking [ˈrekɔːdˌbreɪkɪŋ] ADJ [*person, team*] que bate récords; [*effort, run*] récord

recorded [rɪˈkɔːdɪd] **Ⓐ** ADJ **1** [*music, programme*] grabado **2** [*history*] escrito, documentado **Ⓑ** CPD ➤ **recorded delivery** (*Brit*) servicio *m* de entrega con acuse de recibo

recorder [rɪˈkɔːdəʳ] N **1** (= *instrument*) flauta *f* dulce **2** (*Brit Jur*) juez *mf* municipal

recording [rɪˈkɔːdɪŋ] N [*of sound, images*] grabación *f*; [*of facts*] registro *m*; **to make a** ~ **(of sth)** realizar una grabación (de algo) ➤ **recording artist** artista *mf* dedicado/a a la grabación ➤ **recording equipment** equipo *m* de grabación ➤ **recording session** sesión *f* de grabación ➤ **recording studio** estudio *m* de grabación

recount [ˈriːkaʊnt] VT (= *relate*) contar, relatar

re-count Ⓐ [ˈriːkaʊnt] N [*of votes etc*] recuento *m*; **to have a** ~ someter los votos a un segundo escrutinio **Ⓑ** [riːˈkaʊnt] VT (= *count again*) volver a contar

recoup [rɪˈkuːp] VT recobrar, recuperar

recourse [rɪˈkɔːs] N **to have** ~ **to** recurrir a

recover [rɪˈkʌvəʳ] **Ⓐ** VT **1** (= *regain*) [+ *faculty, balance*] recuperar, recobrar (*frm*); **to** ~ **consciousness** recobrar el conocimiento
2 (= *retrieve*) [+ *bodies, wreck*] rescatar; [+ *debt*] cobrar; [+ *stolen property, costs, losses, money*] recuperar; [+ *property*] reivindicar, recuperar; (*Comput*) [+ *data*] recobrar, recuperar; **to** ~ **damages from sb** ser indemnizado por daños y perjuicios por algn **Ⓑ** VI **1** (*after accident, illness*) reponerse, recuperarse, restablecerse (**from** de); (*after shock, blow*) sobreponerse, reponerse (**from** de)
2 (*Fin*) [*currency*] recuperarse, restablecerse; [*shares, stock market*] volver a subir; [*economy*] reactivarse

re-cover [ˈriːˈkʌvəʳ] VT [+ *chair, sofa*] tapizar de nuevo

recoverable [rɪˈkʌvərəbl] ADJ recuperable; (*at law*) reivindicable

recovery [rɪˈkʌvərɪ] **Ⓐ** N **1** (*after accident, illness*) recuperación *f*, restablecimiento *m*; (*after shock, blow*) recuperación *f*; (*Fin*) [*of currency*] recuperación *f*; (*Econ*) reactivación *f*; **to be in** ~ (*from addiction*) estar en rehabilitación; **to make a (full)** ~ recuperarse *or* restablecerse (completamente); **to be on the road to** ~ (*Med*) estar camino de la recuperación
2 (= *retrieval*) [*of bodies, wreck*] rescate *m*; [*of debt*] cobro *m*; [*of stolen property, money, data*] recuperación *f* **Ⓑ** CPD ➤ **recovery position** posición *f* decúbito lateral; **to put sb in the** ~ **position** poner a algn en posición decúbito lateral ➤ **recovery room** sala *f* de posoperatorio ➤ **recovery service** servicio *m* de rescate ➤ **recovery vehicle** grúa *f*

re-create [ˈriːkrɪˈeɪt] VT recrear, volver a crear

recreation [ˌrekrɪˈeɪʃən] N (= *break, leisure*) recreo *m* ➤ **recreation centre, recreation center** (*US*) centro *m* recreativo ➤ **recreation ground** campo *m* de deportes

recreational [ˌrekrɪˈeɪʃənəl] ADJ [*activity*] recreativo; [*drug*] de placer ➤ **recreational vehicle** (*US*) caravana *f or* rulota *f* pequeña

recrimination [rɪˌkrɪmɪˈneɪʃən] N recriminación *f*

recruit [rɪˈkruːt] Ⓐ N (Mil) recluta mf; (to organization) adquisición f; **new ~** (Mil) nuevo recluta; (to organization) nuevo/a m/f Ⓑ VT (Mil) reclutar; [+ staff] contratar; [+ new members, talent] buscar

recruitment [rɪˈkruːtmənt] N (Mil) reclutamiento m; [of staff] contratación f ➤ **recruitment agency** agencia f de colocaciones

rectangle [ˈrekˌtæŋgl] N rectángulo m

rectangular [rekˈtæŋgjʊləʳ] ADJ rectangular

rectify [ˈrektɪfaɪ] VT rectificar

rectitude [ˈrektɪtjuːd] N rectitud f

rector [ˈrektəʳ] N (Rel) párroco m; (Univ) rector(a) m/f

rectum [ˈrektəm] N recto m

recuperate [rɪˈkuːpəreɪt] Ⓐ VI recuperarse, reponerse; **to be recuperating from sth** estar convaleciente de algo Ⓑ VT [+ losses] recuperar

recuperation [rɪˌkuːpəˈreɪʃən] N (Med) recuperación f, restablecimiento m; [of losses] recuperación f

recur [rɪˈkɜːʳ] VI [pain, illness] producirse de nuevo; [event, mistake, theme] repetirse; [difficulty, opportunity] volver a presentarse

recurrence [rɪˈkʌrəns] N [of event, mistake, theme] repetición f; (Med) reaparición f, recurrencia f

recurrent [rɪˈkʌrənt] ADJ [problem, feature] repetido, constante; (Med) recurrente; **it is a ~ theme** es un tema constante or que se repite a menudo

recurring [rɪˈkɜːrɪŋ] ADJ 1 (Math) **3.3333 ~** 3,3 periódico puro 2 [problem] repetido, constante; (Med) recurrente

recyclable [ˌriːˈsaɪkləbl] ADJ reciclable

recycle [ˌriːˈsaɪkl] VT reciclar

recycling [ˌriːˈsaɪklɪŋ] N reciclado m, reciclaje m ➤ **recycling plant** planta f de reciclado or reciclaje

red [red] Ⓐ ADJ (compar **~der**; superl **~dest**) (gen) rojo; [wine] tinto; **the (traffic) lights are ~** el semáforo está en rojo; **his eyes were ~** (from crying) tenía los ojos rojos; **to be ~ in the face** (from anger, exertion, heat) estar rojo; (from embarrassment) estar rojo or colorado; **to go ~ in the face** (from anger, exertion, heat) ponerse rojo; (with embarrassment) ponerse colorado; (with shame) sonrojarse; **to have ~ hair** ser pelirrojo; ✦ IDIOMS **to go** or **turn as ~ as a beetroot** (Brit) or **beet** (US) ponerse como un tomate; **it's like a ~ rag to a bull** es lo que más le saca de quicio; **to roll out the ~ carpet for sb** recibir a algn por todo lo alto or a bombo y platillo; **not a ~ cent** (US*) ni una gorda* Ⓑ N (color m) rojo m; ✦ IDIOM **to be in the ~** [account, firm] estar en números rojos; **I'm £100 in the ~** tengo un descubierto de 100 libras en el banco; **to see ~** sulfurarse, salirse de sus casillas

Ⓒ CPD ➤ **red alert** alerta f roja; **to be on ~ alert** estar en alerta roja ➤ **the Red Army** el Ejército Rojo ➤ **red blood cell** glóbulo m rojo ➤ **red cabbage** (col f) lombarda f ➤ **red card** (Ftbl) tarjeta f roja; **to show sb the ~ card** sacar a algn la tarjeta roja ➤ **Red Cross** Cruz f Roja ➤ **red deer** ciervo m común ➤ **red herring** (fig) pista f falsa, despiste m ➤ **Red Indian** piel mf roja ➤ **red light** luz f roja; **to go through a ~ light** saltarse un semáforo en rojo ➤ **red meat** carne f roja ➤ **red pepper** (= capsicum) pimiento m rojo, pimiento m morrón, pimentón m rojo (LAm) ➤ **(Little) Red Riding Hood** Caperucita f Roja ➤ **Red Sea** Mar m Rojo ➤ **red squirrel** ardilla f roja ➤ **red tape** trámites mpl, papeleo m ➤ **red wine** vino m tinto, tinto m

red-blooded [ˈredˈblʌdɪd] ADJ (fig) viril

redbrick [ˈredbrɪk] ADJ [building] de ladrillo; (Brit) [university] construido en el siglo XIX y fuera de Londres

redcurrant [ˈredˈkʌrənt] N (Brit) grosella f roja

redden [ˈredn] VI (= blush) ponerse colorado, ruborizarse; (with anger) ponerse rojo

reddish [ˈredɪʃ] ADJ rojizo

redecorate [ˌriːˈdekəreɪt] VT [+ room, house] (gen) redecorar, renovar el decorado de; (= repaint) pintar de nuevo; (= repaper) volver a empapelar

redeem [rɪˈdiːm] VT [+ sinner] redimir; [+ pawned goods]

desempeñar; [+ debt, mortgage] amortizar; **to ~ o.s.** redimirse

redeemable [rɪˈdiːməbl] ADJ (Comm) reembolsable; (Fin) amortizable

Redeemer [rɪˈdiːməʳ] N Redentor m

redeeming [rɪˈdiːmɪŋ] ADJ **I see no ~ feature in it** no le encuentro ninguna cosa buena or ningún punto favorable; **~ virtue** virtud f compensadora

redefine [ˌriːdɪˈfaɪn] VT redefinir

redemption [rɪˈdempʃən] N (Rel) redención f; (Fin) amortización f; **to be beyond** or **past ~** no tener remedio

redeploy [ˈriːdɪˈplɔɪ] VT [+ resources] disponer de otro modo, reorganizar; [+ workers, staff] redistribuir, adscribir; [+ troops, forces] cambiar de destino

redeployment [ˈriːdɪˈplɔɪmənt] N (= rearrangement) disposición f nueva, reorganización f; (= redistribution) redistribución f; (Mil) cambio m de destino

redevelop [ˌriːdɪˈveləp] VT [+ land, site] reurbanizar

redevelopment [ˌriːdɪˈveləpmənt] N [of land, site] reurbanización f

red-faced [ˈredˈfeɪst] ADJ (lit) con la cara roja; (= ashamed) ruborizado, avergonzado

red-haired [ˈredˈhɛəd] ADJ pelirrojo

red-handed [ˈredˈhændɪd] ADJ ✦ IDIOM **to catch sb ~** pillar or coger or (LAm) agarrar a algn con las manos en la masa

redhead [ˈredhed] N pelirrojo/a m/f

red-headed [ˈredˈhedɪd] ADJ pelirrojo

red-hot [ˈredˈhɒt] ADJ [iron, poker] candente; (*) [news, information] de última hora

redial [riːˈdaɪəl] Ⓐ VT volver a marcar Ⓑ VI volver a marcar el número Ⓒ N **automatic ~** marcación f automática

redid [ˈriːˈdɪd] PT, PP of **redo**

redirect [ˈriːdaɪˈrekt] VT [+ letter] remitir; [+ energies] emplear de otro modo

rediscover [ˈriːdɪsˈkʌvəʳ] VT redescubrir, volver a descubrir

rediscovery [ˈriːdɪsˈkʌvərɪ] N redescubrimiento m

redistribute [ˈriːdɪsˈtrɪbjuːt] VT distribuir de nuevo, volver a distribuir

redistribution [ˈriːˌdɪstrɪˈbjuːʃən] N redistribución f

red-letter [ˈredˈletəʳ] ADJ ➤ **red-letter day** día m señalado

red-light district [ˌredˈlaɪtdɪstrɪkt] N zona f de tolerancia, barrio m chino (Sp)

redneck* [ˈrednek] N (esp US) campesino m blanco de los estados del Sur

redness [ˈrednɪs] N rojez f

redo [ˈriːˈduː] (pt **redid**; pp **redone**) VT rehacer, volver a hacer

redolent [ˈredələnt] ADJ **~ of** (= smelling of) con olor or fragancia a; **to be ~ of** (= recall) recordar, hacer pensar en

redouble [riːˈdʌbl] VT redoblar, intensificar

redoubtable [rɪˈdaʊtəbl] ADJ temible

redraft [ˈriːˈdrɑːft] VT redactar de nuevo

redress [rɪˈdres] Ⓐ N (= compensation) compensación f, indemnización f; (for offence) reparación f Ⓑ VT (= compensate for) reparar, indemnizar; [+ fault] remediar; **to ~ the balance** equilibrar la balanza

reduce [rɪˈdjuːs] VT 1 [+ number, costs, inflation] reducir; [+ price] rebajar; [+ speed, visibility, risk] disminuir; [+ temperature, swelling] bajar; [+ stress, tension] reducir, disminuir; **"reduce speed now"** "disminuya la velocidad" 2 **to ~ sb to despair** llevar a algn a la desesperación; **to ~ sb to tears/silence** hacer llorar/callar a algn; **to ~ sth to ashes** reducir algo a cenizas; **we were ~d to begging on the streets** nos vimos obligados a mendigar por las calles

reduced [rɪˈdjuːst] ADJ (gen) reducido; [price] reducido, rebajado; **"reduced to clear"** "rebajas por liquidación"

reduction [rɪˈdʌkʃən] N (gen) reducción f; (in price) rebaja f; **there has been no ~ in demand** no ha disminuido la demanda

redundancy [rɪ'dʌndənsɪ] **Ⓐ** N **1** (*Brit*) (= *dismissal*) despido *m*; (= *unemployment*) desempleo *m* **2** (= *superfluousness*) exceso *m*, superfluidad *f* **Ⓑ** CPD ➤ **redundancy payment** indemnización *f* por despido

redundant [rɪ'dʌndənt] ADJ **1** (*Brit*) [*worker*] sin trabajo, parado; **to be made ~** ser despedido (*por reducción de plantilla*), quedar sin trabajo **2** (= *superfluous*) superfluo; **to be ~** estar de más

redwood ['redwʊd] N secoya *f*

reed [riːd] N (*Bot*) junco *m*, caña *f*; [*of instrument*] lengüeta *f* ➤ **reed bed** juncal *m*, cañaveral *m* ➤ **reed instrument** instrumento *m* de lengüeta

re-educate ['riː'edjʊkeɪt] VT reeducar

reedy ['riːdɪ] ADJ (*compar* **reedier**; *superl* **reediest**) [*voice, tone, instrument*] aflautado

reef [riːf] N (*Geog*) arrecife *m* ➤ **reef knot** nudo *m* de rizo

reefer ['riːfəʳ] N (= *joint*) porro *m* (*Sp**), toque *m* (*Mex***), cacho *m* (*Carib**), pito *m* (*Chi**)

reek [riːk] **Ⓐ** N tufo *m*, hedor *m* (**of** a) **Ⓑ** VI **to ~ of sth** apestar a algo

reel [riːl] **Ⓐ** N **1** (*for cable, hose*) rollo *m*; (*in fishing*) carrete *m*; (*for thread*) carrete *m*, bobina *f*; (*for small camera*) carrete *m*, rollo *m*; [*of cine film*] cinta *f* **2** (= *dance*) baile escocés **Ⓑ** VI (= *sway*) tambalear(se); [*mind, head, brain*] dar vueltas; **he was sent ~ing by a blow to the head** un golpe en la cabeza hizo que se tambaleara; **I'm still ~ing from the shock** todavía no me he recuperado del susto
➤ **reel in** VT + ADV [+ *fish*] sacar del agua (enrollando el sedal); [+ *line*] recoger, ir cobrando
➤ **reel off** VT + ADV recitar de un tirón

re-elect ['riː'lekt] VT reelegir

re-election ['riːr'lekʃən] N reelección *f*

re-emerge ['riːr'mɜːdʒ] VI volver a salir

re-enact ['riːr'nækt] VT [+ *crime, battle*] reconstruir

re-enter ['riːr'entəʳ] **Ⓐ** VI volver a entrar **Ⓑ** VT [+ *room, building, country*] volver a entrar en, entrar de nuevo en; **to ~ the Earth's atmosphere** regresar a o volver a entrar en la atmósfera terrestre

re-entry ['riː'entrɪ] N reentrada *f*

re-establish ['riːɪs'tæblɪʃ] VT restablecer

re-examine ['riːɪg'zæmɪn] VT [+ *facts, evidence*] reexaminar, repasar; (*Jur*) [+ *witness*] volver a interrogar

ref PREP ABBR **1** (= **with reference to**) respecto de **2** (*in letter-head*) (= **reference**) ref.

refectory [rɪ'fektərɪ] N refectorio *m*

refer [rɪ'fɜːʳ] **Ⓐ** VI **to ~ to 1** (= *allude to, relate to*) referirse a; (= *mention*) mencionar; **I ~ to your letter of May 1st** con relación a su carta con fecha del uno de mayo; **this kind of art is often ~red to as "minimal art"** este tipo de arte a menudo se denomina "arte minimalista" **2** (= *consult*) consultar; **she had to ~ to her notes** tuvo que consultar sus apuntes; **please ~ to section three** véase la sección tres **Ⓑ** VT **1** (= *send, direct*) **to ~ sth to sb** remitir algo a algn; **to ~ a dispute to arbitration** someter o remitir una disputa al arbitraje; **to ~ sb to sth/sb: the reader is ~red to page 15** remito al lector a la página 15; **I ~red him to the manager** lo envié a que viera al gerente; **the doctor ~red me to a specialist** el médico me mandó a un especialista **2** (*Brit Univ*) [+ *student*] suspender

referee [,refə'riː] **Ⓐ** N **1** (*in dispute, Sport*) árbitro/a *m/f* **2** (*Brit*) (*for application, post*) avalista *mf*, persona *f* que avala; **Pérez has named you as a ~** Pérez dice que usted está dispuesto a avalarlo **Ⓑ** VT [+ *game*] dirigir, arbitrar en **Ⓒ** VI arbitrar, hacer de árbitro

reference ['refrəns] **Ⓐ** N **1** (= *consultation*) consulta *f*; **I'll keep it for future ~** lo guardo por si hace falta consultarlo en el futuro **2** (= *allusion*) alusión *f*, referencia *f*; **I can't find any ~ to him in the files** no encuentro nada que haga referencia a él en los archivos **3** (= *identifying source*) (*in text*) referencia *f*, remisión *f*; (= *citation*) referencia *f*; (*Comm*) (*in letter, catalogue*) número

m de referencia; (*on map*) indicación *f* **4** (= *testimonial*) referencia *f*, informe *m*; **to take up (sb's) ~s** pedir referencias o informes (de algn) **5** (*US*) (*for application, post*) avalista *mf*, persona *f* que avala **Ⓑ** CPD [*material, room*] de consulta ➤ **reference book** libro *m* de consulta ➤ **reference library** biblioteca *f* de consulta ➤ **reference number** número *m* de referencia

referendum [,refə'rendəm] N (*pl* **~s**, **referenda** [,refə'rendə]) referéndum *m*; **to hold a ~ on sth** someter algo a referéndum

referral [rɪ'fɜːrəl] N remisión *f*; **ask your GP for a ~ to a clinical psychologist** pídale a su médico que le envíe a un psicólogo clínico; **letter of ~** volante *m* médico

refill Ⓐ ['riːfɪl] N (*gen*) recambio *m*; (*for pencil*) mina *f*; **would you like a ~?** ¿te pongo más vino *etc*?, ¿otro vaso? **Ⓑ** [,riː'fɪl] VT [+ *lighter, pen*] recargar; [+ *glass*] volver a llenar

refine [rɪ'faɪn] VT **1** [+ *sugar, oil*] refinar **2** (= *improve*) [+ *design, technique, machine*] perfeccionar; [+ *methods*] refinar; [+ *behaviour, style of writing*] pulir, refinar

refined [rɪ'faɪnd] ADJ **1** [*sugar, flour*] refinado **2** [*manners, humour*] fino, refinado; [*style of writing*] elegante, pulido

refinement [rɪ'faɪnmənt] N **1** [*of person, language*] refinamiento *m*; (= *good manners*) educación *f*, finura *f*; **a person of some ~** una persona fina **2** (= *improvement*) mejora *f*; [*of machine*] perfeccionamiento *m*

refinery [rɪ'faɪnərɪ] N refinería *f*

refit Ⓐ ['riː'fɪt] VT (*gen*) reparar, componer; [+ *ship*] reparar **Ⓑ** VI (*Naut*) repararse

reflect [rɪ'flekt] **Ⓐ** VT **1** [+ *light, image*] reflejar **2** [+ *situation, opinion*] reflejar, hacerse eco de; **the difficulties are ~ed in his report** las dificultades se reflejan en su informe, el informe se hace eco de las dificultades **3** (= *say*) reflexionar **Ⓑ** VI **1 to ~ off sth** [*light, heat*] reflejarse en algo **2** (= *think, meditate*) reflexionar, pensar; **to ~ on sth** reflexionar o meditar sobre algo **3 to ~ well on sb** hacer honor a algn; **to ~ badly on sb** decir poco en favor de algn; **it will ~ badly on the university** eso dará una imagen poco favorable de la universidad

reflection [rɪ'flekʃən] N **1** (*in mirror*) reflejo *m*; **to see one's ~ in a shop window** verse reflejado en un escaparate **2** (= *thought*) meditación *f*, reflexión *f*; **on ~** pensándolo bien; **without due ~** sin pensarlo lo suficiente **3** (= *aspersion, doubt*) tacha *f*, descrédito *m*; **this is no ~ on your work** esto no significa crítica alguna a su trabajo; **this is no ~ on your honesty** esto no dice nada en contra de su honradez, esto no es ningún reproche a su honradez **4** (= *idea*) pensamiento *m*, idea *f*

reflective [rɪ'flektɪv] ADJ **1** [*surface*] brillante, lustroso **2** (= *meditative*) pensativo, reflexivo

reflector [rɪ'flektəʳ] N reflector *m*

reflex ['riːfleks] **Ⓐ** ADJ (*gen*) reflejo; [*angle*] de reflexión **Ⓑ** N reflejo *m*

reflexive [rɪ'fleksɪv] ADJ [*verb, pronoun*] reflexivo

reforestation ['riː,fɒrɪs'teɪʃən] N repoblación *f* forestal

reform [rɪ'fɔːm] **Ⓐ** N reforma *f* **Ⓑ** VT reformar **Ⓒ** VI reformarse **Ⓓ** CPD ➤ **reform school** (*US*) reformatorio *m*

reformat ['riː'fɔːmæt] VT reformatear

reformation [,refə'meɪʃən] N reformación *f*; **the Reformation** la Reforma

reformed [rɪ'fɔːmd] ADJ reformado; **he's a ~ character these days** últimamente se ha reformado

reformer [rɪ'fɔːməʳ] N reformista *mf*, reformador(a) *m/f*

refraction [rɪ'frækʃən] N refracción *f*

refrain¹ [rɪ'freɪn] N (*Mus*) estribillo *m*; **his constant ~ is ...** siempre está con la misma canción ...

refrain² [rɪ'freɪn] VI **to ~ from (doing) sth** abstenerse de (hacer) algo

refresh [rɪ'freʃ] VT (*gen*) refrescar; (*Comput*) actualizar

refresher course [rɪ'freʃə,kɔːs] N curso *m* de actualización

refreshing [rɪ'freʃɪŋ] ADJ [*drink*] refrescante; **it's ~ to hear some new ideas** da gusto escuchar nuevas ideas; **it's a ~**

change to find this es alentador encontrar esto

refreshingly [rɪˈfreʃɪŋlɪ] ADV **she's ~ honest** da gusto ver lo honesta que es; **his style of writing is ~ different** tiene un estilo distinto, lo cual resulta muy grato

refreshment [rɪˈfreʃmənt] N (= *food*) refrigerio *m*, piscolabis *m inv* (*Sp*); (= *drink*) (*non-alcoholic*) refresco *m*; (*alcoholic*) copa *f*; **refreshments** refrigerio *msing*, comida *fsing* liviana; **"refreshments will be served"** "se servirá un refrigerio"

refrigerate [rɪˈfrɪdʒəreɪt] VT refrigerar

refrigeration [rɪˌfrɪdʒəˈreɪʃən] N refrigeración *f*

refrigerator [rɪˈfrɪdʒəreɪtəʳ] N frigorífico *m*, nevera *f*, refrigeradora *f* (*LAm*)

refuel [ˈriːˈfjʊəl] Ⓐ VI repostar, echar gasolina Ⓑ VT llenar de combustible

refuelling, refueling (*US*) [ˈriːˈfjʊəlɪŋ] N reabastecimiento *m* de combustible ➤ **refuelling stop** escala *f* para repostar

refuge [ˈrefjuːdʒ] N (= *shelter*) refugio *m*; (= *hut, shelter for climbers*) albergue *m*; **God is my ~** Dios es mi amparo; **to seek ~** buscar refugio, buscar dónde guarecerse; **to take ~** ponerse al abrigo, guarecerse; **to take ~ in sth** refugiarse en algo; (*fig*) recurrir a algo

refugee [ˌrefjuˈdʒiː] N refugiado/a *m/f* ➤ **refugee camp** campamento *m* para refugiados ➤ **refugee status** estatus *m inv* de refugiado

refund Ⓐ [ˈriːfʌnd] N reembolso *m* Ⓑ [rɪˈfʌnd] VT devolver, reembolsar

refundable [rɪˈfʌndəbl] ADJ reembolsable

refurbish [ˈriːˈfɜːbɪʃ] VT restaurar

refurnish [ˈriːˈfɜːnɪʃ] VT amueblar de nuevo

refusal [rɪˈfjuːzəl] N negativa *f*; **a flat ~** una negativa rotunda; **her request met with a flat ~** su solicitud fue rechazada de plano; **I'm giving you first ~ (on the house)** le daré prioridad en la compra (de la casa)

refuse[1] [rɪˈfjuːz] Ⓐ VT **1** (= *decline*) [+ *offer, chance*] rechazar, rehusar; [+ *applicant*] rechazar; **she ~d their invitation to stay to dinner** rechazó *or* no aceptó su invitación para quedarse a cenar; **she ~d him** lo rechazó; **to ~ to do sth** negarse a hacer algo **2** (= *not grant*) [+ *request, permission*] (*gen*) negar; (*officially*) denegar; **to ~ sb sth** negar algo a algn; (*officially*) denegar algo a algn Ⓑ VI negarse

refuse[2] [ˈrefjuːs] N (= *rubbish*) basura *f*, desperdicios *mpl*; (= *industrial waste*) desechos *mpl*, residuos *mpl*; **household ~** basura *f* doméstica, residuos *mpl* domésticos ➤ **refuse bin** cubo *m* or (*LAm*) bote *m* de la basura ➤ **refuse collection** recogida *f* de basura ➤ **refuse collector** basurero *m* ➤ **refuse dump, refuse tip** vertedero *m*, basural *m* (*LAm*) ➤ **refuse lorry** camión *m* de la basura

refute [rɪˈfjuːt] VT refutar, rebatir

regain [rɪˈɡeɪn] VT recobrar, recuperar; **to ~ consciousness** recobrar el conocimiento, volver en sí

regal [ˈriːɡəl] ADJ regio, real

regale [rɪˈɡeɪl] VT (= *entertain*) entretener; (= *delight*) divertir; **he ~d us with a funny story** para entretenernos nos contó una historia graciosa

regalia [rɪˈɡeɪlɪə] NPL (= *royal trappings*) atributos *mpl*; (= *insignia*) insignias *fpl*

regard [rɪˈɡɑːd] Ⓐ N **1** (= *esteem*) estima *f*, respeto *m*; (= *respect*) respeto *m*; (= *consideration*) consideración *f*; **my ~ for him** la estima *or* el respeto que le tengo; **to have a high ~ for sb** tener a algn en gran estima, tener un gran concepto de algn; **in this/that ~** en este/ese aspecto, a este/ese respecto; **out of ~ for** por respeto a; **with ~ to** con respecto a; **it should be done with a proper ~ for safety** debería hacerse prestándole la atención debida a la seguridad; **without ~ to** sin tener en cuenta **2 regards** recuerdos *mpl*, saludos *mpl*; **(give my) ~s to Yvonne** (dele) recuerdos a Yvonne, salude a Yvonne de mi parte; **(with) kind ~s** (*as letter ending*) saludos; **he sends his ~s** te manda recuerdos *or* saludos Ⓑ VT **1** (= *look at*) contemplar, observar; (*fig*) mirar **2** (= *consider*) considerar; **he is ~ed as Britain's foremost**

composer se le considera *or* está considerado el compositor más importante de Gran Bretaña **3** (= *esteem*) **he was a highly ~ed scholar** era un académico muy respetado *or* de mucha reputación **4** (= *concern*) tratar, tocar; **as ~s** en *or* por lo que respecta a, en *or* por lo que se refiere a, en cuanto a

regarding [rɪˈɡɑːdɪŋ] PREP con respecto a, en relación con; (*introducing sentence*) en *or* por lo que respecta a, en *or* por lo que se refiere a; **and other things ~ money** y otras cosas relativas al dinero

regardless [rɪˈɡɑːdlɪs] Ⓐ ADJ **~ of** sin reparar en; **~ of the cost** cueste lo que cueste/costase lo que costase *etc*, sin reparar en gastos; **we did it ~ of the consequences** lo hicimos sin tener en cuenta las consecuencias *or* sin reparar en las consecuencias Ⓑ ADV a pesar de todo, pase lo que pase

regatta [rɪˈɡætə] N regata *f*

regency [ˈriːdʒənsɪ] N regencia *f*

regenerate [rɪˈdʒenəreɪt] VT regenerar

regeneration [rɪˌdʒenəˈreɪʃən] N regeneración *f*

regent [ˈriːdʒənt] Ⓐ ADJ **prince ~** príncipe *m* regente Ⓑ N regente *mf*

reggae [ˈreɡeɪ] N reggae *m*

régime, regime [reɪˈʒiːm] N régimen *m*

regiment [ˈredʒɪmənt] N regimiento *m*

regimental [ˌredʒɪˈmentl] ADJ de regimiento; (*fig*) militar

region [ˈriːdʒən] N región *f*, zona *f*; **the ~s** (*Brit*) (= *provinces*) las provincias; **in the ~ of £6 million** alrededor de *or* aproximadamente seis millones de libras

regional [ˈriːdʒənl] ADJ regional

register [ˈredʒɪstəʳ] Ⓐ N (*gen*) registro *m*; (*in school*) lista *f*; [*of members*] lista *f*, registro *m*; **the ~ of births, marriages and deaths** el registro civil; **to call** *or* **take the ~** pasar lista Ⓑ VT **1** (= *record*) [+ *fact, figure*] registrar, hacer constar; [+ *birth, marriage, death*] registrar, inscribir; [+ *company, property*] registrar; [+ *car, ship*] matricular, registrar; [+ *letter*] certificar; **are you ~ed with a doctor?** ¿está inscrito en la lista de pacientes de algún médico?; **to be ~ed to vote** estar inscrito en el censo electoral; **to be ~ed blind** estar registrado como ciego **2** (= *show*) marcar, indicar; **the petrol** (*Brit*) **or gas** (*US*) **gauge was ~ing empty** el indicador de gasolina marcaba *or* indicaba que el depósito estaba vacío **3** (= *express*) [+ *emotion*] manifestar, mostrar; [+ *protest, support*] expresar, manifestar; [+ *complaint*] presentar Ⓒ VI (*with agency, for course or conference*) inscribirse; (*at hotel*) registrarse; (*Univ*) matricularse, inscribirse; **to ~ with a doctor** inscribirse en la lista de un médico; **to ~ to vote** inscribirse *or* registrarse en el censo electoral; **to ~ as unemployed** registrarse como parado; **to ~ with the police** dar parte a la policía; **it doesn't seem to have ~ed with her*** no parece haber hecho mella en ella; **when it finally ~ed*** cuando por fin cayó en la cuenta

registered [ˈredʒɪstəd] ADJ [*letter*] certificado; [*student, car*] matriculado; [*voter*] inscrito ➤ **registered charity** sociedad *f* benéfica legalmente constituida ➤ **registered company** sociedad *f* legalmente constituida ➤ **registered mail** (*esp US*) = **registered post** ➤ **registered nurse** (*US*) enfermero/a *m/f* titulado/a ➤ **registered post** (*Brit*) servicio *m* de entrega con acuse de recibo ➤ **registered trademark** marca *f* registrada

registrar [ˌredʒɪsˈtrɑːʳ] N **1** (*Brit*) [*of births, marriages, deaths*] secretario/a *m/f* del registro civil **2** (*Brit Univ*) secretario/a *m/f* general **3** (*Med*) interno/a *m/f*

registration [ˌredʒɪsˈtreɪʃən] N (*for course, conference, of voter*) inscripción *f*; (*Univ*) matriculación *f*, inscripción *f*; [*of company, trademark, gun*] registro *m*; [*of ship*] matriculación *f*, abanderamiento *m*; (*Brit*) [*of car*] matriculación *f* ➤ **registration document** (*Brit*) documento *m* de matriculación ➤ **registration fee** (*Univ*) matrícula *f*; (*for agency*) cuota *f* de inscripción ➤ **registration form** formulario *m* de inscripción ➤ **registration number** (*Brit Aut*) matrícula *f*

registry [ˈredʒɪstrɪ] N registro *m*, archivo *m*; (*Univ*) secretaría f general ➤ **registry office** (*esp Brit*) registro m civil; **to get married at a ~ office** casarse por lo civil

regress [rɪˈgres] VI retroceder

regression [rɪˈgreʃən] N regresión f

regressive [rɪˈgresɪv] ADJ regresivo

regret [rɪˈgret] Ⓐ N 1 (= *sorrow*) pena f, pesar m; **my one ~ is that I didn't see her before she died** lo único que siento *or* lamento es no haberla visto antes de que muriera; **much to my ~** con gran pesar mío
2 (= *remorse*) remordimiento(s) m(pl); **I have no ~s** no me arrepiento de nada
Ⓑ VT 1 (= *be sorry for*) [+ *death, inconvenience, error*] lamentar; **the President ~s (that) he cannot see you today** el presidente lamenta *or* siente no poder recibirlo hoy; **we ~ to inform you that ...** lamentamos tener que informarle que ...
2 (= *rue*) [+ *decision*] arrepentirse de, lamentar; **you won't ~ it!** ¡no te arrepentirás!, ¡no lo lamentarás!

regretfully [rɪˈgretfəlɪ] ADV con pesar

regrettable [rɪˈgretəbl] ADJ lamentable; **it is ~ that** es lamentable que + *subjun*, es de lamentar que + *subjun*

regrettably [rɪˈgretəblɪ] ADV desgraciadamente, lamentablemente

regroup [ˈriːˈgruːp] VI reagruparse

Regt. ABBR (= **Regiment**) regto.

regular [ˈregjʊləʳ] Ⓐ ADJ 1 (= *symmetrical*) [*shape*] regular
2 (= *even*) [*surface, teeth*] uniforme, parejo (*esp LAm*)
3 (= *recurring at even intervals*) [*pulse, flights, breathing, order*] regular; **to take ~ exercise** hacer ejercicio con regularidad; **at ~ intervals** (*in time*) con regularidad; (*in space*) a intervalos regulares; **it's important to eat ~ meals** es importante comer con regularidad; **to be in ~ use** utilizarse de manera regular; ✦ IDIOM **as ~ as clockwork** como un cronómetro, como un reloj
4 (= *habitual, customary*) [*visitor, customer, listener*] habitual, asiduo; [*doctor, partner*] habitual; **they are ~ churchgoers** van a misa con regularidad *or* con asiduidad; **on a ~ basis** con regularidad; **to be in ~ employment** tener un trabajo fijo; **the ~ staff** el personal habitual
5 (= *unvarying*) **a man of ~ habits** un hombre metódico, un hombre ordenado (en sus costumbres); **to keep ~ hours** llevar una vida ordenada
6 (= *frequent*) frecuente; **I have to make ~ trips to France** tengo que viajar a Francia con frecuencia, tengo que hacer viajes frecuentes a Francia; **to be in ~ contact with sb** mantener *or* tener un contacto frecuente con algn; **it's a ~ occurrence** pasa con frecuencia, es algo frecuente
7 (*Mil*) [*soldier, army*] profesional, de carrera
8 (*Ling*) [*verb*] regular
9 (*esp US*) (= *ordinary, normal*) normal; **I'm just a ~ guy** no soy más que un tipo *or* (*Sp*) tío normal (y corriente); **~ fries** porción f mediana de patatas fritas
Ⓑ N 1 (= *customer*) (*in pub, bar*) cliente mf habitual, parroquiano/a m/f; **one of the ~s at the club** un asiduo del club; **he's a ~ on the programme** es un invitado habitual del programa
2 (*Mil*) militar mf de carrera

regularity [ˌregjʊˈlærɪtɪ] N regularidad f

regularize [ˈregjʊləraɪz] VT (= *standardize*) [+ *activities, procedure*] regularizar, estandarizar; (= *make official*) [+ *situation*] formalizar, regularizar

regularly [ˈregjʊləlɪ] ADV (= *at regular arranged times*) regularmente, con regularidad; (= *frequently*) frecuentemente, con frecuencia, a menudo; (= *at evenly spaced intervals*) a intervalos regulares

regulate [ˈregjʊleɪt] VT regular

regulation [ˌregjʊˈleɪʃən] N 1 (= *rule*) norma f; **safety ~s** normas fpl de seguridad; **it's against (the) ~s** va contra las normas *or* el reglamento 2 [*of industry, prices, temperature*] regulación f

regulator [ˈregjʊleɪtəʳ] N 1 (*Tech*) regulador m 2 (= *person, organization*) persona u organización que regula oficialmente un sector de los negocios o la industria

regulatory [ˈregjʊˌleɪtərɪ] ADJ regulador

regurgitate [rɪˈgɜːdʒɪteɪt] VT regurgitar; (*fig*) repetir mecánicamente

rehab** [ˈriːhæb] N rehabilitación f; **to be in ~** estar en tratamiento (de rehabilitación) ➤ **rehab centre, rehab center** (*US*) centro m de rehabilitación

rehabilitate [ˌriːəˈbɪlɪteɪt] VT rehabilitar

rehabilitation [ˈriːəˌbɪlɪˈteɪʃən] N rehabilitación f ➤ **rehabilitation centre, rehabilitation center** (*US*) centro m de rehabilitación

rehash Ⓐ [ˈriːhæʃ] N refrito m Ⓑ [ˌriːˈhæʃ] VT [+ *book, speech*] hacer un refrito de

rehearsal [rɪˈhɜːsəl] N ensayo m

rehearse [rɪˈhɜːs] VT, VI ensayar

rehouse [ˈriːˈhaʊz] VT dar una nueva vivienda a; **200 families have been ~d** 200 familias tienen vivienda nueva ya

reign [reɪn] Ⓐ N reinado m; **in the ~ of** bajo el reinado de; **~ of terror** régimen m de terror Ⓑ VI reinar

reigning [ˈreɪnɪŋ] ADJ [*monarch*] reinante, actual; **~ champion** campeón m actual

reiki [ˈreɪkɪ] N reiki m

reimburse [ˌriːɪmˈbɜːs] VT **to ~ sb for sth** reembolsar a algn por algo

reimbursement [ˌriːɪmˈbɜːsmənt] N reembolso m

rein [reɪn] N rienda f; **we must keep a tight ~ on expenditure** tenemos que restringir los gastos; **to give sb free ~** dar rienda suelta a algn
➤ **rein in** VT + ADV refrenar

reincarnation [ˈriːɪnkɑːˈneɪʃən] N reencarnación f

reindeer [ˈreɪndɪəʳ] N (*pl* ~) reno m

reinforce [ˌriːɪnˈfɔːs] VT (*gen, fig*) reforzar; [+ *concrete*] armar

reinforcement [ˌriːɪnˈfɔːsmənt] N 1 (= *act*) refuerzo m
2 (*Mil*) **reinforcements** refuerzos mpl

reinstate [ˈriːɪnˈsteɪt] VT [+ *passage*] reincorporar, incluir de nuevo (**in** a); [+ *worker*] reincorporar, volver a emplear; [+ *official*] restituir en su puesto *or* cargo

reinstatement [ˈriːɪnˈsteɪtmənt] N [*of passage*] reincorporación f, restitución f (**in** a); [*of worker*] reincorporación f al puesto; [*of official*] restitución f en el puesto

reissue [ˈriːˈɪʃuː] VT [+ *film*] reestrenar; [+ *book*] reimprimir, reeditar

reiterate [riːˈɪtəreɪt] VT [+ *statement*] reiterar, repetir; **I must ~ that ...** quiero recalcar que ...

reject Ⓐ [rɪˈdʒekt] VT (*gen*) rechazar; [+ *suggestion, possibility, solution*] descartar, rechazar; [+ *accusation*] negar; [+ *plea*] ignorar, hacer caso omiso de; **to feel ~ed** (*emotionally*) sentirse rechazado; (*socially*) sentirse marginado, sentirse rechazado Ⓑ [ˈriːdʒekt] N (= *product*) artículo m defectuoso; **society's ~s** los marginados de la sociedad

rejection [rɪˈdʒekʃən] N (*gen*) rechazo m; [*of help*] denegación f ➤ **rejection slip** nota f de rechazo

rejoice [rɪˈdʒɔɪs] Ⓐ VI alegrarse, regocijarse (*liter*) (**at, about** de) Ⓑ VT **to ~ that ...** alegrarse de que ... + *subjun*

rejoicing [rɪˈdʒɔɪsɪŋ] N regocijo m, júbilo m

rejoin [ˈriːˈdʒɔɪn] Ⓐ VT [+ *organization*] reincorporarse a (*also Mil*); [+ *person*] reunirse con Ⓑ VI reincorporarse

rejoinder [rɪˈdʒɔɪndəʳ] N réplica f

rejuvenate [rɪˈdʒuːvɪneɪt] VT rejuvenecer

rekindle [ˈriːˈkɪndl] VT reanimar, revivar

relapse [rɪˈlæps] Ⓐ N (*Med*) recaída f; **to have a ~** sufrir una recaída Ⓑ VI 1 (*Med*) recaer 2 (= *revert*) **he ~d into his usual state of depression** volvió a sumirse en su habitual estado de depresión

relate [rɪˈleɪt] Ⓐ VT 1 (= *tell*) relatar
2 (= *link*) **to ~ sth to sth** relacionar algo con algo
Ⓑ VI relacionarse; **to ~ to** (= *form relationship with, connect with*) relacionarse con; (= *understand, identify with*) identificarse con; (= *appertain to*) referirse a, estar relacionado con, tener que ver con; **he is unable to ~ to other people** no es capaz de relacionarse con otras

personas; **I can ~ to that*** yo eso lo entiendo*, yo me identifico con eso; **most of the enquiries ~ to debt** la mayoría de las preguntas se refieren a deudas or tienen que ver con deudas; **relating to** relativo a, referente a, relacionado con

related [rɪˈleɪtɪd] ADJ 1 [subject] relacionado, afín; [language] afín; [issue, problem, offence] relacionado; **this murder is not ~ to the other** este asesinato no está relacionado con el otro; **pay rises are ~ to performance** los aumentos de sueldo guardan relación con el rendimiento; **the two events are not ~** los dos sucesos no guardan relación
2 (by family) **they are ~ (to each other)** son parientes, están emparentados; **we are closely/distantly ~** somos parientes cercanos/lejanos; **are you ~ to the prisoner?** ¿es usted pariente del prisionero?; **to be ~ to sb by marriage** ser pariente político de algn; **termites are closely ~ to cockroaches** las termitas son de la misma familia que las cucarachas

relation [rɪˈleɪʃən] N 1 (= relationship) relación f (**to, with** con); **to bear little/no ~ to sth** tener poco/no tener nada que ver con algo; **in ~ to** (= compared to) en relación con, con relación a; (= in connection with) en lo que se refiere a
2 (= relative) pariente mf, familiar mf; **all my ~s came** vinieron todos mis parientes, vino toda mi familia; **close/distant ~** pariente mf cercano/a/lejano/a; **what ~ is she to you?** ¿qué parentesco tiene contigo?
3 **relations** (= relationship) relaciones fpl; **to break off ~s with sb** romper (relaciones) con algn

relationship [rɪˈleɪʃənʃɪp] N (gen) relación f; (sexual) relación f, relaciones fpl; (= kinship) parentesco m

relative [ˈrelətɪv] **Ⓐ** ADJ 1 (= comparative) [safety, peace, comfort, ease] relativo; **it's all ~** todo es relativo; **he is a ~ newcomer** es relativamente nuevo; **in ~ terms** relativamente; **petrol** (Brit) or **gasoline** (US) **consumption is ~ to speed** el consumo de gasolina está en relación con la velocidad
2 (= respective) **the ~ merits of the two systems** los méritos de cada uno de los dos sistemas
3 (= relevant) **~ to** relativo a, concerniente a
4 (Gram) relativo; **~ pronoun** pronombre m relativo
Ⓑ N pariente mf, familiar mf; **friends and ~s** amigos mpl y familiares; **a close/distant ~** un pariente cercano/lejano

relatively [ˈrelətɪvlɪ] ADV [few, small, slow] relativamente; **~ speaking** relativamente

relativity [ˌreləˈtɪvɪtɪ] N relatividad f

relaunch [ˈriːˈlɔːntʃ] **Ⓐ** VT [+ organization, scheme] relanzar **Ⓑ** N [of organization, scheme] relanzamiento m

relax [rɪˈlæks] **Ⓐ** VT [+ person, body, rules] relajar; [+ standards] dejar que bajen; **to ~ one's muscles** relajar los músculos **Ⓑ** VI [person] relajarse; **I like to ~ with a book** me gusta relajarme leyendo; **his face ~ed** relajó la cara; **~!** everything's fine ¡tranquilízate! todo está bien

relaxation [ˌriːlækˈseɪʃən] N relajación f, relajamiento m; **to get some ~** esparcirse, expansionarse

relaxed [rɪˈlækst] ADJ relajado

relaxing [rɪˈlæksɪŋ] ADJ relajante

relay [ˈriːleɪ] **Ⓐ** N 1 [of workmen] turno m; **to work in ~s** trabajar por turnos, ir relevándose en el trabajo 2 (also ~ **race**) carrera f de relevos; **the 400 metres ~** los 400 metros relevos **Ⓑ** VT 1 (Rad, TV) retransmitir 2 (= pass on) [+ message] transmitir, pasar

release [rɪˈliːs] **Ⓐ** N 1 (= liberation) [of prisoner of war, hostage] liberación f, puesta f en libertad; [of convict] puesta f en libertad, excarcelación f; **on his ~ from prison he ...** al salir de la cárcel ...; **death came as a merciful ~** la muerte fue una bendición or un gran alivio
2 (= issue) [of film] estreno m; [of album, video] puesta f en venta; [of book] puesta f en venta or circulación; [of news, documentation] publicación f; **to be on general ~** exhibirse en todos los cines
3 (= new item) **their new ~ is called ...** su nuevo álbum se llama ...; **new ~s** (= records) novedades fpl discográficas; (= films) nuevas producciones fpl
4 (= emission) [of gas, smoke] escape m, emisión f
Ⓑ VT 1 (= set free) [+ prisoner of war, hostage] liberar, poner

en libertad; [+ convict] poner en libertad, excarcelar; [+ patient] dar de alta; [+ animal] soltar, dejar en libertad; [+ person] (from obligation) eximir; **the bird was ~d into the wild** el pájaro fue devuelto a su hábitat natural
2 (= issue) [+ film] estrenar; [+ album, video] [group, artist] sacar; [company] poner a la venta; [+ news, report, statement] hacer público, dar a conocer
3 (= make available) [+ documents] facilitar; [+ funds] facilitar, ceder
4 (= emit) [+ gas, smoke, heat, energy] despedir, emitir
5 (= let go) [+ hand, arm, catch, brake] soltar; (Phot) [+ shutter] disparar; **he ~d his grip on my arm** me soltó el brazo

relegate [ˈrelɪgeɪt] VT relegar; **the news had been ~d to the inside pages** la noticia había sido relegada a las páginas interiores; **they were ~d to the second division** (Brit) bajaron or descendieron a segunda división

relent [rɪˈlent] VI ablandarse, aplacarse

relegation [ˌrelɪˈgeɪʃən] N relegación f; (Brit Sport) descenso m

relentless [rɪˈlentlɪs] ADJ (= heartless) [cruelty] cruel, despiadado; (= incessant) incesante; **he is quite ~ about it** en esto se muestra totalmente implacable

relentlessly [rɪˈlentlɪslɪ] ADV (= persistently) sin descanso; **he presses on ~** avanza implacable

relevance [ˈreləvəns] N pertinencia f, relevancia f; **what is the ~ of that?** y eso ¿tiene que ver (con lo que estamos discutiendo)?

relevant [ˈreləvənt] ADJ [information, facts, document, page] pertinente; [authority] competente; **Shakespeare's plays are still ~ today** las obras de Shakespeare tienen aún trascendencia hoy día; **applicants need a year's ~ experience** los solicitantes necesitan tener un año de experiencia en el campo; **details ~ to this affair** detalles relacionados con or concernientes a este asunto; **information which may be ~ to this case** información que puede ser relevante para este caso

reliability [rɪˌlaɪəˈbɪlɪtɪ] N [of person, firm] seriedad f, formalidad f; [of car, method, information, figures, account] fiabilidad f; **they have a reputation for good service and ~** tienen fama de dar un buen servicio y ser formales

reliable [rɪˈlaɪəbl] ADJ [person, firm] digno de confianza, formal; [car] seguro, fiable; [method, memory] de fiar; [information, figures, indicator] fiable; [evidence, report, description, source] fidedigno; **she's very ~** puedes confiar completamente en ella, es una persona muy formal; **a cheap and ~ service** un servicio barato y fiable

reliably [rɪˈlaɪəblɪ] ADV **equipment that works ~ in most conditions** equipo que funciona sin fallos en la mayoría de las condiciones; **I am ~ informed that ...** sé de fuentes fidedignas que ...

reliance [rɪˈlaɪəns] N **~ on sth** dependencia f de algo

reliant [rɪˈlaɪənt] ADJ **to be ~ on** depender de

relic [ˈrelɪk] N (Rel) reliquia f; (fig) vestigio m

relief [rɪˈliːf] **Ⓐ** N 1 (from pain, anxiety) alivio m; **that's a ~!** ¡qué alivio!; **to provide ~ from sth** aliviar algo; **to our (great) ~, she accepted** para (gran) alivio nuestro, aceptó; **it's a ~ to get out of the office once in a while** es una alegría or un alivio trabajar fuera de la oficina de vez en cuando
2 (= aid) auxilio m, ayuda f; **disaster ~** auxilio a las víctimas de una catástrofe
3 (US) (= welfare) **to be on ~** recibir prestaciones de la seguridad social
4 (Mil) [of town] liberación f
5 (Art, Geog) relieve m; **in ~** en relieve
Ⓑ CPD [train, bus] de reemplazo; [typist, secretary] suplente; [work, worker, agency, organization, convoy] de ayuda, de auxilio ➤ **relief driver** conductor(a) m/f de relevo ➤ **relief fund** fondo m de auxilio (a los damnificados) ➤ **relief map** mapa m físico or de relieve; (3-D) mapa m en relieve

relieve [rɪˈliːv] VT 1 (= alleviate) [+ sufferings, pain] aliviar; [+ tension] disipar, aliviar; **to ~ one's feelings** desahogarse
2 (= ease mind of) [+ person] tranquilizar
3 **to ~ o.s.** (= go to lavatory) ir al baño, hacer pis*

4 (= *release*) **to ~ sb of a post** destituir a algn; **he was ~d of his command** fue relevado de su mando; **let me ~ you of your coat** permítame ayudarla con el abrigo; **to ~ sb of his wallet** (*hum*) quitar la cartera a algn, robar la cartera a algn **5** (*Mil*) [+ *city*] descercar, socorrer; [+ *soldier*] relevar

religion [rɪˈlɪdʒən] N religión *f*

religious [rɪˈlɪdʒəs] ADJ [*beliefs, leader, service, reason*] religioso; [*practice*] de la religión, religioso; [*war*] de religión, religioso ➤ **religious education** enseñanza *f* religiosa

religiously [rɪˈlɪdʒəslɪ] ADV **1** (*Rel*) **a ~ diverse country** un país con diversidad religiosa *or* de religiones **2** (= *meticulously*) religiosamente

relinquish [rɪˈlɪŋkwɪʃ] VT [+ *claim, right*] renunciar a; [+ *control*] ceder; [+ *post*] renunciar a, dimitir de

relish [ˈrelɪʃ] **Ⓐ** N **1** (= *enthusiasm*) entusiasmo *m*; **to do sth with ~** hacer algo de buena gana; **to eat sth with ~** comer algo con apetito **2** (= *sauce*) salsa *f* **Ⓑ** VT [+ *meal*] saborear; **I don't ~ the idea of staying up all night** no me hace gracia la idea de estar levantado toda la noche

relive [ˈriːˈlɪv] VT [+ *past*] revivir; [+ *memories*] rememorar

reload [ˈriːˈləʊd] VT recargar, volver a cargar

relocate [ˈriːləʊˈkeɪt] **Ⓐ** VT [+ *factory, employees*] trasladar, reubicar **Ⓑ** VI trasladarse

relocation [ˌriːləʊˈkeɪʃən] N traslado *m*, reubicación *f* ➤ **relocation package** prima *f* de traslado

reluctance [rɪˈlʌktəns] N reticencia *f*, renuencia *f* (*frm*); **to show ~ (to do sth)** mostrarse reacio *or* reticente *or* (*frm*) renuente (a hacer algo), mostrar reticencia *or* (*frm*) renuencia (a hacer algo); **with ~** con reticencia, a regañadientes

reluctant [rɪˈlʌktənt] ADJ [*person*] reacio, reticente, renuente (*frm*); [*praise*] a regañadientes; **he took the ~ decision to stop production** tomó la decisión, muy a su pesar, de parar la producción; **we were ~ to sell the house** éramos reacios *or* nos resistíamos a vender la casa

reluctantly [rɪˈlʌktəntlɪ] ADV de mala gana, a regañadientes

rely [rɪˈlaɪ] VI **to ~ (up)on sth/sb** (= *depend on*) depender de algo/algn; (= *count on*) contar con algo/algn; (= *trust*) confiar en algo/algn, fiarse de algo/algn; **to ~ (up)on sth/sb for sth** depender de algo/algn para algo; **we are ~ing on you to do it** contamos con usted para hacerlo; **you can ~ on him to be late** ten *or* puedes tener por seguro que va a llegar tarde; **can I ~ on you to behave?** ¿puedo confiar en que te vas a comportar?

remain [rɪˈmeɪn] VI **1** (= *be left*) quedar; **much ~s to be done** queda mucho por hacer; **it only ~s to thank you** sólo queda darle las gracias; **that ~s to be seen** eso está por ver **2** (= *continue to be*) seguir, continuar, permanecer; **to ~ seated/standing** permanecer sentado/de pie; **they ~ed silent** permanecieron en silencio; **the fact ~s that ...** no es menos cierto que ..., sigue siendo un hecho que ... **3** (= *stay*) quedarse; **we ~ed there (for) three weeks** nos quedamos allí tres semanas; **to ~ behind** (*gen*) quedarse; (*after school*) quedarse después de las clases

remainder [rɪˈmeɪndə'] N **1** (= *part left over*) resto *m*; **the ~** (= *remaining people*) los otros, los demás **2 remainders** (*Comm*) artículos *mpl* no vendidos; (= *books*) restos *mpl* de edición

remaining [rɪˈmeɪnɪŋ] ADJ **the three ~ hostages** los tres rehenes restantes *or* que quedaban; **he is her only ~ relative** él es el único pariente que le queda; **the ~ passengers** los otros *or* los demás pasajeros

remains [rɪˈmeɪnz] NPL [*of building*] restos *mpl*; [*of food*] sobras *fpl*, restos *mpl*; **human ~** restos *mpl* humanos; **Roman ~** ruinas *fpl* romanas

remake Ⓐ [ˌriːˈmeɪk] VT rehacer, volver a hacer **Ⓑ** [ˈriːmeɪk] N nueva versión *f*

remand [rɪˈmɑːnd] (*Jur*) **Ⓐ** N **to be on ~** estar en prisión preventiva **Ⓑ** VT [+ *case*] remitir; **to ~ sb in custody** poner a algn en prisión preventiva; **to ~ sb on bail** libertar *or* liberar a algn bajo fianza **Ⓒ** CPD ➤ **remand centre** (*Brit*) cárcel *f* transitoria

remark [rɪˈmɑːk] **Ⓐ** N comentario *m*, observación *f*; **to make ~s about sb** hacer comentarios sobre algn **Ⓑ** VT **to ~ that** comentar que, observar que, decir que; **"it's a pity,"** **she ~ed** —es una lástima —dijo **Ⓒ** VI **to ~ on sth** hacer observaciones sobre algo

remarkable [rɪˈmɑːkəbl] ADJ [*person, success, performance*] extraordinario; [*achievement, progress*] notable, extraordinario; [*results*] excelente, extraordinario; [*story*] singular; **~ for sth** notable por algo; **it is ~ that** es sorprendente que + *subjun*; **it was ~ how quickly she recovered** fue sorprendente *or* extraordinario lo pronto que se recuperó

remarkably [rɪˈmɑːkəblɪ] ADV [*similar, beautiful, cheap*] extraordinariamente; [*well, quickly*] increíblemente; **~, the factory had escaped the bombing** la fábrica, increíblemente, no resultó dañada en el bombardeo; **he looked ~ like his father** guardaba un parecido extraordinario con su padre

remarry [ˈriːˈmærɪ] VI volver a casarse

rematch [ˈriːˈmætʃ] N (= *return match*) partido *m* de vuelta

remedial [rɪˈmiːdɪəl] ADJ (*Med*) reparador; (*fig*) correctivo ➤ **remedial education** educación *f* especial ➤ **remedial teaching** enseñanza *f* a niños *etc* con dificultades, enseñanza *f* compensatoria

remedy [ˈremədɪ] **Ⓐ** N remedio *m* **Ⓑ** VT remediar

remember [rɪˈmembə'] **Ⓐ** VT **1** (= *recall*) [+ *person, fact, promise*] acordarse de, recordar; **I can never ~ phone numbers** tengo muy mala memoria para los números de teléfono, soy incapaz de recordar números de teléfono; **I ~ seeing it** me acuerdo de *or* recuerdo haberlo visto, me acuerdo de que *or* recuerdo que lo vi; **I seem to ~ (that) ...** si mal no recuerdo ...; **it was a night to ~** fue una noche memorable *or* inolvidable **2** (= *bear in mind*) recordar, tener presente; **~ that he carries a gun** recuerda *or* ten presente que lleva una pistola **3** (= *not forget*) acordarse de; **have you ~ed your passport?** ¿te has acordado del pasaporte *or* de traer el pasaporte?; **to ~ sb in one's prayers** rezar por algn; **to ~ sb in one's will** mencionar a algn en el testamento; **she ~ed to do it** se acordó de hacerlo; **~ to turn out the light** no te olvides de apagar la luz; **~ what happened before** no te olvides *or* acuérdate de lo que pasó antes **4** (= *commemorate*) recordar **5** (*Brit*) (*with wishes*) **she asks to be ~ed to you all** manda recuerdos a todos; **~ me to your family** dale recuerdos a tu familia, saluda a tu familia de mi parte **Ⓑ** VI **1** (= *recall*) acordarse, recordar; **do you ~?** ¿te acuerdas?, ¿recuerdas?; **try to ~!** ¡haz memoria!, ¡intenta acordarte!; **I don't** *or* **can't ~** no me acuerdo, no recuerdo; **as far as I (can) ~** que yo recuerde; **if I ~ right(ly)** si mal no recuerdo, si la memoria no me falla **2** (= *not forget*) acordarse; **I'll try to ~** intentaré acordarme, intentaré no olvidarme *or* que no se me olvide

remembrance [rɪˈmembrəns] N recuerdo *m*; **in ~ of** en conmemoración de ➤ **Remembrance Day, Remembrance Sunday** (*Brit*) día en el que se recuerda a los caídos en las dos guerras mundiales; ver tb www.britishlegion.org.uk

remind [rɪˈmaɪnd] VT recordar a; **thank you for ~ing me** gracias por recordármelo; **to ~ sb that** recordar a algn que; **to ~ sb to do sth** recordar a algn que haga algo; **to ~ sb about sth** recordar algo a algn; **to ~ sb of sth** recordar algo a algn; **that ~s me!** ¡a propósito!

reminder [rɪˈmaɪndə'] N **1** (*esp Brit*) (= *letter etc*) notificación *f*, aviso *m*; (= *payment reminder*) recordatorio *m* **2** (= *memento*) recuerdo *m*; **it's a ~ of the good old days** recuerda los buenos tiempos pasados

reminisce [ˌremɪˈnɪs] VI recordar, rememorar

reminiscence [ˌremɪˈnɪsəns] N recuerdo *m*

reminiscent [ˌremɪˈnɪsənt] ADJ **to be ~ of** recordar

remiss [rɪˈmɪs] ADJ negligente, descuidado; **it was ~ of me** fue un descuido de mi parte

remission [rɪˈmɪʃən] N **1** (*Rel*) remisión *f*, perdón *m* **2** (*Brit*) (= *reduction of prison sentence*) disminución *f* de pena **3** **to be in ~** [*sick person*] haberse recuperado (temporalmente); [*disease*] remitir, estar en fase de remisión

remit ❶ ['ri:mɪt] N (*Brit*) (= *area of responsibility*) competencia *f*; (= *terms of reference*) [*of committee etc*] cometido *m* **❷** [rɪ'mɪt] VT remitir

remittance [rɪ'mɪtəns] N (= *payment*) pago *m*, giro *m* ➤ **remittance advice** aviso *m* de pago

remnant ['remnənt] N (= *remainder*) resto *m*, remanente *m*; (= *scrap of cloth*) retal *m*

remonstrate ['remənstreɪt] VI (= *protest*) protestar, quejarse; (= *argue*) discutir; **to ~ about sth** protestar contra algo, poner reparos a algo; **to ~ with sb** reconvenir a algn

remorse [rɪ'mɔːs] N remordimiento *m*; **without ~** sin remordimientos; **to feel ~** arrepentirse

remorseful [rɪ'mɔːsfəl] ADJ arrepentido

remorsefully [rɪ'mɔːsfəlɪ] ADV con remordimiento; **he said ~** dijo arrepentido

remorseless [rɪ'mɔːslɪs] ADJ **1** (= *merciless*) despiadado **2** (= *relentless*) [*advance, progress*] implacable, inexorable

remote [rɪ'məʊt] **❶** ADJ (*compar* ~**r**; *superl* ~**st**) **1** (= *distant*) [*village, area*] remoto, apartado; [*galaxy*] lejano, remoto **2** (= *removed*) lejano, remoto; **these events seem ~ from contemporary life** estos sucesos parecen estar alejados de la vida contemporánea **3** (= *aloof*) [*person, manner, voice*] distante **4** (= *slight*) [*possibility, chance, prospect, hope, connection*] remoto; [*risk, resemblance*] ligero; **I haven't the ~st idea** no tengo ni la más remota idea **❷** CPD ➤ **remote access** acceso *m* remoto ➤ **remote control** (= *system*) control *m* remoto; (= *device*) mando *m* a distancia, telemando *m*

remote-controlled [rɪ'məʊtkən'trəʊld] ADJ teledirigido

remotely [rɪ'məʊtlɪ] ADV **1** (= *slightly*) [*connected, possible*] remotamente; **it wasn't even ~ amusing** no era ni por asomo divertido; **he isn't even ~ interested in opera** no está ni siquiera remotamente interesado en la ópera; **I've never seen anything ~ like it** nunca he visto nada (ni) remotamente parecido **2** (= *by remote control*) [*control*] a distancia; [*detonate*] por control remoto

remoteness [rɪ'məʊtnɪs] N lo remoto

remould ['ri:məʊld] N neumático *m* recauchutado, llanta *f* recauchutada (*LAm*)

removable [rɪ'mu:vəbl] ADJ (*gen*) movible; [*collar*] de quita y pon

removal [rɪ'mu:vəl] N (= *transfer*) traslado *m*; [*of word, sentence*] supresión *f*; (*Brit*) (*to new house*) mudanza *f*; (= *elimination*) eliminación *f* ➤ **removal expenses** (*Brit*) gastos *mpl* de traslado de efectos personales ➤ **removal man** (*Brit*) mozo *m* de mudanzas ➤ **removal van** (*Brit*) camión *m* de mudanzas

remove [rɪ'mu:v] VT **1** (= *take away*) [*+ object*] quitar; [*+ documents, evidence*] llevarse; **to ~ a child from school** sacar *or* quitar a un niño de la escuela; **the demonstrators were forcibly ~d by police** (*from building*) la policía echó a los manifestantes a la fuerza; **to ~ sth/sb to** trasladar *or* llevar algo/a algn a **2** (= *take off*) quitar; [*+ one's clothing, make-up*] quitarse; **he ~d his jacket** se quitó la chaqueta **3** (= *take out*) [*+ object*] sacar; (*Med*) [*+ organ, tumour*] extirpar, quitar; [*+ bullet*] extraer, quitar **4** (= *delete*) [*+ word, sentence*] suprimir, quitar; [*+ name from list*] quitar, tachar (**from** de) **5** (= *get rid of*) [*+ obstacle, threat, waste, problem*] eliminar; [*+ doubt, suspicion*] disipar; [*+ stain*] quitar **6** (= *dismiss*) (*from post*) destituir; **to ~ sb from office** destituir a algn de su cargo

remover [rɪ'mu:və'] N **make-up ~** desmaquillador *m*, desmaquillante *m*; **stain ~** quitamanchas *m inv*

remunerate [rɪ'mju:nəreɪt] VT remunerar

remuneration [rɪˌmju:nə'reɪʃən] N remuneración *f*

Renaissance [rə'neɪsəns] N **the ~** el Renacimiento

renal ['ri:nl] ADJ renal ➤ **renal failure** insuficiencia *f* renal

rename ['ri:'neɪm] VT poner nuevo nombre a; **they have ~d it "Mon Repos"** le han puesto el nuevo nombre de "Mon Repos"

render ['rendə'] VT **1** (= *make*) dejar, volver; **the accident ~ed him blind** el accidente lo dejó ciego; **to ~ sth useless** inutilizar algo **2** (= *translate*) traducir

rendering ['rendərɪŋ], **rendition** [ren'dɪʃən] N (= *translation*) traducción *f*; [*of song, role*] interpretación *f*

rendezvous ['rɒndɪvu:] **❶** N (*pl* ~ ['rɒndɪvu:z]) **1** (= *date*) cita *f*; (= *meeting*) reunión *f*; **to have a ~ with sb** tener una cita con algn **2** (= *meeting-place*) lugar *m* de reunión **❸** VI reunirse, encontrarse

renegade ['renɪgeɪd] ADJ, N renegado/a *m/f*

renege [rɪ'ni:g] VI faltar a su palabra; **to ~ on a promise** no cumplir una promesa

renew [rɪ'nju:] VT **1** (= *restore, update*) renovar **2** (= *resume*) [*+ negotiations, relations*] reanudar; **to ~ the attack** (*Mil*) volver al ataque; **to ~ one's efforts (to do sth)** volver a esforzarse (por hacer algo), reanudar sus esfuerzos (por hacer algo) (*frm*)

renewable [rɪ'nju:əbl] ADJ [*contract*] renovable; [*energy, resources*] no perecedero

renewal [rɪ'nju:əl] N **1** [*of contract, passport, subscription*] renovación *f*; **his contract is up for ~** le toca que le renueven el contrato **2** (= *restarting*) [*of negotiations, relations*] reanudación *f*; [*of attack, hostilities*] recrudecimiento *m* **3** (= *improvement*) renovación *f*; **urban ~** renovación *f* urbanística **4** (= *reinvigoration*) renacimiento *m*

renewed [rɪ'nju:d] ADJ [*enthusiasm*] renovado; [*outbreaks*] nuevo; **there have been ~ calls for his resignation** se ha vuelto a pedir su dimisión; **there have been ~ attempts/ efforts to reach agreement** se han reanudado los intentos/ esfuerzos por llegar a un acuerdo

rennet ['renɪt] N cuajo *m*

renounce [rɪ'naʊns] VT [*+ right, inheritance*] renunciar; [*+ plan, post, the world*] renunciar a

renovate ['renəʊveɪt] VT (= *modernize*) remodelar; (= *restore*) restaurar

renovation [ˌrenəʊ'veɪʃən] N (= *modernization*) remodelación *f*; (= *restoration*) restauración *f*

renown [rɪ'naʊn] N renombre *m*, fama *f*

renowned [rɪ'naʊnd] ADJ renombrado, famoso; **it is ~ for ...** es famoso por ..., es célebre por ...

rent [rent] **❶** N alquiler *m*, arriendo *m*; **"for rent"** (*US*) "se alquila" **❷** VT [*owner, tenant*] [*+ house, TV, car*] alquilar, arrendar, rentar (*Mex*); **to ~ a house from sb** alquilar *or* arrendar *or* (*Mex*) rentar una casa a algn; **to ~ a house (out) to sb** alquilar *or* arrendar *or* (*Mex*) rentar una casa a algn **❸** CPD ➤ **rent book** librito *m* del alquiler ➤ **rent boy*** (*Brit*) chapero** *m*, puto** *m* ➤ **rent collector** recaudador(a) *m/f* de alquileres ➤ **rent rebate** devolución *f* de alquiler

rental ['rentl] N [*of car, TV etc*] (= *hire*) alquiler *m*; (= *cost*) alquiler *m*, arriendo *m* (*LAm*) ➤ **rental car** (*esp US*) coche *m* de alquiler

rent-free ['rent'fri:] **❶** ADJ [*house etc*] exento de alquiler **❷** ADV **to live ~** ocupar una casa sin pagar alquiler

renunciation [rɪˌnʌnsɪ'eɪʃən] N renuncia *f*

reopen ['ri:'əʊpən] **❶** VT [*+ shop, theatre, border*] volver a abrir, reabrir; [*+ negotiations, investigation, debate*] reanudar; **to ~ a case** reabrir un caso **❷** VI [*shop, theatre*] volverse a abrir; [*negotiations*] reanudarse

reopening ['ri:'əʊpnɪŋ] N [*of shop, border*] reapertura *f*; [*of negotiations, investigation, debate*] reanudación *f*

reorder ['ri:'ɔːdə'] VT **1** (*Comm*) volver a pedir **2** (= *rearrange*) ordenar de nuevo, volver a poner en orden

reorganization ['ri:'ɔːgənaɪ'zeɪʃən] N reorganización *f*

reorganize ['ri:'ɔːgənaɪz] **❶** VT reorganizar **❷** VI reorganizarse

rep¹* [rep] N (= *salesperson*) viajante *mf*, agente *mf*; [*of union etc*] representante *mf*

rep²* [rep] N (*Theat*) = **repertory**

Rep. ABBR (*US*) **1** = **Republican 2** = **Representative**

repackage [ˌri:'pækɪdʒ] VT [*+ product*] reempaquetar; [*+ parcel*] reembalar; [*+ proposal, scheme*] reformular

repaid [riː'peɪd] PT, PP *of* **repay**

repaint ['riː'peɪnt] VT repintar

repair [rɪ'peə'] **A** N 1 (= *act*) reparación *f*, arreglo *m*; **to be beyond ~** (*lit*, *fig*) no tener arreglo; **she had taken her car in for ~s** había llevado el coche al taller; **"closed for repairs"** "cerrado por obras", "cerrado por reforma" 2 (= *state*) **to be in good/bad ~** estar en buen/mal estado **B** VT (= *mend*) [+ *car*, *machinery*, *roof*] arreglar, reparar; [+ *clothes*, *shoes*, *road*] arreglar **C** CPD ➤ **repair job** arreglo *m*, reparación *f* ➤ **repair shop** taller *m* de reparaciones; **bicycle ~ shop** taller *m* de reparación de bicicletas

repairable [rɪ'peərəbl] ADJ reparable

repairman [rɪ'peəmæn] N (*pl* **repairmen**) (*US*) reparador *m*

reparation [ˌrepə'reɪʃən] N reparación *f*; **to make ~ to sb for sth** indemnizar a algn por algo

repartee [ˌrepɑː'tiː] N réplicas *fpl* agudas

repatriate [riː'pætrɪeɪt] VT repatriar

repay [riː'peɪ] (*pt*, *pp* **repaid**) VT [+ *money*] reembolsar, devolver; [+ *debt*] liquidar, pagar; [+ *person*] reembolsar, pagar; [+ *kindness*] devolver, corresponder a; [+ *visit*] devolver, pagar; **to ~ sb in full** pagar *or* devolver a algn todo lo que se le debe; **I don't know how I can ever ~ you** no sé cómo podré devolverle el favor

repayable [riː'peəbl] ADJ reembolsable; **~ in ten instalments** a pagar en diez cuotas; **£5 deposit not ~** depósito inicial de cinco libras no reembolsable

repayment [riː'peɪmənt] N [*of expenses*] reembolso *m*; **now he asks for ~** ahora pide que se le devuelva el dinero; **in six ~s of £8** en seis cuotas de ocho libras cada uno; **mortgage ~s** los pagos de la hipoteca ➤ **repayment schedule** plan *m* de amortización

repeal [rɪ'piːl] VT revocar, abrogar

repeat [rɪ'piːt] **A** VT 1 (= *say or do again*) repetir (*also Scol*); [+ *thanks*] reiterar, volver a dar; [+ *demand*, *request*, *promise*] reiterar; **the documentary will be ~ed on Monday** el documental se volverá a emitir el lunes; **to ~ o.s.** repetirse 2 (= *divulge*) contar; **don't ~ this to anybody** no le cuentes esto a nadie 3 (= *recite*) recitar **B** N repetición *f* **C** CPD ➤ **repeat offender** delincuente *mf* reincidente ➤ **repeat performance** (*Theat*, *fig*) repetición *f* ➤ **repeat prescription** (*Brit*) receta *f* renovada

repeated [rɪ'piːtɪd] ADJ [*attacks*, *warnings*, *attempts*] repetido; [*requests*, *demands*] reiterado; [*criticism*] constante; **there have been ~ calls for his resignation** se ha pedido su dimisión reiteradamente *or* repetidas veces

repeatedly [rɪ'piːtɪdlɪ] ADV [*tell*, *deny*, *ask for*] repetidamente, reiteradamente, en repetidas ocasiones; **he ~ broke the rules** infringía las reglas constantemente

repel [rɪ'pel] VT (= *force back*) repeler, rechazar; (= *disgust*) repugnar, dar asco a

repellent [rɪ'pelənt] **A** ADJ repugnante, asqueroso **B** N **insect ~** repelente *m* contra insectos

repent [rɪ'pent] **A** VI arrepentirse (**of** de) **B** VT arrepentirse de

repentance [rɪ'pentəns] N arrepentimiento *m*

repentant [rɪ'pentənt] ADJ arrepentido

repercussion [ˌriːpə'kʌʃən] N repercusión *f*

repertoire ['repətwɑː'] N [*of songs*, *jokes*] repertorio *m*

repertory ['repətərɪ] N repertorio *m* ➤ **repertory company** compañía *f* de repertorio ➤ **repertory theatre**, **repertory theater** (*US*) teatro *m* de repertorio

repetition [ˌrepɪ'tɪʃən] N repetición *f*

repetitive [rɪ'petɪtɪv] ADJ repetitivo ➤ **repetitive strain injury** lesión en las muñecas y los brazos sufrida por teclistas

rephrase [riː'freɪz] VT expresar de otro modo

replace [rɪ'pleɪs] VT 1 (= *put back*) volver a colocar; **~ the cap after use** vuelva a colocar la tapa después de usarlo; **he ~d the letter in his pocket** se volvió a meter la carta en el bolsillo; **to ~ the receiver** colgar (el auricular) 2 (= *get replacement for*) [+ *object*] reponer; [+ *person*]

sustituir, reemplazar 3 (= *put in place of*) **to ~ sth with sth** sustituir algo por algo; **the airline is replacing its DC10s with Boeing 747s** la compañía aérea está sustituyendo los DC10 por Boeings 747; **to ~ sb with sth/sb** sustituir a algn por algo/algn, reemplazar a algn por algo/algn 4 (= *take the place of*) [+ *thing*] sustituir; [+ *person*] sustituir, reemplazar 5 (= *change*) cambiar

replaceable [rɪ'pleɪsəbl] ADJ reemplazable, sustituible; **it will not easily be ~** no será fácil encontrar uno igual

replacement [rɪ'pleɪsmənt] N 1 (= *putting back*) reposición *f*; (= *substitution*) sustitución *f* (**by**, **with** por) 2 (= *substitute*) 2.1 (= *person*) sustituto/a *m/f*, suplente *mf* (**for** de) 2.2 (= *thing*) **it took three days to find a ~** tardaron tres días en encontrar un repuesto; **we will give you a ~ if the goods are faulty** le damos uno nuevo si el artículo está defectuoso

replay (*esp Brit*) **A** [ˌriː'pleɪ] VT [+ *tape*] volver a poner; (*esp Brit*) [+ *match*] volver a jugar **B** ['riː'pleɪ] N [*of match*] repetición *f* de un partido; **there will be a ~ on Friday** el partido se volverá a jugar el viernes

replenish [rɪ'plenɪʃ] VT [+ *tank etc*] rellenar, llenar de nuevo; [+ *stocks*] reponer

replete [rɪ'pliːt] ADJ (*liter*) repleto, lleno (**with** de)

replica ['replɪkə] N réplica *f*, reproducción *f*

reply [rɪ'plaɪ] **A** N (*spoken*, *written*) respuesta *f*, contestación *f*; **"reply paid"** "no necesita sello", "a franquear en destino"; **in ~ to your letter** en respuesta a *or* contestando a su carta; **there's no ~** (*Telec*) no contestan **B** VI responder, contestar; **to ~ to sth/sb** contestar *or* responder a algo/algn; **to ~ to a letter** contestar (a) una carta **C** VT responder, contestar

repopulate ['riː'pɒpjʊleɪt] VT repoblar

report [rɪ'pɔːt] **A** N 1 (= *account*) informe *m*; (*Press*, *Rad*, *TV*) reportaje *m*, crónica *f*; (= *piece of news*) noticia *f*; **there were no ~s of casualties** no se anunciaron víctimas; **according to ~(s)** según se dice 2 (*Brit*) (*also* **school ~**) boletín *m* *or* cartilla *f* de notas 3 (*US*) (= *assignment*) trabajo *m* 4 (= *shot*) disparo *m* **B** VT 1 (= *state*, *make known*) **it is ~ed from Berlin that ...** comunican *or* se informa desde Berlín que ... 2 (*Press*, *TV*, *Rad*) [+ *event*] informar acerca de, informar sobre 3 (= *allege*) **she is ~ed to be in Italy** se dice que está en Italia; **he is ~ed to have said that ...** parece que dijo que ... 4 (= *notify*) [+ *crime*] denunciar, dar parte de; [+ *accident*] dar parte de; **13 people were ~ed killed** hubo informes de que murieron 13 personas; **to ~ sb missing** denunciar la desaparición de algn, declarar a algn desaparecido; **nothing to ~** nada nuevo (que contar), sin novedad 5 (= *denounce*) [+ *person*] denunciar (**for sth** por algo) 6 **~ed speech** (*Brit*) estilo *m* indirecto **C** VI 1 (= *make report*) presentar un informe 2 (*Press*, *TV*, *Rad*) (*gen*) informar; (= *be reporter*) ser reportero/a; **to ~ on sth** informar sobre algo 3 (= *present oneself*) presentarse; **he has to ~ to the police every five days** tiene que personarse *or* presentarse en la comisaría cada cinco días 4 **to ~ to sb** (= *be responsible to*) estar bajo las órdenes de algn; **who do you ~ to?** ¿quién es tu superior *or* tu jefe? **D** CPD ➤ **report card** (*US*) boletín *m* *or* cartilla *f* de notas ➤ **report back** VI + ADV 1 (= *give report*) informar; (*officially*) presentar un informe 2 (= *return*) volver (a presentarse)

reportedly [rɪ'pɔːtɪdlɪ] ADV según se dice; **he is ~ living in Australia** se dice que está viviendo en Australia

reporter [rɪ'pɔːtə'] N (*Press*) periodista *mf*, reportero/a *m/f*; (*TV*, *Rad*) locutor(a) *m/f*

reporting [rɪ'pɔːtɪŋ] N (*Press*, *TV*, *Rad*) cobertura *f*, reportajes *mpl* ➤ **reporting restrictions** (*Brit*) restricciones *fpl* informativas

repose [rɪ'pəʊz] N reposo *m*, descanso *m*; **in ~** relajado

repository [rɪ'pɒzɪtərɪ] N depósito *m*

repossess ['riː'pə'zes] VT embargar

repossession [ˌriːpəˈzeʃən] N embargo *m*

reprehensible [ˌreprɪˈhensɪbl] ADJ reprensible, censurable

represent [reprɪˈzent] VT (*gen*) representar; [+ *company*] ser agente de

representation [ˌreprɪzenˈteɪʃən] N 1 (*gen, Pol*) representación *f* 2 (= *protest*) **to make ~s to sb** elevar una protesta a algn; **to make ~s about sth** quejarse de algo

representative [ˌreprɪˈzentətɪv] **Ⓐ** ADJ representativo (**of** de) **Ⓑ** N (*gen*) representante *mf*; (*esp Brit Comm*) viajante *mf*; **Representative** (*US Pol*) ≈ diputado/a *m/f*

repress [rɪˈpres] VT reprimir

repressed [rɪˈprest] ADJ reprimido

repression [rɪˈpreʃən] N represión *f*

repressive [rɪˈpresɪv] ADJ represivo

reprieve [rɪˈpriːv] N 1 (*Jur*) indulto *m*; [*of sentence*] conmutación *f*; **to win a last-minute ~** ser indultado a última hora; **the building got a ~** se retiró la orden de demoler el edificio 2 (= *delay*) aplazamiento *m*, alivio *m* temporal

reprimand [ˈreprɪmɑːnd] **Ⓐ** N reprimenda *f* **Ⓑ** VT reprender, regañar

reprint **Ⓐ** [ˈriːprɪnt] N reimpresión *f*, reedición *f* **Ⓑ** [ˌriːˈprɪnt] VT reimprimir

reprisal [rɪˈpraɪzəl] N represalia *f*; **as a ~ for** como represalia por; **to take ~s** tomar represalias

reproach [rɪˈprəʊtʃ] **Ⓐ** N reproche *m*; **above** or **beyond ~** intachable, irreprochable **Ⓑ** VT **to ~ sb for sth** reprochar algo a algn; **to ~ o.s. for sth** reprocharse algo

reproachful [rɪˈprəʊtʃfəl] ADJ de reproche, de acusación

reproachfully [rɪˈprəʊtʃfəlɪ] ADV [*look*] con reproche; [*speak*] en tono acusador

reprobate [ˈreprəʊbeɪt] N réprobo/a *m/f*

reprocess [ˌriːˈprəʊses] VT reprocesar

reproduce [ˌriːprəˈdjuːs] **Ⓐ** VT reproducir **Ⓑ** VI reproducirse

reproduction [ˌriːprəˈdʌkʃən] N (= *act*) reproducción *f*; (= *copy*) copia *f*, reproducción *f* ➤ **reproduction furniture** muebles *mpl* antiguos de imitación

reproductive [ˌriːprəˈdʌktɪv] ADJ reproductor

reproof [ˌriːˈpruːf] N reprobación *f*, regaño *m*

reprove [rɪˈpruːv] VT **to ~ sb for** reprobar a algn por

reptile [ˈreptaɪl] N reptil *m*

republic [rɪˈpʌblɪk] N república *f*

republican [rɪˈpʌblɪkən] ADJ, N republicano/a *m/f*

repudiate [rɪˈpjuːdɪeɪt] VT [+ *charge*] rechazar, negar; [+ *attitude, violence*] repudiar

repugnance [rɪˈpʌɡnəns] N repugnancia *f*

repugnant [rɪˈpʌɡnənt] ADJ repugnante; **it is ~ to me** me repugna

repulse [rɪˈpʌls] **Ⓐ** VT (*gen*) rechazar **Ⓑ** N rechazo *m*

repulsion [rɪˈpʌlʃən] N 1 (= *disgust*) repulsión *f*, repugnancia *f* 2 (= *rejection*) rechazo *m*

repulsive [rɪˈpʌlsɪv] ADJ repulsivo, repugnante

reputable [ˈrepjʊtəbl] ADJ [*firm, brand*] acreditado, de confianza; [*person*] honroso, formal

reputation [ˌrepjʊˈteɪʃən] N reputación *f*, fama *f*; **to have a bad ~** tener mala fama; **of good ~** de buena fama; **he has a ~ for being awkward** tiene fama de difícil; **the hotel has a ~ for good food** el hotel es célebre por su buena comida

repute [rɪˈpjuːt] N reputación *f*, renombre *m*; **to know sb by ~ only** conocer a algn sólo por su reputación *or* de oídas nada más; **a house of ill ~** una casa de mala fama

reputed [rɪˈpjuːtɪd] ADJ 1 (= *supposed*) supuesto, presunto 2 (= *well known*) renombrado

reputedly [rɪˈpjuːtɪdlɪ] ADV según dicen

request [rɪˈkwest] **Ⓐ** N (*gen*) solicitud *f*; (= *plea*) petición *f*; **at the ~ of** a petición de; **by popular ~** por petición popular, a petición del público; **a ~ for help** una petición de socorro; **to grant sb's ~** acceder al ruego de algn; **to make a ~ for sth** pedir algo; **on ~** a solicitud

Ⓑ VT pedir, solicitar; **to ~ sb to do sth** pedir a algn que haga algo; **"visitors are requested not to talk"** "se ruega a los visitantes respetar el silencio" **Ⓒ** CPD ➤ **request stop** (*Brit*) parada *f* discrecional

requiem [ˈrekwɪem] N réquiem *m*

require [rɪˈkwaɪəʳ] VT 1 (= *need*) necesitar; **this plant ~s watering frequently** esta planta hay que regarla con frecuencia; **as (and when) ~d** cuando haga falta; **I am willing to give evidence if ~d** estoy dispuesto a testificar si se requiere *or* si es necesario 2 (= *call for, take*) [+ *patience, effort*] requerir 3 (= *ask, demand*) exigir; **it's not up to the standard I ~** no tiene el nivel que yo exijo; **the law ~s that safety belts be worn** la ley exige el uso del cinturón de seguridad; **to ~ sb to do sth** exigir que algn haga algo; **as ~d by law** como *or* según exige la ley; **what qualifications are ~d?** ¿qué títulos se requieren?

required [rɪˈkwaɪəd] ADJ 1 (= *necessary*) necesario; **the qualities ~ for the job** las cualidades que se requieren para el puesto 2 (= *fixed*) establecido; **within the ~ time** dentro del plazo establecido 3 (= *compulsory*) [*reading*] obligatorio

requirement [rɪˈkwaɪəmənt] N 1 (= *need*) necesidad *f* 2 (= *condition*) requisito *m*; **to meet all the ~s for sth** reunir todos los requisitos para algo; **Latin is a ~ for the course** el latín es un requisito para este curso, para este curso se exige el latín; **it is one of the ~s of the contract** es una de las estipulaciones del contrato

requisite [ˈrekwɪzɪt] **Ⓐ** ADJ = **required Ⓑ** N requisito *m*

requisition [ˌrekwɪˈzɪʃən] **Ⓐ** N (*Mil*) requisa *f*, requisición *f* **Ⓑ** VT (*Mil*) requisar

reroute [ˌriːˈruːt] VT desviar; **the train was ~d through Burgos** el tren pasó por Burgos al ser desviado de su ruta habitual

rerun [ˈriːrʌn] N repetición *f*

resale [ˌriːˈseɪl] N reventa *f*; **"not for resale"** "prohibida la venta" ➤ **resale value** valor *m* de reventa

resat [ˌriːˈsæt] PT, PP of **resit**

reschedule [ˌriːˈʃedjuːl, (*US*) ˌriːˈskedjuːl] VT [+ *meeting, visit, trip, programme*] cambiar la fecha/hora de; [+ *repayments, debt*] renegociar

rescind [rɪˈsɪnd] VT [+ *contract*] rescindir; [+ *order*] anular; [+ *law*] abrogar

rescue [ˈreskjuː] **Ⓐ** N rescate *m*, salvamento *m*; **to come/ go to sb's ~** acudir en auxilio de algn, socorrer a algn **Ⓑ** VT rescatar, salvar **Ⓒ** CPD ➤ **rescue attempt** intento *m* de rescate ➤ **rescue package** paquete *m* de medidas urgentes ➤ **rescue party** equipo *m* de rescate, equipo *m* de salvamento ➤ **rescue services** servicios *mpl* de rescate, servicios *mpl* de salvamento

rescuer [ˈreskjʊəʳ] N salvador(a) *m/f*, rescatador(a) *m/f*

research [rɪˈsɜːtʃ] **Ⓐ** N investigación *f*, investigaciones *fpl* (**in, into** de); **a piece of ~** una investigación **Ⓑ** VI hacer investigaciones; **to ~ into sth** investigar algo **Ⓒ** VT investigar; **to ~ an article** preparar el material para un artículo, reunir datos para escribir un artículo; **a well ~ed article** un artículo bien documentado **Ⓓ** CPD ➤ **research and development** investigación *f* y desarrollo *m* ➤ **research fellow** investigador(a) *m/f* ➤ **research grant** beca *f* de investigación ➤ **research laboratory** laboratorio *m* de investigación ➤ **research student** estudiante *mf* investigador(a) ➤ **research work** trabajo(s) *m(pl)* de investigación ➤ **research worker** investigador(a) *m/f*

researcher [rɪˈsɜːtʃəʳ] N investigador(a) *m/f*

resell [ˈriːˈsel] (*pt, pp* **resold**) VT revender

resemblance [rɪˈzembləns] N semejanza *f*, parecido *m*; **to bear a strong ~ to sb** parecerse mucho a algn

resemble [rɪˈzembl] VT parecerse a

resent [rɪˈzent] VT **I ~ that!** ¡me molesta *or* me ofende que digas eso!; **he ~ed the fact that I married her** le molestaba que me hubiese casado con ella; **she ~s having to look after her mother** le amarga tener que cuidar de su madre; **I ~ your tone** encuentro tu tono ofensivo; **I ~ed him because**

he was her favourite tenía celos de él porque era su preferido

resentful [rɪˈzentfəl] ADJ [*person*] resentido; [*tone*] resentido, de resentimiento; [*look, air*] de resentimiento; **to be** *or* **feel ~ about/at sth** estar resentido por algo; **he still felt ~ towards her** todavía estaba resentido con ella; **she was ~ of her sister, who was cleverer than her** tenía celos de su hermana, que era más inteligente que ella

resentment [rɪˈzentmənt] N resentimiento *m*, rencor *m* (**about** por); **I feel no ~ towards him** no le guardo rencor, no estoy resentido con él

reservation [ˌrezəˈveɪʃən] **Ⓐ** N **1** (= *booking*) reserva *f*; (= *seat*) plaza *f* reservada; (= *table*) mesa *f* reservada; **to make a ~ in a hotel** reservar una habitación en un hotel **2** (= *doubt*) reserva *f*, duda *f*; **I had ~s about it** tenía ciertas dudas sobre ese punto **3** (= *land*) reserva *f*; (*Brit*) (*on road*) mediana *f*, franja *f* central **Ⓑ** CPD ➤ **reservation desk** (*Brit*) (*in airport, etc*) mostrador *m* de reservas; (*US*) (= *reception desk*) recepción *f*

reserve [rɪˈzɜːv] **Ⓐ** N **1** [*of money, fuel, minerals*] reserva *f*; **to keep sth in ~** guardar algo en reserva **2** (*Mil*) **the ~** la reserva **3** (*esp Brit Sport*) reserva *mf*, suplente *mf* **4** (= *land*) reserva *f*; (*also* **game ~**) coto *m* (de caza); (*also* **nature ~**) reserva *f* natural **5** (= *restriction*) **without ~** sin reserva **6** (*towards others*) reserva *f* **Ⓑ** VT (= *book, set aside*) reservar; **to ~ the right to do sth** reservarse el derecho de hacer algo; **I ~ judgment on this** me reservo la opinión en este asunto **Ⓒ** CPD ➤ **reserve fund** fondo *m* de reserva ➤ **reserve price** (*Brit*) precio *m* mínimo (*fijado en una subasta*) ➤ **reserve team** (*Brit Sport*) equipo *m* de reserva

reserved [rɪˈzɜːvd] ADJ [*person, behaviour, room, table, seat*] reservado; **to be ~ about sth** ser reservado acerca de algo

reservist [rɪˈzɜːvɪst] N reservista *mf*

reservoir [ˈrezəvwɑːˀ] N **1** (= *lake*) embalse *m*, represa *f* (*LAm*); (= *tank*) depósito *m* **2** [*of strength etc*] reserva *f*

reset [ˈriːˈset] (*vb: pt, pp* ~) VT [+ *machine*] reajustar; [+ *bone*] volver a encajar ➤ **reset switch** conmutador *m* de reajuste

reshape [ˈriːˈʃeɪp] VT [+ *policy, constitution*] reformar; [+ *organization*] reorganizar

reshuffle [ˈriːˈʃʌfl] N (*esp Brit Pol*) remodelación *f*; **cabinet ~** remodelación *f* del gabinete

reside [rɪˈzaɪd] VI residir

residence [ˈrezɪdəns] **Ⓐ** N **1** (= *stay*) permanencia *f*, estancia *f* (*LAm*); **after six months' ~** después de seis meses de permanencia; **to take up ~** (*in house*) instalarse; (*in country*) establecerse; **in ~** residente; **artist in ~** artista *mf* residente; **when the students are in ~** cuando están los estudiantes; **there is a doctor in ~** hay un médico interno **2** (= *home*) residencia *f*, domicilio *m* **3** (*also* **hall of ~, ~ hall**) residencia *f*, colegio *m* mayor **Ⓑ** CPD ➤ **residence hall** (*US*) residencia *f*, colegio *m* mayor ➤ **residence permit** permiso *m* de residencia

resident [ˈrezɪdənt] **Ⓐ** ADJ [*person*] residente; [*population*] permanente; [*doctor, servant*] interno; **to be ~ in a town** tener domicilio fijo en una ciudad; **we were ~ there for some years** residimos allí durante varios años **Ⓑ** N [*of hotel, guesthouse*] huésped *mf*; [*of area, in block of flats*] vecino/a *m/f*; (*in country*) residente *mf* **Ⓒ** CPD ➤ **residents' association** asociación *f* de vecinos

residential [ˌrezɪˈdenʃəl] ADJ [*area*] residencial; [*work*] interno ➤ **residential home** (*for old people*) residencia *f* (de ancianos), hogar *m*; (*for handicapped people*) hogar *m* para minusválidos

residual [rɪˈzɪdjʊəl] ADJ residual

residue [ˈrezɪdjuː] N residuo *m*

resign [rɪˈzaɪn] **Ⓐ** VT [+ *post*] dimitir de, renunciar a; **to ~ o.s. to (doing) sth** resignarse a (hacer) algo **Ⓑ** VI dimitir, renunciar; **to ~ in favour of sb** renunciar en favor de algn

resignation [ˌrezɪɡˈneɪʃən] N **1** (= *act*) dimisión *f*, renuncia

f; **to hand in one's ~** presentar la dimisión **2** (= *state*) resignación *f* (**to** a)

resigned [rɪˈzaɪnd] ADJ resignado (**to** a)

resilience [rɪˈzɪlɪəns] N resistencia *f*

resilient [rɪˈzɪlɪənt] ADJ resistente

resin [ˈrezɪn] N resina *f*

resist [rɪˈzɪst] **Ⓐ** VT (= *oppose*) resistir(se) a; (= *be unaffected by*) resistir; **to ~ arrest** resistirse a ser detenido, oponer resistencia a la policía; **I couldn't ~ buying it** no me pude resistir a comprarlo **Ⓑ** VI resistir

resistance [rɪˈzɪstəns] N resistencia *f*; **to offer ~** oponer resistencia (**to** a); **the Resistance** la Resistencia ➤ **resistance fighter** militante *mf* de la Resistencia ➤ **resistance movement** (movimiento *m* de) resistencia *f*

resistant [rɪˈzɪstənt] ADJ resistente (**to** a)

resit (*vb: pt, pp* **resat**) (*Brit*) **Ⓐ** [ˈriːsɪt] N examen *m* de recuperación; **to do a ~** volver a presentarse (a un examen) **Ⓑ** [ˌriːˈsɪt] VT (*Brit*) [+ *exam*] volver a presentarse a; [+ *subject*] recuperar, volver a examinarse de (*Sp*)

reskill [ˈriːˈskɪl] (*Ind*) **Ⓐ** VI reciclarse **Ⓑ** VT reciclar

resold [ˌriːˈsəʊld] PT, PP *of* **resell**

resolute [ˈrezəluːt] ADJ resuelto, decidido

resolutely [ˈrezəluːtlɪ] ADV [*act*] con resolución, con determinación; [*refuse, resist*] firmemente, con firmeza; **to be ~ opposed to sth** oponerse firmemente *or* con firmeza a algo

resolution [ˌrezəˈluːʃən] N **1** (= *determination*) resolución *f*, determinación *f*; **to show ~** mostrarse resuelto *or* determinado **2** (= *solving*) resolución *f* **3** (*Parl*) acuerdo *m*; **to pass a ~** tomar un acuerdo **4** (= *goal*) propósito *m*; **New Year ~s** buenos propósitos *mpl* para el Año Nuevo; **to make a ~ to do sth** resolverse a hacer algo **5** (*Comput*) definición *f*

resolve [rɪˈzɒlv] **Ⓐ** N resolución *f* **Ⓑ** VT resolver, solucionar **Ⓒ** VI **to ~ to do sth** resolverse a hacer algo

resolved [rɪˈzɒlvd] ADJ **to be ~ to do sth** estar resuelto a hacer algo

resonance [ˈrezənəns] N resonancia *f*

resonant [ˈrezənənt] ADJ [*sound*] resonante

resort [rɪˈzɔːt] **Ⓐ** N **1** (= *recourse*) recurso *m*; **as a last ~** ◇ **in the last ~** como último recurso; **without ~ to force** sin recurrir a la fuerza **2** (= *place*) lugar *m* de encuentro; **holiday ~** (= *area, town*) lugar *m* turístico **Ⓑ** VI recurrir (**to** a); **to ~ to violence** recurrir a la violencia; **then they ~ed to throwing stones** pasaron luego a tirar piedras

resound [rɪˈzaʊnd] VI resonar; **the house ~ed with laughter** resonaron las risas por toda la casa

resounding [rɪˈzaʊndɪŋ] ADJ [*noise*] sonoro; [*victory, success*] resonante

resource [rɪˈsɔːs] N recurso *m*; **natural ~s** recursos *mpl* naturales; **to leave sb to his own ~s** dejar que algn se apañe como pueda

resourceful [rɪˈsɔːsfəl] ADJ ingenioso, con iniciativa

resourcefulness [rɪˈsɔːsfəlnɪs] N ingenio *m*, iniciativa *f*

respect [rɪsˈpekt] **Ⓐ** N **1** (= *consideration*) respeto *m*, consideración *f*; **she has no ~ for other people's feelings** no respeta los sentimientos de los demás; **out of ~ for sth/sb** por respeto a algo/algn, por consideración hacia algo/algn **2** (= *admiration, esteem*) respeto *m*; **we have the greatest ~ for him** le respetamos muchísimo; **show some ~!** ¡un poco de respeto!; **with (all due) ~** con el debido respeto **3 respects** respetos *mpl* (*frm*), recuerdos *mpl*, saludos *mpl*; **give my ~s to everyone** da recuerdos *or* saluda a todos de mi parte; **to pay one's ~s to sb** presentar sus respetos a algn **4** (= *point, detail*) aspecto *m*, sentido *m*; **in certain ~s** hasta cierto punto, en cierta medida, en cierto modo; **in other ~s** por lo demás; **in some/many ~s** en algunos/muchos aspectos *or* sentidos; **in this ~** en este sentido **5** (= *reference, regard*) respecto *m*; **in ~ of** (*Brit frm*) respecto a *or* de; **with ~ to** en lo que respecta a, con respecto a **Ⓑ** VT **1** (= *esteem, have consideration for*) respetar **2** (= *observe*) [+ *law, treaty*] acatar

respectability [rɪs,pektə'bɪlɪtɪ] N respetabilidad *f*

respectable [rɪs'pektəbl] ADJ respetable; ~ **people** gente *f* bien; **in ~ society** en la buena sociedad; **at a ~ distance** a una distancia prudente; **my marks were quite ~** mis notas eran bastante decentes

respected [rɪs'pektɪd] ADJ respetado; **a much ~ person** una persona muy respetada

respectful [rɪs'pektfəl] ADJ respetuoso

respectfully [rɪs'pektfəlɪ] ADV respetuosamente

respecting [rɪs'pektɪŋ] PREP en lo que concierne a, con respecto a

respective [rɪs'pektɪv] ADJ respectivo

respectively [rɪs'pektɪvlɪ] ADV respectivamente

respiration [,respɪ'reɪʃən] N respiración *f*

respirator ['respɪreɪtəʳ] N (*Med*) respirador *m*

respiratory [rɪs'pɪrətərɪ] ADJ respiratorio ➤ **respiratory tract** vías *fpl* respiratorias

respite ['respaɪt] N respiro *m* (**from** de); **without ~** sin descanso

resplendent [rɪs'plendənt] ADJ resplandeciente, refulgente; **she looked ~ in that new dress** estaba espléndida con ese vestido nuevo

respond [rɪs'pɒnd] VI **1** (= *answer*) contestar, responder **2** (= *be responsive*) responder, reaccionar (**to** a)

respondent [rɪs'pɒndənt] N (*to questionnaire*) persona *f* que responde a un cuestionario *or* que rellena un cuestionario

response [rɪs'pɒns] Ⓐ N **1** (= *answer*) contestación *f*, respuesta *f*; (*to charity appeal*) acogida *f*; **in ~ to** como respuesta a; **in ~ to many requests ...** accediendo a muchos ruegos ...; **we got a 73% ~** respondió el 73 por ciento **2** (= *reaction*) reacción *f* Ⓑ CPD ➤ **response time** tiempo *m* de respuesta

responsibility [rɪs,pɒnsə'bɪlɪtɪ] N responsabilidad *f*; **that's his ~** eso es responsabilidad suya; **it's my ~ to lock up** cerrar es responsabilidad mía, yo soy el responsable de cerrar; **she wants a position with more ~** quiere un puesto de mayor responsabilidad; **he has admitted ~ for the tragedy** ha aceptado ser responsable de la tragedia; **the group which claimed ~ for the attack** el grupo que reivindicó el atentado; **to have ~ for sth** ser responsable de algo; **the company takes no ~ for objects left here** la empresa no asume responsabilidad *or* no se responsabiliza de los objetos que se dejen aquí; **to take on/ take over (the) ~ for sth** asumir la responsabilidad de algo, responsabilizarse de algo, hacerse responsable de algo

responsible [rɪs'pɒnsəbl] ADJ **1** (= *accountable*) responsable; **those ~ will be punished** se castigará a los responsables; **he is not ~ for his actions** no es responsable de sus actos; **who is ~ for this?** ¿quién es el responsable de esto?; **who was ~ for the delay?** ¿quién tiene la culpa del retraso?; **to hold sb ~ for sth** hacer a algn responsable de algo, responsabilizar a algn de algo **2** (= *in charge of*) **the boys were ~ for tidying their own rooms** los niños tenían la responsabilidad *or* eran responsables de ordenar sus habitaciones; **she is ~ for 40 children** tiene a su cargo 40 niños; **the secretary is ~ for taking the minutes** la secretaria se hace cargo de levantar el acta **3** (= *sensible*) [*person*] serio, responsable; [*behaviour, attitude*] responsable **4** (= *important*) [*post, job*] de responsabilidad

responsibly [rɪs'pɒnsəblɪ] ADV de forma responsable, responsablemente, con responsabilidad

responsive [rɪs'pɒnsɪv] ADJ **1** (= *sensitive*) sensible; **to be ~ to sth** ser sensible a algo **2** (= *interested*) interesado; [*audience*] que reacciona con entusiasmo *or* interés

rest¹ [rest] Ⓐ N **1** (= *break, stop*) descanso *m*; **to be at ~** (= *not moving*) estar en reposo; (= *dead*) descansar; **to come to ~** [*ball, vehicle*] pararse, detenerse; **to give sth a ~** dejar algo (por un tiempo); **why don't you have a ~?** (= *take a break*) ¿por qué no te tomas un descanso?; (= *lie down*) ¿por qué no descansas un rato?; **to lay sth/sb to ~** enterrar algo/ a algn

2 (*Mus*) silencio *m*
3 (= *support*) apoyo *m*, soporte *m*
Ⓑ VT **1** (= *give rest to*) descansar; **God ~ his soul!** ¡Dios le acoja en su seno!
2 (= *support*) apoyar (**on** en, sobre; **against** contra)
3 (= *settle*) **to ~ one's eyes on sth** posar la mirada en algo
4 (*Jur*) **to ~ one's case** concluir su alegato; **I ~ my case** [*lawyer*] concluyo mi alegato; (*hum*) he dicho
Ⓒ VI **1** (= *repose*) descansar; **he won't ~ until he finds out the truth** no descansará hasta que descubra la verdad; **may he ~ in peace** que en paz descanse
2 (= *lean, be supported*) [*person*] apoyarse (**on** en); [*ladder*] estar apoyado (**against** contra); [*roof, structure*] estar sostenido (**on** por); **his head was ~ing on her shoulder** tenía la cabeza apoyada en su hombro
3 (= *be based, depend*) [*argument, case*] basarse (**on** en); [*sb's future*] depender (**on** de)
4 (= *be, remain*) quedar; **we cannot let the matter ~ there** no podemos permitir que la cosa quede ahí; **the decision ~s with her** la decisión la tiene que tomar ella, ella es la que tiene que decidir, la decisión es suya
Ⓓ CPD ➤ **rest area** (*esp US Aut*) área *f* de descanso

> Use **el/un** not **la/una** before feminine nouns beginning with stressed **a** or **ha** like **área**.

➤ **rest room** (*US*) servicios *mpl*, baño(s) *m(pl)* (*LAm*) ➤ **rest stop** (*US*) = **rest area**

rest² [rest] N **the ~** [*of money, food, month*] el resto; [*of people, things*] el resto, los/las demás; **the dog ate the ~** el perro se comió el resto *or* lo que sobró; **you go home — I'll do the ~** tú vete a casa, yo hago lo demás *or* lo que queda; **the ~ of us will wait here** los demás esperaremos aquí; **the ~ of the boys** los otros chicos, los demás chicos; **what shall we give the ~ of them?** ¿qué les daremos a los otros?; **and all the ~ (of it)*** etcétera, etcétera*; **(as) for the ~** por lo demás

restart ['riː'staːt] VT [+ *book, drawing*] empezar de nuevo, volver a empezar; [+ *negotiations, meeting*] reanudar; [+ *engine*] volver a arrancar

restaurant ['restərɒŋ] N restaurante *m* ➤ **restaurant car** (*Brit*) coche-comedor *m*

restaurateur [,restərə'tɜːʳ] N dueño/a *m/f* de un restaurante, restaurador(a) *m/f*

restful ['restfəl] ADJ descansado, tranquilo

restitution [,restɪ'tjuːʃən] N **1** (= *return*) restitución *f*; **to make ~ of sth to sb** restituir algo a algn, devolver algo a algn **2** (= *compensation*) **to make ~ to sb for sth** indemnizar a algn por algo

restive ['restɪv] ADJ inquieto; **to grow ~** impacientarse

restless ['restlɪs] ADJ (= *unsettled, fidgety*) inquieto; (= *discontented*) [*crowd, mob*] agitado; **I had a ~ night** pasé muy mala noche, no dormí bien; **to grow ~** inquietarse, impacientarse

restock ['riː'stɒk] Ⓐ VT [+ *larder*] reabastecer; [+ *pond*] repoblar (**with** de) Ⓑ VI **we ~ed with Brand X** renovamos las existencias con la Marca X

restoration [,restə'reɪʃən] N [*of money, possession*] devolución *f*, restitución *f* (*frm*); [*of relations, links, order*] restablecimiento *m*; [*of building, painting, democracy*] restauración *f*

restore [rɪs'tɔːʳ] VT **1** (= *give back*) [+ *money, possession*] devolver, restituir (*frm*) (**to** a)
2 (= *reinstate*) [+ *relations, links, order*] restablecer; [+ *monarch, democracy*] restaurar; **to ~ sb's sight** devolver la vista a algn; **to ~ sb to health/life** devolver la salud a algn/ reanimar a algn; **his supporters want to ~ him to power** sus partidarios quieren conseguir que vuelva al poder
3 (= *repair*) [+ *building, painting*] restaurar; **to ~ sth to its original condition** restituir *or* devolver algo a su estado original

restrain [rɪs'treɪn] VT [+ *person*] (*physically*) sujetar, retener; (*by talking*) retener; [+ *anger, feelings, impulse, laugh*] contener, reprimir; **to ~ o.s.** contenerse; **to ~ sb from doing sth** (= *dissuade*) disuadir a algn de hacer algo; (= *physically prevent*) impedir a algn hacer algo

restrained [rɪs'treɪnd] ADJ [*person*] cohibido; [*style*] reservado; **he was very ~ about it** estuvo muy comedido

restraint [rɪs'treɪnt] N **1** (= *check*) restricción *f*; (= *control*) control *m*; (= *check on wages*) moderación *f* **2** (= *reserve*) reserva *f*; (= *moderation*) moderación *f* **3** (= *self-control*) autodominio *m*, control *m* de sí mismo; **he showed great ~** mostró poseer un gran autodominio *or* autocontrol

restrict [rɪs'trɪkt] VT [+ *visits, price rise*] limitar; [+ *authority, freedom*] restringir, limitar; **to ~ o.s. to (doing) sth** limitarse a (hacer) algo

restricted [rɪs'trɪktɪd] ADJ (= *prohibited*) vedado, prohibido; (= *limited*) limitado; (= *reduced*) reducido

restriction [rɪs'trɪkʃən] N restricción *f*, limitación *f*

restrictive [rɪs'trɪktɪv] ADJ restringido, limitado; **~ practices** (*Brit*) prácticas *fpl* restrictivas

restructure ['riː'strʌktʃəʳ] (*Comm, Ind*) Ⓐ VT reconvertir Ⓑ VI reconvertirse

restructuring [,riː'strʌktʃərɪŋ] N reestructuración *f*

result [rɪ'zʌlt] Ⓐ N resultado *m*; **as a ~** por consiguiente; **as a ~ of** como *or* a consecuencia de; **her exam ~s were excellent** (*esp Brit*) en los exámenes sacó unas notas excelentes; **to get ~s** obtener resultados; **with disastrous ~s** con consecuencias desastrosas *or* resultados desastrosos; **with the ~ that ...** con la consecuencia de que ... Ⓑ VI **to ~ in sth: it ~ed in a large increase** dio como resultado un aumento apreciable; **it ~ed in his death** le acarreó la muerte, tuvo como resultado su muerte; **such behaviour may ~ in dismissal** semejante comportamiento puede acarrear el despido

resultant [rɪ'zʌltənt] ADJ resultante

resume [rɪ'zjuːm] Ⓐ VT [+ *meeting, negotiations*] reanudar; **"now then," he ~d** —ahora bien —dijo reanudando la conversación *or* su discurso Ⓑ VI [*meeting etc*] reanudarse

⚠ **resume** ≠ *resumir*

résumé ['reɪzjuːmeɪ] N **1** (= *summary*) resumen *m* **2** (*US*) (= *curriculum vitae*) currículum *m* (vitae)

resumption [rɪ'zʌmpʃən] N (*gen*) reanudación *f*; (= *continuation*) continuación *f*

resurface ['riː'sɜːfɪs] Ⓐ VI [*submarine*] volver a la superficie; [*person*] reaparecer Ⓑ VT [+ *road*] rehacer el firme de

resurgence [rɪ'sɜːdʒəns] N resurgimiento *m*

resurrect [,rezə'rekt] VT resucitar

resurrection [,rezə'rekʃən] N resurrección *f*

resuscitate [rɪ'sʌsɪteɪt] VT resucitar

retail ['riːteɪl] Ⓐ N venta *f* al por menor *or* al detalle Ⓑ ADV **to buy/sell sth ~** comprar/vender algo al por menor *or* al detalle Ⓒ VT vender al por menor *or* al detalle Ⓓ VI **to ~ at** tener precio de venta al público de Ⓔ CPD ➤ **retail business** comercio *m* al por menor *or* al detalle ➤ **retail outlet** punto *m* de venta al por menor *or* al detalle ➤ **retail park** (*Brit*) parque *m* comercial ➤ **retail price** precio *m* de venta al público ➤ **retail price index** (*Brit*) índice *m* de precios al consumo ➤ **retail trade** comercio *m* al por menor, comercio *m* detallista

retailer ['riːteɪləʳ] N comerciante *mf* al por menor, detallista *mf*

retain [rɪ'teɪn] VT (= *hold back*) retener; (= *keep*) guardar, quedarse con; (= *remember*) recordar, retener; **~ing wall** muro *m* de contención

retainer [rɪ'teɪnəʳ] N (= *fee*) anticipo *m*; (= *payment on flat, room*) depósito *m*, señal *f* (*para que se guarde el piso etc*)

retake (*vb: pt* **retook**; *pp* **~n**) Ⓐ ['riːteɪk] N (*Cine*) repetición *f*; (*Educ*) examen *m* de recuperación Ⓑ [,riː'teɪk] VT **1** (*Mil*) volver a tomar **2** [+ *exam*] volver a presentarse a; [+ *subject*] recuperar, volver a examinarse de (*Sp*)

retaliate [rɪ'tælɪeɪt] VI (= *respond*) responder; (*Mil*) tomar represalias; **to ~ against sth/sb** tomar represalias contra algo/algn

retaliation [rɪ,tælɪ'eɪʃən] N (*Mil*) represalias *fpl*; (= *revenge*) represalia *f*

retaliatory [rɪ'tælɪətərɪ] ADJ de represalia; **to take ~ action** tomar represalias

retarded [rɪ'tɑːdɪd] ADJ retrasado

retch [retʃ] VI tener arcadas

retention [rɪ'tenʃən] N retención *f*

rethink ['riː'θɪŋk] (*vb: pt, pp* **rethought**) Ⓐ N **to have a ~** volver a pensarlo Ⓑ VT reconsiderar

reticence ['retɪsəns] N reticencia *f*, reserva *f*

reticent ['retɪsənt] ADJ reticente, reservado

retina ['retɪnə] N retina *f*

retinue ['retɪnjuː] N séquito *m*, comitiva *f*

retire [rɪ'taɪəʳ] VI **1** (= *give up work*) (*due to old age, illness*) jubilarse, retirarse; [*soldier, sportsperson*] retirarse; **she ~d on a good pension** se jubiló *or* se retiró con una buena pensión **2** (= *withdraw*) retirarse **3** (= *go to bed*) acostarse, retirarse (*frm*); **to ~ for the night** ir a dormir, ir a acostarse **4** [*competitor*] abandonar, retirarse

retired [rɪ'taɪəd] ADJ (*gen*) jubilado, retirado; [*soldier, sportsperson*] retirado; **I've been ~ since 1996** me jubilé en 1996; **a ~ person** un(a) jubilado/a

retiree [rɪ'taɪə,riː] N (*US*) jubilado/a *m/f*

retirement [rɪ'taɪəmənt] Ⓐ N **1** (= *state of being retired*) retiro *m*; **to spend one's ~ growing roses** dedicarse a cultivar rosas después de la jubilación; **how will you spend your ~?** ¿qué piensa hacer cuando se jubile? **2** (= *act of retiring*) (*gen*) jubilación *f*; [*of soldier, sportsperson*] retiro *m* Ⓑ CPD ➤ **retirement age** edad *f* de jubilación; (*Mil*) edad *f* de retiro ➤ **retirement benefit** prestaciones *fpl* por jubilación ➤ **retirement pension** jubilación *f*; (*Mil*) retiro *m*

retiring [rɪ'taɪərɪŋ] ADJ **1** [*chairman, president*] saliente; [*age*] de jubilación **2** (= *shy*) reservado, retraído

retook [,riː'tʊk] PT *of* **retake**

retort [rɪ'tɔːt] VT replicar; **he ~ed that ...** replicó que ...

retrace [riː'treɪs] VT **to ~ one's steps** desandar lo andado

retract [rɪ'trækt] Ⓐ VT **1** [+ *statement*] retractar, retirar **2** [+ *claws*] retraer Ⓑ VI retractarse, desdecirse

retractable [rɪ'træktəbl] ADJ retractable; (*Tech*) replegable, retráctil

retrain ['riː'treɪn] Ⓐ VT [+ *workers*] reciclar, recapacitar, reconvertir Ⓑ VI reciclarse, reconvertirse; **he ~ed as a programmer** hizo un curso de programación para reciclarse

retraining ['riː'treɪnɪŋ] N reciclaje *m*, recapacitación *f*

retread ['riː'tred] N (= *tyre*) neumático *m* recauchutado, llanta *f* recauchutada, llanta *f* reencauchada (*LAm*)

retreat [rɪ'triːt] Ⓐ N **1** (*Mil*) (= *withdrawal*) retirada *f*; (*fig*) vuelta *f* atrás, marcha *f* atrás; **to beat a hasty ~** (*fig*) batirse en retirada **2** (= *place*) retiro *m*, refugio *m* Ⓑ VI retirarse

retrial ['riː'traɪəl] N [*of person*] nuevo juicio *m*; [*of case*] revisión *f*

retribution [,retrɪ'bjuːʃən] N justo castigo *m*, pena *f* merecida

retrieval [rɪ'triːvəl] N recuperación *f*

retrieve [rɪ'triːv] VT **1** (= *get back*) [+ *object*] recuperar (*also Comput*), recobrar **2** (= *put right*) [+ *error etc*] reparar, subsanar; [+ *fortunes*] reparar; [+ *situation*] salvar

retriever [rɪ'triːvəʳ] N perro *m* cobrador

retro ['retrəʊ] ADJ retro

retrograde ['retrəʊgreɪd] ADJ [*step, measure*] retrógrado

retrospect ['retrəʊspekt] N **in ~** retrospectivamente; **in ~ it seems a happy time** volviendo la vista atrás parece haber sido un período feliz

retrospective [,retrəʊ'spektɪv] Ⓐ ADJ retrospectivo; [*law etc*] retroactivo, de efecto retroactivo Ⓑ N (*Art*) (exposición *f*) retrospectiva *f*

retrovirus ['retrəʊ,vaɪrəs] N retrovirus *m inv*

return [rɪ'tɜːn] Ⓐ N **1** (= *going/coming back*) vuelta *f*, regreso *m*; **on my ~** a mi vuelta, a mi regreso; **the ~ home** la vuelta *or* el regreso a casa; **their ~ to power** su vuelta *or* retorno al poder; **many happy ~s (of the day)!** ¡feliz cumpleaños!, ¡felicidades!; **by ~ (of) post** *or* (*US*) **by ~ mail** a vuelta de correo

2 (= *reappearance*) [*of symptoms, pain*] reaparición *f*; [*of doubts, fears*] resurgimiento *m*

3 (= *giving back*) [*of thing taken*] devolución *f*, restitución *f* (*frm*); [*of thing borrowed*] devolución *f*; [*of merchandise*] devolución *f*; (= *reimbursement*) reembolso *m*, devolución *f*

4 (= *thing returned: merchandise*) devolución *f*

5 (*Sport*) devolución *f*; **~ of serve** *or* **service** devolución *f* del servicio *or* saque, resto *m*

6 (*Fin*) (= *profit*) ganancia *f*; (*from investments, shares*) rendimiento *m* (**on** de)

7 (= *reward, exchange*) **in ~ (for)** a cambio (de)

8 returns (= *election results*) resultados *mpl* (del escrutinio)

9 (*Brit*) (*also ~* **ticket**) billete *m* (*Sp*) *or* boleto *m* (*LAm*) de ida y vuelta, billete *m* redondo (*Mex*)

Ⓑ VT **1** (= *give back*) [+ *item*] devolver, regresar (*LAm*); [+ *favour, visit, call*] devolver; [+ *greeting, look*] devolver, responder a; (*Sport*) [+ *ball*] devolver; **"return to sender"** "devuélvase al remitente"

2 (= *declare*) [+ *income, details*] declarar; **they ~ed a verdict of guilty/not guilty (on him)** lo declararon culpable/inocente

3 (*Brit Pol*) (= *elect*) elegir, votar a; (= *reelect*) reelegir

Ⓒ VI **1** (= *go/come back*) volver, regresar (**to** a); **to ~ home** volver *or* regresar a casa; **things have ~ed to normal** las cosas han vuelto a la normalidad

2 (= *reappear*) [*symptoms*] volver a aparecer, reaparecer; [*doubts, fears, suspicions*] volver a surgir, resurgir

Ⓓ CPD [*journey, flight*] de regreso, de vuelta ➤ **return address** señas *fpl* del remitente ➤ **return fare** (*esp Brit*) billete *m* (*Sp*) *or* boleto *m* (*LAm*) de ida y vuelta, billete *m* redondo (*Mex*) ➤ **return journey** viaje *m* de regreso ➤ **return key** tecla *f* de retorno ➤ **return match** (*Brit*) partido *m* de vuelta ➤ **return ticket** (*esp Brit*) billete *m* (*Sp*) *or* boleto *m* (*LAm*) de ida y vuelta, billete *m* redondo (*Mex*)

returnable [rɪˈtɜːnəbl] ADJ [*deposit*] reintegrable, reembolsable; [*bottle*] retornable; **the deposit is not ~** no se reembolsa el depósito

returning officer [rɪˈtɜːnɪŋˌɒfɪsəʳ] N (*Brit Pol*) escrutador(a) *m/f*

reunification [ˈriːjuːnɪfɪˈkeɪʃən] N reunificación *f*

reunion [riːˈjuːnjən] N reencuentro *m*, reunión *f*

reunite [ˈriːjuːˈnaɪt] VT (volver a) reunir; **eventually the family was ~d** por fin la familia volvió a verse unida; **she was ~d with her husband** volvió a verse al lado de su marido

re-usable [ˌriːˈjuːzəbl] ADJ reutilizable, que se puede volver a emplear

rev* [rev] **Ⓐ** N revolución *f* **Ⓑ** VT [+ *engine*] girar

Rev. ABBR (= **Reverend**) R., Rdo., Rvdo.

revamp [riːˈvæmp] VT modernizar, renovar **Ⓑ** N [ˈriːvæmp] modernización *f*, renovación *f*

Revd. ABBR (= **Reverend**) R., Rdo., Rvdo.

reveal [rɪˈviːl] VT (*gen*) revelar; [*survey, test*] poner de manifiesto; **he ~ed himself to be** *or* **as ...** demostró ser ...

revealing [rɪˈviːlɪŋ] ADJ revelador

reveille [rɪˈvælɪ] N (toque *m* de) diana *f*

revel [ˈrevl] VI (= *make merry*) ir de juerga *or* de parranda; **to ~ in sth** gozar de algo; **to ~ in doing sth** gozar haciendo algo

revelation [ˌrevəˈleɪʃən] N revelación *f*

reveller, reveler (*US*) [ˈrevləʳ] N (= *party-goer*) juerguista *mf*, parrandero/a *m/f*; (= *drunk*) borracho/a *m/f*

revelry [ˈrevlrɪ] N juerga *f*, parranda *f*, jarana *f*; (*organized*) fiestas *fpl*, festividades *fpl*

revenge [rɪˈvendʒ] **Ⓐ** N venganza *f*; **in ~** para vengarse (**for** de); **to get one's ~ (for sth)** vengarse (de algo); **to take ~ on sb for sth** vengarse de algn por algo **Ⓑ** VT vengar, vengarse de; **to ~ o.s. on sb** vengarse de algn

revenue [ˈrevənjuː] N (= *profit, income*) ingresos *mpl*, rentas *fpl*; (*on investments*) rédito *m*; [*of country*] rentas *fpl* públicas

reverberate [rɪˈvɜːbəreɪt] VI [*sound*] resonar, retumbar; [*news, protests etc*] tener amplia resonancia, tener una fuerte repercusión; **the valley ~d with the sound** el ruido resonaba *or* retumbaba por el valle

reverberation [rɪˌvɜːbəˈreɪʃən] N [*of sound*] retumbo *m*, eco *m*; **reverberations** [*of news, protests etc*] consecuencias *fpl*

revere [rɪˈvɪəʳ] VT venerar

reverence [ˈrevərəns] N (= *respect*) reverencia *f*; **Your Reverence** Reverencia

reverend [ˈrevərənd] ADJ reverendo

reverie [ˈrevərɪ] N ensueño *m*; **to be lost in ~** estar absorto, estar ensimismado

reversal [rɪˈvɜːsəl] N [*of order, roles*] inversión *f*; [*of policy*] cambio *m* de rumbo; [*of decision*] revocación *f*

reverse [rɪˈvɜːs] **Ⓐ** ADJ **1** [*order*] inverso; [*direction*] contrario, opuesto; **in ~ order** en orden inverso

2 [*gear*] de marcha atrás

Ⓑ N **1** (= *opposite*) **the ~** lo contrario; **no, quite the ~!** no, ¡todo lo contrario!; **but the ~ is true** pero es al contrario; **it's the same process in ~** es el mismo proceso al revés

2 [*of coin*] reverso *m*; [*of paper*] dorso *m*; [*of cloth*] revés *m*

3 (*also ~* **gear**) marcha *f* atrás; **to go into ~** dar marcha atrás; **to put a car into ~** dar marcha atrás a un coche

Ⓒ VT **1** (= *invert order of*) invertir, invertir el orden de; (= *turn other way*) volver al revés

2 (= *change*) [+ *opinion*] cambiar completamente de; [+ *decision*] revocar, anular, cancelar

3 (*Brit Telec*) **to ~ the charges** cobrar al número llamado, llamar a cobro revertido

4 (*esp Brit*) [+ *car*] dar marcha atrás a; **he ~d the car into the garage** dio marcha atrás para entrar en el garaje; **he ~d the car into a pillarbox** al dar marcha atrás chocó con un buzón

Ⓓ VI (*esp Brit*) dar marcha atrás; **I ~d into a van** al dar marcha atrás choqué con una furgoneta

Ⓔ CPD ➤ **reverse charge call** (*Brit*) llamada *f* a cobro revertido ➤ **reverse discrimination** (*US*) discriminación *f* positiva

reversible [rɪˈvɜːsəbl] ADJ reversible

reversing [rɪˈvɜːsɪŋ] N marcha *f* atrás ➤ **reversing light** (*Brit*) luz *f* de marcha atrás

revert [rɪˈvɜːt] VI (= *return*) volver; **to ~ to a subject** volver a un tema; **to ~ to type** volver por donde solía, volver a ser el mismo/la misma de antes

review [rɪˈvjuː] **Ⓐ** N **1** (= *assessment*) examen *m*, análisis *m inv*; [*of research*] evaluación *f*; [*of case*] revisión *f*; **salaries are under ~** los sueldos están sujetos a revisión; **when the case comes up for ~** cuando el asunto se someta a revisión; **the sentence is subject to ~ in the high court** la sentencia puede revertir a ser vista en el tribunal supremo

2 (= *critique*) crítica *f*, reseña *f*; **the play got good ~s** la obra fue bien recibida por los críticos

3 (*US Scol*) repaso *m*

Ⓑ VT **1** (= *assess*) examinar, analizar; [+ *research*] evaluar; [+ *situation*] estudiar; [+ *case*] revisar; **we shall have to ~ our policy** tendremos que reconsiderar nuestra política

2 (*Mil*) [+ *troops*] pasar revista a

3 (= *write review of*) reseñar, hacer una crítica de

4 (*US Scol*) repasar

Ⓒ VI (*US Scol*) repasar

Ⓓ CPD ➤ **review copy** ejemplar *m* para reseñar

reviewer [rɪˈvjuːəʳ] N crítico/a *m/f*

revile [rɪˈvaɪl] VT insultar, injuriar

revise [rɪˈvaɪz] **Ⓐ** VT **1** [+ *text*] revisar; [+ *estimate, figures*] corregir; [+ *offer*] reconsiderar; [+ *schedule*] ajustar; **to ~ sth upward(s)** ajustar *or* revisar algo al alza **2** (*Brit*) [+ *subject, notes*] repasar **Ⓑ** VI (*Brit*) repasar

revision [rɪˈvɪʒən] N **1** (*Brit*) (*for exams*) repaso *m*; **I need two weeks for ~** necesito dos semanas para repasar **2** [*of text*] revisión *f*; [*of estimate, figures*] corrección *f*; [*of offer*] reconsideración *f*; [*of schedule*] ajuste *m*

revitalize [ˈriːˈvaɪtəlaɪz] VT revitalizar, revivificar

revival [rɪˈvaɪvəl] N **1** (= *bringing back*) [*of custom*] recuperación *f*; [*of old ideas*] resurgimiento *m* **2** (= *coming* back) [of custom] vuelta f; [of old ideas] renacimiento m

revive [rɪ'vaɪv] **Ⓐ** VT [+ person] reanimar; [+ old customs] restablecer, recuperar **Ⓑ** VI [person] (from faint) reanimarse, volver en sí; (from tiredness, shock) reponerse, recuperarse; (from apparent death) revivir; [hope, emotions] renacer; [business, trade] reactivarse; **interest in Gongora has ~d** ha renacido el interés por Góngora; **the pound has ~d** la libra se ha recuperado

revoke [rɪ'vəʊk] VT (gen) revocar; [+ licence] suspender

revolt [rɪ'vəʊlt] **Ⓐ** N (= insurrection) levantamiento m, revuelta f; (= rejection of authority) rebelión f; **to rise (up) in** ~ sublevarse, rebelarse **Ⓑ** VT (= disgust) dar asco a, repugnar **Ⓒ** VI (= rebel) sublevarse, rebelarse (**against** contra)

revolting [rɪ'vəʊltɪŋ] ADJ [smell, taste, sight, habit, person] repugnante, asqueroso; [colour, dress] horroroso, repelente

revolution [ˌrevə'luːʃən] N revolución f

revolutionary [ˌrevə'luːʃənərɪ] ADJ, N revolucionario/a m/f

revolutionize [ˌrevə'luːʃənaɪz] VT revolucionar

revolve [rɪ'vɒlv] **Ⓐ** VT girar, hacer girar **Ⓑ** VI girar, dar vueltas; (Astron) revolverse; **to ~ around** (fig) girar alrededor de; (fig) girar en torno a; **everything ~s around him** todo gira en torno a él; **the discussion ~d around three topics** el debate se centró en tres temas

revolver [rɪ'vɒlvə'] N revólver m

revolving [rɪ'vɒlvɪŋ] ADJ giratorio ➤ **revolving door** puerta f giratoria

revue [rɪ'vjuː] N (teatro m de) revista f or variedades fpl

revulsion [rɪ'vʌlʃən] N (= disgust) repugnancia f, asco m

reward [rɪ'wɔːd] **Ⓐ** N recompensa f, premio m; (for finding sth) gratificación f; **as a ~ for** en recompensa de, como premio a; **"£50 reward"** "50 libras de recompensa"; **a ~ will be paid for information about ...** se recompensará al que dé alguna información acerca de ... **Ⓑ** VT (lit) recompensar; (fig) premiar (**with** con); **to ~ sb for his services** recompensar a algn por sus servicios

rewarding [rɪ'wɔːdɪŋ] ADJ gratificante

rewind ['riː'waɪnd] VT [+ cassette, videotape] rebobinar

rewire ['riː'waɪə'] VT [+ house] rehacer la instalación eléctrica de

reword ['riː'wɜːd] VT expresar en otras palabras

rewrite (pt **rewrote**; pp **rewritten**) **Ⓐ** [ˌriː'raɪt] VT reescribir; [+ text] rehacer, refundir **Ⓑ** ['riːraɪt] N nueva versión f, refundición f

Reykjavik ['reɪkjəviːk] N Reykiavik m

RGN N ABBR (Brit) = **Registered General Nurse**

rhapsody ['ræpsədɪ] N (Mus) rapsodia f; **to go into rhapsodies over** extasiarse por

rhesus ['riːsəs] N ~ **negative** Rh or Rhesus negativo; ~ **positive** Rh or Rhesus positivo ➤ **rhesus factor** factor m Rhesus ➤ **rhesus monkey** macaco m de la India

rhetoric ['retərɪk] N retórica f

rhetorical [rɪ'tɒrɪkəl] ADJ retórico

rheumatic [ruː'mætɪk] ADJ reumático

rheumatism ['ruːmətɪzəm] N reumatismo m

rheumatoid arthritis [ˌruːmətɔɪdɑː'θraɪtɪs] N artritis f reumatoide

rheumatologist [ˌruːmə'tɒlədʒɪst] N reumatólogo/a m/f

Rhine [raɪn] N **the** ~ el Rin

rhino* ['raɪnəʊ] N ABBR rinoceronte m

rhinoceros [raɪ'nɒsərəs] N rinoceronte m

rhododendron [ˌrəʊdə'dendrən] N rododendro m

rhombus ['rɒmbəs] N (pl **-es** or **rhombi** ['rɒmbaɪ]) rombo m

rhubarb ['ruːbɑːb] **Ⓐ** N ruibarbo m **Ⓑ** ADJ de ruibarbo

rhyme [raɪm] **Ⓐ** N **1** (= identical sound) rima f; **✦** IDIOM **without ~ or reason** sin ton ni son **2** (= poem) poesía f, versos mpl; **in** ~ en verso **Ⓑ** VI rimar

rhyming ['raɪmɪŋ] ADJ [couplet, verse] rimado ➤ **rhyming slang** argot m basado en rimas (p.ej, "apples and pears" = "stairs")

rhythm ['rɪðəm] N ritmo m ➤ **rhythm guitar** guitarra f rítmica ➤ **rhythm method** método m de Ogino-Knaus

rhythmic ['rɪðmɪk], **rhythmical** ['rɪðmɪkəl] ADJ rítmico

rhythmically ['rɪðmɪkəlɪ] ADV rítmicamente, de forma rítmica

RI **Ⓐ** N ABBR (= **religious instruction**) religión f, educación f religiosa, ed. religiosa **Ⓑ** ABBR = **Rhode Island**

rib [rɪb] **Ⓐ** N (= bone) costilla f **Ⓑ** VT (*) (= tease) tomar el pelo a, mofarse de **Ⓒ** CPD ➤ **rib cage** tórax m

ribald ['rɪbəld] ADJ [jokes, laughter] verde, colorado (LAm); [person] irreverente, procaz

ribbed [rɪbd] ADJ ~ **sweater** jersey m de cordoncillo

ribbon ['rɪbən] N (gen) cinta f; (for hair) moña f, cinta f; (Mil) galón m

rib-tickler* ['rɪbtɪklə'] N (Brit) chiste m desternillante*

rice [raɪs] N arroz m ➤ **rice paddy** (US) arrozal m ➤ **rice paper** papel m de arroz ➤ **rice pudding** arroz m con leche

rice-growing ['raɪsˌgrəʊɪŋ] ADJ arrocero

rich [rɪtʃ] **Ⓐ** ADJ (compar ~**er**; superl ~**est**) **1** (= wealthy) [person, country] rico; **to get ~(er)** hacerse (más) rico, enriquecerse (más); **to get ~ quick*** hacer fortuna or enriquecerse rápidamente
2 (= abundant) [variety, source] grande; [deposit, harvest] abundante; [reward] generoso
3 (= fertile) [soil] rico, fértil
4 (= heavy, concentrated) [food, sauce] sustancioso (que contiene mucha grasa, azúcar, etc); (pej) pesado, fuerte
5 (= intense) [colour] vivo, cálido; [sound, smell] intenso
6 (*) (= laughable) **that's ~!** ¡mira por dónde!*; **that's ~, coming from her!** ¡ella no es quién para hablar!, ¡tiene gracia que sea ella la que diga eso!
Ⓑ NPL **the ~** los ricos

riches ['rɪtʃɪz] NPL riqueza fsing

richly ['rɪtʃlɪ] ADV [rewarded] generosamente; [illustrated] profusamente; [decorated, furnished] suntuosamente, lujosamente; **she ~ deserves it** se lo tiene bien merecido; **the success they so ~ deserve** el éxito que tanto merecen

richness ['rɪtʃnɪs] N riqueza f

Richter scale ['rɪxtəˌskeɪl] N escala f de Richter

rickets ['rɪkɪts] NSING raquitismo m

rickety ['rɪkɪtɪ] ADJ (= wobbly) tambaleante, inseguro; [old car] desvencijado

rickshaw ['rɪkʃɔː] N carrito de estilo oriental tirado por un hombre

ricochet ['rɪkəʃeɪ] **Ⓐ** N rebote m **Ⓑ** VI rebotar (**off** de)

rid [rɪd] (pt, pp ~) VT **I couldn't ~ myself of the feeling that** no me podía librar de la sensación de que; **I couldn't ~ my mind of these thoughts** no podía quitarme estos pensamientos de la cabeza; **we want to ~ the world of this disease** queremos erradicar esta enfermedad en el mundo, queremos librar a la humanidad de esta enfermedad; **she was glad to be ~ of him** estaba contenta de haberse librado de él, estaba contenta de habérselo quitado de encima*; **to get ~ of** [+ unwanted item] deshacerse de; [+ habit, headache] quitarse; [+ *rats, smell, waste, corruption*] eliminar; (= *sell*) vender, deshacerse de; **to get ~ of sb** (*gen*) librarse de algn; [+ *tedious person*] quitarse a algn de encima*; (*euph*) (= *kill*) deshacerse de algn, eliminar a algn

riddance ['rɪdəns] N **and good ~ to him!** ¡que se pudra!

ridden ['rɪdn] PP *of* **ride**

riddle¹ ['rɪdl] N (= *word puzzle*) acertijo *m*, adivinanza *f*; (= *mystery*) enigma *m*, misterio *m*; **to speak in ~s** hablar en clave

riddle² ['rɪdl] VT **to ~ with** [+ *bullets*] acribillar a; **the house is ~d with damp** la casa tiene humedad por todas partes; **the organization is ~d with communists** el organismo está plagado de comunistas

ride [raɪd] (*vb: pt* **rode**; *pp* **ridden**) Ⓐ N 1 (= *journey*) paseo *m*; (= *car ride*) vuelta *f* en coche; (= *bike ride*) paseo en bicicleta; (= *horse ride*) paseo a caballo; (*esp US*) (= *free ride*) viaje *m* gratuito; **he gave me a ~ into town** (*in car*) me llevó en coche a la ciudad, me dio aventón hasta la ciudad (*Mex*); **to go for a ~** (*in car, on bike, on horse*) dar una vuelta, pasear; ♦ IDIOMS **to give sb a rough ~** hacer pasar un mal rato a algn; **to take sb for a ~*** (= *swindle*) dar gato por liebre a algn; (*US***) (= *kill*) mandar a algn al otro barrio**; **to be taken for a ~*** hacer el primo*
2 (= *distance travelled*) viaje *m*, recorrido *m*; **it's only a short ~** es poco camino; **it's a ten-minute ~ on the bus** son diez minutos en autobús *or* (*Mex*) en camión
3 (*at fairground*) (= *attraction*) atracción *f*; **"50p a ride"** "50 peniques por persona"
Ⓑ VT 1 [+ *horse*] montar; [+ *bicycle*] montar en, ir en, andar en; **a horse ridden by ...** un caballo montado por ...; **he rode his horse into town** fue a caballo hasta la ciudad; **he rode in two races** lo corrió en dos carreras; **to ~ an elephant** ir montado en un elefante; **to ~ the bus** (*US*) tomar el autobús
2 [+ *distance*] **we rode ten km yesterday** recorrimos diez kilómetros ayer
3 **to ~ sb** (*US**) tenerla tomada con algn, no dejar en paz a algn
4 (*Naut*) [+ *waves*] hender, surcar
Ⓒ VI 1 (*on horse*) montar; **she ~s every day** monta todos los días; **can you ~?** ¿sabes montar a caballo?; **to ~ on an elephant** ir montado en un elefante; **to ~ to Jaén** ir (a caballo) a Jaén; **he rode up to me** se me acercó a caballo
2 (*in car*) ir, viajar; **to ~ on a bus/in a train** viajar en autobús/en tren
3 (*in phrases*) ♦ IDIOMS **to be riding high: he's riding high at the moment** por ahora lo va muy bien; **to let things ~** dejar que las cosas sigan su curso
➤ **ride on** Ⓐ VI + ADV seguir adelante Ⓑ VI + PREP (= *depend on*) depender de
➤ **ride out** VT + ADV [+ *crisis*] sobrevivir, sobreponerse a

rider ['raɪdə^r] N 1 (= *horserider*) jinete *mf*; **I'm not much of a ~** apenas sé montar 2 (= *cyclist*) ciclista *mf*; (= *motorcyclist*) motociclista *mf*, motorista *mf*; (*US Aut*) pasajero/a *m/f*, viajero/a *m/f* 3 **with the ~ that ...** a condición de que ...; **I must add the ~ that ...** debo añadir que ...

ridge [rɪdʒ] N [*of hills, mountains*] cadena *f*; [*of roof*] caballete *m*; (= *crest of hill*) cumbre *f*, cresta *f*; **~ of high/low pressure** línea *f* de presión alta/baja

ridicule ['rɪdɪkjuːl] Ⓐ N irrisión *f*, burla *f*; **to hold sth/sb up to ~** poner algo/a algn en ridículo Ⓑ VT dejar *or* poner en ridículo, ridiculizar

ridiculous [rɪ'dɪkjʊləs] ADJ ridículo, absurdo; **to look ~** [*person*] estar ridículo; [*thing*] ser ridículo; **to make o.s. (look) ~** ponerse en ridículo

ridiculously [rɪ'dɪkjʊləslɪ] ADV absurdamente, ridículamente

riding ['raɪdɪŋ] N equitación *f*; **I like ~** me gusta montar a caballo ➤ **riding boots** botas *fpl* de montar ➤ **riding crop** fusta *f* ➤ **riding jacket** chaqueta *f* de montar ➤ **riding school** escuela *f* de equitación ➤ **riding stables** cuadras *fpl*

rife [raɪf] ADJ **to be ~** [*problem*] ser muy común; [*rumours, speculation, fears*] abundar, proliferar; [*disease*] hacer estragos; [*unemployment, crime*] abundar, hacer estragos; [*racism, corruption*] estar muy extendido; **countries ~ with**

Aids países donde el sida hace estragos; **the whole industry is ~ with corruption** la corrupción reina *or* está muy extendida en todo el sector

riff-raff ['rɪfræf] N gentuza *f*, chusma *f*

rifle¹ ['raɪfl] VT [+ *drawers*] (= *search*) rebuscar en, revolver; (= *burgle*) desvalijar; [+ *house, room*] (= *search*) registrar; (= *burgle*) desvalijar, saquear
➤ **rifle through** VI + PREP rebuscar en, revolver

rifle² ['raɪfl] N (= *gun*) rifle *m*, fusil *m* ➤ **rifle range** (*Mil*) campo *m* de tiro; (*at fair*) barraca *f* de tiro al blanco

rift [rɪft] N (*between people*) ruptura *f*; (*in political party*) escisión *f*, cisma *m*

rig [rɪg] Ⓐ N 1 (*also* **oil ~**) (*on land*) torre *f* de perforación; (*at sea*) plataforma *f* petrolífera 2 (*US*) (= *truck*) vehículo *m* articulado Ⓑ VT [+ *election, competition*] amañar; [+ *prices*] manipular; **it was ~ged*** hubo tongo*
➤ **rig up** VT + ADV (= *build*) improvisar; (= *arrange*) organizar, trabar

rigging ['rɪgɪŋ] N jarcia *f*, aparejo *m*

right [raɪt] Ⓐ ADJ 1 (= *just*) justo; **it seems only ~ that she should get the biggest share** me parece justo *or* bien que ella reciba la mayor parte; **it doesn't seem ~ that his contribution should not be acknowledged** parece injusto que no se le reconozca su aportación; **it's not ~!** ¡no hay derecho!; **it is only ~ and proper that people should know what is going on** lo suyo es que la gente sepa lo que pasa; **to do what is ~** hacer lo correcto, actuar correctamente; **to do the ~ thing by sb** portarse como es debido con algn
2 (= *suitable*) [*tool, clothes*] apropiado, adecuado; [*time*] oportuno; **he's the ~ man for the job** es el hombre más indicado para el cargo; **I don't think he's the ~ sort of person for you** me parece que no es la persona que te conviene; **she's just ~ for the job** es la persona perfecta para el puesto; **the flat is just ~ for me** el piso es justo lo que necesito; **"is there too much salt in it?" — "no, it's just ~"** —¿tiene demasiada sal? —no, está en su punto justo; **to know the ~ people** tener enchufes *or* (*LAm*) palanca; **I was in the ~ place at the ~ time** estaba en el lugar adecuado en el momento preciso; **if the price is ~** si el precio es razonable; **he's on the ~ side of 40** tiene menos de 40 años; **we'll do it when the ~ time is ~** lo haremos en el momento oportuno *or* a su debido tiempo; **the ~ word** la palabra exacta *or* apropiada
3 (= *correct*) correcto, exacto; **"she's your sister?" — "that's ~!"** —¿es tu hermana? —¡eso es! *or* ¡así es! *or* ¡exacto!; **and quite ~ too!** ¡y con razón!; **~ you are!** (*Brit**) ¡muy bien!, ¡vale! (*Sp**); **I was beginning to wonder whether I had the ~ day** empezaba a preguntarme si me habría equivocado de día; **to get sth ~** (= *guess correctly*) acertar en algo; (= *do properly*) hacer algo bien; **is this the ~ house?** ¿es ésta la casa?; **are you sure you've got the ~ number?** (*Telec*) ¿seguro que es ése el número?; **to put sb ~** sacar a algn de su error, corregir a algn; (*unpleasantly*) enmendar la plana a algn; **to put a clock ~** poner un reloj en hora; **to put a mistake ~** corregir *or* rectificar un error; **is this the ~ road for Segovia?** ¿es éste el camino de Segovia?, ¿por aquí se va a Segovia?; **is the skirt the ~ size?** ¿va bien la falda de talla?; **it's not the ~ size** no es la talla; **the ~ time** la hora exacta; ♦ IDIOM **to get on the ~ side of sb** congraciarse con algn
4 **to be ~** [*person*] tener razón, estar en lo cierto; **you're quite ~** tienes toda la razón; **how ~ you are!** ¡qué razón tienes!; **you were ~ about there being none left** tenías razón cuando decías que no quedaba ninguno; **you were ~ about Peter** tenías razón en cuanto a Peter *or* con respecto a Peter; **am I ~ in thinking that we've met before?** si no me equivoco ya nos conocemos ¿no?; **to be ~ to do sth** hacer bien en hacer algo
5 (= *well*) **I don't feel quite ~** no me siento del todo bien; **his leg hasn't been ~ since the accident** tiene la pierna mal desde el accidente; **my stereo still isn't ~** mi equipo sigue sin ir bien; **it will all come ~ in the end** todo se arreglará al final; **she's not quite ~ in the head** no está en sus cabales; **to be in one's ~ mind** en su sano juicio; **to put sth ~** (= *fix*) arreglar algo
6 (= *not left*) derecho; **we are a ~ of centre party** somos un partido de centro derecha; ♦ IDIOMS **I'd give my ~ arm to**

know daría cualquier cosa *or* todo el oro del mundo por saberlo; **it's a case of the ~ hand not knowing what the left hand is doing** es uno de esos casos en que la mano derecha no sabe lo que hace la izquierda
7 (*Math*) [*angle*] recto
8 (*Brit**) (*as intensifier*) **he's a ~ idiot** es un auténtico idiota; **she made a ~ mess of it** lo hizo fatal*
9 *see* **all right**
Ⓑ ADV **1** (= *directly, exactly*) **~ away** en seguida, ahora mismo, ahorita (mismo) (*Mex, And*); **she was standing ~ behind/in front of him** estaba justo detrás/delante de él; **~ here** aquí mismo *or* (*CAm*) mero; **~ now** (= *immediately*) ahora mismo; (= *at the moment*) (justo) ahora
2 (= *immediately*) justo, inmediatamente; **I'll do it ~ after dinner** lo haré justo *or* inmediatamente después de cenar; **I'll be ~ back** vuelvo en seguida
3 (= *completely*) **we were sitting ~ at the back** estábamos sentados atrás del todo; **their house is ~ at the end of the street** su casa está justo al final de la calle; **to go ~ to the end of sth** ir hasta el final de algo; **there is a fence ~ round the house** hay una valla que rodea la casa por completo
4 (= *correctly*) bien, correctamente; **you did ~ (not) to invite them** hiciste bien en (no) invitarlos; **if I remember ~** si mal no recuerdo, si no me falla la memoria
5 (= *fairly*) **to do ~ by sb** portarse como es debido con algn; **to treat sb ~** tratar bien a algn
6 (= *properly, satisfactorily*) bien; **I felt nothing was going ~ for me** sentía que nada me iba bien
7 (= *not left*) a la derecha; **he looked neither left nor ~** no miró a ningún lado; **to turn ~** torcer a la derecha
8 (*as linker*) **~, who's next?** a ver, ¿quién va ahora?
9 (*Brit*) (*in titles*) **the Right Honourable Edmund Burke** el Excelentísimo Señor Edmund Burke; **the Right Honourable member for Huntingdon** Su Señoría el diputado por Huntingdon
Ⓒ N **1** (= *not wrong*) **~ and wrong** el bien y el mal; **to know ~ from wrong** saber distinguir el bien del mal; **by ~s the house should go to me** lo suyo *or* lo propio es que la casa me correspondiera a mí; **to be in the ~** tener razón, estar en lo cierto; **to set the world to ~s** arreglar el mundo; **to have ~ on one's side** tener la razón de su parte
2 (= *prerogative*) derecho *m*; **to have a ~ to sth/to do sth** tener derecho a algo/a hacer algo; **you had no ~ to take it** no tenías (ningún) derecho a llevártelo; **what gives you the ~ to criticize me?** ¿qué derecho tienes tú a criticarme?; **to own sth in one's own ~** poseer algo por derecho propio; **he's a person in his own ~** es una persona de pleno derecho; **~ to reply** derecho *m* de réplica; **~ of way** prioridad *f*
3 **rights** derechos *mpl*; **"all rights reserved"** "es propiedad", "reservados todos los derechos"; **film ~s** derechos *mpl* cinematográficos; **you'd be well within your ~s to refuse to cooperate** estarías en tu derecho a negarte a cooperar
4 (= *not left*) derecha *f*; **to keep to the ~** (*Aut*) circular por la derecha; **our house is the second on the ~** nuestra casa es la segunda *a or* de la derecha; **on *or* to my ~** a mi derecha
5 (*Pol*) **the ~** la derecha
6 (= *right turn*) **it's the next ~ after the lights** es la próxima a la derecha después del semáforo
Ⓓ VT [+ *picture, vehicle, person*] enderezar; [+ *injustice*] reparar
Ⓔ CPD **➤ right angle** ángulo *m* recto; **to be at ~ angles (to sth)** estar en *or* formar ángulo recto (con algo) **➤ right triangle** (*US*) triangulo *m* rectángulo **➤ right wing** derecha *f*

right-angled ['raɪtˌæŋgld] ADJ [*bend, turning*] en ángulo recto; (*Brit*) [*triangle*] rectángulo

right-click ['raɪtklɪk] **Ⓐ** VI clicar con el botón derecho del ratón **Ⓑ** VT **to ~ an icon** clicar en un icono con el botón derecho del ratón

righteous ['raɪtʃəs] ADJ **1** (= *virtuous*) [*person, conduct*] honrado, recto **2** (= *self-righteous*) [*tone, manner*] de superioridad moral

rightful ['raɪtfəl] ADJ [*owner, heir*] legítimo

rightfully ['raɪtfəlɪ] ADV legítimamente, por derecho

right-hand ['raɪtˈhænd] ADJ derecho **➤ right-hand drive** conducción *f* por la derecha **➤ right-hand man** brazo *m* derecho **➤ right-hand side** derecha *f* **➤ right-hand turn** giro *m* a la derecha

right-handed ['raɪtˈhændɪd] ADJ que usa la mano derecha, diestro

rightly ['raɪtlɪ] ADV **1** (= *correctly*) [*fear, suspect*] con razón; [*assume*] sin equivocarse; [*act, behave*] correctamente, bien; **quite ~** con toda la razón; **if I remember ~** si mal no recuerdo, si no me falla la memoria; **as he (so) ~ said ...** como bien dijo él ...
2 (= *justifiably*) con (toda) la razón; **they are ~ regarded as the best in the world** se les considera, con (toda) la razón, los mejores del mundo; **and ~ so** y con (toda) la razón; **~ or wrongly** con razón o sin ella, justa o injustamente

right-minded ['raɪtˈmaɪndɪd] ADJ (= *decent*) honrado; (= *sensible*) prudente

right-to-life [ˌraɪttəˈlaɪf] N [*movement, group*] pro derecho a la vida

rightsizing ['raɪtˌsaɪzɪŋ] N reestructuración *f* (*que conlleva recortes de plantilla*)

right-thinking ['raɪtˈθɪŋkɪŋ] ADJ = **right-minded**

right-wing ['raɪtˈwɪŋ] ADJ derechista, de derechas

right-winger ['raɪtˈwɪŋəʳ] N derechista *mf*

rigid ['rɪdʒɪd] ADJ **1** [*material*] rígido, tieso; **to be ~ with fear** estar paralizado de miedo **2** [*rules*] riguroso, estricto
3 [*person, ideas*] inflexible, intransigente

rigidity [rɪˈdʒɪdɪtɪ] N rigidez *f*

rigidly ['rɪdʒɪdlɪ] ADV **1** (= *stiffly*) rígidamente **2** (= *strictly*) estrictamente **3** (= *inflexibly*) con inflexibilidad, con intransigencia

rigmarole ['rɪgmərəʊl] N (= *process*) galimatías *m inv*, lío *m*; (= *paperwork*) trámites *mpl*, papeleo *m*

rigor ['rɪgəʳ] N (*US*) = **rigour**

rigor mortis ['rɪgəˈmɔːtɪs] N rigidez *f* cadavérica

rigorous ['rɪgərəs] ADJ riguroso

rigorously ['rɪgərəslɪ] ADV rigurosamente

rigour, rigor (*US*) ['rɪgəʳ] N rigor *m*; [*of climate*] rigores *mpl*

rile* [raɪl] VT sulfurar*, reventar*; **there's nothing that ~s me more** no hay nada que me reviente más*

Riley ['raɪlɪ] N **✦** IDIOM **to live the life of ~** (*Brit**) darse la buena vida

rim [rɪm] N [*of cup etc*] borde *m*; [*of wheel*] llanta *f*; [*of spectacles*] montura *f*

rind [raɪnd] N [*of fruit*] cáscara *f*; [*of cheese, bacon*] corteza *f*

ring¹ [rɪŋ] **Ⓐ** N **1** (*on finger*) (*plain*) anillo *m*; (*jewelled*) anillo *m*, sortija *f*; (*in nose*) arete *m*, aro *m*; (*on bird's leg, for curtain*) anilla *f*; (*on stove*) quemador *m*, hornillo *m*; **electric ~** (*esp Brit*) quemador *m* eléctrico, hornillo *m* eléctrico; **gas ~** (*esp Brit*) fuego *m* de gas; **onion ~s** aros *mpl* de cebolla rebozados; **pineapple ~s** rodajas *fpl* de piña
2 (= *circle*) [*of people*] círculo *m*; (*in game, dance*) corro *m*; [*of objects*] anillo *m*; **to stand in a ~** ponerse en círculo; **to have ~s round one's eyes** tener ojeras; **the ~s of Saturn** los anillos de Saturno; **✦** IDIOM **to run ~s round sb** dar mil vueltas a algn*
3 (= *group*) [*of criminals, drug dealers*] banda *f*, red *f*; [*of spies*] red *f*; (*Comm*) cartel *m*, cártel *m*
4 (= *arena*) (*Boxing*) cuadrilátero *m*, ring *m*; (*at circus*) pista *f*; (= *bullring*) ruedo *m*, plaza *f*; **the ~** (= *boxing*) el boxeo
Ⓑ VT (= *surround*) rodear, cercar
Ⓒ CPD **➤ ring binder** carpeta *f* de anillas *or* (*LAm*) anillos **➤ ring finger** (*dedo m*) anular *m* **➤ ring road** (*Brit*) carretera *f* de circunvalación, ronda *f*, periférico *m* (*LAm*)

ring² [rɪŋ] (*vb: pt* **rang**; *pp* **rung**) **Ⓐ** N **1** (= *sound*) [*of bell*] toque *m* de timbre; **there was a ~ at the door** llamaron al timbre de la puerta, sonó el timbre de la puerta; **that has the ~ of truth about it** eso suena a cierto
2 (*esp Brit Telec*) **to give sb a ~** llamar a algn (por teléfono), dar un telefonazo *or* un toque a algn*
Ⓑ VT **1** [+ *doorbell, handbell, church bell*] tocar; **✦** IDIOM **that ~s a bell (with me)** eso me suena
2 (*esp Brit Telec*) llamar (por teléfono) a; **you must ~ the hospital** tienes que llamar al hospital
Ⓒ VI **1** [*bell, alarm, telephone*] sonar; **✦** IDIOM **to ~ off the hook** (*US*) sonar constantemente, no parar de sonar
2 (= *use bell*) llamar; **to ~ at the door** llamar a la puerta; **we'll ~ for some sugar** llamaremos para pedir azúcar; **"please ring for attention"** "rogamos toque el timbre para que le atiendan"

3 (*esp Brit*) (= *telephone*) llamar (por teléfono); **could someone ~ for a taxi?** ¿podría alguien llamar a un taxi? **4** (= *echo*) (*gen*) resonar; [*ears*] zumbar; ✦ IDIOM **to ~ true/ false** sonar a cierto/falso; **her story just didn't ~ true** la historia no parecía verdad ⓓ CPD **ring tone** señal *f* or tono *m* de llamada
➤ **ring back** (*esp Brit*) ⓐ VT + ADV (= *ring again*) volver a llamar; (= *return sb's call*) llamar ⓑ VI + ADV (= *ring again*) volver a llamar; (= *return call*) llamar
➤ **ring off** VI + ADV (*esp Brit*) colgar
➤ **ring out** VI + ADV [*bell*] sonar, repicar; [*shot*] oírse, sonar
➤ **ring around** (*esp Brit*), **ring round** (*Brit*) ⓐ VI + ADV llamar (por teléfono); **if you ~ round, you can usually get a good deal** si llamas a varios sitios, generalmente se consiguen gangas ⓑ VI + PREP **I'll ~ round my friends** llamaré a mis amigos
➤ **ring up** ⓐ VI + ADV (*esp Brit*) llamar (por teléfono) ⓑ VT + ADV **1 to ~ sb up** (*esp Brit*) llamar a algn (por teléfono) **2** (*on cash-register*) [+ *amount, purchase*] registrar

ringing ['rɪŋɪŋ] ⓐ ADJ [*phone*] que suena *or* sonaba *etc* ⓑ N [*of large bell*] repique *m*; [*of handbell*] campanilleo *m*; [*of electric bell*] toque *m*; [*of phone*] sonido *m*, timbre *m*; (*in ears*) zumbido *m* ⓒ CPD ➤ **ringing tone** (*Brit*) señal *f* de llamada
ringleader ['rɪŋ,liːdəʳ] N cabecilla *mf*
ringlet ['rɪŋlɪt] N rizo *m*, tirabuzón *m*
ringmaster ['rɪŋ,mɑːstəʳ] N maestro *m* de ceremonias
ring-pull ['rɪŋpʊl] N (*Brit*) anilla *f*
ringworm ['rɪŋwɜːm] N tiña *f*
rink [rɪŋk] N (*for ice-skating*) pista *f* de hielo; (*for roller-skating*) pista *f* de patinaje
rinse [rɪns] ⓐ N [*of dishes, clothes*] enjuague *m*, aclarado *m* (*Sp*); **to give sth a ~** enjuagar algo ⓑ VT [+ *dishes, clothes*] enjuagar, aclarar (*Sp*); **to ~ one's hands/mouth** enjuagarse las manos/la boca
riot ['raɪət] ⓐ N (= *uprising*) disturbio *m*, motín *m*; **there was nearly a ~** hubo casi un motín; ✦ IDIOMS **it was a ~!*** ¡fue divertidísimo!, ¡fue la monda! (*Sp**); **he's a ~!*** ¡es un tipo desternillante!, ¡te mondas de risa con él!; **to run ~** (= *go out of control*) desmandarse; **to let one's imagination run ~** dejar volar la imaginación ⓑ VI amotinarse ⓒ CPD ➤ **riot gear** uniforme *m* antidisturbios ➤ **riot police** policía *f* antidisturbios
rioter ['raɪətəʳ] N amotinado/a *m/f*
riotous ['raɪətəs] ADJ [*party, living*] desenfrenado, alborotado; [*comedy*] divertidísimo; **we had a ~ time*** nos divertimos una barbaridad
RIP ABBR (= *rest in peace*) q.e.p.d., D.E.P., E.P.D.
rip [rɪp] ⓐ N rasgón *m*, desgarrón *m* ⓑ VT rasgar, desgarrar; **to ~ open** abrir desgarrando; **to ~ sth to pieces** hacer algo trizas ⓒ VI [*cloth*] rasgarse, desgarrarse; ✦ IDIOM **to let ~** desenfrenarse; **to let ~ at sb** arremeter contra algn
➤ **rip off** VT + ADV **1** (= *pull off*) arrancar **2** (**) (= *cheat*) estafar; (= *steal*) pulir**, birlar*
➤ **rip up** VT + ADV hacer pedazos
ripe [raɪp] ADJ (*compar* ~**r**; *superl* ~**st**) [*fruit etc*] maduro; **the company is ~ for a takeover** la empresa está en su punto para un cambio de dueño; **to live to a ~ old age** llegar a muy viejo
ripen ['raɪpən] VT, VI madurar
ripeness ['raɪpnɪs] N madurez *f*
rip-off** ['rɪpɒf] N **1** (= *swindle*) **it's a ~!** ¡es una estafa *or* un robo! **2** (= *imitation*) [*of film, song etc*] plagio *m*, copia *f*
riposte [rɪ'pɒst] N réplica *f*
ripple ['rɪpl] N (= *small wave*) onda *f*, rizo *m*; (= *sound*) murmullo *m*; **a ~ of excitement** un susurro *or* murmullo de emoción; **a ~ of applause** unos cuantos aplausos
rise [raɪz] (*vb: pt* **rose**; *pp* ~**n** ['rɪzn]) ⓐ N **1** (= *upward movement*) subida *f*, ascenso *m*; ✦ IDIOM **to give ~ to** [+ *problems, impression*] causar; [+ *speculation, suspicion*] suscitar, dar lugar a
2 (= *increase*) (*in number, rate, value*) aumento *m*; (*in price, temperature*) subida *f*, aumento *m*; (*Brit*) (*in salary*) aumento *m* (de sueldo); **they got a ~ of 50 dollars** les aumentaron el

sueldo en 50 dólares; **a ~ in interest rates** un aumento de los tipos de interés
3 (= *advancement*) ascenso *m*, subida *f*; **Napoleon's ~ to power** el ascenso *or* la subida de Napoleón al poder; **the ~ and fall of the empire** el auge *or* la (la) decadencia del imperio ⓑ VI **1** (= *get up*) (*from bed*) levantarse; (= *stand up*) ponerse de pie, levantarse; **to ~ early** madrugar, levantarse temprano; **~ and shine!** ¡levántate y espabila!; **to ~ to one's feet** ponerse de pie; **to ~ from (the) table** levantarse de la mesa; **to ~ from the dead** resucitar
2 (= *get higher*) [*sun, moon*] salir; [*smoke, balloon*] subir, ascender; [*curtain*] levantarse; [*water, level, aircraft*] subir; [*dough, cake*] aumentar, subir; [*river*] crecer; ✦ IDIOM **to ~ to the surface** [*tensions, contradictions*] surgir, aflorar
3 (= *increase*) [*price, temperature, pressure*] subir, aumentar; [*number, amount, tension*] aumentar; [*stocks, shares*] subir
4 [*ground*] subir (en pendiente); **the mountains rose up before him** las montañas se elevaban *or* se alzaban frente a él
5 (*in rank*) ascender; **he rose to be president** llegó a ser presidente; **she rose to the top of her profession** llegó a la cumbre de su profesión; **to ~ from the ranks** (*Mil*) ascender de soldado raso
6 (= *improve*) [*standards*] mejorar; **our spirits rose** nos animamos
7 (= *originate*) [*river*] nacer
8 (= *rebel*) (*also* ~ **up**) sublevarse, levantarse (**against** contra); **to ~ (up) in revolt** sublevarse, rebelarse
riser ['raɪzəʳ] N **to be an early/late ~** ser madrugador(a)/ dormilón/ona
rising ['raɪzɪŋ] ⓐ ADJ [*number*] creciente; [*prices*] en aumento, en alza; [*sun*] naciente; (= *promising*) prometedor ⓑ N (= *uprising*) rebelión *f*, sublevación *f* ⓒ CPD ➤ **rising star** (= *person*) figura *f* emergente
risk [rɪsk] ⓐ N **1** (*gen*) riesgo *m*; **it's not worth the ~** no merece la pena correr el riesgo; **a health/security ~** un peligro para la salud/la seguridad; **up to 25,000 jobs are at ~** hay hasta 25.000 puestos de trabajo que peligran *or* que están en peligro; **at the ~ of seeming stupid** a riesgo de parecer estúpido; **there is no ~ of his coming** *or* **that he will come** no hay peligro de que venga; **at one's own ~** por su cuenta y riesgo; **I can't take the ~** no me puedo exponer *or* arriesgar a eso, no puedo correr ese riesgo; **that's a ~ you'll have to take** ése es un riesgo que vas a tener que correr
2 (*Fin, Insurance*) riesgo *m*; **insured against all ~s** asegurado contra *or* a todo riesgo; **a good/bad ~** un riesgo admisible/ inadmisible ⓑ VT (= *put at risk*) arriesgar, poner en peligro; (= *run the risk of*) correr el riesgo de, arriesgarse a; **to ~ losing** correr el riesgo de perder, arriesgarse a perder; **shall we ~ it?** ¿nos arriesgamos?; **I can't ~ it** no me puedo arriesgar (a eso) ⓒ CPD ➤ **risk factor** factor *m* de riesgo
risky ['rɪskɪ] ADJ (*compar* **riskier**; *superl* **riskiest**) arriesgado, riesgoso (*LAm*)
risotto [rɪ'zɒtəʊ] N risotto *m*, arroz *m* a la italiana
risqué ['riːskeɪ] ADJ [*humour, joke*] subido de tono
rissole ['rɪsəʊl] N (*Brit*) ≈ croqueta *f*
rite [raɪt] N rito *m* ➤ **rite of passage** rito *m* de paso, rito *m* de tránsito
ritual ['rɪtjʊəl] ⓐ ADJ ritual ⓑ N rito *m*, ritual *m*
rival ['raɪvəl] ⓐ ADJ [*team, firm*] rival, contrario; [*claim, attraction*] competidor ⓑ N rival *mf* ⓒ VT competir con, rivalizar con
rivalry ['raɪvəlrɪ] N rivalidad *f*, competencia *f*
river ['rɪvəʳ] N río *m*; **up/down ~** río arriba/abajo ➤ **river basin** cuenca *f* de río
riverbank ['rɪvəbæŋk] N orilla *f*, ribera *f*
riverbed ['rɪvəbed] N lecho *m* (del río)
River Plate [,rɪvə'pleɪt] ⓐ N Río *m* de la Plata ⓑ ADJ rioplatense
riverside ['rɪvəsaɪd] N orilla *f*, ribera *f*
rivet ['rɪvɪt] ⓐ N remache *m* ⓑ VT **1** (*Tech*) remachar **2** [+ *attention*] captar; **to be ~ed to sth** (*fig*) tener los ojos puestos en algo

riveting, rivetting ['rɪvɪtɪŋ] ADJ fascinante, cautivador

Riviera [ˌrɪvɪ'eərə] N (*French*) Riviera *f* (francesa), Costa *f* Azul; (*Italian*) Riviera *f* italiana

Riyadh [rɪ'yɑːd] N Riyadh *m*

RMT N ABBR (*Brit*) = **National Union of Rail, Maritime and Transport Workers**

RN N ABBR **1** (*Brit*) = **Royal Navy 2** = **registered nurse**

RNA N ABBR (= **ribonucleic acid**) ARN *m*

RNLI N ABBR (*Brit*) (= **Royal National Lifeboat Institution**) *servicio de lanchas de socorro*

roach [rəʊtʃ] N **1** (*pl* ~ *or* ~**es**) (= *fish*) gobio *m* **2** (*US*) (= *cockroach*) cucaracha *f*

road [rəʊd] Ⓐ N **1** (= *street*) calle *f*; (= *main road*) carretera *f*; (= *route*) camino *m*; (= *surface*) firme *m*; **across the** ~ al otro lado de la calle; **she lives across the** ~ **from us** vive en frente de nosotros; **by** ~ por carretera; **to be off the** ~ [*car*] estar fuera de circulación; **to be on the** ~ (= *be travelling*) estar en camino; (*Mus, Theat*) estar de gira; **he shouldn't be allowed on the** ~ no deberían dejarle conducir; **the** ~ **to Teruel** el camino de Teruel **2** (*fig*) **somewhere along the** ~ tarde o temprano; **our relationship has reached the end of the** ~ nuestras relaciones han llegado al punto final; **to be on the right** ~ ir por buen camino; **the** ~ **to success** el camino del éxito; **he's on the** ~ **to recovery** se está reponiendo; ✦ IDIOM **to have one for the** ~* tomarse la penúltima (copa)
Ⓑ CPD ➤ **road accident** accidente *m* de tráfico, accidente *m* de circulación, accidente *m* de tránsito (*LAm*) ➤ **road book** libro *m* de mapas e itinerarios, mapa *m* de carreteras ➤ **road bridge** puente *m* de carretera ➤ **road haulage** transporte *m* por carretera ➤ **road haulier** (= *company*) compañía *f* de transporte por carretera; (= *person*) transportista *mf* ➤ **road junction** empalme *m* ➤ **road map** mapa *m* de carreteras ➤ **road race** carrera *f* en carretera ➤ **road rage*** *conducta agresiva al volante* ➤ **road safety** seguridad *f* vial ➤ **road sign** señal *f* de tráfico ➤ **road sweeper** (= *person*) barrendero/a *m/f*; (= *vehicle*) máquina *f* barrendera ➤ **road tax** (*Brit*) impuesto *m* de rodaje ➤ **road test** prueba *f* en carretera ➤ **road user** usuario/a *m/f* de la vía pública

roadblock ['rəʊdblɒk] N control *m*, barricada *f*, retén *m* (*LAm*)

roadhog ['rəʊdhɒɡ] N loco(a) *m/f* del volante

roadshow ['rəʊdʃəʊ] N programa *m* itinerante

roadside ['rəʊdsaɪd] N borde *m* de la carretera, orilla *f* del camino (*LAm*) ➤ **roadside restaurant** (*US*) café-restaurante *m* (de carretera)

road-test ['rəʊdtest] VT probar en carretera

roadworks ['rəʊdwɜːks] NPL (*Brit*) obras *fpl* (*en la calzada*)

roadworthy ['rəʊdˌwɜːðɪ] ADJ en buen estado (para circular)

roam [rəʊm] Ⓐ VT [+ *streets etc*] rondar, vagar por Ⓑ VI [*person*] vagar, errar; [*thoughts*] divagar

roar [rɔː] Ⓐ N **1** [*of lion, person*] rugido *m*; [*of crowd*] clamor *m*; [*of laughter*] carcajada *f* **2** (= *loud noise*) estruendo *m*, fragor *m*; [*of river, storm*] estruendo *m* Ⓑ VI [*lion*] rugir; [*crowd*] clamar; [*guns, thunder*] retumbar; **to** ~ **(with laughter)** reírse a carcajadas; **the lorry** ~**ed past** el camión pasó ruidosamente

roaring ['rɔːrɪŋ] ADJ **a** ~ **fire** un fuego bien caliente; **it was a** ~ **success** fue un tremendo éxito; **to do a** ~ **trade** hacer muy buen negocio

roast [rəʊst] Ⓐ N asado *m* Ⓑ ADJ asado; [*coffee*] torrefacto, tostado; ~ **beef** rosbif *m* Ⓒ VT [+ *meat*] asar; [+ *coffee*] tostar

roasting ['rəʊstɪŋ] Ⓐ ADJ (*) [*day, heat*] abrasador; **it's** ~ **in here** esto es un horno Ⓑ N **to give sb a** ~ (*Brit**) (= *scold*) desollar vivo a algn

rob [rɒb] VT [+ *person*] robar; [+ *bank etc*] atracar; **to** ~ **sb of sth** robar algo a algn; **I've been** ~**bed!** ¡me han robado!; **we were** ~**bed!** (*Sport**) ¡nos robaron el partido!

robber ['rɒbə'] N ladrón/ona *m/f*; (= *bankrobber*) atracador(a) *m/f*; (= *brigand*) bandido *m*

robbery ['rɒbərɪ] N robo *m*

robe [rəʊb] N (= *ceremonial garment*) traje *m* de ceremonia, túnica *f*; (*lawyer's, academic's etc*) toga *f*; (= *bathrobe*) bata *f*; **robes** traje *msing* de ceremonia, traje *msing* talar

robin ['rɒbɪn] N petirrojo *m*

robot ['rəʊbɒt] N robot *m*

robotic [rəʊ'bɒtɪk] ADJ [*equipment, arm etc*] robótico; (*fig*) de robot, robotizado

robust [rəʊ'bʌst] ADJ [*person, constitution*] robusto, fuerte; [*material, design, object*] resistente, sólido; [*economy*] fuerte; **to be in** ~ **health** tener una salud de hierro

robustly [rəʊ'bʌstlɪ] ADV **to be** ~ **built** [*person*] ser de constitución robusta *or* fuerte; [*thing*] estar sólidamente construido

rock¹ [rɒk] Ⓐ N **1** (= *substance, large stone*) roca *f*; (*US*) (= *small stone*) piedra *f*; **the Rock (of Gibraltar)** el Peñón (de Gibraltar); **an outcrop of** ~ un peñasco, un peñón **2** (*in phrases*) **to be at** ~ **bottom** estar por los suelos, haber tocado fondo; ~ **hard** [*ground*] duro como la roca; [*bed*] duro como una piedra; **whisky on the** ~**s** whisky con hielo; **to run on(to) the** ~**s** (*Naut*) chocar contra los escollos, encallar en las rocas; ~ **solid** (*lit, fig*) sólido como una roca; ✦ IDIOMS **to be on the** ~**s*** [*marriage*] andar fatal*; **to be (caught) between a** ~ **and a hard place** estar entre la espada y la pared **3** (*Brit*) **a stick of** ~ un palo de caramelo
Ⓑ CPD ➤ **rock candy** (*US*) palo *m* de caramelo ➤ **rock climbing** escalada *f* en rocas; **to go** ~ **climbing** ir a escalar en roca ➤ **rock face** vertiente *f* rocosa, pared *f* de roca ➤ **rock formation** formación *f* rocosa ➤ **rock garden** jardín *m* de roca *or* de rocalla ➤ **rock plant** planta *f* rupestre *or* de roca ➤ **rock pool** charca *f* (de agua de mar) entre rocas ➤ **rock salmon** (*Brit*) cazón *m* ➤ **rock salt** sal *f* gema *or* mineral *or* sin refinar

rock² [rɒk] Ⓐ VT **1** (= *swing to and fro*) [+ *child*] acunar; [+ *cradle*] mecer; **to** ~ **a child to sleep** arrullar a un niño **2** (= *shake*) (*lit, fig*) sacudir; **his death** ~**ed the fashion business** su muerte sacudió *or* convulsionó al mundo de la moda; ✦ IDIOM **to** ~ **the boat** hacer olas
Ⓑ VI (*gently*) mecerse, balancearse; (*violently*) sacudirse
Ⓒ N (*also* ~ **music**) rock *m*, música *f* rock
Ⓓ CPD ➤ **rock and roll** rocanrol *m*, rock and roll *m* ➤ **rock band** grupo *m* de rock ➤ **rock concert** concierto *m* de rock ➤ **rock festival** festival *m* de rock ➤ **rock music** rock *m*, música *f* rock ➤ **rock musician** músico/a *m/f* de rock ➤ **rock 'n' roll** rocanrol *m*, rock and roll *m* ➤ **rock star** estrella *f* de rock

rock-bottom [ˌrɒk'bɒtəm] ADJ ~ **prices** precios *mpl* mínimos, precios *mpl* tirados

rockery ['rɒkərɪ] N jardín *m* de roca *or* de rocalla

rocket¹ ['rɒkɪt] Ⓐ N (= *firework, missile*) cohete *m*; (= *space rocket*) cohete *m* espacial Ⓑ VI [*prices*] dispararse Ⓒ CPD ➤ **rocket attack** ataque *m* con cohetes ➤ **rocket launcher** lanzacohetes *m inv* ➤ **rocket science** astronáutica *f*; **this isn't** ~ **science*** para esto no hace falta saber latín ➤ **rocket scientist** ingeniero/a *m/f* astronáutico/a; **it doesn't take a** ~ **scientist to ...*** no hace falta ser una lumbrera para ...

rocket² ['rɒkɪt] N (= *vegetable*) oruga *f*

rocket-propelled ['rɒkɪtprəˌpeld] ADJ propulsado por cohete(s)

Rockies ['rɒkɪz] NPL Montañas *fpl* Rocosas

rocking ['rɒkɪŋ] N balanceo *m* ➤ **rocking chair** mecedora *f*, mecedor *m* (*LAm*) ➤ **rocking horse** caballito *m* de balancín

rock-steady ['rɒkˌstedɪ] ADJ [*hand*] muy firme; [*voice*] muy seguro; [*car*] muy estable

rocky¹ ['rɒkɪ] ADJ (*compar* **rockier**; *superl* **rockiest**) [*substance*] (duro) como la piedra; [*slope etc*] rocoso ➤ **the Rocky Mountains** las Montañas Rocosas

rocky² ['rɒkɪ] ADJ (*compar* **rockier**; *superl* **rockiest**) (= *precarious*) [*situation*] inseguro, inestable; [*government etc*] débil

rod [rɒd] N [*of wood*] vara *f*; [*of metal*] barra *f*; (= *fishing rod*) caña *f*; ✦ IDIOMS **to rule with a** ~ **of iron** gobernar con mano de hierro; **to make a ~ for one's own back** hacer algo que después resultará contraproducente

rode [rəʊd] PT *of* **ride**

rodent ['rəʊdənt] N roedor *m*

rodeo ['rəʊdiəʊ] N rodeo *m*, charreada *f* (*Mex*)

roe[1] [rəʊ] N [*of fish*] hard ~ hueva *f*; **soft** ~ lecha *f*

roe[2] [rəʊ] N (*also* ~ **deer**) corzo/a *m/f*

rogue [rəʊg] Ⓐ N (= *thief etc*) pícaro/a *m/f*, pillo/a *m/f*; (*hum*) granuja *mf* Ⓑ ADJ [*lion, male*] solitario, apartado de la manada; [*gene*] defectuoso; [*company*] sin escrúpulos; ~ **cop*** policía *mf* corrupto/a

roguish ['rəʊgɪʃ] ADJ [*child*] travieso; [*look, smile etc*] pícaro

role [rəʊl] N papel *m* ➤ **role model** modelo *m* a imitar ➤ **role play(ing)** juego *m* de rol(es) ➤ **role reversal** inversión *f* de papeles

roll [rəʊl] Ⓐ N 1 [*of paper, cloth, wire, tobacco*] rollo *m*; [*of banknotes*] fajo *m*; **a ~ of film** un carrete *or* un rollo de fotos; **~s of fat** (*on stomach*) michelines *mpl* (*hum*)
2 [*of bread*] panecillo *m*, bolillo *m* (*Mex*)
3 (= *list*) lista *f*; **to have 500 pupils on the ~** tener inscritos a 500 alumnos; **to call the ~** pasar lista
4 (= *sound*) [*of thunder, cannon*] retumbo *m*; [*of drum*] redoble *m*
5 (= *movement*) [*of ship, plane*] balanceo *m*
6 (= *act of rolling*) revolcón *m*; **the horse was having a ~ on the grass** el caballo se estaba revolcando en la hierba
7 [*of dice*] tirada *f*; ✦ IDIOM **to be on a ~** estar en racha, tener una buena racha
Ⓑ VT **1** [+ *ball*] hacer rodar; [+ *pastry, dough*] estirar; [+ *cigarette*] liar; **to ~ the dice** tirar los dados; **I ~ed her onto her back** la puse boca arriba; **to ~ sth between one's fingers** hacer rodar algo entre los dedos; **she ~ed her sweater into a ball** hizo una bola con el jersey; **she is trainer and rep ~ed into one** es entrenadora y representante, todo a la vez; **to ~ one's eyes** poner los ojos en blanco; **to ~ one's r's** pronunciar fuertemente las erres
2 (*US***) (= *rob*) atracar
Ⓒ VI **1** (= *roll along*) ir rodando; (*on ground, in pain*) revolcarse; **the ball ~ed into the net** el balón entró rodando en la red; **it ~ed under the chair** desapareció *or* rodó debajo de la silla; **the tanks ~ed into the city** los tanques entraron en la ciudad; **the convoy ~ed slowly along the road** el convoy avanzaba lentamente por la carretera; **newspapers were ~ing off the presses** los periódicos estaban saliendo de las prensas; **tears ~ed down her cheeks** las lágrimas le corrían *or* caían por la cara; **his eyes ~ed** los ojos se le pusieron en blanco; **she ~ed onto her back** se puso boca arriba; ✦ IDIOM **they're ~ing in money** *or* **in it**** están forrados*
2 [*camera*] rodar; [*machine*] funcionar, estar en marcha
Ⓓ CPD ➤ **roll bar** (*on car*) barra *f* antivuelco ➤ **roll call** lista *f*; **to take (a) ~ call** pasar lista
➤ **roll around, roll about** (*Brit*) VI + ADV [*ball, coin*] rodar de un lado a otro; [*person, dog*] revolcarse; [*ship*] balancearse
➤ **roll away** VI + ADV [*ball*] alejarse (rodando), irse (rodando); [*clouds, mist*] disiparse
➤ **roll by** VI + ADV [*vehicle, clouds, time, years*] pasar
➤ **roll in** VI + ADV (*) [*money, letters*] llover, llegar a raudales; (*esp Brit*) [*person*] aparecer **2** [*waves, cloud, mist*] llegar
➤ **roll on** VI + ADV [*time*] pasar; **~ on the summer!** (*Brit***) ¡que llegue pronto el verano!
➤ **roll out** VT + ADV **1** (*Comm*) [+ *product*] sacar *or* lanzar (al mercado) **2** [+ *pastry*] extender con el rodillo *or* uslero (*And*); [+ *carpet*] desenrollar
➤ **roll over** Ⓐ VI + ADV [*person, animal*] darse la vuelta; [*object, vehicle*] (*180°*) volcar, voltearse (*LAm*); (*360°*) (*once*) dar una vuelta de campana; (*several times*) dar vueltas de campana; **she ~ed over onto her back** se dio la vuelta poniéndose boca arriba Ⓑ VT + ADV [+ *object*] volver; [+ *body*] poner boca arriba
➤ **roll up** VI + ADV (*) [*person*] presentarse, aparecer; **~ up, ~ up!** ¡acérquense!, ¡vengan todos! Ⓑ VT + ADV enrollar; [+ *car window*] subir; **to ~ up one's sleeves** remangarse, arremangarse; **to ~ o.s. up into a ball** hacerse un ovillo

roller ['rəʊlə'] Ⓐ N **1** (*Agr, Tech*) rodillo *m*; (= *road-roller*)

apisonadora *f*; (= *caster*) ruedecilla *f*; (*for hair*) rulo *m*
2 (= *wave*) ola *f* grande Ⓑ CPD ➤ **roller blind** (*Brit*) persiana *f* enrollable ➤ **roller coaster** montaña *f* rusa ➤ **roller skate** patín *m* (de ruedas)

rollerblades ['rəʊləbleɪdz] NPL patines *mpl* en línea

roller-skate ['rəʊlə‚skeɪt] VI ir en patines de ruedas, patinar

roller-skating ['rəʊlə‚skeɪtɪŋ] N patinaje *m* sobre ruedas

rollicking* ['rɒlɪkɪŋ] Ⓐ ADJ alegre, divertido; **we had a ~ time** nos divertimos una barbaridad Ⓑ N **to give sb a ~** (*Brit*) poner a algn como un trapo*

rolling ['rəʊlɪŋ] ADJ [*waves*] fuerte; [*sea*] agitado; [*countryside, hills*] ondulado; **a ~ programme of privatization** un programa de privatización escalonado ➤ **rolling pin** rodillo *m* (de cocina), uslero *m* (*And*) ➤ **rolling stock** material *m* rodante *or* móvil

roll-neck ['rəʊlnek] N (*Brit*) jersey *m* cuello cisne

roll-on deodorant [‚rəʊlɒndrˈəʊdərənt] N desodorante *m* roll-on, desodorante *m* de bola

roll-on-roll-off [‚rəʊlɒnrəʊlˈɒf] N (*Brit*) ro-ro *m*

ROM [rɒm] N ABBR (= **Read-Only Memory**) ROM *f*

Roman ['rəʊmən] ADJ, N romano/a *m/f* ➤ **Roman numeral** número *m* romano

Roman Catholic [‚rəʊmənˈkæθəlɪk] ADJ, N católico/a *m/f* (apostólico/a y romano/a)

romance [rəʊˈmæns] Ⓐ N **1** (= *love affair*) romance *m*, idilio *m*, amores *mpl* **2** (= *romantic quality*) lo romántico, lo poético **3** (= *tale*) novela *f* (sentimental), cuento *m* (de amor) Ⓑ ADJ [*language*] romance

Romanesque [‚rəʊməˈnesk] ADJ románico

Romania [rəʊˈmeɪnɪə] N Rumania *f*, Rumanía *f*

Romanian [rəʊˈmeɪnɪən] Ⓐ ADJ rumano Ⓑ N **1** (= *person*) rumano/a *m/f* **2** (*Ling*) rumano *m*

romantic [rəʊˈmæntɪk] ADJ, N romántico/a *m/f*

romantically [rəʊˈmæntɪkəlɪ] ADV románticamente, de modo romántico

romanticism [rəʊˈmæntɪsɪzəm] N romanticismo *m*

romanticize [rəʊˈmæntɪsaɪz] Ⓐ VT sentimentalizar Ⓑ VI fantasear

Romany ['rɒmənɪ] Ⓐ ADJ gitano Ⓑ N **1** gitano/a *m/f*
2 (*Ling*) romaní *m*, lengua *f* gitana; (*in Spain*) caló *m*

Rome [rəʊm] N **1** Roma *f* **2** (*Rel*) la Iglesia, el catolicismo

romp [rɒmp] Ⓐ N retozo *m*; **the play was just a ~** la obra era una farsa alegre nada más Ⓑ VI retozar; **she ~ed through the examination** no tuvo problema alguno para aprobar el examen; **to ~ home** ganar fácilmente

roof [ruːf] N [*of building*] tejado *m* (*esp Sp*), techo *m* (*esp LAm*); [*of car*] techo *m*; **flat ~** azotea *f*; **to have a ~ over one's head** tener dónde cobijarse; **the ~ of the mouth** el paladar; **prices are going through the ~** los precios están por las nubes; ✦ IDIOMS **he hit the ~*** se subió por las paredes*; **to raise the ~** (= *protest*) poner el grito en el cielo ➤ **roof rack** (*Brit*) baca *f*, portamaletas *m inv*, portaequipajes *m inv*, parrilla *f* (*LAm*)

roofing ['ruːfɪŋ] CPD ➤ **roofing felt** (*Brit*) fieltro *m* para techar ➤ **roofing material** material *m* para techado

rooftop ['ruːftɒp] N techo *m*; (*with flat roof*) azotea *f*; ✦ IDIOM **we will proclaim it from the ~s** lo proclamaremos a los cuatro vientos

rook[1] [rʊk] N (= *bird*) grajo *m*

rook[2] [rʊk] N (*Chess*) torre *f*

rookie* ['rʊkɪ] (*US*) N novato/a *m/f*

room [rʊm] Ⓐ N **1** (*in house, hotel*) habitación *f*, cuarto *m*, pieza *f* (*esp LAm*), recámara *f* (*Mex*), ambiente *m* (*Arg*); (*large, public*) sala *f*; **double/single ~** habitación *f etc* doble/ individual; **ladies' ~** servicios *mpl* de señoras
2 rooms (= *lodging*) alojamiento *msing*
3 (= *space*) sitio *m*, espacio *m*, campo *m* (*And*); **is there ~?** ¿hay sitio?; **there's plenty of ~** hay sitio de sobra; **is there ~ for this?** ¿cabe esto?, ¿hay cabida para esto?; **is there ~ for me?** ¿quepo yo?, ¿hay sitio para mí?; **to make ~ for sb**

hacer sitio a algn; **there is ~ for improvement** esto se puede mejorar todavía
Ⓑ VI (*US*) **to ~ with three other students** estar en una pensión con otros tres estudiantes, compartir (un) piso *or* (*LAm*) un departamento con otros tres estudiantes
Ⓒ CPD ➤ **room service** servicio *m* de habitaciones ➤ **room temperature** temperatura *f* ambiente

roomful ['rʊmfəl] N **a ~ of priests** un cuarto lleno de curas

rooming house ['ruːmɪŋˌhaʊs] N (*US*) pensión *f*

roommate ['rʊmmeɪt] N (*sharing room*) compañero/a *m/f* de cuarto; (*US*) (*sharing apartment*) compañero/a *m/f* de piso

roomy ['rʊmɪ] ADJ (*compar* **roomier**; *superl* **roomiest**) [*flat, cupboard etc*] amplio, espacioso

roost [ruːst] **Ⓐ** N gallinero *m* **Ⓑ** VI ✦ IDIOM **to come home to ~: now his policies have come home to ~** ahora su política produce su fruto amargo, ahora se están viendo los malos resultados de su política

rooster ['ruːstəʳ] N (*esp US*) gallo *m*

root [ruːt] **Ⓐ** N **1** raíz *f*; **to pull sth up by the ~s** arrancar algo de raíz; **to take ~** (*lit*) echar raíces, arraigar; [*idea*] arraigarse; **the ~ of the problem is that ...** la raíz del problema es que ...; ✦ IDIOM **~ and branch** completamente, del todo
2 (*Math*) **square ~** raíz *f* cuadrada
Ⓑ VT **to be ~ed to the spot** quedar paralizado; **a deeply ~ed prejudice** un prejuicio muy arraigado
Ⓒ CPD ➤ **root beer** (*US*) bebida refrescante elaborada a base de raíces ➤ **root cause** causa *f* primordial ➤ **root crops** cultivos *mpl* de tubérculos ➤ **root ginger** raíz *f* de jengibre ➤ **root vegetable** tubérculo *m* comestible
➤ **root around**, **root about** (*Brit*) VI + ADV [*pig*] hozar, hocicar; [*person*] (= *search*) andar buscando por todas partes; (= *investigate*) investigar; **to ~ around for sth** andar buscando algo
➤ **root for*** VI + PREP [+ *team*] animar (*con gritos y pancartas*)
➤ **root out** VT + ADV (= *find*) desenterrar, encontrar; (= *eliminate*) acabar con, arrancar de raíz, extirpar

rope [rəʊp] N cuerda *f*, soga *f*, mecate *m* (*Mex*); **to jump** *or* **skip ~** (*US*) saltar a la cuerda *or* (*Sp*) comba; ✦ IDIOMS **to be at the end of one's ~** (*US*) no poder soportarlo más, no aguantar más; **to know/learn the ~s** estar/ponerse al tanto; **I'll show you the ~s** te voy a mostrar cómo funciona todo
➤ **rope ladder** escala *f* de cuerda
➤ **rope in*** VT + ADV **to ~ sb in (to do sth)** (*esp Brit*) enganchar a algn (*para que haga algo*)
➤ **rope off** VT + ADV acordonar

ropy*, **ropey*** ['rəʊpɪ] ADJ (*Brit*) (*compar* **ropier**; *superl* **ropiest**) (= *off colour*) indispuesto, pachucho (*Sp**); (= *weak*) [*plan, argument etc*] nada convincente, flojo

rosary ['rəʊzərɪ] N rosario *m*

rose¹ [rəʊz] **Ⓐ** N **1** (= *flower*) rosa *f*; (= *bush*) rosal *m*; (= *colour*) rosa *m*; **life isn't all ~s** la vida no es un lecho de rosas **2** (*on shower, watering can*) alcachofa *f* **3** (*also* **ceiling ~**) roseta *f*, rosetón *m* **Ⓑ** ADJ (= *rose-coloured*) (de color de) rosa *inv*, rosado; **~ pink** rosado, rosa **Ⓒ** CPD
➤ **rose bush** rosal *m* ➤ **rose garden** rosaleda *f* ➤ **rose window** rosetón *m*

rose² [rəʊz] PT *of* **rise**

rosé ['rəʊzeɪ] **Ⓐ** ADJ rosado **Ⓑ** N rosado *m*

rosebud ['rəʊzbʌd] N capullo *m* *or* botón *m* de rosa

rose-coloured, **rose-colored** (*US*) ['rəʊzˌkʌləd] ADJ color de rosa; ✦ IDIOM **to see everything through ~ glasses** *or* (*Brit*) **spectacles** verlo todo color de rosa

rosehip ['rəʊzhɪp] N escaramujo *m*

rosemary ['rəʊzmərɪ] N romero *m*

rosette [rəʊ'zet] N (= *prize*) premio *m*

rosewood ['rəʊzwʊd] N palo *m* de rosa

roster ['rɒstəʳ] N lista *f*; **duty ~** lista *f* de turnos

rostrum ['rɒstrəm] N (*pl* **~s** *or* **rostra** ['rɒstrə]) N tribuna *f*

rosy ['rəʊzɪ] ADJ (*compar* **rosier**; *superl* **rosiest**) **1** [*cheeks*] sonrosado; [*colour*] rosáceo **2** [*future, prospect*] prometedor, halagüeño

rot [rɒt] **Ⓐ** N (= *process*) putrefacción *f*; (= *substance*) podredumbre *f*; ✦ IDIOM **to stop the ~** cortar el problema de raíz, cortar por lo sano **Ⓑ** VI pudrirse, descomponerse; **to ~ in jail** pudrirse en la cárcel

rota ['rəʊtə] N (*Brit*) lista *f* (de tareas)

rotary ['rəʊtərɪ] ADJ [*movement*] giratorio; [*blade*] rotativo, giratorio

rotate [rəʊ'teɪt] **Ⓐ** VT (= *turn*) hacer girar, dar vueltas a; [+ *crops*] alternar, cultivar en rotación **Ⓑ** VI (= *turn*) girar, dar vueltas; [*staff*] alternarse

rotating [rəʊ'teɪtɪŋ] ADJ [*blade*] rotativo, giratorio; [*presidency*] rotatorio

rotation [rəʊ'teɪʃən] N rotación *f*; **orders are dealt with in strict ~** los pedidos se sirven por riguroso orden

rote [rəʊt] N **to learn sth by ~** aprender algo a fuerza de repetirlo ➤ **rote learning ~ learning was the fashion** era costumbre aprender las cosas a fuerza de repetirlas

rotisserie [rəʊ'tɪsərɪ] N asador *m*, grill *m*

rotor ['rəʊtəʳ] N rotor *m* ➤ **rotor blade** paleta *f* de rotor

rotten ['rɒtn] ADJ **1** [*fruit, meat*] podrido; [*tooth*] cariado, picado, podrido; [*wood*] carcomido, podrido **2** (*fig*) [*system, government*] corrompido; (*) (= *of bad quality*) pésimo, fatal*; **he's ~ at chess** para el ajedrez es un desastre; **I feel ~** (= *ill*) me encuentro fatal*; (= *guilty*) me siento culpable; **what a ~ thing to do!** ¡qué maldad!; **what a ~ thing to happen!** ¡qué mala suerte!; **what ~ weather!** ¡qué tiempo de perros!

rotund [rəʊ'tʌnd] ADJ corpulento, rotundo

rouble, **ruble** (*US*) ['ruːbl] N rublo *m*

rouge [ruːʒ] N colorete *m*, carmín *m*

rough [rʌf] **Ⓐ** ADJ (*compar* **~er**; *superl* **~est**) **1** (= *coarse*) [*surface, texture*] áspero, rugoso; [*skin*] áspero; [*cloth*] basto **2** (= *uneven*) [*terrain*] accidentado, escabroso; [*road*] desigual, lleno de baches; [*ground*] desigual; [*edge*] irregular
3 (= *not gentle*) [*behaviour, person, voice, manner*] brusco; [*words, tone*] severo, áspero; [*play, sport, game*] violento; [*neighbourhood, area*] malo, peligroso; **he got ~ justice** recibió un castigo duro pero apropiado
4 (= *stormy*) [*sea*] agitado, encrespado; [*weather*] tormentoso, tempestuoso; **to get ~** [*sea*] embravecerse
5 (= *unpolished*) [*person*] tosco, rudo; [*manners*] tosco
6 (*) (= *hard, tough*) duro; **things are ~ now, but they will get better** las cosas están un poco difíciles ahora pero mejorarán; **to be ~ on sb** [*situation*] ser duro para algn; [*person*] ser duro con algn; ✦ IDIOM **to give sb a ~ ride** hacérselo pasar mal a algn; **to have a ~ time (of it)** pasarlo mal; **7** (*Brit**) (= *ill*) **to feel ~** encontrarse mal
8 (= *approximate*) [*calculation, estimate, description, outline*] aproximado; [*translation*] hecho a grandes rasgos, aproximado; **I would say 50 at a ~ guess** diría que 50 aproximadamente; **can you give me a ~ idea of how long it will take?** ¿puedes darme una idea aproximada *or* más o menos una idea de cuánto tiempo llevará?
9 (= *preparatory*) [*work*] de preparación, preliminar; **~ copy** ◊ **~ draft** borrador *m*; **~ paper** papel *m* de borrador; **~ plan** ◊ **~ sketch** bosquejo *m*, boceto *m*
Ⓑ ADV **to live ~** (*Brit*) vivir sin las comodidades más básicas; **to play ~** jugar duro; **to sleep ~** (*Brit*) dormir a la intemperie
Ⓒ N **1** (*Golf*) rough *m*, zona *f* de matojos
2 (= *draft*) **we'll do it in ~ first** lo haremos primero en borrador
3 ✦ IDIOM **to take the ~ with the smooth** tomar las duras con las maduras
Ⓓ VT **to ~ it** vivir sin comodidades
Ⓔ CPD ➤ **rough and tumble the ~ and tumble of life** los vaivenes de la vida; **the ~ and tumble of politics** los avatares *or* altibajos de la política ➤ **rough book** cuaderno *m* de borrador

roughage ['rʌfɪdʒ] N (*for animals*) forraje *m*; (*for people*) alimentos *mpl* ricos en fibra

rough-and-ready ['rʌfən'redɪ] ADJ [*person*] tosco, burdo, basto; [*accommodation*] humilde, sencillo; [*method*] improvisado

roughly ['rʌflɪ] ADV **1** (= *approximately*) [*equal*] aproximadamente, más o menos; **~ translated** traducido a grandes rasgos *or* de forma aproximada **2** (= *generally*) [*describe, outline*] en líneas generales, más o menos; **they fall ~ into two categories** en términos generales se dividen en dos categorías; **~ speaking** en líneas generales **3** (= *not gently*) [*push*] bruscamente; [*play*] de forma violenta; [*speak*] con brusquedad **4** (= *crudely*) [*constructed, carved*] toscamente

roughness ['rʌfnɪs] N [*of hands, surface*] aspereza *f*, rugosidad *f*; [*of road*] desigualdad *f*; [*of person*] (= *brusqueness*) brusquedad *f*; (= *crudeness*) tosquedad *f*; (= *violence*) violencia *f*

roughshod ['rʌfʃɒd] ADV **to ride ~ over sth/sb** pisotear algo/a algn

roulette [ruːˈlet] N ruleta *f*

round [raʊnd]

> When **round** is an element in a phrasal verb, eg **call round**, look up the verb.

Ⓐ ADJ (*compar* **~er**; *superl* **~est**) redondo
Ⓑ ADV **there is a fence all** ~ está rodeado por un cercado; **it would be better all** ~ **if we didn't go** (*esp Brit*) (= *in every respect*) sería mejor en todos los sentidos que no fuéramos; (= *for all concerned*) sería mejor para todos que no fuéramos; **all year** ~ (durante) todo el año; **we were** ~ **at my sister's** estábamos en casa de mi hermana; **it flew** ~ **and round** voló dando vueltas; **the long way** ~ el camino más largo; **it's a long way** ~ es mucho rodeo; **the other/wrong way** ~ al revés
Ⓒ PREP **1** (*of place etc*) alrededor de; **we were sitting** ~ **the table/fire** estábamos sentados alrededor de la mesa/en torno a la chimenea; **she ignored the people** ~ **her** ignoró a la gente que estaba a su alrededor; **the wall** ~ **the garden** el muro que rodea el jardín; **a walk** ~ **the town** un paseo por la ciudad; **all the people** ~ **about** toda la gente alrededor; **all** ~ **the house** (*inside*) por toda la casa; (*outside*) alrededor de toda la casa; **she's 36 inches** ~ **the bust** tiene 90 de busto *or* de pecho; ~ **the corner** a la vuelta de la esquina; **are you from** ~ **here?** ¿eres de por aquí?; **when you're** ~ **this way** cuando pases por aquí
2 (*esp Brit*) (= *approximately*) alrededor de, más o menos; ~ **four o'clock** a eso de las cuatro; ~ **about £50** alrededor de 50 libras, 50 libras más o menos; **somewhere** ~ **Derby** cerca de Derby
Ⓓ N **1** (= *circle*) círculo *m*; (*Brit*) (= *slice*) tajada *f*, rodaja *f*; **a ~ of sandwiches** (*Brit*) un sandwich
2 (*esp Brit*) [*of postman, milkman etc*] recorrido *m*; [*of watchman*] ronda *f*; **the watchman was doing his** ~ el vigilante estaba de ronda; **the story is doing the ~s that ...** se dice *or* se rumorea que ...; **the doctor's on his ~s** el médico está haciendo sus visitas
3 (*Boxing*) asalto *m*, round *m*; (*Golf*) partido *m*, recorrido *m*, vuelta *f*; (*Showjumping*) recorrido *m*; (*Cards*) (= *game*) partida *f*; (*in tournament*) vuelta *f*
4 [*of drinks, negotiations*] ronda *f*; **it's my** ~ yo invito, me toca a mí; ~ **of ammunition** cartucho *m*, bala *f*, tiro *m*; ~ **of applause** salva *f* de aplausos; **life was one long ~ of parties** la vida consistía en una sucesión constante de fiestas
Ⓔ VT (= *go round*) [+ *corner*] doblar, dar la vuelta a
Ⓕ CPD ➤ **round robin** (= *request*) petición *f* firmada en rueda, circular *f*; (= *protest*) protesta *f* firmada en rueda ➤ **round trip** viaje *m* de ida y vuelta ➤ **round trip ticket** (*US*) billete *m* (*Sp*) *or* boleto *m* (*LAm*) de ida y vuelta
➤ **round down** VT + ADV redondear (rebajando)
➤ **round off** VT + ADV acabar, rematar; **to ~ off the evening** dar el remate a la fiesta
➤ **round on, round upon** VI + PREP volverse en contra de
➤ **round up** VT + ADV **1** [+ *cattle*] acorralar, rodear; [+ *friends*] reunir; [+ *criminals*] coger, agarrar (*LAm*) **2** [+ *figures*] redondear por arriba

roundabout ['raʊndəbaʊt] Ⓐ ADJ indirecto; **by a ~ way** dando un rodeo, por una ruta alternativa Ⓑ N **1** (*Brit*) (*at fair*) caballitos *mpl*, carrusel *m* (*esp LAm*), calesita(s) *f(pl)* (*And, SC*); (*in playground*) carrusel *m* **2** (*Brit Aut*) cruce *m* giratorio, glorieta *f* (*SC*), rotonda *f* (*SC*), redoma *f* (*Carib*)

rounded ['raʊndɪd] ADJ **1** (= *curved*) [*shape, hills, hips*] redondeado; [*face*] redondo, relleno; [*handwriting*] redondo **2** [*style, book*] pulido, maduro; [*education*] completo

rounders ['raʊndəz] NSING (*Brit*) juego similar al béisbol

roundly ['raʊndlɪ] ADV [*condemn, criticize*] duramente; [*reject, deny*] categóricamente, rotundamente; **he was ~ defeated in the election** sufrió una derrota aplastante en las elecciones

round-shouldered ['raʊndˈʃəʊldəd] ADJ cargado de espaldas

round-the-clock ['raʊndðəˈklɒk] ADJ (*Brit*) [*surveillance etc*] de veinticuatro horas

round-up ['raʊndʌp] N [*of suspects etc*] detención *f*; (*by police*) redada *f*; **a ~ of the latest news** un resumen de las últimas noticias

rouse [raʊz] VT [+ *person*] despertar; [+ *interest*] despertar, suscitar; [+ *anger*] provocar; **to ~ sb to action** mover a algn a actuar

rousing ['raʊzɪŋ] ADJ [*applause*] caluroso; [*song*] vivo, lleno de vigor; [*speech*] conmovedor

rout [raʊt] Ⓐ N derrota *f* aplastante Ⓑ VT aplastar, derrotar de forma aplastante

route [ruːt] Ⓐ N **1** (*gen*) ruta *f*, camino *m*; [*of bus*] recorrido *m*; [*of ship*] rumbo *m*, derrota *f*; (= *itinerary*) itinerario *m*; (= *direction*) rumbo *m*; **the ~ to the coast** el camino de la costa; **to go by a new** ~ seguir una ruta nueva **2** (*US*) [ruːt, raʊt] (= *delivery round*) recorrido *m* Ⓑ VT fijar el itinerario de; (*Comput*) encaminar; **the train is now ~d through Derby** ahora el tren pasa por Derby

routine [ruːˈtiːn] Ⓐ N **1** rutina *f*; **the daily ~** la rutina diaria
2 (*esp Theat*) número *m*; **dance ~** número *m* de baile
3 (= *spiel*) **he gave me the old ~ about his wife not understanding him*** me vino con la historia de siempre de que su mujer no le entendía Ⓑ ADJ [*test, check-up, maintenance, inspection*] de rutina; [*matter, problem*] rutinario; [*work*] habitual, de rutina; **to make ~ enquiries** hacer averiguaciones rutinarias *or* de rutina; **it's just** ~ es cosa de rutina; **reports of thefts had become almost** ~ las denuncias de robos se habían convertido en algo casi habitual; **on a ~ basis** de forma rutinaria

routinely [ruːˈtiːnlɪ] ADV de forma rutinaria, rutinariamente

rove [rəʊv] Ⓐ VT vagar *or* errar por, recorrer Ⓑ VI vagar, errar

roving ['rəʊvɪŋ] ADJ errante

row¹ [rəʊ] N (= *line*) fila *f*, hilera *f*; (*Theat etc*) fila *f*; [*of books, houses etc*] hilera *f*, fila *f*; (*in knitting*) pasada *f*, vuelta *f*; **in the front** ~ en primera fila, en la fila uno; **in a** ~ en fila; **he killed four in a** ~ mató a cuatro seguidos, mató a cuatro uno tras otro; **for five days in a** ~ durante cinco días seguidos ➤ **row house** (*US*) casa *f* adosada

row² [rəʊ] Ⓐ VT [+ *boat*] remar; **can you ~ me out to the yacht?** ¿me lleva en bote al yate? Ⓑ VI remar; **to ~ round an island** dar la vuelta a una isla remando *or* a remo

row³ [raʊ] (*esp Brit*) N **1** (= *noise*) ruido *m*, bulla* *f*
2 (= *argument*) bronca *f*, pelea *f*; (= *dispute*) disputa *f*; **to have a** ~ reñir, pelearse (*LAm*) **3** (= *disturbance*) jaleo *m*, escándalo *m*, lío *m*, follón *m* (*Sp*), bronca *f* (*esp LAm*)
4 (= *scolding*) regaño *m*, regañina *f*; **to get into a** ~ ganarse una regañina (**for** por)

rowan ['raʊən] N (*also* ~ **tree**) serbal *m*

rowboat ['rəʊbəʊt] N (*US*) = **rowing boat**

rowdy ['raʊdɪ] ADJ (*compar* **rowdier**; *superl* **rowdiest**) [*person*] escandaloso; [*meeting etc*] alborotado, agitado

rowing ['rəʊɪŋ] N remo *m* ➤ **rowing boat** (*Brit*) barca *f* de remos, bote *m* de remos ➤ **rowing machine** máquina *f* de remo

royal ['rɔɪəl] Ⓐ ADJ real Ⓑ N (*) personaje *m* real, miembro *mf* de la familia real; **the ~s*** la realeza Ⓒ CPD ➤ **the Royal Air Force** (*Brit*) las Fuerzas Aéreas Británicas ➤ **royal blue** azul *m* marino intenso ➤ **the royal family** la familia real

➤ **Royal Highness His/Her Royal Highness** Su Alteza Real
➤ **the Royal Navy** (*Brit*) la Marina Británica

royal-blue [ˌrɔɪəlˈbluː] ADJ azul marino intenso

royalist [ˈrɔɪəlɪst] ADJ, N monárquico/a *m/f*

royalty [ˈrɔɪəltɪ] N **1** (= *people*) realeza *f*, familia *f* real
2 (*also* **royalties**) (*on books*) derechos *mpl* de autor; (*on other items*) regalías *fpl*, royalti(e)s *mpl* (*LAm*)

RP N ABBR (*Brit*) (= **Received Pronunciation**) *pronunciación estándar del inglés*

RPI N ABBR (= **Retail Price Index**) IPC *m*

RSI N ABBR = **repetitive strain injury**

RSPB N ABBR (*Brit*) = **Royal Society for the Protection of Birds**

RSPCA N ABBR (*Brit*) = **Royal Society for the Prevention of Cruelty to Animals**

RSVP ABBR (= **répondez s'il vous plaît**) S.R.C.

Rt Hon. ABBR (*Brit*) (= **Right Honourable**) *título honorífico de diputado*

rub [rʌb] **Ⓐ** N (*gen*) **to give sth a ~** frotar algo; **to give one's shoes a ~ (up)** limpiar los zapatos; ✦ IDIOM **there's the ~** ahí está el problema, ésa es la dificultad **Ⓑ** VT frotar; (*hard*) restregar, estregar; (*Med etc*) friccionar; (= *clean*) limpiar frotando; (= *polish*) sacar brillo a; **to ~ sth dry** secar algo frotándolo; **to ~ a cream into the skin** frotar la piel con una crema; ✦ IDIOM **to ~ sb's nose in sth** restregar algo a algn por las narices **Ⓒ** VI **to ~ against sth** rozar algo
➤ **rub down** VT + ADV **1** [+ *body*] secar frotando; [+ *horse*] almohazar **2** [+ *door, wall etc*] lijar
➤ **rub in** VT + ADV [+ *ointment, cream*] aplicar frotando; ✦ IDIOM **don't ~ it in!** ¡no me lo refriegues por las narices!
➤ **rub off Ⓐ** VI + ADV [*dirt*] quitarse (frotando); [*writing, pattern*] borrarse; **some of their ideas have ~bed off on him** se le han pegado algunas de sus ideas, ha hecho suyas algunas de sus ideas **Ⓑ** VT + ADV [+ *writing, pattern*] borrar; [+ *dirt etc*] quitar (frotando)
➤ **rub out Ⓐ** VT + ADV borrar **Ⓑ** VI + ADV borrarse; **it ~s out easily** es fácil de quitar, se borra fácilmente

rubber [ˈrʌbəʳ] **Ⓐ** N **1** (= *material*) goma *f*, caucho *m*, hule *m* (*LAm*), jebe *m* (*Col, Per*)
2 (*Brit*) (= *eraser*) goma *f* de borrar
3 (*US***) (= *condom*) condón *m*, goma *f*
Ⓑ CPD [*ball, dinghy, gloves, boots*] de goma *etc* ➤ **rubber band** goma *f*, gomita *f* ➤ **rubber boots** (*US*) botas *fpl* de agua, botas *fpl* de goma ➤ **rubber bullet** bala *f* de goma ➤ **rubber dinghy** lancha *f* neumática ➤ **rubber gloves** guantes *mpl* de goma ➤ **rubber plant** ficus *m inv* ➤ **rubber ring** (*esp Brit*) flotador *m* ➤ **rubber stamp** estampilla *f* de goma ➤ **rubber tree** árbol *m* gomero *or* de caucho

rubber-stamp [ˌrʌbəˈstæmp] VT (*officially*) aprobar con carácter oficial; (*fig*) aprobar maquinalmente

rubbery [ˈrʌbərɪ] ADJ gomoso, parecido a la goma

rubbing [ˈrʌbɪŋ] N (= *brass rubbing*) calco *m* ➤ **rubbing alcohol** (*US*) alcohol *m* de 90°

rubbish [ˈrʌbɪʃ] (*esp Brit*) **Ⓐ** N **1** (= *refuse*) basura *f*
2 (= *nonsense*) tonterías *fpl*, disparates *mpl*; (= *goods, film etc*) basura *f*, birria *f*, porquería *f*; **he talks a lot of ~** no dice más que tonterías; **the book is ~** la novela es una basura **Ⓑ** ADJ **to be ~ at sth** (*Brit***) no tener ni idea de algo*, ser un negado* *or* (*Sp***) un manta en algo **Ⓒ** VT (*Brit***) poner por los suelos **Ⓓ** CPD ➤ **rubbish bin** (*Brit*) cubo *m* de la basura, basurero *m* ➤ **rubbish collection** (*Brit*) recogida *f* de basuras, recolección *f* de la basura ➤ **rubbish dump** (*Brit*) basurero *m*, vertedero *m*, basural *m* (*LAm*)

rubbishy* [ˈrʌbɪʃɪ] ADJ (*Brit*) [*goods*] de pacotilla; [*film, novel etc*] que no vale para nada, malísimo

rubble [ˈrʌbl] N escombros *mpl*

rub-down [ˈrʌbdaʊn] N (= *massage*) masaje *m*, friega *f*; **to give o.s. a ~** (= *dry o.s.*) secarse frotándose con una toalla

rubella [ruːˈbelə] N rubéola *f*

ruble [ˈruːbl] N (*US*) = **rouble**

rubric [ˈruːbrɪk] N rúbrica *f*

ruby [ˈruːbɪ] **Ⓐ** N rubí *m* **Ⓑ** ADJ (*in colour*) color rubí *inv* **Ⓒ** CPD [*necklace, ring*] de rubí(es)

RUC N ABBR (= **Royal Ulster Constabulary**) *Policía de Irlanda del Norte*

ruck [rʌk] N (*in clothing etc*) arruga *f*
➤ **ruck up** VI + ADV arrugarse

rucksack [ˈrʌksæk] N (*Brit*) mochila *f*

ructions [ˈrʌkʃənz] NPL lío* *msing*, jaleo *msing*, follón *msing* (*Sp*); **there will be ~** se va a armar la gorda

rudder [ˈrʌdəʳ] N timón *m*

ruddy [ˈrʌdɪ] ADJ (*compar* **ruddier**; *superl* **ruddiest**)
1 [*complexion*] rubicundo, coloradote **2** (*Brit†***) *euph*) maldito, condenado*

rude [ruːd] ADJ (*compar* **~r**; *superl* **~st**) **1** (= *impolite*) [*person*] grosero, maleducado; [*remark*] grosero; **to be ~ to sb** ser grosero con algn; **it's ~ to stare** mirar fijamente es de mala educación; **it was ~ of you to ignore him** ignorarlo fue una grosería por tu parte; **he was ~ about her new dress** hizo comentarios poco halagüeños respecto a su vestido nuevo
2 (*esp Brit*) (= *indecent*) [*gesture*] grosero, obsceno; [*joke, song*] verde, colorado (*LAm*); **a ~ word** una grosería, una mala palabra
3 (= *unexpected*) **a ~ awakening** una sorpresa muy desagradable

rudely [ˈruːdlɪ] ADV [*say, interrupt, stare*] groseramente; [*push*] bruscamente

rudeness [ˈruːdnɪs] N [*of person, behaviour*] grosería *f*, falta *f* de educación; [*of reply, remark*] falta *f* de educación

rudimentary [ˌruːdɪˈmentərɪ] ADJ (*gen*) rudimentario; **he has ~ Latin** sabe un poquito de latín

rudiments [ˈruːdɪmənts] NPL rudimentos *mpl*, primeras nociones *fpl*

rueful [ˈruːfəl] ADJ (= *sorrowful*) triste; (= *repentant*) arrepentido

ruff [rʌf] N **1** (*on clothing*) gorguera *f*, gola *f* **2** (*on bird, animal*) collarín *m*

ruffian [ˈrʌfɪən] N rufián *m*

ruffle [ˈrʌfl] VT [+ *hair*] despeinar; **nothing ~s him** no se altera por nada; **she wasn't at all ~d** no se perturbó en lo más mínimo; ✦ IDIOM **to ~ sb's feathers** herir la susceptibilidad *or* sensibilidad de algn

rug [rʌg] N **1** (*for floor*) alfombrilla *f*, tapete *m*; ✦ IDIOM **to pull the ~ from under sb's feet** *or* **under sb** mover la silla para que algn se caiga **2** (*esp Brit*) (= *blanket*) manta *f*

rugby [ˈrʌgbɪ] **Ⓐ** N (*also* **~ football**) rugby *m* **Ⓑ** CPD [*player, match*] de rugby ➤ **rugby league** rugby *m* a trece ➤ **rugby union** *tipo de rugby en que los equipos tienen quince jugadores*

rugged [ˈrʌgɪd] ADJ **1** [*terrain, landscape*] accidentado, escabroso; [*coastline, mountains*] escarpado; **the ~ beauty of the island** la belleza violenta de la isla **2** [*man*] de rasgos duros; [*features*] duro

ruin [ˈruːɪn] **Ⓐ** N **1** (= *building*) ruina *f*; **the ~s of a castle** las ruinas *or* los restos de un castillo; **the town lay** *or* **was in ~s** la ciudad estaba en ruinas **2** (*fig*) ruina *f*; **my life/career is in ~s** mi vida/carrera está destruida *or* arruinada; **drink will be the ~ of him** el alcohol será su ruina *or* su perdición **Ⓑ** VT [+ *reputation, career, life*] arruinar, destruir; [+ *plans, clothes, car, meal, eyesight*] estropear

ruined [ˈruːɪnd] ADJ [*building*] en ruinas; [*career, life*] arruinado; [*plans*] frustrado; [*person*] (*financially*) arruinado

ruinous [ˈruːɪnəs] ADJ ruinoso

rule [ruːl] **Ⓐ** N **1** (= *regulation*) regla *f*, norma *f*; **rules** [*of competition*] bases *fpl*; **the ~s of the game** las reglas del juego; **it's a ~ that** por norma; **it's against the ~s to run** está prohibido correr; **as a (general) ~** por regla general, en general, normalmente; **to break the ~s** infringir las reglas *or* las normas *or* el reglamento; **he makes it a ~ to get up early** tiene por norma *or* por sistema levantarse temprano; **to play by the ~s** (*fig*) obedecer las reglas *or* las normas; **a life governed by ~s and regulations** una vida llena de cortapisas; **school ~s** reglamento *msing* escolar; **as a ~ of thumb** por regla general

2 (= *government*) gobierno *m*; (= *reign*) reinado *m*; **under British ~** bajo el dominio británico
3 (*for measuring*) regla *f*
Ⓑ VT **1** (= *govern*) gobernar; **✦** IDIOM **to ~ the roost** llevar la batuta
2 (= *control, dominate*) controlar, dominar
3 (= *judge*) dictaminar
4 (= *draw*) [+ *line*] trazar
Ⓒ VI **1** (= *govern*) gobernar; [*monarch*] reinar; **to ~ over sth/sb** gobernar algo/a algn
2 (= *prevail*) reinar
3 (= *decide*) [*chairman, president*] decidir, resolver; [*judge, jury*] fallar; **to ~ against sth/sb** fallar or resolver en contra de algo/algn; **to ~ in favour of sth/sb** fallar en or a favor de algo/algn, resolver en or a favor de algo/algn
Ⓓ CPD **➤ rule book** reglamento *m*
➤ rule out VT + ADV **1** (= *exclude*) [+ *action, possibility*] descartar, excluir; [+ *candidate*] excluir; **the age limit ~s him out** el límite de edad lo excluye, queda excluido por el límite de edad **2** (= *make impossible*) hacer imposible, imposibilitar

ruled [ruːld] ADJ [*paper*] de rayas, pautado
ruler ['ruːləʳ] N **1** (= *person*) gobernante *mf*; (= *monarch*) soberano/a *m/f* **2** (*for measuring*) regla *f*
ruling ['ruːlɪŋ] **Ⓐ** ADJ [*class, body*] dirigente; [*party*] en el poder; [*monarch*] reinante **Ⓑ** N (*Jur*) fallo *m*, resolución *f*; (*Admin, Sport*) decisión *f*; **to give a ~ on a dispute** fallar en una disputa

rum [rʌm] N ron *m*
Rumania *etc* [ruːˈmeɪnɪə] = **Romania** *etc*
rumble¹ ['rʌmbl] **Ⓐ** N [*of traffic etc*] ruido *m* sordo, retumbo *m*, rumor *m*; [*of thunder, heavy vehicle*] estruendo *m* **Ⓑ** VI [*thunder*] retumbar; [*guns*] hacer un ruido sordo; [*stomach*] sonar, hacer ruidos; **the train ~d past** el tren pasó con estruendo **Ⓒ** CPD **➤ rumble seat** (*US*) asiento *m* trasero exterior **➤ rumble strip** banda *f* sonora
rumble²* ['rʌmbl] VT (*Brit*) [+ *person*] calar, pillar
ruminant ['ruːmɪnənt] N rumiante *m*
ruminate ['ruːmɪneɪt] VI rumiar; **to ~ on sth** rumiar algo
rummage ['rʌmɪdʒ] VI hurgar; **to ~ about** revolverlo todo, buscar revolviéndolo todo **➤ rummage sale** (*US*) venta *f* de objetos usados (*con fines benéficos*); ⇨ *JUMBLE SALE/ RUMMAGE SALE*
rummy ['rʌmɪ] N (*Cards*) rummy *m*
rumour, rumor (*US*) ['ruːməʳ] **Ⓐ** N rumor *m*; **~ has it that ...** se rumorea que ..., corre el rumor or la voz de que ... **Ⓑ** VT **it is ~ed that** se rumorea que, corre el rumor or la voz de que **Ⓒ** CPD **➤ rumour mill, rumor mill** (*US*): **the ~ mill says she's getting married in May** se rumorea que se casa en mayo, corre el rumor de que or la voz de que se casa en mayo
rump [rʌmp] N [*of horse etc*] ancas *fpl*, grupa *f*; [*of bird*] rabadilla *f*; (*) [*of person*] trasero *m*; (*Culin*) cuarto *m* trasero, cadera *f* **➤ rump steak** filete *m* de lomo de vaca or (*LAm*) de res
rumpus* ['rʌmpəs] N (*pl* **-es**) lío* *m*, jaleo *m*; **to kick up a ~** armar un lío* or un jaleo

run [rʌn] (*vb: pt* **ran**; *pp* **~**) **Ⓐ** N **1** (= *act of running*) carrera *f*; **at a ~** a corriendo, a la carrera; **to go for a ~** before breakfast (salir a) correr antes del desayuno; **to make a ~ for it** (= *flee*) darse a al fuga, huir; **to be on the ~** (*from police*) estar huido de la justicia, ser fugitivo; **a prisoner on the ~** un preso fugado; **✦** IDIOM **to give sb a ~ for their money** hacer sudar a algn
2 (= *outing*) vuelta *f*, paseo *m*, excursión *f*; **let's go for a ~ down to the coast** vamos a dar una vuelta por la costa
3 (= *journey*) viaje *m*; (= *route*) ruta *f*, línea *f*; **it's a short ~ in the car** es un breve viaje en coche; **it's a 30-minute ~ by bus** en autobús se tarda 30 minutos; **the Calais ~** la ruta de Calais
4 (= *sequence*) serie *f*; **in the long ~** a la larga; **a ~ of luck** una racha de suerte; **a ~ of bad luck** una racha or temporada de mala suerte; **in the short ~** a plazo corto
5 (*Theat, TV*) temporada *f*; **the play had a long ~** la obra se mantuvo mucho tiempo en cartelera

6 (= *trend*) [*of market*] tendencia *f*
7 (*Comm, Fin*) (= *increased demand*) gran demanda *f*; **a ~ on sterling** una gran demanda de libras esterlinas
8 (*for animals*) corral *m*
9 (*Cricket, Baseball*) carrera *f*; **to make** or **score a ~** hacer or anotar(se) una carrera
10 (*in tights*) carrera *f*
11 (= *raid*) ataque *m*; **a bombing ~** un bombardeo
12 (*US Pol*) (= *bid for leadership*) carrera *f*, campaña *f*
13 (= *access, use*) **they gave us the ~ of their garden** nos dejaron usar su jardín
14 (= *track for skiing*) pista *f*; **ski ~** pista *f* de esquí
15 to have the ~s* andar muy suelto*, tener cagalera**
Ⓑ VT **1** (*gen*) correr; **she ran 20km** corrió 20km; **to ~ the 100 metres** participar en or correr los 100 metros lisos; **let things ~ their course** deja que las cosas sigan su curso; **to ~ a race** participar en una carrera; **the race is ~ over four km** la carrera se hace sobre una distancia de cuatro km; **you ran a good race** corriste muy bien; **✦** IDIOMS **to ~ it fine** dejarse muy poco tiempo; **to be ~ off one's feet** estar ocupadísimo
2 (= *take*) [+ *person*] llevar; **I'll ~ you home** te llevo a casa
3 (= *put, move*) **to ~ a comb through one's hair** peinarse rápidamente; **to ~ one's eye over a letter** echar un vistazo a una carta; **to ~ one's fingers through sb's hair** pasar los dedos por el pelo de algn; **let me ~ this idea past you** a ver qué piensas de esta idea; **to ~ water into a bath** hacer correr agua en un baño, llenar un baño de agua
4 (= *organize etc*) [+ *business, hotel etc*] dirigir, llevar; [+ *country*] gobernar; [+ *campaign, competition*] organizar; **a house which is easy to ~** una casa de fácil manejo; **he wants to ~ my life** quiere organizarme la vida; **they ran a series of tests on the product** llevaron a cabo or efectuaron una serie de pruebas con el producto
5 (*esp Brit*) (= *operate, use*) [+ *car*] tener; [+ *machine*] hacer funcionar, hacer andar; [+ *train*] poner; (*Comput*) [+ *program*] ejecutar; **the car is very cheap to ~** el coche gasta muy poco or tiene muy pocos gastos de mantenimiento; **you can ~ it on** or **off the mains** funciona conectado or sin conectar a una toma de corriente
6 (= *publish*) [+ *report, story*] publicar, imprimir
Ⓒ VI **1** (*gen*) correr; (*in race*) competir, correr, tomar parte; (= *flee*) huir; **to ~ across the road** cruzar la calle corriendo; **to ~ down the road** correr (por la) calle abajo; **to ~ downstairs** bajar la escalera corriendo; **to ~ for a bus** correr tras el autobús; **we shall have to ~ for it** (= *move quickly*) tendremos que correr; (= *escape*) habrá que darse a la fuga; **to ~ to help sb** correr al auxilio de algn; **he ran up the stairs** subió la escalera corriendo; **✦** IDIOM **he's trying to ~ before he can walk** (*Brit*) quiere empezar la casa por el tejado
2 (= *go*) **that train does not ~ on Sundays** ese tren no circula los domingos; **the bus ~s every 20 minutes** hay un autobús cada 20 minutos; **there are no trains ~ning to Toboso** no hay servicio de trenes a Toboso
3 (= *be*) **the train is ~ning late** el tren lleva retraso; **I'm ~ning a bit late** se me está haciendo un poco tarde; **the service usually ~s on time** el servicio generalmente es puntual
4 (*Naut*) **to ~ aground** encallar
5 (= *function*) funcionar; **you mustn't leave the engine ~ning** no se debe dejar el motor en marcha; **it ~s on petrol** funciona con gasolina, tiene motor de gasolina; **things did not ~ smoothly for them** las cosas no les fueron bien
6 (= *extend*) **6.1** (*in time*) **the contract has two years left to ~** al contrato le quedan dos años de duración; **the contract ran for seven years** el contrato duró siete años; **it ~s in the family** [*disease*] es algo genético; **the play ran for two years** la obra estuvo dos años en cartelera; **the sentences will ~ concurrently** las condenas se cumplirán al mismo tiempo **6.2** (*in space*) **the road ~s along the river** la carretera va a lo largo del río; **the path ~s from our house to the station** el sendero va de nuestra casa a la estación; **the road ~s past our house** la carretera pasa delante de nuestra casa
7 (= *flow, leak*) correr; [*colour*] correrse, desteñirse; **blood ran from the wound** la sangre manaba de la herida, la herida manaba sangre; **to ~ dry** [*river, well*] secarse; [*resources*] agotarse; **the milk ran all over the floor** la leche

se derramó por todo el suelo; **his nose was ~ning** le moqueaba la nariz; **the river ~s into the sea** el río desemboca en el mar; **you left the tap ~ning** dejaste el grifo abierto (*Sp*) *or* la llave abierta (*LAm*); **the tears ran down her cheeks** las lágrimas le corrían por las mejillas; **the streets were ~ning with water** el agua corría por las calles **8** (*Pol*) (= *stand for election*) presentarse como candidato/a; **to ~ against sb** medirse con algn, enfrentarse a algn; **to ~ for office** presentarse como candidato a un cargo **9** (*Comput*) ejecutarse
➤ **run across** VI + PREP (= *encounter*) [+ *person*] tropezar con, encontrarse con; [+ *object*] encontrar, topar(se) con
➤ **run after** VI + PREP (= *to catch up*) correr tras; (= *chase*) perseguir
➤ **run along** VI + ADV ~ **along now!** (*to child*) ¡anda, márchate!; (*to children*) ¡anda marchaos (*Sp*) *or* márchense (*LAm*)
➤ **run around** VI + ADV ir corriendo de aquí para allá
➤ **run away** VI + ADV escaparse, fugarse; **to ~ away from home** huir de casa
➤ **run away with** VI + PREP **1** (= *control*) **he let his imagination ~ away with him** se dejó llevar por su imaginación **2** (= *win easily*) [+ *race*] ganar fácilmente
➤ **run down** Ⓐ VT + ADV **1** (*Aut*) (= *knock down*) atropellar; (*Naut*) hundir **2** (= *disparage*) menospreciar Ⓑ VI + ADV [*battery*] acabarse, gastarse, agotarse; [*car battery*] descargarse
➤ **run into** VI + PREP **1** (= *encounter*) [+ *person*] tropezar con, encontrarse con; [+ *problems*] tropezar con **2** (= *collide with*) chocar contra **3** (= *amount to*) elevarse a, ascender a
➤ **run off** Ⓐ VI + ADV escaparse, fugarse; **to ~ off with sb** fugarse con algn Ⓑ VT + ADV **1** (= *print*) [+ *copies*] tirar; [+ *photocopies*] hacer, sacar **2** [+ *water*] vaciar, dejar salir
➤ **run out** VI + ADV **1** (= *leave*) salir corriendo **2** (= *come to an end*) [*time, food, money*] acabarse; [*contract*] vencer; [*supplies*] agotarse; **my patience is ~ning out** se me está agotando la paciencia, estoy perdiendo la paciencia; **their luck ran out** se les acabó la suerte
➤ **run out of** VI + PREP [+ *food, money*] quedarse sin; **I've ~ out of petrol** me he quedado sin gasolina, se me acabó la gasolina; **we've ~ out of time** no nos queda más tiempo, se nos ha acabado el tiempo
➤ **run out on** VI + PREP (= *abandon*) abandonar
➤ **run over** Ⓐ VI + ADV (*in time*) durar más de la cuenta, pasarse del tiempo; **the show ran over by five minutes** la función duró cinco minutos más de la cuenta Ⓑ VI + PREP (= *go through again*) repasar; (= *rehearse*) volver a hacer, volver a ensayar Ⓒ VT + ADV (*with vehicle*) atropellar
➤ **run through** VI + PREP **1** (= *read quickly*) leer (por encima), echar un vistazo a **2** (= *rehearse*) [+ *play*] ensayar **3** (= *recapitulate*) repasar
➤ **run to** VI + PREP **1** (= *extend to*) **the book will ~ to 700 pages** el libro tendrá 700 páginas en total **2** (= *amount to*) elevarse a, ascender a **3** (*esp Brit*) (= *afford*) permitirse (el lujo de)
➤ **run up** Ⓐ VT + ADV [+ *debt*] contraer; **she had ~ up a huge bill at the hairdresser's** tenía acumulada una factura enorme de peluquería Ⓑ VI + ADV acercarse corriendo; **he ran up to me** se me acercó corriendo
➤ **run up against** VI + PREP [+ *problem*] tropezar con

runaround ['rʌnəraʊnd] N ✦ IDIOM **to give sb the ~*** traer a algn al retortero

runaway ['rʌnəweɪ] Ⓐ ADJ [*prisoner, slave*] fugitivo; [*soldier*] desertor; [*horse*] desbocado; [*lorry*] sin frenos, fuera de control; [*success*] arrollador; [*victory*] aplastante, abrumador Ⓑ N (= *person*) fugitivo/a *m/f*

rundown ['rʌndaʊn] N (= *résumé*) resumen *m* (**on** de); **to give sb a ~** poner a algn al tanto

run-down ['rʌn'daʊn] ADJ [*building*] destartalado, ruinoso; **to be ~** [*person*] no encontrarse bien, estar pachucho (*Sp**)

rung¹ [rʌŋ] N escalón *m*, peldaño *m*

rung² [rʌŋ] PP *of* **ring²**

run-in* ['rʌnɪn] N (= *argument*) altercado *m*

runner ['rʌnə'] Ⓐ N **1** (= *athlete*) corredor(a) *m/f* **2** [*of sledge, aircraft*] patín *m*; [*of skate*] cuchilla *f* **3** ✦ IDIOM **to do a ~** (*Brit**) largarse* (*sin pagar*) Ⓑ CPD ➤ **runner bean** (*Brit*) judía *f* (escarlata), habichuela *f*

runner-up ['rʌnər'ʌp] N (*pl* **runners-up**) subcampeón/ona *m/f*, segundo/a *m/f*

running ['rʌnɪŋ] Ⓐ ADJ **1** [*water*] corriente; **hot and cold ~ water** agua corriente caliente y fría **2** (= *continuous*) continuo; **a ~ joke** una broma continua; **a ~ commentary (on sth)** (*TV, Rad*) un comentario en directo (sobre algo) Ⓑ ADV **for five days ~** durante cinco días seguidos *or* consecutivos; **for the third year ~** por tercer año consecutivo Ⓒ N **1** [*of business, organization, school*] gestión *f*, dirección *f*; [*of country*] gestión *f* **2** [*of machine, car*] funcionamiento *m*, marcha *f* **3** (*fig*) **she's in the ~ for promotion** tiene posibilidades de que la asciendan; **to be out of the ~** estar fuera de combate Ⓓ CPD ➤ **running costs** (*esp Brit*) [*of business*] gastos *mpl* corrientes; [*of car*] gastos *mpl* de mantenimiento ➤ **running jump** salto *m* con carrerilla; **to take a ~ jump** (*lit*) saltar tomando carrerilla; ✦ IDIOM **he can take a ~ jump!*** ¡puede irse a la porra!* ➤ **running mate** (*US*) [*of presidential candidate*] candidato/a *m/f* a la vicepresidencia ➤ **running shoe** zapatilla *f* de correr *or* de deporte ➤ **running total** suma *f* parcial; **to keep a ~ total (of sth)** llevar la cuenta del total (de algo) ➤ **running track** pista *f* (de atletismo)

runny ['rʌnɪ] ADJ (*compar* **runnier**; *superl* **runniest**) [*substance*] líquido; [*eyes*] lloroso; [*egg*] poco hecho; **I've got a ~ nose** no paro de moquear

run-of-the-mill ['rʌnəvðə'mɪl] ADJ (= *ordinary*) común y corriente, corriente y moliente; (= *mediocre*) mediocre

runt [rʌnt] N (= *animal*) cría más pequeña de la camada; (*pej*) (= *person*) enano *m*

run-through ['rʌnθru:] N ensayo *m*

run-up ['rʌnʌp] N (*Brit*) (*to election*) período *m* previo (**to** a)

runway ['rʌnweɪ] N (*Aer*) pista *f* (de aterrizaje); (*US Theat*) pasarela *f* ➤ **runway lights** balizas *fpl*

rupture ['rʌptʃə'] Ⓐ N (*Med*) hernia *f*; (*fig*) ruptura *f* Ⓑ VT **1** (*Med*) (= *cause rupture in*) causar una hernia en; (= *suffer rupture of*) quebrarse; **to ~ o.s.** causarse una hernia, herniarse **2** (*fig*) romper, destruir

rural ['rʊərəl] ADJ rural; **~ development** desarrollo *m* rural; **~ planning** planificación *f* rural

ruse [ru:z] N ardid *m*, treta *f*, estratagema *f*

rush¹ [rʌʃ] N (= *plant*) junco *m*

rush² [rʌʃ] Ⓐ N **1** (= *act of rushing*) **there was a ~ for the door** se precipitaron todos hacia la puerta; **two were injured in the ~** hubo dos heridos en el tumulto **2** (= *hurry*) prisa *f*, apuro *m* (*LAm*); **what's all the ~ about?** ¿por qué tanta prisa?; **we had a ~ to get it ready** tuvimos que darnos prisa *or* (*LAm*) apurarnos para tenerlo listo; **is there any ~ for this?** ¿corre prisa esto?, ¿tiene apuro esto? (*LAm*); **I'm in a ~** tengo prisa, estoy *or* ando apurado (*LAm*); **I did it in a ~** lo hice deprisa, lo hice muy apurado (*LAm*) **3** (*Comm*) demanda *f*; **we've had a ~ of orders** ha habido una enorme demanda de pedidos; **the Christmas ~** la actividad frenética de las Navidades; **a ~ for tickets** una enorme demanda de entradas **4** (*US Ftbl*) carga *f* Ⓑ VT **1** [+ *person*] meter prisa a, apurar (*LAm*); **he was trying to ~ her into a decision** trataba de meterle prisa *or* (*LAm*) apurarla para que se decidiera; **don't be ~ed into signing anything** no dejes que te hagan firmar deprisa y corriendo, no dejes que te metan prisa *or* (*LAm*) que te apuren para firmar **2** [+ *work, job*] hacer con mucha prisa *or* a la carrera; **I'm not going to ~ things** no voy a precipitarme **3** (= *carry, take*) **reinforcements were ~ed to the scene** mandaron rápidamente refuerzos al lugar del incidente; **he was ~ed (off) to hospital** lo llevaron al hospital con la mayor urgencia Ⓒ VI **1** (= *run*) **to ~ upstairs/downstairs** subir/bajar la escalera corriendo *or* a toda prisa; **to ~ past** pasar a toda velocidad; **everyone ~ed to the windows** todos corrieron *or* se precipitaron hacia las ventanas **2** (= *hurry*) **I must ~** me voy corriendo; **don't ~!** ¡con calma!; **I was ~ing to finish it** me daba prisa *or* (*LAm*) me estaba apurando por terminarlo; **people are ~ing to buy the book** la gente corre a comprar el libro; **the blood ~ed to her cheeks** enrojeció violentamente; **he will not ~ into any decisions** no tomará ninguna decisión precipitada **Ⓓ** CPD ➤ **rush hour** hora *f* punta, hora *f* pico (*LAm*) ➤ **rush hour traffic** tráfico *m* de hora punta *or* (*LAm*) de hora pico ➤ **rush job** (= *urgent*) trabajo *m* urgente; (= *too hurried*) trabajo *m* hecho deprisa y corriendo ➤ **rush around, rush about** (*Brit*) VI + ADV correr de un lado a otro, correr de acá para allá ➤ **rush off** VI + ADV irse corriendo, largarse a toda prisa* ➤ **rush out Ⓐ** VT + ADV [+ *book*] publicar a toda prisa; [+ *statement*] hacer público a toda prisa **Ⓑ** VI + ADV salir corriendo ➤ **rush through** VT + ADV [+ *legislation*] aprobar a toda prisa; [+ *order, supplies*] despachar rápidamente

rushed [rʌʃt] ADJ [*meeting*] rápido, cortísimo; [*meal*] con prisas, rápido; **I didn't feel ~ or under pressure** no sentí que me estuvieran metiendo prisa *or* presionando, no me sentí presionado *or* (*LAm*) apurado*; **we were ~ off our feet** estábamos hasta arriba de trabajo*

rusk [rʌsk] N (*esp Brit*) galleta *f*

russet [ˈrʌsɪt] **Ⓐ** N (= *colour*) color *m* rojizo **Ⓑ** ADJ rojizo

Russia [ˈrʌʃə] N Rusia *f*

Russian [ˈrʌʃən] **Ⓐ** ADJ ruso **Ⓑ** N **1** (= *person*) ruso/a *m/f* **2** (*Ling*) ruso *m* **Ⓒ** CPD ➤ **Russian roulette** ruleta *f* rusa ➤ **Russian salad** ensalada *f* rusa, ensaladilla *f* (rusa) (*Sp*)

rust [rʌst] **Ⓐ** N (= *action*) oxidación *f*; (= *substance*) orín *m*, herrumbre *f*, óxido *m*; (= *colour*) color *m* herrumbre de orín; (*Agr*) roya *f* **Ⓑ** VI oxidarse, aherrumbrarse

rustbelt [ˈrʌstbelt] N (*US*) cinturón *m* industrial; ○ *SUNBELT*

rust-coloured, rust-colored (*US*) [ˈrʌstˌkʌləd] ADJ de color herrumbre *or* de orín

rustic [ˈrʌstɪk] ADJ rústico

rustle¹ [ˈrʌsl] **Ⓐ** N [*of leaves*] susurro *m*; [*of paper*] crujido

m; [*of silk, dress*] frufrú *m*, crujido *m* **Ⓑ** VT [+ *leaves*] hacer susurrar; [+ *paper*] mover ligeramente, hacer crujir **Ⓒ** VI [*leaves*] susurrar; [*paper*] crujir

rustle² [ˈrʌsl] VT (= *steal*) robar, abigear (*Mex*) ➤ **rustle up*** VT + ADV (= *find*) encontrar, dar con; (= *obtain*) conseguir, (lograr) reunir; (= *make*) [+ *meal*] improvisar, preparar; **I'll see what I can ~ up** veré lo que hay; **can you ~ up some coffee?** ¿podrías hacernos un café?

rustler [ˈrʌslər] N (*esp US*) ladrón/ona *m/f* de ganado, abigeo/a *m/f* (*Mex*)

rustproof [ˈrʌstpruːf] ADJ inoxidable

rusty [ˈrʌstɪ] ADJ (*compar* **rustier**; *superl* **rustiest**) **1** (*lit*) oxidado, herrumbrado, herrumbroso; [*colour*] de orín **2** (*fig*) **my Greek is pretty ~** me falta práctica en griego, tengo el griego muy olvidado

rut¹ [rʌt] N surco *m*, rodera *f*, rodada *f*; ✦ IDIOMS **to be in/ get into a ~** ser/hacerse esclavo de la rutina; **I need to change jobs, I'm in a ~ here** necesito cambiar de trabajo, aquí me estoy anquilosando *or* estancando; **to get out of the ~** salir de la rutina

rut² [rʌt] **Ⓐ** N (*Bio*) celo *m* **Ⓑ** VI (= *be in rut*) estar en celo; (= *begin to rut*) caer en celo

rutabaga [ˌruːtəˈbeɪgə] N (*US*) nabo *m* sueco, naba *f*

ruthless [ˈruːθlɪs] ADJ [*person, act*] despiadado, cruel; [*efficiency, determination*] inquebrantable, implacable; [*opponent, enemy*] implacable

ruthlessly [ˈruːθlɪslɪ] ADV [*exploit, suppress, kill*] despiadadamente; [*hunt down*] implacablemente, inexorablemente

ruthlessness [ˈruːθlɪsnɪs] N crueldad *f*

RV N ABBR (*US*) = **recreational vehicle**

Rwanda [rʊˈændə] N Ruanda *f*

Rwandan [rʊˈændən] ADJ, N ruandés/esa *m/f*

rye [raɪ] N (= *grain, grass*) centeno *m* ➤ **rye bread** pan *m* de centeno ➤ **rye (whisky)** whisky *m* de centeno

Ss

S¹, s [es] N (*letter*) S, s *f*; **S for sugar** S de Soria; **S-bend** curva *f* en S

S² ABBR 1 (= **south**) S 2 (= **Saint**) Sto., Sta., S.

SA N ABBR 1 = **South Africa** 2 = **South America**

Sabbath ['sæbəθ] N (*Jewish*) sábado *m*; (*Christian*) domingo *m*

sabbatical [sə'bætɪkəl] N (*also* ~ **year**) año *m* sabático

saber ['seɪbə'] N (*US*) = **sabre**

sable ['seɪbl] N (= *fur*) marta *f* cibelina *or* cebellina

sabotage ['sæbətɑ:ʒ] Ⓐ N sabotaje *m* Ⓑ VT sabotear

saboteur [ˌsæbə'tɜ:'] N saboteador(a) *m/f*

sabre, saber (*US*) ['seɪbə'] N sable *m*

sabre-rattling, saber-rattling (*US*) ['seɪbəˌrætlɪŋ] N alarde *m* de un poder militar que generalmente no se tiene

sac [sæk] N saco *m*

saccharin(e) ['sækərɪn] N sacarina *f*

sachet ['sæʃeɪ] N sobrecito *m*, bolsita *f*

sack [sæk] Ⓐ N 1 (*Brit*) (*for coal, grain*) saco *m*; (*US*) (*for shopping*) bolsa *f* de papel 2 (*) (*from job*) **to get the ~** ser despedido; **to give sb the ~** despedir *or* echar a algn 3 (= *bed*) **the ~** la cama, el sobre* Ⓑ VT 1 (= *put into sacks*) ensacar, meter en sacos 2 (*) (= *dismiss*) despedir; **he was ~ed** lo despidieron

sacking ['sækɪŋ] N 1 (= *cloth*) arpillera *f* 2 (*) (= *dismissal*) despido *m*

sacrament ['sækrəmənt] N sacramento *m*

sacred ['seɪkrɪd] ADJ sagrado; **~ to the memory of ...** consagrado a la memoria de ...; **is nothing ~?** ¿ya no se respeta nada? ➤ **sacred cow** vaca *f* sagrada ➤ **the Sacred Heart** el Sagrado Corazón

sacrifice ['sækrɪfaɪs] Ⓐ N sacrificio *m*; **to make ~s (for sb)** hacer sacrificios (por algn), sacrificarse (por algn) Ⓑ VT sacrificar; **to ~ o.s. (for sb/sth)** sacrificarse (por algn/algo)

sacrificial [ˌsækrɪ'fɪʃəl] ADJ sacrificial ➤ **sacrificial lamb** chivo *m* expiatorio

sacrilege ['sækrɪlɪdʒ] N sacrilegio *m*

sacrilegious [ˌsækrɪ'lɪdʒəs] ADJ sacrílego

sacristan ['sækrɪstən] N sacristán *m*

sacristy ['sækrɪstɪ] N sacristía *f*

sacrosanct ['sækrəʊsæŋkt] ADJ sacrosanto

SAD [sæd] N ABBR = **seasonal affective disorder**

sad [sæd] ADJ (*compar* ~**der**; *superl* ~**dest**)

A common translation of **sad** is **triste**. Note that **triste** generally follows any noun it modifies when **sad** means "unhappy" and precedes it when **sad** means "distressing".

---

1 (= *unhappy*) triste; **he always seemed a ~ little boy** siempre pareció un niño triste; **we were ~ about** *or* **at the news of her illness** nos entristeció *or* nos apenó enterarnos de su enfermedad; **to become ~** entristecerse, ponerse triste; **to make sb ~** entristecer *or* poner triste a algn; **he left a ~der and a wiser man** cuando se marchó era un hombre escarmentado 2 (= *distressing*) triste; **the ~ fact** *or* **truth is that ...** la triste realidad es que ...; **how ~!** ¡qué triste!, ¡qué pena!; **it is my ~ duty to inform you that ...** tengo el penoso deber de informarle de que ... 3 (= *deplorable*) [*state of affairs*] lamentable, penoso; **~ to say** lamentablemente 4 (*pej*) (= *pathetic*) penoso

sadden ['sædn] VT entristecer

saddle ['sædl] Ⓐ N [*of bicycle*] silla *f*; [*of horse*] silla *f* de montar; **to be in the ~** (*fig*) estar en el poder Ⓑ VT 1 (*also* ~ **up**) [+ *horse*] ensillar 2 (*) (= *lumber*) **to ~ sb with sth** cargar a algn con algo; **now we're ~d with it** ahora tenemos que cargar con ello

saddlebag ['sædlbæg] N alforja *f*

saddle-sore ['sædlˌsɔ:'] ADJ **he was ~** le dolían las posaderas de tanto montar

sadism ['seɪdɪzəm] N sadismo *m*

sadist ['seɪdɪst] N sádico/ca *m/f*

sadistic [sə'dɪstɪk] ADJ sádico

sadly ['sædlɪ] ADV 1 (= *sorrowfully*) con tristeza, tristemente 2 (= *regrettably*) desgraciadamente, lamentablemente; **his uncle, who ~ died** su tío, que tristemente *or* desgraciadamente falleció 3 (= *severely*) **to be ~ lacking in sth** ser muy deficiente en algo; **he will be ~ missed** se le echará mucho de menos; **you are ~ mistaken** estás muy equivocado

sadness ['sædnɪs] N tristeza *f*

sadomasochism [ˌseɪdəʊ'mæsə ̩kɪzəm] N sadomasoquismo *m*

sadomasochist [ˌseɪdəʊ'mæsəkɪst] N sadomasoquista *mf*

s.a.e. N ABBR (*Brit*) (= **stamped addressed envelope**) *sobre franqueado con las señas de uno*

safari [sə'fɑ:rɪ] N safari *m*; **to be on ~** estar de safari ➤ **safari jacket** chaqueta *f* de safari, sahariana *f* ➤ **safari park** (*Brit*) safari park *m*

safe [seɪf] Ⓐ ADJ (*compar* ~**r**; *superl* ~**st**) 1 (= *not in danger*) [*person*] a salvo, seguro; [*object*] seguro; **to feel ~** sentirse seguro; **to be ~ from** estar a salvo de; **to keep sth ~** guardar algo (en lugar seguro); **I'll keep it ~ for you** yo te lo guardo; **the secret is ~ with me** guardaré el secreto; ✦ IDIOM **~ and sound** sano y salvo; ✦ PROV **better ~ than sorry** más vale prevenir que curar

2 (= *not dangerous*) [*ladder, vehicle, method, investment*] seguro; [*structure, bridge*] sólido; [*level*] que no entraña riesgo; **it's not ~ to go out after dark** es peligroso salir de noche; **it's ~ to eat** se puede comer sin peligro; **it's ~ to say that ...** se puede decir sin miedo a equivocarse que ...; **to keep a distance from sth** mantenerse a una distancia prudencial de algo; (*when driving*) mantener la distancia de seguridad con algo; **to follow sb at a ~ distance** seguir a algn manteniendo cierta distancia; **to be a ~ driver** conducir con prudencia *or* con cuidado; **keep your alcohol consumption within ~ limits** mantén tu consumo de alcohol dentro de los límites de seguridad; **just to be on the ~ side** para mayor seguridad, por si acaso; **the ~st thing is to ...** lo más seguro es + *infin*; **he's ~ with children** [*dog*] no es un peligro para los niños

3 (= *secure*) [*environment, harbour*] seguro; **to be in ~ hands** estar a salvo, estar en buenas manos; ✦ IDIOM **a ~ pair of hands** (*Brit*) una persona competente

4 (= *trouble-free*) [*arrival, delivery*] sin problemas; [*landing*] sin riesgo, sin peligro; **~ journey!** ¡buen viaje!

Ⓑ N (*for valuables*) caja *f* fuerte

Ⓒ ADV **to play (it) ~** ir a lo seguro, no arriesgarse

Ⓓ CPD ➤ **safe breaker** N ladrón/ona *m/f* de cajas fuertes ➤ **safe deposit box** caja *f* fuerte, caja *f* de seguridad ➤ **safe haven** refugio *m* seguro ➤ **safe house** piso *m* franco ➤ **safe seat** (*Brit Pol*) **it was a ~ Conservative seat** era un escaño prácticamente seguro para los conservadores, el escaño estaba prácticamente asegurado para los conservadores ➤ **safe sex** sexo *m* seguro *or* sin riesgo

safe-conduct ['seɪf'kɒndəkt] N salvoconducto *m*

safeguard ['seɪfgɑ:d] Ⓐ N resguardo *m*; **as a ~ against ...** como defensa contra ... Ⓑ VT proteger, resguardar

safe-keeping [ˌseɪf'ki:pɪŋ] N custodia *f*; **to put into ~** poner a buen recaudo *or* bajo custodia

safely ['seɪflɪ] ADV 1 (= *without danger*) **you can walk about quite ~ in this town** no se corre peligro andando por esta ciudad, no es peligroso andar por esta ciudad; **drive ~!** conduce con prudencia *or* cuidado; **I can ~ say that ...** puedo afirmar con toda seguridad *or* sin miedo a

equivocarme que ...; to put sth away ~ guardar algo en un lugar seguro; **she was** ~ **tucked up in bed** estaba bien metidita en la cama

2 (= *without mishap*) [*land, return*] sin ningún percance; (*in the midst of danger*) sano y salvo; **to arrive** ~ llegar bien, llegar sin ningún percance; **he's** ~ **through to the semi-final** ya se ha asegurado el paso a las semifinales

safety ['seɪftɪ] N seguridad *f*; **for his** (**own**) ~ por su seguridad; **they helped the survivors to** ~ ayudaron a los sobrevivientes *or* supervivientes a ponerse a salvo; ~ **first!** ¡lo primero es la seguridad!; **there's** ~ **in numbers** cuantos más, menos peligro; **in a place of** ~ en un lugar seguro; **to reach** ~ ponerse a salvo; **for** ~**'s sake** para mayor seguridad ➤ **safety belt** cinturón *m* de seguridad ➤ **safety catch** (*on gun*) seguro *m*; (*on bracelet*) cierre *m* de seguridad ➤ **safety curtain** (*in theatre*) telón *m* de seguridad ➤ **safety deposit box** caja *f* fuerte, caja *f* de seguridad ➤ **safety harness** arnés *m* de seguridad ➤ **safety helmet** casco *m* de protección ➤ **safety measure** medida *f* de seguridad *or* de precaución ➤ **safety net** (*in circus*) red *f* de seguridad; (*fig*) protección *f* ➤ **safety pin** imperdible *m* (*Sp*), seguro *m* (*CAm, Mex*) ➤ **safety precaution** medida *f* de seguridad *or* de precaución ➤ **safety razor** maquinilla *f* de afeitar ➤ **safety valve** válvula *f* de seguridad *or* de escape

saffron ['sæfrən] N azafrán *m*

sag [sæg] VI [*roof, awning*] combarse; [*bed*] hundirse; [*shoulders*] encorvarse; **his spirits ~ged** le flaquearon los ánimos, se desanimó

saga ['sɑːɡə] N (*Hist*) saga *f*; (= *novel*) serie *f* (de novelas); (*fig*) epopeya *f*

sage[1] [seɪdʒ] **Ⓐ** ADJ (= *wise*) sabio **Ⓑ** N sabio/a *m/f*

sage[2] [seɪdʒ] N (= *herb*) salvia *f* ➤ **sage green** verde *m* salvia (*also used as invariable adj*)

sagging ['sæɡɪŋ] ADJ [*gate, hemline, breasts*] caído; [*shoulders*] encorvado; [*cheek*] fofo

Sagittarius [ˌsædʒɪˈtɛərɪəs] N **1** (= *sign, constellation*) Sagitario *m* **2** (= *person*) sagitario *mf inv*; **she's (a)** ~ es sagitario

sago ['seɪɡəʊ] N sagú *m*

Sahara [səˈhɑːrə] N **the** ~ el (desierto del) Sáhara

said [sed] **Ⓐ** PT, PP of **say** **Ⓑ** ADJ dicho

Saigon [saɪˈɡɒn] N Saigón *m*

sail [seɪl] **Ⓐ** N **1** (*Naut*) (= *cloth*) vela *f*; **to set** ~ hacerse a la mar, alzar velas, zarpar; **✦** IDIOM **to take the wind out of sb's ~s** bajarle los humos a algn
2 (= *trip*) **to go for a** ~ dar una vuelta *or* un paseo en barco
3 [*of windmill*] aspa *f*

Use **el/un** not **la/una** before feminine nouns beginning with stressed **a** or **ha** like **aspa**.

Ⓑ VT [+ *boat*] gobernar; **to** ~ **the Atlantic** cruzar el Atlántico; **they ~ed the ship to Cadiz** fueron con el barco a Cádiz
Ⓒ VI **1** (*Naut*) [*boat, person*] navegar; **we ~ed into harbour** entramos a puerto; **we ~ed into Lisbon** llegamos a Lisboa; **to** ~ **round the world** dar la vuelta al mundo en barco
2 (*Naut*) (= *leave*) zarpar, salir; **she ~s on Monday** zarpa *or* sale el lunes
3 (*fig*) **she ~ed into the room** entró majestuosamente en la sala; **the plate ~ed over my head** el plato voló por encima de mi cabeza
➤ **sail through** VI + PREP [+ *life, situation*] pasar sin esfuerzo por; [+ *exam, driving test*] no tener problemas para aprobar

sailboard ['seɪlbɔːd] N plancha *f or* tabla *f* de windsurf

sailboat ['seɪlbəʊt] N (*US*) = **sailing boat**

sailing ['seɪlɪŋ] N (*Sport*) vela *f*, navegación *f* a vela; **to go** ~ hacer vela; **✦** IDIOM **to be plain ~: now it's all plain** ~ ahora es coser y cantar ➤ **sailing boat** (*Brit*) velero *m*, barco *m* de vela ➤ **sailing ship** velero *m*, buque *m* de vela

sailor ['seɪlə'] N marinero *m*; **to be a bad/good** ~ marearse fácilmente/no marearse ➤ **sailor suit** traje *m* de marinero (*de niño*)

saint [seɪnt] N santo/a *m/f*; **she's no** ~ (*iro*) ella no es una santa, que digamos

When used before a man's name, the word **Santo** is shortened to **San**, the exceptions being **Santo Tomás** and **Santo Domingo**.

Saint John San Juan; **Saint Theresa** Santa Teresa ➤ **All Saints' Day** día *m* de Todos los Santos (*1 de noviembre*) ➤ **Saint Bernard** (= *dog*) (perro *m*) San Bernardo *m* ➤ **Saint Patrick's Day** el día *or* la fiesta de San Patricio ➤ **saint's day** fiesta *f* (del santo), santo *m*

saintly ['seɪntlɪ] ADJ (*compar* **saintlier**; *superl* **saintliest**) santo

sake [seɪk] N **for the** ~ **of sb/sth** por algn/algo; **for the** ~ **of argument** digamos, pongamos por caso; **art for art's** ~ el arte por el arte; **for God's ~!** ¡por Dios!; **for my** ~ por mí; **for old times'** ~ por los viejos tiempos; **for your own** ~ por tu propio bien; **to talk for the** ~ **of talking** hablar por hablar

salable ['seɪləbl] ADJ (*US*) = **saleable**

salacious [səˈleɪʃəs] ADJ (*frm*) salaz

salad ['sæləd] N ensalada *f*; **fruit** ~ ensalada *f* de frutas, macedonia *f* de frutas (*Sp*) ➤ **salad bowl** ensaladera *f* ➤ **salad cream** (*Brit*) mayonesa *f* ➤ **salad dressing** aliño *m*

salamander ['sælə,mændə'] N salamandra *f*

salami [səˈlɑːmɪ] N salami *m*, salame *m* (*SC*)

salaried ['sælərɪd] ADJ [*person*] asalariado; [*position*] retribuido, con sueldo

salary ['sælərɪ] N salario *m*, sueldo *m* ➤ **salary earner** asalariado/a *m/f* ➤ **salary range** gama *f* de salarios ➤ **salary review** revisión *f* de sueldos ➤ **salary scale** escala *f* salarial

sale [seɪl] **Ⓐ** N **1** [*of item, object, house*] venta *f*; **is it for ~?** ¿está en venta?; **the house is for** ~ la casa está en venta, esta casa se vende; **"for sale"** "se vende"; **to be on** ~ (*Brit*) estar a la venta; (*US*) estar rebajado; **on a** ~ **or return basis** en depósito
2 (= *event*) rebajas *fpl*; (= *auction*) subasta *f*; **there's a** ~ **on at Harrods** en Harrods están de rebajas; **clearance** ~ liquidación *f* (total); **the January ~s** las rebajas de enero **Ⓑ** CPD ➤ **sale price** (= *cost*) precio *m* de venta; (= *reduced cost*) precio *m* rebajado, precio *m* de rebaja ➤ **sales assistant** (*Brit*) dependiente/a *m/f* ➤ **sales campaign** campaña *f* de promoción y venta ➤ **sales clerk** (*US*) dependiente/a *m/f* ➤ **sales conference** conferencia *f* de ventas ➤ **sales department** sección *f* de ventas ➤ **sales executive** ejecutivo/a *m/f* de ventas ➤ **sales figures** cifras *fpl* de ventas ➤ **sales force** personal *m* de ventas ➤ **sales manager** jefe/a *m/f* de ventas ➤ **sales meeting** reunión *f* de ventas ➤ **sales pitch*** rollo *m* publicitario* ➤ **sales rep**, **sales representative** representante *mf*, agente *mf* comercial ➤ **sales revenue** ingresos *mpl* de facturación ➤ **sales slip** (*US*) (= *receipt*) hoja *f* de venta ➤ **sales target** objetivo *m* de ventas ➤ **sales tax** (*US*) impuesto *m* sobre las ventas

saleable, **salable** (*US*) ['seɪləbl] ADJ vendible

saleroom ['seɪlrʊm] N (*Brit*) sala *f* de subastas

salesman ['seɪlzmən] N (*pl* **salesmen**) (*in shop*) dependiente *m*, vendedor *m*; (= *traveller*) viajante *m*, representante *m*

salesmanship ['seɪlzmənʃɪp] N arte *m* de vender

salesperson ['seɪlz,pɜːsn] N (*esp US*) vendedor(a) *m/f*, dependiente/a *m/f*

salesroom ['seɪlzrʊm] N (*US*) sala *f* de subastas

saleswoman ['seɪlzwʊmən] N (*pl* **saleswomen**) (*in shop*) dependienta *f*, vendedora *f*; (= *traveller*) viajante *f*, representante *f*

salient ['seɪlɪənt] ADJ [*angle*] saliente; (*fig*) sobresaliente

saline ['seɪlaɪn] ADJ salino

salinity [səˈlɪnɪtɪ] N salinidad *f*

saliva [səˈlaɪvə] N saliva *f*

salivate ['sælɪveɪt] VI salivar

sallow ['sæləʊ] ADJ amarillento, cetrino

sally ['sælɪ] VI (*liter*) **to** ~ **forth** *or* **out** salir, hacer una salida

salmon ['sæmən] **A** N (pl ~s or ~) salmón m **B** ADJ color salmón inv, asalmonado **C** CPD ➤ **salmon farm** piscifactoría f de salmónidos ➤ **salmon fishing** pesca f del salmón ➤ **salmon pink** color m salmón, color m asalmonado ➤ **salmon steak** filete m de salmón ➤ **salmon trout** trucha f asalmonada

salmonella [ˌsælmə'nelə] N salmonela f ➤ **salmonella poisoning** salmonelosis f

salon ['sælɒn] N salón m; **hair** ~ salón m de peluquería; **beauty** ~ salón m de belleza

saloon [sə'luːn] **A** N **1** (Brit) (= car) turismo m **2** (= room) **billiard/dancing** ~ sala f or salón m de billar/de baile **3** (US) (= bar) taberna f, bar m, cantina f (esp Mex) **4** (on ship) salón m **B** CPD ➤ **saloon car** (Brit) turismo m

salt [sɔːlt] **A** N sal f; ✦ IDIOMS **the** ~ **of the earth** la sal de la tierra; **to take sth with a pinch** (Brit) or **grain** (US) **of** ~ no tomarse algo al pie de la letra; **to rub** ~ **into the wound** poner sal en la llaga
B VT (= flavour) salar; (= preserve) conservar en sal
C ADJ salado
D CPD ➤ **salt cellar** (Brit) salero m ➤ **salt flats** salinas fpl ➤ **salt marsh** saladar m, salina f ➤ **salt mine** mina f de sal ➤ **salt shaker** salero m ➤ **salt water** agua f salina or salobre

> Use **el/un** not **la/una** before feminine nouns beginning with stressed **a** or **ha** like **agua**.

salted ['sɔːltɪd] ADJ salado, con sal

salt-free ['sɔːltfriː] ADJ sin sal

saltiness ['sɔːltɪnɪs] N **1** (= salty flavour) sabor m a sal, salobridad f **2** (= salinity) salinidad f

saltwater ['sɔːltˌwɔːtəʳ] ADJ [fish etc] de agua salada

salty ['sɔːltɪ] ADJ (compar **saltier**; superl **saltiest**) salado

salubrious [sə'luːbrɪəs] ADJ (frm) (= healthy) saludable, salubre; (fig) (= desirable, pleasant) salubre

salutary ['sæljʊtərɪ] ADJ saludable

salute [sə'luːt] **A** N (Mil) (with hand) saludo m; (with guns) salva f; **to fire a 21-gun** ~ **for sb** saludar a algn con una salva de 21 cañonazos **B** VT, VI saludar, hacer un saludo

Salvadoran [ˌsælvə'dɔːrən], **Salvadorean, Salvadorian** [ˌsælvə'dɔːrɪən] ADJ, N salvadoreño/a m/f

salvage ['sælvɪdʒ] VT salvar; (fig) [+ sth from theory, policy etc] rescatar; [+ pride, reputation] (= manage to keep) conservar; (= regain) recuperar, salvar ➤ **salvage operation** operación f de rescate, operación f de salvamento

salvation [sæl'veɪʃən] N salvación f ➤ **Salvation Army** Ejército m de Salvación

salve [sælv] **A** VT (= soothe) **to** ~ **one's conscience** descargar la conciencia **B** N pomada f bálsamica

salver ['sælvəʳ] N bandeja f

salvo ['sælvəʊ] N salva f

Samaritan [sə'mærɪtn] N **the Good** ~ el buen samaritano; **to call the** ~**s** (organization) llamar al teléfono de la esperanza

samba ['sæmbə] N samba f

same [seɪm] **A** ADJ mismo; **he will never be the** ~ **again** nunca volverá a ser el mismo; **the two houses are the** ~ las dos casas son iguales; **for the** ~ **reason** por la misma razón; **if it's all the** ~ **to you** si a ti te da igual or lo mismo; **the carpet was the** ~ **colour as the wall** la moqueta era del mismo color que la pared; **their house is almost the** ~ **as ours** su casa es casi igual a or que la nuestra; **"how's Derek?" — "** ~ **as usual/ever"** —¿qué tal está Derek? —como siempre; **they are much the** ~ son más o menos iguales; **the** ~ **one/ones** el mismo/los mismos; **one and the** ~ **person** la misma persona; **it comes to the** ~ **thing** viene a ser lo mismo; **at the** ~ **time** (= at once) al mismo tiempo, a la vez; (= on the other hand) por otro lado; **the very** ~ **day/person** justo ese mismo día/esa misma persona; **to go the** ~ **way as sth/sb** (fig) (pej) seguir el mismo camino que algo/algn
B PRON **the** ~ lo mismo; **I don't feel the** ~ **about it as I did** ya no lo veo de la misma forma; **all** or **just the** ~ (= even so) de todas formas or maneras; **no, but thanks all the** ~ no,

pero de todas formas, gracias; **the** ~ **goes for you** eso también va por ti; ~ **here!*** ¡yo también!; **one and the** ~ el mismo/la misma; **(and the)** ~ **to you!*** (returning insult) ¡lo mismo digo!; (returning good wishes) ¡igualmente!

sameness ['seɪmnɪs] N (= monotony) monotonía f, uniformidad f

Samoa [sə'məʊə] N Samoa f

samosa [sə'məʊsə] N samosa f

sample ['sɑːmpl] **A** N muestra f; **a blood/urine** ~ una muestra de sangre/orina; **to take a** ~ tomar una muestra; **free** ~ muestra f gratuita **B** VT **1** (= try out) [+ food, drink] probar **2** (= take samples) tomar muestras de **C** CPD ➤ **sample book** muestrario m ➤ **sample pack** paquete m de muestra

sampling ['sɑːmplɪŋ] N muestreo m

sanatorium [ˌsænə'tɔːrɪəm] N (pl ~s or **sanatoria** [ˌsænə'tɔːrɪə]) (Brit) sanatorio m

sanctify ['sæŋktɪfaɪ] VT santificar

sanctimonious [ˌsæŋktɪ'məʊnɪəs] ADJ mojigato, santurrón

sanction ['sæŋkʃən] **A** N **1** (= approval) permiso m, autorización f **2** (= penalty) sanción f; (esp Pol) **sanctions** sanciones fpl; **to impose economic** ~**s on** or **against** imponer sanciones económicas a or contra **B** VT **1** (= approve) sancionar, autorizar **2** (= penalize) sancionar **C** CPD ➤ **sanctions busting** ruptura f de sanciones

sanctity ['sæŋktɪtɪ] N (= sacredness) lo sagrado; (= inviolability) inviolabilidad f

sanctuary ['sæŋktjʊərɪ] N (Rel) santuario m; (fig) (= refuge) asilo m; (for wildlife) reserva f; **to seek** ~ buscar refugio (**in** en)

sanctum ['sæŋktəm] N (also **inner** ~) sanctasanctórum m

sand [sænd] **A** N arena f **B** VT **1** [+ road] echar arena a **2** (also ~ **down**) [+ wood etc] lijar; [+ floor] pulir **C** CPD ➤ **sand dune** duna f

sandal ['sændl] N sandalia f, guarache m or huarache m (Mex)

sandalwood ['sændlwʊd] N sándalo m

sandbag ['sændbæg] N saco m de arena

sandbank ['sændbæŋk] N banco m de arena

sandblast ['sændblɑːst] VT limpiar con chorro de arena

sandbox ['sændbɒks] N (US) cajón m de arena

sandcastle ['sændˌkɑːsl] N castillo m de arena

sander ['sændəʳ] N lijadora f; (for floor) pulidora f

sandlot ['sændlɒt] (US) **A** N terreno m en una ciudad que se usa para el béisbol, etc **B** ADJ de barrio, de vecindad; ~ **baseball** béisbol m de barrio

sandpaper ['sændˌpeɪpəʳ] N papel m de lija

sandpit ['sændpɪt] N (Brit) recinto de arena para juegos infantiles

sandstone ['sændstəʊn] N arenisca f

sandstorm ['sændstɔːm] N tempestad f de arena

sandwich ['sænwɪdʒ] **A** N sándwich m **B** VT (also ~ **in**) [+ person, appointment etc] intercalar **C** CPD ➤ **sandwich bar** sandwichería f ➤ **sandwich board** cartelón m (que lleva el hombre-anuncio) ➤ **sandwich course** (Brit Univ etc) programa que intercala períodos de estudio con prácticas profesionales ➤ **sandwich loaf** pan m de molde

sandy ['sændɪ] ADJ (compar **sandier**; superl **sandiest**) **1** [beach] arenoso **2** (in colour) [hair] rubio

sane [seɪn] ADJ (compar ~**r**; superl ~**st**) [person] cuerdo; [judgment] sabio, sensato

> ⚠ **sane ≠ sano**

sang [sæŋ] PT of **sing**

sang-froid ['sɑːŋ'frwɑː] N sangre f fría

sangria [sæŋ'griːə] N sangría f

sanguine ['sæŋgwɪn] ADJ (fig) optimista

sanitarium [ˌsænɪ'tɛərɪəm] N (pl ~s or **sanitaria** [ˌsænɪ'tɛərɪə]) (esp US) sanatorio m

sanitary ['sænɪtərɪ] ADJ (= clean) higiénico; (= for health protection) de sanidad ➤ **sanitary towel** (Brit), **sanitary napkin** (US) compresa f, paño m higiénico

sanitation [,sænɪ'teɪʃən] N (= science) higiene f; (= plumbing) instalación f sanitaria ➤ **sanitation department** (US) departamento m de limpieza y recogida de basuras

sanitize ['sænɪtaɪz] VT sanear; **to ~ the image of war** dar una imagen aséptica de la guerra

sanity ['sænɪtɪ] N [of person] cordura f, juicio m; [of judgment] sensatez f

sank [sæŋk] PT of **sink**[1]

Sanskrit ['sænskrɪt] N sánscrito m

Santa Claus [,sæntə'klɔːz] N Papá Noel m, San Nicolás m

Santiago [,sæntɪ'ɑːgəʊ] N (in Chile) Santiago m (de Chile); (in Spain) ~ **de Compostela** Santiago m (de Compostela)

sap [sæp] Ⓐ N (Bot) savia f Ⓑ VT (= weaken) debilitar

sapling ['sæplɪŋ] N árbol m joven

sapphire ['sæfaɪəʳ] N zafiro m

Saragossa [,særə'gɒsə] N Zaragoza f

Saran wrap® [sə'rænræp] N (US) film m adherente (para envolver alimentos)

sarcasm ['sɑːkæzəm] N sarcasmo m

sarcastic [sɑː'kæstɪk] ADJ sarcástico

sarcastically [sɑː'kæstɪkəlɪ] ADV con sarcasmo, sarcásticamente

sarcoma [sɑː'kəʊmə] N sarcoma m

sarcophagus [sɑː'kɒfəgəs] N (pl **~es** or **sarcophagi** [sɑː'kɒfəgaɪ]) sarcófago m

sardine [sɑː'diːn] N (pl ~ or **~s**) sardina f

Sardinia [sɑː'dɪnɪə] N Cerdeña f

Sardinian [sɑː'dɪnɪən] ADJ, N sardo/a m/f

sardonic [sɑː'dɒnɪk] ADJ [humour, laugh] sardónico; [person] sarcástico; [tone] burlón

sardonically [sɑː'dɒnɪkəlɪ] ADV con sarcasmo

sari ['sɑːrɪ] N sari m

SARS [sɑːz] N ABBR (= severe acute respiratory syndrome) neumonía f asiática, SARS m

SAS N ABBR (Brit Mil) (= Special Air Service) cuerpo del ejército británico encargado de misiones clandestinas

SASE **s.a.s.e.** N ABBR (US) = **self-addressed stamped envelope**) sobre con las propias señas de uno y con sello

sash [sæʃ] N [of dress etc] faja f ➤ **sash cord** cuerda f de ventana (de guillotina) ➤ **sash window** ventana f de guillotina

sashay [sæ'ʃeɪ] VI (esp US) pasearse; **to ~ off** largarse*

Sask. ABBR (Canada) = **Saskatchewan**

sassy* ['sæsɪ] ADJ (compar **sassier**; superl **sassiest**) (US) fresco, descarado

SAT N ABBR **1** (US) = **Scholastic Aptitude Test 2** (Brit) = **Standard Assessment Task**

sat [sæt] PT, PP of **sit**

Sat. N ABBR (= **Saturday**) Sáb

Satan ['seɪtn] N Satanás m

satanic [sə'tænɪk] ADJ satánico

Satanist ['seɪtənɪst] N satanista mf

satchel ['sætʃəl] N cartera f, mochila f (SC)

sate [seɪt] VT saciar, hartar

satellite ['sætəlaɪt] N satélite m ➤ **satellite broadcasting** retransmisión f vía satélite ➤ **satellite dish** antena f parabólica para TV por satélite ➤ **satellite television** televisión f vía satélite ➤ **satellite town** ciudad f satélite

satiate ['seɪʃɪeɪt] VT (with food) hartar; (with pleasures) saciar

satin ['sætɪn] Ⓐ N satén m, raso m Ⓑ ADJ [dress, blouse etc] de satén; [paper, finish] satinado

satire ['sætaɪəʳ] N sátira f

satirical [sə'tɪrɪkəl] ADJ satírico

satirist ['sætərɪst] N (= writer) escritor(a) m/f satírico/a

satirize ['sætəraɪz] VT satirizar

satisfaction [,sætɪs'fækʃən] N satisfacción f; **has it been done to your ~?** ¿se ha hecho a su gusto?; **it gives me great ~ ...** es para mí una gran satisfacción ...; **to demand ~** exigir satisfacción

satisfactorily [,sætɪs'fæktərɪlɪ] ADV de modo satisfactorio

satisfactory [,sætɪs'fæktərɪ] ADJ (= pleasing) satisfactorio; (= sufficient) adecuado

satisfy ['sætɪsfaɪ] VT **1** (= make content) satisfacer, dejar satisfecho; **you'll have to be satisfied with that** tendrás que contentarte con eso; **to ~ o.s. with sth** contentarse con algo **2** (= convince) convencer; **to ~ sb that ...** convencer a algn de que ... **3** (= fulfil) satisfacer, cumplir; **to ~ the requirements** cumplir los requisitos

satisfying ['sætɪsfaɪɪŋ] ADJ [result] satisfactorio; [food, meal] que satisface, que llena

satsuma [,sæt'suːmə] N satsuma f

saturate ['sætʃəreɪt] VT empapar, saturar (**with** de)

saturated ['sætʃəreɪtɪd] ADJ (= soaking wet) empapado ➤ **saturated fat** grasa f saturada

saturation [,sætʃə'reɪʃən] N saturación f ➤ **saturation point: to reach ~ point** alcanzar el punto de saturación

Saturday ['sætədɪ] N sábado m ➤ **Saturday job: I've got a ~ job** tengo un trabajo los sábados; see **Tuesday**

Saturn ['sætən] N Saturno m

sauce [sɔːs] N (savoury) salsa f; (sweet) crema f

saucepan ['sɔːspən] N cacerola f, cazo m, olla f (esp LAm)

saucer ['sɔːsəʳ] N platillo m

saucy* ['sɔːsɪ] ADJ (compar **saucier**; superl **sauciest**) fresco, descarado

Saudi ['saʊdɪ] ADJ, N saudí mf, saudita mf

Saudi Arabia ['saʊdɪə'reɪbɪə] N Arabia f Saudí or Saudita

sauerkraut ['saʊəkraʊt] N chucrut m

sauna ['sɔːnə] N sauna f (m in SC)

saunter ['sɔːntəʳ] VI pasearse, deambular (LAm); **to ~ in/out** entrar/salir sin prisa

sausage ['sɒsɪdʒ] N (to be cooked) salchicha f; (= salami, mortadella etc) embutido m, fiambre m ➤ **sausage meat** carne f de salchicha ➤ **sausage roll** (Brit) masa de hojaldre con una salchicha en su interior

sauté ['səʊteɪ] Ⓐ ADJ salteado Ⓑ VT saltear

savage ['sævɪdʒ] Ⓐ ADJ **1** (= ferocious) [animal, attack] feroz, salvaje; [person] salvaje; [blow] violento; [war, criticism] despiadado **2** (= primitive) salvaje, primitivo **3** (= drastic) [cuts, reductions] drástico, radical Ⓑ N salvaje mf Ⓒ VT (= injure) atacar salvajemente; (= criticize) atacar ferozmente or despiadadamente

savagely ['sævɪdʒlɪ] ADV **1** [beat, attack] salvajemente, violentamente; [fight] violentamente **2** (= severely) [criticize, attack] despiadadamente **3** [cut, edit] drásticamente, radicalmente

savagery ['sævɪdʒrɪ] N **1** (= violence) [of attack, blow] ferocidad f, violencia f; [of criticism] saña f, ferocidad f **2** (= primitiveness) salvajismo m, estado m salvaje **3** [of cuts, reductions] radicalidad f, carácter m drástico

savannah [sə'vænə] N sabana f, pampa f (SC), llanos mpl (Ven)

save[1] [seɪv] Ⓐ VT **1** (= rescue) [+ person in danger] rescatar, salvar; [+ lives, jobs] salvar; (Rel) [+ soul] salvar; **to ~ the day: reinforcements sent by the Allies ~d the day** los refuerzos que enviaron los Aliados los sacaron del apuro; **to ~ sth/sb from sth/doing sth: he ~d the company from bankruptcy** salvó a la empresa de la bancarrota; **he ~d me from falling** me salvó de caerme, impidió que me cayera; **to ~ sb's life** salvar la vida a algn; **I can't sing to ~ my life** soy una negada para cantar*; **✦** IDIOM **to ~ one's bacon** or **one's (own) skin*** salvar el pellejo*

2 (= preserve) **to ~ o.s. for sth** reservarse para algo; **God ~ the Queen!** ¡Dios salve or guarde a la Reina!; **to ~ one's strength (for sth)** conservar or reservar (las) fuerzas (para algo)

3 (= *keep, put aside*) (*gen*) guardar; [+ *money*] (*also* ~ **up**) ahorrar; **to** ~ **sb sth** ◇ **to** ~ **sth for sb** guardar algo a algn; ~ **me a seat** guárdame un asiento **4** (= *not spend*) [+ *time*] ahorrar, ganar; [+ *money*] ahorrar; [+ *trouble*] evitar, ahorrar; **it** ~**s fuel** economiza *or* ahorra combustible; **to** ~ **sb** (**from**) **sth/doing sth: it** ~**s me** (**from**) **having to make a decision** me ahorra *or* evita tener que tomar una decisión; **I'll take him, it'll** ~ **you the journey** yo lo llevaré, así te ahorras *or* evitas el viaje **5** (*Sport*) [+ *penalty, shot*] parar **6** (*Comput*) archivar, guardar **Ⓑ** VI **1** (*also* ~ **up**) ahorrar; **he's saving for a new bike** está ahorrando (dinero) para (comprarse) una bici nueva **2** (= *economize*) **to** ~ **on sth: to** ~ **on petrol** ahorrar gasolina; **appliances that** ~ **on housework** aparatos que aligeran las tareas domésticas **Ⓒ** N (*Sport*) parada *f*

save² [seɪv] PREP (*liter*) salvo; ~ **that** ... excepto que ...

saver ['seɪvə'] N (= *person with account*) ahorrador(a) *m/f*

saving ['seɪvɪŋ] **Ⓐ** N **1** (= *putting aside*) ahorro *m* **2** (= *economy*) ahorro *m*; **we must make** ~**s** tenemos que economizar *or* hacer economías **3** **savings** ahorros *mpl*; **life** ~**s** los ahorros de toda una vida **Ⓑ** ADJ ~ **grace: his only** ~ **grace was that** ... lo único que lo salvaba era que ... **Ⓒ** PREP (= *apart from*) salvo, excepto **Ⓓ** CPD ➤ **savings account** cuenta *f* de ahorros ➤ **savings and loan association** (*US*) sociedad *f* de ahorro y préstamo ➤ **savings bank** caja *f* de ahorros ➤ **savings bond** bono *m* de ahorros

saviour, savior (*US*) ['seɪvjə'] N salvador(a) *m/f*

savour, savor (*US*) ['seɪvə'] **Ⓐ** N sabor *m*, gusto *m* **Ⓑ** VT saborear

savoury, savory (*US*) ['seɪvərɪ] **Ⓐ** ADJ **1** (= *appetizing*) sabroso **2** (*not sweet*) salado **3** (*fig*) **it's not a very** ~ **district** no es un barrio muy respetable; **it's not a very** ~ **subject** no es un tema muy apto **Ⓑ** N (*Brit*) entremés *m* salado

savvy*** ['sævɪ] N inteligencia *f*

saw¹ [sɔ:] (*vb: pt* ~**ed**; *pp* ~**ed** *or* ~**n**) **Ⓐ** N (= *tool*) sierra *f* **Ⓑ** VT serrar **Ⓒ** VI **to** ~ **through** cortar con (una) sierra ➤ **saw up** VT + ADV cortar con la sierra

saw² [sɔ:] PT *of* **see¹**

sawdust ['sɔ:dʌst] N serrín *m*, aserrín *m*

sawed-off shotgun [ˌsɔ:dɒf'ʃɒtgʌn] N (*US*) escopeta *f* de cañones recortados

sawmill ['sɔ:mɪl] N aserradero *m*

sawn [sɔ:n] PP *of* **saw¹**

sawn-off shotgun [ˌsɔ:nɒf'ʃɒtgʌn] N (*Brit*) escopeta *f* de cañones recortados

sax*** [sæks] N saxo***** *m*

Saxon ['sæksn] **Ⓐ** ADJ sajón **Ⓑ** N **1** (= *person*) sajón/ona *m/f* **2** (*Ling*) sajón *m*

saxophone ['sæksəfəʊn] N saxofón *m*, saxófono *m*

say [seɪ] (*vb: pt, pp* said) **Ⓐ** VT, VI **1** [*person*] (= *speak, tell*) decir; **"hello," he said** —hola —dijo; **to o.s.** decir para sí; **I** ~ (**that**) **we should go** yo digo que nos vayamos; ~ **after me** repite lo que digo yo; **I must** ~ (**that**) **I disapprove of the idea** la verdad es que no me parece bien la idea; **it's difficult, I must** ~ es difícil, lo confieso; **to** ~ **yes/no** decir que sí/no; **to** ~ **yes/no to a proposal** aceptar/rechazar una propuesta; **let's** ~ **no more about it** se acabó el asunto **2** (= *show on dial*) marcar; (= *show in print*) poner, decir; **my watch** ~**s three o'clock** mi reloj marca las tres; **the rules** ~ **that** ... según las reglas ..., en las reglas pone ... **3** (*in phrases*) **when all is said and done** al fin y al cabo, a fin de cuentas; **it's easier said than done** del dicho al hecho hay gran trecho; **she has nothing to** ~ **for herself** no tiene conversación, nunca abre la boca; **there's a lot to be said for it/for doing it** hay mucho que decir a su favor/a favor de hacerlo; **though I** ~ **it** *or* **so myself** aunque soy yo el que lo dice; **there's no** ~**ing what he'll do** quién sabe lo que hará; **to** ~ **nothing of the rest** sin hablar de lo demás; **would you really** ~ **so?** ¿lo crees de veras?; **no sooner said than done** dicho y hecho; **that is to** ~ o sea, es decir; **it**

goes without ~**ing that** ... ni que decir tiene que ..., huelga decir que ...; **that goes without** ~**ing** eso cae de su peso **4** (*in exclamations*) **you don't** ~!***** (*often hum*) ¡no me digas!; **enough said!** ¡basta!; ~ **no more!** ¡basta!, ¡ni una palabra más! **5** (= *suppose*) suponer, poner; **let's** ~ **for instance that** ... supongamos *or* pongamos por ejemplo que ...; **shall we** ~ **Tuesday?** ¿quedamos en el martes?; **shall we** ~ **£5?** ¿convenimos en cinco libras?; **we were going at** ~ **80kph** íbamos a 80kph más o menos **Ⓑ** N **to have one's** ~ dar su opinión; **to have a** ~ **in the matter** tener voz y voto; **to have no** ~ **in the matter** no tener voz en capítulo; **let him have his** ~! ¡que hable él!

saying ['seɪɪŋ] N dicho *m*, refrán *m*

say-so*** ['seɪsəʊ] N (= *authority*) **on whose** ~? ¿autorizado por quién?, ¿con permiso de quién?; **it depends on his** ~ tiene que darle el visto bueno

SC ABBR (*US*) = **South Carolina**

scab [skæb] N **1** (*Med*) costra *f*; (*Vet*) roña *f* **2** (*pej*)***** (= *strikebreaker*) esquirol *mf*, rompehuelgas *mf inv*

scabbard ['skæbəd] N vaina *f*, funda *f*

scabby ['skæbɪ] ADJ [*skin, knee*] lleno de costras; (*Vet*) roñoso

scabies ['skeɪbi:z] NSING sarna *f*

scaffold ['skæfəld] N (*Constr*) (*also* ~**ing**) andamio *m*, andamiaje *m*; (*for execution*) patíbulo *m*, cadalso *m*

scaffolding ['skæfəldɪŋ] N andamio *m*, andamiaje *m*

scald [skɔ:ld] **Ⓐ** N escaldadura *f* **Ⓑ** VT escaldar

scalding ['skɔ:ldɪŋ] ADJ **it's** ~ (**hot**) está hirviendo *or* (*LAm*) que arde; **the soup is** ~ la sopa está muy caliente

scale¹ [skeɪl] **Ⓐ** N [*of fish, reptile, skin*] escama *f*; (*inside kettle, boiler*) costra *f* **Ⓑ** VT [+ *fish*] quitar las escamas a, escamar; [+ *teeth*] quitar el sarro a

scale² [skeɪl] N (= *weighing device*) (*often pl*) balanza *f*; (*for heavy weights*) báscula *f*; **bathroom** ~(**s**) báscula *f* (de baño); **a kitchen** ~ ◇ **a pair of kitchen** ~**s** una balanza de cocina

scale³ [skeɪl] **Ⓐ** N **1** (= *size, extent*) escala *f*; **on a large/small** ~ a gran/pequeña escala **2** (= *graduated system*) escala *f*; ~ **of charges** (lista *f* de) tarifas *fpl* **3** [*of map, model*] escala *f*; **on a** ~ **of 1 to 5km** con una escala de 1cm a 5km; **the drawing is not to** ~ el dibujo no está a escala **4** (*Mus*) escala *f* **Ⓑ** VT [+ *wall*] trepar a, escalar; [+ *tree*] trepar a; [+ *mountain*] escalar **Ⓒ** CPD ➤ **scale drawing** dibujo *m* a escala ➤ **scale model** modelo *m* a escala ➤ **scale back** VT + ADV (= *reduce*) = **scale down 2** ➤ **scale down** VT + ADV **1** (= *make proportionally smaller*) reducir a escala **2** (= *reduce*) [+ *production, operations, demands, plan*] recortar

scallion ['skælɪən] N (*US*) cebolleta *f* (para ensalada), cebollita *f* (*LAm*)

scallop ['skɒləp] N (*Zool*) venera *f*

scalp [skælp] **Ⓐ** N cuero *m* cabelludo; (*as trophy*) cabellera *f* **Ⓑ** VT arrancar la cabellera de

scalpel ['skælpəl] N escalpelo *m*

scaly ['skeɪlɪ] ADJ (*compar* **scalier**; *superl* **scaliest**) escamoso

scam*** [skæm] N estafa *f*, timo *m*

scamp*** [skæmp] N diablillo *m*, pillín/ina *m/f*

scamper ['skæmpə'] VI escabullirse; **to** ~ **in/out** entrar/salir corriendo; **to** ~ **along** ir corriendo ➤ **scamper away, scamper off** VI + ADV escabullirse

scampi ['skæmpɪ] N (*esp Brit*) gambas *fpl* rebozadas

scan [skæn] **Ⓐ** VT **1** (= *inspect closely*) escudriñar; (*Comput*) examinar, explorar **2** (= *glance at*) echar un vistazo a **Ⓑ** VI [*poetry*] estar bien medido **Ⓒ** N (*Med*) exploración *f* con un escáner; **to go for a** ~ ◇ **have a** ~ hacerse un escáner

scandal ['skændl] **Ⓐ** N **1** (= *public furore*) escándalo *m* **2** (= *disgraceful state of affairs*) vergüenza *f* **3** (= *gossip*) chismes *mpl* **Ⓑ** CPD ➤ **the scandal sheets** (*US*) la prensa amarilla

scandalize ['skændəlaɪz] VT escandalizar; **she was** ~**d** se escandalizó

scandalous ['skændələs] ADJ escandaloso; **it's ~ that ...** es vergonzoso que ...

Scandinavia [ˌskændɪ'neɪvɪə] N Escandinavia f

Scandinavian [ˌskændɪ'neɪvɪən] ❶ ADJ escandinavo ❷ N escandinavo/a m/f

scanner ['skænəʳ] N (Med) escáner m, scanner m; (also **ultra-sound ~**) ecógrafo m; (Comput) (in airports) escáner m; (Radar) antena f direccional

scant [skænt] ADJ (compar **~er**; superl **~est**) escaso

scantily ['skæntɪlɪ] ADV insuficientemente; **~ clad** or **dressed** ligero de ropa

scanty ['skæntɪ] ADJ (compar **scantier**; superl **scantiest**) insuficiente; [clothing] ligero

scapegoat ['skeɪpgəʊt] N cabeza f de turco, chivo m expiatorio

scar [skɑːʳ] ❶ N (Med) cicatriz f; (fig) (on building, landscape etc) huella f; **it left a deep ~ on his mind** dejó una huella profunda en su ánimo ❷ VT dejar una cicatriz en; (fig) marcar, rayar; **he was ~red for life** quedó marcado para toda la vida

scarce ['skɛəs] ADJ (compar **~r**; superl **~st**) [reserves, resources] escaso; **to be ~** escasear; **to grow** or **become ~** volverse escaso, escasear; **to make o.s. ~*** largarse*, esfumarse*

scarcely ['skɛəslɪ] ADV apenas; **~ anybody** casi nadie; **we could ~ refuse** ¿cómo podíamos negarnos?, difícilmente podíamos negarnos

scarcity ['skɛəsɪtɪ] N escasez f

scare ['skɛəʳ] ❶ N **1** (= fright) susto m; **to give sb a ~** dar un susto or asustar a algn
2 (= panic, threat) **bomb ~** amenaza f de bomba; **the invasion ~** (= panic) el pánico de la invasión; (= rumours) los rumores alarmistas de una invasión
❷ VT **1** (= frighten) asustar; **to ~ sb stiff*** darle un susto de muerte a algn
2 to be ~d tener miedo, estar asustado; **to be ~d to do sth** tener miedo de hacer algo; **to be ~d to death*** estar muerto de miedo; **to be ~d of sb/sth: he's ~d of women** tiene miedo a las mujeres; **I'm ~d of spiders** les tengo miedo a or me dan miedo las arañas; **to be ~d stiff*** estar muerto de miedo
❸ VI **he doesn't ~ easily** no se asusta fácilmente
❹ CPD ➤ **scare story: it's only a ~ story** se trata de un reportaje alarmista ➤ **scare tactics** tácticas fpl para infundir miedo
➤ **scare away, scare off** VT + ADV espantar, ahuyentar

scarecrow ['skɛəkrəʊ] N espantapájaros m inv

scaremonger ['skɛəmʌŋgəʳ] N alarmista mf

scaremongering ['skɛəˌmʌŋgərɪŋ] N alarmismo m

scarf [skɑːf] N (pl **~s** or **scarves**) (for neck) bufanda f; (= headscarf) pañuelo m

scarlet ['skɑːlɪt] ❶ N escarlata f ❷ ADJ escarlata inv, colorado (LAm) ❸ CPD ➤ **scarlet fever** escarlatina f

scarper** ['skɑːpəʳ] VI (Brit) largarse*

scarves [skɑːvz] NPL of **scarf**

scary* ['skɛərɪ] ADJ (compar **scarier**; superl **scariest**) que da miedo; **that's a ~ thought** ésa es una idea espeluznante

scathing ['skeɪðɪŋ] ADJ mordaz

scatter ['skætəʳ] ❶ VT **1** (= strew around) [+ crumbs, papers etc] esparcir, desparramar; [+ seeds] sembrar a voleo, esparcir **2** (= disperse) [+ clouds, crowd] dispersar ❷ VI dispersarse ❸ N (Math, Tech) dispersión f; **a ~ of houses** unas casas dispersas ❹ CPD ➤ **scatter cushions** almohadones mpl

scatterbrained* ['skætəbreɪnd] ADJ atolondrado, ligero de cascos*

scattered ['skætəd] ADJ disperso; **~ showers** chubascos mpl dispersos

scatty* ['skætɪ] ADJ (compar **scattier**; superl **scattiest**) (Brit) ligero de cascos, atolondrado; **to drive sb ~** volver majareta a algn*

scavenge ['skævɪndʒ] ❶ VT [+ food] rebuscar; [+ streets]

rebuscar por ❷ VI remover basuras, pepenar (Mex); **to ~ for food** andar rebuscando comida (entre la basura)

scavenger ['skævɪndʒəʳ] N (= person) persona f que rebusca en la basura, pepenador(a) m/f (Mex); (= animal) animal m carroñero; (= bird) ave f de carroña

> Use **el/un** not **la/una** before feminine nouns beginning with stressed **a** or **ha** like **ave**.

SCE N ABBR = **Scottish Certificate of Education**

scenario [sɪ'nɑːrɪəʊ] N (Theat) argumento m; (Cine) guión m; (fig) escenario m

scene [siːn] N **1** (Theat, Cine, TV, Literat) escena f; **Act I, Scene 1** acto I, escena 1; **behind the ~s** (lit, fig) entre bastidores; **the ~ is set in a castle** la escena tiene lugar en un castillo
2 (= sight) escena f; **there were ~s of violence** hubo escenas de violencia; **there were unhappy ~s at the meeting** en la reunión pasaron cosas nada agradables
3 (= view) vista f, panorama m; (= landscape) paisaje m
4 (= place) escena m, lugar m; **to appear** or **come on the ~** llegar; **I need a change of ~** necesito un cambio de aires; **the police were soon on the ~** la policía no tardó en acudir al lugar de los hechos
5 (= sphere of activity) **to be part of the Madrid ~** formar parte de la movida madrileña*; **it's not my ~*** no me interesa or llama la atención; **the political ~ in Spain** el panorama político español
6 (*) (= fuss) escena f, escándalo m, bronca f (esp LAm); **to make a ~** hacer una escena, montar un número (Sp*)

scenery ['siːnərɪ] N **1** (= landscape) paisaje m **2** (Theat) decorado m

> ⚠ **scenery** ≠ **escenario**

scenic ['siːnɪk] ADJ (gen) pintoresco; **~ route** carretera f que recorre lugares pintorescos

scent [sent] ❶ N **1** (= smell) [of flowers, perfume] perfume m, fragancia f; [of food] aroma m **2** (esp Brit) (= perfume, toilet water) perfume m, fragancia f **3** (Hunting etc) rastro m, pista f; **to be on the ~** seguir el rastro or la pista; **to put** or **throw sb off the ~** (fig) despistar a algn ❷ VT **1** (= make sth smell nice) perfumar (with de) **2** (= smell) olfatear; (fig) [+ danger etc] presentir, sentir

scepter ['septəʳ] N (US) = **sceptre**

sceptic, skeptic (US) ['skeptɪk] N escéptico/a m/f

sceptical, skeptical (US) ['skeptɪkəl] ADJ escéptico (of, about acerca de)

scepticism, skepticism (US) ['skeptɪsɪzəm] N escepticismo m

sceptre, scepter (US) ['septəʳ] N cetro m

schedule ['ʃedjuːl, (US) 'skedjuːl] ❶ N **1** (= timetable) [of work, visits, events] programa m, calendario m; [of trains, buses] horario m; (TV, Rad) (often pl) programación f; **we are working to a very tight ~** tenemos un programa or calendario de trabajo muy apretado; **everything went according to ~** todo sucedió según se había previsto; **the work is behind/ahead of ~** el trabajo lleva retraso/va adelantado (con respecto al programa or calendario); **I was running one hour behind ~** llevaba una hora de retraso con respecto a mi agenda
2 (= list) lista f
❷ VT [+ meeting] programar, fijar; [+ TV programmes] programar; [+ trains, planes] programar el horario de; **you are ~d to speak for 20 minutes** según el programa hablarás durante 20 minutos; **this building is ~d for demolition** se ha previsto la demolición de este edificio; **as ~d** según lo previsto, de acuerdo con lo previsto

scheduled ['ʃedjuːld, (US) 'skedjuːld] ADJ [date, time] previsto, programado; [meeting, visit] programado; **at the ~ time** a la hora prevista or programada ➤ **scheduled flight** vuelo m regular ➤ **scheduled stop** parada f programada; (Aer) escala f programada

scheduling ['ʃedjuːlɪŋ, (US) 'skedjuːlɪŋ] N [of event, visit, *meeting*] organización *f*; [*of TV programmes*] programación *f*

schematic [skɪ'mætɪk] ADJ esquemático

scheme [skiːm] **Ⓐ** N **1** (= *project*) plan *m*, proyecto *m*; (= *plan*) plan *m*; (= *idea*) idea *f*; **it's some crazy ~ of his** es otro de sus proyectos alocados
2 (= *structure*) esquema *m*; **colour ~** combinación *f* de colores; **pension ~** sistema *m* de pensión; **man's place in the ~ of things** el puesto del hombre en el universo
3 (= *conspiracy*) intriga *f*; **it's a ~ to get him out of the way** es una jugada para quitarle de en medio
Ⓑ VI intrigar (**to do** para hacer); **their opponents were scheming against them** sus adversarios estaban conspirando contra ellos

scheming ['skiːmɪŋ] **Ⓐ** ADJ (*pej*) maquinador, intrigante
Ⓑ N conspiración *f*, maquinación *f*

schism ['sɪzəm, 'skɪzəm] N cisma *m*

schizophrenia [skɪtsəʊ'friːnɪə] N esquizofrenia *f*

schizophrenic [skɪtsəʊ'frenɪk] ADJ, N esquizofrénico/a *m/f*

schmaltz* [ʃmɔːlts] N sentimentalismo *m*, sensiblería *f*

schmaltzy* ['ʃmɔːltsɪ] ADJ sentimental, sensiblero

schmooze* [ʃmuːz] VI (*US*) cascar*, estar de cháchara*

schmuck** [ʃmʌk] N (*US*) imbécil *mf*

schnitzel ['ʃnɪtsəl] N escalope *m*

scholar ['skɒlə'] N **1** (= *learned person*) sabio/a *m/f*; (= *expert*) estudioso/a *m/f*, experto/a *m/f*; **a Dickens ~** un experto en Dickens **2** (= *scholarship holder*) becario/a *m/f*

scholarly ['skɒləlɪ] ADJ erudito, estudioso

scholarship ['skɒləʃɪp] N **1** (= *learning*) erudición *f*
2 (= *money award*) beca *f*

scholastic [skə'læstɪk] ADJ escolar; **Scholastic Aptitude Test** (*US*) examen *m* de acceso a la universidad

school¹ [skuːl] **Ⓐ** N **1** (*for children*) **1.1** (= *institution*) escuela *f*, colegio *m*; **we have to be at ~ by nine** tenemos que estar en el colegio a las nueve; **to go to ~** ir a la escuela; **to leave ~** terminar el colegio **1.2** (= *lessons*) clase *f*; **there's no ~ today** hoy no hay clase
2 (*Univ*) **2.1** (= *faculty*) facultad *f*; **School of Languages** departamento *m* de lenguas modernas; **law ~** Facultad *f* de derecho **2.2** (*US*) (= *university*) universidad *f*; **I went back to ~ at 35** a los 35 años volví a la universidad
3 (= *group of artists, writers, thinkers*) escuela *f*
4 (*in expressions*) **I am not of that ~** yo no soy de esa opinión, yo no pertenezco a esa escuela; **of the old ~** (*fig*) de la vieja escuela; **~ of thought** (*fig*) corriente *f* de opinión
Ⓑ VT [+ *horse*] amaestrar; [+ *person*] educar, instruir
Ⓒ CPD [*age, bus, holiday*] escolar ➤ **school dinner** (*Brit*) comida *f* escolar, comida *f* de colegio ➤ **school fees** matrícula *fsing* (escolar) ➤ **school friend** amigo/a *m/f* de clase ➤ **school hours: during ~ hours** durante las horas de clase ➤ **school inspector** inspector(a) *m/f* de enseñanza ➤ **school kid*** colegial(a) *m/f*, niño/a *m/f* de colegio ➤ **school leaver** (*Brit*) persona *f* que termina la escuela ➤ **school lunch** comida *f* escolar, comida *f* de colegio ➤ **school meal** comida *f* provista por la escuela ➤ **school report** boletín *m* escolar ➤ **school trip: to go on a ~ trip to the zoo** ir de visita al zoo con el colegio ➤ **school uniform** uniforme *m* escolar ➤ **school yard** (*US*) patio *m* de recreo ➤ **school year** año *m* escolar

school² [skuːl] N [*of fish, dolphins, whales*] banco *m*

schoolbag ['skuːlbæg] N bolso *m*, cabás *m*

schoolbook ['skuːlbʊk] N libro *m* de texto (escolar)

schoolboy ['skuːlbɔɪ] N alumno *m* (de escuela), colegial *m*

schoolchild ['skuːltʃaɪld] N (*pl* **~ren**) alumno/a *m/f*, colegial(a) *m/f*

schooldays ['skuːldeɪz] NPL años *mpl* del colegio

schoolgirl ['skuːlgɜːl] N colegiala *f*

schoolhouse ['skuːlhaʊs] N (*US*) (*pl* **~s**) escuela *f*

schooling ['skuːlɪŋ] N (= *education*) instrucción *f*, enseñanza *f*; (= *studies*) estudios *mpl*; **compulsory ~** escolaridad *f* obligatoria; **he had little formal ~** apenas asistió a la escuela

school-leaving age [skuːl'liːvɪŋ,eɪdʒ] N edad *f* en que se termina la escuela; **to raise the ~** aumentar la edad de escolaridad obligatoria

schoolmaster ['skuːl,mɑːstə'] N maestro *m* (de escuela), profesor *m* (de escuela)

schoolmate ['skuːlmeɪt] N (*Brit*) compañero/a *m/f* de clase

schoolmistress ['skuːl,mɪstrɪs] N maestra *f* (de escuela), profesora *f* (de escuela)

schoolroom ['skuːlrʊm] N aula *f*, clase *f*

> Use **el/un** not **la/una** before feminine nouns beginning with stressed **a** or **ha** like **aula**.

schoolteacher ['skuːl,tiːtʃə'] N (*gen*) maestro/a *m/f* (de escuela), profesor(a) *m/f* (de escuela)

schoolwork ['skuːlwɜːk] N trabajo *m* de clase

schooner ['skuːnə'] N (*Naut*) goleta *f*

sciatica [saɪ'ætɪkə] N (*Med*) ciática *f*

science ['saɪəns] N ciencia *f*; **to blind sb with ~** impresionar *or* deslumbrar a algn citándole muchos datos científicos ➤ **science fiction** ciencia-ficción *f*

scientific [,saɪən'tɪfɪk] ADJ científico

scientifically [,saɪən'tɪfɪkəlɪ] ADV científicamente

scientist ['saɪəntɪst] N científico/a *m/f*

scientologist [,saɪən'tɒlədʒɪst] N cienciólogo/a *m/f*

scientology [,saɪən'tɒlədʒɪ] N cienciología *f*

sci-fi* ['saɪfaɪ] N ABBR = **science-fiction**

Scillies ['sɪlɪz], **Scilly Isles** ['sɪlɪ,aɪlz] NPL Islas *fpl* Sorlingas

scintillating ['sɪntɪleɪtɪŋ] ADJ [*conversation, company*] chispeante, brillante

scissors ['sɪzəz] NPL tijeras *fpl*; **a pair of ~** unas tijeras

sclerosis [sklɪ'rəʊsɪs] N (*pl* **scleroses** [sklɪ'rəʊsiːz]) (*Med*) esclerosis *f*

scoff [skɒf] **Ⓐ** VI mofarse, burlarse (**at sb/sth** de algn/algo)
Ⓑ VT (*Brit**) (= *eat*) zamparse*, papearse**

scold [skəʊld] VT reñir, regañar (**for** por)

scolding ['skəʊldɪŋ] N reprimenda *f*, regañina *f*

scone [skɒn] N (*esp Brit*) bollo *m* (inglés)

scoop [skuːp] **Ⓐ** N **1** (*for flour*) pala *f*; (*for ice cream, water*) cucharón *m*; (= *quantity*) palada *f*, cucharada *f* **2** (*by newspaper*) exclusiva *f* **Ⓑ** VT **1** (= *pick up*) recoger **2** [+ *prize, award*] hacerse con, obtener
➤ **scoop out** VT + ADV (*with scoop*) sacar con pala; (*with spoon*) sacar con cuchara; [+ *water*] achicar; [+ *hollow*] excavar, ahuecar
➤ **scoop up** VT + ADV recoger

scoot* [skuːt] VI (*also* **~ away, ~ off**) largarse*, rajarse (*LAm*); **scoot!** ¡lárgate!*

scooter ['skuːtə'] N (*child's*) patinete *m*; (*adult's*) moto *f*, escúter *m*, motoneta *f* (*LAm*)

scope [skəʊp] N (= *opportunity*) libertad *f*, oportunidades *fpl*; (= *range*) [*of law, activity, responsibilities*] ámbito *m*; (= *capacity*) [*of person, mind*] alcance *m*; **the ~ of the new measures must be defined** conviene delimitar el campo de aplicación de las nuevas medidas; **there is plenty of ~ for** hay bastante campo para; **I'm looking for a job with more ~** busco un puesto que ofrezca más posibilidades

scorch [skɔːtʃ] **Ⓐ** VT (= *burn*) quemar; (= *singe*) chamuscar
Ⓑ VI [*linen*] chamuscarse

scorcher* ['skɔːtʃə'] N (= *hot day*) día *m* abrasador

scorching ['skɔːtʃɪŋ] ADJ (*also* **~ hot**) [*heat, day, sun*] abrasador; [*sand*] que quema; **it's ~ hot** hace un calor tremendo

score [skɔː'] **Ⓐ** N **1** (*in game, match*) (= *result*) resultado *m*; (= *goal*) gol *m*, tanto *m*; (*at cards, in test, competition*) puntuación *f*, puntaje *m* (*LAm*); **there's no ~ yet** están a cero; (*in commentary*) no se ha abierto el marcador todavía; **what's the ~?** ¿cómo van?, ¿cómo va el marcador?; **to keep (the) ~** (*Sport*) llevar la cuenta; (*Cards*) sumar los puntos **2 the ~*** (= *situation*) **what's the ~?** ¿qué pasa?, ¿qué hubo?

(*Mex, Chi*); **you know the** ~ ya estás al cabo de la calle *or* de lo que pasa*, ya estás al tanto

3 (= *subject*) **you've got no worries on that** ~ en ese sentido *or* aspecto no tienes por qué preocuparte

4 (= *dispute*) **to have a** ~ **to settle with sb** tener cuentas pendientes con algn; **to settle old** ~**s (with sb)** saldar las cuentas pendientes (con algn)

5 (*Mus*) partitura *f*; [*of show, play*] música *f*; [*of film*] banda *f* sonora (original)

6 (= *line*) (*on card*) raya *f*, línea *f*; (= *scratch*) (*on wood*) marca *f*, muesca *f*

7 (= *twenty*) veintena *f*; **three** ~ **years and ten** (*liter*) 70 años; **bombs were falling by the** ~ caían bombas a mansalva

B VT **1** (*Sport*) [+ *points*] conseguir, anotarse (*LAm*), apuntarse (*LAm*); [+ *runs*] hacer; [+ *goal, try*] marcar

2 (*in exam, test*) [+ *marks, points*] sacar; **to** ~ **points off sb** (*fig*) aventajarse con respecto a algn

3 (*Mus*) [+ *piece*] instrumentar, orquestar

4 (= *cut*) [+ *meat*] hacer unos pequeños cortes en; (= *mark*) [+ *line*] marcar

5 (******) [+ *drugs*] conseguir, comprar, pillar (*Sp*******)

C VI **1** (*Sport*) marcar; **no one has** ~**d yet** aún no ha marcado nadie; **that's where he** ~**s (over the others)** (*fig*) en eso es en lo que tiene más ventaja (sobre los demás)

2 (*in exam, test*) **she** ~**d well in the test** sacó *or* obtuvo buena nota en el test

D CPD ➤ **score draw** (*Brit Ftbl*) empate *m*
➤ **score out, score through** VT + ADV tachar

scoreboard [ˈskɔːbɔːd] N marcador *m*

scorer [ˈskɔːrəʳ] N (= *person keeping score*) persona *f* que va apuntando los resultados; (= *player*) (*also* **goal** ~) él/la *m/f* que marca un gol *etc*

scoring [ˈskɔːrɪŋ] N (= *keeping score*) tanteo *m*

scorn [ˈskɔːn] **A** N desprecio *m*, menosprecio *m*; **to pour** ~ **on sth** (*esp Brit*) ridiculizar algo **B** VT despreciar, menospreciar; **to** ~ **to do sth** no dignarse a hacer algo

scornful [ˈskɔːnfəl] ADJ desdeñoso, despreciativo; **to be** ~ **about sth** desdeñar algo

scornfully [ˈskɔːnfəlɪ] ADV desdeñosamente, con desprecio

Scorpio [ˈskɔːpɪəʊ] N **1** (= *sign, constellation*) Escorpio *m*
2 (= *person*) escorpio *mf inv*; **I'm (a)** ~ soy escorpio

scorpion [ˈskɔːpɪən] N alacrán *m*, escorpión *m*

Scot [skɒt] N escocés/esa *m/f*

Scotch [skɒtʃ] **A** ADJ escocés **B** N (= *whisky*) whisky *m* escocés, scotch *m* **C** CPD ➤ **Scotch broth** sopa *f* de verduras ➤ **Scotch egg** (*esp Brit*) huevo *m* cocido rodeado de carne de salchicha y rebozado ➤ **Scotch mist** neblina *f*
➤ **Scotch tape®** (*esp US*) cinta *f* adhesiva, scotch *m* (*LAm*), durex *m* (*Mex*)

scotch [skɒtʃ] VT [+ *attempt, plan*] frustrar; [+ *rumour*] acallar

scot-free [ˈskɒtˈfriː] ADJ **to get off** ~ salir impune

Scotland [ˈskɒtlənd] N Escocia *f*

Scots [skɒts] **A** ADJ escocés **B** N (*Ling*) escocés *m*

Scotsman [ˈskɒtsmən] N (*pl* **Scotsmen**) escocés *m*

Scotswoman [ˈskɒtsˌwʊmən] N (*pl* **Scotswomen**) escocesa *f*

Scottish [ˈskɒtɪʃ] ADJ escocés

scoundrel [ˈskaʊndrəl] N sinvergüenza *mf*

scour [ˈskaʊəʳ] VT **1** [+ *pan, floor*] fregar, restregar (*esp LAm*)
2 (= *search*) registrar; **we** ~**ed the countryside for him** hicimos una batida por el campo buscándole

scourer [ˈskaʊrəʳ] N (= *pad*) estropajo *m*

scourge [skɜːdʒ] N azote *m*

scouring pad [ˈskaʊrɪŋpæd] N estropajo *m*

scouring powder [ˈskaʊrɪŋpaʊdəʳ] N limpiador *m* (en polvo), quitagrasas *m inv* (en polvo)

Scouse* [skaʊs] **A** ADJ de Liverpool **B** N nativo/a *m/f* de Liverpool, habitante *mf* de Liverpool

scout [skaʊt] N **1** (= *person*) (*Mil*) explorador(a) *m/f*; (*also* **boy** ~) scout *m*, muchacho *m* explorador **2** (*****) (= *reconnaissance*) reconocimiento *m*; (= *search*) búsqueda

f; **to have a** ~ **round** reconocer *or* explorar el terreno
➤ **scout around, scout round** (*Brit*) VI + ADV **to** ~ **around for sth** buscar algo

scoutmaster [ˈskaʊtˌmɑːstəʳ] N jefe *m* de exploradores *or* de scouts

scowl [skaʊl] **A** N ceño *m* fruncido; **he said with a** ~ dijo con el ceño fruncido **B** VI fruncir el ceño, fruncir el entrecejo; **to** ~ **at sb** mirar a algn con el ceño fruncido, mirar a algn frunciendo el ceño *or* el entrecejo

scrabble [ˈskræbl] **A** VI **to** ~ **about** *or* **around for sth** revolver todo buscando algo **B** N **Scrabble®** (*game*) Scrabble® *m*

scraggy [ˈskrægɪ] ADJ (*compar* **scraggier**; *superl* **scraggiest**) (*esp Brit*) flacucho

scram* [skræm] VI **scram!** ¡lárgate!*

scramble [ˈskræmbl] **A** VI **1 to** ~ **up** subir gateando; **to** ~ **down/out** bajar/salir con dificultad; **we** ~**d through the hedge** nos abrimos paso con dificultad a través del seto; **to** ~ **for** [+ *coins, seats*] luchar entre sí por, pelearse por
2 (*Sport*) **to go scrambling** hacer motocross **B** VT **1** (*Culin*) revolver **2** (*Telec*) [+ *message*] cifrar; (*TV*) codificar **C** N (= *rush*) lucha *f*, pelea *f* (**for** por)

scrambled eggs [ˈskræmbldegs] NPL huevos *mpl* revueltos

scrambling [ˈskræmblɪŋ] N (*Sport*) motocross *m* campo a través

scrap¹ [skræp] **A** N **1** (= *small piece*) pedacito *m*; [*of newspaper*] recorte *m*; [*of material*] retal *m*, retazo *m*; (*fig*) pizca *f*; **a** ~ **of paper** un trocito de papel; **a few** ~**s of news** unos fragmentos de noticias; **not a** ~ **of use** sin utilidad alguna
2 scraps (= *leftovers*) restos *mpl*, sobras *fpl*
3 (*also* ~ **metal**) chatarra *f*, desecho *m* de hierro
B VT [+ *car, ship*] chatarrear, convertir en chatarra;
[+ *old equipment*] tirar; [+ *idea, plan*] desechar, descartar
C CPD ➤ **scrap dealer** chatarrero/a *m/f* ➤ **scrap heap** montón *m* de desechos; **to throw sth on the** ~ **heap** (*fig*) desechar *or* descartar algo; **to be/end up on the** ~ **heap** [*person*] no tener nada/quedarse sin nada a que agarrarse
➤ **scrap merchant** chatarrero/a *m/f* ➤ **scrap metal** chatarra *f* ➤ **scrap paper** pedazos *mpl* de papel suelto (*que se utilizan para borrador*) ➤ **scrap value** valor *m* como chatarra
➤ **scrap yard** chatarrería *f*; (*for cars*) cementerio *m* de coches

scrap²* [skræp] **A** N (= *fight*) riña *f*, pelea *f*; **to get into** *or* **have a** ~ **with sb** reñir *or* pelearse con algn **B** VI reñir, pelearse (**with sb** con algn)

scrapbook [ˈskræpbʊk] N álbum *m* de recortes

scrape [skreɪp] **A** N **1 to give sth a** ~ raspar algo, limpiar algo raspándolo; **to give one's knee a** ~ hacerse un rasguño en la rodilla
2 (*fig*) lío *m*, aprieto *m*; **to get into/out of a** ~ meterse en/salir de un lío *or* aprieto
B VT [+ *knee, elbow*] arañarse, hacerse un rasguño; (= *clean*) [+ *vegetables*] raspar, limpiar; **to** ~ **one's plate clean** dejar completamente limpio el plato; **to** ~ **a living** sacar lo justo para vivir; **the ship** ~**d the bottom** el barco rozó el fondo
C VI (= *make sound*) chirriar; (= *rub*) **to** ~ **(against)** pasar rozando; **to** ~ **past** pasar rozando
➤ **scrape by*** VI + ADV (*financially*) sacar lo justo para vivir; (= *live*) ir tirando
➤ **scrape off** VT + ADV raspar, quitar raspando
➤ **scrape out** VT + ADV [+ *contents*] remover raspando
➤ **scrape through** VI + ADV (*in exam*) **I just** ~**d through** aprobé por los pelos
➤ **scrape together** VT + ADV (*fig*) reunir poco a poco

scraper [ˈskreɪpəʳ] N (= *tool*) raspador *m*, rascador *m*; (*on doorstep*) limpiabarros *m inv*

scrappy [ˈskræpɪ] ADJ (*compar* **scrappier**; *superl* **scrappiest**) [*essay*] deshilvanado; [*knowledge*] incompleto

scratch [ˈskrætʃ] **A** N (*on skin*) arañazo *m*, rasguño *m*; (*on surface, record*) raya *f*; **the cat gave her a** ~ el gato la arañó; **he hadn't a** ~ **on him** no tenía ni un arañazo; **to have a good** ~ rascarse con ganas; **to start from** ~ partir de *or* empezar desde cero; **to come up to** ~ cumplir con los requisitos

B VT **1** (*with claw, nail etc*) rasguñar, arañar; (*making sound*) rascar, raspar; [+ *surface, record*] rayar; **he ~ed his hand on a rose bush** se arañó la mano con un rosal; **the lovers ~ed their names on the tree** los amantes grabaron sus nombres en el árbol

2 (*to relieve itch*) rascarse; **he ~ed his head** se rascó la cabeza; ✦ IDIOM **you ~ my back and I'll ~ yours** un favor con favor se paga, hoy por mí y mañana por ti

3 (= *cancel*) [+ *meeting, game*] cancelar; (= *cross off list*) [+ *competitor*] ,tachar borrar; (*Comput*) borrar

C VI [*person, dog*] rascarse; [*hens*] escarbar; **the dog ~ed at the door** el perro arañó la puerta

D CPD [*team, meal*] improvisado ➤ **scratch card** (*Brit*) tarjeta *f* de "rasque y gane" ➤ **scratch paper** (*US*) papel *m* de borrador

➤ **scratch out** VT + ADV **to ~ sb's eyes out** sacarle los ojos a algn

scratchpad ['skrætʃpæd] N (*US*) bloc *m* (*para apuntes o para borrador*)

scratchy ['skrætʃɪ] ADJ (*compar* **scratchier**; *superl* **scratchiest**) [*fabric*] que rasca *or* pica; [*pen*] que rasca

scrawl [skrɔːl] **A** N garabatos *mpl* **B** VT, VI garabatear

scrawny ['skrɔːnɪ] ADJ (*compar* **scrawnier**; *superl* **scrawniest**) [*neck, limb*] flaco; [*animal*] escuálido, descarnado

scream [skriːm] **A** N (= *yell*) grito *m*; (*high-pitched*) chillido *m*; (*stronger*) alarido *m*; **to give a ~** pegar un grito, soltar un grito; **there were ~s of laughter** hubo sonoras carcajadas; **it was a ~*** fue para morirse de la risa, fue la monda (*Sp**); **he's a ~*** es graciosísimo, es de lo más chistoso, es la monda (*Sp**) **B** VT gritar

C VI [*person*] chillar, gritar; [*baby*] berrear; **to ~ for help** pedir ayuda a gritos; **to ~ in** *or* **with pain** pegar *or* soltar un grito de dolor, gritar de dolor; **to ~ with laughter** reírse a carcajada limpia

scree [skriː] N pedregal *m* (*en una ladera*)

screech [skriːtʃ] **A** N [*of brakes, tyres*] chirrido *m*; [*of person*] grito *m*; [*of animal*] chillido *m* **B** VI [*brakes, tyres*] chirriar; [*person*] gritar, chillar; [*animal*] chillar

screen [skriːn] **A** N **1** (= *physical barrier*) (*in room*) biombo *m*; (*on window, door*) (*to keep out mosquitoes*) mosquitera *f*; (*for fire*) pantalla *f*; **a ~ of trees** una pantalla de árboles

2 [*of television, computer, in cinema, for slides*] pantalla *f*; **stars of the ~** estrellas *fpl* de la pantalla, estrellas *fpl* de cine; **the big/small ~** la gran/pequeña pantalla

B VT **1 to ~ (from)** (= *hide*) (*from view, sight*) ocultar *or* tapar (de); (= *protect*) proteger (de); **the house is ~ed (from view) by trees** la casa queda oculta detrás de los árboles; **he ~ed his eyes with his hand** se puso la mano sobre los ojos a modo de pantalla

2 [+ *film*] proyectar; [+ *TV programme*] emitir

3 (= *check*) [+ *suspect, applicant*] investigar; [+ *telephone calls*] filtrar; **he was ~ed by Security** Seguridad le investigó, estuvo sometido a investigaciones de Seguridad; **to ~ sb for sth** (*Med*) hacer una exploración a algn buscando algo

C CPD ➤ **screen door** puerta *f* con mosquitera ➤ **screen rights** derechos *mpl* cinematográficos ➤ **screen saver** salvapantallas *m inv* ➤ **screen test** prueba *f* cinematográfica ➤ **screen writer** guionista *mf*

screenful ['skriːnfʊl] N pantalla *f*

screening ['skriːnɪŋ] N **1** [*of film*] proyección *f*; (*for the first time*) estreno *m* **2** (*for security*) investigación *f*; (*Med*) exploración *f*

screenplay ['skriːnpleɪ] N guión *m*

screenwriting ['skriːnraɪtɪŋ] N escritura *f* de guiones

screw [skruː] **A** N **1** tornillo *m*; ✦ IDIOM **he's got a ~ loose*** le falta un tornillo

2 (= *propeller*) hélice *f*

3 (*Brit***) (= *prison officer*) carcelero/a *m/f*

4 (***) (= *sexual intercourse*) polvo*** *m*

B VT **1** [+ *screw*] atornillar; [+ *nut*] apretar; [+ *lid*] dar vueltas a, enroscar; **to ~ sth down** fijar algo con tornillos; **to ~ sth (in) tight** atornillar algo bien fuerte; **to ~ money out of sb** (*esp Brit***) sacarle dinero a algn

2 (***) (= *have sex with*) joder***

3 (*) (= *defraud*) timar, estafar

C VI (***) joder***, echar un polvo***, coger (*LAm***), chingar (*Mex***)

D CPD ➤ **screw top** tapa *f* de tornillo

➤ **screw around*** VI + ADV ligar*

➤ **screw off** **A** VT + ADV desenroscar **B** VI + ADV desenroscarse; **the lid ~s off** la tapadera se desenrosca

➤ **screw on** **A** VT + ADV ➤ **the lid on tightly** enrosca *or* mete bien la tapa; **he's got his head ~ed on** sabe cuántas son dos más dos **B** VI + ADV **the lid ~s on** la tapa se cierra a rosca *or* enroscándose

➤ **screw together** **A** VI + ADV juntarse con tornillos **B** VT + ADV armar (con tornillos)

➤ **screw up** **A** VT + ADV **1** (*Brit*) [+ *paper, material*] arrugar; **to ~ up one's eyes** arrugar el entrecejo; **to ~ up one's face** torcer la cara; **to ~ up one's courage** armarse de valor **2** (*) (= *ruin*) fastidiar, joder***, fregar (*LAm*), chingar (*Mex***); **the experience really ~ed him up** la experiencia lo dejó completamente hecho polvo **B** VI + ADV (*US**) **he really ~ed up this time** esta vez sí que lo fastidió *or* (*LAm*) fregó

screwball* ['skruːbɔːl] ADJ (*esp US*) excéntrico, estrafalario

screwdriver ['skruːdraɪvəʳ] N destornillador *m*, desarmador *m* (*Mex*)

screw-top ['skruːtɒp] ADJ, **screw-topped** ['skruːtɒpt] ADJ [*bottle, jar*] de rosca

screwy* ['skruːɪ] ADJ (*compar* **screwier**; *superl* **screwiest**) chiflado, tarado (*LAm*)

scribble ['skrɪbl] **A** N garabatos *mpl* **B** VT, VI garabatear; **to ~ sth down** garabatear algo

scribe [skraɪb] N [*of manuscript*] escribiente/a *m/f*, escribano/a *m/f*; (*Bible*) escriba *m*

scrimmage ['skrɪmɪdʒ] N **1** (= *fight*) escaramuza *f* **2** (*US Sport*) = **scrum**

scrimp [skrɪmp] VI **to ~ and save** hacer economías, apretarse el cinturón

script [skrɪpt] **A** N **1** [*of film*] guión *m*; [*of TV programme, play*] argumento *m* **2** (= *system of writing*) escritura *f* **3** (*in exam*) escrito *m* **B** VT [+ *film*] escribir el guión de

scripted ['skrɪptɪd] ADJ escrito

Scripture ['skrɪptʃəʳ] N Sagrada Escritura *f*

scriptwriter ['skrɪptraɪtəʳ] N guionista *mf*

scroll [skrəʊl] **A** N (= *roll of parchment*) rollo *m*; (= *ancient manuscript*) manuscrito *m* **B** VT (*Comput*) desplazar **C** CPD ➤ **scroll bar** (*Comput*) barra *f* de desplazamiento vertical ➤ **scroll key** (*Comput*) tecla *f* de desplazamiento ➤ **scroll down** VI + ADV desplazarse hacia abajo ➤ **scroll up** VI + ADV desplazarse hacia arriba

Scrooge [skruːdʒ] N el avariento típico (*personaje del "Cuento de Navidad" de Dickens*)

scrotum ['skrəʊtəm] N escroto *m*

scrounge* [skraʊndʒ] **A** N **to be on the ~ (for sth)** ir sacando (algo) de gorra **B** VT gorrear*, gorronear (*Sp**); **to ~ sth from sb** gorrear *or* (*Sp*) gorronear algo a algn* **C** VI **to ~ on** *or* **off sb** vivir a costa de algn

scrounger* ['skraʊndʒəʳ] N gorrón/ona *m/f*, garronero/a *m/f* (*RPl*)

scrub¹ [skrʌb] N (= *undergrowth*) monte *m* bajo, maleza *f*; (= *bushes*) matas *fpl*, matorrales *mpl*

scrub² [skrʌb] **A** N **to give sth a (good) ~** fregar *or* (*esp LAm*) restregar algo (bien) **B** VT [+ *floor, hands etc*] fregar; **to ~ sth clean** fregar *or* restregar algo hasta que quede limpio **C** CPD ➤ **scrub brush** (*US*) cepillo *m* de fregar

➤ **scrub away** VT + ADV [+ *dirt*] quitar restregando; [+ *stain*] quitar frotando

➤ **scrub down** VT + ADV [+ *room, wall*] fregar; **to ~ o.s. down** fregarse

➤ **scrub out** VT + ADV [+ *stain*] limpiar restregando; [+ *pan*] fregar; [+ *name*] tachar

➤ **scrub up** VI + ADV [*doctor, surgeon*] lavarse

scrubbing brush ['skrʌbɪŋbrʌʃ] N (*Brit*) cepillo *m* de fregar

scrubland ['skrʌblænd] N monte *m* bajo, maleza *f*

scruff [skrʌf] N **1 by the ~ of the neck** del cogote

2 (*) (= *untidy person*) dejado/a *m/f*

scruffily ['skrʌfɪlɪ] ADV ~ **dressed** mal vestido, vestido con desaliño

scruffy ['skrʌfɪ] ADJ (*compar* **scruffier**; *superl* **scruffiest**) desaliñado

scrum [skrʌm] N (*Rugby*) melé *f* ➤ **scrum half** medio *m* de melé

scrumptious* ['skrʌmpʃəs] ADJ delicioso, sabrosísimo

scrunch [skrʌntʃ] VT (*also* **to** ~ **up**) ronzar

scruple ['skru:pl] N escrúpulo *m*; **to have no** ~**s about ...** no tener escrúpulos acerca de ...

scrupulous ['skru:pjʊləs] ADJ escrupuloso (**about** en cuanto a)

scrupulously ['skru:pjʊləslɪ] ADV escrupulosamente; ~ **honest/clean** sumamente honrado/limpio

scrutinize ['skru:tɪnaɪz] VT [+ *work etc*] escudriñar; [+ *votes*] efectuar el escrutinio de

scrutiny ['skru:tɪnɪ] N (= *examination*) examen *m* detallado; (*Pol*) [*of votes*] escrutinio *m*, recuento *m*; **under the ~ of sb** bajo la mirada de algn; **to keep sb under close** ~ vigilar a algn de cerca; **it does not stand up to** ~ no resiste un examen

scuba diving ['sku:bə,daɪvɪŋ] N submarinismo *m*

scuff [skʌf] VT [+ *shoes, floor*] rayar, marcar ➤ **scuff marks** rozaduras *fpl*

scuffle ['skʌfl] Ⓐ N refriega Ⓑ VI tener una refriega

scull [skʌl] Ⓐ N espadilla *f* Ⓑ VT, VI remar (*con espadilla*)

scullery ['skʌlərɪ] N (*Brit*) trascocina *f*, fregadero *m*

sculpt [skʌlpt] VT, VI esculpir

sculptor ['skʌlptəʳ] N escultor(a) *m/f*

sculpture ['skʌlptʃəʳ] N escultura *f*

scum [skʌm] N (*on liquid*) espuma *f*; (*pej*) (= *people*) escoria *f*; **the ~ of the earth** la escoria de la tierra

scumbag*** ['skʌm,bæg] N cabronazo* *m*

scupper ['skʌpəʳ] VT (*Naut*) abrir los imbornales de, barrenar; (*Brit**) [+ *plan*] echar por tierra

scurrilous ['skʌrɪləs] ADJ [*gossip, article*] difamatorio, calumnioso

scurry ['skʌrɪ] VI (= *run*) ir corriendo; **to** ~ **away** escabullirse

scurvy ['skɜ:vɪ] N escorbuto *m*

scuttle[1] ['skʌtl] VT [+ *ship*] barrenar; [+ *hopes, plans*] dar al traste con, echar por tierra

scuttle[2] ['skʌtl] VI (= *run*) echar a correr

scuttle[3] ['skʌtl] N (*esp Brit*) (*for coal*) cubo *m*, carbonera *f*

scythe [saɪð] N guadaña *f*

SD, **S.Dak.** ABBR (*US*) = **South Dakota**

SDLP N ABBR (*Northern Irl Pol*) = **Social Democratic and Labour Party**

SE ABBR (= **southeast**) SE

sea [si:] Ⓐ N **1** (= *not land*) mar *m* (*or f in some phrases*); (**out**) **at** ~ en alta mar; **to spend three years at** ~ pasar tres años navegando; **to go by** ~ ir por mar; **a house by the** ~ una casa junto al mar *or* a la orilla del mar; **the little boat was swept out to** ~ la barquilla fue arrastrada mar adentro; **to put (out) to** ~ hacerse a la mar, zarpar; ✦ IDIOM **to be all at** ~ (**about** *or* **with sth**) estar en un lío (por algo)
2 (*fig*) **a** ~ **of blood** un río *or* mar de sangre; **a** ~ **of faces** un mar de caras
Ⓑ CPD ➤ **sea air** aire *m* de mar ➤ **sea anemone** anémona *f* de mar ➤ **sea bed** fondo *m* del mar, lecho *m* marino (*frm*) ➤ **sea bird** ave *f* marina

Use **el/un** not **la/una** before feminine nouns beginning with stressed **a** or **ha** like **ave**.

➤ **sea breeze** brisa *f* marina ➤ **sea change** viraje *m*, cambio *m* radical ➤ **sea dog** lobo *m* de mar ➤ **sea fish** pez *m* marino ➤ **sea front** paseo *m* marítimo ➤ **sea horse** caballito *m* de mar, hipocampo *m* ➤ **sea lane** ruta *f* marítima ➤ **sea legs**: **to find one's** ~ **legs** mantener el

equilibrio (en barco) ➤ **sea level** nivel *m* del mar; **800 metres above** ~ **level** 800 metros sobre el nivel del mar ➤ **sea lion** león *m* marino ➤ **sea mist** bruma *f* marina ➤ **sea salt** sal *f* marina ➤ **sea shanty** saloma *f* ➤ **sea trout** trucha *f* marina, reo *m* ➤ **sea turtle** (*US*) tortuga *f* (marina) ➤ **sea urchin** erizo *m* de mar ➤ **sea wall** malecón *m*, rompeolas *m inv* ➤ **sea water** agua *f* de mar

Use **el/un** not **la/una** before feminine nouns beginning with stressed **a** or **ha** like **agua**.

seaboard ['si:bɔ:d] N (*US*) litoral *m*

seafarer ['si:,fɛərəʳ] N marinero *m*

seafaring ['si:,fɛərɪŋ] ADJ [*community*] marinero; [*life*] de marinero

seafood ['si:fu:d] N marisco *m*, mariscos *mpl*

seagoing ['si:,gəʊɪŋ] ADJ marítimo

seagull ['si:gʌl] N gaviota *f*

seal[1] [si:l] N (*Zool*) foca *f*

seal[2] [si:l] Ⓐ N **1** (= *official stamp*) sello *m*; **they have given their** ~ **of approval to the proposed reforms** han dado el visto bueno a *or* han aprobado las reformas que se planean; **this set the** ~ **on their friendship** esto selló su amistad
2 [*of envelope, parcel, exterior of bottle, jar*] precinto *m*; (*inside lid of jar*) aro *m* de goma
Ⓑ VT **1** (= *close*) [+ *envelope*] cerrar; [+ *package, coffin*] precintar; [+ *border*] cerrar
2 (= *stop up, make airtight*) [+ *container*] tapar *or* cerrar herméticamente; [+ *surface*] sellar
3 (*fig*) (= *confirm*) [+ *bargain, deal*] sellar; [+ *victory*] decidir; [+ *sb's fate*] decidir, determinar
➤ **seal in** VT + ADV conservar
➤ **seal off** VT + ADV [+ *building, room*] cerrar; [+ *area, road*] acordonar
➤ **seal up** VT + ADV [+ *letter, parcel, building, tunnel*] precintar; [+ *window, door*] condenar, precintar; [+ *hole*] rellenar, tapar

sealing wax ['si:lɪŋwæks] N lacre *m*

sealskin ['si:lskɪn] N piel *f* de foca

seam [si:m] N **1** (*Sew*) costura *f*; **to fall** *or* **come apart at the** ~**s** descoserse; **to be bursting at the** ~**s*** estar a rebosar
2 (*Geol*) filón *m*, veta *f*

seaman ['si:mən] N (*pl* **seamen**) marinero *m*, marino *m*

seamanship ['si:mənʃɪp] N náutica *f*

seamless ['si:mlɪs] ADJ sin costura(s)

seamstress ['semstrɪs] N costurera *f*

seamy* ['si:mɪ] ADJ (*compar* **seamier**; *superl* **seamiest**) sórdido, insalubre; **the** ~ **side** (*fig*) el revés *or* reverso de la medalla

seance, séance ['seɪɑ:ns] N sesión *f* de espiritismo

seaplane ['si:pleɪn] N hidroavión *m*

seaport ['si:pɔ:t] N puerto *m* de mar

sear [sɪəʳ] VT (= *scorch*) chamuscar, quemar; (= *wither*) secar, marchitar; (*Culin*) soasar; **it was ~ed into my memory** me quedó grabado en la memoria

search [sɜ:tʃ] Ⓐ N **1** (= *hunt*) búsqueda *f* (**for** de); **after a long** ~ **I found the key** después de mucho buscar, encontré la llave; **in** ~ **of** en busca de
2 (= *inspection*) [*of building, place*] registro *m*; [*of records*] inspección *f*; **police made a thorough** ~ **of the premises** la policía registró todo el local
3 (*Comput*) búsqueda *f*
Ⓑ VT **1** [+ *building, luggage, pockets*] registrar, catear (*Mex*); [+ *person*] registrar, cachear, catear (*Mex*); **she ~ed the kitchen drawers for her keys** buscó las llaves en los cajones de la cocina; ~ **me!*** ¡yo qué sé!, ¡ni idea!
2 (= *scan*) [+ *documents, records*] examinar; **to** ~ **one's memory** hacer memoria
3 (*Comput*) buscar en
Ⓒ VI **1** (*gen*) buscar; **to** ~ **for sth/sb** buscar algo/a algn; **rescuers ~ed through the rubble for survivors** los del equipo de rescate buscaron supervivientes entre los escombros

2 (*Comput*) **"search and replace"** "buscar y reemplazar" ⓓ CPD ➤ **search engine** (*Internet*) buscador *m* ➤ **search party** pelotón *m* de búsqueda ➤ **search warrant** orden *f* de registro

searcher ['sɜːtʃəʳ] N buscador(a) *m/f*

searching ['sɜːtʃɪŋ] ADJ [*look*] inquisitivo; [*question*] perspicaz

searchlight ['sɜːtʃlaɪt] N reflector *m*, proyector *m*

searing ['sɪərɪŋ] ADJ [*heat*] ardiente; [*pain*] agudo

seascape ['siːskeɪp] N paisaje *m* marino

seashell ['siːʃel] N concha *f* marina

seashore ['siːʃɔːʳ] N (= *beach*) playa *f*; (*gen*) orilla *f* del mar; **by** or **on the ~** en la playa, a la orilla del mar

seasick ['siːsɪk] ADJ mareado; **to get/be ~** marearse (*en barco*)

seasickness ['siːsɪknɪs] N mareo *m* (*por viajar en barco*)

seaside ['siːsaɪd] ⓐ N (= *beach*) playa *f*; (= *shore*) orilla *f* del mar; **at the ~** en la playa ⓑ CPD [*hotel*] de playa, en la playa; [*town*] costero, costeño ➤ **seaside resort** *lugar de veraneo en la playa*

season ['siːzn] ⓐ N **1** (= *period of the year*) estación *f*; **the four ~s** las cuatro estaciones; **the dry/rainy ~** la temporada de sequía/de lluvias

2 (*for specific activity*) temporada *f*; **we did a ~ at La Scala** (*Theat*) representamos en la Scala durante una temporada; **"Season's Greetings"** "Felices Pascuas"; **the busy ~** la temporada alta; **the closed ~** (*Hunting*) la veda; **the fishing/football ~** la temporada de pesca/de fútbol; **during the holiday ~** (*Brit*) en la temporada de vacaciones; **to be in ~** [*fruit*] estar en sazón; [*animal*] estar en celo; **the open ~** (*Hunting*) la temporada de caza or de pesca; **to be out of ~** estar fuera de temporada; **during the vacation ~** (*US*) en la temporada de vacaciones

ⓑ VT (*Culin*) sazonar, condimentar (**with** con)

ⓒ CPD ➤ **season ticket** abono *m* ➤ **season ticket holder** abonado/a *m/f*

seasonable ['siːznəbl] ADJ [*weather*] propio de la estación

seasonal ['siːzənl] ADJ [*work, migration*] de temporada, estacional; [*fruit, vegetable*] del tiempo, de temporada ➤ **seasonal affective disorder** trastorno *m* afectivo estacional

seasoned ['siːznd] ADJ **she's a ~ campaigner** es una veterana de las campañas, está curtida en mil y una campañas

seasoning ['siːznɪŋ] N (*for food*) aliño *m*, condimentos *mpl*

seat [siːt] ⓐ N **1** (= *place to sit*) asiento *m*; (*in cinema, theatre*) butaca *f*, asiento *m*; (*on cycle*) sillín *m*, asiento *m*; **to take one's ~** sentarse, tomar asiento; ✦ IDIOM **to take a back ~** mantenerse al margen

2 [*of chair, toilet*] asiento *m*

3 (= *ticket*) (*Theat, Cine, Sport*) localidad *f*, entrada *f*; (*for plane, train, bus*) plaza *f*; **are there any ~s left?** (*Theat, Cine, Sport*) ¿quedan localidades or entradas?; (*on plane*) ¿quedan plazas?

4 (*in parliament*) escaño *m*, curul *f* (*Col*)

5 (*on board, committee*) puesto *m*; **to have a ~ on the board** ser miembro de la junta directiva

ⓑ VT **1** [+ *person, child, invalid*] sentar; **please remain ~ed** por favor permanezcan sentados (*frm*); **to ~ o.s.** sentarse, tomar asiento (*frm*)

2 (= *hold*) [*hall, vehicle*] tener cabida para; **the table can ~ 20 comfortably** en la mesa caben 20 personas cómodamente

ⓒ CPD ➤ **seat belt** cinturón *m* de seguridad

seating ['siːtɪŋ] N asientos *mpl* ➤ **seating capacity** número *m* de asientos, cabida *f* ➤ **seating plan** disposición *f* de los asientos

seaway ['siːweɪ] N vía *f* marítima

seaweed ['siːwiːd] N alga *f*

Use **el/un** not **la/una** before feminine nouns beginning with stressed **a** or **ha** like **alga**.

---

seaworthy ['siːwɜːðɪ] ADJ en condiciones de navegar

sec* [sek] N ABBR = **second²**

secateurs [,sekə'tɜːz] NPL (*Brit*) podadera *fsing*

secede [sɪ'siːd] VI separarse, escindirse (**from** de)

secession [sɪ'seʃən] N secesión *f*, separación *f* (**from** de)

secluded [sɪ'kluːdɪd] ADJ retirado, apartado

seclusion [sɪ'kluːʒən] N aislamiento *m*; **to live in ~** vivir aislado

second¹ ['sekənd] ⓐ ADJ segundo; **on his ~ birthday** en su segundo cumpleaños, cuando cumpla/cumplió dos años; **in the ~ century** (*spoken form*) en el siglo segundo or dos; (*in writing*) en el siglo II; **give him a ~ chance** dale otra oportunidad; **in ~ gear** en segunda (velocidad); **they have a ~ home in Oxford** tienen otra casa en Oxford, en Oxford tienen una segunda vivienda; **it's ~ nature to her** lo hace sin pensar; **to ask for a ~ opinion** pedir una segunda opinión; **to be/lie in ~ place** estar/encontrarse en segundo lugar or segunda posición; **to have ~ thoughts (about sth/ about doing sth)** tener sus dudas (sobre algo/si hacer algo); **on ~ thoughts ...** pensándolo bien ...; **to be ~ to none** no tener rival, ser inigualable

ⓑ ADV **1** (*in race, competition, election*) en segundo lugar, en segunda posición; **to come/finish ~** quedar/llegar en segundo lugar or segunda posición

2 (= *secondly*) segundo, en segundo lugar

3 (*before superl adj*) **the ~ tallest building in the world** el segundo edificio más alto del mundo; **this is the ~ largest city in Spain** ocupa la segunda posición entre las ciudades más grandes de España

ⓒ PRON **1** (*in race, competition*) **he came a good/poor ~** quedó segundo a poca/gran distancia del vencedor; **his exams come a poor ~ to playing football** el fútbol es su prioridad y después, los exámenes

2 (*in dates*) dos *m*; **he arrives on May (the) ~** or **the ~ of May** llega el dos de mayo; **it's the ~ of May** ◇ **it's May (the) ~** estamos a dos de mayo, es dos de mayo

3 (*in titles*) **Charles the Second** (*spoken form*) Carlos Segundo; (*in writing*) Carlos II

4 (*also ~ gear*) segunda *f* (velocidad *f*); **in ~** en segunda (velocidad)

5 (= *assistant*) (*in duel*) padrino *m*; (*in boxing*) segundo *m*, cuidador *m*; **~s out!** ¡segundos fuera!

6 (*Brit Univ*) **Lower/Upper Second** calificación que ocupa el tercer/segundo lugar en la escala de las que se otorgan con un título universitario

7 seconds 7.1 (*Comm*) artículos *mpl* con defecto de fábrica; **these dresses are slight ~s** estos vestidos tienen pequeños defectos de fábrica 7.2 (= *second helping*) **will you have ~s?** ¿quieres más?

ⓓ VT **1** [+ *motion, speaker, nomination*] apoyar, secundar; **I'll ~ that*** lo mismo digo yo, estoy completamente de acuerdo

2 [sɪ'kɒnd] (*Brit*) [+ *employee*] trasladar temporalmente

ⓔ CPD ➤ **second name** apellido *m* ➤ **second sight: to have ~ sight** tener clarividencia, ser clarividente

second² ['sekənd] N (*in time*) segundo *m*; **just a ~!*** ¡un momento!, ¡momentito! (*esp LAm*); **in a split ~** en un instante, en un abrir y cerrar de ojos ➤ **second hand** [*of clock*] segundero *m*

secondary ['sekəndərɪ] ⓐ ADJ **1** [*character, role, effect*] secundario; **it is a ~ consideration** es un factor secundario **2** [*education*] secundario; [*student, teacher*] de enseñanza secundaria ⓑ CPD ➤ **secondary modern (school)** (*Brit*) (*formerly*) instituto de enseñanza secundaria que centraba su actividad docente más en conocimientos prácticos y tecnológicos que en la formación académica; ▷ COMPREHENSIVE SCHOOLS ➤ **secondary school** centro *m* de enseñanza secundaria

second-best ['sekənd'best] ⓐ N segundo *m* ⓑ ADV **to come off ~** quedar en segundo lugar ⓒ ADJ segundo mejor

second-class ['sekənd'klɑːs] ⓐ ADJ [*compartment, ticket*] de segunda clase; [*post*] ordinario; **~ citizen** ciudadano/a *m/f* de segunda clase; **~ degree** (*Univ*) licenciatura *f* con media de notable; **~ stamp** sello *m* para correo ordinario ⓑ ADV **to send sth ~** enviar algo por correo ordinario; **to travel ~** viajar en segunda

second-hand ['sekənd'hænd] **Ⓐ** ADJ de segunda mano; [car] usado, de segunda mano; ~ **bookshop** (esp Brit) or **bookstore** (esp US) librería f de viejo; ~ **clothes** (esp Brit) ropa f usada or de segunda mano; ~ **shop** (esp Brit) or **store** (esp US) tienda f de segunda mano, bazar m (Mex), cambalache m (SC) **Ⓑ** ADV **to buy sth** ~ comprar algo de segunda mano; **I heard it only** ~ yo lo supe solamente por otro

second-in-command ['sekəndɪnkə'mɑːnd] N segundo/a m/f de a bordo

secondly ['sekəndlɪ] ADV en segundo lugar

secondment [sɪ'kɒndmənt] N (Brit) **on** ~ trasladado, destacado; **she is on** ~ **to section B** ha sido trasladada temporalmente a la sección B, está destacada en la sección B

second-rate ['sekənd'reɪt] ADJ de segunda fila

secrecy ['siːkrəsɪ] N secreto m; **in** ~ en secreto, a escondidas; **to swear sb to** ~ hacer que algn jure no revelar algo

secret ['siːkrɪt] **Ⓐ** ADJ secreto; [drinker, drug addict] a escondidas; **to keep sth** ~ mantener algo en secreto; **they held a** ~ **meeting** mantuvieron una reunión en secreto **Ⓑ** N secreto m; **to do sth in** ~ hacer algo en secreto or a escondidas; **to be in on the** ~ estar al corriente; **to keep a** ~ guardar un secreto; **to keep sth a** ~ **from sb** ocultar algo a algn; **to let sb into a/the** ~ contar or revelar a algn un/el secreto; **there's no** ~ **about it** esto no tiene nada de secreto; **to make no** ~ **of sth** no ocultar algo; **the** ~: **the** ~ **is to** (+ INFIN) el secreto consiste en + infin **Ⓒ** CPD ➤ **secret agent** agente mf secreto/a, espía mf ➤ **secret service** servicio m secreto

secretarial [ˌsekrə'teərɪəl] ADJ ➤ **secretarial college** colegio m de secretariado ➤ **secretarial course** curso m de secretariado ➤ **secretarial skills** técnicas fpl de secretariado ➤ **secretarial work** trabajo m de secretario

secretariat [ˌsekrə'teərɪət] N secretaría f, secretariado m

secretary ['sekrətrɪ] N secretario/a m/f; (Pol) ministro/a m/f ➤ **Secretary of State** (Brit) Ministro/a m/f (**for** de); (US) Ministro/a m/f de Asuntos Exteriores

secretary-general ['sekrətrɪ'dʒenərəl] N (pl **secretaries-general**) secretario-general/secretaria-general m/f

secrete [sɪ'kriːt] VT **1** (Med) secretar, segregar **2** (= hide) ocultar, esconder

secretion [sɪ'kriːʃən] N secreción f

secretive [sɪ'kriːtɪv] ADJ [person] reservado, callado; [behaviour] reservado; [organization] hermético; **to be** ~ **about sth** ser reservado con respecto a algo

secretly ['siːkrɪtlɪ] ADV [meet, plan, film] en secreto, a escondidas; [marry] en secreto; [hope, want] en el fondo; **she was** ~ **relieved** en su fuero interno sintió alivio

sect [sekt] N secta f

sectarian [sek'teərɪən] ADJ sectario

sectarianism [sek'teərɪənɪzəm] N sectarismo m

section ['sekʃən] **Ⓐ** N **1** (= part) [of pipeline, road] tramo m; [of self-assembly item] pieza f, parte f; [of orange etc] gajo m; [of book, text] parte f; [of code, law] artículo m; [of document, report] apartado m, punto m; [of orchestra] sección f; [of country] región f; [of community, opinion] sector m; [of town] (Brit) sector m, zona f; (US) (= district) barrio m; **the sports/finance** ~ [of newspaper] la sección de deportes/economía **2** (= cut) (in diagram, dissection) sección f, corte m **Ⓑ** VT **1** (= divide) partir, trocear **2** [+ mentally ill person] internar en un psiquiátrico ➤ **section off** VT + ADV cortar, seccionar

sector ['sektəʳ] N sector m

secular ['sekjʊləʳ] ADJ [authority] laico; [music] profano

secure [sɪ'kjʊəʳ] **Ⓐ** ADJ **1** (= firm) [knot, hold] seguro; [door, window, lock] bien cerrado; [structure, foothold] firme; [ladder] bien sujeto; [foundation] sólido **2** (= safe) [job, place, building] seguro; [position] garantizado; [career, future] asegurado; **to be financially** ~ tener seguridad económica **3** (emotionally) [person] seguro; [relationship, environment] estable; ~ **in the knowledge that** seguro de que, confiado

de que **Ⓑ** VT **1** (= make fast) [+ rope] sujetar bien; (to floor etc) afianzar; [+ load] asegurar; [+ door, window] cerrar bien; (= tie up) [+ person, animal] atar, amarrar (LAm) **2** (= make safe) [+ home, building] proteger (**against**, **from** de, contra; [+ future] asegurar **3** (frm) (= obtain) conseguir, obtener; **a win that** ~**d them a place in the final** una victoria que les aseguró un puesto en la final **4** (Fin) [+ loan, debt] garantizar

securely [sɪ'kjʊəlɪ] ADV **1** (= firmly) [fasten, lock, fix, tie] bien **2** (= safely) firmemente; **he remains** ~ **in power** permanece firmemente afincado en el poder

security [sɪ'kjʊərɪtɪ] **Ⓐ** N **1** (= precautions) seguridad f **2** (= safety) **2.1** (from harm or loss) seguridad f; ~ **of tenure** (in one's job) seguridad f en el cargo; [of tenant] derecho m de ocupación (de un inmueble) **2.2** (from worry) seguridad f, estabilidad f **3** (= guarantee) garantía f, aval m **4 securities** valores mpl, títulos mpl **Ⓑ** CPD ➤ **security check** control m de seguridad ➤ **Security Council** Consejo m de Seguridad; **the Security Council of the United Nations** el Consejo de Seguridad de las Naciones Unidas ➤ **security forces** fuerzas fpl de seguridad ➤ **security guard** guarda mf jurado

sedan [sɪ'dæn] N **1** (also ~ **chair**) silla f de manos **2** (US Aut) turismo m, sedán m

sedate [sɪ'deɪt] **Ⓐ** ADJ (compar ~**r**; superl ~**st**) serio, formal **Ⓑ** VT (Med) sedar

sedation [sɪ'deɪʃən] N sedación f; **under** ~ bajo los efectos de sedantes

sedative ['sedətɪv] ADJ, N sedante m

sedentary ['sedntrɪ] ADJ sedentario

sediment ['sedɪmənt] N (in liquids, boiler) sedimento m, poso m; (Geol) sedimento m

sedimentary [ˌsedɪ'mentərɪ] ADJ sedimentario

sedition [sə'dɪʃən] N sedición f

seditious [sə'dɪʃəs] ADJ sedicioso

seduce [sɪ'djuːs] VT seducir; **to** ~ **sb into doing sth** (fig) engatusar or convencer a algn para que haga algo

seduction [sɪ'dʌkʃən] N seducción f

seductive [sɪ'dʌktɪv] ADJ seductor

see[1] [siː] (pt **saw**; pp ~**n**) VT, VI **1** (gen) ver; **I can't** ~ no veo nada; **to** ~ **sb do** or **doing sth** ver a algn hacer algo; **I saw it done in 1988** lo vi hacer en 1988; **"see page eight"** "véase la página ocho"; **he's not at all** está de vuelta de todo; **there was nobody to be** ~**n** no se veía a nadie; **as you can** ~ como ves; **as far as the eye can** ~ hasta donde alcanza la vista; ~ **for yourself** compruébalo tú mismo; **I'll go and** ~ voy a ver; **now** ~ **here!** (in anger) ¡mira!, ¡oiga!, ¡escuche!; **I** ~ **nothing wrong in it** no le encuentro nada malo; **I don't know what she** ~**s in him** no sé lo que encuentra en él; **let me** ~ ◇ **let's** ~ (= show me/us) ¿a ver?; (= let me/us think) vamos a ver; **she's certainly** ~**ing life** es seguro que está viendo muchas cosas; **so I** ~ ya lo veo; **I must be** ~**ing things*** estoy viendo visiones; **I can't** ~ **to read** no veo lo suficiente para leer; **can you** ~ **your way to helping us?** (fig) ¿nos hace el favor de ayudarnos?; **we'll** ~ ya veremos, vamos a ver **2** (= visit, meet) ver, visitar; **I want to** ~ **you about my daughter** quiero hablar con usted acerca de mi hija; **what did he want to** ~ **you about?** ¿qué asunto quería discutir contigo?; **to** ~ **the doctor** ir a ver al médico, consultar al médico; **to go and** ~ **sb** ir a ver a algn; (a friend) visitar a algn; **we don't** ~ **much of them nowadays** ahora les vemos bastante poco; ~ **you!*** chau*; ~ **you on Sunday!** ¡hasta el domingo!; ~ **you tomorrow!** ¡hasta mañana!; ~ **you later!** ¡hasta luego!; ~ **you soon!** ¡hasta pronto! **3** (= understand, perceive) entender; **I** ~ ya entiendo; **this is how I** ~ **it** éste es mi modo de verlo, yo lo entiendo así; **I saw only too clearly that ...** percibí claramente que ...; **I can't** ~ **why/how** etc ... no veo or entiendo por qué/cómo etc ...; **as far as I can** ~ por lo visto, por lo que yo veo; **the way I** ~ **it** a mi parecer **4** (= accompany) acompañar; **he was so drunk we had to** ~ **him to bed** estaba tan borracho que tuvimos que llevarle a la cama; **to** ~ **sb to the door** acompañar a algn a la puerta;

to ~ sb home acompañar a algn a casa
5 (= *try*) procurar; ~ **if ...** ve a ver si ..., mira a ver si ...
6 (= *imagine*) imaginarse; **I don't ~ her as a minister** no la veo *or* no me la imagino de ministra; **I can't ~ him winning** me parece imposible que gane
7 (= *ensure*) **to ~ (to it) that** procurar que + *subjun*
➤ **see about** VI + PREP **1** (= *deal with*) ocuparse de; **he came to ~ about our TV** vino a ver nuestra televisión
2 (= *consider*) pensar; **I'll ~ about it** ya veré, lo pensaré
➤ **see in** VT + ADV [+ *person*] hacer entrar, hacer pasar; **to ~ the New Year in** celebrar *or* festejar el Año Nuevo
➤ **see off** VT + ADV (= *say goodbye to*) despedir, despedirse de
➤ **see out** VT + ADV (= *take to the door*) acompañar hasta la puerta; **I'll ~ myself out*** no hace falta que me acompañe hasta la puerta
➤ **see over** VI + PREP recorrer
➤ **see through** Ⓐ VI + PREP [+ *person, behaviour*] calar; **I can ~ right through him** lo tengo calado Ⓑ VT + ADV [+ *project, deal*] llevar a cabo; **£100 should ~ you through** tendrás bastante con 100 libras
➤ **see to** VI + PREP (= *deal with*) atender a; (= *take care of*) ocuparse de, encargarse de; **please ~ to it that ...** por favor procura que ...

see² [si:] N (*Rel*) sede *f*; **the Holy See** la Santa Sede

seed [si:d] Ⓐ N **1** [*of plant*] semilla *f*, simiente *f*; (*inside fruit*) pepita *f*; [*of grain*] grano *m*; (*fig*) [*of idea etc*] germen *m*; **to go to ~** (*lit*) granar, dar en grana; (*fig*) ir a menos; **to sow ~s of doubt in sb's mind** sembrar la duda en la mente de algn **2** (*Sport*) (= *player, team*) cabeza *mf* de serie; **she's the number one ~** es la cabeza de serie número uno Ⓑ VT **1** (= *plant with seeds*) sembrar (**with** de) **2** (= *remove seed of*) [+ *raisins, grapes*] despepitar **3** (*Sport*) clasificar como cabeza de serie

seedbed [si:dbed] N semillero *m*

seedless [si:dlɪs] ADJ sin semillas

seedling [si:dlɪŋ] N planta *f* de semillero

seedy [si:dɪ] ADJ (*compar* **seedier**; *superl* **seediest**) [*hotel, nightclub*] sórdido, de mala muerte*, cutre (*Sp**); [*person*] de pinta desastrada

seeing [si:ɪŋ] Ⓐ CONJ ~ (**that** *or* **as**) (*esp Brit*) visto que, en vista de que Ⓑ N ✦ PROV ~ **is believing** ver para creer

seeing-eye dog [si:ɪŋ'aɪdɒg] N (*US*) perro *m* guía

seek [si:k] (*pt, pp* **sought**) Ⓐ VT **1** (= *look for*) buscar; **it is much sought after** está muy cotizado **2** (= *ask for*) pedir, solicitar; **to ~ advice from sb** pedir consejo a algn **3** (*frm*) (= *attempt*) **to ~ to do sth** tratar de *or* procurar hacer algo Ⓑ VI (*frm*) **to ~ after** *or* **for** buscar
➤ **seek out** VT + ADV buscar

seem [si:m] VI parecer; **he ~ed to be in difficulty** parecía tener dificultades; **the shop ~ed to be closed** parecía que la tienda estaba cerrada; **what ~s to be the trouble?** ¿qué pasa?; **I ~ to have heard that before** me parece que ya me contaron eso antes; **that ~s like a good idea** parece una buena idea; **it ~s not** parece que no; **it ~s so** parece que sí; **so it ~s** así parece; **there ~s to be a problem/mistake** parece que hay un problema/error; **it ~s to me/him that ...** me/le parece que ...; **how did he ~ to you?** ¿qué te pareció?

seeming [si:mɪŋ] ADJ aparente

seemingly [si:mɪŋlɪ] ADV según parece, aparentemente

seemly [si:mlɪ] ADJ (*compar* **seemlier**; *superl* **seemliest**) (*frm*) [*behaviour, language, dress*] decoroso, decente

seen [si:n] PP *of* **see¹**

seep [si:p] VI filtrarse; **to ~ through/into/from** filtrarse *or* colarse por/en/desde

seer [sɪəʳ] N vidente *mf*

seesaw [si:sɔ:] N subibaja *m*, balancín *m*

seethe [si:ð] VI **he's seething** está furioso; **to ~ with anger** estar furioso

see-through [si:θru:] ADJ transparente

segment Ⓐ [segmənt] N segmento *m*; [*of citrus fruit*] gajo *m* Ⓑ [seg'ment] VT segmentar; [+ *citrus fruit*] desgajar, separar en gajos

segregate [segrɪgeɪt] VT segregar, separar (**from** de)

segregated [segrɪgeɪtɪd] ADJ segregado, separado

segregation [ˌsegrɪ'geɪʃən] N segregación *f*, separación *f*

Seine [seɪn] N Sena *m*

seismic [saɪzmɪk] ADJ (*lit*) sísmico; (*fig*) [*shift, changes*] radical

seize [si:z] VT **1** (= *physically take hold of*) coger, agarrar; **to ~ hold of sth/sb** coger *or* agarrar algo/a algn **2** (= *capture*) [+ *person*] detener; [+ *territory*] apoderarse de; [+ *power*] tomar, hacerse con **3** (*Jur*) (= *confiscate*) [+ *property*] incautar, embargar
➤ **seize up** VI + ADV [*machine, limbs*] agarrotarse
➤ **seize upon** VI + PREP [+ *chance*] aprovechar; [+ *idea*] fijarse en

seizure [si:ʒəʳ] N **1** [*of goods*] embargo *m*, incautación *f* **2** (*Med*) ataque *m*

seldom [seldəm] ADV rara vez, pocas veces, casi nunca; **~, if ever** rara vez *or* pocas veces, si es que alguna

select [sɪ'lekt] Ⓐ VT (= *team, candidate*) seleccionar; [+ *book, gift etc*] escoger, elegir; **~ed works** obras *fpl* escogidas Ⓑ ADJ selecto; **a very ~ neighbourhood** un barrio de muy buen tono; **a ~ few** una minoría privilegiada Ⓒ CPD ➤ **select committee** comité *m* de investigación

selection [sɪ'lekʃən] Ⓐ N **1** (= *act of choosing*) elección *f* **2** (= *person/thing chosen*) elección *f*, selección *f* **3** (= *range, assortment*) surtido *m*, selección *f* Ⓑ CPD ➤ **selection committee** (*esp Pol*) comisión *f* de nombramiento ➤ **selection test** prueba *f* de selección

selective [sɪ'lektɪv] ADJ selectivo

selector [sɪ'lektəʳ] N (= *person*) seleccionador(a) *m/f*

self [self] N (*pl* **selves**) uno/a mismo/a *m/f*; **the ~** el yo; **my true ~** mi verdadero yo; **he's quite his old ~ again** vuelve a ser el que era

self- [self] PREF auto..., ... de sí mismo

self-addressed [ˌselfə'drest] ADJ ➤ **self-addressed envelope** (*Brit*), **self-addressed stamped envelope** (*US*) sobre *m* con el nombre y la dirección del remitente

self-adhesive [ˌselfəd'hi:zɪv] ADJ autoadhesivo, autoadherente

self-appointed [ˌselfə'pɔɪntɪd] ADJ que se ha nombrado a sí mismo, autoproclamado

self-assembly [selfə'semblɪ] ADJ [*furniture etc*] automontable, para montar uno mismo

self-assessment [selfə'sesmənt] N (*gen*) autoevaluación *f*; (*Brit Tax*) autoliquidación *f*

self-assurance [selfə'ʃʊərəns] N confianza *f* en sí mismo

self-assured [ˌselfə'ʃʊəd] ADJ seguro de sí mismo

self-awareness [ˌselfə'weənɪs] N conocimiento *m* or conciencia *f* de sí mismo

self-catering [self'keɪtərɪŋ] ADJ (*Brit*) ~ **apartment** apartamento *m* con acceso a cocina (*p.ej. en unas vacaciones organizadas*); ~ **holiday** vacaciones *fpl* en piso *or* chalet *or* casita con cocina propia

self-centred, self-centered (*US*) [ˌself'sentəd] ADJ egocéntrico

self-cleaning [ˌself'kli:nɪŋ] ADJ autolimpiable

self-composed [ˌselfkəm'pəʊzd] ADJ sereno, dueño de sí mismo

self-confessed [ˌselfkən'fest] ADJ confeso

self-confidence [ˌself'kɒnfɪdəns] N confianza *f* en sí mismo

self-confident [ˌself'kɒnfɪdənt] ADJ seguro de sí mismo, lleno de confianza en sí mismo

self-conscious [ˌself'kɒnʃəs] ADJ cohibido, tímido

self-consciously [ˌself'kɒnʃəslɪ] ADV cohibidamente, tímidamente

self-consciousness [ˌself'kɒnʃəsnɪs] N timidez *f*, inseguridad *f*

self-contained [ˌselfkən'teɪnd] ADJ [*flat*] con entrada propia, independiente; [*person*] autónomo, autosuficiente

self-contradictory [ˌselfkɒntrəˈdɪktərɪ] ADJ que se contradice a sí mismo, que lleva implícita una contradicción

self-control [ˌselfkənˈtrəʊl] N dominio *m* de sí mismo, autocontrol *m*; **to lose one's ~** no poder contenerse *or* dominarse

self-controlled [ˌselfkənˈtrəʊld] ADJ sereno

self-deception [ˌselfdɪˈsepʃən] N autoengaño *m*; **this is mere ~** esto es engañarse a sí mismo

self-defeating [ˌselfdɪˈfiːtɪŋ] ADJ contraproducente

self-defence, self-defense (*US*) [ˌselfdɪˈfens] N autodefensa *f*, defensa *f* propia; **she killed him in ~** lo mató en defensa propia; **to act in ~** obrar en defensa propia ➤ **self-defence classes** clases *fpl* de defensa personal

self-denial [ˌselfdɪˈnaɪəl] N abnegación *f*

self-destruct [ˌselfdɪsˈtrʌkt] VI autodestruirse

self-destructive [ˌselfdɪsˈtrʌktɪv] ADJ autodestructivo

self-discipline [ˌselfˈdɪsɪplɪn] N autodisciplina *f*

self-disciplined [ˌselfˈdɪsɪplɪnd] ADJ autodisciplinado

self-drive [ˈselfdraɪv] ADJ (*Brit*) sin chofer *or* (*Sp*) chófer

self-educated [ˌselfˈedjʊkeɪtɪd] ADJ autodidacta

self-effacing [ˌselfɪˈfeɪsɪŋ] ADJ modesto, humilde

self-employed [ˌselfɪmˈplɔɪd] ADJ autónomo, que trabaja por cuenta propia; **to be ~** ser autónomo, trabajar por cuenta propia

self-esteem [ˌselfɪsˈtiːm] N amor *m* propio

self-evident [ˌselfˈevɪdənt] ADJ manifiesto, patente

self-explanatory [ˌselfɪksˈplænɪtərɪ] ADJ que no necesita explicación

self-expression [ˌselfɪksˈpreʃən] N autoexpresión *f*

self-financing [ˌselffaɪˈnænsɪŋ] ADJ autofinanciado

self-fulfilling [ˌselffʊlˈfɪlɪŋ] ADJ **~ prophecy** profecía *f* que por su propia naturaleza se cumple

self-governing [ˌselfˈgʌvənɪŋ] ADJ autónomo

self-help [ˌselfˈhelp] CPD [*book, method, measures*] de autoayuda ➤ **self-help group** grupo *m* de apoyo mutuo

self-importance [ˌselfɪmˈpɔːtəns] N prepotencia *f*

self-important [ˌselfɪmˈpɔːtənt] ADJ prepotente

self-imposed [ˌselfɪmˈpəʊzd] ADJ [*punishment etc*] autoimpuesto, voluntario

self-indulgence [ˌselfɪnˈdʌldʒəns] N excesos *mpl* (en el comer etc), falta *f* de moderación

self-indulgent [ˌselfɪnˈdʌldʒənt] ADJ que se permite excesos

self-inflicted [ˌselfɪnˈflɪktɪd] ADJ [*wound*] autoinfligido, infligido a sí mismo

self-interest [ˌselfˈɪntrɪst] N interés *m* propio

self-interested [ˌselfˈɪntrɪstɪd] ADJ que actúa en interés propio, egoísta

selfish [ˈselfɪʃ] ADJ egoísta

selfishly [ˈselfɪʃlɪ] ADV con egoísmo, de modo egoísta

selfishness [ˈselfɪʃnɪs] N egoísmo *m*

self-knowledge [ˌselfˈnɒlɪdʒ] N conocimiento *m* de sí mismo

selfless [ˈselflɪs] ADJ desinteresado

selflessly [ˈselflɪslɪ] ADV desinteresadamente

selflessness [ˈselflɪsnɪs] N desinterés *m*

self-locking [ˌselfˈlɒkɪŋ] ADJ de cierre automático

self-made [ˌselfˈmeɪd] ADJ ➤ **self-made man** hombre *m* que ha llegado a su posición actual por sus propios esfuerzos, hijo *m* de sus propias obras

self-opinionated [ˌselfəˈpɪnjəneɪtɪd] ADJ terco

self-perpetuating [ˌselfpəˈpetjʊeɪtɪŋ] ADJ que se autoperpetúa

self-pity [ˌselfˈpɪtɪ] N autocompasión *f*

self-pitying [ˌselfˈpɪtɪŋ] ADJ autocompasivo

self-portrait [ˌselfˈpɔːtrɪt] N autorretrato *m*

self-possessed [ˌselfpəˈzest] ADJ sereno, dueño de sí mismo

self-preservation [ˌselfprezəˈveɪʃən] N autopreservación *f*, supervivencia *f*

self-proclaimed [ˌselfprəˈkleɪmd] ADJ autoproclamado

self-raising flour [ˈselfˌreɪzɪŋˈflaʊəʳ] N (*Brit*) harina *f* con levadura *or* (*And, SC*) leudante

self-reliant [ˌselfrɪˈlaɪənt] ADJ independiente, autosuficiente

self-respect [ˌselfrɪsˈpekt] N amor *m* propio

self-respecting [ˌselfrɪsˈpektɪŋ] ADJ que tiene amor propio

self-restraint [ˌselfrɪsˈtreɪnt] N dominio *m* de sí mismo, autocontrol *m*

self-righteous [ˌselfˈraɪtʃəs] ADJ pretencioso, farisaico, creído (*LAm*)

self-righteousness [ˌselfˈraɪtʃəsnɪs] N pretensión *f*, fariseísmo *m*

self-rising flour [ˈselfˌraɪzɪŋˈflaʊəʳ] N (*US*) harina *f* con levadura *or* (*And, SC*) leudante

self-sacrifice [ˌselfˈsækrɪfaɪs] N abnegación *f*

self-same [ˈselfseɪm] ADJ mismo, mismísimo

self-satisfied [ˌselfˈsætɪsfaɪd] ADJ satisfecho de sí mismo

self-seeking [ˌselfˈsiːkɪŋ] **Ⓐ** ADJ egoísta **Ⓑ** N egoísmo *m*

self-service [ˌselfˈsɜːvɪs], **self-serve** [ˌselfˈsɜːv] (*esp US*) ADJ de autoservicio ➤ **self-service restaurant** autoservicio *m*, self-service *m*

self-serving [ˌselfˈsɜːvɪŋ] ADJ egoísta, interesado

self-starter [ˌselfˈstɑːtəʳ] N **1** (*Aut*) arranque *m* automático **2** (*Comm etc*) persona *f* dinámica

self-styled [ˌselfˈstaɪld] ADJ supuesto, sedicente

self-sufficiency [ˌselfsəˈfɪʃənsɪ] N [*of person*] independencia *f*, confianza *f* en sí mismo; (*economic*) autosuficiencia *f*

self-sufficient [ˌselfsəˈfɪʃənt] ADJ [*person*] independiente; (*economically*) autosuficiente

self-taught [ˌselfˈtɔːt] ADJ autodidacta

sell [sel] (*pt, pp* **sold**) **Ⓐ** VT vender (**to** a); **I was sold this in London** me vendieron esto en Londres; **to ~ sth for £1** vender algo por una libra; **he doesn't ~ himself very well** no es capaz de causar buena impresión, no convence mucho; **to ~ sb an idea** (*fig*) convencer a algn de una idea; **to be sold on sth/sb*** estar cautivado por algo/algn **Ⓑ** VI [*merchandise*] venderse; **these ~ at 15p** éstos se venden a 15 peniques; **this line just isn't ~ing** esta línea no tiene demanda; **it ~s well** se vende bien
➤ **sell back** VT + ADV **to ~ sth back to sb** revender algo a algn
➤ **sell off** VT + ADV [+ *stocks and shares*] vender; [+ *goods*] liquidar
➤ **sell out Ⓐ** VI + ADV **1** [*tickets, goods*] agotarse; **we've sold out of bananas** no nos quedan plátanos, hemos agotado las existencias de plátanos **2** (*fig*) claudicar, transigir, transar (*LAm*) **3** (*US*) liquidarse, venderlo todo **Ⓑ** VT + ADV **1** [+ *goods*] agotar las existencias de, venderlo todo; **the tickets are all sold out** los billetes están agotados **2** [+ *person*] traicionar
➤ **sell up** VI + ADV (*Brit*) liquidar, vender todo

sell-by date [ˈselbaɪˌdeɪt] N (*Brit*) fecha *f* de caducidad

seller [ˈseləʳ] N (= *person who sells*) vendedor(a) *m/f*; (= *dealer*) comerciante *mf* (**of** en); ➤ **seller's market** mercado *m* favorable al vendedor

selling [ˈselɪŋ] N venta *f*, el vender ➤ **selling point** punto *m* fuerte ➤ **selling price** precio *m* de venta *or* (*LAm*) de menudeo

sell-off [ˈselɒf] N (*Econ*) (= *sale*) venta *f*; [*of public company*] privatización *f*

Sellotape® [ˈseləʊteɪp] N (*Brit*) cinta *f* adhesiva, celo *m* (*Sp*), Scotch® *m* (*esp LAm*), Durex® *m* (*LAm*)

sellout [ˈselaʊt] N **1** (*Theat*) lleno *m*, éxito *m* de taquilla **2** (= *betrayal*) claudicación *f*, traición *f*

seltzer water ['seltsə,wɔːtə'] N agua f de seltz

Use **el/un** not **la/una** before feminine nouns beginning with stressed **a** or **ha** like **agua**.

---

selvage, selvedge ['selvɪdʒ] N orillo m, bordo m

selves [selvz] NPL of **self**

semantics [sɪ'mæntɪks] NSING semántica f

semaphore ['seməfɔː'] N semáforo m

semblance ['sembləns] N apariencia f

semen ['siːmən] N semen m

semester [sɪ'mestə'] N (US) semestre m

semi- ['semɪ] N **1** (Brit) (also **--detached house**) casa f con una pared medianera **2** (Brit) = **semi-final 3** (US) = **semi-trailer**

semi-annual ['semɪ'ænjʊəl] ADJ (US) semestral

semibreve ['semɪbriːv] N (Brit) semibreve f

semicircle ['semɪ,sɜːkl] N semicírculo m

semicircular ['semɪ'sɜːkjʊlə'] ADJ semicircular

semi-colon ['semɪ'kəʊlən] N punto y coma m

semiconductor [,semɪkən'dʌktə'] N semiconductor m

semi-conscious ['semɪ'kɒnʃəs] ADJ semiconsciente

semi-detached ['semɪdɪ'tætʃt] (Brit) **🄐** ADJ **~ house** casa f adosada **🄑** N = **semi-detached house**

semi-final ['semɪ'faɪnl] N semifinal f

semi-finalist ['semɪ'faɪnəlɪst] N semifinalista mf

seminal ['semɪnl] ADJ **1** (Physiol) [fluid, liquid] seminal **2** (fig) [idea, work, event, study] seminal

seminar ['semɪnɑː'] N (Univ) clase f, seminario m

seminary ['semɪnərɪ] N seminario m

semi-precious ['semɪ,preʃəs] ADJ semiprecioso

semiquaver ['semɪ,kweɪvə'] N (Brit) semicorchea f

semi-skilled ['semɪ'skɪld] ADJ semicalificado, semicualificado (Sp); [work] para persona semicalificada or (Sp) semicualificada

semi-skimmed milk [,semɪskɪmd'mɪlk] N (Brit) leche f semidesnatada, leche f semidescremada (LAm)

semi-trailer ['semɪ'treɪlə'] N (US) trailer m

semolina [,semə'liːnə] N sémola f

Sen. ABBR (US Pol) = **Senator**

senate ['senɪt] N **1** (Pol) senado m; **the Senate** (US) el Senado; ver tb www.senate.gov; ⊃ CONGRESS **2** (Univ) consejo m universitario

senator ['senɪtə'] N (Pol) senador(a) m/f; ⊃ CONGRESS

send [send] (pt, pp **sent**) VT [+ letter, parcel, money, signal, troops] mandar, enviar; [+ person] mandar; **I wrote the letter but didn't ~ it** escribí la carta pero no la eché al correo; **Jan ~s her apologies** Jan pide que la disculpen or excusen; **I had some flowers sent to her** le mandé or envié unas flores; **to ~ sb one's love** mandar recuerdos a algn; **to ~ a child to bed/to school** mandar a un niño a la cama/a la escuela; **to ~ sb for sth: I sent her for some bread** la mandé a comprar pan or (Sp) a por pan; **to ~ sb home** mandar a algn a casa; (from abroad) repatriar a algn; **to ~ sb to prison** mandar a algn a la cárcel; **to ~ sth/sb flying** mandar algo/a algn volando por los aires; **their music sent the fans wild** su música volvía locos a los fans; **his lessons used to ~ me to sleep** me solía quedar dormido en sus clases; ✦ IDIOMS **to ~ sb to Coventry** hacer el vacío a algn; **to ~ sb packing** mandar a algn a freír espárragos*

➤ **send away 🄐** VI + ADV **to ~ away for sth** escribir pidiendo algo, pedir algo por correo **🄑** VT + ADV **1** [+ person] (= dismiss) despachar; (= send to another place) mandar **2** [+ goods] mandar, enviar

➤ **send back** VT + ADV [+ person] hacer volver, hacer regresar; [+ goods] mandar de vuelta, devolver

➤ **send down** VT + ADV [+ prices] provocar la bajada de, hacer bajar; [+ diver] mandar, enviar

➤ **send for** VT + PREP [+ person] mandar a buscar, mandar llamar; [+ catalogue, information] escribir pidiendo, pedir por correo

➤ **send in** VT + ADV [+ report, application, competition entry] mandar, enviar; [+ resignation] presentar; [+ troops] enviar, mandar; **~ him in!** ¡que pase!

➤ **send off 🄐** VI + ADV = **send away A 🄑** VT + ADV **1** [+ letter, parcel] mandar, enviar; [+ goods] despachar, expedir **2** [+ person] mandar, (= say goodbye to) despedir **3** (Sport) [+ player] expulsar

➤ **send on** VT + ADV **1** [+ letter] remitir, expedir; [+ luggage, document] remitir; [+ person] mandar **2** (Sport) [+ substitute] mandar a jugar

➤ **send out 🄐** VI + ADV **to ~ out for sth: we sent out for sandwiches** mandamos a alguien a traer or (Sp) a por unos sándwiches **🄑** VT + ADV **1** (= dispatch) [+ invitations, circulars, scout] mandar, enviar; [+ person] (on errand) mandar **2** (= dismiss) echar; **she was sent out for talking** la echaron (de clase) por hablar **3** (= emit) [+ smoke] despedir; [+ signal] emitir

➤ **send round** VT + ADV (= dispatch) [+ item] mandar, enviar; [+ person] mandar; **we'll ~ a car round to pick you up** mandaremos un coche a recogerlo

➤ **send up** VT + ADV **1** (= cause to rise) [+ rocket, balloon,] lanzar; [+ smoke, dust, spray] despedir; [+ prices] provocar la subida de, hacer subir **2** (Brit*) (= parody) burlarse de, parodiar

sender ['sendə'] N remitente mf

send-off ['sendɒf] N despedida f

send-up* ['sendʌp] N (Brit) parodia f

Senegal [senɪ'gɔːl] N el Senegal

Senegalese [,senɪgə'liːz] **🄐** ADJ senegalés **🄑** N senegalés/esa m/f

senile ['siːnaɪl] ADJ senil; **to go ~** empezar a chochear

➤ **senile dementia** demencia f senil

senility [sɪ'nɪlɪtɪ] N senilidad f

senior ['siːnɪə'] **🄐** ADJ **1** (in age) mayor **2** (in rank) [position, rank] superior; [partner, executive, officer] mayoritario; (in length of service) de más antigüedad; **~ management** los altos directivos **🄑** N **1** (in age) mayor mf; **he is my ~** es mayor que yo; **he's two years my ~** es dos años mayor que yo, tiene dos años más que yo **2** (in rank) superior mf, socio/a m/f más antiguo/a; **he's my ~** es mi superior **3** (Scol) alumno/a m/f de los cursos más avanzados; (US) estudiante mf del último año **🄒** CPD ➤ **senior citizen** jubilado/a m/f, persona f de la tercera edad ➤ **senior high school** (US) centro m de enseñanza superior, ≈ preparatoria f (Mex) ➤ **senior partner** socio/a m/f mayoritario/a ➤ **senior school** centro m de enseñanza secundaria

seniority [,siːnɪ'ɒrɪtɪ] N antigüedad f

sensation [sen'seɪʃən] N sensación f; **I had the ~ that I was being watched** tenía la sensación de que me estaban observando; **to be a ~** ser un éxito; **to cause a ~** causar sensación

sensational [sen'seɪʃənl] ADJ **1** [event] sensacional **2** [film, novel, newspaper] sensacionalista **3** (*) (= marvellous) sensacional, fantástico

sensationalism [sen'seɪʃnəlɪzəm] N sensacionalismo m

sensationalist [sen'seɪʃnəlɪst] ADJ, N sensacionalista mf

sensationally [sen'seɪʃnəlɪ] ADV [report, describe] sensacionalmente; **it was ~ successful** tuvo un éxito sensacional; **it was ~ popular** era increíblemente popular

sense [sens] **🄐** N **1** (= sight, taste etc) sentido m; **~ of hearing/smell/taste/touch** sentido m del oído/olfato/gusto/tacto; **~ of sight** sentido m de la vista **2** (= feeling) sensación f; **I felt a terrible ~ of loss** sentí un tremendo vacío; **to get/have a ~ that** tener la impresión de que; **I lost all ~ of time** perdí la noción del tiempo **3** (= good judgement) sentido m común; **to talk ~** hablar con sentido común, hablar con juicio; **to make sb see ~** hacer que algn entre en razón **4 to make ~** (= be advisable) ser conveniente; (= be comprehensible, logical) tener sentido; **it makes ~ to me** a mí me parece lógico; **it doesn't make ~** or **it makes no ~** no tiene sentido; **to make ~ of sth: I could make no ~ of what**

1127   seriously

he was saying no entendía nada de lo que decía, no podía sacar nada en claro de lo que decía
5 (= point, use) sentido m; **there's no ~ in making people unhappy** no tiene sentido disgustar a la gente
6 senses (= sanity) **to come to one's ~s** entrar en razón; **have you taken leave of your ~s?** ¿has perdido el juicio?
7 (= meaning) sentido m; (in dictionary) acepción f, significado m; **in every ~ (of the word)** en todos los sentidos (de la palabra); **in the true ~ of the word** en el verdadero sentido de la palabra; **in a ~** en cierto modo
8 (= awareness) sentido m; **~ of direction** sentido m de la orientación; **~ of humour** sentido m del humor; **he has no ~ of timing** es de lo más inoportuno
Ⓑ VT **1** (= suspect, intuit) presentir; **he looked about him, sensing danger** miró a su alrededor, presintiendo peligro; **he ~d that he wasn't wanted** notó que estaba de más **2** (= be conscious of) percibir; **the horse can ~ your fear** el caballo percibe si tienes miedo

senseless ['senslɪs] ADJ **1** [waste, violence etc] sin sentido; **it is ~ to protest** no tiene sentido protestar **2** (= unconscious) sin sentido, inconsciente; **to knock sb ~** derribar a algn y dejarle sin sentido

sensibility [ˌsensɪ'bɪlɪtɪ] N **1** sensibilidad f (**to** a) **2 sensibilities** susceptibilidad fsing

sensible ['sensəbl] ADJ **1** (= having good sense) sensato; **she's a very ~ girl** es una chica muy sensata **2** (= reasonable) [act] prudente; [decision] lógico; [clothing, shoes] práctico; **that is very ~ of you** en eso haces muy bien, me parece muy lógico

⚠ **sensible** ≠ *sensible*

sensibly ['sensəblɪ] ADV (= carefully) con sensatez; (= wisely) prudentemente; **try to behave ~** intenta comportarte como es debido

sensitive ['sensɪtɪv] ADJ **1** (= emotionally aware, responsive) sensible **2** (= touchy) [person] susceptible **3** (= delicate) [issue] delicado; [region] conflictivo **4** [skin] delicado, sensible; [teeth] sensible

sensitivity [ˌsensɪ'tɪvɪtɪ] N **1** (= emotional awareness) sensibilidad f (**to** a) **2** (= touchiness) susceptibilidad f (**to** a) **3** (= delicate nature) [of subject] lo delicado

sensitize ['sensɪtaɪz] VT sensibilizar

sensor ['sensə'] N sensor m

sensory ['sensərɪ] ADJ sensorial, sensorio ➤ **sensory deprivation** aislamiento m sensorial

sensual ['sensjʊəl] ADJ sensual

sensuous ['sensjʊəs] ADJ sensual, sensitivo

sent [sent] PT, PP of **send**

sentence ['sentəns] **Ⓐ** N **1** (Ling) frase f, oración f **2** (Jur) sentencia f, fallo m; **a ~ of ten years** una condena de diez años; **the judge gave him a six-month ~** el juez le condenó a seis meses de prisión; **a long ~** una larga condena; **to pass ~ on sb** condenar a algn (a una pena) **Ⓑ** VT condenar (**to** a); **to ~ sb to death** condenar a muerte a algn

sentiment ['sentɪmənt] N **1** (= feeling) sentimiento m **2** (= opinion, thought) opinión f, juicio m **3** (= sentimentality) sentimentalismo m, sensiblería f

sentimental [ˌsentɪ'mentl] ADJ sentimental; (pej) sentimental, sensiblero

sentimentality [ˌsentɪmen'tælɪtɪ] N sentimentalismo m, sensiblería f

sentry ['sentrɪ] N centinela mf, guardia mf ➤ **sentry box** garita f de centinela ➤ **sentry duty to be on ~ duty** estar de guardia

Seoul [səʊl] N Seúl m

Sep. ABBR (= September) sep., set.

separate Ⓐ ['seprɪt] ADJ (= apart) separado; (= different) distinto, diferente; (= distant) apartado, retirado; **we sat at ~ tables** nos sentamos en mesas distintas; **could we have ~ bills?** queremos cuentas individuales, ¿podemos pagar por separado?; **they live very ~ lives** viven vidas independientes el uno del otro, cada uno vive su vida; **on ~ occasions** en

diversas ocasiones; **they went their ~ ways** fueron cada uno por su lado
Ⓑ ['seprɪt] N **separates** (= clothes) coordinados mpl
Ⓒ ['sepəreɪt] VT (= keep apart) separar; (= set aside) apartar; (= divide) dividir, partir; **he is ~d from his wife** está separado de su mujer
Ⓓ ['sepəreɪt] VI separarse
➤ **separate out** VT + ADV (= set apart) apartar

separately ['seprɪtlɪ] ADV por separado

separation [ˌsepə'reɪʃən] N separación f

separatist ['sepərətɪst] ADJ, N separatista mf

sepia ['siːpɪə] **Ⓐ** N (= colour, ink) sepia f **Ⓑ** ADJ color sepia inv

Sept. ABBR (= September) sep., set.

September [sep'tembə'] N septiembre m, setiembre m; see **July**

septic ['septɪk] ADJ séptico; **to go ~** infectarse ➤ **septic tank** fosa f séptica, pozo m séptico

septicaemia, septicemia (US) [ˌseptɪ'siːmɪə] N septicemia f

sepulchre, sepulcher (US) ['sepəlkə'] N (poet) sepulcro m; **whited ~** sepulcro m blanqueado

sequel ['siːkwəl] N **1** (= film, book) continuación f **2** (= consequence) consecuencia f, resultado m

sequence ['siːkwəns] N **1** (= order) orden m; **in ~** en orden; **to arrange things in ~** ordenar cosas secuencialmente **2** (= series) serie f; **a ~ of events** una serie de acontecimientos **3** (Cine) secuencia f **4** (Cards) escalera f

sequential [sɪ'kwenʃəl] ADJ secuencial

sequester [sɪ'kwestə'] VT **1** (= isolate, shut up) aislar **2** (Jur) [+ property] secuestrar, confiscar

sequestrate [sɪ'kwestreɪt] VT secuestrar

sequin ['siːkwɪn] N lentejuela f

sera ['sɪərə] NPL of **serum**

Serb [sɜːb] N serbio/a m/f

Serbia ['sɜːbɪə] N Serbia f

Serbian ['sɜːbɪən] **Ⓐ** ADJ serbio **Ⓑ** N serbio/a m/f

Serbo-Croat ['sɜːbəʊ'krəʊæt], **Serbo-Croatian** ['sɜːbəʊkrəʊ'eɪʃən] **Ⓐ** ADJ serbocroata **Ⓑ** N **1** (= person) serbocroata mf **2** (Ling) serbocroata m

serenade [serə'neɪd] **Ⓐ** N serenata f, mañanitas fpl (Mex) **Ⓑ** VT dar una serenata a, cantar las mañanitas a (Mex)

serene [sə'riːn] ADJ sereno

serenity [sɪ'renɪtɪ] N serenidad f

serf [sɜːf] N siervo/a m/f (de la gleba)

serge [sɜːdʒ] N sarga f

sergeant ['sɑːdʒənt] **Ⓐ** N **1** (Mil) sargento mf; **yes, ~** sí, mi sargento **2** (Pol) oficial mf de policía **Ⓑ** CPD ➤ **sergeant major** sargento mf mayor

serial ['sɪərɪəl] **Ⓐ** N (in magazine) novela f por entregas; (on TV, radio) serial m (f in SC), serie f; (= soap opera) (on TV) telenovela f; (on radio) radio-novela f **Ⓑ** CPD [printer, interface, access] en serie ➤ **serial killer** asesino/a m/f (que comete crímenes en serie) ➤ **serial number** [of goods, machinery, banknotes etc] número m de serie

serialize ['sɪərɪəlaɪz] VT (= publish) publicar por entregas; (= show on TV) televisar por entregas

series ['sɪəriːz] N (pl ~) serie f; **a ~ of events** una serie de acontecimientos

serious ['sɪərɪəs] ADJ **1** (= not frivolous) serio; **are you ~?** ¿lo dices en serio?; **she's ~ about her studies** se toma sus estudios en serio; **is she ~ about him?** ¿va ella en serio con él?; **they haven't made a ~ attempt to solve the problem** no han intentado realmente resolver el problema
2 [problem, danger, illness, mistake] grave; **the patient's condition is ~** el paciente está grave; **to have ~ doubts about sth** tener serias dudas sobre algo; **she is in ~ trouble** está en serios apuros

seriously ['sɪərɪəslɪ] ADV **1** (= in earnest) seriamente; **we are ~ considering emigrating** estamos considerando seriamente la posibilidad de emigrar; **seriously?** ¿en serio?,

¿de verdad?; **to take sth/sb ~** tomar algo/a algn en serio **2** (= *badly*) [*damage, affect*] seriamente, gravemente; [*injured*] gravemente; **he is ~ ill** está grave, está gravemente enfermo

seriousness ['sɪərɪəsnɪs] N **1** (= *earnestness*) seriedad *f*; **in all ~** hablando en serio **2** (= *gravity*) gravedad *f*

sermon ['sɜːmən] N sermón *m*

serotonin [ˌserəʊ'təʊnɪn] N serotonina *f*

serpent ['sɜːpənt] N (*poet*) serpiente *f*, sierpe *f* (*liter*)

SERPS [sɜːps] N ABBR (*Brit*) = **state earnings-related pension scheme**

serrated [se'reɪtɪd] ADJ serrado, dentellado

serried ['serɪd] ADJ apretado

serum ['sɪərəm] N (*pl* **~s** *or* **sera**) suero *m*

servant ['sɜːvənt] N (*domestic*) criado/a *m/f*, sirviente/a *m/f*, muchacho/a *m/f*, mucamo/a *m/f* (*SC*); (*fig*) servidor(a) *m/f*

serve [sɜːv] **Ⓐ** VT **1** (= *work for*) servir a **2** (= *be used for, be useful as*) servir; **it ~s its/my purpose** viene al caso; **it ~s you right** te lo mereces, te lo tienes merecido **3** (*in shop, restaurant*) servir; **are you being ~d, madam?** ¿la están atendiendo, señora? **4** (= *complete*) cumplir, hacer; **to ~ an apprenticeship** hacer el aprendizaje; **to ~ a prison sentence ◇ ~ time** cumplir una condena *or* una pena de cárcel **5** (*Jur*) [+ *writ, summons*] entregar **6** (*Culin*) (= *be enough for*) **this recipe ~s six** esta receta es (suficiente) para seis personas **7** (*Tennis*) **to ~ the ball** servir (la bola), sacar **Ⓑ** VI **1** [*servant, soldier*] servir; **to ~ on a committee/jury** ser miembro de una comisión/un jurado **2** (*in shop*) atender **3** (= *be useful*) **to ~ for** *or* **as** servir de **4** (*Tennis*) sacar **Ⓒ** N (*Tennis etc*) servicio *m*, saque *m*; **whose ~ is it?** ¿quién saca?, ¿de quién es el servicio?
➤ **serve out** VT + ADV **1** [+ *term of office, sentence*] cumplir **2** [+ *food*] servir
➤ **serve up** VT + ADV servir

server ['sɜːvəʳ] N **1** (*Rel*) monaguillo *m* **2** (*Tennis*) jugador(a) *m/f* que tiene el saque *or* servicio **3** (*Comput*) servidor *m*

service ['sɜːvɪs] **Ⓐ** N **1** (= *period of work*) trabajo *m*; (= *work provided*) servicio *m*; **he retired after 50 years'** ~ se jubiló después de 50 años de servicio; **they provide a 24-hour ~** proporcionan un servicio de 24 horas; **to be in ~** [*maid, servant*] ser criado/a, servir **2** (= *organization, system*) servicio *m*; **the postal ~** el servicio postal; **the train ~ to Pamplona** el servicio de trenes a Pamplona **3** (= *help, use*) servicio *m*; **he died in the ~ of his country** murió en acto de servicio a su patria; **this machine will give years of ~** esta máquina durará años; **I am at your ~** estoy a su disposición; **the new buses were brought into ~ in 1995** los autobuses nuevos entraron en servicio en 1995; **to come into ~** [*vehicle, weapon*] entrar en servicio; **you have done me a great ~** me ha hecho un gran favor, me ha sido de muchísima ayuda; **to be of ~** ayudar, servir; **to be out of ~** no funcionar, estar fuera de servicio **4** (*in hotel, restaurant, shop*) servicio *m*; **"service not included"** "servicio no incluido" **5 services** (*Econ*) (= *tertiary sector*) sector *m* terciario *or* (de) servicios; (*Brit*) (*on motorway*) área *f* de servicio **6** (*Mil*) **the Services** las fuerzas armadas **7** (*Rel*) (= *mass*) misa *f*; (*other*) oficio *m* (religioso) **8** (*Aut, Mech*) revisión *f*; **to send one's car in for a ~** mandar el coche a revisar **9** (= *set of crockery*) vajilla *f*; **dinner ~** vajilla *f* **10** (*Tennis*) servicio *m*, saque *m* **Ⓑ** VT [+ *car*] revisar, hacer la revisión a; [+ *appliance*] realizar el mantenimiento de; [+ *organization, customers*] dar servicio a, proveer de servicios a **Ⓒ** CPD ➤ **service area** (*Brit*) (*on motorway*) área *f* de servicio

---

Use **el/un** not **la/una** before feminine nouns beginning with stressed **a** or **ha** like **área**.

➤ **service charge** (*in restaurant*) servicio *m*; [*of flat*] gastos *mpl* de comunidad, gastos *mpl* comunes (*LAm*) ➤ **service industry** (= *company*) empresa *f* de servicios ➤ **service provider** (*Internet*) proveedor *m* de servicios ➤ **service station** (*Brit*) gasolinera *f*, estación *f* de servicio, bencinera *f* (*Chi*), grifo *m* (*Per*)

serviceable ['sɜːvɪsəbl] ADJ (= *practical*) [*clothes etc*] práctico; (= *usable, working*) utilizable

serviceman ['sɜːvɪsmən] N (*pl* **servicemen**) militar *m*

servicing ['sɜːvɪsɪŋ] N [*of car*] revisión *f*; [*of appliance*] mantenimiento *m*

serviette [ˌsɜːvɪ'et] N (*Brit*) servilleta *f*

servile ['sɜːvaɪl] ADJ servil

serving ['sɜːvɪŋ] **Ⓐ** ADJ [*officer*] en activo **Ⓑ** N [*of meal*] servicio *m* **Ⓒ** CPD ➤ **serving dish** plato *m* de servir

sesame seeds ['sesəmɪˌsiːdz] NPL semillas *fpl* de sésamo

session ['seʃən] N **1** (= *meeting, sitting, Comput*) sesión *f* **2** (*Scol, Univ*) (= *year*) año *m* académico, curso *m* **3** (*Pol, Jur*) sesión *f*; **to be in ~** estar en sesión, estar reunido (*Sp*)

set [set] (*vb*: *pt, pp* **~**) **Ⓐ** N **1** (= *matching series*) [*of golf clubs, pens, keys*] juego *m*; [*of books, works*] colección *f*; [*of tools*] equipo *m*, estuche *m*; [*of gears*] tren *m*; (*Math*) conjunto *m*; **a chess ~** un ajedrez; **I need one more to make up the complete ~** me falta uno para completar la serie; **they are sold in ~s** se venden en juegos completos; **a ~ of kitchen utensils** una batería de cocina **2** (*Tennis*) set *m* **3** (*Elec*) aparato *m*; (*Rad*) aparato *m* de radio; (*TV*) televisor *m*, televisión *f* **4** (*Theat*) decorado *m*; (*Cine*) plató *m*; **to be on the ~** estar en el plató **5** (*often pej*) (= *group*) grupo *m*, pandilla *f* **6** (*Brit Scol*) clase *f* **Ⓑ** ADJ **1** (= *fixed*) [*price, purpose*] fijo; [*opinions*] inflexible, rígido; [*talk*] preparado de antemano; [*expression*] hecho; [*date, time*] señalado; (*Brit Scol*) [*books, subjects*] obligatorio; **to be ~ in one's ways** tener costumbres profundamente arraigadas; **a ~ phrase** una frase hecha; **~ piece** (*Art*) grupo *m*; (*Literat etc*) escena *f* importante **2** (= *determined*) resuelto, decidido; **to be (dead) ~ against (doing) sth** oponerse (completamente) a (hacer) algo; **to be (dead) ~ on (doing) sth** estar (completamente) decidido a *or* empeñado en (hacer) algo **3** (= *ready*) listo; **to be all ~ to do sth** estar listo para hacer algo **Ⓒ** VT **1** (= *place, put*) poner; **the film is ~ in Rome** la película se desarrolla *or* está ambientada en Roma; **a novel ~ in Madrid** una novela ambientada en Madrid; **what value do you ~ on it?** ¿en cuánto lo valoras?; (*fig*) ¿qué valor tiene para ti? **2** (= *arrange*) poner, colocar; (= *adjust*) [+ *clock*] poner en hora; [+ *mechanism*] ajustar; [+ *hair*] marcar, fijar; [+ *trap*] armar; **the alarm clock is ~ for seven** el despertador está puesto para las siete; **to ~ the table** poner la mesa **3** (= *mount*) [+ *gem*] engastar, montar **4** (*Med*) [+ *broken bone*] encajar, reducir **5** (*Typ*) [+ *type*] componer **6** (= *fix, establish*) [+ *date, limit*] fijar, señalar; [+ *record*] establecer; [+ *fashion*] imponer; [+ *dye, colour*] fijar; **to ~ one's heart on sth** tener algo como máximo deseo; **the meeting is ~ for Tuesday** (*US*) la reunión se celebrará el martes; **to ~ a record of ten seconds** establecer un récord de diez segundos; **to ~ a time for a meeting** fijar una hora para una reunión; **to ~ an exam in French** (*Brit*) preparar un examen de francés **7** (= *assign*) [+ *task*] dar; **to ~ sb a task** dar a algn una tarea que hacer **8** (= *cause to start*) **the noise ~ the dogs barking** el ruido hizo ladrar a los perros; **to ~ a fire** (*US*) provocar un incendio; **to ~ sth going** poner algo en marcha; **to ~ sb to work** poner a algn a trabajar **9** (= *cause to pursue*) **to ~ a dog on sb** azuzar un perro contra algn **Ⓓ** VI **1** [*sun, moon*] ponerse **2** [*concrete, glue*] endurecerse **3** (*Med*) [*broken bone*] [*limb*] componerse **4** [*jelly, jam*] cuajarse

5 (= *begin*) **to ~ to work** ponerse a trabajar
🅔 CPD ➤ **set point** (*Tennis*) punto *m* de set ➤ **set square**
escuadra *f*; (*with two equal sides*) cartabón *m*
➤ **set about** VI + PREP [+ *task*] empezar; **to ~ about doing sth**
ponerse a hacer algo
➤ **set against** VT + PREP **1** (= *turn against*) **to ~ sb against sb**
enemistar a algn contra algn **2** (= *balance against*)
comparar con
➤ **set apart** VT + ADV (*lit*) separar (**from** de); **his genius ~ him
apart from his contemporaries** destacó de entre sus
contemporáneos por su genialidad
➤ **set aside** VT + ADV **1** (= *separate*) [+ *book, work*] poner
aparte, apartar **2** (= *save*) [+ *money, time*] reservar, guardar
3 (= *put to one side*) [+ *differences, quarrels*] dejar de lado
➤ **set back** VT + ADV **1** [+ *project, process*] retrasar **2** (= *place
apart*) apartar; **a house ~ back from the road** una casa
apartada de la carretera **3** (*) (= *cost*) costar; **the dinner ~
me back £40** la cena me costó 40 libras
➤ **set down** VT + ADV **1** (= *put down*) [+ *object*] dejar;
[+ *passenger*] bajar, dejar **2** (= *record*) poner por escrito
➤ **set forth 🅐** VT + ADV [+ *theory*] exponer, explicar **🅑** VI
+ ADV = **set out A**
➤ **set in** VI + ADV [*bad weather*] establecerse; **the rain has ~ in
for the night** la lluvia continuará toda la noche; **the
reaction ~ in after the war** la reacción se afianzó después de
la guerra
➤ **set off 🅐** VI + ADV (= *leave*) salir, partir (*esp LAm*); **to ~ off
on a journey** salir de viaje **🅑** VT + ADV **1** (= *start*) provocar,
desencadenar; **that was what ~ off the riot** eso fue lo que
provocó or desencadenó el motín **2** [+ *burglar alarm*] hacer
sonar; [+ *bomb*] hacer estallar, explotar **3** (= *enhance*)
resaltar
➤ **set on** VI + PREP (= *attack*) agredir, atacar
➤ **set out 🅐** VI + ADV salir, partir (*esp LAm*) (**for** para; **from**
de); **to ~ out to do sth** proponerse hacer algo; **we did not ~
out to do that** no teníamos esa intención al principio
🅑 VT + ADV [+ *goods*] exponer; [+ *reasons, ideas*] presentar,
exponer
➤ **set to** VI + ADV (= *start*) empezar; (= *start working*) ponerse
(resueltamente) a trabajar
➤ **set up 🅐** VI + ADV **to ~ up in business** establecerse en un
negocio
🅑 VT + ADV **1** (= *place in position*) [+ *chairs, tables etc*]
disponer, colocar; **to ~ up camp** acampar
2 [+ *school, business, company*] establecer, fundar;
[+ *committee*] poner en marcha; [+ *inquiry*] constituir;
[+ *fund*] crear; [+ *infection*] causar, producir; **to ~ up house**
establecerse, poner casa; **to ~ up shop** (*Comm*) poner (un)
negocio; **to ~ sb up in business** poner un negocio a algn,
establecer a algn; **now he's ~ up for life** ahora tiene el
porvenir asegurado
3 (= *pose*) **to ~ o.s. up as sth** presumir de algo, dárselas de
algo
4 (*) (= *frame*) tender una trampa a
5 (*) (= *lure into a trap*) engañar, llevar al huerto a*
➤ **set upon** VI + PREP = **set on**

set-aside ['sɛtəsaɪd] N (*Agr*) retirada *f* de tierras, abandono
m de tierras; **~ land** tierra *f* en barbecho

setback ['sɛtbæk] N revés *m*

settee [sɛ'tiː] N sofá *m*

setter ['sɛtəʳ] N (= *dog*) setter *m*, perro *m* de muestra

setting ['sɛtɪŋ] **🅐** N **1** [*of novel etc*] escenario *m*; [*of jewels*]
engaste *m*, montura *f* **2** (*Mus*) arreglo *m* **3** [*of controls*]
ajuste *m* **🅑** CPD ➤ **setting lotion** fijador *m* (para el pelo)

settle ['sɛtl] **🅐** VT **1** (= *resolve*) [+ *dispute, problem*] resolver;
the result was ~d in the first half el resultado se decidió en
el primer tiempo; **so that's ~d then** así que ya está
decidido; **the couple have ~d their differences** la pareja ha
resuelto sus diferencias
2 (= *make comfortable*) [+ *person*] poner cómodo,
acomodar; **I'd just got the baby ~d when ...** acababa de
acostar al bebé cuando ...; **it took a long time to get ~d in
our new home** nos costó mucho instalarnos en la nueva
casa
3 (= *colonize*) [+ *land*] colonizar
4 (= *calm*) [+ *nerves*] calmar, sosegar; [+ *doubts*] disipar,
desvanecer; [+ *stomach*] asentar

5 (= *pay*) [+ *bill*] pagar; [+ *debt*] saldar, liquidar
6 (*) (= *deal with*) [+ *person*] **I'll soon ~ him** ya me encargaré
de ponerlo en su sitio*
🅑 VI **1** (= *establish o.s.*) (*in a house*) instalarse; (*in a country*)
establecerse
2 (= *come to rest*) [*bird, insect*] posarse; [*dust*] asentarse;
[*snow*] cuajar
3 (= *sink*) [*sediment*] depositarse; [*building*] asentarse
4 (= *get comfortable*) (*in chair*) arrellanarse; (*in new job,
routine*) adaptarse, establecerse
5 (= *calm down*) [*weather*] estabilizarse, asentarse; [*situation*]
volver a la normalidad, normalizarse
6 (= *reach an agreement*) llegar a un acuerdo or arreglo
7 (= *pay*) **I'll ~ with you on Friday** te pagaré el viernes,
ajustaremos cuentas el viernes
➤ **settle down 🅐** VI + ADV **1** (= *get comfortable*) ponerse
cómodo, acomodarse **2** (= *calm down*) calmarse,
tranquilizarse **3** (= *adopt a stable life*) echar raíces; **why
don't you ~ down and get married?** ¿por qué no sientas
cabeza y te casas?* **4** (= *get back to normal*) [*situation*] volver
a la normalidad, normalizarse **🅑** VT + ADV **1** (= *make
comfortable*) poner cómodo, acomodar; **he ~d the children
down for the night** acostó a los niños **2** (= *calm down*)
calmar, tranquilizar
➤ **settle for** VI + PREP **1** (= *accept*) conformarse con
2 (= *choose*) decidirse por, escoger
➤ **settle in** VI + ADV (*in new home, hotel*) instalarse; (*in new
job, school*) adaptarse
➤ **settle on** VI + PREP (= *choose*) decidirse por, escoger
➤ **settle up** VI + ADV ajustar cuentas (**with sb** con algn)

settled ['sɛtld] ADJ **1** (= *fixed, established*) [*ideas, opinions*]
fijo; [*order, rhythm*] estable; [*team*] fijo, estable; **to feel ~** (*in
a place, job*) sentirse adaptado **2** [*weather*] estable, asentado

settlement ['sɛtlmənt] N **1** (= *payment*) [*of bill, debt*]
liquidación *f* **2** (= *agreement*) acuerdo *m*; **to reach a ~** llegar
a un acuerdo **3** (= *colony, village*) colonia *f*, poblado *m*
4 (= *act of settling persons*) establecimiento *m*; [*of land*]
colonización *f* **5** (*Jur*) (= *sum of money*) **she accepted an
out-of-court ~ of £4,000** aceptó una compensación de
4.000 libras a cambio de no seguir adelante con el juicio

settler ['sɛtləʳ] N colonizador(a) *m/f*

set-to* ['sɛtuː] N (*Brit*) (= *fight*) pelea *f*; (= *quarrel*)
agarrada* *f*, bronca* *f*

setup* ['sɛtʌp] N **1** (= *way sth is organised*) sistema *m*; **it's
an odd ~ here** aquí todo es en un plan raro **2** (*) (= *trick,
trap*) trampa *f*, montaje* *m*

seven ['sɛvn] NUMBER siete *m*; *see* **five**

seventeen ['sɛvn'tiːn] NUMBER diecisiete *m*; *see* **five**

seventeenth ['sɛvn'tiːnθ] **🅐** ADJ decimoséptimo **🅑** PRON
(*in series*) decimoséptimo/a *m/f*; (= *fraction*) decimoséptima
parte *f*, decimoséptimo *m*; *see* **fifteenth**

seventh ['sɛvnθ] **🅐** ADJ séptimo **🅑** PRON (*in series*)
séptimo/a *m/f*; (= *fraction*) séptima parte *f*, séptimo *m*; *see*
fifth

seventieth ['sɛvntɪɪθ] **🅐** ADJ septuagésimo **🅑** PRON (*in
series*) septuagésimo/a *m/f*; (= *fraction*) septuagésima parte
f, septuagésimo *m*; *see* **fiftieth**

seventy ['sɛvntɪ] NUMBER setenta *m*; *see* **fifty**

sever ['sɛvəʳ] **🅐** VT cortar; (*fig*) [+ *relations, communications*]
romper **🅑** VI [*rope etc*] cortarse

several ['sɛvrəl] **🅐** ADJ varios; **~ times** varias veces **🅑** PRON
varios; **~ of them wore hats** varios (de ellos) llevaban
sombrero

severance ['sɛvərəns] CPD ➤ **severance package**
indemnización por despido o jubilación anticipada
➤ **severance pay** indemnización *f* por despido

severe [sɪ'vɪəʳ] ADJ (*compar* **~r**; *superl* **~st**) **1** (= *serious*)
[*problem, consequence, damage*] grave, serio; [*injury, illness*]
grave; [*defeat, shortage*] serio; [*blow, reprimand*] fuerte,
duro; [*pain, headache*] fuerte **2** (= *harsh*) [*weather, conditions,
winter*] duro, riguroso; [*cold*] extremo; [*storm, flooding, frost*]
fuerte **3** (= *strict*) [*person, penalty*] severo; [*discipline*] estricto
4 (= *austere*) [*person, appearance, expression*] severo, adusto;
[*clothes, style*] austero

severely [sɪ'vɪəlɪ] ADV **1** [*damage, disrupt, hamper*] seriamente; [*limit, restrict*] severamente; [*injure, affect*] gravemente **2** [*ill, disabled*] gravemente; [*depressed, disturbed*] profundamente **3** (= *harshly*) [*punish, reprimand, criticize*] duramente, con severidad; [*look*] con severidad

severity [sɪ'verɪtɪ] N **1** (= *seriousness*) [*of illness*] gravedad *f*, seriedad *f*; [*of pain*] intensidad *f*; [*of attack*] dureza *f* **2** (= *strictness*) [*of character, criticism*] severidad *f* **3** (= *harshness*) [*of weather, conditions, winter*] rigor *m*

Seville [sə'vɪl] N Sevilla *f* ➤ **Seville orange** naranja *f* amarga

sew [səʊ] (*pt* ~**ed**; *pp* ~**n**, ~**ed**) **Ⓐ** VT **to ~ a button on** *or* **onto sth** coser un botón a algo **Ⓑ** VI coser
➤ **sew up** VT + ADV (*gen*) coser; (*mend*) remendar; **it's all ~n up*** (*fig*) está todo arreglado

sewage ['sjuːɪdʒ] N aguas *fpl* residuales ➤ **sewage farm, sewage works** SING estación *fsing* depuradora

sewer ['sjʊəʳ] N alcantarilla *f*, albañal *m*, cloaca *f*

sewerage ['sjʊərɪdʒ] N alcantarillado *m*; (*as service on estate etc*) saneamiento *m*

sewing ['səʊɪŋ] N costura *f* ➤ **sewing machine** máquina *f* de coser

sewn [səʊn] PP *of* **sew**

sex [seks] **Ⓐ** N **1** (= *gender*) sexo *m*
2 (= *sexual activities*) sexo *m*; (= *sexual intercourse*) relaciones *fpl* sexuales; **to have ~** tener relaciones sexuales (**with** con) **Ⓑ** VT [+ *animal, bird*] sexar, determinar el sexo de **Ⓒ** CPD ➤ **sex appeal** atractivo *m* sexual, sex-appeal *m* ➤ **sex change operation** operación *f* de cambio de sexo ➤ **sex discrimination** discriminación *f* por cuestión de sexo ➤ **sex drive** libido *f*, líbido *f*, apetito *m* sexual ➤ **sex education** educación *f* sexual ➤ **sex life** vida *f* sexual ➤ **sex maniac** maníaco/a *m/f* sexual ➤ **sex object** objeto *m* sexual ➤ **sex offender** delincuente *mf* sexual ➤ **sex shop** sex-shop *m* ➤ **sex symbol** sex-símbol *mf*
➤ **sex up*** VT + ADV hacer más atractivo

sexism ['seksɪzəm] N sexismo *m*

sexist ['seksɪst] ADJ, N sexista *mf*

sextant ['sekstənt] N sextante *m*

sextet(te) [seks'tet] N (*Mus*) (= *players, composition*) sexteto *m*

sexton ['sekstən] N sacristán *m*

sextuplet ['sekstjʊplɪt] N sextillizo/a *m/f*

sexual ['seksjʊəl] ADJ sexual ➤ **sexual abuse** abuso *m* sexual ➤ **sexual assault** agresión *m* sexual ➤ **sexual discrimination** discriminación *f* a base de sexo ➤ **sexual harassment** acoso *m* sexual ➤ **sexual intercourse** relaciones *fpl* sexuales

sexuality [ˌseksjʊ'ælɪtɪ] N sexualidad *f*

sexually ['seksjʊəlɪ] ADV sexualmente; **to be ~ active** ser sexualmente activo; **to be ~ abused** ser víctima de abusos sexuales ➤ **sexually transmitted disease** enfermedad *f* de transmisión sexual

sexy ['seksɪ] ADJ (*compar* **sexier**; *superl* **sexiest**) sexy; **you look very ~ in that dress** estás muy sexy con ese vestido

Seychelles [seɪ'ʃelz] NPL Seychelles *fpl*

SF N ABBR = **science fiction**

SGML ABBR (*Internet*) (= **Standard Generalized Mark-Up Language**) LEGS *m* (*Lenguaje Estándar Generalizado de Señalamiento*)

Sgt. ABBR = **Sergeant**

shabbily ['ʃæbɪlɪ] ADV **1** [*dress*] desaliñadamente, pobremente **2** [*treat*] fatal, vilmente

shabby ['ʃæbɪ] ADJ (*compar* **shabbier**; *superl* **shabbiest**) **1** [*building*] desvencijado; [*clothes*] andrajoso; (*also* ~-**looking**) [*person*] andrajoso, desaliñado **2** [*treatment*] injusto, vil; [*behaviour*] poco honrado

shack [ʃæk] N choza *f*, jacal *m* (*CAm, Mex*)

shackle ['ʃækl] **Ⓐ** VT [+ *prisoner*] poner grilletes a, poner grillos a; (= *obstruct*) echar trabas a **Ⓑ** **shackles** NPL (= *chains*) grilletes *mpl*, grillos *mpl*; (*fig*) (= *obstruction*) trabas *fpl*

shade [ʃeɪd] **Ⓐ** N **1** (= *area of darkness*) sombra *f*; **in the ~** a la sombra; **35 degrees in the ~** 35 grados a la sombra; **to**

put sb in the ~ (*fig*) hacer sombra a algn; **to put sth in the ~** (*fig*) dejar algo en la sombra
2 [*of colour*] tono *m*, matiz *m*; (*fig*) [*of meaning, opinion*] matiz *m*
3 shades (*esp US***) (= *sunglasses*) gafas *fpl* de sol
4 (= *lampshade*) pantalla *f*; (= *eye-shade*) visera *f*; (*US*) (= *blind*) persiana *f*
5 (= *small quantity*) poquito *m*, tantito *m* (*LAm*) **Ⓑ** VT (= *protect from light*) dar sombra a; **she put up her hand to ~ her eyes (from the sun)** levantó la mano para protegerse los ojos (del sol)
➤ **shade in** VT + ADV sombrear

shading ['ʃeɪdɪŋ] N [*of colour*] sombreado *m*; [*of meaning*] matiz *m*

shadow ['ʃædəʊ] **Ⓐ** N sombra *f*; (= *darkness*) oscuridad *f*, tinieblas *fpl*; **in the ~** a la sombra; **without a ~ of a doubt** sin (la menor) sombra de duda; **to cast a ~ over sth** (*fig*) ensombrecer algo; **to live in the ~ of sth/sb** vivir eclipsado por algo/algn; **a ~ of his former self** la sombra de lo que fue **Ⓑ** VT (= *follow*) seguir y vigilar **Ⓒ** CPD ➤ **shadow boxing** boxeo *m* con un adversario imaginario; (*fig*) disputa *f* con un adversario imaginario ➤ **shadow cabinet** (*Brit Pol*) consejo *m* de ministros de la oposición; ⊃ FRONT BENCH

shadowy ['ʃædəʊɪ] ADJ (= *ill-lit*) oscuro, tenebroso; (= *blurred*) indistinto, vago, indefinido; (= *mysterious*) oscuro, misterioso

shady ['ʃeɪdɪ] ADJ (*compar* **shadier**; *superl* **shadiest**) **1** (= *shaded*) [*place*] sombreado **2** (*) (= *dubious*) [*person*] dudoso; [*deal*] turbio, chueco (*Mex***)

shaft [ʃɑːft] N **1** (= *stem, handle*) [*of arrow, spear*] astil *m*; [*of tool, golf club etc*] mango *m*; [*of cart etc*] vara *f*; **a ~ of light** un rayo de luz **2** [*of mine, lift etc*] pozo *m*

shag*** [ʃæg] VT, VI (*Brit*) joder***

shaggy ['ʃægɪ] ADJ (*compar* **shaggier**; *superl* **shaggiest**) [*hair, beard*] greñudo; [*fur, animal*] peludo ➤ **shaggy dog story** chiste *m* largo y pesado

shake [ʃeɪk] (*vb: pt* **shook**; *pp* ~**n**) **Ⓐ** N **1** (= *act of shaking*) sacudida *f*; **she gave the tin a ~** agitó la lata; **I gave the boy a good ~** zarandeé *or* sacudí bien al chico; ✦ IDIOM **in two ~s*** en un santiamén*, en un abrir y cerrar de ojos*
2 the shakes el tembleque*, la tembladera*; **to have the ~s** tener el tembleque* *or* la tembladera*
3 (*also* **milkshake**) batido *m* **Ⓑ** VT **1** (= *agitate*) [+ *bottle, tin, dice, cocktail*] agitar; [+ *towel, duster*] sacudir; [+ *head*] mover; [+ *building*] hacer temblar, sacudir; [+ *person*] zarandear, sacudir; **to ~ hands** estrecharse la mano; **to ~ hands with sb** estrechar la mano a algn; **to ~ one's head** (*in refusal*) negar con la cabeza; (*in disbelief*) mover la cabeza con gesto incrédulo; (*in dismay*) mover la cabeza con gesto de disgusto; **the dog shook itself** el perro se sacudió
2 (= *wave*) [+ *stick, paper*] blandir, agitar; **to ~ one's fist at sb** amenazar a algn con el puño
3 (*fig*) (= *weaken*) [+ *faith*] debilitar; [+ *resolve*] afectar; (= *impair, upset, shock*) afectar; (= *disconcert*) desconcertar; **he was ~n by the news of her death** la noticia de su muerte le afectó mucho *or* le conmocionó **Ⓒ** VI temblar; **he was shaking with rage/fear/cold** estaba temblando de rabia/miedo/frío; ✦ IDIOM **to ~ like a leaf** temblar como un flan
➤ **shake off** VT + ADV **1** [+ *water, snow, dust*] sacudir
2 [+ *pursuer*] zafarse de, dar esquinazo a; [+ *illness*] deshacerse de, librarse de; [+ *cold, habit*] quitarse (de encima)
➤ **shake out** VT + ADV [+ *tablecloth, bedding, rug*] sacudir; **I took off my boot and shook out a stone** me quité la bota y la sacudí para sacar una piedra
➤ **shake up** VT + ADV **1** [+ *bottle*] agitar; [+ *pillow*] sacudir
2 (= *upset*) conmocionar; **he was ~n up but not hurt** estaba en estado de shock, pero ileso **3** (= *rouse, stir*) [+ *person*] espabilar, despabilar **4** [+ *company*] reorganizar, reestructurar; [+ *system*] reformar

shaken ['ʃeɪkən] PP *of* **shake**

Shakespearean, Shakespearian [ʃeɪks'pɪərɪən] ADJ

shakespeariano

shake-up ['ʃeɪkʌp] N [of company, system] reorganización f, reestructuración f

shakily ['ʃeɪkɪlɪ] ADV [speak] con voz temblorosa; [walk] con paso vacilante; [write] con mano temblorosa

shaky ['ʃeɪkɪ] ADJ (compar **shakier**; superl **shakiest**) **1** (= trembling) [person, legs] tembloroso **2** (= wobbly) inestable, poco firme **3** (= weak) [person] débil **4** (= uncertain) [health, memory] frágil, precario; [finances] precario; [knowledge] deficiente, flojo

shale [ʃeɪl] N esquisto m

shall [ʃæl] AUX VB **I ~ go** yo iré; **no I ~ not (come)** ⋄ **no I shan't (come)** no, yo no (vendré or voy a venir); **~ I go now?** ¿me voy ahora?; **let's go in, ~ we?** ¿entramos?

shallot [ʃə'lɒt] N chalote m

shallow ['ʃæləʊ] **A** ADJ (compar **~er**; superl **~est**) **1** (gen) poco profundo, playo (SC); [dish etc] llano; **the ~ end** (of swimming pool) la parte poco profunda **2** [breathing] superficial **3** (= superficial) superficial **B shallows** NPL bajío msing, bajos mpl

sham [ʃæm] **A** ADJ falso, fingido **B** N (= imposture) farsa f; (= person) impostor(a) m/f

shaman ['ʃæmən] N chamán m

shambles ['ʃæmblz] NSING (= scene of confusion) desorden m, confusión f; **this room is a ~!** ¡esta habitación está hecha un desastre!

shambolic* [ʃæm'bɒlɪk] ADJ (Brit) caótico

shame [ʃeɪm] N **1** (= guilt) vergüenza f, pena f (LAm); **she has no sense of ~** no tiene vergüenza alguna or ninguna; **to put sb to ~** poner a algn en evidencia; **~ (on you)!** ¡qué vergüenza!, ¡vergüenza debería darte! **2** (= loss of respect) deshonra f; **to bring ~ upon sb** deshonrar a algn **3** (= pity) lástima f, pena f; **it's a ~ that ...** es una lástima or pena que + subjun; **what a ~!** ¡qué lástima!, ¡qué pena!

shamefaced ['ʃeɪmfeɪst] ADJ avergonzado, apenado (LAm)

shameful ['ʃeɪmfəl] ADJ vergonzoso

shamefully ['ʃeɪmfəlɪ] ADV vergonzosamente

shameless ['ʃeɪmlɪs] ADJ descarado, desvergonzado

shamelessly ['ʃeɪmlɪslɪ] ADV descaradamente, desvergonzadamente

shampoo [ʃæm'puː] **A** N champú m; **a ~ and set** un lavado y marcado **B** VT [+ carpet] lavar con champú; **I ~ my hair twice a week** me lavo el pelo dos veces por semana

shamrock ['ʃæmrɒk] N trébol m

shandy ['ʃændɪ] N (Brit) cerveza f con gaseosa, clara f (Sp)

shan't [ʃɑːnt] = **shall not**

shanty¹ ['ʃæntɪ] N (Brit) (also **sea ~**) saloma f

shanty² ['ʃæntɪ] N (= hut) chabola f, jacal m (Mex), bohío m (CAm), callampa f (Chi)

shantytown ['ʃæntɪˌtaʊn] N chabolas fpl (Sp), villa f miseria (Mex), (población f) callampa f (Chi), ciudad f perdida (Mex), colonia f proletaria (Mex), pueblo m joven (Per), cantegriles mpl (Uru), ranchitos mpl (Ven)

shape [ʃeɪp] **A** N **1** (= outline) forma f, figura f; (= figure) [of person] silueta f, figura f; **what ~ is it?** ¿de qué forma es?; **all ~s and sizes** todas las formas; **in the ~ of ...** (fig) en forma de ...; **to bend** or **twist sth into ~** dar forma a algo doblándolo; **to lose its ~** [sweater etc] perder la forma; **to bend** or **twist sth out of ~** deformar algo doblándolo; **to take ~** cobrar forma **2** (= undefined object) forma f, bulto m **3** (= nature, appearance) estructura f, configuración f; **the ~ of things to come** lo que nos depara el mañana; **to take ~** tomar forma **4** (= condition) forma f (física), estado m físico; **to be in bad ~** [person] estar en mala forma (física); [object] estar en mal estado; **to be in good ~** [person] estar en buena forma (física); [object] estar en buen estado; **to get o.s. into ~** ponerse en forma; **to keep in ~** mantenerse en forma; **to be out of ~** [person] estar en mala forma **B** VT **1** (= mould) dar forma a, formar **2** (= influence, determine) conformar, determinar

⊳ shape up VI + ADV [person] ir, marchar; [campaign, plan] desarrollarse; **to ~ up well** ir bien, marchar bien; **it's shaping up to be a terrible winter** (esp US) promete ser un invierno muy crudo, ya se perfila como un invierno muy crudo

-shaped ['ʃeɪpt] ADJ (ending in compounds) en forma de ...; **heart-shaped** en forma de corazón

shapeless ['ʃeɪplɪs] ADJ sin forma definida

shapely ['ʃeɪplɪ] ADJ [object] proporcionado, bien formado; [woman] con una bonita figura, con buen cuerpo; **~ legs** piernas torneadas

shard [ʃɑːd] N tiesto m, casco m, fragmento m

share [ʃɛəʳ] **A** N **1** (= portion) parte f, porción f; **a ~ of** or **in the profits** una proporción de las ganancias; **to do one's (fair) ~ (of sth)** hacer lo que a uno le toca or corresponde (de algo); **to have a ~ in sth** participar en algo; **we've had our ~ of misfortunes** hemos sufrido bastante infortunio, hemos sufrido lo nuestro **2** (Fin) acción f **B** VT **1** (= split, divide) [+ resource, benefit] repartir, dividir, partir; **would you like to ~ the bottle with me?** ¿quieres compartir la botella conmigo?; **a ~d room** una habitación compartida **2** (= accept equally) [+ duty, responsibility, task] compartir, corresponsabilizarse de **3** (= have in common) compartir; **I do not ~ that view** no comparto ese criterio; **two nations who ~ a common language** dos naciones que tienen en común or comparten la misma lengua **4** (= tell, relate) [+ piece of news, thought] contar (with sb a algn), compartir (with sb con algn) **C** VI compartir (with con); **to ~ in sth** participar en algo; **✦** IDIOM **~ and ~ alike** todos por igual **D** CPD **▸ share capital** capital m social en acciones **▸ share certificate** (certificado m or título m de una) acción f **▸ share index** índice m de la Bolsa **▸ share issue** emisión f de acciones **▸ share option** plan de compra de acciones de una empresa por sus empleados (a precios ventajosos) **▸ share price** precio m de las acciones **▸ share out** VT + ADV repartir, distribuir

shared [ʃɛəd] ADJ compartido; [facilities etc] comunitario

shareholder ['ʃɛəˌhəʊldəʳ] N accionista mf

share-out ['ʃɛəraʊt] N reparto m

shark [ʃɑːk] N tiburón m

sharp [ʃɑːp] **A** ADJ (compar **~er**; superl **~est**) **1** (= not blunt) [edge] afilado; [needle] puntiagudo; **to have a ~ point** ser muy puntiagudo **2** (= abrupt, acute) [bend, angle] cerrado; [rise, drop, turn by car] brusco **3** (of person) (= alert) avispado, perspicaz; (= unscrupulous) listo, vivo; [mind] agudo, perspicaz; **his ~ eyes spotted a free seat** sus ojos de lince vieron un asiento libre; **~ practice** artimañas fpl **4** (= brusque) [retort] seco, cortante; [rebuke, tone] áspero, severo; **to have a ~ tongue** tener la lengua afilada, tener una lengua viperina **5** (= strong) [taste] ácido; [smell, cheese] fuerte **6** (= clear, well-defined) [outline, image] nítido; [contrast] claro, marcado; [sound] claro; [features] marcado, anguloso **7** (= intense) [pain] agudo; [cold, wind] cortante; [frost] fuerte; **a ~ blow to the head** un fuerte golpe en la cabeza **8** (*) (= stylish) [suit] elegante; **he was a ~ dresser** vestía con mucha elegancia **9** (Mus) (= raised a semitone) sostenido; (= too high) demasiado alto; **C ~** do m sostenido **B** ADV **1** (= quickly, abruptly) **and be** or **look ~ about it!** ¡y date prisa! **2** (= precisely) **at five o'clock ~** a las cinco en punto **3** (Mus) demasiado alto **C** N (Mus) sostenido m

sharpen ['ʃɑːpən] VT **1** [+ tool, blade] afilar; [+ pencil] sacar punta a, afilar **2** [+ reactions] agudizar; [+ resolve] aumentar; [+ contrast] marcar; [+ appetite] abrir; [+ image] definir, hacer más nítido

sharpener ['ʃɑːpnəʳ] N (for pencil) sacapuntas m inv; (for knife) afilador m

sharp-eyed [ˈʃɑːpˈaɪd] ADJ de vista aguda

sharpish* [ˈʃɑːpɪʃ] ADV (*Brit*) rapidito*

sharply [ˈʃɑːplɪ] ADV **1** (= *abruptly*) [*fall, rise, turn, brake*] bruscamente **2** (= *clearly*) marcadamente, claramente **3** (= *brusquely*) con aspereza **4** (= *severely*) [*criticize*] severamente, con dureza **5** (= *hard*) [*strike*] fuertemente

sharpshooter [ˈʃɑːpˌʃuːtəʳ] N (*esp US*) tirador(a) *m/f* de primera

sharp-witted [ˈʃɑːpˈwɪtɪd] ADJ perspicaz, despabilado

shat*** [ʃæt] PT, PP *of* **shit**

shatter [ˈʃætəʳ] VT romper en pedazos *or* añicos, hacer pedazos *or* añicos; **to ~ sb's hopes** frustrar las esperanzas de algn; **she was ~ed by his death** su muerte la dejó destrozada

shattered [ˈʃætəd] ADJ (= *grief-stricken*) trastornado, destrozado; (*Brit**) (= *exhausted*) hecho polvo*

shattering [ˈʃætərɪŋ] ADJ [*attack, defeat*] aplastante; [*experience, news*] pasmoso; **it was a ~ blow to his hopes** deshizo sus esperanzas

shatterproof [ˈʃætəpruːf] ADJ inastillable

shave [ʃeɪv] (*vb: pt* ~**d**; *pp* ~**d, shaven**) **Ⓐ** N **to have a ~** afeitarse, rasurarse (*esp LAm*); **to have a close** *or* **narrow ~** (*fig*) salvarse de milagro *or* por los pelos; **that was a close ~!** ¡qué poco le ha faltado!, ¡(ha sido) por los pelos! **Ⓑ** VT afeitar, rasurar (*esp LAm*) **Ⓒ** VI afeitarse, rasurarse (*esp LAm*) ➤ **shave off** VT + ADV **to ~ off one's beard** afeitarse la barba

shaven [ˈʃeɪvn] ADJ afeitado

shaver [ˈʃeɪvəʳ] N máquina *f* de afeitar, rasuradora *f* eléctrica (*LAm*)

shaving [ˈʃeɪvɪŋ] **Ⓐ** N **1** (= *act of shaving*) afeitado *m*; ~ **is a nuisance** afeitarse es una lata **2** (= *piece of wood, metal etc*) viruta *f* **Ⓑ** CPD ➤ **shaving brush** brocha *f* de afeitar ➤ **shaving cream** crema *f* de afeitar ➤ **shaving foam** espuma *f* de afeitar ➤ **shaving mirror** espejo *m* de tocador (de aumento) ➤ **shaving point** enchufe *m* para máquinas de afeitar

shawl [ʃɔːl] N chal *m*, rebozo *m* (*LAm*)

she [ʃiː] **Ⓐ** PERS PRON (*emphatic, to avoid ambiguity*) ella; **you've got more money than ~ has** tienes más dinero que ella

---

Don't translate the subject pronoun when not emphasizing or clarifying:

~**'s very nice** es muy simpática **Ⓑ** N **it's a ~** (= *animal*) es hembra; (= *baby*) es una niña

sheaf [ʃiːf] N (*pl* **sheaves**) (*Agr*) gavilla *f*; [*of papers*] fajo *m*, manojo *m*

shear [ʃɪəʳ] (*pt* ~**ed**; *pp* ~**ed, shorn**) VT esquilar ➤ **shear off** **Ⓐ** VT + ADV cortar **Ⓑ** VI + ADV partirse, romperse ➤ **shear through** VI + PREP cortar

shears [ʃɪəz] NPL (*for sheep*) tijeras *fpl* de esquilar; (*for hedges, grass*) tijeras *fpl* de podar

sheath [ʃiːθ] N (*pl* ~**s** [ʃiːðz]) (*for sword*) vaina *f*, funda *f* ➤ **sheath dress** vestido *m* (de) tubo ➤ **sheath knife** cuchillo *m* de monte

sheathe [ʃiːð] VT envainar, enfundar (**in** en)

sheaves [ʃiːvz] NPL *of* **sheaf**

shed¹ [ʃed] (*pt, pp* ~) VT **1** (= *lose*) [+ *clothes, fur, leaves, skin*] despojarse de; [+ *jobs*] suprimir, recortar; [+ *tears, blood*] derramar; **the lorry ~ its load** (*Brit*) la carga cayó del camión **2** (= *send out*) [+ *warmth*] dar; [+ *light*] echar; ✦ IDIOM **to ~ light on sth** arrojar luz sobre algo

shed² [ʃed] N (*in garden*) cobertizo *m*, galpón *m* (*SC*); (*for cattle*) establo *m*; (*Ind, Rail*) nave *f*

she'd [ʃiːd] = **she would, she had**

sheen [ʃiːn] N brillo *m*, lustre *m*

sheep [ʃiːp] N (*pl* ~) oveja *f* ➤ **sheep dip** (baño *m*) desinfectante *m* para ovejas ➤ **sheep farmer** criador(a) *m/f* de ganado lanar, ganadero/a *m/f* de ovejas ➤ **sheep farming** ganadería *f* ovina *or* lanar, cría *f* de ganado ovino *or* lanar

sheepdog [ˈʃiːpdɒg] N perro *m* pastor

sheepish [ˈʃiːpɪʃ] ADJ avergonzado

sheepskin [ˈʃiːpskɪn] N piel *f* de carnero

sheer [ʃɪəʳ] **Ⓐ** ADJ (*compar* ~**er**; *superl* ~**est**) **1** (= *absolute*) puro, absoluto; **in ~ desperation** en último extremo **2** (= *transparent*) transparente, fino **3** (= *precipitous*) escarpado **Ⓑ** N (*US*) **sheers** visillos *mpl*

sheet [ʃiːt] **Ⓐ** N **1** (*also* **bedsheet**) sábana *f* **2** [*of metal, glass, plastic*] lámina *f* **3** [*of paper*] hoja *f*; [*of labels, stamps, stickers*] pliego *m*, hoja *f* **4** [*of ice, water*] capa *f*; **the rain was coming down in ~s** estaba cayendo una cortina de agua *or* lluvia, llovía a mares **Ⓑ** CPD ➤ **sheet lightning** fucilazo *m* ➤ **sheet metal** metal *m* en lámina ➤ **sheet music** (hojas *fpl* de) partitura *f*

sheik(h) [ʃeɪk] N jeque *m*

shelf [ʃelf] **Ⓐ** N (*pl* **shelves**) **1** (*fixed to wall, in shop*) estante *m*, balda *f*; (*in cupboard*) tabla *f*, anaquel *m*; (*in oven*) parrilla *f*; ✦ IDIOM **to be (left) on the ~** [*proposal etc*] quedar arrinconado; (*) [*woman*] quedarse para vestir santos **2** (*in rock face*) saliente *m*; (*underwater*) plataforma *f* **Ⓑ** CPD ➤ **shelf life** (*Comm*) tiempo *m* de durabilidad antes de la venta; ✦ IDIOM **most pop stars have a very short ~ life** la mayoría de las estrellas del pop son flor de un día *or* tienen una carrera efímera

she'll [ʃiːl] = **she will, she shall**

shell [ʃel] **Ⓐ** N **1** [*of egg, nut*] cáscara *f*; [*of tortoise, turtle*] caparazón *m*, carapacho *m*; [*of snail, shellfish*] concha *f*, caracol *m* (*LAm*); ✦ IDIOM **to come out of one's ~** salir del caparazón *or* (*LAm*) carapacho **2** [*of building, vehicle, ship*] armazón *m or f*, casco *m* **3** (= *artillery round*) obús *m*, proyectil *m*; (*US*) [*of shotgun*] cartucho *m* **Ⓑ** VT **1** [+ *peas*] pelar, desvainar **2** (*Mil*) bombardear **Ⓒ** CPD ➤ **shell game** (*US*) (= *trick*) juego consistente en adivinar en cuál de tres cubiletes se esconde un objeto, triles** *fpl*; (*fig*) (= *fraud*) artimaña *f* ➤ **shell shock** neurosis *f inv* de guerra ➤ **shell suit** tipo de chandal ➤ **shell out*** **Ⓐ** VI + ADV soltar el dinero; **to ~ out for sth** desembolsar para pagar algo **Ⓑ** VT + ADV [+ *money*] desembolsar

shellfish [ˈʃelfɪʃ] N (*pl* ~) (*Zool*) crustáceo *m*; (*as food*) marisco(s) *m(pl)*

shelling [ˈʃelɪŋ] N bombardeo *m*

shell-shocked [ˈʃelʃɒkt] ADJ que padece neurosis de guerra

shelter [ˈʃeltəʳ] **Ⓐ** N **1** (= *protection*) protección *f*, refugio *m*; **to seek ~ (from)** (*rain, sun*) buscar dónde protegerse (de); (*persecution*) buscar dónde refugiarse (de); **to take ~** refugiarse, guarecerse **2** (= *accommodation*) alojamiento *m* **3** (= *construction*) (*on mountain*) refugio *m*, albergue *m*; (*for homeless people, battered women*) refugio *m*, centro *m* de acogida **Ⓑ** VT **1** (= *protect*) proteger (**from** de) **2** (= *hide*) [+ *fugitive*] esconder, ocultar, dar asilo a **Ⓒ** VI refugiarse, guarecerse (**from** de)

sheltered [ˈʃeltəd] ADJ protegido; ~ **housing** residencia *f* vigilada (*para ancianos*); **she has led a very ~ life** ha tenido una vida muy protegida, ha vivido entre algodones

shelve [ʃelv] **Ⓐ** VT (= *postpone*) dar carpetazo a **Ⓑ** VI (= *slope away*) formar declive

shelves [ʃelvz] NPL *of* **shelf**

shelving [ˈʃelvɪŋ] N estantería *f*

shepherd [ˈʃepəd] **Ⓐ** N pastor *m* **Ⓑ** VT **to ~ sb in/out** acompañar a algn al entrar/salir **Ⓒ** CPD ➤ **shepherd's pie** (*Brit*) pastel *m* de carne con patatas

shepherdess [ˈʃepədɪs] N pastora *f*, zagala *f*

sherbet [ˈʃɜːbət] N **1** (*Brit*) (= *powder*) polvos *mpl* azucarados **2** (*US*) (= *water ice*) sorbete *m*

sheriff [ˈʃerɪf] N (*in US*) alguacil *m*, sheriff *m*

sherry [ˈʃerɪ] N jerez *m*

she's [ʃiːz] = **she is, she has**

Shetland [ˈʃetlənd] CPD ➤ **the Shetland Islands, the Shetlands** las Islas Shetland

shhh [ʃ:] EXCL ¡chitón!

Shia, Shiah [ˈʃiːə] ⓐ N (also ~ **Muslim**) chiíta mf ⓑ ADJ chiíta

shield [ʃiːld] ⓐ N **1** (armour) escudo m **2** (US) (= badge) [of policeman] placa f ⓑ VT proteger (**from** de); **to ~ one's eyes** taparse los ojos

shift [ʃɪft] ⓐ N **1** (= change) cambio m
2 (= period of work) turno m; (= group of workers) tanda f; **day/night ~** turno m de día/noche; **to work (in) ~s** trabajar por turnos; **I work an eight-hour ~** trabajo or hago turnos de ocho horas
3 (US Aut) (= gear shift) palanca f de cambio
4 (= dress) vestido m suelto
ⓑ VT **1** (= move) mover; **to ~ scenery** (Theat) cambiar el decorado; **she ~ed her weight to the other leg** cambió el peso a la otra pierna, volcó su peso sobre la otra pierna
2 (Brit) (= sell) [+ stock] deshacerse de, vender
3 (= get rid of) [+ cold] quitarse (de encima); [+ stain] quitar
4 (US Aut) [+ gear] cambiar de
ⓒ VI **1** (= move) [person] moverse; [load] correr
2 (= change) [wind] cambiar de dirección; [attitudes, mood] cambiar; **the scene ~s to Burgos** la escena se traslada a Burgos; **we couldn't get him to ~** no logramos hacerle cambiar de actitud
3 (Brit*) (= move quickly) volar
4 (US Aut) **to ~ into high/low gear** cambiar a una velocidad or marcha más alta/baja
ⓓ CPD ➤ **shift key** tecla f de mayúsculas ➤ **shift work** trabajo m por turnos ➤ **shift worker** trabajador(a) m/f por turnos
➤ **shift down** VI + ADV (US Aut) cambiar a una velocidad or marcha inferior
➤ **shift up** VI + ADV (US Aut) cambiar a una velocidad or marcha superior

shifting [ˈʃɪftɪŋ] ADJ [sand] movedizo; [winds, values, attitudes] cambiante

shiftless [ˈʃɪftlɪs] ADJ holgazán, perezoso, flojo (esp LAm)

shifty [ˈʃɪftɪ] ADJ (compar **shiftier**; superl **shiftiest**) [look] furtivo; [person, behaviour] sospechoso

Shiite, Shi'ite [ˈʃiːaɪt] ADJ, N chiíta mf

shilling [ˈʃɪlɪŋ] N (Brit) chelín m

shilly-shally [ˈʃɪlɪˌʃælɪ] VI vacilar, titubear

shimmer [ˈʃɪmər] VI rielar, relucir

shimmering [ˈʃɪmərɪŋ], **shimmery** [ˈʃɪmərɪ] ADJ reluciente

shin [ʃɪn] ⓐ N espinilla f ⓑ VI **to ~ up/down a tree** trepar a/bajar de un árbol ⓒ CPD ➤ **shin pad** espinillera f

shinbone [ˈʃɪnbəʊn] N tibia f

shindig [ˈʃɪndɪg] N juerga* f

shine [ʃaɪn] (vb: pt, pp **shone**) ⓐ N brillo m, lustre m; **to give sth a ~** sacar brillo a algo; **to take the ~ off sth** deslustrar algo; (fig) deslucir algo, quitar a algo su encanto; ✦ IDIOM **to take a ~ to sb*** tomar simpatía por algn ⓑ VI [sun, light] brillar; [metal] relucir; **her face shone with happiness** su cara irradiaba felicidad ⓒ VT **1 to ~ a light on sth** echar luz sobre algo **2** (pt, pp **~d**) (= polish) sacar brillo a, pulir

shingle [ˈʃɪŋgl] N (on beach) guijarros mpl; (on roof) tablilla f; (US) (= signboard) placa f

shingles [ˈʃɪŋglz] NPL (Med) herpes msing (zoster)

shinguard [ˈʃɪngɑːd] N espinillera f

shining [ˈʃaɪnɪŋ] ADJ [surface, light] brillante; [face] radiante; [hair] brillante, lustroso; [eyes] brillante, chispeante; ✦ IDIOM **a ~ example** un ejemplo perfecto

Shinto [ˈʃɪntəʊ] N shinto m

shiny [ˈʃaɪnɪ] ADJ (compar **shinier**; superl **shiniest**) brillante

ship [ʃɪp] ⓐ N (gen) barco m; (for cargo, also Mil) buque m, navío m; ✦ IDIOM **~s that pass in the night** personas que pasan por la vida y desaparecen ⓑ VT (= transport) enviar, consignar ⓒ CPD ➤ **ship canal** canal m de navegación
➤ **ship off** VT + ADV expedir

➤ **ship out** VT + ADV enviar, mandar

shipbuilder [ˈʃɪpˌbɪldər] N constructor(a) m/f naval

shipbuilding [ˈʃɪpˌbɪldɪŋ] N construcción f naval

shipload [ˈʃɪpləʊd] N cargamento m

shipmate [ˈʃɪpmeɪt] N compañero/a m/f de tripulación

shipment [ˈʃɪpmənt] N (= act) transporte m, embarque m; (= load) consignación f

shipowner [ˈʃɪpˌəʊnər] N naviero/a m/f, armador(a) m/f

shipper [ˈʃɪpər] N empresa f naviera

shipping [ˈʃɪpɪŋ] ⓐ N **1** (= ships) barcos mpl, buques mpl; (= fleet) flota f; **a danger to ~** un peligro para la navegación **2** (= transporting) transporte m (en barco), embarque m; (= sending) envío m ⓑ CPD ➤ **shipping company, shipping line** compañía f naviera ➤ **shipping lane** ruta f de navegación

shipshape [ˈʃɪpʃeɪp] ADJ en buen orden

shipwreck [ˈʃɪprek] ⓐ N (= event) naufragio m; (= wrecked ship) buque m naufragado, nave f or embarcación f naufragada ⓑ VT **to be ~ed** naufragar; **a ~ed sailor** un marinero náufrago; **a ~ed vessel** un buque naufragado

shipwright [ˈʃɪpraɪt] N carpintero m de navío

shipyard [ˈʃɪpjɑːd] N astillero m

shire [ˈʃaɪər] N (Brit) condado m ➤ **shire horse** (Brit) ≈ percherón/ona m/f

shirk [ʃɜːk] ⓐ VT [+ duty] esquivar, zafarse de ⓑ VI gandulear

shirker [ˈʃɜːkər] N gandul(a) m/f, flojo/a m/f (LAm)

shirt [ʃɜːt] N camisa f ➤ **shirt sleeves: to be in (one's) ~ sleeves** estar en mangas de camisa ➤ **shirt tail** faldón m (de camisa)

shirtwaist [ˈʃɜːtweɪst] N (US) blusa f (de mujer)

shirty [ˈʃɜːtɪ] ADJ (compar **shirtier**; superl **shirtiest**) (Brit) **he was pretty ~ about it*** no le gustó nada, no le cayó en gracia

shit* [ʃɪt] (vb: pt, pp ~ or **shat**) ⓐ N (= excrement) mierda*** f; (= nonsense) gilipolleces*** fpl; (= person) mierda*** m ⓑ VI cagar***

shiver [ˈʃɪvər] ⓐ N (with cold) tiritón m; [of horror etc] escalofrío m; **it sent ~s down my spine** me dio escalofríos ⓑ VI (with cold) tiritar; (with emotion) temblar, estremecerse

shivery [ˈʃɪvərɪ] ADJ (= feverish) destemplado

shoal [ʃəʊl] N [of fish] banco m

shock¹ [ʃɒk] ⓐ N **1** (emotional) conmoción f, golpe m, impresión f; (= start) susto m; **the ~ killed him** la impresión le mató; **to come as a ~** resultar sorprendente or asombroso, causar estupefacción; **to get a ~** llevarse or pegarse un susto
2 (= impact) sacudida f; (= shake-up) choque m, sacudida f; **~ resistant** antichoque; **it was a ~ to the establishment** sacudió el sistema, fue un serio golpe para el sistema
3 (Elec) descarga f; **she got a ~ from the refrigerator** la nevera le dio una descarga or un calambre
4 (Med) shock m, postración f nerviosa; **to be suffering from ~** ◇ **be in (a state of)** ~ estar en estado de shock, padecer una postración nerviosa
ⓑ VT **1** (= startle) sobresaltar, asustar
2 (= affect emotionally) (= upset) conmover, chocar; (= offend) escandalizar; **easily ~ed** que se escandaliza por nada
ⓒ CPD ➤ **shock absorber** (Aut) amortiguador m ➤ **shock jock*** presentador(a) polémico/a de coloquios radiofónicos abiertos al público ➤ **shock tactics** (fig) provocación f ➤ **shock therapy, shock treatment** (Med) (also **electric ~ treatment**) tratamiento m por electrochoque ➤ **shock troops** guardias mpl de asalto ➤ **shock wave** onda f de choque

shock² [ʃɒk] N (also ~ **of hair**) mata f de pelo

shocking [ˈʃɒkɪŋ] ⓐ ADJ **1** (= extremely bad) pésimo, espantoso **2** (= appalling) espeluznante, espantoso; **the ~ truth** la sobrecogedora verdad **3** (= outrageous) escandaloso

B CPD ➤ **shocking pink** rosa *m* estridente, rosa *m* fosforito

shod [ʃɒd] PT, PP *of* **shoe**

shoddy ['ʃɒdɪ] ADJ (*compar* **shoddier**; *superl* **shoddiest**) [*merchandise, product*] de baja calidad, de pacotilla; [*work, service*] chapucero

shoe [ʃuː] (*vb: pt, pp* **shod**) **A** N zapato *m*; (*for horse*) herradura *f*; **to put on one's ~s** ponerse los zapatos, calzarse (*frm*); **to take off one's ~s** quitarse los zapatos, descalzarse (*frm*); ✦ IDIOMS **I wouldn't like to be in his ~s** no quisiera estar en su lugar *or* pellejo; **to step into sb's ~s** pasar a ocupar el puesto de algn
B VT [+ *horse*] herrar
C CPD ➤ **shoe brush** cepillo *m* para zapatos ➤ **shoe polish** betún *m*, lustre *m* (*LAm*) ➤ **shoe repairer** zapatero/a *m/f* remendón/ona ➤ **shoe shop** (*esp Brit*), **shoe store** (*US*) zapatería *f* ➤ **shoe size** número *m* (de zapato) ➤ **shoe tree** horma *f*

shoehorn ['ʃuːhɔːn] N calzador *m*

shoelace ['ʃuːleɪs] N cordón *m*, pasador *m* (*And*)

shoemaker ['ʃuːˌmeɪkəʳ] N zapatero/a *m/f*

shoeshine ['ʃuːʃaɪn] N (*US*) **to have a ~** hacerse limpiar los zapatos ➤ **shoeshine boy**, **shoeshine man** limpiabotas *m inv*, lustrabotas *m inv* (*LAm*), bolero *m* (*Mex*), embolador *m* (*Col*)

shoestring ['ʃuːstrɪŋ] N (*US*) cordón *m*, lazo *m*; ✦ IDIOM **to do sth on a ~** hacer algo con muy poco dinero ➤ **shoestring budget** presupuesto *m* muy limitado

shone [ʃɒn] PT, PP *of* **shine**

shoo [ʃuː] EXCL ¡fuera!, ¡zape!, ¡ándale! (*Mex*)

shoo-in* ['ʃuːɪn] N (*US*) **it's a ~** es (cosa de) coser y cantar; **he's a ~ for the presidency** es el favorito para hacerse con la presidencia, es el más firme candidato a la presidencia

shook [ʃʊk] PT *of* **shake**

shoot [ʃuːt] (*vb: pt, pp* **shot**) **A** N **1** (*Bot*) brote *m*, retoño *m*
2 (*Cine*) rodaje *m*; (*Phot*) sesión *f* fotográfica
3 (= *shooting party*) cacería *f*, partida *f* de caza
B VT **1** (= *wound*) pegar un tiro a; (= *kill*) matar de un tiro; (*more brutally*) matar a tiros; (= *execute*) fusilar; (= *hunt*) cazar; **he was shot as a spy** lo fusilaron por espía; **to ~ sb in the back** disparar a algn por la espalda; **to ~ sb dead** matar a algn de un tiro *or* a tiros; ✦ IDIOM **to ~ o.s. in the foot** cavar su propia fosa sin darse cuenta
2 (= *launch*) [+ *bullet, gun, arrow*] disparar; [+ *missile*] lanzar
3 (= *propel*) [+ *object*] lanzar (**at** hacia); **the impact shot them forward** el impacto hizo que salieran despedidos hacia delante
4 (*fig*) [+ *glance, look*] lanzar; [+ *smile*] dedicar; ✦ IDIOMS **to ~ the breeze** (*US***) darle a la lengua*; **to ~ one's mouth off*** irse de la lengua*, hablar más de la cuenta*
5 (*Cine*) rodar, filmar; (*Phot*) [+ *subject of picture*] tomar, sacar
6 to ~ the lights (*Aut**) saltarse un semáforo en rojo
C VI **1** (*with gun*) disparar, tirar; (*esp Brit*) (= *hunt*) cazar; **to ~ at sth/sb** disparar a algo/algn; **to ~ to kill** disparar a matar, tirar a matar; **to go ~ing** ir de caza
2 (*in ball games*) (*gen*) tirar; (*Ftbl*) disparar, chutar
3 (= *move rapidly*) **to ~ by** pasar como un rayo; **flames shot 100ft into the air** las llamas saltaron por los aires a 100 pies de altura; **to ~ past** pasar como un rayo; **to ~ to fame** lanzarse a la fama; **the pain went ~ing up his arm** un dolor punzante le subía por el brazo
4 (*Cine*) rodar, filmar
➤ **shoot down** VT + ADV [+ *aeroplane*] derribar; [+ *person*] matar a tiros, balear (*LAm*); (*fig*) [+ *argument*] echar por tierra
➤ **shoot out** **A** VT + ADV (= *move rapidly*) [+ *hand*] sacar rápidamente **B** VI + ADV (= *come out suddenly*) [*person, animal*] salir disparado
➤ **shoot up** VI + ADV **1** [*prices, value, temperature*] dispararse; [*hand, head*] alzarse de repente; [*smoke, flames, water*] salir disparado **2** [*plant*] crecer rápidamente; **your son's shot up over the last few months** tu hijo ha dado un estirón en estos últimos meses* **3** (*) [*drug user*] chutarse*, pincharse*

shooter ['ʃuːtəʳ] N (= *person*) tirador(a) *m/f*; (**) (= *gun*)

arma *f* (de fuego)

> Use **el/un** not **la/una** before feminine nouns beginning with stressed **a** or **ha** like **arma**.

shooting ['ʃuːtɪŋ] **A** N **1** (= *shots*) tiros *mpl*, disparos *mpl*; (= *continuous shooting*) tiroteo *m*, balacera *f* (*LAm*)
2 (= *murder*) asesinato *m*; (= *execution*) fusilamiento *m*
3 [*of film*] rodaje *m*, filmación *f* **4** (*esp Brit*) (= *hunting*) caza *f*
B ADJ [*pain*] punzante **C** CPD ➤ **shooting gallery** barraca *f* de tiro al blanco ➤ **shooting star** estrella *f* fugaz
➤ **shooting stick** bastón *m* taburete

shoot-out ['ʃuːtaʊt] N tiroteo *m*, balacera *f* (*LAm*)

shop [ʃɒp] **A** N (*esp Brit*) (= *store*) tienda *f*; (= *workshop*) taller *m*; **he's just gone (round) to the ~s** acaba de salir a comprar; **to set up ~** montar un negocio, establecerse; **to shut up ~** (*Brit*) cerrar; **to talk ~*** hablar de trabajo, hablar de negocios; ✦ IDIOM **all over the ~** (*Brit***) en *or* por todas partes
B VI comprar, hacer compras; **to go ~ping** ir de compras *or* de tiendas
C VT (*Brit***) (= *inform on*) delatar
D CPD ➤ **shop assistant** (*Brit*) dependiente/a *m/f*, empleado/a *m/f* de una tienda ➤ **shop floor** (*Brit*) taller *m*; (*bigger*) planta *f* de producción ➤ **shop front** (*Brit*) fachada *f* de la tienda ➤ **shop steward** (*Brit Ind*) enlace *mf* sindical ➤ **shop talk*** charla *f* sobre el trabajo ➤ **shop window** (*esp Brit*) escaparate *m*, vitrina *f*, vidriera *f* (*SC*)
➤ **shop around** VI + ADV comparar precios

shopaholic* [ʃɒpə'hɒlɪk] N comprador(a) *m/f* obsesivo/a, adicto/a *m/f* a las compras

shopkeeper ['ʃɒpˌkiːpəʳ] N (*Brit*) tendero/a *m/f*

shoplift ['ʃɒplɪft] VI hurtar en tiendas

shoplifter ['ʃɒpˌlɪftəʳ] N ratero/a *m/f*, ladrón/ona *m/f* (de tiendas)

shoplifting ['ʃɒpˌlɪftɪŋ] N ratería *f*

shopper ['ʃɒpəʳ] N (= *person*) comprador(a) *m/f*; (= *customer*) cliente *mf*

shopping ['ʃɒpɪŋ] N (= *act of buying*) compra *f*; (= *goods bought*) compras *fpl*; **I like** ~ me gusta ir de tiendas; **to do the ~** hacer la compra; **to go ~** ir de tiendas *or* de compras ➤ **shopping bag** bolsa *f* de compras ➤ **shopping cart** (*US*) carrito *m* de la compra ➤ **shopping centre** (*Brit*) centro *m* comercial ➤ **shopping channel** canal *m* de televentas ➤ **shopping list** lista *f* de compras ➤ **shopping mall** (*esp US*) centro *m* comercial ➤ **shopping precinct** (*Brit*) centro *m* comercial ➤ **shopping spree to go on a ~ spree** salir de compras (*gastando mucho dinero*) ➤ **shopping trolley** (*Brit*) carrito *m* de la compra

shop-soiled ['ʃɒpsɔɪld] ADJ (*Brit*) deteriorado

shore¹ [ʃɔːʳ] N [*of sea, lake*] orilla *f*; **on ~** en tierra

shore² [ʃɔːʳ] VT **to ~ up** apuntalar; (*fig*) apoyar, reforzar, sostener

shorn [ʃɔːn] PP *of* **shear**

short [ʃɔːt] **A** ADJ (*compar* ~**er**; *superl* ~**est**) **1** (*in length, distance, quantity*) corto; (*in height*) bajo, chaparro (*CAm, Mex*); **the days are getting ~er** los días se vuelven más cortos; **a ~ time ago** hace poco; **a ~ way off** a poca distancia, no muy lejos; ✦ IDIOM **to make ~ work of sth** despachar algo
2 (= *insufficient*) escaso; **I'm a bit ~ at the moment*** en este momento ando un poco corto *or* escaso de dinero; **to be ~ of sth** andar falto *or* escaso de algo; **to give ~ measure to sb** dar de menos a algn; **gold is in ~ supply** escasea el oro, hay escasez de oro
3 ~ of (= *less than*): **~ of blowing it up** a menos que lo volemos, a no ser que lo volemos; **~ of apologizing ...** fuera de pedirle perdón ...; **not far ~ of £100** poco menos de 100 libras; **nothing ~ of a miracle can save him** sólo un milagro le puede salvar, se necesitaría un milagro para salvarle
4 (= *concise*) corto, breve; **"Pat" is ~ for "Patricia"** "Patricia" se abrevia "Pat"; **Rosemary is called "Rose" for ~** a Rosemary le dicen "Rose" para abreviar; **"TV" is ~ for "television"** "TV" es abreviatura de "televisión"

5 (= *curt*) [*reply, manner*] brusco, seco; **to be ~ with sb** tratar a algn con sequedad; *see also* **shrift**
Ⓑ ADV **1** (= *suddenly, abruptly*) en seco; **to stop ~ ⬦ pull up** ~ pararse en seco
2 (*insufficiency*) **to cut sth ~** suspender algo; **to fall ~ of** no alcanzar; **to fall ~ of expectations** no cumplir las esperanzas; **to go ~ of** pasarse sin; **we never went ~ (of anything) as children** no nos faltó nada de niños; **we're running ~ of bread** tenemos poco pan, se nos acaba el pan (*LAm*); **to stop ~ of** (*lit*) detenerse antes de llegar a
Ⓒ N **1** (*Elec*) = **short-circuit A**
2 (*Brit**) (= *drink*) bebida *f* corta
3 in ~ en pocas palabras, en resumen
Ⓓ VT, VI = **short-circuit B, C**
Ⓔ CPD ➤ **short cut** atajo *m* ➤ **short list** lista *f* de candidatos preseleccionados ➤ **short story** cuento *m* ➤ **short wave** (*Rad*) onda *f* corta

shortage [ˈʃɔːtɪdʒ] N escasez *f*, falta *f*; **a water ~** escasez *or* falta de agua; **the housing ~** la crisis de la vivienda; **there is no ~ of advice** no es que falten consejos, no faltan los consejos

shortbread [ˈʃɔːtbred] N *especie de mantecado*

shortcake [ˈʃɔːtkeɪk] N (*Brit*) *especie de mantecada*; (*US*) torta *f* de frutas

short-change [ˈʃɔːtˈtʃeɪndʒ] VT **to ~ sb** no dar el cambio completo a algn; (*fig*) defraudar a algn

short-circuit [ˈʃɔːtˈsɜːkɪt] (*Elec*) **Ⓐ** N cortocircuito *m* **Ⓑ** VT provocar un cortocircuito en **Ⓒ** VI hacer un cortocircuito

shortcomings [ˈʃɔːtkʌmɪŋz] NPL defectos *mpl*

shortcrust pastry [ˈʃɔːtkrʌstˈpeɪstrɪ] N (*Brit*) pasta *f* quebradiza

shorten [ˈʃɔːtn] **Ⓐ** VT acortar **Ⓑ** VI acortarse, reducirse

shortfall [ˈʃɔːtfɔːl] N (*in profits*) déficit *m* (**in** en); (*in payments, savings*) disminución *f* (**in** de); (*in numbers*) insuficiencia *f* (**in** de); **there is a ~ of £5,000** faltan 5.000 libras

short-haired [ˈʃɔːtˈheəd] ADJ pelicorto

shorthand [ˈʃɔːthænd] N taquigrafía *f*; **to take sth down in ~** escribir algo taquigráficamente ➤ **shorthand typist** (*Brit*) taquimecanógrafo/a *m/f*

short-handed [ˈʃɔːtˈhændɪd] ADJ falto de mano de obra/personal

short-haul [ˈʃɔːtˈhɔːl] ADJ de corto recorrido

short-list [ˈʃɔːtˈlɪst] VT (*esp Brit*) **to ~ sb** preseleccionar a algn, poner a algn en la lista de candidatos a entrevistar

short-lived [ˈʃɔːtˈlɪvd] ADJ (*fig*) [*happiness*] efímero

shortly [ˈʃɔːtlɪ] ADV (= *soon*) dentro de poco, en breve (*frm*), ahorita (*Mex*); **~ before/after** poco antes/después

short-range [ˈʃɔːtˈreɪndʒ] ADJ [*gun*] de corto alcance; [*aircraft*] de autonomía limitada, de corto radio en acción

shorts [ʃɔːts] NPL pantalones *mpl* cortos; **a pair of ~** un pantalón corto, unos pantalones cortos

short-sighted [ˈʃɔːtˈsaɪtɪd] ADJ (*esp Brit*) miope, corto de vista; (*fig*) [*person*] miope, con poca visión (de futuro); [*measure etc*] con poca visión (de futuro)

short-sightedness [ˈʃɔːtˈsaɪtɪdnɪs] N miopía *f*; (*fig*) falta *f* de visión (de futuro)

short-sleeved [ˈʃɔːtsliːvd] ADJ de manga corta

short-staffed [ˈʃɔːtˈstɑːft] ADJ (*Brit*) falto de personal

short-stay car park [ˈʃɔːtsteɪˈkɑːpɑːk] N aparcamiento *m* (*para estancias de corta duración*)

short-tempered [ˈʃɔːtˈtempəd] ADJ irritable

short-term [ˈʃɔːttɜːm] ADJ a corto plazo

shot [ʃɒt] **Ⓐ** PT, PP *of* **shoot**
Ⓑ N **1** (= *act of shooting*) tiro *m*; (*causing wound*) balazo *m*; (= *sound*) tiro *m*, disparo *m*; **to fire a ~ at sth/sb** disparar a algo/disparar a *or* sobre algn; **he was off like a ~** salió disparado *or* como un rayo
2 (= *missile*) bala *f*, proyectil *m*; (= *shotgun pellets*) perdigones *mpl*; (*Athletics*) peso *m*; **to put the ~** lanzar el peso
3 (= *person*) tirador(a) *m/f*; **he's a bad/good ~** es un mal/

buen tirador
4 (*Ftbl*) tiro *m*; (*Golf, Tennis*) golpe *m*; (*Snooker*) golpe *m*, jugada *f*; (= *throw*) tirada *f*, echada *f*; **good ~!** ¡buen tiro!; **✦** IDIOM **to call the ~s** mandar, llevar la voz cantante
5 (= *attempt*) tentativa *f*, intento *m*; **just give it your best ~** limítate a hacerlo lo mejor que puedas; **to have a ~ at sth** intentar algo; **✦** IDIOM **a ~ in the dark** un palo de ciego, una tentativa a ciegas
6 (= *injection*) inyección *f*; (= *dose*) dosis *f inv*; [*of alcohol*] trago *m*; (*) [*of drug*] pico* *m*, chute* *m*; **a ~ of rum** un trago de ron; **✦** IDIOM **a ~ in the arm*: the economy needs a ~ in the arm** la economía necesita estímulo
7 (*Phot*) foto *f*; (*Cine*) toma *f*, plano *m*
Ⓒ ADJ **1** (= *suffused*) **his story is ~ through with inconsistencies** su narración está plagada de incongruencias
2 (*Brit**) (= *rid*) **✦** IDIOM **to get ~ of sth/sb** deshacerse *or* librarse de algo/algn
3 (*) [*person, nerves*] deshecho, hecho polvo*
Ⓓ CPD ➤ **shot put** (*Sport*) lanzamiento *m* de pesos ➤ **shot putter** lanzador(a) *m/f* de pesos

shotgun [ˈʃɒtgʌn] N escopeta *f* ➤ **shotgun wedding** casamiento *m* a la fuerza; **to have a ~ wedding** casarse a la fuerza, casarse de penalty*

should [ʃʊd] AUX VB, MODAL AUX VB **1** (*duty, advisability, desirability*) deber; **you ~ take more exercise** deberías hacer más ejercicio; **I ~ have been a doctor** yo debería haber sido médico; **you ~n't do that** no deberías hacerlo, más vale no hacer eso; **he ~ know that ...** debiera *or* debería saber que ...; **all is as it ~ be** todo está en regla; **why ~ I?** ¿por qué lo voy a hacer?, ¿por qué tengo que hacerlo?
2 (*statements of probability*) deber de; **they ~ have arrived by now** deben (de) haber llegado ya; **he ~ be there by now** ya debería estar allí
3 (*used to form conditional tense*) **I ~ go if they sent for me** iría si me llamasen; **~ I be out at the time ⬦ if I ~ be out at the time** si estoy fuera en ese momento; **I ~n't be surprised if ...** no me sorprendería si ...; **I ~ think so** supongo que sí
4 (*subjunctive uses*) **... and who ~ I bump into but Mike?** ... ¿y con quién crees que me encuentro? ¡pues con Mike!

shoulder [ˈʃəʊldə] **Ⓐ** N **1** (*Anat*) hombro *m*; **to carry sth over one's ~** llevar algo en hombros; **to have broad ~s** ser ancho de espaldas; **they carried him ~ high** le llevaron a hombros; **all the responsibilities fell on his ~s** tuvo que cargar con todas las responsabilidades; **✦** IDIOMS **to give sb the cold ~** dar de lado a algn; **to cry on sb's ~** desahogarse con algn
2 (*esp US*) (*on road*) arcén *m*, hombrillo *m*
Ⓑ VT (= *carry*) llevar al hombro; (*pick up*) ponerse al hombro; (*fig*) [+ *burden, responsibility*] cargar con
Ⓒ CPD ➤ **shoulder bag** bolso *m* de bandolera ➤ **shoulder blade** omóplato *m* ➤ **shoulder pad** hombrera *f* ➤ **shoulder strap** tirante *m*; [*of satchel*] bandolera *f*

shoulder-length [ˈʃəʊldəˌleŋθ] ADJ que llega hasta los hombros

shouldn't [ˈʃʊdnt] = **should not**

shout [ʃaʊt] **Ⓐ** N **1** (= *loud cry*) grito *m*; **to give sb a ~** pegar un grito a algn*, avisar a algn **2** (*Brit**) (= *round of drinks*) ronda *f*; **it's my — — what are you drinking?** me toca pagar esta ronda — ¿qué tomáis? **Ⓑ** VT gritar; **to ~ abuse at sb** insultar a algn a gritos **Ⓒ** VI (= *cry out*) gritar; **to ~ at sb** gritar a algn; **I ~ed for help** pedí socorro a gritos; **to ~ with laughter** reírse a carcajadas
➤ **shout down** VT + ADV abuchear, hacer callar a gritos
➤ **shout out Ⓐ** VT + ADV gritar, decir a voz en grito **Ⓑ** VI + ADV gritar, dar un grito, pegar un grito*

shouting [ˈʃaʊtɪŋ] N gritos *mpl*, vocerío *m*; **✦** IDIOM **it's all over bar the ~** ya es asunto concluido ➤ **shouting match*** pelea *f or* riña *f* de gallos

shove [ʃʌv] **Ⓐ** N empujón *m* **Ⓑ** VT **1** (= *push*) empujar; **he ~d everyone aside** apartó a un lado a todo el mundo a empujones; **to ~ sth/sb in** meter a algo/algn a empujones; **they ~d the car over the cliff** fueron empujando el coche hasta que cayó por el acantilado **2** (*) (= *put*) poner, meter; **~ it over to me** trae pa'acá* **Ⓒ** VI empujar, dar empujones; **he ~d past me** se abrió paso dándome empujones, pasó

por mi lado empujando *or* dando empujones
➤ **shove off** VI + ADV **1** (*Naut*) alejarse del muelle *etc* **2** (*)
(= *leave*) largarse, marcharse; ~ **off!** ¡lárgate!*
➤ **shove over, shove up** VI + ADV correrse

shovel [ˈʃʌvl] **A** N pala *f* **B** VT mover con pala; **to ~ coal
on to a fire** añadir carbón a la lumbre con pala; **he was
~ling** *or* (*US*) **~ing food into his mouth*** se zampaba la
comida

show [ʃəʊ] (*vb: pt* **~ed**; *pp* **shown**) **A** N **1** (= *showing*)
demostración *f*, manifestación *f*; ~ **of hands** votación *f* a
mano alzada; **a ~ of strength** una demostración de fuerza
2 (= *exhibition*) exposición *f*; [*of trade*] feria *f*; **fashion ~** pase
m de modelos; **motor ~** salón *m* del automóvil; **to be on ~**
estar expuesto
3 (*Theat*) espectáculo *m*, función *f*; (*Rad, TV*) programa *m*;
to go to a ~ (*esp Brit*) (*in theatre*) ir al teatro; (*US*) (*in movie
theater*) ir al cine; **to put up a good ~*** dar buena cuenta de
sí, hacer un buen papel; ✦ IDIOMS **let's get this ~ on the
road** echémonos a la carretera; **to steal the ~** acaparar toda
la atención
4 (= *outward appearance*) apariencia *f*; **it's just for ~**
(*behaviour*) es para impresionar nada más; (*object*) (= *for
decoration*) es sólo un adorno; (= *not real*) es de adorno
B VT **1** (*gen*) enseñar, mostrar; **he ~ed me his new car** me
enseñó *or* mostró su nuevo coche; **to ~ o.s.: she won't ~
herself here again** no volverá a dejarse ver por aquí; **don't
~ your face here again** no te vuelvas a dejar ver por aquí;
to ~ one's hand (*fig*) descubrir el juego; **he had nothing to ~
for his trouble** no vió recompensado su esfuerzo, no le
lució nada el esfuerzo
2 (= *exhibit*) [+ *paintings*] exhibir; [+ *goods*] exponer; [+ *film*]
proyectar, pasar; [+ *slides*] proyectar
3 (= *indicate*) [*dial, gauge, instrument*] marcar; **the
motorways are ~n in black** las autopistas están marcadas en
negro; **the figures ~ a rise** las cifras arrojan un aumento; **as
~n in the illustration** como se ve en el grabado; **to ~ a loss/
profit** (*Comm*) arrojar un saldo negativo/positivo
4 (= *demonstrate*) demostrar; **it just goes to ~ (that) ...**
queda demostrado (que) ...; **I'll ~ him!*** ¡ya va a ver!, ¡ese se
va a enterar!
5 (= *express*) demostrar; **she ~ed great courage** demostró
gran valentía
6 (= *reveal*) **she's beginning to ~ her age** ya empieza a
aparentar su edad; **white shoes soon ~ the dirt** en los
zapatos blancos se ve pronto la suciedad
7 (= *direct, conduct*) **to ~ sb to the door** acompañar a algn a
la puerta; **to ~ sb into a room** hacer que pase algn, hacer
entrar a algn en un cuarto; **to ~ sb over** *or* **round a house**
enseñar a algn una casa; **to ~ sb to his seat** acompañar a
algn a su asiento
C VI **1** [*stain, emotion, underskirt*] notarse, verse; **it doesn't ~**
no se ve, no se nota
2 (*esp US*) (*also* ~ **up**) (= *arrive*) venir, aparecer
D CPD ➤ **show business** el mundo del espectáculo ➤ **show
home, show house** (*Brit*) casa *f* piloto ➤ **show jumper**
(= *rider*) participante *mf* en concursos de saltos *or* de hípica
➤ **show jumping** concursos *mpl* de saltos *or* de hípica
➤ **show trial** proceso *m* organizado con fines
propagandísticos
➤ **show in** VT + ADV hacer pasar; ~ **him in!** ¡que pase!
➤ **show off A** VI + ADV presumir, darse tono **B** VT + ADV
[+ *beauty etc*] hacer resaltar, destacar; (*pej*) hacer alarde de,
ostentar
➤ **show out** VT + ADV acompañar a la puerta
➤ **show up A** VI + ADV **1** (= *be visible*) verse, notarse **2** (*)
(= *arrive*) venir, aparecer **B** VT + ADV **1** [+ *visitor*] hacer subir
2 (= *reveal*) [+ *defect*] poner de manifiesto; **he was ~n up as
an imposter** se demostró que era un impostor
3 (= *embarrass*) dejar en ridículo, poner en evidencia

showcase [ˈʃəʊkeɪs] **A** N vitrina *f* **B** VT (*fig*) mostrar
C CPD ➤ **showcase project** proyecto *m* modelo

showdown [ˈʃəʊdaʊn] N enfrentamiento *m* (final); **to have
a ~ with sb** enfrentarse con algn

shower [ˈʃaʊəʳ] **A** N **1** [*of rain*] chubasco *m*, chaparrón *m*;
[*of arrows, stones, blows etc*] lluvia *f*
2 (*in bathroom*) ducha *f*, regadera *f* (*Mex*); **to have** *or* **take a ~**
ducharse, tomar una ducha
3 (*Brit* pej*) (= *people*) **what a ~!** ¡que montón de inútiles!

4 (*US*) (= *party*) fiesta *f* de obsequio
B VT (*fig*) **they ~ed gifts (up)on the queen** colmaron a la
reina de regalos; **to ~ sb with honours** colmar a algn de
honores
C VI **1** (= *rain*) caer un chaparrón *or* chubasco
2 (= *take a shower*) ducharse, darse una ducha
D CPD ➤ **shower cap** gorro *m* de baño ➤ **shower curtain**
cortina *f* de ducha ➤ **shower gel** gel *m* de ducha ➤ **shower
unit** ducha *f*

showerproof [ˈʃaʊəpruːf] ADJ impermeable

showery [ˈʃaʊəɪ] ADJ [*weather*] lluvioso; [*day*] lluvioso, de
lluvia; **it will be ~ tomorrow** mañana habrá chubascos *or*
chaparrones*

showground [ˈʃəʊɡraʊnd] N recinto *m* ferial, real *m* de la feria
feria

showing [ˈʃəʊɪŋ] N **1** [*of film*] proyección *f*, pase *m*; [*of
paintings etc*] exposición *f* **2** (= *performance*) actuación *f*;
the poor ~ of the team la pobre actuación del equipo

showing-off [ʃəʊɪŋˈɒf] N (= *displaying*) lucimiento *m*

showman [ˈʃəʊmən] N (*pl* **showmen**) empresario *m*; **he's a
real ~!** (*fig*) ¡es todo un número *or* espectáculo!

showmanship [ˈʃəʊmənʃɪp] N espectacularidad *f*,
teatralidad *f*

shown [ʃəʊn] PP *of* **show**

show-off* [ˈʃəʊɒf] N presumido/a *m/f*, fantasmón/ona *m/f*
(*Sp**)

showpiece [ˈʃəʊpiːs] N (= *centrepiece*) joya *f*, lo mejor; **this
vase is a real ~** este florero es realmente excepcional

showroom [ˈʃəʊrʊm] N (*Comm*) sala *f* de muestras

showy [ˈʃəʊɪ] ADJ (*compar* **showier**; *superl* **showiest**)
ostentoso

shrank [ʃræŋk] PT *of* **shrink**

shrapnel [ˈʃræpnl] N metralla *f*

shred [ʃred] **A** N [*of cloth*] jirón *m*; [*of paper*] tira *f*; **if you
had a ~ of decency** si usted tuviese un mínimo de
honradez; **in ~s** hecho jirones *or* trizas **B** VT [+ *paper*]
hacer trizas, triturar; [+ *food*] despedazar

shredder [ˈʃredəʳ] N (*for documents, papers*) trituradora *f*;
(*for vegetables*) picadora *f*

shrew [ʃruː] N (*Zool*) musaraña *f*

shrewd [ʃruːd] ADJ (*compar* **~er**; *superl* **~est**) [*person,
politician, businessperson*] astuto, sagaz; [*observer, glance*]
perspicaz; [*remark, observation*] sagaz, perspicaz;
[*assessment*] muy acertado; [*investment*] inteligente; **to be a
~ judge of character** tener buen ojo para juzgar a la gente

shrewdly [ˈʃruːdlɪ] ADV [*say, ask, point out*] sagazmente;
[*reason*] con perspicacia, con sagacidad; [*act*] hábilmente,
con astucia; [*invest*] inteligentemente; **she had ~ guessed
the reason for his absence** había adivinado astutamente la
razón de su ausencia, se había dado cuenta hábilmente de
la razón de su ausencia

shrewdness [ˈʃruːdnɪs] N [*of person*] astucia *f*, sagacidad *f*;
[*of remark, observation*] sagacidad *f*, perspicacia *f*; [*of plan*]
lo inteligente

shriek [ʃriːk] **A** N chillido *m*, grito *m* agudo; **with ~s of
laughter** con grandes carcajadas **B** VI chillar; **to ~ with
laughter** reírse histéricamente **C** VT gritar

shrift [ʃrɪft] N **to give sb short ~** despachar a algn sin
rodeos; **he got short ~ from the boss** el jefe se mostró poco
compasivo con él

shrill [ʃrɪl] ADJ (*compar* **~er**; *superl* **~est**) [*voice*] chillón,
agudo; [*sound*] estridente, agudo

shrimp [ʃrɪmp] N (*small*) camarón *m*; (*US*) (*medium*) gamba
f, camarón *m* (*esp LAm*) ➤ **shrimp cocktail** (*US*) cóctel *m* de
gambas

shrine [ʃraɪn] N (= *tomb*) sepulcro *m*; (= *sacred place*) lugar
m sagrado

shrink [ʃrɪŋk] (*pt* **shrank**; *pp* **shrunk**) **A** VI **1** (= *get smaller*)
encogerse; **"will not shrink"** "no (se) encoge",
"inencogible" **2** (*also* ~ **away**, ~ **back**) retroceder, echar
marcha atrás; **he did not ~ from touching it** no vaciló en
tocarlo **B** VT encoger **C** N (**) (= *psychiatrist*) psiquiatra *mf*

shrinkage ['ʃrɪŋkɪdʒ] N [*of clothes, fabric*] encogimiento *m*; (*Tech*) (= *contraction*) contracción *f*

shrinking ['ʃrɪŋkɪŋ] ADJ [*resources etc*] que escasea(n) ➤ **shrinking violet** (*fig*) tímido/a *m/f*, vergonzoso/a *m/f*

shrink-wrapped ['ʃrɪŋkræpt] ADJ empaquetado *or* envasado en plástico

shrivel ['ʃrɪvl] (*also* ~ **up**) VI [*plant etc*] marchitarse, secarse; [*skin etc*] arrugarse

shroud [ʃraʊd] Ⓐ N (*around corpse*) sudario *m*, mortaja *f* Ⓑ VT (*fig*) velar, cubrir; **the whole thing is ~ed in mystery** el asunto está envuelto en un halo de misterio

Shrove Tuesday ['ʃraʊv'tjuːzdɪ] N martes *m inv* de Carnaval (*en que en Inglaterra se sirven hojuelas*)

shrub [ʃrʌb] N arbusto *m*

shrubbery ['ʃrʌbərɪ] N (*Brit*) arbustos *mpl*

shrug [ʃrʌg] Ⓐ N encogimiento *m* de hombros; **he said with a ~** dijo encogiéndose de hombros Ⓑ VT, VI **to ~ (one's shoulders)** encogerse de hombros
➤ **shrug off** VT + ADV no hacer caso de

shrunk [ʃrʌŋk] PP *of* **shrink**

shrunken ['ʃrʌŋkən] ADJ encogido

shudder ['ʃʌdər] Ⓐ VI [*person*] estremecerse (**with** de); [*machinery*] vibrar; **the car ~ed to a halt** el coche paró a sacudidas; **I ~ to think** (*fig*) sólo pensarlo me da horror Ⓑ N [*of person*] estremecimiento *m*, escalofrío *m*; [*of machinery*] vibración *f*, sacudida *f*; **she realized with a ~ that ...** se estremeció al darse cuenta de que ...

shuffle ['ʃʌfl] Ⓐ N **1 to walk with a ~** caminar arrastrando los pies **2** (*Cards*) **to give the cards a ~** barajar (las cartas) Ⓑ VT **1** [+ *feet*] arrastrar **2** (= *mix up*) [+ *cards*] barajar; [+ *papers*] revolver, traspapelar Ⓒ VI (= *walk*) arrastrar los pies; **to ~ in/out** entrar/salir arrastrando los pies

shun [ʃʌn] VT **1** (= *reject*) rechazar **2** (= *avoid*) [+ *work*] evitar; [+ *publicity*] rehuir

shunt [ʃʌnt] Ⓐ VT (*Rail*) cambiar de vía, shuntar; **we were ~ed about all day** (*fig*) nos tuvieron dando vueltas todo el día; **to ~ sb aside** apartar a algn, relegar a algn a un puesto menos importante Ⓑ VI **to ~ to and fro** trajinar de acá para allá

shush [ʃʊʃ] EXCL ¡chis!, ¡chitón!

shut [ʃʌt] (*pt, pp* ~) Ⓐ VT cerrar; **they ~ the door in his face** le dieron con la puerta en las narices; **to ~ one's fingers in the door** pillarse los dedos en la puerta Ⓑ VI cerrarse
➤ **shut away** VT + ADV encerrar; **to ~ o.s. away** encerrarse
➤ **shut down** Ⓐ VI + ADV cerrarse Ⓑ VT + ADV [+ *lid, business, factory*] cerrar; [+ *machine*] apagar; (*by law*) clausurar
➤ **shut in** VT + ADV encerrar
➤ **shut off** VT + ADV **1** (= *stop*) [+ *water, power*] cortar, cerrar; [+ *engine*] apagar; (*US*) [+ *lights*] apagar **2** (= *isolate*) aislar (**from** de); **to be ~ off from** estar aislado de
➤ **shut out** VT + ADV (= *leave outside*) dejar fuera; (= *put outside*) sacar; (= *close door on*) cerrar la puerta a; (= *keep out*) excluir; (= *block*) tapar
➤ **shut up** Ⓐ VI + ADV (*) (= *be quiet*) callarse; ~ **up!** ¡cállate! Ⓑ VT + ADV **1** (= *close*) cerrar **2** (= *enclose*) encerrar **3** (*) (= *silence*) callar, hacer callar

shutdown ['ʃʌtdaʊn] N cierre *m*

shut-eye* ['ʃʌtaɪ] N sueño *m*; **to get some ~** echar un sueñecito*

shutter ['ʃʌtər] N (*on window*) contraventana *f*, postigo *m*; (*Phot*) obturador *m* ➤ **shutter release** (*Phot*) disparador *m* ➤ **shutter speed** (*Phot*) velocidad *f* de obturación

shuttered ['ʃʌtəd] ADJ [*house, window*] (= *fitted with shutters*) con contraventanas; (= *with shutters closed*) con las contraventanas cerradas

shuttle ['ʃʌtl] Ⓐ N **1** (*for weaving, sewing*) lanzadera *f* **2** (*Aer*) puente *m* aéreo; (= *plane, train etc*) servicio *m* regular de enlace; **air ~** puente *m* aéreo **3** (*Space*) (*also* **space ~**) lanzadera *f or* transbordador *m* espacial Ⓑ VI [*person*] (= *go regularly*) ir y venir (**between** entre) Ⓒ VT (= *transport*) transportar, trasladar Ⓓ CPD ➤ **shuttle diplomacy** viajes *mpl* diplomáticos ➤ **shuttle service** servicio *m* regular de enlace

shuttlecock ['ʃʌtlkɒk] N (*Badminton*) volante *m*

shy [ʃaɪ] Ⓐ ADJ (*compar* ~**er**; *superl* ~**est**) **1** (= *nervous*) [*person*] vergonzoso, tímido; [*smile*] tímido; [*animal*] asustadizo, huraño; **she's ~ of cameras** se siente cohibida delante de las cámaras; **don't be ~ of telling them what you think** no tengas miedo de decirles lo que piensas
2 ~ **of** (*esp US*) (= *short of*) **we're $65,000 ~ of the $1 million that's needed** nos faltan 65.000 dólares para el millón de dólares que se necesitan; **he's two months ~ of 70** le faltan dos meses para cumplir 70 años Ⓑ VI [*horse*] asustarse, espantarse (**at** de)
➤ **shy away** VI + ADV **to ~ away from doing sth** tener miedo a hacer algo

shyly ['ʃaɪlɪ] ADV tímidamente, con timidez

shyness ['ʃaɪnɪs] N [*of person, smile*] timidez *f*; [*of animal*] lo asustadizo

Siamese [ˌsaɪə'miːz] Ⓐ N siamés/esa *m/f* Ⓑ ADJ siamés Ⓒ CPD ➤ **Siamese cat** gato *m* siamés ➤ **Siamese twins** hermanos/as *mpl/fpl* siameses/esas

Siberia [saɪ'bɪərɪə] N Siberia *f*

Siberian [saɪ'bɪərɪən] ADJ, N siberiano/a *m/f*

sibling ['sɪblɪŋ] N hermano/a *m/f* ➤ **sibling rivalry** rivalidad *f* entre hermanos

sic [sɪk] ADV sic

Sicily ['sɪsɪlɪ] N Sicilia *f*

sick [sɪk] Ⓐ ADJ (*compar* ~**er**; *superl* ~**est**) **1** (= *ill*) [*person*] enfermo; [*animal*] malo, enfermo; **to get ~** ponerse enfermo; **to be off ~** faltar por estar enfermo (*al colegio, trabajo, etc*); (*with a medical certificate*) estar de baja; **she phoned in ~** llamó para decir que estaba enferma
2 to be ~ (*Brit*) (= *vomit*) devolver, vomitar; **to feel ~** (*Brit*) (= *nauseous*) tener ganas de devolver *or* de vomitar, tener náuseas; **to make sb ~** (*lit*) hacer devolver *or* vomitar a algn
3 (= *fed up*) **to be ~ of (doing) sth** estar harto de (hacer) algo*; **to be ~ and tired of (doing) sth** estar hasta la coronilla de (hacer) algo*, estar más que harto de (hacer) algo*
4 (= *disgusted*) **it makes me ~ the way they waste our money** me pone enferma ver la manera en que malgastan nuestro dinero; **you make me ~!** ¡me das asco!
5 (*pej*) (= *morbid*) [*joke, act*] de mal gusto; [*person, mind, sense of humour*] morboso Ⓑ N **1 the ~** los enfermos
2 (*Brit*) (= *vomit*) vómito *m*, devuelto *m* Ⓒ CPD ➤ **sick bag** bolsa *f* para el mareo ➤ **sick leave to be on ~ leave** tener permiso *or* (*Sp*) baja por enfermedad ➤ **sick list** lista *f* de enfermos; **to be on the ~ list** estar de permiso *or* (*Sp*) de baja por enfermedad ➤ **sick note** justificante *m* por enfermedad ➤ **sick pay** *pago que se percibe mientras se está con permiso por enfermedad*, baja *f* (*Sp*)
➤ **sick up*** VT + ADV (*Brit*) vomitar, devolver

sickbay ['sɪkbeɪ] N enfermería *f*

sickbed ['sɪkbed] N lecho *m* de enfermo

sicken ['sɪkn] Ⓐ VT poner enfermo; (*fig*) dar asco Ⓑ VI caer enfermo, enfermarse; **to be ~ing for** mostrar síntomas de

sickening ['sɪknɪŋ] ADJ [*sight, smell*] nauseabundo, asqueroso; [*cruelty, crime*] espeluznante, repugnante; [*waste*] indignante, escandaloso

sickle ['sɪkl] N hoz *f*

sickle-cell anaemia, sickle-cell anemia (*US*) ['sɪkl,selə'niːmɪə] N anemia *f* de células falciformes, drepanocitosis *f*

sickly ['sɪklɪ] ADJ (*compar* **sicklier**; *superl* **sickliest**) **1** [*person*] (= *unwell*) enfermizo, enclenque; (= *pale*) pálido
2 (= *cloying*) [*taste, smell*] empalagoso; ~ **sweet** dulzón

sick-making* ['sɪkmeɪkɪŋ] ADJ asqueroso

sickness ['sɪknɪs] N (= *illness*) enfermedad *f*; (= *feeling of nausea*) náuseas *fpl*; (= *vomiting*) vómitos *mpl*

sickroom ['sɪkrʊm] N cuarto *m* del enfermo

side [saɪd] Ⓐ N **1** [*of person*] lado *m*, costado *m*; [*of animal*] ijar *m*, ijada *f*; **at** *or* **by sb's ~** al lado de algn; (*fig*) en apoyo a algn; **~ by ~** uno al lado del otro; **to sleep <u>on</u> one's ~** dormir de costado or lado; **to <u>split</u> one's ~s** desternillarse de risa

2 (= edge) [of box, square, building] lado m; [of boat, vehicle] costado m; [of hill] ladera f, falda f; [of lake] orilla f; [of road, pond] borde m; **the car was abandoned at the ~ of the road** el coche estaba abandonado al borde de la carretera; **he was driving on the <u>wrong</u> ~ of the road** iba por el lado contrario de la carretera

3 (= face, surface) [of box, solid figure, paper, record] cara f; **<u>right</u> ~ up** boca arriba; **<u>wrong</u> ~ up** boca abajo; **to be wrong ~ out** estar al revés

4 (= aspect) lado m, aspecto m; **to hear both ~s of the question** escuchar los argumentos en pro y en contra

5 (= part) lado m; **from <u>all</u> ~s** de todas partes, de todos lados; **on all ~s** por todas partes, por todos lados; **to make a bit (of money) <u>on</u> the ~*** ganar algún dinero extra, hacer chapuzas (Sp); **to move to <u>one</u> ~** apartarse, ponerse or hacerse a un lado; **to take sb on** or **to one ~** apartar a algn; **to put sth to** or **on one ~ (for sb)** guardar algo (para algn); **to be on the <u>safe</u> ~ ...** para estar seguro ..., por si acaso ...; **it's <u>this</u> ~ of Segovia** está más acá de Segovia; **from ~ <u>to</u> ~** de un lado a otro; **to be on the <u>wrong</u> ~ of 30** haber cumplido los 30 años; ✦ IDIOMS **to get on the right ~ of sb** procurar congraciarse con algn; **to get on the wrong ~ of sb** ponerse a malas con algn; **to get out of bed on the wrong ~** levantarse con el pie izquierdo

6 (fig) **the weather's on the <u>cold</u> ~** el tiempo es algo frío; **it's a bit on the <u>large</u> ~** es algo or (LAm) tantito grande

7 (Brit) (= team) equipo m; (Pol) (= party) partido m; **to <u>let</u> the ~ down** (Brit Sport) dejar caer a los suyos; (fig) decepcionar; **he's <u>on</u> our ~** (fig) es de los nuestros; **whose ~ are you on?** ¿a quiénes apoyas?; **to be on the ~ of sth/sb** ser partidario de algo/algn; **to have age/justice on one's ~** tener la juventud/la justicia de su lado; **<u>our</u> ~ won** ganaron los nuestros; **to <u>take</u> ~s (with sb)** tomar partido (con algn)

B VI **to ~ with sb** ponerse de parte de algn

C CPD **➤ side dish** plato m adicional (servido con el principal) **➤ side door** puerta f al lado **➤ side effect** efecto m secundario **➤ side issue** cuestión f secundaria **➤ side plate** platito m (para el pan, ensalada, etc) **➤ side road** carretera f secundaria **➤ side street** calle f lateral

sideboard ['saɪdbɔ:d] N aparador m

sideboards (Brit) ['saɪdbɔ:dz], **sideburns** ['saɪdbɜ:nz] NPL patillas fpl

sidecar ['saɪdkɑ:ʳ] N sidecar m

sidekick* ['saɪdkɪk] N secuaz* mf

sidelight ['saɪdlaɪt] N (Aut) (Brit) (at front of car) luz f de posición; (US) (on side of car) luz f lateral; (showing size of big vehicles) luz f de gálibo

sideline ['saɪdlaɪn] **A** N **1** (Ftbl, Tennis etc) línea f de banda; **to be on the ~s** (Sport) estar fuera del terreno de juego, estar en la banda **2** (Comm) actividad f suplementaria; **it's just a ~** (fig) es un pasatiempo, nada más **B** VT (esp US) marginar

sidelong ['saɪdlɒŋ] **A** ADV de costado **B** ADJ [glance] de soslayo, de reojo

side-saddle ['saɪd,sædl] ADV **to ride ~** montar estilo amazona

sideshow ['saɪdʃəʊ] N (at fair) atracción f secundaria

side-splitting* ['saɪd,splɪtɪŋ] ADJ para reírse a carcajadas, para morirse de risa

sidestep ['saɪdstep] **A** VT [+ problem, question] eludir, esquivar **B** VI (Boxing) dar un quiebro, fintar, dar una finta (LAm)

sideswipe ['saɪdswaɪp] N (lit, fig) golpe m de refilón

sidetrack ['saɪdtræk] VT [+ person] despistar; [+ discussion] conducir por cuestiones de poca importancia; **I got ~ed** me despisté

sidewalk ['saɪdwɔ:k] N (US) acera f, vereda f (LAm), andén m (CAm, Col), banqueta f (Mex)

sideways ['saɪd,weɪz] **A** ADJ (gen) de lado, lateral; [look] de reojo, de soslayo **B** ADV **to step ~** hacerse a un lado; **to walk/move ~** andar/moverse de lado; **to look ~** mirar de reojo, mirar de soslayo; **~ on** de perfil

siding ['saɪdɪŋ] N (Rail) apartadero m, vía f muerta

sidle ['saɪdl] VI **to ~ up (to sb)** acercarse furtivamente (a algn); **to ~ in/out** entrar/salir furtivamente

SIDS N ABBR (Med) = **sudden infant death syndrome**

siege [si:dʒ] N cerco m, sitio m; **to lay ~ to** cercar, sitiar **➤ siege mentality to have a ~ mentality** tener manía persecutoria

sienna [sɪˈenə] N siena f

Sierra Leone [sɪˈeərəlɪˈəʊn] N Sierra f Leona

siesta [sɪˈestə] N siesta f; **to have a ~** dormir la siesta

sieve [sɪv] **A** N (for liquids) colador m; (for solids) criba f, tamiz m **B** VT [+ liquid] colar; [+ flour, soil] cribar, tamizar

sift [sɪft] **A** VT [+ flour, soil] cerner, tamizar **B** VI **to ~ through** (fig) examinar cuidadosamente

sigh [saɪ] **A** N suspiro m; **to breathe a ~ of relief** suspirar aliviado, dar un suspiro de alivio **B** VI suspirar

sight [saɪt] **A** N **1** (= eyesight) vista f; **I'm losing my ~** estoy perdiendo la vista

2 (= act of seeing) vista f; **I can't bear the ~ of blood** no aguanto la vista de la sangre; **I can't stand the ~ of him** no le puedo ver; **at first ~** a primera vista; **I know her <u>by</u> ~** la conozco de vista; **it came into ~** apareció; **to <u>catch</u> ~ of sth/sb** divisar algo/a algn; **it was love at <u>first</u> ~** fue un flechazo; **to be <u>in</u> ~** estar a la vista (of de); **to <u>lose</u> ~ of sth/sb** perder algo/a algn de vista; **to shoot <u>on</u> ~** disparar sin previo aviso; **to be <u>out</u> of ~** no estar a la vista; **not to let sb out of one's ~** no perder a algn de vista

3 (= spectacle) espectáculo m; **to see** or **visit the ~s of Madrid** visitar los lugares de interés turístico de Madrid, hacer turismo por Madrid; **it's not a <u>pretty</u> ~** no es precisamente bonito; ✦ IDIOM **it's a ~ for sore eyes** da gusto verlo

4 (on gun) (often pl) mira f, alza f

Use **el/un** not **la/una** before feminine nouns beginning with stressed **a** or **ha** like **alza**.

✦ IDIOM **to set one's ~s on sth/doing sth** aspirar a or ambicionar algo/hacer algo

5 (*) (= a great deal) **he's a ~ too clever** es demasiado listo **B** VT [+ land] ver, divisar; [+ bird, rare animal] observar, ver; [+ person] ver

sighted ['saɪtɪd] ADJ vidente

sighting ['saɪtɪŋ] N observación f

sight-read ['saɪtri:d] (pt, pp ~) (Mus) VT, VI repentizar

sightseeing ['saɪt,si:ɪŋ] N turismo m; **to go ~ ✧ do some ~** hacer turismo

sightseer ['saɪt,sɪəʳ] N turista mf, excursionista mf

sign [saɪn] **A** N **1** (= indication) señal f, indicio m; **it's a good/bad ~** es buena/mala señal; **to show ~s of sth/doing sth** dar muestras or señales de algo/de hacer algo

2 (= gesture) seña f; **to make a ~ to sb** hacer una seña a algn; **to make the ~ of the Cross** hacer la señal de la cruz, santiguarse

3 (= notice) letrero m; (= road sign) señal f (de tráfico); (= direction indicator) indicador m; (= shop sign) letrero m, rótulo m; (US) (carried in demonstration) pancarta f

4 (= written symbol) símbolo m; (Math, Mus, Astrol) signo m; **plus/minus ~** signo de más/menos **B** VT **1** [+ letter, contract] firmar; **to ~ one's name** firmar **2** [+ player] fichar, contratar **C** VI **1** (with signature) firmar

2 (= be recruited) (Sport) firmar un contrato; **he has ~ed for** or **with Arsenal** ha firmado un contrato con el Arsenal, ha fichado por el Arsenal (Sp)

3 (= signal) **to ~ to sb to do sth** hacer señas a algn para que haga algo

4 (= use sign language) hablar con señas **D** CPD **➤ sign language** lenguaje m por señas; **to talk in ~ language** hablar por señas **➤ sign away** VT + ADV [+ rights] ceder **➤ sign for** VI + PREP [+ item] firmar el recibo de **➤ sign in** VI + ADV (at hotel) firmar el registro (al entrar), registrarse; (at work) firmar la entrada

➤ **sign off** VI + ADV (*ending activity*) terminar; (*ending letter*) despedirse; (*Rad, TV*) cerrar el programa, despedirse
➤ **sign on** VI + ADV (*Brit*) (*as unemployed*) registrarse como desempleado
➤ **sign over** VT + ADV [+ *property, rights*] ceder (**to** a)
➤ **sign up** Ⓐ VI + ADV (= *be recruited*) (*as employee*) firmar un contrato; (*Sport*) [*player*] fichar (**with, for** por); **to ~ up for a course** inscribirse en un curso; **to ~ up for welfare** (*US*) inscribirse como desempleado Ⓑ VT + ADV [+ *employee*] contratar; (*Sport*) [+ *player*] fichar, contratar; (*Mil*) [+ *soldier*] reclutar

signal ['sɪɡnl] Ⓐ N señal *f*; (*Telec*) señal *f*, tono *m*; (*TV, Rad*) sintonía *f*; **railway ~s** semáforos *mpl* de ferrocarril; **traffic ~s** semáforo *msing*
Ⓑ VT [+ *message*] comunicar por señales; **to ~ sb on/through** dar a algn la señal de pasar; **to ~ a left-/right-hand turn** (*Aut*) indicar un giro a la izquierda/derecha
Ⓒ VI (*gen*) dar una señal; (*with hands*) hacer señas; **to ~ to sb that ...** comunicar a algn por señas que ...; **to ~ before stopping** hacer una señal antes de parar
Ⓓ CPD ➤ **signal box** (*Rail*) garita *f* de señales

signalman ['sɪɡnlmən] N (*pl* **signalmen**) guardavía *m*

signatory ['sɪɡnətərɪ] N firmante *mf*, signatario/a *m/f*

signature ['sɪɡnətʃəʳ] N firma *f*; **to put one's ~ to sth** firmar algo ➤ **signature tune** (*Brit*) sintonía *f* de apertura (*de un programa*)

signet ring ['sɪɡnɪt,rɪŋ] N sello *m*

significance [sɪɡ'nɪfɪkəns] N **1** (= *meaning*) **she gave him a look full of ~** le dirigió una mirada muy significativa *or* elocuente **2** (= *importance*) importancia *f*; **to be of some/no ~** ser importante/no tener ninguna importancia

significant [sɪɡ'nɪfɪkənt] ADJ **1** (= *important*) [*number, event, achievement, part, development*] importante; [*effect, amount, improvement, sum of money*] considerable; [*contribution, reduction, increase*] significativo, considerable; [*difference*] significativo; [*change*] importante, considerable; [*factor, impact*] significativo, importante **2** (= *meaningful*) significativo, elocuente

significantly [sɪɡ'nɪfɪkəntlɪ] ADV **1** (= *considerably*) (*with adj*) [*higher, lower, better, reduced*] considerablemente; (*with verb*) [*change, improve, reduce, increase*] de forma significativa, considerablemente **2** (= *notably*) **~, most of them are Scottish** es significativo que la mayoría sean escoceses; **they have ~ different ideas** sus ideas son notablemente distintas

signify ['sɪɡnɪfaɪ] VT **1** (= *mean*) querer decir, significar **2** (= *make known*) indicar; **to ~ one's approval** indicar su aprobación

signing ['saɪnɪŋ] N **1** [*of letter, contract, treaty etc*] firma *f* **2** (*Sport*) fichaje *m* **3** (= *sign language*) lenguaje *m* por señas

signpost ['saɪnpəʊst] N poste *m* indicador

Sikh [siːk] ADJ, N sij *mf*

silage ['saɪlɪdʒ] N ensilaje *m*

silence ['saɪləns] Ⓐ N silencio *m*; **a two minutes' ~** dos minutos de silencio; **they stood in ~** permanecieron en silencio Ⓑ VT [+ *person, crowd*] hacer callar, acallar; [+ *bells, guns, cries*] silenciar, acallar; [+ *criticism, fears, doubts*] acallar, silenciar; **he ~d his critics** silenció a sus críticos

silencer ['saɪlənsəʳ] N (*on gun, also Brit Aut*) silenciador *m*

silent ['saɪlənt] Ⓐ ADJ **1** (= *noiseless*) **to be ~** [*person*] quedarse callado; [*place, street*] estar en silencio; **to fall ~** [*person*] quedarse callado; [*room*] quedar en silencio; **the ~ majority** la mayoría silenciosa; **you have the right to remain ~** tiene derecho a permanecer callado, no está obligado a responder **2** (= *wordless*) [*prayer, vigil*] silencioso; [*film, contempt, protest*] mudo **3** [*letter*] mudo; **the "k" in knee is ~** la "k" en "knee" es muda *or* no se pronuncia Ⓑ CPD ➤ **silent partner** (*US*) socio/a *m/f* comanditario/a

silently ['saɪləntlɪ] ADV **1** (= *without speaking*) en silencio **2** (= *without making noise*) silenciosamente

silhouette [,sɪluː'et] Ⓐ N silueta *f* Ⓑ VT **to be ~d against sth** destacarse *or* perfilarse en *or* contra algo

silica ['sɪlɪkə] N sílice *f*

silicon ['sɪlɪkən] N silicio *m* ➤ **silicon chip** chip *m or* plaqueta *f* de silicio

silicone ['sɪlɪkəʊn] N silicona *f*

silk [sɪlk] N seda *f*

silk-screen printing [,sɪlkskriːn'prɪntɪŋ] N serigrafía *f*

silkworm ['sɪlkwɜːm] N gusano *m* de seda

silky ['sɪlkɪ] ADJ (*compar* **silkier**; *superl* **silkiest**) sedoso; [*sound, voice*] suave; **~ smooth** suave como la seda

sill [sɪl] N **1** (= *windowsill*) alféizar *m* **2** (*Aut*) umbral *m*

silliness ['sɪlɪnɪs] N estupidez *f*; (= *act*) tontería *f*

silly ['sɪlɪ] ADJ (*compar* **sillier**; *superl* **silliest**) (= *stupid*) [*person*] tonto, bobo, sonso *or* zonzo (*LAm*); [*act, idea*] absurdo; (= *ridiculous*) ridículo; **that was a ~ thing to do** eso que hiciste fue muy tonto *or* bobo, fue una tontería *or* estupidez por tu parte; **I've done a ~ thing** he hecho una tontería, he sido un tonto

silo ['saɪləʊ] N (*pl* **~s**) silo *m*

silt [sɪlt] N sedimento *m*, aluvión *m*
➤ **silt up** Ⓐ VI + ADV obstruirse (con sedimentos) Ⓑ VT + ADV obstruir (con sedimentos)

silver ['sɪlvəʳ] Ⓐ N **1** (= *metal*) plata *f*; (= *silverware, cutlery*) plata *f*, vajilla *f* de plata
2 (= *money*) monedas *fpl* de plata, monedas *fpl* plateadas Ⓑ ADJ **1** (= *made of silver*) [*ring, cutlery*] de plata
2 (*in colour*) plateado; [*car*] gris plata *inv* Ⓒ CPD ➤ **silver birch** abedul *m* plateado ➤ **silver foil** (*Brit*) papel *m* de aluminio *or* plata ➤ **silver jubilee** vigésimo quinto aniversario *m* ➤ **silver lining** resquicio *m* de esperanza ➤ **silver medal** medalla *f* de plata ➤ **silver medallist** medallero/a *m/f* de plata ➤ **silver paper** papel *m* de plata ➤ **the silver screen** la pantalla cinematográfica ➤ **silver wedding** bodas *fpl* de plata

silver-plated [,sɪlvə'pleɪtɪd] ADJ plateado

silversmith ['sɪlvəsmɪθ] N platero/a *m/f*

silverware ['sɪlvəweəʳ] N plata *f*, vajilla *f* de plata

silvery ['sɪlvərɪ] ADJ [*colour*] plateado; [*sound, voice*] argentino

similar ['sɪmɪləʳ] ADJ parecido, similar, semejante; **they were of a ~ age** eran más o menos de la misma edad; **to be ~ to** parecerse a, ser parecido *or* similar *or* semejante a

similarity [,sɪmɪ'lærɪtɪ] N **1** (*uncountable*) (= *resemblance*) parecido *m*, semejanza *f* **2** (*countable*) (= *feature in common*) semejanza *f*, rasgo *m* común, similitud *f*

similarly ['sɪmɪləlɪ] ADV **1** (= *equally*) igualmente; (= *in a like manner*) de modo parecido, de manera parecida, de modo *or* manera similar

simile ['sɪmɪlɪ] N símil *m*

simmer ['sɪməʳ] Ⓐ VT cocer a fuego lento Ⓑ VI hervir a fuego lento; (*fig*) estar a punto de estallar
➤ **simmer down*** VI + ADV (*fig*) calmarse, tranquilizarse

simper ['sɪmpəʳ] Ⓐ N sonrisa *f* tonta Ⓑ VI sonreír tontamente Ⓒ VT **"yes," she ~ed** —sí —dijo con una sonrisa tonta

simple ['sɪmpl] ADJ (*compar* **~r**; *superl* **~st**)
1 (= *uncomplicated*) sencillo, simple; **nothing could be ~r** no hay nada más simple; **it's as ~ as that** la cosa es así de sencilla; **keep it ~** no lo compliques; **in ~ terms** en lenguaje sencillo; **to be ~ to make/use** ser sencillo de hacer/usar
2 (= *mere*) simple; **for the ~ reason that ...** por la simple razón de que ...; **the ~ fact is ...** la pura realidad es ...; **the ~ truth** la pura verdad
3 (= *not fussy*) [*dress, style, food*] sencillo
4 (= *unsophisticated*) sencillo; **the ~ things in life** las cosas sencillas de la vida
5 (*) (*mentally*) simple

simple-minded ['sɪmpl'maɪndɪd] ADJ ingenuo, simple

simpleton ['sɪmpltən] N inocentón/ona *m/f*, simplón/ona *m/f*

simplicity [sɪm'plɪsɪtɪ] N (= *uncomplicated nature*) sencillez *f*, simplicidad *f*; **it's ~ itself** es la sencillez personificada

simplify ['sɪmplɪfaɪ] VT simplificar

simplistic [sɪm'plɪstɪk] ADJ simplista

simply ['sɪmplɪ] ADV **1** (= in a simple way) [dress, furnish] sencillamente; [speak, explain] en términos sencillos **2** (= merely) simplemente; (emphatic) (= absolutely) simplemente; **it ~ isn't possible** sencillamente no es posible; **you ~ MUST come!** ¡no dejes de venir!

simulate ['sɪmjʊleɪt] VT simular

simulation [ˌsɪmjʊ'leɪʃən] N simulación f

simulator ['sɪmjʊleɪtəʳ] N simulador m

simultaneous [ˌsɪməl'teɪnɪəs] ADJ simultáneo

simultaneously [ˌsɪməl'teɪnɪəslɪ] ADV simultáneamente, a la vez

sin [sɪn] Ⓐ N pecado m; **it would be a ~ to do that** (Rel) sería un pecado hacer eso; (fig) sería un crimen hacer eso; **to live in ~†** (unmarried) vivir amancebados, vivir en pecado Ⓑ VI pecar

Sinai ['saɪnaɪ] N Sinaí m

since [sɪns] Ⓐ ADV desde entonces; **ever ~** desde entonces; **the time for talking has long ~ passed** el tiempo de hablar ya pasó hace tiempo
Ⓑ PREP desde; **~ Monday** desde el lunes; **~ then** desde entonces; **I've been waiting ~ ten** espero desde las diez
Ⓒ CONJ **1** (= from the time that) desde que; **~ I arrived** desde que llegué; **I've been wearing glasses ~ I was three** llevo gafas desde los tres años; **it's a week ~ he left** hace una semana que se fue, se fue hace una semana; **it's a few years ~ I've seen them** hace varios años que no los veo; **ever ~ I've been here** desde que estoy aquí
2 (= as, because) ya que, puesto que, como

sincere [sɪn'sɪəʳ] ADJ sincero (**about sth** sobre algo, con respecto a algo); **it is my ~ belief that ...** creo sinceramente que ...

sincerely [sɪn'sɪəlɪ] ADV **1** [hope, believe, regret, say] sinceramente **2** (in letters) **Yours sincerely** (Brit) ◇ **Sincerely yours** (US) (le saluda) atentamente

sincerity [sɪn'serɪtɪ] N sinceridad f

sine [saɪn] N (Math) seno m

sinecure ['saɪnɪkjʊəʳ] N sinecura f

sine qua non ['saɪnɪkweɪ'nɒn] N sine qua non m

sinew ['sɪnjuː] N tendón m

sinewy ['sɪnjuːɪ] ADJ [person] musculoso, fibroso; [body, arms, muscles] nervudo, fibroso

sinful ['sɪnfəl] ADJ [act, thought] pecaminoso; [person] pecador; [town etc] inmoral, depravado

sing [sɪŋ] (pt **sang**; pp **sung**) Ⓐ VT [+ song, words] cantar; **to ~ a child to sleep** arrullar a un niño, adormecer a un niño cantando; ✦ IDIOM **to ~ sb's praises** cantar las alabanzas de algn Ⓑ VI [person, bird] cantar; [wind, kettle] silbar; [ears] zumbar
➤ **sing along** VI + ADV **he invited the audience to ~ along** invitó al público a cantar (a coro) con él; **to ~ along with** or **to a song** corear una canción

Singapore [ˌsɪŋgə'pɔːʳ] N Singapur m

Singaporean [ˌsɪŋgə'pɔːrɪən] ADJ de Singapur

singe [sɪndʒ] VT chamuscar, quemar

singer ['sɪŋəʳ] N cantante mf

singer-songwriter [ˌsɪŋə'sɒŋraɪtəʳ] N cantautor(a) m/f

singing ['sɪŋɪŋ] N canto m; **his ~ was atrocious** cantaba pésimamente, cantaba fatal*; ➤ **singing lesson** lección f de canto ➤ **singing teacher** profesor(a) m/f de canto

single ['sɪŋgl] Ⓐ ADJ **1** (= one only) solo; **in a ~ day** en un solo día; **it rained every ~ day** no dejó de llover ni un solo día, llovió todos los días sin excepción; **not a** or **one ~ person came to her aid** ni una sola persona fue a ayudarla; **the ~ biggest problem** el problema más grande
2 (= individual) **he gave her a ~ rose** le dio una rosa
3 (= not double) [bed, sheet, room] individual; [garage] para un solo coche, de una plaza; [whisky, gin, etc] sencillo
4 (= unmarried) [person] soltero; [mother, father] sin pareja; [life] de soltero
5 (before noun) (Brit) [ticket, fare] de ida

Ⓑ N **1** (in hotel, also ~ **room**) habitación f individual
2 (Brit) (also ~ **ticket**) billete m de ida
3 (= record) sencillo m, single m
4 singles (Tennis etc) individuales mpl; **the men's ~s** los individuales masculinos
Ⓒ CPD ➤ **single bed** cama f individual ➤ **single cream** (Brit) crema f de leche líquida, nata f líquida (Sp) ➤ **single European currency** moneda f europea ➤ **single figures: interest rates have been in ~ figures since 1992** los tipos de interés no llegan al 10% desde 1992 ➤ **single file: in ~ file** en fila india ➤ **single honours** licenciatura universitaria en la que se estudia una sola especialidad ➤ **single market** mercado m único ➤ **single parent** (= woman) madre f soltera; (= man) padre m soltero ➤ **single room** habitación f individual ➤ **singles bar** bar m para solteros ➤ **single supplement, single person supplement, single room supplement** (in hotel) recargo m por reserva individual ➤ **single out** VT + ADV (= choose) elegir; (= distinguish) hacer resaltar; **he was ~d out for criticism** fue elegido como blanco de las críticas, fue el blanco de las críticas

single-breasted [ˌsɪŋgl'brestɪd] ADJ recto

single-decker [ˌsɪŋgl'dekəʳ] N (Brit) autobús m de un solo piso

single-entry [ˌsɪŋgl'entrɪ] N partida f simple ➤ **single-entry book-keeping** contabilidad f por partida simple

single-handed [ˌsɪŋgl'hændɪd] ADJ, ADV sin ayuda

single-minded [ˌsɪŋgl'maɪndɪd] ADJ resuelto, firme

single-parent ['sɪŋgl,peərənt] CPD ➤ **single-parent family** familia f monoparental

single-sex school [ˌsɪŋglseks'skuːl] N escuela sólo f para niños or niñas

single-sided disk [ˌsɪŋglsaɪdɪd'dɪsk] N disco m de una cara

singlet ['sɪŋglɪt] N (Brit) camiseta f sin mangas, camiseta f de tirantes, playera f (LAm)

single-use ['sɪŋgl,juːs] ADJ [camera, syringe etc] de un solo uso

singly ['sɪŋglɪ] ADV (= separately) por separado; (= one at a time) uno por uno

singsong ['sɪŋˌsɒŋ] Ⓐ ADJ [voice] cantarín Ⓑ N (Brit) concierto m improvisado; **to get together for a ~** reunirse para cantar (canciones populares, folklóricas etc)

singular ['sɪŋgjʊləʳ] Ⓐ ADJ **1** (Ling) singular
2 (= extraordinary) singular, excepcional Ⓑ N singular m; **in the ~** en singular

singularly ['sɪŋgjʊləlɪ] ADV (= extraordinarily) extraordinariamente, singularmente

sinister ['sɪnɪstəʳ] ADJ siniestro

sink¹ [sɪŋk] (pt **sank**; pp **sunk**) Ⓐ VT **1** (= submerge) [+ ship] hundir; (fig) (= destroy) [+ person] hundir; [+ project] acabar con, dar al traste con; [+ theory] destruir, acabar con; **to be sunk in thought** estar absorto en mis etc pensamientos, estar ensimismado; **to be sunk*** estar perdido
2 [+ mineshaft] abrir, excavar; [+ hole] hacer, excavar; [+ well] perforar, abrir; **to ~ money in** or **into sth** invertir dinero en algo
3 (= dig in) [+ knife] hundir, clavar; [+ teeth] hincar
Ⓑ VI **1** [ship, object] hundirse; **the body sank to the bottom of the lake** el cadáver se hundió en el fondo del lago; **to ~ out of sight** desaparecer; ✦ IDIOM **to leave sb to ~ or swim** abandonar a algn a su suerte
2 (= subside) [building, land] hundirse; [flood waters] bajar de nivel; [sun] ponerse
3 (= slump) [person] **to ~ into a chair** arrellanarse en una silla, dejarse caer en una silla; **to ~ to one's knees** caer de rodillas; **to ~ into poverty** hundirse or caer en la miseria; **my heart sank** se me cayó el alma a los pies
4 (= deteriorate) [sick person] **he's ~ing fast** está cada vez peor
5 (= fall) (in amount, value) **the shares have sunk to three dollars** las acciones han bajado a tres dólares; **he has sunk in my estimation** ha bajado en mi estima
Ⓒ ADJ [school, estate] marginal
➤ **sink in** VI + ADV (= penetrate) penetrar; **she paused to let the news ~ in** (fig) hizo una pausa para que pudieran asimilar la noticia

sink² [sɪŋk] N (*in kitchen*) fregadero *m*, pila *f*; (*in bathroom*) lavabo *m* ➤ **sink unit** fregadero *m*

sinking ['sɪŋkɪŋ] ADJ **1** (= *foundering*) **a** ~ **ship** un barco que se hunde; (*fig*) (= *cause*) una causa en declive *or* que va a pique; (= *organization*) una organización en declive *or* que va a pique **2** **that ~ feeling** esa sensación de ansiedad *or* desazón; **with a ~ heart** entristecido

sinner ['sɪnəʳ] N pecador(a) *m/f*

Sinn Fein [ˌʃɪn'feːn] N Sinn Fein *m*

Sino... ['saɪnəʊ] PREF sino...

sinuous ['sɪnjʊəs] ADJ sinuoso

sinus ['saɪnəs] N (*pl* ~**es**) seno *m*

sinusitis [ˌsaɪnə'saɪtɪs] N sinusitis *f*

sip [sɪp] **Ⓐ** N sorbo *m* **Ⓑ** VT sorber, beber a sorbos **Ⓒ** VI (*also* ~ **at**) sorber, beber a sorbitos

siphon ['saɪfən] **Ⓐ** N sifón *m* **Ⓑ** VT (*also* ~ **off**, ~ **out**) sacar con sifón; (*fig*) [+ *traffic, funds*] desviar

sir [sɜːʳ] N señor *m*; **Sirs** (*US*) muy señores nuestros; **yes,** ~ sí, señor; **Dear Sir** (*in letter*) muy señor mío, estimado señor; **Sir Winston Churchill** Sir Winston Churchill

sire ['saɪəʳ] **Ⓐ** N (*Zool*) padre *m*; **Sire**†† (*to monarch*) Señor *m* **Ⓑ** VT ser el padre de; **he ~d 49 children** tuvo 49 hijos

siren ['saɪərən] N (*all senses*) sirena *f*

sirloin ['sɜːlɔɪn] N solomillo *m*

sirup ['sɪrəp] N (*US*) = **syrup**

sissy** ['sɪsɪ] N **1** (= *effeminate*) marica** *m*, mariquita** *m*; **the last one's a ~!** ¡maricón el último!** **2** (= *coward*) gallina* *f*

sister ['sɪstəʳ] **Ⓐ** N **1** (= *relation*) hermana *f* **2** (*Brit Med*) (*also* **nursing ~**) enfermera *f* jefe **3** (*Rel*) hermana *f*; (*before name*) sor *f* **Ⓑ** CPD ➤ **sister city** (*US*) ciudad *f* hermana ➤ **sister organization** organización *f* hermana ➤ **sister ship** barco *m* gemelo

sister-in-law ['sɪstərɪnlɔː] N (*pl* **sisters-in-law**) cuñada *f*

sisterly ['sɪstəlɪ] ADJ de hermana

sit [sɪt] (*pt, pp* **sat**) **Ⓐ** VI **1** (= *be seated*) [*person*] estar sentado; [*bird*] estar posado; [*hen*] (*on eggs*) empollar; **don't just ~ there, do something!** ¡no te quedes ahí sentado, haz algo!; **to ~ at home all day** pasar todo el día en casa (sin hacer nada); **they were ~ting in a traffic jam for two hours** estuvieron dos horas metidos en un atasco sin moverse; **to ~ still/straight** estarse *or* (*LAm*) quedarse quieto/ponerse derecho (en la silla); ✦ IDIOMS **to be ~ting pretty*** estar bien colocado *or* situado; **to ~ tight:** ~ **tight, I'll be right back** no te muevas, ahora vuelvo **2** (= *sit down*) sentarse; (= *alight*) [*bird*] posarse; **sit!** (*to dog*) ¡quieto! **3** (*Art, Phot*) (= *pose*) **to ~ for a painter/a portrait** posar para un pintor/un retrato **4** (= *be in session*) [*assembly*] reunirse, celebrar sesión **5** (= *weigh*) **it sat heavy on his conscience** le pesaba en la conciencia, le producía remordimientos de conciencia **6** (= *to fit*) [*clothing*] sentar; **to ~ well/badly (on sb)** sentar bien/mal (a algn) **Ⓑ** VT **1** [+ *person*] sentar; [+ *object*] colocar **2** (*Brit*) [+ *exam, test*] presentarse a

➤ **sit around, sit about** VI + ADV **I'm tired of ~ting around waiting for him** estoy aburrido de esperar sentado a que venga

➤ **sit back** VI + ADV (*in seat*) recostarse; **just ~ back and enjoy the show** póngase cómodo y disfrute del espectáculo; **we can't just ~ back and do nothing** (*fig*) no podemos quedarnos cruzados de brazos sin hacer nada

➤ **sit down** **Ⓐ** VI + ADV sentarse; **to be ~ting down** estar sentado **Ⓑ** VT + ADV [+ *person*] sentar

➤ **sit in** VI + ADV **1** (= *observe*) estar presente; **they said I could ~ in on the meeting** me dijeron que podía asistir a la reunión (como observador) **2** (= *substitute*) sustituir; **to ~ in for sb** sustituir a algn

➤ **sit on** VI + PREP **1** (= *be member of*) [+ *jury, committee*] ser miembro de, formar parte de **2** (*) (= *keep secret*) [+ *news, information*] ocultar, callar; (= *delay taking action on*) [+ *application, plan*] no dar trámite a, dar carpetazo a*

➤ **sit out** VT + ADV **1** (= *not take part in*) [+ *dance*] no bailar;

(*Sport*) [+ *game, event*] no participar en **2** (= *endure*) aguantar; **he decided to ~ the war out in Brussels** decidió aguantar en Bruselas hasta que terminara la guerra

➤ **sit through** VI + PREP **it was the most boring speech he'd ever had to ~ through** fue el discurso más aburrido que jamás tuvo que escuchar *or* aguantar

➤ **sit up** VI + ADV **1** (= *straighten o.s.*) ponerse derecho, enderezarse; (*after lying*) incorporarse; **he knew the offer of money would make them ~ up and take notice** (*fig*) sabía que la oferta de dinero conseguiría hacerles prestar atención **2** (= *stay up late*) **I sat up all night trying to work it out** me quedé toda la noche levantado intentando resolverlo; **I'll be late back so don't ~ up for me** volveré tarde así que no me esperes levantado; **to ~ up with a child** pasar la noche en vela con un niño

sitcom* ['sɪtkɒm] N comedia *f* de situación

sit-down* ['sɪtdaʊn] N (*Brit*) **I must have a ~*** tengo que sentarme a descansar un rato

site [saɪt] **Ⓐ** N **1** (= *place*) sitio *m*, lugar *m*; (= *location*) situación *f*; (= *scene*) escenario *m*; (*for building*) solar *m*, terreno *m*; (*archaeological*) yacimiento *m*; **the ~ of the accident** el lugar del accidente **2** (*Internet*) = **website** **Ⓑ** VT situar, ubicar (*esp LAm*)

sit-in ['sɪtɪn] N (= *protest, demonstration*) encierro *m*, ocupación *f*; (= *strike*) huelga *f* de brazos caídos, sentada *f*

sitter ['sɪtəʳ] N (*Art*) modelo *mf*; (= *babysitter*) babysitter *mf*, canguro *mf* (*Sp*)

sitting ['sɪtɪŋ] N (*Pol, Art etc*) sesión *f*; (*in canteen*) turno *m*; **to read a book in one ~** leer un libro de un tirón ➤ **sitting duck*** (*fig*) objetivo *m* fácil ➤ **sitting room** (*Brit*) (= *living room*) sala *f*, cuarto *m* de estar, salón *m*, living *m* (*LAm*) ➤ **sitting target** objetivo *m* fácil ➤ **sitting tenant** (*Brit*) inquilino/a *m/f* en posesión

situate ['sɪtjʊeɪt] VT situar, ubicar (*esp LAm*)

situation [ˌsɪtjʊ'eɪʃən] **Ⓐ** N **1** (= *position*) situación *f*, ubicación *f* (*esp LAm*) **2** (= *circumstances*) situación *f*; **to save the** ~ salvar la situación **3** (= *job*) empleo *m*, vacante *f*; **"situations vacant/wanted"** (*Brit*) "ofertas/demandas de empleo" **Ⓑ** CPD ➤ **situation comedy** comedia *f* de situación

sit-up ['sɪtʌp] N abdominal *m*

six [sɪks] NUMBER seis *m*; **to hit a ~** (*Cricket*) batear un seis, hacer seis carreras de un golpe; ✦ IDIOMS ~ **of the best** (*Brit*) seis azotes *mpl* (*castigo escolar*); **it's ~ of one and half a dozen of the other*** da lo mismo, da igual; **to knock sb for** ~ (*Brit**) dejar pasmado a algn; **to be (all) at ~es and sevens** [*person*] estar confuso; [*things*] estar en desorden; *see* **five**

six-pack ['sɪkspæk] N paquete *m* de seis

sixpence ['sɪkspəns] N (*Brit*) (*formerly*) moneda *f* de seis peniques

six-shooter* ['sɪksˈʃuːtəʳ] N (*US*) revólver *m* de seis tiros

sixteen ['sɪksˈtiːn] NUMBER dieciséis *m*; *see* **five**

sixteenth ['sɪksˈtiːnθ] **Ⓐ** ADJ decimosexto **Ⓑ** PRON (*in series*) decimosexto/a *m/f*; (= *fraction*) decimosexta parte *f*, dieciseisavo *m*; *see* **fifteenth**

sixth [sɪksθ] **Ⓐ** ADJ sexto **Ⓑ** PRON (*in series*) sexto/a *m/f*; (= *fraction*) sexta parte *f*, sexto *m* **Ⓒ** CPD ➤ **sixth form** (*Brit*) clase *f* de alumnos del sexto año (*de 16 a 18 años de edad*) ➤ **sixth former** (*Brit*) alumno/a *m/f* de 16 a 18 años ➤ **sixth sense** sexto sentido *m*; *see* **fifth**

sixth-form college [ˌsɪksfɔːmˈkɒlɪdʒ] N instituto *m* para alumnos de 16 a 18 años

sixtieth ['sɪkstɪθ] **Ⓐ** ADJ sexagésimo **Ⓑ** PRON (*in series*) sexagésimo/a *m/f*; (= *fraction*) sexagésima parte *f*, sesentavo *m*; *see* **fiftieth**

sixty ['sɪkstɪ] NUMBER sesenta *m*; *see* **fifty**

sixty-four thousand dollar question* [ˌsɪkstɪfɔːˈθaʊzəndɒləˈkwestʃən] N **that's the ~** ésa es la pregunta del millón (de dólares)

sizable ['saɪzəbl] ADJ = **sizeable**

size [saɪz] N [*of object, place*] tamaño *m*; [*of person*] talla *f*, estatura *f*; [*of garments*] talla *f*, medida *f*; [*of shoes, gloves*] número *m*; [*of problem*] magnitud *f*, envergadura *f*; **it's the** ~ **of a brick** es del tamaño de un ladrillo; **the skirt is two ~s**

too big la falda es dos tallas grande; **try this (on)** <u>for</u> ~ prueba esto a ver si te conviene; **it's** <u>quite a</u> ~ es bastante grande; **I** <u>take</u> ~ **nine** (*shoes*) uso *or* tengo el número nueve; **I take** ~ **14** (*blouse etc*) uso *or* tengo la talla 14; **to cut sth** <u>to</u> ~ cortar algo al tamaño que se necesita; <u>what</u> ~ **is the room?** ¿de qué tamaño *or* (*LAm*) qué tan grande es el cuarto?; **what** ~ **are you?** ¿qué talla usas *or* tienes?, ¿qué talla eres?; **what** ~ **shoes do you take?** ¿qué número (de zapato) calzas *or* gastas?; **he's about** <u>your</u> ~ tiene más o menos tu talla; ✦ IDIOMS **that's about the** ~ **of it** eso es lo que puedo decirle acerca del asunto, es más o menos eso; **to cut sb down to** ~* bajar los humos a algn
➤ **size up** VT + ADV [+ *problem, situation*] evaluar, apreciar; [+ *person*] **they looked at each other, sizing each other up** se miraban el uno al otro, intentando formarse *or* hacerse un juicio; **I can't quite** ~ **him up** no sé muy bien de qué va

sizeable ['saɪzəbl] ADJ [*sum of money etc*] considerable, importante; [*object, building*] bastante grande

sizzle ['sɪzl] VI chisporrotear; (*in frying*) crepitar (al freírse)

sizzling ['sɪzlɪŋ] ADJ [*heat*] sofocante

SK ABBR (*Canada*) = **Saskatchewan**

skate¹ [skeɪt] N (= *fish*) raya *f*

skate² [skeɪt] Ⓐ N patín *m*; ✦ IDIOM **get your ~s on!*** ¡date prisa! Ⓑ VI patinar
➤ **skate around, skate over, skate round** VI + PREP [+ *problem, issue*] pasar por alto de, pasar por encima de

skateboard ['skeɪtbɔːd] N monopatín *m*

skateboarder ['skeɪtbɔːdəʳ] N monopatinador(a) *m/f*

skateboarding ['skeɪtbɔːdɪŋ] N monopatinaje *m*; **to go ~** montar en monopatín

skater ['skeɪtəʳ] N patinador(a) *m/f*

skating ['skeɪtɪŋ] N patinaje *m*; **to go ~** ir a patinar
➤ **skating rink** (*for ice skating*) pista *f* de hielo; (*for roller skating*) pista *f* de patinaje

skein [skeɪn] N madeja *f*

skeletal ['skelɪtl] ADJ [*person, body*] esquelético; [*face*] enjuto

skeleton ['skelɪtn] N esqueleto *m*; [*of novel, report*] esquema *m*, bosquejo *m*; ✦ IDIOM ~ **in the cupboard** (*Brit*) *or* **closet** (*US*) secreto *m* de familia ➤ **skeleton key** llave *f* maestra ➤ **skeleton staff: with a** ~ **staff** con un personal mínimo

skeptic *etc* ['skeptɪk] (*US*) = **sceptic** *etc*

sketch [sketʃ] Ⓐ N **1** (= *drawing*) dibujo *m*; (= *preliminary drawing*) esbozo *m*, bosquejo *m*; (= *rough drawing*) croquis *m inv*; (= *plan*) borrador *m*, esquema *m* **2** (*Theat*) sketch *m* Ⓑ VT dibujar; [+ *preliminary drawing, plan*] bosquejar, esbozar Ⓒ VI hacer bosquejos Ⓓ CPD ➤ **sketch pad** bloc *m* de dibujos
➤ **sketch in** VT + ADV [+ *details*] explicar

sketchbook ['sketʃbʊk] N bloc *m* de dibujos

sketchy ['sketʃi] ADJ (*compar* **sketchier**; *superl* **sketchiest**) incompleto, sin detalles

skew [skjuː] Ⓐ VT sesgar, desviar Ⓑ VI (*also* **to ~ round**) desviarse, ponerse al sesgo, torcerse

skewed [skjuːd] ADJ sesgado, torcido (*also fig*)

skewer ['skjʊəʳ] Ⓐ N pincho *m*, broqueta *f*, brocheta *f* Ⓑ VT ensartar, espetar

skew-whiff* [skjuː'wɪf] ADJ (*Brit*) torcido, chueco (*LAm*)

ski [skiː] Ⓐ N esquí *m* Ⓑ VI esquiar; **to go ~ing** practicar el esquí, (ir a) esquiar; **to ~ down** bajar esquiando
Ⓒ CPD ➤ **ski boot** bota *f* de esquí ➤ **ski instructor** instructor(a) *m/f* de esquí, monitor(a) *m/f* de esquí ➤ **ski jump** (= *action*) salto *m* con esquís; (= *course*) pista *f* de salto ➤ **ski jumper** saltador(a) *m/f* de esquí ➤ **ski jumping** salto *m* de esquí ➤ **ski lift** telesquí *m*, telesilla *m* ➤ **ski pants** pantalones *mpl* de esquí ➤ **ski pole** bastón *m* ➤ **ski resort** estación *f* de esquí ➤ **ski run** pista *f* de esquí ➤ **ski slope** pista *f* de esquí ➤ **ski stick** bastón *m* ➤ **ski suit** traje *m* de esquiar, mono *m* de esquí

skid [skɪd] Ⓐ N patinazo *m*, resbalón *m* Ⓑ VI (*Aut*) patinar; [*person, object*] deslizarse, resbalarse; **I ~ded into a**

tree patiné y di contra un árbol, de un patinazo di contra un árbol; **the car ~ded to a halt** el coche patinó y paró Ⓒ CPD ➤ **skid row*** (*US*) *calles donde se refugian los borrachos, drogadictos etc*

skidmark ['skɪdmɑːk] N huella *f* de un patinazo

skidproof ['skɪdpruːf] ADJ antideslizante

skier ['skiːəʳ] N esquiador(a) *m/f*

skiing ['skiːɪŋ] N esquí *m*; **do you like ~?** ¿te gusta esquiar? ➤ **skiing holiday** vacaciones *fpl* de esquí ➤ **skiing resort** estación *f* de esquí

skilful, skillful (*US*) ['skɪlfəl] ADJ hábil, diestro (**at, in** en)

skilfully, skillfully (*US*) ['skɪlfəli] ADV hábilmente, con destreza

skilfulness, skillfulness (*US*) ['skɪlfəlnɪs] N habilidad *f*, destreza *f*

skill [skɪl] N **1** (= *ability*) habilidad *f*, destreza *f*; **his ~ as a fundraiser came in useful** su habilidad para recaudar fondos resultó útil; **his lack of ~ in dealing with people** su inaptitud *or* falta de capacidad para tratar con la gente **2** (= *technique*) técnica *f*; **the basic ~s of reading and writing** los conocimientos básicos de lectura y escritura; **communication ~s** habilidad *f or* aptitud *f* para comunicarse

skilled [skɪld] ADJ **1** [*person*] (= *specialized*) especializado; (= *skilful*) hábil, diestro; **he is ~ at** *or* **in dealing with children** tiene muy buena mano con los niños **2** [*worker, labour*] cualificado (*esp Sp*), calificado (*esp LAm*), especializado **3** [*job, work*] especializado

skillet ['skɪlɪt] N sartén *f* pequeña, sartén *m* pequeño (*LAm*)

skillful *etc* ['skɪlfəl] ADJ (*US*) = **skilful** *etc*

skim [skɪm] Ⓐ VT **1** [+ *milk*] desnatar, descremar; [+ *soup, liquid*] espumar; **to ~ the cream off the milk** quitar la nata a la leche, desnatar la leche; **~med milk** (*Brit*) ✧ ~ **milk** (*US*) leche *f* descremada *or* desnatada **2** [+ *surface*] rozar; [+ *stone*] hacer cabrillas con, hacer el salto de la rana con Ⓑ VI **to ~ across/along the ground** pasar rozando la tierra; **to ~ through a book** (*fig*) echar una ojeada *or* hojear a un libro
➤ **skim off** VT + ADV [+ *cream, grease*] desnatar; **they ~med off the brightest pupils** separaron a la flor y nata de los alumnos

skimp [skɪmp] VI economizar; **to ~ on fabric/work/food** escatimar tela/trabajo/alimento

skimpy ['skɪmpi] ADJ (*compar* **skimpier**; *superl* **skimpiest**) [*skirt etc*] breve; [*allowance, meal*] escaso, mezquino

skin [skɪn] Ⓐ N **1** [*of person*] piel *f*; [*of face*] cutis *m*; (= *complexion*) tez *f*; ✦ IDIOMS **to be ~ and bone** estar en los huesos; **to jump out of one's ~** llevarse un tremendo susto; **it's no ~ off my nose*** a mí ni me va ni me viene, me da igual *or* lo mismo; **to save one's ~** salvar el pellejo; **by the ~ of one's teeth** por los pelos; **to have a thick/thin ~** ser poco sensible/muy susceptible; **to get under sb's ~** (= *annoy*) irritar *or* molestar a algn; **I've got you under my ~*** no puedo dejar de pensar en ti
2 [*of animal*] piel *f*, pellejo *m*; (*as hide*) piel *f*, cuero *m*
3 [*of fruit, vegetable*] piel *f*, cáscara *f*; (*discarded*) mondaduras *fpl*
4 (= *crust*) (*on paint, milk pudding*) nata *f*
Ⓑ VT [+ *animal*] despellejar, desollar; **I'll ~ him alive!** (*fig*) ¡lo voy a matar!*, ¡lo voy a desollar vivo!; **to ~ one's knee/elbow** desollarse la rodilla/el codo
Ⓒ CPD ➤ **skin cancer** cáncer *m* de piel ➤ **skin disease** enfermedad *f* de la piel ➤ **skin diver** buceador(a) *m/f*, buzo *mf*, submarinista *mf* ➤ **skin diving** buceo *m*, submarinismo *m* ➤ **skin graft** injerto *m* de piel

skin-deep ['skɪn'diːp] ADJ superficial

skinflint ['skɪnflɪnt] N tacaño/a *m/f*, roñoso/a *m/f*

skinful* ['skɪnfəl] N **to have had a ~** estar borracho/a *or* (*LAm*) tomado/a

skinhead ['skɪnhed] N skinhead *mf*, cabeza *mf* rapada

skinny ['skɪni] ADJ (*compar* **skinnier**; *superl* **skinniest**) flaco

skinny-dipping* ['skɪnidɪpɪŋ] N **to go ~** bañarse en bolas*

skint [skɪnt] ADJ **to be ~** (*Brit**) estar sin cuartos, estar pelado

skin-tight ['skɪntaɪt] ADJ muy ajustado

skip[1] [skɪp] **Ⓐ** N salto *m*, brinco *m* **Ⓑ** VI (= *jump*) brincar, saltar; (*esp Brit*) (*with a rope*) saltar a la cuerda *or* (*Sp*) comba; **to ~ in/out** entrar/salir dando brincos; **to ~ over sth** (*fig*) pasar algo por alto, saltarse algo; **to ~ from one thing to another** saltar de un tema a otro; **the book ~s about a lot** el libro da muchos saltos **Ⓒ** VT (*fig*) [+ *meal, lesson, page*] saltarse; **to ~ school** hacer novillos, hacer la rabona **Ⓓ** CPD ➤ **skip rope** (*US*) cuerda *f*, comba *f* (*Sp*)

skip[2] [skɪp] N (*Brit*) (= *container*) contenedor *m* de basura(s)

skipper ['skɪpəʳ] **Ⓐ** N (*Sport*) capitán/ana *m/f*; (*Naut*) capitán/ana *m/f*, patrón/ona *m/f* **Ⓑ** VT [+ *boat*] capitanear, patronear; [+ *team*] capitanear

skipping ['skɪpɪŋ] N (*esp Brit*) saltar a la cuerda *or* (*Sp*) comba ➤ **skipping rope** cuerda *f*, comba *f* (*Sp*)

skirmish ['skɜːmɪʃ] N escaramuza *f*, refriega *f*; (*fig*) roce *m*

skirt [skɜːt] **Ⓐ** N falda *f*, pollera *f* (*LAm*); [*of coat etc*] faldón *m* **Ⓑ** VT (*also* **~ around**) rodear, dar la vuelta a; (*fig*) (= *avoid*) esquivar **Ⓒ** VI **to ~ around = B**

skirting board ['skɜːtɪŋˌbɔːd] N (*Brit*) zócalo *m*, cenefa *f*

skit [skɪt] N (*Theat*) sátira *f* (**on** de)

skitter ['skɪtəʳ] VI **to ~ across the water/along the ground** [*bird*] volar rozando el agua/el suelo

skittish ['skɪtɪʃ] ADJ (= *capricious*) caprichoso, delicado; (= *nervous*) [*horse etc*] nervioso, asustadizo

skittle ['skɪtl] N (*esp Brit*) bolo *m*; **~s** el juego de bolos; **to play ~s** jugar a los bolos ➤ **skittle alley** bolera *f*

skive** [skaɪv] (*Brit*) VI gandulear*, haraganear* ➤ **skive off**** (*Brit*) **Ⓐ** VI + ADV (= *not work*) gandulear*, haraganear* **Ⓑ** VI + PREP **to ~ off school** hacer novillos, hacer la rabona

skiver** ['skaɪvəʳ] N (*Brit*) gandul(a) *m/f*

skivvy* ['skɪvɪ] N (*Brit pej*) esclava *f* del hogar

skulduggery*† [skʌlˈdʌgərɪ] N trampas *fpl*, embustes *mpl*; **a piece of ~** una trampa, un embuste

skulk [skʌlk] VI esconderse

skull [skʌl] N calavera *f*; (*Med*) cráneo *m*; **~ and crossbones** (= *flag*) la bandera pirata

skullcap ['skʌlkæp] N gorro *m*

skunk [skʌŋk] N (*Zool*) mofeta *f*, zorrillo *m* (*LAm**); **you ~!** (*fig*) ¡canalla!

sky [skaɪ] **Ⓐ** N cielo *m*; **the skies over England** el cielo en Inglaterra; **to praise sb to the skies** poner a algn por las nubes; **the ~'s the limit*** (*fig*) no hay límite **Ⓑ** CPD ➤ **sky marshal** agente *mf* de seguridad (*en vuelos comerciales*)

sky-blue ['skaɪ'bluː] ADJ celeste, azul celeste

skydive ['skaɪdaɪv] **Ⓐ** N caída *f* libre **Ⓑ** VI saltar en caída libre

skydiver ['skaɪdaɪvəʳ] N paracaidista *mf* de caída libre, paracaidista *mf* acrobático/a

skydiving ['skaɪdaɪvɪŋ] N caída *f* libre, paracaidismo *m* acrobático

sky-high ['skaɪ'haɪ] ADV por las nubes; **prices have gone ~** los precios están por las nubes

skylark ['skaɪlɑːk] N alondra *f*

skylight ['skaɪlaɪt] N tragaluz *m*, claraboya *f*

skyline ['skaɪlaɪn] N (= *horizon*) horizonte *m*; [*of city*] contorno *m*, perfil *m*

skyrocket ['skaɪˌrɒkɪt] **Ⓐ** N cohete *m* **Ⓑ** VI [*prices etc*] ponerse por las nubes, dispararse

skyscraper ['skaɪˌskreɪpəʳ] N rascacielos *m inv*

skyward ['skaɪwəd], **skywards** ['skaɪwədz] (*esp Brit*) ADV hacia el cielo

slab [slæb] N **1** [*of stone*] losa *f* **2** (*in mortuary*) plancha *f* de mármol, tabla *f* de mármol **3** [*of chocolate*] tableta *f*; [*of cake etc*] buen trozo *m*; [*of meat*] buena tajada *f*

slack [slæk] **Ⓐ** ADJ (*compar* **~er**; *superl* **~est**) **1** (= *not tight or firm*) flojo **2** (= *lax*) descuidado, negligente; (= *lazy*)

perezoso, vago, flojo; **to be ~ about one's work** desatender su trabajo, ser negligente en su trabajo **3** (*Comm*) [*market*] flojo, encalmado; [*period*] de inactividad; **business is ~** hay poco movimiento *or* poca actividad en el negocio **Ⓑ** N (*in rope*) comba *f*; **to take up the ~ in a rope** tensar una cuerda **Ⓒ** VI (*) gandulear, holgazanear; **he's been ~ing** ha sido muy gandul

slacken ['slækn] **Ⓐ** VT [+ *reins*] aflojar; **to ~ one's pace** aflojar el paso **Ⓑ** VI **1** (= *loosen*) [*rope*] aflojarse **2** (*esp Brit*) (= *reduce*) [*activity, demand*] disminuir, bajar; [*trade*] decaer ➤ **slacken off** (*esp Brit*) **Ⓐ** VI + ADV (*esp Brit*) (= *reduce*) [*demand, production*] disminuir, bajar **Ⓑ** VT + ADV [+ *rope*] aflojar

slacker* ['slækəʳ] N holgazán/ana *m/f*, vago/a *m/f*, gandul(a) *m/f*

slackness ['slæknɪs] N [*of rope, market*] flojedad *f*

slacks [slæks] NPL pantalones *mpl*

slag[1] [slæg] N (*Min*) escoria *f* ➤ **slag heap** (*esp Brit*) escorial *m*

slag[2]** [slæg] N (*Brit pej*) (= *slut*) puta* *f*, ramera *f* ➤ **slag off**** VT + ADV (*Brit*) (= *criticize*) poner como un trapo*

slain [sleɪn] PP *of* **slay**

slake [sleɪk] VT [+ *one's thirst*] apagar, aplacar

slalom ['slɑːləm] N eslálom *m*, slalom *m*

slam [slæm] **Ⓐ** N portazo *m* **Ⓑ** VT **to ~ the door** dar un portazo, cerrar (la puerta) de un portazo; **to ~ sth shut** cerrar algo de golpe; **to ~ sth (down) on the table** dejar de golpe algo sobre la mesa, estampar algo sobre la mesa **Ⓒ** VI **1** [*door*] cerrarse de golpe, cerrarse de un portazo; **the door ~med shut** *or* **to** la puerta se cerró de golpe *or* de un portazo **2** **to ~ into/against sth** estrellarse contra algo; **to ~ on the brakes** dar un frenazo

slander ['slɑːndəʳ] **Ⓐ** N calumnia *f*; (*Jur*) difamación *f* **Ⓑ** VT calumniar; (*Jur*) difamar

slanderer ['slɑːndərəʳ] N calumniador(a) *m/f*, difamador(a) *m/f*

slanderous ['slɑːndərəs] ADJ calumnioso, difamatorio

slang [slæŋ] **Ⓐ** N argot *m*, jerga *f*; [*of a group, trade etc*] jerga *f* **Ⓑ** ADJ argótico, jergal; **~ word** palabra *f* del argot, palabra *f* argótica *or* jergal **Ⓒ** VT (*esp Brit**) poner verde a, injuriar; **a ~ing match** (*Brit*) una disputa a voces

slangy* ['slæŋɪ] ADJ (*compar* **slangier**; *superl* **slangiest**) argótico, jergal

slant [slɑːnt] **Ⓐ** N inclinación *f*, sesgo *m*; (= *slope*) pendiente *f*, cuesta *f*; (= *point of view*) punto *m* de vista, interpretación *f*; **what is your ~ on this?** ¿cuál es su punto de vista sobre esto?, ¿cómo interpreta usted esto?; **to get a ~ on a topic** pedir pareceres sobre un asunto **Ⓑ** VT inclinar, sesgar; **to ~ a report** (*fig*) enfocar una cuestión de manera parcial **Ⓒ** VI inclinarse, sesgarse

slanting ['slɑːntɪŋ] ADJ inclinado, sesgado

slap [slæp] **Ⓐ** N palmada *f*, manotazo *m*; **a ~ on the back** un espaldarazo; **a ~ in the face** una bofetada, un bofetón; (*fig*) un desaire; **to give sb a ~ on the wrist** (*fig*) dar un tirón de orejas a algn **Ⓑ** ADV (*Brit**) **it fell ~ in the middle** cayó justo en el medio **Ⓒ** VT **1** (= *strike*) dar manotazos a; (*once*) dar una manotada a; (*in the face*) abofetear, dar una bofetada a; **to ~ sb's face** dar una bofetada a algn, abofetear a algn; **to ~ sb on the back** dar a algn una palmada en la espalda; **to ~ sb down** (*fig*) bajar los humos a algn **2** (= *put*) **the judge ~ped £100 on the fine** el juez aumentó la multa en 100 libras; **to ~ paint on sth** pintar algo a brochazos

slap-bang* ['slæp'bæŋ] ADV (*Brit*) justo, exactamente

slapdash ['slæpdæʃ], **slap-happy** ['slæphæpɪ] ADJ descuidado, chapucero

slapstick ['slæpstɪk] N (*also* **~ comedy**) bufonada *f*

slap-up* ['slæpʌp] CPD (*Brit*) ➤ **slap-up meal** banquete *m*, comilona *f*

slash [slæʃ] **Ⓐ** N **1** (= *cut*) tajo *m*; (*with knife*) cuchillada *f* **2** (*Typ*) barra *f* oblicua **Ⓑ** VT **1** (= *cut*) (*with knife etc*) acuchillar; (*with razor*) hacer *or* dar un tajo a; [+ *tyre*] rajar; **to ~ one's wrists** cortarse las venas (*de la muñeca*)

2 (= *reduce*) [+ *price*] reducir, rebajar; **"prices slashed"** "grandes rebajas"

slat [slæt] N (*wooden*) tablilla *f*, listón *m*; [*of blind*] lama *f*

slate [sleɪt] Ⓐ N (= *substance*) pizarra *f*; (= *tile*) teja *f* de pizarra; (*US Pol*) lista *f* de candidatos; **to wipe the ~ clean** (*fig*) hacer borrón y cuenta nueva Ⓑ ADJ (= *made of slate*) de pizarra; (*in colour*) color pizarra Ⓒ VT **1** (*Brit**) (= *criticize*) vapulear, criticar duro **2** (*US*) anunciar; **it is ~d to start at nine** según el programa comienza a las nueve, deberá comenzar a las nueve Ⓓ CPD ➤ **slate pencil** pizarrín *m* ➤ **slate quarry** pizarral *m* ➤ **slate roof** empizarrado *m*

slate-blue [ˌsleɪtˈbluː] ADJ de color azul pizarra

slaughter [ˈslɔːtəʳ] Ⓐ N [*of animals*] matanza *f*, sacrificio *m*; [*of persons*] matanza *f*, carnicería *f*; **the ~ on the roads** el gran número de muertes en las carreteras Ⓑ VT [+ *animals*] matar, sacrificar; [+ *person, people*] matar brutalmente

slaughterhouse [ˈslɔːtəhaʊs] N matadero *m*

Slav [slɑːv] Ⓐ ADJ eslavo Ⓑ N eslavo/a *m/f*

slave [sleɪv] Ⓐ N esclavo/a *m/f*; **to be a ~ to sth** (*fig*) ser esclavo de algo Ⓑ VI **to ~ (away) at sth/at doing sth** trabajar como un esclavo en algo/haciendo algo Ⓒ CPD ➤ **slave driver** negrero/a *m/f*; (*fig*) tirano/a *m/f* ➤ **slave labour**, **slave labor** (*US*) (= *work*) trabajo *m* de esclavos; (= *persons*) esclavos *mpl* ➤ **slave trade** trata *f* de esclavos, comercio *m* de esclavos, tráfico *m* de esclavos

slaver [ˈslævəʳ] VI (= *dribble*) babear

slavery [ˈsleɪvəri] N esclavitud *f*

Slavic [ˈslɑːvɪk] ADJ eslavo

slavish [ˈsleɪvɪʃ] ADJ servil, de esclavo

slavishly [ˈsleɪvɪʃli] ADV servilmente

Slavonic [sləˈvɒnɪk] ADJ eslavo

slaw [slɔː] N (*US*) ensalada *f* de col

slay [sleɪ] (*pt* **slew** *pp* **slain**) VT (*poet or US*) matar

slaying [ˈsleɪɪŋ] N (*poet or US*) (= *murder*) asesinato *m*; (*large scale*) matanza *f*

sleaze* [sliːz] N (= *sordidness*) sordidez *f*, asco *m*; (*Pol*) (= *corruption*) corrupción *f*

sleazy [ˈsliːzi] ADJ (*compar* **sleazier** *superl* **sleaziest**) [*place*] sórdido, asqueroso; [*person*] desaseado, desaliñado; (= *corrupt*) [*deal etc*] poco limpio, sucio

sled (*US*) [sled], **sledge** (*Brit*) [sledʒ] Ⓐ N trineo *m* Ⓑ VI ir en trineo

sledgehammer [ˈsledʒˌhæməʳ] N almádena *f*

sleek [sliːk] ADJ (*compar* **~er** *superl* **~est**) [*hair, fur*] lustroso; [*person*] impecable

sleep [sliːp] (*vb: pt, pp* **slept**) Ⓐ N sueño *m*; **I couldn't get to ~** no podía dormirme *or* conciliar el sueño; **to go to ~** [*person*] dormirse, quedarse dormido; (= *limb*) dormirse; **to have a ~** dormir; **to have a good night's ~** dormir bien (durante) toda la noche; **I shan't lose any ~ over it** eso no me va a quitar el sueño; **to put an animal to ~** (*euph*) (= *kill*) sacrificar un animal; **to send sb to ~** (= *bore*) dormir a algn; **to talk in one's ~** hablar en sueños Ⓑ VT (= *accommodate*) **we can ~ four** hay cama para cuatro Ⓒ VI dormir; **to ~ on sth** (*fig*) consultar algo con la almohada; **he slept through the alarm clock** no oyó el despertador; **I slept through till the afternoon** dormí hasta la tarde; **~ tight!** ¡que duermas bien!, ¡que descanses!; **to ~ with sb** (*euph*) (= *have sex*) acostarse con algn; ✦ IDIOM **to ~ like a log** dormir como un tronco
➤ **sleep around*** VI + ADV irse a la cama con cualquiera
➤ **sleep in** VI + ADV (*deliberately*) dormir hasta tarde
➤ **sleep off** VT + ADV **to ~ off a big dinner** dormir para reposar una cena grande; **to ~ it off*** ◇ **~ off a hangover** dormir la mona*, dormir la curda*
➤ **sleep over** VI + ADV pasar la noche
➤ **sleep together** VI + ADV (= *have sex*) acostarse juntos

sleeper [ˈsliːpəʳ] N **1** (= *person*) durmiente *mf*; **to be a heavy/light ~** tener el sueño pesado/ligero **2** (*Brit Rail*) (*on track*) traviesa *f*, durmiente *m*; (= *berth*) litera *f*; (= *compartment*) camarín *m*, alcoba *f*

sleepily [ˈsliːpɪli] ADV soñolientamente; **"yes," she said ~** —sí —dijo adormilado *or* soñoliento

sleeping [ˈsliːpɪŋ] ADJ dormido; ✦ PROV **let ~ dogs lie** más vale no meneallo ➤ **sleeping bag** (*camper's*) saco *m* de dormir; (*baby's*) pelele *m* ➤ **Sleeping Beauty** la bella durmiente ➤ **sleeping car** coche-cama *m* ➤ **sleeping draught** soporífero *m* ➤ **sleeping partner** (*Brit*) socio/a *m/f* comanditario/a ➤ **sleeping pill** somnífero *m* ➤ **sleeping policeman** (*Aut*) resalto *m* ➤ **sleeping quarters** dormitorio *msing* ➤ **sleeping sickness** enfermedad *f* del sueño ➤ **sleeping tablet** somnífero *m*

sleepless [ˈsliːplɪs] ADJ [*person*] insomne; **to have a ~ night** pasar la noche en blanco *or* sin dormir

sleeplessness [ˈsliːplɪsnɪs] N insomnio *m*

sleepover [ˈsliːpˌəʊvəʳ] N **we're having a ~ at Jo's** nos vamos a quedar a dormir en casa de Jo

sleepwalk [ˈsliːpˌwɔːk] VI ser sonámbulo, pasearse dormido

sleepwalker [ˈsliːpˌwɔːkəʳ] N sonámbulo/a *m/f*

sleepy [ˈsliːpi] ADJ (*compar* **sleepier** *superl* **sleepiest**) **1** (= *drowsy*) [*person, voice*] soñoliento; **to be** *or* **feel ~** tener sueño **2** (= *quiet*) [*place*] tranquilo; (*pej*) soporífero

sleepyhead [ˈsliːpɪhed] N dormilón/ona *m/f*

sleet [sliːt] Ⓐ N aguanieve *f*, cellisca *f* Ⓑ VI **it was ~ing** caía aguanieve *or* cellisca

sleeve [sliːv] N manga *f*; (*esp Brit*) [*of record*] funda *f*; ✦ IDIOM **to have sth up one's ~** tener algo en reserva

sleeveless [ˈsliːvlɪs] ADJ sin mangas

sleigh [sleɪ] N trineo *m*

sleight [slaɪt] N **~ of hand** prestidigitación *f*, juegos *mpl* de manos

slender [ˈslendəʳ] ADJ [*person*] (= *thin*) delgado, fino; (= *slim*) esbelto; [*waist, neck, hand*] delgado; [*resources*] escaso; [*hope*] lejano, remoto; **by a ~ majority** por escasa mayoría

slept [slept] PT, PP *of* **sleep**

sleuth*† [sluːθ] N (*hum*) detective *mf*, sabueso *mf*

slew¹, **slue** (*US*) [sluː] (*also* **to ~ round**) Ⓐ VT torcer; **to ~ sth to the left** torcer algo a la izquierda Ⓑ VI torcerse

slew² [sluː] PT *of* **slay**

slew³ [sluː] N (*US*) (= *range*) montón* *m*

slice [slaɪs] Ⓐ N **1** [*of bread*] rebanada *f*; [*of salami, sausage*] loncha *f*, raja *f*; [*of cheese, ham*] loncha *f*; [*of beef, lamb etc*] tajada *f*; [*of lemon, cucumber, pineapple*] rodaja *f*; [*of cake, pie*] trozo *m*; (*fig*) (= *portion*) parte *f*; **a ~ of life** un trozo de la vida tal como es
2 (*esp Brit*) (= *utensil*) pala *f*
3 (*Sport*) pelota *f* cortada; (*Golf*) golpe *m* con efecto a la derecha
Ⓑ VT **1** (= *cut into slices*) [+ *bread*] rebanar; [+ *salami, sausage, ham, cheese*] cortar en lonchas; [+ *beef, lamb*] cortar en tajadas; [+ *lemon, cucumber, pineapple*] cortar en rodajas; [+ *cake, pie*] partir en trozos
2 (= *cut*) cortar; **to ~ sth in two** cortar algo en dos; **to ~ sth open** abrir algo de un tajo
➤ **slice through** VI + PREP cortar, partir

sliced [slaɪst] ADJ [*bread*] rebanado, en rebanadas; [*lemon*] en rodajas; ✦ IDIOM **it's the best thing since ~ bread** (*hum**) es la octava maravilla (del mundo)

slicer [ˈslaɪsəʳ] N máquina *f* de cortar

slick [slɪk] Ⓐ ADJ (*compar* **~er** *superl* **~est**) **1** (*pej*) (= *superficial, glib*) hábil **2** (= *polished, skilful*) impecable Ⓑ N **oil ~** (*large*) marea *f* negra; (*small*) mancha *f* de petróleo, capa *f* de petróleo (en el agua) Ⓒ VT alisar; **to ~ down one's hair** alisarse el pelo

slicker [ˈslɪkəʳ] N **1** (= *person*) **city ~*** capitalino/a* *m/f* **2** (*US*) (= *coat*) chubasquero *msing*, impermeable *msing*

slide [slaɪd] (*vb: pt, pp* **slid** [slɪd]) Ⓐ N **1** (*in playground, swimming pool*) tobogán *m*
2 (= *fall*) (*in share prices*) baja *f*, bajón* *m*; **the ~ into chaos/debt** la caída en el caos/en la deuda
3 (*in microscope*) portaobjetos *m inv*, platina *f*
4 (*Phot*) (= *transparency*) diapositiva *f*, filmina *f*, transparencia *f*
5 (*also* **hair ~**) (*esp Brit*) pasador *m*
Ⓑ VI (= *glide*) deslizarse; (= *slip*) resbalar; **they were sliding across the floor/down the banisters** se deslizaban por el

suelo/por la barandilla; **the drawer ~s in and out easily** el cajón se abre y se cierra suavemente; **the book slid off my knee** el libro se me resbaló de la rodilla; **the economy is sliding into recession** la economía está cayendo en la recesión

⊙ VT **he slid his hands into his pockets** metió las manos en los bolsillos; **she slid the key into the keyhole** deslizó la llave en el ojo de la cerradura

⊙ CPD ➤ **slide projector** (*Phot*) proyector *m* de diapositivas ➤ **slide rule** regla *f* de cálculo ➤ **slide show** proyección *f* de diapositivas

sliding ['slaɪdɪŋ] ADJ [*part*] corredizo; [*door*] corredero; ~ **scale** escala *f* móvil

slight [slaɪt] **Ⓐ** ADJ (*compar* ~**er**; *superl* ~**est**) **1** (= *small, minor*) [*difference, change, increase, improvement*] ligero, pequeño; [*injury, problem*] pequeño; **the chances of him winning are very ~** tiene muy pocas posibilidades de ganar; **the wall is at a ~ angle** la pared está ligeramente inclinada; **to have a ~ temperature** tener un poco de fiebre; **not in the ~est** en absoluto; **nobody showed the ~est interest** nadie mostró el menor interés; **he takes offence at the ~est thing** se ofende por la menor cosa *or* por cualquier nimiedad **2** (= *slim*) [*figure, person*] delgado, menudo **Ⓑ** N (*frm*) desaire *m* **Ⓒ** VT (*frm*) desairar a, hacer un desaire a

slightly ['slaɪtlɪ] ADV **1** (= *a little*) ligeramente, un poco; ~ **better** algo mejor, un poco mejor; **he hesitated ever so ~** vaciló apenas un poco; **she was ~ injured** resultó levemente herida; ~ **more/less** un poco más/menos **2** (= *slenderly*) ~ **built** delgado, menudo, de constitución delgada *or* menuda

slim [slɪm] **Ⓐ** ADJ (*compar* ~**mer**; *superl* ~**mest**) [*figure, person*] delgado, fino; **his chances are pretty ~** sus posibilidades son bastante limitadas **Ⓑ** VI adelgazar; **I'm ~ming** estoy haciendo régimen, estoy a régimen ➤ **slim down Ⓐ** VT + ADV (*fig*) ~**med down** [+ *business*] reconvertir, sanear **Ⓑ** VI + ADV bajar de peso, adelgazar

slime [slaɪm] N (*in pond*) cieno *m*, fango *m*; [*of snail*] baba *f*

slimline ['slɪm,laɪn] ADJ **1** [*drink*] light *inv*; [*food*] reductivo, que no engorda **2** [*body, person*] esbelto, delgadísimo; [*screen, calculator*] extraplano; [*fridge, washing machine*] de diseño estrecho; [*book, diary*] finísimo

slimmer ['slɪmə^r] N persona *f* que está a dieta

slimming ['slɪmɪŋ] N adelgazamiento *m*

slimy ['slaɪmɪ] ADJ (*compar* **slimier**; *superl* **slimiest**) **1** [*substance*] viscoso; [*snail*] baboso **2** (*Brit*) (*fig*) [*person*] adulón, zalamero

sling [slɪŋ] (*vb: pt, pp* **slung**) **Ⓐ** N **1** (= *weapon*) honda *f* **2** (*Med*) cabestrillo *m*; **to have one's arm in a ~** llevar el brazo en cabestrillo **Ⓑ** VT **1** (= *throw*) arrojar, lanzar, echar; **to ~ sth over** *or* **across one's shoulder** lanzar algo al hombro **2** (*) (= *throw away*) tirar, botar (*LAm*) ➤ **sling out** VT + ADV **1** (= *throw away*) [+ *rubbish*] echar, tirar, botar (*LAm*) **2** (= *throw out*) [+ *person*] echar, poner de patitas en la calle**

slingshot ['slɪŋʃɒt] N (*US*) tirador *m*, tirachinas *m inv*

slink [slɪŋk] (*pt, pp* **slunk**) VI **to ~ away** ◇ **~ off** escabullirse, zafarse

slinky* ['slɪŋkɪ] ADJ (*compar* **slinkier**; *superl* **slinkiest**) [*clothes*] ajustado, pegado al cuerpo

slip [slɪp] **Ⓐ** N **1** (= *mistake*) error *m*, equivocación *f*; **a ~ of the pen/tongue** un lapsus calami/linguae; **✦** IDIOM **to give sb the ~** escabullirse *or* zafarse de algn, dar esquinazo a algn **2** (= *undergarment*) combinación *f* **3** (*in filing system*) ficha *f*; **I wrote the number on a ~ of paper** escribí el número en un papelito *or* un trocito de papel **4 a ~ of a girl** una chiquilla **Ⓑ** VI **1** (= *slide, shift*) resbalar; **my foot ~ped** se me fue el pie; **the knife ~ped and I cut my hand** se me fue el cuchillo y me hice un corte en la mano; **we let the game ~ through our fingers** dejamos que el partido se nos escapara *or* se nos fuera de las manos; **you're ~ping** (*hum*) estás decayendo

2 (= *move quickly*) **he ~ped into his bathrobe** se puso el albornoz; **I ~ped downstairs to fetch it** bajé a traerlo rápidamente

3 (= *move imperceptibly*) pasar desapercibido; **he ~ped out of the room while my back was turned** salió sigilosamente de la habitación mientras estaba de espaldas; **he soon ~ped back into his old ways** al poco tiempo volvió a las andadas

4 (= *become known*) **he let (it) ~ that he was a Democrat** dejó escapar que era demócrata **Ⓒ** VT **1** (= *move quickly and smoothly*) pasar, deslizar; **I ~ped a note under his door** deslicé *or* le pasé una nota por debajo de la puerta

2 (= *move imperceptibly*) **he ~ped his hand into her bag** le metió disimuladamente la mano en el bolso; **to ~ sth to sb** pasarle disimuladamente algo a algn

3 (= *escape from*) **the dog ~ped its collar** el perro se soltó del collar; **I meant to do it but it ~ped my mind** lo quise hacer pero se me olvidó *or* se me pasó **Ⓓ** CPD ➤ **slip road** (*Brit*) (*on motorway*) vía *f* de acceso ➤ **slip away** VI + ADV [*person*] escabullirse, escurrirse ➤ **slip in Ⓐ** VT + ADV [+ *comment, word*] incluir **Ⓑ** VI + ADV (= *sneak in*) entrar desapercibido; (= *enter quickly*) entrar deprisa *or* rápidamente ➤ **slip out** VI + ADV [*person*] salir un momento; [*remark, secret*] **I didn't mean to say it — it just ~ped out** no quería decirlo, pero se me escapó ➤ **slip up** VI + ADV (= *make a mistake*) equivocarse

slip-on ['slɪpɒn] ADJ, N ➤ **slip-on shoes**, **slip-ons** zapatos *mpl* sin cordones

slipper ['slɪpə^r] N zapatilla *f*, pantufla *f* (*esp LAm*)

slippery ['slɪpərɪ] ADJ **1** (*lit*) [*ground, surface*] resbaladizo, escurridizo; [*object, fish*] escurridizo; **✦** IDIOM **to be on a ~ slope** estar en terreno resbaladizo **2** (*fig*) (*pej*) [*person*] (= *evasive*) escurridizo; (= *unreliable*) poco de fiar

slipshod ['slɪpʃɒd] ADJ descuidado, chapucero

slipstream ['slɪpstriːm] N estela *f*

slip-up ['slɪpʌp] N (= *mistake*) error *m*, desliz *m*, metedura *f* de pata**

slipway ['slɪpweɪ] N gradas *fpl*

slit [slɪt] (*vb: pt, pp* ~) **Ⓐ** N (= *opening*) abertura *f*, hendidura *f*; (= *cut*) corte *m*; (*in dress etc*) raja *f*; **to make a ~ in sth** hacer un corte en algo **Ⓑ** VT cortar, abrir; **to ~ sb's throat** cortarle el pescuezo a algn

slither ['slɪðə^r] VI deslizarse; **to ~ down a slope** ir rodando por una pendiente; **to ~ about on ice** ir resbalando sobre el hielo

sliver ['slɪvə^r] N lonja *f*, tajada *f*; [*of wood*] astilla *f*

slob* [slɒb] N vago/a *m/f*, dejado/a *m/f*

slobber ['slɒbə^r] VI babear

sloe [sləʊ] N (= *fruit*) endrina *f*

slog [slɒg] **Ⓐ** N **it was a ~** me costó trabajo; **it's a hard ~ to the top** cuesta trabajo llegar a la cumbre **Ⓑ** VI **1** (= *work*) afanarse, sudar tinta; **to ~ away at sth** afanarse por hacer algo **2** (= *walk*) caminar trabajosamente, avanzar trabajosamente; **we ~ged on for eight kilometres** seguimos la marcha otros ocho kilómetros más

slogan ['sləʊgən] N slogan *m*, lema *m*

sloop [sluːp] N balandra *f*

slop [slɒp] **Ⓐ** VI (*also* ~ **over**) [*water etc*] derramarse, verterse; **the water was ~ping about in the bucket** el agua se agitaba en el cubo **Ⓑ** VT (= *spill*) derramar, verter; (= *tip carelessly*) derramar, tirar **Ⓒ** **slops** NPL (= *food*) gachas *fpl*; [*of tea*] posos *mpl* de té

slope [sləʊp] **Ⓐ** N (*up*) cuesta *f*, pendiente *f*; (*down*) declive *m*, bajada *f*; [*of hill*] falda *f*, ladera *f*; **the street was on a ~** la calle era en cuesta; **on the eastern ~** en la vertiente este **Ⓑ** VI inclinarse; **the garden ~s down to the stream** el jardín baja hacia el arroyo ➤ **slope off*** VI + ADV escabullirse, largarse, rajarse (*LAm*)

sloping ['sləʊpɪŋ] ADJ inclinado, al sesgo

sloppily ['slɒpɪlɪ] ADV (= *carelessly*) en forma descuidada; **to dress ~** vestirse sin atención

sloppy ['slɒpɪ] ADJ (*compar* **sloppier**; *superl* **sloppiest**) **1** (= *runny*) [*food*] aguado **2** (= *careless*) [*work etc*] descuidado; [*appearance, dress*] desaliñado, desaseado; [*thinking*] poco riguroso **3** (= *sentimental*) sentimentaloide, ñoño

slosh* [slɒʃ] Ⓐ VT (= *splash*) [+ *liquid*] **to ~ some water over sth** echar agua sobre algo Ⓑ VI **the water was ~ing about in the pail** el agua chapoteaba en el cubo

sloshed* [slɒʃt] ADJ (*Brit*) **to be/get ~** tener/agarrarse una buena curda *or* melopea*

slot [slɒt] Ⓐ N **1** (= *hole*) (*in machine etc*) ranura *f*; (= *groove*) muesca *f*; **to put a coin in the ~** meter una moneda en la ranura **2** (= *space*) (*in timetable, programme etc*) hueco *m*; (= *advertising slot*) cuña *f* (publicitaria) Ⓑ VT **to ~ in(to)** [+ *object*] introducir *or* meter en; (*fig*) [+ *activity, speech*] incluir en Ⓒ VI introducirse; **it ~s in here** entra en esta ranura, encaja aquí Ⓓ CPD ➤ **slot machine** (*at funfair*) tragaperras *f inv*; (= *vending machine*) máquina *f* expendedora ➤ **slot meter** contador *m*

sloth [sləʊθ] N **1** (= *idleness*) pereza *f*, indolencia *f* **2** (*Zool*) oso *m* perezoso

slothful ['sləʊθfəl] ADJ perezoso, vago, flojo

slotted spoon [ˌslɒtɪd'spuːn] N cucharón *m* perforado

slouch [slaʊtʃ] Ⓐ N **1 to walk with a ~** andar con un aire gacho **2** (*) **he's no ~** (*in skill*) no es ningún principiante; (*at work*) no es ningún vago Ⓑ VI (*walking*) andar desgarbado

slough off [slʌf'ɒf] VT + ADV mudar, echar de sí; (*fig*) deshacerse de, desechar

Slovak ['sləʊvæk] Ⓐ ADJ eslovaco Ⓑ N eslovaco/a *m/f*

Slovakia [sləʊ'vækɪə] N Eslovaquia *f*

Slovakian [sləʊ'vækɪən] ADJ eslovaco

Slovene ['sləʊviːn], **Slovenian** [sləʊ'viːnɪən] Ⓐ ADJ esloveno Ⓑ N esloveno/a *m/f*

Slovenia [sləʊ'viːnɪə] N Eslovenia *f*

slovenly ['slʌvnlɪ] ADJ [*person*] descuidado; [*appearance*] desaliñado, desaseado; [*work*] chapucero, descuidado

slow [sləʊ] (*compar* ~**er**; *superl* ~**est**) Ⓐ ADJ **1** (= *not speedy*) lento; **business is** ~ hay poco movimiento (en el negocio); **extra lessons for** ~ **learners** clases extra para alumnos con problemas de aprendizaje; **life here is** ~ aquí se vive a un ritmo lento *or* pausado; **bake for two hours in a** ~ **oven** cocer dos horas en el horno a fuego lento; **he's a** ~ **reader** lee despacio; **after a** ~ **start, he managed to end up in third place** después de un comienzo flojo, consiguió llegar en tercer puesto; **to be** ~ **to do sth** tardar *or* (*LAm*) demorar en hacer algo **2** [*clock, watch*] atrasado; **my watch is 20 minutes** ~ mi reloj está 20 minutos atrasado **3** (= *mentally sluggish*) torpe, lento; **he's a bit** ~ **at maths** es algo torpe para las matemáticas Ⓑ ADV despacio, lentamente, lento; **to go** ~ [*driver*] conducir despacio; (*in industrial dispute*) trabajar a ritmo lento, hacer huelga de celo (*Sp*) Ⓒ VT (*also* ~ **down,** ~ **up**) [+ *person*] retrasar; [+ *progress*] retrasar, disminuir el ritmo de Ⓓ VI [*vehicle, runner*] reducir la marcha; [*driver*] reducir la velocidad *or* la marcha; [*growth*] disminuir Ⓔ CPD ➤ **slow lane** (*Aut*) (*in Britain*) carril *m* de la izquierda; (*most countries*) carril *m* de la derecha ➤ **slow motion** (*Cine*) **in** ~ **motion** a *or* (*LAm*) en cámara lenta ➤ **slow worm** lución *m*

➤ **slow down** Ⓐ VI + ADV [*engine, vehicle, runner*] reducir la marcha; [*driver*] reducir la velocidad *or* la marcha; **you must** ~ **down or you'll make yourself ill** tienes que aflojar el ritmo de vida o te pondrás enfermo Ⓑ VT + ADV **1** [+ *vehicle*] reducir la velocidad de; **his injury ~ed him down** su lesión le restaba rapidez **2** (= *cause delay to*) retrasar

slow-acting ['sləʊ,æktɪŋ] ADJ de efecto retardado

slowcoach* ['sləʊkəʊtʃ] N (*Brit*) tortuga *f*

slowdown ['sləʊdaʊn] N [*of productivity, growth*]

disminución *f* del ritmo; (*US*) (= *go-slow*) huelga *f* de manos caídas, huelga *f* de celo (*Sp*)

slowly ['sləʊlɪ] ADV **1** (= *not quickly*) [*move*] lentamente, despacio; [*drive*] despacio; [*say*] pausadamente, lentamente **2** (= *gradually*) poco a poco; ~ **but surely he was killing himself** lenta pero inexorablemente estaba acabando con su vida

slow-motion ['sləʊ'məʊʃən] ADJ ~ **film** película *f* a cámara lenta

slowness ['sləʊnɪs] N lentitud *f*; **he was criticized for his** ~ **to act** le criticaron por la lentitud con la que actuó

slowpoke* ['sləʊ,pəʊk] N (*US*) tortuga *f*

slow-witted ['sləʊ'wɪtɪd] ADJ torpe, lento

sludge [slʌdʒ] N (= *mud*) fango *m*, lodo *m*; (= *sediment*) residuos *mpl*; (= *sewage*) aguas *fpl* residuales

slue [sluː] (*US*) *see* **slew**[1]

slug [slʌg] Ⓐ N **1** (*Zool*) babosa *f* **2** (**) (= *blow*) porrazo *m*; (*with fist*) puñetazo *m*; **a** ~ **of whisky** un trago de whisk(e)y Ⓑ VT (**) pegar, aporrear

sluggish ['slʌgɪʃ] ADJ [*river, engine, car*] lento; [*business, sales*] inactivo

sluggishly ['slʌgɪʃlɪ] ADV lentamente

sluice [sluːs] VT **to** ~ **sth down** *or* **out** regar algo, echar agua sobre algo (para lavarlo)

sluice-gate ['sluːsgeɪt] N esclusa *f*, compuerta *f*

slum [slʌm] Ⓐ N (= *area*) barrio *m* bajo, suburbio *m*, colonia *f* proletaria (*Mex*), barriada *f* (*Per*); (= *house*) casucha *f*, tugurio *m*, chabola *f* (*Sp*); **the ~s** los barrios bajos, los suburbios Ⓑ VI **to** ~ **◇ go ~ming** visitar los barrios bajos Ⓒ CPD ➤ **slum clearance** deschabolización *f*

slumber ['slʌmbər] Ⓐ N (*also* ~**s**) sueño *msing* Ⓑ VI dormir

slump [slʌmp] Ⓐ N (*gen*) baja *f* (repentina), bajón *m*; (*in production, sales*) caída *f*, baja *f*; (*economic*) depresión *f* Ⓑ VI **1** [*price etc*] hundirse; [*production, sales*] bajar, caer; (*fig*) [*morale etc*] desplomarse **2 to** ~ **into a chair** hundirse en una silla; **he ~ed to the floor** se desplomó al suelo; **he was ~ed over the wheel** se había caído sobre el volante

slung [slʌŋ] PT, PP *of* **sling**

slunk [slʌŋk] PT, PP *of* **slink**

slur [slɜː^r] Ⓐ N (= *stigma*) mancha *f*, calumnia *f*; **to cast a** ~ **on sb** manchar la reputación de algn Ⓑ VT [+ *word etc*] pronunciar mal, tragar

slurp [slɜːp] VT, VI sorber ruidosamente

slurred [slɜːd] ADJ [*pronunciation*] mal articulado, borroso

slurry ['slʌrɪ] N (= *mud*) lodo *m* líquido; (*Agr*) estiércol *m* líquido

slush [slʌʃ] N (= *melting snow*) aguanieve *f*, nieve *f* medio derretida; (*) (= *bad poetry etc*) sentimentalismo *m* ➤ **slush fund** fondos *mpl* para sobornar

slushy ['slʌʃɪ] ADJ (*compar* **slushier**; *superl* **slushiest**) [*snow*] medio derretido; (*) [*poetry etc*] sentimentaloide, sensiblero

slut** [slʌt] N (*immoral*) puta* *f*; (*dirty, untidy*) marrana* *f*, guarra** *f*

sly [slaɪ] Ⓐ ADJ (*compar* ~**er**; *superl* ~**est**) **1** (= *wily*) [*person*] astuto, taimado; **he's a** ~ **one!** ¡es un zorro! **2** (= *mischievous*) [*person*] pícaro, travieso; [*look, smile*] pícaro, malicioso Ⓑ N **on the** ~ a hurtadillas, a escondidas

slyly ['slaɪlɪ] ADV **1** (= *cunningly*) con astucia, astutamente **2** (= *mischievously*) [*smile, say*] pícaramente

smack[1] [smæk] VI **to** ~ **of** (*fig*) oler a

smack[2] [smæk] Ⓐ N (= *slap*) bofetada *f*, tortazo *m*; **to give a child a** ~ dar una bofetada a *or* abofetear a un niño Ⓑ VT (= *slap*) dar una bofetada a, abofetear; **she ~ed the child's bottom** le pegó al niño en el trasero *or* culo; **to** ~ **one's lips** relamerse, chuparse los labios Ⓒ ADV **it fell** ~ **in the middle*** cayó justo en medio; **she ran** ~ **into the door** chocó contra la puerta, dio de lleno con la puerta

smacker* ['smækər] N **1** (= *kiss*) besazo *m*, besucón *m* **2** (*Brit*) (= *pound*) libra *f*; (*US*) (= *dollar*) dólar *m*

small [smɔːl] **A** ADJ (*compar* ~**er**; *superl* ~**est**) **1** (= *not big*) [*object, building, room, animal, group*] pequeño, chico (*LAm*); (*in height*) bajo, pequeño, chaparro (*LAm*); [*family, population*] pequeño, poco numeroso; [*stock, supply*] reducido, escaso; [*clothes*] de talla pequeña; **the dress is too ~ for her** el vestido le viene pequeño *or* chico; **the ~er of the two** el menor (de los dos); **with a ~ "e"** con "e" minúscula; **to cut sth up** ~ cortar algo en trocitos; **to get** *or* **grow ~er** [*income, difficulties, supply, population, amount*] disminuir, reducirse; [*object*] hacerse más pequeño; **to make sb look** ~ rebajar a algn; **to make sth ~er** [+ *income, difficulties, supply, amount*] reducir algo; [+ *object, garment*] reducir algo de tamaño, hacer algo más pequeño
2 (= *minor*) [*problem, mistake, job*] pequeño, de poca importancia; [*contribution*] pequeño; [*difference, increase, improvement*] pequeño, ligero; **to start in a ~ way** empezar desde abajo
3 (= *young*) [*child, baby*] pequeño, chico (*esp LAm*)
B N **the ~ of the back** la región lumbar
C CPD ➤ **small ad** (*Brit*) anuncio *m* por palabras ➤ **small arms** armas *fpl* ligeras de bajo calibre ➤ **small business** pequeña empresa *f* ➤ **small change** suelto *m*, cambio *m*, calderilla *f*, sencillo *m* (*LAm*), feria *f* (*Mex**) ➤ **small claims court** tribunal *m* de instancia (*que se ocupa de asuntos menores*) ➤ **small fry***: **to be** ~ **fry** ser de poca monta ➤ **small intestine** intestino *m* delgado ➤ **small print** letra *f* menuda ➤ **small screen** pequeña pantalla *f*, pantalla *f* chica (*LAm*) ➤ **small talk** charla *f*, charloteo* *m*

smallholder [ˈsmɔːlˌhəʊldəʳ] N (*Brit*) cultivador(a) *m/f* de una granja pequeña, minifundista *mf*

smallholding [ˈsmɔːlˌhəʊldɪŋ] N (*Brit*) parcela *f*, minifundio *m*, chacra *f* (*SC*)

smallish [ˈsmɔːlɪʃ] ADJ más bien pequeño, más bien chico

small-minded [ˈsmɔːlˈmaɪndɪd] ADJ mezquino, de miras estrechas

small-mindedness [ˈsmɔːlˈmaɪndɪdnɪs] N mezquindad *f*, estrechez *f* de miras

smallness [ˈsmɔːlnɪs] N [*of object, animal, room, hand, foot*] pequeñez *f*, lo chico (*LAm*)

smallpox [ˈsmɔːlpɒks] N (*Med*) viruela *f*

small-scale [ˈsmɔːlˈskeɪl] ADJ (*gen*) en pequeña escala

small-time* [ˈsmɔːlˈtaɪm] ADJ de poca categoría, de poca monta; **a ~ criminal** un delincuente menor

small-town [ˈsmɔːlˈtaʊn] ADJ (*esp US*) provinciano, pueblerino

smarmy* [ˈsmɑːmɪ] ADJ (*compar* **smarmier**; *superl* **smarmiest**) (*Brit*) zalamero

smart [smɑːt] **A** ADJ (*compar* ~**er**; *superl* ~**est**) **1** (*esp Brit*) (= *elegant*) [*person, clothes, car*] elegante; [*garden*] bien arreglado; [*house*] bien puesto; **to look** ~ [*person*] estar elegante
2 (= *chic*) elegante; **the ~ set** la buena sociedad, la gente de buen tono
3 (= *clever*) [*person*] listo, inteligente; [*idea*] inteligente, bueno; [*bombs, missiles*] inteligente; **that wasn't very** ~ no ha sido una idea muy buena; **he was too ~ for me** era muy listo y me ganó la batalla
4 (*pej*) (= *cocky*) **don't get** ~ **with me!** ¡no te las des de listo conmigo!; **she's got a ~ answer to everything** tiene respuesta para todo
5 (= *brisk*) [*pace, action*] rápido
B VI (= *sting*) [*wound, eyes*] escocer, picar, arder (*esp LAm*); [*iodine etc*] escocer; (*fig*) dolerse; **my eyes are ~ing** me escuecen *or* me pican los ojos; **to ~ under an insult** sentirse dolido por una injuria
C CPD ➤ **smart alec***, **smart aleck*** (*esp US*) sabelotodo* *mf*, sabihondo/a* *m/f* ➤ **smart bomb** bomba *f* con mecanismo inteligente ➤ **smart card** tarjeta *f* electrónica, tarjeta *f* inteligente

smart-arse* (*Brit*) [ˈsmɑːtɑːs] , **smart-ass*** (*US*) [ˈsmɑːtæs] N sabelotodo* *mf*, sabihondo/a* *m/f*

smarten up [ˈsmɑːtənʌp] **A** VT + ADV arreglar **B** VI + ADV [*person*] arreglarse, adecentarse; [*town*] mejorar de aspecto

smartly [ˈsmɑːtlɪ] ADV **1** (= *elegantly*) [*dressed, furnished*] con elegancia, elegantemente **2** (= *cleverly*) inteligentemente

3 (= *briskly*) rápidamente; **to tap sth** ~ dar un golpe seco a algo

smarty* [ˈsmɑːtɪ] N (*also* ~-**pants**) sabelotodo* *mf*

smash [smæʃ] **A** N **1** (= *breakage*) rotura *f*, quiebra *f* (*LAm*); (= *sound of breaking*) estruendo *m*; **the cup fell with a** ~ la taza cayó con gran estruendo
2 (*) (= *collision*) choque *m*; **he died in a car** ~ murió en un accidente de coche
3 (*Tennis*) smash *m*, remate *m*, remache *m*
4 (*) (= *success*) exitazo *m*
B VT **1** (= *break*) romper, quebrar (*esp LAm*); (= *shatter*) hacer pedazos, hacer trizas; **I've ~ed my watch** he estropeado mi reloj; **to ~ sth to pieces** *or* **bits** hacer pedazos *or* añicos algo
2 (= *wreck*) dar al traste con; (= *ruin*) arruinar, minar; **we will ~ this crime ring** acabaremos con esta banda de delincuentes
3 (*Tennis*) [+ *ball*] rematar, remachar
C VI romperse, hacerse pedazos, quebrarse (*esp LAm*); **the car ~ed into the wall** el coche se estrelló contra la pared
D CPD ➤ **smash hit** exitazo *m*
➤ **smash down** VT + ADV [+ *door*] echar abajo
➤ **smash in** VT + ADV [+ *door, window*] forzar; **to ~ sb's face in*** romper la cara a algn
➤ **smash up*** VT + ADV [+ *car, person, place*] pulverizar, hacer pedazos; **he was all ~ed up in the accident** salió destrozado del accidente

smash-and-grab [ˌsmæʃənˈgræb] N robo *m* relámpago (*con rotura de escaparate*)

smashed** [smæʃt] ADJ (= *drunk*) como una cuba*

smashing* [ˈsmæʃɪŋ] ADJ (*Brit*) estupendo (*Sp*), bárbaro, macanudo (*LAm*); **we had a ~ time** lo pasamos estupendamente *or* de maravilla *or* (*SC*) regio

smash-up [ˈsmæʃʌp] N (*Brit*) colisión *f* violenta , grave accidente *m* de tráfico

smattering [ˈsmætərɪŋ] N **to have a ~ of** tener cierta idea *or* algunas nociones de

smear [smɪəʳ] **A** N **1** (= *mark*) mancha *f* **2** (*fig*) (= *libel*) calumnia *f* **3** (*Brit Med*) frotis *m* **B** VT **1** (= *wipe*) untar; **to ~ one's face with blood** untarse la cara de sangre **2** (*fig*) (= *libel*) calumniar, difamar; **to ~ sb because of his past** tachar a algn por su pasado **C** VI [*paint, ink etc*] correrse
D CPD ➤ **smear campaign** campaña *f* de difamación ➤ **smear tactics** tácticas *fpl* de difamación ➤ **smear test** (*Brit Med*) frotis *m*, citología *f*

smell [smel] (*vb*: *pt, pp* ~**ed**, **smelt**) **A** N **1** (= *sense*) olfato *m*; **to have a keen sense of** ~ tener buen olfato, tener un buen sentido del olfato
2 (= *odour*) olor *m*; **it has a nice** ~ tiene un olor agradable, huele bien; **there's a ~ of gas/of burning** huele a gas/a quemado, hay olor a gas/a quemado
B VT oler; **I can ~ gas/burning** huele a gas/a quemado; **to ~ danger** (*fig*) olfatear el peligro
C VI oler; **it ~s good** huele bien; **that flower doesn't ~** esa flor no tiene olor; **to ~ of sth** oler a algo; **her breath ~s** le huele el aliento
➤ **smell out** VT + ADV **1** (= *find by scent*) [*dog*] olfatear
2 (= *cause to smell*) **it's ~ing the room out** está haciendo oler mal el cuarto

smelling salts [ˈsmelɪŋsɔːlts] NPL sales *fpl* aromáticas

smelly* [ˈsmelɪ] ADJ (*compar* **smellier**; *superl* **smelliest**) maloliente, apestoso; **he's got ~ feet** le huelen los pies

smelt[1] [smelt] (*esp Brit*) PT, PP *of* **smell**

smelt[2] [smelt] VT fundir

smidgen, smidgin [ˈsmɪdʒən] N **a ~ of*** un poquito de, un poquitín de

smile [smaɪl] **A** N sonrisa *f*; **to give sb a** ~ sonreír a algn; **his jokes failed to raise a** ~ sus chistes no hicieron reír a nadie; **to wipe the ~ off sb's face** quitar a algn las ganas de reír **B** VI sonreír; **to ~ at sb** sonreír a algn; **to ~ at sth** reírse de algo; **to keep smiling** seguir sonriendo, no decaer ; **fortune ~d on him** le sonrió la fortuna **C** VT **"of course!"** **she ~d** —¡por supuesto! —dijo sonriente *or* sonriendo

smiley [ˈsmaɪlɪ] **A** ADJ **1** (*) [*person, face*] sonriente
2 [*badge, symbol, email*] smiley **B** N (*in email etc*) smiley *m*, emoticón *m*

smiling ['smaɪlɪŋ] ADJ sonriente

smirk [smɜ:k] **Ⓐ** N sonrisa f de satisfacción **Ⓑ** VI sonreír de satisfacción

smite [smaɪt] VT (pt **smote**; pp **smitten**) (††) golpear; **my conscience smote me** me remordió la conciencia

smith [smɪθ] N herrero/a m/f

smithereens [ˌsmɪðəˈriːnz] NPL **to smash sth to ~** hacer añicos or trizas algo

smithy ['smɪðɪ] N herrería f, fragua f

smitten ['smɪtn] ADJ **to be ~ (with sb)** estar locamente enamorado (de algn); **to be ~ with an idea** entusiasmarse por una idea

smock [smɒk] N (for artist) bata f, guardapolvo m; (for expectant mother) bata f corta, tontón m

smog [smɒg] N smog m, niebla f tóxica

smoke [sməʊk] **Ⓐ** N **1** (from fire, cigarette etc) humo m; **to go up in ~** [building] quemarse (totalmente); [plans] quedar en agua de borrajas; [hopes] esfumarse; **♦** PROV **there's no ~ without fire** cuando el río suena, agua lleva

2 (*) (= cigarette) **to have a ~** fumar(se) un pitillo* or cigarrillo or un cigarro

Ⓑ VT **1** [+ cigarette, cigar, pipe] fumar; **she wouldn't let him ~ his pipe** no le dejaba fumar en pipa

2 [+ bacon, fish, cheese] ahumar

Ⓒ VI **1** (= emit smoke) echar humo

2 [person] fumar; **to ~ like a chimney*** fumar como un carretero or como una chimenea*

Ⓓ CPD **➤ smoke alarm** detector m de humo, alarma f contra incendios **➤ smoke bomb** bomba f or granada f de humo **➤ smoke detector** detector m de humo **➤ smoke ring** anillo m or aro m de humo; **to blow ~ rings** hacer anillos or aros de humo **➤ smoke screen** cortina f de humo **➤ smoke signal** señal f de humo

➤ smoke out VT + ADV [+ animal, demonstrators] hacer salir con humo; (fig) (= expose) poner al descubierto

smoked [sməʊkt] ADJ ahumado

smoke-filled ['sməʊkfɪld] ADJ lleno de humo

smokeless ['sməʊklɪs] ADJ **~ fuel** combustible m sin humo; **~ zone** zona f libre de humos

smoker ['sməʊkəʳ] N fumador(a) m/f; **~'s cough** tos f de fumador; **to be a heavy ~** fumar mucho

smokescreen ['sməʊkskriːn] N cortina f de humo

smokestack ['sməʊkstæk] N chimenea f **➤ smokestack industries** industrias fpl con chimeneas

smoking ['sməʊkɪŋ] N **~ is bad for you** el fumar te perjudica; **~ or non-~?** ¿fumador o no fumador?; **to give up ~** dejar de fumar; **"no smoking"** "prohibido fumar" **➤ smoking car** (US) coche m de fumadores **➤ smoking compartment** compartimento m de fumadores **➤ smoking jacket** batín m corto **➤ smoking room** sala f de fumadores

smoky ['sməʊkɪ] ADJ (compar **smokier**; superl **smokiest**) [chimney, fire] humeante, que humea; [room, atmosphere] lleno de humo; [flavour, surface] ahumado

smolder etc ['sməʊldəʳ] VI (US) = **smoulder** etc

smooch* [smuːtʃ] VI besuquearse

smoochy* ['smuːtʃɪ] ADJ [record, song] sentimental

smooth [smuːð] **Ⓐ** ADJ (compar **~er**; superl **~est**) **1** (= not rough) [surface, stone] liso; [skin] suave, terso; [hair] suave; [road] llano, parejo (esp LAm); [sea, lake] tranquilo, en calma; **♦** IDIOM **to be as ~ as silk** or **satin** ser suave como la seda

2 (= not lumpy) [paste, sauce] sin grumos

3 (= not jerky) [running of engine, motion] suave, parejo (esp LAm); [crossing, flight] bueno

4 (= trouble-free) [transition] sin problemas, poco conflictivo; [journey] sin problemas, sin complicaciones

5 (= mellow) [flavour, whisky, sound] suave

6 (= polished) [style] fluido, suave; [performance] fluido

7 (pej) (= slick) [person] zalamero; [manner] experimentado; **to be a ~ talker** tener un pico de oro

Ⓑ VT **1** (= flatten) alisar; **she ~ed her skirt** se alisó la falda

2 (= polish) [+ wood, surface] lijar, pulir

3 (= make easy) [+ transition] facilitar; [+ process] suavizar; **to ~ the way for sth/sb** allanar el camino para algo/a algn

4 to ~ cream into one's skin untarse crema en la piel **➤ smooth down** VT + ADV [+ hair, sheet, clothes] alisar; [+ wood] lijar, pulir

➤ smooth out VT + ADV [+ creases, dress] alisar; (fig) [+ problem] solucionar, resolver; [+ difficulties] allanar

➤ smooth over VT + ADV [+ soil] allanar; (fig) **to ~ things over** limar las asperezas

smoothie ['smuːðɪ] N (pej) zalamero/a m/f

smoothly ['smuːðlɪ] ADV [move] suavemente; **to run ~** [engine] funcionar muy bien; [event] transcurrir sin contratiempos or complicaciones or problemas

smooth-shaven ['smuːðˈʃeɪvn] ADJ bien afeitado

smooth-talking ['smuːðˈtɔːkɪŋ] ADJ afable; (pej) zalamero, meloso

smoothy** ['smuːðɪ] N = **smoothie**

smote [sməʊt] PT of **smite**

smother ['smʌðəʳ] VT **1** (= stifle) [+ person] ahogar, asfixiar; [+ fire] apagar; [+ yawn, sob, laughter] contener **2** (= cover) cubrir; **fruit ~ed in cream** fruta cubierta de crema; **they ~ed him with kisses** le colmaron or abrumaron de besos

smoulder, smolder (US) ['sməʊldəʳ] VI [fire] arder sin llama; (fig) [passion etc] arder

smouldering, smoldering (US) ['sməʊldərɪŋ] ADJ que arde lentamente; (fig) latente; **she gave me a ~ look** me miró con aire provocativo

SMS N ABBR (= **short message service**) (servicio m) SMS m; (also ~ **message**) SMS m

smudge [smʌdʒ] **Ⓐ** N borrón m **Ⓑ** VT manchar **Ⓒ** VI correrse

smug [smʌg] ADJ (compar **~ger**; superl **~gest**) creído, engreído

smuggle ['smʌgl] **Ⓐ** VT pasar de contrabando; **to ~ goods in/out** meter/sacar mercancías de contrabando; **to ~ sth past** or **through Customs** pasar algo de contrabando por la aduana; **to ~ sb out in disguise** pasar a algn disfrazado **Ⓑ** VI hacer contrabando, dedicarse al contrabando

smuggler ['smʌgləʳ] N contrabandista mf

smuggling ['smʌglɪŋ] N contrabando m

smugly ['smʌglɪ] ADV con engreimiento, con suficiencia

smugness ['smʌgnɪs] N engreimiento m, suficiencia f

smut [smʌt] N (= crudity) obscenidades fpl

smutty ['smʌtɪ] ADJ (compar **smuttier**; superl **smuttiest**) (= crude) obsceno, verde, colorado (LAm)

snack [snæk] N tentempié m; **to have a ~** picar algo, tomar un tentempié **➤ snack bar** cafetería f, lonchería f (LAm)

snag [snæg] **Ⓐ** N (= difficulty) inconveniente m, problema m; **that's the ~** ahí está el problema; **to run into** or **hit a ~** encontrar inconvenientes, dar con un obstáculo **Ⓑ** VT enganchar, coger (**on** en)

snail [sneɪl] N caracol m; **♦** IDIOM **at a ~'s pace** a paso de tortuga **➤ snail mail*** (hum) correo m ordinario

snake [sneɪk] **Ⓐ** N serpiente f; (harmless) culebra f; **a ~ in the grass** (fig) un traidor **Ⓑ** VI **the road ~d down the mountain** la carretera serpenteaba montaña abajo **Ⓒ** CPD **➤ snake charmer** encantador(a) m/f de serpientes **➤ snakes and ladders** SING ≈ (juego m de) la oca

snakebite ['sneɪkbaɪt] N mordedura f de serpiente, picadura f de serpiente

snakeskin ['sneɪkskɪn] N piel f de serpiente

snap [snæp] **Ⓐ** N **1** (= sound) golpe m, ruido m seco; [of sth breaking, of whip, of fingers] chasquido m

2 (Brit) (= photograph) foto f

3 (= short period) **a cold ~** una ola de frío **Ⓑ** ADJ (= sudden) repentino, sin aviso; **~ decision** decisión f instantánea; **~ judgement** juicio m instantáneo **Ⓒ** VT **1** (= break) partir, quebrar (esp LAm)

2 (= click) chasquear; **to ~ one's fingers** chasquear los dedos; **to ~ one's fingers at sb/sth** (fig) burlarse de algn/ algo; **to ~ a box shut** cerrar una caja de golpe

3 **"be quiet!" she ~ped** —¡cállate! —espetó ella enojada

4 (Phot) sacar una foto de **Ⓓ** VI **1** (= break) romperse

2 (= *make sound*) [*whip*] chasquear; **it ~ped shut** se cerró de golpe; **to ~ into place** meterse de golpe
3 to ~ at sb [*person*] regañar a algn; [*dog*] intentar morder a algn
E EXCL (*Brit*) ¡lo mismo!; (= *me too*) ¡yo también!
F CPD ➤ **snap bean** (*US*) judía *f* verde, ejote *m* (*Mex*), poroto *m* verde (*And, SC*), chaucha *f* (*Arg*) ➤ **snap fastener** (*US*) cierre *m* (automático)
➤ **snap off** **A** VT + ADV separar, quebrar; **to ~ sb's head off** (*fig*) regañar a algn, echar un rapapolvo a algn (*Sp*) **B** VI + ADV **it ~ped off** se desprendió, se partió
➤ **snap out*** VI + ADV **to ~ out of sth** [+ *gloom, lethargy*] sacudirse algo; [+ *self-pity*] dejarse de algo; [+ *bad temper*] quitarse algo de encima
➤ **snap up** VT + ADV **to ~ up a bargain** (*fig*) agarrar una ganga; **our stock was ~ped up at once** nuestras existencias quedaron agotadas al instante

snapdragon ['snæp,drægən] N dragón *m*

snappy* ['snæpɪ] ADJ (*compar* **snappier**; *superl* **snappiest**)
1 (= *quick*) rápido; (= *energetic*) enérgico, vigoroso; **make it ~!** ¡date prisa!, ¡apúrate! (*esp LAm*) **2** (= *smart*) elegante; **he's a ~ dresser** se viste con elegancia **3** (= *punchy*) [*slogan*] conciso

snapshot ['snæpʃɒt] N (*Phot*) foto *f*

snare [snɛəʳ] **A** N lazo *m* **B** VT coger *or* (*LAm*) agarrar con lazo **C** CPD ➤ **snare drum** tambor *m* militar pequeño

snarl [snɑːl] **A** N (= *noise*) gruñido *m*; **he said with a ~** dijo gruñendo **B** VI gruñir; **to ~ at sb** [*person, dog*] gruñir a algn **C** VT gruñir, decir gruñendo

snarl-up ['snɑːlʌp] N (*Brit*) (*in plans etc*) enredo *m*, maraña *f*

snatch [snætʃ] **A** N (= *snippet*) trocito *m*; **to whistle ~es of Mozart** silbar fragmentos de Mozart; **~es of conversation** fragmentos *mpl* de conversación
B VT **1** (= *grab*) arrebatar; **to ~ sth from sb** arrebatar algo a algn; **he ~ed the keys from my hand** me arrebató las llaves de la mano; **to ~ a meal** comer a la carrera; **to ~ some sleep** buscar tiempo para dormir **2** (= *steal*) robar; (= *kidnap*) secuestrar
C VI **don't ~!** ¡no me lo quites!; **to ~ at sth** (*lit, fig*) intentar agarrar algo
➤ **snatch away, snatch off** VT + ADV **to ~ sth away from** *or* **off sb** arrebatar algo a algn
➤ **snatch up** VT + ADV agarrar (*rápidamente*)

snazzy* ['snæzɪ] ADJ (*compar* **snazzier**; *superl* **snazziest**) **a ~ dress** un vestido vistoso

sneak [sniːk] **A** VT **to ~ sth out of a place** sacar algo furtivamente de un lugar; **to ~ a look at sth** mirar algo de reojo *or* soslayo
B VI **1** (= *move*) **to ~ about** ir a hurtadillas, moverse furtivamente; **to ~ in/out** entrar/salir a hurtadillas; **to ~ away** *or* **off** escabullirse; **to ~ up on sb** acercarse sigilosamente a algn
2 (= *tell tales*) **to ~ on sb*** delatar a algn, dar el soplo sobre algn*, chivarse de algn (*Sp**)
C N (*) (= *tale-teller*) chivato/a *m/f*, soplón/ona *m/f*
D CPD ➤ **sneak preview** [*of film*] preestreno *m* ➤ **sneak thief** ratero/a *m/f*

sneakers ['sniːkəz] NPL (*esp US*) zapatillas *fpl* de deporte

sneaking ['sniːkɪŋ] ADJ **I have a ~ feeling that ...** tengo la sensación de que ...; **to have a ~ regard for sb** respetar a algn a pesar de todo, respetar a algn sin querer confesarlo abiertamente

sneaky* ['sniːkɪ] ADJ (*compar* **sneakier**; *superl* **sneakiest**) soplón

sneer [snɪəʳ] **A** N (= *expression*) cara *f* de desprecio; (= *remark*) comentario *m* desdeñoso; **he said with a ~** dijo con desprecio **B** VI hablar con desprecio, hablar con desdén; **to ~ at sb/sth** (= *laugh*) mofarse de algn/algo; (= *scorn*) despreciar a algn/algo

sneeze [sniːz] **A** N estornudo *m* **B** VI estornudar

snide* [snaɪd] ADJ bajo, sarcástico

sniff [snɪf] **A** N **1** (= *act*) sorbo *m* (por la nariz); (*by dog*) husmeo *m* **2** (= *faint smell*) olorcillo *m* **B** VT [+ *snuff etc*] sorber (por la nariz), aspirar; [+ *smell*] oler; [*dog etc*] olfatear, husmear; **to ~ glue** esnifar *or* inhalar pegamento

C VI [*person*] aspirar por la nariz, sorber, sorberse la nariz; [*dog etc*] oler, husmear, olfatear; **to ~ at sth** oler algo; (*fig*) despreciar algo, desdeñar algo; **an offer not to be ~ed at** una oferta que no es de despreciar *or* desdeñar
➤ **sniff out** VT + ADV (= *discover*) encontrar husmeando

sniffer dog ['snɪfədɒg] N perro *m* rastreador; (*for drugs*) perro *m* antidroga; (*for explosives*) perro *m* antiexplosivos

sniffle ['snɪfl] **A** N **to have the ~s** estar resfriado *or* constipado **B** VI sorber haciendo ruido

sniffy* ['snɪfɪ] ADJ (= *disdainful*) estirado, desdeñoso; **he was pretty ~ about it** trató el asunto con bastante desdén

snifter* ['snɪftəʳ] N (*Brit*) (= *drink*) copa *f*, trago *m*

snigger ['snɪgəʳ] **A** N risilla *f*, risita *f* **B** VI reír disimuladamente; **to ~ at sth** reírse tontamente de algo

snip [snɪp] VT tijeretear; **to ~ sth off** cortar algo con tijeras

snipe [snaɪp] **A** N (= *bird*) agachadiza *f* **B** VI **to ~ at sb** disparar a algn desde un escondite; **to ~ at one's critics** responder ante las críticas

sniper ['snaɪpəʳ] N francotirador(a) *m/f*

snippet ['snɪpɪt] N [*of cloth, paper*] pedacito *m*, recorte *m*; [*of information, conversation*] retazo *m*, fragmento *m*

snitch** [snɪtʃ] **A** VI **to ~ on sb** chivarse *or* soplar a algn **B** N (= *informer*) soplón/ona* *m/f*

snivel ['snɪvl] VI lloriquear

snivelling, sniveling (*US*) ['snɪvlɪŋ] **A** ADJ llorón **B** N lloriqueo *m*

snob [snɒb] N snob *mf*, esnob *mf*; **he's an intellectual ~** presume de intelectual

snobbery ['snɒbərɪ] N snobismo *m*, esnobismo *m*

snobbish ['snɒbɪʃ] ADJ snob, esnob

snobby* ['snɒbɪ] ADJ (*compar* **snobbier**; *superl* **snobbiest**) snob, esnob

snog** [snɒg] (*Brit*) **A** N **to have a ~** besuquearse* **B** VI besuquearse*

snooker ['snuːkəʳ] **A** N snooker *m*, billar *m* inglés **B** VT **to be properly ~ed** (*Brit**) (*fig*) estar en un aprieto serio

snoop [snuːp] **A** N **1** (= *person*) fisgón/ona *m/f* **2** (= *act*) **to have a ~ round** fisgar, fisgonear; **I had a ~ round the kitchen** estuve fisgando *or* fisgoneando *or* husmeando por la cocina **B** VI (*also ~ about, ~ around*) (= *pry*) fisgar, fisgonear; (= *interfere*) entrometerse

snooper ['snuːpəʳ] N fisgón/ona *m/f*

snooty* ['snuːtɪ] ADJ (*compar* **snootier**; *superl* **snootiest**) presumido

snooze [snuːz] **A** N cabezada *f*; (*in the afternoon*) siestecita *f*; **to have a ~** dar *or* echar una cabezada *or* cabezadita; (*in the afternoon*) echar una siestecita **B** VI dormitar

snore [snɔːʳ] **A** N ronquido *m* **B** VI roncar

snorer ['snɔːrəʳ] N persona *f* que ronca mucho

snoring ['snɔːrɪŋ] N ronquidos *mpl*

snorkel ['snɔːkl] **A** N [*of swimmer*] tubo *m* de respiración; [*of submarine*] snorquel *m*, esnorquel *m* **B** VI bucear con tubo para respirar

snort [snɔːt] **A** N [*of horse, person*] resoplido *m*, bufido *m* **B** VI [*horse, person*] resoplar, bufar; **he ~ed with anger** bufó enojado **C** VT **1** (= *say*) bufar; **"no!" he ~ed** —¡no! —bufó él **2** (*Drugs**) [+ *cocaine etc*] inhalar, esnifar*

snot* [snɒt] N mocos *mpl*, mocarro *m*

snotty* ['snɒtɪ] ADJ (*compar* **snottier**; *superl* **snottiest**) [*nose, handkerchief*] lleno de mocos; (*Brit*) (= *snooty*) presumido

snotty-nosed* ['snɒtɪ,nəʊzd] ADJ mocoso; (*fig*) presumido

snout [snaʊt] N hocico *m*

snow [snəʊ] **A** N nieve *f* **B** VT **1** (*Met*) **to be ~ed in** *or* **up** quedar aislado por la nieve **2** (*fig*) **to be ~ed under with work** estar agobiado de trabajo **C** VI nevar; **it's ~ing** está nevando **D** CPD ➤ **snow blindness** (*Med*) ceguera *f* de nieve ➤ **snow pea** (*US, Australia*) arveja *f* china ➤ **snow report** (*Met*) informe *m* sobre el estado de la nieve ➤ **snow tyre, snow tire** (*US*) neumático *m* antideslizante ➤ **Snow White** Blancanieves *f*

snowball ['snəʊbɔːl] Ⓐ N bola *f* de nieve Ⓑ VI (*fig*) aumentar progresivamente, ir aumentándose

snow-bound ['snəʊbaʊnd] ADJ aislado por la nieve, bloqueado por la nieve

snow-capped ['snəʊkæpt] ADJ cubierto de nieve, nevado

snow-covered ['snəʊ'kʌvəd] ADJ cubierto de nieve, nevado

snowdrift ['snəʊdrɪft] N *montón de nieve que queda acumulada después de una ventisca*

snowdrop ['snəʊdrɒp] N campanilla *f* de invierno

snowfall ['snəʊfɔːl] N nevada *f*

snowflake ['snəʊfleɪk] N copo *m* de nieve

snowman ['snəʊmæn] N (*pl* **snowmen**) muñeco *m* de nieve; **the abominable ~** el abominable hombre de las nieves

snowmobile ['snəʊməˌbiːl] N motonieve *f*

snowplough, snowplow (*US*) ['snəʊplaʊ] N quitanieves *m inv*

snowshoe ['snəʊʃuː] N raqueta *f* (de nieve)

snowstorm ['snəʊstɔːm] N temporal *m* de nieve, ventisca *f*, nevasca *f*

snowsuit ['snəʊsuːt] N mono *m* acolchado de nieve

snow-white ['snəʊ'waɪt] ADJ blanco como la nieve

snowy ['snəʊɪ] ADJ (*compar* **snowier**; *superl* **snowiest**) **1** [*climate, region*] de mucha nieve; [*day etc*] de nieve; [*countryside etc*] cubierto de nieve; **it was very ~ yesterday** ayer nevó mucho, ayer cayó mucha nieve **2** (= *white as snow*) blanco como la nieve

SNP N ABBR (*Brit Pol*) = **Scottish National Party**

Snr ABBR (*esp Brit*) = **Senior**

snub[1] [snʌb] Ⓐ N desaire *m* Ⓑ VT [+ *person*] desairar, volver la espalda a; [+ *offer*] rechazar

snub[2] [snʌb] ADJ **~ nose** nariz *f* respingona

snuff[1] [snʌf] N rapé *m*; **to take ~** tomar rapé

snuff[2] [snʌf] VT apagar; **to ~ it** (*Brit**) estirar la pata*, liar el petate*
➤ **snuff out** VT + ADV [+ *candle*] apagar; (*fig*) extinguir

snuffbox ['snʌfbɒks] N caja *f* de rapé, tabaquera *f*

snuffle ['snʌfl] N, VI = **sniffle**

snug [snʌg] Ⓐ ADJ (*compar* **~ger**; *superl* **~gest**) **1** (= *cosy*) [*house, room*] acogedor; [*bed*] confortable; **it's nice and ~ here** aquí se está bien; **to be ~ in bed** estar calentito y a gusto en la cama, estar arrebujado en la cama **2** (= *close-fitting*) ajustado, ceñido, justo (*esp LAm*); **it's a ~ fit** [*garment*] ciñe bien; [*object*] cabe justito Ⓑ N (*Brit*) (*in pub*) salón *m* pequeño

snuggle ['snʌgl] VI **to ~ down in bed** acurrucarse en la cama; **to ~ up to sb** arrimarse a algn

snugly ['snʌglɪ] ADV **1** (= *cosily*) **wrap your baby ~ in a blanket** abrigue bien a su bebé con una manta; **the children were ~ tucked up in bed** los niños estaban bien abrigados en la cama, los niños estaban bien tapaditos en la cama* **2** (= *tightly*) **it fits ~** [*jacket*] (= *well*) queda bien ajustado *or* ceñido *or* (*esp LAm*) justo; [*one object in another*] encaja perfectamente

so [səʊ] Ⓐ ADV **1** (= *to such an extent*) tan; **1.1** (*with adj/adv*) tan; **I'm so worried** estoy tan preocupado; **he was talking so fast I couldn't understand** hablaba tan rápido que no lo entendía; **"how's your father?" — "not so good"** —¿cómo está tu padre? —no muy bien; **it's about so high/long** es más o menos así de alto/largo; **she's not so clever as him** no es tan lista como él; **he's not so silly as to do that** no es bastante tonto para hacer eso, no es tan tonto como para hacer eso; **so many** tantos/as; **so much** tanto/a; **I've got so much to do** tengo tantísimo que hacer; **it's not so very difficult** no es tan difícil **1.2** (*with vb*) tanto; **I love you so** te quiero tanto
2 (= *thus, in this way, likewise*) así, de esta manera, de este modo; **so it was that ...** así fue que ..., de esta manera *or* de este modo fue como ...; **so it is!** ◊ **so it does!** ¡es verdad!, ¡es cierto!, ¡correcto! **is that so?** ¿de veras?, **isn't that so?** ¿no es así?; **so be it** así sea; **by so doing** haciéndolo así;

I expect so supongo que sí, a lo mejor; **so far** hasta aquí *or* ahora; **and so forth** y así sucesivamente, etcétera; **I hope so** eso espero yo, espero que sí; **and so on (and so forth)** y así sucesivamente, etcétera; **so he says** eso dice él; **so to speak** por decirlo así; **I think so** creo que sí; **I told you so** ya te lo dije
3 (= *also*) **he's wrong and so are you** se equivocan tanto usted como él; **so do I** (y) yo también; **"I work a lot" — "so do I"** —trabajo mucho —(y) yo también; **so would I** yo también
4 (*phrases*) **she didn't so much as send me a birthday card** no me mandó ni (siquiera) una tarjeta para mi cumpleaños; **I haven't so much as a penny** no tengo ni un peso; **ten or so** unos diez, diez más o menos; **at five o'clock or so** a las cinco o así *or* o por ahí *or* más o menos Ⓑ CONJ **1** (*expressing purpose*) para; **I left early so I'd catch my train** me fui pronto para poder tomar el tren; **he took her upstairs so they wouldn't be overheard** la subió al piso de arriba para que nadie los oyera; **so as to do sth** para hacer algo, a fin de hacer algo; **we hurried so as not to be late** nos dimos prisa para no llegar tarde *or* a fin de no llegar tarde; **so that** para que + *subjun*, a fin de que + *subjun*; **I bought it so that you should see it** lo compré para que lo vieras
2 (*expressing result*) así que, de manera que; **it rained and so we could not go out** llovió, así que no pudimos salir, llovió y no pudimos salir; **so that** de modo que, de manera que; **he stood so that he faced west** se puso de tal modo *or* de manera que miraba al oeste, se puso mirando al oeste
3 (= *therefore*) así que; **the shop was closed, so I went home** la tienda estaba cerrada, así que me fui a casa
4 (*in questions, exclamations*) entonces, así que; **so you're Spanish?** entonces *or* así que ¿eres español?; **so?*** ¿y?, ¿y qué?; **so what?*** ¿y?, ¿y qué?

soak [səʊk] Ⓐ VT **1** (= *immerse*) poner en remojo **2** (= *make wet*) empapar; **to get ~ed (to the skin)** empaparse *or* quedar empapado, calarse hasta los huesos Ⓑ VI remojarse; **to leave sth to ~** dejar algo en *or* al remojo Ⓒ N (= *rain*) diluvio *m*; **to have a good ~ in the bath** darse un buen baño; **give your shirt a ~ overnight** deja la camisa en remojo toda la noche
➤ **soak in** VI + ADV penetrar
➤ **soak through** Ⓐ VT + ADV **to be ~ed through** [*person*] estar calado hasta los huesos, estar empapado Ⓑ VI + PREP calar, penetrar
➤ **soak up** VT + ADV absorber

soaking ['səʊkɪŋ] Ⓐ ADJ (*also* **~ wet**) [*person*] calado hasta los huesos, empapado; [*object*] empapado, calado Ⓑ N (*in liquid*) remojo *m*; [*of rain*] diluvio *m*; **to get a ~** calarse hasta los huesos, empaparse

so-and-so ['səʊənsəʊ] N (*pl* **~s**) fulano/a *m/f*; **Mr ~** don Fulano (de Tal); **he's a ~** (*pej*) es un tal, es un hijo de su madre*

soap [səʊp] Ⓐ N **1** jabón *m* **2** = **soap opera** Ⓑ VT jabonar Ⓒ CPD ➤ **soap dish** jabonera *f* ➤ **soap flakes** jabón *msing* en escamas ➤ **soap opera** (*TV*) telenovela *f*; (*Rad*) radionovela *f* ➤ **soap powder** polvos *mpl* de jabón, detergente *m* en polvo

soapbox ['səʊpbɒks] N tribuna *f* improvisada

soapsuds ['səʊpsʌdz] NPL espuma *fsing* de jabón

soapy ['səʊpɪ] ADJ (*compar* **soapier**; *superl* **soapiest**) cubierto de jabón

soar [sɔːr] VI [*birds etc*] remontar el vuelo; [*tower etc*] elevarse; [*price etc*] subir vertiginosamente, ponerse por las nubes; [*hopes*] aumentar; [*spirits*] renacer, reanimarse

soaring ['sɔːrɪŋ] ADJ [*flight*] planeador, que vuela; [*building*] altísimo; [*prices*] en alza, en aumento; [*hopes, imagination*] expansivo; [*ambition*] inmenso

sob [sɒb] Ⓐ N sollozo *m*; **she said with a ~** dijo sollozando, dijo entre sollozos Ⓑ VI sollozar Ⓒ VT **"no,"** **she ~bed** —no —dijo sollozando, —no —dijo entre sollozos; **to ~ one's heart out** llorar a lágrima viva Ⓓ CPD ➤ **sob story*** tragedia *f*

sobbing ['sɒbɪŋ] N sollozos *mpl*

sober ['səʊbər] ADJ **1** (= *not drunk*) sobrio; ✦ IDIOM **to be as**

~ as a judge ◇ **be stone-cold ~*** estar perfectamente sobrio **2** (= *serious, calm*) [*person*] serio, formal; [*expression*] grave; [*attitude, assessment*] serio, sobrio; [*fact*] cruel; [*reality*] crudo, duro; **upon ~ reflection** después de una seria reflexión **3** (= *plain*) [*clothes, style*] sobrio, discreto
➤ **sober up** Ⓐ VT + ADV (= *stop being drunk*) despejar, quitar la borrachera a Ⓑ VI + ADV (= *stop being drunk*) **when she had ~ed up** cuando se hubo despejado, cuando se le hubo pasado la borrachera

sobering ['səʊbərɪŋ] ADJ **it had a ~ effect on me** fue aleccionador; **it's a ~ thought** da que pensar

soberly ['səʊbəlɪ] ADV **1** (= *seriously*) [*say, look*] con seriedad, sobriamente **2** (= *plainly*) [*decorated, dressed*] sobriamente, discretamente; **he was ~ dressed in a dark suit** vestía un traje oscuro y sobrio or discreto

sobriety [səʊ'braɪətɪ] N **1** (= *not being drunk*) **~ test** (*US*) prueba *f* de alcoholemia **2** (= *seriousness, sedateness*) seriedad *f*, sobriedad *f* **3** (= *subdued nature*) sobriedad *f*, discreción *f*

Soc ABBR = **society**

so-called ['səʊ'kɔːld] ADJ supuesto, presunto

soccer ['sɒkə'] N fútbol *m*; **to play ~** jugar al fútbol
➤ **soccer player** (*US*) futbolista *mf*

sociability [ˌsəʊʃə'bɪlɪtɪ] N sociabilidad *f*

sociable ['səʊʃəbl] ADJ [*person*] sociable, tratable; [*occasion*] social; **I don't feel very ~** no estoy para hacer vida social; **I'll have one drink, just to be ~** para hacerles compañía, tomaré una copa

sociably ['səʊʃəblɪ] ADV sociablemente; **to live ~ together** vivir juntos amistosamente

social ['səʊʃəl] Ⓐ ADJ **1** (= *relating to society*) social; **the ~ order** el orden social
2 (= *in society*) [*engagements, life*] social; **he has little ~ contact with his business colleagues** apenas trata con sus colegas fuera del trabajo; **I'm a ~ drinker only** sólo bebo cuando estoy con gente; **to have a good ~ life** hacer or tener buena vida social; **this isn't a ~ visit** ésta no es una visita de cortesía
3 (= *interactive*) [*person, animal, behaviour*] social; **he has poor ~ skills** no tiene aptitud para el trato social, no tiene mucho don de gentes
Ⓑ N reunión *f* (social)
Ⓒ CPD ➤ **social climber** arribista *mf* ➤ **social club** club *m* social ➤ **Social Democrat** socialdemócrata *mf* ➤ **social drinker** bebedor(a) *m/f* social ➤ **social insurance** (*US*) seguro *m* social ➤ **social science** ciencias *fpl* sociales ➤ **social security** (*Brit*) seguridad *f* social; **to be on ~ security** (*Brit*) vivir de la seguridad social ➤ **social skills** comportamiento *m*sing social; **to learn ~ skills** aprender a comportarse socialmente ➤ **social welfare** asistencia *f* social ➤ **social work** asistencia *f* social ➤ **social worker** asistente/a *m/f* social, trabajador(a) *m/f* social (*Mex*), visitador(a) *m/f* social (*Chi*)

socialism ['səʊʃəlɪzəm] N socialismo *m*

socialist ['səʊʃəlɪst] ADJ, N socialista *mf*

socialite ['səʊʃəlaɪt] N famosillo/a* *m/f* (*pej*), vividor(a) *m/f*

socialize ['səʊʃəlaɪz] VI alternar, salir

socially ['səʊʃəlɪ] ADV [*integrate, interact*] socialmente; [*inferior, necessary*] socialmente, desde el punto de vista social; **~ acceptable** aceptado por la sociedad; **to be ~ unacceptable** ser mal visto; **to be ~ aware** tener conciencia social; **I didn't really get to know him ~** apenas tuve trato con él; **I don't really mix with him ~** no suelo alternar con él

society [sə'saɪətɪ] Ⓐ N **1** (= *social community*) sociedad *f* **2** (= *high society*) alta sociedad *f*; **in polite ~** entre gente educada **3** (= *club, organization*) asociación *f*, sociedad *f*
Ⓑ CPD ➤ **society column** ecos *mpl* de sociedad, notas *fpl* sociales (*LAm*) ➤ **society wedding** boda *f* de sociedad

socioeconomic ['səʊsɪəʊˌiːkə'nɒmɪk] ADJ socioeconómico

sociological [ˌsəʊsɪə'lɒdʒɪkəl] ADJ sociológico

sociologist [ˌsəʊsɪ'ɒlədʒɪst] N sociólogo/a *m/f*

sociology [ˌsəʊsɪ'ɒlədʒɪ] N sociología *f*

sock¹ [sɒk] N calcetín *m*, media *f* (*LAm*); ✦ IDIOMS **to pull** **one's ~s up** (*Brit**) hacer esfuerzos, despabilarse; **put a ~ in it!** (*Brit**) ¡a callar!, ¡cállate!; **this will knock your ~s off*** esto es para quitarse el sombrero

sock²* [sɒk] Ⓐ N (= *blow*) puñetazo *m*; **to give sb a ~ on the jaw** pegar a algn en la cara Ⓑ VT pegar

socket ['sɒkɪt] N **1** [*of eye*] cuenca *f*; [*of joint*] glena *f* **2** (*Brit Elec*) enchufe *m*, toma *f* de corriente, tomacorriente *m* (*LAm*)

sod*** [sɒd] (*Brit*) Ⓐ N cabrón/ona*** *m/f*; **some poor ~** algún pobre diablo; **this job is a real ~** este trabajo es una jodienda*** Ⓑ VT **~ it!** ¡mierda!***; **~ him!** ¡que se joda!***
➤ **sod off***** VI + ADV (*Brit*) **~ off!** ¡vete a la porra!*

soda ['səʊdə] Ⓐ N **1** (*Chem*) sosa *f*; (*Culin*) bicarbonato *m* (sódico) **2** (= *drink*) soda *f*; **whisky and ~** whisky *m* con soda **3** (*US*) (= *pop*) refresco *m* Ⓑ CPD ➤ **soda bread** pan hecho con levadura de bicarbonato ➤ **soda fountain** (*US†*) (= *place*) café-bar *m* ➤ **soda pop** (*US*) refresco *m* ➤ **soda siphon** sifón *m* ➤ **soda water** soda *f*

sodden ['sɒdn] ADJ empapado

sodding*** ['sɒdɪŋ] (*Brit*) ADJ jodido***, puñetero (*Sp***)

sodium ['səʊdɪəm] N sodio *m* ➤ **sodium bicarbonate** bicarbonato *m* sódico ➤ **sodium chloride** cloruro *m* sódico, cloruro *m* de sodio

sodomy ['sɒdəmɪ] N sodomía *f*

sofa ['səʊfə] N sofá *m* ➤ **sofa bed** sofá-cama *m*

Sofia ['səʊfɪə] N Sofía *f*

soft [sɒft] Ⓐ ADJ (*compar* **~er**; *superl* **~est**) **1** (= *not hard*) [*ground, water, contact lens, fruit*] blando; [*bed, mattress, pillow*] blando, mullido; [*metal*] maleable, dúctil; (*pej*) [*muscles, flesh*] blando; **to go ~** [*biscuits etc*] ablandarse
2 (= *smooth*) [*skin, hair, fur, fabric, texture*] suave; **to make ~** [+ *skin, clothes*] suavizar; [+ *leather*] ablandar
3 (= *gentle, not harsh*) [*breeze, landing, music*] suave; [*light*] tenue; [*colour*] delicado; [*drug*] blando
4 (= *quiet*) [*whisper, laugh*] suave; [*whistle*] flojo; [*voice*] suave, tenue
5 (= *kind*) [*smile, person*] dulce; (= *lenient, weak*) blando; **to have a ~ heart** ser todo corazón; **to be (too) ~ on/with sb** ser (demasiado) blando or indulgente con algn; **to have a ~ spot for sb** tener debilidad por algn
6 (= *easy*) fácil; **~ option** camino *m* fácil
7 (*) (= *foolish*) bobo*, tonto; **to be ~ in the head** ser un poco bobo*
Ⓑ CPD ➤ **soft centre** relleno *m* blando ➤ **soft drink** bebida *f* refrescante, refresco *m* ➤ **soft furnishings**, **soft goods** (*US*) textiles *mpl* ➤ **soft pedal** (*Mus*) pedal *m* suave ➤ **soft porn** pornografía *f* blanda ➤ **soft sell** venta *f* por persuasión ➤ **soft skills** habilidades *fpl* interpersonales ➤ **soft top** (*esp US*) descapotable *m* ➤ **soft toy** (*Brit*) juguete *m* de peluche

softback ['sɒftbæk] ADJ, N **~ (book)** libro *m* en rústica

softball ['sɒftbɔːl] N sófbol *m*, softball *m*

soft-boiled ['sɒftˌbɔɪld] ADJ [*egg*] pasado (por agua)

softcover ['sɒftkʌvə'] ADJ, N (*US*) = **softback**

soften ['sɒfn] Ⓐ VT **1** (= *make less hard*) ablandar **2** (= *make smooth*) [+ *fabric, skin, hair*] suavizar **3** (= *make gentle*) [+ *sound, outline*] suavizar; [+ *lights, lighting*] hacer más tenue; [+ *person*] ablandar **4** (= *mitigate*) [+ *effect, reaction*] mitigar, atenuar; **to ~ the blow** (*fig*) amortiguar el golpe
Ⓑ VI **1** (= *become less hard*) ablandarse **2** (= *become smooth*) suavizarse **3** (= *become gentle*) [*voice, outline*] suavizarse; [*lighting*] hacerse más tenue; [*person*] ablandarse; [*attitude*] suavizarse, moderarse
➤ **soften up** Ⓐ VT + ADV [+ *resistance*] debilitar Ⓑ VI + ADV **to ~ up on sb** volverse menos severo con algn

softener ['sɒfnə'] N (= *water softener*) descalcificador *m*, decalcificador *m*; (= *fabric softener*) suavizante *m*

soft-hearted ['sɒft'hɑːtɪd] ADJ compasivo, bondadoso

softie* ['sɒftɪ] N = **softy**

softly ['sɒftlɪ] ADV **1** (= *quietly*) [*walk, move*] silenciosamente, sin hacer ruido; [*say*] bajito, en voz baja; [*whistle*] bajito; **he closed the door ~** cerró la puerta silenciosamente; **he swore ~** dijo una palabrota en voz baja, susurró una palabrota; **a ~ spoken young man** un joven de voz suave **2** (= *gently*) [*touch, tap, kiss*] suavemente **3** (= *not brightly*) [*glow, gleam, shine*] tenuemente; **~ lit** iluminado con luz tenue

softness ['sɒftnɪs] N **1** [*of ground, bread, water*] blandura *f*, lo blando; [*of bed, pillow*] lo mullido; [*of muscles, flesh*] blandura *f* **2** [*of skin, hair, fabric*] suavidad *f* **3** [*of breeze, touch, voice, light, colour*] suavidad *f*; [*of light*] lo tenue **4** [*of sound, laugh*] suavidad *f* **5** (= *kindness*) ternura *f* **6** (= *leniency*) [*of person, approach*] indulgencia *f*, blandura *f* **7** (= *weakness*) debilidad *f* **8** (= *stupidity*) estupidez *f*

soft-pedal ['sɒft'pedl] VT (*esp US*) (*fig*) minimizar la importancia de

soft-soap* [ˌsɒft'səʊp] VT dar coba a*

soft-spoken ['sɒft'spəʊkən] ADJ de voz suave

software ['sɒftwɛəʳ] N (*Comput*) software *m* ➤ **software engineer** ingeniero/a *m/f* de software ➤ **software house** compañía *f* especializada en programación ➤ **software package** paquete *m* de programas

softy* ['sɒftɪ] N blandengue* *mf*

soggy ['sɒgɪ] ADJ (*compar* **soggier**; *superl* **soggiest**) [*paper*] mojado; [*clothes, ground*] empapado; [*bread, biscuits*] revenido; [*vegetables*] pasado

soil [sɔɪl] Ⓐ N (= *earth*) tierra *f*; **his native ~** su tierra natal, su patria; **on British ~** en suelo británico Ⓑ VT ensuciar; (*fig*) [+ *reputation, honour etc*] manchar

soiled [sɔɪld] ADJ (= *dirty*) sucio; (= *stained*) manchado

soirée ['swɑːreɪ] N velada *f*

sojourn ['sɒdʒɜːn] N (*liter*) estancia *f*

solace ['sɒlɪs] N consuelo *m*

solar ['səʊləʳ] ADJ solar ➤ **solar cell** célula *f* solar ➤ **solar panel** panel *m* solar ➤ **solar plexus** (*Anat*) plexo *m* solar ➤ **solar power** energía *f* solar ➤ **solar system** sistema *m* solar

solarium [səˈlɛərɪəm] N (*pl* **~s** *or* **solaria** [səˈlɛərɪə]) solárium *m*, solario *m*

sold [səʊld] PT, PP *of* **sell**

solder ['səʊldəʳ] Ⓐ N soldadura *f* Ⓑ VT soldar

soldering iron ['səʊldərɪŋˌaɪən] N soldador *m*

soldier ['səʊldʒəʳ] N soldado *mf*, militar *mf*; **an old ~** un veterano *or* excombatiente; **to play at ~s** jugar a los soldados
➤ **soldier on** VI + ADV seguir adelante

sole¹ [səʊl] Ⓐ N [*of foot*] planta *f*; [*of shoe*] suela *f* Ⓑ VT poner suela a

sole² [səʊl] N (*pl* **~** *or* **~s**) (= *fish*) lenguado *m*

sole³ [səʊl] ADJ (= *only*) único; (= *exclusive*) exclusivo, en exclusividad ➤ **sole trader** empresario/a *m/f* individual

solely ['səʊllɪ] ADV (= *only*) únicamente, solamente, sólo; (= *exclusively*) exclusivamente

solemn ['sɒləm] ADJ [*person, face*] serio, adusto; [*warning*] serio; [*occasion, promise*] solemne

solemnity [səˈlemnɪtɪ] N [*of occasion, promise*] solemnidad *f*; [*of person's expression*] seriedad *f*, adustez *f*

solemnize ['sɒləmnaɪz] VT solemnizar

solemnly ['sɒləmlɪ] ADV [*nod, look*] seriamente, con gesto adusto; [*say*] con seriedad, con tono solemne; [*promise, declare, swear*] solemnemente

sol-fa ['sɒl'fɑː] N (*Mus*) solfeo *m*

solicit [səˈlɪsɪt] Ⓐ VT (= *request*) solicitar; (= *demand*) exigir; (= *beg for*) pedir; **to ~ sb for sth** ◇ **~ sth of sb** solicitar algo a algn Ⓑ VI [*prostitute*] ejercer la prostitución abordando a clientes

soliciting [səˈlɪsɪtɪŋ] N (*by prostitute*) ejercicio *m* de la prostitución (*abordando a los clientes*)

solicitor [səˈlɪsɪtəʳ] N **1** (*Brit Jur*) (= *lawyer*) procurador(a) *m/f*, abogado/a *m/f*; (*for wills*) notario/a *m/f*; ▷ LAWYERS **2** (*US*) (= *officer*) representante *mf*, agente *mf*; (*Jur*) abogado/a *m/f* asesor(a) adscrito/a a un municipio

solicitous [səˈlɪsɪtəs] ADJ solícito (**about, for** por)

solid ['sɒlɪd] Ⓐ ADJ **1** (= *not liquid*) sólido; **~ food** alimentos *mpl* sólidos; **to be frozen ~** estar completamente congelado; **to go ~** solidificarse **2** (= *not hollow*) [*rock*] sólido; [*wood, steel*] macizo, puro; [*tyre, ball, block*] macizo; **~ gold** oro *m* puro **3** (= *continuous*) [*line, rain*] ininterrumpido; **we waited two ~ hours** esperamos dos horas enteras **4** (= *substantial*) [*building, understanding, basis*] sólido; [*argument*] sólido, bien fundamentado; [*relationship*] sólido, firme; **~ ground** tierra *f* firme; **a ~ meal** una comida sustanciosa **5** (= *compact, dense*) [*layer, crowd*] compacto; **a man of ~ build** un hombre fornido *or* de constitución robusta; **a ~ mass of colour** una masa de color sólida; **he's six feet of ~ muscle** mide uno ochenta y cinco de puro músculo; **the traffic was ~ going into town** había una caravana tremenda en dirección a la ciudad* **6** (= *reliable*) [*person, relationship*] serio; [*evidence, reason, values*] sólido; [*information*] fiable; [*work*] concienzudo; [*advice*] útil; **he's a good ~ worker** es un trabajador responsable Ⓑ ADV **flights to Israel are booked ~** los vuelos a Israel están completamente llenos; **the taps are jammed ~** los grifos se han atascado y es imposible hacerlos girar; **the streets were packed ~ with people** las calles estaban abarrotadas de gente; **I've been working on this for eight hours ~** he estado trabajando sobre esto durante ocho horas ininterrumpidas, llevo trabajando sobre esto ocho horas sin parar Ⓒ N **1** (*Phys, Chem, Geom*) sólido *m* **2 solids** (= *solid food*) (alimentos *mpl*) sólidos *mpl* Ⓓ CPD ➤ **solid fuel** (*Brit*) combustible *m* sólido

solidarity [ˌsɒlɪˈdærɪtɪ] N solidaridad *f*

solidify [səˈlɪdɪfaɪ] Ⓐ VI solidificarse Ⓑ VT solidificar

solidity [səˈlɪdɪtɪ] N solidez *f*

solidly ['sɒlɪdlɪ] ADV **1** (= *firmly*) con firmeza **2** (= *sturdily*) **~ made** *or* **built** *or* **constructed** de construcción sólida **3** (= *without pause*) [*drive, rain*] ininterrumpidamente, sin parar; [*work*] sin descanso, sin parar; **it rained ~ for two days** llovió ininterrumpidamente durante dos días, llovió dos días sin parar **4** (= *unanimously*) [*vote*] unánimemente; **to be ~ behind sth/sb** apoyar algo/a algn unánimemente **5** (= *thoroughly*) **a ~ middle-class neighbourhood** un barrio totalmente de clase media

soliloquy [səˈlɪləkwɪ] N soliloquio *m*

solitaire [ˌsɒlɪˈtɛəʳ] N **1** (= *gem*) solitario *m* **2** (= *game*) solitario *m*

solitary ['sɒlɪtərɪ] Ⓐ ADJ **1** (= *lonely, lone*) [*person, life, childhood*] solitario; **to feel ~** sentirse solo *or* aislado **2** (= *secluded*) [*place*] apartado **3** (= *sole*) solo, único; **there has been one ~ case** ha habido un caso único Ⓑ N (*) = **solitary confinement** Ⓒ CPD ➤ **solitary confinement to be in ~ confinement** estar incomunicado

solitude ['sɒlɪtjuːd] N soledad *f*

solo ['səʊləʊ] Ⓐ N (*pl* **~s**) solo *m*; **a guitar ~** un solo de guitarra Ⓑ ADJ **~ flight** vuelo *m* en solitario; **~ trip round the world** vuelta *f* al mundo en solitario Ⓒ ADV [*fly*] en solitario

soloist ['səʊləʊɪst] N solista *mf*

solstice ['sɒlstɪs] N solsticio *m*; **summer ~** solsticio *m* de verano; **winter ~** solsticio *m* de invierno

soluble ['sɒljʊbl] ADJ soluble; **~ in water** soluble en agua

solution [səˈluːʃən] N **1** (*to problem*) solución *f* (**to** de, a) **2** (*Chem*) solución *f*

solve [sɒlv] VT [+ *problem, puzzle*] resolver, solucionar; [+ *mystery, crime*] resolver, esclarecer

solvency ['sɒlvənsɪ] N (*Fin*) solvencia *f*

solvent ['sɒlvənt] Ⓐ ADJ solvente Ⓑ N disolvente *m* Ⓒ CPD ➤ **solvent abuse** (*Brit*) abuso *m* de los disolventes

Somali [səˈmɑːlɪ] ADJ, N somalí *mf*

Somalia [səˈmɑːlɪə] N Somalia *f*

Somalian [səˈmɑːlɪən] ADJ, N somalí *mf*

sombre, somber (*US*) ['sɒmbəʳ] ADJ **1** (= *sober*) [*prospect, colour*] sombrío **2** (= *pessimistic*) pesimista **3** (= *melancholy*) melancólico

---

some

ⓐ ADJECTIVE   **ⓒ** ADVERB
ⓑ PRONOUN

some [sʌm] **ⓐ** ADJECTIVE
1 (= *an amount of*)

> When **some** refers to something you can't count, it usually isn't translated:

would you like ~ tea? ¿quieres té?; **have ~ more cake** toma *or* sírvete más pastel; *BUT* **we gave them ~ food** les dimos comida *or* algo de comida
2 (= *a little*) algo de, un poco de; **all I have left is ~ chocolate** solamente me queda algo de *or* un poco de chocolate
3 (= *a number of*) unos; **~ boys were shouting at him** unos chicos le estaban gritando; **you need ~ new trousers** necesitas unos pantalones nuevos; *BUT* **would you like ~ sweets/grapes?** ¿quieres caramelos/uvas?; **surely she has SOME friends?** debe de tener por lo menos algún amigo
4 (*as opposed to others*) **~ people say that ...** algunos dicen que ..., algunas personas dicen que ..., hay gente que dice que ...; **~ people hate fish** algunas personas odian el pescado, hay gente que odia el pescado; **~ people have all the luck!** ¡los hay que tienen suerte!, ¡algunos parece que nacen de pie!*; **I paid for mine, unlike ~ people I could mention** yo pagué el mío, no como ciertas personas *or* algunos a los que no quiero nombrar; **~ mushrooms are poisonous** ciertos tipos de setas son venenosas; **in ~ ways he's right** en cierto modo *or* sentido, tiene razón
5 (*indefinite*) algún + *masc noun*, alguna + *fem noun*; **~ day** algún día; **~ day next week** algún día de la semana que viene; **~ idiot of a driver** algún imbécil de conductor; **I read it in ~ book (or other)** lo he leído en algún libro; **for ~ reason (or other)** por alguna razón, por una u otra razón; **there must be SOME solution** alguna solución tiene que haber; *BUT* **~ man was asking for you** un hombre estuvo preguntando por ti; **this will give you ~ idea of ...** esto te dará una idea de ...; **let's make it ~ other time** hagámoslo otro día
6 (= *a considerable amount/number of*) bastante; **it took ~ courage to do that** hacer eso exigió bastante valor; **I haven't seen him for ~ time/years** hace bastante (tiempo)/bastantes años que no lo veo; **I posted it ~ days ago (now)** lo mandé por correo hace (ya) varios días
7 (*) (*admiring*) **that's ~ fish!** ¡eso sí que es un pez!, ¡eso es lo que se llama un pez!, ¡vaya pez!; **it was ~ party!** ¡vaya fiesta!, ¡menuda fiesta!
8 (*iro**) **~ friend!** ¡menudo amigo!; **you're ~ help, you are!** ¡vaya ayuda das!, ¡menuda ayuda eres tú!; **~ expert!** ¡valiente experto!
9 (*) (*in annoyance*) **~ people!** ¡qué gente!
ⓑ PRONOUN
1 (= *a certain amount, a little*) un poco; **have ~!** ¡toma un poco!; **could I have ~ of that cheese?** ¿me das un poco de ese queso?; *BUT* **thanks, I've got ~** gracias, ya tengo; **"I haven't got any paper" — "I'll give you ~"** —no tengo nada de papel —yo te doy; **it would cost twice that much and then ~*** costaría el doble de eso y algo más de propina*
2 (= *a part*) una parte; **I've read ~ of the book** he leído (una) parte del libro; **~ of what he said was true** parte de lo que dijo era cierto
3 (= *a number*) algunos/as *mpl/fpl*; **would you like ~?** ¿quieres algunos?, ¿quieres unos pocos *or* cuantos?; **~ of them have been sold** algunos de ellos se han vendido; **~ of my friends came** vinieron algunos de mis amigos
4 (= *certain people*) algunos, algunas personas; **~ believe that ...** algunos creen que ..., algunas personas creen que ..., hay gente que cree que ...
ⓒ ADVERB
1 (= *about*) **~ 20 people** unas 20 personas, una veintena de personas; **~ £30** unas 30 libras
2 (*US**) (= *a lot*) mucho; **we laughed ~** nos reímos mucho
3 (*US**) (= *a little*) un poco; **you'll feel better when you've**

slept **~** te sentirás mejor cuando hayas dormido un poco
somebody ['sʌmbədɪ] **ⓐ** PRON alguien; **there's ~ coming** viene alguien; **~ knocked at the door** alguien llamó a la puerta; **~ speak to me!** ¡que alguien me diga algo!; **~ Italian** un italiano; **~ from the audience** alguien del público; **we need ~ strong for that** necesitamos a alguien fuerte para eso; **you must have seen SOMEBODY!** ¡a alguien tienes que haber visto!; **let ~ else try** deja que otro *or* otra persona *or* alguien más lo intente; **~ or other** alguien
ⓑ N **to be ~** ser un personaje, ser alguien; **he really thinks he's ~** realmente se cree alguien

somehow ['sʌmhaʊ] ADV **1** (= *by some means*) de algún modo, de alguna manera; **I'll do it ~** de algún modo *or* de alguna manera lo haré; **it has to be done ~ or other** de un modo u otro *or* de una manera u otra tiene que hacerse
2 (= *for some reason*) por alguna razón; **~ I don't think he believed me** no sé porqué, pero me parece que no me creyó; **~ or other I never liked him** por alguna razón u otra nunca me cayó bien

someone ['sʌmwʌn] PRON = **somebody**

someplace ['sʌmpleɪs] ADV (*US*) = **somewhere**

somersault ['sʌməsɔːlt] **ⓐ** N (*by person*) voltereta *f*, salto *m* mortal; (*by car*) vuelco *m*, vuelta *f* de campana; **to do a ~** dar una voltereta, dar un salto mortal **ⓑ** VI [*person*] dar una voltereta, dar un salto mortal; [*car*] dar una vuelta de campana

something ['sʌmθɪŋ] **ⓐ** PRON **1** algo; **cook ~ nice** haz algo que esté rico; **there's ~ about him I don't like** hay algo que no me gusta de él; **let me ask you ~** déjame hacerte una pregunta, deja que te pregunte algo; **it's ~ to come to ~ when ...** llegamos a un punto grave cuando ...; **~ else** otra cosa; **I think you may have ~ there** puede que estés en lo cierto; **there's ~ in what you say** hay algo de verdad en lo que dices; **~ of the kind** algo por el estilo; **do you want to make ~ of it?** ¿quieres hacer un problema de esto?; **there's ~ the matter** pasa algo; **you can't get ~ for nothing** las cosas no las regalan; **it's ~ of a problem** es de algún modo *or* en cierto modo un problema, en cierto sentido representa un problema; **the play proved to be ~ of a letdown** la obra resultó ser un tanto decepcionante; **I hope to see ~ of you** espero que nos sigamos viendo, nos estaremos viendo, espero (*LAm*); **well, that's ~** eso ya es algo; **will you have ~ to drink?** ¿quieres tomar algo?; **I need ~ to eat** necesito comer algo; **it gives her ~ to live for** le da un motivo para vivir; **that has ~ to do with accountancy** eso tiene que ver *or* está relacionado con la contabilidad; **he's got ~ to do with it** está metido *or* involucrado en eso
2 (*) (= *something special or unusual*) **he thinks he's ~*** se cree alguien; **that's really ~!*** ¡eso sí que es fenomenal *or* estupendo!
3 (*in guesses, approximations*) **he's called John ~** se llama John no sé qué, se llama John algo; **there were 30 ~** había 30 y algunos más; **the four ~ train** el tren de las cuatro y pico; **her name is Camilla or ~** se llama Camilla o algo así, se llama algo así como Camilla, se llama Camilla o algo por el estilo; **he's got flu or ~** tiene gripe o algo parecido; **~ or other** algo, alguna cosa
ⓑ ADV **1** (= *a little, somewhat*) **there were ~ like 80 people there** había algo así como 80 personas allí, había como unas 80 personas allí; **it cost £100, or ~ like that** costó 100 libras, o algo así; **he looks ~ like me** se parece algo *or* un poco a mí; **~ over 200** algo más de 200, un poco más de 200
2 (*Brit dialect**) **they pull her leg ~ chronic** le toman el pelo una barbaridad*, le toman el pelo que es una cosa mala*; **it hurts ~ awful** duele un montón*
ⓒ N **she has a certain ~** tiene un algo, tiene un no sé qué; **that certain ~ that makes all the difference** ese no sé qué que importa tanto; **it's just a little ~ I picked up in a sale** es una tontería que compré en las rebajas; **would you like a little ~ before dinner?** ¿quieres tomar *or* picar algo antes de la cena?

sometime ['sʌmtaɪm] **ⓐ** ADV **1** (*in future*) algún día; **you must come and see us ~** tienes que venir a vernos algún día; **I'll finish it ~** lo voy a terminar un día de estos; **~ soon** un día de estos, antes de que pase mucho tiempo; **~ next**

year en algún momento el año que viene, el año que viene, no sé cuándo exactamente **2** (*in past*) **~ last month** (en algún momento) el mes pasado, el mes pasado, no sé cuándo exactamente
B ADJ **1** (= *former*) ex ..., antiguo **2** (*US*) (= *occasional*) intermitente

sometimes ['sʌmtaɪmz] ADV a veces; **I ~ drink beer** a veces bebo cerveza; **~ I lose interest** hay veces que pierdo el interés

somewhat ['sʌmwɒt] ADV algo, un tanto; **he was ~ puzzled** se quedó algo *or* un tanto perplejo; **it was done ~ hastily** se hizo con demasiada prisa

somewhere ['sʌmwɛəʳ] **A** ADV **1** (*location*) en alguna parte, en algún lugar, en algún sitio; (*direction*) a alguna parte, a algún lugar, a algún sitio; **I left my keys ~** me he dejado las llaves en alguna parte *or* en algún sitio; **let's go ~ private** vamos a algún sitio *or* lugar donde podamos estar solos; **I'd like to go ~ exotic** me gustaría irme a algún sitio *or* lugar exótico; **he's ~ around** anda por ahí; **~ else** (*location*) en otra parte; (*direction*) a otra parte, a otro sitio; **she lives ~ in Wales** vive en algún lugar *or* en alguna parte de Gales; **~ near Huesca** cerca de Huesca, en algún lugar *or* sitio cerca de Huesca; ✦ IDIOMS **~ along the line they changed the title** en algún momento cambiaron el título; **now we're getting ~*** ahora sí que estamos haciendo progresos *or* consiguiendo algo
2 (= *approximately*) **~ around** three o'clock alrededor de las tres, a eso de las tres; **he paid ~ in the region of £1,000** pagó alrededor de 1.000 libras
B PRON algún lugar, algún sitio; **you'll have to find ~ else to live** tendrás que buscarte otro sitio *or* lugar para vivir; **they broadcast from ~ in Europe** emiten desde algún lugar de Europa

somnolent ['sɒmnələnt] ADJ soñoliento

son [sʌn] N hijo *m*; **come here, ~*** ven, hijo; **~ of a bitch***** hijo *m* de puta***, hijo *m* de la chingada (*Mex***)

sonar ['səʊnɑːʳ] N sonar *m*

sonata [sə'nɑːtə] N sonata *f*

son et lumière [ˌsɒneɪˈluːmjɛəʳ] N luz *f* y sonido *m*

song [sɒŋ] **A** N **1** (= *ballad etc*) canción *f*; **give us a ~!** ¡cántanos algo!; ✦ IDIOMS **to make a ~ and dance about sth** (*Brit*) hacer aspavientos por algo; **there's no need to make a ~ and dance about it** no es para tanto; **I got it for a ~** lo compré regalado **2** [*of birds*] canto *m* **B** CPD ➤ **song and dance routine** número *m* de canción y baile ➤ **song book** cancionero *m* ➤ **Song of Solomon, Song of Songs** Cantar *m* de los Cantares

songbird ['sɒŋbɜːd] N pájaro *m* cantor

songwriter ['sɒŋˌraɪtəʳ] N compositor(a) *m/f* (de canciones)

sonic ['sɒnɪk] ADJ sónico ➤ **sonic boom** estampido *m* sónico

son-in-law ['sʌnɪnlɔː] N (*pl* **sons-in-law**) yerno *m*, hijo *m* político

sonnet ['sɒnɪt] N soneto *m*

sonny* ['sʌnɪ] N hijo *m*

sonorous ['sɒnərəs] ADJ sonoro

soon [suːn] ADV **1** (= *before long*) pronto, dentro de poco; **they'll be here ~** pronto llegarán, llegarán dentro de poco; **it will ~ be summer** pronto llegará el verano, falta poco para que llegue el verano; **~ afterwards** poco después; **come back ~** vuelve pronto
2 (= *early*) pronto, temprano; **how ~ can you come?** ¿cuándo puedes venir?; **Friday is too ~** el viernes es muy pronto; **we got there too ~** llegamos demasiado pronto *or* temprano; **it's too ~ to tell** es demasiado pronto para saber; **all too ~ it was over** terminó demasiado pronto; **not a minute** *or* **moment too ~** ya era hora
3 as ~ as en cuanto, tan pronto como; **I'll do it as ~ as I can** lo haré en cuanto pueda, lo haré tan pronto como pueda; **as ~ as possible** cuanto antes, lo antes posible, lo más pronto posible
4 (*expressing preference*) **I would just as ~ not go** preferiría no ir; **I would just as ~ he didn't know** preferiría que él no

lo supiera

sooner ['suːnəʳ] ADV **1** (*of time*) antes, más temprano; **can't you come a bit ~?** ¿no puedes venir un poco antes *or* un poco más temprano?; **the ~ we start the ~ we finish** cuanto antes empecemos, antes acabaremos; **the ~ the better** cuanto antes mejor; **~ or later** tarde o temprano; **no ~ had we left than they arrived** apenas nos habíamos marchado cuando llegaron; ✦ IDIOM **no ~ said than done** dicho y hecho
2 (*of preference*) **I'd** *or* **I would ~ not do it** preferiría no hacerlo; **I'd ~ die!*** ¡antes morir!

soot [sʊt] N hollín *m*

soothe [suːð] VT [+ *person, baby*] calmar, tranquilizar; [+ *nerves*] calmar; [+ *mind*] relajar; [+ *anger*] aplacar; [+ *doubts*] acallar; [+ *pain, cough*] aliviar

soothing ['suːðɪŋ] ADJ [*ointment, lotion*] balsámico, calmante; [*massage, bath, music*] relajante; [*tone, words, voice, manner*] tranquilizador

soothsayer ['suːθˌseɪəʳ] N adivino/a *m/f*

sooty ['sʊtɪ] ADJ (*compar* **sootier**; *superl* **sootiest**) hollinoso; (*fig*) negro como el hollín

sop [sɒp] N (*fig*) (= *pacifier*) compensación *f*; **as a ~ to his pride** para que su orgullo no quedara/quede herido

sophisticated [sə'fɪstɪkeɪtɪd] ADJ [*person, lifestyle, tastes, clothes, idea*] sofisticado; [*equipment*] sofisticado, complejo, altamente desarrollado; [*technique*] sofisticado, muy elaborado, complejo; [*play, film, book*] muy elaborado, complejo

sophistication [səˌfɪstɪˈkeɪʃən] N (= *refinement*) sofisticación *f*; (= *complexity*) complejidad *f*

sophistry ['sɒfɪstrɪ] N sofistería *f*; **a ~** un sofisma

sophomore ['sɒfəmɔːʳ] N (*US*) estudiante *mf* de segundo año

soporific [ˌsɒpəˈrɪfɪk] ADJ soporífero

sopping ['sɒpɪŋ] ADJ **to be ~ (wet)** estar empapado

soppy* ['sɒpɪ] ADJ (*compar* **soppier**; *superl* **soppiest**) **1** (= *mushy*) sentimentaloide **2** (= *foolish*) bobo, tonto

soprano [sə'prɑːnəʊ] **A** N (*pl* **~s** *or* **soprani** [sə'prɑːniː]) (*female*) soprano *f*; (*male*) tiple *m*; (= *voice, part*) soprano *m* **B** ADJ [*part*] de soprano, para soprano; [*voice*] de soprano **C** ADV **to sing ~** cantar soprano

sorbet ['sɔːbeɪ] N (*Brit*) sorbete *m*; **lemon ~** sorbete *m* de limón

sorcerer ['sɔːsərəʳ] N hechicero *m*, brujo *m*

sorceress ['sɔːsərɪs] N hechicera *f*, bruja *f*

sorcery ['sɔːsərɪ] N hechicería *f*, brujería *f*

sordid ['sɔːdɪd] ADJ [*place, room etc*] miserable, sórdido; [*deal, motive etc*] mezquino; **it's a pretty ~ business** es un asunto de lo más desagradable

sore [sɔːʳ] **A** ADJ (*compar* **~r**; *superl* **~st**) **1** (= *painful*) [*part of body*] dolorido; [*cut, graze*] doloroso; **I'm ~ all over** me duele todo el cuerpo; **I have a ~ throat** me duele la garganta; ✦ IDIOM **it's a ~ point** es un tema delicado *or* espinoso **2** (*esp US**) (= *angry, upset*) **to be ~ about sth** estar resentido por algo; **to be ~ at sb** estar enfadado (*Sp*) *or* enojado con algn; **don't get ~!** ¡no te vayas a ofender!, ¡no te enojes! (*LAm*)
B N (*Med*) llaga *f*, úlcera *f*; ✦ IDIOM **to open up old ~s** abrir viejas heridas

sorehead* ['sɔːhed] N (*US*) persona *f* resentida

sorely ['sɔːlɪ] ADV (= *very*) muy; (= *much*) mucho; (= *deeply*) profundamente; (= *seriously*) seriamente; **I am ~ tempted** estoy muy tentado

soreness ['sɔːnɪs] N dolor *m*

sorority [sə'rɒrɪtɪ] N (*US Univ*) hermandad *f* de mujeres

sorrel[1] ['sɒrəl] N (= *tree*) acedera *f*

sorrel[2] ['sɒrəl] N (= *horse*) alazán *m*, caballo *m* alazán

sorrow ['sɒrəʊ] N pena *f*, pesar *m*, dolor *m*; **her ~ at the death of her son** su pena por la muerte de su hijo; **more in ~ than in anger** con más pesar que enojo; **this was a great ~ to me** esto me causó mucha pena; ✦ IDIOM **to drown one's ~s** ahogar las penas (en alcohol)

sorrowful ['sɒrəfəl] ADJ afligido, triste, apenado

sorry ['sɒrɪ] ADJ (*compar* **sorrier**; *superl* **sorriest**)
1 (= *apologetic*) **I'm ~, she's busy at the moment** lo siento, en este momento está ocupada; **I'm so ~!** ¡lo siento mucho!, ¡perdón!; **sorry!** ¡perdón!, ¡perdone!, ¡disculpe! (*esp LAm*); **~ I'm late!** ¡siento llegar tarde!; **I'm ~ to bother you but ...** siento or (*frm*) lamento molestarle, pero ...; **I'm ~ about** what I said last night siento lo que dije anoche; **we are ~ for** any inconvenience caused lamentamos cualquier molestia ocasionada; **to say ~ (to sb) (for sth)** pedir perdón or (*esp LAm*) disculpas (a algn) (por algo) **2** (= *repentant*) arrepentido; **he wasn't in the least bit ~** no estaba arrepentido en lo más mínimo; **you'll be ~ for this!** ¡me las pagarás!, ¡te arrepentirás de esto)! **3** (= *regretful, sad*) **I can't say I'm ~** no puedo decir que lo sienta; **I'm ~ he didn't get the job** siento que no consiguiera el trabajo; **I'm ~ to hear that you're leaving** me da pena saber que te vas; **we are ~ to have to tell you that ...** lamentamos tener que decirle que ...; **I was ~ to hear of your accident** siento or lamento lo de tu accidente; **it was a failure, I'm ~ to say** me duele reconocerlo, pero fue un fracaso; **no one seemed very ~ to see him go** nadie parecía sentir or lamentar mucho que se fuera; **I'm ~ about your mother** siento or (*frm*) lamento lo de tu madre
4 (= *pitying*) **I feel ~ for him** lo compadezco; **I feel ~ for the child** el niño me da lástima or pena; **it's no good feeling ~ for yourself** no sirve de mucho lamentarte de tu suerte
5 (= *pitiful*) **the garden was a ~ sight** el jardín estaba en un estado lamentable, el jardín estaba hecho una pena*; **to be in a ~ state** encontrarse en un estado lamentable
6 (*when sb has not heard*) **~, I didn't catch what you said** perdón, no entendí lo que dijiste
7 (*when correcting o.s.*) **it's the third, sorry, the fourth on the left** es la tercera, perdón, la cuarta a la izquierda

sort [sɔːt] **Ⓐ** N **1** (= *kind*) clase *f*, tipo *m*; **all ~s of books** libros de toda clase or de todo tipo, toda clase or todo tipo de libros; **I know his ~** conozco el paño, conozco a esacindym,it clase de gente; **he's not the ~ of man to say that** no es de los que dicen eso; **he's a painter of ~s** se puede decir que es pintor; **something of the ~** algo por el estilo; **I shall do nothing of the ~** no lo haré bajo ningún concepto, ni se me ocurriría hacerlo; **he's some ~ of painter** es pintor de algún tipo; **that's the ~ of person I am** así soy yo; **he's not that ~ of person** no es capaz de hacer eso, no es ese tipo de persona; **I'm not that ~ of girl** yo no soy de esas; **he's the ~ who will cheat you** es de esa clase or de ese tipo de personas que te engañará, es de esos que or de los que te engañan; **that's the ~ of thing I need** eso es lo que me hace falta; **that's just the ~ of thing I mean** eso es precisamente lo que quiero decir; **and all that ~ of thing** y otras cosas por el estilo; **this ~ of house** una casa de este estilo; **what ~ do you want?** (= *make*) ¿qué marca quieres?; (= *type*) ¿de qué tipo lo quieres?; **what ~ of man is he?** ¿qué clase de hombre es?; **◆ PROV it takes all ~s (to make a world)** de todo hay en la viña del Señor
2 a ~ of: **it's a ~ of dance** es una especie de baile; **he's a ~ of agent** es algo así como un agente
3 ~ of: **it's ~ of awkward** es bastante or (*LAm*) medio difícil; **it's ~ of blue** es más bien azul; **I'm ~ of lost** estoy como perdido; **it's ~ of finished** está más o menos terminado; **I have a ~ of idea that ...** tengo cierta idea de que ...; **I ~ of thought that ...** quedé con la idea de que ...; **"aren't you pleased?" — "~ of"** —¿no te alegras? —en cierto sentido
4 (= *person*) **he's a good ~** es buena persona or (*esp LAm*) buena gente; **he's an odd ~** es un tipo raro
5 (*Brit*) **◆ IDIOM to be out of ~s** (= *unwell*) estar indispuesto, no estar del todo bien; (= *in bad mood*) estar de mal humor, estar de malas
Ⓑ VT **1** (= *classify, arrange*) clasificar; **to ~ the good apples from the bad ones** separar las manzanas malas de las buenas
2 (*Comput*) ordenar
3 (*) (= *resolve, settle*) arreglar; **we've got it ~ed now** ya se arregló
Ⓒ CPD **➤ sort code** [*of bank*] número *m* de sucursal
➤ sort out VT + ADV **1** (= *organize*) ordenar, organizar; **to ~**

out the bad ones separar or quitar los malos **2** (= *resolve*) [+ *problem, situation etc*] arreglar, solucionar; **things will ~ themselves out eventually** al final, todo se arreglará **3 to ~ sb out** (*esp Brit**) ajustar cuentas con algn **4** (= *explain*) **to ~ sth out for sb** explicar or aclarar algo a algn
➤ sort through VI + ADV revisar

sortie ['sɔːtɪ] N (*Aer, Mil*) salida *f*

sorting ['sɔːtɪŋ] N clasificación *f*; (*Comput*) ordenación *f*
➤ sorting office (*Brit*) sala *f* de batalla

sort-out* ['sɔːtaʊt] N **to have a ~** ordenar las cosas

SOS N (= *signal*) SOS *m*

so-so ['səʊsəʊ] ADV regular, así así

soufflé ['suːfleɪ] N soufflé *m*, suflé *m*

sought [sɔːt] PT, PP *of* **seek**

sought-after ['sɔːtˌɑːftəʳ] ADJ [*person*] solicitado; [*object*] codiciado; **this much ~ title** este codiciado título

soul [səʊl] **Ⓐ** N **1** [*of person*] alma *f*; [*of nation*] espíritu *m*

> Use **el/un** not **la/una** before feminine nouns beginning with stressed **a** or **ha** like **alma**.

with all one's ~ con todo el alma; **God rest his ~** que Dios lo acoja en su seno; **to be the ~ of discretion** ser la discreción personificada or en persona; **◆ IDIOM like a lost ~** como alma en pena
2 (= *feeling*) **the music lacks ~** a la música le falta sentimiento; **these places have no ~** estos sitios no tienen vida
3 (= *person*) alma *f*; **there was not a ~ in sight** no se veía (ni) un alma; **a few brave ~s ventured out** unos cuantos valientes se aventuraron a salir; **poor ~!** ¡pobrecito!; **I won't tell a ~** no se lo diré a nadie
4 (*also* ~ **music**) música *f* soul
Ⓑ CPD **➤ soul food** cocina negra del Sur de EE.UU. **➤ soul music** música *f* soul

soul-destroying ['səʊldɪsˌtrɔɪɪŋ] ADJ de lo más aburrido

soulful ['səʊlfʊl] ADJ [*gaze, look, eyes*] conmovedor; [*music*] lleno de sentimiento

soulless ['səʊllɪs] ADJ [*person*] sin alma, desalmado; [*work*] mecánico, monótono

soulmate ['səʊlmeɪt] N compañero/a *m/f* del alma, alma *f* gemela

> Use **el/un** not **la/una** before feminine nouns beginning with stressed **a** or **ha** like **alma**.

soul-searching ['səʊlˌsɜːtʃɪŋ] N **after a lot of ~** después de repensarlo muchas veces

sound[1] [saʊnd] **Ⓐ** N **1** (*Phys*) sonido *m*
2 (= *noise*) ruido *m*; **the ~ of footsteps** el ruido de pasos; **I didn't hear a ~** no oí ni un ruido; **don't make a ~!** ¡no hagas el menor ruido!; **he opened the door without a ~** abrió la puerta sin hacer nada de ruido
3 (= *volume*) volumen *m*
4 (= *impression*) **by the ~ of it** según parece; **I don't like the ~ of it** (*film etc*) por lo que he oído, no me gusta nada; (*situation*) me preocupa, me da mala espina
Ⓑ VT [+ *horn, trumpet*] tocar, hacer sonar; [+ *alarm, warning*] dar; **to ~ a note of warning** dar la señal de alarma
Ⓒ VI **1** [*bell, cannon*] sonar
2 (= *suggest by sound*) sonar; **it ~s hollow** suena a hueco; **he ~s Italian to me** por la voz, diría que es italiano; **he ~ed angry** parecía enfadado; **it ~s like French** suena a francés; **that ~s like them arriving now** parece que llegan ahora
3 (= *seem*) sonar, parecer; **that ~s interesting** eso suena interesante; **it ~s as if she won't be coming** parece que no va a venir; **that ~s like a good idea** eso parece buena idea
Ⓓ CPD **➤ sound barrier** barrera *f* del sonido **➤ sound bite** cita *f* jugosa **➤ sound card** (*Comput*) tarjeta *f* de sonido **➤ sound effect** efecto *m* sonoro **➤ sound engineer** (*Brit*), **sound mixer** ingeniero/a *m/f* de sonido **➤ sound file** (*Comput*) fichero *m* de sonido **➤ sound system** (= *hi-fi*) cadena *f* de sonido **➤ sound truck** (*US*)

furgón *m* publicitario ➤ **sound wave** (*Phys*) onda *f* sonora
➤ **sound off*** VI + ADV discursear* (**about** sobre)
➤ **sound out** VT + ADV **to ~ sb out about sth** sondear *or* tantear a algn sobre algo, tratar de averiguar lo que piensa algn sobre algo

sound² [saʊnd] **Ⓐ** ADJ (*compar* **~er**; *superl* **~est**) **1** (= *in good condition*) sano; [*constitution*] robusto; [*structure*] sólido, firme; **to be of ~ mind** estar en su cabal juicio; ✦ IDIOM **to be as ~ as a bell** [*person*] gozar de perfecta salud; [*thing*] estar en perfectas condiciones
2 (= *well-founded*) [*argument*] bien fundado, sólido; [*ideas, opinions*] válido, razonable; [*investment*] bueno, seguro; [*training*] sólido; [*decision, choice*] acertado; **she gave me some ~ advice** me dio un buen consejo; **he's ~ enough on the theory** tiene una preparación sólida en cuanto a la teoría; **he's a ~ worker** es buen trabajador, trabaja con seriedad
3 (= *deep*) [*sleep*] profundo
Ⓑ ADV **to be ~ asleep** estar profundamente dormido

sounding board ['saʊndɪŋ,bɔːd] N caja *f* de resonancia(s)

soundings ['saʊndɪŋz] NPL **to take ~** (*fig*) sondear la opinión

soundly ['saʊndlɪ] ADV [*built*] sólidamente; [*argued*] lógicamente; [*invested*] con cordura, con prudencia; **to sleep ~** dormir profundamente

soundness ['saʊndnɪs] N [*of structure*] firmeza *f*, solidez *f*; [*of ideas, opinions*] validez *f*; [*of argument*] solidez *f*; [*of investment*] prudencia *f*; [*of business*] solvencia *f*

soundproof ['saʊndpruːf] **Ⓐ** ADJ insonorizado, a prueba de ruidos **Ⓑ** VT insonorizar

soundtrack ['saʊndtræk] N banda *f* sonora

soup [suːp] N (*thin*) caldo *m*, consomé *m*; (*thick*) sopa *f*; **vegetable ~** sopa *f* de verduras; ✦ IDIOM **to be in the ~*** estar en apuros ➤ **soup kitchen** comedor *m* popular, olla *f* común ➤ **soup plate** plato *m* sopero ➤ **soup spoon** cuchara *f* sopera ➤ **soup tureen** sopera *f*

soupçon ['suːpsɔ̃] N (*Culin*) pizca *f*; **with a ~ of ginger** con una pizca de jengibre; **with a ~ of cream** con un chorrito de nata (*Sp*) *or* crema (*LAm*)

souped-up* ['suːptˌʌp] ADJ [*car*] trucado

sour ['saʊəʳ] **Ⓐ** ADJ (*compar* **~er**; *superl* **~est**) **1** (= *not sweet*) [*fruit, flavour*] agrio, ácido; [*smell*] acre; ✦ IDIOM **~ grapes** envidia *f*; **that's just ~ grapes** eso es simplemente envidia
2 (= *bad*) [*milk*] cortado, agrio; [*wine*] agrio; **does this milk taste ~ to you?** ¿te sabe esta leche a cortada?, ¿te sabe esta leche agria?; **to turn ~** [*milk*] cortarse; [*wine*] agriarse; [*plan*] venirse abajo; [*marriage, relationship*] deteriorarse
3 (= *surly*) [*person*] avinagrado; [*expression, look, mood, comment*] avinagrado, agrio
Ⓑ VT [+ *person*] agriar, amargar; [+ *relationship*] deteriorar; [+ *atmosphere*] agriar; [+ *success*] empañar
Ⓒ VI [*milk*] cortarse; [*mood, attitude*] avinagrarse, agriarse; [*relationship*] deteriorarse
Ⓓ CPD ➤ **sour cream** nata *f* (*Sp*) *or* crema *f* (*LAm*) agria

source [sɔːs] N **1** (= *origin*) fuente *f*; [*of gossip*] procedencia *f*; **I have it from a reliable ~ that ...** sé de fuente fidedigna que ...; **what is the ~ of this information?** ¿de dónde proceden estos informes?; **his antics were a ~ of much amusement** sus gracias fueron motivo de diversión; **at ~** en su origen **2** [*of river*] nacimiento *m*

sourdough bread [ˌsaʊədəʊ'bred] N (*esp US*) pan *m* de masa fermentada

sour-faced ['saʊəfeɪst] ADJ con cara de pocos amigos, con cara avinagrada

sourly ['saʊəlɪ] ADV [*say, complain, look*] agriamente; [*think*] con amargura

souse [saʊs] VT (*Culin*) (= *pickle*) escabechar, adobar (*LAm*); ✦ IDIOM **to be ~d**** estar mamado*, estar tomado (*LAm*)

south [saʊθ] **Ⓐ** N (= *direction*) sur *m*; (= *region*) sur *m*, mediodía *m*; **the South of France** el sur de Francia, el mediodía francés, la Francia meridional; **in the ~** en el sur; **to the ~ of** al sur de
Ⓑ ADJ [*side, part*] sur, del sur; [*coast, border*] sur, del sur, meridional; [*wind*] del sur

Ⓒ ADV (= *southward*) hacia el sur; **~ of the border** al sur de la frontera; **it's ~ of London** está al sur de Londres
Ⓓ CPD ➤ **South Africa** Suráfrica *f*, Sudáfrica *f*; *ver tb* www.gov.za ➤ **South America** América *f* del Sur, Sudamérica *f* ➤ **South Atlantic** Atlántico *m* Sur ➤ **South Carolina** Carolina *f* del Sur ➤ **South Dakota** Dakota *f* del Sur ➤ **South Georgia** Georgia *f* del Sur ➤ **South Korea** Corea *f* del Sur ➤ **South Pacific** Pacífico *m* Sur ➤ **the South Pole** el Polo sur ➤ **the South Sea Islands** las Islas de los mares del Sur ➤ **the South Seas** los mares del Sur, el mar austral ➤ **South Vietnam** Vietnam *m* del Sur

South African [ˌsaʊθ'æfrɪkən] ADJ, N sudafricano/a *m/f*

South American [ˌsaʊθə'merɪkən] ADJ, N sudamericano/a *m/f*

southbound ['saʊθbaʊnd] ADJ en dirección sur

southeast ['saʊθ'iːst] **Ⓐ** N sureste *m* **Ⓑ** ADJ [*side, part*] sureste, del sureste; [*coast*] sureste, del sureste, suroriental; [*wind*] del sureste **Ⓒ** ADV (= *southeastward*) hacia el sureste; **it's ~ of London** está al sureste de Londres

southeasterly [saʊθ'iːstəlɪ] ADJ [*wind*] del sureste; **in a ~ direction** hacia el sureste, en dirección sureste

southeastern [saʊθ'iːstən] ADJ [*side, part*] sureste, del sureste; [*coast, border*] sureste, del sureste, suroriental; [*wind, front, town*] del sureste; **in ~ Spain** al *or* en el sureste de España

southerly ['sʌðəlɪ] ADJ [*wind*] del sur; **in a ~ direction** hacia el sur, en dirección sur; **the most ~ point in Europe** el punto más meridional *or* más al sur de Europa

southern ['sʌðən] ADJ [*side, part*] sur, del sur; [*coast, border*] sur, del sur, meridional; [*wind, front, town*] del sur; [*person*] sureño; **in ~ Spain** al *or* en el sur de España, en la España meridional; **the ~ coast** la costa meridional *or* (del) sur ➤ **Southern Cone** Cono *m* Sur ➤ **the southern hemisphere** el hemisferio sur, el hemisferio austral

southerner ['sʌðənəʳ] N persona *f* del sur, habitante *mf* del sur, sureño/a *m/f*; **she's a ~** es del sur

southernmost ['sʌðənməʊst] ADJ más meridional, más al sur

south-facing ['saʊθˌfeɪsɪŋ] ADJ de cara al sur, orientado hacia el sur; **~ slope** vertiente *f* sur

southward ['saʊθwəd] **Ⓐ** ADJ [*movement, migration, journey*] hacia el sur, en dirección sur **Ⓑ** ADV (*also* **~s**) hacia el sur, en dirección sur

southwest ['saʊθ'west] **Ⓐ** N suroeste *m* **Ⓑ** ADJ [*side, part*] suroeste, del suroeste; [*coast*] suroeste, del suroeste, suroccidental; [*wind*] del suroeste **Ⓒ** ADV (= *toward southwest*) hacia el suroeste; **it's ~ of London** está al suroeste de Londres

southwesterly [saʊθ'westəlɪ] ADJ [*wind*] del suroeste; **in a ~ direction** hacia el suroeste, en dirección suroeste

southwestern [saʊθ'westən] ADJ [*side, part*] suroeste, del suroeste; [*coast, border*] suroeste, del suroeste, suroccidental; [*wind, front, town*] del suroeste; **in ~ Spain** al *or* en el suroeste de España; **the ~ coast** la costa suroeste *or* suroccidental

souvenir [ˌsuːvəˈnɪəʳ] N recuerdo *m*, souvenir *m* ➤ **souvenir shop** tienda *f* de recuerdos

sou'wester [saʊ'westəʳ] N sueste *m*

sovereign ['sɒvrɪn] **Ⓐ** ADJ soberano **Ⓑ** N (= *monarch*) soberano/a *m/f*

sovereignty ['sɒvrəntɪ] N soberanía *f*

soviet ['səʊvɪət] (*Hist*) **Ⓐ** N soviet *m*; **the Soviets** (= *people*) los soviéticos **Ⓑ** ADJ soviético **Ⓒ** N ➤ **Soviet Russia** Rusia *f* Soviética ➤ **the Soviet Union** la Unión Soviética

sow¹ [səʊ] VT (*pt* **~ed**; *pp* **~n**) [+ *seed*] sembrar; **to ~ doubt in sb's mind** sembrar dudas en algn

sow² [saʊ] N (= *pig*) puerca *f*, marrana *f*

sown [səʊn] PP *of* **sow¹**

soy [sɔɪ] N (*US*) = **soya**

soya ['sɔɪə] N (*Brit*) soja *f* ➤ **soya bean** semilla *f* de soja ➤ **soya sauce** salsa *f* de soja

sozzled** ['sɒzld] ADJ (*Brit*) **to be ~** estar mamado*, estar tomado (*LAm*); **to get** ~ coger una trompa*, agarrarse una borrachera (*LAm*)

spa [spɑː] N balneario *m*

space [speɪs] **Ⓐ** N **1** (*Phys, Astron*) espacio *m*; **in** ~ en el espacio; **outer** ~ el espacio exterior; **to stare into** ~ estar con la mirada perdida, mirar al vacío
2 (= *room*) espacio *m*, sitio *m*; **there isn't enough** ~ no hay espacio *or* sitio suficiente; **to take up a lot of** ~ ocupar mucho sitio *or* espacio
3 (= *gap*) espacio *m*; **blank** ~ espacio *m* en blanco; **to leave a ~ for sth** dejar sitio *or* lugar para algo; **we couldn't find a parking** ~ no pudimos encontrar aparcamiento, no pudimos encontrar un sitio para aparcar *or* (*LAm*) estacionar; **wide open ~s** campo *m* abierto
4 [*of time*] espacio *m*, lapso *m*; **in a short ~ of time** en un corto espacio *or* lapso de tiempo; **in the ~ of one hour** en el espacio de una hora
5 (= *freedom*) espacio *m*
Ⓑ CPD [*centre, exploration, flight, platform, helmet*] espacial ➤ **space age** era *f* espacial ➤ **space bar** (*on keyboard*) espaciador *m*, barra *f* espaciadora *or* de espacios ➤ **space capsule** cápsula *f* espacial ➤ **space lab** laboratorio *m* espacial ➤ **space probe** sonda *f* espacial ➤ **space programme, space program** (*US*) programa *m* de investigaciones espaciales ➤ **space race** carrera *f* espacial ➤ **space research** investigaciones *fpl* espaciales ➤ **space shot** (= *vehicle*) vehículo *m* espacial; (= *launch*) lanzamiento *m* de un vehículo espacial ➤ **space shuttle** transbordador *m* espacial, lanzadera *f* espacial ➤ **space station** estación *f* espacial ➤ **space travel** viajes *mpl* espaciales
➤ **space out** VT + ADV espaciar, separar; **well ~d out** bastante espaciados; **to be ~d out**** (= *on drugs*) estar volado *or* (*Sp*) colocado*

spacecraft [ˈspeɪskrɑːft] N (*pl* ~) nave *f* espacial, astronave *f*

spaceman [ˈspeɪsmæn] N (*pl* **spacemen**) astronauta *m*, cosmonauta *m*

space-saving [ˈspeɪsˌseɪvɪŋ] ADJ que economiza espacio, que ahorra espacio

spaceship [ˈspeɪsʃɪp] N nave *f* espacial, astronave *f*

spacesuit [ˈspeɪssuːt] N traje *m* espacial

spacewalk [ˈspeɪswɔːk] **Ⓐ** N paseo *m* por el espacio **Ⓑ** VI pasear por el espacio

spacewoman [ˈspeɪswʊmən] N (*pl* **spacewomen**) astronauta *f*, cosmonauta *f*

spacing [ˈspeɪsɪŋ] N espaciamiento *m*; (*Typ*) espaciado *m*; **in double** ~ a doble espacio; **in single** ~ a un solo espacio

spacious [ˈspeɪʃəs] ADJ espacioso, amplio

spade [speɪd] N **1** (= *tool*) pala *f*; ✦ IDIOM **to call a ~ a ~** (*Brit*) llamar al pan pan y al vino vino **2 spades** (*Cards*) picas *fpl*, picos *mpl*

⚠ **spade ≠ espada**

spadeful [ˈspeɪdfʊl] N pala *f*

spadework [ˈspeɪdwɜːk] N (*fig*) trabajo *m* preliminar

spaghetti [spəˈɡetɪ] N espaguetis *mpl* ➤ **spaghetti western** spaghetti-western *m*, película de vaqueros hecha por un director italiano

Spain [speɪn] N España *f*

Spam® [spæm] N carne *f* de cerdo en conserva

spam [spæm] (*Internet*) **Ⓐ** N correo *m* basura, spam *m* **Ⓑ** VT enviar spam *or* correo basura por Internet a

spammer [ˈspæməʳ] N (*Internet*) spammer *mf*

span [spæn] **Ⓐ** N **1** [*of wing*] envergadura *f* **2** [*of road*] tramo *m*; [*of arch*] luz *f*; [*of roof*] vano *m* **3** [*of time*] lapso *m*, espacio *m*; **for a brief** ~ durante un breve lapso **Ⓑ** VT [+ *river*] extenderse sobre, cruzar; [+ *period of time*] abarcar; **his life ~ned four reigns** su vida abarcó cuatro reinados

spangle [ˈspæŋɡl] N lentejuela *f*

Spanglish [ˈspæŋɡlɪʃ] N (*hum*) espanglish *m*

Spaniard [ˈspænjəd] N español(a) *m/f*

spaniel [ˈspænjəl] N spaniel *m*

Spanish [ˈspænɪʃ] **Ⓐ** ADJ español **Ⓑ** N **1 the** ~ (= *people*) los españoles **2** (= *language*) español *m*, castellano *m* **Ⓒ** CPD ➤ **Spanish America** Hispanoamérica *f* ➤ **the Spanish Armada** la Armada invencible ➤ **Spanish guitar** guitarra *f* española

Spanish American [ˈspænɪʃəˈmerɪkən] ADJ, N hispanoamericano/a *m/f*

Spanish-speaking [ˈspænɪʃˈspiːkɪŋ] ADJ hispanohablante, de habla española

spank [spæŋk] **Ⓐ** N azote *m*, manotazo *m* (en las nalgas); **to give sb a** ~ dar un azote a algn (en las nalgas) **Ⓑ** VT zurrar*

spanking [ˈspæŋkɪŋ] N zurra *f*; **to give sb a** ~ zurrar a algn*

spanner [ˈspænəʳ] N (*esp Brit*) llave *f* de tuercas, llave *f* de tubo; (*adjustable*) llave *f* inglesa; ✦ IDIOM **to throw** *or* **put a** ~ **in the works** (*Brit*) meter un palo en la rueda

spar [spɑːʳ] VI **1** (*Boxing*) entrenarse en el boxeo; **~ring match** combate *m* con spárring; **~ring partner** sparring *m* **2** (= *argue*) discutir (*amistosamente*)

spare [speəʳ] **Ⓐ** ADJ **1** (= *extra*, de más, de sobra; (= *reserve*) de reserva; (= *free*) libre; **there's a ~ blanket if you're cold** hay una manta de más *or* de sobra si tienes frío; **take a ~ pair of socks** llévate otro par de calcetines; **I leave a ~ key with the neighbours** dejo una llave de reserva en casa de los vecinos; **I always keep a bit of ~ cash for emergencies** siempre guardo un poco de dinero extra para emergencias; **have you got a ~ jacket I could borrow?** ¿tienes otra chaqueta para prestarme?; **I do it whenever I get a ~ moment** lo hago cuando tengo un momento libre; **there are two tickets going** ~ quedan *or* sobran dos entradas
2 (= *lean*) [*body, build*] enjuto (*liter*)
3 (*Brit***) (= *crazy*) **to go** ~ ponerse como loco*
Ⓑ N (= *part*) (pieza *f* de) recambio *m*, (pieza *f* de) repuesto *m*, refacción *f* (*Mex*); (= *wheel*) rueda *f* de repuesto *or* recambio
Ⓒ VT **1** (= *make available*) **I can ~ you five minutes** le puedo conceder *or* dedicar cinco minutos; **to ~ a thought for sb** pensar un momento en algn; **can you ~ the time?** ¿dispones del tiempo?, ¿tienes tiempo?; **we completed the job with three days to** ~ terminamos el trabajo con tres días de antelación; **I arrived with time to** ~ llegué con tiempo de sobra
2 (= *do without*) **can you ~ this for a moment?** ¿me puedo llevar esto un momento?; **if you can ~ it** si no lo vas a necesitar; **we can't ~ him now** ahora no podemos prescindir de él
3 (= *be grudging with*) **she ~d no effort in helping me** no escatimó esfuerzos para ayudarme; **they ~d no expense in refurbishing the house** no repararon en *or* escatimaron gastos a la hora de renovar la casa
4 (= *show mercy to*) perdonar; **to ~ sb's feelings** no herir los sentimientos de algn; **to ~ sb's life** perdonar la vida a algn
5 (= *save*) ahorrar, evitar; **I'll ~ you the gory details** me ahorraré los detalles escabrosos, te evitaré los detalles escabrosos; **I could have ~d myself the trouble** podía haberme ahorrado *or* evitado la molestia
Ⓓ CPD ➤ **spare part** (pieza *f* de) repuesto *m*, (pieza *f* de) recambio *m*, refacción *f* (*Mex*) ➤ **spare room** cuarto *m* de invitados, cuarto *m* para las visitas ➤ **spare time** tiempo *m* libre ➤ **spare tyre, spare tire** (*US*) neumático *m* de recambio, llanta *f* de recambio (*LAm*); (*Brit hum*) michelín *m* ➤ **spare wheel** (*esp Brit*) rueda *f* de repuesto *or* recambio

sparerib [ˌspeəˈrɪb] N (*Culin*) costilla *f* de cerdo

sparing [ˈspeərɪŋ] ADJ **to be ~ in one's use of sth** usar algo con moderación; **he was ~ with the wine** (*frm*) no fue muy generoso con el vino

sparingly [ˈspeərɪŋlɪ] ADV [*use, apply*] con moderación, en pequeñas cantidades

spark [spɑːk] **Ⓐ** N **1** (*from fire, Elec*) chispa *f*; ✦ IDIOM **to make the ~s fly** provocar una bronca **2** (= *trace*) pizca *f*; **the book hasn't a ~ of interest** el libro no tiene ni pizca de interés **Ⓑ** VT (*also* ~ **off**) provocar **Ⓒ** VI chispear, echar chispas **Ⓓ** CPD ➤ **spark plug** (*Aut*) bujía *f*

sparkle ['spɑːkl] **Ⓐ** N centelleo *m*, destello *m* **Ⓑ** VI (= *flash*) centellear, echar chispas; (= *shine*) brillar; (= *stand out*) relucir

sparkler ['spɑːklə^r] N **1** (= *firework*) bengala *f* **2** (*) (= *diamond*) diamante *m*

sparkling ['spɑːklɪŋ] ADJ **1** [*glass, crystal*] brillante, centelleante; [*eyes*] chispeante **2** (= *fizzy*) [*wine*] espumoso; ~ **water** agua con gas **3** [*person, wit, conversation*] chispeante

sparkly* ['spɑːklɪ] ADJ [*necklace, eyes*] brillante, centelleante

sparrow ['spærəʊ] N gorrión *m*

sparrowhawk ['spærəʊhɔːk] N gavilán *m*

sparse [spɑːs] ADJ (*compar* ~**r**; *superl* ~**st**) (= *thin*) escaso; (= *dispersed*) disperso, esparcido; [*hair*] ralo; [*vegetation*] escaso, ralo; ~ **population** poca densidad *f* de población

sparsely ['spɑːslɪ] ADV (= *thinly*) escasamente; (= *in scattered way*) en forma dispersa; ~ **populated** escasamente poblado; ~ **furnished** con pocos muebles

spartan ['spɑːtən] ADJ espartano

spasm ['spæzəm] N **1** (*Med*) espasmo *m* **2** (= *fit*) ataque *m*, acceso *m*; **a** ~ **of coughing** un ataque *or* acceso de tos; **to work in** ~**s** trabajar a rachas

spasmodic [spæz'mɒdɪk] ADJ (= *intermittent*) irregular, intermitente

spasmodically [spæz'mɒdɪkəlɪ] ADV (= *intermittently*) de forma irregular, de forma intermitente

spastic ['spæstɪk] ADJ, N espástico/a *m/f*

spat [spæt] PT, PP *of* **spit¹**

spate [speɪt] N **1** (= *series*) torrente *m*, avalancha *f*; [*of burglaries*] serie *f* **2** (*esp Brit*) **to be in (full)** ~ [*river*] estar (muy) crecido

spatial ['speɪʃəl] ADJ espacial

spatter ['spætə^r] VT salpicar (**with** de)

spatula ['spætjʊlə] N espátula *f*

spawn [spɔːn] **Ⓐ** N **1** [*of fish, frogs*] freza *f*, huevas *fpl* **2** (*pej*) (= *offspring*) prole *f* **Ⓑ** VT (*pej*) engendrar, producir

spay [speɪ] VT [+ *animal*] sacar los ovarios a

SPCA N ABBR (*US*) = **Society for the Prevention of Cruelty to Animals**

SPCC N ABBR (*US*) = **Society for the Prevention of Cruelty to Children**

speak [spiːk] (*pt* **spoke**; *pp* **spoken**) **Ⓐ** VI **1** hablar (**to** con); **she never spoke to me again** no volvió a dirigirme la palabra; **I don't know him to** ~ **to** no lo conozco bastante como para hablar con él; **technically/biologically** ~**ing** en términos técnicos/biológicos, desde el punto de vista técnico/biológico; **I'll** ~ **to him about it** (= *discuss it with him*) lo hablaré con él; (= *point it out to him*) se lo diré; ~**ing as a student myself** hablando desde mi experiencia como estudiante; **we're not** ~**ing** no nos hablamos; ~**ing of holidays ...** a propósito de las vacaciones ...; **it's nothing to** ~ **of** no tiene importancia; **he has no money to** ~ **of** no tiene dinero que digamos; ~**ing personally ...** en cuanto a mí ..., yo por mi parte ...; **roughly** ~**ing** en términos generales; **so to** ~ por decirlo así, por así decir; **to** ~ **well of sb** hablar bien de algn
2 (= *make a speech*) hablar (**on** sobre)
3 (*Telec*) **speaking!** ¡al habla!, ¡soy yo!; **this is Peter** ~**ing** ¡soy Peter!, ¡habla Peter!; **may I** ~ **to Mr Jones?** ¿me pone con el Sr. Jones, por favor?; **who's** ~**ing?** ¿con quién hablo?, ¿quién es?; (*taking message*) ¿de parte de (de quién)? **Ⓑ** VT **1** (= *talk*) [+ *language*] hablar; **do you** ~ **English?** ¿hablas inglés?; **he can** ~ **seven languages** habla siete idiomas; **"English spoken here"** "se habla inglés"
2 (= *say*) decir; **to** ~ **one's mind** hablar claro *or* con franqueza; **to** ~ **the truth** decir la verdad; **nobody spoke a word** nadie habló, nadie dijo palabra
➤ **speak for** VI + PREP **1** **to** ~ **for sb** (*as representative*) hablar por algn, hablar en nombre de algn; (*as defender*) interceder por algn; ~**ing for myself** en cuanto a mí, yo por mi parte; ~ **for yourself!** ¡eso lo dirás tú!; **let her** ~ **for herself** déjala que hable **2 the facts** ~ **for themselves** los

datos hablan por sí solos **3 to be spoken for: that's already been spoken for** eso ya está reservado *or* apartado; **she's already spoken for*** ya está comprometida
➤ **speak out** VI + ADV **he's not afraid to** ~ **out** no tiene miedo a decir lo que piensa; **to** ~ **out against sth** denunciar algo
➤ **speak up** VI + ADV **1** (= *raise voice*) hablar más fuerte *or* alto; ~ **up!** ¡más fuerte! **2** (= *give one's opinion*) **don't be afraid to** ~ **up** no tengas miedo de decir lo que piensas; **to** ~ **up for sb** defender a algn

speakeasy* ['spiːkˌiːzɪ] N (*US*) taberna *f* clandestina

speaker ['spiːkə^r] N **1** (*gen*) el/la *m/f* que habla; (*in public*) orador(a) *m/f*; (*at conference*) ponente *mf*, orador(a) *m/f*; (= *lecturer*) conferenciante *mf*; **he's a good** ~ es buen orador, habla bien
2 [*of language*] hablante *mf*; **French** ~**s** los hablantes de francés, los francoparlantes; **he's a French** ~ habla francés; **all** ~**s of Spanish** todos los que hablan español, todos los hispanohablantes; **Catalan has several million** ~**s** el catalán es hablado por varios millones
3 (= *loud-speaker*) altavoz *m*, altoparlante *m* (*LAm*); **speakers** [*of hi-fi system*] bafles *mpl*, parlantes *mpl*
4 (*Pol*) **the Speaker** (*Brit*) el Presidente/la Presidenta de la Cámara de los Comunes; (*US*) el Presidente/la Presidenta de la Cámara de los Representantes; ⊃ *FRONT BENCH*

speaking ['spiːkɪŋ] ADJ (= *talking*) que habla, parlante ➤ **speaking clock** (*Brit*) servicio *f* telefónico de información horaria ➤ **speaking part** papel *m* hablado ➤ **speaking terms: to be on** ~ **terms with sb** hablarse con algn; **we're not on** ~ **terms** no nos hablamos ➤ **speaking voice: a pleasant** ~ **voice** una voz agradable

-speaking ['spiːkɪŋ] ADJ (*ending in compounds*) **English-speaking** de habla inglesa, anglohablante; **French-speaking** de habla francés, francoparlante; **Spanish-speaking people** los hispanohablantes, los de habla española *or* (*esp LAm*) castellana

spear [spɪə^r] **Ⓐ** N lanza *f* **Ⓑ** VT (*with spear*) alancear, herir con lanza; **he** ~**ed a carrot with his fork** atravesó *or* pinchó una zanahoria con el tenedor

speargun ['spɪəɡʌn] N harpón *m* submarino

spearhead ['spɪəhed] **Ⓐ** N punta *f* de lanza **Ⓑ** VT encabezar

spearmint ['spɪəmɪnt] N menta *f* verde, hierbabuena *f* ➤ **spearmint chewing gum** chicle *m* de menta

spec* [spek] N **to go along on** ~ ir a ver lo que sale; **to turn up on** ~ presentarse por si acaso

special ['speʃəl] **Ⓐ** ADJ **1** (= *important, exceptional*) [*occasion, day, permission, price, attention, diet*] especial; **what's so** ~ **about that?** y eso ¿qué tiene de especial?; **is there anyone** ~ **in your life?** ¿hay alguien especial en tu vida?; ~ **arrangements will be made for disabled people** se tomarán medidas especiales para las personas discapacitadas; **to take** ~ **care of sth** cuidar especialmente de algo; **in** ~ **cases** en casos especiales *or* extraordinarios; **to make a** ~ **effort to do sth** esforzarse especialmente *or* hacer un esfuerzo extra para hacer algo; **you're extra** ~ tú eres lo mejor de lo mejor; **to make sb feel** ~ hacer que algn se sienta especial; **my** ~ **friend** mi amigo del alma; **his** ~ **interest was always music** siempre tuvo especial interés por la música; **there's nothing** ~ **about being a journalist** ser periodista no tiene nada de especial; **it's nothing** ~* no es nada especial, no es nada del otro mundo; **I've cooked something** ~ **for dinner** he preparado algo especial para cenar; **she's very** ~ **to us** la apreciamos mucho; ~ **to that country** exclusivo de ese país; **as a** ~ **treat** como algo especial; **to expect** ~ **treatment** esperar un trato especial
2 (= *specific*) especial; **a** ~ **tool for working leather** una herramienta especial para trabajar el cuero; **is there anything** ~ **you would like?** ¿hay algo que quieras en especial?; **I had no** ~ **reason for suspecting him** no tenía ningún motivo en especial para sospechar de él; **"why do you say that?" — "oh, no** ~ **reason"** —¿por qué dices eso? —por nada en especial; **I've no-one** ~ **in mind** no tengo en mente a nadie en concreto *or* en especial; **"what are you doing this weekend?" — "nothing** ~**"** —¿qué haces este fin de semana? —nada (en) especial *or* nada en particular;

Britain has its <u>own</u> ~ problems Gran Bretaña tiene sus propios problemas particulares
B N 1 **the chef's ~** ◇ **today's ~** la especialidad del día
2 (*US**) (= *special offer*) oferta *f* especial
C CPD ➤ **special agent** agente *mf* especial ➤ **Special Branch** (*Brit*) Servicio *m* de Seguridad del Estado ➤ **special delivery** correo *m* exprés ➤ **special edition** edición *f* especial ➤ **special effects** efectos *mpl* especiales ➤ **special needs** (*Brit*): **children with ~ needs** niños que requieren una atención diferenciada ➤ **special offer** oferta *f* especial, oferta *f* de ocasión ➤ **special school** (*Brit*)·colegio *m* de educación especial

specialism ['speʃə,lızəm] N especialidad *f*

specialist ['speʃəlɪst] **A** N especialista *mf*; **heart ~** especialista *mf* del corazón **B** ADJ especializado; **~ knowledge** conocimientos *mpl* especializados

speciality [,speʃɪ'ælɪtɪ], **specialty** (*US*) ['speʃəltɪ] N especialidad *f*

specialization [,speʃəlaɪ'zeɪʃən] N (= *act*) especialización *f*; (= *subject*) especialidad *f*

specialize ['speʃəlaɪz] VI especializarse (**in** en)

specialized ['speʃəlaɪzd] ADJ **~ knowledge** conocimientos *mpl* especializados

specially ['speʃəlɪ] ADV 1 (= *specifically*) [*designed, made, adapted, trained, selected*] especialmente, expresamente; **we asked for it ~** lo pedimos a propósito
2 (= *particularly*) especialmente, en especial, en particular; **we would ~ like to see the orchard** nos gustaría especialmente *or* en especial ver el huerto, nos gustaría ver el huerto en particular; **~ the yellow ones** especialmente *or* sobre todo los amarillos
3 (= *exceptionally*) especialmente, particularmente; **her job is not ~ important to her** su trabajo no es especialmente *or* particularmente importante para ella

specialty ['speʃəltɪ] N (*US*) = **speciality**

species ['spiːʃiːz] N (*pl ~*) especie *f*

specific [spə'sɪfɪk] **A** ADJ 1 (= *definite, particular*) [*need, plan*] específico; [*issue, area, problem*] específico, concreto; [*question, reason, example*] concreto; **with the ~ aim of ...** con el propósito expreso de ...; **problems which are ~ to a particular group of people** problemas que son específicos *or* propios de un grupo particular de personas
2 (= *precise*) [*description, instructions*] preciso; [*meaning*] exacto; **can you be more ~?** ¿puedes ser más concreto?, ¿puedes puntualizar?
B NPL **specifics** (= *particulars*) aspectos *mpl* concretos, detalles *mpl*; **to get down to ~s** ir a los aspectos concretos *or* los detalles

specifically [spə'sɪfɪkəlɪ] ADV 1 (= *especially*) [*design, aim*] específicamente, expresamente 2 (= *more precisely*) en concreto, concretamente 3 (= *explicitly*) [*mention, refer to*] explícitamente; [*ask, authorize*] expresamente, explícitamente; **he ~ asked us not to mention the fact** nos pidió expresamente *or* explícitamente que no mencionáramos ese hecho 4 (= *uniquely*) específicamente

specification [,spesɪfɪ'keɪʃən] N 1 especificación *f*; **the computers are customized to your ~(s)** los ordenadores *or* (*LAm*) computadoras se diseñan de acuerdo con sus especificaciones 2 **specifications** (= *plan*) especificaciones *fpl*, plan *msing* detallado

specify ['spesɪfaɪ] **A** VT especificar; **at a specified time** a una hora determinada **B** VI precisar; **he did not ~** no precisó; **unless otherwise specified** salvo indicaciones en sentido contrario

specimen ['spesɪmɪn] N [*of blood, urine, tissue, rock*] muestra *f*; [*of species*] ejemplar *m*, espécimen *m*
➤ **specimen copy** ejemplar *m* de muestra ➤ **specimen signature** muestra *f* de firma

specious ['spiːʃəs] ADJ especioso

speck [spek] N 1 (= *small stain*) pequeña mancha *f*
2 (= *particle*) [*of dust*] mota *f*; **it's just a ~ on the horizon** es un punto en el horizonte nada más

speckled ['spekld] ADJ moteado, con puntos

specs* [speks] NPL 1 (= *spectacles*) gafas *fpl*, anteojos *mpl*

(*LAm*), lentes *mpl* (*LAm*) 2 (= *specifications*) especificaciones *fpl*, plan *msing* detallado

spectacle ['spektəkl] **A** N 1 (= *sight*) espectáculo *m*; **to make a ~ of o.s.** hacer el ridículo, ponerse en ridículo
2 **spectacles** gafas *fpl*, lentes *mpl* (*LAm*), anteojos *mpl* (*LAm*); **a pair of ~s** unas gafas **B** CPD ➤ **spectacle case** estuche *m* de gafas

spectacular [spek'tækjʊləʳ] **A** ADJ espectacular, impresionante; [*failure, defeat*] espectacular, estrepitoso
B N show *m* espectacular

spectacularly [spek'tækjʊlələ] ADV [*increase, improve*] de modo *or* manera espectacular, espectacularmente; [*crash, fail*] de modo espectacular, estrepitosamente; [*good*] verdaderamente, realmente; [*bad*] terriblemente; **~ beautiful** de una belleza impresionante; **everything went ~ wrong** todo salió terriblemente mal

spectator [spek'teɪtəʳ] N espectador(a) *m/f* ➤ **spectator sport** deporte *m* espectáculo

spectre, specter (*US*) ['spektəʳ] N espectro *m*, fantasma *m*

spectrum ['spektrəm] N (*pl* **spectra** ['spektrə]) [*of colours*] espectro *m*; [*of emotions*] espectro *m*, gama *f*; [*of opinions*] espectro *m*, abanico *m*, gama *f*; **the political ~** el espectro político

specula ['spekjʊlə] NPL *of* **speculum**

speculate ['spekjʊleɪt] VI 1 (= *conjecture*) especular; **to ~ about/on** especular sobre, hacer conjeturas acerca de
2 (*Fin*) especular (**on** en)

speculation [,spekjʊ'leɪʃən] N especulación *f* (*also Fin*); **it is pure ~** es pura especulación; **it is the subject of much ~** se está especulando mucho sobre el tema, es un tema sobre el que se está especulando mucho

speculative ['spekjʊlətɪv] ADJ especulativo

speculator ['spekjʊleɪtəʳ] N especulador(a) *m/f*

speculum ['spekjʊləm] N (*pl* **~s** *or* **specula**) espéculo *m*

sped [sped] PT, PP *of* **speed**

speech [spiːtʃ] **A** N 1 (= *faculty*) habla *f*; (= *words*) palabras *fpl*; (= *language*) lenguaje *m*; (= *manner of speaking*) lenguaje *m*, forma *f* de hablar

> Use **el/un** not **la/una** before feminine nouns beginning with stressed **a** or **ha** like **habla**.

to lose the power of ~ perder el habla; **his ~ was slurred** arrastraba las palabras, farfullaba al hablar; **he expresses himself better in ~ than in writing** se expresa mejor hablando *or* de palabra que por escrito; **freedom of ~** libertad *f* de expresión; **direct/indirect ~** estilo *m* directo/indirecto
2 (= *address*) discurso *m*; **to make a ~** pronunciar un discurso; **speech, speech!** ¡que hable! ¡que hable!
B CPD ➤ **speech bubble** bocadillo *m* ➤ **speech day** (*Brit*) reparto *m* de premios ➤ **speech defect, speech impediment** defecto *m* del habla ➤ **speech recognition** (*Comput*) reconocimiento *m* de voz ➤ **speech therapist** logopeda *mf* ➤ **speech therapy** terapia *f* de la palabra

speechless ['spiːtʃlɪs] ADJ **to be ~** quedarse estupefacto *or* sin habla; **I'm ~!** no sé qué decir, estoy estupefacto; **to be ~ with rage** enmudecer de rabia

speed [spiːd] (*vb: pt, pp* **sped** *or* **~ed**) **A** N 1 (= *rate of movement*) velocidad *f*, rapidez *f*; (= *rapidity, haste*) rapidez *f*, prisa *f*; **at ~** a gran velocidad; **at a ~ of 70km/h** a una velocidad de 70km por hora; **what ~ were you doing?** (*in car*) ¿a qué velocidad ibas?; **at full ~** a toda velocidad, a máxima velocidad; **to gather ~** acelerar, cobrar velocidad; **the ~ of light** la velocidad de la luz; **to pick up ~** acelerar, cobrar velocidad; **the ~ of sound** la velocidad del sonido
2 (*Aut, Tech*) (= *gear*) velocidad *f*
3 (*Phot*) velocidad *f*
4 (*Drugs***) speed *m*, anfetamina *f*
B VI 1 (*pt, pp* **sped**) (= *go fast*) correr a toda prisa; (= *hurry*) darse prisa, apresurarse; **he sped down the street** corrió a toda prisa por la calle; **to ~ along** ir a gran velocidad
2 (*pt, pp* **~ed**) (*Aut*) (= *exceed speed limit*) conducir *or* (*LAm*) manejar por encima del límite de velocidad permitido

Ⓒ CPD ➤ **speed bump** banda *f* sonora ➤ **speed dating** *citas a ciegas rápidas* ➤ **speed limit** velocidad *f* máxima, límite *m* de velocidad ➤ **speed trap** (*Aut*) *sistema policial para detectar infracciones de velocidad*
➤ **speed up** (*pt, pp* ~**ed up**) **Ⓐ** VI + ADV [*person*] apresurarse, apurarse (*LAm*); [*process*] acelerarse **Ⓑ** VT + ADV [+ *object*] acelerar; [+ *person*] apresurar, apurar (*LAm*)

speedboat [ˈspiːdˌbəʊt] N lancha *f* motora

speedily [ˈspiːdɪlɪ] ADV (= *quickly*) rápidamente, con la mayor prontitud; (= *promptly*) prontamente, en seguida

speeding [ˈspiːdɪŋ] N (*Aut*) exceso *m* de velocidad

speedometer [spɪˈdɒmɪtəʳ] N velocímetro *m*, cuentakilómetros *m inv*

speedway [ˈspiːdweɪ] N 1 (= *sport*) carreras *fpl* de motos 2 (= *track*) pista *f* de carreras 3 (*US*) autopista *f*

speedwell [ˈspiːdwel] N verónica *f*

speedy [ˈspiːdɪ] ADJ (*compar* **speedier**; *superl* **speediest**) veloz, rápido; [*answer*] pronto

speleologist [ˌspiːlɪˈɒlədʒɪst] N espeleólogo/a *m/f*

spell[1] [spel] N encanto *m*, hechizo *m*; **to be under sb's ~** estar hechizado por algn; **to break the ~** romper el hechizo *or* encanto; **to cast a ~ on sb** hechizar a algn

spell[2] [spel] (*pt, pp* ~**ed** *or* **spelt**) **Ⓐ** VT 1 (= *write*) escribir; (*letter by letter*) deletrear; **how do you ~ your name?** ¿cómo se escribe tu nombre?; **can you ~ that please?** ¿me lo deletrea, por favor? 2 (= *denote*) significar, representar; **it ~s disaster for us** significa *or* representa un desastre para nosotros **Ⓑ** VI (= *write correctly*) escribir correctamente; **she can't ~** no sabe escribir correctamente, sabe poco de ortografía
➤ **spell out** VT + ADV 1 (= *letter by letter*) deletrear 2 (= *explain*) **to ~ sth out for sb** explicar algo a algn en detalle

spell[3] [spel] N 1 (= *period*) racha *f*; **a cold ~** una racha de frío 2 (= *shift, turn*) turno *m*; **we each took a ~ at the wheel** nos turnamos al volante; **a ~ of duty** una temporada

spellbinding [ˈspelˌbaɪndɪŋ] ADJ cautivador, fascinante

spellbound [ˈspelbaʊnd] ADJ embelesado, hechizado; **to hold sb ~** tener a algn embelesado

spellchecker [ˈspelˌtʃekəʳ] N corrector *m* ortográfico

spelling [ˈspelɪŋ] N ortografía *f*; **my ~ is terrible** cometo muchas faltas de ortografía ➤ **spelling checker** corrector *m* ortográfico ➤ **spelling mistake** falta *f* de ortografía

spelt [spelt] (*esp Brit*) PT, PP *of* **spell**[2]

spelunker [spɪˈlʌŋkəʳ] N (*US*) espeleólogo/a *m/f*

spelunking [spɪˈlʌŋkɪŋ] N (*US*) espeleología *f*

spend [spend] (*pt, pp* **spent**) **Ⓐ** VT 1 (= *pay out*) [+ *money*] gastar (**on** en); **she ~s too much money on clothes** gasta demasiado dinero en ropa; **it's money well spent** es dinero bien empleado; ✦ IDIOM **to ~ a penny** (*Brit euph*) cambiar de agua al canario
2 (= *devote*) [+ *effort, time*] dedicar; **we ~ time, money and effort training these people** dedicamos tiempo, dinero y trabajo a formar a estas personas
3 (= *pass*) [+ *period of time*] pasar; **where are you ~ing your holiday?** ¿dónde vas a pasar las vacaciones?; **he ~s all his time sleeping** se pasa la vida durmiendo
Ⓑ VI gastar

spender [ˈspendəʳ] N gastador(a) *m/f*; **big ~** persona *f* generosa; (*pej*) derrochador(a) *m/f*

spending [ˈspendɪŋ] N gastos *mpl*; **to keep one's ~ down** mantener los gastos bajos; **to reduce government** *or* **public ~** reducir el gasto público ➤ **spending cuts** recortes *mpl* presupuestarios ➤ **spending money** (*for holiday*) dinero *m* para gastar; (= *allowance*) dinero *m* para gastos (personales) ➤ **spending power** poder *m* de compra, poder *m* adquisitivo ➤ **spending spree** derroche *m* de dinero; **we went on a ~ spree** salimos a gastar dinero

spendthrift [ˈspendθrɪft] **Ⓐ** ADJ derrochador, pródigo **Ⓑ** N derrochador(a) *m/f*, pródigo/a *m/f*

spent [spent] **Ⓐ** PT, PP *of* **spend** **Ⓑ** ADJ [*match, lightbulb, battery*] gastado; [*bullet, cartridge, ammunition*] usado; **he's a ~ force** ya no es lo que era

sperm [spɜːm] N esperma *m or f* ➤ **sperm bank** banco *m* de esperma ➤ **sperm count** recuento *m* de espermas ➤ **sperm whale** cachalote *m*

spermicide [ˈspɜːmɪsaɪd] N espermicida *m*

spew [spjuː] **Ⓐ** VT (*also* ~ **up**) vomitar; (*fig*) arrojar, vomitar **Ⓑ** VI vomitar

sphere [sfɪəʳ] N esfera *f*; **~ of influence** esfera *f* de influencia; **his ~ of interest** el ámbito de sus intereses; **that's outside my ~** eso no es de mi competencia

spherical [ˈsferɪkəl] ADJ esférico

sphinx [sfɪŋks] N (*pl* ~**es**) esfinge *f*

spice [spaɪs] **Ⓐ** N 1 (*for cooking*) especia *f*; **mixed ~(s)** especias *fpl* mixtas; ✦ PROV **variety is the ~ of life** en la variedad está el gusto
2 (= *excitement*) **the papers like stories with some ~** a los periódicos les gustan los reportajes con algo de picante; **the details add ~ to the story** los detalles dan sabor a la historia **Ⓑ** VT 1 [+ *food*] condimentar, sazonar
2 (*fig*) **a highly ~d account** un relato de mucho picante; **gossip ~d with scandal** cotilleos acompañados por el morbo del escándalo
Ⓒ CPD ➤ **spice rack** especiero *m*

spick-and-span [ˈspɪkənˈspæn] ADJ [*house, room*] impecable, como los chorros del oro*; [*person*] acicalado

spicy [ˈspaɪsɪ] ADJ (*compar* **spicier**; *superl* **spiciest**) 1 [*food*] muy condimentado, muy sazonado; (= *hot*) picante, picoso (*LAm*) 2 [*joke*] picante, colorado (*LAm*)

spider [ˈspaɪdəʳ] N araña *f* ➤ **spider plant** cinta *f* ➤ **spider's web** telaraña *f*

spidery [ˈspaɪdərɪ] ADJ delgado; [*writing*] de patas de araña

spiel* [spiːl] N (= *speech*) arenga *f*, discurso *m*; [*of salesman*] rollo* *m*, material *m* publicitario

spigot [ˈspɪgət] N (*US*) espita *f*, bitoque *m*

spike [spaɪk] **Ⓐ** N 1 (= *point*) punta *f*; (*on railing*) barrote *m*; (*on sports shoes*) clavo *m*; [*of hedgehog etc*] púa *f* 2 **spikes** (= *shoes*) zapatillas *fpl* con clavos **Ⓑ** VT (= *fix*) clavar; (= *impale*) atravesar; **a ~d drink*** (*with added alcohol*) una bebida con alcohol añadido a escondidas *or* (*Sp*) de extranjis; ✦ IDIOM **to ~ sb's guns** (*Brit*) poner trabas a los planes de algn **Ⓒ** CPD ➤ **spike heel** (*US*) tacón *m* de aguja

spiky [ˈspaɪkɪ] ADJ (*compar* **spikier**; *superl* **spikiest**) (= *sharp, pointed*) puntiagudo; (= *thorny*) cubierto de púas; [*animal*] erizado; [*hair*] de punta

spill[1] [spɪl] (*pt, pp* ~**ed** *or* **spilt**) **Ⓐ** VT [+ *water, salt*] derramar, verter; **you've spilt coffee on your shirt** te ha caído café en la camisa; ✦ IDIOM **to ~ the beans*** descubrir el pastel*, contarlo todo **Ⓑ** VI derramarse, verterse **Ⓒ** N 1 (= *fall*) caída *f* 2 (= *spillage*) vertido *m*
➤ **spill out Ⓐ** VI + ADV [*liquid*] derramarse; [*contents, objects*] desparramarse; [*people*] salir en avalancha; **the crowd ~ed out into the streets** la gente salió a la calle en avalancha; **the audience ~ed out of the cinema** el público salió en masa del cine **Ⓑ** VT + ADV volcar; (*fig*) soltar
➤ **spill over** VI + ADV [*liquid*] derramarse; [*cup, pan*] desbordarse; **these problems ~ed over into his private life** estos problemas llegaron a afectar su vida privada

spill[2] [spɪl] N (*for lighting fire*) pajuela *f*

spillage [ˈspɪlɪdʒ] N vertido *m*

spilt [spɪlt] (*esp Brit*) PT, PP *of* **spill**

spin [spɪn] (*vb: pt, pp* **spun**) **Ⓐ** N 1 (= *rotating motion*) vuelta *f*, revolución *f*; **give the towels another ~** (*in washing machine*) vuelve a centrifugar las toallas (en la lavadora); **to put (a) ~ on a ball** dar efecto a una pelota; **to go into a ~** [*plane*] entrar en barrena; [*car*] hacer un trompo 2 (*Brit**) (*in car*) **to go for a ~** dar una vuelta *or* un paseo, darse un garbeo (*Sp**) 3 (*esp Pol*) (= *presentation*) presentación *f*; (*pej*) manipulación *f*; **it depends on the ~ you put on it** depende de cómo lo quieras interpretar **Ⓑ** VT 1 (= *rotate*) hacer girar; [+ *top*] hacer bailar; [+ *ball*] dar efecto a; **to ~ a coin** (*to decide sth*) echar una moneda a cara o cruz 2 (= *spin-dry*) [+ *clothes*] centrifugar 3 [+ *thread*] hilar; [+ *web*] tejer; ✦ IDIOM **to ~ a yarn*** inventar una historia

⊙ VI **1** (= *rotate*) girar, dar vueltas; **she spun around to face him** se dio la vuelta para tenerlo de frente; **my head is ~ning** me da vueltas la cabeza; **the car spun out of control** el coche se descontroló y empezó a dar vueltas; **the blow sent him ~ning** el golpe le hizo rodar por el suelo **2** [*washing machine*] centrifugar **3** (*with spinning wheel*) hilar **⊙** CPD ➤ **spin doctor*** (*Pol*) asesor(a) *m/f* político(a) ➤ **spin out*** VT + ADV [+ *process, story*] alargar, prolongar

spina bifida [ˌspaɪnəˈbɪfɪdə] N espina *f* bífida

spinach [ˈspɪnɪdʒ] N **1** (= *cut leaves*) espinacas *fpl* **2** (= *plant*) espinaca *f*

spinal [ˈspaɪnl] ADJ espinal, vertebral ➤ **spinal column** columna *f* vertebral ➤ **spinal cord** médula *f* espinal

spindle [ˈspɪndl] N (*for spinning*) huso *m*

spindly [ˈspɪndlɪ] ADJ (*compar* **spindlier**; *superl* **spindliest**) [*person, plant*] alto y delgado; [*legs*] largo y delgado

spin-dry [ˌspɪnˈdraɪ] VT centrifugar

spin-dryer [ˈspɪnˈdraɪəʳ] N (*Brit*) secadora-centrifugadora *f*

spine [spaɪn] N **1** (= *backbone*) columna *f* (vertebral), espina *f* dorsal **2** (= *spike*) púa *f*, pincho *m*; (= *thorn*) espina *f*, pincho *m* **3** [*of book*] lomo *m*

spine-chilling [ˈspaɪnˌtʃɪlɪŋ] ADJ escalofriante

spineless [ˈspaɪnlɪs] ADJ (*fig*) débil

spinner [ˈspɪnəʳ] N **1** [*of cloth*] hilandero/a *m/f* **2** (*) (= *spin-dryer*) secadora-centrifugadora *f*

spinney [ˈspɪnɪ] N (*Brit*) bosquecillo *m*

spinning [ˈspɪnɪŋ] N (= *act*) hilado *m*; (= *art*) hilandería *f*, arte *m* de hilar ➤ **spinning top** peonza *f*, trompo *m* ➤ **spinning wheel** rueca *f* or torno *m* de hilar

spin-off [ˈspɪnɒf] N (= *product*) derivado *m*, producto *m* secundario; (= *incidental benefit*) beneficio *m* incidental, beneficio *m* indirecto

spinster [ˈspɪnstəʳ] N soltera *f*; (*pej*) solterona *f*

spiral [ˈspaɪərəl] **Ⓐ** ADJ espiral, en espiral; **a ~ staircase** una escalera de caracol **Ⓑ** N espiral *f*, hélice *f* **⊙** VI **to ~ up** [*plane*] subir en espiral; [*smoke*] subir formando una espiral; [*prices*] subir vertiginosamente

spire [ˈspaɪəʳ] N aguja *f*

spirit [ˈspɪrɪt] **Ⓐ** N **1** (= *soul*) espíritu *m*; **young in ~** joven de espíritu **2** (= *supernatural being*) espíritu *m*; **evil ~** espíritu *m* maligno **3** (= *courage*) espíritu *m*; (= *liveliness*) ímpetu *m*, energía *f*; **to break sb's ~** quebrantar el espíritu a algn; **a woman of ~** una mujer con espíritu *or* brío; **to do sth with ~** hacer algo con energía **4** [*of agreement, law*] espíritu *m*; **a ~ of adventure** un espíritu aventurero; **the ~ of the age** el espíritu de la época; **community ~** civismo *m*; **in a ~ of cooperation** con espíritu de cooperación; **to enter into the ~ of things** entrar en ambiente; **festive ~** espíritu *m* festivo; **public ~** civismo *m*; **to take sth in the right/wrong ~** interpretar bien/mal algo; **that's the ~!** ¡así me gusta!, ¡ánimo! **5** (= *person*) alma *f*

> Use **el/un** not **la/una** before feminine nouns beginning with stressed **a** or **ha** like **alma**.

the leading ~ in the party el alma del partido, la figura más destacada del partido; **she was a free ~** era una persona que estaba más allá de los convencionalismos **6** (= *alcohol*) alcohol *m* **7** spirits 7.1 (= *state of mind*) **to be in good ~s** tener la moral alta; **to be in high ~s** estar animadísimo, estar muy alegre; **we kept our ~s up by singing** mantuvimos la moral alta cantando; **to be in low ~s** tener la moral baja, estar bajo de moral; **my ~s rose** se me levantó el ánimo *or* la moral 7.2 (= *alcohol*) licores *mpl* **Ⓑ** VT **to ~ sth away** llevarse algo como por arte de magia, hacer desaparecer algo **⊙** CPD ➤ **spirit level** nivel *m* de burbuja

spirited [ˈspɪrɪtɪd] ADJ (= *lively*) [*person*] animado, lleno de vida; [*horse*] fogoso; [*debate, discussion*] animado, enérgico;

[*attack*] enérgico

spiritual [ˈspɪrɪtjʊəl] **Ⓐ** ADJ espiritual **Ⓑ** N (*Mus*) canción *f* religiosa

spiritualism [ˈspɪrɪtjʊəlɪzəm] N espiritismo *m*

spiritualist [ˈspɪrɪtjʊəlɪst] N espiritista *mf*

spirituality [ˌspɪrɪtjʊˈælɪtɪ] N espiritualidad *f*

spit¹ [spɪt] (*vb*: *pt, pp* **spat**) **Ⓐ** N saliva *f*, esputo *m* **Ⓑ** VT **1** [+ *blood, crumb*] escupir **2** (= *exclaim*) espetar, soltar **⊙** VI **1** [*person*] escupir (**at** a; **on** en); [*cat*] bufar; **to ~ in sb's face** escupir a la cara a algn; **it's ~ting with rain** (*Brit*) están cayendo algunas gotas **2** [*fat, fire*] chisporrotear ➤ **spit out** VT + ADV [+ *pip, pill*] escupir; **I spat it out** lo escupí; **~ it out!*** ¡dilo!, ¡habla!

spit² [spɪt] **Ⓐ** N **1** (*for meat*) asador *m*, espetón *m* **2** (*Geog*) [*of land*] lengua *f* **Ⓑ** VT espetar

spite [spaɪt] **Ⓐ** N **1** (= *ill will*) rencor *m*, ojeriza *f*; **to do sth out of ~** hacer algo por inquina **2** **in ~ of** (= *despite*) a pesar de, pese a; **in ~ of the fact that** a pesar de que, pese a que; **in ~ of herself** a pesar de sí misma **Ⓑ** VT herir, dañar; **she just does it to ~ me** lo hace solamente para causarme pena

spiteful [ˈspaɪtfəl] ADJ [*person*] (= *resentful*) rencoroso; (= *malicious*) malicioso; [*action*] malintencionado

spitefully [ˈspaɪtfəlɪ] ADV (= *out of resentment*) por despecho; **she said ~** dijo, con malicia

spitting [ˈspɪtɪŋ] ADJ **it's within ~ distance*** está muy cerca; ✦ IDIOM **to be the ~ image of sb** ser la viva imagen *or* el vivo retrato de algn

spittle [ˈspɪtl] N saliva *f*, baba *f*

spiv* [spɪv] N (*Brit*) chanchullero* *m*, caballero *m* de industria; (= *black marketeer*) estraperlista *mf*

splash [splæʃ] **Ⓐ** N (= *spray*) salpicadura *f*; (= *splashing noise*) chapoteo *m*; **whisky with a ~ of water** whisky *m* con un poquitín de agua; **a ~ of colour** una mancha de color; ✦ IDIOM **to make a ~*** causar sensación **Ⓑ** VT salpicar; **to ~ sb with water** salpicar a algn de agua; **he ~ed water on his face** se echó agua en la cara; **to ~ paint on the floor** manchar el suelo de pintura; **the story was ~ed across the front page*** el reportaje apareció con grandes titulares en primera plana **⊙** VI **1** [*liquid, mud etc*] **mud ~ed all over his trousers** el barro le salpicó los pantalones **2** [*person, animal*] (*in water*) chapotear ➤ **splash out*** VI + ADV (*Brit*) derrochar dinero; **so we ~ed out and bought it** decidimos echar la casa por la ventana y comprarlo

splashdown [ˈsplæʃdaʊn] N amaraje *m*, amerizaje *m*

splashy* [ˈsplæʃɪ] ADJ (*US*) (*compar* **splashier**; *superl* **splashiest**) (= *showy*) ostentoso

splat [splæt] **Ⓐ** N **with a ~** con un plaf **Ⓑ** EXCL ¡plaf!

spleen [spliːn] N (= *organ*) bazo *m*; ✦ IDIOM **to vent one's ~** descargar la bilis

splendid [ˈsplendɪd] ADJ magnífico; **splendid!** ¡magnífico!, ¡estupendo!

splendidly [ˈsplendɪdlɪ] ADV (= *magnificently*) espléndidamente, magníficamente; (= *wonderfully*) estupendamente; **everything went ~** todo fue de maravilla; **we get along ~** nos llevamos muy bien

splendour, splendor (*US*) [ˈsplendəʳ] N esplendor *m*

splice [splaɪs] VT [+ *rope, tape*] empalmar, juntar; ✦ IDIOM **to get ~d*** casarse

splint [splɪnt] N tablilla *f*; **to put sb's arm in ~s** entablillar el brazo a algn; **to be in ~s** estar entablillado

splinter [ˈsplɪntəʳ] **Ⓐ** N [*of wood, metal*] astilla *f*; [*of glass*] fragmento *m*; [*of bone*] esquirla *f*, fragmento *m* **Ⓑ** VI astillarse, hacerse astillas; (*fig*) [*party*] escindirse **⊙** CPD ➤ **splinter group** grupo *m* disidente, facción *f*

split [splɪt] (*vb*: *pt, pp* **~**) **Ⓐ** N **1** (= *crack*) (*in wood, rock*) hendidura *f*, grieta *f* **2** (= *rift*) ruptura *f*, escisión *f* **3** (= *division*) división *f*; **a three-way ~** una división en tres partes **4** (*in skirt*) abertura *f* **5** **to do the ~s** (*Gymnastics*) hacer el spagat

B ADJ **1** (= *cracked*) [*wood, rock*] partido, hendido; **he had a ~ lip** tenía un labio partido
2 (= *divided*) dividido; **the government is ~ on this question** el gobierno está dividido en este asunto; **it was a ~ decision** la decisión no fue unánime
C VT **1** (= *break*) partir; **to ~ the atom** desintegrar el átomo; **to ~ sth open** abrir algo; **✦** IDIOMS **to ~ hairs** hilar muy fino *or* delgado, buscarle tres pies al gato, buscarle mangas al chaleco (*LAm*); **to ~ one's sides laughing** partirse de risa, morirse de (la) risa
2 (= *divide, share*) repartir; **let's ~ the money between us** repartámonos el dinero; **to ~ the difference** repartir la diferencia (a partes iguales); **the children were ~ into two groups** dividieron a los niños en dos grupos
3 [+ *government, group*] dividir; [+ *party*] escindir, dividir
D VI **1** (= *come apart*) [*stone*] henderse, rajarse; **her jeans ~** los vaqueros se le abrieron por las costuras; **to ~ open** abrirse; **✦** IDIOM **my head is ~ting** me va a estallar la cabeza
2 [*government, group*] dividirse; [*party*] escindirse, dividirse
3 (*Brit**) (= *tell tales*) chivatear**, soplar*; **to ~ on sb** chivatear contra algn**, soplar contra algn*
4 (*esp US**) (= *leave*) largarse*, irse
E CPD ➤ **split ends** puntas *fpl* partidas ➤ **split infinitive** infinitivo en el que un adverbio o una frase se intercala entre "*to*" y el verbo ➤ **split personality** personalidad *f* desdoblada ➤ **split screen** pantalla *f* partida ➤ **split second** fracción *f* de segundo; **in a ~ second** en un instante, en un abrir y cerrar de ojos
➤ **split off** VI + ADV separarse
➤ **split up** **A** VI + ADV [*partners, couple*] separarse; [*meeting, crowd*] dispersarse; **let's ~ up for safety** separémonos para mayor seguridad; **we ~ up into two groups** nos dividimos en dos grupos **B** VT + ADV **1** (= *break up*) partir **2** (= *divide up*) repartir; **we'll ~ the work up among us** nos repartiremos *or* dividiremos el trabajo **3** (= *separate*) dividir; **~ the children up into small groups** divide a los niños en grupos pequeños

split-level ['splɪtˌlevl] ADJ [*room*] a desnivel; [*house*] dúplex

splitting ['splɪtɪŋ] **A** ADJ [*headache*] terrible **B** N **~ of the atom** desintegración *f* del átomo

split-up ['splɪtʌp] N ruptura *f*; [*of couple*] separación *f*

splodge (*Brit*) [splɒdʒ], **splotch** (*US*) [splɒtʃ] N mancha *f*, borrón *m*

splurge* [splɜːdʒ] **A** N (= *excess*) derroche *m* **B** VI **to ~ on sth** derrochar dinero comprando algo

splutter ['splʌtəʳ] **A** VI **1** [*person*] (= *spit*) escupir, echar saliva; (= *stutter*) farfullar, balbucear **2** [*fire, fat*] chisporrotear; [*engine*] renquear **B** VT farfullar, balbucear

spoil [spɔɪl] (*vb: pt, pp* **~ed** *or* **~t**) **A** VT **1** (= *ruin*) estropear, arruinar; (= *harm*) dañar; (*Brit*) (= *invalidate*) [+ *voting paper*] invalidar; **it ~ed our holiday** nos estropeó las vacaciones; **it will ~ your appetite** te quitará el apetito; **to ~ sb's fun** aguar la fiesta a algn **2** (= *pamper*) mimar, consentir (*LAm*) **B** VI **1** [*food*] estropearse, echarse a perder **2 to be ~ing for a fight** estar con ganas de luchar *or* (*LAm*) pelear

spoiler ['spɔɪləʳ] N **1** (*Aut, Aer*) alerón *m*, spoiler *m* **2** (*Press*) **a rival paper brought out a ~** un periódico rival publicó otra exclusiva para quitarles parte de las ventas

spoils [spɔɪlz] NPL botín *msing*; **the ~ of war** el botín de la guerra

spoilsport* ['spɔɪlspɔːt] N aguafiestas *mf inv*

spoilt [spɔɪlt] **A** PT, PP *of* **spoil** **B** ADJ **1** (= *ruined*) [*meal*] estropeado, echado a perder; [*vote*] nulo **2** (= *pampered*) [*child*] mimado, consentido **3** (*US*) (= *gone bad*) [*food*] pasado, malo; [*milk*] cortado

spoke[1] [spəʊk] N [*of wheel*] rayo *m*, radio *m*; **✦** IDIOM **to put a ~ in sb's wheel** (*Brit**) ponerle trabas a algn

spoke[2] [spəʊk] PT *of* **speak**

spoken ['spəʊkən] **A** PP *of* **speak** **B** ADJ hablado; **the ~ language** la lengua hablada

spokesman ['spəʊksmən] N (*pl* **spokesmen**) portavoz *mf*, vocero *mf* (*LAm*)

spokesperson ['spəʊkspɜːsn] N (*pl* **spokespeople**) portavoz *mf*, vocero *mf* (*LAm*)

spokeswoman ['spəʊkswʊmən] N (*pl* **spokeswomen**) portavoz *f*, vocero *f* (*LAm*)

sponge [spʌndʒ] **A** N **1** (*for washing*) esponja *f*; **✦** IDIOM **to throw in the ~*** darse por vencido, tirar la toalla
2 (*also* **~ cake**) bizcocho *m*, queque *m*, pastel *m* (*LAm*)
B VT **1** (= *wash*) lavar/limpiar con esponja
2 (*) (= *scrounge*) **he ~d £15 off me** me sacó 15 libras de gorra*
C VI (*) (= *scrounge*) dar sablazos*, vivir de gorra*; **to ~ off** *or* **on sb** (= *depend on*) vivir de algn; (*on occasion*) dar sablazos a algn*
D CPD ➤ **sponge bag** (*Brit*) esponjera *f* ➤ **sponge cake** bizcocho *m*, queque *m*, pastel *m* (*LAm*) ➤ **sponge rubber** gomaespuma *f*
➤ **sponge down** VT + ADV limpiar/lavar con esponja

sponger* ['spʌndʒəʳ] N gorrón/ona* *m/f*, garronero/a* *m/f* (*RPl*)

spongy ['spʌndʒɪ] ADJ (*compar* **spongier**; *superl* **spongiest**) esponjoso

sponsor ['spɒnsəʳ] **A** N (*Sport, Rad, TV*) patrocinador(a) *m/f*, sponsor *mf*; (*for participant in charity event*) patrocinador(a) *m/f* **B** VT **1** (= *fund*) [+ *event*] patrocinar, auspiciar; [+ *studies, research*] financiar; (*Brit*) [+ *participant in charity event*] respaldar *or* avalar mediante un donativo a favor de una obra benéfica; **~ed walk** (*Brit*) marcha benéfica que cuenta con algún patrocinio **2** (= *support*) respaldar, apoyar

sponsorship ['spɒnsəʃɪp] N [*of event*] patrocinio *m*, auspicio *m*; [*of studies, research*] financiación *f*

spontaneity [ˌspɒntəˈneɪtɪ] N espontaneidad *f*

spontaneous [spɒnˈteɪnɪəs] ADJ espontáneo

spontaneously [spɒnˈteɪnɪəslɪ] ADV espontáneamente

spoof* [spuːf] **A** N (= *parody*) burla *f*, parodia *f*; (= *hoax*) trampa *f*, truco *m* **B** VT (= *parody*) parodiar; (= *trick*) engañar

spook* [spuːk] **A** N **1** (*hum**) (= *ghost*) espectro *m*, aparición *f* **2** (*US***) (= *secret agent*) espía *mf*, agente *mf* secreto/a **B** VT (*US*) (= *frighten*) asustar, pegar un susto a

spooky* ['spuːkɪ] ADJ (*compar* **spookier**; *superl* **spookiest**) espeluznante, horripilante

spool [spuːl] N (*Phot*) carrete *m*; (*Sew*) bobina *f*, carrete *m*; (*on fishing line*) cucharilla *f*

spoon [spuːn] **A** N **1** (*gen*) cuchara *f*; (= *teaspoon*) cucharita *f* **2** (= *spoonful*) cucharada *f* **B** VT **to ~ sth onto a plate** echar cucharadas de algo en un plato

spoonerism ['spuːnərɪzəm] N trastrueque *m* verbal, trastrueque *m* de palabras

spoon-feed ['spuːnfiːd] (*pt, pp* **spoon-fed**) VT (*fig*) dar todo hecho a, poner todo en bandeja a

spoonful ['spuːnfəl] N cucharada *f*

spoor [spʊəʳ] N pista *f*, rastro *m*

sporadic [spəˈrædɪk] ADJ esporádico

sporadically [spəˈrædɪkəlɪ] ADV esporádicamente

spore [spɔː] N espora *f*

sporran ['spɒrən] N escarcela *f*

sport [spɔːt] **A** N **1** (= *game*) deporte *m*; (= *games in general*) deporte(s) *m(pl)*; **to be good at ~** ser buen deportista
2 (*) (= *person*) persona *f* amable; **she's a good ~** es buena persona, es buena gente (*esp LAm*); **be a ~!** ¡no seas malo!
B VT lucir, ostentar
C CPD ➤ **sports car** coche *m* deportivo ➤ **sports centre** polideportivo *m* ➤ **sports day** (*Brit*) día *m* de competiciones deportivas (de un colegio) ➤ **sports desk** sección *f* de deportes ➤ **sports facilities** instalaciones *fpl* deportivas ➤ **sports ground** (*Brit*) campo *m* deportivo, centro *m* deportivo ➤ **sports jacket** chaqueta *f* sport, saco *m* sport (*LAm*) ➤ **sports page** página *f* de deportes ➤ **sport(s) utility vehicle** todoterreno *m inv*

sporting ['spɔːtɪŋ] ADJ **1** [*activity, career*] deportivo **2** (= *fair*) [*conduct, spirit*] deportivo, caballeroso; **that's very ~ of you** eres muy amable, es muy amable de su parte; **there's a ~ chance that ...** existe la posibilidad de que ...

sportsman ['spɔːtsmən] N (*pl* **sportsmen**) deportista *m*

sportsmanlike ['spɔːtsmənlaɪk] ADJ caballeroso

sportsmanship ['spɔːtsmənʃɪp] N espíritu *m* deportivo

sportswear ['spɔːtsweəʳ] N ropa *f* deportiva

sportswoman ['spɔːtswʊmən] N (*pl* **sportswomen**) deportista *f*

sporty* ['spɔːtɪ] ADJ (*compar* **sportier**; *superl* **sportiest**) deportivo, aficionado a los deportes

spot [spɒt] **Ⓐ** N **1** (= *dot*) lunar *m*; **a red dress with white ~s** un vestido rojo con lunares blancos; **to have ~s before one's eyes** tener la vista nublada
2 (= *stain, mark*) mancha *f*
3 (= *pimple*) grano *m*, granito *m*; **she <u>came out</u> in ~s** le salieron granos en la piel; **he's <u>covered</u> in ~s** está lleno de granos
4 (= *place*) sitio *m*, lugar *m*; (= *scene*) escena *f*, escenario *m*; **it's a lovely ~ for a picnic** es un sitio *or* lugar precioso para un picnic; **a tender ~ on the arm** un punto *or* lugar sensible en el brazo; **on the ~** (= *immediately*) en el acto; (= *there*) en el mismo sitio; **they gave her the job on the ~** le dieron el trabajo en el acto; **they were able to mend the car on the ~** consiguieron arreglar el coche allí mismo; **the firemen were on the ~ in three minutes** los bomberos acudieron *or* llegaron en tres minutos; **to run on the ~** correr en parada; **to pay cash on the ~** (*US*) pagar al contado; **his <u>soft</u> ~** su debilidad, su punto flaco, su lado flaco (*LAm*); **to have a soft ~ for sb** tener debilidad por algn; **his <u>weak</u> ~** su debilidad, su punto flaco, su lado flaco (*LAm*)
5 (*Brit**) (= *small quantity*) poquito *m*, pizca *f*; **a ~ of <u>bother</u>** un pequeño disgusto; **we had a ~ of <u>rain</u> yesterday** ayer se sintieron gotas de lluvia
6 (= *difficulty*) apuro *m*, aprieto *m*; **to be <u>in</u> a (tight) ~** estar en un apuro *or* aprieto; **to put sb <u>on</u> the ~** (= *put in difficulty*) poner a algn en un apuro *or* aprieto; (= *compromise*) comprometer a algn
7 (*in show*) espacio *m*; (= *advertisement*) espacio *m* publicitario
8 (*) (= *spotlight*) foco *m*
Ⓑ VT (= *notice*) darse cuenta de, notar; (= *see*) observar, darse cuenta de; (= *recognize*) reconocer; (= *catch out*) coger, pillar; **I ~ted a mistake** descubrí un error
Ⓒ CPD ➤ **spot check** comprobación *f* en el acto, reconocimiento *m* rápido ➤ **spot price** precio *m* de entrega inmediata

spot-check ['spɒttʃek] VT revisar en el acto

spotless ['spɒtlɪs] ADJ inmaculado, sin mancha; [*appearance*] impecable, pulcro; [*house*] limpísimo; [*reputation*] impecable, intachable

spotlessly ['spɒtlɪslɪ] ADV **~ clean** limpísimo

spotlight ['spɒtlaɪt] **Ⓐ** N (= *beam, lamp*) foco *m*, reflector *m*; (*Theat*) proyector *m*; **to be in the ~** (*fig*) ser el centro de atención; **✦** IDIOM **to turn the ~ on sth/sb** exponer algo/a algn a la luz pública **Ⓑ** VT (*fig*) destacar, subrayar

spotlit ['spɒtlɪt] ADJ iluminado

spot-on* [ˌspɒt'ɒn] ADJ (*Brit*) **what he said was ~** dio en el claro con lo que dijo

spotted ['spɒtɪd] ADJ [*dress*] de lunares, con motas; [*animal*] con manchas; **~ with mud** salpicado *or* manchado de lodo

spotter ['spɒtəʳ] N (*Brit*) *see* **trainspotter**

spotting ['spɒtɪŋ] N (*Brit*) *see* **trainspotting**

spotty* ['spɒtɪ] ADJ (*compar* **spottier**; *superl* **spottiest**)
1 (= *pimply*) con granos **2** (*) (= *patterned*) [*dress, material*] de lunares, con motas; [*dog*] con manchas

spouse [spaʊs] N cónyuge *mf*

spout [spaʊt] **Ⓐ** N [*of jug*] pico *m*; [*of teapot*] pitón *m*, pitorro *m*; (= *jet of water*) surtidor *m*, chorro *m*; **to be up the ~** (*Brit**) [*person*] (= *in a jam*) estar en un apuro; **my holiday's up the ~*** mis vacaciones se han ido al garete*
Ⓑ VT **1** [+ *water*] arrojar en chorro **2** (*) [+ *poetry etc*] declamar **Ⓒ** VI **1** [*water*] brotar, salir en chorros **2** (*) (= *declaim*) hablar incansablemente

sprain [spreɪn] **Ⓐ** N torcedura *f* **Ⓑ** VT torcer; **to ~ one's wrist/ankle** torcerse la muñeca/el tobillo

sprang [spræŋ] PT *of* **spring**

sprawl [sprɔːl] **Ⓐ** VI **1** (*person*) (= *sit down, lie down*) tumbarse, echarse; (*untidily*) despatarrarse; (= *fall down*) derrumbarse; **the body was ~ed on the floor** el cadáver estaba tumbado en el suelo; **he was ~ed** *or* **~ing in a chair** estaba tumbado de modo poco elegante en un sillón; **the jolt sent him ~ing** la sacudida le hizo ir rodando por el suelo **2** [*plant, town*] extenderse **Ⓑ** N [*of town etc*] extensión *f*; **urban ~** crecimiento *m* urbano descontrolado

sprawling ['sprɔːlɪŋ] ADJ [*person*] tumbado; [*city, town*] en crecimiento rápido; [*handwriting*] desgarbado

spray¹ [spreɪ] **Ⓐ** N **1** (= *liquid*) rociada *f*; [*of sea*] espuma *f*; (*from atomizer, aerosol*) pulverización *f* **2** (= *aerosol, atomizer*) atomizador *m*, spray *m*; (*Med*) rociador *m* **Ⓑ** VT [+ *water, perfume*] rociar; **to ~ sth/sb with water/bullets** rociar algo/a algn de agua/balas; **to ~ the roses with insecticide** rociar las rosas de insecticida **Ⓒ** CPD ➤ **spray can** spray *m*, pulverizador *m* ➤ **spray gun** pistola *f* rociadora, pulverizador *m* ➤ **spray paint** pintura *f* spray ➤ **spray out** VI + ADV [*liquid etc*] salir a chorro

spray² [spreɪ] N (*of flowers*) ramita *f*, ramo *m*

spray-on ['spreɪɒn] ADJ en aerosol, en spray

spread [spred] (*vb: pt, pp* **~**) **Ⓐ** N **1** [*of infection, disease, fire*] propagación *f*; [*of idea, information*] difusión *f*, divulgación *f*; [*of nuclear weapons*] proliferación *f*
2 (= *extent*) [*of wings, sails*] envergadura *f*
3 (*) (= *meal*) comilona* *f*, banquetazo* *m*
4 (= *cover*) (*for bed*) cubrecama *m*, sobrecama *m or f*
5 (*for bread*) pasta *f* para untar; **cheese ~** queso *m* para untar
6 (*Press, Typ*) **a double-page ~** una página doble, una doble plana
Ⓑ VT **1** (*also* **~ out**) [+ *tablecloth, blanket*] extender, tender; [+ *map*] extender, desplegar; [+ *arms, fingers, legs*] extender; [+ *sails, wings*] desplegar; [+ *net*] tender; **she lay ~ out on the floor** estaba tendida en el suelo; **to ~ one's wings** desplegar las alas; **her clothes were ~ all over the floor** (*untidily*) su ropa estaba esparcida *or* desparramada por todo el suelo
2 [+ *butter*] untar; **to ~ butter on one's bread** untar mantequilla en el pan, untar el pan con mantequilla; **to ~ cream on one's face** untarse *or* ponerse crema en la cara
3 (= *distribute*) distribuir; **you are advised to ~ the workload** le aconsejamos que se distribuya el trabajo; **repayments will be ~ over 18 months** los pagos se efectuarán a lo largo de 18 meses; **✦** IDIOM **don't ~ yourself too thin** no intentes abarcar más de la cuenta
4 (= *disseminate*) [+ *news, information, gossip*] divulgar, difundir; [+ *rumour*] hacer correr, difundir; [+ *disease*] propagar
Ⓒ VI **1** (= *extend, advance*) [*fire*] propagarse, extenderse; [*disease*] propagarse; [*panic, fear*] cundir; [*information, news, ideas*] difundirse; **the cancer had ~ to his lungs** el cáncer se había extendido a los pulmones; **a smile ~ over** *or* **across his face** sonrió de oreja a oreja; **✦** IDIOM **the rumours ~ like wildfire** los rumores corrieron como la pólvora
2 (= *stretch*) extenderse; **the city ~s several miles to the north** la ciudad se extiende varias millas hacia el norte
3 [*butter*] untarse
➤ **spread out** VI + ADV **1** (= *disperse*) [*people*] dispersarse
2 (= *extend*) [*city, liquid*] extenderse; (= *widen*) [*river*] ensancharse **Ⓑ** VT + ADV *see* **spread B1**

spread-eagled [spred'iːgld] ADJ a pata tendida

spreadsheet ['spredʃiːt] N hoja *f* de cálculo, hoja *f* electrónica

spree* [spriː] N juerga *f*, parranda *f*, farra *f* (*esp SC*); **to go on a ~** (*spending money*) salir a gastar dinero

sprig [sprɪg] N [*of heather etc*] espiga *f*

sprightly ['spraɪtlɪ] ADJ (*compar* **sprightlier**; *superl* **sprightliest**) enérgico

spring [sprɪŋ] (*vb: pt* **sprang**; *pp* **sprung**) **Ⓐ** N **1** (= *season*) primavera *f*; **in ~** en primavera; **~ morning** una mañana de primavera; **~ is in the air** se siente la llegada de la primavera
2 (*in watch*) muelle *m*, resorte *m*; (*in mattress*) muelle *m*
3 [*of water*] fuente *f*, manantial *m*
4 (= *leap*) salto *m*, brinco *m*

5 (= *elasticity*) elasticidad *f*
Ⓑ VT **to ~ sth on sb** soltar algo a algn (de buenas a primeras)*; **to ~ a surprise on sb** dar una sorpresa a algn; **to ~ a leak** [*boat*] empezar a hacer agua
Ⓒ VI **1** (= *leap*) saltar; **to ~ out of bed** saltar de la cama; **the cat sprang onto the roof** el gato dio un salto y se puso en el tejado; **to ~ at sb** abalanzarse sobre algn; **to ~ back** [*person, animal*] saltar para atrás; **the branch sprang back** la rama volvió hacia atrás como un látigo; **where did you ~ from?*** ¿de dónde diablos has salido?*; **to ~ into action** entrar en acción; **to ~ open/shut** abrirse/cerrarse de golpe; **to ~ to one's feet** levantarse de un salto; **a number of examples ~ to mind** se me vienen a la mente *or* se me ocurren varios ejemplos
2 (= *originate*) **the idea sprang from a TV programme he saw** la idea surgió de un programa de televisión que vio; **to ~ into existence** surgir de la noche a la mañana, aparecer repentinamente
Ⓓ CPD [*flowers, weather*] primaveral, de primavera ➤ **spring break** (*US Educ*) vacaciones *fpl* de Semana Santa ➤ **spring chicken** ✦ IDIOM **she's no ~ chicken*** no es ninguna niña ➤ **spring onion** (*Brit*) cebolleta *f*, cebollino *m* ➤ **spring roll** rollito *m* de primavera ➤ **spring tide** marea *f* viva ➤ **spring water** agua *f* de manantial

> Use **el/un** not **la/una** before feminine nouns beginning with stressed **a** or **ha** like **agua**.

➤ **spring up** VI + ADV **1** [*building, settlement*] surgir; [*plant, weeds*] brotar **2** [*person*] (*from chair*) levantarse de un salto
springboard ['sprɪŋbɔːd] N trampolín *m*; (*fig*) plataforma *f* de lanzamiento
spring-clean [ˌsprɪŋ'kliːn] VT limpiar completamente
spring-cleaning [ˌsprɪŋ'kliːnɪŋ] N limpieza *f* general; **to do the ~** limpiar toda la casa
spring-loaded [ˌsprɪŋ'ləʊdɪd] ADJ con resorte
springtime ['sprɪŋtaɪm] N primavera *f*
springy ['sprɪŋɪ] ADJ (*compar* **springier**; *superl* **springiest**) [*mattress, carpet, turf*] mullido; [*rubber*] elástico; [*step*] ligero
sprinkle ['sprɪŋkl] VT rociar (**with water** de agua); **to ~ sugar over a cake** ◇ **~ a cake with sugar** espolvorear un bizcocho con azúcar; **they are ~d about here and there** están esparcidos aquí y allá
sprinkler ['sprɪŋklər] **Ⓐ** N **1** (*for lawn*) aspersor *m*; (*Agr*) rociadera *f*, aparato *m* de lluvia artificial **2** (= *fire safety device*) aparato *m* de rociadura automática **Ⓑ** CPD ➤ **sprinkler system** (*Agr*) sistema *m* de regadío por aspersión
sprinkling ['sprɪŋklɪŋ] N **a ~ of rain** unas gotitas de lluvia; **there was a ~ of young people** había unos cuantos jóvenes
sprint [sprɪnt] **Ⓐ** N (*in race*) sprint *m*, esprint *m*; (= *dash*) carrera *f* sprint; **the women's 100 metres ~** los 100 metros lisos femeninos **Ⓑ** VI (*in race*) sprintar, esprintar; (= *dash*) correr a toda velocidad; **he ~ed for the bus** corrió tras el autobús
sprinter ['sprɪntər] N velocista *mf*, (e)sprínter *mf*
spritzer ['sprɪtsər] N vino *m* blanco con soda
sprocket ['sprɒkɪt] N rueda *f* de espigas
sprog* * [sprɒg] N (*Brit*) rorro* *m*, bebé *m*
sprout [spraʊt] **Ⓐ** N **1** (*from bulb, seeds*) brote *m*, retoño *m* **2** (*also* **Brussels ~**) col *f* de Bruselas **Ⓑ** VT **to ~ new leaves** echar hojas nuevas **Ⓒ** VI (= *bud*) brotar, retoñar, echar retoños; (= *grow quickly*) crecer rápidamente; **skyscrapers are ~ing up** se están levantando rascacielos por todos lados
spruce¹ [spruːs] N (= *tree*) pícea *f*
spruce² [spruːs] ADJ (= *neat*) pulcro
➤ **spruce up** VT + ADV arreglar; **to ~ o.s. up** arreglarse; **all ~d up** muy acicalado
sprung [sprʌŋ] **Ⓐ** PP *of* **spring** **Ⓑ** ADJ de muelles
spry [spraɪ] ADJ ágil, activo
spud* [spʌd] N patata *f*, papa *f* (*LAm*)
spun [spʌn] **Ⓐ** PT, PP *of* **spin** **Ⓑ** ADJ [*silk*] hilado

spunk [spʌŋk] N **1** (**) (= *spirit*) ánimo *m*, valor *m*, agallas* *fpl* **2** (***) (= *sperm*) leche*** *f*
spunky* * ['spʌŋkɪ] ADJ (*compar* **spunkier**; *superl* **spunkiest**) valiente, arrojado
spur [spɜːr] **Ⓐ** N (*on boot*) espuela *f*; [*of cock, mountain, hill*] espolón *m*; ✦ IDIOMS **on the ~ of the moment** sin pensar; **it was a ~ of the moment decision** fue una decisión tomada al instante; **to win one's ~s** pasar pruebas **Ⓑ** VT (*also* **~ on**) [+ *horse*] espolear, picar con las espuelas; **to ~ sb (on) to do sth** incitar a algn a hacer algo; **this ~red him on to greater efforts** esto lo animó a hacer mayores esfuerzos; **~red on by greed** bajo el aguijón de la codicia
spurious ['spjʊərɪəs] ADJ falso, espurio
spurn [spɜːn] VT desdeñar, rechazar
spurt [spɜːt] **Ⓐ** N **1** [*of water, blood*] chorro *m*, borbotón *m* **2** [*of energy*] **to put on a ~** hacer un gran esfuerzo; **final ~** esfuerzo *m* final (*para ganar una carrera*) **Ⓑ** VI (*also* **~ out**) salir a chorros, borbotar, chorrear **Ⓒ** VT hacer salir a chorros, arrojar un chorro de
sputter ['spʌtər] = **splutter**
spy [spaɪ] **Ⓐ** N espía *mf* **Ⓑ** VT (= *catch sight of*) divisar; **to play I ~** jugar al veo-veo **Ⓒ** VI espiar, ser espía; **to ~ on sb** espiar a algn, observar a algn clandestinamente **Ⓓ** CPD ➤ **spy plane** avión *m* espía ➤ **spy ring** red *f* de espionaje ➤ **spy satellite** satélite *m* espía ➤ **spy story** novela *f* de espionaje
spying ['spaɪɪŋ] N espionaje *m*
Sq. ABBR (*in address*) = **square**
sq. ABBR (*Math*) = **square**
squabble ['skwɒbl] **Ⓐ** N riña *f*, pelea *f*, pleito *m* (*esp LAm*) **Ⓑ** VI reñir, pelearse (**over, about** por, sobre)
squabbling ['skwɒblɪŋ] N riñas *fpl*, peleas *fpl*, pleitos *mpl* (*esp LAm*)
squad [skwɒd] N (*Mil*) pelotón *m*; [*of police*] brigada *f*; [*of workmen*] cuadrilla *f*; [*of players*] equipo *m* ➤ **squad car** (*US*) coche-patrulla *m*
squadron ['skwɒdrən] N (*Mil*) escuadrón *m*; (*Aer*) escuadrilla *f*, escuadrón *m*; (*Naut*) escuadra *f* ➤ **squadron leader** (*Brit*) comandante *m* (de aviación)
squalid ['skwɒlɪd] ADJ [*boarding house, conditions*] miserable; [*affair*] asqueroso; [*motive*] vil
squall [skwɔːl] N (= *wind*) ráfaga *f*; (= *rain*) chubasco *m*
squalor ['skwɒlər] N miseria *f*, vileza *f*; **to live in ~** vivir en la miseria, vivir en la sordidez
squander ['skwɒndər] VT [+ *money*] derrochar, despilfarrar; [+ *opportunity*] desperdiciar; [+ *time, resources*] emplear mal
square [skweər] **Ⓐ** N **1** (= *shape*) cuadrado *m*, cuadro *m*; (*on graph paper, chessboard*) casilla *f*; [*of material, paper*] cuadrado *m*; **to cut into ~s** cortar en cuadros *or* cuadrados; ✦ IDIOM **to go back to ~ one*** volver a empezar desde cero **2** (*in town*) plaza *f*; **the town ~** la plaza del pueblo **3** (*Math*) cuadrado *m* **4** (*) **he's a real ~** es un carca *or* (*Sp*) un carroza *or* (*Chi*) un momio*
Ⓑ ADJ **1** (*in shape*) cuadrado; ✦ IDIOM **to be a ~ peg in a round hole** estar como un pulpo en un garaje **2** (*forming right angle*) en ángulo recto, en escuadra **3** (*Math*) cuadrado; **a ~ kilometre** un kilómetro cuadrado; **a kilometre ~** un kilómetro por un kilómetro **4** (= *substantial*) [*meal*] decente, como Dios manda **5** (= *fair*) justo, equitativo; **to give sb a ~ deal** ser justo con algn **6** (= *even*) **now we're all ~** (*Sport*) ahora vamos iguales *or* (*LAm*) parejos, ahora estamos empatados; (*financially*) ahora estamos en paz; **to get ~ with sb** ajustar las cuentas con algn **7** (*) (= *conventional*) anticuado*, carca*, carroza (*Sp*)
Ⓒ ADV **in the middle** justo en el centro, justo en el medio; **to look sb ~ in the eye** mirar a algn directamente a los ojos; **the blow caught him ~ on the chin** el golpe le dio en plena barbilla *or* de lleno en la barbilla
Ⓓ VT **1** (= *make square*) cuadrar; **to ~ one's shoulders** ponerse derecho

2 (= *settle*) [+ *accounts*] ajustar; [+ *debts*] pagar; **I'll ~ it with him*** yo lo arreglo con él
3 (*Math*) elevar al cuadrado
E VI cuadrar (**with** con)
F CPD ➤ **square brackets** corchetes *mpl* ➤ **square dance** cuadrilla *f* (*baile*) ➤ **the Square Mile** (*in London*) zona de alta concentración de entidades financieras ➤ **square root** raíz *f* cuadrada
➤ **square up** VI + ADV **to ~ up with sb** ajustar cuentas con algn

squarely ['skwɛəlɪ] ADV **1** (= *directly*) directamente; **responsibility rests ~ with the President** la responsabilidad recae directamente sobre el presidente; **to look sb ~ in the eye** mirar a algn directamente a los ojos; **it caught him ~ on the chin** le dio en plena barbilla *or* de lleno en la barbilla **2** (= *honestly, fairly*) justamente

squash¹ [skwɒʃ] **A** N **1** (*Brit*) (= *drink*) **orange ~** naranjada *f* (*sin burbujas*)
2 (*Brit*) (= *crowd*) apiñamiento *m*, agolpamiento *m*; **there was such a ~ in the doorway** había tantísima gente apiñada en la puerta, se apiñaba tanto la gente en la puerta
B VT **1** (= *flatten*) aplastar; **you're ~ing me** me estás aplastando; **to ~ sth** meter algo a la fuerza; **can you ~ two more in the car?** ¿caben dos más en el coche?; **to be ~ed together** ir apretujados
2 [+ *argument*] dar al traste con; [+ *person*] apabullar
C VI **to ~ in** entrar con dificultad; **to ~ up** arrimarse

squash² [skwɒʃ] N (= *vegetable*) calabaza *f*

squash³ [skwɒʃ] N (= *sport*) squash *m* ➤ **squash court** cancha *f* de squash ➤ **squash racket** raqueta *f* de squash

squashy ['skwɒʃɪ] ADJ (*compar* **squashier**; *superl* **squashiest**) blando y algo líquido, muelle y húmedo

squat [skwɒt] **A** ADJ [*person*] rechoncho, achaparrado; [*building*] desproporcionadamente bajo **B** VI **1** (*also ~ down*) agacharse, sentarse en cuclillas **2** (*on property*) ocupar un inmueble ilegalmente **C** N *piso etc ocupado ilegalmente*

squatter ['skwɒtə'] N ocupante *mf* ilegal, okupa *mf* (*Sp*)

squaw [skwɔː] N india *f*, piel roja *f*

squawk [skwɔːk] **A** N graznido *m*, chillido *m* **B** VI graznar, chillar

squeak [skwiːk] **A** N [*of hinge, wheel*] chirrido *m*; [*of mouse, person*] chillido *m*; [*of shoe*] crujido *m*; [*of pen*] raspeo *m*; **I don't want to hear another ~ out of you** y no vuelvas a abrir la boca, y sin rechistar; **✦** IDIOM **to have a narrow ~** escaparse por los pelos **B** VI [*hinge, wheel*] chirriar, rechinar; [*mouse*] chillar; [*shoes*] crujir; [*pen*] raspear **C** VT chillar

squeaky ['skwiːkɪ] ADJ (*compar* **squeakier**; *superl* **squeakiest**) [*hinge, door*] chirriante; [*voice*] chillón; [*shoes*] crujiente; **~ clean** relimpio; (*fig*) perfectamente honrado

squeal [skwiːl] **A** N chillido *m*; **a ~ of tyres** un chillido de ruedas **B** VI **1** [*person, animal*] chillar; [*brakes, tyres*] chirriar **2** (**) (= *inform*) cantar, soplar

squeamish ['skwiːmɪʃ] ADJ **I'm ~ about having needles stuck in me** me da aprensión que me claven agujas; **don't be so ~** no seas tan delicado *or* tiquismiquis

squeegee ['skwiːdʒiː] N enjugador *m*

squeeze [skwiːz] **A** N **1** (= *handclasp*) apretón *m*; (= *hug*) estrujón *m*; **to give sth a ~** apretar algo
2 (= *crush*) **it was a tight ~ in the bus** íbamos muy apretados en el autobús; **it was a tight ~ to get through** había muy poco espacio para pasar
3 (= *restriction*) restricciones *fpl*; **small businesses are feeling the ~** las restricciones están afectando sobre todo a la pequeña empresa
4 (= *small amount*) [*of liquid*] chorrito *m*; [*of toothpaste*] poquito *m*, pizca *f*; **a ~ of lemon** un chorrito de zumo de limón, unas gotas de limón
5 (*) (= *difficult situation*) aprieto *m*; **to be in a (tight) ~** encontrarse en un aprieto
B VT **1** [+ *pimple, tube, trigger*] apretar; [+ *lemon, orange*]

exprimir; **freshly ~d orange juice** zumo *m* de naranjas recién exprimidas; **I ~d her tightly** la estreché entre mis brazos; **to ~ sb's hand** apretar la mano a algn; **to ~ money/information out of sb** sacar dinero/información a algn
2 (= *cram, fit*) meter; **can you ~ two more in?** ¿puedes hacer hueco para dos más?, ¿puedes meter a dos más?; **I could ~ you in on Thursday** le podría hacer un hueco para el jueves; **she ~d herself into the dress** se enfundó el vestido
C VI **they all ~d into the car** se metieron todos apretujados en el coche; **he ~d past me** me pasó rozando; **to ~ through a hole** pasar por un agujero con dificultad

squelch [skwɛltʃ] VI chapotear; **to ~ through the mud** ir chapoteando por el lodo

squib [skwɪb] N buscapiés *m inv*

squid [skwɪd] N (*pl* ~) calamar *m*, sepia *f*

squiggle ['skwɪgl] N garabato *m*

squiggly ['skwɪglɪ] ADJ garrapatoso

squint [skwɪnt] **A** N **1** (= *eye condition*) estrabismo *m*; **to have a ~** tener estrabismo, ser bizco **2** (= *sidelong look*) mirada *f* de soslayo, mirada *f* de reojo; **let's have a ~*** déjame ver **B** VI **1** (*Med*) bizquear, ser bizco **2 to ~ at sth** (*quickly*) echar un vistazo a algo; (*with half-closed eyes*) mirar algo con los ojos entreabiertos; **he ~ed in the sunlight** entrecerró los ojos por el sol

squire ['skwaɪə'] N (*esp Brit†*) (= *landowner*) terrateniente *m*, hacendado *m* (*LAm*), estanciero *m* (*LAm*); **the ~** (*in relation to villagers etc*) el señor; **yes, ~!** (*Brit**) ¡sí, jefe!

squirm [skwɜːm] VI retorcerse; **to ~ with embarrassment** estar violento, avergonzarse mucho

squirrel ['skwɪrəl] N ardilla *f*

squirt [skwɜːt] **A** N **1** (= *jet, spray*) chorro *m* **2** (*) (= *person*) farolero/a *m/f*, presumido/a *m/f* **B** VT [+ *liquid*] lanzar; [+ *person, car*] mojar; **to ~ water at sb** lanzar un chorro de agua hacia algn **C** VI **to ~ out** salir a chorros; **the water ~ed into my eyes** salió un chorro de agua que me dio en los ojos

Sr ABBR = **Senior**

Sri Lanka [ˌsriːˈlæŋkə] N Sri Lanka *m*

Sri Lankan [ˌsriːˈlæŋkən] **A** ADJ de Sri Lanka **B** N nativo/a *m/f* de Sri Lanka, habitante *mf* de Sri Lanka

SRN N ABBR (*Brit*) (*formerly*) = **State Registered Nurse**

SS ABBR (*Brit*) = **steamship**

SSSI N ABBR = **Site of Special Scientific Interest**

St ABBR **1** (= **Saint**) Sto., Sta., S. **2** (= **Street**) C/

stab [stæb] **A** N (*with knife*) puñalada *f*, navajazo *m*; **a ~ of pain** una punzada de dolor; **✦** IDIOMS **~ in the back** puñalada *f* por la espalda, puñalada *f* encubierta; **to have a ~ at sth** intentar hacer algo
B VT apuñalar, dar una puñalada a; **to ~ sb in the back** apuñalar a algn por la espalda; (*fig*) clavar a algn un puñal por la espalda; **to ~ sb to death** matar a algn a puñaladas **C** VI **to ~ at sb** tratar de apuñalar a algn; **he ~bed at the picture with his finger** señaló el cuadro con un movimiento brusco del dedo
D CPD ➤ **stab wound** puñalada *f*

stabbing ['stæbɪŋ] **A** N apuñalamiento *m* **B** ADJ [*pain, ache*] punzante

stability [stəˈbɪlɪtɪ] N estabilidad *f*

stabilization [ˌsteɪbəlaɪˈzeɪʃən] N estabilización *f*

stabilize ['steɪbəlaɪz] **A** VT estabilizar **B** VI estabilizarse

stabilizer ['steɪbəlaɪzə'] N **1** (*on bike*) estabilizador *m* **2** (*Culin*) estabilizante *m*

stable¹ ['steɪbl] ADJ (*compar* **~r**; *superl* **~st**) estable; (*Med*) [*condition*] estacionario; (*Psych*) [*person, character*] equilibrado; **that ladder's not very ~** esa escalera no está muy firme

stable² ['steɪbl] **A** N cuadra *f*; **✦** IDIOM **to shut** *or* **close the ~ door after the horse has bolted** a buenas horas, mangas verdes **B** VT (= *put in stable*) poner en una cuadra

staccato [stəˈkɑːtəʊ] ADV, ADJ staccato

stack [stæk] **A** N 1 (= *pile*) montón *m*, pila *f* 2 **stacks of*** (= *lots of*) un montón* *or* una gran cantidad de; **we've got ~s of time** nos sobra tiempo **B** VT (= *pile up*) amontonar, apilar; ♦ IDIOM **the cards are ~ed against us** todo va en contra nuestra

stadium ['steɪdɪəm] N estadio *m*

staff [stɑːf] **A** N 1 (= *personnel*) personal *m*, empleados *mpl*; **the teaching ~** el cuerpo docente, el profesorado; **to be on the ~** ser parte del personal, estar en plantilla (*Sp*); **to join the ~** entrar a formar parte del personal, entrar en plantilla (*Sp*) 2 (= *stick*) bastón *m*, vara *f* 3 (*esp US Mus*) pentagrama *m* **B** VT proveer de personal; **to be fully ~ed** tener el personal completo *or* (*Sp*) la plantilla completa; **the centre is ~ed by qualified lawyers** el centro cuenta con abogados titulados **C** CPD ➤ **staff meeting** reunión *f* de personal ➤ **staff nurse** (*Brit*) enfermero/a *m/f* titulado/a ➤ **staff room** sala *f* de profesores ➤ **staff training** formación *f* de personal

staff-student ratio [ˌstɑːfˌstjuːdənt'reɪʃɪəʊ] N proporción *f* alumno-profesor

stag [stæg] N (= *deer*) ciervo *m*, venado *m* ➤ **stag night** despedida *f* de soltero

stage [steɪdʒ] **A** N 1 (= *platform*) tablado *m*; (*in conference hall*) estrado *m* 2 (*Theat*) escenario *m*; **to go on ~** salir a escena *or* al escenario; **the ~** (*as profession*) el teatro; **to go on the ~** hacerse actor/actriz; ♦ IDIOM **to set the ~ for sth** crear el marco idóneo para algo 3 (= *step*) (*in process*) etapa *f*, fase *f*; **at this ~ in the negotiations** en esta etapa *or* a estas alturas de las negociaciones; **at a later ~** más adelante; **in its early ~s** en su fase *or* etapa inicial; **to go through a difficult ~** pasar por una etapa difícil; **it's just a ~ he's going through** no es más que una fase que está atravesando; **in ~s** por etapas; **in** *or* **by easy ~s** en etapas *or* fases cortas **B** VT [+ *play*] representar, poner en escena; [+ *concert*] organizar, montar; [+ *protest*] organizar; [+ *demonstration, strike*] hacer; [+ *attack*] lanzar; [+ *comeback*] preparar; **that was no accident, it was ~d** eso no fue ningún accidente, estaba montado *or* organizado **C** CPD ➤ **stage door** entrada *f* de artistas ➤ **stage fright** miedo *m* a las tablas *or* al escenario, miedo *m* escénico; **to get ~ fright** ponerse nervioso al salir a las tablas *or* al escenario ➤ **stage manager** director(a) *m/f* de escena ➤ **stage name** nombre *m* artístico ➤ **stage whisper** aparte *m*

stagecoach ['steɪdʒkəʊtʃ] N diligencia *f*

stagehand ['steɪdʒhænd] N tramoyista *mf*, sacasillas *m*

stage-manage ['steɪdʒˌmænɪdʒ] VT [+ *play, production*] dirigir; (*fig*) [+ *event, confrontation etc*] orquestar

stagestruck ['steɪdʒstrʌk] ADJ enamorado del teatro, fascinado por el teatro

stagger ['stægəʳ] **A** N tambaleo *m* **B** VI tambalear; **he ~ed to the door** fue tambaleándose hasta la puerta; **he was ~ing about** iba tambaleándose **C** VT 1 (= *amaze*) dejar anonadado, dejar pasmado; **we were ~ed by the number of letters we received** nos dejó anonadados *or* pasmados la cantidad de cartas que recibimos 2 [+ *hours, holidays, payments*] escalonar

staggering ['stægərɪŋ] ADJ (= *astonishing*) asombroso, pasmoso

stagnant ['stægnənt] ADJ estancado

stagnate [stæg'neɪt] VI estancarse

stagnation [stæg'neɪʃən] N estancamiento *m*

staid [steɪd] ADJ [*person*] serio; [*clothes*] sobrio, serio

stain [steɪn] **A** N (= *mark*) mancha *f*; **without a ~ on one's character** sin una sola mancha en la reputación **B** VT (= *mark*) manchar; (= *dye*) teñir, colorar; **~ed with blood** manchado de sangre **C** VI manchar **D** CPD ➤ **stain remover** quitamanchas *m inv*

stained glass [ˌsteɪnd'glɑːs] N vidrio *m* de color

stained-glass window [ˌsteɪndˌglɑːs'wɪndəʊ] N vidriera *f*

(de colores)

stainless steel [ˌsteɪnlɪs'stiːl] N acero *m* inoxidable

stair [stɛəʳ] N (= *single step*) escalón *m*, peldaño *m*; (*also ~s*) escalera *f* ➤ **stair lift** (plataforma *f*) salvaescaleras *m inv*

staircase ['stɛəkeɪs], **stairway** ['stɛəweɪ] N escalera *f*

stairwell ['stɛəwel] N hueco *m or* caja *f* de la escalera

stake [steɪk] **A** N 1 (= *bet*) apuesta *f*; **the company's reputation is at ~** la reputación de la empresa está en juego; **he has got a lot at ~** ◇ **there is a lot at ~ for him** es mucho lo que se está jugando; **the ~s are high** (*fig*) es mucho lo que está en juego, hay mucho en juego; **to raise the ~s** (*Gambling*) subir la apuesta 2 (= *interest*) (*Fin*) participación *f*; **he bought a 12 per cent ~ in the company** compró un 12 por ciento de participación en la compañía; **every employee has a ~ in the success of the firm** a todos los empleados les interesa que la empresa sea un éxito 3 (= *post*) poste *m*; (*for plant*) rodrigón *m*; **to be burned at the ~** morir en la hoguera 4 **stakes: he is still in front in the popularity ~s** sigue siendo el más popular de todos **B** VT 1 (= *bet*) [+ *money, jewels*] jugarse, apostar; [+ *one's reputation, life*] jugarse 2 ♦ IDIOM **to ~ one's claim to sth** reivindicar algo, reclamar algo 3 (*also ~ up*) [+ *plants*] arrodrigar ➤ **stake out** VT + ADV 1 [+ *piece of land, path, line*] marcar *or* señalar con estacas; **you have to ~ out your place on the beach early** tienes que ir temprano para poder pillar sitio en la playa 2 [+ *house*] [*journalist, criminal*] vigilar; [*police*] poner bajo vigilancia, mantener vigilado

stakeout ['steɪkaʊt] N operación *f* de vigilancia

stalactite ['stæləktaɪt] N estalactita *f*

stalagmite ['stæləgmaɪt] N estalagmita *f*

stale [steɪl] ADJ (*compar* **~r**; *superl* **~st**) 1 [*cheese, sweat, cigarette smoke*] rancio; [*breath*] maloliente; [*air*] viciado; [*biscuit, beer*] pasado; [*cake*] seco; [*bread*] correoso; **to go ~** [*biscuit, beer*] pasarse; [*cake*] secarse; [*bread*] ponerse correoso 2 [*news, joke*] viejo; [*idea*] marchito; **to become ~** [*person, relationship*] estancarse, anquilosarse

stalemate ['steɪlmeɪt] N (*Chess*) ahogado *m*; **there is ~ between the two powers** las relaciones entre las dos potencias están en un punto muerto; **to reach ~** estancarse

stalk¹ [stɔːk] **A** VT [+ *animal*] [*hunter*] cazar al acecho; [*animal*] acechar; [+ *suspect*] seguir los pasos de **B** VI **to ~ off** irse con paso airado; **she ~ed out of the room** salió airada del cuarto

stalk² [stɔːk] N [*of plant*] tallo *m*, caña *f*; [*of cabbage*] troncho *m*; [*of apple, tomato, strawberry*] rabillo *m*

stalker ['stɔːkəʳ] N *persona que está obsesionada con otra y la acosa constantemente con llamadas telefónicas o siguiéndola a todas partes*

stall [stɔːl] **A** N 1 (= *stable*) establo *m*; (= *manger*) pesebre *m*; (*for single horse etc*) casilla *f* 2 (*in market*) puesto *m*; (*in fair*) caseta *f*, casilla *f* 3 (*Brit Theat*) **the ~s** el patio de butacas **B** VT 1 [+ *car, plane*] parar, calar 2 [+ *person*] entretener **C** VI 1 [*car*] pararse; [*plane*] perder velocidad 2 (= *delay*) andar con rodeos, esquivar

stallholder ['stɔːlˌhəʊldəʳ] N dueño/a *m/f* de un puesto, puestero/a *m/f* (*LAm*)

stallion ['stælɪən] N semental *m*, padrillo *m* (*LAm*)

stalwart ['stɔːlwət] **A** ADJ [*person*] (*in spirit*) fuerte, robusto; (*in build*) fornido, robusto; [*supporter, opponent*] leal, fiel; [*belief*] empedernido **B** N partidario/a *m/f* incondicional

stamen ['steɪmen] N estambre *m*

stamina ['stæmɪnə] N resistencia *f*, aguante *m*

stammer ['stæməʳ] **A** N tartamudeo *m*; **to have a ~** tartamudear **B** VI tartamudear **C** VT decir tartamudeando

stamp [stæmp] **Ⓐ** N **1** (= *postage stamp*) sello *m*, estampilla *f* (*LAm*)
2 (= *rubber stamp*) estampilla *f*; (*for metal*) cuño *m*
3 (= *mark*) sello *m*; **it bears the ~ of genius** tiene el sello del genio
4 (*with foot*) **with a ~ of her foot** dando un taconazo **Ⓑ** VT **1 to ~ one's foot** patear, patalear; (*in dancing*) zapatear
2 [+ *letter*] sellar, poner el sello a
3 (= *mark with rubber stamp*) marcar con sello; (= *emboss*) grabar; [+ *passport*] sellar
4 (= *impress mark etc on*) estampar, imprimir; [+ *coin, design*] estampar; **to ~ sth on one's memory** grabar algo en la memoria de uno **Ⓒ** VI patear, patalear; **to ~ on sth** pisotear algo, hollar algo; **ouch, you ~ed on my foot!** ¡ay, me has pisado el pie!; **to ~ in/out** entrar/salir dando fuertes zancadas **Ⓓ** CPD ➤ **stamp album** álbum *m* de sellos ➤ **stamp collecting** filatelia *f* ➤ **stamp collection** colección *f* de sellos ➤ **stamp collector** filatelista *mf* ➤ **stamp duty** (*Brit*) impuesto *m or* derecho *m* del timbre
➤ **stamp out** VT + ADV [+ *rhythm*] marcar con los pies; [+ *fire, cigarette*] apagar con el pie; [+ *crime, corruption*] erradicar, acabar con; [+ *rebellion*] sofocar; [+ *epidemic*] erradicar

stamped addressed envelope
[ˌstæmptəˌdrestˈenvələʊp] N (*Brit*) sobre *m* franqueado con las señas de una persona

stampede [stæmˈpiːd] **Ⓐ** N estampida *f*, desbandada *f*; **there was a sudden ~ for the door** todo el mundo corrió en estampida hacia la puerta **Ⓑ** VT [+ *cattle*] provocar la estampida *or* desbandada de **Ⓒ** VI (*lit*) ir en estampida *or* desbandada; (*fig*) precipitarse

stamping-ground* [ˈstæmpɪŋˌɡraʊnd] N territorio *m*

stance [stæns] N **1** (*lit*) postura *f* **2** (*fig*) actitud *f*, postura *f*; **to take up a ~** adoptar una actitud *or* postura

stand [stænd] (*vb: pt, pp* **stood**) **Ⓐ** N **1** (= *stance*) actitud *f*, postura *f*; **to take a ~ on an issue** adoptar una actitud hacia una cuestión; **✦** IDIOM **to make a ~** hacer parada, plantarse
2 (*for taxis*) parada *f* (de taxis)
3 (= *lamp stand*) pie *m*; (= *music stand*) atril *m*
4 (= *newspaper stand*) quiosco *m*, puesto *m* (*esp LAm*); (= *market stall*) puesto *m*; (*in shop*) estante *m*, puesto *m*; (*at exhibition*) caseta *f*, stand *m*; (= *bandstand*) quiosco *m*
5 (= *seating area*) tribuna *f*; **I've got a ticket for the ~s** tengo una entrada de tribuna
6 (*Jur*) estrado *m*; **to take the ~** (*esp US*) (= *go into witness box*) subir a la tribuna de los testigos; (= *give evidence*) prestar declaración **Ⓑ** VT **1** (= *place*) poner, colocar; **to ~ sth against the wall** apoyar algo en la pared
2 (= *withstand*) resistir; **it won't ~ serious examination** no resistirá un examen detallado; **his heart couldn't ~ the shock** su corazón no resistió el *or* al choque; **✦** IDIOM **to ~ one's ground** mantenerse firme, plantarse
3 (= *tolerate*) aguantar; **I can't ~ it any longer!** ¡no aguanto más!; **I can't ~ Debussy** no aguanto a Debussy; **I can't ~ (the sight of) him** no lo aguanto, no lo puedo tragar; **I can't ~ waiting for people** no aguanto *or* soporto que me hagan esperar
4 (*Brit**) (= *pay for*) **to ~ sb a drink/meal** invitar a algn a una copa/a comer **Ⓒ** VI **1** (= *be upright*) estar de pie *or* derecho, estar parado (*LAm*); **he could hardly ~** hasta tenía problemas para ponerse de pie; **the house is still ~ing** la casa sigue en pie; **✦** IDIOM **to ~ on one's own two feet** valerse por sí mismo, defenderse solo (*LAm*)
2 (= *get up*) levantarse, pararse (*LAm*); **all ~!** ¡levántense!
3 (= *stay*) **to ~ in the doorway** estar en la puerta; **don't just ~ there, do something!** ¡no te quedes ahí parado, haz algo!; **✦** IDIOM **he left the others ~ing** dejó a todos atrás *or* (*LAm*) parados
4 (= *tread*) **to ~ on sth** pisar algo; **you're ~ing on my foot** me estás pisando
5 (= *measure*) medir; **he ~s a good six feet** mide seis pies largos; **the tower ~s 50m high** la torre tiene 50m de alta
6 (= *have reached*) **the thermometer ~s at 40°** el termómetro marca 40 grados; **the record ~s at ten minutes** el record está en diez minutos, el tiempo récord sigue siendo de

diez minutos; **sales are currently ~ing at two million** las ventas ya han alcanzado los dos millones
7 (= *be situated*) encontrarse, ubicarse (*LAm*); **it ~s beside the town hall** está junto al ayuntamiento
8 (= *be mounted, based*) apoyarse
9 (= *remain valid*) [*offer, argument, decision*] seguir en pie *or* vigente; **the theory ~s or falls on this** de allí depende la teoría entera
10 (= *be placed*) **as things ~** tal como están las cosas; **I'd like to know where I ~** quisiera saber a qué atenerme; **how do we ~?** ¿cómo estamos?; **nothing ~s between you and success** no tienes ningún obstáculo en el camino al éxito
11 (= *be in a position*) **he ~s to gain a great deal** tiene la posibilidad de ganar mucho; **what do we ~ to gain by it?** ¿qué posibilidades hay para nosotros de ganar algo?, ¿qué ventaja nos daría esto?; **we ~ to lose a lot** para nosotros supondría una pérdida importante, estamos en peligro de perder bastante
12 (= *be*) **to ~ accused of murder** estar acusado de asesinato; **it ~s to reason that ...** es evidente que ..., no cabe duda de que ...
13 (= *remain undisturbed*) estar; **to allow a liquid to ~** dejar estar un líquido; **let it ~ for three days** déjelo reposar durante tres días
14 (*Brit Pol*) presentarse (como candidato); **to ~ against sb in an election** presentarse como oponente a algn en unas elecciones; **to ~ for Parliament/president** presentarse como candidato a diputado/a la presidencia
➤ **stand around** VI + ADV estar, esperar, seguir en un sitio sin propósito fijo
➤ **stand aside** VI + ADV apartarse, mantenerse al margen
➤ **stand back** VI + ADV **1** [*person*] retirarse; (*fig*) tomar una posición más objetiva **2** [*building*] estar apartado (**from** de)
➤ **stand by Ⓐ** VI + ADV **1** (= *do nothing*) mantenerse aparte **2** (= *be ready*) estar preparado *or* listo; **~ by for further news** seguirán más noticias; **the Navy is ~ing by to help** unidades de la Flota están listas para prestar ayuda **Ⓑ** VI + PREP [+ *person*] apoyar *or* respaldar a; [+ *promise*] cumplir con; [+ *decision*] mantener; **we ~ by what we said** nos atenemos a lo dicho
➤ **stand down** VI + ADV [*official, chairman*] dimitir; [*candidate, witness*] retirarse
➤ **stand for** VI + PREP **1** (= *represent*) [*abbreviation*] significar; **MP ~s for Member of Parliament** MP significa Miembro del Parlamento **2** (= *support*) [+ *principle, honesty*] representar **3** (= *permit*) permitir; (= *tolerate*) admitir; **I won't ~ for that** eso no lo admito
➤ **stand in** VI + ADV sustituir; **to ~ in for sb** sustituir a algn
➤ **stand off** VI + ADV apartarse, guardar las distancias
➤ **stand out** VI + ADV **1** (= *project*) [*ledge, vein*] sobresalir, salir **2** (= *be conspicuous*) destacar (**against** contra); **✦** IDIOM **it ~s out a mile*** se ve a la legua **3** (= *be outstanding*) destacar; **he ~s out from all the other students** destaca del resto de los alumnos **4** (= *be firm*) mantenerse firme, aferrarse; **to ~ out for sth** insistir en algo
➤ **stand up Ⓐ** VI + ADV **1** (= *rise*) levantarse, ponerse de pie; (= *be standing*) estar de pie; **✦** IDIOM **to ~ up and be counted** declararse abiertamente
2 [*argument etc*] ser sólido, ser lógico, convencer; **the case did not ~ up in court** la acusación no se mantuvo en el tribunal
3 to ~ up for sb (*fig*) respaldar a algn; **to ~ up for sth** defender algo; **to ~ up for o.s.** defenderse solo
4 to ~ up to sb hacer frente a algn; **it ~s up to hard wear** es muy resistente **Ⓑ** VT + ADV **1** (= *place upright*) colocar de pie **2** (*) [+ *girlfriend, boyfriend*] dejar plantado*, dar plantón a*

stand-alone [ˈstændələʊn] ADJ autónomo

standard [ˈstændəd] **Ⓐ** N **1** (= *measure*) estándar *m*; (= *level*) nivel *m*; (= *quality*) calidad *f*; **his ~s are high/low** sus estándares son altos/bajos, los niveles que requiere son altos/bajos; **of (a) high/low ~** de alto/bajo nivel; **the ~ of service** el nivel de servicio; **the ~ of medical care** la calidad de atención médica; **by any ~** desde cualquier punto de vista; **to be below ~** no tener la suficiente calidad; **~s of conduct** normas *fpl* de conducta; **moral ~s** valores *mpl* morales; **society sets impossible ~s for feminine beauty** la sociedad impone unos patrones de belleza femenina

imposibles; **her work was not up to** ~ su trabajo no estaba a la altura (requerida); **the product is not up to** ~ el producto no tiene la calidad requerida
2 (= *flag*) estandarte *m*, bandera *f*
3 (= *pole*) (*for flag*) poste *m*; (*for lamp*) pie *m*
B ADJ (= *normal*) [*design, length, spelling, pronunciation*] estándar *inv*; [*amount, size*] normal; [*feature*] normal, corriente; [*charge*] fijo; [*procedure, medical treatment*] habitual; [*measure*] legal; **it has become** ~ **practice for many surgeons** se ha convertido en una norma entre muchos cirujanos; **it's a** ~ **text** es un texto clásico
C CPD ➤ **standard class** clase *f* turista ➤ **standard English** inglés *m* estándar *or* normativo ➤ **Standard Grade** (*Scot Scol*) *certificado obtenido tras aprobar los exámenes al final de la educación secundaria obligatoria* ➤ **standard lamp** (*Brit*) lámpara *f* de pie ➤ **standard of living** nivel *m* de vida ➤ **standard price** precio *m* oficial ➤ **standard time** hora *f* oficial ➤ **standard weight** peso *m* legal

standardize ['stændədaɪz] VT normalizar, estandar(d)izar

stand-by ['stændbaɪ] N (= *person*) suplente *mf*; (= *spare*) repuesto *m*; (= *stand-by ticket*) billete *m* (*Sp*) *or* pasaje *m* (*LAm*) para pasajeros en lista de espera, billete *m* (*Sp*) *or* pasaje *m* (*LAm*) de stand-by; **to be on** ~ [*troops*] estar preparado para el ataque; [*doctor*] estar listo para acudir; [*passenger*] estar en lista de espera ➤ **stand-by passenger** (*Aer*) pasajero/a *m/f* de la lista de espera

stand-in ['stændɪn] N sustituto/a *m/f* (**for** por); (*Cine*) doble *mf*

standing ['stændɪŋ] **A** ADJ **1** (= *not sitting*) de pie, parado (*LAm*); (= *upright*) derecho, recto
2 (= *permanent*) [*committee, rule etc*] permanente; [*joke*] constante, eterno
B N **1** (= *social position*) rango *m*, estatus *m inv*; (= *reputation*) reputación *f*, fama *f*; **to be in good** ~ tener buena reputación; (*Fin*) gozar de buen crédito; **of high** ~ de categoría; **social** ~ posición *f* social
2 (= *duration*) duración *f*; (= *seniority*) antigüedad *f*; **of six months'** ~ que lleva seis meses; **of long** ~ de mucho tiempo (acá), viejo
3 (*US Aut*) **"no standing"** "prohibido estacionar"
C CPD ➤ **standing order** (*Brit*) (*at bank*) giro *m or* pedido *m* regular ➤ **standing ovation** ovación *f* en pie; **he got a** ~ **ovation** todos se pusieron en pie para darle una ovación ➤ **standing room** sitio *m* para estar de pie; ~ **room only** ya no quedan asientos

stand-off ['stændɒf] N (= *deadlock*) punto *m* muerto, callejón *m* sin salida; (*Sport*) empate *m*

stand-offish [ˌstænd'ɒfɪʃ] ADJ distante, reservado

standpipe ['stændpaɪp] N (*in street*) fuente *f* provisional

standpoint ['stændpɔɪnt] N punto *m* de vista

standstill ['stændstɪl] N parada *f*; **to be at a** ~ [*vehicle*] estar parado; [*industry, negotiations*] estar paralizado; **to bring to a** ~ [+ *car*] parar; [+ *industry, traffic*] paralizar; **to come to a** ~ [*person*] pararse, hacer un alto; [*vehicle*] pararse; [*industry etc*] estancarse

stand-up ['stændʌp] ADJ ~ **fight** (*lit*) pelea *f* violenta; (*fig*) altercado *m* violento; ~ **comedian** cómico/a *m/f*; ~ **comedy** comedia *f*

stank [stæŋk] PT *of* **stink**

Stanley knife® ['stænlɪˌnaɪf] N cuchilla *f* para moqueta

stanza ['stænzə] N estrofa *f*

staple¹ ['steɪpl] **A** N (= *fastener*) grapa *f*, corchete *m* (*SC*)
B VT sujetar con grapa

staple² ['steɪpl] **A** ADJ [*product*] de primera necesidad; **their** ~ **food** *or* **diet** su comida cotidiana, su alimento de primera necesidad **B** N (= *chief product*) artículo *m* de primera necesidad; (= *food*) alimento *m* de primera necesidad; (= *raw material*) materia *f* prima

stapler ['steɪplə'] N grapadora *f*

star [stɑː'] **A** N **1** (*in sky*) estrella *f*, astro *m*; (= *asterisk*) asterisco *m*; **the** ~**s** (= *horoscope*) el horóscopo; ✦ IDIOMS **to have** ~**s in one's eyes** estar ilusionado; **to see** ~**s** ver (las) estrellas; **you can thank your lucky** ~**s that** ... da gracias que ...

2 (= *famous person*) estrella *f*
B VT (*Cine etc*) presentar como estrella; **a film** ~**ring Greta Garbo** una película con Greta Garbo en el papel principal
C VI (*Cine etc*) tener el papel principal; **to** ~ **in a film** ser el/la protagonista de una película, protagonizar una película
D CPD ➤ **star attraction** atracción *f* principal ➤ **star player** estrella *f* ➤ **star prize** (*in competition*) premio *m* estrella ➤ **the Stars and Stripes** (*US*) las barras y las estrellas ➤ **star sign** signo *m* del Zodíaco

-star [stɑː'] ADJ (*ending in compounds*) **four-star hotel** hotel *m* de cuatro estrellas; **four-star (petrol)** gasolina *f* extra, súper *f*

starboard ['stɑːbɔːd] **A** N estribor *m* **B** ADJ [*lights*] de estribor; **on the** ~ **side** a estribor

starch [stɑːtʃ] **A** N (*for clothes etc*) almidón *m*; (*in food*) fécula *f* **B** VT almidonar

starchy ['stɑːtʃɪ] ADJ (*compar* **starchier**; *superl* **starchiest**) [*food*] con fécula

stardom ['stɑːdəm] N estrellato *m*; **to rise to** ~ alcanzar el estrellato

stare [steə'] **A** N mirada *f* fija; **to give sb a** ~ mirar fijamente a algn **B** VT **to** ~ **sb out** *or* **down** mirar a algn fijamente hasta que aparte la vista; ✦ IDIOM **it's staring you in the face** salta a la vista **C** VI mirar fijamente; **don't** ~**!** ¡no mires tan fijo!; **to** ~ **at sth/sb** mirar algo/a algn fijamente, mirar algo/a algn de hito en hito; **it's rude to** ~ **at people** está mal visto fijar la mirada en la gente; **to** ~ **into space** estar con la mirada perdida, mirar al vacío

starfish ['stɑːfɪʃ] N (*pl* ~ *or* ~**es**) estrella *f* de mar

stargazer ['stɑːˌgeɪzə'] N astrónomo/a *m/f*

stargazing ['stɑːˌgeɪzɪŋ] N **1** (= *astronomy*) astronomía *f* **2** (= *astrology*) astrología *f*

staring ['steərɪŋ] ADJ que mira fijamente, curioso; [*eyes*] saltón; (*in fear*) lleno de espanto

stark [stɑːk] **A** ADJ (*compar* ~**er**; *superl* ~**est**) [*simplicity, colour, beauty, décor, outline*] austero; [*conditions*] severo, duro; [*landscape*] inhóspito; [*reality, poverty*] crudo, sin adornos; [*choice, warning, reminder*] duro; [*terror, folly*] absoluto; **to be in** ~ **contrast to sth** contrastar brutalmente con algo **B** ADV ~ **raving mad*** loco de remate*; ~ **naked*** en cueros*, en pelotas**, encuerado (*LAm**), pilucho (*Chi**), calato (*Per, Bol**)

starkers** ['stɑːkəz] ADJ **to be** ~ (*Brit*) estar en cueros*, estar en pelotas**, estar encuerado (*LAm**), estar pilucho (*Chi**), estar calato (*Per, Bol**)

starkly ['stɑːklɪ] ADV **1** [*furnished*] austeramente; [*describe*] escuetamente, sucintamente **2** [*illustrate*] crudamente; [*outline*] claramente; [*stand out*] con claridad; [*different, apparent, evident*] completamente; **to contrast** ~ **with sth** contrastar brutalmente con algo

starlet ['stɑːlɪt] N (*Cine*) joven aspirante *f* a estrella

starlight ['stɑːlaɪt] N luz *f* de las estrellas; **by** ~ a la luz de las estrellas

starling ['stɑːlɪŋ] N estornino *m*

starlit ['stɑːlɪt] ADJ iluminado por las estrellas

starring role [ˌstɑːrɪŋ'rəʊl] N papel *m* estelar

starry ['stɑːrɪ] ADJ (*compar* **starrier**; *superl* **starriest**) sembrado de estrellas

starry-eyed ['stɑːrɪ'aɪd] ADJ (= *idealistic*) idealista, ingenuo; (= *in love*) sentimentaloide

star-studded ['stɑːˌstʌdɪd] ADJ [*sky*] estrellado; **a** ~ **cast** (*Cine, Theat*) un elenco *m* estelar

START [stɑːt] N ABBR = **Strategic Arms Reduction Talks**

start [stɑːt] **A** N **1** (= *beginning*) principio *m*, comienzo *m*; **at the** ~ al principio, en un principio; **at the** ~ **of the century** a principios del siglo; **for a** ~ en primer lugar, para empezar; **from the** ~ desde el principio; **from** ~ **to finish** desde el principio hasta el fin; **to get a good** ~ **in life** disfrutar de una infancia privilegiada; **to get off to a good/bad/slow** ~ empezar bien/mal/lentamente; **to make a** ~ empezar; **to make a** ~ **on the painting** empezar a pintar; **to make an early** ~ (*on journey*) ponerse en camino temprano;

(with job) empezar temprano
2 (= *departure*) salida *f* (*also Sport*)
3 (= *advantage*) ventaja *f*; **to give sb a five-minute ~** dar a algn cinco minutos de ventaja
4 (= *fright etc*) susto *m*, sobresalto *m*; **to give sb a ~** asustar *or* dar un susto a algn; **what a ~ you gave me!** ¡qué susto me diste!; **to give a sudden ~** sobresaltarse; **to wake with a ~** despertarse sobresaltado
B VT **1** (= *begin*) empezar, comenzar; [+ *discussion etc*] abrir, iniciar; [+ *bottle*] abrir; [+ *quarrel, argument*] empezar; [+ *journey*] iniciar; **don't ~ that again!** ¡no vuelvas a eso!; **to ~ doing sth** ◇ **to do sth** empezar a hacer algo; **to ~ sth again** comenzar *or* empezar algo de nuevo; **he always ~s the day with a glass of milk** lo primero que toma cada mañana es un vaso de leche; **he ~ed life as a labourer** empezó de *or* como peón; **to ~ a new life** comenzar una vida nueva; **to ~ school** empezar a ir al colegio; **he ~ed work yesterday** entró a trabajar ayer
2 (= *cause*) [+ *fire*] provocar; [+ *war*] [*person, country*] empezar, iniciar; [*incident*] desencadenar; [+ *fashion*] empezar, iniciar; [+ *rumour*] iniciar, dar comienzo a; **you ~ed it!** ¡tú diste el primer golpe!; **to ~ a family** (empezar a) tener hijos
3 to **get ~ed** empezar, ponerse en marcha; **let's get ~ed** empecemos; **to get sth ~ed** [+ *engine, car*] poner algo en marcha, arrancar algo; [+ *project*] poner algo en marcha; **to get sb ~ed** (*on activity*) poner a algn en marcha; (*in career*) iniciar a algn en su carrera; **to get ~ed on sth** empezar a hacer algo; **to get sb ~ed on sth** poner a algn a hacer algo
4 (*also* **~ up**) [+ *business*] montar, poner
5 (*also* **~ up**) [*car, engine*] arrancar, poner en marcha
C VI **1** (= *begin*) empezar, comenzar; [*conversation, discussion*] iniciarse; [*quarrel, argument*] producirse; [*fashion*] empezar, iniciar; [*war*] estallar, empezar; [*rumour, tradition*] originarse; [*fire*] empezar, iniciarse; [*music*] empezar; **that's when the trouble ~ed** entonces fue cuando empezaron los problemas; **it all ~ed when he refused to pay** todo empezó cuando se negó a pagar; **to ~ again** volver a empezar, comenzar de nuevo; **he ~ed as an office boy** empezó como chico de los recados; **to ~ at the beginning** empezar desde el principio; **he ~ed by saying ...** empezó por decir *or* diciendo ...; **~ing from Tuesday** a partir del martes; **to ~ with ...** (= *firstly*) en primer lugar ..., para empezar ...; (= *at the beginning*) al principio ..., en un principio ...; **he ~ed with the intention of ...** empezó con la intención de ...
2 (= *set out*) [*person*] partir, ponerse en camino; [*bus, train, runner*] salir; **to ~ from London/for Madrid** salir de Londres/partir con rumbo a *or* para Madrid
3 (*also* **~ up**) [*car, engine*] arrancar, ponerse en marcha
4 (= *jump nervously*) asustarse, sobresaltarse (**at** a)
➤ **start back** VI + ADV **1** (= *return*) emprender el viaje de regreso (**for** a); **it's time we ~ed back** es hora de volvernos
2 (= *recoil*) retroceder
➤ **start off** ❶ VI + ADV **1** (= *begin*) empezar; **it ~ed off well/badly** [*film, match*] empezó bien/mal; **he ~ed off by saying ...** empezó por decir *or* diciendo ...; **he ~ed off as a postman/Marxist** empezó como cartero/marxista; **to ~ off with ...** (= *firstly*) en primer lugar ..., para empezar ...; (= *at the beginning*) al principio ...; **he ~ed off with the intention of ...** empezó con la intención de ...
2 (= *set out*) [*person*] partir, ponerse en camino; [*bus, train, runner*] salir; **to ~ off from London/for Madrid** salir de Londres/partir con rumbo a *or* para Madrid; **he ~ed off down the street** empezó a caminar calle abajo
B VT + ADV **don't ~ him off on that!** ¡no le des cuerda!; **that ~ed him off sneezing** eso le hizo empezar a estornudar
➤ **start on*** VI + PREP **1** (= *scold*) regañar **2** (= *begin*) empezar; **to ~ on a book** (= *begin reading*) empezar a leer un libro; (= *begin writing*) empezar a escribir un libro; **to ~ on a task** emprender una tarea; **to ~ on something new** emprender algo nuevo
➤ **start out** VI + ADV **1** (= *begin*) empezar; **he ~ed out as a teacher/communist** empezó siendo profesor/comunista; **he ~ed out with the intention of ...** empezó con la intención de ... **2** (= *set out*) [*person*] partir, ponerse en camino; [*bus, train, runner*] salir; **to ~ out from London/for Madrid** salir de Londres/partir con rumbo a *or* para Madrid
➤ **start over** (*esp US*) ❶ VI + ADV volver a empezar **B** VT + ADV comenzar *or* empezar de nuevo

➤ **start up** ❶ VI + ADV [*car, engine*] arrancar, ponerse en marcha; **to ~ up in business** montar *or* poner un negocio **B** VT + ADV [+ *car, engine*] arrancar, poner en marcha; [+ *business*] montar, poner

starter ['stɑːtəʳ] ❶ N **1** (*Sport*) (= *judge*) juez *mf* de salida; (= *competitor*) corredor(a) *m/f*; **to be under ~'s orders** (*Horse racing*) estar listos para la salida **2** (= *button*) botón *m* de arranque; (*Aut*) (= *motor*) motor *m* de arranque **3** (*Brit*) (= *first course*) entrada *f*; **for ~s*** (*fig*) en primer lugar **B** CPD ➤ **starter home** primera vivienda *f* ➤ **starter motor** (*Aut*) motor *m* de arranque

starting ['stɑːtɪŋ] CPD ➤ **starting block** taco *m* de salida ➤ **starting gate** (*US*) cajón *m* de salida, parrilla *f* de salida ➤ **starting grid** parrilla *f* de arranque ➤ **starting line** línea *f* de salida ➤ **starting point** (*fig*) punto *m* de partida ➤ **starting post** poste *m* de salida ➤ **starting price** (*St Ex*) cotización *f* ➤ **starting salary** sueldo *m* inicial

startle ['stɑːtl] VT asustar, sobresaltar; **you ~d me!** ¡vaya susto que me has dado!

startled ['stɑːtld] ADJ [*animal*] asustado, espantado; [*person*] sorprendido; [*expression, voice*] de sobresalto, sobresaltado

startling ['stɑːtlɪŋ] ADJ [*news*] alarmante; [*discovery*] inesperado; [*appearance*] llamativo

start-up ['stɑːtʌp] ADJ [*costs, loan*] de puesta en marcha

starvation [stɑːˈveɪʃən] N hambre *f*, inanición *f*, hambruna *f* (*LAm*); (*fig*) privación *f*; **to die of ~** morir de hambre ➤ **starvation diet** régimen *m* de hambre

---

Use **el/un** not **la/una** before feminine nouns beginning with stressed **a** or **ha** like **hambre**.

---

starve [stɑːv] ❶ VT **1** (= *deprive of food*) privar de comida; **to ~ sb to death** hacer que algn muera de hambre **2** (= *deprive*) **to ~ sb of sth** privar a algn de algo; **to be ~d of affection** estar privado de afecto **B** VI pasar hambre, padecer hambre; **to ~ to death** morirse de hambre

starving ['stɑːvɪŋ] ADJ hambriento; **I'm ~!*** estoy muerto de hambre

stash* [stæʃ] ❶ N escondite *m*, alijo *m* **B** VT (*also* **~ away**) (= *hide*) esconder; (= *save up, store away*) guardar

state [steɪt] ❶ N **1** (= *condition*) estado *m*; **the ~ of affairs continues** si las cosas siguen así; **to be in a bad ~** estar en mal estado; **to be in a good ~** estar en buenas condiciones; **he's not in a fit ~ to do it** no está en condiciones para hacerlo; **he arrived home in a shocking ~** llegó a casa hecho una pena; **she was in no ~ to talk** no estaba en condiciones para hablar; **~ of mind** estado *m* de ánimo; **what's the ~ of play?** (*fig*) ¿cuál es la situación?; **~ of repair** estado *m*
2 (*) (= *poor condition*) **you should have seen the ~ the car was in** tenías que haber visto cómo estaba el coche; **just look at the ~ of this room!** ¡mira cómo está esta habitación!; **the flat was in a right ~ after the party** el piso estaba hecho un asco después de la fiesta*
3 (*) (= *agitated condition*) **to be in a ~** estar nervioso; **to get into a ~** ponerse nervioso
4 (= *region, country*) estado *m*; **the States*** (= *USA*) los Estados Unidos
5 (= *government*) **the State** el Estado
B VT [+ *intention*] declarar; [+ *views*] dar, expresar; [+ *facts, case, problem*] exponer; **he has publicly ~d that ...** ha declarado públicamente que ...; **I'm simply stating the facts** simplemente estoy exponiendo los hechos; **~ your address and telephone number** (*on form*) escriba su dirección y número de teléfono; (*orally*) diga su dirección y número de teléfono
C CPD [*policy, documents, security*] del estado; [*visit, funeral, business*] de estado; [*control*] público, estatal; [*aid, sector, subsidy*] estatal; [*tax, police*] (*in US*) del estado ➤ **state apartments** *apartamentos destinados a visitas de mandatarios* ➤ **state banquet** banquete *m* de gala ➤ **State Capitol** (*US*) *edificio donde tiene su sede el poder legislativo de un estado* ➤ **State Department** (*US*) Ministerio *m* de Asuntos Exteriores ➤ **state education** enseñanza *f* pública ➤ **state line** (*US*) frontera *f* de estado ➤ **State of the Union**

Address (*US Pol*) informe *m* sobre el estado de la nación ➤ **state pension** pensión *f* del estado, pensión *f* estatal ➤ **State Registered Nurse** (*Brit*) (*formerly*) enfermero/a *m/f* diplomado/a (*con tres años de estudios*) ➤ **State Representative** (*US Pol*) representante *mf* del estado ➤ **state school** (*Brit*) colegio *m* público, escuela *f* pública ➤ **state secret** (*lit, fig*) secreto *m* de estado ➤ **state trooper** (*US*) [*of specific state*] policía *mf* del estado

state-controlled ['steɪtkən'trəʊld] ADJ controlado por el Estado, estatal

stated ['steɪtɪd] ADJ **1** (= *indicated*) indicado, señalado; **do not exceed the ~ dose** no exceda la dosis indicada *or* señalada **2** (= *declared*) [*aim, purpose*] expresado **3** (= *fixed*) [*limit*] establecido

stateless ['steɪtlɪs] ADJ desnacionalizado, apátrida

stately ['steɪtlɪ] ADJ (*compar* **statelier**; *superl* **stateliest**) [*person, manner*] imponente; [*pace, music*] majestuoso ➤ **stately home** (*esp Brit*) casa *f* solariega

statement ['steɪtmənt] N **1** (= *declaration*) (*also Jur*) declaración *f*; **to make a ~** (*Jur*) prestar declaración; **he made a ~ to the press** hizo una declaración a la prensa; **an official ~** un comunicado oficial; **to issue a press ~** emitir un comunicado de prensa **2** (= *exposition*) [*of views, facts, problem, theory*] exposición *f* **3** (*also* **bank ~**) extracto *m* de cuenta

state-of-the-art [,steɪtəvðɪ'ɑːt] ADJ [*equipment*] de lo más moderno *or* reciente; [*technology*] de vanguardia

STATE OF THE UNION ADDRESS

Se denomina **State of the Union Address** al discurso que el presidente de Estados Unidos dirige cada mes de enero al Congreso y al pueblo estadounidense, en que muestra su visión de la nación y la economía y explica sus planes para el futuro. Como el discurso recibe una amplia cobertura informativa, el mensaje del presidente va dirigido no sólo a los parlamentarios sino a todo el país. Esta tradición de dirigirse al Congreso tras las vacaciones de Navidad se debe a que es un requisito de la Constitución que el presidente informe al Congreso de vez en cuando sobre **the State of the Union**.

state-owned [,steɪt'əʊnd] ADJ nacional, estatal

stateroom ['steɪtrʊm] N (*esp Brit*) (*in palace etc*) salón *m* de gala

stateside★ ['steɪtsaɪd] ADV (*esp US*) [*be*] en Estados Unidos; [*go*] a Estados Unidos, hacia Estados Unidos

statesman ['steɪtsmən] N (*pl* **statesmen**) estadista *m*, hombre *m* de estado

statesmanlike ['steɪtsmənlaɪk] ADJ (digno) de estadista

statesmanship ['steɪtsmənʃɪp] N habilidad *f* política, capacidad *f* para gobernar

STATES' RIGHTS

En EE.UU., **States' Rights** son los derechos de los estados (como por ejemplo la recaudación de impuestos, la aprobación de leyes o el control sobre la educación pública) frente a los del gobierno federal. En la Décima Enmienda de la Constitución se dice que los poderes que la Constitución no concede a los Estados Unidos se reservan a cada estado particular o al pueblo y este polémico principio sirvió para justificar la secesión de los estados sureños antes de la Guerra Civil y se convirtió en una consigna contra la integración racial en el sur durante los años 50. Debido a la actual falta de confianza en el gobierno federal, que acapara cada vez más poderes a costa de un aumento del gasto, este principio tiene cada vez más seguidores.

state-subsidized [,steɪt'sʌbsɪdaɪzd] ADJ subvencionado por el Estado

static ['stætɪk] **Ⓐ** ADJ estático **Ⓑ** N **1** (*Rad etc*) parásitos *mpl* **2** (*Phys*) (*also* **~s**) estática *f* **Ⓒ** CPD ➤ **static electricity** estática *f*

station ['steɪʃən] **Ⓐ** N **1** (*Rail*) estación *f* (de ferrocarril); (= *police station*) comisaría *f*; (*US*) (= *gas station*) gasolinera *f*, fuente *f*, grifo *m* (*Per*) **2** (*esp Mil*) (= *post*) puesto *m*; **to take up one's ~** colocarse, ir a su puesto **3** (*Rad*) emisora *f* **4** (= *social position*) rango *m*; **to have ideas above one's ~** darse aires de superioridad **Ⓑ** VT [+ *troops*] estacionar, apostar; (*fig*) colocar, situar **Ⓒ** CPD ➤ **station house** (*US Rail*) estación *f* de ferrocarril; (*US Police*) comisaría *f* ➤ **station master** (*Rail*) jefe *m* de estación ➤ **station wag(g)on** (*US Aut*) furgoneta *f*, camioneta *f*

stationary ['steɪʃənərɪ] ADJ (= *not moving*) inmóvil; (= *not movable*) parado, estacionario; **to remain ~** quedarse inmóvil

stationer ['steɪʃənəʳ] N papelero/a *m/f*; **~'s (shop)** papelería *f*

stationery ['steɪʃənərɪ] N artículos *mpl* de escritorio *or* de papelería

statistic [stə'tɪstɪk] N estadística *f*, número *m*

statistical [stə'tɪstɪkəl] ADJ estadístico

statistically [stə'tɪstɪkəlɪ] ADV según las estadísticas

statistician [,stætɪs'tɪʃən] N estadístico/a *m/f*

statistics [stə'tɪstɪks] **Ⓐ** NSING (= *subject*) estadística *f* **Ⓑ** NPL (= *numbers*) estadísticas *fpl*

stats★ [stæts] NPL ABBR = **statistics**

statuary ['stætjʊərɪ] N (= *art*) estatuaria *f*; (= *statues*) estatuas *fpl*

statue ['stætjuː] N estatua *f*; **the Statue of Liberty** la estatua de la libertad

statuesque [,stætjʊ'esk] ADJ escultural

statuette [,stætjʊ'et] N figurilla *f*, estatuilla *f*

stature ['stætʃəʳ] N **1** (= *size*) estatura *f*, talla *f* **2** (*fig*) rango *m*, estatus *m inv*; **he lacks moral ~** le falta carácter

status ['steɪtəs] N (*pl* **~es**) [*of person*] (*legal*) estado *m*; **marital ~** estado *m* civil; **social ~** posición *f* social, estatus *m inv*; **what is his official ~?** ¿qué rango oficial tiene?, ¿qué rango ocupa oficialmente? ➤ **status quo** (e)statu quo *m* ➤ **status report** informe *m* situacional ➤ **status symbol** símbolo *m* de rango

statute ['stætjuːt] N ley *f*, estatuto *m* ➤ **statute book** (*esp Brit*) código *m* de leyes ➤ **statute law** derecho *m* escrito

statutory ['stætjʊtərɪ] ADJ reglamentario, estatutario; [*holiday, right etc*] legal ➤ **statutory rape** (*US Jur*) relaciones sexuales con un(a) menor

staunch¹ [stɔːntʃ] ADJ (*compar* **~er**; *superl* **~est**) leal, firme

staunch² [stɔːntʃ] VT [+ *bleeding*] restañar

staunchly ['stɔːntʃlɪ] ADV lealmente, firmemente

stave [steɪv] N (*esp Brit Mus*) pentagrama *m* ➤ **stave in** VT + ADV (*pt, pp* **stove in**) desfondar ➤ **stave off** VT + ADV (*pt, pp* **~d off**) [+ *attack, crisis*] evitar; [+ *threat*] evitar, conjurar; (*temporarily*) aplazar, posponer

stay [steɪ] **Ⓐ** VI **1** (= *remain*) quedarse; **to ~ at home** quedarse en casa; **to ~ in bed** guardar cama; **you ~ right there** no te muevas de ahí, quédate ahí; **video recorders are here to ~** los vídeos no son una simple moda pasajera; **can you ~ to** *or* **for dinner?** ¿puedes quedarte a cenar?; **to ~ ahead of the competition** mantenerse a la cabeza de la competencia; **to ~ awake** quedarse despierto; **I tried to ~ calm** intenté mantener la calma; **if it ~s fine** si continúa el buen tiempo, si el tiempo sigue siendo bueno; **I hope we can ~ friends** espero que podamos seguir siendo amigos; **to ~ healthy** mantenerse en buen estado de salud; **the shops ~ open until eight** las tiendas están abiertas hasta las ocho; **to ~ put** (*on spot*) no moverse; (*in same house, city, job*) quedarse; **to ~ together** seguir juntos **2** (*with friends, relatives*) quedarse, alojarse; (*in hotel*) alojarse, hospedarse; **to ~ with friends** quedarse *or* hospedarse *or* alojarse en casa de unos amigos; **I'm ~ing with my aunt for a few days** estoy pasando unos días en casa de mi tía; **where are you ~ing?** ¿dónde te alojas *or* hospedas?; **I'm ~ing at the**

Europa Hotel estoy *or* me alojo *or* me hospedo en el Hotel Europa; **did he ~ the night?** ¿se quedó a pasar la noche?, ¿se quedó a dormir?
Ⓑ VT **1** (*Jur*) (= *delay*) [+ *execution, proceedings*] suspender **2** (= *last out*) [+ *distance*] aguantar, resistir; [+ *race*] terminar; **to ~ the course** terminar la carrera; (*fig*) aguantar hasta el final
Ⓒ N estancia *f*, estadía *f* (*LAm*); **during our ~ in London** durante nuestra estancia en Londres
Ⓓ CPD ➤ **stay of execution** aplazamiento *m* de la sentencia
➤ **stay away** VI + ADV (*from person, building*) no acercarse (**from** a); (*from event*) no acudir (**from** a); **~ away from here** no vuelvas por aquí; **tourists were warned to ~ away from the beaches** se aconsejó a los turistas que no fueran a las playas
➤ **stay behind** VI + ADV (*after work, school*) quedarse
➤ **stay down** VI + ADV **1** (= *not increase*) [*prices, inflation*] mantenerse al mismo nivel, no subir **2** (= *not get up*) no levantarse; (= *remain lying*) permanecer tendido; **~ down!** ¡no te levantes! **3** (= *remain under water*) permanecer bajo el agua **4** (*Scol*) (*in lower class*) repetir el curso **5** [*food*] **nothing he eats will ~ down** no retiene nada de lo que come, vomita todo lo que come
➤ **stay in** VI + ADV **1** (*at home*) quedarse en casa, no salir **2** (*after school*) quedarse (depués de las clases) **3** (*in place*) **the nail doesn't seem to want to ~ in** parece que el clavo no quiere quedarse en su sitio; **this paragraph must ~ in** hay que dejar este párrafo
➤ **stay off** VI + PREP **to ~ off school/work** no ir al colegio/trabajo; **to ~ off drink** (= *stop taking*) dejar de beber; (= *avoid taking*) no beber
➤ **stay on** VI + ADV **1** [*person*] (*in job, at school*) seguir, quedarse; (*after party*) quedarse; **fewer teenagers are ~ing on at school** cada vez menos adolescentes siguen *or* se quedan en la escuela **2** [*lid, top*] quedarse en su sitio; **her wig wouldn't ~ on** no había forma de que la peluca se quedara en su sitio
➤ **stay out** VI + ADV **1** (= *not come home*) **she ~ed out all night** pasó *or* estuvo toda la noche fuera, no volvió a casa en toda la noche; **get out and ~ out!** ¡vete y no vuelvas! **2** (= *remain outside*) quedarse fuera **3** (*esp Brit*) (*on strike*) seguir en huelga **4** **to ~ out of** [+ *trouble, discussion*] no meterse en; **~ out of this!** ¡no te metas!; **try to ~ out of sight** procura pasar desapercibido; **to ~ out of the sun** quedarse a la sombra
➤ **stay over** VI + ADV quedarse a la noche, quedarse a dormir
➤ **stay up** VI + ADV **1** (= *not fall*) [*tent*] mantenerse de pie; **my trousers won't ~ up** los pantalones se me caen **2** (= *not go to bed*) quedarse levantado; **we ~ed up late** nos quedamos levantados hasta tarde; **he ~ed up all night working** se quedó toda la noche trabajando

stay-at-home ['steɪəthəʊm] ADJ casero, hogareño

staying power ['steɪɪŋˌpaʊə^r] N aguante *m*, resistencia *f*

stays [steɪz] NPL (= *corset*) corsé *msing*

STD N ABBR (= **sexually transmitted disease**) ETS *f*

stead [sted] N **in sb's ~** en lugar de algn; **to stand sb in good ~** ser muy útil a algn

steadfast ['stedfəst] ADJ [*person*] firme, resuelto; [*gaze*] fijo; **~ in love** constante en el amor

steadfastly ['stedfəstlɪ] ADV firmemente, resueltamente

steadily ['stedɪlɪ] ADV **1** [*improve, grow, move, advance*] a un ritmo constante, de manera *or* forma continuada, de manera *or* forma constante; [*increase, rise*] a un ritmo constante; [*work*] a un ritmo constante; (*without stopping*) sin parar; [*rain*] ininterrumpidamente; [*breathe, beat*] regularmente; **it gets ~ worse** se pone cada vez peor; **a ~ increasing number of people** un número cada vez mayor de gente
2 [*speak*] con firmeza; [*look*] fijamente, sin pestañear **3** [*walk*] con paso seguro; [*hold, grasp*] firmemente

steady ['stedɪ] **Ⓐ** ADJ (*compar* **steadier**; *superl* **steadiest**) **1** (= *continuous*) [*decline, increase, improvement, flow*] continuo; [*rain*] constante, ininterrumpido; [*breathing, beat*] regular; [*temperature*] constante, uniforme; **he doesn't have a ~ income** no tiene ingresos regulares *or* estables; **a ~ job** un empleo fijo; **at a ~ pace** a paso regular *or* constante; **we have been making ~ progress** hemos ido mejorando de forma continuada *or* constante; **we have a ~ stream of visitors** tenemos un flujo constante de visitantes

2 (= *calm*) [*voice*] firme; [*gaze*] fijo; [*nerves*] templado **3** (= *stable*) [*chair, table*] firme, seguro; [*relationship*] estable; [*boyfriend, girlfriend*] formal; **a ~ hand** pulso firme; **hold the camera ~** no muevas la cámara; **to be ~ on one's feet** caminar con paso seguro
Ⓑ EXCL **~ on!** [*calm down*] ¡tranquilo!
Ⓒ ADV (*) **to go ~ with sb** ser novio formal de algn
Ⓓ VT **1** (= *stabilize*) [+ *wobbling object*] estabilizar; [+ *chair, table*] (*with hands*) sujetar para que no se mueva; (*with wedge*) poner un calzo a (para que no cojee) **2** (= *compose*) [+ *nervous person*] calmar, tranquilizar; [+ *horse*] tranquilizar; **to ~ o.s.** calmarse, tranquilizarse; **she smokes to ~ her nerves** fuma para calmar los nervios
Ⓔ VI **1** (= *stop moving*) dejar de moverse
2 (= *grow calm*) [*voice*] calmarse; [*prices, market*] estabilizarse, hacerse más estable; **to have a ~ing influence on sb** ejercer una buena influencia sobre algn

steak [steɪk] N (= *one piece*) filete *m or* bistec *m* de vaca, filete *m or* bistec *m* de res (*LAm*), bife *m* (*And, SC*); (*for stewing etc*) carne *f* de vaca *or* res; (= *barbecued steak*) churrasco *m* (*And, SC*) ➤ **steak and kidney pie** pastel *m* de carne y riñones ➤ **steak knife** cuchillo *m* para la carne

steal [stiːl] (*pt* **stole**; *pp* **stolen**) **Ⓐ** VT [+ *object, money, kiss, idea*] robar; **to ~ sth from sb** robar algo a algn; **he stole it from school** lo robó del colegio; **to ~ a glance at sb** mirar a algn de soslayo, echar una mirada de soslayo a algn; **✦** IDIOMS **to ~ the show** llevarse todos los aplausos, acaparar la atención de todos; **to ~ sb's thunder** eclipsar a algn
Ⓑ VI **1** (= *take things*) robar; **to ~ from sb** robar a algn **2** (= *creep*) **to ~ into a room** entrar sigilosamente en una habitación, entrar en una habitación a hurtadillas; **to ~ up on sb** acercarse a algn sigilosamente; **a smile stole across her lips** una sonrisa se escapó de sus labios
Ⓒ N (*US**) (= *bargain*) **it's a ~** es una ganga* *or* un regalo*

stealing ['stiːlɪŋ] N robo *m*, hurto *m* (*frm*); **~ is wrong** robar *or* (*frm*) hurtar está mal

stealth [stelθ] N sigilo *m*; **by ~** a hurtadillas, sigilosamente

stealthy ['stelθɪ] ADJ (*compar* **stealthier**; *superl* **stealthiest**) cauteloso, sigiloso

steam [stiːm] **Ⓐ** N vapor *m*; **to pick up ~** dar presión; **full ~ ahead!** (*Naut*) ¡a todo vapor!; **✦** IDIOMS **to go full ~ ahead with sth** avanzar a toda marcha con algo; **to let off ~** desahogarse; **under one's own ~** por sus propios medios *or* propias fuerzas; **to run out of ~** quedar sin fuerza
Ⓑ VT **1** (= *cook*) cocer al vapor
2 **to ~ open an envelope** abrir un sobre con vapor
Ⓒ VI (= *give off steam*) echar vapor
Ⓓ CPD ➤ **steam engine** máquina *f* de vapor ➤ **steam iron** plancha *f* de vapor ➤ **steam shovel** (*US*) pala *f* mecánica de vapor, excavadora *f*
➤ **steam up** **Ⓐ** VI + ADV [*window*] empañarse **Ⓑ** VT + ADV [+ *window*] empañar; **to get ~ed up** empañarse; **✦** IDIOM **to get ~ed up about sth*** (= *angry*) ponerse negro por algo; (= *worried*) preocuparse por algo

steamboat ['stiːmbəʊt] N vapor *m*, buque *m* de vapor

steam-driven ['stiːmˌdrɪvn] ADJ impulsado por vapor, a vapor

steamer ['stiːmə^r] N **1** (= *saucepan*) olla *f* de estofar **2** (= *ship*) vapor *m*, buque *m* de vapor

steaming ['stiːmɪŋ] ADJ **1** (= *steaming hot*) humeante **2** (*) (= *angry*) negro*, furioso **3** (*Scot***) (= *drunk*) mamado*

steamroller ['stiːmˌrəʊlə^r] **Ⓐ** N apisonadora *f* **Ⓑ** VT (*fig*) aplastar, arrollar; **to ~ a bill through Parliament** hacer aprobar un proyecto de ley por mayoría aplastante *or* arrolladora

steamship ['stiːmʃɪp] N vapor *m*, buque *m* de vapor

steamy ['stiːmɪ] ADJ (*compar* **steamier**; *superl* **steamiest**) **1** [*room*] lleno de vapor; [*atmosphere*] húmedo y caluroso; [*window*] empañado **2** (*) [*film, novel*] erótico; [*relationship*] apasionado

steed [stiːd] N (*liter*) corcel *m*

steel [stiːl] **Ⓐ** N acero *m*; **nerves of ~** nervios *mpl* de acero **Ⓑ** VT **to ~ one's heart** endurecer el corazón; **to ~ o.s.**

fortalecerse (**against** contra); **to ~ o.s. for sth/to do sth** cobrar ánimo para algo/para hacer algo **⊙** CPD de acero ➤ **steel band** (*Mus*) *banda de percusión del Caribe* ➤ **steel guitar** guitarra *f* de cordaje metálico ➤ **steel industry** industria *f* siderúrgica ➤ **steel mill** fundición *f*, fundidora *f* (*LAm*) ➤ **steel wool** estropajo *m* de aluminio

steel-plated [,stiːlˈpleɪtɪd] ADJ chapado en acero

steelworker [ˈstiːlˌwɜːkə'] N trabajador(a) *m/f* siderúrgico/a

steelworks [ˈstiːlwɜːks] NSING fundición *f*, fundidora *f* (*LAm*)

steely [ˈstiːlɪ] ADJ (*compar* **steelier**; *superl* **steeliest**) [*determination*] inflexible; [*gaze*] duro, de acero

steely-eyed [,stiːlɪˈaɪd] ADJ de mirada penetrante

steep[1] [stiːp] ADJ (*compar* **~er**; *superl* **~est**) **1** [*hill, cliff*] empinado, escarpado; [*stairs, slope*] empinado; **it's a ~ climb to the top** hay una subida empinada hasta la cumbre **2** (= *sharp*) [*drop*] abrupto, brusco; [*increase*] pronunciado **3** (*) (= *expensive*) [*price*] excesivo **4** (*Brit*) (= *unreasonable*) **that's pretty ~!** ¡eso es demasiado!, ¡no hay derecho!

steep[2] [stiːp] VT (= *soak*) remojar, poner a *or* en remojo (**in** en); **a town ~ed in history** una ciudad cargada *or* impregnada de historia

steeple [ˈstiːpl] N aguja *f*, chapitel *m*

steeplechase [ˈstiːplˌtʃeɪs] N carrera *f* de obstáculos

steeplejack [ˈstiːplˌdʒæk] N *reparador de chimeneas, torres etc*

steeply [ˈstiːplɪ] ADV **the mountain rises ~** la montaña está cortada a pico; **the road climbs ~** la carretera sube muy empinada; **prices have risen ~** los precios han subido muchísimo

steer[1] [stɪə'] **Ⓐ** VT (+ *car*) conducir, manejar (*LAm*); (+ *ship*) gobernar; (+ *person*) dirigir, llevar; (+ *conversation*) llevar; **to ~ one's way through a crowd** abrirse paso por entre una multitud **Ⓑ** VI [*car*] conducir, manejar (*LAm*); [*ship*] gobernar; **to ~ for sth** dirigirse hacia algo; **✦** IDIOM **to ~ clear of sb/sth** esquivar a algn/evadir algo **⊙** N (*US**) (= *tip*) **to sell sb a bum ~** dar información falsa a algn

steer[2] [stɪə'] N (= *bull*) novillo *m*

steering [ˈstɪərɪŋ] N dirección *f*, conducción *f* ➤ **steering column** columna *f* de dirección ➤ **steering committee** comité *m* de dirección ➤ **steering lock** (*Aut*) (= *anti-theft device*) dispositivo *m* antirrobo ➤ **steering wheel** volante *m*, manubrio *m* (*LAm*)

stellar [ˈstelə'] ADJ estelar

stem[1] [stem] **Ⓐ** N [*of plant*] tallo *m*; [*of leaf*] pedúnculo *m*; [*of glass*] pie *m*; [*of word*] tema *m* **Ⓑ** VI **to ~ from sth** ser el resultado de algo

stem[2] [stem] VT (= *check, stop*) [+ *blood*] restañar; [+ *attack, flood*] detener; **to ~ the tide of events** detener el curso de los acontecimientos

stench [stentʃ] N hedor *m*

stencil [ˈstensl] **Ⓐ** N (*for lettering etc*) plantilla *f*; (*for typing*) cliché *m*, clisé *m* **Ⓑ** VT [+ *lettering etc*] estarcir

stenographer [steˈnɒɡrəfə'] N (*US*) taquígrafo/a *m/f*, estenógrafo/a *m/f*

step [step] **Ⓐ** N **1** (= *movement*) (*lit, fig*) paso *m*; (= *sound*) paso *m*, pisada *f*; **to take a ~ back/forward** dar un paso atrás/adelante; **it's a big ~ for him** es un gran paso *or* salto para él; **~ by ~** (*lit, fig*) poco a poco; **to be a ~ closer to doing sth** estar más cerca de hacer algo; **I'll fight this decision every ~ of the way** voy a oponerme a esta decisión hasta el final; **the first ~ is to decide ...** el primer paso es decidir ...; **to follow in sb's ~s** seguir los pasos de algn; **I would go one ~ further and make all guns illegal** yo iría aún más lejos y prohibiría todo tipo de armas de fuego; **what's the next ~?** ¿cuál es el siguiente paso?; **it's a ~ in the right direction** es un paso adelante; **to turn one's ~s towards sth** dirigir los pasos hacia algo; **it's a ~ up in his career** es un ascenso en su carrera profesional; **to watch one's ~** (*lit, fig*) ir con cuidado; **✦** IDIOMS **to be one ~ ahead of sb** llevar ventaja a *or* sobre algn; **to keep one ~ ahead (of)** mantenerse en una posición de ventaja (con respecto

a); **it's a case of one ~ forward, two ~s back** es un caso típico de un paso adelante y dos hacia atrás **2** (*in dancing, marching*) paso *m*; **he quickly fell into ~ beside me** no tardó en ajustar su paso al mío; **to be/keep in ~ (with)** (*in marching*) llevar el paso (de); (*in dance*) llevar el compás *or* ritmo (de); **to be out of ~** (*in marching*) no llevar el paso; (*in dance*) no llevar el compás *or* el ritmo; **to get out of ~** (*in march*) perder el paso; (*in dance*) perder el ritmo *or* compás; **✦** IDIOMS **to be out of ~ with sth/sb** no estar sintonizado con algo/algn; **to fall** *or* **get out of ~ with sth/sb** desconectarse de algo/algn **3** (= *footprint*) huella *f* **4** (= *measure*) medida *f*; **to take ~s (to do sth)** tomar medidas (para hacer algo) **5** (= *stair*) peldaño *m*, escalón *m*; (*also* **doorstep**) escalón *m* de la puerta; **"mind the step"** "cuidado con el escalón"; **I'll meet you on the library ~s** quedamos en los escalones *or* la escalinata de la biblioteca; **a flight of stone ~s** un tramo de escalera *or* de escalones de piedra **6** (*also* **aerobics**) step *m*

Ⓑ VI **1** (= *walk*) **to ~ aside** hacerse a un lado, apartarse; **to ~ back** dar un paso hacia atrás, retroceder; **to ~ down (from sth)** bajar (de algo); **to ~ forward** dar un paso hacia adelante; **to ~ in** entrar; **won't you ~ inside?** ¿no quiere pasar?; **he ~ped into the room** entró en la habitación; **he ~ped into his slippers** se puso las zapatillas; **to ~ off sth** bajarse de algo; **as he ~ped onto the pavement ...** al poner el pie en la acera ...; **to ~ out** (= *go outside*) salir; **as she ~ped out of the car** al bajar del coche; **she ~ped out of her dress** se quitó el vestido (por abajo); **I had to ~ outside for a breath of fresh air** tuve que salir fuera a tomar el aire; **to ~ over sth** pasar por encima de algo; **~ this way** haga el favor de pasar por aquí; **✦** IDIOM **to ~ out of line** desobedecer, romper las reglas **2** (= *tread*) **to ~ in/on sth** pisar algo; **don't ~ in that puddle** no te metas en ese charco; **~ on it!*** (= *hurry up*) ¡date prisa!, ¡ponte las pilas!*, ¡apúrate! (*LAm*); (*Aut*) ¡acelera!; **to ~ on the accelerator** (*Brit*) ◊ **~ on the gas** (*US*) pisar el acelerador

⊙ CPD ➤ **step aerobics** step *m* ➤ **step aside** VI + ADV (= *withdraw*) **he ~ped aside in favour of a younger person** renunció *or* dimitió para dejar paso a alguien más joven ➤ **step back** VI + ADV **1** (= *go back*) **it's like ~ping back in time** es como viajar hacia atrás *or* retroceder en el tiempo **2** (= *detach o.s.*) distanciarse un poco; **I needed to ~ back from the situation** necesitaba distanciarme un poco de la situación ➤ **step down** VI + ADV (= *resign*) renunciar, dimitir ➤ **step forward** VI + ADV (= *volunteer*) ofrecerse ➤ **step in** VI + ADV (= *intervene*) intervenir; (= *volunteer*) ofrecerse ➤ **step out** **Ⓐ** VI + ADV (= *go outside*) salir **Ⓑ** VT + ADV (= *measure*) [+ *distance*] medir a pasos ➤ **step up** **Ⓐ** VI + ADV **to ~ up to sth/sb** acercarse a algo/ algn **Ⓑ** VT + ADV [+ *production, sales, current*] aumentar; [+ *campaign*] intensificar; [+ *attacks, attempts, efforts*] intensificar, redoblar

stepbrother [ˈstepˌbrʌðə'] N hermanastro *m*

step-by-step [ˌstepbaɪˈstep] ADJ ➤ **step-by-step instructions** instrucciones *fpl* paso a paso

stepchild [ˈsteptʃaɪld] N (*pl* **~ren**) hijastro/a *m/f*

stepdaughter [ˈstepˌdɔːtə'] N hijastra *f*

stepfather [ˈstepˌfɑːðə'] N padrastro *m*

stepladder [ˈstepˌlædə'] N escalera *f* de mano, escalera *f* de tijera

stepmother [ˈstepˌmʌðə'] N madrastra *f*

step-parent [ˈstepˌpɛərənt] N (= *father*) padrastro *m*; (= *mother*) madrastra *f*

steppe [step] N (*also* **~s**) estepa *f*

stepping stone [ˈstepɪŋstəʊn] N **1** (*lit*) pasadera *f* **2** (*fig*) trampolín *m* (**to** para llegar a)

stepsister [ˈstepˌsɪstə'] N hermanastra *f*

stepson [ˈstepsʌn] N hijastro *m*

step-up [ˈstepʌp] N (*in production, sales*) aumento *m*; (*in campaign, attempts, efforts*) intensificación *f*

stereo ['steriəʊ] **Ⓐ** N (= *hi-fi equipment*) equipo *m* estereofónico; (= *sound*) estéreo *m*; **in** ~ en estéreo **Ⓑ** ADJ estereofónico

stereotype ['steriətaip] N estereotipo *m*

stereotyped ['steriətaipt] ADJ estereotipado

stereotypical [,stiəriə'tipikl] ADJ estereotípico

sterile ['sterail] ADJ **1** (= *germ-free*) esterilizado **2** (= *infertile*) estéril

sterility [ste'rɪlɪtɪ] N esterilidad *f*

sterilization [,sterilai'zeiʃən] N esterilización *f*

sterilize ['sterilaiz] VT esterilizar

sterling ['stɜːlɪŋ] **Ⓐ** ADJ **1** (*Econ*) **pound** ~ libra *f* esterlina **2** [*quality etc*] destacado; **a ~ character** una persona de toda confianza **Ⓑ** N (= *currency*) (libras *fpl*) esterlinas *fpl* **Ⓒ** CPD ➤ **sterling silver** plata *f* de ley

stern¹ [stɜːn] ADJ (*compar* ~**er**; *superl* ~**est**) [*person, look*] severo; [*reprimand*] duro; [*warning*] serio; **but he was made of ~er stuff** pero él tenía un carácter más fuerte

stern² [stɜːn] N (*Naut*) popa *f*

sternly ['stɜːnlɪ] ADV [*look*] severamente; [*reprimand*] severamente, con dureza; [*warn*] con seriedad

sternum ['stɜːnəm] N esternón *m*

steroid ['stɪərɔɪd] N esteroide *m*

stethoscope ['steθəskəʊp] N estetoscopio *m*

stevedore ['stiːvɪdɔːˈ] N estibador *m*

stew [stjuː] **Ⓐ** N estofado *m*, guisado *m* (*esp LAm*); ✦ IDIOM **to be in a ~*** sudar la gota gorda* **Ⓑ** VT [+ *meat*] estofar, guisar; [+ *fruit*] cocer, hacer una compota de; ~**ed apples** compota *f* de manzanas **Ⓒ** VI [*tea*] quedarse reposando demasiado; ✦ IDIOM **to let sb ~ in his own juice** dejar a algn que cueza en su propia salsa **Ⓓ** CPD ➤ **stew meat** (*US*) carne *f* de vaca, res *f* para estofar (*LAm*)

steward ['stjuːəd] N (*on estate*) administrador(a) *m/f*, mayordomo *m*; (= *butler*) mayordomo *m*; (*in plane*) auxiliar *m* de vuelo, auxiliar *m* de cabina, aeromozo *m* (*LAm*), sobrecargo *m* (*Mex*), cabinero *m* (*Col*); (*on ship*) camarero *m*

stewardess ['stjuːədes] N (*in plane*) azafata *f*, auxiliar *f* de vuelo or de cabina, aeromoza *f* (*LAm*), sobrecargo *f* (*Mex*), cabinera *f* (*Col*); (*on ship*) camarera *f*

stewing steak ['stjuːɪŋˌsteɪk] N (*Brit*) carne *f* de vaca, res *f* para estofar (*LAm*)

stick¹ [stɪk] **Ⓐ** N **1** (= *length of wood*) (trozo *m* de) madera *f*; (*shaped*) palo *m*, vara *f*; (*as weapon*) palo *m*, porra *f*; (= *walking stick*) bastón *m*; (*Hockey, Ice Hockey etc*) palo *m*; (= *drumstick*) palillo *m*; ~ **of furniture** mueble *m*; ✦ IDIOMS **policy of the ~ and carrot** política *f* de incentivos y amenazas; **a ~ to beat sb with** un arma con la que atacar a algn **2** [*of gum*] barra *f*; [*of celery*] rama *f*; [*of dynamite*] cartucho *m* **3** (*Brit*) (= *criticism*) **the critics gave him a lot of ~** los críticos le dieron una buena paliza* **4 sticks 4.1** (= *firewood*) astillas *fpl*, leña *f* **4.2** (*Horse racing**) (= *hurdles*) obstáculos *mpl* **4.3** ✦ IDIOM **to live in the ~s*** vivir en el quinto pino or infierno **Ⓑ** CPD ➤ **stick insect** insecto *m* palo ➤ **stick shift** (*US*) palanca *f* de marchas

stick² [stɪk] (*vb: pt, pp* **stuck**) **Ⓐ** VT **1** (*with glue etc*) pegar, encolar; **to ~ a poster on the wall** pegar un póster a la pared **2** (= *thrust*) meter; [+ *sth pointed*] clavar, hincar; **he stuck his hand in his pocket** metió la mano en el bolsillo; **I've stuck the needle into my finger** me he clavado la aguja en el dedo **3** (*) (= *put*) poner; (= *insert*) meter; ~ **it on the shelf** ponlo en el estante; ~ **it in your case** métdelo en la maleta; ✦ IDIOM **she told him he could ~ his job**** le dijo que se metiera el trabajo donde le cupiera** **4** (*Brit*) (= *tolerate*) aguantar; **I can't ~ him** no lo aguanto; **I can't ~ it any longer** no aguanto más **5 to be stuck 5.1** (= *jammed*) estar atascado, estar atorado (*esp LAm*); (*in mud etc*) estar atascado; [*sth pointed*] estar clavado; **the window is stuck** se ha atrancado la ventana;

the lift is stuck at the ninth floor el ascensor se ha quedado parado or colgado or atrancado en el piso nueve **5.2** (= *trapped*) **to be stuck in the lift** quedarse atrapado en el ascensor; **the car was stuck between two trucks** el coche estaba atrapado entre dos camiones; **I'm stuck at home all day** estoy metida en casa todo el día; **he's stuck in France** sigue en Francia sin poder moverse; **he's stuck in a boring job** tiene un trabajo muy aburrido (y no puede buscarse otro) **5.3** (*) (= *have a problem*) estar en un apuro or aprieto; **I'm stuck** (*in crossword puzzle, guessing game, essay etc*) estoy atascado; **he's never stuck for an answer** no le falta nunca una respuesta **5.4 to be stuckwith sth/sb*** tener que aguantar algo/a algn; **and now we're stuck with it*** y ahora no lo podemos quitar de encima, y ahora no hay manera de deshacernos de eso **5.5 to be stuck on sb*** estar enamorado de algn **6 to get stuck: to get stuck in the snow** quedar sin poderse mover en la nieve; **a bone got stuck in my throat** se me había clavado una espina en la garganta; **we got stuck with this problem*** nos quedamos con este problema **Ⓑ** VI **1** (= *adhere*) [*glue, stamp, sticky object etc*] pegarse; **it stuck to the wall** quedó pegado a la pared; **the name seems to have stuck** el apodo se le pegó; **to make a charge ~** hacer que una acusación tenga efecto **2** (= *get jammed*) atascarse, atorarse (*esp LAm*); (*in mud etc*) atascarse; [*sth pointed*] quedar clavado, clavarse; **the door ~s in wet weather** en tiempo de lluvia la puerta se pega; ✦ IDIOM **that really ~s in my throat** eso me indigna **3** (= *extend, protrude*) **the nail was ~ing through the plank** el clavo sobresalía del tablón **4** (= *be embedded*) **he had a knife ~ing into his back** tenía una navaja clavada en la espalda **5** (*fig*) (*set expressions*) **just ~ at it and I'm sure you'll manage it** no te amedrentes y al fin llegarás; **we'll all ~ by you** (= *support you*) te apoyaremos todos; (= *stay with you*) no te abandonaremos; **it stuck in my mind** se me quedó grabado; **to ~ to one's principles** seguir fiel a sus principios, aferrarse a sus principios; **to ~ to a promise** cumplir una promesa; **she stuck to her decision** se plantó en su decisión; **decide what you're going to do, then ~ to it!** ¡decídete y no te dejes desviar!; **he stuck to his story** se mantuvo firme en su versión de los hechos; **let's ~ to the matter in hand** ciñámonos al asunto, no perdamos de vista el tema principal; **I'd better ~ to fruit juice** creo que seguiré con el zumo de frutas; **let's ~ to the main roads** vamos a seguir por carreteras principales; ~ **with us and you'll be all right** quédate con nosotros y todo saldrá bien; **I'll ~ with the job for another few months** seguiré con el trabajo unos meses más; ✦ IDIOM **to ~ to sb like a leech** pegarse a algn como una lapa **6** (= *balk*) **she will ~ at nothing to get what she wants** no se para en barras para conseguir lo que quiere

➤ **stick around*** VI + ADV quedarse

➤ **stick in** VT + ADV **1** (= *thrust in*) [+ *knife, fork etc*] clavar, hincar; [+ *one's hand*] meter, introducir; (*) (= *add, insert*) introducir, añadir **2** (*Brit**) **get stuck in!** (= *work*) ¡manos a la obra!; (= *eat*) ¡atacar!; **to get stuck into sth** meterse de lleno en algo

➤ **stick on Ⓐ** VT + ADV **1** [+ *stamp, label*] pegar **2** (*) (= *put on*) [+ *coat, hat etc*] ponerse; [+ *tape, CD*] meter, poner; **they've stuck ten pence on a litre*** han subido el precio del litro diez peniques **Ⓑ** VI + ADV [*label, stamp*] adherirse, pegarse

➤ **stick out Ⓐ** VI + ADV **1** (= *protrude*) [*balcony, nail*] sobresalir; **her feet stuck out over the end of the bed** sus pies asomaban por la punta de la cama; **his teeth ~ out** tiene los dientes salidos; **his ears ~ out** tiene las orejas de soplillo **2** (= *be noticeable*) destacarse, resaltar; ✦ IDIOMS **it ~s out a mile** salta a la vista; **to ~ out like a sore thumb** llamar la atención **3** (= *insist, persevere*) **to ~ out for sth** empeñarse en conseguir algo **Ⓑ** VT + ADV **1** [+ *tongue*] asomar, sacar; [+ *leg*] extender; [+ *chest*] sacar; [+ *head*] asomar **2** (*) (= *tolerate, endure*) aguantar; **to ~ it out** aguantar

➤ **stick together Ⓐ** VT + ADV (*with glue etc*) pegar, unir con cola *etc* **Ⓑ** VI + ADV **1** (= *adhere*) pegarse, quedar pegados

2 [*people*] mantenerse unidos, no separarse; (*fig*) cerrar las filas
➤ **stick up** Ⓐ VT + ADV [+ *notice, poster*] pegar; [+ *hand*] levantar; **~ 'em up!*** ¡arriba las manos! Ⓑ VI + ADV
1 (= *protrude*) sobresalir; [*hair*] ponerse de punta, pararse (*LAm*) **2** (*) **to ~ up for sb** defender a algn; **to ~ up for o.s.** hacerse valer; **to ~ up for one's rights** hacer valer sus derechos, defender sus derechos

sticker ['stɪkəʳ] N (= *label*) etiqueta *f*; (*with slogan*) pegatina *f*

sticking plaster ['stɪkɪŋ,plɑːstəʳ] N (*Brit*) tirita *f* (*Sp*), curita *f* (*LAm*)

sticking point ['stɪkɪŋ,pɔɪnt] N (*fig*) punto *m* de fricción

stick-in-the-mud* ['stɪkɪnðəmʌd] N (*Brit*) persona rutinaria *y poco aventurera*

stickleback ['stɪklbæk] N espinoso *m*

stickler ['stɪkləʳ] N **to be a ~ for** insistir mucho en

stick-on ['stɪkɒn] ADJ [*label*] adhesivo

stickpin ['stɪkpɪn] N (*US*) alfiler *m* de corbata

stick-up** ['stɪkʌp] N atraco *m*, asalto *m*

sticky ['stɪkɪ] Ⓐ ADJ (*compar* **stickier**; *superl* **stickiest**)
1 (= *gooey*) [*substance, object*] pegajoso; [*fingers*] pegajoso, pringoso; (= *adhesive*) [*label*] engomado, adhesivo;
✦ IDIOM **to have ~ fingers** (*Brit**) tener la mano larga*
2 (= *sweaty*) sudado; [*weather, day*] bochornoso; **to feel hot and ~** sudar y pasar calor
3 (*) (= *awkward*) [*situation*] difícil, delicado; [*problem, moment*] difícil; **to go through a ~ patch** pasar por una mala racha; ✦ IDIOM **to come to a ~ end** (*Brit*) acabar mal
Ⓑ CPD ➤ **sticky tape** (*Brit*) cinta *f* adhesiva

stiff [stɪf] Ⓐ ADJ (*compar* **-er**; *superl* **-est**) **1** (= *rigid*) [*card, paper, chair*] rígido, duro; [*collar, fabric*] duro, tieso; [*brush, boots*] duro; [*corpse*] rígido
2 (= *firm*) [*paste, mixture*] compacto, consistente; **beat the egg whites until ~** bata las claras de huevo a punto de nieve
3 [*joints, limbs, muscles*] entumecido, agarrotado; [*fingers*] rígido, agarrotado; [*movement*] rígido; **to become ~** [*joints, limbs, muscles*] entumecerse, agarrotarse; **to feel ~** (= *because of cold, injury etc*) sentirse agarrotado; (*after exercise*) tener agujetas; **to have a ~ neck** tener tortícolis; ✦ IDIOM **to keep a ~ upper lip** mantener el tipo, poner a mal tiempo buena cara
4 [*door, drawer, lock*] duro, que no abre bien, atorado (*esp LAm*)
5 (= *formal*) [*smile*] frío; [*person, manner*] estirado, frío; **he gave a ~ bow** se inclinó con frialdad *or* con formalidad
6 (= *tough*) [*climb, test*] difícil, duro; [*penalty, sentence, fine*] severo; [*challenge*] difícil; [*opposition, competition*] duro
7 (= *high*) [*price*] excesivo, exorbitante; [*price rise*] fuerte
8 (= *strong*) [*breeze*] fuerte; [*drink*] cargado
Ⓑ ADV **to be bored ~** aburrirse como una ostra; **to be frozen ~** estar muerto de frío; **to be scared ~** estar muerto de miedo; **to be worried ~** estar muy preocupado, estar preocupadísimo
Ⓒ N (**) (= *corpse*) cadáver *m*, fiambre* *m* (*hum*)

stiffen ['stɪfn] Ⓐ VT **1** [+ *card, fabric etc*] reforzar; (*with starch*) almidonar **2** (*also* **~ up**) [+ *limb, muscle*] contraer, poner tieso; [+ *joint*] agarrotar **3** (*fig*) [+ *morale, resistance etc*] fortalecer Ⓑ VI **1** [*card, fabric*] hacerse más rígido, atiesarse
2 (*also* **~ up**) [*limb, muscle*] contraerse, ponerse tieso; [*joint*] agarrotarse **3** (*fig*) [*person, manner*] endurecerse

stiffly ['stɪflɪ] ADV **1** (= *uncomfortably*) [*walk, move, bend*] con rigidez **2** (= *formally*) [*smile, greet*] con formalidad; [*say*] con frialdad, fríamente; [*nod, bow*] fríamente, con formalidad

stiffness ['stɪfnɪs] N **1** (= *rigidness*) [*of card, paper, chair, collar, fabric*] rigidez *f*, dureza *f*; [*of boots, brush*] dureza *f*
2 (= *firmness*) [*of paste, mixture*] lo compacto, consistencia *f*
3 [*of joints, muscles, limbs*] entumecimiento *m*, agarrotamiento *m*; [*of fingers*] agarrotamiento *m*; **~ of the neck** tortícolis *f* (*sometimes m*); **the ~ you feel after exercise** las agujetas que sientes después de hacer ejercicio
4 [*of door, drawer, lock*] dificultad *f* en abrirse
5 (= *formality*) [*of smile, bow, person, manner*] frialdad *f*

6 (= *toughness*) [*of climb, test*] dificultad *f*; [*of penalty, sentence, fine*] severidad *f*; [*of opposition, competition*] dureza *f*

stifle ['staɪfl] Ⓐ VT **1** [+ *person*] ahogar, sofocar **2** (*fig*) suprimir; **to ~ a yawn** contener un bostezo Ⓑ VI ahogarse, sofocarse

stifling ['staɪflɪŋ] ADJ (*lit, fig*) agobiante; **it's ~ in here!** ¡hace un calor agobiante *or* sofocante aquí dentro!

stigma ['stɪgmə] N estigma *m*

stile [staɪl] N escalones *mpl* para saltar una cerca

stiletto [stɪ'letəʊ] N (*esp Brit*) (= *shoe*) zapato *m* con tacón de aguja ➤ **stiletto heel** tacón *m* de aguja

still¹ [stɪl] Ⓐ ADJ (*compar* **-er**; *superl* **-est**) **1** (= *motionless*) [*person, hands*] inmóvil, quieto; [*air*] en calma, manso; [*water*] quieto, manso; **try to hold it ~** intenta que no se te mueva; **to keep ~** quedarse quieto; **keep ~!** ¡no te muevas!, ¡quédate quieto!; **she lay ~** estaba tendida sin moverse; **to sit/stand ~** estarse quieto; **time stood ~** el tiempo se detuvo; **her heart stood ~** se le paró el corazón
2 (= *quiet, calm*) [*place, night*] tranquilo, silencioso
3 (= *not fizzy*) [*drink, water*] sin gas
Ⓑ N (*Cine*) fotograma *m*
Ⓒ VT [+ *protest, voice*] acallar; [+ *waves*] calmar; [+ *storm*] calmar, apaciguar; [+ *doubt, fear*] disipar
Ⓓ VI apagarse
Ⓔ CPD ➤ **still life** naturaleza *f* muerta, bodegón *m*

still² [stɪl] ADV **1** (= *up to this/that time*) todavía, aún; **she ~ lives in London** todavía *or* aún vive en Londres, sigue viviendo en Londres; **I ~ don't understand** sigo sin entender, todavía *or* aún no lo entiendo; **there are ~ two more** quedan dos más, todavía *or* aún quedan dos
2 (= *nevertheless, all the same*) aún así, de todas formas; **I didn't win, still, it's been a good experience** no he ganado, pero aun así *or* de todas formas *or* con todo, ha sido una buena experiencia; **I'm ~ going, even if it rains** iré de todas formas, incluso si llueve; **~, it was worth it** pero en fin, valió la pena; **whatever they have done, they are ~ your parents** a pesar de todo lo que han hecho, siguen siendo tus padres
3 (= *besides, in addition*) todavía, aún; **the next day there were ~ more problems** al día siguiente había todavía *or* aún más problemas
4 (= *even*) todavía, aún; **you need a rest, better ~, have a holiday** necesitas un descanso, mejor todavía *or* aún, tómate unas vacaciones; **worse ~, the disease seems to be spreading** (lo que es) peor todavía *or* aún, la enfermedad parece propagarse

still³ [stɪl] N (*for alcohol*) alambique *m*

stillbirth ['stɪl,bɜːθ] N mortinato *m*

stillborn ['stɪl,bɔːn] ADJ nacido muerto; **the child was ~** el niño nació muerto

stillness ['stɪlnɪs] N **1** (= *motionlessness*) quietud *f*
2 (= *quiet, calm*) tranquilidad *f*, calma *f*

stilt [stɪlt] N (*for stiltwalker*) zanco *m*; (*Archit*) pilar *m*, soporte *m*

stilted ['stɪltɪd] ADJ [*conversation, style, manner*] forzado, poco natural; **her English is rather ~** su inglés no suena muy natural

stimulant ['stɪmjʊlənt] N estimulante *m*

stimulate ['stɪmjʊleɪt] VT estimular; [+ *growth etc*] favorecer; **to ~ sb to do sth** alentar a algn a que haga algo

stimulating ['stɪmjʊleɪtɪŋ] ADJ estimulante

stimulation [,stɪmjʊ'leɪʃən] N (= *stimulus*) estímulo *m*; (= *act*) estimulación *f*; (= *state*) excitación *f*

stimulus ['stɪmjʊləs] N (*pl* **stimuli** ['stɪmjʊlaɪ]) estímulo *m*, incentivo *m*

sting [stɪŋ] (*vb: pt, pp* **stung**) Ⓐ N **1** (*by insect, nettle*) picadura *f*; (= *sharp pain*) punzada *f*; ✦ IDIOM **to take the ~ out of sth** restar fuerza a algo
2 (*in bee, wasp*) aguijón *m*; ✦ IDIOM **but there's a ~ in the tail** pero viene algo no tan agradable al final
3 (*esp US**) (= *confidence trick*) timo *m*
Ⓑ VT [*insect, nettle*] picar; (= *make smart*) escocer, picar, arder (*esp LAm*); [*conscience*] remorder; [*remark, criticism*]

herir; **they stung me for four pounds**** me clavaron cuatro libras*
ⓒ VI [*insect*] picar; **my eyes ~** me pican los ojos

stinging nettle ['stɪŋɪŋnetl] N ortiga *f*

stingy ['stɪndʒɪ] ADJ (*compar* **stingier**; *superl* **stingiest**) [*person*] tacaño; [*meal*] parco, escaso

stink [stɪŋk] (*vb: pt* **stank**; *pp* **stunk**) **Ⓐ** N **1** (= *smell*) peste *f*, hedor *m* **2** (*) (*fig*) (= *row, trouble*) lío* *m*, follón *m* (*Sp**); **to kick up a ~** armar un escándalo **Ⓑ** VI **1 to ~ (of)** apestar (a), heder (a) **2** (**) (= *be very bad*) **the idea ~s** es una pésima idea **ⓒ** VT **to ~ the place out** (*Brit**) **or up** (*US**) infestar el lugar de olor **Ⓓ** CPD ➤ **stink bomb** bomba *f* fétida

stinker** ['stɪŋkə'] N (= *person*) mal bicho* *m*, canalla* *mf*; **this problem is a ~** es un problema peliagudo

stinking ['stɪŋkɪŋ] **Ⓐ** ADJ **1** (= *smelly*) hediondo, fétido **2** (*) (= *horrible*) horrible, bestial, asqueroso; **to have a ~ cold** tener un resfriado muy fuerte **Ⓑ** ADV **they're ~ rich** (*Brit**) son unos ricachones*

stint [stɪnt] **Ⓐ** N **1** (= *amount of work*) **I've done my ~** he hecho lo que me corresponde **2** (= *period*) periodo *m*, período *m*; **she did a two-year ~ on the committee** fue miembro del comité durante un periodo *or* período de dos años **Ⓑ** VT **to ~ o.s.** estrecharse, privarse de cosas; **don't ~ yourself!** ¡no te prives de nada! **ⓒ** VI **to ~ on** [+ *food, luxuries*] no escatimar en

stipend ['staɪpend] N (*esp Brit*) salario *m*, estipendio *m*

stipulate ['stɪpjʊleɪt] VT estipular, poner como condición, especificar

stipulation [ˌstɪpjʊ'leɪʃən] N estipulación *f*, condición *f*

stir[1] [stɜː'] **Ⓐ** N **1 to give sth a ~** remover algo **2 to cause a ~** causar conmoción; **it didn't make much of a ~** apenas despertó interés alguno **Ⓑ** VT **1** [+ *liquid etc*] remover, revolver **2** (= *move*) mover; **a breeze ~red the leaves** una brisa agitó las hojas; **come on, ~ yourself*** ¡venga, muévete! **3** (*fig*) [+ *interest*] despertar; [+ *imagination*] estimular, avivar; **we were all ~red by the speech** el discurso nos conmovió a todos; **to ~ sb to do sth** incitar a algn a hacer algo **ⓒ** VI **1** (= *move*) moverse; **she hasn't ~red all day** no se ha movido en todo el día; **they are not ~ring yet** están todavía en la cama **2** (*) (= *make trouble*) acizañar, meter cizaña ➤ **stir up** VT + ADV [+ *liquid*] remover, revolver; [+ *memories*] traer a la memoria; [+ *hatred*] provocar, despertar; [+ *trouble*] provocar; [+ *the past*] remover; **he's always trying to ~ things up** siempre anda provocando

stir[2]** [stɜː'] N (*esp US*) (= *prison*) chirona** *f*

stir-fry ['stɜːfraɪ] **Ⓐ** VT sofreír **Ⓑ** N sofrito *m* (chino)

stirring ['stɜːrɪŋ] **Ⓐ** ADJ [*speech, music*] emocionante, conmovedor **Ⓑ** N **I sense no ~ of interest** no creo que esté despertando ningún interés; **there were ~s of protest** la gente empezó a protestar

stirrup ['stɪrəp] N estribo *m*

stitch [stɪtʃ] **Ⓐ** N **1** (*Sew*) puntada *f*, punto *m*; ✦ IDIOM **she hadn't a ~ on** andaba en cueros *or* (*LAm*) encuerada* **2** (*Med*) punto *m* de sutura; **to put ~es in a wound** suturar una herida **3** (= *pain*) punto *m*, punzada *f*; **to have a ~** tener flato; ✦ IDIOMS **we were in ~es*** nos moríamos *or* (*LAm*) partíamos de (la) risa; **she had us in ~es*** nos partimos de risa con ella **Ⓑ** VT (*also ~ up*) **1** (*Sew*) coser **2** (*Med*) suturar ➤ **stitch up** VT + ADV **1** (*esp Brit**) (= *finalize*) [+ *agreement, deal*] concertar **2** (*Brit***) (= *frame*) vender*, incriminar dolosamente

stitching ['stɪtʃɪŋ] N (*Sew*) puntadas *fpl*

stoat [stəʊt] N armiño *m*

stock [stɒk] **Ⓐ** N **1** (*Comm*) (= *quantity for sale*) existencias *fpl*; (= *selection*) surtido *m*; **to have sth in ~** tener algo en existencia; **we have a large ~ of sportswear** tenemos un amplio surtido de ropa deportiva; **to be out of ~** estar agotado; **to take ~ of** [+ *situation, prospects*] evaluar; [+ *person*] formarse una opinión sobre **2** (= *supply*) reserva *f*; **I always keep a ~ of tinned food** siempre estoy bien abastecido de latas de comida; **to lay in**

a ~ of sth abastecerse de algo **3** (*Fin*) (= *capital*) capital *m* social, capital *m* en acciones; (= *shares*) acciones *fpl*; (= *government securities*) bonos *mpl* del estado; **~s and shares** acciones *fpl* **4** (= *livestock*) ganado *m* **5** (= *descent*) **of Mediterranean ~** de ascendencia mediterránea **6** (*for soup*) caldo *m*; **beef/chicken ~** caldo de vaca/pollo **7 the stocks** (*Hist*) el cepo **Ⓑ** VT **1** (= *sell*) [+ *goods*] vender; **we ~ a wide range of bicycles** tenemos un gran surtido de bicicletas **2** (= *fill*) [+ *shop*] surtir, abastecer (**with** de); [+ *shelves*] reponer; [+ *library*] surtir, abastecer (**with** de); [+ *farm*] abastecer (**with** con); [+ *freezer, cupboard*] llenar (**with** de); [+ *lake, river*] poblar (**with** de); **a well ~ed shop/library** una tienda/biblioteca bien surtida **ⓒ** ADJ [*argument, joke, response*] típico; **a ~ phrase** una frase hecha **Ⓓ** CPD ➤ **stock car** (*Aut, Sport*) stock-car *m* ➤ **stock car racing** carreras *fpl* de stock-car, carreras *fpl* de choque ➤ **stock control** control *m* de existencias ➤ **stock cube** (*Culin*) pastilla *f or* cubito *m* de caldo ➤ **Stock Exchange** (*Fin*) Bolsa *f*; **prices on the Stock Exchange** ◊ **Stock Exchange prices** cotizaciones *fpl* en bolsa ➤ **stock management** gestión *f* de existencias ➤ **stock market** (*Fin*) bolsa *f*, mercado *m* bursátil ➤ **stock up** **Ⓐ** VI + ADV [*shopkeeper*] proveerse de existencias; [*private individual*] abastecerse; **to ~ up on** *or* **with sth** [*shopkeeper*] proveerse de algo; [*private individual*] abastecerse de algo **Ⓑ** VT + ADV (= *fill*) [+ *larder, cupboard, freezer*] llenar (**with** de); [+ *shelves*] reponer (**with** con)

stockade [stɒ'keɪd] N (= *fencing*) estacada *f*

stockbroker ['stɒkˌbrəʊkə'] N corredor(a) *m/f* de Bolsa, bolsista *mf*

stockholder ['stɒkˌhəʊldə'] N (*US*) accionista *mf*

Stockholm ['stɒkhəʊm] N Estocolmo *m*

stocking ['stɒkɪŋ] N media *f*; **a pair of ~s** unas medias, un par de medias ➤ **stocking filler, stocking stuffer** (*US*) pequeño regalo *m* de Navidad

stock-in-trade ['stɒkɪn'treɪd] N repertorio *m*

stockist ['stɒkɪst] N (*Brit*) distribuidor(a) *m/f*, proveedor(a) *m/f*

stockman ['stɒkmən] N (*pl* **stockmen**) (*US*) ganadero *m*

stockpile ['stɒkpaɪl] **Ⓐ** N reservas *fpl* **Ⓑ** VT (= *accumulate*) acumular; (= *store*) almacenar

stockroom ['stɒkrʊm] N almacén *m*, depósito *m*

stock-still ['stɒk'stɪl] ADV **to be** *or* **stand ~** mantenerse *or* quedarse inmóvil

stocktaking ['stɒkˌteɪkɪŋ] N (*Brit*) inventario *m*, balance *m*; **to do the ~** hacer el inventario

stocky ['stɒkɪ] ADJ (*compar* **stockier**; *superl* **stockiest**) fornido

stodgy ['stɒdʒɪ] ADJ (*compar* **stodgier**; *superl* **stodgiest**) **1** [*food*] indigesto **2** [*book, person*] pesado

stoic ['stəʊɪk] **Ⓐ** ADJ estoico **Ⓑ** N estoico *m*

stoical ['stəʊɪkəl] ADJ estoico

stoicism ['stəʊɪsɪzəm] N estoicismo *m*

stoke [stəʊk] VT (*also ~ up*) [+ *fire, furnace*] atizar

stole[1] [stəʊl] N (= *garment*) estola *f*

stole[2] [stəʊl] PT *of* **steal**

stolen ['stəʊlən] **Ⓐ** PP *of* **steal** **Ⓑ** ADJ robado

stolid ['stɒlɪd] ADJ impasible, imperturbable; (*pej*) terco

stomach ['stʌmək] **Ⓐ** N estómago *m*; (= *belly*) barriga *f*; **I've got a pain in my ~** me duele el estómago, tengo dolor de estómago; **to hold one's ~ in** meter estómago; **to lie on one's ~** estar tumbado boca abajo **Ⓑ** VT (*) (= *stand*) aguantar, soportar **ⓒ** CPD ➤ **stomach ache** dolor *m* de estómago, dolor *m* de barriga ➤ **stomach pump** bomba *f* gástrica ➤ **stomach ulcer** úlcera *f* gástrica ➤ **stomach upset** trastorno *m* estomacal

stomp [stɒmp] VI pisar fuerte; **to ~ in/out** entrar/salir dando fuertes pisotones

stone [stəʊn] **Ⓐ** N **1** (gen) piedra f; (= gravestone) lápida f; (= gemstone) piedra f, gema f; ✦ IDIOMS **within a ~'s throw** a un tiro de piedra; **to leave no ~ unturned** no dejar piedra por mover **2** (Brit) [of fruit] hueso m **3** (in kidney) cálculo m, piedra f **4** (Brit) (= weight) ≈ 6.350kg; **he weighs 12 ~(s)** ≈ pesa 76 kilos; ◌ IMPERIAL SYSTEM **Ⓑ** VT **1** [+ person] apedrear, lapidar (Brit) [+ fruit] deshuesar **Ⓒ** CPD ➤ the **Stone Age** la Edad de Piedra

stone-broke* ['stəʊn'brəʊk] ADJ (US) = **stony-broke**

stone-cold [ˌstəʊn'kəʊld] ADJ como un témpano; **to be ~ sober*** estar completamente sobrio

stoned** [stəʊnd] ADJ (on drugs) fumado, colocado (Sp*)

stone-deaf ['stəʊn'def] ADJ sordo como una tapia, sordo del todo

stoneground ['stəʊnˌɡraʊnd] ADJ molido por piedras

stonemason ['stəʊnˌmeɪsn] N albañil mf; (in quarry) cantero m

stonewall ['stəʊn'wɔːl] VI (in answering questions) negarse a contestar

stonewashed ['stəʊnˌwɒʃt] ADJ lavado a la piedra

stonework ['stəʊnwɜːk] N cantería f

stony ['stəʊnɪ] ADJ (compar **stonier**; superl **stoniest**)
1 [ground, beach] pedregoso; [material] pétreo
2 [glance, silence] glacial, frío; [heart] empedernido; [stare] duro

stony-broke* ['stəʊnɪ'brəʊk] ADJ **to be ~** (Brit) estar sin un duro*, estar pelado*, estar sin un peso (LAm*)

stony-faced [ˌstəʊnɪ'feɪst] ADJ de expresión pétrea

stood [stʊd] PT, PP of **stand**

stooge [stuːdʒ] N [of comedian] compañero/a m/f; (*) (= lackey) secuaz mf, siervo/a m/f

stool [stuːl] **Ⓐ** N **1** (= seat) taburete m, escabel m; ✦ IDIOM **to fall between two ~s** quedarse sin lo uno y sin lo otro, quedarse nadando entre dos aguas y no llegar a ningún lado **2** (= faeces) deposición f **Ⓑ** CPD ➤ **stool pigeon*** (= informer) chivato/a* m/f, soplón/ona* m/f; (= decoy) señuelo m

stoop[1] [stuːp] **Ⓐ** N **to walk with a ~** andar encorvado **Ⓑ** VI **1** (= bend) (also ~ **down**) inclinarse, agacharse; (permanently, as defect) andar encorvado **2** (fig) **to ~ to sth/ doing sth** rebajarse a algo/hacer algo; **I wouldn't ~ so low!** ¡a eso no llegaría!, ¡no me rebajaría tanto!

stoop[2] [stuːp] N (US) (= verandah) pórtico m, pequeña veranda f

stop [stɒp] **Ⓐ** N **1** (= halt) parada f, alto m; **to bring to a ~** [+ vehicle] parar, detener; [+ production, process] paralizar, interrumpir; **to come to a ~** [vehicle] parar(se), detenerse; [production, progress] interrumpirse; **to put a ~ to sth** poner fin or término a algo, acabar con algo
2 (= break, pause) descanso m, pausa f; (overnight) estancia f, estadía f (LAm), estada f (LAm); (for refuelling) escala f; **to make a ~ at Bordeaux** hacer escala en Burdeos; **without a ~** sin parar
3 (= stopping place) (for bus etc) parada f; (Aer, Naut) escala f
4 ✦ IDIOM **to pull out all the ~s** tocar todos los registros **Ⓑ** VT **1** (= block) [+ hole] tapar; [+ leak, flow of blood] restañar
2 (= put an end to) [+ rumour, activity, injustice] poner fin a, poner término a, acabar con
3 (= prevent) evitar; **to ~ sth happening** evitar que algo ocurra; **to ~ sb doing sth** impedir a algn hacer algo, impedir que algn haga algo; **there is nothing to ~ him** y no hay nada que se lo impida; **I can't ~ myself doing it** no puedo dejar de hacerlo; **I ~ped myself in time** me detuve a tiempo
4 (= cease) **to ~ doing sth** dejar de hacer algo; **it has ~ped raining** ha dejado de llover, ya no llueve; **she never ~s talking** habla sin parar; **~ it!** ¡basta ya!; **~ that noise!** ¡basta ya de ruido!
5 (= suspend) [+ payments, wages, subscription] suspender; [+ cheque] invalidar; [+ supply] cortar, interrumpir; **to ~ sb's electricity** cortar la electricidad a algn; **to ~ ten pounds from sb's wages** (Brit) retener diez libras del sueldo de algn
Ⓒ VI **1** (= stop moving) [person, vehicle] pararse, detenerse;

[clock, watch] pararse; **where does the bus ~?** ¿dónde para el autobús?; **stop!** ¡pare!
2 (= pause, take a break) parar, hacer alto; **to ~ to do sth** detenerse a hacer algo; **without ~ping** sin parar
3 (= come to an end) [fighting, production] acabar, terminar; [supply etc] cortarse, interrumpirse; **the pain ~ped** el dolor se le quitó; **the rain has ~ped** ha dejado de llover; **he doesn't know when to ~** no sabe cuándo conviene hacer alto; ✦ IDIOM **to ~ at nothing (to do sth)** no detenerse ante nada (para hacer algo)
4 (*) (= stay) quedarse; **I'm not ~ping** no me quedo
5 (*) (= live temporarily) hospedarse; **she's ~ping with her aunt** se hospeda en casa de su tía
Ⓓ CPD ➤ **stop press** (Brit) noticias fpl de última hora; **"stop press"** (as heading) "al cierre de la edición" ➤ **stop sign** (Aut) stop m, señal f de stop
➤ **stop by** **Ⓐ** VI + ADV **I'll ~ by on the way to school** me asomaré de paso al colegio **Ⓑ** VI + PREP [+ sb's house] pasar por
➤ **stop in*** VI + ADV quedarse en casa, no salir
➤ **stop off** VI + ADV interrumpir el viaje; **to ~ off at** (= drop by) pasar por; (= stop at) parar en
➤ **stop out*** VI + ADV (= remain outside) quedarse fuera; (= not come home) no volver a casa
➤ **stop over** VI + ADV (= stay the night) pasar la noche; (Aer) (for refuelling etc) hacer escala
➤ **stop up** **Ⓐ** VT + ADV [+ hole] tapar **Ⓑ** VI + ADV (Brit*) velar, no acostarse, seguir sin acostarse; **don't ~ up for me** no os quedéis esperándome hasta muy tarde

stopcock ['stɒpkɒk] N llave f de paso

stopgap ['stɒpɡæp] N (= thing) recurso m provisional, expediente m; (= person) sustituto/a m/f ➤ **stopgap measure** medida f provisional

stoplights ['stɒplaɪts] NPL **1** (= brake lights) luces fpl de freno **2** (US) (= traffic lights) luces fpl de tráfico, semáforo msing

stop-off ['stɒpɒf], **stopover** ['stɒpəʊvəʳ] N (Aer) escala f

stoppage ['stɒpɪdʒ] N **1** [of work] paro m, suspensión f; (= strike) huelga f; [of pay] suspensión f; (from wages) deducción f **2** (= blockage) obstrucción f

stopper ['stɒpəʳ] N tapón m

stopwatch ['stɒpwɒtʃ] N cronómetro m

storage ['stɔːrɪdʒ] N almacenaje m, almacenamiento m (also Comput); **to put into ~** almacenar; [+ furniture] llevar a un guardamuebles ➤ **storage heater** acumulador m
➤ **storage space** lugar m para los trastos ➤ **storage unit** armario m

store [stɔːʳ] **Ⓐ** N **1** (= supply) [of food, candles, paper] reserva f; [of jokes, stories] repertorio m; [of information] cúmulo m; **to keep a ~ of sth** tener una reserva de algo; **to lay in a ~ of sth** hacer una reserva de algo, proveerse de algo; **he possessed a vast ~ of knowledge** tenía una cultura muy amplia; **little did I know what the future had in ~** qué poco sabía lo que nos deparaba el futuro; **there's a surprise in ~ for you!** ¡te espera una sorpresa!; **to set great/little ~ by sth** tener algo en mucho/poco, dar mucho/poco valor a algo; **I wouldn't set much ~ by that** yo no le daría mucho valor
2 (= depository) almacén m, depósito m; **furniture ~** guardamuebles m inv
3 **stores** (= provisions) provisiones fpl, existencias fpl; (esp Mil) (= equipment) pertrechos mpl
4 (US) (= shop) tienda f; **book ~** librería f
5 (also **department ~**) grandes almacenes mpl
Ⓑ VT **1** (= keep) [+ food] conservar, guardar; [+ water, fuel, electricity] almacenar; [+ documents] archivar; (Comput) [+ information] almacenar, guardar; (Physiol) [+ fat, energy] almacenar, acumular; **~ in an airtight tin** consérvense en un frasco hermético
2 (also ~ **away**) guardar; **I've got the camping things ~d away till we need them** tengo las cosas de acampar guardadas hasta que las necesitemos
3 (= place in store) [+ furniture] depositar en un guardamuebles; [+ goods, crop, waste] almacenar
Ⓒ CPD ➤ **store card** (esp Brit) tarjeta f de compra ➤ **store detective** vigilante mf jurado (de paisano en grandes almacenes) ➤ **store window** (US) escaparate m, vitrina f, vidriera f (SC)

➤ **store away** VT + ADV (*in bulk*) almacenar; [+ *individual items*] guardar

➤ **store up** VT + ADV [+ *fat, energy*] almacenar, acumular; **to ~ up problems for the future** ir acumulando problemas para el futuro

storefront ['stɔːfrʌnt] N (*US*) escaparate *m*

storehouse ['stɔːhaʊs] N almacén *m*, depósito *m*; [*of information*] mina *f*, tesoro *m*

storekeeper ['stɔːˌkiːpəʳ] N (*US*) (= *shopkeeper*) tendero/a *m/f*

storeroom ['stɔːrʊm] N despensa *f*; (*Naut*) pañol *m*

storey, **story** (*US*) ['stɔːrɪ] N piso *m*; **a nine-~ building** un edificio de nueve pisos *or* plantas

stork [stɔːk] N cigüeña *f*

storm [stɔːm] Ⓐ N **1** (*gen*) tormenta *f*, tempestad *f*; (= *gale*) vendaval *m*; (= *hurricane*) huracán *m*

2 (= *uproar*) escándalo *m*, bronca *f*; **there was a political ~** hubo un gran revuelo político; **a ~ of abuse** un torrente de injurias; **a ~ of applause** una salva de aplausos; **a ~ of criticism** un aluvión *or* vendaval de críticas; ✦ IDIOM **a ~ in a teacup** (*Brit*) una tormenta *or* tempestad en un vaso de agua

3 to take by ~ (*Mil*) tomar por asalto; **the play took Paris by ~** la obra cautivó a todo París

Ⓑ VT asaltar

Ⓒ VI **he ~ed out of the meeting** salió de la reunión como un huracán; **to ~ at sb** tronar contra algn, enfurecerse con algn

Ⓓ CPD [*signal*] de temporal ➤ **storm cloud** nubarrón *m* ➤ **storm door** contrapuerta *f* ➤ **storm troops** (*Mil*) tropas *fpl* de asalto, guardia *fsing* de asalto

stormproof ['stɔːmpruːf] ADJ a prueba de tormentas

stormy ['stɔːmɪ] ADJ (*compar* **stormier**; *superl* **stormiest**)
1 [*weather, night, skies*] tormentoso
2 [*meeting, scene*] tumultuoso, turbulento; [*relationship*] tormentoso

story¹ ['stɔːrɪ] Ⓐ N **1** (= *account*) historia *f*; (= *tale*) cuento *m*, relato *m*; (= *joke*) chiste *m*; **but that's another ~** pero eso es otro cantar; **the ~ goes that ...** se dice *or* se cuenta que ...; **that's the ~ of my life!** ¡siempre me pasa lo mismo!; **it's a long ~** es *or* sería largo de contar; **to cut (**Brit**) or make (**US**) a long ~ short** en resumidas cuentas, en pocas palabras; **it's the same old ~** es la historia de siempre; **that's not the whole ~** eso no es todo
2 (= *plot*) argumento *m*, trama *f*
3 (*Press*) artículo *m*, reportaje *m*
4 (*euph*) (= *lie*) mentira *f*, cuento *m*; **a likely ~!** ¡puro cuento!

Ⓑ CPD ➤ **story writer** narrador(a) *m/f*

story² ['stɔːrɪ] N (*US*) = **storey**

storybook ['stɔːrɪbʊk] Ⓐ N libro *m* de cuentos Ⓑ ADJ **a ~ ending** un final como el de una novela

storyline ['stɔːrɪlaɪn] N argumento *m*

storyteller ['stɔːrɪˌtelə'] N **1** (*gen*) cuentista *mf* **2** (*) (= *liar*) cuentista *mf*, embustero/a *m/f*

stout [staʊt] Ⓐ ADJ (*compar* **~er**; *superl* **~est**) **1** (= *sturdy*) [*stick, shoes etc*] fuerte, sólido **2** (= *fat*) [*person*] gordo, robusto **3** (= *determined*) [*supporter, resistance*] resuelto, empedernido Ⓑ N (*Brit*) (= *beer*) cerveza *f* negra

stout-hearted ['staʊt'hɑːtɪd] ADJ valiente, resuelto

stove¹ [stəʊv] N (*for heating*) estufa *f*; (*for cooking*) cocina *f*, horno *m* (*LAm*)

stove² [stəʊv] PT, PP *of* **stave**; *see* **stave in**

stow [stəʊ] VT **1** (*Naut*) [+ *cargo*] estibar, arrumar **2** (= *put away*) guardar

➤ **stow away** Ⓐ VT + ADV (= *put away*) guardar; (= *hide*) esconder Ⓑ VI + ADV viajar de polizón

stowaway ['stəʊəweɪ] N polizón *m*, llovido *m*

straddle ['strædl] VT [+ *horse*] montar a horcajadas, ponerse a horcajadas sobre; [*town*] [+ *river etc*] hacer puente sobre

strafe [strɑːf] VT ametrallar, abalear (*LAm*)

straggle ['strægl] VI **1** (= *lag behind*) rezagarse **2** (= *spread*

untidily) [*plant*] lozanear; [*hair*] caer lacio

straggler ['stræglə'] N rezagado/a *m/f*

straggling ['stræglɪŋ], **straggly** ['stræglɪ] ADJ [*plants*] extendido; [*hair*] despeinado, desordenado

straight [streɪt] Ⓐ ADJ (*compar* **~er**; *superl* **~est**) **1** (= *not bent or curved*) [*line, road, nose, skirt*] recto; [*hair*] lacio, liso; **he couldn't even walk in a ~ line** ni siquiera podía caminar en línea recta; **to have a ~ back** tener la espalda erguida *or* recta; **I couldn't keep a ~ face** no podía mantener la cara seria; **she said it with a completely ~ face** lo dijo con la cara totalmente seria

2 (= *not askew*) [*picture, rug, hat, hem*] derecho; **your tie isn't ~** tienes la corbata torcida, tu corbata no está bien

3 (= *honest, direct*) [*answer*] franco, directo; [*question*] directo; [*refusal, denial*] categórico, rotundo; **it's time for some ~ talking** es hora de hablar con franqueza *or* claramente

4 (= *unambiguous*) claro; **let's get that ~** vamos a dejar eso claro; **have you got that ~?** ¿lo has entendido?, ¿está claro?; **to get things ~ in one's mind** aclararse las ideas; **he hasn't got his facts ~** no tiene la información correcta; **to put sth ~** aclarar algo; **he soon set me ~** enseguida me aclaró las cosas; **to put** *or* **set the record ~** aclarar las cosas

5 (= *tidy, in order*) [*house, room*] arreglado, ordenado; [*books, affairs, accounts*] en orden; **to put sth ~** arreglar algo

6 (= *clear-cut, simple*) [*choice, swap*] simple; **her latest novel is ~ autobiography** su última novela es una simple autobiografía

7 (= *consecutive*) [*victories, defeats, games*] consecutivo; **to get ~ As** sacar sobresaliente en todo; **she lost in ~ sets** (*in tennis*) perdió sin ganar ningún set; **we had ten ~ wins** ganamos diez veces seguidas, tuvimos diez victorias consecutivas

8 (= *neat*) [*whisky, vodka*] solo

9 (*Theat*) (= *not comic*) dramático, serio

10 (*) (= *conventional*) [*person*] de cabeza cuadrada*

11 (*) (= *not owed or owing money*) **if I give you a fiver, then we'll be ~** si te doy cinco libras, estamos en paz

12 (*) (= *heterosexual*) heterosexual, hetero*

13 (*) (= *not criminal*) **he's been ~ for two years** ha llevado una vida honrada durante dos años

14 (**) (= *not using drugs*) **I've been ~ for 13 years** hace 13 años que dejé las drogas, llevo 13 años desenganchado de las drogas

Ⓑ ADV **1** (= *in a straight line*) [*walk, shoot, fly*] en línea recta; [*grow*] recto; **stand up ~!** ¡ponte derecho *or* erguido!; **~ above us** directamente encima de nosotros; **it's ~ across the road** está justo al otro lado de la calle; **to go ~ ahead** ir todo recto, ir todo derecho; **to look ~ ahead** mirar al frente, mirar hacia adelante; **to look ~ at sb** mirar derecho hacia algn; **he came ~ at me** vino derecho hacia mí; **to look sb ~ in the eye** mirar directamente a los ojos de algn; **to look sb ~ in the face** mirar a algn directamente a la cara; **to go ~ on** ir todo recto, ir todo derecho; **the bullet went ~ through his chest** la bala le atravesó limpiamente el pecho; **I saw a car coming ~ towards me** vi un coche que venía derecho hacia mí; **the cork shot ~ up in the air** el corcho salió disparado hacia arriba

2 (= *level*) **to hang ~** [*picture*] estar derecho

3 (= *directly*) directamente; (= *immediately*) inmediatamente; **I went ~ home/to bed** fui derecho a casa/ a la cama; **come ~ back** vuelve directamente aquí; **to come ~ to the point** ir al grano; **~ after this** inmediatamente después de esto; **~ away** inmediatamente, en seguida, al tiro (*Chi*); **~ off** (= *without hesitation*) sin vacilar; (= *immediately*) inmediatamente; (= *directly*) directamente, sin rodeos; ✦ IDIOM **I heard it ~ from the horse's mouth** se lo oí decir a él mismo (*or* a ella misma)

4 (= *frankly*) francamente, con franqueza; **just give it to me or tell me ~** dímelo francamente *or* con franqueza; **to tell sb sth ~ out** decir algo a algn sin rodeos *or* directamente; ✦ IDIOM **I let him have it ~ from the shoulder** se lo dije sin rodeos

5 (= *neat*) [*drink*] solo

6 (= *clearly*) [*think*] con claridad; **I was so drunk I couldn't see ~** estaba tan borracho que no veía

7 (*) **to go ~** [*criminal*] enmendarse; [*drug addict*] dejar de tomar drogas, desengancharse

8 (= *consecutively*) **for three days** ~ durante tres días seguidos
ⓖ N **1 ✦** IDIOM **to keep to the** ~ **and narrow** ir por buen camino; **to keep sb on the** ~ **and narrow** mantener a algn por el buen camino
2 (*Brit*) (*on racecourse*) **the** ~ la recta
3 (*) (= *heterosexual*) heterosexual *mf*
ⓓ CPD ➤ **straight man** actor *m* que da pie al cómico ➤ **straight ticket** (*US Pol*) **to vote a** ~ **ticket** votar a candidatos del mismo partido para todos los cargos

straighten ['streɪtn] **ⓐ** VT [+ *wire, nail*] (*also* ~ **out**) enderezar; [+ *picture, tie, hat*] poner derecho, enderezar; (*also* ~ **up**) [+ *room, house*] ordenar, arreglar; [+ *papers*] ordenar; **to** ~ **one's shoulders** poner la espalda erguida *or* recta *or* derecha **ⓑ** VI = **straighten out B**
➤ **straighten out ⓐ** VT + ADV [+ *wire, nail*] enderezar; [+ *problem*] resolver; **I soon** ~**ed him out on that point** enseguida le aclaré las cosas a ese respecto; **they sent me to a psychoanalyst to try and** ~ **me out** me mandaron a un psicoanalista para ver si resolvía mis problemas **ⓑ** VI + ADV [*road*] **after the crossroads the road** ~**s out** tras el cruce ya no hay más curvas
➤ **straighten up ⓐ** VI + ADV enderezarse, ponerse derecho **ⓑ** VT + ADV [+ *room, house*] ordenar, arreglar

straight-faced ['streɪt'feɪst] **ⓐ** ADJ serio; **a** ~ **newsreader** un locutor de expresión seria **ⓑ** ADV con cara seria

straightforward [ˌstreɪt'fɔːwəd] ADJ **1** (= *honest*) honrado; (= *sincere*) sincero **2** (= *simple*) sencillo; [*answer*] claro, franco

strain¹ [streɪn] **ⓐ** N **1** (= *physical pressure*) (*on rope, cable*) tensión *f*; (*on beam, bridge, structure*) presión *f*; **that puts a great** ~ **on the beam** esto pone mucha presión sobre la viga; **to take the** ~ (*lit*) aguantar el peso; **to take the** ~ **off** [+ *rope, cable*] disminuir la tensión de; **to take the** ~ [+ *beam, bridge, structure*] disminuir la presión sobre; **to break under the** ~ [*rope, cable*] romperse debido a la tensión; **to collapse under the** ~ [*bridge, ceiling*] venirse abajo debido a la presión
2 (*fig*) (= *burden*) carga *f*; (= *pressure*) presión *f*; (= *stress*) tensión *f*; **it was a** ~ **on the economy/his purse** suponía una carga para la economía/su bolsillo; **the** ~**s of modern life** las tensiones de la vida moderna; **mental** ~ cansancio *m* mental; **to put a** ~ **on** [+ *resources*] suponer una carga para; [+ *system*] forzar al límite; [+ *relationship*] crear tirantez *or* tensiones en; **it put a great** ~ **on their friendship** creó mucha tirantez en su amistad; **his illness has put a terrible** ~ **on the family** su enfermedad ha creado mucha tensión *or* estrés para la familia; **he has been under a great deal of** ~ ha estado sometido a mucha presión
3 (= *effort*) esfuerzo *m*; **the** ~ **of climbing the stairs** el esfuerzo de subir las escaleras
4 (= *injury*) (*from pull*) esguince *m*; (*involving twist*) esguince *m*, torcedura *f*; **muscle** ~ esguince muscular
5 (= *wear*) (*on eyes, heart*) esfuerzo *m*; **tennis put a** ~ **on his heart** el tenis le sometía el corazón a un esfuerzo *or* le forzaba el corazón
6 strains (= *sound*) compases *mpl*; **the gentle** ~**s of a Haydn quartet** los suaves compases de un cuarteto de Haydn
ⓑ VT **1** (= *stretch beyond reasonable limits*) [+ *system*] forzar al límite; [+ *friendship, marriage*] crear tensiones en, crear tirantez en; [+ *resources, budget*] suponer una carga para
2 (= *damage, tire*) [+ *back*] dañar(se), hacer daño en; [+ *eyes*] cansar; **to** ~ **a muscle** hacerse un esguince; **to** ~ **o.s.** (= *work too hard*) hacer (demasiados) esfuerzos; (= *hurt o.s.*) hacerse daño; **don't** ~ **yourself!** (*iro*) ¡no te vayas a quebrar *or* herniar!
3 (= *make an effort with*) [+ *voice, eyes*] forzar; **to** ~ **one's ears to hear sth** aguzar el oído para oír algo; **to** ~ **every nerve to do sth** esforzarse mucho por hacer algo, hacer grandes esfuerzos por hacer algo
4 (*in cooking*) [+ *gravy, soup, custard*] colar; [+ *vegetables*] escurrir; ~ **the mixture through a sieve** pase la mezcla por un tamiz
ⓒ VI (= *make an effort*) **to** ~ **to do sth** esforzarse por hacer algo; **to** ~ **at sth** tirar de algo; **to** ~ **at the leash** [*dog*] tirar de la correa; **to** ~ **under a weight** ir agobiado por un peso
➤ **strain off** VT + ADV [+ *liquid*] escurrir

strain² [streɪn] N **1** (= *breed*) (*of animal*) raza *f*; (*of plant*)

variedad *f*; (*of virus*) tipo *m* **2** (= *streak, element*) vena *f*

strained [streɪnd] ADJ **1** (= *tense*) [*person*] tenso; [*face*] crispado; [*voice, laugh, politeness*] forzado; [*atmosphere, relations, silence*] tirante, tenso **2** [*wrist, ankle*] torcido; [*eyes, voice*] cansado; **a** ~ **muscle** un esguince; **he has a** ~ **shoulder/back** tiene una lesión en un hombro/en la espalda **3** (= *overtaxed*) [*economy*] debilitado **4** [*baby food*] pasado por el pasapurés *or* el tamiz; [*soup, gravy*] colado

strainer ['streɪnəʳ] N (*Culin*) colador *m*

strait [streɪt] N **1** (*Geog*) (*also* ~**s**) estrecho *m*; **the Straits of Dover** el estrecho de Dover **2 straits** (*fig*) situación *f* apurada, apuro *m*; **to be in dire** ~**s** estar en un gran apuro

straitened ['streɪtnd] ADJ **in** ~ **circumstances** en condiciones difíciles *or* de apuro

straitjacket ['streɪtˌdʒækɪt] N camisa *f* de fuerza

strait-laced ['streɪt'leɪst] ADJ puritano

strand¹ [strænd] N [*of thread*] hebra *f*, hilo *m*; [*of hair*] pelo *m*; [*of rope*] ramal *m*; [*of story*] hilo *m* argumental

strand² [strænd] **ⓐ** N (*liter*) (= *beach, shore*) playa *f* **ⓑ** VT [+ *ship*] varar, encallar; **to be (left)** ~**ed** [*ship, fish*] quedar varado; [*person*] (*without money*) quedar desamparado; (*without transport*) quedar tirado; **✦** IDIOM **to leave sb** ~**ed** (*in the lurch*) dejar a algn plantado

strange [streɪndʒ] ADJ (*compar* ~**r**; *superl* ~**st**) **1** (= *odd*) [*person, event, behaviour, feeling*] extraño, raro; [*experience, place, noise*] extraño; **it's** ~ **that he should come today of all days** es extraño *or* raro que venga precisamente hoy; **there's something** ~ **about him** hay algo extraño *or* raro en él; **I felt rather** ~ **at first** al principio me sentía bastante raro; **I find it** ~ **that we never heard anything about this** me parece raro *or* me extraña que nunca hayamos oído hablar de esto; **for some** ~ **reason** por alguna razón inexplicable; ~ **as it may seem ◇** ~ **to say** por extraño que parezca, aunque parezca mentira; **the** ~ **thing is that ...** lo extraño *or* lo curioso es que ...
2 (= *unknown, unfamiliar*) [*person, house, car, country*] desconocido; [*language*] desconocido, extranjero; **I never sleep well in a** ~ **bed** nunca duermo bien en una cama que no sea la mía; **don't talk to any** ~ **men** no hables con ningún desconocido; **I was** ~ **to this part of town** esta parte de la ciudad me era desconocida

strangely ['streɪndʒlɪ] ADV [*act, behave*] de una forma extraña *or* rara; **the room was** ~ **quiet** en la habitación había un silencio extraño; **her voice sounded** ~ **familiar** su voz me resultaba extrañamente familiar; ~ **(enough), ...** por extraño que parezca, ..., aunque resulte extraño, ...

strangeness ['streɪndʒnɪs] N **1** (= *oddness*) lo extraño, rareza *f* **2** (= *unfamiliarity*) novedad *f*

stranger ['streɪndʒəʳ] N (= *unknown person*) desconocido/a *m/f*, extraño/a *m/f*; (*from another area etc*) forastero/a *m/f*; **he's a** ~ **to me** es un desconocido para mí; **I'm a** ~ **here** yo soy nuevo aquí; **hello,** ~**!** ¡cuánto tiempo sin vernos!; **he is no** ~ **to vice** conoce bien los vicios

> ⚠ **stranger** ≠ **extranjero**

strangle ['stræŋgl] VT estrangular; (*fig*) [+ *sob*] ahogar; **a** ~**d cry** un grito entrecortado

stranglehold ['stræŋglhəʊld] N **to have a** ~ **on sb** tener dominio completo sobre algn; **to have a** ~ **on sth** monopolizar algo

strangler ['stræŋgləʳ] N estrangulador(a) *m/f*

strap [stræp] **ⓐ** N correa *f*, tira *f*; (= *shoulder strap*) tirante *m*, bretel *m* (*LAm*); (= *safety strap*) cinturón *m* **ⓑ** VT (= *fasten*) atar con correa; **to** ~ **sb/o.s. in** (*with seatbelt*) poner a algn/ponerse el cinturón de seguridad; **he isn't properly** ~**ped in** no está bien atado

strapless ['stræplɪs] ADJ [*dress, bra*] sin tirantes

strapped* [stræpt] ADJ **to be** ~ **for cash** andar escaso de dinero

strapping ['stræpɪŋ] ADJ [*person*] fornido, robusto

Strasbourg ['stræzbɜːg] N Estrasburgo *m*

strata ['strɑːtə] NPL *of* **stratum**

stratagem ['strætɪdʒəm] N estratagema *f*

strategic [strə'tiːdʒɪk], **strategical** [strə'tiːdʒɪkəl] ADJ estratégico

strategically [strə'tiːdʒɪkəlɪ] ADV estratégicamente

strategist ['strætɪdʒɪst] N estratega *mf*

strategy ['strætɪdʒɪ] N estrategia *f*

stratified ['strætɪfaɪd] ADJ estratificado

stratosphere ['strætəsfɪəʳ] N estratosfera *f*

stratum ['strɑːtəm] N (*pl* **~s** *or* **strata**) estrato *m*

straw [strɔː] Ⓐ N 1 (*Agr*) paja *f*; ✦ IDIOMS **to clutch at ~s** agarrarse a un clavo ardiendo; **I always draw the short ~** siempre me toca a mí la china*; **it's the last ~!** ¡es el colmo!, ¡sólo faltaba eso! 2 (= *drinking straw*) pajita *f*, caña *f*, popote *m* (*Mex*); **to drink through a ~** beber con pajita Ⓑ CPD [*hat*] de paja ➤ **straw man** hombre *m* de paja ➤ **straw poll, straw vote** votación *f* de tanteo

strawberry ['strɔːbərɪ] Ⓐ N (= *fruit, plant*) fresa *f*, frutilla *f* (*LAm*); (*large, cultivated*) fresón *m* Ⓑ CPD [*jam, ice cream, tart*] de fresa ➤ **strawberry mark** (*on skin*) mancha *f* de nacimiento

strawberry-blonde [ˌstrɔːbərɪ'blɒnd] ADJ bermejo

straw-coloured, straw-colored (*US*) ['strɔːkʌləd] ADJ pajizo, (de) color de paja

stray [streɪ] Ⓐ ADJ 1 (= *errant*) [*bullet*] perdido; [*sheep*] descarriado; [*cat, dog, cow*] extraviado 2 (= *isolated, occasional*) aislado; **in a few ~ cases** en algunos casos aislados; **a few ~ cars** algún que otro coche Ⓑ N (= *animal*) animal *m* extraviado; (= *child*) niño/a *m/f* sin hogar, niño/a *m/f* desamparado/a Ⓒ VI [*animal*] extraviarse; [*person*] vagar, ir sin rumbo fijo; [*speaker, thoughts*] desvariar; **to ~ from** (*also fig*) apartarse de; **they ~ed into the enemy camp** erraron el camino y se encontraron en el campamento enemigo; **my thoughts ~ed to the holidays** empecé a pensar en las vacaciones

streak [striːk] Ⓐ N 1 (= *line*) raya *f*; [*of mineral*] veta *f*, vena *f*; **to have ~s in one's hair** tener mechas en el pelo; ✦ IDIOM **like a ~ of lightning** como un rayo 2 (*fig*) [*of madness etc*] vena *f*; [*of luck*] racha *f*; **he had a cruel ~ (in him)** tenía un rasgo cruel Ⓑ VT rayar (**with** de) Ⓒ VI 1 (= *rush*) **to ~ in/out/past** entrar/salir/pasar como un rayo 2 (*) (= *run naked*) correr desnudo

streaky ['striːkɪ] ADJ rayado, listado ➤ **streaky bacon** (*Brit*) beicon *m*, bacon *m* (*Sp*)

stream [striːm] Ⓐ N 1 (= *brook*) arroyo *m*, riachuelo *m* 2 (= *current*) corriente *f*; **to go with/against the ~** (*lit, fig*) ir con/contra la corriente 3 (= *jet, gush*) [*of liquid*] chorro *m*; [*of light*] raudal *m*; [*of air*] chorro *m*, corriente *f*; [*of lava*] río *m*; [*of insults, abuse*] sarta *f*; [*of letters, questions, complaints*] lluvia *f*; **a thin ~ of water** un chorrito de agua; **a steady ~ of cars** un flujo constante *or* ininterrumpido de coches; **we had a constant ~ of visitors** recibíamos visitas continuamente *or* sin parar; **~ of consciousness** monólogo *m* interior 4 (*Brit Scol*) grupo *m* de alumnos de la misma edad y aptitud académica; **the top/middle/bottom ~** la clase de nivel superior/medio/inferior Ⓑ VI 1 (= *pour*) **tears were ~ing down her face** le corrían las lágrimas por la cara; **rain ~ed down the windows** la lluvia chorreaba por las ventanas; **blood ~ed from a cut on his knee** le chorreaba sangre de un corte en la rodilla; **his head was ~ing with blood** la cabeza le chorreaba sangre; **people ~ed into the hall** la gente entró en tropel a la sala; **bright sunlight ~ed in through the window** la fuerte luz del sol entraba a raudales por la ventana 2 (= *water, run*) **her eyes were ~ing** le lloraban los ojos; **my nose was ~ing** (*Brit*) me moqueaba la nariz Ⓒ VT 1 **his face ~ed blood** la sangre le corría *or* chorreaba por la cara 2 (*Brit Scol*) [+ *pupils*] agrupar, clasificar (*según su aptitud académica*)

streamer ['striːməʳ] N [*of paper, at parties etc*] serpentina *f*

streaming ['striːmɪŋ] Ⓐ ADJ **to have a ~ cold** (*Brit*) tener un resfriado muy fuerte Ⓑ N (*Scol*) división *f* de alumnos por grupos (*según su aptitud académica*)

streamline ['striːmlaɪn] VT (*lit*) aerodinamizar; (*fig*) racionalizar

streamlined ['striːmlaɪnd] ADJ [*air*] aerodinámico; (*fig*) racionalizado

street [striːt] N calle *f*, jirón *m* (*Per*); **to be on the ~s** (= *homeless*) estar sin vivienda; ✦ IDIOMS **to be ~s ahead of sb** (*Brit**) sacarle mucha ventaja a algn; **they're ~s apart** (*Brit**) los separa un abismo; **they're not in the same ~ as us** (*Brit**) no están a nuestra altura, no admiten comparación con nosotros; **it's right up my ~** (*Brit**) esto es lo que me va, esto es lo mío ➤ **street cleaner** (*esp US*) barrendero/a *m/f* ➤ **street cred*, street credibility** (*Brit*) dominio *m* de la contracultura urbana ➤ **street fighting** peleas *fpl* callejeras ➤ **street lamp** farola *f*, faro *m* (*LAm*) ➤ **street level: at ~ level** en el nivel de la calle ➤ **street light** farola *f*, faro *m* (*LAm*) ➤ **street map** plano *m* (de la ciudad) ➤ **street musician** músico *m* ambulante ➤ **street plan** plano *m*, callejero *m* ➤ **street sweeper** barrendero/a *m/f* ➤ **street theatre, street theater** (*US*) teatro *m* en la calle, teatro *m* de calle ➤ **street value** valor *m* en la calle ➤ **street vendor** (*US*) vendedor/a *mf* callejero/a

streetcar ['striːtkɑːʳ] N (*US*) tranvía *m*, tren *m*

street-smart ['striːtsmɑːt] ADJ (*US*) despabilado

streetwalker ['striːtˌwɔːkəʳ] N mujer *f* de la vida

streetwise ['striːtwaɪz] ADJ despabilado

strength [streŋθ] N 1 (= *might, energy*) (*for particular task*) fuerzas *fpl*; (= *general attribute*) fuerza *f*; **he hadn't the ~ to lift it** no tenía fuerzas para levantarlo; **his ~ failed him** le fallaron las fuerzas; **you don't know your own ~** no controlas tu propia fuerza; **you'll soon get your ~ back** pronto recobrarás las fuerzas *or* te repondrás; **to save one's ~** ahorrar las energías; **with all my ~** con todas mis fuerzas 2 (= *fortitude*) fortaleza *f*, fuerzas *fpl*; (= *firmness*) [*of belief, conviction*] firmeza *f*; **his help gives me the ~ to carry on** su ayuda me da fortaleza *or* fuerzas para seguir adelante; **~ of character** fortaleza *f* *or* firmeza *f* de carácter; **~ of purpose** determinación *f* 3 (= *sturdiness*) [*of material, structure, frame*] resistencia *f* 4 (= *power*) [*of argument*] lo convincente, solidez *f*; [*of claim, case, evidence*] peso *m*; [*of magnet, lens, drug*] potencia *f*; [*of wind*] fuerza *f*; [*of alcohol*] graduación *f*; **on the ~ of that success she applied for promotion** en base a ese éxito, solicitó un ascenso; **he was recruited on the ~ of his communication skills** lo contrataron en virtud de *or* debido a su aptitud para comunicarse 5 (= *intensity*) intensidad *f* 6 [*of currency*] (= *value*) valor *m*; (= *high value*) solidez *f*, fuerza *f* 7 (= *good point, asset*) punto *m* fuerte; ✦ IDIOM **to go from ~ to ~** tener un éxito tras otro; **the company has gone from ~ to ~** la empresa ha ido teniendo un éxito tras otro 8 (*in number*) número *m*; (*Mil, Police*) efectivos *mpl*; **to increase the ~ of the police force** incrementar los efectivos de la policía; **to be at full ~** [*army*] disponer de todos sus efectivos; [*team*] contar con todos sus jugadores; [*office*] contar con todo el personal; **his supporters had come in ~** sus partidarios habían acudido en masa; **the team was under ~ due to injuries** el equipo contaba con pocos jugadores debido a las lesiones

strengthen ['streŋθən] Ⓐ VT [+ *wall, roof, building, argument, case*] reforzar; [+ *back, muscle, limb*] fortalecer; [+ *currency, economy, bond, relationship, character*] fortalecer, consolidar; [+ *government*] consolidar; [+ *resolve, belief*] hacer más firme; [+ *opposition*] afianzar Ⓑ VI [*muscle, arm, back*] fortalecerse; [*wind, storm*] hacerse más fuerte; [*currency, economy*] fortalecerse, consolidarse; [*desire, determination*] redoblarse, intensificarse

strenuous ['strenjʊəs] ADJ 1 (= *physically demanding*) [*efforts*] intenso, arduo; [*work*] agotador, arduo; [*exercise, walk*] agotador, fatigoso 2 (= *vigorous*) [*objections, protest, opposition*] enérgico; [*denial*] enérgico, rotundo

strenuously ['strenjʊəslɪ] ADV [*deny, object, protest, oppose*] enérgicamente; [*resist*] tenazmente, con tenacidad; [*exercise*] con intensidad

strep throat* [ˌstrepˈθrəʊt] N infección f de garganta (*por estreptococos*)

stress [stres] **Ⓐ** N **1** (*Tech*) tensión f, carga f
2 (*psychological etc*) estrés m, tensión f (nerviosa); **the ~es and strains of modern life** las presiones de la vida moderna; **to be under ~** estar estresado, tener estrés
3 (= *emphasis*) hincapié m, énfasis m; **to lay great ~ on sth** recalcar algo
4 (*Ling, Poetry*) acento m (tónico); **the ~ is on the second syllable** lleva el acento (tónico) en la segunda sílaba
Ⓑ VT **1** (= *emphasize*) subrayar, insistir en, recalcar
2 (*Ling, Poetry*) acentuar
Ⓒ CPD ➤ **stress mark** (*Ling*) tilde f

stressed [strest] ADJ **1** (= *tense*) [*person*] estresado, agobiado **2** (*Ling, Poetry*) [*syllable*] acentuado

stressful [ˈstresfəl] ADJ estresante

stretch [stretʃ] **Ⓐ** N **1** (= *elasticity*) elasticidad f
2 (= *act of stretching*) **to have a ~** [*person*] estirarse; **by a ~ of the imagination** con un esfuerzo de imaginación; **by no ~ of the imagination** bajo ningún concepto
3 (= *distance*) trecho m
4 (= *expanse*) extensión f; [*of road etc*] tramo m; [*of time*] periodo m, tiempo m; **in that ~ of the river** en aquella parte del río; **for a long ~ of time** durante mucho tiempo; **for hours at a ~** durante horas enteras
5 (**) (*in prison*) **a five-year ~** una condena de cinco años
Ⓑ VT **1** (= *pull out*) [+ *elastic*] estirar; [+ *rope etc*] tender (**between** entre)
2 (= *make larger*) [+ *pullover, shoes*] ensanchar; (= *make longer*) alargar; (= *spread on ground etc*) extender
3 (= *exercise*) **to ~ one's legs** estirar las piernas; (*after stiffness*) desentumecerse las piernas; (*fig*) (= *go for a walk*) dar un paseíto; **to ~ o.s.** (*after sleep etc*) desperezarse
4 (= *money, resources, meal*) hacer que llegue or alcance; **our resources are fully ~ed** nuestros recursos están aprovechados al máximo
5 [+ *meaning, law, truth*] forzar, violentar; **that's ~ing it too far** eso va demasiado lejos; **to ~ a point** hacer una excepción
6 [+ *athlete, student etc*] exigir el máximo esfuerzo a; **the course does not ~ the students enough** el curso no exige bastante esfuerzo a los estudiantes; **to be fully ~ed** llegar a sus límites; **to ~ o.s.** esforzarse; **to ~ sb to the limits** sacar el máximo provecho de algn
Ⓒ VI **1** (= *be elastic*) estirar(se), dar (de sí)
2 (= *become larger*) [*clothes, shoes*] ensancharse
3 (= *stretch one's limbs, reach out*) estirarse; (*after sleep etc*) desperezarse
4 (= *reach, extend*) [*rope, area of land*] llegar (**to** a); [*power, influence*] permitir (**to** que); [*money, food*] alcanzar (**to** para)
Ⓓ CPD [*fabric*] elástico ➤ **stretch limo*** limusina f americana ➤ **stretch marks** estrías fpl
➤ **stretch out Ⓐ** VT + ADV **1** [+ *arm*] extender; [+ *hand*] tender, alargar; [+ *leg*] estirar **2** (= *lengthen*) [+ *essay, discussion*] alargar **Ⓑ** VI + ADV **1** [*person*] estirarse; (= *lie down*) tumbarse, tenderse **2** [*space, time*] extenderse

stretcher [ˈstretʃəʳ] **Ⓐ** N camilla f **Ⓑ** VT llevar en camilla **Ⓒ** CPD ➤ **stretcher bearer** camillero/a m/f ➤ **stretcher case** enfermo o herido que tiene que ser llevado en camilla

stricken [ˈstrɪkən] ADJ **1** (= *distressed, upset*) afligido, acongojado; **to be ~ with grief** estar agobiado por el dolor; **she was ~ with remorse** le remordía la conciencia
2 (= *damaged*) [*ship etc*] destrozado, dañado; (= *wounded*) herido; (= *ill*) enfermo; (= *suffering*) afligido con; (= *doomed*) condenado; **the ~ city** la ciudad condenada or destrozada; **drought-~** aquejado de sequía, afectado por la sequía

strict [strɪkt] ADJ (*compar* ~**er**; *superl* ~**est**) **1** (= *severe*) estricto, severo; **to be ~ with sb** ser estricto or severo con algn
2 (= *stringent*) [*rules*] estricto; [*control*] estricto, riguroso; [*limit*] riguroso; **to be under ~ orders (not) to do sth** tener órdenes estrictas de (no) hacer algo
3 (= *precise*) [*meaning*] estricto; **in ~ order of precedence** por riguroso or estricto orden de precedencia; **in the ~ sense of the word** en el sentido estricto de la palabra
4 (= *absolute*) [*secrecy*] absoluto; **I told you that in ~ confidence** te lo dije en la más absoluta reserva; **to treat sth in the ~est confidence** tratar algo con la reserva más absoluta

strictly [ˈstrɪktlɪ] ADV **1** (= *severely*) severamente
2 (= *stringently*) estrictamente, rigurosamente
3 (= *absolutely*) [*forbidden*] terminantemente; [*necessary*] absolutamente; [*confidential*] estrictamente; **it is not ~ accurate to say that ...** no es del todo preciso decir que ...; **~ speaking** en (el) sentido estricto (de la palabra); **that's not ~ true** eso no es del todo cierto, eso no es rigurosamente cierto
4 (= *exclusively*) exclusivamente; **this is ~ business** esto es exclusivamente una cuestión de trabajo; **the car park is ~ for the use of residents** el aparcamiento es para uso exclusivo de los residentes

strictness [ˈstrɪktnɪs] N **1** (= *severity*) severidad f
2 (= *stringency*) [*of rules, control, security*] lo riguroso

stricture [ˈstrɪktʃəʳ] N (= *criticism*) censura f, crítica f

stride [straɪd] (*vb*: *pt* **strode**; *pp* **stridden** [ˈstrɪdn]) **Ⓐ** N zancada f, tranco m; **to make great ~s** (*fig*) hacer grandes progresos; **✦** IDIOMS **to get into one's ~** coger or (*LAm*) agarrar el ritmo; **to take things in one's ~** or (*US*) **in ~** tomar las cosas con calma; **to put sb off their ~** (*Brit*) hacer perder los papeles a algn **Ⓑ** VI (*also* **~ along**) andar a zancadas

strident [ˈstraɪdənt] ADJ [*voice, sound*] estridente; [*colour, person*] chillón, estridente; [*protest*] fuerte, ruidoso

strife [straɪf] N conflictos mpl; **domestic ~** riñas fpl domésticas; **internal ~** conflictos mpl internos

strife-ridden [ˈstraɪfˌrɪdn] ADJ conflictivo

strike [straɪk] (*vb*: *pt*, *pp* **struck**) **Ⓐ** N **1** (*by workers*) huelga f, paro m; **to be on ~** estar en huelga; **to come out** or **go on ~** declarar la huelga
2 (= *discovery*) [*of oil, gold*] descubrimiento m
3 (*Baseball*) golpe m; (*Bowling*) strike m; **you have two ~s against you** (*esp US*) (*fig*) tienes dos cosas en contra
4 (= *attack*) ataque m; (*by air*) ataque m aéreo, bombardeo m
Ⓑ VT **1** (= *hit*) golpear; (*with fist etc*) pegar, dar una bofetada a; [+ *ball*] golpear; [+ *chord, note*] tocar; **the president was struck by two bullets** dos balas alcanzaron al presidente; **the clock struck the hour** el reloj dio la hora; **the tower was struck by lightning** la torre fue alcanzada por un rayo, cayó un rayo en la torre; **✦** IDIOMS **to ~ a blow for sth** romper una lanza a favor de algo; **to ~ a blow against sth** socavar algo; **that ~s a chord!** ¡eso me suena!
2 (= *collide with*) [+ *iceberg, rocks, landmine*] chocar con, chocar contra; [+ *difficulty, obstacle*] encontrar, dar con, tropezar con; **he struck his head on the beam** dio con la cabeza contra or en la viga; **the light ~s the window** la luz hiere la ventana; **disaster struck us** el desastre nos vino encima
3 [+ *coin, medal*] acuñar; [+ *a light, match*] encender, prender (*LAm*); **to ~ terror into sb's heart** infundir terror a algn
4 (= *appear to, occur to*) **it ~s me as being most unlikely** me parece poco factible, se me hace poco probable (*LAm*); **how did it ~ you?** ¿qué te pareció?, ¿qué impresión te causó?; **it ~s me that ...** se me ocurre que ...; **has it ever struck you that ...?** ¿has pensado alguna vez que ...?
5 (= *impress*) **I was struck by his sincerity** su sinceridad me impresionó
6 (= *find*) [+ *gold, oil*] descubrir; **✦** IDIOMS **to ~ it lucky** tener suerte; **he struck it rich** le salió el gordo
7 (= *arrive at*) [+ *agreement*] alcanzar, llegar a; **to ~ a balance** encontrar el equilibrio; **to ~ a bargain** cerrar un trato
8 (= *assume, adopt*) **to ~ an attitude** adoptar una actitud
9 (= *cause to become*) **to ~ sb blind** cegar a algn; **to ~ sb dead** matar a algn; **to be struck dumb** (*lit, fig*) quedarse sin habla
10 (= *cross out*) suprimir (**from** de)
Ⓒ VI **1** (= *attack*) atacar; [*disaster*] sobrevenir; [*disease*] golpear; [*snake etc*] morder, atacar; **to ~ against sth** dar con algo, dar contra algo, chocar contra algo; **to ~ at sb** (*with fist*) tratar de golpear a algn; (*Mil*) atacar a algn; **this ~s at our very existence** esto amenaza nuestra existencia misma; **to be within striking distance of** [+ *place*] estar a poca

distancia or a un paso de; ✦ IDIOM **to ~ lucky** tener suerte **2** [*workers*] declarar la huelga, declararse en huelga; **to ~ for sth** hacer una huelga para conseguir algo **3** [*clock*] dar la hora
🄓 CPD [*committee, fund*] de huelga ➤ **strike pay** subsidio *m* de huelga
➤ **strike back** VI + ADV (*gen*) devolver el golpe (**at** a); (*Mil*) contraatacar
➤ **strike down** VT + ADV [*illness*] (= *incapacitate*) fulminar; (= *kill*) matar; **he was struck down in his prime** se lo llevó la muerte en la flor de la vida
➤ **strike off** VT + ADV [+ *name from list*] tachar; (*Brit*) [+ *doctor*] suspender
➤ **strike out** 🄰 VT + ADV (= *cross out*) tachar 🄱 VI + ADV **1** (= *hit out*) arremeter (**at** contra) **2** (= *set out*) dirigirse; **he struck out for the shore** se dirigió nadando hacia la playa; **to ~ out on one's own** (*in business*) volar con sus propias alas
➤ **strike up** 🄰 VT + ADV **1** [+ *friendship, conversation*] entablar, empezar **2** [+ *tune*] atacar 🄱 VI + ADV [*band*] empezar a tocar
strikebreaker [ˈstraɪkˌbreɪkəʳ] N esquirol(a) *m/f*, rompehuelgas *mf inv*
striker [ˈstraɪkəʳ] N **1** (*in industry*) huelguista *mf* **2** (*Sport*) delantero/a *m/f*, ariete *m*
striking [ˈstraɪkɪŋ] ADJ [*picture, clothes, colour*] llamativo; [*contrast*] notable; [*similarity, difference*] sorprendente; [*woman*] imponente; **her ~ good looks** su imponente or impresionante belleza; **to bear a ~ resemblance to sb** parecerse muchísimo a algn; **the most ~ feature of the house** el detalle que más llama la atención de la casa
strikingly [ˈstraɪkɪŋlɪ] ADV [*similar, different, bold*] sorprendentemente; [*attractive*] extraordinariamente; **to contrast ~ with sth** contrastar notablemente con algo
Strimmer® [ˈstrɪməʳ] N cortacésped *m inv* (*especial para los bordes*)
string [strɪŋ] (*vb: pt, pp* **strung**) 🄰 N **1** (= *cord*) cuerda *f*, cordel *m*, cabuya *f* (*LAm*), mecate *m* (*Mex*); ✦ IDIOMS **to have sb on a ~** dominar a algn completamente, tener a algn en un puño; **to pull ~s** mover palancas; **there are no ~s attached** esto es sin compromiso alguno; **with no ~s attached** sin compromiso
2 [*of onions, garlic*] ristra *f*; [*of beads*] hilo *m*, sarta *f*; [*of vehicles*] caravana *f*, fila *f*; [*of people*] hilera *f*, desfile *m*; [*of excuses, lies*] sarta *f*, serie *f*
3 (*on musical instrument, racket*) cuerda *f*; **the ~s** (= *instruments*) los instrumentos de cuerda; ✦ IDIOM **to have more than one ~ to one's bow** ser una persona de recursos
4 (*Comput*) cadena *f*
🄱 VT **1** [+ *pearls etc*] ensartar; **he can't even ~ two sentences together** ni sabe conectar dos frases seguidas **2** [+ *violin, tennis racket, bow*] encordar
🄲 CPD ➤ **string bag** (*esp Brit*) bolsa *f* de red ➤ **string bean** judía *f* verde, ejote *m* (*Mex*), poroto *m* verde (*Chi*)
➤ **string(ed) instrument** instrumento *m* de cuerda ➤ **string quartet** cuarteto *m* de cuerda(s) ➤ **string section** (*Mus*) sección *f* de cuerda(s), cuerda(s) *f(pl)* ➤ **string vest** camiseta *f* de malla
➤ **string along*** 🄰 VT + ADV (= *give false hope to*) dar falsas esperanzas a; (= *con*) embaucar 🄱 VI + ADV ir también, venir también
➤ **string out** VT + ADV (= *space out*) **to be strung out along sth** hacer fila a lo largo de algo
stringent [ˈstrɪndʒənt] ADJ [*controls, standards*] riguroso, severo, estricto; **~ rules** reglas *fpl* estrictas
strip [strɪp] 🄰 N **1** [*of paper etc*] tira *f*; [*of metal*] fleje *m*; [*of land*] franja *f*, faja *f*; ✦ IDIOM **to tear sb off a ~** (*Brit**) echar una bronca a algn*
2 (*Brit Ftbl*) (= *clothes*) uniforme *m*; (= *colours*) colores *mpl* **3** (*) (= *striptease*) striptease *m*, despelote* *m* **4** (*esp US*) (= *strip cartoon*) tira *f* cómica, historieta *f*, caricatura *f* (*LAm*)
🄱 VT **1** [+ *person*] desnudar
2 [+ *bed*] quitar la ropa de; [+ *wall*] desempapelar; [+ *wallpaper*] quitar; **to ~ the bark off sth** descortezar algo **3** (= *deprive*) **to ~ sb of sth** despojar a algn de algo **4** [+ *engine*] desmontar

🄲 VI desnudarse; [*striptease artist*] hacer striptease; **to ~ naked** quitarse toda la ropa; **to ~ to the waist** desnudarse hasta la cintura
🄓 CPD ➤ **strip cartoon** (*Brit*) tira *f* cómica, historieta *f*, caricatura *f* (*LAm*) ➤ **strip club, strip joint*** (*US*) club *m* de striptease ➤ **strip light** (*Brit*) lámpara *f* fluorescente ➤ **strip lighting** (*Brit*) alumbrado *m* fluorescente, alumbrado *m* de tubos ➤ **strip search** registro *m* integral ➤ **strip show** espectáculo *m* de striptease
➤ **strip down** VT + ADV [+ *engine*] desmontar
➤ **strip off** 🄰 VT + ADV [+ *paint etc*] quitar; (*violently*) arrancar 🄱 VI + ADV [*person*] desnudarse
stripe [straɪp] N **1** (= *line*) raya *f*, lista *f*; (*on flag*) franja *f* **2** (*on uniform*) galón *m*
striped [straɪpt] ADJ [*clothes, trousers*] de rayas, a rayas; [*pattern, wallpaper*] rayado, listado, de rayas
stripper [ˈstrɪpəʳ] N stripper *mf*, *persona que hace striptease*
strip-search [ˈstrɪpsɜːtʃ] VT **he was ~ed at the airport** lo desnudaron para cachearlo en el aeropuerto
striptease [ˈstrɪptiːz] N striptease *m*
strive [straɪv] (*pt* **strove** [strəʊv] *pp* **striven** [ˈstrɪvn]) VI esforzarse, procurar; **to ~ to do sth** esforzarse por hacer algo
strobe [strəʊb] CPD ➤ **strobe light** luz *f* estroboscópica ➤ **strobe lighting** luces *fpl* estroboscópicas
strode [strəʊd] PT *of* **stride**
stroke [strəʊk] 🄰 N **1 a ~ of genius** una ocurrencia genial; **~ of lightning** rayo *m*; **a ~ of luck** un golpe de suerte; **he hasn't done a ~ of work** no ha dado golpe; ✦ IDIOM **at a ~** de un solo golpe
2 (= *caress*) **she gave the cat a ~** acarició el gato **3** [*of pen*] trazo *m*, plumada *f*; [*of brush*] pincelada *f* **4** (*Swimming*) (= *single movement*) brazada *f*; (= *type of stroke*) estilo *m*; (*Rowing*) remada *f*; (*Cricket, Golf*) golpe *m*, jugada *f*; **good ~!** ¡buen golpe!, ¡muy bien!; **to put sb off his ~** (= *distract*) hacer perder la concentración a algn, distraer a algn
5 [*of bell, clock*] campanada *f*; **on the ~ of 12** al dar las 12 **6** (*Med*) derrame *m* cerebral, apoplejía *f*; **to have a ~** tener un derrame cerebral, tener un ataque de apoplejía
🄱 VT [+ *cat, sb's hair*] acariciar; [+ *chin*] pasar la mano sobre, pasar la mano por
stroll [strəʊl] 🄰 N paseo *m*, vuelta *f*; **to go for** or **have a ~** dar un paseo, dar una vuelta 🄱 VI dar un paseo, pasear, dar una vuelta
stroller [ˈstrəʊləʳ] N (*US*) (= *pushchair*) cochecito *m*, sillita *f* de paseo
strong [strɒŋ] 🄰 ADJ (*compar* **~er**; *superl* **~est**)
1 (= *physically tough*) [*person, material, structure*] fuerte; **to have ~ nerves** tener nervios de acero; **to have a ~ stomach** (*lit, fig*) tener un buen estómago; ✦ IDIOM **to be as ~ as an ox** ser fuerte como un toro
2 (= *healthy*) [*teeth, bones*] sano; [*heart*] fuerte, sano; **she has never been very ~** nunca ha tenido una constitución fuerte
3 (= *powerful*) [*drug, wine, cheese, wind, currency*] fuerte; [*coffee*] fuerte, cargado; [*argument, evidence*] sólido, de peso; [*magnet, lens*] potente; [*impression, influence*] grande; **music with a ~ beat** música *f* con mucho ritmo; **we have a ~ case** las razones que nosotros exponemos son muy sólidas
4 (= *firm*) [*opinion, belief, supporter*] firme; **I am a ~ believer in tolerance** creo firmemente en or soy gran partidario de la tolerancia
5 (= *mentally*) fuerte; **he has a ~ personality** tiene un carácter or una personalidad fuerte; **he tries to be ~ for the sake of his children** intenta mostrarse fuerte por el bien de sus hijos; **he's the ~ silent type** es de los muy reservados
6 (= *intense*) [*emotion, colour, smell*] fuerte, intenso; [*light*] potente, intenso
7 (= *good*) [*team*] fuerte; [*candidate*] bueno, firme; [*marriage, relationship, cast*] sólido; **he's not very ~ on grammar** no está muy fuerte en gramática; **geography was never my ~ point** la geografía nunca fue mi fuerte; **to be in a ~ position** encontrarse en una buena posición; **there is a ~ possibility that ...** hay muchas posibilidades de que ...; **he is a ~ swimmer** es un buen nadador

8 (= *severe, vehement*) [*words*] subido de tono, fuerte; [*denial*] tajante; **there has been ~ criticism of the regime** se ha criticado duramente el régimen; **~ language** (= *swearing*) lenguaje *m* fuerte; (= *frank*) lenguaje *m* muy directo; **in the ~est possible terms** enérgicamente
9 (= *noticeable*) [*resemblance*] marcado; **he had a ~ German accent** tenía un fuerte *or* marcado acento alemán
10 [*features*] pronunciado, marcado
11 (*in number*) **they are 20 ~** son 20 en total
Ⓑ ADV (*) **to be going ~** [*firm, company*] mantenerse próspero; [*marriage*] seguir viento en popa; [*person*] conservarse en forma

strong-arm ['strɒŋɑːm] ADJ [*tactics, methods*] represivo

strongbox ['strɒŋbɒks] N caja *f* fuerte

stronghold ['strɒŋhəʊld] N fortaleza *f*, plaza *f* fuerte; (*fig*) baluarte *m*, centro *m*

strongly ['strɒŋlɪ] ADV **1** (= *sturdily*) **~ built** [*person*] de constitución fuerte *or* robusta; [*furniture, structure*] de construcción sólida
2 [*recommend, advise*] encarecidamente; [*believe, suspect, defend, argue*] firmemente; [*criticize*] duramente; [*oppose, support, protest, react*] enérgicamente; [*deny*] tajantemente, rotundamente; [*indicate*] claramente; **~ anti-British** profundamente antibritánico; **to be ~ against sth** estar totalmente en contra de algo, oponerse enérgicamente a algo; **she was ~ attracted to him** sentía una fuerte atracción hacia él, se sentía fuertemente atraída hacia él; **I ~ disagree with the decision** estoy totalmente en desacuerdo con la decisión; **if you feel ~ about this issue ...** si este tema te parece que es importante ...; **I feel very ~ that ...** creo firmemente que ...; **he is a man with ~ held views** es un hombre de convicciones firmes; **to be ~ in favour of sth** estar totalmente a favor de algo; **~ influenced by** muy influenciado por; **to be ~ opposed to sth** estar totalmente en contra de algo, oponerse enérgicamente a algo; **~ recommended** [*book, film*] muy recomendado; **to smell ~ of sth** tener un fuerte olor a algo, oler mucho a algo; **I would ~ urge you to reconsider** le ruego encarecidamente que recapacite; **a ~ worded letter** una carta subida de tono

strongman ['strɒŋmæn] N (*pl* **strongmen**) (*Circus*) forzudo *m*, hércules *m*; (*Pol etc*) hombre *m* fuerte

strongroom ['strɒŋrʊm] N cámara *f* acorazada

strong-willed ['strɒŋ'wɪld] ADJ resuelto, decidido; (*pej*) obstinado

strontium ['strɒntɪəm] N estroncio *m*; **~ 90** estroncio *m* 90

stroppy* ['strɒpɪ] ADJ (*Brit*) insolente, borde (*Sp***); **to get ~** ponerse insolente *or* (*Sp***) borde

strove [strəʊv] PT *of* **strive**

struck [strʌk] PT, PP *of* **strike**

structural ['strʌktʃərəl] ADJ estructural

structurally ['strʌktʃərəlɪ] ADV **~ sound** de estructura sólida

structure ['strʌktʃəʳ] Ⓐ N **1** (= *organization*) estructura *f*
2 (= *thing constructed*) construcción *f* Ⓑ VT estructurar

struggle ['strʌgl] Ⓐ N **1** (*physical*) pelea *f*, forcejeo *m*; **there were signs of a ~** había señales de haberse producido una pelea *or* un forcejeo; **he lost his glasses in the ~** perdió las gafas en la pelea *or* refriega; **to put up a ~** oponer resistencia, forcejear; **without a ~** sin oponer resistencia
2 (*fig*) lucha *f* (**for** por); **her ~ to feed her children** su lucha por poder dar de comer a sus hijos; **I had a ~ to persuade her** me costó trabajo persuadirla; **his ~ against cancer** su lucha contra el cáncer; **to give up without a ~** rendirse sin luchar
Ⓑ VI **1** (= *scuffle*) forcejear (**with sb** con algn); **stop struggling!** ¡deja de forcejear!; **he ~d to get free** forcejeó para soltarse
2 (= *move with difficulty*) **I ~d into my costume** logré ponerme el disfraz como pude; **she ~d to her feet** logró ponerse de pie; **the bus was struggling up the hill** el autobús subía con dificultad la cuesta
3 (= *fight*) luchar; **to ~ to do sth** luchar por hacer algo, esforzarse por hacer algo; **he ~d against the disease for 20 years** luchó contra la enfermedad durante 20 años; **to ~ for breath** respirar con dificultad
4 (= *have difficulties*) tener problemas; **they were struggling**

to pay their bills tenían problemas *or* iban apurados para pagar las facturas
➤ **struggle on** VI + ADV **1** (= *keep moving*) **we ~d on for another kilometre** conseguimos avanzar otro kilómetro a duras penas **2** (*fig*) seguir bregando; **many old people choose to ~ on alone** muchas personas mayores prefieren seguir bregando solas

strum [strʌm] VT [+ *guitar*] rasguear

strung [strʌŋ] PT, PP *of* **string**

strut[1] ['strʌt] Ⓐ VI (*also* **~ about, ~ along**) pavonearse, contonearse Ⓑ VT ✦ IDIOM **to ~ one's stuff*** pavonearse, darse pisto (*Sp*)

strut[2] [strʌt] N (= *beam*) puntal *m*, riostra *f*

strychnine ['strɪkniːn] N estricnina *f*

stub [stʌb] Ⓐ N [*of cigarette*] colilla *f*, pitillo *m*; [*of pencil*] cabo *m*; [*of cheque, receipt*] talón *m* Ⓑ VT **to ~ one's toe (on sth)** dar con el dedo del pie (contra algo)
➤ **stub out** VT + ADV [+ *cigarette*] apagar

stubble ['stʌbl] N **1** (*in field*) rastrojo *m* **2** (*on chin*) barba *f* (incipiente)

stubborn ['stʌbən] ADJ **1** (= *obstinate*) [*person*] testarudo, terco, tozudo; [*animal*] terco; [*nature, attitude, silence, refusal*] obstinado; [*resistance, insistence, determination*] obstinado, pertinaz **2** (= *hard to deal with*) [*problem*] pertinaz; [*stain, lock*] difícil, resistente; **a ~ cold** un resfriado persistente

stubbornly ['stʌbənlɪ] ADV (= *pig-headedly*) obstinadamente; (= *steadfastly*) tenazmente; **he was ~ determined** su resolución era obstinada; **interest rates have remained ~ high** perduran los tipos altos de interés

stubbornness ['stʌbənnɪs] N [*of person*] testarudez *f*, terquedad *f*, tozudez *f*

stubby ['stʌbɪ] ADJ (*compar* **stubbier**; *superl* **stubbiest**) achaparrado

stucco ['stʌkəʊ] Ⓐ N estuco *m* Ⓑ ADJ de estuco Ⓒ VT estucar

stuck [stʌk] PT, PP *of* **stick**[2]

stuck-up* ['stʌk'ʌp] ADJ presumido, engreído

stud[1] [stʌd] Ⓐ N (*decorative*) tachón *m*, clavo *m* (de adorno); (*Brit*) (*on boots*) taco *m*; (= *collar stud, shirt stud*) corchete *m* Ⓑ VT tachonar; **~ded with** (*fig*) salpicado de

stud[2] [stʌd] N (*also* **~ farm**) caballeriza *f*, cuadra *f*; (*also* **~ horse**) caballo *m* semental

student ['stjuːdənt] Ⓐ N (*at school*) alumno/a *m/f*; (*at university*) estudiante *mf*, universitario/a *m/f*; (= *researcher*) investigador(a) *m/f*; **a medical ~** un(a) estudiante de medicina
Ⓑ CPD [*life, unrest*] estudiantil ➤ **student driver** (*US*) persona que está sacando el carnet de conducir ➤ **student grant** beca *f* ➤ **student loan** crédito *m* personal para estudiantes ➤ **student nurse** estudiante *mf* de enfermería ➤ **student teacher** (*at college*) estudiante *mf* de magisterio; (*doing teaching practice*) (*in secondary school*) profesor(a) *m/f* en prácticas; (*in primary school*) maestro/a *m/f* en prácticas ➤ **student(s') union** (= *building*) centro *m* estudiantil; (*Brit*) (= *association*) federación *f* de estudiantes

studied ['stʌdɪd] ADJ (*gen*) estudiado, pensado; [*calm, insult*] calculado, premeditado; [*pose, style*] estudiado, afectado

studio ['stjuːdɪəʊ] N (*TV, Mus*) estudio *m*; [*of artist*] estudio *m*, taller *m* ➤ **studio apartment** (*US*) estudio *m* ➤ **studio audience** público *m* de estudio ➤ **studio flat** (*Brit*) estudio *m*

studious ['stjuːdɪəs] ADJ **1** (= *devoted to study*) estudioso **2** (= *thoughtful*) atento; [*effort*] asiduo

studiously ['stjuːdɪəslɪ] ADV [*research*] con aplicación; [*avoid*] cuidadosamente; [*ignore*] deliberadamente

study ['stʌdɪ] Ⓐ N **1** (*gen*) estudio *m*; [*of text, evidence etc*] investigación *f*, estudio *m*; **to make a ~ of sth** realizar una investigación de algo **2** (= *room*) biblioteca *f*, despacho *m* Ⓑ VT **1** [+ *subject*] estudiar **2** (= *examine*) [+ *evidence, painting*] examinar, investigar Ⓒ VI estudiar; **to ~ to be an agronomist** estudiar para agrónomo; **to ~ for an exam**

estudiar *or* preparar un examen **D** CPD ➤ **study tour** viaje *m* de estudios

stuff [stʌf] **A** N **1** (*) **what's that ~ in the bucket?** ¿qué es eso que hay en el cubo?; **beetroot? I hate the ~** ¿remolacha? me da asco; **it's dangerous ~** [*substance*] es una sustancia peligrosa; **there's some good ~ in that book** ese libro tiene cosas buenas; **that's the ~!** ¡muy bien!, ¡así se hace!; **he was busy writing letters and ~*** estaba ocupado escribiendo cartas y tal*; ✦ IDIOM **to know one's ~*** ser un experto **2** (*) (= *things*) cosas *fpl*, bártulos* *mpl*, chismes *mpl* (*Sp**); **where have you put my ~?** ¿dónde has puesto mis bártulos *or* (*Sp*) chismes?*; **he brought back a lot of ~ from China** trajo muchas cosas de China **3** (*) (= *nonsense*) historias *fpl*; **all that ~ about how he wants to help us** todas esas historias *or* todo el cuento ese de que quiere ayudarnos; **don't give me that ~!** ¡no me vengas con esas historias *or* ese cuento! **4** (= *essence*) **the pleasures and pains that are the ~ of human relationships** las alegrías y las penas que constituyen la esencia de las relaciones humanas; **his feats on the tennis court are the ~ of legend** sus proezas en la cancha de tenis son legendarias **B** VT **1** (= *fill, pack*) [+ *chicken, peppers, cushion, toy*] rellenar (**with** con); [+ *sack, box, pockets*] llenar (**with** de); [+ *animal*] disecar, embalsamar; **to ~ one's head with useless facts*** llenarse la cabeza de información que no vale para nada; **to ~ one's face*** ✧ **~ o.s. (with food)*** atracarse *or* atiborrarse de comida*, darse un atracón* **2** (*) (= *put*) **to ~ sth in** *or* **into sth** meter algo en algo; **he ~ed it into his pocket** se lo metió de prisa en el bolsillo; ✦ IDIOM **to ~ sth down sb's throat*** meter a algn algo por la fuerza* **C** VI (*) (= *guzzle*) atracarse de comida*, atiborrarse de comida*, darse un atracón*

stuffed [stʌft] **A** ADJ **1** (*in taxidermy*) disecado, embalsamado **2** (*Culin*) **~ peppers/tomatoes** pimientos *mpl*/tomates *mpl* rellenos **3** (*) (= *full*) **I'm ~** estoy hasta arriba* **B** CPD ➤ **stuffed animal** (*US*), **stuffed toy** (*US*) muñeco *m* de peluche

stuffing [ˈstʌfɪŋ] N [*of furniture, stuffed animal*] relleno *m*, borra *f*; (*for chicken etc*) relleno *m*; ✦ IDIOM **to knock the ~ out of sb*** dejar a algn para el arrastre

stuffy [ˈstʌfɪ] ADJ (*compar* **stuffier**; *superl* **stuffiest**) **1** [*room*] mal ventilado; [*atmosphere*] cargado, sofocante; **it's ~ in here** aquí huele a cerrado, el ambiente está un poco cargado aquí **2** [*person*] (= *narrow-minded*) remilgado, de miras estrechas; (= *prudish*) remilgado; (= *stiff, starchy*) tieso; (= *dull, boring*) pesado, poco interesante **3** (= *congested*) [*nose*] taponado, atascado

stultifying [ˈstʌltɪfaɪɪŋ] ADJ [*work, regime, routine*] embrutecedor; [*atmosphere*] sofocante, agobiante

stumble [ˈstʌmbl] **A** N tropezón *m*, traspié *m* **B** VI tropezar, dar un traspié; **to ~ against sth** tropezar contra algo; **to ~ over sth** tropezar en algo; **to ~ through a speech** pronunciar un discurso de cualquier manera, pronunciar un discurso atracándose; **to ~ (up)on** *or* **across sth** (*fig*) tropezar con algo

stumbling block [ˈstʌmblɪŋblɒk] N (*fig*) tropiezo *m*, escollo *m*

stump [stʌmp] **A** N **1** (*gen*) cabo *m*; [*of limb*] muñón *m*; [*of tree*] tocón *m* **2** (*Cricket*) palo *m* **3** **to be** *or* **go on the ~** (*US Pol*) hacer campaña electoral **B** VT **1** (*) (= *perplex*) dejar perplejo *or* confuso; **I'm completely ~ed** estoy totalmente perplejo; **to be ~ed for an answer** no tener respuesta **2** (*Cricket*) eliminar
➤ **stump up*** (*Brit*) **A** VT + ADV **to ~ up five pounds** apoquinar cinco libras, desembolsar cinco libras (**for sth** para comprar algo *or* por algo) **B** VI + ADV apoquinar, soltar la guita* (**for sth** para pagar algo)

stumpy [ˈstʌmpɪ] ADJ [*person etc*] achaparrado; [*pencil etc*] corto, reducido a casi nada, muy gastado

stun [stʌn] VT **1** (= *render unconscious*) dejar sin sentido; (= *daze*) aturdir, atontar **2** (= *amaze*) dejar pasmado; (= *shock*) dejar anonadado; **the family were ~ned by his death** la familia quedó anonadada a raíz de su muerte

stung [stʌŋ] PT, PP *of* **sting**

stunk [stʌŋk] PP *of* **stink**

stunned [stʌnd] ADJ **1** (= *unconscious*) sin sentido; (= *dazed*) aturdido, atontado **2** (= *amazed*) pasmado; (= *shocked*) anonadado; **I sat in ~ silence** me senté en silencio, anonadado

stunner* [ˈstʌnəʳ] N (= *person*) persona *f* maravillosa; **she's a real ~** está buenísima *or* como un tren*, es una mujer despampanante*

stunning [ˈstʌnɪŋ] ADJ **1** (= *fabulous*) [*dress, girl*] imponente, deslumbrante, despampanante*; [*film, performance*] impresionante, sensacional; **you look absolutely ~** estás deslumbrante **2** (= *startling*) [*news*] asombroso; **his death came as a ~ blow** su muerte fue un golpe tremendo

stunt¹ [stʌnt] VT [+ *tree, growth*] impedir (el crecimiento de), atrofiar

stunt² [stʌnt] N **1** (= *feat*) proeza *f*, hazaña *f*; (*for film*) escena *f* peligrosa, toma *f* peligrosa; (*in plane*) vuelo *m* acrobático, ejercicio *m* acrobático; **to pull a ~** hacer algo peligroso (y tonto) **2** (= *publicity stunt*) truco *m* publicitario

stunted [ˈstʌntɪd] ADJ enano, mal desarrollado

stuntman [ˈstʌntmæn] N (*pl* **stuntmen**) doble *m* (*especializado en escenas peligrosas*)

stupefaction [ˌstjuːpɪˈfækʃən] N estupefacción *f*

stupefy [ˈstjuːpɪfaɪ] VT **1** (*through tiredness, alcohol*) atontar **2** (= *astound*) dejar estupefacto *or* pasmado

stupendous* [stjuːˈpendəs] ADJ (= *wonderful*) estupendo; (= *extraordinary*) extraordinario

stupid [ˈstjuːpɪd] **A** ADJ **1** (= *unintelligent*) [*person, question, remark, idea*] estúpido, tonto; [*mistake, game*] tonto, bobo; **I'll never do anything so ~ again** nunca volveré a cometer semejante estupidez; **it's ~ to leave money lying around** es una estupidez *or* es de tontos dejar el dinero a la vista de todos; **to act ~*** (= *pretend to be stupid*) hacerse el tonto; (= *behave stupidly*) hacer el tonto; **she looks ~ in that hat** está ridícula con ese sombrero; **to make sb look ~** dejar a algn en ridículo; **it was ~ of me to say that** fui tonto al decir eso, cometí una estupidez al decir eso; **it was a ~ thing to do** fue una tontería *or* una estupidez; **she gets annoyed by ~ little things** se molesta por cualquier tontería *or* (*Sp**) chorrada **2** (*) (*expressing irritation*) maldito*, condenado*; **I hate these ~ shoes** odio estos malditos *or* condenados zapatos*; **you ~ idiot!** ¡idiota!, ¡imbécil! **B** N (*) **don't do that, ~!** ¡no hagas eso, imbécil!* **C** ADV (*) **don't talk ~!** ¡no digas tonterías *or* estupideces!*

stupidity [stjuːˈpɪdɪtɪ] N estupidez *f*

stupidly [ˈstjuːpɪdlɪ] ADV [*behave, act*] como un idiota; [*stare, grin*] como un bobo, como un tonto; **~, I said I would help her** como un tonto, dije que la ayudaría, cometí la estupidez de decir que la ayudaría

stupor [ˈstjuːpəʳ] N estupor *m*

sturdily [ˈstɜːdɪlɪ] ADV **~ built** [*house*] de construcción sólida; [*person*] robusto; [*furniture*] sólido

sturdy [ˈstɜːdɪ] ADJ (*compar* **sturdier**; *superl* **sturdiest**) [*person, tree*] robusto, fuerte; [*table, furniture*] sólido

sturgeon [ˈstɜːdʒən] N esturión *m*

stutter [ˈstʌtəʳ] **A** N tartamudeo *m*; **to have a ~** tartamudear **B** VI tartamudear **C** VT decir tartamudeando

sty¹ [staɪ] N [*of pigs*] pocilga *f*, chiquero *m* (*SC*)

sty², stye [staɪ] N (*on eye*) orzuelo *m*

style [staɪl] **A** N **1** (*Mus, Art, Literat, Clothing etc*) estilo *m*; **I want something in that ~** quiero algo de ese estilo; **the present ~ of leadership** el estilo actual de liderazgo; **that's not her ~*** eso no es su estilo **2** (= *elegance*) estilo *m*; **to have ~** tener estilo; **to live/travel in ~** vivir/viajar por todo lo alto; **he won in fine ~** ganó de manera impecable **3** (= *fashion*) moda *f*; **to go out of ~** pasar de moda; **they spent money like it was going out of ~*** (*hum*) gastaban dinero a troche y moche *or* como si fuera agua **4** (*also* **hairstyle**) peinado *m*

B VT [+ *clothes, car, model*] diseñar; **to ~ sb's hair** peinar a algn

styling ['staɪlɪŋ] N estilización *f*

stylish ['staɪlɪʃ] ADJ (= *elegant*) elegante; (= *modern*) moderno

stylishly ['staɪlɪʃlɪ] ADV (= *elegantly*) con estilo, con elegancia; (= *fashionably*) a la moda

stylist ['staɪlɪst] N **1** (*also* **hair ~**) peluquero/a *m/f* **2** (*Literat*) estilista *mf*

stylistic [staɪ'lɪstɪk] ADJ [*device*] estilístico; [*improvement*] del estilo

stylized ['staɪlaɪzd] ADJ estilizado

stymie* ['staɪmɪ] VT bloquear, poner obstáculos infranqueables delante de; **now we're ~d!** ¡la hemos pringado *or* liado!*

Styrofoam® ['staɪrəfəʊm] (*US*) **A** N poliestireno *m* **B** CPD de poliestireno

suave [swɑːv] ADJ fino; (*pej*) hábil

sub* [sʌb] N (= *advance on wages*) avance *m*, anticipo *m*

subaqua [sʌb'ækwə] ADJ subacuático, de submarinismo

subcommittee ['sʌbkə,mɪtɪ] N subcomisión *f*, subcomité *m*

subconscious ['sʌb'kɒnʃəs] **A** ADJ subconsciente **B** N **the ~** el subconsciente; **in one's ~** en el subconsciente

subconsciously ['sʌb'kɒnʃəslɪ] ADV subconscientemente

subcontinent ['sʌb'kɒntɪnənt] N **the (Indian) ~** el subcontinente (de la India)

subcontract **A** [sʌb'kɒntrækt] N subcontrato *m* **B** [sʌbkən'trækt] VT subcontratar

subcontractor [sʌbkən'træktəʳ] N subcontratista *mf*

subculture ['sʌb,kʌltʃəʳ] N subcultura *f*

subdivide ['sʌbdɪ'vaɪd] **A** VT subdividir **B** VI subdividirse

subdivision ['sʌbdɪ,vɪʒən] N subdivisión *f*

subdue [sʌb'djuː] VT [+ *enemy*] someter, sojuzgar; [+ *children*] calmar, tranquilizar; [+ *passions*] dominar

subdued [sʌb'djuːd] ADJ [*colours, lighting*] tenue, suave; [*voice*] suave; [*mood*] apagado; [*person*] (= *quiet*) apagado; (= *passive*) sumiso, manso; (= *depressed*) deprimido; **you were very ~ last night** anoche se te veía muy apagado

sub-editor ['sʌb'edɪtəʳ] N (*Brit*) redactor(a) *m/f*

subhead(ing) ['sʌb,hed(ɪŋ)] N subtítulo *m*

subhuman ['sʌb'hjuːmən] ADJ infrahumano

subject **A** ['sʌbdʒɪkt] N **1** (= *topic, theme*) tema *m*; **to change the ~** cambiar de tema; **it's a delicate ~** es un asunto delicado; **on the ~ of ...** a propósito de ...; **(while we're) on the ~ of money ...** ya que de dinero se trata ... **2** (*Scol, Univ*) asignatura *f* **3** (= *citizen*) súbdito/a *m/f*; **British ~** súbdito/a *m/f* británico/a
B ['sʌbdʒɪkt] ADJ **subject to** (= *liable to*) [+ *law, tax, delays*] sujeto a; [+ *disease*] propenso a; [+ *flooding*] expuesto a; (= *conditional on*) [+ *approval, confirmation*] sujeto a; **these prices are ~ to change without notice** estos precios están sujetos a cambio sin previo aviso
C [sʌb'dʒekt] VT **to ~ sb to sth** someter a algn a algo; **she was ~ed to much indignity** tuvo que aguantar muchas afrentas
D ['sʌbdʒɪkt] CPD ➤ **subject heading** título *m* de materia ➤ **subject index** (*in book*) índice *m* de materias; (*in library*) catálogo *m* de materias ➤ **subject matter** (= *topic*) tema *m*, asunto *m*; [*of letter*] contenido *m* ➤ **subject pronoun** pronombre *m* (de) sujeto

subjection [sʌb'dʒekʃən] N sometimiento *m* (**to** a); **to bring a people into ~** subyugar a un pueblo

subjective [sʌb'dʒektɪv] ADJ subjetivo

subjectivity [sʌbdʒek'tɪvɪtɪ] N subjetividad *f*

sub judice [sʌb'dju:dɪsɪ] ADJ (*Jur*) **the matter is ~** el asunto está en manos del tribunal

subjugate ['sʌbdʒʊgeɪt] VT subyugar, sojuzgar

subjunctive [sʌb'dʒʌŋktɪv] **A** ADJ subjuntivo **B** N

subjuntivo *m*; **in the ~** en subjuntivo

sublet ['sʌb'let] (*pt, pp ~*) VT subarrendar

sub-lieutenant ['sʌblefˈtenənt] N (*esp Brit Naut*) alférez *mf* de fragata; (*Mil*) subteniente *mf*

sublimate ['sʌblɪmeɪt] VT sublimar

sublime [sə'blaɪm] **A** ADJ sublime; (*iro*) [*indifference, contempt*] supremo, total **B** N **to go from the ~ to the ridiculous** pasar de lo sublime a lo ridículo

sublimely [sə'blaɪmlɪ] ADV [*play, sing*] maravillosamente; [*unaware, ignorant*] completamente, absolutamente; [*funny*] terriblemente, tremendamente; **~ beautiful** de una belleza sublime

subliminal [sʌb'lɪmɪnl] ADJ **~ advertising** publicidad *f* subliminal

submachine gun ['sʌbmə'fiːngʌn] N ametralladora *f*, pistola *f* ametralladora, metralleta *f*

submarine [sʌbmə'riːn] N **1** (= *vessel*) submarino *m* **2** (*US**) *sándwich mixto de tamaño grande*

submerge [səb'mɜːdʒ] **A** VT **1** (= *plunge*) hundir (**in** en) **2** (= *flood*) inundar **B** VI sumergirse

submerged [səb'mɜːdʒd] ADJ sumergido

submission [səb'mɪʃən] N **1** (= *submissiveness*) sumisión *f*; **to beat sb into ~** (*lit*) someter a algn a base de golpes **2** (= *handing in*) [*of proposal, application*] presentación *f*, entrega *f* **3** (= *plan, proposal*) propuesta *f*

submissive [səb'mɪsɪv] ADJ sumiso

submit [səb'mɪt] **A** VT **1** (= *put forward*) [+ *proposal, claim, report, evidence*] presentar; [+ *account*] rendir; **to ~ that ...** proponer que ..., sugerir que ... **2** (= *subject*) **to ~ o.s. to sth/sb** someterse a algo/algn **B** VI (= *give in*) rendirse, someterse; **to ~ to sth** someterse a algo

subnormal ['sʌb'nɔːməl] ADJ subnormal

subordinate **A** [sə'bɔːdɪnɪt] N subordinado/a *m/f* **B** [sə'bɔːdɪnɪt] ADJ subordinado; **to be ~ to sb** (*in rank*) ser subordinado de algn **C** [sə'bɔːdɪneɪt] VT subordinar

subordination [sə,bɔːdɪ'neɪʃən] N subordinación *f*

subplot ['sʌb,plɒt] N intriga *f* secundaria

subpoena [səb'piːnə] (*Jur*) **A** N citación *f* **B** VT [+ *witness*] citar; [+ *document*] reclamar como pruebas

sub post-office [sʌb'pəʊst,ɒfɪs] N (*Brit*) subdelegación *f* de correos

subscribe [səb'skraɪb] **A** VI **1 to ~ to** [+ *magazine, newspaper*] su(b)scribirse *or* abonarse a; [+ *charity, good cause*] contribuir con; **I've never ~d to that view** yo nunca he sido de esa opinión; **I don't ~ to the idea that money should be given to ...** yo no soy partidario de que se dé dinero a ... **2** (*Internet*) apuntarse **B** VT **1** (= *contribute*) [+ *money*] donar **2** (= *apply for*) **the course is fully ~d** el curso está completo, ya no quedan plazas en el curso

subscriber [səb'skraɪbəʳ] N (*to magazine, newspaper*) su(b)scriptor(a) *m/f*, abonado/a *m/f*; (*to telephone*) abonado/a *m/f*

subscription [səb'skrɪpʃən] N **1** (= *act of subscribing*) (*to magazine, newspaper*) su(b)scripción *f*; (*to club, telephone service*) abono *m* **2** (= *fee*) (*to magazine, newspaper*) su(b)scripción *f*, tarifa *f* de su(b)scripción; (*to club*) cuota *f*; **to take out a ~ to sth** (*to club, telephone service*) abonarse a algo; (*to magazine, newspaper*) su(b)scribirse a algo

subsequent ['sʌbsɪkwənt] ADJ posterior, subsiguiente (*more frm*); **~ to** con posterioridad a; **~ to that** posteriormente

subsequently ['sʌbsɪkwəntlɪ] ADV posteriormente

subservience [səb'sɜːvɪəns] N (= *submissiveness*) sumisión *f* (**to sb** a algn); (= *servility*) servilismo *m*

subservient [səb'sɜːvɪənt] ADJ (= *submissive*) sumiso; (= *servile*) servil; **to be ~ to sb** someterse a algn

subset ['sʌb,set] N subconjunto *m*

subside [səb'saɪd] VI [*floods*] bajar, descender; [*road, land, house*] hundirse; [*wind*] amainar; [*anger, laughter, excitement*] apagarse; [*threat, violence, pain*] disminuir

subsidence [səb'saɪdəns, 'sʌbsɪdəns] N [*of road, land, house*] hundimiento *m*; [*of floods*] bajada *f*, descenso *m*; **"road liable to subsidence"** "firme en mal estado"

subsidiarity [səbsɪdɪˈærɪtɪ] N (*Pol*) subsidiariedad *f*

subsidiary [səbˈsɪdɪərɪ] **Ⓐ** ADJ **1** [*interest, importance, role, question*] secundario **2** [*company, bank*] filial **3** [*subject, course*] complementario **Ⓑ** N (= *company*) filial *f*

subsidize [ˈsʌbsɪdaɪz] VT subvencionar

subsidy [ˈsʌbsɪdɪ] N subvención *f*; **state ~** subvención *f* estatal

subsist [səbˈsɪst] VI subsistir (**on** a base de)

subsistence [səbˈsɪstəns] N (= *nourishment*) sustento *m*, subsistencia *f*; (= *existence*) existencia *f*; **means of ~** medios *mpl* de subsistencia ➤ **subsistence level to live at ~ level** vivir muy justo, poderse sustentar apenas

subsoil [ˈsʌbsɔɪl] N subsuelo *m*

subsonic [ˈsʌbˈsɒnɪk] ADJ subsónico

substance [ˈsʌbstəns] **Ⓐ** N **1** (= *solution, chemical*) sustancia *f*; **a sticky ~** una sustancia pegajosa **2** (= *solid quality*) corporeidad *f*; [*of fabric*] cuerpo *m*; **to lack ~** [*claim, allegation*] carecer de base *or* fundamento; [*book, argument*] no tener mucha sustancia; **the rumours are completely without ~** los rumores no tienen ninguna base *or* ningún fundamento **3** (= *essence*) [*of speech, writing*] esencia *f*; **in ~** en esencia **4** (= *wealth*) **a woman of ~** una mujer de fortuna **Ⓑ** CPD ➤ **substance abuse** abuso *m* de estupefacientes, toxicomanía *f*

substandard [ˈsʌbˈstændəd] ADJ **1** (= *inferior*) [*products, material*] de calidad inferior; [*service, work, performance*] poco satisfactorio; **~ housing** viviendas *fpl* que no reúnen condiciones de habitabilidad **2** [*language*] no estándar

substantial [səbˈstænʃəl] ADJ **1** (= *significant*) [*amount, progress, improvement, damage*] considerable, importante; [*difference*] importante, sustancial; [*evidence*] sustancial, de peso; [*document, book*] sustancioso **2** (= *solid*) [*building*] sólido **3** (= *filling*) [*meal, dish*] sustancioso

substantially [səbˈstænʃəlɪ] ADV **1** (= *significantly*) [*increase, contribute*] sustancialmente, considerablemente; **~ higher/lower** bastante más alto/bajo **2** (= *largely*) [*correct, true*] básicamente

substantiate [səbˈstænʃɪeɪt] VT confirmar, corroborar

substantive [ˈsʌbstəntɪv] ADJ [*role*] fundamental; [*talks, progress, difference*] sustancial; **the two sides remain divided on several ~ issues** las dos partes permanecen divididas en varios puntos fundamentales *or* de importancia

substitute [ˈsʌbstɪtjuːt] **Ⓐ** N **1** (= *thing, artificial product*) sucedáneo *m*; **it may replace saccharin as a sugar ~** puede reemplazar a la sacarina como sucedáneo del azúcar; **he uses honey as a ~ for sugar** usa miel como sustituto del azúcar; **a correspondence course is no** *or* **a poor ~ for personal tuition** un curso por correspondencia no puede sustituir a la enseñanza cara a cara **2** (= *person*) sustituto/a *m/f*, suplente *mf*; (*Sport*) suplente *mf*; **friends are no ~ for parents** los amigos no pueden sustituir a los padres **Ⓑ** VT sustituir; **to ~ margarine for butter** sustituir la mantequilla por margarina **Ⓒ** VI **to ~ for sth/sb** sustituir a algo/algn **Ⓓ** CPD ➤ **substitute teacher** (*US*) profesor(a) *m/f* suplente

substitution [ˌsʌbstɪˈtjuːʃən] N sustitución *f*; **to make a ~** (*Sport*) hacer una suplencia *or* sustitución

subtenant [ˈsʌbˈtenənt] N subarrendatario/a *m/f*

subterfuge [ˈsʌbtəfjuːdʒ] N subterfugio *m*

subterranean [ˌsʌbtəˈreɪnɪən] ADJ subterráneo

subtext [ˈsʌbtekst] N subtexto *m*

subtitle [ˈsʌbtaɪtl] **Ⓐ** N subtítulo *m* **Ⓑ** VT subtitular

subtitling [ˈsʌbtaɪtlɪŋ] N subtitulado *m*

subtle [ˈsʌtl] ADJ (*compar* **~r**; *superl* **~st**) [*perfume, flavour*] suave, sutil; [*colour*] tenue; [*charm, beauty, reminder, person, difference*] sutil; [*humour, irony*] sutil, fino; **the ~ fragrance of the violet** la suave fragancia *or* la fragancia sutil de la violeta; **a ~ hint of pink** un ligero toque de rosa

subtlety [ˈsʌtltɪ] N sutileza *f*; **his performance lacked ~** su

actuación carecía de matices; **the subtleties of English** los matices del inglés

subtly [ˈsʌtlɪ] ADV [*imply, remind, suggest*] sutilmente, de manera sutil; [*change*] ligeramente, levemente; **~ different** ligeramente distinto

subtotal [ˈsʌbˌtəʊtl] N subtotal *m*

subtract [səbˈtrækt] VT (*gen*) restar; (*fig*) sustraer; **to ~ five from nine** restar cinco de nueve

subtraction [səbˈtrækʃən] N resta *f*

subtropical [ˈsʌbˈtrɒpɪkəl] ADJ subtropical

suburb [ˈsʌbɜːb] N **1** (*affluent*) **a London ~** una zona residencial de las afueras de Londres; **I live in the ~s** vivo en una zona residencial de las afueras (de la ciudad) **2** (*poor*) suburbio *m*

suburban [səˈbɜːbən] ADJ **1** [*train*] de cercanías; **~ areas** las zonas residenciales de las afueras de una ciudad **2** (= *middle-class*) de clase media

suburbanite [səˈbɜːbənaɪt] N *habitante de una zona residencial de las afueras de una ciudad*

suburbia [səˈbɜːbɪə] N *zonas residenciales de las afueras de las ciudades*

subversion [səbˈvɜːʃən] N subversión *f*

subversive [səbˈvɜːsɪv] ADJ subversivo

subvert [sʌbˈvɜːt] VT (*frm*) subvertir, trastornar

subway [ˈsʌbweɪ] **Ⓐ** N **1** (*Brit*) (= *underpass*) paso *m* subterráneo **2** (*US Rail*) metro *m*, subterráneo *m* (*Arg*), subte *m* (*Arg**) **Ⓑ** CPD ➤ **subway station** (*US*) estación *f* de metro

sub-zero [ˈsʌbˈzɪərəʊ] ADJ **~ temperatures** temperaturas *fpl* por debajo del cero

succeed [səkˈsiːd] **Ⓐ** VI **1** (= *be successful*) [*person*] (*in business, career*) tener éxito, triunfar (**in** en); [*plan, strategy, experiment*] dar resultado, salir bien; [*business*] prosperar; [*film*] tener éxito; **she tried to smile but did not ~** intentó sonreír pero no lo consiguió *or* no lo logró; **to ~ in doing sth** conseguir hacer algo, lograr hacer algo; **he only ~ed in making it worse** lo único que consiguió *or* logró fue empeorar las cosas; ✦ PROV **if at first you don't ~, try, try again** si no lo consigues a la primera, sigue intentándolo **2** (= *take over*) **if she dies, who will ~?** si muere, ¿quién la sucederá?; **to ~ to the throne** subir al trono **Ⓑ** VT (= *follow*) suceder a; **his eldest son ~ed him** su hijo mayor lo sucedió; **he ~ed Lewis as Olympic champion** sucedió a Lewis como campeón olímpico

succeeding [səkˈsiːdɪŋ] ADJ sucesivo

success [səkˈses] **Ⓐ** N **1** (*at task*) éxito *m* (**at, in** en); **she tried without ~ to get a loan from the bank** intentó, sin éxito, obtener un préstamo del banco; **we have had some ~ in reducing the national debt** hemos conseguido *or* logrado reducir en parte la deuda pública; **to make a ~ of sth** [+ *project*] hacer de algo un éxito, conseguir *or* lograr que algo sea un éxito; **to meet with ~** tener éxito; **to wish sb every ~** desear a algn todo lo mejor **2** (= *sensation, hit*) éxito *m*; **to be a ~** [*product, event*] ser un éxito; [*person*] tener éxito; **he was a great ~** tuvo un gran éxito **Ⓑ** CPD ➤ **success story** éxito *m*

⚠️ **success** ≠ *suceso*

successful [səkˈsesfʊl] ADJ **1 to be ~** [*person, campaign, scheme, attempt, book*] tener éxito; [*plan, strategy, experiment*] salir bien; **the campaign was very ~** la campaña tuvo mucho éxito; **the company has been very ~ over the past five years** a la empresa le ha ido muy bien en los últimos cinco años; **the film is ~ at capturing the atmosphere of the time** la película consigue *or* logra captar el ambiente de la época; **we have not been very ~ at** *or* **in attracting new contracts** no hemos tenido mucho éxito a la hora de atraer nuevos contratos **2** [*product, film, novelist*] de éxito; [*company, businessperson*] próspero; [*treatment, remedy*] eficaz; [*conclusion, end*] satisfactorio; [*deal*] favorable; **one of the most ~ movies of all time** una de las películas de más éxito de todos los tiempos; **he had a ~ operation for an eye problem** lo operaron con éxito de un problema en el ojo; **to bring sth to a ~ conclusion** llevar algo a buen término; **we've had a very ~ day** nos han salido muy bien las cosas hoy; **the ~ candidate will be notified by post** se notificará al candidato elegido por correo

successfully [sək'sesfəlɪ] ADV (= *effectively*) con éxito; (= *satisfactorily*) satisfactoriamente; **he ~ defended his title** defendió con éxito su título; **Pam ~ evaded the police** Pam consiguió *or* logró evadir a la policía; **the problem has been ~ resolved** el problema se ha resuelto satisfactoriamente

succession [sək'seʃən] N 1 (= *series*) sucesión *f*, serie *f*; **after a ~ of disasters** después de una sucesión *or* serie de catástrofes; **he was my tutor two years in ~** fue mi tutor dos años seguidos *or* consecutivos; **in rapid ~** uno tras de otro, en rápida sucesión; **four times in ~** cuatro veces seguidas 2 (*to a post*) sucesión *f*

successive [sək'sesɪv] ADJ [*governments, generations, owners*] sucesivo; [*nights, days*] seguido, consecutivo; **on four ~ nights** cuatro noches seguidas *or* consecutivas; **for the third ~ time** por tercera vez consecutiva; **the percentage increased with each ~ year** el porcentaje aumentaba año tras año

successively [sək'sesɪvlɪ] ADV sucesivamente; **~ higher levels of unemployment** niveles de desempleo cada vez más altos

successor [sək'sesəʳ] N (*in office*) sucesor(a) *m/f*

succinct [sək'sɪŋkt] ADJ sucinto, conciso

succulent ['sʌkjʊlənt] Ⓐ ADJ 1 [*meat, fruit, vegetable*] suculento 2 [*plant, leaves*] carnoso Ⓑ N planta *f* carnosa

succumb [sə'kʌm] VI sucumbir (**to** a)

such [sʌtʃ] Ⓐ ADJ 1 (= *of that kind*) tal; **in ~ cases** en tales casos, en semejantes casos; **we had ~ a case last year** tuvimos un caso parecido el año pasado; **on just ~ a day in June** justo en un día parecido de junio; **~ a plan is most unwise** un proyecto así es poco aconsejable, un proyecto de ese tipo no es aconsejable; **did you ever see ~ a thing?** ¿has visto alguna vez cosa semejante?, ¿se vio jamás tal cosa?; **writers ~ as Updike** autores como Updike; **books ~ as these** semejantes libros; **~ money as I have** el dinero que tengo; **this is my car ~ as it is** aunque valga poco, es mi coche; **~ as?** ¿por ejemplo?; **~ is <u>life</u>** así es la vida; **there's <u>no</u> ~ thing** no existe tal cosa; **there's <u>no</u> ~ thing as a unicorn** el unicornio no existe; **or <u>some</u> ~ idea** o algo por el estilo 2 (= *so much*) tanto; **I was in ~ a hurry** tenía tanta prisa Ⓑ ADV tan; **~ good food** comida tan buena; **~ a clever girl** una muchacha tan inteligente; **it's ~ a long time now** hace tanto tiempo Ⓒ PRON los que, las que; **we took ~ as we wanted** tomamos los que queríamos; **rabbits and hares <u>and</u> ~** conejos y liebres y tal; **and <u>as</u> ~ he was promoted** y así fue ascendido; **there are no trees as ~** no hay árboles propiamente dichos, no hay árboles que digamos

such-and-such ['sʌtʃənsʌtʃ] ADJ tal o cual; **she lives in ~ a street** vive en tal o cual calle; **on ~ a day in May** a tantos de mayo

suchlike ['sʌtʃlaɪk] PRON **buses, lorries and ~** autobuses, camiones y vehículos por el estilo

suck [sʌk] Ⓐ VT [*person*] sorber; [*machine*] aspirar; **to ~ one's thumb** chuparse el dedo; **we were ~ed into the controversy** nos vimos envueltos en la polémica; ✦ IDIOM **to ~ sb dry** exprimir a algn Ⓑ VI 1 (*gen*) chupar; [*baby*] (*at breast*) mamar; **to ~ on/at sth** chupar algo 2 (*esp US*) **this ~s**** es una mierda**
➤ **suck down** VT + ADV [*current, mud*] tragar
➤ **suck in** VT + ADV 1 [*machine*] [+ *dust, air*] aspirar 2 [*person*] [+ *air*] tomar; **he heard her ~ in her breath sharply** le oyó aspirar sobresaltada; **to ~ one's stomach in** meter el estómago
➤ **suck out** VT + ADV succionar
➤ **suck up** Ⓐ VT + ADV [+ *dust, liquid*] aspirar Ⓑ VI + ADV **to ~ up to sb*** dar coba a algn

sucker ['sʌkəʳ] Ⓐ N 1 (*Zool, Tech*) ventosa *f*; (*Bot*) serpollo *m*, mamón *m* 2 (*) (= *gullible person*) primo/a *m/f*, bobo/a *m/f*; **to be a ~ for sth** no poder resistirse a algo Ⓑ VT (*US***) **to ~ sb into doing sth** embaucar a algn para que haga algo;

they ~ed him out of six grand le estafaron *or* timaron 6.000 dólares

suckle ['sʌkl] Ⓐ VT amamantar, dar de mamar Ⓑ VI mamar

sucrose ['su:krəʊz] N sucrosa *f*

suction ['sʌkʃən] N succión *f*, aspiración *f* ➤ **suction disc** ventosa *f* ➤ **suction pump** bomba *f* de aspiración, bomba *f* de succión

Sudan [su'dɑ:n] N Sudán *m*

Sudanese [,su:də'ni:z] ADJ, N (*pl* ~) sudanés(esa) *m/f*

sudden ['sʌdn] Ⓐ ADJ 1 (= *hasty, swift*) repentino; (= *unexpected*) inesperado; **a ~ drop in temperature** un descenso repentino de la temperatura; **this is all so ~!** ¡todo esto es tan repentino!; **she looked startled by his ~ appearance** parecía asustada cuando él apareció de repente; **all of a ~** de pronto, de repente 2 (= *abrupt*) [*movement*] brusco Ⓑ CPD ➤ **sudden death: they had to go to ~ death** (*Tennis*) tuvieron que recurrir a la muerte súbita; (*Ftbl*) (*penalty shoot-out*) tuvieron que recurrir a los goles; (*extra time*) tuvieron que recurrir a la prórroga de desempate ➤ **sudden infant death syndrome** síndrome *m* de la muerte súbita infantil

suddenly ['sʌdnlɪ] ADV 1 (= *all at once*) de repente, de pronto; **~, the door opened** de repente *or* de pronto se abrió la puerta 2 (= *abruptly*) [*cease, die*] repentinamente, de repente; [*move*] bruscamente; **the rain stopped as ~ as it had begun** la lluvia paró tan repentinamente *or* de repente como había empezado

suds [sʌdz] NPL espuma *fsing* de jabón

sue [su:] Ⓐ VT demandar (**for** por); **to ~ sb for damages** demandar *or* poner pleito a algn por daños y perjuicios Ⓑ VI (*Jur*) presentar una demanda; **to ~ for divorce** solicitar el divorcio

suede, suède [sweɪd] Ⓐ N ante *m* Ⓑ CPD [*gloves, shoes*] de ante

suet ['suɪt] N sebo *m*; **~ pudding** pudín *m* a base de sebo

Suez ['su:ɪz] CPD ➤ **the Suez Canal** el Canal de Suez

suffer ['sʌfəʳ] Ⓐ VT 1 (= *experience*) [+ *pain, hardship*] sufrir, padecer; (+ *loss, decline, setback*] sufrir, experimentar; **to ~ the consequences** sufrir las consecuencias 2 (= *tolerate*) [+ *opposition, rudeness*] soportar, aguantar; **I can't ~ it a moment longer** no lo soporto *or* aguanto un minuto más; ✦ IDIOM **he doesn't ~ fools gladly** no soporta a los imbéciles Ⓑ VI 1 (= *experience pain*) sufrir; **to ~ for sth** sufrir las consecuencias de algo; **you'll ~ for this!** ¡me las pagarás!; **to make sb ~** hacer sufrir a algn; **to ~ in silence** sufrir en silencio 2 (= *be afflicted by*) **to ~ from** [+ *illness*] padecer; **the house is ~ing from neglect** la casa está en un cierto estado de abandono; **they were ~ing from shock** se encontraban en estado de shock; **to ~ from the effects of** [+ *a fall*] resentirse de; [+ *alcohol*] sufrir los efectos de 3 (= *worsen*) [*studies, business, eyesight, health*] verse afectado, resentirse

sufferance ['sʌfərəns] N **on ~** a disgusto, a regañadientes

sufferer ['sʌfərəʳ] N (*from illness*) enfermo/a *m/f*; **~s from diabetes** los enfermos de diabetes, los diabéticos; **asthma ~s** las personas que sufren de asma, los asmáticos

suffering ['sʌfərɪŋ] N sufrimiento *m*, padecimiento *m*; **after months of ~** después de sufrir durante meses, después de meses de sufrimiento

suffice [sə'faɪs] (*frm*) Ⓐ VI ser suficiente, bastar; **a short letter will ~** una carta breve será suficiente *or* bastará Ⓑ VT **~ it to say** basta con decir

sufficient [sə'fɪʃənt] ADJ suficiente; **given ~ time** con suficiente tiempo; **to be ~** bastar, ser suficiente; **ten minutes is quite ~** con diez minutos basta *or* es suficiente

sufficiently [sə'fɪʃəntlɪ] ADV **~ large/high to do sth** (lo) suficientemente *or* (lo) bastante grande/alto (como) para hacer algo; **he had recovered ~ to ...** se había recuperado lo suficiente como para ...

suffix ['sʌfɪks] N sufijo *m*

suffocate ['sʌfəkeɪt] **Ⓐ** VT asfixiar, ahogar **Ⓑ** VI asfixiarse, ahogarse

suffocating ['sʌfəkeɪtɪŋ] ADJ [*heat*] sofocante, agobiante; [*fumes, smell*] asfixiante; [*atmosphere, life, relationship*] agobiante; **it's ~ in here** hace un calor sofocante *or* agobiante aquí dentro

suffocation [ˌsʌfə'keɪʃən] N asfixia *f*, ahogo *m*

suffrage ['sʌfrɪdʒ] N sufragio *m*

suffragette [ˌsʌfrə'dʒet] N (*Brit*) sufragista *f*

suffuse [sə'fju:z] VT [*light*] bañar; [*colour, flush*] teñir; [*delight, relief*] inundar; **~d with light** bañado de luz

sugar ['ʃʊgəʳ] **Ⓐ** N azúcar *m or f*; **oh ~!*** ¡miércoles! (*euph**), ¡mecachis! (*Sp**) **Ⓑ** VT [+ *tea etc*] azucarar, echar azúcar a **Ⓒ** CPD ➤ **sugar basin** (*Brit*) azucarero *m* ➤ **sugar beet** remolacha *f* azucarera ➤ **sugar bowl** azucarero *m* ➤ **sugar cane** caña *f* de azúcar ➤ **sugar cube** terrón *m* de azúcar ➤ **sugar daddy*** *viejo adinerado amante o protector de una joven* ➤ **sugar lump** terrón *m* de azúcar

sugar-coated ['ʃʊgə'kəʊtɪd] ADJ azucarado

sugar-free [ˌʃʊgə'fri:], **sugarless** ['ʃʊgəlɪs] ADJ sin azúcar

sugary ['ʃʊgərɪ] ADJ **1** (= *sweet*) [*food, taste*] dulce **2** (*pej*) [*film, smile, words*] empalagoso; [*voice*] meloso

suggest [sə'dʒest] VT **1** (= *propose*) sugerir, proponer; **I ~ed to him that we go out for a drink** le sugerí *or* propuse ir a tomar algo; **I ~ed taking her out to dinner** propuse llevarla a cenar **2** (= *advise*) aconsejar; **we ~ you contact him** le aconsejamos que contacte con él; **to ~ doing sth** aconsejar que se haga algo **3** (= *imply*) insinuar; **what are you trying to ~?** ¿qué insinúas? **4** (= *indicate*) parecer indicar; **the coins ~ a Roman settlement** las monedas parecen indicar *or* nos hacen pensar que era una colonia romana

suggestible [sə'dʒestɪbl] ADJ sugestionable

suggestion [sə'dʒestʃən] **Ⓐ** N **1** (= *proposal, recommendation*) sugerencia *f*; **have you any ~s?** ¿tienes alguna sugerencia?, ¿se te ocurre algo?; **if I may make a ~** si se me permite proponer algo; **to be open to ~s** estar abierto a cualquier sugerencia **2** (= *implication*) insinuación *f*; **we reject any ~ that the law needs amending** rechazamos cualquier insinuación de que la ley necesite una modificación **3** (= *indication*) indicio *m*; **there is no ~ that the two sides are any closer** no hay indicios de que ambas partes se hayan acercado **4** (= *trace*) [*of doubt*] sombra *f*; [*of garlic*] pizca *f* **5** (*Psych*) **the power of ~** el poder de la sugestión **Ⓑ** CPD ➤ **suggestion box** buzón *m* de sugerencias

suggestive [sə'dʒestɪv] ADJ **1** (= *improper*) [*remark, look, clothing*] provocativo, insinuante **2** (= *indicative*) **to be ~ of sth: symptoms which were ~ of heart failure** síntomas que sugerían que pod(r)ía tratarse de un fallo cardíaco, síntomas que parecían indicar que se trataba de un fallo cardíaco

suicidal [ˌsʊɪ'saɪdl] ADJ [*feeling, tendency*] suicida; **to be ~** estar al borde del suicidio; **to feel ~** tener ganas de suicidarse; **it would be ~ to do that** sería suicida hacer eso

suicide ['sʊɪsaɪd] N suicidio *m*; **to commit ~** suicidarse; **a case of attempted ~** un caso de intento de suicidio; **it would be political ~** sería un suicidio político ➤ **suicide bomber** terrorista *mf* suicida ➤ **suicide bombing** atentado *m* suicida ➤ **suicide mission** misión *f* suicida ➤ **suicide note** *carta en que se explica el motivo del suicidio*

suit [su:t] **Ⓐ** N **1** (for man) traje *m*, terno *m* (*LAm*); (for woman) traje *m* (de chaqueta); **~ of armour** armadura *f* **2** (in court) pleito *m*; **to bring a ~ (against sb)** entablar un pleito (contra algn) **3** (*Cards*) palo *m*; **✦ IDIOM to follow ~** seguir el ejemplo **Ⓑ** VT **1** (= *look good on*) [*clothes, shoes, hairstyle*] quedar bien a, sentar bien a; **the coat ~s you** el abrigo te queda *or* te sienta bien **2** (= *be acceptable to, please*) [*date, time, arrangement*] venir bien a, convenir; **when would ~ you?** ¿cuándo te viene bien *or* te conviene?; **I'll do it when it ~s me** lo haré cuando

me venga bien *or* cuando me convenga; **that ~s me fine** eso me va bien *or* me conviene; **~ yourself!*** ¡como quieras!; **✦ IDIOM to ~ sb down to the ground** (*esp Brit*) [*plan, situation*] venir de perlas a algn; [*house, job*] ser perfecto para algn **Ⓒ** VI (= *be convenient*) **will tomorrow ~?** ¿te viene bien mañana?

suitability [ˌsu:tə'bɪlɪtɪ] N [*of person, tool*] idoneidad *f*; [*of clothes*] lo apropiado

suitable ['su:təbl] ADJ [*training, job*] adecuado, apropiado; [*product, reply, clothing*,] apropiado; **the shortage of ~ housing** la escasez de viviendas adecuadas *or* apropiadas; **both courses are ~ for beginners** ambos cursos son apropiados para principiantes; **dishes that are ~ for freezing** platos preparados que se pueden congelar; **the most ~ man for the job** el hombre más indicado *or* adecuado para el puesto; **"suitable for children"** "apto para niños"; **a ~ moment to talk** un momento oportuno *or* apropiado para hablar

suitably ['su:təblɪ] ADV [*dressed*] apropiadamente, adecuadamente; [*equipped*] adecuadamente; **he tried to look ~ impressed** intentó parecer todo lo impresionado que la ocasión requería

suitcase ['su:tkeɪs] N maleta *f*, valija *f* (*LAm*), veliz *m* (*Mex*)

suite [swi:t] N **1** (*Mus*) suite *f* **2** (= *rooms*) suite *f* **3** [*of furniture*] juego *m*; **three-piece ~** tresillo *m*

suitor ['su:təʳ] N (= *lover*) pretendiente *m*

sulfate ['sʌlfeɪt] N (*US*) = **sulphate**

sulfide ['sʌlfaɪd] N (*US*) = **sulphide**

sulfur ['sʌlfəʳ] N (*US*) = **sulphur**

sulfuric [sʌl'fjʊərɪk] ADJ (*US*) = **sulphuric**

sulk [sʌlk] **Ⓐ** VI (= *get sulky*) enfurruñarse; (= *be sulky*) estar enfurruñado **Ⓑ** N **to have the ~s** enfurruñarse

sulky ['sʌlkɪ] ADJ (*compar* **sulkier**; *superl* **sulkiest**) [*person, voice*] malhumorado, enfurruñado; [*expression*] ceñudo, malhumorado; **to be ~ about sth** estar malhumorado *or* enfurruñado por algo, estar de mal humor por algo

sullen ['sʌlən] ADJ [*person, expression, voice*] hosco, huraño; [*sky, landscape*] plomizo, triste

sully ['sʌlɪ] VT (*poet*) [+ *name, reputation*] manchar, mancillar

sulphate, sulfate (*US*) ['sʌlfeɪt] N sulfato *m*

sulphide, sulfide (*US*) ['sʌlfaɪd] N sulfuro *m*

sulphur, sulfur (*US*) ['sʌlfəʳ] N azufre *m*

sulphuric, sulfuric (*US*) [sʌl'fjʊərɪk] ADJ **~ acid** ácido *m* sulfúrico

sultan ['sʌltən] N sultán *m*

sultana [sʌl'tɑ:nə] N (*Brit*) pasa *f* sultana

sultry ['sʌltrɪ] ADJ **1** (= *muggy*) [*day, weather*] bochornoso, sofocante; [*heat, air*] sofocante, agobiante **2** (= *seductive*) [*woman*] seductor, sensual

sum [sʌm] N **1** (= *piece of arithmetic*) suma *f*, adición *f*; **to do one's ~s** hacer cuentas **2** (= *total*) suma *f*, total *m*; (= *amount of money*) suma *f*, importe *m*; **~ total** total *m* (completo); **in ~** en suma, en resumen
➤ **sum up Ⓐ** VI + ADV (= *summarize*) resumir; **to ~ up, I would say ...** en resumidas cuentas, yo diría ... **Ⓑ** VT + ADV **1** (= *summarize*) [+ *speech, facts, argument, situation*] resumir **2** (= *assess*) [+ *person*] calar; **he ~med up the situation quickly** se dio cuenta rápidamente de la situación

summarize ['sʌməraɪz] VT, VI resumir; **to ~, ...** en resumen, ..., en resumidas cuentas ...

summary ['sʌmərɪ] **Ⓐ** N resumen *m*; **in ~** en resumen **Ⓑ** ADJ [*trial, execution, justice*] sumario

summer ['sʌməʳ] **Ⓐ** N verano *m*, estío *m* (*liter, poet*); **in ~** en verano; **a ~'s day** un día de verano; **to spend the ~ in Spain** veranear *or* pasar el verano en España **Ⓑ** CPD [*clothing, residence, holiday*] de verano; [*weather, heat*] veraniego ➤ **summer camp** colonia *f or* campamento *m* de vacaciones ➤ **summer holidays** vacaciones *fpl* de verano, veraneo *msing* ➤ **summer school** (*esp Brit*) escuela *f* de verano ➤ **summer time** (*Brit*) (*daylight saving*) hora *f* de verano

summerhouse ['sʌməhaʊs] N cenador *m*, glorieta *f*

summertime ['sʌmətaɪm] N (= *season*) verano *m*

summery ['sʌmərɪ] ADJ [*day*] veraniego; [*clothes, colour*] veraniego, de verano; [*weather*] estival

summing-up ['sʌmɪŋ'ʌp] N (*Jur*) resumen *m*

summit ['sʌmɪt] Ⓐ N **1** [*of mountain, career*] cima *f*, cumbre *f* **2** (*also* ~ **conference**) cumbre *f*, conferencia *f* al más alto nivel Ⓑ CPD ➤ **summit conference** cumbre *f*, conferencia *f* al más alto nivel

summon ['sʌmən] VT [+ *servant, doctor etc*] llamar; [+ *meeting*] convocar; [+ *aid*] pedir; (*Jur*) citar, emplazar ➤ **summon up** VT + ADV [+ *courage*] armarse de, cobrar; [+ *memory*] evocar; [+ *energy, strength*] reunir

summons ['sʌmənz] Ⓐ N (*pl* ~**es**) (*Jur*) citación *f* judicial, emplazamiento *m*; (*fig*) llamada *f*; **she received a ~ to appear in court** recibió una citación para presentarse en el juzgado Ⓑ VT citar, emplazar

sumo ['suːməʊ] N (*also* ~ **wrestling**) sumo *m*

sump [sʌmp] N (*Brit Aut*) cárter *m*

sumptuous ['sʌmptjʊəs] ADJ suntuoso

sun [sʌn] Ⓐ N sol *m*; **the** ~ **is shining** brilla el sol, hace sol; **the ~ is in my eyes** me da el sol en los ojos; **you've caught the ~** te ha cogido el sol; **to be (out) in the ~** estar al sol; ✦ IDIOM **under the ~: they have everything under the ~** no les falta de nada; **he called me all the names under the ~** me llamó de todo; ✦ PROV **there is nothing new under the ~** no hay nada nuevo bajo el sol Ⓑ VT **to ~ o.s.** tomar el sol, asolearse (*LAm*), tomar sol (*SC*) Ⓒ CPD ➤ **sun dress** vestido *m* de playa ➤ **sun hat** pamela *f*, sombrero *m* de ala ancha ➤ **sun lamp** lámpara *f* solar ultravioleta ➤ **sun lotion** bronceador *m* ➤ **sun lounger** tumbona *f* (*Sp*), perezosa *f* (*LAm*) ➤ **sun umbrella** sombrilla *f*

Sun. ABBR (= **Sunday**) dom.º

sunbathe ['sʌnbeɪð] VI tomar el sol, asolearse (*LAm*), tomar sol (*SC*)

sunbathing ['sʌnbeɪðɪŋ] N baños *mpl* de sol

sunbeam ['sʌnbiːm] N rayo *m* de sol

sunbed ['sʌnbed] N cama *f* solar

sunbelt ['sʌnbelt] N (*US*) franja del sur de Estados Unidos caracterizada por su clima cálido

SUNBELT

A los estados del sur de EE.UU. que van desde Carolina del Norte hasta California se les denomina **sunbelt** (cinturón del sol) por su clima cálido. Este nombre también se asocia con el reciente desarrollo económico de la zona, lo cual ha dado lugar a un aumento de población (por el movimiento demográfico de norte a sur) y a un mayor poder político. Por oposición a este término, a los estados del norte se les llama a veces **frostbelt** (cinturón de escarcha) o **rustbelt** (cinturón de óxido), por el número de fábricas ya en declive que hay en la zona.

sunblock ['sʌnblɒk] N filtro *m* solar

sunburn ['sʌnbɜːn] N quemaduras *fpl* del sol

sunburned ['sʌnbɜːnd], **sunburnt** ['sʌnbɜːnt] ADJ (*painfully*) quemado por el sol; (= *tanned*) bronceado; **to get ~** (*painfully*) quemarse

sundae ['sʌndeɪ] N helado *m* con frutas y nueces

Sunday ['sʌndɪ] N domingo *m* ➤ **Sunday best: in one's ~ best** en traje de domingo, endomingado ➤ **Sunday newspaper, Sunday paper** periódico *m* del domingo, (*periódico m*) dominical *m* ➤ **Sunday school** escuela *f* dominical, catequesis *f*; *see* **Tuesday**

sundial ['sʌndaɪəl] N reloj *m* de sol

sundown ['sʌndaʊn] N (*US*) anochecer *m*

sun-drenched ['sʌndrentʃt] ADJ bañado de sol

sun-dried ['sʌndraɪd] ADJ secado al sol

sundry ['sʌndrɪ] Ⓐ ADJ diversos, varios; **all and ~** todos sin excepción Ⓑ N **sundries** (*Comm*) artículos *mpl* diversos; (= *expenses*) gastos *mpl* diversos

sunflower ['sʌnˌflaʊəʳ] N girasol *m* ➤ **sunflower oil** aceite *m* de girasol ➤ **sunflower seeds** pipas *fpl*

sung [sʌŋ] PP *of* **sing**

sunglasses ['sʌnˌglɑːsɪz] NPL gafas *fpl* de sol, anteojos *mpl* de sol (*LAm*)

sunk [sʌŋk] PP *of* **sink**

sunken ['sʌŋkən] ADJ [*ship, treasure, cheeks, eyes*] hundido; [*garden, road, bath*] que está a un nivel inferior *or* más bajo

sunlight ['sʌnlaɪt] N sol *m*, luz *f* del sol; **those plants must be kept out of direct ~** a esas plantas no las debe dar el sol directamente

sunlit ['sʌnlɪt] ADJ iluminado por el sol

Sunni ['sʌnɪ] ADJ, N sunita *mf*, suní *mf*

sunny ['sʌnɪ] ADJ (*compar* **sunnier**; *superl* **sunniest**) **1** [*weather, climate, morning, place*] soleado; **it's a lovely ~ day** hace un día de sol precioso; **it's ~** hace sol; ~ **intervals** intervalos *mpl* soleados; **the outlook is ~** el pronóstico es soleado; ✦ IDIOM **eggs ~ side up** huevos fritos sin cubrir la yema con aceite **2** [*person*] risueño, alegre; [*smile, disposition*] alegre

sunrise ['sʌnraɪz] N salida *f* del sol; **at ~** al amanecer; **from ~ to sunset** de sol a sol

sunroof ['sʌnruːf] N (*on car*) techo *m* solar

sunscreen ['sʌnskriːn] N bronceador *m* con filtro solar

sunset ['sʌnset] N puesta *f* del sol; **at ~** al atardecer, al ponerse el sol

sunshade ['sʌnʃeɪd] N (*portable*) sombrilla *f*; (= *awning*) toldo *m*

sunshine ['sʌnʃaɪn] N sol *m*, luz *f* del sol; **in the ~** al sol; **hours of ~** (*Met*) horas *fpl* de sol; **hello, ~!*** (*to little girl*) ¡hola, nena!*

sunspot ['sʌnspɒt] N **1** (= *resort*) centro turístico muy soleado **2** (*Astron*) mancha *f* solar

sunstroke ['sʌnstrəʊk] N insolación *f*; **to get ~** coger *or* agarrar una insolación; **to have ~** tener una insolación

suntan ['sʌntæn] N bronceado *m*, moreno *m* (*Sp*); **to get a ~** broncearse, ponerse moreno (*Sp*) ➤ **suntan lotion** bronceador *m*

suntanned ['sʌntænd] ADJ bronceado, moreno (*Sp*)

suntrap ['sʌntræp] N lugar muy soleado y protegido

sun-up ['sʌnʌp] N (*US*) salida *f* del sol

super* ['suːpəʳ] ADJ (*esp Brit*) bárbaro, estupendo (*Sp*), tremendo, macanudo (*LAm*), regio (*SC***), chévere (*Ven*) ➤ **Super Bowl** (*US Sport*) supercopa de fútbol americano

superannuation [ˌsuːpəˌrænjʊ'eɪʃən] N (*Brit*) (= *pension*) jubilación *f*, pensión *f*

superb [suː'pɜːb] ADJ estupendo, magnífico

superbug* ['suːpəbʌg] N bacteria *f* asesina

supercilious [ˌsuːpə'sɪlɪəs] ADJ desdeñoso, altanero

supercharged ['suːpətʃɑːdʒd] ADJ **1** (*Aut*) sobrealimentado **2** [*atmosphere, environment*] sobrecargado

supercomputer ['suːpəkəmˌpjuːtəʳ] N superordenador *m* (*Sp*), supercomputadora *f* (*LAm*), supercomputador *m* (*LAm*)

superconductor [ˌsuːpəkən'dʌktəʳ] N superconductor *m*

superego ['suːpərˌiːgəʊ] N superego *m*

superficial [ˌsuːpə'fɪʃəl] ADJ [*person, damage, cut*] superficial

superficially [ˌsuːpə'fɪʃəlɪ] ADV **1** (= *in a shallow way*) [*deal with, treat, know, discuss*] superficialmente, de manera superficial, por encima **2** (= *at first glance*) a primera vista

superfluous [sʊ'pɜːfluəs] ADJ superfluo; **to be ~** [*comment, detail, explanation*] ser superfluo, sobrar; [*object, person*] sobrar; **I feel ~** me siento de más, me parece que sobro

superglue ['suːpəˌgluː] N supercola *f*

supergrass* ['suːpəgrɑːs] N (*Brit*) soplón/ona *m/f*

superhero ['suːpəˌhɪərəʊ] N superhéroe *m*

superhuman [ˌsuːpə'hjuːmən] ADJ sobrehumano

superimpose ['su:pərɪm'pəʊz] VT sobreponer (**on** en)

superintend [,su:pərɪn'tend] VT supervisar

superintendent [,su:pərɪn'tendənt] N [*of institution, orphanage*] director(a) *m/f*; (*in swimming pool*) vigilante *mf*; (*US*) (= *porter*) conserje *mf*; **police ~** (*Brit*) subjefe *mf* de policía; (*US*) superintendente *mf*

superior [sʊ'pɪərɪəʳ] **Ⓐ** ADJ **1** (= *better*) superior (**to** a); **the enemy's ~ numbers** la superioridad numérica del enemigo **2** (= *high quality*) [*product*] de primera calidad; **a very ~ model** un modelo de primerísima calidad, un modelo muy superior; **thanks to its ~ design** gracias a la supremacía del diseño **3** (*in hierarchy, rank*) superior (**to** a) **4** (= *smug*) [*person*] altanero, desdeñoso; [*tone, expression, smile*] de superioridad, de suficiencia **Ⓑ** N (*in rank, organization*) superior *m*

superiority [sʊ,pɪərɪ'ɒrɪtɪ] N **1** (*in quality, amount*) superioridad *f* **2** (= *smugness*) superioridad *f*, altanería *f*

superlative [sʊ'pɜ:lətɪv] **Ⓐ** ADJ **1** (= *outstanding*) excepcional **2** (*Gram*) superlativo **Ⓑ** N superlativo *m*; **he tends to talk in ~s** tiende a hablar en términos muy elogiosos de todo

superman ['su:pəmæn] N (*pl* **supermen**) superhombre *m*

supermarket ['su:pə,mɑ:kɪt] N supermercado *m*

supermodel ['su:pəmɒdl] N supermodelo *mf*

supernatural [,su:pə'nætʃərəl] **Ⓐ** ADJ sobrenatural **Ⓑ** N **the ~** lo sobrenatural

superpower ['su:pə,paʊəʳ] N superpotencia *f*

supersede [,su:pə'si:d] VT desbancar, suplantar

supersonic ['su:pə'sɒnɪk] ADJ supersónico

superstar ['su:pəstɑ:ʳ] N superestrella *f*

superstition [,su:pə'stɪʃən] N superstición *f*

superstitious [,su:pə'stɪʃəs] ADJ supersticioso

superstore ['su:pəstɔ:ʳ] N (*Brit*) hipermercado *m*

superstructure ['su:pə,strʌktʃəʳ] N superestructura *f*

supertanker ['su:pə,tæŋkəʳ] N superpetrolero *m*

supertax ['su:pətæks] N sobretasa *f*, sobreimpuesto *m*

supervise ['su:pəvaɪz] VT [+ *work, people*] supervisar

supervision [,su:pə'vɪʒən] N supervisión *f*; **to work under the ~ of** trabajar bajo la supervisión de

supervisor ['su:pəvaɪzəʳ] N (*gen*) supervisor(a) *m/f*

supervisory ['su:pəvaɪzərɪ] ADJ [*body, staff, powers*] de supervisión; [*role*] de supervisor

supine ['su:paɪn] ADJ (*frm*) (= *prostrate*) de espaldas, sobre el dorso, supino (*more frm*)

supper ['sʌpəʳ] N (= *evening meal*) cena *f*; **what's for ~?** ¿qué hay de cena?; **to have ~** cenar

suppertime ['sʌpətaɪm] N hora *f* de cenar

supplant [sə'plɑ:nt] VT suplantar, reemplazar

supple ['sʌpl] ADJ [*body, leather*] flexible; [*joint, limb*] ágil; [*skin*] suave

supplement Ⓐ ['sʌplɪmənt] N (*gen*) suplemento *m* **Ⓑ** [sʌplɪ'ment] VT [+ *diet*] complementar; [+ *income*] aumentar

supplementary [,sʌplɪ'mentərɪ] ADJ suplementario

suppleness ['sʌplnɪs] N [*of body, leather*] flexibilidad *f*; [*of joint, limb*] agilidad *f*; [*of skin*] suavidad *f*

supplication [,sʌplɪ'keɪʃən] N súplica *f*

supplier [sə'plaɪəʳ] N (= *distributor*) distribuidor(a) *m/f*; (= *provider*) abastecedor(a) *m/f*, proveedor(a) *m/f*

supply [sə'plaɪ] **Ⓐ** N **1** (= *stock, amount*) [*of oil, coal, water*] reservas *fpl*, existencias *fpl*; [*of goods, merchandise*] existencias *fpl*; **we need a fresh ~ of coffee** nos hace falta proveernos de café; **to lay in a ~ of sth** proveerse de algo, hacer provisión de algo; **to be in short ~** escasear **2 supplies** (= *provisions*) provisiones *fpl*, víveres *mpl*; (*Mil*) pertrechos *mpl*; **food supplies** víveres *mpl*, provisiones *fpl*; **medical supplies** suministros *mpl* médicos **3** (= *act of supplying*) suministro *m*; **electricity/gas ~** suministro de electricidad/gas; **~ and demand** la oferta y la demanda

Ⓑ VT (= *provide*) [+ *merchandise, goods, materials, food, arms*] suministrar, proporcionar; [+ *information*] facilitar, proporcionar; **to ~ sb with** [+ *merchandise, equipment*] suministrar algo a algn, proporcionar algo a algn; [+ *services*] proveer a algn de algo; [+ *information*] facilitar algo a algn; **they kept us supplied with vegetables** nos fueron abasteciendo de verduras

Ⓒ CPD **► supply teacher** (*Brit*) profesor(a) *m/f* suplente, profesor(a) *m/f* sustituto/a

support [sə'pɔ:t] **Ⓐ** N **1** (= *help, backing*) apoyo *m* (*also Mil*); **I've had a lot of ~ from my family** mi familia me ha apoyado mucho *or* me ha dado mucho apoyo; **do I have I your ~ in this?** ¿puedo contar con tu apoyo para esto?; **history offers some ~ for this view** la historia respalda en cierta medida esta opinión; **financial ~** ayuda *f* económica, respaldo *m* económico; **they depend on him for financial ~** económicamente dependen de él; **to give sb ~** dar apoyo a algn, apoyar a algn; **he has given his ~ to the programme** ha apoyado *or* respaldado el programa, ha dado su apoyo *or* respaldo al programa; **he spoke in ~ of the motion** habló en apoyo de la moción; **in ~ of this argument he states that ...** para apoyar *or* respaldar este argumento aduce que ...; **evidence in ~ of a particular theory** pruebas que confirman una determinada teoría; **a man with no visible means of ~** (*financial*) un hombre sin una fuente de ingresos aparente; **moral ~** apoyo moral **2** (*esp Comm*) (= *backup*) servicio *m* de asistencia (al cliente); **technical ~** servicio *m* de asistencia técnica **3** (= *capacity to support*) soporte *m*; **a good bed should provide adequate ~ for your back** una buena cama debe ofrecerle un soporte adecuado para su espalda; **to lean on sb for ~** apoyarse en algn **4** (= *object*) soporte *m* (*also Med*); **use the stool as a ~ for your feet** usa el taburete como soporte para los pies; **steel ~s** soportes *mpl* de acero **Ⓑ** VT **1** (= *hold up*) sostener; **his knees wouldn't ~ him any more** sus rodillas ya no lo sostenían; **that chair won't ~ your weight** esa silla no resistirá *or* aguantará tu peso **2** (*financially*) [+ *person*] mantener; [+ *organization, project*] financiar; **he has a wife and three children to ~** tiene una mujer y tres hijos que mantener; **to ~ o.s.** ganarse la vida **3** [+ *proposal, project, person*] apoyar **4** [+ *team*] **he ~s Manchester United** es hincha del Manchester United **5** (= *corroborate*) [+ *theory, view*] respaldar, confirmar **6** (= *sustain*) **an environment capable of ~ing human life** un medio en que existen las condiciones necesarias para que se desarrolle la vida humana **Ⓒ** CPD **► support band** (*Mus*) teloneros *mpl* **► support group** grupo *m* de apoyo

supporter [sə'pɔ:təʳ] N [*of proposal, party*] partidario/a *m/f*; [*of team*] hincha *mf*; **football ~s** hinchas *mpl* de fútbol

supporting [sə'pɔ:tɪŋ] ADJ **1** [*documents*] acreditativo; **there is no ~ evidence for this theory** no hay pruebas que confirmen esta teoría **2** (*Theat*) [*role, cast*] secundario; [*actor*] secundario, de reparto

supportive [sə'pɔ:tɪv] ADJ [*role*] de apoyo; **I have a very ~ family** tengo una familia que me apoya mucho

suppose [sə'pəʊz] VT **1** (= *imagine*) suponer; **let us ~ that ...** supongamos que ..., pongamos por caso que ...; **but just ~ he's right** y ¿si tiene razón?; **supposing it rains, what shall we do?** pongamos que llueve, entonces ¿qué hacemos?; **always supposing he comes** siempre y cuando venga; **even supposing that were true** aun en el caso de que fuera verdad **2** (= *assume, believe*) suponer, creer; **I ~ she'll come** supongo que vendrá; **I don't ~ she'll come** no creo que venga; **who do you ~ was there?** ¿quién crees tú que estaba allí?; **you don't ~ they'd start without us, do you?** no empezarán sin nosotros, ¿verdad?; **I ~ so/not** supongo que sí/no **3 to be ~d to do sth: you're ~d to be in bed by ten** tendrías que estar acostado a las diez; **you're not ~d to do that** no deberías hacer eso; **you're ~d to be my friend!** ¡yo creía que eras mi amigo!; **what am I ~d to have done wrong now?** ¿qué se supone que he hecho mal ahora?; **what's that ~d to mean?** ¿qué quieres decir con eso?; **he's ~d to be an expert** se le supone un experto; **he was ~d to telephone this morning** tendría que haber llamado esta mañana

4 (*in requests*) **do you ~ you could wrap this up for me?** ¿podrías envolverme esto?; **I don't ~ you could lend me ten pounds?** ¿no podrías prestarme diez libras?

supposed [sə'pəʊzd] ADJ [*ally, benefit, threat*] supuesto

supposedly [sə'pəʊzɪdlɪ] ADV supuestamente; **he had ~ gone to Scotland** según se suponía había ido a Escocia, supuestamente había ido a Escocia

supposition [ˌsʌpə'zɪʃən] N suposición *f*; **that is pure ~** eso es una suposición or hipótesis nada más; **the report was based on ~** el informe estaba basado en suposiciones; **it's based on the ~ that ...** se basa en la hipótesis de que ...

suppository [sə'pɒzɪtərɪ] N supositorio *m*

suppress [sə'pres] VT [+ *opposition, publication*] suprimir; [+ *feelings*] reprimir; [+ *emotion*] contener, dominar; [+ *yawn, smile*] contener; [+ *news, the truth*] callar, ocultar; [+ *revolt, uprising*] sofocar, reprimir

suppression [sə'preʃən] N [*of symptoms, dissent, opposition, publication*] supresión *f*; [*of feelings*] represión *f*; [*of news, the truth*] ocultación *f*; [*of revolt*] represión *f*

suppressor [sə'presəʳ] N supresor *m*

suppurate ['sʌpjʊəreɪt] VI supurar

supremacy [sʊ'preməsɪ] N supremacía *f*

supreme [sʊ'priːm] ADJ [*effort, sacrifice*] supremo; [*heroism, confidence, importance, indifference*] sumo; [*champion*] absoluto ➤ **Supreme Court** Tribunal *m* Supremo, Corte *f* Suprema (*LAm*)

supremo [sʊ'priːməʊ] N (*Brit*) jefe *m*

Supt ABBR (*Brit*) = **Superintendent**

surcharge ['sɜːtʃɑːdʒ] Ⓐ N recargo *m* Ⓑ VT cobrar un recargo a

sure [ʃʊəʳ] ADJ (*compar* ~**r**; *superl* ~**st**) Ⓐ ADJ **1** (= *certain*) seguro; **I'm not ~** no sé, no estoy seguro; **"I know my duty" — "I'm ~ you do"** —sé cuál es mi deber —de eso estoy seguro; **to be ~ that** estar seguro de que; **I'm not ~ that I can help you** no estoy seguro de que te pueda ayudar, no estoy seguro de poder ayudarte; **are you ~ you won't have another drink?** ¿seguro que no quieres tomarte otra copa?; **to be ~ about sth** estar seguro de algo; **to be ~ of sth** estar seguro de algo; **we can't be ~ of winning** no podemos estar seguros de que vayamos a ganar; **to be ~ of one's facts** estar seguro de lo que se dice; **to be ~ of sb** confiar en algn; **he was not quite ~ of Flora** tenía sus dudas acerca de Flora; **to be ~ of o.s.** estar seguro de sí mismo; **to be ~ what/whether/who** estar seguro de qué/(de) si/quién

2 (+ INFIN) **it is ~ to rain** seguro que llueve, seguramente lloverá; **be ~ to close the window** asegúrate de que cierras la ventana; **be ~ to tell me** que no se te olvide contármelo

3 to make ~ (that) asegurarse (de que); **make ~ it doesn't happen again** asegúrate de que no vuelva a ocurrir; **please make ~ that your children get to school on time** consiga de la forma que sea que sus hijos lleguen a la escuela a tiempo; **better get a ticket beforehand, just to make ~** mejor compre el billete de antemano, más que nada para ir sobre seguro or para tener esa seguridad

4 for ~* seguro*; **you'll get it tomorrow for ~** lo recibirás mañana seguro; **nobody knows for ~** nadie lo sabe con seguridad; **that's for ~** eso desde luego; **one thing's for ~** una cosa está clara

5 (= *reliable*) [*sign*] claro; **one ~ way to lose is ...** una forma segura de perder es ...; **to do sth in the ~ knowledge that** hacer algo sabiendo bien que or con la seguridad de que

Ⓑ ADV **1** (= *of course*) claro; **"can I go with you?" — "sure!"** —¿puedo ir contigo? —¡por supuesto! or —¡claro que sí!

2 ~ enough efectivamente, en efecto; **he said he'd be here, and ~ enough, there he is** dijo que estaría aquí y efectivamente or en efecto, aquí está

3 (*US**) (= *certainly*) **I ~ am bored** no veas si estoy aburrido*; **"know what I mean?" — "~ do"** —sabes, ¿no? —claro que sí or claro que lo sé

sure-fire* ['ʃʊə'faɪəʳ] ADJ [*way, success*] seguro; [*method*] infalible; **he's a ~ winner** tiene el éxito asegurado

sure-footed ['ʃʊə'fʊtɪd] ADJ (*lit*) de pie firme; **to be ~** (*lit, fig*) conocer el terreno que se pisa

surely ['ʃʊəlɪ] ADV **1** (*emphatic*) **~ there must be something**

we can do? algo habrá que podemos hacer, ¿no?; **~ it's better to steal than to starve** mejor será robar que pasar hambre, digo or creo yo; **~ it's obvious?** pero si es obvio, ¿no?; **you ~ don't think it was me!** ¡no pensarás que fui yo!; **~ not** no puede ser

2 (= *undoubtedly*) sin duda; **his time will ~ come** no cabe duda de que le llegará su momento

3 (= *safely, confidently*) con seguridad; **slowly but ~** lento pero seguro

4 (*US*) (= *of course*) por supuesto, ¡cómo no! (*LAm*)

surety ['ʃʊərətɪ] N (= *sum*) garantía *f*, fianza *f*, caución *f*; (= *person*) fiador(a) *m/f*, garante *mf*; **to stand ~ for sb** ser fiador de algn, salir garante de algn

surf [sɜːf] Ⓐ N (= *waves*) olas *fpl*, rompientes *mpl*; (= *foam*) espuma *f*; (= *swell*) oleaje *m* Ⓑ VT [+ *waves*] hacer surf en; **to ~ the Net** navegar por Internet

surface ['sɜːfɪs] Ⓐ N **1** [*of table, skin, lake, sun*] superficie *f*; [*of road*] firme *m*; **beneath** or **below the ~: the box was buried two metres beneath** or **below the ~** la caja estaba enterrada a dos metros por debajo de la superficie; **she appeared calm, but beneath** or **below the ~ she was seething with rage** parecía estar tranquila pero en el fondo or por dentro hervía de rabia; **her grief was still close to the ~** su dolor estaba todavía a flor de piel; **on the ~ it seems that ...** a primera vista parece que ...; **these feelings may come** or **rise to the ~** estos sentimientos pueden aflorar (a la superficie); **under the ~ = beneath the surface**; ✦ IDIOM **to scratch** or **touch the ~ (of sth)** arañar la superficie (de algo)

2 (*also* **~ area**) superficie *f*

3 (= *side*) [*of solid*] cara *f*

Ⓑ VT [+ *road*] revestir, asfaltar

Ⓒ VI [*swimmer, diver, whale*] salir a la superficie; [*submarine*] emerger; [*information, news*] salir a la luz; [*feeling*] salir, aflorar; [*issue*] salir a relucir; [*problem*] presentarse, surgir; [*person*] (*in place*) dejarse ver; (*hum*) (= *get up*) salir de la cama

Ⓓ CPD ➤ **surface area** área *f* (de la superficie)

> Use **el/un** not **la/una** before feminine nouns beginning with stressed **a** or **ha** like **área**.

➤ **surface mail by ~ mail** por vía terrestre

surface-(to-)air ['sɜːfɪs(tuː)'eəʳ] ADJ ➤ **surface-(to-)air missile** misil *m* tierra-aire

surfboard ['sɜːfbɔːd] N plancha *f* de surf, tabla *f* de surf

surfeit ['sɜːfɪt] N exceso *m*

surfer ['sɜːfəʳ] N surfista *mf*, tablista *mf* de surf

surfing ['sɜːfɪŋ] N surf *m*

surge [sɜːdʒ] Ⓐ N [*of sea*] oleaje *m*, oleada *f*; [*of people, sympathy*] oleada *f*; **a power ~** (*Elec*) una subida de tensión Ⓑ VI [*water*] levantarse, hincharse; [*people, crowd*] **to ~ in/out** entrar/salir en tropel; **the blood ~d to her cheeks** se le subió la sangre a las mejillas

surgeon ['sɜːdʒən] N cirujano/a *m/f*; (*Mil, Naut*) médico *m*, oficial *m* médico ➤ **Surgeon General** (*US*) jefe del servicio federal de sanidad

surgery ['sɜːdʒərɪ] Ⓐ N **1** (= *branch of medicine, operation*) cirugía *f*; **to have ~** ser operado, someterse a una operación (quirúrgica)

2 (*Brit*) (= *consulting room of doctor, vet*) consultorio *m*

3 (*Brit*) (*with doctor, vet*) consulta *f*; **she has a Wednesday afternoon ~** tiene or pasa consulta los miércoles por la tarde

4 (*US*) (*for operations*) quirófano *m*, sala *f* de operaciones

5 (*Brit Pol*) sesión de consulta y atención de reclamaciones de un diputado con los electores de su circunscripción Ⓑ CPD ➤ **surgery hours** (*Brit*) horas *fpl* de consulta

surgical ['sɜːdʒɪkəl] ADJ quirúrgico ➤ **surgical spirit** (*Brit*) alcohol *m* de 90°

surgically ['sɜːdʒɪklɪ] ADV quirúrgicamente

Surinam [ˌsʊərɪ'næm] N Surinam *m*

surly ['sɜːlɪ] ADJ (*compar* **surlier**; *superl* **surliest**) hosco, malhumorado

surmise [sɜː'maɪz] **Ⓐ** N conjetura *f*, suposición *f* **Ⓑ** VT conjeturar, suponer; **I ~d as much** ya me lo suponía *or* imaginaba

surmount [sɜː'maʊnt] VT [+ *difficulty*] superar, vencer

surmountable [sɜː'maʊntəbl] ADJ superable

surname ['sɜːneɪm] N apellido *m*

surpass [sɜː'pɑːs] VT [+ *amount, level, record*] superar, sobrepasar; [+ *expectations*] rebasar, superar; **to ~ o.s.** superarse a sí mismo; (*iro*) pasarse (de la raya)

surplice ['sɜːpləs] N sobrepelliz *f*

surplus ['sɜːpləs] **Ⓐ** N (*pl* **~es**) **1** (= *excess*) exceso *m*; (*from overproduction*) excedente *m* **2** (*Fin, Econ*) superávit *m* **Ⓑ** ADJ sobrante; (*from overproduction*) excedentario, excedente; **~ energy** energía *f* sobrante; **to be ~ to requirements** no ser ya necesario, sobrar **Ⓒ** CPD ➤ **surplus store** tienda *f* de excedentes

surprise [sə'praɪz] **Ⓐ** N sorpresa *f*; **imagine my ~ when ...** puedes imaginarte la sorpresa que me llevé cuando ...; **"what?" George asked in ~** —¿qué? —preguntó George, sorprendido; **there was a look of ~ on his face** tenía cara de sorpresa; **surprise, surprise!** (*iro*) ¡menuda sorpresa! (*iro*); **much to my ~, he agreed** para gran sorpresa mía, accedió; **to take sb by ~** coger *or* (*LAm*) tomar a algn por sorpresa; **what a lovely ~!** ¡qué sorpresa más *or* tan agradable!; **it came as a ~ to me to learn that ...** me llevé una sorpresa al enterarme de que ...; **to give sb a ~** dar una sorpresa a algn **Ⓑ** ADJ [*party, present, visit*] sorpresa *inv*; [*announcement, defeat, decision*] inesperado; [*attack*] por sorpresa **Ⓒ** VT sorprender; **go on, ~ me!** (*iro*) ¡venga, sorpréndeme! (*iro*); **it ~d her to hear John sounding so angry** le sorprendió oír a John hablar tan enfadado; **no one will be ~d by her appointment** a nadie le extrañará *or* sorprenderá su nombramiento; **I was ~d by his ignorance** me sorprendió su ignorancia, me quedé sorprendido de lo ignorante que era; **it wouldn't ~ me if he ended up in jail** no me extrañaría *or* sorprendería que terminara en la cárcel; **it ~s me that ...** me sorprende que + *subjun*; **to ~ o.s.** sorprenderse (a sí mismo)

surprised [sə'praɪzd] ADJ [*look, expression, smile*] de sorpresa; **he was ~ to hear that ...** se sorprendió *or* quedó sorprendido al enterarse de que ...; **they were ~ that she hadn't told them about her new job** se sorprendieron de que no les hubiera dicho nada de su nuevo trabajo; **I'm ~ at you!** ¡me sorprendes!; **you'd be ~ how many people ...** te sorprenderías de la cantidad de gente que ..., te quedarías sorprendido si supieras la cantidad de gente que ...; **don't be ~ if he doesn't recognize you** no te sorprendas si no te reconoce; **I wouldn't be ~ if he won** no me sorprendería que ganara

surprising [sə'praɪzɪŋ] ADJ sorprendente; **it is ~ that ...** es sorprendente que ... + *subjun*; **it is hardly ~ that some teachers are leaving the profession** no es de extrañar que algunos profesores estén dejando la profesión

surprisingly [sə'praɪzɪŋlɪ] ADV [*good, large, easy*] sorprendentemente; **~ enough this is her first film** esta es su primera película, lo cual es bastante sorprendente; **not ~ he didn't come** como era de esperar, no vino

surreal [sə'rɪəl] ADJ surrealista, surreal

surrealism [sə'rɪəlɪzəm] N surrealismo *m*

surrealist [sə'rɪəlɪst] ADJ, N surrealista *mf*

surrealistic [sə,rɪə'lɪstɪk] ADJ surrealista

surrender [sə'rendəʳ] **Ⓐ** N **1** (*Mil*) rendición *f*; (*fig*) claudicación *f* **2** (= *handover*) [*of weapons*] entrega *f* **3** [*of insurance policy*] rescate *m* (previo al vencimiento) **Ⓑ** VI rendirse; **to ~ to the police** entregarse a la policía **Ⓒ** VT [+ *weapons*] rendir, entregar; [+ *territory, city*] entregar; [+ *claim, right*] renunciar a; [+ *passport, ticket*] entregar, hacer entrega de (*more frm*)

surreptitious [ˌsʌrəp'tɪʃəs] ADJ subrepticio

surreptitiously [ˌsʌrəp'tɪʃəslɪ] ADV [*glance, signal*] subrepticiamente

surrogate ['sʌrəgeɪt] N sustituto *m*; (= *substance, material*) sucedáneo *m* ➤ **surrogate mother** madre *f* de alquiler

surround [sə'raʊnd] **Ⓐ** VT rodear; **the house was ~ed by a** high wall la casa estaba rodeada por un muro muy alto; **she was ~ed by children** estaba rodeada de niños; **the uncertainty ~ing the future of the project** la incertidumbre que envuelve *or* rodea al proyecto; **you are ~ed!** ¡estáis rodeados! **Ⓑ** N (= *border*) marco *m*, borde *m*; (*esp Brit*) [*of fireplace*] marco *m*

surrounding [sə'raʊndɪŋ] ADJ [*countryside*] circundante; [*hills*] circundante, de alrededor

surroundings [sə'raʊndɪŋz] NPL (= *environment*) ambiente *msing*; (= *setting*) entorno *msing*; **he'll soon get used to his new ~** pronto se acostumbrará al nuevo ambiente *or* entorno que le rodea; **a hotel set in peaceful ~** un hotel situado en un apacible entorno; **he looked around at his ~** miró a su alrededor, miró en torno suyo

surtax ['sɜːtæks] N sobretasa *f*, sobreimpuesto *m*

surveillance [sɜː'veɪləns] N **to be under ~** estar vigilado, estar bajo vigilancia; **to keep sb under ~** vigilar a algn, tener vigilado a algn

survey Ⓐ ['sɜːveɪ] N **1** (= *study*) estudio *m* **2** (= *poll*) encuesta *f*; **to carry out a ~** realizar una encuesta **3** [*of land*] inspección *f*, reconocimiento *m*; (*in topography*) medición *f*; (*esp Brit*) [*of building, property*] tasación *f*, peritaje *m*; (= *report to purchaser*) informe *m* de tasación, informe *m* de peritaje **4** (= *general view*) visión *f* global, vista *f* de conjunto; **he gave a general ~ of the situation** dio una visión global *or* de conjunto de la situación **Ⓑ** [sɜː'veɪ] VT **1** (= *contemplate*) contemplar, mirar; **he ~ed the desolate scene** miró detenidamente la triste escena **2** (= *study*) estudiar, hacer un estudio de **3** (= *poll*) [+ *person, group*] encuestar; [+ *town*] hacer una encuesta en, pulsar la opinión de; [+ *reactions*] sondear; **95% of those ~ed believed that ...** el 95% de los encuestados creía que ... **4** (= *inspect*) [+ *building*] inspeccionar; [+ *land*] hacer un reconocimiento de; (*in topography*) medir; (= *map*) [+ *town*] levantar el plano de **5** (= *take general view of*) pasar revista a

surveying [sɜː'veɪɪŋ] N agrimensura *f*, topografía *f*

surveyor [sə'veɪəʳ] N (*Brit*) [*of land*] agrimensor(a) *m/f*, topógrafo/a *m/f*; [*of property*] tasador(a) *m/f* (de la propiedad), perito *mf* tasador(a)

survival [sə'vaɪvəl] N **1** (= *act*) supervivencia *f*; **the ~ of the fittest** la ley del más fuerte **2** (= *relic*) vestigio *m*, reliquia *f* **Ⓑ** CPD ➤ **survival course** curso *m* de supervivencia ➤ **survival kit** equipo *m* de emergencia

survive [sə'vaɪv] **Ⓐ** VI [*person, species*] sobrevivir; [*painting, building, manuscript*] conservarse; [*custom*] pervivir; **I'll ~!** ¡de ésta no me muero!, ¡sobreviviré!; **he ~d on nuts for several weeks** logró sobrevivir durante varias semanas comiendo nueces; **Jim ~s on £65 a fortnight** Jim se las arregla para vivir con 65 libras a la quincena **Ⓑ** VT [+ *accident, illness, war*] sobrevivir a; **he is ~d by a wife and two sons** deja una mujer y dos hijos

surviving [sə'vaɪvɪŋ] ADJ (= *living*) vivo; (*after catastrophe, also Jur*) sobreviviente; **the last ~ member of the band** el último miembro vivo del grupo

survivor [sə'vaɪvəʳ] N superviviente *mf*, sobreviviente *mf*; **I'm a ~, I'll get by** soy de los que no se hunden, me las arreglaré

susceptibility [sə,septə'bɪlɪtɪ] N (*to attack*) susceptibilidad *f*; (*to illness, infection*) propensión *f* (**to** a); (*to persuasion, flattery*) sensibilidad *f* (**to** a)

susceptible [sə'septəbl] ADJ (*to attack*) susceptible (**to** a); (*to illness, infection*) propenso (**to** a); (*to persuasion, flattery*) sensible (**to** a); (= *easily moved*) impresionable

sushi ['suːʃɪ] N sushi *m*

suspect Ⓐ ['sʌspekt] ADJ [*person, package*] sospechoso; [*motives*] dudoso, sospechoso **Ⓑ** ['sʌspekt] N sospechoso/a *m/f* **Ⓒ** [səs'pekt] VT **1** (= *have suspicions about*) [+ *person*] sospechar de; **I ~ her of having stolen it** sospecho que ella lo ha robado; **he ~s nothing** no sospecha nada **2** (= *believe*) **I ~ it's not paid for** sospecho que *or* me temo que no está remunerado; **I ~ed as much** ya me lo figuraba *or* imaginaba

suspend [səs'pend] **Ⓐ** VT **1** (= *hang*) suspender, colgar

2 (*from job*) suspender (**from** de); (*from school*) expulsar temporalmente (**from** de); (*from team*) excluir (**from** de) **3** [+ *hostilities, aid, flights*] suspender; [+ *licence*] retirar **4** (= *defer*) [+ *judgement, decision*] aplazar, posponer Ⓑ CPD ➤ **suspended sentence: he was given a two-year ~ed sentence** fue condenado a dos años en libertad condicional

suspender [səs'pendə^r] N (*Brit*) (*for stocking*) liga *f*; **~s** (*US*) (= *braces*) tirantes *mpl*, tiradores *mpl* (*SC*) ➤ **suspender belt** (*Brit*) portaligas *m inv*, liguero *m*

suspense [səs'pens] N incertidumbre *f*; (*Theat, Cine*) intriga *f*, suspense *m*; **to keep sb in** ~ mantener a algn en vilo; **the ~ is killing me!** ¡no puedo con tanta emoción!

suspension [səs'penʃən] Ⓐ N **1** (*from job*) suspensión *f*; (*from school*) expulsión *f* temporal; (*from team*) exclusión *f* **2** (*in car*) suspensión *f* Ⓑ CPD ➤ **suspension bridge** puente *m* colgante

suspicion [səs'pɪʃən] N sospecha *f*; **to be above** ~ estar por encima de toda sospecha; **to arouse sb's ~s** despertar los recelos de algn; **to have one's ~s (about sth)** tener sus sospechas (acerca de algo); **I have a sneaking ~ that ...** tengo la ligera sospecha de que ...; **he was arrested on ~ of spying** fue arrestado bajo sospecha de espionaje, fue arrestado como sospechoso de espionaje; **to lay o.s. open to ~** hacerse sospechoso; **to regard sb/sth with ~** desconfiar de algn/algo; **to be under ~** estar bajo sospecha

suspicious [səs'pɪʃəs] ADJ **1** (= *mistrustful*) [*person, nature*] desconfiado; [*glance*] receloso; **many people are ~ that ...** mucha gente tiene la sospecha de que ...; **to be ~ about sth** desconfiar de algo; **to become ~ (of sth/sb)** empezar a desconfiar (de algo/algn); **that made him ~** eso le hizo sospechar; **to have a ~ mind** tener una mente desconfiada *or* recelosa **2** (= *causing suspicion*) [*person, behaviour, package*] sospechoso; **did you see anything ~?** ¿viste algo sospechoso?; **in ~ circumstances** en circunstancias sospechosas

suspiciously [səs'pɪʃəslɪ] ADV **1** (= *mistrustfully*) [*look, ask*] con recelo, con desconfianza **2** (= *causing suspicion*) [*behave, act*] de modo sospechoso; **their essays were ~ similar** sus trabajos se parecían sospechosamente; **he arrived ~ early** llegó sospechosamente pronto; **the stain looked ~ like blood** la mancha tenía todo el aspecto de ser de sangre

suss* [sʌs] VT (*esp Brit*) (*also* ~ **out**) [+ *person*] calar*; **she's got you ~ed** te tiene calado*; **we couldn't ~ it out at all** no logramos sacar nada en claro; **they never ~ed what was going on** no llegaron a percatarse *or* coscarse* de lo que pasaba

sustain [səs'teɪn] VT **1** (= *keep going*) [+ *interest, relationship, marriage*] mantener; [+ *effort*] sostener, continuar; [+ *life*] sustentar; [+ *note*] sostener **2** (*frm*) (= *suffer*) [+ *attack, loss, damage*] sufrir; [+ *injury*] recibir, sufrir; [+ *defeat*] padecer

sustainable [səs'teɪnəbl] ADJ [*growth, development, agriculture*] sostenible; [*charge*] sustentable ➤ **sustainable develpoment** desarrollo *m* sostenible

sustained [səs'teɪnd] ADJ [*growth, note*] sostenido; [*effort*] constante, ininterrumpido; [*applause*] prolongado

sustenance ['sʌstɪnəns] N sustento *m*; **they get their ~ from** se sustentan *or* alimentan de

suture ['suːtʃə^r] Ⓐ N sutura *f* Ⓑ VT suturar, coser

SUV N ABBR (= **sport(s) utility vehicle**) todoterreno *m inv*

SVQ N ABBR = **Scottish Vocational Qualification**

SW ABBR **1** (= **southwest**) SO **2** (*Rad*) (= **short wave**) OC *f*

swab [swɒb] Ⓐ N (*for cleaning wound*) algodón *m*, tampón *m*; (*for specimen*) frotis *m* Ⓑ VT limpiar

swaddle ['swɒdl] VT envolver (**in** en)

swag* [swæg] N botín *m*

swagger ['swægə^r] Ⓐ N **1** (*in walk*) paso *m* decidido y arrogante; **to walk with a ~** andar con paso decidido y arrogante, pavonearse al caminar **2** (= *bravado*) fanfarronería *f*, pavoneo *m* Ⓑ VI (*also* ~ **about, ~ along**) pavonearse, andar pavoneándose; **he ~ed out** salió con paso firme y arrogante

swaggering ['swægərɪŋ] ADJ [*person*] fanfarrón,

jactancioso; [*gait*] importante, jactancioso

Swahili [swɑː'hiːlɪ] N swahili *m*, suajili *m*

swallow¹ ['swɒləʊ] Ⓐ N trago *m*; **with one ~** de un trago Ⓑ VT [+ *food, drink*] tragar; [+ *pill*] tomar; [+ *insult, story*] tragarse; **he ~ed the lot** se lo tragó todo; ✦ IDIOM **to ~ one's pride** tragarse el orgullo Ⓒ VI tragar; **to ~ hard** (*fig*) tragar saliva
➤ **swallow down** VT + ADV tragar
➤ **swallow up** VT + ADV [+ *savings*] agotar, consumir; [*sea*] tragar; **the mist ~ed them up** la niebla los envolvió

swallow² ['swɒləʊ] N (= *bird*) golondrina *f*

swam [swæm] PT *of* **swim**

swamp [swɒmp] Ⓐ N pantano *m*, ciénaga *f*, marisma *f* Ⓑ VT [+ *land*] inundar; [+ *boat*] hundir; **they have been ~ed with applications** se han visto abrumados *or* desbordados por las solicitudes; **we're ~ed with work** estamos agobiados de trabajo

swampy ['swɒmpɪ] ADJ pantanoso, cenagoso

swan [swɒn] Ⓐ N cisne *m* Ⓑ VI (*Brit**) **to ~ around** pavonearse; **to ~ off to New York** escaparse a Nueva York Ⓒ CPD ➤ **swan song** canto *m* del cisne

swanky* ['swæŋkɪ] ADJ (*compar* **swankier**; *superl* **swankiest**) [*person*] fanfarrón*, presumido; [*car*] despampanante; [*restaurant, hotel*] elegante, de postín (*Sp**)

swap [swɒp] Ⓐ N trueque *m*, canje *m* Ⓑ VT [+ *cars, stamps*] trocar, canjear, intercambiar; **will you ~ your hat for my jacket?** ¿quieres cambiar tu sombrero por mi chaqueta?; **to ~ places (with sb)** cambiar(se) de sitio (con algn); **I wouldn't mind ~ping places with him!** (*fig*) ¡ya me gustaría a mí estar en su pellejo! Ⓒ VI hacer un intercambio; **do you want to ~?** ¿quieres que cambiemos?
➤ **swap around, swap over, swap round** VT + ADV, VI + ADV cambiar de sitio

swarm [swɔːm] Ⓐ N [*of bees, mosquitoes*] enjambre *m*; [*of people*] multitud *f*; **they came in ~s** vinieron en tropel Ⓑ VI [*bees*] enjambrar; **Stratford is ~ing with tourists** Stratford está plagado de turistas; **journalists ~ed around her** los periodistas se arremolinaban alrededor de ella

swarthy ['swɔːðɪ] ADJ (*compar* **swarthier**; *superl* **swarthiest**) moreno

swashbuckling ['swɒʃˌbʌklɪŋ] ADJ [*hero*] de historia de aventuras, bravucón; [*film*] de aventuras, de capa y espada

swastika ['swɒstɪkə] N esvástica *f*, cruz *f* gamada

swat [swɒt] Ⓐ VT [+ *fly*] aplastar, matar Ⓑ N **to take a ~ at sth/sb** intentar darle un zurriagazo a algo/algn

swathe [sweɪð] Ⓐ N **to cut a ~ through sth** avanzar por algo a guadañadas Ⓑ VT (= *wrap*) envolver; (= *bandage*) vendar; **~d in sheets** envuelto en sábanas

swatter ['swɒtə^r] N palmeta *f* matamoscas

sway [sweɪ] Ⓐ N **1** (*also* ~**ing**) (= *movement*) balanceo *m* **2** (= *rule*) dominio *m* (**over** de); (= *influence*) influencia *f* (**over** en); (= *power*) poder *m*; **to hold ~ over a nation** gobernar *or* dominar una nación; **this theory held ~ during the 1970s** esta teoría se impuso durante la década de los setenta Ⓑ VI (= *swing*) balancearse, oscilar; (*gently*) mecerse; (*violently*) bambolearse; (= *totter*) tambalearse Ⓒ VT **1** (= *move*) balancear; (*gently*) mecer **2** (= *influence*) mover, influir en; **I allowed myself to be ~ed** me dejé influir; **these factors finally ~ed me** estos factores terminaron por *or* por convencerme

swear [sweə^r] (*pt* **swore**; *pp* **sworn**) Ⓐ VT jurar; **I ~ it!** ¡lo juro!; **to ~ to do sth** jurar hacer algo; **I could have sworn that it was Janet** juraría que fue Janet; **to ~ sb to secrecy** hacer que algn jure guardar el secreto; **to ~ allegiance to** jurar lealtad a; **they swore an oath of allegiance to him** le prestaron juramento de fidelidad Ⓑ VI **1** (*solemnly*) jurar; **I could ~ to it** juraría que fue así; **I can't ~ to it** no lo juraría **2** (= *use swearwords*) decir palabrotas, soltar tacos (*Sp*); **to ~ at sb** insultar a algn, mentar la madre a algn (*Mex*)
➤ **swear by** VI + PREP tener plena confianza en, creer ciegamente en
➤ **swear in** VT + ADV [+ *witness, president*] tomar juramento

a, juramentar a; **to be sworn in** prestar juramento

swearword ['sweəwɜːd] N palabrota f, taco m

sweat [swet] **Ⓐ** N sudor m; **to be in a ~** estar sudando, estar todo sudoroso; (*) (fig) estar en un apuro; **to be in a ~ about sth*** estar muy preocupado por algo; **no ~!*** ¡ningún problema! **Ⓑ** VI sudar, transpirar; (*) (= work hard) sudar la gota gorda (**over sth** por algo); **✦** IDIOM **he was ~ing like a pig*** estaba sudando tinta or como un pollo **Ⓒ** VT **✦** IDIOM **to ~ blood** sudar tinta
➤ **sweat out** VT + ADV **to ~ a cold out** quitarse un resfriado sudando; **✦** IDIOM **to ~ it out*** aguantar, aguantarse; **they left him to ~ it out** no hicieron nada para ayudarlo

sweatband ['swetbænd] N (round forehead) banda f elástica; (round wrist) muñequera f

sweater ['swetəʳ] N suéter m, jersey m, chompa f (Per)

sweatpants ['swetpænts] NPL (US) pantalón m de equipo de deportes, pantalón m de (Sp) chándal or (CS) buzo or (RPl) jogging or (Col) sudadera, pants mpl (Mex)

sweatshirt ['swetʃɜːt] N sudadera f

sweatshop ['swetʃɒp] N fábrica donde se explota al obrero

sweatsuit ['swetsuːt] N (US) equipo m de deportes, chandal m (Sp), buzo m (Chi, Per), sudadera f (Col), jogging m (RPl), sudadera f (Col), pants mpl (Mex)

sweaty ['sweti] ADJ (compar **sweatier**; superl **sweatiest**) [face, hands, person, horse] sudoroso; [clothes] sudado

Swede [swiːd] N sueco/a m/f

swede [swiːd] N (esp Brit) (= vegetable) nabo m sueco

Sweden ['swiːdn] N Suecia f

Swedish ['swiːdɪʃ] **Ⓐ** ADJ sueco **Ⓑ** N (= language) sueco m

sweep [swiːp] (vb: pt, pp **swept**) **Ⓐ** VT **1** (= clean) [+ floor, room, street] barrer; [+ chimney] deshollinar; **the floor had been swept clean** el suelo estaba limpio porque lo habían barrido; **he swept the leaves off the path** barrió las hojas del camino; **✦** IDIOM **to ~ sth under the carpet** (Brit) or (US) **rug** ocultar algo
2 (= touch) rozar; **her long dress swept the ground as she walked** su vestido largo rozaba el suelo al caminar
3 (= spread through) [disease, idea, craze] arrasar; [rumours] correr por, extenderse por
4 (= lash) [storm, rain, waves] azotar, barrer; **torrential storms swept the country** lluvias torrenciales azotaron or barrieron el país
5 (= scan) [searchlight, eyes] recorrer; **he swept the horizon with his binoculars** recorrió el horizonte con sus prismáticos
6 (with hand, arm) **she swept her hair back with a flick of her wrist** se echó el pelo hacia atrás con un movimiento rápido de muñeca; **to ~ sb into one's arms** coger or tomar a algn en brazos
7 (forcefully) **she was swept along by the crowd** la multitud la arrastró; **landslides that swept cars into the sea** corrimientos de tierra que arrastraron algunos coches hasta el mar; **the water swept him off his feet** la fuerza del agua lo derribó; **he swept her off her feet** (fig) la conquistó totalmente; **a wave swept him overboard** una ola lo arrastró por encima de la borda; **✦** IDIOM **to ~ all before one** arrasar con todo
8 (= win decisively) arrasar en; **✦** IDIOM **to ~ the board** (= win prizes) arrasar con todo; **the socialists swept the board at the election** los socialistas arrasaron en las elecciones
Ⓑ VI **1** (= clean) barrer
2 (= spread, move quickly) **the convoy swept along the road** la caravana pasó por la carretera a toda velocidad; **the war/ hurricane which swept through the country** la guerra/el huracán que arrasó el país; **the fire swept through the forest** el fuego se propagó or extendió rápidamente por el bosque; **panic swept through the city** en la ciudad cundió el pánico
3 (= move majestically) **to ~ past/in/out** [person, car] pasar/entrar/salir majestuosamente
Ⓒ N **1** (with broom, brush) barrido m, barrida f; **to give sth a ~** darle un barrido or una barrida a algo
2 (Brit) (also **chimney ~**) deshollinador(a) m/f
3 (= movement) **with a ~ of his arm** con un amplio movimiento del brazo; **with one ~ of his scythe** con un

golpe de guadaña; **with a ~ of her hand she indicated the desk** extendió la mano indicando el pupitre con un gesto amplio
4 (= search) (for criminals, drugs) batida f, rastreo m
5 (= curve) [of coastline, river] curva f; [of land] extensión f
➤ **sweep aside** VT + ADV [+ object] apartar bruscamente; [+ objections, protest, suggestion] desechar, descartar; [+ obstacle] pasar por alto; [+ difficulty] sortear
➤ **sweep away** VT + ADV **1** (= remove with brush) barrer
2 (= wash away) [river, storm] [+ building, car, person] llevarse por delante; **he was swept away by strong currents** fuertes corrientes se lo llevaron por delante **3** (= rush away) llevar a (toda) prisa (**to** a)
➤ **sweep out** **Ⓐ** VT + ADV [+ room] barrer **Ⓑ** VI + ADV salir (con paso majestuoso)
➤ **sweep up** **Ⓐ** VI + ADV **1** (with broom, brush) barrer
2 **to ~ up to sth: the car swept up to the house** (majestically) el coche subió majestuosamente hasta la casa; (fast) el coche subió a toda velocidad hasta la casa
Ⓑ VT + ADV **1** (with brush) recoger con un cepillo; (with broom) recoger con una escoba
2 [person] coger, agarrar (LAm); [storm] arrastrar; **I swept her up in my arms** la levanté en mis brazos; **her hair was swept up in a bun** tenía el pelo recogido en un moño; **she had been swept up in an exciting relationship** se había dejado arrastrar por una relación apasionada

sweeper ['swiːpəʳ] N (= cleaner) barrendero/a m/f; (= machine) (for streets) barredora f; (also **carpet ~**) cepillo m mecánico

sweeping ['swiːpɪŋ] ADJ [gesture, movement] amplio; [generalization] excesivo; [curve] abierto; [view] magnífico; [change] radical; [victory] arrollador, aplastante; **that's rather a ~ statement** eso es generalizar demasiado

sweepstake ['swiːpsteɪk] N, **sweepstakes** (US) N (= lottery) lotería f (esp de carreras de caballos); (= race) carrera de caballos en que el ganador recibe el dinero de las apuestas del resto de los participantes

sweet [swiːt] **Ⓐ** ADJ (compar **~er**; superl **~est**) **1** (= sugary) [taste, drink, wine, food] dulce; **I love ~ things** me encanta lo dulce, me encantan las cosas dulces; **~ and sour** agridulce; **to taste ~** tener un sabor dulce
2 (= agreeable) [smell, perfume] agradable; [sound] melodioso, dulce; **~ dreams!** (Brit) (gen) que duermas bien; (to child) ¡que sueñes con los angelitos!; **to smell ~** tener un olor fragante or aromático; **the ~ smell of success** las mieles del éxito; **✦** IDIOM **to whisper ~ nothings in sb's ear** decirle cariñitos al oído
3 (= gentle, kind) [nature, smile] dulce; [face] dulce, lindo (esp LAm); **she is a very ~ person** es un verdadero encanto, es una persona muy linda (LAm); **that's very ~ of you** es muy amable de tu parte, ¡qué amable!
4 (= enchanting) [child, animal, hat] mono, lindo (esp LAm)
5 (= fresh) [water] dulce; [air] fresco; [breath] sano
6 (iro) **to do sth in one's own ~ time** hacer algo a su aire, hacer algo cuando le parece a uno; **he carried on in his own ~ way** siguió a su aire
Ⓑ N **1** (Brit) (= piece of confectionery) (of any sort) golosina f; (= boiled sweet, toffee) caramelo m
2 (Brit) (= dessert) postre m
Ⓒ CPD ➤ **sweet chestnut** castaño m dulce ➤ **sweet pea** guisante m de olor (Sp), chícharo m de olor (CAm, Mex), clarín m (Chi), arvejilla f (RPl) ➤ **sweet pepper** pimiento m (dulce), pimentón m (SAm) ➤ **sweet potato** batata f, boniato m, camote m (And, Mex) ➤ **sweet shop** (Brit) tienda f de chucherías (Sp), dulcería f (esp LAm) ➤ **sweet talk*** zalamerías fpl ➤ **sweet tooth: to have a ~ tooth** ser goloso ➤ **sweet trolley** (Brit) carrito m de los postres

sweet-and-sour [ˌswiːtənˈsaʊəʳ] ADJ agridulce

sweetbreads ['swiːtbredz] NPL mollejas fpl, lechecillas fpl (Sp)

sweetcorn ['swiːtkɔːn] N maíz m dulce (Sp), maíz m tierno (esp LAm), elote m (Mex), choclo m (And, SC)

sweeten ['swiːtn] VT **1** [+ tea, coffee, dish] endulzar
2 (= freshen) [+ breath] refrescar; [+ room] ambientar
3 (= placate, soften) [+ temper] aplacar, calmar; (also **~ up**) [+ person] ablandar **4** (with financial incentives) [+ deal] hacer más atractivo; [+ person] (= bribe) sobornar; (= win over) ganarse a

sweetener ['swiːtnəʳ] N **1** (*for coffee, food*) dulcificante *m*; (*artificial*) edulcorante *m* **2** (*) (= *incentive*) incentivo *m*

sweetening ['swiːtnɪŋ] N dulcificante *m*

sweetheart ['swiːthɑːt] N novio/a *m/f*, amor *mf*; **yes,** ~ sí, mi amor

sweetie* ['swiːtɪ] N **1** (*also* ~**-pie**) **he's/she's a** ~ es un cielo*; **yes,** ~ si, cielo* **2** (*Brit*) (= *sweet*) (*of any sort*) golosina *f*; (= *boiled sweet, toffee*) caramelo *m*

sweetly ['swiːtlɪ] ADV [*sing*] dulcemente; [*smile, answer, act*] con dulzura; (= *kindly*) (muy) amablemente

sweet-natured [ˌswiːt'neɪtʃəd] ADJ dulce, amable

sweetness ['swiːtnɪs] N [*of food*] sabor *m* dulce, dulzor *m*; [*of smell*] fragancia *f*, buen olor *m*; [*of person, character*] dulzura *f*; (= *kindness*) simpatía *f*; **he was all** ~ **and light yesterday** ayer estuvo la mar de amable

sweet-scented ['swiːtˌsentɪd] ADJ fragante, de aroma agradable

sweet-talk* ['swiːttɔːk] VT engatusar*, camelar*

swell [swel] (*vb: pt* ~**ed**; *pp* **swollen**) **🅐** N [*of sea*] oleaje *m* **🅑** ADJ (*US†*) (= *fine, good*) fenomenal*, bárbaro* **🅒** VI **1** (*physically*) [*ankle, eye etc*] (*also* ~ **up**) hincharse; [*sails*] (*also* ~ **out**) inflarse, hincharse; [*river*] crecer; **her arm** ~**ed up** se le hinchó el brazo; **to** ~ **with pride** hincharse de orgullo
2 (*in size, number*) aumentar, crecer; **the little group soon** ~**ed into a crowd** el pequeño grupo se transformó pronto en multitud
🅓 VT **1** [+ *river*] hacer crecer; **to have a swollen hand** tener la mano hinchada; **her eyes were swollen with tears** tenía los ojos hinchados de lágrimas; **the river is swollen** el río está crecido; ✦ IDIOM **you'll give him a swollen head** le vas a hacer que se lo crea
2 [+ *numbers, sales*] aumentar; **to** ~ **the ranks of the unemployed** engrosar la cifra de desempleados

swelling ['swelɪŋ] N (*Med*) hinchazón *f*

swelter ['sweltəʳ] VI abrasarse, sofocarse de calor

sweltering ['sweltərɪŋ] ADJ [*day*] de calor sofocante, de muchísimo calor; [*heat*] sofocante; **it's** ~ **in here** hace un calor sofocante aquí; **I'm** ~ me ahogo de calor

swept [swept] PT, PP *of* **sweep**

swerve [swɜːv] **🅐** N (*by car, driver*) viraje *m* brusco **🅑** VI [*vehicle, driver*] virar bruscamente

swift [swɪft] **🅐** ADJ (*compar* ~**er**; *superl* ~**est**) [*runner, animal, vehicle, current*] rápido, veloz; [*reaction*] pronto, rápido; [*decision, response, journey, victory*] rápido; [*river*] de corriente rápida; **we must be** ~ **to act** tenemos que obrar con prontitud **🅑** N (= *bird*) vencejo *m*

swiftly ['swɪftlɪ] ADV [*run*] rápidamente, velozmente; [*react, act*] con prontitud, rápidamente; [*become, walk*] rápidamente; [*spread, rise, flow*] con rapidez; **the company has moved** *or* **acted** ~ **to deny the rumours** la empresa ha actuado con prontitud para desmentir los rumores; **a** ~ **flowing river** un río de corriente rápida

swiftness ['swɪftnɪs] N [*of runner*] rapidez *f*, velocidad *f*; [*of reaction*] prontitud *f*, rapidez *f*

swig* [swɪg] **🅐** VT beber (a tragos) **🅑** N trago *m*; **he took a** ~ **from his flask** se echó un trago de la botella

swill [swɪl] **🅐** N **1** (= *food for pigs*) comida *f* para los cerdos; (= *revolting food, drink*) bazofia *f*, basura *f* **2** (= *wash*) **to give sth a** ~ **(out)** limpiar algo con agua **🅑** VT (*also* ~ **out**) (*esp Brit*) lavar, limpiar con agua

swim [swɪm] (*vb: pt* **swam**; *pp* **swum**) **🅐** N **to have a** ~ darse un baño, nadar; **after a two-kilometre** ~ después de nadar dos kilómetros; **to go for a** ~ ir a nadar *or* a bañarse
🅑 VT **1** (*also* ~ **across**) pasar a nado, cruzar a nado; **he was the first man to** ~ **the English channel** fue el primer hombre que cruzó a nado el Canal de la Mancha
2 [+ *length, race*] nadar; **he can** ~ **two lengths** puede nadar dos largos; **she can't** ~ **a stroke** no sabe nadar en absoluto; **she swam the 400 metres medley** nadó los 400 metros a cuatro estilos
🅒 VI **1** [*person, fish*] nadar; **I can't** ~ no sé nadar; **to go** ~**ming** ir a nadar *or* bañarse; **to** ~ **across a river** pasar *or*

cruzar un río a nado; **to** ~ **under water** nadar debajo del agua, bucear; ✦ IDIOM **to** ~ **against the tide** nadar contra corriente
2 (= *float*) flotar; **the meat was** ~**ming in gravy** la carne flotaba *or* nadaba en la salsa; **her eyes were** ~**ming with tears** tenía los ojos inundados de lágrimas
3 (*dizzily*) (= *reel*) [*room, head*] dar vueltas; **my head is** ~**ming** me estoy mareando, me da vueltas la cabeza; **everything swam before my eyes** todo parecía que daba vueltas ante mis ojos

swimmer ['swɪməʳ] N nadador(a) *m/f*

swimming ['swɪmɪŋ] N natación *f* ➤ **swimming bath(s)** (*Brit*) = **swimming pool** ➤ **swimming cap** (*Brit*) gorro *m* de baño ➤ **swimming costume** (*Brit*) traje *m* de baño, bañador *m* (*Sp*) ➤ **swimming pool** piscina *f*, alberca *f* (*Mex*), pileta *f* (de natación) (*SC*) ➤ **swimming trunks** (*Brit*) bañador *m*sing (*Sp*)

swimsuit ['swɪmsuːt] N traje *m* de baño, bañador *m* (*Sp*)

swindle ['swɪndl] **🅐** N estafa *f*, timo *m*; **it's a** ~! ¡nos han estafado *or* timado! **🅑** VT estafar, timar; **to** ~ **sb out of sth** estafar algo a algn, quitar algo a algn estafándolo

swindler ['swɪndləʳ] N estafador(a) *m/f*, timador(a) *m/f*

swine [swaɪn] N **1** (= *pig*) (*pl* ~) cerdo *m*, puerco *m* **2** (*fig*) (*) (= *person*) canalla *mf*, cochino/a *m/f*, marrano/a *m/f*

swing [swɪŋ] (*vb: pt, pp* **swung**) **🅐** N **1** (= *movement*) [*of pick, axe*] movimiento *m* (amplio); [*of pendulum*] oscilación *f*, movimiento *m*; (*Boxing, Cricket, Golf*) (= *technique*) swing *m*; **to take a** ~ **at sb*** (*with fist*) intentar darle un puñetazo a algn; (*with weapon*) intentar darle un golpe a algn; **the golfer took a** ~ **at the ball** el golfista intentó darle a la pelota
2 (= *change*) (*in opinion*) cambio *m*; (*in vote*) desplazamiento *m*; **a** ~ **to the left** un viraje *or* desplazamiento hacia la izquierda
3 ✦ IDIOMS **to go with a** ~ (*Brit*) [*evening, party*] estar muy animado; [*business*] ir a las mil maravillas; **to be in full** ~ [*party, election, campaign*] estar en pleno apogeo; [*business*] estar en pleno desarrollo; **to get into the** ~ **of things** coger el tranquillo a algo, captar el ritmo de las cosas (*LAm*)
4 (*also* ~ **music**) swing *m*, música *f* swing
5 (= *garden swing*) columpio *m*; ✦ IDIOM **it's** ~**s and roundabouts** (*Brit*) lo que se pierde aquí, se gana allá
🅑 VI **1** (= *move to and fro*) [*hanging object, hammock*] balancearse; [*pendulum*] oscilar; [*person*] (*on swing, hammock*) columpiarse; **to** ~ **to and fro** [*hanging object*] balancearse de un lado para otro; [*pendulum*] oscilar *or* moverse de un lado para otro; **he was** ~**ing from a trapeze** se columpiaba colgado de un trapecio; **the orang-utang swung from tree to tree** el orangután se columpiaba de árbol en árbol; ✦ IDIOM **to** ~ **into action** ponerse en marcha
2 (= *pivot*) girar; **the door** ~**s on its hinges** la puerta gira sobre sus goznes; **to** ~ **open/shut** abrirse/cerrarse
3 **to** ~ **at sb** (*with one's fist*) intentar dar un puñetazo a algn; **he swung at the ball** intentó dar a la pelota
4 (= *turn*) **the car swung into the square** el coche viró *or* dio un viraje y entró en la plaza; **to** ~ **to the left/right** (*politically*) dar un viraje hacia la izquierda/derecha
5 (= *move rhythmically*) **a group of schoolchildren were** ~**ing along up the road** un grupo de colegiales subían por la calle, andando al compás; **music that really** ~**s** música que tiene mucho ritmo
6 (*) (= *be lively*) [*entertainment, party*] ambientarse; [*place*] tener ambiente
🅒 VT **1** (= *move to and fro*) [+ *bag, arms, legs*] columpiar, balancear; **to** ~ **one's hips** andar contoneándose
2 (= *move*) [+ *weapon*] blandir; **he swung the box up onto the roof of the car** con un amplio movimiento de brazos, puso la caja en el techo del coche; **to** ~ **o.s. (up) into the saddle** subirse a la silla de montar de un salto
3 (= *turn*) **he swung the car off the road** viró con el coche y se salió de la carretera
4 (= *influence*) [+ *opinion, decision, vote, voters*] decidir; [+ *outcome*] determinar, decidir; **this could** ~ **the vote in our favour** esto podría cambiar el sentido del voto a nuestro favor; **she managed to** ~ **it so that we could all go** consiguió arreglarlo para que todos pudiéramos ir
5 (*Mus*) [+ *tune*] tocar con swing

ⓓ CPD ➤ **swing bin** cubo *m* de la basura (con tapa oscilante) ➤ **swing bridge** puente *m* giratorio ➤ **swing door** *(Brit)* puerta *f* de batiente, puerta *f* de vaivén ➤ **swing voter** *(US)* elector(a) *m/f* indeciso

swingeing ['swɪndʒɪŋ] ADJ *(Brit) [increase]* vertiginoso; *[cut]* fulminante, drástico; *[majority]* abrumador

swinging ['swɪŋɪŋ] **ⓐ** ADJ (†*) (= *lively*) *[city, party]* con mucha marcha*; **the Swinging Sixties** los marchosos años sesenta* **ⓑ** N vaivén *m*, oscilación *f* **ⓒ** CPD ➤ **swinging door** *(US)* puerta *f* de vaivén, puerta *f* de batiente

swipe [swaɪp] **ⓐ** N **to take a ~ at sb** asestar un golpe a algn **ⓑ** VT **1** (= *hit*) golpear, pegar **2** (*) (= *steal*) birlar*, afanar* **3** *(Comput) [+ card]* pasar *(por un lector de tarjetas)* **ⓒ** VI **to ~ at sth/sb** asestar un golpe a algo/algn **ⓓ** CPD ➤ **swipe card** tarjeta *f* magnética deslizante, tarjeta *f* swipe

swirl [swɜːl] **ⓐ** N (= *movement*) remolino *m*, torbellino *m*; **a ~ of water** un remolino de agua **ⓑ** VI *[water, dust, mist]* arremolinarse; *[person]* dar vueltas, girar

swish [swɪʃ] **ⓐ** N *[of cane]* silbido *m*; *[of skirt]* frufrú *m*; *[of water]* susurro *m* **ⓑ** ADJ *(Brit*)* (= *smart*) muy elegante **ⓒ** VT *[+ cane]* agitar, blandir *(produciendo un silbido)*; *[+ skirt]* hacer frufrú con; *[+ tail]* agitar, menear **ⓓ** VI *[skirts]* hacer frufrú; *[long grass]* silbar; *[water]* susurrar

Swiss [swɪs] **ⓐ** ADJ suizo **ⓑ** N suizo/a *m/f* **ⓒ** CPD ➤ **Swiss army knife** navaja *f* multiuso(s), navaja *f* suiza ➤ **Swiss roll** *(Brit Culin)* brazo *m* de gitano

switch [swɪtʃ] **ⓐ** N **1** *(electrical)* interruptor *m*, suich(e) *m* *(LAm)*, switch *m* *(LAm)*; **the ~ was on/off** el interruptor estaba encendido/apagado
2 (= *change*) cambio *m* **(from** de; **to** a); **a ~ in US policy** un cambio en la política estadounidense; **to make the ~ from X to Y** pasar de X a Y
3 (= *swap*) cambio *m*; **to make a ~** hacer un cambio **ⓑ** VT **1** (= *change*) *[+ tactics]* cambiar de; **if you ~ allegiance from one party to another ...** si cambias de bando y vas de un partido a otro ...
2 (= *move*) *[+ production]* trasladar **(from** de; **to** a); **she quickly ~ed the conversation to another topic** rápidamente desvió la conversación hacia otro tema
3 (= *swap, exchange*) cambiar; **we had to ~ taxis when the first broke down** tuvimos que cambiar de taxi cuando el primero tuvo una avería
4 *(Elec)* **he ~ed the heater to "low"** puso el calentador en "bajo"
ⓒ VI (= *change*) cambiar **(from** de; **to** a); **I've ~ed to a cheaper brand of washing powder** (me) he cambiado a una marca de detergente más barata; **he had ~ed with another driver** había hecho un cambio con otro conductor, se había cambiado con otro conductor
➤ **switch off** **ⓐ** VT + ADV *[+ light, television, gas]* apagar; *[+ ignition, engine]* parar; **the oven ~es itself off** el horno se apaga solo **ⓑ** VI + ADV **1** *[washing-machine, light, heating]* apagarse; **the dryer ~es off automatically** la secadora se apaga automáticamente **2** (*) (= *stop listening*) desconectar(se)
➤ **switch on** **ⓐ** VT + ADV *[+ light, television, gas, electricity]* encender, prender *(LAm)*; *[+ alarm clock, burglar alarm]* poner; **to leave the television ~ed on** dejar la televisión puesta *or* encendida **ⓑ** VI + ADV *[washing-machine, light, heating]* encenderse; *[viewer]* encender la televisión, poner la televisión, prender la televisión *(LAm)*; **the lights ~ on automatically** las luces se encienden automáticamente
➤ **switch over** VI + ADV *(TV, Rad)* cambiar de canal; **we've ~ed over to gas** (nos) hemos cambiado *or* pasado a gas

switchback ['swɪtʃbæk] N *(Brit) (at fair)* montaña *f* rusa; (= *road*) camino *m* de fuertes altibajos

switchblade ['swɪtʃbleɪd] N *(US)* navaja *f* de muelle *or* de resorte

switchboard ['swɪtʃbɔːd] N *(Telec) (at exchange)* central *f*; *(in offices)* centralita *f*, conmutador *m* *(LAm)* ➤ **switchboard operator** telefonista *mf*

switch-over ['swɪtʃəʊvəʳ] N cambio *m* **(from** de; **to** a)

Switzerland ['swɪtsələnd] N Suiza *f*

swivel ['swɪvl] **ⓐ** N eslabón *m* giratorio **ⓑ** VI (*also* ~ **round**) girar; *[person]* volverse, girar sobre los talones **ⓒ** VT (*also* ~ **round**) girar **ⓓ** CPD ➤ **swivel chair** silla *f* giratoria

swollen ['swəʊlən] PP *of* **swell**

swoon [swuːn] **ⓐ** N desmayo *m*, desvanecimiento *m* **ⓑ** VI desmayarse, desvanecerse

swoop [swuːp] **ⓐ** N *[of bird]* descenso *m* súbito; *(by police)* redada *f* **(on** de); ✦ IDIOM **at one fell ~** de un solo golpe **ⓑ** VI *[bird] (also ~ down)* abatirse, lanzarse en picado *(Sp) or* en picada *(LAm)* **(on** sobre); *[police]* hacer una redada **(on** en)

swop [swɒp] = **swap**

sword [sɔːd] N espada *f*; ✦ IDIOM **to cross ~s with sb** habérselas con algn

swordfish ['sɔːdfɪʃ] *(pl* ~**)** N pez *m* espada

swordsman ['sɔːdzmən] N *(pl* **swordsmen)** espada *f*, espadachín *m*; **a good ~** una buena espada

sword-swallower ['sɔːdˌswɒləʊəʳ] N tragasables *mf inv*

swore [swɔːʳ] PT *of* **swear**

sworn [swɔːn] **ⓐ** PP *of* **swear** **ⓑ** ADJ *[enemy]* declarado; *[testimony]* dado bajo juramento, jurado

swot* [swɒt] *(Brit)* **ⓐ** N empollón/ona *m/f (Sp*)*, mateo/a *m/f (Chi)*, pilo/a *m/f (Col)*, matado/a *m/f (Mex*)*, chancón/ona *m/f (Per*)*, traga *mf (RPl*)* **ⓑ** VT **to ~ up (on)** sth matarse estudiando algo, empollar algo *(Sp*)*, clavarse algo *(Col*)*, chancar algo *(Per*)*, tragar algo *(RPl*)*

swum [swʌm] PP *of* **swim**

swung [swʌŋ] PT, PP *of* **swing**

sycamore ['sɪkəmɔːʳ] N sicomoro *m*, sicómoro *m*

sycophant ['sɪkəfənt] N adulador(a) *m/f*

sycophantic [ˌsɪkə'fæntɪk] ADJ *[person]* servil, sobón; *[speech]* adulatorio; *[manner]* servil

syllable ['sɪləbl] N sílaba *f*

syllabus ['sɪləbəs] N *(esp Brit)* plan *m* de estudios; *(specific)* programa *m* (de estudios)

symbiosis [ˌsɪmbɪ'əʊsɪs] N simbiosis *f*

symbiotic [ˌsɪmbɪ'ɒtɪk] ADJ simbiótico

symbol ['sɪmbəl] N *(gen)* símbolo *m*; *(Math)* signo *m*

symbolic [sɪm'bɒlɪk] ADJ simbólico **(of** de)

symbolism ['sɪmbəlɪzəm] N simbolismo *m*

symbolize ['sɪmbəlaɪz] VT simbolizar

symmetrical [sɪ'metrɪkəl] ADJ simétrico

symmetry ['sɪmɪtrɪ] N simetría *f*

sympathetic [ˌsɪmpə'θetɪk] ADJ (= *showing pity*) compasivo **(to** con); (= *kind, understanding*) comprensivo; **he wasn't in the least ~** no mostró compasión alguna; **they were ~ but could not help** estaban de nuestra parte pero no podían ayudarnos; **to be ~ to a cause** solidarizarse con *or* apoyar una causa

sympathetically [ˌsɪmpə'θetɪkəlɪ] ADV (= *showing pity*) con compasión; (= *with understanding*) con comprensión; **she looked at me ~** me miró compasiva

sympathize ['sɪmpəθaɪz] VI (= *feel pity*) compadecerse; (= *understand*) comprender; **to ~ with sb** compadecerse de algn, compadecer a algn; **those who ~ with our demands** los que apoyan nuestras reclamaciones

sympathizer ['sɪmpəθaɪzəʳ] N simpatizante *mf*, partidario/a *m/f* **(with** de)

sympathy ['sɪmpəθɪ] N **1** (= *compassion*) compasión *f*; **you have my deepest ~** te compadezco; **a letter of ~** un pésame; **I have no ~ for him** no siento ninguna compasión *or* pena por él **2** (= *agreement*) solidaridad *f*; **they came out in ~ with their colleagues** se declararon en huelga por solidaridad con sus colegas; **I have some ~ with this point of view** comparto en parte este punto de vista; **she has expressed Republican sympathies** ha expresado sus simpatías por los republicanos

symphonic [sɪm'fɒnɪk] ADJ sinfónico

symphony ['sɪmfənɪ] N sinfonía *f* ➤ **symphony orchestra** orquesta *f* sinfónica

symposium [sɪm'pəʊzɪəm] N simposio *m*

symptom ['sɪmptəm] N síntoma *m*

symptomatic [ˌsɪmptə'mætɪk] ADJ sintomático **(of** de)

synagogue ['sɪnəgɒg] N sinagoga f

sync* [sɪŋk] N ABBR (= **synchronization**); **in ~** en sincronización; **out of ~** (fig) desincronizado

synchronization [ˌsɪŋkrənaɪ'zeɪʃən] N sincronización f

synchronize ['sɪŋkrənaɪz] VT sincronizar (**with** con); **~d swimming** natación f sincronizada

syncopate ['sɪŋkəpeɪt] VT sincopar

syncopation [ˌsɪŋkə'peɪʃən] N síncopa f

syndicate Ⓐ ['sɪndɪkɪt] N **1** (Comm) sindicato m, corporación f **2** (US) (= news agency) agencia f de prensa; (= chain of papers) cadena f de periódicos **3** (*) **crime ~** banda f de malhechores, cuadrilla f de bandidos **Ⓑ** ['sɪndɪkeɪt] VT (US) [+ article, interview] sindicar

syndrome ['sɪndrəʊm] N síndrome m

synergy ['sɪnədʒɪ] N sinergia f

synod ['sɪnəd] N sínodo m

synonym ['sɪnənɪm] N sinónimo m

synonymous [sɪ'nɒnɪməs] ADJ sinónimo (**with** con)

synopsis [sɪ'nɒpsɪs] N (pl **synopses** [sɪ'nɒpsiːz]) sinopsis f inv

syntactic [sɪn'tæktɪk] ADJ sintáctico

syntax ['sɪntæks] N sintaxis f **➤ syntax error** error m sintáctico

synthesis ['sɪnθəsɪs] N (pl **syntheses** ['sɪnθəsiːz]) síntesis f inv

synthesize ['sɪnθəsaɪz] VT sintetizar

synthesizer ['sɪnθəsaɪzəʳ] N sintetizador m

synthetic [sɪn'θetɪk] **Ⓐ** ADJ (= man-made) sintético **Ⓑ** N **synthetics** fibras fpl sintéticas

syphilis ['sɪfɪlɪs] N sífilis f

syphon ['saɪfən] = **siphon**

Syria ['sɪrɪə] N Siria f

Syrian ['sɪrɪən] ADJ, N sirio/a m/f

syringe [sɪ'rɪndʒ] N jeringa f, jeringuilla f

syrup ['sɪrəp] N (also **golden ~**) almíbar m, jarabe m

syrupy ['sɪrəpɪ] ADJ parecido a jarabe, espeso como jarabe

system ['sɪstəm] **Ⓐ** N **1** (gen) sistema m; **a political/social ~** un sistema político/social; **the metric ~** el sistema métrico; **the nervous/immune ~** el sistema nervioso/inmunitario; **the digestive ~** el aparato digestivo; **the ~'s down** (Comput) el sistema no funciona; **to beat the ~** burlar el sistema **2** (= order) método m; **he lacks ~** carece de método **3** (= body) organismo m, cuerpo m; **it was quite a shock to the ~** (fig) fue un buen golpe para el organismo; **✦** IDIOM **to get sth out of one's ~** quitarse algo de encima **Ⓑ** CPD **➤ system disk** disco m del sistema **➤ systems analysis** análisis m inv de sistemas **➤ systems analyst** (Comput) analista mf de sistemas **➤ systems engineer** (Comput) ingeniero/a m/f de sistemas **➤ systems software** software m del sistema

systematic [ˌsɪstə'mætɪk] ADJ sistemático, metódico

systematically [ˌsɪstə'mætɪkəlɪ] ADV sistemáticamente, metódicamente

Tt

T, t [tiː] N (= *letter*) T, t *f*; **T for Tommy** T de Tommy

TA N ABBR (*Brit Mil*) = **Territorial Army**

ta* [tɑː] EXCL (*Brit*) gracias

tab [tæb] Ⓐ N **1** (*on garment*) (= *flap*) oreja *f*, lengüeta *f*; (= *loop*) presilla *f*; (= *label*) etiqueta *f*; ✦ IDIOM **to keep ~s on sb*** vigilar a algn **2** (*US*) (= *bill*) cuenta *f*; **to pick up the ~** (*also Brit**) pagar la cuenta; (*fig*) asumir la responsabilidad **3** (*also* **tabulator**) tabulador *m* Ⓑ CPD ➤ **tab key** tecla *f* de tabulación

tabby ['tæbɪ] N (*also* ~ **cat**) gato/a *m/f* atigrado/a

table ['teɪbl] Ⓐ N **1** mesa *f*; **don't read at the ~** no leas en la mesa; **to clear the ~** quitar *or* recoger *or* levantar la mesa; **to set** *or* (*Brit*) **lay the ~** poner la mesa; ✦ IDIOMS **to turn the ~s** dar la vuelta a la tortilla; **under the ~*: he was accepting money under the ~** aceptaba dinero bajo cuerda *or* bajo mano **2** (*for discussion*) mesa *f* de negociaciones; **he managed to get all the parties around the ~** consiguió que todos los interesados se sentaran a la mesa de negociaciones; **to put sth on the ~** poner algo sobre el tapete; **there are two proposals on the ~** hay dos propuestas sobre el tapete **3** (= *chart*) tabla *f*, cuadro *m*; **~ of contents** índice *m* de materias **4** (*Math*) (*also* **multiplication** ~) tabla *f* de multiplicar; **the six-times ~** la tabla del seis Ⓑ VT **1** (*Brit*) [+ *motion, amendment*] presentar **2** (*US*) (= *postpone*) aplazar, posponer Ⓒ CPD ➤ **table football** futbolín *m* ➤ **table lamp** lámpara *f* de mesa ➤ **table manners** comportamiento *msing* en la mesa, modales *mpl* en la mesa ➤ **table napkin** servilleta *f* ➤ **table tennis** ping-pong *m*, pimpón *m*, tenis *m* de mesa ➤ **table wine** vino *m* de mesa

tableau ['tæbləʊ] N (*pl* ~**x** ['tæbləʊz]) cuadro *m* (vivo)

tablecloth ['teɪblklɒθ] N mantel *m*

table d'hôte ['tɑːbl'dəʊt] N menú *m*, comida *f* (corrida) (*Mex*)

tablemat ['teɪblmæt] N salvamanteles *m inv*

tablespoon ['teɪblspuːn] N (= *spoon*) cuchara *f* grande, cuchara *f* de servir; (= *quantity*) cucharada *f* grande

tablet ['tæblɪt] N (*Med*) pastilla *f*; (= *round pill*) comprimido *m*

tabloid ['tæblɔɪd] N tabloide *m*, periódico *m* popular; **the ~s** la prensa amarilla; ⊃ *BROADSHEETS AND TABLOIDS*

taboo [tə'buː] Ⓐ ADJ tabú *inv* Ⓑ N tabú *m*

tabulate ['tæbjʊleɪt] VT exponer en forma de tabla; (*Comput*) tabular

tabulator ['tæbjʊleɪtə'] N tabulador *m*

tachograph ['tækəgrɑːf] N (*Brit*) tacógrafo *m*

tachometer [tæ'kɒmɪtə'] N taquímetro *m*

tacit ['tæsɪt] ADJ tácito

taciturn ['tæsɪtɜːn] ADJ taciturno

tack [tæk] Ⓐ N **1** (= *nail*) tachuela *f*; (*esp US*) (*also* **thumbtack**) chincheta *f*, chinche *m or f* **2** (*fig*) rumbo *m*, dirección *f*; ✦ IDIOMS **to change ~** cambiar de rumbo *or* sentido; **to try a different ~** abordar un problema desde otro punto de partida; **to be on the right ~** ir por buen camino **3** (*for horse*) arreos *mpl* Ⓑ VT **1** (= *nail*) clavar con tachuelas **2** (*Brit Sew*) (*also* ~ **up**) hilvanar Ⓒ VI (*Naut*) dar bordadas; (= *change course*) virar, cambiar de bordada ➤ **tack on** VT + ADV añadir

tackle ['tækl] Ⓐ N **1** (= *lifting gear*) aparejo *m*, polea *f*; (= *ropes*) jarcia *f*, cordaje *m* **2** (= *equipment*) equipo *m*, avíos *mpl*; (= *bits and pieces*) cosas *fpl*, trastos *mpl*; (*also* **fishing** ~) equipo *m* de pesca **3** (*Ftbl*) entrada *f*; (*Rugby*) placaje *m* Ⓑ VT **1** [+ *problem*] abordar, enfrentar; [+ *task*] enfrentar, emprender; [+ *fire*] luchar contra **2** [+ *thief, intruder*] enfrentarse con; (= *confront*) encararse con; **I'll have to ~ him about that money he owes me** voy a tener que encararme con él y plantearle lo del dinero que me debe **3** (*Brit Ftbl*) entrar a; (*Rugby*) placar, taclear

tacky ['tækɪ] ADJ (*compar* **tackier**; *superl* **tackiest**) **1** (*) (= *cheap*) [*furniture*] chabacano, hortera (*Sp**); [*restaurant, hotel*] destartalado **2** (= *sticky*) pegajoso

tact [tækt] N tacto *m*

tactful ['tæktfʊl] ADJ diplomático, discreto; **she's very ~** tiene mucho tacto, es muy diplomática *or* discreta

tactfully ['tæktfəlɪ] ADV con mucho tacto, discretamente

tactic ['tæktɪk] N táctica *f*

tactical ['tæktɪkəl] ADJ táctico ➤ **tactical voting** (*Brit*) votación *f* táctica

tactile ['tæktaɪl] ADJ táctil

tactless ['tæktlɪs] ADJ [*person*] falto de tacto, poco diplomático; [*comment, behaviour*] indiscreto, poco diplomático

tactlessly ['tæktlɪslɪ] ADV con poco tacto

tactlessness ['tæktlɪsnɪs] N falta *f* de tacto

tad* [tæd] N **a ~ big/small** un poco grande/pequeño

tadpole ['tædpəʊl] N renacuajo *m*

taffeta ['tæfɪtə] N tafetán *m*

taffy ['tæfɪ] N (*US*) (= *toffee*) melcocha *f*

tag [tæg] Ⓐ N **1** (= *label*) etiqueta *f*, marbete *m*; (*for identification*) chapa *f* **2** (= *game*) **to play ~** jugar al cogecoge *or* (*LAm*) a la pega **3** (*also* ~ **question**) cláusula *f* final interrogativa Ⓑ VT [+ *criminal*] controlar electrónicamente Ⓒ VI **to ~ after sb** seguir a algn Ⓓ CPD ➤ **tag line** remate *m* ➤ **tag along** VI + ADV **we don't want your brother ~ging along** no queremos que tu hermano se nos pegue

Tahiti [tɑː'hiːtɪ] N Tahití *m*

tail [teɪl] Ⓐ N **1** [*of bird, horse, fish, plane*] cola *f*; [*of dog, bull, ox*] cola *f*, rabo *m*; [*of shirt*] faldón *m*; ✦ IDIOM **to turn ~** huir **2** tails (= *coat*) frac *msing*; [*of coin*] cruz *fsing*; **heads or ~s** cara o cruz; **~s you lose** si sale cruz pierdes **3** (= *person following*) sombra *f*; **to put a ~ on sb** hacer seguir a algn Ⓑ VT (= *follow*) seguir la pista a Ⓒ CPD ➤ **tail end** [*of procession, queue*] cola *f*, tramo *m* final; [*of party, storm*] final *m* ➤ **tail light** (*US*) piloto *m*, luz *f* trasera, calavera *f* (*Mex*) ➤ **tail back** VI + ADV (*Brit*) **the traffic ~ed back to the bridge** la cola de coches se extendía atrás hasta el puente ➤ **tail off** VI + ADV **1** [*production, demand*] disminuir; **business has ~ed off lately** el negocio ha decaído *or* empeorado últimamente **2** [*voice, sound*] ir apagándose

tailback ['teɪlbæk] N (*Brit*) caravana *f*, cola *f*

tailcoat ['teɪlkəʊt] N frac *m*

tailgate ['teɪlgeɪt] N (*Aut*) puerta *f* trasera

tailor ['teɪlə'] Ⓐ N sastre *m*; **~'s (shop)** sastrería *f* Ⓑ VT [+ *suit*] confeccionar, hacer; (*fig*) adaptar

tailor-made ['teɪləmeɪd] ADJ **1** [*suit*] hecho a (la) medida **2** [*computer program*] hecho según los requisitos del usuario; **it's ~ for you** te viene al pelo; **the part could have been ~ for her** parece que el papel se ha escrito para ella

tailpipe ['teɪlpaɪp] N (*US*) tubo *m* de escape

tailplane ['teɪlpleɪn] N (*Aer*) plano *m* de cola

tailspin ['teɪlspɪn] N [*of plane*] barrena *f*

tailwind ['teɪlwɪnd] N viento *m* de cola

taint [teɪnt] Ⓐ N (*liter*) mancha *f*, mácula *f* (*liter*) Ⓑ VT [+ *food, medicine*] contaminar; [+ *reputation*] mancillar

tainted ['teɪntɪd] ADJ [*food, air, blood, medicine*] contaminado; [*reputation*] mancillado

Taiwan [ˌtaɪ'wɑːn] N Taiwán *m*

Taiwanese [ˌtaɪwə'niːz] ADJ, N taiwanés/esa *m/f*

take [teɪk] (*vb: pt* **took**; *pp* **taken**) Ⓐ VT **1** (= *remove*) llevarse; (= *steal*) robar, llevarse; **I'll ~ the blue one** me llevaré el azul; **I picked up the letter but he took it <u>from</u> me**

cogí la carta pero él me la quitó; ~ **37 from 51** resta 37 de 51

2 (= *grab*) tomar, coger, agarrar (*LAm*); **she took the spade** cogió la pala; **let me ~ your coat** permíteme tu abrigo; **to ~ sb's arm** tomar del brazo a algn; **to ~ sb in one's arms** abrazar a algn; **~ five!** (*esp US**) ¡hagan una pausa!, ¡descansen un rato!; **~ a seat** tome asiento; **is this seat ~n?** ¿está ocupado este asiento?; **it took me by surprise** me cogió desprevenido, me pilló *or* agarró desprevenido (*LAm*)

3 (= *transport, guide*) llevar (**to** a); **he took me home in his car** me llevó a casa en su coche; **they took me over the factory** me mostraron la fábrica, me acompañaron en una visita a la fábrica; **he took his suitcase upstairs** subió su maleta; **to ~ sb for a walk** llevar a algn de paseo; **it took us out of our way** nos hizo desviarnos

4 [+ *bus, taxi*] (= *travel by*) ir en; (*at specified time*) coger, tomar (*esp LAm*); [+ *road, short cut*] ir por; **we decided to ~ the train** decidimos ir en tren; **we took the five o'clock train** cogimos *or* tomamos el tren de las cinco; **~ the first on the right** vaya por *or* tome la primera calle a la derecha; **we took the wrong road** nos equivocamos de camino

5 (= *capture*) [+ *person*] coger, agarrar (*LAm*); [+ *town*] tomar

6 (= *obtain, win*) [+ *prize*] ganar, llevarse; [+ *first place*] conseguir, obtener; **we took £500 today** (*Brit Comm*) hoy hemos ganado 500 libras

7 (= *accept, receive*) [+ *money, cheque*] aceptar; [+ *advice*] seguir; [+ *responsibility*] asumir; **he took it badly** le afectó mucho; **~ it from me!** ¡escucha lo que te digo!; **you can ~ it from me that ...** puedes tener la seguridad de que ...; **losing is hard to ~** es difícil aceptar la derrota; **it's £50, ~ it or leave it** son 50 libras, lo toma o lo deja; **~ that!** ¡toma!

8 (= *rent*) alquilar, tomar; (= *buy*) [+ *newspaper*] comprar, leer

9 (= *have room for*) tener cabida para; (= *support weight of*) aguantar; **a car that ~s five passengers** un coche con cabida para *or* donde caben cinco personas; **can you ~ two more?** ¿puedes llevar dos más?, ¿caben otros dos?

10 (= *wear*) [+ *clothes size*] gastar, usar (*LAm*); [+ *shoe size*] calzar; **what size do you ~?** (*clothes*) ¿qué talla usas?; (*shoes*) ¿qué número calzas?

11 (= *require*) necesitar, requerir; **it took three policemen to hold him down** se necesitaron tres policías para sujetarlo; **it ~s a lot of courage** exige *or* requiere gran valor; **that will ~ some explaining** a ver cómo explicas eso; **she's got what it ~s*** tiene lo que hace falta

12 (*of time*) **it ~s an hour to get there** se tarda una hora en llegar; **it will only ~ me five minutes** sólo tardo cinco minutos; **the job will ~ a week** el trabajo llevará una semana; **it won't ~ long** no tardaré *or* no me llevará mucho tiempo; **it ~s time** lleva tiempo

13 (= *teach*) [+ *course, class*] enseñar; [+ *pupils*] tomar; (= *study*) [+ *course*] hacer; [+ *subject*] dar, estudiar; (= *sit*) [+ *exam, test*] presentarse a, pasar; **what are you taking next year?** ¿qué vas a hacer *or* estudiar el año que viene?; **the teacher who took us for economics** (*Brit*) el profesor que nos daba clase de económicas

14 (= *record*) [+ *sb's name, address*] anotar, apuntar; [+ *measurements*] tomar

15 (= *assume*) **I ~ it that ...** supongo que ..., me imagino que ...; **I took him for a doctor** lo tenía por médico, creí que era médico; **what do you ~ me for?** ¿por quién me has tomado?; **I don't quite know how to ~ that** no sé muy bien cómo tomarme eso

16 (= *consider*) [+ *case, example*] tomar; **~ John, he never complains** por ejemplo John, él nunca se queja

17 (= *endure*) aguantar, soportar; **I can't ~ any more!** ¡no aguanto más!, ¡no soporto más!

18 (= *ingest*) tomar; **"to be taken three times a day"** "a tomar tres veces al día"; **"not to be taken (internally)"** "para uso externo"; **to ~ drugs** (*narcotics*) tomar drogas

19 (= *negotiate*) [+ *bend*] tomar; [+ *fence*] saltar, saltar por encima de

20 to be ~n with sth/sb (= *attracted*): **he's very ~n with her** le gusta mucho; **I'm not at all ~n with the idea** la idea no me gusta nada *or* no me hace gracia

Ⓑ VI [*dye*] coger, agarrar (*LAm*); [*vaccination, fire*] prender

Ⓒ N **1** (*Cine*) toma *f*

2 (= *takings*) ingresos *mpl*; (= *proceeds*) recaudación *f*; (*US Comm*) caja *f*, ventas *fpl* del día

3 ✦ IDIOM to be on the ~* estar dispuesto a dejarse sobornar

4 (***) (= *opinion*) opinión *f*; **what's your ~ on the new government?** ¿qué piensas del nuevo gobierno?, ¿qué opinión te merece el nuevo gobierno?

➤ **take after** VI + PREP (*in looks*) parecerse a, salir a

➤ **take along** VT + ADV [+ *person, thing*] llevar (consigo)

➤ **take apart** VT + ADV **1** [+ *clock, machine*] desmontar, desarmar **2** (= *search*) **the police took the place apart** la policía registró el local de arriba abajo

➤ **take aside** VT + ADV llevar aparte, llevar a un lado

➤ **take away Ⓐ** VT + ADV **1** (= *remove*) [+ *person, thing*] llevarse; [+ *privilege*] quitar; (= *carry away, transport*) llevar; **she took her children away from the school** sacó a los niños del colegio **2** (= *subtract*) restar; **~ nine away from 12** reste nueve de 12; **seven ~ away is three** siete menos cuatro son tres **Ⓑ** VI + ADV **this does not ~ away from their achievement** esto no quita mérito *or* resta valor a su éxito

➤ **take back** VT + ADV **1** (= *return*) [+ *book, goods*] devolver; [+ *person*] llevar (de vuelta); **can you ~ him back home?** ¿le puedes acompañar a su casa?

2 (= *accept back*) [+ *purchase, gift*] aceptar la devolución de; [+ *one's wife, husband*] aceptar que vuelva; **the company took him back** la compañía volvió a emplearlo *or* lo restituyó a su puesto

3 (= *retract*) [+ *statement, words*] retirar; **I ~ it all back!** ¡retiro lo dicho!

4 (= *get back, reclaim*) [+ *territory*] retomar

5 (= *recall*) **it ~s me back to my childhood** me recuerda a mi niñez

➤ **take down** VT + ADV **1** (*off shelf*) bajar; [+ *decorations, curtains*] quitar; [+ *picture*] descolgar, bajar; [+ *poster*] despegar; [+ *trousers*] bajar; [+ *scaffolding*] desmantelar, desmontar **2** (= *write down*) anotar

➤ **take in** VT + ADV **1** (= *bring in*) [+ *person*] hacer entrar; [+ *chairs, toys*] recoger, meter para dentro

2 (= *give home to*) [+ *orphan, stray dog*] acoger, recoger

3 (= *receive*) [+ *laundry, sewing*] coger para hacer en casa

4 [+ *skirt, dress, waistband*] achicar

5 (= *include*) [+ *possibilities, cases*] abarcar, incluir; **we took in Florence on the way** pasamos por Florencia en el camino; **to ~ in a movie*** ir al cine

6 (= *understand*) [+ *situation*] comprender; [+ *surroundings*] captar; **that child ~s everything in** a esa criatura no se le escapa nada; **it's so incredible you can't quite ~ it in** es tan increíble que es difícil de asimilar

7 (= *deceive, cheat*) engañar; **to be ~n in by appearances** dejarse engañar por las apariencias

➤ **take off Ⓐ** VT + ADV **1** (= *remove*) [+ *lid, wrapping, label, stain, menu item*] quitar; [+ *clothes*] quitarse, sacarse (*LAm*)

2 (= *deduct*) (*from bill, price*) descontar; **she took 50p off** hizo un descuento de *or* descontó 50 peniques

3 (= *lead away*) [+ *person, object*] llevarse; **she was ~n off to hospital** la llevaron al hospital; **to ~ o.s. off** irse, largarse*

4 (= *not work*) **I'm going to ~ two weeks off at Christmas** me voy a tomar dos semanas de vacaciones en Navidad

5 (*Brit*) (= *imitate*) imitar

Ⓑ VI + ADV **1** [*plane, passengers*] despegar, decolar (*LAm*) (**for** con rumbo a)

2 (= *succeed*) empezar a tener éxito; **the style really took off among young people** el estilo se puso muy de moda entre los jóvenes

Ⓒ VT + PREP **1** (= *remove*) quitar de, sacar de (*LAm*); **she's been ~n off the case** le han hecho dejar el caso; **to ~ sth off sb*** quitar algo a algn; **~ your hands off me!** ¡no me toques!; **her new hairstyle ~s ten years off her** ese peinado nuevo le quita diez años de encima

2 (= *deduct*) (*from bill, price*) descontar de

➤ **take on Ⓐ** VT + ADV **1** [+ *work*] aceptar, encargarse de; [+ *responsibility, risk*] asumir; [+ *challenger*] enfrentarse a, aceptar el reto de **2** [+ *worker*] contratar; [+ *passengers*] recoger **3** (= *assume*) [+ *form, qualities*] asumir **Ⓑ** VI + ADV (*Brit†**) (= *become upset*) **don't ~ on so!** ¡no te pongas así!, ¡no te agites!

➤ **take out** VT + ADV **1** (= *bring, carry out*) sacar; **he took the dog out for a walk** sacó el perro a pasear; **can I ~ you out to lunch?** ¿le puedo invitar a almorzar?

2 (= *remove*) (*gen*) sacar; [+ *tooth*] extraer, sacar; [+ *stain*] quitar, limpiar; [+ *target, enemy position*] eliminar; **it took**

me out of myself* me hizo olvidar mis propios problemas; **it ~s it out of you*** te deja hecho pedazos*
3 (= *procure*) [+ *patent, licence*] obtener; [+ *policy*] sacar; **to ~ out insurance** hacerse un seguro
4 to ~ it out on sb desquitarse con algn
➤ **take over △** VT + ADV [+ *responsibility*] asumir; [+ *job*] encargarse de; [+ *building, country*] tomar; [+ *company*] adquirir; **he took over the business from his father** se hizo cargo del negocio cuando lo dejó su padre; **to ~ over sb's job** sustituir a algn
⑤ VI + ADV **1** (= *take charge*) [*new president, official*] entrar en funciones; [*government*] entrar en poder; [*driver*] tomar el volante; [*pilot*] tomar los mandos; **to ~ over from sb** (*in job*) (*temporarily*) hacer de suplente para algn; (*permanently*) reemplazar a algn; (= *cover for*) cubrir a algn
2 (= *seize control*) [*dictator, political party*] tomar el poder
➤ **take to** VI + PREP **1** (= *form liking for*) [+ *person*] tomar cariño a algn, encariñarse con algn; [+ *sport*] aficionarse a; [+ *surroundings, idea*] hacerse a; **she didn't ~ kindly to the idea** no le gustó or no le hizo gracia la idea; **I didn't much ~ to him** no me resultó simpático
2 (= *form habit of*) **she took to inviting them round every Sunday** empezó a invitarles a casa todos los domingos; **she took to telling everyone that ...** le dio por contar a todos que ...; **to ~ to drink** darse a la bebida
3 (= *escape to*) **to ~ to one's bed** guardar cama
➤ **take up** VT + ADV **1** (= *raise, lift*) levantar, recoger; [+ *carpet, floorboards*] quitar; [+ *dress, hem*] acortar
2 (= *lead, carry upstairs*) subir
3 (= *pick up*) [+ *pen, one's work*] coger, agarrar (*LAm*); [+ *passengers*] recoger
4 (= *continue*) [+ *story*] continuar con
5 (= *occupy*) [+ *time*] ocupar; [+ *space*] llenar, ocupar
6 (= *raise question of*) **I shall ~ the matter up with the manager** hablaré del asunto con el gerente
7 (= *take issue with*) **I feel I must ~ you up on that** siento que debo contestar a lo que has dicho
8 (= *start*) [+ *hobby, sport*] dedicarse a; [+ *career*] emprender
9 (= *accept*) [+ *offer, challenge*] aceptar; **I'll ~ you up on that some day** algún día recordaré lo que has dicho
10 (= *adopt*) [+ *cause*] apoyar; [+ *case*] ocuparse de
⑤ VI + ADV **to ~ up with sb** (*as friend*) hacerse amigo de algn; (*romantically*) juntarse con algn
➤ **take upon** VT + PREP **to ~ sth upon o.s.** tomar algo sobre sí; **to ~ it upon o.s. to do sth** atreverse a hacer algn

takeaway ['teɪkəweɪ] N (*Brit*) (= *restaurant*) tienda *f* de comida para llevar; (= *meal*) comida *f* para llevar

take-home pay [ˌteɪkhəʊm'peɪ] N sueldo *m* neto, sueldo *m* líquido

taken ['teɪkən] PP of **take**

takeoff ['teɪkɒf] N [*of plane, economy*] despegue *m*

takeout ['teɪkaʊt] N (*US*) (= *meal*) comida *f* para llevar; (= *food shop*) tienda *f* de comida para llevar

takeover ['teɪkˌəʊvəʳ] N adquisición *f*, compra *f*
➤ **takeover bid** oferta *f* pública de adquisición (de acciones), OPA *f*

taker ['teɪkəʳ] N **at £5 there were no ~s** a un precio de cinco libras nadie se ofreció a comprarlo; **the challenge found no ~s** no hubo nadie que quisiera aceptar el desafío

take-up ['teɪkʌp] N (*Brit*) acogida *f*, tasa *f* de aceptación; **this benefit has a low ~ rate** la oferta de esta prestación ha tenido muy mala acogida; **there was an enthusiastic public ~ of these shares** hubo muchísima demanda para comprar estas acciones, esta oferta de acciones ha tenido muy buena acogida entre el público

taking ['teɪkɪŋ] N **1 the job's yours for the ~** el trabajo es tuyo si lo quieres **2 takings** (*Brit Comm*) recaudación *fsing*; (*at show*) taquilla *fsing*

talc [tælk] N talco *m*

talcum powder ['tælkəmˌpaʊdəʳ] N polvos *mpl* de talco, talco *m*

tale [teɪl] N cuento *m*, historia *f*; **few people who get caught in an avalanche live to tell the ~** muy poca gente sobrevive una avalancha; ✦ IDIOM **to tell ~s** chivarse, chismear

talent ['tælənt] N talento *m* (**for** para); **he's got a real ~ for languages** tiene verdadera facilidad para los idiomas; **she**

had a ~ for making people laugh tenía el don de saber hacer reír a la gente; **he encourages young ~** promociona a los jóvenes talentos ➤ **talent competition** concurso *m* de talentos ➤ **talent spotter** cazatalentos *mf inv*

talented ['tæləntɪd] ADJ talentoso, de talento

Taliban ['tælɪbæn] **△** ADJ talibán **⑤** N **the T~** los talibanes, el talibán

talisman ['tælɪzmən] N (*pl* **~s**) talismán *m*

talk [tɔːk] **△** N **1** (= *conversation*) conversación *f*, charla *f*, plática *f* (*Mex*); **to have a ~ (with sb)** hablar (con algn), tener una conversación (con algn)
2 (= *lecture*) charla *f*; **to give a ~ (on sth)** dar una charla (sobre algo)
3 talks (= *negotiations*) (*gen*) conversaciones *fpl*, pláticas *fpl* (*Mex*); (*with defined aim*) negociaciones *fpl*
4 (= *rumours*) rumores *mpl*; **there is some ~ of his resigning** se habla de *or* corren rumores sobre su posible dimisión
5 (= *remarks*) **that's the kind of ~ we could do without** esos comentarios sobran
6 (= *hot air*) (*pej*) palabrería *f*, cuento *m*; **it's just ~** es pura palabrería, es todo cuento
⑤ VI **1** (= *speak, gossip*) hablar (**about** de); **it's easy for you to ~** para ti es fácil hablar; **I wasn't ~ing about you** no hablaba de ti; **everyone's ~ing about him** anda en boca de todos; **~ about a stroke of luck!*** ¡qué suerte!; **you can ~!** ◆ **look** who's ~ing! ¡mira quién habla!, ¡mira quién fue a hablar!; **now you're ~ing!** ¡así se habla!; **~ing of films, have you seen ...?** hablando de películas, ¿has visto ...?; **don't ~ to your mother like that!** ¡no le hables así a tu madre!; **I'm not ~ing to him any more** ya no me hablo con él; ✦ IDIOM **~ of the devil!** ¡hablando del rey de Roma!
2 (= *converse*) hablar, platicar (*Mex*) (**to** con); **stop ~ing!** ¡callaos!, ¡dejad de hablar!; **they ~ed about old times** hablaron de los viejos tiempos; **to get ~ing** empezar a hablar, entablar conversación; **to ~ to sb** hablar con algn; **she had no one to ~ to** no tenía con quién hablar; **were you ~ing to me?** ¿me hablas a mí?; **to ~ to o.s.** hablar solo; **to ~ with sb** hablar con algn
3 (= *have discussion*) hablar, hablar seriamente; **we really need to ~** tenemos que hablar (seriamente); **to ~ (to sb) about sth** discutir algo (con algn); **the two companies are ~ing about a possible merger** las dos empresas están discutiendo *or* negociando una posible fusión
⑥ VT **1** (= *speak*) hablar; **they were ~ing Arabic** hablaban (en) árabe; **we're ~ing big money here*** estamos hablando de mucho dinero; **to ~ nonsense** decir tonterías
2 (= *discuss*) hablar de; **we were ~ing politics** hablábamos de política; ✦ IDIOM **to ~ shop** hablar del trabajo
3 (= *persuade*) **to ~ sb sth into doing sth** convencer a algn de que haga algo; **to ~ sb out of doing sth** convencer a algn de que no haga algo, disuadir a algn de que haga algo
⑩ CPD ➤ **talk radio** radio *f* hablada ➤ **talk show** programa *m* de entrevistas
➤ **talk back** VI + ADV replicar
➤ **talk down △** VI + ADV **to ~ down to sb** hablar con aires de superioridad a algn **⑤** VT + ADV **1** [+ *pilot*] dirigir por radio el aterrizaje a **2** (*esp Brit*) [+ *currency, shares*] hacer bajar; **I ~ed him down another thousand** hice que rebajara el precio otras mil libras
➤ **talk over** VT + ADV (= *discuss*) hablar, discutir; **let's ~ it/things over** vamos a hablarlo *or* discutirlo; **to ~ sth over with sb** consultar algo con algn
➤ **talk round** VT + ADV **to ~ sb round** (*esp Brit*) llegar a convencer a algn
➤ **talk through △** VT + ADV [+ *plan, problem*] discutir detenidamente **⑤** VT + PREP **to ~ sb through sth** explicar algo a algn
➤ **talk up** VT + ADV (= *exaggerate*) exagerar

talkative ['tɔːkətɪv] ADJ hablador, platicón (*Mex*)

talker ['tɔːkəʳ] N hablador(a) *m/f*; **I'm not much of a ~** no soy buen conversador

talking ['tɔːkɪŋ] **△** ADJ [*bird, doll*] que habla **⑤** N **she does all the ~** ella es quien habla siempre; **I'll do the ~** yo seré el que hable; **no ~, please!** ¡silencio, por favor! **⑥** CPD ➤ **talking book** audiolibro *m* ➤ **talking point** tema *m* de conversación

talking-to ['tɔːkɪŋtuː] N **I gave him a good ~** le llamé al orden, le leí la cartilla

tall [tɔːl] ADJ (compar **~er**; superl **~est**) alto; **a six-foot ~ man** ≈ un hombre de uno ochenta; **how ~ are you?** ¿cuánto mides?, ¿qué altura tienes?; **I'm 1.6 metres ~** mido 1,60m (de alto); **she's 5cm ~er than me** es cinco centímetros más alta que yo, mide cinco centímetros más que yo, me saca cinco centímetros; **to get ~er** crecer, ponerse más alto ➤ **tall order* it's a bit of a ~ order, but we'll try** no es fácil, pero lo intentaremos; **it was a ~ order to expect us to finish in three days** esperar que terminásemos en tres días era mucho pedir* ➤ **tall ship** gran buque m de regata ➤ **tall story*** cuento m chino*

talliboy ['tɔːlbɔɪ] N (Brit) cómoda f alta

tallow ['tæləʊ] N sebo m

tally ['tælɪ] Ⓐ N cuenta f, total m; **to keep a ~ of** llevar la cuenta de Ⓑ VI [stories, accounts] concordar, coincidir (**with** con)

Talmud ['tælmʊd] N Talmud m

talon ['tælən] N garra f

tamarind ['tæmərɪnd] N tamarindo m

tambourine [,tæmbə'riːn] N pandereta f

tame [teɪm] Ⓐ ADJ (compar **~r**; superl **~st**) **1** [lion, tiger] domesticado, manso; [hedgehog, fox] dócil, manso **2** (= boring) [book, film, match, performance] soso, insulso; **the report was pretty ~ stuff** el informe era bastante anodino Ⓑ VT domar, amansar

Tamil ['tæmɪl] ADJ, N tamil mf

Tampax® ['tæmpæks] N tampax® m, támpax m

tamper ['tæmpə'] VI **to ~ with** [+ machinery, brakes] manipular; [+ lock] tratar de forzar; [+ evidence] falsificar; [+ witness] sobornar

tampon ['tæmpən] N tampón m

tan [tæn] Ⓐ N bronceado m; **to get a ~** broncearse Ⓑ ADJ color canela inv, color café claro inv (esp LAm); [shoes] marrón Ⓒ VI [person] broncearse, ponerse moreno (Sp) Ⓓ VT **1** [+ person, skin] broncear, poner moreno (Sp), quemar (LAm) **2** [+ leather] curtir

tandem ['tændəm] Ⓐ N (= bicycle) tándem m Ⓑ ADV **in ~** conjuntamente; **the two systems will run in ~** los dos sistemas funcionarán conjuntamente or en tándem; **in ~ with** conjuntamente con

tang [tæŋ] N (= taste) sabor m fuerte y picante; (= smell) olor m acre

tangent ['tændʒənt] N tangente f; ✦ IDIOM **to go off at a ~** salirse por la tangente

tangerine [,tændʒə'riːn] N mandarina f, tangerina f

tangible ['tændʒəbl] ADJ tangible

Tangier(s) [tæn'dʒɪə(z)] N Tánger m

tangle ['tæŋgl] Ⓐ N (in hair) enredo m, maraña f; [of streets] laberinto m; (= muddle) enredo m, lío m; **to be in a ~** [hair, thread] estar enredado; **to get into a ~** [hair, thread] enredarse; **I got into a ~ with the police** me metí en un lío con la policía Ⓑ VT (also **~ up**) enredar, enmarañar Ⓒ VI (also **~ up**) enredarse, enmarañarse; **to ~ with sth/sb*** (fig) meterse en algo/con algn

tangled ['tæŋgld] ADJ [hair, wool] enredado, enmarañado; (fig) enmarañado, complicado

tango ['tæŋgəʊ] Ⓐ N (pl **~s**) tango m Ⓑ VI bailar el tango; ✦ IDIOM **it takes two to ~*** es cosa de dos

tangy ['tæŋɪ] ADJ fuerte y picante

tank [tæŋk] Ⓐ N **1** (for liquid) tanque m, depósito m; (large) cisterna f; **fuel ~** depósito m (de combustible); (also **fish ~**) acuario m; **petrol** or (US) **gas ~** depósito m (de gasolina); **water ~** (for village, in house) depósito m de agua; (on lorry) cisterna f **2** (also **~ful**) depósito m **3** (Mil) tanque m, carro m (de combate) **4** (also **swimming ~**) (US) piscina f, alberca f (Mex), pileta f (de natación) (SC) Ⓒ CPD ➤ **tank truck** (US) camión m cisterna

tankard ['tæŋkəd] N (esp Brit) bock m, pichel m

tanked* [tæŋkt], **tanked up*** (Brit) [,tæŋkt'ʌp] ADJ **to be ~ (up)** estar borracho

tanker ['tæŋkə'] N (= ship) buque-cisterna m; (carrying oil)

petrolero m; (= lorry) camión m cisterna; **an oil ~** un petrolero; **a petrol ~** un camión cisterna

tanned [tænd] ADJ bronceado, moreno (Sp)

tannin ['tænɪn] N tanino m

tanning ['tænɪŋ] CPD ➤ **tanning lotion** bronceador m

Tannoy® ['tænɔɪ] N (Brit) sistema m de anuncios por altavoces; **on** or **over the ~** por los altavoces

tantalize ['tæntəlaɪz] VT (= torment) **to ~ sb (with sth)** atormentar a algn (con algo)

tantalizing ['tæntəlaɪzɪŋ] ADJ [aroma, sight, offer] tentador

tantamount ['tæntəmaʊnt] ADJ **~ to** equivalente a; **this is ~ to a refusal** esto equivale a una negativa

tantrum ['tæntrəm] N rabieta* f, berrinche* m; **she had** or **threw a ~** le dio una rabieta or un berrinche*

Tanzania [,tænzə'niːə] N Tanzania f

Tanzanian [,tænzə'nɪən] ADJ, N tanzano/a m/f

Taoiseach ['tiːʃæx] N (Irl) Primer(a) Ministro/a m/f

Taoist ['taʊɪst] ADJ, N taoísta mf

tap¹ [tæp] Ⓐ N **1** (Brit) (= water tap) grifo m (Sp), llave f (LAm), canilla f (SC); (= gas tap) llave f; **cold/hot water ~** grifo m (Sp) or llave f (LAm) or canilla f (SC) del agua fría/caliente **2** [of barrel] espita f, canilla f; **beer on ~** cerveza f de barril; **to have sth on ~** disponer de algo **3** (Telec) micrófono m; **to put a ~ on sb's phone** intervenir or pinchar el teléfono de algn* Ⓑ VT **1** [+ resource, situation] explotar **2** [+ telephone] intervenir, pinchar* Ⓒ CPD ➤ **tap water** agua f corriente, agua f del grifo (Sp)

> Use **el/un** not **la/una** before feminine nouns beginning with stressed **a** or **ha** like **agua**.

➤ **tap into** VI + PREP **they are trying to ~ into the youth market** están intentando introducirse en el mercado juvenil; **to ~ into one's potential** aprovechar al máximo su capacidad

tap² [tæp] Ⓐ N **1** (on door) toque m; (on back, shoulder) golpecito m, toque m; **there was a ~ at** or **on the door** llamaron or tocaron suavemente a la puerta **2** (also **~ dancing**) claqué m Ⓑ VT (= hit lightly) [+ table, surface] golpear suavemente; **he was ~ping his fingers on the steering wheel** estaba repiqueteando or tamborileando sobre el volante con los dedos; **to ~ one's foot** (impatiently) taconear (impacientemente); **they were ~ping their feet in time to the music** seguían el compás de la música con el pie Ⓒ VI dar golpecitos; **she ~ped at the door** llamó suavemente a la puerta Ⓓ CPD ➤ **tap dance** claqué m ➤ **tap dancer** bailarín/ina m/f de claqué ➤ **tap dancing** claqué m

tap-dance ['tæpdɑːns] VI bailar claqué

tape [teɪp] Ⓐ N **1** (= adhesive tape) cinta f adhesiva, Scotch® m; (Sport) meta f; (also **~ measure**) cinta f métrica, metro m **2** (= cassette, recording) cinta f Ⓑ VT **1** (= record) grabar (en cinta) **2** (= seal) (also **~ up**) cerrar con cinta, poner una cinta a **3** (= stick) **to ~ sth to sth** pegar algo a algo con cinta adhesiva Ⓒ CPD ➤ **tape deck** pletina f, unidad f de cinta ➤ **tape machine** casete m, magnetofón m ➤ **tape measure** cinta f métrica, metro m ➤ **tape recorder** casete m (Sp), grabadora f (esp LAm) ➤ **tape recording** grabación f (en cinta)

taper ['teɪpə'] VI afilarse, estrecharse; **to ~ to a point** rematar en punta ➤ **taper off** VI + ADV [spending, fighting, violence] ir disminuyendo

tape-record ['teɪprɪ,kɔːd] VT grabar (en cinta)

tapered ['teɪpəd], **tapering** ['teɪpərɪŋ] ADJ [shape] ahusado, que termina en punta; [finger] afilado; [table leg] que se va estrechando

tapestry ['tæpɪstrɪ] N (= object) tapiz m; (= art) tapicería f

tapeworm ['teɪpwɜːm] N tenia *f*, solitaria *f*

tapioca [ˌtæpɪˈəʊkə] N tapioca *f* ➤ **tapioca pudding** postre *m* de tapioca

tar [tɑːʳ] **Ⓐ** N alquitrán *m*, brea *f*, chapopote *m* (*Mex*) **Ⓑ** VT [+ *road, surface*] alquitranar; ✦ IDIOM **to be ~red with the same brush** estar cortado por el mismo patrón

tarantula [təˈræntjʊlə] N tarántula *f*

tardy ['tɑːdɪ] ADJ (*compar* **tardier**; *superl* **tardiest**) (*frm*) (= *late*) tardío; (= *slow*) lento

target ['tɑːgɪt] **Ⓐ** N 1 (*Sport*) blanco *m*, diana *f*; (*Mil*) objetivo *m*; **he missed the ~** no dio en el blanco *or* la diana; **the bombs were way off ~** las bombas cayeron muy lejos del objetivo; **the shot was on ~** (*Ftbl, Hockey, etc*) el tiro iba directo a gol
2 [*of criticism, remark*] blanco *m*; [*of advertising*] objetivo *m*
3 (= *objective*) objetivo *m*, meta *f*; **the project is on ~ for completion** el proyecto lleva camino de terminarse dentro del plazo previsto; **to set a ~ for sth** fijar un objetivo para algo; **to set o.s. a ~** fijarse un objetivo
Ⓑ VT 1 (*Mil*) [+ *positions, installations*] fijar como objetivo
2 (= *select, single out*) [*advertiser*] dirigir su publicidad a; **a mugger who ~ed elderly women** un atracador que asaltaba en particular a ancianas; **the factory is ~ed for closure** se propone cerrar la fábrica
3 (= *aim*) **products ~ed at children** productos dirigidos a los niños; **programs ~ed at reducing infant deaths** programas que tienen como objetivo reducir el número de muertes infantiles
Ⓒ CPD ➤ **target audience** público *m* objetivo ➤ **target group** grupo *m* objetivo, grupo *m* destinatario ➤ **target market** mercado *m* objetivo ➤ **target practice** tiro *m* al blanco, prácticas *fpl* de tiro

tariff ['tærɪf] N (*Brit*) tarifa *f*

Tarmac®, **tarmac** ['tɑːmæk] (*vb: pt, pp* **tarmacked**) (*esp Brit*) **Ⓐ** N (= *substance*) asfalto *m*, alquitranado *m*; **the ~** (= *runway*) la pista de despegue; (= *road*) el asfalto **Ⓑ** VT asfaltar, alquitranar

tarnish ['tɑːnɪʃ] **Ⓐ** VT [+ *metal*] deslustrar, quitar el brillo a; [+ *reputation*] manchar, empañar **Ⓑ** VI [*metal*] deslustrarse, perder el brillo

tarnished ['tɑːnɪʃt] ADJ [*metal*] deslustrado, sin brillo; [*reputation*] manchado, empañado

tarot ['tærəʊ] N tarot *m* ➤ **tarot card** carta *f* de tarot

tarp* [tɑːp] N (*US*) = **tarpaulin**

tarpaulin [tɑːˈpɔːlɪn] N lona *f* alquitranada

tarragon ['tærəgən] N estragón *m*

tarry ['tɑːrɪ] ADJ [*substance*] alquitranado, embreado; (= *covered with tar*) cubierto de alquitrán; (= *stained with tar*) manchado de alquitrán

tart¹ [tɑːt] ADJ [*flavour, fruit*] ácido, agrio; [*expression, remark*] áspero

tart² [tɑːt] N 1 (*Culin*) (*large*) tarta *f*; (*small*) pastelillo *m*
2 (*esp Brit***) (= *prostitute*) puta*** *f*, furcia *f* (*Sp***); (*pej*) (= *promiscuous woman*) fulana* *f*
➤ **tart up**** VT + ADV (*Brit*) [+ *house*] pintar, remodelar, renovar; **to ~ o.s. up** vestirse y pintarse

tartan ['tɑːtən] N tartán *m*, tela *f* a cuadros escoceses; **a ~ scarf** una bufanda escocesa

Tartar ['tɑːtəʳ] ADJ, N tártaro/a *m/f*

tartar ['tɑːtəʳ] N 1 (*on teeth*) sarro *m*, tártaro *m* 2 (*Chem*) tártaro *m* 3 (*also* **cream of ~**) crémor *m* tartárico
4 (= *woman*) fiera *f*

tartar(e) sauce ['tɑːtəˈsɔːs] N salsa *f* tártara

tarty* ['tɑːtɪ] ADJ putesco*

task [tɑːsk] **Ⓐ** N 1 (= *job*) tarea *f*; **to set sb the ~ of doing sth** pedir a algn que haga algo; ✦ IDIOM **to take sb to ~ (for sth)** reprender *or* regañar a algn (por algo) 2 (= *function, stated aim*) cometido *m*; **it was the ~ of the army to maintain order** mantener el orden era el cometido del ejército **Ⓑ** CPD ➤ **task force** (*Mil*) destacamento *m* especial; (= *working group*) grupo *m* de trabajo

taskmaster ['tɑːskˌmɑːstəʳ] N **he's a hard ~** es muy exigente, es un tirano

Tasmania [tæzˈmeɪnɪə] N Tasmania *f*

Tasmanian [tæzˈmeɪnɪən] ADJ, N tasmanio/a *m/f*

tassel ['tæsəl] N borla *f*

taste [teɪst] **Ⓐ** N 1 (= *sense*) gusto *m*
2 (= *flavour*) sabor *m*, gusto *m*; ✦ IDIOM **to leave a bad** *or* **nasty ~ in the mouth** dejar mal sabor de boca; **his jokes leave a bad** *or* **nasty ~ in the mouth** sus chistes te dejan mal sabor de boca
3 (= *small amount*) **"more wine?" — "just a ~"** —¿más vino? —sólo un poco *or* un poquito; **would you like a ~?** ¿quieres probarlo?; ✦ IDIOM **to give sb a ~ of their own medicine** pagar a algn con la misma moneda
4 (= *experience*) experiencia *f*; (= *sample*) muestra *f*; **her first ~ of freedom** su primera experiencia de la libertad, su primer contacto con la libertad; **he's had a ~ of prison** ha conocido *or* probado la cárcel; **to give sb a ~ of sth** dar una idea de algo a algn; **it was a ~ of things to come** era una muestra de lo que estaba por venir
5 (= *liking*) gusto *m*; **~s differ** los gustos cambian; **to develop a ~ for sth** tomar gusto a algo; **it gave him a ~ for reading** esto hizo que le tomara gusto a la lectura; **she has a ~ for adventure** le gusta la aventura; **we have the same ~s in music** tenemos el mismo gusto para la música; **season to ~** sazonar al gusto; **is it to your ~?** ¿te gusta?, ¿es de su gusto?; ✦ IDIOM **there's no accounting for ~** sobre gustos no hay nada escrito
6 (= *discernment*) gusto *m*; **people of ~** la gente con gusto; **to be in bad/poor ~** ser de mal gusto; **she has very good ~** tiene muy buen gusto; **to have ~** tener gusto
Ⓑ VT 1 (= *try*) [+ *food, drink*] probar; (*at tasting*) degustar, catar
2 (= *perceive flavour of*) **I can't ~ the rum in this** no noto el sabor del ron en esto, esto apenas me sabe a ron
3 (= *eat*) comer, probar
4 (= *experience*) [+ *success, power*] saborear; [+ *poverty, loneliness*] conocer
Ⓒ VI saber; **the brandy ~d bitter** el brandy sabía amargo, el brandy tenía un sabor *or* un gusto amargo; **it ~s good** está rico *or* bueno; **to ~ like/of sth** saber a algo
Ⓓ CPD ➤ **taste bud** papila *f* gustativa

tasteful ['teɪstfʊl] ADJ de buen gusto

tastefully ['teɪstfəlɪ] ADV con buen gusto

tasteless ['teɪstlɪs] ADJ 1 (= *without flavour*) (*by nature*) insípido; (*pej*) (*through cooking*) soso, insípido 2 (= *vulgar*) [*object*] de mal gusto, ordinario; [*remark, joke*] de mal gusto

taster ['teɪstəʳ] N 1 (= *person*) catador(a) *m/f*, degustador(a) *m/f* 2 (*Brit*) (= *sample*) muestra *f*

tasty ['teɪstɪ] ADJ (*compar* **tastier**; *superl* **tastiest**) 1 [*food, dish*] sabroso, apetitoso; **this is very ~** esto sabe muy rico
2 (*Brit***) **he/she's very ~!** ¡está buenísimo/a!*

tat* [tæt] N (*Brit*) basura* *f*

ta-ta* ['tæˈtɑː] EXCL (*Brit*) adiós, adiosito*

tattered ['tætəd] ADJ [*clothes, flag*] en jirones; [*book*] destrozado; [*reputation*] hecho trizas

tatters ['tætəz] NPL (= *shreds*) jirones *mpl*; **to be in ~** [*clothes*] estar hecho jirones; [*reputation*] estar hecho trizas; [*marriage, coalition*] andar muy mal

tattoo [təˈtuː] **Ⓐ** N tatuaje *m* **Ⓑ** VT tatuar

tatty* ['tætɪ] ADJ (*compar* **tattier**; *superl* **tattiest**) (*Brit*) [*clothes*] raído, deshilachado; [*furniture*] estropeado

taught [tɔːt] PT, PP *of* **teach**

taunt [tɔːnt] **Ⓐ** N (= *jeer*) pulla *f*, mofa *f*; (= *insult*) insulto *m* **Ⓑ** VT (= *jeer at*) mofarse de; (= *insult*) insultar; **to ~ sb (with sth)** mofarse de algn (por algo)

Taurus ['tɔːrəs] N 1 (= *sign, constellation*) Tauro *m*
2 (= *person*) tauro *mf inv*; **she's (a) ~** es tauro

taut [tɔːt] ADJ 1 (= *tight*) [*rope*] tirante, tenso; **to pull sth ~** tensar algo 2 (= *tense*) tenso 3 (= *firm*) [*body, legs, muscles*] firme 4 (= *tightly written*) [*novel, film*] compacto

tauten ['tɔːtn] **Ⓐ** VT tensar **Ⓑ** VI tensarse

tautology [tɔːˈtɒlədʒɪ] N tautología *f*

tavern† ['tævən] N taberna *f*

tawdry ['tɔːdrɪ] ADJ (*compar* **tawdrier**; *superl* **tawdriest**) [*jewellery*] de oropel, de relumbrón; [*clothes*] chabacano, hortera (*Sp**); [*decor*] charro, hortera (*Sp**); [*place, town*] chabacano; [*affair, business*] sórdido

tawny ['tɔ:nɪ] ADJ leonado; [*wine*] ámbar oscuro, tostado ➤ **tawny owl** cárabo *m*

tax [tæks] **Ⓐ** N impuesto *m*; **~ on petrol** impuesto *m* sobre la gasolina; **profits before/after ~** beneficios antes de/después de impuestos; **free of ~** exento *or* libre de impuestos; **to pay one's ~es** pagar los impuestos; **I paid £3,000 in ~ last year** el año pasado pagué 3.000 libras de impuestos; **for ~ purposes** a efectos fiscales; **to put a ~ on sth** gravar algo con un impuesto
Ⓑ VT **1** (*Fin*) [+ *income, profit*] gravar; [+ *person*] cobrar impuestos a, imponer cargas fiscales a; **household goods are ~ed at the rate of 15%** los artículos del hogar se gravan con el 15% *or* llevan un impuesto del 15%
2 (*Brit*) **I haven't got my car ~ed yet** aún no he pagado el impuesto de circulación
3 (= *try*) [+ *person*] poner a prueba
4 (= *accuse*) **to ~ sb with sth** acusar a algn de algo
Ⓒ CPD ➤ **tax allowance** desgravación *f* fiscal ➤ **tax avoidance** evasión *f* legal de impuestos ➤ **tax code** código *m* impositivo ➤ **tax collector** recaudador(a) *m/f* de impuestos ➤ **tax cuts** reducciones *fpl* en los impuestos ➤ **tax disc** (*Brit*) pegatina *f* del impuesto de circulación ➤ **tax evasion** evasión *f* fiscal ➤ **tax exemption** exención *f* de impuestos, exención *f* tributaria ➤ **tax exile** (= *person*) persona autoexiliada para evitar los impuestos; (= *state*) exilio *m* voluntario para evitar los impuestos ➤ **tax haven** paraíso *m* fiscal ➤ **tax inspector** (*Brit*) inspector(a) *m/f* fiscal, inspector(a) *m/f* de Hacienda ➤ **tax law** derecho *m* tributario ➤ **tax rate** tasa *f* impositiva ➤ **tax rebate** devolución *f* de impuestos ➤ **tax relief** desgravación *f* fiscal ➤ **tax return** declaración *f* fiscal *or* de la renta ➤ **tax shelter** refugio *m* fiscal ➤ **tax year** año *m* fiscal, ejercicio *m* fiscal

taxable ['tæksəbl] ADJ gravable, imponible

taxation [tæk'seɪʃən] N (= *taxes*) impuestos *mpl*, contribuciones *fpl*; (= *system*) sistema *m* tributario

tax-deductible ['tæksdɪ'dʌktəbl] ADJ desgravable

tax-exempt (*US*) [,tæksɪg'zempt], **tax-free** (*Brit*) ['tæks'fri:] ADJ exento *or* libre de impuestos

taxi ['tæksɪ] **Ⓐ** N (= *cab*) taxi *m* **Ⓑ** VI (*Aer*) rodar por la pista **Ⓒ** CPD ➤ **taxi driver** taxista *mf* ➤ **taxi fare** tarifa *f* de taxi ➤ **taxi rank** (*Brit*), **taxi stand** (*US*) parada *f* de taxis

taxidermist ['tæksɪdɜ:mɪst] N taxidermista *mf*

taximeter ['tæksɪ,mi:tə^r] N taxímetro *m*

taxing ['tæksɪŋ] ADJ **1** (*mentally*) [*problem, task*] dificilísimo; [*period, time*] muy duro **2** (*physically*) [*task, journey*] agotador, duro

taxman* ['tæksmæn] N (*pl* **taxmen**) recaudador *m* de impuestos; **the ~** (= *tax authorities*) Hacienda *f*

taxpayer ['tæks,peɪə^r] N contribuyente *mf*

TB N ABBR = **tuberculosis**

tbc ABBR (= **to be confirmed**) por confirmar

T-bar ['ti:bɑ:^r] N hierro *m* en T; (*also* = **lift**) (*Ski*) telesquí *m*

T-bone (steak) ['ti:bəʊn('steɪk)] N chuleta *f* en forma de T

tbs, tbsp, tblsp ABBR = **tablespoon(ful)**

T-cell ['ti:sel] N célula *f* T

tea [ti:] **Ⓐ** N **1** (= *drink, plant*) té *m*; **would you like some ~?** ¿te apetece un té?; **lemon ~** té con limón
2 (*Brit*) (= *meal*) (*afternoon*) té *m*, merienda *f*; (*evening*) cena *f*
Ⓑ CPD ➤ **tea bag** bolsita *f* de té ➤ **tea break** (*Brit*) descanso *m* para el té ➤ **tea caddy** (*Brit*) tarro *m* *or* bote *m* para el té ➤ **tea chest** (*Brit*) caja *f* grande de madera ➤ **tea cloth** (*Brit*) (*for trolley, tray*) mantelito *m*, pañito *m*; (*for dishes*) paño *m* de cocina, trapo *m* de cocina (*LAm*) ➤ **tea cosy, tea cozy** (*US*) cubretetera *m* ➤ **tea lady** (*Brit*) señora que prepara y sirve el té en una fábrica u oficina ➤ **tea leaf** hoja *f* de té ➤ **tea party** té *m*, merienda *f* ➤ **tea service, tea set** servicio *m* de té, juego *m* de té ➤ **tea strainer** colador *m* de té ➤ **tea towel** (*Brit*) paño *m* de cocina, trapo *m* de cocina (*LAm*) ➤ **tea tray** bandeja *f* del té ➤ **tea trolley** (*Brit*) carrito *m* del té

teacake ['ti:keɪk] N (*Brit*) *bollo con pasas que generalmente se come tostado y untado con mantequilla*

teach [ti:tʃ] (*pt, pp* **taught**) **Ⓐ** VT **1** (*in class*) [+ *subject*] dar clases de, enseñar; **to ~ school** (*US*) (*primary*) dar clases en un colegio de enseñanza primaria; (*secondary*) dar clases en un colegio de enseñanza secundaria; **she taught English to businessmen** enseñaba inglés *or* daba clases de inglés a ejecutivos
2 (*not in class*) enseñar; **to ~ sb to do sth** enseñar a algn a hacer algo; **he taught himself Arabic** aprendió árabe por su cuenta; **my mother taught me how to cook** mi madre me enseñó a cocinar; **that'll ~ you!** ¡eso te servirá de lección!, ¡te está bien empleado!; ✦ IDIOM **to ~ sb a lesson*** darle una lección a algn
Ⓑ VI (= *give classes*) dar clases; **he has always wanted to ~** siempre ha querido ser profesor *or* dedicarse a la enseñanza

teacher ['ti:tʃə^r] N (*in secondary school*) profesor(a) *m/f*; (*in primary school*) maestro/a *m/f*; **French ~** profesor(a) *m/f* de francés ➤ **teacher training** (*Brit*) formación *f* pedagógica ➤ **teacher training college** (*for primary schools*) escuela *f* normal; (*for secondary schools*) ≈ Instituto *m* de Ciencias de la Educación, ICE *m*

teacher-pupil ratio [,ti:tʃə,pju:pl'reɪʃɪəʊ] N proporción *f* profesor-alumno

teaching ['ti:tʃɪŋ] **Ⓐ** N **1** (= *profession, activity*) enseñanza *f*; **her son's gone into ~** su hijo se ha metido a profesor; **I like ~** me gusta dar clases *or* enseñar
2 (*also* **~s**) [*of philosopher, prophet*] enseñanzas *fpl*
Ⓑ CPD ➤ **teaching hospital** (*Brit*) hospital *m* clínico ➤ **teaching material** material *m* didáctico, material *m* de enseñanza ➤ **teaching post** puesto *m* de profesor, puesto *m* docente ➤ **teaching practice** (*Brit*) prácticas *fpl* de enseñanza ➤ **the teaching profession** la profesión docente, la docencia ➤ **the teaching staff** el profesorado, el cuerpo docente

teacup ['ti:kʌp] N taza *f* para el té

teak [ti:k] N teca *f*, madera *f* de teca

teakettle ['ti:ketl] N (*US*) hervidor *m*, caldera *f* (*Bol, Uru*), pava *f* (*SC*)

team [ti:m] N (*gen*) equipo *m*; **the national ~** la selección nacional; **home/away ~** equipo *m* de casa/visitante ➤ **team game** juego *m* de equipo ➤ **team member** miembro *mf* del equipo ➤ **team player** (*fig*) persona que trabaja bien en equipo ➤ **team spirit** espíritu *m* de equipo, compañerismo *m* ➤ **team up** VI + ADV juntarse, asociarse (**with** con); (*Sport*) formar un equipo (**with** con)

team-mate ['ti:mmeɪt] N compañero/a *m/f* de equipo

teamster ['ti:mstə^r] N (*US*) camionero *m*, camionista *m*

teamwork ['ti:mwɜ:k] N labor *f* de equipo, trabajo *m* en *or* de equipo

teapot ['ti:pɒt] N tetera *f*

tear¹ [teə^r] (*vb: pt* **tore**; *pp* **torn**) **Ⓐ** N (*in fabric, paper*) roto *m*, desgarrón *m*; (*in muscle*) desgarro *m*; (*in ligament*) rotura *f*; **the dress had a ~ in it** el vestido tenía un roto *or* desgarrón *or* estaba rasgado
Ⓑ VT **1** (= *rip*) [+ *fabric, paper*] romper, rasgar; [+ *muscle*] desgarrarse; [+ *ligament*] romperse; **you've torn your trousers** te has roto *or* rasgado el pantalón; **to ~ a hole in sth** hacer un agujero en algo; **she tore open the envelope** abrió el sobre rápidamente; **to ~ sth to pieces** *or* **bits** (*lit*) hacer pedazos algo, destrozar algo; [+ *argument, essay, idea*] echar algo por tierra; ✦ IDIOM **that's torn it!** (*Brit**) ¡ya la hemos fastidiado!*, ¡buena la hemos hecho!*
2 (= *pull, remove*) **to ~ o.s. free** *or* **loose** soltarse; **to ~ sth from/off sth** arrancar algo de algo
3 (*fig*) **a country torn by war** un país desgarrado por la guerra; **she is torn between her job and her family** se debate entre su trabajo y su familia; **she was torn between the two men in her life** no se decidía entre los dos hombres que formaban parte de su vida
Ⓒ VI **1** (= *get torn*) [*fabric, paper*] rasgarse, romperse; [*muscle, tissue*] desgarrarse; [*ligament*] romperse
2 (*pull*) **to ~ at sth: he tore at the wrapping paper** tiró del papel de regalo; **the brambles tore at his face** las zarzas le arañaron la cara
3 (= *rush*) **she tore up the stairs** subió las escaleras embalada *or* a toda velocidad; **we were ~ing along the motorway**

íbamos embalados por la autopista, íbamos por la autopista a toda velocidad *or* a toda pastilla*
➤ **tear apart** VT + ADV **1** (= *rip to pieces*) [+ *object*] hacer pedazos, hacer trizas; [+ *prey*] descuartizar **2** (*in search*) [+ *room, house*] destrozar **3** (= *damage*) [+ *family, organization, person*] desgarrar; **it ~s me apart to know you're unhappy** me desgarra el corazón saber que no eres feliz **4** (= *criticize*) echar por tierra
➤ **tear away** VT + ADV **eventually we tore him away from the party** por fin conseguimos arrancarlo de la fiesta; **if you can ~ yourself away from that book/the television** si puedes dejar ese libro/despegarte del televisor un momento
➤ **tear down** VT + ADV [+ *building, statue*] derribar; [+ *poster, flag*] arrancar
➤ **tear off** Ⓐ VT + ADV **1** [+ *sheet of paper, label, wrapping, roof*] arrancar; **he tore off his clothes** se quitó la ropa a tirones **2** (*) [+ *letter*] escribir deprisa y corriendo, garrapatear Ⓑ VI + ADV (*at speed*) salir embalado, salir a toda velocidad
➤ **tear out** VT + ADV [+ *cheque, page*] arrancar; **to ~ one's hair (out)** (*in exasperation, worry*) tirarse de los pelos
➤ **tear up** VT + ADV **1** [+ *letter, photo*] romper, hacer pedazos; (*fig*) [+ *contract*] romper, anular **2** [+ *plant, tree*] arrancar, arrancar de cuajo; [+ *forest*] talar, despoblar

tear² [tɪəʳ] N (= *teardrop*) lágrima *f*; **to burst into ~s** echarse a llorar; **she was close to ~s** estaba a punto de llorar; **to be in ~s** estar llorando; **it'll end in ~s** acabará mal; **to be moved to ~s** llorar de la emoción; ✦ IDIOM **I was bored to ~s** me aburrí soberanamente *or* como una ostra* ➤ **tear duct** conducto *m* lacrimal ➤ **tear gas** gas *m* lacrimógeno

tearaway* ['tɛərəweɪ] N (*Brit*) alborotador(a) *m/f*, gamberro/a *m/f* (*Sp*)

teardrop ['tɪədrɒp] N lágrima *f*

tearful ['tɪəfʊl] ADJ [*eyes, voice*] lloroso; [*farewell, reunion*] emotivo; **she was surrounded by ~ children** estaba rodeada de niños que lloraban; **she felt a bit ~** se le saltaron las lágrimas; **to become ~** ponerse a llorar

tearing ['tɛərɪŋ] ADJ **to be in a ~ hurry** (*esp Brit*) estar muy de prisa

tear-jerker* ['tɪə,dʒɜːkəʳ] N (= *film*) película *f* lacrimógena

tearoom ['tiːrʊm] N salón *m* de té

tear-stained ['tɪəsteɪnd] ADJ manchado de lágrimas

tease [tiːz] Ⓐ N **1** (= *joker*) bromista *mf*, guasón/ona* *m/f* **2** (= *flirt*) **he's a dreadful ~** le gusta mucho flirtear Ⓑ VT (= *make fun of*) tomar el pelo a, mofarse de; (*cruelly*) atormentar; **they ~ her about her hair** la molestan con chistes acerca de su pelo
➤ **tease out** VT + ADV [+ *information*] sonsacar, ir sacando

teaser* ['tiːzəʳ] N (= *problem*) rompecabezas *m inv*

teashop ['tiːʃɒp] N (*Brit*) café *m*, cafetería *f*; (*strictly*) salón *m* de té

teasing ['tiːzɪŋ] Ⓐ ADJ burlón, guasón* Ⓑ N burlas *fpl*, guasa* *f*

teaspoon ['tiːspuːn] N (= *spoon*) cucharilla *f*, cucharita *f* (*de postre*); (= *quantity*) cucharadita *f*

teaspoonful ['tiːspuːnfʊl] N cucharadita *f*

teat [tiːt] N [*of animal*] teta *f*; (*Brit*) [*of bottle*] tetina *f*

teatime ['tiːtaɪm] N (*Brit*) (*for afternoon tea*) hora *f* del té; (= *suppertime*) hora *f* de cenar

tech [tek] N ABBR (*Brit*) = **technical college**

technical ['teknɪkəl] ADJ técnico; **a ~ hitch** un fallo técnico (*Sp*), una falla técnica (*LAm*); **a ~ point** un detalle técnico ➤ **technical college** (*esp Brit*) ≈ escuela *f* politécnica, ≈ instituto *m* de formación profesional (*Sp*) ➤ **technical drawing** dibujo *m* técnico ➤ **technical support** (servicio *m* de) asistencia *f* técnica

technicality [,teknɪ'kælɪtɪ] N **1** (= *technical detail*) detalle *m* (técnico) **2** (= *nature*) tecnicidad *f*, carácter *m* técnico

technically ['teknɪkəlɪ] ADV técnicamente, desde el punto de vista técnico

technician [tek'nɪʃən] N técnico/a *m/f*

technique [tek'niːk] N técnica *f*

technocrat ['teknəkræt] N tecnócrata *mf*

technological [,teknə'lɒdʒɪkəl] ADJ tecnológico

technologically [,teknə'lɒdʒɪkəlɪ] ADV tecnológicamente

technology [tek'nɒlədʒɪ] N tecnología *f*

technophobe ['teknəʊˌfəʊb] N tecnófobo/a *m/f*

teddy ['tedɪ] N (*also ~ bear*) osito *m* (de peluche)

tedious ['tiːdɪəs] ADJ pesado, aburrido

tedium ['tiːdɪəm] N pesadez *f*, lo aburrido

tee [tiː] N (*Golf*) (= *object*) tee *m*; (= *area*) punto *m* de salida
➤ **tee off** VI + ADV dar el primer golpe

teem [tiːm] VI **to ~ (with)** [+ *insects, fish*] abundar (en); **through streets ~ing with people** por calles atestadas de gente; **it's ~ing (with rain)** está lloviendo a mares *or* a cántaros

teen* [tiːn] Ⓐ ADJ = **teenage** Ⓑ N (*esp US*) = **teenager**

teenage ['tiːneɪdʒ] ADJ [*fashion*] para adolescentes, juvenil; **a ~ boy/girl** un/una adolescente; **the number of ~ pregnancies** el número de embarazos entre las jóvenes adolescentes

teenager ['tiːnˌeɪdʒəʳ] N adolescente *mf*

teens [tiːnz] NPL adolescencia *fsing*; **to be in one's ~** ser adolescente

teeny(-weeny)* ['tiːnɪ('wiːnɪ)] ADJ chiquito, chiquitín

tee-shirt ['tiːʃɜːt] N = **T-shirt**

teeter ['tiːtəʳ] VI (*unsteadily*) bambolearse, tambalearse; (= *hesitate*) vacilar, titubear; **to ~ on the edge of** estar al borde de

teeth [tiːθ] NPL *of* **tooth**

teethe [tiːð] VI **he's teething** le están saliendo los dientes, está echando los dientes

teething ['tiːðɪŋ] N dentición *f* ➤ **teething troubles**, **teething problems** (*Brit*) problemas *mpl* iniciales

teetotal ['tiːtəʊtl] ADJ [*person*] abstemio

teetotaller, **teetotaler** (*US*) ['tiːtəʊtləʳ] N abstemio/a *m/f*

TEFL ['tefl] N ABBR = **Teaching of English as a Foreign Language**

Teflon ® ['teflɒn] N teflón® *m*

Teheran, **Tehran** [tɛə'rɑːn] N Teherán *m*

tel. ABBR (= **telephone**) tel., tfno.

telebanking ['telɪˌbæŋkɪŋ] N telebanco *m*, banca *f* telefónica

telecast ['telɪkɑːst] (*US*) Ⓐ N programa *m* de televisión Ⓑ VT, VI transmitir (por televisión)

telecommunications ['telɪkəˌmjuːnɪ'keɪʃənz] N telecomunicaciones *fpl*

telecommuter ['telɪkəmˌjuːtəʳ] N teletrabajador(a) *m/f*, trabajador(a) *m/f* a distancia

teleconference ['telɪkɒnfərəns] N teleconferencia *f*

telegenic [,telɪ'dʒenɪk] ADJ televisivo, telegénico

telegram ['telɪgræm] N telegrama *m*

telegraph pole ['telɪgrɑːfpəʊl] N (*Brit*) poste *m* de teléfonos

telemarketing ['telɪmɑːkɪtɪŋ] N telemárketing *m*

Telemessage ® ['telɪmesɪdʒ] N (*Brit*) telegrama *m*

telepathic [,telɪ'pæθɪk] ADJ telepático

telepathy [tɪ'lepəθɪ] N telepatía *f*

telephone ['telɪfəʊn] Ⓐ N teléfono *m*; **to be on the ~** (= *be speaking*) estar hablando por teléfono; (*Brit*) (= *be connected*) tener teléfono; **you're wanted on the ~** le llaman al teléfono
Ⓑ VI telefonear; **I'll ~ for an ambulance** llamaré a una ambulancia
Ⓒ VT llamar por teléfono, telefonear
Ⓓ CPD ➤ **telephone answering machine** contestador *m* automático ➤ **telephone book** guía *f* telefónica ➤ **telephone booth** (*US*), **telephone box** (*Brit*) cabina *f* telefónica ➤ **telephone call** llamada *f* (telefónica) ➤ **telephone directory** guía *f* telefónica ➤ **telephone exchange** (*esp Brit*) central *f* (telefónica) ➤ **telephone number** número *m* de teléfono, fono *m* (*Chi*) ➤ **telephone pole** (*US*) poste *m* de teléfonos

telephonist [tɪ'lefənɪst] N (*Brit*) telefonista *mf*

telephoto lens ['telɪ,fəʊtəʊ'lenz] N teleobjetivo *m*

teleprinter ['telɪ,prɪntə'] N teletipo *m*

teleprompter ® ['telɪ,prɒmptə'] N (*esp US*) teleprompter *m*

telesales ['telɪ,seɪlz] NPL televenta(s) *f(pl)* ➤ **telesales person** televendedor(a) *m/f*

telescope ['telɪskəʊp] N telescopio *m*

telescopic [,telɪ'skɒpɪk] ADJ telescópico ➤ **telescopic lens** teleobjetivo *m* ➤ **telescopic sight** mira *f* telescópica, visor *m* telescópico

teleshopping ['telɪ,ʃɒpɪŋ] N (*US*) telecompra(s) *f(pl)*

Teletext ® ['telɪtekst] N teletex(to) *m*

telethon ['teləθɒn] N telemaratón *m* (con fines benéficos)

televangelist [,telɪ'vændʒəlɪst] N (*esp US*) evangelista *mf* de la tele

televise ['telɪvaɪz] VT transmitir (por televisión), televisar

television ['telɪ,vɪʒən] **Ⓐ** N (= *broadcast, broadcasting industry*) televisión *f*; (*also* ~ **set**) televisor *m*, aparato *m* de televisión; **to be on** ~ [*person*] salir por la televisión **Ⓑ** CPD [*broadcast, play, report, serial*] televisivo; [*camera, aerial*] de televisión; [*personality*] de la televisión ➤ **television announcer** locutor(a) *m/f* de televisión ➤ **television broadcast** emisión *f* televisiva ➤ **television licence** (*Brit*) *licencia que se paga por el uso del televisor, destinada a financiar la BBC* ➤ **television programme** programa *m* de televisión ➤ **television screen** pantalla *f* de televisión ➤ **television set** televisor *m*, aparato *m* de televisión

teleworker ['telɪwɜ:kə'] N teletrabajador(a) *m/f*

teleworking ['telɪwɜ:kɪŋ] N teletrabajo *m*

telex ['teleks] **Ⓐ** N télex *m inv* **Ⓑ** VT enviar un télex a

tell [tel] (*pt, pp* **told**) **Ⓐ** VT **1** [+ *story, experiences*] contar; [+ *truth*] decir; [+ *secret*] contar, divulgar (*frm*); (*formally*) comunicar, informar; **to** ~ **sb sth** decir algo a algn; **to** ~ **sb how/why** decir a algn cómo/por qué; **to** ~ **sb that ...** decir a algn que ...; **there were three, I** ~ **you, three!** había tres, ¿me oyes?, tres; **I told him about the missing money** le dije lo del dinero que faltaba, le informé acerca del dinero que faltaba (*frm*); **me all about it** cuéntame todo; **I'll** ~ **you all about it** te (lo) diré todo; ~ **me another!** ¡cuéntaselo a tu abuela!*; **he's no saint, I can** ~ **you!** ¡no es ningún santo, te lo aseguro!; **I cannot** ~ **you how pleased I am** no encuentro palabras para expresarle lo contento que estoy; **to** ~ **a lie** mentir; **you're** ~**ing me!*** ¡a quién se lo cuentas!, ¡a mí no me lo vas a contar!; **I told you so!** ¡ya lo decía yo!; **I** ~ **you what!** ¡se me ocurre una idea!

2 (= *order*) **to** ~ **sb to do sth** decir a algn que haga algo, mandar a algn a hacer algo; **do as you are told!** ¡haz lo que te digo!

3 (= *distinguish*) distinguir; **I couldn't** ~ **them apart** no podría distinguirlos; **to** ~ **the difference between A and B** distinguir entre A y B; **I can't** ~ **the difference** no veo la diferencia

4 (= *know, be certain*) saber; **you can** ~ **he's a German** se (le) nota que es alemán; **you can't** ~ **much from his letter** su carta nos dice bien poco; **I couldn't** ~ **how it was done** no sabía cómo se hizo; **there is no** ~**ing what he will do** es imposible saber qué va a hacer

Ⓑ VI **1** (= *speak*) **to** ~ (**of**) hablar (de)

2 (*) (= *sneak, tell secrets*) **please don't** ~! ¡no vayas contándolo o soplándolo* por ahí!; **he told on me to my parents** se chivó de mí a mis padres (*Sp**); **that would be** ~**ing!** ¡es un secreto!

3 (= *know, be certain*) saber; **how can I** ~? ¿cómo lo voy a saber?, ¿yo qué sé?; **I can't** ~ (me) es imposible saberlo, no le puedo decir, no sabría decirle; **who can** ~? ¿quién sabe?; **you never can** ~ nunca se sabe

4 (= *have an effect*) **the strain is beginning to** ~ **on him** la tensión está empezando a afectarle

➤ **tell off*** VT + ADV **to** ~ **sb off** (**for sth/for doing sth**) regañar a algn (por algo/por haber hecho algo)

teller ['telə'] N (*US, Scot*) (*in bank*) cajero/a *m/f*; (*at election*) escrutador(a) *m/f*

telling ['telɪŋ] **Ⓐ** ADJ [*blow*] certero; [*argument*] contundente, eficaz; [*figures, remark*] revelador **Ⓑ** N narración *f*; **the story did not lose in the** ~ la historia no perdió nada al ser narrada

telling-off* [,telɪŋ'ɒf] N bronca *f*, reprimenda *f*; **to give sb a** ~ echar una bronca *or* regañar a algn

telltale ['telteɪl] ADJ [*sign*] revelador, indicador

telly* ['telɪ] N (*Brit*) tele* *f* ➤ **telly addict*** teleadicto/a *m/f*

temerity [tɪ'merɪtɪ] N temeridad *f*; **to have the** ~ **to** (+ INFIN) atreverse a + *infin*

temp* [temp] **Ⓐ** N empleado/a *m/f* eventual, temporero/a *m/f* **Ⓑ** VI trabajar como empleado/a eventual, trabajar de temporero/a

temper ['tempə'] **Ⓐ** N (= *nature*) carácter *m*, genio *m*; (= *mood*) humor *m*; **in a fit of** ~ en un acceso de furia *or* ira; **to fly into a** ~ ponerse furioso, montar en cólera; **to be in a** ~ estar furioso; **to be in a good/bad** ~ estar de buen/mal humor; **to keep one's** ~ no perder la calma, contenerse; **to lose one's** ~ perder los estribos **Ⓑ** VT (= *moderate*) [+ *remarks*] suavizar, atenuar; [+ *energy, enthusiasm*] atemperar; **to** ~ **justice with mercy** templar la justicia con la compasión

temperament ['tempərəmənt] N temperamento *m*, disposición *f*

temperamental [,tempərə'mentl] ADJ caprichoso

temperance ['tempərəns] **Ⓐ** N **1** (= *moderation*) templanza *f* (*frm*), moderación *f* **2** (= *teetotalism*) abstinencia *f* de bebidas alcohólicas **Ⓑ** CPD ➤ **temperance movement** campaña *f* antialcohólica

temperate ['tempərɪt] ADJ [*climate, zone*] templado; [*person*] moderado; (*in drinking*) abstemio

temperature ['temprɪtʃə'] N (*Met*) temperatura *f*; **to have** *or* **run a** ~ tener fiebre *or* calentura; **she has a** ~ **of 103°** ≈ tiene 39° de fiebre

tempest ['tempɪst] N (*poet*) tempestad *f*; ✦ IDIOM **a** ~ **in a teapot** (*US*) una tormenta *or* tempestad en un vaso de agua

tempestuous [tem'pestjʊəs] ADJ tempestuoso

template ['templɪt] N plantilla *f*

temple ['templ] N **1** (= *building*) templo *m* **2** (= *forehead*) sien *f*

templet ['templɪt] N (*US*) ≈ template

tempo ['tempəʊ] N tempo *m*

temporarily ['tempərərɪlɪ] ADV temporalmente

temporary ['tempərərɪ] ADJ [*accommodation, solution, licence, measure*] provisional, temporal; [*secretary, job, staff*] temporal, eventual; [*problem*] pasajero, temporal

temporize ['tempəraɪz] VI tratar de ganar tiempo

tempt [tempt] VT **1** (*gen*) tentar; **to** ~ **sb to do sth** tentar a algn a hacer algo **2** (*Rel*) tentar, poner a prueba; **to** ~ **fate** tentar a la suerte

temptation [temp'teɪʃən] N tentación *f*; **there is always a** ~ **to ...** existe siempre la tentación de ...; **to put** ~ **in sb's way** exponer a algn a la tentación

tempting ['temptɪŋ] ADJ [*food*] apetitoso; [*offer*] tentador

temptress ['temptrɪs] N tentadora *f*

ten [ten] NUMBER diez *m*; ~**s of thousands** decenas de miles; ✦ IDIOMS ~ **to one**: ~ **to one he'll be late*** te apuesto que llega tarde; **they're** ~ **a penny*** se encuentran en todas partes; *see* **five**

tenable ['tenəbl] ADJ [*argument*] sostenible, defendible

tenacious [tɪ'neɪʃəs] ADJ [*person*] tenaz; [*belief, idea*] firme

tenacity [tɪ'næsɪtɪ] N tenacidad *f*

tenancy ['tenənsɪ] N (= *possession, period*) tenencia *f*, inquilinato *m*; (= *lease*) arriendo *m*, alquiler *m*

tenant ['tenənt] N inquilino/a *m/f*, arrendatario/a *m/f* ➤ **tenant farmer** agricultor(a) *m/f* arrendatario/a

tend¹ [tend] VI **to** ~ **to do sth** tender a hacer algo, soler hacer algo; **I** ~ **to agree** me inclino a pensar lo mismo

tend² [tend] **Ⓐ** VT **1** (= *care for*) [+ *patient*] cuidar, atender; [+ *sheep, horses*] cuidar, ocuparse de; [+ *garden*] ocuparse de **2 to** ~ **bar** (*US*) servir en el bar **Ⓑ** VI **to** ~ **to** [+ *patient*] cuidar, atender; [+ *sheep, horses*] cuidar, ocuparse de; [+ *housework, wounds, needs*] ocuparse de

tendency ['tendənsı] N tendencia *f*; **to have a ~ to do sth** [*person*] tener tendencia a hacer algo

tendentious [ten'denʃəs] ADJ tendencioso

tender[1] ['tendə[r]] **ⒶⒶ** N **1** (*Comm*) oferta *f*; **to put in a ~ (for)** presentarse a concurso *or* a una licitación (para); **to put sth out to ~** sacar algo a concurso *or* a licitación **2 legal ~** moneda *f* corriente *or* de curso legal **Ⓑ** VT **to ~ one's resignation** presentar su dimisión **Ⓒ** VI **to ~ (for)** presentarse a concurso *or* a una licitación (para)

tender[2] ['tendə[r]] ADJ **1** (= *gentle*) [*person, kiss, word*] tierno; [*voice*] lleno de ternura **2** (= *young*) tierno; **in spite of his ~ years** a pesar de su tierna edad **3** (= *sensitive, sore*) sensible, dolorido **4** [*meat, vegetables*] tierno

tender-hearted ['tendə'hɑːtɪd] ADJ compasivo, bondadoso, tierno de corazón

tenderize ['tendəraɪz] VT ablandar

tenderloin ['tendəlɔɪn] N **1** (= *meat*) lomo *m*, filete *m* **2** (*US**) barrio de vicio y corrupción reconocidos

tenderly ['tendəlɪ] ADV tiernamente, con ternura

tenderness ['tendənɪs] N **1** (= *gentleness*) ternura *f* **2** (= *soreness*) dolor *m* **3** [*of meat, vegetables*] lo tierno

tendon ['tendən] N tendón *m*

tendril ['tendrɪl] N zarcillo *m*

tenement ['tenɪmənt] N (= *building*) bloque *m* de viviendas (*esp de alquiler*); (*Scot*) (= *flat*) piso *m* (*Sp*), departamento *m* (*LAm*)

tenet ['tenət] N principio *m*

ten-gallon hat [,tengælən'hæt] N sombrero *m* tejano

Tenn. ABBR (*US*) = **Tennessee**

tenner* ['tenə[r]] N (*Brit*) (= £10) diez libras; (£10 *note*) billete *m* de diez libras; (*US*) (= $10) diez dólares; (= $10 *note*) billete *m* de diez dólares

tennis ['tenɪs] N tenis *m* ➤ **tennis ball** pelota *f* de tenis ➤ **tennis court** pista *f* de tenis (*Sp*), cancha *f* de tenis (*LAm*) ➤ **tennis elbow** sinovitis *f* del codo, codo *m* de tenista ➤ **tennis match** partido *m* de tenis ➤ **tennis player** tenista *mf* ➤ **tennis racket, tennis racquet** raqueta *f* de tenis ➤ **tennis shoe** zapatilla *f* de tenis

tenor ['tenə[r]] **Ⓐ** ADJ [*instrument, voice*] de tenor; [*aria*] para tenor **Ⓑ** N **1** (*Mus*) tenor *m* **2** [*of speech*] tenor *m*

tenpin bowling [,tenpɪn'bəʊlɪŋ] N, **tenpins** ['tenpɪnz] NPL (*Brit*) bolos *mpl*, bolera *fsing*

tense[1] [tens] N tiempo *m*; **in the present ~** en presente

tense[2] [tens] **Ⓐ** ADJ (*compar* **~r**; *superl* **~st**) **1** (= *nervous*) tenso; **to become ~** ponerse tenso; **her voice was ~** se le notaba la tensión en la voz **2** [*body, muscles, neck*] tenso, en tensión **3** (= *strained*) [*atmosphere, silence*] tenso; [*relations*] tenso, tirante; [*moment, situation*] de tensión **4** (= *taut*) [*rope, wire*] tenso, tirante **Ⓑ** VI (*also* **~ up**) ponerse tenso **Ⓒ** VT (*also* **~ up**) tensar, poner tenso

tensely ['tenslɪ] ADV [*say, wait*] tensamente

tenseness ['tensnɪs] N tensión *f*

tension ['tenʃən] N tensión *f*

tent [tent] N tienda *f* de campaña, carpa *f* (*LAm*) ➤ **tent peg** (*Brit*) estaca *f* de tienda, estaquilla *f*

tentacle ['tentəkl] N tentáculo *m*

tentative ['tentətɪv] ADJ **1** (= *provisional*) provisional, provisorio (*LAm*) **2** (= *hesitant*) [*gesture*] vacilante, tímido; [*smile, attempt*] tímido; **he made a ~ suggestion that ...** sugirió tímidamente que ...

tentatively ['tentətɪvlɪ] ADV **1** (= *provisionally*) provisionalmente, provisoriamente (*LAm*) **2** (= *hesitantly*) tímidamente

tenterhooks ['tentəhʊks] NPL ✦ IDIOMS **to be on ~** estar sobre ascuas, tener el alma en vilo; **to keep sb on ~** tener a algn sobre ascuas

tenth [tenθ] **Ⓐ** ADJ décimo **Ⓑ** PRON (*in series*) décimo *m*; (= *fraction*) décima parte *f*, décimo *m*; *see* **fifth**

tenuous ['tenjʊəs] ADJ [*connection, link*] vago, ligero;

[*evidence*] poco sólido; [*alliance, peace*] frágil, endeble; **he has only a ~ grasp of reality** sólo tiene una escasa conciencia de la realidad

tenure ['tenjʊə[r]] N **1** [*of land*] posesión *f*, tenencia *f*, ocupación *f*; [*of office*] ocupación *f*, ejercicio *m* **2** (= *guaranteed employment*) puesto *m* asegurado, permanencia *f*

tepee ['tiːpiː] N tipi *m*

tepid ['tepɪd] ADJ tibio

Ter. ABBR = **Terrace**

term [tɜːm] **Ⓐ** N **1** (= *period*) periodo *m*, período *m*; (*as President, governor, mayor*) mandato *m*; **in the long ~** a largo plazo; **in the longer ~** a un plazo más largo; **in the medium ~** a medio plazo; **during his ~ of office** bajo su mandato; **in the short ~** a corto plazo; **she carried the baby to ~** llevó el embarazo a término

2 (*Educ*) trimestre *m*; **in the autumn** *or* (*US*) **fall/spring/summer ~** en el primer/segundo/tercer trimestre

3 (= *period of validity*) plazo *m*; **the policy is near the end of its ~** el plazo de la póliza está a punto de vencer

4 (= *word*) término *m*; **a ~ of abuse** un término ofensivo, un insulto; **in simple ~s** de forma sencilla

5 terms **5.1** (= *conditions*) condiciones *fpl*, términos *mpl*; **we offer easy ~s** ofrecemos facilidades de pago; **~s of employment** condiciones *fpl* de empleo; **they accepted him on his own ~s** lo aceptaron con las condiciones que él había puesto; **~s of reference** [*of committee, inquiry*] cometido *msing*, instrucciones *fpl*; [*of study*] ámbito *msing*; (= *area of responsibility*) responsabilidades *fpl*, competencia *fsing*; ✦ IDIOM **to come to ~s with sth** asumir *or* asimilar algo **5.2** (= *relations*) **to be on bad ~s with sb** llevarse mal con algn, no tener buenas relaciones con algn; **we're on first name ~s with all the staff** ≈ nos tuteamos con todos los empleados; **to be on good ~s with sb** llevarse bien con algn, tener buenas relaciones con algn **5.3** (= *sense*) **in political ~s** desde el punto de vista político, en términos políticos; **in ~s of production we are doing well** en cuanto a la producción vamos bien, por lo que se refiere *or* por lo que respecta a la producción vamos bien; **we were thinking more in ~s of an au pair** nuestra idea era más una au pair, teníamos en mente a una au pair

Ⓑ VT (= *designate*) calificar de

Ⓒ CPD ➤ **term paper** (*US*) trabajo *m* escrito trimestral

terminal ['tɜːmɪnl] **Ⓐ** ADJ [*cancer, patient, case*] terminal, en fase terminal; **the government's problems may be ~** los problemas del gobierno pueden no tener solución; **to be in (a state of) ~ decline** estar en un estado de declive irreversible **Ⓑ** N **1** (*Comput*) terminal *m* **2** [*of bus, train*] terminal *f*

terminally ['tɜːmɪnəlɪ] ADV **to be ~ ill** estar en fase terminal

terminate ['tɜːmɪneɪt] **Ⓐ** VT [+ *meeting*] concluir; [+ *conversation, relationship*] poner fin a; [+ *contract*] finalizar; [+ *pregnancy*] interrumpir **Ⓑ** VI [*contract*] finalizar, concluir; [*train, bus*] terminar

termination [,tɜːmɪ'neɪʃən] N [*of contract*] terminación *f*; [*of pregnancy*] interrupción *f*; **~ of employment** baja *f*, cese *m*

terminology [,tɜːmɪ'nɒlədʒɪ] N terminología *f*

terminus ['tɜːmɪnəs] N (= *last station*) (*Rail*) estación *f* terminal; [*of bus route*] última parada *f*, final *f* del recorrido; (= *building*) terminal *m*; (*for buses*) terminal *f*

termite ['tɜːmaɪt] N termita *f*, comején *m*

termtime ['tɜːmtaɪm] N **in ~** durante el trimestre

Terr. ABBR = **Terrace**

terrace ['terəs] N **1** (= *patio, verandah*) terraza *f* (*also Agr*); (= *roof*) azotea *f* **2** (*Brit*) [*of houses*] hilera *f* de casas (adosadas); (= *name of street*) calle *f* **3** (*Brit Sport*) **the ~s** las gradas *fpl*, el graderío

terraced ['terəst] ADJ [*hillside, garden*] en terrazas, terraplenado; (*Brit*) [*house, cottage*] alineado, adosado (*Sp*)

terracotta ['terə'kɒtə] **Ⓐ** N terracota *f* **Ⓑ** ADJ (= *clay*) de terracota; (*in colour*) terracota *inv*

terrain [te'reɪn] N terreno *m*

terrestrial [tɪ'restrɪəl] ADJ **1** [*life, plant*] terrestre **2** (*Brit*) [*broadcasting, channel*] de transmisión (por) vía terrestre

terrible ['terəbl] ADJ **1** [*experience, accident, disease*] terrible, espantoso
2 (*) [*weather, food*] horrible, espantoso; **her French is ~** habla fatal el francés, habla un francés espantoso; **I'm ~ at cooking** se me da fatal la cocina*; **I'm ~ at remembering names** se me da fatal recordar (los) nombres, soy malísimo para recordar (los) nombres; **I've had a ~ day at the office** he tenido un día malísimo *or* horrible en la oficina; **to feel ~** (= *guilty, ill*) sentirse fatal *or* muy mal; **to look ~** (= *ill*) tener muy mal aspecto; **I've got a ~ memory** tengo una memoria malísima; **we had a ~ time** lo pasamos fatal
3 (*) (*as intensifier*) [*pity, shame*] verdadero; **I've made a ~ mistake** he cometido un terrible error; **it was a ~ shock** fue un golpe terrible

terribly ['terəblɪ] ADV **1** (= *extremely*) [*worried, difficult, important*] terriblemente, tremendamente; **it's ~ good/bad** es buenísimo/malísimo; **it's ~ hard for me to make a decision** me resulta dificilísimo *or* terriblemente difícil tomar una decisión; **I'm ~ sorry** lo siento muchísimo; **we aren't doing ~ well at the moment** ahora no nos va muy bien que digamos
2 (*) (= *very much*) **I miss him ~** le echo muchísimo de menos; **to suffer ~** sufrir horrores*, pasarlo fatal*
3 (= *very poorly*) [*play, perform, behave*] muy mal, fatal

terrier ['terɪəʳ] N terrier *m*

terrific [təˈrɪfɪk] ADJ **1** (= *great*) [*explosion, disappointment*] tremendo, enorme; [*noise, heat*] terrible, tremendo **2** (*) (= *excellent*) [*idea, news, person*] genial*, estupendo; **terrific!** ¡genial!, ¡estupendo!; **you look ~!** ¡estás guapísimo/a!; **to have a ~ time** pasárselo estupendamente *or* fenomenal*

terrified ['terɪfaɪd] ADJ **to be ~** estar aterrorizado, estar aterrado; **to be ~ of sth/sb** tener terror *or* pavor a algo/algn; **he was ~ of catching Aids** le aterrorizaba *or* le daba terror (la idea de) coger el sida; **I was ~ that he might follow me** tenía terror de que pudiera seguirme

terrify ['terɪfaɪ] VT (= *terrorize*) aterrorizar; (= *horrify*) aterrar; **it terrifies me to think that I might lose her** me aterra pensar que podría perderla

terrifying ['terɪfaɪɪŋ] ADJ [*experience, sound, sight*] espantoso, aterrador; [*person*] aterrador; **I still find it ~ to walk along that street** todavía me da muchísimo miedo caminar por esa calle

territorial [ˌterɪˈtɔːrɪəl] ADJ territorial ➤ **Territorial Army** (*Brit*) ejército *m* de reserva ➤ **territorial waters** aguas *fpl* jurisdiccionales *or* territoriales

territory ['terɪtərɪ] N territorio *m*

terror ['terəʳ] Ⓐ N **1** (= *fear*) terror *m*; **to live in ~ of sth** vivir aterrorizado por algo; **he was in ~ of his life** temía por su vida; **he had a ~ of flying** le daba miedo volar **2** (*) (= *person, child*) **she's a ~ on the roads** es un peligro conduciendo; **you little ~!** ¡eres un diablillo!* Ⓑ CPD ➤ **terror attack** atentado *m* (terrorista)

terrorism ['terərɪzəm] N terrorismo *m*

terrorist ['terərɪst] ADJ, N terrorista *mf*

terrorize ['terəraɪz] VT (= *terrify*) aterrorizar; (= *threaten, coerce*) atemorizar

terror-stricken ['terəˌstrɪkən], **terror-struck** ['terəˌstrʌk] ADJ aterrorizado

terse [tɜːs] ADJ (*compar* ~**r**; *superl* ~**st**) [*reply, tone, person*] lacónico, seco; [*statement*] escueto

tertiary ['tɜːʃərɪ] ADJ [*sector, rocks, deposits*] terciario ➤ **tertiary education** (*Brit*) enseñanza *f* superior

Terylene® ['terəliːn] N (*Brit*) terylene® *m*

TESL ['tesəl] N ABBR = **Teaching (of) English as a Second Language**

TESOL ['tesɒl] N ABBR = **Teaching of English to Speakers of Other Languages**

test [test] Ⓐ N **1** (*Scol, Univ*) examen *m*; (*multiple-choice*) test *m*; (*esp for job*) prueba *f*; **to give sb a ~** (**in sth**) examinar a algn (de algo), poner a algn un examen (de algo); **to take a ~** (*Scol, Univ*) hacer un examen; (*multiple choice*) hacer un test; (*for job*) hacer una prueba; **a written ~** un examen escrito
2 (*also* **driving ~**) examen *m* de conducir; **to fail/pass one's ~** suspender (*Sp*) *or* reprobar (*LAm*)/aprobar el examen de conducir
3 (*Med*) [*of organs, functioning*] prueba *f*; [*of sample, substance*] análisis *m inv*; **AIDS ~** prueba *f* del sida; **blood ~** análisis *m inv* de sangre; **eye ~** revisión *f* de la vista; **it was sent to the laboratory for ~s** lo mandaron al laboratorio para que lo analizaran
4 (= *trial*) [*of aircraft, new product, drug*] prueba *f* (*also fig*); **to put sth to the ~** poner *or* someter algo a prueba; **to stand the ~ of time** resistir el paso del tiempo
5 (*Brit Cricket, Rugby*) (*also* **~ match**) partido *m* internacional Ⓑ VT **1** [+ *student, pupil*] examinar; [+ *candidate*] (*for job*) hacer una prueba a; [+ *knowledge*] evaluar; (= *try out*) (*Scol, Univ*) examinar a algn de algo; (*esp for job*) hacer una prueba de algo a algn; (*for revision*) hacer preguntas de algo a algn (para repasar)
2 (*Med*) [+ *blood, urine, sample*] analizar; **to have one's eyes ~ed** hacerse una revisión de la vista; **to ~ sb for AIDS** hacer la prueba del SIDA a algn; **to ~ sb for drugs** (*gen*) realizar pruebas a algn para comprobar si ha consumido drogas; [+ *sportsperson*] realizar el control antidoping a algn
3 (= *conduct trials on*) [+ *aircraft, weapon, new product, drug*] probar; **the drug was ~ed in clinical trials** se sometió el medicamento a pruebas clínicas; **all our products are ~ed for quality** probamos la calidad de todos nuestros productos; **to ~ sth on sth/sb** probar algo con *or* en algo/algn
4 (= *check*) probar; **~ the water temperature with your elbow** pruebe la temperatura del agua con el codo; ✦ IDIOM **to ~ the water(s)** tantear el terreno
5 (*fig*) (= *put to the test*) [+ *person, courage*] poner a prueba Ⓥ VI (= *conduct a test*) **it is a method used to ~ for allergies** es un método utilizado en pruebas de alergia; **to ~ negative/positive (for sth)** dar negativo/positivo (en la prueba de algo) Ⓓ CPD ➤ **(nuclear) test ban** prohibición *f* de pruebas nucleares ➤ **test bed** (= *equipment*) banco *m* de pruebas; (*fig*) conejillo *m* de indias ➤ **test case** (*Jur*) juicio *m* que sienta jurisprudencia ➤ **test drive** (*by potential buyer*) prueba *f* en carretera; (*by mechanic, technician*) prueba *f* de rodaje; **to take sth for a ~ drive** probar algo en carretera ➤ **test flight** vuelo *m* de prueba, vuelo *m* de ensayo ➤ **test match** (*Brit*) partido *m* internacional ➤ **test paper** (*Scol, Univ*) examen *m*; (*multiple-choice*) test *m* ➤ **test pilot** piloto *mf* de pruebas ➤ **test tube** probeta *f*, tubo *m* de ensayo ➤ **test tube baby** bebé *mf* probeta
➤ **test out** VT + ADV probar

testament ['testəmənt] N **1** (= *will*) testamento *m* **2** **the Old/New Testament** el Antiguo/Nuevo Testamento
3 (= *proof*) testimonio *m*; **the building is a ~ to his skills as an architect** el edificio es testimonio de su competencia como arquitecto

testator [tesˈteɪtəʳ] N testador *m*

test-drive ['testˌdraɪv] (*vb: pt* **test-drove**; *pp* **test-driven**) VT [+ *car*] [*prospective buyer*] probar en carretera; [*mechanic, technician*] hacer la prueba de rodaje a

tester ['testəʳ] N (= *person*) ensayador(a) *m/f*; (= *sample, trial product*) muestra *f*, artículo *m* de muestra

testicle ['testɪkl] N testículo *m*

testify ['testɪfaɪ] Ⓐ VI (*Jur*) prestar declaración, declarar; **to ~ to sth** declarar algo, testificar algo Ⓑ VT **to ~ that ...** declarar *or* testificar que ...

testimonial [ˌtestɪˈməʊnɪəl] N **1** (= *certificate*) certificado *m*; (= *reference*) carta *f* de recomendación, recomendación *f* **2** (= *gift*) obsequio *m* **3** (*Sport*) partido *m* homenaje

testimony ['testɪmənɪ] N testimonio *m*, declaración *f*

testing ['testɪŋ] Ⓐ ADJ (= *difficult*) duro; **it was a ~ time** fue un período difícil Ⓑ N pruebas *fpl* Ⓒ CPD ➤ **testing ground** zona *f* de pruebas, terreno *m* de pruebas

testosterone [teˈstɒstərəʊn] N testosterona *f*

testy ['testɪ] ADJ (*compar* **testier**; *superl* **testiest**) irritable

tetanus ['tetənəs] Ⓐ N tétanos *m* Ⓑ CPD [*injection*] del tétanos, contra el tétanos; [*vaccine*] contra el tétanos, antitetánica

tetchy* ['tetʃɪ] ADJ (*compar* **tetchier**; *superl* **tetchiest**) (*esp Brit*) irritable

tête-à-tête [ˈteɪtɑːˈteɪt] N (pl ~ or ~s) conversación f íntima

tether [ˈteðəʳ] Ⓐ N ronzal m, soga f; ✦ IDIOM **to be at the end of one's ~** (Brit) no aguantar más, no poder más Ⓑ VT [+ animal] atar (con una cuerda) (**to** a)

Tex. ABBR (US) = **Texas**

Texan [ˈteksən] ADJ, N tejano/a m/f

Texas [ˈteksəs] N Tejas m

text [tekst] Ⓐ N texto m; (= text message) mensaje m (de texto) Ⓑ VT **to ~ sb*** enviar un mensaje a algn Ⓒ CPD ➤ **text editor** (Comput) editor m de texto ➤ **text message** mensaje m de texto ➤ **text messaging** (envío m de) mensajes mpl de texto

textbook [ˈtekstbʊk] N libro m de texto; **a ~ case of ...** un caso clásico de ...

textile [ˈtekstaɪl] N textil m, tejido m ➤ **textile industry** industria f textil

texting [ˈtekstɪŋ] N = **text messaging**

textual [ˈtekstjʊəl] ADJ textual ➤ **textual notes** notas fpl al pie de página

texture [ˈtekstʃəʳ] N textura f

TGWU N ABBR (Brit) = **Transport and General Workers' Union**

Thai [taɪ] Ⓐ ADJ tailandés Ⓑ N **1** (= person) tailandés/esa m/f **2** (Ling) tailandés m

Thailand [ˈtaɪlænd] N Tailandia f

Thames [temz] N **the ~** el Támesis

than [ðæn] CONJ **1** (in comparisons) que; **I have more ~ you** tengo más que usted; **nobody is more sorry ~ I (am)** nadie lo siente más que yo; **they have more money ~ we have** tienen más dinero que nosotros; **the car went faster ~ we had expected** el coche alcanzó una velocidad mayor de lo que habíamos esperado; **it is better to phone ~ to write** más vale llamar por teléfono que escribir **2** (with numerals) de; **more/less ~ 90** más/menos de 90; **more ~ once** más de una vez **3** (stating preference) antes que; **rather you ~ me** tú antes que yo

thank [θæŋk] VT **1 to ~ sb** dar las gracias or agradecer a algn; **I cannot ~ you enough!** ¡cuánto te lo agradezco!; **to ~ sb for sth** agradecer algo a algn, dar las gracias a algn por algo; **he has only himself to ~ for that** él mismo tiene la culpa de eso; **I have John to ~ for that** eso se lo tengo que agradecer a John; (iro) John tiene la culpa de eso; **he won't ~ you for telling her** no te agradecerá de que se lo hayas dicho; **~ heavens/goodness (for that)!** ¡gracias a Dios!, ¡menos mal! **2 ~ you!** ¡gracias!; **~ you very much** muchas gracias; **~ you for the present** muchas gracias por el regalo; **~ you for letting me know** gracias por contármelo or decírmelo; **~ you for having me** gracias por invitarme; **no ~ you** no, gracias; **did you say ~ you?** ¿has dado las gracias?

thankful [ˈθæŋkfʊl] ADJ agradecido; **to be ~ for sth** estar agradecido por algo; **let's be ~ that it's over** demos gracias que haya terminado; **she was ~ to be alive** daba gracias por estar viva; ✦ IDIOM **to be ~ for small mercies** dar gracias por que la cosa no sea peor

thankfully [ˈθæŋkfəlɪ] ADV **1** (= fortunately) gracias a Dios, afortunadamente **2** (= gratefully) **he accepted the drink ~** aceptó la bebida agradecido

thankless [ˈθæŋklɪs] ADJ ingrato

thanks [θæŋks] Ⓐ NPL **1** (= gratitude) agradecimiento msing, gratitud fsing; **that's all the ~ I get!** ¡y así se me agradece!; **she murmured her ~** dio las gracias murmurando **2 ~ to:** ~ **to you ...** gracias a ti ...; (iro) por culpa tuya ...; **small/no ~ to you** no fue gracias a ti; **I got the job ~ to him** conseguí el trabajo a or por mediación suya; **~ to the rain the game was abandoned** debido a la lluvia el partido fue anulado

Ⓑ EXCL (*) **thanks!** ¡gracias!; **many ~!** ◇ **~ very much!** ◇ **~ a lot!** ¡muchas gracias!; **~ for letting me know** gracias por contármelo or decírmelo; **you went and told her? ~ a lot!** (iro) ¡y se lo dijiste!, ¡gracias, hombre!

thanksgiving [ˈθæŋksˌgɪvɪŋ] N acción f de gracias, voto m

de gracias ➤ **Thanksgiving Day** (US) día m de Acción de Gracias

---

THANKSGIVING

Desde 1621, el cuarto jueves de noviembre se celebra en Estados Unidos el Día de Acción de Gracias **Thanksgiving** o **Thanksgiving Day** para conmemorar la fecha en que los primeros colonos norteamericanos (**Pilgrim Fathers**) celebraron un acto de acción de gracias por el éxito de su primera cosecha en suelo americano. La celebración suele reunir a toda la familia alrededor de la comida típica del Día de Acción de Gracias (**Thanksgiving meal**), que consiste en pavo asado y pastel de calabaza.

En Canadá se celebra una fiesta semejante el segundo lunes de octubre, aunque no está relacionada con dicha fecha histórica. ⇨ PILGRIM FATHERS

---

thank-you, thankyou [ˈθæŋkjuː] N **now a big ~ to John** ahora, nuestro más sincero agradecimiento a John

---

that

Ⓐ DEMONSTRATIVE ADJECTIVE	Ⓓ ADVERB
Ⓑ DEMONSTRATIVE PRONOUN	Ⓔ CONJUNCTION
Ⓒ RELATIVE PRONOUN	

Those is treated as a separate entry.

---

that [(strong form) ðæt, (weak form) ðət] (pl **those**) Ⓐ DEMONSTRATIVE ADJECTIVE (nearer) ese m, esa f; (more remote) aquel m, aquella f;

You can generally use **ese** etc when pointing to something near the person you are speaking to. Use **aquel** etc for something which is distant from both of you:

~ hill over there aquella colina de allí; **~ lad of yours** ese chico tuyo; **what about ~ cheque?** ¿y el cheque ese?; **~ one** ése m, ésa f; (more remote) aquél m, aquélla f

---

Aquel is used to refer to a time in the distant past. Use **ese** if you mention a concrete date, month, year etc:

---

do you remember ~ holiday we had in Holland? ¿te acuerdas de aquellas vacaciones que pasamos en Holanda?; **May! we can't come ~ month** ¿en mayo? ese mes no podemos ir Ⓑ DEMONSTRATIVE PRONOUN (nearer) ése m, ésa f, eso neuter; (more remote) aquél m, aquélla f, aquello neuter;

You can generally use **ése** etc when pointing to something near the person you are speaking to. Use **aquél** etc for something which is distant from both of you. Note that the masculine and feminine pronouns carry accents to distinguish them from the masculine and feminine adjectives, though these can be omitted if there is no ambiguity. Neuter pronouns never carry an accent.

---

who's ~? ¿quién es ése?; **what's ~?** ¿qué es eso?, ¿eso qué es?; **~'s my French teacher over there** aquél es mi profesor de francés; **~'s my sister over by the window** aquélla de la ventana es mi hermana; **is ~ you, Paul?** ¿eres tú, Paul?; **£5? it must have cost more than ~** ¿cinco libras? debe haber costado más (que eso); **~'s impossible** eso es imposible; **~'s odd!** ¡qué raro!, ¡qué cosa más rara!; **~ was the year you graduated** ése fue el año en que acabaste la carrera; **after ~** después de eso; **bees and wasps and all ~** abejas, avispas y cosas así; **~'s all I can tell you** eso es todo lo que puedo decirte; **is ~ all?** ¿eso es todo?, ¿nada más?; **she's not as**

stupid as (all) ~ no es tan estúpida como para eso; **and it was broken at** ~ y además estaba roto; **at** ~ **I panicked** entonces me entró el pánico, en esto me entró el pánico; **what do you mean by** ~? ¿qué quieres decir con eso?; **it will cost 20 dollars, if** ~ costará 20 dólares, si es que llega; ~ **is ...** (= i.e.) es decir ...; ~'**s it, we've finished** ya está, hemos terminado; **they get their wages and** ~'**s it** tienen un sueldo y eso es todo; ~'**s it! she can find her own gardener!** ¡se acabó! ¡que se busque un jardinero por su cuenta!; **do it like** ~ hazlo así; **a hurricane like** ~ **of 1987** un huracán como el de 1987; ~ **is to say ...** es decir ...; ~'**s what he said** eso es lo que dijo; ~ **which** (frm) lo que, aquello que; **with** ~ con eso; ✦ IDIOMS **that's that: you can't go and that's** ~ no puedes irte sin más, no puedes ir y no hay más qué decir, no puedes ir y sanseacabó; **so** ~ **was** ~ y no había más que hacer, y ahí terminó la cosa
ⓒ RELATIVE PRONOUN

Unlike **that**, **que** cannot be omitted.

que; **the man** ~ **came in** el hombre que entró; **the book – I read** el libro que leí; **the girl** ~ **met on holiday and later married** la chica que conoció durante las vacaciones y con la que después se casó; **the evening** ~ **we went to the theatre** la tarde (en) que fuimos al teatro; **all – I have** todo lo que tengo; **fool – I am!** ¡tonto que soy!

If the **that** clause ends in a preposition, you can either translate **that** as **que** (usually preceded by the definite article) or as ARTICLE + **cual/cuales**.

the actor ~ **I was telling you about** el actor del que te hablaba; **the box – I put it in** la caja donde lo puse, la caja en la que or en la cual lo puse
ⓓ ADVERB tan; **I didn't know he was** ~ **ill** no sabía que estuviera tan enfermo; **it's about** ~ **big** (with gesture) es más o menos así de grande; ~ **much money** tanto dinero; **it was** ~ **cold!*** ¡hacía tanto frío!
ⓔ CONJUNCTION

Unlike **that**, **que** cannot be omitted.

1 (AFTER VERB) que; **he said** ~ **he was going to London and would be back in the evening** dijo que se iba a Londres y (que) volvería por la tarde
2 (AFTER NOUN)

Translate as **de que** in phrases like **the idea/belief/hope that:**

any hope ~ **they might have survived was fading** toda esperanza de que hubiesen sobrevivido se estaba desvaneciendo
3 (= in order that) para que + subjun; **those who died** ~ **we might live** los que lucharon para que nosotros pudiésemos vivir
4 (in expressions)
✦ **in that** en el sentido de que; **it's an attractive investment in** ~ **it is tax-free** es una inversión atractiva en el sentido de que está exenta de impuestos
✦ **not that: ..., not** ~ **I want to, of course** ..., no es que yo quiera, por supuesto; **not** ~ **I know of** que yo sepa, no

thatched [θætʃt] ADJ ~ **cottage** casita f con techo de paja; ~ **roof** techo m de paja

Thatcherite ['θætʃəraɪt] ADJ, N thatcheriano/a m/f

thaw [θɔː] **ⓐ** N deshielo m; [of snow] derretimiento m; **the** ~ **in East-West relations** la distensión en las relaciones Este-Oeste **ⓑ** VT (also ~ **out**) [+ frozen food] descongelar **ⓒ** VI [snow] derretirse; [ice] deshelarse; [frozen food] (also ~ **out**) descongelarse; [relations] distenderse; **I sat by the fire to** ~ **out** me senté junto al fuego para entrar en calor; **he began to** ~ (= get friendlier) empezó a relajarse or perder su reserva inicial

the [(strong form) ðiː, (weak form) ðə] **ⓐ** DEF ART **1** (singular) el/la; (plural) los/las

Note: **a** + **el** changes to **al** and **de** + **el** changes to **del**

we went to ~ **theatre** fuimos al teatro; ~ **soup of** ~ **day** la sopa del día; **do you know** ~ **Smiths?** ¿conoce a los Smith?; **how's** ~ **leg?** ¿cómo va la pierna?; **to play** ~ **piano** tocar el piano; **in this age of** ~ **computer ...** en esta época del ordenador ...
2 (+ adjective to form noun) (denoting sing) lo; (denoting plural) los/las; **to attempt** ~ **impossible** intentar lo imposible; ~ **rich** los ricos
3 (+ comparative, superlative) el/la; **she was** ~ **oldest** era la mayor
4 (= per) por; **they are sold by** ~ **dozen** se venden por docena; **paid by** ~ **hour** pagado por hora; **700 lire to** ~ **dollar** 700 liras por dólar
5 (emphatic) **you don't mean THE professor Bloggs?** ¿quieres decir el profesor Bloggs del que tanto se habla?; **it was THE colour of 1995** fue el color que estaba tan de moda en 1995
6 (in titles) **Richard** ~ **Second** Ricardo Segundo
ⓑ ADV ~ **more he works** ~ **more he earns** cuanto más trabaja más gana; ~ **sooner** ~ **better** cuanto antes mejor

theatre, theater (US) ['θɪətə'] N **1** teatro m; **to go to the** ~ ir al teatro **2** (Brit) (in hospital) sala f de operaciones

theatre-goer, theater-goer (US) ['θɪətə,ɡəʊə'] N aficionado/a m/f al teatro

theatrical [θɪ'ætrɪkəl] ADJ **1** [production, performance, tradition] teatral; **the** ~ **world** el mundo del teatro or de las tablas **2** (= melodramatic) teatral, histriónico, teatrero (pej)

thee [ðiː] PRON (†poet) te; (after prep) ti; **with** ~ contigo

theft [θeft] N robo m

their [ðeə'] POSS ADJ (with singular noun) su; (with plural noun) sus; ~ **house** su casa; ~ **sisters** sus hermanas

Their is usually translated by the definite article **el/los** or **la/las** when its clear from the sentence who the possessor is, particularly when referring to clothing or parts of the body:

they took off ~ **coats** se quitaron los abrigos; **after washing** ~ **hands** después de lavarse las manos; **they had** ~ **car stolen** alguien les robó el coche; **somebody left** ~ **jacket behind** alguien se ha dejado la chaqueta

theirs [ðeəz] POSS PRON **1** (referring to singular possession) (el/la) suyo/a; (referring to plural possession) (los/las) suyos/as

Only use the article with **suyo/suyos** etc when you mean the one(s) belonging to them.

it's not our car, it's ~ no es nuestro coche, es suyo or es de ellos; **Emma is a friend of** ~ Emma es amiga suya; **it's one of** ~ es suyo, es de ellos, es uno de los suyos; **that stupid son of** ~ el imbécil de su hijo; **the house became** ~ la casa pasó a ser suya or de su propiedad; **"is this their house?" — "no,** ~ **is a bit further on"** —¿es ésta su casa? —no, la suya or la de ellos está un poco más lejos; **my parents and** ~ mis padres y los suyos; ~ **is a happy home** el suyo es un hogar feliz
2 (= his or hers) **if anyone takes one that isn't** ~ si alguien toma uno que no sea suyo

them [ðem, ðəm] PRON **1** (direct object) los/las; **I didn't know** ~ no los conocía; **look at** ~! ¡míralos!; **I had to give** ~ **to her** tuve que dárselos
2 (indirect object) les; (combined with direct object pron) se; **I gave** ~ **some brochures** les di unos folletos; **you must tell** ~ **the truth** tienes que decirles la verdad; **yes, of course I gave it to** ~ sí, claro que se la; **I gave the money to** ~, **not their parents** les di el dinero a ellos, no a sus padres; **give it to** ~ **tomorrow** dáselo mañana
3 (after prepositions, in comparisons, with verb "to be") ellos/ellas; **it's for** ~ es para ellos; **we are older than** ~ somos mayores que ellos; **it must be** ~ deben de ser ellos; BUT

they were carrying them on ~ los llevaban encima *or* consigo
4 (*referring back to "someone", "anyone" etc: direct object*) lo *or* (*Sp*) le/la; (*indirect object*) le; **if anyone tries to talk to you, ignore ~** si alguien trata de hablar contigo, no le hagas caso

theme [θi:m] N tema *m* ➤ **theme park** parque *m* de atracciones temático ➤ **theme song** tema *m* musical ➤ **theme tune: he was humming the ~ James Bond theme tune** tarareaba la música de James Bond

themselves [ðəm'selvz] PRON **1** (*reflexive*) se; **did they hurt ~?** ¿se hicieron daño?
2 (*for emphasis*) ellos mismos/ellas mismas; **they built it ~** lo construyeron ellos mismos
3 (*after prep*) sí mismos/as, ellos/as mismos/as; **they talked mainly about ~** hablaron principalmente de sí mismos *or* ellos mismos
4 by ~: she left the children at home by ~ dejó a los niños solos en casa; **the girls did it all by ~** (= *completed task*) las chicas lo hicieron todo ellas solas; (= *achieved sth big*) las chicas lo hicieron todo por sí mismas

then [ðen] **Ⓐ** ADV **1** (= *at that time*) entonces; (= *on that occasion*) en aquel momento, en aquella ocasión; (= *at that period in time*) en aquel entonces, en aquella época; **it was ~ that ...** fue entonces cuando ...; **by ~** para entonces; **even ~ it didn't work** aún así, no funcionaba; **from ~ on** desde aquel momento, desde entonces, a partir de entonces; **just ~ he came in** entró justo entonces; **I wasn't doing anything just ~** justo en ese momento no estaba haciendo nada; **(every) now and ~** de vez en cuando; **since ~** desde entonces; **he wanted it done there and ~** quería que lo hicieran en el acto *or* en ese mismo momento; **until ~** hasta entonces
2 (= *afterwards, next*) después, luego; **what happened ~?** ¿qué pasó después *or* luego?; **and ~ what?** ¿y luego qué?
3 (= *in that case*) entonces; **what do you want me to do ~?** ¿entonces, qué quieres que haga?; **~ you don't want it?** ¿así que no lo quieres?; **but ~ we shall lose money** pero en ese caso perderemos dinero
4 (= *furthermore*) además; **and ~ there's the family** y además tengo que pensar en la familia
5 (*in summarizing*) **this, ~, was the situation** esta era, pues, *or* esta era, por (lo) tanto, la situación
6 (= *having said that*) **and ~ again** por otra parte; **I like it, but ~ I'm biased** a mí sí me gusta, pero yo no soy objetivo
Ⓑ ADJ entonces, de entonces; **the ~ king** el entonces rey

thence [ðens] ADV (*frm*) **1** (= *from that place*) de allí, desde allí **2** (= *consequently*) por lo tanto, por eso, por consiguiente

thenceforth [ˌðens'fɔ:θ], **thenceforward** [ˌðens'fɔ:wəd] ADV (*frm*) desde entonces, de allí en adelante, a partir de entonces

theologian [θɪə'ləʊdʒən] N teólogo/a *m/f*

theological [θɪə'lɒdʒɪkəl] ADJ teológico ➤ **theological college** seminario *m*

theology [θɪ'ɒlədʒɪ] N teología *f*

theorem ['θɪərəm] N teorema *m*

theoretical [θɪə'retɪkəl] ADJ teórico

theoretically [θɪə'retɪkəlɪ] ADV teóricamente, en teoría

theorize ['θɪəraɪz] VI teorizar (**about** cerca de)

theory ['θɪərɪ] N teoría *f*; **in ~** en teoría, teóricamente

therapeutic [ˌθerə'pju:tɪk] ADJ terapéutico

therapist ['θerəpɪst] N terapeuta *mf*

therapy ['θerəpɪ] N terapia *f*

there [ðeəʳ] **Ⓐ** ADV **1** (*place*) (= *there near you*) ahí; (*less precisely*) allí; (*further away*) allá; **put it ~** ponlo ahí; **I don't know how to get ~** no sé cómo llegar allí; **~ he is!** ¡allí está!; **~'s the bus** ahí viene el autobús, ya viene el autobús; **~ we were, stuck** así que nos encontramos sin podernos mover de allí; **to go ~ and back** ir y volver; **12 kilometres ~ and back** 12 kilómetros ida y vuelta; **we left him back ~ at the crossroads** lo dejamos allí atrás, en el cruce; **to be ~ for sb** (= *supportive*) estar al lado de algn, apoyar a algn; **down ~ on the floor** ahí en el suelo; **let's go down ~ by the river** vamos

allí por el río; **it's in ~** está ahí dentro; **it's on ~** está ahí encima; **it's over ~ by the TV** está allí, junto al televisor; **~ and then** en el acto, en seguida; **up ~** ahí arriba; ✦ IDIOM **he's not all ~** le falta un tornillo*
2 (= *in existence*) **if the demand is ~, the product will appear** si existe la demanda, aparecerá el producto; **the money just isn't ~** sencillamente (es que) no hay dinero; **the old church is still ~ today** la vieja iglesia todavía está en pie *or* existe hoy
3 (= *present*) **all the family were ~** la familia al completo estaba allí; **is John ~, please?** (*on phone*) ¿está John?
4 (= *on that point*) en eso; **I agree with you ~** en eso estoy de acuerdo contigo
5 (= *at that point*) **we'll leave it ~ for today** lo dejaremos aquí por hoy; **could I just stop you ~ and say something?** ¿puedo interrumpirle para decir algo al respecto?
6 (*other uses*) **~ again** por otra parte; **~ you are** (*offering sth*) ahí lo tienes; **ah ~ you are!** (= *I've found you*) ¡ah! ¿estabas aquí?; **~ you are, what did I tell you!** ¿ves? es lo que te dije; **you press this switch and ~ you are!** tienes que pulsar este interruptor y ya está; **~ you go again, upsetting the children** ¿vuelta a las andadas, molestando a los niños?, ¿ya estamos otra vez molestando a los niños?; **it wasn't what I wanted, but ~ you go*** no era lo que buscaba, pero ¿qué le vamos a hacer?; **hurry up ~!** ¡menearse!; **you ~!** ¡oye, tú!, ¡eh, usted! (*more frm*)
Ⓑ PRON **~ is/are** hay; **~ will be** habrá; **~ were** había *or* (*esp LAm*) habían; **how many are ~?** ¿cuántos hay?; **~ was laughter at this** en esto hubo risas; **~ was singing and dancing** se cantó y se bailó; **~ has been an accident** ha habido un accidente; **is ~ any coffee?** ¿hay café?

If **there is/are** is followed by **the**, you should generally use **estar** instead of **hay** *etc*:

and then ~ are the neighbours to consider están también los vecinos, a los que hay que tener en cuenta

Use **ser** not **hay** *etc* to translate phrases like **there are four of us**:

~ are four of us somos cuatro; **~ will be six of them** serán seis; **~ is no wine left** no queda vino
Ⓒ EXCL **~, now look what you've done!** desde luego, ¡mira lo que has hecho!; **~, what did I tell you?** ¿lo ves? ¿no te lo había dicho?; **there, there** (*comforting*) no te preocupes, no pasa nada

thereabouts ['ðeərəbaʊts] ADV **1** (*place*) por ahí, allí cerca **2** (*number*) **12 or ~** 12 más o menos, alrededor de 12; **£5 or ~** cinco libras o así

thereafter [ðeər'ɑːftəʳ] ADV (*frm*) después de eso, de allí en adelante, a partir de entonces

thereby ['ðeə'baɪ] ADV así, de ese modo

therefore ['ðeəfɔ:ʳ] ADV por tanto, por lo tanto

therein [ðeər'ɪn] ADV (*frm*) en eso, en esto; **~ lies the danger** ahí está el peligro, en eso consiste el peligro

there's [ðeəz] = **there is**, **there has**

thereupon ['ðeərə'pɒn] ADV (*frm*) **1** (= *at that point*) acto seguido, en eso, con eso **2** (= *on that subject*) sobre eso

thermal ['θɜ:məl] **Ⓐ** ADJ [*current*] termal; [*underwear, blanket*] térmico **Ⓑ** N térmica *f*, corriente *f* térmica **Ⓒ** CPD ➤ **thermal baths, thermal springs** baños *mpl* termales, termas *fpl*

thermodynamics ['θɜ:məʊdaɪ'næmɪks] NSING termodinámica *f*

thermometer [θə'mɒmɪtəʳ] N termómetro *m*

thermonuclear ['θɜ:məʊ'nju:klɪəʳ] ADJ termonuclear

Thermos® ['θɜ:məs] N (*also* **~ flask** (*Brit*) *or* **~ bottle** (*US*)) termo *m*

thermostat ['θɜ:məstæt] N termostato *m*

thesaurus [θɪ'sɔ:rəs] N (*pl* **~es** *or* **thesauri** [θɪ'sɔ:raɪ]) tesauro *m*

these [ði:z] **Ⓐ** DEM ADJ éstos/éstas; **~ ones over here** éstos/éstas de aquí, éstos/éstas que están aquí; **how are you**

getting on ~ days? ¿cómo le va últimamente? **B** DEM PRON éstos/éstas; **what are ~?** ¿qué son éstos?; **~ are my friends** éstos son mis amigos

thesis ['θiːsɪs] N (pl **theses** ['θiːsiːz]) tesis f inv

thespian ['θespɪən] N (esp hum) actor m, actriz f

they [ðeɪ] PRON **1** (emphatic, to avoid ambiguity) ellos/ellas; **we went to the cinema but ~ didn't** nosotros fuimos al cine pero ellos no; **we work harder than ~ do** trabajamos más que ellos

> Don't translate the subject pronoun when not emphasizing or clarifying:

~'re yellow son amarillos **2** (= he or she) **if anyone tells you otherwise, ~'re mistaken** si alguien te dice lo contrario, no tiene razón **3** (generalizing) **~ say that ...** se dice que ..., dicen que ...; **~ are making it illegal** lo van a hacer ilegal

they'd [ðeɪd] = **they would, they had**

they'll [ðeɪl] = **they will, they shall**

they're [ðeəʳ] = **they are**

they've [ðeɪv] = **they have**

thick [θɪk] **A** ADJ (compar **~er**; superl **~est**) **1** (= not thin) [wall, line, slice, neck] grueso; [lips] grueso, carnoso; [sweater] gordo; [spectacles] de lente gruesa; **a ~ layer of snow/dust** una espesa capa de nieve/polvo; **a ~ layer of potatoes** una capa gruesa de patatas; **it's 2 metres ~** tiene 2 metros de grosor; **to give sb a ~ ear*** dar un sopapo a algn*; **how ~ is it?** ¿qué grosor tiene?, ¿cómo es de grueso?; **that's a bit ~*** eso ya pasa de castaño oscuro* **2** (= dense) [beard, eyebrows] poblado; [carpet, fur] tupido; [forest] tupido, poblado; [vegetation, dust] espeso; [smoke, clouds, night] denso; [fog] espeso, denso; **to be ~ with** (gen) estar lleno de; **the air was ~ with smoke** el aire estaba cargado or lleno de humo **3** (= not runny) [yoghurt, sauce] espeso **4** (Brit*) (= stupid) corto*, burro*; **I finally got it into his ~ head** por fin conseguí que le entrase en esa cabeza hueca* **5** (= strong) [accent] fuerte, marcado **6** [voice] pastoso; **I woke up with a ~ head** me desperté con la cabeza embotada **7** ✦ IDIOM **to be (as) ~ as thieves*** ser uña y carne* **B** ADV **slice the bread nice and ~** corte el pan en rebanadas bien gruesas; ✦ IDIOMS **to come/follow ~ and fast** llegar/sucederse con rapidez; **to lay it on ~*** cargar or recargar las tintas* **C** N **he likes to be in the ~ of the action** le gusta estar metido en el meollo del asunto or en el ajo; **he was in the ~ of the fighting** estaba en lo más intenso de la lucha; ✦ IDIOM **through ~ and thin** en las duras y en las maduras

thicken ['θɪkən] **A** VT espesar, hacer más espeso **B** VI [mixture, sauce] espesarse; ✦ IDIOM **the plot ~s** la cosa se complica

thicket ['θɪkɪt] N matorral m

thickly ['θɪklɪ] ADV **1** (= densely) densamente; **the snow was falling ~** la nieve caía con fuerza or copiosamente **2** (= in a thick layer) **she spread the butter ~ on the toast** untó una gruesa capa de mantequilla en la tostada **3** (= in thick pieces) **to cut/slice sth ~** [+ vegetable, fruit] cortar algo en rodajas gruesas; [+ bread] cortar algo en rebanadas gruesas **4** [say, reply] con voz pastosa

thickness ['θɪknɪs] N **1** [of wall, door, layer] grosor m, espesor m; [of cream, sauce] lo espeso **2** (= layer) capa f

thickset [θɪk'set] ADJ robusto, fornido

thick-skinned [ˌθɪk'skɪnd] ADJ [person] insensible, duro

thief [θiːf] N (pl **thieves** [θiːvz]) ladrón/ona m/f; **stop ~!** ¡al ladrón!

thieving ['θiːvɪŋ] **A** ADJ ladrón **B** N robo m, hurto m

thigh [θaɪ] N muslo m ➤ **thigh bone** fémur m

thimble ['θɪmbl] N dedal m

thin [θɪn] **A** ADJ (compar **~ner**; superl **~nest**) **1** (= not fat) [person, legs, arms] delgado, flaco (pej); [face] delgado; [lips] fino; [animal] flaco; **to get ~(ner)** adelgazar; ✦ IDIOM **to be**

as ~ as a rake* estar en los huesos* **2** (= not thick) [layer, sheet] fino, delgado; [wall] delgado; [slice, line, fabric] fino; **a ~ layer of paint** una capa fina de pintura; **my patience is wearing ~** se me está agotando or acabando la paciencia; ✦ IDIOM **to walk on ~ ice** estar pisando terreno resbaladizo or peligroso **3** (= watery) [custard, sauce, paint] poco espeso **4** (= not dense) [smoke, fog, rain] fino **5** (= sparse) [beard, hair] ralo, escaso; [eyebrows] fino, delgado; [crowd] escaso, poco numeroso; ✦ IDIOMS **to be ~ on the ground** (esp Brit) escasear; **to be ~ on top** estar casi calvo, tener poco pelo (en la cabeza) **6** (= feeble) [excuse] pobre, poco convincente; [evidence] poco concluyente; [argument] pobre, flojo; [majority] escaso **7** (= weak) [voice] aflautado **8** [air, atmosphere] enrarecido, rarificado; ✦ IDIOM **to produce sth out of ~ air** sacar algo de la nada; **he vanished into ~ air** desapareció como por arte de magia, se lo tragó la tierra **B** ADV [cut] en rodajas finas **C** VT [+ sauce, soup] aclarar; [+ paint] diluir **D** VI (also **~ out**) [fog] aclararse; [ozone layer] hacerse menos espeso; [crowd] disminuir

thine [ðaɪn] (poet†) **A** POSS PRON (sing) (el) tuyo, (la) tuya; (pl) (los) tuyos, (las) tuyas **B** ADJ (sing) tu; (pl) tus

thing [θɪŋ] N **1** (= object) cosa f; **what's that ~ called?** ¿cómo se llama eso?; **a ~ of beauty** una belleza, un objeto bello; **~s of value** objetos mpl de valor; ✦ IDIOM **you must be seeing ~s** estás viendo visiones **2** (= matter) cosa f, asunto m, cuestión f; **as ~s are** tal como están las cosas; **that's how ~s are** así están las cosas; **how are ~s (with you)?** ¿qué tal (te va)?; **the ~ is ...** lo que pasa es que ..., el caso es que ...; **what a ~ to say!** ¡qué dices!, ¡cómo se te ocurre!; **I haven't done a ~ about it** no he hecho nada de nada al respecto; **I don't know a ~ about cars** no sé nada en absoluto de coches; **all ~s considered** bien mirado; **and for another ~ ...** y además ..., y por otra parte ...; **the best ~ would be to wait** lo mejor sería esperar; **it's a good ~ he didn't see you** menos mal que no te vio; **the good ~ about it is that ...** lo bueno es que ...; **it's just the ~!** ¡es justo lo que me faltaba!; **the main ~** lo más importante, lo principal; **for one ~** en primer lugar; **it's one ~ to buy it, quite another to make it work** es fácil comprarlo, pero no es tan fácil hacerlo funcionar; **did you ever see such a ~?** ¿se vio jamás tal cosa?; **there's no such ~!** ¡no hay tal!; **it's just one of those ~s** son cosas que pasan, son cosas de la vida; **he knows a ~ or two** sabe de qué va; **I could tell you a ~ or two about her** podría decirte unas cuantas cosas sobre ella; ✦ IDIOM **to make a (big) ~ (out) of sth***: **he made a big ~ out of the accident** exageró mucho el accidente **3 things** (= belongings) cosas fpl; (= clothes) ropa fsing; (= luggage) equipaje msing; **she had brought her painting ~s with her** se había traído sus utensilios de pintura **4** (*) (= person) **you mean ~!** ¡mira que eres tacaño!; **(you) poor ~!** ¡pobrecito!; **she's a sweet little ~** es monísima **5** (*) (= activity, preference) **his ~ is fast cars** lo suyo son los coches rápidos; **it's not my ~** no es lo mío **6** (*) (= obsession) obsesión f; (= phobia) fobia f; **he has a ~ about cleanliness** está obsesionado con la limpieza, tiene obsesión or manía con la limpieza; **she has a ~ about snakes** le tiene fobia a las serpientes

thingamajig* ['θɪŋəmɪdʒɪg], **thingummy*** ['θɪŋəmɪ], **thingy*** ['θɪŋɪ] N (= object) chisme m, cosa f; (= person) fulano/a m/f

think [θɪŋk] (vb: pt, pp **thought**) **A** VI **1** (gen) pensar; (= ponder) reflexionar; **to act without ~ing** actuar sin pensar; **~ before you reply** piénselo antes de contestar; **now let me ~** a ver, déjame pensar; **give me time to ~** dame tiempo para reflexionar; **I'm sorry, I wasn't ~ing** lo siento, estaba distraído; **to ~ about sth** (= occupy one's thoughts with) pensar en algo; (= consider) pensar algo; **what are you ~ing about?** ¿en qué estás pensando?; **I'll ~ about it** lo voy a pensar; **to ~ aloud** pensar en voz alta; **~ carefully before you reply** piénsalo bien antes de responder; **to ~ for o.s.** pensar por sí mismo; **I'll be ~ing of you** me acordaré de ti; **to ~ straight** concentrarse; **to ~ twice before doing sth**

pensar algo dos veces antes de hacerlo
2 (= *imagine*) imaginarse; **just ~!** ¡fíjate!, ¡imagínate!, ¡te das cuenta!; ~ **of the expense** imagínate lo que costaría; **and to ~ of her going there alone!** ¡y pensar que ella fue allí sola!
3 (= *remember*) **now I come to ~ of it ...** ahora que lo pienso ...; **I couldn't ~ of the right word** no pude acordarme de la palabra exacta
4 (= *have opinion*) **what do you ~ of him?** ¿qué opinas de él?, ¿qué te parece (él)?; **I told him what I thought of him** le dije lo que pensaba de él; **to ~ highly of sb** tener muy buena opinión de algn, tener a algn en muy buen concepto; **I didn't ~ much of the play** la obra no me convenció, la obra no me gustó mucho
5 (= *consider*) **to ~ of other people's feelings** pensar en *or* tener en cuenta los sentimientos de los demás; **he ~s of nobody but himself** no piensa más que en sí mismo; **have you ever thought of going to Cuba?** ¿has pensado alguna vez en ir a Cuba?; **whatever were you ~ing of?** ¿cómo se te ocurrió hacer eso?; **I was the one who thought of it first** fui yo quien tuve la idea primero
Ⓑ VT **1** (*gen*) pensar; (= *consider*) pensar en; **to ~ great thoughts** pensar cosas profundas, tener pensamientos profundos; ~ **what you've done** piense en lo que hizo
2 (= *believe*) creer; **I ~ (that) it is true** creo que es verdad; **I don't ~ it can be done** no creo que se pueda hacer; **I don't ~ it likely** lo creo *or* me parece muy poco probable; **I ~ (that) you're wrong** me parece que estás equivocado; **I ~ so** creo que sí, me parece que sí; **I don't ~ so** creo que no; **what do you ~ I should do?** ¿qué crees que debo hacer?; **who do you ~ you are?** ¿quién te crees que eres?; **anyone would ~ she was dying** cualquiera diría que se estaba muriendo
3 (= *imagine*) imaginar(se); ~ **what we could do with that house!** ¡imagina lo que podríamos hacer con esa casa!; **I thought as much** ya me lo figuraba, ya lo sabía; **who'd have thought it?** ¿quién lo diría?
4 (= *be of opinion*) opinar; **this is my new dress, what do you ~?** éste es mi vestido nuevo, ¿qué te parece? *or* ¿qué opinas?
5 (= *envisage*) **I didn't ~ to tell him** no se me ocurrió decírselo; **I'd thought I might go swimming** había pensado en ir a nadar
6 (= *expect*) pensar, esperar; **I didn't ~ to see you here** no pensaba *or* esperaba verte aquí; **"I paid him for it" — "I should ~ so too!"** —se lo he pagado —¡faltaría más!
Ⓒ N **I'll have a ~ about it** lo pensaré
Ⓓ CPD ➤ **think tank** grupo *m* de expertos; (*in government*) gabinete *m* de estrategia
➤ **think back** VI + ADV recordar; **I ~ back to that moment when ...** recuerdo ese momento cuando ...
➤ **think out** VT + ADV [+ *plan*] elaborar; [+ *problem*] meditar a fondo; [+ *solution, response*] encontrar; **a well thought out answer** una respuesta muy elaborada
➤ **think over** VT + ADV pensar, considerar; **I'll ~ it over** pensaré; ~ **it over!** ¡piénsatelo!, ¡piénsalo!
➤ **think through** VT + ADV [+ *plan*] planear detenidamente, planear cuidadosamente; [+ *implications*] considerar detenidamente, examinar detenidamente
➤ **think up** VT + ADV [+ *plan*] idear; [+ *idea*] tener; [+ *solution*] idear, inventar

thinker ['θɪŋkə'] N pensador(a) *m/f*

thinking ['θɪŋkɪŋ] **Ⓐ** N pensamiento *m*, ideas *fpl*; **to my way of ~** en mi opinión, bajo mi punto de vista; **good ~!** ¡buena idea!; **I'll have to do some serious ~** voy a tener que pensar *or* reflexionar seriamente **Ⓑ** ADJ [*person, machine*] inteligente; **the ~ mind** la mente racional

thinly ['θɪnlɪ] ADV **1** = *cut/sliced* [*vegetable, fruit*] cortado en rodajas finas; [*bread*] cortado en rebanadas finas; [*ham, bacon*] cortado en lonchas finas **2** (= *in a thin layer*) **roll out the pastry very ~** estirar la masa hasta que quede muy fina; **spread the butter ~** untar una capa fina de mantequilla; **a ~ veiled threat/warning** una amenaza/advertencia mal disimulada

thinner ['θɪnə'] N disolvente *m; see also* **thin**

thinness ['θɪnnɪs] N **1** [*of person, arms, face*] delgadez *f*; [*of animal*] flacura *f* **2** [*of layer, sheet, wall*] delgadez *f*; [*of slice, line*] lo fino **3** [*of air, atmosphere*] lo enrarecido

thin-skinned ['θɪn'skɪnd] ADJ sensible, susceptible

third [θɜːd] **Ⓐ** ADJ tercero; (*before m sing noun*) tercer; **on his ~ birthday** en su tercer cumpleaños, cuando cumpla/cumplió tres años; **in the ~ century** (*spoken form*) en el siglo tercero *or* tres; (*in writing*) en el siglo III; ~ **time lucky!** ¡a la tercera va la vencida!
Ⓑ PRON **1** (*in series*) tercero/a *m/f*
2 (= *fraction*) tercera parte *f*, tercio *m*
3 (*in dates*) tres *m*; **he arrives on June (the) ~** *or* **the ~ of June** llega el tres de junio; **it's June (the) ~** *or* **the ~ of June** estamos a tres de junio, es tres de junio
4 (*in titles*) **Henry the ~** (*spoken form*) Enrique tercero; (*in writing*) Enrique III
5 (*also* ~ **gear**) tercera *f* (velocidad *f*); **in ~** en tercera
6 (*Brit Univ*) tercera clase *f*
7 (*Mus*) tercera *f*
Ⓒ ADV (*in third place*) en tercer lugar, en tercera posición; **to finish ~** (*in race*) llegar el tercero, llegar en tercer lugar *or* en tercera posición
Ⓓ CPD ➤ **third party** tercero *m*, tercera persona *f* ➤ **third party insurance** (*Brit*) seguro *m* contra terceros, seguro *m* de responsabilidad social (*Sp*) ➤ **third person** (*Gram*) tercera persona *f* ➤ **Third World** Tercer Mundo *m*

third-class [,θɜːd'klɑːs] **Ⓐ** ADJ de tercera clase; (*pej*) de tercera **Ⓑ** ADV **to travel ~** viajar en tercera **Ⓒ** N (*US Post*) tarifa *f* de impreso

thirdly ['θɜːdlɪ] ADV en tercer lugar

third-rate [,θɜːd'reɪt] ADJ (*pej*) de tercera

third-world ['θɜːdwɜːld] ADJ tercermundista

thirst [θɜːst] **Ⓐ** N sed *f*; **to have a ~ for sth** (*fig*) tener sed *or* ansias de algo **Ⓑ** VI **to ~ after** *or* **for sth** tener sed *or* ansias de algo, estar sediento de algo (*liter*)

thirstily ['θɜːstɪlɪ] ADV con avidez

thirsty ['θɜːstɪ] ADJ (*compar* **thirstier**; *superl* **thirstiest**) (*lit*) [*person, animal*] que tiene sed, sediento (*liter*); **to be ~** tener sed; **all this work is making me ~** todo este trabajo me está dando sed; **it's ~ work** da sed

thirteen ['θɜː'tiːn] NUMBER trece *m; see* **five**

thirteenth ['θɜː'tiːnθ] **Ⓐ** ADJ (*in series*) decimotercero/a *m/f*; (= *fraction*) decimotercera parte *f*, decimotercio *m; see* **fifteenth**

thirtieth ['θɜːtɪɪθ] **Ⓐ** ADJ trigésimo **Ⓑ** N (*in series*) trigésimo/a *m/f*, (= *fraction*) trigésima parte *f*, treintavo *m; see* **fifteenth**

thirty ['θɜːtɪ] NUMBER treinta *m; see* **fifty**

this [ðɪs] **Ⓐ** DEM ADJ (*pl* **these**) este/a; ~ **evening** esta tarde; ~ **one** éste/ésta; ~ **time** esta vez; ~ **time next week** de hoy en una semana; ~ **time last year** hoy hace un año; ~ **way** por aquí; ~ **week** esta semana
Ⓑ DEM PRON (*pl* **these**) éste/a; (*neuter*) esto; **who is ~?** ¿quién es?; **what is ~?** ¿qué es esto?; ~ **is Mr Brown** (*in introductions*) le presento al señor Brown; (*in photo*) éste es el señor Brown; (*on phone*) soy *or* al habla el señor Brown; **I prefer ~ to that** prefiero esto a aquello; ~ **is where I live** aquí vivo; ~ **is it** (= *that's the problem*) ahí está la dificultad; **what's all ~?** ¿qué pasa?; **what's all ~ I hear about you leaving?** ¿qué es eso de que te vas?; **do it like ~** hágalo así; **it was like ~ ...** te diré lo que pasó ...; **they were talking about ~ and that** hablaban de esto y lo otro; *see also* **these**
Ⓒ DEM ADV **I didn't know it was ~ far** no sabía que estaba tan lejos; **I've never been ~ far before** nunca había llegado hasta aquí; **the wall is ~ high** la pared es así de alta; **I've never seen ~ much money** nunca había visto tanto dinero junto; **I can tell you ~ much ...** lo que sí te puedo decir es ...

thistle ['θɪsl] N cardo *m*

tho' [ðəʊ] CONJ = **though**

thong [θɒŋ] N **1** (= *strap*) correa *f* **2** thongs (*US*) (= *sandals*) chancletas *fpl*

thorax ['θɔːræks] N (*pl* **-es** *or* **thoraces** ['θɔːrəsiːz]) tórax *m*

thorn [θɔːn] N espina *f*; ✦ IDIOM **to be a ~ in sb's side** *or* **flesh** ser una espina para algn

thorny ['θɔːnɪ] ADJ (*compar* **thornier**; *superl* **thorniest**) espinoso

thorough ['θʌrə] ADJ **1** (= *meticulous*) [*person, teacher*] concienzudo, meticuloso; [*examination, search, investigation*] riguroso, minucioso; [*training*] riguroso, a fondo; [*knowledge, understanding*] profundo, sólido; **to give sth a ~ clean** limpiar algo bien *or* a fondo **2** (*as intensifier*) **to make a ~ nuisance of o.s.** dar la lata a base de bien*

thoroughbred ['θʌrəbred] Ⓐ ADJ [*horse*] de pura sangre Ⓑ N pura sangre *mf*

thoroughfare ['θʌrəfɛəʳ] N (= *public highway*) vía *f* pública, carretera *f*; (= *street*) calle *f*; **"no thoroughfare"** "prohibido el paso"

thoroughgoing ['θʌrəɡəʊɪŋ] ADJ [*analysis*] minucioso; [*restructuring*] concienzudo, a fondo; [*conservative, revolutionary*] convencido, auténtico

thoroughly ['θʌrəlɪ] ADV **1** (= *meticulously*) [*clean, rinse, search, check*] a fondo; [*research*] minuciosamente, meticulosamente **2** (= *utterly*) **2.1** (*with verb*) [*deserve*] totalmente; [*discredit*] totalmente, por completo; **he ~ enjoyed himself** se divirtió muchísimo, se lo pasó en grande* **2.2** (*with adj*) [*enjoyable, unpleasant, miserable*] realmente, verdaderamente; [*modern*] totalmente

thoroughness ['θʌrənɪs] N [*of examination, search, research*] rigurosidad *f*, minuciosidad *f*; [*of person*] meticulosidad *f*

those [ðəʊz] Ⓐ DEM ADJ esos/esas; (*further away*) aquellos/aquellas; **~ ones over there** aquéllos de allí, aquéllos que están allí; **it's not these chocolates but ~ ones I like** no son estos bombones los que me gustan sino aquéllos Ⓑ DEM PRON ésos/ésas; (*further away*) aquéllos/aquéllas; **~ who** los que, las que, quienes; **~ of you/us who ...** los/las que ...; **I prefer these to ~** prefiero éstos a aquéllos; *see also* **that**

thou [ðaʊ] PRON (*poet†*) tú, vos††

though [ðəʊ] Ⓐ CONJ aunque; **~ it was raining** aunque llovía; **~ small, it's good** aunque (es) pequeño, es bueno, si bien es pequeño, es bueno; **as ~** como si + *subjun*; **even ~** aunque; **strange ~ it may appear** aunque parezca extraño, por muy extraño que parezca; **young ~ she is** aunque es joven, por muy joven que sea Ⓑ ADV sin embargo, aun así; **it's not so easy, ~** sin embargo *or* pero no es tan fácil; **it's difficult, ~, to put into practice** pero es difícil llevarlo a la práctica

thought [θɔːt] Ⓐ PT, PP *of* **think** Ⓑ N **1** pensamiento *m*; **Western** ~ el pensamiento occidental; **after much** ~ después de mucho pensarlo *or* pensarlo mucho; **I'll give it some ~ over the next few days** lo pensaré durante los próximos días; **I didn't give it another** ~ no volví a pensar en ello; **don't give it another** ~ no te preocupes, no lo pienses más; **with no ~ for o.s.** sin pensar en sí mismo **2** (= *idea*) idea *f*; (= *intention*) intención *f*; **the ~ crossed my mind that ...** se me ocurrió que ...; **I've just had a ~** se me acaba de ocurrir una idea; **never mind, it was just a ~** no importa, no era más que una idea; **that's a ~!** ¡no es mala idea!, ¡qué buena idea!; **"she might still be there"** — **"that's a ~"** —puede que todavía esté allí —es una posibilidad; ✦ IDIOM **it's the ~ that counts** la intención es lo que cuenta Ⓒ CPD ➤ **thought police** policía *f* política ➤ **thought process** proceso *m* mental ➤ **thought reader** adivino/a *m/f*

thoughtful ['θɔːtfʊl] ADJ **1** (= *pensive*) pensativo, meditabundo; **he looked ~** estaba pensativo *or* meditabundo **2** (= *considerate*) [*person*] atento, considerado; [*gesture*] amable, atento; **it was very ~ of you** fue muy amable de tu parte; **how ~ of him to invite me!** ¡qué detalle tuvo al invitarme!, ¡qué detalle por su parte el invitarme!

thoughtfully ['θɔːtfəlɪ] ADV **1** (= *pensively*) pensativamente, con aire pensativo **2** (= *considerately*) **she very ~ left out some food for us** tuvo el detalle de dejarnos algo de comida

thoughtless ['θɔːtlɪs] ADJ [*person*] poco considerado, desconsiderado; [*remark*] desconsiderado

thoughtlessly ['θɔːtlɪslɪ] ADV desconsideradamente

thoughtlessness ['θɔːtlɪsnɪs] N **1** (= *lack of consideration*) falta *f* de consideración, desconsideración *f* **2** (= *carelessness*) irreflexión *f*, inconsciencia *f*

thought-provoking ['θɔːtprəˌvəʊkɪŋ] ADJ que hace reflexionar

thousand ['θaʊzənd] NUMBER mil *m*; **a ~ ◇ one ~** mil; **two/five ~** dos/cinco mil; **a ~ and one/two** mil uno/dos; **they sell them by the ~** los venden a millares; **in their ~s** a millares; **~s of ...** miles de ...

thousandth ['θaʊzəntθ] Ⓐ ADJ milésimo Ⓑ PRON (*in classification*) número mil *m*; (= *fraction*) milésima parte *f*, milésimo *m*

thrash [θræʃ] Ⓐ VT **1** (= *beat*) apalear, dar una paliza a; (*as punishment*) azotar **2** (*) (= *defeat*) dar una paliza a*, cascar* Ⓑ VI (*also* ~ **about**, ~ **around**) revolverse; (*in water*) revolcarse
➤ **thrash out** VT + ADV [+ *problem, difficulty*] discutir a fondo; [+ *plan*] idear; [+ *deal*] alcanzar; **to ~ out an agreement** llegar a un acuerdo

thrashing ['θræʃɪŋ] N zurra *f*, paliza *f*; **to give sb a ~** (*lit*) zurrar a algn, dar una paliza a algn; (*Sport*) dar una paliza a algn*, cascar a algn*

thread [θred] Ⓐ N hilo *m*; **to lose the ~ (of what sb is saying)** perder el hilo (de lo que algn está diciendo) Ⓑ VT [+ *needle*] enhebrar; [+ *beads*] ensartar

threadbare ['θredbɛəʳ] ADJ [*clothes, carpet*] raído, gastado

threat [θret] N amenaza *f*; **to be a ~ to sth/sb** ser una amenaza para algo/algn; **to be under ~ from sth** verse amenazado por algo

threaten ['θretn] VT amenazar (**to do sth** con hacer algo); **to ~ sb with sth** amenazar a algn con algo; **to be ~ed with extinction** estar amenazado de extinción

threatening ['θretnɪŋ] ADJ (= *menacing*) amenazador; **to find sb ~** sentirse intimidado por algn

three [θriː] NUMBER tres *m*; **~ cheers!** ¡tres hurras! ➤ **the three Rs** lectura, escritura y aritmética; *see* **five**

La expresión **the three Rs** hace referencia a los tres aspectos que se consideran fundamentales en educación: **reading, writing and arithmetic** (lectura, escritura y aritmética). La expresión, que tiene su origen en la forma humorística en la que se escribe a veces la frase: **reading, 'riting, and 'rithmetic**, se menciona a menudo cuando se habla de la necesidad de mejorar la calidad de la enseñanza.

three-D, **3-D** ['θriː'diː] = **three-dimensional** Ⓐ ADJ tridimensional Ⓑ N in ~ en tres dimensiones

three-dimensional ['θriːdɪ'menʃənl] ADJ tridimensional

threefold ['θriːfəʊld] Ⓐ ADJ triple Ⓑ ADV tres veces

three-piece ['θriːpiːs] ADJ ➤ **three-piece suit** terno *m*, traje *m* de tres piezas ➤ **three-piece suite** (*esp Brit*) tresillo *m*, juego *m* de living (*LAm*)

three-point turn [ˌθriːpɔɪnt'tɜːn] N cambio *m* de sentido haciendo tres maniobras

three-quarters [ˌθriː'kwɔːtəz] Ⓐ N tres cuartos *mpl*, tres cuartas partes *fpl*; **in ~ of an hour** en tres cuartos de hora Ⓑ ADV **the tank is ~ full** el depósito está lleno en sus tres cuartas partes

threesome ['θriːsəm] N grupo *m* de tres, trío *m*

three-way ['θriːweɪ] ADJ [*conversation*] entre tres personas; **~ split** división *f* en tercios

three-wheeler ['θriː'wiːləʳ] N (= *car*) coche *m* de tres ruedas; (= *tricycle*) triciclo *m*

thresh [θreʃ] VT, VI trillar

threshold ['θreʃhəʊld] N **1** (= *doorway*) umbral *m* **2** (*fig*) umbral *m*, puertas *fpl*; **to be on the ~ of** estar en el umbral *or* a las puertas de; **to have a low pain ~** tener poca tolerancia del dolor

threw [θruː] PT *of* **throw**

thrift [θrɪft], **thriftiness** ['θrɪftɪnɪs] N economía *f*, frugalidad *f* ➤ **thrift shop** (*US*), **thrift store** (*US*) tienda de *artículos de segunda mano que dedica su recaudación a causas benéficas*

thrifty ['θrɪftɪ] ADJ (*compar* **thriftier**; *superl* **thriftiest**) económico, frugal, ahorrativo

thrill [θrɪl] N emoción *f*; **it was a great ~ to meet her** fue muy emocionante conocerla, me hizo muchísima ilusión conocerla (*Sp*); **he gets a real ~ out of parachuting** hacer paracaidismo le resulta muy emocionante *or* excitante

thrilled [θrɪld] ADJ **to be ~ (to bits** *or* (*esp US*) **pieces)** estar contentísimo (**with** con); **I was ~ to meet him** fue muy emocionante conocerlo, me hizo mucha ilusión conocerlo (*Sp*)

thriller ['θrɪləʳ] N (= *novel*) novela *f* de suspense *or* (*LAm*) de suspenso, novela *f* de misterio; (= *film*) película *f* de suspense *or* (*LAm*) de suspenso, thriller *m*

thrilling ['θrɪlɪŋ] ADJ emocionante

thrive [θraɪv] VI [*economy, business*] prosperar; [*plant*] crecer muy bien, prosperar; [*animal, child*] desarrollarse; (*fig*) prosperar, medrar; **she seems to ~ on adversity** parece que se crece en la adversidad

thriving ['θraɪvɪŋ] ADJ [*industry, business*] próspero, floreciente

throat [θrəʊt] N 1 (*interior*) garganta *f*; **to clear one's ~** aclararse la voz, carraspear; [*animal*] cuello *m*; **they are at each other's ~s all the time** se atacan uno a otro todo el tiempo

throaty ['θrəʊtɪ] ADJ (*compar* **throatier**; *superl* **throatiest**) [*person, voice*] ronco, afónico; [*laugh*] gutural

throb [θrɒb] 🅐 N [*of engine*] vibración *f* 🅑 VI [*heart*] latir, palpitar; [*engine*] vibrar; [*wound, sore finger*] dar punzadas; **my head was ~bing** la cabeza estaba a punto de estallarme

throes [θrəʊz] NPL [*of death*] agonía *fsing*; **she was in the ~ of an unpleasant divorce** estaba en medio de los trámites de un divorcio nada agradable; **we're in the ~ of a major restructuring at work** en el trabajo estamos en plena reestructuración

thrombosis [θrɒm'bəʊsɪs] N (*pl* **thromboses** [θrɒm'bəʊsiːz]) trombosis *f*

throne [θrəʊn] N trono *m*

throng [θrɒŋ] 🅐 N multitud *f*, muchedumbre *f* 🅑 VT atestar; **the streets are ~ed with tourists** las calles están atestadas de turistas 🅒 VI **the schoolchildren came ~ing in** los escolares entraron en tropel; **to ~ round sb** apiñarse en torno a algn

throttle ['θrɒtl] N acelerador *m*; **at full ~** a toda marcha, a toda pastilla*

through [θruː] 🅐 PREP 1 (*place*) por;

> When **through** is an element in a phrasal verb, eg **break through, fall through**, look up the verb.

---

to look ~ a telescope mirar por un telescopio; **to walk ~ the woods** pasear por el bosque; **to go ~ a tunnel** atravesar un túnel; **the bullet went ~ three layers** la bala penetró tres capas

2 (*time, process*) (**from**) **Monday ~ Friday** (*US*) de lunes a viernes; **right ~ the year** durante el año entero *or* todo el año

3 (*means*) por; **~ lack of resources** por falta de recursos; **~ him I found out that ...** por *or* a través de él supe que ...; **he got the job ~ friends** consiguió el trabajo por mediación de *or* a través de unos amigos

4 (*Brit Telec*) **you're ~!** ¡ya puede hablar!, ¡hable!

🅑 ADV 1 (*place*) **does this train go ~ to London?** ¿este tren va directamente a Londres?; **he went straight ~ to the dining room** pasó directamente al comedor; **the nail went right ~** el clavo penetró de parte a parte; **it's frozen (right) ~** está completamente helado

2 (*time, process*) **to sleep the whole night ~** dormir la noche entera; **did you stay right ~ to the end?** (*Brit*) ¿te quedaste hasta el final?; **he is ~ to the finals of the competition** pasó a la final del concurso

3 **~ and ~** [*be*] hasta la médula, completamente

4 (= *finished*) **we'll be ~ at seven** terminaremos a las siete; **she told him they were ~** ella le dijo que todo había

acabado entre ellos; **I'm ~ with my girlfriend** he roto *or* terminado con mi novia

🅒 ADJ [*road, train*] directo; [*traffic*] de paso; **"no through road"** "calle sin salida"

throughout [θruː'aʊt] 🅐 PREP 1 (*place*) por todo; **we have branches ~ the country** tenemos sucursales por todo el país; **the company is known ~ the world** la compañía es conocida en todo el mundo 2 (*time, process*) durante todo; **~ his life** durante toda su vida 🅑 ADV 1 (= *fully*) completamente; (= *everywhere*) en todas partes, por todas partes 2 (*time, process*) de principio a fin

throughput ['θruːpʊt] N (= *production*) producción *f*; (= *total quantity*) [*of applicants, patients*] movimiento *m*, número *m*; (*Comput*) capacidad *f* de procesamiento

throughway ['θruːweɪ] N (*US*) autopista *f* (*de peaje*)

throw [θrəʊ] (*vb*: *pt* **threw**; *pp* **thrown**) 🅐 VT 1 (= *toss*) [+ *ball, stone, dice*] tirar, echar; (*violently*) tirar, arrojar, lanzar; [+ *javelin, discus, grenade*] lanzar; **he threw a double six** sacó dos seises; **to ~ sb sth** tirar *or* echar algo a algn; **to ~ sth at sb** tirar *or* arrojar algo a algn; **they think they can solve problems by ~ing money at them** piensan que metiendo dinero pueden solucionar cualquier problema; **she threw the letters in the bin** tiró *or* echó las cartas a la basura

2 (= *hurl to the ground*) [+ *rider*] desmontar

3 (= *send, hurl*) **the blast threw her across the room** la explosión la lanzó *or* arrojó al otro lado de la sala; **he was ~n clear of the car** salió despedido del coche; **she threw herself into the river** se tiró al río; **the country was ~n into turmoil** el país se sumió en el caos; **to ~ sb into prison** meter a algn en la cárcel; **he threw himself into his work** se metió de lleno en el trabajo; **he threw me to the ground** me arrojó al suelo

4 (= *direct*) [+ *light, shadow*] proyectar; [+ *look, smile*] lanzar; **this new information ~s doubt on their choice** esta nueva información pone en duda su elección

5 (= *disconcert*) desconcertar

6 (= *put*) **she threw her arms around his neck** le echó los brazos al cuello, le abrazó por el cuello; **to ~ open** [+ *doors, windows*] abrir de par en par; [+ *house, gardens*] abrir al público; [+ *competition, race*] abrir a todos

7 (= *have*) **to ~ a party** dar *or* hacer una fiesta

8 (= *move*) [+ *lever, switch*] dar a

9 (*Pottery*) **to ~ a pot** tornear un tiesto, hacer un tiesto con el torno

10 (*) (= *lose on purpose*) [+ *contest, game*] perder a posta 🅑 N 1 [*of ball, stone*] tiro *m*; [*of javelin, discus*] lanzamiento *m*; [*of dice*] tirada *f*; (*in judo, wrestling*) derribo *m*; **it's your ~** te toca tirar (a ti)

2 (*) (= *each*) **"how much are they?"** — **"50 quid a ~"** —¿cuánto cuestan? —50 libras cada uno

3 (*for sofa*) cubresofá *m*; (*for bed*) cubrecama *m*, colcha *f*

➤ **throw around, throw about** VT + ADV 1 (*lit*) **they were ~ing a ball around** jugaban con una pelota; **don't ~ it around or it might break** no lo manosees para arriba y para abajo, que se puede romper; **they were ~n around in the back of the lorry** se zarandeaban de un lado para otro en la parte trasera del camión 2 [+ *ideas*] intercambiar; **to ~ (one's) money around** derrochar *or* despilfarrar el dinero, tirar el dinero; ✦ IDIOM **to ~ one's weight around*** ir de sargento*

➤ **throw away** VT + ADV [+ *rubbish*] tirar, botar (*LAm*); [+ *chance, opportunity*] desperdiciar; [+ *one's life, health, happiness*] echar a perder

➤ **throw back** VT + ADV [+ *ball*] devolver; [+ *fish*] devolver al agua; [+ *head*] echar para atrás, echar hacia atrás

➤ **throw in** VT + ADV 1 (*Sport*) [+ *ball*] sacar; ✦ IDIOM **to ~ in the towel** tirar la toalla 2 (= *include*) incluir; **pay for extra prints and they ~ in a photo album** pague copias extra y le regalan un álbum de fotos

➤ **throw off** VT + ADV [+ *clothes, disguise*] quitarse a toda prisa; [+ *depression*] salir de; [+ *cold, infection, habit*] quitarse

➤ **throw out** VT + ADV 1 (= *throw away*) [+ *rubbish, old clothes*] tirar, botar (*LAm*) 2 (= *expel*) (*from organization, team*) echar; (*from country*) expulsar, echar 3 (= *reject*) [+ *proposal, bill*] rechazar; [+ *case, claim*] desestimar, rechazar 4 (= *make wrong*) [+ *calculation*] desbaratar, dar al traste con

➤ **throw together** VT + ADV 1 (= *make hastily*) [+ *costume,*

plan, essay] hacer a la carrera, pergeñar; [+ *meal*] preparar a la carrera, improvisar **2** (= *gather together*) [+ *clothes*] juntar rápidamente; [+ *people*] juntar; **fate had ~n them together** el destino les había juntado
➤ **throw up** Ⓐ VI + ADV (*) (= *vomit*) devolver*, vomitar Ⓑ VT + ADV **1** (*lit*) [+ *object*] lanzar *or* echar al aire **2** (*Brit*) [+ *result*] dar, producir; [+ *dilemma*] producir; [+ *problem*] crear **3** [+ *building*] construir rápidamente **4** (*) (= *vomit*) devolver*, vomitar **5** (*) (= *abandon*) [+ *job, task, studies*] dejar

throwaway ['θrəʊəweɪ] ADJ [*bottle, container*] desechable, para usar y tirar; [*remark*] dicho de paso; **our ~ society** nuestra sociedad de consumo

throwback ['θrəʊbæk] N salto *m* atrás; **it's like a ~ to the old days** es como un salto atrás a los viejos tiempos

throw-in ['θrəʊɪn] N (*Ftbl*) saque *m* (de banda)

thrown [θrəʊn] PP *of* **throw**

thru [θruː] (*US*) = **through**

thrush¹ [θrʌʃ] N (= *bird*) zorzal *m*, tordo *m*

thrush² [θrʌʃ] N (= *infection*) afta *f*

Use **el/un** not **la/una** before feminine nouns beginning with stressed **a** or **ha** like **afta**.

---

thrust [θrʌst] (*vb: pt, pp* ~) Ⓐ N **1** (*Mech*) empuje *m*; (*Aer, Naut*) propulsión *f*; **forward/reverse** ~ empuje *m* de avance/de marcha atrás **2** [*of speech*] idea *f* clave Ⓑ VT (= *push*) empujar; (= *insert*) introducir, meter (**into** en); (= *insert piercingly*) clavar, hincar (**into** en); **to ~ one's hands into one's pockets** meter las manos en los bolsillos; **he ~ a book into my hands** me metió un libro entre las manos

thruway ['θruːweɪ] N (*US*) autopista *f* de peaje

Thu. ABBR (= **Thursday**) juev.

thud [θʌd] Ⓐ N ruido *m* sordo, golpe *m* sordo Ⓑ VI hacer un ruido sordo

thug [θʌg] N matón/ona *m/f*; (*fig, as term of abuse*) bruto *m*, bestia *f*

thumb [θʌm] Ⓐ N pulgar *m*; ✦ IDIOMS **to be all ~s** ser un manazas; **to be under sb's ~** estar dominado por algn; **they gave it the ~s down** lo rechazaron, lo desaprobaron; **they gave it the ~s up** lo aprobaron Ⓑ VT **1** [+ *book*] manosear **2 to ~ a lift** *or* **a ride** hacer autostop, hacer dedo, pedir aventón (*LAm*); **to ~ a lift to London** viajar en autostop a Londres Ⓒ VI **to ~ through a book** hojear un libro

thumbnail ['θʌmneɪl] N uña *f* del pulgar ➤ **thumbnail sketch** pequeño esbozo *m*

thumbprint ['θʌmprɪnt] N impresión *f* del pulgar

thumbs-up sign [ˌθʌmz'ʌpˌsaɪn] N **he gave me a ~** me indicó con el pulgar que todo iba bien

thumbtack ['θʌmtæk] N (*US*) chincheta *f*, chinche *m or f* (*LAm*)

thump [θʌmp] Ⓐ N golpetazo *m* Ⓑ VT (= *hit hard*) golpear; (*accidentally*) [+ *head etc*] dar *or* topar con; **to ~ sb** (*esp Brit**) pegar un puñetazo a algn; **he ~ed me on the back** me dio un golpetazo en la espalda Ⓒ VI [*heart*] latir con fuerza; **someone was ~ing on the door** había alguien dando golpes a *or* aporreando la puerta

thumping* ['θʌmpɪŋ] (*Brit*) ADJ enorme; **a ~ headache** una jaqueca terrible

thunder ['θʌndə'] Ⓐ N (*Met*) truenos *mpl*; [*of traffic, applause*] estruendo *m*; [*of hooves*] estampido *m*; **a clap of ~** un trueno; **there is ~ in the air** amenaza tronar; **with a face like ~** con cara de furia, con cara de pocos amigos Ⓑ VI (*Met*) tronar; **the guns ~ed in the distance** los cañones tronaban a lo lejos; **the train ~ed by** el tren pasó con gran estruendo Ⓒ VT **to ~ out an order** dar una orden a gritos; **"yes!", he ~ed** —¡sí! —rugió

thunderbolt ['θʌndəbəʊlt] N rayo *m*; (*fig*) rayo *m*, bomba *f*

thunderclap ['θʌndəklæp] N trueno *m*

thunderous ['θʌndərəs] ADJ estruendoso, atronador

thunderstorm ['θʌndəstɔːm] N tormenta *f*

thunderstruck ['θʌndəstrʌk] ADJ atónito, pasmado, estupefacto

thundery ['θʌndərɪ] ADJ [*weather, shower, sky*] tormentoso

Thur(s). ABBR (= **Thursday**) juev.

Thursday ['θɜːzdɪ] N jueves *m inv; see* **Tuesday**

thus [ðʌs] ADV (= *in this way*) así, de este modo; (= *as a result*) por eso, así que, de modo que; ~ **it is that ...** así es que ..., es por eso que ...; ~, **when he got home ...** así que, cuando llegó a casa ...; ~ **far** hasta ahora *or* aquí

thwart [θwɔːt] VT [+ *plan*] frustrar, desbaratar; [+ *attempt*] frustrar; **there's no knowing what she'll do if she's ~ed** quién sabe qué hará si alguien se interpone en su camino

thyme [taɪm] N tomillo *m*

thyroid ['θaɪrɔɪd] Ⓐ N (*also* ~ **gland**) tiroides *m or f inv* Ⓑ ADJ tiroideo

tiara [tɪ'ɑːrə] N (*royal*) diadema *f*; (*pope's*) tiara *f*

Tibet [tɪ'bet] N el Tíbet

Tibetan [tɪ'betən] ADJ, N tibetano/a *m/f*

tibia ['tɪbɪə] N (*pl* ~**s** *or* ~**e** ['tɪbɪiː]) tibia *f*

tic [tɪk] N tic *m*; **a nervous ~** un tic nervioso

tick¹ [tɪk] Ⓐ N **1** (*also* ~**-tock**) tictac *m* **2** (*Brit**) (= *moment*) momentito *m*, segundito *m*; **just a ~!** ¡un momentito *or* segundito!; **I shan't be a ~** en seguida voy, no tardo, ahorita voy (*LAm*) **3** (*esp Brit*) (= *sign*) señal *f*, visto *m*; (*on work*) bien *m*; **place a ~ in the appropriate box** marque la casilla correspondiente/correcta Ⓑ VT (*esp Brit*) (= *mark as correct*) poner una señal de correcto a; (= *indicate*) [+ *item on list, name*] marcar, poner una señal contra Ⓒ VI [*clock*] hacer tictac
➤ **tick away, tick by** VI + ADV **time is ~ing away** *or* **by** el tiempo pasa
➤ **tick off** VT + ADV **1** (*Brit*) (= *mark with tick*) [+ *name, item on list*] marcar, poner una señal contra **2** (= *count*) contar en los dedos **3** (*Brit**) (= *reprimand*) **to ~ sb off** echar una bronca a algn, regañar *or* reñir a algn **4** (*US**) (= *annoy*) fastidiar, dar la lata a*
➤ **tick over** VI + ADV (*Brit Aut, Mech*) marchar al ralentí; [*business*] ir tirando

tick² [tɪk] N (*Zool*) garrapata *f*

ticker tape ['tɪkəˌteɪp] N cinta *f* de teletipo

ticket ['tɪkɪt] Ⓐ N **1** (*for bus, train*) billete *m* (*Sp*), boleto *m* (*LAm*); (*for plane*) billete *m* (*Sp*), pasaje *m* (*LAm*); (*for concert, film, play*) entrada *f*; (*for library membership*) carné *m*, carnet *m*; (= *label*) etiqueta *f*; (*at dry-cleaner's etc*) resguardo *m*; (*in lottery*) boleto *m*; **return ~** (*esp Brit*) ◇ **round-trip ~** (*US*) billete *m* (*Sp*) *or* boleto *m* (*LAm*) de ida y vuelta, billete *m* redondo (*Mex*); **that holiday was just the ~*** esas vacaciones eran justo lo que necesitaba
2 (*for parking offence*) multa *f* (por estacionamiento indebido); **to get a (parking) ~** ser multado por aparcar mal *or* por estacionamiento indebido
3 (*US Pol*) (= *list of candidates*) lista *f* (de candidatos), candidatura *f*, planilla *f* (*LAm*); **to run on a republican ~** presentarse como candidato republicano
Ⓑ VT **1** (= *fine*) [+ *person*] multar; [+ *vehicle*] dejar la papeleta de una multa en
2 (*US*) [+ *passenger*] expedir un billete (*Sp*) *or* boleto (*LAm*)
Ⓒ CPD ➤ **ticket agency** (*Rail etc*) agencia *f* de viajes; (*Theat*) agencia *f* de localidades, boletería *f* (*LAm*) ➤ **ticket barrier** (*Brit Rail*) barrera más allá de la cual se necesita billete/boleto ➤ **ticket collector, ticket inspector** revisor(a) *m/f*, controlador(a) *m/f* de boletos (*LAm*) ➤ **ticket holder** poseedor(a) *m/f* de billete (*Sp*) *or* boleto (*LAm*); (*of travelcard etc*) titular *mf* ➤ **ticket machine** máquina *f* de billetes (*Sp*) *or* boletos (*LAm*) ➤ **ticket office** (*Rail*) despacho *m* de billetes (*Sp*) *or* boletos (*LAm*); (*Theat, Cine*) taquilla *f*, boletería *f* (*LAm*) ➤ **ticket tout** revendedor *m* (de entradas) ➤ **ticket window** ventanilla *f*; (*Rail etc*) despacho *m* de billetes (*Sp*) *or* boletos (*LAm*); (*Theat etc*) taquilla *f*

ticking ['tɪkɪŋ] N [*of clock*] tictac *m*

ticking-off* ['tɪkɪŋ'ɒf] N (*Brit*) bronca *f*; **to give sb a ~** echar una bronca a algn, regañar *or* reñir a algn

tickle ['tɪkl] Ⓐ VT **1** [+ *person*] hacer cosquillas a **2** (*) (= *amuse*) divertir, hacer gracia a; ✦ IDIOM **to be ~d pink***

estar encantado *or* como unas castañuelas **B** VI it ~**s**
[*material*] pica; **don't, it ~s!** ¡no, que me hace cosquillas!
C N **to give sb a** ~ hacer cosquillas a algn; **to have a** ~ **in one's throat** tener picor de garganta

ticklish ['tıklıʃ], **tickly** ['tıklı] ADJ **1** (*lit*) [*person*]
cosquilloso; [*blanket*] que pica; [*cough*] irritante; **to be** ~
[*person*] tener cosquillas, ser cosquilloso **2** [*situation, problem*] peliagudo, delicado

tic-tac-toe [ˌtıktæk'təʊ] N (*US*) tres *m* en raya

tidal ['taɪdl] ADJ de (la) marea ➤ **tidal wave** maremoto *m*;
(*fig*) ola *f* gigantesca

tidbit ['tıdbıt] N (*US*) = **titbit**

tiddler ['tıdlə'] N (*Brit*) (= *fish*) pececillo *m*

tiddly[*]* ['tıdlı] ADJ (*compar* **tiddlier**; *superl* **tiddliest**) (*Brit*)
1 (= *drunk*) alegre, achispado, tomado (*LAm*[*]) **2** (= *tiny*)
pequeñito, pequeñín

tiddlywinks ['tıdlıwıŋks] NSING juego *m* de las pulgas

tide [taɪd] N [*of sea*] marea *f*; **high** ~ marea *f* alta, pleamar
f; **low** ~ marea *f* baja, bajamar *f*; **it is possible to walk
across at low** ~ es posible cruzar cuando la marea está
baja; ✦ IDIOMS **the** ~ **has turned** han cambiado las cosas; **to
go against the** ~ ir contra la corriente; **to go with the** ~
seguir la corriente
➤ **tide over** VT + ADV **can you lend me some money to** ~ **me
over till the end of the month?** ¿puedes dejarme algo de
dinero para que pueda llegar a final de mes *or* para
sacarme de apuros hasta final de mes?

tidemark ['taɪdmɑːk] N (*lit*) línea *f* de la marea alta; (*hum*)
(*in bath*) cerco *m* (de suciedad)

tidily ['taɪdɪlı] ADV [*arranged, piled, stacked*]
ordenadamente; [*dressed*] bien, perfectamente

tidiness ['taɪdɪnıs] N [*of room, house, desk*] orden *m*; [*of
person's appearance*] pulcritud *f*

tidings ['taɪdıŋz] NPL († *or liter*) noticias *fpl*

tidy ['taɪdı] **A** ADJ (*compar* **tidier**; *superl* **tidiest**) **1** [*house,
room*] ordenado, arreglado; [*garden*] cuidado; [*cupboard,
desk, pile*] ordenado; [*appearance*] aseado, pulcro; [*hair*]
arreglado; [*schoolwork*] limpio; **he likes to keep the house**
~ le gusta tener la casa ordenada *or* arreglada **2** [*person,
child*] ordenado **3** (*) (= *sizeable*) [*sum*] bonito[*]; [*income,
profit*] bueno **B** VI (*also* ~ **up**) ordenar
➤ **tidy away** VT + ADV (*Brit*) guardar, poner en su sitio

tie [taɪ] **A** N **1** (= *necktie*) corbata *f*
2 (= *fastening*) (*for plastic bags*) atadura *f*; (*on garment*) lazo *m*
3 (= *bond*) lazo *m*, vínculo *m*; **to maintain close ~s with**
mantener unos vínculos *or* lazos estrechos con; **family ~s**
lazos *mpl* familiares
4 (= *hindrance, obligation*) atadura *f*
5 (*Sport*) (= *draw*) empate *m*; (*Brit*) (*also* **cup** ~) partido *m* (de
copa), eliminatoria *f* (de copa)
B VT **1** (= *fasten*) atar, amarrar (*LAm*); [+ *one's shoelaces*] atarse,
amarrarse (*LAm*); [+ *one's necktie*] hacerse el nudo de; **her hands
were ~d behind her back** tenía las manos atadas a la espalda;
to ~ sth in a bow hacer un lazo con algo; **to ~ a knot in sth**
hacer un nudo en *or* con algo; ✦ IDIOM **our hands are ~d**
tenemos atadas las manos
2 (= *link*) relacionar (**to** con)
3 (= *restrict*) atar; **she didn't want to be ~d to a long-term
contract** no quería atarse a un contrato a largo plazo
C VI (*in match, competition, election*) empatar
D CPD ➤ **tie clip** pinza *f* de corbata ➤ **tie rack** corbatero *m*
➤ **tie tack** (*US*) alfiler *m* de corbata
➤ **tie back** VT + ADV [+ *curtains*] recoger; **to ~ one's hair back**
recogerse el pelo
➤ **tie down** VT + ADV **1** (*with rope*) [+ *object, person, animal*]
sujetar, amarrar (*LAm*) **2** (= *restrict*) atar; **we didn't want to ~
ourselves down to a mortgage** no queríamos atarnos a la
obligación de una hipoteca **3** (= *commit*) **to ~ sb down** hacer
que algn se comprometa
➤ **tie in** VI + ADV **to ~ in with sth** (*with facts*) concordar *or*
cuadrar con algo
➤ **tie on** VT + ADV atar
➤ **tie up** **A** VT + ADV **1** (= *fasten, secure*) [+ *parcel, person, horse,
sb's shoelaces*] atar, amarrar (*LAm*); [+ *one's shoelaces*] atarse,
amarrarse (*LAm*); [+ *boat*] amarrar

2 (= *make inaccessible*) [+ *money, capital*] inmovilizar
3 (= *conclude*) [+ *business deal*] concluir, cerrar
4 (= *link*) **to be ~d up with sth** estar vinculado con algo,
estar vinculado a algo
5 (= *occupy*) **to be ~d up (with sth/sb)** estar ocupado (con
algo/algn)
6 (*esp US*) (= *obstruct, hinder*) [+ *traffic*] paralizar, inmovilizar;
[+ *production*] paralizar; [+ *programme*] interrumpir
B VI + ADV (= *be linked*) **to ~ up with sth** estar relacionado con
algo, estar vinculado a algo

tie-break ['taɪbreɪk] (*esp Brit*), **tie-breaker** ['taɪbreɪkə'] N
muerte *f* rápida, desempate *m*

tie-in ['taɪɪn] N (= *link*) vinculación *f*, relación *f*

tiepin ['taɪpın] N alfiler *m* de corbata

tier [tɪə'] N **1** (*in stadium, amphitheatre*) grada *f*; [*of cake*]
piso *m*; **to arrange in ~s** disponer en gradas *or* pisos **2** (*fig*)
(*in management, system*) nivel *m*; **a two-~ health service** un
sistema sanitario que hace distinciones entre dos grupos

tie-up ['taɪʌp] N **1** (= *connection*) enlace *m*, vínculo *m*;
(*Comm*) (*between companies*) acuerdo *m* (*para llevar a cabo
un proyecto*) **2** (*US*) [*of traffic*] embotellamiento *m*

tiff[*]* [tıf] N pelea *f*, riña *f* (sin trascendencia)

tiger ['taɪgə'] N tigre *m* ➤ **tiger economy** economía *f*
emergente

tight [taɪt] **A** ADJ (*compar* **~er**; *superl* **~est**) **1** [*clothes, jeans*]
(= *close-fitting*) ajustado, ceñido; (= *too tight*) apretado,
estrecho; **my shoes are too** ~ me aprietan los zapatos
2 (= *taut*) [*rope, skin*] tirante; **to pull sth** ~ tensar algo;
✦ IDIOM **to keep a** ~ **rein on sth/sb** mantener un control
estricto sobre algo/algn
3 (= *not loose*) [*screw, knot, curl*] apretado; [*seal*] hermético;
[*embrace, grip*] fuerte; **the insect curled up in a** ~ **ball** el
insecto se enroscó formando una pequeña bola; ✦ IDIOMS
to have a ~ **grip on sth** (*on power, economy*) ejercer un firme
control sobre algo; **to keep a** ~ **grip on sth** (*on finances,
discipline*) mantener un firme control de algo; **to keep a** ~
hold of sth agarrar algo con fuerza; **to keep a** ~ **lid on sth**
controlar bien algo, mantener algo bajo control
4 (= *tense*) [*voice, throat, smile*] tenso; [*muscle*] tenso, tirante;
my chest feels ~ siento una opresión en el pecho
5 (= *strict*) [*schedule*] apretado; [*budget*] ajustado, limitado;
[*control*] estricto; **security will be** ~ habrá fuertes medidas de
seguridad
6 (= *sharp*) [*bend*] cerrado
7 (*) (= *scarce*) [*space, resources*] limitado, escaso; **when we
first got married money was** ~ al principio de casarnos
estábamos bastante escasos de dinero
8 (*) (= *difficult*) [*situation*] apurado, difícil; ✦ IDIOM **to be in
a ~ corner**[*]* estar en una situación apurada *or*
comprometida
9 (*) (= *drunk*) mamado[*], tomado (*LAm*[*]); **to get** ~ agarrarse
una moña[*], cogérsela[*]
10 (*) (= *mean*) agarrado[*]
B ADV [*hold, grip*] bien, con fuerza; [*squeeze*] con fuerza;
[*shut, seal, tie*] bien; **hold (on) ~!** ¡agárrate *or* sujétate bien!,
¡agárrate *or* sujétate fuerte!; ✦ IDIOM **sleep ~!** ¡que duermas
bien!, ¡que descanses!

tighten ['taɪtn] VT (*also* ~ **up**) [+ *rope*] estirar, tensar;
[+ *nut, belt, shoes*] apretar; [+ *regulations*] hacer más severo;
[+ *restrictions, discipline, security*] reforzar
➤ **tighten up on** VI + PREP **to ~ up on sth** ser más estricto
con algo; **they have decided to ~ up on this type of import**
han decidido controlar más este tipo de importaciones

tight-fisted ['taɪt'fıstıd] ADJ tacaño, agarrado[*]

tight-fitting ['taɪt'fıtıŋ] ADJ muy ajustado, muy ceñido

tight-knit ['taɪt'nıt] ADJ muy unido

tight-lipped ['taɪt'lıpt] ADJ **to be/remain ~ about sth**
mantener la boca cerrada respecto a algo

tightly ['taɪtlı] ADV **1** (= *firmly*) [*hold*] bien, con fuerza;
[*close, tie, wrap*] bien; [*bind*] firmemente **2** (= *strictly*)
[*controlled, enforced*] estrictamente

tightness ['taɪtnıs] N **I can feel a ~ in my chest** siento una
opresión en el pecho

tightrope ['taɪtrəʊp] N cuerda *f* floja; ✦ IDIOM **to be
walking a ~** andar en la cuerda floja ➤ **tightrope walker**

equilibrista *mf*, funámbulo/a *m/f*

tights [taɪts] NPL **1** (*Brit*) (= *everyday clothes*) pantis *mpl*, medias *fpl* **2** (*for sport, ballet*) leotardos *mpl*

tigress ['taɪgrɪs] N tigresa *f*

tile [taɪl] **A** N (= *roof tile*) teja *f*; (= *floor tile*) baldosa *f*; (= *wall tile, decorative tile*) azulejo *m* **B** VT [+ *floor*] embaldosar; [+ *wall*] revestir de azulejos, alicatar (*Sp*); [+ *roof*] tejar

tiled [taɪld] ADJ [*floor*] embaldosado; [*wall*] revestido de azulejos, alicatado (*Sp*); ~ **roof** tejado *m*

tiling ['taɪlɪŋ] N (*on roof*) tejas *fpl*, tejado *m*; (*on floor*) baldosas *fpl*, embaldosado *m*; (*on wall*) azulejos *mpl*

till[1] [tɪl] PREP, CONJ = **until**

till[2] [tɪl] N (*for money*) (*Brit*) (= *machine*) caja *f*, caja *f* registradora; (*US*) (= *drawer*) cajón *m* ➤ **till receipt** ticket *m* de caja

tiller ['tɪləʳ] N (*Naut*) caña *f* del timón, timón *m*

tilt [tɪlt] **A** N (= *slant*) inclinación *f*; (**at**) **full** ~ a toda velocidad *or* carrera **B** VT inclinar; **he** ~**ed his chair back** inclinó la silla hacia atrás

timber ['tɪmbəʳ] N (= *wood*) madera *f*; (= *trees*) árboles *mpl* (productores de madera); (= *beam*) viga *f*, madero *m*; (*Naut*) cuaderna *f* ➤ **timber merchant** (*Brit*) maderero *m* ➤ **timber yard** (*Brit*) almacén *m* de madera

time [taɪm] **A** N **1** (*gen*) tiempo *m*; **as** ~ **goes on** *or* **by** con el (paso del) tiempo, a medida que pasa el tiempo; **race against** ~ carrera *f* contra (el) reloj; **to find (the)** ~ **for sth** encontrar tiempo para algo; **half the** ~ **he's drunk** la mayor parte del tiempo está borracho; **to have (the)** ~ **(to do sth)** tener tiempo (para hacer algo); **we have plenty of** ~ tenemos tiempo de sobra; **to make** ~ (*US**) ganar tiempo, apresurarse; **it's only a matter of** ~ sólo es cuestión de tiempo; **I've no** ~ **for him** (*too busy*) no tengo tiempo para él; (*contemptuous*) no le aguanto; **I've no** ~ **for sport** odio los deportes; **there is no** ~ **to lose** no hay tiempo que perder; ~ **is on our side** el tiempo obra a nuestro favor; **it'll take** ~ **to get over the loss of her family** le llevará tiempo superar la pérdida de su familia; **it took him all his** ~ **to find it** sólo encontrarlo le ocupó bastante tiempo; **take your** ~ tómate el tiempo que necesites, ¡no hay prisa!; ✦ PROV ~ **is money** el tiempo es oro

2 (= *period of time*) tiempo *m*, período *m*; (*short*) rato *m*; **have you been here all this** ~? ¿has estado aquí todo este tiempo?; **for the** ~ **being** por ahora, de momento; **for a** ~ durante un rato; (*longer*) durante una temporada; **a long** ~ mucho tiempo; **he hasn't been seen for a long** ~ hace mucho tiempo que no se le ve; **to take a long** ~ **to do sth** tardar mucho en hacer algo; **in no** ~ **at all** en un abrir y cerrar de ojos; **a short** ~ **ago** hace poco; **a short** ~ **after** poco (tiempo) después, al poco tiempo; **after some** ~ después de cierto tiempo, pasado algún tiempo; **in a week's** ~ dentro de una semana; **in two weeks'** ~ en dos semanas, al cabo de dos semanas; ✦ IDIOM **to do** ~* cumplir una condena

3 (*at work*) **on Saturdays they pay** ~ **and a half** los sábados pagan lo normal más la mitad

4 (= *moment*) momento *m*; **I was watching TV at the** ~ en ese momento estaba viendo la televisión; **about** ~ **too!** ¡ya era hora!; **it's about** ~ **you had a haircut** ya es hora de que te cortes el pelo; **come (at) any** ~ **(you like)** ven cuando quieras; **it might happen (at) any** ~ podría ocurrir de un momento a otro *or* en cualquier momento; **any** ~ **now** de un momento a otro; **at** ~**s** a veces, a ratos; **at all** ~**s** siempre, en todo momento; **by the** ~ **we got there he'd left** cuando llegamos allí ya se había ido; **by this** ~ ya, antes de esto; **the** ~ **has come to leave** ha llegado el momento de irse; **when the** ~ **comes** cuando llegue el momento; **from** ~ **to** ~ de vez en cuando; **at my** ~ **of life** a mi edad, con los años que yo tengo; **(by) this** ~ **next year** el año que viene por estas fechas; **this is no** ~ **for jokes** éste no es momento para bromas; **now is the** ~ ahora es el momento de irse; **from that** ~ **on** a partir de entonces, desde entonces; **at one** ~ en cierto momento, en cierta época; **this is neither the** ~ **nor the place to discuss it** éste no es ni el momento ni el lugar oportuno para hablar de eso; **there's a** ~ **and a place for everything** todo tiene su momento y su

lugar; **at that** ~ por entonces, en aquel entonces, en aquella época; **at this** ~ **of the year** en esta época del año; **it's a lovely** ~ **of year** es una estación encantada

5 (*by clock*) hora *f*; **what's the** ~? ¿qué hora es?; **the** ~ **is 2.30** son las dos y media; **it's** ~ **to go** es hora de irse; **at any** ~ **of the day or night** en cualquier momento *or* a cualquier hora del día o de la noche; **it's coffee** ~ es la hora del café; **at this** ~ **of day** a esta hora; **it's** ~ **for lunch** es (la) hora de comer; **make sure you get there in good** ~ asegúrate de que llegas allí con tiempo; **he'll come in his own good** ~ vendrá cuando le parezca conveniente; **all in good** ~ todo a su (debido) tiempo; **have you got the (right)** ~? ¿tiene la hora (exacta)?; **we were just in** ~ **to see it** llegamos justo a tiempo para verlo; **just look at the** ~! ¡fíjate qué hora es ya!, ¡mira qué tarde es!; **what** ~ **do you make it?** ¿qué hora es *or* tiene?; **we made good** ~ **on the journey** el viaje ha sido rápido; **to be on** ~ [*person*] ser puntual, llegar puntualmente; [*train, plane*] llegar puntual; **to tell the** ~ [*clock*] dar la hora; **he can't tell the** ~ **yet** todavía no sabe decir la hora

6 (= *era, period*) tiempo *m*, época *f*; **in Elizabethan** ~**s** en tiempos isabelinos, en la época isabelina; **in our own** ~**(s)** en nuestra época; **in my** ~**(s)** en mis tiempos; **one of the greatest footballers of our** ~ uno de los mejores futbolistas de nuestros tiempos; **to be ahead of one's** ~ adelantarse a su época; **that was all before my** ~ todo eso fue antes de mis tiempos; **to be behind the** ~**s** [*person*] estar atrasado de noticias; [*thing, idea*] estar fuera de moda, haber quedado anticuado; **how** ~**s change!** ¡cómo cambian las cosas!; ~**s were hard** fueron tiempos duros; **the** ~**s we live in** los tiempos en que vivimos; **to move with the** ~**s** ir con los tiempos, mantenerse al día

7 (= *experience*) **to have a bad** ~ **(of it)** pasarlo mal, pasarlas negras; **to have a good** ~ pasarlo bien, divertirse; **we have a lovely** ~ lo pasamos la mar de bien*; **have a nice** ~! ¡que lo pases/paséis *etc* bien!

8 (= *occasion*) vez *f*; **three** ~**s** tres veces; **I remember the** ~ **he came here** recuerdo la ocasión en que vino por aquí, me acuerdo de cuando vino por aquí; **to carry three boxes at a** ~ llevar tres cajas a la vez; **for weeks at a** ~ durante semanas enteras *or* seguidas; **the first** ~ **I did it** la primera vez que lo hice; **for the first** ~ por primera vez; **last** ~ la última vez; **for the last** ~ por última vez; **many** ~**s** muchas veces; **many's the** ~ **...** no una vez, sino muchas ...; **next** ~ la próxima vez, a la próxima (*esp LAm*); **this** ~ esta vez; ✦ IDIOMS **ninety-nine** ~**s out of a hundred** casi siempre; **third** ~ **lucky!** ¡a la tercera va la vencida!

9 (*Mus*) compás *m*; **in** ~ **to the music** al compás de la música; **to keep** ~ llevar el compás

10 (*Math*) **four** ~**s three is 12** cuatro por tres son 12; **it's five** ~**s faster than** *or* **as fast as yours** es cinco veces más rápido que el tuyo

B VT **1** (= *schedule*) planear, calcular; (= *choose time of*) [+ *remark, request*] elegir el momento para; **the race is** ~**d for 8.30** el comienzo de la carrera está previsto para las 8.30; **you** ~**d that perfectly** elegiste a la perfección el momento para hacerlo

2 (= *calculate time of*) [+ *call, journey*] calcular la duración de; (*with stopwatch*) cronometrar; **to** ~ **o.s.** cronometrarse

C CPD ➤ **time bomb** bomba *f* de relojería ➤ **time deposit** (*US*) depósito *m* a plazo ➤ **time frame** margen *m* de tiempo; **to set a** ~ **frame for sth** poner fecha a algo ➤ **time lag** (= *delay*) retraso *m*; (= *lack of synchronization*) desfase *m* ➤ **time limit** plazo *m*, límite *m* de tiempo; (= *closing date*) fecha *f* tope; **to set a** ~ **limit (for sth)** fijar un plazo (para algo) ➤ **time loan** (*US*) préstamo *m* a plazo fijo ➤ **time machine** máquina *f* de transporte a través del tiempo ➤ **time out** (*esp US Sport, also fig*) tiempo *m* muerto; **to take** ~ **out (from sth/from doing sth)** descansar (de algo/de hacer algo) ➤ **time sheet** hoja *f* de registro horario ➤ **time signal** (*Brit*) señal *f* horaria ➤ **time switch** interruptor *m* horario ➤ **time zone** huso *m* horario

time-consuming ['taɪmkənˌsjuːmɪŋ] ADJ que requiere mucho tiempo

time-honoured, time-honored (*US*) ['taɪmˌɒnəd] ADJ consagrado

timekeeper ['taɪmˌkiːpəʳ] N (= *official*) cronometrador/a *m/f*; **to be a good** ~ (*Brit*) (= *punctual*) ser puntual

timekeeping ['taɪmˌkiːpɪŋ] N (gen) cronometraje m; (in factory etc) control m; **her ~ has always been very good** siempre ha sido muy puntual

timeless ['taɪmlɪs] ADJ intemporal

timely ['taɪmlɪ] ADJ oportuno

timer ['taɪməʳ] N (Aut) distribuidor m; (Tech) reloj m automático; (= regulator) temporizador m

time-saving ['taɪmˌseɪvɪŋ] ADJ que ahorra tiempo

timescale ['taɪmskeɪl] N escala f de tiempo

time-share ['taɪmʃɛəʳ] **Ⓐ** N 1 (for holiday) multipropiedad f 2 (Comput) tiempo m compartido **Ⓑ** CPD ➤ **time-share apartment** apartamento m en multipropiedad

timetable ['taɪmˌteɪbl] **Ⓐ** N (Brit) (for trains, buses; at school) horario m; (= programme of events etc) programa m, agenda f **Ⓑ** VT programar

timid ['tɪmɪd] ADJ [person] tímido; [animal] huraño, asustadizo

timidity [tɪˈmɪdɪtɪ] N timidez f

timidly ['tɪmɪdlɪ] ADV tímidamente

timing ['taɪmɪŋ] N **the ~ of the meeting was inconvenient** la hora fijada para la reunión no era muy conveniente; **it's all a matter of ~** todo es cuestión de elegir el momento oportuno; **that was good/bad ~** (= opportunity) lo hiciste en buen/mal momento; (= on time) lo hiciste a tiempo/destiempo

timpani ['tɪmpənɪ] NPL (Mus) tímpanos mpl, timbales mpl

tin [tɪn] **Ⓐ** N 1 (= ore) estaño m; (= metal) hojalata f 2 (Brit) (= can) lata f, bote m **Ⓑ** CPD [roof, tray, trunk] de hojalata ➤ **tin can** lata f, bote m ➤ **tin mine** mina f de estaño ➤ **tin opener** (Brit) abrelatas m inv ➤ **tin soldier** soldadito m de plomo ➤ **tin whistle** pito m

tinfoil ['tɪnfɔɪl] N papel m de estaño

tinge [tɪndʒ] **Ⓐ** N 1 [of colour] tinte m, matiz m 2 [of irony, sadness] deje m, matiz m; **not without a ~ of regret** no sin cierto arrepentimiento **Ⓑ** VT 1 (= colour) teñir, matizar (**with** de) 2 (fig) matizar (**with** de); **pleasure ~d with sadness** placer m matizado or no exento de tristeza

tingle ['tɪŋgl] **Ⓐ** N (= sensation) hormigueo m; (= thrill) estremecimiento m **Ⓑ** VI **your skin will ~ a bit when you apply the cream** te escocerá un poco al aplicar la crema; **my fingers are tingling** tengo un cosquilleo or un hormigueo en los dedos, me hormiguean los dedos

tingling ['tɪŋglɪŋ] **Ⓐ** N hormigueo m **Ⓑ** ADJ **a ~ sensation** una sensación de hormigueo

tinker ['tɪŋkəʳ] **Ⓐ** N (esp Brit) (= mender) calderero m; (pej) (= gipsy) gitano m **Ⓑ** VI (also ~ **about**) **to ~ with** toquetear, jugar con; **he's been ~ing with the car all day** ha pasado todo el día tratando de reparar el coche

tinkle ['tɪŋkl] **Ⓐ** N [of bell etc] tintín m, tintineo m; (Brit Telec*) llamada f; **give me a ~ some time** llámame algún día **Ⓑ** VI tintinear **Ⓒ** VT hacer tintinear

tinned [tɪnd] ADJ (Brit) en or de lata; **~ peaches** melocotones mpl en or de lata

tinnitus [tɪˈnaɪtəs] N tinnitus m, zumbido m

tinny ['tɪnɪ] ADJ (compar **tinnier**; superl **tinniest**) (= metallic) [sound] metálico; [taste] que sabe a lata

tinsel ['tɪnsəl] N oropel m

tint [tɪnt] N (gen) tono m, matiz m; (for hair) tinte m

tinted ['tɪntɪd] ADJ [glass] tintado; [spectacles] ahumado

tiny ['taɪnɪ] ADJ (compar **tinier**; superl **tiniest**) diminuto, minúsculo

tip¹ [tɪp] N [of knife, paintbrush, finger, nose] punta f; [of shoe, boot] puntera f; **he stood on the ~s of his toes** se puso de puntillas; **the southern ~ of Florida** el extremo sur de Florida; ✦ IDIOMS **it's only the ~ of the iceberg** no es más que la punta del iceberg; **it was on the ~ of my tongue** lo tenía en la punta de la lengua

tip² [tɪp] **Ⓐ** N 1 (= gratuity) propina f 2 (= hint) consejo m; (Racing, Gambling) pronóstico m; **to give sb a ~** dar un consejo a algn **Ⓑ** VT 1 [+ driver, waiter] dar una propina a; **she ~ped the barman ten dollars** le dio diez dólares de propina or una

propina de diez dólares al barman
2 (Racing, Gambling) **to ~ the winner** pronosticar quién va a ganar; **her horse was ~ped to win** se pronosticaba que su caballo sería el ganador; **they are ~ped to win the next election** (Brit) son los favoritos para ganar las próximas elecciones
➤ **tip off** VT + ADV (= forewarn) (gen) avisar; [+ police] dar el soplo a*, dar el chivatazo a (Sp*)

tip³ [tɪp] **Ⓐ** N (Brit) (= rubbish dump) vertedero m, basurero m, basural m (LAm), tiradero(s) m(pl) (Mex); **this room is a ~*** este cuarto es una pocilga* **Ⓑ** VT 1 (= tilt) inclinar; **to ~ sb off their seat** quitar a algn de su asiento (inclinándolo); **he ~s the scales at 70kg** pesa 70 kilos; ✦ IDIOM **to ~ the balance** or **scale (in sb's favour/against sb)** inclinar la balanza (a favor de algn/en contra de algn)
2 (= pour) **~ the vegetables into a bowl** eche las verduras en un cuenco; **they ~ the rubbish into the river** vierten or tiran la basura en el río; **she ~ped her things out of the suitcase** volcó la maleta y sacó sus cosas **Ⓒ** VI 1 (= incline) inclinarse, ladearse; (also ~ **over**) volcarse, voltearse (LAm)
2 (Brit) (= dump rubbish) tirar or (LAm) botar basura; **"no tipping"** "prohibido arrojar basura"
3 (= rain) ✦ IDIOM **it's ~ping (down)*** está diluviando*
➤ **tip out** VT + ADV [+ contents] verter; [+ container] vaciar
➤ **tip over** **Ⓐ** VI + ADV [chair, vehicle] volcar, volcarse, voltearse (LAm) **Ⓑ** VT + ADV volcar
➤ **tip up** **Ⓐ** VI + ADV [seat] levantarse; [lorry] bascular **Ⓑ** VT + ADV [+ chair] levantar, alzar; [+ container] volcar

tip-off ['tɪpɔf] N (= warning) (gen) información f, advertencia f; (to police) soplo* m, chivatazo m (Sp*)

Tipp-Ex® ['tɪpeks] **Ⓐ** N Tippex® m, corrector m **Ⓑ** VT (also ~ **out**, ~ **over**) borrar con Tippex

tipple* ['tɪpl] N (Brit) **his ~ is Cointreau** él bebe Cointreau; **what's your ~?** ¿qué quieres tomar?

tipster ['tɪpstəʳ] N pronosticador(a) m/f

tipsy ['tɪpsɪ] ADJ (compar **tipsier**; superl **tipsiest**) achispado, piripi (Sp*), tomado (LAm*)

tiptoe ['tɪptəʊ] **Ⓐ** N **on ~** de puntillas **Ⓑ** VI ir de puntillas; **to ~ in/out** entrar/salir de puntillas

tiptop ['tɪpˈtɒp] ADJ de primera, excelente; **in ~ condition** [car] en excelentes condiciones; [person] en plena forma

tip-up ['tɪpʌp] ADJ [truck] con volquete; [seat] abatible

tirade [taɪˈreɪd] N diatriba f

tire¹ ['taɪəʳ] **Ⓐ** VT cansar **Ⓑ** VI cansarse; **he ~s easily** se cansa fácilmente; **to ~ of** cansarse or aburrirse de
➤ **tire out** VT + ADV agotar, dejar rendido

tire² ['taɪəʳ] N (US) = **tyre**

tired ['taɪəd] ADJ 1 [person, eyes] cansado; **to get ~** cansarse; **to be ~ of sb/sth** estar cansado or aburrido de algn/algo; **to get ~ of (doing) sth** cansarse or aburrirse de (hacer) algo; **to be ~ out** estar agotado or rendido 2 (= old) **a ~ lettuce leaf** una hoja de lechuga mustia

tiredness ['taɪədnɪs] N cansancio m

tireless ['taɪəlɪs] ADJ [person, work] incansable, infatigable

tiresome ['taɪəsəm] ADJ pesado, aburrido

tiring ['taɪərɪŋ] ADJ cansado, cansador (SC)

tissue ['tɪʃuː] N (= handkerchief) pañuelo m de papel, klínex m inv; (in body) tejido m; **a ~ of lies** una sarta de mentiras ➤ **tissue paper** papel m de seda

tit¹ [tɪt] N (= bird) paro m, herrerillo m

tit² [tɪt] N ✦ IDIOM **~ for tat** ojo por ojo

tit³*** [tɪt] N (= breast) teta* f

titanium [tɪˈteɪnɪəm] N titanio m

titbit ['tɪtbɪt], **tidbit** ['tɪdbɪt] (US) N (= food) golosina f; (= gossip) cotilleo m

tit-for-tat ['tɪtfəˌtæt] ADJ **~ killing** asesinato m en represalia, (asesinato m por) ajuste m de cuentas

titillate ['tɪtɪleɪt] VT [+ audience, reader] despertar el interés de; (sexually) excitar

title ['taɪtl] **Ⓐ** N 1 [of book, chapter, person] título m;

(= *headline*) titular *m*, cabecera *f*; **what's your job ~?** ¿cómo se llama *or* qué nombre recibe tu puesto?; **to hold a ~** (*Sport*) ser campeón/ona *m/f*, tener un título
2 titles (*Cine, TV*) créditos *mpl*; **the opening/closing ~s** créditos *mpl* iniciales/finales
Ⓑ vt titular, intitular (*frm*)
Ⓒ CPD ➤ **title deed** título *m* de propiedad ➤ **title fight** combate *m* por el título ➤ **title holder** (*Sport*) campeón/ona *m/f* ➤ **title page** portada *f* ➤ **title role** papel *m* principal ➤ **title track** corte *m* que da nombre al álbum

titled ['taɪtld] ADJ [*person*] con título de nobleza

titter ['tɪtəʳ] Ⓐ N risa *f* tonta Ⓑ vi reírse tontamente

tittle-tattle* ['tɪtl,tætl] N chismes *mpl*

tizzy* ['tɪzɪ] N **to be in/get into a ~ (about sth)** estar/ponerse nervioso (por algo)

T-junction ['tiːdʒʌŋkʃən] N (*Brit*) cruce *m* en T

TN ABBR (*US*) = **Tennessee**

TNT N ABBR (= **trinitrotoluene**) TNT *m*

to	
Ⓐ PREPOSITION	Ⓒ ADVERB
Ⓑ INFINITIVE PARTICLE	

When **to** is the second element in a phrasal verb, eg **set to**, look up the phrasal verb. When **to** is part of a set combination, eg **nice to**, **to my mind**, **to all appearances**, **appeal to**, look up the other word.

to [tʊ, tuː, tə] Ⓐ PREPOSITION **1** (*destination*) a

Note: a + el = al

it's 90 kilometres to Lima de aquí a Lima hay 90 kilómetros, hay 90 kilómetros a Lima; **a letter to his wife** una carta a su mujer; **to go to Paris/Spain** ir a París/España; **to go to school** ir al colegio; **to go to the doctor's** ir al médico; *BUT* **we're going to John's** vamos a casa de John; **have you ever been to India?** ¿has estado alguna vez en la India?; **flights to Heathrow** vuelos a *or* con destino a Heathrow; **the road to Edinburgh** la carretera de Edimburgo
2 (= *towards*) hacia; **he walked slowly to the door** caminó despacio hacia la puerta; **move it to the left** muévelo hacia la izquierda
3 (= *as far as*) hasta; **I'll see you to the door** te acompaño hasta la puerta
4 (= *up to*) hasta; **to count to ten** contar hasta diez; *BUT* **we are expecting 40 to 50 people** esperamos entre 40 y 50 personas; **he didn't stay to the end** no se quedó hasta el final; **from Monday to Friday** de lunes a viernes; **from morning to night** de la mañana a la noche, desde la mañana hasta la noche
5 (= *located at*) a; **the airport is to the west of the city** el aeropuerto está al oeste de la ciudad
6 (= *against*) contra; **he stood with his back to the wall** estaba con la espalda contra la pared; *BUT* **to turn a picture to the wall** volver un cuadro mirando a la pared
7 (*when telling time*) **it's a quarter to three** son las tres menos cuarto, es *or* (*LAm*) falta un cuarto para las tres
8 (*introducing indirect object*) a; **to give sth to sb** dar algo a algn; **the man I sold it to** *or* (*frm*) **to whom I sold it** el hombre a quien se lo vendí
9 (*in ratios*) por; **there were three men to a cell** había tres hombres por celda; **it does 30 miles to the gallon** hace 30 millas por galón; **five pesos to the dollar** cinco pesos por dólar; *BUT* **the odds are eight to one** las probabilidades son de ocho a uno; **they won by four goals to two** ganaron por cuatro goles a dos
10 (= *about*) **what do you say to that?** ¿qué te parece (eso)?
11 (= *according to*) según; **to my way of thinking** a mi modo de ver, según mi modo de pensar
12 (= *to the accompaniment of*) **we danced to the music of the band** bailamos con la música de la orquesta; **it is sung to the tune of "Tipperary"** se canta con la melodía de "Tipperary"
13 (= *of, for*) de; **the key to the front door** la llave de la puerta principal; **assistant to the manager** asistente del gerente; *BUT* **he was a good father to the children** fue un buen padre para sus hijos
Ⓑ INFINITIVE PARTICLE
1 (*infinitive*) **to come** venir; **to sing** cantar; **I don't want to go** no quiero ir

Following another verb, a preposition may be required with the Spanish infinitive: look up the verb.

she refused to listen se negó a escuchar; **to try to do sth** tratar de hacer algo, intentar hacer algo

Note the use of the subjunctive when translating the English object + INFINITIVE construction:

he'd like me to give up work le gustaría que dejase de trabajar; **I want you to do it** quiero que lo hagas; **there was no one for me to ask** no había nadie a quien yo pudiese preguntar
2 (*purpose*) para; **he did it to help you** lo hizo para ayudarte; *BUT* **he came to see you** vino a verte; **he's gone to get the paper** ha ido a por el periódico
3 (*result*) **I arrived to find she had gone** cuando llegué me encontré con que se había ido
4 (*standing in for verb*)

to is not translated when it stands in for the infinitive:

we didn't want to sell it but we had to no queríamos venderlo pero tuvimos que hacerlo *or* no hubo más remedio; **I don't want to** no quiero; **I forgot to** se me olvidó
5 (*after adjective, noun or pronoun*)

For combinations like **difficult/easy/ready to** *etc*, look up the adjective.

he's young to be a grandfather es joven para ser abuelo; **I have things to do** tengo cosas que hacer; **he has a lot to lose** tiene mucho que perder; **that book is still to be written** ese libro está todavía por escribir
6 to see him now one would never think that ... al verlo *or* viéndolo ahora nadie creería que ...
Ⓒ ADVERB **to push the door to** empujar la puerta para cerrarla, cerrar la puerta empujando

toad [təʊd] N sapo *m*

toad-in-the-hole [,təʊdɪnðə'həʊl] N (*Brit Culin*) salchichas *fpl* en pasta

toadstool ['təʊdstuːl] N hongo *m* venenoso

toady ['təʊdɪ] (*pej*) Ⓐ N adulador(a) *m/f*, pelotilla* *mf*, pelota* *mf* Ⓑ vi **to ~ to sb** adular *or* hacer la pelotilla a algn*, dar coba a algn*

toast [təʊst] Ⓐ N **1** (= *bread*) pan *m* tostado, tostada *f*; **a piece of ~** una tostada **2** (= *drink*) brindis *m inv* (**to** por); **to drink a ~ to sb** brindar por algn; **to propose a ~ to sb** proponer un brindis por algn Ⓑ vt **1** [+ *bread*] tostar **2** (= *drink to*) brindar por; **we ~ed the victory in champagne** celebramos la victoria con champán Ⓒ CPD ➤ **toast rack** rejilla *f* para tostadas

toaster ['təʊstəʳ] N tostadora *f*

toastie, toasty (*Brit*) ['təʊstɪ] N sándwich *m* tostado

tobacco [tə'bækəʊ] N tabaco *m* ➤ **tobacco industry** industria *f* tabacalera

tobacconist [tə'bækənɪst] N (*Brit*) estanquero/a *m/f*, tabaquero/a *m/f*; **~'s (shop)** estanco *m*, tabaquería *f*

Tobago [tə'beɪgəʊ] N Tobago *f*

-to-be [tə'biː] ADJ (*ending in compounds*) futuro; **mothers-to-be** futuras madres

toboggan [tə'bɒgən] N tobogán *m*

today [tə'deɪ] ADV, N **1** hoy *m*; **from ~** desde hoy, a partir de hoy; **~ is Monday** hoy es lunes; **~ is the 4th of March** hoy es el cuatro de marzo; **what day is it ~?** ¿qué día es hoy?, ¿a cuántos estamos?; **what date is it ~?** ¿a qué fecha estamos?; **~ week** ◇ **a week ~** de hoy en ocho días, dentro de una semana; **a year ago ~** hoy hace un año **2** (= *these days*) hoy (en) día; **the writers of ~** los escritores de hoy

toddle ['tɒdl] VI (= *begin to walk*) empezar a andar, dar los primeros pasos; (= *walk unsteadily*) caminar sin seguridad; (= *depart*) (*also* **~ off**) irse, marcharse

toddler ['tɒdlə'] N niño/a *m/f* pequeño/a (que empieza a caminar *or* en edad de aprender a andar)

toddy ['tɒdɪ] N **hot ~** ponche *m*

to-do* [tə'du:] N (*pl* **~s**) (= *fuss*) lío *m*, follón *m* (*Sp**)

toe [təʊ] Ⓐ N (*Anat*) dedo *m* del pie; [*of shoe*] puntera *f*; [*of sock*] punta *f*; **big/little ~** dedo *m* gordo/pequeño del pie; **to tread on sb's ~** pisar el pie a algn; ◆ IDIOMS **to keep sb on his ~s** mantener a algn sobre ascuas; **to keep on one's ~s** estar alerta, mantenerse bien despierto; **to tread on sb's ~s** meterse con algn Ⓑ VT tocar con la punta del pie; ◆ IDIOM **to ~ the line** conformarse

TOEFL ['təʊfəl] N ABBR = **Test of English as a Foreign Language**

toenail ['təʊneɪl] N uña *f* del dedo del pie

toffee ['tɒfɪ] N (*Brit*) caramelo *m*, dulce *m* de leche; ◆ IDIOM **he can't do it for ~*** no tiene ni idea de cómo hacerlo ➤ **toffee apple** manzana *f* de caramelo

toffee-nosed* ['tɒfɪ'nəʊzd] ADJ (*Brit*) presumido, engreído

tofu ['təʊ.fu:] N tofu *m*, tofú *m*

together [tə'geðə']

> When **together** is an element in a phrasal verb, eg **bring together**, **get together**, **sleep together**, look up the verb.

ADV **1** (= *in company*) [*live, work, be*] juntos/as; **~ they managed it** entre los dos lo lograron; **they belong ~** [*couple*] están hechos el uno para el otro; [*socks*] esos van juntos; **let's get it ~*** (*fig*) organicémonos, pongamos manos a la obra; **we're in this ~** estamos metidos todos por igual; **~ with** junto con
2 (= *simultaneously*) a la vez; **don't all talk ~** no habléis todos a la vez; **all ~ now!** (*singing*) ¡todos en coro!; (*pulling*) ¡todos a la vez!

togetherness [tə'geðənɪs] N compañerismo *m*

toggle ['tɒgl] N (*on coat*) botón *m* (*alargado de madera*) ➤ **toggle key** (*Comput*) tecla *f* de conmutación binaria

toil [tɔɪl] (*liter*) Ⓐ N trabajo *m*, esfuerzo *m* Ⓑ VI trabajar duro

toilet ['tɔɪlɪt] N (= *installation*) wáter *m*, retrete *m*, inodoro *m* (*euph, frm*); (*Brit*) (= *room*) servicio *m*, wáter *m*, lavabo *m*, baño *m* (*esp LAm*); **"Toilets"** "Servicios", "Baño"; **to go to the ~** (*Brit*) ir al servicio *or* al baño ➤ **toilet bag** (*Brit*) neceser *m* ➤ **toilet bowl** taza *f* (de retrete) ➤ **toilet paper** papel *m* higiénico ➤ **toilet roll** rollo *m* de papel higiénico ➤ **toilet seat** asiento *m* de retrete ➤ **toilet water** agua *f* de colonia, colonia *f*

> Use **el/un** not **la/una** before feminine nouns beginning with stressed **a** or **ha** like **agua**.

toiletries ['tɔɪlɪtrɪz] NPL artículos *mpl* de tocador

toilet-train ['tɔɪlɪttreɪn] VT **to ~ a child** acostumbrar a un niño a ir solo al baño

to-ing ['tu:ɪŋ] N **~ and fro-ing** (*Brit*) ir y venir *m*, idas y vueltas *fpl*

token ['təʊkən] Ⓐ N **1** (= *metal disc*) ficha *f*; (*Brit*) (= *voucher*) vale *m* **2** (= *sign, symbol*) muestra *f*, señal *f*; (= *remembrance*) prenda *f*, recuerdo *m*; [*of one's appreciation etc*] detalle *m*; **as a ~ of friendship** como prueba de amistad; **by the same ~** por la misma razón Ⓑ ADJ simbólico; **~ woman** representación *f* femenina

Tokyo ['təʊkjəʊ] N Tokio *m*, Tokío *m*

told [təʊld] PT, PP *of* **tell**

tolerable ['tɒlərəbl] ADJ **1** (= *bearable*) soportable, tolerable **2** (= *adequate*) pasable

tolerably ['tɒlərəblɪ] ADV (= *moderately*) medianamente; **a ~ good player** un jugador pasable

tolerance ['tɒlərəns] N tolerancia *f*

tolerant ['tɒlərənt] ADJ **1** [*person, society, attitude*] tolerante (**of** con) **2** (*Med*) **to be ~ to sth** tolerar algo

tolerate ['tɒləreɪt] VT [+ *heat, pain*] aguantar, soportar; [+ *person*] tolerar, soportar

toll[1] [təʊl] Ⓐ N **1** (*on road, bridge*) peaje *m*, cuota *f* (*Mex*) **2** (= *losses, casualties*) número *m* de víctimas, mortandad *f*; **the death ~ on the roads** el número de víctimas de accidentes de tráfico; **the effort took its ~ on all of us** el esfuerzo tuvo un grave efecto en todos nosotros Ⓑ CPD ➤ **toll booth** cabina *f* de peaje ➤ **toll bridge** puente *m* de peaje *or* (*Mex*) de cuota ➤ **toll call** (*US Telec*) llamada *f* interurbana, conferencia *f* (*Sp*) ➤ **toll road** carretera *f* de peaje

toll[2] [təʊl] VI [*bell*] tañer, doblar

toll-free [,təʊl'fri:] ADV (*US*) **to call ~** llamar gratuitamente

Tom [tɒm] N ◆ IDIOM **any ~, Dick or Harry** un fulano cualquiera

tom [tɒm] N (*also* **~ cat**) gato *m* (macho)

tomato [tə'mɑ:təʊ, (*US*) tə'meɪtəʊ] N (*pl* **~es**) (= *fruit*) tomate *m*, jitomate *m* (*Mex*); (= *plant*) tomatera *f* ➤ **tomato juice** jugo *m* de tomate ➤ **tomato ketchup** salsa *f* de tomate, ketchup *m* ➤ **tomato plant** tomatera *f* ➤ **tomato purée** puré *m* de tomate, concentrado *m* de tomate ➤ **tomato sauce** salsa *f* de tomate; (*Brit*) (*in bottle, sachet*) salsa *f* de tomate, ketchup *m*

tomb [tu:m] N tumba *f*, sepulcro *m*

tombola [tɒm'bəʊlə] N (*Brit*) tómbola *f*

tomboy ['tɒmbɔɪ] N marimacho *m*

tombstone ['tu:mstəʊn] N lápida *f* (sepulcral)

tomcat ['tɒmkæt] N gato *m* (macho)

tome [təʊm] N (*hum*) mamotreto* *m*

tomorrow [tə'mɒrəʊ] ADV, N mañana; **~ is Sunday** mañana es domingo; **the day after ~** pasado mañana; **~ afternoon/ evening** mañana por la tarde; **~ morning** mañana por la mañana; **a week ~** de mañana en ocho días; **the writers of ~** los escritores del mañana; ◆ IDIOM **~ is another day** mañana será otro día

tom-tom ['tɒmtɒm] N (= *drum*) tantán *m*

ton [tʌn] N **1** (= *weight*) tonelada *f* (*GB = 1016.06kg; Can, EEUU etc. = 907.20kg*); **metric ~** tonelada *f* métrica; ◆ IDIOM **to weigh a ~*** pesar un quintal* **2** (*) **~s of** montones *mpl* de*

tone [təʊn] N **1** tono *m*; **in an angry ~** en tono de enojo; **~ of voice** tono *m* de voz; **to raise/lower the ~ of sth** levantar/bajar el nivel de algo **2** (*Telec*) señal *f*; **dialling ~** (*Brit*) ◇ **dial ~** (*US*) señal *f* para marcar; **please speak after the ~** (*Telec*) por favor, hable después de oír la señal **3** (= *shade*) tono *m*, matiz *m*; **two-~ colour scheme** combinación *f* de dos tonalidades **4** **muscle ~** tono *m* muscular
➤ **tone down** VT + ADV [+ *colour*] atenuar, suavizar; [+ *noise*] reducir, disminuir; [+ *language, criticism*] moderar
➤ **tone up** VT + ADV [+ *muscles*] tonificar, fortalecer

tone-deaf ['təʊn'def] ADJ que no tiene oído musical

toner ['təʊnə'] N (*for photocopier*) tóner *m*; (*Phot*) virador *m*

Tonga ['tɒŋə] N Tonga *f*

tongs [tɒŋz] NPL tenazas *fpl*

tongue [tʌŋ] Ⓐ N **1** (*Anat, Culin*) lengua *f*; **to put one's ~ out (at sb)** sacar la lengua (a algn); **she has a quick/nasty ~** tiene mucha labia/una lengua viperina; ◆ IDIOMS **to hold one's ~** callarse; **hold your ~!** ¡cállate la boca!; **have you lost your ~?** ¿te has tragado la lengua? **2** [*of shoe*] lengüeta *f* **3** (= *language*) lengua *f*, idioma *m* Ⓑ CPD ➤ **tongue twister** trabalenguas *m inv*

tongue-in-cheek ['tʌŋɪn'tʃi:k] ADJ [*remark*] irónico

tongue-tied ['tʌŋtaɪd] ADJ tímido, premioso, cortado (*Sp**)

tonic ['tɒnɪk] **Ⓐ** N **1** (*reviving*) tónico *m* **2** (*also* ~ **water**) agua *f* tónica, tónica *f* **3** (*Mus*) tónica *f*

> Use **el/un** not **la/una** before feminine nouns beginning with stressed **a** or **ha** like **agua**.

Ⓑ ADJ (*all senses*) tónico

tonight [tə'naɪt] ADV, N esta noche

tonnage ['tʌnɪdʒ] N (= *weight of ship*) tonelaje *m*

tonne [tʌn] N tonelada *f* (métrica) (*1.000kg*)

tonsil ['tɒnsl] N amígdala *f*, angina *f* (*Mex*); **to have one's ~s out** quitarse las amígdalas

tonsillitis [ˌtɒnsɪ'laɪtɪs] N amigdalitis *f*

too [tuː] ADV **1** (= *excessively*) demasiado, muy; **it's ~ sweet** está demasiado *or* muy dulce; **it's ~ hot to drink** está demasiado *or* muy caliente para beberlo; **it's ~ heavy for me to lift** no puedo levantarlo porque es demasiado *or* muy pesado; **it's not ~ difficult** no es muy difícil; **~ bad!** ¡mala suerte!, ¡qué le vamos a hacer!, ¡ni modo! (*Mex*); **it's ~ good to be true** no puede ser; **I'm not ~ keen on the idea** la idea no me hace gracia que digamos; **~ many** demasiados; **~ many difficulties** demasiadas dificultades; **~ much** demasiado; **~ much jam** demasiada mermelada; **~ often** con demasiada frecuencia, muy a menudo; **~ right!** ¡muy bien dicho!, ¡y cómo!
2 (= *also*) también; (= *moreover*) además

took [tʊk] PT *of* **take**

tool [tuːl] N (*carpenter's, mechanic's etc*) herramienta *f*; (*gardener's*) útil *m*, utensilio *m*; **the book is an essential ~** el libro es indispensable, el libro es instrumento imprescindible ➤ **tool box, tool chest** caja *f* de herramientas ➤ **tool kit** juego *m* de herramientas, estuche *m* de herramientas ➤ **tool shed** cobertizo *m* para herramientas

toolbar ['tuːlbɑː'] N (*Comput*) barra *f* de herramientas

toot [tuːt] **Ⓐ** N toque *m*, bocinazo *m* **Ⓑ** VT **to ~ the horn** tocar la bocina

tooth [tuːθ] **Ⓐ** N (*pl* **teeth**) **1** (*Anat*) diente *m*; (*esp molar*) muela *f*; **to clean one's teeth** lavarse los dientes; **to cut a ~** echar un diente; **to have a ~ out** sacarse una muela; **◆** IDIOMS **to cut one's teeth on sth** foguearse con *or* en algo, dar los primeros pasos con algo; **to be fed up to the (back) teeth with sth/sb** estar hasta la coronilla de algo/algn; **to get one's teeth into sth** hincarle el diente a algo, meterse de lleno en algo; **to lie through one's teeth** mentir descaradamente; **to fight ~ and nail** luchar a brazo partido; **it sets my/his teeth on edge** me/le da dentera; **by the skin of one's teeth** por un pelo
2 (*of saw*) diente *m*; (*of comb*) púa *f*
Ⓑ CPD ➤ **tooth fairy** ≈ ratoncito *m* Pérez ➤ **tooth powder** polvos *mpl* dentífricos

toothache ['tuːθeɪk] N dolor *m* de muelas; **to have ~** tener dolor de muelas

toothbrush ['tuːθbrʌʃ] N cepillo *m* de dientes

toothless ['tuːθlɪs] ADJ desdentado, sin dientes

toothpaste ['tuːθpeɪst] N pasta *f* de dientes, dentífrico *m*

toothpick ['tuːθpɪk] N palillo *m* (de dientes)

toothy* ['tuːθɪ] ADJ (*compar* **toothier**; *superl* **toothiest**) dentudo; **to give sb a ~ smile** sonreír a algn enseñando mucho los dientes

top¹ [tɒp] **Ⓐ** N **1** (= *highest point, peak*) cumbre *f*, cima *f*; (*of hill*) cumbre *f*; (*of tree*) copa *f*; (*of wall*) coronamiento *m*; (*of stairs, ladder*) lo alto; (*of page*) cabeza *f*; (*of list, table*) cabeza *f*, primer puesto *m*, primera posición *f*; **to reach the ~ ◊ make it to the ~** (*of career etc*) alcanzar la cumbre (del éxito); **the men at the ~** los que mandan; **~ of the charts** el número uno; **to be at the ~ of the class** ser el/la mejor de la clase; **Liverpool are at the ~ of the league** Liverpool encabeza la liga; **at the ~ of the page** a la cabeza de la página; **~ of the range** lo mejor de la gama
2 (= *upper part*) parte *f* superior, parte *f* de arriba; (*of bus*) piso *m* superior; **he lives at the ~ of the house** ocupa el piso más alto de la casa; **the ~ of the milk** la nata
3 (= *surface*) superficie *f*; **oil comes** *or* **floats** *or* **rises to the ~**

el aceite sube a la superficie
4 (= *lid*) (*of pen, bottle, jar*) tapa *f*, cubierta *f*, tapón *m*
5 (= *blouse*) blusa *f*; (= *sweater*) suéter *m*, jersey *m*, chompa *f* (*Per, Bol*); **pyjama ~** parte *f* de arriba del pijama
6 (*Brit Aut*) = **top gear**
7 (*US Aut*) capota *f*
8 **it's (the) ~s*** es tremendo*, es fabuloso*; **she's (the) ~s** es la reoca*
9 (*in phrases*) **from ~ to bottom** de arriba abajo; **the system is rotten from ~ to bottom** el sistema entero está podrido; **on ~** encima, arriba; **to be on ~** estar encima, (*fig*) (= *winning etc*) llevar ventaja, estar ganando; **on ~ of** (= *on*) sobre, encima de; **on ~ of (all) that** y encima *or* además de (todo) eso; **on ~ of which** y para colmo, más encima; **to be/ get on ~ of things** estar/ponerse a la altura de las cosas; **things are getting on ~ of me** ya no puedo más; **to come out on ~** salir ganando *or* con éxito; **to be/feel on ~ of the world** estar/sentirse en el paraíso *or* en el séptimo cielo; **over the ~** (*Brit**) (= *excessive*) excesivo, desmesurado; **to go over the ~** (*Brit**) (*fig*) pasarse (de lo razonable), desbordarse; **at the ~ of one's voice** a voz en grito; **◆** IDIOM **speaking off the ~ of my head, I would say ...** hablando así sin pensarlo, yo diría que ...
Ⓑ ADJ **1** (= *highest*) (*drawer, shelf*) de arriba, más alto; (*edge, side*) superior, de arriba; (*floor, step*) último; **at the ~ end of the scale** en el extremo superior de la escala
2 (= *maximum*) (*price*) máximo; **~ priority** principal prioridad *f*, asunto *m* primordial; **at ~ speed** a máxima velocidad, a toda carrera
3 (*in rank etc*) más importante; **a ~ executive** un(a) alto/a ejecutivo/a; **a ~ job** un puesto de importancia; **~ management** alta gerencia *f*
4 (= *best, leading*) mejor; **a ~ surgeon** uno de los mejores cirujanos; **the ~ ten** (*Mus*) los diez mejores, los diez principales; **to be** *or* **come ~** ganar, ganar el primer puesto; **he was** *or* **came ~ in maths** sacó la mejor nota de la clase en matemáticas; **~ scorer** máximo/a goleador(a) *m/f*, pichichi *mf* (*Sp**)
5 (= *final*) (*coat of paint*) último
6 (= *farthest*) **the ~ right-hand corner** la esquina superior derecha
7 (*Brit**) (= *super*) super*
Ⓒ ADV **~s*** (= *maximum, at most*) como mucho
Ⓓ VT **1** (= *form top of*) (+ *building*) coronar; (+ *cake*) cubrir, recubrir
2 (= *be at top of*) (+ *class, list*) encabezar, estar a la cabeza de; **to ~ the bill** (*Theat*) encabezar el reparto
3 (= *exceed, surpass*) exceder, superar; **and to ~ it all ...** y para colmo ..., como remate ..., y para rematar las cosas ...; **how are you going to ~ that?** (+ *joke, story*) ¿cómo vas a superar eso?
4 (= *remove top from*) (+ *vegetables, fruit, plant*) descabezar; (+ *tree*) desmochar; **to ~ and tail fruit** (*Brit*) quitar los extremos de la fruta
5 (**) (= *kill*) colgar; **to ~ o.s.** suicidarse
Ⓔ CPD ➤ **top banana** (*US*) pez *m* gordo* ➤ **top dog*: she's ~ dog at work** ella es mandamás en el trabajo ➤ **top dollar*** (*US*) **to pay ~ dollar for sth** pagar algo a precio de oro ➤ **top gear** (*Brit Aut*) **in ~ gear** (*four-speed box*) en cuarta, en la directa; (*five-speed box*) en quinta, en la directa ➤ **top hat** sombrero *m* de copa, chistera *f*
➤ **top up** (*Brit*) VT + ADV llenar; **to ~ sb's glass up** rellenar el vaso de algn; **shall I ~ you up?** ¿te doy más?

top² [tɒp] N (= *spinning top*) peonza *f*, peón *m*; (= *humming top, musical top*) trompa *f*

topaz ['təʊpæz] N topacio *m*

top-heavy [ˌtɒp'hevɪ] ADJ (*lit*) demasiado pesado en la parte superior; **the army was ~ with officers** el ejército tenía demasiados oficiales

topic ['tɒpɪk] N tema *m*, asunto *m*

topical ['tɒpɪkəl] ADJ **1** (= *of current interest*) de interés actual, de actualidad **2** (*US*) local

topless ['tɒplɪs] **Ⓐ** ADJ topless **Ⓑ** ADV **to go ~** ir en topless

top-level [ˌtɒp'levl] ADJ del más alto nivel

topmost ['tɒpməʊst] ADJ más alto

top-of-the-range [ˌtɒpəvðə'reɪndʒ], **top-of-the-line** [ˌtɒpəvðə'laɪn] ADJ más alto de la gama

topography [tə'pɒɡrəfɪ] N topografía f

topping ['tɒpɪŋ] N (*Culin*) cubierta f

topple ['tɒpl] Ⓐ VT 1 (*also* ~ **over**) volcar 2 (= *overthrow*) derribar, derrocar Ⓑ VI (*also* ~ **down**) caerse, venirse abajo; (*also* ~ **over**) volcarse

top-ranked ['tɒp'ræŋkt] ADJ [*player, team*] primero en el ránking

top-ranking [ˌtɒp'ræŋkɪŋ] ADJ de alto rango; [*officer*] de alta graduación

top-secret [ˌtɒp'siːkrɪt] ADJ de alto secreto

top-security [ˌtɒpsɪ'kjʊərɪtɪ] ADJ de alta seguridad, de máxima seguridad

topsy-turvy [ˌtɒpsɪ'tɜːvɪ] ADJ en desorden, revuelto; **everything is** ~ todo está patas arriba

top-up ['tɒpʌp] N (*Brit**) (= *refill*) **can I give you a** ~? ¿te sirvo un poco más? ➤ **top-up loan** (*Brit*) préstamo m gubernamental a estudiantes

torch [tɔːtʃ] Ⓐ N 1 (*flaming*) antorcha f, tea f 2 (*Brit*) (*electric*) linterna f 3 (*also* **blow** ~) soplete m Ⓑ VT prender fuego a, incendiar

tore [tɔːʳ] PT *of* **tear**

torment Ⓐ ['tɔːment] N tormento m; **to be in** ~ estar atormentado Ⓑ [tɔː'ment] VT (= *hurt*) atormentar, torturar; (= *annoy*) fastidiar, molestar; **she was** ~**ed by doubts** la atormentaban las dudas

tormentor [tɔː'mentəʳ] N atormentador(a) m/f

torn [tɔːn] PP *of* **tear**

tornado [tɔː'neɪdəʊ] N (*pl* ~**s** *or* ~**es**) tornado m

torpedo [tɔː'piːdəʊ] Ⓐ N (*pl* ~**es**) torpedo m Ⓑ VT torpedear

torpid ['tɔːpɪd] ADJ aletargado

torpor ['tɔːpəʳ] N letargo m

torrent ['tɒrənt] N torrente m

torrential [tɒ'renʃəl] ADJ torrencial

torrid ['tɒrɪd] ADJ tórrido

torso ['tɔːsəʊ] N torso m

tortilla [tɔː'tiːə] N tortilla f

tortoise ['tɔːtəs] N tortuga f

tortoiseshell ['tɔːtəʃel] N 1 (*shell*) carey m, concha f 2 (= *cat*) gato m pardo

tortuous ['tɔːtjʊəs] ADJ [*path, road, process*] tortuoso; [*sentence, essay, logic*] enrevesado

torture ['tɔːtʃəʳ] Ⓐ N tortura f; **it was sheer** ~! ¡era una verdadera tortura! Ⓑ VT torturar; **to be** ~**d by doubts** ser atormentado por las dudas Ⓒ CPD ➤ **torture chamber** cámara f de tortura

torturer ['tɔːtʃərəʳ] N torturador(a) m/f

Tory ['tɔːrɪ] ADJ, N (*Brit*) conservador(a) m/f

toss [tɒs] Ⓐ N (= *throw*) echada f, tirada f; [*of head*] sacudida f; [*of coin*] tirada f, echada f (*esp LAm*); **to win/lose the** ~ ganar/perder (a cara o cruz); ✦ IDIOMS **to argue the** ~ (*Brit**) machacar el asunto*; **I don't give a** ~ (*Brit***) me importa un bledo* Ⓑ VT (= *shake*) sacudir; (= *throw*) tirar, lanzar, echar, aventar (*Mex*); [*bull*] coger (y lanzar al aire); **to** ~ **a coin** echar a cara o cruz; **I'll** ~ **you for it** lo echamos a cara o cruz; **to** ~ **a pancake** dar la vuelta a *or* voltear una tortita; **to** ~ **a salad** mezclar una ensalada Ⓒ VI 1 (*also* ~ **about**, ~ **around**) [*boat*] (*gently*) balancearse sobre las ondas; (*violently*) ser sacudido por las ondas; **to** ~ **and turn** dar vueltas *or* revolverse (en la cama) 2 (*also* ~ **up**) echar a cara o cruz; (*Sport*) sortear (**for sth** algo); **we'll** ~ (**up**) **to see who does it** echaremos a cara o cruz quién lo hace ➤ **toss off** VT + ADV (*) [+ *poem etc*] escribir rapidísimamente

toss-up ['tɒsʌp] N **we'll settle it by a** ~ nos lo jugaremos *or* lo echaremos a cara o cruz; **it was a** ~ **between me and him** la cosa estaba entre él y yo (al cincuenta por ciento); **it's a** ~ **whether I go or stay** no me decido si irme o quedarme

tot [tɒt] N 1 (= *child*) nene/a m/f, chiquillo/a m/f, niñito/a m/f 2 (*esp Brit*) (= *drink*) trago m, traguito m; **a** ~ **of rum** un dedo de ron

total ['təʊtl] Ⓐ ADJ 1 (= *complete*) [*lack, commitment*] total, absoluto; [*failure*] rotundo, absoluto; **a** ~ **stranger** un completo desconocido; **the car was a** ~ **write-off** el coche quedó totalmente destrozado 2 (= *overall*) [*amount, number, cost*] total; [*effect, policy*] global; ~ **sales/losses** el total de ventas/pérdidas Ⓑ N total m; **in** ~ en total; **a** ~ **of** un total de Ⓒ VT 1 (= *add up*) [+ *figures*] sacar el total de, sumar el total de 2 (= *amount to*) **that** ~**£20** el total asciende a 20 libras; **the class now** ~**s 20 students** en la clase hay ahora un total de 20 alumnos; **prizes** ~**ling £300** premios por un (valor) total de 300 libras 3 (*US**) (= *wreck*) destrozar, hacer fosfatina*

totalitarian [ˌtəʊtælɪ'teərɪən] ADJ totalitario

totalitarianism [ˌtəʊtælɪ'teərɪənɪzəm] N totalitarismo m

totality [təʊ'tælɪtɪ] N totalidad f

totally ['təʊtəlɪ] ADV totalmente

tote[1] [təʊt] N (*Brit Racing*) totalizador m

tote[2] [təʊt] VT (*) (= *carry*) cargar con

totem ['təʊtəm] N tótem m ➤ **totem pole** tótem m

totter ['tɒtəʳ] VI (= *stagger*) bambolearse, tambalearse; (= *be about to fall*) tambalearse, estar para desplomarse

tot up* [tɒt'ʌp] VT + ADV (*Brit*) sumar, hacer la cuenta de

toucan ['tuːkən] N tucán m

touch [tʌtʃ] Ⓐ N 1 (= *sense*) tacto m; **sense of** ~ sentido m del tacto, tacto m
2 (= *pressure*) **the merest** ~ **might break it** el más mínimo roce podría romperlo; **at the** ~ **of a button** con sólo dar a un botón; **it's soft to the** ~ es blando al tacto; ✦ IDIOM **to be an easy** *or* **a soft** ~* ser fácil de convencer
3 (= *technique, manner*) **to lose one's** ~ perder facultades
4 (= *stamp*) toque m; **the personal** ~ el toque personal
5 (= *detail*) detalle m; **that was a nice** ~ eso fue un bonito detalle
6 (= *small quantity*) **6.1 a** ~ **of** [*of milk, water*] un chorrito de; [*of salt, pepper*] una pizca de; [*of irony, sarcasm*] un toque *or* un dejo de; **there was a** ~ **of frost this morning** había algo de *or* un poco de escarcha esta mañana; **it needs a** ~ **of paint** le hace falta un poquito de pintura **6.2** (*esp Brit*) (*with adjective*) **it's a** ~ (*too*) **expensive** es algo *or* un poquito caro
7 (= *contact*) **to be in** ~ (**with sb**) estar en contacto (con algn); **I'll be in** ~ (*writing*) te escribiré; (*phoning*) te llamaré; **to get in** ~ (**with sb**) ponerse en contacto (con algn); **to keep in** ~ (**with sb**) mantener el contacto (con algn); **well, keep in** ~! ¡bueno, no pierdas contacto!, ¡bueno, no dejes de llamar o escribir!; **to lose** ~ (**with sth/sb**) perder el contacto (con algo/algn); **the party has lost** ~ **with the voters** el partido está desconectado de los votantes; **to be out of** ~ no estar al corriente (**with sth** de algo); **to put sb in** ~ **with sb** poner a algn en contacto con algn
8 (*Rugby*) **to kick the ball into** ~ poner el balón fuera de juego Ⓑ VT 1 tocar; **she** ~**ed his arm** le tocó el brazo; **they can't** ~ **you** no te pueden hacer nada
2 (= *try*) [+ *food, drink*] probar; **I never** ~ **gin** no pruebo la ginebra; **you haven't** ~**ed your dinner** no has probado bocado, no has tocado la cena
3 (= *move*) conmover; **her faith** ~**ed me** su fe me conmovió *or* me llegó al alma; **she was** ~**ed by his gift** el regalo la emocionó mucho
4 (= *compare with*) igualar; **no artist in the country can** ~ **him** no hay artista en todo el país que (se) le iguale; **nobody can** ~ **him as a pianist** como pianista es inigualable
5 (*esp Brit*) (= *reach*) **he was** ~**ing 290mph** alcanzaba las 290 millas por hora Ⓒ VI 1 (*with hand*) tocar; **"please do not touch"** "se ruega no tocar"
2 (= *come into contact*) [*hands*] encontrarse; [*lips*] rozarse; [*wires*] hacer contacto ➤ **touch down** VI + ADV (*on land*) aterrizar ➤ **touch off** VT + ADV [+ *violence, riot, fire*] provocar ➤ **touch on, touch upon** VI + PREP (= *deal with*) tocar; (= *mention*) mencionar (de pasada)

➤ **touch up** VT + ADV **1** (= *improve*) [+ *photograph, painting, make-up*] retocar **2** (*Brit**) (*sexually*) meter mano a*, sobar*

touch-and-go ['tʌtʃən'gəʊ] N **it's ~ whether he'll survive** no se sabe si sobrevivirá; **we made it, but it was ~** lo conseguimos, pero por los pelos*

touchdown ['tʌtʃdaʊn] N (*on land*) aterrizaje *m*

touched* [tʌtʃt] ADJ (= *crazy*) tocado*, majara (*Sp**)

touching ['tʌtʃɪŋ] ADJ conmovedor, patético

touchline ['tʌtʃlaɪn] N línea *f* de banda

touchpad ['tʌtʃpæd] N touchpad *m*

touchpaper ['tʌtʃpeɪpə'] N mecha *f*

touch-sensitive ['tʌtʃ'sensɪtɪv] ADJ sensible al tacto

touchstone ['tʌtʃstəʊn] N (*lit, fig*) piedra *f* de toque

touch-tone ['tʌtʃtəʊn] ADJ (*Telec*) digital, por tonos

touch-type ['tʌtʃtaɪp] VI mecanografiar al tacto

touchy ['tʌtʃi] ADJ (*compar* **touchier**; *superl* **touchiest**) (= *sensitive*) [*person*] susceptible; [*subject*] delicado; **he's ~ about his weight** su peso es un tema delicado

tough [tʌf] **Ⓐ** ADJ (*compar* **~er**; *superl* **~est**) **1** (= *robust*) fuerte
2 (= *hard, uncompromising*) [*person*] duro; [*neighbourhood*] peligroso; **~ customer*** ◇ **~ nut*** tipo/a *m/f* or (*Sp*) tío/a *m/f* duro/a*; **~ guy*** tipo *m* duro; **to do some ~ talking** hablar sin rodeos
3 (= *resistant*) [*substance, material*] fuerte, resistente; [*skin*] duro
4 (= *not tender*) [*meat*] duro
5 (= *harsh*) [*policies*] duro, de mano dura; [*measures*] duro; [*teacher, parent*] severo; **to take a ~ line on sth** adoptar una línea dura con respecto a algo; **to take a ~ line with sb** ponerse duro con algn
6 (= *difficult*) [*way of life, situation, day*] duro, difícil; [*choice, question*] difícil; [*competition*] fuerte; **it was ~ trying to raise the cash** fue difícil conseguir el dinero; **he has found it ~ going this year** este año se le ha hecho muy cuesta arriba, este año le ha resultado muy difícil; **to have a ~ time (of it)** pasarlo mal or fatal*, pasar las de Caín*
7 (*set expressions*) **tough!** ◇ **~ luck!*** ¡mala suerte!; **that's your ~ luck!** ¡te fastidias!
Ⓑ N (*) (= *thug*) matón *m*, macarra *m* (*Sp**)
Ⓒ VT (*) **to ~ it out** aguantar el tipo*
Ⓓ ADV (*) **to act/talk ~** hacerse el duro*; **to hang ~** (*US*) mantenerse firme

toughen ['tʌfn] (*also* **~ up**) VT [+ *material*] endurecer; [+ *person*] fortalecer, hacer más fuerte

tough-minded ['tʌf'maɪndɪd] ADJ duro, nada sentimental

toughness ['tʌfnɪs] N dureza *f*; **she has a reputation for ~** tiene fama de dura

toupée, toupee ['tu:peɪ] N peluca *f*, postizo *m*

tour ['tʊə'] **Ⓐ** N **1** (*by tourist*) [*of country*] gira *f*, viaje *m*; [*of city*] recorrido *m*; [*of building, exhibition*] visita *f*; **they went on a ~ of the Lake District** hicieron una excursión or un viaje por la Región de los Lagos; **to go on a walking/cycling ~** hacer una excursión a pie/en bicicleta; **we went on a ~ around London** hicimos un recorrido por Londres; **guided ~** [*of building*] visita *f* guiada or con guía; [*of city*] recorrido *m* turístico (con guía)
2 (*by musician, team, statesman*) gira *f*; **concert ~** gira *f* de conciertos; **to be/go on ~** estar/ir de gira
3 (*Mil*) **~ of duty** periodo *m* de servicio
Ⓑ VT **1** (*as tourist*) [+ *country, region*] recorrer, viajar por; [+ *town*] recorrer
2 (*officially*) ir de gira por; **the England team will be ~ing South Africa this winter** el equipo inglés hará una gira por Sudáfrica este invierno; **the Prince ~ed the factory** el Príncipe visitó la fábrica
Ⓒ VI **1** [*tourist*] viajar; **they went ~ing in Italy** se fueron de viaje por Italia
2 (*officially*) [*musician, team*] ir de gira; **he's currently ~ing in the States** actualmente está de gira por Estados Unidos
Ⓓ CPD ➤ **tour director** (*US*) guía *mf* turístico/a ➤ **tour guide** guía *mf* turístico/a ➤ **tour operator** touroperador(a) *m/f*

tour de force ['tʊədə'fɔ:s] N (*pl* **tours de force**) proeza *f*, hazaña *f*

touring ['tʊərɪŋ] N (*by tourist*) turismo *m*; (*by band, statesman etc*) giras *fpl* ➤ **touring holiday** viaje *m* turístico

tourism ['tʊərɪzəm] N turismo *m*

tourist ['tʊərɪst] **Ⓐ** N turista *mf* **Ⓑ** CPD [*attraction, season*] turístico ➤ **tourist industry** industria *f* del turismo ➤ **tourist office** oficina *f* de turismo, oficina *f* de información turística ➤ **tourist season** temporada *f* del turismo ➤ **the tourist trade** el turismo ➤ **tourist trap** sitio *m* para turistas

touristy* ['tʊərɪsti] ADJ (*demasiado*) turístico, turistizado

tournament ['tʊənəmənt] N torneo *m*

tourniquet ['tʊənɪkeɪ] N torniquete *m*

tousled ['taʊzld] ADJ [*appearance, style*] desaliñado, desarreglado; [*hair*] despeinado

tout [taʊt] **Ⓐ** N (*Brit*) revendedor(a) *m/f* **Ⓑ** VI (*Brit*) **to ~ for business** or **custom** tratar de captar clientes **Ⓒ** VT [+ *wares*] ofrecer, pregonar; (*Brit*) [+ *tickets*] revender

tow [təʊ] **Ⓐ** N **to give sb a ~** dar remolque or remolcar a algn; **on ~** (*Brit*) ◇ **in ~** (*US*) a remolque; **he arrived with a friend in ~*** llegó acompañado de un amigo **Ⓑ** VT [+ *car, caravan*] remolcar **Ⓒ** CPD ➤ **tow bar** barra *f* de remolque ➤ **tow car** (*US*) grúa *f*, coche *m* de remolque ➤ **tow truck** (*US*) camión *m* grúa, grúa *f*, coche *m* de remolque ➤ **tow away** VT + ADV remolcar, quitar remolcando; **to ~ a car away** llevar un coche a la comisaría

toward [tə'wɔ:d], **towards** [tə'wɔ:dz] PREP **1** (*direction*) hacia **2** (*time*) alrededor de, a eso de; **~ noon** alrededor de mediodía **3** (*attitude*) para con, con respecto a, hacia; **his attitude ~ the church** su actitud para con or con respecto a or hacia la iglesia; **to feel friendly ~ sb** sentir simpatía hacia or por algn **4** (*purpose*) para; **we're saving ~ our holiday** ahorramos dinero para nuestras vacaciones

towaway zone ['təʊəweɪˌzəʊn] N (*US*) zona de aparcamiento prohibido donde la grúa procede a retirar los vehículos

towel ['taʊəl] **Ⓐ** N (*gen*) toalla *f*; (*for hands*) paño *m*, toalla *f*; ✦ IDIOM **to throw in the ~*** darse por vencido **Ⓑ** VT frotar con toalla **Ⓒ** CPD ➤ **towel rail** toallero *m*

towelling, toweling (*US*) ['taʊəlɪŋ] N felpa *f*

tower ['taʊə'] **Ⓐ** N **1** [*of castle*] torre *f*; **a ~ of strength** una gran ayuda **2** (*also* **bell ~**) campanario *m* **Ⓑ** VI **to ~ above** or **over sth** dominar algo; **to ~ above** or **over sb** destacar or descollar sobre algn **Ⓒ** CPD ➤ **tower block** (*Brit*) bloque *m* de pisos, torre *f* de pisos

towering ['taʊərɪŋ] ADJ [*building*] muy alto, imponente por su altura; **in a ~ rage** con una rabia terrible

town [taʊn] N ciudad *f*; (*smaller*) pueblo *m*, población *f*; **Jake's back in ~!** ¡ha vuelto Jake!; **to be out of ~** [*building, amenity*] estar fuera de la ciudad; [*person*] estar de viaje; **he's from out of ~** (*US*) es forastero, no es de aquí; **to go into ~** ir al centro; ✦ IDIOMS **to go out on the ~*** salir de juerga or de parranda*; **to go to ~ (on sth)*** dedicarse con entusiasmo (a algo), no cortarse nada (con algo); (*spending*) no reparar en gastos (con algo) ➤ **town centre, town center** (*US*) centro *m* urbano ➤ **town clerk** secretario/a *m/f* del ayuntamiento ➤ **town council** (*Brit*) ayuntamiento *m* ➤ **town councillor, town councilor** (*US*) concejal(a) *m/f* ➤ **town hall** (*Brit*) ayuntamiento *m*, municipalidad *f* ➤ **town meeting** (*US*) pleno *m* municipal ➤ **town planner** (*Brit*) urbanista *mf* ➤ **town planning** (*Brit*) urbanismo *m*

townee* [taʊ'ni:], **townie*** ['taʊni] N habitante *mf* de la ciudad

townsfolk ['taʊnzfəʊk] NPL ciudadanos *mpl*

township ['taʊnʃɪp] N (= *small town*) pueblo *m*; (*US*) municipio *m*; (*South Africa*) asentamiento urbano creado en Sudáfrica en tiempos del apartheid para personas de raza negra

townspeople ['taʊnzˌpi:pl] NPL ciudadanos *mpl*

towpath ['təʊpɑ:θ] N camino *m* de sirga

towrope ['təʊrəʊp] N remolque *m*, cable *m* de remolque

toxic ['tɒksɪk] ADJ tóxico ➤ **toxic waste** desechos *mpl* tóxicos

toxicology [ˌtɒksɪˈkɒlədʒɪ] N toxicología f

toxin [ˈtɒksɪn] N toxina f

toy [tɔɪ] Ⓐ N juguete m Ⓑ VI **to ~ with** [+ object, sb's affections] jugar con, juguetear con; [+ food] comiscar; [+ idea] acariciar Ⓒ CPD ► **toy car** coche m de juguete ► **toy dog** (= small breed) perrito m, perro m faldero ► **the toy industry** la industria juguetera ► **toy poodle** (= small breed of poodle) caniche mf enano/a ► **toy soldier** soldadito m de juguete ► **toy train** tren m de juguete

toybox [ˈtɔɪbɒks] N caja f de juguetes

toyboy* [ˈtɔɪbɔɪ] N (Brit) amante m (de una mujer mayor)

toyshop (Brit) [ˈtɔɪʃɒp], **toystore** (US) [ˈtɔɪstɔːʳ] N juguetería f

trace [treɪs] Ⓐ N 1 (= sign) rastro m, señal f; **she had no ~ of an accent** no tenía ni pizca de acento; **to vanish without (a) ~** desaparecer sin dejar huella or rastro 2 (= remains) **they found ~s of an ancient settlement** encontraron vestigios de un antiguo poblado 3 (= small amount) rastro m; **~s of poison** rastros de veneno Ⓑ VT [+ document, fault] localizar, encontrar; [+ missing person, suspect] averiguar el paradero de, localizar, ubicar (LAm); (= find source of) [+ phone call] averiguar el origen de; **they ~d the van to a car rental agency** averiguaron que la furgoneta era de una agencia de alquiler de automóviles; **I can ~ my family back to Elizabethan times** las raíces de mi familia se remontan a la época isabelina Ⓒ CPD ► **trace element** oligoelemento m

trachea [trəˈkɪə] N (pl **~s** or **~e** [trəˈkiːiː]) tráquea f

tracing paper [ˈtreɪsɪŋˌpeɪpəʳ] N papel m de calco

track [træk] Ⓐ N 1 [of animal, person] rastro m, pista f; [of vehicle] rastro m; [of wheel] huellas fpl, rodada f; **to cover one's ~s** borrar las huellas; **to keep ~ of: they prefer him to live at home where they can keep ~ of him** prefieren que viva en casa donde le pueden seguir la pista; **to lose ~ of: I lost all ~ of time** perdí la noción del tiempo por completo; **to lose ~ of what sb is saying** perder el hilo de lo que está diciendo algn; **it's time we were making ~s** es hora de irse marchando or de que empecemos a irnos; **it will take time to get the economy back on ~** se tardará un tiempo en volver a encarrilar la economía; **to throw sb off the ~** despistar a algn 2 ✦ IDIOM **to be on the right/wrong ~** ir por buen/mal camino 3 (= path) camino m, sendero m 4 (Sport) pista f; **~ and field** atletismo m; **~ and field events** pruebas fpl de atletismo 5 (Rail) vía f; **single ~** vía f única; ✦ IDIOM **she was born on the wrong side of the ~s** (esp US*) nació en los barrios bajos 6 (Audio) pista f; **four/eight ~ recording system** equipo m de grabación de cuatro/ocho pistas 7 (Comput) pista f 8 (= song, piece) tema m; **title ~** tema m que da título or nombre al álbum 9 (US Educ) agrupamiento de alumnos según su capacidad Ⓑ VT [+ animal] seguir las huellas de, seguir el rastro de; [+ person, suspect] seguir la pista a Ⓒ CPD ► **track events** (Sport) pruebas fpl en pista ► **track meet** (US) concurso m de atletismo ► **track record** historial m; **he had a good ~ record** su historial era bueno ► **track shoes** zapatillas fpl para pista de atletismo (claveteadas) ► **track down** VT + ADV [+ suspect, information] localizar, ubicar (LAm); [+ missing person] averiguar el paradero de, localizar

trackball [ˈtrækbɔːl] N bola f rastreadora, trackball m

tracked [trækt] ADJ **~ vehicle** vehículo m de oruga

tracker dog [ˈtrækəˌdɒg] N perro m rastreador

tracker fund [ˈtrækəˌfʌnd] N (esp Brit) fondo m (de inversión) indexado, fondo m (de inversión) en índices

trackman [ˈtrækmən] N (pl **trackmen**) (US) obrero m de ferrocarril

tracksuit [ˈtræksuːt] N (Brit) equipo m de deportes, chandal m (Sp), buzo m (CS), jogging m (RPl), sudadera f (Col), pants mpl (CAm, Mex)

tract¹ [trækt] N (= area of land, sea) extensión f

tract² [trækt] N (= pamphlet) folleto m, panfleto m; (= treatise) tratado m

tractable [ˈtræktəbl] ADJ [person] tratable; [problem] soluble

traction [ˈtrækʃən] N tracción f ► **traction engine** locomotora f de tracción

tractor [ˈtræktəʳ] N tractor m

trade [treɪd] Ⓐ N 1 (= buying and selling) comercio m; **domestic/foreign/world ~** comercio m interior/exterior/ internacional; **to do ~ with sb** comerciar con algn; **to do a good ~ (in sth)** (Brit) hacer (un) buen negocio (con algo) 2 (= industry) industria f; **the building ~** la industria de la construcción; **the arms ~** el tráfico de armas 3 (= profession) oficio m; **he's a butcher by ~** es carnicero de oficio 4 (= people in trade) **to sell to the ~** vender al por mayor or (LAm) al mayoreo; **"trade only"** "sólo mayoristas" 5 (esp US) (= exchange) cambio m; **it was fair ~** fue un cambio justo; **I'm willing to do** or **make a ~ with you** estoy dispuesto a hacerte un cambio or a hacer un cambio contigo Ⓑ VT (esp US) (= exchange) [+ goods] cambiar; [+ blows, insults, jokes] intercambiar; **to ~ sth for sth** cambiar algo por algo; **to ~ sth with sb** intercambiar algo con algn; **managers ~d places with cleaners for a day** los gerentes y el personal de limpieza se cambiaron los trabajos por un día Ⓒ VI 1 (= do business) comerciar; **to cease trading** cerrar; **to ~ in sth** comerciar con algo 2 (= exchange) (esp US) hacer un cambio 3 (= sell) [currency, shares] cotizarse (**at** a) 4 (US Sport) [+ player] traspasar Ⓓ CPD ► **trade agreement** acuerdo m comercial, convenio m comercial ► **trade balance** balance m comercial ► **trade barriers** barreras fpl arancelarias ► **trade deficit** déficit m comercial ► **Trade Descriptions Act** ► **trade fair** feria f de muestras, feria f comercial ► **trade figures** estadísticas fpl comerciales ► **trade gap** déficit m comercial ► **trade name** nombre m comercial ► **trade secret** secreto m comercial; (fig) secreto m profesional ► **trades union** (esp Brit) = **trade union** ► **trade surplus** balanza f comercial favorable, superávit m (en balanza) comercial ► **trade union** (esp Brit) sindicato m ► **trade unionism** (esp Brit) sindicalismo m ► **trade unionist** (esp Brit) sindicalista mf, miembro mf de un sindicato ► **trade war** guerra f comercial ► **trade in** VT + ADV (= exchange) cambiar; [+ car, appliance] ofrecer como parte del pago ► **trade up** VI + ADV **they buy a house and then ~ up as their income rises** compran una casa y luego, cuando aumentan sus ingresos, la venden para comprar otra mejor

trade-in [ˈtreɪdɪn] N sistema de devolver un artículo usado al comprar uno nuevo ► **trade-in value** valor de un artículo usado que se descuenta del precio de otro nuevo

trademark [ˈtreɪdmɑːk] N (Comm) marca f de fábrica, marca f comercial; (fig) marca f personal

trade-off [ˈtreɪdɒf] N **there is always a ~ between risk and return** siempre existe un elemento de compensación entre el riesgo y las ganancias

trader [ˈtreɪdəʳ] N comerciante mf, negociante mf

tradesman [ˈtreɪdzmən] N (pl **tradesmen**) (= shopkeeper) tendero m; (= roundsman) repartidor m, proveedor m

trading [ˈtreɪdɪŋ] N (Comm) comercio m, actividad f comercial; (St Ex) operaciones fpl bursátiles ► **trading estate** (Brit) zona f industrial, polígono m industrial (Sp) ► **trading loss** pérdidas fpl comerciales, pérdidas fpl de explotación ► **trading partner** socio/a m/f comercial ► **trading profits** beneficios mpl comerciales, beneficios mpl de explotación

tradition [trəˈdɪʃən] N tradición f

traditional [trəˈdɪʃənl] ADJ tradicional

traditionalist [trəˈdɪʃənəlɪst] ADJ, N tradicionalista mf

traditionally [trəˈdɪʃənəlɪ] ADV (= by tradition) tradicionalmente; (= in the traditional way) de forma tradicional, a la manera tradicional

traffic [ˈtræfɪk] (vb: pt, pp **~ked**) Ⓐ N 1 (Aut, Aer, Naut, Rail)

tráfico *m*, circulación *f*, tránsito *m* (*esp LAm*); **~ is heavy** hay mucho tráfico
2 (= *trade*) tráfico *m*, comercio *m* (**in** en); **drug ~** narcotráfico *m*, tráfico *m* de drogas
Ⓑ VI **to ~ (in)** traficar (en)
Ⓒ CPD (*Aut*) [*regulations*] de circulación, de tránsito (*esp LAm*)
➤ **traffic accident** accidente *m* de tráfico, accidente *m* de circulación, accidente *m* de tránsito (*LAm*) ➤ **traffic circle** (*US*) rotunda *f*, glorieta *f* ➤ **traffic cone** cono *m* señalizador ➤ **traffic cop*** guardia *mf* de tráfico *or* (*LAm*) tránsito
➤ **traffic flow** flujo *m* de tráfico ➤ **traffic island** refugio *m*
➤ **traffic jam** embotellamiento *m*, atasco *m*; **a five-mile ~ jam** un atasco de cinco millas ➤ **traffic light, traffic lights** semáforo *msing* ➤ **traffic offence** (*Brit*) infracción *f* de tráfico ➤ **traffic police** policía *f* de tráfico, policía *f* de tránsito ➤ **traffic violation** (*US*) infracción *f* de tráfico
➤ **traffic warden** (*esp Brit*) guardia *mf* de tráfico *or* tránsito

trafficker ['træfɪkəʳ] N traficante *mf* (**in** en)

tragedy ['trædʒɪdɪ] N tragedia *f*; **it is a ~ that ...** es una tragedia que ...; **the ~ of it is that ...** lo trágico del asunto es que ...

tragic ['trædʒɪk] ADJ trágico

tragically ['trædʒɪkəlɪ] ADV trágicamente; **he died ~ young** murió terriblemente joven

tragicomedy ['trædʒɪ'kɒmɪdɪ] N tragicomedia *f*

trail [treɪl] **Ⓐ** N **1** (*of dust, smoke*) estela *f*; [*of blood*] reguero *m*; [*of comet, meteor*] cola *f*; **the hurricane left a ~ of destruction** el huracán dejó una estela de estragos
2 (= *track*) (*left by animal, person*) rastro *m*, pista *f*; **to be on sb's ~** seguir la pista a algn
3 (= *path*) camino *m*, sendero *m*
Ⓑ VT **1** (= *drag*) arrastrar; **he was ~ing his schoolbag behind him** iba arrastrando la cartera (de la escuela); **to ~ one's fingers in the water** hacer surcos en el agua con los dedos
2 (= *deposit*) **the children ~ed dirt all over the carpet** los niños iban dejando suciedad por toda la moqueta
3 (*esp Brit*) (= *track*) [+ *animal, person*] seguir la pista a, seguir el rastro a; [+ *suspect*] seguir de cerca
4 (= *lag behind*) ir rezagado con respecto a, ir a la zaga de
Ⓒ VI **1** (= *drag*) arrastrarse; **your coat is ~ing in the mud** se te está arrastrando *or* vas arrastrando el abrigo por el barro
2 (= *spread*) **wires ~ing across the floor are dangerous** los cables sueltos por el suelo son peligrosos
3 (= *trudge*) **I spent the afternoon ~ing around the shops** pasé la tarde pateándome las tiendas
4 (= *lag behind*) ir rezagado, ir a la zaga; **he's ~ing in the polls** va por detrás *or* a la zaga en las encuestas
➤ **trail away, trail off** VI + ADV [*sound*] irse apagando; **her voice ~ed away** se le fue la voz

trailblazer ['treɪlbleɪzəʳ] N pionero/a *m/f*

trailblazing ['treɪlbleɪzɪŋ] ADJ pionero

trailer ['treɪləʳ] **Ⓐ** N **1** (*Aut*) remolque *m*; (*esp US*) (*of truck*) tráiler *m*, remolque *m*; (*US*) (= *caravan*) caravana *f*, rulot *f*
2 (*Cine*) tráiler *m*, avance *m* **Ⓑ** CPD ➤ **trailer park** (*US*) camping *m* para caravanas ➤ **trailer truck** (*US*) camión *m* articulado

train [treɪn] **Ⓐ** N **1** (*Rail*) tren *m*; **to change ~s** cambiar de tren, hacer tra(n)sbordo; **to go by ~** ir en tren; **to take the ~** coger *or* (*LAm*) tomar el tren; **to travel by ~** viajar en tren
2 (= *line*) [*of people, vehicles*] fila *f*; [*of mules, camels*] recua *f*, reata *f*
3 (= *series*) serie *f*; **to set sth in ~** (= *esp Brit*) poner algo en marcha; **you're interrupting my ~ of thought** me cortas el hilo de mis pensamientos
4 (= *entourage*) séquito *m*, comitiva *f*
5 [*of dress*] cola *f*
Ⓑ VT **1** (= *instruct*) [+ *staff*] formar; [+ *worker*] (*in new technique*) capacitar; [+ *soldier, pilot*] adiestrar; [+ *athlete, team, racehorse*] entrenar; [+ *animal*] (= *house-train*) enseñar; (*for task*) adiestrar; (*to do tricks*) amaestrar; **he was ~ed in Salamanca** (*for qualification*) estudió en Salamanca; (*for job*) recibió su formación profesional en Salamanca; **to ~ sb to do sth** enseñar a algn a hacer algo; **the dogs were ~ed to attack intruders** se adiestraba a los perros para que atacaran a los intrusos
2 (= *develop*) [+ *voice, mind*] educar

3 (= *direct*) [+ *gun*] apuntar (**on** a); [+ *camera*] enfocar (**on** a)
4 [+ *plant*] guiar (**up, along** por)
Ⓒ VI **1** (= *learn a skill*) estudiar; **where did you ~?** (*for qualification*) ¿dónde estudió?; (*for job*) ¿dónde se formó?; **she was ~ing to be a teacher** estudiaba para (ser) maestra, estudiaba magisterio
2 (*Sport*) entrenar, entrenarse
Ⓓ CPD ➤ **train crash** accidente *m* ferroviario ➤ **train driver** maquinista *mf* ➤ **train journey** viaje *m* en tren ➤ **train service** servicio *m* de trenes ➤ **train set** tren *m* de juguete (*con vías, estaciones, etc*)
➤ **train up*** VT + ADV (*Brit*) [+ *new staff*] empezar a formar a partir de cero

trained [treɪnd] ADJ [*teacher, nurse*] titulado; [*worker, staff*] cualificado; [*animal*] (= *house-trained*) enseñado; (*for tasks*) adiestrado; (*to do tricks*) amaestrado; [*eye, ear, voice*] educado; **she is a ~ singer** ha recibido formación de cantante, ha estudiado canto; **we have counsellors ~ to deal with these sorts of problems** tenemos asesores capacitados para llevar este tipo de problemas; **a well-~ army** un ejército disciplinado, un ejército bien entrenado

trainee [treɪ'ni:] N aprendiz(a) *m/f*; (*US Mil*) recluta *mf* en período de aprendizaje ➤ **trainee manager** aprendiz(a) *m/f* de administración

trainer ['treɪnəʳ] N **1** [*of athletes, gymnasts, footballers*] entrenador(a) *m/f*; [*of horses*] preparador(a) *m/f*; [*of circus animals*] domador(a) *m/f* **2** (*Brit*) **trainers** (= *shoes*) zapatillas *fpl* de deporte

training ['treɪnɪŋ] **Ⓐ** N **1** (*for job*) formación *f*; (*Mil*) instrucción *f*; [*of animals*] adiestramiento *m*; (= *teaching*) enseñanza *f*, instrucción *f*; (= *period of training*) aprendizaje *m*, periodo *m* de formación; **staff ~** formación *f* de empleados **2** (*Sport*) entrenamiento *m*; **to be in ~ for sth** estar entrenando *or* entrenándose para algo; **to be out of ~** estar desentrenado *or* bajo de forma **Ⓑ** CPD ➤ **training scheme** plan *m* de formación profesional ➤ **training shoes** zapatillas *fpl* de deporte

trainspotter ['treɪnspɒtəʳ] N (*Brit*) *persona cuyo hobby es apuntar los números de serie de los trenes que pasan*

trainspotting ['treɪnspɒtɪŋ] N (*Brit*) **to go ~** *ir a apuntar el número de serie de los trenes que pasan*

traipse* [treɪps] VI **we ~d about all morning** pasamos toda la mañana yendo de acá para allá

trait [treɪt] N rasgo *m*

traitor ['treɪtəʳ] N traidor(a) *m/f*; **to be a ~ to one's country** traicionar a la patria; **to turn ~** volverse traidor

trajectory [trə'dʒektərɪ] N trayectoria *f*, curso *m*

tram [træm] N (*Brit*) tranvía *m*

tramlines ['træmlaɪnz] NPL (*Brit*) **1** (*for tram*) rieles *mpl* de tranvía **2** (*Tennis*) líneas *fpl* laterales

tramp [træmp] **Ⓐ** N **1** (= *sound of feet*) ruido *m* de pasos
2 (= *hike*) caminata *f*; **to go for a ~ in the hills** ir de paseo por la montaña **3** (= *homeless person*) vagabundo/a *m/f*
4 (*esp US**) (= *loose woman*) **she's a ~** es una zorra*, es una golfa* **Ⓑ** VT **to ~ the streets** andar por las calles, callejear **Ⓒ** VI **to ~ (along)** caminar (con pasos pesados); **the soldiers ~ed past** los soldados pasaron marchando

trample ['træmpl] **Ⓐ** VT pisar, pisotear **Ⓑ** VI **to ~ on sth** pisar algo, pisotear algo; **to ~ on sb** (*fig*) tratar a algn sin miramientos

trampoline ['træmpəlɪn] N cama *f* elástica

tramway ['træmweɪ] N (*esp Brit*) tranvía *m*

trance [trɑːns] N trance *m*; **to go into a ~** entrar en trance

tranquil ['træŋkwɪl] ADJ tranquilo, calmo

tranquillity, tranquility (*US*) [træŋ'kwɪlɪtɪ] N tranquilidad *f*, calma *f*

tranquillize, tranquilize (*US*) ['træŋkwɪlaɪz] VT tranquilizar

tranquillizer, tranquilizer (*US*) ['træŋkwɪlaɪzəʳ] N tranquilizante *m*

transact [træn'zækt] VT negociar, tramitar

transaction [træn'zækʃən] N operación *f*, transacción *f*; **cash ~s** operaciones *fpl* al contado

transatlantic ['trænzət'læntık] ADJ transatlántico

transcend [træn'send] VT sobrepasar, rebasar

transcendence [træn'sendəns] N trascendencia f

transcendent [træn'sendənt] ADJ transcendente

transcendental [,trænsen'dentl] ADJ trascendental ➤ **transcendental meditation** meditación f trascendental

transcribe [træn'skraıb] VT transcribir, copiar

transcript ['trænskrıpt] N **1** (= copy) transcripción f **2** (US Scol) expediente m

transcription [træn'skrıpʃən] N transcripción f

transept ['trænsept] N crucero m

transfer Ⓐ ['trænsfə'] N **1** (of job, papers) traslado m; (of power) traspaso m; **I've applied for a ~ to head office** he solicitado el traslado a la oficina central
2 (Jur, Fin) (of property) transmisión f, traspaso m; (of funds) transferencia f; **bank ~** transferencia f bancaria; **~ of ownership** traspaso m de propiedad
3 (Brit Sport) traspaso m; **to ask for a ~** pedir el traspaso
4 (= picture) calcomanía f
Ⓑ [træns'fз:'] VT **1** (+ person) trasladar (**from** de; **to** a); (+ power) traspasar; (+ allegiance) mudar; **~ the chops to a serving dish** pase las chuletas a una fuente; **the disease can be ~red to humans** la enfermedad puede transmitirse or contagiarse a seres humanos
2 (Jur, Fin) (+ property) traspasar, transmitir; (+ funds) transferir
3 (Brit Sport) (+ player) traspasar
4 (Telec) (+ call) pasar; **please hold while I ~ you** no cuelgue, que ahora mismo le paso
5 (= copy) (+ design) pasar, trasladar; **the documents were ~red to microfilm** los documentos se pasaron or se trasladaron a microfilm
Ⓒ [træns'fз:'] VI **1** (= change) (from job) trasladarse; (= change trains, buses) hacer transbordo; **she ~red from French to Spanish** se cambió or se trasladó del curso de francés al de español; **we had to ~ to another coach** tuvimos que pasarnos a otro autobús
Ⓓ ['trænsfə'] CPD ➤ **transfer fee** (Brit) traspaso m ➤ **transfer list** (Brit) lista f de posibles traspasos

transferable [træns'fз:rəbl] ADJ transferible

transference ['trænsfərəns] N (of information) transferencia f, transmisión f; (of power) traspaso m

transfigure [træns'fıgə'] VT transfigurar

transfix [træns'fıks] VT traspasar, paralizar; **he stood ~ed with fear** se quedó paralizado por el miedo

transform [træns'fɔ:m] VT transformar (**into** en)

transformation [,trænsfə'meıʃən] N transformación f

transformer [træns'fɔ:mə'] N transformador m

transfuse [træns'fju:z] VT transfundir; (+ blood) hacer una transfusión de

transfusion [træns'fju:ʒən] N transfusión f; **to give sb a blood ~** hacer a algn una transfusión de sangre

transgress [træns'gres] Ⓐ VT (= go beyond) traspasar; (= violate) violar, infringir Ⓑ VI pecar, cometer una transgresión

transgression [træns'greʃən] N transgresión f, infracción f; (Rel) pecado m

transgressor [træns'gresə'] N transgresor(a) m/f, infractor(a) m/f; (Rel) pecador(a) m/f

transience ['trænzıəns] N lo pasajero, transitoriedad f

transient ['trænzıənt] Ⓐ ADJ transitorio, pasajero Ⓑ N (US) transeúnte mf

transistor [træn'zıstə'] N transistor m

transit ['trænzıt] N tránsito m; **in ~** en tránsito ➤ **transit camp** campo m de tránsito ➤ **transit lounge** (Brit) sala f de tránsito ➤ **transit system** (US) transportes fpl

transition [træn'zıʃən] N transición f ➤ **transition period** período m de transición

transitional [træn'zıʃənəl] ADJ transicional, de transición

transitive ['trænzıtıv] ADJ transitivo

transitory ['trænzıtərı] ADJ transitorio

translate [trænz'leıt] Ⓐ VT **1** (Ling) traducir (**from** de; **into** a) **2** (= convert) convertir (**into** en); **to ~ words into deeds** convertir palabras en acción Ⓑ VI (person) traducir; (word, expression) traducirse

translation [trænz'leıʃən] N traducción f

translator [trænz'leıtə'] N traductor(a) m/f

translucent [trænz'lu:snt] ADJ translúcido

transmissible [trænz'mısəbl] ADJ transmisible

transmission [trænz'mıʃən] N transmisión f

transmit [trænz'mıt] VT transmitir (**to** a)

transmitter [trænz'mıtə'] N (Rad, TV, Telec) emisora f

transmute [trænz'mju:t] VT transmutar (**into** en)

transparency [træns'pærənsı] N **1** (of material) transparencia f; (of statement) claridad f **2** (for overhead projector) transparencia f; (= slide) diapositiva f

transparent [træns'pærənt] ADJ (material) transparente; (situation, system) claro, transparente; (lie) obvio; (attempt, device) claro; **he's so ~** se le ve venir, es una persona sin tapujos*; **it is ~ that** está claro que, se ve claramente que

transparently [træns'pærəntlı] ADV claramente; **it is ~ clear** or **obvious that** está meridianamente claro que; **the reason is ~ obvious** la razón está clarísima, la razón está más clara que el agua

transpire [træns'paıə'] VI **1** (= become known) **it finally ~d that ...** al final se supo que ... **2** (= happen) ocurrir, suceder

transplant Ⓐ [træns'plɑ:nt] VT trasplantar Ⓑ ['trænsplɑ:nt] N trasplante m; **she had a heart ~** le hicieron un trasplante de corazón

transplantation [,trænsplɑ:n'teıʃən] N trasplante m

transport Ⓐ ['trænspɔ:t] N (esp Brit) transporte m; **air ~** transporte m aéreo; **means of ~** medio m de transporte; **road ~** transporte m por carretera; **I haven't got any ~** no tengo transporte Ⓑ [træns'pɔ:t] VT transportar Ⓒ ['trænspɔ:t] CPD ➤ **transport café** (Brit) cafetería f de carretera ➤ **transport police** policía f de tráfico

transportation [,trænspɔ:'teıʃən] N (esp US) (= transport) transporte m; **mass ~** (US) transporte m público **2** (Hist) (of criminal) deportación f

transporter [træns'pɔ:tə'] N (esp Brit) transportador m

transpose [træns'pəuz] VT **1** (+ words) transponer **2** (Mus) transportar

transposition [,trænspə'zıʃən] N **1** (of words) transposición f **2** (Mus) transporte m

transsexual [trænz'seksjuəl] ADJ, N transexual mf

transshipment [træns'ʃıpmənt] N transbordo m

transverse ['trænzvз:s] ADJ transverso, transversal

transvestism [trænz'vestızəm] N travestismo m

transvestite [trænz'vestaıt] N travesti mf, travestido/a m/f

trap [træp] Ⓐ N **1** (= snare) (also fig) trampa f; **to fall into a ~** caer en una trampa; **to set a ~ (for sb)** tender una trampa (a algn)
2 (**) (= mouth) **shut your ~!** ¡cierra el pico!*, ¡cállate la boca!*; **to keep one's ~ shut** cerrar el pico*, callar la boca*
3 (Brit) (= carriage) coche ligero de dos ruedas
Ⓑ VT **1** (= snare) (+ animal) atrapar, cazar con trampa; (+ criminal) atrapar, coger, agarrar (LAm)
2 (= dupe) hacer caer en la trampa, engañar; **to ~ sb into sth** tender una trampa a algn para que haga algo; **they ~ped her into confessing** le tendieron una trampa y confesó
3 (= immobilize) atrapar; **they tied a rope around his body, ~ping his arms** le ataron una cuerda alrededor del cuerpo, inmovilizándole los brazos; **to ~ one's finger in sth** pillarse or cogerse or (LAm) atraparse el dedo con algo
4 (Sport) (+ ball) parar (con el pie)
Ⓒ CPD ➤ **trap door** trampilla f; (Theat) escotillón m

trapeze [trə'pi:z] N trapecio m ➤ **trapeze artist** trapecista mf

trapper ['træpə'] N trampero m, cazador m

trappings ['træpıŋz] NPL (fig) adornos mpl; **with all the ~ of kingship** con todo el boato de la monarquía

trash [træʃ] **A** N **1** (US) (= *rubbish*) basura *f*, desperdicios *mpl*
2 (*) (*fig*) tonterías *fpl*, babosadas *fpl* (*LAm*); **he talks a lot of** ~ no dice más que tonterías; **the book is** ~ el libro es una basura
3 (= *people*) **(human)** ~ gente *f* inútil, gentuza *f*
B VT **1** (= *wreck*) hacer polvo*, destrozar
2 (*esp US*) (= *criticize*) [+ *person*] poner verde*; [+ *ideas*] poner por los suelos
C CPD (US) ➤ **trash bag** bolsa *f* de basura ➤ **trash can** cubo *m* de la basura, bote *m* de la basura, tarro *m* de la basura (*LAm*) ➤ **trash heap** basurero *m*

trashy ['træʃɪ] ADJ malo, barato

trauma ['trɔːmə] N (*Psych*) trauma *m*; (*Med*) traumatismo *m*, trauma *m* ➤ **trauma centre, trauma center** (US) departamento *m* (hospitalario) de urgencias

traumatic [trɔːˈmætɪk] ADJ traumatizante, traumático

traumatize ['trɔːmətaɪz] VT traumatizar

travel ['trævl] **A** N **1** (= *travelling*) viajes *mpl*; ~ **broadens the mind** viajar te abre más a la mente *or* te da más amplitud de miras; **air** ~ viajes *mpl* en avión
2 travels viajes *mpl*; **to set off on one's ~s** emprender el viaje; **you'll never guess who I met on my ~s today!** ¡no te vas a imaginar *or* a que no sabes con quién me he topado en la calle hoy!
B VI **1** (= *make a journey*) viajar; **to ~ by car/train/bus** (*short journeys*) ir en coche/tren/autobús; (*longer journeys*) viajar en coche/tren/autobús; **to ~ to work by train** voy al trabajo en tren; **to ~ light** viajar con poco equipaje; **we'll be ~ling round Italy** recorreremos Italia; **we'll be ~ling through France** viajaremos *or* pasaremos por Francia
2 (= *move*) ir; **we were ~ling at 30mph** íbamos a 30 millas por hora; **light ~s at a speed of ...** la luz viaja *or* se desplaza a una velocidad de ...; **news ~s fast** las noticias vuelan
C VT [+ *country*] viajar por, recorrer; [+ *road*] recorrer; [+ *distance*] recorrer, hacer; **he has ~led the world** ha viajado por *or* ha recorrido todo el mundo
D CPD ➤ **travel agency** agencia *f* de viajes ➤ **travel agent** agente *mf* de viajes ➤ **travel expenses** gastos *mpl* de viaje, gastos *mpl* de desplazamiento ➤ **travel insurance** seguro *m* de viaje ➤ **travel sickness** mareo *m* (*por el viaje*)

travelator ['trævəleɪtə'] N (US) cinta *f* transbordadora, pasillo *m* móvil

traveller, traveler (US) ['trævlə'] N (*gen*) viajero/a *m/f*; (*also* **commercial** ~) viajante *mf* ➤ **traveller's cheque, traveler's check** (US) cheque *m* de viajero

travelling, traveling (US) ['trævlɪŋ] **A** ADJ [*circus*] ambulante; [*exhibition*] itinerante **B** **I've always loved** ~ siempre me ha encantado viajar, siempre me han encantado los viajes **C** CPD ➤ **travelling bag** bolso *m* de viaje ➤ **travelling companion** compañero/a *m/f* de viaje ➤ **travelling expenses** gastos *mpl* de viaje, gastos *mpl* de desplazamiento ➤ **travelling salesman** viajante *m* (de comercio), representante *m*

travelogue, travelog (US) ['trævəlɒg] N (= *lecture*) charla *f* sobre viajes; (= *film*) película *f* de viajes; (= *documentary*) documental *m* de viajes

travel-sick ['trævəlsɪk] ADJ mareado (*por el viaje*); **to get** ~ marearse al viajar

traverse ['trævəs] VT (*frm*) atravesar

travesty ['trævɪstɪ] N parodia *f*, farsa *f*

trawl [trɔːl] **A** VT [+ *area*] rastrear; [+ *river, lake*] dragar **B** VI **to ~ through the files** (*Brit*) rastrear los archivos; **to ~ for evidence** rastrear buscando pruebas

trawler ['trɔːlə'] N trainera *f*, barco *m* pesquero de arrastre

tray [treɪ] N bandeja *f*, charola *f* (*Mex*)

treacherous ['tretʃərəs] ADJ [*person*] traidor; [*road, bend, condition*] peligroso; [*current*] traicionero

treacherously ['tretʃərəslɪ] ADV traidoramente, a traición; **the roads are** ~ **icy** el hielo que cubre las carreteras hace peligrosa la conducción

treachery ['tretʃərɪ] N traición *f*; **an act of** ~ una traición

treacle ['triːkl] N (*Brit*) melaza *f* ➤ **treacle tart** tarta *f* de melaza

treacly ['triːklɪ] ADJ (= *like treacle*) parecido a melaza; (= *covered in treacle*) cubierto de melaza

tread [tred] (*vb: pt* **trod**; *pp* **trodden**) **A** N **1** (= *footsteps*) paso *m*; **with (a) heavy** ~ con paso pesado **2** [*of stair*] huella *f*; [*of shoe*] suela *f*; [*of tyre*] rodadura *f*, banda *f* rodante (*LAm*) **B** VT [+ *ground, grapes*] pisar; [+ *path*] (= *make*) marcar; (= *follow*) seguir; **to ~ water** flotar en el agua en posición vertical **C** VI (= *walk*) andar, caminar (*LAm*); **to ~ on** pisar; ✦ IDIOMS **to ~ carefully** *or* **warily** andar con pies de plomo; **to ~ on sb's toes** meterse con algn
➤ **tread down** VT + ADV pisar

treadle ['tredl] N pedal *m*

treadmill ['tredmɪl] N rueda *f* de andar; (*fig*) rutina *f*; **back to the ~!** ¡volvamos al trabajo!

treason ['triːzn] N traición *f*; **high** ~ alta traición *f*

treasonable ['triːzənəbl] ADJ traidor, desleal

treasure ['treʒə'] **A** N tesoro *m*; **he's a real** ~ es una verdadera joya; **yes, my** ~ sí, mi tesoro **B** VT **1** (= *value*) valorar **2** (= *keep*) [+ *memories, mementos*] guardar, atesorar **C** CPD ➤ **treasure chest** cofre *m* del tesoro; (*fig*) tesoro *m* ➤ **treasure house** (*fig*) mina *f* ➤ **treasure hunt** caza *f* del tesoro ➤ **treasure trove** tesoro *m* hallado

treasured ['treʒəd] ADJ [*memory*] entrañable; [*possession*] preciado

treasurer ['treʒərə'] N tesorero/a *m/f*

treasury ['treʒərɪ] **A** N **1 the Treasury** (*Pol*) la Secretaría de Hacienda **2** (= *anthology*) antología *f* **B** CPD ➤ **the Treasury Department** (US) la Secretaría de Hacienda

treat [triːt] **A** N **1** (= *something special*) **I've bought a few little ~s for the children** les he comprado unas cosillas a los niños; **a birthday/Christmas** ~ un regalo de cumpleaños/Navidad; **as a (special)** ~ como algo (muy) especial; **to give sb a** ~ obsequiar a algn con algo especial; **I wanted to give myself a** ~ quería darme un gusto *or* permitirme un lujo; **viewers are in for a** ~ **this weekend** los televidentes se llevarán una agradable sorpresa este fin de semana; **"I'll pay" — "no, this is my ~"** —yo pago —no, invito yo
2 a ~ (*Brit**) (= *wonderfully*) **the garden is coming on a** ~ el jardín va de maravilla*; **this powder works a~** estos polvos hacen milagros *or* son mano de santo*
B VT **1** (= *behave towards*) [+ *person, animal, subject*] tratar; (= *handle*) [+ *object*] manejar; **this chemical should be ~ed with caution** este producto químico debería manejarse con cuidado; **to ~ sb like a child** tratar a algn como a un niño; **to ~ sth as a joke** tomarse algo a risa
2 (= *invite*) invitar; **I'm ~ing you** yo te invito; **to ~ sb to sth** invitar *or* convidar a algn a algo; **to ~ o.s to sth** darse el gusto *or* permitirse el lujo de (hacer) algo; **we ~ed ourselves to a meal out** nos dimos el gusto *or* nos permitimos el lujo de comer fuera
3 (*Med*) [+ *patient*] tratar, atender; [+ *illness*] tratar; **to ~ sth successfully with** curar algo con; **they were ~ed for shock** recibieron tratamiento por shock
4 (= *process*) [+ *wood, crops, sewage*] tratar

treatable ['triːtəbl] ADJ [*condition, illness*] tratable

treatise ['triːtɪz] N tratado *m*

treatment ['triːtmənt] **A** N **1** (= *handling*) [*of people*] trato *m*; [*of object*] trato *m*, manejo *m*; [*of subject, idea*] tratamiento *m*; **our ~ of foreigners** el trato que damos a los extranjeros; **to give sb preferential** ~ dar a algn un trato preferente
2 (*Med*) tratamiento *m*; **he needs medical** ~ le hace falta atención médica *or* tratamiento médico; **I am still receiving ~ for the injury** todavía estoy en tratamiento por la lesión
3 (= *processing*) [*of sewage, waste*] tratamiento *m*
B CPD ➤ **treatment room** sala *f* de curas

treaty ['triːtɪ] N tratado *m*

treble ['trebl] **A** N (= *boy*) tiple *m*; (= *voice*) voz *f* de tiple **B** ADJ **1** (= *triple*) triple **2** (*Mus*) [*voice, note, instrument*] de tiple **C** VT triplicar **D** VI triplicarse **E** ADV (= *three times*) tres veces **F** CPD ➤ **treble clef** clave *f* de sol

tree [triː] N árbol *m*; ~ **of knowledge** árbol *m* de la ciencia; ✦ IDIOMS **to be at the top of the** ~ (*Brit*) estar en la cumbre de su carrera profesional; **we can't see the wood** *or* (US) **the**

forest for the ~s los árboles no dejan ver el bosque, aún no encuentran el chiste (*LAm*) ➤ **tree house** casita *f* en un árbol ➤ **tree surgeon** arboricultor(a) *m/f* ➤ **tree trunk** tronco *m* (de árbol)

tree-lined ['tri:laɪnd] ADJ bordeado de árboles

treetop ['tri:tɒp] N copa *f* (de árbol)

trek [trek] Ⓐ N **1** (= *hike*) expedición *f* **2** (*) (= *tiring walk*) caminata *f*; **it's quite a ~ to the shops*** las tiendas quedan muy lejos Ⓑ VI caminar; **I had to ~ up to the top floor*** tuve que subir hasta el último piso

trellis ['trelɪs] N espaldera *f*

tremble ['trembl] Ⓐ N temblor *m*; **to be all of a ~** estar tembloroso Ⓑ VI **to ~ (with)** temblar (de); **to ~ at the thought of sth** temblar ante la idea de algo

trembling ['tremblɪŋ] Ⓐ ADJ tembloroso Ⓑ N temblor *m*, estremecimiento *m*

tremendous [trə'mendəs] ADJ **1** (= *huge*) [*pressure, success, explosion, problem*] tremendo, enorme; **it cost a ~ amount of money** costó muchísimo dinero, costó una enorme *or* tremenda cantidad de dinero; **you've been a ~ help** me has ayudado enormemente *or* muchísimo **2** (= *wonderful*) [*person, goal, performance, achievement*] formidable, extraordinario; [*opportunity*] tremendo, estupendo; **she has done a ~ job** ha hecho un trabajo formidable *or* magnífico *or* estupendo

tremendously [trə'mendəslɪ] ADV [*important, useful*] tremendamente, enormemente; [*improve, vary*] enormemente, muchísimo; **he was ~ helpful** nos ayudó enormemente *or* muchísimo

tremor ['tremə'] N **1** (= *earthquake*) temblor *m* **2** (= *tremble*) estremecimiento *m*

tremulous ['tremjʊləs] ADJ trémulo

trench [trentʃ] N (*gen*) zanja *f*; (*Mil*) trinchera *f* ➤ **trench coat** trinchera *f* ➤ **trench warfare** guerra *f* de trincheras

trenchant ['trentʃənt] ADJ mordaz

trend [trend] N (= *tendency*) tendencia *f*; (= *fashion*) moda *f*; **to set the ~** marcar la pauta

trendy* ['trendɪ] ADJ (*compar* **trendier**; *superl* **trendiest**) a la moda, moderno

trepidation [,trepɪ'deɪʃən] N (= *fear*) temor *m*; (= *anxiety*) inquietud *f*, agitación *f*; **in some ~** algo turbado, agitado

trespass ['trespəs] Ⓐ VI entrar ilegalmente (**on** en); **"no trespassing"** "prohibida la entrada" Ⓑ N entrada *f* ilegal, invasión *f* (de propiedad ajena); **forgive us our ~es** perdónanos nuestras deudas

trespasser ['trespəsə'] N intruso/a *m/f*; **"trespassers will be prosecuted"** "entrada terminantemente prohibida"

tress [tres] N trenza *f*; **tresses** cabellera *fsing*, pelo *msing*

trestle ['tresl] N caballete *m* ➤ **trestle table** mesa *f* de caballete

trial ['traɪəl] Ⓐ N **1** (*Jur*) juicio *m*, proceso *m*; **to bring sb to ~** llevar a algn a juicio, procesar a algn; **the case never came to ~** el caso nunca se llevó a juicio; **~ by jury** proceso *m or* juicio *m* ante jurado; **new ~** revisión *f* (de juicio); **he is on ~ for murder** se lo está procesando por asesinato; **to go on/ stand ~** ser procesado **2** (= *test*) [*of drug, machine*] prueba *f*; **clinical ~s** ensayos *mpl* clínicos; **by ~ and error** a base de probar y cometer errores; **to give sb a ~** (*for job*) ofrecer a algn un periodo de prueba; **to be on ~** (*lit, fig*) estar a prueba; **a ~ of strength** una prueba de fuerza **3** (= *hardship*) **the interview was a great ~** la entrevista fue todo un suplicio; **the ~s of old age** los padecimientos de la vejez; **a movie about the ~s of family life** una película sobre las dificultades de la vida familiar; **the child is a great ~ to them** el niño les hace sufrir mucho **4 trials** (*Sport*) pruebas *fpl* de selección; **time ~s** pruebas *fpl* contrarreloj Ⓑ VT poner a prueba Ⓒ CPD ➤ **trial basis: on a ~ basis** (en periodo) de prueba ➤ **trial flight** vuelo *m* de prueba ➤ **trial jury** (*US*) jurado *m* de juicio ➤ **trial offer** oferta *f* de prueba ➤ **trial period** periodo *m* de prueba ➤ **trial run** prueba *f*; **I took the car out for a ~ run** saqué el coche para probarlo *or* ponerlo a prueba

triangle ['traɪæŋgl] N (*also Mus*) triángulo *m*

triangular [traɪ'æŋgjʊlə'] ADJ triangular

triathlon [traɪ'æθlən] N triatlón *m*

tribal ['traɪbəl] ADJ tribal, de tribu

tribe [traɪb] N tribu *f*

tribesman ['traɪbzmən] N (*pl* **tribesmen**) miembro *m* de una tribu

tribulation [,trɪbjʊ'leɪʃən] N **trials and ~s** tribulaciones *fpl*

tribunal [traɪ'bju:nl] N tribunal *m*

tributary ['trɪbjʊtərɪ] Ⓐ ADJ tributario Ⓑ N afluente *m*

tribute ['trɪbju:t] N homenaje *m*, tributo *m*; **to pay ~ to sth/sb** rendir homenaje a algo/algn; **that is a ~ to his loyalty** eso hace honor a *or* acredita su lealtad

trice [traɪs] N **in a ~** en un santiamén

tricentenary [,traɪsen'ti:nərɪ] Ⓐ ADJ (de) tricentenario Ⓑ N tricentenario *m*

triceps ['traɪseps] N (*pl* ~) tríceps *m*

trick [trɪk] Ⓐ N **1** (= *joke, hoax*) broma *f*; (= *mischief*) travesura *f*; (= *ruse*) truco *m*, ardid *m*; **dirty** *or* **mean ~** mala pasada *f*, jugada *f* sucia; **the ~s of the trade** los trucos del oficio; **to play a ~ on sb** gastar una broma a algn; **it must be a ~** aquí seguro que hay trampa; **~ or treat!** *frase amenazante que pronuncian en tono jocoso los niños que rondan las casas en la noche de Halloween; quiere decir:* —¡*danos algo o te hacemos una trastada!*; ⋄ HALLOWE'EN ✦ IDIOMS **he's up to his old ~s again** ha vuelto a hacer de las suyas; **how's ~s?*** ¿cómo te va?; **he/she knows a ~ or two** se lo sabe todo; **that should do the ~** esto servirá; **to try every ~ in the book** emplear todos los trucos; **that's the oldest ~ in the book** eso es un viejo truco; **the whole bag of ~s*** todo el rollo* **2** (= *card trick*) baza *f*; (= *conjuring trick*) truco *m*; (*in circus*) número *m*; ✦ IDIOM **he/she doesn't miss a ~** no se pierde nada **3** (= *special knack*) truco *m*; **there's a ~ to opening this door** esta puerta tiene truco para abrirla **4** (= *peculiarity, strange habit*) manía *f*, peculiaridad *f*; **history has a ~ of repeating itself** la historia tiene tendencia a repetirse; **it's a ~ of the light** es una ilusión óptica Ⓑ VT (= *deceive*) engañar; (= *swindle*) estafar, timar; **to ~ sb into doing sth** engañar a algn para que haga algo, conseguir con engaños que algn haga algo; **to ~ sb out of sth** quitar algo a algn con engaños Ⓒ CPD ➤ **trick photography** trucaje *m* ➤ **trick question** pregunta *f* de pega

trickery ['trɪkərɪ] N engaño *m*; **by ~** fraudulentamente

trickle ['trɪkl] Ⓐ N (*gen*) chorrito *m*; [*of blood*] hilo *m*; **a ~ of people** un goteo de personas Ⓑ VI escurrir; **blood ~d down his cheek** la sangre le caía a gotas por la mejilla; **people kept trickling in** la gente seguía entrando poco a poco

trickster ['trɪkstə'] N estafador(a) *m/f*, embustero/a *m/f*

tricky ['trɪkɪ] ADJ (*compar* **trickier**; *superl* **trickiest**) [*situation*] complicado, difícil; [*problem*] delicado

tricolour, tricolor (*US*) ['trɪkələ'] N bandera *f* tricolor, tricolor *f*

tricycle ['traɪsɪkl] N triciclo *m*

trident ['traɪdənt] N tridente *m*

tried [traɪd] Ⓐ PT, PP of **try** Ⓑ ADJ **~ and tested** ◇ **~ and trusted** probado

trier ['traɪə'] N (*Brit*) persona *f* aplicada

trifle ['traɪfl] N **1** (= *cheap object*) baratija *f* **2** (= *unimportant issue*) pequeñez *f*, nimiedad *f* **3** (= *small amount*) insignificancia *f*; **£5 is a mere ~** cinco libras son una insignificancia *f*; **4** (*Culin*) dulce *m* de bizcocho borracho **5 a ~** (= *somewhat*) algo, un poquito ➤ **trifle with** VI + PREP jugar con; **to ~ with sb** jugar con algn, tratar a algn con poca seriedad; **to ~ with sb's affections** jugar con los sentimientos de algn; **he's not a person to be ~d with** con ése (es) mejor no meterse

trifling ['traɪflɪŋ] ADJ sin importancia, frívolo

trigger ['trɪgəʳ] **Ⓐ** N [*of gun*] gatillo *m*; [*of bomb, machine*] disparador *m*; **to pull the** ~ apretar el gatillo, disparar **Ⓑ** VT (*also* ~ **off**) [*+ bomb*] hacer estallar; [*+ fight, explosion*] provocar; [*+ mechanism*] hacer funcionar, poner en movimiento; [*+ chain of events*] desencadenar

trigger-happy* ['trɪgə,hæpɪ] ADJ pronto a disparar, que dispara a la mínima

trigonometry [,trɪgə'nɒmɪtrɪ] N trigonometría *f*

trike* [traɪk] N triciclo *m*

trilby ['trɪlbɪ] N (*Brit*) sombrero *m* flexible, sombrero *m* tirolés

trill [trɪl] **Ⓐ** N [*of bird*] gorjeo *m*, trino *m*; (*Mus*) trino *m* **Ⓑ** VI [*bird*] gorjear, trinar

trillion ['trɪlɪən] NUMBER (= 10^{12}) billón *m*

trilogy ['trɪlədʒɪ] N trilogía *f*

trim [trɪm] **Ⓐ** ADJ (*compar* **~mer**; *superl* **~mest**) **1** (= *neat*) [*garden, beard*] bien cuidado; [*person*] arreglado **2** (= *slim*) [*person, figure*] esbelto; [*waist*] delgado **Ⓑ** N **1** (= *cut*) **to get** *or* **have a** ~ cortarse un poco el pelo; **to give one's beard a** ~ recortarse la barba **2** (*Brit*) **in (good)** ~ [*person*] en buena forma, en buen estado físico; [*car, house*] en buen estado, en buenas condiciones; **to get into** ~ ponerse en forma **3** (= *decoration*) (*Sew*) adorno *m*; (*on edge*) ribete *m*, reborde *m*; (*on outside of car*) embellecedor *m* (*Sp*) **Ⓒ** VT **1** (= *clip*) [*+ hair, beard, moustache*] recortar; [*+ hedge*] cortar, podar **2** (= *reduce*) [*+ costs, prices, profits, workforce*] recortar; [*+ programme, policy*] hacer recortes en **3** (= *decorate*) [*+ dress, hat*] adornar; [*+ Xmas tree*] decorar **➤ trim away, trim off** VT + ADV cortar, quitar

trimester [trɪ'mestəʳ] N trimestre *m*

trimming ['trɪmɪŋ] N **1** (= *edging*) adorno *m*, guarnición *f* **2** trimmings **2.1** (= *cuttings*) recortes *mpl* **2.2** (= *extras, embellishments*) **turkey with all the ~s** pavo con su guarnición; **without all the ~s** sin los adornos

Trinidad ['trɪnɪdæd] N Trinidad *f*

Trinity ['trɪnɪtɪ] N Trinidad *f*

trinket ['trɪŋkɪt] N chuchería *f*, baratija *f*

trio ['trɪəʊ] N trío *m*

trip [trɪp] **Ⓐ** N **1** (= *journey*) viaje *m*; (= *excursion*) excursión *f*; (= *visit*) visita *f*; (= *outing*) salida *f*; **it's her first** ~ **abroad** es su primer viaje al extranjero; **fishing** ~ excursión *f* de pesca; **she went on a** ~ **to Tasmania** (se) fue de viaje a Tasmania; **he's away on a** ~ está de viaje; **school** ~ excursión *f* del colegio **2** (*Drugs**) viaje *m*; **she had a bad** ~ tuvo un mal viaje* **3** (*also* ~ **switch**) interruptor *m* de desconexión **Ⓑ** VI (= *stumble*) tropezar; **he ~ped and fell** tropezó y se cayó al suelo; **to** ~ **on/over sth** tropezar con algo **2** (= *step lightly*) **to** ~ **along** ir con paso ligero; **➤ IDIOM it doesn't exactly** ~ **off the tongue** no se puede decir que sea fácil de pronunciar **3** (*) (*on drugs*) **to be ~ping** estar volado *or* (*Sp*) colocado* **Ⓒ** VT **1** (*also* ~ **up**) (*intentionally*) poner *or* echar la zancadilla a; (*accidentally*) hacer tropezar **2** (= *set off*) [*+ mechanism, switch*] activar **Ⓓ** CPD **➤ trip switch** interruptor *m* de desconexión **➤ trip over** VI + ADV tropezar y caerse **➤ trip up** **Ⓐ** VI + ADV (= *stumble*) tropezar; (= *make a mistake*) equivocarse **Ⓑ** VT + ADV **1** (= *cause to stumble*) (*intentionally*) poner *or* echar la zancadilla a; (*accidentally*) hacer tropezar **2** (= *cause to make a mistake*) **she tried to** ~ **him up** intentó que se equivocase *or* que se confundiese

tripartite ['traɪ'pɑ:taɪt] ADJ tripartito

tripe [traɪp] N (*Culin*) callos *mpl*; **what utter ~!*** ¡tonterías!

triple ['trɪpl] **Ⓐ** ADJ triple **Ⓑ** ADV el triple, tres veces; **~ the sum** el triple **Ⓒ** N triple *m* **Ⓓ** VT triplicar **Ⓔ** VI triplicarse **Ⓕ** CPD **➤ triple jump** triple salto *m*

triplet ['trɪplɪt] N trillizo/a *m/f*, triate *mf* (*Mex*)

triplicate ['trɪplɪkɪt] N **in** ~ por triplicado

tripod ['traɪpɒd] N trípode *m*

Tripoli ['trɪpəlɪ] N Trípoli *m*

tripper ['trɪpəʳ] N (*Brit*) turista *mf*, excursionista *mf*

tripwire ['trɪpwaɪəʳ] N cuerda *f* de trampa

trite [traɪt] ADJ trillado, manido

triumph ['traɪʌmf] **Ⓐ** N **1** (= *victory*) triunfo *m* (**over** sobre); **a new ~ for industry** otro éxito para la industria **2** (= *emotion*) júbilo *m*; **in** ~ con júbilo **Ⓑ** VI triunfar (**over** sobre)

triumphal [traɪ'ʌmfəl] ADJ triunfal, de triunfo

triumphalism [traɪ'ʌmfəlɪzəm] N (*esp Brit*) triunfalismo *m*

triumphant [traɪ'ʌmfənt] ADJ (= *victorious*) victorioso, vencedor; (= *jubilant*) triunfante

triumphantly [traɪ'ʌmfəntlɪ] ADV triunfalmente, de modo triunfal; **he said** ~ dijo en tono triunfal

trivia ['trɪvɪə] NPL trivialidades *fpl*, nimiedades *fpl*, banalidades *fpl*

trivial ['trɪvɪəl] ADJ [*details, matter*] trivial, banal; [*sum*] insignificante, nimio

triviality [,trɪvɪ'ælɪtɪ] N **1** (= *trivial nature*) trivialidad *f*, banalidad *f* **2** (= *trivial detail*) trivialidad *f*

trivialize ['trɪvɪəlaɪz] VT minimizar, trivializar

trod [trɒd] PT *of* **tread**

trodden ['trɒdn] PP *of* **tread**

troglodyte ['trɒglədaɪt] N troglodita *mf*

troika ['trɔɪkə] N troica *f*

Trojan ['trəʊdʒən] **Ⓐ** ADJ troyano **Ⓑ** N troyano/a *m/f*; **✦ IDIOM to work like a** ~ trabajar como un mulo/una mula **Ⓒ** CPD **➤ Trojan horse** (*lit*) caballo *m* de Troya; (*fig*) tapadera *f*

troll [trəʊl] N gnomo *m*, duende *m*

trolley ['trɒlɪ] **Ⓐ** N **1** (*Brit*) (*in station, supermarket*) carrito *m*; (*in hospital*) camilla *f*; (= *tea trolley*) carrito *m*; **✦ IDIOM to be off one's ~*** estar chiflado* **2** (*US*) (= *tram*) tranvía *m* **Ⓑ** CPD **➤ trolley bus** trolebús *m* **➤ trolley car** (*US*) tranvía *m*

trombone [trɒm'bəʊn] N trombón *m*

trombonist [trɒm'bəʊnɪst] N (*orchestral*) trombón *mf*; (*jazz etc*) trombonista *mf*

troop [tru:p] **Ⓐ** N **1** (*gen*) banda *f*, grupo *m* **2** (*Mil*) **troops** tropas *fpl* **Ⓑ** VI (= *walk*) **to** ~ **in/out** entrar/salir en tropel *or* atropelladamente **Ⓒ** VT **to** ~ **the colour** (*Brit*) presentar la bandera **Ⓓ** CPD **➤ troop carrier** transporte *m* (militar) **➤ troop ship** (buque *m* de) transporte *m*

trooper ['tru:pəʳ] N **1** (*Mil*) soldado *mf* (de caballería); **✦ IDIOM to swear like a** ~ (*Brit**) jurar *or* hablar como un carretero **2** (*US*) (= *policeman*) policía *mf* montado/a

trophy ['trəʊfɪ] N trofeo *m*

tropic ['trɒpɪk] N trópico *m*; **the ~s** el trópico; **the Tropic of Cancer/Capricorn** el Trópico de Cáncer/Capricornio

tropical ['trɒpɪkəl] ADJ tropical

trot [trɒt] **Ⓐ** N **1** (= *step*) trote *m*; **to break into a** ~ echar a trotar; **to go for a** ~ ir a montar a caballo **2** (*Brit*) **for five days on the ~*** durante cinco días seguidos; **Barcelona won five times on the ~*** Barcelona ganó cinco veces seguidas **3** **the ~s**** diarrea *fsing*; **to have the ~s** tener diarrea **Ⓑ** VI [*horse, rider*] trotar, ir al trote; [*person*] ir trotando **➤ trot out*** VT + ADV [*+ excuse, reason*] ensartar, recitar

trotter ['trɒtəʳ] N (*Brit*) **pig's ~s** manitas *fpl* (de cerdo *or* (*LAm*) chancho)

troubadour ['tru:bədɔ:ʳ] N trovador *m*

trouble ['trʌbl] **Ⓐ** N **1** (= *problem*) problema *m*, dificultad *f*; (= *difficult situation*) apuro *m*, aprieto *m*; **what's the ~?** ¿cuál es el problema?, ¿qué pasa?; **the ~ is ...** el problema es ..., lo que pasa es ...; **that's just the ~** ahí está (la madre del cordero); **heart/back ~** problemas *mpl* de corazón/espalda; **engine ~** problemas *mpl* con el motor; **it's just asking for** ~ eso es buscarse problemas; **there'll <u>be</u> ~ if she finds out** se armará una buena si se entera; **to <u>get</u> into ~**: **he got into ~ with the police** se metió en un lío con la policía; **he got into ~ for saying that** se mereció una bronca diciendo eso; **to get sb into** ~ meter a algn en un lío *or* problemas; **to get out of** ~ salir del apuro; **to <u>give</u> ~:**

she never gave us any ~ nunca nos causó problemas; **to
have** ~ **doing sth: I had no** ~ **finding the house** encontré la
casa sin problemas; **we had** ~ **getting here in time** nos
costó trabajo llegar aquí a tiempo; **to be in** ~ (= having
problems) estar en un apuro or aprieto; (for doing wrong)
tener problemas; **don't go looking for** ~ no busques
camorra or problemas; **to make** ~ **for sb** crear un lío a algn;
money ~**s** dificultades fpl económicas
2 (= effort, bother) molestia f; **to go to (all) the** ~ **of doing
sth** tomarse la molestia de hacer algo; **I went to a lot of** ~
to get it for her me tomé muchas molestias para
conseguírselo; **it's no** ~ no es molestia; **I fear I am putting
you to a lot of** ~ me temo que se te vaya a molestar
bastante; **to take the** ~ **to do sth** tomarse la molestia de
hacer algo; **to take a lot of** ~ **over sth** esmerarse en algo,
hacer algo con el mayor cuidado; **nothing is too much** ~
for her para ella todo es poco; **it's more** ~ **than it's worth** no
vale la pena
3 (= unrest, fighting) conflicto m, disturbio m
Ⓑ VT **1** (= worry) preocupar
2 (= bother) molestar; **I'm sorry to** ~ **you** disculpe la
molestia; **don't** ~ **yourself!** ¡no te molestes!, ¡no te
preocupes!; **may I** ~ **you for a light?** ¿le molestaría darme
fuego, por favor?; **if the tooth** ~**s you again call the dentist**
si vuelves a tener molestias en el diente llama al dentista
Ⓒ VI molestarse; **don't** ~ **to write** no te molestes en
escribir; **he didn't** ~ **to shut the door** no se tomó la
molestia de cerrar la puerta
Ⓓ CPD ➤ **trouble spot** zona f conflictiva

troubled ['trʌbld] ADJ **1** (= worried) [person] preocupado;
[expression] de preocupación; [sleep] inquieto, agitado
2 (= beset by problems) [life, marriage, relationship] lleno de
problemas, aquejado de problemas; [region] conflictivo;
[industry] aquejado de problemas

trouble-free ['trʌblfri:] ADJ sin problemas; [demonstration]
sin disturbios, pacífico

troublemaker ['trʌbl,meɪkəʳ] N agitador(a) m/f

troubleshooter ['trʌblʃuːtəʳ] N apagafuegos mf inv
(profesional o consultor experto en la detección de problemas y
el desarrollo de soluciones empresariales o administrativas)

troubleshooting ['trʌblʃuːtɪŋ] N detección de problemas y
desarrollo de soluciones empresariales o administrativas

troublesome ['trʌblsəm] ADJ [person] fastidioso, molesto,
latoso; [ache] molesto; [dispute, problem] difícil, penoso

troubling ['trʌblɪŋ] ADJ inquietante, alarmante

trough [trɒf] N **1** (= feeding trough) comedero m, pesebre
m; (= drinking trough) abrevadero m, bebedero m
2 (= depression) depresión f, hoyo m

trounce [traʊns] VT dar una paliza a

troupe [truːp] N troupe f

trouser ['traʊzəʳ] N (Brit) **trousers** pantalón msing,
pantalones mpl; **a pair of** ~**s** un pantalón, unos
pantalones; ✦ IDIOM **to wear the** ~**s** llevar los pantalones
➤ **trouser press** prensa f para pantalones ➤ **trouser suit**
traje-pantalón m

trousseau ['truːsəʊ] N ajuar m

trout [traʊt] (pl ~) N trucha f

trowel ['traʊəl] N **1** (for gardening) desplantador m
2 (builder's) paleta f, llana f

truancy ['trʊənsɪ] N ausencia f sin permiso

truant ['trʊənt] Ⓐ N ausente mf; **to play** ~ hacer novillos,
hacer la rabona* Ⓑ VI hacer novillos, hacer la rabona*

truce [truːs] N tregua f; **to call a** ~ acordar una tregua

truck¹ [trʌk] Ⓐ N **1** (esp US) (= lorry) camión m **2** (Brit Rail)
vagón m Ⓑ VT (US) llevar, transportar Ⓒ CPD ➤ **truck
driver** (esp US) camionero/a m/f ➤ **truck stop** (US)
restaurante m de carretera

truck² [trʌk] N ✦ IDIOM **to have no** ~ **with** no tener nada
que ver con; ➤ **truck farm** (US) huerto m de hortalizas
➤ **truck farmer** (US) hortelano/a m/f ➤ **truck farming** (US)
horticultura f

trucker ['trʌkəʳ] N (US) camionero/a m/f, transportista mf

trucking ['trʌkɪŋ] N (US) acarreo m, transporte m (en camión)

truckload ['trʌkləʊd] N carga f de camión; **by the** ~ (fig) a
carretadas

truculence ['trʌkjʊləns] N agresividad f, mal humor m

truculent ['trʌkjʊlənt] ADJ agresivo, malhumorado

trudge [trʌdʒ] Ⓐ VT recorrer a pie (penosamente) Ⓑ VI **to**
~ **up/down/along** subir/bajar/caminar penosamente

true [truː] Ⓐ ADJ (compar ~r; superl ~st) **1** (= not false)
[story] real, verídico; [account] verídico; [statement] cierto,
verídico; [rumour] cierto, verdadero; **it is** ~ **that ...** es
verdad or cierto que ...; **is it** ~? ¿es (eso) verdad?; **it can't be**
~! ¡no me lo creo!; **I'm quite tired, it's** ~ es verdad or cierto
que estoy bastante cansado; **he's so jealous it's not** ~* es
tan celoso que resulta difícil creerlo; **is it** ~ **about Harry?**
¿es verdad or cierto lo de Harry?; ~, **but ...** cierto, pero ...;
to come ~ [dream] hacerse realidad; [wish, prediction]
cumplirse, hacerse realidad; ~ **or false?** ¿verdadero o
falso?; **it is** ~ **to say that ...** puede afirmarse que ...; **the film
is based on a** ~ **story** la película está basada en un hecho
real or verídico; **that's** ~ es cierto, es verdad; **too** ~ eso es
totalmente cierto
2 (= real) verdadero; **this helps us to discover our** ~ **selves**
esto nos ayuda a descubrir nuestra verdadera identidad; **in
the** ~ **sense (of the word)** en el sentido estricto (de la
palabra), propiamente dicho; **her** ~ **love**† su gran amor m
3 (= applicable) cierto; **this is particularly** ~ **for** single women
esto es cierto particularmente en el caso de las mujeres
solteras; **to hold** ~ ser válido (for para); **this is** ~ **of** any new
business venture éste es el caso con cualquier empresa
nueva; **the same is** ~ **of nuclear power stations** el caso es el
mismo con las centrales nucleares
4 (= faithful) **to be** ~ **to sb/sth** ser fiel a algn/algo; **to be** ~
to o.s. ser fiel a sí mismo; ~ **to form** como es/era de
esperar; **to be** ~ **to life** ser como la vida real; **to be** ~ **to
one's word** ser fiel a su palabra, cumplir con su palabra
5 (= accurate) **his aim was** ~ dio en el blanco
6 (= straight) derecho
7 (Mus) afinado
Ⓑ N **the doorframe is out of** ~ el marco de la puerta no cae
a plomo; **the top of the window was out of** ~ la parte
superior de la ventana no estaba nivelada
Ⓒ CPD ➤ **true colours, true colors** (US) **to show one's** ~
colours mostrarse tal y como se es en realidad ➤ **true
north** norte m geográfico

true-blue ['truː'bluː] ADJ rancio, de lo más rancio

true-born ['truː'bɔːn] ADJ auténtico, verdadero

truffle ['trʌfl] N trufa f

truism ['truːɪzəm] N (= well-known truth) perogrullada f;
(= cliché) tópico m

truly ['truːlɪ] ADV [happy, democratic, amazing, grateful]
verdaderamente, realmente; [understand, love] de verdad; **I**
~ **believe this** me lo creo de verdad, realmente me lo creo;
really and ~ de verdad; **yours** ~ le saluda atentamente

trump [trʌmp] Ⓐ N (Cards) triunfo m; **hearts are** ~**s**
triunfan corazones, pintan corazones; ✦ IDIOM **to turn up**
~**s** (Brit) (= come out all right) salir or resultar bien; **he always
turns up** ~**s** no nos falla nunca Ⓑ VT (Cards) fallar; (fig)
superar Ⓒ VI (Cards) triunfar Ⓓ CPD ➤ **trump card**
triunfo m; ✦ IDIOM **to play one's** ~ **card** jugar su mejor
carta

trumped-up ['trʌmpt'ʌp] ADJ fabricado, inventado

trumpet ['trʌmpɪt] Ⓐ N trompeta f Ⓑ VT pregonar,
anunciar (a son de trompeta)

trumpeter ['trʌmpɪtəʳ] N (orchestral) trompetero m,
trompeta mf; (jazz) trompetista mf

truncate [trʌŋ'keɪt] VT [+ report, speech] truncar

truncheon ['trʌntʃən] N (Brit) porra f

trundle ['trʌndl] Ⓐ VT (= push) empujar; (= pull) tirar, jalar
(LAm) Ⓑ VI [cart etc] rodar

trunk [trʌŋk] Ⓐ N **1** [of tree, human] tronco m **2** [of
elephant] trompa f **3** (= case) baúl m **4** (US) [of car] maletero
m, baúl m (LAm), cajuela f (Mex), maletera f (SC) Ⓑ CPD
➤ **trunk road** (Brit) carretera f principal

trunks [trʌŋks] NPL (also **swimming** or **bathing** ~) bañador
msing, slip msing

truss [trʌs] N braguero *m*
➤ **truss up** VT + ADV **to ~ sb up** atar a algn (*con cuerdas*)

trust [trʌst] Ⓐ N **1** (= *faith*) confianza *f* (**in** en); **you've**
betrayed their ~ has traicionado la confianza que tenían
puesta en ti; **to take sth/sb on** = fiarse de algo/algn; **to put**
one's ~ in sth/sb depositar su confianza en algo/algn
2 (*Jur*) (*for third party*) fondo *m* fiduciario, fondo *m* de
fideicomiso; (= *investment*) fondo *m* de inversiones;
(= *institution*) fundación *f*; **charitable** ~ fundación *f*
benéfica; **in** ~ en fideicomiso; **to set up a** ~ crear un fondo
fiduciario *or* de fideicomiso
Ⓑ VT **1** (= *consider honest, reliable*) [+ *person, judgment,*
instincts] fiarse de; (= *have confidence in*) confiar en, tener
confianza en; **~ me, I know what I'm doing** confía en mí, sé
lo que estoy haciendo; **I ~ you to keep this secret** confío
en que guardes este secreto; **her parents ~ her to make her**
own decisions sus padres confían en ella y la dejan que
tome sus propias decisiones; **he did not ~ himself to speak**
no se atrevió a hablar; **she is not to be ~ed** ella no es de
fiar; **I'd ~ him with my life** pondría mi vida en sus manos;
you can't ~ a word he says es imposible creer ninguna
palabra suya, no se puede uno fiar de nada de lo que dice;
"I forgot" — "~ you!" —se me olvidó —¡mira por dónde! *or*
—¡cómo no!; **~ you to break it!** ¡era de esperar que lo
rompieses!; ✦ IDIOM **I wouldn't ~ him an inch** *or* **as far as I**
could throw him no me fío de él ni un pelo
2 (= *hope*) esperar; **I ~ you are all well** espero que estéis
todos bien; **I ~ not** espero que no
Ⓒ VI **to ~ in sth/sb** confiar en algo/algn; **to ~ to luck/fate**
encomendarse a la suerte/al destino
Ⓓ CPD ➤ **trust company** compañía *f* fiduciaria, compañía *f*
de fideicomiso ➤ **trust fund** fondo *m* fiduciario, fondo *m*
de fideicomiso

trusted ['trʌstɪd] ADJ [*friend, adviser, servant*] de confianza;
[*formula*] probado

trustee [trʌs'tiː] N (*in bankruptcy*) síndico *m*; (= *holder of*
property for another) fideicomisario/a *m/f*, depositario/a
m/f, administrador(a) *m/f*; [*of college*] regente/a *m/f*

trustful ['trʌstfʊl] ADJ confiado

trusting ['trʌstɪŋ] ADJ confiado

trustworthiness ['trʌst,wɜːðɪnɪs] N formalidad *f*

trustworthy ['trʌst,wɜːðɪ] ADJ [*person*] formal, de
confianza; [*source of news*] fidedigno, fiable

trusty ['trʌstɪ] ADJ (*compar* **trustier**; *superl* **trustiest**) [*servant*]
fiel, leal; [*weapon*] seguro, bueno

truth [truːθ] N (*pl* **~s** [truːðz]) N verdad *f*; **there is some ~ in**
this hay una parte de verdad en esto; **there is no ~ in the**
rumour that ... no hay nada de verdad en el rumor de que
...; **in** ~ en verdad, a la verdad; **to tell the** ~ decir la verdad;
to tell (you) the ~ a decir verdad; ✦ PROV **~ is stranger than**
fiction la realidad sobrepasa a la ficción

truthful ['truːθfʊl] ADJ [*account*] verídico, veraz; [*person*]
veraz; **are you being ~?** ¿es esto la verdad?

truthfully ['truːθfəlɪ] ADV sinceramente; **now tell me ~**
ahora dime, dime la verdad

truthfulness ['truːθfəlnɪs] N veracidad *f*

try [traɪ] Ⓐ N **1** (= *attempt*) intento *m*, tentativa *f*; **it was a**
good ~ — better luck next time no lo conseguiste pero no
estuvo mal — otra vez será; **nice ~ Dave, but I know you're**
lying no cuela, Dave, sé que estás mintiendo; **to give sth a**
~ intentar (hacer) algo; **let me have a ~** déjame intentarlo;
it's worth a ~ vale *or* merece la pena intentarlo
2 (= *trial*) **to give sth a ~** [+ *product, food, experience*] probar
algo; **to give sb a ~** darle una oportunidad a algn, poner a
algn a prueba; **we'll give her a ~ for a week** le daremos una
semana de prueba
3 (*Rugby*) ensayo *m*; **to score a ~** marcar un ensayo
Ⓑ VT **1** (= *attempt*) **to ~ to do sth** intentar hacer algo,
tratar de hacer algo; **he was ~ing his best not to laugh**
estaba haciendo todo lo posible por no reírse
2 (= *try out, sample*) probar; **have you tried these olives?**
¿has probado estas aceitunas?; **to ~ doing sth** probar a
hacer algo; **~ turning the key** da vuelta a la llave y a ver
qué pasa, prueba a *or* intenta darle la vuelta a la llave
3 (= *attempt to work*) [+ *door handle*] tirar de; [+ *telephone*
number] intentar llamar a; [+ *phone*] intentar usar;

[+ *door*] intentar abrir
4 (= *inquire at*) **we tried three hotels but they had no room**
preguntamos en tres hoteles pero no tenían habitación;
have you tried the local music shops? ¿lo has buscado en
las tiendas de música del barrio?
5 (= *put to the test*) [+ *person, strength, patience*] poner a
prueba; **to ~ one's luck** probar suerte; **they haven't tried the**
drug on humans yet todavía no han probado la droga con
personas; ✦ PROV **these things are sent to ~ us** estas cosas
nos las manda el Señor para ponernos a prueba
6 (*Jur*) **to ~ sb (for sth)** procesar *or* enjuiciar a algn (por
algo); **to ~ a case** ver una demanda
Ⓒ VI **~ again!** ¡vuelve a intentarlo!; **he didn't even ~** ni
siquiera lo intentó; **you're not ~ing!** ¡no estás poniendo
todo tu empeño!; **I couldn't have done that (even) if I'd**
tried no podría haber hecho eso ni (siquiera) queriendo;
(just) you ~! ¡hazlo y verás!, ¡atrévete (y verás)!; **to ~ and**
do sth* intentar hacer algo, tratar de hacer algo; **it is not**
for lack *or* **want of ~ing** no será porque no se ha intentado;
~ as I might I couldn't persuade her por más que intenté
persuadirla no lo conseguí
➤ **try for** VI + PREP intentar conseguir, tratar de conseguir
➤ **try on** VT + ADV **1** [+ *clothes, shoes*] **would you like me**
to ~ it on? ¿quiere probárselo? **2** (*Brit**) **she's ~ing it on to see**
how far she can push you lo está haciendo para ver hasta
cuánto aguantas; **take no notice, he's just ~ing it on** no le
hagas caso, sólo está intentando quedarse contigo*; **don't ~**
anything on with me! ¡no intentes quedarte conmigo!*
➤ **try out** VT + ADV [+ *machine, new product, method*] probar;
[+ *new employee*] poner a prueba

trying ['traɪɪŋ] ADJ [*time, situation*] difícil; [*experience, day*]
duro; [*person*] latoso, pesado

try-on* ['traɪɒn] N camelo* *m*

tryst [trɪst] N cita *f*

tsar [zɑː^r] N zar *m*

tsarina [zɑːˈriːnə] N zarina *f*

tsetse fly ['tsetsɪflaɪ] N mosca *f* tsetsé

T-shirt ['tiːʃɜːt] N camiseta *f* de manga corta, playera *f*,
remera *f* (*Arg*), polera *f* (*Chi, Bol*)

tsp. ABBR = **teaspoon(ful)**

tub [tʌb] N **1** (= *large vessel*) cubo *m*, cuba *f*; (*for margarine*
etc) tarrina *f*; (= *washtub*) tina *f* **2** (*US*) (= *bathtub*) bañera *f*,
tina *f* (*esp LAm*)

tuba ['tjuːbə] N tuba *f*

tubby* ['tʌbɪ] ADJ (*compar* **tubbier**; *superl* **tubbiest**) gordito,
rechoncho

tube [tjuːb] Ⓐ N **1** [*of toothpaste, paint, TV*] tubo *m*; [*of*
tyre] cámara *f* de aire; ✦ IDIOM **it's all gone down the ~*****
todo se ha perdido **2** **the ~** (*US**) (= *television*) la tele*
3 (*Brit*) (= *underground*) metro *m*; **let's take the ~** vamos en
(el) metro Ⓑ CPD ➤ **tube station** (*Brit*) estación *f* de metro
➤ **tube top** (*US*) camiseta-tubo *f*

tuber ['tjuːbə^r] N (*Bot*) tubérculo *m*

tuberculosis [tjuˌbɜːkjʊˈləʊsɪs] N tuberculosis *f*, tisis *f*

tubular ['tjuːbjʊlə^r] ADJ tubular, en forma de tubo
➤ **tubular bells** campanas *fpl* tubulares

TUC N ABBR (*Brit*) = **Trades Union Congress**; *ver tb*
www.tuc.org.uk

tuck [tʌk] Ⓐ N **1** (*Sew*) (= *fold*) pinza *f*, pliegue *m* **2** (*Brit**)
(= *food*) comida *f*; (= *sweets*) dulces *fpl*, golosinas *fpl* Ⓑ VT
1 (= *put*) meter **2** (*Sew*) plegar Ⓒ CPD ➤ **tuck shop** (*Brit Scol*)
tienda *f* de golosinas
➤ **tuck away** VT + ADV (= *hide*) esconder, ocultar; **the village**
is ~ed away among the woods la aldea se esconde en el
bosque; **he ~ed it away in his pocket** se lo guardó en el
bolsillo; **she has her money safely ~ed away** tiene su dinero
bien guardado
➤ **tuck in** Ⓐ VI + ADV (*Brit**) (= *eat*) comer con apetito; **~ in!**
¡a comer!, ¡a ello! Ⓑ VT + ADV **1** [+ *shirt, blouse*] remeter,
meter dentro; **to ~ in a flap** meter una solapa para dentro;
to ~ the bedclothes in remeter la ropa de la cama
2 [+ *child*] (*in bed*) arropar
➤ **tuck into*** VI + PREP (*Brit*) [+ *meal*] comer con buen apetito
➤ **tuck up** VT + ADV **1** [+ *skirt, sleeves*] remangar **2** (*Brit*)

[+ *child*] (*in bed*) arropar

tucker* ['tʌkəʳ] VT (*US*) **to be ~ed (out)** estar molido *or* rendido*

Tue(s). ABBR (= **Tuesday**) mart.

Tuesday ['tjuːzdɪ] N martes *m inv*; **the date today is ~ 23rd March** *or* **March 23rd** hoy es martes, 23 de marzo; **on ~** (*past or future*) el martes; **on ~s** los martes; **every ~** todos los martes; **every other ~** cada otro martes, un martes sí y otro no; **last ~** el martes pasado; **next ~** el martes próximo, el martes que viene; **this ~** este martes; **the following ~** el martes siguiente; **the ~ before last** el martes antepasado; **the ~ after next** el martes próximo no, el siguiente, el martes que viene no, el siguiente; **a week on ~** ◇ **~ week** del martes en una semana; **a fortnight on ~** ◇ **~ fortnight** del martes en una quincena; **~ morning/night** el martes por la mañana/por la noche; **~ afternoon/evening** el martes por la tarde; **~ lunchtime** el martes a mediodía; **the ~ film** la película del martes; **~'s newspaper** el periódico del martes

tuft [tʌft] N [*of hair*] copete *m*, mechón *m*; [*of grass*] mata *f*; [*of feathers*] cresta *f*; (*on top of head*) copete *m*

tug [tʌg] Ⓐ N 1 (= *pull*) tirón *m*, jalón *m* (*LAm*); **to give sth a (good) ~** dar a algo un tirón (fuerte) 2 (*also* **~boat**) remolcador *m* Ⓑ VT 1 (= *pull*) tirar de, jalar (*LAm*); **to ~ sth along** arrastrar algo, llevar algo arrastrándolo 2 [+ *boat*] remolcar Ⓒ VI tirar, jalar (*LAm*); **to ~ at sth** tirar de algo

tug-of-war ['tʌgəv'wɔːʳ] N (*Sport*) juego *m* de tiro de cuerda; (*fig*) lucha *f*, tira y afloja *m*

tuition [tjʊ'ɪʃən] N enseñanza *f*, instrucción *f*; (*US*) matrícula *f*; **private ~** clases *fpl* particulares (**in** de); ➤ **tuition fees** matrícula *fsing*, tasas *fpl* de matriculación

tulip ['tjuːlɪp] N tulipán *m*

tulle [tjuːl] N tul *m*

tumble ['tʌmbl] Ⓐ N (= *fall*) caída *f*; (= *somersault*) voltereta *f*, rodada *f* (*LAm*); **to take a ~** caerse Ⓑ VI 1 (= *fall*) caerse; (= *stumble*) tropezar; **to ~ downstairs** rodar por la escalera, rodar escaleras abajo 2 [*water*] correr con fuerza; [*prices*] desplomarse 3 (= *rush*) **to ~ into/out of bed** tirarse en/saltar de la cama; **the children ~d out of the room/car** los niños salieron de la habitación/del coche en tropel 4 (*Brit**) (= *realize*) **to ~ to sth** caer en la cuenta de algo Ⓒ CPD ➤ **tumble dryer** (*esp Brit*) secadora *f*

tumbledown ['tʌmbldaʊn] ADJ ruinoso, desvencijado

tumble-dry [ˌtʌmbl'draɪ] VT meter en la secadora

tumbler ['tʌmbləʳ] N (= *glass*) vaso *m*

tummy* ['tʌmɪ] N barriga* *f*, tripa* *f* ➤ **tummy ache** dolor *m* de barriga*, dolor *m* de tripa*

tumour, tumor (*US*) ['tjuːməʳ] N tumor *m*

tumult ['tjuːmʌlt] N (= *uproar*) tumulto *m*; **to be in a ~** [*person*] estar agitado *or* alborotado; **her emotions were in a ~** tenía un conflicto emocional

tumultuous [tjuː'mʌltjʊəs] ADJ [*applause*] tumultuoso

tuna ['tjuːnə] N (*pl ~*) (*also* **~ fish**) atún *m*

tune [tjuːn] Ⓐ N 1 (= *melody*) melodía *f*; (= *piece*) tema *m*; (= *song*) canción *f*; **it hasn't got much ~** no es muy melódico, no tiene mucha melodía; **come on, give us a ~!** (= *sing*) ¡vamos, cántanos algo!; **he gave us a ~ on the piano** nos tocó un tema al piano; **to the ~ of** (*lit*) con la música de; **he was in debt to the ~ of £4,000** tenía deudas que llegaban a 4.000 libras; ✦ IDIOMS **to call the ~** llevar la voz cantante; **to change one's ~** cambiar de parecer; **to sing a different ~** bailar a un son distinto 2 (= *accurate pitch*) **to be in/out of ~** [*instrument*] estar afinado/desafinado; **he can't sing in ~** no sabe cantar sin desafinar, no sabe cantar afinado; **he is in/out of ~ with the people** sintoniza con/está desconectado con el pueblo; **his ideas were in/out of ~ with the spirit of his age** sus ideas estaban a tono/desentonaban con el espíritu de su época Ⓑ VT [+ *piano, guitar*] afinar; [+ *engine, machine*] poner a punto, afinar; [+ *radio, TV*] sintonizar ➤ **tune in** Ⓐ VI (*Rad, TV*) sintonizar; **to ~ in to** (*Rad, TV*) sintonizar (con); [+ *needs, feelings*] conectar con Ⓑ VT + ADV 1 (*Rad, TV*) **you are ~d in to ...** está usted

sintonizando (la cadena) ... 2 (*fig*) **to be ~d in to** [+ *new developments*] estar al corriente de; [+ *sb's feelings*] estar conectado con ➤ **tune up** VT + ADV, VI + ADV (*Mus*) afinar

tuneful ['tjuːnfəl] ADJ [*voice, song*] melodioso, armonioso

tuneless ['tjuːnlɪs] ADJ poco melodioso

tuner ['tjuːnəʳ] N (*Rad*) (= *knob, equipment*) sintonizador *m*

tungsten ['tʌŋstən] N tungsteno *m*

tunic ['tjuːnɪk] N túnica *f*; (*Brit Mil*) guerrera *f*, blusa *f*

tuning fork ['tjuːnɪŋfɔːk] N diapasón *m*

Tunis ['tjuːnɪs] N Túnez *m*

Tunisia [tjuː'nɪzɪə] N Túnez *m*

Tunisian [tjuː'nɪzɪən] ADJ, N tunecino/a *m/f*

tunnel ['tʌnl] Ⓐ N (*gen*) túnel *m*; (*Min*) galería *f*; (= *underpass*) paso *m* subterráneo Ⓑ VI construir un túnel Ⓒ CPD ➤ **tunnel vision** visión *f* periférica restringida; (*fig*) estrechez *f* de miras

tuppence* ['tʌpəns] N = **twopence**

turban ['tɜːbən] N turbante *m*

turbine ['tɜːbaɪn] N turbina *f*

turbo ['tɜːbəʊ] N (= *fan*) turboventilador *m*; (*in cars*) turbo(compresor) *m*

turbo-charged ['tɜːbəʊtʃɑːdʒd] ADJ turbocargado, turboalimentado

turbojet ['tɜːbəʊ'dʒet] Ⓐ N turborreactor *m* Ⓑ CPD turborreactor

turbot ['tɜːbət] N (*pl ~*) rodaballo *m*

turbulence ['tɜːbjʊləns] N turbulencia *f*

turbulent ['tɜːbjʊlənt] ADJ turbulento

turd** [tɜːd] N 1 (= *excrement*) cagada*** *f*, zurullo*** *m* 2 (= *person*) mierda*** *mf*

tureen [tə'riːn] N sopera *f*

turf [tɜːf] N (= *grass*) césped *m*; (= *peat*) turba *f*; (*) [*of gang etc*] territorio *m*, zona *f* de influencia; **the Turf** el turf, el hipódromo ➤ **turf out*** VT + ADV (*Brit*) echar (de la casa), plantar en la calle

turgid ['tɜːdʒɪd] ADJ [*prose etc*] inflado, rimbombante

Turk [tɜːk] N turco/a *m/f*; **young ~** (*Pol*) joven reformista *mf*

Turkey ['tɜːkɪ] N Turquía *f*

turkey ['tɜːkɪ] N 1 (= *bird*) pavo *m*, guajolote *m* (*Mex*), jolote *m* (*CAm*), chompipe *m* (*CAm*); ✦ IDIOM **to talk ~** (*US**) hablar en serio 2 (*esp US Cine, Theat**) (= *flop*) fiasco* *m*, fracaso *m*

Turkish ['tɜːkɪʃ] Ⓐ ADJ turco Ⓑ N (= *language*) turco *m* Ⓒ CPD ➤ **Turkish bath** baño *m* turco ➤ **Turkish coffee** café *m* turco ➤ **Turkish delight** lokum *m*, capricho *m* de reina ➤ **Turkish towel** (*US*) toalla *f*

Turkmenistan [tɜːkˌmenɪs'tɑːn] N Turkmenistán *m*

turmeric ['tɜːmərɪk] N cúrcuma *f*

turmoil ['tɜːmɔɪl] N confusión *f*, desorden *m*; (*mental*) trastorno *m*; **to be in ~** [*house*] estar alborotado

turn [tɜːn] Ⓐ N 1 (= *rotation*) vuelta *f*, revolución *f*; **he gave the handle a ~** dio vuelta a la palanca 2 (= *bend*) vuelta *f*, curva *f* 3 (= *turn-off*) salida *f*; **I think we've missed our ~** creo que nos hemos pasado de la salida; **"no left turn"** "prohibido girar a la izquierda"; **to do a left ~** (*Aut*) doblar *or* girar a la izquierda 4 (*Swimming*) vuelta *f* 5 (= *change of direction*) **at the ~ of the century** a finales del siglo; **this was a surprising ~ of events** esto suponía un giro inesperado de los acontecimientos; **at every ~** (*fig*) a cada paso; **~ of the tide** (*lit, fig*) cambio *m or* vuelta *f* de la marea; **then things took a ~ for the better** entonces las cosas empezaron a mejorar; **the patient took a ~ for the worse** el paciente empeoró 6 (*in series, etc*) turno *m*, vez *f*; **whose ~ is it?** ¿a quién le toca?; **it's your ~** te toca a ti; **your ~ will come** ya te tocará; **by ~s** por turnos, sucesivamente; **in ~** por turnos, sucesivamente; **and they, in ~, said ...** y ellos a su vez

dijeron ...; **to speak <u>out</u> of** ~ (*fig*) hablar fuera de lugar; **to take ~s** *or* (*Brit*) **take it in ~(s) to do sth** turnarse para hacer algo
7 (*Brit Med*) (= *fainting fit*) vahído *m*, desmayo *m*; (= *crisis*) crisis *f inv*, ataque *m*; **he had a bad ~ last night** anoche tuvo un ataque
8 (*) (= *fright*) susto *m*; **the news gave me quite a** ~ la noticia me asustó *or* dejó de piedra
9 (= *act*) número *m*, turno *m*
10 (= *deed*) **to do sb a <u>good</u>** hacerle un favor a algn; ✦ PROV **one good ~ deserves another** amor con amor se paga
11 (*in phrases*) **to be of a scientific ~ of <u>mind</u>** ser más dado a las ciencias; **~ of <u>phrase</u>** forma *f* de hablar, giro *m*; **it's done <u>to</u> a ~** está en su punto
Ⓑ VT **1** (= *rotate*) [+ *wheel, handle*] girar, dar vueltas a; [+ *screw*] atornillar, destornillar; **to ~ the key in the lock** dar vuelta a la llave en la cerradura; **~ it to the left** dale una vuelta hacia la izquierda
2 (*also* **~ over**) [+ *record, mattress, steak*] dar la vuelta a, voltear (*LAm*); [+ *page*] pasar; ✦ IDIOM **it ~s my stomach** (*lit, fig*) me revuelve el estómago
3 (= *direct*) dirigir, volver; **they ~ed him <u>against</u> us** le pusieron en contra nuestra; **we managed to ~ his argument against him** pudimos volver su argumento contra él mismo; **to ~ a <u>gun</u> on sb** apuntar una pistola a algn; ✦ IDIOMS **to ~ the other cheek** ofrecer la otra mejilla; **without ~ing a hair** sin inmutarse; **he didn't ~ a hair** ni se inmutó; **to ~ sb's head: earning all that money has ~ed his head** se le han subido los humos con lo de ganar tanto dinero
4 (= *pass*) doblar, dar la vuelta a; **the car ~ed the corner** el coche dobló la esquina; **when he ~s 18** cuando cumpla los 18 (años); ✦ IDIOM **to have ~ed the corner** haber salido del apuro, haber pasado lo peor
5 (= *change*) **the heat ~ed the walls black** el calor volvió negras las paredes, el calor ennegreció las paredes; **an actor ~ed writer** un actor metido a escritor; **to ~ sth <u>into</u> sth** convertir algo en algo; **she ~ed her dreams into reality** hizo sus sueños realidad, realizó sus sueños
Ⓒ VI **1** (= *rotate*) [*wheel etc*] girar, dar vueltas; **the earth ~s on its axis** la Tierra gira sobre su propio eje; ✦ IDIOMS **his stomach ~ed at the sight** al verlo se le revolvió el estómago, se le revolvieron las tripas al verlo*; **she would ~ in her grave if she knew** le daría un síncope si supiera
2 (= *change direction*) [*person*] dar la vuelta, voltearse (*LAm*); [*tide*] repuntar; **to ~ and go back** volverse *or* dar la vuelta y regresar; **to ~ <u>against</u> sb** volverse contra algn; **to ~ <u>for</u> home** volver hacia casa; **then our <u>luck</u> ~ed** luego nuestra suerte cambió; **he ~ed <u>to</u> me and smiled** se volvió hacia mí y sonrió; **to ~ to sb for help** acudir a algn en busca de ayuda; **she has no-one to ~ to** no tiene a quién recurrir; **our thoughts ~ to those who ...** pensamos ahora en los que ...; **please ~ to page 34** vamos a la página 34; **he ~ed to drink** se dio a la bebida, le dio por el alcohol; **the conversation ~ed to religion** la conversación viró hacia la religión; **I don't know which <u>way</u> to ~** (*fig*) no sé qué hacer; ✦ IDIOM **the tide is ~ing** las cosas están cambiando
3 (*Aut*) torcer, girar; (*Aer, Naut*) virar; **to ~ left** (*Aut*) torcer *or* girar *or* doblar a la izquierda; **the car ~ed <u>into</u> a lane** el coche se metió en una bocacalle
4 (= *change*) **to ~ <u>into</u> sth** convertirse *or* transformarse en algo
5 (= *become*) **it has ~ed <u>cold</u>** el tiempo se ha puesto frío, se ha echado el frío; **to ~ <u>nasty</u>** [*person*] ponerse *or* volverse antipático; **to ~ <u>professional</u>** hacerse profesional; **to ~ <u>red</u>** ponerse rojo
6 (= *depend*) **everything ~s <u>on</u> his decision** todo depende de su decisión
Ⓓ CPD ➤ **turn signal** (*esp US*) intermitente *m*, direccional *f* (*LAm*)
➤ **turn around Ⓐ** VI + ADV **1** [*person*] volverse, darse la vuelta; **as soon as I ~ed around they were quarrelling** *or* (*US*) **quarreling again** en cuanto les volví la espalda se pusieron otra vez a reñir
2 (= *rotate*) girar, dar vueltas; **to ~ around and around** dar vueltas y más vueltas
3 (= *improve*) [*business, economy*] recuperarse
Ⓑ VT + ADV **1** [+ *object*] dar la vuelta a, voltear (*LAm*);

[+ *vehicle, ship etc*] dar la vuelta a, girar
2 (*Comm*) **to ~ an order around** tramitar un pedido
3 (= *make successful*) [+ *business*] sacar a flote, hacer despegar; (= *make profitable*) [+ *company, school*] rentabilizar, sanear (las finanzas de); [+ *the economy*] sanear
➤ **turn aside Ⓐ** VI + ADV desviarse, apartarse (**from** de) **Ⓑ** VT + ADV desviar, apartar
➤ **turn away Ⓐ** VI + ADV apartarse (**from** de) **Ⓑ** VT + ADV [+ *eyes, head, gun*] desviar, apartar; [+ *person, offer, business, customer*] rechazar
➤ **turn back Ⓐ** VI + ADV volverse (atrás), desandar el camino; **there can be no ~ing back now** (*fig*) ahora no vale volverse atrás **Ⓑ** VT + ADV **1** (= *send back*) hacer volver, hacer regresar; **they were ~ed back at the frontier** en la frontera les hicieron volver *or* regresar **2** [+ *clock*] retrasar; **we can't ~ the clock back** no podemos dar marcha atrás *or* volver al pasado
➤ **turn down** VT + ADV **1** (= *fold down*) [+ *bedclothes, collar*] doblar **2** (= *reduce*) [+ *gas, heat, volume*] bajar **3** (= *refuse*) [+ *offer, suitor, candidate*] rechazar; **he was ~ed down for the job** no le dieron el puesto
➤ **turn in Ⓐ** VI + ADV **1** [*car, person*] entrar **2** (*) (= *go to bed*) acostarse **Ⓑ** VT + ADV (= *hand over*) entregar; **to ~ sb in** entregar a algn a la policía; **to ~ o.s. in** entregarse
➤ **turn off Ⓐ** VI + ADV **1** (*Aut*) [*person, vehicle*] doblar; **~ off at the next exit** toma la próxima (salida de la autopista)
2 [*appliance etc*] apagarse **Ⓑ** VT + ADV **1** [+ *light*] apagar; [+ *appliance*] apagar; (*at mains*) desconectar, cortar; [+ *tap*] cerrar; [+ *engine*] parar; [+ *gas*] cerrar la llave de; [+ *TV programme, radio programme*] quitar **2** (*) [+ *person*] (= *fail to interest*) dejar frío; (*sexually*) matar el deseo a
➤ **turn on Ⓐ** VI + ADV **1** [*appliance*] encenderse, prender (*LAm*) **2** (*TV, Rad*) [*viewer, listener*] encender *or* (*LAm*) prender el receptor **Ⓑ** VT + ADV **1** [+ *appliance, electricity*] encender, prender (*LAm*); [+ *tap*] abrir **2** (*) (= *excite*) interesar, despertar; (*sexually*) excitar **Ⓒ** VI + PREP **to ~ on sb** volverse contra algn
➤ **turn out Ⓐ** VI + ADV **1** (= *appear*) aparecer; (= *attend*) [*doctor*] atender
2 (= *prove*) resultar; **it ~ed out that ...** resultó (ser) que ...; **it ~ed out well/badly** salió bien/mal
3 (= *transpire*) salir; **how are things ~ing out?** ¿cómo van las cosas?; **as it ~s out I already have one** da la casualidad de que ya tengo uno; **it's ~ed out nice again** vuelve a hacer bueno
Ⓑ VT + ADV **1** [+ *appliance, light*] apagar; [+ *gas*] cortar
2 (= *produce*) [+ *goods, secretaries*] producir
3 (= *empty*) [+ *pockets*] vaciar; [+ *cake*] sacar
4 (= *expel*) [+ *person*] expulsar, echar
5 to be well ~ed out [*person*] ir elegante *or* bien vestido
➤ **turn over Ⓐ** VI + ADV **1** [*person, car etc*] volverse, voltearse (*LAm*); [*boat*] volcar(se)
2 (*in reading*) pasar a la siguiente página; (*in letter*) volver la página; (*TV*) cambiar de canal
Ⓑ VT + ADV **1** [+ *page*] volver; [+ *container, vehicle*] volcar; [+ *patient, mattress, card*] dar la vuelta a; [+ *tape, record*] dar la vuelta a, poner la otra cara de; **to ~ over an idea in one's mind** darle vueltas a una idea en la cabeza
2 (= *hand over*) [+ *person*] entregar (**to** a)
3 (*Comm*) [+ *sum*] mover, facturar; **they ~ over a million a year** su volumen de ventas/producción es de un millón al año
➤ **turn round** VI + ADV, VT + ADV = **turn around**
➤ **turn up Ⓐ** VI + ADV **1** (= *be found*) aparecer **2** (= *arrive, show up*) [*person*] llegar, aparecer; **something will ~ up** algo saldrá **Ⓑ** VT + ADV **1** [+ *collar, sleeve, hem*] subir **2** [+ *heat, gas, sound*] subir; [+ *radio etc*] poner más fuerte, subir; ✦ IDIOM **to ~ up the heat (on sth/sb)*** meter más presión (a algo/algn) **3** (= *find*) descubrir, desenterrar; [+ *evidence, information*] sacar a la luz, revelar

turnabout ['tɜːnəbaʊt] N cambio *m* de rumbo, giro *m* radical

turnaround ['tɜːnəraʊnd] N **1** (= *change*) cambio *m* de rumbo, giro *m* radical **2** (= *improvement*) despegue *m* **3** (*also* **~ time**) [*of goods*] plazo *m*

turncoat ['tɜːnkəʊt] N renegado/a *m/f*, chaquetero/a *m/f*

turning ['tɜːnɪŋ] N (= *side road*) bocacalle *f*; **the first ~ on**

the right la primera bocacalle a la derecha ➤ **turning point** momento *m* decisivo, punto *m* de inflexión

turnip ['tɜːnɪp] N nabo *m*

turn-off ['tɜːnɒf] N **1** (*in road*) desvío *m*, empalme *m* **2** (*) **he's a real ~** ese me cae gordo*; **his breath is a big ~** su aliento me repugna

turn-on* ['tɜːnɒn] N (= *person*) tipo/a *m/f* bueno/a*, tío/a *m/f* bueno/a (*Sp**)

turnout ['tɜːnaʊt] N (= *attendance*) concurrencia *f*, asistencia *f*; (= *paying spectators*) entrada *f*, público *m*; (*at election*) número *m* de votantes; **there was a poor ~** asistió poca gente

turn-out ['tɜːnaʊt] N (*US Aut*) área *f* de descanso, área *f* de estacionamiento

> Use **el/un** not **la/una** before feminine nouns beginning with stressed **a** or **ha** like **área**.

turnover ['tɜːnˌəʊvəʳ] N **1** (*of stock, goods*) renovación *f* de existencias; (= *total business*) movimiento *m* de mercancías; **a ~ of £6,000 a week** una facturación de 6.000 libras a la semana; **there is a rapid ~ in staff** el personal cambia muy a menudo **2** (*Culin*) empanada *f*

turnpike ['tɜːnpaɪk] N (*US Aut*) autopista *f* de peaje

turnround ['tɜːnraʊnd] N = **turnaround**

turnstile ['tɜːnstaɪl] N torniquete *m*

turntable ['tɜːnˌteɪbl] N (*for record player*) plato *m* (giratorio), giradiscos *m inv*

turn-up ['tɜːnʌp] N (*Brit*) (*of trousers*) vuelta *f*; ✦ IDIOM **that was a ~ for the books** eso sí que no se esperaba

turpentine ['tɜːpəntaɪn] N trementina *f* ➤ **turpentine substitute** aguarrás *m*

turquoise ['tɜːkwɔɪz] Ⓐ N (= *stone*) turquesa *f*; (= *colour*) azul *m* turquesa Ⓑ ADJ azul turquesa *inv*

turret ['tʌrɪt] N (*of castle*) torreón *m*; (*of tank etc*) torreta *f*

turtle ['tɜːtl] N (*Brit*) tortuga *f* (marina); ✦ IDIOM **to turn ~*** volverse patas arriba; (*boat, car*) volcar(se)

turtledove ['tɜːtldʌv] N tórtola *f*

turtleneck ['tɜːtlnek] N (*also* **~ sweater**) (*US*) (*high*) jersey *m* de cuello alto; (*Brit*) (*low*) jersey *m* de cuello vuelto *or* de tortuga

tusk [tʌsk] N colmillo *m*

tussle ['tʌsl] Ⓐ N (= *struggle*) lucha *f* (**for** por); (= *scuffle*) pelea *f*, agarrada *f* Ⓑ VI pelearse (**with** con; **about, over** por)

tut [tʌt] (*also* **tut-tut**) Ⓐ EXCL ¡vaya! Ⓑ VI chasquear la lengua en señal de desaprobación

tutor ['tjuːtəʳ] Ⓐ N (= *private teacher*) profesor(a) *m/f* particular; (*Brit Univ*) tutor(a) *m/f* Ⓑ VT **to ~ sb in Latin** dar clases particulares de latín a algn Ⓒ CPD ➤ **tutor group** (*Brit*) grupo *m* de tutoría

tutorial [tjuːˈtɔːrɪəl] N seminario *m*

tutu ['tuːtuː] N tutú *m*

tuxedo [tʌkˈsiːdəʊ], **tux*** ['tʌks] N (*esp US*) smoking *m*, esmoquin *m*

TV N ABBR (= **television**) tele *f*, TV *f* ➤ **TV dinner** *cena precocinada que se vende en la misma bandeja de la que se come* ➤ **TV licence** = **television licence**

twaddle* ['twɒdl] N tonterías *fpl*, chorradas* *fpl*, babosadas *fpl* (*LAm**), pendejadas *fpl* (*LAm**)

twang [twæŋ] Ⓐ N (*of wire, bow etc*) tañido *m*; (*of voice*) deje *m*; **to speak with a ~** ganguear Ⓑ VT (*Mus*) tañer; (+ *bowstring*) estirar y soltar repentinamente

tweak [twiːk] Ⓐ N **1** (= *pull*) pellizco *m* **2** (*) (= *alteration*) pequeño retoque *m* Ⓑ VT **1** (= *pull*) pellizcar **2** (*) (= *alter*) retocar ligeramente

twee* [twiː] ADJ (*Brit pej*) cursi, afectado

tweed [twiːd] N **1** (= *cloth*) tweed *m* **2 tweeds** (= *suit*) traje *msing* de tweed

tweet [twiːt] Ⓐ N (*of bird*) pío pío *m* Ⓑ VI piar

tweezers ['twiːzəz] NPL pinzas *fpl*; **a pair of ~** unas pinzas

twelfth [twelfθ] Ⓐ ADJ duodécimo Ⓑ PRON (*in series*) duodécimo/a *m/f*; (= *fraction*) duodécima parte *f*, doceavo *m* Ⓒ CPD ➤ **Twelfth Night** Día *m* de Reyes, Reyes *mpl*; *see* **fifteenth**

twelve [twelv] NUMBER doce *m*; *see* **five**

twentieth ['twentɪɪθ] Ⓐ ADJ vigésimo Ⓑ PRON (*in series*) vigésimo/a *m/f*; (= *fraction*) vigésima parte *f*, veinteavo *m*; *see* **fifteenth**

twenty ['twentɪ] NUMBER veinte *m*; **to be in one's twenties** tiene más de veinte años, tener veintitantos (años), ser un veinteañero; *see* **fifty**

twenty-first ['twentɪfɜːst] PRON (= *birthday*) veintiún cumpleaños *m inv*; (= *party*) fiesta *f* del veintiún cumpleaños

twenty-four ['twentɪˈfɔːʳ] ADJ **"twenty-four hour service"** "abierto 24 horas"

24/7 ['twentɪˌfɔːˈsevn] ADV ABBR (= **24 hours a day, 7 days a week**) 24 horas al día, 7 días a la semana; **we are on call 24/7** estamos de guardia las 24 horas

twenty-twenty vision [ˌtwentɪˌtwentɪˈvɪʒən] N visión *f* normal

twerp* [twɜːp] N idiota *mf*, bruto/a *m/f*; **you ~!** ¡imbécil!

twice [twaɪs] ADV dos veces; **~ as much/many** dos veces más; **~ a week** dos veces a la *or* por semana; **she is ~ your age** ella tiene dos veces tu edad, es dos veces mayor que tú; **~ the sum** ◇ **~ the quantity** el doble; **A is ~ as big as B** A es el doble de B, A es dos veces más grande que B; **he didn't have to be asked ~** no se hizo de rogar, no se lo tuve que pedir dos veces

twiddle ['twɪdl] Ⓐ VT dar vueltas a; ✦ IDIOM **to ~ one's thumbs** estar de brazos cruzados, estar mano sobre mano Ⓑ VI **to ~ with sth** jugar con algo (entre los dedos)

twig¹ [twɪg] N ramita *f*

twig²* [twɪg] (*Brit*) VI caer en la cuenta

twilight ['twaɪlaɪt] N anochecer *m*, crepúsculo *m*; **at ~** al anochecer; **in the ~** a media luz

twill [twɪl] N tela *f* cruzada

twin [twɪn] Ⓐ N (*identical*) gemelo/a *m/f*; (*non-identical*) mellizo/a *m/f* Ⓑ ADJ **1** (*brother, sister*) (*identical*) gemelo; (*non-identical*) mellizo **2** (*Brit*) (*town, city*) hermano **3** (*towers, peaks, engines*) gemelo Ⓒ VT **1** (*Brit*) (*towns, cities, institutions*) hermanar (**with** con) **2** (= *combine*) (+ *clothes*) combinar Ⓓ CPD ➤ **twin beds** camas *fpl* gemelas

twin-bedded ['twɪn'bedɪd] ADJ (*esp Brit*) (*room*) con camas gemelas

twine [twaɪn] Ⓐ N bramante *m* Ⓑ VI (*spiral, plant*) enroscarse; (*fingers*) entrelazarse

twin-engined ['twɪn'endʒɪnd] ADJ bimotor

twinge [twɪndʒ] N (*also* **~ of pain**) dolor *m* agudo; **~s of conscience** remordimientos *mpl* de conciencia

twinkle ['twɪŋkl] Ⓐ N centelleo *m*, parpadeo *m*; **he had a ~ in his eye** tenía un brillo en sus ojos Ⓑ VI (*light*) centellear, parpadear; (*eyes*) brillar

twirl [twɜːl] Ⓐ N vuelta *f*, pirueta *f* Ⓑ VT dar vueltas rápidas a; (+ *baton*) dar vueltas a; (+ *moustache*) atusarse

twist [twɪst] Ⓐ N **1** (= *coil*) (*of paper*) cucurucho *m*; (*of smoke*) voluta *f*

2 (= *kink, bend*) (*in wire, cord, hose*) vuelta *f*; (*in road*) recodo *m*, curva *f*; ✦ IDIOM **to drive sb round the ~*** volver loco a algn*

3 (= *action*) **with a quick ~ of the wrist** torciendo *or* girando rápidamente la muñeca; **to give sth a ~** (+ *lid, top*) girar algo

4 (*in plot, story*) giro *m*; **the plot has an unexpected ~** el argumento tiene un giro inesperado; **by a strange ~ of fate** por una de esas extrañas vueltas que da la vida

5 (= *dance*) twist *m*; **to do the ~** bailar el twist

Ⓑ VT **1** (= *coil*) enroscar, enrollar; ✦ IDIOM **to ~ sb round one's little finger** tener a algn en el bolsillo, hacer con algn lo que le da la gana

2 (= *turn*) (+ *knob, handle, lid*) girar; (*repeatedly*) (+ *ring*) dar vueltas a; ✦ IDIOM **to ~ sb's arm** apretarle las tuercas a algn

3 (= *injure*) torcerse; **he ~ed his ankle** se torció el tobillo

4 (= *distort, contort*) [+ *girder, metal*] retorcer; [+ *words, argument*] tergiversar
⊙ VI **1** (= *coil*) enroscarse
2 (= *bend*) [*road, river*] serpentear
➤ **twist off ⓐ** VI + ADV [*top, lid*] desenroscarse **ⓑ** VT + ADV [+ *top, lid*] desenroscar

twisted ['twɪstɪd] ADJ **1** [*metal, roots, cables, smile*] retorcido; [*face, features, ankle, wrist*] torcido **2** (= *warped*) [*person, mind, logic*] retorcido

twister* ['twɪstəʳ] N (*US*) (= *tornado*) huracán *m*

twit* [twɪt] N (*Brit*) imbécil *mf*

twitch [twɪtʃ] **ⓐ** N tic *m*, contracción *f* nerviosa **ⓑ** VI [*face, muscles*] crisparse; [*nose, tail*] moverse nerviosamente

twitchy* ['twɪtʃɪ] ADJ (= *nervous*) nervioso, inquieto

twitter ['twɪtəʳ] VI [*bird*] piar

two [tuː] NUMBER dos *m*; **to break sth in ~** romper algo en dos, partir algo por la mitad; **~ by ~** ◇ **in ~s** de dos en dos; **that makes ~ of us** ya somos dos; ✦ IDIOM **to put ~ and ~ together** atar cabos; *see* **five**

two-bit* ['tuːbɪt] ADJ (*US*) de poca monta, de tres al cuarto

two-door ['tuːdɔːʳ] ADJ [*car*] de dos puertas

two-faced ['tuːfeɪst] ADJ falso, hipócrita

twofold ['tuːfəʊld] **ⓐ** ADV dos veces **ⓑ** ADJ doble

two-legged ['tuːlegɪd] ADJ bípedo, de dos piernas

two-party ['tuːpɑːtɪ] ADJ [*state, country*] bipartidista

twopence ['tʌpəns] N dos peniques; (= *coin*) moneda *f* de dos peniques; ✦ IDIOM **it's not worth ~*** no vale una perra gorda

two-percent milk ['tuːpəˌsentˈmɪlk] N (*US*) leche *f* semidesnatada

two-piece ['tuːpiːs] **ⓐ** ADJ [*suit*] de dos piezas **ⓑ** N (= *suit*) conjunto *m* de dos piezas

two-seater ['tuːsiːtəʳ] **ⓐ** ADJ biplaza, de dos plazas **ⓑ** N (= *car, plane*) biplaza *m*

twosome ['tuːsəm] N pareja *f*

two-star (petrol) ['tuːstɑːˈpetrəl)] N (*Brit*) gasolina *f* normal

two-stroke ['tuːstrəʊk] N (*also* **~ engine**) motor *m* de dos tiempos

two-time* ['tuːtaɪm] VT engañar con otro/a a, ser infiel con otro/a a

two-way ['tuːweɪ] ADJ [*radio*] emisor y receptor; [*street*] de doble sentido ➤ **two-way mirror** luna *f* de efecto espejo ➤ **two-way switch** conmutador *m* de dos direcciones ➤ **two-way traffic** circulación *f* en dos sentidos

TX ABBR (*US*) = **Texas**

tycoon [taɪˈkuːn] N magnate *m*

type [taɪp] **ⓐ** N **1** (= *class, kind*) tipo *m*, clase *f*; **I'm not the ~ to get carried away** no soy del tipo *or* de la clase de personas que se dejan llevar; **she's/he's not my ~** no es mi tipo; **it's my ~ of film** es una película de las que a mí me gustan; **a moisturizer suitable for all skin ~s** una crema hidratante apropiada para todo tipo de pieles
2 (*) (= *individual*) tipo/a* *m/f*
3 (= *typeface*) tipo *m*; (= *printed characters*) letra *f*; **in bold ~** en negrita; **in large/small ~** en letra grande/pequeña
ⓑ VT (*also* **~ up**) escribir a máquina, pasar a máquina
ⓒ VI escribir a máquina

typecast ['taɪpkɑːst] ADJ [*actor*] encasillado

typeface ['taɪpfeɪs] N tipo *m*, tipo *m* de letra, letra *f*

typescript ['taɪpskrɪpt] N texto *m* mecanografiado

typeset ['taɪpset] VT componer

typesetter ['taɪpˌsetəʳ] N cajista *mf*, compositor(a) *m/f*

typewriter ['taɪpˌraɪtəʳ] N máquina *f* de escribir

typewritten ['taɪpˌrɪtn] ADJ escrito a máquina, mecanografiado

typhoid ['taɪfɔɪd] N tifoidea *f*, fiebre *f* tifoidea

typhoon [taɪˈfuːn] N tifón *m*

typhus ['taɪfəs] N tifus *m*

typical ['tɪpɪkəl] ADJ típico; **that's ~ of him!** ¡eso es típico de él!

typically ['tɪpɪkəlɪ] ADV **1** (= *characteristically*) [*defiant, flamboyant, Spanish*] típicamente **2** (= *usually*) por regla general, generalmente **3** (= *predictably*) (*iro*) como era de esperar, como suele ocurrir

typify ['tɪpɪfaɪ] VT [+ *thing*] representar, tipificar; [+ *person*] ser ejemplo de

typing ['taɪpɪŋ] N mecanografía *f* ➤ **typing error** error *m* mecanográfico ➤ **typing paper** papel *m* para máquina de escribir ➤ **typing pool** servicio *m* de mecanografía ➤ **typing speed** palabras *fpl* por minuto (mecanografiadas)

typist ['taɪpɪst] N mecanógrafo/a *m/f*

typo* ['taɪpəʊ] N errata *f*

typography [taɪˈpɒgrəfɪ] N tipografía *f*

tyrannical [tɪˈrænɪkəl] ADJ tiránico, tirano

tyranny ['tɪrənɪ] N tiranía *f*

tyrant ['taɪərənt] N tirano/a *m/f*

tyre, tire (*US*) ['taɪəʳ] N neumático *m* (*Sp*), llanta *f* (*LAm*), caucho *m* (*SC*) ➤ **tyre pressure** presión *f* de los neumáticos

Tyrol [tɪˈrəʊl] N el Tirol

tzar [zɑːʳ] N zar *m*

Uu

U¹, u [ju:] N (= *letter*) U, u *f*; **U for Uncle** U de Uruguay

U² ADJ ABBR (*Brit Cine*) (= *universal*) todos los públicos

UAE N ABBR (= **United Arab Emirates**) EAU *mpl*

U-bend ['ju:bend] N (*Brit*) codo *m*, curva *f* en U

ubiquitous [ju:'bɪkwɪtəs] ADJ ubicuo, omnipresente

U-boat ['ju:bəʊt] N submarino *m* alemán

UCAS ['ju:kæs] N ABBR (*Brit*) = **Universities and Colleges Admissions Service**

udder ['ʌdəʳ] N ubre *f*

UDR N ABBR (= **Ulster Defence Regiment**) *fuerza de seguridad de Irlanda del Norte*

UEFA [jʊ'eɪfə] N ABBR (= **Union of European Football Associations**) UEFA *f*

UFO N ABBR (= **unidentified flying object**) OVNI *m*

Uganda [ju:'gændə] N Uganda *f*

Ugandan [ju:'gændən] ADJ, N ugandés/esa *m/f*

ugh [ɜ:h] EXCL ¡uf!, ¡puf!

ugliness ['ʌglɪnɪs] N fealdad *f*

ugly ['ʌglɪ] ADJ (*compar* **uglier**; *superl* **ugliest**) **1** [*appearance, person*] feo **2** (= *unpleasant*) [*mood*] peligroso, violento; [*situation, wound*] peligroso; [*rumour*] nada grato, inquietante; [*custom, vice etc*] feo, repugnante; **to grow** or **turn ~** ponerse violento, amenazar violencia

UHF N ABBR (= **ultra high frequency**) UHF *f*

uh-huh ['ʌ,hʌ] EXCL (*agreeing*) ajá

UHT ADJ ABBR (*Brit*) (= **ultra heat-treated**) uperizado

UK N ABBR (= **United Kingdom**) Reino *m* Unido; **in the UK** en el Reino Unido; **the UK government** el gobierno del Reino Unido

Ukraine [ju:'kreɪn] N Ucrania *f*

Ukrainian [ju:'kreɪnɪən] ADJ, N ucranio/a *m/f*

ukulele [,ju:kə'leɪlɪ] N ukelele *m*

ulcer ['ʌlsəʳ] N **1** (*Med*) (*internal*) úlcera *f*; (*external*) llaga *f* **2** (*fig*) llaga *f*

ulcerated ['ʌlsəreɪtɪd] ADJ ulcerado

Ulster ['ʌlstəʳ] N Ulster *m*

ulterior [ʌl'tɪərɪəʳ] ADJ **~ motive** segunda intención *f*, motivo *m* oculto

ultimate ['ʌltɪmɪt] **Ⓐ** ADJ **1** (= *final*) [*aim, decision, destination*] final **2** (= *greatest*) [*power, sacrifice, responsibility*] máximo; [*control*] total; [*insult*] peor; **the ~ deterrent** (*Mil*) el mayor disuasivo **3** (= *best*) **the ~ sports car** lo último en coches deportivos **Ⓑ** N **the ~ in luxury** lo último en lujos

ultimately ['ʌltɪmɪtlɪ] ADV (= *eventually*) al final, finalmente; (= *in the final analysis*) en última instancia; (= *in the long run*) a la larga; (= *deep down*) en el fondo; **they were ~ responsible for his death** eran responsables en última instancia de su muerte; **~, that's what people want** en el fondo, eso es lo que la gente quiere

ultimatum [,ʌltɪ'meɪtəm] N ultimátum *m*; **to issue an ~** dar un ultimátum

ultramodern ['ʌltrə'mɒdən] ADJ ultramoderno

ultrasonic ['ʌltrə'sɒnɪk] ADJ ultrasónico

ultrasound ['ʌltrəsaʊnd] N ultrasonido *m* ➤ **ultrasound scan** ecografía *f*

ultraviolet ['ʌltrə'vaɪəlɪt] ADJ ultravioleta *inv* ➤ **ultraviolet rays** rayos *mpl* ultravioleta

umber ['ʌmbəʳ] N ocre *m*, pardo *m* oscuro

umbilical [,ʌmbɪ'laɪkəl] ADJ umbilical ➤ **umbilical cord** cordón *m* umbilical

umbrage ['ʌmbrɪdʒ] N **to take ~ (at sth)** ofenderse or quedarse resentido (por algo)

umbrella [ʌm'brelə] N paraguas *m inv*; **beach/sun ~** sombrilla *f*; **under the ~ of** (= *protected*) al abrigo de; (= *incorporating*) comprendido en ➤ **umbrella organization**

organización *f* paraguas ➤ **umbrella stand** paragüero *m*

umpire ['ʌmpaɪəʳ] **Ⓐ** N árbitro/a *m/f* **Ⓑ** VT arbitrar **Ⓒ** VI arbitrar, hacer de árbitro

umpteen* ['ʌmpti:n] ADJ tropecientos*; **~ times** tropecientas veces*, miles de veces

umpteenth* ['ʌmpti:nθ] ADJ enésimo; **for the ~ time** por enésima vez

UN N ABBR (= **United Nations**) ONU *f*; *ver tb* www.un.org

'un* [ʌn] PRON **he did well, for an old ~** lo hizo bien, para ser un viejo; **she's got two little ~s** tiene dos críos

unabashed ['ʌnə'bæʃt] ADJ (= *shameless*) descarado, desvergonzado; (= *unperturbed*) impertérrito; **"yes," he said quite ~** —sí —dijo sin alterarse

unabated ['ʌnə'beɪtɪd] ADJ sin disminución, no disminuido; **the storm continued ~** la tormenta siguió sin amainar

unable ['ʌn'eɪbl] ADJ **to be ~ to do sth** (*gen*) no poder hacer algo; (= *be incapable of*) ser incapaz de hacer algo; (= *be prevented from*) verse imposibilitado de hacer algo

unabridged ['ʌnə'brɪdʒd] ADJ íntegro

unacceptable ['ʌnək'septəbl] ADJ inaceptable

unaccompanied ['ʌnə'kʌmpənɪd] ADJ solo, no acompañado; (*Mus*) sin acompañamiento

unaccountable ['ʌnə'kaʊntəbl] ADJ (= *inexplicable*) inexplicable

unaccountably ['ʌnə'kaʊntəblɪ] ADV (= *inexplicably*) inexplicablemente; (= *strangely*) extrañamente

unaccounted ['ʌnə'kaʊntɪd] ADJ **two passengers are still ~ for** aún (nos) faltan dos pasajeros

unaccustomed ['ʌnə'kʌstəmd] ADJ **1 to be ~ to sth** no estar acostumbrado a algo, no tener costumbre de algo; **to be ~ to doing sth** no tener costumbre de hacer algo, no acostumbrar hacer algo; **as I am to public speaking** aunque no tengo experiencia de hablar en público **2** (= *unusual*) **with ~ zeal** con un entusiasmo insólito

unacquainted ['ʌnə'kweɪntɪd] ADJ **to be ~ with** desconocer, ignorar

unadulterated ['ʌnə'dʌltəreɪtɪd] ADJ sin mezcla, puro

unadventurous ['ʌnəd'ventʃərəs] ADJ poco atrevido

unaffected ['ʌnə'fektɪd] ADJ **1** (= *sincere*) sin afectación, sencillo **2** (*emotionally*) no afectado, inmutable; **to be ~ by ...** no verse afectado por ...

unafraid ['ʌnə'freɪd] ADJ sin temor or miedo; **to be ~ of (doing) sth** no temer (hacer) algo, no tener miedo de (hacer) algo

unaided ['ʌn'eɪdɪd] ADV sin ayuda, por sí solo

unalloyed ['ʌnə'lɔɪd] ADJ [*pleasure*] en estado puro

unalterable ['ʌn'ɒltərəbl] ADJ inalterable

unaltered ['ʌn'ɒltəd] ADJ inalterado, sin cambiar; **his appearance was ~** no había cambiado

unambiguous ['ʌnæm'bɪgjʊəs] ADJ inequívoco

unanimous [ju:'nænɪməs] ADJ [*group, decision, vote*] unánime; **the committee was ~ in its condemnation of** or **in condemning this** el comité condenó esto unánimemente

unanimously [ju:'nænɪməslɪ] ADV unánimemente, por unanimidad

unannounced ['ʌnə'naʊnst] **Ⓐ** ADJ [*visitor, visit*] inesperado **Ⓑ** ADV **to arrive ~** llegar sin dar aviso

unanswerable [ʌn'ɑ:nsərəbl] ADJ [*question*] incontestable

unanswered [ʌn'ɑ:nsəd] ADJ [*question*] incontestado, sin contestar; [*letter*] sin contestar

unappealing ['ʌnə'pi:lɪŋ] ADJ poco atractivo

unappetizing ['ʌn'æpɪtaɪzɪŋ] ADJ poco apetitoso, poco apetecible; (*fig*) poco apetecible, nada atractivo

unapproachable ['ʌnə'prəʊtʃəbl] ADJ **1** (= *inaccessible*) inaccesible **2** (= *aloof*) [*person*] intratable, inasequible

unarguably [ʌnˈɑːgjʊəblɪ] ADV indiscutiblemente

unarmed [ʌnˈɑːmd] ADJ desarmado

unashamed [ʌnəˈʃeɪmd] ADJ desvergonzado, descarado; **she was quite ~ about it** no se avergonzó en lo más mínimo

unashamedly [ʌnəˈʃeɪmɪdlɪ] ADV desvergonzadamente; **to be ~ proud of sth** enorgullecerse desvergonzadamente de algo

unasked [ʌnˈɑːskt] **A** ADJ [guest] no invitado; [question] no formulado; **~ for** [advice] no solicitado **B** ADV **to do sth ~** hacer algo motu propio

unassailable [ʌnəˈseɪləbl] ADJ [position, influence] inatacable

unassisted [ʌnəˈsɪstɪd] ADJ, ADV sin ayuda, por sí solo

unassuming [ʌnəˈsjuːmɪŋ] ADJ modesto, sin pretensions

unattached [ʌnəˈtætʃt] ADJ (= unmarried) soltero, libre

unattainable [ʌnəˈteɪnəbl] ADJ [record, objective] inalcanzable

unattended [ʌnəˈtendɪd] ADJ [shop, machine, luggage] desatendido, sin atender; **to leave sth ~** dejar algo desatendido; **please do not leave your luggage ~** por favor, no abandonen su equipaje

unattractive [ʌnəˈtræktɪv] ADJ poco atractivo

unauthorized [ʌnˈɔːθəraɪzd] ADJ (gen) no autorizado; **this was ~** esto no estaba autorizado

unavailable [ʌnəˈveɪləbl] ADJ (gen) no disponible; (= out of stock) agotado; **the Minister was ~ for comment** el ministro no se prestó a hacer comentarios

unavoidable [ʌnəˈvɔɪdəbl] ADJ inevitable, ineludible

unavoidably [ʌnəˈvɔɪdəblɪ] ADV inevitablemente; **he was ~ detained** no pudo evitar retrasarse, se retrasó por causas ajenas a su voluntad

unaware [ʌnəˈweəʳ] ADJ **to be ~ that ...** ignorar que ...; **to be ~ of sth** ignorar algo

unawares [ʌnəˈweəz] ADV **to catch sb ~** pillar a algn desprevenido

unbalanced [ʌnˈbælənst] ADJ (physically) desequilibrado; (mentally) trastornado, desequilibrado

unbearable [ʌnˈbɛərəbl] ADJ inaguantable, insoportable

unbearably [ʌnˈbɛərəblɪ] ADV insoportablemente; **it is ~ hot** hace un calor insoportable

unbeatable [ʌnˈbiːtəbl] ADJ [team, opponent, army] invencible; [price, offer] inmejorable

unbeaten [ʌnˈbiːtn] ADJ [team, opponent] imbatido, invicto; [army] invicto; [price] insuperable

unbecoming [ʌnbɪˈkʌmɪŋ] ADJ [behaviour etc] indecoroso, impropio; [dress etc] poco favorecedor

unbeknown(st) [ʌnbɪˈnəʊn(st)] ADJ **~ to me** sin yo saberlo

unbelievable [ʌnbɪˈliːvəbl] ADJ 1 (= incredible) increíble; **it is ~ that** es increíble que + subjun 2 (*) (= fantastic) increíble

unbelievably [ʌnbɪˈliːvəblɪ] ADV increíblemente; **they're ~ lucky** tienen una suerte increíble

unbeliever [ʌnbɪˈliːvəʳ] N no creyente mf

unbend [ʌnˈbend] (pt, pp unbent) **A** VT enderezar **B** VI (fig) [person] relajarse

unbending [ʌnˈbendɪŋ] ADJ [person, attitude] inflexible

unbias(s)ed [ʌnˈbaɪəst] ADJ imparcial

unblemished [ʌnˈblemɪʃt] ADJ sin tacha, sin mancha

unblinking [ʌnˈblɪŋkɪŋ] ADJ imperturbable; (pej) desvergonzado

unblock [ʌnˈblɒk] VT [+ sink, pipe] desatascar

unbolt [ʌnˈbəʊlt] VT desatrancar, quitar el cerrojo de

unborn [ʌnˈbɔːn] ADJ no nacido aún, nonato; **the ~ child** el feto

unbounded [ʌnˈbaʊndɪd] ADJ ilimitado, sin límites

unbreakable [ʌnˈbreɪkəbl] ADJ irrompible

unbridgeable [ʌnˈbrɪdʒəbl] ADJ insalvable, infranqueable

unbridled [ʌnˈbraɪdld] ADJ desenfrenado

unbroken [ʌnˈbrəʊkən] ADJ 1 (= intact) entero, intacto 2 (= continuous) ininterrumpido, continuo 3 (= unbeaten) no batido; **his spirit remained ~** no se hundió

unbuckle [ʌnˈbʌkl] VT desabrochar

unburden [ʌnˈbɜːdn] VT **to ~ o.s. to sb** desahogarse con algn

unbusinesslike [ʌnˈbɪznɪslaɪk] ADJ poco profesional; (in appearance etc) poco formal

unbutton [ʌnˈbʌtn] VT desabrochar, desabotonar

uncalled-for [ʌnˈkɔːldfɔːʳ] ADJ gratuito, impropio; **that was quite ~** eso fue totalmente gratuito or impropio

uncanny [ʌnˈkænɪ] ADJ (compar **uncannier**; superl **uncanniest**) (= peculiar) raro, extraño; **it's quite ~** es extraordinario; **an ~ resemblance** un asombroso parecido

uncared-for [ʌnˈkɛədfɔːʳ] ADJ [person, building] abandonado; [appearance] desaseado, de abandono

uncaring [ʌnˈkɛərɪŋ] ADJ poco compasivo

unceasing [ʌnˈsiːsɪŋ] ADJ incesante

unceasingly [ʌnˈsiːsɪŋlɪ] ADV incesantemente, sin cesar

unceremonious [ʌnˌserɪˈməʊnɪəs] ADJ brusco, hosco

unceremoniously [ʌnˌserɪˈməʊnɪəslɪ] ADV bruscamente, sin cortesías

uncertain [ʌnˈsɜːtn] ADJ 1 (= unsure) **for a moment he looked ~** por un momento pareció no estar seguro; **to be ~ about/of sth** no estar seguro de algo; **she is ~ about the future/what to do next** no está segura sobre el futuro/de qué hacer ahora; **I am ~ whether to accept** no estoy seguro si aceptar

2 (= doubtful) [future, outcome, destiny] incierto; **in no ~ terms** sin dejar lugar a dudas, claramente 3 (= changeable) [conditions] inestable; **we live in ~ times** vivimos unos tiempos muy inestables 4 (= indecisive) [voice] indeciso; [smile] tímido, indeciso

uncertainty [ʌnˈsɜːtntɪ] N (= doubt) duda f, incertidumbre f; **in view of these uncertainties** teniendo en cuenta estas dudas or este grado de incertidumbre; **he heard the ~ in her voice** notó la indecisión en su voz

unchallenged [ʌnˈtʃælɪndʒd] ADV **his ideas went ~** sus ideas no fueron cuestionadas; **we cannot let that go ~** eso no lo podemos dejar pasar sin protesta

unchangeable [ʌnˈtʃeɪndʒəbl] ADJ inalterable, inmutable

unchanged [ʌnˈtʃeɪndʒd] ADJ igual, sin cambiar

unchanging [ʌnˈtʃeɪndʒɪŋ] ADJ inalterable, inmutable

uncharacteristic [ʌnkærəktəˈrɪstɪk] ADJ [hostility, politeness etc] inusitado, nada típico; **it's very ~ of her** no es nada propio de ella

uncharacteristically [ʌnkærəktəˈrɪstɪklɪ] ADV **~ rude/ generous** de una grosería/generosidad inusitada; **to behave ~** comportarse de manera inusual

uncharitable [ʌnˈtʃærɪtəbl] ADJ poco caritativo

uncharted [ʌnˈtʃɑːtɪd] ADJ inexplorado, desconocido

unchecked [ʌnˈtʃekt] **A** ADV [continue] libremente, sin estorbo or restricción; **left ~, the virus could spread throughout Africa** si no se controla, el virus podría extenderse por toda África **B** ADJ 1 [growth, power, emotion, anger] desenfrenado 2 [data, statement] no comprobado

unchristian [ʌnˈkrɪstɪən] ADJ poco cristiano, impropio de un cristiano

uncivil [ʌnˈsɪvɪl] ADJ descortés (**to sb** con algn)

uncivilized [ʌnˈsɪvɪlaɪzd] ADJ 1 (= primitive) [people, country] poco civilizado 2 (= socially unacceptable) [conditions, activity] inaceptable; [person, behaviour] grosero; **at this ~ hour*** a estas horas tan intempestivas

unclaimed [ʌnˈkleɪmd] ADJ sin reclamar

unclassified [ʌnˈklæsɪfaɪd] ADJ 1 (= not ordered) [items, papers, waste, football results] sin clasificar 2 (= not secret) [information, document] no confidencial

uncle [ˈʌŋkl] N tío m; **my ~ and aunt** mis tíos; ✦ IDIOM **to cry ~** (US*) rendirse, darse por vencido

unclean [ʌnˈkliːn] ADJ 1 (= dirty) [person, hands, room] sucio **2** (= *impure*) [*person, animal, thoughts*] impuro

unclear [ʌn'klɪə'] ADJ **1** (= *not obvious*) **the reasons for this behaviour are** ~ las razones de este comportamiento no están claras; **it is** ~ **what effect this will have** no se sabe muy bien qué efectos tendrá esto **2** (= *not specific*) **he was ~ about how much he would pay us** no fue muy claro respecto a cuánto nos pagaría **3** (= *confusing*) poco claro **4** (= *unsure*) **to be** ~ **about sth** no tener algo muy claro

unclothed ['ʌn'kləʊðd] ADJ desnudo

uncoil ['ʌn'kɔɪl] Ⓐ VT desenrollar Ⓑ VI desenrollarse; [*snake*] desenroscarse

uncombed ['ʌn'kəʊmd] ADJ despeinado, sin peinar

uncomfortable [ʌn'kʌmfətəbl] ADJ **1** (*physically*) incómodo; **to be/feel** ~ [*chair, shoes, position*] ser *or* resultar incómodo; [*person*] estar/sentirse incómodo **2** (= *uneasy*) incómodo; **I had an** ~ **feeling that ...** tenía la incómoda sensación de que ...; **to be** ~ **about sth** estar incómodo *or* a disgusto con algo; **to make sb** ~ hacer a algn sentirse incómodo, hacer que algn se sienta incómodo **3** (= *disagreeable*) [*truth, fact*] desagradable

uncomfortably [ʌn'kʌmfətəblɪ] ADV **1** (*lit*) **she felt ~ hot** se encontraba incómoda del calor que tenía; **I'm feeling ~ full** estoy tan lleno que me siento incómodo **2** (= *uneasily*) **he shifted ~ in his chair** se removía incómodo *or* inquieto en su silla

uncommitted ['ʌnkə'mɪtɪd] ADJ no comprometido

uncommon [ʌn'kɒmən] ADJ **1** (= *unusual*) poco común, nada frecuente **2** (= *outstanding*) insólito, extraordinario

uncommonly [ʌn'kɒmənlɪ] ADV **1** (†) (= *exceptionally*) [*gifted, pretty, hot*] extraordinariamente **2 not** ~ con cierta frecuencia

uncommunicative ['ʌnkə'mju:nɪkətɪv] ADJ poco comunicativo, reservado

uncomplaining ['ʌnkəm'pleɪnɪŋ] ADJ resignado, sumiso

uncompleted ['ʌnkəm'pli:tɪd] ADJ incompleto, inacabado

uncomplicated [ʌn'kɒmplɪkeɪtɪd] ADJ sin complicaciones, sencillo

uncomplimentary ['ʌn,kɒmplɪ'mentərɪ] ADJ poco halagüeño *or* halagador

uncomprehending ['ʌn,kɒmprɪ'hendɪŋ] ADJ incomprensivo

uncompromising [ʌn'kɒmprəmaɪzɪŋ] ADJ intransigente, inflexible; ~ **loyalty** lealtad *f* absoluta

unconcealed ['ʌnkən'si:ld] ADJ evidente, no disimulado

unconcerned ['ʌnkən'sɜ:nd] ADJ (= *unworried*) despreocupado; (= *indifferent*) indiferente, despreocupado; **to be** ~ **about sth** no inquietarse *or* preocuparse por algo, mostrarse indiferente a algo

unconditional ['ʌnkən'dɪʃənl] ADJ incondicional, sin condiciones; ~ **surrender** rendición *f* sin condiciones

unconditionally ['ʌnkən'dɪʃnəlɪ] ADV incondicionalmente

unconfirmed ['ʌnkən'fɜ:md] ADJ no confirmado, sin confirmar

uncongenial ['ʌnkən'dʒi:nɪəl] ADJ [*person*] antipático, poco amigable; [*company, work, surroundings*] desagradable, poco agradable

unconnected ['ʌnkə'nektɪd] ADJ **1** (= *unrelated*) no relacionado **2** (= *incoherent*) inconexo

unconscious [ʌn'kɒnʃəs] Ⓐ ADJ **1** (= *out cold*) sin sentido, inconsciente; **to be** ~ estar sin sentido *or* inconsciente; **to be ~ for three hours** pasar tres horas sin sentido **2** (= *unaware*) inconsciente, insensible; **to be ~ of sth** no ser consciente de algo **3** (= *unintentional*) inconsciente Ⓑ N **the** ~ el inconsciente

unconsciously [ʌn'kɒnʃəslɪ] ADV inconscientemente

unconsciousness [ʌn'kɒnʃəsnɪs] N inconsciencia *f*

unconstitutional ['ʌn,kɒnstɪ'tju:ʃənl] ADJ inconstitucional, anticonstitucional

unconsummated [ʌn'kɒnsəmeɪtɪd] ADJ no consumado

uncontested ['ʌnkən'testɪd] ADJ (*Parl*) [*seat*] ganado sin oposición, no disputado

uncontrollable ['ʌnkən'trəʊləbl] ADJ **1** (= *irrepressible*) [*rage, desire*] incontenible, incontrolable; [*urge*] irrefrenable, incontenible; [*laughter*] incontenible **2** (= *involuntary*) [*movement, spasm*] incontrolable **3** (= *unmanageable*) [*person, animal, situation*] incontrolable

uncontrollably ['ʌnkən'trəʊləblɪ] ADV [*spread, increase*] incontrolablemente; [*laugh, cry, shake*] sin poder controlarse, inconteniblemente

uncontrolled ['ʌnkən'trəʊld] ADJ (= *out of control*) descontrolado; [*passion*] desenfrenado

unconventional ['ʌnkən'venʃnl] ADJ poco convencional; [*person*] original, poco convencional

unconvinced ['ʌnkən'vɪnst] ADJ poco convencido

unconvincing ['ʌnkən'vɪnsɪŋ] ADJ poco convincente

uncooked ['ʌn'kʊkt] ADJ crudo, sin cocer

uncooperative ['ʌnkəʊ'ɒpərətɪv] ADJ poco dispuesto a cooperar, nada colaborador

uncoordinated ['ʌnkəʊ'ɔ:dɪneɪtɪd] ADJ no coordinado, sin coordinar

uncork ['ʌn'kɔ:k] VT descorchar, destapar

uncorroborated ['ʌnkə'rɒbəreɪtɪd] ADJ no confirmado, sin corroborar

uncountable ['ʌn'kaʊntəbl] ADJ incontable

uncouth [ʌn'ku:θ] ADJ (= *unrefined*) grosero, inculto; (= *clumsy*) torpe, desmañado

uncover [ʌn'kʌvə'] VT descubrir

uncritical ['ʌn'krɪtɪkəl] ADJ falto de sentido crítico

uncrossed ['ʌn'krɒst] ADJ [*cheque*] sin cruzar

unction ['ʌŋkʃən] N (= *ointment*) unción *f*; **extreme** ~ (*Rel*) extremaunción *f*

unctuous ['ʌŋktjʊəs] ADJ empalagoso, afectado

uncultivated ['ʌn'kʌltɪveɪtɪd] ADJ sin cultivar

uncultured ['ʌn'kʌltʃəd] ADJ [*person*] inculto, sin cultura; [*voice*] no cultivado; [*accent*] poco culto

uncut ['ʌn'kʌt] ADJ **1** [*grass, tree, hair, nails*] sin cortar; [*diamond*] en bruto, sin tallar **2** (= *unabridged*) [*film, text*] integral, sin cortes

undamaged [ʌn'dæmɪdʒd] ADJ (*gen*) en buen estado; (= *intact*) intacto

undated ['ʌn'deɪtɪd] ADJ sin fecha

undaunted ['ʌn'dɔ:ntɪd] ADJ **to be ~ by** no dejarse desanimar por; **he carried on quite** ~ siguió sin inmutarse

undecided ['ʌndɪ'saɪdɪd] ADJ [*person*] indeciso; [*question*] pendiente, no resuelto; **we are still ~ whether to go** aún no sabemos si ir o no; **that is still** ~ eso queda por resolver

undefeated ['ʌndɪ'fi:tɪd] ADJ invicto, imbatido

undelete ['ʌndɪ'li:t] VT (*Comput*) restaurar

undelivered [ʌndɪ'lɪvəd] ADJ no entregado al destinatario

undemanding [ʌndɪ'mɑ:ndɪŋ] ADJ [*person*] poco exigente; [*job*] que exige poco esfuerzo

undemocratic [ʌndemə'krætɪk] ADJ antidemocrático

undemonstrative ['ʌndɪ'mɒnstrətɪv] ADJ poco expresivo

undeniable [ʌndɪ'naɪəbl] ADJ innegable, indudable

undeniably [ʌndɪ'naɪəblɪ] ADV innegablemente, indudablemente; **it is ~ true that ...** es innegable *or* indudable que ...

under ['ʌndə'] Ⓐ ADV **1** (= *beneath*) por debajo; **he lifted the rope and crawled** ~ levantó la cuerda y se deslizó por debajo; **he stayed ~ for three minutes** (= *underwater*) estuvo sumergido durante tres minutos **2** (*) (= *under anaesthetic*) **he's been ~ for three hours** lleva tres horas bajo los efectos de la anestesia **3** (= *less*) menos; **children of 15 and** ~ niños de 15 años y menores; **ten degrees** ~ diez grados bajo cero Ⓑ PREP **1** (= *beneath*) (*position*) debajo de; (*movement*) por debajo de; **it's ~ the bed** está debajo de la cama; **what's ~ there?** ¿qué hay ahí debajo?; **to swim ~ the water** nadar por debajo del agua; **the tunnel goes ~ the river** el túnel pasa por debajo del río; ~ **the microscope** bajo el microscopio

2 (= *less than*) menos de; **in ~ a minute** en menos de un minuto; **children ~ ten** niños menores de diez años; **it sells at ~ £20** se vende a menos de 20 libras
3 (= *subject to*) bajo; **~ Ferdinand VII** bajo Fernando VII, durante el reinado de Fernando VII; **he has 30 workers ~ him** tiene 30 obreros a su cargo; **to study ~ sb** estudiar con algn, tener a algn por profesor
4 (*with names*) **~ a false name** con nombre falso; **you'll find him ~ "plumbers" in the phone book** lo encontrarás en la sección de "fontaneros" en la guía
5 (= *according to, by*) de acuerdo con, según; **~ Article 25 of the Code** conforme al Artículo 25 del Código; **his rights ~ the contract** sus derechos según el contrato

under- ['ʌndəʳ] PREF (= *insufficiently*) poco, insuficientemente

underachiever [ʌndərə'tʃiːvəʳ] N (*Brit*) persona *f* que no desarrolla su potencial, persona *f* que no rinde (como podría)

underage [ʌndər'eɪdʒ] ADJ menor de edad; **he's ~** es menor de edad

underarm ['ʌndərɑːm] **ⓐ** ADV (*Brit*): **to serve ~** sacar sin levantar el brazo por encima **ⓑ** N axila *f*, sobaco *m* **ⓒ** CPD ➤ **underarm deodorant** desodorante *m*

underbelly ['ʌndəbelɪ] N (*Anat*) panza *f*; **the soft ~** (*fig*) la parte indefensa

underbrush ['ʌndəbrʌʃ] N (*US*) maleza *f*, monte *m* bajo

undercapitalized ['ʌndə'kæpɪtəlaɪzd] ADJ descapitalizado, subcapitalizado

undercarriage ['ʌndə,kærɪdʒ] N (*esp Brit*) [*of plane*] tren *m* de aterrizaje

undercharge ['ʌndə'tʃɑːdʒ] VT cobrar de menos a; **he ~d me by £2** me cobró dos libras de menos

underclass ['ʌndəklɑːs] N clase *f* inferior

underclothes ['ʌndəkləʊðz] NPL, **underclothing** ['ʌndə,kləʊðɪŋ] N ropa *fsing* interior *or* (*esp LAm*) íntima

undercoat ['ʌndəkəʊt] N [*of paint*] primera capa *f*, primera mano *f*; (= *paint*) pintura *f* preparatoria

undercooked ['ʌndə'kʊkt] ADJ medio crudo, a medio cocer

undercover ['ʌndə,kʌvəʳ] **ⓐ** ADJ [*operation, activity*] clandestino; [*agent, etc*] secreto **ⓑ** ADV **she was working ~ for the FBI** trabajaba como agente secreto para el FBI

undercurrent ['ʌndə,kʌrənt] N (*in sea*) corriente *f* submarina, contracorriente *f*; [*of feeling etc*] trasfondo *m*; **an ~ of criticism** un trasfondo de críticas calladas

undercut ['ʌndəkʌt] (*pt, pp ~*) VT (= *sell cheaper than*) vender más barato que

underdeveloped ['ʌndədɪ'veləpt] ADJ [*country, society, economy*] subdesarrollado

underdog ['ʌndədɒg] N **the ~ 1** (*in game, fight*) el/la más débil **2** (*economically, socially*) el/la desvalido/a, el/la desamparado/a

underdone ['ʌndə'dʌn] ADJ [*food*] a medio cocer; (*deliberately*) [*steak*] poco hecho

underemployed ['ʌndərɪm'plɔɪd] ADJ subempleado

underestimate ['ʌndər'estɪmeɪt] VT [+ *strength, importance, value, person*] subestimar, menospreciar

underexposed ['ʌndərɪks'pəʊzd] ADJ (*Phot*) subexpuesto

underfed ['ʌndə'fed] ADJ subalimentado

underfelt ['ʌndəfelt] N arpillera *f*

underfinanced [ʌndəfaɪ'nænst] ADJ insuficientemente financiado

underfoot ['ʌndə'fʊt] ADV debajo de los pies; **it's wet ~** el suelo está mojado

underfunded [ʌndə'fʌndɪd] ADJ infradotado

undergarments ['ʌndə,gɑːmənts] N (*frm*) ropa *fsing* interior, ropa *fsing* íntima (*LAm*)

undergo ['ʌndə'gəʊ] (*pt* **underwent**; *pp* **undergone**) VT sufrir, experimentar; [+ *treatment*] recibir; [+ *operation*] someterse a

undergraduate ['ʌndə'grædjʊɪt] **ⓐ** N estudiante *mf*

universitario/a **ⓑ** ADJ [*student*] no licenciado; [*course*] para universitarios (no licenciados)

underground ['ʌndəgraʊnd] **ⓐ** ADJ **1** [*building, cave, mine*] subterráneo; **an ~ car park** un parking subterráneo
2 (*fig*) [*newspaper, movement*] clandestino
3 (= *alternative*) [*film, magazine, artist, culture*] underground *inv*
ⓑ ADV **1** (= *under the ground*) bajo tierra; **it's six feet ~** está a seis pies bajo tierra
2 to go ~ (= *hide*) esconderse; (*Pol*) pasar a la clandestinidad
ⓒ N **1** (*Brit*) (= *railway*) metro *m*, subterráneo *m* (*Arg*), subte *m* (*Arg**)
2 (*Mil*) resistencia *f* clandestina; (*Pol*) movimiento *m* clandestino

undergrowth ['ʌndəgrəʊθ] N (*Brit*) maleza *f*, matorrales *mpl*

underhand ['ʌndəhænd] **ⓐ** ADJ **1** (= *dishonest*) [*person*] solapado; [*behaviour, deals, tactics*] turbio, poco limpio
2 (*Sport*) [*throw*] por debajo del hombro **ⓑ** ADV **to serve ~** sacar sin levantar el brazo por encima

underhanded ['ʌndə'hændɪd] ADJ (*US*) = **underhand**

underinsure [ʌndərɪn'ʃʊəʳ] VT asegurar por debajo del valor real; **to be ~d** estar asegurado por debajo del valor real

underlay ['ʌndəleɪ] N (*Brit*) refuerzo *m*

underlie [ʌndə'laɪ] (*pt* **underlay**; *pp* **underlain**) VT **1** (= *lie under*) estar debajo de, extenderse debajo de **2** (*fig*) sustentar

underline [ʌndə'laɪn] VT (*lit, fig*) subrayar

underling ['ʌndəlɪŋ] N (*pej*) subordinado/a *m/f*, subalterno/a *m/f*

underlying [ʌndə'laɪɪŋ] ADJ [*cause, theme*] subyacente; **the ~ problem is that ...** el problema subyacente *or* de fondo es que ...

undermanned ['ʌndə'mænd] ADJ **to be ~** no tener (el) personal suficiente

undermentioned ['ʌndə'menʃənd] ADJ abajo citado

undermine [ʌndə'maɪn] VT minar, socavar

underneath [ʌndə'niːθ] **ⓐ** PREP (*position*) debajo de, bajo (*more frm*); (*movement*) por debajo de; **it's ~ the sofa** está debajo del sofá, está bajo el sofá (*more frm*); **I walked ~ a ladder** pasé por debajo de una escalera **ⓑ** ADV (*position*) debajo; (*movement*) por debajo

undernourished ['ʌndə'nʌrɪʃt] ADJ subalimentado, desnutrido

underpaid ['ʌndə'peɪd] ADJ mal pagado; **teachers are ~** los profesores están mal pagados

underpants ['ʌndəpænts] NPL calzoncillos *mpl*, calzones *mpl* (*LAm*); **a pair of ~** unos calzoncillos

underpass ['ʌndəpɑːs] N (*for cars*) paso *m* a desnivel; (*for pedestrians*) paso *m* subterráneo

underpin [ʌndə'pɪn] VT **1** (*Archit*) apuntalar **2** [+ *argument, case*] sustentar, respaldar

underplay ['ʌndə'pleɪ] VT (*esp Brit*) [+ *importance*] minimizar; [+ *issue*] quitar *or* restar importancia a

underpopulated ['ʌndə'pɒpjʊleɪtɪd] ADJ poco poblado, con baja densidad de población

underprice ['ʌndə'praɪs] VT poner un precio demasiado bajo a; **at £10 this book is ~d** el precio de diez libras es demasiado bajo para este libro

underprivileged ['ʌndə'prɪvɪlɪdʒd] **ⓐ** ADJ menos privilegiado, desfavorecido **ⓑ** NPL **the ~** los menos privilegiados, los desfavorecidos

underqualified ['ʌndə'kwɒlɪfaɪd] ADJ **to be ~** no estar suficientemente cualificado (**for** para)

underrate [ʌndə'reɪt] VT subestimar, menospreciar; **he's very ~d** no se lo valora debidamente

underscore [ʌndə'skɔːʳ] VT subrayar, recalcar

underseal ['ʌndəsiːl] VT (*Brit*) impermeabilizar (*por debajo*), proteger contra la corrosión

under-secretary ['ʌndə'sekrətərɪ] N subsecretario/a *m/f*

undersell [ˌʌndəˈsel] (pt, pp **undersold**) VT **to ~ o.s.** subestimarse, infravalorarse

undershirt [ˈʌndəʃɜːt] N (US) camiseta f

undershorts [ˈʌndəʃɔːts] NPL (US) calzoncillos mpl, calzones mpl (LAm)

underside [ˈʌndəsaɪd] N parte f inferior

undersigned [ˈʌndəsaɪnd] ADJ **the ~** el/la abajofirmante; **we, the ~** nosotros, los abajofirmantes

undersized [ˈʌndəˈsaɪzd] ADJ demasiado pequeño

underskirt [ˈʌndəskɜːt] N (Brit) enaguas fpl

undersold [ˈʌndəˈsəʊld] PT, PP of **undersell**

understaffed [ˈʌndəˈstɑːft] ADJ **to be ~** no tener (el) personal suficiente, estar falto de personal

understand [ˌʌndəˈstænd] (pt, pp **understood**) Ⓐ VT **1** (= comprehend) (gen) entender; (more formal, esp complex issues) comprender; **I can't ~ it!** ¡no lo entiendo!; **I can't ~ your writing** no entiendo tu letra; **that's what I can't ~** eso es lo que no logro entender or comprender; **I don't want to hear another word about it, (is that) understood?** no quiero que se hable más del tema, ¿entendido or comprendido?; **the process is still not fully understood** el proceso todavía no se comprende or entiende del todo; **to ~ how/why** entender or comprender cómo/por qué **2** (= follow, interpret) entender; **to make o.s. understood** hacerse entender; **do I make myself understood?** ¿queda claro? **3** (= empathize with) [+ person, point of view, attitude] comprender, entender **4** (= know) [+ language] entender **5** (= believe) tener entendido; **I ~ you have been absent** tengo entendido que usted ha estado ausente; **as I ~ it, he's trying to set up a meeting** según tengo entendido or según creo está intentando convocar una reunión; **am I to ~ that ...?** ¿debo entender que ...?; **it was understood that he would pay for it** se dio por sentado que él lo pagaría; **he let it be understood that ...** dio a entender que ... Ⓑ VI **1** (= comprehend) entender; (esp more emphatic) comprender; **don't worry, I quite ~** no te preocupes, lo entiendo or comprendo perfectamente **2** (= believe) **she was, I ~, a Catholic** según tengo entendido era católica

understandable [ˌʌndəˈstændəbl] ADJ comprensible; **it is very ~ that ...** se comprende perfectamente que ...

understandably [ˌʌndəˈstændəblɪ] ADV (= naturally) **~, he was very upset** tenía un disgusto muy grande, y era comprensible; **he's ~ reluctant to talk about the affair** se muestra reacio a hablar del asunto, y es comprensible

understanding [ˌʌndəˈstændɪŋ] Ⓐ ADJ [person] comprensivo; [smile] de comprensión; **to be ~ about sth** ser comprensivo (respecto a algo); **she was very ~ about it** fue muy comprensiva Ⓑ N **1** [of sth] (= comprehension) comprensión f; (= awareness) conciencia f; **our ~ of these processes is still poor** todavía no comprendemos muy bien estos procesos; **a basic ~ of computers is essential** se necesitan unos conocimientos básicos de informática **2** (= interpretation) interpretación f; **that's my ~ of the situation** esa es mi interpretación de la situación, así es como veo or interpreto la situación **3** (= sympathy) comprensión f; **thank you for your kindness and ~** te agradezco su amabilidad y comprensión **4** (= belief) **my ~ was that ...** tenía entendido que ..., según yo creía ... **5** (= agreement) acuerdo m; **to come to an ~ (with sb)** llegar a un acuerdo (con algn); **on the ~ that** a condición de que + subjun

understate [ˌʌndəˈsteɪt] VT **1** (= underestimate) [+ rate, level, growth] subestimar **2** (= underplay) quitar importancia a

understated [ˌʌndəˈsteɪtɪd] ADJ [style, clothes, elegance] sencillo, discreto; [writing, manner] sencillo; [performance, acting] comedido

understatement [ˈʌndəˌsteɪtmənt] N **I think that's something of an ~** creo que eso es quedarse corto; **to say I'm disappointed is an ~** decir que estoy desilusionado es quedarse corto; **interesting? that's the ~ of the year!**

¿interesante? ¡eso es quedarse corto!; **typical British ~** la típica moderación británica

understood [ˌʌndəˈstʊd] PT, PP of **understand**

understudy [ˈʌndəˌstʌdɪ] N suplente mf

undertake [ˌʌndəˈteɪk] (pt **undertook**; pp **~n**) Ⓐ VT [+ task] emprender; [+ responsibility] asumir; **to ~ to do sth** comprometerse a hacer algo; **to ~ that ...** comprometerse a que ... Ⓑ VI, VT (Brit Aut*) adelantar por el lado contrario or el carril indebido

undertaker [ˈʌndəˌteɪkəʳ] N (= director) director(a) m/f de funeraria or pompas fúnebres; (= employee) empleado/a m/f de una funeraria; **the ~'s** la funeraria

undertaking [ˌʌndəˈteɪkɪŋ] N **1** (= enterprise) empresa f; (= task) tarea f **2** (= pledge) garantía f; **to give an ~ that ...** garantizar que ...

undertone [ˈʌndətəʊn] N **1** (= low voice) voz f baja **2** (= suggestion, hint) matiz m; [of criticism] trasfondo m **3** [of perfume, taste, colour] matiz m

undertook [ˌʌndəˈtʊk] PT of **undertake**

undertow [ˈʌndətəʊ] N resaca f

underused [ˌʌndəˈjuːzd] ADJ infrautilizado

underutilized [ˌʌndəˈjuːtəlaɪzd] ADJ infrautilizado

undervalue [ˌʌndəˈvæljuː] VT **1** [+ goods] valorizar por debajo de su precio **2** (fig) subestimar; **he has been ~d as a writer** como escritor no se lo ha valorado debidamente

underwater [ˈʌndəˈwɔːtəʳ] Ⓐ ADV debajo del agua, bajo el agua Ⓑ ADJ [exploration, fishing] submarino; [archaeology, photography] submarino, subacuático

underway [ˌʌndəˈweɪ] ADJ **to be ~** estar en marcha; **the job is now well under way** el trabajo ya está muy avanzado; **to get ~** [work, project] ponerse en marcha, empezar a moverse

underwear [ˈʌndəweəʳ] N ropa f interior, ropa f íntima (LAm)

underweight [ˌʌndəˈweɪt] ADJ de peso insuficiente; **to be ~** [person] pesar menos de lo debido; **she's 20lb ~** pesa 20 libras menos de lo que debiera

underwent [ˌʌndəˈwent] PT of **undergo**

underwhelm* [ˈʌndəˈwelm] VT (hum) impresionar muy poco; **this left us somewhat ~ed** eso apenas nos impresionó

underworld [ˈʌndəwɜːld] Ⓐ N **1** (= hell) **the ~** el infierno **2** (criminal) **the ~** el hampa Ⓑ ADJ (= criminal) [organization] delictivo; [personality] del mundo del hampa; [connections] con el hampa

underwrite [ˈʌndəraɪt] (pt **underwrote**; pp **underwritten**) VT **1** (Insurance) asegurar (contra riesgos); (on second insurance) reasegurar; (Fin) subscribir **2** (= support) aprobar, respaldar

underwriter [ˈʌndəˌraɪtəʳ] N (Insurance) asegurador(a) m/f, reasegurador(a) m/f

undeserved [ˈʌndɪˈzɜːvd] ADJ inmerecido

undeserving [ˈʌndɪˈzɜːvɪŋ] ADJ [person] de poco mérito; [cause] poco meritorio; **to be ~ of sth** no ser digno de algo, no merecer algo

undesirable [ˈʌndɪˈzaɪərəbl] Ⓐ ADJ indeseable; **it is ~ that** no es recomendable que + subjun, es poco aconsejable que + subjun Ⓑ N indeseable mf

undetected [ˈʌndɪˈtektɪd] ADJ no descubierto; **to go ~** pasar inadvertido

undeterred [ˈʌndɪˈtɜːd] ADJ **he was ~ by ...** no se dejó intimidar por ...; **he carried on ~** siguió sin inmutarse

undeveloped [ˈʌndɪˈveləpt] ADJ [country, nation] no desarrollado; [land, area, resources] sin explotar

undid [ʌnˈdɪd] PT of **undo**

undies* [ˈʌndɪz] NPL ropa fsing interior, ropa fsing íntima (LAm)

undignified [ʌnˈdɪgnɪfaɪd] ADJ [behaviour] indecoroso, poco digno; [posture, position] indecoroso; [person] poco digno

undiluted [ˈʌndaɪˈluːtɪd] ADJ **1** [fruit juice, chemical] sin diluir, puro **2** [pleasure, accent] puro

undiminished [ˌʌndɪ'mɪnɪʃt] ADJ no disminuido

undiplomatic [ˌʌnˌdɪplə'mætɪk] ADJ poco diplomático

undischarged [ˌʌndɪs'tʃɑːdʒd] ADJ [*debt*] impagado, por pagar ➤ **undischarged bankrupt** (*Brit*) quebrado/a *m/f* no rehabilitado/a, persona *f* que sigue en estado de quiebra

undisciplined [ʌn'dɪsɪplɪnd] ADJ indisciplinado

undisclosed [ˌʌndɪs'kləʊzd] ADJ no revelado, sin revelar

undiscovered [ˌʌndɪs'kʌvəd] ADJ (= *undetected*) [*treasure, country*] sin descubrir, no descubierto; (= *unknown*) desconocido; **to lie** ~ estar sin descubrir; **he remained ~ for three days** estuvo *or* permaneció tres días sin ser descubierto

undisguised [ˌʌndɪs'ɡaɪzd] ADJ 1 (= *with no disguise*) sin disfraz ➤ (*fig*) [*pleasure, relief, hostility*] manifiesto, indisimulado

undisputed [ˌʌndɪs'pjuːtɪd] ADJ 1 (= *irrefutable*) [*fact, authority, right*] innegable 2 (= *unchallenged*) [*champion, leader*] indiscutible

undistinguished [ˌʌndɪs'tɪŋɡwɪʃt] ADJ mediocre

undisturbed [ˌʌndɪs'tɜːbd] Ⓐ ADJ 1 (= *untouched*) **to leave sth ~** dejar algo como está 2 (= *uninterrupted*) [*sleep*] ininterrumpido; **you need a quiet place where you will be ~** necesitas un lugar tranquilo donde no se te moleste Ⓑ ADV [*work, play, sleep*] sin ser molestado; **he went on with his work ~** continuó su trabajo sin interrupciones

undivided [ˌʌndɪ'vaɪdɪd] ADJ (= *wholehearted*) **I want your ~ attention** quiero que me prestes toda tu atención

undo [ʌn'duː] (*pt* **undid**; *pp* **undone**) VT 1 [+ *button, blouse*] desabrochar; [+ *knot, parcel, shoe laces*] desatar; [+ *zipper*] abrir 2 (= *reverse*) deshacer; [+ *damage etc*] reparar 3 (*Comput*) [+ *command*] cancelar

undoing [ʌn'duːɪŋ] N ruina *f*, perdición *f*; **that was his ~** aquello fue su ruina *or* perdición

undomesticated [ˌʌndə'mestɪkeɪtɪd] ADJ indomado, no domesticado

undone [ʌn'dʌn] Ⓐ PP *of* **undo** Ⓑ ADJ 1 (= *unfastened*) [*clasp, blouse*] desabrochado; [*zip, flies*] abierto; [*tie, shoelace, knot*] desatado; **to come ~** [*button*] desabrocharse; [*parcel, shoelace*] desatarse 2 (= *not done*) **to leave sth ~** dejar algo sin hacer

undoubted [ʌn'daʊtɪd] ADJ indudable

undoubtedly [ʌn'daʊtɪdlɪ] ADV indudablemente, sin duda; **he is ~ the best man for the job** es sin duda alguna el mejor para el trabajo

undreamed-of [ʌn'driːmdɒv], (*Brit*) **undreamt-of** [ʌn'dremtɒv] ADJ inimaginable, nunca soñado

undress [ʌn'dres] Ⓐ VT desnudar, desvestir (*LAm*); **to get ~ed** desnudarse, desvestirse (*LAm*) Ⓑ VI desnudarse, desvestirse (*LAm*)

undrinkable [ʌn'drɪŋkəbl] ADJ (= *unpalatable*) imbebible; (= *poisonous*) no potable

undue [ʌn'djuː] ADJ indebido, excesivo

undulating [ˈʌndjʊleɪtɪŋ] ADJ ondulante, ondeante; [*land*] ondulado

unduly [ʌn'djuːlɪ] ADV (= *excessively*) excesivamente; **we are not ~ worried** no estamos demasiado preocupados

undying [ʌn'daɪɪŋ] ADJ (*fig*) imperecedero, inmarcesible

unearned [ʌn'ɜːnd] ADJ no ganado ➤ **unearned income** renta *f* (no salarial) ➤ **unearned increment** plusvalía *f*

unearth [ʌn'ɜːθ] VT 1 (= *dig up*) desenterrar 2 (= *uncover*) (*fig*) desenterrar, descubrir

unearthly [ʌn'ɜːθlɪ] ADJ 1 (= *otherworldly*) sobrenatural 2 (***) [*noise*] tremendo*; **at some ~ hour** a unas horas intempestivas

unease [ʌn'iːz] N (= *tension*) malestar *m*; (= *apprehension*) inquietud *f*, desasosiego *m*

uneasily [ʌn'iːzɪlɪ] ADV [*look, say*] con inquietud, inquietamente; **I noted ~ that ...** noté con inquietud que ...; **he shifted ~ in his chair** se removió inquieto en su silla; **she laughed ~** se rió nerviosa

uneasiness [ʌn'iːzɪnɪs] N inquietud *f*, desasosiego *m*

uneasy [ʌn'iːzɪ] ADJ (= *worried*) inquieto; (= *ill at ease*) incómodo, molesto; **people are ~ about their future** la gente está preocupada por el futuro; **I felt ~ about doing it on my own** me inquietaba la idea de hacerlo solo

uneconomic [ˌʌnˌiːkə'nɒmɪk] ADJ [*business, factory*] poco rentable, no económico; **it's ~ to put on courses for so few students** no es rentable organizar cursos para tan pocos alumnos

uneconomical [ˌʌnˌiːkə'nɒmɪkəl] ADJ antieconómico, poco económico

unedifying [ʌn'edɪfaɪɪŋ] ADJ indecoroso, poco edificante

unedited [ʌn'edɪtɪd] ADJ inédito

uneducated [ʌn'edjʊkeɪtɪd] ADJ inculto, ignorante

unemotional [ˌʌnɪ'məʊʃənl] ADJ (*gen*) impasible, insensible; [*account*] objetivo

unemployable [ˌʌnɪm'plɔɪəbl] ADJ inútil para el trabajo

unemployed [ˌʌnɪm'plɔɪd] Ⓐ ADJ [*person*] desempleado, parado (*Sp*), en paro (*Sp*), cesante (*Chi*) Ⓑ NPL **the ~** los desempleados, los parados (*Sp*), los cesantes (*Chi*)

unemployment [ˌʌnɪm'plɔɪmənt] N desempleo *m*, paro *m* (*Sp*), cesantía *f* (*Chi*) ➤ **unemployment benefit** (*Brit*) subsidio *m* de desempleo *or* (*Sp*) paro, subsidio *m* de cesantía (*Chi*) ➤ **unemployment figures** cifras *fpl* del desempleo *or* (*Sp*) paro, cifras *fpl* de cesantía (*Chi*) ➤ **unemployment line** (*US*) cola *f* de desempleados, cola *f* del paro (*Sp*), cola *f* de cesantes (*Chi*)

unencumbered [ˌʌnɪn'kʌmbəd] ADJ **~ by** sin el estorbo de

unending [ʌn'endɪŋ] ADJ interminable, sin fin

unendurable [ˌʌnɪn'djʊərəbl] ADJ inaguantable, insoportable

unenthusiastic [ˌʌnɪnˌθuːzɪ'æstɪk] ADJ poco entusiasta

unenviable [ʌn'envɪəbl] ADJ poco envidiable

unequal [ʌn'iːkwəl] ADJ 1 (= *unfair*) desigual 2 (= *differing*) [*size, length*] distinto 3 (= *inadequate*) **to be ~ to a task** no estar a la altura de una tarea

unequalled, unequaled (*US*) [ʌn'iːkwəld] ADJ inigualado, sin par

unequivocal [ˌʌnɪ'kwɪvəkəl] ADJ [*response, message, proof*] inequívoco, claro

unequivocally [ˌʌnɪ'kwɪvəkəlɪ] ADV inequívocamente, de manera inequívoca

unerring [ʌn'ɜːrɪŋ] ADJ infalible

UNESCO [juː'neskəʊ] N ABBR (= **United Nations Educational, Scientific and Cultural Organization**) UNESCO *f*

unethical [ʌn'eθɪkəl] ADJ poco ético

uneven [ʌn'iːvən] ADJ 1 (= *not flat or straight*) [*surface, wall, road*] desigual, irregular; [*teeth*] desigual 2 (= *irregular*) [*breathing, rate*] irregular; **it was an ~ performance** fue una actuación irregular 3 (= *unfair*) [*distribution*] desigual, poco equitativo; [*contest*] desigual

unevenly [ʌn'iːvənlɪ] ADV 1 (= *not regularly*) desigualmente, irregularmente 2 (= *unfairly*) de manera poco equitativa; **the country's new wealth was ~ distributed** la nueva riqueza del país estaba distribuida de manera poco equitativa

uneventful [ˌʌnɪ'ventfʊl] ADJ sin incidentes

unexceptional [ˌʌnɪk'sepʃənl] ADJ sin nada de extraordinario, común y corriente

unexciting [ˌʌnɪk'saɪtɪŋ] ADJ sin interés

unexpected [ˌʌnɪks'pektɪd] ADJ inesperado; **it was all very ~** fue todo muy inesperado

unexpectedly [ˌʌnɪks'pektɪdlɪ] ADV [*arrive*] de improviso, sin avisar; [*happen*] inesperadamente, de repente; [*die*] repentinamente, inesperadamente; **there was an ~ high turnout of voters** se produjo una asistencia de votantes inesperadamente alta

unexplained [ˌʌnɪks'pleɪnd] ADJ inexplicado

unexploded [ˌʌnɪks'pləʊdɪd] ADJ sin explotar

unexplored [ˌʌnɪks'plɔːd] ADJ inexplorado

unexpressed [ˈʌnɪksˈprest] ADJ no expresado, tácito

unexpurgated [ˈʌnˈekspɜːˈɡeɪtɪd] ADJ sin expurgar, íntegro

unfailing [ʌnˈfeɪlɪŋ] ADJ (gen) indefectible, infalible; [supply] inagotable

unfailingly [ʌnˈfeɪlɪŋlɪ] ADV **to be ~ courteous** ser siempre cortés, no faltar en ningún momento a la cortesía

unfair [ˈʌnˈfeəʳ] ADJ (compar ~**er**; superl ~**est**) [system, treatment, decision] injusto; [comment, criticism] injusto, improcedente; [play] sucio; [tactics, practice, methods] antirreglamentario; [competition] desleal; **you're being ~** estás siendo injusto; **how ~!** ¡no hay derecho!; **it's ~ to expect her to do that** no es justo or es injusto esperar que ella haga eso; **it's ~ on those who have paid** es injusto para los que han pagado; **to be ~ to sb** ser injusto con algn, no ser justo con algn ➤ **unfair dismissal** despido m improcedente, despido m injustificado

unfairly [ˈʌnˈfeəlɪ] ADV [treat, dismiss, judge, penalize] injustamente; [compete] deslealmente

unfairness [ˈʌnˈfeənɪs] N injusticia f

unfaithful [ˈʌnˈfeɪθfʊl] ADJ infiel (**to** a)

unfamiliar [ˈʌnfəˈmɪlɪəʳ] ADJ desconocido, extraño; **I heard an ~ voice** oí una voz desconocida or extraña; **to be ~ with sth** no estar familiarizado con algo

unfashionable [ˈʌnˈfæʃnəbl] ADJ pasado de moda; **it is now ~ to talk of ...** no está de moda ahora hablar de ...

unfasten [ˈʌnˈfɑːsn] VT [+ button etc] desabrochar; [+ rope etc] desatar, aflojar (LAm)

unfathomable [ʌnˈfæðəməbl] ADJ insondable

unfavourable, unfavorable (US) [ˈʌnˈfeɪvərəbl] ADJ **1** (= adverse) [conditions] poco propicio, desfavorable; [outlook, weather] poco propicio **2** (= negative) [impression, opinion] negativo, malo; [comparison] poco favorable

unfavourably, unfavorably (US) [ˈʌnˈfeɪvərəblɪ] ADV [react, impress] de forma negativa; **he reviewed your book very ~** hizo una crítica muy negativa de tu libro; **he was compared ~ with his predecessors** se lo comparó desfavorablemente con sus predecesores

unfazed* [ˈʌnˈfeɪzd] ADJ **her criticism left him quite ~** sus críticas le dejaban tan pancho*; **she was completely ~ by the extraordinary events** se quedó como si nada ante unos sucesos tan extraordinarios

unfeeling [ʌnˈfiːlɪŋ] ADJ insensible

unfilled [ˈʌnˈfɪld] ADJ [post, vacancy] sin cubrir; **~ orders** pedidos mpl pendientes

unfinished [ˈʌnˈfɪnɪʃt] ADJ inacabado, sin terminar; **we have ~ business** tenemos asuntos pendientes

unfit [ˈʌnˈfɪt] ADJ **1** (= unsuitable) no apto (**for** para); (= incompetent) incapaz; (= unworthy) indigno (**to** de); **to be ~ for human consumption** no ser apto para el consumo; **to be ~ for habitation** ser inhabitable; **complaints that he was ~ for the job** quejas fpl de que no estaba capacitado para el trabajo
2 (= not physically fit) en mala forma (física), bajo de forma; **he is very ~** está en muy mala forma (física), está muy bajo de forma; **two of their players are ~** dos de sus jugadores no se encuentran en condiciones de jugar; **~ for military service** no apto para el servicio militar; **she is ~ to drive** no está en condiciones de conducir or (LAm) manejar

unflagging [ʌnˈflægɪŋ] ADJ incansable

unflappable* [ˈʌnˈflæpəbl] ADJ imperturbable

unflattering [ˈʌnˈflætərɪŋ] ADJ [description] poco halagüeño; [clothes, haircut] poco favorecedor

unflinching [ˈʌnˈflɪntʃɪŋ] ADJ impávido, resuelto

unfocused, unfocussed [ˈʌnˈfəʊkəst] ADJ [eyes] desenfocado; [desires] sin objetivo concreto, nada concreto; [energies] que carece de dirección

unfold [ʌnˈfəʊld] **Ⓐ** VT [+ map, etc] desplegar, desdoblar **Ⓑ** VI (lit) desplegarse, desdoblarse; [view etc] revelarse

unforeseeable [ˈʌnfɔːˈsiːəbl] ADJ imprevisible

unforeseen [ˈʌnfɔːˈsiːn] ADJ imprevisto

unforgettable [ˈʌnfəˈɡetəbl] ADJ inolvidable

unforgivable [ˈʌnfəˈɡɪvəbl] ADJ imperdonable

unforgiving [ˈʌnfəˈɡɪvɪŋ] ADJ implacable

unformatted [ˈʌnˈfɔːmætɪd] ADJ (Comput) [disk, text] sin formatear

unfortunate [ʌnˈfɔːtʃnɪt] ADJ **1** (= deserving of pity, unlucky) **we must help these ~ people** debemos ayudar a estas personas tan desafortunadas; **how very ~!** ¡qué mala suerte!, ¡qué desgracia!; **you have been most ~** ha tenido usted muy mala suerte; **he was ~ enough to be caught** tuvo la desgracia or mala suerte de que lo cogieran or pillaran; **it is most ~ that he left** es una lástima or muy de lamentar que se haya ido
2 (= unsuitable, regrettable) [remark] poco acertado, inoportuno; [incident, consequences, tendency] lamentable

unfortunately [ʌnˈfɔːtʃnɪtlɪ] ADV (= unluckily) desgraciadamente, por desgracia; **~ for you** desgraciadamente para ti, por desgracia para ti; **the statement was rather ~ phrased** la declaración estaba formulada con muy poco acierto

unfounded [ˈʌnˈfaʊndɪd] ADJ infundado, sin fundamento

unfriendly [ˈʌnˈfrendlɪ] ADJ (compar **unfriendlier**; superl **unfriendliest**) [person] poco amistoso; (stronger) antipático; [act, gesture] poco amistoso; (stronger) hostil; **to be ~ to** or **towards sb** ser or mostrarse antipático or poco amistoso con algn

unfulfilled [ˈʌnfʊlˈfɪld] ADJ [ambition, hope] frustrado; [desire] no hecho realidad; [promise] no cumplido; [need] insatisfecho; [potential] sin desarrollar; **to feel ~** sentirse insatisfecho, no sentirse realizado

unfunny* [ˈʌnˈfʌnɪ] ADJ nada divertido

unfurl [ʌnˈfɜːl] VT desplegar

unfurnished [ˈʌnˈfɜːnɪʃt] ADJ sin amueblar

ungainly [ʌnˈɡeɪnlɪ] ADJ [person] desgarbado; [gait] torpe, desgarbado

ungenerous [ˈʌnˈdʒenərəs] ADJ **1** (= uncharitable) mezquino; **to be ~ in one's thoughts** tener pensamientos mezquinos **2** (= miserly) poco generoso

unglued [ˈʌnˈɡluːd] ADJ (US) = **unstuck**

ungodly [ʌnˈɡɒdlɪ] ADJ **at this ~ hour** a estas horas tan intempestivas

ungovernable [ʌnˈɡʌvənəbl] ADJ ingobernable

ungracious [ˈʌnˈɡreɪʃəs] ADJ descortés; **it would be ~ to refuse** sería descortés no aceptar

ungrammatical [ˈʌnɡrəˈmætɪkəl] ADJ incorrecto desde el punto de vista gramatical

ungrateful [ʌnˈɡreɪtfʊl] ADJ desagradecido, ingrato

unguarded [ˈʌnˈɡɑːdɪd] ADJ **1** (Mil etc) indefenso, sin protección **2** (fig) (= open, careless) descuidado; (= thoughtless) imprudente; **in an ~ moment** en un momento de descuido

unhappily [ʌnˈhæpɪlɪ] ADV **1** (= miserably) tristemente, con tristeza; **he was ~ married** no fue feliz or fue infeliz en su matrimonio **2** (= unfortunately) lamentablemente; (stronger) desgraciadamente, por desgracia

unhappiness [ʌnˈhæpɪnɪs] N **1** (= sadness) desdicha f, tristeza f; (= absence of happiness) infelicidad f **2** (= dissatisfaction) descontento m; **they expressed their ~ with** or **over the decision** expresaron su descontento con respecto a la decisión

unhappy [ʌnˈhæpɪ] ADJ (compar **unhappier**; superl **unhappiest**) **1** (= sad) [person] infeliz; (stronger) desdichado; [childhood] infeliz; (stronger) desgraciado, desdichado; [marriage] infeliz; [memory] desagradable; **she looked so ~** se la veía tan triste; **I had an ~ time at school** lo pasé muy mal en la escuela
2 (= not pleased) descontento; **to be ~ about/with sth/sb** no estar contento con algo/algn, estar descontento con algo/algn
3 (= uneasy, worried) **I'm ~ about leaving him on his own** no estoy a gusto dejándolo solo, me preocupa dejarlo solo
4 (= unfortunate) [remark] poco acertado, inoportuno; [experience, situation] lamentable

unharmed [ˈʌnˈhɑːmd] ADJ [person, animal] ileso; [thing] intacto; **to escape ~** escapar ileso

UNHCR N ABBR (= **United Nations High Commission for Refugees**) ACNUR *m*

unhealthy [ʌnˈhelθɪ] ADJ (*compar* **unhealthier**; *superl* **unhealthiest**) **1** (= *unwell*) [*person*] poco sano, enfermizo; [*complexion*] poco saludable **2** (= *harmful*) [*climate, place, environment*] malsano, insalubre; [*diet, lifestyle, food*] poco sano **3** (= *unwholesome*) [*interest, fascination, curiosity*] malsano, morboso

unheard-of [ʌnˈhɜːdɒv] ADJ (= *unprecedented*) inaudito; (= *outrageous*) escandaloso

unheeded [ʌnˈhiːdɪd] ADJ [*plea, warning*] desatendido

unhelpful [ʌnˈhelpfʊl] ADJ [*person*] poco servicial, poco dispuesto a ayudar; [*remark*] inútil; [*advice*] poco útil; **it is ~ to pretend the problem does not exist** no se consigue nada pretendiendo que el problema no existe; **to be ~ to sth/sb** no ayudar a algo/algn

unhesitating [ʌnˈhezɪteɪtɪŋ] ADJ (= *steadfast*) resuelto, decidido; (= *prompt*) inmediato, pronto

unhesitatingly [ʌnˈhezɪteɪtɪŋlɪ] ADV sin vacilar

unhindered [ʌnˈhɪndəd] ADJ libre, sin estorbos; **~ by** no estorbado por

unhinge [ʌnˈhɪndʒ] VT [+ *mind*] trastornar; [+ *person*] trastornar el juicio de

unhinged [ʌnˈhɪndʒd] ADJ (= *mad*) trastornado

unhitch [ʌnˈhɪtʃ] VT desenganchar

unholy* [ʌnˈhəʊlɪ] ADJ [*mess, row*] tremendo*; [*noise*] tremendo, de mil demonios*

unhook [ʌnˈhʊk] VT **1** (= *remove*) desenganchar, descolgar **2** (= *undo*) [+ *garment*] desabrochar

unhoped-for [ʌnˈhəʊptfɔːˈ] ADJ inesperado

unhurried [ʌnˈhʌrɪd] ADJ [*pace*] pausado, lento; [*atmosphere, person*] tranquilo; [*activity*] tranquilo, pausado

unhurt [ʌnˈhɜːt] ADJ ileso; **to escape ~** salir ileso

unhygienic [ʌnhaɪˈdʒiːnɪk] ADJ antihigiénico

UNICEF [ˈjuːnɪsef] N ABBR (= **United Nations International Children's Emergency Fund**) UNICEF *m*

unicorn [ˈjuːnɪkɔːn] N unicornio *m*

unidentified [ˈʌnaɪˈdentɪfaɪd] ADJ sin identificar, no identificado ➤ **unidentified flying object** objeto *m* volante no identificado

unification [ˌjuːnɪfɪˈkeɪʃən] N unificación *f*

uniform [ˈjuːnɪfɔːm] **(A)** ADJ [*shape, size, colour*] uniforme; [*speed*] constante; [*rate, tariff*] fijo, invariable **(B)** N uniforme *m*; **school ~** uniforme *m* escolar *or* de colegio; **to be in/out of ~** ir con/sin uniforme; **to wear (a) ~** llevar uniforme, ir de uniforme

uniformity [ˌjuːnɪˈfɔːmɪtɪ] N uniformidad *f*

uniformly [ˈjuːnɪfɔːmlɪ] ADV [*spread, distributed, applied*] uniformemente; **the book has had ~ bad reviews** el libro obtuvo malas críticas en general

unify [ˈjuːnɪfaɪ] VT unificar, unir

unifying [ˈjuːnɪfaɪɪŋ] ADJ [*factor etc*] unificador

unilateral [ˈjuːnɪˈlætərəl] ADJ unilateral

unimaginable [ʌnɪˈmædʒɪnəbl] ADJ inimaginable, inconcebible

unimaginative [ˈʌnɪˈmædʒɪnətɪv] ADJ falto de imaginación, poco imaginativo

unimpaired [ˈʌnɪmˈpeəd] ADJ [*mental powers*] en perfecto estado; [*relationship*] intacto

unimportant [ˈʌnɪmˈpɔːtənt] ADJ sin importancia; **the problem itself is relatively ~** el problema en sí tiene relativamente poca importancia

unimpressed [ˈʌnɪmˈprest] ADJ **I am ~ by the new building** el nuevo edificio no me impresiona; **they were ~ by such arguments** tales argumentos les resultaron muy poco convincentes; **he remained ~** siguió sin convencerse

unimpressive [ˈʌnɪmˈpresɪv] ADJ poco impresionante, poco convincente

uninformed [ˈʌnɪnˈfɔːmd] ADJ [*comment, rumour, criticism*] infundado; [*attitudes, prejudice*] ignorante; **I did not want to**

appear **~** no quería parecer ignorante; **well-meaning but ~ people** personas *fpl* de buenas intenciones pero sin conocimientos; **to be ~ about sth** no estar informado sobre algo, no estar al corriente *or* al tanto de algo; **the ~ observer** el observador profano

uninhabitable [ˈʌnɪnˈhæbɪtəbl] ADJ inhabitable

uninhabited [ˈʌnɪnˈhæbɪtɪd] ADJ (= *deserted*) desierto, despoblado; [*house*] desocupado

uninhibited [ˈʌnɪnˈhɪbɪtɪd] ADJ [*person*] desinhibido, sin inhibiciones; [*behaviour*] desinhibido, desenfadado; **to be ~ about doing sth** no tener inhibiciones a la hora de hacer algo

uninitiated [ˈʌnɪˈnɪʃɪeɪtɪd] **(A)** ADJ no iniciado **(B)** NPL **the ~** los no iniciados

uninjured [ˈʌnˈɪndʒəd] ADJ ileso; **to escape ~** salir ileso

uninspired [ˈʌnɪnˈspaɪəd] ADJ [*person*] poco inspirado, sin inspiración; [*book, film, performance*] sin inspiración, falto de inspiración; [*food*] poco original

uninspiring [ˈʌnɪnˈspaɪərɪŋ] ADJ [*person, film, book, play*] poco estimulante, aburrido; [*view*] monótono

uninsured [ˈʌnɪnˈʃʊəd] ADJ no asegurado

unintelligent [ˈʌnɪnˈtelɪdʒənt] ADJ poco inteligente

unintelligible [ˈʌnɪnˈtelɪdʒəbl] ADJ ininteligible, incomprensible

unintended [ˈʌnɪnˈtendɪd], **unintentional** [ˈʌnɪnˈtenʃənl] ADJ involuntario, no intencionado

unintentionally [ˈʌnɪnˈtenʃnəlɪ] ADV sin querer, involuntariamente

uninterested [ˈʌnˈɪntrɪstɪd] ADJ (= *indifferent*) indiferente, desinteresado; **I am quite ~ in what he thinks** me es igual *or* indiferente lo que piensa; **to be ~ in a subject** no tener interés en un tema

uninteresting [ˈʌnˈɪntrɪstɪŋ] ADJ [*person, book, film, speech*] poco interesante; [*city, building*] sin interés

uninterrupted [ˈʌnˌɪntəˈrʌptɪd] ADJ ininterrumpido

uninvited [ˈʌnɪnˈvaɪtɪd] ADJ [*guest etc*] sin invitación; [*criticism, comment*] gratuito; **they came to the party ~** vinieron a la fiesta sin haber sido invitados

uninviting [ˈʌnɪnˈvaɪtɪŋ] ADJ [*appearance, offer*] poco atractivo; [*food*] poco apetitoso

union [ˈjuːnjən] **(A)** N **1** [*of countries etc*] unión *f*; (= *marriage*) enlace *m*; **the Union** (*US*) la Unión **2** (= *trade union*) sindicato *m*, gremio *m* **3** (= *club, society*) club *m*, sociedad *f* **(B)** CPD (*Ind*) [*leader, movement, headquarters*] sindical ➤ **union card** carnet *m* de afiliado ➤ **Union Jack** bandera *f* del Reino Unido ➤ **union member** miembro *mf* del sindicato, sindicalista *mf* ➤ **union shop** (*US*) taller *m* de afiliación (sindical) obligatoria ➤ **union suit** (*US*) prenda *f* interior de cuerpo entero

Unionist [ˈjuːnjənɪst] N (*Brit Pol*) unionista *mf*

unionize [ˈjuːnjənaɪz] VT sindicar, sindicalizar

unique [juːˈniːk] ADJ **1** (= *exclusive*) [*style, collection, combination*] único; **the experience is ~ to each individual** la experiencia es única (e irrepetible) en cada individuo; **it is a species ~ to these islands** es una especie que se da únicamente en estas islas **2** (= *exceptional*) [*opportunity*] único; [*ability, talent*] sin igual, excepcional; [*insight*] único, de excepción

uniquely [juːˈniːklɪ] ADV **she is ~ qualified for the job** está excepcionalmente capacitada para el puesto; **to be ~ placed to do sth** encontrarse en una posición de excepción para hacer algo; **a ~ British characteristic** una característica exclusivamente británica

uniqueness [juːˈniːknɪs] N singularidad *f*

unisex [ˈjuːnɪseks] ADJ unisex *inv*

UNISON [ˈjuːnɪsn] N ABBR (*Brit*) gran sindicato de funcionarios

unison [ˈjuːnɪzn] N **in ~** al unísono

unit [ˈjuːnɪt] **(A)** N **1** (*Admin, Elec, Math*) unidad *f*; **a ~ of measurement** una unidad de medida **2** (*in course, textbook*) unidad *f* **3** (= *piece of furniture*) mueble *m*; **a kitchen ~** un mueble de cocina

4 (*Tech*) (= *device*) aparato *m*; (= *mechanism*) conjunto *m*
5 (*in hospital*) unidad *f*; **intensive care** ~ unidad *f* de cuidados intensivos
6 (= *group of people*) unidad *f* (*also Mil*); (*in firm*) centro *m*; **family** ~ núcleo *m* familiar, familia *f*
Ⓑ CPD ➤ **unit charge, unit cost** (*Brit Fin*) costo *m* unitario *or* por unidad ➤ **unit price** precio *m* unitario *or* por unidad ➤ **unit trust** (*Brit*) (= *fund*) fondo *m* de inversión mobiliaria; (= *company*) sociedad *f* de inversiones

unite [juːˈnaɪt] **Ⓐ** VT [+ *people, organizations*] unir; [+ *parts of country*] unificar, unir **Ⓑ** VI unirse; **to ~ against sb** unirse para hacer frente a algn

united [juːˈnaɪtɪd] ADJ [*country, group, front*] unido; [*effort*] conjunto; **they were ~ by a common enemy** los unía un enemigo común; **the family was ~ in grief** la familia estaba unida por el dolor; **they are ~ in their belief that ...** comparten la creencia de que ...; **they are ~ in their opposition to the plan** los une su oposición al plan ➤ **the United Arab Emirates** los Emiratos Árabes Unidos ➤ **the United Arab Republic** la República Árabe Unida ➤ **the United Kingdom** el Reino Unido (*Inglaterra, Gales, Escocia, Irlanda del Norte*) ➤ **the United Nations (Organization)** la Organización de las Naciones Unidas, las Naciones Unidas ➤ **the United States (of America)** los Estados Unidos (de América)

unity [ˈjuːnɪtɪ] N unidad *f*

Univ. ABBR (= **University**) U.

universal [ˌjuːnɪˈvɜːsəl] ADJ [*agreement, acceptance*] general, global; [*law, language*] universal; **the closures met with ~ condemnation** los cierres provocaron la condena general *or* unánime; **her writing has ~ appeal** su forma de escribir atrae a todo el mundo; **a ~ truth** una verdad universal, una verdad aceptada por todos *or* por todo el mundo; **to become ~** generalizarse ➤ **universal product code** (*US*) código *m* de barras

universally [ˌjuːnɪˈvɜːsəlɪ] ADV [*accepted, acknowledged*] universalmente, generalmente; [*popular, available*] en todas partes

universe [ˈjuːnɪvɜːs] N universo *m*

university [ˌjuːnɪˈvɜːsɪtɪ] **Ⓐ** N universidad *f*; **to be at ~** estar en la universidad; **to go to ~** ir a la universidad; **he has a ~ education** ha cursado estudios universitarios; **Lancaster University** la Universidad de Lancaster **Ⓑ** CPD [*degree, year, professor, student*] universitario; [*library*] de la universidad ➤ **university entrance examination** examen *m* de ingreso a la universidad ➤ **university place** plaza *f* universitaria

unjust [ˈʌnˈdʒʌst] ADJ injusto; **to be ~ to sb** ser injusto con algn

unjustifiable [ʌnˈdʒʌstɪfaɪəbl] ADJ injustificable

unjustified [ʌnˈdʒʌstɪfaɪd] ADJ [*attack, reputation*] injustificado

unjustly [ˈʌnˈdʒʌstlɪ] ADV injustamente

unkempt [ˈʌnˈkempt] ADJ [*clothes, appearance, beard, garden*] descuidado; [*hair*] despeinado, descuidado

unkind [ʌnˈkaɪnd] ADJ (*compar* ~**er**; *superl* ~**est**) (= *cruel, nasty*) [*person*] poco amable; (*stronger*) cruel; [*criticism*] duro; [*remark*] cruel; [*words*] desagradable; **that was very ~ of him** eso fue muy poco amable de su parte; **to be ~ to sb** portarse mal con algn

unkindly [ʌnˈkaɪndlɪ] ADV [*say, behave*] cruelmente, con crueldad; **it wasn't meant ~** no iba con malas intenciones; **to treat sb ~** tratar mal a algn

unknowing [ˈʌnˈnəʊɪŋ] ADJ inconsciente; **she was the ~ cause** ella fue la causa, inconscientemente

unknowingly [ˈʌnˈnəʊɪŋlɪ] ADV (= *involuntarily*) inconscientemente, sin querer; (= *in ignorance*) sin darse cuenta, sin saberlo

unknown [ˈʌnˈnəʊn] **Ⓐ** ADJ [*identity, destination, territory, writer*] desconocido; **for some ~ reason** por alguna razón desconocida; **the Unknown Soldier** el soldado desconocido; **the Cazorla Sierra is almost ~ outside Spain** la Sierra de Cazorla casi no se conoce fuera de España; **a substance ~ to science** una sustancia no conocida por la

ciencia, una sustancia que la ciencia desconoce; **it's ~ for him to refuse a sweet** nunca ha dicho que no a un caramelo que se sepa; **she's a bit of an ~ quantity** ella es una incógnita
Ⓑ ADV ~ **to me** sin yo saberlo
Ⓒ N **a journey into the ~** un viaje a lo desconocido

unladen [ˈʌnˈleɪdn] ADJ vacío, sin cargamento

unladylike [ˈʌnˈleɪdɪlaɪk] ADJ impropio de una dama

unlawful [ˈʌnˈlɔːfʊl] ADJ ilegal, ilícito

unleaded [ˌʌnˈledɪd] **Ⓐ** ADJ [*petrol*] sin plomo **Ⓑ** N gasolina *f* sin plomo

unleash [ˈʌnˈliːʃ] VT [+ *dog*] desatar, soltar; [+ *anger, imagination*] desencadenar, desatar

unleavened [ˈʌnˈlevnd] ADJ ázimo, sin levadura

unless [ənˈles] CONJ a menos que + *subjun*, a no ser que + *subjun*; ~ **I hear to the contrary** a menos que me digan lo contrario, a no ser que me digan lo contrario; ~ **I am mistaken, we're lost** si no me equivoco, estamos perdidos; ~ **otherwise stated** de no especificarse lo contrario

unlicensed [ˈʌnˈlaɪsənst] ADJ sin permiso, sin licencia

unlike [ˈʌnˈlaɪk] PREP a diferencia de; ~ **him, I really enjoy flying** a diferencia de él, a mí me encanta viajar en avión; **it's quite ~ him** no es nada característico de él; **the photo is quite ~ him** la foto no se le parece en absoluto

unlikely [ʌnˈlaɪklɪ] ADJ (*compar* **unlikelier**; *superl* **unlikeliest**) **1** (= *improbable*) poco probable, improbable; **it is most ~** es muy poco probable; **it is ~ that he will come** ◊ **he is ~ to come** es poco probable que venga, no es probable que venga; **he's ~ to survive** tiene pocas posibilidades de sobrevivir, es poco probable que sobreviva; **in the ~ event that we win** en el caso improbable de que ganáramos
2 (= *implausible*) [*explanation, excuse*] inverosímil, increíble **3** (= *odd*) insólito, extraño; **he and Paula made an ~ couple** él y Paula hacían una pareja insólita *or* extraña; **they turn up in the most ~ places** aparecen en los lugares más insospechados *or* extraños

unlimited [ʌnˈlɪmɪtɪd] ADJ [*travel, amount, access, use*] ilimitado; [*patience*] inagotable

unlisted [ˈʌnˈlɪstɪd] ADJ **1** (*St Ex*) ~ **company** sociedad *f* sin cotización oficial, compañía *f* no cotizable **2** (*US Telec*) ~ **number** número *m* que no figura en la guía telefónica

unlit [ˈʌnˈlɪt] ADJ [*fire, cigarette, pipe*] sin encender, apagado; [*place*] no iluminado, oscuro

unload [ˈʌnˈləʊd] VT, VI descargar

unlock [ˈʌnˈlɒk] VT **1** [+ *door, box*] abrir (con llave); **the door is ~ed** la puerta no está cerrada con llave **2** (*fig*) [+ *secret*] descubrir; [+ *potential*] liberar

unlovable [ˈʌnˈlʌvəbl] ADJ antipático

unluckily [ʌnˈlʌkɪlɪ] ADV lamentablemente, desgraciadamente; ~ **for her** lamentablemente *or* desgraciadamente para ella

unlucky [ʌnˈlʌkɪ] ADJ (*compar* **unluckier**; *superl* **unluckiest**) **1** (= *luckless*) [*person*] desafortunado; **the ~ ones** los menos afortunados; **to be ~** [*person*] tener mala suerte; **she was ~ enough to meet him** tuvo la mala suerte *or* la desgracia de encontrarse con él; **to be ~ in love** no tener suerte en el amor
2 (= *causing bad luck*) [*number, object*] que trae mala suerte; **it's ~ to break a mirror** romper un espejo trae mala suerte **3** (= *ill-omened*) [*day, omen*] funesto, nefasto; **1990 was an ~ year for me** 1990 fue un año de mala suerte para mí

unmade [ˈʌnˈmeɪd] ADJ [*bed*] sin hacer

unmanageable [ʌnˈmænɪdʒəbl] ADJ (= *overwhelming*) [*problem, system, situation, size, number*] imposible de controlar; [*hair*] difícil de peinar, rebelde

unmanned [ˈʌnˈmænd] ADJ no tripulado

unmarked [ˈʌnˈmɑːkt] ADJ **1** (= *anonymous*) [*grave*] sin nombre; [*police car*] particular, camuflado (*Sp*); [*container, envelope*] sin marcar **2** (= *uncorrected*) [*essay, exam etc*] sin corregir

unmarried ['ʌn'mærɪd] ADJ soltero; **an ~ mother** una madre soltera; **an ~ couple** una pareja no casada

unmask ['ʌn'mɑːsk] VT (*lit, fig*) desenmascarar

unmatched ['ʌn'mætʃt] ADJ incomparable, sin par

unmistakable ['ʌnmɪs'teɪkəbl] ADJ inconfundible, inequívoco

unmistakably ['ʌnmɪs'teɪkəblɪ] ADV de modo inconfundible; **it is ~ mine** sin duda alguna es mío

unmitigated [ʌn'mɪtɪɡeɪtɪd] ADJ [*disaster, failure*] auténtico, verdadero; **it was an ~ disaster** fue un auténtico *or* verdadero desastre

unmoved ['ʌn'muːvd] ADJ impasible; **to remain ~ by** seguir indiferente ante, permanecer impasible frente a

unnamed ['ʌn'neɪmd] ADJ (= *nameless*) sin nombre; (= *anonymous*) anónimo

unnatural [ʌn'nætʃrəl] ADJ **1** (= *unusual, abnormal*) poco normal, poco natural; **it's ~ to eat so much** no es normal comer tanto; **it is not ~ to think that ...** es normal pensar que ... **2** (= *perverted*) [*habit, vice, practice*] antinatural

unnaturally [ʌn'nætʃrəlɪ] ADV (= *unusually, abnormally*) extrañamente; **not ~, he was cross** como es natural *or* lógico se enfadó

unnecessarily [ʌn'nesɪsərɪlɪ] ADV innecesariamente, sin necesidad

unnecessary [ʌn'nesɪsərɪ] ADJ innecesario; **it is ~ to add that ...** no hace falta *or* no es necesario añadir que ...

unnerve ['ʌn'nɜːv] VT desconcertar

unnerving ['ʌn'nɜːvɪŋ] ADJ desconcertante

unnoticed ['ʌn'nəʊtɪst] ADJ inadvertido, desapercibido; **to go ~** pasar inadvertido *or* desapercibido

UNO N ABBR (= **United Nations Organization**) ONU *f*

unobservant ['ʌnəb'zɜːvənt] ADJ [*person etc*] distraído, poco atento

unobserved ['ʌnəb'zɜːvd] ADJ (= *not seen*) inadvertido, desapercibido; **to get away ~** lograr pasar inadvertido *or* desapercibido

unobstructed ['ʌnəb'strʌktɪd] ADJ [*pipe etc*] despejado; [*view etc*] perfecto

unobtainable ['ʌnəb'teɪnəbl] ADJ **1** [*goods*] imposible de conseguir; [*goal, objective*] inalcanzable, imposible de conseguir *or* realizar **2** (*Brit Telec*) [*number*] desconectado

unobtrusive ['ʌnəb'truːsɪv] ADJ discreto, modesto

unoccupied ['ʌn'ɒkjʊpaɪd] ADJ **1** (= *empty*) [*building*] desocupado, vacío; [*room*] vacío; [*seat, table*] libre; [*post*] vacante **2** (*Mil*) [*country, zone*] no ocupado

unofficial ['ʌnə'fɪʃl] ADJ **1** (= *informal*) [*visit, tour*] no oficial, extraoficial; **in an ~ capacity** de forma *or* manera extraoficial *or* no oficial; **from an ~ source** de fuente oficiosa; **~ strike** huelga *f* no oficial **2** (= *de facto*) [*leader, spokesperson*] no oficial **3** (= *unconfirmed*) [*report, results*] no oficial

unofficially ['ʌnə'fɪʃlɪ] ADV extraoficialmente

unopened ['ʌn'əʊpənd] ADJ sin abrir

unopposed ['ʌnə'pəʊzd] ADJ sin oposición; (*Mil*) sin encontrar resistencia

unorthodox ['ʌn'ɔːθədɒks] ADJ (= *unconventional*) poco ortodoxo, poco convencional

unpack ['ʌn'pæk] **Ⓐ** VT deshacer, desempacar (*LAm*); **I ~ed my suitcase** deshice la maleta; **I haven't ~ed my clothes yet** todavía no he sacado la ropa de la maleta **Ⓑ** VI deshacer la(s) maleta(s), desempacar (*LAm*)

unpaid ['ʌn'peɪd] ADJ [*staff, worker, overtime*] no remunerado, no retribuido; [*leave*] sin paga, sin sueldo; [*debts, bills*] sin pagar, pendiente; [*taxes, rent*] sin pagar

unpalatable [ʌn'pælɪtəbl] ADJ [*food*] de mal sabor; [*truth, fact*] difícil de aceptar

unparalleled [ʌn'pærəleld] ADJ [*opportunity, prosperity, event*] sin precedentes, sin paralelo; [*beauty, wit*] sin par, incomparable

unpardonable [ʌn'pɑːdnəbl] ADJ imperdonable, indisculpable

unpatriotic ['ʌn,pætrɪ'ɒtɪk] ADJ antipatriótico, poco patriótico

unperturbed ['ʌnpɜː'tɜːbd] ADJ impertérrito; **he carried on ~** siguió sin inmutarse *or* (*LAm*) alterarse; **~ by this disaster ...** sin dejarse desanimar por esta catástrofe ...

unpick ['ʌn'pɪk] VT descoser

unpin ['ʌn'pɪn] VT desprender, quitar los alfileres a

unplanned ['ʌn'plænd] ADJ [*pregnancy*] sin planear; [*visit*] imprevisto

unpleasant [ʌn'pleznt] ADJ (*gen*) desagradable; [*person*] desagradable, antipático; **to be ~ to sb** ser desagradable *or* antipático con algn

unpleasantness [ʌn'plezntnɪs] N (*gen*) lo desagradable; (= *bad feeling, quarrel*) disgusto *m*, desavenencia *f*; **there has been a lot of ~** ha habido muchos disgustos *or* muchas desavenencias

unplug ['ʌn'plʌɡ] VT desenchufar, desconectar

unpolished ['ʌn'pɒlɪʃt] ADJ **1** (*lit*) (*gen*) sin pulir; [*diamond*] en bruto **2** (*fig*) tosco, inculto

unpolluted ['ʌnpə'luːtɪd] ADJ no contaminado, impoluto

unpopular ['ʌn'pɒpjʊləʳ] ADJ (*gen*) impopular, poco popular; (= *unacceptable*) inaceptable, mal visto; **she's an ~ child** tiene muy pocos amigos; **it is ~ with the miners** los mineros no lo aceptan, los mineros lo ven mal

unpopulated ['ʌn'pɒpjʊleɪtɪd] ADJ deshabitado, desierto

unprecedented [ʌn'presɪdəntɪd] ADJ sin precedentes

unpredictable ['ʌnprɪ'dɪktəbl] ADJ [*situation*] impredecible, incierto; [*weather*] variable; [*person*] caprichoso, de reacción imprevisible

unprejudiced [ʌn'predʒʊdɪst] ADJ (= *not biased*) imparcial; (= *having no prejudices*) sin prejuicios

unprepared ['ʌnprɪ'peəd] ADJ (= *unready*) **the student who comes to an exam ~** el estudiante que viene al examen sin estar preparado *or* sin preparación; **to catch sb ~** pillar a algn desprevenido; **to be ~ for sth** (= *not expect*) no contar con algo, no esperar algo; (= *be unequipped for*) no estar preparado para algo

unprepossessing ['ʌn,priː'pə'zesɪŋ] ADJ poco atractivo

unpretentious ['ʌnprɪ'tenʃəs] ADJ sin pretensiones, modesto

unprincipled [ʌn'prɪnsɪpld] ADJ sin escrúpulos, cínico

unprintable ['ʌn'prɪntəbl] ADJ [*story*] impublicable; [*remark, comment*] irrepetible

unproductive ['ʌnprə'dʌktɪv] ADJ [*capital, soil etc*] improductivo; [*meeting etc*] infructuoso

unprofessional ['ʌnprə'feʃnl] ADJ [*person, behaviour, attitude*] poco profesional; **it was ~ of her** fue poco profesional de su parte; **~ conduct** comportamiento *m* contrario a la ética profesional

unprofitable [ʌn'prɒfɪtəbl] ADJ [*business*] poco rentable

unpronounceable ['ʌnprə'naʊnsəbl] ADJ impronunciable

unprotected ['ʌnprə'tektɪd] **Ⓐ** ADJ **1** (= *defenceless*) [*person*] indefenso **2** (= *uncovered*) [*skin, eyes, plants*] sin protección **Ⓑ** CPD ► **unprotected sex, unprotected intercourse** relaciones *fpl* sexuales sin protección

unproved ['ʌn'pruːvd], **unproven** [ʌn'pruːvən] ADJ no probado

unprovoked ['ʌnprə'vəʊkt] ADJ no provocado, sin provocación

unpublished ['ʌn'pʌblɪʃt] ADJ inédito, no publicado

unpunished ['ʌn'pʌnɪʃt] ADJ **to go ~** [*crime*] quedar sin castigo, quedar impune; [*person*] escapar sin castigo, salir impune

unqualified ['ʌn'kwɒlɪfaɪd] ADJ **1** (= *without qualifications*) [*staff, pilot*] no calificado, no cualificado; [*teacher*] sin título, no titulado; **to be ~ to do sth** no estar capacitado para hacer algo **2** (= *unmitigated*) [*success, disaster*] rotundo, total y absoluto; [*acceptance, support*] incondicional

unquestionable [ʌn'kwestʃənəbl] ADJ indiscutible, incuestionable

unquestionably [ʌn'kwestʃənəblɪ] ADV

indiscutiblemente, incuestionablemente

unquestioning [ʌnˈkwestʃənɪŋ] ADJ [*faith*] ciego; [*acceptance*] incondicional, ciego; [*loyalty*] incondicional

unquote [ˈʌnˈkwəʊt] N *see* **quote**

unquoted [ˈʌnˈkwəʊtɪd] ADJ [*share etc*] no cotizado, sin cotización oficial

unravel [ʌnˈrævəl] **A** VT desenredar, desenmarañar **B** VI desenredarse, desenmarañarse

unread [ˈʌnˈred] ADJ **to leave sth ~** dejar algo sin leer

unreadable [ʌnˈriːdəbl] ADJ **1** [*book*] imposible de leer; **I found the book ~** el libro me resultó pesadísimo **2** (= *illegible*) ilegible (*also Comput*)

unreal [ʌnˈrɪəl] ADJ **1** [*situation, world*] irreal **2** (*) (= *excellent*) increíble*; (= *unbelievable*) increíble

unrealistic [ˈʌnrɪəˈlɪstɪk] ADJ poco realista; **it is ~ to expect that …** no es realista esperar que …

unrealistically [ˈʌnrɪəˈlɪstɪkəlɪ] ADV **the prices are ~ high** los precios son tan altos que no son realistas

unreality [ˈʌnrɪˈælɪtɪ] N irrealidad *f*

unrealized [ˈʌnˈrɪəlaɪzd] ADJ [*ambition*] no realizado, que ha quedado sin realizar; [*objective*] no logrado

unreasonable [ʌnˈriːznəbl] ADJ [*person, behaviour*] irrazonable, poco razonable; [*price, amount*] excesivo; **he was most ~ about it** reaccionó en forma irracional

unrecognizable [ʌnˈrekəgnaɪzəbl] ADJ irreconocible

unrecognized [ʌnˈrekəgnaɪzd] ADJ **1** (= *unnoticed*) [*talent, genius*] desapercibido, no reconocido; **to go ~** pasar desapercibido; **he walked along the road ~ by passers-by** fue por la calle sin que los transeúntes le reconocieran **2** (*Pol*) [*government, party, country*] no reconocido

unrecorded [ˈʌnrɪˈkɔːdɪd] ADJ no registrado, ignorado

unrefined [ˈʌnrɪˈfaɪnd] ADJ **1** [*oil, sugar*] crudo, sin refinar **2** [*person, manners*] poco refinado

unrehearsed [ˈʌnrɪˈhɜːst] ADJ (= *spontaneous*) improvisado

unrelated [ˈʌnrɪˈleɪtɪd] ADJ **1** (= *unconnected*) inconexo **2** (*by family*) no emparentado

unrelenting [ˈʌnrɪˈlentɪŋ] ADJ [*rain, heat, attack*] implacable; [*person*] despiadado

unreliability [ˈʌnrɪˌlaɪəˈbɪlɪtɪ] N falta *f* de fiabilidad

unreliable [ˈʌnrɪˈlaɪəbl] ADJ [*person*] informal, poco de fiar; [*machine, service*] poco fiable, que no es de fiar; [*information, statistics*] poco fiable

unrelieved [ˈʌnrɪˈliːvd] ADJ **three hours of ~ boredom** tres horas de aburrimiento total

unremarkable [ˈʌnrɪˈmɑːkəbl] ADJ ordinario, corriente

unremitting [ˈʌnrɪˈmɪtɪŋ] ADJ incansable; (= *continuous*) continuo

unrepeatable [ˈʌnrɪˈpiːtəbl] ADJ **what he said is quite ~** no me atrevo a repetir lo que dijo; **an ~ bargain** una ganga única

unrepentant [ˈʌnrɪˈpentənt] ADJ impenitente

unreported [ˌʌnrɪˈpɔːtɪd] ADJ [*crime*] no denunciado, sin denunciar; **the news went ~** la noticia no fue comunicada

unrepresentative [ˈʌnˌreprɪˈzentətɪv] ADJ poco representativo; **to be ~ of sth** no ser representativo de algo

unrequited [ˈʌnrɪˈkwaɪtɪd] ADJ no correspondido

unreserved [ˈʌnrɪˈzɜːvd] ADJ **1** (= *not booked*) no reservado **2** (= *frank*) franco, directo **3** (= *complete*) total, completo

unreservedly [ˈʌnrɪˈzɜːvɪdlɪ] ADV sin reserva, incondicionalmente

unresolved [ˈʌnrɪˈzɒlvd] ADJ [*problem*] no resuelto, pendiente

unresponsive [ˈʌnrɪˈspɒnsɪv] ADJ insensible, sordo (**to** a)

unrest [ʌnˈrest] N (*Pol*) malestar *m*; (= *riots*) disturbios *mpl*; **the ~ in the Congo** los disturbios del Congo

unrestrained [ˈʌnrɪˈstreɪnd] ADJ **1** [*joy, laughter, violence*] desenfrenado, incontrolado; [*enthusiasm*] desbordante; **to be ~ by morality** no estar frenado por la moralidad **2** (= *not held physically*) [*car passenger*] sin cinturón; [*patient, prisoner*] sin maniatar

unrestricted [ˈʌnrɪˈstrɪktɪd] ADJ (= *unlimited*) [*use, right*] ilimitado; **~ access** libre acceso *m*

unrewarded [ˈʌnrɪˈwɔːdɪd] ADJ sin recompensa; **to go ~** quedar sin recompensa

unrewarding [ˈʌnrɪˈwɔːdɪŋ] ADJ ingrato; (*financially*) improductivo

unripe [ˈʌnˈraɪp] ADJ verde

unrivalled, unrivaled (*US*) [ʌnˈraɪvəld] ADJ sin par, incomparable

unroadworthy [ˈʌnˈrəʊdˌwɜːðɪ] ADJ no apto para circular

unroll [ˈʌnˈrəʊl] **A** VT desenrollar **B** VI desenrollarse

unruffled [ˈʌnˈrʌfld] ADJ [*person*] sereno, imperturbable

unruly [ʌnˈruːlɪ] ADJ (*compar* **unrulier**; *superl* **unruliest**) [*behaviour*] rebelde; [*child*] revoltoso; [*mob*] alterado

unsafe [ˈʌnˈseɪf] ADJ **1** (= *dangerous*) [*building, neighbourhood, machine, vehicle, wiring*] peligroso, poco seguro; **the car is ~ to drive** el coche no está en condiciones de conducirlo; **it is ~ to walk there at night** es peligroso caminar por ahí de noche **2** (*Jur*) [*evidence, conviction, verdict*] abierto a revisión judicial

unsaid [ˈʌnˈsed] ADJ sin decir; **to leave sth ~** callar algo, dejar de decir algo; **much was left ~** muchas cosas se quedaron por decir

unsaleable, unsalable (*US*) [ˈʌnˈseɪləbl] ADJ invendible

unsatisfactory [ˈʌnˌsætɪsˈfæktərɪ] ADJ poco satisfactorio; [*work*] insatisfactorio

unsatisfied [ˈʌnˈsætɪsfaɪd] ADJ insatisfecho

unsatisfying [ˈʌnˈsætɪsfaɪɪŋ] ADJ poco satisfactorio

unsavoury, unsavory (*US*) [ˈʌnˈseɪvərɪ] ADJ [*person*] indeseable; [*remark etc*] desagradable, repugnante

unscathed [ˈʌnˈskeɪðd] ADJ ileso; **to escape/get out ~** salir ileso

unscheduled [ˈʌnˈʃedjuːld, (*US*) ˈʌnˈskedjuld] ADJ no programado

unscientific [ˈʌnˌsaɪənˈtɪfɪk] ADJ poco científico

unscramble [ˈʌnˈskræmbl] VT [+ *message*] descifrar; (*TV*) descodificar

unscrew [ˈʌnˈskruː] **A** VT destornillar; [+ *lid*] desenroscar **B** VI destornillarse; [*lid*] desenroscar

unscrupulous [ʌnˈskruːpjʊləs] ADJ sin escrúpulos, poco escrupuloso

unseasonably [ʌnˈsiːznəblɪ] ADV **we had an ~ warm spring** tuvimos una primavera calurosa para esa época del año; **it was ~ mild for late January** hacía un tiempo muy moderado para estar a últimos de enero

unseat [ʌnˈsiːt] VT **1** (= *bring down*) [+ *government*] derrocar; [+ *person*] derribar; [+ *MP*] hacer perder su escaño **2** [+ *rider*] derribar, desarzonar

unsecured [ˈʌnsɪˈkjʊəd] ADJ (*Fin*) no respaldado, sin aval

unseeded [ˈʌnˈsiːdɪd] ADJ [*player, team*] que no es cabeza de serie

unseemly [ʌnˈsiːmlɪ] ADJ (*gen*) mal visto; [*behaviour*] impropio, indecoroso

unseen [ˈʌnˈsiːn] **A** ADJ (= *hidden*) oculto; (= *unknown*) desconocido; (*esp Brit*) [*translation*] hecho a primera vista; **he managed to get through ~** logró pasar inadvertido **B** N (*esp Brit*) traducción *f* hecha a primera vista

unselfconscious [ˈʌnˌselfˈkɒnʃəs] ADJ natural

unselfish [ˈʌnˈselfɪʃ] ADJ desinteresado

unselfishly [ˈʌnˈselfɪʃlɪ] ADV desinteresadamente

unsentimental [ˈʌnsentɪˈmentəl] ADJ nada sentimental

unsettle [ʌnˈsetl] VT (= *worry*) inquietar; [+ *opponent*] desconcertar; **don't let her comments ~ you** no dejes que sus comentarios te pongan nervioso

unsettled [ʌnˈsetld] ADJ **1** (= *restless*) [*person*] intranquilo; [*sleep, night*] agitado; **he's feeling ~ in his job** no está del todo contento *or* a gusto en su trabajo **2** (= *undecided*) [*matter, question*] pendiente, sin resolver **3** (= *changeable*) [*weather*] inestable, variable; [*situation, market*] inestable

unsettling [ʌnˈsetlɪŋ] ADJ [*influence, effect*]

desestabilizador; [*experience, dream*] perturbador

unshak(e)able [ʌnˈʃeɪkəbl] ADJ [*belief*] inquebrantable; **he was ~ in his resolve** se mostró totalmente resuelto

unshaven [ʌnˈʃeɪvn] ADJ sin afeitar

unshockable [ʌnˈʃɒkəbl] ADJ **she's ~** no se escandaliza por nada

unsightly [ʌnˈsaɪtlɪ] ADJ feo

unsigned [ʌnˈsaɪnd] ADJ [*letter, article, contract*] sin firmar

unsinkable [ʌnˈsɪŋkəbl] ADJ insumergible

unskilled [ʌnˈskɪld] ADJ [*work*] no especializado; [*worker*] no cualificado, no calificado

unsmiling [ʌnˈsmaɪlɪŋ] ADJ adusto

unsociable [ʌnˈsəʊʃəbl] ADJ insociable, poco sociable

unsocial [ʌnˈsəʊʃəl] ADJ antisocial; **to work ~ hours** (*Brit*) trabajar fuera de las horas normales

unsold [ˈʌnˈsəʊld] ADJ por vender, sin venderse

unsolicited [ˈʌnsəˈlɪsɪtɪd] ADJ no solicitado

unsolved [ˈʌnˈsɒlvd] ADJ no resuelto, sin resolver

unsophisticated [ˈʌnsəˈfɪstɪkeɪtɪd] ADJ sencillo, cándido; (*pej*) burdo

unsound [ˈʌnˈsaʊnd] ADJ (*in health*) malo; (*in construction*) defectuoso; (= *unstable*) poco sólido *or* estable; [*argument*] poco sólido; **of ~ mind** (*Jur*) mentalmente incapacitado; **the book is ~ on some points** el libro yerra en algunos puntos, no hay que fiarse del libro en ciertos aspectos

unspeakable [ʌnˈspiːkəbl] ADJ (= *terrible*) [*pain*] horrible; (= *dreadful*) incalificable

unspecified [ˈʌnˈspesɪfaɪd] ADJ no especificado

unspoiled [ˈʌnˈspɔɪld], **unspoilt** [ˈʌnˈspɔɪlt] ADJ [*place*] que no ha perdido su belleza natural; [*child*] nada mimado; **~ by tourism** no echado a perder por el turismo

unspoken [ˈʌnˈspəʊkən] ADJ tácito, sobreentendido

unsporting [ˈʌnˈspɔːtɪŋ] ADJ antideportivo

unstable [ˈʌnˈsteɪbl] ADJ inestable

unsteady [ˈʌnˈstedɪ] ADJ [*chair, ladder structure*] inestable, inseguro; [*walk*] vacilante; **to be ~ on one's feet** caminar con paso vacilante

unstick [ˈʌnˈstɪk] VT despegar

unstinting [ʌnˈstɪntɪŋ] ADJ pródigo; **to be ~ in one's praise** no escatimar las alabanzas, prodigar las alabanzas; **to be ~ in one's efforts to** (+ INFIN) no regatear esfuerzo por + *infin*

unstoppable [ˈʌnˈstɒpəbl] ADJ incontenible, irrefrenable; (*Sport*) [*shot etc*] imparable

unstressed [ˈʌnˈstrest] ADJ (*Ling*) átono, inacentuado

unstuck [ˈʌnˈstʌk] ADJ **to come ~** [*label etc*] despegarse, desprenderse; (*Brit**) (= *fail*) fracasar, sufrir un revés

unsubscribe [ˈʌnsəbˈskraɪb] VI (*Internet*) borrarse

unsubstantial [ˈʌnsəbˈstænʃəl] ADJ insustancial

unsubstantiated [ˈʌnsəbˈstænʃɪeɪtɪd] ADJ no comprobado, no demostrado

unsuccessful [ˈʌnsəkˈsesfʊl] ADJ [*attempt, effort*] inútil, infructuoso; [*appeal, search, job application*] infructuoso; **he embarked on an ~ business venture** se embarcó en un negocio que no tuvo éxito *or* que fracasó; **to be ~** no tener éxito, fracasar; **we regret to inform you that your application for the post has been ~** lamentamos informarle que no ha sido seleccionado para el puesto de trabajo solicitado; **he was ~ in getting a job** no consiguió *or* logró encontrar trabajo

unsuccessfully [ˈʌnsəkˈsesfəlɪ] ADV sin éxito

unsuitable [ˈʌnˈsuːtəbl] ADJ [*clothes, shoes*] inadecuado, inapropiado; [*accommodation, job, site*] inadecuado; [*moment*] inoportuno, inconveniente; **these shoes are ~ for walking** estos zapatos no son los adecuados *or* apropiados para caminar; **the film is ~ for children** la película no es apta para menores; **he is ~ for the post** no es la persona indicada para el puesto; **she always went for ~ men** siempre escogía a hombres que no le convenían

unsuited [ˈʌnˈsuːtɪd] ADJ **to be ~ for/to sth** no estar hecho para algo, no servir para algo; **they are ~ to each other** son

incompatibles (el uno con el otro)

unsung [ˈʌnˈsʌŋ] ADJ [*hero, heroine*] olvidado

unsupported [ˈʌnsəˈpɔːtɪd] ADJ **1** (= *unsubstantiated*) [*allegation*] sin pruebas que lo respalden; [*claim, statement*] sin base **2** (*physically*) [*person*] sin ayuda; **he was too weak to walk ~** estaba demasiado débil para andar sin ayuda

unsure [ˈʌnˈʃʊə*] ADJ **1** (= *doubtful, undecided*) **to be ~ about/of sth** no estar seguro de algo; **I was ~ what to expect** no estaba seguro de qué esperar; **I was ~ whether he would be able to do it** no estaba seguro de si sería capaz de hacerlo **2** (= *lacking confidence*) inseguro, poco seguro; **to be ~ of o.s.** no estar seguro de uno mismo, no tener confianza en sí mismo

unsurpassed [ˈʌnsəˈpɑːst] ADJ no superado, sin par

unsurprising [ˈʌnsəˈpraɪzɪŋ] ADJ nada sorprendente

unsuspected [ˈʌnsəsˈpektɪd] ADJ insospechado

unsuspecting [ˈʌnsəsˈpektɪŋ] ADJ confiado

unsweetened [ˈʌnˈswiːtnd] ADJ sin azúcar

unswerving [ʌnˈswɜːvɪŋ] ADJ [*resolve*] inquebrantable; [*loyalty*] inquebrantable, firme

unsympathetic [ˈʌnˌsɪmpəˈθetɪk] ADJ poco comprensivo; **he was totally ~** no mostró la más mínima comprensión; **they were ~ to my plea** no hicieron caso de mi ruego

unsystematic [ˈʌnˌsɪstɪˈmætɪk] ADJ poco sistemático, poco metódico

untangle [ʌnˈtæŋgl] VT desenredar, desenmarañar

untapped [ˈʌnˈtæpt] ADJ sin explotar

untaxed [ˈʌnˈtækst] ADJ libre de impuestos, no sujeto a contribuciones

untenable [ˈʌnˈtenəbl] ADJ insostenible

untested [ˈʌnˈtestɪd] ADJ no probado

unthinkable [ʌnˈθɪŋkəbl] **Ⓐ** ADJ **1** (= *inconceivable*) inconcebible, impensable; **it is ~ that** es inconcebible *or* impensable que + *subjun* **2** (= *unbearable*) insoportable **Ⓑ** N **the ~** lo inconcebible

unthinkingly [ʌnˈθɪŋkɪŋlɪ] ADV irreflexivamente, sin pensar

untidily [ʌnˈtaɪdɪlɪ] ADV [*piled, stacked*] sin orden, de manera desordenada; [*dressed*] de forma desaliñada

untidiness [ʌnˈtaɪdɪnɪs] N (*gen*) desorden *m*; [*of appearance*] desaliño *m*

untidy [ʌnˈtaɪdɪ] ADJ (*compar* **untidier**; *superl* **untidiest**) [*room, desk, heap, person*] desordenado; [*appearance*] desaliñado, descuidado; [*hair*] despeinado, descuidado; [*work, writing*] poco metódico, descuidado

untie [ˈʌnˈtaɪ] VT [+ *shoelace, shoe, animal*] desatar; [+ *knot, parcel*] deshacer

until [ənˈtɪl] **Ⓐ** PREP hasta; **he won't be back ~ tomorrow** no volverá hasta mañana **Ⓑ** CONJ **1** (*in future*) hasta que + *subjun*; **wait ~ I get back** espera hasta que yo vuelva; **I don't get up ~ eight o'clock** no me levanto antes de las ocho **2** (*in past*) hasta que + *indic*; **we stayed there ~ the doctor came** nos quedamos allí hasta que vino el médico; **we didn't stop ~ we reached York** no paramos hasta llegar a York

untimely [ʌnˈtaɪmlɪ] ADJ (= *premature*) prematuro; (= *inopportune*) inoportuno

untiring [ʌnˈtaɪərɪŋ] ADJ incansable

untold [ˈʌnˈtəʊld] ADJ (= *indescribable, incalculable*) [*suffering*] indecible; [*loss, wealth*] incalculable, fabuloso

untouchable [ʌnˈtʌtʃəbl] ADJ, N intocable *mf*

untouched [ˈʌnˈtʌtʃt] ADJ **1** (= *not used*) intacto, sin tocar; **she left her breakfast ~** no tocó el desayuno **2** (= *safe*) indemne, incólume **3** (= *unaffected*) insensible, indiferente; **he is ~ by any plea** es insensible a cualquier súplica; **those peoples ~ by civilization** esos pueblos no alcanzados por la civilización

untoward [ˌʌntəˈwɔːd] ADJ (= *adverse*) adverso; (= *inapt*) impropio; (= *unfortunate*) desafortunado

untrained [ˈʌnˈtreɪnd] ADJ [*person*] sin formación, no

capacitado; [*teacher etc*] sin título; (*Sport*) no entrenado; [*animal*] sin amaestrar; **to the ~ ear/eye** para el oído/ojo de alguien que no es experto

untranslatable ['ʌntrænz'leɪtəbl] ADJ intraducible

untreated [ʌn'tri:tɪd] ADJ **1** [*patient, injury, illness*] sin tratar **2** [*sewage, wood, cotton*] no tratado, sin tratar

untried ['ʌn'traɪd] ADJ (= *untested*) [*product, method*] no probado

untroubled ['ʌn'trʌbld] ADJ tranquilo; **she was ~ by the news** la noticia no pareció preocuparle

untrue ['ʌn'tru:] ADJ falso; **it is ~ that** no es cierto *or* verdad que + *subjun*, es falso que + *subjun*

untrustworthy ['ʌn'trʌstˌwɜ:ðɪ] ADJ [*person*] de poca confianza, no muy de fiar

untruth ['ʌn'tru:θ] N (*pl* **~s** ['ʌn'tru:ðz]) mentira *f*

unusable ['ʌn'ju:zəbl] ADJ inservible, inútil

unused¹ ['ʌn'ju:zd] ADJ (= *new*) nuevo, sin estrenar; (= *not made use of*) sin usar *or* utilizar

unused² ['ʌn'ju:st] ADJ (= *unaccustomed*) **to be ~ to (doing) sth** no estar acostumbrado a (hacer) algo

unusual [ʌn'ju:ʒʊəl] ADJ **1** (= *uncommon*) [*sight, circumstances, name*] poco común, poco corriente; [*amount, number*] fuera de lo normal, fuera de lo corriente; **I didn't feel hungry, which was ~ for me** no me sentía con hambre, lo cual era raro en mí; **it's ~ for him to be late** no suele llegar tarde; **it's not ~ to see snow in June here** no es raro ver nieve aquí en junio; **there's nothing ~ in that** no hay nada de raro *or* extraordinario en ello **2** (= *odd*) raro, extraño **3** (= *exceptional*) excepcional, poco común *or* corriente

unusually [ʌn'ju:ʒʊəlɪ] ADV **1** (= *unaccustomedly*) **he arrived ~ late** llegó más tarde que de costumbre; **the streets were ~ quiet** las calles estaban extrañamente silenciosas; **~ for her, she didn't say goodbye** no se despidió, lo cual es raro en ella **2** (= *exceptionally*) excepcionalmente, extraordinariamente

unvarnished ['ʌn'vɑ:nɪʃt] ADJ sin barnizar

unveil [ʌn'veɪl] VT quitar el velo a; [+ *statue, painting etc*] descubrir

unwanted ['ʌn'wɒntɪd] ADJ [*item*] superfluo; [*visitor, guest*] poco grato, inoportuno; [*child, pregnancy, advances, attention*] no deseado; **to feel ~** sentirse de más; **to remove ~ hair** quitar el vello superfluo

unwarranted [ʌn'wɒrəntɪd] ADJ injustificado

unwary [ʌn'wɛərɪ] ADJ imprudente, incauto

unwashed ['ʌn'wɒʃt] ADJ sin lavar, sucio

unwavering [ʌn'weɪvərɪŋ] ADJ [*loyalty, resolve*] inquebrantable, firme; [*course*] firme; [*gaze*] fijo

unwelcome [ʌn'welkəm] ADJ [*news, surprise*] desagradable, poco grato; [*visitor, guest, intruder*] poco grato, inoportuno; **I felt ~** sentí que allí sobraba; **to make sb feel ~** hacer que algn sienta que sobra

unwelcoming [ʌn'welkəmɪŋ] ADJ [*person*] nada simpático, poco cordial; [*place*] poco acogedor

unwell ['ʌn'wel] ADJ **to feel ~** sentirse mal

unwholesome ['ʌn'həʊlsəm] ADJ **1** (= *unhealthy*) [*food*] poco sano, poco saludable **2** (*morally*) malsano

unwieldy [ʌn'wi:ldɪ] ADJ [*object*] difícil de manejar; [*system, structure, bureaucracy*] rígido

unwilling ['ʌn'wɪlɪŋ] ADJ poco dispuesto; **to be ~ to do sth** estar poco dispuesto a hacer algo, no estar dispuesto a hacer algo

unwillingly ['ʌn'wɪlɪŋlɪ] ADV de mala gana, a regañadientes

unwind ['ʌn'waɪnd] (*pt, pp* **unwound**) Ⓐ VT desenrollar Ⓑ VI **1** desenrollarse **2** (*) (= *relax*) relajarse

unwise ['ʌn'waɪz] ADJ (= *careless*) imprudente; (= *inadvisable*) poco aconsejable; **it would be ~ to** (+ INFIN) sería poco aconsejable + *infin*; **that was most ~ of you** en eso has sido muy imprudente

unwisely ['ʌn'waɪzlɪ] ADV imprudentemente

unwitting [ʌn'wɪtɪŋ] ADJ involuntario; **I was the ~ cause** sin querer, yo fui la causa

unwittingly [ʌn'wɪtɪŋlɪ] ADV inconscientemente, sin darse cuenta

unworkable ['ʌn'wɜ:kəbl] ADJ impracticable, no viable

unworldly ['ʌn'wɜ:ldlɪ] ADJ **1** (= *unmaterialistic*) nada materialista **2** (= *naïve*) ingenuo, poco realista

unworthy [ʌn'wɜ:ðɪ] ADJ **1** (= *undeserving*) [*person*] indigno, poco digno; **he felt himself ~ of her** sentía que no era digno de ella, sentía que no se la merecía; **it is ~ of attention** no merece atención **2** (= *ignoble*) impropio; **his accusations are ~ of a gentleman** sus acusaciones no son dignas *or* son impropias de un caballero

unwound [ʌn'waʊnd] PT, PP *of* **unwind**

unwrap ['ʌn'ræp] VT abrir

unwritten ['ʌn'rɪtn] ADJ no escrito; **~ law** ley *f* consuetudinaria

unyielding [ʌn'ji:ldɪŋ] ADJ inflexible

unzip ['ʌn'zɪp] VT **1** (= *unfasten*) abrir la cremallera *or* (*LAm*) el cierre de; **can you ~ me?** ¿me puedes bajar la cremallera? **2** (*Comput*) descomprimir

---

up

Ⓐ ADVERB	Ⓓ ADJECTIVE
Ⓑ PREPOSITION	Ⓔ INTRANSITIVE VERB
Ⓒ NOUN	Ⓕ TRANSITIVE VERB

*When **up** is the second element in a phrasal verb, eg **come up**, **throw up**, look up the verb. When it is part of a set combination, eg **the way up**, **close up**, look up the other word.*

up [ʌp] Ⓐ ADVERB
1 (*direction*) hacia arriba, para arriba; **he looked up** (*towards sky*) miró hacia *or* para arriba; **to walk up and down** pasearse de un lado para otro *or* de arriba abajo; **she's still a bit up and down** (*fig*) todavía tiene sus altibajos; **to stop halfway up** pararse a mitad de la subida; **to throw sth up in the air** lanzar algo al aire; **he walked/ran up to the house** caminó/corrió hasta la casa
2 (*position*) **the people three floors up (from me)** los que viven tres pisos más arriba; **up above (us) we could see a ledge** por encima (de nosotros) *or* sobre nuestras cabezas podíamos ver una cornisa; **from up above** desde arriba; **my office is five floors up** mi oficina está en el quinto piso; **higher up** más arriba; **up in the mountains** montaña arriba; **up in the sky** en lo alto del cielo; **the jug's up there** la jarra está ahí arriba; **the castle's up there** el castillo está allí arriba
3 (*in northern place, capital etc*) **we're up for the day** hemos venido a pasar el día; **when you're next up this way** la próxima vez que pases por aquí; **how long have you lived up here?** ¿cuánto tiempo llevas viviendo aquí?; **he lives up in Scotland** vive en Escocia; **up in London** (allá) en Londres; **up north** en el norte; **how long did you live up there?** ¿cuánto tiempo estuviste viviendo allí *or* allá?; **to go up to London** ir a Londres
4 (= *standing*) de pie; **while you're up, can you get me a glass of water?** ya que estás de pie, ¿me puedes traer un vaso de agua?; **the ladder was up against the wall** la escalera estaba apoyada en *or* contra la pared
5 (= *out of bed*) **to be up** (= *get up*) levantarse; (= *be active*) estar levantado; **we were up at seven** nos levantamos a las siete; **is Peter up yet?** ¿está levantado Peter?; **we were still up at midnight** a medianoche seguíamos sin acostarnos, a medianoche todavía estábamos levantados; **she was up and about at 6 a.m.** estaba en pie a las seis de la mañana; **to be up and about again** [*sick person*] estar repuesto; **to be up all night** no acostarse en toda la noche
6 (= *raised*) **with his head up (high)** con la cabeza bien levantada *or* erguida; **several children had their hands up** varios niños habían levantado la mano; **the blinds were up** las persianas estaban subidas *or* levantadas; **"this side up"** "este lado hacia arriba"
7 (*in price, value*) **potatoes are up** han subido las patatas; **the temperature was up in the forties** la temperatura estaba

por encima de los cuarenta; **prices are up on** last year los precios han subido desde el año pasado, del año pasado a éste los precios han subido

8 (*in score*) **we're a goal up** llevamos un tanto de ventaja

9 (*in terms of excellence*) **to be up among** *or* **with the leaders** estar a la altura de los líderes

10 (= *built, installed*) **the new building isn't up yet** el nuevo edificio no está construido todavía, no han levantado el nuevo edificio todavía; **the tent isn't up yet** la tienda todavía no está puesta; **the notice about the outing is up** el cartel de la excursión está puesto; **the curtains are up** las cortinas están colocadas

11 (= *finished*) [*contract etc*] vencido, caducado; **when the period is up** cuando termine el plazo, cuando venza el plazo; **time is up, put down your pens** se ha acabado el tiempo, dejen los bolígrafos sobre la mesa

12 (= *and over*) **from £2 up** de 2 libras para arriba; **from the age of 13 up** a partir de los 13 años

13 (= *knowledgeable*) **he's well up in** *or* **on British politics** está muy al corriente *or* al día en lo referente a la política británica

14 (*) (= *wrong*) **there's something up with him** algo le pasa; **what's up?** ¿qué pasa?; **what's up with him?** ¿que le pasa?

15 (*in running order*) **first up** el primero (de la lista); **next up** el siguiente (de la lista)

16 (*Jur*) **to be up before the judge/board** [*person*] (tener que) comparecer ante el juez/el consejo; [*case, matter*] verse ante el juez/en el consejo

17 (= *risen*) **the sun is up** ha salido el sol; **the tide is up** la marea está alta

18 (*Brit*) (= *under repair*) **the road is up** la calle está en obras

19 (*US Culin**) **two fried eggs, up** un par de huevos fritos boca arriba; **a bourbon (straight) up** un bourbon sin hielo

20 (*in exclamations*) **up (with) Celtic!** ¡arriba el Celtic!

21 (*in set expressions*)

✦ **up against: he's really up against it** ahora sí que está en un aprieto; **to be up against sb** tener que habérselas con algn, tener que enfrentarse a algn

✦ **up and running: to be up and running** estar en funcionamiento

✦ **up for sth: three seats are up for election** tres escaños salen a elecciones; **most politicians up for reelection know this** (= *seeking*) la mayoría de los políticos que se presentan a la reelección lo saben; **are you up for it?*** ¿estás dispuesto?

✦ **up to¹** (= *till, as far as*) hasta; **up to now** hasta ahora, hasta la fecha; **up to here** hasta aquí; **to count up to 100** contar hasta 100; **we were up to our knees/waist in water** el agua nos llegaba por *or* hasta las rodillas/la cintura

✦ **up to²** (= *capable of*) **to be up to a task** estar a la altura de una tarea, estar en condiciones de realizar una tarea; **to be up to doing sth** estar en condiciones de hacer algo; **are you (feeling) up to going for a walk?** ¿te sientes con ganas de dar un paseo?; **I don't feel up to going out** no tengo ánimos para salir

✦ **up to³** (= *equal to*) **it isn't up to his usual standard** no está a su nivel de siempre; **the book isn't up to much** (*Brit**) el libro no vale mucho

✦ **up to⁴** (*) (= *doing*) **what are you up to?** ¿qué andas haciendo?; **what are you up to with that knife?** ¿qué haces con ese cuchillo?; **he's up to something** está tramando algo; **I see what you're up to** te veo venir; **what have you been up to lately?** ¿qué has estado haciendo últimamente?

✦ **it's up to** (= *it depends on*) **it's up to you to decide** te toca (a ti) decidir; **I feel it is up to me to tell him** creo que me corresponde a mí decírselo; **I wouldn't do it but it's up to you** yo (que tú) no lo haría, pero allá tú *or* tú verás; **I'd go, but it's up to you** por mí iría, pero depende de ti; **if it were** *or* **was up to me** si dependiera de mí

Ⓑ PREPOSITION

1 (= *on top of*) en lo alto de, arriba de (*LAm*); **he was up a ladder pruning the apple trees** estaba subido a una escalera *or* en lo alto de una escalera podando los manzanos; **to be up a tree** estar en lo alto de *or* (*LAm*) arriba de un árbol

2 (= *along, towards the top*) **he went off up the road** se fue calle arriba; **put your handkerchief up your sleeve** guárdate el pañuelo dentro de la manga; **the heat disappears straight up the chimney** el calor se escapa chimenea arriba,

el calor se escapa por lo alto de la chimenea; **to travel up and down the country** viajar por todo el país; **they live further up the road** viven en esta calle pero más arriba; **further up the page** en la misma página, más arriba; **halfway up the stairs** a mitad de la escalera

Ⓒ NOUN

1 ups and downs altibajos *mpl*, vicisitudes *fpl*

2 it's on the up and up (*Brit*) (= *improving*) va cada vez mejor; (*US*) (= *above board*) está en regla

Ⓓ ADJECTIVE

1 (*Rail*) [*train, line*] ascendente

2 (= *elated*) **to be up*** estar en plena forma

Ⓔ INTRANSITIVE VERB (*) **she upped and left** (= *stood up*) se levantó y se marchó, se levantó y se largó*; (= *went*) fue y se marchó, fue y se largó*

Ⓕ TRANSITIVE VERB (= *raise*) [+ *price, offer*] subir, aumentar

up-and-coming ['ʌpənd'kʌmɪŋ] ADJ prometedor, con futuro

up-and-down ['ʌpən'daʊn] ADJ [*career, progress, relationship*] inestable

upbeat* ['ʌp'biːt] ADJ (= *positive*) optimista

upbraid [ʌp'breɪd] VT censurar, reprender

upbringing ['ʌp,brɪŋɪŋ] N educación *f*

upchuck* ['ʌptʃʌk] VI (*US*) echar los hígados por la boca*

upcoming ['ʌpkʌmɪŋ] ADJ [*elections, holidays*] próximo

upcountry ['ʌp'kʌntrɪ] **Ⓐ** ADV **to go** ~ ir hacia el interior, ir tierra adentro; **to be** ~ estar tierra adentro, estar en el interior **Ⓑ** ADJ [*town, school, accent*] del interior

update Ⓐ [ʌp'deɪt] VT poner al día; **to** ~ **sb on sth** poner a algn al corriente *or* al tanto de algo **Ⓑ** ['ʌpdeɪt] N puesta *f* al día; (= *updated version*) versión *f* actualizada; **news** ~ últimas noticias *fpl*; **he gave me an** ~ **on ...** me puso al día con respecto a ..., me puso al corriente *or* al tanto de ...

upend [ʌp'end] VT (= *stand on its end*) poner vertical

upfront [ʌp'frʌnt] **Ⓐ** ADJ **1** (*) (= *frank*) abierto, franco **2** [*payment*] inicial **Ⓑ** ADV (= *in advance*) por adelantado; **to pay** ~ **for sth** pagar algo por adelantado

upgrade Ⓐ ['ʌpgreɪd] N [*of system*] mejora *f*, mejoramiento *m*; (*Comput*) [*of hardware*] upgrade *m*, mejora *f* (del equipo informático) **Ⓑ** [ʌp'greɪd] VT [+ *hardware, machinery, building, road, area, facilities*] mejorar; [+ *passenger*] cambiar a una clase superior **Ⓒ** VI (= *buy new computer*) cambiar de ordenador (*Sp*), cambiar de computador *or* computadora (*LAm*); (= *buy new software*) añadir más software; (*Travel*) cambiar el asiento/el billete (*Sp*) *or* pasaje (*LAm*) *etc* por otro de una clase superior

upheaval [ʌp'hiːvəl] N **1** (*emotional*) trastorno *m* **2** (*in home, office etc*) trastorno *m* **3** (*Pol*) agitación *f*

upheld [ʌp'held] PT, PP *of* **uphold**

uphill ['ʌp'hɪl] **Ⓐ** ADV **to go** ~ ir cuesta arriba; **the road goes** ~ **for two miles** la carretera sube durante dos millas **Ⓑ** ADJ en cuesta, en pendiente; (*fig*) arduo, penoso; **it's an** ~ **task** es una tarea laboriosa *or* ardua *or* penosa; **it was an** ~ **struggle** fue una lucha llena de dificultades; **it was** ~ **all the way** (*fig*) fue todo cuesta arriba, se nos hizo todo cuesta arriba

uphold [ʌp'həʊld] (*pt, pp* **upheld**) VT **1** (= *sustain*) mantener, sostener; (= *support*) apoyar, defender **2** (*Jur*) confirmar

upholstery [ʌp'həʊlstərɪ] N **1** (= *cushioning etc*) tapizado *m*; (*in car*) tapizado *m* **2** (= *trade*) tapicería *f*

upkeep ['ʌpkiːp] N **1** (= *care*) mantenimiento *m* **2** (= *cost*) gastos *mpl* de mantenimiento

upmarket [ʌp'mɑːkɪt] (*Brit*) **Ⓐ** ADJ [*image, shop, hotel, person*] de categoría; [*product*] de primera calidad, de calidad superior; [*magazine*] para un público de categoría **Ⓑ** ADV **to go/move up-market** subir de categoría, buscar una clientela más selecta

upon [ə'pɒn] PREP **1** (*with place, position*) sobre; ~ **the table** sobre la mesa **2** (*with time*) **he emigrated** ~ **the death of his son** emigró tras la muerte de su hijo; ~ **hearing this she wept** al oir esto, lloró **3** (*with numbers*) **row** ~ **row of women** hilera tras hilera de mujeres; **thousands** ~ **thousands of people were arriving** iban llegando miles y miles de personas

upper [ˈʌpəʳ] **Ⓐ** ADJ **1** (*in level*) [*deck, floor*] de arriba; (*more frm*) superior; **the ~ atmosphere** la atmósfera superior; **the ~ slopes of Illimani** las pendientes más altas del Illimani
2 (*in importance, rank*) [*echelons, ranks, caste*] superior; **~ management** los altos cargos de la administración
3 (*on scale*) [*limit*] máximo; **properties at the ~ end of the market** inmuebles de la sección más cara del mercado; **people in the ~ income bracket** las personas con un nivel de ingresos superior
4 (*in Geog names*) alto; **the Upper Nile** el alto Nilo
Ⓑ N **1** (*of shoe*) pala *f*; ✦ IDIOM **to be (down) on one's ~s** estar en las últimas *or* (*Sp*) sin un duro
2 (*) (= *drug*) anfeta* *f*
Ⓒ CPD ➤ **upper arm** brazo *m* superior ➤ **upper case** (*Typ*) mayúsculas *fpl*; **in ~ case** en mayúsculas ➤ **the upper circle** (*Theat*) la galería superior ➤ **the upper classes** la(s) clase(s) alta(s) **Upper Egypt** alto Egipto *m* ➤ **upper house** (*Pol*) cámara *f* alta ➤ **upper lip** labio *m* superior ➤ **upper school** cursos *mpl* superiores

upper-case [ˈʌpəˈkeɪs] ADJ mayúsculo, de letra mayúscula

upper-class [ˈʌpəˈklɑːs] ADJ de clase alta; **an ~ twit** un señorito de clase alta

upper-crust* [ˈʌpəˈkrʌst] ADJ de categoría (social) superior, de buen tono

uppermost [ˈʌpəməʊst] ADJ **1** (= *topmost*) el/la más alto/a
2 (*fig*) principal, predominante; **it was ~ in my mind** me preocupaba más que cualquier otra cosa

upright [ˈʌpraɪt] **Ⓐ** ADJ **1** (*lit*) derecho, recto **2** (*fig*) honrado, íntegro **Ⓑ** ADV erguido, derecho, recto; **to hold o.s. ~** mantenerse erguido; **to sit bolt ~** sentarse muy derecho, sentarse muy erguido **Ⓒ** CPD ➤ **upright piano** piano *m* vertical *or* recto

uprising [ˈʌpraɪzɪŋ] N alzamiento *m*, sublevación *f*

uproar [ˈʌprɔːʳ] N alboroto *m*, jaleo *m*; **this caused an ~** (= *shouting*) en esto se armó un alboroto; (= *protesting*) en esto estallaron ruidosas las protestas

uproarious [ʌpˈrɔːrɪəs] ADJ [*laughter*] escandaloso; [*meeting*] alborotado, ruidoso; [*success*] clamoroso

uproot [ʌpˈruːt] VT desarraigar, arrancar (de raíz)

upscale* [ˈʌpskeɪl] ADJ (*US*) [*image, store, hotel, person*] de categoría; [*product*] de primera calidad, de calidad superior

upset (*vb: pt, pp ~*) **Ⓐ** [ʌpˈset] VT **1** (= *knock over*) [+ *object*] volcar, tirar; [+ *liquid*] derramar, tirar; [+ *boat*] volcar
2 (= *distress*) afectar; (= *hurt, make sad*) disgustar; (= *offend*) ofender, disgustar
3 (= *disrupt*) [+ *plans, calculations*] dar al traste con, desbaratar
4 (= *make ill*) sentar mal a, enfermar (*LAm*); **garlic ~s me/my stomach** el ajo no me sienta bien
Ⓑ ADJ [ʌpˈset] **1** (= *distressed*) alterado; (= *hurt, sad*) disgustado; (= *offended*) ofendido, disgustado; (= *annoyed*) molesto; **he's ~ that you didn't tell him** se disgustó *or* se molestó porque no se lo dijiste; **she's ~ about failing** está disgustada por haber suspendido; **what are you so ~ about?** ¿qué es lo que te ha disgustado tanto?; **to get ~** (= *distressed*) alterarse; (= *hurt*) disgustarse; (= *offended*) ofenderse; (= *annoyed*) enfadarse (*Sp*), enojarse (*esp LAm*)
2 [ˈʌpset] (= *sick*) **I have an ~ stomach** tengo el estómago revuelto
Ⓒ [ˈʌpset] N **1** (= *disturbance*) contratiempo *m*; (= *disappointment*) disgusto *m*; (*emotional*) trastorno *m*
2 (= *illness*) malestar *m*; **stomach ~** malestar *m* de estómago; **to have a stomach ~** tener el estómago revuelto

upsetting [ʌpˈsetɪŋ] ADJ (= *distressing*) [*experience, incident*] terrible; [*image*] sobrecogedor; (= *saddening*) triste; (= *offending*) [*language, remark*] ofensivo; (= *annoying*) fastidioso, molesto; **the whole incident was very ~ for me** todo el incidente me afectó *or* disgustó mucho

upshot [ˈʌpʃɒt] N resultado *m*; **the ~ of it all was ...** el resultado fue que ...

upside-down [ˈʌpsaɪdˈdaʊn] ADJ, ADV al revés; (= *untidily*) patas arriba; **to turn sth ~** (*lit*) volver algo al revés; (*fig*) revolverlo todo; **the room was ~** reinaba el desorden en el cuarto, en el cuarto todo estaba patas arriba*

upstage [ʌpˈsteɪdʒ] VT **to ~ sb** (*fig*) eclipsar a algn

upstairs [ˈʌpˈsteəz] **Ⓐ** ADV arriba; **"where's your coat?" — "it's ~"** —¿dónde está tu abrigo? —está arriba; **the people ~** los de arriba; **to go ~** subir (al piso superior) **Ⓑ** ADJ de arriba; **an ~ window** una ventana del piso superior *or* de arriba **Ⓒ** N piso *m* superior *or* de arriba

upstanding [ʌpˈstændɪŋ] ADJ **1** (= *respectable*) honrado
2 (*Jur*) **be ~!** ¡pónganse de pie!

upstart [ˈʌpstɑːt] N (*pej*) **1** (= *arrogant person*) presuntuoso/a *m/f* **2** (= *social climber*) arribista *mf*, advenedizo/a *m/f*

upstate [ˈʌpsteɪt] (*US*) **Ⓐ** ADJ interior, septentrional **Ⓑ** ADV [*be*] en el interior; [*go*] al interior

upstream [ˈʌpˈstriːm] ADV río arriba; **to go ~** ir río arriba; **to swim ~** nadar contra la corriente

uptake [ˈʌpteɪk] N **1** (= *understanding*) **to be quick on the ~*** ser muy listo, agarrar las cosas al vuelo*; **to be slow on the ~*** ser corto (de entendederas)* **2** (= *intake*) consumo *m*
3 (= *acceptance*) aceptación *f*

uptight* [ʌpˈtaɪt] ADJ nervioso, tenso; **to get ~ about sth** ponerse nervioso por algo

up-to-date [ˈʌptəˈdeɪt] ADJ [*information, edition, report*] al día, actualizado; [*clothes, equipment, technology*] moderno; **to be ~ with one's payments** llevar sus pagos al día; **to bring/keep sth/sb ~** poner/mantener algo/a algn al día *or* al corriente; **we'll keep you ~ with any news** le mantendremos al día *or* al corriente de las noticias

up-to-the-minute [ˈʌptəðəˈmɪnɪt] ADJ de última hora

uptown [ˈʌpˈtaʊn] (*US*) **Ⓐ** ADV hacia las afueras, hacia los barrios exteriores **Ⓑ** ADJ exterior, de las afueras

upturn Ⓐ [ˈʌptɜːn] N (= *improvement*) mejora *f*, aumento *m* (**in** de); (*Econ etc*) repunte *m* **Ⓑ** [ʌpˈtɜːn] VT (= *turn over*) volver hacia arriba; (= *overturn*) volcar

upturned [ʌpˈtɜːnd] [*box etc*] vuelto hacia arriba; [*nose*] respingón

upward [ˈʌpwəd] **Ⓐ** ADJ [*slope*] ascendente, hacia arriba; [*tendency*] al alza **Ⓑ** ADV (*also esp Brit* **~s**) **1** (*gen*) hacia arriba; **to look ~** mirar hacia arriba; **face ~** boca arriba
2 (*with numbers*) **£50 and ~** de 50 libras para arriba; **from the age of 13 ~** desde los 13 años; **~ of 500** más de 500

upwardly [ˈʌpwədlɪ] ADV **~ mobile** [*person*] ambicioso

upwards [ˈʌpwədz] ADV (*esp Brit*) = **upward B**

uranium [jʊəˈreɪnɪəm] N uranio *m*

Uranus [jʊəˈreɪnəs] N Urano *m*

urban [ˈɜːbən] ADJ urbano ➤ **urban myth** leyenda *f* urbana ➤ **urban renewal** renovación *f* urbana ➤ **urban sprawl** extensión *f* urbana

urbane [ɜːˈbeɪn] ADJ urbano, cortés

urbanization [ˈɜːbənaɪˈzeɪʃən] N urbanización *f*

urchin [ˈɜːtʃɪn] N pilluelo/a *m/f*, golfillo/a *m/f*

Urdu [ˈʊədu:] N (*Ling*) urdu *m*

urge [ɜːdʒ] **Ⓐ** N impulso *m*; (*sexual*) deseo *m*; **to feel an ~ to do sth** sentir fuertes deseos *or* ganas de hacer algo; **when you get *or* have the ~ to eat something exotic ...** cuando te entren ganas de comer algo exótico ... **Ⓑ** VT **1** (= *try to persuade*) **to ~ sb to do sth** animar *or* instar a algn a hacer algo; **to ~ that sth should be done** recomendar encarecidamente que se haga algo **2** (= *advocate*) recomendar, abogar por; **to ~ sth on** *or* **upon sb** insistir en algo con algn
➤ **urge on** VT + ADV animar, alentar; (*fig*) animar, instar

urgency [ˈɜːdʒənsɪ] N urgencia *f*; **it is a matter of ~** es un asunto urgente; **with a note of ~ in his voice** con un tono de urgencia

urgent [ˈɜːdʒənt] ADJ (= *imperative*) [*matter, business, case, message*] urgente; **is this ~?** ¿es urgente?, ¿corre prisa esto?; **to be in ~ need of sth** necesitar algo urgentemente

urgently [ˈɜːdʒəntlɪ] ADV [*need, seek*] urgentemente, con urgencia

urinal [jʊəˈraɪnl] N (= *place*) urinario *m*; (= *vessel*) orinal *m*

urinate ['jʊərɪneɪt] VI orinar(se)

urine ['jʊərɪn] N orina *f*, orines *mpl*

urn [ɜːn] N (= *vase*) urna *f*

urologist [jʊə'rɒlədʒɪst] N urólogo/a *m/f*

urology [jʊə'rɒlədʒɪ] N urología *f*

Uruguay ['jʊərəgwaɪ] N Uruguay *m*

Uruguayan [jʊərə'gwaɪən] ADJ, N uruguayo/a *m/f*

US N ABBR (= **United States**) **the US** EE.UU., Estados Unidos; **in the US** en Estados Unidos; **the US Army/ government** el Ejército/gobierno estadounidense

us [ʌs] PRON **1** (*direct/indirect object*) nos; **they helped us** nos ayudaron; **look at us!** ¡míranos!; **give it to us** dánoslo; **they gave us some brochures** nos dieron unos folletos **2** (*after prepositions, in comparisons, with the verb to be*) nosotros/as; **why don't you come with us?** ¿por qué no vienes con nosotros?; **both of us** los dos; **they are older than us** son mayores que nosotros; **as for us English, we ...** en cuanto a nosotros los ingleses, ...; **it's us** somos nosotros

USA N ABBR **1** (= **United States of America**) **the ~** EE.UU., Estados Unidos; **in the ~** en Estados Unidos **2** = **United States Army**

usable ['juːzəbl] ADJ utilizable; **~ space** espacio *m* útil; **it is no longer ~** ya no sirve

USAF N ABBR = **United States Air Force**

usage ['juːzɪdʒ] N **1** (= *custom*) costumbre *f*, usanza *f* **2** (*Ling*) uso *m* **3** (= *handling*) manejo *m*; (= *treatment*) tratos *mpl*; **it's had some rough ~** ha sido manejado con bastante dureza

use ⓐ [juːs] N **1** (= *act of using*) uso *m*, empleo *m*, utilización *f*; **the ~ of steel in industry** el empleo *or* la utilización *or* el uso del acero en la industria; **for ~ in case of emergency** para uso en caso de emergencia; **"directions for use"** "modo de empleo"; **fit for ~** servible, en buen estado; **word in ~** palabra *f* en uso *or* que se usa; **to be no longer in ~** estar fuera de uso; **it is not now in ~** ya no se usa; **to make ~ of** hacer uso de, usar; **to make good ~ of** sacar partido *or* provecho de; **out of ~** en desuso; **to go out of ~** caer en desuso; **to put sth to good ~** hacer buen uso de algo, sacar partido *or* provecho de algo; **ready for ~** listo (para ser usado)
2 (= *way of using*) modo *m* de empleo; (= *handling*) manejo *m*; **we were instructed in the ~ of firearms** se nos instruyó en el manejo de armas de fuego
3 (= *function*) uso *m*; **can you find a ~ for this?** ¿te sirve esto? **4** (= *usefulness*) utilidad *f*; **it has its ~s** tiene su utilidad; **to be of ~** servir, tener utilidad; **can I be of any ~?** ¿puedo ayudar?; **he's no ~ as a teacher** no vale para profesor, no sirve como profesor; **it's (of) no ~** es inútil, no sirve para nada; **it's no ~ discussing it further** es inútil *or* no vale la pena seguir discutiendo; **I have no further ~ for it** ya no lo necesito, ya no me sirve para nada; **what's the ~ of all this?** ¿de qué sirve todo esto?
5 (= *ability to use, access*) **he gave me the ~ of his car** me dejó que usara su coche; **to have the ~ of a garage** tener acceso a un garaje; **I have the ~ of it on Sundays** me permiten usarlo los domingos, lo puedo usar los domingos; **he lost the ~ of his arm** se le quedó inútil el brazo
ⓑ [juːz] VT **1** (*gen*) usar, emplear, utilizar; **are you using this book?** ¿te hace falta este libro?; **have you ~d a gun before?** ¿has manejado alguna vez una escopeta?; **"use only in emergencies"** "usar sólo en caso de emergencia"; **to ~ sth as a hammer** emplear *or* usar algo como martillo; **I could ~ a drink!*** ¡no me vendría mal un trago!; **what's this ~d for?** ¿para qué sirve esto?, ¿para qué se utiliza esto?; **the money is ~d for the poor** el dinero se dedica a los pobres; **the word is no longer ~d** la palabra ya no se usa; **to ~ force** emplear la fuerza; **to ~ every means** emplear todos los medios a su alcance (**to do sth** para hacer algo)
2 (= *make use of*) usar, utilizar; **he wants to ~ the bathroom** quiere entrar en *or* usar el cuarto de baño; (= *go to the toilet*) quiere ir al lavabo *or* (*LAm*) al baño; **~ your head *or* brains!*** ¡usa el coco!*
3 (= *consume*) [+ *fuel*] consumir; **have you ~d all the milk?** ¿has terminado toda la leche?
ⓒ [juːs] AUX VB (*gen*) soler, acostumbrar (a); **I ~d to go camping as a child** de pequeño solía *or* acostumbraba ir de

acampada; **I ~d to live in London** (antes) vivía en Londres; **I didn't ~ to like maths, but now I love it** antes no me gustaban las matemáticas, pero ahora me encantan; **but I didn't ~ to** pero antes no; **things aren't what they ~d to be** las cosas ya no son lo que eran
➤ use up VT + ADV [+ *supplies*] agotar; [+ *money*] gastar; **we've ~d up all the paint** hemos acabado toda la pintura

used¹ [juːzd] ADJ **1** (= *finished with*) [*stamp, syringe*] usado; [*battery, tyre*] gastado, usado **2** (= *second-hand*) [*clothing*] usado; **a ~ car** un coche de segunda mano; **a ~-car salesman** un vendedor de coches de segunda mano

used² [juːst] ADJ **to be ~ to (doing) sth** estar acostumbrado a (hacer) algo; **don't worry, I'm ~ to it** no te preocupes, estoy acostumbrado; **to get ~ to** acostumbrarse a

useful ['juːsfʊl] ADJ [*information, advice, tool*] útil; [*discussion, meeting*] fructífero; [*experience*] provechoso, útil; **a ~ player** un buen jugador, un jugador que vale; **he's a ~ person to know** es una persona que conviene conocer; **it is very ~ to be able to drive** es muy útil saber conducir; **to come in ~** ser útil, venir bien; **the machine has reached the end of its ~ life** la máquina ha llegado al final de su periodo de funcionamiento; **to make o.s. ~** ayudar, echar una mano*; **this discussion is not serving any ~ purpose** esta discusión no está sirviendo para nada útil *or* provechoso

usefully ['juːsfəlɪ] ADV de manera provechosa, provechosamente; **the staff are not being ~ employed** no se está empleando al personal de manera provechosa *or* provechosamente

usefulness ['juːsfəlnɪs] N utilidad *f*

useless ['juːslɪs] ADJ **1** (= *ineffective*) [*object*] que no sirve para nada; [*person*] inútil; **this can opener's ~** este abrelatas no sirve para nada; **she's ~ es una inútil; **he's ~ as a forward** no vale para delantero, no sirve como delantero; **I was always ~ at maths** siempre fui (un) negado *or* un inútil para las matemáticas **2** (= *unusable*) [*object, vehicle*] inservible; [*limb*] inutilizado, inútil **3** (= *pointless*) inútil; **it's ~ to shout** de nada sirve gritar, es inútil gritar

Usenet ['juːznet] N Usenet *f or m*

user ['juːzəʳ] N usuario/a *m/f*; **drug ~** drogadicto/a *m/f*; **heroin ~** heroinómano/a *m/f* **➤ user identification** identificación *f* del usuario

user-friendly [juːzə'frendlɪ] ADJ [*computer, software, system, dictionary*] fácil de utilizar *or* usar *or* manejar

usher ['ʌʃəʳ] **ⓐ** N (*in court etc*) ujier *mf*; (*in theatre, cinema etc*) acomodador(a) *m/f*; (*at public meeting etc*) guardia *mf* de sala, encargado/a *m/f* del orden **ⓑ** VT **to ~ sb into a room** hacer pasar a algn a un cuarto
➤ usher in VT + ADV [+ *person*] hacer pasar a

usherette [ʌʃə'ret] N acomodadora *f*

USN N ABBR = **United States Navy**

USS N ABBR = **United States Ship** *or* **Steamer**

USSR N ABBR (*Hist*) (= **Union of Soviet Socialist Republics**) URSS *f*; **in the ~** en la URSS, en la Unión Soviética

usu. ABBR = **usual(ly)**

usual ['juːʒʊəl] **ⓐ** ADJ [*method, answer*] acostumbrado, habitual, usual; [*place, time, excuse*] de siempre; **more than ~** más que de costumbre; **it's ~ to give a tip** es costumbre *or* (*esp LAm*) se acostumbra dar una propina; **as (per) ~** como de costumbre, como siempre; **it's not ~ for her to be late** no suele llegar tarde; **in the ~ sense of the word** en el sentido normal de la palabra; **boil the potatoes in the ~ way** cueza las patatas como de costumbre *or* como siempre
ⓑ N **the ~ please!*** (= *drink*) lo de siempre, por favor

usually ['juːʒʊəlɪ] ADV normalmente, por lo general; **not ~** normalmente *or* por lo general no; **what do you ~ do?** ¿qué hacen ustedes normalmente?

usurp [juː'zɜːp] VT usurpar

usurper [juː'zɜːpəʳ] N usurpador(a) *m/f*

usury ['juːʒʊrɪ] N usura *f*

UT ABBR (*US*) = **Utah**

utensil [juːˈtensl] N utensilio *m*

uterus [ˈjuːtərəs] N (*pl* **uteri** [ˈjuːtəraɪ]) útero *m*

utilitarian [ˌjuːtɪlɪˈtɛərɪən] ADJ utilitario

utility [juːˈtɪlɪtɪ] **Ⓐ** N **1** (= *usefulness*) utilidad *f* **2** (*also* **public ~**) servicio *m* público **Ⓑ** CPD ➤ **utility room** trascocina *f*

utilization [ˌjuːtɪlaɪˈzeɪʃən] N utilización *f*

utilize [ˈjuːtɪlaɪz] VT utilizar, aprovecharse de

utmost [ˈʌtməʊst] **Ⓐ** ADJ **1** (= *greatest*) sumo; **of the ~ importance** de la mayor importancia, de suma importancia; **with the ~ ease** con suma facilidad **2** (= *furthest*) más lejano **Ⓑ** N **to do one's ~ (to do sth)** hacer todo lo posible (por hacer algo); **to the ~ of one's ability** lo mejor que pueda *or* sepa uno

Utopia [juːˈtəʊpɪə] N Utopía *f*

Utopian [juːˈtəʊpɪən] ADJ [*dream etc*] utópico; [*person*] utopista

utter¹ [ˈʌtəʳ] ADJ completo, total; [*madness*] puro; **~ nonsense!** ¡tonterías!; **he was in a state of ~ depression** estaba completamente deprimido

utter² [ˈʌtəʳ] VT [+ *words*] pronunciar; [+ *cry*] dar, soltar; [+ *threat, insult etc*] proferir; **she never ~ed a word** no dijo nada *or* (ni una) palabra

utterly [ˈʌtəlɪ] ADV totalmente, completamente

U-turn [ˈjuːtɜːn] N (*lit, fig*) cambio *m* de sentido, giro *m* de 180 grados; **to do a ~** (*lit*) dar media vuelta, cambiar de sentido; (*fig*) dar un giro; **"no U-turns"** "prohibido cambiar de sentido"

UV ADJ ABBR (= **ultraviolet**) UV, UVA

Uzbekistan [ˌʊzbekɪsˈtɑːn] N Uzbekistán *m*

V¹, v¹ [viː] N (= *letter*) V, v *f*

V² ABBR **1** (= **volt(s)**) v **2 = very**

v² ABBR **1** (= **versus**) vs. **2** (*Bible*) (= **verse**) vers.º **3** (= **vide**) vid., v. **4 = very**

VA, Va. (*US*) ABBR = **Virginia**

vac* [væk] N (*Brit Univ*) = **vacation**

vacancy ['veɪkənsɪ] N **1** (= *job*) vacante *f*; **"vacancies"** "ofertas de trabajo" **2** (*in hotel*) habitación *f* libre, cuarto *m* libre; **"no vacancies"** "completo"

vacant ['veɪkənt] ADJ **1** [*seat*] libre, desocupado; [*room*] libre, disponible; [*house*] desocupado, vacío; [*space*] vacío; **~ lot** (*US*) solar *m*; **~ post** vacante *f* **2** [*look*] ausente, vacío

vacantly ['veɪkəntlɪ] ADV [*look*] con gesto ausente, distraídamente

vacate [və'keɪt] VT (*frm*) [+ *seat, room*] dejar libre; [+ *premises*] desocupar, desalojar; [+ *post*] dejar

vacation [və'keɪʃən] N **1** (*Univ*) **the long ~** las vacaciones de verano **2** (*US*) (= *holiday*) vacaciones *fpl*; **to be on ~** estar de vacaciones; **to take a ~** tomarse unas vacaciones

vacationer [və'keɪʃənəʳ] N (*US*) (*gen*) turista *mf*; (*in summer*) veraneante *mf*

vaccinate ['væksɪneɪt] VT vacunar

vaccination [,væksɪ'neɪʃən] N vacunación *f*

vaccine ['væksiːn] N vacuna *f*

vacillate ['væsɪleɪt] VI (= *hesitate*) vacilar, dudar; (= *waver*) oscilar (**between** entre)

vacillating ['væsɪleɪtɪŋ] ADJ vacilante, irresoluto

vacuity [væ'kjuːɪtɪ] N (*frm*) vacuidad *f*

vacuous ['vækjʊəs] ADJ (*frm*) [*expression*] vacío, ausente; [*comment*] vacuo, vacío; [*person*] alelado, bobo

vacuum ['vækjʊm] **A** N **1** vacío *m*; **it can't exist in a ~** no puede existir en el vacío **2** (= *hoover*) **to give a room a ~** limpiar un cuarto con aspiradora **B** VT pasar la aspiradora por **C** VI pasar la aspiradora **D** CPD ➤ **vacuum bottle** (*US*) termo *m* ➤ **vacuum cleaner** aspiradora *f* ➤ **vacuum flask** (*Brit*) termo *m*

vacuum-packed ['vækjʊm'pækt] ADJ envasado al vacío

vagabond ['vægəbɒnd] N vagabundo/a *m/f*

vagary ['veɪgərɪ] N (= *whim*) capricho *m*, antojo *m*; (= *strange idea*) manía *f*, capricho *m*

vagina [və'dʒaɪnə] N vagina *f*

vaginal [və'dʒaɪnəl] ADJ vaginal

vagrant ['veɪgrənt] N vagabundo/a *m/f*

vague [veɪg] ADJ (*compar* **~r**; *superl* **~st**) **1** (= *imprecise*) [*concept*] impreciso, vago; [*description*] impreciso, [*outline*] borroso; [*feeling*] indefinido, indeterminado; [*person*] (*in giving details etc*) impreciso; (*by nature*) de ideas poco precisas; **he made some ~ promises** hacía promesas, pero sin concretar; **he was ~ about the date** no quiso precisar la fecha; **I'm a bit ~ on that subject** sé poco en concreto sobre ese tema **2** (= *absent-minded*) [*person*] despistado, distraído; [*expression, look*] ausente

vaguely ['veɪglɪ] ADV **1** (= *imprecisely*) [*define, remember*] vagamente; [*embarrassed, guilty*] ligeramente, levemente; **she was ~ aware of someone else in the room** tenía la ligera *or* vaga impresión de que había alguien más en la habitación; **his face looked ~ familiar** su rostro me resultaba ligeramente familiar **2** (= *absent-mindedly*) distraídamente; **she looked at me ~** me miró distraída

vagueness ['veɪgnɪs] N **1** (= *imprecision*) vaguedad *f*, imprecisión *f* **2** (= *absent-mindedness*) distracción *f*

vain [veɪn] ADJ **1** (= *useless*) vano, inútil; [*hope*] vano; **in ~** [*try, struggle*] en vano, inútilmente; [*search*] sin éxito, en vano; **all our efforts were in ~** todos nuestros esfuerzos fueron en vano *or* resultaron inútiles **2** (*compar* **~er**; *superl* **~est**) (= *conceited*) vanidoso, presumido

vainglorious [veɪn'glɔːrɪəs] ADJ vanaglorioso

vainly ['veɪnlɪ] ADV **1** (= *to no effect*) [*try, struggle*] en vano, inútilmente; [*search*] sin éxito, en vano **2** (= *conceitedly*) vanidosamente

valance ['væləns] N (*on bed*) cenefa *f*; (*US*) (*on curtains*) [*of wood*] galería *f*; [*of fabric*] cenefa *f*

vale [veɪl] N (*liter*) valle *m*

valediction [,vælɪ'dɪkʃən] N despedida *f*

valedictory [,vælɪ'dɪktərɪ] **A** ADJ [*address*] de despedida **B** N (*US*) oración *f* de despedida

valentine ['væləntaɪn] N **1 (St) Valentine's Day** día *m* de San Valentín, día *m* de los enamorados (*14 de febrero*) **2** (*also ~ card*) tarjeta *f* del día de San Valentín, tarjeta *f* de los enamorados (*enviada sin firmar, de tono amoroso o jocoso*)

valet ['væleɪ] **A** N **1** (*in hotel or household*) ayuda *m* de cámara **2** (*for car*) lavado *m* y limpieza, lavado *m* completo (*por dentro y por fuera*) **B** VT [+ *car*] lavar y limpiar **C** CPD ➤ **valet parking** (*US*) servicio *m* de aparcamiento a cargo del hotel

valiant ['vælɪənt] ADJ (*poet*) [*person*] valiente, valeroso; [*effort*] valeroso

valiantly ['vælɪəntlɪ] ADV valientemente, con valor

valid ['vælɪd] ADJ **1** [*argument, point, question*] válido; [*excuse, claim, objection*] válido, legítimo **2** [*ticket, passport, contract*] válido, valedero; **~ for three months** válido *or* valedero para tres meses; **that ticket is no longer ~** ese billete (*Sp*) *or* boleto (*LAm*) ya no tiene validez

validate ['vælɪdeɪt] VT (*gen*) validar, dar validez a; [+ *document*] convalidar

validation [,vælɪ'deɪʃən] N convalidación *f*

validity [və'lɪdɪtɪ] N validez *f*

valley ['vælɪ] N valle *m*

valour, valor (*US*) ['væləʳ] N (*frm*) valor *m*, valentía *f*

valuable ['væljʊəbl] **A** ADJ **1** (*in monetary terms*) valioso; **is it ~?** ¿vale mucho? **2** (= *extremely useful*) [*information, lesson, advice*] valioso; [*time*] valioso, precioso; **your ~ time** su precioso tiempo **B** N **valuables** objetos *mpl* de valor

valuation [,væljʊ'eɪʃən] N [*of property, house, antique*] tasación *f*, valoración *f*

value ['væljuː] **A** N valor *m*; **it's good ~ (for money)** sale a cuenta, está bien de precio; **to go down in ~** bajar de valor, depreciarse; **to go up in ~** subir de valor, revalorizarse; **market ~** valor *m* en el mercado; **her education has been of no ~ to her** su educación no le ha servido de *or* para nada; **you can't put a ~ on it** no se le puede poner precio; **to put a high ~ on sth** valorar mucho algo; **sentimental ~** valor *m* sentimental; **goods to the ~ of £100** bienes por valor de 100 libras **B** VT **1** [+ *property, jewellery, painting*] valorar, tasar; **to ~ sth at £200** valorar *or* tasar algo en 200 libras **2** [+ *health, life, independence,*] valorar; [+ *opinion, friendship*] valorar, apreciar **C** CPD ➤ **value judgment** juicio *m* de valor

value-added tax ['væljuː'ædɪdtæks] N (*Brit*) impuesto *m* sobre el valor añadido (*Sp*), impuesto *m* sobre el valor agregado (*LAm*)

valued ['væljuːd] ADJ [*friend, customer*] estimado, apreciado; [*contribution*] valioso

valueless ['væljʊlɪs] ADJ sin valor

valuer ['væljʊəʳ] N (*Brit*) tasador(a) *m/f*

valve [vælv] N (*Anat, Mech*) válvula *f*; (*Rad, TV*) lámpara *f*, válvula *f*; [*of musical instrument*] llave *f*

vampire ['væmpaɪəʳ] N vampiro *m* ➤ **vampire bat** vampiro *m*

van [væn] N (*Brit Aut*) camioneta *f*, furgoneta *f*; (*for removals*) camión *m* de mudanzas; (*Brit Rail*) furgón *m*

vandal ['vændəl] N vándalo/a *m/f*, gamberro/a *m/f* (*Sp*)

vandalism ['vændəlɪzəm] N vandalismo *m*

vandalize ['vændəlaɪz] VT destrozar

vane [veɪn] N *see* **weather**

vanguard ['væŋgɑːd] N vanguardia *f*; **to be in the ~** ir a la vanguardia, estar en la vanguardia

vanilla [vəˈnɪlə] Ⓐ N vainilla *f* Ⓑ ADJ de vainilla

vanish ['vænɪʃ] VI desaparecer; **to ~ without trace** desaparecer sin dejar rastro; **to ~ into thin air** esfumarse

vanishing ['vænɪʃɪŋ] CPD ➤ **vanishing cream** crema *f* de día ➤ **vanishing point** punto *m* de fuga ➤ **vanishing trick** truco *m* de desaparecer

vanity ['vænɪtɪ] Ⓐ N 1 (= *conceit*) vanidad *f* 2 (= *pride*) orgullo *m* Ⓑ CPD ➤ **vanity case** neceser *m* ➤ **vanity plate** (*Aut*) matrícula *f* personalizada

vanquish ['væŋkwɪʃ] VT (*poet*) vencer, derrotar

vantage point ['vɑːntɪdʒpɔɪnt] N posición *f* ventajosa, lugar *m* estratégico; (*for views*) punto *m* panorámico

vapid ['væpɪd] ADJ insípido, soso

vapor ['veɪpəʳ] N (*US*) = **vapour**

vaporize ['veɪpəraɪz] Ⓐ VT vaporizar, volatilizar Ⓑ VI vaporizarse, volatilizarse

vapour, vapor (*US*) ['veɪpəʳ] N vapor *m*; (*on breath, window*) vaho *m* ➤ **vapour trail** estela *f* (de humo)

variability [ˌvɛərɪəˈbɪlɪtɪ] N variabilidad *f*

variable ['vɛərɪəbl] Ⓐ ADJ variable Ⓑ N variable *f*

variance ['vɛərɪəns] N **to be at ~ (with sb over sth)** estar en desacuerdo *or* discrepar (con algn en algo)

variant ['vɛərɪənt] N variante *f*

variation [ˌvɛərɪˈeɪʃən] N variación *f*

varicose veins ['værɪkəʊsˈveɪnz] NPL varices *fpl*

varied ['vɛərɪd] ADJ variado

variegated ['vɛərɪgeɪtɪd] ADJ [*plant, plumage, markings*] multicolor; [*colour*] abigarrado; [*leaf*] jaspeado, abigarrado

variety [vəˈraɪətɪ] Ⓐ N 1 variedad *f*; (= *range, diversity*) diversidad *f*; [*of stock*] surtido *m*; **for a ~ of reasons** por varias *or* diversas razones; **for ~** por variar 2 (= *type, kind*) clase *f* Ⓑ CPD ➤ **variety show** espectáculo *m* de variedades

various ['vɛərɪəs] ADJ (*gen*) varios, diversos; (= *different*) distintos; **for ~ reasons** por diversas razones; **in ~ ways** de diversos modos

variously ['vɛərɪəslɪ] ADV **the caravan served ~ as an office, bedroom and changing room** según los casos la caravana hacía de oficina, dormitorio o vestuario

varnish ['vɑːnɪʃ] Ⓐ N (*for wood*) barniz *m*; (*for nails*) esmalte *m* (para las uñas), laca *f* (para las uñas) Ⓑ VT [+ *wood*] barnizar; [+ *nails*] pintar, laquear

vary ['vɛərɪ] Ⓐ VT [+ *routine, diet*] variar; [+ *temperature, speed*] cambiar, modificar Ⓑ VI 1 (= *differ*) [*amounts, sizes, conditions*] variar; **they ~ in price** los hay de diversos precios; **it varies** depende, según; **designs may ~ from the illustration on the box** los diseños pueden diferir de la ilustración del paquete; **opinions ~ on this point** las opiniones varían en este punto 2 (= *fluctuate*) [*weight, temperature, number*] oscilar

varying ['vɛərɪɪŋ] ADJ [*amounts*] distinto; [*periods of time*] variado; [*ages, shades, sizes*] diverso; **with ~ degrees of success** con más o menos éxito

vase [vɑːz, (*US*) veɪs] N florero *m*, jarrón *m*

⚠ **vase** ≠ ***vaso***

---

vasectomy [væˈsektəmɪ] N vasectomía *f*

Vaseline® ['væsɪliːn] N vaselina® *f*

vast [vɑːst] ADJ (*compar* **~er**; *superl* **~est**) [*building, quantity, organization*] enorme, inmenso; [*area*] vasto, extenso; [*range, selection*] enorme, amplísimo; [*knowledge, experience*] vasto; **it's a ~ improvement** es muchísimo mejor; **the ~ majority** la inmensa mayoría

vastly ['vɑːstlɪ] ADV [*different, overrated*] enormemente; [*superior*] infinitamente

vastness ['vɑːstnɪs] N inmensidad *f*

VAT [viːeɪˈtiː, væt] N ABBR (*Brit*) (= **value-added tax**) IVA *m* ➤ **VAT man** recaudador *m* del IVA ➤ **VAT return** declaración *f* del IVA

vat [væt] N tina *f*, tinaja *f*; [*of cider*] cuba *f*

Vatican ['vætɪkən] N **the ~** el Vaticano ➤ **Vatican City** Ciudad *f* del Vaticano

vaudeville ['vəʊdəvɪl] N (*esp US*) vodevil *m*

vault[1] [vɔːlt] N (*Archit*) bóveda *f*; (= *cellar*) sótano *m*; (*for wine*) bodega *f*; [*of bank*] cámara *f* acorazada; (= *tomb*) panteón *m*; [*of church*] cripta *f*

vault[2] [vɔːlt] Ⓐ N (= *jump*) salto *m* Ⓑ VI saltar; **to ~ over a stream** cruzar un arroyo de un salto, saltar un arroyo Ⓒ VT saltar

vaulted ['vɔːltɪd] ADJ abovedado

vaulting horse ['vɔːltɪŋˌhɔːs] N potro *m* (de madera)

vaunt [vɔːnt] Ⓐ VT (= *boast of*) jactarse de, hacer alarde de; (= *display*) lucir, ostentar Ⓑ VI jactarse

vaunted ['vɔːntɪd] ADJ **much ~** tan cacareado

VC N ABBR (*Brit Mil*) = **Victoria Cross**

VCR N ABBR = **video cassette recorder**

VD N ABBR (= **venereal disease**) enfermedad *f* venérea

VDT N ABBR (*esp US*) (= **visual display terminal**) UDV *f* ➤ **VDT operator** operador(a) *m/f* de UDV

VDU N ABBR (*Brit*) (= **visual display unit**) UDV *f* ➤ **VDU operator** operador(a) *m/f* de UDV

veal [viːl] N ternera *f*

V-E Day [ˌviːˈiːdeɪ] N ABBR (= **Victory in Europe Day**) día *m* de la victoria en Europa

veep** [viːp] N (*US*) = **vice-president**

veer [vɪəʳ] VI (*also* **to ~ round**) [*ship*] virar; [*car*] girar, torcer; [*wind*] cambiar de dirección; **the car ~ed off the road** el coche se salió de la carretera; **the country has ~ed to the left** el país ha dado un giro hacia *or* a la izquierda

veg* [vedʒ] N ABBR (*esp Brit*) (= **vegetable(s)**) verdura *f* ➤ **veg out**** VI + ADV relajarse

vegan ['viːgən] N vegeteriano/a *m/f* estricto/a

vegeburger ['vedʒɪˌbɜːgəʳ] N hamburguesa *f* vegetariana

vegetable ['vedʒtəbl] Ⓐ N hortaliza *f*, verdura *f*; **green ~s** verdura(s) *f(pl)*; **~s are an important part of the diet** la verdura es *or* las hortalizas son una parte importante de la dieta Ⓑ CPD [*fat, matter, oil*] vegetal ➤ **vegetable garden** (*big*) huerta *f*; (*small*) huerto *m* ➤ **vegetable patch** huerto *m* pequeño ➤ **vegetable soup** sopa *f* de verduras

vegetarian [ˌvedʒɪˈtɛərɪən] ADJ, N vegetariano/a *m/f*

vegetarianism [ˌvedʒɪˈtɛərɪənɪzəm] N vegetarianismo *m*

vegetate ['vedʒɪteɪt] VI vegetar

vegetation [ˌvedʒɪˈteɪʃən] N vegetación *f*

veggie* ['vedʒɪ] Ⓐ ADJ vegetariano; **~ burger** hamburguesa *f* vegetariana Ⓑ N (*esp Brit*) (= *person*) vegetariano/a *m/f*; **veggies** (*esp US*) (= *vegetables*) verdura *f*

vehemence ['viːɪməns] N [*of words, person, protest*] vehemencia *f*; [*of attack*] violencia *f*; [*of denial*] rotundidad *f*

vehement ['viːɪmənt] ADJ [*person, tone, criticism, protest*] vehemente; [*denial*] rotundo, categórico; [*dislike*] intenso; [*attack*] violento

vehemently ['viːɪməntlɪ] ADV [*say*] vehementemente, con vehemencia; [*deny*] rotundamente, categóricamente; [*reject, shake one's head*] ostensiblemente; [*oppose*] radicalmente; [*attack*] violentamente; **to be ~ opposed to sth** oponerse radicalmente a algo, estar radicalmente en contra de algo

vehicle ['viːɪkl] N vehículo *m*; **the programme was a ~ for promoting himself** el programa era un vehículo *or* medio *or* instrumento para promocionarse

veil [veɪl] Ⓐ N velo *m*; **under a ~ of secrecy** en el mayor secreto; **to draw a ~ over sth** (*fig*) correr un (tupido) velo sobre algo Ⓑ VT [+ *face*] cubrir *or* tapar con un velo; [+ *truth, facts*] velar, encubrir; [+ *dislike, hatred*] disimular

veiled [veɪld] ADJ [*threat, criticism, insult*] velado; **thinly-~ dislike** antipatía *f* apenas disimulada

vein [veɪn] N **1** (*in body, leaf*) vena *f* **2** [*of ore*] filón *m*, veta *f*; (*in stone*) vena *f* **3** (= *streak*) vena *f*; **there is a ~ of anti-semitism running through his writing** hay una vena antisemita en todos sus escritos **4** (= *mood, tone*) vena *f*; **she went on in this ~ for some time** continuó de esta guisa *or* en este tono durante un rato; **the next two speakers continued in the same ~** los dos siguientes conferenciantes se expresaron en la misma línea

veined [veɪnd] ADJ [*hands, eyes*] venoso

Velcro® ['velkrəʊ] N velcro® *m*

velocity [vɪ'lɒsɪtɪ] N velocidad *f*

velvet ['velvɪt] Ⓐ N terciopelo *m* Ⓑ ADJ (= *of velvet*) de terciopelo; (= *velvety*) aterciopelado

velvety ['velvɪtɪ] ADJ aterciopelado

venal ['viːnl] ADJ [*person*] venal, sobornable; [*action*] corrupto, corrompido

vendetta [ven'detə] N vendetta *f*

vending machine ['vendɪŋməˌʃiːn] N máquina *f* expendedora, vendedora *f* automática

vendor ['vendɔː'] N vendedor(a) *m/f*

veneer [və'nɪə'] N chapa *f*, enchapado *m*; **a ~ of respectability** un barniz *or* una apariencia de respetabilidad

venerable ['venərəbl] ADJ venerable

venerate ['venəreɪt] VT venerar, reverenciar

veneration [ˌvenə'reɪʃən] N veneración *f*

venereal disease [vɪ'nɪərɪəldɪˌziːz] N enfermedad *f* venérea

Venetian [vɪ'niːʃən] ADJ veneciano ➤ **Venetian blind** persiana *f*

Venezuela [ˌvene'zweɪlə] N Venezuela *f*

Venezuelan [ˌvene'zweɪlən] ADJ, N venezolano/a *m/f*

vengeance ['vendʒəns] N venganza *f*; **to take ~ on sb** vengarse de algn; **it began to rain with a ~** empezó a llover de verdad, empezó a llover de lo lindo*

vengeful ['vendʒfʊl] ADJ vengativo

venial ['viːnɪəl] ADJ venial; [*error, fault*] leve

Venice ['venɪs] N Venecia *f*

venison ['venɪzn] N carne *f* de venado

venom ['venəm] N veneno *m*; **he spoke with ~** habló con veneno *or* malicia, habló con palabras envenenadas

venomous ['venəməs] ADJ [*snake*] venenoso; [*look*] maligno

venomously ['venəməslɪ] ADV con malignidad

vent [vent] Ⓐ N (*Mech*) agujero *m*; (= *valve*) válvula *f*; (= *airhole*) respiradero *m*; (= *grille*) rejilla *f* de ventilación; (= *pipe*) ventosa *f*, conducto *m* de ventilación; **to give ~ to one's feelings** desahogarse Ⓑ VT [+ *feelings*] desahogar, descargar; **to ~ one's anger on sth/sb** desahogar la ira con algo/algn

ventilate [ventɪleɪt] VT ventilar, airear

ventilation [ˌventɪ'leɪʃən] N ventilación *f* ➤ **ventilation shaft** pozo *m* de ventilación

ventilator ['ventɪleɪtə'] N **1** (*Constr*) ventilador *m* **2** (*Med*) respirador *m*

ventriloquism [ven'trɪləkwɪzəm] N ventriloquia *f*

ventriloquist [ven'trɪləkwɪst] N ventrílocuo/a *m/f*

venture ['ventʃə'] Ⓐ N (= *enterprise*) empresa *f*; (= *exploit, adventure*) aventura *f*; **a business ~** una empresa comercial Ⓑ VT [+ *money, reputation, life*] arriesgar, jugar(se); [+ *opinion, guess*] aventurar; **to ~ to do sth** osar *or* atreverse a hacer algo; ✦ PROV **nothing ~d, nothing gained** quien no se arriesga no pasa la mar Ⓒ VI **to ~ out** aventurarse a salir Ⓓ CPD ➤ **venture capital** capital-riesgo *m* ➤ **venture forth** VI + ADV (*liter*) aventurarse a salir

venue ['venjuː] N (*for concert*) local *m*; **there has been a change of ~ for the rehearsal** se ha cambiado de lugar para el ensayo

Venus ['viːnəs] N (*Myth*) Venus *f*; (*Astron*) Venus *m*

veracity [və'ræsɪtɪ] N (*frm*) veracidad *f*

veranda(h) [və'rændə] N galería *f*, veranda *f*, terraza *f*

verb [vɜːb] N verbo *m*

verbal ['vɜːbəl] ADJ verbal; **~ diarrhoea*** verborrea *f*

verbalize ['vɜːbəlaɪz] Ⓐ VT expresar verbalmente, expresar en palabras Ⓑ VI expresarse en palabras

verbally ['vɜːbəlɪ] ADV [*communicate, abuse*] verbalmente; [*agree*] de palabra

verbatim [vɜː'beɪtɪm] Ⓐ ADJ textual, literal Ⓑ ADV textualmente, palabra por palabra

verbiage ['vɜːbɪɪdʒ] N verborrea *f*, palabrería *f*

verbose [vɜː'bəʊs] ADJ verboso

verdict ['vɜːdɪkt] N (*Jur*) (= *judgment*) veredicto *m*, fallo *m*; [*of judge*] sentencia *f*; **to return a ~** emitir *or* pronunciar un veredicto, emitir un fallo; **what's your ~?** ¿qué opinas de esto?

verge [vɜːdʒ] N **1** (*esp Brit*) [*of road*] borde *m*; [*of motorway*] arcén *m* **2** (*fig*) borde *m*, margen *m*; **to be on the ~ of disaster/a nervous breakdown** estar al borde de la catástrofe/de una crisis nerviosa; **to be on the ~ of a great discovery** estar en la antesala de un gran descubrimiento; **she was on the ~ of tears** estaba a punto de llorar; **to be on the ~ of doing sth** estar a punto *or* al borde de hacer algo ➤ **verge on, verge upon** VI + PREP rayar en

verger ['vɜːdʒə'] N sacristán *m*

verifiable ['verɪfaɪəbl] ADJ verificable, comprobable

verification [ˌverɪfɪ'keɪʃən] N verificación *f*, comprobación *f*; [*of result*] confirmación *f*

verify ['verɪfaɪ] VT verificar, comprobar; [+ *result*] confirmar; (*Comput*) verificar

veritable ['verɪtəbl] ADJ verdadero, auténtico

vermilion [və'mɪlɪən] Ⓐ N bermellón *m* Ⓑ ADJ bermejo

vermin ['vɜːmɪn] N (= *insects*) bichos *mpl*, sabandijas *fpl*; (= *mammals*) alimañas *fpl*; (*pej*) (= *people*) chusma *f*

vermouth ['vɜːməθ] N vermut *m*, vermú *m*

vernacular [və'nækjʊlə'] Ⓐ ADJ **1** (*Ling*) vernáculo, vulgar **2** [*architecture*] típico, local, regional Ⓑ N (*Ling*) lengua *f* vernácula; (*fig*) lenguaje *m* corriente

verruca [və'ruːkə] N (*Brit*) verruga *f*

versatile ['vɜːsətaɪl] ADJ [*person*] polifacético, versátil; [*material*] versátil, que se presta a usos distintos

versatility [ˌvɜːsə'tɪlɪtɪ] N [*of person*] carácter *m* polifacético, versatilidad *f*; [*of tool, machine, material*] versatilidad *f*, múltiple funcionalidad *f*

verse [vɜːs] N **1** (= *stanza*) estrofa *f*; [*of Bible*] versículo *m* **2** (= *poetry*) verso *m*, poesía *f*; **in ~** en verso

versed [vɜːst] ADJ **to be well ~ in** ser *or* estar versado en, ser experto en

versification [ˌvɜːsɪfɪ'keɪʃən] N versificación *f*

version ['vɜːʃən] N versión *f*; (= *translation*) traducción *f*; [*of car etc*] modelo *m*

versus ['vɜːsəs] PREP contra

vertebra ['vɜːtɪbrə] N (*pl* **~e** ['vɜːtɪbriː]) vértebra *f*

vertebrate ['vɜːtɪbrɪt] Ⓐ ADJ vertebrado Ⓑ N vertebrado *m*

vertical ['vɜːtɪkəl] Ⓐ ADJ vertical Ⓑ N vertical *f*

vertically ['vɜːtɪkəlɪ] ADV verticalmente

vertigo ['vɜːtɪɡəʊ] N vértigo *m*

verve [vɜːv] N (= *drive*) energía *f*; (= *vitality*) brío *m*; (= *enthusiasm*) entusiasmo *m*

very ['verɪ] Ⓐ ADV **1** (= *extremely*) muy; **it is ~ cold** [*object*] está muy frío; [*weather*] hace mucho frío; **~ much** mucho; **I didn't like it ~ much** no me gustó mucho; **he ~ nearly missed the bus** por muy poco pierde el autobús; **it's not so ~ difficult** no es tan difícil; **~ well, I'll do what I can** muy bien *or* bueno, haré lo que pueda; **he couldn't ~ well refuse** no pudo negarse a hacerlo

2 (= *absolutely*) **she eats nothing but the ~ best** sólo come lo mejor de lo mejor; **at the ~ earliest** como muy pronto; **the ~ first/last** el primero/último de todos; **at the ~ latest** a más tardar, como muy tarde; **at the ~ least** como mínimo; **at the ~ most** a lo sumo, como mucho, como máximo; **the**

~ **next day** precisamente el día siguiente; **it's my ~ own** es el mío; **the ~ same hat** el mismísimo sombrero
B ADJ **1** (= *precise*) mismo; **from the ~ beginning** desde el comienzo mismo; **at that ~ moment** en ese mismo momento; **those were his ~ words** eso fue exactamente lo que dijo
2 (= *mere*) **the ~ idea!** ¡qué cosas dices!, ¡cómo se te ocurre!; **the ~ thought (of it) makes me feel sick** con sólo pensarlo me da náuseas
3 (= *extreme*) **at the ~ bottom** abajo del todo; **at the ~ end** justo al final, al final de todo

vessel ['vesl] N **1** (= *ship*) barco *m*, buque *m*, embarcación *f* **2** (= *receptacle*) vasija *f*, recipiente *m*

vest [vest] N **1** (*Brit*) (= *undergarment*) camiseta *f* (*sin mangas*) **2** (*US*) (= *waistcoat*) chaleco *m*

vested ['vestɪd] ADJ [*right*] inalienable; **to have a ~ interest in sth** tener un interés personal en algo

vestibule ['vestɪbjuːl] N vestíbulo *m*

vestige ['vestɪdʒ] N (= *trace*) vestigio *m*, rastro *m*; **a ~ of truth** un elemento *or* un tanto de verdad

vestments ['vestmənts] N vestiduras *fpl*

vestry ['vestrɪ] N sacristía *f*

Vesuvius [vɪ'suːvɪəs] N Vesubio *m*

vet¹ [vet] N ABBR **1** (*esp Brit*) (= **veterinary surgeon, veterinarian**) veterinario/a *m/f* **2** (*US**) (= **veteran**) excombatiente *mf*

vet² [vet] (*esp Brit*) VT **1** [+ *article, speech*] repasar, revisar **2** (= *examine*) [+ *application*] examinar, investigar; **he was ~ted by Security** fue sometido a una investigación por los servicios de seguridad

veteran ['vetərən] **A** ADJ (*gen*) veterano; (= *battleworn*) aguerrido **B** N (= *war veteran, experienced person*) veterano/a *m/f*; (= *ex-serviceman*) excombatiente *mf* **C** CPD ➤ **veteran car** (*Brit*) coche fabricado antes de 1919, especialmente antes de 1905 ➤ **Veterans' Day** (*US*) fecha del aniversario del armisticio de 1918 en que se recuerda a los caídos en las dos guerras mundiales (11 de noviembre)

veterinarian [ˌvetərɪ'neərɪən] N (*US*) veterinario/a *m/f*

veterinary ['vetərɪnərɪ] ADJ veterinario ➤ **veterinary surgeon** (*Brit*) veterinario/a *m/f*

veto ['viːtəʊ] **A** N (*pl* **~es**) veto *m* **B** VT [+ *bill, application*] vetar, prohibir; [+ *suggestion, idea*] rechazar; **the president ~ed it** el presidente lo vetó *or* le puso su veto

vetting ['vetɪŋ] N (= *check*) examen *m* previo; (= *investigation*) investigación *f*

vexation [vek'seɪʃən] N **1** (= *anger*) irritación *f* **2** (= *trouble*) aflicción *f*, disgusto *m*

vexed [vekst] ADJ **1** (= *angry*) enfadado (*Sp*), enojado (*LAm*); **to get ~** enfadarse (*Sp*), enojarse (*LAm*); **in a ~ tone** en tono ofendido, en tono de enojo **2** [*question*] reñido, controvertido **3** (= *puzzled*) perplejo, confuso

vexing ['veksɪŋ] ADJ fastidioso, molesto, enojoso (*LAm*)

VG, v.g. ABBR (= **very good**) S

VHF N ABBR (= **very high frequency**) VHF

VHS N ABBR = **video home system**

via ['vaɪə] PREP por; (*esp by plane*) vía; **we drove to Lisbon ~ Salamanca** fuimos a Lisboa por Salamanca

viability [ˌvaɪə'bɪlɪtɪ] N viabilidad *f*

viable ['vaɪəbl] ADJ viable

viaduct ['vaɪədʌkt] N viaducto *m*

vibes** [vaɪbz] NPL ABBR (= **vibrations**) vibraciones *fpl*, ambiente *msing*; **I got good ~ from her** me cayó muy bien

vibrancy ['vaɪbrənsɪ] N [*of colour*] viveza *f*; [*of person*] dinamismo *m*, vitalidad *f*; [*of voice*] sonoridad *f*

vibrant ['vaɪbrənt] ADJ [*colour*] vivo; [*person*] animado; [*personality*] vibrante; [*voice*] vibrante, sonoro

vibraphone ['vaɪbrəfəʊn] N vibráfono *m*

vibrate [vaɪ'breɪt] **A** VI vibrar **B** VT hacer vibrar

vibration [vaɪ'breɪʃən] N vibración *f*

vibrator [vaɪ'breɪtər] N vibrador *m*

vicar ['vɪkər] N vicario *m*; (*Anglican*) cura *m*, párroco *m*

vicarage ['vɪkərɪdʒ] N (*Brit*) casa *f* del párroco

vicarious [vɪ'keərɪəs] ADJ (= *indirect*) indirecto; [*substitute*] por referencias; **to get ~ pleasure out of sth** disfrutar indirectamente de algo

vicariously [vɪ'keərɪəslɪ] ADV indirectamente

vice¹ [vaɪs] N (= *habit, activity*) vicio *m* ➤ **vice ring** asociación *f* criminal ➤ **vice squad** brigada *f* antivicio

vice², vise (*US*) [vaɪs] N (= *tool*) torno *m or* tornillo *m* de banco

vice-chancellor ['vaɪs'tʃɑːnsələr] N (*Univ*) rector(a) *m/f*

vice-presidency ['vaɪs'prezɪdənsɪ] N vicepresidencia *f*

vice-president ['vaɪs'prezɪdənt] N vicepresidente/a *m/f*

vice-principal ['vaɪs'prɪnsɪpəl] N subdirector(a) *m/f*

viceroy ['vaɪsrɔɪ] N virrey *m*

vice versa ['vaɪsɪ'vɜːsə] ADV viceversa, al revés

vicinity [vɪ'sɪnɪtɪ] N (= *neighbourhood*) cercanías *fpl*, alrededores *mpl*, inmediaciones *fpl*; **in the ~ of Tel Aviv** en las cercanías or en los alrededores or en las inmediaciones de Tel Aviv; **houses in the immediate ~ of the blast** las viviendas más cercanas a la explosión; **and other towns in the ~** y otras ciudades de las inmediaciones or de la zona or cercanas

vicious ['vɪʃəs] ADJ [*person, gang*] despiadado; [*attack, crime*] atroz, brutal; [*animal*] agresivo, fiero; [*criticism, campaign*] despiadado, cruel; [*remark*] malicioso ➤ **vicious circle** círculo *m* vicioso

viciously ['vɪʃəslɪ] ADV [*attack, beat, stab*] brutalmente, con saña; [*say, speak*] con malicia

viciousness ['vɪʃəsnɪs] N [*of person, attack*] brutalidad *f*; [*of animal*] fiereza *f*, agresividad *f*; [*of words*] malicia *f*, malevolencia *f*; [*of criticism, campaign*] lo despiadado, crueldad *f*

vicissitudes [vɪ'sɪsɪtjuːdz] NPL vicisitudes *fpl*, peripecias *fpl*

victim ['vɪktɪm] N (= *subject of attack*) víctima *f*; **the ~s** (= *survivors of disaster*) los damnificados; **to be the ~ of** [+ *attack, hoax*] ser víctima de ➤ **Victim Support** (*Brit*) organización de ayuda a las víctimas de actos delictivos

victimization [ˌvɪktɪmaɪ'zeɪʃən] N persecución *f*

victimize ['vɪktɪmaɪz] VT (= *pursue*) perseguir; (= *punish*) escoger y castigar, tomar represalias contra; **to be ~d** ser víctima de una persecución

victimless ['vɪktɪmlɪs] ADJ sin víctimas

victor ['vɪktər] N vencedor(a) *m/f*

Victoria Cross [vɪk'tɔːrɪə'krɒs] N (*Brit*) la condecoración más alta de las fuerzas armadas británicas y de la Commonwealth

Victorian [vɪk'tɔːrɪən] ADJ, N victoriano/a *m/f*

VICTORIAN

El adjetivo **Victorian** se usa tanto en Gran Bretaña como en EE.UU. para referirse a las personas, la arquitectura y la cultura de la época de la reina Victoria (1837-1901). Asimismo, las actitudes o cualidades llamadas victorianas son las que se consideran características de su época, tales como el interés por el respeto social y la moral estricta acompañada de la falta de sentido del humor, la intolerancia y la hipocresía. El término **Victorian values** (valores victorianos) se usa positivamente en política para referirse a la honestidad, la superación personal, el respeto a la autoridad y la importancia de la familia.

Victoriana [vɪkˌtɔːrɪ'ɑːnə] NPL objetos *mpl* victorianos, antigüedades *fpl* victorianas

victorious [vɪk'tɔːrɪəs] ADJ [*army*] victorioso, triunfante; [*person, team*] vencedor, triunfador

victory ['vɪktərɪ] N victoria *f*, triunfo *m* (**over** sobre)

video ['vɪdɪəʊ] **A** N **1** (*esp Brit*) (*also* ~ **(cassette) recorder**) vídeo *m* (*Sp*), video *m* (*LAm*)
2 (*also* ~ **cassette**) vídeo *m* (*Sp*), video *m* (*LAm*); **it's out on ~**

ha salido en vídeo (*Sp*) *or* video (*LAm*)
B VT (*esp Brit*) grabar en vídeo (*Sp*) *or* video (*LAm*)
C CPD ➤ **video camera** videocámara *f* ➤ **video club**
videoclub *m* ➤ **video conferencing** videoconferencia *f*
➤ **video diary** (*TV*) diario *m* en vídeo (*Sp*) *or* video (*LAm*)
➤ **video disk** videodisco *m* ➤ **video film** película *f* de vídeo
(*Sp*) *or* video (*LAm*), videofilm *m* ➤ **video game** videojuego
m ➤ **video library** videoteca *f* ➤ **video nasty*** (= *horror film*)
película *f* de terror en vídeo (*Sp*) *or* video (*LAm*);
(= *pornography*) vídeo *m* (*Sp*) *or* video *m* (*LAm*) porno*
➤ **video piracy** videopiratería *f* ➤ **video shop** videoclub *m*

videophone ['vɪdɪəʊˌfəʊn] N videófono *m*, videoteléfono *m*

videotape ['vɪdɪəʊˌteɪp] **A** N (= *tape*) cinta *f* de vídeo *or*
(*LAm*) video; (= *recording*) vídeo *m*, video *m* (*LAm*) **B** VT
grabar en vídeo (*Sp*) *or* video (*LAm*)

vie [vaɪ] VI **to ~ for sth** disputarse algo; **to ~ with sb**
competir con algn, rivalizar con algn

Vienna [vɪ'enə] N Viena *f*

Viennese [ˌvɪə'niːz] ADJ, N vienés/esa *m/f*

Vietnam, Viet Nam ['vjet'næm] N Vietnam *m*

Vietnamese [ˌvjetnə'miːz] **A** ADJ vietnamita
B N **1** (= *person*) vietnamita *mf* **2** (*Ling*) vietnamita *m*

view [vjuː] **A** N **1** (= *sight*) vista *f*; **he stood up to get a
better ~** se puso de pie para ver mejor; **am I blocking your
~?** ¿te estoy tapando?; **to come into ~** aparecer; **to
disappear from ~** perderse de vista; **in full ~ of the crowd**
bien a la vista de la multitud; **to be on ~** estar expuesto al
público; **with a ~ to doing sth** con miras *or* vistas a hacer
algo
2 (= *picture*) vista *f*; **50 ~s of Venice** 50 vistas de Venecia
3 (= *opinion*) opinión *f*; **in my ~** a mi parecer, en mi
opinión; **to express one's ~s** expresar su opinión; **to hold**
or **take the ~ that** opinar que
4 (= *way of understanding*) visión *f*; **an idealistic ~ of the
world** una visión idealista del mundo
5 in ~ of (the fact that) en vista de (que)
B VT [+ *house, goods, slides*] ver; [+ *accounts*] examinar;
London ~ed from the air Londres vista desde arriba; **he is
~ed with suspicion by many MPs** muchos parlamentarios lo
miran *or* tratan con recelo

viewer ['vjuːə'] N **1** (*TV*) televidente *mf*, telespectador(a)
m/f **2** (*for viewing slides*) visor *m*

viewfinder ['vjuːˌfaɪndə'] N (*Phot*) visor *m* (de imagen),
objetivo *m*

viewing ['vjuːɪŋ] **A** N **1** [*of property, gallery*] visita *f*; (*prior to
auction*) exposición *f*, inspección *f* **2** (*TV*) **your weekend ~**
sus programas *or* su programación para el fin de semana;
"unsuitable for family viewing" "no apto para ver en
familia" **B** CPD ➤ **TV viewing figures** cifras *fpl* de audiencia
televisiva ➤ **viewing habits** hábitos *mpl* de los
telespectadores *or* televidentes

viewpoint ['vjuːpɔɪnt] N **1** (*on hill etc*) mirador *m*, punto *m*
panorámico **2** (*fig*) punto *m* de vista

vigil ['vɪdʒɪl] N vigilia *f*, vela *f*; **to keep ~ (over sth/sb)** velar
(algo/a algn)

vigilance ['vɪdʒɪləns] N vigilancia *f*

vigilant ['vɪdʒɪlənt] ADJ vigilante, alerta

vigilante [ˌvɪdʒɪ'læntɪ] N vigilante *mf*

vigilantly ['vɪdʒɪləntlɪ] ADV vigilantemente

vigor ['vɪɡə'] N (*US*) = **vigour**

vigorous ['vɪɡərəs] ADJ [*exercise, debate, campaign*]
enérgico; [*denial*] categórico, rotundo; [*growth*] vigoroso;
[*economy*] pujante

vigorously ['vɪɡərəslɪ] ADV [*nod, shake*] enérgicamente,
vigorosamente; [*deny*] categóricamente, rotundamente;
[*exercise, defend, oppose, protest*] enérgicamente; **to grow ~**
crecer con vigor

vigour, vigor (*US*) ['vɪɡə'] N vigor *m*, energía *f*

Viking ['vaɪkɪŋ] ADJ, N vikingo/a *m/f*

vile [vaɪl] ADJ **1** (= *base, evil*) vil, infame **2** (*) (= *disgusting*)
[*conditions*] miserable, infame; [*weather*] pésimo, infame;
[*smell, taste*] repugnante; **it tasted ~** tenía un sabor
repugnante; **he has a ~ temper** tiene un genio muy

violento *or* (*) de mil demonios

vilify ['vɪlɪfaɪ] VT vilipendiar

villa ['vɪlə] N (*Roman*) villa *f*; (= *country house*) casa *f* de
campo, quinta *f*; (*for holiday*) chalet *m*

village ['vɪlɪdʒ] N pueblo *m*; (= *small*) aldea *f*, pueblito *m*
(*LAm*) ➤ **village green** prado *m* comunal, campo *m*
comunal ➤ **village hall** sala *f* del pueblo

villager ['vɪlɪdʒə'] N (= *inhabitant*) vecino/a *m/f* del pueblo;
[*of small village*] aldeano/a *m/f*

villain ['vɪlən] N **1** (*) (= *wrongdoer*) maleante *mf*,
delincuente *mf* **2** (*in novel, film*) malo/a *m/f*

villainous ['vɪlənəs] ADJ malvado, vil

villainy ['vɪlənɪ] N maldad *f*, vileza *f*

vinaigrette [ˌvɪneɪ'gret] N vinagreta *f*

vindaloo [ˌvɪndə'luː] N *plato indio muy picante*

vindicate ['vɪndɪkeɪt] VT [+ *decision, action*] justificar;
[+ *claim, right*] reivindicar, hacer valer; **I feel ~d by this
decision** me siento resarcido por esta decisión, siento que
con esta decisión se me hace justicia

vindication [ˌvɪndɪ'keɪʃən] N justificación *f*; [*of claim, right*]
reivindicación *f*, defensa *f*; (= *means of exoneration*)
vindicación *f* (*frm*)

vindictive [vɪn'dɪktɪv] ADJ vengativo

vindictively [vɪn'dɪktɪvlɪ] ADV vengativamente, con afán
de venganza

vine [vaɪn] N vid *f*; (= *climbing, trained*) parra *f*; (= *climber*)
enredadera *f* ➤ **vine growing** viticultura *f* ➤ **vine leaf** (*pl ~
leaves*) hoja *f* de parra, hoja *f* de vid, pámpana *f*

vinegar ['vɪnɪɡə'] N vinagre *m*

vinegary ['vɪnɪɡərɪ] ADJ vinagroso

vine-growing ['vaɪnˌɡrəʊɪŋ] ADJ [*region*] viticultor

vineyard ['vɪnjəd] N viña *f*, viñedo *m*

vintage ['vɪntɪdʒ] N (= *season, harvest*) vendimia *f*; (= *year*)
cosecha *f*, añada *f*; **the 1970 ~** la cosecha de 1970; **it will be
a good ~** la cosecha será buena; **this film is ~ Chaplin** esta
película es un clásico de Chaplin ➤ **vintage car** coche *m* de
época, coche *m* antiguo (*fabricado entre 1919 y 1930*)
➤ **vintage wine** vino *m* añejo ➤ **vintage year: it has been a
~ year for plays** ha sido un año destacado en lo que a
teatro se refiere

vinyl ['vaɪnl] **A** N vinilo *m* **B** ADJ de vinilo, vinílico

viola [vɪ'əʊlə] N viola *f* ➤ **viola player** viola *mf*

violate ['vaɪəleɪt] VT **1** [+ *law*] violar, infringir, quebrantar;
[+ *constitution, agreement, treaty*] violar, infringir, vulnerar;
[+ *sanctions*] incumplir, desobedecer; [+ *contract*] no
cumplir, incumplir; [+ *rights*] violar, vulnerar; [+ *privacy*]
invadir **2** [+ *grave*] profanar

violation [ˌvaɪə'leɪʃən] N **1** [*of law*] violación *f*, infracción *f*;
[*of rights*] violación *f*; **~ of privacy** entrometimiento *m*,
intromisión *f* **2** (*US*) (= *minor offence*) infracción *f*, falta *f*
leve

violence ['vaɪələns] N violencia *f*; **an act of ~** un acto de
violencia; **to resort to ~** recurrir a la violencia *or* a la
fuerza

violent ['vaɪələnt] ADJ [*person, quarrel, storm, language*]
violento; [*kick*] violento, fuerte; [*pain*] intenso, agudo; **he
has a ~ temper** tiene un genio terrible; **to take a ~ dislike
to sb** coger *or* (*LAm*) agarrar una profunda antipatía a algn

violently ['vaɪələntlɪ] ADV [*act*] con violencia, de manera
violenta; [*tremble*] violentamente; [*brake*] bruscamente;
she shook the child ~ sacudió al niño con violencia; **to be
~ opposed to sth** oponerse a algo; **to be ~
sick** vomitar mucho

violet ['vaɪəlɪt] **A** N **1** (= *flower*) violeta *f* **2** (= *colour*)
violado *m*, violeta *f* **B** ADJ violado, violeta

violin [ˌvaɪə'lɪn] N violín *m* ➤ **violin case** estuche *m* de
violín ➤ **violin concerto** concierto *m* para violín ➤ **violin
player** violinista *mf*

violinist [ˌvaɪə'lɪnɪst] N violinista *mf*

VIP N ABBR (= **very important person**) vip *mf*, persona *f* de
categoría; **to give sb the ~ treatment** tratar a algn como a

un vip ➤ **VIP lounge** sala *f* de vips

viper ['vaɪpəʳ] N (*lit, fig*) víbora *f*

viral ['vaɪərəl] ADJ vírico

virgin ['vɜːdʒɪn] **Ⓐ** N virgen *mf*; **to be a** ~ ser virgen **Ⓑ** ADJ [*forest, soil*] virgen **Ⓒ** CPD ➤ **virgin birth** partenogénesis *f inv* ➤ **the Virgin Isles** las Islas Vírgenes ➤ **virgin oil** aceite *m* virgen

virginity [vɜː'dʒɪnɪtɪ] N virginidad *f*

Virgo ['vɜːgəʊ] N **1** (= *sign, constellation*) Virgo *m* **2** (= *person*) virgo *mf inv*; **she's (a)** ~ es virgo

virile ['vɪraɪl] ADJ [*man*] viril; [*looks*] varonil

virility [vɪ'rɪlɪtɪ] N virilidad *f*

virtual ['vɜːtjʊəl] ADJ real, verdadero; **it was a** ~ **failure** en realidad fue un fracaso ➤ **virtual memory** memoria *f* virtual ➤ **virtual memory storage** memoria *f* virtual ➤ **virtual reality** realidad *f* virtual

virtually ['vɜːtjʊəlɪ] ADV prácticamente; **it** ~ **destroyed the building** destruyó prácticamente el edificio; **I've** ~ **finished the work** casi he terminado el trabajo

virtue ['vɜːtjuː] N **1** (= *good quality*) virtud *f* **2** (= *advantage*) virtud *f*, ventaja *f*; **it has the** ~ **being simple** tiene la virtud *or* ventaja de ser sencillo **3** (= *chastity*) castidad *f*, honra *f* **4 by** ~ **of** en virtud de, debido a

virtuosity [vɜːtjʊ'ɒsɪtɪ] N virtuosismo *m*

virtuoso [vɜːtjʊ'əʊzəʊ] **Ⓐ** N virtuoso/a *m/f* **Ⓑ** ADJ de virtuoso/a; **a** ~ **performance** una interpretación de auténtico virtuoso *or* llena de virtuosismo

virtuous ['vɜːtjʊəs] ADJ virtuoso

virtuously ['vɜːtjʊəslɪ] ADV virtuosamente

virulent ['vɪrʊlənt] ADJ virulento

virulently ['vɪrʊləntlɪ] ADV con virulencia

virus ['vaɪərəs] N (*pl* ~**es**) (*Med, Comput*) virus *m inv*; **the AIDS** ~ el virus del SIDA; **a computer** ~ un virus informático

visa ['viːzə] N (*pl* ~**s**) visado *m*, visa *f* (*LAm*)

vis-à-vis ['viːzəviː] PREP (= *with regard to*) con respecto a, en relación con, con relación a

visceral ['vɪsərəl] ADJ (*liter*) visceral

viscose ['vɪskəʊs] N (*esp Brit*) viscosa *f*

viscosity [vɪs'kɒsɪtɪ] N viscosidad *f*

viscount ['vaɪkaʊnt] N vizconde *m*

viscous ['vɪskəs] ADJ viscoso

vise [vaɪs] N (*US*) = **vice²**

visibility [vɪzɪ'bɪlɪtɪ] N (*Met*) visibilidad *f*; **good/poor** ~ buena/poca visibilidad *f*

visible ['vɪzɪbl] ADJ **1** (= *able to be seen*) ~ **to the human eye** perceptible a simple vista, visible al ojo humano; **the house is** ~ **from the road** la casa puede verse desde la carretera **2** (= *obvious*) [*effect, sign, result*] evidente; **with a** ~ **effort** con un esfuerzo evidente; **there was no** ~ **damage** no se veía ningún daño aparente

visibly ['vɪzɪblɪ] ADV visiblemente

vision ['vɪʒən] N **1** (= *eyesight*) vista *f* **2** (= *farsightedness*) clarividencia *f*, visión *f* de futuro; (= *imagination*) imaginación *f*; **a man of (broad)** ~ un hombre de miras amplias **3** (= *dream, hope*) visión *f*; **his** ~ **of the future** su visión del futuro **4** (= *image*) **I had** ~**s of having to walk home** ya me veía volviendo a casa a pie **5** (*Rel*) visión *f*; **to have a** ~ tener una visión

visionary ['vɪʒənərɪ] **Ⓐ** N **1** (= *original thinker*) visionario/a *m/f* **2** (= *dreamer*) soñador(a) *m/f* **Ⓑ** ADJ **1** (= *farsighted*) con visión de futuro, visionario **2** (= *impractical*) utópico, quimérico

visit ['vɪzɪt] **Ⓐ** N visita *f*; **to pay sb a** ~ hacer una visita *or* visitar a algn, pasar a ver a algn (*esp LAm*); **on a private** ~ de *or* en visita privada; **he was taken ill during a** ~ **to Amsterdam** cayó enfermo durante una visita a Amsterdam **Ⓑ** VT (= *go and see*) [+ *person*] visitar, hacer una visita a; [+ *place*] ir a, visitar **Ⓒ** VI **1** (= *make a visit*) hacer una visita; (= *make visits*) hacer visitas; **to go** ~**ing** hacer visitas **2** (*US*): **to** ~ **with sb** (= *go*

and see) visitar a algn; (= *chat with*) charlar con algn

visitation [vɪzɪ'teɪʃən] N **1** (*by official*) inspección *f*; (*by bishop, cardinal*) visita *f* pastoral; **we had a** ~ **from her** (*hum*) nos cayó encima una de sus visitas **2** (*Rel*) visitación *f*

visiting ['vɪzɪtɪŋ] ADJ [*speaker, professor*] invitado; [*team*] visitante, de fuera ➤ **visiting card** tarjeta *f* de visita ➤ **visiting hours** horas *fpl* de visita ➤ **visiting nurse** (*US*) enfermera *f* que visita a domicilio ➤ **visiting time** horas *fpl* de visita

visitor ['vɪzɪtəʳ] **Ⓐ** N **1** (*to one's home*) visita *f*; **we've got** ~**s** tenemos visita **2** (*to place*) (= *tourist*) turista *mf*, visitante *mf*; (= *tripper*) excursionista *mf*; (*to zoo, exhibition*) visitante *mf*; (*to hospital, prison*) visita *f*; ~**s to this country** los que visitan este país; **the museum had 900** ~**s** el museo recibió a 900 visitantes; **we're just** ~**s here** estamos aquí de visita nada más **Ⓑ** CPD ➤ **visitor centre, visitor center** (*US*) centro *m* de información ➤ **visitors' book** libro *m* de visitas

visor ['vaɪzəʳ] N visera *f*

VISTA ['vɪstə] N ABBR (*US*) (= **Volunteers in Service to America**) *programa de ayuda voluntaria a los necesitados*

vista ['vɪstə] N (*lit*) vista *f*, panorama *m*; (*fig*) perspectiva *f*, horizonte *m*

visual ['vɪzjʊəl] ADJ visual ➤ **visual aids** medios *mpl* visuales ➤ **the visual arts** las artes plásticas ➤ **visual display unit** unidad *f* de despliegue visual, monitor *m* ➤ **visual effects** efectos *mpl* visuales

visualization [vɪzjʊəlaɪ'zeɪʃən] N visualización *f*

visualize ['vɪzjʊəlaɪz] VT **1** (= *imagine*) imaginarse; **he tried to** ~ **the scene** intentó imaginarse la escena **2** (= *call to mind*) [+ *person, sb's face*] recordar **3** (= *foresee*) prever

visually ['vɪzjʊəlɪ] ADV visualmente

vital ['vaɪtl] **Ⓐ** ADJ **1** (= *crucial*) [*part, component, element*] vital, indispensable; [*ingredient*] esencial, indispensable, imprescindible; [*factor*] decisivo; [*link, role*] fundamental; [*question*] vital; [*information*] vital, esencial; **it is** ~ **to keep accurate records** es imprescindible *or* esencial llevar un registro detallado; **to be of** ~ **importance (to sth/sb)** ser de suma *or* vital importancia (para algo/algn); **these meetings are** ~ **to a successful outcome** estas reuniones son esenciales para un resultado positivo **2** (= *dynamic*) vital, lleno de vitalidad **3** (*Physiol*) [*organ, function*] vital **Ⓑ** CPD ➤ **vital signs** (*Med*) signos *mpl* vitales ➤ **vital statistics** (*) [*of woman's body*] medidas *fpl*

vitality [vaɪ'tælɪtɪ] N vitalidad *f*

vitally ['vaɪtəlɪ] ADV [*interested, concerned*] sumamente; [*affect*] de forma vital; **it is** ~ **important that ...** es de vital *or* suma importancia que ... + *subjun*; ~ **needed** [*food, tents, money*] indispensable

vitamin ['vɪtəmɪn] **Ⓐ** N vitamina *f*; **with added** ~**s** vitaminado, reforzado con vitaminas **Ⓑ** CPD [*content, supplement*] vitamínico ➤ **vitamin deficiency** avitaminosis *f*, déficit *m* vitamínico ➤ **vitamin pill, vitamin tablet** pastilla *f* de vitaminas

vitamin-enriched [vɪtəmɪnɪn'rɪtʃt] ADJ enriquecido con vitaminas

vitreous ['vɪtrɪəs] ADJ vítreo

vitriol ['vɪtrɪəl] N vitriolo *m*

vitriolic [vɪtrɪ'ɒlɪk] ADJ [*attack, criticism*] corrosivo, mordaz

vituperative [vɪ'tjuːpərətɪv] ADJ (*frm*) injurioso

viva ['vaɪvə] N (*Brit*) (*also* = **voce**) examen *m* oral

vivacious [vɪ'veɪʃəs] ADJ vivaz, animado

vivacity [vɪ'væsɪtɪ] N vivacidad *f*, animación *f*

vivid ['vɪvɪd] ADJ [*colour*] vivo, intenso; [*impression, recollection, memory*] vivo, fuerte; [*dream*] clarísimo; [*description*] gráfico, realista; **to have a** ~ **imagination** tener una imaginación muy viva *or* despierta

vividly ['vɪvɪdlɪ] ADV vivamente; [*describe*] gráficamente

vividness ['vɪvɪdnɪs] N [*of colours*] intensidad *f*, viveza *f*; [*of description*] lo gráfico; [*of impression, recollection*] fuerza *f*

vivisection [vɪvɪ'sekʃən] N vivisección *f*

vixen ['vɪksn] N zorra f, raposa f

viz. [vɪz] ADV ABBR (= *namely*) v.g., v.gr.

V-neck ['viːnek] Ⓐ N (= *neckline*) cuello m de pico; (= *sweater*) jersey m de cuello de pico Ⓑ ADJ (*also* ~**ed**) de cuello de pico

vocab* ['vəʊkæb] N ABBR = **vocabulary**

vocabulary [vəʊˈkæbjʊlərɪ] N 1 [*of person, language, subject*] vocabulario m, léxico m 2 (= *glossary*) glosario m

vocal ['vəʊkəl] Ⓐ ADJ vocal; **a small but ~ minority** una minoría pequeña pero ruidosa Ⓑ NPL vocals voz f*sing*, canto m*sing*; **lead ~s** voz f principal; **backing ~s** coros mpl Ⓒ CPD ➤ **vocal cords** cuerdas fpl vocales ➤ **vocal organs** órganos mpl vocales

vocalist ['vəʊkəlɪst] N vocalista mf; (*in pop group*) cantante mf

vocation [vəʊˈkeɪʃən] N (= *calling*) vocación f; (= *profession*) profesión f, carrera f; **he has missed his ~** se ha equivocado de carrera

vocational [vəʊˈkeɪʃənl] ADJ [*subject, course*] de formación profesional; [*qualification, skill*] profesional ➤ **vocational guidance** orientación f profesional ➤ **vocational training** formación f or capacitación f profesional

vocative ['vɒkətɪv] N (*also* ~ **case**) vocativo m

vociferous [vəʊˈsɪfərəs] ADJ 1 (= *forceful, energetic*) ruidoso 2 (= *noisy*) vociferante

vodka ['vɒdkə] N vodka m

vogue [vəʊg] N moda f; **to be in ~** estar en boga or de moda; **the ~ for short skirts** la moda de la falda corta

voice [vɔɪs] Ⓐ N 1 (= *sound, faculty of speech*) voz f; **in a deep ~** en tono grave; **in a loud ~** en voz alta; **keep your ~ down!** ¡no levantes la voz!; **to lose one's ~** quedarse afónico or sin voz; **to raise one's ~** alzar or levantar la voz; **at the top of one's ~** a voz en grito, a voz en cuello; **+ IDIOMS to speak with one ~ (about sth)** expresar una opinión unánime (con respecto a algo); **he likes the sound of his own ~** cómo le gusta oírse hablar

2 (*Mus*) voz f; **she has a beautiful (singing) ~** tiene una voz preciosa (para el canto), canta muy bien

3 (= *opinion*) voz f; **to have a ~ in the matter** tener voz en el asunto; **there were no dissenting ~s** no hubo opiniones en contra

4 (*Gram*) **active/passive ~** voz f activa/pasiva Ⓑ VT [+ *opinion, feelings, concern, support*] expresar Ⓒ CPD ➤ **voice box** laringe f ➤ **voice mail** (*Telec*) buzón m de voz ➤ **voice training** educación f de la voz

voice-activated ['vɔɪsˈæktɪveɪtəd] ADJ activado por voz

voiced [vɔɪst] ADJ [*consonant*] sonoro

voiceless ['vɔɪslɪs] ADJ [*Ling*] [*consonant*] sordo

voice-over ['vɔɪsˌəʊvəʳ] N voz f en off

void [vɔɪd] Ⓐ ADJ 1 (*Jur*) (= *invalid*) nulo, inválido 2 (*frm*) (= *empty*) vacío; **~ of interest** carente or desprovisto de interés Ⓑ N vacío m; **the ~** la nada; **to fill the ~** llenar el hueco or vacío

vol. ABBR (= *volume*) vol.

volatile ['vɒlətaɪl] ADJ 1 (*Chem*) volátil 2 [*person*] voluble; [*situation, atmosphere, market*] inestable, volátil

volatility [vɒləˈtɪlɪtɪ] N 1 (*Chem*) volatilidad f 2 [*of person*] volubilidad f; [*of situation, atmosphere, market*] inestabilidad f, volatilidad f

vol-au-vent ['vɒləvɑ̃] N volován m

volcanic [vɒlˈkænɪk] ADJ volcánico

volcano [vɒlˈkeɪnəʊ] N volcán m

vole [vəʊl] N campañol m, ratón m de campo

volition [vəˈlɪʃən] N **of one's own ~** (*frm*) por voluntad (propia), de libre albedrío

volley ['vɒlɪ] Ⓐ N 1 [*of shots*] descarga f (cerrada); [*of applause*] salva f; [*of stones, objects*] lluvia f; [*of insults*] torrente m 2 (*Tennis*) volea f Ⓑ VT 1 [+ *abuse, insults*] dirigir (**at** a) 2 (*Tennis*) volear

volleyball ['vɒlɪbɔːl] N balonvolea m, voleibol m, volibol m (*LAm*)

volt [vəʊlt] N voltio m

voltage ['vəʊltɪdʒ] N voltaje m, tensión f

volte-face ['vɒltˈfɑːs] N viraje m, cambio m súbito de opinión

voluble ['vɒljʊbl] ADJ [*person*] locuaz; [*speech*] prolijo

volume ['vɒljuːm] Ⓐ N 1 (= *book*) libro m, volumen m; (= *one of series*) volumen m, tomo m 2 (= *sound*) volumen m; **to turn the ~ up** subir el volumen or sonido 3 (= *size, amount*) volumen m; (*when measuring liquids*) capacidad f 4 **volumes** (= *great quantities*) **~s of smoke** gran cantidad de humo; **to write ~s** escribir mucho; **his expression spoke ~s** su expresión lo decía todo Ⓑ CPD ➤ **volume control** control m de volumen

voluminous [vəˈluːmɪnəs] ADJ (= *large, capacious*) voluminoso; (= *prolific*) prolífico; (= *overlong*) prolijo

voluntarily ['vɒləntərɪlɪ] ADV 1 (= *freely*) voluntariamente, por voluntad propia 2 (= *for no payment*) [*helper*] como voluntario

voluntary ['vɒləntərɪ] Ⓐ ADJ 1 (= *not compulsory*) voluntario; **attendance is on a ~ basis** la asistencia es voluntaria

2 (= *unpaid*) [*helper*] voluntario; **he does ~ work in his spare time** trabaja de voluntario en su tiempo libre; **he works at the school on a ~ basis** trabaja en el colegio como voluntario

Ⓑ CPD ➤ **voluntary liquidation** liquidación f voluntaria, disolución f; **to go into ~ liquidation** entrar en liquidación voluntaria, disolverse voluntariamente ➤ **voluntary redundancy** (*esp Brit*), **voluntary layoff** (*US*) retiro m voluntario, baja f voluntaria (*Sp*) ➤ **the voluntary sector** el voluntariado ➤ **Voluntary Service Overseas** (*Brit*) Servicio m de Voluntarios en el Extranjero ➤ **voluntary worker** voluntario/a m/f

volunteer [ˌvɒlənˈtɪəʳ] Ⓐ N voluntario/a m/f Ⓑ VT [+ *one's help, services*] ofrecer; [+ *remark, suggestion*] hacer; [+ *information*] dar Ⓒ VI (*for a task*) ofrecerse; (*for the army*) alistarse como voluntario; **to ~ to do sth** ofrecerse (voluntario) para hacer algo

voluptuous [vəˈlʌptjʊəs] ADJ voluptuoso

voluptuously [vəˈlʌptjʊəslɪ] ADV voluptuosamente

vomit ['vɒmɪt] Ⓐ N vómito m Ⓑ VI devolver, vomitar Ⓒ VT (*also* ~ **up**) vomitar

vomiting ['vɒmɪtɪŋ] N vómito m

voodoo ['vuːduː] N vudú m

voracious [vəˈreɪʃəs] ADJ [*appetite, person, animal*] voraz; [*reader*] insaciable, ávido

voraciously [vəˈreɪʃəslɪ] ADV [*eat*] vorazmente; [*read*] con avidez

vortex ['vɔːteks] N (*pl* ~**es** *or* **vortices** ['vɔːtɪsiːz]) 1 (*lit*) vórtice m, torbellino m 2 (*fig*) [*of activity*] torbellino, remolino m

vote [vəʊt] Ⓐ N 1 (= *single vote*) voto m (**for** a favor de; **against** en contra de)

2 (= *votes cast*) votos mpl; **they captured 13 per cent of the ~** se hicieron con un 13 por ciento de los votos

3 (= *right to vote*) derecho m al voto or a votar, sufragio m; **to have the ~** tener (el) derecho al voto

4 (= *act*) votación f; **to have** or **take a ~ on sth** decidir algo por votación, someter algo a votación (*more frm*); **a ~ of confidence** un voto de confianza; **a ~ of no confidence** un voto de censura; **to put sth to the ~** someter algo a votación; **a ~ of thanks** un voto de gracias

Ⓑ VT 1 (= *cast one's vote for*) votar; **to ~ Labour** votar por or a los laboristas

2 (= *elect*) elegir (por votación)

3 (*) (= *suggest*) **I ~ we turn back*** sugiero or propongo que regresemos

Ⓒ VI votar; **the country ~s in three weeks** el país acudirá a las urnas dentro de tres semanas; **to ~ to do sth** votar por hacer algo; **to ~ against sth** votar en contra de algo; **to ~ in favour of sth** votar a favor de algo; **to ~ for sb** votar por or a algn; **to ~ on sth** someter algo a votación

Ⓓ CPD ➤ **vote loser*** política f perdedora de votos ➤ **vote winner*** política f ganadora de votos

➤ **vote in** VT + ADV [+ *candidate, party*] elegir (por votación); [+ *law*] aprobar (por votación)
➤ **vote out** VT + ADV [+ *person, party*] no reelegir
➤ **vote through** VT + ADV [+ *bill, motion*] aprobar

voter ['vəʊtəʳ] N votante *mf*; (*in election*) elector(a) *m/f*

voting ['vəʊtɪŋ] N votación *f* ➤ **voting booth** cabina *f* electoral ➤ **voting paper**, **voting slip** papeleta *f* de votación ➤ **voting right** derecho *m* a voto ➤ **voting share** acción *f* con derecho a voto

votive ['vəʊtɪv] ADJ votivo ➤ **votive offering** ofrenda *f* votiva, exvoto *m*

vouch [vaʊtʃ] VI **to ~ for sth** responder de algo, garantizar algo; **to ~ for sb** responder por *or* salir como fiador de algn

voucher ['vaʊtʃəʳ] N vale *m*; (*Comm*) bono *m*

vow [vaʊ] **Ⓐ** N (*Rel*) voto *m*; (= *promise*) promesa *f*, compromiso *m*; **to make a ~ to do sth** jurar hacer algo, comprometerse a hacer algo; **to break one's ~** faltar a un compromiso **Ⓑ** VT [+ *obedience, allegiance*] jurar, prometer; **to ~ to do sth** jurar hacer algo, comprometerse a hacer algo; **to ~ that ...** jurar *or* prometer que ...

vowel [vaʊəl] N vocal *f* ➤ **vowel sound** sonido *m* vocálico

vox pop* ['vɒks'pɒp] N (*Brit*) voz *f* de la calle

voyage ['vɔɪɪdʒ] N viaje *m* (*por mar, por el espacio*); (= *crossing*) travesía *f*

voyager ['vɔɪədʒəʳ] N (*liter*) viajero/a *m/f* (*por mar*)

voyeur [vwɑː'jɜːʳ] N voyeur *mf*, voyer *mf*, mirón/ona *m/f*

voyeurism [vwɑː'jɜːrɪzəm] N voyeurismo *m*, voyerismo *m*, mironismo *m*

voyeuristic [vwɑːjə'rɪstɪk] ADJ voyeur

V.P. N ABBR (= **Vice-President**) V.P. *mf*

VR N ABBR (= **virtual reality**) realidad *f* virtual

vs ABBR (= **versus**) vs

V-sign ['viːsaɪn] N V *f* de la victoria; (*obscene*) (*in Brit*): **to give sb the ~** ≈ hacer un corte de mangas a algn

VSO N ABBR (*Brit*) = **Voluntary Service Overseas**

VT, Vt. ABBR (*US*) = **Vermont**

vulgar ['vʌlɡəʳ] ADJ **1** (= *unrefined*) [*person, taste*] ordinario, vulgar **2** (= *tasteless*) de mal gusto, vulgar **3** (= *indecent*) [*joke*] verde, colorado (*LAm*); [*person, comedian*] grosero, ordinario **4** [*Latin*] vulgar

vulgarity [vʌl'ɡærɪtɪ] N **1** (= *lack of refinement*) ordinariez *f*, vulgaridad *f* **2** (= *tastelessness*) mal gusto *m*, vulgaridad *f* **3** (= *indecency*) grosería *f*, obscenidad *f*

vulnerability [ˌvʌlnərə'bɪlɪtɪ] N vulnerabilidad *f*

vulnerable ['vʌlnərəbl] ADJ vulnerable

vulture ['vʌltʃəʳ] N (= *bird*) buitre *m*, zopilote *m* (*CAm, Mex*), aura *f* (*Carib*), carancho *m* (*SC*), gallinazo *m* (*Col, And*), urubú *m* (*Per, Uruguay*), zamuro *m* (*Ven*); **they're like a lot of ~s** son una panda de buitres

vulva ['vʌlvə] N vulva *f*

vying ['vaɪɪŋ] *see* **vie**

Ww

W¹, w [ˈdʌbljʊ] N (= *letter*) W, w f; **W for William** W de Washington

W² ABBR **1** (= **west**) O **2** (= **watt(s)**) W

WA ABBR (*US*) = **Washington**

wacky* [ˈwækɪ] ADJ (*compar* **wackier**; *superl* **wackiest**) [*person*] chiflado*; [*idea*] disparatado

wad [wɒd] N [*of cotton wool*] bolita f; [*of papers*] fajo m, lío m; [*of banknotes*] fajo m; **~s of money** un dineral

wadding [ˈwɒdɪŋ] N (*for packing*) relleno m; (*for quilting*) entretela f, forro m; (*Med*) algodón m hidrófilo

waddle [ˈwɒdl] 🅐 N andares mpl de pato 🅑 VI andar como un pato; **to ~ out** salir andando como un pato

wade [weɪd] 🅐 VI **1** (= *paddle*) **to ~ across a river** vadear un río; **to ~ ashore** llegar a tierra vadeando; **to ~ through the water/mud** caminar por el agua/el barro; **to ~ through a book** leer(se) un libro con dificultad (*por lo aburrido/lo difícil que es*) **2** **to ~ into sb** (*physically*) abalanzarse sobre algn; (*fig*) emprenderla con algn, arremeter contra algn 🅑 VT [+ *river*] vadear

wader [ˈweɪdəʳ] N **1** (= *bird*) ave f zancuda

> Use **el/un** not **la/una** before feminine nouns beginning with stressed **a** or **ha** like **ave**.

2 waders (= *boots*) botas fpl altas de goma

wading pool [ˈweɪdɪŋˌpuːl] N (*US*) piscina f para niños

wafer [ˈweɪfəʳ] N **1** (= *biscuit*) galleta f; (*Rel*) hostia f; (*eaten with ice cream*) barquillo m **2** (*Comput*) oblea f

wafer-thin [ˈweɪfəˈθɪn] ADJ finísimo

waffle [ˈwɒfl] N **1** (*Culin*) gofre m **2** (*Brit**) (= *talk*) palabrería f; (*in essay*) paja f 🅑 VI (*Brit**) (*also* **~ on**) parlotear*, enrollarse (*Sp**); (*in essay*) poner mucha paja

waft [wɑːft] 🅐 N soplo m, ráfaga f 🅑 VT llevar por el aire 🅒 VI flotar, moverse

wag [wæg] 🅐 N [*of tail*] sacudida f, meneo m; [*of finger*] movimiento m 🅑 VT [+ *tail*] sacudir, menear; **the dog ~ged its tail** el perro sacudió *or* meneó la cola; **he ~ged a finger at me** me apuntó agitando el dedo 🅒 VI [*tail*] sacudirse, menearse; **tongues were ~ging about their relationship** las malas lenguas hablaban de sus relaciones

wage [weɪdʒ] 🅐 N **1** (= *rate per week, year, etc*) sueldo m, salario m (*more frm*); **a basic ~ of £55 a week** un sueldo *or* (*more frm*) salario base de 55 libras semanales; **minimum ~** salario mínimo
2 wages (= *money received*) paga fsing, sueldo msing 🅑 VT [+ *war*] hacer; [+ *campaign*] llevar a cabo, hacer; **to ~ war against** *or* **on inflation** luchar contra la inflación, hacer la guerra a la inflación
🅒 CPD ➤ **wage claim** (*Brit*) reivindicación f salarial ➤ **wage earner** asalariado/a m/f ➤ **wage freeze** congelación f salarial ➤ **wage increase** aumento m salarial ➤ **wage packet** (*esp Brit*) (= *envelope with pay*) sobre m de la paga; (*fig*) paga f ➤ **wage restraint** moderación f salarial ➤ **wage rise** aumento m salarial ➤ **wages bill** (*Brit*) gastos mpl de nómina ➤ **wage scale** escala f salarial ➤ **wages clerk** (*Brit*) habilitado/a m/f ➤ **wage settlement** acuerdo m salarial ➤ **wage slip** nómina f, hoja f salarial ➤ **wages snatch** robo m de nóminas ➤ **wage worker** (*US*) asalariado/a m/f

waged [weɪdʒd] ADJ [*person*] asalariado; [*employment*] remunerado

wager [ˈweɪdʒəʳ] 🅐 N apuesta f (**on** a) 🅑 VT [+ *sum of money*] apostar

waggle [ˈwægl] VT [+ *finger*] agitar; [+ *tail*] sacudir, menear

waggon [ˈwægən] N (*Brit*) = **wagon**

wagon [ˈwægən] N **1** (*horse-drawn*) carro m; (= *truck*) camión m; (*Brit Rail*) vagón m; (*US*) (*also* **station ~**) furgoneta f, camioneta f; (*US*) (= *police van*) furgón m policial; ◆ IDIOM **to be on the ~*** no beber; **he decided to**

go on the ~ se resolvió a no beber **2** (*also* **tea ~**) carrito m

waif [weɪf] N (= *child*) niño/a m/f abandonado/a, niño/a m/f desamparado/a; (= *animal*) animal m abandonado; **~s and strays** (= *children*) niños mpl abandonados *or* desamparados; (= *animals*) animales mpl abandonados

wail [weɪl] 🅐 N **1** (= *moan*) lamento m, gemido m **2** [*of siren, wind*] gemido m 🅑 VI **1** (= *moan*) lamentarse, gemir; [*child*] llorar **2** [*siren, wind, gunfire*] gemir

wailing [ˈweɪlɪŋ] N **1** (= *moaning*) lamentaciones fpl, gemidos mpl; [*of child*] llanto m **2** [*of siren, wind*] gemido m

waist [weɪst] N [*of person*] cintura f, talle m; [*of skirt*] talle m

waistband [ˈweɪstbænd] N pretina f, cinturilla f

waistcoat [ˈweɪskəʊt] N (*Brit*) chaleco m

waist-deep [ˈweɪstˈdiːp] ADJ hasta la cintura

-waisted [ˈweɪstɪd] ADJ (*ending in compounds*) **slim-waisted** de cintura delgada, de talle delgado; **high-/low-waisted** de talle alto/bajo

waistline [ˈweɪstlaɪn] N [*of person*] cintura f, talle m; [*of dress*] talle m

wait [weɪt] 🅐 VI **1** (= *hold on*) esperar; **just ~ a moment while I fetch you a chair** espere un momento que voy a traerle una silla; **"repairs while you wait"** "reparaciones en el acto"; **reporters were ~ing to interview her** los reporteros estaban esperando para entrevistarla; **I can't ~ to see his face** estoy deseando ver su cara; **to ~ for sth/sb** esperar algo/a algn; **they ~ed for him to finish** esperaron (a) que terminara; **to keep sb ~ing** hacer esperar a algn; **~ a minute!** ¡un momento!, ¡momentito! (*esp LAm*), ¡aguarde! (*LAm*); **~ and see!** ¡espera, ya verás!; **~ till you're asked** espera a que te inviten; **just you ~ till your father finds out!** ¡ya verás cuando se entere tu padre!
2 (*Brit*) **to ~ at table** servir a la mesa, atender la mesa 🅑 VT **1** (= *await*) **to ~ one's chance** esperar la oportunidad; **~ your turn!** ¡espere a que llegue su turno!
2 (*US*) **to ~ table** servir a la mesa, atender la mesa 🅒 N espera f; **it was a long ~** fue una larga espera; **to lie in ~ (for sb)** andar *or* estar al acecho (de algn)
➤ **wait around, wait about** VI + ADV quedarse esperando; **to ~ around for sb** quedarse esperando a algn
➤ **wait behind** VI + ADV esperarse; **to ~ behind for sb** quedarse para esperar a algn
➤ **wait in** VI + ADV (*esp Brit*) quedarse en casa (esperando); **to ~ in for sb** quedarse en casa esperando a algn
➤ **wait on** VI + PREP servir, atender (*esp LAm*); ◆ IDIOM **to ~ on sb hand and foot** atender el menor deseo de algn
➤ **wait up** VI + ADV **1** (= *stay up*) **to ~ up for sb** quedarse despierto esperando a algn **2** (*US**) (= *wait*) esperar

waiter [ˈweɪtəʳ] N camarero m, mesero m (*Mex*), garzón m (*SC*), mesonero m (*Ven*)

waiting [ˈweɪtɪŋ] N espera f; **"no waiting"** "prohibido aparcar", "prohibido estacionarse" (*esp LAm*) ➤ **waiting game**: **to play a ~ game** esperar la ocasión apropiada ➤ **waiting list** lista f de espera; **to be on a ~ list** estar en lista de espera ➤ **waiting room** sala f de espera

waitress [ˈweɪtrɪs] N camarera f, mesera f (*Mex*), mesonera f (*Ven*)

waitressing [ˈweɪtrɪsɪŋ] N **to do ~** trabajar de camarera

waive [weɪv] VT [+ *right, claim, fee*] renunciar a; [+ *regulation*] no aplicar; [+ *condition, restriction*] no exigir

waiver [ˈweɪvəʳ] N [*of right, claim, fee*] renuncia f; (*from payment*) exoneración f; [*of regulation, condition, restriction*] exención f

wake¹ [weɪk] N [*of ship*] estela f; **the tornado brought a trail of destruction in its ~** el tornado dejó una estela de destrucción a su paso; **in the ~ of the storm/riots** tras la tormenta/los disturbios

wake² [weɪk] N (*over corpse*) velatorio m, vela f, velorio m (*esp LAm*)

wake³ [weɪk] (*vb*: *pt* **woke** *or* (*US*) **~d**; *pp* **woken** *or* (*US*) **~d**)

Ⓐ VI (*also* ~ **up**) despertar, despertarse (**from** de) **Ⓑ** VT (*also* ~ **up**) despertar

wakeful ['weɪkfʊl] ADJ **1** (= *unable to sleep*) desvelado **2** (= *sleepless*) **to have a** ~ **night** pasar la noche en vela

waken ['weɪkən] (*liter*) **Ⓐ** VT despertar **Ⓑ** VI despertar, despertarse

wake-up call ['weɪkʌp,kɔːl] N **ask the hotel staff for a** ~ pídele al personal del hotel que te despierten

wakey-wakey ['weɪkɪ'weɪkɪ] EXCL ¡despierta!

waking ['weɪkɪŋ] ADJ **one's** ~ **hours** las horas en que se está despierto

Wales [weɪlz] N (el país de) Gales *m*

walk [wɔːk] **Ⓐ** N **1** (= *stroll, ramble*) paseo *m*; (= *hike*) caminata *f*, excursión *f* a pie; **it's only a ten-minute** ~ **from here** está a sólo diez minutos de aquí a pie; **to go for** or **take a** ~ ir de paseo
2 (= *pace*) paso *m*; **at a quick** ~ a (un) paso rápido
3 (= *gait*) modo *m* de andar
4 ~ **of life: people from all ~s of life** gente de todas las profesiones y condiciones sociales
Ⓑ VT **1** [+ *distance*] andar, caminar (*esp LAm*); **to** ~ **the streets** andar por las calles; (*aimlessly*) vagar por las calles; (= *be homeless*) no tener hogar, estar sin techo; [*prostitute*] hacer la calle or la carrera; **I had to** ~ **it** tuve que ir a pie or ir andando
2 (= *lead*) [+ *dog*] pasear, sacar a pasear; [+ *horse*] llevar al paso; **I'll** ~ **you to the station** te acompaño a la estación;
✦ IDIOM **to** ~ **sb off his feet** dejar a algn rendido de tanto caminar
Ⓒ VI **1** andar, caminar (*esp LAm*); (*as opposed to riding etc*) ir a pie, ir andando, ir caminando (*esp LAm*); (= *stroll*) pasear; (*Sport*) marchar; **you can** ~ **there in five minutes** está a cinco minutos andando de aquí; **are you ~ing or going by bus?** ¿vas a ir a pie o en autobús?; **we had to** ~ tuvimos que ir a pie or ir andando; **"walk"** (*US*) (*on traffic signal*) "cruzar"; **"don't walk"** (*US*) (*on traffic signal*) "no cruzar"; **to** ~ **in one's sleep** ser sonámbulo, andar dormido; **to** ~ **downstairs/upstairs** bajar/subir la escalera; **to** ~ **home** ir or volver andando a casa; **to** ~ **across sth** cruzar algo; **to** ~ **up and down** pasearse (de acá para allá)
2 (*) (= *disappear*) volar*; **my camera's ~ed** mi cámara ha volado or desaparecido
➤ walk around, walk about VI + ADV pasearse (de acá para allá)
➤ walk away VI + ADV irse, marcharse; **to** ~ **away unhurt** salir ileso; **to** ~ **away from a problem** huir de un problema; **to** ~ **away with** (= *take, win*) llevarse
➤ walk back VI + ADV volver a pie, regresar andando
➤ walk in VI + ADV entrar; **to** ~ **in on sb** interrumpir a algn
➤ walk into VI + PREP **1** (= *enter*) [+ *room*] entrar en **2** (= *fall into*) [+ *trap*] caer en **3** (= *collide with*) chocar con, dar con, dar contra **4** (*) (= *get easily*) [+ *job*] conseguir fácilmente
➤ walk off VI + ADV irse, marcharse **Ⓑ** VT + ADV **we ~ed off our lunch** dimos un paseo para bajar la comida
➤ walk off with VI + PREP (= *take, win*) llevarse
➤ walk out VI + ADV salir; (*on strike*) abandonar el trabajo
➤ walk out on VI + PREP [+ *spouse, family*] abandonar, dejar; [+ *business partner*] dejar
➤ walk over VI + PREP **to** ~ **all over sb** (= *dominate*) tratar a algn a patadas*, atropellar a algn; (= *defeat*) dar una paliza a algn*
➤ walk up VI + ADV (= *ascend*) subir (a pie); (= *approach*) acercarse (**to** a)

walkabout ['wɔːkəbaʊt] N (*esp Brit*) baño *m* de multitudes; **to go on a** ~ (*Brit*) [*monarch, politician*] darse un baño de multitudes, pasearse entre el público

walkaway ['wɔːkəweɪ] N (*US*) victoria *f* fácil, paseo *m*, pan *m* comido*

walker ['wɔːkə'] N paseante *mf*, transeúnte *mf*; (= *pedestrian*) peatón *m*; (= *hiker*) excursionista *mf*

walkie-talkie ['wɔːkɪ'tɔːkɪ] N transmisor-receptor *m* portátil, walkie-talkie *m*

walk-in ['wɔːkɪn] CPD **➤ walk-in clinic** *clínica donde no hay que pedir hora para ver al médico* **➤ walk-in closet** (*US*) alacena *f* ropera

walking ['wɔːkɪŋ] **Ⓐ** N (= *act*) andar *m*, caminar *m*; (*as*

pastime) excursionismo *m*; (= *hill walking*) senderismo *m*; (*Sport*) marcha *f* (atlética)
Ⓑ ADJ ambulante; **he's a** ~ **encyclopaedia** es una enciclopedia ambulante
Ⓒ CPD **➤ walking distance: it's within** ~ **distance** se puede ir andando **➤ walking frame** andador *m* **➤ walking pace: at a** ~ **pace** a paso de peatón, a paso normal **➤ walking papers** (*US*) pasaporte* *msing*, aviso *msing* de despido **➤ walking shoes** zapatos *mpl* para andar or (*esp LAm*) caminar **➤ walking stick** bastón *m*

Walkman® ['wɔːkmən] N (*pl* ~**s** ['wɔːkmənz]) Walkman® *m*

walk-on ['wɔːkɒn] ADJ ~ **part** (*Theat*) papel *m* de figurante or de comparsa; (*Cine*) papel *m* de extra

walkout ['wɔːkaʊt] N (*from conference*) retirada *f*, abandono *m* (de la sala); (= *strike*) abandono *m* del trabajo

walkover ['wɔːk,əʊvə'] N paseo *m*, pan *m* comido*

walk-up ['wɔːkʌp] N (*US*) (= *building*) edificio *m* sin ascensor; (= *flat*) piso *m* or (*LAm*) departamento *m* en un edificio sin ascensor

walkway ['wɔːkweɪ] N (*raised*) pasarela *f*; (= *passageway*) pasaje *m* (entre edificios)

wall [wɔːl] **Ⓐ** N (*interior*) pared *f*; (*outside*) muro *m*; [*of city*] muralla *f*; (= *garden wall*) tapia *f*; **✦** IDIOMS **to come up against a brick** ~ tener por delante una barrera infranqueable; **it's like talking to a brick** ~ es como hablarle a la pared; **to do sth off the** ~ (*esp US*) hacer algo espontáneamente or de improviso; **it drives me up the ~*** me saca de quicio; **to go up the ~*** ponerse furioso; **to go to the** ~ ir a la bancarrota, quebrar
Ⓑ CPD [*socket, light, clock*] de pared **➤ wall bars** espalderas *fpl* **➤ wall hanging** tapiz *m* **➤ wall socket** enchufe *m*, toma *f* de corriente, tomacorriente *m* (*LAm*)
➤ wall in VT + ADV [+ *area of land*] cerrar con muro; [+ *garden*] tapiar, cercar con tapia
➤ wall up VT + ADV [+ *person*] emparedar; [+ *opening, entrance*] tapiar, cerrar con muro, tabicar; [+ *window*] condenar

wallaby ['wɒləbɪ] N ualabí *m*

walled [wɔːld] ADJ [*city*] amurallado; [*garden*] tapiado

wallet ['wɒlɪt] N cartera *f*, billetera *f* (*esp LAm*)

wallflower ['wɔːl,flaʊə'] N alhelí *m*; **✦** IDIOM **to be a** ~ comer pavo, ser la fea del baile

wallop* ['wɒləp] **Ⓐ** N golpe *m* fuerte, golpazo* *m*; **to give sb a** ~ pegar fuerte a algn **Ⓑ** VT (*esp Brit*) (= *strike*) golpear fuertemente; (= *punish*) dar una paliza a, zurrar*

walloping* ['wɒləpɪŋ] N **to give sb a** ~ dar una paliza a algn, zurrar a algn*

wallow ['wɒləʊ] VI (*in water, mud*) revolcarse (**in** en); **to** ~ **in self-pity** regodearse en la autocompasión, disfrutar autocompadeciéndose

wallpaper ['wɔːl,peɪpə'] **Ⓐ** N (*for walls*) papel *m* pintado; (*Comput*) fondo *m* de escritorio **Ⓑ** VT empapelar

wall-to-wall ['wɔːltə'wɔːl] ADJ ~ **carpeting** moqueta *f*, alfombra *f* de pared a pared

wally* ['wɒlɪ] N (*Brit*) memo/a* *m/f*

walnut ['wɔːlnʌt] **Ⓐ** N (= *nut*) nuez *f*; (= *tree, wood*) nogal *m* **Ⓑ** ADJ (= *wooden*) de nogal

walrus ['wɔːlrəs] N morsa *f*

waltz [wɔːls] **Ⓐ** N vals *m* **Ⓑ** VI bailar el vals; **to** ~ **in/out*** entrar/salir tan fresco*

WAN [wæn] N ABBR (*Comput*) = **wide area network**

wan [wɒn] ADJ [*complexion, face*] pálido; [*light*] tenue, pálido; [*smile*] lánguido

wand [wɒnd] N (= *magic wand*) varita *f* mágica

wander ['wɒndə'] **Ⓐ** N paseo *m*; **to go for a** ~ pasearse, dar un paseo, dar una vuelta
Ⓑ VI **1** (*for pleasure*) pasear; (*aimlessly*) deambular, vagar, errar; **we spent the morning ~ing** pasamos la mañana paseando por el casco antiguo
2 (= *stray*) **to** ~ **from the path** desviarse or alejarse del camino; **to** ~ **from the point** salirse del tema; **to let one's mind** ~ dejar vagar la imaginación; **his eyes ~ed round the room** paseó la mirada por la habitación; **his attention ~ed**

for a moment se distrajo *or* despistó un momento **C** VT [+ *streets, hills*] recorrer, vagar por ➤ **wander around, wander about** VI + ADV deambular ➤ **wander off** VI + ADV **the children ~ed off into the woods** los niños se alejaron sin rumbo *or* entraron en el bosque; **don't go ~ing off** no te alejes demasiado

wanderer ['wɒndərəʳ] N (= *traveller*) viajero/a *m/f*; (= *nomad*) nómada *mf*; **the ~ returns!** (*hum*) ¡ha vuelto el viajero!

wandering ['wɒndərɪŋ] ADJ [*person*] errante; [*path, river*] sinuoso; [*eyes, mind*] distraído

wanderings ['wɒndərɪŋz] NPL (= *travels*) viajes *mpl*, andanzas *fpl*; **let me know if you see one on your ~** avísame si encuentras uno por ahí

wanderlust ['wɒndəlʌst] N pasión *f* de viajar

wane [weɪn] **A** VI [*moon*] menguar; [*strength*] decaer; [*popularity, enthusiasm, interest*] disminuir **B** N **to be on the ~** [*moon*] estar menguando; [*strength*] estar decayendo; [*popularity, interest*] estar disminuyendo

wangle* ['wæŋgl] VT [+ *job, ticket*] agenciarse; **he ~d his way in** se las arregló para entrar

waning ['weɪnɪŋ] ADJ [*moon*] menguante; [*popularity, power, enthusiasm, interest*] decreciente

wank*** [wæŋk] (*Brit*) **A** N **to have a ~** hacerse una paja*** **B** VI hacerse una paja***

wanker*** ['wæŋkəʳ] N (*Brit*) mamón/ona*** *m/f*, gilipollas*** *mf inv* (*Sp*)

wanly ['wɒnlɪ] ADV [*look, smile, say*] lánguidamente

wanna* ['wɒnə] = **want to**

want [wɒnt] **A** VT **1** (= *desire, wish for*) querer; **what do you ~ for your birthday?** ¿qué quieres por tu cumpleaños?; **don't ~ you interfering!** ¡no quiero que te entrometas!; **I ~ my son alive** quiero a mi hijo vivo; **to ~ sb** (*sexually*) desear a algn; **you ~ her back, don't you?** quieres que vuelva, ¿no?; **what I ~ from a computer is ...** lo que quiero de un ordenador es ...; **I ~ an explanation from you** quiero que me des una explicación; **I know when I'm not ~ed** sé muy bien cuando sobro *or* estoy de más; ✦ IDIOM **you've got him where you ~ him** lo tienes donde tú quieres **2** (*with infinitive*) **to ~ to do sth** querer hacer algo; **I don't ~ to** no quiero; **to ~ sb to do sth** querer que algn haga algo **3** (= *ask for*) querer, pedir; **she ~s £500 for the car** quiere *or* pide 500 libras por el coche; **how much do you ~ for it?** ¿cuánto quiere *or* pide? **4** (= *seek*) [*police*] buscar; **he is ~ed for robbery** se le busca por robo; **you're ~ed in the kitchen** te buscan en la cocina; **you're ~ed on the phone** te llaman al teléfono; **"wanted: general maid"** "se necesita asistenta" **5** (= *need*) **this car ~s cleaning** (*esp Brit*) a este coche le hace falta una limpieza, a este coche hay que limpiarlo; **you ~ to be more careful when you're driving** tienes que tener más cuidado al conducir; **what do you ~ with a house that size?** ¿para qué quieres una casa tan grande? **B** VI **1** (= *wish*) querer; **you're welcome to stay if you ~** te puedes quedar si quieres **2** (= *lack*) **they ~ for nothing** no les falta de nada **C** N **1** (= *lack*) falta *f*; **for ~ of a better word** a falta de una palabra más apropiada; **it was not for ~ of trying** no fue por falta de intentos **2** (= *need*) necesidad *f*; **my ~s are few** necesito poco **3** (= *poverty*) necesidad *f*, penuria *f* **D** CPD ➤ **want ad*** (*US*) anuncio *m* clasificado

wanting ['wɒntɪŋ] ADJ **all the applicants proved ~ in some respect** todos los aspirantes resultaron deficientes en algún aspecto; **he looked at his life and found it ~** examinó su vida y se dio cuenta de que faltaba algo; **to be ~ in sth** carecer de algo

wanton ['wɒntən] ADJ (= *wilful*) [*destruction*] sin sentido, gratuito; [*violence*] gratuito

WAP [wæp] N ABBR (*Comput*) (= **wireless application protocol**) WAP *f* ➤ **WAP phone** teléfono *m* WAP

war [wɔːʳ] **A** N guerra *f*; (*fig*) lucha *f*; **the ~ against inflation** la lucha contra la inflación; **to be at ~ (with)** estar en guerra (con); **the period between the ~s** el período de entreguerras; **to declare ~ (on)** declarar la guerra (a); **to go**

to ~ (with sb) (over sth) entrar en guerra (con algn) (por algo); **to wage ~ with sb** hacer la guerra a algn; ✦ IDIOM **you've been in the ~s!** (*hum*) (*to child*) ¡parece que vienes de la guerra! **B** CPD de guerra ➤ **war correspondent** corresponsal *mf* de guerra ➤ **war crime** crimen *m* de guerra ➤ **war criminal** criminal *mf* de guerra ➤ **war cry** grito *m* de guerra ➤ **war dance** danza *f* guerrera ➤ **war effort** esfuerzo *m* bélico ➤ **war game** (*Mil*) simulacro *m* de guerra; (= *game*) juego *m* de guerra ➤ **war hero** héroe *m* de guerra ➤ **war memorial** monumento *m* a los caídos ➤ **war paint** pintura *f* de guerra; (*hum*) (= *make-up*) maquillaje *m* ➤ **war widow** viuda *f* de guerra ➤ **war zone** zona *f* de guerra

warble ['wɔːbl] **A** N [*of bird*] trino *m*, gorjeo *m* **B** VT cantar trinando, cantar gorjeando **C** VI gorjear, trinar

ward [wɔːd] N **1** (*in hospital*) sala *f*, pabellón *m* **2** (*Pol*) distrito *m* electoral **3** (*Jur*) (= *person*) pupilo/a *m/f*; **to make sb a ~ of court** poner a algn bajo la protección *or* el amparo del tribunal ➤ **ward off** VT + ADV [+ *attack*] rechazar; [+ *blow*] parar, desviar; [+ *infection*] protegerse de; [+ *danger*] protegerse contra, conjurar; [+ *evil spirits*] conjurar

warden ['wɔːdn] N (*Univ*) rector(a) *m/f*; (*Aut*) (*also* **traffic ~**) controlador(a) *m/f* de estacionamiento; (*also* **church ~**) coadjutor(a) *m/f*; [*of prison*] (*Brit*) (= *guard*) celador(a) *m/f*; (*US*) (= *governor*) director(a) *m/f*

warder ['wɔːdəʳ] N (*Brit*) celador(a) *m/f*

wardrobe ['wɔːdrəʊb] N **1** (= *cupboard*) guardarropa *m*, armario *m* (ropero), ropero *m* (*LAm*) **2** (= *clothes*) vestuario *m*

wardroom ['wɔːdrʊm] N (*Naut*) cámara *f* de oficiales

warehouse ['wɛəhaʊs] N almacén *m*, depósito *m*; **at ~ prices** a precios de mayorista

wares [wɛəz] NPL mercancías *fpl*

warfare ['wɔːfɛəʳ] N (= *fighting*) guerra *f*; (= *techniques*) artes *mpl* militares

warfarin ['wɔːfərɪn] N warfarina *f*

warhead ['wɔːhed] N [*of torpedo*] cabeza *f* explosiva; [*of rocket*] cabeza *f* de guerra; **nuclear ~** cabeza *f* nuclear

warhorse ['wɔːhɔːs] N (= *soldier*) veterano *m*

warily ['wɛərɪlɪ] ADV con cautela, cautelosamente

wariness ['wɛərɪnɪs] N cautela *f*, recelo *m*

warlike ['wɔːlaɪk] ADJ [*people*] guerrero, belicoso

warlock ['wɔːlɒk] N brujo *m*, hechicero *m*

warlord ['wɔːlɔːd] N caudillo *m*

warm [wɔːm] **A** ADJ (*compar* **~er**; *superl* **~est**) **1** (= *hot*) [*bath, hands, feet*] caliente; [*water*] templado, tibio; [*air*] templado, cálido; [*room, weather, colour*] cálido; **to be ~** [*person*] tener calor; **it's very ~ today** hace calor hoy; **to get ~** [*person*] entrar en calor; [*object, surface*] calentarse; **it's getting ~er** [*weather*] ya empieza a hacer más calor; **to keep (o.s.) ~** mantenerse abrigado; **wear thick gloves to keep your hands ~** usa guantes gruesos para mantener las manos calientes; **keep the sauce ~** mantén la salsa caliente; ✦ IDIOM **to be as ~ as toast** estar bien calentito* **2** (= *thick*) [*clothes*] de abrigo, abrigado (*SC*) **3** (= *kindly*) [*person, smile, face*] simpático, afable, cálido; **to give sb a ~ welcome** dar a algn una cordial *or* calurosa bienvenida; **with ~est wishes** (*in letter*) con mis/nuestros mejores deseos **B** VT [+ *food, room, engine*] calentar; **I ~ed my hands on the radiator** me calenté las manos en el radiador; **to ~ o.s.** calentarse **C** VI [*room*] calentarse; **I began to ~ to him** empecé a encontrarle agradable; **she was beginning to ~ to the idea** estaba empezando a gustarle la idea; **he began to ~ to his subject** *or* **theme** empezó a entusiasmarse con su tema **D** N **come into the ~!** ¡entra aquí que hace calorcito!* **E** ADV **to wrap up ~*** abrigarse bien ➤ **warm up A** VI + ADV [*person*] entrar en calor; [*room, engine, athlete, singer*] calentarse; [*party, game*] animarse **B** VT + ADV [+ *food, engine*] calentar; [+ *party, audience*] animar

warm-blooded ['wɔːm'blʌdɪd] ADJ de sangre caliente

warm-hearted ['wɔːm'hɑːtɪd] ADJ cariñoso, afectuoso

warming ['wɔːmɪŋ] ADJ [*drink*] que hace entrar en calor

warmly ['wɔːmlɪ] ADV **1** (= *cosily*) **to be ~ dressed** ir *or* estar bien abrigado; **to wrap up ~** abrigarse bien **2** [*greet, smile*] calurosamente, afectuosamente; [*say, speak*] cariñosamente; [*thank*] cordialmente; [*congratulate*] efusivamente; [*welcome*] calurosamente; [*recommend*] sin reservas

warmonger ['wɔːˌmʌŋgəʳ] N belicista *mf*

warmongering ['wɔːˌmʌŋgərɪŋ] N belicismo *m*

warmth [wɔːmθ] N **1** [*of sun, fire*] calor *m*; **a blanket will provide extra ~** una manta proporcionará más abrigo **2** [*of greeting, welcome*] cordialidad *f*; [*of smile*] simpatía *f*, afabilidad *f*

warm-up ['wɔːmʌp] N (*Sport*) precalentamiento *m*, ejercicios *mpl* de calentamiento

warn [wɔːn] VT (= *put on guard, urge caution to*) advertir; (= *notify, tell*) avisar, advertir; **I did ~ you that this would happen** ya te avisé *or* advertí que esto pasaría; **you have been ~ed!** ¡ya estás avisado!, ¡quedas advertido!; **she ~ed me not to go out alone** me advirtió *or* me aconsejó que no saliera sola; **children must be ~ed about the dangers of smoking** debe advertirse a los niños de los peligros que conlleva fumar; **I've ~ed you about your behaviour before** ya te he llamado la atención por tu comportamiento antes; **to ~ sb against sth** prevenir a algn contra algo; **to ~ sb against doing sth** aconsejar a algn que no haga algo ➤ **warn off** VT + PREP **to ~ sb off doing sth** advertir a algn que no haga algo; **I was ~ed off trying to help her** me advirtieron que no intentara ayudarla

warning ['wɔːnɪŋ] 🅐 N (= *caution*) advertencia *f*; (= *advance notice*) aviso *m*, advertencia *f*; **this is a final ~** ésta es la última advertencia; **let this be a ~ to you** que te sirva de advertencia; **his employer gave him a ~ about lateness** el patrón le advirtió que no debía seguir llegando tarde; **you could have given me a bit more ~** me podrías haber avisado *or* advertido con más tiempo; **without (any) ~** sin previo aviso 🅑 ADJ [*sign, signal*] de aviso, de advertencia; [*look, label*] de advertencia 🅒 CPD ➤ **warning light** señal *f* luminosa ➤ **warning shot** disparo *m* de advertencia ➤ **warning triangle** triángulo *m* de advertencia

warp [wɔːp] 🅐 VT [+ *wood*] alabear, combar 🅑 VI [*wood*] alabearse, combarse

warpath ['wɔːpɑːθ] N ✦ IDIOM **to be on the ~*** estar dispuesto a armar un lío*

warped [wɔːpt] ADJ **1** [*wood*] alabeado, combado **2** [*mind, sense of humour*] pervertido

warplane ['wɔːpleɪn] N avión *m* de combate

warrant ['wɒrənt] 🅐 N (*also* **search ~**) orden *f* de registro; (*also* **arrest ~**) orden *f* de detención; **there is a ~ out for his arrest** se ha ordenado su detención 🅑 VT (= *justify, merit*) merecer; **her condition did not ~ calling the doctor** su condición no justificaba llamar al médico 🅒 CPD ➤ **warrant officer** (*Mil*) suboficial *mf*; (*Naut*) contramaestre *mf*

warranted ['wɒrəntɪd] ADJ (= *justified*) [*action, remark*] justificado; **that wasn't ~!** ¡ese comentario está de sobra!

warranty ['wɒrəntɪ] N (*Comm*) garantía *f*

warren ['wɒrən] N **1** (*also* **rabbit ~**) madriguera *f* (de conejos) **2** (= *place*) laberinto *m*; (= *house*) conejera *f*

warring ['wɔːrɪŋ] ADJ [*nations, armies*] en guerra; [*factions, parties, families*] enfrentados

warrior ['wɒrɪəʳ] N guerrero/a *m/f*

Warsaw ['wɔːsɔː] N Varsovia *f*

warship ['wɔːʃɪp] N buque *m* or barco *m* de guerra

wart [wɔːt] N (*Med*) verruga *f*

warthog ['wɔːthɒg] N jabalí *m* verrugoso, facochero *m*

wartime ['wɔːtaɪm] N **in ~** en tiempos de guerra

war-torn ['wɔːtɔːn] ADJ destrozado por la guerra, devastado por la guerra

war-weary ['wɔːwɪərɪ] ADJ cansado de la guerra

wary ['wɛərɪ] ADJ (*compar* **warier**; *superl* **wariest**) [*person*] receloso; [*manner*] cauteloso, precavido; **to be ~ of sth/sb**

desconfiar de algo/algn, no fiarse de algo/algn

was [wɒz, wəz] PT *of* **be**

wash [wɒʃ] 🅐 N **1** (= *act of washing*) **to give sth a ~** lavar algo; **to give one's face a ~** lavarse la cara; **to have a ~** lavarse **2** (*in washing machine*) lavado *m* **3** (= *laundry*) **your jeans are in the ~** (= *being washed*) tus vaqueros se están lavando; (= *with dirty clothes*) tus vaqueros están con la ropa sucia; ✦ IDIOM **it'll all come out in the ~** al final, todo se arreglará **4** [*of ship, plane*] estela *f* 🅑 VT **1** (= *clean*) [+ *clothes, car*] lavar; [+ *floor*] fregar; **to ~ the dishes** fregar (los platos), lavar los platos; **to get ~ed** lavarse; **to ~ one's hands** lavarse las manos; ✦ IDIOMS **to ~ one's hands of sth** lavarse las manos de algo, desentenderse de algo; **to ~ one's hands of sb** despreocuparse de algn **2** (= *sweep*) arrastrar; **the sea ~ed it ashore** el mar lo arrastró hasta la playa; **he was ~ed overboard** cayó del barco arrastrado por las olas 🅒 VI **1** (= *have a wash*) lavarse **2** (= *be washable*) **a fabric that ~es well** una tela que se lava bien; ✦ IDIOM **that excuse won't ~!** (*Brit**) ¡esa excusa no cuela!* ➤ **wash away** VT + ADV [+ *bridge, house, vehicle*] llevarse por delante, arrastrar; [+ *dirt*] quitar (lavando) ➤ **wash down** VT + ADV **1** (= *clean*) [+ *walls, car*] lavar **2 a sandwich ~ed down with a bottle of beer** un bocadillo acompañado con una botella de cerveza ➤ **wash off** 🅐 VT + ADV [+ *stain, dirt*] quitar (lavando) 🅑 VI + ADV (= *disappear*) quitarse, limpiarse; **it ~es off easily** se quita *or* se limpia fácilmente ➤ **wash out** 🅐 VT + ADV **1** [+ *stain*] quitar (lavando); [+ *container*] lavar; [+ *paintbrush*] lavar, enjuagar **2** (*Sport*) **the game was ~ed out** el partido fue cancelado debido a la lluvia **3 to feel ~ed out** sentirse rendido *or* agotado; **to look ~ed out** tener aspecto de estar rendido *or* agotado 🅑 VI + ADV **1** (= *disappear*) [*stain, mark*] quitarse, limpiarse **2** (= *fade*) [*dye, colour*] descolorarse, desteñirse ➤ **wash up** 🅐 VI + ADV **1** (*Brit*) (= *wash dishes*) fregar (los platos), lavar los platos **2** (*US*) (= *have a wash*) lavarse 🅑 VT + ADV **1** (*Brit*) [+ *dishes*] fregar, lavar **2** (*onto beach*) arrastrar **3** (*) ✦ IDIOM **to be all ~ed up** [*person, marriage*] estar acabado

Wash. ABBR (*US*) = **Washington**

washable ['wɒʃəbl] ADJ lavable

washbasin ['wɒʃˌbeɪsn] N (= *bowl*) palangana *f*, jofaina *f*; (*esp Brit*) (= *sink*) lavabo *m*, lavamanos *m inv*, lavatorio *m* (*SC*)

washbowl ['wɒʃˌbəʊl] N (*US*) = **washbasin**

washcloth ['wɒʃklɒθ] N (*US*) paño *m* para lavarse, manopla *f*

washday ['wɒʃdeɪ] N día *m* de lavado *or* (*Sp*) de colada

washer ['wɒʃəʳ] N **1** (*Tech*) arandela *f* **2** (= *washing machine*) lavadora *f*; (= *dishwasher*) lavavajillas *m inv*

washer-dryer, washer-drier ['wɒʃəˈdraɪəʳ] N lavadora-secadora *f*

washing ['wɒʃɪŋ] 🅐 N **1** (= *act*) lavado *m*; **to do the ~** lavar la ropa, hacer la colada (*Sp*) **2** (= *clothes*) (*dirty*) ropa *f* sucia; (*hung to dry*) colada *f* 🅑 CPD ➤ **washing line** tendedero *m* ➤ **washing machine** lavadora *f* ➤ **washing powder** (*Brit*) jabón *m* en polvo, detergente *m*

Washington ['wɒʃɪŋtən] N Washington *m*

washing-up ['wɒʃɪŋ'ʌp] N (*Brit*) (= *act*) fregado *m*; (= *dishes*) platos *mpl* (para fregar); **to do the ~** fregar (los platos), lavar los platos ➤ **washing-up bowl** (*Brit*) barreño *m*, palangana *f* ➤ **washing-up liquid** (*Brit*) lavavajillas *m inv*

washout* ['wɒʃaʊt] N **it was a ~** [*match*] se suspendió debido a la lluvia; [*plan, party etc*] fue un fracaso *or* desastre

washroom ['wɒʃrʊm] N servicios *mpl*, aseos *mpl*, baño *m*

wasn't ['wɒznt] = **was not**

WASP [wɒsp] N ABBR (*US**) = **White Anglo-Saxon Protestant**

wasp [wɒsp] N avispa *f*; **~s' nest** (*also fig*) avispero *m*

waspish ['wɒspɪʃ] ADJ [*character, person*] irritable, irascible;

[*remark*] mordaz, punzante

wasp-waisted [ˈwɒspˈweɪstɪd] ADJ (*fig*) con talle de avispa

wastage [ˈweɪstɪdʒ] N (= *loss*) desperdicio *m*; (= *amount wasted*) pérdidas *fpl*; (= *wear and tear*) desgaste *m*

waste [weɪst] Ⓐ N 1 (= *misuse*) desperdicio *m*, derroche *m*; **what a ~!** ¡qué desperdicio *or* derroche!; **to go to ~** echarse a perder, desperdiciarse; **it's a ~ of money** es dinero perdido, es tirar *or* derrochar el dinero; **it's a ~ of time** es una pérdida de tiempo; **it's a ~ of effort** es un esfuerzo inútil

2 (= *rubbish*) basura *f*, desperdicios *mpl*; (= *waste material, substance*) desechos *mpl*, residuos *mpl*; **household ~** basura *f* doméstica; **human ~** excrementos *mpl*; **nuclear/toxic ~** desechos *mpl or* residuos *mpl* nucleares/tóxicos

Ⓑ VT 1 (= *use inefficiently, squander*) [+ *water, electricity, gas*] derrochar; [+ *money*] malgastar, derrochar; [+ *time*] perder; [+ *life*] echar a perder; [+ *space, opportunity*] desaprovechar, desperdiciar; [+ *food*] desperdiciar, echar a perder; **don't ~ your time trying to persuade her** no pierdas el tiempo intentando persuadirla; **to ~ no time in doing sth** no tardar en hacer algo; **sarcasm is ~d on him** con él el sarcasmo es inútil; **caviar is ~d on him** no sabe apreciar el caviar; **nothing is ~d** no se desperdicia nada, no se echa a perder nada; ✦ IDIOM **you're wasting your breath!** ¡estás gastando saliva!

2 (*US***) (= *kill*) liquidar*, cargarse (*Sp**)

Ⓒ ADJ 1 (= *for disposal*) [*material*] de desecho

2 (= *leftover*) [*paper, fabric*] sobrante

3 (= *unused*) [*ground*] baldío, yermo

4 **to lay ~ to sth** devastar algo, asolar algo

Ⓓ CPD ➤ **waste bin** (*Brit*) cubo *m* de la basura ➤ **waste disposal** (*industrial*) eliminación *f* de los desechos *or* residuos; [*of household waste*] eliminación *f* de la basura doméstica ➤ **waste disposal unit** (*Brit*) triturador *m* de basura ➤ **waste matter** (*industrial*) residuos *mpl*; (*from body*) excrementos *mpl* ➤ **waste paper** papel *m* de desecho ➤ **waste pipe** tubería *f* de desagüe ➤ **waste products** (*industrial*) residuos *mpl*; (*from body*) excrementos *mpl* ➤ **waste away** VI + ADV [*person*] consumirse; [*muscles*] atrofiarse

wastebasket [ˈweɪstbɑːskɪt] N (*US*) (*gen*) cesto *m* de los papeles, papelera *f*; (*Comput*) papelera *f* de reciclaje

wasted [ˈweɪstɪd] ADJ 1 (= *lost, useless*) [*opportunity*] desaprovechado, desperdiciado; [*effort*] inútil; [*years*] perdido; **I'm afraid you've had a ~ journey** me temo que has hecho un viaje inútil *or* en vano 2 (= *thin*) [*person*] consumido; [*muscle*] atrofiado; [*arm, leg, hand*] atrofiado, inútil 3 (*) (*from drugs*) destrozado; (*from drink*) borracho

wasteful [ˈweɪstfəl] ADJ [*person*] despilfarrador, derrochador; [*process, method*] antieconómico; [*expenditure*] pródigo, excesivo; **to be ~ with sth** despilfarrar algo, desperdiciar algo

wastefulness [ˈweɪstfəlnɪs] N [*of system*] derroche *m*, despilfarro *m*; [*of person*] falta *f* de economía, prodigalidad *f*

wasteland [ˈweɪstlænd] N (*undeveloped*) terreno *m* baldío *or* yermo, tierra *f* baldía *or* yerma; (*uncultivated*) erial *m*; **a cultural ~** un desierto cultural

wastepaper basket [ˌweɪstˈpeɪpəˌbɑːskɪt], **wastepaper bin** [ˌweɪstˈpeɪpəbɪn] N cesto *m* de los papeles, papelera *f*

waster [ˈweɪstəʳ] N 1 (= *good-for-nothing*) gandul *mf* 2 (= *spendthrift*) derrochador(a) *m/f*

wasting [ˈweɪstɪŋ] ADJ [*disease*] debilitante

watch¹ [wɒtʃ] N (= *wristwatch*) reloj *m* (de pulsera)

watch² [wɒtʃ] Ⓐ N 1 (= *vigilance*) vigilancia *f*; **to keep ~** hacer guardia, vigilar; **to keep a (close) ~ on sth/sb** vigilar algo/a algn (de cerca); **to keep ~ over sth/sb** (= *keep a check on*) vigilar algo/a algn; (= *look after*) cuidar algo/a algn 2 (= *period of duty*) guardia *f*; **to take the first ~** montar *or* hacer la primera guardia; **to be on ~** estar de guardia, hacer guardia 3 (*Mil*) (= *individual guard*) centinela *mf*, guardia *mf*; (= *pair, group*) guardia *f*

Ⓑ VT 1 [+ *television, programme, game, play*] ver; **~ this space** estén pendientes, les mantendremos informados 2 (= *observe, look at*) mirar; (*more attentively*) observar; **we ~ed the car disappear from view** vimos cómo el coche

desaparecía de nuestra vista; **just ~ him run!** ¡mira cómo corre!; **"you can't do that"** — **"just you ~ (me)!"** —no puedes hacer eso —¿que no? ¡ya verás (como puedo)!; ✦ IDIOMS **to ~ the clock** estar pendiente del reloj; **to ~ sb like a hawk** no quitar el ojo *or* la vista de encima a algn; **it's about as exciting as ~ing paint dry** *or* **grass grow** es para morirse de aburrimiento

3 (= *mind*) [+ *children, luggage, shop*] cuidar; [+ *soup, frying pan*] echar un ojo a; **~ that knife/your head/your language!** ¡(ten) cuidado con ese cuchillo/la cabeza/esas palabrotas!; **~ you don't burn yourself** ten cuidado de no quemarte; **~ how you go!** ¡ve con cuidado!; **~ what you're doing!** ¡cuidado con lo que haces!; **~ it!** (= *careful!*) ¡ojo!*, ¡cuidado!, ¡abusado! (*Mex**); (*threatening*) ¡cuidadito!*; **to ~ one's step** ir con cuidado

4 (= *be mindful of*) [+ *weight, health*] cuidar; [+ *time*] estar pendiente de; **I have to ~ what I eat** tengo que tener cuidado con lo que como

5 (= *monitor*) [+ *situation, developments*] seguir; [+ *suspect, house, sb's movements*] vigilar; **we are being ~ed** nos están vigilando

Ⓒ VI 1 (= *observe*) mirar; (*attentively*) observar

2 (= *wait, be alert*) **I was ~ing for the plumber** estaba atento esperando a que llegara el fontanero; **~ to see what you're going to do** está pendiente de lo que vas a hacer ➤ **watch out** VI + ADV tener cuidado, ir con cuidado; **~ out!** (= *be careful*) ¡(ten) cuidado!, ¡abusado! (*Mex**); (*threatening*) ¡cuidadito!; **~ out for thieves** cuidado con los (ladrones) ➤ **watch over** VI + PREP 1 (= *look after*) [+ *person*] velar por; [+ *sb's rights, safety*] velar por, mirar por 2 (= *monitor*) supervisar 3 (= *guard*) vigilar

watchable [ˈwɒtʃəbl] ADJ [*programme*] que se deja ver; **the film is eminently ~** la película es sumamente entretenida

watchband [ˈwɒtʃbænd] N (*US*) correa *f* de reloj

watchdog [ˈwɒtʃdɒg] N 1 (= *guard dog*) perro *m* guardián 2 (= *person*) guardián/ana *m/f*; **a consumer ~** un organismo que protege los intereses del consumidor

watchful [ˈwɒtʃfʊl] ADJ [*eyes, face*] atento; (*stronger*) vigilante; **to keep a ~ eye on sth/sb** vigilar algo/a algn de cerca; **under the ~ eye of** bajo la atenta mirada de, bajo la mirada vigilante de

watchmaker [ˈwɒtʃˌmeɪkəʳ] N relojero/a *m/f*

watchman [ˈwɒtʃmən] N (*pl* **watchmen**) (= *security guard*) guardián *m*, vigilante *m*; (*also* **night ~**) (*in factory*) vigilante *m* nocturno; (*in street*) sereno *m*

watchstrap [ˈwɒtʃstræp] N correa *f* de reloj

watchtower [ˈwɒtʃˌtaʊəʳ] N atalaya *f*, torre *f* de vigilancia

watchword [ˈwɒtʃwɜːd] N (*Mil, Pol*) contraseña *f*; (= *motto*) lema *m*, consigna *f*

water [ˈwɔːtəʳ] Ⓐ N 1 agua *f*

Use **el/un** not **la/una** before feminine nouns beginning with stressed **a** or **ha** like **agua**.

fresh ~ agua *f* dulce; **hard ~** agua *f* dura; **high/low ~** marea *f* alta/baja; **salt ~** agua *f* salada; **soft ~** agua *f* blanda; **to turn on the ~** (*at main*) hacer correr el agua; (*at tap*) abrir el grifo (*Sp*) *or* la llave (*LAm*); ✦ IDIOMS **that's all ~ under the bridge now** todo eso ya ha pasado a la historia; **to pour cold ~ on an idea** echar un jarro de agua fría a una idea; **like ~ off a duck's back** como si nada, como quien oye llover; **that theory doesn't hold ~** esa teoría carece de fundamento; **to be in hot ~** estar metido en un lío*; **to spend money like ~** despilfarrar *or* tirar el dinero

2 **waters** (*at spa, of sea, river*) aguas *fpl*; **British ~s** aguas británicas

3 (= *urine*) aguas *fpl* menores, orina *f*; **to pass ~** orinar, hacer aguas (menores)

4 (*Med*) **~ on the brain** hidrocefalia *f*; **her ~s broke** rompió aguas; **~ on the knee** derrame *m* sinovial

Ⓑ VT [+ *garden, plant*] regar; [+ *horses, cattle*] abrevar, dar de beber a

Ⓒ VI (*Physiol*) **her eyes started ~ing** empezaron a llorarle los ojos; **her mouth ~ed** se le hizo agua la boca

D CPD ➤ **water bed** cama *f* de agua ➤ **water bird** ave *f* acuática

---

Use **el/un** not **la/una** before feminine nouns beginning with stressed **a** or **ha** like **ave**.

➤ **water bottle** (*for drinking*) cantimplora *f*; (*also* **hot-~ bottle**) bolsa *f* de agua caliente, guatona *f* (*Chi*) ➤ **water cannon** cañón *m* de agua ➤ **water carrier** aguador *m* ➤ **water chestnut** castaña *f* de agua ➤ **water closet** (*frm*) wáter *m*, baño *m* ➤ **water diviner** zahorí *mf* ➤ **water divining** arte *m* del zahorí ➤ **water heater** calentador *m* de agua ➤ **water hole** (*for animals*) abrevadero *m* ➤ **water jump** foso *m* (de agua) ➤ **water level** nivel *m* del agua; (*Naut*) línea *f* de agua ➤ **water lily** nenúfar *m* ➤ **water line** línea *f* de flotación ➤ **water main** cañería *f* principal ➤ **water meter** contador *m* de agua ➤ **water pipe** caño *m* de agua ➤ **water pistol** pistola *f* de agua ➤ **water plant** planta *f* acuática ➤ **water polo** waterpolo *m*, polo *m* acuático ➤ **water power** energía *f* hidráulica ➤ **water pressure** presión *f* del agua ➤ **water pump** bomba *f* de agua ➤ **water rat** rata *f* de agua ➤ **water snake** culebra *f* de agua ➤ **water softener** ablandador *m* de agua ➤ **water sports** deportes *mpl* acuáticos ➤ **water supply** abastecimiento *m* de agua ➤ **water tank** (*for village, in house*) depósito *m* de agua ➤ **water tower** depósito *f* de agua ➤ **water wheel** rueda *f* hidráulica; (*Agr*) noria *f* ➤ **water wings** manguitos *mpl*, flotadores *mpl* para los brazos

➤ **water down** VT + ADV [+ *wine*] aguar, bautizar*; [+ *juice, paint*] diluir; [+ *proposal, report*] suavizar

waterborne [ˈwɔːtəbɔːn] ADJ [*disease*] transmitido a través del agua; [*traffic, trade*] (*by river*) fluvial; (*by sea*) marítimo

watercolour, watercolor (*US*) [ˈwɔːtəˌkʌləʳ] N acuarela *f*

watercourse [ˈwɔːtəkɔːs] N (= *river bed*) lecho *m*, cauce *m*; (= *canal*) canal *m*, conducto *m*

watercress [ˈwɔːtəkres] N berro *m*

waterfall [ˈwɔːtəfɔːl] N cascada *f*, salto *m* de agua; (*larger*) catarata *f*

waterfront [ˈwɔːtəfrʌnt] N puerto *m*, muelle *m*

watering [ˈwɔːtərɪŋ] N riego *m*; **frequent ~ is needed** hay que regar con frecuencia ➤ **watering can** regadera *f* ➤ **watering hole** (*for animals*) abrevadero *m*

waterlogged [ˈwɔːtəlɒgd] ADJ [*ground*] anegado, inundado; [*pitch*] encharcado, inundado; [*wood, paper*] empapado

Waterloo [ˌwɔːtəˈluː] N Waterloo *m*; ♦ IDIOM **he met his ~** se le llegó su San Martín

watermark [ˈwɔːtəmɑːk] N (*on paper*) filigrana *f*; (*left by tide*) marca *f* del nivel del agua

watermelon [ˈwɔːtəˌmelən] N sandía *f*

waterproof [ˈwɔːtəpruːf] **A** ADJ [*material*] impermeable; [*watch, torch*] sumergible; [*mascara, sunscreen, glue*] resistente al agua **B** N (*Brit*) impermeable *m*

water-resistant [ˈwɔːtərɪˈzɪstənt] ADJ [*material*] impermeable; [*sunscreen*] a prueba de agua

watershed [ˈwɔːtəʃed] N **1** (*Geog*) línea *f* divisoria de las aguas; (= *basin*) cuenca *f* **2** (= *decisive moment*) momento *m* clave, momento *m* decisivo; (= *landmark*) hito *m*

waterside [ˈwɔːtəsaɪd] **A** N (= *river, lake*) orilla *f*, ribera *f*; (= *harbour*) muelle *m* **B** ADJ ribereño

water-ski [ˈwɔːtəskiː] VI esquiar en el agua

water-skier [ˈwɔːtəˌskiːəʳ] N esquiador(a) *m/f* acuático/a

water-skiing [ˈwɔːtəˌskiːɪŋ] N esquí *m* acuático

water-soluble [ˈwɔːtəˈsɒljʊbl] ADJ soluble en agua

watertight [ˈwɔːtətaɪt] ADJ **1** [*bottle, container, seal*] hermético; [*compartment, boat, ship*] estanco **2** [*alibi*] perfecto; [*argument, theory*] irrefutable

waterway [ˈwɔːtəweɪ] N vía *f* fluvial *or* navegable; (= *inland waterway*) canal *m* (navegable)

waterworks [ˈwɔːtəwɜːks] NSING central *f* depuradora; ♦ IDIOM **to turn on the ~*** echarse a llorar

watery [ˈwɔːtərɪ] ADJ **1** [*fluid, discharge, solution*] acuoso;

[*paint, ink*] aguado; **to go to a ~ grave** (*liter*) encontrar su lecho de muerte en el fondo del mar (*liter*) **2** [*tea, soup*] aguado **3** [*eyes*] lloroso **4** [*sun*] débil; [*light*] desvaído, tenue; [*colour*] pálido, desvaído

watt [wɒt] N vatio *m*

wattage [ˈwɒtɪdʒ] N vatiaje *m*

wave [weɪv] **A** N **1** (*in sea, lake*) ola *f*; ♦ IDIOM **to make ~s** (= *stir up trouble*) crear problemas **2** (*in hair*) onda *f* **3** (*Phys, Rad*) onda *f*; **long/medium/short ~** onda larga/media/corta **4** [*of strikes, refugees, enthusiasm*] oleada *f* **5** (= *wave of hand*) gesto *m* de la mano; **to give sb a ~** (*in greeting*) saludar a algn con la mano; (*saying goodbye*) decir adiós a algn con la mano **B** VT [+ *flag, handkerchief*] agitar; [+ *weapon, stick*] blandir, agitar; **he was waving his arms in the air** agitaba los brazos en el aire; **he saw Jarvis, and ~d a hand** (*to catch attention*) vio a Jarvis y le hizo señas con la mano; **he ~d the ticket under my nose** agitó el billete delante de mis narices; **to ~ goodbye to sb** decir adiós a algn con la mano; **he ~d the car through the gates** le indicó al coche que entrara por el portón **C** VI **1** [*person*] **I saw her and ~d** la vi y la saludé con la mano; **to ~ to** *or* **at sb** (= *sign to*) hacer señas a algn con la mano; (= *greet*) saludar a algn con la mano; (= *say goodbye to*) decir adiós a algn con la mano **2** (= *sway*) [*flag*] ondear; [*branches, grass*] mecerse **D** CPD ➤ **wave power** energía *f* mareomotriz

➤ **wave around, wave about** VT + ADV agitar

➤ **wave aside** VT + ADV [+ *suggestion, objection*] (*verbally*) rechazar, desechar; (*with gesture*) rechazar con (un gesto de) la mano

➤ **wave away** VT + ADV [+ *sth offered*] rechazar con (un gesto de) la mano; **he ~d the waiter away** con un gesto de la mano le indicó al camarero que se fuera

➤ **wave down** VT + ADV **to ~ a car down** (= *sign to stop*) hacer señales a un coche para que pare; **we ~d down a passing car** paramos a un coche que pasaba haciéndole señas con las manos

➤ **wave off** VT + ADV **to ~ sb off** decir adiós a algn con la mano; **she came to the pier to ~ us off** vino al muelle para decirnos adiós

➤ **wave on** VT + ADV **to ~ sb on** indicar a algn que siga adelante, hacer señas a algn para que siga adelante

waveband [ˈweɪvbænd] N banda *f* de frecuencia

wavelength [ˈweɪvleŋθ] N longitud *f* de onda; ♦ IDIOM **we're not on the same ~** no estamos en la misma onda

waver [ˈweɪvəʳ] VI **1** (= *oscillate*) [*needle*] oscilar; [*flame*] temblar **2** (= *hesitate*) vacilar, dudar (**between** entre); (= *weaken*) [*courage, support*] flaquear; (= *falter*) [*voice*] temblar

waverer [ˈweɪvərəʳ] N indeciso/a *m/f*, irresoluto/a *m/f*

wavy [ˈweɪvɪ] ADJ (*compar* **wavier**; *superl* **waviest**) [*hair, surface, line*] ondulado

wax¹ [wæks] **A** N cera *f*; (*in ear*) cera *f* (de los oídos), cerumen *m*, cerilla *f* **B** VT [+ *furniture, car*] encerar **C** CPD ➤ **wax paper** (*US*) papel *m* encerado

wax² [wæks] VI [*moon*] crecer; **to ~ and wane** crecer y decrecer

waxed [wækst] ADJ [*paper*] encerado; [*jacket*] impermeabilizado

waxwork [ˈwækswɜːk] N figura *f* de cera

waxworks [ˈwækswɜːks] NSING (*pl* **~**) museo *m* de cera

waxy [ˈwæksɪ] ADJ (*compar* **waxier**; *superl* **waxiest**) ceroso

way [weɪ] **A** N **1** (= *route*) camino *m*; **I don't know the ~ to his house** no sé el camino a su casa, no sé cómo se va *or* llega a su casa; **which is the ~ to the station?** ¿cómo se va *or* cómo se llega a la estación?; **this isn't the ~ to Lugo!** ¡por aquí no se va a Lugo!; **he walked all the ~ home** hizo todo el camino andando; **it rained all the ~ there** llovió durante todo el viaje; **he ran all the ~ home** hizo todo el camino a casa corriendo; **to ask one's ~ to the station** preguntar el camino *or* cómo se va a la estación; **if the chance comes my ~** si se me presenta la oportunidad; **to take the easy ~**

out optar por la solución más fácil; **he's still feeling his ~ in the new job** todavía se está familiarizando con el nuevo trabajo; **to find one's ~** orientarse, ubicarse (*esp LAm*); **I had to find my own ~ home** me las tuve que arreglar para volver a casa; **to go out of one's ~ to help sb** desvivirse por ayudar a algn; **the ~ in** (= *entrance*) la entrada; **I know my ~ about town** conozco la ciudad; **to lead the ~** (*lit*) ir primero; (*fig*) marcar la pauta, abrir el camino; **to go the long ~ round** ir por el camino más largo; **to lose one's ~** extraviarse; **to make one's ~ home** volver a casa; **on the ~ here** de camino hacia aquí, mientras veníamos aquí; **it's on the ~ to Murcia** está en la carretera de Murcia; **he's on his ~** está de camino; **your house is on my ~** tu casa me viene de camino; **the ~ out** la salida; **you'll find it on the ~ out** lo encontrarás cerca de la salida; **I'll find my own ~ out** no hace falta que me acompañen a la puerta; **there's no ~ out** (*fig*) no hay salida or solución, esto no tiene solución; **there's no other ~ out** (*fig*) no hay más remedio; **it's on its ~ out** está en camino de desaparecer, ya está pasando de moda; **I don't want to take you out of your ~** no quiero apartarle del camino; **the village I live in is rather out of the ~** mi pueblo está un poco retirado; **to pay one's ~** (*in restaurant*) pagar su parte; **to see one's ~ (clear) to helping sb** ver la forma de ayudar a algn; **~** subida *f*, ruta *f* para subir; ✦ IDIOMS **I'm with you all the ~** te apoyo en todo; **to go one's own ~** seguir su propio camino

2 (= *path*) camino *m*; **to clear a ~ for** abrir camino para; **to force one's ~ in** introducirse a la fuerza; **to be/get in sb's ~** estorbar a algn; **to get in the ~** estorbar; **to stand in sb's ~** (*lit*) cerrar el paso a algn; (*fig*) ser un obstáculo para algn; **now nothing stands in our ~** ahora no hay obstáculo alguno; **to make ~ (for sth/sb)** dejar paso (a algo/algn); **make ~!** ¡abran paso!; **to get out of the ~** quitarse de en medio; **I try to keep out of his ~** procuro evitar cualquier contacto con él; **to move sth out of the ~** quitar algo de en medio or del camino; **as soon as I've got this essay out of the ~** en cuanto termine este ensayo; **to push one's ~ through the crowd** abrirse paso por la multitud a empujones; **he worked his ~ up in the company** ascendió en la compañía a fuerza de trabajo

3 (= *direction*) **are you going my ~?** ¿vas por dónde voy yo?; **everything is going my ~** (*fig*) todo me está saliendo a pedir de boca; **to look the other ~** (*fig*) mirar para otro lado, hacer la vista gorda; **turn it the other ~ round** vuélvelo del revés; **turn the map the right ~ up** pon el mapa mirando hacia arriba; **to split sth three ~s** dividir algo en tres partes iguales; **come this ~** pase por aquí; **this ~ and that** por aquí y por allá; **which ~ did it go?** ¿hacia dónde fue?, ¿por dónde se fue?; **she didn't know which ~ to look** no sabía dónde mirar or dónde poner los ojos

4 (= *distance*) **a little ~ off** no muy lejos, a poca distancia; **it's a long ~ away** esto está muy lejos; **spring is a long ~ off** la primavera queda muy lejos; **it's a long ~ es** mucho camino; **we have a long ~ to go** tenemos mucho camino por delante; **he'll go a long ~** (*fig*) llegará lejos; **a little of that flavouring goes a long ~** un poco de ese condimento cunde mucho; **we've come a long ~ since those days** hemos avanzado mucho desde entonces; **not by a long ~** ni con mucho

5 (= *means*) manera *f*, forma *f*, modo *m*; **we'll find a ~ of doing it** encontraremos la manera or forma or el modo de hacerlo; **that's the ~!** ¡así!, ¡eso es!; **that ~ it won't disturb anybody** así no molestará a nadie; **every which ~** (*esp US*) (= *in every manner*) de muchísimas maneras; (= *in every direction*) por todas partes; **~s and means** medios *mpl*; **that's not the right ~** así no se hace; ✦ IDIOM **there are no two ~s about it** no hay vuelta de hoja

6 (= *manner*) manera *f*, forma *f*, modo *m*; **the ~ things are going ...** si esto continúa así ...; **she looked at me in a strange ~** me miró de manera or forma extraña or de modo extraño; **without any ~ wishing to** (+ INFIN) sin querer en lo más mínimo + *infin*, sin tener intención alguna de + *infin*; **in a big ~*** en grande*; **you can't have it both ~s** tienes que optar por lo uno o lo otro; **either ~ I can't help you** de todas formas no puedo ayudarle; **I will help you in every ~ possible** haré todo lo posible por ayudarte; **the British ~ of life** el estilo de vida británico; **no ~!*** ¡ni pensarlo!, ¡ni hablar!; **there is no ~ I am going to agree*** de ninguna manera or forma or de ningún modo lo voy a

consentir; **(in) one ~ or another** de una u otra manera or otra forma, de un modo u otro; **it doesn't matter to me one ~ or the other** me es igual, me da lo mismo; **he has his own ~ of doing it** tiene su manera or forma or modo de hacerlo; **in the same ~** de la misma manera or forma, del mismo modo; **she's clever that ~** para esas cosas es muy lista; **to my ~ of thinking** a mi parecer, a mi manera or forma or modo de ver; **do it this ~** hazlo así; **in this ~** así, de esta manera or forma or de este modo

7 [*of will*] **to get one's own ~** salirse con la suya; **have it your own ~!** ¡como quieras!; **they've had it all their own ~ too long** hace tiempo que hacen lo que les da la gana

8 (= *custom*) costumbre *f*; **he has his little ~s** tiene sus manías or rarezas; **to get into/out of the ~ of doing sth** adquirir/perder la costumbre de hacer algo

9 (= *gift*) **he has a ~ with people** tiene don de gentes; **he has a ~ with children** sabe manejar a los niños

10 (= *respect, aspect*) sentido *m*; **in a ~** en cierto sentido; **in many ~s** en muchos sentidos; **in no ~** de ninguna manera, de manera alguna; **in some ~s** en algunos sentidos

11 (= *state*) estado *m*; **the ~ things are** tal como están or van las cosas; **to leave things the ~ they are** dejar las cosas como están; **things are in a bad ~** las cosas van or marchan mal; **he's in a bad ~** (= *sick*) está grave; **it looks that ~** así parece; ✦ IDIOM **to be in the family ~*** estar embarazada

12 (*in set expressions with preposition*) **by the ~** a propósito, por cierto; **by ~ of a warning** a modo de advertencia; **that was all I got by ~ of an answer** eso es todo lo que conseguí por respuesta; **he had little in the ~ of formal education** tuvo poca educación formal; **to be under ~** estar en marcha; **the job is now well under ~** el trabajo ya está muy avanzado; **to get under ~** [*person, group*] partir, ponerse en camino; [*work, project*] ponerse en marcha, empezar a moverse

Ⓑ ADV (*) **~ back in 1900** allá en 1900; **~ down (below)** muy abajo; **it's ~ out in Nevada** está allá en Nevada; **he was ~ out in his estimate** se equivocó (en) mucho en su presupuesto; **it's ~ past your bedtime** hace rato que deberías estar en la cama; **it's ~ too big** es demasiado grande; **~ up high** muy alto

wayfarer[†] ['weɪˌfɛərəʳ] N caminante *mf*, viajero/a *m/f*

waylay [weɪˈleɪ] (*pt, pp* **waylaid**) VT abordar, detener; **I was waylaid by the manager** me detuvo el gerente

way-out* ['weɪˈaut] ADJ ultramoderno

wayside ['weɪsaɪd] N borde *m* del camino; **by the ~** al borde del camino; ✦ IDIOM **to fall by the ~** [*project*] quedarse en aguas de borraja; [*person*] quedarse a mitad de camino

wayward ['weɪwəd] ADJ [*person*] rebelde; [*behaviour*] díscolo, rebelde

WC N ABBR (*Brit*) (= *water closet*) wáter *m*, WC *m*

w/e ABBR (= *week ending*) **~ 28 Oct** semana que termina el día 28 de octubre

we [wiː] PRON (*for emphasis, to avoid ambiguity*) nosotros/as; **you've got kids but we haven't** ustedes tienen hijos pero nosotros no; **we English** nosotros los ingleses; **they work harder than we do** trabajan más que nosotros

> Don't translate the subject pronoun when not emphasizing or clarifying:

we were in a hurry teníamos prisa

weak [wiːk] ADJ (*compar* **~er**; *superl* **~est**) [*person, limb, sun, signal, voice, smile, government*] débil; [*structure*] endeble, frágil; [*material*] endeble; [*pulse, economy*] débil, flojo; [*student, team, current*] flojo; [*coffee, tea*] poco cargado; [*beer*] flojo; [*solution*] diluido; [*argument, evidence*] poco sólido, poco convincente; [*case*] poco sólido; [*excuse, answer*] poco convincente; **he was too ~ to stand up** estaba demasiado débil para levantarse, no tenía fuerzas para levantarse; **to feel ~** sentirse débil; **to grow ~(er)** debilitarse; **to have a ~ heart** padecer del corazón; **the film had a ~ plot** el argumento de la película era muy flojo; **~ point** punto *m* débil; **geography is my ~ subject** estoy flojo en geografía, la geografía es mi asignatura floja; **to be ~ with hunger** estar debilitado por el hambre; ✦ IDIOMS **to be**

~ in the head* ser cortito de arriba*; **I went ~ at the knees** se me flaquearon las piernas

weaken ['wiːkən] **A** VT [+ *person, heart, structure, economy*] debilitar; [+ *power, influence, resolve*] menguar, debilitar; [+ *case, argument*] quitar fuerza a; [+ *solution, mixture*] diluir **B** VI **1** (= *grow weaker*) [*person, muscle, structure, economy*] debilitarse; [*power, influence, resolve*] menguarse, debilitarse **2** (= *give way*) flaquear; **we must not ~ now** no debemos flaquear, ahora menos que nunca

weak-kneed ['wiːk'niːd] ADJ sin carácter, débil

weakling ['wiːklɪŋ] N (*physical*) debilucho/a *m/f*; (*moral*) pelele *m*

weakly ['wiːklɪ] ADV [*move, lean*] sin fuerzas; [*say, smile*] débilmente, tímidamente

weakness ['wiːknɪs] N **1** (*in body*) debilidad *f*; [*of structure*] falta *f* de solidez, lo endeble **2** (= *ineffectuality*) [*of person*] falta *f* de carácter; [*of government, management*] flaqueza *f*, debilidad *f* **3** (= *weak point*) punto *m* débil **4** (= *soft spot*) debilidad *f*; **to have a ~ for sth** tener debilidad por algo

weak-willed ['wiːk'wɪld] ADJ sin voluntad, indeciso

weal [wiːl] N (*Brit*) verdugón *m*

wealth [welθ] **A** N **1** riqueza *f*; **the country's mineral ~** las riquezas minerales del país **2** (= *abundance*) abundancia *f* (**of** de); **a ~ of information** una abundancia de información **B** CPD ➤ **wealth tax** impuesto *m* sobre el patrimonio

wealthy ['welθɪ] ADJ (*compar* **wealthier**; *superl* **wealthiest**) rico, acaudalado

wean [wiːn] VT [+ *child*] destetar; **to ~ sb (away) from sth** (*fig*) alejar a algn de algo

weapon ['wepən] N arma *f*

Use **el/un** not **la/una** before feminine nouns beginning with stressed **a** or **ha** like **arma**.

---

a secret ~ un arma secreta; **~s of mass destruction** armas *fpl* de destrucción masiva

weaponry ['wepənrɪ] N armas *fpl*

wear [weəʳ] (*vb: pt* **wore**; *pp* **worn**) **A** N **1** (= *use*) uso *m*; **this material will stand up to a lot of ~** este tejido resistirá mucho uso; **there is still some ~ left in it** todavía le queda vida; **clothes for everyday ~** ropa *fsing* para todos los días, ropa *fsing* para uso diario **2** (= *deterioration through use*) desgaste *m*; **to show signs of ~** [*clothes, furniture, tyres*] dar muestras de desgaste, mostrar señales de desgaste; **~ and tear** desgaste natural; **to be the worse for ~***: **his suit looked decidedly the worse for ~*** el traje se le veía muy deslucido; **she looks the worse for ~** se la ve algo desmejorada **3** (= *dress, clothing*) ropa *f*; **casual ~** ropa *f* informal; **children's ~** ropa *f* de niños; **evening ~** ropa *f* para la noche; **summer ~** ropa *f* de verano **B** VT **1** (= *have on*) [+ *clothing, jewellery*] llevar, llevar puesto; [+ *spectacles, hairstyle, perfume*] llevar; [+ *beard*] tener; [+ *smile*] lucir; (= *put on*) [+ *clothes, shoes, perfume*] ponerse; **she wore blue** iba de azul; **what shall I ~?** ¿qué me pongo?; **I have nothing to ~** no tengo qué ponerme, no tengo nada que ponerme; **I never ~ make-up** nunca llevo *or* me pongo maquillaje; **does she ~ glasses?** ¿usa gafas?; **to ~ one's hair long** llevar el pelo largo; ✦ IDIOM **she's the one who ~s the trousers** *or* (*US*) **pants in that house*** en esa casa los pantalones los lleva ella* **2** (= *make worn*) **to ~ a path across the lawn** hacer un camino pisando la hierba; **the carpet had been worn threadbare** la alfombra estaba muy desgastada del uso; **to ~ a hole in sth** hacer un agujero en algo; **the flagstones had been worn smooth by centuries of use** tantos siglos de uso habían alisado las losas **C** VI **1** (= *last*) durar, aguantar; **that dress has worn well** ese vestido ha durado *or* aguantado mucho; **she's worn well*** se ha conservado muy bien **2** (= *become worn*) desgastarse; **the trousers have worn at the knees** los pantalones se han desgastado por la rodillas; **to ~ thin** [*fabric*] desgastarse; **that excuse is ~ing a bit thin** esa excusa está ya muy pasada; **my patience is ~ing thin** se me está agotando la paciencia, estoy perdiendo la paciencia

3 [*day, year, sb's life*] **to ~ to its end** acercarse a su fin ➤ **wear away A** VT + ADV [+ *rock*] erosionar; [+ *pattern*] desgastar, borrar **B** VI + ADV [*wood, metal*] desgastarse, gastarse; [*cliffs*] erosionarse; [*inscription, design*] borrarse ➤ **wear down A** VT + ADV [+ *heels, pencil*] gastar, desgastar; [+ *opposition, resistance, patience*] agotar; [+ *person*] (*physically*) agotar, cansar; (*mentally*) cansar **B** VI + ADV [*heels*] desgastarse, gastarse ➤ **wear off A** VI + ADV [*anaesthetic, effects, pain*] pasarse; [*colour, design, inscription*] borrarse; **when the novelty ~s off** cuando pase la novedad **B** VT + ADV [+ *design, inscription*] quitar, borrar ➤ **wear on** VI + ADV [*year, war*] transcurrir, pasar; **as the evening wore on** a medida que transcurría la noche ➤ **wear out A** VT + ADV **1** [+ *clothes, battery, engine, clutch*] gastar, desgastar **2** (= *exhaust*) agotar; **I'm worn out** estoy agotado *or* rendido; **to ~ o.s. out** agotarse, matarse* **B** VI + ADV [*clothes, battery, engine*] gastarse, desgastarse ➤ **wear through** VI + ADV [*clothing*] romperse con el uso

wearer ['weərəʳ] N **contact lens/spectacle ~s** personas que usan lentillas/llevan gafas

wearily ['wɪərɪlɪ] ADV (= *with tiredness*) con cansancio; (= *dispiritedly*) con desaliento; **she smiled ~** sonrió cansada

weariness ['wɪərɪnɪs] N (*physical, mental*) cansancio *m*, fatiga *f*; (*emotional*) hastío *m*

wearing ['weərɪŋ] ADJ (= *exhausting*) [*journey*] cansado, pesado; [*activity*] pesado

wearisome ['wɪərɪsəm] ADJ (*frm*) (= *tiring*) fatigoso, pesado; (= *boring*) aburrido

weary ['wɪərɪ] **A** ADJ (*compar* **wearier**; *superl* **weariest**) [*person*] cansado; [*sigh, smile, voice*] de cansancio; **to grow ~ of (doing) sth** [*person*] cansarse de (hacer) algo **B** VI (*frm*) **to ~ of sth** cansarse *or* hartarse de algo

weasel ['wiːzl] N comadreja *f*

weather ['weðəʳ] **A** N tiempo *m*; **in this ~** con el tiempo que hace, con este tiempo; **in hot ~** cuando hace calor; **what's the ~ like?** ¿qué tiempo hace?; **to go out in all ~s** salir haga el tiempo que haga; ✦ IDIOMS **to make heavy ~ of sth** (*Brit**) complicar algo, hacer algo más difícil de lo que es; **to be under the ~** (= *ill*) estar indispuesto, estar pachucho (*Sp**) **B** VT [+ *rock*] erosionar; [+ *wood*] curar; [+ *skin, face*] curtir; ✦ IDIOM **to ~ the storm** capear el temporal **C** VI [*rocks*] erosionarse; [*wood*] curarse; [*face*] curtirse **D** CPD [*bureau, map, station*] meteorológico ➤ **weather conditions** estado *m* del tiempo ➤ **weather forecast** pronóstico *m* del tiempo, boletín *m* meteorológico ➤ **weather forecaster** meteorólogo/a *m/f* ➤ **weather report** boletín *m* meteorológico ➤ **weather vane** veleta *f*

weather-beaten ['weðəˌbiːtn] ADJ [*skin, face*] curtido; [*wood*] deteriorado; [*stone*] erosionado

weathercock ['weðəkɒk] N veleta *f*

weathered ['weðəd] ADJ [*rocks*] erosionado; [*skin, face*] curtido; [*wood*] curado, maduro

weatherman ['weðəmæn] N (*pl* **weathermen**) hombre *m* del tiempo

weatherproof ['weðəpruːf] ADJ [*house*] impermeabilizado; [*clothing*] impermeable, impermeabilizado

weatherwoman ['weðəwʊmən] N (*pl* **weatherwomen**) mujer *f* del tiempo

weave [wiːv] (*vb: pt* **wove**; *pp* **woven**) **A** VT [+ *fabric, basket*] tejer; [+ *story*] urdir **B** VI **1** (*with thread*) tejer **2** (*pt, pp* **~d**) (= *move in and out*) zigzaguear; **the motorbike was weaving in and out of the traffic** la motocicleta zigzagueaba *or* se abría paso entre los coches; ✦ IDIOM **let's get weaving!**† ¡pongamos manos a la obra!

weaver ['wiːvəʳ] N tejedor(a) *m/f*

weaving ['wiːvɪŋ] N tejido *m*; **basket ~** cestería *f*

Web, web¹* [web] (*Internet*) N **the ~** el *or* la Web ➤ **web address** dirección *f* de Internet ➤ **web page** página *f* web ➤ **web surfer** internauta *mf*

web² [web] N [*of spider*] telaraña *f*; [*of deceit, lies*] maraña *f*; **a ~ of intrigue** una red *or* un tejido de intrigas

webbed [webd] ADJ palmeado

webbing ['webɪŋ] N (= *material*) cincha *f*; [*of chair*] cinchas *fpl*

webcam ['webkæm] N webcam *f*

webcast ['webkɑːst] N *transmisión por Internet*

web-footed [,web'fʊtɪd] ADJ palmípedo

webmail ['webmeɪl] N correo *m* web

webmaster ['webmɑːstəʳ] N webmaster *mf*

website ['websaɪt] N web site *m*, sitio *m* web

webspace ['webspeɪs] N espacio *m* disponible en la Red

webzine ['webziːn] N revista *f* digital

we'd [wiːd] = **we would**, **we had**

wed [wed] († *or* Journalism) **Ⓐ** VT (= *get married to*) desposarse con, casarse con **Ⓑ** VI desposarse, casarse

Wed. ABBR (= **Wednesday**) miérc.

wedded ['wedɪd] ADJ **1** (*frm*) [*wife, husband*] desposado, casado; [*bliss*] conyugal; **his lawful ~ wife** su legítima esposa **2 to be ~ to an idea** aferrarse *or* estar aferrado a una idea; **she's ~ to her work** está casada con su trabajo

wedding ['wedɪŋ] **Ⓐ** N boda *f*, casamiento *m*; **to have a quiet ~** casarse en la intimidad **Ⓑ** CPD [*invitation, cake, present*] de boda ➤ **wedding anniversary** aniversario *m* de boda ➤ **wedding breakfast** (*frm*) banquete *m* de bodas ➤ **wedding day** día *m* de la boda; **on her ~ day** el día de su boda ➤ **wedding dress** traje *m* de novia ➤ **wedding reception** banquete *m* de bodas ➤ **wedding ring** alianza *f*, anillo *m* de boda

wedge [wedʒ] **Ⓐ** N **1** (*for keeping in position*) cuña *f*, calza *f*; ✦ IDIOM **this is the thin end of the ~** (*Brit*) esto puede ser el principio de muchos males **2** (= *piece*) [*of cheese, cake*] porción *f*, pedazo *m* (grande) **Ⓑ** VT **to ~ a door open** mantener abierta una puerta con una cuña *or* una calza; **I was ~d between two other passengers** me estuve apretado *or* inmovilizado entre otros dos pasajeros; **it's ~d** no se puede mover

wedge-shaped ['wedʒʃeɪpt] ADJ en forma de cuña

wedlock ['wedlɒk] N (*frm*) matrimonio *m*

Wednesday ['wenzdeɪ] N miércoles *m inv*; *see* **Tuesday**

Weds. ABBR (= **Wednesday**) miérc.

wee¹ [wiː] ADJ (*compar* **~r**; *superl* **~st**) (*Scot*) pequeñito, chiquito (*LAm*); **the ~ small hours (of the morning)** (*Brit*) las altas horas de la madrugada

wee² [wiː] (*Brit*) **Ⓐ** N pipí *m* **Ⓑ** VI hacer pipí*

weed [wiːd] **Ⓐ** N **1** mala hierba *f*, hierbajo *m* **2** (*) (= *person*) pelele* *m* **Ⓑ** VT, VI desherbar ➤ **weed out** VT + ADV [+ *plant*] arrancar; (*fig*) eliminar

weeding ['wiːdɪŋ] N **to do the ~** desherbar

weedkiller ['wiːd,kɪləʳ] N herbicida *m*

weedy ['wiːdɪ] ADJ (*compar* **weedier**; *superl* **weediest**) (*Brit* pej*) [*person*] debilucho*, desmirriado*, enclenque

week [wiːk] N semana *f*; **twice a ~** dos veces a la semana; **a ~ today** de hoy en ocho días, dentro de ocho días; **Tuesday ~** ◇ **a ~ on Tuesday** del martes en ocho días, este martes no, el otro; **in a ~ or so** dentro de una semana; **I don't have time during the ~** entre semana no tengo tiempo; **it changes from ~ to ~** esto cambia cada semana; **in, ~ out** semana tras semana; **I haven't seen her for ~s** hace tiempo que no la veo

weekday ['wiːkdeɪ] N día *m* laborable; **on ~s** entre semana

weekend ['wiːk'end] N fin *m* de semana; **a long ~** un puente

weekly ['wiːklɪ] **Ⓐ** ADJ semanal **Ⓑ** ADV semanalmente, cada semana; **I am paid ~** me pagan semanal *or* por semana; **£15 ~** 15 libras por semana; **twice/three times ~** dos/tres veces por semana *or* a la semana **Ⓒ** N (= *magazine*) semanario *m*

weeny* ['wiːnɪ] ADJ chiquitito*, minúsculo*

weep [wiːp] (*vb*: *pt*, *pp* **wept**) **Ⓐ** VI **1** (= *cry*) llorar **2** (*Med*) [*wound*] supurar **Ⓑ** VT [+ *tears*] llorar **Ⓒ** N **to have a good ~** llorar a lágrima viva

weeping ['wiːpɪŋ] N llanto *m* ➤ **weeping willow** sauce *m* llorón

weepy ['wiːpɪ] **Ⓐ** ADJ **1** (= *tearful*) [*person*] llorón; **to feel ~** sentir *or* tener ganas de llorar **2** (*) (= *sentimental*) [*film, novel, song*] lacrimógeno **Ⓑ** N (*) (= *film*) película *f* lacrimógena, melodrama *m*

wee-wee* ['wiːwiː] **Ⓐ** N pipí* *m* **Ⓑ** VI hacer pipí*

weigh [weɪ] **Ⓐ** VT [+ *person, apples*] pesar; [+ *evidence, risks*] sopesar, considerar; **to ~ o.s.** pesarse; **the advantages have to be ~ed against possible risks** las ventajas se tienen que contraponer a los posibles riesgos
Ⓑ VI pesar; **it ~s four kilos** pesa cuatro kilos; **how much** *or* **what do you ~?** ¿cuánto pesas?; **to ~ against sth/sb** ser un factor en contra de algo/algn; **to ~ on sb's conscience** pesar sobre la conciencia de algn; **it ~s (heavily) on her mind** le preocupa (mucho)
➤ **weigh down** VT + ADV (*to keep from blowing away*) sujetar (con un peso/una piedra *etc*); **don't take anything with you that will ~ you down** no te lleves nada que te suponga demasiado peso; **she was ~ed down with parcels** iba muy cargada de paquetes; **a branch ~ed down with fruit** una rama muy cargada de fruta; **he felt ~ed down with** *or* **by responsibilities** se sentía agobiado por las responsabilidades
➤ **weigh in** VI + ADV [*boxer, jockey*] pesarse; **to ~ in at 65 kilos** pesar 65 kilos
➤ **weigh out** VT + ADV [+ *goods, ingredients, kilo*] pesar
➤ **weigh up** (*esp Brit*) VT + ADV [+ *situation, risks, alternatives, evidence*] sopesar, considerar; [+ *person*] sondear, tantear

weighbridge ['weɪbrɪdʒ] N báscula-puente *f*, báscula *f* de puente

weigh-in ['weɪɪn] N pesaje *m*

weighing machine ['weɪɪŋməˌʃiːn] N báscula *f*

weight [weɪt] N peso *m*; (*for scales*) pesa *f*; **it's not good for you to lift heavy ~s** no te conviene levantar peso(s) *or* cosas pesadas; **sold by ~** vendido a peso; **those arguments carry no ~ with him** esos argumentos no influyen en él *or* no le influyen; **a package three kilos in ~** un paquete que pesa tres kilos, un paquete de tres kilos; **to lose ~** adelgazar, perder peso; **to put on ~** engordar, ganar peso; **to take the ~ off one's feet** sentarse a descansar; ✦ IDIOM **to throw one's ~ about*** ir de sargento*; **it is worth its ~ in gold** vale su peso en oro; **that's a ~ off my mind** eso me quita un peso de encima; **he doesn't pull his ~** no hace su parte *or* lo que le corresponde ➤ **weight limit** límite *m* de peso ➤ **weight training** entrenamiento *m* con pesas ➤ **weight watcher** persona *f* que vigila el peso *or* cuida la línea

weighted [weɪtɪd] ADJ [*clothing, object*] con peso; **to be ~ in favour of sb** favorecer a algn; **to be ~ against sb** perjudicar a algn

weightless ['weɪtlɪs] ADJ ingrávido

weightlessness ['weɪtlɪsnɪs] N ingravidez *f*

weightlifter ['weɪt,lɪftəʳ] N levantador(a) *m/f* de pesas, halterófilo/a *m/f*

weightlifting ['weɪt,lɪftɪŋ] N levantamiento *m* de pesas, halterofilia *f*

weight-train ['weɪt,treɪn] VI entrenar con pesas

weighty ['weɪtɪ] ADJ (*compar* **weightier**; *superl* **weightiest**) [*load*] pesado; [*volume*] de peso; [*matter, problem*] grave; [*argument*] importante, de peso; [*burden*] pesado

weir [wɪəʳ] N (= *dam*) presa *f*

weird [wɪəd] ADJ (*compar* **~er**; *superl* **~est**) raro, extraño; **all sorts of ~ and wonderful things** todo tipo de cosas extraordinarias

weirdo* ['wɪədəʊ] N persona *f* rara

welcome ['welkəm] **Ⓐ** VT [+ *person*] dar la bienvenida a; [+ *news*] alegrarse de; **we'd ~ your suggestions** nos alegraría recibir sus sugerencias; ✦ IDIOM **to ~ sb with open arms** recibir a algn con los brazos abiertos **Ⓑ** N bienvenida *f*, recibimiento *m*; **to give sb a warm ~** dar a algn una calurosa bienvenida *or* un caluroso recibimiento **Ⓒ** ADJ **1** [*person, guest, visitor*] bienvenido, bien recibido; **he's not ~ here any more** aquí ya no es bienvenido; **you're ~** (*in reply to thanks*) de nada, no hay de qué; **you're ~ to it!** (*iro*) ¡te lo puedes quedar!; **I didn't feel very ~** no me sentí

muy bien recibido; **to make sb ~** hacer que algn se sienta acogido; **you're ~ to try** puedes probar si quieres; **you're ~ to use my car** puedes usar mi coche con toda libertad, el coche está a tu disposición
2 [*decision, change*] bienvenido; **a cup of tea is always ~** una taza de té siempre se agradece; **to be ~ news** ser una noticia grata; **shelters provide ~ relief from the sun** los refugios proporcionan un grato alivio del sol
Ⓓ EXCL **welcome!** ¡bienvenido!

> If you're addressing a woman remember to use the feminine form: **¡Bienvenida!** If you're addressing more than one person use the plural form **¡Bienvenidos!** or **¡Bienvenidas!**

~ back! ¡bienvenido!; **~ home!** ¡bienvenido a casa!

welcoming ['welkəmɪŋ] ADJ **1** [*smile*] amable, cordial; (*esp Brit*) [*place, atmosphere*] acogedor **2** [*ceremony, banquet, speech*] de bienvenida

weld [weld] Ⓐ N soldadura *f* Ⓑ VT soldar

welder ['weldəʳ] N soldador(a) *m/f*

welding ['weldɪŋ] N soldadura *f* ➤ **welding torch** soplete *m* soldador

welfare ['welfɛəʳ] Ⓐ N **1** (= *well-being*) bienestar *m*; **child ~** la protección a *or* de la infancia **2** (*US*) (= *social aid*) asistencia *f* social; **to be on ~** recibir asistencia social Ⓑ CPD ➤ **welfare state** estado *m* de bienestar social ➤ **welfare worker** asistente *mf* social

well¹ [wel] Ⓐ N (*for water, oil*) pozo *m* Ⓑ VI (*also ~ out, ~ up*) brotar, manar

well² [wel] (*compar* **better**; *superl* **best**) Ⓐ ADV **1** (= *in a good manner*) bien; **I remember it ~** lo recuerdo bien; **to do ~ at school** sacar buenas notas en el colegio; **to do ~ in an exam** sacar buena nota en un examen; **the patient is doing ~** el paciente evoluciona bien; **you did ~ to come at once** hizo bien en venir enseguida; **~ done!** ¡bien hecho!; **to go ~** ir bien; **~ and good** muy bien; **to speak ~ of sb** hablar bien de algn; **to think ~ of sb** tener una buena opinión de algn
2 (= *thoroughly, considerably*) bien; **it was ~ deserved** estuvo bien merecido; **to be ~ in with sb** llevarse muy bien con algn; **it continued ~ into 1996** siguió hasta bien entrado 1996; **~ over a thousand** muchos más de mil, los mil bien pasados; **it's ~ past ten o'clock** son las diez y mucho; **as we know only too ~** como sabemos perfectamente; **~ and truly** (*esp Brit*) de verdad, realmente; **it was ~ worth the trouble** realmente valió la pena
3 (= *probably, reasonably*) **you may ~ be surprised to learn that ...** puede que te sorprenda mucho saber que ...; **it may ~ be that ...** es muy posible que ... + *subjun*; **they may ~ be lying** es muy posible que mientan; **we may as ~ begin now** ya podemos empezar, ¿no?; **you might as ~ tell me the truth** más valdría decirme la verdad; **we might (just) as ~ have stayed at home** para lo que hemos hecho, nos podíamos haber quedado en casa; **she cried, as ~ she might** lloró, y con razón; **you may ~ ask!** ¡buena pregunta!; **I couldn't very ~ leave** me resultaba imposible marcharme
4 (*in set expressions*) **to leave ~ alone**: **my advice is to leave ~ alone** te aconsejo que no te metas; **as ~** (= *in addition*) también; **I'll take those as ~** me llevo esos también; **and it rained as ~!** ¡y además llovió!; **I had Paul with me as ~ as Lucy** Paul estaba conmigo, además de Lucy; **could you eat mine as ~ as yours?** ¿podrías comerte el mío y el tuyo?
Ⓑ ADJ **1** (= *healthy*) bien; **I'm very ~, thank you** estoy muy bien, gracias; **I hope you're ~** espero que te encuentres bien; **get ~ soon!** ¡que te mejores!
2 (= *acceptable, satisfactory*) bien; **that's all very ~, but ...** todo eso está muy bien, pero ...; **it would be as ~ to ask** más vale *or* valdría preguntar; **it's just as ~ we asked** menos mal que preguntamos; ✦ PROV **all's ~ that ends ~** bien está lo que bien acaba
Ⓒ EXCL **1** (*introducing topic, resuming*) bueno; **~, it was like this** bueno, pues así ocurrió
2 (*dismissive*) pues; **~, I think she's a fool** pues yo pienso que es tonta
3 (*expressing surprise*) ¡vaya!; **~, what do you know!*** ¡anda,

quién lo diría!; **well, well!** ¡vaya, vaya!

we'll [wi:l] = **we will, we shall**

well- [wel] PREF bien

well-adjusted [ˌwelə'dʒʌstɪd] ADJ equilibrado

well-appointed [ˌwelə'pɔɪntɪd] ADJ bien amueblado

well-attended [ˌwelə'tendɪd] ADJ muy concurrido

well-balanced [ˌwel'bælənsd] ADJ bien equilibrado

well-behaved [ˌwelbɪ'heɪvd] ADJ que se porta bien

well-being ['wel'biːɪŋ] N bienestar *m*

well-bred [ˌwel'bred] ADJ [*person*] educado, cortés; [*animal*] de raza; [*horse*] (de) pura sangre

well-brought-up [ˌwelbrɔːt'ʌp] ADJ educado

well-built [ˌwel'bɪlt] ADJ [*house*] de construcción sólida; [*person*] fornido

well-chosen [ˌwel'tʃəʊzn] ADJ [*remark, words*] acertado

well-cooked [ˌwel'kʊkt] ADJ (= *tasty*) bien preparado; (= *well-done*) muy hecho

well-defined [ˌweldɪ'faɪnd] ADJ bien definido

well-deserved [ˌweldɪ'zɜːvd] ADJ merecido

well-developed [ˌweldɪ'veləpt] ADJ [*arm, muscle*] bien desarrollado; [*sense*] agudo, fino

well-disposed [ˌweldɪs'pəʊzd] ADJ bien dispuesto (**to, towards** hacia)

well-dressed [ˌwel'drest] ADJ bien vestido

well-earned [ˌwel'ɜːnd] ADJ merecido

well-educated [ˌwel'edjʊkeɪtɪd] ADJ instruido, culto

well-equipped [ˌwelɪ'kwɪpt] ADJ bien equipado

well-established [ˌwelɪ'stæblɪʃt] ADJ [*custom*] muy arraigado; [*firm*] (= *of long standing*) sólido; (= *with good reputation*) de buena reputación

well-fed [ˌwel'fed] ADJ bien alimentado

well-founded [ˌwel'faʊndɪd] ADJ fundamentado

well-groomed [ˌwel'gruːmd] ADJ acicalado

well-heeled* [ˌwel'hiːld] ADJ ricacho*

well-informed [ˌwelɪn'fɔːmd] ADJ bien informado, al corriente

Wellington ['welɪŋtən] N Wellington *m*

wellington (boot) ['welɪŋtən('buːt)] N (*Brit*) bota *f* de goma

well-intentioned [ˌwelɪn'tenʃnd] ADJ [*person*] con buenas intenciones; [*act*] bienintencionado

well-judged [ˌwel'dʒʌdʒd] ADJ bien calculado

well-kept [ˌwel'kept] ADJ [*secret,*] bien guardado; [*garden*] bien cuidado; [*house*] bien conservado

well-known [ˌwel'nəʊn] ADJ [*person, brand*] muy conocido, famoso; **it's a ~ fact that ...** es bien sabido que ...

well-liked [ˌwel'laɪkt] ADJ querido

well-loved [ˌwel'lʌvd] ADJ muy querido, amado

well-made [ˌwel'meɪd] ADJ bien hecho, fuerte

well-managed [ˌwel'mænɪdʒd] ADJ bien administrado

well-mannered [ˌwel'mænəd] ADJ educado, cortés

well-meaning [ˌwel'miːnɪŋ] ADJ bienintencionado

well-meant [ˌwel'ment] ADJ bienintencionado

well-nigh ['welnaɪ] ADV **~ impossible** casi imposible

well-off [ˌwel'ɒf] ADJ acomodado, pudiente; **you don't know when you're ~** no sabes los muchos beneficios que tienes

well-paid [ˌwel'peɪd] ADJ bien pagado, bien retribuido

well-preserved [ˌwelprɪ'zɜːvd] ADJ [*person*] bien conservado

well-read [ˌwel'red] ADJ culto, instruido

well-spoken [ˌwel'spəʊkən] ADJ bienhablado, con acento culto

well-stocked [ˌwel'stɒkt] ADJ bien surtido *or* provisto

well-timed [ˌwel'taɪmd] ADJ oportuno

well-to-do [ˌweltə'duː] ADJ acomodado

well-wisher ['wel,wɪʃə^r] N admirador(a) *m/f*

well-woman clinic ['welwʊmən,klɪnɪk] N clínica *f* de salud (*para mujeres*)

well-worn [,wel'wɔːn] ADJ [*garment*] raído; [*path, cliché*] trillado

well-written [,wel'rɪtn] ADJ bien escrito

welly* ['welɪ] N (*Brit*) ~ **boots** ◇ **wellies** botas *fpl* de goma

Welsh [welʃ] **Ⓐ** ADJ galés **Ⓑ** N **1** (= *language*) galés *m* **2 the** ~ (= *people*) los galeses **Ⓒ** CPD ➤ **Welsh rabbit, Welsh rarebit** pan *m* con queso tostado

welsh [welʃ] VI **to** ~ **on a promise** no cumplir una promesa; **they ~ed on the agreement** no respetaron el acuerdo

Welshman ['welʃmən] N (*pl* **Welshmen**) galés *m*

Welshwoman ['welʃ,wʊmən] N (*pl* **Welshwomen**) galesa *f*

welt [welt] N (= *weal*) verdugón *m*

welterweight ['weltəweɪt] N wélter *m*; **light** ~ wélter *m* ligero

wench†† [wentʃ] N moza *f*

wend [wend] VT **to** ~ **one's way home** (*hum*) encaminarse a casa

Wendy house ['wendɪhaʊs] N (*Brit*) casa *f* de juguete (*suficientemente grande para jugar dentro*)

went [went] PT *of* **go**

wept [wept] PT, PP *of* **weep**

we're [wɪə^r] = **we are**

were [wɜː^r] PT *of* **be**

weren't [wɜːnt] = **were not**

werewolf ['wɪəwʊlf] N (*pl* **werewolves**) hombre *m* lobo

west [west] **Ⓐ** N oeste *m*, occidente *m*; **the West** (*Pol*) el Oeste, (el) Occidente; **in the** ~ en el oeste; **to the** ~ **of** al oeste de
Ⓑ ADJ [*side, part*] oeste, del oeste; [*coast*] oeste, del oeste, occidental; [*wind*] del oeste
Ⓒ ADV (= *westward*) hacia el oeste; **it's** ~ **of London** está al oeste de Londres
Ⓓ CPD ➤ **West Africa** África *f* Occidental ➤ **the West Bank** Cisjordania *f* ➤ **the West Country** (*Brit*) el West Country (*el sudoeste de Inglaterra, esp. los condados de Cornualles, Devon y Somerset*) ➤ **the West End** (*of London*) el West End (de Londres) (*zona del centro de Londres donde hay muchas tiendas y locales de ocio*) ➤ **West Germany** (*formerly*) Alemania *f* Occidental ➤ **West Indies** Antillas *fpl*

westbound ['westbaʊnd] ADJ en dirección oeste

westerly ['westəlɪ] ADJ [*wind*] del oeste; **in a** ~ **direction** hacia el oeste, en dirección oeste; **the most** ~ **point in Europe** el punto más occidental *or* más al oeste de Europa

western ['westən] **Ⓐ** ADJ [*side, part*] oeste, del oeste; [*coast, border*] oeste, del oeste, occidental; [*wind, front, town*] del oeste; **Western** (*Pol*) occidental, del Oeste; **in** ~ **Spain** en la España occidental **Ⓑ** N (= *film*) western *m*, película *f* del oeste

westerner ['westənə^r] N (*Pol*) occidental *mf*

westernization ['westənaɪ'zeɪʃən] N occidentalización *f*

westernize ['westənaɪz] VT occidentalizar; **to become** ~**d** occidentalizarse

West German [,west'dʒɜːmən] ADJ (*formerly*) de Alemania Occidental

West Indian [,west'ɪndɪən] ADJ, N antillano/a *m/f*

Westminster ['west,mɪnstə^r] N (*Brit*) Westminster *m*

westward ['westwəd] **Ⓐ** ADJ [*movement, migration, journey*] hacia el oeste, en dirección oeste **Ⓑ** ADV (*also* ~**s**) hacia el oeste, en dirección oeste

wet [wet] **Ⓐ** ADJ (*compar* ~**ter**; *superl* ~**test**) **1** [*person, clothes, nappy, bed*] mojado; (= *sopping*) calado; [*paint, ink, plaster*] fresco; **"wet paint"** "recién pintado"; **to get** ~ mojarse; **to get one's feet** ~ mojarse los pies; **to be** ~ **through** estar empapado, estar calado; **the grass was** ~ **with dew** la hierba estaba mojada de rocío; **her cheeks were** ~ **with tears** las lágrimas le corrían por las mejillas; ✦ IDIOM **to be** ~ **behind the ears*** estar verde*
2 (= *rainy*) [*weather, month, winter, climate*] lluvioso; **it's been very** ~ ha llovido mucho

3 (*Brit* pej*) (= *feeble*) soso, blandengue
Ⓑ N **the** ~ (= *rain, wet weather*) la lluvia
Ⓒ VT mojar; **to** ~ **one's lips** humedecerse los labios; **to** ~ **the bed** orinarse en la cama, hacerse pis en la cama*, mearse en la cama**; **to** ~ **o.s.** orinarse encima, hacerse pis encima*, mearse encima**; ✦ IDIOM **to** ~ **o.s. (laughing)*** mearse de risa**
Ⓓ CPD ➤ **wet blanket*** aguafiestas* *mf inv* ➤ **wet dream** polución *f* nocturna ➤ **wet fish** ✦ IDIOM **he's a bit of a** ~ **fish** es un poco soso ➤ **wet nurse** nodriza *f*, ama *f* de cría

> Use **el/un** not **la/una** before feminine nouns beginning with stressed **a** or **ha** like **ama**.

wetness ['wetnɪs] N [*of surface, road*] estado *m* mojado; [*of substance*] lo mojado; [*of weather*] lo lluvioso

wetsuit ['wetsuːt] N traje *m* isotérmico

we've [wiːv] = **we have**

whack [wæk] **Ⓐ** N **1** (= *blow*) golpe *m* fuerte, porrazo *m*; **to give sb a** ~ dar un golpe fuerte *or* un porrazo a algn; **to give sth a** ~ golpear algo ruidosamente **2** (*) (= *attempt*) **to have a** ~ **at sth** intentar *or* probar algo **3** (*Brit**) (= *share*) parte *f*, porción *f*; **you'll get your** ~ recibirás tu parte **4** (*) **the car does 200kph top** ~ a toda máquina, el coche alcanza una velocidad de 200km/h **Ⓑ** VT golpear, aporrear

whacked* ['wækt] ADJ (*Brit*) **to be** ~ estar agotado, estar hecho polvo*

whacking ['wækɪŋ] **Ⓐ** ADJ (*esp Brit**) (*also* ~ **great**) grandote*, enorme **Ⓑ** N zurra *f*

whale [weɪl] N ballena *f*; ✦ IDIOM **to have a** ~ **of a time*** pasarlo bomba *or* (*SC*) regio

whaler ['weɪlə^r] N (= *person, ship*) ballenero *m*

whaling ['weɪlɪŋ] N pesca *f* de ballenas

wham [wæm] EXCL **wham!** ¡zas!

wharf [wɔːf] N (*pl* ~**s** *or* **wharves** [wɔːvz]) muelle *m*, embarcadero *m*

---

what

Ⓐ PRONOUN   **Ⓒ** EXCLAMATION
Ⓑ ADJECTIVE

what [wɒt] **Ⓐ** PRONOUN
1 (*in direct questions*) qué; ~ **do you want?** ¿qué quieres?; **what?** (= *pardon?*) ¿cómo?, ¿qué?; ~ **did you say?** ¿cómo *or* qué dices?, ¿qué has dicho?, ¿qué dijiste? (*LAm*); ~ **are capers?** ¿qué son las alcaparras?

> Only use ¿**qué es...?**/¿**qué son...?** to translate **what is/are** when asking for a **definition**. In other contexts use ¿**cuál es?**/¿**cuáles son?**:

~**'s her telephone number?** ¿cuál es su número de teléfono?

> Some expressions with **what** require **qué** used adjectivally:

~ **is the difference?** ¿qué diferencia hay?; ~ **are your plans?** ¿qué planes tienes?; *BUT* ~**'s the Spanish for "pen"?** ¿cómo se dice "pen" en español?; ~**'s your name?** ¿cómo te llamas?
2 (= *how much*) cuánto; ~ **will it cost?** ¿cuánto va a costar?; ~ **does it weigh?** ¿cuánto pesa?; **he asked her** ~ **she had paid for it** le preguntó cuánto había pagado por ello
3 (*in indirect questions*) qué, lo que; **he asked her** ~ **she thought of the new plan** le preguntó qué *or* lo que pensaba de ello; **I asked him** ~ **DNA was** le pregunté qué *or* lo que era el ADN

> Use **cuál era/cuáles son** *etc* instead of **lo que era/lo que son** *etc* if **what was/are** *etc* does not relate to a definition:

she asked me ~ **my hobbies were** me preguntó cuáles eran mis aficiones

4 *(before an infinitive)* qué; **I don't know ~ to do** no sé qué hacer
5 *(relative use)* lo que; **~ I want is a cup of tea** lo que quiero es una taza de té; **it wasn't ~ I was expecting** no era lo que yo me esperaba; **do ~ you like** haz lo que quieras; **business isn't ~ it was** los negocios ya no son lo que eran; **I saw ~ happened** vi lo que pasó; ✦ PROV **~'s done is done** lo hecho hecho está
6 *(in set expressions)*
✦ **and what have you, and what not*** y qué sé yo qué más, y qué sé yo cuántas cosas
✦ **to give sb what for*** regañar a algn
✦ **to know what's what*** saber cuántas son cinco*
✦ **or what?*: do you want it or ~?** ¿lo quieres o qué?; **are you coming or ~?** entonces ¿vienes o no?; **is this luxury or ~?** esto sí que es lujo, ¿eh?
✦ **say what you like, ...** digas lo que digas, ..., se diga lo que se diga, ...
✦ **so what?*** ¿y qué?; **so ~ if it does rain?** ¿y qué, si llueve?
✦ **(I'll) tell you what** se me ocurre una idea, tengo una idea
✦ **what about: ~ about me?** y yo ¿qué?; **~ about next week?** ¿qué te parece la semana que viene?; **"your car ..." — "~ about it?"*** —tu coche ... —¿qué pasa con mi coche?; **~ about going to the cinema?** ¿qué tal si vamos al cine?, ¿y si vamos al cine?; **~ about people who haven't got cars?** ¿y la gente que no tiene coche?
✦ **what for?** *(= why)* ¿por qué?; *(= to what purpose)* ¿para qué?; **~ are you doing that for?** ¿por or para qué haces eso?; **~'s that button for?** ¿para qué es ese botón?
✦ **what if ...?** ¿y si ...?; **~ if he says no?** ¿y si dice que no?
✦ **what of: but ~ of the political leaders?** pero, ¿y qué hay de los líderes políticos?; **~ of it?*** y eso ¿qué importa?
✦ **what's ...: ~'s surprising is that we hadn't heard of this before** lo sorprendente es que no nos habíamos enterado antes
✦ **¿what's it like?** *(asking for description)* ¿cómo es?; *(asking for evaluation)* ¿qué tal es?; **~'s their new house like?** ¿cómo es su nueva casa?; **~'s his first novel like?** ¿qué tal es su primera novela?; **~ will the weather be like tomorrow?** ¿qué tal tiempo va a hacer mañana?
✦ **and what's more ...** y, además, ...
✦ **what's that?** *(asking about sth)* ¿qué es eso?; *(= what did you say?)* ¿qué has dicho?; **~'s that to you?*** ¿eso qué tiene que ver contigo?, ¿a ti qué te importa?
✦ **what's worse: and ~'s worse ...** y lo que es peor ...
✦ **what with: ~ with one thing and another** entre una cosa y otra; **~ with the stress and lack of sleep ...** entre la tensión y la falta de sueño ...
🅑 ADJECTIVE
1 *(in questions)* qué; **~ dress shall I wear?** ¿qué vestido me pongo?; **~ colour is it?** ¿de qué color es?; **she asked me ~ day she should come** me preguntó qué día tenía que venir; **did they tell you ~ time they'd be arriving?** ¿te dijeron a qué hora llegarían?
2 *(relative)* **~ savings we had are now gone** los ahorros que teníamos ya han desaparecido; **I will give you ~ information we have** te daré la información que tenemos; **~ little I had** lo poco que tenía
3 *(in exclamations)*

> Remember to put an accent on **qué** in exclamations as well as in direct and indirect questions:

~ a nuisance! ¡qué lata!; **~ an ugly dog!** ¡qué perro más or tan feo!; **~ a lot of people!** ¡qué cantidad de gente!
🅒 EXCLAMATION ¡qué!; **~! you sold it!** ¿qué? ¡lo has vendido!; **you told him WHAT?** ¿que le has dicho QUÉ?

whatever [wɒt'evəʳ] **🅐** PRON **1** *(= no matter what)* **~ it may be** sea lo que sea; **~ happens** pase lo que pase; **~ the weather** haga el tiempo que haga; **~ that means** lo que quiera que eso signifique
2 *(= anything that)* lo que; *(= everything that)* todo lo que; **~ you like** lo que quieras; **we'll do ~'s necessary** haremos lo que haga falta; **~ you say** *(acquiescing)* lo que quieras; **"I tell you I'm ill" — "~ you say"** *(iro)* —te digo que estoy enfermo —sí, sí or —sí, lo que tú quieras; **or ~ they're called** o como quiera que se llamen

3 *(= what on earth)* qué; **~ do you mean?** ¿qué quieres decir?; **~ did you do?** ¿pero qué hiciste?
4 *(= other similar things)* **you can put your pyjamas, sponge bag and ~ in here** aquí puedes guardar el pijama, el neceser y todas esas cosas
🅑 ADJ **1** *(= any)* cualquier; *(= all)* todo; **~ book you choose** cualquier libro que elijas; **~ books you choose** cualquier libro de los que elijas; **give me ~ change you've got** dame todo el cambio que tengas
2 *(= no matter what)* **~ problems you've got, we'll help** nosotros te ayudaremos, tengas el problema que tengas
3 *(in questions)* qué; **~ time is it?** ¿qué hora podrá ser?
🅒 ADV *(with negative)* **nothing ~** nada en absoluto; **it's no use ~** no sirve para nada

whatnot ['wɒtnɒt] **🅐** N (*) *(whatsit)* chisme m **🅑** PRON **and ~*** y qué sé yo, y todas esas cosas

what's-her-name* ['wɒtsəneɪm] PRON fulana f, cómo-se-llame f

what's-his-name* ['wɒtsɪzneɪm] PRON fulano m, cómo-se-llame m

whatsit* ['wɒtsɪt] N chisme m

whatsoever [ˌwɒtsəʊ'evəʳ] ADV **it's no use ~** no sirve para nada; **nothing ~** nada en absoluto

wheat [wiːt] N trigo m; ✦ IDIOM **to separate the ~ from the chaff** separar la cizaña or la paja del buen grano

wheatgerm ['wiːtdʒɜːm] N germen m de trigo

wheedle ['wiːdl] VT **to ~ sth out of sb** sonsacar algo a algn

wheedling ['wiːdlɪŋ] **🅐** ADJ mimoso **🅑** N mimos mpl, halagos mpl

wheel [wiːl] **🅐** N rueda f; *(= steering wheel)* volante m; **to be at** or **behind the ~** estar al volante; **to take the ~** tomar el volante; **do you have ~s?*** ¿tienes coche? **🅑** VT [+ bicycle] empujar; [+ child] pasear en cochecito **🅒** VI [bird] revolotear; **to ~ round** [person] girar sobre los talones **🅓** CPD ➤ **wheel clamp** cepo m

wheelbarrow ['wiːlˌbærəʊ] N carretilla f

wheelchair ['wiːltʃeəʳ] N silla f de ruedas

wheeler-dealer ['wiːləˌdiːləʳ] N chanchullero/a m/f

wheelhouse ['wiːlhaʊs] N timonera f, cámara f del timonel

wheeling ['wiːlɪŋ] N **~ and dealing** trapicheos* mpl, chanchullos* mpl

wheeze [wiːz] **🅐** VI resollar, respirar con silbido **🅑** N **1** resuello m (asmático), respiración f sibilante **2** *(Brit*)* *(= trick)* truco m, treta f; *(= idea)* idea f

whelk [welk] N buccino m

---

when

🅐 ADVERB	**🅑** CONJUNCTION

when [wen] **🅐** ADVERB
1 *(in questions and reported speech)*

> **When** in direct and indirect questions as well as after expressions of (un)certainty and doubt (e.g. **no sé**) translates as **cuándo** (with an accent) and is used with the indicative:

cuándo; **~ did it happen?** ¿cuándo ocurrió?; **do you know ~ he died?** ¿sabes cuándo murió?
✦ **say when!** *(when serving food, drink)* ¡dime cuánto!
✦ **since when: since ~ do you like** or **have you liked Indian food?** ¿desde cuándo te gusta la comida india?
✦ **till when?** ¿hasta cuándo?
2 *(= the time, day, moment etc)* cuando; **that was ~ the trouble started** entonces fue cuando empezaron los problemas; **that's ~ the programme starts** a esa hora es cuando empieza el programa; **1958: that's ~ I was born** 1958: (en) ese año nací yo

3 (*relative use*)

> If **when** follows a noun (e.g. **day**, **time**) and defines the noun, translate using (**en**) **que** not **cuando**:

(en) que; **the year ~ you were born** el año (en) que naciste

> If the **when** clause following a noun provides additional information which does not define or restrict the noun - in English as in Spanish, commas are obligatory here - translate using **cuando**:

cuando; **some days, ~ we're very busy, we don't finish work till very late** algunos días, cuando tenemos mucho trabajo, no acabamos hasta muy tarde
B CONJUNCTION
1 (= *at, during or after the time that*)

> As a conjunction, **when** can be translated by **cuando** (without an accent) followed by either the indicative or the subjunctive. Use the indicative when talking about the past or making general statements about the present. Use the subjunctive when the action is or was in the future at the time of speaking:

cuando; **~ I was young** cuando era joven; **he had just sat down ~ the phone rang** acababa de sentarse cuando sonó el teléfono; **call me ~ you get there** llámame cuando llegues; **he said he'd tell me ~ I was older** dijo que me lo diría cuando fuera mayor

> If **when** + VERB can be substituted by **on** + -ING in English and describes an action that takes place at the same time as another one or follows it very closely, you can use **al** + INFINITIVE:

be careful ~ crossing or **~ you cross the road** ten cuidado al cruzar la calle; **the floor is slippery ~ wet** el suelo resbala cuando está mojado
2 (= *if*) si, cuando; **this sounds expensive ~ compared with other cars** éste parece caro si or cuando se compara con otros coches
3 (= *whereas*) cuando; **he thought he was recovering, ~ in fact ...** pensaba que se estaba recuperando, cuando de hecho ...

whence [wens] ADV **1** (*poet*) (= *from where*) de donde
2 (*frm*) (= *from which*) por lo cual; (= *therefore*) y por consiguiente

whenever [wen'evəʳ] **A** CONJ **1** (= *at whatever time*) cuando; **come ~ you like** ven cuando quieras
2 (= *every time*) siempre que, cuando, cada vez que, cada que (*Mex**); **~ I smell roses I think of Mary** siempre que or cada vez que or cuando huele a rosas me acuerdo de Mary; **I go ~ I can** voy siempre que puedo; **we will help ~ possible** ayudaremos siempre cuando or que sea posible
B ADV **1 Monday, Tuesday, or ~** el lunes o el martes o cuando sea
2 (*in questions*) cuándo; **~ can he have done it?** ¿cuándo demonios ha podido hacerlo?

where

A ADVERB	**B** CONJUNCTION

where [weəʳ] **A** ADVERB
1 (*in questions and reported speech*) dónde; **~ am I?** ¿dónde estoy?; **~ are you going (to)?** ¿a dónde or adónde vas?, ¿dónde vas?; **~ would we be if ...?** ¿a dónde or adónde habríamos ido a parar si ...?; **~ did we go wrong?** ¿en qué nos equivocamos?; **I don't know ~ she lives** no sé dónde vive
2 (*in other statements*) donde (*without an accent*); **this is ~ we found it** aquí es donde lo encontramos; **that's just ~ you're wrong!** ¡en eso te equivocas!, ¡ahí es donde te

equivocas!; **the house ~ Diego was born** la casa (en) donde nació Diego
B CONJUNCTION
1 (= *if*) **~ husband and wife both work, benefits are ...** en el caso de que los dos esposos trabajen, los beneficios son ...; **~ possible** en lo posible
2 (= *whereas*) mientras que, cuando; **sometimes a teacher will be listened to ~ a parent might not** a veces a un maestro se le hace caso, mientras que or cuando a un padre tal vez no

whereabouts **A** [ˌweərəˈbaʊts] ADV dónde; **~ did you first see it?** ¿dónde lo viste por primera vez? **B** [ˈweərəbaʊts] NSING or NPL paradero *msing*; **nobody knows his ~** se desconoce su paradero actual

whereas [weərˈæz] CONJ mientras

whereby [weəˈbaɪ] ADV (*frm*) por lo cual, por donde

whereupon [ˈweərəpɒn] ADV (*frm or liter*) con lo cual, después de lo cual

wherever [weərˈevəʳ] **A** CONJ **1** (= *no matter where*) dondequiera que; **he follows me ~ I go** me sigue dondequiera que or por donde vaya; **~ I am** (esté) donde esté; **I'll buy them ~ they come from** los compraré no importa su procedencia, los compraré vengan de donde vengan
2 (= *anywhere*) donde; **sit ~ you like** siéntate donde te parezca bien; **~ possible** donde sea posible
B ADV **1 in Madrid, London, or ~** en Madrid, Londres o donde sea; **he comes from Laxey, ~ that is** es de Laxey, a saber dónde está eso
2 (*in questions*) ¿dónde demonios or diablos?; **~ did you put it?** ¿dónde demonios lo pusiste?

wherewithal [ˈweəwɪðɔːl] N **the ~ (to do sth)** los medios (para hacer algo), los recursos (para hacer algo)

whet [wet] VT [+ *appetite, curiosity*] estimular, despertar

whether [ˈweðəʳ] CONJ si; **I don't know ~ ...** no sé si ...; **I doubt ~ ...** dudo que ... + *subjun*; **~ you like it or not** tanto si quieres como si no; **~ they come or not** vengan o no (vengan)

whew [hwjuː] EXCL ¡vaya!, ¡caramba!

whey [weɪ] N suero *m*

which

A PRONOUN	**B** ADJECTIVE

which [wɪtʃ] **A** PRONOUN
1 (*in questions and reported speech*) cuál; **~ do you want?** (*offering one*) ¿cuál quieres?; (*offering two or more*) ¿cuáles quieres?; **I can't tell ~ is ~** no sé cuál es cuál; **~ of you is Kathleen?** ¿cuál de vosotras es Kathleen?
2 (*relative*) (= *that*) que; **the letter ~ came this morning** la carta que llegó esta mañana
3 (*giving additional information*) que, lo/la cual; **your letter, ~ I received this morning, cheered me up** tu carta, que or (*more frm*) la cual he recibido esta mañana, me ha levantado el ánimo
4 (*replacing clause*) lo que, lo cual; **it rained hard, ~ upset her** llovió mucho, lo que or lo cual le disgustó
5 (*after preposition*) lo cual; **after ~ we went to bed** después de lo cual nos acostamos
B ADJECTIVE
1 (*in questions and reported speech*) qué; (*when the possibilities are limited*) cuál/cuáles de; **~ picture do you prefer?** ¿qué cuadro prefieres?, ¿cuál de los cuadros prefieres?; **I don't know ~ tie he wants** no sé qué corbata quiere; **~ one?** ¿cuál?; **~ way did she go?** ¿por dónde se fue?
2 (*relative*) **in ~ case** en cuyo caso; **he didn't get here till ten, by ~ time Jane had already left** no llegó hasta las diez y para entonces Jane ya se había ido

whichever [wɪtʃˈevəʳ] **A** PRON **1** (= *no matter which*) **~ of the methods you choose** cualquiera de los métodos que escojas, no importa el método que escojas
2 (= *the one which*) el/la que; **choose ~ is easiest** elige el que sea más fácil
B ADJ **1** (= *no matter which*) **~ system you have there are**

difficulties no importa el sistema que tengas *or* cualquiera que sea el sistema que tengas, hay problemas; **~ way you look at it** se mire como se mire
2 (= *any, the ... which*) el ... que/la ... que; **you can choose ~ system you want** puedes elegir el sistema que quieras

whiff [wɪf] Ⓐ N **1** (= *smell*) olorcito *m*; (= *nasty*) tufillo; **to catch a ~ of sth** oler algo; **what a ~!** ¡qué tufo! **2** (= *sniff*) **to go out for a ~ of air** salir a tomar el fresco Ⓑ VI (*) oler (mal)

while [waɪl] Ⓐ N **1 a ~** (= *some moments*) un ratito; (= *some minutes, hours*) un rato; (= *some weeks, months*) un tiempo; **after a ~** al cabo de un rato, al rato; **I lived in Paris for a ~** viví un tiempo en París; **let it simmer for a ~** deje que hierva un rato a fuego lento; **a little ~ ago** hace poco; **a long ~ ago** hace mucho; **once in a ~** de vez en cuando; **it takes quite a ~** lleva tiempo; **in a short ~** dentro de poco, al rato (*LAm*)
2 it is worth ~ to ask whether ... vale la pena preguntar si ...; **we'll make it worth your ~** te compensaremos generosamente; **it's not worth my ~** no me vale la pena
Ⓑ CONJ **1** (= *during the time that*) mientras; **~ this was happening** mientras pasaba esto; **~ you are away** mientras estés fuera
2 (= *as long as*) mientras (que); **it won't happen ~ I'm here** no pasará mientras (que) yo esté aquí
3 (= *although*) aunque; **~ I admit it is awkward** aunque reconozco que es difícil
4 (= *whereas*) mientras que; **I enjoy sport, ~ he prefers reading** a mí me gusta el deporte, mientras que él prefiere la lectura
➤ **while away** VT + ADV **to ~ away the time** *or* **the hours** pasar el tiempo *or* el rato

whilst [waɪlst] CONJ (*esp Brit*) = **while B**

whim [wɪm] N capricho *m*, antojo *m*; **a passing ~** un capricho pasajero, un antojo

whimper ['wɪmpəʳ] Ⓐ N [*from dog, sick person*] gemido *m*, quejido *m*; **without a ~** sin un quejido, sin una queja Ⓑ VI [*dog*] gemir, gimotear; [*sick person*] gemir; [*child*] lloriquear

whimpering ['wɪmpərɪŋ] ADJ [*dog*] que gime, que gimotea; [*sick person*] que gime; [*child*] que lloriquea

whimsical ['wɪmzɪkəl] ADJ [*person*] caprichoso; [*idea, suggestion*] caprichoso, fantástico; [*smile*] enigmático

whine [waɪn] Ⓐ N [*of dog*] gemido *m*; (*louder*) gañido *m*; [*of child*] quejido *m*; [*of siren, bullet*] silbido *m* Ⓑ VI **1** (= *make noise*) [*dog*] gemir; (*louder*) gañir; [*child*] lloriquear, gimotear; [*siren, bullet*] silbar **2** (*) (= *complain*) quejarse

whinge* [wɪndʒ] VI (*Brit*) quejarse (**about** de)

whining ['waɪnɪŋ] N **1** (= *complaining*) quejidos *mpl*, gimoteo *m* **2** [*of engine*] chirrido *m* [*of siren*] silbido *m*; [*of dog*] gemido(s) *m(pl)*; (*louder*) gañido(s) *m(pl)*

whinny ['wɪnɪ] Ⓐ N relincho *m* Ⓑ VI relinchar

whip [wɪp] Ⓐ N (*for training animals*) látigo *m*; (= *riding crop*) fusta *f*, fuete *m* (*LAm*); (*for punishment*) azote *m* Ⓑ VT **1** [+ *horse*] fustigar; [+ *person*] azotar; [+ *child*] dar un azote a, dar una paliza a **2** [+ *cream*] batir, montar (*Sp*); [+ *egg white*] batir **3** (*) (= *take quickly*) **he ~ped a gun out of his pocket** en un abrir y cerrar de ojos sacó un revólver del bolsillo **4** (*Brit**) (= *steal*) mangar*, birlar*
Ⓒ CPD ➤ **whip hand** ✦ IDIOM **to have the ~ hand** llevar la voz cantante
➤ **whip around** VI + ADV (= *turn*) [*person*] volverse *or* darse la vuelta de repente
➤ **whip out** VT + ADV sacar de repente
➤ **whip round** VI + ADV = **whip around**
➤ **whip up** VT + ADV **1** (*) (= *make*) [+ *meal*] preparar rápidamente; [+ *dress*] hacer rápidamente
2 [+ *cream*] batir, montar (*Sp*); [+ *egg white*] batir
3 (= *stir up*) [+ *support*] procurar, conseguir;

[+ *enthusiasm, interest, excitement*] despertar

whiplash ['wɪplæʃ] N (*also ~ injury*) traumatismo *m* cervical

whipped [wɪpt] ADJ batido ➤ **whipped cream** nata *f* (*Sp*) *or* crema *f* (*LAm*) montada

whippersnapper†* ['wɪpəˌsnæpəʳ] N (*also* **young ~**) mequetrefe *m*

whippet ['wɪpɪt] N perro *m* lebrel

whipping ['wɪpɪŋ] Ⓐ N **1** (= *hiding*) tunda* *f*, azotaina* *f*; (*more serious*) paliza* *f*; **to give sb a ~** dar una tunda *or* azotaina a algn **2** (*) (= *defeat*) paliza* *f* Ⓑ CPD ➤ **whipping boy** cabeza *f* de turco, chivo *m* expiatorio ➤ **whipping cream** nata *f* para montar (*Sp*), crema *f* para batir (*LAm*)

whip-round* ['wɪpraʊnd] N (*esp Brit*) colecta *f*; **to have a ~ (for sb)** hacer una colecta (para algn)

whirl [wɜːl] Ⓐ N (= *spin*) giro *m*, vuelta *f*; [*of dust, water etc*] remolino *m*; **my head is in a ~** la cabeza me está dando vueltas; **the social ~** la actividad social; ✦ IDIOM **let's give it a ~*** ¡nada se pierde con intentar! Ⓑ VT hacer girar Ⓒ VI [*wheel, merry-go-round*] girar; [*leaves, dust, water*] arremolinarse; **my head was ~ing** me daba vueltas la cabeza

whirlpool ['wɜːlpuːl] N remolino *m*; (*fig*) vorágine *f*

whirlwind ['wɜːlwɪnd] Ⓐ N torbellino *m*; ✦ IDIOM **like a ~** como un torbellino, como una tromba Ⓑ CPD [*romance*] apasionado, arrollador; **they took us on a ~ tour** nos llevaron de gira relámpago

whirr [wɜːʳ] Ⓐ N [*of machine*] (*quiet*) zumbido *m*, runrún *m*; (*louder*) rechino *m* Ⓑ VI [*machine*] (*quietly*) zumbar, runrunear; (*more loudly*) rechinar

whisk [wɪsk] Ⓐ N (= *hand whisk*) batidor *m*; (= *electric whisk*) batidora *f* Ⓑ VT **1** [+ *egg white*] batir **2** (*) (= *move quickly*) **they ~ed him off to a meeting** se lo llevaron volando a una reunión

whisker ['wɪskəʳ] N [*of animal*] bigote *m*; (= *hair*) pelo *m*; **~s** (= *side whiskers*) patillas *fpl*; (= *beard*) barba *fsing*; (= *moustache*) bigote(s) *m(pl)*; ✦ IDIOM **by a ~** por un pelo

whisky, whiskey (*US, Irl*) ['wɪskɪ] N whisky *m*

whisper ['wɪspəʳ] Ⓐ N cuchicheo *m*, susurro *m*; [*of leaves*] susurro *m*; **to speak in a ~** hablar en voz baja, susurrar Ⓑ VT decir en voz baja, susurrar; **to ~ sth to sb** decir algo al oído de algn, susurrar algo a algn Ⓒ VI cuchichear, susurrar, hablar muy bajo; [*leaves*] susurrar; **to ~ to sb** cuchichear a algn; **it's rude to ~ in company** es de mala educación cuchichear en compañía, secretos en reunión es falta de educación

whispering ['wɪspərɪŋ] N (= *talking*) cuchicheo *m*

whist [wɪst] N whist *m*

whistle ['wɪsl] Ⓐ N **1** (= *sound*) silbido *m*, chiflido *m* (*esp LAm*); **final ~** pitido *m* final **2** (= *instrument*) silbato *m*, pito *m*; **the referee blew his ~** el árbitro pitó; ✦ IDIOM **to blow the ~ on sb** (= *denounce*) delatar a algn Ⓑ VT silbar; **to ~ a tune** silbar una melodía Ⓒ VI silbar, chiflar (*esp LAm*); (*Sport*) pitar, silbar; **the boys ~ at the girls** los chicos silban a las chicas; **the bullet ~d past my ear** la bala pasó silbando muy cerca de mi oreja

whistle-stop ['wɪslstɒp] N (*US*) (= *station*) apeadero *m*
➤ **whistle-stop tour** (*by tourist*) recorrido *m* rápido; (*by*

politician) visita *f* relámpago

Whit [wɪt] (*Brit*) **Ⓐ** N Pentecostés *m*; **Ⓑ** CPD [*holiday, weekend*] de Pentecostés ➤ **Whit Monday** (*Brit*) lunes *m* de Pentecostés ➤ **Whit Sunday** (*Brit*) día *m* de Pentecostés

whit [wɪt] N († *or liter*) **not a** ~ ni un ápice

white [waɪt] **Ⓐ** ADJ (*compar* ~**r**; *superl* ~**st**) blanco; **to go** *or* **turn** ~ (*in face*) ponerse blanco *or* pálido, palidecer; **he went** ~ **at the age of 30** el pelo se le puso blanco a los 30 años, encaneció a los 30 años; **she was** ~ **with rage** estaba pálida de la rabia; ✦ IDIOM **to be as** ~ **as a sheet** *or* **ghost** estar pálido como la muerte

Ⓑ N **1** (= *colour*) blanco *m*; **the sheets were a dazzling** ~ las sábanas eran de un blanco deslumbrante; **to be dressed in** ~ ir vestido de blanco

2 (= *white person*) blanco/a *m/f*

3 [*of egg*] clara *f*

4 [*of eye*] blanco *m*

Ⓒ CPD ➤ **white blood cell** glóbulo *m* blanco ➤ **white bread** pan *m* blanco ➤ **white chocolate** chocolate *m* blanco ➤ **white Christmas** Navidades *fpl* blancas *or* con nieve ➤ **white coffee** (*Brit*) (*milky*) café *m* con leche; (*with dash of milk*) café *m* cortado ➤ **white elephant** (*fig*) elefante *m* blanco ➤ **white flag** bandera *f* blanca ➤ **white gold** oro *m* blanco ➤ **white goods** electrodomésticos *mpl* ➤ **white horses** (*on waves*) cabrillas *fpl* ➤ **the White House** (*in US*) la Casa Blanca; *ver tb* www.whitehouse.gov ➤ **white knight** (*Fin*) caballero *m* blanco ➤ **white lie** mentira *f* piadosa ➤ **white meat** (*Culin*) carne *f* blanca ➤ **White Pages** (*US Telec*) Páginas *fpl* Blancas ➤ **White Paper** (*Brit, Australia, Canada Parl*) libro *m* blanco ➤ **white pepper** pimienta *f* blanca ➤ **white sauce** salsa *f* bechamel, besamel *f* (*Sp*) ➤ **white spirit** (*Brit*) trementina *f* ➤ **white tie** (= *tie*) pajarita *f* blanca (*Sp*), corbata *f* de moño blanca (*LAm*); (= *outfit*) traje *m* de etiqueta con pajarita (*Sp*) *or* corbata *f* de moño (*LAm*) blanca ➤ **white water** aguas *fpl* rápidas ➤ **white water rafting** piragüismo *m* en aguas rápidas, rafting *m* ➤ **white wedding** (*esp Brit*) **to have a** ~ **wedding** casarse de blanco (y por la iglesia) ➤ **white wine** vino *m* blanco

whitebait ['waɪtbeɪt] N morralla *f*, pescadito *m* frito

white-collar worker ['waɪtˌkɒlə'wɜ:kə'] N oficinista *mf*

white-haired ['waɪt'heəd] ADJ canoso, con canas

Whitehall [ˌwaɪt'hɔ:l] N *calle de Londres en la cual hay muchos ministerios*; (*fig*) el gobierno británico

white-hot ['waɪt'hɒt] ADJ calentado al blanco, candente

whiten ['waɪtn] **Ⓐ** VT blanquear **Ⓑ** VI [*person*] palidecer, ponerse pálido

whiteness ['waɪtnɪs] N blancura *f*

whitewash ['waɪtwɒʃ] **Ⓐ** N **1** (*for walls*) cal *f*, jalbegue *m* **2** (*fig*) encubrimiento *m* **Ⓑ** VT **1** [+ *wall*] encalar, enjalbegar **2** (*Sport**) dejar en blanco, dar un baño a*

whiting ['waɪtɪŋ] N (*pl* ~) (= *fish*) pescadilla *f*

Whitsun ['wɪtsn] N (*Brit*) Pentecostés *m*

whittle ['wɪtl] VT [+ *wood, shape*] tallar (con cuchillo) ➤ **whittle away** **Ⓐ** VT + ADV (= *reduce*) [+ *savings, amount*] ir reduciendo **Ⓑ** VI + ADV **to** ~ **away at sth** [+ *wood, shape*] tallar algo; [+ *amount*] ir reduciendo algo ➤ **whittle down** VT + ADV [+ *workforce, amount*] reducir; **the short-list has been** ~**d down to three** hemos reducido el número de candidatos preseleccionados a tres

whiz(z) [wɪz] **Ⓐ** N (*) (= *genius*) as* *m*; **he's a** ~ **at tennis** es un as del tenis* **Ⓑ** VI **to** ~ **by** *or* **past** [*bullet, arrow*] pasar zumbando; [*car*] pasar a gran velocidad **Ⓒ** CPD ➤ **whiz(z) kid*** prodigio *m*

WHO N ABBR (= **World Health Organization**) OMS *f*; *ver tb* www.who.int/en/

who [hu:] PRON **1** (*in questions, exclamations*) quién *sing*, quiénes *pl*; ~ **is it?** ¿quién es?; ~ **are they?** ¿quiénes son?; ~ **does she think she is?*** ¿quién se cree que es?; **guess** ~! ¡a ver si adivinas quién soy! **2** (*relative*) que; (*after preposition*) el/la que, quien, el/la cual (*more frm*); **my cousin** ~ **lives in New York** mi primo que vive en Nueva York; **the girl** ~ **you spoke to** la chica con la que *or* con quien *or* (*more frm*) con la cual hablaste; **those** ~ **can swim** los que saben nadar

whodun(n)it* [hu:'dʌnɪt] N novela *f* policíaca

whoever [hu:'evə'] PRON **1** (= *no matter who*) **it won't be**

easy, ~ **does it** no será fácil, no importa quién lo haga; **I'll talk to** ~ **it is** hablaré con quien sea

2 (= *anyone that*) ~ **finds it can keep it** quienquiera que lo encuentre puede quedarse con él, el/la que lo encuentre que se lo quede; **ask** ~ **you like** pregúntaselo a cualquiera

3 (= *the person that*) ~ **said that is an idiot** quien haya dicho eso es un imbécil, quienquiera que haya dicho eso es un imbécil

4 (*in questions*) quién; ~ **told you that?** ¿quién te dijo eso?

whole [həʊl] **Ⓐ** N (= *complete unit*) todo *m*; **four quarters make a** ~ cuatro cuartos hacen una unidad; **the estate is to be sold as a** ~ la propiedad va a venderse como una unidad; **the** ~ **of** todo; **the** ~ **of Glasgow was talking about it** todo Glasgow hablaba de ello; **the** ~ **of July** todo el mes de julio; **the** ~ **of Europe** toda Europa, Europa entera; **on the** ~ en general

Ⓑ ADJ **1** (= *entire*) todo; **a** ~ **hour** toda una hora, una hora entera; **it rained for three** ~ **days** llovió durante tres días enteros *or* seguidos; ~ **towns were destroyed** pueblos enteros fueron destruidos; **he took the** ~ **lot*** se lo llevó todo; **the** ~ **point was to avoid that happening** el propósito era evitar que eso pasara; **let's forget the** ~ **thing** olvidemos todo el asunto, olvidémoslo todo; **the** ~ **world** todo el mundo, el mundo entero; ✦ IDIOM **to go the** ~ **hog*** liarse la manta a la cabeza*

2 (= *intact*) entero; **keep the egg yolks** ~ procure que no se rompan las yemas de huevo; **he swallowed it** ~ se lo tragó entero

Ⓒ CPD ➤ **whole milk** leche *f* entera ➤ **whole note** (*US*) semibreve *f* ➤ **whole number** número *m* entero

wholefood(s) ['həʊlfu:d(z)] N(PL) (*Brit*) comida *f* naturista, alimentos *mpl* integrales

wholegrain ['həʊlgreɪn] ADJ [*bread, cereal*] integral

wholehearted ['həʊl'hɑ:tɪd] ADJ incondicional

wholeheartedly ['həʊl'hɑ:tɪdlɪ] ADV incondicionalmente

wholemeal ['həʊlmi:l] ADJ (*Brit*) integral

wholesale ['həʊlseɪl] **Ⓐ** ADJ [*price, trade*] al por mayor; [*destruction*] total, sistemático **Ⓑ** ADV [*buy, sell*] al por mayor **Ⓒ** N venta *f* al por mayor, mayoreo *m* (*Mex*)

wholesaler ['həʊlˌseɪlə'] N comerciante *mf* al por mayor, mayorista *mf*

wholesome ['həʊlsəm] ADJ sano, saludable

wholewheat ['həʊlwi:t] ADJ (*esp US*) de trigo integral, hecho con trigo entero

wholly ['həʊlɪ] ADV totalmente, completamente

whom [hu:m] PRON (*frm*) **1** (*in questions*) ~ **did you see?** ¿a quién viste?; **from** ~ **did you receive it?** ¿de quién lo recibiste? **2** (*relative*) **the gentleman** ~ **I saw** el señor a quien *or* al cual *or* al que vi, el señor que vi (*less frm*); **the lady with** ~ **I was talking** la señora con la que *or* con la cual *or* con quien hablaba; **three policemen, none of** ~ **wore a helmet** tres policías, ninguno de los cuales llevaba casco; **three policemen, all of** ~ **were drunk** tres policías, que estaban todos borrachos

whoop [hu:p] **Ⓐ** N grito *m*, alarido *m* **Ⓑ** VI gritar, dar alaridos **Ⓒ** VT **to** ~ **it up**†* (= *make merry*) divertirse ruidosamente; (= *let hair down*) echar una cana al aire

whooping cough ['hu:pɪŋˌkɒf] N tos *f* ferina, coqueluche *f*

whoops [wu:ps] EXCL ¡epa!, ¡ep!

whoosh [wʊʃ] N *ruido del agua que sale bajo presión, o del viento fuerte*

whopper* ['wɒpə'] N **1** (= *big thing*) monstruo *m*; **that fish is a** ~ ese pez es enorme **2** (= *lie*) bola *f*

whopping* ['wɒpɪŋ] ADJ (*also* ~ **great**) enorme, grandísimo

whore ['hɔ:'] N (*pej*) puta *f*

whorl [wɜ:l] N [*of fingerprint*] espiral *m*

whose [hu:z] **Ⓐ** PRON de quién; ~ **is this?** ¿de quién es esto?; ~ **are these?** (*one owner expected*) ¿de quién son éstos?; (*two or more owners expected*) ¿de quiénes son éstos?; **I don't know** ~ **it is** no sé de quién es

Ⓑ ADJ **1** (*in questions*) de quién; ~ **purse is this?** ¿de quién es este monedero?; ~ **cars are these?** (*one owner expected*) ¿de quién son estos coches?; (*two or more owners expected*)

¿de quiénes son estos coches?
2 (*relative*) cuyo; **the man ~ hat I took** el hombre cuyo sombrero tomé; **the man ~ seat I sat in** el hombre en cuya silla me senté

why [waɪ] **Ⓐ** ADV por qué; **~ not?** ¿por qué no?; **I know ~ you did it** sé por qué lo hiciste; **that's ~ I couldn't come** por eso no pude venir; **which is ~ I am here** que es por lo que estoy aquí **Ⓑ** EXCL (*esp US*) ¡toma!, ¡anda!

WI Ⓐ ABBR **1** = **West Indies 2** (*US*) = **Wisconsin Ⓑ** N ABBR (*Brit*) (= **Women's Institute**) ≈ IM *m*

wick [wɪk] N mecha *f*; ✦ IDIOM **he gets on my ~** (*Brit**) me hace subir por las paredes*

wicked ['wɪkɪd] **Ⓐ** ADJ **1** (= *evil*) malvado, cruel **2** (= *naughty*) [*look, suggestion*] pícaro; [*sense of humour*] socarrón **3** (*) [*price, waste*] escandaloso; [*temper*] terrible **4** (*Brit***) (= *brilliant*) estupendo*, guay (*Sp**) **Ⓑ** N ✦ IDIOM **there's no rest** *or* **peace for the ~** no hay descanso para los malvados

wickedness ['wɪkɪdnɪs] N (= *evil*) maldad *f*, crueldad *f*

wicker ['wɪkəʳ] **Ⓐ** N mimbre *m or f* **Ⓑ** ADJ de mimbre

wicket ['wɪkɪt] N (*Cricket*) (= *stumps*) palos *mpl*; (= *pitch*) terreno *m*; (= *fallen wicket*) entrada *f*, turno *m* ➤ **wicket keeper** guardameta *mf*

wide [waɪd] **Ⓐ** ADJ (*compar* **~r**; *superl* **~st**) **1** [*street, river, trousers*] ancho; [*area*] extenso; [*ocean, desert*] vasto; [*space, circle, valley*] amplio; **it's ten centimetres ~** tiene diez centímetros de ancho *or* de anchura; **how ~ is it?** ¿cuánto tiene de ancho?, ¿qué anchura tiene?; **her eyes were ~ with amazement** tenía los ojos como platos de asombro* **2** (= *extensive*) [*support, variety*] gran; [*range, selection*] amplio; **there is a ~ choice of colours** hay muchos colores para escoger; **to win by a ~ margin** ganar por un margen amplio **3** (= *off target*) **his first shot was ~** (*Ftbl*) su primer tiro *or* chute pasó de largo; (*Shooting*) su primer disparo no dio en el blanco **Ⓑ** ADV **1** (= *fully*) **he opened the window ~** abrió la ventana de par en par; **~ apart** bien separados; **to be ~ awake** estar completamente despierto; **~ open** [*window, door*] de par en par, completamente abierto; **with his eyes (open) ~** *or* **~ open** con los ojos muy abiertos **2** (= *off target*) **the shot went ~** (*Ftbl*) el tiro *or* chute pasó de largo; (*Shooting*) el disparo no dio en el blanco

wide-angle ['waɪdˌæŋgl] ADJ ➤ **wide-angle lens** gran angular *m*

wide-awake ['waɪdə'weɪk] ADJ **1** (= *fully awoken*) completamente *or* bien despierto **2** (= *on the ball*) despabilado; (= *alert*) vigilante, alerta

wide-eyed ['waɪd'aɪd] ADJ con los ojos muy abiertos, con los ojos como platos*; (*fig*) inocente, cándido

widely ['waɪdlɪ] ADV [*travel, vary, differ*] mucho; **to be ~ available** poder conseguirse con facilidad; **it is ~ believed that ...** mucha gente cree que ...; **to be ~ read** [*reader*] tener una amplia cultura, haber leído mucho; [*author*] contar con un gran número de lectores; **it is ~ regarded as ... as** es considerado por la mayoría como ...; **to be ~ travelled** haber viajado mucho; **to be ~ used** ser de uso extendido *or* generalizado

widen ['waɪdn] **Ⓐ** VT [+ *road, river*] ensanchar **Ⓑ** VI [*road, river*] (*also* **~ out**) ensancharse; **the gap between rich and poor has ~ed** ha aumentado la diferencia entre ricos y pobres

wide-ranging ['waɪdˌreɪndʒɪŋ] ADJ [*survey, report*] de gran alcance; [*interests*] muy diversos

wide-screen ['waɪdskriːn] ADJ [*film*] para pantalla ancha; [*television set*] de pantalla ancha, con pantalla panorámica

widespread ['waɪdspred] ADJ [*use*] generalizado, extendido; [*belief, concern*] generalizado; [*support, criticism*] a nivel general; **to become ~** extenderse, generalizarse

widow ['wɪdəʊ] **Ⓐ** N viuda *f*; **I'm a golf ~** paso mucho tiempo sola mientras mi marido juega al golf **Ⓑ** VT **to be ~ed** enviudar, quedar viudo/a; **she has been ~ed for five years** enviudó hace cinco años, quedó viuda hace cinco años; **his ~ed mother** su madre viuda

widower ['wɪdəʊəʳ] N viudo *m*

width [wɪdθ] N **1** [*of street, river*] ancho *m*, anchura *f*; **what ~ is the room?** ¿qué ancho *or* anchura tiene la habitación?; **it is five metres in ~** tiene cinco metros de ancho *or* anchura, tiene un ancho *or* una anchura de cinco metros **2** [*of swimming pool*] ancho *m*

widthways ['wɪdθweɪz] ADV, **widthwise** ['wɪdθwaɪz] ADV a lo ancho

wield [wiːld] VT [+ *sword, axe, pen*] manejar; [+ *power, influence*] ejercer

wife [waɪf] N (*pl* **wives**) mujer *f*, esposa *f*

wig [wɪg] N peluca *f*

wiggle ['wɪgl] **Ⓐ** N meneo *m* **Ⓑ** VT [+ *toes, fingers*] mover (mucho); [+ *hips*] contonear, menear

wiggly ['wɪglɪ] ADJ [*line*] ondulado

wigwam ['wɪgwæm] N tipi *m*, tienda *f* india

wild [waɪld] **Ⓐ** ADJ (*compar* **-er**; *superl* **-est**) **1** (= *not domesticated*) [*animal, bird*] salvaje; [*plant, strawberry*] silvestre; [*countryside*] salvaje, agreste; **~ flowers** flores *fpl* silvestres; ✦ IDIOMS **~ horses wouldn't drag me there** tendrían que llevarme a rastras, no iría ni por todo el oro del mundo; **to sow one's ~ oats** correrla* **2** (= *fierce*) [*animal*] feroz **3** (= *stormy*) [*wind*] furioso, violento; [*weather*] tormentoso; [*sea*] bravo **4** (= *unrestrained*) [*party, person*] loco; [*enthusiasm*] desenfrenado; [*hair*] revuelto; [*appearance*] desastrado; [*look, eyes*] de loco; **he had a ~ youth** hizo muchas locuras en su juventud; **we had some ~ times together!** ¡hicimos cada locura juntos! **5** (*) (= *angry*) **it makes me ~** me saca de quicio **6** (*) (= *distraught*) **I was ~ with jealousy** estaba loco de celos **7** (*) (= *ecstatic*) [*cheers, applause*] exaltado, apasionado; **he's ~ about her** está loco por ella; **I'm not exactly ~ about the idea** no es que la idea me entusiasme demasiado; **the crowd went ~ (with excitement)** la multitud se puso loca de entusiasmo **8** (= *crazy, rash*) [*idea, plan, rumour*] descabellado, disparatado; **it's a ~ exaggeration** es una enorme exageración; **they made some ~ promises** hicieron unas promesas disparatadas; **they have succeeded beyond their ~est dreams** han tenido más éxito del que jamás habían soñado; **it's just a ~ guess** no es más que una conjetura al azar *or* una suposición muy aventurada **9** (*Cards*) **aces are ~** los ases sirven de comodines **Ⓑ** ADV **to grow ~** crecer en estado silvestre; **to run ~** [*animal*] correr libremente; [*child*] corretear libremente; **the garden had run ~** las plantas del jardín habían crecido de forma descontrolada; **you've let your imagination run ~** te has dejado llevar por la imaginación **Ⓒ** N **animals caught in the ~** animales capturados en su hábitat natural; **the call of the ~** el atractivo de lo salvaje *or* de la naturaleza; **the ~s of Canada** las tierras inexploradas de Canadá; **to live out in the ~s** (*hum*) vivir en el quinto pino* **Ⓓ** CPD ➤ **wild beast** fiera *f*, bestia *f* salvaje ➤ **wild boar** jabalí *m* ➤ **wild card** (*Comput, Cards*) comodín *m* ➤ **wild goose chase: he sent me off on a ~ goose chase** me mandó de la Ceca a la Meca* ➤ **wild rice** arroz *m* silvestre ➤ **the Wild West** el oeste americano

wildcat ['waɪld'kæt] **Ⓐ** N (= *animal*) gato *m* montés **Ⓑ** CPD [*scheme, venture*] descabellado ➤ **wildcat strike** huelga *f* salvaje *or* no autorizada

wilderness ['wɪldənɪs] N (= *desert*) desierto *m*; (= *hills*) monte *m*; (= *virgin land*) tierra *f* virgen

wildfire ['waɪldˌfaɪəʳ] N **to spread like ~** correr como un reguero de pólvora

wildlife ['waɪldlaɪf] N fauna *f* ➤ **wildlife reserve, wildlife sanctuary** reserva *f* natural

wildly ['waɪldlɪ] ADV **1** (= *ecstatically*) [*shout*] como loco; [*applaud*] a rabiar, como loco **2** (= *frantically*) [*stare, look*] con cara de espanto; [*gesture*] como loco, violentamente **3** (= *extremely*) [*exaggerated*] muy; [*fluctuate, vary*] muchísimo; **a ~ inaccurate estimate** un cálculo que dista muchísimo de la realidad; **~ enthusiastic** loco de entusiasmo

wiles [waɪlz] NPL artimañas *fpl*, ardides *mpl*

wilful, willful (*US*) ['wɪlfʊl] ADJ **1** (= *obstinate*) testarudo, terco **2** (= *deliberate*) intencionado, deliberado, premeditado; [*murder etc*] premeditado

will¹ [wɪl] (*pt* **would**) **Ⓐ** AUX VB, MODAL AUX VB **1** (*future*) **I ~ or I'll finish it tomorrow** lo terminaré mañana; **you won't lose it, ~ you?** no lo perderás ¿verdad?; (*stronger*) no lo vayas a perder; **you ~ come to see us, won't you?** vendrás a vernos, ¿no?; **it won't take long** no llevará mucho tiempo; **what ~ you do?** ¿qué vas a hacer?; **we'll be having lunch late** vamos a comer tarde; **we'll talk about it later** hablamos luego; **I WILL do it!** ¡sí lo haré!
2 (*future perfect*) **will have** (+ PAST PARTICIPLE): **I ~ or I'll have finished it by tomorrow** lo habré terminado para mañana
3 (*in conjectures*) **he'll be there by now** ya debe de haber llegado *or* ya habrá llegado; **that ~ be the postman** será el cartero
4 (*expressing unwillingness*) **Tom won't help me** Tom no me quiere ayudar; **I won't put up with it!** ¡no lo voy a consentir!
5 (*in commands, insistence*) **~ you sit down!** ¡siéntate!; **~ you be quiet!** ¿te quieres callar?; **"I won't go" — "oh yes you ~"** —no voy —¿cómo que no?
6 (*in offers*) **come on, I'll help you** venga, te ayudo
7 (*in requests*) **~ you help me?** ¿me ayudas?; **wait a moment, ~ you?** espera un momento, ¿quieres?
8 (*in invitations*) **~ you have some tea?** ¿quieres tomar un té?; **~ you sit down?** ¿quiere usted sentarse?, tome usted asiento (*more frm*); **won't you come with us?** ¿no quieres venir con nosotros?
9 (*expressing habits*) soler, acostumbrar a; **she ~ read for hours on end** suele leer *or* acostumbra a leer durante horas y horas
10 (*expressing persistence*) **she WILL smoke, despite what the doctor says** a pesar de lo que dice el médico, se empeña en fumar; **accidents WILL happen** son cosas que pasan; **he WILL keep leaving the door open** siempre tiene que dejar la puerta abierta
11 (*expressing capability*) **the car won't start** el coche no arranca; **a man who ~ do that ~ do anything** un hombre que es capaz de eso es capaz de todo
Ⓑ VI (= *wish*) querer

will² [wɪl] **Ⓐ** N **1** (= *inclination, wish*) voluntad *f*; **against sb's ~** contra la voluntad de algn; **at ~** a voluntad; **to do sth of one's own free ~** hacer algo por voluntad propia; **to have a ~ of one's own** tener voluntad propia; **the ~ to live** el deseo de vivir; **with the best ~ in the world** por mucho que se quiera; **✦** PROV **where there's a ~ there's a way** querer es poder
2 (= *testament*) testamento *m*; **the last ~ and testament of ...** la última voluntad de ...; **to make a ~** hacer testamento
Ⓑ VT **1** (= *urge on by willpower*) **I was ~ing you to win** estaba deseando que ganaras
2 (= *leave in one's will*) **to ~ sth to sb** legar algo a algn, dejar algo (en herencia) a algn

willful ['wɪlfʊl] ADJ (*US*) = **wilful**

willie* [wɪlɪ] N (*Brit Anat*) pito* *m*, colita *f* (*Sp**)

willies* ['wɪlɪz] NPL **it gives me the ~** me da horror; **I get the ~ whenever I think about it** me horroriza pensar en ello

willing ['wɪlɪŋ] ADJ **1** (= *enthusiastic*) [*helper*] voluntarioso **2** (= *disposed*) **to be ~ to do sth** estar dispuesto a hacer algo

willingly ['wɪlɪŋlɪ] ADV **1** (= *with pleasure*) con gusto, de buena gana **2** (= *voluntarily*) por voluntad propia

willingness ['wɪlɪŋnɪs] N buena voluntad *f*, buena disposición *f*

will-o'-the-wisp ['wɪləðə'wɪsp] N fuego *m* fatuo

willow ['wɪləʊ] N (*also* ~ **tree**) sauce *m* ➤ **willow pattern** dibujos de aspecto chinesco para la cerámica

willowy ['wɪləʊɪ] ADJ esbelto

willpower ['wɪlpaʊəʳ] N fuerza *f* de voluntad

willy* ['wɪlɪ] N **1** (*Brit Anat*) pito* *m*, colita *f* (*Sp**) **2 the willies** *see* **willies**

willy-nilly ['wɪlɪ'nɪlɪ] ADV (= *unsystematically*) de cualquier manera

wilt [wɪlt] VI [*flower*] marchitarse; **we were beginning to ~ in the heat** el calor estaba empezando a hacernos desfallecer

wily ['waɪlɪ] ADJ (*compar* **wilier**; *superl* **wiliest**) astuto, taimado

wimp* [wɪmp] N **he's a ~** (*physically*) es un debilucho*; (*in character*) es un parado*

win [wɪn] (*vb: pt, pp* **won**) **Ⓐ** N victoria *f*, triunfo *m*; **last Sunday's ~ against** *or* **over Pakistan** la victoria del domingo frente a *or* sobre Pakistán; **I had a ~ on the lottery** gané la lotería
Ⓑ VT **1** [+ *competition, bet, war, election*] ganar; **✦** IDIOMS **you can't ~ them all** no siempre se puede ganar; **to ~ the day** triunfar, imponerse
2 [+ *cup, award, prize, title*] ganar; [+ *contract, order*] obtener, conseguir; [+ *pay rise, promotion*] conseguir, ganarse; [+ *support, friendship, recognition, reputation*] ganarse; **it won him first prize** le valió *or* le ganó el primer premio; **he won five pounds from her at cards** le ganó cinco libras jugando a cartas
Ⓒ VI (*in war, sport, competition*) ganar; **who's ~ning?** ¿quién va ganando?; **OK, you ~*** vale (*Sp*) *or* okey (*LAm*), ganas tú*; **she always ~s at cards** siempre gana a las cartas; **to play to ~** jugar a ganar; **✦** IDIOMS **you can't ~: whatever you say, you're always wrong, you can't ~** digas lo que digas, ellos siempre tienen razón, ¡no hay manera!; **to ~ hands down** ganar de forma aplastante
➤ win back VT + ADV [+ *trophy*] recobrar; [+ *support, confidence*] volver a ganarse; [+ *gambling loss, job*] recuperar; [+ *voters, girlfriend, boyfriend*] volver a conquistar a
➤ win out VI + ADV triunfar, imponerse
➤ win over, win round (*Brit*) VT + ADV convencer; **eventually we won him over to our point of view** por fin lo convencimos de que teníamos razón

wince [wɪns] **Ⓐ** N [*of revulsion*] mueca *f*; [*of pain*] mueca *f* de dolor **Ⓑ** VI (= *shudder*) estremecerse; **he ~d in pain** hizo una mueca de dolor

winch [wɪntʃ] **Ⓐ** N torno *m*, cabrestante *m* **Ⓑ** VT **to ~ sth up/down** levantar/bajar algo (con un torno *or* cabrestante)

wind¹ [wɪnd] **Ⓐ** N **1** viento *m*; **which way is the ~ blowing?** ¿de dónde sopla el viento?; **against the ~** contra el viento; **✦** IDIOMS **to see which way the ~ blows** esperar para ver por dónde van los tiros; **~s of change** aires *mpl* de cambio, aires *mpl* nuevos; **to get ~ of sth** enterarse de algo; **to get the ~ up** (*Brit**) preocuparse; **there's something in the ~** algo se está cociendo; **to put the ~ up sb** (*Brit**) dar un susto a algn; **to take the ~ out of sb's sails** cortar las alas a algn
2 (= *flatulence*) gases *mpl*; [*of baby*] flato *m*; **to break ~** ventosear; **to bring up** [*baby*] eructar
3 (= *breath*) aliento *m*; **to be short of ~** estar sin aliento **Ⓑ** VT (*Brit*) **to ~ sb** (*with punch etc*) dejar a algn sin aliento; **to ~ a baby** hacer eructar a un niño
Ⓒ CPD **➤ wind chimes** móvil *msing* de campanillas **➤ wind farm** parque *m* eólico **➤ wind instrument** instrumento *m* de viento **➤ wind power** energía *f* eólica *or* del viento **➤ wind tunnel** túnel *m* aerodinámico *or* de pruebas aerodinámicas

wind² [waɪnd] (*pt, pp* **wound**) **Ⓐ** VT **1** (= *roll, coil*) [+ *rope, wire*] enrollar; **to ~ one's arms round sb** rodear a algn con los brazos, abrazar a algn estrechamente **2** [+ *clock, watch*] dar cuerda a **3** (= *twist*) **the road ~s its way through the valley** la carretera serpentea por el valle **Ⓑ** VI (= *snake*) serpentear; **the road ~s up the valley** el camino serpentea por el valle; **the car wound slowly up the hill** el coche subió lentamente la sinuosa colina **Ⓒ** N (= *bend*) curva *f*, recodo *m*
➤ wind down **Ⓐ** VT + ADV [+ *car window*] bajar
2 [+ *production, business*] disminuir poco a poco, reducir poco a poco **Ⓑ** VI + ADV **1** [*clock*] pararse **2** (*) (= *relax*) relajarse **3** (*) (= *come to an end*) tocar a su fin
➤ wind up **Ⓐ** VT + ADV **1** [+ *car window*] subir; [+ *clock, toy*] dar cuerda a **2** (= *close*) [+ *meeting, debate*] cerrar, dar por terminado; [+ *company*] liquidar; [+ *speech*] terminar **3 to be wound up** (= *tense*) estar tenso **4** (*Brit**) **to ~ sb up** (= *provoke*) provocar a algn; (= *tease*) tomar el pelo a algn **Ⓑ** VI + ADV **1** (= *finish*) [*meeting, debate, speaker*] concluir, terminar **2** (*) (= *end up*) acabar; **we wound up in Rome** acabamos en Roma, fuimos a parar a Roma

windbag* ['wɪndbæg] N (= *person*) charlatán(a) *m/f*

windborne ['wɪndbɔːn] ADJ llevado por el viento

windbreak ['wɪndbreɪk] N (*for plants*) pantalla *f* cortavientos; (*at seaside*) cortavientos *m inv*

windcheater ['wɪndtʃiːtə'] N (*Brit*) cazadora *f*

windchill ['wɪndtʃɪl] CPD ➤ **the windchill factor** *factor que determina la sensación térmica producida por un viento frío y una baja temperatura*

winder ['waɪndə'] N (*on watch etc*) cuerda *f*

windfall ['wɪndfɔːl] **Ⓐ** N 1 (= *apple etc*) fruta *f* caída 2 (= *money*) dinero *m* caído del cielo **Ⓑ** CPD ➤ **windfall tax** *impuesto sobre determinados beneficios extraordinarios*

winding ['waɪndɪŋ] ADJ [*road, path*] tortuoso, serpenteante ➤ **winding staircase** escalera *f* de caracol

windmill ['wɪndmɪl] N molino *m* de viento

window ['wɪndəʊ] **Ⓐ** N 1 (*gen, Comput*) ventana *f*; (= *shop window*) escaparate *m*, vitrina *f* (*LAm*), vidriera *f* (*SC*); (*of booking office, car, envelope*) ventanilla *f*; **to look out of the ~** mirar por la ventana; **to break a ~** romper un cristal (*Sp*) *or* un vidrio (*LAm*) 2 (= *period of time*) espacio *m* **Ⓑ** CPD ➤ **window box** jardinera *f* de ventana ➤ **window cleaner** (= *liquid*) limpiacristales *m inv* (*Sp*), limpiavidrios *m inv* (*LAm*); (= *person*) limpiacristales *mf inv* (*Sp*), limpiavidrios *mf inv* (*LAm*) ➤ **window display** escaparate *m* ➤ **window dresser** escaparatista *mf*, decorador(a) *m/f* de escaparates ➤ **window dressing** escaparatismo *m*, decoración *f* de escaparates; ✦ IDIOM **it's just ~ dressing** es pura fachada ➤ **window frame** marco *m* de ventana ➤ **window ledge** antepecho *m*, alféizar *m* de la ventana ➤ **window of opportunity** excelente oportunidad *f*, oportunidad *f* única ➤ **window pane** cristal *m* (*Sp*), vidrio *m* (*LAm*) ➤ **window seat** asiento *m* junto a la ventana; (*Rail etc*) asiento *m* junto a una ventanilla ➤ **window shade** (*US*) persiana *f*

window-shopping ['wɪndəʊʃɒpɪŋ] N **to go ~** ir a mirar escaparates

windowsill ['wɪndəʊsɪl] N antepecho *m*, alféizar *m* de la ventana

windpipe ['wɪndpaɪp] N tráquea *f*

windscreen ['wɪndskriːn] N (*Brit*) parabrisas *m inv* ➤ **windscreen washer** lavaparabrisas *m inv* ➤ **windscreen wiper** limpiaparabrisas *m inv*

windshield ['wɪndʃiːld] N (*US*) parabrisas *m inv* ➤ **windshield washer** lavaparabrisas *m inv* ➤ **windshield wiper** limpiaparabrisas *m inv*

windsock ['wɪndsɒk] N (*Aer*) manga *f* (de viento)

windsurfing ['wɪndsɜːfɪŋ] N windsurf *m*; **to go ~** hacer windsurf

windswept ['wɪndswept] ADJ [*place*] azotado por el viento

wind-up ['waɪndʌp] N (*Brit*) (= *joke*) tomadura *f* de pelo*

windy ['wɪndɪ] ADJ (*compar* **windier**; *superl* **windiest**) [*day*] de mucho viento, ventoso; **it's ~ today** hoy hace viento; **Edinburgh's a very ~ city** en Edimburgo hace mucho viento

wine [waɪn] **Ⓐ** N vino *m* **Ⓑ** VT **to ~ and dine sb** agasajar a algn **Ⓒ** CPD ➤ **wine bar** bar *m* especializado en servir vinos ➤ **wine bottle** botella *f* de vino ➤ **wine cask** tonel *m* de vino, barril *m* de vino ➤ **wine cellar** bodega *f* ➤ **wine glass** copa *f* (de vino) ➤ **wine grower** viñador(a) *m/f* ➤ **wine growing** viticultura *f* ➤ **wine list** lista *f* *or* carta *f* de vinos ➤ **wine merchant** (*Brit*) vinatero/a *m/f* ➤ **wine press** prensa *f* de uvas, lagar *m* ➤ **wine rack** botellero *m* ➤ **wine taster** catador(a) *m/f* de vinos ➤ **wine tasting** cata *f* de vinos ➤ **wine vinegar** vinagre *m* de vino ➤ **wine waiter** (*Brit*) sumiller *m*, escanciador *m*

wing [wɪŋ] **Ⓐ** N 1 [*of bird*] ala *f*

Use **el/un** not **la/una** before feminine nouns beginning with stressed **a** or **ha** like **ala**.

---

to be on the ~ estar volando; **to take ~** (*liter*) irse volando, alzar el vuelo; ✦ IDIOMS **to clip sb's ~s** cortar las alas a algn; **to stretch** *or* **spread one's ~s** empezar a volar; **to take sb under one's ~** dar amparo a algn, tomar a algn bajo su protección 2 (*Sport*) (= *position*) extremo *m*, ala *f*; (= *player*) extremo/a *m/f*, alero/a *m/f*

3 (*of building*) ala *f*; **the east/west ~** el ala este/oeste 4 (*of political party*) ala *f*; **the left ~ of the party** el ala izquierda del partido 5 (*Brit*) (*of vehicle*) aleta *f* 6 **wings** (*Theat*) bastidores *mpl*; ✦ IDIOM **to be waiting in the ~s** esperar entre bastidores **Ⓑ** VT 1 **to ~ one's way: soon they were airborne and ~ing their way south** poco tiempo después iban (transportados) por aire en dirección sur 2 **to ~ it*** improvisar sobre la marcha **Ⓒ** CPD ➤ **wing commander** (*Brit*) teniente *mf* coronel de aviación ➤ **wing mirror** retrovisor *m* ➤ **wing nut** tuerca *f* mariposa

winger ['wɪŋə'] N (*Sport*) extremo/a *m/f*, alero/a *m/f*

wingspan ['wɪŋspæn] N envergadura *f*

wink [wɪŋk] **Ⓐ** N (= *blink*) pestañeo *m*; (*meaningful*) guiño *m*; **to give sb a ~** guiñar el ojo a algn; **he said with a ~** dijo guiñando el ojo; **I didn't get a ~ of sleep** no pegué ojo; ✦ IDIOM **to have 40 ~s** echarse una siesta *or* cabezada **Ⓑ** VI guiñar el ojo; **to ~ at sb** guiñar el ojo a algn **Ⓒ** VT [+ *eye*] guiñar

winner ['wɪnə'] N (*in race, competition*) vencedor(a) *m/f*, ganador(a) *m/f*; [*of prize, lottery*] ganador(a) *m/f*; **I think you're on to a ~ there*** creo que con esto tienes la ganancia asegurada

winning ['wɪnɪŋ] **Ⓐ** ADJ 1 [*person, horse, team*] ganador, vencedor; [*number, entry*] ganador; [*goal, shot*] de la victoria, decisivo 2 (= *engaging*) [*smile*] encantador, irresistible; [*personality*] encantador, cautivador **Ⓑ** CPD ➤ **winning post** meta *f*

winnings ['wɪnɪŋz] NPL ganancias *fpl*

wino* ['waɪnəʊ] N alcohólico/a *m/f*

winter ['wɪntə'] N invierno *m*; **in ~** en invierno; **a ~'s day** un día de invierno ➤ **winter clothes** ropa *f* de invierno ➤ **Winter Olympics** Olimpiada *f* de invierno, Juegos *mpl* Olímpicos de invierno ➤ **winter sports** deportes *mpl* de invierno

wintertime ['wɪntətaɪm] N invierno *m*; **in (the) ~** en invierno

wintry, wintery ['wɪntrɪ] ADJ invernal; (*fig*) glacial

wipe [waɪp] **Ⓐ** N **to give sth a ~** pasar un trapo a algo, dar una pasada con un trapo a algo; **baby ~s** toallitas *fpl* húmedas para el bebé **Ⓑ** VT 1 (= *clean, dry*) [+ *table, floor, surface*] pasar un trapo a, limpiar (con un trapo); [+ *blackboard*] borrar, limpiar; [+ *dishes*] secar; [+ *one's nose, shoes*] limpiarse; [+ *one's face, hands*] secarse; **~ your feet before you come in** límpiate los pies antes de entrar; **to ~ sth clean** limpiar algo; **she ~d the tears from her eyes** se secó *or* se limpió las lágrimas de los ojos; ✦ IDIOMS **to ~ the floor with sb*** dar una paliza a algn*; **to ~ the slate clean** hacer borrón y cuenta nueva; **that will ~ the smile off her face!*** ¡eso le quitará las ganas de sonreír!, ¡con eso se le quitarán las ganas de sonreír! 2 (= *erase*) [+ *tape, disk, data*] borrar **Ⓒ** VI secar; **you wash, I'll ~** tú friega, yo seco ➤ **wipe away** VT + ADV 1 [+ *one's tears*] enjugarse, secarse; [+ *sb's tears*] enjugar, secar; [+ *marks*] quitar, limpiar; **he ~d away the blood with a handkerchief** limpió la sangre con un pañuelo 2 [+ *guilt, hurt, memory*] borrar ➤ **wipe off** **Ⓐ** VT + ADV [+ *stain, marks*] quitar, limpiar; [+ *recording, data*] borrar **Ⓑ** VI + ADV [*stain, marks*] salir, limpiarse ➤ **wipe out** VT + ADV 1 (= *clean*) [+ *container*] limpiar 2 (= *eliminate*) [+ *town, people, army*] aniquilar; [+ *species*] exterminar; [+ *disease*] erradicar 3 (= *erase*) [+ *past, memory*] borrar 4 (*) (= *exhaust*) dejar hecho polvo* 5 (*) (= *kill*) liquidar*, borrar del mapa* ➤ **wipe up** VT + ADV limpiar

wiper ['waɪpə'] N (*Brit*) (*also* **windscreen ~**) limpiaparabrisas *m inv*

wire ['waɪə'] **Ⓐ** N 1 (*metal*) alambre *m*; (*Elec*) cable *m*; ✦ IDIOMS **to get one's ~s crossed*** tener un malentendido; **to pull ~s** (*US**) tocar resortes 2 (*US Telec*) telegrama *m* 3 (*Police*) (= *hidden microphone*) micrófono *m* oculto **Ⓑ** VT 1 (*also* **~ up**) (*Elec*) [+ *house*] poner la instalación eléctrica en; [+ *fence*] electrificar; **it's ~d to the alarm** está conectado a la alarma

2 (*US Telec*) **to ~ sb** comunicar con algn (por telegrama) **⊙** CPD ➤ **wire brush** cepillo *m* de alambre ➤ **wire cutters** cortaalambres *msing inv*, cizalla *fsing* ➤ **wire fence** alambrado *m* ➤ **wire mesh**, **wire netting** tela *f* metálica, malla *f* metálica ➤ **wire wool** (*Brit*) lana *f* de alambre

wireless ['waɪəlɪs] **Ⓐ** N (*esp Brit*†) radio *f* **Ⓑ** ADJ (= *without wires*) inalámbrico **⊙** CPD➤ **Wireless Application Protocol** (*Telec*) Protocolo *m* de aplicaciones inalámbricas ➤ **wireless operator** radiotelegrafista *mf*, radio *mf* ➤ **wireless set** radio *f*, receptor *m* de radio, transistor *m* ➤ **wireless technology** tecnología *f* inalámbrica

wiretapping ['waɪətæpɪŋ] N (*US*) intervención *f* de la línea

wiring ['waɪərɪŋ] N (*Elec*) (= *wiring system*) instalación *f* eléctrica; (= *wires*) cables *mpl*

wiry ['waɪərɪ] ADJ (*compar* **wirier**; *superl* **wiriest**) [*person*] enjuto y fuerte; [*hair*] áspero, tieso; [*hand*] nervudo

Wis., Wisc. ABBR (*US*) = **Wisconsin**

wisdom ['wɪzdəm] N sabiduría *f*; **I question the ~ of that decision** dudo que sea una decisión acertada ➤ **wisdom tooth** muela *f* del juicio

wise [waɪz] **Ⓐ** ADJ (*compar* **~r**; *superl* **~st**) **1** (= *learned*) [*person*] sabio; [*words*] sabio, acertado; **the Three Wise Men** los Reyes Magos; **to get ~** (*esp US**) darse cuenta, caer en la cuenta*; **the police got ~ to them** la policía los caló*; **a ~ move** una idea acertada; **I'm none the wiser** me he quedado igual; **nobody will be any the ~r** nadie se dará cuenta; ✦ IDIOM **to be ~ after the event** criticar una vez que las cosas ya han pasado, criticar a posteriori

2 (= *prudent*) [*precaution*] sabio; [*decision, choice*] sabio, acertado; **it would be ~ to** (+ INFIN) sería prudente + *infin*, sería aconsejable + *infin*; **he was ~ enough to refuse** tuvo la suficiente sensatez como para negarse

Ⓑ CPD ➤ **wise guy*** (*esp US*) listo/a *m/f*, listillo/a *m/f* (*Sp pej**) ➤ **wise man** (= *sage*) sabio *m*

➤ **wise up** VI + ADV (*) espabilarse*, avisparse*; **~ up!*** ¡espabílate!; **to ~ up to sth*** caer en la cuenta de algo

wisecrack* ['waɪzkræk] N salida *f* graciosa

wisely ['waɪzlɪ] ADV **1** (= *prudently*) [*choose*] sabiamente, prudentemente; **he had ~ brought an umbrella with him** había tenido la prudencia de traerse un paraguas **2** (= *sagaciously*) sabiamente

wish [wɪʃ] **Ⓐ** N **1** (= *desire, will*) deseo *m*; **he did it against my ~es** lo hizo en contra de mis deseos *or* mi voluntad; **to go against sb's ~es** ir en contra de los deseos *or* la voluntad de algn; **your ~ is my command** (*liter or hum*) sus deseos son órdenes para mí; **I have no great ~ to go** no tengo muchas ganas de ir, no me apetece mucho ir; **to make a ~** pedir un deseo

2 (*in letters*) **with best ~es from Jo** recuerdos de Jo; (*with*) **best ~es for Christmas and the New Year** (*con*) nuestros mejores deseos *or* (*frm*) augurios para la Navidad y el Año Nuevo; **please give him my best ~es** dale recuerdos míos

Ⓑ VT **1** (*in unrealizable or unlikely situations*) **I ~ I were rich** ojalá fuese rico; **I ~ I could!** ¡ojalá pudiera!; **I ~ I hadn't said that** siento haber dicho eso, ojalá no hubiera dicho eso; **she ~es that she could go to school like other children** le gustaría poder ir a la escuela como otros niños **2** (*when change is possible*) **I ~ you'd hurry up** a ver si te das prisa; **I ~ you wouldn't shout** me gustaría que no gritaras, a ver si dejas de gritar

3 **to ~ sb sth: to ~ sb good luck/a happy Christmas** desear buena suerte/felices pascuas a algn; **~ me luck!** ¡deséame suerte!; **I ~ you all possible happiness** os/te deseo la más completa felicidad; **to ~ sb goodbye** despedirse de algn; **I wouldn't ~ that on anybody** eso no se lo desearía a nadie; **we ~ her well in her new job** le deseamos todo lo mejor en su nuevo trabajo

4 (*frm*) (= *want*) querer, desear (*frm*); **I ~ to be alone** quiero *or* (*frm*) deseo estar solo

Ⓒ VI (= *make a wish*) pedir un deseo; **to ~ for sth** desear algo; **she has everything she could ~ for** tiene todo lo que pudiera desear; **I couldn't have ~ed for a nicer birthday** no podía haber soñado con un día de cumpleaños mejor

wishbone ['wɪʃbəʊn] N espoleta *f*

wishful ['wɪʃfʊl] ADJ **~ thinking** ilusiones *fpl*; **that's just ~ thinking** eso es querer hacerse ilusiones

wishing well ['wɪʃɪŋ,wel] N pozo *m* de los deseos

wishy-washy* ['wɪʃɪ'wɒʃɪ] ADJ [*colour*] soso; [*answer*] a medias; [*ideas*] vago; [*person*] sin carácter

wisp [wɪsp] N [*of hair*] mechón *m*; [*of cloud*] voluta *f*

wistful ['wɪstfʊl] ADJ (= *thoughtful*) pensativo; (= *sad*) melancólico, triste

wit¹ [wɪt] N **1** (= *understanding*) inteligencia *f*; **a battle of ~s** una contienda entre dos inteligencias; **to be at one's ~s' end** no saber qué hacer, estar desesperado; **to have one's ~s about one** no perder la cabeza; **to be out of one's ~s** estar fuera de sí; **to be scared out of one's ~s** estar profundamente asustado; **to use one's ~s** usar su sentido común **2** (= *humour, wittiness*) ingenio *m*, agudeza *f* **3** (= *person*) persona *f* ingeniosa; (*Hist*) ingenio *m*

wit² [wɪt] N (*frm, also Jur*) **to wit ...** a saber ..., esto es ...

witch [wɪtʃ] N bruja *f* ➤ **witch doctor** hechicero *m* ➤ **witch hunt** caza *f* de brujas

witchcraft ['wɪtʃkrɑːft] N brujería *f*

---

with

When **with** is part of a set combination, eg **good with**, **pleased with**, **to agree with**, look up the other word.

with [wɪð, wɪθ] PREPOSITION

The commonest translation of **with** is **con**. Note that whenever it combines with **mí**, **ti** or **sí** the forms **conmigo**, **contigo**, **consigo** are used.

1 con; **she mixed the sugar ~ the eggs** mezcló el azúcar con los huevos; **come ~ me** ven conmigo; **he took it away ~ him** se lo llevó consigo

✦ **to be with sb** (= *in the company of*) estar con algn; **I was ~ him** yo estaba con él; **I'll be ~ you in a moment** en un momento *or* enseguida estoy con ustedes; **I'm ~ you there** en eso estoy de acuerdo contigo; *BUT* **are you ~ us or against us?** ¿estás a favor nuestro o en contra?; **I'm not ~ you*** (= *able to understand*) no te entiendo *or* sigo; **are you ~ me?*** ¿me entiendes?

✦ **to be with it*** (= *up-to-date*) estar al tanto *or* al día; (= *fashionable*) [*person*] estar al tanto de lo que se lleva; [*thing*] estar de moda; (= *mentally alert*) estar lúcido *or* despabilado; **sorry, I'm just not ~ it today** lo siento, hoy estoy atontado

2 (= *along with*) junto con; *BUT* **~ the Alcántara it is the biggest ship of its class** junto con el Alcántara es el mayor buque de esa clase

✦ **along** *or* **together with** junto con; **he was arrested along** *or* **together ~ four other terrorists** fue detenido junto con otros cuatro terroristas

3 (*in descriptions*) con; **a house ~ a garden** una casa con jardín; **I don't like men ~ beards** no me gustan los hombres con barba; **a man ~ checked trousers** un hombre con pantalones de cuadros; *BUT* **passengers ~ tickets** los pasajeros con *or* que tienen billetes; **~ his hat on** con el sombrero puesto

Note: when the **with** description pinpoints the particular person or thing you are talking about, **with** is usually translated by **de**:

the man ~ the checked trousers el hombre de los pantalones de cuadros; **the girl ~ the blue eyes** la chica de los ojos azules

4 (*indicating manner, means*) con; **to walk ~ a stick** andar con bastón; **to cut wood ~ a knife** cortar madera con uncuchillo; *BUT* **... and ~ these words of advice, he left us ...** y tras darnos este consejo nos dejó; **~ no trouble at all** sin dificultad alguna, sin ninguna dificultad; **~ that, he closed the door** luego *or* a continuación, cerró la puerta

5 (*indicating cause*) de; **to shiver ~ cold** tiritar *or* temblar de

frío; **to shake ~ fear** temblar de miedo; **the hills are white ~ snow** las colinas están cubiertas de nieve; *BUT* **I spent a week in bed ~ flu** estuve una semana en (la) cama con la gripe
6 (= *owing to*) con; **I couldn't see him ~ so many people there** no lo vi con tanta gente como había; **~ so much happening ...** con todo lo que estaba pasando ...; *BUT* **the approach of winter** al acercarse el invierno
7 (= *according to*) [*increase, change, improve*] con; **the risk of developing heart disease increases ~ the number of cigarettes smoked** el riesgo de sufrir enfermedades coronarias aumenta con el número de cigarrillos que se fume
8 (= *in the house of*) con; **he lives ~ his aunt** vive con su tía; **she stayed ~ friends** se quedó con *or* en casa de unos amigos
9 (= *working for*) **he's ~ IBM** trabaja para *or* en IBM; **a scientist ~ ICI** un científico de ICI; **I've been ~ this company for eight years** llevo ocho años en esta empresa
10 (= *in the care of*) **to leave sth ~ sb** dejar algo en manos de algn *or* con algn; **to leave a child ~ sb** dejar a un niño al cuidado de algn *or* con algn
11 (*on, about*) **he had no money ~ him** no llevaba dinero (encima)
12 (= *in the same direction as*) con; **I was swimming ~ the current** nadaba con *or* a favor de la corriente
13 (= *in spite of*) con; **~ all his faults** con todos sus defectos

withdraw [wɪθˈdrɔː] (*pt* **withdrew**; *pp* **~n**) Ⓐ VT [+ *money*] retirar, sacar (**from** de); [+ *troops, team, product, banknotes*] retirar (**from** de); [+ *application, support, licence, charge*] retirar; [+ *words, remark*] retractarse de, retirar Ⓑ VI
1 (= *move away*) apartarse, alejarse; (= *leave room*) retirarse; [*troops, forces, police*] retirarse (**from** de); **to ~ into o.s.** retraerse, encerrarse en sí mismo **2** [*competitor, negotiator, candidate*] retirarse (**from** de)

withdrawal [wɪθˈdrɔːəl] Ⓐ N **1** [*of troops, team, services, support*] retirada *f* (**from** de); [*of banknote*] retirada *f* de la circulación; [*of application, support, licence, charge*] retirada *f*; [*of allegation, remark*] retractación *f*; **to make a ~** (*from bank*) retirar dinero *or* fondos **2** (*Psych*) retraimiento *m* (**from** de) **3** (*after drug addiction*) síndrome *m* de abstinencia Ⓑ CPD ➤ **withdrawal symptoms** síndrome *msing* de abstinencia

withdrawn [wɪθˈdrɔːn] Ⓐ PP of **withdraw** Ⓑ ADJ (= *introverted*) reservado, introvertido; (= *detached, absent*) retraído, encerrado en sí mismo

withdrew [wɪθˈdruː] PT of **withdraw**

wither [ˈwɪðəʳ] VI [*flower, plant, beauty*] marchitarse; [*limb*] atrofiarse; [*person*] debilitarse
➤ **wither away** VI + ADV [*plant*] marchitarse; [*hope*] desvanecerse

withered [ˈwɪðəd] ADJ [*flower, plant*] marchito; [*limb*] atrofiado

withering [ˈwɪðərɪŋ] ADJ [*tone, look, remark*] fulminador

withhold [wɪθˈhəʊld] (*pt, pp* **withheld**) VT [+ *information*] ocultar; [+ *money*] retener; [+ *decision*] aplazar; [+ *consent, permission*] negar; **to ~ the truth from sb** no revelar la verdad a algn

within [wɪðˈɪn] Ⓐ PREP dentro de; **I want it back ~ three days** quiero que me lo devuelvas dentro de tres días; **here ~ the town** aquí dentro de la ciudad; **to live ~ one's income** vivir conforme a los ingresos; **to be ~ the law** no rebasar los límites de la ley, atenerse a la legalidad; **the police arrived ~ minutes** la policía llegó a los pocos minutos; **the village is ~ a mile of the river** el pueblo dista poco menos de una milla del pueblo; **we were ~ 100 metres of the summit** faltaban 100 metros para que llegáramos a la cumbre; **~ a year of her death** a poco menos de un año de su muerte; **~ the week** antes de terminar la semana;
✦ IDIOM **to be ~ an inch of** estar a dos dedos de
Ⓑ ADV dentro; **from ~** desde dentro, desde el interior

without [wɪðˈaʊt]

When **without** is an element in a phrasal verb, eg **do without, go without,** look up the verb.

Ⓐ PREP sin; **~ a coat** sin abrigo; **~ speaking** sin hablar, sin decir nada; **~ my noticing it** sin verlo yo, sin que yo lo

notase; **not ~ some difficulty** no sin cierta dificultad Ⓑ ADV (*liter*) fuera; **from ~** desde fuera

with-profits [ˈwɪθˈprɒfɪts] ADJ **~ endowment assurance** seguro *m* dotal con beneficios

withstand [wɪθˈstænd] (*pt, pp* **withstood**) VT resistir, aguantar

witness [ˈwɪtnɪs] Ⓐ N **1** (= *person*) testigo *mf*; **eye ~** testigo ocular; **~ for the prosecution/defence** (*Brit*) *or* (*US*) **defense** testigo de cargo/descargo; **there were no ~es** no hubo testigos; **to call sb as a ~** citar a algn como testigo; **I was (a) ~ to this event** yo presencié este suceso, yo fui testigo de este suceso
2 (= *evidence*) **to bear ~ to sth** (*lit*) atestiguar algo; (*fig*) demostrar *or* probar algo
Ⓑ VT **1** (= *see*) ver; **to ~ sb doing sth** ver a algn hacer algo, ver cómo algn hace algo; **the accident was ~ed by two people** hay dos testigos del accidente; **this period ~ed important changes** este periodo fue testigo de cambios importantes
2 [*Jur*] [+ *document*] (= *sign*) firmar como testigo; (= *attest by signature*) atestiguar la veracidad de
Ⓒ CPD ➤ **witness box** (*Brit*), **witness stand** (*US*) tribuna *f* de los testigos, estrado *m*

witticism [ˈwɪtɪsɪzəm] N dicho *m* ingenioso, agudeza *f*, ocurrencia *f*

witty [ˈwɪtɪ] ADJ (*compar* **wittier**; *superl* **wittiest**) [*person, remark, speech*] agudo, ingenioso

wives [waɪvz] NPL of **wife**

wizard [ˈwɪzəd] N mago *m*, brujo *m*, hechicero *m*; **he's a financial ~*** es un genio de las finanzas

wizened [ˈwɪznd] ADJ arrugado, marchito

wk ABBR (= *week*) sem.

WMD(s) NPL ABBR = **weapons of mass destruction**

wobble [ˈwɒbl] VI (= *move unsteadily*) tambalearse, bambolearse; [*voice*] temblar

wobbly [ˈwɒblɪ] ADJ (*compar* **wobblier**; *superl* **wobbliest**) [*chair, table*] cojo, que se tambalea; [*tooth, wheel*] flojo, que se mueve; [*cyclist*] inseguro; [*voice, jelly*] temblón; [*line*] irregular; **he's a bit ~ on his legs** tiene las piernas un poco flojas

woe [wəʊ] N (*poet, hum*) desgracia *f*, aflicción *f*; **~ is me!** ¡ay de mí!; **~ betide you if you're lying!** ¡pobre de ti como sea mentira!; **a tale of ~** una historia triste

woeful [ˈwəʊfʊl] ADJ **1** [*lack, ignorance*] lamentable, deplorable **2** (*liter*) [*expression*] de desconsuelo, de congoja

woefully [ˈwəʊfəlɪ] ADV **1** (= *lamentably*) **the level of funding is ~ inadequate** el nivel de financiación es de una insuficiencia lamentable *or* deplorable **2** (*liter*) (= *sadly*) tristemente

wog*** [wɒg] N (*Brit offensive*) negro/a *m/f*

wok [wɒk] N *cazuela china de base redonda*

woke [wəʊk] PT of **wake**³

woken [ˈwəʊkn] PP of **wake**³

wolf [wʊlf] Ⓐ N (*pl* **wolves** [wʊlvz]) lobo *m*; ✦ IDIOMS **to cry ~** dar una falsa alarma; **to keep the ~ from the door** defenderse de *or* contra la miseria; **a ~ in sheep's clothing** un lobo disfrazado de cordero Ⓑ VT (*also* **~ down**) zamparse*, engullir Ⓒ CPD ➤ **wolf cub** lobato *m* ➤ **wolf whistle** silbido *m* de admiración

woman [ˈwʊmən] N (*pl* **women**) mujer *f*; **~ to ~** de mujer a mujer; **women's doubles** dobles *mpl* femeninos; **women's football** fútbol *m* femenino; **women's group** grupo *m* femenino; **women's lib*** la liberación de la mujer; **women's movement** movimiento *m* feminista; **women's page** sección *f* femenina; **women's refuge** hogar *m* para mujeres maltratadas; **women's rights** derechos *mpl* de la mujer; **women's room** (*US*) servicio *m* de señoras; **women's studies** (*Univ*) estudios *mpl* de la mujer; **women's team** equipo *m* femenino; **it's women's work** es un trabajo de mujeres; **a ~ of the world** una mujer de mundo; **young ~** joven *f* ➤ **woman doctor** doctora *f* ➤ **woman driver** conductora *f*

womanize [ˈwʊmənaɪz] VI dedicarse a la caza de mujeres

womanizer [ˈwʊmənaɪzəʳ] N mujeriego *m*, donjuán *m*

womanly [ˈwʊmənlɪ] ADJ femenino

womb [wuːm] N matriz *f*, útero *m*; (*fig*) cuna *f*

women ['wɪmɪn] NPL *of* **woman**

womenfolk ['wɪmɪnfəʊk] NPL mujeres *fpl*

won [wʌn] PT, PP *of* **win**

wonder ['wʌndə'] **Ⓐ** N **1** (= *feeling*) asombro *m*; **in ~** asombrado, maravillado
2 (= *sth wonderful*) maravilla *f*; **the ~s of science** las maravillas de la ciencia; **a nine-day ~** un prodigio que deja pronto de serlo; **it's a ~ that ...** es un milagro que ...; **~s will never cease!** ¡todavía hay milagros!; **it did ~s for her health** obró milagros en su salud; **no ~!** ¡no me extraña!; **to work ~s** obrar milagros
Ⓑ VT preguntarse; **I was just ~ing if you knew ...** me preguntaba si tu sabrías ...; **I ~ what he'll do now** me pregunto qué hará ahora; **I ~ where Caroline is** ¿dónde estará Caroline?, ¿me pregunto dónde estará Caroline?; **I ~ whether the milkman's been** a ver si el lechero ha venido; **I ~ why she said that** ¿por qué diría eso?, me pregunto por qué dijo eso
Ⓒ VI **1** (= *ask o.s.*, *speculate*) preguntarse, pensar; **I ~ about that for a long time** le di muchas vueltas a eso; **I was ~ing if you could help** te agradecería que me ayudaras
2 (= *be surprised*) asombrarse, maravillarse; **I shouldn't ~ if ...** no me sorprendería que ... + *subjun*
Ⓓ CPD ➤ **wonder drug** remedio *m* milagroso

wonderful ['wʌndəfʊl] ADJ **1** (= *excellent*) maravilloso; **it would be ~ to be able to sing well** sería maravilloso tener buena voz; **we had a ~ time** (nos) lo pasamos de maravilla *or* estupendamente **2** (= *amazing*) [*memory*, *achievement*] increíble

wonderfully ['wʌndəfəlɪ] ADJ **1** (= *extremely*) **~ kind/funny** amabilísimo/divertidísimo; **he looks ~ well** está de maravilla, tiene un aspecto estupendo **2** (= *very well*) [*sleep*, *adapt*, *work*] de maravilla

wonky* ['wɒŋkɪ] ADJ (*compar* **wonkier**; *superl* **wonkiest**) (*Brit*)
1 (= *wobbly*) [*chair*, *table*] cojo, que se tambalea
2 (= *crooked*) torcido, chueco (*LAm*) **3** (= *broken down*) estropeado, descompuesto (*esp Mex*)

won't [wəʊnt] = **will not**

wont [wəʊnt] N (*frm*) **as was my ~** como era mi costumbre, como solía hacer *or* acostumbraba a hacer

woo [wu:] VT [+ *woman*] cortejar; [+ *voters*] captar

wood [wʊd] **Ⓐ** N **1** (= *material*) madera *f*; **it's made of ~** es de madera; **touch ~!** (*Brit*) ◇ **knock on ~!** (*US*) ¡toca madera!
2 (*Brit*) (= *forest*) bosque *m*; **woods** (*also US*) bosque *msing*; **we went for a walk in the ~(s)** fuimos a pasear por el bosque; ✦ IDIOMS **we're not out of the ~(s) yet** aún no estamos fuera de peligro; **he can't see the ~ for the trees** (*Brit*) los árboles no le dejan ver el bosque, aún no le encuentra el chiste (*LAm*)
Ⓑ CPD ➤ **wood carving** talla *f* de madera ➤ **wood shavings** virutas *fpl*

woodcock ['wʊdkɒk] N chocha *f* perdiz

woodcut ['wʊdkʌt] N grabado *m* en madera

woodcutter ['wʊd,kʌtə'] N leñador *m*

wooded ['wʊdɪd] ADJ arbolado

wooden ['wʊdn] **Ⓐ** ADJ **1** (= *made of wood*) de madera
2 (*fig*) (= *lacking expression*) [*actor*, *performance*] acartonado, inexpresivo; [*face*, *person*] rígido, inexpresivo **Ⓑ** CPD
➤ **wooden leg** pierna *f* de madera, pata *f* de palo*
➤ **wooden spoon** cuchara *f* de palo

woodland ['wʊdlənd] N bosque *m*

woodlouse ['wʊdlaʊs] N (*pl* **woodlice**) cochinilla *f*

woodpecker ['wʊd,pekə'] N pájaro *m* carpintero

woodshed ['wʊdʃed] N leñera *f*

woodwind ['wʊdwɪnd] N **the ~s** ◇ **the ~ section** los instrumentos *mpl* de viento de madera

woodwork ['wʊdwɜ:k] N **1** (= *craft*) carpintería *f*
2 (= *wooden parts*) enmaderado *m*, maderaje *m*; **they come crawling out of the ~** (*fig*) aparecen de no se sabe dónde

woodworm ['wʊdwɜ:m] N carcoma *f*; **the table has ~** la mesa está carcomida

woof [wʊf] **Ⓐ** N (= *bark*) ladrido *m* **Ⓑ** EXCL ¡guau! **Ⓒ** VI ladrar

wool [wʊl] **Ⓐ** N lana *f*; ✦ IDIOM **to pull the ~ over sb's eyes** dar a algn gato por liebre **Ⓑ** ADJ de lana

woollen, woolen (*US*) ['wʊlən] **Ⓐ** ADJ de lana
Ⓑ **woollens** NPL géneros *mpl* de lana

woolly, wooly (*US*) ['wʊlɪ] ADJ (*compar* **woollier**; *superl* **woolliest**) **1** [*jumper*] de lana; [*animal*] lanudo **2** (= *vague*) [*ideas*, *thinking*, *essay*] vago, impreciso; [*person*] confuso

woozy* ['wu:zɪ] ADJ (*compar* **woozier**; *superl* **wooziest**) mareado

wop* [wɒp] N (*offensive*) italiano/a *m/f*

word [wɜ:d] **Ⓐ** N **1** palabra *f*; **I remember every ~ he said** recuerdo todas y cada una de sus palabras; **that's not the ~ I would have chosen** yo no me hubiera expresado así; **the ~s** (= *lyrics*) la letra; **I won't hear a ~ against him** no permito que se le critique; **~s failed me** me quedé sin habla; **a man of few ~s** un hombre nada locuaz; **I can't find (the) ~s to tell you ...** no encuentro palabras para decirte ...; **~ for ~** palabra por palabra; **too stupid for ~s** de lo más estúpido; **what's the ~ for "shop" in Spanish?** ¿cómo se dice "shop" en español?; **there is no other ~ for it** no se puede llamar de otro modo; **silly isn't the ~ for it!** ¡llamarle estúpido es poco!; **I can't get a ~ out of him** no logro sacarle una palabra; **in a ~** en pocas palabras, en una palabra; **in other ~s** en otros términos, es decir, esto es; **in the ~s of Calderón** con palabras de Calderón, como dice Calderón; **she didn't say so in so many ~s** no lo dijo exactamente así, no lo dijo así concretamente; **to have the last ~ in an argument** decir la última palabra en una discusión; **by ~ of mouth** verbalmente, de palabra; **a ~ of advice** un consejo; **a ~ of thanks** unas palabras de agradecimiento; **a ~ of warning** una advertencia; **I can't put my feelings into ~s** no tengo palabras para expresar lo que siento; **to put in a (good) ~ for sb** avalar a algn, interceder por algn; **don't say a ~ about it** no digas nada de eso; **he never said a ~** no dijo una sola palabra; **he didn't say a ~ about it to me** ni me lo mencionó; **nobody had a good ~ to say about him** nadie quería defenderle, nadie habló en su favor; **with these ~s, he sat down** y tras pronunciar estas palabras se sentó; **without a ~** sin decir palabra *or* ni pío; ✦ IDIOMS **from the ~ go** desde el principio mismo; **it's the last ~ in luxury** es el último grito en lo que a lujo se refiere; **you're putting ~s into my mouth** te refieres a cosas que yo no he dicho; **you took the ~s right out of my mouth** me quitaste la palabra de la boca
2 (= *talk*) **to have a ~ with sb** hablar (dos palabras) con algn, tener unas palabras con algn; **I'll have a ~ with him about it** lo hablaré con él, se lo mencionaré
3 (= *angry words*) **to have ~s with sb** reñir *or* (*esp LAm*) pelear(se) con algn
4 (= *news*) noticia *f*, aviso *m*; **to bring ~ of sth to sb** informar a algn de algo; **~ came that ...** llegó noticia de que ..., se supo que ...; **if ~ gets out that ...** si sale a la luz que ..., si llega a saberse que ...; **the ~ is that ...** se dice que ...; **there's still no ~ from John** todavía no sabemos nada de John; **pass the ~ that ...** diles que es hora de marcharnos; **to send ~** mandar recado; **to spread the ~** propagar la noticia; **the ~ on the street is that ...** corre el rumor de que ...
5 (= *promise*, *assurance*) palabra *f* (de honor); **it's his ~ against mine** es su palabra contra la mía; **to take sb at his ~** aceptar lo que algn dice; **to break one's ~** faltar a *or* no cumplir la palabra; **to give sb one's ~ (that ...)** dar la palabra a algn (de que ...); **to go back on one's ~** faltar a la palabra; **you have my ~** tienes mi palabra; **we only have *or* we've only got her ~ for it** todo lo que sabemos es lo que ella dice; **~ of honour** palabra *f*, palabra *f* de honor; **to keep one's ~** cumplir (lo prometido); **he's a man of his ~** es hombre de palabra; **I take your ~ for it** te creo, ¡basta con que me lo digas!**; take my ~ for it** te lo aseguro;
✦ IDIOM **to be as good as one's ~** cumplir (lo prometido)
6 (= *command*) orden *f*; **to give the ~ to do sth** dar la orden de hacer algo; **you have only to say the ~** solamente hace falta que des la orden
7 (*Rel*) verbo *m*, palabra *f*; **the Word of God** el Verbo de Dios
Ⓑ VT [+ *letter etc*] redactar; **it's not very clearly ~ed** está mal redactado
Ⓒ CPD ➤ **word association** (*Psych*) asociación *f* de

palabras ➤ **word game** juego *m* de formación de palabras ➤ **word order** orden *m* de palabras ➤ **word processing** procesamiento *m* de textos ➤ **word processor** procesador *m* de textos

wording ['wɜːdɪŋ] N **the ~ is unclear** está mal redactado

word-perfect ['wɜːd'pɜːfɪkt] ADJ (*Brit*) sin falta de expresión; **to be ~** saber perfectamente su papel

wordy ['wɜːdɪ] ADJ (*compar* **wordier**; *superl* **wordiest**) verboso, prolijo

wore [wɔːʳ] PT *of* **wear**

work [wɜːk] **Ⓐ** N **1** (= *activity*) trabajo *m*; (= *effort*) esfuerzo *m*; **to be at ~ on sth** estar trabajando sobre algo; **~ has begun on the new dam** se han comenzado las obras del nuevo embalse; **~ has begun on the new project** ha comenzado el trabajo en el nuevo proyecto; **it's all in a day's ~** es pan de cada día; **to do one's ~** hacer su trabajo; **he did some good ~ at head office** hizo un buen trabajo en la oficina central; **to get some ~ done** hacer algo (de trabajo); **to get on with one's ~** seguir trabajando; **good ~!** (= *well done*) ¡buen trabajo!; **it's hard ~** es mucho trabajo, cuesta (trabajo); **a piece of ~** un trabajo; **she's put a lot of ~ into it** le ha puesto grandes esfuerzos; **to make short ~ of sth/sb** despachar algo/a algn con rapidez; **to start ~** ponerse a trabajar; **✦** IDIOM **I have my ~ cut out** tengo trabajo hasta por encima de las cejas

2 (= *employment, place of employment*) trabajo *m*; **to be at ~** estar trabajando; **to go to ~** ir a trabajar; **to go out to ~** (= *have a job*) tener un trabajo; **to be in ~** tener trabajo; **she's looking for ~** está buscando trabajo; **I'm off ~ for a week** tengo una semana de permiso; **a day off ~** un día libre; **to take time off ~** tomarse tiempo libre; **to be out of ~** estar desempleado *or* (*Sp*) parado

3 (= *product, deed*) obra *f*; **this is the ~ of a professional/madman** esto es trabajo de un profesional/loco; **good ~s** obras *fpl* de caridad; **his life's ~** el trabajo al que ha dedicado su vida

4 (*Art, Literat etc*) obra *f*; **the ~s of Dickens** las obras de Dickens

5 **works** [*of machine, clock etc*] mecanismo *msing*; **road ~s** obras *fpl*; **Ministry of Works** Ministerio *m* de Obras Públicas

Ⓑ VI **1** trabajar; (= *be in a job*) tener trabajo; **he is ~ing at his German** está dándole al alemán; **to ~ hard** trabajar mucho *or* duro; **he ~s in publishing** trabaja en el campo editorial; **to ~ towards sth** trabajar *or* realizar esfuerzos para conseguir algo

2 (= *function*) [*machine, car*] funcionar; **the heating isn't ~ing** la calefacción no funciona; **it won't ~** no funciona; **it may ~ against us** podría volverse en contra de nosotros; **this can ~ both ways** esto puede ser un arma de doble filo; **this may ~ in our favour** puede que esto nos venga bien; **it ~s off the mains** funciona con la electricidad de la red

3 (= *be effective*) [*plan*] salir, marchar; [*drug, medicine, spell*] surtir efecto, ser eficaz; **it won't ~, I tell you!** ¡te digo que no se puede (hacer)!

4 (= *move gradually*) **to ~ loose** desprenderse; **to ~ round to a question** preparar el terreno para preguntar algo

Ⓒ VT **1** (= *make work*) hacer trabajar; **he ~s his staff too hard** hace trabajar demasiado al personal; **to ~ o.s. to death** matarse trabajando

2 (= *operate*) **I don't know how to ~ the microwave** no sé cómo funciona el microondas

3 (= *achieve*) [= *miracle*] hacer; **they ~ed it so that she could come*** lo arreglaron para que viniera

4 (= *shape*) [+ *dough, clay*] trabajar

5 (= *exploit*) [+ *mine*] explotar; [+ *land*] cultivar

6 (= *manoeuvre*) **he gradually ~ed the rope through the hole** poco a poco fue metiendo la cuerda por el agujero; **to ~ one's hands free** lograr soltar las manos; **to ~ one's way along** ir avanzando poco a poco; **he ~ed his way up in the firm** ascendió en la compañía mediante sus propios esfuerzos

7 (= *finance*) **to ~ one's way through college** costearse los estudios universitarios trabajando

Ⓓ CPD ➤ **work ethic** ética *f* del trabajo ➤ **work experience** experiencia *f* laboral ➤ **work force** (= *labourers*) mano *f* de obra; (= *personnel*) personal *m* ➤ **work of art** obra *f* de arte ➤ **work permit** permiso *m* de trabajo ➤ **work station** estación *f* de trabajo ➤ **work surface** encimera *f* ➤ **work**

week (*US*) semana *f* laboral

➤ **work off** VT + ADV **1** [+ *debt*] pagar con su trabajo **2 to ~ off surplus fat** quitarse las grasas excesivas trabajando; **I must try to ~ off all the weight I've put on** tengo que moverme para ver si adelgazo lo que he engordado

➤ **work out Ⓐ** VT + ADV **1** (= *calculate*) [+ *cost, profit*] calcular; [+ *answer*] encontrar

2 (= *solve*) [+ *problem*] resolver; **things will ~ themselves out** al final, todo saldrá bien *or* se solucionará

3 (= *devise*) [+ *plan*] idear

4 (= *understand*) lograr entender; **I just couldn't ~ it out** no lograba entenderlo; **can you ~ out where we are on the map?** ¿puedes determinar *or* averiguar dónde estamos en el mapa?; **I can't ~ him out*** no lo entiendo

Ⓑ VI + ADV **1** (= *amount to*) **how much does it ~ out at?** ¿cuánto suma?, ¿a cuánto sale?; **it ~s out at ten pounds each** sale a diez libras esterlinas por persona

2 (= *turn out*) salir; **I hope it will ~ out well** *or* **all right** espero que salga bien; **how did it ~ out?** ¿qué tal salió?; **it hasn't ~ed out that way** no ha sido así

3 (= *exercise*) hacer ejercicio

➤ **work up** VT + ADV **1** (= *develop*) [+ *energy, courage*] conseguir; **I can't ~ up much enthusiasm for the plan** no consigo entusiasmarme con el plan; **to ~ up an appetite** abrir el apetito **2** (= *excite*) **he ~ed the crowd up into a frenzy** exaltó los ánimos de la multitud; **to get ~ed up** excitarse, exaltarse, emocionarse (*esp LAm*)

workable ['wɜːkəbl] ADJ práctico, factible

workaholic [ˌwɜːkə'hɒlɪk] N trabajador(a) *m/f* obsesivo/a, adicto/a *m/f* al trabajo

workbench ['wɜːkbentʃ] N banco *m* de trabajo, mesa *f* de trabajo

workbook ['wɜːkbʊk] N libro *m* de ejercicios

workday ['wɜːkdeɪ] N (*US*) día *m* laborable

worker ['wɜːkəʳ] N trabajador(a) *m/f*; (*Agr, Ind*) obrero/a *m/f*; **he's a fast/good ~** trabaja deprisa/bien; **she's a hard ~** es muy trabajadora ➤ **worker ant** hormiga *f* obrera ➤ **worker bee** abeja *f* obrera

workhouse ['wɜːkhaʊs] N (*Brit*) asilo *m* de pobres

working ['wɜːkɪŋ] **Ⓐ** ADJ [*person, mother*] trabajador, que trabaja; [*population*] activo; [*conditions, practice, environment, week*] laboral; [*life*] laboral, activo; [*lunch*] de trabajo; [*clothes*] de faena, de trabajo; **within three ~ days** (*Brit*) en un plazo de tres días laborables; **my ~ day begins at eight a.m.** mi jornada (laboral *or* de trabajo) empieza a las ocho de la mañana; **during ~ hours** durante horas de trabajo; **~ hypothesis** hipótesis *f inv* de trabajo; **to have a ~ knowledge of sth** tener conocimientos básicos de algo; **to be in ~ order** funcionar perfectamente

Ⓑ N **1** [*of machine, computer*] funcionamiento *m*

2 **workings** [*of organization, parliament*] forma *fsing* de funcionar; [*of machine, computer*] (= *operation, way of working*) funcionamiento *msing*; (= *mechanism*) mecanismo *msing*

Ⓒ CPD ➤ **the working class(es)** la clase obrera, la clase trabajadora ➤ **working holiday** (*Brit*) vacaciones en las que se combina el trabajo con el ocio ➤ **working model** modelo *m* articulado ➤ **working relationship** relación *f* de trabajo; **they have a good ~ relationship** tienen una buena relación de trabajo, trabajan bien juntos ➤ **working vacation** (*US*) = **working holiday**

working-class ['wɜːkɪŋklɑːs] ADJ [*person, family*] de clase obrera, de clase trabajadora; [*neighbourhood*] obrero; **he's from a ~ background** es de clase obrera *or* trabajadora; **to be ~** ser de clase obrera *or* trabajadora

workload ['wɜːkləʊd] N cantidad *f* de trabajo, trabajo *m*

workman ['wɜːkmən] N (*pl* **workmen**) obrero *m*

workmanship ['wɜːkmənʃɪp] N [*of craftsman*] (= *work*) trabajo *m*; (= *skill*) habilidad *f*; [*of artefact*] factura *f*, fabricación *f*; **of fine ~** esmerado, exquisito

workmate ['wɜːkmeɪt] N (*esp Brit*) compañero/a *m/f* de trabajo

workout ['wɜːkaʊt] N (*Sport*) sesión *f* de ejercicios, sesión *f* de entrenamiento

workplace ['wɜːkˌpleɪs] N lugar *m* de trabajo

works [wɜːks] N (pl ~) **1** (Brit) (= factory etc) fábrica f **2 the ~*** (= the lot) todo, la totalidad

worksheet ['wɜːkʃiːt] N (Scol) hoja f de ejercicios

workshop ['wɜːkʃɒp] N taller m

workshy ['wɜːkʃaɪ] ADJ (Brit) perezoso, flojo (esp LAm)

workstation ['wɜːksteɪʃən] N terminal f de trabajo

worktable ['wɜːkteɪbl] N mesa f de trabajo

worktop ['wɜːktɒp] N (Brit) encimera f

work-to-rule ['wɜːktə'ruːl] N huelga f de brazos caídos

world [wɜːld] **Ⓐ** N **1** (= planet) mundo m; **the ~'s worst cook** el peor cocinero del mundo; **it's not the end of the ~!*** ¡no es el fin del mundo!; **the tallest man in the ~** el hombre más alto del mundo; **she has travelled all over the ~** ha viajado por todo el mundo; **people came from all over the ~** vino gente de todas partes del mundo; **it's the same the ~ over** es igual en todo el mundo, es igual vayas a donde vayas; **you have to start living in the real ~** tienes que empezar a afrontar la vida or la realidad; **to go round the ~** dar la vuelta al mundo; **to see the ~** ver mundo; ◆ IDIOMS **it's out of this ~*** es una maravilla; **to live in a ~ of one's own** vivir en su propio mundo; **the ~ is your oyster** tienes el mundo a tus pies; **it's a small ~!** ¡el mundo es un pañuelo!; **to feel on top of the ~** sentirse de maravilla

2 (= realm) mundo m; **the business ~** el mundo de los negocios; **the English-speaking ~** el mundo de habla inglesa; **the ~ of sport** el mundo deportivo, el mundo de los deportes; **the Western ~** el mundo occidental

3 (= society) mundo m; **to be alone in the ~** estar solo en el mundo, no tener a nadie en el mundo; ◆ IDIOMS **to come down in the ~** (esp Brit) venir a menos; **to go up in the ~** (esp Brit) prosperar, medrar

4 (= life) mundo m; **in this ~** en esta vida, en este mundo; **to bring a child into the ~** traer a un niño al mundo; **to come into the ~** venir al mundo; **in the next ~** en la otra vida, en el otro mundo; ◆ IDIOM **to have the best of both ~s** tenerlo todo

5 (in emphatic expressions) **for all the ~ as if it had never happened** como si nunca hubiera ocurrido; **she looked for all the ~ as if she were dead** cualquiera hubiera dicho que estaba muerta; **not for all the ~** por nada del mundo; **they're ~s apart** son totalmente opuestos or diferentes, no tiene nada que ver el uno con el otro; **there's a ~ of difference between ...** hay un mundo or abismo entre ...; **it did him the ~ of good** le sentó de maravilla, le hizo la mar de bien*; **nothing in the ~ would make me do it** no lo haría por nada del mundo; **where in the ~ has he got to?*** ¿dónde demonios or diablos se ha metido?*; **why in the ~ did you do that?*** ¿por qué demonios or diablos hiciste eso?*; **she means the ~ to me** ella significa muchísimo para mí; **to think the ~ of sb** tener a algn en gran estima

Ⓑ CPD [economy, proportions] mundial; [events, news] internacional; [trade] internacional, mundial; [tour] mundial, alrededor del mundo ➤ **World Bank** Banco m Mundial ➤ **world champion** (Brit) campeón/ona m/f del mundo, campeón/ona m/f mundial ➤ **world championship** (Brit) campeonato m mundial, campeonato m del mundo ➤ **the World Cup** (Ftbl) la Copa Mundial, la Copa del Mundo ➤ **world fair** feria f universal ➤ **the World Health Organization** la Organización Mundial de la Salud ➤ **world leader** [of country, company] líder m mundial; (= politician) jefe/a m/f de estado ➤ **world order** orden m mundial ➤ **world power** (= country) potencia f mundial ➤ **world record** récord m mundial ➤ **world's champion** (US) campeón/ona m/f del mundo, campeón/ona m/f mundial ➤ **World Series** (US) campeonato m mundial de béisbol ➤ **world title** título m mundial ➤ **world war** guerra f mundial; **World War One/Two** ◇ **the First/Second World War** la Primera/Segunda Guerra Mundial ➤ **the World Wide Web** el World Wide Web, el WWW

world-class ['wɜːldklɑːs] ADJ de talla mundial

world-famous ['wɜːld'feɪməs] ADJ de fama mundial, mundialmente conocido

worldly ['wɜːldlɪ] ADJ (compar **worldlier**; superl **worldliest**) **1** (= material) [success, pleasures] mundano, material; **all my ~ goods** todos mis bienes materiales **2** (= experienced) (mucho) mundo **3** (= sophisticated) sofisticado

worldly-wise ['wɜːldlɪ'waɪz] ADJ de mundo, que conoce mundo

worldwide ['wɜːld'waɪd] **Ⓐ** ADJ mundial, universal **Ⓑ** ADV mundialmente, en todo el mundo; **to travel ~** viajar por todo el mundo

worm [wɜːm] **Ⓐ** N (= earthworm) gusano m, lombriz f; (in fruit, vegetable) gusano m (also Comput); **to have ~s** tener lombrices **Ⓑ** VT **1** (= wriggle) **to ~ one's way into a group** infiltrarse en un grupo; **to ~ a secret out of sb** arrancarle un secreto a algn **2** [+ dog, cat, horse] desparasitar **Ⓒ** CPD ➤ **worm tablet** pastilla f contra los parásitos

worn [wɔːn] **Ⓐ** PP of **wear** **Ⓑ** ADJ [garment, furniture, tyre, component] gastado; [steps, stone, surface] desgastado

worn-out ['wɔːn'aʊt] ADJ **1** [garment, furniture, tyre, component] gastado **2** (= exhausted) rendido, agotado

worried ['wʌrɪd] ADJ [person] preocupado; [look] de preocupación; **to be ~ about sth** estar preocupado por algo; **I was getting ~** estaba empezando a preocuparme; **you had me ~** me tenías preocupado; **to be ~ sick (about sth)*** estar preocupadísimo or muy preocupado (por algo); **he was ~ that she would report him to the police** tenía miedo de que ella lo delatase a la policía; **I'm not ~*** me da igual*, me tiene sin cuidado

worrier ['wʌrɪə*] N **to be a ~** preocuparse por nada

worrisome ['wʌrɪsəm] ADJ (esp US) preocupante, inquietante

worry ['wʌrɪ] **Ⓐ** N preocupación f; **it's a great ~ to us all** es una gran preocupación para todos nosotros, nos preocupa mucho a todos; **she has caused me a lot of ~** me ha tenido muy preocupado or inquieto, me ha dado muchas preocupaciones; **that's the least of my worries** eso es lo que menos me preocupa, eso es lo de menos; **to be sick with ~*** estar preocupadísimo; **source of ~** motivo m de preocupación

Ⓑ VT **1** (= cause concern to) preocupar; **that phone call has been ~ing me all day** esa llamada de teléfono me ha tenido preocupado todo el día; **to ~ o.s. sick about sth*** preocuparse muchísimo por algo

2 (= bother) molestar; **the cold doesn't ~ me** el frío no me molesta; **that doesn't ~ me in the least** eso me trae absolutamente sin cuidado

Ⓒ VI **1** (= be anxious) preocuparse; **don't ~!** ¡no te preocupes!; **to ~ about sth/sb** preocuparse por algo/algn; **she worries about her health** le preocupa su salud; **not to ~!*** ¡no pasa nada!, ¡no te preocupes!

2 (= bother) molestarse; **don't ~, I'll do it** no te molestes, yo lo haré

worrying ['wʌrɪɪŋ] ADJ (esp Brit) preocupante, inquietante

worse [wɜːs] **Ⓐ** ADJ COMPAR of **bad** peor (**than** que); **it could be ~** podría ser peor; **to get ~** [weather, situation] empeorar; [patient] empeorar, ponerse peor; **my cold is getting ~** mi resfriado va a peor; **my eyesight is getting ~** mi vista va a peor, cada vez veo peor, cada vez tengo peor vista); **his behaviour is getting ~** su comportamiento es cada vez peor; **to get ~ and ~** ponerse cada vez peor, ir de mal en peor; **to make sth ~** empeorar algo; **it'll only make matters ~** sólo empeorará las cosas; **and, to make matters ~, ...** y, para colmo de desgracia, ...; **he appeared none the ~ for his ordeal** no parecía desmejorado a pesar de su terrible experiencia; **there's nothing ~ than ...** no hay nada peor que ...; **what was ~** para colmo (de males)

Ⓑ ADV COMPAR of **badly** peor; **I sang ~ than he did** or **than him** yo cantaba peor que él; **you could do ~ than give her a call** sería aconsejable que la llamarás

Ⓒ N **it's a change for the ~** es un cambio a peor; **there was ~ to come** ◇ **~ was to come** lo peor todavía estaba por venir, aún quedaba lo peor

worsen ['wɜːsn] VT, VI empeorar

worsening ['wɜːsnɪŋ] **Ⓐ** ADJ [situation] que empeora, que va de mal en peor **Ⓑ** N empeoramiento m

worship ['wɜːʃɪp] **Ⓐ** N **1** (= adoration) adoración f; (= reverence) veneración f; (= organized worship) culto m; **place of ~** lugar m de culto **2** (Brit) (in titles) **Your Worship** (to judge) su Señoría **Ⓑ** VT [+ God, money, success] adorar, rendir culto a; [+ film star, singer] adorar, idolatrar; **she ~s her children** adora a sus hijos; ◆ IDIOM **he ~ped the ground**

she walked on besaba la tierra que ella pisaba, sentía verdadera adoración por ella **G** VI (*Rel*) hacer sus devociones

worst [wɜːst] **A** ADJ SUPERL *of* **bad** peor; **it was the ~ film I've ever seen** fue la peor película de mi vida, fue la película más mala que he visto en mi vida; **~ of** all lo que es peor; **the ~ storm** in **years** la peor tormenta en años; **at the ~ possible** time en el peor momento posible; **it was the ~ thing he ever did** fue lo peor que hizo nunca **B** ADV SUPERL *of* **badly** peor; **the ~-dressed man in England** el hombre peor vestido de Inglaterra; **he visited some of the ~ affected areas** visitó algunas de las zonas más afectadas **G** N **the ~ that can happen is that ...** lo peor que puede pasar es que ...; **at ~,** **they can only say no** en el peor de los casos, nos dirán que no; **the situation is at its ~ in urban centres** en los núcleos urbanos es donde la situación es más grave; **to** fear **the ~** temerse lo peor; **it's ~ the ~ of it is that ...** lo peor de todo es que ...; **that's not the ~ of it** eso no es lo peor; **♦** IDIOMS **if the ~ comes to the ~** ◇ **if ~ comes to ~** (*US*) en el peor de los casos

worth [wɜːθ] **A** ADJ **1** (= *equal in value to*) **to be ~ sth** valer algo; **it's ~ five pounds** vale cinco libras; **what is it ~?** ¿cuánto vale?; **it's not ~ much** no vale mucho; **it's ~ a great deal to me** (*sentimentally*) para mí tiene gran valor sentimental; **what's the old man ~?** ¿cuánto dinero tiene el viejo?; **it must be ~ a** fortune debe valer una fortuna; **it's more than my** job's **~ to tell you** me costaría mi empleo decirte eso; **it's not ~ the** paper **it's written on** vale menos que el papel en que está escrito; **I tell you this for** what **it's ~** te digo esto por si te interesa **2** (= *deserving of*) **it's ~ reading** vale *or* merece la pena leerlo; **it's not ~ it** no vale *or* merece la pena; **it's ~ the** effort vale *or* merece la pena molestarse en hacerlo; **life isn't ~** living la vida no tiene sentido para mí; **the cathedral is ~ a** look la catedral merece la pena, merece la pena ver la catedral; **it's ~** thinking **about** vale *or* merece la pena pensarlo; **it's not ~ the** trouble no vale *or* merece la pena; **it's** well **~ doing** bien vale *or* merece la pena hacerlo **B** N [*of thing*] valor *m*; [*of person*] valía *f*; **ten pounds' ~ of books** libros por valor de diez libras, diez libras de libros; **he had no chance to show his true ~** no tuvo oportunidad de mostrar su valía

worthless [ˈwɜːθlɪs] ADJ (= *of no monetary value*) sin ningún valor; (= *useless*) inútil; **the painting was quite ~** el cuadro no tenía valor alguno *or* no tenía ningún valor

worthwhile [ˈwɜːθˈwaɪl] ADJ [*activity, job*] que vale la pena; [*cause*] loable; **it makes it all ~** le da sentido a todo; **to be ~** (= *worthy*) valer *or* merecer la pena

worthy [ˈwɜːðɪ] ADJ (*compar* **worthier**; *superl* **worthiest**) [*winner, champion*] merecido; [*successor*] digno; [*person*] respetable; [*motive, aim*] encomiable; **~ cause** buena causa *f*, causa *f* noble; **to be ~ of sth/sb** ser digno de algo/algn

would [wʊd] AUX VB, MODAL AUX VB **1** (*conditional tense*) **if you asked him he ~ do it** si se lo pidieras lo haría; **if you had asked him he ~ have done it** si se lo hubieras pedido lo habría hecho; **you ~ never know she was not a native Spanish speaker** nadie diría que el español no es su lengua materna; **~ you go there by yourself?** ¿irías allí sola?; **I ~n't worry too much if I were you** yo en tu lugar no me preocuparía demasiado **2** (*indirect speech*) **I said I ~ do it** te dije que lo haría *or* hacía; **I thought you ~ want to know** pensé que querrías saber **3** (*emphatic*) **he ~ say that,** **~n't he?** es lógico que dijera eso **4** (*conjecture*) **it ~ have been about eight o'clock** serían las ocho; **it ~ seem so** así parece ser **5** (*invitations*) querer; **~ you like some tea?** ¿quiere tomar un té? **6** (*requests*) **~ you close the door please?** ¿puedes cerrar la puerta, por favor?; **~ you mind?** si no le importa, si no tiene inconveniente **7** (*insistence*) **I told her not to but she ~ do it** le dije que no, pero insistió en hacerlo; **try as he ~** por mucho que se esforzara, por más que intentase **8** (*refusal*) **he ~n't do it** no quería hacerlo, se negó a hacerlo; **the car ~n't start** el coche se negó *or* negaba a arrancar, el coche no quería arrancar

9 (*past habit*) **he ~ paint it each year** solía pintarlo cada año, lo pintaba cada año

would-be [ˈwʊdbiː] ADJ **a ~ poet** un aspirante a poeta

wouldn't [ˈwʊdnt] = **would not**

wound[1] [wuːnd] **A** N herida *f*; **a bullet ~** una herida de bala; **a chest ~** una herida en el pecho; **✦** IDIOM **to open up old ~s** abrir viejas heridas **B** VT herir; **he was ~ed in the leg** fue herido en la pierna; **she was deeply ~ed by this remark** su comentario la hirió profundamente

wound[2] [waʊnd] PT, PP *of* **wind**[2]

wounded [ˈwuːndɪd] ADJ herido; **there were six dead and fifteen ~** hubo seis muertos y quince heridos

wove [wəʊv] PT *of* **weave**

woven [ˈwəʊvən] PP *of* **weave**

wow* [waʊ] EXCL ¡vaya!, ¡anda!, ¡mira nomás! (*LAm*)

WPC N ABBR (*Brit*) = **Woman Police Constable**

WRAF [ræf] N ABBR (*Brit*) = **Women's Royal Air Force**

wrangle [ˈræŋgl] N riña *f*, disputa *f*, pleito *m* (*esp LAm*); **legal ~** disputa *f* legal

wrap [ræp] **A** N **1** (= *garment*) chal *m*, rebozo *m* (*LAm*) **2 to keep sth under ~s** (*fig*) guardar algo en secreto **B** VT envolver; **shall I ~ it for you?** ¿se lo envuelvo?; **she ~ped the child in a blanket** envolvió al niño en una manta; **~ the rug round your legs** enróllate la manta alrededor de las piernas
➤ **wrap up A** VT + ADV **1** (= *cover*) [+ *gift*] envolver; [+ *abrigar*] **2** (*) (= *conclude*) concluir, poner punto final a; **to ~ up a deal** cerrar un trato **3 to be ~ped up in sb/sth** estar embelesado con algn/absorto en algo **B** VI + ADV **1** (= *dress warmly*) abrigarse; **~ up warm!** ¡abrígate bien! **2** (*) (= *be quiet*) callarse; **~ up!*** ¡cállate!

wraparound [ˈræpəˌraʊnd] CPD ➤ **wraparound skirt** falda *f* cruzada ➤ **wraparound sunglasses** gafas *fpl* de sol envolventes

wrapper [ˈræpəʳ] N [*of goods*] envoltura *f*, envase *m*; [*of sweet*] envoltorio *m*; [*of book*] sobrecubierta *f*

wrapping [ˈræpɪŋ] N envoltura *f*, envase *m* ➤ **wrapping paper** (*gen*) papel *m* de envolver; (= *gift-wrap*) papel *m* de regalo

wrath [rɒθ] N (*poet*) cólera *f*

wreak [riːk] VT [+ *destruction, vengeance*] hacer, causar; **to ~ havoc** causar estragos

wreath [riːθ] N (*pl* **~s** [riːðz]) [*of flowers*] guirnalda *f*; (*for funeral*) corona *f*; [*of smoke, mist*] espiral *m*

wreathe [riːð] VT (*esp liter*) **a face ~d in smiles** una cara muy risueña *or* sonriente; **trees ~d in mist** árboles *mpl* envueltos en niebla

wreck [rek] **A** N **1** (= *destruction*) [*of ship*] naufragio *m* **2** (= *wrecked ship*) restos *mpl* de un naufragio, buque *m* hundido **3** (*) **the car was a complete ~** el coche estaba hecho polvo*; **she's a nervous ~** estoy hecho polvo*; **she's a nervous ~** tiene los nervios destrozados **4** (*US*) (= *accident*) accidente *m*; **he died in a car ~** murió en un accidente de coche **B** VT **1** (*Naut*) [+ *ship*] hundir, hacer naufragar; **to be ~ed** naufragar **2** (= *break*) estropear, destrozar; (*into pieces*) destruir, hacer pedazos; **he ~ed the car** dejó el coche destrozado **3** (= *ruin*) [+ *health, happiness*] arruinar, hundir; [+ *marriage*] destrozar; **it ~ed my life** me arruinó la vida

wreckage [ˈrekɪdʒ] N (= *remains*) [*of ship*] restos *mpl* de un naufragio; [*of car, aeroplane, train*] restos *mpl*; [*of building*] escombros *mpl*, ruinas *fpl*

wrecker [ˈrekəʳ] N **1** (= *destroyer*) (*gen*) destructor(a) *m/f* **2** (*US*) (= *breaker, salvager*) demoledor *m*

Wren* [ren] N (*Brit Navy*) *mujer que presta servicio en la marina británica*

wren [ren] N (= *bird*) reyezuelo *m*, troglodito *m*

wrench [rentʃ] **A** N **1** (= *tug*) tirón *m*, jalón *m* (*LAm*); **it was a ~ to see her go** (*Brit*) dolió mucho verla partir **2** (= *tool*) (*Brit*) (*adjustable*) llave *f* inglesa; (*US*) (*non-adjustable*) llave *f* fija (de tuercas) Ⓑ VT **to ~ sth off/from/out of** arrancar algo de; **he ~ed himself free** haciendo un gran esfuerzo se soltó

wrestle ['resl] Ⓐ VI luchar (a brazo partido); (*Sport, fig*) luchar (**with** con); **the pilot ~d with the controls** el piloto luchaba con los mandos Ⓑ VT [+ *opponent*] luchar con, luchar contra

wrestler ['reslə'] N (*Sport*) luchador(a) *m/f*

wrestling ['reslɪŋ] N (*Sport*) lucha *f* libre ➤ **wrestling match** partido *m* de lucha libre

wretch [retʃ] N desgraciado/a *m/f*, miserable *mf*

wretched ['retʃɪd] ADJ **1** (= *unhappy*) desdichado, desgraciado **2** (= *poor*) [*conditions*] miserable, lamentable; [*life, existence*] miserable, desgraciado, infeliz **3** (*) (*expressing annoyance*) maldito*, condenado*; **where's that ~ dog!*** ¡dónde está ese maldito *or* condenado perro!*

wriggle ['rɪgl] Ⓐ VT mover; **to ~ one's toes/fingers** mover los dedos de los pies/de las manos Ⓑ VI (*also ~ about or around*) [*person, animal*] (*restlessly*) moverse, revolverse; (*in pain*) retorcerse; [*worm, snake, eel*] serpentear; [*fish*] colear; **to ~ away** escaparse serpenteando; **to ~ free** escaparse, escurrirse; **to ~ through a hole** deslizarse por un agujero; **to ~ out of a difficulty** escabullirse, escaparse de un apuro

wring [rɪŋ] (*pt, pp* **wrung**) VT **1** (*also ~ out*) [+ *clothes*] escurrir **2** (= *twist*) torcer, retorcer; **I'll ~ your neck for that!*** ¡te voy a retorcer el pescuezo!*; **to ~ money out of sb** sacar dinero a algn; ✦ IDIOM **to ~ one's hands** (*in distress*) retorcerse las manos

wringing ['rɪŋɪŋ] ADJ (*also ~ wet*) empapado

wrinkle ['rɪŋkl] Ⓐ N arruga *f* Ⓑ VT (*also ~ up*) [+ *clothes*] arrugar; [+ *brow*] fruncir Ⓒ VI (*also ~ up*) arrugarse

wrinkled ['rɪŋkld] ADJ arrugado

wrist [rɪst] N muñeca *f* ➤ **wrist rest** reposamuñecas *m inv*

wristwatch ['rɪstwɒtʃ] N reloj *m* de pulsera

writ [rɪt] N (*Jur*) mandato *m* judicial; **to issue a ~ against sb** demandar a algn

write [raɪt] (*pt* **wrote**; *pp* **written**) Ⓐ VT **1** [+ *letter, book, essay*] escribir; [+ *music, song*] escribir, componer; **~ your name here** escribe *or* pon tu nombre aquí; **how do you ~ his name?** ¿cómo se escribe su nombre?; **to ~ sb a cheque** hacer un cheque a algn, extender un cheque a algn (*more frm*); **to ~ sb a letter** escribir (una carta) a algn; **to ~ sb a prescription** hacer una receta a algn; ✦ IDIOM **you're lying, it's written all over your face!*** estás mintiendo, se te nota a la legua *or* en la cara

2 (*US*) **to ~ sb** escribir a algn

3 (*Comput*) [+ *program, software*] escribir; **to ~ sth to disk** pasar algo a un disco

Ⓑ VI escribir (**to** a); **she wrote to say that she'd be late** escribió para avisar que llegaría tarde; **he ~s for "The Times"** escribe *or* colabora en el "Times"; ✦ IDIOM **it's nothing to ~ home about*** no es nada del otro mundo*

➤ **write away** VI + ADV **to ~ away for sth** escribir pidiendo algo

➤ **write back** VI + ADV **to ~ back to sb** contestar a algn

➤ **write down** VT + ADV [+ *address, number, details*] apuntar, anotar

➤ **write in** Ⓐ VI + ADV escribir, mandar una carta; **a lot of people have written in to complain** mucha gente ha escrito *or* ha mandado cartas quejándose; **to ~ in for sth** escribir pidiendo algo Ⓑ VT + ADV (= *include*) [+ *word, item, part, scene*] añadir, agregar; [+ *clause in contract*] incluir

➤ **write off** Ⓐ VI + ADV **to ~ off for sth** escribir pidiendo algo Ⓑ VT + ADV [+ *debt*] cancelar (al darla por incobrable); **he's just written off his new car** (*Brit**) acaba de tener un accidente con el coche nuevo y ha quedado destrozado; **I've written off the whole thing as a dead loss** ese asunto lo considero un fracaso que es mejor olvidar

➤ **write out** VT + ADV **1** (= *write*) [+ *name, list, prescription*] escribir; [+ *cheque, receipt*] hacer **2** (= *copy*) [+ *notes, essay*] pasar en limpio, pasar a limpio (*Sp*)

➤ **write up** VT + ADV **1** (= *make*) [+ *report*] redactar; [+ *notes*] pasar en limpio, pasar a limpio (*Sp*) **2** (= *record*) [+ *experiment, one's findings, visit*] describir (por escrito) **3** (= *report on*) [+ *event*] escribir una crónica sobre, hacer un reportaje sobre

write-off ['raɪtɒf] N **1** (*Brit*) (= *vehicle*) siniestro *m* total; **his car was a complete ~** el coche fue declarado siniestro total, el coche quedó siniestro total **2** (= *disaster*) desastre *m*, fracaso *m*; **the whole afternoon was a ~** la tarde entera fue un desastre *or* fracaso

write-protect ['raɪtprə'tekt] VT proteger contra escritura

writer ['raɪtə'] N [*of letter, report*] escritor(a) *m/f*; (*as profession*) escritor(a) *m/f*, autor(a) *m/f*; **~'s cramp** calambre *m* de los escribientes

write-up ['raɪtʌp] N **1** (= *report*) crónica *f*, reportaje *m* **2** (= *review*) crítica *f*, reseña *f*

writhe [raɪð] VI retorcerse; **to ~ with *or* in pain** retorcerse de dolor

writing ['raɪtɪŋ] Ⓐ N **1** (= *handwriting*) letra *f*; **I can't read your ~** no entiendo tu letra

2 (= *letters, words*) **there was some ~ on the page** había algo escrito en la página; **I'd like to have that in ~** me gustaría tenerlo por escrito; **to put sth in ~** poner algo por escrito

3 (= *written work*) **it's a brilliant piece of ~** está maravillosamente escrito

4 (= *activity*) escritura *f*; **~ is his hobby** su hobby es la escritura, su hobby es escribir; **he earns quite a lot from ~** gana bastante escribiendo

Ⓑ CPD ➤ **writing pad** bloc *m* ➤ **writing paper** papel *m* de escribir

written ['rɪtn] Ⓐ PP of **write** Ⓑ ADJ [*agreement, exam, statement*] escrito; [*permission, guarantee, offer*] por escrito; **her ~ English is excellent** su inglés escrito es excelente; **the power of the ~ word** el poder de la palabra escrita

WRNS [renz] N ABBR (*Brit formerly*) = **Women's Royal Naval Service**

wrong [rɒŋ] Ⓐ ADJ **1** (*morally*) (= *bad*) malo; (= *unfair*) injusto; **it's ~ to steal** ◇ **stealing is ~** robar está mal; **that was very ~ of you** ahí *or* en eso has hecho muy mal; **there's nothing ~ with that** no hay nada malo en eso

2 (= *incorrect*) [*answer, information*] incorrecto; [*calculation, belief*] equivocado; **that clock is ~** ese reloj anda *or* marcha mal; **the letter has the ~ date on it** la carta tiene la fecha equivocada; **you've opened the packet at the ~ end** has abierto el paquete por el lado que no es, has abierto el paquete al revés; **I'm in the ~ job** tengo un puesto que no me conviene; **he's got the ~ kind of friends** no tiene los amigos apropiados; **that's the ~ kind of plug** se necesita otro tipo de enchufe; **she married the ~ man** se equivocó al casarse con él; **you have the ~ number** (*Telec*) se ha equivocado de número; **it's the ~ one** no es el/la que hace falta; **I think you're talking to the ~ person** creo que no es conmigo con quien debería hablar; **it's in the ~ place** está mal situado, está mal colocado; **he was driving on the ~ side** (of the road) iba por el carril contrario; **to say/do the ~ thing** decir/hacer algo inoportuno; **at the ~ time** inoportunamente; **we were on the ~ train** nos habíamos equivocado de tren; **the ~ way round** al revés; **to go the ~ way** (*on route*) equivocarse de camino; **that's the ~ way to go about it** ésa no es la forma de enfocarlo; **a piece of bread went down the ~ way** se me fue un pedazo de pan por el otro camino *or* por el camino viejo

3 (= *mistaken*) **to be ~** [*person*] equivocarse, estar equivocado; **you're ~ about that** ahí *or* en eso estás equivocado; **I was ~ in thinking that …** me equivoqué al pensar que …

4 (= *amiss*) **is anything** *or* **something ~?** ¿pasa algo?; **what's ~?** ¿qué pasa?; **what's ~ with you?** ¿qué te pasa?; **what's ~ with the car?** ¿qué le pasa al coche?; **nothing's ~** ◇ **there's nothing ~** no pasa nada; **there's nothing ~ with it/him** no le pasa nada; **something's ~** ◇ **there's something ~** hay algo mal *or* que no está bien; **there's something ~ with my lights** algo les pasa a mis faros; **something was very ~** había algo que no iba nada bien

Ⓑ ADV mal; **you've done it ~** lo has hecho mal; **to get sth ~** equivocarse en algo; **don't get me ~*** no me malinterpretes; **you've got it all ~*** (= *misunderstood*) no has entendido nada; **to go ~** [*person*] (*on route*) equivocarse de camino; (*in calculation*) equivocarse; [*plan*] salir mal, malograrse (*Per*), cebarse (*Mex**); (*Mech*) fallar, estropearse; **you can't go ~** (*with choice*) no te equivocarás, puedes estar seguro (**with** con); (*in directions*) no tiene pérdida; **well, in that case you thought ~** bueno, en ese caso pensaste mal

Ⓒ N mal *m*; **he can <u>do</u> no** ~ es incapaz de hacer mal a nadie; **to be <u>in</u> the** ~ (= *guilty*) obrar mal; (= *mistaken*) estar equivocado; **to <u>right</u> a** ~ deshacer un agravio, acabar con un abuso; ✦ PROV **two ~s don't make a right** no se subsana un error cometiendo otro
Ⓓ VT ser injusto con; **to feel that one has been ~ed** sentirse agraviado

wrongdoer ['rɒŋ,duːəʳ] N malhechor(a) *m/f*, delincuente *mf*

wrongful ['rɒŋfʊl] ADJ **1** (= *unjust*) injusto; ~ **dismissal** despido *m* improcedente **2** (= *unlawful*) ilegal; ~ **arrest** arresto *m* ilegal

wrongly ['rɒŋlɪ] ADV **1** (= *incorrectly*) [*believe, diagnose*] equivocadamente; [*spell*] mal; **you have been ~ informed** le han informado mal **2** (= *unjustly*) [*accuse,* *convict*] injustamente

wrote [rəʊt] PT *of* **write**

wrought-iron [,rɔːt'aɪən] ADJ de hierro forjado

wrung [rʌŋ] PT, PP *of* **wring**

WRVS N ABBR (*Brit*) = **Women's Royal Voluntary Service**

wry [raɪ] ADJ [*person, sense of humour, remark*] irónico; **to make a ~ face** hacer una mueca, torcer el gesto

WV, W. Va. ABBR (*US*) = **West Virginia**

WWI N ABBR = **World War One**

WWII N ABBR = **World War Two**

WWW N ABBR (= **World Wide Web**) **the** ~ el Web

WY, Wyo. ABBR (*US*) = **Wyoming**

Xx

X, x [eks] N (= *letter*) (*also Math*) X, x *f*; **X for X-rays** X de rayos X; **X marks the spot** el sitio está señalado con una X; **if you have X dollars a year** si uno tiene X dólares al año ➤ **X chromosome** cromosoma *m* X

xenophobe ['zenəfəʊb] N xenófobo/a *m/f*

xenophobic [ˌzenə'fəʊbɪk] ADJ xenófobo

Xerox® ['zɪərɒks] VT fotocopiar

XL ABBR = **extra large**

Xmas ['eksməs] N ABBR = **Christmas**

X-rated ['eks'reɪtɪd] ADJ (*Cine*) no apto para menores de 18 años

X-ray ['eks'reɪ] **Ⓐ** N (= *ray*) rayo *m* X; (= *photo*) radiografía *f*; **I had an ~** me hicieron una radiografía **Ⓑ** VT [+ *person*] hacer una radiografía a; **they ~ed my arm** me hicieron una radiografía del brazo, me radiografiaron el brazo

xylophone ['zaɪləfəʊn] N xilófono *m*

Yy

Y, y [waɪ] N (= *letter*) Y, y *f*; **the Y** (*US**) el albergue juvenil ➤ **Y chromosome** cromosoma *m* Y; *see also* **Y-fronts**

Y2K [ˌwaɪtuːˈkeɪ] ABBR = **Year 2000**

yacht [jɒt] Ⓐ N (*Sport*) barco *m* de vela, velero *m*; (*luxury*) yate *m*; (*small*) balandro *m*, balandra *f* Ⓑ VI **to go ~ing** ir a pasear *or* navegar a vela Ⓒ CPD ➤ **yacht club** club *m* náutico ➤ **yacht race** regata *f* de veleros

yachting [ˈjɒtɪŋ] N navegación *f* a vela, balandrismo *m*

yachtsman [ˈjɒtsmən] N (*pl* **yachtsmen**) balandrista *m*, deportista *m* náutico

yachtswoman [ˈjɒtswʊmən] N (*pl* **yachtswomen**) balandrista *f*, deportista *f* náutica

yak [jæk] N yac *m*, yak *m*

Yale® [jeɪl] CPD ➤ **Yale key** llave *f* de seguridad ➤ **Yale lock** cerradura *f* de cilindro

yam [jæm] N ñame *m*; (*US*) (= *sweet potato*) batata *f*, camote *m* (*LAm*)

Yank* [jæŋk] N yanqui *mf*, gringo/a *m/f* (*LAm*)

yank [jæŋk] Ⓐ N tirón *m*, jalón *m* (*LAm*) Ⓑ VT tirar de, jalar (*LAm*)

Yankee [ˈjæŋkɪ] ADJ, N yanqui *mf*

YANKEE

El término **Yankee** o el peyorativo **Yank** se utilizan fuera de EE.UU. para referirse a los estadounidenses en general. Sin embargo, desde la guerra de Secesión, en el sur de Estados Unidos un **Yankee** es un habitante de un estado del norte, y a su vez, en el norte se considera un verdadero **Yankee** al oriundo de Nueva Inglaterra. El nombre procede de la canción **Yankee Doodle**, escrita inicialmente por un inglés para burlarse de los colonos americanos y adoptada después como himno patriótico por los soldados del general Washington durante la lucha por la independencia.

---

yap [jæp] Ⓐ N pequeño ladrido *m* Ⓑ VI dar pequeños ladridos

yard¹ [jɑːd] N (= *measure*) yarda *f* (*91,44cm*)

yard² [jɑːd] N (= *courtyard, farmyard*) patio *m*; (*US*) (= *garden*) jardín *m*; (*for livestock*) corral *m*; (*Scol*) patio *m* (de recreo); (= *worksite*) taller *m*; (*for storage*) depósito *m*, almacén *m*; (*for boats*) astillero *m*; (*Rail*) estación *f* ➤ **yard sale** (*US*) venta *f* de objetos usados (*en mercadillo improvisado*), mercadillo *m* de cosas viejas

yardstick [ˈjɑːdstɪk] N patrón *m*, criterio *m*, medida *f*

yarn [jɑːn] N 1 (= *wool*) hilo *m* 2 (= *tale*) cuento *m*, historia *f*; ✦ IDIOM **to spin a ~** soltar una historia

yawn [jɔːn] Ⓐ N bostezo *m* Ⓑ VI bostezar; [*gap, abyss*] abrirse

yawning [ˈjɔːnɪŋ] ADJ enorme; **there is a ~ gap between the moderates and the left wing of the party** existe un enorme abismo entre los moderados y el ala izquierda del partido

yd ABBR = **yard**

yeah* [jeə] ADV = **yes**

year [jɪəʳ] N 1 (= *twelve months*) año *m*; **it takes ~s** es cosa de años, se tarda años; **he died in his 89th** = murió a los 89 años; **he got ten ~s** le condenaron a diez años de prisión; **three times a ~** tres veces al año; **~ in, ~ out** año tras año, todos los años sin falta; **last ~** el año pasado; **next ~** el año que viene; **she's three ~s old** tiene tres años; **an eight-~-old child** un niño de ocho años; **the work has put ~s on him** el trabajo lo ha envejecido; **all (the) ~ round** durante todo el año; **that hairstyle takes ~s off you*** ese peinado te quita un montón de años*; ✦ IDIOM **the ~ dot** el año de la nana* 2 (= *age*) **he looks young for his ~s** aparenta menos años de los que tiene; **he's getting on in ~s** va para viejo 3 (*Brit Scol, Univ*) curso *m*, año *m*; **she's in the fifth ~** está en

quinto; **the kids in my ~** los chicos de mi curso 4 (*of wine*) cosecha *f*, vendimia *f*; **1982 was a good ~** 1982 fue una buena cosecha *or* vendimia, 1982 fue un buen año

yearbook [ˈjɪəbʊk] N anuario *m*

yearly [ˈjɪəlɪ] Ⓐ ADJ anual; **~ payment** anualidad *f* Ⓑ ADV anualmente, cada año; **(once) ~** una vez al año

yearn [jɜːn] VI **to ~ for** [+ *native land, person*] añorar; **to ~ to do sth** anhelar *or* ansiar hacer algo

yearning [ˈjɜːnɪŋ] N (= *desire*) ansia *f*, anhelo *m*; (= *longing*) añoranza *f* (**for** de)

Use **el/un** not **la/una** before feminine nouns beginning with stressed **a** or **ha** like **ansia**.

---

yeast [jiːst] N levadura *f*

yell [jel] Ⓐ N grito *m*, chillido *m*; **to let out a ~** soltar *or* pegar un grito Ⓑ VI, VT (*also ~ out*) gritar, chillar

yellow [ˈjeləʊ] Ⓐ ADJ (*compar* **~er**; *superl* **~est**) 1 (*in colour*) amarillo; [*hair*] rubio; [*teeth, fingers*] amarillo, amarillento; **to go** *or* **turn ~** volverse *or* ponerse amarillo 2 (*) (= *cowardly*) gallina*, miedica* Ⓑ N 1 (= *colour*) amarillo *m* 2 (= *yolk*) yema *f* Ⓒ VI volverse amarillo, ponerse amarillo; **~ing leaves/pages** hojas *fpl* amarillentas Ⓓ VT **~ed newspapers** periódicos amarillentos (por el paso del tiempo); **grass ~ed by weeks of sunshine** la hierba seca y amarillenta tras semanas de sol Ⓔ CPD ➤ **yellow card** tarjeta *f* amarilla ➤ **yellow fever** fiebre *f* amarilla ➤ **yellow line** línea *f* amarilla (de estacionamiento limitado); **a double ~ line** una línea amarilla doble ➤ **Yellow Pages®** páginas *fpl* amarillas ➤ **the yellow press** la prensa amarilla *or* sensacionalista ➤ **the Yellow Sea** el Mar Amarillo

yelp [jelp] Ⓐ N [*of animal*] gañido *m*; [*of person*] grito *m*, chillido *m* Ⓑ VI [*animal*] gañir; [*person*] gritar, chillar

Yemen [ˈjemən] N Yemen *m*

Yemeni [ˈjemənɪ] ADJ, N yemenita *mf*

yen [jen] N 1 (= *currency*) yen *m* 2 (*) **to have a ~ to do sth** morirse de ganas de hacer algo*

yes [jes] ADV sí; **"I didn't say that!" — "oh, ~, you did"** —¡yo no he dicho eso! —sí, sí que lo has dicho; **to say ~** decir que sí, aceptar; (*to marriage proposal*) dar el sí; **~ ~, but what if it doesn't?** de acuerdo, pero ¿y si no es así? ➤ **yes man*** adulador *m*, pelotillero *m* (*Sp**)

yesterday [ˈjestədeɪ] Ⓐ ADV ayer; **~ morning/afternoon** ayer por la mañana/tarde; **all day ~** todo el día de ayer; ✦ IDIOM **I wasn't born ~** no me chupo el dedo* Ⓑ N ayer *m*; **the day before ~** anteayer

yet [jet] Ⓐ ADV 1 (= *now, up to now, by now*) todavía, aún; **he hasn't come ~** todavía *or* aún no ha llegado, no ha llegado todavía *or* aún; **we haven't heard anything as ~** todavía *or* por ahora no sabemos nada; **not ~** todavía *or* aún no 2 (= *to date*) hasta ahora; **this is his best film ~** es su mejor película hasta ahora 3 (= *still*) todavía, aún; **that question is ~ to be decided** está todavía por *or* sin decidir, aún está por *or* sin decidir 4 (= *even*) todavía, aún; **the queues are likely to grow longer** es probable que las colas se hagan aún *or* todavía más largas; **~ again** otra *or* una vez más; **they are celebrating ~ another victory** están celebrando otra *or* una victoria más Ⓑ CONJ (= *in spite of everything*) sin embargo, con todo; (= *but*) pero; **a powerful ~ fragile piece of equipment** un equipo potente pero frágil

yeti [ˈjetɪ] N yeti *m*

yew [juː] N (*also ~ tree*) tejo *m*

Y-fronts® ['waɪfrʌnts] NPL (Brit) calzoncillos mpl

YHA N ABBR (Brit) = **Youth Hostels Association**

Yiddish ['jɪdɪʃ] N yíd(d)ish m

yield [ji:ld] **Ⓐ** N (from crop, mine, investment) rendimiento m
Ⓑ VT **1** (= produce) [+ crop, minerals, results] producir; [+ interest] rendir, producir; [+ profit, benefits] producir, reportar; **the shares ~ five per cent** las acciones producen or reportan or rinden un cinco por ciento de beneficios **2** (= surrender) [+ territory, power, control] ceder (**to** a) **Ⓒ** VI **1** (= produce) **land that ~s well** una tierra que produce mucho
2 (= surrender) rendirse, ceder; **to ~ to sth** ceder a or ante algo
3 (= give way) [ice, door, branch] ceder; **to ~ under pressure** ceder or hundirse ante la presión
4 (US Aut) ceder el paso; **"yield"** "ceda el paso"

yippee* [jɪ'pi:] EXCL yupi*

YMCA N ABBR = **Young Men's Christian Association**

yo ['jəʊ] EXCL (as greeting) ¡hola!; (to attract attention) ¡eh!, ¡oye!

yob* ['jɒb], **yobbo*** ['jɒbəʊ] N (Brit) vándalo m, gamberro m (Sp)

yodel, yodle ['jəʊdl] VI, VT cantar a la tirolesa

yoga ['jəʊgə] N yoga m

yogurt ['jəʊgət] N yogur(t) m

yoke [jəʊk] **Ⓐ** N **1** (of oxen) yunta f; (carried on shoulder) balancín m, percha f; (fig) yugo m **2** (on dress, blouse) canesú m **Ⓑ** VT (also ~ **together**) [+ oxen] uncir; (fig) unir

yokel ['jəʊkəl] N palurdo/a m/f, pueblerino/a m/f

yolk [jəʊk] N yema f (de huevo)

Yom Kippur [ˌjɒmkɪ'pʊəʳ] N Yom Kip(p)ur m

yonder ['jɒndəʳ] **Ⓐ** ADJ aquel **Ⓑ** ADV allá, a lo lejos; **(over) ~** allá

yonks* [jɒŋks] N (Brit) **for ~** hace siglos*

Yorkshire pudding ['jɔ:kʃɪə'pʊdɪŋ] N (Brit) especie de buñuelo que se sirve acompañando al rosbif

you [ju:] PRON

Note that subject pronouns are used less in Spanish than in English – mainly for emphasis or to avoid ambiguity.

1 (sing, familiar) (as subject) tú, vos (CAm, River Plate); (as direct/indirect object) te; (after prep) ti, vos (CAm, River Plate); **what do ~ think about it?** ¿y tú qué piensas?; **~'re very strong** eres muy fuerte; **I know ~** te conozco; **I gave the letter to ~ yesterday** te di la carta ayer; **I gave it to ~** te lo di; **I told ~ to do it** te dije que lo hicieras ti; **it's for ~** es para ti; **she's taller than ~** es más alta que tú; **can I come with ~?** ¿puedo ir contigo?
2 (sing, formal) (as subject) usted, Ud, Vd; (as direct object) lo/la, le (Sp); (as indirect object) le; (after prep) usted, Ud, Vd; **~'re very kind** es usted muy amable; **I saw ~, Mrs Jones** la vi, señora Jones; **I gave ~ the keys** le di las llaves

Change **le** to **se** before a direct object pronoun:

I gave it to ~ se lo di; **this is for ~** esto es para usted; **they're taller than ~** son más altos que usted
3 (pl, familiar) (as subject) vosotros/as (Sp), ustedes (LAm); (as direct object) os (Sp), los/las (LAm); (as indirect object) os (Sp), les (LAm); (after prep) vosotros/as (Sp), ustedes (LAm); **~'ve got kids but we haven't** vosotros tenéis (Sp) or ustedes tienen (LAm) hijos pero nosotros no; **all know why we are here** todos sabéis (Sp) or saben (LAm) por qué estamos aquí; **~ stay here, and I'll go and get the key** quedaos (Sp) or quédense (LAm) aquí, que yo iré a por la llave; **I know ~ two** yo os (Sp) or los (LAm) conozco a los dos; **I gave it to ~** os (Sp) or se (LAm) lo di; **they've done it better than ~** lo han hecho mejor que vosotros (Sp) or ustedes (LAm); **they'll go without ~** irán sin vosotros (Sp) or ustedes (LAm)
4 (pl, formal) (as subject) ustedes, Uds, Vds; (as direct object)

los/las, les (Sp); (as indirect object) les; (after prep) ustedes, Uds, Vds; **~ are very kind** son ustedes muy amables; **are ~ brothers?** ¿son (ustedes) hermanos?; **may I help ~?** ¿puedo ayudarlos?; **I gave ~ the keys** les di las llaves

Change **les** to **se** before a direct object pronoun:

I gave it to ~ se lo di; **we arrived after ~** llegamos después de ustedes
5 (general)

When **you** means one or people in general, the impersonal **se** is often used:

~ can't smoke here no se puede fumar aquí, está prohibido fumar aquí; **~ never know** nunca se sabe

A further possibility is **uno/una**:

~ never know whether ... uno nunca sabe si ...

Impersonal constructions are also used:

~ need to check it every day conviene or hay que comprobarlo cada día; **~ must paint it** hace falta pintarlo
6 (phrases and special uses) **~ Spaniards** vosotros/ustedes los españoles; **~ and I** tú y yo; **between ~ and me** entre tú y yo; **~ fool!** ¡no seas tonto!; **that's lawyers for ~!** ¡para que te fíes de los abogados!; **if I were ~** yo de ti, yo que tú, si yo fuera tú, yo en tu lugar; **~ there!** ¡oye, tú!; **that dress just isn't ~** ese vestido no es tu estilo; **poor ~!** ¡pobrecito!

you'd [ju:d] = **you would, you had**

you'll [ju:l] = **you will, you shall**

young [jʌŋ] **Ⓐ** ADJ (compar **~er** ['jʌŋgəʳ]; superl **~est** ['jʌŋgɪst]) **1** (= not old) [person, animal, wine, country] joven; [plant, spinach, wheat] tierno; [child] pequeño, de corta edad; **my ~er brother** mi hermano menor or pequeño; **she is two years ~er than me** es dos años más joven que yo, tiene dos años menos que yo; **I'm not so ~ as I was** los años no perdonan or no pasan en balde; **at a very ~ age** (child) siendo muy joven; (adult) siendo muy pequeño; **in my ~(er) days** cuando era joven, en mi juventud; **they have a ~ family** tienen niños pequeños; **she looks quite ~ for her age** aparenta bastante menos edad de la que tiene, parece bastante más joven de lo que es; **the ~er generation** la generación de los más jóvenes; **a ~ lady** una joven; **now look here, ~ lady!** ¡atiende, jovencita!; **a ~ man** un joven; **you've done well, ~ man** muy bien hecho, muchacho; **to marry ~** casarse joven; **it is enjoyed by millions, ~ and old** millones lo disfrutan, grandes y pequeños; **✦** IDIOMS **~ as ~ as you feel** la edad se lleva dentro; **~ at heart** joven de espíritu; **the night is ~** la noche es joven; **you're only ~ once** sólo se vive una vez
2 (= youthful) **that dress is too ~ for her** ese vestido es para alguien más joven; **he has a very ~ outlook** piensa como los jóvenes, tiene mentalidad de joven
Ⓑ NPL **1** [of animals] crías fpl
2 (= young people) **the ~** los jóvenes, la juventud
Ⓒ CPD ➤ **young offender** (Brit) delincuente mf juvenil

youngster ['jʌŋstəʳ] N joven mf

your ['jʊəʳ] POSS ADJ **1** (belonging to one person) **1.1** (familiar) (with singular noun) tu; (with plural noun) tus; **~ book/table** tu libro/mesa; **~ friends** tus amigos; **have you washed ~ hair?** ¿te has lavado la cabeza? **1.2** (formal) (with singular noun) su; (with plural noun) sus; **~ book/table** su libro/mesa; **~ friends** sus amigos; **is this ~ luggage?** ¿es de usted este equipaje?
2 (belonging to more than one person) **2.1** (familiar) (with singular noun) vuestro/a (Sp), su (LAm); (with plural noun) vuestros/as (Sp), sus (LAm); **~ house** vuestra casa (Sp), su casa (LAm); **would you like to wash ~ hands?** ¿queréis lavaros las manos? **2.2** (formal) su; **~ house** su casa; **~ friends** sus amigos; **is this ~ dog?** ¿es de ustedes este perro?
3 (= one's) **it's bad for ~ health** perjudica la salud

you're [ˈjʊəʳ] = **you are**

yours [ˈjʊəz] POSS PRON **1** (*belonging to one person*) **1.1** (*familiar*) (*referring to singular possession*) (el/la) tuyo/a; (*referring to plural possession*) (los/las) tuyos/as; **is that box ~?** ¿esa caja es tuya?; **I've lost my pen, can I use ~?** he perdido el bolígrafo, ¿puedo usar el tuyo?; **that dog of ~!** ¡ese perro tuyo!, ¡ese perro que tienes tú!; **which is ~?** ¿cuál es el tuyo? **1.2** (*formal*) (*referring to singular possession*) (el/la) suyo/a, (el/la) de usted; (*referring to plural possession*) (los/las) suyos/as, (los/las) de usted; **is that box ~?** ¿esa caja es suya?; **I've lost my pen, can I use ~?** he perdido el bolígrafo, ¿puedo usar el suyo?; **Yours** (*in letter*) un abrazo **2** (*belonging to more than one person*) **2.1** (*familiar*) (*referring to singular possession*) (el/la) vuestro/a (*Sp*), (el/la) suyo/a (*LAm*), (el/la) de ustedes (*LAm*); (*referring to plural possession*) (los/las) vuestros/as (*Sp*), (los/las) suyos/as (*LAm*), (los/las) de ustedes (*LAm*) **2.2** (*formal*) (*referring to singular possession*) (el/la) suyo/a, (el/la) de ustedes; (*referring to plural possession*) (los/las) suyos/as, (los/las) de ustedes

> Only use the article with **tuyo/tuyos** and **suyo/suyos** *etc* when you mean "the one(s) belonging to you".

yourself [jəˈself] PRON **1** (*reflexive*) te (*familiar*), se (*formal*); **have you hurt ~?** ¿te has hecho daño? (*familiar*), ¿se ha hecho daño? (*formal*) **2** (*for emphasis*) tú mismo/a (*familiar*), usted mismo/a (*formal*); **you did it ~** tú mismo lo hiciste (*familiar*), usted mismo lo hizo (*formal*); **be ~** sé tú mismo, sé como tú eres **3** (*after a preposition*) ti mismo/a (*familiar*), usted mismo/a (*formal*); **you did it for ~** lo hiciste para ti mismo (*familiar*), lo hizo para usted mismo (*formal*); **you did it (all) by ~** lo hiciste sin ayuda de nadie; **did you come by ~?** ¿viniste solo? **4** (= *oneself*) (*emphatic*) uno/a mismo/a; (*reflexive*) se; (*after preposition*) sí (mismo/a); **to talk to ~** hablar consigo mismo *or* con uno mismo

yourselves [jəˈselvz] PRON **1** (*reflexive*) **1.1** (*familiar*) os (*Sp*), se (*LAm*); **did you enjoy ~?** ¿os divertisteis?, ¿se divirtieron?

(*LAm*); **help ~ to vegetables** servíos las verduras **1.2** (*formal*) se; **help ~ to vegetables** sírvanse las verduras **2** (*after prep, for emphasis*) **2.1** (*familiar*) vosotros/as mismos/as, ustedes mismos/as (*LAm*); **you'll have to pay for taxis ~** los taxis los tendréis que pagar vosotros (mismos) **2.2** (*formal*) ustedes mismos/as; **you'll have to pay for taxis ~** los taxis los tendrán que pagar ustedes (mismos)

youth [juːθ] **Ⓐ** N **1** (= *young age*) juventud *f*; **in my ~** en mi juventud **2** (*pl* **~s** [juːðz]) (= *boy*) joven *m* **3** (= *young people*) jóvenes *mpl*, juventud *f* **Ⓑ** CPD ➤ **youth club** club *m* juvenil ➤ **youth hostel** albergue *m* juvenil ➤ **youth worker** (*Brit*) (= *social worker*) asistente social que se encarga de adolescentes menores de 18 años; (= *community worker*) empleado del municipio que trabaja con grupos de jóvenes en la comunidad

youthful [ˈjuːθfʊl] ADJ [*looks, appearance*] joven, juvenil; [*enthusiasm, energy*] juvenil; [*ambition, indiscretion, inexperience*] de juventud

youthfulness [ˈjuːθfəlnɪs] N juventud *f*

you've [juːv] = **you have**

yowl [jaʊl] **Ⓐ** N [*of animal*] aullido *m*; [*of person*] alarido *m* **Ⓑ** VI [*animal*] aullar; [*person*] dar alaridos

yo-yo ® [ˈjəʊjəʊ] N (*pl* **~s**) (= *toy*) yoyó ® *m*

yucca [ˈjʌkə] N yuca *f*

yuck* [jʌk] EXCL ¡puaj!*

Yugoslav [ˈjuːgəʊˈslɑːv] ADJ, N yugoeslavo/a *m/f*, yugoslavo/a *m/f*

Yugoslavia [ˈjuːgəʊˈslɑːvɪə] N Yugoslavia *f*

Yugoslavian [ˈjuːgəʊˈslɑːvɪən] ADJ yugoeslavo, yugoslavo

Yuletide [ˈjuːltaɪd] N († *or liter*) Navidad *f*

yummy* [ˈjʌmɪ] ADJ (*compar* **yummier**; *superl* **yummiest**) de rechupete*

yuppie* [ˈjʌpɪ] N ABBR = **young upwardly mobile professional**) yuppie *mf*

YWCA N ABBR = **Young Women's Christian Association**

Zz

Z, z [zed, (US) ziː] N (= letter) Z, z f; **Z for Zebra** Z de Zaragoza

Zaïre [zɑːˈiːəʳ] N (formerly) Zaire m

Zambia [ˈzæmbɪə] N Zambia f

zany [ˈzeɪnɪ] ADJ (compar **zanier**; superl **zaniest**) estrafalario, surrealista

zap* [zæp] **Ⓐ** VT **1** (= destroy) [+ person] liquidar, cargarse (Sp*) **2** (Comput) (= delete) [+ word, data] borrar **Ⓑ** VI (= move quickly) ir corriendo; **to ~ through the TV channels** zapear

zeal [ziːl] N celo m, entusiasmo m (**for** por)

zealot [ˈzelət] N fanático/a m/f

zealous [ˈzeləs] ADJ entusiasta (**for** de)

zebra [ˈziːbrə] **Ⓐ** N (pl **~s** or **~**) cebra f **Ⓑ** CPD ➤ **zebra crossing** (Brit) paso m de peatones, paso m de cebra

zenith [ˈzenɪθ] N **1** (Astron) cenit m **2** (fig) cenit m, apogeo m; **to be at the ~ of one's power** estar en el apogeo de su poder

zeppelin [ˈzeplɪn] N zepelín m

zero [ˈzɪərəʊ] **Ⓐ** N cero m; **5° below ~** 5 grados bajo cero **Ⓑ** CPD [altitude] cero; (*) [interest, hope] nulo ➤ **zero gravity** gravedad f nula ➤ **zero hour** hora f cero, hora f H ➤ **zero rating** tasa f cero ➤ **zero tolerance: a policy of ~ tolerance** una política de mano dura (en el mantenimiento del orden público)
➤ **zero in on** VI + PREP **1** (Mil) [+ target] apuntar a **2** (= concentrate on) dirigir todos sus esfuerzos a

zest [zest] N **1** (= enthusiasm) gusto m, entusiasmo m (**for** por); **to eat with ~** comer con gusto; **her ~ for life** sus ganas de vivir, su gusto por la vida **2** (= excitement) ánimo m

zigzag [ˈzɪgzæg] **Ⓐ** N zigzag m **Ⓑ** VI zigzaguear, serpentear **Ⓒ** ADJ en zigzag

zillion* [ˈzɪljən] N **a ~ dollars** ◇ **~s of dollars** tropecientos dólares*

Zimbabwe [zɪmˈbɑːbwɪ] N Zimbabue m

Zimmer® [ˈzɪməʳ] N (Brit) (also **~ frame**) andador m

zinc [zɪŋk] N zinc m, cinc m

Zionist [ˈzaɪənɪst] ADJ, N sionista mf

zip [zɪp] **Ⓐ** N **1** (Brit) (also **~ fastener**) cremallera f, cierre m relámpago (LAm) **2** (*) (= energy) vigor m, energía f **3** (= sound of bullet) silbido m, zumbido m **Ⓑ** VT **1** [+ dress, bag] cerrar la cremallera de; **to ~ sth open** abrir la cremallera de algo **2** (Comput) comprimir **Ⓒ** VI **to ~ in/past** entrar/pasar volando or zumbando **Ⓓ** CPD ➤ **zip code** (US) código m postal ➤ **zip fastener** cremallera f, cierre m relámpago (LAm) ➤ **zip gun** (US) arma f de fuego de fabricación casera

> Use **el/un** not **la/una** before feminine nouns beginning with stressed **a** or **ha** like **arma**.

➤ **zip up** **Ⓐ** VT + ADV [+ dress, bag] cerrar la cremallera de; **can you ~ me up please?** ¿me subes or cierras la cremallera, por favor? **Ⓑ** VI + ADV cerrar

zipper [ˈzɪpəʳ] N (esp US) cremallera f, cierre m relámpago (LAm)

zit* [zɪt] N (esp US) grano m

zither [ˈzɪðəʳ] N cítara f

zodiac [ˈzəʊdɪæk] N zodíaco m

zombie [ˈzɒmbɪ] N (= monster) zombi m; (fig) zombi mf

zone [zəʊn] N zona f; **postal ~** (US) zona f postal

zoo [zuː] N (parque m) zoológico m, zoo m

zookeeper [ˈzuːkiːpəʳ] N guardián/ana m/f del (parque) zoológico, guardián/ana m/f del zoo

zoological [zəʊəˈlɒdʒɪkəl] ADJ zoológico

zoologist [zəʊˈɒlədʒɪst] N zoólogo/a m/f

zoology [zəʊˈɒlədʒɪ] N zoología f

zoom [zuːm] VI ir zumbando*; **he ~ed past at 120kph*** pasó zumbando a 120kph* ➤ **zoom lens** zoom m

zucchini [zuːˈkiːnɪ] N (pl **~** or **~s**) (US) calabacín m, calabacita f (LAm)

Zulu [ˈzuːlʊ] ADJ, N zulú mf